COMPLETE TELEVISION, RADIO & CABLE INDUSTRY DIRECTORY

2013

COMPLETE TELEVISION, RADIO & CABLE INDUSTRY DIRECTORY

GREY HOUSE PUBLISHING

PUBLISHER: Leslie Mackenzie
EDITOR: Richard Gottlieb
EDITORIAL DIRECTOR: Laura Mars
ASSOCIATE EDITOR: Joseph Esser

PRODUCTION MANAGER & COMPOSITION: Kristen Thatcher
PRODUCTION ASSISTANTS: Diana Delgado, Chad Dewey, Cathy Hughes, Dawn Jenkins, Nicole Palumbo, Alfredo Proietti

MARKETING DIRECTOR: Jessica Moody

Grey House Publishing, Inc.
4919 Route 22
Amenia, NY 12501
518.789.8700
FAX 845.373.6390
www.greyhouse.com
e-mail: books@greyhouse.com

Printed in Canada
1st edition published 2013

Publisher's Cataloging-In-Publication Data
(Prepared by The Donohue Group, Inc.)

Complete television, radio & cable industry directory / [editor: Richard Gottlieb].

v. ; cm.
Annual
Began with 2013.
Description based on: 2013; title from title page.
"An earlier version of a similar work was published by Bowker as Broadcasting & Cable Yearbook"--P. vii.
Includes index.
ISBN: 978-1-61925-103-8 (2013 ed.)

1. Television broadcasting--United States--Directories. 2. Radio broadcasting--United States--Directories. 3. Cable television--United States--Directories. 4. Television broadcasting--Canada--Directories. 5. Radio broadcasting--Canada--Directories. 6. Cable television--Canada--Directories. I. Gottlieb, Richard. II. Grey House Publishing, Inc. III. Title: Broadcasting & cable yearbook. New Providence, N.J.: R.R. Bowker, c1993- IV. Title: Complete television, radio and cable industry directory

HE8689 .C66
384.54/097

Table of Contents

Introduction

This is Grey House Publishing's first edition of the retitled *Complete Television, Radio & Cable Industry Directory.* First published more than 70 years ago as *Broadcasting Yearbook,* and later as *Broadcasting & Cable Yearbook,* this reference work has consistently filled the need for current, comprehensive television, radio and cable industry information for both U.S. and Canadian markets. Grey House acquired the database from Bowker, and is pleased to continue to offer authoritative information in both print and online formats.

New Features

This 2013 edition covers the same valuable data fields researchers are used to, with a number of significant differences to the content—there is more of it, it is more current, and it is presented in a fresh, new look. This edition has a new name, a new cover design, and important changes to the arrangement of data and the page design, so that even the smallest of details—and there are lots of them—are easier to find.

Previous editions interspersed U.S. and Canadian data. This edition clearly separates U.S. and Canadian material for television, radio and cable, so that users interested in either market will find a comprehensive section with everything from market areas, call letter lists and station profiles in one place.

Instead of all station data running together in one paragraph, we have separated important elements, such as web sites, ownership, and programming. Not only are key contact names indented for quick recognition, but there are nearly 5,000 more names in this edition, for a total of 72,549. And each station profile includes new, relevant data, like television's virtual channel and radio's Arbitron market area.

The *Complete Television, Radio & Cable Industry Directory* includes eight major sections, with the "big three"—television, radio and cable—arguably the most detailed and most significant. But this directory is so much more than station data, with all the professional services from producers to engineers, from equipment manufacturers to legal services, including those who produce, distribute, manufacture, engineer, consult, and advocate for this diverse industry.

Television

U.S. television starts with TV statistics—ranking of TV markets, top TV programs, growth and transactions of TV stations, and television sales.

Following these statistics are detailed listings of national and regional networks, and group owners. Detailed listings of 1,909 TV stations are arranged by DMA (Designated Market Area). These station listings include dozens of technical details direct from the FCC, such as digital and virtual channel numbers, hours of operation, frequency, and antenna height. Corporate information follows, including licensee, owner and network—plus names of important decision makers, such as President, Station Manager, Program Director and more. Users will find thousands more names than in the previous edition.

Following the U.S. stations are informative lists—TV stations by call letters, by digital and virtual channels, and a list of U.S. stations that broadcast in Spanish.

Comprehensive Canadian TV information follows the U.S. sections—including networks, group owners, detailed station listings, and lists by call letters and channels.

Radio

U.S. radio starts with an updated Arbitron Metro Survey Area Ranking, which ranks each of the 300 U.S. radio markets by its population.

Following radio market information are detailed listings of national and regional radio networks, and group owners, all with current key contact names. Detailed listings of 15,725 radio stations are arranged by state of license, then city within the state. Like the television stations, these listings include dozens of technical details direct from the FCC, such as power, frequency and hours of operation. New to this section is the station's market area. Users will find type of programming and special programming, including hours of news programming, and target audience. Long lists of key contacts follow, many more than the previous edition, assuring you will always be able to reach the right person.

Following the detailed station listings is information on international radio, satellite radio, and call letters listed by AM and FM and frequency. The U.S. radio section ends with detailed programming information—putting each radio station into one or more of 48 total categories, from Adult Contemporary to Vietnamese. This programming index is followed by special programming, where you will find specifics, like which stations in Portland, Oregon offer jazz as part of their program mix.

Comprehensive Canadian radio information follows the U.S. sections—including networks, group owners, detailed station listings, lists by call letters and frequency, and programming.

Cable

This section starts with a variety of updated statistics on U.S. cable programming, followed by detailed listings of national and regional cable networks, with a separate section on regional cable sports networks.

Cable data for Canada follows, with detailed listings of Canadian cable networks. New to this section are industry statistics.

Technical Equipment and Services

Following the detailed station listings, the *Complete Television, Radio & Cable Industry Directory* goes on to include current, comprehensive information on those who provide services, materials and equipment to the industry. From major television syndicators to radio news services, from producers to distributors, from equipment manufacturers to cable audio services, this edition will help you find the product or service you need.

Professional Services and More

This comprehensive directory goes on to include more valuable industry information, from employment services to technical consultants, from legal services to talent agents. There is a separate section on associations, trade shows and vocational schools and, finally, complete listings for the FCC and other regulatory agencies. New to this edition is Canadian agency information.

This directory is your key to this dynamic industry, all in one place, with more than 22,600 listings, valuable lists and indexes. Find out specifics of any station in the U.S. and Canada, including their audience, how to reach them, what school offers industry training, where to find the latest studio sound board, and how to keep up on the latest industry regulations.

Online Database

For even easier access to this information, the *Compete Television, Radio & Cable Industry Directory* is available by subscription to our online database—G.O.L.D. For more information or a free trial, call 800-562-2139 or visit www.greyhouse.com.

From Isaac Newton to the iPad: A Chronology of the Electronic Media

1666
Sir Isaac Newton performs basic experiments on the spectrum.

1794
Allessandro Volta of Italy invents the voltaic cell, a primitive battery.

1827
George Ohm of Germany shows the relationship between resistance, amperage and voltage. Sir Charles Wheatstone of England invents an acoustic device to amplify sounds that he calls a "microphone."

1844
Samuel F.B. Morse tests the first telegraph with "What hath God wrought?" message sent on link between Washington and Baltimore.

1858
First trans-Atlantic cable completed. President James Buchanan and Queen Victoria exchange greetings.

1867
James Clerk Maxwell of Scotland develops the electromagnetic theory.

1875
George R. Carey of Boston proposes a system that would transmit and receive moving visual images electrically.

1876
Alexander Graham Bell invents the telephone.

1877
Thomas A. Edison applies for a patent on a "phonograph or talking machine."

1878
Sir William Cooke of England passes high voltage through a wire in a sealed glass tube, causing a pinkish glow—evidence of cathode rays. It's the first step toward the development of the vacuum tubes.

1884
Paul Nipkow of Germany patents a mechanical, rotating facsimile scanning disk.

1886
Heinrich Hertz of Germany proves that electromagnetic waves can be transmitted through space at the speed of light and can be reflected and refracted.

1895
Wilheim Conrad Roentgen of Germany discovers X-rays.

Guglielmo Marconi sends and receives his first wireless signals across his father's estate at Bologna, Italy.

1896
Marconi applies for British patent for wireless telegraphy. He receives an American patent a year later.

1899
Marconi flashes the first wireless signals across the English Channel.

1900
Constantin Perskyi (France) coins the word television at the International Electricity Congress, part of the 1900 Paris Exhibition.

1901
Marconi at Newfoundland, Canada, receives the first trans-Atlantic signal, the letter "S," transmitted from Poldhu, England.

1906
Dr. Lee de Forest invents the audion, a three-element vacuum tube, having a filament, plate and grid, which leads to the amplification of radio signals.

1910
Enrico Caruso and Emmy Destinn, singing backstage at the Metropolitan Opera House in New York, broadcast through the De Forest radiophone and are heard by an operator on the SS Avon at sea and by wireless amateurs in Connecticut.

United States approves an act requiring certain passenger ships to carry wireless equipment and operators.

1912
The Titanic disaster proves the value of wireless at sea; 705 lives saved. Jack Phillips and Harold Bride are the ship's wireless operators.

1920
On August 20, 8MK (later, WWJ) in Detroit, owned by the Detroit News, starts what is later claimed to be regular broadcasting.

The Westinghouse Co.'s KDKA(AM) Pittsburgh broadcasts the Harding-Cox election on returns November 2 as the country's first licensed commercial radio station.

1921
The Dempsey-Carpentier fight is broadcast from Boyle's Thirty Acres in Jersey City through a temporarily installed transmitter at Hoboken, New Jersey. Major J. Andrew White was the announcer. This event gave radio a tremendous boost.

1922
The superheterodyne circuit is demonstrated by its inventor, Edwin H. Armstrong. It dramatically improves AM radio reception.

WEAF(AM) New York broadcasts what is claimed to be the first commercially sponsored program on September 7. The advertiser is the Queensborough Corp., a real estate organization.

WOI(AM) Ames, Iowa, goes on air as the country's first licensed educational station.

1923
Dr. Vladimir K. Zworykin files for a U.S. patent for an all-electronic television system.

A "chain" broadcast features a telephone tie-up between WEAF(AM) New York and WNAC(AM) Boston.

1924
The Republican convention in Cleveland and the Democratic convention in New York are broadcast over networks.

1925
President Calvin Coolidge's inaugural ceremony is broadcast by 24 stations in a transcontinental network.

1926
President Coolidge signs the Dill-White Radio Bill creating the Federal Radio Commission and ending the chaos on the radio dial caused by the wild growth of broadcasting.

National Broadcasting Co. is organized on November 1 with WEAF(AM) and WJZ(AM) in New York as key stations and Merlin Hall Aylesworth as president. Headquarters are at 711 Fifth Ave., New York.

1927
The Columbia Broadcasting System goes on the air with a basic network of 16 stations. Major J. Andrew White is president.

Philo T. Farnsworth applies for a patent on his image dissector television camera tube.

1928
NBC establishes a permanent coast-to-coast radio network.

1929
William S. Paley, 27, is elected president of the Columbia Broadcasting System.

Vladimir Zworykin demonstrates his kinescope or cathode ray television receiver before a meeting of the Institute of Radio Engineers on November 19.

1930
Experimental TV station W2XBS is opened by National Broadcasting Co. in New York.

1931
Experimental television station W2XAB is opened by Columbia Broadcasting System in New York.

The first issue of Broadcasting magazine appears on October 15.

The National Association of Broadcasters reports that more than half of the nation's radio stations are operating without a profit.

1932
CBS, NBC, and New York area stations, notably WOR(AM), go into round-the-clock operations to cover the Lindbergh kidnapping, radio's biggest spot-news reporting job to date.

NBC lifts its ban on recorded programs for its owned-and-operated stations, but continues to bar them from network use.

NBC withdraws prohibitions against price mentions on the air during daytime hours; two months later, both NBC and CBS allow price mentions at nighttime as well.

1933
Associated Press members vote to ban network broadcasts of AP news and to restrict local broadcasts to bulletins to stipulated times with air credit to member newspapers.

The American Newspaper Publishers Association declares radio program schedules are advertising and should be published only if paid for.

CBS assigns publicity director Paul White to organize a nationwide staff to collect news for network broadcast. General Mills agrees to sponsor twice-daily newscasts.

1934
Congress passes the Communication Act, which, among other things, replaces the Federal Radio Commission with the Federal Communications Commission.

1935
RCA announces that it is taking television out of the laboratory for a $1 million field-test program.

1936
A year of TV demonstrations begins in June with the Don Lee Broadcasting System's first public exhibition of cathode ray television in the U.S., using a system developed by Don Lee TV director Harry Lubcke. One month later, RCA demonstrates its system of TV with transmissions from the Empire State Building, and Philco follows with a seven-mile transmission in August.

FM (frequency modulation) broadcasting, a new radio system invented by Major Edwin H. Armstrong, is described at an FCC hearing as static-free, free from fading and cross-talk, having uniformity day and night in all seasons and greater fidelity of reproduction.

A.C. Nielsen, revealing his firm's acquisition of the MIT-developed "Audimeter," proposes a metered tuning method of measuring radio audience size.

1937
WLS(AM) Chicago recording team of Herb Morrison, announcer, and Charles Nehlsen, engineer, on a routine assignment at Lakehurst, New Jersey, records an on-the-spot account of the explosion of the German dirigible Hindenburg. NBC breaks its rigid rule against recordings to put it on the network.

1938
Broadcasting publishes the first facsimile newspaper in a demonstration at the National Association of Broadcasters convention.

1939
After 15 years of litigation, the patent for iconoscope-kinescope tubes, the basis for electronic television, is granted to Dr. Vladimir Zworykin.

A telecast of the opening ceremonies of the New York World's Fair marks the start of a regular daily television schedule by RCA-NBC in New York.

The first baseball game ever televised—Princeton vs. Columbia—appears on NBC.

1940
The FCC authorizes commercial operation of FM, but puts TV back into the laboratory until the industry reaches an agreement on technical standards.

CBS demonstrates a system of color TV developed by its chief TV engineer, Dr. Peter Goldmark.

1941
Bulova Watch Co., Sun Oil Co., Lever Bros. and Procter & Gamble sign as sponsors of the first commercial telecasts on July 1 over NBC's WNBT(TV) New York (until then W2XBS).

President Roosevelt's broadcast to the nation on December 9, the day after war is declared, has the largest audience in radio history—about 90 million listeners.

1942
The Advertising Council is organized by advertisers, agencies, and media to put the talents and techniques of advertising at the disposal of the government to inspire and instruct the public concerning the war effort.

1943
Edward J. Noble buys the Blue Network from RCA for $8 million in cash. RCA had two networks, NBC Red and NBC Blue.

1944
With the FCC approval of the transfer of owned stations, the Blue Network assumes the name of its holding company, the American Broadcasting Co.

1945
Pooled coverage of the Nazi surrender in May brings the American people full details of the end of the war in Europe. Peace heralds a communications boom: Not only will programming restrictions end, but new station construction, frozen for the duration, will proceed at an explosive pace soon after V-J Day in August.

1946
A telecast of the Louis-Conn heavyweight title fight, sponsored by Gillette Safety Razor Co. on a four-city hookup, reaches an estimated 100,000 viewers and convinces skeptics that television is here to stay.

RCA demonstrates its all-electronic system of color TV.

Bristol-Myers is the first advertiser to sponsor a television network program—Geographically Speaking—which debuted October 27 on NBC TV's two-station network.

1947
Radio comedian Fred Allen uses a gag, which NBC had ruled out, about network vice presidents, and is cut off the air while he tells it. The story is front-page news across the country as the sponsor's ad agency demands a rebate for 35 seconds of dead air.

1948
Texaco puts an old-style vaudeville show on NBC TV; the hour-long series stars Milton Berle.

1949
The Academy of Television Arts & Sciences presents the first Emmy Awards at ceremonies televised by KTSL(TV) Los Angeles.

1950
General Foods drops actress Jean Muir, who denies any communist affiliations or sympathies, from the cast of The Aldrich Family (NBC TV) after protests against her appearance by "a number of groups." The Joint Committee Against Communism claims credit for her removal, announcing a drive to "cleanse" radio and television of pro-communist actors, directors, and writers.

The FCC approves CBS's color TV system, effective November 20. The network promises 20 hours of color programming a week within two months. TV set manufacturers are divided, however, over whether to make sets, since the CBS system is incompatible with black-and-white broadcasts. In the meantime, RCA continues work on its color system.

1951
Witness Frank Costello's hands provide TV's picture of the week as he refuses to expose his face to cameras covering New York hearings on organized crime of the Senate Crime Investigation Committee, chaired by Senator Estes Kefauver (D-Tenn.)

Sixteen advertisers sponsor the first commercial color telecast, an hour-long program on a five-station East Coast CBS TV hook-up.

Bing Crosby Enterprises announces the development of a system for recording video and audio programs on magnetic tape. The pictures shown at demonstrations are described as "hazy" but "viewable." A year later the images are described as improved "more than 20-fold."

1952
By rushing equipment across the country, from Bridgeport, Connecticut, to Portland, Oregon, KPTV(TV) Portland goes on the air as the first commercial UHF TV station.

1953
With the end of daylight-saving time, CBS TV and NBC TV inaugurate "hot kinescope" systems to put programs on the air on the West Coast at the same clock hour as in the East.

RCA demonstrates black-and-white and color TV programs recorded on magnetic tape. RCA-NBC Board Chairman David Sarnoff says two years of finishing touches are needed before the system is ready for market.

The FCC approves RCA's compatible (with black-and-white transmission) color TV standards. System supplants the incompatible CBS system.

1954
CBS President Frank Stanton broadcasts the first network editorial, urging that radio and TV be allowed to cover congressional hearings.

1955
A contract between the DuMont TV network and Jackie Gleason Enterprises calls for Gleason's The Honeymooners to be done as a filmed program for CBS TV on Saturday nights.

1956
Ampex Corp. unveils the first practical videotape recorder at the National Association of Radio and Television Broadcasters convention in Chicago. The company takes in $4 million in orders.

1957
Videotape recorders are seen as the solution to the TV networks' daylight-saving time problems.

1958
Subliminal TV messages are put under the spotlight at hearings in Los Angeles and Washington.

The BBDO ad agency converts live commercials to videotape.

1959
Sixty-eight TV stations defy the broadcasters' code of conduct by refusing to drop Preparation H commercials.

The quiz show scandal climaxes when famed Twenty-One prizewinner Charles Van Doren admits to a House committee that he had been provided with answers and strategies in advance. The sad ending to the quiz show era prompts cancellation of big-prize shows and vows by NBC and CBS to end deceptive practices.

1960
A satellite sends weather reports back from a 400-mile-high orbit.

RKO-Zenith plans a $10 million test of an on-air pay TV system in Hartford, Connecticut.

Sam Goldwyn offers a package of movies to television.

The last daytime serial on network radio ends.

The opening Kennedy-Nixon debate attracts the largest TV audience to date.

1961
FCC Chairman Newton Minnow shakes up the National Association of Broadcasters convention with his assessment of TV programming: Although it occasionally shines with programs like Twilight Zone and CBS Reports, it is, more than anything, from sign-on to sign-off "a vast wasteland."

Off-network shows become popular as syndicated fare.

The Ampex "electronic editor" permits inserts and additions to be made in videotape without physical splices.

ABC TV engineers develop a process for the immediate playback of videotape recordings in slow motion.

1962
John Glenn's orbital space flight is seen by 135 million TV viewers.

Telstar, AT&T's orbiting satellite, provides a glamorous debut for global television.

1963
Astronaut Gordon Cooper sends back the first TV pictures from space.

All radio and TV network commercials and entertainment programming are canceled following the assassination of President Kennedy. In the same week, the first trans-Pacific broadcast via satellite previews live TV coverage of the 1964 Olympics in Tokyo.

1964
The government and the tobacco companies each ponder their next move after the surgeon general's report links cigarette smoking and lung cancer. Within weeks, American Tobacco drops sports broadcasts, radio stations begin to ban cigarette ads and CBS TV orders a de-emphasis of cigarette use on programs.

1965
Early Bird, the first commercial communications satellite, goes into stationary orbit, opening trans-Atlantic circuits for TV use.

1966
Fred W. Friendly quits as president of CBS News when his new boss, John Schneider, CBS group vice president for broadcasting, cancels coverage of a Senate hearing on the Vietnam War and runs a rerun of I Love Lucy instead.

Network TV viewers see live close-up pictures of the moon—sent back by Surveyor I—as they come into the Jet Propulsion Laboratory.

1967
ABC Radio introduces a radical plan: four networks instead of one, each tailored to suit different station formats.

President Johnson signs the Public Broadcasting Act into law, establishing the Corporation for Public Broadcasting, federal funding mechanism.

1968
The Children's Television Workshop is created by the Ford Foundation, the Carnegie Corp., and the Office of Education to develop a 26-week series of hour-long color programs for preschool children. Sesame Street is the result.

The U.S. Supreme Court gives the FCC jurisdiction over all cable TV systems.

Pictures taken inside Apollo 7 in flight and sent back to Earth revive public interest in the space program.

NBC TV earns the life-long ire of sports fans when it cuts off the end of a Jets-Raiders game to air its made-for-TV movie Heidi. Viewers miss the Raiders' two-touch-downs-in-nine-seconds defeat of the Jets.

1969
The Corporation for Public Broadcasting plans the creation of the Public Broadcasting Service to distribute programming to noncommercial TV stations.

In the same week that ABC-TV announces its $8 million Monday Night Football deal (games to begin in 1970), Apollo 10 sends back the first color TV pictures of the moon and of Earth from the moon.

The world watches live coverage of Neil Armstrong's walk on the moon.

1970
House and Senate conferees agree on legislation to outlaw cigarette advertising on radio and TV, but change the bill's effective date from January 1, 1971, to January 2, so commercials can appear on New Year's Day football telecasts.

The FCC rules that TV stations in the top 50 markets cannot accept more than three hours of network programming between 7 and 11 p.m., and bars them from domestic syndication and from acquiring subsidiary rights in independently produced programs.

1971
National Public Radio debuts with a 90-station interconnected lineup.

1972
Judge Benjamin Hooks of Memphis, Tennessee, is nominated to the FCC. He becomes the first black to serve on a federal regulatory agency.

Home Box Office Inc., New York, is formed as a subsidiary of Sterling Communications to provide pay-cable TV systems with live and film programming.

1973
Western Union becomes the first company to receive federal permission to launch a commercial communications satellite in the U.S.

Broadcast media around the world open their coverage of the Senate select committee's investigation of the Watergate scandal.

1974
RCA inaugurates the nation's first domestic satellite communications service, using a Canadian satellite.

More than 110 million viewers watch President Nixon announce his resignation.

1975
Home Box Office, Time Inc.'s pay cable subsidiary, announces that it will inaugurate a satellite delivery network in the fall.

1976
Ampex Corp. and CBS develop the electronic still-store system, which uses a digital recording technique to store 1,500 frames in random mode, each accessible in 100 milliseconds.

Cable network launches include Showtime and Univision.

1977
ABC's eight-day telecast of the miniseries Roots becomes the most watched program in television history, with ratings in the mid-40s and shares in the mid-60s. Eighty million people watch at least some part of the final episode.

Sony unveils its Betamax videocassette in August and later the same month RCA introduces its SelectaVision home videotape recorder.

1978
The U.S. Supreme Court upholds the FCC in the "seven dirty words" case involving Pacifica's WBAI(FM) New York. The ruling says the FCC may regulate and punish for the broadcasting of "indecent material."

1979
Ampex demonstrates its digital videotape recorder at the Society of Motion Picture and Television Engineers conference in San Francisco in February. Sony unveils its version two months later.

Cable network launches include C-SPAN, ESPN, The Movie Channel, and Nickelodeon.

1980
"Who Shot J.R.?" episode of Dallas garners the highest rating for any program in modern TV history, with a 53.3 rating and a 76 share.

Cable network launches include Cable News Network, Black Entertainment Television, the Learning Channel, Bravo, and USA Network.

1981
With five ENG cameras rolling, the shooting of President Reagan becomes history's most heavily covered assassination attempt.

The first U.S. demonstration of high-definition television (HDTV) takes place at the annual convention of the Society of Motion Picture and Television Engineers. The Japanese Broadcasting Corp.'s (NHK) 1,125-line analog system draws raves from engineers and filmmakers.

Cable network launches include MTV: Music Television and the Eternal Word Television Network.

1982
Having reached a settlement with the Justice Department to divest itself of its 23 local telephone companies, communications giant AT&T hopes to lead the country into the "information age." The National Cable Television Association, Congress, and the FCC wonder what the agreement has wrought.

Cable network launches include the Weather Channel and the Playboy Channel.

1983
Reagan appointee Mark Fowler, chairman of the FCC, tells a common carrier conference that the U.S. is heading toward a regulation-free telecommunications marketplace.

In February, the two-and-a-half-hour final episode of CBS's M*A*S*H is the most watched program in TV history, garnering a 60.3 rating and a 77 share.

Cable network launches include the Disney Channel and Country Music Television.

1984
The U.S. Supreme Court rules that home videotaping is legal.

Congress passes the Cable Telecommunications Act of 1984, landmark legislation deregulating cable. Law accelerates the growth of cable.

Cable network launches include the Arts & Entertainment Network (A&E), American Movie Classics, and Lifetime.

1985
Ted Turner makes inquiries at the FCC about a possible takeover of CBS. Later, in March, media company Capital Cities Communications purchases ABC for $3.5 billion. Turner's efforts to acquire CBS fail by the end of July, when a federal judge approves the network's stock buyback plan.

The Advanced Television Services Committee (ATSC) votes in favor of the NHK HDTV standard: 1,125 lines, 60 fields, 2:1 interlace, 5.33:3 ratio. This standard is put forward by the U.S. to the International Radio Consultative Committee (CCIR) for consideration as the international standard. The CCIR adopts the recommendation later in the year.

Having lost his bid to buy CBS, Ted Turner makes a $1.5 billion offer for MGM/UA.

Cable network launches include The Discovery Channel, Home Shopping Network, and VH-1.

1986
MGM and Color Systems Technology sign an agreement for the conversion of 100 of the studio's black-and-white films to color.

Cable network launches include C-SPAN2 and QVC.

1987
Fox Broadcasting Co. introduces its primetime lineup with 108 affiliates in its bid to become the fourth major U.S. commercial television network.

The National Association of Broadcasters and the Association for Maximum Service Television broadcast HDTV over standard TV channels during public demonstrations in Washington.

President Reagan vetoes legislation to write the fairness doctrine into law. The doctrine required broadcast stations to allow opposing views of issues, but critics claimed that it discouraged open debate.

Cable network launches include Movietime (renamed E! Entertainment Television in 1990), The Travel Channel, and Telemundo.

1988
The FCC adopts preliminary ground rules for HDTV. It tentatively decides to require HDTV broadcasts to be compatible with NTSC sets and says it will not make additional spectrum available outside the VHF and UHF bands for HDTV because there is enough already available to accommodate the service.

Cable network launches include Turner Network Television.

Max Robinson, first African American broadcast news anchor, dies.

1989
Time Inc. and Warner Communications agree to swap stock and merge into what will be world's largest media and entertainment company.

1990
Digital audio broadcasting is demonstrated at the National Association of Broadcasters convention and is heralded as the HDTV of radio.

General Instrument revolutionizes the development of high-definition television by proposing an all-digital system. The video compression system also has implications for satellite transmissions.

Cable network launches include CNBC and The Inspiration Network (INSP).

1991
The U.S. air attack on Iraq begins January 16 with dramatic live coverage from network reporters in Baghdad. CNN is the lone network to maintain contact with its Baghdad reporters through the night.

Free to move around Moscow and ready to commit resources to coverage, television and radio provide gripping details of the short-lived Soviet coup and the collapse of communism in the Soviet Union. During his detention in the Crimea, Soviet President Mikhail Gorbachev keeps track of events by listening to the BBC, Voice of America, and Radio Liberty.

Cable network launches include Court TV, Comedy Central, and Encore.

1992

In March, the Supreme Court let stand an appeals court ruling that struck down the FCC's around-the-clock ban on broadcast indecency as unconstitutional and requiring the commission to establish a safe harbor—a part of the day when few children are tuning in and during which radio and TV stations may broadcast without fear of FCC sanctions for indecency.

General Instrument and MIT show the first over-the-air digital HDTV transmission to Washington lawmakers and regulators. The 12-minute transmission of 1,050-line video was broadcast by noncommercial WETA-TV Washington.

The FCC raises the limit on radio stations a single company may own from 12 AM and 12 FM to 30 of each, then backpedals and lowers the caps to 18 each, with no more than two AMs and two FMs in large markets and three stations—only two in the same service—in small markets.

Fox expands its programming lineup to seven nights a week, ending its status as a "weblet" and becoming the fourth full-fledged commercial TV network in the U.S.

The FCC unanimously approves allowing broadcast TV networks to purchase cable systems that serve no more than 10 percent of U.S. homes and up to 50 percent of a particular market's homes.

The FCC tells TV broadcasters they will have five years to begin broadcasting in HDTV once the agency adopts a standard and makes channels available.

Cable network launches include The Cartoon Network and the Sci Fi Channel.

1993

Warner Bros. announces it will launch a fifth broadcast TV network in 1994.

The FCC expands the AM band's upper limit from 1605 kHz to 1705 kHz.

General Instrument, Zenith, AT&T, and the ATRC join forces as the "Grand Alliance" to develop a single HDTV system. Later in the year, the Grand Alliance announces its support of the emerging MPEG-2 digital compression HD system: six-channel, CD-quality Dolby AC-3 music system; 1,920-pixel by 1,080-line interlaced scanning picture; and progressive scanning.

Paramount Communications begins talks with TV stations about forming a fifth broadcast TV network.

Southwestern Bell and Cox Cable form a $4.9-billion partnership.

Cable network launches include ESPN2 and the Television Food Network.

1994

Two companies, Hubbard's United States Satellite Broadcasting and Hughes's DirecTV, begin direct broadcast satellite transmissions to 18-inch home dish antennas from a shared satellite.

Paramount and Viacom merge in a deal worth $9.2 billion, forming the world's most powerful entertainment company. Viacom's Sumner Redstone becomes the new company's chairman. Later in the year, Viacom adds Blockbuster Entertainment to its portfolio.

Cable network launches include FX, Home & Garden TV, the International Film Channel, Starz!, Trio, the Game Show Network, and Turner Classic Movies.

1995

Seagram pays $7 billion for the 80 percent of Hollywood studio MCA Inc. owned by Matsushita Electric Industrial Co. Seagram is controlled by the Bronfman family and is headed by President/CEO Edgar Bronfman Jr.

The Megamedia Age begins when, in the same week, Walt Disney Co. announces it is buying Capital Cities/ABC for $18.5 billion and then Westinghouse Electric Co. releases word of its purchase of CBS Inc. for $5.4 billion.

Time Warner and Turner Broadcasting System agree to merge in an $8 billion stock swap deal.

Live television coverage of the verdict in the O.J. Simpson murder trial sets viewing records when 150 million people watch the jury return a "not guilty" verdict.

Microsoft buys 50 percent stake in NBC's cable channel America's Talking for $250 million. AT's talk format will be dropped and the network will become a news operation after being rechristened MSNBC.

The FCC repeals its Prime Time Access and Fin-Syn rules. These rules restricted the major broadcast networks from owning interest in their own primetime programming.

Cable network launches include CNN/fn, The Golf Channel, Great American Country, the History Channel, and the Outdoor Life Network.

1996

Congress passes—and President Clinton signs—the Telecommunications Act of 1996, the first major overhaul of telecommunication legislation since 1934. Its key provisions include: replacing the 12-station TV ownership limit with a national home coverage cap of 35 percent; eliminating the national ownership limits on radio stations and allowing one company to own different numbers of stations locally, depending on the market size; requiring TV sets sold in the U.S. to be equipped with a V-chip to enable blocking of channels based on encoded ratings; deregulating cable rates.

Westinghouse/CBS buys Infinity Broadcasting for $4.9 billion, creating the country's largest radio station group in terms of earnings. The deal results in Westinghouse/CBS owning 83 radio stations in 15 markets.

The FCC releases its first list of proposed digital TV channel assignments for all U.S. analog television stations.

In July, WRAL-HD Raleigh, North Carolina, begins HDTV transmission on channel 32 under an experimental FCC license, making it the first HDTV station to broadcast in the U.S.

The Washington-based Model HDTV Station Project demonstrates live, over-the-air digital TV transmission and reception. A few months later, it bounces digital signals off a satellite and displays them on a receiver.

Cable network launches include Animal Planet, Fox News Channel, MSNBC, the Sundance Channel, and TVLand.

1997

After several starts and stops, the TV industry unveils content-based V-chip ratings to mixed reviews. Recalcitrant NBC maintains it will not implement the new ratings.

Paxson Communications chief Bud Paxson announces plans to launch a new television network, Pax Net, using his 73 owned UHF stations as a base and airing family friendly off-network programming.

ABC Television Network President Preston Padden and Sinclair Broadcasting President David Smith say broadcasters ought to consider using DTV channels for broadcasting multiple channels of conventional TV rather than a single channel of HDTV.

Hearst Corp. (8 TVs) and Argyle Television (6 TVs) join their TV stations and create a new company, Hearst-Argyle Television Inc., that is valued at $1.8 billion.

The FCC gives TV broadcasters a second channel for the delivery of HDTV and other digital services and said that all network affiliates in the top 10 markets have 24 months to start broadcasting a digital signal; those in markets 11-30 have 30 months; all other commercial stations have five years. Noncommercial broadcasters have six.

DTV service provider EchoStar plans to launch two satellites that will give it the ability to provide local broadcast TV signals to about 43 percent of the U.S.

Cable network launches include WE.

1998

The National Association of Broadcasters agrees to support plans by satellite TV providers to retransmit local TV station signals into their markets as long as the satellite services carry all a market's signals.

At 2:17 p.m. on February 27, WFAA-TV Dallas broadcast what it claims is the first non-experimental HDTV signal (in 1080i, 16:9 format). The broadcast began with a half-hour of taped HD programming, followed by a live simulcast of the station's NTSC programming that was upconverted to HDTV. The next month, Sinclair Broadcasting becomes the first TV group owner to broadcast multiple digital channels.

AT&T pays $50 billion for cable system giant Tele-Communications Inc.

Paxson Communications launches its broadcast television network, now called Pax TV, with a lineup of 90 stations covering about 75 percent of U.S. TV homes.

Radio group owner Clear Channel Communications purchases competitor Jacor Communications for $4.4 billion. The deal gives Clear Channel 453 stations in 101 markets. The year's other big deals include: Chancellor Media's purchase of Capstar Broadcasting for $3.9 billion; Hearst-Argyle Television's purchase of Pulitzer Broadcasting for $1.85 billion; Chancellor's purchase of LIN Television for $1.5 billion; and Sinclair Broadcast Group's purchase of Sullivan Broadcasting for $1 billion.

CBS is the first broadcast TV network to air a live HDTV sports event with its Nov. 8 telecast of the New York Jets-Buffalo Bills NFL game. It is carried by CBS stations in New York; Philadelphia; Washington; Cincinnati; Charlotte, North Carolina; Raleigh, North Carolina; and Columbus, Ohio.

Hughes Electronics Corp., parent of DBS provider DirecTV, announces deal to buy rival U.S. Satellite Broadcasting from Hubbard Broadcasting for $1.3 billion. The DBS business now has three providers: DirecTV, EchoStar, and Primestar.

Cable network launches include BBC America, the Biography Channel, Cinemax, Tech TV, and Toon Disney.

1999
Hughes Electronics Corp., parent of DBS provider DirecTV, buys rival Primestar for $1.1 billion plus stock. The DBS business now has two providers: DirecTV and EchoStar.

Paxson Broadcasting sells its 30 percent interest in The Travel Channel to the cable channel's 70 percent owner, Discovery Channel.

MSO Comcast offers $58 billion for MediaOne Group's cable systems. AT&T then comes in with a $69 billion offer that has AT&T swapping and selling Comcast systems with 2 million subscribers for roughly $9 billion. In return, Comcast agrees to withdraw its $58 billion offer.

CBS pays $2.5 billion for syndication giant King World Productions, whose properties include the hit shows Oprah, Wheel of Fortune, and Jeopardy!

FCC votes to allow a broadcaster to own two TV stations in a market under certain conditions and liberalizes its radio/TV cross-ownership restrictions. A flood of station deals follow.

Viacom Inc. buys CBS Corp. for $36 billion, merging Viacom's Paramount Station Group, UPN network, cable networks, and other properties, with those of CBS.

Clear Channel Communications pays $23.5 billion in stock and assumption of debt for the 443 radio stations of AMFM Inc., the country's largest radio broadcaster. Clear Channel will have to divest about 100 stations to comply with FCC and Justice Department regulations. Those spinoffs will bring Clear Channel $4.3 billion.

Legislation takes affect allowing satellite delivery of local television stations in their markets, increasing DBS providers' ability to compete with cable.

Digital recorders are introduced, allowing a viewer to watch one TV show while taping another.

2000
America Online Inc. and Time Warner merge in a deal worth $181 billion. The merged company, AOL Time Warner, combines the company that serves the largest number of Internet users with the largest producer of TV shows and movies and cable programming, plus cable systems passing 20 percent of U.S. homes.

Tribune Co. buys Times Mirror Co. for $6.5 billion, acquiring seven daily newspapers and various magazines. The deal will give Tribune co-ownership of TV stations and major daily newspapers in the top three markets and the assets to sell packages of multimedia advertising to clients on national, regional, and local levels.

Harry Pappas, head of Pappas Television, the country's largest privately held TV station group, announces plans to launch Azteca America, the third U.S. Hispanic television network (Univision and Telemundo are the others) in 2001.

Cable network launches include Oxygen.

2001
FCC approves the $5.4-billion sale of Chris-Craft Broadcasting's ten TV stations to Fox Television.

DBS operator EchoStar Communications engineers a $26-billion bid for competitor DirecTV, owned by GM's Hughes Corp. The move follows attempts by Rupert Murdoch's News Corp. to acquire DirecTV. But regulatory reviews keep the deal in limbo.

XM Satellite Radio begins broadcasting a nationwide radio service of 200 channels from two satellites—"Rock" and "Roll"—in orbit above the equator. The Washington-based company charges subscribers $9.95 a month for the service. A rival, New York-based Sirius Satellite Radio, plans to launch a similar service later in the year.

The September 11 terrorist attacks on New York and Washington result in around-the-clock news coverage, dropping commercials. It's estimated that the networks lost $200 million-$300 million in the first four days of coverage. Four FM and nine New York TV stations whose antennas were on top of the World Trade Center are knocked off the air and several stations lost employees who had been manning the transmitters in Tower 1. Across the country, broadcasters raised money and arranged blood drives. The fall TV season is delayed, late-night talk/comedy shows are put on hiatus, the Emmy Awards are postponed, and several industry gatherings are canceled.

NBC buys Telemundo, the No. 2 U.S. Spanish-language TV network, for $2.7 billion.

Comcast negotiates $72 billion merger with rival cable operator AT&T Broadband, topping bids by AOL Time Warner and Cox Communications.

Cable network launches include ABC Family, Hallmark Channel, and National Geographic Television.

2002
Sirius Satellite Radio launches its satellite-delivered subscription radio service in four markets in February, then rolls out nationally in July. Sirius follows XM Satellite Radio to become the second U.S. satellite radio programmer.

Prompted by lawsuits from Fox, Viacom, NBC, and Time Warner, a three-judge panel of the federal appeals court in Washington refuses to uphold an FCC rule limiting a TV station group owner's audience reach to 35 percent of U.S. TV households and strikes down a rule barring a cable system from owning TV stations in its market. The court orders the FCC to rewrite or justify the ownership limit rule.

Tom Brokaw of NBC News announces he will step down as evening news anchor after the 2004 presidential election, to be succeeded by NBC's Brian Williams. Brokaw will then focus on in-depth reporting projects.

The Securities and Exchange Commission begins a formal investigation into the accounting practices of cable MSO Adelphia Communications. Five of Adelphia's top executives—including founder John Rigas and his two sons, Michael and Tim—are arrested on fraud charges, alleging that the family used the company as a "personal piggy bank," financing various personal transactions, including $3.1 billion in loans for stock and family businesses.

The FCC mandates that all TV sets must be equipped with digital tuners by 2007 and proposes strong copy-protection measures intended to prevent widespread copying and streaming of content over the Internet.

Lifestyle mogul Martha Stewart, whose media empire included TV, magazines, and books, is investigated by the Justice Department for allegedly lying to federal authorities looking into insider trading involving Stewart's sale of ImClone Systems stock the day before it became public that the Food and Drug Administration had denied the company's application to market a new cancer drug.

In October, both the FCC and the Department of Justice reject DBS operator EchoStar Communications' proposed $26-billion purchase of competitor DirecTV, and a revised agreement fails to sway either agency. In December, EchoStar withdrew its merger request from the FCC. Rupert Murdoch's News Corp., whose previous bid for DirecTV had been rebuffed, puts together a new deal.

2003
Rupert Murdoch's News Corp. receives FCC and Justice Department approval of its deal to acquire 34 percent of DBS operator DirecTV's parent company Hughes Electronics for $6.6 billion in cash and stock.

New York City's Metropolitan Television Alliance agrees to place a new broadcast tower for New York-area television stations on top of the Freedom Tower, a 1,776-foot office tower that will be built on the site of the World Trade Center, where the stations' towers were located prior to 9/11. The MTVA comprises all the city's major TV broadcasters. After the terrorist attacks, most of the stations operated from backup facilities atop the Empire State Building. Ground is expected to be broken on the Freedom Tower in the summer of 2004, and broadcasters should begin operating from the tower by 2008.

The FCC releases new media ownership rules in response to a federal appeals court ruling in 2002. Among the changes: raising the national coverage cap for TV groups from 35 percent to 45 percent; allowing ownership of two TV stations (duopoly) in markets with five or more commercial stations; allowing ownership of three TV stations (triopoly) in markets with at least 18 stations; newspaper-TV cross-ownership is permitted in markets with at least four TV stations; radio-TV cross-ownership now include newspapers in the formula—owners in markets with nine or more TV stations face no cross-ownership restrictions per se but are limited by individual radio and TV limits applicable to specific markets. TV-duopoly owners would not be permitted to own newspapers in markets with fewer than nine TV stations. In markets with three or fewer TV stations, no cross-ownership of TV, radio, or newspapers is permitted. In markets with four to eight TV stations, an owner may form one of the following combos: (1) A daily newspaper, one TV station, up to one-half the number of radio stations permitted to one owner in that market.

(2) A daily newspaper, the total number of radio stations permitted to one owner there, no TV stations.

(3) Two TV stations and the total number of radio stations permitted there.

Congress quickly reacts with legislation introduced by Rep. John Dingell (D-Mich.), which would restore the 35 percent cap. Other critics of the new rules challenge them in federal court.

Liberty Media pays $7.9 billion for Comcast's 56 percent stake in home shopping giant QVC. With 2002 sales of $4.4 billion, QVC is not just the largest shopping network, it's the second-largest television network of any kind.

A panel of federal appeals court judges in Philadelphia agrees with public advocacy groups and imposes a stay of the FCC's new broadcast-ownership rules scheduled to take effect on September 4. The stay will remain in effect until lawsuits to overturn the new rules are settled. The Philadelphia court then decides to retain the case attacking the new FCC broadcast-ownership limits rather than granting broadcast networks' pleas to transfer it to a court in Washington.

The Bush White House brokered a surprise compromise over media deregulation by agreeing to permanently set the national TV station ownership cap at 39 percent of U.S. television households. That percentage allows Fox and Viacom to retain all their stations. Wielding a threat to veto a catch-all spending bill over a provision that would roll the limit back to 35 percent, aides to President Bush persuaded Senate Appropriations Committee Chairman Ted Stevens (R-Alaska) to back down from the tighter limit. Stevens's action came less than a week after he had persuaded reluctant House leadership to go along with the old level. The compromise splits the difference between the 45 percent limit set by the FCC in June and the previous 35 percent level that rank-and-file lawmakers on both sides of Capitol Hill had been pushing to reinstate. The agreement is part of a spending bill that funds the FCC and many other agencies in fiscal 2004.

After a 36-year run, the California Cable Telecommunications Association's annual Western Cable Show makes its curtain call in December, citing consolidation in the cable industry and economic pressure.

Cable network launches include Spike TV.

2004
NBC gets Federal Trade Commission approval for its $14 billion purchase of Vivendi Universal Entertainment, its last regulatory hurdle. The FCC was not required to review the deal because it involved no station licenses. Among other things, NBC acquires USA Network and the Sci Fi Network. The new entity will be called NBC Universal.

Congress and the FCC react swiftly to the "wardrobe malfunction" that bared Janet Jackson's breast during the MTV-produced half-time entertainment in CBS TV's Super Bowl broadcast. Congress passes legislation that dramatically increases the limits on FCC fines for indecency violations.

Congress and the FCC take the first steps toward punishing stations that air "excessively" violent shows. Under orders from leaders of the House Commerce Committee, FCC Chairman Michael Powell by the end of the year will start investigating whether the commission should restrict onscreen violence. Cable can't count on immunity either. Growing ranks of lawmakers say cable must do more to make sure that children aren't exposed to potentially traumatizing content.

A panel of federal appeals court judges in Philadelphia concludes that the FCC wasn't justified in its June 2003 decision relaxing ownership restrictions in the newspaper, television, and radio industries. The rules, which were blocked from taking effect in September 2003, have been sent back to the FCC for a rewrite. A frustrated FCC Chairman Michael Powell criticized the decision, claiming that it created a "clouded and confused state of media law" and makes it nearly impossible for his agency to design standards for ownership limits.

Cable network launches include TV One.

2005
George W. Bush, on January 20, becomes the first president to have his inauguration covered in HDTV. ABC News deploys 36 HD cameras and four HD production vehicles throughout the parade route to give viewers an unparalleled view of American history.

President Bush chooses FCC commissioner Kevin Martin to be chairman of the agency.

In a King Solomon-like answer to critics that Viacom has become too big to grow, Chairman Sumner Redstone proposes cleaving it in half. The resulting companies would be Viacom and CBS Corp.

Longtime ABC World News Tonight anchor Peter Jennings, 67, died August 7 at his home in Manhattan, four months after being diagnosed with lung cancer.

Following Hurricane Katrina, local TV broadcasters and cable operators in the Gulf Coast area say rebuilding their stations and plants could take several months.

The Disney-ABC Television Group announces that three ABC shows, Desperate Housewives, Lost, and Night Stalker will be available for purchase from the Apple iTunes store for $1.99 an episode. The announcement prompts the other big media companies to begin "repurposing" primetime programming on the Internet. It's soon clear that the Web is the next big TV medium.

2006
In January, PBS dips into the ranks of its member stations and selects Paula Kerger of WNET New York to succeed Pat Mitchell as president of the noncommercial "network."

After battling to be the broadcasting fifth network for 11 years and mostly lackluster years, WB and UPN stun the broadcasting industry in January by deciding to merger into The CW. To fill the vacuum created by the loss of one network, Fox creates My Network Television, a mini network built around telenovelas, a popular Spanish TV format. Both CW and MNT debut in September.

Two years after the Janet Jackson "wardrobe malfunction" at the Super Bowl, broadcasters are still feeling the fallout. In March, the FCC issues another round of fines topped by $3.6 million against CBS affiliates for airing an episode of Without a Trace. A few months later, Congress increases ten-fold the base indecency fine to $325,000 per incident.

Ending a year of speculation, CBS announces in March the hiring of Katie Couric, the popular co-host of NBC's Today Show, to anchor the CBS Evening News. With new set and features, she begins her reign as anchor on September 5, becoming the first solo female news anchor. Longtime anchor Dan Rather resigned from the job in March 2005 after botching a 60 Minutes story critical of President Bush's military record. CBS News's Washington Bureau Chief Bob Schieffer anchored the news during the Rather-Couric interregnum.

2007
On January 29 ION Media Networks Inc. changed the name of its TV network from "I" to ION Television.

In 2007 The Sopranos ended an eight-year run on HBO. There was much speculation about the final moments of the finale when the show faded to black.

After years of acquiring stations, on April 20 Clear Channel Communications Inc. entered into an agreement to sell its Television Group. And, as of June 30, the company had entered into definitive agreements to sell 389 radio stations in 77 markets.

2008
On July 25 the FCC approved the merger of Sirius Satellite Radio Inc. and XM Satellite Holdings Inc. On July 29 the two companies announced they had completed their merger, and that the new company would change its name to Sirius XM Radio Inc.

The FCC announced that Wilmington, NC, would be the first market to test the transition to digital television before the nationwide transition to DTV on February 17, 2009. The commercial broadcasters serving the Wilmington market agreed to turn off their analog signals at noon on September 8, 2008. Beginning at noon on September 8 WWAY (ABC), WECT (NBC), WSFX-TV (Fox), WILM-LP (CBS) and W51CW (Trinity Broadcasting) planned to broadcast only digital signals to their viewers in the five North Carolina counties that comprise the Wilmington, NC, market.

Election night viewership sets a ratings record as 71.5 million watch Barack Obama become the nation's first African American president.

2009
The nationwide transition from analog to digital television, scheduled for February 17, 2009, was delayed until June 12, 2009 to allow more time to get ready for the digital transition. The National Telecommunications and Information Administration (NTIA) provided consumers with a TV converter box coupon program to help the consumers make the switch to digital TV. Both the FCC and TV stations across the U.S. made a mighty effort to inform consumers about, and make, the switch. Some TV stations made the switch to digital television early. Notably Hawaii's full-power stations made the switch to digital TV on January 15, 2009. Finally on June 12, 2009 full-power TV stations all over the U.S. became all-digital, when the FCC reported 971 full-power TV stations made the switch.

Later in June 2009 the FCC adopted an order allowing AM radio stations to use FB radio translators to increase their reach within a local community. The FCC action gave AM stations an opportunity to overcome technical problems in their coverage areas.

Walter Cronkite, anchor and managing editor of the CBS Evening News from 1962 to 1981, died on July 17, 2009. A memorial service was held on September 9 at Lincoln Center in New York.

2010
Apple, Inc. introduces the iPad, the first mobile computer tablet to achieve worldwide commercial success. Many manufacturers followed with their own tablet.

After 25 years on the air, Larry King announces his departure from his nightly CNN talk show "Larry King Live."

2011
"The Oprah Winfrey Show" ends after 25 seasons, and Oprah Winfrey launches OWN—Oprah Winfrey Network.

Satellite TV provider DISH Network acquires Blockbuster LLC.

Axel Technologies releases Fuugo Video 1.0, which aggregates online video content from multiple sources into a single application, and Fuugo TV, a broadcast digital TV application for computer tablets, smart phones, and other portable devices.

Steve Jobs, influential head of Apple, Inc., dies.

2012
Satellite TV provider DISH Network announces its remote access application, which provides the capability of streaming on-demand movies and TV shows to the iPad.

The FCC and the Rules of Broadcasting

The following is the FCC's own overview of the laws and regulations that govern TV and radio stations. It is edited and printed here with the permission of the FCC. The agency invites those with questions about its rules and how it operates to visit its web site (www.fcc.gov) or to call 1-888-CALLFCC (1-888-225-5322).

THE FCC AND ITS REGULATORY AUTHORITY

The Communications Act

The FCC was created by Congress in the Communications Act of 1934 for the purpose, in part, of "regulating interstate and foreign commerce in communication by wire and radio so as to make available, so far as possible, to all the people of the United States a rapid, efficient, Nation-wide, and worldwide wire and radio communications service...." The Communications Act authorizes the FCC to "make such regulations not inconsistent with law as it may deem necessary to prevent interference between stations and to carry out the provisions of [the] Act.

How the FCC Adopts Regulations

Like most other federal agencies, the FCC cannot adopt regulations without first notifying and seeking comment from the public. The agency releases a document called a Notice of Proposed Rulemaking, where it explains the specific regulations being proposed and set a deadline for public comment. After receiving the comments, the FCC has several options: (1) adopt the proposed rules; (2) adopt a modified version of the proposed rules; (3) ask for public comment on additional issues relating to the proposals; or (4) end the rulemaking proceeding without adopting any rules at all. The FCC also establishes broadcast regulatory policies through individual cases that it decides.

The FCC and the Media Bureau

The FCC has five commissioners who are appointed by the President and confirmed by the Senate. Under the commissioners are various operating bureaus, one of which is the Media Bureau. The Media Bureau has day-to-day responsibility for developing, recommending and administering the rules governing radio and television stations. These rules are in Title 47 of the Code of Federal Regulations ("CFR"), Parts 73 and 74. The rules of practice and procedure are in Part 1 of Title 47.

FCC Regulation of Broadcast Radio and Television

The FCC allocates new stations based both on the relative needs of communities for additional broadcast outlets and on engineering standards that prevent interference between stations. Whenever it looks at a broadcast station application—whether to build, modify, renew or sell—it must determine if granting it would serve the public interest. The FCC expects stations to be aware of the important problems or issues in their communities and to foster public understanding by presenting some programs and/or announcements about local issues. However, broadcasters—not the FCC or any other government agency—are responsible for selecting all the material they air. The Communications Act prohibits the FCC from censoring broadcast matter and, therefore, its role in overseeing the content of programming is limited. It is authorized to fine a station or revoke its license if it has, among other things, aired obscene language, broadcast indecent language when children are likely to be in the audience, broadcast some types of lottery information, or solicited money under false pretenses.

THE LICENSING OF TV AND RADIO STATIONS

Commercial and Noncommercial-Educational Stations

The FCC licenses radio and TV stations to be either commercial or noncommercial-educational. Commercial stations generally support themselves by advertising. In contrast, noncommercial-educational stations (including public stations) generally support themselves by contributions from listeners and viewers, and they may also receive government funding. Noncommercial-educational stations may also receive contributions from for-profit entities, and they may acknowledge such contributions or underwriting donations with announcements naming and generally describing the entity. However, noncommercial-educational stations may not broadcast promotional announcements or commercials on behalf of for-profit entities.

Applications to Build New Stations; Length of the License Period

To build a new TV or radio station, a citizen must first apply to the FCC for a construction permit. The applicant must demonstrate that he is qualified to construct and operate as proposed in the application. After the applicant has built the station, he must file a license application, where he certifies that he has constructed the station consistently with the construction permit. The FCC licenses radio and TV stations for a period of up to eight years. Before the FCC renews a station's license, it must first determine whether it has served the public interest. In addition, to have its license renewed, a station must certify that: (1) it has sent us certain specified reports that we require;

(2) its ownership is consistent with Section 310(b) of the Communications Act, which restricts interests held by foreign governments and non-citizens;

(3) there has not been a judgment against it by a court or administrative body under federal, state, or local law; and

(4) it has placed certain specified material in its public inspection file (see below).

Employment Discrimination and Equal Employment Opportunity (EEO)

The FCC requires all radio and TV stations to afford equal opportunity in employment. We also prohibit employment discrimination on the basis of race, color, religion, national origin, or sex.

Public Participation in Licensing Process

Renewal Applications. Citizens can file a formal protest against a station by filing a formal petition to deny its renewal application, or by sending us an informal objection to the application. The citizen must file a petition to deny the application by the end of the first day of the last full calendar month of the expiring license term. (For example, if the license expires on December 31, the petition must be filed by the end of the day on December 1.) Before a citizen files a petition to deny an application, he should check the FCC's rules and policies to make sure that the petition complies with the procedural requirements. Before their licenses expire, stations have to broadcast announcements giving the date the license will expire, the date on which a renewal application must be filed, and the date by which formal petitions against it must be filed. A citizen can file an informal objection at any point until the FCC grant or deny the application.

Other Types of Applications. Citizens may also participate formally in the application process when a station is sold (technically called an assignment of the license), undergoes a major stock transfer (technically called a transfer of control), or proposes major construction. The station owner is required to run a series of advertisements in the closest local newspaper when it files these types of applications. Later, the FCC will also run a Public Notice (all FCC Public Notices are placed on our Internet home page at www.fcc.gov) and open a 30-day period during which you may file petitions to deny these applications. As with renewal applications, you can also file an informal objection at any point until we either grant or deny the application.

BROADCAST PROGRAMMING

The FCC and Freedom of Speech

The First Amendment and federal law generally prohibit us from censoring broadcast material and from interfering with freedom of expression in broadcasting. Individual radio and TV stations are responsible for selecting everything they broadcast and for determining how they can best serve their communities. Stations are responsible for choosing their entertainment programming, as well as their programs concerning local issues, news, public affairs, religion, sports events, and other subjects. They also decide how their programs (including call-in shows) will be conducted and whether to edit or reschedule material for broadcasting. The FCC does not substitute its judgment for that of the station, and it does not advise stations on artistic standards, format, grammar, or the quality of their programming. This also applies to a station's commercials, with the exception of commercials for political candidates during an election (see below).

Access to Station Facilities

Stations are not required to broadcast everything that is offered or suggested to them. Except as required by the Communications Act, stations have no obligation to have any particular person participate in a broadcast or to present that person's remarks. Further, no federal law or rule requires stations to broadcast "public service announcements" of any kind. The FCC generally does not require stations to keep the material they broadcast.

Station Identification

Stations must make identification announcements when they sign on and off for the day. They must also make the announcements hourly, as close to the hour as possible, at a natural programming break. TV stations may make these announcements on-screen or by voice only. Official station identification includes the station's call letters followed by the community or communities specified in its license as the station's location. Between the call letters and its community, the station may insert the name of the licensee, the station's channel number, and/or its frequency. However, we do not allow any other insertion.

Broadcast Journalism

Under the First Amendment and the Communications Act, the FCC cannot tell stations how to select material for news programs, and we cannot prohibit the broadcasting of an opinion on any subject. We also do not review anyone's qualifications to gather, edit, announce, or comment on the news; these decisions are the station's responsibility.

Broadcasts by Candidates for Public Office (Equal Time)

When a qualified candidate for public office has been permitted to use a station, the law requires the station to "afford equal opportunities to all other such candidates for that office." The Act also states that the station "shall have no power of censorship over the material broadcast" by the candidate. The FCC exempts the following: (1) An appearance by a legally qualified candidate on a bona fide newscast, interview or documentary (if the appearance of the candidate is incidental to the presentation of the subject covered by the documentary); or (2) on-the-spot coverage of bona fide news events, including political conventions and related incidental activities.

Children's Television Programming

Throughout its license term, every TV station must serve the educational and informational needs of children both through its overall programming. It must also broadcast programming that is specifically designed to serve those needs. The FCC considers programming to be educational and informational if it furthers the educational and informational needs of children 16 years old and under (this includes their intellectual/cognitive or social/emotional needs). A program is considered to be "specifically designed to serve educational and information needs of children" if (1) that it its principal purpose; (2) it is aired between the hours of 7:00 a.m. and 10:00 p.m.; (3) it is a regularly scheduled weekly program; and (4) it is at least 30 minutes in length. Commercial TV stations must identify programs specifically designed to educate and inform children at the beginning of the program, in a form left to their discretion, and must provide information identifying such programs to publishers of program guides. Additionally, in TV programs aimed at children 12 and under, advertising may not exceed 10.5 minutes an hour on weekends and 12 minutes an hour on weekdays.

Criticism, Ridicule, and Humor Concerning Individuals, Groups, and Institutions

The First Amendment's guarantee of freedom of speech protects programming that stereotypes or otherwise offends people with regard to their religion, race, national background, gender, or other characteristics. It also protects broadcasts that criticize or ridicule established customs and institutions, including the government and its officials.

Clear and Present Danger

The First Amendment protects advocacy of using force or of violating the law. However, the Supreme Court has said that the government may curtail speech if it is both: (1) intended to incite or produce dangerous activity; and (2) likely to succeed in achieving that result. Even where this "clear and present danger" test is met, the FCC believes that any review that might lead to a curtailment of speech should be performed by the appropriate criminal law enforcement authorities, and not by the FCC.

Obscenity and Indecency

Federal law prohibits the broadcasting of obscene programming and regulates the broadcasting of "indecent" language and images. Obscene speech is not protected by the First Amendment and cannot be broadcast at any time. To be obscene, material must have all three of the following characteristics: (1) an average person, applying contemporary community standards, must find that the material, as a whole, appeals to the prurient interest; (2) the material must depict or describe, in a patently offensive way, sexual conduct specifically defined by applicable law; and (3) the material, taken as a whole, must lack serious literary, artistic, political, or scientific value. Indecent speech is protected by the First Amendment and cannot be outlawed. However, the courts have upheld Congress's prohibition of the broadcast of indecent speech during times of the day when there is a reasonable risk that children may be in the audience. The FCC has decided that those times fall between 6:00 a.m. and 10:00 p.m. In other words, stations may only broadcast indecent material between 10 p.m. and 6 a.m. Indecent speech is defined as "language or material that, in context, depicts or describes, in terms patently offensive as measured by contemporary community standards for the broadcast medium, sexual or excretory organs or activities." Profanity that does not fall under one of the above two categories is fully protected by the First Amendment and cannot be regulated.

Violent Programming

Neither the law nor FCC rules regulate violent programming. However, the law requires TV sets with screens 13 inches or larger to be equipped with V-chip technology, which allows parents to program their TV sets to block display of TV programming that carries a certain rating. The rating system, voluntarily created by the television industry, tags programming that contains sexual, violent, or other indecent material programmers believe may be harmful to children.

Station-Conducted Contests

Stations that broadcast or advertise information about a contest that they conduct must fully and accurately disclose the material terms of the contest, and they must conduct the contest substantially as announced or advertised. Contest descriptions may not be false, misleading, or deceptive with respect to any material term. Material terms include the factors that define the operation of the contest and affect participation.

Broadcast Hoaxes

Broadcasting false information concerning a crime or a catastrophe violates the FCC's rules if: (1) the station knew the information was false; (2) broadcasting the false information directly caused substantial public harm; (3) and it was foreseeable that broadcasting the false information would cause substantial public harm. In this context, a "crime" is an act or omission that makes the offender subject to criminal punishment by law, and a "catastrophe" is a disaster or imminent disaster involving violent or sudden events affecting the public. "Public harm" must begin immediately; it must cause direct and actual damage to property or to the health or safety of the general public, or diversion of law enforcement or other public health and safety authorities from their duties.

Lotteries

The law prohibits broadcasting any advertisement for a lottery or any information concerning a lottery. A lottery is any game, contest, or promotion that contains the elements of prize, chance, and "consideration" (a legal term that means an act or promise that is made to induce someone into an agreement). There are a number of exceptions to this prohibition. Some of the exceptions are: (1) lotteries conducted by a state acting under the authority of state law, where the advertisement or information is broadcast by a radio or TV station licensed to a location in that state or in any other state that conducts such a lottery; (2) gaming conducted by an Indian Tribe under the Indian Gaming Regulatory Act; (3) lotteries authorized or not otherwise prohibited by the state in which they are conducted, and which are conducted by a not-for-profit organization or a governmental organization; and (4) lotteries conducted as a promotional activity by commercial organizations that are clearly occasional and ancillary to the primary business of that organization, as long as the lotteries are authorized or not otherwise prohibited by the state in which they are conducted.

Soliciting Funds

No federal law prohibits broadcast requests for funds for legal purposes (including appeals by stations for contributions to meet their operating expenses) if the money or other valuable things contributed are used for the announced purposes. It is up to an individual station to decide whether to permit fund solicitations. Fraud by wire, radio or television is prohibited by federal law and may lead to FCC sanctions, as well as to criminal prosecution by the U.S. Department of Justice.

Broadcasting Telephone Conversations

Before recording a telephone conversation for broadcast, or broadcasting a telephone conversation live, a station must inform any party to the call of its intention to broadcast the conversation. However, this does not apply to conversations whose broadcast can reasonably be presumed (for example, telephone calls to programs where the station customarily broadcasts the calls).

BROADCASTING AND ADVERTISING

Business Practices, Advertising Rates, and Profits

Except with respect to political advertisements, the FCC does not regulate a station's advertising rates or its profits. Rates charged for broadcast time are matters for negotiation between sponsors and stations. Further, except for certain classes of political advertisements, stations are free to accept or reject any advertising.

Sponsorship Identification

Sponsorship identification or disclosure must accompany any material that is broadcast in exchange for money, service, or anything else of value paid to a station, either directly or indirectly. This announcement must clearly say that the time was purchased and by whom. In the case of advertisements for commercial products or services, it is sufficient to announce the sponsor's corporate or trade name, or the name of the sponsor's product when it is clear that the mention of the product constitutes a sponsorship identification.

Underwriting Announcements on Noncommercial-Educational Stations

Noncommercial educational stations may acknowledge contributions over the air, but they may not promote the goods and services of for-profit donors or underwriters. Acceptable "enhanced underwriting" acknowledgements may include (1) logograms and slogans that identify but do not promote; (2) location information; (3) value-neutral descriptions of a product line or service; and (4) brand names, trade names, and product service listings. However, such acknowledgements may not interrupt a noncommercial station's regular programming.

Amount of Advertising

Except with respect to children's television programming, no law or regulation limits the amount of commercial matter that a station may broadcast. In TV programs aimed at children 12 and under, advertising may not exceed 10.5 minutes an hour on weekends and 12 minutes an hour on weekdays.

Loud Commercials

In surveys and technical studies of broadcast advertising, the FCC has found that loudness is a judgment that varies with each listener and is influenced by many factors (such as an announcement's content and style). We have also found no evidence that stations deliberately raise audio and modulation levels to emphasize commercial messages. Broadcast licensees have primary responsibility for the adoption of equipment and procedures to avoid objectionably loud commercials. Citizens should address any complaint about such messages to the station. They should identify each message by the sponsor or product's name and by the date and time of the broadcast.

False or Misleading Advertising

The Federal Trade Commission has primary responsibility for determining whether an advertisement is false or deceptive and for taking action against the sponsor. Also, the Food and Drug Administration has primary responsibility for the safety of food and drug products. Citizens should contact these agencies regarding advertisements that they believe may be false or misleading.

Offensive Advertising

Unless a broadcast advertisement is found to be in violation of a specific law or regulation, the government cannot take action against it. If a citizen thinks that an advertisement is offensive because of the kind of item advertised, the scheduling of the announcement, or the way the message is presented, then he should address his complaint directly to the stations and networks involved. This will help them become better informed about audience opinion.

Tobacco and Alcohol

The law prohibits advertising for cigarettes, little cigars, smokeless tobacco, or chewing tobacco on radio, TV, or any other medium of electronic communication under the FCC's jurisdiction. The law does not ban the advertising of smoking accessories, cigars, pipes, pipe tobacco, or cigarette-making machines. Congress has not enacted any law prohibiting broadcast advertising for any kind of alcoholic beverage. Also, the FCC does not have a rule or policy regulating advertisements for alcoholic beverages. Most broadcasters have voluntarily abstained from advertising hard liquor, although they accept beer and wine advertising.

Subliminal Programming

The FCC sometimes receives complaints regarding the alleged use of subliminal techniques in radio and TV programming. Subliminal programming is designed to be perceived on a subconscious level only. Regardless of whether it is effective, the use of subliminal perception is inconsistent with a station's obligation to serve the public interest because the broadcast is intended to be deceptive. However, it is not specifically prohibited.

INTERFERENCE

Blanketing Interference

Some people who are close to a radio station's transmitting antenna may experience impaired reception of other stations. This is called "blanketing" interference. The FCC requires the station causing the interference to resolve most interference complaints received within the first year of operation at no cost to the person complaining. However, stations are not required to resolve interference complaints based on malfunctioning or mistuned receivers, improperly installed antenna systems, or the use of high gain antennas or antenna booster amplifiers. Mobile receivers and non-radio frequency (RF) devices such as tape recorders or CD players are also excluded. Stations are not financially responsible for resolving interference complaints located outside the blanketing contour.

THE LOCAL PUBLIC INSPECTION FILE

Requirement to Maintain a Public Inspection File

The FCC requires all TV and radio stations and applicants for new stations to maintain a file available for public inspection containing documents relevant to the station's operation. The public inspection file generally must be maintained at the station's main studio. The station must make its public inspection file available at its main studio at any time during regular business hours. A station that chooses to maintain all or part of its public file in a computer database must provide a computer terminal to those who wish to review the file. Stations must keep the following materials in their public inspection file:

The License. Stations must keep a copy of their current FCC license in the public file, together with any material documenting FCC-approved modifications to the license. The license reflects the station's technical parameters (authorized frequency, call letters, operating power, transmitter location, etc.), as well as any special conditions imposed by the FCC on the station's operation. The license also indicates when it was issued and when it will expire.

Applications and Related Materials. The public file must contain copies of all applications that are pending before either the FCC or the courts. These include applications to sell the station or to modify its facilities (for example, to increase power, change the antenna system, or change the transmitter location); copies of any construction or sales application whose grant required the FCC to waive our rules; applications that required the FCC to waive its rules; renewal applications granted for less than a full license term (the FCC grants short-term renewals when it is concerned about the station's performance over the previous term).

Citizen Agreements. Stations must keep a copy of any written agreements they make with local viewers or listeners. These "citizen agreements" deal with programming, employment, or other issues of community concern. The station must keep these agreements in the public file for as long as they are in effect.

Contour Maps. The public file must contain copies of any service contour maps or other information submitted with any application filed with the FCC that reflects the station's service area and/or its main studio and transmitter location. These documents must stay in the file for as long as they remain accurate.

Material Relating to an FCC Investigation or a Complaint. The station must keep this material until the FCC notifies it that the material may be discarded. Since the FCC is not involved in disputes regarding matters unrelated to the Communications Act or our rules, stations do not have to keep material relating to such matters in the public file.

Ownership Reports and Related Material. The public file must contain a copy of the most recent, complete Ownership Report filed for the station. This report has the names of the owners of the station and their ownership interests, lists any contracts related to the station that are required to be filed with the FCC, and identifies any interest held by the station licensee in other broadcast stations.

List of Contracts Filed with the FCC. Stations have to keep either a copy of all the contracts that they have to file with the FCC, or an up-to-date list identifying all such contracts. If the station keeps a list and you ask to see copies of the actual contracts, the station must give them to you within seven days. Such contracts include network affiliation contracts; contracts relating to ownership or control of the licensee or permittee or its stock. Examples include articles of incorporation, bylaws, agreements providing for the assignment of a license or permit or affecting stock ownership or voting rights (stock options, pledges, or proxies), and mortgage or loan agreements that restrict the licensee or permittee's freedom of operation; management consultant agreements with independent contractors, and station management contracts that provide for a percentage of profits or sharing of losses.

Political File. Stations must keep a file containing records of all requests for broadcast time made by or for a candidate for public office. The file must identify how the station responded to such requests and (if the request was granted) the charges made, a schedule of the time purchased, the times the spots actually aired, the rates charged, and the classes of time purchased. The file must also reflect any free time provided to a candidate. The station must keep the political records for two years after the spot airs. You can find the political broadcasting rules elsewhere in this manual.

Letters and E-Mail from the Public. Commercial stations must keep written comments and suggestions received from the public regarding their operation for at least three years. Noncommercial stations are not subject to this requirement.

Issues/Programs List. Every three months, all stations must prepare and place in their file a list of programs that have provided their most significant treatment of community issues during the preceding three months. The list must briefly describe both the issue and the programming where the issue was discussed. The stations must keep these lists for the entire license term.

Children's Television Programming Reports. The Children's Television Act of 1990 and our rules require all TV stations to air programming that serves the educational and informational needs of children 16 and under, including programming that is specifically designed to serve such needs. In addition, commercial TV stations must make and retain Children's Television Programming Reports identifying the educational and informational programming for children aired by the station. (Noncommercial stations are not required to prepare these reports.) The report must include the name of the person at the station responsible for collecting comments on the station's compliance with the law. The station has to prepare these reports each calendar quarter, and it must place them in the public file separately from the file's other material. Stations must keep the reports for the remainder of their license terms. You can also view each station's reports on our web site at http://www.fcc.gov/mb/policy/kidstv.html.

Records Regarding Children's Programming Commercial Limits. The Children's Television Act of 1990 and our rules limit the type and amount of advertising that may be aired in TV programming directed to children 12 and under. On weekends, commercial television stations may air no more than 10.5 minutes of commercials per hour during children's programming, and no more than 12 minutes on weekdays. Stations must keep records that substantiate compliance with these limits.

Radio Time Brokerage Agreements. A time brokerage agreement is a type of contract that generally involves a station's sale of discrete blocks of air time to a broker, who then supplies the programming to fill that time and sells the commercial spot announcements to support the programming. Commercial radio stations must keep a copy of every agreement involving: (1) time brokerage of that station; or (2) time brokerage by any other station owned by the same licensee.

List of Donors. Noncommercial TV and radio stations must keep a list of donors supporting specific programs for two years after the program airs.

Local Public Notice Announcements. When someone files an application to build a new station or to renew, sell, or modify an existing station, the FCC often requires the applicant to make a series of local announcements to inform the public of the application's existence and nature.

Must-Carry or Retransmission Consent Election. There are two ways that a broadcast TV station can choose to be carried on a cable TV system: "must-carry" and "retransmission consent." All TV stations are generally entitled to be carried on cable television systems in their local markets. A station that chooses to exercise this must-carry right receives no compensation from the cable system. Instead of exercising their must-carry rights, TV stations may choose to receive compensation from a cable system in return for granting permission to the cable system to carry the station. This option is available only to commercial TV stations. Every three years, commercial TV stations must decide whether their relationship with each local cable system will be governed by must-carry or by retransmission consent agreements. Each commercial station must keep a copy of its decision in the public file for the three-year period to which it pertains. Noncommercial stations are not entitled to compensation in return for carriage on a cable system, but they may request mandatory carriage on the system. A noncommercial station making this request must keep a copy of the request in the public file for the duration of the period to which it applies.

Glossary of Terms

AM—Amplitude modulation. Also referring to audio service broadcast over 535 khz-1705 khz.

Analog—AA continuous electrical signal that carries information in the form of variable physical values, such as amplitude or frequency modulation.

Basic cable service—Package of programming on cable systems eligible for regulation by local franchising authorities under 1992 Cable Act, including all local broadcast signals and PEG (public, educational and government) access channels.

Cable television—System that transmits original programming, and programming of broadcast television stations, to consumers over wired network.

CC—Closed captioning. Method of transmitting textual information over television channel's vertical blanking interval; transmissions are deciphered with decoders; decoded transmissions appear as text superimposed over television image.

Clear channel—AM radio station allowed to dominate its frequency with up to 50 kw of power; their signals are generally protected for distance of up to 750 miles at night.

Closed circuit—The method of transmission of programs or other material that limits its target audience to a specific group rather than the general public.

Coaxial cable—Cable with several common axis lines under protective sheath used for television signal transmissions.

Common carrier—Telecommunication company that provides communications transmission services to the public.

DAB—Digital audio broadcasting. Modulations for sending digital rather than analog audio signals by either terrestrial or satellite transmitter with audio response up to compact disc quality (20 khz).

DBS—Direct broadcast satellite. High powered satellite authorized to broadcast direct to homes.

Digital—A discontinuous electrical signal that carries information in binary fashion. Data is represented by a specific sequence of off-on electrical pulses.

Directional antenna—An antenna that directs most of its signal strength in a specific direction rather than at equal strength in all directions. Used chiefly in AM radio operation.

Downlink—Earth station used to receive signals from satellites.

Earth station—Equipment used for transmitting or receiving satellite communications.

EDTV—Enhanced-definition television. Proposed intermediate systems for evolution to full HDTV, usually including slightly improved resolution and sound, with a wider (16:9) aspect ratio.

Effective competition—Market status under which cable TV systems are exempt from regulation of basic tier rates by local franchising authorities, as defined in 1992 Cable Act. To claim effective competition, a cable system must compete with at least one other multichannel provider that is available to at least 50\% of an area's households and is subscribed to by more than 15\% of the households.

Encryption—System for scrambling signals to prevent unauthorized reception.

ENG—Electronic news gathering.

ETV—Educational television.

Fiber-optic cable—Wires made of glass fiber used to transmit video, audio, voice or data providing vastly wider bandwidth than standard coaxial cable.

Field—Half of the video information in the frame of a video picture. The NTSC system displays 59.94 fields per second.

FM—Frequency modulation. Also referring to audio service broadcast over 88 mhz-108 mhz.

Footprint—Area on earth within which a satellite's signal can be received.

Frame—A full video picture. The NTSC system displays 29.97 525-line frames per second.

Frequency—The number of cycles a signal is transmitted per second, measured in hertz.

Geostationary orbit—Orbit 22,300 miles above earth's equator where satellites circle earth at same rate earth rotates.

ghz—Gigahertz. One billion hertz (cycles) per second.

HDTV—High-definition television.

Headend—Facility in cable system from which all signals originate. (Local and distant television stations, and satellite programming, are picked up and amplified for retransmission through system.)

Hertz—A measurement of frequency. One cycle per second equals one hertz (hz).

Independent television—Television stations that are not affiliated with networks and that do not use the networks as a primary source of their programming.

Information services—Broad term used to describe full range of audio, video and data transmission services that can be transmitted over the air or by cable.

Interactive—Allowing two-way data flow.

Interlaced scanning—Television transmission technique in which each frame is divided into two fields. NTSC system interleaves odd-numbered lines with even-numbered lines at a transmission rate of 59.94 fields per second.

ITFS—Instructional Television Fixed Service.

khz—Kilohertz. One thousand hertz (cycles) per second.

LED—Light emitting diode. Type of semiconductor that lights up when activated by voltage.

LO—Local origination channel.

MDS—Multipoint distribution service.

mhz—Megahertz. One million hertz (cycles) per second.

Microwave—Frequencies above 1,000 mhz.

MSO—Multiple cable systems operator.

Must carry—Legal requirement that cable operators carry local broadcast signals. Cable systems with 12 or fewer channels must carry at least three broadcast signals; systems with 12 or more channels must carry up to one-third of their capacity; systems with 300 or fewer subscribers are exempt. The 1992 Cable Act requires broadcast station to waive must-carry rights if it chooses to negotiate retransmission compensation (see "Retransmission consent").

NTSC—National Television System Committee. Committee that recommended current American standard color television.

PCM—Pulse code modulation. Conversion of voice signals into digital code.

PPV—Pay-per-view.

Progressive scanning—TV system where video frames are transmitted sequentially, unlike interlaced scanning in which frames are divided into two fields.

PSA—Public service announcement.

PTV—Public television.

Public radio—Radio stations and networks that are operated on a noncommercial basis.

Public television—Television stations and networks that operate as noncommercial ventures.

RCC—Radio common carrier. Common carriers whose major businesses include radio paging and mobile telephone services.

Retransmission consent—Local TV broadcasters' right to negotiate a carriage fee with local cable operators, as provided in 1992 Cable Act.

SCA—Subsidiary communications authorizations. Authorizations granted to FM broadcasters for using subcarriers on their channels for other communications services.

Shortwave—Transmissions on frequencies of 6-25 mhz.

SHF—Super high frequency.

Signal-to-noise ratio—The ratio between the strength of an electronically produced signal to interfering noises in the same bandwidth.

SMATV—Satellite master antenna television.

STV—Subscription television.

Superstation—Local television station whose signal is retransmitted via satellite to cable systems beyond reach of over-the-air signal.

Teletext—A one-way electronic publishing service that can be transmitted over the vertical blanking interval of a standard television signal or the full channel of a television station or cable television system. The major use today is for closed-captioning.

Translator—Broadcast station that rebroadcasts signals of other stations without originating its own programming.

Transponder—Satellite transmitter/receiver that picks up signals transmitted from earth, translates them into new frequencies and amplifies them before retransmitting them back to ground.

UHF—Ultra high frequency band (300 mhz-3,000 mhz), which includes TV channels 14-83.

Uplink—Earth station used for transmitting to satellite.

VHF—Very high frequencies (30 mhz-300 mhz), which include TV channels 2-13 and FM radio.

Videotext—Two-way interactive service that uses either two-way cable or telephone lines to connect a central computer to a television screen.

List of Abbreviations

* .... noncommercial
a .... annual
A&E .... Arts & Entertainment
actg .... acting
admin .... administrative
adv .... advertising
affil .... affiliate
affrs .... affairs
AFRTS .... Armed Forces Radio and TV Service
alt .... alternate
ant .... antenna
AOR .... album-oriented rock
AP .... Associated Press
assn .... association
assoc .... associate
asst .... assistant
atty .... attorney
aur .... aural
aux .... auxiliary
bcst .... broadcast
bcstg .... broadcasting
bcstr .... broadcaster
bd .... board
BET .... Black Entertainment Television
bi-m .... every two months
bk rev .... book reviews
bldg .... building
bor .... borough
btfl .... beautiful
C-SPAN .... Cable Satellite Public Affairs Network
CATV .... community antenna television
CBC .... Canadian Broadcasting Corp.
CEO .... chief executive officer
ch .... channel
CH .... critical hours
chg .... charge
CHR .... contemporary hit radio
chmn .... chairman
circ .... circulation
coml .... commercial
contemp .... contemporary
COO .... chief operating officer
coord .... coordinator
CP .... construction permit
CRTC .... Canadian Radio-television and Telecommunications Commission
C&W .... country & western
D .... day
d .... daily
DA .... directional antenna
dance rev .... dance reviews
DBS .... direct broadcast satellite
dev .... development
dir .... director
div .... diverse
DMA .... Designated Market Area
dups .... duplicates
Eds .... editors
Ed Bd .... Editorial Board
educ .... educational
engr .... engineer
engrg .... engineering
EPG .... Electronic Program Guide
ERP .... effective radiated power
ESPN Entertainment & Sports Programming Network
ETV .... educational television
exec .... executive
FCC .... Federal Communications Commission
film rev .... film reviews
fortn .... fortnightly
Fr .... French
g .... ground
gen .... general
Ger .... German
govt .... government
HAAT .... height above average terrain
HBO .... Home Box Office
horiz .... horizontal polarization
hqtrs .... headquarters
ind .... independent
info .... information
instal .... installation
ISBN .... International Standard Book Number
ISSN .... International Standard Serial Number
Illus .... illustrations
Irreg .... irregular
It .... Italian
khz .... kilohertz
kw .... kilowatts
loc .... local
LPTV .... low power television
LS .... local sunset
lstng .... listening
lw .... long wave
m .... meters
MDS .... Multipoint Distribution Service
mdse .... merchandising
mfg .... manufacturing
mgng .... managing
mgr .... manager
mgmt .... management
mhz .... megahertz
mi .... miles
mktg .... marketing
MMDS .. Multichannel Multipoint Distribution Service
mo .... month
mod .... modification
MOR .... middle of the road
MSO .... multiple system operator
Mthy .... monthly
MTV .... Music Television
mus .... music
music rev .... music reviews
mw .... medium wave
N .... night
na .... not available
NAB .... National Association of Broadcasters
natl .... national
net .... network
NPR .... National Public Radio
nwspr .... newspaper
off .... officer
opns .... operations
per .... personnel
play rev .... play reviews (theatre reviews)
Pol .... Polish
pop .... population
PR .... public relations
pres .... president
PRI .... Public Radio International
progmg .... programming
progsv .... progressive
prom .... promotion

PSA .... presunrise authority, public service announcement
ptnr .... partner
pub affrs......................... public affairs
publ .... publicity
q .... quarterly
quad .... quadraphonic
record rev .... record reviews
rel .... relations
relg .... religion
rep .... representative
RFE....................... Radio Free Europe
rgn .... region
rgnl .... regional
RL .... Radio Liberty
rsch .... research
s-a .... twice annually
s-m .... twice monthly
s-w .... twice weekly
sec .... secretary
sep .... separate
sh.................................. shares
SH......................... specified hours
sls .... sales
SMATV .... satellite master antenna television
Sp .... Spanish
sr................................... senior
ST.............................. shares time
stn .... station
sub............................. subscriber
supt......................... superintendent
supvr .... supervisor
svcs.............................. services
sw .... short wave
t .... terrain
tech .... technical
tele rev .... television reviews
3/m .... three times a month
3/y .... three times a year
TNN................... The Nashville Network
traf................................. traffic
trans .... translators
treas............................ treasurer
twp .... township
TWX................. Teletypewriter Exchange
U................................ unlimited
UHF .... ultra high frequency
UPI................. United Press International
UPN .... United Paramount Network
var .... variety
vert...................... vertical polarization
VHF .... very high frequency
video rev...................... video reviews
vis .... visual
VOA....................... Voice of America
vp .... vice president
w.................................... watts
wkly .... weekly

Index to Advertisers

Local Television Market Universe Estimates

Estimates as of January 1, 2012 and used throughout the 2011-2012 television season

Estimates are effective September 24, 2011

Rank	Designated Market Area (DMA)	TV Homes	% of US
1	New York	7,387,810	6.444
2	Los Angeles	5,569,780	4.858
3	Chicago	3,493,480	3.047
4	Philadelphia	2,993,370	2.611
5	Dallas-Ft. Worth	2,571,310	2.243
6	San Francisco-Oak-San Jose	2,506,510	2.186
7	Boston (Manchester)	2,379,690	2.076
8	Washington, DC (Hagrstwn)	2,360,180	2.059
9	Atlanta	2,292,640	2.000
10	Houston	2,185,260	1.906
11	Detroit	1,842,650	1.607
12	Seattle-Tacoma	1,811,420	1.580
13	Phoenix (Prescott)	1,811,330	1.580
14	Tampa-St. Pete (Sarasota)	1,788,240	1.560
15	Minneapolis-St. Paul	1,721,940	1.502
16	Miami-Ft. Lauderdale	1,583,800	1.381
17	Denver	1,548,570	1.351
18	Cleveland-Akron (Canton)	1,514,170	1.321
19	Orlando-Daytona Bch-Melbrn	1,465,460	1.278
20	Sacramnto-Stkton-Modesto	1,388,570	1.211
21	St. Louis	1,253,920	1.094
22	Portland, OR	1,190,010	1.038
23	Pittsburgh	1,171,490	1.022
24	Raleigh-Durham (Fayetvlle)	1,143,420	0.997
25	Charlotte	1,140,900	0.995
26	Indianapolis	1,109,970	0.968
27	Baltimore	1,097,310	0.957
28	San Diego	1,077,600	0.940
29	Nashville	1,024,560	0.894
30	Hartford & New Haven	1,006,280	0.878
31	Kansas City	939,740	0.820
32	Columbus, OH	932,680	0.814
33	Salt Lake City	927,540	0.809
34	Milwaukee	907,660	0.792
35	Cincinnati	896,090	0.782
36	San Antonio	880,690	0.768
37	Greenvll-Spart-Ashevll-And	860,930	0.751
38	West Palm Beach-Ft. Pierce	788,020	0.687
39	Birmingham (Ann and Tusc)	738,790	0.644
40	Las Vegas	737,300	0.643

Rank	Designated Market Area (DMA)	TV Homes	% of US
41	Harrisburg-Lncstr-Leb-York	729,440	0.636
42	Grand Rapids-Kalmzoo-B.Crk	722,150	0.630
43	Norfolk-Portsmth-Newpt Nws	718,750	0.627
44	Oklahoma City	712,630	0.622
45	Albuquerque-Santa Fe	710,050	0.619
46	Greensboro-H.Point-W.Salem	691,200	0.603
47	Austin	686,830	0.599
48	Louisville	674,050	0.588
49	Memphis	669,940	0.584
50	Jacksonville	669,840	0.584
51	Buffalo	645,190	0.563
52	New Orleans	643,660	0.561
53	Providence-New Bedford	620,010	0.541
54	Wilkes Barre-Scranton-Hztn	590,740	0.515
55	Fresno-Visalia	574,800	0.501
56	Little Rock-Pine Bluff	571,630	0.499
57	Richmond-Petersburg	559,390	0.488
58	Albany-Schenectady-Troy	551,120	0.481
59	Tulsa	529,100	0.461
60	Mobile-Pensacola (Ft Walt)	527,930	0.460
61	Knoxville	527,790	0.460
62	Ft. Myers-Naples	504,240	0.440
63	Dayton	493,600	0.431
64	Lexington	488,850	0.426
65	Charleston-Huntington	465,030	0.406
66	Roanoke-Lynchburg	455,860	0.398
67	Wichita-Hutchinson Plus	454,590	0.397
68	Flint-Saginaw-Bay City	451,880	0.394
69	Green Bay-Appleton	445,760	0.389
70	Tucson (Sierra Vista)	442,020	0.386
71	Honolulu	434,730	0.379
72	Des Moines-Ames	431,300	0.376
73	Spokane	426,690	0.372
74	Toledo	426,280	0.372
75	Springfield, MO	423,010	0.369
76	Omaha	415,510	0.362
77	Columbia, SC	404,830	0.353
78	Portland-Auburn	401,370	0.350
79	Rochester, NY	398,790	0.348
80	Huntsville-Decatur (Flor)	394,010	0.344

Rank	Designated Market Area (DMA)	TV Homes	% of US
81	Paducah-Cape Girard-Harsbg	393,330	0.343
82	Champaign&Sprngfld-Decatur	386,160	0.337
83	Shreveport	386,150	0.337
84	Syracuse	386,090	0.337
85	Madison	378,290	0.330
86	Chattanooga	366,790	0.320
87	Harlingen-Wslco-Brnsvl-McA	361,820	0.316
88	Waco-Temple-Bryan	353,190	0.308
89	Cedar Rapids-Wtrlo-IWC&Dub	344,150	0.300
90	Colorado Springs-Pueblo	343,160	0.299
91	El Paso (Las Cruces)	336,570	0.294
92	Savannah	335,080	0.292
93	Jackson, MS	334,530	0.292
94	Baton Rouge	333,010	0.290
95	Burlington-Plattsburgh	323,750	0.282
96	Tri-Cities, TN-VA	323,640	0.282
97	South Bend-Elkhart	322,090	0.281
98	Charleston, SC	311,260	0.271
99	Greenville-N.Bern-Washngtn	307,610	0.268
100	Davenport-R.Island-Moline	307,050	0.268
101	Ft. Smith-Fay-Sprngdl-Rgrs	301,120	0.263
102	Johnstown-Altoona-St Colge	294,770	0.257
103	Myrtle Beach-Florence	289,060	0.252
104	Evansville	287,880	0.251
105	Lincoln & Hastings-Krny	280,310	0.244
106	Tallahassee-Thomasville	272,520	0.238
107	Tyler-Longview(Lfkn&Ncgd)	271,400	0.237
108	Reno	271,020	0.236
109	Ft. Wayne	267,710	0.234
110	Youngstown	263,850	0.230
111	Augusta-Aiken	262,560	0.229
112	Boise	261,810	0.228
113	Sioux Falls(Mitchell)	261,530	0.228
114	Springfield-Holyoke	257,080	0.224
115	Lansing	252,890	0.221
116	Peoria-Bloomington	247,850	0.216
117	Fargo-Valley City	246,780	0.215
118	Macon	245,910	0.214
119	Montgomery-Selma	245,100	0.214
120	Traverse City-Cadillac	244,050	0.213

Rank	Designated Market Area (DMA)	TV Homes	% of US
121	Eugene	241,270	0.210
122	SantaBarbra-SanMar-SanLuOb	230,830	0.201
123	Yakima-Pasco-Rchlnd-Knnwck	230,010	0.201
124	Lafayette, LA	229,320	0.200
125	Monterey-Salinas	223,620	0.195
126	Bakersfield	221,920	0.194
127	Columbus, GA (Opelika, AL)	215,410	0.188
128	La Crosse-Eau Claire	213,660	0.186
129	Corpus Christi	203,550	0.178
130	Amarillo	195,650	0.171
131	Chico-Redding	194,590	0.170
132	Wilmington	190,730	0.166
133	Columbus-Tupelo-W Pnt-Hstn	189,910	0.166
134	Rockford	184,360	0.161
135	Wausau-Rhinelander	181,280	0.158
136	Topeka	177,710	0.155
137	Monroe-El Dorado	177,410	0.155
138	Columbia-Jefferson City	176,470	0.154
139	Duluth-Superior	173,710	0.152
140	Medford-Klamath Falls	170,670	0.149
141	Beaumont-Port Arthur	168,420	0.147
142	Wichita Falls & Lawton	160,540	0.140
143	Lubbock	160,160	0.140
144	Salisbury	159,640	0.139
145	Palm Springs	158,440	0.138
146	Erie	157,730	0.138
147	Sioux City	157,060	0.137
148	Anchorage	155,600	0.136
149	Joplin-Pittsburg	153,910	0.134
150	Albany, GA	151,620	0.132
151	Odessa-Midland	146,040	0.127
152	Minot-Bsmrck-Dcknsn(Wlstn)	145,480	0.127
153	Rochestr-Mason City-Austin	145,450	0.127
154	Terre Haute	142,780	0.125
155	Bangor	141,580	0.123
156	Bluefield-Beckley-Oak Hill	137,380	0.120
157	Binghamton	136,730	0.119
158	Wheeling-Steubenville	133,120	0.116
159	Panama City	132,120	0.115
160	Idaho Fals-Pocatllo(Jcksn)	128,940	0.112

Rank	Designated Market Area (DMA)	TV Homes	% of US
161	Sherman-Ada	128,790	0.112
162	Biloxi-Gulfport	128,150	0.112
163	Gainesville	124,730	0.109
164	Abilene-Sweetwater	115,630	0.101
165	Missoula	114,590	0.100
166	Yuma-El Centro	112,850	0.098
167	Hattiesburg-Laurel	111,560	0.097
168	Billings	109,940	0.096
169	Dothan	109,080	0.095
170	Clarksburg-Weston	108,980	0.095
171	Quincy-Hannibal-Keokuk	104,790	0.091
172	Utica	104,750	0.091
173	Rapid City	100,120	0.087
174	Elmira (Corning)	96,600	0.084
175	Lake Charles	94,850	0.083
176	Jackson, TN	94,650	0.083
177	Watertown	93,090	0.081
178	Harrisonburg	91,620	0.080
179	Alexandria, LA	90,160	0.079
180	Marquette	85,230	0.074
181	Jonesboro	81,300	0.071
182	Bowling Green	79,990	0.070
183	Charlottesville	74,630	0.065
184	Grand Junction-Montrose	72,970	0.064
185	Laredo	72,060	0.063
186	Meridian	70,190	0.061
187	Greenwood-Greenville	67,730	0.059
188	Lafayette, IN	67,260	0.059
189	Butte-Bozeman	66,910	0.058
190	Great Falls	66,190	0.058
191	Twin Falls	65,800	0.057
192	Parkersburg	63,120	0.055
193	Bend, OR	62,620	0.055
194	Eureka	61,180	0.053
195	Cheyenne-Scottsbluff	56,640	0.049
196	Casper-Riverton	56,460	0.049
197	San Angelo	55,570	0.048
198	Mankato	53,720	0.047
199	Ottumwa-Kirksville	47,810	0.042
200	St. Joseph	46,690	0.041

Rank	Designated Market Area (DMA)	TV Homes	% of US
201	Lima	39,350	0.034
202	Fairbanks	37,010	0.032
203	Zanesville	33,140	0.029
204	Victoria	31,540	0.028
205	Presque Isle	29,850	0.026
206	Helena	28,050	0.024
207	Juneau	25,500	0.022
208	Alpena	17,100	0.015
209	North Platte	15,180	0.013
210	Glendive	4,180	0.004
	NSI Total U.S.	**114,649,310**	**100.000**

TV Sets in Use

	In Home (000)	Avg. Sets Per HH
1970	81,040	1.39
1971	85,290	1.42
1972	89,770	1.45
1973	95,330	1.47
1974	100,020	1.51
1975	105,460	1.54
1976	108,890	1.56
1977	113,440	1.59
1978	118,630	1.63
1979	124,570	1.67
1980	128,190	1.68
1981	132,260	1.70
1982	142,460	1.75
1983	148,910	1.79
1984	149,180	1.78
1985	155,410	1.83
1986	157,500	1.83
1987	162,750	1.86
1988	168,260	1.90
1989	175,580	1.94
1990	193,320	2.10
1991	193,200	2.08
1992*	192,480	2.09
1993	200,565	2.15
1994	211,443	2.24
1995	217,067	2.28
1996	222,753	2.32
1997	228,740	2.36
1998	235,010	2.40
1999	240,320	2.42
2000	244,990	2.43
2001	248,160	2.43
2002	254,360	2.41
2003	260,230	2.44
2004	268,260	2.47
2005	287,000	2.62
2006	301,380	2.73
2007	310,840	2.79
2008	319,420	2.83
2009	330,930	2.86
2010	336,770	2.93
2011	343,810	2.97
2012	327,370	3.01

1970-79, as of September of prior year; 1980 to date as of January of calendar year; excludes Alaska and Hawaii prior to 1989.

* Reflects adjustments to conform to the 1990 census.

55 Years of Station Transactions

YEAR	RADIO ONLY*	GROUPS*	TV ONLY	TOTAL
1954	$10,224,047 (187)	$26,213,323 (18)	$23,906,760 (27)	$60,344,130
1955	27,333,104 (242)	22,351,602 (11)	23,394,660 (29)	$73,079,366
1956	32,563,378 (316)	65,212,055 (24)	17,830,395 (21)	$115,605,828
1957	48,207,470 (357)	47,490,884 (28)	28,489,206 (38)	$124,187,560
1958	49,868,123 (407)	60,872,618 (17)	16,796,285 (23)	$127,537,026
1959	65,544,653 (436)	42,724,727 (15)	15,227,201 (21)	$123,496,581
1960	51,763,285 (345)	24,648,400 (10)	22,930,225 (21)	$99,341,910
1961	55,532,516 (282)	42,103,708 (13)	31,167,943 (24)	$128,804,167
1962	59,912,520 (306)	18,822,745 (8)	23,007,638 (16)	$101,742,903
1963	43,457,584 (305)	25,045,726 (3)	36,799,768 (16)	$105,303,078
1964	52,296,480 (430)	67,185,762 (20)	86,274,494 (36)	$205,756,736
1965	55,933,300 (389)	49,756,993 (15)	29,433,473 (32)	$135,123,766
1966	76,633,762 (367)	28,510,500 (11)	30,574,054 (31)	$135,718,316
1967	59,670,053 (316)	32,086,297 (9)	80,316,223 (30)	$172,072,573
1968	71,310,709 (316)	47,556,634 (9)	33,588,069 (20)	$152,455,412
1969	108,866,538 (343)	35,037,000 (5)	87,794,032 (32)	$231,697,570
1970	86,292,899 (268)	1,038,465 (3)	87,454,078 (19)	$174,785,442
1971	125,501,514 (270)	750,000 (2)	267,296,410 (27)	$393,547,924
1972	114,424,673 (239)	0 (0)	156,905,864 (37)	$271,330,537
1973	160,933,557 (352)	2,812,444 (4)	66,635,144 (25)	$230,381,145
1974	168,998,012 (369)	19,800,000 (5)	118,983,462 (24)	$307,781,474
1975	131,065,860 (363)	0 (0)	128,420,101 (22)	$259,485,961
1976	180,663,820 (413)	1,800,000 (3)	108,459,657 (32)	$290,923,477
1977	161,236,169 (344)	0 (0)	128,635,435 (25)	$289,871,604
1978	331,557,239 (586)	30,450,000 (5)	289,721,159 (51)	$651,728,398
1979	335,597,000 (546)	463,500,000 (52)	317,581,000 (47)	$1,116,678,000
1980	339,634,000 (424)	27,000,000 (3)	534,150,000 (35)	$900,784,000
1981	447,838,060 (625)	78,400,000 (6)	227,950,000 (24)	$754,188,060
1982	470,722,833 (597)	0 (0)	527,675,411 (30)	$998,398,244
1983	621,077,876 (669)	332,000,000 (10)	1,902,701,830 (61)	$2,855,779,706
1984	977,024,266 (782)	234,500,000 (2)	1,252,023,787 (82)	$2,463,548,053
1985	1,414,816,073 (1,558)	962,450,000 (218)	3,290,995,000 (99)	$5,668,261,073
1986	1,490,131,426 (959)	1,993,021,955 (192)	2,709,516,490 (128)	$6,192,669,871
1987	1,236,355,748 (775)	4,610,965,000 (132)	1,661,832,724 (59)	$7,509,153,472
1988	1,841,630,156 (845)	1,326,250,000 (106)	1,779,958,042 (70)	$4,947,838,198
1989	1,148,524,765 (663)	533,599,078 (40)	1,541,055,033 (84)	$3,223,178,876
1990	868,636,700 (1,045)	411,037,150 (60)	696,952,350 (75)	$1,976,626,200
1991	534,694,500 (793)	206,995,500 (61)	273,365,000 (38)	$1,015,055,000
1992	603,192,980 (667)	318,176,050 (24)	124,004,000 (41)	$1,045,373,030
1993	815,450,000 (633)	756,722,000 (NA)	1,728,711,000 (101)	$3,300,883,000
1994	970,400,000 (494)	1,800,000,000 (154)	2,200,000,000 (89)	$4,970,400,000
1995	792,440,000 (524)	2,790,000,000 (213)	4,740,000,000 (112)	$8,322,440,000
1996	2,840,820,000 (671)	12,034,000,000 (345)	10,488,000,000 (99)	$25,362,820,000
1997	2,461,570,000 (630)	14,580,000,000 (329)	6,400,000,000 (108)	$23,441,570,000
1998	1,596,210,000 (589)	14,080,000,000 (271)	7,120,000,000 (90)	$22,796,210,000
1999	1,718,000,000 (382)	26,880,000,000 (196)	4,720,000,000 (86)	$33,318,000,000
2000**	24,900,000,000 (1,794)	0 (0)	8,800,000,000 (154)	$33,700,000,000
2001**	3,800,000,000 (1,000)	0 (0)	4,900,000,000 (108)	$8,700,000,000
2002**	5,594,141,000 (836)	0 (0)	2,529,039,000 (249)	$8,123,180,000
2003**	2,400,000,000 (950)	0 (0)	520,000,000 (97)	$2,920,000,000
2004**	1,897,422,000 (901)	0 (0)	871,923,000 (66)	$2,769,345,000
2005**	2,791,531,000 (895)	0 (0)	2,842,439,000 (86)	$5,633,970,000
2006**	22,871,247,000 (2101)	0 (0)	18,127,686,000 (180)	$40,998,933,000
2007**	1,488,628,000 (1,187)	0 (0)	4,616,018,000 (295)	$6,104,646,000
2008	642,344,000 (749)	0 (0)	745,511,000 (48)	$1,387,855,000
2009	345,487,000 (638)		713,490,000 (80)	$1,058,977,000
2010	339,317,000 (816)		199,288,000 (60)	$538,605,000
2011	4,275,300,000 (1,067)		1,098,971,000 (49)	$5,374,271,000
2012YTD	1,019,889,000 (772)		1,805,316,000 (89)	$2,825,205,000
TOTAL	$92,239,870,648	$85,110,886,616	$100,129,129,403	$277,479,886,667

Dollar Volume of Transactions (number of stations changing hands)

Note: Dollar volume figures represent total considerations reported for all transactions with exception of minority interest transfers in which control of stations did not change hands and stations sold as part of larger company transactions. Although all states have been approved by the FCC, they may not necessarily have reached final closing. Prior to 1978, combined AM-FM facilities were counted as one station in computing total number of stations traded. Now AM-FM combinations are counted as two stations.

*Starting in 1993, the Radio only column includes only stand alone AM and FM deals and the Groups column contains AM-FM combos and all other multiple station deals. In previous years the AM-FM combos were included under Radio only.

**Figures for 2000 to 2008 courtesy of BIA Financial Network.

Record of Television Station Growth

	Authorized	On Air
Jan. 1, 1946*	9	6
Jan. 1, 1947*	52	
Jan. 1, 1948*	73	17
Jan. 1, 1949	124	50
Jan. 1, 1950	111	97
Jan. 1, 1951	109	107
Jan. 1, 1952	108	108
Jan. 1, 1953*	273	129
Jan. 1, 1954	567	356
Jan. 1, 1955	576	439 (1)
Jan. 1, 1956	590	482 (2)
Jan. 1, 1957	631	511
Jan. 1, 1958	657	544 (3)
Jan. 1, 1959	666	562 (4)
Jan. 1, 1960	673	573 (5)
Jan. 1, 1961	634	583
Jan. 1, 1962	654	563
Jan. 1, 1963	662	579
Jan. 1, 1964	661	582
Jan. 1, 1965	676	586
Jan. 1, 1966	702	596
Jan. 1, 1967	769	623
Jan. 1, 1968	818	644
Jan. 1, 1969	834	672
Jan. 1, 1970	1,038	872
Jan. 1, 1971	1,025	892
Jan. 1, 1972	1,004	905
Jan. 1, 1973	1,001	922
Jan. 1, 1974	1,002	938
Jan. 1, 1975	1,010	952
Jan. 1, 1976	1,030	962
Jan. 1, 1977	1,029	984
Jan. 1, 1978	1,045	986
Jan. 1, 1979	1,059	992
Jan. 1, 1980	1,094	1,013
Jan. 1, 1981	1,143	1,019
Jan. 1, 1982	1,168	1,020
Jan. 1, 1983	1,276	1,090
Jan. 1, 1984	1,318	1,149
Jan. 1, 1985	1,505	1,194
Oct. 30, 1986	1,493	1,220
Oct. 31, 1987	1,558	1,285
Jan. 1, 1988	1,615	1,342
Jan. 1, 1989	1,683	1,395
Jan. 1, 1990	1,684	1,436

Jan. 1, 1991	1,690	1,469
Jan. 1, 1992	1,688	1,488
Jan. 1, 1993	1,688	1,505
Jan. 1, 1994		1,518
Jan. 1, 1995		1,520
Jan. 1, 1996		1,544
Jan. 1, 1997		1,554
Jan. 1, 1998		1,564
Jan. 1, 1999		1,589
Jan. 1, 2000		1,616
Jan. 1, 2001		1,663
Jan. 1, 2002		1,686
Jan. 1, 2003		1,719
Jan. 1, 2004		1,733
Jan. 1, 2005		1,748
Jan. 1, 2006		1,750
Jan. 1, 2007		1,756
Jan. 1, 2008		1,759
Jan. 1, 2009		1,759
Jan. 1, 2011		1,781
Sep. 30, 2012		1,782

*Comparable figures for all services not available at this date.
(1) Includes stations with Special Temporary Authorizations (STAs), which either had not started operations as of this date, had started but had gone dark, or had received authorizations but turned them back with or without operating.
(2) Includes 2 licenses that had suspended operation and 37 stations with STAs in same category as footnote 1.
(3) Includes 7 licenses that had suspended operation and 40 stations with STAs in same category as footnote 1.
(4) Includes 6 licenses that had suspended operation and 38 stations with STAs in same category as footnote 1.
(5) Includes 10 licenses that had suspended operation and 38 stations with STAs in same category as footnote 1.

Top 100 TV Programs 2011-2012

Rank	Program	Network	HHLD Live+SD US AA%
1	Super Bowl XLVI	NBC	47.0
2	NFC Championship	FOX	30.6
3	AFC Championship	CBS	27.4
4	NFC Playoff-Sun	FOX	25.3
5	AFC Wildcard Playoff	CBS	24.0
6	Academy Awards	ABC	22.6
7	Grammy Awards	CBS	21.7
8	NFC Playoff-Sat	FOX	20.5
9	AFC Divisional Playoff-Su	CBS	19.0
10	AFC Divisional Playoff-Sa	CBS	18.5
11	NFL Playoff Game 2	NBC	18.2
12	NFC Wildcard Game	FOX	17.3
13	Super Bowl Pre Game 530P	NBC	16.9
14	NFL Sunday-National	FOX	15.4
15	NFL-Thursday	FOX	14.8
16	World Series Game 7	FOX	14.7
17	NFL National	CBS	14.5
18	NFL Single - Thursday	CBS	14.3
19	Oscar's Red Carpet Live-3	ABC	14.3
20	BCS Championship	ESPN	14.0
21	NFL Playoff Game 1	NBC	13.5
22	NFL Sat-National	FOX	12.9
23	World Series Game 6	FOX	12.7
24	NBC Sunday Night Football	NBC	12.4
25	NCAA Bskbl Champships	CBS	12.3
26	NFL Sunday-Single	FOX	12.1
27	Macy's Thanksgiving Parade	NBC	11.7
28	Super Bowl Pre Game 5P	NBC	11.6
29	Home Depot Prime Clg Ftbl-11/05/11	CBS	11.5
30	Dancing With The Stars	ABC	11.2
31	American Idol Aud Sp-1/22	FOX	11.1
32	NFC Championship-Pre	FOX	10.9
33	NCIS	CBS	10.8
34	American Idol-Wednesday	FOX	10.6
35	New Year's Rockin Eve Pt.1	ABC	10.5
36	NFL Single	CBS	10.5
37	Rose Bowl	ESPN	10.2
38	Oscar's Red Carpet Live-2	ABC	10.2
39	Golden Globe Awards	NBC	10.2
40	Dancing W/Stars Results	ABC	10.1

41	CMA Awards	ABC	9.9
42	American Idol-Thursday	FOX	9.8
43	AFC Wildcard Pre Game	CBS	9.8
44	NCAA Bskbl Champ Sa-2	CBS	9.6
45	American Idol Tue Sp-2/28(S)	FOX	9.4
46	NFC Playoff-Pre-Sun	FOX	9.4
47	World Series Game 4	FOX	9.2
48	Kentucky Derby	NBC	9.0
49	NCIS: Los Angeles	CBS	8.9
50	World Series Game 2	FOX	8.9
51	World Series Game 5	FOX	8.8
52	The Big Bang Theory- Sp(S)-9/22	CBS	8.8
53	Super Bowl Pre Game 430P	NBC	8.8
54	60 Minutes - Sp 1/1	CBS	8.7
55	World Series Game 1	FOX	8.7
56	American Idol Tue Sp-5/22	FOX	8.7
57	Betty White 90th Birthday	NBC	8.5
58	Modern Family Sp-9/21	ABC	8.5
59	NCAA Bskbl Champ-Sa-1	CBS	8.4
60	NFL Regular Season	ESPN	8.4
61	Fiesta Bowl	ESPN	8.4
62	20/20 Sp Edition-11/14	ABC	8.4
63	NFL Single-Spc(S)	CBS	8.3
64	CBS Sunday Movie-Special	CBS	8.3
65	NCIS 9P-Special	CBS	8.2
66	NFL Sunday-Regional	FOX	8.2
67	The Big Bang Theory	CBS	8.2
68	AFC Championship Pre-Game	CBS	8.2
69	60 Minutes	CBS	8.1
70	Masters Golf Tourn.-Sun	CBS	8.0
71	NFL Sat-Regional	FOX	8.0
72	Nascar Daytona 500 Monday	FOX	8.0
73	The Voice	NBC	8.0
74	ACM Awards	CBS	7.9
75	Oscar's Red Carpet Live-1	ABC	7.8
76	World Series Game 7-Post	FOX	7.8
77	NCAA Bskbl-Bridge	CBS	7.8
78	NFL Regional	CBS	7.8
79	Super Bowl Pre Game 4P	NBC	7.7
80	Two And A Half Men	CBS	7.7
81	The Big Bang Theory: Sp 3/8/12	CBS	7.6
82	The Mentalist	CBS	7.6
83	Person Of Interest	CBS	7.5
84	Daytona 500 Red Flag-Begins	FOX	7.5
85	DWTS: Meet The Cast	ABC	7.5
86	Off Their Rockers	NBC	7.4

87	The Big Bang Theory: Sp 10/13/11	CBS	7.3
88	SEC Champ: Dr Pepper	CBS	7.3
89	How I Met Your Mother 830(S)-09/19/11	CBS	7.3
90	AFC-NFC Pro Bowl	NBC	7.3
91	Survivor: S. Pacific Final	CBS	7.3
92	Dancing W/Stars: Story(S)-03/27/12	ABC	7.3
93	Modern Family Sp-11/23	ABC	7.2
94	60 Minutes Special-04/08/2012	CBS	7.1
95	20/20 Sp Edition-4/23	ABC	7.1
96	Touch Preview 1/25	FOX	7.1
97	The Mentalist Friday-Sp	CBS	7.1
98	Criminal Minds	CBS	7.1
99	NCAA Bskbl Chmp Su-2	CBS	7.1
100	American Music Awards	ABC	6.8

Source: Television Bureau of Advertising, based on data from Nielsen Galaxy Lightning. Ranked by average audience percentage of the total number of homes in the U.S. with TV sets.

Full Season: 9/19/11-5/23/12

Sales of Television Receivers

Year	Analog Color TV*			Digital TV Sets & Displays			HDTV**		
	Units (Thousands)	Dollars (Million)	Average Price	Units (Thousands)	Dollars (Million)	Average Price	Units (Thousand	Dollars (Million)	Average Price
1981	11157	$4,123	$370.00						
1982	11366	$4,141	$364.00						
1983	13986	$4,728	$338.00						
1984	16083	$5,359	$333.00						
1985	16829	$5,522	$328.00						
1986	18204	$5,836	$321.00						
1987	19330	$6,148	$318.00						
1988	20216	$5,907	$292.00						
1989	21706	$6,490	$299.00						
1990	20384	$6,197	$304.00						
1991	19474	$5,979	$307.00						
1992	21056	$6,591	$313.00						
1993	23005	$7,316	$318.00						
1994	24715	$7,225	$292.00						
1995	23231	$6,798	$293.00						
1996	22384	$6,492	$290.00						
1997	21293	$6,036	$283.00						
1998	22204	$6,122	$276.00	14	$43	$3,147.00			
1999	23218	$6,199	$267.00	121	$295	$2,433.00			
2000	24175	$6,140	$254.00	625	$1,422	$2,275.00			
2001	21167	$5,130	$242.00	1460	$2,648	$1,812.00			
2002	22469	$5,782	$257.00	2535	$4,280	$1,688.00			
2003	20791	$4,756	$229.00	5532	$8,692	$1,571.00	3735	$6,253	$1,674.00
2004	19934	$3,526	$177.00	8002	$12,300	$1,537.00	6091	$9,212	$1,512.00
2005	16934	$2,790	$165.00	10719	$15,043	$1,403.00	8803	$11,547	$1,312.00
2006	8761	$1,000	$114.00	22366	$22,696	$1,015.00	17268	$18,410	$1,066.00
2007	1166	$115	$99.00	24966	$24,519	$982.00	20722	$19,439	$938.00
2008				31153	$25,827	$829.00	26192	$23,677	$904.00
2009				34799	$22,407	$644.00	29662	$21,670	$731.00
2010				34659	$20,120	$581.00	33619	$19,600	$583.00
2011				33781	$18,150	$537.00	33781	$18,151	$537.00

**CEA stopped tracking sales after 2007.*

***HDTV is a subset of Digital TV Sets & Displays*

Consumer Electronics Association Market Research 2012

Major Broadcast TV Networks

ABC
Mailing Address: 77 West 66th Street, New York, NY 10023
Second Address: 500 S Bueana Vista Street, Burbank, CA 91521
(212) 456-7777
www.abcgo.com
Anne Sweeney, Co-Chairman/President
George Bodenheimer, Executive Chairman
John Skipper, President, ESPN Inc
Rebecca Campbell, President, ABC Televisions Stations Group
ABC Daytime:
2300 Riverside Drive, Burbank, CA 91506; Vicki Dummer, EVP, Times Square Studio.
Ownership:
The Walt Disney Company, 500 Buena Vista Street, Burbank, CA 91521-9722; Tel:(818) 560-1000; Website: www.disney.com
Primetime and Late Night
Castle, Dancing with the Stars, Private Practice, The Middle, The Neighbors, Last Resort, Grey's Anatomy, Scandal, Shark Tank, Once Upon a Time, Revenge, 666 Park Avenue, Nashville, Modern Family and Late Night: Jimmy Kimmel Live.

CBS
Mailing Address: CBS Television Network, 51 West 52nd Street, New York, NY 10019
Second Address: 7800 Beverly Blvd, Los Angeles, CA 90036
(212) 975-4321
www.cbs.com
Louis Briskman, EVP/General Counsel
Gil Schwartz, EVP/Chief Communications Officer
Adam Townsend, EVP/Investor Relations
Martin Franks, EVP/Planning and Policy
Jospeh Ianniello, EVP/Chief Financial Officer
Ownership:
CBS Corporation, 51 West 52ns Street, New York, NY 10019-6188; Tel:(212) 975-4321; Website: www.cbscorporation.com; Sumner M Redstone, Executive Chairman; Leslie Moonves, President/CEO.
Primetime:
2 Broke Girls, 48 Hours Mystery, The Amazing Race, The Big Bang Theory, Big Brother, Blue Bloods, Criminal Minds, CSI, Dogs int he City, Elementary, The Good Wife, Hawaii Five-O, How I Met Your Mother, Made in Jersey, The Mentalist, Mike andMolly, NCIS, Person of Interest, Rules of Engagement, Survivor, Two and a Half Men, Undercover Boss, Unforgettable, Vegas, The Bold and the Beautiful, CBS this Morning, Let's Make a Deal, The Price is Right, The Talk, The Young and the Restless,Late Show with David Letterman, The Late Show with Craig Ferguson.

The CW Television Network
Mailing Address: 4000 Warner Blvd, Burbank, CA 81522
Second Address: 3300 West Olive Street, Burbank, CA 91505
(818) 977-2500 (818) 977-2500, *Fax:* (818) 954-7667
www.cwtv.com
John Maata, COO
Mark Pedowitz, President
Thom Sherman, EVP/Development
Rick Haskins, EVP/Marketing and Digital Programming
Rob Tuck, EVP/National Sales
The CW is a joint venture betweeen CBS corporation and Warner Brothers Entertainment, a subsidiary of Time Warner.
Ownership:
CBS Corporation, Warner Bros. Entertainment Inc. (Time Warner)
Programming:
America's Next Top Model, Arrow, Beauty and the Beast, Breaking Pointe, Cult, Emily Owens M.D., Gossip Girl, Hart of Dixie, Nikita, Oh Sit!, One Tree Hill, Remodeled, Supernatural, The Carrie Diaries, The Catalina, The L.A. Complex, The Next,The Vampire Diaries.

FOX Broadcasting Company
10201 West Pico Blvd, Los Angeles, CA 90035
(310) 369-3553
www.fox.com
Peter Rice, Chairman/CEO
Kevin Reilly, Chairman of Entertainment
Joe Early, COO
David Wertheimer, President/Digital
Emiliano Saccone, President/Mundo Fox
Gaude Lydia Paez, VP/Corporate Communications
Ownership:
News Corp., 1211 Avenue of the Americas, New York, NY 10036; Tel: (212) 852-7000; Website: www.newscorp.com
Programming:
American Dad, American Idol, Ben and Kate, Bob's Burgers, Bones, The Choice, The Cleveland Show, Comic Con 2012, Cops, Famiy Guy, Fringe, Glee, Hell's Kitchen, Hotel Hell, Kitchen Nightmares, MasterChef, The Mindy Project, The Mob Doctor,Mobbed, New Girl, Q'Viva: The Chosen, Raising Hope, The Simpsons, So You Think You Can Dance, Take Me Out, Touch, The X Factor.

ION Television
601 Claerwater Park Road, West Palm Beach, FL 33401
(561) 682-4100
www.ionmedianetowrks.com
Brandon Burgess, Chairman/CEO
William Watson, Vice President/Assistant Secretary
Marc Zand, Vice President
Jeffrey Quinn, Treasurer
Ownership:
ION Media Networks Inc., 601 Clearwater Park Road, West Palm Beach, FL 33401; Tel: (888) 467-2988.

NBC
Mailing Address: 30 Rockefeller Plaza, Suite 2, New York, NY 10112
Second Address: 3000 West Almeda Avenue, Burbank, CA 91523
(818) 840-4444 (212) 664-4444
www.nbc.com
Ted Harbert, Chairman
Stephen Burke, CEO
Matt Bond, EVP
Richard Cotton, EVP/General Counsel
Stuart Epstein, EVP/CFO
Ownership:
Owned 51% by Comcast Corp. and 49% by General Electric; NBCUniversal, 30 Rockefeller Plaza, New York, NY 10112; Tel: (212) 664-4444; Website: www.nbcuni.com; Comcast Corp, One Comcast Center, Philadelphia, PA 19103; Tel: (215) 286-1700;Website: www.comcast.com.
Primetime:
30 Rock, America's Got Talent, Animal Practice, Chicago Fire. Community Dateline, Go On, Grimm, Guys with Kids, Last Call: Carson, Law & Order SVU, The New Normal, The Office, Parenthood, Parks and Recreation, Revolution, Rock Center withBrian Williams, Tonight Show: Leno Up All Night, The Voice, Whitney.

Regional Broadcast TV Networks

ALIN-TV
149 Madison Ave., Suite 602, New York, NY 10016
(212) 889-1327
http://www.alintv.com
ALIN-TV offers locally originated progmg on a line-up of leading ind stns providing natl participation on a daily basis. Specific networks are provided to zero in on target audience progmg: prime, prime access, teen/young adult, late nightentertainment, daytime, weekend entertainment, news & kids.

American Public Television
55 Summer St. 4th Fl., Boston, MA 2110
(617) 338-4455, *Fax:* (617) 338-5369
www.aptonline.org
info@aptonline.org
Comprises WETA-TV, WHMM, both Washington, DC; WEDW(TV) Bridgeport, WEDY(TV) New Haven, WEDH(TV) Hartford, WEDN(TV) Norwich, all Connecticut; WCBB(TV) Augusta, WMED-TV Calais, WMEB-TV Orono, WMEM-TV Presque Isle, all Maine; WGBH-TV Boston,WGBX-TV Boston, WGBY-TV Springfield, all Massachusetts; WENH-TV Durham, WEKW-TV Keene, WLED-TV Littleton, all New Hampshire; WNJT-TV Trenton, New Jersey; WSKG(TV) Binghamton, WNED-TV Buffalo, WNET(TV) New York, WLIW-TV Plainview, WXXI(TV) Rochester,WMHT(TV) Schenectady, WCNY-TV Syracuse, WNPE-TV Watertown, all New York; WCET-TV Cincinnati, WVIZ-TV Cleveland, WPTD-TV Dayton, all Ohio; WLVT-TV Bethlehem-Allentown, WPSX-TV Clearfield, WITF-TV Harrisburg, WHYY-TV Philadelphia, WQED(TV) Pittsburgh,WVIA(TV) Scranton-Wilkes Barre, WQLN Erie, all Pennsylvania; WSBE-TV Providence, Rhode Island; WMPT-TV Annapolis, WMPB(TV) Baltimore, WWPB(TV) Hagerstown, WCPB-TV Salisbury, all Maryland. Service virtually all Public Television stations in the U.S.

California Farm Network
2300 River Plaza Dr., Sacramento, CA 95833
(916) 561-5550, *Fax:* (916) 561-5695
www.cfbf.com
cfbf@cfbf.com
Comprises KUVI-TV Bakersfield, KAEF-TV Eureka, KSEE-TV Fresno, KIXE-TV Redding, KRCR-TV Redding, KSBW-TV Salinas, KSBY-TV San Luis Obispo, K26AY Lakeport, KXTV-TV Sacramento, KPXN-TV Los Angeles, KFTY-TV Santa Rosa, KBHAA-TV San Francisco,all California; KYMA(TV) Yuma, Arizona; RFD-TV dish net direct TV.

California-Oregon Broadcasting Inc.
Box 1489, Medford, OR 97501
(541) 779-5555, *Fax:* (541) 779-1151
www.localnewscomesfirst.com
kobi@kobi5.com
Comprises KLSR-TV & KEVU-TV Eugene, KOTI(TV) Klamath Falls, KOBI(TV) Medford, all Oregon. Represented by John Blair & Co., Northwest.

4X Network
Box 1686, 3425 S. Broadway, Minot, ND 58701
(701) 852-2104, *Fax:* (701) 838-9360
www.kxmc.com
webmaster@kxmcnews.com
Comprises KXMB-TV Bismarck, KXMA-TV Dickinson, KXMC-TV Minot, KXMD-TV Williston, all North Dakota. Represented by Katz Continental.

Kansas Television Network
1500 N. West St., Wichita, KS 67203
(316) 943-4221, *Fax:* (316) 943-5493
www.kake.com
Comprises KLBY-TV Colby, KUPK-TV Garden City, KAKE-TV Wichita, all Kansas. Represented by Katz.

Keloland TV Young Broadcasting of Sioux Falls Inc.
KELO TV Bldg., 501 S. Phillips Ave., Sioux Falls, SD 57104
(605) 336-1100, *Fax:* (605) 334-3447, (605) 336-0202
www.keloland.com
Comprises KDLO-TV Florence, KPLO-TV Reliance, KELO-TV Sioux Falls, KCLO-TV Rapid City, all South Dakota. Represented by Adam Young Inc.

KMWB
Div/DBA: (Sinclair Communication Inc.)
1640 Como Ave., St. Paul, MN 55108
(651) 646-2300, *Fax:* (651) 646-1220
www.kmwb23.com
sales@kmwb23.com
Minnesota, Wisconsin. Represented by Millenium.

KSN Television Group
Box 333, 833 N. Main St., Wichita, KS 67201
(316) 265-3333, *Fax:* (316) 292-1197
www.ksn.com
Comprises KSNG Garden City, KSNC Great Bend, KSNT Topeka, KSNW Wichita, KSNK Oberlin, all Kansas. Represented by TeleRep. Above TV stns affiliated with NBC Television Network. Owned by SJL of KS.

KWCH-TV, Sunflower Broadcasting Inc.
Div/DBA: (formerly KWCH-TV Schurz Communications Inc.)
2815 E. 37th St., N., Wichita, KS 67219
(316) 838-1212, *Fax:* (316) 831-6198
www.kwch.com
Comprises KBSD-TV Ensign-Dodge City, KBSL-TV Goodland, KBSH-TV Hays, KWCH-TV Wichita-Hutchinson, all Kansas. Represented by HRP.

National Educational Telecommunications Association
Box 50008, Columbia, SC 29250
(803) 799-5517, *Fax:* (803) 771-4831
www.netaonline.org
skip@netaonline.org
Comprises Alabama PTV Birmingham, Alabama; KUAC Fairbanks, KYUK Bethel, Alaska; KUAT Tucson, Arizona; Arkansas ETV Conway, Arkansas; KOCE Huntington Beach, KLCS Los Angeles, both California; WBCC Cocoa, WCEU Daytona Beach, WFSU Tallahassee,WGCU Fort Myers, WLRN Miami, WSRE Pensacola, WUFT Gainesville, WUSF Tampa, WXEL West Palm Beach, all Florida; Georgia Public Broadcasting Atlanta, WPBA Atlanta, both Georgia; Idaho PTV Boise, Idaho; WNIT, Elkhart, WYIN Merrillville, both Indiana;Iowa PTV Johnston, Iowa; KOOD Bunker Hill, Kansas; Kentucky ETV Lexington, WKYU Bowling Green, both Kentucky; LA Public Broadcasting Baton Rouge, WLAE New Orleans, both Louisiana; Maryland Public Broadcasting Owings Mills, Maryland; WKAR, E. Lansing,WGVU Grand Rapids, Michigan; Minnesota, Twin Cities PTV St. Paul, Minnesota; Mississippi EB Jackson, Mississippi; KCPT Kansas City, KETC St. Louis, KMOS Warrensburg, KOZK Ozarks Public TV Springfield, all Missouri; Montana PTV Bozeman, Montana;Nebraska ETV Lincoln, Nebraska; KLVX La

Nebraska Television Network (NTV)
Box 220, Kearney, NE 68848

(308) 743-2494, *Fax:* (308) 743-2644
www.nebraska.tv
news@nebraskatv.net
Comprises KTVG(TV) Grand Island; KHGI-TV13, Kearney, Hastings, Grand Island; KWNB-TV North Platte & KSNB-TV Superior and the translators of K02HB, K17CI, K11KV, K12KW, K13OM, K13NP, K13VO, K06EY. Represented by Petry.

North Dakota Television
200 N. 4th St., Bismarck, ND 58501
(701) 255-5757, *Fax:* (701) 255-8220
www.kfyrtv.com
kfyrtv@kfyrtv.com
Comprises KFYR-TV Bismarck, KQCD-TV Dickinson, KMOT-TV Minot, KUMV-TV Williston, all North Dakota; KVLY-TV, serving North Dakota, South Dakota & Montana. Represented by Blair.

Ohio Educational Telecommunications Network Commission
2470 North Star Rd., Columbus, OH 43221
(614) 644-1714, *Fax:* (614) 644-3112
www.oet.edu
christofi@oet.state.oh.us
Comprises WEAO Akron, WNEO-TV Alliance, WOUB-TV Athens, WBGU-TV Bowling Green, WOUC-TV Cambridge, WCET Cincinnati, WVIZ-TV Cleveland, WOSU-TV Columbus, WPTD Dayton, WPTO Oxford, WPBO-TV Portsmouth, WGTE-TV Toledo, all Ohio.

Pennsylvania Public Television Network
24 Northeast Dr., Hershey, PA 17033
(717) 533-6011, *Fax:* (717) 533-4236
www.pptn.pa.us
sstrobel@state.pa.us
PPTN provides leadership & acountablity in guiding, supporting & advocating public telecommunications to educate, enlighten, inspire & connect the citizens of PA. Public stns operating across PA : WQLN-TV Erie; WITF-TV Harrisburg; WHYY-TV &WYBE-TV Philadelphia; WQED-TV Pittsburgh; WVIA-TV Scranton; WPSU-TV University Park.

Wisconsin Educational Communications Board
3319 W. Beltline Hwy., Madison, WI 53713-4296
(608) 264-9600, *Fax:* (608) 264-9664
www.ecb.org
Comprises WPNE(TV) Green Bay, WHLA-TV La Crosse, WHWC-TV Menomonie/Eau Claire, WLEF-TV Park Falls, WHRM-TV Wausau, all Wisconsin. Affils: Wisconsin: WMVS(TV) Milwaukee; WDSE-TV Duluth, Minnesota.

US TV Group Ownership

ABC Inc.
2300 Riverside Dr., Burbank CA 91521
(818) 249-9999
www.abc.go.com
Ownership: ABC Enterprises Inc., 100%. Note: ABC Enterprises Inc. is 100% owned by Disney Enterprises Inc.

TV Stns: 10 TV.
KABC-TV Los Angeles, CA; KFSN-TV Fresno, CA; KGO-TV San Francisco, CA; KTRK-TV Houston, TX; WABC-TV New York, NY; WJRT-TV Flint, MI; WLS-TV Chicago, IL; WPVI-TV Philadelphia, PA; WTVD Durham, NC; WTVG Toledo, OH;

Radio Stns: 41 AM. 3 FM.
KWDZ Salt Lake City, UT; KDDZ Arvada, CO; KSPN Los Angeles, CA; KDIZ Golden Valley, MN; KRDY San Antonio, TX; KKDZ Seattle, WA; KDZR Lake Oswego, OR; KMIK Tempe, AZ; KMKI Plano, TX; KMKY Oakland, CA; KPHN Kansas City, MO; KQAM Wichita, KS; KIID Sacramento, CA; KDIS Pasadena, CA; KMIC Houston, TX; WBOB(AM) Jacksonville, FL; WCOG Greensboro, NC; WDWD Atlanta, GA; WSDK Bloomfield, CT; WDZY Colonial Heights, VA; WEPN New York, NY; WMYM Miami, FL; WFDF Farmington Hills, MI; WGFY Charlotte, NC; WDDY Albany, NY; WHKT Portsmouth, VA; WDYZ Orlando, FL; WKSH Sussex, WI; WDDZ Pittsburgh, PA; WMVP Chicago, IL; WHBE Newburg, KY; WNTT Tazewell, TN; WPMH Portsmouth, VA; WHTY(AM) Riviera Beach, FL; WMKI Boston, MA; WQEW New York, NY; WRDZ La Grange, IL; WSDZ Belleville, IL; WWJZ Mount Holly, NJ; WWMI St. Petersburg, FL; WWMK Cleveland, OH; KESN Allen, TX; KDIS-FM Little Rock, AR; WRDZ-FM Plainfield, IN;

Phillip J. Meek, President
Robert A. Iger, Vice President
Lawrence J. Pollock, Chairman/Owner

Access.1 Communications Corp.
11 Penn Plaza, 16th Fl., New York NY 10001
(212) 714-1000; *Fax:*(212) 714-1563;

TV Stns: 1 TV.
WMGM-TV Wildwood, NJ;

Radio Stns: 5 AM. 10 FM.
KCUL Marshall, TX; KFRO Longview, TX; KOKA Shreveport, LA; WGYM Hammonton, NJ; WWRL New York, NY; KCUL-FM Marshall, TX; KBTT Haughton, LA; KKUS Tyler, TX; KOYE Frankston, TX; KSYR Benton, LA; KOOI Jacksonville, TX; KDKS-FM Blanchard, LA; KLKL Minden, LA; KTAL-FM Texarkana, TX; KYKX Longview, TX;

Sydney Small, CEO

ACME Communications Inc.
2101 E. Fourth St., Suite 202A, Santa Ana CA 92705
(714) 245-9499; *Fax:*(714) 245-9494
www.acmecommunications.com
t.allen@acmecomm.com

TV Stns: 7 TV.
KASY-TV Albuquerque, NM; KWBQ Santa Fe, NM; WBDT Springfield, OH; WBUI Decatur, IL; WBXX-TV/DT Crossville, TN; WBUW Janesville, WI; KRWB-TV Roswell, NM;

Jamie Kellner, Chairman
Tom Allen, CFO
Doug Gealy, President

Allbritton Communications Co.
1000 Wilson Blvd., Suite 2700, Arlington VA 22209
(703) 647-8700; *Fax:*(703) 647-8707;

TV Stns: 8 TV.
KATV Little Rock, AR; KTUL Tulsa, OK; WCFT-TV Tuscaloosa, AL; WCIV Charleston, SC; WHTM-TV Harrisburg, PA; WJLA-TV Washington, DC; WJSU-TV Anniston, AL; WSET-TV Lynchburg, VA;

Robert Allbritton, CEO
Frederick Ryan Jr., President

American Spirit Media LLC
2131 Ayrsley Town Blvd., Suite 300, Charlotte NC 28273
(704) 643-4148
Ownership: Thomas B. Henson, 100%.

TV Stns: 5 TV.
KYOU-TV Ottumwa, IA; WSFX-TV Wilmington, NC; WUPV Ashland, VA; WUPW Toledo, OH; WXTX Columbus, GA;

Bahakel Communications
Box 32488, Charlotte NC 28232
(704) 372-4434; *Fax:*(704) 335-9904
Ownership: Bahakel Communications

TV Stns: 7 TV.
WAKA Selma, AL; WBBJ-TV Jackson, TN; WCCB Charlotte, NC; WCCU Urbana, IL; WFXB Myrtle Beach, SC; WOLO-TV Columbia, SC; WRSP-TV Springfield, IL;

Radio Stns: 3 AM. 5 FM.
KWLO Waterloo, IA; KXEL Waterloo, IA; WDEF Chattanooga, TN; KFMW Waterloo, IA; KILO Colorado Springs, CO; KOKZ Waterloo, IA; KRXP Pueblo West, CO; WDEF-FM Chattanooga, TN;

Beverly B. Poston, President
Russell Schwartz, General Counsel
John Hutchinson, SVP/Television
Jim Babb, Executive Vice President

Barrington Broadcasting Group, LLC.
2500 W. Higgins Rd., Suite 155, Hoffman Estates IL 60169-7275
(847) 884-1877; *Fax:*(847) 755-3045
www.barringtontv.com
info@barringtontv.com

TV Stns: 18 TV.
KGBT-TV Harlingen, TX; KHQA-TV Hannibal, MO; KRCG Jefferson City, MO; KTVO Kirksville, MO; KVIH-TV Clovis, NM; KVII-TV Amarillo, TX; KXRM-TV Colorado Springs, CO; WACH Columbia, SC; WEYI-TV Saginaw, MI; WFXL Albany, GA; WHOI Peoria, IL; WLUC-TV Marquette, MI; WNWO-TV Toledo, OH; WPBN-TV Traverse City, MI; WPDE-TV Florence, SC; WSTM-TV Syracuse, NY; WTOM-TV Cheboygan, MI; WBSF Bay City, MI;

K. James Yager, CEO
Chris Cornelius, President
Keith Bland, Operations Dir
Warren Spector, CFO
Paul McNicol, Secretary
Mary Flodin, Senior VP

Beach TV Properties Inc.
Box 9556, Panama City Beach FL 32407

TV Stns: 2 TV.
WAWD Fort Walton Beach, FL; WPCT Panama City Beach, FL

Byron Colley, President

Bell Media Inc.
299 Queen Street West, Toronto ON M5V 2Z5
(416) 384-8000
www.bellmedia.ca
bellmediacommunications@bellmedia.ca

TV Stns: 9 TV.
CFPL-DT London, ON; CHROTV Pembroke, ON; CHWI-DT Wheatley, ON; CIVT-DT Vancouver, BC; CKVR-DT Barrie, ON; CKX-TV Brandon, MB; CIVI-DT Victoria, BC; CIANTV Calgary, AB; CHRO-DT-43 Ottawa, ON;

Radio Stns: 10 AM. 21 FM.
CFAX Victoria, BC; CFGO Ottawa, ON; CFRA Ottawa, ON; CFTE Vancouver, BC; CHUM Toronto, ON; CFRW Winnipeg, MB; CKGM Montreal, QC; CKLW Windsor, ON; CKST Vancouver, BC; CKWW Windsor, ON; CFCAFM Kitchener, ON; CFLYFM Kingston, ON; CFWM-FM Winnipeg, MB; CHIQFM Winnipeg, MB; CHQMFM Vancouver, BC; CHUMFM Toronto, ON; CJPT-FM Brockville, ON; CIDR-FM Windsor, ON; CIMX Windsor, ON; CIOOFM Halifax, NS; CJMJ Ottawa, ON; CKKL Ottawa, ON; CKLY-FM Lindsay (city of Kawartha Lakes), ON; CKQMFM Peterborough, ON; CHBE-FM Victoria, BC; CFBT-FM Vancouver, BC; CKCE-FM Calgary, AB; CKPT-FM Peterborough, ON; CKLC-FM Kingston, ON; CJCH-FM Halifax, NS; CKKW-FM Kitchener, ON;

Kevin Crull, President
Gary Anderson, Senior Vice President
Steven Bickley, EVP Marketing/Development
Rita Fabian, General Sales Mgr

Belo Corp
400 S. Record St., Dallas TX 75202
(214) 977-6600; *Fax:*(214) 977-6603
www.belo.com
Ownership: Belo Corp.

TV Stns: 19 TV.
KASW Phoenix, AZ; KENS San Antonio, TX; KGW Portland, OR; KHOU Houston, TX; KING-TV Seattle, WA; KMOV St. Louis, MO; KMSB Tucson, AZ; KONG Everett, WA; KREM Spokane, WA; KSKN Spokane, WA; KTTU Tucson, AZ; KTVB Boise, ID; KTVK Phoenix, AZ; KVUE Austin, TX; WCNC-TV Charlotte, NC; WFAA Dallas, TX; WHAS-TV Louisville, KY; WVEC Hampton, VA; WWL-TV New Orleans, LA;

Robert Decherd, Chairman
Dunia Shive, President/COO

Better Life Ministries
8320 W. 66th Ave., Arvada CO 80004
(303) 431-0103;

TV Stns: 1 TV.
KTVC Roseburg, OR;

Claud Pettit, President

Block Communications Inc.
6450 Monroe St., Sylvania OH 43560
(419) 724-6448; *Fax:*(419) 724-6167
www.blockcommunications.com
Ownership: Estate of William Block, Allan Block, John R. Block.

TV Stns: 5 TV.
KTRV-TV Nampa, ID; WAND Decatur, IL; WDRB Louisville, KY; WMYO Salem, IN; WLIO Lima, OH;

Allan Block, Chairman
David Huey, President
Gary J. Blair, EVP
Jodi Miehls, Treasurer

Bonneville International Corporation
Broadcast House, Box 1160, Salt Lake City UT 84110-1160
(801) 575-7500; *Fax:*(801) 575-7521
www.bonnint.com
Ownership: Deseret Management Corp. Deseret Management Corp. owns The Deseret Morning News, a Salt Lake City, UT, daily.

TV Stns: 1 TV.
KSL-TV Salt Lake City, UT;

Radio Stns: 8 AM. 21 FM.
KIRO Seattle, WA; KMVP Phoenix, AZ; KTTH Seattle, WA; KSL Salt Lake City, UT; KTAR Phoenix, AZ; WBQH(AM) Silver Spring, MD; WFED Washington, DC; WWFD Frederick, MD; KIRO-FM Tacoma, WA; KSWD Los Angeles, CA; KTAR-FM Glendale, AZ; KPKX Phoenix, AZ; KSL-FM Midvale, UT; KRSP-FM Salt Lake City, UT; KSFI Salt Lake City, UT; WTOP-FM Washington, DC; WIL-FM St. Louis, MO; WARH Granite City, IL; WKRQ Cincinnati, OH; WYGY Fort Thomas, KY; WDRV Chicago, IL; WWDV Zion, IL; WILV Chicago, IL; WTMX Skokie, IL; WWWT-FM Manassas, VA; WUBE-FM Cincinnati, OH; WXOS East St. Louis, IL; WTLP Braddock Heights, MD; WYGY(FM) Fort Thomas, KY;

Robert Johnson, COO
Bruce Reese, President

Bonten Media Group LLC
675 Third Ave., Suite 2521, New York NY 10017
(212) 710-7771; *Fax:*(212) 949-0909
www.bontenmedia.com
invest@bontenmedia.com

TV Stns: 7 TV.
KAEF-TV Arcata, CA; KCFW-TV Kalispell, MT; KECI-TV Missoula, MT; KRCR-TV Redding, CA; KTVM-TV Butte, MT; KTXS-TV Sweetwater, TX; WCYB-TV Bristol, VA;

Randall Bongarten, Chairman

Cadillac Telecasting Co.
7669 S. 45 Rd., Cadillac MI 49601
(231) 775-9813; *Fax:*(231) 775-1898
www.fox33.com
info@fox33.com

TV Stns: 2 TV.
WFQX-TV Cadillac, MI; WFUP Vanderbilt, MI;

Alexander Bolea, President

California Oregon Broadcasting Inc.
Box 1489, Medford OR 97501
(541) 779-5555; *Fax:*(541) 779-1151
cobiadmin@kobi5.com
Ownership: Patricia C. Smullin and Carol Anne Smullin Brown. Other interests: Cable TV: Crestview Cable TV (systems in Oregon).

TV Stns: 3 TV.
KLSR-TV Eugene, OR; KOBI Medford, OR; KOTI Klamath Falls, OR;

Patricia Smullin, Owner

Capital Community Broadcasting Inc.
360 Egan Dr., Juneau AK 99801-1748
(907) 586-1670; *Fax:*(907) 586-3612;

TV Stns: 1 TV.
KTOO-TV Juneau, AK;

Radio Stns: 3 FM.
KRNN Juneau, AK; KXLL Juneau, AK; KTOO Juneau, AK;

Capitol Broadcasting Co. Inc.
Box 12000, Raleigh NC 27605
(919) 821-8555; *Fax:*(919) 821-8733
www.cbc-raleigh.com
Ownership: Capitol Holding Co. Inc.

TV Stns: 4 TV.
WMYT-TV Rock Hill, SC; WJZY Belmont, NC; WRAL-TV Raleigh, NC; WRAZ Raleigh, NC;

Radio Stns: 1 AM. 8 FM.
WMFD Wilmington, NC; WUIN Oak Island, NC; WCMC-FM Holly Springs, NC; WRMR(FM) Jacksonville, NC; WKXB Boiling Spring

Lakes, NC; WRAL Raleigh, NC; WILT Wilmington, NC; WAZO Southport, NC; WLQC Sharpsburg, NC;
James R. Hefner, III, VP, TV
Michael D. Hill, VP/General Counsel
Daniel P. McGrath, Vp/CFO
James Goodmon, President
Vicke S. Murray, Secretary

CaribeVision Station Group LLC
1401 Brickell Ave., Suite 500, Miami FL 33131
(305) 381-8500; *Fax:*(305) 381-6225;
TV Stns: 4 TV.
WIRS Yauco, PR; WJPX San Juan, PR; WJWN-TV San Sebastian, PR; WKPV Ponce, PR;
Carlos Barba, CEO

CBS Television Stations Group
524 W. 57th St., 3rd Fl., New York NY 10019
(212) 975-4321
cbslocal.com
Ownership: Viacom Inc., 100%.
TV Stns: 30 TV.
KBCW San Francisco, CA; KCAL Redlands, CA; KCBS-TV Los Angeles, CA; KCCO-TV Alexandria, MN; KCCW-TV Walker, MN; KCNC-TV Denver, CO; KDKA-TV Pittsburgh, PA; KMAX-TV Sacramento, CA; KOVR Stockton, CA; KPIX-TV San Francisco, CA; KSTW Tacoma, WA; KTVT Fort Worth, TX; KTXA Fort Worth, TX; KYW-TV Philadelphia, PA; WBBM-TV Chicago, IL; WBFS-TV Miami, FL; WBZ-TV Boston, MA; WCBS-TV New York, NY; WCCO-TV Minneapolis, MN; WFOR-TV Miami, FL; WGNT Portsmouth, VA; WJZ-TV Baltimore, MD; WKBD-TV Detroit, MI; WPCW Jeannette, PA; WPSG Philadelphia, PA; WSBK-TV Boston, MA; WTOG St. Petersburg, FL; WUPA Atlanta, GA; WUPL Slidell, LA; WWJ-TV Detroit, MI;
Radio Stns: 1 AM.
KCAL Redlands, CA;
Tom Kane, President

Chambers Communications Corp.
Box 7009, Eugene OR 97401
(541) 485-5611; *Fax:*(541) 342-1568
www.cmc.net/chambers
kezi@kezi.com
Ownership: Carolyn S. Chambers. Other interests: Oregon cable TV.
TV Stns: 4 TV.
KDKF Klamath Falls, OR; KDRV Medford, OR; KEZI Eugene, OR; KOHD Bend, OR;
Carolyn Chambers, CEO
Scott Chambers, President

Christian Television Corporation Inc.
6922 142nd Ave. N., Largo FL 33771
(727) 535-5622; *Fax:*(727) 531-2497
www.ctnonline.com
TV Stns: 2 TV.
KFXB-TV Dubuque, IA; WCLF Clearwater, FL;
Robert D'Andrea, President

Citadel Communications Co. LTD.
44 Pondfield Rd., Suite 12, Bronxville NY 10708
(914) 793-3400; *Fax:*(914) 793-3693
citnyltd@aol.com
Ownership: (Coronet Communications, Capital Communications, Citadel Comm. LLC.)
TV Stns: 4 TV.
KCAU-TV Sioux City, IA; KLKN Lincoln, NE; WHBF-TV Rock Island, IL; WOI-TV Ames, IA;
Philip Lombardo, CEO

Cocola Broadcasting Companies LLC
706 W. Herndon Ave., Fresno CA 93650
(559) 435-7000; *Fax:*(559) 435-3201
www.cocolatv.com
info@cocolatv.com
TV Stns: 3 TV.
KGMC Clovis, CA; KKJB Boise, ID; KVME-TV Bishop, CA;
Gary Cocola, CEO

Commonwealth Broadcasting Corp.
113 W. Public Sq., Suite 400, Glasgow KY 42141
(270) 659-2002; *Fax:*(270) 651-1771;
TV Stns: 1 TV.
WABG-TV Greenwood, MS;
Radio Stns: 8 AM. 13 FM.
WGRK Jeffersontown, KY; WWKU Plum Springs, KY; WIEL Elizabethtown, KY; WLUE Eminence, KY; WLBN Lebanon, KY; WPKY Princeton, KY; WTCO Campbellsville, KY; WTTL Madisonville, KY; WYSB Springfield, KY; WAVJ Princeton, KY; WCKQ Campbellsville, KY; WGRK-FM Greensburg, KY; WHHT Horse Cave, KY; WWKY Providence, KY; WRZI Hodgenville, KY; WLSK Lebanon, KY; WKMO Lebanon Junction, KY; WOVO Glasgow, KY; WHHT(FM) Cave City, KY; WTHX Vine Grove, KY; WTTL-FM Madisonville, KY;
Steven Newberry, CEO
W. Dale Thornhill, President

Communications Corp. of America
Box 53708, Lafayette LA 70505-3708
(337) 237-1142; *Fax:*(337) 237-1373;
TV Stns: 10 TV.
KADN-TV Lafayette, LA; KETK-TV Jacksonville, TX; KMSS-TV Shreveport, LA; KPEJ-TV Odessa, TX; KTSM-TV El Paso, TX; KVEO-TV Brownsville, TX; KWKT-TV Waco, TX; KYLE-TV Bryan, TX; WEVV-TV Evansville, IN; WGMB-TV Baton Rouge, LA;
Thomas Galloway, Chairman
Wayne Elmore, CEO

Cordillera Communications Inc.
600 E. Superior St., Suite 203, Duluth MN 55802
(218) 625-3045; *Fax:*(218) 625-3047
www.cordillera.tv
Ownership: Evening Post Publishing Co., 100%.
TV Stns: 11 TV.
KATC Lafayette, LA; KBZK Bozeman, MT; KOAA-TV Pueblo, CO; KPAX-TV Missoula, MT; KRIS-TV Corpus Christi, TX; KRTV Great Falls, MT; KSBY San Luis Obispo, CA; KTVQ Billings, MT; KVOA Tucson, AZ; KXLF-TV Butte, MT; WLEX-TV Lexington, KY;
Terrance Hurley, President
Lamont Wallis, VP
Andrew Suk, VP/Technology

Cornerstone TeleVision Inc.
1 Signal Hill Dr., Wall PA 15148-1499
(412) 824-3930; *Fax:*(412) 824-5442
www.ctvn.org
info@ctvn.org
Ownership: Nonprofit.
TV Stns: 2 TV.
WKBS-TV Altoona, PA; WPCB-TV Greensburg, PA;
Ron Hembree, President

Cowles California Media Co.
W. 999 Riverside Ave., Spokane WA 99201
(509) 459-5520; *Fax:*(509) 459-3815;
TV Stns: 2 TV.
KCOY-TV Santa Maria, CA; KION-TV Monterey, CA;
Elizabeth Allison Cowles, President

Cox Media Group
6205 Peachtree Dunwoody Rd., Atlanta GA 30328
(678) 645-0000; *Fax:*(678) 645-5002
www.coxmediagroup.com
Ownership: Cox Enterprises Inc., 100%.
TV Stns: 13 TV.
KFOX-TV El Paso, TX; KICU-TV San Jose, CA; KIRO-TV Seattle, WA; KRXI-TV Reno, NV; KTVU Oakland, CA; WAXN-TV Kannapolis, NC; WFTV Orlando, FL; WJAC-TV Johnstown, PA; WPXI Pittsburgh, PA; WRDQ Orlando, FL; WSB-TV Atlanta, GA; WSOC-TV Charlotte, NC; WTOV-TV Steubenville, OH;
Radio Stns: 1 FM.
WHIO-FM Pleasant Hill, OH;
Doug Franklin, Chairman
Bill Hoffman, EVP
Jane Williams, SVP

Cox Television
Box 105357, Atlanta GA 30348-5357
(678) 645-0000; *Fax:*(678) 645-5250
www.coxenterprises.com
TV Stns: 1 TV.
WHIO-TV Dayton, OH;
Bruce Baker, President

CP Media LLC
1181 Hwy. 315, Wilkes-Barre PA 18702
(570) 970-5600;
TV Stns: 4 TV.
WGFL High Springs, FL; WQMY Williamsport, PA; WOLF-TV Hazleton, PA; WTLH Bainbridge, GA;
John Parente, President

Cunningham Broadcasting Corporation
2000 W. 41st St., Baltimore MD 21211
(410) 662-9688; *Fax:*(410) 662-0816;
TV Stns: 5 TV.
WMYA-TV Anderson, SC; WNUV Baltimore, MD; WRGT-TV Dayton, OH; WTAT-TV Charleston, SC; WTTE Columbus, OH;
Robert Simmons, CEO

Dispatch Broadcast Group
770 Twin Rivers Dr., Columbus OH 43215
(614) 460-3700; *Fax:*(614) 460-2809
www.10tv.com
Ownership: Dispatch Printing Company
TV Stns: 2 TV.
WBNS-TV Columbus, OH; WTHR Indianapolis, IN;
Radio Stns: 1 AM. 1 FM.
WBNS Columbus, OH; WBNS-FM Columbus, OH;
Michael Fiorile, President
Tamara Clapsaddle, Controller

Diversified Communications
121 Free St., Box 7437, Portland ME 04112-7437
(207) 842-5400; *Fax:*(207) 842-5405
www.divbusiness.com
Ownership: Horace A. Hildreth Jr., Josephine H. Detmer. See Cross-Ownership, Sect. A. Cable TV: New England Cablevision Inc.
TV Stns: 2 TV.
WABI-TV Bangor, ME; WCJB-TV Gainesville, FL;
David H. Lowell, President

Duhamel Broadcasting Enterprises
Box 1760, Rapid City SD 57709
(605) 342-2000; *Fax:*(605) 342-7305
www.kotatv.com
Ownership: William F. Duhamel, 63%; Peter A. and Lois G. Duhamel, 37%.
TV Stns: 4 TV.
KDUH-TV Scottsbluff, NE; KHSD-TV Lead, SD; KOTA-TV Rapid City, SD; KSGW-TV Sheridan, WY;
Radio Stns: 1 AM. 1 FM.
KOTA Rapid City, SD; KDDX Spearfish, SD;
William Duhamel, President

Eagle Creek Broadcasting LLC
2111 University Park Dr., Suite 650, Okemos MI 48864
(517) 347-4141,
bradybw1@comcast.net
TV Stns: 2 TV.
KVTV Laredo, TX; KZTV Corpus Christi, TX;
Brian Brady, CEO

Entravision Communications Corp.
2425 Olympic Blvd., Suite 6000W, Santa Monica CA 90404
(310) 447-3872; *Fax:*(310) 447-3899
www.entravision.com
kthompson@entravision.com
TV Stns: 20 TV.
KCEC Denver, CO; KINC Las Vegas, NV; KINT-TV El Paso, TX; KTFN El Paso, TX; KLDO-TV Laredo, TX; KLUZ-TV Albuquerque, NM; KNVO McAllen, TX; KORO Corpus Christi, TX; KPMR Santa Barbara, CA; KREN-TV Reno, NV; KSMS-TV Monterey, CA; KUPB Midland, TX; KVYE El Centro, CA; WVEA-TV Venice, FL; WUVN Hartford, CT; WJAL Hagerstown, MD; WVEN-TV Daytona Beach, FL; WUNI Worcester, MA; KVSN-DT Pueblo, CO; KDCU-DT Derby, KS;
Radio Stns: 12 AM. 36 FM.
KWST El Centro, CA; KSVE El Paso, TX; KBZO Lubbock, TX; KCVR Lodi, CA; KGOL Humble, TX; KMXA Aurora, CO; KRZY Albuquerque, NM; KHRO El Paso, TX; KBMB Black Canyon City, AZ; KMBX Soledad, CA; WACA Wheaton, MD; WLQY Hollywood, FL; KDLD Santa Monica, CA; KYSE El Paso, TX; KDLE Newport Beach, CA; KBMB(FM) Sacramento, CA; KFRQ Harlingen, TX; KXSE Davis, CA; KINT-FM El Paso, TX; KJMN Castle Rock, CO; KKPS Brownsville, TX; KLNZ Glendale, AZ; KLOB Thousand Palms, CA; KLOK-FM Greenfield, CA; KSSE Arcadia, CA; KMIX Tracy, CA; KDVA Buckeye, AZ; KMXX Imperial, CA; KOFX El Paso, TX; KRCX-FM Marysville, CA; KRRN Moapa Valley, NV; KRNV-FM Reno, NV; KNTY Shingle Springs, CA; KLYY Riverside, CA; KSSD Fallbrook, CA; KCVR-FM Columbia, CA; KQRT Las Vegas, NV; KVLY Edinburg, TX; KNVO-FM Port Isabel, TX; KSES-FM Seaside, CA; KVVA-FM Apache Junction, AZ; KSSC Ventura, CA; KSEH Brawley, CA; KXPK Evergreen, CO; KTSE-FM Patterson, CA; WNUE-FM Deltona, FL; KAIQ Wolfforth, TX; KPVW Aspen, CO;
Philip Wilkinson, President
Walter Ulloa, Chairman/CEO

Equity Media Holdings Corp.
1 Shackleford Dr., Suite 400, Little Rock AR 72211
(501) 219-2400; *Fax:*(501) 221-1101
www.emdaholdings.com
TV Stns: 12 TV.

KEYU Borger, TX; KQUP Pullman, WA; KQCK Cheyenne, WY; KMYA-DT Camden, AR; KWBM Harrison, AR; KXNW Eureka Springs, AR; WPXS Mount Vernon, IL; KWWF Waterloo, IA; KUTF Logan, UT; DKBTZ Butte, MT; WNYI Ithaca, NY; KUTH-DT Provo, UT;

John Oxendine, CEO
Larry Morton, President
Emilia Chastain, Operations Dir
Lori Withrow, Secretary
Greg Fess, Vice President
James Hearnsberger, Vice President
Max Hooper, Vice President

Esteem Broadcasting
13865 E. Elliott Dr., Marshall IL 62441
(217) 826-6095;

TV Stns: 3 TV.
WEMT Greeneville, TN; WFXI Morehead City, NC; WYDO Greenville, NC;
David L. Bailey, President

Family Stations Inc.
290 Hegenberger Rd., Oakland CA 94621
(510) 568-6200; *Fax:*(510) 568-6190
Ownership: Nonprofit corporation.

TV Stns: 1 TV.
WFME-TV West Milford, NJ;

Radio Stns: 12 AM. 54 FM.
KARR Kirkland, WA; KEBR Rocklin, CA; KECR El Cajon, CA; KEAR San Francisco, CA; KFRN Long Beach, CA; KKAA Aberdeen, SD; KQKD Redfield, SD; KYFR Shenandoah, IA; WFSI Baltimore, MD; WBMD Baltimore, MD; WCTF Vernon, CT; WCUE Cuyahoga Falls, OH; KDFR Des Moines, IA; KEAR-FM Sacramento, CA; KEFR Le Grand, CA; KFNO Fresno, CA; KFRB Bakersfield, CA; KFRS Soledad, CA; KHAP Chico, CA; KJVH Longview, WA; KPHF Phoenix, AZ; KPOR Emporia, KS; KPRA Ukiah, CA; KQFE Springfield, OR; KTXB Beaumont, TX; KUFR Salt Lake City, UT; WBFR Birmingham, AL; WEFR Erie, PA; WFBF Buffalo, NY; WFCH Charleston, SC; WFME Newark, NJ; WFRC Columbus, GA; WFRH Kingston, NY; WFRJ Johnstown, PA; WFRS Smithtown, NY; WFRW Webster, NY; WLZL Annapolis, MD; WFTI-FM St. Petersburg, FL; WJCH Joliet, IL; WMFL Florida City, FL; WMWK Milwaukee, WI; WOTL Toledo, OH; WQLZ Taylorville, IL; WWFR Stuart, FL; WYTN Youngstown, OH; WOFR Schoolcraft, MI; KBFR Bismarck, ND; KEDR(FM) Butte, MT; KEGR Fort Dodge, IA; KPFR Pine Grove, OR; KFRJ China Lake, CA; KHFR Santa Maria, CA; WFRP Americus, GA; KQFR Rapid City, SD; KFRP Coalinga, CA; KEDR Bay City, TX; KFRW Great Falls, MT; KFRY Pueblo, CO; KFRD Butte, MT; KYOR Newport, OR; WUFR Bedford, PA; WKDN(FM) State College, PA; KXFR Socorro, NM; KEAF Fort Smith, AR; KXBC Garberville, CA; KIFR Alice, TX;
Harold Camping, President

Fisher Communications Inc.
100 4th Ave. N., Suite 440, Suite 1525, Seattle WA 98109
(206) 404-7000; *Fax:*(206) 404-7050
www.fsci.com

TV Stns: 12 TV.
KATU Portland, OR; KBOI-TV Boise, ID; KUNS-TV Bellevue, WA; KUNP La Grande, OR; KCBY-TV Coos Bay, OR; KEPR-TV Pasco, WA; KIDK Idaho Falls, ID; KIMA-TV Yakima, WA; KLEW-TV Lewiston, ID; KOMO-TV Seattle, WA; KPIC Roseburg, OR; KVAL-TV Eugene, OR;

Radio Stns: 3 AM. 4 FM.
KOMO Seattle, WA; KQDI Great Falls, MT; KVI Seattle, WA; KPLZ-FM Seattle, WA; KQDI-FM Great Falls, MT; KINX Fairfield, MT; KIKF Cascade, MT;
Collen Brown, President/CEO

Fort Myers Broadcasting Co.
2824 Palm Beach Blvd., Fort Myers FL 33916
(239) 334-1111; *Fax:*(239) 334-0744
winktv.com
manaager@winktv.com

TV Stns: 1 TV.
WINK-TV Fort Myers, FL;

Radio Stns: 1 AM. 2 FM.
WNPL Golden Gate, FL; WTLQ-FM Punta Rassa, FL; WINK-FM Fort Myers, FL;
Brian McBride, CEO
Gary Gardner, Operations Dir

Forum Communications Co.
Box 2020, Fargo ND 58107
(701) 235-7311; *Fax:*(701) 241-5406
www.in-forum.com

TV Stns: 4 TV.
KBMY Bismarck, ND; KMCY Minot, ND; WDAY-TV Fargo, ND; WDAZ-TV Devil's Lake, ND;

Radio Stns: 1 AM. 1 FM.
WDAY Fargo, ND; WZUU Mattawan, MI;
William Marcil, President

Four Points Media Group
299 S. Main St., Suite 150, Salt Lake City UT 84111
(801) 973-3000; *Fax:*(801) 973-3387;

TV Stns: 5 TV.
KEYE-TV Austin, TX; KMYU Saint George, UT; KUTV Salt Lake City, UT; WLWC New Bedford, MA; WTVX Fort Pierce, FL;
Mark Ploof, COO

Fox Television Stations Inc.
1999 S. Bundy Dr., Los Angeles CA 90025-5235
(310) 584-2000
www.newscorp.com
Ownership: Fox Entertainment Group Inc., 85.2% voting interest. Note: Fox Entertainment Group Inc. is a wholly-owned subsidiary of News Corp.

TV Stns: 28 TV.
KCOP-TV Los Angeles, CA; KDFI Dallas, TX; KDFW Dallas, TX; KFTC Bemidji, MN; KMSP-TV Minneapolis, MN; KRIV Houston, TX; KTBC Austin, TX; KTTV Los Angeles, CA; KTXH Houston, TX; KUTP Phoenix, AZ; WAGA-TV Atlanta, GA; WDAF-TV Kansas City, MO; WDCA Washington, DC; WFLD Chicago, IL; WFTC Minneapolis, MN; WFXT Boston, MA; WHBQ-TV Memphis, TN; WJBK Detroit, MI; WNYW New York, NY; WOFL Orlando, FL; WOGX Ocala, FL; WPWR-TV Gary, IN; WRBW Orlando, FL; WTTG Washington, DC; WTVT Tampa, FL; WTXF-TV Philadelphia, PA; WUTB Baltimore, MD; WWOR-TV Secaucus, NJ;
Jack Abernethy, CEO
Roger Ailes, Chairman
Dennis Swanson, Presidant
Kevin Hale, General Manager

Gannett Broadcasting
7950 Jones Branch Dr., Mclean VA 22107
(703) 854-6760; *Fax:*(703) 854-2005
www.gannett.com
Ownership: (Division of Gannett Co. Inc.)

TV Stns: 23 TV.
KARE Minneapolis, MN; KNAZ-TV Flagstaff, AZ; KPNX Mesa, AZ; KSDK St. Louis, MO; KTHV Little Rock, AR; KTVD Denver, CO; KUSA Denver, CO; KXTV Sacramento, CA; WATL Atlanta, GA; WBIR-TV Knoxville, TN; WCSH Portland, ME; WFMY-TV Greensboro, NC; WGRZ Buffalo, NY; WJXX Orange Park, FL; WKYC-DT Cleveland, OH; WLBZ Bangor, ME; WLTX Columbia, SC; WMAZ-TV Macon, GA; WTLV Jacksonville, FL; WTSP St. Petersburg, FL; WUSA Washington, DC; WXIA-TV Atlanta, GA; WZZM Grand Rapids, MI;
Dave Lougee, President

Granite Broadcasting Corp.
767 Third Ave., 34th Fl., New York NY 10017
(212) 826-2530; *Fax:*(212) 826-2858
www.granitetv.com

TV Stns: 10 TV.
KBJR-TV Superior, WI; KOFY-TV San Francisco, CA; KSEE Fresno, CA; WBNG-TV Binghamton, NY; WMYD Detroit, MI; WEEK-TV Peoria, IL; WKBW-TV Buffalo, NY; WISE-TV Fort Wayne, IN; WTVH Syracuse, NY; KRII Chisholm, MN;
Ellen McClain, CEO
John Deushane, COO
Stuart Beck, President
Larry Willis, CFO

Grant Communications Inc.
915 Middle River Dr., Suite 409, Fort Lauderdale FL 33304
(954) 568-2000; *Fax:*(954) 568-2015
Ownership: The Milton Grant Living Trust, Jack L. Lewis, business trustee.

TV Stns: 7 TV.
KGCW Burlington, IA; KLJB Davenport, IA; WEUX Chippewa Falls, WI; WFXR Roanoke, VA; WWCW Lynchburg, VA; WLAX La Crosse, WI; WZDX Huntsville, AL;
Mark Ryan, CFO

Gray Television Inc.
Box 1867, Albany GA 31702-1867
(229) 888-9390; *Fax:*(229) 888-9374
www.graytvinc.com
cindy.holden@gcslink.com
Ownership: Bull Run Corp., Datasouth Computer Corp. and affiliated companies. Other interests: Porta Phone Paging Inc. and Lynqx.

TV Stns: 34 TV.
KAKE Wichita, KS; KBTX-TV Bryan, TX; KGIN Grand Island, NE; KKCO Grand Junction, CO; KKTV Colorado Springs, CO; KLBY Colby, KS; KOLN Lincoln, NE; KOLO-TV Reno, NV; KUPK Garden City, KS; KWTX-TV Waco, TX; KXII Sherman, TX; WBKO Bowling Green, KY; WCTV Thomasville, GA; WEAU-TV Eau Claire, WI; WSWG Valdosta, GA; WHSV-TV Harrisonburg, VA; WIBW-TV Topeka, KS; WIFR Freeport, IL; WILX-TV Onondaga, MI; WITN-TV Washington, NC; WJHG-TV Panama City, FL; WKYT-TV Lexington, KY; WMTV Madison, WI; WNDU-TV South Bend, IN; WOWT Omaha, NE; WRDW-TV Augusta, GA; WSAW-TV Wausau, WI; WSAZ-TV Huntington, WV; WTAP-TV Parkersburg, WV; WTOK-TV Meridian, MS; WTVY Dothan, AL; WVLT-TV Knoxville, TN; WYMT-TV Hazard, KY; WCAV Charlottesville, VA;
James Ryan, VP/CFO
Robert Prather Jr., President/COO
J. Mack Robinson, Chairman

Griffin Communications L.L.C.
7401 N. Kelley Ave., Oklahoma City OK 73111
(405) 843-6641; *Fax:*(405) 841-9135
www.griffincommunications.net

TV Stns: 3 TV.
KOTV-DT Tulsa, OK; KQCW-DT Muskogee, OK; KWTV-DT Oklahoma City, OK;
Ted Strickland, CFO
David Griffin, President
Dick Dutton, Operations Dir
Joyce Reed, Vice President
Kathy Haney, Vice President
Steve Foerster, Vice President

Hearst Corporation
300 West 57th Street, New York NY 10019
(212) 649-2000
www.hearst.com
contact@hearst.com

TV Stns: 5 TV.
KOCO-TV Oklahoma City, OK; WBAL-TV Baltimore, MD; WLKY-TV Louisville, KY; WMUR-TV Manchester, NH; WPTZ North Pole, NY;
Frank Bennack, Chief Executive Officer
Steven Scwartz, Chief Operating Officer
Ronald Doerfler, Senior Vice President

Hearst Television Inc.
300 W. 57th St., 39th Fl., New York NY 10019
(212) 887-6800; *Fax:*(212) 887-6855
www.hearstargyle.com
Ownership: The Hearst Corp., 65%.

TV Stns: 26 TV.
KCCI Des Moines, IA; KCRA-TV Sacramento, CA; KCWE Kansas City, MO; KETV Omaha, NE; KHBS Fort Smith, AR; KHOG-TV Fayetteville, AR; KHVO Hilo, HI; KITV Honolulu, HI; KMAU Wailuku, HI; KMBC-TV Kansas City, MO; KOAT-TV Albuquerque, NM; KQCA Stockton, CA; KSBW Salinas, CA; WAPT Jackson, MS; WCVB-TV Boston, MA; WDSU New Orleans, LA; WGAL Lancaster, PA; WISN-TV Milwaukee, WI; WKCF Clermont, FL; WLWT Cincinnati, OH; WMTW Poland Spring, ME; WNNE Hartford, VT; WPBF Tequesta, FL; WTAE-TV Pittsburgh, PA; WXII-TV Winston-Salem, NC; WYFF Greenville, SC;
David Barrett, President/CEO

Heritage Broadcasting Co of MI
Box 627, Cadillac MI 49601
(231) 775-3478; *Fax:*(231) 775-3671
www.9and10news.com
Ownership: Heritage Broadcasting Group Inc., 100%.

TV Stns: 2 TV.
WWTV Cadillac, MI; WWUP-TV Sault Ste. Marie, MI;
Mario Lacobelli, President
William Kring, VP/General Manager

High Plains Broadcasting Inc.
Box 288, Kaw City OK 74641
(580) 269-2215;

TV Stns: 4 TV.
KEMO-TV Santa Rosa, CA; WOAI-TV San Antonio, TX; KUCW Ogden, UT; WTEV-TV Jacksonville, FL;
James Martin, President

HITV License Subsidiary Inc.
1100 Wilson Blvd., Suite 3000, Arlington VA 22209
(703) 247-7500; *Fax:*(703) 247-7505
www.mcgcapital.com

TV Stns: 3 TV.
KGMB Honolulu, HI; KGMD-TV Hilo, HI; KGMV Wailuku, HI;
Michael McHugh, President

Hoak Media Corporation
500 Crescent Ct., Suite 220, Dallas TX 75201
(972) 960-4848; *Fax:*(972) 960-4899
www.hoakmedia.com

TV Stns: 16 TV.
KALB-TV Alexandria, LA; KAUZ-TV Wichita Falls, TX; KFYR-TV Bismarck, ND; KHAS-TV Hastings, NE; KMOT Minot, ND; KNOE-TV Monroe, LA; KNOP-TV North Platte, NE; KPRY-TV Pierre, SD; KQCD-TV Dickinson, ND; KREG-TV Glenwood Springs, CO; KREX-TV Grand Junction, CO; KREY-TV Montrose, CO; KSFY-TV Sioux Falls, SD; KUMV-TV Williston, ND; KVLY-TV Fargo, ND; WMBB Panama City, FL;
Eric Van den Branden, President

Holston Valley Broadcasting Corp.
222 Commerce St., Kingsport TN 37660
(423) 246-9578; *Fax:*(423) 247-9836
hvbcgroup.com
Ownership: Glenwood Communications Corp., 100%.
TV Stns: 1 TV.
WKPT-TV Kingsport, TN;
Radio Stns: 4 AM. 4 FM.
WKPT Kingsport, TN; WKTP Jonesborough, TN; WUKZ(AM) Marion, VA; WOPI Bristol, TN; WMEV-FM Marion, VA; WRZK Colonial Heights, TN; WVEK-FM Weber City, VA; WTFM Kingsport, TN;
George DeVault Jr., President

Hubbard Broadcasting Inc.
3415 University Ave., St. Paul MN 55114
(651) 646-5555; *Fax:*(651) 642-4103
jmahoney@hbi.com
TV Stns: 12 TV.
KAAL Austin, MN; KOB Albuquerque, NM; KOBF Farmington, NM; KOBR Roswell, NM; KRWF Redwood Falls, MN; KSAX Alexandria, MN; KSTP-TV St. Paul, MN; KSTC-TV Minneapolis, MN; WDIO-DT Duluth, MN; WHEC-TV Rochester, NY; WIRT Hibbing, MN; WNYT Albany, NY;
Radio Stns: 3 AM. 2 FM.
KSTP St. Paul, MN; WIXK New Richmond, WI; WBQH Silver Spring, MD; KSTP-FM St. Paul, MN; WTMY(FM) Coon Rapids, MN;
Gerald Deeney, SVP/CFO
Edward Aiken, Vice President
Harold Crump, Vice President
Julia Coyte, Vice President
Linda Tremere, Vice President
Robert Hubbard, Vice President
Stanley Hubbard II, Vice President

Independent Communications Inc.
2817 W. 11th St., Sioux Falls SD 57104
(605) 338-0017; *Fax:*(605) 338-7173
fox17@kttw.com
Ownership: Independent Communications Inc.
TV Stns: 2 TV.
KTTM Huron, SD; KTTW Sioux Falls, SD;
Ed Hoffman, General Manager

InterMedia Partners L.P.
405 Lexington Ave., 48th Fl., New York NY 10174
(212) 503-2855
www.intermediaadvisors.com
Ownership: HK Capital Partners LLC, 100% of votes, 7% of equity.
TV Stns: 3 TV.
WAPA-TV San Juan, PR; WNJX-TV Mayaguez, PR; WTIN-TV Ponce, PR;

Intermountain West Communications
1500 Foremaster Lane, Las Vegas NV 89101
(702) 642-3333; *Fax:*(702) 657-3423
www.sunbelt.com
TV Stns: 1 TV.
KPVI-DT Pocatello, ID;

International Broadcasting Corp.
1554 Bori St., San Juan PR 00927-6113
(787) 274-1800; *Fax:*(787) 281-9758;
TV Stns: 3 TV.
WTCV San Juan, PR; WVEO Aguadilla, PR; WVOZ-TV Ponce, PR;
Radio Stns: 7 AM. 1 FM.
WIBS Guayama, PR; WDNO Quebradillas, PR; WEKO Morovis, PR; WRSJ Bayamon, PR; WTIL Mayaguez, PR; WXRF Guayama, PR; WGIT Canovanas, PR; WVOZ-FM Carolina, PR;
Pedro Callazo, President
Margarita Nazario, General Manager

ION Media Networks Inc.
601 Clearwater Park Rd., West Palm Beach FL 33401-6233
(561) 659-4122; *Fax:*(561) 655-7246,
www.ionmedianetworks.com
ionaffiliates@ionmedia.com
Ownership: ION Media Networks, Inc. owns and operates the largest U.S. broadcast television station group and ION Television, thecountry's only independent broadcast television network. The Company owns 59 of its 60 full-power broadcast television stations, including stations in each of the top 20 U.S. market
TV Stns: 57 TV.
KGPX-TV Spokane, WA; KKPX-TV San Jose, CA; KOPX-TV Oklahoma City, OK; KPPX-TV Tolleson, AZ; KPXB-TV Conroe, TX; KPXC-TV Denver, CO; KPXD Arlington, TX; KPXE-TV Kansas City, MO; KPXG-TV Salem, OR; KPXL-TV Uvalde, TX; KPXM-TV Saint Cloud, MN; KPXN-TV San Bernardino, CA; KPXO-TV Kaneohe, HI; KPXR-TV Cedar Rapids, IA; KSPX-TV Sacramento, CA; KTPX-TV Okmulgee, OK; KUPX-TV Provo, UT; KWPX-TV Bellevue, WA; WUPX-TV Morehead, KY; WBPX-TV Boston, MA; WPXC-TV Brunswick, GA; WCPX-TV Chicago, IL; WDPX-TV Vineyard Haven, MA; WEPX-TV Greenville, NC; WFPX-TV Fayetteville, NC; WPXU-TV Jacksonville, NC; WGPX-TV Burlington, NC; WHPX-TV New London, CT; WIPX-TV Bloomington, IN; WLPX-TV Charleston, WV; WNPX-TV Cookeville, TN; WOPX-TV Melbourne, FL; WPPX-TV Wilmington, DE; WPXA-TV Rome, GA; WPXD-TV Ann Arbor, MI; WPXE-TV Kenosha, WI; WPXG-TV Concord, NH; WPXH-TV Gadsden, AL; WPXJ-TV Batavia, NY; WPXK-TV Jellico, TN; WPXM-TV Miami, FL; WPXN-TV New York, NY; WPXP-TV Lake Worth, FL; WPXQ-TV Block Island, RI; WPXR-TV Roanoke, VA; WPXV-TV Norfolk, VA; WPXW-TV Manassas, VA; WPXX-TV Memphis, TN; WQPX-TV Scranton, PA; WRPX-TV Rocky Mount, NC; WSPX-TV Syracuse, NY; WTPX-TV Antigo, WI; WVPX-TV Akron, OH; WWPX-TV Martinsburg, WV; WXPX-TV Bradenton, FL; WYPX-TV Amsterdam, NY; WZPX-TV Battle Creek, MI;
R. Brandon Burgess, CEO
Eleo Hensleigh, CMO
Leslie Chesloff, Executive Vice President, Programming
John Lawson, Executive Vice President
Stephen Appel, President, Sales & Marketing
Marc Zand, Senior Vice President Business Affairs

Journal Communications Inc.
333 W. State St., Milwaukee WI 53203
(414) 224-2616; *Fax:*(414) 224-2469
www.jc.com
TV Stns: 12 TV.
KGUN-TV Tucson, AZ; KIVI-TV Nampa, ID; KMIR-TV Palm Springs, CA; KMTV-TV Omaha, NE; KNIN-TV Caldwell, ID; KTNV-TV Las Vegas, NV; KWBA-TV Sierra Vista, AZ; WACY-TV Appleton, WI; WFTX-TV Cape Coral, FL; WGBA-TV Green Bay, WI; WSYM-TV Lansing, MI; WTMJ-TV Milwaukee, WI;
Radio Stns: 9 AM. 26 FM.
KCID Caldwell, ID; KLIO Wichita, KS; KFFN Tucson, AZ; KGEM Boise, ID; KSGF Springfield, MO; KFAQ Tulsa, OK; KXSP Omaha, NE; WKTI Powell, TN; WTMJ Milwaukee, WI; KTHI Caldwell, ID; KXBL Henryetta, OK; KEZO-FM Omaha, NE; KFDI-FM Wichita, KS; KRVB Nampa, ID; KTGV Oracle, AZ; KRVI Mount Vernon, MO; KICT-FM Wichita, KS; KJOT Boise, ID; KKCD Omaha, NE; KFXJ Augusta, KS; KSPW Sparta, MO; KMXZ-FM Tucson, AZ; KFTI-FM Newton, KS; KQXR Payette, ID; KSRZ Omaha, NE; KTTS-FM Springfield, MO; KVOO-FM Tulsa, OK; KYQQ Arkansas City, KS; KQTH Tucson, AZ; KSGF-FM Ash Grove, MO; WLWK-FM Milwaukee, WI; WWST Sevierville, TN; KQCH Omaha, NE; WKHT Knoxville, TN; WCYQ Karns, TN;
Douglas Kiel, President

KEVN Inc.
Box 677, Rapid City SD 57709
(605) 394-7777; *Fax:*(605) 348-9128
www.blackhillsfox.com
news@blackhillsfox.com
TV Stns: 2 TV.
KEVN-TV Rapid City, SD; KIVV-TV Lead, SD;
Robert Slocum, CFO
Bill Reyner, President
Cindy McNeill, Operations Dir
Kathy Silk, General Sales Mgr

KHQ Inc.
Box 600, Spokane WA 99210-4102
(509) 448-6000; *Fax:*(509) 448-3231;
TV Stns: 3 TV.
KHQ-TV Spokane, WA; KNDO Yakima, WA; KNDU Richland, WA;
Lon Lee, President

KM Communications Inc.
3654 Jarvis Ave., Skokie IL 60076
(847) 674-0864; *Fax:*(847) 674-9188
www.kmcommunications.com
TV Stns: 1 TV.
KWKB Iowa City, IA;
Radio Stns: 1 AM. 7 FM.
KQMG Independence, IA; KQMG-FM Independence, IA; KWKM St. Johns, AZ; WLCN Atlanta, IL; WPNG Pearson, GA; WMKB Earlville, IL; KHMR Lovelady, TX; KBDK Leakey, TX;
Myoung Hwa Bae, President
Kevin Bae, Operations Dir

Lake Superior Community Broadcasting Corp.
1390 Bagley St., Alpena MI 49707
(989) 356-3434;
TV Stns: 2 TV.
WBKP Calumet, MI; WBUP Ishpeming, MI;

Landmark Communications Inc.
150 W. Brambleton Ave., Norfolk VA 23510
(757) 446-2000; *Fax:*(757) 446-2179
www.landmarkcommunications.com
Ownership: (Landmark Broadcast Division.)
TV Stns: 2 TV.
KLAS-TV Las Vegas, NV; WTVF Nashville, TN;
Frank Batten, Chairman
Decker Anstrom, President

Le Sea Broadcasting
Box 12, South Bend IN 46624
(574) 291-8200; *Fax:*(574) 291-9043
www.lesea.com
leseabroadcasting@lesea.com
TV Stns: 8 TV.
KWHB Tulsa, OK; KETD Castle Rock, CO; KWHE Honolulu, HI; KWHD Hilo, HI; KWHM Wailuku, HI; WHMB-TV Indianapolis, IN; WHME-TV South Bend, IN; WHNO New Orleans, LA;
Radio Stns: 3 FM.
WHME South Bend, IN; WHPZ Bremen, IN; WHPD Dowagiac, MI;
Peter Sumrall, President

Liberman Broadcasting Inc.
1845 Empire Ave., Burbank CA 91504
(818) 729-5300; *Fax:*(818) 729-5678
www.lbimedia.com
LBIinfo@lbimedia.com
TV Stns: 4 TV.
KPNZ Ogden, UT; KMPX Decatur, TX; KRCA Riverside, CA; KZJL Houston, TX;
Radio Stns: 7 AM. 15 FM.
KEYH Houston, TX; KJOZ Conroe, TX; KHJ Los Angeles, CA; KQUE Houston, TX; KSEV Tomball, TX; KVNR Santa Ana, CA; KZMP University Park, TX; KBOC Bridgeport, TX; KBUA San Fernando, CA; KBUE Long Beach, CA; KNOR Krum, TX; KEBN Garden Grove, CA; KXBJ El Campo, TX; KJOJ-FM Freeport, TX; KZMP-FM Pilot Point, TX; KTJM Port Arthur, TX; KWIZ Santa Ana, CA; KRQB San Jacinto, CA; KNTE Bay City, TX; KZZA Muenster, TX; KQQK Beaumont, TX; KTCY Azle, TX;
Brett Zane, CEO
Lenard Liberman, President

Liberty Media Corp.
12300 Liberty Blvd., Englewood CO 80112
(720) 875-5400
www.libertymedia.com
TV Stns: 2 TV.
WFRV-TV Green Bay, WI; WJMN-TV Escanaba, MI;
John Malone, Chairman
Gregory Maffei, CEO

LIN Media
One West Exchange St., Suite 5A, Providence RI 02903
(401) 454-2880; *Fax:*(401) 454-6990
www.linmedia.com
courtney.guertin@linmedia.com
Ownership: Hicks, Muse, Tate & Furst 47%.
TV Stns: 39 TV.
KAII-TV Wailuku, HI; KASA-TV Santa Fe, NM; KBIM-TV Roswell, NM; KHAW-TV Hilo, HI; KIMT Mason City, IA; KOIN Portland, OR; KREZ-TV Durango, CO; KRQE Albuquerque, NM; KSNC Great Bend, KS; KSNG Garden City, KS; KSNK McCook, NE; KSNT Topeka, KS; KSNW Wichita, KS; KXAN-TV Austin, TX; WALA-TV Mobile, AL; WANE-TV Fort Wayne, IN; WAVY-TV Portsmouth, VA; WCTX New Haven, CT; WDTN Dayton, OH; WIAT Birmingham, AL; WISH-TV Indianapolis, IN; WIVB-TV Buffalo, NY; WCWF Suring, WI; WJCL Savannah, GA; WKBN-TV Youngstown, OH; WLFI-TV Lafayette, IN; WLUK-TV Green Bay, WI; WNDY-TV Marion, IN; WNLO Buffalo, NY; WOOD-TV Grand Rapids, MI; WOTV Battle Creek, MI; WPRI-TV Providence, RI; WTHI-TV Terre Haute, IN; WTNH New Haven, CT; WVBT Virginia Beach, VA; WWHO Chillicothe, OH; WWLP Springfield, MA; WFNA Gulf Shores, AL; KBVO Llano, TX;
Vincent L. Sadusky, President
Scott M. Blumenthal, EVP, television

Richard J. Schmaeling, SVP/CFO
Denise M. Parent, SVP, Chief Legal Advisor

Local TV LLC
1717 Dixie Hwy., Suite 650, Ft. Wright KY 41011
(859) 448-2700; *Fax:*(859) 331-6014
www.localtvllc.com

TV Stns: 18 TV.
KAUT-TV Oklahoma City, OK; KDVR Denver, CO; KFCT Fort Collins, CO; KFOR-TV Oklahoma City, OK; KFSM-TV Fort Smith, AR; KSTU Salt Lake City, UT; KTVI St. Louis, MO; WGHP High Point, NC; WHNT-TV Huntsville, AL; WHO-DT Des Moines, IA; WITI Milwaukee, WI; WJW Cleveland, OH; WNEP-TV Scranton, PA; WQAD-TV Moline, IL; WREG-TV Memphis, TN; WTKR Norfolk, VA; WTVR-TV Richmond, VA; KFCT Fort Collins, CO;
Bobby Lawrence, CEO
Pam Taylor, CFO

Malara Broadcast Group Inc.
9257 Bailey Ln., Fairfax VA 22031
(703) 253-2020;

TV Stns: 2 TV.
KDLH Duluth, MN; WPTA Fort Wayne, IN;

Manship Stations
Box 2906, Baton Rouge LA 70821
(225) 387-2222; *Fax:*(225) 336-2246
www.2theadvocate.com

TV Stns: 2 TV.
KRGV-TV Weslaco, TX; WBRZ-TV Baton Rouge, LA;
Richard Manship, President

Mark III Media Inc.
2312 Sagewood, Casper WY 82601
(307) 235-3962
Ownership: Julie Jaffe, 35%; Jennifer Lechter, 35%; and Mark R. Nalbone, 30%.

TV Stns: 3 TV.
KGWC-TV Casper, WY; KGWL-TV Lander, WY; KGWR-TV Rock Springs, WY;
Julie Jaffe, President

MAX Media L.L.C.
900 Laskin Rd., Virginia Beach VA 23451
(757) 437-9800; *Fax:*(757) 437-0034
www.maxmediallc.com
Ownership: MBG-GG LLC, 42.0345%; MBG Quad-C Investors I Inc., 41.4124%; Aardvarks Also LLC, 6.1967%; Colonnade Max Investors Inc., 4.8671%; Quad-C Max Investors Inc., 4.6799%; MBG Quad-C Investors II Inc., 0.6221%; and Quad-C Max Investors II Inc., 0.1872%.

TV Stns: 6 TV.
KTMF Missoula, MT; KULR-TV Billings, MT; KWYB Butte, MT; WNKY Bowling Green, KY; WMEI Arecibo, PR; WPFO Waterville, ME;

Radio Stns: 12 AM. 25 FM.
KCAB Dardanelle, AR; KGIR Cape Girardeau, MO; KSIM Sikeston, MO; KMAL Malden, MO; KVOM Morrilton, AR; KWOC Poplar Bluff, MO; KZIM Cape Girardeau, MO; WCIL Carbondale, IL; WGAI Elizabeth City, NC; WGH Newport News, VA; WJPF Herrin, IL; WVSL(AM) Selinsgrove, PA; KCGQ-FM Gordonville, MO; KCJC Dardanelle, AR; KEZS-FM Cape Girardeau, MO; KGKS Scott City, MO; KJEZ Poplar Bluff, MO; KKLR-FM Poplar Bluff, MO; KLSC Malden, MO; KVLD Atkins, AR; KONN-FM Bennett, CO; KVOM-FM Morrilton, AR; KWKK Russellville, AR; WVHT Norfolk, VA; WCXL Kill Devil Hills, NC; WVBW Suffolk, VA; WGH-FM Newport News, VA; WFYY Bloomsburg, PA; WVSL-FM Riverside, PA; WOOZ-FM Harrisburg, IL; WQDK Gatesville, NC; WXLT Christopher, IL; WWBE Mifflinburg, PA; WCMS-FM Hatteras, NC; WVSP-FM Yorktown, VA; WUEZ Carterville, IL; WYGL-FM Elizabethville, PA;
John A. Trinder, President

McKinnon Broadcasting Co.
5002 S. Padre Island Dr., Corpus Christi TX 78411
(361) 986-8300; *Fax:*(361) 986-8411
Ownership: Michael McKinnon.

TV Stns: 3 TV.
KBMT Beaumont, TX; KIII Corpus Christi, TX; KUSI-TV San Diego, CA;
Michael McKinnon, President/CEO

Media General Broadcast Group
111 N. 4th St., Richmond VA 23219
(804) 775-4600; *Fax:*(804) 775-4601
www.mgbg.com
Ownership: Media General Inc.

TV Stns: 18 TV.
WYCW Asheville, NC; WBTW Florence, SC; WCBD-TV Charleston, SC; WCMH-TV Columbus, OH; WFLA-TV Tampa, FL; WHLT Hattiesburg, MS; WJAR Providence, RI; WJBF Augusta, GA; WJHL-TV Johnson City, TN; WJTV Jackson, MS; WKRG-TV Mobile, AL; WNCN Goldsboro, NC; WNCT-TV Greenville, NC; WRBL Columbus, GA; WSAV-TV Savannah, GA; WSLS-TV Roanoke, VA; WSPA-TV Spartanburg, SC; WVTM-TV Birmingham, AL;
James Zimmerman, Chairman
Catherine Gugerty, Marketing Director
Paul Gaulke, Marketing Vice President
Daniel Bradley, Vice President
James Conschafter, Vice President
Richard Roberts, Vice President
Tom Conway, Vice President

Mel Wheeler Inc.
3934 Electric Rd., Roanoke VA 24018-4513
(540) 989-4591; *Fax:*(540) 774-5667
melwheelerinc.com
Ownership: Leonard E. Wheeler, 35%; Steve Wheeler, 34%; and Clark Wheeler, 31%.

TV Stns: 2 TV.
KPOB-TV Poplar Bluff, MO; WSIL-TV Harrisburg, IL;

Radio Stns: 2 AM. 4 FM.
WFIR Roanoke, VA; WVBE Roanoke, VA; WVBE-FM Lynchburg, VA; WSLC-FM Roanoke, VA; WSLQ Roanoke, VA; WXLK Roanoke, VA;
Leonard Wheeler, President
Gretchen Cummings, Sec/Treasurer

Meredith Broadcasting Group, Meredith Corp.
1716 Locust St., Des Moines IA 50309-3023
(515) 284-2159; *Fax:*(515) 284-2514
www.meredith.com
Ownership: Meredith Broadcasting is an operating group of Meredith Corp., Des Moines, IA.

TV Stns: 11 TV.
KCTV Kansas City, MO; KPDX Vancouver, WA; KPHO-TV Phoenix, AZ; KPTV Portland, OR; KSMO-TV Kansas City, MO; KVVU-TV Henderson, NV; WFSB Hartford, CT; WGCL-TV Atlanta, GA; WHNS Greenville, SC; WNEM-TV Bay City, MI; WSMV-TV Nashville, TN;

Radio Stns: 1 AM.
WNEM Bridgeport, MI;
Paul Karpowic, President
Douglas Lowe, EVP

Mission Broadcasting Inc.
7650 Chippewa Rd., Suite 305, Brecksville OH 44141
(440) 526-2227; *Fax:*(330) 336-8454,
dpthatcher@sbcglobal.net

TV Stns: 14 TV.
KSAN-TV San Angelo, TX; KAMC Lubbock, TX; KCIT Amarillo, TX; KHMT Hardin, MT; KJTL Wichita Falls, TX; KODE-TV Joplin, MO; KOLR Springfield, MO; KFTA-TV Fort Smith, AR; KRBC-TV Abilene, TX; WAWV-TV Terre Haute, IN; WFXP Erie, PA; WTVO Rockford, IL; WUTR Utica, NY; WYOU Scranton, PA;
Dennis Thatcher, COO
David Smith, President
Nancie Smith, Operations Dir

Morgan Murphy Media (Evening Telegram Co)
7025 Raymond Rd., Madison WI 53719
(608) 271-4321; *Fax:*(608) 271-6111
www.channel3000.com
talkback@wisctv.com
Ownership: Evening Telegram Co. owns 100% of KVEW(TV), KXLY-AM-FM-TV, KXLY-DT and KAPP(TV). Evening Telegram Co. owns 84.4% of TelevisionWisconsin Inc., with an additional 15.2% of the stn held by Evening Telegram stockholders.

TV Stns: 5 TV.
KAPP Yakima, WA; KVEW Kennewick, WA; KXLY-TV Spokane, WA; WISC-TV Madison, WI; WKBT La Crosse, WI;

Radio Stns: 4 AM. 4 FM.
KXLX Airway Heights, WA; KXLY Spokane, WA; WGLR Lancaster, WI; WPVL Platteville, WI; KEZE Spokane, WA; KZZU-FM Spokane, WA; WGLR-FM Lancaster, WI; WPVL-FM Platteville, WI;
Brian Lubanski, Gen Mgr
George Nelson, Executive Vice President
Steve Herling, Executive Vice President
Elizabeth Murphy Burns, President

Morris Multimedia Inc.
27 Abercorn St., Savannah GA 31401
(912) 233-1281; *Fax:*(912) 238-2059
www.morrismultimedia.com
Ownership: Charles H. Morris.

TV Stns: 6 TV.
WCBI-TV Columbus, MS; WDEF-TV Chattanooga, TN; WMGT-TV Macon, GA; WTVQ-DT Lexington, KY; WWAY Wilmington, NC; WXXV-TV Gulfport, MS;
Charles Morris, President

Mountain Broadcasting Corp.
99 Clinton Rd., West Caldwell NJ 7006
(973) 852-0300; *Fax:*(973) 808-5516;

TV Stns: 1 TV.
WMBC-TV Newton, NJ;

Radio Stns: 3 AM.
WPWA Chester, PA; WBTK Richmond, VA; WWGB Indian Head, MD;
Sun Young Joo, President

Multicultural Capital Trust
c/o 11077 Swansfield Rd., Columbia MD 21044-2724
(202) 350-9658; *Fax:*(703) 991-7120;

TV Stns: 4 TV.
KCNS San Francisco, CA; WMFP Lawrence, MA; WRLM Canton, OH; WRAY-TV Wilson, NC;

NBC Owned Television Stations
30 Rockefeller Plaza, New York NY 10112
(212) 664-4444; *Fax:*(212) 664-5830
www.nbcuni.com
Ownership: Comcast Corp., 51%; General Electric Co., 49%.

TV Stns: 10 TV.
KNBC Los Angeles, CA; KNSD San Diego, CA; KNTV San Jose, CA; KXTX-TV Dallas, TX; WCAU Philadelphia, PA; WMAQ-TV Chicago, IL; WNBC New York, NY; WRC-TV Washington, DC; WTVJ Miami, FL; WVIT New Britain, CT;
Valari Dobson Staab, Chairman

Neuhoff Family L.P.
1501 N. Washington, Danville IL 61832
(217) 442-1700,; *Fax:*(217) 431-1489
neuhoffmedia.com
mhulvey@cooketech.net
Ownership: Neuhoff Corp., North Palm Beach, FL, 100% of votes.

TV Stns: 1 TV.
KMVT Twin Falls, ID;

Radio Stns: 4 AM. 8 FM.
WDAN Danville, IL; WDZ Decatur, IL; WFMB Springfield, IL; WSOY Decatur, IL; WCVS-FM Virden, IL; WCZQ Monticello, IL; WDNL Danville, IL; WDZQ Decatur, IL; WFMB-FM Springfield, IL; WRHK Danville, IL; WSOY-FM Decatur, IL; WXAJ Hillsboro, IL;
Geoff Neuhoff, President
Mike Hulvey, General Manager

Newport Television LLC
460 Nichols Rd., Suite 250, Kansas City MO 64112
(816) 751-0200; *Fax:*(816) 751-0250
www.newporttv.com
info@newporttv.com
Ownership: Newport Television Holdings LLC, 100%.

TV Stns: 26 TV.
KAAS-TV Salina, KS; KASN Pine Bluff, AR; KOCW Hoisington, KS; KLRT-TV Little Rock, AR; KMTR Eugene, OR; KTCW Roseburg, OR; KMCB Coos Bay, OR; KOKI-TV Tulsa, OK; KSAS-TV Wichita, KS; KMYT-TV Tulsa, OK; KTVF Fairbanks, AK; KTVX Salt Lake City, UT; WAWS Jacksonville, FL; WETM-TV Elmira, NY; WHP-TV Harrisburg, PA; WIVT Binghamton, NY; WSYR-TV Syracuse, NY; WJTC Pensacola, FL; WKRC-TV Cincinnati, OH; WLMT Memphis, TN; WJKT Jackson, TN; WHAM-TV Rochester, NY; WPMI-TV Mobile, AL; WPTY-TV Memphis, TN; WWTI Watertown, NY; WXXA-TV Albany, NY;
Sandy DiPasquale, CEO
Craig Millar, SVP
Jim Martin, Senior VP

News-Press & Gazette Co.
Box 29, St. Joseph MO 64502
(816) 271-8500; *Fax:*(816) 271-8695;

TV Stns: 7 TV.
KECY-TV El Centro, CA; KESQ-TV Palm Springs, CA; KIFI-TV Idaho Falls, ID; KJCT Grand Junction, CO; KRDO-TV Colorado Springs, CO; KTVZ Bend, OR; KVIA-TV El Paso, TX;

Radio Stns: 2 AM. 1 FM.
KESQ Indio, CA; KRDO Colorado Springs, CO; KUNA-FM La Quinta, CA;
John Kueneke, President

Newsweb Corp.
1645 W. Fullerton Ave., Chicago IL 60614

(773) 975-0401; *Fax:*(773) 975-1301
Ownership: Fred Eychaner, 100%.
TV Stns: 1 TV.
KCDO-TV Sterling, CO;
Radio Stns: 5 AM. 4 FM.
WAIT Crystal Lake, IL; WCFJ Chicago Heights, IL; WNDZ Portage, IN; WSBC Chicago, IL; WCPT Willow Springs, IL; WCPY Dekalb, IL; WCPT-FM Arlington Heights, IL; WKIF Kankakee, IL; WCPQ Park Forest, IL;
Fred Eychaner, CEO
Charley Gross, COO

Nexstar Broadcasting Group Inc.
909 Lake Carolyn Pkwy., Suite 1450, Irving TX 75039
(972) 373-8800; *Fax:*(972) 373-8888
www.nexstar.tv
TV Stns: 37 TV.
KAMR-TV Amarillo, TX; KARD West Monroe, LA; KARK-TV Little Rock, AR; KBTV-TV Port Arthur, TX; KOZL-TV Springfield, MO; KNWA-TV Rogers, AR; KFDX-TV Wichita Falls, TX; KGET-TV Bakersfield, CA; KGPE Fresno, CA; KLBK-TV Lubbock, TX; KLST San Angelo, TX; KMID Midland, TX; KQTV St. Joseph, MO; KSNF Joplin, MO; KSVI Billings, MT; KTAB-TV Abilene, TX; KTAL-TV Texarkana, TX; KTVE El Dorado, AR; KARZ-TV Little Rock, AR; WBRE-TV Wilkes-Barre, PA; WCIX Springfield, IL; WCIA Champaign, IL; WDHN Dothan, AL; WFFF-TV Burlington, VT; WFFT-TV Fort Wayne, IN; WFXV Utica, NY; WHAG-TV Hagerstown, MD; WJET-TV Erie, PA; WCWJ Jacksonville, FL; WLYH-TV Lancaster, PA; WMBD-TV Peoria, IL; WQRF-TV Rockford, IL; WROC-TV Rochester, NY; WTAJ-TV Altoona, PA; WTVW Evansville, IN; WTWO Terre Haute, IN; WVNY Burlington, VT;
Brian Jones, COO
Perry Sook, President
Matt Devine, CFO
Timothy Busch, COO

Northwest Broadcasting Inc.
2111 University Park Dr., Suite 650, Okemos MI 48864
(517) 347-4141; *Fax:*(517) 347-4675
bradybw1@comcast.net
Ownership: LPTV: WBPN-LP Morris, NY; and KCYU-LP Yakima, WA.
TV Stns: 4 TV.
KAYU-TV Spokane, WA; KFFX-TV Pendleton, OR; KMVU-DT Medford, OR; WICZ-TV Binghamton, NY;
Leann Brady, CEO

NRJ Holdings LLC
722 S. Denton Tap Road, Suite 130, Coppell TX 75019
(972) 947-3391
Ownership: Ted B. Bartley, 100% votes, 35% of total assets.
TV Stns: 3 TV.
KIKU Honolulu, HI; KSCI Long Beach, CA; WZME Bridgeport, CT;
Ted B. Bartley, President

Oceania Christian Church
Box 15667, Honolulu HI 96830
(808) 440-1350
info@oceaniachurch.org
TV Stns: 1 TV.
KUPU Waimanalo, HI;
James Gustafson, President

OTA Broadcasting
12011 Lee Jackson Hwy., Suite 301, Fairfax VA 22033
(703) 865-4442
otabroadcasting.com
Ownership: MSDC Management L.P. Group also owns class A TV stn WEBR-CD Manhattan, NY.
TV Stns: 3 TV.
KFFV Seattle, WA; KTLN-TV Novato, CA; KVOS-TV Bellingham, WA;

Pappas Telecasting Companies
500 S. Chinowth Rd., Visalia CA 93277
(559) 733-7800; *Fax:*(559) 733-7878
www.pappastv.com
Ownership: Harry J. Pappas.
TV Stns: 14 TV.
KCWK North Las Vegas, NV; KDBC-TV El Paso, TX; KQSL Fort Bragg, CA; KHGI-TV Kearney, NE; KAZA-TV Avalon, CA; KPTH Sioux City, IA; KCWI-TV Ames, IA; KSWT Yuma, AZ; KTNC-TV Concord, CA; KUBE-TV Baytown, TX; KWNB-TV Hayes Center, NE; WCWG Lexington, NC; WLGA Opelika, AL; KDMI Des Moines, IA;
Radio Stns: 3 AM.
KTRB San Francisco, CA; KCWK North Las Vegas, NV; KMPH Modesto, CA;
Bruce Yeager, EVP/CFO
Harry J. Pappas, CEO
Dennis J. Davis, COO

Parker Broadcasting Inc.
5341 Tate Ave., Plano TX 75093
(214) 704-7559;
TV Stns: 2 TV.
KFQX Grand Junction, CO; KXJB-TV Valley City, ND;

Pollack Broadcasting Co.
5500 Poplar Ave. #1, Memphis TN 38119
(901) 685-3993; *Fax:*(901) 685-3995
wpollack@midsouth.rr.com
TV Stns: 2 TV.
KIEM-TV Eureka, CA; KLAX-TV Alexandria, LA;
Radio Stns: 4 AM. 3 FM.
KBOA Kennett, MO; KCRV Caruthersville, MO; KMIS Portageville, MO; KXIQ(AM) Turrell, AR; KBOA-FM Piggott, AR; KCRV-FM Caruthersville, MO; KTMO New Madrid, MO;
William Pollack, President

Post-Newsweek Stations Inc.
550 W. Lafayette Blvd., Detroit MI 48226
(313) 223-2260; *Fax:*(313) 223-2263
Ownership: Post-Newsweek Stations is a subsidiary of the publicly traded Washington Post Co.
TV Stns: 5 TV.
KPRC-TV Houston, TX; KSAT-TV San Antonio, TX; WJXT Jacksonville, FL; WKMG-TV Orlando, FL; WPLG Miami, FL;
Alan W. Frank, President

Prime Cities Broadcasting Inc.
Box 4026, 3130 E. Broadway Ave, Bismarck ND 58502-4026
(701) 355-0026; *Fax:*(701) 250-7244
www.myfoxbis.com, kndx@fox26.tv
TV Stns: 2 TV.
KNDX Bismarck, ND; KXND Minot, ND;
John Tupper, CEO
Gary O'Halloran, General Manager

Quincy Newspapers Inc.
130 S. Fifth St., Quincy IL 62301
(217) 223-5100; *Fax:*(217) 223-5019
www.qni.biz
TV Stns: 12 TV.
KTIV Sioux City, IA; KTTC Rochester, MN; KWWL Waterloo, IA; WAOW Wausau, WI; WGEM-TV Quincy, IL; WKOW Madison, WI; WQOW-DT Eau Claire, WI; WREX-TV Rockford, IL; WSJV Elkhart, IN; WVVA Bluefield, WV; WXOW La Crosse, WI; WYOW Eagle River, WI;
Radio Stns: 1 AM. 1 FM.
WGEM Quincy, IL; WGEM-FM Quincy, IL;
Thomas Oakley, President

R.H. Drewry Group
Box 708, Lawton OK 73502
(580) 353-0820; *Fax:*(580) 357-3811
Ownership: R.H. Drewry owns 69% of KSWO-TV. KFDA-TV is a joint venture owned by Lawton Cablevision (50%), KSWD-TV (45%), KSWO(AM) (2 1/2%) and KRHD-AM-FM (2 1/2%). KWAB(TV) and KWES-TV areowned by KSWO Television Inc. (50%) and Lawton Cablevision Inc. (50%). KXXV(TV) is owned by Centrex Television L.P. Cable
TV Stns: 5 TV.
KFDA-TV Amarillo, TX; KSWO-TV Lawton, OK; KWAB-TV Big Spring, TX; KWES-TV Odessa, TX; KXXV Waco, TX;
Robert Drewry, President
Larry Patton, VP

Ramar Communications II Ltd.
Box 3757, Lubbock TX 79452
(806) 745-3434; *Fax:*(806) 748-1949
www.ramarcom.com, bmoran@ramarcom.com
TV Stns: 4 TV.
KRTN-TV Durango, CO; KUPT Hobbs, NM; KJTV-TV Lubbock, TX; KTEL-TV Carlsbad, NM;
Radio Stns: 1 AM. 3 FM.
KJTV Lubbock, TX; KLZK New Deal, TX; KSTQ(FM) Brownfield, TX; KXTQ-FM Lubbock, TX;
Ray Moran, Chairman
Brad Moran, President

Raycom Media Inc.
201 Monroe St., RSA Tower, 20th Fl, Montgomery AL 36104
(334) 206-1400; *Fax:*(334) 206-1555
www.raycommedia.com
Ownership: Raycom Media Inc. Other interests: Raycom Sports, New York, NY; Charlotte, NC; Ft. Lauderdale, FL; Nashville, TN; and Chicago, IL.
TV Stns: 39 TV.
KAIT Jonesboro, AR; KCBD Lubbock, TX; KFVE Honolulu, HI; KFVS-TV Cape Girardeau, MO; KHBC-TV Hilo, HI; KHNL Honolulu, HI; KLTV Tyler, TX; KOGG Wailuku, HI; KOLD-TV Tucson, AZ; KPLC Lake Charles, LA; KSLA Shreveport, LA; KTRE Lufkin, TX; WAFB Baton Rouge, LA; WAFF Huntsville, AL; WALB Albany, GA; WAVE Louisville, KY; WBRC Birmingham, AL; WBTV Charlotte, NC; WCSC-TV Charleston, SC; WDAM-TV Laurel, MS; WDFX-TV Ozark, AL; WECT Wilmington, NC; WFIE Evansville, IN; WFLX West Palm Beach, FL; WIS Columbia, SC; WLBT Jackson, MS; WLOX Biloxi, MS; WMC-TV Memphis, TN; WOIO Shaker Heights, OH; WPGX Panama City, FL; WSFA Montgomery, AL; WTNZ Knoxville, TN; WTOC-TV Savannah, GA; WTOL Toledo, OH; WTVM Columbus, GA; WUAB Lorain, OH; WWBT Richmond, VA; WXIX-TV Newport, KY; WMBF-TV Myrtle Beach, SC;
Paul McTear, President/CEO

Red River Broadcast Co. L.L.C.
Box 9115, Fargo ND 58106
(701) 277-1515; *Fax:*(701) 277-1830
Ownership: Curtis Squire Inc., 100%. Myron Kunin owns 100% of Curtis Squire Inc.
TV Stns: 7 TV.
KBRR Thief River Falls, MN; KDLT-TV Sioux Falls, SD; KDLV-TV Mitchell, SD; KJRR Jamestown, ND; KNRR Pembina, ND; KQDS-TV Duluth, MN; KVRR Fargo, ND;
Radio Stns: 1 AM.
KQDS Duluth, MN;
Ro Grignon, President
Kathy Lau, VP

Reiten Television Inc.
Box 1686, Minot ND 58702-1686
(701) 852-2104; *Fax:*(701) 838-9360
www.kxmc.com, dreiten@kxnet.com
TV Stns: 4 TV.
KXMA-TV Dickinson, ND; KXMB-TV Bismarck, ND; KXMC-TV Minot, ND; KXMD-TV Williston, ND;
David Reiten, Chairman

Roberts Broadcasting Co.
1408 N. Kingshighway Blvd., St. Louis MO 63113
(314) 367-4600; *Fax:*(314) 367-0174
www.upn46stl.com
TV Stns: 3 TV.
WRBU East St. Louis, IL; WRBJ Magee, MS; WZRB Columbia, SC;
Michael Roberts, CEO
Steven Roberts, President

Rockfleet Broadcasting Inc.
575 Madison Ave., 10th Fl., New York NY 10022
(212) 605-0401,; *Fax:*(212) 605-0402,
Ownership: Rockfleet Holdings, 100%.
TV Stns: 2 TV.
WJFW-TV Rhinelander, WI; WVII-TV Bangor, ME;
R. Joseph Fuchs, President

Saga Communications Inc.
73 Kercheval Ave., Suite 201, Grosse Pointe Farms MI 48236
(313) 886-7070; *Fax:*(313) 886-7150
www.sagacommunications.com, chapsburg@sagacom.com
Ownership: Edward K. Christian, 56.5% of the voting stock. Other Interests: Illinois Radio Network, Michigan Radio Network, Michigan FarmRadio Network.
TV Stns: 3 TV.
KAVU-TV Victoria, TX; KOAM-TV Pittsburg, KS; WXVT Greenville, MS;
Radio Stns: 28 AM. 59 FM.
KGMI Bellingham, WA; KICD Spencer, IA; KBAI Bellingham, WA; KPUG Bellingham, WA; KRNT Des Moines, IA; KPSZ Des Moines, IA; WEGI Fort Campbell, KY; WBAE Portland, ME; WBCO Bucyrus, OH; WKFN Clarksville, TN; WFEA Manchester, NH; WGAN Portland, ME; WHMQ Greenfield, MA; WHCU Ithaca, NY; WHMP Northampton, MA; WVAE Biddeford, ME; WINA Charlottesville, VA; WJOI Norfolk, VA; WJYI Milwaukee, WI; WZBK Keene, NH; WKBK Keene, NH; WKVT Brattleboro, VT; WHNP East Longmeadow, MA; WTAX Springfield, IL; WNYY Ithaca, NY; WYSE Canton, NC; WZAN Portland, ME; WVAX Charlottesville, VA; KAZR Pella, IA; KEGI Jonesboro, AR; KDXY Lake City, AR; KUQL Ethan, SD; KICD-FM Spencer, IA; KLLT Spencer, IA; KIOA Des Moines, IA; KISM Bellingham, WA; KJBX Cash, AR; KLTI-FM Ames, IA; KMIT Mitchell, SD; KSTZ Des Moines, IA; WAFX Suffolk, VA; WAQY Springfield, MA; WCNR Keswick, VA; WCLZ North Yarmouth, ME; WTMT Weaverville, NC; WCVQ Fort Campbell, KY; WEGI-FM Oak Grove, KY; WDBR Springfield, IL; WJMR-FM Menomonee Falls, WI; WHAI Greenfield, MA; WLZX Northampton, MA; WYXY(FM) Danville, IL; WIII Cortland, NY; WSNI Keene, NH; WIXY

Champaign, IL; WJZX(FM) Brookfield, WI; WNND Pickerington, OH; WCFF Urbana, IL; WKLH Milwaukee, WI; WKNE Keene, NH; WKVT-FM Brattleboro, VT; WLRW Champaign, IL; WHQG Milwaukee, WI; WMGX Portland, ME; WNOR Norfolk, VA; WPOR Portland, ME; WRSI Turners Falls, MA; WQEL Bucyrus, OH; WMLL Bedford, NH; WQMZ Charlottesville, VA; WQNY Ithaca, NY; WQQL Springfield, IL; WPVQ Greenfield, MA; WSNY Columbus, OH; WRSY Marlboro, VT; WVVR Hopkinsville, KY; WWWV Charlottesville, VA; WINQ Winchester, NH; WVMX Westerville, OH; WYMG Chatham, IL; WYNZ South Portland, ME; WYXL Ithaca, NY; WABZ Sherman, IL; WZID Manchester, NH; WNNP Richwood, OH; WZZP Hopkinsville, KY; WOXL-FM Biltmore Forest, NC;

Sam Bush, CFO
Edward Christian, CEO
Marcia Lobaito, VP
Warren Lada, VP Operations

SagamoreHill Broadcasting LLC
3825 Inverness Way, Augusta GA 30901
(706) 855-8506;
TV Stns: 6 TV.
WBMM Tuskegee, AL; KGNS-TV Laredo, TX; KGWN-TV Cheyenne, WY; KSTF Scottsbluff, NE; WLTZ Columbus, GA; WNCF Montgomery, AL;

Louis Wall, President

SagamoreHill Midwest LLC
3825 Inverness Way, Augusta GA 30907
(706) 855-8506;
TV Stns: 2 TV.
KXLT-TV Rochester, MN; WWMB Florence, SC;

Sainte Partners II L.P.
Box 4159, Modesto CA 95352-4159
(209) 523-0777; *Fax:*(209) 523-0839
kcso33gm@sainte.tv
Ownership: Naomi Smith, gen ptnr; & other limited ptnrs.
TV Stns: 2 TV.
KBVU Eureka, CA; KCVU Paradise, CA;

Robert Castro, CEO

Sarkes Tarzian Inc.
Box 62, Bloomington IN 47402
(812) 332-7251; *Fax:*(812) 331-4575
Ownership: Tom Tarzian; Gray Television Inc.
TV Stns: 2 TV.
KTVN Reno, NV; WRCB-DT Chattanooga, TN;
Radio Stns: 1 AM. 3 FM.
WGCL Bloomington, IN; WAJI Fort Wayne, IN; WLDE Fort Wayne, IN; WTTS Bloomington, IN;

Tom Tarzian, Chairman
Bob Davis, CFO
Geoff Vargo, Pres, Radio
Tom Tolar, Pres, TV

Schurz Communications Inc.
225 W. Colfax Ave., South Bend IN 46626
(574) 287-1001; *Fax:*(574) 287-2257
www.schurz.com, mburdick@schurz.com
Ownership: Franklin D. Schurz Jr., James M. Schurz, Scott C. Schurz and Mary Schurz, trustees.
TV Stns: 6 TV.
KTUU-TV Anchorage, AK; KSCW-DT Wichita, KS; KYTV Springfield, MO; WAGT Augusta, GA; WDBJ Roanoke, VA; WSBT-TV South Bend, IN;
Radio Stns: 4 AM. 8 FM.
KBHB Sturgis, SD; KKLS Rapid City, SD; WASK Lafayette, IN; WSBT South Bend, IN; KFXS Rapid City, SD; KKMK Rapid City, SD; KOUT Rapid City, SD; KRCS Sturgis, SD; WASK-FM Battle Ground, IN; WKOA Lafayette, IN; WXXB Delphi, IN; WNSN South Bend, IN;

Franklin Schurz Jr., Chairman
Todd Schurz, President
Marcia Burdick, SVP

Shaw Communications
2055 Flavelle Boulevard, Mississauga ON L5K 1Z8
(800) 268-2943; *Fax:*(905) 403-2022
www.shawbroadcast.com, support@shawbroadcast.com
TV Stns: 1 TV.
CFRE-DT Regina, SK;

Karen Baglole, Operations Dir

Sinclair Broadcast Group Inc.
10706 Beaver Dam Rd., Hunt Valley MD 21030
(410) 568-1500; *Fax:*(410) 568-1533
www.sbgi.net
ir@sbgnet.com
Ownership: Smith brothers (major shareholders).
TV Stns: 47 TV.
KABB San Antonio, TX; KBSI Cape Girardeau, MO; KDNL-TV St. Louis, MO; KDSM-TV Des Moines, IA; KVCW Las Vegas, NV; KGAN Cedar Rapids, IA; WUCW Minneapolis, MN; KOCB Oklahoma City, OK; KOKH-TV Oklahoma City, OK; KMYS Kerrville, TX; KVMY Las Vegas, NV; WABM Birmingham, AL; WBFF Baltimore, MD; WCGV-TV Milwaukee, WI; WCHS-TV Charleston, WV; WPMY Pittsburgh, PA; WDKY-TV Danville, KY; WEAR-TV Pensacola, FL; WFGX Fort Walton Beach, FL; WGME-TV Portland, ME; WICD Champaign, IL; WKEF Dayton, OH; WLFL Raleigh, NC; WLOS Asheville, NC; WMMP Charleston, SC; WMSN-TV Madison, WI; WNYO-TV Buffalo, NY; WPGH-TV Pittsburgh, PA; WRDC Durham, NC; WRLH-TV Richmond, VA; WSMH Flint, MI; WSTR-TV Cincinnati, OH; WSYT Syracuse, NY; WSYX Columbus, OH; WTTA St. Petersburg, FL; WTTO Homewood, AL; WTVZ-TV Norfolk, VA; WTWC-TV Tallahassee, FL; WUHF Rochester, NY; WMYV Greensboro, NC; WUTV Buffalo, NY; WUXP-TV Nashville, TN; WVAH-TV Charleston, WV; WVTV Milwaukee, WI; WXLV-TV Winston-Salem, NC; WYZZ-TV Bloomington, IL; WZTV Nashville, TN;

Frederick Smith, VP
David Amy, EVP/CFO
David Smith, President/CEO

Smith Media License Holdings LLC
1215 Cole St., St. Louis MO 63106
(314) 853-7736
Ownership: Smith Media LLC, 100%.
TV Stns: 5 TV.
KATN Fairbanks, AK; KEYT-TV Santa Barbara, CA; KYUR Anchorage, AK; KJUD Juneau, AK; WKTV Utica, NY;

South Central Communications Corp.
Box 3848, Evansville IN 47736
(812) 463-7950; *Fax:*(812) 463-7915
www.southcentralcommunications.net
Ownership: John D. Engelbrecht, 80%, J.P. Engelbrecht, 20%.
TV Stns: 1 TV.
WMAK Knoxville, TN;
Radio Stns: 1 AM. 11 FM.
WEOA Evansville, IN; WABX Evansville, IN; WLYT(FM) Norris, TN; WEJK Boonville, IN; WIKY-FM Evansville, IN; WIMZ-FM Knoxville, TN; WLFW Chandler, IN; WJXA Nashville, TN; WJXB-FM Knoxville, TN; WCJK Murfreesboro, TN; WSTO Owensboro, KY; WQJK Maryville, TN;

John D. Engelbrecht, President
J.P. Engelbrecht, VP

Southern Broadcast Corp. of Sarasota
1477 10th St., Sarasota FL 34236
(941) 923-8840; *Fax:*(941) 924-3971;
TV Stns: 3 TV.
WAAY-TV Huntsville, AL; WTXL-TV Tallahassee, FL; WWSB Sarasota, FL;

Spanish Broadcasting System Inc.
2601 South Bayshore Dr., PH 2, Coconut Grove FL 33133
(305) 441-6901; *Fax:*(305) 446-5148
www.spanishbroadcasting.com
Ownership: Raul Alarcon Jr., Jose Grimalt.
TV Stns: 1 TV.
WSBS-TV Key West, FL;
Radio Stns: 20 FM.
KXOL-FM Los Angeles, CA; KLAX-FM East Los Angeles, CA; KRZZ San Francisco, CA; WCMQ-FM Hialeah, FL; WODA Bayamon, PR; WEGM San German, PR; WRXD Fajardo, PR; WZET Hormigueros, PR; WIOA San Juan, PR; WIOB Mayaguez, PR; WIOC Ponce, PR; WLEY-FM Aurora, IL; WMEG Guayama, PR; WNOD Mayaguez, PR; WPAT-FM Paterson, NJ; WRMA Fort Lauderdale, FL; WSKQ-FM New York, NY; WXDJ North Miami Beach, FL; WZMT Ponce, PR; WZNT San Juan, PR;

Jose Grimalt, EVP
Raul Alarcon, CEO

Sunbeam Television Corp.
1401 79th St. Causeway, Miami FL 33141
(305) 751-6692; *Fax:*(305) 757-2266
www.wsvn.com, 7news@wsvn.com
TV Stns: 3 TV.
WHDH Boston, MA; WLVI Cambridge, MA; WSVN Miami, FL;

Edmund Ansin, President
Deisy Bermudez, Programming Director

Sunbelt Communications Co.
c/o KVBC(TV), 1500 Foremaster Ln., Las Vegas NV 89101
(702) 642-3333; *Fax:*(702) 657-3423
www.kvbc.com
ch3@kvbc.com
Ownership: James E. Rogers.
TV Stns: 6 TV.
KENV-DT Elko, NV; KJWY Jackson, WY; KRNV-DT Reno, NV; KTVH-DT Helena, MT; KXTF Twin Falls, ID; KYMA-DT Yuma, AZ;

Ralph Toddre, President

Surtsey Media LLC
73 Kercheval Ave., Suite 100, Grosse Pointe Farms MI 48236
(313) 884-7878;
TV Stns: 2 TV.
KVCT Victoria, TX; KFJX-DT Pittsburg, KS;

Tanana Valley Television Co.
3650 Braddock St., Suite 2, Fairbanks AK 99701
(907) 452-3697; *Fax:*(907) 456-3428
Ownership: William St. Pierre, 85%.
TV Stns: 2 TV.
KFXF Fairbanks, AK; KNLT(FM) Palmer, AK;
Radio Stns: 3 FM.
KYSC Fairbanks, AK; KDJF Ester, AK; KNLT(FM) Palmer, AK;

Telemundo Television Stations
2290 W. 8th Ave., Hialeah FL 33010
(305) 884-8200; *Fax:*(305) 889-7950
www.telemundo.com
Ownership: Comcast Corp., 51%; General Electric Co., 49%. See also NBC Owned Television Stations (see listing).
TV Stns: 12 TV.
KDEN-TV Longmont, CO; KHRR Tucson, AZ; KNSO Merced, CA; KSTS San Jose, CA; KTMD Galveston, TX; KVEA Corona, CA; KWHY-TV Los Angeles, CA; WKAQ-TV San Juan, PR; WNJU Linden, NJ; WNEU Merrimack, NH; WSCV Fort Lauderdale, FL; WSNS-TV Chicago, IL;

Manuel Abud, Chairman
Juan Antunez, VP General Counsel
Vincent Sadusky, CFO

The Curators of the University of Missouri
University of Missouri, 316 University Hall, Columbia MO 65211
(573) 882-2388; *Fax:*(573) 882-0010
www.umsystem.edu
Ownership: (Business Services Division).
TV Stns: 1 TV.
KOMU-TV Columbia, MO;
Radio Stns: 6 FM.
KBIA Columbia, MO; KCUR-FM Kansas City, MO; KMNR Rolla, MO; KMST Rolla, MO; KWMU St. Louis, MO; KAUD Mexico, MO;

Michael Dunn, General Manager

The E. W. Scripps Co.
Box 5380, 312 Walnut St., 28th Fl., Cincinnati OH 45202
(513) 977-3000; *Fax:*(513) 977-3728
www.scripps.com
Ownership: The E.W. Scripps Co.
TV Stns: 10 TV.
KJRH-TV Tulsa, OK; KMCI-TV Lawrence, KS; KNXV-TV Phoenix, AZ; KSHB-TV Kansas City, MO; WCPO-TV Cincinnati, OH; WEWS-TV Cleveland, OH; WFTS-TV Tampa, FL; WMAR-TV Baltimore, MD; WPTV-TV West Palm Beach, FL; WXYZ-TV Detroit, MI;

Brian G. Lawlor, SVP, Television

The Victory Television Network
Box 22007, Little Rock AR 72221-2007
(501) 223-2525; *Fax:*(501) 221-3837
www.vtntv.com
jim.grant@vtntv.com
TV Stns: 3 TV.
KVTH-DT Hot Springs, AR; KVTJ-DT Jonesboro, AR; KVTN-DT Pine Bluff, AR;

Pastor Happy Caldwell, President
Jim Grant, General Manager

Tri-State Christian Television
Box 1010, Marion IL 62959
(618) 997-9333; *Fax:*(618) 997-1859
www.tct.tv
Ownership: Nonprofit corporation. LPTV: WDWO-CA Detroit, MI; and WDYR-CA Dyersburg, TN.
TV Stns: 6 TV.
WAQP Saginaw, MI; WINM Angola, IN; WLXI Greensboro, NC; WNYB Jamestown, NY; WTCT Marion, IL; WTLJ Muskegon, MI;

Garth Coonce, President
Shane Chaney, CFO

Tribune Broadcasting Co.
435 N. Michigan Ave., Suite 1800, Chicago IL 60611
(312) 222-3333; *Fax:*(312) 329-0611
www.tribune.com

Ownership: The Tribune Employee Stock Ownership Plan as implemented through the Tribune Employee Stock Ownership Trust, Oak Brook, IL, 100%.

TV Stns: 24 TV.
KCPQ Tacoma, WA; KDAF Dallas, TX; KIAH Houston, TX; KPLR-TV St. Louis, MO; KSWB-TV San Diego, CA; KTLA Los Angeles, CA; KZJO Seattle, WA; KTXL Sacramento, CA; KRCW-TV Salem, OR; KWGN-TV Denver, CO; WDCW Washington, DC; WSFL-TV Miami, FL; WGN Chicago, IL; WGNO New Orleans, LA; WNOL-TV New Orleans, LA; WPHL-TV Philadelphia, PA; WPIX New York, NY; WPMT York, PA; WTIC-TV Hartford, CT; WTTK Kokomo, IN; WTTV Bloomington, IN; WCCT-TV Waterbury, CT; WXIN Indianapolis, IN; WXMI Grand Rapids, MI;

Radio Stns: 2 AM.
WGN(AM) Chicago, IL; WGN Chicago, IL;
Ed Wilson, President
Nils Larsen, CEO

Trinity Broadcasting Network
2442 Michelle Dr., Tustin CA 92780
(714) 832-2950; *Fax:*(714) 730-0657
www.tbn.org, comments@tbn.org
Ownership: Nonprofit corporation.

TV Stns: 25 TV.
KAAH-TV Honolulu, HI; KDOR-TV Bartlesville, OK; KDTX-TV Dallas, TX; KNAT-TV Albuquerque, NM; KPAZ-TV Phoenix, AZ; KTAJ-TV St. Joseph, MO; KTBN-TV Santa Ana, CA; KTBO-TV Oklahoma City, OK; KTBW-TV Tacoma, WA; WBUY-TV Holly Springs, MS; WCLJ-TV Bloomington, IN; WDLI-TV Canton, OH; WELF-TV Dalton, GA; WGTW-TV Burlington, NJ; WHFT-TV Miami, FL; WHSG-TV Monroe, GA; WKOI-TV Richmond, IN; WMCF-TV Montgomery, AL; WMPV-TV Mobile, AL; WPGD-TV Hendersonville, TN; WSFJ-TV Newark, OH; WTBY-TV Poughkeepsie, NY; WTJP-TV Gadsden, AL; WWTO-TV La Salle, IL; KPJR-DT Greeley, CO;
Paul Crouch, President
Ben Miller, VP Engineering
Janice Crouch, VP Programming
Rod Henke, VP Sales

Tucker Broadcasting of Traverse City Inc.
9434 N. Sunset Ridge, Fountain Hills AZ 85268
(480) 836-2181
bentucker13@cox.net

TV Stns: 2 TV.
WGTQ Sault Ste. Marie, MI; WGTU Traverse City, MI;

Tyler Media Broadcasting Corp.
5101 S. Shields Blvd., Oklahoma City OK 73129
(405) 616-5500; *Fax:*(405) 616-5505
www.kkng.com

TV Stns: 1 TV.
KTUZ-TV Shawnee, OK;

Radio Stns: 2 AM. 3 FM.
KTLR Oklahoma City, OK; KEBC Del City, OK; KTUZ-FM Okarche, OK; KJKE Newcastle, OK; KKNG-FM Blanchard, OK;
Robert De Negri, CFO
Skip Stow, Promotions Manager

United Communications Corp.
5800 7th Ave., Kenosha WI 53140
(262) 657-1000; *Fax:*(262) 657-6226
www.kenoshanews.com
hbrown@kenoshanews.com
Ownership: Howard J. Brown, Lucy Brown Minn, Sarah Brown Russ, Amy Brown Tuchler. Note: Group also owns LPTV stn WNYF-CA Watertown, NY.

TV Stns: 2 TV.
KEYC-TV CBS & NEYC FOX Mankato, MN; WWNY-TV Carthage, NY;
Howard Brown, President
Kenneth Dowdell, Vice President
Ronald Montemurro, Vice President

Univision Communications Inc.
5999 Center Dr., Los Angeles CA 90045
(310) 216-3434; *Fax:*(310) 556-3568
www.univision.net/corp/en/overview.jsp
Ownership: Broadcasting Media Partners Inc.

TV Stns: 30 TV.
KTFQ-TV Albuquerque, NM; KFTU-DT Douglas, AZ; KFPH-DT Flagstaff, AZ; KDTV-DT San Francisco, CA; KFTV-DT Hanford, CA; KFTR-DT Ontario, CA; KFTH-DT Alvin, TX; KMEX-DT Los Angeles, CA; KFSF-DT Vallejo, CA; KTFF-DT Porterville, CA; KUVI-DT Bakersfield, CA; KUVN-DT Garland, TX; KUVS-DT Modesto, CA; KWEX-DT San Antonio, TX; WFTT-DT Tampa, FL; WOTF-DT Melbourne, FL; WXFT-DT Aurora, IL; WUVG-DT Athens, GA; WFUT-DT Newark, NJ; WUTF-DT Marlborough, MA; WFTY-DT Smithtown, NY; WUVP-DT Vineland, NJ; WUVC-DT Fayetteville, NC; WLII Caguas, PR; WLTV-DT Miami, FL; WQHS-DT Cleveland, OH; WSTE-DT Ponce, PR; WSUR-DT Ponce, PR; WFDC-DT Arlington, VA; WXTV-DT Paterson, NJ;
Ray Rodriguez, President

Vaughan Media LLC
c/o Vaughan Acquisition LLC, 14429 Bridgeview Land, Port Charlotte FL 33953
(217) 521-3702; *Fax:*(941) 764-6867
Ownership: Thomas J. Vaughan, 100%.

TV Stns: 3 TV.
KTKA-TV Topeka, KS; WTGS Hardeeville, SC; WYTV Youngstown, OH;
Thomas J. Vaughan, Manager

VCY America Inc.
3434 W. Kilbourn Ave., Milwaukee WI 53208
(414) 935-3000; *Fax:*(414) 935-3015
www.vcyamerica.org, vcy@vcyamerica.org
Ownership: VCY America, Inc.

TV Stns: 1 TV.
WVCY-TV Milwaukee, WI;

Radio Stns: 1 AM. 18 FM.
WVCY Oshkosh, WI; KCVS Salina, KS; KVCX Gregory, SD; KVCY Fort Scott, KS; WVCN Baraga, MI; WEGZ Washburn, WI; WJIC Zanesville, OH; WVCF Eau Claire, WI; WVCX Tomah, WI; WVCY-FM Milwaukee, WI; WVCM Iron Mountain, MI; WVFL Fond Du Lac, WI; KVCF Freeman, SD; WVRN Wittenberg, WI; KVFL Pierre, SD; KVCS Spring Valley, MN; KVCH Huron, SD; WQRN Cook, MN; WVCS Owen, WI;
Vic Eliason, VP/Gen Mgr
Jim Schneider, Programming Director

Waterman Broadcasting Corp.
Box 7578, Fort Myers FL 33911-7578
(239) 939-2020; *Fax:*(239) 939-7903
www.water.net,www.nbc-2.com
Ownership: Bernard Waterman, Edith Waterman.

TV Stns: 2 TV.
WBBH-TV Fort Myers, FL; WVIR-TV Charlottesville, VA;
Bernard Waterman, President
Steve Pontius, EVP
Joe Ernest, VP

Weigel Broadcasting Co.
26 N. Halsted St., Chicago IL 60661
(312) 705-2600; *Fax:*(312) 705-2656
www.wciu.com
Ownership: Howard Shapiro Remainder Trust, 51% equity; Norman Shapiro Rem Children's Trust, 10% equity.

TV Stns: 3 TV.
WCIU-TV Chicago, IL; WDJT-TV Milwaukee, WI; WMLW-TV Racine, WI;
Norman H. Shapiro, President

West Virginia Media Holdings LLC
Box 11848, Charleston WV 25339-1848
(304) 720-6527; *Fax:*(304) 345-7280
www.wvmh.com

TV Stns: 4 TV.
WBOY-TV Clarksburg, WV; WOWK-TV Huntington, WV; WTRF-TV Wheeling, WV; WVNS-TV Lewisburg, WV;
Marty Becker, Chairman
Bray Cary, CEO

White Knight Broadcasting of Longview Inc
4300 Richmond Road, Tyler TX 75703
(903) 581-5656; *Fax:*(903) 561-1648
www.myklpn.com, info@klpn.com

TV Stns: 1 TV.
KFXK-TV Longview, TX;
Drew Balch, Operations Dir

White Knight Holdings Inc.
9257 Bailey Ln., Fairfax VA 22031-1903
(703) 253-2027;

TV Stns: 2 TV.
KSHV-TV Shreveport, LA; WVLA-TV Baton Rouge, LA;
Anthony Malara III, President

Wilderness Communications LLC
3501 Northwest Evangeline Thruway, Carencro LA 70520
(337) 896-1600; *Fax:*(337) 896-2695;

TV Stns: 2 TV.
KBCA Alexandria, LA; KLWB New Iberia, LA;

Radio Stns: 1 AM.
WROD Daytona Beach, FL;

Withers Broadcasting Co.
Box 1508, Mount Vernon IL 62864
(618) 242-3500; *Fax:*(618) 242-4444
Ownership: W. Russell Withers Jr., 100%.

TV Stns: 3 TV.
WDHS Iron Mountain, MI; WDTV Weston, WV; WVFX Clarksburg, WV;

Radio Stns: 13 AM. 20 FM.
KAPE Cape Girardeau, MO; KOKX Keokuk, IA; KRHW Sikeston, MO; KJXX Jackson, MO; WAYE Birmingham, AL; WEBQ Harrisburg, IL; WFRX West Frankfort, IL; WILY Centralia, IL; WMIX Mount Vernon, IL; WMOK Metropolis, IL; WQUL Woodruff, SC; WROY Carmi, IL; WSDR Sterling, IL; KBXB Sikeston, MO; KGMO Cape Girardeau, MO; KOKX-FM Keokuk, IA; KRNQ Keokuk, IA; WDDD-FM Johnston City, IL; WEBQ-FM Eldorado, IL; WGKY Wickliffe, KY; WKIB Anna, IL; WMIX-FM Mount Vernon, IL; WREZ Metropolis, IL; WRUL Carmi, IL; WRXX Centralia, IL; WSSQ Sterling, IL; WTAO-FM Herrin, IL; WYNG Mount Carmel, IL; WVZA Murphysboro, IL; WZZL Reidland, KY; WZZT Morrison, IL; WISH-FM Galatia, IL; WCEZ Carthage, IL;
W. Russell Withers, President

Woods Communications Corp.
One WCOV Ave., Montgomery AL 36111
(334) 288-7020; *Fax:*(334) 288-5414
www.wcov.com

TV Stns: 2 TV.
KLCW-TV Wolfforth, TX; WCOV-TV Montgomery, AL;
David Woods, CEO

Wooster Republican Printing Co.
212 E. Liberty St., Wooster OH 44691
(330) 264-3511; *Fax:*(330) 263-5013
www.dixcom.com
Ownership: (dba Dix Communications).

TV Stns: 1 TV.
KFBB-TV Great Falls, MT;

Radio Stns: 3 AM. 6 FM.
WFRB Frostburg, MD; WKVX Wooster, OH; WTBO Cumberland, MD; WFRB-FM Frostburg, MD; WKGO Cumberland, MD; WNDD Silver Springs, FL; WNDT Alachua, FL; WOGK Ocala, FL; WQKT Wooster, OH;
Dale Gerber, CFO
G. Charles Dix, VP
Robert Dix, TV Division Chairman

Word Broadcasting Network Inc.
Box 19229, Louisville KY 40259
(502) 964-3304; *Fax:*(502) 966-9692
www.wbna21.com

TV Stns: 1 TV.
WBNA Louisville, KY;

Radio Stns: 3 AM.
WYRM Norfolk, VA; WYMM Jacksonville, FL; WVHI Evansville, IN;
Bob Rogers, President
Greg Holt, Operations Dir

Wyomedia Corp.
1856 Skyview Dr., Casper WY 82601
(307) 577-5923; *Fax:*(307) 234-4005;

TV Stns: 4 TV.
KFNB Casper, WY; KFNE Riverton, WY; KFNR Rawlins, WY; KLWY Cheyenne, WY;
Marvin Gussman, Chairman

Young Broadcasting Inc.
599 Lexington Ave., 47th Fl., New York NY 10022
(212) 754-7070; *Fax:*(212) 758-1229
www.youngbroadcasting.com
Ownership: Vincent J. Young, Gabelli Asset Management Inc., New South Capital Management Inc.

TV Stns: 14 TV.
KCLO-TV Rapid City, SD; KDLO-TV Florence, SD; KELO-TV Sioux Falls, SD; KLFY-TV Lafayette, LA; KPLO-TV Reliance, SD; KRON-TV San Francisco, CA; KWQC-TV Davenport, IA; WATE-TV Knoxville, TN; WBAY-TV Green Bay, WI; WCDC-TV Adams, MA; WKRN-TV Nashville, TN; WLNS-TV Lansing, MI; WRIC-TV Petersburg, VA; WTEN Albany, NY;
Vincent Young, Chairman
Deborah McDermott, CEO/COO
James Morgan, CFO

ZGS Communications
2000 North 14th Street, Suite 400, Arlington VA 22201
(703) 528-5656; *Fax:*(703) 526-0878
www.zgsgroup.com
info@zgsgroup.com

TV Stns: 1 TV.
WWSI Atlantic City, NJ;
Julissa Marenco, President

Key to TV Listings

Television listings include TV stations in the United States, its territories and Canada. All collected data for these listings include information current to fall 2012. To use the television key, see boldface numbers and corresponding explanations.

(1) WOF-TV (2) Digital Channel: 53 Virtual Channel: 17 hrs: 24 2,200 kw vis , 20 kw aur, ant 500t/300g. TL: N36 49 21 W108 47 32 (CP: Ant 750t/550g) **(3)** On air date: Apr 13, 1952. **(4)** Box 100, Dothan, AL 36301. Phone: (909) 555-1000 FAX: (909) 999-9999. Web Site www.wot.tv. **(5)** Licensee: WOF Broadcasting Co. **(6)** Group Owner: Acme Stations (acq 7-20-69; $2 million. **(7)** Population served: 230,000 **(8)** Natl. Network: CBS. **(9)** Natl. Rep: Jones, Tri-State. Washington Atty: Goltz & Stick. **(10)** News staff: 3; 10 hrs wkly.
(11) Key Personnel:
Jud Jones . . . . Pres & Gen Mgr
D. Spark . . . . Chief Engineer

(1) Station call letters as assigned by the Federal Communications Commission (FCC) or Canadian Radio-television and Telecommunications Commission (CRTC)

(2) Virtual channel and digital channels, hours of operation, power, antenna, location and construction permit. WOF-TV operates with 2,200 kilowatts (effective radiated power) visual and 20 kilowatts aural. Its antenna is 500 feet above average terrain and 300 feet above ground. N36 49 21 W108 47 32 refers to the geographical coordinates (latitude and longitude) of the transmitter location, WOF-TV holds a construction permit for an antenna height change to 750 feet above average terrain, 550 feet above ground.

(3) Date station first went on the air (regardless of subsequent ownership changes)

(4) Address and zip code, telephone and fax number, web site and e-mail address.

(5) Licensee name.

(6) Ownership and date of acquisition (if not original owner). If a station has been sold, any available sale information is listed following the acquisition date. WOF-TV is owned by Acme Stations.

(7) Population served refers to the station's potential market.

(8) Network programming. WOF-TV's national network is CBS.

(9) Representatives and Washington attorney. Sales representatives are listed with the national rep first, then regional.

(10) Number of staff providing local news and number of local news aired weekly.

(11) Key personnel.

An asterisk (*) preceding station call letters indicates noncommercial stations

DMA Cross Reference List

The following cities are in hyphenated markets, but are not the first city given in such a market; i.e., Troy in Albany-Schenectady-Troy, NY. They are listed alphabetically.

Ada, OK	See Sherman-Ada
Akron, OH	See Cleveland-Akron (Canton)
Altoona, PA	See Johnstown-Altoona
Ames, IA	See Des Moines-Ames
Anderson, SC	See Greenville-Spartanburg-Asheville-Anderson
Anniston, AL	See Birmingham (Anniston, Tuscaloosa)
Appleton, WI	See Green Bay-Appleton
Asheville, NC	See Greenville-Spartanburg-Asheville-Anderson
Auburn, ME	See Portland-Auburn
Austin, MN	See Rochester-Mason City-Austin
Battle Creek, MI	See Grand Rapids-Kalamazoo-Battle Creek
Bay City, MI	See Flint-Saginaw-Bay City
Beckley, WV	See Bluefield-Beckley-Oak Hill
Bismarck, ND	See Minot-Bismarck-Dickinson
Bloomington, IL	See Peoria-Bloomington
Bozeman, MT	See Butte-Bozeman
Brownsville, TX	See Harlingen-Weslaco-Brownsville-McAllen
Bryan, TX	See Waco-Temple-Bryan
Cadillac, MI	See Traverse City-Cadillac
Canton, OH	See Cleveland-Akron (Canton)
Cape Girardeau, MO	See Paducah-Cape Girardeau-Harrisburg-Mount Vernon
Daytona Beach, FL	See Orlando-Daytona Beach-Melbourne
Decatur, AL	See Huntsville-Decatur-Florence
Decatur, IL	See Champaign & Springfield-Decatur
Dickinson, ND	See Minot-Bismarck-Dickinson
Dubuque, IA	See Cedar Rapids-Waterloo-Iowa City & Dubuque
Durham, NC	See Raleigh-Durham
Eau Claire, WI	See La Crosse-Eau Claire
El Centro, CA	See Yuma-El Centro
El Dorado, AR	See Monroe-El Dorado
Elkhart, IN	See South Bend-Elkhart
Fayetteville, AR	See Ft. Smith-Fayetteville-Springdale-Rogers
Fayetteville, NC	See Raleigh-Durham (Fayetteville)
Florence, AL	See Huntsville-Decatur-Florence
Florence, SC	See Myrtle Beach-Florence
Ft. Lauderdale, FL	See Miami-Ft. Lauderdale
Ft. Pierce, FL	See West Palm Beach-Ft. Pierce
Ft. Walton Beach, FL	See Mobile-Pensacola (Ft. Walton Beach)
Ft. Worth, TX	See Dallas-Ft. Worth
Greenville, MS	See Greenwood-Greenville
Gulfport, MS	See Biloxi-Gulfport
Hagerstown, MD	See Washington, DC (Hagerstown)
Hannibal, MO	See Quincy-Hannibal-Keokuk
Harrisburg, IL	See Paducah-Cape Girardeau-Harrisburg-Mount Vernon
Hastings, NE	See Lincoln & Hastings-Kearney Plus
High Point, NC	See Greensboro-High Point-Winston Salem
Holyoke, MA	See Springfield-Holyoke
Huntington, WV	See Charleston-Huntington
Hutchinson, KS	See Wichita-Hutchinson Plus
Iowa City, IA	See Cedar Rapids-Waterloo-Iowa City & Dubuque
Jefferson City, MO	See Columbia-Jefferson City
Kalamazoo, MI	See Grand Rapids-Kalamazoo-Battle Creek

Kearney, NE	See Lincoln & Hastings-Kearney Plus
Kennewick, WA	See Yakima-Pasco-Richland-Kennewick
Keokuk, IA	See Quincy-Hannibal-Keokuk
Kirksville, MO	See Ottumwa-Kirksville
Klamath Falls, OR	See Medford-Klamath Falls
Lancaster, PA	See Harrisburg-Lancaster-Lebanon-York
Laurel, MS	See Hattiesburg-Laurel
Lawton, OK	See Wichita Falls & Lawton
Lebanon, PA	See Harrisburg-Lancaster-Lebanon-York
Longview, TX	See Tyler-Longview (Lufkin & Nacogdoches)
Lufkin, TX	See Tyler-Longview (Lufkin & Nacogdoches)
Lynchburg, VA	See Roanoke-Lynchburg
Manchester, NH	See Boston (Manchester)
Mason City, IA	See Rochester-Mason City-Austin
McAllen, TX	See Harlingen-Weslaco-Brownsville-McAllen
Melbourne, FL	See Orlando-Daytona Beach-Melbourne
Midland, TX	See Odessa-Midland
Mitchell, SD	See Sioux Falls (Mitchell)
Modesto, CA	See Sacramento-Stockton-Modesto
Moline, IL	See Davenport-Rock Island-Moline
Montrose, CO	See Grand Junction-Montrose
Nacogdoches, TX	See Tyler-Longview (Lufkin & Nacogdoches)
Naples, FL	See Ft. Myers-Naples
New Bedford, MA	See Providence-New Bedford
New Bern, NC	See Greenville-New Bern-Washington
New Haven, CT	See Hartford & New Haven
Newport News, VA	See Norfolk-Portsmouth-Newport News
Oak Hill, WV	See Bluefield-Beckley-Oak Hill
Oakland, CA	See San Francisco-Oakland-San Jose
Pasco, WA	See Yakima-Pasco-Richland-Kennewick
Pensacola, FL	See Mobile-Pensacola
Petersburg, VA	See Richmond-Petersburg
Pine Bluff, AR	See Little Rock-Pine Bluff
Pittsburg, KS	See Joplin-Pittsburg
Plattsburgh, NY	See Burlington-Plattsburgh
Pocatello, ID	See Idaho Falls-Pocatello
Port Arthur, TX	See Beaumont-Port Arthur
Portsmouth, VA	See Norfolk-Portsmouth-Newport News
Pueblo, CO	See Colorado Springs-Pueblo
Redding, CA	See Chico-Redding
Rhinelander, WI	See Wausau-Rhinelander
Richland, WA	See Yakima-Pasco-Richland-Kennewick
Riverton, WY	See Casper-Riverton
Rock Island, IL	See Davenport-Rock Island-Moline
Rogers, AR	See Ft. Smith-Fayetteville-Springdale-Rogers
Saginaw, MI	See Flint-Saginaw-Bay City
St. Paul, MN	See Minneapolis-St. Paul
St. Petersburg, FL	See Tampa-St. Petersburg-Sarasota
Salinas, CA	See Monterey-Salinas
San Jose, CA	See San Francisco-Oakland-San Jose
San Luis Obispo, CA	See Santa Barbara-Santa Maria-San Luis Obispo
Santa Fe, NM	See Albuquerque-Santa Fe

Santa Maria, CA	See Santa Barbara-Santa Maria-San Luis Obispo
Sarasota, FL	See Tampa-St. Petersburg-Sarasota
Schenectady, NY	See Albany-Schenectady-Troy
Scottsbluff, NE	See Cheyenne-Scottsbluff
Scranton, PA	See Wilkes Barre-Scranton
Selma, AL	See Montgomery (Selma)
Sierra Vista, AZ	See Tucson (Sierra Vista)
Spartanburg, SC	See Greenville-Spartanburg-Asheville-Anderson
Springdale, AR	See Ft. Smith-Fayetteville-Springdale-Rogers
Springfield, IL	See Champaign & Springfield-Decatur
Steubenville, OH	See Wheeling-Steubenville
Stockton, CA	See Sacramento-Stockton-Modesto
Superior, WI	See Duluth-Superior
Sweetwater, TX	See Abilene-Sweetwater
Tacoma, WA	See Seattle-Tacoma
Temple, TX	See Waco-Temple-Bryan
Thomasville, GA	See Tallahassee-Thomasville
Troy, NY	See Albany-Schenectady-Troy
Tupelo, MS	See Columbus-Tupelo-West Point
Tuscaloosa, AL	See Birmingham (Anniston, Tuscaloosa)
Valley City, ND	See Fargo-Valley City
Visalia, CA	See Fresno-Visalia
Washington, NC	See Greenville-New Bern-Washington
Waterloo, IA	See Cedar Rapids-Waterloo-Iowa City & Dubuque
Weslaco, TX	See See Harlingen-Weslaco-Brownsville-McAllen
Weston, WV	See Clarksburg-Weston
West Point, MS	See Columbus-Tupelo-West Point
Winston Salem, NC	See Greensboro-High Point-Winston Salem
York, PA	See Harrisburg-Lancaster-Lebanon-York

TV Stations in the United States

Alabama

Birmingham (Anniston, Tuscaloosa), AL (DMA 40)

WABM *Digital Channel:* 36 *Virtual Channel:* 68; 885 kw; 1332 ft.; N33 29 4 W86 48 25
3474 William Penn Highway, Pittsburgh, PA 15235 US
(205) 943-2168, *Fax:* (205) 290-2115
www.wabm68.com
License: Birmingham, Jefferson County, AL held by Birmingham (WABM-TV) Licensee Inc.
Group Owner: Sinclair Broadcast Group Inc.; (acq 2-1-2002).
Nat'l Network: MYTV
Steve Marks, CEO
J. C. Lowe, General Manager
Theresa Cottrell, General Sales Mgr
Lucrecia Rubio, Programming Director
John Batson, Chief Engineer
Matt Morris, Traffic Manager

***WBIQ** *Digital Channel:* 10 *Virtual Channel:* 10; 3 kw; 1398 ft.; N33 29 4 W86 48 25
2112 11th Ave, S., #400, Birmingham, AL 35256 US
(205) 328-8756, *Fax:* (205) 251-2192
www.aptv.org
License: Birmingham, Jefferson County, AL held by Alabama ETV Commission
Washington Law Firm: Dow, Lohnes & Albertson, PLLC
Nat'l Network: PBS *Regional Network:* Alabama Public Television
Allan Pizzato, CEO
Gary Stokes, General Sales Mgr
Pauline Howland, CFO
Charles Grantham, COO

WBRC *Digital Channel:* 50 *Virtual Channel:* 6; 912 kw; 1385 ft.; N33 29 19 W86 47 58
Mailing Address: 5151 Wisconsin Ave., N.W, Washington, DC 20016 US
Second Address: 1720 Valley View Dr., Birmingham, AL 35209
(205) 322-6666, *Fax:* (205) 583-4386
www.myfoxal.com
License: Birmingham, Jefferson County, AL held by WBRC License Subsidiary LLC.
Group Owner: Raycom Media Inc.; (acq 3-31-2009; exchange for WTVR-TV Richmond, VA)
Nat'l Network: FOX *Nat'l Reps:* TeleRep
Size of News Staff: 53; *Hours of Local News Weekly:* news progmg 21 hrs wkly
Lou Kirchen, Operations Dir
Jay Abbattista, General Sales Mgr
Wayne Farrell, Programming Director
Andy Cook, Chief Engineer
Roy Gardner, Operations Manager

WCFT-TV *Digital Channel:* 33 *Virtual Channel:* 33; 300 kw; 2162 ft.; N33 28 48 W87 25 50
Mailing Address: 800 Concourse Parkway, Suite 200, Birmingham, AL 35244 US
Second Address: 800 Concourse Pkwy., Suite 200, Birmingham, AL 35244
(205) 403-3340, *Fax:* (205) 403-3329
www.abc3340.com
License: Tuscaloosa, Tuscaloosa County, AL held by TV Alabama Inc.
Group Owner: Allbritton Communications Co.; (acq 1996; $20 million); *Washington Law Firm:* Hogan & Hartson
Nat'l Network: ABC
Mike Murphy, General Manager
Ron Thomas, Chief Engineer

***WCIQ** *Digital Channel:* 7 *Virtual Channel:* 7; 34.8 kw; 1889 ft.; N33 29 6 W85 48 32
2112 11th Ave, S., #400, Birmingham, AL 35256 US
(205) 328-8756, *Fax:* (205) 251-2192
www.aptv.org
License: Mount Cheaha, Talladega County, AL held by Alabama ETV Commission
Washington Law Firm: Dow, Lohnes & Albertson, PLLC
Nat'l Network: PBS *Regional Network:* Alabama Public Television
Allan Pizzato, CEO
Gary Stokes, General Sales Mgr
Pauline Howland, CFO
Charles Grantham, COO

WDBB *Digital Channel:* 18 *Virtual Channel:* 17; 350 kw; 2215 ft.; N33 28 51 W87 24 3; *Rebroadcasting:* Satellite of WTTO Homewood
5455 Jug Factory Road, Tuscaloosa, AL 35405 US
(205) 943-2168, *Fax:* (205) 290-2115
www.wtto21.com
License: Bessemer, Jefferson County, AL held by WDBB-TV Inc (acq 1-19-95; $1.5 million); *Washington Law Firm:* Fletcher, Heald & Hildreth
Nat'l Network: CW *Nat'l Reps:* Adam Young *Wire Services:* NOAA Weather; Weather Wire
Size of News Staff: 20; *Hours of Local News Weekly:* news progmg 15 hrs wkly
Steve Marks, CEO
J. C. Lowe, General Manager
Theresa Cottrell, General Sales Mgr
Lucrecia Rubio, Programming Director
John Batson, Chief Engineer
Matt Morris, Traffic Manager

WIAT *Digital Channel:* 30 *Virtual Channel:* 42; 2,163 kw vis, 216 kw aur; ant 1,382t/1,134g; N33 29 02 W86 48 21; *Population Served:* 700,000
Mailing Address: 2075 Goldencrest Dr., Birmingham, AL 35209
Second Address: P.O. Box 59496, Birmingham, AL 35259
(205) 322-4200, *Fax:* (205) 320-2710
www.cbs42.com
License: Birmingham, Jefferson County, AL held by LIN Licensing Company LLC
Group Owner: LIN Media; (acq 10-6-2006; $35 million with KIMT(TV) Mason City, IA).; *Washington Law Firm:* Dow, Lohnes & Albertson
Nat'l Network: CBS *Nat'l Reps:* TeleRep
Hours of Local News Weekly: News progmg 6 hrs wkly
Bill Ballard, General Manager
Allison Lindsey, General Sales Mgr
Alex Morrow, Promotions Manager
Bill Payer, News Director
Scott Sarkinson, Engineering Dir
Greg Butler, Operations Director

WJSU-TV *Digital Channel:* 9 *Virtual Channel:* 40; 15.6 kw; 1178 ft.; N33 36 24 W86 25 3
P.O. Box 90406, San Antonio, TX 78209 US
(205) 403-3340, *Fax:* (205) 403-3329
www.abc3340.com
License: Anniston, Calhoun County, AL held by TV Alabama Inc.
Group Owner: Allbritton Communications Co.; (acq 1-24-2000).; *Washington Law Firm:* Haley, Bader & Potts
Nat'l Network: ABC
Size of News Staff: 16; *Hours of Local News Weekly:* news progmg 9 hrs wkly
Mike Murphy, General Manager
Ron Thomas, Chief Engineer

WPXH-TV *Digital Channel:* 45; 1,750 kw vis, 175 kw aur; 1,000t/500g; N33 57 11 W86 13 00; *Population Served:* 1,000,000
2085 Goldencrest Dr., Birmingham, AL 35209
(205) 870-4404, *Fax:* (205) 870-0744
www.ionmedia.com
License: Gadsden, Etowah County, AL held by ION Media License Company, LLC, Debtor-in-possession
Group Owner: ION Media Networks Inc.; *Washington Law Firm:* Fletcher, Heald & Hildreth
Nat'l Network: ION Television
Hours of Local News Weekly: News progmg 8 hrs wkly
Debra Perry, General Manager
Angela Head, Programming Director

WTJP-TV *Digital Channel:* 26 *Virtual Channel:* 60; 1000 kw; 1079 ft.; N33 48 53 W86 26 55
313 Rosedale Avenue, Gadsden, AL 35901 US
(256) 546-8860, *Fax:* (256) 543-8623
www.tbn.org
License: Gadsden, Etowah County, AL held by Trinity Christian Center of Santa Ana Inc. dba Trinity Broadcasting Network.
Group Owner: Trinity Broadcasting Network; (acq 5-8-2000).
Nat'l Network: TRINITY BROADCA
Paul Crouch, CEO
Gary Hodges, General Manager
Curtiss Kemp, Chief Engineer
Terry Hickey, Executive Vice President

WTTO *Digital Channel:* 28 *Virtual Channel:* 21; 765 kw; 1402 ft.; N33 29 4 W86 48 25
10706 Beaver Dam Road, Cockeysville, MD 21030 US
(205) 943-2168, *Fax:* (205) 250-6788
www.wtto21.com
License: Homewood, Jefferson County, AL held by WTTO Licensee LLC
Group Owner: Sinclair Broadcast Group Inc.; *Washington Law Firm:* Arter & Hadden
Nat'l Network: CW *Nat'l Reps:* Millennium Sales & Marketing
Chris Hummel, Operations Dir
J. C. Lowe, General Manager
Justin Hoekstra, General Sales Mgr
Lucrecia Rubio, Programming Director
Tim Costley, Chief Engineer
Matt Morris, Traffic Manager

WUOA *Digital Channel:* 6 *Virtual Channel:* 23; 26 kw; 1296 ft.; N33 29 2 W86 48 21; *Rebroadcasting:* Rebroadcasts WVUA Tuscaloosa/Northport 100%
Mailing Address: C/O Allstate Leasing, 9428 Reinsterstown Road, Owings Mills, MD 21117 US
Second Address: Reese Phifer Hall, Univ of Alabama, 901 University Blvd., Tuscaloosa, AL 35401
(205) 943-2168, *Fax:* (205) 250-6788
www.wvuatv.com
news@wvua7.com
License: Tuscaloosa, Tuscaloosa County, AL held by The Board of Trustees of the University of Alabama
Nat'l Network: NONE
Scott Spence, Operations Dir
Roy Clem, General Manager
Camille Shotts, General Sales Mgr
Vicki Richardson, Programming Director
Lynn Brooks, News Director
Dave Baughn, Chief Engineer
Dan Bradley, General Sales Manager

WVTM-TV *Digital Channel:* 13 *Virtual Channel:* 13; 20 kw; 1322 ft.; N33 29 26 W86 47 48
Ms Diane Zipursky, 1299 Pennsylvania Ave, Washngton, DC 20004 US
(205) 558-7311; (205) 933-1313, *Fax:* (205) 933-7516 (sales)
www.nbc13.com
newscomments@nbc13.com
License: Birmingham, Jefferson County, AL held by Media General Communications Holdings, LLC
Group Owner: Media General Broadcast Group; (acq 6-26-2006; grpsl).
Nat'l Network: NBC *Nat'l Reps:* Harrington, Righter & Parsons
Size of News Staff: 70; *Hours of Local News Weekly:* news progmg 24 hrs wkly
Minea Baker, General Sales Mgr
Domini Jones, Programming Director
Cil Frazier, Promotions Manager
Tim Gardner, News Director
Chuck Blackwood, Engineering Dir
Rhonda Garvin, General Sales Manager
Don Hawes, Sports Commentator

Columbus, GA (DMA 128)

***WGIQ** *Digital Channel:* 44 *Virtual Channel:* 43; 925 kw; 860 ft.; N31 43 4 W85 26 3
2112 11th Ave, So., #400, Birmingham, AL 35256 US
(205) 328-8756, *Fax:* (205) 251-2192
www.aptv.org
License: Louisville, Barbour County, AL held by Alabama ETV Commission
Washington Law Firm: Dow, Lohnes & Albertson, PLLC
Nat'l Network: PBS *Regional Network:* Alabama Public Television
Allan Pizzato, CEO
Gary Stokes, General Sales Mgr
Pauline Howland, CFO
Charles Grantham, COO

WLGA *Digital Channel:* 47; 794.3 kw vis, 79.43 kw aur; ant 679t; N32 38 33 W85 14 13
1800 Pepperell Pkwy., Opelika, AL 93277
(334) 745-0066, *Fax:* (334) 749-5768
www.wlgatv.com
wdix@wlgatv.com
License: Opelika, Lee County, AL held by Pappas Telecasting of Opelika L.P. (a Delaware limited partnership).
Group Owner: Pappas Telecasting Companies; (acq 1996; $1.6 million); *Washington Law Firm:* Paul, Hastings, Janofsky & Walker
Harry Pappas, President
Walter Dix, General Manager
Bill Brooks, General Sales Mgr
Mike Carroll, Chief Engineer

Dothan, AL (DMA 172)

WDFX-TV *Digital Channel:* 33 *Virtual Channel:* 34; 15 kw; 495 ft.; N31 12 28 W85 36 49
13906 Gold Circle, Suite 201, Omaha, NE 68144 US

(334) 794-3434, *Fax:* (334) 794-0034
www.myfox34.tv
myfox34.tv
License: Ozark, Dale County, AL held by WDFX License Subsidiary, LLC.
Group Owner: Raycom Media Inc.; (acq 10-14-2003; grpsl).; *Ownership:* WDFX,LLC.; *Washington Law Firm:* Covington & Burling
Nat'l Network: FOX *Nat'l Reps:* Harrington, Righter & Parsons
Wire Services: AP
Hours of Local News Weekly: 7
Rebecca Jones, Operations Dir
Erick Steffens, General Sales Mgr
Megan Anderson, Promotions Manager
Denise Holley, News Director
Ken McCrimmon, Chief Engineer
Melinda Chaney, Regional Sales Manager

WDHN *Digital Channel:* 21 *Virtual Channel:* 18; 1000 kw; 625 ft.; N31 14 25 W85 18 43
Mailing Address: PO Box 6237, Dothan, AL 36302 US
Second Address: 5274 E. Hwy. 52, Webb, AL 36376
(334) 793-1818, *Fax:* (334) 793-2623
www.dothanfirst.com
jhinson@wdhn.com
License: Dothan, Houston County, AL held by Nexstar Broadcasting Inc.
Group Owner: Nexstar Broadcasting Group Inc.; (acq 8-1-2003; $40 million with KARK-TV Little Rock, AR).; *Washington Law Firm:* Fletcher, Heald & Hildreth
Nat'l Network: ABC *Nat'l Reps:* Millennium Sales & Marketing
Size of News Staff: 8; *Hours of Local News Weekly:* news progmg 7 hrs wkly
Janie Hinson, Operations Dir
Kim Allen, Promotions Manager
Ken Curtis, News Director
Neal Riddle, Chief Engineer
Lynn Adkinson, Public Affairs Director

WTVY *Digital Channel:* 36 *Virtual Channel:* 4; 100 kw vis, 20 kw aur; 1,670t/1,909g; N30 55 10 W85 44 28; *Population Served:* 230,000
Mailing Address: Box 1089, Dothan, AL 36302
Second Address: 285 N. Foster St., Dothan, AL 36303
(334) 792-3195, *Fax:* (334) 793-3947
www.wtvy.com
License: Dothan, Houston County, AL held by Gray Television Licensee Inc.
Group Owner: Gray Television Inc.; (acq 8-29-2002; grpsl).
Nat'l Network: CBS WTVY 1; MyNetworkTV WTVY 2; CW WTVY 3 *Nat'l Reps:* Continental Television Sales *Wire Services:* AP
Size of News Staff: 26; *Hours of Local News Weekly:* news progmg 20.5 hrs wkly
Mike Smith, General Manager
Marc Stover, General Sales Mgr
Julia Bassett, Programming Director
Jeff Raker, News Director
Tom Johnson, Chief Engineer
Olivia Ware, Business Manager
Millicent Smith, National Sales Manager
LauraClark, Regional Sales Account Rep

Huntsville-Decatur (Florence), AL (DMA 82)

WAAY-TV *Digital Channel:* 32 *Virtual Channel:* 31; 468 kw; 1764 ft.; N34 44 12 W86 31 59
307 Clinton Avenue, Suite 100, Huntsville, AL 35801 US
(256) 533-3131, *Fax:* (256) 533-6616
www.waaytv.com
License: Huntsville, Madison County, AL held by WAAY-TV License LLC.
Group Owner: Southern Broadcast Corp. of Sarasota; (acq 1-31-2007; $41.645 million); *Washington Law Firm:* Cohn & Marks
Nat'l Network: ABC
Tracy Slayton, Operations Dir
Art Lanham, General Manager
Ed Groves, General Sales Mgr
Dave Keller, Programming Director
Keith Lowhorne, News Director
Don Roden, Chief Engineer
Robin Dorning, Traffic Manager

WAFF *Digital Channel:* 48 *Virtual Channel:* 48; 48 kw; 1890 ft.; N34 42 39 W86 32 7
Rsa Tower, 20th Floor, 201 Monroe Street, Montgomery, AL 36104 US
(256) 533-4848, *Fax:* (256) 533-1337
www.waff.com
webmaster@waff.com
License: Huntsville, Madison County, AL held by Raycom America License Subsidiary LLC.
Group Owner: Raycom Media Inc.; (acq 3-16-97; grpsl).; *Washington Law Firm:* Covington & Burling
Nat'l Network: NBC *Nat'l Reps:* Harrington, Righter & Parsons
Wire Services: AP
Size of News Staff: 43; *Hours of Local News Weekly:* news progmg 26 hrs wkly
Vanessa Oubre, Operations Dir
Dale Stafford, General Sales Mgr
Leigh Michal, Programming Director
Becky Shores, Promotions Manager
Adam Henning, News Director
J.T. Harriman, Engineering Dir
Susan Craft, Local Sales Manager
Catherine Young, Traffic Manager

***WFIQ** *Digital Channel:* 22 *Virtual Channel:* 36; 418.8 kw; 681 ft.; N34 34 41 W87 47 2
2112 11th Avenue, #400, Birmingham, AL 35256 US
(205) 328-8756, *Fax:* (205) 251-2192
www.aptv.org
License: Florence, Lauderdale County, AL held by Alabama ETV Commission
Washington Law Firm: Dow, Lohnes & Albertson, PLLC
Nat'l Network: PBS *Regional Network:* Alabama Public Television
Allan Pizzato, CEO
Gary Stokes, General Sales Mgr
Pauline Howland, CFO
Charles Grantham, COO

WHDF *Digital Channel:* 14 *Virtual Channel:* 15; 1000 kw; 1414 ft.; N35 0 9 W87 8 9
Mailing Address: 200 Galleria Parkway, Suite 1740, Atlanta, GA 30339 US
Second Address: 840 Cypress Mill Rd., Florence, AL 35630
(256) 767-1515;(256) 536-1550, *Fax:* (256) 764-7750
www.thevalleyscw.tv
License: Florence, Lauderdale County, AL held by Huntsville TV L.L.C
Nat'l Network: CW *Nat'l Reps:* Blair Television
Louann Thomson, General Manager
Shanda Love, General Sales Mgr
Tim Rovere, Chief Engineer

***WHIQ** *Digital Channel:* 24 *Virtual Channel:* 25; 396 kw; 1110 ft.; N34 44 13 W86 31 45
2112-11th Ave, So., #400, Birmingham, AL 35256 US
(205) 328-8756, *Fax:* (205) 251-2192
www.aptv.org
License: Huntsville, Madison County, AL held by Alabama ETV Commission
Washington Law Firm: Dow, Lohnes & Albertson, PLLC
Nat'l Network: PBS *Regional Network:* Alabama Public Television
Allan Pizzato, CEO
Gary Stokes, General Sales Mgr
Pauline Howland, CFO
Charles Grantham, COO

WHNT-TV *Digital Channel:* 19 *Virtual Channel:* 19; 250 kw; 1742 ft.; N34 44 19 W86 31 56
229 West 43rd Street, New York, NY 10036 US
(256) 533-1919, *Fax:* (256) 533-4503,(256) 536-9468 (news)
www.whnt.com
feedback@whnt19.com
License: Huntsville, Madison County, AL held by Local TV Alabama License LLC.
Group Owner: Local TV LLC; (acq 5-7-2007; grpsl); *Washington Law Firm:* Koteen & Naftalin
Nat'l Network: CBS
Stan Pylant, General Manager
Heather Carlton, General Sales Mgr
Jean Nance, Programming Director
Lori Miller, Promotions Manager
Denise Vickers, News Director
Richard Hunter, Engineering Dir
Nathan McGee, Regional SalesManager

WZDX *Digital Channel:* 41 *Virtual Channel:* 54; 2,400 kw vis, 240 kw aur; ant 1,699t/906g; N34 44 12 W86 31 59
Mailing Address: Box 3889, Huntsville, AL 33304
Second Address: 1309 N. Memorial Pkwy, Huntsville, AL 35801
(256) 533-5454, *Fax:* (256) 533-5315
www.fox54.com
License: Huntsville, Madison County, AL held by Huntsville Television Acquisition Licensing LLC.
Group Owner: Grant Communications Inc.; (acq 4-90; $6.1 million)
Nat'l Network: Fox; MyNetworkTV *Nat'l Reps:* TeleRep
Charlene Brueggeman, Operations Dir
Bill Ambrose, General Sales Mgr
Elizabeth Zaideman, Programming Director
Bob Boyer, Promotions Manager
Wes Hall, Chief Engineer
Everett Lawrence, National Sales Manager
Emily Parsons, TrafficManager

Mobile, AL-Pensacola (Ft. Walton Beach), FL (DMA 60)

WALA-TV *Digital Channel:* 9 *Virtual Channel:* 10; 29 kw; 1250 ft.; N30 41 17 W87 47 54
950 North Meridian Street, Suite 1200, Indianapolis, IN 46204 US
(251) 434-1010, *Fax:* (251) 434-1073 / 1061
www.fox10tv.com
info@fox10tv.com
License: Mobile, Mobile County, AL held by LIN of Alabama LLC.
Group Owner: LIN Media; (acq 11-30-2005; grpsl).; *Washington Law Firm:* Fisher, Wayland, Cooper, Leader & Zaragoza
Nat'l Network: FOX *Nat'l Reps:* TeleRep
Size of News Staff: 45; *Hours of Local News Weekly:* 23 hrs
Michael Strickler, General Sales Mgr
Kyle Claude, Promotions Manager
Bob Cashen, News Director
Roland Fields, Chief Engineer
Carrie Laughlin, National Sales Manager

***WEIQ** *Digital Channel:* 41 *Virtual Channel:* 42; 464 kw; 590 ft.; N30 39 33 W87 53 33
2112 11th Ave, S., #400, Birmingham, AL 35256 US
(205) 328-8756, *Fax:* (205) 251-2192
www.aptv.org
License: Mobile, Mobile County, AL held by Alabama ETV Commission
Washington Law Firm: Dow, Lohnes & Albertson, PLLC
Nat'l Network: PBS *Regional Network:* Alabama Public Television
Allan Pizzato, CEO
Gary Stokes, General Sales Mgr
Pauline Howland, CFO
Charles Grantham, COO

WFNA *Digital Channel:* 25; 1510 kw vis; ant 1,010t; N30 36 37 W87 36 26; *Population Served:* 1,200,000
1501 Satchel Paige Dr., Mobile, AL 20006
(251) 434-1010, *Fax:* (251) 434-1073 / 1061
License: Gulf Shores, Baldwin County, AL held by LIN of Alabama LLC.
Group Owner: LIN Media; (acq 7-7-2006; grpsl).
Nat'l Network: CW *Nat'l Reps:* TeleRep
Michael Strickler, General Sales Mgr
Kyle Claude, Promotions Manager
Roland Fields, Chief Engineer
Carrie Laughlin, National Sales Manager

WKRG-TV *Digital Channel:* 27 *Virtual Channel:* 5; 1000 kw; 1880 ft.; N30 41 20 W87 49 49
250 International Drive, Spartanburg, SC 29301 US
(251) 479-5555, *Fax:* (251) 473-8130
www.wkrg.com
License: Mobile, Mobile County, AL held by Media General Communications Holdings, LLC
Group Owner: Media General Broadcast Group; (acq 3-27-2000; grpsl).; *Washington Law Firm:* Wiley, Rein & Fielding
Nat'l Network: CBS
Joe Goleniowski, Operations Dir
Mark Bunting, General Sales Mgr
Beverly Hartman, Programming Director
David Mooney, News Director
Keith Brazel, Chief Engineer

WMPV-TV *Digital Channel:* 20 *Virtual Channel:* 21; 700 kw; 1736 ft.; N30 36 40 W87 36 26
758 St. Michaels Street, Mobile, AL 36602 US
(251) 661-2101, *Fax:* (251) 661-7121
www.tbn.org
wmpv@tbn.org
License: Mobile, Mobile County, AL held by Trinity Broadcasting Network
Group Owner: Trinity Broadcasting Network; (acq 5-8-2000; grpsl).; *Washington Law Firm:* Fisher, Wayland, Cooper, Leader & Zaragoza
Nat'l Network: TRINITY BROADCA
Linda Dixon, General Manager
LaTrynnda Hollis, Programming Director
Alvin Goins, Chief Engineer
Joseph Mass, Traffic Manager

WPMI-TV *Digital Channel:* 15 *Virtual Channel:* 15; 1000 kw; 1847 ft.; N30 36 40 W87 36 26
200 Concord Plaza, Suite 600, San Antonio, TX 78216 US

(251) 602-1500, *Fax:* (251) 602-1547
www.local15tv.com
local15@local15tv.com
License: Mobile, Mobile County, AL held by Newport Television License LLC.
Group Owner: Newport Television LLC; (acq 3-14-2008; grpsl);
Washington Law Firm: Covington & Burling
Nat'l Network: NBC *Nat'l Reps:* Millennium Sales & Marketing
Size of News Staff: 50; *Hours of Local News Weekly:* news progmg 5 hrs wkly
Jared Quijas, Operations Dir
Shea Grandquest, General Manager
Ric Phillips, General Sales Mgr
Chuck Reeves, Programming Director
Wes Finley, News Director
Tim Reid, Chief Engineer
Chris Delaporte, General Sales Manager
CareyGolden, Local Sales Manager

Montgomery-Selma, AL (DMA 118)

***WAIQ** *Digital Channel:* 27 *Virtual Channel:* 26; 600 kw; 586 ft.; N32 22 55 W86 17 33
2112 11th Ave, S., #400, Birmingham, AL 35256 US
(205) 328-8756, *Fax:* (205) 251-2192
www.aptv.org
License: Montgomery, Montgomery County, AL held by Alabama ETV Commission
Washington Law Firm: Dow, Lohnes & Albertson, PLLC
Nat'l Network: PBS *Regional Network:* Alabama Public Television
Allan Pizzato, CEO
Gary Stokes, General Sales Mgr
Pauline Howland, CFO
Charles Grantham, COO

WAKA *Digital Channel:* 42 *Virtual Channel:* 8; 1000 kw; 1627 ft.; N32 8 58 W86 46 51
3020 Eastern Boulevard, Montgomery, AL 36123 US 36123
(334) 271-8888, *Fax:* (334) 272-6444
www.waka.com
License: Selma, Dallas County, AL held by Alabama Broadcasting Partners.
Group Owner: Bahakel Communications; (acq 8-85)
Nat'l Network: CBS *Wire Services:* AP
Size of News Staff: 22; *Hours of Local News Weekly:* news progmg 9 hrs wkly
Jim Caruthers, General Manager
Steffanie Patterson, General Sales Mgr
Mark Smith, Programming Director
Rob Martin, News Director
Thomas Mayberry, Chief Engineer
Richard Baker, Traffic Manager

WBIH *Digital Channel:* 29 *Virtual Channel:* 29; 1000 kw; 1339 ft.; N32 32 26 W86 50 33
188 South Bellevue, Suite 222, Memphis, TN 38104 US
(334) 491-2900, *Fax:* (334) 491-2929
License: Selma, Dallas County, AL held by Flinn Broadcasting Corp
Nat'l Network: TBN
Dirk Freeman, General Manager

WBMM *Digital Channel:* 22 *Virtual Channel:* 22; 65 kw; 1119 ft.; N32 4 5 W85 56 41
1059 Bolton Road, Columbus, GA 31906 US
(334) 270-3200, *Fax:* (334) 271-6348
www.cwmontgomery.com
License: Tuskegee, Macon County, AL held by SagamoreHill Broadcasting of Alabama LLC.
Group Owner: SagamoreHill Broadcasting LLC; (acq 7-26-2006; $2 million); *Washington Law Firm:* Wiley, Rhein
Nat'l Network: CW *Nat'l Reps:* Blair Television
Hours of Local News Weekly: 3
Jesse Grear, Station Manager
Mitchell Maund, General Sales Mgr
Austin Saunders, Local Sales Manager

WCOV-TV *Digital Channel:* 20 *Virtual Channel:* 20; 460 kw; 1699 ft.; N31 58 28 W86 9 44
Mailing Address: One Wcov Avenue, Montgomery, AL 36111 US
Second Address: c/o WCOV-TV, One WCOV Ave., Montgomery, AL 36111
(334) 288-7020, *Fax:* (334) 288-5414
www.wcov.com
mail@wcov.com
License: Montgomery, Montgomery County, AL held by Woods Communications Corp.
Group Owner: Woods Communications Corp.; (acq 12-1-85; $4 million;; *Washington Law Firm:* Kenkel, Barnard & Edmundson
Nat'l Network: FOX *Nat'l Reps:* Millennium Sales & Marketing
David Woods, General Manager

***WDIQ** *Digital Channel:* 10 *Virtual Channel:* 2; 30 kw; 738 ft.; N31 33 16 W86 23 32
2112 11th Ave, S., #400, Birmingham, AL 35256 US
(205) 328-8756, *Fax:* (205) 251-2192
www.aptv.org
License: Dozier, Crenshaw County, AL held by Alabama ETV Commission
Washington Law Firm: Dow, Lohnes & Albertson, PLLC
Nat'l Network: PBS *Regional Network:* Alabama Public Television
Allan Pizzato, CEO
Gary Stokes, General Sales Mgr
Pauline Howland, CFO
Charles Grantham, COO

***WIIQ** *Digital Channel:* 19 *Virtual Channel:* 41; 1000 kw; 1067 ft.; N32 21 45 W87 52 30.5
2112 11th Ave. So.,#400, Birmingham, AL 35256 US
(205) 328-8756, *Fax:* (205) 251-2192
www.aptv.org
License: Demopolis, Marengo County, AL held by Alabama ETV Commission
Washington Law Firm: Dow, Lohnes & Albertson, PLLC
Nat'l Network: PBS
Allan Pizzato, CEO
Gary Stokes, General Sales Mgr
Pauline Howland, CFO
Charles Grantham, COO

WMCF-TV *Digital Channel:* 46 *Virtual Channel:* 45; 851 kw; 427 ft.; N32 24 13 W86 11 49
250 West Arrow Highway, San Dimas, CA 91773 US
(334) 272-0045, *Fax:* (334) 277-6635
www.tbn.org
License: Montgomery, Montgomery County, AL held by Christian Center of Santa Ana, Inc.
Group Owner: Trinity Broadcasting Network; (acq 5-8-2000; grpsl).; *Washington Law Firm:* Baraff, Keorner, Olender & Hochberg
Nat'l Network: TRINITY BROADCA
P. Crouch, President
Aaron Motley, General Manager
Larry Dean, Chief Engineer
Rick Hall, Public Affairs Director

WNCF *Digital Channel:* 32 *Virtual Channel:* 32; 35 kw; 1788 ft.; N32 8 30 W86 44 42
6120 Wettropicana Avenue, A-16, Suite 329, Las Vegas, NV 89103 US
(334) 270-3200, *Fax:* (334) 271-6348
www.wncftv.com
gsingleton@wncftv.com
License: Montgomery, Montgomery County, AL held by Channel 32 Montgomery L.L.C.
Group Owner: SagamoreHill Broadcasting LLC; (acq 1999; $8 million); *Washington Law Firm:* Wiley, Rein & Fielding
Nat'l Network: ABC *Nat'l Reps:* Blair Television
Size of News Staff: 2; *Hours of Local News Weekly:* news progmg one hr wkly
Jesse Grear, General Manager
Mitchell Maund, General Sales Mgr
Lois Crenshaw, Programming Director
Clie Waller, Promotions Manager
Ed Cole, Chief Engineer
Linda Babers, Traffic Manager

WRJM *Digital Channel:* 48; 2,820 kw vis; ant 1066t/913g; N32 03 37 W85 57 02; *Population Served:* 611,750
Mailing Address: Josie Park Broadcasting Inc., 285 E. Broad St., Ozark, AL 36360
Second Address: 315 S. Three Notch St., Troy, AL 36081
(334) 670-6766, *Fax:* (334) 670-6717
www.wrjm.net
info@wrjm.com
License: Troy, Pike County, AL held by Walter P. Lunsford, Receiver for Josie Park Broadcasting Inc.
Washington Law Firm: Borsari and Assoc, PLC
Nat'l Network: MyNetworkTV
Jack Misell, CEO
Walter Lunsford, Operations Dir
Nicky Vull, Station Manager
Buddy Johnson, General Sales Mgr
Don Hess, Programming Director
Vincent Hodges, Promotions Manager
Boyd Mizell, Operations Manager
Jenny Dykes,Public Affairs Director
Sonny Strassburger, Regional Sales Manager

WSFA *Digital Channel:* 12 *Virtual Channel:* 12; 31.6 kw; 1962 ft.; N31 58 28 W86 9 44
12 E. Delano Ave., Montgomery, AL 36105 US
(334) 288-1212, *Fax:* (334) 613-8303
www.wsfa.com
License: Montgomery, Montgomery County, AL held by WSFA License Subsidiary LLC.
Group Owner: Raycom Media Inc.; (acq 1-31-2006; grpsl);
Washington Law Firm: Dow, Lohnes & Albertson
Nat'l Network: NBC *Nat'l Reps:* Harrington, Righter & Parsons
Mark Wilder, Operations Dir
Ken Selvaggi, General Manager
Marnie Jackson, General Sales Mgr
Alicia Briscoe, Promotions Manager
Scott Duff, News Director
Morris Pollock, Chief Engineer
Collin Gaston, Regional Sales Manager

Alaska

Anchorage, AK (DMA 150)

***KAKM** *Digital Channel:* 8 *Virtual Channel:* 7; 50 kw; 787 ft.; N61 25 22 W149 52 20
3877 University Drive, Anchorage, AK 99508 US
(907) 550-8400, *Fax:* (907)550-8401
www.kakm.org
questions@kakm.org
License: Anchorage, Anchorage County, AK held by Alaska Public Telecommunications Inc
Washington Law Firm: Dow, Lohnes & Albertson
Nat'l Network: PBS
Steve Lindbeck, General Manager
Bede Trantina, Programming Director
Constance Huff, Operations Manager

KDMD *Digital Channel:* 33 *Virtual Channel:* 33; 17.2 kw; 985 ft.; N61 20 10.8 W149 30 48.2
P. O. Box 255, Evergreen, CO 80439 US
(907) 562-5363, *Fax:* (907) 562-5346
www.kdmd.tv
stationmail@kdmd.tv
License: Anchorage, Anchorage County, AK held by Ketchikan TV LLC
Nat'l Network: IND
David Drucker, CEO
Bill Vanderpoel, President
Andy Tierney, General Manager
Don Nelson, Chief Engineer

KTBY *Digital Channel:* 20 *Virtual Channel:* 4; 234.4 kw; 148 ft.; N61 13 11 W149 53 24
The Pinnacle, Suite 875, 3455 Peachtree Rd., N.E., Atlanta, GA 30326 US
(907) 274-0404, *Fax:* (907) 264-5180
License: Anchorage, Anchorage County, AK held by Coastal Television Broadcasting Company LLC
Nat'l Network: FOX
Hours of Local News Weekly: 4.5
Kirsten Bolton, General Manager
Kyle Keller, Programming Director

KTUU-TV *Digital Channel:* 10 *Virtual Channel:* 2; 50 kw; 787 ft.; N61 25 22 W149 52 20
1802 - 136th Place, N.E., Bellevue, WA 98005 US
(907) 762-9202, *Fax:* (907) 561-0882
www.ktuu.com
ktuu@ktuu.com
License: Anchorage, Anchorage County, AK held by Northern Lights Media Inc
Group Owner: Schurz Communications Inc.; 7/1/2008
Nat'l Network: NBC *Nat'l Reps:* Blair Television *Wire Services:* AP
Size of News Staff: 40; *Hours of Local News Weekly:* news progmg 19.5 hrs wkly
Susan Lucas, President
Margo Russ, Operations Dir
Andy MacLeod, General Sales Mgr
Steve MacDonald, News Director
Leland Verschueren, Chief Engineer
Elisa Fleener, Advertising Director
Nancy Johnson, National Sales Manager
TrentMcNelly, Operations Manager

KTVA *Digital Channel:* 28 *Virtual Channel:* 11; 28.9 kw; 199 ft.; N61 11 33 W149 54 1.1
1007 West 32nd Avenue, Anchorage, AK 99503 US
(907) 273-3192, *Fax:* (907) 273-3189
www.ktva.com
11news@ktva.com
License: Anchorage, Anchorage County, AK held by Alaska Broadcasting Company Inc

(acq 5-25-2000; grpsl).; *Washington Law Firm:* Wilkinson, Barker, Knauer & Quinn
Nat'l Network: CBS *Regional Reps:* Art Moore
Size of News Staff: 16; *Hours of Local News Weekly:* news progmg 7 hrs wkly
Bush Houston, Operations Dir
Jerry Bever, General Manager
Laurie Bruce, General Sales Mgr
Cyd Terhune, Programming Director
Staci Chil, News Director
Tom Lambert, Chief Engineer
Monica Bouvier, Traffic Manager

KUBD *Digital Channel:* 13 *Virtual Channel:* 4; 0.413 kw; -233 ft.; N55 20 59 W131 40 12
770 Se Summerfield Pl, Corvallis, AK 97333 US
(907) 225-4613, *Fax:* (907) 247-5365
License: Ketchikan, Ketchikan Gateway County, AK held by Ketchikan TV LLC
Nat'l Network: CBS
Jack Gibson, General Manager
Rudy Casillas, Programming Director
Michael Serres, Promotions Manager
Peter Michaels, News Director
David Ross, Chief Engineer

KYES-TV *Digital Channel:* 6; 5.9 kw vis, 50 kw aur; ant 820t/160g; N61 20 10 W149 30 49; *Population Served:* 254,479
3700 Woodland Dr., Suite 800, Anchorage, AK 99517
(907) 248-5937, *Fax:* (907) 339-3889
www.yes.com
License: Anchorage, Anchorage County, AK held by Fireweed Communications LLC
(acq 12-11-91; $100 & assumption of debt;; *Washington Law Firm:* Benjamin Perez
Nat'l Network: MyNetworkTV
Hours of Local News Weekly: News progmg one hr wkly
Jeremy Lansman, President
Roy Nederbrock, Operations Dir
Carol Schatz, General Manager
Lori Erickson, Station Manager
Maryann Spinella, Promotions Manager
Amy Simonson, Traffic Manager

KYUR *Digital Channel:* 12 *Virtual Channel:* 13; 316 kw vis, 31.6 kw aur; ant 781t; N61 25 22 W149 52 20; *Population Served:* 250,000
2700 E. Tudor Rd., Anchorage, AK 33703
(907) 561-1313, *Fax:* (907) 561-1377
www.aksuperstation.com
info@aksuperstation.com
License: Anchorage, Anchorage County, AK held by Smith Media License Holdings LLC.
Group Owner: Smith Media License Holdings LLC; (acq 11-8-2004; grpsl).
Nat'l Network: ABC; CW *Nat'l Reps:* Continental Television Sales
Sean Bradley, Operations Dir
Terri Bradley, Programming Director
Nate Kimmell, Promotions Manager
Ty Hardt, News Director
George Heacock, Chief Engineer
Stephanie Lewis, Marketing Coordinator

Fairbanks, AK (DMA 202)

KATN *Digital Channel:* 18 *Virtual Channel:* 2; 28.2 kw vis, 5.5 kw aur; ant 200t/151g; N64 50 42 W147 42 52; *Rebroadcasting:* Rebroadcasts KIMO-TV Anchorage 99%.; *Population Served:* 84,800
516 2nd Ave., Suite 400, Fairbanks, AK 33703
(907) 452-2125, *Fax:* (907) 456-8225
www.aksuperstation.com
info@aksuperstation.com
License: Fairbanks, Fairbanks North Star County, AK held by Smith Media License Holdings LLC.
Group Owner: Smith Media License Holdings LLC; (acq 11-8-2004; grpsl).
Nat'l Network: ABC
Hours of Local News Weekly: News progmg 6p - 11p wkly
Sean Bradley, Operations Dir
Jeff Glaser, General Sales Mgr
Terri Bradley, Programming Director
Rita Corwin, Promotions Manager
Ty Hardt, News Director
George Heacock, Engineering Dir
George Heacock, Chief Engineer
GerilynneBuonocore, Public Affairs Director

KFXF *Digital Channel:* 7 *Virtual Channel:* 7; 6.1 kw; 879 ft.; N64 55 20 W147 42 55
3650 Bradock Street, Suite 2, Fairbanks, AK 99701 US
(907) 452-3697, *Fax:* (907) 456-3428
www.TVTV.com
License: Fairbanks, Fairbanks North Star County, AK held by Tanana Valley Television Co
Group Owner: Tanana Valley Television Co.; *Washington Law Firm:* Baker & Hostetler
Nat'l Network: FOX
Size of News Staff: 4; *Hours of Local News Weekly:* news progmg 10 hr wkly
John Hoff, General Manager
Christine Fry, Station Manager
Darryl Lewis, News Director
Dave Sala, Chief Engineer
Trent Heineken, Traffic Manager

KJNP-TV *Digital Channel:* 20; 18.66 kw vis, 2.8 kw aur; 1,619t/191g; N64 52 44 W148 03 10; *Population Served:* 8,100
Box 56359, 2501 Mission Rd., North Pole, AK 99705
(907) 488-2216, *Fax:* (907) 488-5246
www.mosquitonet.com/~kjnp
kjnp@mosquitonet.com
License: North Pole, Fairbanks North Star County, AK held by Evangelistic Alaska Missionary Fellowship
Washington Law Firm: Fletcher, Heald & Hildreth
Yvonne Carriker, President
Richard Olson, Operations Dir
Julie Beaver, Station Manager
Dave Castor, Chief Engineer

KTVF *Digital Channel:* 26 *Virtual Channel:* 11; 50 kw vis, 5 kw aur; 50t/168g; N64 50 36 W147 42 48; *Population Served:* 85,000
3528 International Way, Fairbanks, AK 20036
(907) 458-1800, *Fax:* (907) 458-1820
www.webcenter11.com
License: Fairbanks, Fairbanks North Star County, AK held by Cheryl Broadcasting LLC.
Group Owner: Newport Television LLC; (acq 3-14-2008; grpsl);
Washington Law Firm: Covington & Burling
Nat'l Network: NBC *Nat'l Reps:* Blair Television
Size of News Staff: 6; *Hours of Local News Weekly:* news progmg 9 hrs wkly
David Castor, Operations Dir
DeeDee Caciari, General Manager
Deedee Caciari, General Sales Mgr
Celia Vissers, Programming Director
Monte Bowen, News Director
David Castor, Engineering Dir
Trent Heineken, Traffic Manager

***KUAC-TV** *Digital Channel:* 9 *Virtual Channel:* 9; 30 kw; 554 ft.; N64 54 42 W147 46 38
Fine Arts Complex, Fairbanks, AK 99775 US
(907) 474-7491, *Fax:* (907) 474-5064
www.kuac.org
comments@kuac.org
License: Fairbanks, Fairbanks North Star County, AK held by University of Alaska
Nat'l Network: PBS
Size of News Staff: 1; *Hours of Local News Weekly:* 2
Patty Dyer-Smith, CFO
Jerry Evans, Operations Dir
John C 'Jake' Poole, General Manager
Gretchen Gordon, General Sales Mgr
Claudia Clark, Programming Director
Keith Martin, Engineering Dir
Wanda Peros, Sales

Juneau, AK (DMA 207)

KJUD *Digital Channel:* 11 *Virtual Channel:* 8; 0.14 kw; -951 ft.; N58 18 5 W134 26 26
3839 Fourth St. North, Suite 420, St. Petersburg, FL 33703 US
(907) 561-1313 / (907) 586-3145, *Fax:* (907) 561-1377 / (907) 463-3041
www.aksuperstation.com
info@aksuperstation.com
License: Juneau, Juneau County, AK held by Smith Media License Holdings LLC.
Group Owner: Smith Media License Holdings LLC; (acq 11-8-2004; grpsl).; *Washington Law Firm:* Kaye, Scholer, Fierman, Hays & Handler
Nat'l Network: ABC; CW
Size of News Staff: 9; *Hours of Local News Weekly:* news progmg 5 hrs wkly
John Bradley, General Manager
Jeff Glaser, General Sales Mgr
Terri Bradley, Programming Director
Ty Hardt, News Director
George Heacock, Chief Engineer
Gerilynne Buonocore, Traffic Manager

KTNL-TV *Digital Channel:* 7 *Virtual Channel:* 13; 0.35 kw; -709 ft.; N57 3 1 W135 20 4
803 Sirstad Street, Sitka, AK 99835 US
(907) 747-5749, *Fax:* (907) 747-8440
www.ktnl.tv
stationmail@ktnl.tv
License: Sitka, Sitka County, AK held by Ketchikan TV LLC (acq 6-19-2002).; *Washington Law Firm:* Wilkinson, Barker, Knauer L.L.P.
Nat'l Network: CBS
David Drucker, CEO
Bill Vanderpoel, Operations Dir
Charlene Nelson, General Manager
Amanda McMellon, General Sales Mgr
Garrett Leighton, Operations Manager

***KTOO-TV** *Digital Channel:* 10 *Virtual Channel:* 3; 1 kw; -1191 ft.; N58 17 56 W134 24 7; *Rebroadcasting:* Rebroadcasts KUAC-TV Fairbanks 95%.
360 Egan Drive, Juneau, AK 99801 US
(907) 586-1670, *Fax:* (907) 586-3612
www.ktoo.org
ktoo@ktoo.org
License: Juneau, Juneau County, AK held by Capital Community Broadcasting Inc
Group Owner: Capital Community Broadcasting Inc.; *Washington Law Firm:* Schwartz, Woods & Miller
Nat'l Network: PBS
Size of News Staff: 1; *Hours of Local News Weekly:* news progmg one hr wkly
Bill Legere, President
Jim Mahan, Station Manager
Cheryl Levitt, General Sales Mgr
William Judy, Engineering Dir

American Samoa

Pago Pago

***KVZK-2** ; 60 kw vis, 6.0 kw aur; 2,000t/400g; N14 16 14 W170 41 12
Box 2567, Pago Pago, AS 96799
(684) 633-4191, *Fax:* (684) 633-1044
www.asg-gov.com/agencies/opi.asg.htm
paolosivia@ymail.com
License: Pago Pago, American Samoa County, AS held by The Government of American Samoa
Nat'l Network: PBS
Foreign Language Programming
Paolo Sivia, General Manager
Jeff Alwin, Chief Engineer

***KVZK-4** ; 72 kw vis, 7.2 kw aur
Box 2567, Pago Pago, AS 96799
(684) 633-4191, *Fax:* (684) 633-1044
www.asg-gov.com/agencies/opi.asg.htm
siviapaolo@yahoo.com
License: Pago Pago, American Samoa County, AS held by The Government of American Samoa
Nat'l Network: ABC; CBS
Sivia Paolo, General Manager

***KVZK-5** *Digital Channel:* 5; 72 kw vis, 7.2 kw aur; 2,000t/400g
Box 2567, Pago Pago, AS 96799
(684) 633-4191, *Fax:* (684) 633-1044
www.asg-gov.com/agencies/opi.asg.htm
paolosivia@ymail.com
License: Pago Pago, American Samoa County, AS held by The Government of American Samoa
Nat'l Network: ABC; CBS
Paolo Sivia, General Manager
Jeff Alwin, Chief Engineer

Arizona

Phoenix (Prescott), AZ (DMA 12)

***KAET** *Digital Channel:* 8 *Virtual Channel:* 8; 40 kw; 1801 ft.; N33 20 0 W112 3 49
Mailing Address: Arizona State University, P.O. Box 871405, Tempe, AZ 85281 US

Second Address: Stauffer Hall B-Wing, Arizona State Univ., Tempe, AZ 85287
(480) 965-8888, *Fax:* (480) 965-1000
www.kaet.asu.edu
eight@asu.edu
License: Phoenix, Maricopa County, AZ held by Arizona Board of Regents
Washington Law Firm: Covington & Burling
Nat'l Network: PBS
Foreign Language Programming; Size of News Staff: 7; *Hours of Local News Weekly:* news progmg 3 hrs wkly
John Martinez, Operations Dir
Kelly McCullough, General Manager
Nancy Southgate, Associate General Manager
Michael Philipsen, News Director
Gilbert Akroyd, Engineering Dir
John Menzies, Promotions Manager

KASW *Digital Channel:* 49 *Virtual Channel:* 61; 531 kw; 1631 ft.; N33 20 2 W112 3 44
5555 North Seventh Ave., Suite 61, Phoenix, AZ 85013 US
(602) 207-3333, *Fax:* (602) 207-3477
www.azfamily.com
feedback@azfamily.com
License: Phoenix, Maricopa County, AZ held by KASW-TV Inc.
Group Owner: Belo Corp; (acq 1-24-2000).
Nat'l Network: CW
Dean Apostalides, General Manager
Skip Cass, Station Manager
Rick Soltesz, General Sales Mgr
Mark Demopoulos, Programming Director
Mike Stone, Chief Engineer
Brock Kruzie, National Sales Manager
Scott Rein, Regional SalesManager
Shana Crane, Traffic Manager

KAZT-TV *Digital Channel:* 7 *Virtual Channel:* 7; 3.2 kw; 2598 ft.; N34 41 15 W112 7 1
3211 Tower Road, Prescott, AZ 86301 US
(602) 977-7700, *Fax:* (602) 224-2214
www.aztv.com
jburnton@aztv.com
License: Prescott, Yavapai County, AZ held by KAZT L.L.C (acq 4-1-2002; $7.336 million); *Washington Law Firm:* Shaw Pittman
Nat'l Network: IND *Nat'l Reps:* Petry Television Inc. *Wire Services:* AP
Size of News Staff: 6; *Hours of Local News Weekly:* 11
John Ryan, CFO
Jeff Burnton, General Manager
Richard Howe, Station Manager
Eric Cohen, Programming Director
Cheryl Strong, Traffic Manager

KCFG *Digital Channel:* 32 *Virtual Channel:* 9; 1000 kw; 1116 ft.; N34 58 6 W111 30 29
3654 West Jarvis Avenue, Skokie, IL 60076 US
(928) 526-5234, *Fax:* (928) 526-1172
www.kcfg.net
License: Flagstaff, Coconino County, AZ held by KM Television of Flagstaff L.L.C
Nat'l Network: AMER1
John Banker, General Manager

***KDTP** *Digital Channel:* 11 *Virtual Channel:* 11; 3.2 kw; 177 ft.; N34 55 5 W110 8 25
C/O Marcus Lamb, PO Box 6102066, Dallas, TX 75261 US
(602) 207-3939
www.daystar.com
License: Holbrook, Navajo County, AZ held by Community Television Educators Inc
Nat'l Network: IND
Elevra Weigand, Station Manager

KFPH-DT *Digital Channel:* 27; 316 kw vis; ant 1,555t/239g; N34 58 05 W111 30 29
2158 North 4th Street, Flagstaff, AZ 86004
(928) 527-1300, *Fax:* (928) 527-1394
www.univision.com
License: Flagstaff, Coconino County, AZ held by TeleFutura Partnership of Flagstaff.
Group Owner: Univision Communications Inc.; (acq 10-2-2001; $19.113 million plus assumption of liabilities with KFTU-TV Douglas).
Nat'l Network: TeleFutura (Spanish)
Foreign Language Programming
Jose Luis Padilla, General Manager
Virginia Luna, Assistant

KMOH-TV *Digital Channel:* 19 *Virtual Channel:* 6; 100 kw vis, 10 kw aur; ant 1,920t; N35 01 57 W114 21 56; *Population Served:* 138,000
2332 Kingman Avenue, Kingman, AZ 22234
928-753-2724, *Fax:* 305-863-5709
www.tr3sphx.com
License: Kingman, Mohave County, AZ held by Hero Licenseco, LLC
Robert Behar, President
Jerry Albers, Operations Dir
Mara Rankin, General Manager
Loren Blumberg, General Sales Mgr
Charlie Trice, Engineering Dir
Jason Gassner, Account Executive

KNAZ-TV *Digital Channel:* 22 *Virtual Channel:* 2; 283 kw; 1526 ft.; N34 58 6 W111 30 28
Mailing Address: 1100 Wilson Boulevard, Arlington, VA 22234 US
Second Address: Box 3360, Flagstaff, AZ 86004
(928) 526-2232, *Fax:* (928) 526-8110
2news@knaztv2.com
License: Flagstaff, Coconino County, AZ held by Multimedia Holdings Corp.
Group Owner: Gannett Broadcasting; (acq 1997; $6.25 million with KMOH-TV Kingman).; *Washington Law Firm:* Dow, Lohnes & Albertson
Nat'l Network: NBC
Scott Jones, Operations Dir
Jerome Parra, General Manager
Stan Pierce, General Sales Mgr
Marge Divine, Programming Director
Mark Casey, News Director
Jon Koger, Chief Engineer

KNXV-TV *Digital Channel:* 15 *Virtual Channel:* 15; 458 kw; 1709 ft.; N33 20 0 W112 3 46
312 Walnut Street, Cincinnati, OH 45202 US
(602) 273-1500, *Fax:* (602) 685-3000
www.abc15.com
news15@abc15.com
License: Phoenix, Maricopa County, AZ held by Scripps Howard Broadcasting Co.
Group Owner: The E. W. Scripps Co.; (acq 1-9-85; $26.6 million); *Washington Law Firm:* Baker & Hostetler
Nat'l Network: ABC *Nat'l Reps:* Eagle Television Sales
Flor Polanco, Operations Dir
Janice Todd, General Manager
Adam Weyne, General Sales Mgr
Trish Greening, Programming Director
Jim Hart, Promotions Manager
Joe Hengemuehler, News Director
Ryan Steward, Chief Engineer
Craig Fouhy,Sports Commentator
Janet Taylor, Traffic Manager
Bill Bellis, Weather Director

KPAZ-TV *Digital Channel:* 20 *Virtual Channel:* 21; 500 kw; 1604 ft.; N33 20 2.5 W112 3 42
3551 E. McDowell Road, Phoenix, AZ 85008 US
(602) 273-1477, *Fax:* (602) 267-9427
License: Phoenix, Maricopa County, AZ held by Trinity Broadcasting of Arizona Inc.
Group Owner: Trinity Broadcasting Network; (acq 1977).; *Washington Law Firm:* Joseph E. Dunne III
Nat'l Network: TRINITY BROADCA
Oralena Valero, Station Manager
Gary Nichols, Chief Engineer

KPHO-TV *Digital Channel:* 17 *Virtual Channel:* 5; 1000 kw; 1663 ft.; N33 20 2 W112 3 40
C/O Haley, Bader & Potts, 4350 North Fairfax Drive, Arlington, VA 22203 US
(602) 264-1000, *Fax:* (602) 650-5510,(602) 650-5545
www.kpho.com
cbs5news@kpho.com
License: Phoenix, Maricopa County, AZ held by Meredith Corp.
Group Owner: Meredith Broadcasting Group, Meredith Corp.; (acq 6-25-52; grpsl;; *Washington Law Firm:* Dow Lohnes
Nat'l Network: CBS *Nat'l Reps:* Harrington, Righter & Parsons
Wire Services: Weather Wire
Size of News Staff: 60; *Hours of Local News Weekly:* news progmg 30.5 hrs wkly
Mitch Nye, General Sales Mgr
Seth Parker, Programming Director
Tom Bell, News Director

KPNX *Digital Channel:* 12 *Virtual Channel:* 12; 39 kw; 1821 ft.; N33 20 0 W112 3 48
Mailing Address: 1101 N. Central Avenue, Phoenix, AZ 85004 US
Second Address: 1101 N. Central Ave., Phoenix, AZ 85001
(602) 257-1212, *Fax:* (602) 261-6135,(602) 257-6619 (news)
webmaster@12news.com
License: Mesa, Maricopa County, AZ held by Multimedia Holdings Corp.
Group Owner: Gannett Broadcasting; (acq 6-7-79; grpsl;
Nat'l Network: NBC
Size of News Staff: 70
John Misner, General Manager
Dan Mayasich, General Sales Mgr

KPPX-TV ; 4,875 kw vis, 487 kw aur; 1,749t/354g; N33 20 03 W112 03 38
1101 N. Central Ave., Phoenix, AZ 85004
(602) 808-0729, *Fax:* (602) 808-8864
www.ionline.tv
License: Tolleson, Maricopa County, AZ held by America 51 L.P.
Group Owner: ION Media Networks Inc.; (acq 1-2-01; $6.6 million for 51%); *Washington Law Firm:* Skadden, Arps, Slate, Meagher & Flom
Nat'l Network: ION Television
Kathy Lawrence, General Manager
Maureen Rowe, Programming Director

KTVK *Digital Channel:* 24 *Virtual Channel:* 3; 1000 kw; 1644 ft.; N33 20 1 W112 3 45
5555 N. 7th Avenue, Phoenix, AZ 85013 US
(602) 207-3333
www.azfamily.com
feedback@azfamily.com
License: Phoenix, Maricopa County, AZ held by KTVK Inc.
Group Owner: Belo Corp; (acq 9-3-99; $315 million cash including 50% of Arizona News Channel).
Nat'l Network: CW *Nat'l Reps:* TeleRep *Wire Services:* AP
Size of News Staff: 100; *Hours of Local News Weekly:* 48 hrs news progmg wkly
Greg Lechowski, CFO
Mark Higgins, President
Lea-Ann Clement, Operations Dir
Jamie Aitken, Station Manager
Marie McGlynn, General Sales Mgr
Mark Demopoulos, Programming Director
Teri Lane, Promotions Manager
Sandy Breland, NewsDirector
Jim Cole, Engineering Dir

KUTP *Digital Channel:* 26 *Virtual Channel:* 45; 1000 kw; 1696 ft.; N33 20 1 W112 3 32
4630 South 33rd Street, Phoenix, AZ 85040 US
(602) 257-1234, *Fax:* (602) 262-5123
www.kutp.com
License: Phoenix, Maricopa County, AZ held by Fox Television Stations Inc.
Group Owner: Fox Television Stations Inc.; (acq 7-31-2001; grpsl).; *Washington Law Firm:* Wilmer, Cutler & Pickering
Nat'l Network: MY NETWORK
Jim Kauffman, Operations Dir
Patrick Nevin, General Manager
Mellynda Hartel, General Sales Mgr
David Saline, Programming Director
Doug Bannard, News Director
Jamie Fischer, Traffic Manager

Tucson (Sierra Vista), AZ (DMA 68)

KFTU-DT ; 100 kw vis; ant 30t/180g; N31 22 08 W109 31 45
1111 G Avenue, Douglas, AZ 85607
(520) 805-1773, *Fax:* (520) 805-1768
www.univisionarizona.univision.com
ktfupublicfile@univision.net
License: Douglas, Cochise County, AZ held by Univision Partnership of Douglas.
Group Owner: Univision Communications Inc.; (acq 10-2-2001; $19.113 million plus assumption of liabilities with KFPH-TV Flagstaff).
Foreign Language Programming
Jose Luis Padilla, General Manager
Virginia Luna, Assistant
Alfonso Romero, General Sales Mgr
Salvador Ocano, Programming Director
Javier Ramis, Promotions Manager
Marco Flores, News Director
Tom Foy, Chief Engineer
NeldaChavarria, Traffic Manager

KGUN-TV *Digital Channel:* 35; 110 kw vis, 21.94 kw aur; ant 3,739t/220g; N32 24 53 W110 42 58; *Population Served:* 1,050,000
7280 East Rosewood Street, Tucson, AZ 85710
(520) 722-5486, *Fax:* (520) 733-7099,(520) 733-7070
www.kgun9.com

License: Tucson, Pima County, AZ held by Journal Broadcast Corp.
Group Owner: Journal Communications Inc.; (acq 12-5-2005; grpsl); *Washington Law Firm:* Reed Smith LLP
Nat'l Network: ABC *Nat'l Reps:* MMT *Wire Services:* NOAA Weather
Size of News Staff: 47; *Hours of Local News Weekly:* news progmg 22 hrs wkly
Kelly Donnell, Operations Dir
Julie Brinks, General Manager
Adam Johnston, General Sales Mgr
Sue Bock, Programming Director
Thor Wasbotten, News Director
Stephen Somerville, Chief Engineer
Kara Quintela, National Sales Manager

KHRR *Digital Channel:* 40 *Virtual Channel:* 40; 396 kw; 2037 ft.; N32 14 55 W111 6 57
4444 Lakeside Drive, Suite 340, Burbank, CA 91505 US
(602) 648-3807, *Fax:* (602) 648-3970
www.telemundo.com
jeff.lovetinsky@nbcuni.com
License: Tucson, Pima County, AZ held by NBC Telemundo License Co.
Group Owner: Telemundo Television Stations; (acq 1-1-2003; $20 million with KDRX-CA Phoenix)
Nat'l Network: TELEMUNDO
Foreign Language Programming; Size of News Staff: 7; *Hours of Local News Weekly:* news progmg 5 hrs wkly
Jeff Lovetinsky, Operations Dir
Araceli De Leon, General Manager
Martha Muniz, Promotions Manager
Sergio Pedroza, News Director
Pablo Sierra, Film Director
Abelardo Oquita, News Commentator

KMSB *Digital Channel:* 25; 316 kw vis, 31.6 kw aur; ant 1,662t/200g; N31 42 18 W110 55 26
1855 N. 6th Ave., Tucson, AZ 85705-5061
(520) 770-1123, *Fax:* (520) 629-7185
www.kmsb.com
License: Tucson, Pima County, AZ held by Belo TV Inc.
Group Owner: Belo Corp; (acq 2-28-97; grpsl).; *Washington Law Firm:* Wiley, Rein & Fielding
Nat'l Network: Fox *Nat'l Reps:* TeleRep
Lou Medran, Operations Dir
Tod Smith, General Manager
John Stringer, General Sales Mgr
Bob Richardson, Programming Director
Brian Baltosewicz, Promotions Manager
Walcott Denison III, Engineering Dir
Jim Watson/Brian Gee,Local/Natl Sales Manager
Lynn Bernadett, Program Director
Bob Lee, Public Service Director
Tricia Terrell/Dale Warshaw, Traffic Assistant

KOLD-TV *Digital Channel:* 32 *Virtual Channel:* 13; 302 kw vis, 3 kw aur; ant 2,040t/187g; N32 14 56 W110 06 58; *Population Served:* 1,100,000
7831 N. Business Park Dr., Tucson, AZ 36104
(520) 744-1313, *Fax:* (520) 744-5233
www.kold.com
License: Tucson, Pima County, AZ held by KOLD License Subsidiary LLC.
Group Owner: Raycom Media Inc.; (acq 9-12-96); *Washington Law Firm:* Covington & Burling
Nat'l Network: CBS *Nat'l Reps:* Harrington, Righter & Parsons
Wire Services: NWS (National Weather Service); AP
Hours of Local News Weekly: News progmg 27 hrs wkly
Debbie Bush, General Manager
David Rash, General Sales Mgr
Alyson Stogol, Programming Director
Craig Fleming, Promotions Manager
Michelle Germano, News Director
Sonny Reschka, Chief Engineer
Bob Gaff, Operations Manager
BobDuffy, Regional Sales Manager

KTTU *Digital Channel:* 19; 2510 kw vis, 251 kw aur; ant 1,970t/200g; N32 14 55 W111 06 57; *Population Served:* 750,000
1855 N. 6th Ave., Tucson, AZ 85705
(520) 624-0180, *Fax:* (520) 629-7185
www.kttu.com
License: Tucson, Pima County, AZ held by KTTU-TV Inc.
Group Owner: Belo Corp; (acq 2-28-2002; $18 million);
Washington Law Firm: Hogan & Hartson
Nat'l Network: MyNetworkTV *Nat'l Reps:* TeleRep
Foreign Language Programming
Lou Medran, Operations Dir
Tod Smith, General Manager
John Stringer, General Sales Mgr
Bob Richardson, Programming Director
Brian Baltosewicz, Promotions Manager
Walcott Denison III, Engineering Dir
Jim Watson/Brian Gee,Local/Natl Sales Manager
Lynn Bernadettq, Program Coordinator
Bob Lee, Public Service Director
Tricia Terrell/Dale Walcott, Traffic Assistant

***KUAS-TV** *Digital Channel:* 28 *Virtual Channel:* 27; 50 kw; 584 ft.; N32 12 53 W111 0 21
University of Arizona, P.O. Box 210067, Tucson, AZ 85721 US
(520) 621-5828, *Fax:* (520) 621-4122 (news)
www.azpm.org
contactarizonapublicmedia@azpm.org
License: Tucson, Pima County, AZ held by Arizona Board of Regents for Benefit of University of Arizona.
Washington Law Firm: Dow, Lohnes & Albertson
Nat'l Network: PBS
Foreign Language Programming
Jack Gibson, General Manager
Susie Hernandez, Programming Director
Peter Michaels, News Director
David Ross, Chief Engineer
Lili Bell, Traffic Manager

***KUAT-TV** *Digital Channel:* 30 *Virtual Channel:* 6; 667.5 kw; 3583 ft.; N32 24 55 W110 42 51
Mailing Address: Univerity of Arizona, P.O. Box 210067, Tucson, AZ 85721 US
Second Address: 1423 E. University Blvd., Tucson, AZ 85721-0067
(520) 621-5828, *Fax:* (520) 621-4122 (news)
www.azpm.org
contactarizonapublicmedia@azpm.org
License: Tucson, Pima County, AZ held by Arizona Board of Regents, University of Arizona
Washington Law Firm: Dow, Lohnes & Albertson
Nat'l Network: PBS
Foreign Language Programming
Jack Gibson, General Manager
Susie Hernandez, Programming Director
Wendy Erica Werden, Promotions Manager
Peter Michaels, News Director
David Ross, Chief Engineer
Lili Bell, Traffic Manager

KVOA *Digital Channel:* 23 *Virtual Channel:* 4; 35 kw vis, 18 kw aur; 3,610t/223g; N32 12 53 W111 00 20; *Population Served:* 1,061,000
Mailing Address: Box 5188, Tucson, AZ 85703
Second Address: 209 W. Elm St., Tucson, AZ 85705-6538
(520) 792-2270, *Fax:* (520) 620-1309
www.kvoa.com
License: Tucson, Pima County, AZ held by KVOA Communications Inc.
Group Owner: Cordillera Communications Inc.; (acq 12-31-93; $13.25 million;; *Washington Law Firm:* Dow, Lohnes & Albertson
Nat'l Network: NBC *Nat'l Reps:* HRP
Hours of Local News Weekly: News progmg 27 hrs wkly
Bill Shaw, President
Dave Kerrigan, Operations Dir
Bill Shaw, General Manager
Jeff Green, General Sales Mgr
Jeff Clemons, Promotions Manager
Cathie Batbie, News Director
Dave Kerrigan, Engineering Dir

KWBA-TV *Digital Channel:* 44; 5,000 kw vis, 500 kw aur; ant 1,086t; N31 45 33 W110 48 02
7280 E. Rosewood St., Tucson, AZ 85710
(520) 722-5486, *Fax:* (520) 733-7050
www.kwba.com
soundoff@kwba.com
License: Sierra Vista, Cochise County, AZ held by Journal Broadcast Corp.
Group Owner: Journal Communications Inc.; (acq 7-22-2008; $11.885 million); *Washington Law Firm:* Leventhal Senter & Lerman PLLC
Nat'l Network: CW
Julie Brinks, General Manager

Yuma, AZ-El Centro, CA (DMA 164)

KSWT *Digital Channel:* 13 *Virtual Channel:* 13; 50 kw; 1575 ft.; N33 3 18 W114 49 39
1891 West Serenade Street, Tucson, AZ 85737 US
(928) 782-5113, *Fax:* (928) 783-0866
www.kswt.com
kswt@adelphia.net
License: Yuma, Yuma County, AZ held by Pappas Arizona License LLC.
Group Owner: Pappas Telecasting Companies; (acq 9-8-2000; $5.375 million); *Washington Law Firm:* Paul, Hastings, Janofsky & Walker
Nat'l Network: CBS AND CW; CW
Size of News Staff: 8; *Hours of Local News Weekly:* news progmg 5 hrs wkly
Larry Patton, General Manager
Joe Bartnik, Chief Engineer

KYMA-DT ; 316 kw vis, 31.6 kw aur; 518t/1,617g; N33 03 10 W114 49 40; *Population Served:* 86,900
1385 S. Pacific Ave., Yuma, AZ 85365-1725
(928) 782-1111, *Fax:* (928) 782-5401
www.kyma.com
License: Yuma, Yuma County, AZ held by Yuma Broadcasting Co.
Group Owner: Sunbelt Communications Co.; (acq 6-6-89; $60,000;; *Washington Law Firm:* Dow, Lohnes & Albertson
Nat'l Network: NBC
Size of News Staff: 24; *Hours of Local News Weekly:* news progmg 12 hrs wkly
Paul Heebink, General Manager
Barbara Monroy, Programming Director
Luis Cruz, News Director
Robbie Decorse, Chief Engineer

Arkansas

Ft. Smith-Fayetteville-Springdale-Rogers, AR (DMA 100)

***KAFT** *Digital Channel:* 9 *Virtual Channel:* 13; 37.9 kw; 1650 ft.; N35 48 53 W94 1 41
Mailing Address: 350 Donaghey, Conway, AR 72032 US
Second Address: 350 S. Donaghey, Conway, AR 72034
(501) 682-2386,(800) 662-2386, *Fax:* (501) 682-4122
www.aetn.org
info@aetn.org
License: Fayetteville, Washington County, AR held by Arkansas Educational Television Commission
Washington Law Firm: Dow, Lohnes & Albertson
Nat'l Network: PBS
DeWayne Wilbur, Operations Dir
Allen Weatherly, Executive Director
Tony Brooks, Deputy Director

KFSM-TV *Digital Channel:* 18 *Virtual Channel:* 5; 100 kw vis, 12.7 kw aur; 1,086t/1,173g; N35 30 43 W94 21 38; *Population Served:* 883,500
Box 369, 318 N. 13th St. (72901), Fort Smith, AR 10036
(479) 783-3131, *Fax:* (479) 783-3295
www.5newsonline.com
License: Fort Smith, Sebastian County, AR held by Local TV Arkansas License LLC.
Group Owner: Local TV LLC; (acq 5-7-2007; grpsl); *Washington Law Firm:* DowLohnes, PLLC
Nat'l Network: CBS
Size of News Staff: 36; *Hours of Local News Weekly:* news progmg 28 hrs wkly
Patty Jewell, CFO
Robert Lawrence, President
John-Mark Scales, Operations Dir
Van Comer, General Manager
Mark LaCrue, General Sales Mgr
Debby Etzkorn, Programming Director
John-Mark Scales, Promotions Manager
TBA, ChiefEngineer
Rose Smith, Traffic Manager

KFTA-TV *Digital Channel:* 27 *Virtual Channel:* 24; 600 kw; 1001 ft.; N35 42 36 W94 8 15
PO Box 4610, Ft. Smith, AR 72914 US
(479) 571-5100, *Fax:* (479) 571-8914
www.nwahomepage.com
news@knwa.com
License: Fort Smith, Sebastian County, AR held by Mission Broadcasting, Inc.
Group Owner: Mission Broadcasting Inc.; (acq 12-21-2004; $10 million with KNWA-TV Rogers); *Washington Law Firm:* Holland & Knight
Nat'l Network: NBC/FOX *Nat'l Reps:* TeleRep
Size of News Staff: 45; *Hours of Local News Weekly:* news progmg 20.5 hrs wkly
Mike Vaughn, Operations Dir
Marty Houston, Station Manager
Lisa Kelsey, General Sales Mgr
Brook Thomas, News Director
Mike Cleveland, Chief Engineer
Travis Spieth, Local Sales Manager

KHBS *Digital Channel:* 21 *Virtual Channel:* 40; 325 kw; 1975 ft.; N35 4 15 W94 40 43
888 Seventh Aven, New York, NY 10106 US
(479) 783-4040, (479) 631-4029, *Fax:* (479) 785-5375, (479) 878-6079
www.4029tv.com
news@4029tv.com
License: Fort Smith, Sebastian County, AR held by KHBS Hearst-Argyle Television Inc.
Group Owner: Hearst-Argyle Television Inc.; (acq 7-16-97; grpsl).; *Washington Law Firm:* Wiley, Rein & Fielding
Nat'l Network: ABC; CW
Size of News Staff: 30; *Hours of Local News Weekly:* news progmg 15 hrs wkly
Jim Prestwood, General Manager
John McCormick, General Sales Mgr
Larry Friddle, Chief Engineer

KHOG-TV *Digital Channel:* 15 *Virtual Channel:* 29; 180 kw; 873 ft.; N36 0 57 W94 4 59
888 Seventh Avenue, New York, NY 10106 US
(479) 783-4040 / (479) 631-4029, *Fax:* (479) 785-5375 / (479) 878-6079
www.4029tv.com
news@4029tv.com
License: Fayetteville, Washington County, AR held by KHBS Hearst-Argyle Television Inc.
Group Owner: Hearst-Argyle Television Inc.; (acq 7-16-97; grpsl).; *Washington Law Firm:* Wiley, Rein & Fielding
Nat'l Network: ABC; CW
Jim Prestwood, General Manager
John McCormick, General Sales Mgr
Larry Friddle, Chief Engineer

KNWA-TV *Digital Channel:* 50 *Virtual Channel:* 51; 1000 kw; 876 ft.; N36 24 47.8 W93 57 16.8; *Rebroadcasting:* Satellite of KFTA-TV Fort Smith.
P.O. Box 4610, Fort Smith, AR 72914 US
(479) 571-5100, *Fax:* (479) 571-8914
www.nwahomepage.com
news@knwa.com
License: Rogers, Benton County, AR held by Nexstar Broadcasting Inc.
Group Owner: Nexstar Broadcasting Group Inc.; (acq 12-21-2004; $10 million with KFTA-TV Fort Smith).; *Washington Law Firm:* Drinker, Biddle & Reath
Nat'l Network: NBC *Nat'l Reps:* Blair Television
Size of News Staff: 27; *Hours of Local News Weekly:* 17 hrs news progmg wkly
Mike Vaughn, Operations Dir
Chad Beckham, General Sales Mgr
Brook Thomas, News Director
Mike Cleveland, Chief Engineer
Lisa Kelsey, General Sales Manager
Deborah Palmer, Local Sales Manager

KWOG *Digital Channel:* 39 *Virtual Channel:* 57; 35 kw; 374 ft.; N36 11 7 W94 17 49
P.O. Box 6968, Springdale, AR 72766 US
(817) 571-1229, *Fax:* (817) 571-8962
ww2.daystar.com
License: Springdale, Washington County, AR held by Word of God Fellowship Inc.
Nat'l Network: IND
Marcus Lamb, President
Harvey Rogers, Chief Engineer

Jonesboro, AR (DMA 181)

KAIT *Digital Channel:* 8 *Virtual Channel:* 8; 28.2 kw; 1742 ft.; N35 53 22 W90 56 8
Mailing Address: P.O. Box 790, Jonesboro, AR 72403 US
Second Address: 472 Country Rd. 766, Jonesboro, AZ 72401
(870) 931-8888, *Fax:* (870) 933-8058 (news),(870) 931-1371(sales)
www.kait8.com
License: Jonesboro, Craighead County, AR held by KAIT License Subsidiary LLC.
Group Owner: Raycom Media Inc.; (acq 1-31-2006; grpsl);
Washington Law Firm: Covington & Burling
Nat'l Network: ABC *Nat'l Reps:* Harrington, Righter & Parsons
Wire Services: Weather Wire; AP
Size of News Staff: 32; *Hours of Local News Weekly:* news progmg 17 hrs wkly
Tracey Rigers, General Manager
Joe Sciortino, General Sales Mgr
Ronnie Weston, Programming Director
Jeremy Shirley, Promotions Manager
Halton Weeks, News Director
Gerald Erickson, Chief Engineer
Ralph Caudill, National SalesManager
Ronnie Weston, Operations Director
Debi Gann, Traffic Manager

***KTEJ** *Digital Channel:* 20 *Virtual Channel:* 19; 322.9 kw; 1017 ft.; N35 54 14 W90 46 14
Mailing Address: 350 South Donaghey St., Conway, AR 72032 US
Second Address: 350 S. Donaghey, Conway, AR 72034
(501) 682-2386,(800) 662-2386, *Fax:* (501) 682-4122
www.aetn.org
info@aetn.org
License: Jonesboro, Craighead County, AR held by Arkansas Educational Television Commission
Washington Law Firm: Dow, Lohnes & Albertson
Nat'l Network: PBS
DeWayne Wilbur, Operations Dir
Allen Weatherly, General Manager
Tony Brooks, Station Manager
Mona Dixon, General Sales Mgr

KVTJ-DT *Digital Channel:* 48; 1,000 kw vis; 1,023t/1,791g; N35 53 17 W90 56 09
701 Napa Valley Dr., Little Rock, AR 72211
(501) 223-2525, *Fax:* (501) 221-3837
www.vtntv.com
jim.grant@vtntv.com
License: Jonesboro, Craighead County, AR held by Agape Church Inc.
Group Owner: The Victory Television Network; (acq 1995).;
Washington Law Firm: Wiley Rein
Jimmie Rushing, Operations Dir
Jim Grant, General Manager
Kim Worden, Programming Director
Andrea Qualls, Promotions Manager
Ron Brown, Engineering Dir
Sharon Case, Traffic Director

Little Rock-Pine Bluff, AR (DMA 56)

KARK-TV *Digital Channel:* 32 *Virtual Channel:* 4; 100 kw vis, 20 kw aur; 1,650t/1,175g; N34 47 57 W92 29 59; *Population Served:* 1,177,000
1401 W. Capitol Ave., Suite 104, Little Rock, AR 72203
(501) 340-4444, *Fax:* (501) 376-1852
www.kark.com
License: Little Rock, Pulaski County, AR held by Nexstar Broadcasting Inc.
Group Owner: Nexstar Broadcasting Group Inc.; (acq 8-1-2003; $40 million with WDHN(TV) Dothan, AL)
Nat'l Network: NBC *Nat'l Reps:* Petry Television Inc. *Wire Services:* Photofax
Size of News Staff: 40; *Hours of Local News Weekly:* news progmg 22 hrs wkly
Gayle Kiger, Operations Dir
Craig Castrellon, General Sales Mgr
Mary Mobbs, Programming Director
Ed Tudor, Promotions Manager
Mike Moravec, Chief Engineer
Cindy Rochelle, National Sales Manager

KARZ-TV *Digital Channel:* 44 *Virtual Channel:* 42; 1000 kw; 1471 ft.; N34 47 57 W92 29 59
601 Clearwater Park Road, West Palm Beach, FL 33401 US
(501) 340-4444, *Fax:* (501) 376-1852
www.arkansasmatters.com
License: Little Rock, Pulaski County, AR held by Nexstar Broadcasting Inc.
Group Owner: Nexstar Broadcasting Group Inc.; (acq 3-12-2009; $4 million)
Nat'l Network: MNT
Gayle Kiger, General Manager

KASN *Digital Channel:* 39; 5,000 kw vis, 500 kw aur; ant 2,008t/1,910g; N34 26 31 W92 13 03; *Population Served:* 481,000
10800 Colonel Glenn, Little Rock, AR 78209
(501) 225-0016, *Fax:* (501) 224-6162
www.fox16.com
captioning@fox16.com
License: Pine Bluff, Jefferson County, AR held by Newport Television License LLC.
Group Owner: Newport Television LLC; (acq 3-14-2008; grpsl)
Nat'l Network: CW
Chuck Spohn, General Manager
Vicki McRae, General Sales Mgr
Suzanne Spearman, Programming Director
Allan Snyder, Promotions Manager
Ed Trauschke, News Director
Dean Wetherbee, Assistant News Director
Errett Porter, ChiefEngineer

KATV *Digital Channel:* 22 *Virtual Channel:* 7; 1000 kw; 1690 ft.; N34 47 49 W92 29 19.5
401 South Main Street, Little Rock, AR 72201 US
(501) 324-7777, *Fax:* (501) 324-7899
www.katv.com
dhook@katv.com
License: Little Rock, Pulaski County, AR held by KATV L.L.C.
Group Owner: Allbritton Communications Co.; (acq 2-14-83; grpsl).; *Washington Law Firm:* Hogan & Hartson
Nat'l Network: ABC
Jim Church, Vice President
Dale Nicholson, General Manager
Mark Rose, General Sales Mgr
Richard Farrester, Programming Director
Randy Dixon, News Director
Fred Anderson, Chief Engineer
Laura Story, Traffic Manager

***KEMV** *Digital Channel:* 13 *Virtual Channel:* 6; 12.1 kw; 1398 ft.; N35 48 47 W92 17 24
Mailing Address: 350 South Donaghey, Conway, AR 72032 US
Second Address: 350 South Donaghey, Conway, AR 72034
(501) 450-1727,(501) 682-2386,(800) 662-2386, *Fax:* (501) 682-4122
www.aetn.org
info@aetn.org
License: Mountain View, Stone County, AR held by Arkansas Educational Television Commission
Washington Law Firm: Dow, Lohnes & Albertson
Nat'l Network: PBS
DeWayne Wilbur, Operations Dir
Allen Weatherly, General Manager
Tony Brooks, Station Manager
Mona Dixon, General Sales Mgr
Darbi Blencowe, Viewer Services Coordinator

***KETG** *Digital Channel:* 13 *Virtual Channel:* 9; 13.85 kw; 1030 ft.; N33 54 26 W93 6 46
Mailing Address: 350 South Donaghey, Conway, AR 72032 US
Second Address: 350 S Donaghey Street, Conway, AR 72034
(501) 682-2386,(800) 662-2386, *Fax:* (501) 682-4122
www.aetn.org
info@aetn.org
License: Arkadelphia, Clark County, AR held by Arkansas Educational Television Commission
Washington Law Firm: Dow, Lohnes & Albertson
Nat'l Network: PBS
DeWayne Wilbur, Operations Dir
Allen Weatherly, General Manager
Tony Brooks, Station Manager
Mona Dixon, General Sales Mgr
Darbi Blencowe, Viewer Services Coordinator

***KETS** *Digital Channel:* 7 *Virtual Channel:* 2; 26.73 kw; 1795 ft.; N34 26 31 W92 13 3
Mailing Address: 350 South Donaghey St., Conway, AR 72032 US
Second Address: 350 South Donaghey, Conway, AR 72034
(501) 682-2386,(800) 662-2386, *Fax:* (501) 682-4122
www.aetn.org
info@aetn.org
License: Little Rock, Pulaski County, AR held by Arkansas Eucational Television Commission
Washington Law Firm: Dow, Lohnes & Albertson
Nat'l Network: PBS
DeWayne Wilbur, Operations Dir
Allen Weatherly, General Manager
Tony Brooks, Station Manager
Mona Dixon, General Sales Mgr

***KKAP** *Digital Channel:* 36 *Virtual Channel:* 36; 50 kw; 1293 ft.; N34 47 56 W92 29 45
#1 Shackleford Drive, Suite 400, Little Rock, AR 72211 US
(817) 571-1229, *Fax:* (817) 571-7458
www.daystart.com
License: Little Rock, Pulaski County, AR held by Educational Broadcasting Corp
Nat'l Network: IND
William Alatini, General Manager
Arnold Torres, Chief Regulatory Officer

KLRT-TV *Digital Channel:* 30 *Virtual Channel:* 16; 1000 kw; 1473 ft.; N34 47 57 W92 29 29
200 Concord Plaza, Suite 600, San Antonio, TX 78216 US
(501) 225-0016, *Fax:* (501) 224-6162
www.fox16.com
info@fox16.com
License: Little Rock, Pulaski County, AR held by Newport Television License LLC.

Group Owner: Newport Television LLC; (acq 3-14-2008; grpsl);
Washington Law Firm: Covington & Burling
Nat'l Network: FOX
Chuck Spohn, General Manager
Vicki McRae, General Sales Mgr
Suzanne Spearmen, Programming Director
Allan Snyder, Promotions Manager
Ed Trauschke, News Director
Errett Porter, Chief Engineer

KMYA-DT *Digital Channel:* 49 *Virtual Channel:* 49; 1,000 kw vis; ant 600t/571g; N33 16 15 W92 42 14
1 Shackelford Dr., Little Rock, AR 72211
(501) 219-2400, *Fax:* (501) 604-8004
License: Camden, Ouachita County, AR held by Arkansas 49 Inc., debtor in possession.
Group Owner: Equity Media Holdings Corp.; (acq 9-15-99)
Tammy Graham, Operations Dir
Neal Ardman, General Manager
Aaron Rothberg, General Sales Mgr
Chuck Stanely, Chief Engineer

KTHV *Digital Channel:* 12 *Virtual Channel:* 11; 316 kw vis, 38 kw aur; 1,709t; N34 47 57 W92 29 59; *Population Served:* 152,483
Mailing Address: 720 S. Izard Street, Little Rock, AR 72203
Second Address: AR
(501) 376-1111, *Fax:* (501) 376-3324
www.todaysthv.com
programming@todaysthv.com
License: Little Rock, Pulaski County, AR held by Arkansas Television Co.
Group Owner: Gannett Broadcasting; (acq 11-30-94; $27 million;;
Washington Law Firm: Wiley, Rein & Fielding
Nat'l Network: CBS *Nat'l Reps:* TeleRep
Size of News Staff: 45; *Hours of Local News Weekly:* news progmg 27 hrs wkly
Larry Audas, President
Dale Remy, General Sales Mgr
David Craft, Promotions Manager
Alison Fletcher, Chief Engineer
Chad Kelley, National Sales Manager
Joanne Canelli, Regional Sales Manager

KVTH-DT *Digital Channel:* 26; 245 kw vis, 24.5 kw aur; 941t; N32 22 20 W93 02 47; *Rebroadcasting:* Satellite of KVTN(TV) Pine Bluff.
701 Napa Valley Dr., Little Rock, AR 72211
(501) 223-2525, *Fax:* (501) 221-3837
www.vtntv.com
jim.grant@vtntv.com
License: Hot Springs, Garland County, AR held by Agape Church.
Group Owner: The Victory Television Network; (acq 1994).;
Washington Law Firm: Wiley Rein
Jim Grant, General Manager
Kim Worden, Programming Director
Andrea Qualls, Promotions Manager
Ron Brown, Engineering Dir
Sharon Case, Traffic Director

KVTN-DT *Digital Channel:* 24; 4,370 kw vis, 43.7 kw aur; ant 594t/594g; N34 31 55 W92 02 41
701 Napa Valley Dr., Little Rock, AR 72211
(501) 223-2525, *Fax:* (501) 221-3837
www.vtntv.com
jim.grant@vtntv.com
License: Pine Bluff, Jefferson County, AR held by Agape Church Inc.
Group Owner: The Victory Television Network; (acq 6-87; $41,000;; *Washington Law Firm:* Wiley, Rein
Jim Grant, General Manager
Kim Worden, Programming Director
Andrea Qualls, Promotions Manager
Ron Brown, Engineering Dir
Sharon Case, Traffic Manager

Monroe, LA-El Dorado, AR (DMA 136)

***KETZ** *Digital Channel:* 10 *Virtual Channel:* 12; 16.2 kw; 1765 ft.; N33 4 41 W92 13 30
Mailing Address: C/O Susan Howarth, 350 S. Donaghey, Conway, AR 72032 US
Second Address: 350 S. Donaghey, Conway, AR 72034
(501) 682-2386, *Fax:* (501) 682-4122
www.aetn.org
info@aetn.org
License: El Dorado, Union County, AR held by Arkansas Educational Television Commission.
Nat'l Network: PBS

Allen Weatherly, General Manager

KTVE *Digital Channel:* 27 *Virtual Channel:* 10; 822.8 kw; 1909 ft.; N33 4 41 W92 13 41
7621 Little Avenue, Suite 506, Charlotte, NC 28266 US
(318) 323-1972, *Fax:* (318) 322-0926
www.myarklamiss.com
License: El Dorado, Union County, AR held by Nexstar Broadcasting Group
Group Owner: Nexstar Broadcasting Group Inc.; *Washington Law Firm:* Cohn & Marks
Nat'l Network: NBC *Nat'l Reps:* Continental Television Sales
Size of News Staff: 26; *Hours of Local News Weekly:* news progmg 13 hrs wkly
Cheryl Olive, General Manager
Susie Cumpton, General Sales Mgr
Irma Campbell, Programming Director
Esther Phillips, Promotions Manager
Melissa Klinzing, News Director
Billy Brown, Chief Engineer
Bob Dowden, Sales Manager

Springfield, MO (DMA 74)

KWBM *Digital Channel:* 31 *Virtual Channel:* 31; 191 kw; 1112 ft.; N36 42 18 W93 3 45
C/O Richard Baker, Treas, 2535 Success Drive, Odessa, FL 33556 US
(417) 877-9231, *Fax:* (417) 877-9015
www.my31tv.com
License: Harrison, Boone County, AR held by EBC Harrison Inc., debtor in possession
Group Owner: Equity Media Holdings Corp.; (acq 9-21-2004; $8,666,670)
Nat'l Network: DAYSTAR *Nat'l Reps:* Roslin Television Sales
Regional Reps: Susan Cochran
S. Lanken, General Manager

KXNW *Digital Channel:* 34 *Virtual Channel:* 34; 1,000 kw vis; ant 736t/322g; N36 24 41 W93 57 12
1 Shackleford Dr., Suite 400, Little Rock, AR 72211
(501) 219-2400, *Fax:* (501) 221-7908
License: Eureka Springs, Carroll County, AR held by TV 34 Inc., debtor in possession.
Group Owner: Equity Media Holdings Corp.; (acq 8-23-99)
Glenn Charlesworth, CFO
Greg Fess, President
James Hearnsberger, Operations Dir
Terrill Weiss, Station Manager
Debbie James, General Sales Mgr
Nathan Stamp, Programming Director
Frank White, Promotions Manager
Doug Krile, NewsDirector
Max Hooper, Executive Vice President

California

Bakersfield, CA (DMA 125)

KBAK-TV *Digital Channel:* 33 *Virtual Channel:* 29; 110 kw; 3701 ft.; N35 27 11 W118 35 25
Mailing Address: 980 North Michigan Ave., Suite 1200, Chicago, IL 60611 US
Second Address: 1901 Westwind Drive, Bakersfield, CA 93301
(661) 327-7955, *Fax:* (661) 327-5603
bakersfieldnow.com
License: Bakersfield, Kern County, CA held by Fisher Communications, Inc.
(acq 1-2008; *Washington Law Firm:* Brooks, Pierce, McLendon, Humphrey & Leonard
Nat'l Network: CBS *Nat'l Reps:* Continental Television Sales
Wire Services: AP
Size of News Staff: 40; *Hours of Local News Weekly:* news progmg 30.5 hrs wkly
Pete Capra, Operations Dir
Teresa Burgess, General Manager
Yvette Graves, Program Administrator
Cindi Dias, General Sales Mgr
Nancy Clarke, Programming Director
Tracy Peoples, Promotions Manager
Doug Barden, News Director
JulieCarter, Local Sales Manager
Janice Curliss, Traffic Manager

KERO-TV *Digital Channel:* 10 *Virtual Channel:* 23; 10.8 kw; 3632 ft.; N35 27 14 W118 35 37
321 21st St, Bakersfield, CA 93301 US
(661) 637-2323, *Fax:* (661) 322-1701
www.thebakersfieldchannel.com
License: Bakersfield, Kern County, CA held by McGraw-Hill Broadcasting Co.
Group Owner: McGraw-Hill Broadcasting Co.; (acq 3-8-72; grpsl;;
Washington Law Firm: Holland & Knight
Nat'l Network: ABC *Nat'l Reps:* Harrington, Righter & Parsons
Steve McEvoy, General Manager
Craig Jahelka, Programming Director
Steve Taylor, Promotions Manager
Todd Karli, News Director
Tom Wimberly, Chief Engineer
Lesley Kirk, Edit Director
Maxcine Cole, Traffic Manager

KGET-TV *Digital Channel:* 25 *Virtual Channel:* 17; 135 kw; 1329 ft.; N35 26 17 W118 44 22
1333 New Hampshire, N.W., Suite 100, Washington, DC 20036 US
(661) 283-1700, *Fax:* (661) 283-1794
www.kget.com
shirleysanford@kget.com
License: Bakersfield, Kern County, CA held by High Plains Broadcasting License Co. LLC.
Group Owner: Nexstar Broadcasting; (acq 9-15-2008; grpsl)
Nat'l Network: NBC-CW
Size of News Staff: 33; *Hours of Local News Weekly:* news progmg 27 hrs wkly
Kristi Spitzer, General Sales Mgr
Shirley Sanford, Programming Director
Jim Tripeny, Promotions Manager
John Pilios, News Director
Tom Ballew, Chief Engineer
Kathleen McNeil, Public Affairs Director

KUVI-DT *Digital Channel:* 55; 5,000 kw vis, 500 kw aur; ant 1,325t/144g; N36 26 20 W118 44 24; *Population Served:* 508,000
5801 Truxtun Ave., Bakersfield, CA 93309
(661) 324-0045, *Fax:* (661) 334-2693
www.kuvi45.com
License: Bakersfield, Kern County, CA held by KUVI License Partnership G.P.
Group Owner: Univision Communications Inc.; (acq 2-4-98; $14,010,800).; *Washington Law Firm:* Shaw Pittman
Nat'l Network: MyNetworkTV
Teresa Ford, General Manager
Denise Snanoudt, General Sales Mgr
Ken Richter, Chief Engineer
Maria Herrandez, Public Affairs Director
Maria Hernandez, Public Service Director
Maritere Alvarez-Jackson, Regional Sales Manager
Clerinda Briones, Traffic Manager

Chico-Redding, CA (DMA 130)

KCVU *Digital Channel:* 20 *Virtual Channel:* 30; 172 kw; 1473 ft.; N39 57 49 W121 42 38
P.O. Box 4159, Modesto, CA 95352 US
(530) 893-1234, *Fax:* (530) 899-5475
www.fox30.com
info@fox30.com
License: Paradise, Butte County, CA held by Sainte Partners II L.P.
Group Owner: Sainte Partners II L.P.; *Washington Law Firm:* Fletcher, Heald & Hildreth
Nat'l Network: FOX *Nat'l Reps:* Millennium Sales & Marketing
Hours of Local News Weekly: News progmg 0 hrs wkly
Doug Holroyd, General Manager
Bert Westhoff, General Sales Mgr
Paula Murphy, Programming Director
Betsy Brewer, Promotions Manager
Ken Rice, Chief Engineer
Glenn Taylor, Regional Sales Manager

KHSL-TV *Digital Channel:* 43 *Virtual Channel:* 12; 235 kw; 1539 ft.; N39 57 29 W121 42 49
3460 Silverbell Road, Chico, CA 95973 US
(530) 342-0141, *Fax:* (530) 342-4905
www.khsltv.com
khsltv@khsltv.com
License: Chico, Butte County, CA held by Catamount Broadcasting of Chico-Redding Inc.
(acq 7-30-98; $10 million); *Ownership:* Catamount Holdings LLC, 100% votes; *Washington Law Firm:* Haley, Bader & Potts
Nat'l Network: CBS; CW *Nat'l Reps:* Continental Television Sales
Size of News Staff: 34; *Hours of Local News Weekly:* news progmg 20 hrs wkly
Stev Siorenson, Operations Dir
John Stall, General Manager
Marnie McDonald, General Sales Mgr

Shannon Bomar, Programming Director
Morgan Schmidt, Promotions Manager
Trisha Coder, News Director
Dave Sien, Chief Engineer

***KIXE-TV** *Digital Channel:* 9 *Virtual Channel:* 9; 15 kw; 3579 ft.; N40 36 9 W122 39 1
603 North Market St., Redding, CA 96003 US
(530) 243-5493, *Fax:* (530) 243-7443
www.kixe.org
channel9@kixe.org
License: Redding, Shasta County, CA held by Northern California Educational TV Association Inc
Washington Law Firm: Schwartz, Woods & Miller
Nat'l Network: PBS
Hours of Local News Weekly: News progmg one hr wkly
Renee Cooper, CFO
Myron Tisdel, President
Mike Lampella, Operations Dir
Anne Kerns, General Sales Mgr
Rob Keenan, Programming Director
Sue Maxey, Chief Engineer
Fred Gaines, Regional Sales Manager
Ken Simmon, Traffic Manager

KNVN *Digital Channel:* 24 *Virtual Channel:* 24; 321 kw; 1772 ft.; N40 15 31 W122 5 24
The Pinnacle, Suite 875, 3455 Peachtree Rd., N.E., Atlanta, GA 30326 US
(530) 894-6397, *Fax:* (530) 342-2405
www.knvn.com
news@knvn.com
License: Chico, Butte County, CA held by Chico License L.L.C (acq 6-2000; $9.2 million); *Washington Law Firm:* Leventhal, Senter & Lerman
Nat'l Network: NBC
John Stall, General Manager
Steve Sorenson, Station Manager
Scott Howard, News Director

KRCR-TV *Digital Channel:* 7 *Virtual Channel:* 7; 84 kw; 3593 ft.; N40 36 10 W122 39 0
755 Auditorium Drive, Redding, CA 96099 US
(530) 243-7777, *Fax:* (530) 243-0217
www.krcrtv.com
info@krcrtv.com
License: Redding, Shasta County, CA held by BlueStone License Holdings Inc.
Group Owner: Bonten Media Group LLC; (acq 5-31-2007; grpsl)
Nat'l Network: ABC *Nat'l Reps:* Petry Television Inc.
Size of News Staff: 21; *Hours of Local News Weekly:* news progmg 16 hrs wkly
Arisl Roblin, General Sales Mgr
Penny Loll, Programming Director
Kirstin Moran, Promotions Manager
Jennifer Scarbrough, News Director
Lance Cratty, Chief Engineer
Jeremy Alexander, Traffic Manager

Eureka, CA (DMA 195)

KAEF-TV ; 141 kw vis, 14 kw aur; 1,672t; N40 43 36 W123 58 18
755 Auditorium Drive, Redding, CA 96001
(530) 232-5700, *Fax:* (530) 243-0217
kaeftv@kadf.com
License: Arcata, Humboldt County, CA held by BlueStone License Holdings Inc.
Group Owner: Bonten Media Group LLC; (acq 5-31-2007; grpsl); *Washington Law Firm:* Covington & Burling LLP
Nat'l Network: ABC
Size of News Staff: 2; *Hours of Local News Weekly:* news progmg 2 hrs wkly
Leslie Lollich, General Manager
Brian Anderson, Chief Engineer

KBVU *Digital Channel:* 28 *Virtual Channel:* 29; 50 kw; 1683 ft.; N40 43 39 W123 58 17
P.O. Box 4159, Modesto, CA 95352 US
(707) 442-2999, *Fax:* (707) 441-0111
www.eurekatelevision.tv
engineering@eurekatelevision.tv
License: Eureka, Humboldt County, CA held by Sainte Partners II L.P.
Group Owner: Sainte Partners II L.P.; acq 7-24-97).; *Washington Law Firm:* Womble, Carlyle, Sandrige & Rice
Nat'l Network: FOX *Nat'l Reps:* Millennium Sales & Marketing
Chester Smith, CEO
Don Smullin, General Manager
Mark Dare, Chief Engineer

***KEET** *Digital Channel:* 11 *Virtual Channel:* 13; 38.4 kw; 1803 ft.; N40 43 38.9 W123 58 17
Mailing Address: PO Box 13, Eureka, CA 95502 US
Second Address: 7246 Humboldt Hill Rd., Eureka, CA 95503
(707) 445-0813, *Fax:* (707) 445-8977
www.keet.com
letters@keet.pbs.org
License: Eureka, Humboldt County, CA held by Redwood Empire Pub TV Inc
Nat'l Network: PBS
Foreign Language Programming
Ronald Schoenherr, CEO
Seth Frankel, Operations Dir
Karen Barnes, General Sales Mgr
Claire Reynolds, Promotions Manager
Joel Householter, Chief Engineer
Therese Buck, Traffic Manager

KIEM-TV *Digital Channel:* 3 *Virtual Channel:* 3; 12.5 kw; 1591 ft.; N40 43 50 W123 57 7
5650 So. Broadway, Eureka, CA 95503 US
(707) 443-3123, *Fax:* (707) 442-6084
www.kiem-tv.com
kiem-tv@hotmail.com
License: Eureka, Humboldt County, CA held by Pollack/Belz Broadcasting Co. L.L.C.
Group Owner: Pollack Broadcasting Co.; (acq 5-1-96; $3 million)
Nat'l Network: NBC *Regional Reps:* KATZ
Size of News Staff: 8
Phil Wright, Operations Dir
Roy Frostenson, General Manager
Hank Ingham, General Sales Mgr
Shawna Brisco, Programming Director
Joseph Lowe, Chief Engineer
Marsha Kane, Traffic Manager

KVIQ *Digital Channel:* 17 *Virtual Channel:* 6; 30 kw; 1804 ft.; N40 43 39 W123 58 17
1333 New Hampshire Ave., N.W., Suite 1000, Washington, DC 20036 US
(707) 443-3061, *Fax:* (707) 441-0111
www.kviq.com
License: Eureka, Humboldt County, CA held by Raul Broadcasting Co. of Eureka Inc.
(acq 4-25-2005; $2 million); *Ownership:* Raul Palazuelos, 100%
Nat'l Network: CBS
John Burgess, General Manager
Penny King, Station Manager
Lauren Faucett, Programming Director
Rick St. Charles, Promotions Manager
Deve Silurrbrand, News Director
Jim Mixou, Chief Engineer

Fresno-Visalia, CA (DMA 55)

KAIL *Digital Channel:* 7; 2,510 kw vis, 251 kw aur; ant 1,906t/140g; N37 04 23 W119 15 52; *Population Served:* 1,700,000
1590 Alluvial Ave., Clovis, CA 93611
(559) 299-9753, *Fax:* (559) 299-1523
www.kail.tv
License: Fresno, Fresno County, CA held by Trans-America Broadcasting Corp.
(acq 12-23-66; $236,500;; *Washington Law Firm:* Miller & Fields
Nat'l Network: MyNetworkTV
G. Borrego, President
Mike Nicassio, Operations Dir
Charles Williams, General Manager
Dave Hetrick, General Sales Mgr
Robert Jenkins, Programming Director
Angela Bartley, Traffic Manager

KFRE-TV *Digital Channel:* 36 *Virtual Channel:* 59; 360 kw; 1991 ft.; N37 4 37 W119 26 1
706 W. Herndon Avenue, Fresno, CA 93650 US
(559) 252-5900, *Fax:* (559) 255-0275
www.kfre.com
License: Sanger, Fresno County, CA held by KFRE(TV) License LLC.
(acq 10/2009).; *Ownership:* TTBG Fresno OpCo, LLC; *Washington Law Firm:* Cohn & Marks
Nat'l Network: CW
Size of News Staff: 5; *Hours of Local News Weekly:* news progmg 2 hrs wkly
Jack Peck, General Manager
Darrell Jennings, General Sales Mgr
Norm Wright, Chief Engineer

KFSN-TV *Digital Channel:* 30 *Virtual Channel:* 30; 260 kw; 2051 ft.; N37 4 38 W119 26 0
77 West 66th Street, 16th Floor, New York, NY 10023 US
(559) 442-1170, *Fax:* (559) 233-5844 (sls),(559) 266-5024 (news)
www.abc30.com
License: Fresno, Fresno County, CA held by KFSN Television LLC.
Group Owner: ABC Inc.; *Washington Law Firm:* ABC Legal
Nat'l Network: ABC *Nat'l Reps:* ABC National Television Sales
Size of News Staff: 50; *Hours of Local News Weekly:* news progmg 30 hrs wkly
Dan Adams, President
Beth Marney, Operations Dir
Susan Blaze, General Sales Mgr
Charlene Ciavaglia, Programming Director
Jeff Aiello, Promotions Manager
Tracey Watkowski, News Director
Ron Neil, Engineering Dir

KFTV-DT *Digital Channel:* 20; 5,000 kw vis, 605 kw aur; ant 1,984t/216g; N37 04 22 W119 25 50; *Population Served:* 637,000
601 West Univision Plaza, Fresno, CA 93722
(559) 222-2121, *Fax:* (559) 222-2890,(559) 222-0917
www.univision.net
kftvpublicfile@univision.net
License: Hanford, Kings County, CA held by KFTV L.P., G.P.
Group Owner: Univision Communications Inc.; (acq 8-87).; *Washington Law Firm:* Shaw Pittman LLP
Nat'l Network: Univision (Spanish)
Foreign Language Programming; Size of News Staff: 58; *Hours of Local News Weekly:* news progmg 8 hrs wkly
Brett Covish, Operations Dir
Maria Gutierrez, General Manager
Angelica Freitas, Assistant General Manager
Ken Holden, Chief Engineer

KGMC *Digital Channel:* 43 *Virtual Channel:* 43; 283 kw; 2106 ft.; N36 44 46 W119 16 57
706 W.Herndon Avenue, Fresno, CA 93650 US
(559) 432-4300,(559) 435-7000, *Fax:* (559) 435-3201
www.cocolatv.com
info@cocolatv.com
License: Clovis, Fresno County, CA held by Gary M. Cocola
Group Owner: Cocola Broadcasting Companies LLC; (acq 11-19-92).; *Washington Law Firm:* Dow, Lohnes & Albertson
Nat'l Network: IND
Gary Cocola, CEO
John Her, Operations Dir
Kevin Mosesian, Station Manager
Al Kinney, Chief Engineer

KGPE *Digital Channel:* 34 *Virtual Channel:* 47; 2,500 kw vis; ant 1,958t/226g; N37 04 14 W119 25 31; *Population Served:* 1,453,000
4880 N. First St., Fresno, CA 98109
(559) 222-2411, *Fax:* (559) 222-5593
www.cbs47.tv
programming@cbs47.tv
License: Fresno, Fresno County, CA held by High Plains Broadcasting License Co. LLC.
Group Owner: Nexstar Broadcasting; (acq 9-15-2008; grpsl); *Ownership:* Newport Television LLC; *Washington Law Firm:* Pillsbury Winthrop Shaw Pittman LLP
Nat'l Network: CBS *Nat'l Reps:* Continental Television Sales
Size of News Staff: 50; *Hours of Local News Weekly:* news progmg 28hrs wkly
Linda Danna, Operations Dir
Linda Danna, General Manager
Robert Torres, General Sales Mgr
Alex Ruiz, Programming Director
Chad McCollum, News Director
Gary Temple, Chief Engineer
Suzanne DiPasquale, Business Manager
MatthewDamore, Creative Services Director
David King, National Sales Manager

KMPH-TV *Digital Channel:* 28 *Virtual Channel:* 26; 219 kw; 2503 ft.; N36 40 2 W118 52 42
500 South Chinowth Road, Visalia, CA 93277 US
(559) 255-2600, *Fax:* (559) 255-0275
www.kmph.com
viewercomments@kmph.com
License: Visalia, Tulare County, CA held by KMPH(TV) License LLC.
(acq 10/2009); *Ownership:* TTBG Fresno OpCo, LLC; *Washington Law Firm:* Fletcher, Heald & Hildreth
Nat'l Network: FOX *Nat'l Reps:* TeleRep
Size of News Staff: 21; *Hours of Local News Weekly:* news progmg 7 hrs wkly
Jack Peck, General Manager
Darrell Jennings, General Sales Mgr

Debbie Sweeney, Programming Director
Mark Hodorowski, Promotions Manager
Norm Wright, Chief Engineer
Janet Williams, Traffic Manager

KNSO *Digital Channel:* 11 *Virtual Channel:* 51; 45 kw; 2041 ft.; N37 4 19 W119 25 49
P.O. Box 4159, Modesto, CA 95352 US
(559) 252-5101, *Fax:* (559) 252-2747
www.holaciudad.com
License: Merced, Merced County, CA held by NBC Telemundo License Co.
Group Owner: Telemundo Television Stations; (acq 4-30-2003; $33 million)
Nat'l Network: TELEMUNDO
Foreign Language Programming
Manuel Cervantes, General Manager

***KNXT** *Digital Channel:* 50 *Virtual Channel:* 49; 185 kw; 2736 ft.; N36 17 14 W118 50 17
1550 N.Fresno St., Fresno, CA 93703 US
(559) 488-7440, *Fax:* (559) 488-7444
www.dioceseoffresno.org
knxt49@hotmail.com
License: Visalia, Tulare County, CA held by Board of Directors Diocese of Fresno Education Corp
Nat'l Network: ETV
Foreign Language Programming
Bishop John Steinback, President
Colin Dougherty, General Manager

KSEE *Digital Channel:* 38 *Virtual Channel:* 24; 1,600 kw vis, 320 kw aur; 2,350t/321g; N36 44 45 W119 16 53; *Population Served:* 165,972
5035 E. McKinley Ave., Fresno, CA 93727
(559) 454-2424, *Fax:* (559) 454-2487
www.ksee24.com
License: Fresno, Fresno County, CA held by Ksee License, Inc.
Group Owner: Granite Broadcasting Corp.; (acq 12-93; $32 million with WTVH(TV) Syracuse, NY;; *Washington Law Firm:* Dow Lohnes
Nat'l Network: NBC *Nat'l Reps:* Continental Television
Matthew Rosenfeld, President
Don Osika, General Sales Mgr
Matthew Rosenfeld, Programming Director
Jim Grovina, Promotions Manager
Chris Manson, News Director
Carlton Simmonds, Chief Engineer
Layne Ryan, Local Sales Manager
DeanSchiro, Production Manager

KTFF-DT *Digital Channel:* 48; 2,510 kw vis, 251 kw aur; 1,443t; N36 17 14 W118 50 17
3239 W. Ashlan Ave., Fresno, CA 93722-4402
(559) 439-6100, *Fax:* (559) 439-5950
www.telefutura.com
License: Porterville, Tulare County, CA held by TeleFutura Fresno LLC.
Group Owner: Univision Communications Inc.; (acq 2-7-2003; $35 million)
Nat'l Network: TeleFutura (Spanish)
Brett Covish, Operations Dir
Maria Gutierrez, General Manager
Jose Elgorriga, General Sales Mgr
Azucena Gomez, Programming Director
Samuel Belilty, News Director
Ken Holden, Chief Engineer
Darrell Jennings, Regional SalesManager

***KVPT** *Digital Channel:* 40 *Virtual Channel:* 18; 250 kw; 2290 ft.; N36 44 45 W119 16 51
733 ""L"" St, Fresno, CA 93721 US
(559) 266-1800, *Fax:* (559) 650-1880
www.kvpt.org
web@kvpt.org
License: Fresno, Fresno County, CA held by Valley Public Television Inc
(acq 11-1-87); *Washington Law Firm:* Fletcher, Heald & Hildreth
Nat'l Network: PBS
Foreign Language Programming; Size of News Staff: 35
Douglas Noll, Chairman
Paula Castadio, CEO
Andrea Bressel, Operations Dir
Eva Torres, General Sales Mgr
Jerry Lee, Programming Director
Jim Page, Promotions Manager
Rodger Hixon, Chief Engineer
Phyllis Brotherton, CFO

Los Angeles (DMA 2)

KABC-TV *Digital Channel:* 7 *Virtual Channel:* 7; 28.7 kw; 3209 ft.; N34 13 37 W118 3 58
4151 Prospect Avenue, Los Angeles, CA 90027 US
(818) 863-7777, *Fax:* (818) 863-7080
www.abc7.com
abc7@abc.com
License: Los Angeles, Los Angeles County, CA held by ABC Inc.
Group Owner: ABC Inc.; (acq 1-6-86; grpsl;
Nat'l Network: ABC *Wire Services:* UPI
Arnold Kleiner, General Manager

KAZA-TV *Digital Channel:* 47 *Virtual Channel:* 54; 350 kw; 3073 ft.; N34 13 37 W118 3 57
500 S. Chinowth Road, Visalia, CA 93277 US
(559) 733-7800,(818) 241-5400, *Fax:* (559) 733-7878
pappastv.com
License: Avalon, Los Angeles County, CA held by Southern California License LLC.
Group Owner: Pappas Telecasting Companies
Nat'l Network: AZTECA AMERICA
Foreign Language Programming
Fernando Acosta, Operations Dir
Eduardo Urbiola, General Manager
Alberto Ezquerro, General Sales Mgr
Ramon Delgado, Programming Director
Oscar Salcedo, News Director
Bruce Yeager, Chief Operator
Joe Berardi, Chief Engineer
Yolanda Williamson, Traffic Manager

KBEH *Digital Channel:* 24 *Virtual Channel:* 63; 1000 kw; 2867 ft.; N34 12 48 W118 3 41
Mailing Address: 950 Flynn Road, Camarillo, CA 93012 US
Second Address: 5757 W Century Blvd, #490, Los Angeles, CA 90045
(805) 388-0081, *Fax:* (305) 863-5709
www.canal63.com
License: Oxnard, Ventura County, CA held by Hero License Co LLC
4/11/2008; *Washington Law Firm:* Fletcher Heald & Hildreth, PLC
Nat'l Network: MTV TR3S
Bob Behar, President
Mara Rankin, General Manager
Barbara Alvarez, Traffic Director
Charlie Trice, Engineering Dir

KCAL *Digital Channel:* 43; 5 kw-D, DAN; 4 kw-N, DAN; 3,184t/464g; N34 4 8 W117 12 6; N34 6 39 W117 9 11
2905 South King Road, San Jose, CA 95122 US
(818) 655-2563, *Fax:* (818) 655-2693
www.kcal.com
kcalnews@cbs.com
License: Redlands, CA held by Viacom Television Stations Group of Los Angeles LLC.
Group Owner: CBS Television Stations Group; (acq 5-3-2002; $650 million)
Nat'l Network: CBS *Nat'l Reps:* Adam Young *Wire Services:* Conus; World Television News Service
Patrick McClenahan, General Manager
Debra Hurd, Engineering Dir

KCBS-TV *Digital Channel:* 43 *Virtual Channel:* 2; 36.3 kw vis, 7.26 kw aur; 3,632t/974g; N34 13 57 W118 04 18; *Population Served:* 14,400,000
4200 Radford Ave, Studio City, CA 20037
818-655-2000, *Fax:* 818-655-2664
www.cbs2.com
License: Los Angeles, Los Angeles County, CA held by CBS Inc.
Group Owner: CBS Television Stations Group; (acq 12-27-50; $3.6 million;
Nat'l Network: CBS
Size of News Staff: 95; *Hours of Local News Weekly:* news progmg 31 hrs wkly
Steve Mauldin, President
Justin Draper, Finance Operations Director
Leslie Keane, Programming Director
Otto Petersen, Promotions Manager
Scott Diener, News Director
Dan Haight, Engineering Dir
Olivia Campos-Bergeron, CommunityAffairs
Lorraine Velona, Traffic Manager
Melanie Steensland, VP-Broadcast Operations

***KCET** *Digital Channel:* 59 *Virtual Channel:* 28; 2,455 kw vis, 245.5 kw au; ant 3,038t/330g; N34 13 26 W118 03 44; *Population Served:* 4,600,000
4401 Sunset Blvd., Los Angeles, CA 90027
(323) 666-6500, *Fax:* (323) 953-5523
www.kcet.org
License: Los Angeles, Los Angeles County, CA held by Community TV of Southern California
Washington Law Firm: Arent, Fox, Kintner, Plotkin & Kahn
Debbie Hinton, CFO
Al Jerome, President
Roger Terracina, Operations Dir

KCOP-TV *Digital Channel:* 13; 161 kw vis, 32.4 kw aur; ant 2,972t/187g; N34 13 29 W118 03 48; *Population Served:* 149,000
1999 South Bundy Drive, Los Angeles, CA 90025
(310) 584-2000, *Fax:* (310) 584-2024
www.myfoxla.com
vivia-rodriguez@foxtv.com
License: Los Angeles, Los Angeles County, CA held by Fox Television Stations Inc.
Group Owner: Fox Television Stations Inc.; (acq 7-31-2001; grpsl).; *Washington Law Firm:* Wilmer, Cutler & Pickering
Nat'l Network: MyNetworkTV
Kevin Hale, General Manager
Jill Brow-Weller, Programming Director

KDOC-TV *Digital Channel:* 32 *Virtual Channel:* 56; 1000 kw; 3114 ft.; N34 13 35 W118 3 58
18021 Cowan, Irvine, CA 92614 US
(949) 442-9800, *Fax:* (949) 261-5956/(949) 221-4171
www.kdoctv.net
mmerker@kdoctv.net
License: Anaheim, Orange County, CA held by Ellis Communications KDOC Licensee LLC
(acq 2006; $149.5 million); *Washington Law Firm:* Cohn & Marks
Nat'l Network: NONE
Foreign Language Programming
Pat Boone, President
Calvin Brack, Operations Dir
John Manzi, General Manager
Tom Jimenez, General Sales Mgr
John Atkinson, Programming Director
Michelle Merker, Promotions Manager
Roger Knipp, Chief Engineer
Dale Foshee,Regional Sales Manager

KFTR-DT ; 2,450 kw vis, 372 kw aur; 3,040t/323g; N34 13 37 W118 03 58
5999 Center Drive, Los Angeles, CA 90045
(310) 348-3411, *Fax:* (310) 348-4849
License: Ontario, San Bernardino County, CA held by Univision Partnership of Southern California.
Group Owner: Univision Communications Inc.; (acq 5-21-2001; grpsl).; *Washington Law Firm:* Wiley, Rein & Fielding
Nat'l Network: TeleFutura (Spanish)
Foreign Language Programming
Beatriz Gomez, Operations Dir
Maelia Macin, General Manager
Mark Dante, General Sales Mgr
Amy Rico, Programming Director
Luis De La Parra, Promotions Manager
Chris Homer, Chief Engineer

KILM *Digital Channel:* 44 *Virtual Channel:* 64; 3,160 kw vis, 627 kw aur; ant 1,699t/203g; N34 36 34 W117 17 11; *Population Served:* 5,000,000
Mailing Address: Box 1468, Victorville, CA 92393-1468
Second Address: 15605 Village Dr., Victorville, CA 92394
(760) 241-6464, *Fax:* (760) 241-0056
www.khiztv.com
License: Barstow, San Bernardino County, CA held by KAZN-TV Licensee LLC.
(acq 11-1-2007; $7.95 million); *Washington Law Firm:* Wilkinson, Barker & Knauer
Size of News Staff: 10; *Hours of Local News Weekly:* news progmg 5 hrs wkly
Arthur Liu, President
Garrett Law, General Manager
Stella Montoya, Programming Director

KJLA *Digital Channel:* 49 *Virtual Channel:* 57; 1000 kw; 3074 ft.; N34 13 35 W118 3 57
15304 Sunset Blvd., Suite 204, Pacific Palisades, CA 90272 US
(310) 943-5288, *Fax:* (310) 943-5299
www.kjla.com
kjlainfo@kjla.com
License: Ventura, Ventura County, CA held by KJLA LLC
(acq 11-14-94;; *Washington Law Firm:* Thompson Hine & Flory
Nat'l Network: IND
Foreign Language Programming
Ed Safa, CFO
Walter Ulloa, President
Mike Seros, Operations Dir
Richard Deanda, General Sales Mgr

Daniel Crowe, Executive Vice President
Francis Wilkinson, Executive Vice President
Daniela Nuno, Traffic Assistant

***KLCS** *Digital Channel:* 41 *Virtual Channel:* 58; 1000 kw; 2958 ft.; N34 13 26 W118 3 45
1061 West Temple Street, Los Angeles, CA 90012 US
(213) 625-6958/(213) 241-4000, *Fax:* (213) 481-1019
www.klcs.org
info@klcs.org
License: Los Angeles, Los Angeles County, CA held by Los Angeles Unified School District
Washington Law Firm: Cohn & Marks
Nat'l Network: PBS
Hours of Local News Weekly: News progmg 5 hrs wkly
Sabrina Thomas, Operations Dir
Dr. Janalyn Glymph, General Manager
Myles Jang, General Sales Mgr
Alan Popkin, Engineering Dir

KMEX-DT *Digital Channel:* 35; 1,950 kw vis, 195 kw aur; ant 2,940t/170g; N34 13 35 W118 03 56; *Population Served:* 281,606
5999 Center Dr., Los Angeles, CA 90045
(310) 216-3434, *Fax:* (310) 348-3459
www.univision.com (keyword: Los Angeles)
License: Los Angeles, Los Angeles County, CA held by KMEX License Partnership G.P.
Group Owner: Univision Communications Inc.
Nat'l Network: Univision (Spanish) *Wire Services:* UPI
Foreign Language Programming; Hours of Local News Weekly: News progmg 17 hrs wkly
A. Jerrold Perenchio, CEO
Jose Delgado, President
Christina Sanchez-Camino, Operations Dir
Maelia Macin, General Manager
Mark Dante, General Sales Mgr
Antoinette Gill, Programming Director
Luis De la Parra, Promotions Manager
Jorge Mattey, News Director
George Blank, CFO

KNBC *Digital Channel:* 36 *Virtual Channel:* 4; 665 kw; 3251 ft.; N34 13 32 W118 3 52
Ms Diane Zipursky, 1299 Pennsylvania Ave, Washington, DC 20004 US
(818) 840-4444, *Fax:* (818) 840-3003
www.nbclosangeles.com
License: Los Angeles, Los Angeles County, CA held by NBC Telemundo License Co.
Group Owner: NBC Owned Television Stations; (acq 6-5-86).
Nat'l Network: NBC *Nat'l Reps:* NBC TV Stations Sales *Wire Services:* Reuters; UPI
Robert Long, Operations Dir
Craig Robinson, General Manager
Christa Morris, Programming Director

***KOCE-TV** *Digital Channel:* 48 *Virtual Channel:* 50; 1000 kw; 3114 ft.; N34 13 35 W118 3 57
15751 Gothard Street, Huntington Beach, CA 92647 US
(714) 842-5797, *Fax:* (714) 895-0852
www.koce.org
kmische@koce.org
License: Huntington Beach, Orange County, CA held by KOCE-TV Foundation
(acq 11-1-2004; $25.5 million).; *Washington Law Firm:* Vorys, Sater, Seymour & Pease
Nat'l Network: PBS
Size of News Staff: 4; *Hours of Local News Weekly:* News progmg 12.5 hrs wkly
JoEllen Allen, Chairman
Susan Truesdale, CFO
Mel Rogers, President
Kurt Mische, Operations Dir
Ed Miskevich, Station Manager
Pat Petrick, Programming Director
Mike Taylor, News Director
Gordon Smith, Chief Engineer

KPXN-TV *Digital Channel:* 38; 3,800 kw vis, 251 kw aur; ant 2,345t; N34 11 15 W117 41 58; *Population Served:* 13,000,000
3000 W. Alameda Ave., Suite 32622, Burbank, CA 91523
(818) 840-4444, *Fax:* (818) 840-2129
www.ionline.tv
License: San Bernardino, San Bernardino County, CA held by Paxson Los Angeles License Inc.
Group Owner: ION Media Networks Inc.; (acq 3-22-95; $18 million;
Nat'l Network: ION Television
Paula Madison, General Manager
Mark Douglas, General Sales Mgr
Rob Word, Programming Director

Steve Vinke, Chief Engineer
Alisha Wofford, Traffic Manager

KRCA *Digital Channel:* 35 *Virtual Channel:* 62; 1000 kw; 2972 ft.; N34 12 48 W118 3 41
5724 Hollywood Boulevard, Los Angeles, CA 90028 US
(818) 563-5722, *Fax:* (818) 972-2694
info@lbimedia.com
License: Riverside, Riverside County, CA held by KRCA License LLC.
Group Owner: Liberman Broadcasting Inc.; (acq 6-18-90)
Nat'l Network: IND
Foreign Language Programming
Winter Horton, General Manager
Michael Sheron, General Sales Mgr
Chris Buchanan, Chief Engineer

KSCI *Digital Channel:* 18 *Virtual Channel:* 18; 2,583 kw vis; ant 2,949t/164g; N34 12 47.8 W118 03 41; *Population Served:* 6,000,000
1990 S. Bundy Dr., Suite 850, Los Angeles, CA 90025
(310) 478-1818, *Fax:* (310) 479-8118
www.la18.tv
info@la18.tv
License: Long Beach, Los Angeles County, CA held by NRJ TV LA OpCo LLP
Group Owner: NRJ Holdings LLC; (acq 8-10-2012); *Washington Law Firm:* Goldberg, Godles, Wiener & Wright
Foreign Language Programming; Size of News Staff: 12; *Hours of Local News Weekly:* news progmg 27 hrs wkly
Dennis J. Davis, CEO/COO
Armando Villalpando, Operations Dir
Larry Potter, General Sales Mgr
Eva McKeown, Programming Director
Alice Lee, Promotions Manager
April Kuan, News Director (Mandarin)
Jeff Kim, News Director(Korean)
Scott Chestnut, Chief Engineer
Bill Welty, Engineering Director

KTBN-TV *Digital Channel:* 33 *Virtual Channel:* 40; 1000 kw; 2871 ft.; N34 13 27 W118 3 44
Mailing Address: 2442 Michelle Drive, Santa Ana, CA 92680 US
Second Address: 2442 Michelle Dr., Tustin, CA 92780
(714) 832-2950, *Fax:* (714) 665-2191
www.tbn.org
License: Santa Ana, Orange County, CA held by Trinity Broadcasting Network.
Group Owner: Trinity Broadcasting Network; (acq 8-2-74; $1,266,400;; *Washington Law Firm:* Joseph E. Dunne III
Nat'l Network: TRINITY BROADCA
Phyllis Smith, General Manager

KTLA *Digital Channel:* 31 *Virtual Channel:* 5; 44.7 kw vis, 6.7 kw aur; 6,176t/473g; N34 13 36 W118 03 56; *Population Served:* 14,443,000
5800 Sunset Blvd., Los Angeles, CA 90028
(323) 460-5500, *Fax:* (323) 460-5405
www.ktla.com
License: Los Angeles, Los Angeles County, CA held by KTLA, Inc.
Group Owner: Tribune Broadcasting Co.; (acq 12-20-2007; grpsl); *Washington Law Firm:* Dow Lohnes PLLC
Nat'l Network: CW *Nat'l Reps:* TeleRep *Wire Services:* Reuters; NWS (National Weather Service)
Hours of Local News Weekly: News progmg 43 hrs wkly
Mike Weiner, CFO
Don Corsini, President
Chris Reilly, Operations Dir
John Moczulski, Station Manager
Troy Arce, General Sales Mgr
Gretchen Dible, Programming Director
Steve Poitras, Promotions Manager
Jason Ball, NewsDirector
Dave Cox, Chief Engineer
Vickie Prothro, Community Affairs

KTTV *Digital Channel:* 11 *Virtual Channel:* 11; 115 kw; 2963 ft.; N34 13 29 W118 3 48
5151 Wisconsin Ave., Washington, DC 20016 US
(310) 584-2000, *Fax:* (310) 584-2024
www.myfoxla.com
License: Los Angeles, Los Angeles County, CA held by Fox Television Stations Inc.
Group Owner: Fox Television Stations Inc.; (acq 11-14-86; grpsl).
Nat'l Network: FOX
Hours of Local News Weekly: News progmg 25 hrs wkly
Kevin Hale, General Manager

***KVCR-DT** *Digital Channel:* 26; 1,318 kw vis, 131.8 kw aur; 3,166t/215g; N30 57 57 W117 17 05; *Population Served:* 17,000,000
701 S. Mt. Vernon Ave., San Bernardino, CA 92410
(909) 384-4444, *Fax:* (909) 885-2116
www.kvcr.org
info@kvcr.org
License: San Bernardino, San Bernardino County, CA held by San Bernardino Community College District
Nat'l Network: PBS
Larry Ciecalone, General Manager
Kenn Couch, Station Manager
Don Leiffer, Programming Director
Lillian Vasquez, Promotions Manager
Thomas Guptill, Chief Engineer
Al Gondos, Producer/Director
Patty Littlejohn, Traffic Manager

KVEA *Digital Channel:* 39 *Virtual Channel:* 52; 1000 kw; 2989 ft.; N34 12 48 W118 3 41
2290 West 8th Avenue, Hialeah, FL 33010 US
(818) 260-5700, *Fax:* (818) 260-5222
www.telemundo52.com
angelnews@ibsys.com
License: Corona, Riverside County, CA held by NBC Telemundo License Co.
Group Owner: Telemundo Television Stations; (acq 4-12-2002; grpsl).
Nat'l Network: TELEMUNDO
Foreign Language Programming
Jose Valle, President

KVMD *Digital Channel:* 23 *Virtual Channel:* 31; 150 kw; 2572 ft.; N34 2 17 W116 48 47
22720 S.E. 410 Street, Enumclaw, WA 98022 US
(949) 365-5710, *Fax:* (949) 365-5709
www.kumd-tv.com
License: Twentynine Palms, San Bernardino County, CA held by KVMD Licensee Co. LLC
Nat'l Network: IND
Larry Peterson, General Manager
Ken Brown, Chief Engineer
Sherrie Karr, Public Service Director

KVME-TV *Digital Channel:* 20 *Virtual Channel:* 20; 4.2 kw vis; ant 3,031t/30g; N37 24 43 W118 11 06
Cocola Broadcasting Companies, 706 W. Herndon Ave., Fresno, CA 93650
(559) 435-7000, *Fax:* (559) 435-3201
www.cocolatv.com
License: Bishop, Inyo County, CA held by Bellagio Broadcasting LLC.
Group Owner: Cocola Broadcasting Companies LLC
Lawrence Rogow, General Manager

KWHY-TV *Digital Channel:* 42 *Virtual Channel:* 22; 486 kw; 892 meters; N34 13 36 W118 03 59; *Population Served:* 5,000,000
1201 West 5th Street, 9th Floor, Los Angeles, CA 90024
(818) 260-5822, *Fax:* (818) 260-5805
www.canal22.tv
License: Los Angeles, Los Angeles County, CA held by NBC Telemundo License Co.
Group Owner: Telemundo Television Stations; (acq 4-12-2002; grpsl); *Washington Law Firm:* Wiley Rein LLP
Nat'l Network: MundoFox *Wire Services:* Reuters
Foreign Language Programming; Size of News Staff: 6; *Hours of Local News Weekly:* news progmg 12 hrs wkly
Otto Padron, General Manager

KXLA *Digital Channel:* 51 *Virtual Channel:* 44; 1000 kw; 3074 ft.; N34 13 35.3 W118 3 57.7
15304 Sunset Boulevard, Suite 204, Pacific Palisades, CA 90272 US
(310) 478-0055, *Fax:* (310) 478-8070
www.kxlatv.com
License: Rancho Palos Verdes, Los Angeles County, CA held by Rancho Palos Verdes Broadcasters Inc
Nat'l Network: IND
Ron Ulloa, President
Ken Brown, Chief Engineer

Monterey-Salinas, CA (DMA 124)

KCBA *Digital Channel:* 13 *Virtual Channel:* 35; 19.75 kw; 2362 ft.; N36 45 22 W121 30 6
1333 New Hampshire, N.W., Suite 100, Washington, DC 20036 US
(831) 422-3500, *Fax:* (831) 754-1120
www.kcba.com
kimmeyenberg@kionrightnow.com
License: Salinas, Monterey County, CA held by Seal Rock Broadcasters LLC

(acq 1-5-00; $11 million); *Washington Law Firm:* Rubin, Winston, Diercks, Harris & Cooke
Nat'l Network: FOX
Hours of Local News Weekly: News progmg 10 hrs wkly
Paul Dughie, General Manager
Greta Richards, General Sales Mgr
Kim Meyenberg, Programming Director
Raymond Ochs, Promotions Manager
Traciann Zeravica, News Director
Adam Perez, Engineering Dir
Monica Escobedo, Traffic Manager

KION-TV *Digital Channel:* 32 *Virtual Channel:* 46; 46 kw; 2487 ft.; N36 32 5 W121 37 14
70 East Lancaster Avenue, Frazer, PA 19355 US
(831) 784-1702/(831) 422-3500, *Fax:* (831) 784-6395
www.kion46.com
License: Monterey, Monterey County, CA held by Cowles California Media Co.
Group Owner: Cowles California Media Co.; (acq 5-7-2008; $41 million with KCOY-TV Santa Maria); *Washington Law Firm:* Skadden, Arps, Slate, Meagher & Flom LLP
Nat'l Network: CBS *Wire Services:* UPI
Size of News Staff: 25; *Hours of Local News Weekly:* news progmg 8 hrs wkly
Mark Faylor, Operations Dir
Lonlee, Station Manager

***KQET** *Digital Channel:* 25; 52.5 kw vis; ant 2,198t; N36 45 23 W121 30 05
Mailing Address: c/o KQED, 2601 Mariposa St., San Francisco, CA 93905
Second Address: 50 W. San Fernando St., Ste. 110, San Jose, CA 95113-2415
(415) 864-2000, *Fax:* (415) 553-2333
www.kqed.org
rdana@kqed.org
License: Watsonville, Santa Cruz County, CA held by KQED Inc.
Nat'l Network: PBS
John Boland, CEO/COO

KSBW *Digital Channel:* 8 *Virtual Channel:* 8; 20.6 kw; 2493 ft.; N36 45 23 W121 30 5
959 Eighth Avenue, New York, NY 10019 US
(831) 758-8888, *Fax:* (831) 424-3750
www.theksbwchannel.com
License: Salinas, Monterey County, CA held by Hearst-Argyle Stations Inc.
Group Owner: Hearst-Argyle Television Inc.; (acq 6-1-98).; *Washington Law Firm:* Brooks, Pierce, McLendon, Humphrey & Leonard
Nat'l Network: NBC *Nat'l Reps:* Eagle Television Sales
Size of News Staff: 31; *Hours of Local News Weekly:* news progmg 31 hrs wkly
Joseph Heston, President
Jose Camacho, Operations Dir
Wendy Hillan, General Sales Mgr
Karen Pren, Programming Director
Bill Mushrush, Promotions Manager
Britt Govea, Marketing Manager

KSMS-TV *Digital Channel:* 31 *Virtual Channel:* 67; 1000 kw; 2299 ft.; N36 45 23 W121 30 5
11900 Olympic Boulevard, Suite 590, Los Angeles, CA 90064 US
(831) 373-6767, *Fax:* (831) 373-6700
www.entravision.com
License: Monterey, Monterey County, CA held by Entravision Holdings L.L.C.
Group Owner: Entravision Communications Corp.; (acq 4-25-97)
Nat'l Network: UNIVISION
Foreign Language Programming
Philip Wilkinson, President
Aaron Scoby, General Manager
Jeanie Harrison, General Sales Mgr

Palm Springs, CA (DMA 142)

KESQ-TV *Digital Channel:* 42 *Virtual Channel:* 42; 42 kw; 745 ft.; N33 51 58 W116 26 8
42-650 Malanie Place, Palm Desert, CA 92211 US
(760) 773-0342, *Fax:* (760) 773-5107
www.kesq.com
micheal.stutz@kesq.com
License: Palm Springs, Riverside County, CA held by Gulf-California Broadcast Co.
Group Owner: News-Press & Gazette Co.; (acq 4-24-96; $19.4 million); *Washington Law Firm:* Smithwick & Belendiuk
Nat'l Network: ABC; CW *Nat'l Reps:* Continental Television Sales *Wire Services:* News 1; AP
Size of News Staff: 40; *Hours of Local News Weekly:* news progmg 17 hrs wkly
Mike O'Malley, CFO
Bob Allen, President
Todd Graham, Operations Dir
Mike Stutz, General Sales Mgr
Ken Spalding, Programming Director
Bob Smith, News Director

KMIR-TV *Digital Channel:* 46 *Virtual Channel:* 36; 120 kw; 697 ft.; N33 52 0 W116 25 59
72-920 Parkview Drive, Palm Desert, CA 92260 US
(760) 568-3636/(760) 340-1623, *Fax:* (760) 568-1176
www.kmir6.com
news@kmir6.com
License: Palm Springs, Riverside County, CA held by Journal Broadcast Corp.
Group Owner: Journal Communications Inc.; (acq 6-11-99; $28.1 million); *Washington Law Firm:* Koteen & Naftalin
Nat'l Network: NBC
Size of News Staff: 30; *Hours of Local News Weekly:* news progmg 27 hrs wkly
Lyle Schulze, Operations Dir
Tony Billett, General Sales Mgr
Mayra Mancilla, Programming Director
Russ Kilgore, News Director
Tim Balint, Chief Engineer
Steve Schill, News Commentator
Frank Keller, Operations Manager
ScottJohnson, Regional Sales Manager

Sacramento-Stockton-Modesto, CA (DMA 20)

***KBSV** *Digital Channel:* 15 *Virtual Channel:* 23; 0.421 kw; 1888 ft.; N37 30 28 W121 22 20.2; *Not on Air/Target Date:* unknown
P.O. Box 4116, Modesto, CA 95352 US
(209) 538-9801, *Fax:* (209) 538-2795
www.betnahrain.org/kbsv
kssv@aol.com
License: Ceres, Stanislaus County, CA held by Bet-Nahrain
Nat'l Network: ETV
Dr. Sargon Dadesho, President
Shemiran Daniel, Operations Dir

KCRA-TV *Digital Channel:* 35 *Virtual Channel:* 3; 1000 kw; 1900 ft.; N38 15 54 W121 29 24
888 Seventh Avenue, New York, NY 10106 US
(916) 446-3333, *Fax:* (916) 441-4050 (news)
www.thekcrachannel.com
License: Sacramento, Sacramento County, CA held by Hearst-Argyle Stations Inc.
Group Owner: Hearst-Argyle Television Inc.; (acq 2-18-99).; *Washington Law Firm:* Koteen & Naftalin
Nat'l Network: NBC *Nat'l Reps:* Petry Television Inc.
Hours of Local News Weekly: News progmg 55 hrs wkly
Elliott Troshinsky, General Manager
Shirley Sullivan, Programming Director

KMAX-TV *Digital Channel:* 21; 5,000 kw vis, 500 kw aur; ant 1,830t/2,000g; N38 15 52 W121 29 22; *Population Served:* 254,413
2713 KOVR Dr., West Sacramento, CA 20005
(916) 374-1313, *Fax:* (916) 374-1304
www.cw31.com
License: Sacramento, Sacramento County, CA held by Sacramento Television Stations Inc.
Group Owner: CBS Television Stations Group; (acq 3-24-98; $100 million)
Nat'l Network: CW
Foreign Language Programming
Kevin Walsh, Operations Dir
Gavin Joe, General Sales Mgr
Rita Gazitano, Programming Director
Drew Fowler, Promotions Manager
Brent Baader, News Director
Bob Hess, Chief Engineer
Diane Mielenz, Traffic Manager

KOVR *Digital Channel:* 25 *Virtual Channel:* 13; 1000 kw; 1946 ft.; N38 14 24 W121 30 3
10706 Beaver Dam Road, Cockeysville, MD 21030 US
(916) 374-1313, *Fax:* (916) 374-1462
www.cbs13.com
License: Stockton, San Joaquin County, CA held by Sacramento Television Stations Inc.
Group Owner: CBS Television Stations Group; (acq 4-29-2005; $285 million)
Nat'l Network: CBS
Size of News Staff: 120; *Hours of Local News Weekly:* news progmg 21 hrs wkly
Kevin Walsh, General Manager
Rita Gazitano, Programming Director
Bob Hess, Chief Engineer
Denise Dituri, Traffic Manager

KQCA *Digital Channel:* 46 *Virtual Channel:* 58; 600 kw; 1903 ft.; N38 15 54 W121 29 24
58 Television Circle, Sacramento, CA 95814 US
(916) 446-3333, *Fax:* (916) 554-4658
www.my58.com
License: Stockton, San Joaquin County, CA held by Hearst-Argyle Stations Inc.
Group Owner: Hearst-Argyle Television Inc.; (acq 1-24-2000; less than $1 million); *Washington Law Firm:* Skadden, Arps, Slate, Meagher & Flom
Nat'l Network: MNT
Elliot Troshinsky, General Manager
Jerry Brehm, General Sales Mgr
Lori Kesler, Programming Director
Jim Caselli, Promotions Manager
Dan Weiser, News Director
Stefan Hadl, Engineering Dir
Patrick Donnelly, General SalesManager
Gene Robinson, Promotions Manager

KSPX-TV *Digital Channel:* 48; 5,000 kw vis, 500 kw aur; ant 1,296t/1,300g; N38 37 49 W120 51 20
3352 Mather Field Rd., Rancho Cordova, CA 95670
(916) 368-2929, *Fax:* (916) 368-0225
License: Sacramento, Sacramento County, CA held by Paxson Sacramento License Inc.
Group Owner: ION Media Networks Inc.; (acq 5-25-2000; $17.725 million); *Washington Law Firm:* Wiley, Rein & Fielding
Nat'l Network: ION Television
Size of News Staff: 75; *Hours of Local News Weekly:* news progmg 7 hrs wkly
Lee Roberts, Operations Dir
Jim Eaton, General Sales Mgr
Frank Ernandes, Engineering Dir

KTXL *Digital Channel:* 40 *Virtual Channel:* 40; 1000 kw; 1972 ft.; N38 16 18 W121 30 18
4655 Fruitridge Road, Sacramento, CA 95820 US
(916) 454-4422, *Fax:* (916) 739-1079
www.fox40.com
License: Sacramento, Sacramento County, CA held by Channel 40 Inc.
Group Owner: Tribune Broadcasting Co.; (acq 12-20-2007; grpsl); *Washington Law Firm:* Sidley Austin LLP
Nat'l Network: FOX *Nat'l Reps:* TeleRep
Hours of Local News Weekly: News progmg 29.5 hrs wkly
Bob Ramsey, Operations Dir
Mike Armstrong, General Sales Mgr
Natalie Grant, Programming Director
Brandon Mercer, News Director
Jack Davis, Chief Engineer
Phil Melchers, National Sales Manager
Lori Misika, National SalesManager
Bill Gee, Operations Manager
Candace Shropshire, Research Director

KUVS-DT *Digital Channel:* 18; 5,000 kw vis, 560 kw aur; 1,877t/250g; N38 14 20 W121 28 52; *Population Served:* 3,480,000
Mailing Address: 1710 Arden Way, Sacramento, CA 95815
Second Address: 1150 9th St., Suite 1505, Modesto, CA 95354
(916) 927-1900, *Fax:* (916) 614-1902
www.univision.com
License: Modesto, Stanislaus County, CA held by KUVS License Partnership G.P.
Group Owner: Univision Communications Inc.; (acq 3-6-97; $40 million); *Washington Law Firm:* Shaw Pittman
Nat'l Network: Univision (Spanish)
Foreign Language Programming; Size of News Staff: 30; *Hours of Local News Weekly:* news progmg 12 hrs wkly
Steve Stuck, General Manager

***KVIE** *Digital Channel:* 9 *Virtual Channel:* 6; 33 kw; 1958 ft.; N38 16 18 W121 30 18
P.O. Box 6, Sacramento, CA 95801 US
(916) 929-5843, *Fax:* (916) 929-7215
www.kvie.org
publicinfo@kvie.org
License: Sacramento, Sacramento County, CA held by KVIE Inc
Washington Law Firm: Dow, Lohnes & Albertson
Nat'l Network: PBS
David Hosley, President
David Lowe, General Manager
Jan Tilmon, Programming Director
Michael Wall, Chief Engineer

KXTV *Digital Channel:* 10 *Virtual Channel:* 10; 28.6 kw; 2008 ft.; N38 14 24 W121 30 3
1100 Wilson Boulevard, Arlington, VA 22234 US
(916) 441-2345, *Fax:* (916) 321-3384
www.news10.net
License: Sacramento, Sacramento County, CA held by KXTV Inc.
Group Owner: Gannett Broadcasting; (acq 1999; swap with KVUE(TV) Austin, TX); *Washington Law Firm:* Wiley, Rein & Fielding
Nat'l Network: ABC *Nat'l Reps:* Blair Television
Russell Postell, President
Kelly Bradley, General Sales Mgr
Ron Comings, News Director
Rod Robinson, Chief Engineer
Dustin Snyder, National Sales Manager

San Diego, CA (DMA 28)

KFMB-TV *Digital Channel:* 8; 316 kw vis, 63.2 kw aur; ant 745t/249g; N32 50 17 W117 14 57; *Population Served:* 2,896,000
7677 Engineer Rd., San Diego, CA 92186
(858) 571-8888, *Fax:* (858) 495-9363
www.cbs8.com
License: San Diego, San Diego County, CA held by Midwest Television Inc
(acq 4-17-2007; with KFMB-AM-FM San Diego); *Ownership:* Midwest Television Inc; *Washington Law Firm:* Dow Lohnes
Nat'l Network: CBS; Me-TV 8.2 *Nat'l Reps:* TeleRep *Wire Services:* UPI
Size of News Staff: 85; *Hours of Local News Weekly:* 24
Elisabeth Kimmel, Owner & President
Pat Nevin, Vice President & General Manager
Adam Weyne, General Sales Mgr
Elyse Sensabaugh, Programming Director
Donna Dube, Promotions Manager
Dean Elwood, News Director
Rich Lochman,Engineering Dir
Rich Lochman, Chief Engineer
Jan Gross, Local Sales Manager
Thelma Presichi, Traffic Manager

KGTV *Digital Channel:* 10 *Virtual Channel:* 10; 20.7 kw; 745 ft.; N32 50 20 W117 14 56
P.O. Box 85347, San Diego, CA 92186 US
(619) 237-1010, *Fax:* (619) 262-1302
www.10news.com
linda.blake@10news.com
License: San Diego, San Diego County, CA held by McGraw-Hill Broadcasting Co.
Group Owner: McGraw-Hill Broadcasting Co.; (acq 6-1-72; grpsl;; *Washington Law Firm:* DowLohnes, PLLC
Nat'l Network: ABC *Nat'l Reps:* Harrington, Righter & Parsons
Size of News Staff: 65; *Hours of Local News Weekly:* news progmg 35 hrs wkly
Mike Biltucci, Operations Dir
Jeffrey Block, General Manager
Ken Rycyzn, General Sales Mgr
Jason Maloney, Promotions Manager
John Jorgenson, Closed Caption Supervisor
Andrew Lombard, Chief Engineer
Paul Kaderabek, BusinessManager
Joel Davis, News Director

KNSD *Digital Channel:* 40 *Virtual Channel:* 39; 370 kw; 1857 ft.; N32 41 48 W116 56 6
C/O Nbc, Inc., 11th Flr., 1299 Pennsylvania Ave., N.W., Washington, DC 20004 US
(619) 231-3939, *Fax:* (619) 578-0225
www.nbcsandiego.com
feedback@nbcsandiego.com
License: San Diego, San Diego County, CA held by Station Venture Operations LP.
Group Owner: NBC Owned Television Stations; (acq 3-2-98; with KXAS-TV Fort Worth, TX).; *Washington Law Firm:* Pepper & Corazzini
Nat'l Network: NBC
Foreign Language Programming
Jackie Bradford, President
Randy Mickler, Operations Dir

***KPBS** *Digital Channel:* 30 *Virtual Channel:* 15; 350 kw; 1862 ft.; N32 41 53 W116 56 3
5200 Campanile Drive, San Diego, CA 92182 US
(619) 594-1515, *Fax:* (619) 594-3812
www.kpbs.org
letters@kpbs.org
License: San Diego, San Diego County, CA held by Board of Trustees, California State University for San Diego State University
Nat'l Network: PUBLIC BROADCAS *Wire Services:* AP
Doug Myrland, General Manager
Keith York, Programming Director
Nancy Worlie, Promotions Manager
John Decker, News Director
Tammy Carpowich, Director of New Media
Anna Bunge, Traffic Manager

KSWB-TV *Digital Channel:* 19 *Virtual Channel:* 69; 4,790 kw vis, 479 kw aur; 1,950t/151g; N32 41 47 W116 56 07; *Population Served:* 943,500
7191 Engineer Rd., San Diego, CA 91911
(858) 492-9269, *Fax:* (858) 268-0401
www.fox5sandiego.com
License: San Diego, San Diego County, CA held by KSWB Inc.
Group Owner: Tribune Broadcasting Co.; (acq 12-20-2007; grpsl); *Washington Law Firm:* Dow Lohnes PLLC
Nat'l Network: Fox *Nat'l Reps:* TeleRep
Hours of Local News Weekly: News progmg 44.5 hrs wkly
Ray Schonbak, Operations Dir
Ray Schonbak, General Manager
Scott Heath, General Sales Mgr
Will Givens, Promotions Manager
Rich Goldner, News Director
Kyle Majors, Technology Director

KUSI-TV *Digital Channel:* 18 *Virtual Channel:* 51; 355 kw; 1890 ft.; N32 41 50 W116 56 4
Mailing Address: 4575 Viewridge Avenue, San Diego, CA 92123 US
Second Address: 4575 Viewridge Ave., San Diego, CA 92123
(858) 571-5151, *Fax:* (858) 505-5050
www.kusi.com
License: San Diego, San Diego County, CA held by Channel 51 of San Diego Inc.
Group Owner: McKinnon Broadcasting Co.; (acq 6-29-90;; *Washington Law Firm:* Cohn & Marks
Nat'l Network: IND
Size of News Staff: 70; *Hours of Local News Weekly:* news progmg 51 hrs wkly
Michael D. McKinnon, CEO
Michael Dean McKinnon, President
Steve Cohen, News Director
Richard Large, Chief Engineer

XETV-DT *Digital Channel:* 23; 100 kw vis, 50 kw aur; 1,000t/550g; *Population Served:* 920,570
8253 Ronson Rd., San Diego, CA 92111
(858) 279-6666, *Fax:* (858) 268-9388
www.sandiego6.com
License: Tijuana, MX held by Radio-Television SA
Washington Law Firm: Leventhal, Senter & Lerman
Nat'l Network: CW
Hours of Local News Weekly: News progmg 20 hrs wkly
Rodrigo Salazar, CFO
Richard Jones, Operations Dir
Chuck Dunning, General Sales Mgr
Judy Albrecht, Promotions Manager
Harry Melkerson, National Sales Manager
Bob Anderson, Operations Director
Lynda DiLorenzo, Regional SalesManager
Scott Dillon, Regional Sales Manager

XEWT-DT *Digital Channel:* 32; 325 kw vis, 32.5 kw aur; 1,000t/200g; N32 30 06 W117 02 23; *Population Served:* 2,200,000
Mailing Address: Box 434537, San Diego, CA 92143
Second Address: 637 Third Ave., Suite B, Chulavista, CA 91910
(800) TELEV 12,(619) 585-9398, *Fax:* (619) 585-9463
www.televisa.com
License: Tijuana, MX held by Televisora de Calimex, SA
Washington Law Firm: Leventhal, Senter & Lerman
Foreign Language Programming; Size of News Staff: 50; *Hours of Local News Weekly:* news progmg 11 hrs wkly
Lourdes Numez, Operations Dir
Ricardo Azcarraga, General Manager

San Francisco-Oakland-San Jose (DMA 6)

KBCW *Digital Channel:* 45 *Virtual Channel:* 44; 1000 kw; 1609 ft.; N37 45 19 W122 27 6
650 California Street, 7th Floor, San Francisco, CA 94108 US
(415) 765-8144, *Fax:* (415) 765-8844
www.cwbayarea.com
feedback@kbcwtv.com
License: San Francisco, San Francisco County, CA held by San Francisco Television Station KBCW Inc.
Group Owner: CBS Television Stations Group; (acq 11-6-2001; swap with WDCA(TV) Washington, DC; and KTXH(TV) Houston, TX).; *Washington Law Firm:* Hogan & Hartson
Nat'l Network: THE CW NETWORK
Ron Longinotti, President
Arturo Riera, General Sales Mgr
Tom Spitz, Programming Director
Akilal Bolden-Monifa, Promotions Manager

KCNS *Digital Channel:* 39 *Virtual Channel:* 38; 1000 kw; 1679 ft.; N37 45 19 W122 27 6
102 Woodmont Boulevard, Suite 200-228, Nashville, TN 37205 US
(415) 863-3800, *Fax:* (415) 863-3998
www.kcnstv.com
kcnstv@pacbell.net
License: San Francisco, San Francisco County, CA held by MTB San Francisco Licensee LLC.
Group Owner: Multicultural Capital Trust; (acq 2-2-2009)
Nat'l Network: IND
Luis Mendoza, Operations Dir
Andrea Yamazaki, General Manager
Alan Ng, Station Manager

***KCSM-TV** *Digital Channel:* 43 *Virtual Channel:* 60; 500 kw; 1678 ft.; N37 45 19 W122 27 6
1700 West Hillsdale Blvd, San Mateo, CA 94402 US
(650) 574-6586, *Fax:* (650) 524-6975
www.kcsm.org
License: San Mateo, San Mateo County, CA held by San Mateo County Community College District
Washington Law Firm: Tierney & Swift
Nat'l Network: PBS
Foreign Language Programming
Alisa Clancy, Operations Dir
Marilyn Lawrence, General Manager
Shelly Rogers, General Sales Mgr
Michelle Muller, Engineering Dir

KDTV-DT *Digital Channel:* 51; 3,980 kw vis, 398 kw aur; 2,509t/439g; N37 29 57 W121 52 16; *Population Served:* 1,023,300
50 Fremont Street, 41st Floor, San Francisco, CA 94105
(415) 538-8000, *Fax:* (415) 538-8053
www.univison.com
kdtvpublicfile@univision.com
License: San Francisco, San Francisco County, CA held by KDTV L.P., GP
Group Owner: Univision Communications Inc.; *Washington Law Firm:* Fisher, Wayland, Cooper, Leader & Zaragoza
Nat'l Network: Univision (Spanish)
Foreign Language Programming; Size of News Staff: 15; *Hours of Local News Weekly:* news progmg 5 hrs wkly
Jim VanTassell, Operations Dir
Marcela Medina, General Manager
Ernie Rizzuti, General Sales Mgr
Carolina Echeverria, Public Affairs Manager
Sandra Thomas, News Director
Mike Roberts, Chief Engineer
Maria Rodriguez, TrafficManager

KEMO-TV *Digital Channel:* 32; 302 kw vis, 60.4 kw aur; ant 3,080t/172g; N38 40 10 W122 37 52; *Population Served:* 1,500,000
533 Mendocino Avenue, Santa Rosa, CA 20036
(707) 526-5050, *Fax:* (707) 526-7429
www.aztecaamericasf.com
License: Santa Rosa, Sonoma County, CA held by High Plains Broadcasting License Co. LLC.
Group Owner: High Plains Broadcasting Inc.; (acq 2-20-2009; $1 million); *Washington Law Firm:* Pillsbury Winthrop Shaw Pittman LLP
Nat'l Network: Azteca America
Hours of Local News Weekly: 0
Richard Starkey, Operations Dir
John Burgess, General Manager
Corinne Flushman, General Sales Mgr
Elizabeth Quinn, News Director

KFSF-DT *Digital Channel:* 34; 3,470 kw vis, 346 kw aur; ant 1,528t/797g; N37 45 19 W122 27 16; *Population Served:* 5,500,000
50 Fremont St., 41st Fl., San Francisco, CA 94105
(415) 538-6466, *Fax:* (415) 538-8053
License: Vallejo, Solano County, CA held by Telefutura San Francisco, LLC
Group Owner: Univision Communications Inc.; (acq 12-18-2001; $39 million)
Nat'l Network: TeleFutura (Spanish)
Foreign Language Programming
Jim VanTassell, Operations Dir
Marcela Medina, General Manager

Ernie Rizzuti, General Sales Mgr
Maria Rodriguez, Programming Director
Sandra Thomas, News Director
Mike Roberts, Chief Engineer

KGO-TV *Digital Channel:* 7 *Virtual Channel:* 7; 23.8 kw; 1703 ft.; N37 45 19 W122 27 6
900 Front Street, San Francisco, CA 94111 US
(415) 954-7777, *Fax:* (415) 956-6402
www.abc7news.com
License: San Francisco, San Francisco County, CA held by KGO-TV Inc.
Group Owner: ABC Inc.; (acq 6-27-86; grpsl;
Nat'l Network: ABC
Valari Staab, General Manager
Kevin Keeshan, News Director
Stephanie Adrouny, Assistant News Director

KICU-TV *Digital Channel:* 36 *Virtual Channel:* 36; 550 kw; 2251 ft.; N37 29 17 W121 51 59
2102 Commerce Dr, San Jose, CA 95131 US
(408) 953-3636
www.kicu.com
License: San Jose, Santa Clara County, CA held by KTVU Partnership.
Group Owner: Cox Media Group; (acq 2-18-00; $130 million);
Washington Law Firm: Leventhal, Senter & Lerman
Nat'l Network: IND
Size of News Staff: 3; *Hours of Local News Weekly:* news progmg .5 hr wkly
Tom Raponi, General Manager
Robert Martinez, General Sales Mgr
Carolyn Chang, Programming Director
Don Thompson, Engineering Dir
Chuck Pracna, Chief Engineer

KKPX-TV ; 3,060 kw vis, 1,179 kw aur; 2,667t/223g; N37 06 41 W121 50 30
660 Price Avenue, Suite B, San Francisco, CA 94111
(415) 276-1400, *Fax:* (415) 276-1401
www.pax.tv
License: San Jose, Santa Clara County, CA held by Paxson San Jose License Inc.
Group Owner: ION Media Networks Inc.; (acq 3-22-95; $5 million;; *Washington Law Firm:* Joseph E. Dunne III
Nat'l Network: ION Television
William Watson, Vice President
Carol Denham, General Manager
Mark Faris, Programming Director
Bob Getsla, Chief Engineer

***KMTP-TV** *Digital Channel:* 33 *Virtual Channel:* 32; 480 kw; 1696 ft.; N37 45 19 W122 27 6
211 Brannan Street, San Francisco, CA 94107 US
(415) 777-3232, *Fax:* (415) 552-3209
www.kmtp.org
kmtpgm@pacbell.net
License: San Francisco, San Francisco County, CA held by Minority Television Project
Nat'l Network: ETV
Booker Wade Jr., General Manager
Arlene Stevens, Programming Director

KNTV *Digital Channel:* 12 *Virtual Channel:* 11; 103.1 kw; 1236 ft.; N37 41 7 W122 26 1
C/O Granite Broadcasting, 767 Third Ave, 34th Flr., New York, NY 10017 US
(408) 432-6221, *Fax:* (408) 432-4425
www.nbcbayarea.com
License: San Jose, Santa Clara County, CA held by NBC Telemundo License Co.
Group Owner: NBC Owned Television Stations; (acq 4-30-2002; $230 million); *Washington Law Firm:* Akin, Gump, Strauss, Hauer & Feld
Nat'l Network: NBC *Nat'l Reps:* NBC TV Stations Sales
Hours of Local News Weekly: News progmg 20 hrs wkly
Rich Cerussi, President
Jim Monroe, Promotions Manager
Susan Sullivan, News Director

KOFY-TV *Digital Channel:* 19 *Virtual Channel:* 20; 3,470 kw vis, 347 kw aur; ant 1,548t/820g; N37 45 19 W122 27 06;
Population Served: 1,200,000
2500 Marin St., San Francisco, CA 21030
(415) 821-2020, *Fax:* (415) 821-1518
kofytv.com
License: San Francisco, San Francisco County, CA held by KBWB License Inc.
Group Owner: Granite Broadcasting Corp.; (acq 7-20-98; $173.75 million)
Nat'l Reps: Katz

Craig Coane, President
Chris Flynn, General Sales Mgr
Warren Holybee, Chief Engineer

KPIX-TV *Digital Channel:* 29 *Virtual Channel:* 5; 1000 kw; 1679 ft.; N37 45 19 W122 27 6
600 New Hampshire Ave NW, Suite 1200, Washington, DC 20037 US
(415) 362-5550, *Fax:* (415) 765-8844
www.cbs5.com
newsdesk@kpix.com
License: San Francisco, San Francisco County, CA held by CBS Broadcasting Inc.
Group Owner: CBS Television Stations Group; (acq 5—4-2000; grpsl).; *Washington Law Firm:* Wilkes, Artis, Hedrick & Lane
Nat'l Network: CBS *Nat'l Reps:* CBS TV Stations National Sales
Wire Services: Reuters
Size of News Staff: 87; *Hours of Local News Weekly:* news progmg 20 hrs wkly
Ron Longinotti, President
Rosemary Roach, Operations Dir
Tom Spitz, Programming Director
Dee Joyce, Promotions Manager
Dan Rosenheim, News Director
Mike Englehaupt, Chief Engineer
Akilal Bolden-Monifa, Communications Director

***KQED** *Digital Channel:* 30 *Virtual Channel:* 9; 710 kw; 1679 ft.; N37 45 19 W122 27 6
2601 Mariposa Street, San Franciso, CA 94110 US
(415) 864-2000, *Fax:* (415) 553-2241
www.kqed.org
(name)@kqed.org
License: San Francisco, San Francisco County, CA held by Northern California Public Broadcasting Inc
Washington Law Firm: Arnold & Porter LLP
Nat'l Network: PBS
Size of News Staff: 8; *Hours of Local News Weekly:* news progmg 1/2 hr wkly
Jeff Clarke, CEO
Jo-Anne Wallace, General Manager
Traci Eckels, General Sales Mgr
Linda O'Bryon, Programming Director
Donald Derheim, VP, Sales
Michael Isip, TV Content Vice President

***KQEH** *Digital Channel:* 50; 661 kw vis, 132 kw aur; 1,922t/137g; N37 29 07 W121 51 57; *Population Served:* 453,000
Mailing Address: 2601 Mariposa St., San Francisco, CA 94110
Second Address: 50 W San Fernando St., Ste. 110, San Jose, CA 95113-2415
(415) 864-2000, *Fax:* (415) 553-2333
www.kqed.org
rdana@kqed.org
License: San Jose, Santa Clara County, CA held by KQED Inc.
Nat'l Network: PBS
John Boland, CEO/COO

KQSL *Digital Channel:* 15 *Virtual Channel:* 8; 225 kw vis, 22.5 kw aur; ant 2,446t/186g; N39 41 38 W123 34 43
500 S. Chinowth Rd., Visalia, CA 93277
(707) 964-8888, *Fax:* (707) 964-8150
License: Fort Bragg, Mendocino County, CA held by Concord License LLC.
Group Owner: Pappas Telecasting Companies; (acq 6-12-97; $1.75 million)
Nat'l Reps: Blair Television
Ricardo Pineda, General Manager

***KRCB** *Digital Channel:* 23 *Virtual Channel:* 22; 105 kw; 2068 ft.; N38 20 54.7 W122 34 37.5
5850 Labath Ave., Rohnert Park, CA 94928 US
(707) 584-2000, *Fax:* (707) 585-1363
www.krcb.org
viewer@krcb.org
License: Cotati, Sonoma County, CA held by Rural California Broadcasting Corp
Nat'l Network: PBS
Foreign Language Programming; Size of News Staff: 1
Nancy Dobbs, CEO
Larry Stratton, COO

KRON-TV *Digital Channel:* 38 *Virtual Channel:* 4; 1000 kw; 1679 ft.; N37 45 19 W122 27 6
1001 Van Ness Avenue, San Francisco, CA 94109 US
(415) 441-4444, *Fax:* (415) 561-8142
www.kron.com
4listens@kron4.com
License: San Francisco, San Francisco County, CA held by Young Broadcasting of San Francisco Inc.
Group Owner: Young Broadcasting Inc.; (acq 6-26-2000; $823 million); *Washington Law Firm:* Brooks, Pierce
Nat'l Network: MNT *Nat'l Reps:* Adam Young *Wire Services:* AP
Hours of Local News Weekly: News progmg 53 hrs wkly
Brian Greif, General Manager
Rich DiPilla, General Sales Mgr
Pat Patton, Programming Director
Kevin Adler, Promotions Manager
Aaron Pero, News Director
Craig Porter, Chief Engineer
Mark Sowinski, Sales Manager
Jim Swanson,Local Programming Director
Lori Gravino, Local Sales Manager
Kathy King, Traffic Manager

KSTS *Digital Channel:* 49 *Virtual Channel:* 48; 257 kw; 2257 ft.; N37 29 57 W121 52 16
2290 West 8th Avenue, Hialeah, FL 33010 US
(408) 435-8848 / (408) 944-4848, *Fax:* (408) 432-4423
www.ksts.com
License: San Jose, Santa Clara County, CA held by NBC Telemundo License Co.
Group Owner: Telemundo Television Stations; (acq 4-12-2002; grpsl).; *Washington Law Firm:* Hogan & Hartson
Nat'l Network: TELEMUNDO *Wire Services:* Reuters; UPI
Foreign Language Programming; Size of News Staff: 10; *Hours of Local News Weekly:* news progmg 3 hrs wkly
Eduardo Dominuez, General Manager

KTLN-TV *Digital Channel:* 47 *Virtual Channel:* 68; 1000 kw; 1319 ft.; N38 9 0 W122 35 31
38 South Peoria, Chicago, IL 60607 US
(415) 924-7500, *Fax:* (415) 924-0264
www.ktln.tv
ktln@tln.com
License: Novato, Marin County, CA
Group Owner: OTA Broadcasting; (acq 12-10-98; $500,000)
Nat'l Network: IND
Jerry Rose, CEO
Debra Fraser, General Manager
Brian Avery, Station Manager
James Nichols, CFO

KTNC-TV *Digital Channel:* 14 *Virtual Channel:* 42; 47.3 kw; 3091 ft.; N37 52 54 W121 55 5
500 South Chinowth Road, Visalia, CA 93277 US
(415) 398-4242, *Fax:* (415) 352-1800
www.ktnc.com
rpineda@ktnc.com
License: Concord, Contra Costa County, CA held by KTNC License LLC.
Group Owner: Pappas Telecasting Companies; (acq 10-29-97).;
Washington Law Firm: Fletcher, Heald & Hildreth
Nat'l Network: TUVISION
Foreign Language Programming
Harry Pappas, Chairman
Dennis Davis, CEO
Fernando Acosta, General Manager
LeBon Abercrombie, General Sales Mgr
Roberto Pineda, General Sales Manager

KTSF *Digital Channel:* 27 *Virtual Channel:* 26; 858 kw; 1323 ft.; N37 41 12 W122 26 3
100 Valley Drive, Brisbane, CA 94005 US
(415) 468-2626, *Fax:* (415) 467-7559
www.ktsf.com
admin@ktsftv.com
License: San Francisco, San Francisco County, CA held by Lincoln Broadcasting Co., a California L.P
Washington Law Firm: Law Office of Michael D. Berg
Nat'l Network: IND *Wire Services:* Bay City News Service; AP; CNN
Foreign Language Programming; Size of News Staff: 40; *Hours of Local News Weekly:* news progmg 24 hrs wkly
Lillian Howell, Chairman
Lincoln Howell, President
Michael Sherman, General Manager
Victor Marino, Programming Director
Lisa Yokota, Promotions Manager
Rose Shirinian, News Director
Mike Fusaro, Engineering Dir

KTVU *Digital Channel:* 44 *Virtual Channel:* 2; 1000 kw; 1680 ft.; N37 45 19 W122 27 6
Two Jack London Square, Oakland, CA 94607 US
(510) 834-1212, *Fax:* (510) 874-0463
www.ktvu.com
License: Oakland, Alameda County, CA held by KTVU Partnership.
Group Owner: Cox Media Group; (acq 10-16-63; $12.36 million;;
Washington Law Firm: Dow, Lohnes & Albertson

Nat'l Network: FOX *Nat'l Reps:* TeleRep *Wire Services:* Reuters; NWS (National Weather Service)
Jeff Block, Operations Dir
Tim McVay, General Manager
Tom Raponi, General Sales Mgr
Caroline Chang, Programming Director
Ed Chapuis, News Director
Don Thompson, Engineering Dir
Greg Bilte, General Sales Manager
Dan Haass,National Sales Manager
Phil Adams, National Sales Manager
Rosy Chu, Public Affairs Director

Santa Barbara-Santa Maria-San Luis Obispo, CA (DMA 121)

KCOY-TV *Digital Channel:* 19 *Virtual Channel:* 12; 115 kw vis, 22.9 kw aur; 1,940t/140g; N34 54 37 W120 11 08; *Population Served:* 462,000
1211 W. McCoy Ln., Santa Maria, CA 20036
(805) 925-1200, *Fax:* (805) 349-2740
www.kcoy.com
Kevinharlan@kcoy.com
License: Santa Maria, Santa Barbara County, CA held by Cowles California Media Co.
Group Owner: Cowles California Media Co.; (acq 5-7-2008; $41 million iwith KION-TV Monterey); *Washington Law Firm:* Skadden, Arps, Slate, Meagher & Flom LLP
Nat'l Network: CBS *Nat'l Reps:* Continental Television Sales
Size of News Staff: 42; *Hours of Local News Weekly:* news progmg 28 hrs wkly
Kevin Harlan, Operations Dir
Tracy Reiner, Local Sales Manager
Monica Esconbido, Programming Director
Donald Weiting, Promotions Manager
Jimmy Sprague, Chief Engineer

KEYT-TV *Digital Channel:* 27 *Virtual Channel:* 3; 250 kw; 3012 ft.; N34 31 32 W119 57 28
730 Miramonte, Santa Barbara, CA 93102 US
(805) 882-3933, *Fax:* (805) 882-3934
www.keyt.com
keyt@aol.com
License: Santa Barbara, Santa Barbara County, CA held by Smith Media License Holdings LLC.
Group Owner: Smith Media License Holdings LLC; (acq 11-8-2004; grpsl).; *Washington Law Firm:* Hogan & Hartson
Nat'l Network: ABC *Nat'l Reps:* Continental Television Sales
Wire Services: AP; CNN
Size of News Staff: 25; *Hours of Local News Weekly:* news progmg 21 hrs wkly
Michael Granados, General Manager
Renee Foley, Programming Director
Jeff Martin, Promotions Manager
Jim Bunner, News Director
Dave Williams, Chief Engineer
Gerry Fall, Sports Commentator
Caryn Meager, Traffic Manager
AllenRose, Weather Director

KPMR *Digital Channel:* 21 *Virtual Channel:* 38; 1000 kw; 3051 ft.; N34 31 28 W119 57 35
122 East Arrellaga St., Santa Barbara, CA 93101 US
(805) 685-3800 / (310) 447-3870, *Fax:* (805) 685-6892
www.entravision.com
License: Santa Barbara, Santa Barbara County, CA held by Entravision Holdings LLC.
Group Owner: Entravision Communications Corp.; (acq 11-2-2000; $4.75 million)
Nat'l Network: UNIVISION
Foreign Language Programming
Gabe Quiroz, General Manager
Michael Scanlon, General Sales Mgr
Angelique Caabrera, Programming Director
Andres Angulo, News Director

KSBY *Digital Channel:* 15 *Virtual Channel:* 6; 1000 kw; 1690 ft.; N35 21 37 W120 39 18
1772 Callie Joaquin, San Luis Obispo, CA 93405 US
(805) 541-6666, *Fax:* (805) 541-5142
www.ksby.com
ksby@ksby.com
License: San Luis Obispo, San Luis Obispo County, CA held by KSBY Communications Inc.
Group Owner: Cordillera Communications Inc.; (acq 2-18-2005; $67.75 million); *Washington Law Firm:* Dow Lohnes
Nat'l Network: NBC; CW *Nat'l Reps:* Harrington, Righter & Parsons *Wire Services:* AP
Evan Pappas, President
Dorothy Rivera, Operations Dir
Madeline Palaszewski, Promotions Manager
Tricia Rittger, News Director
Bill Ingram, Chief Engineer
Dave Hovde, Chief Meteorologist
Brandon Downing, Creative Director
DaveSchermer, News Director

KTAS *Digital Channel:* 34 *Virtual Channel:* 33; 80.3 kw vis; ant 1,443t/75g; N35 21 38 W120 39 21; *Rebroadcasting:* Telemundo
Mailing Address: Box 172, Santa Maria, CA 93030
Second Address: 330 W. Carmen Ln., Santa Maria, CA 93458
(805) 928-7700, *Fax:* (805) 928-8606
ktastv@fix.net
License: San Luis Obispo, San Luis Obispo County, CA held by Raul and Consuelo Palazuelos
(acq 7-3-97).; *Washington Law Firm:* Wiley, Rein & Fielding, LLC
Nat'l Network: Telemundo (Spanish) *Nat'l Reps:* Telemundo National Sales
Foreign Language Programming; Size of News Staff: 6; *Hours of Local News Weekly:* news progmg 3 hrs wkly
Sandy Keefer, General Manager
Sandy Keefer, Station Manager
Sandy Keefer, General Sales Mgr
Sandy Keefer, Programming Director
Sandy Keefer, Promotions Manager
Roy Keefer, Engineering Dir
Roy Keefer, Chief Engineer

Yuma, AZ-El Centro, CA (DMA 164)

KECY-TV *Digital Channel:* 9 *Virtual Channel:* 9; 50 kw; 1568 ft.; N33 3 19 W114 49 44
646 Main Street, El Centro, CA 92243 US
(928) 539-9990, *Fax:* (928) 343-0218
License: El Centro, Imperial County, CA held by Gulf-California Broadcast Co.
Group Owner: News-Press & Gazette Co.; (acq 5-5-2008; $2 million); *Washington Law Firm:* Smithwick & Belendiuk
Nat'l Network: FOX; ABC *Nat'l Reps:* Millennium Sales & Marketing
Deborah Weekes, General Manager
Darin Coragata, General Sales Mgr
Adriana Sanchez, Programming Director
Jesus Corona, Promotions Manager
Deborah Weeks, National Sales Manager
Linda Young, Traffic Manager

KVYE *Digital Channel:* 22 *Virtual Channel:* 7; 1000 kw; 1566 ft.; N33 3 2 W114 49 38
11900 Olympic Boulevard, Suite 590, Los Angeles, CA 90064 US
(760) 482-7777, *Fax:* (760) 482-0099
www.kvyetv.com
avaldez@entravision.com
License: El Centro, Imperial County, CA held by Entravision Holdings L.L.C.
Group Owner: Entravision Communications Corp.; (acq 2-19-98; $500,000 for CP).; *Washington Law Firm:* Thompson, Hine & Flory L
Nat'l Network: UNVISION
Foreign Language Programming; Size of News Staff: 8; *Hours of Local News Weekly:* news progmg 5 hrs wkly
Walter Ulloa, CEO
Albert Valdez, Operations Dir
Ray Nieves, General Manager
Philip Wilkinson, COO

Colorado

Albuquerque-Santa Fe, NM (DMA 44)

KREZ-TV *Digital Channel:* 15 *Virtual Channel:* 6; 46 kw; 297 ft.; N37 15 46 W107 53 58; *Rebroadcasting:* Satellite of KRQE(TV) Albuquerque, NM
Mailing Address: P. O. Box 789, Grand Junction, CO 81502 US
Second Address: 158 Bodo Dr., Durango, CO 81303
(970) 259-6666, *Fax:* (970) 247-8472
License: Durango, La Plata County, CO held by LIN of Colorado LLC.
Group Owner: LIN Television Corporation; (acq 11-30-2005; grpsl)
Nat'l Network: CBS; NBC
Bill Anderson, General Manager
Christopher Bartsh, General Manager

***KRMU** *Digital Channel:* 20 *Virtual Channel:* 20; 12.6 kw; 427 ft.; N37 15 46 W107 53 58; *Rebroadcasting:* Rebroadcasts KRMJ-TV Grand Junction 100%.
Network, Inc., 1089 Bannock St, Denver, CO 80204 US
(303) 892-6666, *Fax:* (303) 620-5600
www.rmpbs.org
License: Durango, La Plata County, CO held by Rocky Mountain Public Broadcasting Network, Inc.
Permitee: Rocky Moun; Washington Law Firm: Dow, Lohnes & Albertson
Nat'l Network: PBS
Scott Long, CFO
Doug Price, President
Donna Sanford, Programming Director
Tom Craig, Chief Engineer

KRTN-TV *Digital Channel:* 33; 50 kw vis; ant 400t/66g; N37 15 46 W107 53 45
Box 3757, Ramar Communications, Lubbock, TX 79452
(806) 745-3434, *Fax:* (806) 748-1949
License: Durango, La Plata County, CO held by Ramar Communications, Inc.
Group Owner: Ramar Communications II Ltd.; (acq 1-24-2001).
Foreign Language Programming
Brad Moran, President

Colorado Springs-Pueblo, CO (DMA 91)

KKTV *Digital Channel:* 49 *Virtual Channel:* 11; 550 kw; 2375 ft.; N38 44 42 W104 51 43
Mailing Address: 100 Park Avenue, Rockford, IL 61101 US
Second Address: 3100 N Nevada Avenue, Colorado Springs, CO 80901
(719) 634-2844, *Fax:* (719) 632-0808,(719) 442-6981
www.kktv.com
License: Colorado Springs, El Paso County, CO held by WEAU Licensee Corp.
Group Owner: Gray Television Inc.; (acq 10-25-02; grpsl).
Nat'l Network: CBS; MyNetworkTV *Nat'l Reps:* Continental Television Sales
Size of News Staff: 42; *Hours of Local News Weekly:* news progmg 27 hrs wkly
Robert Prather, President
Charles Peterson, Operations Dir
Tim Merritt, General Manager
Marion Houghton, General Sales Mgr
Becky Tomek, Programming Director
Michelle Hughes, Promotions Manager
Nick Matesi, News Director
MarkDoan, Chief Engineer
Deborah Bullock, Business Manager
Emily Edwards, Operations Manager

KOAA-TV *Digital Channel:* 42 *Virtual Channel:* 5; 880 kw; 2165 ft.; N38 44 42 W104 51 39
Mailing Address: 2200 Seventh Avenue, Pueblo, CO 81003 US
Second Address: 530 Communications Cir., Colorado Springs, CO 81003
(719) 544-5781,(719) 632-5030, *Fax:* (719) 295-6677
www.koaa.com
License: Pueblo, Pueblo County, CO held by Sangre De Cristo Communications Inc.
Group Owner: Cordillera Communications Inc.; (acq 8-6-76; $4.5 million;; *Washington Law Firm:* Dow, Lohnes & Albertson
Nat'l Network: NBC *Nat'l Reps:* Harrington, Righter & Parsons
Size of News Staff: 23; *Hours of Local News Weekly:* news progmg 7 hrs wkly
David Whitaker, President
Patricia Cone, Operations Dir
Tom Wright, General Sales Mgr
Ron Eccher, Programming Director
Cindy Aubrey, News Director
Quentin Henry, Chief Engineer
Lisa Lyden, News Commentator
Pauline Quintana,Traffic Manager

KRDO-TV *Digital Channel:* 24 *Virtual Channel:* 13; 200 kw; 2215 ft.; N38 44 45.2 W104 51 37.2
P. O. Box 1457, Colorado Springs, CO 80901 US
(719) 632-1515, *Fax:* (719) 475-0815
www.krdo.com
License: Colorado Springs, El Paso County, CO held by Pikes Peak Television Inc.
Group Owner: News-Press & Gazette Co.; (acq 6-26-2006; $45 million with KJCT(TV) Grand Junction).
Nat'l Network: ABC *Nat'l Reps:* Airtime TV *Regional Reps:* Blair Television
David Bradley Jr., President
Neil Klockziem, General Manager

***KTSC** *Digital Channel:* 8 *Virtual Channel:* 8; 22.4 kw; 2362 ft.; N38 44 43 W104 51 39
2200 Bonforte Blvd., Pueblo, CO 81001 US

(719) 543-8800, *Fax:* (719) 549-2208
www.rmpbs.org
ktsc@rmpbs.org
License: Pueblo, Pueblo County, CO held by Rocky Mountain Public Broadcasting Network Inc
Nat'l Network: PBS
Tom Scheel, Chairman
James Morgese, President
Wynona Sullivan, Station Manager
Donna Sanford, Programming Director
Tiffany Tyson, Promotions Manager
Ian Hartley, Chief Engineer

KVSN-DT *Digital Channel:* 48; 950 kw vis; ant 2,280t/271g; N38 44 42 W104 51 37
777 Grant St., Suite 500, Denver, CO 80203
(303) 832-0050, *Fax:* (303) 832-3410
www.entravision.com
yvillavicencio@entravision.com
License: Pueblo, Pueblo County, CO held by Entravision Holdings L.L.C.
Group Owner: Entravision Communications Corp.; *Ownership:* Univision (Spanish)
Walter Ulloa, CEO
Mario Carrera, General Manager

KXRM-TV *Digital Channel:* 22 *Virtual Channel:* 21; 51 kw; 2103 ft.; N38 44 43 W104 51 40
560 Wooten St, Colorado Springs, CO 80915 US
(719) 596-2100, *Fax:* (719) 591-4180
www.coloradoconnection.com
info@kxrm.com
License: Colorado Springs, El Paso County, CO held by Barrington Colorado Springs License LLC.
Group Owner: Barrington Broadcasting Group, LLC.; (acq 8-11-2006; grpsl); *Washington Law Firm:* Covington & Durling
Nat'l Network: FOX *Nat'l Reps:* TeleRep *Wire Services:* CNN
Hours of Local News Weekly: News progmg 3.5 hrs wkly
K. James Yager, CEO
Steve Dant, President
Dan Corken, General Sales Mgr
Patti Clements, Programming Director
Joe Cole, News Director
Matt Gerstner, Director of Technical Operations
Leanne Franke, Natl & Regional Sales Manager
Mike Silecchia, VP/Retail Sales Manager

Denver, CO (DMA 18)

***KBDI-TV** *Digital Channel:* 13 *Virtual Channel:* 12; 33.6 kw; 2421 ft.; N39 40 55 W105 29 49
1531 Stout Street, Denver, CO 80202 US
(303) 296-1212, *Fax:* (303) 296-6650
www.kbdi.org
bhaug@kbdi.org
License: Broomfield, Boulder County, CO held by Colorado Public Television Inc.
Washington Law Firm: Mintz, Levin, Cohn, Ferris, Glovsky & Popeo
Nat'l Network: PBS
Dr. Willard Rowland, President
Kim Johnson, Operations Dir
Darrow Hodges, General Sales Mgr
Brad Haug, Programming Director

KCDO-TV *Digital Channel:* 23; 1,000 kw; N40 34 02-01.2 W103 56 18.9; *Population Served:* 1,400,000
3001 S. Jamaica Ct, Ste. 210, Aurora, CO 80014
(303) 925-0303, *Fax:* (303) 925-7461
www.k3colorado
garmstrong@ch3tv.com
License: Sterling, Logan County, CO held by Channel 3 TV Co.
Group Owner: Newsweb Corp.; (acq 8-31-99; $240,000); *Ownership:* Channel 3 TV Company; *Washington Law Firm:* Skadlen, Arps, Slate, Meagher, Flom LLP
Nat'l Network: Independent *Regional Reps:* none
Size of News Staff: 0; *Hours of Local News Weekly:* none
Greg Armstrong, President
Ron Anderson, Operations Dir
Greg Armstrong, General Manager
Greg Armstrong, Station Manager
Greg Armstrong, General Sales Mgr
Greg Armstrong, Programming Director
Greg Armstrong, Promotions Manager
N/A, News Director
Ron Anderson, Engineering Dir

KCEC *Digital Channel:* 51 *Virtual Channel:* 50; 900 kw; 763 ft.; N39 43 58 W105 14 8
11900 Olympic Boulevard, Suite 590, Los Angeles, CA 90064 US
(303) 832-0050, *Fax:* (303) 832-3410
www.entravision.com
yvillavicencio@entravision.com
License: Denver, Denver County, CO held by Entravision Holdings LLC
Group Owner: Entravision Communications Corp.; (acq 4-25-97)
Nat'l Network: UNIVISION
Foreign Language Programming
Walter Ulloa, CEO
Mario Carrera, General Manager
Don Daboub, General Sales Mgr
Erma Atencio, Programming Director
Rafael Medina, Promotions Manager
Luisa Collins, News Director
Carl Cutforth, Engineering Dir
Michelle Morawiec,National Sales Manager
Jamie Moreno, Research Director

KCNC-TV *Digital Channel:* 35 *Virtual Channel:* 4; 1000 kw; 1227 ft.; N39 43 51 W105 13 54
600 New Hampshire Ave.NW, Suite 1200, Washington, DC 20037 US
(303) 861-4444, *Fax:* (303) 830-6537
www.cbs4denver.com
wholmes@cbs.com
License: Denver, Denver County, CO held by CBS Television Stations Inc.
Group Owner: CBS Television Stations Group; (acq 9-10-95; grpsl).
Nat'l Network: CBS *Nat'l Reps:* CBS TV Stations National Sales
Wire Services: Conus; PR Newswire; Medialink
Size of News Staff: 90; *Hours of Local News Weekly:* news progmg 28.5 hrs wkly
Marge Smelt, CFO
David Layne, Operations Dir
Walt DeHaven, General Manager
David Rash, General Sales Mgr
Wendy Holmes, Programming Director
Ed Cushing, Promotions Manager
Cathy Considine, Local Sales Manager
Aaron Inman,National Sales Manager

KDEN-TV *Digital Channel:* 29; 5,000 kw vis; ant 1,066t/964g; N40 05 47 W104 54 04
2851 South Parker Road, Suite 1130, Aurora, CO 80014
(303) 832-0402 (Denver), *Fax:* (303) 832-0777
License: Longmont, Boulder County, CO held by NBC Telemundo License Co.
Group Owner: Telemundo Television Stations; (acq 7-13-2006; $42 million); *Washington Law Firm:* NBC Legal
Nat'l Network: Telemundo (Spanish)
Foreign Language Programming; Size of News Staff: 1; *Hours of Local News Weekly:* news progmg one hr wkly
Don Brown, CEO
Clara Rivas, Operations Dir
Nora Grisanti, Assistant

KDVR *Digital Channel:* 32 *Virtual Channel:* 31; 1000 kw; 1030 ft.; N39 43 45 W105 14 12
5151 Wisconsin Ave., NW, Washington, DC 20016 US
(303) 595-3131,(888) 595-3131, *Fax:* (303) 566-2931,(303) 566-7631(news)
www.kdvr.com
news@denvernewshd.com
License: Denver, Denver County, CO held by Community Television of Colorado License LLC.
Group Owner: Local TV LLC; (acq 7-14-2008; grpsl)
Nat'l Network: FOX
Dennis Leonard, President
John Strassner, General Sales Mgr
Garrett Sailor, Programming Director
Hayley Hearst, Promotions Manager
Carolyn Kane, News Director
Patti Brady, Traffic Director
Rick Wheeler, VP Technology

KETD *Digital Channel:* 46 *Virtual Channel:* 53; 5,000 kw vis, 1,000 kw au; 713t; N39 25 58 W104 39 18; *Population Served:* 1,578,660
12999 E. Adam Aircraft, Englewood, CO 46624
(303) 799-8853, *Fax:* (303) 792-5303
www.mykwhd.com
License: Castle Rock, Douglas County, CO held by LeSea Broadcasting.
Group Owner: Le Sea Broadcasting
Foreign Language Programming
Pete Sumrall, CEO
Dan Smith, General Manager
Ron Vincent, Chief Engineer

KFCT *Digital Channel:* 21 *Virtual Channel:* 22; 50 kw; 764 ft.; N40 38 32 W104 49 5; *Rebroadcasting:* Satellite of KDVR(TV) Denver.
501 Wazee Street, Denver, CO 80204 US
(303) 595-3131, *Fax:* (303) 566-2931
www.kdvr.com
news@denvernewshd.com
License: Fort Collins, Larimer County, CO held by Community Television of Colorado License LLC.
Group Owner: Local TV LLC; (acq 7-14-2008; grpsl)
Nat'l Network: FOX
Dennis Leonard, General Manager
John Strassner, General Sales Mgr
Garrett Sailor, Programming Director
Carolyn Kane, News Director
Rick Wheeler, VP Technology

KFCT *Digital Channel:* 21; 1,860 kw vis; ant 840t/705g; N40 38 23 W104 49 05; *Rebroadcasting:* Satellite of KDVR(TV) Denver.
c/o TV Station KDVR, 100 East Speer Blvd, Denver, CO 80203
(303) 595-3131, *Fax:* (303) 566-2931
www.kdvr.com
news@denvernewshd.com
License: Fort Collins, Larimer County, CO held by Community Television of Colorado License LLC.
Group Owner: Local TV LLC; (acq 7-14-2008; grpsl)
Nat'l Network: Fox
Dennis Leonard, General Manager
John Strassner, General Sales Mgr
Garrett Sailor, Programming Director
Carolyn Kane, News Director
Rick Wheeler, VP Technology

KMGH-TV *Digital Channel:* 7 *Virtual Channel:* 7; 54 kw; 1178 ft.; N39 43 51 W105 13 54
123 Speer Boulevard, Denver, CO 80203 US
(303) 832-7777, *Fax:* (303) 832-0119
www.thedenverchannel.com
License: Denver, Denver County, CO held by McGraw-Hill Broadcasting Co. Inc.
Group Owner: McGraw-Hill Broadcasting Co.; (acq 6-1-72; grpsl;
Nat'l Network: ABC *Nat'l Reps:* Harrington, Righter & Parsons
Byron Grandy, Operations Dir
John Curry, General Sales Mgr
Laura Horgis, National Sales Manager
Barry Edmond, Operations Manager

KPJR-DT *Digital Channel:* 38; 1,000 kw vis; ant 1,187t/23g; N40 05 59 W104 54 02; *Not on Air/Target Date:* unknown
Box C-11949, Santa Ana, CA 92711
(714) 832-2950, *Fax:* (714) 730-0657
www.tbn.org
License: Greeley, Weld County, CO
Group Owner: Trinity Broadcasting Network; (acq 9-16-2008; $37.5 million for CP)
Paul Crouch, President

KPXC-TV *Digital Channel:* 43 *Virtual Channel:* 59; 1000 kw; 1188 ft.; N40 5 59 W104 54 2
601 Clearwater Park Road, West Palm Beach, FL 33401 US
(303) 751-5959, *Fax:* (303) 751-5993
www.ionline.tv/stations/list.cfm
License: Denver, Denver County, CO held by Paxson Denver License Inc.
Group Owner: ION Media Networks Inc.; (acq 7-1-96; grpsl).; *Washington Law Firm:* Cole, Raywid & Braverman
Nat'l Network: ION
Foreign Language Programming; Hours of Local News Weekly: News progmg 24 hrs wkly
Bud Paxson, President
Mark Cornetta, General Sales Mgr
Geri Crawley, Programming Director
Brian Schauer, Chief Engineer
Christy Bradford, Regional Sales Manager

KREG-TV *Digital Channel:* 23 *Virtual Channel:* 3; 16.1 kw; 2530 ft.; N39 25 7 W107 22 6; *Rebroadcasting:* Rebroadcasts KREX-TV Grand Junction
Mailing Address: P.O. Box 1508, Mount Vernon, IL 62864 US
Second Address: 345 Hillcrest Dr., Grand Junction, CO 81501
(970) 963-3333, *Fax:* (970) 242-0886
www.krextv.com
rtillery@krextv.com
License: Glenwood Springs, Garfield County, CO held by Hoak Media of Colorado LLC.
Group Owner: Hoak Media Corporation; (acq 10-10-2003; grpsl).; *Washington Law Firm:* Gardner, Carton & Douglas
Nat'l Network: CBS *Nat'l Reps:* Petry Television Inc.
Ron Tillery, General Manager

***KRMA-TV** *Digital Channel:* 18 *Virtual Channel:* 6; 1000 kw; 1263 ft.; N39 40 17 W105 13 6
Broadcasting Network, 1089 Bannock St, Denver, CO 80204 US
(303) 892-6666, *Fax:* (303) 620-5600
www.rmpbs.org
License: Denver, Denver County, CO held by Rocky Mountain Public Broadcasting Network Inc.
Washington Law Firm: Dow & Lohnes
Nat'l Network: PBS
Hours of Local News Weekly: News progmg one hr wkly
Scott Long, CFO
Doug Price, President
Donna Sanford, Programming Director
Tom Craig, Chief Engineer

***KRMT** *Digital Channel:* 40 *Virtual Channel:* 41; 74.8 kw; 1129 ft.; N39 35 59 W105 12 35
12014 West 64th Ave., Arvada, CO 80004 US
(303) 423-4141, *Fax:* (303) 424-0571
www.daystar.com
License: Denver, Denver County, CO held by Word of God Fellowship Inc.
(acq 5-29-97; $1.95 million); *Ownership:* Word Of God Fellowship; *Washington Law Firm:* Hogan & Hartson
Nat'l Network: IND
Foreign Language Programming
Marcus Lamb, CEO
Joni Lamb, President
Kevin Russell, General Manager
Trish Lord, Programming Director
James Barnes, Promotions Manager
Judy Nelson, Office Manager

***KRMZ** *Digital Channel:* 10 *Virtual Channel:* 24; 0.481 kw; 575 ft.; N40 27 43 W106 50 57; *Rebroadcasting:* Rebroadcasts KRMA-TV Denver 100%
P.O. Box 255, Evergreen, CO 80439 US
(303) 892-6666, *Fax:* (303) 620-5600
www.rmpbs.org
License: Steamboat Springs, Routt County, CO held by Rocky Mountain Public Broadcasting Network Inc.
Nat'l Network: PBS *Regional Network:* Rocky Mountain PBS
Scott Long, CFO
Doug Price, President
Donna Sanford, Programming Director
Tom Craig, Chief Engineer

KTVD *Digital Channel:* 19; 5,000 kw vis, 500 kw aur; ant 1,256t/243g; N39 40 18 W105 13 12
500 Speer Blvd., Denver, CO 60614
(303) 871-9999, *Fax:* (303) 871-1819
www.mytvdenver.com
feedback@ktvd.com
License: Denver, Denver County, CO held by Multimedia Holdings Corp.
Group Owner: Gannett Broadcasting; *Washington Law Firm:* Fletcher, Heald & Hildreth
Nat'l Network: MyNetworkTV
Mark Cornetta, President
Dean Ditmer, General Sales Mgr
Robbie Gutierrez, Programming Director
Robert Springer, Promotions Manager
Patti Dennis, News Director
Scott Gill, Chief Engineer

KUSA *Digital Channel:* 16; 316 kw vis, 45.3 kw aur; ant 918t/246g; N39 43 46 W105 14 08; *Population Served:* 3,535,000
500 Speer Blvd., Denver, CO 80203
(303) 871-9999, *Fax:* (303) 698-4719 (sales)
www.9news.com
kusa@9news.com
License: Denver, Denver County, CO held by Multimedia Cablevision Inc
Group Owner: Gannett Broadcasting; (acq 6-7-79; grpsl;;
Washington Law Firm: Wiley, Rein & Fielding
Nat'l Network: NBC
Mark Cornetta, President
Patricia Wilson, General Sales Mgr
Patti Dennis, News Director
Don Perez, Engineering Dir

KWGN-TV *Digital Channel:* 34 *Virtual Channel:* 2; 1000 kw; 1102 ft.; N39 43 58 W105 14 8
6160 South Wabash Way, Englewood, CO 80111 US
(303) 740-2222, *Fax:* (303) 740-2847
www.cw2.com
License: Denver, Denver County, CO held by KWGN Inc.
Group Owner: Tribune Broadcasting Co.; (acq 12-20-2007; grpsl); *Washington Law Firm:* Dow Lohnes PLLC
Nat'l Network: CW *Nat'l Reps:* TeleRep
Hours of Local News Weekly: News progmg 29.5 hrs wkly
Dennis O'Brien, CFO
Beverly Martinez, Operations Dir
Dennis Leonard, General Manager
John Strassner, General Sales Mgr
Natalie Grant, Programming Director
Rob Venusti, Promotions Manager
Carl Bilek, News Director
Donna Laboy,Traffic Manager

Grand Junction-Montrose, CO (DMA 184)

KFQX *Digital Channel:* 15 *Virtual Channel:* 4; 71.5 kw; 1335 ft.; N39 3 58 W108 44 46
Mailing Address: 800 Gold Creek Rd., Ohio City, CO 81237 US
Second Address: 345 Hillcrest Dr., Grand Junction, CO 81501
(970) 242-5000, *Fax:* (970) 242-0886
www.krextv.com
rtillery@krextv.com
License: Grand Junction, Mesa County, CO held by Parker Broadcasting of Colorado LLC.
Group Owner: Parker Broadcasting Inc.; (acq 12-27-2004)
Nat'l Network: FOX
Ron Tillery, General Manager
Randy Stone, General Sales Mgr
Shelley Moore, Programming Director
Scot Stewart, Promotions Manager
Keira Bresnahan, News Director
Phil Mowbray, Engineering Dir

KJCT *Digital Channel:* 7 *Virtual Channel:* 8; 9.7 kw; 2927 ft.; N39 2 55 W108 15 6
PO Box 3788, Grand Junction, CO 81505 US
(970) 245-8880, *Fax:* (970) 245-8249
www.kjct8.com
kristy.santiago@kjct8.com
License: Grand Junction, Mesa County, CO held by Pikes Peak Television Inc.
Group Owner: News-Press & Gazette Co.; (acq 6-26-2006; $45 million with KRDO-TV Colorado Springs).; *Washington Law Firm:* Smithwick & Belendiuk, P.C.
Nat'l Network: ABC *Nat'l Reps:* Millennium Sales & Marketing
Regional Reps: Kristy Santiago *Wire Services:* AP
Size of News Staff: 18; *Hours of Local News Weekly:* news progmg 19.5 wkly
David Bradley Jr., CEO
Kristy Santiago, General Manager

KKCO *Digital Channel:* 12 *Virtual Channel:* 11; 5.3 kw; 1483 ft.; N39 4 0 W108 44 45
2325 Interstate Ave, Grand Junction, CO 81505 US
(970) 243-1111, *Fax:* (970) 243-1770
www.nbc11news.com
billv@nbc11news.com
License: Grand Junction, Mesa County, CO held by Gray Television Licensee Inc.
Group Owner: Gray Television Inc.; (acq 1-31-2005; $13.5 million with translator K50EZ Montrose).; *Washington Law Firm:* Wood, Maines & Brown, Chartered
Nat'l Network: NBC; CW *Nat'l Reps:* Millennium Sales & Marketing
Size of News Staff: 35; *Hours of Local News Weekly:* news progmg 28 hrs wkly
Paul Varecha, Operations Dir
William Varecha, General Manager
Sandy Moore, Programming Director
Jason Duran, IT Manager

KREX-TV *Digital Channel:* 2 *Virtual Channel:* 5; 0.8 kw; 91 ft.; N39 5 17 W108 33 58
Mailing Address: P. O. Box 789, Grand Junction, CO 81502 US
Second Address: 345 Hillcrest Dr., Grand Junction, CO 81501
(970) 242-5000, *Fax:* (970) 242-0886
www.krextv.com
rtillery@krextv.com
License: Grand Junction, Mesa County, CO held by Hoak Media of Colorado LLC.
Group Owner: Hoak Media Corporation; (acq 11-12-2003; grpsl).
Nat'l Network: CBS *Nat'l Reps:* Petry Television Inc.
Size of News Staff: 15; *Hours of Local News Weekly:* news progmg 30 hrs wkly
Dave Colvin, Operations Dir
Ron Tillery, General Manager

KREY-TV *Digital Channel:* 13 *Virtual Channel:* 10; 2.6 kw; 115 ft.; N38 31 2 W107 51 12
345 Hillcrest Manor, Grand Junction, CO 81502 US
(970) 249-9601, *Fax:* (970) 249-9610
kreytv@gwe.net
License: Montrose, Montrose County, CO held by Hoak Media of Colorado LLC.
Group Owner: Hoak Media Corporation; (acq 10-10-2003; grpsl).
Nat'l Network: CBS; NBC
Chris Larum, Station Manager

***KRMJ** *Digital Channel:* 18 *Virtual Channel:* 18; 21 kw; 1342 ft.; N39 3 58 W108 44 43; *Rebroadcasting:* Rebroadcasts KRMA-TV Denver 99.9%.
Broadcasting Network, 1089 Bannock St, Denver, CO 80217 US
(970) 245-1818, *Fax:* (303) 620-5600
www.rmpbs.org
License: Grand Junction, Mesa County, CO held by Rocky Mountain Public Broadcasting Network Inc
Washington Law Firm: Dow, Lohnes & Albertson
Nat'l Network: PBS
James Morgese, President
Angie Salazar, Station Manager
Suzanne Banning, General Sales Mgr
Donna Sanford, Programming Director
John Anderson, Engineering Dir

Connecticut

Hartford & New Haven, CT (DMA 30)

WCCT-TV *Digital Channel:* 20; 2,239 kw vis, 223.9 kw au; ant 1,200t/1,013g; N41 31 04 W73 01 07; *Population Served:* 1,000,000
285 Broad St., Hartford, CT 06712
(860) 527-6161, *Fax:* (860) 727-0158
www.wtxx.com
newsteam@fox61.com
License: Waterbury, New Haven County, CT held by WTXX Inc., Debtor-in-possession
Group Owner: Tribune Broadcasting Co.; (acq 12-20-2007; grpsl)
Nat'l Network: CW *Nat'l Reps:* MMT
Richard Graziano, General Manager
Mark Oxton, General Sales Mgr
Dean Maluski, Chief Engineer

WCTX *Digital Channel:* 39 *Virtual Channel:* 59; 170 kw; 988 ft.; N41 25 22 W72 57 6
210 Skokie Valley Road, Highland Park, IL 60035 US
(203) 784-8888, *Fax:* (203) 789-2010
www.myzone.tv
License: New Haven, New Haven County, CT held by WTNH Broadcasting Inc.
Group Owner: LIN Television Corporation; (acq 3-2002)
Nat'l Network: MY NETWORK *Nat'l Reps:* Petry Television Inc.
Hours of Local News Weekly: News progmg 8.5 hrs wkly
Jamie Holowaty, Operations Dir
Roger Hess, General Sales Mgr
Judi Mickmac, Programming Director
Mary Lee Weber, Promotions Manager
Kirk Varner, News Director
Karen Rorke, Local Sales Manager
Roger Megroz, National SalesManager

***WEDH** *Digital Channel:* 45 *Virtual Channel:* 24; 490 kw; 1657 ft.; N41 42 13 W72 49 57
24 Summit Street, Hartford, CT 06106 US
(860) 278-5310, *Fax:* (860) 275-7500
www.cptv.org
License: Hartford, Hartford County, CT held by Connecticut Public Broadcasting Inc
Washington Law Firm: Schwartz, Woods & Miller
Nat'l Network: PBS
Jerry Franklin, CEO
Haig Papasian, Operations Dir
Dean Orton, General Sales Mgr
Larry Rifkin, Programming Director
Joseph Zareski, Chief Engineer
Meg Sakellarides, CFO

***WEDN** *Digital Channel:* 9 *Virtual Channel:* 53; 4.2 kw; 630 ft.; N41 31 14 W72 10 3
24 Summit Street, Hartford, CT 06106 US
(860) 278-5310, *Fax:* (860) 275-7402
www.cptv.org
License: Norwich, New London County, CT held by Connecticut Public Broadcasting
Nat'l Network: PBS
Jerry Franklin, CEO
Haig Papasian, Operations Dir
Dean Orton, General Sales Mgr
Meg Sakellarides, CFO

***WEDY** *Digital Channel:* 6 *Virtual Channel:* 65; 0.4 kw; 289 ft.; N41 19 42 W72 54 25; *Rebroadcasting:* Rebroadcasts WEDH(TV) Hartford 100%.
24 Summit Street, Hartford, CT 06106 US
(860) 278-5310, *Fax:* (860) 275-7500
www.cptv.org
License: New Haven, New Haven County, CT held by Connecticut Public Broadcasting Inc
Nat'l Network: PBS
Jerry Franklin, CEO
Haig Papasian, Operations Dir
Dean Orton, General Sales Mgr
Larry Rifkin, Programming Director
Joseph Zareski, Chief Engineer
Meg Sakellarides, CFO

WFSB *Digital Channel:* 33 *Virtual Channel:* 3; 1000 kw; 948 ft.; N41 46 30 W72 48 20
1716 Locust Street, Des Moines, IA 50309 US
(860) 728-3333, *Fax:* (860) 247-8940,(860) 728-0263 (News Room)
www.wfsb.com
License: Hartford, Hartford County, CT held by Meredith Corp. dba WFSB.
Group Owner: Meredith Broadcasting Group, Meredith Corp.; (acq 9-4-97; $159 million); *Washington Law Firm:* Garvey, Schubert & Barer
Nat'l Network: CBS *Nat'l Reps:* Harrington, Righter & Parsons
Hours of Local News Weekly: News progmg 36 hrs wkly
John Ahearn, Operations Dir
Klarn DePalma, General Manager
Bill Whittle, General Sales Mgr
Rob Luciano, Programming Director
Stephanie Turner, Promotions Manager
Gary Brown, News Director
Victor Zarrillio, Engineering Dir
Shelly Smith, Promotions Manager

WHPX-TV *Digital Channel:* 26; 2,792 kw vis, 279 kw aur; 1,251t; N41 25 05 W72 11 55
3 Shaws Cove, Suite 226, New London, CT 6320
(860) 444-2626, *Fax:* (860) 440-2601
www.ionline.tv
License: New London, New London County, CT held by ION Media Hartford License, Inc.
Group Owner: ION Media Networks Inc.; (acq 2-25-00; grpsl).
Nat'l Network: ION Television
Dianne Sullivan, General Sales Mgr
Aaron Kaplan, Programming Director
Bob Tiodor, Chief Engineer

WTIC-TV *Digital Channel:* 31 *Virtual Channel:* 61; 495 kw; 1660 ft.; N41 42 13 W72 49 57
One Corporate Center, Hartford, CT 06103 US
(860) 527-6161, *Fax:* (860) 727-0158
www.fox61.com
newsteam@fox61.com
License: Hartford, Hartford County, CT held by Tribune Television, Co., Debtor-in-possession
Group Owner: Tribune Broadcasting Co.; (acq 12-20-2007; grpsl)
Nat'l Network: FOX *Nat'l Reps:* TeleRep
Size of News Staff: 31; *Hours of Local News Weekly:* news progmg 6 hrs wkly
Richard Graziano, Operations Dir
Mark Oxton, General Sales Mgr
Dean Maluski, Chief Engineer

WTNH *Digital Channel:* 10; 166 kw vis, 16.6 kw aur; 1,210t/909g; N41 25 23 W72 57 06; *Population Served:* 1,000,000
8 Elm St., New Haven, CT 6510
(203) 784-8888, *Fax:* (203) 789-2010
www.wtnh.com
wtnh@wtnh.com
License: New Haven, New Haven County, CT held by LIN Television Inc.
Group Owner: LIN Television Corporation; (acq 12-94; $120.17 million;); *Washington Law Firm:* Lin Legal
Nat'l Network: ABC *Nat'l Reps:* Petry Television Inc.
Size of News Staff: 77; *Hours of Local News Weekly:* news progmg 32 hrs wkly
Jamie Holowaty, Operations Dir
Roger Hess, General Sales Mgr
Judi Mickmac, Programming Director
Mary Lee Weber, Promotions Manager
Kirk Varner, News Director
Phil Jermain, Local Sales Manager
Roger Megroz, National SalesManager
Connie Fitch, Public Service Director
Tony Marnaio, Research Director

WUVN *Digital Channel:* 46 *Virtual Channel:* 18; 217 kw; 883 ft.; N41 46 30 W72 48 4
Town Center, 29 South, Maine Street, Room 215, West Hartford, CT 06107 US
(860) 278-1818, *Fax:* (860) 278-1811
www.wuvntv.com
License: Hartford, Hartford County, CT held by Entravision Holdings LLC.
Group Owner: Entravision Communications Corp.; (acq 1-4-01; $18 million); *Washington Law Firm:* Wiley, Rein & Fielding
Nat'l Network: UNIVISION; TeleFutura (Spanish)
Hours of Local News Weekly: News progmg 5 hrs wkly
Robert Smith, Operations Dir
Ulysses Arrigoitia, General Manager
Renee Barbour, Programming Director
Meg Godin, Promotions Manager
Sara Suarez, News Director
Dania Alexandrino, Music Director
Rob Donner, National Sales Manager

WVIT *Digital Channel:* 35 *Virtual Channel:* 30; 250 kw; 1424 ft.; N41 42 2 W72 49 57
Nbc, 11th Fl, 1299 Pennsylvania Ave, NW, Washington, DC 20004 US
(860) 521-3030, *Fax:* (860) 521-4860(news),(860) 521-3110
www.nbcconnecticut.com
news@nbcconnecticut.com
License: New Britain, Hartford County, CT held by NBC Telemundo License Co.
Group Owner: NBC Owned Television Stations; (acq 12-07-97; trade).
Nat'l Network: NBC *Nat'l Reps:* NBC TV Stations Sales
Dave Doebler, President
Keith Barbaria, Operations Dir
Pat DeRico, General Sales Mgr
Ronni Attenello, Programming Director
Lowell Briggs, Promotions Manager
Mike St. Peter, News Director
LaVerne Jefferys, Public AffairsDirector
Colleen Green, Traffic Manager

New York (DMA 1)

***WEDW** *Digital Channel:* 49 *Virtual Channel:* 49; 170 kw; 722 ft.; N41 16 44 W73 11 8
240 New Britain Avenue, Hartford, CT 06106 US
(860) 278-5310, *Fax:* (860) 275-7500
www.cptv.org
License: Bridgeport, Fairfield County, CT held by Connecticut Public Broadcasting
Nat'l Network: PBS
Meg Sakellarides, CFO
Jerry Franklin, President
Haig Papasian, Operations Dir
Dean Orton, General Sales Mgr
Larry Rifkin, Programming Director
Joseph Zareski, Chief Engineer

WZME *Digital Channel:* 42; 2.5 kw vis, 2 kw aur; ant 620t/300g; N41 21 43 W73 06 48
7 Wakely St., Seymour, CT 37230
(203) 881-1153, *Fax:* (203) 881-1302
License: Bridgeport, Fairfield County, CT held by NRJ TV NY License Co. LLC
Group Owner: NRJ Holdings LLC; (acq 3-26-2012); *Washington Law Firm:* Goldberg, Godles, Wiener & Wright
Ronald Barnes, General Manager

Delaware

Philadelphia (DMA 4)

***WHYY-TV** *Digital Channel:* 12; 30 kw; 960t/1,148g; N40 02 30 W75 14 24; *Population Served:* 9,297,178
Mailing Address: Independence Mall W., 150 N. 6th St., Philadelphia, PA 19106
Second Address: 625 Orange St., Wilmington, DE 19801
(215) 351-1200,(302) 888-1200, *Fax:* (215) 351-0398,(302) 575-0346
www.whyy.org
talkback@whyy.org
License: Wilmington, New Castle County, DE held by WHYY Inc
Washington Law Firm: Schwartz, Woods & Miller
Nat'l Network: PBS
Size of News Staff: 10; *Hours of Local News Weekly:* news progmg 1 hr wkly
Gerard W. Sweeney, Chairman
William Marrazzo, President & CEO
Kyra G. McGrath, Executive Vice President & COO
Christine Dempsey, Vice President & CCO
Roseann Oleyn, Vice President Institutional Advancement
Chris Satullo, VicePresident of News & Civic Dialogue
William J. Weber, Vice President & CTO
A. William Dana, Vice President & CTO
John Doran, Chief Engineer
Art Ellis, Executive Director of Communications & Management
Jeffrey M. Bundy, Director of MemberRelations

Salisbury, MD (DMA 144)

***WDPB** *Digital Channel:* 44 *Virtual Channel:* 64; 98 kw; 643 ft.; N38 39 15 W75 36 42; *Rebroadcasting:* Satellite of WHYY-TV (Wilmington, DE)
5th & Scott St., Wilmington, DE 19805 US
(302) 888-1200, *Fax:* (302) 575-0346
www.whyy.org
whyydbc@whyy.org
License: Seaford, Sussex County, DE held by WHYY Inc (acq 2-28-86); *Washington Law Firm:* Schwartz, Woods & Miller
Nat'l Network: PBS
Size of News Staff: 10; *Hours of Local News Weekly:* news progmg 3 hrs wkly
Gerard H. Sweeney, Chairman
William Marrazzo, President

District of Columbia

Washington, DC (Hagerstown, MD) (DMA 9)

WDCA *Digital Channel:* 35 *Virtual Channel:* 20; 500 kw; 745 ft.; N38 57 22 W77 4 59
1501 M Street, N.W., Suite 1100, Washington, DC 20005 US
(202) 895-3050, *Fax:* (202) 895-3340
www.upn20wdca.com
upn20wdca@paramount.com
License: Washington, DC County, DC held by Fox Television Stations Inc.
Group Owner: Fox Television Stations Inc.; (acq 11-6-2001; with KTXH(TV) Houston, TX in swap for KBHK-TV San Francisco, CA).; *Washington Law Firm:* Leventhal, Senter & Lerman
Nat'l Network: MY NETWORK *Nat'l Reps:* Fox Stations Sales
Duffy Dyer, Station Manager
Mike Lewis, General Sales Mgr

WDCW *Digital Channel:* 50 *Virtual Channel:* 50; 1000 kw; 830 ft.; N38 57 44 W77 1 36
2121 Wisconsin Ave.,N.W., Suite 350, Washington, DC 20007 US
(202) 965-5050, *Fax:* (202) 965-0050
thecwdc.trb.com
License: Washington, DC County, DC held by WDCW Broadcasting Inc.
Group Owner: Tribune Broadcasting Co.; (acq 12-20-2007; grpsl)
Nat'l Network: CW *Nat'l Reps:* Harrington, Righter & Parsons
Dennis Fitzsimons, CEO
Eric Meyrowitz, Operations Dir
Chip Shenkan, General Sales Mgr
Jim Byrne, Promotions Manager
John Handley, Chief Engineer
Brett Burke, National Sales Manager

***WETA-TV** *Digital Channel:* 27 *Virtual Channel:* 26; 73 kw; 833 ft.; N38 57 1 W77 4 47
2775 South Quincy Street, Arlington, VA 22206 US
(703) 998-2600, *Fax:* (703) 998-3401
www.weta.org
License: Washington, DC County, DC held by Greater Washington Educational Telecommunications Association Inc
Washington Law Firm: Dow, Lohnes & Albertson
Nat'l Network: PBS
Sharon Rockefeller, President
Karen Fritz, General Manager
Kevin Harris, Programming Director
Joe Bruns, Executive Vice President

WFDC-DT *Digital Channel:* 15; 2,680 kw vis; ant 567t/407g; N38 56 24 W77 04 54
101 Constitution Ave. N.W., # L100, Washington, DC 20001
(202) 522-8640, *Fax:* (202) 898-1960
www.entravision.com
rguernica@entravisiondc.com
License: Arlington, Arlington County, VA held by TeleFutura D.C. LLC.
Group Owner: Univision Communications Inc.; (acq 6-1-2001; $30 million)
Nat'l Network: Univision (Spanish)
Foreign Language Programming

Rudy Guernica, General Manager
Ernesto Clavijo, News Director
Fred Willard, Chief Engineer

***WHUT-TV** *Digital Channel:* 33 *Virtual Channel:* 32; 100 kw; 833 ft.; N38 57 1 W77 4 47
2600 Fourth St., N. W., Washington, DC 20001 US
(202) 806-3200, *Fax:* (202) 806-3300
www.whut.org
j_lawson@howard.edu
License: Washington, DC County, DC held by Howard University
Washington Law Firm: Arnold & Porter
Nat'l Network: PBS *Wire Services:* Bloomberg Financial
Harold Burris, Operations Dir
Jennifer Lawson, General Manager
Luma Haj, General Sales Mgr

WJLA-TV *Digital Channel:* 7 *Virtual Channel:* 7; 52 kw; 773 ft.; N38 57 1 W77 4 47
3007 Tilden Street, NW, Washington, DC 20008 US
(703) 236-9552, *Fax:* (703) 236-2345
www.wjla.com
License: Washington, DC County, DC held by ACC Licensee Inc.
Group Owner: Allbritton Communications Co.; (acq 1-76; grpsl).; *Washington Law Firm:* Dow, Lohnes & Albertson, PLLC
Nat'l Network: ABC
Hours of Local News Weekly: News progmg 24 hrs wkly
Frederick Ryan Jr., General Manager
Robert Scutari, General Sales Mgr
Mark Olingy, Chief Engineer

WPXW-TV *Digital Channel:* 34; 5,000 kw vis, 500 kw aur; 560t/455g; N38 47 16 W77 19 49
6199 Old Arrington Ln., Fairfax Stn., VA 22039
(703) 503-7966, *Fax:* (703) 503-1225
www.ionline.tv
License: Manassas, Manassas City County, VA held by ION Media Washington License Inc., Debtor in Possession
Group Owner: ION Media Networks Inc.; (acq 4-16-97; $30 million); *Washington Law Firm:* Wilmer, Cutler & Pickering
Nat'l Network: ION Television
Anthony Polcaro, General Manager
David Weaver, Chief Engineer

WRC-TV *Digital Channel:* 48 *Virtual Channel:* 4; 813 kw; 794 ft.; N38 56 24 W77 4 54
1299 Pennsylvania Ave NW, 11th Floor, Washington, DC 20004 US
(202) 885-4000, *Fax:* (202) 885-4104
www.nbc4.com
License: Washington, DC County, DC held by NBC Telemundo License Co.
Group Owner: NBC Owned Television Stations
Nat'l Network: NBC *Nat'l Reps:* NBC TV Stations Sales *Wire Services:* UPI
Michael Jack, President

WTTG *Digital Channel:* 36 *Virtual Channel:* 5; 1000 kw; 745 ft.; N38 57 22 W77 4 59
5151 Wisconsin Ave.,N.W., Washington, DC 20015 US
(202) 244-5151, *Fax:* (202) 244-1745
www.fox5dc.com
License: Washington, DC County, DC held by Fox Television Stations Inc.
Group Owner: Fox Television Stations Inc.; (acq 3-86; grpsl).; *Washington Law Firm:* Hogan & Hartson
Nat'l Network: FOX *Nat'l Reps:* TeleRep
Duffy Dyer, Operations Dir
Carla Pregnolato, General Sales Mgr

WUSA *Digital Channel:* 9 *Virtual Channel:* 9; 52 kw; 773 ft.; N38 57 1 W77 4 47
4100 Wisconsin Ave, N.W., Washington, DC 20016 US
(202) 895-5999, *Fax:* (202) 364-6163
www.wusatv9.com
9news@wusatv9.com
License: Washington, DC County, DC held by The Detroit News Inc.
Group Owner: Gannett Broadcasting; (acq 2-18-86).; *Washington Law Firm:* Reed Smith LLP
Nat'l Network: CBS *Nat'l Reps:* Blair Television
Hours of Local News Weekly: News progmg 39 hrs wkly
Darryll Green, President
Allans Horlick, Station Manager

WWPX-TV *Digital Channel:* 12; 2,040 kw vis; ant 984t/200g; N39 27 27 W78 03 52; *Rebroadcasting:* Satellite of WPXW Manassas, Virginia 100%
Mailing Address: 6199 Old Arrington Ln., Fairfax Stn., VA 22039
Second Address: 74 Swinging Bridge Rd., Martinsburg, WV 25401
(703) 503-7966, *Fax:* (703) 503-1225
www.ionline.tv
License: Martinsburg, Berkeley County, WV held by ION Media Martinsburg License Inc., Debtor-in-possession
Group Owner: ION Media Networks Inc.; (acq 6-1-2000).; *Washington Law Firm:* Cohn & Marks
Nat'l Network: ION Television
Faye Williams, Station Manager

Florida

Ft. Myers-Naples, FL (DMA 62)

WBBH-TV *Digital Channel:* 15 *Virtual Channel:* 20; 1000 kw; 1489 ft.; N26 49 21 W81 45 54
3719 Central Avenue, Fort Myers, FL 33901 US
(239) 939-2020, *Fax:* (239) 939-3244(news);(239) 939-4801
www.nbc-2.com
comments@nbc-2.com
License: Fort Myers, Lee County, FL held by Waterman Broadcasting Corp. of Fla.
Group Owner: Waterman Broadcasting Corp.; *Washington Law Firm:* Cohn & Marks
Nat'l Network: NBC *Nat'l Reps:* Continental Television Sales
Size of News Staff: 80; *Hours of Local News Weekly:* news progmg 32 hrs wkly
Gerry Poppe, CFO
Bernard Waterman, President
Chris Rhodes, Operations Dir
Bob Beville, General Sales Mgr
Dan Billings, Chief Engineer
Steven Pontius, Executive Vice President

WFTX-TV *Digital Channel:* 35; 4,550 kw vis, 450 kw aur; ant 1,503t/1,450g; N26 47 43 W81 48 04; *Population Served:* 413,000
621 S.W. Pine Island Rd., Cape Coral, FL 33991
(239) 574-3636, *Fax:* (239) 574-2025
www.fox4florida.com
License: Cape Coral, Lee County, FL held by Journal Broadcast Corp.
Group Owner: Journal Communications Inc.; (acq 12-5-2005; grpsl).; *Washington Law Firm:* Dow, Lohnes & Albertson
Nat'l Network: Fox
Judy Kenney, Operations Dir
Brent Struense, Promotions Manager
Forrest Carr, News Director

***WGCU** *Digital Channel:* 30; 1,321 kw vis, 158 kw aur; 963t/992g; N26 48 54 W81 45 44; *Population Served:* 1,217,000
10501 FGCU Blvd. S., Fort Meyers, FL 33965
(239) 590-2300, *Fax:* (239) 590-7088
www.wgcu.org
License: Fort Myers, Lee County, FL held by Board of Trustees, Florida Gulf Coast University
(acq 11-16-01).; *Washington Law Firm:* Schwartz Woods Miller
Nat'l Network: PBS
Iris Gerstle, CFO
Barbara Linstrom, Operations Dir
Rick Johnson, General Manager
Taby Cooke, Programming Director
Barbara Steinhoff, Promotions Manager
Amy Tardiff, News Director
Rick Carroll, Engineering Dir
Michael Stepf,Chief Engineer
Muriel Olsen, Administrative Assistant
Terry Brennen, Director of Corporate Affairs
Toby Cooke, Director of Programming

WINK-TV *Digital Channel:* 50 *Virtual Channel:* 11; 1000 kw; 1,478t/1,519g; N26 48 01 W81 45 48; *Population Served:* 1,061,000
2824 Palm Beach Blvd., Fort Myers, FL 33916
(239) 334-1111, *Fax:* (239) 334-0744
www.winktv.com
webmaster@winktv.com
License: Fort Myers, Lee County, FL held by Fort Myers Broadcasting Co.
Group Owner: Fort Myers Broadcasting Co.; *Washington Law Firm:* Leibowitz & Associates
Nat'l Network: CBS *Nat'l Reps:* Eagle Television Sales
Size of News Staff: 55; *Hours of Local News Weekly:* news progmg 32 hrs wkly
Brian McBride, CEO
Wayne Simons, Operations Dir
Jesse Daniels, National Sales Manager

WRXY-TV *Digital Channel:* 33 *Virtual Channel:* 49; 1000 kw; 1407 ft.; N26 47 8 W81 47 41
Mailing Address: 40000 Horseshoe Acres Rd, Punta Gorda, FL 33955 US
Second Address: 40000 Horseshoe Rd., Punta Gorda, FL 33982
(239) 543-7200, *Fax:* (239) 543-6800
wrxy@wrxytv.com
License: Tice, Lee County, FL held by West Coast Christian Television Inc
Nat'l Network: REL
Steven Speheger, Operations Dir
Paul Lodato, General Manager

WXCW *Digital Channel:* 45 *Virtual Channel:* 46; 1000 kw; 1496 ft.; N26 47 8 W81 47 40
3451 Bonita Bay Blvd., Bonita Springs, FL 34134 US
(239) 338-1111, *Fax:* (239) 479-5592
www.wb6tv.com
License: Naples, Collier County, FL held by Sun Broadcasting Inc.
(acq 2-16-2007; $45 million); *Ownership:* Joseph C. Schwartzel, 100%; *Washington Law Firm:* Dickstein Shapiro Morin & Oshinsky L.L.P.
Nat'l Network: CW *Nat'l Reps:* Millennium Sales & Marketing
Hours of Local News Weekly: News progmg 13.5 hrs wkly
Jack Spiess, Operations Dir
Joe Schwartzel, General Manager
Jim Schwartzel, General Sales Mgr

WZVN-TV *Digital Channel:* 41 *Virtual Channel:* 26; 1000 kw; 1489 ft.; N26 49 21 W81 45 54
3719 Central Ave., Ft. Myers, FL 33901 US
(239) 939-2020, *Fax:* (239) 939-3244 (news),(239) 939-4801
www.abc-7.com
comments@nbc-2.com
License: Naples, Collier County, FL held by Montclair Communications Inc
(acq 10-10-1996; $21.3 million); *Washington Law Firm:* Irwin, Campbell & Tannenwald
Nat'l Network: ABC *Nat'l Reps:* Continental Television Sales
Size of News Staff: 85; *Hours of Local News Weekly:* news progmg 19.5 hrs wkly
Lara Kunkler, President
Chris Rhodes, Operations Dir
Dan Billings, Chief Engineer

Gainesville, FL (DMA 160)

WCJB-TV *Digital Channel:* 16; 2,818 kw vis, 282 kw aur; ant 1,049t/985g; N29 32 11 W82 24 00; *Population Served:* 370,710
6220 N.W. 43rd St., Gainesville, FL 32653
(352) 377-2020, *Fax:* (352) 373-6516
www.wcjb.com
tv20news@wcjb.com
License: Gainesville, Alachua County, FL held by Diversified Broadcasting Inc.
Group Owner: Diversified Communications; (acq 12-1-76;; *Washington Law Firm:* Irwin, Campbell & Tannenwald
Nat'l Network: ABC; CW
Size of News Staff: 35; *Hours of Local News Weekly:* news progmg 17 hrs wkly
Carolyn Barrett, General Manager
Alan Chatman, General Sales Mgr
Sean Kaplan, Promotions Manager
Andrea Crenney, News Director
Steve Ingam, Chief Engineer

WGFL *Digital Channel:* 28; 5,000 kw vis, 53 kw aur; 911t; N29 37 47 W82 34 24; *Population Served:* 400,000
1703 N.W. 80th Blvd., Gainesville, FL 32652
(352) 332-1128, *Fax:* (352) 332-1506
www.mygainesville.tv
License: High Springs, Alachua County, FL held by New Age Media of Gainesville License LLC
Group Owner: CP Media LLC; (acq 3-31-2007; grpsl)
Nat'l Network: CBS
Sue Edwards, Operations Dir
Todd Senter, General Manager

WNBW-DT *Digital Channel:* 9 *Virtual Channel:* 9; 4.9 kw; 919 ft.; N29 37 47 W82 34 25
Of Gainesville, 415 E 37th St, New York, NY 10016 US
(352) 332-1128, *Fax:* (352) 332-1506
www.mygainesville.tv
License: Gainesville, Alachua County, FL held by MPS Media of Gainesville LLC
Nat'l Network: N/A *Nat'l Reps:* Petry Television Inc.
Todd Senter, General Manager

WOGX *Digital Channel:* 31 *Virtual Channel:* 51; 500 kw; 850 ft.; N29 21 32 W82 19 43

Mailing Address: 1716 Locust Street, Des Moines, IA 50309 US
Second Address: 35 Skyline Dr., Lake Mary, FL 32746
(407) 644-3535, *Fax:* (352) 237-5423
www.myfoxorlando.com
License: Ocala, Marion County, FL held by Fox Television Stations Inc.
Group Owner: Fox Television Stations Inc.; (acq 6-17-2002; with WOFL(TV) Orlando).; *Washington Law Firm:* Skadden, Arps, Slate, Meagher & Flom
Nat'l Network: FOX *Nat'l Reps:* Fox Stations Sales
Size of News Staff: 35; *Hours of Local News Weekly:* news progmg 7 hrs wkly
Stan Knott, General Manager

***WUFT** *Digital Channel:* 36 *Virtual Channel:* 5; 1000 kw; 863 ft.; N29 42 34 W82 23 40
2000 Weimer Hall, Gainsville, FL 32611 US
(352) 392-5551, *Fax:* (352) 392-5731
www.wuft.org
info@wuft.tv
License: Gainesville, Alachua County, FL held by Board of Trustees, University of Florida
Washington Law Firm: Schwartz, Woods & Miller
Nat'l Network: PBS
Hours of Local News Weekly: News progmg 3 hrs wkly
Larry Bankner, General Manager
Titus Rush, Station Manager
Brent Williams, General Sales Mgr
Rob Carr, Chief Engineer

Greenville-Spartanburg, SC-Asheville, NC-Anderson, SC (DMA 36)

***DWUNW** *Digital Channel:* 27; 50 kw; ant 1,555t/68g; N35 34 06 W82 54 25
Mailing Address: Box 14900, Research Triangle Park, NC 33040
Second Address: 10 TW Alexander Dr, Research Triangle Park, NC 27709
(919) 549-7000, *Fax:* (919) 549-7201
www.unctv.org
License: Canton, Haywood County, NC held by University of North Carolina
Tom Howe, General Manager

Jacksonville, FL (DMA 47)

WAWS *Digital Channel:* 32 *Virtual Channel:* 30; 1000 kw; 955 ft.; N30 16 51 W81 34 12
200 Concord Plaza, Suite 600, San Antonio, TX 78216 US
(904) 642-3030, *Fax:* (904) 642-5665
www.fox30jax.com
info@fox30online.com
License: Jacksonville, Duval County, FL held by Newport Television License LLC.
Group Owner: Newport Television LLC; (acq 3-14-2008; grpsl);
Washington Law Firm: Covington & Burling
Nat'l Network: FOX; MyNetworkTV *Nat'l Reps:* Continental Television Sales
Jack Potter, General Sales Mgr

WCWJ *Digital Channel:* 34 *Virtual Channel:* 17; 863 kw; 927 ft.; N30 16 36 W81 33 47
Mailing Address: 333 East Grace Street, Richmond, VA 23219 US
Second Address: 9117 Hogan Rd., Jacksonville, FL 32216
(904) 641-1700, *Fax:* (904) 642-7201
www.yourjax.com
License: Jacksonville, Duval County, FL held by Nexstar Broadcasting Inc.
Group Owner: Nexstar Broadcasting Group Inc.; (acq 5-1-2009);
Washington Law Firm: Drinker Biddle & Reath LLP
Nat'l Network: CW
Marc Hefner, General Sales Mgr
Mark Marshman, Chief Engineer

***WJCT** *Digital Channel:* 7 *Virtual Channel:* 7; 18 kw; 991 ft.; N30 16 51 W81 34 12
100 Festival Park Ave., Jacksonville, FL 32202 US
(904) 353-7770, *Fax:* (904) 358-6331
www.wjct.org
wjct@wjct.org
License: Jacksonville, Duval County, FL held by WJCT Inc
Washington Law Firm: Schwartz, Woods & Miller
Nat'l Network: PBS
Foreign Language Programming
Steven Wallace, Chairman
Jocelyn Enriquez, CFO
Michael Boylan, President
Jeri Cirillo, General Sales Mgr
Stanley Cleiland, Programming Director

***WJEB-TV** *Digital Channel:* 44 *Virtual Channel:* 59; 1000 kw; 945 ft.; N30 16 34 W81 33 52
3101 Emerson Expressway, Jacksonville, FL 32207 US
(904) 399-8413, *Fax:* (904) 399-8423
www.wjeb.org
prayer@wjeb.org
License: Jacksonville, Duval County, FL held by Jacksonville Educators Broadcasting Inc
Nat'l Network: TRINITY BROADCA
Colette Snowden, General Manager
Clayton Roney, Engineering Dir

WJXT *Digital Channel:* 42 *Virtual Channel:* 4; 976 kw; 965 ft.; N30 16 24 W81 33 13
4 Broadcast Place, Jacksonville, FL 32207 US
(904) 399-4000, *Fax:* (904) 393-9822
www.news4jax.com,www.wjxt.com
jaxnews@news4jax.com
License: Jacksonville, Duval County, FL held by Post-Newsweek Stations, Fla. Inc.
Group Owner: Post-Newsweek Stations Inc.; (acq 1-28-53; grpsl;; *Washington Law Firm:* Covington & Burling
Nat'l Network: IND *Nat'l Reps:* TeleRep *Wire Services:* AP; CNN
Size of News Staff: 75; *Hours of Local News Weekly:* 47
Tina Schultz, Operations Dir
Bob Ellis, General Manager
Wayne Reid, General Sales Mgr
Mike Guerrieri, Promotions Manager
Mo Ruddy-Baker, News Director

WJXX *Digital Channel:* 10 *Virtual Channel:* 25; 29.5 kw; 954 ft.; N30 16 24 W81 33 13
Box 551000, 7025 A.C. Skinner Pkwy., Jacksonville, FL 32255 US
(904) 354-1212, *Fax:* (904) 633-8899
www.firstcoastnews.com
news@firstcoastnews.com
License: Orange Park, Clay County, FL held by Gannett River States Publishing Corp.
Group Owner: Gannett Broadcasting; (acq 3-15-00; $81 million)
Nat'l Network: ABC
Dodie Cantrell, President
Sam Folley, General Sales Mgr
Glenn Sebold, Programming Director
Mike Garber, News Director

WTEV-TV *Digital Channel:* 19 *Virtual Channel:* 47; 1000 kw; 955 ft.; N30 16 51 W81 34 12
115 East Travis, Suite 1427, San Antonio, TX 78205 US
(904) 642-3030, *Fax:* (904) 642-5665
ActionNewsJax.com
info@cbs47.com
License: Jacksonville, Duval County, FL held by High Plains Broadcasting License Co. LLC.
Group Owner: High Plains Broadcasting Inc.; (acq 9-15-2008; grpsl); *Washington Law Firm:* Pillsbury Winthrop Shaw Pittman LLP
Nat'l Network: CBS *Nat'l Reps:* Millennium Sales & Marketing
Size of News Staff: 72; *Hours of Local News Weekly:* news progmg 22 hrs wkly
Adrian West, Programming Director

WTLV *Digital Channel:* 13 *Virtual Channel:* 12; 53.3 kw; 954 ft.; N30 16 24 W81 33 13
P.O. Box Tv12, Jacksonville, FL 32231 US
(904) 354-1212, *Fax:* (904) 633-8899
www.firstcoastnews.com
news@firstcoastnews.com
License: Jacksonville, Duval County, FL held by Multimedia Holdings Corporation
Group Owner: Gannett Broadcasting; (acq 5-12-75; $11,401,217;; *Washington Law Firm:* Reed, Smith, Shaw & McClay
Nat'l Network: NBC *Nat'l Reps:* Blair Television
Size of News Staff: 54; *Hours of Local News Weekly:* news progmg 17 hrs wkly
Dodie Cantrell, President
Sam Folley, General Sales Mgr

Miami-Ft. Lauderdale, FL (DMA 16)

***WBEC-TV** *Digital Channel:* 40 *Virtual Channel:* 63; 1000 kw; 935 ft.; N25 59 8.7 W80 11 37.1
4035 N. 29th Avenue, Hollywood, FL 33020 US
(754) 321-1000, *Fax:* (754) 321-1180
www.becon.tv
feedback@becon.tv
License: Boca Raton, Palm Beach County, FL held by The School Board of Broward County, Florida
Nat'l Network: ETV
Chris Bartch, Station Manager
Tom Ford, Programming Director

WBFS-TV *Digital Channel:* 32 *Virtual Channel:* 33; 1000 kw; 861 ft.; N25 58 2 W80 12 34
C/O Viacom/D.C., 1501, M St., N.W., Suite 1100, Washington, DC 20005 US
(305) 621-3333, *Fax:* (305) 471-7843
www.upn33.com
upn33@wbfs.com
License: Miami, Dade County, FL held by Miami Television Station WBFS Inc.
Group Owner: CBS Television Stations Group
Nat'l Network: IND
Shaun McDonald, General Manager
Tom Cury, General Sales Mgr

WFOR-TV *Digital Channel:* 22 *Virtual Channel:* 4; 1000 kw; 978 ft.; N25 58 7 W80 13 20
600 New Hampshire Ave NW, Suite 1200, Washington, DC 20037 US
(305) 591-4444, *Fax:* (305) 477-3040 (news)
www.cbs4news.com
License: Miami, Dade County, FL held by CBS Television Stations Inc.
Group Owner: CBS Television Stations Group
Nat'l Network: CBS *Nat'l Reps:* CBS TV Stations National Sales
Wire Services: NWS (National Weather Service)
Size of News Staff: 90; *Hours of Local News Weekly:* news progmg 30 hrs wkly
Shaun McDonald, President
Tom Cury, General Sales Mgr
Tracy Letize, Programming Director
Adrienne Roark, News Director
Juan Andrea, Engineering Dir
Franklin Anderson, Chief Engineer
Michael Applebaum, General Sales Manager

WGEN-TV *Digital Channel:* 8 *Virtual Channel:* 8; 7 kw; 183 ft.; N24 33 18 W81 48 5
5420 Mac Donald Avenue, Key West, FL 33040 US
(305) 293-4333, *Fax:* (305) 293-4007
www.wgent.tv.com
amonge@wegentv.com
License: Key West, Monroe County, FL held by Sonia Licensed Subsidiary LLC
Nat'l Network: IND
Alberto Monge, Station Manager

WHFT-TV *Digital Channel:* 46 *Virtual Channel:* 45; 1000 kw; 1010 ft.; N25 59 34 W80 10 27
3324 Pembroke Road, Pembroke Park, FL 33021 US
(954) 962-1700, *Fax:* (954) 962-2817
www.tbn.org
License: Miami, Dade County, FL held by Trinity Broadcasting of Florida Inc.
Group Owner: Trinity Broadcasting Network; (acq 5-14-80; $10 million); *Washington Law Firm:* Colby M. May
Nat'l Network: TRINITY BROADCA
Foreign Language Programming
Paul Crouch, President
T. Hines, General Manager

***WLRN-TV** *Digital Channel:* 20 *Virtual Channel:* 17; 870 kw; 988 ft.; N25 58 46 W80 11 46
172 N.E. 15th St., Miami, FL 33132 US
(305) 995-1717, *Fax:* (305) 995-2299
www.wlrn.org
info@wlrn.org
License: Miami, Dade County, FL held by The School Board of Miami-Dade County, FL
Washington Law Firm: Leibowitz & Associates
Nat'l Network: PBS
Mario Barrios, Operations Dir
John LaBonia, General Manager
Bernadette Siy, Station Manager
Ginette Grey, Promotions Manager
Adrienne Kennedy, Special Projects Manager

WLTV-DT ; 4,470 kw vis; 974t; N25 58 07 W80 13 20;
Population Served: 4,600,000
9405 N.W. 41st St., Miami, FL 33178
(305) 470-2323, *Fax:* (305) 471-3959
www.univision.net
License: Miami, Dade County, FL held by WLTV L.P.
Group Owner: Univision Communications Inc.; (acq 8-7-88);
Washington Law Firm: Wiley, Rein & Fielding
Nat'l Network: Univision (Spanish)

Foreign Language Programming; Size of News Staff: 70; *Hours of Local News Weekly:* 24
Luis Fernandez-Rocha, President
Bert Delgado, Operations Dir
Teri Vila Caballero, General Sales Mgr
Carlos Espinosa, Programming Director
Evi Fabrega, Promotions Manager
Emilio Marrero, News Director
Douglas Petersen, ChiefEngineer
Leonor Guerrero, Business Manager
Angela Ramos, Community Affairs
Mary Fuentes, Traffic Manager

***WPBT** *Digital Channel:* 18 *Virtual Channel:* 2; 1000 kw; 1014 ft.; N25 57 30 W80 12 44
Mailing Address: 14901 N.E. 20th Avenue, Miami, FL 33181 US
Second Address: 14901 N.E. 20th Ave., Miami, FL 33261-0002
(305) 949-8321, *Fax:* (305) 944-4211
www.channel2.org
channel2@channel2.org
License: Miami, Dade County, FL held by Community Television Foundation of South Florida Inc
Washington Law Firm: Wilmer, Cutler & Pickering
Nat'l Network: PBS
Foreign Language Programming
Rick Schneider, CEO
Dave Mullins, Promotions Manager
Jody Rafkind, Promotions Manager

WPLG *Digital Channel:* 10 *Virtual Channel:* 10; 127.7 kw; 1014 ft.; N25 58 0 W80 12 43
3900 Biscayne Blvd., Miami, FL 33137 US
(954) 364-2500, *Fax:* (954) 364-2935
www.local10.com
License: Miami, Dade County, FL held by Post-Newsweek Stations, Fla. Inc.
Group Owner: Post-Newsweek Stations Inc.; (acq 9-27-69; grpsl;; *Washington Law Firm:* Covington & Burling
Nat'l Network: ABC *Nat'l Reps:* MMT
David Boylan, Operations Dir
Paul Wasserman, General Sales Mgr
Melinda Harper, Programming Director
Darren Alline, Chief Engineer
Sharon Harrison, Operations Manager

WPXM-TV *Digital Channel:* 35; 3,240 kw vis, 324 kw aur; 335t; N24 41 05 W80 18 52
13801 N. W. 14th St., Sunrise, FL 33323
(954) 703-1920, *Fax:* (954) 858-1848
www.ionmedia.tv
License: Miami, Dade County, FL held by ION Media License Company, LLC, Debtor-in-possession
Group Owner: ION Media Networks Inc.; (acq 12-12-97)
Nat'l Network: ION Television
Frank Tenore, General Sales Mgr
Robert Ford, Chief Engineer

WSBS-TV *Digital Channel:* 3 *Virtual Channel:* 22; 1 kw; 177 ft.; N24 33 18 W81 48 7
P.O. Box 255, Evergreen, CO 80439 US
(305) 644-4800, *Fax:* (786) 470-1667
www.mega.tv
info@mega.tv
License: Key West, Monroe County, FL held by WSBS Licensing Inc.
Group Owner: Spanish Broadcasting System Inc.; (acq 2-28-2006; $37.25 million with WSBS-CA Miami).
Nat'l Network: MEGA TV
Foreign Language Programming
Alex Aleman, Operations Dir
Cynthia Hudson, Station Manager

WSCV *Digital Channel:* 30 *Virtual Channel:* 51; 1000 kw; 997 ft.; N25 59 9 W80 11 37
2290 West 8th Avenue, Hialeah, FL 33010 US
(954) 622-6000, *Fax:* (954) 622-6107
www.telemundo51.com
wtvjdesk@nbc.com
License: Fort Lauderdale, Broward County, FL held by NBC Telemundo License Co.
Group Owner: Telemundo Television Stations; (acq 4-12-2002; grpsl).
Nat'l Network: TELEMUNDO
Foreign Language Programming; Size of News Staff: 70; *Hours of Local News Weekly:* news progmg 16 hrs wkly
Don Browne, CEO
Manuel Martinez, General Manager
Jorge Carballo, General Sales Mgr
Maria Christina Barros, Programming Director
Migdalia Figueroa, News Director

WSFL-TV *Digital Channel:* 19 *Virtual Channel:* 39; 5,000 kw vis, 500 kw aur; ant 905t/905g; N25 58 07 W80 13 20; *Population Served:* 3,247,000
500 E. Broward Blvd., 9th Fl., Fort Lauderdale, FL 33020
(954) 627-7300, *Fax:* (954) 355-5200
wsfltv.sun-sentinel.com
License: Miami, Dade County, FL held by Channel 39 Inc.
Group Owner: Tribune Broadcasting Co.; (acq 12-20-2007; grpsl)
Nat'l Network: CW *Nat'l Reps:* TeleRep
Jen Dekarz, CFO
Howard Greenberg, General Manager
Marilyn Hansen, Station Manager
Natalie Grant, Programming Director
Felicia Blanski, Promotions Manager
Rudy Morris, Chief Engineer
Joe Ryan, Traffic Manager

WSVN *Digital Channel:* 7 *Virtual Channel:* 7; 158 kw; 1008 ft.; N25 58 0 W80 12 43
1401 79th St. Causeway, Miami, FL 33141 US
(305) 751-6692, *Fax:* (305) 757-2266
www.wsvn.com
License: Miami, Dade County, FL held by Sunbeam Television Corp
Group Owner: Sunbeam Television Corp.; (acq 10-4-67;;
Washington Law Firm: Koteen & Naftalin
Nat'l Network: FOX *Nat'l Reps:* Harrington, Righter & Parsons
Edmund Ansin, President
Anby Ansin, Operations Dir
Robert Leider, General Manager
Steven Cejas, Executive Producer

WTVJ *Digital Channel:* 31 *Virtual Channel:* 6; 1000 kw; 1020 ft.; N25 58 7 W80 13 20
Ms Diane Zipursky, 1299 Pennsylvania Ave, Washington, DC 20004 US
(954) 622-6000
www.nbcmiami.com
wtvjdesk@nbc.com
License: Miami, Dade County, FL held by NBC Telemundo License Co.
Group Owner: NBC Owned Television Stations; (acq 1995).
Nat'l Network: NBC *Nat'l Reps:* NBC TV Stations Sales *Wire Services:* NWS (National Weather Service)
Amanda Calpin, CFO
Ardyth Diercks, General Manager

Mobile, AL-Pensacola (Ft. Walton Beach), FL (DMA 60)

WAWD *Digital Channel:* 49 *Virtual Channel:* 58; 32 kw; 200 ft.; N30 27 14.1 W86 51 59.4
Mailing Address: 5580 NW 75th Avenue, Ocala, FL 34482 US
Second Address: 8317 Front Beach Rd., Suite 23, Panama City, FL
(850) 234-2773, *Fax:* (850) 234-1179
www.tripsmarter.com
License: Fort Walton Beach, Okaloosa County, FL held by Beach TV Properties Inc.
Group Owner: Beach TV Properties Inc.; (acq 10-29-99; $175,000); *Washington Law Firm:* Baraff, Koerner, Olender & Hochberg
Nat'l Network: IND
Jud Colley, General Manager
Brad Skaret, Chief Engineer

WEAR-TV *Digital Channel:* 17 *Virtual Channel:* 3; 1000 kw; 1900 ft.; N30 36 45 W87 38 43
10706 Beaver Dam Road, Cockeysville, MD 21030 US 32506
(850) 456-3333, *Fax:* (850) 455-0159
www.weartv.com
comments@wear.sbgnet.com
License: Pensacola, Escambia County, FL held by WEAR Licensee L.L.C.
Group Owner: Sinclair Broadcast Group Inc.; (acq 10-8-97).;
Washington Law Firm: Shaw Pittman LLP
Nat'l Network: ABC *Nat'l Reps:* Millennium Sales & Marketing
Size of News Staff: 30; *Hours of Local News Weekly:* news progmg 14 hrs wkly
Terry Cole, General Manager
Debra Curry, General Sales Mgr
Kyle Brinkman, News Director
David Brown, Chief Engineer

WFBD *Digital Channel:* 48 *Virtual Channel:* 48; 1000 kw; 1044 ft.; N30 59 52 W86 43 13
1 Shackleford Drive, Little Rock, AR 72211 US
(251) 809-3013, *Fax:* (251) 809-3014
License: Destin, Okaloosa County, FL held by George S. Flinn, Jr.
Nat'l Network: IND
Dirk Freeman, General Manager
Tammy Elliott, Programming Director
Brian Walton, Chief Engineer

WFGX *Digital Channel:* 50 *Virtual Channel:* 35; 1000 kw; 1912 ft.; N30 36 45 W87 38 42
Mailing Address: 7602-4 Congress Street, New Port Richey, FL 34653 US
Second Address: 4990 Mobile Hgwy., Fort Walton Beach, FL 32506
(850) 456-3333, *Fax:* (850) 453-4335
www.wfgxtv.com
wfgx@wfgxtv.com
License: Fort Walton Beach, Okaloosa County, FL held by WFGX Licensee LLC.
Group Owner: Sinclair Broadcast Group Inc.; (acq 3-31-2004; $520,000).; *Washington Law Firm:* Shaw Pittman LLP
Nat'l Network: MYTV
David Smith, President
Joe Smith, Operations Dir
Carl Leahy, General Manager

WHBR *Digital Channel:* 34 *Virtual Channel:* 33; 1000 kw; 1362 ft.; N30 36 45 W87 38 43
Mailing Address: P. O. Box 2633, Pensacola, FL 32513 US
Second Address: 6500 Pensacola Blvd., Pensacola, FL 32505
(850) 473-8633, *Fax:* (850) 473-8631
www.whbr.org
dmayo@whbr.org
License: Pensacola, Escambia County, FL held by Christian Television of Pensacola/Mobile Inc
(acq 12-16-97).; *Washington Law Firm:* Gammon & Grange
Nat'l Network: IND
Bob D'Andrea, President
Wayne Wetzel, Operations Dir
David Mayo, General Manager

WJTC *Digital Channel:* 45 *Virtual Channel:* 44; 1000 kw; 1499 ft.; N30 35 16 W87 33 13
661 Azalea Road, Mobile, AL 36691 US
(251) 602-1544, *Fax:* (251) 602-1547
www.utv44.com
utv44@online.com
License: Pensacola, Escambia County, FL held by Newport Television License LLC.
Group Owner: Newport Television LLC; (acq 3-14-2008; grpsl);
Washington Law Firm: Covington & Burling
Nat'l Network: IND *Nat'l Reps:* Millennium Sales & Marketing
Jared Quijas, Operations Dir
Shea Grandquest, General Manager
Chris Delaporte, General Sales Mgr
Chuck Reeves, Programming Director
Kristen Mosley, Promotions Manager
Tim Reid, Chief Engineer

WPAN *Digital Channel:* 40 *Virtual Channel:* 53; 33.5 kw; 719 ft.; N30 24 9 W86 59 35
Mailing Address: 2105 West Gregory Street, Pensacola, FL 32505 US
Second Address: 2105 W. Gregory St., Pensacola, FL 32523
(850) 433-1766, *Fax:* (850) 433-1641
License: Fort Walton Beach, Okaloosa County, FL held by Franklin Media Inc
(acq 5-23-88).; *Washington Law Firm:* Pepper & Corazzini
Nat'l Network: IND
John Franklin, General Manager

***WSRE** *Digital Channel:* 31 *Virtual Channel:* 23; 1000 kw; 1801 ft.; N30 36 40.3 W87 36 26.9
1000 College Blvd., Pensacola, FL 32504 US
(850) 484-1200, *Fax:* (850) 484-1255
www.wsre.org
rolandphillips@wsre.pbs.org
License: Pensacola, Escambia County, FL held by District Board of Trustees of Pensacola Junior College
Nat'l Network: PBS
Sandy Cesartiray, General Manager

Orlando-Daytona Beach-Melbourne, FL (DMA 19)

WACX-DT *Digital Channel:* 40; 1,000 kw vis; ant 1,619t/1,591g; N28 35 11.6 W81 04 58.2; *Population Served:* 3,500,000
Mailing Address: Box 608040, Orlando, FL 32860
Second Address: 285 W. Central Pkwy., Altamonte Springs, FL 32714
(407) 263-4040
www.wacxtv.com
superchannel@superchannel.com
License: Leesburg, Lake County, FL held by Associated Christian Television System Inc

(acq 6-8-83;; *Washington Law Firm:* Koerner & Olender
Foreign Language Programming
Claud Bowers, CEO
Carol Gentry, General Sales Mgr
Linda Jarrel, Programming Director

***WBCC** *Digital Channel:* 30 *Virtual Channel:* 68; 182 kw; 1611 ft.; N28 36 35 W81 3 35
1519 Clearlake Road, Cocoa, FL 32922 US
(321) 433-7110, *Fax:* (321) 433-7154
www.wbcctv.org
wbcc@brevardcc.edu
License: Cocoa, Brevard County, FL held by Brevard Community College.
Nat'l Network: PBS
Dr. James Drake, President
Philip T. Wallace, General Manager

***WDSC-TV** *Digital Channel:* 33 *Virtual Channel:* 15; 708 kw vis, 201.4 kw aur; ant 577t/567g; N29 10 24 W81 09 24; *Population Served:* 3,500,000
Mailing Address: Box 9245, Daytona Beach, FL 32120
Second Address: 1200 W. International Speedway Blvd., Daytona Beach, FL 32114
(386) 506-4415, *Fax:* (386) 506-4427
www.wceu.org
channel15@dbc.edu
License: New Smyrna Beach, Volusia County, FL held by Daytona State College Inc.
(acq 6-30-2002); *Washington Law Firm:* Fletcher, Heald & Hildreth
Bruce Dunn, General Manager
Bill Schwartz, Engineering Dir

WESH *Digital Channel:* 11 *Virtual Channel:* 2; 100 kw vis, 10 kw aur; 1,650t/1,670g; N28 56 17 W81 18 58; *Population Served:* 1,735,900
1021 N. Wymore Rd., Winter Park, FL 10106
(407) 645-2222, *Fax:* (407) 539-7812
www.wesh.com
License: Daytona Beach, Volusia County, FL held by WESH-TV Broadcasting.
Group Owner: Hearst Corporation; (acq 1999; grpsl).;
Washington Law Firm: Brooks, Pierce, McLendon, Humphrey & Leonard
Nat'l Network: NBC *Nat'l Reps:* Eagle Television Sales *Wire Services:* AP
Size of News Staff: 80; *Hours of Local News Weekly:* 7.5
James Carter, President
Rick Scharf, Operations Dir
James Carter, General Manager
N/A, Station Manager
Rob Halpern, General Sales Mgr
Lenora Boutte, Programming Director
Steve Rifkin, Promotions Manager
Bob Longo, NewsDirector
N/A, Engineering Dir
Richard Monn, Chief Engineer
Justin Jones, National Sales Manager
Veronica Serrano, Traffic

WFTV *Digital Channel:* 39 *Virtual Channel:* 9; 1000 kw; 1608 ft.; N28 34 7 W81 3 16
Mailing Address: 3773 Howard Hughes Parkway, Suite 300n, Las Vegas, NV 89109 US
Second Address: 490 E. South St., Orlando, FL 32801-2841
(407) 841-9000, *Fax:* (407) 841-8529(sales),(407) 481-2891 (news)
www.wftv.com
License: Orlando, Orange County, FL held by WFTV, Inc.
Group Owner: Cox Media Group; (acq 8-85; $185 million)
Nat'l Network: ABC
Size of News Staff: 80; *Hours of Local News Weekly:* news progmg 25 hrs wkly
Shawn Bartelt, Operations Dir
Bill Funke, General Sales Mgr
Bob St. Charles, Promotions Manager
Bob Jordan, News Director
Chip Reif, Operations Manager

WKCF *Digital Channel:* 17 *Virtual Channel:* 18; 1000 kw; 1549 ft.; N28 35 12 W81 4 58
1350 Campus Parkway, Suite 106, Wall, NJ 07753 US
(407) 645-1818, *Fax:* (407) 647-4163
www.wb18.com
wb18wkcf@wb18.com
License: Clermont, Lake County, FL held by Orlando Hearst-Argyle Television Inc.
Group Owner: Hearst-Argyle Television Inc.; (acq 7-7-2006; $217.5 million)
Nat'l Network: CW *Nat'l Reps:* Harrington, Righter & Parsons
James Carter, President
John Soapes, General Sales Mgr
Steve Rifkin, Promotions Manager
Joe Addalia, Engineering Dir

WKMG-TV *Digital Channel:* 26 *Virtual Channel:* 6; 944 kw; 1693 ft.; N28 36 35 W81 3 35
Wkmg-Tv, 4466 John Young Parkway, Orlando, FL 32804 US
(407) 291-6000
www.local6.com; www.clickorlando.com
License: Orlando, Orange County, FL held by Post-Newsweek Stations Orlando Inc.
Group Owner: Post-Newsweek Stations Inc.; (acq 9-4-97);
Washington Law Firm: Covington & Burling
Nat'l Network: CBS *Nat'l Reps:* MMT
Size of News Staff: 80; *Hours of Local News Weekly:* news progmg 24 hrs wkly
Alan Frank, President
Skip Valet, General Manager

***WMFE-TV** *Digital Channel:* 24; 1,350 kw vis; ant 1,246t/1,220g; N28 36 08 W81 05 37; *Population Served:* 1,301,000
12443 Research Parkway, Suite 301, Orlando, FL 32817
(407) 823-1300, *Fax:* (407) 206-2791
wucflv.org
wucftv@ucf.edu
License: Orlando, Orange County, FL held by University of Central Florida
Washington Law Firm: Dow Lohnes PLLC
Nat'l Network: PBS
Ana Tangel-Rodriguez, Chairman
Grant J Heston, Operations Dir
Associate VP, General Manager
Nancy Zappa, Programming Director

WOFL *Digital Channel:* 22 *Virtual Channel:* 35; 607 kw; 1473 ft.; N28 36 13 W81 5 11
1716 Locust Street, Des Moines, IA 50309 US
(407) 644-3535
www.myfoxorlando.com
License: Orlando, Orange County, FL held by Fox Television Stations Inc.
Group Owner: Fox Television Stations Inc.; (acq 6-17-2002; with WOGX(TV) Ocala).
Nat'l Network: FOX
Stan Knott, General Manager
Terry Walden, Programming Director

WOPX-TV *Digital Channel:* 48; 5,000 kw vis; ant 1,548t/1,522g; N28 05 37 W81 07 28; *Population Served:* 685,000
7091 Grand Natl Dr., Suite 100, Orlando, FL 32819
(407) 370-5600, *Fax:* (407) 363-1757
www.iontelevision.com
License: Melbourne, Brevard County, FL held by Paxson Orlando License Inc.
Group Owner: ION Media Networks Inc.; (acq 12-12-97; $13,161,274).; *Washington Law Firm:* Dow, Lohnes & Albertson
Nat'l Network: ION Television
Conny Fiala, Operations Dir
Frank Tenore, General Sales Mgr

WOTF-DT *Digital Channel:* 43; 4,170 kw vis, 854 kw aur; 1,049t/1,005g; N28 18 26 W80 54 48
3010 Dill Rd., Orlando, FL 32820
(321) 254-4343, *Fax:* (321) 254-9343
www.univision.com
License: Melbourne, Brevard County, FL held by Univision of Melbourne Inc.
Group Owner: Univision Communications Inc.; (acq 5-21-2001; grpsl).; *Washington Law Firm:* Dow, Lohnes & Albertson
Foreign Language Programming
Rolo Duartes, General Manager
Frank Banos, Chief Engineer

WRBW *Digital Channel:* 41 *Virtual Channel:* 65; 763 kw; 1691 ft.; N28 36 35 W81 3 35
132 South Rodeo Drive, Fourth Floor, Beverly Hills, CA 90212 US
(407) 644-3535, *Fax:* (407) 333-3535 (sales)
www.wrbw.com
wrbw@wrbw.com
License: Orlando, Orange County, FL held by Fox Television Stations Inc.
Group Owner: Fox Television Stations Inc.; (acq 7-31-2001; grpsl).
Nat'l Network: MYTV
Stan Knott, General Manager
Terry Walden, Programming Director

WRDQ *Digital Channel:* 27 *Virtual Channel:* 27; 1000 kw; 1608 ft.; N28 34 7 W81 3 16
P.O. Box 1968, Orlando, FL 32802 US
(407) 841-9000, *Fax:* (407) 422-1414
www.wrdq.com
License: Orlando, Orange County, FL held by WFTV, Inc.
Group Owner: Cox Media Group; (acq 2-1-2001).
Nat'l Network: ABC
Shawn Bartelt, General Manager
Mario Mendosa, General Sales Mgr
Bob Jordan, News Director

***WTGL** *Digital Channel:* 45; 4,680 kw vis, 468 kw aur; ant 934t/1,005g; N28 18 26 W80 54 48; *Population Served:* 3,068,000
31 Skyline Dr., Lake Mary, FL 32746
(407) 215-6745, *Fax:* (407) 215-6789
www.tv45.org
kathy@tv45.org
License: Cocoa, Brevard County, FL held by Good Life Broadcasting
1982; *Washington Law Firm:* Lerman & Senter
Regional Reps: Ken Mikesell
Foreign Language Programming; Hours of Local News Weekly: 0
Ed Griffis, Operations Dir
Ken Mikesell, General Manager
Eileen Kelly, Programming Director
Michael Flynn, Chief Engineer

WVEN-TV *Virtual Channel:* 26; 2,750 kw vis, 2,750 kw au; 1,063t; N29 17 10 W81 29 37
523 Douglas Ave., Suite 100, Altamonte Springs, FL 32714
(407) 774-2626, *Fax:* (407) 774-3384
License: Daytona Beach, Volusia County, FL held by Entravision Holdings L.L.C.
Group Owner: Entravision Communications Corp.; (acq 9-15-00; $22.55 million)
Nat'l Network: Univision (Spanish)
Foreign Language Programming
Ulysses Arrigoitia, General Manager

Panama City, FL (DMA 151)

WBIF *Digital Channel:* 51 *Virtual Channel:* 51; 50 kw; 833 ft.; N30 30 42 W85 29 17; *Station Currently Dark*
Mailing Address: 11849 N Dragoon Springs, Tucson, AZ 85737 US
Second Address: 3901 Hwy 121, Bedford, TX 76021
(817) 571-1229, *Fax:* (817) 799-2396
License: Marianna, Jackson County, FL held by Word of God Fellowship, Inc.
Nat'l Network: DAYSTAR
Marcus D. Lamb, President

***WFSG** *Digital Channel:* 38 *Virtual Channel:* 56; 49.2 kw; 449 ft.; N30 22 2 W85 55 28; *Rebroadcasting:* Rebroadcasts WFSU-TV Tallahassee.
2565 Pottsdamer Street, Tallahassee, FL 32304 US
(850) 487-3170, *Fax:* (850) 487-3093
www.wfsu.org
mail@wfsu.org
License: Panama City, Bay County, FL held by Florida State University
(acq 2-28-86).; *Washington Law Firm:* Cohn & Marks
Nat'l Network: PBS
Mike Dunn, Operations Dir
Patrick Keating, General Manager
John Kwak, General Sales Mgr
Jannie Whitt, Promotions Manager
David Lauther, Chief Engineer

WJHG-TV *Digital Channel:* 7 *Virtual Channel:* 7; 67 kw; 859 ft.; N30 25 59 W85 24 51
P.O. Box 2349, Panama City, FL 32402 US
(850) 234-7777, *Fax:* (850) 233-6647
www.wjhg.com
License: Panama City, Bay County, FL held by Gray Television License, LLC
Group Owner: Gray Television Inc.; (acq 6-29-60; $340,000;;
Washington Law Firm: Venable, Baetjer, Howard & Civiletti
Nat'l Network: NBC; CW; MyNetworkTV *Nat'l Reps:* Continental Television Sales
Jon McKee, Operations Dir
Curt Molander, General Manager
Steve Morabito, General Sales Mgr
Mark Gilland, Chief Engineer

WMBB *Digital Channel:* 13 *Virtual Channel:* 13; 42 kw; 1424 ft.; N30 21 8 W85 23 28
250 International Drive, Spartanburg, SC 29304 US

(850) 769-2313, *Fax:* (850) 769-8231
www.wmbb.com
wmbbnews@wmbb.com
License: Panama City, Bay County, FL held by Hoak Media of Panama City License LLC.
Group Owner: Hoak Media Corporation; (acq 7-15-2008; $60 million with KALB-TV Alexandria, LA); *Washington Law Firm:* Akin Gump Strauss Hauer & Feld LLP
Nat'l Network: ABC *Nat'l Reps:* Blair Television
Size of News Staff: 24; *Hours of Local News Weekly:* news progmg 143 hrs wkly
Terry Cole, General Manager
Christopher M. Golden, Promotions Manager

WPCT *Digital Channel:* 47 *Virtual Channel:* 46; 132 kw; 194 ft.; N30 10 59 W85 46 42
8317 W. Hwy 98, Suite 23, Panama City, FL 32407 US
(850) 234-2773, *Fax:* (850) 234-1179
www.tripsmarter.com
License: Panama City Beach, Bay County, FL held by Beach TV Properties Inc.
Group Owner: Beach TV Properties Inc.
Nat'l Network: IND
Jud Colley, President

WPGX *Digital Channel:* 9 *Virtual Channel:* 28; 34 kw vis, 126 kw aur; ant 748t; N30 23 42 W85 32 02; *Population Served:* 250,000
Fox 28, 700 W. 23 St. C-28, Panama City, FL 68144
(850) 215-6500, *Fax:* (850) 784-1773
www.myfox28.com
License: Panama City, Bay County, FL held by WPGX License Subsidiary LLC.
Group Owner: Raycom Media Inc.; (acq 12-15-2003; grpsl)
Nat'l Network: Fox *Nat'l Reps:* Harrington, Righter & Parsons
Heather Moore, General Manager
Sharon Davlin, General Sales Mgr
Al Shook, Operations Manager

Tallahassee, FL-Thomasville, GA (DMA 105)

***WFSU-TV** *Digital Channel:* 32 *Virtual Channel:* 11; 937.8 kw; 778 ft.; N30 21 31 W84 36 38
1600 Red Barber Plaza, Tallhasee, FL 32310 US
(850) 487-3170, *Fax:* (850) 487-3093
www.wfsu.org
mail@wfsu.org
License: Tallahassee, Leon County, FL held by Florida State University
Nat'l Network: ETV
Patrick Keating, General Manager
John Kwak, General Sales Mgr
Sarah Schuetz, Programming Director
Ray Chamberlain, Chief Engineer

WFXU *Digital Channel:* 48 *Virtual Channel:* 57; 22 kw; 438 ft.; N30 33 0 W83 0 48
2130 Greenbrier Drive, Vallanova, PA 19085 US
(352) 371-7772
License: Live Oak, Suwannee County, FL held by Budd Broadcasting Co. Inc.
Nat'l Network: PBS
Harvey Budd, CEO

WTLF *Digital Channel:* 24 *Virtual Channel:* 24; 24 kw; 128 ft.; N30 29 40 W84 25 3
Mailing Address: 103 Springer Building, 3411 Silverside Rd, Wilmington, DE 19810 US
Second Address: 950 Commerce Blvd., Midway, FL 32343
(850) 576-4990, *Fax:* (850) 576-0200
License: Tallahassee, Leon County, FL held by MPS Media of Tallahassee License LLC.
(acq 3-31-2007; $3.044 million with WSWB(TV) Scranton, PA); *Ownership:* Eugene J. Brown, 100% votes
Nat'l Network: CW *Nat'l Reps:* Petry Television Inc.
doris jones, Operations Dir
Dan Mecca, General Manager
nirmal singh, Engineering Dir
Don Abel, Creative Services Director
nathan mears, National Sales Manager
tyrone hayes, Office Manager

WTWC-TV *Digital Channel:* 40 *Virtual Channel:* 40; 462 kw; 1969 ft.; N30 40 50 W83 58 21
10706 Beaver Dam Road, Cockeysville, MD 21030 US
(850) 893-4140, *Fax:* (850) 893-6974
www.wtwc40.com
License: Tallahassee, Leon County, FL held by WTWC Licensee L.L.C.
Group Owner: Sinclair Broadcast Group Inc.; (acq 1999; grpsl).; *Washington Law Firm:* Dow, Lohnes & Albertson
Nat'l Network: NBC *Nat'l Reps:* Millennium Sales & Marketing
Size of News Staff: 30; *Hours of Local News Weekly:* news progmg 14 hrs wkly
Bebe Francis, General Manager
Halley Stinchfield, General Sales Mgr
Steve Sheridan, Chief Engineer

WTXL-TV *Digital Channel:* 27 *Virtual Channel:* 27; 1000 kw; 1699 ft.; N30 40 6 W83 58 10
8927 Thomasville Rd., Tallahassee, FL 32312 US
(850) 893-3127, *Fax:* (850) 575-7838
www.wtxl.tv
abc27news@wtxl.tv
License: Tallahassee, Leon County, FL held by WTXL-TV License LLC
Group Owner: Southern Broadcast Corp. of Sarasota; (acq 11-30-2005; $12 million); *Washington Law Firm:* Keck, Mahin & Cate
Nat'l Network: ABC
Size of News Staff: 26; *Hours of Local News Weekly:* news progmg 24 hrs wkly
Gary Wordlaw, General Manager
Marc Stover, General Sales Mgr
Bill Cummings, News Director
David Long, Chief Engineer

Tampa-St Petersburg (Sarasota), FL (DMA 13)

WCLF *Digital Channel:* 21 *Virtual Channel:* 22; 1000 kw; 1342 ft.; N27 49 10 W82 15 39
Mailing Address: P.O. Box 6922, Clearwater, FL 33758 US
Second Address: 6922 142nd Ave., Largo, FL 33771
(727) 535-5622, *Fax:* (727) 531-2497
www.ctnonline.com
License: Clearwater, Pinellas County, FL held by Christian Television Corporation Inc.
Group Owner: Christian Television Corporation Inc.; (acq 12-16-97).; *Washington Law Firm:* Gammon & Grange
Nat'l Network: IND
Foreign Language Programming
Robert DeAndrea, President

***WEDU** *Digital Channel:* 13 *Virtual Channel:* 3; 25 kw; 1545 ft.; N27 50 50 W82 15 50
Mailing Address: P.O. Box 4033, Tampa, FL 33677 US
Second Address: 1300 North Blvd., Tampa, FL 33607
(813) 254-9338, *Fax:* (813) 253-0826
www.wedu.org
License: Tampa, Hillsborough County, FL held by Florida West Coast Pub Broadcasting Inc
Washington Law Firm: Schwartz, Woods & Miller
Nat'l Network: PBS
Foreign Language Programming
Richard Lobo, CEO
Frank Wolynski, Operations Dir
Susanna Grady, General Sales Mgr
Ellyne Lonergan, Programming Director
Patrick Perkins, CFO
Mike Seymour, Programming Director

WFLA-TV *Digital Channel:* 7 *Virtual Channel:* 8; 32 kw; 1526 ft.; N27 50 32 W82 15 45
Mailing Address: 333 East Grace Street, Richmond, VA 23219 US
Second Address: 200 South Parker St., Tampa, FL 33608
(813) 228-8888, *Fax:* (813) 221-5787
www.wfla.com
License: Tampa, Hillsborough County, FL held by Media General Communications Inc.
Group Owner: Media General Broadcast Group; (acq 1965; $17.5 million); *Washington Law Firm:* Dow, Lohnes & Albertson
Nat'l Network: NBC *Nat'l Reps:* Harrington, Righter & Parsons
Wire Services: UPI
Michael Pumo, President
Rick McEwen, Operations Dir

WFTS-TV *Digital Channel:* 29; 2.63 kw vis, 260 w aur; 1,546t/1,649g; N27 50 32 W82 15 46
4045 N. Himes Ave., Tampa, FL 33607
(813) 354-2828, *Fax:* (813) 354-3001
www.abcactionnews.com
License: Tampa, Hillsborough County, FL held by Tampa Bay Television Inc.
Group Owner: The E. W. Scripps Co.; (acq 1-2-86; grpsl).; *Washington Law Firm:* Baker & Hostetler
Nat'l Network: ABC *Nat'l Reps:* Eagle Television Sales
Rich Pegram, Operations Dir
Sarah Tyrrell, General Sales Mgr
Donna Wilson, Promotions Manager
Jack Winter, Operations Manager

WFTT-DT *Digital Channel:* 47; 4,200 kw vis, 420 kw aur; 1,600t/1,580g; N27 50 32 W82 15 46; *Population Served:* 1,600,000
2610 W. Hillsborough Ave., Tampa, FL 33614
(813) 872-6262, *Fax:* (813) 998-3600
univision.com
info@univision.com
License: Tampa, Hillsborough County, FL held by TeleFutura Tampa LLC.
Group Owner: Univision Communications Inc.; (acq 5-21-2001; grpsl).; *Washington Law Firm:* Wiley, Rein & Fielding
Nat'l Network: TeleFutura (Spanish)
Foreign Language Programming
Lilly Gonzalez, General Manager
Nelson Castillo, General Sales Mgr
Carol Davis, Programming Director
Steve Hess, Chief Engineer

WTOG *Digital Channel:* 44 *Virtual Channel:* 44; 550 kw; 1490 ft.; N27 49 46 W82 15 59
1501 M Street N.W., Suite. 1100, Washington, DC 20005 US
(727) 576-4444, *Fax:* (727) 570-4458
www.cw44.com
License: St. Petersburg, Pinellas County, FL held by CBS Operations Inc.
Group Owner: CBS Television Stations Group; (acq 9-19-96)
Nat'l Network: THE CW NETWORK *Nat'l Reps:* TeleRep *Wire Services:* NWS (National Weather Service)
Laura Caruso, Operations Dir
Steve Soldinger, General Manager

WTSP *Digital Channel:* 10 *Virtual Channel:* 10; 69 kw; 1565 ft.; N27 49 9.7 W82 15 38.7
11450 Gandy Boulevard, St. Petersburg, FL 33702 US
(727) 577-1010, *Fax:* (727) 578-7637
www.10connects.com
desk@10connects.com
License: St. Petersburg, Pinellas County, FL held by Pacific and Southern Co.
Group Owner: Gannett Broadcasting; (acq 12-31-96).; *Washington Law Firm:* Wiley, Rein & Fielding
Nat'l Network: CBS *Nat'l Reps:* Blair Television
Lee Griffin, Operations Dir
Ken Tonning, General Manager
Pete Nikiel, Promotions Manager

WTTA *Digital Channel:* 32 *Virtual Channel:* 38; 1000 kw; 1531 ft.; N27 50 32 W82 15 45
10706 Beaver Dam Road, Cockeysville, MD 21030 US
(813) 886-9882, *Fax:* (813) 880-8100 (sales)/ 8154
www.wtta38.com; www.mytvtampabay.com
comments@wtta38.com
License: St. Petersburg, Pinellas County, FL held by Bay Television Inc.
Group Owner: Sinclair Broadcast Group Inc.; *Washington Law Firm:* Shaw Pittman
Nat'l Network: MYTV
Julie Nelson, General Manager
Jeanne McGuiness, General Sales Mgr

WTVT *Digital Channel:* 12 *Virtual Channel:* 13; 72.3 kw; 1430 ft.; N27 49 8 W82 14 26
Mailing Address: 5151 Wisconsin Ave., NW, Washington, DC 20016 US
Second Address: 3213 W. Kennedy Blvd., Tampa, FL 33609
(813) 876-1313, *Fax:* (813) 871-3135
www.wtvt.com
news@wtvt.com
License: Tampa, Hillsborough County, FL held by TVT License Inc.
Group Owner: Fox Television Stations Inc.; (acq 11-96; grpsl); *Washington Law Firm:* Hogan & Hartson
Nat'l Network: FOX *Wire Services:* Conus
Size of News Staff: 100; *Hours of Local News Weekly:* news progmg 46 hrs wkly
Bill Schneider, President
Jim Benedict, Operations Dir

***WUSF-TV** *Digital Channel:* 34 *Virtual Channel:* 16; 475 kw; 1486 ft.; N27 50 52 W82 15 48
4202 Fowler Ave., Tampa, FL 33620 US
(813) 905-6900, *Fax:* (813) 974-4806
www.wusf.org
news@wusf.org
License: Tampa, Hillsborough County, FL held by University of South Florida
Washington Law Firm: Cohn & Marks
Nat'l Network: PBS

Jo Ann Urofsky, General Manager
Tom Dollenmayer, Station Manager
Cathy Coccia, General Sales Mgr
Susan Geiger, Programming Director

WVEA-TV *Digital Channel:* 25 *Virtual Channel:* 62; 750 kw; 1549 ft.; N27 49 10 W82 15 39
2065 Cantu Court, Sarasota, FL 34232 US
(813) 872-6262, *Fax:* (813) 998-3600
www.wvea.entravision.com
info@wvea.entravision.com
License: Venice, Sarasota County, FL held by Entravision Holdings L.L.C.
Group Owner: Entravision Communications Corp.; (acq 1999; $17 million); *Washington Law Firm:* Thompson Hine, LLP
Nat'l Network: UNIVISION *Wire Services:* AP
Foreign Language Programming; Size of News Staff: 14; *Hours of Local News Weekly:* news progmg 3.5 hrs wkly
Lilly Gonzalez, General Manager
Nelson Castillo, General Sales Mgr
Margaret Stanfield, Programming Director
Pilar Ortiz, News Director
Bill Mierisch, Chief Engineer

WWSB *Digital Channel:* 24 *Virtual Channel:* 40; 90 kw; 768 ft.; N27 33 21 W82 21 48
5725 Lawton Drive, Sarasota, FL 33583 US
(941) 923-8840, *Fax:* (941) 924-3971/ (941) 923-8709
www.mysuncoast.com
generalmanager@wwsb.tv
License: Sarasota, Sarasota County, FL held by WWSB License LLC
Group Owner: Southern Broadcast Corp. of Sarasota; (acq 3-26-86; $40,500); *Washington Law Firm:* Leibowitz & Associates
Nat'l Network: ABC
Size of News Staff: 45; *Hours of Local News Weekly:* news progmg 21 hrs wkly
Ken Long, CEO
J. Manuel Calvo, President
Jason Wildanstein, Operations Dir

WXPX-TV *Digital Channel:* 42; 2,240 kw vis, 224 kw aur; ant 1,525t/1,496g; N27 24 30 W82 15 00
4444 66th St N., Clearwater, FL 33764-7204
(813) 314-5462, *Fax:* (813) 314-5464
www.ionline.tv
License: Bradenton, Manatee County, FL held by Paxson Communications License Co. L.L.C.
Group Owner: ION Media Networks Inc.; (acq 12-15-97).
Nat'l Network: ION Television
David Booth, General Manager
Sean Dwyer, News Director
Dave White, Chief Engineer

West Palm Beach-Ft. Pierce, FL (DMA 38)

WFGC *Digital Channel:* 49 *Virtual Channel:* 61; 800 kw; 410 ft.; N26 45 47 W80 12 19
2406 South Congress Ave., Building #2, West Palm Beach, FL 33406 US
(561) 642-3361, *Fax:* (561) 967-5961
www.wfgc.com
comments@wfgc.com
License: Palm Beach, Palm Beach County, FL held by Christian TV of Palm Beach County Inc.
(acq 12-16-97).; *Washington Law Firm:* Gammon & Grange
Nat'l Network: IND
Neville Chankersingh, CFO
Wayne Wetzel, President
Mike Gonzalez, General Manager
Chris Mavros, Chief Engineer

WFLX *Digital Channel:* 28 *Virtual Channel:* 29; 630 kw; 1503 ft.; N26 34 37 W80 14 32
1660 West Second Street, Cleveland, OH 44113 US
(561) 845-2929, *Fax:* (561) 863-1238
www.wflx.com
License: West Palm Beach, Palm Beach County, FL held by WFLX License Subsidiary, LLC
Group Owner: Raycom Media Inc.; (acq 1998).
Nat'l Network: FOX *Nat'l Reps:* Harrington, Righter & Parsons
John Spinola, Operations Dir
John Heislman, General Sales Mgr

WPBF *Digital Channel:* 16 *Virtual Channel:* 25; 1000 kw; 1490 ft.; N27 7 17 W80 23 42
959 Eighth Avenue, New York, NY 10019 US
(561) 694-2525, *Fax:* (561) 624-1089
www.wpbf.com
License: Tequesta, Palm Beach County, FL held by WPBF-TV Co.
Group Owner: Hearst-Argyle Television Inc.; (acq 8-1-97).
Nat'l Network: ABC *Nat'l Reps:* Continental Television Sales
Size of News Staff: 48; *Hours of Local News Weekly:* news progmg 25 hrs wkly
Caroline Scollard-Taplett, Operations Dir
Russ Larish, Programming Director

WPEC *Digital Channel:* 13 *Virtual Channel:* 12; 90 kw; 1014 ft.; N26 35 18 W80 12 30
Mailing Address: 1100 Fairfield Drive, West Palm Beach, FL 33407 US
Second Address: 1100 Fairfield Dr., West Palm Beach, FL 33419-8512
(561) 844-1212, *Fax:* (561) 842-1212
www.wpecnews12.com
License: West Palm Beach, Palm Beach County, FL held by Freedom Broadcasting of Florida Licensee L.L.C.
Group Owner: Freedom Communications Inc., Broadcast Division; (acq 2-1-96; $150 million); *Washington Law Firm:* Latham & Watkins
Nat'l Network: CBS *Nat'l Reps:* TeleRep
Hours of Local News Weekly: News progmg 24 hrs wkly
Doreen Wade, President
Diana Wilkin, Operations Dir
Donn Colee, Station Manager
Doug Wolfmueller, General Sales Mgr
Steve Hunsicker, News Director
Keith Betts, Engineering Dir
Mary Gregg, National Sales Manager
Jim Posey,Regional Sales Manager

WPTV-TV *Digital Channel:* 12; 100 kw vis, 20 kw aur; 990t/1,031g; N26 35 20 W80 12 43; *Population Served:* 1,200,000
1100 Banyan Blvd., West Palm Beach, FL 33401
(561) 655-5455, *Fax:* (561) 653-5719 (news)
www.wptv.com
newstips@wptv.com
License: West Palm Beach, Palm Beach County, FL held by Scripps Howard Broadcasting Co.
Group Owner: The E. W. Scripps Co.; (acq 12-27-61; $2 million;;
Washington Law Firm: Baker & Hostetler
Nat'l Network: NBC *Nat'l Reps:* Harrington, Righter & Parsons
Wire Services: Reuters
Size of News Staff: 75; *Hours of Local News Weekly:* news progmg 27 hrs wkly
Richard Boehne, CEO
Steve Wasserman, Operations Dir
Joseph Ne Castro, CFO

WPXP-TV *Digital Channel:* 36; 1,000 kw vis, 200 kw aur; 492t; N26 47 59 W80 04 33
13801 N. W. 14th St., Sunrise, FL 33323
(954) 703-1920, *Fax:* (954) 858-1848
www.ionmedia.tv
License: Lake Worth, Palm Beach County, FL held by ION Media West Palm Beach License, Inc., Debtor-in-possession
Group Owner: ION Media Networks Inc.; (acq 1998).; *Ownership:* Paxson Communications Corp., 90%; Betti Lidsky, 10%.
Nat'l Network: ION Television
Frank Tenore, General Sales Mgr
Julio Bonet, Chief Engineer

***WTCE-TV** *Digital Channel:* 38 *Virtual Channel:* 21; 1000 kw; 974 ft.; N27 1 31 W80 10 43
PO Box 721582, Houston, TX 77272 US
(772) 489-2701, *Fax:* (772) 489-6833
www.wtcebellsouth.net
License: Fort Pierce, Saint Lucie County, FL held by Jacksonville Educators Broadcasting Inc
Nat'l Network: TRINITY BROADCA
Charles Massi, General Manager

WTVX *Digital Channel:* 34 *Virtual Channel:* 34; 1000 kw; 1495 ft.; N27 7 19 W80 23 20
630 Fifth Avenue, 27th Floor, New York, NY 10111 US
(561) 841-3434, *Fax:* (561) 848-9150
www.wtvx.com
License: Fort Pierce, Saint Lucie County, FL held by WPB TV Licensee Corp.
Group Owner: Four Points Media Group; (acq 11-21-2007; grpsl); *Washington Law Firm:* Wiley Rein LLP
Nat'l Network: CW *Nat'l Reps:* TeleRep
Shaun McDonald, General Manager

***WXEL-TV** *Digital Channel:* 27 *Virtual Channel:* 42; 400 kw; 1444 ft.; N26 34 37 W80 14 32
Mailing Address: 11300 NESecond Avenue, Miami Shores, FL 33161 US
Second Address: 3401 South Congress Ave., Boynton Beach, FL 33426
(561) 737-8000, *Fax:* (561) 369-3067
www.wxel.org
jcarr@wxel.org
License: West Palm Beach, Palm Beach County, FL held by Barry Telecommunications Inc
(acq 4-16-97).; *Washington Law Firm:* Schwartz, Woods & Miller
Nat'l Network: PBS
Jerry Carr, CEO
Jerry Carr, General Manager
Fred Flaxman, General Sales Mgr
Bernard Henneberg, CFO
Lee Rowand, Promotions Director
Ross Cooper, Sales Director

Georgia

Albany, GA (DMA 147)

***WABW-TV** *Digital Channel:* 6 *Virtual Channel:* 14; 10.5 kw; 1243 ft.; N31 8 5 W84 6 16
260 - 14th Street, N.W., Atlanta, GA 30318 US
(404) 685-2400, *Fax:* (404) 685-2591
www.gpb.org
ask@gpb.org
License: Pelham, Mitchell County, GA held by Georgia Public Telecommunications Commission
Nat'l Network: PBS
Bonnie Bean, CFO
Bob Olive, General Manager
Jack Watts, Chief Engineer

***WACS-TV** *Digital Channel:* 8 *Virtual Channel:* 25; 4.7 kw; 1093 ft.; N31 56 15 W84 33 15
260 - 14th Street, N.W., Atlanta, GA 30318 US
(404) 685-2400, *Fax:* (404) 685-2591
www.gpb.org
ask@gpb.org
License: Dawson, Terrell County, GA held by Georgia Public Telecommunications Commission
Washington Law Firm: Arent, Fox, Kintner, Plotkin & Kahn
Nat'l Network: PBS
Bob Olive, General Manager

WALB *Digital Channel:* 10 *Virtual Channel:* 10; 22 kw; 974 ft.; N31 19 52 W83 51 43
Mailing Address: 2000 Wade Hampton Blvd., Greenville, SC 29615 US
Second Address: 1709 Stuart Ave., Albany, GA 30707
(229) 446-1010, *Fax:* (229) 446-4000
www.walb.com
walb@walb.com
License: Albany, Dougherty County, GA held by WALB License Subsidiary LLC.
Group Owner: Raycom Media Inc.; (acq 1-31-2006; grpsl)
Nat'l Network: NBC *Nat'l Reps:* Continental Television Sales
Size of News Staff: 5; *Hours of Local News Weekly:* news progmg 15 hrs wkly
James Wilcox, President
Rick Williams, News Director

WFXL *Digital Channel:* 12; 1,580 kw vis, 150 kw aur; ant 991t/968g; N31 19 52 W83 51 43; *Population Served:* 385,000
Mailing Address: Box 4050, Albany, GA 68144
Second Address: 1201 Stuart Ave., Albany, GA 31707
(229) 435-3100, *Fax:* (229) 903-8240
www.mysouthwestga.com
License: Albany, Dougherty County, GA held by Barrington Albany License LLC.
Group Owner: Barrington Broadcasting Group, LLC.; (acq 8-11-2006; grpsl); *Washington Law Firm:* Covington & Burling
Nat'l Network: Fox *Nat'l Reps:* HRP
Size of News Staff: 14; *Hours of Local News Weekly:* news progmg 26 hrs wkly
Pat Coffman, Operations Dir
Brenda Holloway, General Manager
Deborah Gay, Station Manager
Lennie Philyaw, General Sales Mgr
Josh Boutwell, Promotions Manager
Jenna McWilliams, News Director
Ken Clubb, Chief Engineer

WSST-TV *Digital Channel:* 51; 91 kw vis; ant 361t/374g; N31 53 35 W83 48 18; *Population Served:* 600,000
Box 917, 112 S. 7th St., Detroit, GA 31015
(229) 273-0001, *Fax:* (229) 273-8894
www.wsst.com
License: Cordele, Crisp County, GA held by Sunbelt-South Telecommunications Ltd

Washington Law Firm: Law Offices of Scott Cinnamon
Phillip Streetman, Operations Dir
Phillip Streetman, General Manager
Sara Howell, General Sales Mgr
Lee Wright, Programming Director
Ricky Smart, Chief Engineer
Barbara Dennis, Traffic Manager

Atlanta (DMA 8)

WAGA-TV *Digital Channel:* 27; 100 kw vis, 20 kw aur; 1,076t/1,103g; N33 47 51 W84 20 02; *Population Served:* 4,000,000
1551 Briarcliff Rd. N.E., Atlanta, GA 30306
(404) 875-5555, *Fax:* (404) 898-0238
www.myfoxatlanta.com
License: Atlanta, DeKalb County, GA held by New World Communications of Atlanta, Inc.
Group Owner: Fox Television Stations Inc.; (acq 11-96; grpsl).
Nat'l Network: Fox
Hours of Local News Weekly: News progmg 38 hrs wkly
Neil Mazur, Operations Dir
Gene McHugh, General Manager

***WATC-DT** *Digital Channel:* 41; 398 kw vis, 39.8 kw aur; 423t; N33 48 40 W84 21 51
1862 Enterprise Dr., Norcross, GA 30093
(770) 300-9828, *Fax:* (770) 300-9838
www.watc.tv
License: Atlanta, Gwinnett County, GA held by Community Television Inc
James Thompson, President
Joanne Thompson, Operations Dir
John Broomall, General Sales Mgr
Greg West, Promotions Manager
Pat Mathis, Business Manager
Vincent Thompson, Production Manager

WATL *Digital Channel:* 25 *Virtual Channel:* 36; 500 kw; 1089 ft.; N33 48 26 W84 20 22
One Monroe Place, Atlanta, GA 30324 US
(404) 892-1611, *Fax:* (404) 881-0675
www.myatltv.com
License: Atlanta, Fulton County, GA held by Pacific and Southern Company, Inc.
Group Owner: Gannett Broadcasting; (acq 8-7-2006; $180 million); *Washington Law Firm:* Wiley, Rein & Fielding
Nat'l Network: MY NETWORK TV *Nat'l Reps:* TeleRep
Robert Walker, General Manager
Tom Hager, General Sales Mgr
Laura Hale, Programming Director
Mark Miller, National Sales Manager

WGCL-TV *Digital Channel:* 19; 2,333 kw vis, 233 kw aur; 1,089t/1,145g; N33 48 27 W84 20 26; *Population Served:* 5,725,787
Mailing Address: Box 93524, Atlanta, GA 50309
Second Address: 425 14th St. NW, Atlanta, GA 30318
(404) 325-4646, *Fax:* (404) 327-3004,(404) 327-3003
www.cbsatlanta.com
news@cbsatlanta.com
License: Atlanta, Fulton County, GA held by Meredith Corp.
Group Owner: Meredith Broadcasting Group, Meredith Corp.; (acq 2-22-99; $370 million swap with KCPQ(TV) Tacoma, WA).; *Washington Law Firm:* Dow, Lohnes & Albertson, PLLC
Nat'l Network: CBS *Nat'l Reps:* Harrington, Righter & Parsons
Size of News Staff: 80
Paul Karpowicz, Meredith Local Media Group
TBA, General Manager
Mark Turner, Director of Sales
Kenny Lawrence, Director of Programming & Audience Development
Eric Ludgood, News Director
Gary Watkins, Chief Engineer

***WGTV** *Digital Channel:* 8 *Virtual Channel:* 8; 21 kw; 1083 ft.; N33 48 18 W84 8 40
260 - 14th Street, N.W., Atlanta, GA 30318 US
(404) 685-2400, *Fax:* (404) 685-2591
www.gpb.org
ask@gpb.org
License: Athens, Clarke County, GA held by Georgia Public Telecommunications Commission
Washington Law Firm: Arent, Fox, Kintner, Plotkin & Kahn
Nat'l Network: PBS
Teya Ryan, President

WHSG-TV *Digital Channel:* 44 *Virtual Channel:* 63; 1000 kw; 1018 ft.; N33 48 26 W84 20 22
P. O. Box C-11949, Santa Ana, CA 92711 US
(404) 288-1156, *Fax:* (404) 288-5613
www.tbn.org
License: Monroe, Walton County, GA held by Trinity Broadcasting Network Inc.
Group Owner: Trinity Broadcasting Network; (acq 11-21-89).
Nat'l Network: TRINITY BROADCA
Dorothy Casoria, General Manager

***WPBA** *Digital Channel:* 21 *Virtual Channel:* 30; 55.4 kw; 872 ft.; N33 45 32 W84 20 7
740 Bismark Rd. Ne, Atlanta, GA 30324 US
(678) 686-0321, *Fax:* (678) 686-0356
www.WPBA.org
License: Atlanta, Fulton County, GA held by Board of Education of the City of Atlanta
Washington Law Firm: Schwartz, Woods & Miller
Nat'l Network: PBS
Hours of Local News Weekly: News progmg 1.5 hrs wkly
Milton Clipper, General Manager

WPCH-TV *Digital Channel:* 20 *Virtual Channel:* 17; 1000 kw; 1018 ft.; N33 48 26 W84 20 22
1050 Techwood Drive, NW, Atlanta, GA 30318 US
(404) 827-1717, *Fax:* (404) 575-9720
www.peachtreetv.com
information@peachtreetv.com
License: Atlanta, Fulton County, GA held by Superstation Inc.
Nat'l Network: IND
Jonathan Katz, General Manager
Walter Naar, General Sales Mgr
Tracy Underwood, Promotions Manager
Barbara Linebarger, Engineering Dir
Bob Hudson, Traffic Manager

WPXA-TV *Digital Channel:* 51; 3,890 kw vis; 2,021t/787g; N34 18 47 W84 38 55; *Population Served:* 3,900,000
200 Cobb Pkwy North, Marietta, GA 30062
(770) 919-0575, *Fax:* (770) 919-9621
www.ionmedia.tv
License: Rome, Floyd County, GA held by ION Media Atlanta License, Inc., Debtor-in-possession
Group Owner: ION Media Networks Inc.; (acq 7-13-94; $9.5 million); *Washington Law Firm:* Dow, Lohnes & Albertson
Nat'l Network: ION Television
Jeanette McNair, Station Manager
Rhonda Schulik, General Sales Mgr
John Swisher, Chief Engineer

WSB-TV *Digital Channel:* 39 *Virtual Channel:* 2; 1000 kw; 1037 ft.; N33 45 51 W84 21 42
3773 Howard Hughes Parkway, Suite 300n, Las Vegas, NV 89109 US
(404) 897-7000, *Fax:* (404) 897-6246 (gen mgr)
www.wsbtv.com
talk2us@wsbtv.com
License: Atlanta, Fulton County, GA held by Georgia Television Company.
Group Owner: Cox Media Group; *Washington Law Firm:* Dow, Lohnes & Albertson
Nat'l Network: ABC *Nat'l Reps:* TeleRep
Bill Hoffman, Operations Dir
Deborah Denechaud, General Sales Mgr
Art Rogers, Programming Director
Steve Riley, Promotions Manager
Marian Pittman, News Director
Gary Alexander, Engineering Dir
David Lamothe, OperationsDirector
Jocelyn Dorsey, Public Affairs Director

WUPA *Digital Channel:* 43 *Virtual Channel:* 69; 1000 kw; 1081 ft.; N33 48 26 W84 20 22
C/O Viacom/D.C., 1501, M St., N.W., Suite 1100, Washington, DC 20005 US
(404) 325-6969, *Fax:* (404) 633-4567
www.cwatlantatv.com
License: Atlanta, Fulton County, GA held by Atlanta Television Station WUPA Inc.
Group Owner: CBS Television Stations Group; (acq 5-4-2000; grpsl).; *Washington Law Firm:* Wiley, Rein & Fielding
Nat'l Network: THE CW NETWORK
Tom Canedo, General Manager
Dana Beifus, Chief Engineer

WUVG-DT *Digital Channel:* 48; 1,258 kw vis, 125.8 kw aur; 1,351t/1,236g; N34 12 27 W83 47 38; *Population Served:* 750,000
3350 Peach Tree Rd., Suite 1250, Atlanta, GA 33026
(404) 926-2300, *Fax:* (404) 926-2320
www.univision.com
License: Athens, Clarke County, GA held by Univision Atlanta LLC
Group Owner: Univision Communications Inc.; (acq 6-6-01; grpsl).; *Washington Law Firm:* William M. Barnard
Nat'l Network: Univision (Spanish)
Foreign Language Programming
Josh Melnick, General Manager

WXIA-TV *Digital Channel:* 10 *Virtual Channel:* 11; 80 kw; 994 ft.; N33 45 24 W84 19 55
1100 Wilson Boulevard, Arlington, VA 22234 US
(404) 892-1611, *Fax:* (404) 881-0675
www.11alive.com
news@11alive.com
License: Atlanta, Fulton County, GA held by Pacific and Southern Company, Inc.
Group Owner: Gannett Broadcasting; (acq 6-7-79; grpsl;; *Washington Law Firm:* Reed Smith LLP
Nat'l Network: NBC *Nat'l Reps:* TeleRep
Robert Walker, President
Tom Hager, General Sales Mgr
Laura Hale, Programming Director
Julie Short, Local Sales Manager
Michael Clifford, Local Sales Manager

Augusta, GA (DMA 115)

WAGT *Digital Channel:* 30 *Virtual Channel:* 26; 400 kw; 1585 ft.; N33 24 20 W81 50 1
905 Broad Street, Augusta, GA 30901 US
(706) 826-0026, *Fax:* (706) 724-4028
www.cwaugusta.com
License: Augusta, Richmond County, GA held by WAGT Television Inc.
Group Owner: Schurz Communications Inc.; (acq 7-1-80; $5 million); *Washington Law Firm:* Hogan & Hartson
Nat'l Network: NBC/CW; CW *Nat'l Reps:* Petry Television Inc.
Size of News Staff: 28; *Hours of Local News Weekly:* news progmg 8 hrs wkly
Mike Bell, Station Manager
Mariah Gardner, Promotions Manager
Greg Baldwin, News Director
Dave DeFrehn, Chief Engineer

***WCES-TV** *Digital Channel:* 6 *Virtual Channel:* 20; 7.9 kw; 1409 ft.; N33 15 33 W82 17 9
260 - 14th Street, N.W., Atlanta, GA 30318 US
(706) 547-0293, *Fax:* (706) 547-0293
www.gpb.org
viewerservices@gpb.org
License: Wrens, Jefferson County, GA held by Georgia Public Telecommunications Commission.
Nat'l Network: PBS
Juanita Rachels, General Manager

WFXG *Digital Channel:* 51 *Virtual Channel:* 54
Mailing Address: 100 - 4th Avenue, North, Seattle, WA 98109 US
Second Address: Box 204540, Augusta, GA 30917-4540
(706) 650-5400, *Fax:* (706) 650-8411
www.wfxg.com
gtomlinson@wfxg.com
License: Augusta, Richmond County, GA held by Southeastern Media Holdings Inc.
Group Owner: Southeastern Media Holdings Inc.; (acq 12-1-2003; $40 million with WXTX(TV) Columbus).; *Washington Law Firm:* Miller & Fields
Nat'l Network: FOX
Barry Barth, General Manager
Paul Brewer, General Sales Mgr

WJBF *Digital Channel:* 42 *Virtual Channel:* 6; 1000 kw; 1663 ft.; N33 24 20.2 W81 50 1.07
Mailing Address: 250 International Drive, Spartanburg, SC 29304 US
Second Address: 1001 Reynolds St., Augusta, GA 30901
(706) 722-6664, *Fax:* (706) 722-0022
www.wjbf.com
License: Augusta, Richmond County, GA held by Media General Operations, Inc.
Group Owner: Media General Broadcast Group; (acq 3-27-2000; grpsl).; *Washington Law Firm:* Dow, Lohnes & Albertson, PLLC
Nat'l Network: ABC
Hours of Local News Weekly: News progmg 22 hrs wky
Mary Gadson, Operations Dir
Bill Stewart, General Manager
Scot Seabolt, General Sales Mgr
Mary Jones, Programming Director
Robert Pippin, Promotions Manager
Mark Rosen, News Director
Cary Hale, Chief Engineer

Roberto Vasquez,Director of Results
Carter Murphy, Local Sales Manager
Michael Schwartz, National Sales Manager

WRDW-TV *Digital Channel:* 12 *Virtual Channel:* 12; 316 kw vis, 30.2 kw aur; ant 1,590t/1,506g; N33 24 29 W81 50 36; *Population Served:* 604,000
Mailing Address: Box 1212, Augusta, GA 20005
Second Address: 1301 Georgia Ave., North Augusta, SC 29841
(803) 278-1212, *Fax:* (803) 279-8316
www.wrdw.com
wrdw@wrdw.com
License: Augusta, Richmond County, GA held by Gray Television Licensee Inc.
Group Owner: Gray Television Inc.; (acq 1-4-96; $34 million)
Nat'l Network: CBS; MyNetworkTV *Nat'l Reps:* Continental Television Sales
Size of News Staff: 35; *Hours of Local News Weekly:* news progmg 20 hrs wkly
John Ray, President
Estelle Parsley, Vice President of News & Operations
Michael Oates, General Sales Mgr
Judi Tredore, Programming Director
Mark Hodges, Creative Services Director
Edward Elser, Chief Engineer

Chattanooga, TN (DMA 86)

WELF-TV *Digital Channel:* 16 *Virtual Channel:* 23; 300 kw; 1394 ft.; N34 57 7 W85 22 58
250 West Arrow Highway, San Dimas, CA 91773 US
(706) 820-1663, *Fax:* (706) 820-1735
www.tbn.org
welf@tbn.org
License: Dalton, Whitfield County, GA held by Trinity Broadcasting Network
Group Owner: Trinity Broadcasting Network; (acq 5-8-2000; grpsl).
Nat'l Network: TRINITY BROADCA
Onya Richter, Station Manager

***WNGH-TV** *Digital Channel:* 33 *Virtual Channel:* 18; 426 kw; 1762 ft.; N34 45 6 W84 42 54
260 - 14th Street, N.W., Atlanta, GA 30318 US
(706) 422-1947
www.gpb.org
viewerservices@gpb.org
License: Chatsworth, Murray County, GA held by Georgia Public Telecommunications Commission
Washington Law Firm: Arent, Fox, Kintner, Plotkin & Kahn
Nat'l Network: PBS
Hugh Pearson, Station Manager

Columbus, GA (DMA 128)

***WJSP-TV** *Digital Channel:* 23 *Virtual Channel:* 28; 177 kw; 1457 ft.; N32 51 8 W84 42 4
260 - 14th Street, N.W., Atlanta, GA 30318 US
(404) 685-2400, *Fax:* (404) 685-2591
www.gpb.org
ask@gpb.org
License: Columbus, Muscogee County, GA held by Georgia Public Telecommunications Commission
Nat'l Network: PBS
Teya Ryan, President
Alfons Pynenburg, Chief Engineer

WLTZ *Digital Channel:* 35 *Virtual Channel:* 38; 50 kw; 1238 ft.; N32 27 28 W84 53 8
6140 Buena Vista Road, Columbus, GA 31907 US
(706) 561-3838, *Fax:* (706) 561-3880 (sales)
www.wltz.com
wltz@wltz.com
License: Columbus, Muscogee County, GA held by SagamoreHill Broadcasting of Georgia LLC.
Group Owner: SagamoreHill Broadcasting LLC; (acq 8-10-2007; $10.6 million); *Washington Law Firm:* Wiley, Rein & Fielding
Nat'l Network: NBC *Nat'l Reps:* Blair Television
Louis Wall, President
Drew Rhodes, General Manager

WRBL *Digital Channel:* 15 *Virtual Channel:* 3; 1000 kw; 1663 ft.; N32 19 16 W84 47 28
Mailing Address: 250 International Drive, Spartanburg, SC 29304 US
Second Address: 1350 13th Ave., Columbus, GA 31902-0270
(706) 323-3333, *Fax:* (706) 327-6655
www.wrbl.com
License: Columbus, Muscogee County, GA held by Media General Broadcasting of South Carolina Holdings Inc.
Group Owner: Media General Broadcast Group; (acq 3-27-2000; grpsl).; *Washington Law Firm:* Dow, Lohnes & Albertson
Nat'l Network: CBS *Nat'l Reps:* MMT
Otis Pickett, Operations Dir

WTVM *Digital Channel:* 11 *Virtual Channel:* 9; 50 kw; 1663 ft.; N32 19 25 W84 46 46
Rsa Tower, 20th Floor, 201 Monroe Street, Montgomery, AL 36104 US
(706) 324-6471, *Fax:* (706) 322-7527
www.wtvm.com
newsleader@wtvm.com
License: Columbus, Muscogee County, GA held by WTVM License Subsidiary, LLC
Group Owner: Raycom Media Inc.; (acq 1996; grpsl).; *Washington Law Firm:* Powell, Goldstein, Frazer & Murphy
Nat'l Network: ABC *Nat'l Reps:* Harrington, Righter & Parsons
Lee Brantley, Operations Dir
Adelaide Kirk, General Sales Mgr
Anne Holmes, News Director
David Williams, Chief Engineer

WXTX *Digital Channel:* 49 *Virtual Channel:* 54; 499.4 kw; 1024 ft.; N32 27 39 W84 52 43
100 - 4th Avenue, North, Seattle, WA 98109 US
(706) 324-6471, *Fax:* (706) 322-7527
www.wxtx.com
programming@wxtx.com
License: Columbus, Muscogee County, GA
Group Owner: American Spirit Media; (acq 12-1-2003; $40 million with WFXG(TV) Augusta).; *Washington Law Firm:* Fisher, Wayland, Cooper, Leader & Zaragoza
Nat'l Network: FOX
Lee Brantley, General Manager
Mark Kirkland, General Sales Mgr
Anne Holmes, News Director
David Williams, Chief Engineer

Greenville-Spartanburg, SC-Asheville, NC-Anderson, SC (DMA 36)

WUGA-TV *Digital Channel:* 24; 647 kw vis, 129 kw aur; ant 835t/600g; N34 36 44 W83 22 05
802 E. Doyle Street, Toccoa, GA 29304
(706) 886-0032, *Fax:* (706) 886-7033
www.wnegtv.com
License: Toccoa, Stephens County, GA held by UGARF Media Holdings LLC.
(acq 8-18-2008; $1,437,500); *Ownership:* University of Georgia Research Foundation Inc., 100% equity owner; *Washington Law Firm:* Fletcher, Heald & Hildreth
Nat'l Reps: MMT
Size of News Staff: 6; *Hours of Local News Weekly:* news progmg 13 hrs wkly
Michael Castengera, Station Manager
Jim Sanders, General Sales Mgr
Tony Garrison, Promotions Manager
Kevin Moss, Chief Engineer

Jacksonville, FL (DMA 47)

WPXC-TV *Digital Channel:* 24 *Virtual Channel:* 21; 790 kw; 1368 ft.; N30 49 39 W81 44 27
7434 Blythe Island Hwy., Brunswick, GA 31523 US
(912) 267-0021, *Fax:* (912) 261-9582
www.ionline.tv
License: Brunswick, Glynn County, GA held by ION Media Brunswick License, Inc., Debtor-in-possession
Group Owner: ION Media Networks Inc.; (acq 12-6-2000; $3.07 million); *Washington Law Firm:* Fleischman & Walsh
Nat'l Network: ION
Joseph Koker, Operations Dir
Nancy O'Connor, Station Manager
Frank Tenore, General Sales Mgr

***WXGA-TV** *Digital Channel:* 8 *Virtual Channel:* 8; 35.3 kw; 1010 ft.; N31 13 17 W82 34 24
260 - 14th Street, N.W., Atlanta, GA 30318 US
(912) 338-5200, *Fax:* (912) 338-5201
www.gpb.org
viewerservices@gpb.org
License: Waycross, Ware County, GA held by Georgia Public Telecommunications Commission
Nat'l Network: PBS
Chris Allen, Station Manager

Macon, GA (DMA 122)

WGNM *Digital Channel:* 45 *Virtual Channel:* 64; 1000 kw; 732 ft.; N32 45 51 W83 33 32
2525 Beech Avenue, Macon, GA 31204 US
(478) 474-8400, *Fax:* (478) 474-4777
www.wgnm.com
wgnm@wgnm.com
License: Macon, Bibb County, GA held by Christian Television Network Inc
(acq 12-31-2003; $3 million); *Washington Law Firm:* Allen & Harold
Nat'l Network: IND
Hours of Local News Weekly: News progmg one hr wkly
Robert D'Andrea, President
Rip Kenley, General Manager
Edie Spradley, Programming Director

WGXA *Digital Channel:* 16 *Virtual Channel:* 24; 1000 kw; 709 ft.; N32 44 58 W83 33 35
Mailing Address: 7621 Little Avenue, Suite 506, Charlotte, NC 28266 US
Second Address: 599 Martin Luther King Blvd., Macon, GA 31201
(478) 745-2424, *Fax:* (478) 745-6057 (news)
www.fox24.com
License: Macon, Bibb County, GA held by Fox24 of Macon License LLC
(acq 9-25-2007; $18.8 million); *Ownership:* Frontier Television Investors L.L.C., 100%; *Washington Law Firm:* Leibowitz & Spencer
Nat'l Network: FOX
Keith True, General Manager

WMAZ-TV *Digital Channel:* 13 *Virtual Channel:* 13; 52.6 kw; 781 ft.; N32 45 10 W83 33 32
1100 Wilson Boulevard, Arlington, VA 22234 US
(478) 752-1313, *Fax:* (478) 752-1331
www.13wmaz.com
License: Macon, Bibb County, GA held by Gannett Georgia L.P.
Group Owner: Gannett Broadcasting; (acq 12-4-95).; *Washington Law Firm:* Wiley, Rein & Fielding
Nat'l Network: CBS
Size of News Staff: 39; *Hours of Local News Weekly:* news progmg 27 hrs wkly
Jeff Dudley, Operations Dir
Frank Shurling, General Sales Mgr
Donna Reeves, Programming Director

WMGT-TV *Digital Channel:* 40 *Virtual Channel:* 41; 760 kw vis, 154 kw aur; ant 893t/837g; N32 45 12 W83 33 46; *Population Served:* 531,000
Mailing Address: Box 4328, Macon, GA 31213
Second Address: 301 Poplar St., Macon, GA 31201
(478) 745-4141, *Fax:* (478) 742-2626
www.wmgt.com
info@wmgt.com
License: Macon, Bibb County, GA held by Morris Network Inc.
Group Owner: Morris Multimedia Inc.; (acq 11-30-78; $2.8 million;; *Washington Law Firm:* McFadden, Evans & Sill
Nat'l Network: NBC *Nat'l Reps:* Millennium Sales & Marketing
Dean Hinson, President
Derek Rogers, General Manager
Damon Boyette, General Sales Mgr
Debbie Wright, Programming Director
Ryan Pope, Promotions Manager
Brandon Long, News Director
Scott Fussell, Chief Engineer

***WMUM-TV** *Digital Channel:* 7 *Virtual Channel:* 29; 31 kw; 1088 ft.; N32 28 11 W83 15 17
260 - 14th Street, N.W., Atlanta, GA 30318 US
(478) 934-3095
www.gpb.org
viewerservices@gpb.org
License: Cochran, Bleckley County, GA held by Georgia Public Telecommunications Commission
Nat'l Network: PBS
Randy Cranford, Station Manager

WPGA-TV *Digital Channel:* 32 *Virtual Channel:* 58; 100 kw; 609 ft.; N32 45 4 W83 33 27
P.O. Box 980, Perry, GA 31069 US
(478) 745-5858, *Fax:* (478) 745-5800
www.wpga.tv
License: Perry, Houston County, GA held by Radio Perry Inc
Washington Law Firm: Brown, Nietert & Kaufman
Nat'l Network: ABC
Hours of Local News Weekly: News progmg 3 hrs wkly

Lowell Register, President
Len Register, Operations Dir
Debbie Hart, General Manager
Julie Register, Promotions Manager

Savannah, GA (DMA 96)

WGSA *Digital Channel:* 35 *Virtual Channel:* 34; 1000 kw; 1145 ft.; N32 2 48 W81 20 27
9661 - 82nd Avenue, North, Seminole, FL 33777 US
(912) 692-8000, *Fax:* (912) 692-0400
www.wgsa.tv
info@wgsa.tv
License: Baxley, Appling County, GA held by Southern TV Corp (acq 6-3-98; $3.2 million); *Washington Law Firm:* Irwin, Campbell & Tannenwald
Nat'l Network: CW
Dan Johnson, CEO
Charles Robb, CFO
Jo Johnson, Executive Vice President

WJCL *Digital Channel:* 22 *Virtual Channel:* 22; 350 kw; 1430 ft.; N32 3 29 W81 20 19
The Pinnacle, Suite 875, 3455 Peachtree Rd., N.E., Atlanta, GA 30326 US
(912) 925-0022, *Fax:* (912) 921-2235
www.abc22tv.com
comments@wjcl.com
License: Savannah, Chatham County, GA held by LIN Licensing Company LLC
.
Group Owner: LIN Media; (acq 9-19-2007; $17.5 million); *Washington Law Firm:* Wiley Rein LLP
Nat'l Network: ABC *Nat'l Reps:* Petry Television Inc.
Size of News Staff: 14; *Hours of Local News Weekly:* news progmg 5 hrs wkly
Jason Elkin, CEO
Chris Hays, Operations Dir
Lynn Fairbanks, General Manager

WSAV-TV *Digital Channel:* 39 *Virtual Channel:* 3; 1000 kw; 1450 ft.; N32 3 31 W81 17 55
333 East Grace Street, Richmond, VA 23219 US
(912) 651-0300, *Fax:* (912) 651-0304
www.wsav.com
License: Savannah, Chatham County, GA held by Media General Communications Holdings, LLC
Group Owner: Media General Broadcast Group; (acq 7-25-97; grpsl).; *Washington Law Firm:* Dow, Lohnes & Albertson
Nat'l Network: NBC; MyNetworkTV
Brad Moses, Operations Dir
Debbi Thompson, General Sales Mgr
Dave Stagnitto, Programming Director
Kevin Brennan, News Director

WTOC-TV *Digital Channel:* 11 *Virtual Channel:* 11; 24.4 kw; 1447 ft.; N32 3 14 W81 21 1
Mailing Address: Rsa Tower, 20th Floor, 201 Monroe Street, Montgomery, AL 36104 US
Second Address: 11 The News Place-Chatham Center, Savannah, GA 31405
(912) 234-1111, *Fax:* (912) 238-5133
www.wtoc.com
License: Savannah, Chatham County, GA held by WTOC License Subsidiary, LLC
Group Owner: Raycom Media Inc.; (acq 4-15-97; grpsl).; *Washington Law Firm:* Covinton & Burling
Nat'l Network: CBS *Nat'l Reps:* Harrington, Righter & Parsons
William Cathcart, Operations Dir
Craig Harney, Operations Manager

***WVAN-TV** *Digital Channel:* 9 *Virtual Channel:* 9; 20 kw; 1274 ft.; N32 8 48 W81 37 5
260 - 14th Street, N.W., Atlanta, GA 30318 US
(404) 685-2400, *Fax:* (404) 685-2591
www.gpb.org
ask@gpb.org
License: Savannah, Chatham County, GA held by Georgia Public Telecommunications Commission
Nat'l Network: PBS
Bob Olive, General Manager

Tallahassee, FL-Thomasville, GA (DMA 105)

WCTV *Digital Channel:* 46 *Virtual Channel:* 6; 1000 kw; 1857 ft.; N30 40 13 W83 56 26
1201 New York Avenue, NW, Suite 1000, Washington, DC 20005 US
(850) 893-6666, *Fax:* (850) 893-5193
www.wctv6.com
License: Thomasville, Leon County, GA held by Gray Television Licensee Inc.
Group Owner: Gray Television Inc.; (acq 1996; $165 million with WVLT-TV Knoxville, TN).; *Washington Law Firm:* Wiley-Rein, LLC
Nat'l Network: CBS; MyNetworkTV *Nat'l Reps:* Continental Television Sales *Wire Services:* AP; CBS; CNN
Nick Waller, President
Ella Paris, General Sales Mgr
Joan Palos, Programming Director
Mike Smith, News Director
Heather Pryor, General Sales Manager

WSWG *Digital Channel:* 43 *Virtual Channel:* 44; 50 kw; 830 ft.; N31 10 18 W83 21 57
Mailing Address: P.O. Box 5391, Valdosta, GA 31603 US
Second Address: 107 2nd Ave. S.W., Moultrie, GA 31768
(229) 985-1340, *Fax:* (229) 985-7549
wswgtv.com
License: Valdosta, Lowndes County, GA held by Gray Television Licensee LLC
Group Owner: Gray Television Inc.; (acq 11-10-2005; $3.75 million); *Washington Law Firm:* Robert Bizer
Nat'l Network: CBS; MyNetworkTV
Nick Waller, General Manager
Chris Mossman, General Sales Mgr
Chris Stanley, Promotions Manager
Jim Killinger, Chief Engineer
Kacey Creech, Office Manager
Jared Yost, Regional Sales Manager

WTLH *Digital Channel:* 50 *Virtual Channel:* 49; 665 kw; 1959 ft.; N30 40 51 W83 58 21
Pegasus Corp. Office, 225 Cty Lne Ave. Ste.200, Bala Cynwyd, PA 19004 US
(850) 576-4990, *Fax:* (850) 576-0200
www.myfoxtallahassee.com
fox49@fox49.com
License: Bainbridge, Decatur County, GA held by New Age Media of Tallahassee License LLC.
Group Owner: CP Media LLC; (acq 3-31-2007; grpsl)
Nat'l Network: FOX; CW *Nat'l Reps:* Petry Television Inc.
Hours of Local News Weekly: 2.5
John Parente, CEO
Mike Yanuzzi, President
Tyrone Hayes, Operations Dir
Dan Mecca, General Manager
Don Abel, Programming Director
Nirmal Singh, Chief Engineer
Doris Jones, Business Manager
Nathan Mears, National Sales Manager

Tampa-St Petersburg (Sarasota), FL (DMA 13)

DWMDE *Digital Channel:* 5; 10 kw; 144 m; N38 57 17 W76 05 35
400 North Ashley Drive, Suite 310, Tampa, FL 31636
(813) 579-4491
License: Seaford, Sussex County, DE held by Western Pacific Broadcast LLC
Dale A. West, Vice President

Guam

Tamuning

KTGM *Digital Channel:* 14 *Virtual Channel:* 14; 12.5 kw; 551 ft.; N13 29 17 E144 49 30
692 N. Marine Drive, Tamuning, GU 96911 US
(671) 477-5700 xt 171, *Fax:* (671) 477-3982
License: Tamuning, Guam County, GU held by Sorensen Television Systems Inc
(acq 10-26-2005; $500,000); *Washington Law Firm:* Kaye, Scholer LLP
Nat'l Network: ABC
Size of News Staff: 10; *Hours of Local News Weekly:* news progmg 20 hrs wkly
Rex Sorensen, President

Hawaii

Honolulu, HI (DMA 72)

KAAH-TV *Digital Channel:* 27 *Virtual Channel:* 26; 262 kw; 1903 ft.; N21 23 45 W158 5 58; *Rebroadcasting:* Satellite of KTBN-TV Los Angeles (Santa Ana), CA 95%.
250 West Arrow Highway, San Dimas, CA 91773 US
(808) 521-5826, *Fax:* (808) 599-6238
www.tbn.org
tbnkaahtv26@hotmail.com
License: Honolulu, Honolulu County, HI held by Trinity Christian Center of Santa Ana Inc. dba Trinity Broadcasting Network.
Group Owner: Trinity Broadcasting Network; (acq 7-1-2000; grpsl).; *Washington Law Firm:* Colby May
Nat'l Network: TRINITY BROADCA
Cheryl Rzonca, General Manager
Paul Crouch Jr., Executive Vice President

KAII-TV *Digital Channel:* 7 *Virtual Channel:* 7; 3.69 kw; 2470 ft.; N20 39 37 W156 21 46; *Rebroadcasting:* Satellite of KHON(TV) Honolulu 100%.
4444 Lakeside Drive, Suite 320, Burbank, CA 46204 US
(808) 591-2222, *Fax:* (808) 593-8479
www.khon.com
news@khon.com
License: Wailuku, Maui County, HI held by LIN License Company LLC
Group Owner: LIN Media; (acq 11-1-2007; grpsl); *Washington Law Firm:* Wiley Rein LLP
Nat'l Network: FOX *Nat'l Reps:* Harrington, Righter & Parsons
Joseph McNamara, President
Alexander Rogers, Operations Dir
Susii Hearst, General Sales Mgr
Gelene Welch, Programming Director
Kyle Funasaki, Promotions Manager
Lori Silva, News Director
Bob Vaillancourt, Engineering Dir

***KALO** *Digital Channel:* 38 *Virtual Channel:* 38; 96.6 kw; 1893 ft.; N21 23 45 W158 5 58; *Rebroadcasting:* Christian programming
875 Waimaua Street, Suite 632, Honolulu, HI 96813 US
(808) 596-4417, *Fax:* (808) 593-2427
www.kalo-tv.com
info@kalo-tv.com
License: Honolulu, Honolulu County, HI held by Pacifica Broadcasting Co
Washington Law Firm: Fletcher, Heald & Hildreth, P.L.C., Harry F. Cole, Esq.
Nat'l Network: IND
Donald Laidlaw, General Manager
Lani Kaaa, Station Manager

KBFD-DT *Digital Channel:* 33; 146 kw vis, 14.6 kw aur; ant 405t/428g; N21 18 49 W157 51 43; *Population Served:* 1,200,000
Century Square, 1188 Bishop Street, Honolulu, HI 96813
(808) 521-8066, *Fax:* (808) 521-5233
www.kbfd.com
jeffchung@kbfd.com
License: Honolulu, Honolulu County, HI held by Allen Broadcasting Corp
Washington Law Firm: Wilkinson, Barker, Knauer L.L.P.
Size of News Staff: 4; *Hours of Local News Weekly:* news progmg 6 hrs wkly
Kea Sung Chung, CEO
June Ho Chung, Director
Jeff Chung, General Manager
June Ho Chung, Executive Vice President

KFVE *Digital Channel:* 22; 5.9 kw; 12.2 meters above ground; N21 24 03 W158 06 10
420 Waiakamilo Road #205, Honolulu, HI 52801
(808) 847-3246, *Fax:* (808) 845-3616
www.k5thehometeam.com
news8@khnl.com
License: Honolulu, Honolulu County, HI held by KHNL/KFVE License Subsidiary LLC.
Group Owner: Raycom Media Inc.; (acq 12-28-99); *Washington Law Firm:* Covington & Burling
Nat'l Network: MyNetworkTV *Nat'l Reps:* TeleRep *Wire Services:* CNN
Hours of Local News Weekly: News progmg 7 hrs wkly
John Fink, Operations Dir

KGMB *Digital Channel:* 23; 209 kw vis, 29.5 kw aur; ant -50t/436g; N21 17 46 W157 50 36; *Population Served:* 1,150,000
1534 Kapiolani Blvd., Honolulu, HI 96910
(808) 973-5462, *Fax:* (808) 973-9354
www.kgmb9.com
kgmb9news@kgmb9.com
License: Honolulu, Honolulu County, HI held by HITV License Subsidiary Inc.
Group Owner: HITV License Subsidiary Inc.; (acq 5-25-2007; grpsl)
Nat'l Network: CBS *Nat'l Reps:* Harrington, Righter & Parsons
Rick Blangiardi, President

KGMD-TV *Digital Channel:* 9 *Virtual Channel:* 9; 2 kw; 102 ft.; N19 43 0 W155 8 13
1534 Kapiolani Blvd., Honolulu, HI 96814 US
(808) 973-5462, *Fax:* (808) 941-8153
www.kgmb.com
kgmbnews@kgmb9.com
License: Hilo, Hawaii County, HI held by HITV License Subsidiary Inc.
Group Owner: HITV License Subsidiary Inc.; (acq 5-25-2007; grpsl)
Nat'l Network: CBS *Nat'l Reps:* Harrington, Righter & Parsons
Rick Blangiardi, President
John Fink, General Manager

KGMV *Digital Channel:* 24 *Virtual Channel:* 3; 77 kw; 2477 ft.; N20 39 37 W156 21 46
1534 Kapiolani Boulevard, Honolulu, HI 96814 US
(808) 973-5462, *Fax:* (808) 973-9354
www.kgmb9.com
kgmb9news@kgmb9.com
License: Wailuku, Maui County, HI held by HITV License Subsidiary Inc.
Group Owner: HITV License Subsidiary Inc.; (acq 5-25-2007; grpsl)
Nat'l Network: CBS *Nat'l Reps:* Harrington, Righter & Parsons
Rick Blangiardi, President
John Fink, General Manager

KHAW-TV *Digital Channel:* 11 *Virtual Channel:* 11; *Rebroadcasting:* Satellite of KHON-TV Honolulu.
4444 Lakeside Drive, Suite 320, Burbank, CA 46204 US
(808) 591-2222, *Fax:* (808) 591-9085
www.khon.com
khan@khon.emmis.com
License: Hilo, Hawaii County, HI held by LIN License Company LLC
Group Owner: LIN Media; (acq 11-1-2007; grpsl); *Washington Law Firm:* Wiley Rein LLP
Nat'l Network: FOX *Nat'l Reps:* Harrington, Righter & Parsons
Size of News Staff: 45; *Hours of Local News Weekly:* news progmg 25 hrs wkly
Joseph McNamara, President
Alexander Rogers, Operations Dir
Susii Hearst, General Sales Mgr
Kyle Funasaki, Promotions Manager
Lori Silva, News Director
Bob Vaillancourt, Engineering Dir
Gelene Welch, General Sales Manager

KHBC-TV *Digital Channel:* 22 *Virtual Channel:* 2; 8 kw; -558 ft.; N19 43 51 W155 4 11; *Rebroadcasting:* Rebroadcasts KHNL(TV) Honolulu 100%.
400 South Record Street, Dallas, TX 75202 US
(808) 847-3246, *Fax:* (808) 845-3616
www.khnl.com
news8@khnl.com
License: Hilo, Hawaii County, HI held by KHNL/KFVE License Subsidiary LLC.
Group Owner: Raycom Media Inc.; (acq 9-2-99; grpsl).; *Washington Law Firm:* Covington & Burling
Nat'l Network: NBC *Nat'l Reps:* TeleRep *Wire Services:* CNN; NBC
John Fink, Operations Dir
Rick Blangiardi, General Manager

***KHET** *Digital Channel:* 11 *Virtual Channel:* 11; 15.7 kw; 2051 ft.; N21 24 3 W158 6 10
Mailing Address: 2350 Dole St., Honolulu, HI 96822 US
Second Address: 2350 Dole Street, Honolulu, HI 96822
(808) 973-1000, *Fax:* (808) 973-1090
www.pbshawaii.org
email@pbshawaii.org
License: Honolulu, Honolulu County, HI held by Hawaii Public Television Foundation
Washington Law Firm: Wilkes, Artis, Hedrick & Lane
Nat'l Network: PBS
Leslie Wilcox, CEO
John Nakahira, Engineering Dir

KHNL *Digital Channel:* 35 *Virtual Channel:* 13; 25 kw; 2064 ft.; N21 24 3 W158 6 10
400 South Record Street, Dallas, TX 75202 US
(808) 847-3246, *Fax:* (808) 845-3616
www.khnl.com
news8@khnl.com
License: Honolulu, Honolulu County, HI held by KHNL/KFVE License Subsidiary LLC.
Group Owner: Raycom Media Inc.; (acq 9-2-99; grpsl).; *Washington Law Firm:* Covington & Burling
Nat'l Network: NBC *Nat'l Reps:* TeleRep *Wire Services:* CNN; NBC
Hours of Local News Weekly: News progmg 19.5 hrs wkly
Rick Blangiardi, General Manager

KHON-TV *Digital Channel:* 8 *Virtual Channel:* 2; 7.2 kw; 56 ft.; N21 17 39 W157 50 18
4444 Lakeside Drive, Suite 320, Burbank, CA 46204 US
(808) 591-2222, *Fax:* (808) 591-9085
www.khon.com
news@khon.com
License: Honolulu, Honolulu County, HI held by NVT Hawaii Licensee LLC.
Group Owner: New Vision Television LLC; (acq 11-1-2007; grpsl)
Nat'l Network: FOX; CW *Nat'l Reps:* Harrington, Righter & Parsons
Size of News Staff: 45; *Hours of Local News Weekly:* news progmg 25 hrs wkly
Joe McNamara, President
Alexander Rogers, Operations Dir
Susii Hearst, General Sales Mgr
Gelene Welch, Programming Director
Kyle Funasaki, Promotions Manager
Lori Silva, News Director
Bob Vaillancourt, Engineering Dir

KHVO *Digital Channel:* 13 *Virtual Channel:* 13; 2 kw; -302 ft.; N19 43 0 W155 8 13; *Rebroadcasting:* Satellite of KITV Honolulu.
888 Seventh Avenue, New York, NY 10106 US
(808) 535-0400
www.kitv.com
acjackson@kitv.com
License: Hilo, Hawaii County, HI held by Hearst-Argyle Stations Inc.
Group Owner: Hearst-Argyle Television Inc.; (acq 7-16-97; grpsl).
Nat'l Network: ABC
Michael Rosenberg, General Manager
Jan Dawson, Traffic Manager

KIKU *Digital Channel:* 19; 467 kw vis, 46.7 kw aur; ant 2,040t; N21 23 51 W158 06 01
737 Bishop St., Suite 1430, Honolulu, HI 96813
(808) 847-2021, *Fax:* (808) 841-3326
www.kikutv.com
License: Honolulu, Honolulu County, HI held by NRJ TV Hawaii License Co. LLC
Group Owner: NRJ Holdings LLC; (acq 8-10-2012); *Washington Law Firm:* Goldberg, Godles, Wiener & Wright
Nat'l Reps: Petry Television Inc.
Foreign Language Programming
Phyllis Kihara, General Manager

KITV *Digital Channel:* 40 *Virtual Channel:* 4; 85 kw; 3 ft.; N21 17 37 W157 50 34
888 Seventh Avenue, New York, NY 10106 US
(808) 535-0400, *Fax:* (808) 536-8777
www.thehawaiichannel.com
acjackson@kitv.com
License: Honolulu, Honolulu County, HI held by Hearst-Argyle Stations Inc.
Group Owner: Hearst-Argyle Television Inc.; (acq 7-16-97; grpsl).; *Washington Law Firm:* Brooks, Pierce, McLendon, Humphrey & Leonard
Nat'l Network: ABC *Nat'l Reps:* Eagle Television Sales
Size of News Staff: 40; *Hours of Local News Weekly:* news progmg 20 hrs wkly
Michael Rosenberg, General Manager
Jan Dawson, Traffic Manager

KKAI *Digital Channel:* 50 *Virtual Channel:* 50; 19 kw vis; ant 1,115t/107g; N21 19 23 W157 40 53
875 Waimanu St., Suite 638, Honolulu, HI 96734
(808) 593-5524, *Fax:* (808) 441-0092
www.kkai.tv
info@kkai.tv
License: Kailua, Honolulu County, HI held by Kailua Television LLC
Ownership: Kailua Television LLC; *Washington Law Firm:* Fletcher, Heald & Hildreth
Nat'l Network: RETRO TV
Foreign Language Programming; Hours of Local News Weekly: 14
Dr. Christopher Racine, President
Dr. Christopher Racine, General Manager
Kirt Caldwell, Chief Engineer

KLEI-TV *Digital Channel:* 25 *Virtual Channel:* 6; 52.5 kw vis, 6.7 kw aur; ant 2,910t; N19 42 56 W155 55 00
Box 143, Honolulu, HI 93108
(808) 329-8120, *Fax:* (808) 443-0424
www.klei.tv
info@klei.tv
License: Kailua-Kona, Hawaii County, HI held by Pacific Christian Church
(acq 10-1-2011; donation); *Ownership:* Mauna Kea Broadcasting Inc.; *Washington Law Firm:* Fletcher, Heald & Hildreth
Foreign Language Programming; Hours of Local News Weekly: 14 hrs
Dr. Christopher Racine, CEO/COO
Chip Begay, General Manager
Kirk Caldwell, Engineering Dir
Kirk Caldwell, Chief Engineer

KMAU *Digital Channel:* 12 *Virtual Channel:* 12; 9 kw; 2451 ft.; N20 39 37 W156 21 46; *Rebroadcasting:* Satellite of KITV Honolulu.
888 Seventh Avenue, New York, NY 10106 US
(808) 535-0400
License: Wailuku, Maui County, HI held by Hearst-Argyle Stations Inc.
Group Owner: Hearst-Argyle Television Inc.; (acq 7-16-97; grpsl).
Nat'l Network: ABC
Michael Rosenberg, General Manager

***KMEB** *Digital Channel:* 10 *Virtual Channel:* 10; 21.13 kw; 2451 ft.; N20 39 37 W156 21 46; *Rebroadcasting:* Satellite of *KHET Honolulu.
Mailing Address: 2350 Dole St., Wailuku, HI 96822 US
Second Address: 2350 Dole St., Honolulu, HI 96822
(808) 973-1000, *Fax:* (808) 973-1090
www.pbshawaii.org
email@pbshawaii.org
License: Wailuku, Maui County, HI held by Hawaii Public Television Foundation
Nat'l Network: PBS
Leslie Wilcox, CEO

KOGG *Digital Channel:* 16 *Virtual Channel:* 15; 50 kw; 2684 ft.; N20 39 37 W156 21 46; *Rebroadcasting:* 100% rebroadcast satellite of KHNL(TV) Honolulu.
400 South Record Street, Dallas, TX 75202 US
(808) 847-3246, *Fax:* (808) 845-3616
www.khnl.com
news8@khnl.com
License: Wailuku, Maui County, HI held by KHNL/KFVE License Subsidiary LLC.
Group Owner: Raycom Media Inc.; (acq 9-2-99; grpsl).; *Washington Law Firm:* Covington & Burling
Nat'l Network: NBC *Nat'l Reps:* TeleRep *Wire Services:* CNN; NBC
Hours of Local News Weekly: 19.5 hrs.
John Fink, Operations Dir

KPXO-TV *Digital Channel:* 41; 95.5 kw vis; ant 2,073t; N21 19 49 W157 45 24
875 Waimanu St., Suite 630, Honolulu, HI 96813
(808) 591-1275, *Fax:* (808) 591-1409
www.ionmedia.tv
License: Kaneohe, Honolulu County, HI held by Paxson Hawaii License Inc.
Group Owner: ION Media Networks Inc.; (acq 8-12-98; $6.9 million)
Nat'l Network: ION Television
Jeff Maguire, General Manager

KUPU *Digital Channel:* 15 *Virtual Channel:* 56; 12 kw; 1224 ft.; N21 19 23 W157 40 53
2525 Date St, #2503, Honolulu, HI 96826 US
(808) 943-0007, *Fax:* (808) 440-1375
www.kupu.tv
info@oceaniachurch.org
License: Waimanalo, Honolulu County, HI held by Oceania Christian Church.
Group Owner: Oceania Christian Church; (acq 9-28-2006); *Washington Law Firm:* Fletcher Heal & Hildreth
Nat'l Network: IND
Size of News Staff: 12; *Hours of Local News Weekly:* news progmg 14 hrs wkly
James Gustafson, President

***KWBN** *Digital Channel:* 43 *Virtual Channel:* 44; 6.46 kw; 1893 ft.; N21 23 45 W158 5 58
875 Waimuau Street, Suite 634, Honolulu, HI 96813 US
(817) 571-1229, *Fax:* (817) 571-7458
www.daystar.com
License: Honolulu, Honolulu County, HI held by Ho'ona'auao Community Television Inc
Nat'l Network: IND
Marcus Lamb, President

KWHD *Digital Channel:* 23 *Virtual Channel:* 14; 14.9 kw; 108 ft.; N19 43 0 W155 8 13; *Rebroadcasting:* Rebroadcasts KWHE Honolulu 100%.
P. O. Box 12, South Bend, IN 46624 US

(808) 538-1414, *Fax:* (808) 526-0326
www.lesea.com,www.kwhe.com
kwhe@lesea.com
License: Hilo, Hawaii County, HI held by Le Sea Broadcasting Corp.
Group Owner: Le Sea Broadcasting; (acq 10-1-89; $8,277;;
Washington Law Firm: Gardner, Carton & Douglas
Nat'l Network: IND
Anthony Hale, CFO
Peter Sumrall, President
T. J. Malievsky, General Manager

KWHE *Digital Channel:* 31 *Virtual Channel:* 14; 20.1 kw; 16 ft.; N21 18 49 W157 51 43
P.O. Box 12, South Bend, IN 46624 US
(808) 538-1414, *Fax:* (808) 526-0326
www.kwhe.com; www.lesea.com
kwhe@lesea.com
License: Honolulu, Honolulu County, HI held by LeSea Broadcasting Corp.
Group Owner: Le Sea Broadcasting; (acq 8-15-86; $825,000;;
Washington Law Firm: Gardner, Carton & Douglas
Nat'l Network: IND
Anthony Hale, CFO
Peter Sumrall, President
T. J. Malievsky, General Manager
Michael Kemmerling, Chief Engineer

KWHM *Digital Channel:* 21 *Virtual Channel:* 21; 23.5 kw; 2477 ft.; N20 39 37 W156 21 46; *Rebroadcasting:* Rebroadcasts KWHE Honolulu 100%
Post Office Box 12, South Bend, IN 46624 US
(808) 538-1414, *Fax:* (808) 526-0326
www.kwhe.com; www.lesea.com
kwhe@lesea.com
License: Wailuku, Maui County, HI held by Le Sea Broadcasting Corp.
Group Owner: Le Sea Broadcasting; *Washington Law Firm:* Gardner, Carton & Douglas
Nat'l Network: IND
Anthony Hale, CFO
Peter Sumrall, President
T. J. Malievsky, General Manager
Michael Kemmerling, Chief Engineer

Idaho

Boise, ID (DMA 112)

***KAID** *Digital Channel:* 21; 57.2 kw vis, 5.7 kw aur; 2,474t/142g; N43 45 16 W116 05 56; *Population Served:* 157,000
1455 N. Orchard St., Boise, ID 83706
(208) 373-7220, *Fax:* (208) 373-7245
www.idahoptv.org
idptv@idahoptv.org
License: Boise, Ada County, ID held by Idaho State Board of Education
Washington Law Firm: Fletcher, Heald & Hildreth
Nat'l Network: PBS
Size of News Staff: 5; *Hours of Local News Weekly:* news progmg 3 hrs wkly
Peter Morrill, General Manager
Ron Pisaneschi, Programming Director
Megan Griffin, Promotions Manager
Rich Van Genderen, Engineering Dir
Craig Koster, Chief Engineer

KBOI-TV *Digital Channel:* 28 *Virtual Channel:* 2; 65 kw vis, 7.0l kw aur; 2,550t/100g; N43 45 17 W116 05 53; *Population Served:* 604,000
140 N. 16th St., Boise, ID 98109
(208) 472-2222, *Fax:* (208) 472-2212
www.2news.tv.com
comments@kbcitv.com
License: Boise, Ada County, ID held by Fisher Broadcasting - Idaho TV L.L.C.
Group Owner: Fisher Communications Inc.; (acq 7-1-99; grpsl).;
Washington Law Firm: Shaw Pittman
Nat'l Network: CBS; CW *Nat'l Reps:* Continental Television Sales
Size of News Staff: 37; *Hours of Local News Weekly:* news progmg 19 hrs wkly
Colleen Brown, CEO
Larry Roberts, Operations Dir
Eric Jordan, General Sales Mgr
Tina Morris, Programming Director
Sean McBride, Promotions Manager
Yvonne Simons, News Director

KIVI-TV ; 60.3 kw vis, 12.0 kw aur; ant 2,660t/210g; N43 45 20 W116 05 55; *Population Served:* 580,000
1866 E Chisholm Drive, Nampa, ID 83687
(208) 336-0500, *Fax:* (208) 381-6682
www.kivitv.com
License: Nampa, Canyon County, ID held by Journal Broadcast Corp.
Group Owner: Journal Communications Inc.; (acq 11-15-2001).
Nat'l Network: ABC
Size of News Staff: 45; *Hours of Local News Weekly:* news progmg 19.5 hrs wkly
Bob Rosenthal, Operations Dir
Ken Richie, General Sales Mgr
Brian Perkins, Programming Director
Jason Knose, Promotions Manager
Scott Picken, News Director
Rick Kemp, Engineering Dir
Jeff Hoffert, Chief Engineer
Kevin Eslinger,Chief Photographer
Kendra Martinez, Chief Producer
Norma Petty, Regional Sales Manager

KKJB *Digital Channel:* 39 *Virtual Channel:* 39; 35 kw; 1752 ft.; N43 44 23 W116 8 15
1320 Eighteenth St NW400, Washington, DC 20036 US
(208) 331-3900, *Fax:* (559) 435-3201
www.cocolatv.com
info@cocolatv.com
License: Boise, Ada County, ID held by Boise Telecasters L.P.
Group Owner: Cocola Broadcasting Companies LLC; (acq 5-7-2004; $3 million for CP).; *Washington Law Firm:* Dow, Lohnes & Albertson, LLPC
Nat'l Network: IND
Gary Cocola, CEO
John Her, Operations Dir
Kevin Mosesian, Station Manager
Seth Diviney, General Sales Mgr
Ralph Malerich, Engineering Dir

KNIN-TV *Digital Channel:* 10 *Virtual Channel:* 9; 162 kw vis; ant 2,690t/210g; N43 45 18 W116 05 52
816 W. Bannock St., Suite 402, Boise, ID 93942
(208) 331-0909, *Fax:* (208) 344-0119
www.knin.com
License: Caldwell, Canyon County, ID held by Journal Broadcast Corp.
Group Owner: Journal Communications Inc.; (acq 4-23-2009; $6.6 million); *Washington Law Firm:* Leventhal Senter & Lerman PLLC
Nat'l Network: Fox *Nat'l Reps:* Blair Television
James Prather, President
Larry Newton, General Manager

KTRV-TV *Digital Channel:* 13 *Virtual Channel:* 12; 17 kw; 2720 ft.; N43 45 18 W116 5 52
679 6th St. N. Extension, Nampa, ID 83651 US
(208) 466-1200, *Fax:* (208) 467-6958
www.fox12idaho.com
comments@ktrv.com
License: Nampa, Canyon County, ID held by Idaho Independent Television Inc.
Group Owner: Block Communications Inc.; (acq 4-23-85; $4.9 million;; *Washington Law Firm:* Dow, Lohnes & Albertson
Nat'l Network: FOX
Size of News Staff: 12; *Hours of Local News Weekly:* news progmg 7 hrs wkly
Rick Joseph, President
Ed Crampton, Operations Dir
Ken Hunter, General Sales Mgr
C.J. Gish, Programming Director
Kelly Cross, News Director
Daniel Paixao, Chief Engineer
Bob Jaundalderis, Manager, Digital Media

KTVB *Digital Channel:* 7 *Virtual Channel:* 7; 42.1 kw; 2644 ft.; N43 45 16 W116 5 56
Mailing Address: 400 South Record Street, Dallas, TX 75202 US
Second Address: 5407 Fairview Ave, Boise, ID 83706
(208) 375-7277, *Fax:* (208) 378-1762
www.ktvb.com
info@ktvb.com
License: Boise, Ada County, ID held by KTVB-TV Inc.
Group Owner: Belo Corp; (acq 1997; grpsl).; *Washington Law Firm:* Wiley, Rein & Fielding
Nat'l Network: NBC *Nat'l Reps:* TeleRep
Hours of Local News Weekly: News progmg 27 hrs wkly
Kyle Morrell, CFO
Douglas Armstrong, President
Paul Budell, Operations Dir
Kristi Edmunds, General Sales Mgr
Richard Strack, Programming Director
Jim Gilchriest, News Director
Brad Bond, Local Sales Manager
Tom Zito, NationalSales Manager

Idaho Falls-Pocatello, ID (DMA 162)

KFXP *Digital Channel:* 31 *Virtual Channel:* 31; 68.5 kw; 1467 ft.; N42 55 15 W112 20 44
103 Entrance Drive, Suite 1, Livingston, ID 77351 US
(208) 232-6666, *Fax:* (208) 232-6678
www.kpvi.com
License: Pocatello, Bannock County, ID held by Compass Communications of Idaho Inc
Shelley Goings, General Manager
Patrick Anderson, General Sales Mgr
Rockky Hansen, Promotions Manager
Brenda Baumgartner, News Director
Robin Estopinal, Chief Engineer

KIDK ; 100 kw vis, 14.4 kw aur; 1,600t/200g; N43 29 51 W112 39 50; *Population Served:* 275,000
Mailing Address: 1915 Yellowstone Highway, Idaho Falls, ID 83401
Second Address: 145 S Arthur, Pocatello, ID 83204
(208) 522-5100, *Fax:* (208) 535-0946
www.kidk.com
comments@kidk.com
License: Idaho Falls, Bonneville County, ID held by Fisher Broadcasting - S.E. Idaho TV L.L.C.
Group Owner: Fisher Communications Inc.; (acq 12-4-01 grpsl).;
Washington Law Firm: Shaw, Pittman
Nat'l Network: CBS *Nat'l Reps:* Millennium Sales & Marketing
Size of News Staff: 35; *Hours of Local News Weekly:* news progmg 15 hrs wkly
Jim Wareham, General Manager
Gary Smith, Chief Engineer

KIFI-TV *Digital Channel:* 8 *Virtual Channel:* 8; 63 kw; 1522 ft.; N43 30 4 W112 39 43
PO Box 21488, Idaho Falls, ID 83401 US
(208) 525-8888, *Fax:* (208) 522-1930,(208) 529-2443 (news)
www.localnews8.com
License: Idaho Falls, Bonneville County, ID held by NPG of Idaho Inc.
Group Owner: News-Press & Gazette Co.; (acq 6-15-2005; $12.5 million); *Washington Law Firm:* SMITHWICK & BELENDIUK, P.C.
Nat'l Network: ABC; Telemundo (Spanish); CW
Size of News Staff: 35; *Hours of Local News Weekly:* news progmg 30 hrs wkly
Russ Haack, Operations Dir
Mark Danielson, General Manager
Monte Young, General Sales Mgr

***KISU-TV** *Virtual Channel:* 10; 122 kw vis, 12.2 kw aur; 1,527t/144g; N43 30 02 W112 39 36
Mailing Address: Campus Box 8111, Pocatello, ID 83706
Second Address: 1455 N. Orchard St., Boise, ID 83706
(208) 282-2857, *Fax:* (208) 282-2848
www.idahoptv.org
idptv@idahoptv.org
License: Pocatello, Bannock County, ID held by Idaho State Board of Education
Nat'l Network: PBS
Peter Morrill, General Manager
Ron Pisaneschi, Programming Director
Rich Van Genderen, Engineering Dir
Dave Turnmire, Chief Engineer

KPVI-DT ; 100 kw vis, 17.4 kw aur; 1,530t/619g; N42 55 15 W112 20 44; *Rebroadcasting:* Rebroadcasts: KJWY Jackson Hole, WY; *Population Served:* 309,000
Box 667, 902 E Sherman, Pocatello, ID 83204
(208) 232-6666, *Fax:* (208) 233-6678
www.kpvi.com
License: Pocatello, Bannock County, ID held by Oregon Trail Broadcasting Co.
Group Owner: Intermountain West Communications; (acq 11-15-95).
Nat'l Network: NBC *Nat'l Reps:* Blair Television *Wire Services:* AP
Size of News Staff: 23; *Hours of Local News Weekly:* news progmg 17 hrs wkly
Shelley Goings, General Manager
Barb Monroy, Programming Director
Scott Larkin, Promotions Manager
Todd Blackinton, News Director
Robin Estopinal, Chief Engineer

Spokane, WA (DMA 75)

KLEW-TV *Digital Channel:* 32 *Virtual Channel:* 3; 133 kw; 1145 ft.; N46 27 27 W117 5 56; *Rebroadcasting:* Satellite of KIMA-TV Yakima Wash.
Mailing Address: 100 - 4th Avenue, North, Seattle, WA 98109 US
Second Address: 2626 17th Street, Lewiston, ID 83501
(208) 746-2636, *Fax:* (208) 746-4819
www.klewtv.com
info@klewtv.com
License: Lewiston, Nez Perce County, ID held by Fisher Broadcasting - Washington TV L.L.C.
Group Owner: Fisher Communications Inc.; (acq 12-4-2001; grpsl).; *Washington Law Firm:* Shaw Pittman
Nat'l Network: CBS *Nat'l Reps:* Petry Television Inc. *Wire Services:* AP
Size of News Staff: 4; *Hours of Local News Weekly:* news progmg 12 hrs wkly
Margo Aragon, Operations Dir
Dan Stellmon, Station Manager
Greg Meyer, News Director
Bill Dunlap, Chief Engineer
Ann Fickenwirth, Operations Manager

***KUID-TV** *Digital Channel:* 12 *Virtual Channel:* 35; 44 kw vis; ant 971t/148g; N46 40 54 W116 58 13; *Population Served:* 151,000
Mailing Address: c/o KAID, 1455 N. Orchard St., Boise, ID 83706
Second Address: PO Box 443101, University of Idaho, Moscow, ID 83844-3101
(208) 885-1226, *Fax:* (208) 885-5711
www.idahoptv.org
idptv@idahoptv.org
License: Moscow, Latah County, ID held by State Board of Education, State of Idaho
Washington Law Firm: Fletcher, Heald & Hildreth
Nat'l Network: PBS
Peter Morrill, General Manager
Kris Freeland, Station Manager
Megan Griffin, General Sales Mgr
Ron Pisaneschi, Programming Director
Rich Van Genderen, Engineering Dir
Ken Segota, Chief Engineer

Topeka, KS (DMA 138)

DKSQA *Digital Channel:* 12; 5,000 kw vis; ant 738t/26g; N39 03 50 W95 45 49; *Not on Air/Target Date:* unknown
1155 Connecticut Ave. N.W., Suite 600, Washington, DC 83847
(202) 861-0870, *Fax:* (202) 429-0657
License: Topeka, Shawnee County, KS
James Winston, General Manager

Twin Falls, ID (DMA 194)

***KIPT** *Digital Channel:* 22; 22.4 kw vis; 528t/69g; N42 43 47 W114 24 52; *Rebroadcasting:* Rebroadcasts KAID Boise 100%.
c/o KAID, 1455 N. Orchard St., Boise, ID 83706
(208) 373-7220, *Fax:* (208) 373-7245
www.idahoptv.org
idptv@idahoptv.org
License: Twin Falls, Twin Falls County, ID held by State Board of Education, State of Idaho
Washington Law Firm: Fletcher, Heald & Hildreth
Nat'l Network: PBS
Peter Morrill, General Manager
Ron Pisaneschi, Programming Director
Rich Van Genderen, Engineering Dir
Craig Koster, Chief Engineer

KMVT *Digital Channel:* 11 *Virtual Channel:* 11; 40 kw; 1060 ft.; N42 43 47 W114 24 52
71 East Avenue, Norwalk, CT 06851 US
(208) 733-1100, *Fax:* (208) 733-4649
www.kmvt.com
License: Twin Falls, Twin Falls County, ID held by Neuhoff Family L.P.
Group Owner: Neuhoff Family L.P.; (acq 8-3-2004; $17.3 million);
Washington Law Firm: Schwartz, Woods & Miller
Nat'l Network: CBS *Nat'l Reps:* Continental Television Sales
Wire Services: AP
Size of News Staff: 14; *Hours of Local News Weekly:* news progmg 10 hrs wkly
Lee Wagner, General Manager
Lisa Collins, General Sales Mgr
Paul Johnson, Promotions Manager
Joe Martin, News Director
Rodger Martin, Chief Engineer
Deborah Flores, Traffic Manager

KXTF *Digital Channel:* 34 *Virtual Channel:* 35; 49.4 kw; 499 ft.; N42 43 42 W114 24 43
1500 Foremaster Lane, Las Vegas, NV 89101 US
(208) 733-0035, *Fax:* (208) 733-0160
www.kxtf.com
License: Twin Falls, Twin Falls County, ID held by Sunbelt Broadcasting Co.
Group Owner: Sunbelt Communications Co.; *Washington Law Firm:* Hamel & Park
Nat'l Network: FOX
Hours of Local News Weekly: News progmg 2 hrs wkly
Bill Fouch, General Manager
Joe Nielsen, Station Manager
Patrick Anderson, General Sales Mgr
Scott Larkin, Promotions Manager
Brenda Baumgartner, News Director
Robin Estopinal, Chief Engineer

Illinois

Champaign & Springfield-Decatur, IL (DMA 83)

WAND *Digital Channel:* 17 *Virtual Channel:* 17; 1000 kw; 1281 ft.; N39 57 7 W88 49 55
200 Crescent Court, Suite 1600, Dallas, TX 75201 US
(217) 424-2500, *Fax:* (217) 422-8203
www.wandtv.com
License: Decatur, Macon County, IL held by WAND Television Inc.
Group Owner: Block Communications Inc.; 11/1/2007;
Washington Law Firm: Dow Lohnes
Nat'l Network: NBC
Ron Pulera, General Manager
Tracey Cole, Station Manager
Carol Barnes, Promotions Manager

WBUI *Digital Channel:* 22 *Virtual Channel:* 23; 325 kw; 1316 ft.; N39 56 56 W88 50 12
10829 Olive Boulevard, Suite 202, St. Louis, MO 63141 US
(217) 428-2323, *Fax:* (217) 428-6455
www.centralillinoiscw.com
promotions@centralillinoiscw.com
License: Decatur, Macon County, IL held by Acme TV Licenses of Illinois L.L.C.
Group Owner: ACME Communications Inc.; (acq 6-14-99; $13.3 million)
Nat'l Network: CW *Nat'l Reps:* MMT
Bill Snider, General Manager
Chad Happersett, Station Manager
Allen White, General Sales Mgr
Jim Cloney, Promotions Manager
Scott Washburn, Chief Engineer

WCCU *Digital Channel:* 26 *Virtual Channel:* 27; 507 kw; 374 ft.; N40 18 46 W87 55 0; *Rebroadcasting:* Rebroadcasts WRSP-TV Springfield 100%
712 Killarney St., Urbana, IL 61801 US
(217) 403-9927, *Fax:* (217) 403-1007
www.myfoxchampaign.com
License: Urbana, Champaign County, IL held by Springfield Broadcasting Partners.
Group Owner: Bahakel Communications; (acq 7-20-92).
Nat'l Network: FOX
Peter O'Brien, General Manager
Randy Stone, General Sales Mgr
Jeff Kaufmann, Promotions Manager
Jack Richardson, Chief Engineer

WCIA *Digital Channel:* 48; 100 kw vis, 20 kw aur; 940t/981g; N40 06 23 W88 26 59
Mailing Address: Box 20, Champaign, IL 61824-0020
Second Address: 509 S. Neil St., Champaign, IL 61820
(217) 356-8333, *Fax:* (217) 373-3680
www.illinoishomepage.net
webmaster@wcia.com
License: Champaign, Champaign County, IL held by Nexstar Broadcasting, Inc.
Group Owner: Nexstar Broadcasting Group Inc.; (acq 5-19-2000; grpsl).; *Washington Law Firm:* Covington & Burling
Nat'l Network: CBS
Russ Hamilton, General Manager
Don Osika, General Sales Mgr
Angela Smith, Programming Director
Peter Carlson, Promotions Manager
Darren Martin, Chief Engineer

WCIX *Digital Channel:* 13; 200 kw vis, 20 kw aur; ant 620t/655g; N39 47 27 W89 30 53
509 S. Neil St., Champaign, IL 61824-0020
(217) 356-8333, *Fax:* (217) 373-3680
www.illinoishomepage.net
webmaster@wcia.com
License: Springfield, Sangamon County, IL held by Nexstar Broadcasting, Inc.
Group Owner: Nexstar Broadcasting Group Inc.; (acq 5-19-2000; grpsl).; *Washington Law Firm:* Drinker-Biddle-Reath
Nat'l Network: MyNetworkTV *Nat'l Reps:* Katz Continental
Coby Cooper, General Manager
Dale Stafford, Director of Sales
Angela Smith, Programming Director
Peter Carlson, Promotions Manager
Darren Martin, Chief Engineer

***WEIU-TV** *Digital Channel:* 50 *Virtual Channel:* 51; 255 kw; 479 ft.; N39 34 15 W88 18 25.5
Mailing Address: Radio and Tv Center, Charleston, IL 61920 US
Second Address: Radio & TV Ctr., Eastern Illinois Univ., Charleston, IL 61920
(217) 581-5956,(877) 727-9348, *Fax:* (217) 581-6650
www.weiu.net
weiu@weiu.net
License: Charleston, Coles County, IL held by Eastern Illinois University
Washington Law Firm: Cohn & Marks
Nat'l Network: PBS
Size of News Staff: 25; *Hours of Local News Weekly:* news progmg 3 hrs wkly
Denis Roche, General Manager
Jeff Owens, General Sales Mgr
Linda Kingery, Programming Director
Ke'an Rogers, Promotions Manager
Kelly Runyon, News Director
Kevin Armstrong, Chief Engineer

WICD *Digital Channel:* 41; 358 kw vis, 35 kw aur; ant 1,300t/1,338g; N40 04 11 W87 54 45; *Population Served:* 332,000
250 S. Country Fair Dr., Champaign, IL 61821-2920
(217) 351-8500, *Fax:* (217) 351-6056
www.wicd15.com
License: Champaign, Champaign County, IL held by WICD License L.L.C.
Group Owner: Sinclair Broadcast Group Inc.; (acq 7-2-99; $81 million with WICS(TV) Springfield).; *Washington Law Firm:* Wiley, Rein & Fielding
Nat'l Network: ABC
Size of News Staff: 20; *Hours of Local News Weekly:* news progmg 17 hrs wkly
David Smith, CEO
Tim Mathis, President
Erik Snell, Promotions Manager
Deana Reece, News Director
Jim Wnek, Chief Engineer

***WILL-TV** *Digital Channel:* 9 *Virtual Channel:* 12; 30 kw; 991 ft.; N40 2 18 W88 40 10
300 North Goodwin Avenue, Urbana, IL 61801 US
(217) 333-1070, *Fax:* (217) 244-6386
www.will.illinois.edu
will-tv@uiuc.edu
License: Urbana, Champaign County, IL held by University of Illinois Board of Trustees
Washington Law Firm: Dow, Lohnes & Albertson
Nat'l Network: PBS
Carl Caldwell, Station Manager
David Thiel, Programming Director
Rick Finnie, Chief Engineer

WRSP-TV *Digital Channel:* 44 *Virtual Channel:* 55; 335 kw; 1362 ft.; N39 47 57 W89 26 46
3003 Old Rochester Road, Springfield, IL 62703 US
(217) 523-8855, *Fax:* (217) 523-4410
www.myfoxillinois.com
License: Springfield, Sangamon County, IL held by Gocom Media of Illinois, LLC
Group Owner: Bahakel Communications; (acq 7-20-92).;
Ownership: Gocom
Nat'l Network: FOX *Nat'l Reps:* Continental Television Sales
Hours of Local News Weekly: 3.5
Peter O'Brien, General Manager
Chad Happersett, General Sales Mgr
Jeff Kaufmann, Promotions Manager
Scott Washburn, Chief Engineer

***WSEC** *Digital Channel:* 15 *Virtual Channel:* 14; 75 kw; 968 ft.; N39 36 9 W90 2 47
P.O.Box 6248, Springfield, IL 62708 US

(217) 483-7887, *Fax:* (217) 483-1112
www.wsec.tv
License: Jacksonville, Morgan County, IL held by West Central Illinois Educational Telecommunication Corp
Washington Law Firm: Dow, Lohnes & Albertson
Nat'l Network: PBS
Jerold Gruebel, CEO
Richard Plotkin, Operations Dir
Ed Strong, General Sales Mgr

Chicago (DMA 3)

WBBM-TV *Digital Channel:* 12 *Virtual Channel:* 2; 8 kw; 1631 ft.; N41 52 44 W87 38 8
600 New Hampshire Ave., NW, Suite 1200, Washington, DC 20037 US
(312) 849-2801, *Fax:* (312) 849-7801
www.cbs2chicago.com
License: Chicago, Cook County, IL held by CBS Broadcasting Inc.
Group Owner: CBS Television Stations Group; (acq 2-9-53; $6 million;
Nat'l Network: CBS *Nat'l Reps:* CBS TV Stations National Sales
Wire Services: Reuters
Bruno Cohen, General Manager
Al Connor, General Sales Mgr
Fran Preston, Programming Director
Will Sliger, Promotions Manager
Jeff Kiernan, News Director
Tom Schnecke, Chief Engineer

WCIU-TV *Digital Channel:* 27 *Virtual Channel:* 26; 550 kw; 1552 ft.; N41 52 44 W87 38 10
26 North Halsted Street, Chicago, IL 60661 US
(312) 705-2600, *Fax:* (312) 705-2656
www.wciu.com
License: Chicago, Cook County, IL held by WCIU-TV L.P.
Group Owner: Weigel Broadcasting Co.; *Washington Law Firm:* Covington & Burling
Nat'l Network: IND *Nat'l Reps:* Harrington, Righter & Parsons
Norman Shapiro, President
Neal Sabin, President, Digital Networks
John Hendricks, EVP, Sales
Robert Ramsey, General Manager
Molly Kelly, Station Manager
Brad Lesak, General Sales Mgr
Sean Long, Programming Director
Kyle Walker,Chief Engineer
Harvey Moshman, Executive Producer

WCPX-TV *Digital Channel:* 43; 3,630 kw vis; ant 1,673t/1,667g; N41 52 44 W87 38 08; *Population Served:* 10,000,000
333 S. Desplains St., Suite 101, Chicago, IL 60661-8735
(312) 376-8520, *Fax:* (312) 575-8735
www.ionline.tv
License: Chicago, Cook County, IL held by ION Media Chicago License Inc.
Group Owner: ION Media Networks Inc.; (acq 8-11-98; $120 million including all interest in KWOK(TV) Novato, CA and other telecasting progmg rights).; *Washington Law Firm:* Dow, Lohnes & Albertson
Nat'l Network: ION Television
Rich Lindsey, Operations Dir
Allen Dagher, Chief Engineer

WFLD *Digital Channel:* 31 *Virtual Channel:* 32; 1000 kw; 1558 ft.; N41 52 44 W87 38 10
5151 Wisconsin Ave., NW, Washington, DC 20016 US
(312) 565-5532, *Fax:* (312) 565-5517
www.myfoxchicago.com
License: Chicago, Cook County, IL held by Fox Television Stations Inc.
Group Owner: Fox Television Stations Inc.; (acq 11-14-86; grpsl).
Nat'l Network: FOX *Nat'l Reps:* Fox Stations Sales
Hours of Local News Weekly: News progmg 35.5 hrs wkly
John Nuck, CFO
Patrick Mullen, General Manager
Judd Beck, General Sales Mgr
Carol Fowler, News Director
John Baich, Chief Engineer

WGN *Digital Channel:* 19; 50 kw-U, ND1; 1,568 ft AAT; N42 0 42 W88 2 7
Wgn(Am), 435 N. Michigan Avenue, Chicago, IL 60611 US
(773) 528-2311, *Fax:* (773) 528-6857
WGNtv.com
License: Chicago, IL held by WGN Continental Broadcasting Co., debtor-in-possession
Group Owner: Tribune Broadcasting Co.; (acq 12-20-2007; grpsl)
Nat'l Network: CW *Nat'l Reps:* TeleRep *Wire Services:* AP
Hours of Local News Weekly: 34.5
Sheau-ming Ross, CFO
Marty Wilke, Operations Dir
Errol Gerber, General Sales Mgr
Tom Boyd, Programming Director
Joanne Stern, Promotions Manager
Greg Caputo, News Director
Marc Drazin, Engineering Dir
Bob Vorwald, Director ofProduction
Jane Hayden, Director of Traffic

WJYS *Digital Channel:* 36; 5,000 kw vis, 300 kw aur; 741; N41 33 10 W87 47 09; *Population Served:* 7,100,000
18600 S. Oak Park Ave., Tinley Park, IL 60477
(708) 633-0001, *Fax:* (708) 633-0040
cs@wjystv62.net
License: Hammond, Lake County, IN held by Jovon Broadcasting Corp
Joseph Stroud, General Manager
Eric Ferguson, Station Manager

WLS-TV *Digital Channel:* 7 *Virtual Channel:* 7; 4.75 kw; 1690 ft.; N41 52 44 W87 38 8
190 North State Street, Chicago, IL 60601 US
(312) 750-7777, *Fax:* (312) 750-7015
www.abc7chicago.com
License: Chicago, Cook County, IL held by WLS Television Inc.
Group Owner: ABC Inc.; (acq 6-27-86; grpsl;
Nat'l Network: ABC *Wire Services:* PR Newswire; Dow Jones Financial News Services; Sports Wire
Size of News Staff: 151; *Hours of Local News Weekly:* news progmg 8 hrs wkly
Emily Barr, President
Joseph Trimarco, Operations Dir
Ed Pearson, General Sales Mgr
Ellen Crawley, Programming Director
Tom Hebel, Promotions Manager
Jennifer Graves, News Director
Kal Hassan, Engineering Dir
Mike Ozog, TrafficManager

WMAQ-TV *Digital Channel:* 29 *Virtual Channel:* 5; 350 kw; 1667 ft.; N41 52 44 W87 38 10
Ms Diane Zipursky, 1299 Pennsylvania Ave, Washingotn, DC 20004 US
(312) 836-5555
www.nbc5.com
License: Chicago, Cook County, IL held by NBC Telemundo License Co.
Group Owner: NBC Owned Television Stations; (acq 6-5-86).
Nat'l Network: NBC *Nat'l Reps:* NBC TV Stations Sales
Larry Wert, President
Patrica Golden, General Sales Mgr
Toni Falvo, Promotions Manager
Jan Jaros, Engineering Dir

WSNS-TV ; 4,260 kw vis, 500 kw aur; 1,420t/1,456g; N41 53 56 W87 37 23; *Population Served:* 1,800,000
454 N. Columbus Dr., Chicago, IL 60611
(312) 836-3000, *Fax:* (312) 836-3034
www.telemundochicago.com
License: Chicago, Cook County, IL held by NBC Telemundo License Co.
Group Owner: Telemundo Television Stations; (acq 4-12-2002; grpsl).; *Washington Law Firm:* Cohn & Marks
Nat'l Network: Telemundo (Spanish)
Foreign Language Programming; Size of News Staff: 12; *Hours of Local News Weekly:* news progmg 5 hrs wkly
Ed Fernandez, Operations Dir

***WTTW** *Digital Channel:* 47; 60.3 kw vis, 12 kw aur; 1,630t/1,710g; N41 52 44 W87 38 10; *Population Served:* 10,000,000
5400 N. St. Louis Ave., Chicago, IL 60625
(773) 583-5000, *Fax:* (773) 583-3046
www.networkchicago.com
License: Chicago, Cook County, IL held by Window to the World Communications Inc
Washington Law Firm: Schwartz, Woods & Miller
Nat'l Network: PBS
Size of News Staff: 15; *Hours of Local News Weekly:* news progmg 5 hrs wkly
Daniel Schmidt, CEO
Donna Davies, General Sales Mgr
Dan Soles, Programming Director
Reese Marcusson, CFO
Farrell Frentress, Executive Vice President
Howard Fisher, General Sales Manager

WWTO-TV *Digital Channel:* 10 *Virtual Channel:* 35; 80 kw; 1362 ft.; N41 16 51 W88 56 13
420 E. Stevenson Rd., Ottawa, IL 61350 US
(815) 434-2700, *Fax:* (815) 434-2458
www.tbn.org
License: La Salle, LaSalle County, IL held by Trinity Broadcasting Network
Group Owner: Trinity Broadcasting Network; (acq 7-1-2000; grpsl).; *Washington Law Firm:* Joseph E. Dunne III
Nat'l Network: TRINITY BROADCA
Marlene Zepeda, Station Manager
Charlie Boyd, Chief Engineer

WXFT-DT ; 5,000 kw vis, 500 kw aur; 1,600t/1,621g; N41 52 44 W87 38 10
541 N. Fairbanks Ct., Suite 1100, Chicago, IL 60611
(312) 670-1000, *Fax:* (312) 467-5821
www.univision.com
License: Aurora, Kane County, IL held by TeleFutura Chicago LLC.
Group Owner: Univision Communications Inc.; (acq 5-21-2001; grpsl).; *Washington Law Firm:* Wiley, Rein & Fielding
Nat'l Network: TeleFutura (Spanish) *Wire Services:* City News Bureau
Vincent Cordero, General Manager
Sean Delahunty, General Sales Mgr
Francisco Garcia, Promotions Manager
Yolanda Lopez De Otero, News Director
George Molnar, Chief Engineer

***WYCC** *Virtual Channel:* 20; 2,421 kw vis, 242.1 kw au; 1,239t/1,110g; N41 53 56 W87 37 23
6258 S Union, Chicago, IL 60606
(773) 838-7878, *Fax:* (773) 581-2071
www.wycc.org
comments@wycc.org
License: Chicago, Cook County, IL held by College Dist. #508, County of Cook
(acq 11-3-81).; *Washington Law Firm:* Dow, Lohnes & Albertson
Nat'l Network: PBS
Foreign Language Programming
Phyllis Stevens, Operations Dir
Arthur Wood, General Manager
Jill Ittersagen, General Sales Mgr
Cynthia Syperek, Programming Director
James Kirwan, Promotions Manager
Mark Jahnke, Engineering Dir

Davenport, IA-Rock Island-Moline, IL (DMA 97)

WHBF-TV *Digital Channel:* 4 *Virtual Channel:* 4; 33.7 kw; 1342 ft.; N41 32 49 W90 28 35
99 Pondfield Road, Bronxville, NY 10708 US
(309) 786-5441, *Fax:* (309) 788-4975
www.cbs4qc.com
sales@cbs4qc.com
License: Rock Island, Rock Island County, IL held by Coronet Communications Co.
Group Owner: Citadel Communications Co. LTD.; (acq 3-16-87; grpsl;; *Washington Law Firm:* Latham & Watkins
Nat'l Network: CBS *Nat'l Reps:* Continental Television Sales
Size of News Staff: 22; *Hours of Local News Weekly:* news progmg 7 hrs wkly
Martha Huggins, Operations Dir
Todd Grady, General Sales Mgr
Patty Gilbert, Promotions Manager
Arthur Steadman, News Director
Ron Schmidt, Chief Engineer
J.D. Walls, Operations Director
Steve Garman, Sales

WQAD-TV *Digital Channel:* 38 *Virtual Channel:* 8; 1000 kw; 1096 ft.; N41 18 44 W90 22 46
3003 Park 16th Street, Moline, IL 61265 US
(309) 764-8888, *Fax:* (309) 764-5763
www.wqad.com
wqad@wqad.com
License: Moline, Rock Island County, IL held by Local TV Illinois License LLC.
Group Owner: Local TV LLC; (acq 5-7-2007; grpsl)
Nat'l Network: ABC
Size of News Staff: 75; *Hours of Local News Weekly:* news progmg 22.5 hrs wkly
Larry Rosmilso, President
Bill Carey, Station Manager
Trent Poindexter, General Sales Mgr
Lisa Short, Promotions Manager
Rick Serre, Engineering Dir
Lori Evans, Creative Services Manager
Jennifer McGivern, Local Sales Manager

***WQPT-TV** *Digital Channel:* 23 *Virtual Channel:* 24; 80 kw; 883 ft.; N41 18 44 W90 22 45
6600 - 34th Avenue, Moline, IL 61265 US
(309) 796-2424, *Fax:* (309) 796-2484
www.wqpt.org
wqpt@bhc.edu
License: Moline, Rock Island County, IL held by Black Hawk College
Washington Law Firm: Drinker, Biddle & Reath
Nat'l Network: ETV
Foreign Language Programming; Hours of Local News Weekly: 0
Cathryn Lass, Operations Dir
Rick Best, General Manager
Lora Adams, General Sales Mgr
Jerry Myers, Programming Director
Terry Wynn, Engineering Dir

Paducah, KY-Cape Girardeau, MO-Harrisburg-Mount Vernon, IL (DMA 78)

WPXS *Digital Channel:* 21 *Virtual Channel:* 13; 350 kw; 299 ft.; N38 41 19 W89 33 38
231 Bradley Place, Suite 204, Palm Beach, FL 33480 US
(618) 822-6900, *Fax:* (618) 822-6526
wpxs@mvn.net
License: Mount Vernon, Jefferson County, IL held by EBC St. Louis Inc.
Group Owner: Equity Media Holdings Corp.; (acq 4-26-2001; $17.75 million with KDUO(TV) Flagstaff, AZ).
Nat'l Network: IND
Dee Rose, Station Manager

WSIL-TV *Digital Channel:* 34 *Virtual Channel:* 3; 1000 kw; 955 ft.; N37 36 50 W88 52 20
5009 South Hulen, Suite 101, Fort Worth, TX 76132 US
(618) 985-2333, *Fax:* (618) 985-3709
www.wsiltv.com
License: Harrisburg, Saline County, IL held by WSIL TV Inc.
Group Owner: Mel Wheeler Inc.; (acq 5-12-83; grpsl;;
Washington Law Firm: Brooks, Pierce, McLendon, Humprey & Leonard
Nat'l Network: ABC *Nat'l Reps:* Continental Television Sales
Steve Wheeler, President
Dave Cisco, General Sales Mgr
Mike Snuffer, News Director

***WSIU-TV** *Digital Channel:* 8 *Virtual Channel:* 8; 53 kw vis; ant 890t/861g; N38 06 11 W89 14 40; *Rebroadcasting:* Rebroadcasts WUSI-TV Olney 99%.; *Population Served:* 326,000
1003 Communications Bldg., 1100 Lincoln Dr., Carbondale, IL 62901
(618) 453-4343, *Fax:* (618) 453-6186
www.wsiu.org
License: Carbondale, Jackson County, IL held by Board of Trustees of Southern Illinois University
Washington Law Firm: Cohn & Marks
Nat'l Network: PBS *Wire Services:* AP
Size of News Staff: 1; *Hours of Local News Weekly:* news progmg 2 hrs wkly
Greg Petrovich, CEO
Delores Kerstein, CFO
Renee Dillard, Aasociate Director/Marketing
Trina Thomas, Programming Director
Monica Tichenor, Promotions Manager
Vacant, Engineering Dir
Vacant, Chief Engineer

WTCT *Digital Channel:* 17 *Virtual Channel:* 27; 2,600 kw vis, 260 kw aur; 775t/500g; N37 33 26 W89 01 24
Box 698, 11717 Rt. 37 N., Marion, IL 62959
(618) 997-4700, *Fax:* (618) 993-9778
www.tct.tv
License: Marion, Williamson County, IL held by Tri-State Christian TV.
Group Owner: Tri-State Christian Television; (acq 5-29-84; $1.2 million)
Peggy Carter, Station Manager
Todd Creamer, Chief Engineer

Peoria-Bloomington, IL (DMA 116)

WAOE *Digital Channel:* 39 *Virtual Channel:* 59; 26 kw; 696 ft.; N40 37 46 W89 32 53
124 Monterey Road #304, South Pasadena, CA 91030 US
(309) 674-5900, *Fax:* (309) 674-5959
my59.tv
License: Peoria, Peoria County, IL held by Four Seasons Peoria LLC
Nat'l Network: MY NETWORK TV
Mark DeSantis, Operations Dir
Sara Horn, Station Manager
Pete Russell, General Sales Mgr
Tim Campbell, Promotions Manager
Jim Garrott, News Director

WEEK-TV *Digital Channel:* 25 *Virtual Channel:* 25; 246 kw; 694 ft.; N40 37 45.9 W89 32 52.6
767 Third Avenue, 34th Floor, New York, NY 10017 US
(309) 698-2525, *Fax:* (309) 698-9663 (sales),(309) 698-3737 (news)
www.week.com
news25@week.com
License: Peoria, Peoria County, IL held by WEEK-TV License Inc.
Group Owner: Granite Broadcasting Corp.; (acq 10-31-88; $33 million); *Washington Law Firm:* Akin, Gump, Strauss, Hauer & Feld
Nat'l Network: NBC
Size of News Staff: 26; *Hours of Local News Weekly:* news progmg 16 hrs wkly
Mark DeSantis, General Manager
Dennis Riley, Chief Engineer

WHOI *Digital Channel:* 19 *Virtual Channel:* 19; 195 kw; 666 ft.; N40 39 11 W89 35 14
500 North Stewart Street, Creve Coeur, IL 61610 US
(309) 698-1919, *Fax:* (309) 698-1910
www.hoinews.com
License: Peoria, Peoria County, IL held by Barrington Broadcasting Peoria Corp.
Group Owner: Barrington Broadcasting Group, LLC.; (acq 4-30-2004; $23.5 million with KHQA-TV Hannibal, MO).;
Washington Law Firm: Covington & Burling
Nat'l Network: ABC; CW *Nat'l Reps:* Harrington, Righter & Parsons
Hours of Local News Weekly: News progmg 7 hrs wkly
Tom Stemmler, Operations Dir
Leo Henning, General Manager
Jon Skorburg, Station Manager
Valerie Bricka, General Sales Mgr
Donna Thompson, Programming Director
Jolie Alois, News Director
Jim Malone, Chief Engineer

WMBD-TV *Digital Channel:* 30 *Virtual Channel:* 31; 800 kw; 633 ft.; N40 38 6 W89 32 19
3131 North University, Peoria, IL 61604 US
(309) 688-3131, *Fax:* (309) 686-8650
www.wmbd.com
License: Peoria, Peoria County, IL held by Nexstar Broadcasting, Inc.
Group Owner: Nexstar Broadcasting Group Inc.; (acq 1999);
Washington Law Firm: Covington & Burling
Nat'l Network: CBS
Coby Cooper, Operations Dir
Steve Mason, General Sales Mgr
David Tomlianovich, Promotions Manager
Rick Moll, News Director
Herman Marvel, Chief Engineer
Nancy Linebaugh, Local Sales Manager

***WTVP** *Digital Channel:* 46 *Virtual Channel:* 47; 190 kw; 709 ft.; N40 37 44 W89 34 12
1501 West Bradley Avenue, Peoria, IL 61625 US
(309) 677-4747, *Fax:* (309) 677-4730
www.wtvp.org
wtvpmail@wtvp.pbs.org
License: Peoria, Peoria County, IL held by Illinois Valley Public Telecommunication Corp
Washington Law Firm: Dow, Lohnes PLLC
Nat'l Network: PBS
Chet Tomczyk, CEO
Jackie Luebcke, Operations Dir
Linda Miller, Programming Director

WYZZ-TV *Digital Channel:* 28 *Virtual Channel:* 43; 1000 kw; 961 ft.; N40 38 45 W89 10 45
10706 Beaver Dam Road, Cockeysville, MD 21030 US
(309) 688-3131, *Fax:* (309) 686-8650
www.cicrowd.com
License: Bloomington, McLean County, IL held by WYZZ Licensee Inc.
Group Owner: Sinclair Broadcast Group Inc.; (acq 1996; $23 million); *Washington Law Firm:* Shaw Pittman LLP
Nat'l Network: FOX *Nat'l Reps:* Harrington, Righter & Parsons
Coby Cooper, General Manager
Steve Mason, General Sales Mgr
Beau Pillet, Promotions Manager
Rick Moll, News Director
Herman Marvel, Chief Engineer
Nik Adams, Local Sales Manager

Quincy, IL-Hannibal, MO-Keokuk, IA (DMA 171)

WGEM-TV *Digital Channel:* 10 *Virtual Channel:* 10; 26 kw; 781 ft.; N39 57 4 W91 19 53
513 Hampshire Street, Quincy, IL 62301 US
(217) 228-6600, *Fax:* (217) 228-6670
wgem.com
License: Quincy, Adams County, IL held by Quincy Broadcasting Co.
Group Owner: Quincy Newspapers Inc.; *Washington Law Firm:* Wilkinson, Barker, Knauer & Quinn
Nat'l Network: NBC; CW; Fox *Nat'l Reps:* Petry Television Inc.
Wire Services: AP
Size of News Staff: 20; *Hours of Local News Weekly:* News progmg 20 hrs wkly
Ralph Oakley, CEO
Carlos Fernandez, General Manager

***WMEC** *Digital Channel:* 21; 24.15 kw vis, 2.42 kw aur; 519t/535g; N40 25 40 W90 40 58; *Population Served:* 915,000
Box 6248, Springfield, IL 62708
(217) 483-7887,(800) 232-3605, *Fax:* (217) 483-1112
www.wmec.tv
License: Macomb, McDonough County, IL held by West Central Illinois Educational Telecommunications Corp
Washington Law Firm: Dow, Lohnes & Albertson
Nat'l Network: PBS
Jerold Gruebel, CEO
Richard Plotkin, Operations Dir
Ed Strong, General Sales Mgr

***WQEC** *Digital Channel:* 34 *Virtual Channel:* 27; 58.6 kw; 502 ft.; N39 58 41 W91 18 32
Brk 432,Sangamon State U, Springfield, IL 62708 US
(217) 483-7887,(800) 232-3605, *Fax:* (217) 483-1112
www.wqec.tv
License: Quincy, Adams County, IL held by West Central Illinois Educational Telecommunications Corp
Washington Law Firm: Dow, Lohnes & Albertson
Nat'l Network: PBS
Jerold Gruebel, CEO
Richard Plotkin, Operations Dir
Ed Strong, General Sales Mgr

WTJR *Digital Channel:* 32 *Virtual Channel:* 16; 1000 kw; 1010 ft.; N39 58 19 W91 19 40
Box 1189, Quincy, IL 62306 US
(217) 228-1616
www.wtjr.org
tv16@wtjr.org
License: Quincy, Adams County, IL held by Christian Television Network Inc
Nat'l Network: N/A
Donette Douglas, Station Manager
Jim Wilson, Engineering Dir

Rockford, IL (DMA 132)

WIFR *Digital Channel:* 41 *Virtual Channel:* 23; 100 kw; 577 ft.; N42 17 48 W89 10 15
Mailing Address: P.O. Box 123, Rockford, IL 61105 US
Second Address: 2523 N. Meridian Rd., Rockford, IL 61101
(815) 987-5300, *Fax:* (815) 987-0981
www.wifr.com
talkto23@wifr.com
License: Freeport, Winnebago County, IL held by WEAU Licensee Corp.
Group Owner: Gray Television Inc.; (acq 8-29-2002; grpsl).;
Washington Law Firm: Covington & Burling
Nat'l Network: CBS *Nat'l Reps:* Continental Television Sales
Size of News Staff: 19; *Hours of Local News Weekly:* news progmg 19 hrs wkly
Greg Graber, Operations Dir
Tim Myers, General Sales Mgr
Dave Smith, News Director
Jeff Clark, Operations Manager

WQRF-TV *Digital Channel:* 42 *Virtual Channel:* 39; 900 kw; 486 ft.; N42 17 14 W89 10 15
Mailing Address: 18 Newbury Street, Boston, MA 02116 US
Second Address: 1917 N. Meridian Rd., Rockford, IL 61101
(815) 963-5413, *Fax:* (815) 963-6113
www.mystateline.com
newsdesk@wtvo.com
License: Rockford, Winnebago County, IL held by Nexstar Broadcasting, Inc.

Group Owner: Nexstar Broadcasting Group Inc.; (acq 12-31-03; grpsl).; *Washington Law Firm:* Arter & Hadden
Nat'l Network: FOX
Joseph Denk, Operations Dir
Kelly Lattimer, General Sales Mgr
Jose Cabezas, Programming Director
Sean Anderson, Promotions Manager
Kent Harrell, News Director
Mike Real, Chief Engineer

WREX-TV *Digital Channel:* 13; 316 kw vis, 39.8 kw aur; 710t/652g; N42 17 50 W89 14 24; *Population Served:* 452,000
Mailing Address: Box 530, Rockford, IL 61105
Second Address: 10322 W. Auburn Rd., Rockford, IL 61103
(815) 335-2213, *Fax:* (815) 335-7230
www.wrex.com
wrex@wrex.com
License: Rockford, Winnebago County, IL held by WREX Television LLC.
Group Owner: Quincy Newspapers Inc.; (acq 5-22-2001; grpsl).; *Washington Law Firm:* Wilkinson, Barker & Knauer
Nat'l Network: NBC; CW *Nat'l Reps:* Blair Television
John Chadwick, Operations Dir
Joe Viglietta, General Sales Mgr
Trista Truesdale, Programming Director
Maggie Hradecky, News Director
Gerry Meinders, Chief Engineer
Kim Carney, National Sales Manager

WTVO *Digital Channel:* 16 *Virtual Channel:* 17; 196 kw; 659 ft.; N42 17 14 W89 10 15
Mailing Address: P. O. Box 472, Rockford, IL 61105 US
Second Address: 1917 N. Meridian Rd., Rockford, IL 61101
(815) 963-5413, *Fax:* (815) 963-6113
www.mystateline.com
newsdesk@wtvo.com
License: Rockford, Winnebago County, IL held by Mission Broadcasting Inc.
Group Owner: Mission Broadcasting Inc.; (acq 1-4-2005; $20,750,000).; *Washington Law Firm:* Wiley, Rein & Fielding
Nat'l Network: ABC; MyNetworkTV
Size of News Staff: 16; *Hours of Local News Weekly:* news progmg 7 hrs wkly
Joseph Denk, Operations Dir
Kelly Lattimer, General Sales Mgr
Eileen Boucek, Programming Director
Sean Anderson, Promotions Manager
Kent Harrell, News Director
Mike Real, Chief Engineer

St. Louis, MO (DMA 21)

WRBU *Digital Channel:* 47 *Virtual Channel:* 46; 109.4 kw; 1043 ft.; N38 23 18 W90 29 16
1408 North Kings Highway, Suite 300, St. Louis, MO 63113 US
(314) 256-4600, *Fax:* (314) 256-4655
www.my46stl.com
contest@my46stl.com
License: East St. Louis, St. Clair County, IL held by Roberts Broadcasting Co.
Group Owner: Roberts Broadcasting Co.; *Washington Law Firm:* Dow, Lohnes & Albertson
Nat'l Network: MYTV *Nat'l Reps:* Harrington, Righter & Parsons
Size of News Staff: 4
Toby Miller, Operations Dir
Bonni Burns, General Manager
Robin Jackson, General Sales Mgr
Monica Nettles-Johnson, Programming Director
Aliah Baker, Promotions Manager
Chris Meisch, Chief Engineer
Stan Marinoff, PromotionsDirector

Terre Haute, IN (DMA 152)

***WUSI-TV** *Digital Channel:* 19 *Virtual Channel:* 16; 46 kw; 931 ft.; N38 50 19 W88 7 47; *Rebroadcasting:* Rebroadcasts WSIU-TV Carbondale 100%.
Mailing Address: Tv Station Wusi-Tv, Carbondale, IL 62903 US
Second Address: 1003 Communications Bldg., Caarbondale, IL 62901-6602
(618) 453-4343, *Fax:* (618) 453-6186
www.wsiu.org
License: Olney, Richland County, IL held by Board of Trustees, Southern Illinois University.
Washington Law Firm: Cohn & Marks
Nat'l Network: ETV *Wire Services:* AP
Delores Kerstein, CFO
Trina Thomas, Programming Director
Terry Harvey, Engineering Dir

Indiana

Chicago (DMA 3)

WPWR-TV *Digital Channel:* 51 *Virtual Channel:* 50; 1000 kw; 1716 ft.; N41 52 44 W87 38 10
2151 North Elston Ave., Chicago, IL 60614 US
(312) 565-5533, *Fax:* (312) 565-5517
www.my50chicago.com
License: Gary, Lake County, IN held by Fox Television Stations Inc.
Group Owner: Fox Television Stations Inc.; (acq 8-21-2002; $425 million)
Nat'l Network: MY NETWORK *Nat'l Reps:* Fox Stations Sales
John Nuck, CFO
Patrick Mullen, General Manager
Judd Beck, General Sales Mgr
Carol Fowler, News Director
John Baich, Chief Engineer

***WYIN** *Digital Channel:* 17 *Virtual Channel:* 56; 300 kw; 951 ft.; N41 20 56 W87 24 2
8625 Indiana Place, Merrillville, IN 46410 US
(219) 756-5656, *Fax:* (219) 755-4312
www.lakeshoreptv.com
news@lakeshoreptv.com
License: Gary, Lake County, IN held by Northwest Indiana Public Broadcasting Inc
Washington Law Firm: Schwartz, Woods & Miller
Nat'l Network: PBS
Thomas Carroll, CEO

Dayton, OH (DMA 64)

WKOI-TV *Digital Channel:* 39 *Virtual Channel:* 43; 500 kw; 909 ft.; N39 30 44 W84 38 9
Mailing Address: PO Box 1057, Richmond, IN 47375 US
Second Address: 1702 S. 9th St., Richmond, IN 47374-7203
(765) 935-2390
www.tbn.org
License: Richmond, Wayne County, IN held by Trinity Broadcasting of Indiana, Inc.
Group Owner: Trinity Broadcasting Network; (acq 9-81).; *Washington Law Firm:* Gammon & Grange
Nat'l Network: TRINITY BROADCA
Mark Crouch, General Manager

Evansville, IN (DMA 102)

WEHT *Digital Channel:* 7 *Virtual Channel:* 25; 12.5 kw; 1037 ft.; N37 51 56 W87 34 4
Mailing Address: P.O. Box 25, Evansville, IN 47701 US
Second Address: 800 Marywood Dr., Henderson, KY 42420
(800) 879-8542, *Fax:* (270) 827-0561
www.news25.us
contactus@news25.us
License: Evansville, Vanderburgh County, IN held by Gilmore Broadcasting Corp
(acq 1-15-2003).; *Washington Law Firm:* Wiley, Rein & Fielding
Nat'l Network: ABC
Doug Padgett, General Manager
Mike Riley, Station Manager
Ginny Powers, Programming Director
Melisse Marks, Promotions Manager
Mark Glover, News Director
Darren Gibson, Chief Engineer

WEVV-TV *Digital Channel:* 45 *Virtual Channel:* 44; 1,250 kw vis, 125 kw aur; 1,000t/1,000g; N37 53 17 W87 32 37
44 Main St., Evansville, IN 70505
(812) 464-4444, *Fax:* (812) 465-4559
www.wevv.com
License: Evansville, Vanderburgh County, IN held by Comcorp of Indiana License Corp.
Group Owner: Communications Corp. of America; (acq 1999; $27.5 million); *Washington Law Firm:* Leventhal, Senter & Lerman
Nat'l Network: CBS; Fox; MyNetworkTV
Size of News Staff: 30; *Hours of Local News Weekly:* news progmg 9 hrs wkly
Jim Barondt, General Manager
Tim Black, Station Manager
Sandy Eickhoff, General Sales Mgr
Joanne Provenzano, Programming Director
John Bennett, Chief Engineer

WFIE *Digital Channel:* 46; 2,510 kw vis; ant 1,017t/905g; N37 53 14 W87 31 07; *Population Served:* 290,000
Mailing Address: Box 1414, Evansville, IN 47701
Second Address: 1115 Mt. Auburn Rd., Evansville, IN 47720
(812) 426-1414, *Fax:* (812) 426-1945
www.14wfie.com
wfie@14wfie.com
License: Evansville, Vanderburgh County, IN held by WFIE License Subsidiary LLC.
Group Owner: Raycom Media Inc.; (acq 1-31-2006; grpsl); *Washington Law Firm:* Dow, Lohnes & Albertson
Nat'l Network: NBC
Size of News Staff: 35
Debbie Bush, General Manager
Laura Lovejoy, General Sales Mgr
Kirk Williams, Programming Director
Adam Frary, Promotions Manager
C.J. Hoyt, News Director
Bobby Barnett, Chief Engineer

***WKMA-TV** *Digital Channel:* 42; 617 kw vis, 61.7 kw aur; 1,040t/998g; N37 11 25 W87 30 47
600 Cooper Dr., Lexington, KY 40502
(606) 258-7000, *Fax:* (606) 258-7399
www.ket.org
License: Madisonville, Hopkins County, KY held by Kentucky Authority for Educational TV
Nat'l Network: PBS *Regional Network:* Kentucky Educational Television
Mike Brower, Operations Dir
Malcolm Wall, Station Manager
Craig Cornwell, Programming Director
Tim Bischoff, Promotions Manager

***WNIN** *Digital Channel:* 9; 282 kw vis, 56.2 kw aur; 570t/570g; N38 01 27 W87 21 43; *Population Served:* 138,764
405 Carpenter St., Evansville, IN 47708
(812) 423-2973, *Fax:* (812) 428-7548
www.wnin.org
wnin@wnin.org
License: Evansville, Vanderburgh County, IN held by WNIN Tri-State Public Media, Inc
(acq 9-12-73).; *Washington Law Firm:* Dow, Lohnes PLLC
Nat'l Network: PBS
David Dial, President
Bonnie Rheinhardt, Operations Dir
Tonya Wolf, General Sales Mgr
Don Hollingsworth, Chief Engineer

WTVW *Digital Channel:* 28; 316 kw vis, 63.2 kw aur; 1,013t/880g; N38 01 27 W87 21 43; *Population Served:* 686,500
477 Carpenter St., Evansville, IN 02116
(812) 424-7777, *Fax:* (812) 421-4040
www.tristatehomepage.com
License: Evansville, Vanderburgh County, IN held by Nexstar Broadcasting Inc.
Group Owner: Nexstar Broadcasting Group Inc.; (acq 10-30-2003; grpsl).; *Washington Law Firm:* Arter & Hadden
Nat'l Reps: Blair Television
Hours of Local News Weekly: News progmg 22.5 hrs wkly
Pam Miller, Operations Dir
Mike Smith, General Manager
Jeff Fisher, General Sales Mgr
Bob Walters, News Director
Dan Jordan, Chief Engineer
Jay Hiett, Local Sales Manager

Ft. Wayne, IN (DMA 107)

WANE-TV *Digital Channel:* 31 *Virtual Channel:* 15; 1000 kw; 761 ft.; N41 5 38 W85 10 48
Mailing Address: 200 Crescent Court, Suite 1600, Dallas, TX 75201 US
Second Address: 2915 W. State Blvd., Fort Wayne, IN 46808
(260) 424-1515, *Fax:* (260) 407-1607
www.wane.com
License: Fort Wayne, Allen County, IN held by Indiana Broadcasting L.L.C.
Group Owner: LIN Television Corporation; (acq 11-14-94;
Nat'l Network: CBS *Nat'l Reps:* Blair Television *Wire Services:* CNN; CBS; NWS (National Weather Ser; NOAA Weather Wire Service
Size of News Staff: 35; *Hours of Local News Weekly:* news progmg 22 hrs wkly
Jim Riecken, Operations Dir
Alan Riebe, General Manager
Mike Luckett, General Sales Mgr
Nancy Applegate, Programming Director
Jerry Grider, Promotions Manager
Ted Linn, News Director
Jeff Kracium, Engineering Dir

Tom Antisdel,Local Sales Manager
April McCampbell, Public Affairs Director

WFFT-TV *Digital Channel:* 36 *Virtual Channel:* 55; 600 kw vis, 38 kw aur; 780t/805g; N41 06 33 W85 11 44; *Population Served:* 1,855,000
Mailing Address: 3707 Hillegas Rd., Fort Wayne, IN 02116
Second Address: Box 8655, Fort Wayne, IN 46808
(260) 471-5555, *Fax:* (260) 484-4331
www.wfft.com
fox55@wfft.com
License: Fort Wayne, Allen County, IN held by Nexstar Finance Inc.
Group Owner: Nexstar Broadcasting Group Inc.; (acq 12-31-2003; grpsl); *Washington Law Firm:* Drinker, Biddle & Reath
Nat'l Reps: Blair Television
Perry Sook, CEO
Tim Busch, Operations Dir
William Richhart, General Manager
Matt Devine, CFO
Bill Ritchhart, Vice President

***WFWA** *Digital Channel:* 40 *Virtual Channel:* 39; 90 kw; 725 ft.; N41 6 13 W85 11 28
P. O. Box 39, Fort Wayne, IN 46801 US
(260) 484-8839, *Fax:* (260) 482-3632
www.wfwa.org
info@wfwa.org
License: Fort Wayne, Allen County, IN held by Fort Wayne Public Television
Washington Law Firm: Wiley Rein LLP
Nat'l Network: PBS
Bruce Haines, President
Todd Grimes, Operations Dir
Kris Hensler, Programming Director
Mark Ryan, Promotions Manager
Matt Kyle, Engineering Dir
Rich Bienz, Administration

WINM *Digital Channel:* 12 *Virtual Channel:* 63; 16.5 kw; 433 ft.; N41 27 15 W84 48 10
Mailing Address: P.O.Box 159, Butler, IN 46721 US
Second Address: PO Box 159, Butler, IN 46721
(260) 483-9809, *Fax:* (419) 298-3707
winm@tct.tv
License: Angola, Steuben County, IN held by Tri-State Christian TV.
Group Owner: Tri-State Christian Television; (acq 1-24-91; $400,000;
Nat'l Network: IND
Leo Vogt, Station Manager

WISE-TV *Digital Channel:* 19; 594 kw vis, 59 kw aur; ant 770t/793g; N41 05 40 W85 10 36; *Population Served:* 222,480
Mailing Address: 3401 Butler Rd., Fort Wayne, IN 46808
Second Address: Box 2121, Fort Wayne, IN 46801-2121
(260) 422-7474, *Fax:* (260) 483-2568
www.indianasnewscenter.com
indianasnewscenter@indianasnewscenter.com
License: Fort Wayne, Allen County, IN held by WISE-TV License LLC.
Group Owner: Granite Broadcasting Corp.; (acq 3-8-2005; $44.2 million); *Washington Law Firm:* Dow Lohnes PLLC
Nat'l Network: NBC; Fox; MyNetworkTV
Size of News Staff: 32; *Hours of Local News Weekly:* news progmg 14 hrs wkly
Jerry Giesler, President
Jim Turcovsky, Operations Dir
Dan Hoffman, General Sales Mgr
Bill Schneider, Programming Director
Tad Frank, Promotions Manager
Peter Neumann, News Director
Bret Angel, Engineering Dir
Debbie Sand,Business Manager

WPTA *Digital Channel:* 24 *Virtual Channel:* 21; 335 kw; 736 ft.; N41 6 7.9 W85 11 4.9
3401 Butler Rd., Ft.Wayne, IN 46801 US
(260) 483-0584, *Fax:* (260) 483-2568
www.indianasnewscenter.com
news@indianasnewscenter.com
License: Fort Wayne, Allen County, IN held by Malara Broadcast Group of Fort Wayne License LLC.
Group Owner: Malara Broadcast Group Inc.; (acq 12-8-2004; $45.9 million); *Washington Law Firm:* Akin, Gump, Strauss, Hauer & Feld
Nat'l Network: ABC
Size of News Staff: 31; *Hours of Local News Weekly:* news progmg 31 hrs wkly
Anthony Malara, CEO
Jerry Giesler, President
Doug Barrow, Station Manager
Dan Hoffman, General Sales Mgr
Tad Frank, Promotions Manager
Peter Neumann, News Director

Indianapolis, IN (DMA 25)

WCLJ-TV *Digital Channel:* 42 *Virtual Channel:* 42; 850 kw; 1030 ft.; N39 24 12 W86 8 50
2528 Us 31 South, Greenwood, IN 46143 US
(317) 535-5542, *Fax:* (317) 535-8584
License: Bloomington, Monroe County, IN held by Trinity Broadcasting of Indiana Inc.
Group Owner: Trinity Broadcasting Network
Nat'l Network: TRINITY BROADCA
Mark Crouch, General Manager
Ken Harl, Chief Engineer

***WDTI** *Digital Channel:* 44 *Virtual Channel:* 69; 28 kw; 961 ft.; N39 53 40 W86 12 21
4600 Sunset Avenue, Indianapolis, IN 46208 US
(817) 571-1229,(817) 571-7458
www.daystar.com/schedules.htm
License: Indianapolis, Marion County, IN held by Indianapolis Community Television Inc
(acq 8-2-2004; $4 million); *Washington Law Firm:* Koerner & Olender
Nat'l Network: IND
Marcus Lamb, President

***WFYI** *Digital Channel:* 21; 1,135 kw vis, 114 kw aur; 847t/867g; N39 53 59 W86 12 01; *Population Served:* 792,500
1630 N. Meridian St., Indianapolis, IN 46202
(317) 636-2020, *Fax:* (317) 283-6645
www.wfyi.org
sjensen@wfyi.org
License: Indianapolis, Marion County, IN held by Metropolitan Indianapolis Public Broadcasting, Inc.
Nat'l Network: PBS
Anthony Lorenz, CFO
Lloyd Wright, President
Kristina Uland, General Sales Mgr
Steve Jensen, Engineering Dir
Jeanelle Adamak, Executive Vice President
Alan Cloe, Executive Vice President

WHMB-TV *Digital Channel:* 20; 2,090 kw vis, 209 kw aur; 991t/1,007g; N39 53 39 W86 12 19; *Population Served:* 2,700,000
10511 Greenfield Ave., Noblesville, IN 46250
(317) 773-5050, *Fax:* (317) 776-4051
www.whmbtv.com
kpasson@lesea.com
License: Indianapolis, Marion County, IN held by LeSea Broadcasting of Indianapolis Inc.
Group Owner: Le Sea Broadcasting; (acq 8-15-72; $354,618;;
Washington Law Firm: Gardner, Carton & Douglas
Hours of Local News Weekly: News progmg one hr wkly
Brian Coyne, CFO
Pete Sumrall, President
Keith Passon, General Manager

***WIPB** *Digital Channel:* 23 *Virtual Channel:* 49; 250 kw; 807 ft.; N40 5 37 W85 23 32
Edmund F. Ball Building, 2000 Univ. Avenue, Muncie, IN 47306 US
(765) 285-1249, *Fax:* (765) 285-5548
www.bsu.edu/wipb
wipb@bsu.edu
License: Muncie, Delaware County, IN held by Ball State University
(acq 10-31-71; $125,000;; *Washington Law Firm:* Schwartz, Woods & Miller
Nat'l Network: PBS
Foreign Language Programming
Alice Cheney, General Manager
Bob Fairchild, Chief Engineer

WIPX-TV *Digital Channel:* 27; 2,000 kw vis, 200 kw aur; ant 1,053t/2,300g; N39 24 16 W86 08 37; *Population Served:* 825,000
2441 Production Dr., Suite 104, Indianapolis, IN 46241
(317) 486-0633, *Fax:* (317) 486-0298
www.ionmedia.tv
License: Bloomington, Monroe County, IN held by ION Media Indianapolis License, Inc., Debtor-in-possession
Group Owner: ION Media Networks Inc.; (acq 2-18-2000; grpsl).;
Washington Law Firm: Fisher, Wayland, Cooper, Leader & Zaragoza
Nat'l Network: ION Television
John Kowalke, Station Manager
Robert Getze, General Sales Mgr
Dexter Wilson, Chief Engineer

WISH-TV *Digital Channel:* 9 *Virtual Channel:* 8; 22.8 kw; 932 ft.; N39 53 25 W86 12 20
P.O. Box7088, Indianapolis, IN 46207 US
(317) 923-8888, *Fax:* (317) 926-1144 (sales)
www.wishtv.com
newsdesk@wishtv.com
License: Indianapolis, Marion County, IN held by Indiana Broadcasting L.L.C.
Group Owner: LIN Television Corporation; (acq 11-14-94;;
Washington Law Firm: Covington & Burling
Nat'l Network: CBS *Nat'l Reps:* Petry Television Inc. *Wire Services:* AP
Jeff White, President
Tina Cosby, Operations Dir
Julie Zoumbaris, General Sales Mgr
Lance Carwile, Programming Director
Scott Hainey, Promotions Manager
Patti McGettigan, News Director
Terry Van Bibber, Engineering Dir
JasonCrundwell, Internet Director
Marilyn Fernandez, Office Administrator
Becky Hardy, Production Manager

WNDY-TV *Digital Channel:* 32 *Virtual Channel:* 23; 1000 kw; 889 ft.; N40 8 56 W85 56 7
1501 M Street, N.W., Suite 1100, Washington, DC 20005 US
(317) 923-8888, *Fax:* (317) 926-1144 (sales)
www.indytv.com
newsdesk@MyINDYtv.com
License: Marion, Grant County, IN held by Indiana Broadcasting LLC.
Group Owner: LIN Television Corporation; (acq 3-31-2005; $85 million with WWHO(TV) Chillicothe, OH).; *Washington Law Firm:* Covington & Burling
Nat'l Network: MYNETWORK *Nat'l Reps:* Blair Television
Jeff White, President
Tina Cosby, Operations Dir
Marilyn Fernandez, General Manager
Julie Zoumbaris, General Sales Mgr
Lance Carwile, Programming Director
Scott Hainey, Promotions Manager
Patti McGettigan, News Director
TerryVanBibber, Engineering Dir
Jason Crundwell, Internet Director
Becky Hardy, Production Manager

WRTV *Digital Channel:* 25 *Virtual Channel:* 6; 1000 kw; 965 ft.; N39 53 56.5 W86 12 3.7
1330 N. Meridian Street, Indianapolis, IN 46202 US
(317) 635-9788,(317) 269-1440, *Fax:* (317) 269-1400 (sales)
www.theindychannel.com
newstips@theindychannel.com
License: Indianapolis, Marion County, IN held by McGraw-Hill Broadcasting Co. Inc.
Group Owner: McGraw-Hill Broadcasting Co.; (acq 6-1-72).;
Washington Law Firm: Holland & Knight
Nat'l Network: ABC *Nat'l Reps:* Harrington, Righter & Parsons
Don Lundy, General Manager
Sally Kohn, General Sales Mgr
Paul Montgomery, Promotions Manager
Sheldon Ripson, News Director
Brian Vetor, Chief Engineer

WTHR *Digital Channel:* 13 *Virtual Channel:* 13; 42.1 kw; 981 ft.; N39 55 43 W86 10 55
Mailing Address: 1000 North Meridian St., Indianapolis, IN 46204 US
Second Address: 1000 N. Meridian St., Indianapolis, IN 46204
(317) 636-1313, *Fax:* (317) 636-3717,(317) 632-6720
www.wthr.com
License: Indianapolis, Marion County, IN held by VideoIndiana Inc.
Group Owner: Dispatch Broadcast Group; (acq 10-1-75; $17.65 million;; *Washington Law Firm:* Sidley & Austin
Nat'l Network: NBC
Jim Tellus, President
Tim Warner, General Sales Mgr
Jeff Dutton, Promotions Manager
Roger Bishop, Chief Engineer

***WTIU** *Digital Channel:* 14 *Virtual Channel:* 30; 224 kw; 725 ft.; N39 8 31 W86 29 43
Imu, M-19 Indiana Unvi., Bloomington, IN 47405 US
(812) 855-5900,(812) 855-8000, *Fax:* (812) 855-0729
www.wtiu.indiana.edu
wtiu@indiana.edu
License: Bloomington, Monroe County, IN held by Trustees of Indiana University.

Ownership: Trustees of IU; *Washington Law Firm:* Crowell & Moring
Nat'l Network: PBS
Size of News Staff: 5; *Hours of Local News Weekly:* 3 hours plus online
Perry Metz, CEO
Brad Howard, Operations Dir
Phil Meyer, Station Manager
Brent Molnar, Programming Director
Ann Wesley, Promotions Manager
Ann Shea, News Director
Marianne Woodruff, Corporate Underwriting
Eva Zogorski,Membership
Mary Ducette, Outreach Coordinator

WTTK *Digital Channel:* 29 *Virtual Channel:* 29; 550 kw; 984 ft.; N39 53 20 W86 12 7; *Rebroadcasting:* Satellite of WTTV(TV) Bloomington.
10706 Beaver Dam Road, Cockeysville, MD 21030 US
(317)632-5900, *Fax:* (317) 687-6531, (317) 687-65
www.indianas4.com
License: Kokomo, Howard County, IN held by Tribune Broadcast Holdings Inc.
Group Owner: Tribune Broadcasting Co.; (acq 12-20-2007; grpsl)
Nat'l Network: CW *Nat'l Reps:* TeleRep
Jerry Martin, General Manager
Tim McNamara, General Sales Mgr
Cindy Wilhite, Programming Director
Kurt Tovey, Promotions Manager
Rich Kittlestved, Engineering Dir

WTTV *Digital Channel:* 48 *Virtual Channel:* 4; 870 kw; 1043 ft.; N39 24 27 W86 8 52
10706 Beaver Dam Road, Cockeysville, MD 21030 US
(317) 632-5900, *Fax:* (317) 687-6532
www.indianas4.com
newsreleases@tribune.com
License: Bloomington, Monroe County, IN held by Tribune Broadcast Holdings Inc., Debtor-in-possession
Group Owner: Tribune Broadcasting Co.; (acq 12-20-2007; grpsl); *Washington Law Firm:* Dow Lohnes PLLC
Nat'l Network: CW *Nat'l Reps:* TeleRep
Jerry Martin, Operations Dir
Tim McNamara, General Sales Mgr
Kurt Tovey, Promotions Manager
Rich Kittilsvted, Chief Engineer

WXIN *Digital Channel:* 45 *Virtual Channel:* 59; 1000 kw; 984 ft.; N39 53 20 W86 12 7
1440 North Meridian St., Indianapolis, IN 46202 US
(317) 632-5900, *Fax:* (317) 687-6532
www.fox59.com
newsreleases@tribune.com
License: Indianapolis, Marion County, IN held by Tribune Television Co., Debtor-in-possession
Group Owner: Tribune Broadcasting Co.; (acq 12-20-2007; grpsl); *Washington Law Firm:* Dow Lohnes PLLC
Nat'l Network: FOX *Nat'l Reps:* TeleRep
Hours of Local News Weekly: News progmg 19 hrs wkly
Jerry Martin, Operations Dir
Tim McNamara, General Sales Mgr
Kurt Tovey, Promotions Manager
Rich Kittilsvted, Chief Engineer

Lafayette, IN (DMA 189)

WLFI-TV *Digital Channel:* 11 *Virtual Channel:* 18; 30 kw; 702 ft.; N40 23 20 W86 36 46
Post Office Box 2618, West Lafayette, IN 47906 US
(765) 463-1800, *Fax:* (765) 463-7979 (news)
www.wlfi.com
newsroom@wlfi.com
License: Lafayette, Tippecanoe County, IN held by Primeland Television Inc.
Group Owner: LIN Television Corporation; (acq 4-1-2000; in exchange for 67% of WAND(TV) Decatur, IL).
Nat'l Network: CBS *Nat'l Reps:* Petry Television Inc. *Wire Services:* UPI
Size of News Staff: 30; *Hours of Local News Weekly:* news progmg 22 hrs wkly
Baron Brendel, Operations Dir
Tom Combs, Station Manager
Jenny Olszewski, General Sales Mgr
Rick Thedwall, Programming Director
Kurt Lahrman, Promotions Manager
Chris Morisse, News Director
Mark Brooks, Chief Engineer

Louisville, KY (DMA 50)

WMYO *Digital Channel:* 51 *Virtual Channel:* 58; 1000 kw; 1281 ft.; N38 21 0 W85 50 57
5257 Skyline Drive, Floyd's Knob, IN 47119 US
(502) 585-0700, *Fax:* (502) 589-5559
www.fox41.com
License: Salem, Washington County, IN held by Independence Television Co.
Group Owner: Block Communications Inc.; (acq 3-30-2001).;
Washington Law Firm: Dow, Lohnes & Albertson
Nat'l Network: MYNETWORKTV *Nat'l Reps:* TeleRep
Steve Ballard, CFO
Bill Lamb, President
Harry Beam, Operations Dir
Marti Hazel, General Sales Mgr
Gary Schroder, Chief Engineer
Rick Burrice, National Sales Manager

South Bend-Elkhart, IN (DMA 89)

WHME-TV *Digital Channel:* 48 *Virtual Channel:* 46; 300 kw; 968 ft.; N41 35 43 W86 9 38
P. O. Box 12, South Bend, IN 46624 US
(574) 291-8200, *Fax:* (574) 291-9043
www.whme.com
License: South Bend, Saint Joseph County, IN held by Le Sea Broadcasting of South Bend, Inc.
Group Owner: Le Sea Broadcasting; (acq 6-10-77; $496,000;;
Washington Law Firm: Gardner, Carton & Douglas
Nat'l Network: IND
Mike Swinehart, Operations Dir
Peter Sumrall, General Manager
Anna Riblet, General Sales Mgr
Wes Hylton, Chief Engineer

WNDU-TV *Digital Channel:* 42 *Virtual Channel:* 16; 800 kw; 1023 ft.; N41 36 20 W86 12 46
Mailing Address: PO Box 1616, South Bend, IN 46634 US
Second Address: 54516 State Rd. 933, SouthBend, IN 46634
(574) 284-3000, *Fax:* (574) 284-3009
www.wndu.com
newscenter16@wndu.com
License: South Bend, Saint Joseph County, IN held by Gray Television, Inc
Group Owner: Gray Television Inc.; (acq 3-6-2006; $85 million)
Nat'l Network: NBC
Mick Wright, Operations Dir
John O'Brien, General Manager
Howard Voss, General Sales Mgr
Michael Fowler, Promotions Manager
CJ Beutein, News Director
George Molnar, Chief Engineer

***WNIT** *Digital Channel:* 35; 708 kw vis, 77 kw aur; 530t/500g; N41 36 59 W86 11 43; *Population Served:* 478,000
Mailing Address: Box 3434, Elkhart, IN 46515
Second Address: 2300 Charger Blvd., Elkhart, IN 46514
(574) 675-9648, *Fax:* (574) 262-8497
www.wnit.org
wnit@wnit.org
License: South Bend, Saint Joseph County, IN held by Michiana Public Broadcasting Corp
Washington Law Firm: Dow, Lohnes & Albertson
Nat'l Network: PBS
Amy Cassidy, CFO
Mary Pruess, President
Brian Hoover, Operations Dir
Diane Marlow, Programming Director

WSBT-TV *Digital Channel:* 22 *Virtual Channel:* 22; 266 kw; 1091 ft.; N41 37 0 W86 13 1
300 W. Jefferson Blvd., South Bend, IN 46601 US
(574) 233-3141, *Fax:* (574) 288-6630
www.wsbt.com
wsbtnews@wsbt.com
License: South Bend, Saint Joseph County, IN held by WSBT Inc.
Group Owner: Schurz Communications Inc.; *Washington Law Firm:* Wilmer Hale
Nat'l Network: CBS *Nat'l Reps:* Harrington, Righter & Parsons
Size of News Staff: 34; *Hours of Local News Weekly:* news progmg 22 hrs wkly
John Mann, President
Bob Johnson, Operations Dir
Beth Young, General Sales Mgr
Scott Leiter, Promotions Manager
Meg Sauer, News Director
C. Eugene Hale, Chief Engineer

Rhonda Malone, Human Resources
Chris Dautel, VicePresident, Finance

WSJV *Digital Channel:* 28 *Virtual Channel:* 28; 311 kw; 1099 ft.; N41 36 58 W86 11 38
58096 County Rd 7 S, Elkhart, IN 46517 US
(574) 679-9758, *Fax:* (574) 294-1267
www.fox28.com
fox28@fox28.com
License: Elkhart, Elkhart County, IN held by WSJV Television Inc.
Group Owner: Quincy Newspapers Inc.; (acq 3-31-75; $3.2 million;; *Washington Law Firm:* Wilkinson, Barker, Knauer & Quinn
Nat'l Network: FOX
Size of News Staff: 22; *Hours of Local News Weekly:* news progmg 16 hrs wkly
Ed Kral, Station Manager
Heather Stewart, Programming Director

Terre Haute, IN (DMA 152)

WAWV-TV *Digital Channel:* 39; 2,140 kw vis, 214 kw aur; ant 976t/1,004g; N39 13 58 W87 23 49; *Population Served:* 70,286
Mailing Address: Box 9268, Terre Haute, IN 47808
Second Address: 10849 US Hwy. 41, Farmersburg, IN 47850
(812) 696-2121, *Fax:* (812) 696-2755
www.mywabashvalley.com
License: Terre Haute, Vigo County, IN held by Mission Broadcasting Inc.
Group Owner: Mission Broadcasting Inc.
Nat'l Network: ABC
Hours of Local News Weekly: News progmg 2 hrs wkly
Lois Mathis, Station Manager
Jeremiah Turner, General Sales Mgr
Tim Sanders, Promotions Manager
Tom McClanahan, News Director
Bruce Yowell, Chief Engineer

WTHI-TV *Digital Channel:* 10; 316 kw vis, 31.6 kw aur; ant 960t/993g; N39 14 36 W87 23 07; *Population Served:* 164,800
Mailing Address: PO Box 9606, Terre Haute, IN 91505
Second Address: 918 Ohio St., Terre Haute, IN 47807
(812) 232-9481, *Fax:* (812) 232-8953
www.wthitv.com
License: Terre Haute, Vigo County, IN held by Indiana Broadcasting LLC.
Group Owner: LIN Television Corporation; (acq 11-30-2005; grpsl).
Nat'l Network: CBS (10.1); FOX (10.2) *Nat'l Reps:* Petry Television Inc.
Todd Weber, General Manager
Nick Telezyn, General Sales Mgr
Jeff Tucker, Chief Engineer

WTWO *Digital Channel:* 36; 100 kw vis, 19.5 kw aur; 950t/999g; N39 14 33 W87 23 29; *Population Served:* 162,320
Mailing Address: Box 9268, Terre Haute, IN 47808
Second Address: 10849 N. U.S. Hwy. 41, Farmersburg, IN 47850
(812) 696-2121, *Fax:* (812) 696-2755
www.mywabashvalley.com
station@wtwo.com
License: Terre Haute, Vigo County, IN held by Nexstar Broadcasting Inc.
Group Owner: Nexstar Broadcasting Group Inc.; (acq 2-14-97; with KQTV(TV) Saint Joseph, MO); *Washington Law Firm:* Drinker, Biddle & Reath LLP
Nat'l Network: NBC
Size of News Staff: 25; *Hours of Local News Weekly:* news progmg 20 hrs wkly
Timothy Sturgess, General Manager
Jeremiah Turner, General Sales Mgr
Tim Sanders, Promotions Manager
Tom McClanahan, News Director
Bruce Yowell, Chief Engineer

***WVUT** *Digital Channel:* 22 *Virtual Channel:* 22; 57 kw; 538 ft.; N38 39 6 W87 28 37
1002 North First Street, Vincennes, IN 47591 US
(812) 888-4345, *Fax:* (812) 882-2237
www.vubroadcasting.org
wvut@vinu.edu
License: Vincennes, Knox County, IN held by Board of Trustees for the Vincennes Univ
(acq 9-16-76;; *Washington Law Firm:* Fletcher, Heald & Hildreth
Nat'l Network: PBS *Wire Services:* UPI
Size of News Staff: 4; *Hours of Local News Weekly:* news progmg 5 hrs wkly

Jill Ballinger, Operations Dir
Al Rerko, General Manager
Sharon Keifer, Programming Director

Iowa

Cedar Rapids-Waterloo-Iowa City & Dubuque, IA (DMA 88)

KCRG-TV *Digital Channel:* 9 *Virtual Channel:* 9; 30.4 kw; 1991 ft.; N42 18 59 W91 51 31
Mailing Address: 2nd Ave, 5th Sttreet Se, Cedar Rapids, IA 52401 US
Second Address: 501 2nd Ave SE, Cedar Rapids, IA 52401
(319) 395-9999, *Fax:* (319) 398-8378
www.kcrg.com
License: Cedar Rapids, Linn County, IA held by Cedar Rapids TV Co.
(acq 8-12-54; $101,500;; *Ownership:* The Gazette Co., 100%; *Washington Law Firm:* Wiley, Rein & Fielding
Nat'l Network: ABC
Joseph Hladky III, CEO
John Phelan III, General Manager
John Phelan, Station Manager
Kevin Schrader, Programming Director

KFXA *Digital Channel:* 27 *Virtual Channel:* 28; 1000 kw; 1473 ft.; N42 5 25 W92 5 13
One Radio Lane, Cleveland, OH 44114 US
(319) 393-2800, *Fax:* (319) 395-7028
www.kfxa.tv
kfxa@kfxa.tv
License: Cedar Rapids, Linn County, IA held by Second Generation of Iowa Ltd
Nat'l Network: FOX
Size of News Staff: 6; *Hours of Local News Weekly:* news progmg 13.5 hrs wkly
Larry Blum, President
Greg Stuart, Operations Dir

***KRIN** *Digital Channel:* 35 *Virtual Channel:* 32; 250 kw; 1916 ft.; N42 18 59 W91 51 31
Mailing Address: P.O.Box 6450, Johnston, IA 50131 US
Second Address: 6450 Corporate Dr., Johnston, IA 50131-6450
(515) 242-3100
www.iptv.org
public_information@iptv.org
License: Waterloo, Black Hawk County, IA held by Iowa Public Broadcasting Board
Washington Law Firm: Dow, Lohnes PLLC
Nat'l Network: PBS
Daniel Miller, General Manager

KWKB *Digital Channel:* 25 *Virtual Channel:* 20; 1000 kw; 1374 ft.; N41 43 29 W91 21 10
3654 West Jarvis Avenue, Skokie, IL 60076 US
(319) 643-5952, *Fax:* (319) 643-3124
www.kwkb.com
License: Iowa City, Johnson County, IA held by KM Television of Iowa L.L.C.
Group Owner: KM Communications Inc.
Nat'l Network: CW; MyNetworkTV
Jeff Hoffman, Operations Dir
Donald Bae, General Manager
Scott Ireland, General Sales Mgr
Trish Wethington, Programming Director
Chris Andrews, Promotions Manager
Dawn Neal, National Sales Manager

KWWF *Digital Channel:* 22 *Virtual Channel:* 22; 11.85 kw; 1084 ft.; N42 17 17.33 W91 52 53.86
Mailing Address: 224 Amberglow Place, Cary, NC 27513 US
Second Address: 501 Sycamore St., Suite 710, Waterloo, IA 50703
(319) 287-5841
License: Waterloo, Black Hawk County, IA held by EBC Waterloo Inc., debtor in possession
Group Owner: Equity Media Holdings Corp.; (acq 8-6-2004; $5 million with WNYI(TV) Ithaca, NY)
Nat'l Network: RTN
Ken Musgrave, Operations Dir
Jason Effinger, General Manager
Bob Bunch, General Sales Mgr

KWWL *Digital Channel:* 7 *Virtual Channel:* 7; 49 kw; 1972 ft.; N42 24 2 W91 50 36
Rsa Tower, 20th Floor, 201 Monroe Street, Montgomery, AL 36104 US
(319) 291-1200, *Fax:* (319) 291-1255
www.kwwl.com
kwwl@kwwl.com
License: Waterloo, Black Hawk County, IA held by KWWL Television Inc.
Group Owner: Quincy Newspapers Inc.; (acq 7-1-2006; $63 million); *Washington Law Firm:* Covington & Burling
Nat'l Network: NBC *Nat'l Reps:* Petry Television Inc. *Wire Services:* AP
Size of News Staff: 35; *Hours of Local News Weekly:* news progmg 22 hrs wkly
Beth Blake, Operations Dir
Tom Allen, General Manager
Kim Leer, Station Manager
Don Morehead, General Sales Mgr
Chris Hussey, Promotions Manager
Nathan Leding, News Director
Jarrett Liddicoat, Chief Engineer
John Huff, GeneralSales Manager
Shelly Davis, Local Sales Manager

Davenport, IA-Rock Island-Moline, IL (DMA 97)

KWQC-TV *Digital Channel:* 36 *Virtual Channel:* 6; 1000 kw; 1079 ft.; N41 18 44 W90 22 46
599 Lexington Avenue, 47th Floor, New York, NY 10022 US
(563) 383-7000, *Fax:* (563) 383-7129
www.kwqc.com
License: Davenport, Scott County, IA held by Young Broadcasting of Davenport, Inc., Debtor-in-possession
Group Owner: Young Broadcasting Inc.; (acq 4-15-96; $55 million); *Washington Law Firm:* Wiley, rein & Fielding
Nat'l Network: NBC *Nat'l Reps:* Adam Young
Mark Antonitis, General Manager
Allen Wiese, General Sales Mgr
Joydene Koresko, Programming Director
Michelle Makelbust, Promotions Manager
Doug Bierman, Chief Engineer

Des Moines-Ames, IA (DMA 71)

KCCI *Digital Channel:* 8 *Virtual Channel:* 8; 28.3 kw; 1959 ft.; N41 48 35 W93 37 16
888 Seventh Avenue, New York, NY 10106 US
(515) 247-8888, *Fax:* (515) 244-0202,(515) 471-8910
www.kcci.com
newschannel18@kcci.com
License: Des Moines, Polk County, IA held by KCCI Television Inc.
Group Owner: Hearst-Argyle Television Inc.; (acq 1999; grpsl).; *Washington Law Firm:* Brooks, Pierce, McLendon, Humprey & Leonard, LLP
Nat'l Network: CBS *Nat'l Reps:* Eagle Television Sales
Size of News Staff: 50; *Hours of Local News Weekly:* news progmg 30 hrs wkly
Paul Fredericksen, President
Bob Day, Operations Dir
Dave Porepp, General Sales Mgr
Sue Knudson, Programming Director
Nanci Elder, Promotions Manager
Dave Busiek, News Director
Steve Houg, Chief Engineer
Mike Cunningham,Creative Services Director
Anne Marie Caudron, National Sales Manager

KCWI-TV *Digital Channel:* 23; 5,000 kw vis; ant 2,011t; N41 49 47 W93 36 56
500 SW 7th Street, Suite 300, Des Moines, IA 93277
(515) 283-2323, *Fax:* (515) 289-4323
www.kcwi23.com
yourstation@kcwi23.com
License: Ames, Story County, IA held by KPWB License LLC.
Group Owner: Pappas Telecasting Companies
Nat'l Network: CW
Ted Stephens, General Manager
Larry Schuler, Chief Engineer

***KDIN-TV** *Digital Channel:* 11 *Virtual Channel:* 11; 22.5 kw; 1969 ft.; N41 48 33 W93 36 53
Mailing Address: 6450 Corporate Drive, Johnston, IA 50131 US
Second Address: 6450 Corporate Drive, Johnston, IA 50131
(515) 242-3100
www.iptv.org
public_information@iptv.org
License: Des Moines, Polk County, IA held by Iowa Public Broadcasting Board
Washington Law Firm: Dow, Lohnes PLLC
Nat'l Network: PBS
Daniel Miller, General Manager
Bill Hayes, Engineering Dir

KDMI *Digital Channel:* 19 *Virtual Channel:* 56; 839 kw; 2001 ft.; N41 49 48 W93 36 54
9279 Dutch Hill Rd, West Valley, NY 14171 US
(515) 964-2323, *Fax:* (515) 965-6900
yourstation@kcwi23.com
License: Des Moines, Polk County, IA held by KDMI License LLC.
Group Owner: Pappas Telecasting Companies; (acq 12-15-2005; $1 million for CP).
Nat'l Network: CW
Ted Stephens, General Manager
Larry Schuler, Chief Engineer

KDSM-TV *Digital Channel:* 16 *Virtual Channel:* 17; 1000 kw; 2008 ft.; N41 49 48 W93 36 54
10706 Beaver Dam Road, Cockeysville, MD 21030 US
(515) 287-1717, *Fax:* (515) 287-0064
www.kdsm.com
programming@kdsm17.com
License: Des Moines, Polk County, IA held by KDSM Licensee L.L.C.
Group Owner: Sinclair Broadcast Group Inc.; *Washington Law Firm:* Dow, Lohnes & Albertson
Nat'l Network: FOX *Nat'l Reps:* Millennium Sales & Marketing
Size of News Staff: 7; *Hours of Local News Weekly:* news progmg 4 hrs wkly
Mike Wilson, General Manager
Carolyn Lawrence, General Sales Mgr
Roni Dixon, Programming Director
Doug Hammond, Chief Engineer
Mike Denison, Local Sales Manager

***KEFB** *Digital Channel:* 34 *Virtual Channel:* 34; 37.23 kw; 505 ft.; N41 58 49 W93 44 23
109 Oak, Huxley, IA 50124 US
(515) 597-3138
License: Ames, Story County, IA held by Family Educational Broadcasting Inc
Nat'l Network: TBN
Doug Sheldahl, President

***KTIN** *Digital Channel:* 25 *Virtual Channel:* 21; 600 kw; 1165 ft.; N42 49 3 W94 24 41
Mailing Address: Post Office Box 6450, Johnston, IA 50131 US
Second Address: 6450 Corporate Dr., Johnston, IA 50131
(515) 242-3100
www.iptv.org
public_information@iptv.org
License: Fort Dodge, Webster County, IA held by Iowa Public Broadcasting Board
Washington Law Firm: Dow, Lohnes PLLC
Nat'l Network: PBS
Daniel Miller, General Manager

Omaha, NE (DMA 76)

***KHIN** *Digital Channel:* 35 *Virtual Channel:* 36; 600 kw; 1558 ft.; N41 20 40 W95 15 21
Mailing Address: P.O.Box 6450, Johnston, IA 50131 US
Second Address: 6450 Corporate Drive, Johnston, IA 50131
(515) 242-3100
www.iptv.org
public_information@iptv.org
License: Red Oak, Montgomery County, IA held by Iowa Public Broadcasting Board
Washington Law Firm: Dow, Lohnes PLLC
Nat'l Network: PBS
Daniel Miller, General Manager
Bill Hayes, Engineering Dir

Ottumwa, IA-Kirksville, MO (DMA 200)

KYOU-TV *Digital Channel:* 15 *Virtual Channel:* 15; 249 kw; 1181 ft.; N41 11 42 W91 57 15
13906 Gold Circle, Suite 201, Omaha, NE 68144 US
(641) 684-5415, *Fax:* (641) 682-5173
www.kyoutv.com
reception@kyoutv.com
License: Ottumwa, Wapello County, IA held by Ottumwa Media Holdings LLC
Group Owner: American Spirit Media; (acq 12-15-2003; $4 million); *Washington Law Firm:* Covington & Burling
Nat'l Network: FOX *Nat'l Reps:* MMT
Dianne Little, General Manager
Phil Benjamin, Chief Engineer

Rochester, MN-Mason City, IA-Austin, MN (DMA 154)

KIMT *Digital Channel:* 42 *Virtual Channel:* 3; 800 kw; 1519 ft.; N43 28 32 W92 42 29
250 International Drive, Spartanburg, SC 29304 US
(641) 423-2540, *Fax:* (641) 423-9309
www.kimt.com
mail@kimt.com
License: Mason City, Cerro Gordo County, IA held by LIN License Company LLC
Group Owner: LIN Media; (acq 10-6-2006; $35 million with WIAT-TV Birmingham, AL).; *Washington Law Firm:* Covington & Burling
Nat'l Network: CBS *Nat'l Reps:* Harrington, Righter & Parsons
Size of News Staff: 21; *Hours of Local News Weekly:* news progmg 19 hrs wkly
Steve Martinson, Operations Dir
Michael Fitzgerald, General Sales Mgr
Jerome Risting, Programming Director
Jerome Risting, Promotions Manager
John Murray, News Director
Larry Eckblad, Chief Engineer
Wayne Kohlhaas, Sales

***KYIN** *Digital Channel:* 18 *Virtual Channel:* 24; 533 kw; 1471 ft.; N43 28 32 W92 42 29
Mailing Address: P.O.Box 6450, Johnston, IA 50131 US
Second Address: 6450 Corporate Dr., Johnston, IA 50131
(515) 242-3100
www.iptv.org
public_information@iptv.org
License: Mason City, Cerro Gordo County, IA held by Iowa Public Broadcasting Board
Washington Law Firm: Dow, Lohnes PLLC
Nat'l Network: PBS
Daniel Miller, General Manager

Sioux City, IA (DMA 149)

KCAU-TV *Virtual Channel:* 9; 245 kw vis, 49 kw aur; 2,020t/2,000g; N42 35 12 W96 13 57; *Population Served:* 166,000
625 Douglas St., Sioux City, IA 51101
(712) 277-2345, *Fax:* (712) 277-3733
www.kcautv.com
License: Sioux City, Woodbury County, IA held by Citadel Communications Co. Ltd.
Group Owner: Citadel Communications Co. LTD.; (acq 10-1-85; $15 million); *Washington Law Firm:* Latham & Watkins
Nat'l Network: ABC
Daniele Feenstra, Operations Dir
Mary Ann Johnson, General Manager
Dan Marsh, General Sales Mgr
Karen Arndt, Programming Director
Brian Plantenberg, Promotions Manager
Carla Kreegan, News Director
Dan Ackerman, Chief Engineer

KMEG *Digital Channel:* 39 *Virtual Channel:* 14; 1000 kw; 2005 ft.; N42 35 12 W96 13 19
13906 Gold Circle, Suite 201, Omaha, NE 68144 US
(712) 277-3554, *Fax:* (712) 277-4732
www.kmeg.com
kmegtv@kmeg.com
License: Sioux City, Woodbury County, IA held by Waitt Broadcasting Inc.
(acq 6-23-98; $12.25 million); *Ownership:* Waitt Media Inc., 100% of total assets; *Washington Law Firm:* Wilkinson, Barker, Knauer & Quinn
Nat'l Network: CBS *Nat'l Reps:* Harrington, Righter & Parsons
Scott Eymer, General Manager
Dan Marsh, General Sales Mgr
Ed Bok, Chief Engineer

KPTH *Digital Channel:* 49 *Virtual Channel:* 44; 1000 kw; 1926 ft.; N42 35 12 W96 13 18
500 South Chinowth Road, Visalia, CA 93277 US
(712) 277-3554, (402) 241-4400, *Fax:* (712) 277-4732
www.kpth.com
yourstation@kpth.com
License: Sioux City, Woodbury County, IA held by KPTH License, LLC
Group Owner: Pappas Telecasting Companies
Nat'l Network: FOX; MyNetworkTV *Nat'l Reps:* Harrington, Righter & Parsons
Scott Eymer, General Manager
Dan Marsh, General Sales Mgr
Ed Bok, Chief Engineer

KTIV *Digital Channel:* 41 *Virtual Channel:* 4; 873 kw; 1998 ft.; N42 35 12 W96 13 18
3135 Floyd Boulevard, Sioux City, IA 51105 US
(712) 239-4100, *Fax:* (712) 239-2621
www.ktiv.com
ktiv4@ktiv.com
License: Sioux City, Woodbury County, IA held by KTIV Television Inc.
Group Owner: Quincy Newspapers Inc.; (acq 11-20-89).; *Washington Law Firm:* Wilkinson, Barker, Knauer & Quinn
Nat'l Network: NBC; CW *Nat'l Reps:* Blair Television
Hours of Local News Weekly: News progmg 19.5 hrs wkly
Jerry Watson, Operations Dir
David Madsen, Station Manager
Adrian Wisner, General Sales Mgr
David Washburn, Promotions Manager
Bridget Breen, News Director
Richard Herr, Chief Engineer

Kansas

Joplin, MO-Pittsburg, KS (DMA 148)

KOAM-TV *Digital Channel:* 7 *Virtual Channel:* 7; 14.8 kw; 1102 ft.; N37 13 15 W94 42 25
Mailing Address: Box 659, Pittsburg, KS 66762 US
Second Address: 2950 N.E. Hwy. 69, Pittsburg, KS 66762-0659
(417) 624-0233, *Fax:* (417) 624-3115, sls & admin
www.koamtv.com
email@koamtv.com
License: Pittsburg, Crawford County, KS held by Saga Quad States Communications LLC.
Group Owner: Saga Communications Inc.; (acq 10-12-94; $8.55 million)
Nat'l Network: CBS *Nat'l Reps:* Continental Television Sales
Hours of Local News Weekly: News progmg 19 hrs wkly
Danny Thomas, President
Vance Lewis, Promotions Manager
Kristi Spencer, News Director
Larry White, Chief Engineer

Topeka, KS (DMA 138)

KSNT *Digital Channel:* 27 *Virtual Channel:* 27; 77.9 kw; 1050 ft.; N39 5 34 W95 47 4
Mailing Address: P.O. Box 2700, Topeka, KS 66601 US
Second Address: 6835 N.W. Hwy. 24, Topeka, KS 66618
(785) 582-4000, *Fax:* (785) 582-5283,(785) 582-4783
www.ksnt.com
27news@ksnt.com
License: Topeka, Shawnee County, KS held by LIN License Company LLC
Group Owner: LIN Media; (acq 11-1-2007; grpsl)
Nat'l Network: NBC; CW *Nat'l Reps:* Harrington, Righter & Parsons *Wire Services:* AP
Size of News Staff: 30; *Hours of Local News Weekly:* news progmg 25 hrs wkly
Jean Turnbough, General Manager
Nate Hill, News Director
Charlie Good, Chief Engineer
Matt Broxterman, Regional Sales Manager

KTKA-TV *Digital Channel:* 49 *Virtual Channel:* 49; 89.1 kw; 1480 ft.; N39 1 34 W95 55 1
Mailing Address: 2121 S.W. Chelsea Avenue, Topeka, KS 66614 US
Second Address: 2121 S.W. Chelsea Dr., Topeka, KS 66614
(785) 273-4949, *Fax:* (785) 273-7811
www.ktka.com
49email@ktka.tv
License: Topeka, Shawnee County, KS held by Free State Communications LLC.
Group Owner: Vaughan Media LLC; (acq 8-29-2005; $6.2 million); *Ownership:* Free State Communications, LLC; *Washington Law Firm:* Cohn & Marks
Nat'l Network: ABC; CW *Nat'l Reps:* Millennium Sales & Marketing *Wire Services:* AP
Size of News Staff: 21; *Hours of Local News Weekly:* news progmg 15 hrs wkly
Ann Niccum, General Manager
Christy Gurney, Programming Director
Denise Eck, News Director

***KTWU** *Digital Channel:* 11 *Virtual Channel:* 11; 38 kw; 991 ft.; N39 3 50 W95 45 49
19th and Jewell Streets, Topeka, KS 66621 US
(785) 670-1111, *Fax:* (785) 670-1112
ktwu.washburn.edu
ktwu-press@lists.washburn.edu
License: Topeka, Shawnee County, KS held by Washburn University of Topeka
Nat'l Network: PBS
Dave Kendall, Operations Dir
Eugene Williams, General Manager
Cindy Barry, General Sales Mgr
Val VanDerSluis, Programming Director
Kevin Goodman, Promotions Manager
Duane Loyd, Chief Engineer
Mary Livingston, Traffic Manager

WIBW-TV *Digital Channel:* 13 *Virtual Channel:* 13; 42 kw; 1355 ft.; N39 0 22 W96 2 57
P.O. Box 119, Topeka, KS 66601 US
(785) 272-6397, *Fax:* (785) 271-1938
www.wibw.com
13news@wibw.com
License: Topeka, Shawnee County, KS held by WEAU Licensee Corp.
Group Owner: Gray Television Inc.; (acq 8-29-2002; grpsl).; *Washington Law Firm:* Wiley Rein LLP
Nat'l Network: CBS; MyNetworkTV *Nat'l Reps:* Continental Television Sales
Size of News Staff: 26; *Hours of Local News Weekly:* news progmg 30.5 hrs wkly
Mike Turner, Operations Dir
Jim Ogle, General Manager
Lisa Chapman, General Sales Mgr
Sharon Cole, Programming Director
Jon Janes, News Director
Cary Lahnum, Chief Engineer
Roger Brokke, General Sales Manager

Wichita-Hutchinson Plus, KS (DMA 69)

KAAS-TV *Digital Channel:* 17 *Virtual Channel:* 18; 65 kw; 1030 ft.; N39 6 16 W97 23 15; *Rebroadcasting:* Satellite of KSAS-TV Wichita.
200 Concord Plaza, Suite 600, San Antonio, TX 78216 US
(316) 942-2424, *Fax:* (316) 942-8927
www.foxkansas.com
programming@foxkansas.com
License: Salina, Saline County, KS held by Newport Television License LLC.
Group Owner: Newport Television LLC; (acq 3-14-2008; grpsl); *Washington Law Firm:* Covington & Burling
Nat'l Network: FOX
Jeff McClausland, General Manager
Ken Whitney, Production Manager
Chuck Reid, General Sales Mgr
Michelle Cleaton, Programming Director
Mike Haden, Promotions Manager
David Caruso, Chief Engineer
Kari Barrett, National SalesManager

KAKE *Digital Channel:* 21; 316 kw vis, 44.7 kw aur; 1,030t/1,079g; N37 46 54 W97 31 10; *Population Served:* 300,000
1500 North West Street, Wichita, KS 67203
(316) 943-4221, *Fax:* (316) 943-5493
www.kake.com
License: Wichita, Sedgwick County, KS held by Gray Television Licensee, Inc.
Group Owner: Gray Television Inc.; (acq 8-29-2002; grpsl).; *Washington Law Firm:* Covington & Burling
Nat'l Network: ABC *Nat'l Reps:* Continental Television Sales
Size of News Staff: 40; *Hours of Local News Weekly:* news progmg 16 hrs wkly
Terry Cole, President
Patrick Myers, Operations Dir
Dan Wall, General Sales Mgr
Bryan Frye, Promotions Manager
Dave Grant, News Director
Ben Bradley, Assistant News Director

***KDCK** *Digital Channel:* 21 *Virtual Channel:* 21; 8.423 kw; 325 ft.; N37 49 33 W100 10 40
604 Elm Street, Bunker Hill, KS 67626 US
(785) 483-6990, *Fax:* (785) 483-4605
www.shptv.org
shptv@shptv.org
License: Dodge City, Ford County, KS held by Smoky Hills Public Television
Washington Law Firm: Dow, Lohnes PLLC
Nat'l Network: PBS
Lynn Meredith, CEO
Terry Cutler, Operations Dir
Terry Cutler, Chief Engineer

KDCU-DT *Digital Channel:* 31; 570 kw vis; ant 905t/909g; N37 48 01 W97 31 29; *Not on Air/Target Date:* unknown
2425 Olympic Blvd., Suite 6000 West, Santa Monica, CA 90404
(310) 447-3870, *Fax:* (310) 447-3899
www.entravision.com
License: Derby, Sedgwick County, KS
Group Owner: Entravision Communications Corp.
Walter Ulloa, CEO

KLBY *Digital Channel:* 17 *Virtual Channel:* 4; 625 kw; 732 ft.; N39 15 9 W101 21 9; *Rebroadcasting:* Satellite of KAKE-TV Wichita.
990 South Range, Colby, KS 67701 US
(316) 946-1369, *Fax:* (316) 945-0599
www.kake.com
closed.captioning@kake.com
License: Colby, Thomas County, KS held by Gray Television Licensee Inc.
Group Owner: Gray Television Inc.; (acq 8-29-2002; grpsl).;
Washington Law Firm: Covington & Burling
Nat'l Network: ABC
Foreign Language Programming; Size of News Staff: 2
Patrick Myers, Operations Dir
Bryce Baker, General Manager

KMTW *Digital Channel:* 35 *Virtual Channel:* 36; 1000 kw; 1017 ft.; N37 56 23 W97 30 42
2750 S. 167th West, Goddard, KS 67052 US
(316) 942-2424, *Fax:* (316) 942-8927
www.mytvwichita.com
License: Hutchinson, Reno County, KS held by Mercury Broadcasting Co. Inc.
(acq 7-1-2001).; *Ownership:* Van H. Archer III, 100%;
Washington Law Firm: Fletcher, Heald & Hildreth
Nat'l Network: MYTV *Nat'l Reps:* Millennium Sales & Marketing
Jeff McClausland, General Manager
Chuck Reid, General Sales Mgr
Michelle Cleaton, Programming Director
David Caruso, Chief Engineer
Kari Barrett, National Sales Manager

KOCW *Digital Channel:* 14 *Virtual Channel:* 14; 40 kw; 535 ft.; N38 37 53 W98 50 52; *Rebroadcasting:* Satellite of KSAS-TV Wichita 100%.
200 Concord Plaza, Suite 600, San Antonio, TX 78216 US
(316) 942-2424, *Fax:* (316) 942-8927
www.foxkansas.com
programming@foxkansas.com
License: Hoisington, Barton County, KS held by Newport Television License LLC.
Group Owner: Newport Television LLC; (acq 3-14-2008; grpsl);
Washington Law Firm: Covington & Burling
Nat'l Network: FOX
Jon Deeble, Operations Dir
Jeff McClausland, General Manager
Chuck Reid, General Sales Mgr
Tom Gdisis, Programming Director
Mike Haden, Promotions Manager
Kari Barrett, National Sales Manager

***KOOD** *Digital Channel:* 16 *Virtual Channel:* 9; 496 kw; 997 ft.; N38 46 16 W98 44 16
P. O. Box 9, Bunker Hill, KS 67626 US
(785) 483-6990, *Fax:* (785) 483-4605
www.shptv.org
License: Hays, Ellis County, KS held by Smoky Hills Public Television Corp
Washington Law Firm: Dow, Lohnes & Albertson
Nat'l Network: PBS
Foreign Language Programming
Lynn Meredith, CEO
Mary-Pat Waymaster, Operations Dir
Jayne Heller, General Sales Mgr
Glenna Letsch, Programming Director
Jane Habiger, Promotions Manager
Terry Cutler, Chief Engineer

***KPTS** *Digital Channel:* 29; 32 kw; 785; N38 03 21 W97 46 35; *Population Served:* 120,250
320 W. 21st St. N., Wichita, KS 67203
(316) 838-3090, *Fax:* (316) 838-8586
www.kpts.org
tv8@kpts.org
License: Hutchinson, Reno County, KS held by Kansas Public Telecommunications Service Inc
(acq 1979).; *Washington Law Firm:* Dow, Lohnes PLLC
Nat'l Network: PBS
Michelle Gors, CEO/COO
Michelle Gors, President
Dave McClintock, Operations Dir
Chris Freshour, General Sales Mgr
David Brewer, Programming Director
Bob Locke, Chief Engineer
Pat Moyer, Content Director

KSAS-TV *Digital Channel:* 26 *Virtual Channel:* 24; 350 kw; 994 ft.; N37 46 40 W97 30 37
200 Concord Plaza, Suite 600, San Antonio, TX 78216 US
(316) 942-2424, *Fax:* (316) 942-8927
www.foxkansas.com
programming@foxkansas.com
License: Wichita, Sedgwick County, KS held by Newport Television License LLC.
Group Owner: Newport Television LLC; (acq 3-14-2008; grpsl);
Washington Law Firm: Covington & Burling
Nat'l Network: FOX *Nat'l Reps:* Millennium Sales & Marketing
Jon Deeble, Operations Dir
Jeff McClausland, General Manager
Chuck Reid, General Sales Mgr
Michelle Cleaton, Programming Director
Mike Haden, Promotions Manager
David Caruso, Chief Engineer
Kari Barrett, National Sales Manager

KSCW-DT *Digital Channel:* 19; 1,000 kw vis; ant 1,381t/1,320g; N38 03 38 W97 45 49; *Population Served:* 443,690
2815 E. 37th N, Wichita, KS 67219
(316) 303-0700, *Fax:* (316) 303-0160 (sales; traffic),(316) 303-9807
www.kansascw.com
programming@kansascw.com
License: Wichita, Sedgwick County, KS held by Sunflower Broadcasting Inc.
Group Owner: Schurz Communications Inc.; (acq 7-20-2007; $6.8 million)
Nat'l Network: CW
Joan Barrett, President
Marty Heffner, Operations Dir
Marcus Wilkerson, General Sales Mgr
Lisa Bryce, Programming Director
Shawn Hilferty, Promotions Manager

KSNC *Digital Channel:* 22 *Virtual Channel:* 2; 500 kw; 932 ft.; N38 25 54 W98 46 18
833 North Main, Wichita, KS 67203 US
(316) 265-3333, *Fax:* (316) 292-1197
www.ksn.com
ksnc@ksn.com
License: Great Bend, Barton County, KS held by LIn License Company LLC
.
Group Owner: LIN Media; (acq 11-1-2007; grpsl)
Nat'l Network: NBC *Nat'l Reps:* TeleRep
Al Buck, General Manager
Dan Shurtz, General Sales Mgr
Betty Erickson, Programming Director
Gregg Cox, Promotions Manager
Jason Kravarik, News Director
Warren Kunkle, Chief Engineer
Kevin White, New Media Manager

KSNG *Digital Channel:* 11 *Virtual Channel:* 11; 56.8 kw; 784 ft.; N37 46 40 W100 52 8
833 North Main, Wichita, KS 67203 US
(316) 265-3333, *Fax:* (316) 292-1197
www.ksn.com
License: Garden City, Finney County, KS held by LIN License Company LLC
Group Owner: LIN Media; (acq 11-1-2007; grpsl); *Washington Law Firm:* Wiley Rein LLP
Nat'l Network: NBC *Nat'l Reps:* TeleRep
Al Buck, General Manager
Dan Shurtz, General Sales Mgr
Betty Erickson, Programming Director
Gregg Cox, Promotions Manager
Jason Kravarik, News Director
Warren Kunkle, Chief Engineer
Kevin White, New Media Manager

KSNW *Digital Channel:* 45 *Virtual Channel:* 3; 891 kw; 1024 ft.; N37 46 26 W97 30 51
833 North Main, Wichita, KS 67203 US
(316) 265-3333, *Fax:* (316) 292-1197
www.ksn.com
news@ksn.com
License: Wichita, Sedgwick County, KS held by LIN License Company LLC
Group Owner: LIN Media; (acq 11-1-2007; grpsl); *Washington Law Firm:* Wiley Rein LLP
Nat'l Network: NBC *Nat'l Reps:* TeleRep
Al Buch, General Manager
Dan Shurtz, General Sales Mgr
Betty Erickson, Programming Director
Greg Cox, Promotions Manager
Jason Kravarik, News Director
Warren Kunkle, Chief Engineer
Kevin White, New Media Manager

***KSWK** *Digital Channel:* 8 *Virtual Channel:* 3; 33 kw; 502 ft.; N37 49 40 W101 6 35
6th & Elm Street, Bunker Hill, KS 67626 US
(785) 483-6990, *Fax:* (785) 483-4605
www.shptv.org
License: Lakin, Kearny County, KS held by Smoky Hills Public Television Corp
Washington Law Firm: Dow, Lohnes PLLC
Nat'l Network: PBS
Lynn Meredith, CEO
Mary-Pat Waymaster, Operations Dir
Jayne Heller, General Sales Mgr
Terry Cutler, Chief Engineer

KUPK *Digital Channel:* 18; 225 kw vis, 45 kw aur; ant 870t/881g; N37 39 01 W100 40 06; *Rebroadcasting:* Satellite of KAKE-TV Wichita.; *Population Served:* 435,000
2900 E. Schulman Ave., Garden City, KS 67846-9064
(620) 275-1560
www.kake.com
License: Garden City, Finney County, KS held by Gray Television Licensee Inc.
Group Owner: Gray Television Inc.; (acq 8-29-2002; grpsl).;
Washington Law Firm: Covington & Burling
Nat'l Network: ABC
Size of News Staff: 2; *Hours of Local News Weekly:* news progmg 7 hrs wkly
Bryce Baker, General Manager

***KWKS** *Digital Channel:* 19 *Virtual Channel:* 19; 464 kw; 1257 ft.; N39 14 31 W101 21 38
US
(785) 483-6990, *Fax:* (785) 483-4605
www.shptv.org
License: Colby, Thomas County, KS held by Smoky Hills Public Television Corp.
Washington Law Firm: Dow, Lohnes, LLC
Nat'l Network: PBS
Lynn Meredith, General Manager
Terry Cutler, Chief Engineer

Kentucky

Bowling Green, KY (DMA 182)

WBKO *Digital Channel:* 13; 22 kw vis; ant 723t/543g; N37 03 49 W86 26 07; *Population Served:* 67,300
2727 Russellville Rd, Bowling Green, KY 42102
(270) 781-1313, *Fax:* (270) 781-1814
www.wbko.com
License: Bowling Green, Warren County, KY held by WEAU Licensee Corp.
Group Owner: Gray Television Inc.; (acq 8-29-2002; grpsl).;
Washington Law Firm: Covington & Burling
Nat'l Network: ABC; CW; Fox *Nat'l Reps:* Continental Television Sales
Size of News Staff: 22; *Hours of Local News Weekly:* news progmg 17 hrs wkly
Rick McCue, Operations Dir
Rick McCue, Vice President
Brad Odil, Station Manager
Brad Odil, Vice President Sales
Barbara Powell, Programming Director
Cliff Cothern, Promotions Manager
Henry Chu, News Director
Wilbum England,Chief Engineer

***WKGB-TV** *Digital Channel:* 48 *Virtual Channel:* 53; 54.8 kw; 768 ft.; N37 5 22 W86 38 5
600 Cooper Dr., Lexington, KY 40502 US
(859) 258-7000, *Fax:* (859) 258-7399
www.ket.org
License: Bowling Green, Warren County, KY held by Kentucky Authority for Educational TV
Nat'l Network: PBS
Mike Brower, Operations Dir
Malcolm Wall, Station Manager
Craig Cornwell, Programming Director
Tim Bischoff, Promotions Manager

***WKYU-TV** *Digital Channel:* 18 *Virtual Channel:* 24; 61 kw; 580 ft.; N37 3 49 W86 26 7
1526 Russellville Road, Bowling Green, KY 42101 US

(270) 745-2400, *Fax:* (270) 745-2084
www.wkyu.org
wkyupbs@wkyu.edu
License: Bowling Green, Warren County, KY held by Western Kentucky University
Washington Law Firm: Leventhal, Senter & Lerman
Nat'l Network: PBS
Size of News Staff: 1; *Hours of Local News Weekly:* news progmg one hr wkly
Gary Ransdell, President
Jack Hanes, General Manager
Linda Gerossky, Station Manager

WNKY *Digital Channel:* 16 *Virtual Channel:* 40; 120 kw; 582 ft.; N37 2 3.8 W86 10 40.9
810 Chestnut Street, Bowling Green, KY 42101 US
(270) 781-2140, *Fax:* (270) 842-7140
wnky.net
wnky@nbc40.tv
License: Bowling Green, Warren County, KY held by MMKentucky License LLC.
Group Owner: MAX Media L.L.C.; (acq 3-1-2003; $7 million);
Washington Law Firm: Williams & Mullen, P.C.
Nat'l Network: NBC; CBS *Nat'l Reps:* Millennium Sales & Marketing
Jeff Cash, President
Heather Davison, Operations Dir
Greg Fotos, General Sales Mgr
Trisha Lackey, Programming Director
Gerald Keith, Promotions Manager
Ross Baize, Business Manager
Andrew Miladin, Research Director
KathyWerner, Traffic Manager

Charleston-Huntington, WV (DMA 65)

***WKAS** *Digital Channel:* 26 *Virtual Channel:* 25; 61.3 kw; 449 ft.; N38 27 44 W82 37 12
600 Cooper Dr., Lexington, KY 40502 US
(859) 258-7000, *Fax:* (859) 258-7399
www.ket.org
License: Ashland, Boyd County, KY held by Kentucky Authority for Educational TV
Nat'l Network: PBS *Regional Network:* Kentucky Educational Television
Mike Brower, Operations Dir
Malcolm Wall, Station Manager
Craig Cornwell, Programming Director
Tim Bischoff, Promotions Manager

WTSF *Digital Channel:* 44 *Virtual Channel:* 61; 50 kw; 571 ft.; N38 25 11 W82 24 6
Mailing Address: 3100 Bath Avenue, Ashland, KY 41101 US
Second Address: 3100 Bath Ave., Ashland, KY 41101
(606) 329-2700, *Fax:* (606) 324-9256
www.wtsftv.com
License: Ashland, Boyd County, KY held by Word of God Fellowship Inc
Nat'l Network: IND
Richard Clifton, General Manager
Virgil Adkins, Chief Engineer

Cincinnati, OH (DMA 34)

***WCVN-TV** *Digital Channel:* 24 *Virtual Channel:* 54; 53.5 kw; 384 ft.; N39 1 50 W84 30 23
600 Cooper Dr., Lexington, KY 40502 US
(859) 258-7000, *Fax:* (859) 258-7399
www.ket.org
License: Covington, Kenton County, KY held by Kentucky Authority for Educational TV
Nat'l Network: PBS *Regional Network:* Kentucky Educational Television
Donna Verhoezen, CFO
Craig Cornwell, Programming Director
Tim Bischoff, Promotions Manager

***WKON** *Digital Channel:* 44 *Virtual Channel:* 52; 49.7 kw; 702 ft.; N38 31 31 W84 48 39
600 Cooper Dr., Lexington, KY 40502 US
(859) 258-7000, *Fax:* (859) 258-7399
www.ket.org
License: Owenton, Owen County, KY held by Kentucky Authority for Educational TV
Nat'l Network: PBS *Regional Network:* Kentucky Educational Television
Mike Brower, Operations Dir
Malcolm Wall, Station Manager
Craig Cornwell, Programming Director
Tim Bischoff, Promotions Manager

WXIX-TV *Digital Channel:* 29; 4,680 kw vis, 468 kw aur; 1,004t/984g; N39 07 19 W84 32 52; *Population Served:* 1,946,000
19 Broadcast Plaza, 635 W. 7th St., Cincinnati, OH 45203
(513) 421-1919, *Fax:* (513) 421-2829
www.fox19.com
fox19@fox19.com
License: Newport, Campbell County, KY held by wxix License Subsidiary, LLC
Group Owner: Raycom Media Inc.; (acq 1998; $45 million; grpsl).; *Washington Law Firm:* Covington & Burling
Nat'l Network: Fox *Nat'l Reps:* TeleRep
Size of News Staff: 57; *Hours of Local News Weekly:* news progmg 32 hrs wkly
Paul McTear, CEO
Rick Oliver, Operations Dir
Bill Lanesey, General Manager
Branden Frantz, General Sales Mgr
Rick Oliver, Programming Director
Kevin Goryl, Creative Services Director
Matt Miller, News Director
Jim Gilbert,Chief Engineer
Amy Goetz, National Sales Manager
Chris Piennert, Regional Sales Manager

Evansville, IN (DMA 102)

***WKOH** *Digital Channel:* 30 *Virtual Channel:* 31; 63.3 kw; 407 ft.; N37 51 7 W87 19 44
600 Cooper Dr., Lexington, KY 40502 US
(859) 258-7000, *Fax:* (606) 258-7399
www.ket.org
License: Owensboro, Daviess County, KY held by Kentucky Authority for Educational TV
Washington Law Firm: Kenkel, Barnard & Edmundson
Nat'l Network: PBS *Regional Network:* Kentucky Educational Television
Mike Brower, Operations Dir
Malcolm Wall, Station Manager
Craig Cornwell, Programming Director
Tim Bischoff, Promotions Manager

Knoxville, TN (DMA 59)

WAGV *Digital Channel:* 51 *Virtual Channel:* 44; 550 kw; 1893 ft.; N36 48 0 W83 22 36; *Rebroadcasting:* Satellite of WLFG(TV) Grundy, VA.
Mailing Address: P.O. Box 151, Vansant, VA 24656 US
Second Address: 8594 Hidden Valley Rd., Abingdon, VA 24210
(276) 676-3806, *Fax:* (276) 676-3572
www.livingfaithtv.com
lisa@livingfaithtv.com
License: Harlan, Harlan County, KY held by Living Faith Ministries Inc
Nat'l Network: IND
Michael Smith, CEO
Lisa Smith, CFO

Lexington, KY (DMA 63)

WDKY-TV *Digital Channel:* 31 *Virtual Channel:* 56; 1000 kw; 1155 ft.; N37 52 51 W84 19 16
10706 Beaver Dam Road, Cockeysville, MD 21030 US
(859) 269-5656, *Fax:* (859) 269-3774
www.foxlexington.com
License: Danville, Boyle County, KY held by WDKY Licensee L.L.C.
Group Owner: Sinclair Broadcast Group Inc.; (acq 1996; $63 million with KOCB(TV) Oklahoma City, OK).; *Washington Law Firm:* Fisher, Wayland, Cooper, Leader & Zaragoza
Nat'l Network: FOX *Nat'l Reps:* Millennium Sales & Marketing
Hours of Local News Weekly: News progmg 7 hrs wkly
Michael Brickey, General Manager
Kevin Neumann, General Sales Mgr
Rick White, Programming Director
Marvin Bartlett, News Director
Dave Kollar, Chief Engineer
Ronna Haskins, Local Sales Manager

***WKHA** *Digital Channel:* 16 *Virtual Channel:* 35; 53.2 kw; 1211 ft.; N37 11 35 W83 11 17
600 Cooper Dr., Lexington, KY 40502 US
(859) 258-7000, *Fax:* (859) 258-7399
www.ket.org
License: Hazard, Perry County, KY held by Kentucky Authority for Educational TV
Nat'l Network: PBS *Regional Network:* Kentucky Educational Television
Mike Brower, Operations Dir
Malcolm Wall, Station Manager
Craig Cornwell, Programming Director
Tim Bischoff, Promotions Manager

***WKLE** *Digital Channel:* 42 *Virtual Channel:* 46; 45.8 kw; 845 ft.; N37 52 45 W84 19 33
600 Cooper Dr., Lexington, KY 40502 US
(859) 258-7000, *Fax:* (859) 258-7399
www.ket.org
License: Lexington, Fayette County, KY held by Kentucky Authority for Educational TV
Washington Law Firm: Kenkel, Barnard & Edmundson
Nat'l Network: PBS *Regional Network:* Kentucky Educational Television
Malcolm Wall, Station Manager
Craig Cornwell, Programming Director

***WKMR** *Digital Channel:* 15 *Virtual Channel:* 38; 51.4 kw; 948 ft.; N38 10 38 W83 24 17
600 Cooper Dr., Lexington, KY 40502 US
(859) 258-7000
www.ket.org
License: Morehead, Rowan County, KY held by Kentucky Authority for Educational TV
Nat'l Network: PBS *Regional Network:* Kentucky Educational Television
Mike Brower, Operations Dir
Malcolm Wall, Station Manager
Craig Cornwell, Programming Director
Tim Bischoff, Promotions Manager

***WKSO-TV** *Digital Channel:* 14 *Virtual Channel:* 29; 53.3 kw; 1407 ft.; N37 10 3 W84 49 30
600 Cooper Dr., Lexington, KY 40502 US
(606) 258-7000, *Fax:* (606) 258-7399
www.ket.org
License: Somerset, Casey County, KY held by Kentucky Authority for Educational TV
Nat'l Network: PBS *Regional Network:* Kentucky Educational Television
Mike Brower, Operations Dir
Malcolm Wall, Station Manager
Craig Cornwell, Programming Director
Tim Bischoff, Promotions Manager

WKYT-TV *Digital Channel:* 13; 1,510 kw vis, 151 kw aur; ant 984t/992g; N38 02 22 W84 24 11; *Population Served:* 871,000
Mailing Address: Box 55037, Lexington, KY 20005
Second Address: 2851 Winchester Rd., Lexington, KY 40509
(859) 299-0411, *Fax:* (859) 299-5531
www.wkyt.com
wmartin@wkyt.com
License: Lexington, Fayette County, KY held by Gray Television Licensee, Inc.
Group Owner: Gray Television Inc.; (acq 1-21-76;; *Washington Law Firm:* Venable, Baetjer, Howard & Civiletti
Nat'l Network: CBS *Nat'l Reps:* Harrington, Righter & Parsons
Wire Services: AP
Size of News Staff: 50; *Hours of Local News Weekly:* news progmg 43 hrs wkly
Wayne Martin, President
Michael Kanarek, Operations Dir
Kevin Kidd, General Sales Mgr
Barbara Howard, Programming Director
Kellen Dargle, Promotions Manager
Robert Thomas, News Director
Tom Bennett, Engineering Dir
Jamie Pyles,Chief Engineer

WLEX-TV *Digital Channel:* 39 *Virtual Channel:* 18; 475 kw; 938 ft.; N38 2 3 W84 23 39
Mailing Address: 134 Columbus Street, Charleston, SC 29403 US
Second Address: 1065 Russell Cave Rd., Lexington, KY 40505
(859) 259-1818, *Fax:* (859) 255-2418,TWX: 859-254-1272
www.wlextv.com
wlextv@wlextv.com
License: Lexington, Fayette County, KY held by WLEX Communications L.L.C.
Group Owner: Cordillera Communications Inc.; (acq 7-8-99; $99.1 million); *Washington Law Firm:* Dow, Lohnes PLLC
Nat'l Network: NBC
Sandra Byron, CFO
Tim Gilbert, President
Sean Franklin, Operations Dir
Chris Fedele, General Sales Mgr

Chip Alfred, Promotions Manager
Bruce Carter, News Director
Mary West, General Sales Manager
Sandy Stevenson, National SalesManager

WLJC-TV *Digital Channel:* 7 *Virtual Channel:* 65; 185 kw; 1055 ft.; N37 36 47 W83 40 18
P. O. Box 1129, Beattyville, KY 41311 US
(606) 464-3600, *Fax:* (606) 464-5021
www.wljc.com
wljc@wljc.com
License: Beattyville, Lee County, KY held by Hour of Harvest Inc
Washington Law Firm: Fletcher, Heald & Hildreth
Nat'l Network: REL *Nat'l Reps:* Rgnl Reps
Margaret Drake, President
Rachel Bogale, Operations Dir
Jonathan Drake, General Manager
Kim Mitchell, General Sales Mgr
Allan Mulford, Chief Engineer

WTVQ-DT *Digital Channel:* 40 *Virtual Channel:* 36; 1,580 kw vis, 158 kw aur; 994t/1,000g; N38 02 03 W84 23 39;
Population Served: 1,981,200
6940 Man-O-War Blvd., Lexington, KY 40509-8412
(859) 294-3636, *Fax:* (859) 293-5002
www.wtvq.com
programming@wtvq.com
License: Lexington, Fayette County, KY held by WTVQ-TV LLC
Group Owner: Morris Multimedia Inc.; (acq 5-13-2008; $16.5 million); *Washington Law Firm:* Fletcher, Heald & Hildreth
Nat'l Network: ABC; My Netwrok TV; Antenna TV *Nat'l Reps:* Telerep *Wire Services:* UPI
Size of News Staff: 25; *Hours of Local News Weekly:* news progmg 27 hrs wkly
Charles H Morris, Chairman
H Dean Hinson, President
Chris Aldridge, General Manager
Jeff Scott, General Sales Mgr
Steve France, News Director
Jerry May, Chief Engineer
Trey Eckerle, Production Manager
Don Sparks, National SalesManager
Cindy Smith, Traffic Manager

WUPX-TV *Digital Channel:* 21 *Virtual Channel:* 67; 719 kw; 1404 ft.; N37 54 26 W83 38 1
9279 Dutch Hill Road, West Valley, NY 14171 US
(606) 784-7932, *Fax:* (606) 768-9278
License: Morehead, Rowan County, KY
Group Owner: ION Media Networks Inc.; (acq 4-27-2001; $8 million)
Nat'l Network: ION

WYMT-TV *Digital Channel:* 12 *Virtual Channel:* 57; 50 kw; 1304 ft.; N37 11 38 W83 10 52
1201 New York Avenue, NW, Suite 1000, Washington, DC 20005 US
(606) 436-5757, *Fax:* (606) 439-3760
www.wymtnews.com
License: Hazard, Perry County, KY held by Gray Television Licensee LLC
Group Owner: Gray Television Inc.; (acq 9-2-94).
Nat'l Network: CBS *Nat'l Reps:* Harrington, Righter & Parsons
Size of News Staff: 15
Ernestine Cornett, General Manager
James Boggs, General Sales Mgr
Edna Eldridge, Promotions Manager
Neil Middleton, News Director
Phillip Hayes, Chief Engineer

Louisville, KY (DMA 50)

WAVE *Digital Channel:* 47 *Virtual Channel:* 3; 1000 kw; 1286 ft.; N38 22 8 W85 49 48
Mailing Address: 725 S. Floyd Street, Louisville, KY 40203 US
Second Address: 725 S. Floyd St., Louisville, KY 40203
(502) 585-2201, *Fax:* (502) 561-4115
www.wave3.com
License: Louisville, Jefferson County, KY held by WAVE License Subsidiary LLC.
Group Owner: Raycom Media Inc.; (acq 1-31-2006; grpsl);
Washington Law Firm: Covington & Burling
Nat'l Network: NBC *Nat'l Reps:* Harrington, Righter & Parsons
Steve Langford, General Manager
Nick Ulmer, Station Manager
Dan Foos, Programming Director
Bob Mack, Promotions Manager
Jim Sears, Chief Engineer

WBKI-TV *Digital Channel:* 19 *Virtual Channel:* 34; 1000 kw; 1119 ft.; N37 31 51 W85 26 45
218 North Third Street, Bardstown, KY 40004 US
(502) 809-3400, *Fax:* (502) 266-6262
www.cwlouisville.com
hr@wb34.com
License: Campbellsville, Taylor County, KY held by WBKISLG LLC.
(acq 6-9-2000); *Ownership:* Cascade Broadcasting Group L.L.C., 100%; *Washington Law Firm:* Shaw Pittman
Nat'l Network: CW *Nat'l Reps:* Harrington, Righter & Parsons
Craig Hoffman, Operations Dir
Terry Glaser, General Sales Mgr
Myrna Jane Jaspan, Programming Director

WBNA *Digital Channel:* 8 *Virtual Channel:* 21; 27 kw; 656 ft.; N38 1 59 W85 45 17
P. O. Box 19859, Louisville, KY 40259 US
(502) 964-2121
www.wbna-21.com
License: Louisville, Jefferson County, KY held by Word Broadcasting Network Inc.
Group Owner: Word Broadcasting Network Inc.; *Washington Law Firm:* Pepper & Corazzini
Nat'l Network: ION
Tom Fawbush, General Manager
Calvin Bader, Chief Engineer

WDRB *Digital Channel:* 49 *Virtual Channel:* 41; 1000 kw; 1281 ft.; N38 21 0 W85 50 57
624 W. Muhammad Ali Blvd, Louisville, KY 40203 US
(502) 585-0700, *Fax:* (502) 589-5559
www.fox41.com
License: Louisville, Jefferson County, KY held by Independence Television Co.
Group Owner: Block Communications Inc.; (acq 3-84; $10 million;; *Washington Law Firm:* Dow, Lohnes & Albertson
Nat'l Network: FOX *Nat'l Reps:* TeleRep
Size of News Staff: 45; *Hours of Local News Weekly:* news progmg 35 hrs wkly
Steve Ballard, CFO
Bill Lamb, President
Harry Beam, Operations Dir
Marti Hazel, General Sales Mgr
Barry Fulmer, News Director
Gary Schroder, Chief Engineer
Rick Burrice, National Sales Manager

WHAS-TV *Digital Channel:* 11 *Virtual Channel:* 11; 16.4 kw; 1286 ft.; N38 21 23 W85 50 52
400 South Record Street, Dallas, TX 75202 US
(502) 582-7711, *Fax:* (502) 582-7279
www.whas11.com
whasprogramming@whas11.com
License: Louisville, Jefferson County, KY held by Belo Kentucky Inc.
Group Owner: Belo Corp; (acq 2-97; grpsl).; *Washington Law Firm:* Covington & Burling
Nat'l Network: ABC
Mark Pimentel, General Manager
Chuck Wolfertz, General Sales Mgr
Joy Pritchett, Programming Director
Kirk Szesny, Promotions Manager
Genie Garner, News Director
Bill Brown, Chief Engineer

***WKMJ-TV** *Digital Channel:* 38; 1,170 kw vis, 230 kw aur; 835t/550g; N38 22 02 W85 49 53
600 Cooper Dr., Lexington, KY 40502
(859) 258-7000, *Fax:* (859) 258-7399
www.ket.org
License: Louisville, Jefferson County, KY held by Kentucky Authority for Educational TV
Nat'l Network: PBS *Regional Network:* Kentucky Educational Television
Mike Brower, Operations Dir
Malcolm Wall, Station Manager
Craig Cornwell, Programming Director
Tim Bischoff, Promotions Manager

***WKPC-TV** *Digital Channel:* 17 *Virtual Channel:* 15; 60.3 kw; 778 ft.; N38 22 1 W85 49 54
600 Cooper Drive, Lexington, KY 40502 US
(859) 258-7000, *Fax:* (859) 258-7399
www.ket.org
License: Louisville, Jefferson County, KY held by Kentucky Authority for Educational Television
Washington Law Firm: Schwartz, Woods & Miller
Nat'l Network: PBS *Regional Network:* Kentucky Educational Television
Mike Brower, Operations Dir
Malcolm Wall, Station Manager
Craig Cornwell, Programming Director
Tim Bischoff, Promotions Manager

***WKZT-TV** *Digital Channel:* 43 *Virtual Channel:* 23; 61 kw; 584 ft.; N37 40 55 W85 50 31
600 Cooper Dr., Lexington, KY 40502 US
(859) 258-7000, *Fax:* (859) 258-7399
www.ket.org
License: Elizabethtown, Hardin County, KY held by Kentucky Authority for Educational TV
Nat'l Network: PBS *Regional Network:* Kentucky Educational Television
Mike Brower, Operations Dir
Malcolm Wall, Station Manager
Craig Cornwell, Programming Director
Tim Bischoff, Promotions Manager

WLKY-TV *Digital Channel:* 26 *Virtual Channel:* 32; 4,300 kw vis, 430 kw aur; 1,260t/989g; N38 22 10 W85 50 02
, 1918 Mellwood Ave., Louisville, KY 10106
(502) 893-3671, *Fax:* (502) 897-2384
www.wlky.com
License: Louisville, Jefferson County, KY held by Hearst Properties Inc.
Group Owner: Hearst Television Inc.; (acq 3-18-99; grpsl);
Washington Law Firm: Brooks, Pierce, McLendon, Humphrey & Leonard
Nat'l Network: CBS *Wire Services:* UPI
Hours of Local News Weekly: News progmg 37.5 hrs wkly
Glenn Haygood, President
Glenn Haygood, General Manager
Greg Baird, General Sales Mgr
Debbie Roberson, Program Coordinator
Michael Neelly, News Director
Bill Greep, Engineering Dir

Paducah, KY-Cape Girardeau, MO-Harrisburg-Mount Vernon, IL (DMA 78)

WDKA *Digital Channel:* 49 *Virtual Channel:* 49; 1000 kw; 1073 ft.; N37 23 42 W88 56 23
200 College Place, Suite 118, Norfolk, VA 23510 US
(573) 334-1223, *Fax:* (573) 334-1208
www.mywdka.com
License: Paducah, McCracken County, KY held by WDKA Acquisition Corp
Nat'l Network: MYTV
Rob Chronister, Operations Dir
Tom Tipton, General Manager
Jennifer Chronister, General Sales Mgr
Alan Muster, Programming Director
Chuck Moffitt, Promotions Manager
Chris Girard, Chief Engineer
Glenn Ralston, National SalesManager

***WKMU** *Digital Channel:* 36 *Virtual Channel:* 21; 56.9 kw; 614 ft.; N36 41 34 W88 32 11
600 Cooper Dr., Lexington, KY 40502 US
(859) 258-7000, *Fax:* (859) 258-7399
www.ket.org
License: Murray, Calloway County, KY held by Kentucky Authority for Educational TV
Nat'l Network: PBS *Regional Network:* Kentucky Educational Television
Mike Brower, Operations Dir
Malcolm Wall, Station Manager
Craig Cornwell, Programming Director
Tim Bischoff, Promotions Manager

***WKPD** *Digital Channel:* 41 *Virtual Channel:* 29; 55.7 kw; 469 ft.; N37 5 39 W88 40 20
600 Cooper Drive, Lexington, KY 40502 US
(859) 258-7000, *Fax:* (859) 258-7399
www.ket.org
License: Paducah, McCracken County, KY held by Kentucky Authority for Educational TV
(acq 2-28-78).; *Washington Law Firm:* Kenkel, Barnard & Edmundson
Nat'l Network: PBS *Regional Network:* Kentucky Educational Television
Mike Brower, Operations Dir
Malcolm Wall, Station Manager
Craig Cornwell, Programming Director
Tim Bischoff, Promotions Manager

WPSD-TV *Digital Channel:* 32 *Virtual Channel:* 6; 906 kw; 1614 ft.; N37 11 31 W88 58 53

Mailing Address: 100 Television Lane, P.O. Box 1197, Paducah, KY 42002 US
Second Address: 100 Television Ln., Paducah, KY 42003
(270) 415-1900, *Fax:* (270) 415-2020
www.wpsdtv.com
djernigan@wpsdlocal6.com;bevans@wpsdlocal6.com;jgill@wpsdlocal6.com
License: Paducah, McCracken County, KY held by WPSD-TV LLC
(acq 12-3-01).; *Washington Law Firm:* Covington & Burling
Nat'l Network: NBC *Nat'l Reps:* Continental Television Sales
Size of News Staff: 49; *Hours of Local News Weekly:* news progmg 23 hrs wkly
Richard Paxton, President
Bill Evans, Operations Dir
David Jernigan, General Sales Mgr
Cathy Crecelius, Promotions Manager
Griff Potter, News Director
Joey Gill, Chief Engineer
Mark Hall, Operations Manager
Carolyn Fox,Regional Sales Manager

Louisiana

Alexandria, LA (DMA 179)

KALB-TV *Digital Channel:* 35 *Virtual Channel:* 5; 820 kw; 1578 ft.; N31 2 15 W92 29 45
Mailing Address: 333 East Grace Street, Richmond, VA 23219 US
Second Address: 605 Washington St., Alexandria, LA 70301
(318) 445-2456, *Fax:* (318) 442-7427
www.kalb.com
news@kalb.com
License: Alexandria, Rapides County, LA held by Hoak Media of Alexandria License LLC.
Group Owner: Hoak Media Corporation; (acq 7-15-2008; $60 million with WMBB(TV) Panama City, FL); *Washington Law Firm:* Akin Gump Strauss Hauer & Feld LLP
Nat'l Network: NBC & CBS; CBS
Eric Van den Branden, President
Rusty Kirkland, General Sales Mgr
Mitch Pederson, Programming Director
Keith Weiss, News Director

KBCA *Digital Channel:* 41 *Virtual Channel:* 41; 1000 kw; 993 ft.; N30 54 17 W92 37 28
1107 Marie Antoinette, Lafayette, LA 70506 US
(337) 896-1600, *Fax:* (337) 896-2695
www.cwtv41.com
info@cwtv41.com
License: Alexandria, Rapides County, LA held by Wilderness Communications LLC.
Group Owner: Wilderness Communications LLC; (acq 4-1-2006); *Washington Law Firm:* Fletcher, Heald & Hildreth
Nat'l Network: CW *Nat'l Reps:* Roslin Television Sales
Charles Chatelain, President
Eddie Blanchard, General Manager
Dave Pierce, General Sales Mgr

KLAX-TV *Digital Channel:* 31 *Virtual Channel:* 31; 200 kw; 1093 ft.; N31 33 54 W92 33 0
105 Mysen Circle, Cordova, TN 38018 US
(318) 473-0031, *Fax:* (318) 442-9984
www.klax-tv.com
License: Alexandria, Rapides County, LA held by Pollack-Belz Communication Co. Inc.
Group Owner: Pollack Broadcasting Co.; (acq 6-3-88; $1.1 million); *Washington Law Firm:* Wood, Maines & Brown
Nat'l Network: ABC
Size of News Staff: 4; *Hours of Local News Weekly:* news progmg 5.5 hrs wkly
William Pollack, President
David Carlson, General Manager
Lisa Ballance, General Sales Mgr
Vernilla Brooks, Programming Director
Frances Yeager, Promotions Manager
D. Herbert, Chief Engineer

***KLPA-TV** *Digital Channel:* 26 *Virtual Channel:* 25; 500 kw; 1355 ft.; N31 33 56.4 W92 32 50.5
7733 Perkins Rd, Baton Rouge, LA 70810 US
(225) 767-5660,(800) 272-8161, *Fax:* (225) 767-4299
www.lpb.org
License: Alexandria, Rapides County, LA held by Louisiana Educational Television Authority
Washington Law Firm: Schwartz, Woods & Miller
Nat'l Network: PBS
Beth Courtney, CEO
William Woodside Jr, Operations Dir
Jennifer Howze, Programming Director
Bob Neese, Promotions Manager
Randy Ward, Engineering Dir

Baton Rouge, LA (DMA 95)

WAFB *Digital Channel:* 9 *Virtual Channel:* 9; 5.57 kw; 1677 ft.; N30 21 58 W91 12 47
Rsa Tower, 20th Floor, 201 Monroe Street, Montgomery, AL 36104 US
(225) 383-9999, *Fax:* (225) 379-7891,TWX: 510-993-3406
www.wafb.com
news@wafb.com
License: Baton Rouge, East Baton Rouge County, LA held by WAFB License Subsidiary LLC.
Group Owner: Raycom Media Inc.; (acq 12-31-96; grpsl).; *Washington Law Firm:* Covington & Burling
Nat'l Network: CBS *Nat'l Reps:* Harrington, Righter & Parsons
Sandy Breland, General Manager
Vicki Kellum, General Sales Mgr
Brent Ledet, Promotions Manager
Vicki Zimmerman, News Director
Dale Russell, Chief Engineer
Ellen Salmon, Regional Sales Manager

WBRZ-TV *Digital Channel:* 13; 100 kw vis, 10 kw aur, DTV Power 30kw; 1,689t; N30 17 48 W91 11 36; *Rebroadcasting:* DTV 2.2-News, DTV 2.3-Weather; *Population Served:* 723,000
Mailing Address: Box 2906, Baton Rouge, LA 70821
Second Address: 1650 Highland Rd., Baton Rouge, LA 70802
(225) 387-2222, *Fax:* (225) 336-2246
www.wbrz.com
news@wbrz.com
License: Baton Rouge, East Baton Rouge County, LA held by Louisiana Television Broadcasting LLC.
Group Owner: Manship Stations; (acq 1958; $548,000).; *Washington Law Firm:* Pillsbury
Nat'l Network: ABC *Nat'l Reps:* Petry Television Inc.
Size of News Staff: 62; *Hours of Local News Weekly:* 30.5
Ed Ball, Operations Dir
James Daboval, General Manager
Denise Murrell, General Sales Mgr
Michelle Martone, Programming Director
Denise Akers, Promotions Manager
Chuck Bark, News Director
Clyde Pierce, Chief Engineer
BobbyBernard, Traffic Manager

WGMB-TV *Digital Channel:* 45; 3,871 kw vis; ant 1,164t; N30 19 35 W91 16 36; *Population Served:* 710,500
10000 Perkins Rd, Baton Rouge, LA 70810
(225) 769-0044, *Fax:* (225) 769-9462
www.fox44.com
License: Baton Rouge, East Baton Rouge County, LA held by Comcorp of Baton Rouge.
Group Owner: Communications Corp. of America; (acq 2-13-95;; *Washington Law Firm:* Fletcher, Heald & Hildreth
Nat'l Network: Fox
Karen Mire, Operations Dir
Phil Waterman, General Manager
Tom Poehler, General Sales Mgr
Destiny Kelley, Programming Director
Meisie Pacris, Promotions Manager
Cecil Connella, Chief Engineer
Lee Stolf, Regional Sales Manager

***WLPB-TV** *Digital Channel:* 25 *Virtual Channel:* 27; 355 kw; 1013 ft.; N30 22 22 W91 12 16
7733 Perkins Rd, Baton Rouge, LA 70810 US
(225) 767-5660,(800) 272-8161, *Fax:* (225) 767-4299
www.lpb.org
License: Baton Rouge, East Baton Rouge County, LA held by Louisiana Educational Television Authority
Washington Law Firm: Schwartz, Woods & Miller
Nat'l Network: PBS
Foreign Language Programming; Size of News Staff: 3; *Hours of Local News Weekly:* news progmg one hr wkly
Beth Courtney, CEO
Bob Graziano, General Manager
Jennifer Howze, Programming Director
Randy Ward, Engineering Dir

WVLA-TV *Digital Channel:* 34; 5,000 kw vis, 1,000 kw aur; ant 1,750t; N30 19 35 W91 16 36; *Population Served:* 773,400
10000 Perkins Rd., Baton Rouge, LA 70810
(225) 766-3233, *Fax:* (225) 768-9200
www.nbc33tv.com
License: Baton Rouge, East Baton Rouge County, LA held by Knight Broadcasting of Baton Rouge.
Group Owner: White Knight Holdings Inc.; (acq 1996; $23.975 million); *Washington Law Firm:* Pillsbury, Winthrop, Shaw & Pittman LLP
Nat'l Network: NBC
Size of News Staff: 3; *Hours of Local News Weekly:* news progmg 6 hrs wkly
Elaine Harrison, Operations Dir
Phil Waterman, Station Manager
Brooks Hogg, General Sales Mgr
Suzanne Marva, Programming Director
Doreen Morgan, Promotions Manager
Jeff Hamburger, News Director
Terry Freeman, Engineering Dir
Cecil Connella, Chief Engineer
Tom Poehler, National Sales Manager
Scott Thomson, Promotions Manager

Lafayette, LA (DMA 123)

KADN-TV *Digital Channel:* 16; 2,630 kw vis, 231 kw aur; ant 1,181t/1,282g; N30 21 44 W92 12 53; *Population Served:* 650,000
1500 Eraste Landry Road, Lafayette, LA 70506
(337) 237-1500, *Fax:* (337) 237-2526
www.kadn.com
tshannon@kadn.com
License: Lafayette, Lafayette County, LA held by Comcorp of Louisiana License Corp.
Group Owner: Communications Corp. of America; (acq 12-9-2004; $13,125,000).; *Washington Law Firm:* Fletcher, Heald & Hildreth
Nat'l Network: Fox
Foreign Language Programming
Tom Poehler, General Manager
Vikki Chapman, Programming Director
Katie Flash, Promotions Manager
Tony Guillory, Chief Engineer
Morgan Polito, Regional Sales Manager

KATC *Digital Channel:* 28 *Virtual Channel:* 3; 1000 kw; 1762 ft.; N30 19 25 W92 17 24
Mailing Address: 1103 Eraste Landry Road, Lafayette, LA 70506 US
Second Address: 1103 Eraste Landry Rd., Lafayette, LA 70596-3333
(337) 235-3333, *Fax:* (337) 235-9363
www.katc.com
webmaster@katctv.com
License: Lafayette, Lafayette County, LA held by KATC Communications Inc.
Group Owner: Cordillera Communications Inc.; (acq 1995; $24.5 million); *Washington Law Firm:* Dow, Lohnes
Nat'l Network: ABC *Nat'l Reps:* Continental Television Sales
Wire Services: AP; CNN
Size of News Staff: 45; *Hours of Local News Weekly:* news progmg 19.5 hrs wkly
Andrew Shenkan, General Manager
Bonnie Will, General Sales Mgr
Joy Bernard, Programming Director
Arte Richard, Promotions Manager
Letitia Walker, News Director
Don Mouton, Chief Engineer

KLFY-TV *Digital Channel:* 10 *Virtual Channel:* 10; 20.3 kw; 1729 ft.; N30 19 19 W92 16 59
PO Box 90665, Lafayette, LA 70509 US
(337) 981-4823, *Fax:* (337) 984-8323
www.klfy.com
sbienvenu@klfy.com
License: Lafayette, Lafayette County, LA held by Young Broadcasting of Louisiana Inc.
Group Owner: Young Broadcasting Inc.; (acq 5-28-88; $51 million;; *Washington Law Firm:* Brooks, Pierce
Nat'l Network: CBS *Nat'l Reps:* Adam Young
Foreign Language Programming; Size of News Staff: 24; *Hours of Local News Weekly:* news progmg 14 hrs wkly
Nanette Lavergne, Operations Dir
Mike Barras, General Manager
Spencer Bienvenu, General Sales Mgr
Carolyn Chretien, Programming Director
Dwight Dugas, News Director
Rodney Evans, Chief Engineer

***KLPB-TV** *Digital Channel:* 23 *Virtual Channel:* 24; 50 kw; 1520 ft.; N30 19 19 W92 16 58
7733 Perkins Rd, Baton Rouge, LA 70810 US
(225) 767-5660,(800) 272-8161, *Fax:* (225) 767-4299
www.lpb.org
License: Lafayette, Lafayette County, LA held by Louisiana Educational Television Authority

Washington Law Firm: Schwartz, Woods & Miller
Nat'l Network: PBS
Beth Courtney, CEO
William Woodside Jr, Operations Dir
Steve Graziano, General Manager
Jennifer Howze, Programming Director
Randy Ward, Engineering Dir

KLWB *Digital Channel:* 50 *Virtual Channel:* 50; 1000 kw; 995 ft.; N30 20 32 W91 57 46
516 St. Landry Street, Lafayette, LA 70506 US
(337) 896-1600, *Fax:* (337) 896-2695
www.cwtv50.com
info@cwtv50.com
License: New Iberia, Iberia County, LA held by Wilderness Communications LLC.
Group Owner: Wilderness Communications LLC; (acq 8-1-2006).; *Washington Law Firm:* Fletcher, Heald & Hildreth
Nat'l Network: CW *Nat'l Reps:* Roslin Television Sales
Eddie Blanchard, General Manager
Dave Pierce, General Sales Mgr
Layla Mouton, Programming Director

Lake Charles, LA (DMA 176)

***KLTL-TV** *Digital Channel:* 20 *Virtual Channel:* 18; 131.4 kw; 981 ft.; N30 23 46 W93 0 3
7733 Perkins Rd, Baton Rouge, LA 70810 US
(225) 767-5660,(800) 272-8161, *Fax:* (225) 767-4299
www.lpb.org
bawilliams@lpb.org
License: Lake Charles, Calcasieu County, LA held by Louisiana Educational Television Authority
Washington Law Firm: Schwartz, Woods & Miller
Nat'l Network: PBS
Beth Courtney, CEO
William Woodside Jr, Operations Dir
Steve Graziano, General Manager
Jennifer Howze, Programming Director
Randy Ward, Engineering Dir

KPLC *Digital Channel:* 7 *Virtual Channel:* 7; 62 kw; 1480 ft.; N30 23 46 W93 0 3
Mailing Address: P.O. Box 1488, Lake Charles, LA 70601 US
Second Address: 320 Division St., Lake Charles, LA 70602
(337) 439-9071, *Fax:* (337) 437-7600
www.kplctv.com
jserra@kplctv.com
License: Lake Charles, Calcasieu County, LA held by KPLC License Subsidiary LLC.
Group Owner: Raycom Media Inc.; (acq 1-31-2006; grpsl);
Washington Law Firm: Covington & Burling LP
Nat'l Network: NBC *Nat'l Reps:* Harrington, Righter & Parsons
Size of News Staff: 37
Dianna Mayo, Operations Dir
Jim Serra, General Manager
John Ware, General Sales Mgr
Agnes DeRouen, Programming Director
Scott Flannagan, News Director
John Scott, Chief Engineer
Veronica Bilbo, EEO Coordinator
Robin Daugereau,Programming Director
Mari Wilson, Public Service Director
Bridget Courtney, Traffic Manager

KVHP *Digital Channel:* 30 *Virtual Channel:* 29; 1000 kw; 1033 ft.; N30 17 26 W93 34 35
129 West Prien Lake Road, Lake Charles, LA 70601 US
(337) 474-1316, *Fax:* (337) 477-0715
www.watchfox.com
info@watchfox.com
License: Lake Charles, Calcasieu County, LA held by National Communications Inc
(acq 10-3-96).; *Washington Law Firm:* Baraff, Koerner, Olender & Hochberg
Nat'l Network: FOX
Size of News Staff: 20; *Hours of Local News Weekly:* news progmg 9 hrs wkly
Carol Kalna, Operations Dir
Madelyn Bonnot, General Manager
Gary Mutchler, General Sales Mgr
Kim Anderson, Programming Director
Crystal Miller, Promotions Manager
Mark Ewing, Chief Engineer
Madelyn Bennet, General SalesManager
Paul Imbragulio, National Sales Manager
Mary Stevens, National Sales Manager
Robin Killmer, Traffic Manager

Monroe, LA-El Dorado, AR (DMA 136)

KAQY *Digital Channel:* 11 *Virtual Channel:* 11; 12.3 kw; 1699 ft.; N32 11 50 W92 4 14
Mailing Address: P.O. Box 2738, Monroe, LA 71207 US
Second Address: 3100 Sterlington Rd., Monroe, LA 71203
(318) 325-3011, *Fax:* (318) 327-7519
www.abc-11.com
License: Columbia, Caldwell County, LA held by Monroe Broadcasting Inc
Nat'l Network: ABC
Joe Currie, General Manager
Carolyn Clampit, General Sales Mgr
Doug Ginn, Programming Director
Mike Halbrook, Promotions Manager
Pat O'Brien, Chief Engineer

KARD *Digital Channel:* 36 *Virtual Channel:* 14; 1000 kw; 1709 ft.; N32 5 42 W92 10 34
18 Newbury Street, Boston, MA 02116 US
(318) 323-1972, *Fax:* (318) 322-0926
www.myarklamiss.com
License: West Monroe, Ouachita County, LA held by Nexstar Finance Inc.
Group Owner: Nexstar Broadcasting Group Inc.; (acq 12-31-03; grpsl).; *Washington Law Firm:* Arter & Hadden
Nat'l Network: FOX *Nat'l Reps:* Continental Television Sales
Size of News Staff: 24; *Hours of Local News Weekly:* 22
Cheryl Olive, General Manager
Bob Dowden, General Sales Mgr
Irma Campbell, Programming Director
Esther Phillips, Promotions Manager
Melissa Klinzing, News Director
susie cumpton, Sales Manager

***KLTM-TV** *Digital Channel:* 13 *Virtual Channel:* 13; 17.2 kw; 1785 ft.; N32 11 50 W92 4 14
7733 Perkins Rd, Baton Rouge, LA 70810 US
(225) 767-5660,(800) 272-8161, *Fax:* (225) 767-4299
www.lpb.org
bawilliams@lpb.org
License: Monroe, Ouachita County, LA held by Louisiana Educational Television Authority
Washington Law Firm: Schwartz, Woods & Miller
Nat'l Network: PBS
Beth Courtney, CEO
William Woodside Jr, Operations Dir
Steve Graziano, General Manager
Jennifer Howze, Programming Director
Randy Ward, Engineering Dir

KMCT-TV *Digital Channel:* 38 *Virtual Channel:* 39; 14 kw; 472 ft.; N32 30 21 W92 8 55
701 Parkwood Dr, West Monroe, LA 71291 US
(318) 322-1399, *Fax:* (318) 323-3783
www.lambbroadcasting.org
lamb@lambbroadcasting.org
License: West Monroe, Ouachita County, LA held by Louisiana Christian Broadcasting Inc.
(acq 7-13-2004).; *Washington Law Firm:* Hardy, Chautin & Balkin
Nat'l Network: IND
Hours of Local News Weekly: News progmg 6 hrs wkly
Mike Reed, President
David Thompson, Chief Engineer

KNOE-TV *Digital Channel:* 8 *Virtual Channel:* 8; 22.3 kw; 1890 ft.; N32 11 50 W92 4 14
Mailing Address: P.O. Box 4067, Monroe, LA 71211 US
Second Address: 1400 Oliver Rd., Monroe, LA 71201
(318) 388-8888, *Fax:* (318) 388-0070,(318) 322-8774
www.knoe.com
knoetv@knoe.com
License: Monroe, Ouachita County, LA held by Hoak Media of Louisiana License LLC.
Group Owner: Hoak Media Corporation; (acq 10-3-2007; $47 million); *Washington Law Firm:* Cohn & Marks
Nat'l Network: CBS; CW *Nat'l Reps:* Blair Television *Wire Services:* CBS; AP; CNN
Size of News Staff: 28; *Hours of Local News Weekly:* news progmg 22 hrs wkly
Eric Van den Branden, President
Tom Cole, Operations Dir
Roy Frostenson, General Manager
Tom Peas, Station Manager
John Matherne, General Sales Mgr
Taylor Henry, News Director
Jerry Harkins, Chief Engineer

New Orleans, LA (DMA 53)

KGLA-AM *Digital Channel:* 42; 1,000 kw vis; ant 964t/964g; N29 58 41 W89 56 26
Box 50790, New Orleans, LA 70150
(504) 913-1540, *Fax:* (504) 340-4737
www.mayavision.tv
License: Hammond, Tangipahoa County, LA held by Mayavision Inc.
Nat'l Network: Telemundo (Spanish)
Foreign Language Programming
Ernesto Schweikert III, President

WDSU *Digital Channel:* 43 *Virtual Channel:* 6; 1000 kw; 938 ft.; N29 56 59 W89 57 28
888 Seventh Avenue, New York, NY 10106 US
(504) 679-0600, *Fax:* (504) 679-0745
www.wdsu.com
feedback6@wdsu.com
License: New Orleans, Orleans County, LA held by New Orleans Hearst-Argyle Television Inc.
Group Owner: Hearst-Argyle Television Inc.; (acq 1999; grpsl);
Washington Law Firm: Brooks, Pierce, McLendon, Humphrey & Leonard
Nat'l Network: NBC *Nat'l Reps:* Eagle Television Sales *Wire Services:* AP
Size of News Staff: 60; *Hours of Local News Weekly:* news progmg 32 hrs. wkly
Joel Vilmenay, President
Wendy Walters, General Sales Mgr
Joy Maurice, Programming Director
Joseph Schiltz, Promotions Manager
Johnathan Shelley, News Director
Chet Guillot, Chief Engineer
Frank Raterman, General SalesManager
Greg Turner, Research Director

WGNO *Digital Channel:* 26 *Virtual Channel:* 26; 1000 kw; 938 ft.; N29 56 59 W89 57 28
Two Canal Street, World Trd Cen. Sute 2800, New Orleans, LA 70130 US
(504) 525-3838, *Fax:* (504) 569-0908
www.abc26.com
License: New Orleans, Orleans County, LA held by Tribune Television New Orleans Inc.
Group Owner: Tribune Broadcasting Co.; (acq 12-20-2007; grpsl); *Washington Law Firm:* Dow Lohnes PLLC
Nat'l Network: ABC *Nat'l Reps:* TeleRep
Phil Waterman, General Manager
John Cruse, General Sales Mgr
Rick Erbach, News Director
Steve Zanolini, Chief Engineer

WHNO *Digital Channel:* 21 *Virtual Channel:* 20; 300 kw; 833 ft.; N29 55 11 W90 1 29
P.O. Box 12, South Bend, IN 46624 US
(504) 681-0210, *Fax:* (504) 681-0180
www.whno.com
whno@lesea.com
License: New Orleans, Orleans County, LA held by Le Sea Broadcasting Corp.
Group Owner: Le Sea Broadcasting
Nat'l Network: IND
Hours of Local News Weekly: News progmg 10 hrs wkly
David Vasquez, General Sales Mgr
Steve Warnecke, Programming Director
Bob Lawrence, Chief Engineer
Ivan Hinson, Sales
Sue Bosio, Traffic Manager

***WLAE-TV** *Digital Channel:* 31 *Virtual Channel:* 32; 200 kw; 899 ft.; N29 58 57 W89 57 9
2929 S. Carrollton Ave., New Orleans, LA 70118 US
(504) 866-7411, *Fax:* (504) 840-9838
www.pbs.org/wlae
License: New Orleans, Orleans County, LA held by Educational Broadcasting Foundation Inc
Washington Law Firm: Marmet & McCombs
Nat'l Network: PBS
Foreign Language Programming
Ron Yager, General Manager
Barbara Wick, Programming Director

WNOL-TV *Digital Channel:* 15 *Virtual Channel:* 38; 775 kw; 938 ft.; N29 56 59 W89 57 28
1400 Poydras Street, Suite 745, New Orleans, LA 70112 US
(504) 525-3838, *Fax:* (504) 569-0908
www.nola38.com
License: New Orleans, Orleans County, LA held by Tribune Television New Orleans Inc.

Group Owner: Tribune Broadcasting Co.; (acq 12-20-2007; grpsl)
Nat'l Network: CW *Nat'l Reps:* MMT
Phil Waterman, General Manager
John Cruse, General Sales Mgr
Rick Erbach, News Director
Steve Zanolini, Chief Engineer

WPXL-TV *Digital Channel:* 50; 5,000 kw vis, 500 kw aur; ant 945t/948g; N29 55 11 W90 01 29
3900 Veterans Memorial Blvd., Suite 202, Metairie, LA 70002
(504) 887-9795, *Fax:* (504) 887-1518
www.ionline.tv
License: New Orleans, Orleans County, LA held by Flinn Broadcasting Corp
Ami Jenkins, General Manager
Matt Pate, General Sales Mgr
Ernie Harvey, Chief Engineer

WUPL *Digital Channel:* 24 *Virtual Channel:* 54; 1000 kw; 892 ft.; N29 55 11 W90 1 29
1501 M Street, N.W., Suite 1100, Washington, DC 20005 US
(504) 529-4444
wupltv.com
License: Slidell, St. Tammany County, LA held by CBS Radio Stations Inc.
Group Owner: CBS Television Stations Group
Nat'l Network: MYNETWORK TV
Bud Brown, General Manager
Mike Zikmund, General Sales Mgr
Carol St.Martin, Programming Director
Christopher Merrifield, Promotions Manager
Robert Gass, Chief Engineer

WVUE-DT *Digital Channel:* 29; 316 kw vis, 31.6 kw aur; ant 990t/1,046g; N29 57 14 W89 56 58; *Population Served:* 1,648,000
1025 S. Jefferson Davis Pkwy., New Orleans, LA 70125
(504) 486-6161, *Fax:* (504) 483-1101
www.fox8live.com
info@fox8live.com
License: New Orleans, Orleans County, LA held by Louisiana Media Co. LLC.
(acq 7-18-2008; $41 million); *Ownership:* Benson Football L.L.C.
Nat'l Network: Fox *Nat'l Reps:* Harrington, Righter & Parsons
Size of News Staff: 54; *Hours of Local News Weekly:* news progmg 21 hrs wkly
Patrice Gunter, CFO
Joe Cook, General Manager
Johnny Faith, General Sales Mgr
Kelly Donnell, Promotions Manager
Mimi Strawn, News Director
Michelle Kehoe Ogden, National Sales Manager
Dee Dee Indovina, Regional Sales Manager

WWL-TV *Digital Channel:* 36 *Virtual Channel:* 4; 1000 kw; 1020 ft.; N29 54 22 W90 2 22
1024 North Rampart St., New Orleans, LA 70116 US
(504) 529-4444, *Fax:* (504) 529-6483
www.wwltv.com
License: New Orleans, Orleans County, LA held by WWL-TV Inc.
Group Owner: Belo Corp; (acq 1994).; *Washington Law Firm:* Holland & Knight
Nat'l Network: CBS *Nat'l Reps:* TeleRep
Bud Brown, General Manager
Mike Zikmund, General Sales Mgr
Carol St. Martin, Programming Director
Christopher Merrifield, Promotions Manager
Robert Gass, Chief Engineer

***WYES-TV** *Digital Channel:* 11 *Virtual Channel:* 12; 104 kw; 1004 ft.; N29 57 13 W89 56 58
PO Box 24026, New Orleans, LA 70184 US
(504) 486-5511
www.wyes.org
info@wyes.org
License: New Orleans, Orleans County, LA held by Greater New Orleans Educational TV Foundation
Washington Law Firm: Schwartz, Woods & Miller
Nat'l Network: PBS
Randall Feldman, CEO

Shreveport, LA (DMA 84)

***KLTS-TV** *Digital Channel:* 24 *Virtual Channel:* 24; 350 kw; 1070 ft.; N32 40 39.6 W93 55 30.1
7733 Perkins Rd, Baton Rouge, LA 70810 US
(225) 767-5660, *Fax:* (225) 767-4299
www.lpb.org
License: Shreveport, Caddo County, LA held by Louisiana Education Television Authority
Washington Law Firm: Schwartz, Woods & Miller
Nat'l Network: PBS
Beth Courtney, President/CEO
Joanne Gaudet, Director, Business
Barbara Williams, Executive Services Assistant
Ken Miller, General Manager
Jason Viso, Programming Director
Charlie Winham, News/Producer
Shauna Sanford,News/Producer
Randy Ward, Engineering Dir

KMSS-TV *Digital Channel:* 34 *Virtual Channel:* 33; 4,570 kw vis, 457 kw aur; 1,813t/1,781g; N32 36 51 W93 48 59
3519 Jewella Ave., Shreveport, LA 70505
(318) 631-5677, *Fax:* (318) 631-4194
www.kmsstv.com
License: Shreveport, Caddo County, LA held by Comcorp of Texas License Corp.
Group Owner: Communications Corp. of America; (acq 10-94).; *Washington Law Firm:* Fletcher, Heald & Hildreth, PLC
Nat'l Network: Fox
Paula Hayward, General Manager
Susan Newman, General Sales Mgr
N/A, Programming Director
Jim Dull, Promotions Manager
Steve Henry, Chief Engineer

KPXJ *Digital Channel:* 21 *Virtual Channel:* 21; 1000 kw; 1647 ft.; N32 41 8 W93 56 0
Mailing Address: 601 Clearwater Park Road, West Palm Beach, FL 33401 US
Second Address: 312 E. Kings Hwy, Shreveport, LA 71104
(318) 861-5800, *Fax:* (318) 219-4680
www.kpxj21.com
License: Minden, Webster County, LA held by Minden Television Co. LLC
(acq 5-7-2004; $10 million); *Washington Law Firm:* Garvey, Schubert & Barer
Nat'l Network: CW
Lauren Wray Ostendorff, President
George Sirven, General Manager

KSHV-TV *Digital Channel:* 44; 1,660 kw vis; 662t; N32 35 38 W93 51 39; *Population Served:* 410,000
3519 Jewella Ave., Shreveport, LA 71109
(318) 631-4545, *Fax:* (318) 631-4194
www.kshv.com
License: Shreveport, Caddo County, LA held by White Knight Broadcasting of Shreveport License Corp.
Group Owner: White Knight Holdings Inc.; (acq 1995; $3.8 million); *Washington Law Firm:* Pillsbury, Winthrop, Shaw Pittman, LLC
Nat'l Network: MyNetworkTV
Paula Hayward, General Manager
Susan Newman, General Sales Mgr
Issac Turner, Programming Director
Jim Dull, Promotions Manager
Steve Henry, Chief Engineer

KSLA *Digital Channel:* 17; 316 kw vis, 40.7 kw aur; 1,800t/1,800g; N32 40 29 W93 55 59; *Population Served:* 461,600
1812 Fairfield Ave., Shreveport, LA 71101
(318) 222-1212, *Fax:* (318) 677-6703
ksla.com
ksla@ksla.com
License: Shreveport, Caddo County, LA held by KSLA License Subsidiary LLC.
Group Owner: Raycom Media Inc.; (acq 9-1-96; grpsl).
Nat'l Network: CBS *Nat'l Reps:* TeleRep *Wire Services:* AP
Size of News Staff: 32
James Smith, Operations Dir
John Clark, General Sales Mgr
Barbara Bennett, Promotions Manager
Jayne Ruben, News Director
Ted Small, Chief Engineer
Delena Leary, Public Service Director

KTBS-TV *Digital Channel:* 28 *Virtual Channel:* 3; 1000 kw; 1847 ft.; N32 41 8 W93 56 0
Mailing Address: PO Box 44227, Shreveport, LA 71104 US
Second Address: 312 E. Kings Hwy., Shreveport, LA 71104-3554
(318) 861-5800, *Fax:* (318) 219-4680
www.ktbs.com
ktbsnews@ktbs.com
License: Shreveport, Caddo County, LA held by KTBS Inc
Washington Law Firm: Fletcher, Heald & Hildreth
Nat'l Network: ABC *Wire Services:* AP
Lauren Wray Ostendorff, President
George Sirven, General Manager
Linda Howard, General Sales Mgr
Bernadette Collier, Programming Director
Cheryl May, Promotions Manager
Randy Bain, News Director
Dale Cassidy, Chief Engineer

Maine

Bangor, ME (DMA 153)

WABI-TV *Digital Channel:* 13 *Virtual Channel:* 5; 12 kw; 1284 ft.; N44 42 11.7 W69 4 46.8
35 Hildreth Street, Bangor, ME 04401 US
(207) 947-8321, *Fax:* (207) 941-9378
www.wabi.tv
wabi@wabi.tv
License: Bangor, Penobscot County, ME held by Community Broadcasting Service.
Group Owner: Diversified Communications; (acq 10-7-53; $125,000;; *Washington Law Firm:* Irwin, Campbell & Tannenwald
Nat'l Network: CBS/CW; CW *Nat'l Reps:* Continental Television Sales *Wire Services:* AP
Size of News Staff: 30; *Hours of Local News Weekly:* news progmg 25 hrs wkly
Michael Young, Operations Dir
Tom Gass, General Sales Mgr
Steve Hiltz, Programming Director
Paul Saliwanchik, Promotions Manager
Jim Morris, News Director
Dale Carter, Chief Engineer
Keith Allen, Operations Manager

WLBZ *Digital Channel:* 2 *Virtual Channel:* 2; 3 kw; 630 ft.; N44 44 10 W68 40 17
1100 Wilson Boulevard, Arlington, VA 22234 US
(207) 942-4821
www.wlbz2.com
License: Bangor, Penobscot County, ME held by Pacific and Southern Co. Inc.
Group Owner: Gannett Broadcasting; (acq 1998; $110 million with WCSH(TV) Portland).; *Washington Law Firm:* Wiley, Rein & Fielding
Nat'l Network: NBC
Size of News Staff: 22; *Hours of Local News Weekly:* news progmg 33 hrs wkly
Charlene Belanger, Operations Dir
Judy Horan, General Manager
Bud Cushman, General Sales Mgr
Mike Marshall, Programming Director
Mark Parent, Promotions Manager
John Smist, News Director
Dave Mundee, Chief Engineer
HeatherSeavey, Edit Manager
Debbie Briggs, Traffic Manager
Steve McKay, Weather Director

***WMEB-TV** *Digital Channel:* 9 *Virtual Channel:* 12; 15 kw; 1230 ft.; N44 42 11 W69 4 47
65 Texas Avenue, Bangor, ME 04401 US
(800) 884-1717,(207) 783-9101, *Fax:* (207) 783-5193,(207) 942-2857
www.mpbn.org
comments@mpbn.org
License: Orono, Penobscot County, ME held by Maine Public Broadcasting Corp
(acq 6-23-92;; *Washington Law Firm:* Dow, Lohnes PLLC
Nat'l Network: PBS
Foreign Language Programming
Jim Dowe, General Manager
Charles Beck, Programming Director
Jeff Pierce, Promotions Manager
Keith Shortall, News Director
Gil Maxwell, Chief Engineer

***WMED-TV** *Digital Channel:* 10 *Virtual Channel:* 13; 3.5 kw; 436 ft.; N45 1 45 W67 19 25
Mailing Address: 65 Texas Avenue, Bangor, ME 04401 US
Second Address: 65 Texas Ave, Bangor, ME 4401
(800) 884-1717,(207) 783-9101, *Fax:* (207) 783-5193,(207) 942-2857
www.mpbn.org
comments@mpbn.net
License: Calais, Washington County, ME held by Maine Public Broadcasting Corp
(acq 6-23-92;; *Washington Law Firm:* Dow, Lohnes PLLC
Nat'l Network: PBS
Foreign Language Programming
Jim Dowe, General Manager
Charles Beck, Programming Director
Jeff Pierce, Promotions Manager
Keith Shortall, News Director
Gil Maxwell, Chief Engineer

WVII-TV *Digital Channel:* 7 *Virtual Channel:* 7; 14 kw; 751 ft.; N44 45 35 W68 34 1
371 Target Indust. Cir., Bangor, ME 04401 US
(207) 945-6457, *Fax:* (207) 942-0511
www.wvii.com
tv7news@wvii.com
License: Bangor, Penobscot County, ME held by Bangor Communications LLC.
Group Owner: Rockfleet Broadcasting Inc.; *Washington Law Firm:* Mullin, Rhyne, Emmons & Topel
Nat'l Network: ABC; Fox *Nat'l Reps:* Continental Television Sales
Size of News Staff: 15; *Hours of Local News Weekly:* news progmg 6 hrs wkly
Mike Palmer, Operations Dir
Mike Palmer, General Manager
Keryn Smith, General Sales Mgr
Gene Hardin, Promotions Manager
George Thomas, News Director
Mike Staples, Engineering Dir
Sue Lovell, Regional Sales Manager

Portland-Auburn, ME (DMA 77)

***WCBB** *Digital Channel:* 10 *Virtual Channel:* 10; 30 kw; 997 ft.; N44 9 15 W70 0 37
1450 Lisbon St., Lewiston, ME 04240 US
(800) 884-1717,(207) 783-9101, *Fax:* (207) 783-5193,(207) 942-2857
www.mpbn.net
comments@mpbn.net
License: Augusta, Kennebec County, ME held by Maine Public Broadcasting Corp
(acq 6-23-92;; *Washington Law Firm:* Dow, Lohnes PLLC
Nat'l Network: PBS
Foreign Language Programming
Jim Dowe, General Manager
Charles Beck, Programming Director
Jeff Pierce, Promotions Manager
Keith Shortall, News Director
Gil Maxwell, Chief Technology Officer

WCSH *Digital Channel:* 44 *Virtual Channel:* 6; 1000 kw; 1929 ft.; N43 51 30 W70 42 41
1100 Wilson Boulevard, Arlington, VA 22234 US
(207) 828-6666, *Fax:* (207) 828-6620
www.wcsh6.com
wcsh6@wcsh6.com
License: Portland, Cumberland County, ME held by Pacific and Southern Co. Inc.
Group Owner: Gannett Broadcasting; (acq 1-98).; *Washington Law Firm:* Wiley, Rein & Fielding
Nat'l Network: NBC
Steve Thaxton, President
Dave Abel, General Sales Mgr
Mike Marshall, Promotions Manager
Mike Curry, News Director
Dave Mundee, Chief Engineer

WGME-TV *Digital Channel:* 38 *Virtual Channel:* 13; 1000 kw; 1526 ft.; N43 55 28 W70 29 28
10706 Beaver Dam Road, Cockeysville, MD 21030 US
(207) 797-1313, *Fax:* (207) 878-3505
www.wgme.com
tvmail@wgme.com
License: Portland, Cumberland County, ME held by WGME Licensee L.L.C.
Group Owner: Sinclair Broadcast Group Inc.; (acq 5-3-99; grpsl).; *Washington Law Firm:* Dow, Lohnes PLLC
Nat'l Network: CBS
Size of News Staff: 55; *Hours of Local News Weekly:* news progmg 25 hrs wkly
Don Barr, General Sales Mgr
Alisa Burris, Promotions Manager
Robb Atkinson, News Director
Craig Clark, Engineering Dir

***WMEA-TV** *Digital Channel:* 45 *Virtual Channel:* 26; 50 kw; 758 ft.; N43 25 0 W70 48 17
Mailing Address: Post Office Box 1628, Portland, ME 04104 US
Second Address: 63 Texas Ave., Bangor, ME 4401
(207) 783-9101, *Fax:* (207) 942-2857,(207) 783-5193
www.mpbn.net
comments@mpbn.net
License: Biddeford, York County, ME held by Maine Public Broadcastig Corp
(acq 6-23-92;; *Washington Law Firm:* Dow, Lohnes PLLC
Nat'l Network: PBS
John Isacke, CFO
P. James Dowe, President
Gil Maxwell, Programming Director

WMTW *Digital Channel:* 8; 316 kw vis; ant 1,994t/1,630g; N43 50 44 W70 45 43
99 Danville Corner Rd, Auburn, ME 04210
(207) 782-1800,(207) 775-1800, *Fax:* (207) 783-7371,(207) 782-2165
www.wmtw.com
wmtw@wmtw.com
License: Poland Spring, Androscoggin County, ME held by Hearst Properties Inc.
Group Owner: Hearst Television Inc.; (acq 5-11-2004; $37.5 million); *Washington Law Firm:* Brooks, Pierce, McLendon, Humphrey & Leonard LLP
Nat'l Network: ABC *Nat'l Reps:* Eagle Television Sales *Wire Services:* AP
Hours of Local News Weekly: News progmg 25.5 hrs wkly
David J. Barrett, President
David W. Abel, General Manager
Micahel Grant, General Sales Mgr
Gloria Shallcross, Programming Director
Matt Earl, Promotions Manager
Amy Beveridge, News Director
Greg Roehr, Engineering Dir
JackConnor, Chief Engineer
John Gregory
Donna Rideout
Leianne M. Gervais

WPFO *Digital Channel* 23 *Virtual Channel:* 23; 5,000 kw vis; 1,086t; N44 09 15 W70 00 37; *Population Served:* 400,000
233 Oxford St., Suite 35, Portland, ME 20036
(207) 828-0023, *Fax:* (207) 347-7330
www.myfoxmaine.com
License: Waterville, Kennebec County, ME held by CMCG Portland License LLC.
Group Owner: MAX Media L.L.C.; (acq 4-7-2003; $10 million with WVIF(TV) Christiansted, VI); *Washington Law Firm:* Williams Mullen & Garvey, Schubert & Barer
Nat'l Network: Fox *Nat'l Reps:* TeleRep
Size of News Staff: 1; *Hours of Local News Weekly:* news progmg 18.5 hrs wkly
Tom MacArthur, General Manager
Rob Barry, General Sales Mgr
Torrey Ham, Programming Assistant
Jen Flint, Promotions Manager
Dave Cox, Chief Engineer
Ann Gagne, Business Manager
Eric Turner, Local Sales Manager
Barry Dodd,Production Manager

WPME *Digital Channel:* 35 *Virtual Channel:* 35; 14.35 kw; 912 ft.; N43 51 6 W70 19 40
545 Pool Road, Biddeford, ME 04005 US
(207) 774-0051, *Fax:* (207) 774-6849
www.ourmaine.com
comments@ourmaine.com
License: Lewiston, Androscoggin County, ME held by MPS Media of Portland License LLC.
(acq 3-31-2007; $4 million); *Ownership:* Eugene J. Brown, 100% votes; *Washington Law Firm:* Fletcher, Heald & Hildreth
Nat'l Network: MYTV *Nat'l Reps:* Petry Television Inc.
Jeff McDonald, Operations Dir
Jeff Christenbury, Station Manager
Douglas Finck, General Sales Mgr
Cory Culleton, Local Sales Manager

WPXT *Digital Channel:* 43 *Virtual Channel:* 51; 137.4 kw; 833 ft.; N43 51 6 W70 19 40
Pegasus Corp. Office, 225 Cty Lne Ave. Str 200, Bala Cynwyd, PA 19004 US
(207) 774-0051, *Fax:* (207) 774-6849
www.ourmaine.com
comments@ourmaine.com
License: Portland, Cumberland County, ME held by New Age Media of Maine License LLC.
(acq 3-31-2007; grpsl); *Ownership:* Sedgwick Media LLC, 65%; Frank M. Henry, 33.64%; Michael Yanuzzi, 1.36%; *Washington Law Firm:* Fletcher, Heald & Hildreth
Nat'l Network: CW *Nat'l Reps:* Petry Television Inc.
Emily Lamoureux, Operations Dir
Douglas Finck, General Manager
Jeff Christenbury, Programming Director
John Marshall, Promotions Manager
Jim Ledger, Chief Engineer
Chet Cook, IT Manager
Cory Culleton, Regional Sales Manager
JenParadis, Traffic/Operations Manager

Presque Isle, ME (DMA 204)

WAGM-TV *Digital Channel:* 8 *Virtual Channel:* 8; 10 kw; 1148 ft.; N46 33 4 W67 48 34
P.O. Box 1149, Presque Isle, ME 04769 US
(207) 764-4461, *Fax:* (207) 764-5329
www.wagmtv.com
wagmtv@wagmtv.com
License: Presque Isle, Aroostook County, ME held by NEPSK Inc
(acq 3-8-91; grpsl;; *Washington Law Firm:* Holland & Knight
Nat'l Network: CBS/FOX; Fox *Nat'l Reps:* Continental Television Sales *Wire Services:* AP
Size of News Staff: 12; *Hours of Local News Weekly:* news progmg 14 hrs wkly
Gordon Wark, General Manager
Linda Connolly, General Sales Mgr
Jon Gulliver, News Director
Brett Lovley, Chief Engineer

***WMEM-TV** *Digital Channel:* 10 *Virtual Channel:* 10; 14.5 kw; 1158 ft.; N46 33 6 W67 48 38
Mailing Address: 1450 Lisbon Street, Lewiston, ME 04240 US
Second Address: 65 Texas Ave., Bangor, ME 4401
(800) 884-1717,(207) 783-9101, *Fax:* (207) 783-5193,(207) 942-2857
www.mpbc.net
comments@mpbn.net
License: Presque Isle, Aroostook County, ME held by Maine Public Broadcasting Network
(acq 6-23-92;; *Washington Law Firm:* Dow, Lohnes PLLC
Nat'l Network: PBS
Foreign Language Programming
P. James Dowe, CEO

Maryland

Baltimore, MD (DMA 26)

WBAL-TV *Digital Channel:* 59 *Virtual Channel:* 11; 316 kw vis, 31.6 kw aur; 1,000t/998g; N39 20 05 W76 39 03; *Population Served:* 905,759
3800 Hooper Ave., Baltimore, MD 10106
(410) 467-3000, *Fax:* (410) 338-6238
www.wbaltv.com
License: Baltimore, Baltimore County, MD held by WBAL Hearst Television Inc.
Group Owner: Hearst Television Inc.; *Washington Law Firm:* Brooks, Pierce, McLendon, Humphrey & Leonard
Nat'l Network: NBC *Nat'l Reps:* Eagle Television Sales *Wire Services:* UPI
Size of News Staff: 63; *Hours of Local News Weekly:* news progmg 24 hrs wkly
Dan Joerres, General Manager
Barbara Anderson, General Sales Mgr
Wanda Draper, Programming Director
Steve Bamonti, Promotions Manager
Michelle Butt, News Director
Jeff=Halapin, Engineering Dir

WBFF *Digital Channel:* 46 *Virtual Channel:* 45; 655 kw; 1223 ft.; N39 20 10 W76 38 59
10706 Beaver Dam Road, Cockeysville, MD 21030 US
(410) 467-4545, *Fax:* (410) 467-5090
www.foxbaltimore.com
License: Baltimore, Baltimore County, MD held by Chesapeake Television Licensee L.L.C.
Group Owner: Sinclair Broadcast Group Inc.; (acq 9-10-90; grpsl;; *Washington Law Firm:* Shaw Pittman
Nat'l Network: FOX *Nat'l Reps:* TeleRep
Steve Moretz, Operations Dir
William Fanshawe, General Manager
Jennifer Furbay, Programming Director
Sharon Wylie, Promotions Manager
Scott Livingston, News Director
David Hackney, Chief Engineer
Peter Ferraro, PromotionsManager

WJZ-TV *Digital Channel:* 13 *Virtual Channel:* 13; 33.8 kw; 968 ft.; N39 20 5 W76 39 3
600 New Hampshire Ave NW, Suite 1200, Washington, DC 20037 US
(410) 466-0013, *Fax:* (410) 578-0642
www.wjz.com
newsroom@wjz.com
License: Baltimore, Baltimore County, MD held by CBS Corporation

Group Owner: CBS Television Stations Group; (acq 6-28-57; $4.4 million;; *Washington Law Firm:* Wilkes, Artis, Hedrick & Lane
Nat'l Network: CBS *Wire Services:* UPI
Jay Newman, Operations Dir
Bridget Hartman, General Sales Mgr
Michelle Dowd-Wood, Programming Director
Gail Bending, News Director
Rick Seaby, Engineering Dir
Susan Otradovec, Public Affairs Director

WMAR-TV *Digital Channel:* 38 *Virtual Channel:* 2; 1000 kw; 1024 ft.; N39 20 5 W76 39 3
312 Walnut Street, 28th Floor, Cincinnati, OH 45202 US
(410) 377-2222, *Fax:* (410) 377-0493
www.abc2news.com
hooper@wmar.com
License: Baltimore, Baltimore County, MD held by Scripps Howard Broadcasting Co.
Group Owner: The E. W. Scripps Co.; (acq 1991; $125 million;;
Washington Law Firm: Baker & Hostetler
Nat'l Network: ABC *Nat'l Reps:* Harrington, Righter & Parsons
Wire Services: AP
Bill Hooper, Operations Dir
Andrew Kinkead, General Sales Mgr
Darlene Dorman, Programming Director
Maria Mager, Promotions Manager
Kelly Groft, News Director
Paul Wilkerson, Chief Engineer

***WMPB** *Digital Channel:* 29 *Virtual Channel:* 67; 42.6 kw; 1014 ft.; N39 26 50 W76 46 48
11767 Owings Mills Blvd, Owing Mills, MD 21117 US
(410) 356-5600, *Fax:* (410) 581-6579
www.mpt.org
comments@mpt.org
License: Baltimore, Baltimore County, MD held by Maryland Public Broadcasting Commission
Washington Law Firm: Schwartz, Woods & Miller
Nat'l Network: PBS
Robert Shuman, President
Kirby Storms, General Manager
George Beneman, Programming Director
Larry Unger, Executive Vice President/Chief

***WMPT** *Digital Channel:* 42 *Virtual Channel:* 22; 516 kw; 951 ft.; N39 0 36 W76 36 33; *Rebroadcasting:* Rebroadcasts WMPB(TV) Baltimore 100%.
11767 Owings Mills Blvd, Owings Mills, MD 21117 US
(410) 356-5600, *Fax:* (410) 581-6579
www.mpt.org
comments@mpt.org
License: Annapolis, Anne Arundel County, MD held by Maryland Public Broadcasting Commission
Washington Law Firm: Schwartz, Woods & Miller
Nat'l Network: PBS
Robert Shuman, President
Kirby Storms, General Manager
George Beneman, Programming Director
Larry Unger, Executive Vice President/Chief

WNUV *Digital Channel:* 40 *Virtual Channel:* 54; 845 kw; 1223 ft.; N39 20 10 W76 38 59
3474 William Penn Highway, Pittsburgh, PA 15235 US
(410) 467-8854, *Fax:* (410) 467-5093
www.cwbaltimore.com
License: Baltimore, Baltimore County, MD held by Baltimore (WNUV-TV) Licensee Inc.
Group Owner: Cunningham Broadcasting Corporation; (acq 1-9-2002).; *Washington Law Firm:* Arter & Hadden
Nat'l Network: CW
Steve Moretz, Operations Dir
William Fanshawe, General Manager
Billy Robbins, General Sales Mgr
Jennifer Furbay, Programming Director
Sharon Wylie, Promotions Manager
David Hackney, Chief Engineer
Peter Ferraro, PromotionsManager

WUTB *Digital Channel:* 41 *Virtual Channel:* 24; 290 kw; 1027 ft.; N39 17 15 W76 45 38
132 South Rodeo Drive, 4th Floor, Beverly Hills, CA 90212 US
(410) 358-2400, *Fax:* (410) 764-7232
www.my24wutb.com
wttg-hr@foxtv.com
License: Baltimore, Baltimore County, MD held by Fox Television Stations Inc.
Group Owner: Fox Television Stations Inc.; (acq 7-31-2001; grpsl).; *Washington Law Firm:* Law Offices of Hogan & Hartson
Nat'l Network: MY NETWORK *Nat'l Reps:* Fox Stations Sales
Alan Sawyer, Operations Dir
Brock Abernathy, General Sales Mgr
Dan Carlin, Programming Director
Michael O'Toole, Promotions Manager
Duane Myers, Chief Engineer
Martha Palmer, National Sales Manager
Eduardo Zuniga, TrafficManager

Pittsburgh, PA (DMA 23)

***WGPT** *Digital Channel:* 36 *Virtual Channel:* 36; 100 kw; 935 ft.; N39 24 14 W79 17 37; *Rebroadcasting:* Rebroadcasts WMPB(TV) Baltimore 100%.
11767 Owings Mills Blvd., Owings Mills, MD 21117 US
(410) 356-5600, *Fax:* (410) 581-6579
www.mpt.org
comments@mpt.org
License: Oakland, Garrett County, MD held by Maryland Public Broadcasting Commission
Washington Law Firm: Schwartz, Woods & Miller
Nat'l Network: PBS
Robert Shuman, President
Kirby Storms, General Manager
George Beneman, Programming Director
Larry Unger, Executive Vice President/Chief

Salisbury, MD (DMA 144)

WBOC-TV *Digital Channel:* 21 *Virtual Channel:* 16; 740 kw; 915 ft.; N38 30 17 W75 38 37
Mailing Address: 1729 N.Salisbury Blvd., Salisbury, MD 21801 US
Second Address: 1729 N. Salisbury Blvd., Salisbury, MD 21801
(410) 749-1111, *Fax:* (410) 749-2361
www.wboc.com
wboc@wboc.com
License: Salisbury, Wicomico County, MD held by WBOC Inc (acq 9-80; $8 million); *Washington Law Firm:* Covington & Burling
Nat'l Network: CBS AND FOX; Fox
Size of News Staff: 40; *Hours of Local News Weekly:* news progmg 31 hrs wkly
Craig Jahelka, Operations Dir
K. Jahelka, Station Manager
David Speicher, General Sales Mgr
Mary Borger, Promotions Manager
John Dearing, News Director
Danny Panicella, Chief Engineer
Steve Bach, Regional Sales Manager
BobBachman, Regional Sales Manager

***WCPB** *Digital Channel:* 28 *Virtual Channel:* 28; 132 kw; 509 ft.; N38 23 9 W75 35 33; *Rebroadcasting:* Rebroadcasts WMPB(TV) Baltimore 100%.
11767 Owings Mills Blvd, Owings Mills, MD 21117 US
(410) 356-5600, *Fax:* (410) 581-6579
www.mpt.org
comments@mpt-org
License: Salisbury, Wicomico County, MD held by Maryland Public Broadcasting Commission
Washington Law Firm: Schwartz, Woods & Miller
Nat'l Network: PBS
Robert Shuman, President
Kirby Storms, Operations Dir
George Beneman, Programming Director
Larry Unger, Executive Vice President/Chief

WMDT *Digital Channel:* 53 *Virtual Channel:* 47; 350 KW ERP Digital; TFU-20GTH-R C170SP; N38 30 06 W76 44 09;
Population Served: 248,969
Mailing Address: Box 4009, Salisbury, MD 32853
Second Address: 202 Downtown Plaza, Salisbury, MD 21801
(410) 742-4747, *Fax:* (410) 742-5767
www.wmdt.com
wmdt@wmdt.com
License: Salisbury, Wicomico County, MD held by Delmarva Broadcast Service LLC.
(acq 1982); *Washington Law Firm:* Fletcher, Heath, Hildreth
Nat'l Network: ABC; CW
Size of News Staff: 23; *Hours of Local News Weekly:* news progmg 23 hrs wkly
Kathleen McLain, General Manager
Phil Bankert, General Sales Mgr
Kathleen McLain, Programming Director
Kathleen McLain, Promotions Manager
Sarah Truitt, News Director
Bill Hoctor, Chief Engineer

Washington, DC (Hagerstown, MD) (DMA 9)

***WFPT** *Digital Channel:* 28 *Virtual Channel:* 62; 41.2 kw; 518 ft.; N39 15 37 W77 18 44; *Rebroadcasting:* Rebroadcasts WMPB(TV) Baltimore 100%.
11767 Owings Mills Blvd, Owings Mills, MD 21117 US
(410) 356-5600, *Fax:* (410) 581-6579
www.mpt.org
comments@mpt.org
License: Frederick, Frederick County, MD held by Maryland Public Broadcasting Commission
Washington Law Firm: Schwartz, Woods & Miller
Nat'l Network: PBS
Robert Shuman, President
Kirby Storms, General Manager
George Beneman, Programming Director
Larry Unger, Executive Vice President/Chief

WHAG-TV *Digital Channel:* 26 *Virtual Channel:* 25; 575 kw; 1234 ft.; N39 39 45 W77 57 54
18 Newbury Street, Boston, MA 02116 US
(301) 797-4400, *Fax:* (301) 733-1735,(301) 745-4093
www.your4state.com
hbreslin@ nbc25.com
License: Hagerstown, Washington County, MD held by Nexstar Broadcasting Inc.
Group Owner: Nexstar Broadcasting Group Inc.; (acq 12-31-2003; grpsl).; *Washington Law Firm:* Drinker Biddle & Reath L.L.P.
Nat'l Network: NBC *Nat'l Reps:* Continental Television Sales
Hours of Local News Weekly: News progmg 20 hrs wkly
Hugh Breslin, Operations Dir
Melissa Fountain, Promotions Manager
Mark Kraham, News Director
Michael Doty, Chief Engineer
Daniel McCarty, Traffic Manager

WJAL *Digital Channel:* 39 *Virtual Channel:* 68; 105 kw; 1220 ft.; N39 53 25 W77 58 5
Mailing Address: 262 Swamp Fox Road, State Highway 914, Chambersburg, PA 17201 US
Second Address: 262 Swamp Fox Rd., Chambersburg, PA 17201
(717) 375-4000, *Fax:* (717) 375-4052
www.wjal.com
adsales@wjal.com
License: Hagerstown, Washington County, MD held by Entravision Holdings LLC.
Group Owner: Entravision Communications Corp.; (acq 6-20-2001; $10.7 million including $400,000 bridge loan).;
Washington Law Firm: Leventhal, Senter & Lerman
Nat'l Network: UNIVISION
Hours of Local News Weekly: 5 hrs local news wkly
Steve Ullom, Station Manager
C. Griffen, Engineering Dir

***WWPB** *Digital Channel:* 44 *Virtual Channel:* 31; 500 kw; 1211 ft.; N39 39 4 W77 58 15; *Rebroadcasting:* Rebroadcasts WMPB(TV) Baltimore 100%.
11767 Owings Mills Blvd, Owings Mills, MD 21117 US
(410) 356-5600, *Fax:* (410) 581-6579
www.mpt.org
comments@mpt.org
License: Hagerstown, Washington County, MD held by Maryland Public Broadcasting Commission
Washington Law Firm: Schwartz, Woods & Miller
Nat'l Network: PBS
Robert Shuman, President
Kirby Storms, General Manager
George Beneman, Programming Director
Larry Unger, Executive Vice President/Chief

Massachusetts

Albany-Schenectady-Troy, NY (DMA 57)

WNYA *Digital Channel:* 13 *Virtual Channel:* 51; 12.69 kw; 988 ft.; N42 38 13 W73 59 45
US
(518) 381-3751, *Fax:* (518) 381-3740
www.my4albany.com
License: Pittsfield, Berkshire County, MA held by Venture Technologies Group LLC.
(acq 7-30-2003).; *Washington Law Firm:* Wiley, Rein LLP
Nat'l Network: MY NETWORK TV
Duncan Brown, General Manager
Alisha Siligato, Programming Director
progmg dir, Promotions Manager

Boston (Manchester, NH) (DMA 7)

WBPX-TV *Digital Channel:* 32; 1,000 kw vis; ant 1,184t/1,175g; N42 18 10 W71 13 07; *Population Served:* 6,366,400
1120 Soldiers Field Rd., Boston, MA 2134
(617) 787-6868, *Fax:* (617) 787-4114
www.ionline.tv
License: Boston, Suffolk County, MA held by ION Media Boston License, Inc., Debtor-in-possession
Group Owner: ION Media Networks Inc.; (acq 5-2-2000; grpsl).
Nat'l Network: ION Television *Wire Services:* Reuters
Hours of Local News Weekly: News progmg 20 hrs wkly
Dianne McLaughlin, Operations Dir
Dianne Sullivan, General Sales Mgr
Paul Strieby, Chief Engineer

WBZ-TV *Digital Channel:* 30 *Virtual Channel:* 4; 825 kw; 1280 ft.; N42 18 37 W71 14 14
600 New Hampshire Ave NW, Suite 1200, Washington, DC 20037 US
(617) 787-7000, *Fax:* (617) 787-5969
www.wbztv.com
webmaster@wbztv.com
License: Boston, Suffolk County, MA held by CBS Corporation
Group Owner: CBS Television Stations Group; *Washington Law Firm:* Wilkes, Artis, Hedrick & Lane
Nat'l Network: CBS *Nat'l Reps:* CBS TV Stations National Sales
Foreign Language Programming; Size of News Staff: 81; *Hours of Local News Weekly:* news progmg 20 hrs wkly
Ed Piette, President
Helen Wynyard, General Sales Mgr
Christine Ferrara, Programming Director
Peter Masucci, Promotions Manager
Jack Barry, Engineering Dir

WCVB-TV *Digital Channel:* 20 *Virtual Channel:* 5; 625 kw; 1280 ft.; N42 18 37 W71 14 14
888 Seventh Avenue, New York, NY 10106 US
(781) 449-0400, *Fax:* (781) 433-4510(news)/(781) 433-4022
www.thebostonchannel.com
wcvbnews@thebostonchannel.com
License: Boston, Suffolk County, MA held by WCVB Hearst-Argyle TV Inc.
Group Owner: Hearst-Argyle Television Inc.; (acq 7-16-97; grpsl)
Nat'l Network: ABC *Nat'l Reps:* Eagle Television Sales *Wire Services:* AP
Foreign Language Programming; Hours of Local News Weekly: News progmg 30 hrs wkly
Gloria Spence, CFO
Bill Fine, President
Joseph Rebelo, Operations Dir
Andy Hoffman, General Sales Mgr
Elizabeth Cheng, Programming Director
Andrew Vrees, News Director

WFXT *Digital Channel:* 31 *Virtual Channel:* 25; 780 kw; 1191 ft.; N42 18 10 W71 13 7
5151 Wisconsin Ave., NW, Washington, DC 20016 US
(781) 467-2525, *Fax:* (781) 467-7213
www.myfoxboston.com
newsdesk@myfoxboston.com
License: Boston, Suffolk County, MA held by Fox Television Stations Inc.
Group Owner: Fox Television Stations Inc.; (acq 7-95;
Nat'l Network: FOX
Size of News Staff: 70; *Hours of Local News Weekly:* news progmg 7 hrs wkly
Gregg Kelley, Operations Dir
Peter Hennessey, General Sales Mgr
Tricia Maloney, Programming Director
Lisa Hall, News Director
Steve Harrington, Engineering Dir

***WGBH** *Digital Channel:* 19; 98 kw; 650 ft.; N42 12 42 W71 6 51
125 Western Avenue, Boston, MA 02134 US
(617) 300-2000, *Fax:* (617) 300-1013
www.wgbh.org
feedback@wgbh.org
License: Boston, Suffolk County, MA held by WGBH Educational Foundation
Washington Law Firm: Covington & Burling
Nat'l Network: PBS
Foreign Language Programming
Henry Becton Jr., Chairman
Jonathan Abbott, CEO
Benjamin Godley, President
Marita Rivero, General Manager

***WGBH-TV** *Digital Channel:* 19 *Virtual Channel:* 2; 700 kw; 1227 ft.; N42 18 37 W71 14 14
125 Western Avenue, Boston, MA 02134 US
(617) 300-5400, *Fax:* (617) 300-1026
www.wgbh.org
feedback@wgbh.org
License: Boston, Suffolk County, MA held by WGBH Educational Foundation
Washington Law Firm: Covington & Burling
Nat'l Network: PBS
Foreign Language Programming
Henry Becton Jr., Chairman
Jonathan Abbott, CEO
Marita Rivero, Operations Dir

WHDH *Digital Channel:* 42; 316 kw vis, 63.2 kw aur; 1,000t/1,069g; N42 18 40 W71 13 00; *Population Served:* 5,330,400
7 Bulfinch Pl., Boston, MA 2114
(617) 725-0777, *Fax:* (617) 723-6117
www.whdh.com
License: Boston, Suffolk County, MA held by WHDH-TV Co
Group Owner: Sunbeam Television Corp.; (acq 6-3-93; $204 million;; *Washington Law Firm:* Holland & Knight
Nat'l Network: NBC *Nat'l Reps:* TeleRep
Chris Wayland, General Manager
Robert Burns, General Sales Mgr
Joan McCready, Programming Director
Linda Miele, News Director
Jim Shultis, Chief Engineer
Paul Magnes, Local Sales Manager
Marcy Burt, National Sales Manager

WLVI *Digital Channel:* 41; 2,240 kw vis, 166 kw aur; ant 1,186t/1,201g; N42 18 12 W71 13 08; *Population Served:* 641,071
7 Bulfinch Pl., Boston, MA 2114
(617) 725-0777, *Fax:* (617) 723-6117
www.cw56.com
License: Cambridge, Middlesex County, MA held by WHDH-TV
Group Owner: Sunbeam Television Corp.; (acq 12-19-2006; $113.7 million); *Washington Law Firm:* Holland & Knight
Nat'l Network: CW *Nat'l Reps:* TeleRep
Size of News Staff: 44; *Hours of Local News Weekly:* news progmg 7 hrs wkly
Chris Wayland, General Manager
Robert Burns, General Sales Mgr
Joan McCready, Programming Director
Linda Miele, News Director
Jim Shultis, Chief Engineer
Heather Hazelton, Local Sales Manager
James DePaul, National SalesManager

WMFP *Digital Channel:* 18 *Virtual Channel:* 62; 1000 kw; 949 ft.; N42 18 27 W71 13 27
P.O. Box 305249, Nashville, TN 37230 US
(617) 720-1062
License: Lawrence, Essex County, MA held by MTB Boston Licensee LLC.
Group Owner: Multicultural Capital Trust; (acq 2-2-2009);
Washington Law Firm: Sciarrino & Shubert PLLC
Nat'l Network: IND
Bill Desmond, Station Manager
Stephen Marra, Chief Engineer

WPXG-TV *Digital Channel:* 33; 190 kw vis; ant 1,128t/259g; N43 11 04 W71 19 12; *Rebroadcasting:* Satellite of WBPX Boston.
1120 Soldiers Field Rd., Boston, MA 2134
(617) 787-6868, *Fax:* (617) 787-4114
www.ionline.tv
License: Concord, Merrimac County, NH held by ION Media Boston License, Inc., Debtor-in-possession
Group Owner: ION Media Networks Inc.; (acq 5-2-2000; grpsl)
Dianne McLaughlin, Operations Dir
Dianne Sullivan, General Sales Mgr
Paul Strieby, Chief Engineer

WSBK-TV *Digital Channel:* 39; 3,160 kw vis, 316 kw aur; ant 1,161t/1,013g; N42 18 12 W71 13 08; *Population Served:* 2,140,000
1170 Soldiers Field Rd., Boston, MA 20005
(617) 787-7000, *Fax:* (617) 787-5969
www.wbztv.com/tv38
webmaster@tv38.com
License: Boston, Suffolk County, MA held by CBS Corporation
Group Owner: CBS Television Stations Group; (acq 2-27-95;
Nat'l Network: MyNetworkTV
Hours of Local News Weekly: News progmg 4 hrs wkly
Ed Piette, President
Helen Wynyard, General Sales Mgr
Christine Ferrara, Programming Director
Peter Masucci, Promotions Manager
Jack Barry, Engineering Dir

WUNI *Digital Channel:* 29 *Virtual Channel:* 27; 270 kw; 1535 ft.; N42 20 9 W71 42 55
C/O Fletcher Et Al, 1300 N. 17th Street, Arlington, VA 22209 US
(781) 433-2727, *Fax:* (781) 433-2750,(781) 433-2701
www.wunitv.com
feedback@wunitv.com
License: Worcester, Worcester County, MA held by Entravision 27 L.L.C.
Group Owner: Entravision Communications Corp.; (acq 1-4-01; $47.5 million); *Washington Law Firm:* Thompson Hine LLP
Nat'l Network: UNIVISION *Wire Services:* AP
Foreign Language Programming; Size of News Staff: 13; *Hours of Local News Weekly:* news progmg 3 hrs wkly
Pam Dias, CFO
Bob Kerrigan, Operations Dir
Alexander von Lichtenberg, General Manager
Scott McGavick, General Sales Mgr
Renee Barbour, Programming Director
Meg Godin, Promotions Manager
Sara Suarez, News Director
Fran Vaccari,Chief Engineer
Rob Donner, National Sales Manager

WUTF-DT *Digital Channel:* 27; 3,311 kw vis; ant 1,168t/1,227g; N42 23 02 W71 29 37; *Population Served:* 2,200,000
71 Parmenter Rd., Hudson, MA 1749
(978) 562-0660, *Fax:* (978) 562-1166
www.univision.com
License: Marlborough, Middlesex County, MA held by Univision Partnership of Massachusetts.
Group Owner: Univision Communications Inc.; (acq 5-21-2001; grpsl).
Nat'l Network: TeleFutura (Spanish)
Foreign Language Programming
Rolo Duartes, General Manager
Scott McGavick, General Sales Mgr
Renee Barbour, Programming Director
Richard Peper, Chief Engineer

WWDP *Digital Channel:* 10 *Virtual Channel:* 46; 5 kw; 466 ft.; N42 0 38 W71 2 42
231 Bradley Place, Suite 204, Palm Beach, FL 33480 US
(952) 943-6000, *Fax:* (952) 943-6566
www.shopnbc.com
License: Norwell, Plymouth County, MA held by Norwell Television LLC
Nat'l Network: N/A
Jon Stoltz, Operations Dir

***WYDN** *Digital Channel:* 47 *Virtual Channel:* 48; 365 kw; 712 ft.; N42 18 27 W71 13 27
Mailing Address: P.O Box 2684, Worcester, MA 01613 US
Second Address: 99Asnebumskit Rd., Paxton, MA 1612
(817) 571-1229, *Fax:* (817) 571-7458
www.daystar.com
comments@daystar.com
License: Worcester, Worcester County, MA held by Educational Public TV Corp
Nat'l Network: IND
Arnold Toraz, General Manager

Providence, RI-New Bedford, MA (DMA 52)

WLWC *Digital Channel:* 22 *Virtual Channel:* 28; 350 kw; 666 ft.; N41 46 39 W70 55 41
630 Fifth Avenue, 27th Floor, New York, NY 10111 US
(401) 351-8828, *Fax:* (401) 351-0222
www.cw28tv.com
License: New Bedford, Bristol County, MA held by Providence TV Licensee Corp.
Group Owner: Four Points Media Group; (acq 11-21-2007; grpsl); *Washington Law Firm:* Wiley Rein LLP
Nat'l Network: CW *Nat'l Reps:* TeleRep
Tina Castano, General Manager
Joe Mulvey, General Sales Mgr

Springfield-Holyoke, MA (DMA 111)

***WGBY-TV** *Digital Channel:* 22 *Virtual Channel:* 57; 50 kw; 1004 ft.; N42 14 29 W72 38 56
44 Hampden Street, Springfield, MA 01103 US
(413) 781-2801, *Fax:* (413) 731-5093
www.wgby.org
feedback@wgby.org

License: Springfield, Hampden County, MA held by WGBH Educational Foundation
Washington Law Firm: Covington & Burling
Nat'l Network: PBS
Russell Peotter, Operations Dir
Lynn Page, Programming Director
Charley Rose, Promotions Manager
Ray Miller, Chief Engineer

WGGB-TV *Digital Channel:* 40 *Virtual Channel:* 40; 460 kw; 1063 ft.; N42 14 30 W72 38 57
10706 Beaver Dam Road, Cockeysville, MD 21030 US
(413) 733-4040, *Fax:* (413) 781-5733
www.wggb.com
License: Springfield, Hampden County, MA held by Gormally Broadcasting Licenses LLC
(acq 11-1-2007; $21.15 million); *Ownership:* Gormally Broadcasting LLC, 100%
Nat'l Network: ABC; Fox *Nat'l Reps:* Millennium Sales & Marketing *Regional Reps:* Millennium
Dean Davidson, Operations Dir
Dave Kaufman, General Manager
Gerry Dunn, General Sales Mgr
Carol Moran, Programming Director
David Baer, News Director
Jason Brusa, Production Manager

WWLP *Digital Channel:* 11 *Virtual Channel:* 22; 4,170 kw vis, 417 kw aur; 877t/530g; N42 05 05 W72 42 14
Mailing Address: Box 2210, Springfield, MA 01102
Second Address: One Broadcast Ctr., Chicopee, MA 1013
(413) 377-2200, *Fax:* (413) 377-2261
www.wwlp.com
License: Springfield, Hampden County, MA held by WWLP Broadcasting L.L.C.
Group Owner: LIN Television Corporation; (acq 10-20-2000; about $128 million); *Washington Law Firm:* Covington & Burling
Nat'l Network: NBC *Nat'l Reps:* Petry *Wire Services:* AP
William Pepin, General Manager
John Baran, Station Manager
Lowell McLane, Director of Sales
Anna Giza, Promotions Manager
Michael Garreffi, News Director
Dave Cote, Chief Engineer

Michigan

Alpena, MI (DMA 208)

WBKB-TV *Digital Channel:* 11 *Virtual Channel:* 11; 20 kw; 662 ft.; N44 42 11 W83 31 26
1390 Bagley Street, Alpena, MI 49707 US
(989) 356-3434, *Fax:* (989) 356-4188
www.wbkb11.com
License: Alpena, Alpena County, MI held by Thunder Bay Broadcasting Corp
Washington Law Firm: Cohn & Marks
Nat'l Network: CBS; Fox *Nat'l Reps:* Millennium Sales & Marketing *Wire Services:* UPI
Size of News Staff: 6; *Hours of Local News Weekly:* news progmg 5.5 hrs wkly
Stephen Marks, President
Cher Allen, General Manager
Robert Race, Promotions Manager
Mark Nowak, Chief Engineer

***WCML** *Digital Channel:* 24 *Virtual Channel:* 6; 300 kw vis, 15.1 kw aur; ant 1,289t/1,148g; N45 08 18 W84 09 45;
Rebroadcasting: Satellite of WCMU-TV Mt. Pleasant.
Central Michigan Univ., 1999 E. Campus Dr., Mt. Pleasant, MI 48859
(989) 774-3105, *Fax:* (989) 774-4427
www.wcmu.org
schud1ra@cmich.edu
License: Alpena, Alpena County, MI held by Central Michigan University
Washington Law Firm: Dow, Lohnes & Albertson
Nat'l Network: PBS
Ed Grant, General Manager
Rick Schudiske, Station Manager
Kurt Wilson, General Sales Mgr
Linda Dielman, Programming Director
David Nichols, News Director
Wayne Henderson, Chief Engineer

Detroit (DMA 11)

WADL *Digital Channel:* 39 *Virtual Channel:* 38; 1000 kw; 558 ft.; N42 33 15 W82 53 15
35000 Adell Drive, Mt. Clemens, MI 48043 US
(586) 790-3838, *Fax:* (586) 790-3841
www.wadldetroit.com
License: Mount Clemens, Macomb County, MI held by Adell Broadcasting Corp
Nat'l Network: IND *Nat'l Reps:* Blair Television
Kevin Adell, CEO
Lewis Gibbs, President
Fredrica Crowe, General Sales Mgr
Jamie Harrington, Programming Director
Tom Ponsart, Chief Engineer
Evelyn Brown, Traffic Manager

WJBK *Digital Channel:* 7 *Virtual Channel:* 2; 27.2 kw; 1030 ft.; N42 27 38 W83 12 50
Mailing Address: 5151 Wisconsin Ave., NW, Washington, DC 20016 US
Second Address: 16550 W. Nine Mile Rd., Southfield, MI 48075
(248) 557-2000, *Fax:* (248) 557-6343(sls); (248) 557-1199(news)
www.myfoxdetroit.com
fox2newsdesk@foxtv.com
License: Detroit, Wayne County, MI held by New World Communications of Detroit, Inc.
Group Owner: Fox Television Stations Inc.; (acq 1-22-97; grpsl).
Nat'l Network: FOX *Wire Services:* Reuters
Size of News Staff: 140; *Hours of Local News Weekly:* news progmg 36 hrs wkly
Jeff Murri, Operations Dir
Sheila Bruce, General Sales Mgr
Kelly Collins, Programming Director
Terry D'Esposito, Promotions Manager
Dana Hahn, News Director
Tim Redmond, Engineering Dir
Keith Stironek, Creative Services VicePresident
Ann Marie Carlton, National Sales Manager
Katie Fehr, Public Affairs Director

WKBD-TV *Digital Channel:* 14; 2,340 kw vis, 209 kw aur; ant 960t/1,053g; N42 29 01 W83 18 44; *Population Served:* 5,521,787
26905 W. 11 Mile Rd., Southfield, MI 48034
(248) 355-7000, *Fax:* (248) 359-7494
www.cw50detroit.com
shows@wkbdtv.com
License: Detroit, Wayne County, MI held by Detroit Television Station WKBD Inc.
Group Owner: CBS Television Stations Group; (acq 9-1-93; $105 million;
Nat'l Network: CW *Nat'l Reps:* TeleRep
Trey Fabacher, Operations Dir
Stephen Danowski, General Sales Mgr
Paul Prange, Programming Director
Pam Baumann, Promotions Manager
Chuck Davis, Engineering Dir

WMYD *Digital Channel:* 21 *Virtual Channel:* 20; 500 kw; 1063 ft.; N42 26 53 W83 10 23
767 Third Avenue, 34th Floor, New York, NY 10017 US
(248) 355-2020, *Fax:* (248) 355-0368
www.tv20detroit.com
License: Detroit, Wayne County, MI held by WXON License Inc.
Group Owner: Granite Broadcasting Corp.; (acq 1-31-97; $175 million); *Washington Law Firm:* Akin, Gump, Strauss, Hauer & Feld
Nat'l Network: MYTV
David Bangura, General Manager
Dan Riley, Chief Engineer
Denny Vinchook, National Sales Manager

WPXD-TV *Digital Channel:* 31; 1,230 kw vis, 217 kw aur; ant 1,080t/1,044g; N42 22 25 W84 04 10
3975 Varsity Dr., Ann Arbor, MI 48108
(734) 973-7900, *Fax:* (734) 973-7906
www.iontelevision.com
helenskinner@ionmedia.com
License: Ann Arbor, Washtenaw County, MI held by Paxson Communications License Co. L.L.C.
Group Owner: ION Media Networks Inc.; (acq 12-11-97; $35 million including LPTV ch); *Washington Law Firm:* Verner, Liipfert, Bernhard, McPherson & Hand
Nat'l Network: ION Television
Helen Skinner, Operations Dir
Robert Thompson, Engineering Dir

***WTVS** *Digital Channel:* 43; 2,200 kw vis, 200 kw aur; 961t/1,020g; N42 29 01 W83 18 44; *Population Served:* 4,500,000
(dba/Detroit Public Television)
Riley Broadcast Ctr, 1 Clover Ct, Wixom, MI 48202
(248) 305-3788, *Fax:* (248) 305-3980
www.dptv.org
email@dptv.org
License: Detroit, Wayne County, MI held by Detroit Educational Television Foundation
Ownership: Detroit Educational Television Foundation;
Washington Law Firm: Schwartz, Woods & Miller
Nat'l Network: PBS *Regional Reps:* Karole White
Melanie Colaianne, Chairman
Rich Homberg, CEO
Daniel Gaitens, Programming Director
John Mark, Chief Engineer
John Wenzel, CFO
Dan Alpert, Sr Vice President Development/Communications
Jeff Forster, Sr Vice PresidentProduction/Station Enterprises
Georgeann Herbert, Sr Vice President Content/Engagement

WWJ-TV *Digital Channel:* 44 *Virtual Channel:* 62; 425 kw; 1060 ft.; N42 26 53 W83 10 23
600 New Hampshire Ave,NW, Suite 1200, Washington, DC 20037 US
(248) 355-7000, *Fax:* (248) 359-7499
www.wwjtv.com
shows@wwjtv.com
License: Detroit, Wayne County, MI held by CBS Broadcasting Inc.
Group Owner: CBS Television Stations Group; (acq 1995; $24 million); *Washington Law Firm:* Hogan & Hartson
Nat'l Network: CBS *Nat'l Reps:* CBS TV Stations National Sales
Trey Fabacher, Operations Dir
Mike Montano, General Sales Mgr
Paul Prange, Programming Director
Pam Shecter, Promotions Manager
Chuck Davis, Engineering Dir
Carol Cain, Community Affairs
Pam Baumann, Creative ServicesDirector
Jennifer Purtan, Vice President

WXYZ-TV *Digital Channel:* 41 *Virtual Channel:* 7; 1000 kw; 1001 ft.; N42 28 14 W83 15 1
20777 West Ten Mile Road, Southfield, MI 48037 US
(248) 827-7777, *Fax:* (248) 827-9444
www.wxyz.com
wxyzdesk@wxyz.com
License: Detroit, Wayne County, MI held by Channel 7 of Detroit Inc.
Group Owner: The E. W. Scripps Co.; (acq 1-2-86; grpsl);
Washington Law Firm: Baker & Hostetler
Nat'l Network: ABC *Nat'l Reps:* Eagle Television Sales *Wire Services:* Reuters
Robert Silva, Operations Dir
Mike Murri, General Sales Mgr
Gary Schlaff, Programming Director
Andrea Parquet-Taylor, News Director
Ray Thurber, Engineering Dir
Steve Kopicki, National Sales Manager
Mike MacLean, Regional SalesManager

Flint-Saginaw-Bay City, MI (DMA 66)

WAQP *Digital Channel:* 48 *Virtual Channel:* 49; 851 kw; 942 ft.; N43 13 18 W84 3 14
P.O. Box 1010, Marion, IL 62959 US
(989) 249-5969
waqp@tct.tv,waqp@.tct.tv
License: Saginaw, Saginaw County, MI held by TCT of Michigan Inc.
Group Owner: Tri-State Christian Television
Nat'l Network: IND
Shane Chaney, CFO
Garth Coonce, President
Tina Coonce, Operations Dir
Chris Gabriel, General Manager
John W. Dady, Chief Engineer

WBSF *Virtual Channel:* 46; 1,600 kw vis; ant 1,004t/1,023g; N43 28 26.75 W83 50 44.65; *Population Served:* 104,868
2225 W. Willard Rd., Clio, MI 60045
(810) 687-1000,(989) 755-0525, *Fax:* (810) 687-4925
www.miNBCnews.com
mail@nbc25.net
License: Bay City, Bay County, MI held by Barrington Bay City License LLC.

Group Owner: Barrington Broadcasting Group, LLC.; (acq 4-14-2005; $4.5 million for CP); *Washington Law Firm:* Covington & Burling LLP
Nat'l Network: CW *Nat'l Reps:* HRP *Wire Services:* AP
Becky Butcher, President
Jeff Reinarz, Operations Dir
Becky Butcher, General Manager
Becky Butcher, General Sales Mgr
Sherry Cudd, Programming Director
Jeff Reinarz, Promotions Manager
Kathy Reynolds, News Director
Mark Olson,Chief Engineer

***WCMU-TV** *Digital Channel:* 26 *Virtual Channel:* 14; 450 kw vis; ant 981t/941g; N43 45 11 W85 12 40; *Population Served:* 151,000
Central Michigan Univ., 1999 E. Campus Dr., Mount Pleasant, MI 48859
(989) 774-3105, *Fax:* (989) 774-4427
www.wcmu.org
schud1ra@cmich.edu
License: Mount Pleasant, Isabella County, MI held by Central Michigan University
Washington Law Firm: Dow, Lohnes & Albertson
Nat'l Network: PBS
Ed Grant, General Manager
Rick Schudiske, Station Manager
Kurt Wislon, General Sales Mgr
Linda Dielman, Programming Director
David Nicholas, News Director
Wayne Henderson, Engineering Dir

***WDCQ-TV** *Digital Channel:* 15 *Virtual Channel:* 35; 200 kw; 1014 ft.; N43 32 33 W83 39 37
Delta Rd., University Center, MI 48710 US
(877) 472-7677, (989) 686-9362, *Fax:* (989) 686-0155
www.deltabroadcasting.org
wdcq@delta.edu
License: Bad Axe, Huron County, MI held by Delta College
Washington Law Firm: Cohn & Marks
Nat'l Network: PBS
Jean Goodnow, CEO
Barry Baker, General Manager
Tom Garnett, Chief Engineer

WEYI-TV *Digital Channel:* 30 *Virtual Channel:* 25; 2,040 kw vis, 203 kw aur; ant 1,296t/1,292g; N43 13 01 W83 43 17; *Population Served:* 104,868
2225 W. Willard Rd., Clio, MI 75201
(810) 687-1000,(989) 755-0525, *Fax:* (810) 687-4925
www.miNBCnews.com
mail@nbc25.net
License: Saginaw, Saginaw County, MI held by Barrington Broadcasting Flint Corp.
Group Owner: Barrington Broadcasting Group, LLC.; (acq 5-14-2004; $24 million); *Washington Law Firm:* Covington & Burling LLP
Nat'l Network: NBC *Nat'l Reps:* HRP *Wire Services:* AP
Hours of Local News Weekly: News progmg 19.5 hrs wkly
Becky Butcher, President
Jeff Reinarz, Operations Dir
Becky Butcher, General Manager
Becky Butcher, General Sales Mgr
Sherry Cudd, Programming Director
Jeff Reinarz, Promotions Manager
Kathy Reynolds, News Director
Mark Olson,Chief Engineer

***WFUM** *Digital Channel:* 28; 17.5 kw; 489 ft.; N42 53 57 W83 27 42
5000 Ls&A Building, 5th Floor, Flint, MI 48109 US
(810) 762-3028, *Fax:* (810) 233-6017
www.michigantelevision.org
information@michigantelevision.org
License: Flint, Genesee County, MI held by Board of Regents, University of Michigan
Washington Law Firm: Dow, Lohnes PLLC
Nat'l Network: PBS
Steve Schram, General Manager
Jennifer White, Station Manager
Wayne Henderson, Chief Engineer

WJRT-TV *Digital Channel:* 12 *Virtual Channel:* 12; 30 kw; 938 ft.; N43 13 49 W84 3 32
2302 Lapeer Road, Flint, MI 48503 US
(810) 233-3130, *Fax:* (810) 257-2834
www.abc12.com
wjrt@abc.com
License: Flint, Genesee County, MI held by Flint License Subsidiary Corp., a wholly owned subsidiary of WJRT Inc.
Group Owner: ABC Inc.; (acq 1995; $155 million with WTVG(TV) Toledo, OH).
Nat'l Network: ABC *Nat'l Reps:* ABC National Television Sales
Wire Services: ESSA Weather Service; AP
Size of News Staff: 49; *Hours of Local News Weekly:* news progmg 34 hrs wkly
Thomas Bryson, President
Rick Roffman, Operations Dir
Daniel Aube, General Sales Mgr
Sara Jo Gallock, Programming Director
James Bleicher, News Director
Skip Orvis, Engineering Dir
Diane Parker, Business Manager
Brock Rice,Local Sales Manager
Cheri Foss, National Sales Manager

WNEM-TV *Digital Channel:* 22 *Virtual Channel:* 5; 100 kw vis, 20 kw aur; ant 1,029t/1,049g; N43 28 13 W83 50 35; *Population Served:* 1,251,000
Mailing Address: Box 531, Saginaw, MI 48606
Second Address: 107 N. Franklin St., Saginaw, MI 48607
(989) 755-8191, *Fax:* (989) 758-2111,(989) 758-2112
www.wnem.com
wnem@wnem.com
License: Bay City, Bay County, MI held by Meredith Corp.
Group Owner: Meredith Broadcasting Group, Meredith Corp.; (acq 4-16-69; $11.5 million;; *Washington Law Firm:* Haley, Bader & Potts
Nat'l Network: CBS; MyNetworkTV *Nat'l Reps:* TeleRep
Al Blinke, Operations Dir
Jeff Guilbert, General Sales Mgr
Karen Frey, Promotions Manager
Ian Rubin, News Director
Garth Sims, Chief Engineer
Ken Frierson, Local Sales Manager

WSMH *Digital Channel:* 16 *Virtual Channel:* 66; 245 kw; 1199 ft.; N43 13 31 W84 4 33
10706 Beaver Dam Road, Cockeysville, MD 21030 US
(810) 785-8866, *Fax:* (810) 785-8963
www.wsmh.com
SEE WEB SITE
License: Flint, Genesee County, MI held by WSMH Licensee L.L.C.
Group Owner: Sinclair Broadcast Group Inc.; (acq 2-28-96; $33 million)
Nat'l Network: FOX *Nat'l Reps:* Millennium Sales & Marketing
Hours of Local News Weekly: News progmg 7 hrs wkly
John Hummel, General Manager
Chad Conklin, General Sales Mgr
Pete Glass, Chief Engineer

Grand Rapids-Kalamazoo-Battle Creek, MI (DMA 39)

***WGVK** *Digital Channel:* 5 *Virtual Channel:* 52; 10 kw; 554 ft.; N42 18 23 W85 39 25; *Rebroadcasting:* Rebroadcasts WGVU-TV Grand Rapids 100%.
College Landing, Allendale, MI 49401 US
(616) 331-6666, *Fax:* (616) 331-6625
www.wgvu.org
wgvu@gvsu.edu
License: Kalamazoo, Kalamazoo County, MI held by Grand Valley State University
Washington Law Firm: Mark Van Bergh
Nat'l Network: PBS
Size of News Staff: 15; *Hours of Local News Weekly:* news progmg one hr wkly
Michael Walenta, General Manager
Gary Hunt, General Sales Mgr
Carrie Corbin, Programming Director
Patrick Center, News Director
Robert Lumbert, Engineering Dir
Ken Kolbe, Asst General Manager
Scott VanderWerf, Music Critic
EdSpier, Traffic Manager

***WGVU-TV** *Digital Channel:* 11 *Virtual Channel:* 35; 41.5 kw; 853 ft.; N42 57 34.9 W85 53 44.9
301 West Fulton Street, Grand Rapids, MI 49504 US
(616) 331-6666, *Fax:* (616) 331-6625
www.wgvu.org
wgvu@gvsu.edu
License: Grand Rapids, Kent County, MI held by Grand Valley State University
Washington Law Firm: Mark Van Bergh
Nat'l Network: PBS
Michael Walenta, General Manager
Gary Hunt, General Sales Mgr
Carrie Corbin, Programming Director
Robert Lumbert, Engineering Dir
Ken Kolbe, Asst General Manager
Scott VanderWerf, Music Critic
Ed Spier, Traffic Manager

WLLA *Digital Channel:* 45 *Virtual Channel:* 64; 440 kw; 1085 ft.; N42 33 52 W85 27 31
Mailing Address: PO Box 3157, Kalamazoo, MI 49003 US
Second Address: 7048 N Ave., Kalamazoo, MI 49048
(269) 345-6421, *Fax:* (269) 345-5665
www.wlla.com
deloris@wlla.com
License: Kalamazoo, Kalamazoo County, MI held by Christian Faith Broadcast, Inc.
Group Owner: Christian Faith Broadcasting Inc.; (acq 1-13-86; $35,000;
Nat'l Network: IND
Richard Hawkins, General Manager
Barb Hawkins, Programming Director
Jacob Potter, Promotions Manager

WOOD-TV *Digital Channel:* 7 *Virtual Channel:* 8; 30 kw; 945 ft.; N42 41 14 W85 30 34
Mailing Address: 4 Richmond Square, Suite 200, Providence, RI 02906 US
Second Address: 120 College Ave. S.E., Grand Rapids, MI 49503
(616) 456-8888, *Fax:* (616) 456-5755 (news)
www.woodtv.com
woodtv@woodtv.com
License: Grand Rapids, Kent County, MI held by Wood License Co. LLC.
Group Owner: LIN Television Corporation; (acq 6-30-99).;
Washington Law Firm: Covington & Burling
Nat'l Network: NBC
Diane Kniowski, President
Eva Cooper, Operations Dir
Barb Klap, General Sales Mgr
Craig Cole, Programming Director
Kurtis Kaechele, Promotions Manager
Ken Selvig, Chief Engineer

WOTV *Digital Channel:* 20 *Virtual Channel:* 41; 270 kw; 1020 ft.; N42 34 15 W85 28 7
Mailing Address: 5200 West Dickman Road, Battle Creek, MI 49016 US
Second Address: 120 College Ave. S.E., Grand Rapids, MI 49503
(269) 968-9341, *Fax:* (269) 660-1222
www.wotv.com
wotv@wotv.com
License: Battle Creek, Calhoun County, MI held by Wood License Co. LLC
Group Owner: LIN Television Corporation; (acq 12-6-2001; $2.25 million); *Washington Law Firm:* Covington & Burling
Nat'l Network: ABC
Size of News Staff: 25; *Hours of Local News Weekly:* news progmg 13 hrs wkly
Diane Kniowski, President
Ann Young, General Sales Mgr
Craig Cole, Programming Director
Molly Kelly, Promotions Manager
Patti McGethgain, News Director
Dave Morse, Chief Engineer
Swaina Noble, National Sales Manager
EthanBeute, Promotions Manager

WTLJ *Digital Channel:* 24 *Virtual Channel:* 54; 310 kw; 928 ft.; N42 57 25 W85 54 7
10290 48th Avenue, Allendale, MI 49401 US
(616) 895-4154, *Fax:* (616) 892-4401
www.tct.tv
wtlj@tct.tv
License: Muskegon, Muskegon County, MI held by TCT of Michigan Inc.
Group Owner: Tri-State Christian Television; (acq 1-15-92; $1.5 million;
Nat'l Network: IND
Vic VanDeventer, General Manager
Frank Ayre, Chief Engineer

WWMT *Digital Channel:* 8 *Virtual Channel:* 3; 25 kw; 843 ft.; N42 37 56 W85 32 16
17666 Fitch, Irvine, CA 92614 US
(269) 388-3333, *Fax:* (269) 388-8228
www.wwmt.com
newschannel3@wwmt.com
License: Kalamazoo, Kalamazoo County, MI held by Freedom Broadcasting of Michigan Licensee L.L.C.
Group Owner: Freedom Communications Inc., Broadcast Division; (acq 7-18-98; $170 million with WLAJ(TV) Lansing).;
Washington Law Firm: Akin, Gump, Strauss, Hauer & Feld
Nat'l Network: CBS; CW *Nat'l Reps:* TeleRep

Hours of Local News Weekly: News progmg 25 hrs wkly
James Lutton, Operations Dir
James Wagner, General Sales Mgr
Susan Abraham, Programming Director
Mark Bishop, Promotions Manager
Kathy Younkin, News Director
Jim Steffey, Chief Engineer

WXMI *Digital Channel:* 19 *Virtual Channel:* 17; 725 kw; 1004 ft.; N42 41 15 W85 31 57
Wxmi(Tv), 3117 Plaza Drive, Ne, Grand Rapids, MI 49525 US
(616) 364-8722, *Fax:* (616) 364-8506
www.fox17online.com
feedback@wxmi.com
License: Grand Rapids, Kent County, MI held by Tribune Television Holdings, Inc., Debtor-in-possession
Group Owner: Tribune Broadcasting Co.; (acq 12-20-2007; grpsl)
Nat'l Network: FOX *Nat'l Reps:* Harrington, Righter & Parsons
Size of News Staff: 30; *Hours of Local News Weekly:* news progmg 4 hrs wkly
Patricia Kolb, Operations Dir
Jeff Cartwright, General Sales Mgr
Mark Krause, Programming Director
Travis Henkaline, Promotions Manager
Tim Dye, News Director
Dale Scholten, Chief Engineer
Rick Sarata, Regional Sales Manager

WZPX-TV *Digital Channel:* 44; 5,000 kw vis, 500 kw aur; 1,058t; N42 40 45 W85 03 57; *Population Served:* 4,500,000
2610 Horizon Dr. S.E., Suite E, Grand Rapids, MI 49546
(616) 222-4343, *Fax:* (616) 493-2677
www.ionline.tv
License: Battle Creek, Calhoun County, MI held by ION Media Battle Creek License, Inc., Debtor-in-possession
Group Owner: ION Media Networks Inc.; (acq 3-13-00; grpsl).
Nat'l Network: ION Television
Tina Hill, Station Manager
Richard Castanie, Chief Engineer

WZZM *Digital Channel:* 13; 295 kw vis, 63 kw aur; ant 1,000t/991g; N43 18 34 W85 54 44; *Population Served:* 635,000
645 Three Mile Rd, NW, Grand Rapids, MI 49544
(616) 785-1313, *Fax:* (616) 785-1301
www.wzzm13.com
management@wzzm13.com
License: Grand Rapids, Kent County, MI held by Combined Communications Corporation of Oklahoma Inc.
Group Owner: Gannett Broadcasting; (acq 1-27-97; grpsl).
Nat'l Network: ABC *Nat'l Reps:* TeleRep *Wire Services:* AP
Hours of Local News Weekly: 22
Janet Mason, President
Karen Kriscunas, Operations Dir
Kim Krause, General Sales Mgr
Chuck Mikowski, Programming Director
Pam Rankin, Promotions Manager
Stanton Tang, News Director
Catherine Behrendt, Programming & Commun

Lansing, MI (DMA 114)

WHTV *Digital Channel:* 34 *Virtual Channel:* 18; 13.6 kw; 863 ft.; N42 41 19 W84 22 35
23642 Calabasas Rd. #104, Calabasas, CA 91302 US
(517) 372-9497, *Fax:* (517) 372-9499
www.my18.tv
info@my18.tv
License: Jackson, Jackson County, MI held by Spartan-TV LLC
Nat'l Network: MY NETWORK TV
Lori Harper, Station Manager
Corey Cummings, Chief Engineer

WILX-TV *Digital Channel:* 10 *Virtual Channel:* 10; 30 kw; 979 ft.; N42 26 33 W84 34 21
500 American Road, Lansing, MI 48911 US
(517) 393-0110, *Fax:* (517) 393-8555
www.wilx.com
news@wilx.com
License: Onondaga, Ingham County, MI held by Gray Television Licensee, LLC
Group Owner: Gray Television Inc.; (acq 8-29-2002; grpsl).
Nat'l Network: NBC *Nat'l Reps:* Continental Television Sales
Size of News Staff: 45
Mike King, General Manager
Jim Beck, General Sales Mgr
Nicole Lenik, Programming Director
Craig Tucker, Promotions Manager
Kevin Ragan, News Director
Mike Winsky, Chief Engineer
Paul Crockett, Local Sales Manager

***WKAR-TV** *Digital Channel:* 40 *Virtual Channel:* 23; 425 kw; 969 ft.; N42 42 7 W84 24 48
283 Comm. Arts Bldg., East Lansing, MI 48824 US
(517) 432-9527, *Fax:* (517) 353-7124
www.wkar.org
mail@wkar.org
License: East Lansing, Ingham County, MI held by Michigan State University
Washington Law Firm: Schwartz, Woods & Miller
Nat'l Network: PBS
De Anne Hamilton, General Manager
Kent Wieland, Station Manager
Cindy Herfindahl, General Sales Mgr
Jeanie Croope, Promotions Manager
Gary Blievernicht, Engineering Dir

WLAJ *Digital Channel:* 51 *Virtual Channel:* 53; 900 kw; 984 ft.; N42 25 13 W84 31 25
17666 Fitch, Irvine, CA 92614 US
(517) 394-5300, *Fax:* (517) 887-0077
www.wlaj.com
License: Lansing, Ingham County, MI held by WLAJ License Inc.
Group Owner: Freedom Communications Inc., Broadcast Division; (acq 6-22-98; $170 million with WWMT(TV) Kalamazoo).
Nat'l Network: ABC; CW
Size of News Staff: 10; *Hours of Local News Weekly:* news progmg 5 hrs wkly
Jim Wareham, Operations Dir
Susan Angel, General Sales Mgr
Jim Fordyce, News Director
Mike Winsky, Chief Engineer

WLNS-TV *Digital Channel:* 36 *Virtual Channel:* 6; 984 kw; 945 ft.; N42 41 19 W84 22 35
2820 East Saginaw, Lansing, MI 48901 US
(517) 372-8282, *Fax:* (517) 374-7610
www.wlns.com
wlns@wlns.com
License: Lansing, Ingham County, MI held by Young Broadcasting of Lansing, Inc., Debtor-in-possession
Group Owner: Young Broadcasting Inc.; (acq 9-15-86; $72 million;; *Washington Law Firm:* Wiley, Rein & Fielding
Nat'l Network: CBS
Gene Shanahan, Operations Dir
Don Carmichael, General Manager
Doug Powers, Station Manager
Clay Koenig, General Sales Mgr
Teresa Morton, Programming Director
Jam Sardar, News Director
Cory Cumming, Chief Engineer

WSYM-TV *Digital Channel:* 38 *Virtual Channel:* 47; 933 kw; 922 ft.; N42 28 3 W84 39 6
P.O. Box 693, Milwaukee, WI 53201 US
(517) 484-7747, *Fax:* (517) 484-9750
www.fox47news.com
fox47news@fox47news.com
License: Lansing, Ingham County, MI held by Journal Broadcast Corp.
Group Owner: Journal Communications Inc.; (acq 11-9-85;;
Washington Law Firm: Crowell & Moring
Nat'l Network: FOX *Nat'l Reps:* Harrington, Righter & Parsons
Size of News Staff: 22; *Hours of Local News Weekly:* news progmg 10 hrs wkly
Gary Baxter, Operations Dir
Jami Anderson, General Sales Mgr
Kip Bohne, Promotions Manager

Marquette, MI (DMA 180)

WBKP *Digital Channel:* 5 *Virtual Channel:* 5; 6.4 kw; 988 ft.; N47 2 11 W88 41 43
1122 Calumet Ave #5, Calumet, MI 49913 US
(906) 204-2436, *Fax:* (906) 204-2433
www.tv5and20.com
510@lscbc.com
License: Calumet, Houghton County, MI held by Lake Superior Community Broadcasting Corp.
Group Owner: Lake Superior Community Broadcasting Corp.; (acq 1-15-2004; $500,000 with WBUP(TV) Ishpeming)
Nat'l Network: CW TELEVISION N
Size of News Staff: 7; *Hours of Local News Weekly:* news progmg 10 hrs wkly
Cher Allen, General Manager
Tim Thompson, General Sales Mgr
Burns Severson, Promotions Manager
Gerry Heyn, Chief Engineer

WBUP *Digital Channel:* 10 *Virtual Channel:* 10; 4.8 kw; 344 ft.; N46 21 10 W87 51 15
201 E. Front Street, Traverse City, MI 49684 US
(906) 204-2436, *Fax:* (906) 204 2433
www.tv5and10.com
510@lscbc.com
License: Ishpeming, Marquette County, MI held by Lake Superior Community Broadcasting Corp.
Group Owner: Lake Superior Community Broadcasting Corp.; (acq 1-15-2004; $500,000 with WBKP(TV) Calumet).;
Washington Law Firm: Latham and Watkins
Nat'l Network: ABC
Cher Allen, General Manager
Tim Thompson, General Sales Mgr
Burns Severson, Promotions Manager
Gerry Heyn, Chief Engineer

WDHS *Digital Channel:* 8 *Virtual Channel:* 8; 22 kw; 561 ft.; N45 49 10 W88 2 35
3501 Broadway, Mount Vernon, IL 62864 US
(906) 776-8888, *Fax:* (906) 776-8888
License: Iron Mountain, Dickinson County, MI held by W. Russell Withers Jr.
Group Owner: Withers Broadcasting Co.
Nat'l Network: N/A
Sue Quadrani, General Manager

WJMN-TV *Digital Channel:* 48 *Virtual Channel:* 3; 1000 kw; 1165 ft.; N46 8 5 W86 56 55; *Rebroadcasting:* Satellite of WFRV-TV Green Bay, WI.
600 New Hampshire Ave, NW, Ste 1200, Washington, DC 20037 US
(920) 437-5411,(906) 226-3023 (sales), *Fax:* (920) 437-5769 (news)
www.wjmntv.com
License: Escanaba, Delta County, MI held by WFRV and WJMN Television Station Inc.
Group Owner: Liberty Media Corp.; (acq 4-16-2007; with WFRV-TV Green Bay, WI)
Nat'l Network: CBS *Nat'l Reps:* TeleRep
R. Perry Kidder, President
Dale Mitchell, Operations Dir
Jackie Stewart, General Sales Mgr
Jaci Haakonson, Programming Director
Kristen Kent, Promotions Manager
H. Lee Hitter, News Director
Mike Smith, National Sales Manager
Erin Davisson, News Commentator
Kit Overlock, Regional Sales Manager
Jill Harkoff, Traffic Manager

WLUC-TV *Digital Channel:* 35 *Virtual Channel:* 6; 100 kw vis, 20 kw aur; ant 978t/1,018g; N46 20 11 W87 50 55; *Population Served:* 292,600
177 U.S. 41 East, Negaunee, MI 36104
(906) 475-4161, *Fax:* (906) 475-4824
www.UpperMichigansSource.com
tv6@wluctv6.com
License: Marquette, Marquette County, MI held by Barrington Marquette License LLC.
Group Owner: Barrington Broadcasting Group, LLC.; (acq 8-11-2006; grpsl); *Washington Law Firm:* Covington & Burling
Nat'l Network: NBC *Nat'l Reps:* Harrington, Righter & Parsons
Wire Services: AP
Foreign Language Programming; Size of News Staff: 17; *Hours of Local News Weekly:* news progmg 16 hrs wkly
Rob Jamros, President
Sonny Reschka, Operations Dir
Dan Di Loreto, General Sales Mgr
Kim Parker, Programming Director
Brian Cabell, News Director

***WNMU** *Digital Channel:* 33; 316 kw vis, 63.1 kw aur; 1,090t/1,000g; N46 21 09 W87 51 32; *Population Served:* 250,000
Northern Michigan Univ., 1401 Presque Isle Ave., Marquette, MI 49855-5301
(906) 227-9668, *Fax:* (906) 227-2905
www.nmu.edu/wnmutv
tv13@nmu.edu
License: Marquette, Marquette County, MI held by Board of Control of Northern Michigan University
Washington Law Firm: Cohn & Marks
Nat'l Network: PBS *Wire Services:* UPI
Hours of Local News Weekly: News progmg one hr wkly
Eric Smith, General Manager
Bruce Turner, Station Manager

WZMQ *Digital Channel:* 19 *Virtual Channel:* 19; 31 kw; 577 ft.; N46 30 8 W87 38 52
1146 19th St.NW Ste 200, Washington, DC 20036 US

(906) 360-9699, *Fax:* (920) 785-0480
gm@wzmqtv.com
License: Marquette, Marquette County, MI held by MMMRC, LLC (acq 4-15-2009); *Ownership:* MMMRC, LLC
Nat'l Network: FOX
Paul Belschner, President
Danny Hood, General Manager

Traverse City-Cadillac, MI (DMA 117)

***WCMV** *Digital Channel:* 17 *Virtual Channel:* 27; 338 kw; 1289 ft.; N44 44 53 W85 4 8; *Rebroadcasting:* Rebroadcasts WCMU(TV) Mt. Pleasant 100%.
3965 E. Broomfield Rd, Mt. Pleasant, MI 48859 US
(989) 774-3105, *Fax:* (989) 774-4427
www.wcmu.org
schud1r@cmich.edu
License: Cadillac, Wexford County, MI held by Central Michigan University
Washington Law Firm: Dow, Lohnes & Albertson
Nat'l Network: PBS
Rick Schudiske, Operations Dir
Edwards Grant, General Manager

***WCMW** *Digital Channel:* 21 *Virtual Channel:* 21; 50 kw vis; ant 305t/277g; N44 03 57 W86 19 58; *Rebroadcasting:* Satellite of WCMU-TV Mt. Pleasant
Central Michigan Univ., 1999 E. Campus Dr., Mt. Pleasant, MI 48859
(989) 774-3105, *Fax:* (989) 774-4427
www.wcmu.org
schud1ra@cmich.edu
License: Manistee, Manistee County, MI held by Central Michigan University
Washington Law Firm: Dow, Lohnes & Albertson
Nat'l Network: PBS
Ed Grant, General Manager
Rick Schudiske, Station Manager
Kurt Wilson, General Sales Mgr
Linda Dielman, Programming Director
David Nicholas, News Director
Wayne Henderson, Chief Engineer

WFQX-TV *Digital Channel:* 32 *Virtual Channel:* 33; 200 kw; 1385 ft.; N44 8 12 W85 20 33
Mailing Address: 7400 South 45 Road, Cadillac, MI 49601 US
Second Address: 7669 S. 45 Rd., Cadillac, MI 49601
(231) 775-9813, *Fax:* (231) 775-3671
www.mifox32.com
info@mifox32.com
License: Cadillac, Wexford County, MI held by Cadillac Telecasting Co.
Group Owner: Cadillac Telecasting Co.; (acq 10-31-2007; $11 million with WFUP(TV) Vanderbilt); *Washington Law Firm:* Womble, Carlyle, Sandridge & Rice PLLC
Nat'l Network: FOX
Hours of Local News Weekly: News progmg 3 hrs wkly
William Kring, General Manager

WFUP *Digital Channel:* 45 *Virtual Channel:* 45; 108 kw; 1063 ft.; N45 10 12 W84 45 4; *Rebroadcasting:* Satellite of WFQX-TV Cadillac
Mailing Address: 7669 South 45 Road, Cadillac, MI 49601 US
Second Address: 7669 S. 45 Rd., Cadillac, MI 49601
(231) 775-9813, *Fax:* (231) 775-3671
www.fox33.com
info@fox33.com
License: Vanderbilt, Otsego County, MI held by Cadillac Telecasting Co.
Group Owner: Cadillac Telecasting Co.; (acq 10-31-2007; $11 million with WFQX-TV Cadillac); *Washington Law Firm:* Womble, Carlyle, Sandridge & Rice PLLC
Nat'l Network: FOX
Size of News Staff: 5; *Hours of Local News Weekly:* news progmg 3 hrs wkly
William Kring, General Manager

WGTQ *Digital Channel:* 8 *Virtual Channel:* 8; 15 kw; 945 ft.; N46 3 8 W84 6 38; *Rebroadcasting:* Satellite of WGTU(TV) Traverse City, rebroadcast 100%.
201 East Front St, Traverse City, MI 49684 US
(231) 946-2900, *Fax:* (231) 946-0945
www.upnorthlive.com
wgtu@wgtu.com
License: Sault Ste. Marie, Chippewa County, MI held by Tucker Broadcasting of Traverse City Inc.
Group Owner: Tucker Broadcasting of Traverse City Inc.; (acq 4-1-2008; $10 million with WGTU(TV) Traverse City); *Washington Law Firm:* Pillsbury Winthrop Shaw Pittman LLP
Nat'l Network: ABC
Jill Saarela, President
Betsy Bard, General Sales Mgr
Mary Speck, Programming Director
David Pistor, Local Sales Manager
Kim St. Mary, Media Operations Manager

WGTU *Digital Channel:* 29 *Virtual Channel:* 29; 68.4 kw; 1289 ft.; N44 44 53 W85 4 8
201 East Front Street, Traverse City, MI 49684 US
(231) 946-2900, *Fax:* (231) 946-0945
www.upnorthlive.com
wgtu@wgtu.com
License: Traverse City, Grand Traverse County, MI held by Tucker Broadcasting of Traverse City Inc.
Group Owner: Tucker Broadcasting of Traverse City Inc.; (acq 4-1-2008; $10 million with WGTQ(TV) Sault Ste. Marie); *Washington Law Firm:* Pillsbury Winthrop Shaw Pittman LLP
Nat'l Network: ABC
Jill Saarela, President
Betsy Bard, General Sales Mgr
Mary Speck, Programming Director
David Pistor, Local Sales Manager
Kim St. Mary, Media Operations Manager

WPBN-TV *Digital Channel:* 47 *Virtual Channel:* 7; 500 kw; 1289 ft.; N44 44 53 W85 4 8
Mailing Address: Rsa Tower Suite 710, 201 Monroe Street, Montgomery, AL 36104 US
Second Address: 8513 M-72 West, Traverse City, MI 49684-5562
(231) 947-7770, *Fax:* (231) 947-0354,(231) 947-1229
www.tv7-4.com
tv7-4@tv7-4.com
License: Traverse City, Grand Traverse County, MI held by Barrington Traverse City License LLC.
Group Owner: Barrington Broadcasting Group, LLC.; (acq 8-11-2006; grpsl).; *Washington Law Firm:* Covington & Burling
Nat'l Network: NBC *Nat'l Reps:* Harrington, Righter & Parsons
Jill Saarela, General Manager
Thom Pritz, General Sales Mgr
Mary Speck, Programming Director
Kim St. Mary, Promotions Manager
Doug DeYoung, News Director
Mike Miller, Chief Engineer

WTOM-TV *Digital Channel:* 35 *Virtual Channel:* 4; 78 kw; 551 ft.; N45 39 1 W84 20 37; *Rebroadcasting:* Satellite of WPBN-TV Traverse City
8518 M72 West, Traverse City, MI 49685 US
(231) 947-7770, *Fax:* (231) 947-1229,(231) 947-0354
www.tv7-4.com
tv7-4@tv7-4.com
License: Cheboygan, Cheboygan County, MI held by Barrington Traverse City License LLC.
Group Owner: Barrington Broadcasting Group, LLC.; (acq 8-11-2006; grpsl); *Washington Law Firm:* Covington & Burling
Nat'l Network: NBC
Jill Saarela, General Manager
Thom Pritz, General Sales Mgr
Mary Speck, Programming Director
Kim St. Mary, Promotions Manager
Doug DeYoung, News Director
Mike Miller, Chief Engineer

WWTV *Digital Channel:* 9 *Virtual Channel:* 9; 45 kw; 1631 ft.; N44 8 12 W85 20 33; *Rebroadcasting:* Satellite of WWUP-TV Sault Ste. Marie.
P. O. Box 627, Cadillac, MI 49601 US
(231) 775-3478, *Fax:* (231) 775-3671
www.9and10news.com
info@9and10news.com
License: Cadillac, Wexford County, MI held by Heritage Broadcasting Co. of Michigan.
Group Owner: Heritage Broadcasting Co of MI; (acq 3-3-89; grpsl;; *Ownership:* .; *Washington Law Firm:* Wamble Carlyle
Nat'l Network: CBS *Wire Services:* UPI
William Kring, General Manager
Sherri Magiera, Programming Director
Tessia Klix, Promotions Manager
Kevin Dunaway, News Director
Lowell Shore, Chief Engineer

WWUP-TV *Digital Channel:* 10 *Virtual Channel:* 10; 25 kw; 1214 ft.; N46 3 36 W84 5 57; *Rebroadcasting:* Satellite of WWTV-TV Cadillac
P.O. Box 627, Cadillac, MI 49601 US
(231) 775-3478, *Fax:* (231) 775-3671
www.9and10news.com
info@9and10news.com
License: Sault Ste. Marie, Chippewa County, MI held by Heritage Broadcasting Co. of Michigan.
Group Owner: Heritage Broadcasting Co of MI; (acq 3-3-89; grpsl;; *Washington Law Firm:* Wamble Carlyle
Nat'l Network: CBS
William Kring, General Manager
Sherri Magiera, Programming Director
Tessia Klix, Promotions Manager
Kevin Dunaway, News Director
Lowell Shore, Chief Engineer

Minnesota

Duluth, MN-Superior, WI (DMA 139)

KCWV *Digital Channel:* 27 *Virtual Channel:* 27; 40 kw; 679 ft.; N46 47 7 W92 7 15; *Not on Air/Target Date:* unknown
US
(901) 375-9324
License: Duluth, Saint Louis County, MN held by George S. Flinn III
George Flinn III, General Manager

KDLH *Digital Channel:* 33 *Virtual Channel:* 3; 381 kw; 1023 ft.; N46 47 21.3 W92 6 50.7
425 West Superior Street, Duluth, MN 55802 US
(218) 733-0303, *Fax:* (218) 720-9699
www.kdlh.com
news@kdlh.com; sales@kdlh.com
License: Duluth, Saint Louis County, MN held by Malara Broadcast Group of Duluth Licensee LLC.
Group Owner: Malara Broadcast Group Inc.; (acq 3-14-2005; $10.8 million); *Washington Law Firm:* Wolf Bloch
Nat'l Network: CBS; CW *Nat'l Reps:* Harrington, Righter & Parsons
Size of News Staff: 17; *Hours of Local News Weekly:* news progmg 12 hrs wkly
Anthony Malara, President
Kelli Latuska, Station Manager
Carl Keller, General Sales Mgr
Nate Stoltman, Promotions Manager
Barbara Reyelts, News Director
Larry Erickson, Engineering Dir
Todd Wentworth, General Sales Manager
JoeBiondi, Local Sales Manager
Mary Rhodes, Traffic Manager

KQDS-TV *Digital Channel:* 17 *Virtual Channel:* 21; 1000 kw; 981 ft.; N46 47 37 W92 7 3
2154 Highland Avenue, S., Birmingham, AL 35205 US
(218) 728-1622, *Fax:* (218) 728-1557
www.fox21online.com
dhileman@kqdsfox21.tv
License: Duluth, Saint Louis County, MN held by KQDS Acquisition Corp.
Group Owner: Red River Broadcast Co. L.L.C.; (acq 10-21-98; grpsl).
Nat'l Network: FOX *Nat'l Reps:* Harrington, Righter & Parsons
Wire Services: AP
Size of News Staff: 20; *Hours of Local News Weekly:* news progmg 2.5 hrs wkly
Ro Grignon, President
Kathy Lau, Operations Dir
Dave Hileman, General Manager
Julie Moravchik, News Director

KRII *Digital Channel:* 11 *Virtual Channel:* 11; 63 kw; 657 ft.; N47 51 39 W92 56 46; *Rebroadcasting:* Satellite of KBJR-TV Superior, WI.
C/O Granite B/C Corp, 767 Third Ave, 28th Fl, New York, NY 10017 US
(218) 720-9600, *Fax:* (218) 720-9660
www.news6.tv
news6@kbjr.com
License: Chisholm, St. Louis County, MN held by Channel 11 License Inc.
Group Owner: Granite Broadcasting Corp.; (acq 5-9-2001; grpsl).
Nat'l Network: NBC
David Jensch, Station Manager
Vincent Nelson, General Sales Mgr
Barb Wentworth, Programming Director
Chris Hussey, Promotions Manager
Derrick Hinds, News Director
Larry Erickson, Engineering Dir

WDIO-DT *Digital Channel:* 10; 316 kw vis, 105 kw aur; 987t/836g; N46 47 13 W92 07 17; *Population Served:* 176,000
Mailing Address: Box 16897, Duluth, MN 55816-0897
Second Address: 10 Observation Rd., Duluth, MN 55811-3506
(218) 727-6864, *Fax:* (218) 727-4415
www.wdio.com
news@wdio.com

License: Duluth, Saint Louis County, MN held by WDIO-TV L.L.C.
Group Owner: Hubbard Broadcasting Inc.; (acq 12-87; grpsl).; *Washington Law Firm:* Fletcher, Heald & Hildreth
Nat'l Network: ABC
Size of News Staff: 18; *Hours of Local News Weekly:* news progmg 9 hrs wkly
George Couture, General Manager
Deb Messer, General Sales Mgr
Dave Poirier, Programming Director
Jeff Laumdergan, Promotions Manager
Steve Goodspeed, News Director
Mike Hatlestad, Chief Engineer

***WDSE** *Digital Channel:* 8 *Virtual Channel:* 8; 34 kw; 968 ft.; N46 47 30 W92 7 21
1202 E. University Cir., Duluth, MN 55811 US
(218) 724-8567, *Fax:* (218) 724-4269
www.wdse.org
email@wdse.org
License: Duluth, Saint Louis County, MN held by Duluth-Superior Area Educ TV Corp
Washington Law Firm: Arnold & Porter
Nat'l Network: PBS
Allen Harmon, General Manager
Cheryl Leeper, General Sales Mgr
Juli Kellner, Programming Director
Brita Edgerton, Promotions Manager
Rex Greenwell, Chief Engineer

WIRT *Digital Channel:* 13; 125 kw vis, 21.6 kw aur; 670t/476g; N47 22 52 W92 57 18; *Rebroadcasting:* Satellite of WDIO-TV Duluth.
Mailing Address: Box 16897, Duluth, MN 55816-0897
Second Address: 10 Observation Rd., Duluth, MN 55811-3506
(218) 727-6864, *Fax:* (218) 727-4415
www.wdio.com
news@wdio.com
License: Hibbing, Saint Louis County, MN held by WDIO-TV L.L.C.
Group Owner: Hubbard Broadcasting Inc.; (acq 12-87; grpsl).
Nat'l Network: ABC
George Couture, General Manager
Deb Messer, General Sales Mgr
Dave Poirier, Programming Director
Jeff Laumdergan, Promotions Manager
Steve Goodspeed, News Director
Mike Hatlestad, Chief Engineer

Fargo-Valley City, ND (DMA 120)

KBRR *Digital Channel:* 10 *Virtual Channel:* 10; 9.3 kw; 650 ft.; N47 58 38 W96 36 18; *Rebroadcasting:* Satellite of KVRR(TV) Fargo, ND
P.O. Box 9115, Fargo, ND 58106 US
(701) 277-1515, *Fax:* (701) 277-1830
news@kvrr.com
License: Thief River Falls, Pennington County, MN held by Red River Broadcast Co. L.L.C.
Group Owner: Red River Broadcast Co. L.L.C.; *Washington Law Firm:* Crowell & Moring
Nat'l Network: FOX
Kathy Lau, General Manager
Ed Beiswenger, General Sales Mgr
Jim Shaw, News Director
Darren Bjerke, Chief Engineer

Mankato, MN (DMA 199)

KEYC-TV CBS & NEYC FOX *Digital Channel:* 12 *Virtual Channel:* 12; 316 kw vis, 63 kw aur; 1,045t/1,116g; N43 56 14 W94 24 41; *Population Served:* 352,000
Mailing Address: Box 128, Mankato, MN 56002
Second Address: 1570 Lookout Dr., N. Mankato, MN 56003
(507) 625-7905, *Fax:* (507) 625-5745
www.keyc.tv
keyc@keyc.com
License: Mankato, Blue Earth County, MN held by United Communications Corp.
Group Owner: United Communications Corp.; (acq 10-14-77; $5 million); *Washington Law Firm:* Wood, Maines & Nolan
Nat'l Network: CBS; Fox *Nat'l Reps:* Continental Television Sales *Wire Services:* AP; CBS; NWS (National Weather Service); Bloomberg Financial; NWS (National Weather Service)
Size of News Staff: 19; *Hours of Local News Weekly:* news progmg 13 hrs wkly
Dennis Wahlstrom, Operations Dir
John Ginther, General Sales Mgr
Sue Briggs, Programming Director
Dan Ruiter, News Director
Terry Rudenick, Chief Engineer
Sharon Freitag, Business Manager
Jan Ellanson, Operations Manager
JeffPoole, Production Manager
Perry Dyke, Sports Commentator
Mark Tarello, Weather Director

Minneapolis-St. Paul, MN (DMA 15)

KARE *Digital Channel:* 11; 316 kw vis, 31.6 kw aur; 1,440t/1,375g; N45 03 44 W93 08 21; *Population Served:* 2,500,000
8811 Olson Memorial Hwy., Minneapolis, MN 55427
(763) 546-1111, *Fax:* (763) 546-8590
www.kare11.com
License: Minneapolis, Hennepin County, MN held by Multimedia Holdings Corp.
Group Owner: Gannett Broadcasting; (acq 4-13-83; $75 million;
Nat'l Network: NBC
John Remes, President
Diana Pierce, Anchor
Tom Lindner, News Director
Jeff Phillips, Chief Engineer

***KAWB** *Digital Channel:* 28 *Virtual Channel:* 22; 137.5 kw; 745 ft.; N46 25 21 W94 27 41
Box 9 Bsu, Bemidji, MN 56601 US
(218) 751-3407, *Fax:* (218) 751-3142
www.lakelandptv.org
viewerservices@lakelandptv.org
License: Brainerd, Crow Wing County, MN held by Northern Minnesota Public TV Inc
Washington Law Firm: Dow, Lohnes PLLC
Nat'l Network: PBS
Hours of Local News Weekly: News progmg 2.5 hrs wkly
Travis Annette, President
Jess Skala, Operations Dir
Bill Sanford, General Manager
Dan Hegstad, Station Manager
Sharon Pugh, General Sales Mgr
Tom Lembrick, Chief Engineer

***KAWE** *Digital Channel:* 9 *Virtual Channel:* 9; 27 kw; 1098 ft.; N47 42 3 W94 29 14
Box 9 B.S.U., Bemidji, MN 56601 US
(218) 751-3407, *Fax:* (218) 751-3142
www.lakelandptv.org
viewerservices@lakelandptv.org
License: Bemidji, Beltrami County, MN held by Northern Minnesota Public TV Inc
Washington Law Firm: Dow, Lohnes PLLC
Nat'l Network: PBS
Size of News Staff: 7; *Hours of Local News Weekly:* news progmg 2.5 hrs wkly
Travis Annette, President
Jess Skala, Operations Dir
Bill Sanford, General Manager
Sharon Pugh, General Sales Mgr
Tom Lembrick, Chief Engineer

KCCO-TV *Digital Channel:* 7 *Virtual Channel:* 7; 29 kw; 1114 ft.; N45 41 10 W95 8 3; *Rebroadcasting:* Rebroadcasts WCCO-TV Minneapolis 100%
600 New Hampshire Ave NW, Suite 1200, Washington, DC 20037 US
(612) 339-4444, *Fax:* (612) 330-2627
www.wcco.com
wcconewstips@wcco.com
License: Alexandria, Douglas County, MN held by CBS Broadcasting Inc.
Group Owner: CBS Television Stations Group; *Washington Law Firm:* Rosenman & Colin
Nat'l Network: CBS *Nat'l Reps:* CBS TV Stations National Sales
Wire Services: NOAA Weather
Susan Adams Loyd, Operations Dir
Kevin Argall, General Sales Mgr
Scott Libin, News Director
Gary Kroger, Engineering Dir

KCCW-TV *Digital Channel:* 12 *Virtual Channel:* 12; 59 kw; 940 ft.; N46 56 5 W94 27 19; *Rebroadcasting:* Rebroadcasts WCCO-TV Minneapolis 100%
600 New Hampshire Ave NW, Suite 1200, Washington, DC 20037 US
(612) 339-4444, *Fax:* (612) 330-2627
www.wcco.com
wcconewstips@wcco.com
License: Walker, Cass County, MN held by CBS Broadcasting Inc.
Group Owner: CBS Television Stations Group; *Washington Law Firm:* Rosenman & Colin
Nat'l Network: CBS
Susan Adams Loyd, Operations Dir
Kevin Argall, General Sales Mgr
Scott Libin, News Director
Gary Kroger, Engineering Dir

KFTC *Digital Channel:* 26 *Virtual Channel:* 26; 4.5 kw; 512 ft.; N47 33 21 W94 48 4; *Rebroadcasting:* Satellite of WFTC-TV Minneapolis 100%; *Not on Air/Target Date:* 2000
11840 N. Dragoon Springs, Tucson, AZ 85737 US
(952) 944-9999, *Fax:* (952) 942-0286
www.my29tv.com
fox9news@foxtv.com
License: Bemidji, Beltrami County, MN held by Fox Television Stations Inc.
Group Owner: Fox Television Stations Inc.; (acq 9-21-2001; grpsl).
Nat'l Network: FOX
Carol Rueppel, General Manager
Sheila Oliver, General Sales Mgr
Bill Dallman, News Director
Marc Majerus, Chief Engineer

KMSP-TV *Digital Channel:* 9 *Virtual Channel:* 9; 30 kw; 1421 ft.; N45 3 30 W93 7 27
11358 Viking Drive, Eden Prairie, MN 55344 US
(952) 944-9999, *Fax:* (952) 942-0286
www.myfox9.com
fox9news@foxtv.com
License: Minneapolis, Hennepin County, MN held by Fox Television Stations Inc.
Group Owner: Fox Television Stations Inc.; (acq 7-31-2001; grpsl).
Nat'l Network: FOX *Wire Services:* AP
Size of News Staff: 64; *Hours of Local News Weekly:* news progmg 19.5 hrs wkly
Carol Rueppel, General Manager
Sheila Oliver, General Sales Mgr
Bill Dallman, News Director
Marc Majerus, Chief Engineer

KPXM-TV *Digital Channel:* 40; 2,750 kw vis, 275 kw aur; 1,469t/1,498g; N45 23 00 W93 42 30; *Population Served:* 1,100,000
22601 176th St. NW, Big Lake, MN 55309
(763) 263-8666, *Fax:* (763) 263-6600
www.ionline.tv
License: Saint Cloud, Stearns County, MN held by Paxson Communications of Minneapolis/41 Inc.
Group Owner: ION Media Networks Inc.; (acq 10-1-96; $12 million); *Washington Law Firm:* Mullin, Rhyne, Emmons & Topel
Nat'l Network: ION Television
Sherry Black, Operations Dir
Robert Getze, General Sales Mgr
Corey Ziegler, News Director
Joe Brunke, Chief Engineer

KRWF *Digital Channel:* 27 *Virtual Channel:* 43; 58 kw; 495 ft.; N44 29 3 W95 29 27
Mailing Address: 3415 University Ave.West, St. Paul, MN 55114 US
Second Address: 415 Fillmore St., Alexandria, MN 56308
(320) 763-5729, *Fax:* (320) 763-4627
ksax.com
ksax@ksax.com
License: Redwood Falls, Redwood County, MN held by KSAX-TV Inc.
Group Owner: Hubbard Broadcasting Inc.; *Washington Law Firm:* Holland & Knight
Nat'l Network: ABC *Wire Services:* AP
Robert Hubbard, General Manager
Edward Smith, Station Manager

KSAX *Digital Channel:* 42 *Virtual Channel:* 42; 80 kw; 1168 ft.; N45 41 59 W95 10 35
Mailing Address: 3415 University Ave.West, St. Paul, MN 55114 US
Second Address: 415 Fillmore St., Alexandria, MN 56308
(320) 763-5729, *Fax:* (320) 763-4627
www.ksax.com
ksax@ksax.com
License: Alexandria, Douglas County, MN held by KSAX-TV Inc.
Group Owner: Hubbard Broadcasting Inc.; *Washington Law Firm:* Holland & Knight
Nat'l Network: ABC *Nat'l Reps:* Petry Television Inc. *Wire Services:* AP
Melissa Mathews, Operations Dir
Robert Hubbard, General Manager
Edward Smith, Station Manager

KSTC-TV *Digital Channel:* 45 *Virtual Channel:* 45; 1000 kw; 1404 ft.; N45 3 45 W93 8 21
1080 W County Rd E, Shoreview, MN 55126 US
(651) 645-4500, *Fax:* (651) 523-7320
www.kstc45.com
License: Minneapolis, Hennepin County, MN held by KSTC.TV LLC.
Group Owner: Hubbard Broadcasting Inc.; (acq 4-24-2000).; *Washington Law Firm:* Holland & Knight LLP
Nat'l Network: IND
Susan Wenz, General Manager
Andy Stavast, General Sales Mgr
Michael Smith, Programming Director
Joe Johnston, Promotions Manager
Christopher Berg, News Director
Dick Rice, Chief Engineer

KSTP-TV *Digital Channel:* 35 *Virtual Channel:* 5; 755 kw; 1421 ft.; N45 3 44 W93 8 21
3415 University Avenue, St. Paul, MN 55114 US
(651) 646-5555, *Fax:* (651) 642-4172
www.kstp.com
License: St. Paul, Ramsey County, MN held by KSTP-TV LLC.
Group Owner: Hubbard Broadcasting Inc.; *Washington Law Firm:* Holland and Knight
Nat'l Network: ABC *Nat'l Reps:* Petry Television Inc. *Wire Services:* AP
Hours of Local News Weekly: 37 hrs weekly
Robert Hubbard, President
Monica Doyle, Operations Dir
Ray Mirabella, General Sales Mgr
Michael Smith, Programming Director
Paul Gaulke, Promotions Manager
Lindsay Radford, News Director
Dick Rice, Chief Engineer
Dixie Hansen,Business Manager

***KTCA-TV** *Digital Channel:* 34 *Virtual Channel:* 2; 662 kw; 1349 ft.; N45 3 30 W93 7 27
172 East 4th Street, St. Paul, MN 55101 US
(651) 222-1717, *Fax:* (651) 229-1282
www.tpt.org
viewerservices@tpt.org
License: St. Paul, Ramsey County, MN held by Twin Cities Public TV Inc
Nat'l Network: PBS
Jim Pagliarini, CEO
Stephen Usery, Promotions Manager
Bruce Jacobs, Chief Engineer

***KTCI-TV** *Digital Channel:* 23 *Virtual Channel:* 17; 325 kw; 1349 ft.; N45 3 30 W93 7 27
172 East 4th Street, St Paul, MN 55101 US
(651) 222-1717, *Fax:* (651) 229-1282
www.tpt.org
viewerservices@tpt.org
License: St. Paul, Ramsey County, MN held by Twin Cities Public Television Inc
Nat'l Network: PBS
Jim Pagliarini, CEO
Stephen Usery, Promotions Manager
Bruce Jacobs, Chief Engineer

***KWCM-TV** *Digital Channel:* 10 *Virtual Channel:* 10; 50 kw; 1250 ft.; N45 10 3 W96 0 2
120 West Schleiman Avenue, Appleton, MN 56208 US
(800) 726-3178, *Fax:* (320) 289-2634
www.pioneer.org
yourtv@pioneer.org
License: Appleton, Swift County, MN held by West Central Minnesota Educational TV Co
Washington Law Firm: Fletcher, Heald & Hildreth
Nat'l Network: PBS
Les Heen, President
Janet Suckow, Operations Dir
Jon Panzer, Station Manager
Shirley Schwarz, Programming Director

WCCO-TV *Digital Channel:* 32 *Virtual Channel:* 4; 1000 kw; 1417 ft.; N45 3 44 W93 8 21
600 New Hampshire Ave., NW, Suite 1200, Washington, DC 20037 US
(612) 339-4444, *Fax:* (612) 330-2627
www.wcco.com
wcconewstips@wcco.com
License: Minneapolis, Hennepin County, MN held by CBS Broadcasting Inc.
Group Owner: CBS Television Stations Group; (acq 2-92; grpsl; *Nat'l Network:* CBS *Nat'l Reps:* CBS TV Stations National Sales *Wire Services:* WU; Reuters
Size of News Staff: 75; *Hours of Local News Weekly:* news progmg 23 hrs wkly
Susan Adams Loyd, Operations Dir
Kevin Argall, General Sales Mgr
Scott Libin, News Director
Gary Kroger, Engineering Dir

WFTC *Digital Channel:* 29 *Virtual Channel:* 29; 1000 kw; 1276 ft.; N45 3 30 W93 7 27
200 Concord Plaza, Suite 600, San Antonio, TX 78216 US
(952) 944-9999, *Fax:* (952) 942-0286
www.my29tv.com
fox9news@foxtv.com
License: Minneapolis, Hennepin County, MN held by Fox Television Stations Inc.
Group Owner: Fox Television Stations Inc.; (acq 10-1-2001; grpsl).
Nat'l Network: MY NETWORK *Wire Services:* AP
Hours of Local News Weekly: News progmg 3.5 hrs wkly
Carol Rueppel, General Manager
Sheila Oliver, General Sales Mgr
Bill Dallman, News Director
Marc Majerus, Chief Engineer

WUCW *Digital Channel:* 22 *Virtual Channel:* 23; 1000 kw; 1345 ft.; N45 3 44 W93 8 21
10706 Beaver Dam Road, Cockeysville, MD 21030 US
(651) 646-2300, *Fax:* (651) 646-1220
www.thecwtc.com
License: Minneapolis, Hennepin County, MN held by KLGT Licensee L.L.C.
Group Owner: Sinclair Broadcast Group Inc.; (acq 3-16-98; $52.5 million)
Nat'l Network: CW
Joe Tracy, General Manager
Laura Crane, General Sales Mgr
Cece Smith, Programming Director
Steve Lunde, Chief Engineer
Tom Burke, Regional Sales Manager

Rochester, MN-Mason City, IA-Austin, MN (DMA 154)

KAAL *Digital Channel:* 36 *Virtual Channel:* 6; 620 kw; 1070 ft.; N43 38 34 W92 31 35
Mailing Address: The Pinnacle, Suite 875, 3455 Peachtree Rd., N.E., Atlanta, GA 30326 US
Second Address: 1701 10th Pl. N.E., Austin, MN 55912
(507) 437-6666, *Fax:* (507) 433-9560
www.kaaltv.com
License: Austin, Mower County, MN held by KAAL-TV LLC.
Group Owner: Hubbard Broadcasting Inc.; (acq 12-13-00; $9.5 million); *Washington Law Firm:* Schwartz, Woods & Miller
Nat'l Network: ABC
Size of News Staff: 18; *Hours of Local News Weekly:* news progmg 11 hrs wkly
Deb Nerud, Operations Dir
David Harbert, General Manager
Bill Klein, General Sales Mgr
Sheryl Barlow, Programming Director
Heather Holmes, Promotions Manager
David Springer, News Director
Wendell Nelson, Chief Engineer
JanThompson, Programming Director
Harlan Carlson, Traffic Manager

***KSMQ-TV** *Digital Channel:* 20 *Virtual Channel:* 15; 319.2 kw; 993 ft.; N43 38 34 W92 31 35
2000 8th Ave. NW, Austin, MN 55912 US
(507) 433-0678, *Fax:* (507) 433-0670
www.ksmq.org
ksmq@ksmq.org
License: Austin, Mower County, MN held by KSMQ Public Service Media, Inc
(acq 5-27-2005); *Washington Law Firm:* Schwartz, Woods & Miller
Nat'l Network: PBS
Marianne Potter, CEO
Suzi Stone, Programming Director
Stefan Olson, Chief Engineer

KTTC *Digital Channel:* 10 *Virtual Channel:* 10; 43.1 kw; 1250 ft.; N43 34 15 W92 25 37
601 First Avenue, S. W., Rochester, MN 55901 US
(507) 288-4444, *Fax:* (507) 288-6324,(507) 288-6278 (news)
www.kttc.com
kttc@kttc.com
License: Rochester, Olmsted County, MN held by KTTC Television, Inc.
Group Owner: Quincy Newspapers Inc.; (acq 7-1-76; $4.25 million;; *Washington Law Firm:* Wilkinson, Barker, Knauer & Quinn
Nat'l Network: NBC; CW *Nat'l Reps:* Blair Television *Wire Services:* AP; CNN; NBC
Size of News Staff: 15; *Hours of Local News Weekly:* news progmg 11 hrs wkly
Jerry Watson, General Manager
Elizabeth Dahlen, Station Manager
Dave Ferber, General Sales Mgr
Vickie Broughton, Programming Director
Rita Duda, Promotions Manager
Tim Morgan, Chief Engineer

KXLT-TV *Digital Channel:* 46 *Virtual Channel:* 47; 220 kw; 1125 ft.; N43 38 34 W92 31 35
5727 Tokay Boulevard, Madison, WI 53719 US
(507) 252-4747, *Fax:* (507) 252-5050
www.fox47kxlt.com
comments@fox47kxlt.com
License: Rochester, Olmsted County, MN held by SagamoreHill of Minnesota Licenses LLC
Group Owner: SagamoreHill Midwest LLC; (acq 3-31-2005; $2.05 million); *Washington Law Firm:* Rosenman & colin
Nat'l Network: FOX
Hours of Local News Weekly: News progmg 7 hrs wkly
Louis Wall, General Manager
Kristopher Lake, General Sales Mgr
Danika Stagemeyer, Programming Director
Rita Duda, Promotions Manager
Tim Morgan, Engineering Dir

Sioux Falls (Mitchell), SD (DMA 113)

***KSMN** *Digital Channel:* 15 *Virtual Channel:* 20; 200 kw; 952 ft.; N43 53 52 W95 56 50; *Rebroadcasting:* Rebroadcasts KWCM-TV Appleton 100%
120 W. Schlieman, Appleton, MN 56208 US
(800) 726-3178, *Fax:* (320) 289-2634
www.pioneer.org
yourtv@pioneer.org
License: Worthington, Nobles County, MN held by West Central Minnesota Educational TV Co
Nat'l Network: PBS
Les Heen, President
Janet Suckow, Operations Dir
Shirley Schwarz, Programming Director
Jon Panzer, Chief Engineer

Mississippi

Biloxi-Gulfport, MS (DMA 163)

WLOX *Digital Channel:* 39 *Virtual Channel:* 13; 715 kw; 1201 ft.; N30 43 22 W89 5 28
Box 4596,W.Biloxi Stat., Biloxi, MS 39531 US
(228) 896-1313, *Fax:* (228) 896-0749
www.wlox.com
wlox@wlox.com
License: Biloxi, Harrison County, MS held by WLOX License Subsidiary LLC.
Group Owner: Raycom Media Inc.; (acq 1-31-2006; grpsl); *Washington Law Firm:* Covington & Burling
Nat'l Network: ABC *Wire Services:* AP
Size of News Staff: 44; *Hours of Local News Weekly:* news progmg 18 hrs wkly
Leon Long, Operations Dir
Dave Vincent, Station Manager
Linda Sherman, General Sales Mgr
Darlene Duffano, Programming Director
David Vincent, News Director
John Armstrong, Chief Engineer
Roger Garrett, Operations Manager
DonMoore, Regional Sales Manager

***WMAH-TV** *Digital Channel:* 16 *Virtual Channel:* 19; 540 kw; 1556 ft.; N30 45 18 W88 56 44
3825 Ridgewood Road, Jackson, MS 39211 US
(601) 432-6565, *Fax:* (601) 432-6654 / (601) 432-6311
www.mpbonline.org
License: Biloxi, Harrison County, MS held by Mississippi Authority for Educational TV
Washington Law Firm: Schwartz, Woods & Miller
Nat'l Network: PBS *Regional Network:* Mississippi Educational Broadcasting
Cy Vance, Operations Dir
Dr. Judy Lewis, General Manager
Teresa Collier, News Director

WXXV-TV *Digital Channel:* 48 *Virtual Channel:* 25; 2,240 kw vis, 224 kw aur; 1,780t/1,540g; N30 44 48 W89 03 30; *Population Served:* 128,150
Mailing Address: P.O. Box 2500, Gulfport, MS 31412
Second Address: 14351 Hwy. 49 N., Gulfport, MS 39503
(228) 832-2525, *Fax:* (228) 314-9223
www.wxxv25.com
info@wxxv25.com
License: Gulfport, Harrison County, MS held by Morris Network of Mississippi Inc.
Group Owner: Morris Multimedia Inc.; (acq 5-22-97; $17.475 million); *Washington Law Firm:* Fletcher, Heald & Hildroth
Nat'l Network: FOX; NBC *Nat'l Reps:* Millennium Sales & Marketing
Dean Hinson, President
Ray Luke, Operations Dir
Bobby Edwards, General Manager
Scott Wilson, General Sales Mgr
Jimmy Spears, National Sales Associate
Leah Mays, Promotions Manager
Ray Luke, Chief Engineer
Donna Ingram, BusinessManager
Cory Hardy, Creative Services

Columbus-Tupelo-West Point, MS (DMA 133)

WCBI-TV *Digital Channel:* 35; 100 kw vis, 10 kw aur; 1,996t/1,800g; N33 45 06 W88 52 40; *Population Served:* 165,000
201 5th St. S., Columbus, MS 77903
(662) 327-4444, *Fax:* (662) 328-5222
www.wcbi.com
comments@wcbi.com
License: Columbus, Lowndes County, MS held by WCBI-TV LLC.
Group Owner: Morris Multimedia Inc.; (acq 12-31-03; $20 million); *Washington Law Firm:* Fletcher, Heald & Hildreth
Nat'l Network: CBS; CW; MyNetworkTV *Wire Services:* Weather Wire
Bobby Berry, General Manager
Derek Rogers, General Sales Mgr
Susan Bell, Promotions Manager
Russ Geller, News Director
Chris Horton, Chief Engineer
Donna Hitchcock, Traffic Manager
Rob Smith, Weather Director

WKDH *Digital Channel:* 45 *Virtual Channel:* 45; 537 kw vis; ant 1,610t/1,368g; N33 47 39.6 W89 05 15.8
Box 1645, Tupelo, MS 39302
(662) 842-7620, *Fax:* (662) 842-6342,(662) 844-7061
www.wkdh.com
License: Houston, Chickasaw County, MS held by Southern Broadcasting Inc
Washington Law Firm: Garvey, Schubert & Barer
Walter Spain, President
Gerald Stanford, Chief Engineer

WLOV-TV *Digital Channel:* 16 *Virtual Channel:* 27; 390 kw; 1670 ft.; N33 47 39.6 W89 5 15.8
1828 L Street, NW, Suite 1111, Washington, DC 20036 US
(662) 842-2227, *Fax:* (662) 844-7061
www.wlov.com
manager@wlov.com
License: West Point, Clay County, MS held by Lingard Broadcasting Corp
(acq 4-12-94).; *Ownership:* John R. Lingard; *Washington Law Firm:* Robert E. Levine, Esq.
Nat'l Network: FOX *Nat'l Reps:* Continental Television Sales
Wire Services: FNS
Hours of Local News Weekly: 5.5 hrs
Jennifer Dennington, General Manager
Marty Davis, Chief Engineer

***WMAB-TV** *Digital Channel:* 10 *Virtual Channel:* 2; 8 kw; 1145 ft.; N33 21 14 W89 9 0
3825 Ridgewood Road, Jackson, MS 39211 US
(601) 432-6565, *Fax:* (601) 432-6654
www.mpbonline.org
License: Mississippi State, Choctaw County, MS held by Mississippi Authority for Educational TV
Washington Law Firm: Schwartz, Woods & Miller
Nat'l Network: PBS
Size of News Staff: 4
Cy Vance, Operations Dir
Dr. Judy Lewis, Station Manager
Mari Irby, Promotions Manager
Teresa Collier, News Director

***WMAE-TV** *Digital Channel:* 12 *Virtual Channel:* 12; 31 kw; 732 ft.; N34 40 0 W88 45 5
3825 Ridgewood Road, Jackson, MS 39211 US
(601) 432-6565, *Fax:* (601) 432-6654,(601) 432-6311
www.mpbonline.org
License: Booneville, Prentiss County, MS held by Mississippi Authority for Educational TV
Washington Law Firm: Schwartz, Woods & Miller
Nat'l Network: PBS *Regional Network:* Mississippi Educational Broadcasting
Dr. Judy Lewis, General Manager
Teresa Collier, News Director

WTVA *Digital Channel:* 8; 16kw; 1,800t/1,561g; N33 47 40 W89 05 16
Mailing Address: 1359 Beech Springs Road, Saltillo, MS 38802
Second Address: PO Box 350, Tupelo, MS 38802
(662) 842-7620, *Fax:* (662) 844-7061
www.wtva.com
manager@wtva.com
License: Tupelo, Lee County, MS held by WTVA Inc.
Ownership: Mary Jane Spain, 51%; Margaret Spain, 40%; and estate of Frank K. Spain, 9%.; *Washington Law Firm:* Garvey, Schubert & Barer
Nat'l Network: NBC *Nat'l Reps:* Continental Television Sales
Wire Services: AP; NBC
Size of News Staff: 22; *Hours of Local News Weekly:* news progmg 17 hrs wkly
Mary Jane Spain, President
Jon Ball, Operations Dir
John P Sullivan, Station Manager
Larry Harris, General Sales Mgr
Jeff Houston, News Director
Rodney Gray, Chief Engineer

Greenwood-Greenville, MS (DMA 187)

WABG-TV *Digital Channel:* 32 *Virtual Channel:* 6; 1000 kw; 1877 ft.; N33 22 23 W90 32 25
2001 Garrard Ave., Greenwood, MS 38930 US 38930
(662) 332-0949, *Fax:* (662) 344-1814
www.wabg.com
License: Greenwood, Leflore County, MS held by Commonwealth Broadcasting Group, Inc.
Group Owner: Commonwealth Broadcasting Corp.
Nat'l Network: ABC; Fox *Nat'l Reps:* Continental Television Sales
Size of News Staff: 16; *Hours of Local News Weekly:* news progmg 13 hrs wkly
Charles Harker, President
Sherry Nelson, General Manager
Sarah Zepponi, General Sales Mgr
Donnie Reid, Programming Director
Pam Chatman, News Director

WMAI *Digital Channel:* 31; *Not on Air/Target Date:* unknown
C/O Larry Miller, 3825 Ridgewood Rd, Jackson, MS 39211 US
(601) 432-6565, *Fax:* (610) 432-6392
www.mpbonline.org
License: Cleveland, Bolivar County, MS held by Mississippi Authority for Educational Television
Regional Network: Mississippi Educational Broadcasting
Marie Antoon, General Manager

***WMAO-TV** *Digital Channel:* 25 *Virtual Channel:* 23; 815 kw; 1041 ft.; N33 22 34 W90 32 32
3825 Ridgewood Road, Jackson, MS 39211 US
(601) 432-6565, *Fax:* (601) 432-6654,(601) 432-6311
www.mpbonline.org
License: Greenwood, Leflore County, MS held by Mississippi Authority for Educational TV
Washington Law Firm: Schwartz, Woods & Miller
Nat'l Network: PBS *Regional Network:* Mississippi Educational Broadcasting
Cy Vance, Operations Dir
Dr. Judy Lewis, General Manager
Teresa Collier, News Director

WXVT *Digital Channel:* 15 *Virtual Channel:* 15; 330 kw; 883 ft.; N33 39 26 W90 42 18
73 Kercheval Avenue, Grosse Pointe Farms, MI 48236 US
(662) 334-1500, *Fax:* (662) 378-8122
www.wxvt.com
License: Greenville, Washington County, MS held by Saga Broadcasting LLC.
Group Owner: Saga Communications Inc.; (acq 7-1-99; $5.2 million)
Nat'l Network: CBS
Darren Lehrmann, General Manager
Larry Cazavan, General Sales Mgr
Carolyn Byars, Programming Director
Stephen Ross, Promotions Manager
Earl Phelps, News Director
Paul Serio, Chief Engineer

Hattiesburg-Laurel, MS (DMA 167)

WDAM-TV *Digital Channel:* 7 *Virtual Channel:* 7; 75 kw; 509 ft.; N31 27 12 W89 17 5
Mailing Address: Rsa Tower Suite 710, 201 Monroe Street, Montgomery, AL 36104 US
Second Address: 2362 Hwy. 11 N., Moselle, MS 39459
(601) 544-4730, *Fax:* (601) 584-9302
www.wdam.com
info@wdam.com
License: Laurel, Jones County, MS held by WDAM License Subsidiary Inc.
Group Owner: Raycom Media Inc.; (acq 9-24-96; grpsl).;
Washington Law Firm: Covington & Burling
Nat'l Network: NBC *Nat'l Reps:* Harrington, Righter & Parsons
Size of News Staff: 26; *Hours of Local News Weekly:* news progmg 20 hrs wkly
Jim Cameron, Operations Dir
Ted Palmer, General Sales Mgr
Betty Young, Programming Director
Pam McGovern, Promotions Manager
Randy Swan, News Director
Jim Wilkinson, Chief Engineer
Wanda Morrison, National Sales Manager
NickOrtego, Weather
Steve Taylor, Weather

WHLT *Digital Channel:* 22 *Virtual Channel:* 22; 1000 kw; 797 ft.; N31 24 20 W89 14 13
333 East Grace Street, Richmond, VA 23219 US
(601) 545-2077, *Fax:* (601) 545-3589
www.cbs22thehub.com
wbabbidge@whlt.com
License: Hattiesburg, Forrest County, MS held by Media General Broadcasting Inc.
Group Owner: Media General Broadcast Group; (acq 7-25-97; grpsl).
Nat'l Network: CBS *Nat'l Reps:* MMT
Robert Romine, General Manager
Wally Babbidge, Station Manager
Jackie McDonald, Programming Director
Gary Wolverton, Promotions Manager
Gary Wright, Chief Engineer

Jackson, MS (DMA 90)

WAPT *Digital Channel:* 21 *Virtual Channel:* 16; 1000 kw; 1089 ft.; N32 16 41 W90 17 40
888 Seventh Avenue, New York, NY 10106 US
(601) 922-1607, *Fax:* (601) 922-1663
www.wapt.com
License: Jackson, Hinds County, MS held by WAPT Hearst-Argyle Television Inc.
Group Owner: Hearst-Argyle Television Inc.; (acq 7-16-97; grpsl).
Nat'l Network: ABC
Size of News Staff: 26; *Hours of Local News Weekly:* news progmg 14 hrs wkly
Stuart Kellogg, General Manager
Jeff Wolfe, General Sales Mgr
Linda Bozone, Programming Director
Cory McRae, Promotions Manager
Bruce Barkley, News Director
Tom Bondurant, Chief Engineer
Teresia Gray, Digital Sales Manager
CarlGustafson, National Sales Manager
Nichole Davis, Programming
David Hartman, Weather Director

WDBD *Digital Channel:* 40 *Virtual Channel:* 40; 981.2 kw; 1962 ft.; N32 12 49.4 W90 22 56.2
Mailing Address: Pegasus Corp. Office, 225 City Ln Ave., Ste200, Bala Cynwyd, PA 19004 US
Second Address: One Great Place, Jackson, MS 39209
(601) 922-1234, *Fax:* (601) 922-0268
www.fox40first.com
License: Jackson, Hinds County, MS held by Jackson Broadcasting, L.L.C
(acq 9-30-2003; $13.4 million with WXMS-LP Jackson).;
Washington Law Firm: Fisher, Wayland, Cooper, Leader & Zaragoza
Nat'l Network: FOX *Nat'l Reps:* Millennium Sales & Marketing
Bonnie Alaimo, Operations Dir
Marc Jaromin, General Manager
Will Hammond, General Sales Mgr

Mike Ingalls, News Director
Mark Wade, Chief Engineer

WJTV *Digital Channel:* 12 *Virtual Channel:* 12; 316 kw vis, 63.1 kw aur; 1,630t/1,615g; N32 14 26 W90 24 15; *Population Served:* 477,300
1820 TV Rd., Jackson, MS 23219
(601) 372-6311, *Fax:* (601) 969-4601
www.wjtv.com
License: Jackson, Hinds County, MS held by Media General Broadcasting Inc.
Group Owner: Media General Broadcast Group; (acq 7-25-97; grpsl); *Washington Law Firm:* Dow Lohnes LLC
Nat'l Network: CBS *Nat'l Reps:* HRP
Size of News Staff: 34; *Hours of Local News Weekly:* news progmg 21 hrs wkly
William Cromwell, Operations Dir
Bob Romine, General Manager
Al Evans, General Sales Mgr
Jackie McDonald, Programming Director
Rick Russell, Promotions Manager
Steve Schrader, Chief Engineer
Stephen Patton, Promotions Director

WLBT *Digital Channel:* 30 *Virtual Channel:* 3; 535 kw; 2047 ft.; N32 12 49 W90 22 56
715 South Jefferson Street, Jackson, MD 39205 US
(601) 948-3333, *Fax:* (601) 355-7830 (news)
www.wlbt.com
news@wlbt.com
License: Jackson, Hinds County, MS held by WLBT License Subsidiary, LLC
Group Owner: Raycom Media Inc.; (acq 1-13-2006; grpsl).; *Washington Law Firm:* Dow, Lohnes & Albertson
Nat'l Network: NBC *Nat'l Reps:* Continental Television Sales
Wire Services: AP
Dan Modisett, General Manager
Frankie Thomas, General Sales Mgr
Teresa White, Programming Director
Dennis Smith, News Director
Curtis McKnight, Chief Engineer

***WMAU-TV** *Digital Channel:* 18 *Virtual Channel:* 17; 682 kw; 1115 ft.; N31 22 22 W90 45 4
3825 Ridgewood Road, Jackson, MS 39211 US
(601) 432-6565, *Fax:* (610) 432-6654 / (601) 432-6311
www.mpbonline.org
License: Bude, Franklin County, MS held by Mississippi Authority for Educational TV
Washington Law Firm: Schwartz, Woods & Miller
Nat'l Network: PBS *Regional Network:* Mississippi Educational Broadcasting
Judith Lewis, General Manager
Jason Klein, Programming Director
Teresa Collier, News Director

***WMPN-TV** *Digital Channel:* 20 *Virtual Channel:* 29; 400 kw; 1581 ft.; N32 11 29 W90 24 22
3825 Ridgewood Road, Jackson, MS 39211 US
(601) 432-6565, *Fax:* (601) 432-6654,(601) 432-6311
www.mpbonline.org
License: Jackson, Hinds County, MS held by Mississippi Authority for Educational TV
Washington Law Firm: Schwartz, Woods & Miller
Nat'l Network: PBS
Cy Vance, Operations Dir
Dr. Judy Lewis, General Manager
Teresa Collier, News Director

WNTZ-TV *Digital Channel:* 49; 1,170 kw vis, 117 kw aur; ant 843t/848g; N31 30 33 W91 24 19
4615 Parliament Dr., Suite 103, Alexandria, LA 71303
(318) 443-4700, *Fax:* (318) 443-4899
www.fox48tv.com
License: Natchez, Adams County, MS held by ComCorp of Alexandria License Corp.
(acq 6-22-98); *Ownership:* ComCorp Broadcasting Inc.; *Washington Law Firm:* Shaw Pittman L.L.P.
Nat'l Network: Fox; MyNetworkTV *Nat'l Reps:* Millennium Sales & Marketing
Mona Dauzat, Operations Dir
Sharon Rachal, General Manager
Vikki Chapman, Programming Director
Ron Taylor, Chief Engineer

WRBJ *Virtual Channel:* 34; 1,400 kw vis; ant 1,229t/1,242g; N32 07 18 W89 32 52
745 N. State St., Jackson, MS 0
(601) 974-5700, *Fax:* (601) 974-5711
cw34jackson.com
License: Magee, Simpson County, MS held by Roberts Broadcasting of Jackson, MS, LLC.
Group Owner: Roberts Broadcasting Co.; *Washington Law Firm:* Fletcher, Heald & Hildreth
Nat'l Network: CW *Nat'l Reps:* Harrington, Righter & Parsons
Gregory McCoy, Operations Dir
Monica Johnson, Programming Director
Tambra Cooper, Promotions Manager
Charles Flowers, Chief Engineer
Terrill Weiss, General Sales Manager

WUFX *Digital Channel:* 41 *Virtual Channel:* 35; 981 kw; 1962 ft.; N32 12 49.4 W90 22 56.2
Mailing Address: Fisher, Wayland, Cooper, 2001 Penn Ave, NW, Washington, DC 20006 US
Second Address: One Great Place, Jackson, MS 39209
(601) 922-1234, *Fax:* (601) 922-0268
www.gomiss.com
License: Vicksburg, Warren County, MS held by Vicksburg Broadcasting, LLC.
Nat'l Network: MY NETWORK
Tracy Day, Operations Dir
Marc Jaromin, General Manager
Will Hammond, General Sales Mgr
Mike Ingalls, News Director
Mark Wade, Chief Engineer

WWJX *Digital Channel:* 23 *Virtual Channel:* 51; 20 kw; 492 ft.; N32 3 13 W90 20 23; *Not on Air/Target Date:* unknown US
(901) 516-8970; (901) 375-9324
License: Jackson, Hinds County, MS held by George S. Flinn, Jr.
George Flinn Jr., General Manager

Memphis, TN (DMA 48)

WBUY-TV *Digital Channel:* 41 *Virtual Channel:* 40; 1000 kw; 1040 ft.; N35 16 33 W89 46 38
250 West Arrow Highway, San Dimas, CA 91773 US
(901) 396-9541, *Fax:* (901) 396-9585
www.tbn.org
wbuy@tbn.org
License: Holly Springs, Marshall County, MS held by Trinity Broadcasting Network.
Group Owner: Trinity Broadcasting Network; (acq 5-8-2000; grpsl).
Nat'l Network: TRINITY BROADCA
Tamela Calvin, Station Manager
Cliff Pickell, Programming Director
Douglas Puryear, Chief Engineer

***WMAV-TV** *Digital Channel:* 36 *Virtual Channel:* 18; 272.5 kw; 1399 ft.; N34 17 28 W89 42 21
3825 Ridgewood Road, Jackson, MS 39211 US
(601) 432-6565, *Fax:* (601) 432-6654,(601) 432-6311
www.mpbonline.org
License: Oxford, Lafayette County, MS held by Mississippi Authority for Educational TV
Nat'l Network: PBS
Size of News Staff: 4
Cy Vance, Operations Dir
Dr. Judy Lewis, General Manager
Teresa Collier, News Director

Meridian, MS (DMA 185)

WGBC *Digital Channel:* 31 *Virtual Channel:* 30; 828 kw; 542 ft.; N32 19 39.5 W88 41 30.8
425 26th Avenue, Meridian, MS 39301 US
(601) 485-3030, *Fax:* (601) 693-9889
www.wgbctv.com
License: Meridian, Lauderdale County, MS held by WGBC-TV, LLC
1/23/2008; *Ownership:* Michael Reed; *Washington Law Firm:* Akin Gump Strauss Hauer & Feld
Nat'l Network: NBC; NBC *Nat'l Reps:* Millennium Sales & Marketing
Mike Reed, President
Susan Ross, General Sales Mgr
Clyde Walker, Engineering Dir

***WMAW-TV** *Digital Channel:* 44 *Virtual Channel:* 14; 880 kw; 1211 ft.; N32 8 18 W89 5 36
3825 Ridgewood Road, Jackson, MS 39211 US
(601) 432-6565, *Fax:* (601) 432-6654,(601) 432-6311
www.mpbonline.org
License: Meridian, Lauderdale County, MS held by Mississippi Authority for Educational TV
Washington Law Firm: Schwartz, Woods & Miller
Nat'l Network: PBS *Regional Network:* Mississippi Educational Broadcasting
Size of News Staff: 4
Dr. Judy Lewis, General Manager
Teresa Collier, News Director

WMDN *Digital Channel:* 24 *Virtual Channel:* 24; 616 kw; 597 ft.; N32 19 40 W88 41 31
Mailing Address: P.O. Box 2424, Meridian, MS 39302 US
Second Address: 1151Crestview Cir., Meridian, MS 39301
(601) 693-2424, *Fax:* (601) 693-7126
www.wmdntv.com
administration@wmdn.net
License: Meridian, Lauderdale County, MS held by Meridian Media LLC.
(acq 1-23-2008; $5.8 million); *Ownership:* Sharlyn Threadgill, 50%; and Wade Threadgill, 50%; *Washington Law Firm:* Fletcher, Heald & Hildreth
Nat'l Network: CBS *Nat'l Reps:* Millennium Sales & Marketing
Susan Ross, General Manager
Mike Reed, Station Manager

WTOK-TV *Digital Channel:* 11 *Virtual Channel:* 11; 90 kw; 525 ft.; N32 19 38 W88 41 28
Mailing Address: P.O. Box 2988, Meridian, MS 39301 US
Second Address: 815 23rd Ave., Meridian, MS 39301
(601) 693-1441, *Fax:* (601) 483-3266
www.wtok.com
License: Meridian, Lauderdale County, MS held by Gray Television Licensee LLC
Group Owner: Gray Television Inc.; (acq 8-29-2002; grpsl).; *Washington Law Firm:* Wiley, Rein & Fielding, LLP
Nat'l Network: ABC; CW; Fox *Nat'l Reps:* Continental Television Sales *Wire Services:* AP
Size of News Staff: 15; *Hours of Local News Weekly:* news progmg 15 hrs wkly
Tim Walker, General Manager
Matt Willis, Programming Director
Julie Walker, Promotions Manager
John Johnson, News Director
Brad LeBrun, Chief Engineer
Lindsey Hall, Sports Commentator

Missouri

Cedar Rapids-Waterloo-Iowa City & Dubuque, IA (DMA 88)

KFXB-TV *Digital Channel:* 43; 646 kw vis, 64.6 kw aur; ant 841t; N42 31 05 W90 37 16; *Population Served:* 90,000
744 Main Street, Dubuque, IA 52001
(563) 690-1704, *Fax:* (563) 557-9383
www.kfxb.net
ctnofiowa@mchsi.com
License: Dubuque, Dubuque County, IA held by Christian Television Network of Iowa Inc.
Group Owner: Christian Television Corporation Inc.; (acq 8-2-2004).
Tom Bond, General Manager
Tamie Cook, Business Manager

KGAN *Digital Channel:* 51; 100 kw vis, 20 kw aur; ant 1,450t/1,355g; N42 17 39 W91 53 10; *Population Served:* 117,040
Mailing Address: Box 3131, Cedar Rapids, IA 52406
Second Address: 600 Old Marion Rd, Cedar Rapids, IA 52406
(319) 395-9060, *Fax:* (319) 395-7028
www.kgan.com
kgan@kgan.com
License: Cedar Rapids, Linn County, IA held by KGAN Licensee L.L.C.
Group Owner: Sinclair Broadcast Group Inc.; (acq 1999; grpsl).; *Washington Law Firm:* Shaw Pittman
Nat'l Network: CBS *Nat'l Reps:* Millennium Sales & Marketing
Wire Services: AP; CBS
Size of News Staff: 35; *Hours of Local News Weekly:* news progmg 12 hrs wkly
Ruth Barnett, Operations Dir
Peter Paisley, Station Manager
David Bell, Promotions Manager
Randy Schildmeyer, Chief Engineer

***KIIN** *Digital Channel:* 12; 316 kw vis, 31.6 kw aur; 1,440t/1,449g; N41 43 14 W91 20 29
Mailing Address: Box 6450, Iowa Public TV, Johnston, IA 50131-6450
Second Address: 6450 Corporate Drive, Johnston, IA 50131
(515) 242-3100
www.iptv.org
public_information@iptv.org

License: Iowa City, Johnson County, IA held by Iowa Public Broadcasting Board
Washington Law Firm: Dow, Lohnes PLLC
Nat'l Network: PBS
Daniel Miller, General Manager
Bill Hayes, Engineering Dir

KPXR-TV ; 5,000 kw vis, 500 kw aur; 466t; N42 04 51 W91 41 45; *Population Served:* 442,400
1957 Blairs Ferry Rd. N.E., Cedar Rapids, IA 52402-5819
(319) 378-1260, *Fax:* (319) 378-0076
www.ionline.tv
License: Cedar Rapids, Linn County, IA held by Paxson Communications License Co. L.L.C.
Group Owner: ION Media Networks Inc.; (acq 7-15-97; $5 million)
Vikki Steele, Station Manager

Columbia-Jefferson City, MO (DMA 137)

KMIZ *Digital Channel:* 17 *Virtual Channel:* 17; 120 kw; 1142 ft.; N38 46 29 W92 33 22.3
501 Business Loop, 70 East, Columbia, MO 65201 US
(573) 449-0917, *Fax:* (573) 875-7078
www.kmiz.com
info@kmiz.com
License: Columbia, Boone County, MO held by JW Broadcasting LLC
(acq 10-21-03).; *Washington Law Firm:* Covington & Burling
Nat'l Network: ABC; MyNetworkTV; Fox *Nat'l Reps:* Petry Television Inc. *Wire Services:* AP
Size of News Staff: 12; *Hours of Local News Weekly:* news progmg 19 hrs wkly
Randy Wright, Operations Dir
Mark Hotchkiss, General Sales Mgr
Cynthia Clark, Programming Director
Sean Stone, Promotions Manager
Curtis Varns, News Director
Rick Hartford, Chief Engineer
Donna Farmer, Human Resources Director

KNLJ *Digital Channel:* 20 *Virtual Channel:* 25; 1000 kw; 1037 ft.; N38 42 15 W92 5 21
Mailing Address: Route 2, Box 72 Hwy 54, New Bloomfiled, MO 63103 US
Second Address: 9810 State Rd. AE, New Bloomfield, MO 65603
(573) 896-5105, *Fax:* (573) 896-4376
www.knlj.tv
traffic@knlj.tv
License: Jefferson City, Cole County, MO held by New Life Evangelistic Center Inc
Washington Law Firm: John H. Midlen Jr
Nat'l Network: REL
Larry Rice, General Manager
Charles Hale, General Sales Mgr
James Shackleford, Programming Director
Shawn Baker, Chief Engineer

KOMU-TV *Digital Channel:* 8 *Virtual Channel:* 8; 13.6 kw; 794 ft.; N38 53 17 W92 15 48
Highway 63 South, Columbia, MO 65201 US
(573) 882-8888, *Fax:* (573) 884-8888
www.komu.com
License: Columbia, Boone County, MO held by The Curators of the University of Missouri.
Group Owner: The Curators of the University of Missouri;
Washington Law Firm: Shaw Pittman
Nat'l Network: NBC; CW *Nat'l Reps:* Millennium Sales & Marketing
Size of News Staff: 23; *Hours of Local News Weekly:* news progmg 20 hrs wkly
Martin Siddall, General Manager
Tom Dugan, General Sales Mgr
Matt Garrett, Promotions Manager
Stacey Woelfel, News Director
Chris Swisher, Chief Engineer
John Parker, National Sales Manager

KRCG *Digital Channel:* 12 *Virtual Channel:* 13; 15.1 kw; 1010 ft.; N38 41 30 W92 5 44
Mailing Address: 5009 South Hulen, Suite 101, Fort Worth, TX 76132 US
Second Address: 10188 Old Hwy. 54 N., New Bloomfield, MO 65063
(573) 896-5144, *Fax:* (573) 896-5193
www.krcg.com
info@krcg.com
License: Jefferson City, Cole County, MO held by Barrington Broadcasting Missouri Corp.
Group Owner: Barrington Broadcasting Group, LLC.; (acq 12-27-2004; $38 million); *Washington Law Firm:* Pepper & Corazzini
Nat'l Network: CBS
Size of News Staff: 14; *Hours of Local News Weekly:* news progmg 14 hrs wkly
Betsy Farris, General Manager
Lee Gordon, Station Manager
Wendy Gustofson, General Sales Mgr
K.J. Lambein, Promotions Manager
Gregg Palermo, News Director
Jim Malone, Chief Engineer
Roger Hulett, Regional Sales Manager

Davenport, IA-Rock Island-Moline, IL (DMA 97)

KGCW *Digital Channel:* 41; 54.3 kw vis, 5.43 kw aur; ant 315t; N40 49 25 W91 08 22; *Population Served:* 590,000
937 E 53rd Street, Suite D, Davenport, IA 52807
(563) 386-1818, *Fax:* (563) 386-8543
www.kgcwtv.com
qandc@kgcwtv.com
License: Burlington, Des Moines County, IA held by Burlington Television Acquisition Licensing LLC.
Group Owner: Grant Communications Inc.; (acq 1995; $400,000); *Washington Law Firm:* Wilkinson, Barker, Knauer & Quinn
Nat'l Network: CW *Nat'l Reps:* TeleRep
Kathy DeBoeuf, Station Manager
Jaime Horowitz, General Sales Mgr
John Bain, Programming Director
Tim Emmerson, Promotions Manager
Tony Wilkins, Local Sales Manager

KLJB *Digital Channel:* 49; 3,000 kw vis, 300 kw aur; ant 1,010t/993g; N41 19 17 W90 22 47; *Population Served:* 737,000
937 E. 53rd St., Suite D, Davenport, IA 52807
(563) 386-1818, *Fax:* (563) 386-8543
www.kljb.com
qandc@kljb.com
License: Davenport, Scott County, IA held by Quad Cities Television Acquisition Licensing LLC
Group Owner: Grant Communications Inc.; *Washington Law Firm:* Wilkinson, Barker, Knauer & Quinn
Nat'l Network: Fox *Nat'l Reps:* TeleRep
Hours of Local News Weekly: News progmg 3.5 hrs wkly
Kathy DeBoeuf, Station Manager
Jaime Horowitz, General Sales Mgr
John Bain, Programming Director
Tim Emmerson, Promotions Manager
Tony Wilkins, Local Sales Manager

***KQIN** ; 6.76 kw vis, 676 w aur; 213t; N41 31 58 W90 34 40; *Rebroadcasting:* Satellite of *WQPT-TV Moline IL 100%.
6600 34th Ave., Moline, IA 61265
(309) 796-2424, *Fax:* (309) 796-2484
www.wqpt.org
wqpt@bhc.edu
License: Davenport, Scott County, IA held by Iowa Public Broadcasting Board
Cathryn Lass, Operations Dir
Rick Best, General Manager
Lora Adams, General Sales Mgr
Jerry Myers, Programming Director
Lora Adams, Promotions Manager
Steve Ellis, Chief Engineer

Des Moines-Ames, IA (DMA 71)

WHO-DT *Digital Channel:* 13; 316 kw vis, 47.9 kw aur; ant 1,970t/2,000g; N41 48 33 W93 36 53; *Population Served:* 500,000
1801 Grand Ave., Des Moines, IA 50309
(515) 242-3500, *Fax:* (515) 242-3796
www.whotv.com
License: Des Moines, Polk County, IA held by Local TV Iowa License LLC
Group Owner: Local TV LLC; (acq 5-7-2007; grpsl); *Washington Law Firm:* Covington & Burling
Nat'l Network: NBC *Nat'l Reps:* Millennium Sales & Marketing
Size of News Staff: 50; *Hours of Local News Weekly:* news progmg 30 hrs wkly
Robert Lawrence, President
Rebecca Jess, Operations Dir
Dale R. Wood, General Manager
Mark McGeary, General Sales Mgr
Tim Gardner, Promotions Manager
Rod Petersen, News Director
Brad Olk, Chief Engineer

WOI-TV *Digital Channel:* 5; 100 kw vis, 20 kw aur; 1,850t/2,000g; N41 48 33 W93 36 53; *Population Served:* 559,700
3903 Westown Pkwy., West Des Moines, IA 50266
(515) 457-9645, *Fax:* (515) 457-1034
www.myabc5.com
info@myabc5.com
License: Ames, Story County, IA held by Capital Communications Co. Inc.
Group Owner: Citadel Communications Co. LTD.; (acq 3-1-94; $12.7 million); *Washington Law Firm:* Latham & Watkins
Nat'l Network: ABC *Nat'l Reps:* Continental Television Sales
Wire Services: AP
Size of News Staff: 25; *Hours of Local News Weekly:* news progmg 15 hrs wkly
Philip Lombardo, CEO
Ray Cole, President
Randy Shelton, Operations Dir

Joplin, MO-Pittsburg, KS (DMA 148)

KFJX-DT ; 5,000 kw vis; ant 1,112t/1,069g; N37 18 46 W94 48 59; *Population Served:* 350,000
Box 659, Pittsburg, KS 66762-0659
(417) 782-1414, *Fax:* (417) 206-4081
www.fox14tv.com
ddishman@fox14tv.com
License: Pittsburg, Crawford County, KS held by Surtsey Media LLC
Group Owner: Surtsey Media LLC; (acq 3-7-2003).
Nat'l Network: Fox
Size of News Staff: 4; *Hours of Local News Weekly:* news progmg 3 hrs wkly
Darren Dishman, General Manager

KODE-TV *Digital Channel:* 43 *Virtual Channel:* 12; 1000 kw; 881 ft.; N37 4 37 W94 32 15
Mailing Address: The Pinnacle, Suite 875, 3455 Peachtree Rd., N.E., Atlanta, GA 30326 US
Second Address: 1928 W. 13th St., Joplin, MO 64802
(417) 623-7260, *Fax:* (417) 782-2417
www.kode-tv.com
License: Joplin, Jasper County, MO held by Mission Broadcasting of Joplin Inc.
Group Owner: Mission Broadcasting Inc.; (acq 2-27-2002; $6 million); *Washington Law Firm:* Cohn
Nat'l Network: ABC
Size of News Staff: 18; *Hours of Local News Weekly:* news progmg 16 hrs wkly
Shirley Morton, Station Manager
Gary Hood, General Sales Mgr
Janice Rohman, Programming Director
Larry Young, News Director
Jeff Hadley, Chief Engineer

***KOZJ** *Digital Channel:* 25 *Virtual Channel:* 26; 55 kw vis; ant 922t/850g; N37 04 37 W94 32 15; *Rebroadcasting:* Satellite of *KOZK Springfield.
Mailing Address: Box 1226, Joplin, MO 65801
Second Address: 403 S. Main St., Joplin, MO 64801
(417) 782-2226, *Fax:* (417) 782-7222
www.optv.org
mail@optv.org
License: Joplin, Jasper County, MO held by Board of Governors of Southwest Missouri State University
(acq 4-25-2001; $1.3 million assumption of debt with KOZK(TV) Springfield).; *Washington Law Firm:* Dow, Lohns PLLC
Nat'l Network: PBS
Tammy Wiley, General Manager
Norma Scott, General Sales Mgr
Tom Carter, Programming Director
Rebecca Scott, Promotions Manager
Brent Moore, Chief Engineer

KSNF *Digital Channel:* 46 *Virtual Channel:* 16; 175 kw; 1057 ft.; N37 4 33 W94 33 16
Mailing Address: 200 Abington Executive Park, Suite 201, Clarks Summit, PA 18411 US
Second Address: 1502 Cleveland, Joplin, MO 64801
(417) 781-2345, *Fax:* (417) 782-2417
www.ksntv.com
License: Joplin, Jasper County, MO held by Nexstar Finance Inc.
Group Owner: Nexstar Broadcasting Group Inc.; (acq 11-6-97; grpsl).; *Washington Law Firm:* Arter & Hadden
Nat'l Network: NBC
John Hoffman, General Manager
Debra Palmer, General Sales Mgr
Robin Richey, Programming Director
Larry Young, News Director
Jeff Hadley, Chief Engineer

Kansas City, MO (DMA 31)

***KCPT** *Digital Channel:* 18 *Virtual Channel:* 19; 1000 kw; 1165 ft.; N39 4 59 W94 28 49
125 East 31st Street, Kansas City, MO 64108 US
(816) 756-3580, *Fax:* (816) 931-2500
www.kcpt.org
kcpt@kcpt.org
License: Kansas City, Jackson County, MO held by Public TV 19 Inc
(acq 1-1-72; $22,226;; *Washington Law Firm:* Arter & Hadden
Nat'l Network: PBS
Victor Hogstrom, CEO
Jeff Evans, Chief Technical Officer

KCTV *Digital Channel:* 24 *Virtual Channel:* 5; 1000 kw; 1129 ft.; N39 4 14 W94 34 57
Mailing Address: 4500 Shawnee Mission Pwy, Fairway, KS 66205 US
Second Address: 4500 Shawnee Mission Pkwy, Fairway, KS 66205
(913) 677-5555, *Fax:* (913) 677-7109
www.kctv5.com
kctv5@kctv5.com
License: Kansas City, Clay County, MO held by Meredith Corp.
Group Owner: Meredith Broadcasting Group, Meredith Corp.; (acq 10-1-53; $2 million)
Nat'l Network: CBS *Nat'l Reps:* TeleRep
Kirk Black, Operations Dir
Dave Duncan, General Sales Mgr
Beth Green, Programming Director
Tracy Brogden-Miller, News Director
Tom Casey, Engineering Dir
Michael Cornette, National Sales Manager
Pam Carder, Regional SalesManager
Jason Mullenix, Regional Sales Manager

KCWE *Digital Channel:* 31 *Virtual Channel:* 29; 1000 kw; 1089 ft.; N39 5 1 W94 30 57
4700 Belleview, Suite 300, Kansas City, MO 64112 US
(816) 221-2900, *Fax:* (816) 760-9149
www.KCWE.com
License: Kansas City, Jackson County, MO held by KCWE-TV Company
Group Owner: Hearst-Argyle Television Inc.; (acq 8-15-2006; $10.96 million)
Nat'l Network: CW *Nat'l Reps:* Harrington, Righter & Parsons
Hours of Local News Weekly: 10
C. Wayne Godsey, General Manager
Shannon Hart, General Sales Mgr
Karen King, Programming Director
Paul Tranisi, Promotions Manager
Jerry Agresti, Engineering Dir

KMBC-TV *Digital Channel:* 29 *Virtual Channel:* 9; 1000 kw; 1175 ft.; N39 5 1 W94 30 57
888 Seventh Avenue, New York, NY 10106 US
(816) 221-9999, *Fax:* (816) 760-9245
www.kmbc.com
License: Kansas City, Jackson County, MO held by KMBC Hearst-Argyle Television Inc.
Group Owner: Hearst-Argyle Television Inc.; (acq 7-16-97; grpsl).; *Washington Law Firm:* Brooks, Pierce, McLendon, Humphrey & Leonard
Nat'l Network: ABC *Nat'l Reps:* Eagle Television Sales *Wire Services:* AP; CNN; ABC
Size of News Staff: 55; *Hours of Local News Weekly:* 28 hrs wkly
Wayne Godsey, Operations Dir
Peggy Madigan, General Sales Mgr
Sherrie Brown, News Director
Jerry Agresti, Engineering Dir

KMCI-TV *Digital Channel:* 36; 5,000 kw vis, 494 kw aur; ant 1,069t/1,128g; N38 58 42 W94 32 01; *Population Served:* 2,182,000
4720 Oak St., Kansas City, MO 64112
(816) 753-4141, *Fax:* (816) 932-4122
www.38thespot.com
comments@38thespot.com
License: Lawrence, Douglas County, KS held by Scripps Howard Broadcasting Co.
Group Owner: The E. W. Scripps Co.; (acq 2-3-2000).
Nat'l Reps: Harrington, Righter & Parsons
Craig Allison, Operations Dir
Alan Fuchsman, General Sales Mgr
Dana Boyd, Programming Director
Randy Thurman, Promotions Manager
Peggy Phillip, News Director
Jay Nix, Chief Engineer

***KMOS-TV** *Digital Channel:* 15 *Virtual Channel:* 6; 322 kw vis; ant 1,978t/1,965g; N38 37 36 W92 52 03; *Population Served:* 1,500,000
University of Central Missouri, Wood 11, Warrensburg, MO 64093
(660) 543-4155, *Fax:* (660) 543-8863
www.kmos.org
kmos@kmos.org
License: Sedalia, Pettis County, MO held by Central Missouri State University
(acq 6-6-78; $1,000); *Washington Law Firm:* Shaw Pittman
Nat'l Network: PBS
Josh Tomlinson, Operations Dir
Rosemary Olas, General Manager
Mark Pearce, General Sales Mgr
Michael O'Keefe, Programming Director
John Long, Chief Engineer
Sarah Bailey, Finance Manager
Dorothy McGrath, Product AffairsDirector

KPXE-TV *Digital Channel:* 51; 678 kw vis, 67.8 kw aur; 1,119t/1,164g; N39 01 19 W94 30 50; *Population Served:* 750,000
4720 Oak St., Kansas City, MO 64112
(816) 924-5050, *Fax:* (816) 931-1818
www.ionline.tv
License: Kansas City, Jackson County, MO held by Paxson Kansas City License Inc.
Group Owner: ION Media Networks Inc.; (acq 3-3-97; $16.4 million); *Washington Law Firm:* Wiley, Rein & Fielding
Nat'l Network: ION Television
Foreign Language Programming
Frank Barajas, General Manager
Alan Fuchsman, General Sales Mgr
Dave Campbell, Chief Engineer

KSHB-TV *Digital Channel:* 42 *Virtual Channel:* 41; 730 kw; 1062 ft.; N38 58 42 W94 32 1
P. O. Box 5610, 28th Floor, Cincinnati, OH 45201 US
(816) 753-4141, *Fax:* (816) 932-4122
www.nbcactionnews.com
programming@nbcactionnews.com
License: Kansas City, Jackson County, MO held by Scripps Howard Broadcasting Co.
Group Owner: The E. W. Scripps Co.; (acq 10-28-77;
Nat'l Network: NBC *Nat'l Reps:* Harrington, Righter & Parsons
Size of News Staff: 75; *Hours of Local News Weekly:* news progmg 32 hrs wkly
Craig Allison, Operations Dir
John McKenna, General Sales Mgr
Dana Boyd, Programming Director
Dominick Nardo, Promotions Manager
Debbie Bush, News Director
Jay Nix, Chief Engineer

KSMO-TV *Digital Channel:* 47 *Virtual Channel:* 62; 1000 kw; 1168 ft.; N39 5 26 W94 28 18
10706 Beaver Dam Road, Cockeysville, MD 21030 US
(913) 621-6262, *Fax:* (913) 621-4703
www.myksmotv.com
ksmo@myKSMOtv.com
License: Kansas City, Jackson County, MO held by Meredith Corp.
Group Owner: Meredith Broadcasting Group, Meredith Corp.; (acq 9-29-2005; $26.8 million)
Nat'l Network: MYTV *Nat'l Reps:* Millennium Sales & Marketing
Kirk Black, Operations Dir
Darrin McDonald, General Sales Mgr
Beth Green, Programming Director
Tom Casey, Chief Engineer

WDAF-TV *Digital Channel:* 34 *Virtual Channel:* 4; 1000 kw; 1138 ft.; N39 4 21 W94 35 45
5151 Wisconsin Ave., NW, Washington, DC 20016 US
(816) 753-4567, *Fax:* (816) 931-3984
www.myfoxkc.com
License: Kansas City, Jackson County, MO held by WDAF License Inc.
Group Owner: Fox Television Stations Inc.; (acq 1-23-97; grpsl).
Nat'l Network: FOX *Nat'l Reps:* Fox Stations Sales
Size of News Staff: 115; *Hours of Local News Weekly:* news progmg 49 hrs wkly
Cheryl McDonald, Operations Dir
Kelly Satalowich, General Sales Mgr
Matt Rankin, Programming Director
Damon Bryant, Promotions Manager
Bryan McGruder, News Director
Jim Moore, Engineering Dir

Ottumwa, IA-Kirksville, MO (DMA 200)

KTVO *Digital Channel:* 33 *Virtual Channel:* 3; 87 kw; 951 ft.; N40 31 47 W92 26 29
Mailing Address: Rsa Tower Suite 710, 201 Monroe Street, Montgomery, AL 36104 US
Second Address: 15518 Hwy. 63 N., Kirksville, MO 63501
(660) 627-3333,(641) 682-3333, *Fax:* (641) 682-1572
www.ktvo.com
License: Kirksville, Adair County, MO held by Barrington Kirksville License LLC.
Group Owner: Barrington Broadcasting Group, LLC.; (acq 8-11-2006; grpsl); *Washington Law Firm:* Covington & Burling
Nat'l Network: ABC *Nat'l Reps:* Harrington, Righter & Parsons
Size of News Staff: 16; *Hours of Local News Weekly:* news progmg 14 hr wkly
Crystal Amini-Rad, General Manager
Merle Snyder, General Sales Mgr
Melissa Billington, Programming Director
Teresa Johnson, Promotions Manager
Marlene Speas, News Director
John Wise, Chief Engineer

Paducah, KY-Cape Girardeau, MO-Harrisburg-Mount Vernon, IL (DMA 78)

KBSI *Digital Channel:* 22 *Virtual Channel:* 23; 705 kw; 1781 ft.; N37 24 23 W89 33 44
10706 Beaver Dam Road, Cockeysville, MD 21030 US
(573) 334-1223, *Fax:* (573) 334-1208
www.kbsi23.com
License: Cape Girardeau, Cape Girardeau County, MO held by KBSI Licensee L.P.
Group Owner: Sinclair Broadcast Group Inc.; (acq 1998; grpsl).
Nat'l Network: FOX *Nat'l Reps:* Millennium Sales & Marketing
Rob Chronister, Operations Dir
Tom Tipton, General Manager
Jennifer Chronister, General Sales Mgr
Alan Muster, Programming Director
Chuck Moffitt, Promotions Manager
Chris Girard, Chief Engineer
Glenn Ralston, National SalesManager
Mary Robbins, Public Service Director
John Schreiner, Traffic Manager

KFVS-TV *Digital Channel:* 12 *Virtual Channel:* 12; 6.8 kw; 1998 ft.; N37 25 46 W89 30 14
Mailing Address: Rsa Tower, 20th Floor, 201 Monroe Street, Montgomery, AL 36104 US
Second Address: 310 Broadway, Cape Girardeau, MT 63702
(573) 335-1212, *Fax:* (573) 335-6303
www.kfvs12.com
manager@kfvs12.com
License: Cape Girardeau, Cape Girardeau County, MO held by Kfvs Licensing Subsidiary LLC
Group Owner: Raycom Media Inc.; (acq 4-97; grpsl).;
Washington Law Firm: Covington & Burling
Nat'l Network: CBS *Nat'l Reps:* Harrington, Righter & Parsons
Size of News Staff: 45; *Hours of Local News Weekly:* news progmg 28 hrs wkly
Mike Wunderlich, Operations Dir
Tim Ingram, General Manager
Joe Trepasso, General Sales Mgr
Kathy Cowan, Programming Director
Paul Keener, Promotions Manager
Mark Little, News Director
Brad Zaruba, National Sales Manager
DanTimpe, Promotions Director
Karen Wade, Regional Sales Manager

KPOB-TV *Digital Channel:* 15 *Virtual Channel:* 15; 34.5 kw; 604 ft.; N36 48 4 W90 27 6; *Rebroadcasting:* Satellite of WSIL-TV Harrisburg IL.
5009 South Hulen, Suite 101, Fort Worth, TX 76132 US
(618) 985-2333, *Fax:* (618) 985-3709
www.wsiltv.com
License: Poplar Bluff, Butler County, MO held by Mel Wheeler Inc.
Group Owner: Mel Wheeler Inc.; (acq 5-12-83; $6.6 million;;
Washington Law Firm: Brooks, Pierce, McLendon, Humphrey & Leonard
Nat'l Network: ABC
Steve Wheeler, General Manager
Pat Victoria, Chief Engineer

Quincy, IL-Hannibal, MO-Keokuk, IA (DMA 171)

KHQA-TV *Digital Channel:* 7 *Virtual Channel:* 7; 13.6 kw; 889 ft.; N39 58 22 W91 19 54
301 South 36th Street, Quincy, IL 62301 US
(217) 222-6200, *Fax:* (217) 228-3164/(217) 222-5078
www.khqa.com
khqa@khqa.com
License: Hannibal, Marion County, MO held by Barrington Broadcasting Quincy Corp.
Group Owner: Barrington Broadcasting Group, LLC.; (acq 4-30-2004; $23.5 million with WHOI(TV) Peoria, IL).; *Washington Law Firm:* Covington & Burling
Nat'l Network: CBS; ABC *Nat'l Reps:* Continental Television Sales
Size of News Staff: 12; *Hours of Local News Weekly:* news progmg 13 hrs wkly
Carol Kellum, President
Leo Henning, General Manager
Jon Van Ness, Station Manager
Mava Clingingsmith, General Sales Mgr
Jim Malone, Chief Engineer
Cindy Johnson, Regional Sales Manager

Sioux City, IA (DMA 149)

***KSIN-TV** *Digital Channel:* 28; 4,070 kw vis, 407 kw aur; 1070; N42 30 53 W96 18 13
Mailing Address: Box 6450, Iowa Public TV, Johnston, IA 50131-6450
Second Address: 6450 Corporate Dr., Joohnston, IA 50131
(515) 242-3100
www.iptv.org
public_information@iptv.org
License: Sioux City, Woodbury County, IA held by Iowa Public Broadcasting Board
Washington Law Firm: Dow, Lohnes PLLC
Nat'l Network: PBS
Daniel Miller, General Manager

Springfield, MO (DMA 74)

KOLR *Digital Channel:* 52; 316 kw vis, 31.6 kw aur; 2,070t/1,887g; N37 13 08 W92 56 56; *Population Served:* 1,472,000
2650 E. Division, Springfield, MO 65803
(417) 862-1010, *Fax:* (417) 862-6439
www.ozarksfirst.com
dwasson@kolr10.com
License: Springfield, Greene County, MO held by Mission Broadcasting Inc.
Group Owner: Mission Broadcasting Inc.; (acq 12-17-2003).
Nat'l Network: CBS
Size of News Staff: 30; *Hours of Local News Weekly:* news progmg 22 hrs wkly
Mark Gordon, General Manager
Dean Wasson, Station Manager
Dave Thomason, General Sales Mgr
Dave Bowen, Promotions Manager
Polly Van Doren-Orr, News Director
David Smith, Engineering Dir

***KOZK** *Digital Channel:* 23 *Virtual Channel:* 21; 100 kw vis; ant 2,024t/1,925g; N37 10 11 W92 56 30; *Population Served:* 650,000
901 S. National, Springfield, MO 65801
(417) 836-3500, *Fax:* (417) 863-3569
www.optv.org
mail@optv.org
License: Springfield, Greene County, MO held by Board of Governors of Missouri State University
Washington Law Firm: Dow, Lohnes PLLC
Nat'l Network: PBS
Tammy Wiley, General Manager
Barb McMeekin, General Sales Mgr
Tom Carter, Programming Director
Brent Moore, Chief Engineer
Rachel Knight, Assistant To General Manager

KOZL-TV *Digital Channel:* 28 *Virtual Channel:* 27; 5,000 kw vis, 500 kw aur; ant 1,694t/1,569g; N37 13 08 W92 56 56; *Population Served:* 890,000
2650 E. Division St., Springfield, MO 02116
(417) 862-2727, *Fax:* (417) 831-4209
www.ozarksfirst.com
License: Springfield, Greene County, MO held by Nexstar Broadcasting Inc.
Group Owner: Nexstar Broadcasting Group Inc.; (acq 12-31-2003; grpsl)
Hours of Local News Weekly: News progmg 12 hrs wkly
Mark Gordon, General Manager
Dave Thomason, General Sales Mgr
Nancy Bingaman, Programming Director
Dave Bowen, Promotions Manager
Polly Van Doren-Orr, News Director
David Smith, Engineering Dir

KRBK *Virtual Channel:* 49; 5,000 kw vis; ant 1,519t/1,375g; N37 49 10 W92 44 52; *Not on Air/Target Date:* unknown
1 S. Memorial Dr., 20th Fl., St. Louis, MO
(314) 345-1000
License: Osage Beach, Camden County, MO
Nat'l Network: Fox
Edward Koplar, President

KSPR *Digital Channel:* 19 *Virtual Channel:* 33; 1000 kw; 1886 ft.; N37 10 26 W92 56 27
Mailing Address: 7621 Little Avenue, Suite 506, Charlotte, NC 28266 US
Second Address: 1359 St. Louis St., Springfield, MO 65802
(417) 831-1333, *Fax:* (417) 831-4125
www.springfield33.com
License: Springfield, Greene County, MO held by Perkin Media LLC.
(acq 2007; $20.629 million); *Ownership:* William N. Perkin, 100%; *Washington Law Firm:* Sciarrino and Associates PLLC
Nat'l Network: ABC
Size of News Staff: 21; *Hours of Local News Weekly:* news progmg 9 hrs wkly
Brad Belote, News Director
Neal Evans, Chief Engineer

KYTV *Digital Channel:* 44 *Virtual Channel:* 3; 967 kw; 2060 ft.; N37 10 26 W92 56 27
999 West Sunshine Street, Springfield, MO 65807 US
(417) 268-3000, *Fax:* (417) 268-3100
www.ky3.com
ky3@ky3.com
License: Springfield, Greene County, MO held by KY-3 Inc.
Group Owner: Schurz Communications Inc.; (acq 2-19-87; $50.8 million;; *Washington Law Firm:* Wilmer Hale
Nat'l Network: NBC; CW *Nat'l Reps:* Harrington, Righter & Parsons
Size of News Staff: 40; *Hours of Local News Weekly:* news progmg 24 hrs wkly
Mike Scott, General Manager
Mary Chalender, General Sales Mgr
Trenna Underhill, Programming Director
Dan McGrane, Promotions Manager
Scott Brady, News Director
Kirk Lemons, Chief Engineer

St. Joseph, MO (DMA 201)

KQTV *Digital Channel:* 7 *Virtual Channel:* 2; 40 kw; 587 ft.; N39 46 12 W94 47 53
Mailing Address: 200 Abington Exe. Park, Suite 201, Clarks Summit, PA 18411 US
Second Address: 4000 & Faraon St., Saint Joseph, MO 64506
(816) 364-2222, *Fax:* (816) 364-3787,TWX: 910-777-7872
www.kq2.com
kq2@kq2.com
License: St. Joseph, Buchanan County, MO held by Nexstar Broadcasting Inc.
Group Owner: Nexstar Broadcasting Group Inc.; (acq 2-14-97; with WTWO(TV) Terre Haute, IN).; *Washington Law Firm:* Drinker, Biddle & Reath
Nat'l Network: ABC *Nat'l Reps:* Blair Television; Petry Television Inc.
Size of News Staff: 18; *Hours of Local News Weekly:* news progmg 16 hrs wkly
Heather Shearin, Operations Dir
Dirk Allsbury, General Sales Mgr
Jim Conlon, Promotions Manager
Bridget Blevins, News Director
Steve Hendrix, Chief Engineer
Steve Cline, Operations Manager

KTAJ-TV *Digital Channel:* 21 *Virtual Channel:* 16; 1000 kw; 1036 ft.; N39 1 20 W94 30 49
4410-B, South 40th St., St. Joseph, MO 64503 US
(816) 364-1616, *Fax:* (816) 364-6729
www.tbn.org
ktaj@tbn.org
License: St. Joseph, Buchanan County, MO held by Trinity Christian Center of Santa Ana Inc. dba Trinity Broadcasting Network.
Group Owner: Trinity Broadcasting Network; (acq 5-8-2000; grpsl).
Nat'l Network: TRINITY BROADCA
Paul Crouch, President
Jan Crouch, Operations Dir
Julie Cluck, Station Manager
Jeff Landers, Engineering Dir
Andrae Hannon, Public Affairs Director

St. Louis, MO (DMA 21)

KDNL-TV *Digital Channel:* 31 *Virtual Channel:* 30; 1000 kw; 1052 ft.; N38 34 50 W90 19 45
Mailing Address: 10706 Beaver Dam Road, Cockeysville, MD 21030 US
Second Address: Promotions/Tape Delivery, 1261 Dublin Rd., Columbus, OH 43215
(314) 436-3030
www.abcstlouis.com
License: St. Louis, Saint Louis City County, MO held by KDNL Licensee L.L.C.
Group Owner: Sinclair Broadcast Group Inc.; (acq 5-30-96);
Washington Law Firm: Shaw, Pittman
Nat'l Network: ABC *Nat'l Reps:* Millennium Sales & Marketing
Jim Wright, Operations Dir
Tom Tipton, General Manager
Mike Held, General Sales Mgr
Sandra Habeck, Programming Director
Andrea Schaffer, Gen/Natl Sls Mgr
Martha Perry, Research Director
Frankie Horan, Traffic Manager

***KETC** *Digital Channel:* 39 *Virtual Channel:* 9; 142.5 kw; 1064 ft.; N38 28 55.8 W90 23 52.6
3655 Olive Street, St. Louis, MO 63108 US
(314) 512-9000, *Fax:* (314) 512-9005
www.ketc.org
License: St. Louis, Saint Louis City County, MO held by St. Louis Regional Educational and Public Television Commission
Washington Law Firm: Dow, Lohnes & Albertson
Nat'l Network: ETV
Jack Galmiche, CEO
Patricia Kistler, Programming Director
Patrick Murphy, Promotions Manager
Richard Skalski, CFO
Dick Skalski, COO
Chrys Marlow, Operations Vice President

KMOV *Digital Channel:* 24 *Virtual Channel:* 4; 1000 kw; 1119 ft.; N38 31 47 W90 17 58
1 Memorial Drive, St. Louis, MO 63102 US
(314) 621-4444, *Fax:* (314) 444-3367,(314) 621-4755
www.kmov.com
channel4@kmov.com
License: St. Louis, Saint Louis City County, MO held by KMOV-TV Inc.
Group Owner: Belo Corp; (acq 6-02-97; grpsl); *Washington Law Firm:* Wiley, Rein & Fielding
Nat'l Network: CBS *Nat'l Reps:* TeleRep
Size of News Staff: 70; *Hours of Local News Weekly:* news progmg 29 hrs wkly
Peggy Milner, CFO
Allan Cohen, President
Jim Rothschild, Operations Dir
Robert Totsch, General Sales Mgr
Liz Mullen, Programming Director
Sean McLaughlin, News Director
Walt Nichol, Chief Engineer
Mike Cukyne, Local SalesManager
Paul Conaty, National Sales Manager

KNLC *Digital Channel:* 14 *Virtual Channel:* 24; 900 kw; 1300 ft.; N38 21 40 W90 32 55
Mailing Address: 1411 Locust Street, St. Louis, MO 63103 US
Second Address: 1411 Locust St., St. Louis, MO 63188
(314) 436-2424, *Fax:* (314) 436-2434
www.knlc.tv
judy@knlc.tv
License: St. Louis, Saint Louis City County, MO held by New Life Evangelistic Center Inc
Washington Law Firm: Midlen & Guillot
Nat'l Network: NONE
Larry Rice, President
Ray Redlich, Operations Dir
Judy Redlich, General Sales Mgr
Victor Anderson, Programming Director
Jim Barnes, Chief Engineer

KPLR-TV *Digital Channel:* 26 *Virtual Channel:* 11; 1000 kw; 945 ft.; N38 34 24 W90 19 30

2101 East Fourth Street, Suite 202, Santa Ana, CA 92705 US
(314) 447-1111, *Fax:* (314) 447-6404
www.cb11tv.com
administration4@tribune.com
License: St. Louis, Saint Louis City County, MO held by KPLR Inc.
Group Owner: Tribune Broadcasting Co.; (acq 12-20-2007; grpsl)
Nat'l Network: CW *Nat'l Reps:* TeleRep
Hours of Local News Weekly: News progmg 4 hrs wkly
Glen Callanan, General Sales Mgr
Gwen Moore, Programming Director
Suzi Schrappen, Promotions Manager
Sheldon Ripson, News Director
Greg Boling, Chief Engineer

KSDK *Digital Channel:* 35 *Virtual Channel:* 5; 838 kw; 1112 ft.; N38 34 5 W90 19 55
Television Plaza, 1000 Market Street, St. Louis, MO 63101 US
(314) 421-5055, *Fax:* (314) 444-5164
www.ksdk.com
comments@ksdk.com
License: St. Louis, Saint Louis City County, MO held by Multimedia KSDK Inc.
Group Owner: Gannett Broadcasting; (acq 11-30-95; grpsl).;
Washington Law Firm: Wiley, Rein & Fielding
Nat'l Network: NBC *Nat'l Reps:* Blair Television
Lynn Beall, President
Julie Heskett, Operations Dir
Mike Meara, General Sales Mgr
Rebecca Rahm, Programming Director
Jeff Winget, Promotions Manager
Mike Shipley, News Director
Dave Hummert, Chief Engineer

KTVI *Digital Channel:* 43 *Virtual Channel:* 2; 1000 kw; 1106 ft.; N38 32 7 W90 22 23
5151 Wisconsin Ave., NW, Washington, DC 20016 US
(314) 213-7462, *Fax:* (314) 213-7461
www.myfoxstl.com
License: St. Louis, Saint Louis City County, MO held by Community Television of Missouri License LLC.
Group Owner: Local TV LLC; (acq 7-14-2008; grpsl); *Washington Law Firm:* Dow Lohnes PLLC
Nat'l Network: FOX
Hours of Local News Weekly: News progmg 37.5 hrs wkly
Spencer Koch, Operations Dir
Kurt Krueger, General Sales Mgr
Elaine Claspill, Programming Director
Kathryn Collett, Promotions Manager
Ernie Dachel, Chief Engineer
Cindy Solomon, National Sales Manager
Steve Mills, Regional SalesManager

Montana

Billings, MT (DMA 170)

KHMT *Digital Channel:* 22; 1,000 kw vis; ant 812t/368g; N45 44 24 W108 08 18; *Population Served:* 150,000
445 S. 24th St. W., Billings, MT 59105
(406) 652-4743, *Fax:* (406) 652-6963
www.yourbigsky.com
jschaefer@ksvi.com
License: Hardin, Big Horn County, MT held by Mission Broadcasting Inc.
Group Owner: Mission Broadcasting Inc.; (acq 12-30-2003).;
Washington Law Firm: Drinker, Biddle & Reath L.L.P.
Nat'l Network: Fox
Sandra Zoldowski, General Manager
Patricia King, Programming Director
Ron Walden, Chief Engineer

KSVI *Digital Channel:* 18 *Virtual Channel:* 6; 1000 kw; 746 ft.; N45 48 26 W108 20 25
18 Newbury Street, Boston, MA 02116 US
(406) 652-4743, *Fax:* (406) 652-6963
www.yourbigsky.com
jschaefer@ksvi.com
License: Billings, Yellowstone County, MT held by Nexstar Broadcasting Inc.
Group Owner: Nexstar Broadcasting Group Inc.; (acq 12-31-2003; grpsl); *Washington Law Firm:* Drinker, Biddle & Reath L.L.P.
Nat'l Network: ABC
Sandra Zoldowski, General Manager
Patricia King, Programming Director
Ron Walden, Chief Engineer

KTVQ *Digital Channel:* 10 *Virtual Channel:* 2; 26.1 kw; 591 ft.; N45 46 1 W108 27 26
3203 3rd Ave. North, Billings, MT 59101 US
(406) 252-5611, *Fax:* (406) 252-9938
www.ktvq.com
news@ktvq.com
License: Billings, Yellowstone County, MT held by Evening Post Publishing Co.
Group Owner: Cordillera Communications Inc.; (acq 1994; $8.5 million); *Washington Law Firm:* Dow, Lohnes & Albertson
Nat'l Network: CBS; CW *Nat'l Reps:* Harrington, Righter & Parsons *Wire Services:* AP
Size of News Staff: 21; *Hours of Local News Weekly:* news progmg 17 hrs wkly
Monty Wallis, President
Jon Stepanek, News Director
John Webber, Chief Engineer

KULR-TV *Digital Channel:* 11 *Virtual Channel:* 8; 16 kw; 627 ft.; N45 45 35 W108 27 14; *Rebroadcasting:* Rebroadcasts KYUS(TV) Miles City.
2045 Overland Avenue, Billings, MT 59108 US
(406) 656-8000, *Fax:* (406) 652-8207
www.kulr8.com
generalmanager@kulr.com
License: Billings, Yellowstone County, MT held by MMM License II LLC.
Group Owner: MAX Media L.L.C.; (acq 6-9-2004; $11 million)
Nat'l Network: NBC *Wire Services:* AP
Size of News Staff: 24; *Hours of Local News Weekly:* news progmg 20 hrs wkly
John Trinder, President
Kris Aschim, Operations Dir
Bruce Cummings, General Manager
Rafael Archille, General Sales Mgr
Blaire Martin, News Director
John Langeliers, National Sales Manager

KYUS-TV *Digital Channel:* 3 *Virtual Channel:* 3; 1.03 kw; 99 ft.; N46 25 34 W105 51 38; *Rebroadcasting:* Satellite of KULR-TV Billings 100% (LMA)
210 South Douglas, Glendive, MT 59330 US
(406) 377-3377, *Fax:* (406) 365-2181
kxgnkdzn@midrivers.com
License: Miles City, Custer County, MT held by KYUS-TV Broadcasting Corp
Nat'l Network: NBC *Nat'l Reps:* Adam Young
Stephen Marks, President
Paul Sturlaugson, General Manager

Butte-Bozeman, MT (DMA 190)

DKBTZ *Digital Channel:* 24 *Virtual Channel:* 24
Mailing Address: 1146 19th St.NW Ste 200, Washington, DC 20036 US
Second Address: 5115 US Hwy. 93 S., Missoula, MT 59804
(406) 542-8900, *Fax:* (501) 604-8004
License: Butte, Silver Bow County, MT held by Montana License Sub, Inc., debtor in possession.
Group Owner: Equity Media Holdings Corp.
Nat'l Network: FOX; MyNetworkTV
Greg Fess, President
Neal Ardman, General Manager
Angie Hughs, General Sales Mgr
Jeff Timpa, Programming Director
Sid Weathorford, Chief Engineer
Terry Cudderford, Regional Sales Manager

KBZK *Digital Channel:* 13 *Virtual Channel:* 7; 18.9 kw; 889 ft.; N45 40 24 W110 52 2
Mailing Address: 445 S.24th Street West, Billings, MT 59102 US
Second Address: 1128 East Main, Bozeman, MT 59715
(406) 586-3280, *Fax:* (406) 586-4135
kbzk.com
receptionist@kbzk.com
License: Bozeman, Gallatin County, MT held by KCTZ Communications Inc.
Group Owner: Cordillera Communications Inc.; (acq 12-93).;
Washington Law Firm: Dow, Lohnes & Albertson
Nat'l Network: CBS; CW *Wire Services:* AP
Size of News Staff: 3
Terry Hurley, President
Pat Cooney, General Manager
Tim Gazy, Station Manager
John Sherer, News Director
Andy Suk, Engineering Dir
Mike Warner, Chief Engineer

KTVM-TV *Digital Channel:* 33; 100 kw vis, 10 kw aur; ant 1,940t/213g; N46 00 29 W112 26 30; *Population Served:* 59,300
201 S. Wallace, Suite A5, Bozeman, MT 59715
(406) 586-0296, *Fax:* (406) 586-0554
www.ktvm.com
news@ktvm.com
License: Butte, Silver Bow County, MT held by BlueStone License Holdings Inc.
Group Owner: Bonten Media Group LLC; (acq 5-31-2007; grpsl);
Washington Law Firm: Covington & Burling LLP
Nat'l Network: NBC *Nat'l Reps:* Continental Television Sales
Charlie Henrich, General Manager
Swan Beck, Station Manager
Scott Bruce, General Sales Mgr
Jean Zosel, Promotions Manager
Charlie Cannaliato, Chief Engineer

KUKL-TV *Digital Channel:* 46; 23.4 kw; 830 m; N48 0 48.2 W114 21 54.5
Visual Communications Bldg 183, Montana State University, Bozeman, MT
(406) 994-3437, *Fax:* (406) 756-0317
www.montanapbs.org
info@montanapbs.org
License: Kalispell, Flathead County, MT held by Board of Regents of the Montana University System
Angela McLean, Chair
Todd Buchanan, Vice Chair

***KUSM-TV** *Digital Channel:* 8; 44 kw vis; ant 817t/305g; N45 40 24 W110 52 02; *Population Served:* 46,000
Box 173340, Visual Communications, Bldg. 183, Montana State Univ., Bozeman, MT 59717-3340
(406) 994-3437, *Fax:* (406) 994-6545
www.montanapbs.org
kusm@montanapbs.org
License: Bozeman, Gallatin County, MT held by Montana State University
Nat'l Network: PBS
Eric Hyyppa, General Manager
Lisa Titus, General Sales Mgr
Aaron Pruitt, Programming Director
Amy Colson, Promotions Manager
Dean Lawver, Engineering Dir
Paul Heitt-Rennie, Traffic Manager

KWYB *Digital Channel:* 19 *Virtual Channel:* 18; 110.7 kw; 1920 ft.; N46 0 24 W112 26 30
118 6th Street South, Great Falls, MT 59405 US
(406) 782-7185, *Fax:* (406) 723-9269
www.kwyb.com
License: Butte, Silver Bow County, MT held by MMM License LLC.
Group Owner: MAX Media L.L.C.; (acq 2-5-2001; grpsl).;
Washington Law Firm: Reddy, Begley & McCormick
Nat'l Network: ABC
Linda Gray, President
Leslie Stoll, General Sales Mgr
Linda Julius, Programming Director
Mike Warner, Chief Engineer
Terry Cuddeford, Regional Sales Manager

KXLF-TV *Digital Channel:* 5; 100 kw vis, 20 kw aur; ant 1,890t/202g; N46 00 27 W112 26 30; *Population Served:* 134,400
Mailing Address: 1003 S. Montana, Butte, MT 59701
Second Address: Box 3500, Butte, MT 59702
(406) 496-8400, *Fax:* (406) 782-8906
www.kxlf.com
License: Butte, Silver Bow County, MT held by KXLF Communications Inc.
Group Owner: Cordillera Communications Inc.; (acq 12-15-86; grpsl;; *Washington Law Firm:* Dow, Lohnes & Albertson
Nat'l Network: CBS; CW *Nat'l Reps:* Harrington, Righter & Parsons *Wire Services:* AP
Size of News Staff: 6+; *Hours of Local News Weekly:* news progmg 20 hrs wkly
Jon Saunders, General Manager
Jon Saunders, Station Manager
Bill Evans, General Sales Mgr
Lynn Hopewell, Programming Director
Lynn Hopewell, Promotions Manager
John Sherer, News Director
Mike Warner, Chief Engineer

Glendive, MT (DMA 210)

KXGN-TV *Digital Channel:* 5 *Virtual Channel:* 5; 1 kw; 500 ft.; N47 2 39 W104 40 52.5
210 South Douglas, Glendive, MT 59330 US

(406) 377-3377, *Fax:* (406) 365-2181
www.kxgn.com
kxgnkdzn@midrivers.com
License: Glendive, Dawson County, MT held by Glendive Broadcasting Corp.
Ownership: Stephen A. Marks.; *Washington Law Firm:* Davis Wright Tremaine LLP
Nat'l Network: CBS/NBC; NBC *Wire Services:* UPI
Stephen Marks, President
Paul Sturlaugson, General Sales Mgr
Andrew Sturlaugson, Programming Director
Mike Huseby, Chief Engineer
Tonya Bruner, Traffic Manager

Great Falls, MT (DMA 191)

KFBB-TV *Digital Channel:* 8 *Virtual Channel:* 5; 100 kw vis, 20 kw aur; 590t/540g; N47 32 08 W111 17 02; *Population Served:* 161,800
Mailing Address: Box 1139, Great Falls, MT 59403
Second Address: 3200 Old Havre Hwy., Black Eagle, MT 59414
(406) 453-4377, *Fax:* (406) 727-9703
www.kfbb.com
kfbb@kfbb.com
License: Great Falls, Cascade County, MT held by KFBB L.L.C.
Group Owner: Wooster Republican Printing Co.; (acq 7-1-82; $5.2 million;; *Washington Law Firm:* Baker & Hostetler
Nat'l Network: ABC; Fox *Wire Services:* Direct Line Weather Wire
Size of News Staff: 6; *Hours of Local News Weekly:* news progmg 6 hrs wkly
Danette Sukut, Station Manager
Linda Julius, Programming Director
Julie Klesh, News Director
Roy Davis, Chief Engineer

KRTV *Digital Channel:* 7 *Virtual Channel:* 3; 28.5 kw; 492 ft.; N47 32 9 W111 17 2
Mailing Address: Post Office Box 2989, Great Falls, MT 59403 US
Second Address: 3300 Old Havre Hwy., Black Eagle, MT 59414
(406) 791-5400, *Fax:* (406) 791-5479
www.montanasnewsstation.com
krtv@krtv.com
License: Great Falls, Cascade County, MT held by KRTV Communications Inc.
Group Owner: Cordillera Communications Inc.; (6-86).; *Washington Law Firm:* Dow, Lohnes & Albertson
Nat'l Network: CBS; CW *Nat'l Reps:* Harrington, Righter & Parsons *Wire Services:* AP; CNN
Size of News Staff: 15; *Hours of Local News Weekly:* news progmg 15 hrs wkly
Jon Saunders, General Manager
Roxie Rattray, Programming Director
Art Taft, Promotions Manager
Jerry Howard, News Director
Marlowe Rames, Engineering Dir

KTGF *Digital Channel:* 45 *Virtual Channel:* 16
118 6th Street South, Great Falls, MT 59405 US
(406) 761-8816, *Fax:* (406) 454-3484
www.ktgf.com
ktgf@ktgf.com
License: Great Falls, Cascade County, MT held by Destiny Licenses LLC.
(acq 11-24-2004; $3 million with translator K47DP Lewistown);
Ownership: Destiny Communications LLC, 100%; *Washington Law Firm:* Garvey, Schubert & Barer
Nat'l Network: IND
Darnell Washington, CEO
Andrea Dean, Station Manager
Jennifer Rimmel, Programming Director

***KUGF** *Digital Channel:* 21 *Virtual Channel:* 21; 23.4 kw; 501 ft.; N47 32 9.2 W111 17 2.1
US
(866) 832-0829, *Fax:* (406) 994-6545
www.montanapbs.org
info@montanapbs.org
License: Great Falls, Cascade County, MT held by Board of Regents of the Montana University System
Eric Hyppa, General Manager of Montana PBS

Helena, MT (DMA 206)

KMTF *Digital Channel:* 29 *Virtual Channel:* 10; 43.4 kw; 2287 ft.; N46 49 35 W111 42 33
455 Capitol Mall, Suite 604, Sacramento, CA 95814 US
(406) 457-1010, *Fax:* (406) 457-2758
www.cwhelena.com
cw10@surewest.net
License: Helena, Lewis and Clark County, MT held by Rocky Mountain Broadcasting Co
Nat'l Network: CW
Jon Gibson, General Manager
Paul Albertson, Station Manager

KTVH-DT *Digital Channel:* 12; 17.5 kw vis; ant 2,339t/144g; N46 49 35 W111 42 33; *Population Served:* 140,000
100 W. Lyndale Ave., Suite A, Helena, MT 59601
(406) 457-1212, *Fax:* (406) 442-5106
www.beartoothnbc.com
kaernst@ktvh.com
License: Helena, Lewis and Clark County, MT held by Beartooth Communications Co.
Group Owner: Sunbelt Communications Co.; (acq 7-9-97).; *Washington Law Firm:* Gerald S. Rourke
Nat'l Network: NBC
Size of News Staff: 8; *Hours of Local News Weekly:* news progmg 7 hrs wkly
Kathy Ernst, General Manager
Don Dunwell, News Director
Mike Anderson, Chief Engineer

Missoula, MT (DMA 166)

KCFW-TV *Digital Channel:* 9 *Virtual Channel:* 9; 2.5 kw; 2789 ft.; N48 0 48 W114 21 55
Mailing Address: 340 West Main Street, Missoula, MT 59802 US
Second Address: 401 First Ave East, Kalispell, MT 59901
(406) 755-5239, *Fax:* (406) 752-8002
www.nbcmontana.com
news@kcfw.com
License: Kalispell, Flathead County, MT held by BlueStone License Holdings Inc.
Group Owner: Bonten Media Group LLC; (acq 5-31-2007; grpsl); *Washington Law Firm:* Covington & Burling LLP
Nat'l Network: NBC
Size of News Staff: 5; *Hours of Local News Weekly:* news progmg 6 hrs wkly
Rebecca Swan, General Manager
Wade Muehlhof, Station Manager
Jacque Walawander, General Sales Mgr
Jean Zosel, Promotions Manager
Robert Owen, Engineering Dir
Chris Neuhausen, Chief Engineer

KECI-TV *Digital Channel:* 13 *Virtual Channel:* 13; 41.3 kw; 2001 ft.; N47 1 4 W114 0 47
Mailing Address: 340 West Main Street, Missoula, MT 59802 US
Second Address: Box 5268, Missoula, MT 59806-5268
(406) 721-2063, *Fax:* (406) 721-2083/(406) 549-6507
www.nbcmontana.com
news@keci.tv
License: Missoula, Missoula County, MT held by BlueStone License Holdings Inc.
Group Owner: Bonten Media Group LLC; (acq 5-31-2007; grpsl); *Washington Law Firm:* Covington & Burling LLP
Nat'l Network: NBC *Nat'l Reps:* Continental Television Sales
Hours of Local News Weekly: News progmg 14 hrs wkly
Charlie Henrich, General Manager
Jean Zosel, Promotions Manager
Jim Harmon, News Director
Robert Owen, Engineering Dir
Charlie Cannaliato, Chief Engineer
Jacque Walawander, Regional Sales Manager
Sharikay Austin, TrafficManager

KPAX-TV *Digital Channel:* 7 *Virtual Channel:* 8; 22.5 kw; 2144 ft.; N47 1 6 W114 0 41
P. O. Box 4827, Missoula, MT 59806 US
(406) 542-4400, *Fax:* (406) 543-7111
www.kpax.com
office@kpax.com
License: Missoula, Missoula County, MT held by KPAX-TV Communications Inc.
Group Owner: Cordillera Communications Inc.; *Washington Law Firm:* Dow, Lohnes & Albertson
Nat'l Network: CBS/CW; CW
Hours of Local News Weekly: News progmg 15 hrs wkly
Bob Hermes, General Manager
Jim McLean, General Sales Mgr
Tammy Engle, Programming Director
James Rafferty, Promotions Manager
Joel Lundstad, News Director
Larry Arbaugh, Chief Engineer

KTMF *Digital Channel:* 23 *Virtual Channel:* 23; 92.6 kw; 2106 ft.; N47 1 10 W114 0 46; *Rebroadcasting:* Rebroadcasts KTMF (LP) Kalispell 90%.
118 Sixth Street South, Great Falls, MT 59405 US
(406) 542-8900, *Fax:* (406) 728-4800
www.abcmontana.com
License: Missoula, Missoula County, MT held by MMM License LLC.
Group Owner: MAX Media L.L.C.; (acq 2-5-2001; grpsl).; *Washington Law Firm:* Reddy, Begley & McCormick
Nat'l Network: ABC; Fox
Linda Gray, President
Craig Toomey, General Sales Mgr
Linda Julius, Programming Director
Mark Huller, Chief Engineer

***KUFM-TV** *Digital Channel:* 11 *Virtual Channel:* 11; 125 kw vis; 2,116t/259g; Missoula, MT; *Rebroadcasting:* Rebroadcasts KUSM(TV) Bozeman 85%.
PARTV 180, 32 Campus Dr., Univ. of Montana, Missoula, MT 59812
(406) 243-4101, *Fax:* (406) 243-3299
www.montanapbs.org
kufm@montanapbs.org
License: Missoula, Missoula County, MT held by The University of Montana
Nat'l Network: PBS
Size of News Staff: 1; *Hours of Local News Weekly:* 0
Daniel Dauterive, Operations Dir
William Marcus, General Manager
Drew Jenkins, General Sales Mgr
Saxon Holbrook, Engineering Dir
Jeff Croonenberghs, Chief Engineer

Nebraska

Cheyenne, WY-Scottsbluff, NE (DMA 198)

KDUH-TV *Digital Channel:* 7 *Virtual Channel:* 4; 32 kw; 1558 ft.; N41 50 28 W103 4 27
Mailing Address: PO Box 1760, Rapid City, SD 57709 US
Second Address: 1523 First Avenue, Scottsbluff, NE 69361
(308) 632-3071, *Fax:* (308) 632-3596
www.kduhtv.com
License: Scottsbluff, Scotts Bluff County, NE held by Duhamel Broadcasting Enterprises.
Group Owner: Duhamel Broadcasting Enterprises; *Washington Law Firm:* Fisher, Wayland, Cooper, Leader & Zaragoza
Nat'l Network: ABC
Size of News Staff: 6; *Hours of Local News Weekly:* news progmg 2 hrs wkly
Patrick Maag, General Manager
Doug Loos, Programming Director
Jerry Dishong, News Director
Teddy Johnson, Chief Engineer

KSTF *Digital Channel:* 29 *Virtual Channel:* 10; 2.7 kw; 764 ft.; N41 59 58 W103 39 55
2923 East Lincolnway, Cheyenne, WY 82001 US
(308) 632-6107, *Fax:* (308) 632-3470
www.kgwn.tv
License: Scottsbluff, Scotts Bluff County, NE held by SagamoreHill Broadcasting Co. of Wyoming/Northern Colorado LLC.
Group Owner: SagamoreHill Broadcasting LLC; (acq 3-19-2004; $6.5 million with KGWN-TV Cheyenne, WY).; *Washington Law Firm:* Dow, Lohnes & Albertson
Nat'l Network: CBS; Fox
Size of News Staff: 6; *Hours of Local News Weekly:* news progmg 8 hrs wkly
Joan Turner-Doyle, General Manager
Dusty Thein, General Sales Mgr
Barbara Parenti, Programming Director
Tricia Murphy, Promotions Manager
Jon Martin, News Director
Tony Schaefer, Chief Engineer

***KTNE-TV** *Digital Channel:* 13 *Virtual Channel:* 13; 27 kw; 1529 ft.; N41 50 27 W103 3 18; *Rebroadcasting:* Satellite of *KUON-TV Lincoln.
P. O. Box 83111, Lincoln, NE 88501 US
(402) 472-3611, *Fax:* (402) 472-1785
www.netnebraska.org
net1@unl.edu
License: Alliance, Box Butte County, NE held by Nebraska Educational Telecommunications Commission
Washington Law Firm: Dow, Lohnes & Albertson
Nat'l Network: PBS *Regional Network:* National Educational Telecommunications Association

Joe Turco, Operations Dir
Rod Bates, General Manager
Michael Winkle, General Sales Mgr
David Feingold, Programming Director
Terry Dugas, Programming & Promotion

Lincoln & Hastings-Kearney, NE (DMA 106)

KGIN *Digital Channel:* 11 *Virtual Channel:* 11; 25 kw; 1032 ft.; N40 35 14 W98 48 10; *Rebroadcasting:* Satellite of KOLN Lincoln.
Mailing Address: 40th and W Street, Lincoln, NE 68503 US
Second Address: 840 N 40th Street, Lincoln, NE 98503
(402) 467-9265, *Fax:* (402) 467-9210
www.kolnkgin.com
kgin1011@hotmail.com
License: Grand Island, Hall County, NE held by WEAU Licensee Corp.
Group Owner: Gray Television Inc.; (acq 7-30-98; grpsl).; *Washington Law Firm:* Pepper & Corazzini
Nat'l Network: CBS; MyNetworkTV *Nat'l Reps:* Continental Television Sales
Troy Frankforter, Operations Dir
Clint Simmons, General Sales Mgr

KHAS-TV *Digital Channel:* 5 *Virtual Channel:* 5; 45 kw; 712 ft.; N40 39 6 W98 23 4
P.O. Box 578, Hastings, NE 68902 US
(402) 463-1321, *Fax:* (402) 463-6551
www.khastv.com
khas@khastv.com
License: Hastings, Adams County, NE held by Hoak Media of Nebraska License LLC.
Group Owner: Hoak Media Corporation; (acq 11-7-2005; with KNOP-TV North Platte).; *Washington Law Firm:* Fletcher, Heald & Hildreth
Nat'l Network: NBC *Wire Services:* Skycom
Alan Uerling, Operations Dir
Ulysses Carlini, General Manager
Connie Caldwell, General Sales Mgr
Jackie Arkerman, Programming Director
Jackie Ackerman, Promotions Manager
Dennis Kellogg, News Director
Connie Cardwell, RegionalSales Manager

KHGI-TV *Digital Channel:* 13 *Virtual Channel:* 13; 19.8 kw; 1115 ft.; N40 39 28 W98 52 4
Mailing Address: P.O. Box 220, Kearney, NE 68848 US
Second Address: 1078 25th Road, Axtell, NE 68924
(308) 743-2494, *Fax:* (308) 743-2644
www.nebraska.tv
comments@nebraska.tv
License: Kearney, Buffalo County, NE held by Pappas Telecasting of Central Nebraska L.P. (DE limited partnership).
Group Owner: Pappas Telecasting Companies; (acq 7-1-96; grpsl).
Nat'l Network: ABC *Nat'l Reps:* Harrington, Righter & Parsons
Size of News Staff: 26; *Hours of Local News Weekly:* news progmg 17.5 hrs wkly
Vincent Barresi, General Manager
Dallas Nau, General Sales Mgr
Scott Swenson, Programming Director
Anita Wragge, Promotions Manager
Mark Baumert, News Director
Jerry Fuehrer, Chief Engineer

***KHNE-TV** *Digital Channel:* 28 *Virtual Channel:* 29; 200 kw; 1201 ft.; N40 46 20 W98 5 21; *Rebroadcasting:* Satellite of *KUON-TV Lincoln.
P.O. Box 83111, Lincoln, NE 88501 US
(402) 472-3611, *Fax:* (402) 472-1785
www.netnebraska.org
net1@unl.edu
License: Hastings, Adams County, NE held by Nebraska Educational Telecommunications Commission
Washington Law Firm: Dow, Lohnes & Albertson
Nat'l Network: PBS *Regional Network:* National Educational Telecommunications Association
Size of News Staff: 3
Joe Turco, Operations Dir
Rod Bates, General Manager
Michael Winkle, General Sales Mgr
David Feingold, Programming Director
Terry Dugas, Programming & Promotion

KLKN *Digital Channel:* 8 *Virtual Channel:* 8; 25.9 kw; 1434 ft.; N40 52 59 W97 18 19
7th and Douglas Street, Sioux City, IA 51101 US
(402) 434-8000, *Fax:* (402) 436-2236
www.klkntv.com
8@klkntv.com
License: Lincoln, Lancaster County, NE held by Citadel Communications Co. L.L.C.
Group Owner: Citadel Communications Co. LTD.; (acq 11-15-86;; *Washington Law Firm:* Latham & Watkins
Nat'l Network: ABC *Nat'l Reps:* Millennium Sales & Marketing
Wire Services: AP
Size of News Staff: 22; *Hours of Local News Weekly:* news progmg 22 hrs wkly
Jeff Swanson, Operations Dir
Roger Moody, General Manager
Kay Wunderlich, General Sales Mgr
Mark Haggar, News Director
Dan Ackerman, Chief Engineer
Phil Maddern, Regional Sales Manager

***KLNE-TV** *Digital Channel:* 26 *Virtual Channel:* 3; 375 kw; 1086 ft.; N40 23 5 W99 27 30; *Rebroadcasting:* Satellite of *KUON-TV Lincoln.
P. O. Box 83111, Lincoln, NE 88501 US
(402) 472-3611, *Fax:* (402) 472-1785
www.netnebraska.org
net1@unl.edu
License: Lexington, Dawson County, NE held by Nebraska Educational Telecommunications Commission
Washington Law Firm: Dow, Lohnes & Albertson
Nat'l Network: PBS *Regional Network:* National Educational Telecommunications Association
Joe Turco, Operations Dir
Rod Bates, General Manager
Michael Winkle, General Sales Mgr
David Feingold, Programming Director
Terry Dugas, Promotions Manager

***KMNE-TV** *Digital Channel:* 7 *Virtual Channel:* 7; 27 kw; 1486 ft.; N42 20 5 W99 29 2; *Rebroadcasting:* Satellite of *KUON-TV Lincoln.
1800 North 33rd St, Lincoln, NE 68501 US
(402) 472-3611, *Fax:* (402) 472-1785
www.netnebraska.org
net1@unl.edu
License: Bassett, Rock County, NE held by Nebraska Educational Telecommunications Commission
Washington Law Firm: Dow, Lohnes & Albertson
Nat'l Network: PBS *Regional Network:* National Educational Telecommunications Association
Joe Turco, Operations Dir
Rod Bates, General Manager
Michael Winkle, General Sales Mgr
David Feingold, Programming Director
Terry Dugas, Promotions Manager

KOLN *Digital Channel:* 10 *Virtual Channel:* 10; 28 kw; 1489 ft.; N40 48 11 W97 10 52
Mailing Address: 40th and W Street, Lincoln, NE 68503 US
Second Address: , Lincoln, NE
(402) 467-4321, *Fax:* (402) 467-9210
www.1011now.com
info@1011now.com
License: Lincoln, Lancaster County, NE held by Gray Television Licensee Inc.
Group Owner: Gray Television Inc.; (acq 7-30-98; grpsl).; *Washington Law Firm:* Holland & Knight, LLP
Nat'l Network: CBS; MyNetworkTV *Nat'l Reps:* Continental Television Sales *Wire Services:* AP
Jason Effinger, President
Troy Frankforter, Operations Dir
Kris Ryan, General Sales Mgr
Stephanie McGowen, Programming Director
Nikki Bates, Promotions Manager
Jerry Howard, News Director
Brent Haun, Chief Engineer
ClintSimmons, Grand Island Sales Manager
Heath Miller, Graphics Manager
Marty Winters, National Sales Manager

KTVG-TV *Digital Channel:* 19; 3,890 kw vis, 21.9 kw aur; 610t/270g; N40 43 44 W98 34 13
Mailing Address: Box 220, Kearney, NE 68848
Second Address: 1078 25th Rd., Axtell, NE 68924
(308) 734-2794, *Fax:* (308) 743-2644
www.nebraska.tv
comments@nebraska.tv
License: Grand Island, Hall County, NE held by Hill Broadcasting Inc
Nat'l Network: Fox *Nat'l Reps:* Harrington, Righter & Parsons
Vince Barresi, General Manager
Dalla Nau, General Sales Mgr
Scott Swenson, Programming Director
Anita Wragge, Promotions Manager
Mark Baumert, News Director
Jerry Fuehrer, Chief Engineer

***KUON-TV** *Digital Channel:* 12 *Virtual Channel:* 12; 75 kw; 830 ft.; N41 8 18 W96 27 20
P. O. Box 83111, Lincoln, NE 68501 US
(402) 472-3611, *Fax:* (402) 472-1785
www.netnebraska.org
net1@unl.edu
License: Lincoln, Lancaster County, NE held by University of Nebraska
(acq 7-28-54;; *Washington Law Firm:* Dow, Lohnes & Albertson
Nat'l Network: PBS *Regional Network:* National Educational Telecommunications Association
Size of News Staff: 3; *Hours of Local News Weekly:* 30 min. wkly
Joe Turco, Operations Dir
Rod Bates, General Manager
Michael Winkle, General Sales Mgr
David Feingold, Programming Director
Terry Dugas, Programming & Promotion

KWNB-TV *Digital Channel:* 6 *Virtual Channel:* 6; 11.9 kw; 725 ft.; N40 37 32 W101 1 45; *Rebroadcasting:* Rebroadcasts KHGI-TV, Kearney, 100%.
Mailing Address: P.O. Box 220, Kearney, NE 68840 US
Second Address: 1078 25th Rd., Axtell, NE 68924
(308) 743-2794, *Fax:* (308) 743-2644
www.nebraska.tv
comments@nebraska.tv
License: Hayes Center, Hayes County, NE held by Pappas Telecasting of Central Nebraska L.P. (DE limited partnership).
Group Owner: Pappas Telecasting Companies; (acq 7-1-96; grpsl).
Nat'l Network: ABC *Nat'l Reps:* Harrington, Righter & Parsons
Size of News Staff: 26; *Hours of Local News Weekly:* news progmg 17.5 hrs wkly
Vince Barresi, General Manager
Dalla Nau, General Sales Mgr
Scott Swensen, Programming Director
Anita Wragge, Promotions Manager
Mark Baumert, News Director
Jerry Fuehrer, Chief Engineer

North Platte, NE (DMA 209)

KNOP-TV *Digital Channel:* 2 *Virtual Channel:* 2; 16 kw; 643 ft.; N41 12 13 W100 43 58
Mailing Address: P. O. Box 749, North Platte, NE 69101 US
Second Address: N. Hwy. 83, North Platte, NE 69101
(308) 532-2222, *Fax:* (308) 532-9579
www.knopnews2.com
lewysknop@knoptv.com
License: North Platte, Lincoln County, NE held by Hoak Media of Nebraska License LLC.
Group Owner: Hoak Media Corporation; (acq 11-7-2005; with KHAS-TV Hastings).; *Washington Law Firm:* Fletcher, Heald & Hildreth
Nat'l Network: NBC *Nat'l Reps:* Blair Television *Wire Services:* AP
Size of News Staff: 10; *Hours of Local News Weekly:* news progmg 15 hrs wkly
Lewys Carlini, General Manager
Darlene Lyman, General Sales Mgr
Gregg Hoover, Promotions Manager
Jacques Harms, News Director
Mike McNeil, Chief Engineer

***KPNE-TV** *Digital Channel:* 9 *Virtual Channel:* 9; 85 kw; 1096 ft.; N41 1 22 W101 9 14; *Rebroadcasting:* Satellite of *KUON-TV Lincoln.
P. O. Box 83111, Lincoln, NE 88501 US
(402) 472-3611, *Fax:* (402) 472-1785
www.netnebraska.org
net1@unl.edu
License: North Platte, Lincoln County, NE held by Nebraska Educational Telecommunications Commission
Washington Law Firm: Dow, Lohnes & Albertson
Nat'l Network: PBS *Regional Network:* National Educational Telecommunications Association
Joe Turco, Operations Dir
Rod Bates, General Manager
Michael Winkle, General Sales Mgr
David Feingold, Programming Director
Terry Dugas, Programming & Promotion

Omaha, NE
(DMA 76)

***KBIN-TV** *Digital Channel:* 33; 575 kw vis, 57.5 kw aur; ant 317t/163g; N41 15 14 W95 50 07
Mailing Address: Box 6450, Iowa Public TV, Johnston, IA 50131-6450
Second Address: 6450 Corporate Dr., Johnston, IA 50131
(515) 242-3100
www.iptv.org
public_information@iptv.org
License: Council Bluffs, Pottawattamie County, IA held by Iowa Public Broadcasting Board
Washington Law Firm: Dow, Lohnes PLLC
Nat'l Network: PBS
Daniel Miller, General Manager
Bill Hayes, Engineering Dir

KETV *Digital Channel:* 20 *Virtual Channel:* 7; 700 kw; 1299 ft.; N41 18 32 W96 1 33
888 Seventh Avenue, New York, NY 10106 US
(402) 345-7777, *Fax:* (402) 522-7755,(402) 522-7761
www.ketv.com
wbehrens@hearst.com
License: Omaha, Douglas County, NE held by KETV Hearst Television Inc.
Group Owner: Hearst-Argyle Television Inc.; (acq 3-18-99; grpsl)
Nat'l Network: ABC *Nat'l Reps:* Eagle Television Sales *Wire Services:* AP
Hours of Local News Weekly: News progmg 28 hrs wkly
Sarah Smith, President
Brian Sather, General Sales Mgr
Linda Hood, Programming Director
Rose Ann Shannon, News Director
Warren Behrens, Chief Engineer

KMTV-TV *Digital Channel:* 45; 100 kw vis, 20 kw aur; ant 1,371t/1,409g; N41 18 25 W96 01 37; *Population Served:* 357,800
10714 Mockingbird Dr., Omaha, NE 68127
(402) 592-3333
www.action3news.com
feedback@action3news.com
License: Omaha, Douglas County, NE held by Journal Broadcast Corp.
Group Owner: Journal Communications Inc.; (acq 3-27-2007)
Nat'l Network: CBS
Hours of Local News Weekly: News progmg 23 hrs wkly
Rob Burton, General Manager
Eric Hanneman, General Sales Mgr
Renee Rich, Programming Director
Willie Garrett, Promotions Manager
Ken Dudzik, News Director
Scott Krayenhagen, Chief Engineer

KPTM *Digital Channel:* 43 *Virtual Channel:* 42; 700 kw; 1558 ft.; N41 4 14 W96 13 33
500 South Chinowth Road, Visalia, CA 93277 US
(402) 558-4200, *Fax:* (402) 554-4290
www.kptm.com
contact42@kptm.com
License: Omaha, Douglas County, NE held by KPTM (TV) License LLC.
(acq 3-14-86).; *Washington Law Firm:* Paul, Hastings, Janofsky & Walker
Nat'l Network: FOX; MyNetworkTV *Nat'l Reps:* TeleRep *Wire Services:* FNS
Size of News Staff: 20; *Hours of Local News Weekly:* news progmg 7 hrs wkly
Randy Oswald, President
Chris McDade, Operations Dir
Jeff Miller, General Sales Mgr
John King, Programming Director
Sam Lawson, Promotions Manager
Joe Radske, News Director
Tim Moan, Regional Sales Manager

KXVO *Digital Channel:* 38 *Virtual Channel:* 15; 490 kw; 1558 ft.; N41 4 16 W96 13 31
706 W. Herndon Avenue, Pinedale, CA 93650 US
(402) 554-1500, *Fax:* (402) 554-4290
www.kxvo.com
contact42@kptm.com
License: Omaha, Douglas County, NE held by Mitts Telecasting Co
(acq 6-13-2000; $972,000); *Washington Law Firm:* Bryan Cave
Nat'l Network: CW *Nat'l Reps:* TeleRep
Randy Oswald, President
Chris McDade, Operations Dir
Jeff Miller, General Sales Mgr
John King, Programming Director
Sam Lawson, Promotions Manager
Tim Moan, Regional Sales Manager

***KYNE-TV** *Digital Channel:* 17 *Virtual Channel:* 26; 200 kw; 384 ft.; N41 15 28 W96 0 32; *Rebroadcasting:* Satellite of *KUON-TV Lincoln.
1800 North 33rd, Lincoln, NE 68501 US
(402) 472-3611, *Fax:* (402) 472-1785
www.netnebraska.org
net1@unl.edu
License: Omaha, Douglas County, NE held by Nebraska Educational Telecommunications Commission
Washington Law Firm: Dow, Lohnes & Albertson
Nat'l Network: PBS *Regional Network:* National Educational Telecommunications Association
Size of News Staff: 3; *Hours of Local News Weekly:* 30 min. wkly
Joe Turco, Operations Dir
Rod Bates, General Manager
Michael Winkle, General Sales Mgr
David Feingold, Programming Director
Terry Dugas, Programming & Promotion

WOWT *Digital Channel:* 22 *Virtual Channel:* 6; 1000 kw; 1371 ft.; N41 18 40 W96 1 37
3501 Farnam Street, Omaha, NE 68131 US
(402) 346-6666, *Fax:* (402) 233-7880
www.wowt.com
sixonline@wowt.com
License: Omaha, Douglas County, NE held by Gray Television Licensee Inc.
Group Owner: Gray Television Inc.; (acq 10-2002; grpsl).;
Washington Law Firm: Fletcher, Heald & Hildreth
Nat'l Network: NBC *Nat'l Reps:* Continental Television Sales
Size of News Staff: 52; *Hours of Local News Weekly:* news progmg 37 hrs wkly
Frank Jonas, General Manager
Don Felton, General Sales Mgr
Gail Backer, Programming Director
Vic Richards, Promotions Manager
John Clark, News Director
Rick Klutts, Chief Engineer

Sioux City, IA
(DMA 149)

***KXNE-TV** *Digital Channel:* 19 *Virtual Channel:* 19; 475 kw; 1056 ft.; N42 14 15 W97 16 41; *Rebroadcasting:* Satellite of *KUON-TV Lincoln.
P.O. Box 83111, Lincoln, NE 68501 US
(402) 472-3611, *Fax:* (402) 472-1785
www.netnebraska.org
net1@unl.edu
License: Norfolk, Madison County, NE held by Nebraska Educational Telecommunications Commission.
Washington Law Firm: Dow, Lohnes & Albertson
Nat'l Network: PBS *Regional Network:* National Educational Telecommunications Association
Size of News Staff: 3; *Hours of Local News Weekly:* 30 min.wkly
Joe Turco, Operations Dir
Rod Bates, General Manager
Michael Winkle, General Sales Mgr
David Feingold, Programming Director
Terry Dugas, Programming & Promotion

Sioux Falls (Mitchell), SD
(DMA 113)

***KRNE-TV** *Digital Channel:* 12 *Virtual Channel:* 12; 75 kw; 1056 ft.; N42 40 37 W101 42 39; *Rebroadcasting:* Satellite of KUON-TV Lincoln.
1800 North 33rd., Lincoln, NE 68501 US
(402) 472-3611, *Fax:* (402) 472-1785
www.netnebraska.org
net1@unl.edu
License: Merriman, Cherry County, NE held by Nebraska Educational Telecommunications Commission
Washington Law Firm: Dow, Lohnes & Albertson
Nat'l Network: PBS *Regional Network:* National Educational Telecommunications Association
Joe Turco, Operations Dir
Rod Bates, General Manager
Michael Winkle, General Sales Mgr
David Feingold, Programming Director
Terry Dugas, Programming & Promotion

Wichita-Hutchinson Plus, KS
(DMA 69)

KSNK *Digital Channel:* 12 *Virtual Channel:* 8; 10.4 kw; 715 ft.; N39 49 48 W100 42 4
833 North Main Street, P.O. Box 333, Wichita, KS 67201 US
(316) 265-3333, *Fax:* (316) 292-1197
www.ksn.com
License: McCook, Red Willow County, NE held by LIN Licensing Company LLC
Group Owner: LIN Media; (acq 11-1-2007; grpsl); *Washington Law Firm:* Wiley Rein LLP
Nat'l Network: NBC *Nat'l Reps:* TeleRep
Al Buch, General Manager
Dan Shurtz, General Sales Mgr
Betty Erickson, Programming Director
Gregg Cox, Promotions Manager
Jason Kravarik, News Director
Warren Kunkle, Chief Engineer
Kevin White, New Media Manager

Nevada

Las Vegas, NV
(DMA 42)

KBLR *Digital Channel:* 40 *Virtual Channel:* 39; 1000 kw; 1191 ft.; N36 0 36 W115 0 20
5000 W Oakey Blvd, Suite B-2, Las Vegas, NV 89102 US
(702) 258-0039, *Fax:* (702) 258-0556
www.telemundo.yahoo.com
License: Paradise, Clark County, NV held by Summit Media Limited Partnership
(acq 1993; $1.5 million;; *Washington Law Firm:* KMZ Rosenman
Nat'l Network: TELEMUNDO
Foreign Language Programming; Size of News Staff: 8; *Hours of Local News Weekly:* news progmg 2 hrs wkly
Carlos Sanchez, Operations Dir
Julie Sanchez, Station Manager
Bill George, General Sales Mgr
Brenda Macias, News Director
Juan Jose Quintana, Chief Engineer

KINC *Digital Channel:* 16 *Virtual Channel:* 15; 1000 kw; 1872 ft.; N35 56 46 W115 2 34
11900 Olympic Boulevard, Suite 590, Los Angeles, CA 90064 US
(702) 434-0015, *Fax:* (702) 434-0527
www.kinc.entravision.com
License: Las Vegas, Clark County, NV held by Entravision Holdings L.L.C.
Group Owner: Entravision Communications Corp.; *Washington Law Firm:* Thompson Hine L.L.P.
Nat'l Network: UNIVISION
Foreign Language Programming; Hours of Local News Weekly: News progmg 5 hrs wkly
Chris Roman, General Manager
J.R. Des Amours, General Sales Mgr
Erin Thomas, Programming Director
Karina Barcena, Promotions Manager

KLAS-TV *Digital Channel:* 7 *Virtual Channel:* 8; 30.1 kw; 1998 ft.; N35 56 44 W115 2 33
PO Box 15047, Las Vegas, NV 89114 US
(702) 792-8888, *Fax:* (702) 792-9034
www.8newsnow.com
thobaica@8nesnow.com
License: Las Vegas, Clark County, NV held by KLAS Inc., a Nevada Corp.
Group Owner: Landmark Communications Inc.; (acq 7-1-78; $8 million).; *Washington Law Firm:* Wiley, Rein Fielding, LLP
Nat'l Network: CBS *Nat'l Reps:* Continental Television Sales
Emily Neilson, President
Linda Bonnici, General Sales Mgr
Kathy Kramer, Programming Director
Doug Kramer, Chief Engineer

***KLVX** *Digital Channel:* 11 *Virtual Channel:* 10; 105 kw; 1206 ft.; N36 0 27 W115 0 24
4210 Channel 10 Dr., Las Vegas, NV 89119 US
(702) 799-1010, *Fax:* (702) 799-5586
www.klvx.org
License: Las Vegas, Clark County, NV held by Clark County School District Board of Trustees
Washington Law Firm: Wiley, Rein & Fielding
Nat'l Network: ETV *Wire Services:* Accu-Weather
Barbara Mirman, Operations Dir
Tom Axtell, General Manager
Cyndy Robbins, Programming Director
Lee Solonche, Distance Learning Manager
Martin Vodovoz, TV Technical Manager

KMCC *Digital Channel:* 32 *Virtual Channel:* 34; 1000 kw; 1991 ft.; N35 39 7 W114 18 42
455 Capitol Mall, Suite 604, Sacramento, CA 95814 US
(702) 298-2222, *Fax:* (702) 298-3495

License: Laughlin, Clark County, NV held by Mojave Broadcasting Co
Washington Law Firm: Wiley, Rein & Fielding
Nat'l Network: RTN *Nat'l Reps:* Blair Television
Bruce Clark, General Manager

KSNV-DT *Digital Channel:* 2 *Virtual Channel:* 3; 100 kw vis, 10 kw aur; ant 1,263t/226g; N36 00 32 W115 00 19; *Population Served:* 1,101,000
1500 Foremaster Ln., Las Vegas, NV 89101
(702) 642-3333, *Fax:* (702) 657-3152 (news)
www.mynews3.com
news3@kvbc.com
License: Las Vegas, Clark County, NV held by Valley Broadcasting Co
Washington Law Firm: Dow, Lohnes & Albertson
Nat'l Network: NBC
Size of News Staff: 55; *Hours of Local News Weekly:* news progmg 29 hrs wkly
James Rogers, CEO
Ralph Toddre, President
Lisa Howfield, General Manager
Joanne Nasby, General Sales Mgr
Pam Sewell, Programming Director
Dale Wyman, Promotions Manager
Dick Tuiniga, News Director
Mark Guranik, ChiefEngineer

KTNV-TV *Digital Channel:* 12; 316 kw vis, 31.6 kw aur; 2,001t/259g; N35 56 43 W115 02 32; *Population Served:* 1,564,000
3355 S. Valley View Blvd., Las Vegas, NV 89102
(702) 876-1313, *Fax:* (702) 871-1961
www.ktnv.com
desk@ktnv.com
License: Las Vegas, Clark County, NV held by Journal Broadcast Corp.
Group Owner: Journal Communications Inc.; (acq 6-29-79);
Washington Law Firm: Crowell & Moring
Nat'l Network: ABC *Nat'l Reps:* Petry Television Inc.
Size of News Staff: 60; *Hours of Local News Weekly:* news progmg 22 hrs wkly
Jim Prather, President
Thom Poterfield, General Sales Mgr
Marie Shea, Programming Director
Jim Koonce, Promotions Manager
Greg Rogers, Chief Engineer
Karin Movesian, Promotions Manager
Loretta Seitz, Traffic Manager

KVCW *Digital Channel:* 29 *Virtual Channel:* 33; 1000 kw; 1256 ft.; N36 0 28 W115 0 24
3840 South Jones Blvd., Las Vegas, NV 89103 US
(702) 952-4600, *Fax:* (702) 873-1233
www.thecwlasvegas.tv
License: Las Vegas, Clark County, NV held by Channel 33 Inc.
Group Owner: Sinclair Broadcast Group Inc.; (acq 2-23-2000; $33 million for stock).; *Washington Law Firm:* Fletcher, Heald & Hildreth
Nat'l Network: CW
Rob Weisbord, General Manager
Tom Anderson, General Sales Mgr
Tommie Gonzalez, Programming Director
Mike Brown, Chief Engineer

KVMY *Digital Channel:* 22 *Virtual Channel:* 21; 1000 kw; 1256 ft.; N36 0 28 W115 0 24
2000 West 41st Street, Baltimore, MD 21211 US
(702) 382-2121, *Fax:* (702) 382-1351
www.mylvtv.com
License: Las Vegas, Clark County, NV held by KUPN Licensee L.L.C.
Group Owner: Sinclair Broadcast Group Inc.; (acq 5-30-97; $87 million); *Washington Law Firm:* Dow, Lohnes & Albertson
Nat'l Network: MYTV
David Smith, CEO
Rob Weisbord, General Manager
Chris Cohen, General Sales Mgr
Mike Brown, Chief Engineer

KVVU-TV *Digital Channel:* 9 *Virtual Channel:* 5; 86 kw; 1261 ft.; N36 0 26 W115 0 22
25 Tv5 Drive, Henderson, NV 89014 US
(702) 435-5555, *Fax:* (702) 436-2507
www.fox5vegas.com
License: Henderson, Clark County, NV held by KVVU Broadcasting Corp.
Group Owner: Meredith Broadcasting Group, Meredith Corp.; (acq 5-85; $36 million); *Washington Law Firm:* Haley, Bader & Potts
Nat'l Network: FOX *Nat'l Reps:* TeleRep
Darrin McDonald, General Manager

Reno, NV (DMA 108)

KAME-TV *Digital Channel:* 20 *Virtual Channel:* 21; 53 kw; 577 ft.; N39 35 3 W119 47 51
1888 Emory Street, Building 2, Third Floor, Atlanta, GA 30318 US
(775) 856-2121, *Fax:* (775) 856-2100
www.foxreno.com
License: Reno, Washoe County, NV held by Broadcast Development Corp.
(acq 2-28-94).; *Washington Law Firm:* Bryan Cave
Nat'l Network: MYTV *Nat'l Reps:* TeleRep
Peter Grimm, Operations Dir
Ray Stofer, General Sales Mgr
Ray Stofer, Chief of Operations

***KNPB** *Digital Channel:* 15 *Virtual Channel:* 5; 32.3 kw; 490 ft.; N39 35 2 W119 47 55
P.O. Box 14730, Reno, NV 89507 US
(775) 784-4555, *Fax:* (775) 784-1438
www.knpb.org
info@knpb.org
License: Reno, Washoe County, NV held by Channel 5 Public Broadcasting Inc
Washington Law Firm: Schwartz, Woods & Miller
Nat'l Network: PBS
Kliff Kuehl, President
Barbara Harmon, Programming Director
Tony Manfredi, Promotions Manager
Pat Miller, VP Programming/Promotions
Fred Ihlow, VP Technology

KOLO-TV *Digital Channel:* 8; 15 kw; 2,929t/119g; N39 18 49 W119 53 00; *Population Served:* 432,400
4850 Ampere Dr., Reno, NV 72917
(775) 858-8888, *Fax:* (775) 858-8855
www.kolotv.com
License: Reno, Washoe County, NV held by Gray Television Licensee Corp.
Group Owner: Gray Television Inc.; (acq 12-10-2002; $41.5 million with K12IX Austin, K58AO Crystal Bay, K03DN Ely/McGill and K49CK Stead/Lawton, all NV).; *Washington Law Firm:* Wiley Rein LL
Nat'l Network: ABC *Nat'l Reps:* Millennium Sales & Marketing
Hours of Local News Weekly: News progmg 22 hrs wkly
Matt Eldredge, General Manager
Laura Newman, General Sales Mgr
Doug Tepe, Promotions Manager
Miriam Gonzalez, News Director
Herb Primosch, Chief Engineer
Jennifer Hardy, News Director

KREN-TV *Digital Channel:* 26 *Virtual Channel:* 27; 1000 kw; 2940 ft.; N39 18 47 W119 52 59
500 South Chinowth Road, Visalia, CA 93277 US
(775) 333-2727, *Fax:* (775) 327-6868
www.kren.com
renofrontdesk@kren.com
License: Reno, Washoe County, NV held by Entravision Holdings LLC.
Group Owner: Entravision Communications Corp.; (acq 4-1-2009; $4 million); *Washington Law Firm:* Thompson Hine LLP
Nat'l Network: CW *Nat'l Reps:* Harrington, Righter & Parsons
Harry Pappas, CEO
Leslie SAdley, Operations Dir
Easter Dominquez, General Manager
Alan Plotkin, General Sales Mgr
Debbie Sweeney, Programming Director
Leslie Sadley, Promotions Manager
James Ocon, Chief Engineer
Bill May,Research Director
Miriam Carbajal, Traffic Manager

KRNV-DT *Digital Channel:* 7; 17.4 kw vis, 3.4 kw aur; 420t/92g; N39 35 03 W119 48 06; *Population Served:* 172,863
Mailing Address: Box 7160, Reno, NV 89510
Second Address: 1790 Vassar St., Reno, NV 89502
(775) 322-4444, *Fax:* (775) 785-1208,(775) 785-1206(news)
www.mynews4.com
comments@krnv.com
License: Reno, Washoe County, NV held by Sierra Broadcasting Co.
Group Owner: Sunbelt Communications Co.; (acq 9-13-89).;
Ownership: James E. Rogers.; *Washington Law Firm:* Gerald S. Rourke
Nat'l Network: NBC
Size of News Staff: 26; *Hours of Local News Weekly:* news progmg 14 hrs wkly
James E Rogers, Chairman
Ralph Toddre, President
John Finkbohner, Operations Dir
Marybeth Sewald, General Manager
Patrick Fisher, Station Manager
Mark Murakami, General Sales Mgr
Barbara Monroy, Programming Director
DividFisher, Engineering Dir
Steve Galvan, Chief Engineer

KRXI-TV *Digital Channel:* 44 *Virtual Channel:* 11; 500 kw; 2743 ft.; N39 35 23 W119 55 37
4920 Brookside Court, Reno, NV 89502 US
(775) 856-1100, *Fax:* (775) 856-1101
www.foxreno.com
License: Reno, Washoe County, NV held by KTVU Partnership
Group Owner: Cox Media Group; *Washington Law Firm:* Dow, Lohnes & Albertson
Nat'l Network: FOX *Nat'l Reps:* TeleRep
Steve Cmmings, General Manager
Steve Cummings, General Sales Mgr
Mike Arnold, Chief Engineer
Mandy Anderson, Regional Sales Manager

KTVN *Digital Channel:* 13 *Virtual Channel:* 2; 16.1 kw; 2874 ft.; N39 18 57 W119 53 2
Mailing Address: P.O. Box 7220, Reno, NV 89510 US
Second Address: 4925 Energy Way, Reno, NV 89502
(775) 858-2222, *Fax:* (775) 861-4298
www.ktvn.com
ktvn@ktvn.com
License: Reno, Washoe County, NV held by Sarkes Tarzian Inc.
Group Owner: Sarkes Tarzian Inc.; (acq 8-13-80; $12.5 million);
Washington Law Firm: Lerman Senter PLLC
Nat'l Network: CBS
Size of News Staff: 31; *Hours of Local News Weekly:* news progmg 23.5 hrs wkly
Tom Tarzian, Chairman
Bob Davis, CFO
Tom Tolar, President
John Richardson, General Sales Mgr
Pat Hall, Programming Director
Ann Burns, Promotions Manager
Jason Pasco, News Director
Jack Antonio, Chief Engineer
Sharon Facque,National Sales Manager

Salt Lake City, UT (DMA 33)

KVNV *Digital Channel:* 3 *Virtual Channel:* 3; 1.2 kw; 908 ft.; N39 14 46 W114 55 36; *Rebroadcasting:* Rebroadcasts KVBC(TV) Las Vegas
#1 Shackelford Drive, Suite 400, Little Rock, AR 72211 US
(702) 642-3333, *Fax:* (702) 657-3256
www.kvbc.com
License: Ely, White Pine County, NV held by PMCM TV LLC (acq 11-12-2008; $200,000); *Ownership:* Richard T. Morena, 25%; Robert E. McAllan, 25%; Alfred D. Colantoni, 25%; Jules L. Plangere Jr., 25%
Nat'l Network: NBC
Karen Livingston, General Manager
Joanne Nasby, General Sales Mgr
Mark Guranik, Chief Engineer

Yakima-Pasco-Richland-Kennewick, WA (DMA 126)

KCWK *Digital Channel:* 9; ant 577t
US
(509) 575-0999, *Fax:* (509) 575-9562
www.kcwk9.com
License: North Las Vegas, NV held by KAZW License LLC.
Group Owner: Pappas Telecasting Companies; (acq 11-7-2002; $3 million)
Nat'l Network: CW
Robert Powers, Operations Dir
Mike Dunlop, General Sales Mgr

New Hampshire

Boston (Manchester, NH) (DMA 7)

WBIN-TV *Digital Channel:* 50; 4,790 kw vis, 479 kw aur; ant 699t; N42 44 07 W71 23 36; *Population Served:* 5,200,000
11 A Street, Derry, NH 03038
(603) 845-1000, *Fax:* (603) 434-8627
www.wbintv.com
info@wbintv.com
License: Derry, Rockingham County, NH held by WBIN Inc.

5-17-2011; *Ownership:* Carlisle One Media, Inc., 100%
Nat'l Network: Independent *Nat'l Reps:* Petry Television Inc.
Wire Services: AP
Hours of Local News Weekly: News progmg 20-22 hrs wkl
Bill Binnie, President
Gerry McGavick, General Manager
Alvin Turner, Vice President of Sales
Lee Kinberg, Senior Vice President, Programming
Matt Mayberry, Expeditor
Martin Morenz, News Director
Keith Webb, Chief Engineer
Angela Bianchi, Traffic Manager
Steven Pomeroy, Office Manager
Kristina Letourneau, Local Sales Manager
Brian O'Keefe, National Sales Manager

***WEKW-TV** *Digital Channel:* 49 *Virtual Channel:* 52; 43 kw; 1083 ft.; N43 2 0 W72 22 4
P.O. Box 1100, Durham, NH 03824 US
(603) 868-1100, *Fax:* (603) 868-7552
www.nhptv.org
themailbox@nhptv.org
License: Keene, Cheshire County, NH held by University of New Hampshire
Washington Law Firm: Schwartz, Woods & Miller
Nat'l Network: PBS
Peter Frid, General Manager
Dennis Malloy, General Sales Mgr
Hazel Molin, Programming Director
Brian Shepperd, Chief Engineer
Jeff Morris, Advertising Manager

***WENH-TV** *Digital Channel:* 11 *Virtual Channel:* 11; 30 kw; 998 ft.; N43 10 33 W71 12 29
PO Box 1100, Durham, NH 03824 US
(603) 868-1100, *Fax:* (603) 868-7552
www.nhptv.org
themailbox@nhptv.org
License: Durham, Strafford County, NH held by University of New Hampshire
Washington Law Firm: Schwartz, Woods & Miller
Nat'l Network: PBS
Hours of Local News Weekly: News progmg 2 hrs wkly
Peter Frid, General Manager

WMUR-TV *Digital Channel:* 59; 282 kw vis, 33.5 kw aur; 1,030t/227g; N42 58 59 W71 35 19; *Population Served:* 1,100,000
100 S. Commercial St., Manchester, NH 03101
(603) 669-9999, *Fax:* (603) 641-9005 (admin)
www.wmur.com
storyideas@wmur.com
License: Manchester, Hillsborough County, NH held by Hearst Television Inc.
Group Owner: Hearst Television Inc.; (acq 3-28-01; $185 million); *Washington Law Firm:* Brooks, Pierce, McLendon, Humphrey & Leonard
Nat'l Network: ABC *Regional Network:* MeTV *Nat'l Reps:* Eagle Television Sales *Wire Services:* AP
Size of News Staff: 54; *Hours of Local News Weekly:* news progmg 29 hrs wkly
Jeff Bartlett, President
Jeff Bartlett, General Manager
David Parker, General Sales Mgr
Betsey Braun, Programming Director
Alex Jasiukowicz, Promotions Manager
Alisha McDevitt, News Director
Roger Rosendahl, Chief Engineer
AhniMalachi, Public Service Manager
Patrick McCarthy, Business Manager

WNEU *Digital Channel:* 34 *Virtual Channel:* 60; 80 kw; 961 ft.; N42 59 2 W71 35 20
601 Clearwater Park Road, West Palm Beach, FL 33401 US
(603) 647-6060
wneu@comcast.net
License: Merrimack, Hillsborough County, NH held by NBC Telemundo License Co.
Group Owner: Telemundo Television Stations; (acq 10-22-2002; $26 million); *Washington Law Firm:* Davis Wright Tremaine L.L.P.
Nat'l Network: TELEMUNDO; Telemundo (Spanish)
Foreign Language Programming
Donna Sill, Station Manager
David Raymond, Chief Engineer

Portland-Auburn, ME (DMA 77)

***WLED-TV** *Digital Channel:* 48 *Virtual Channel:* 49; 45 kw; 1273 ft.; N44 21 10 W71 44 15; *Rebroadcasting:* Rebroadcasts *WENH Durham 100%.
PO Box 1100, Durham, NH 03824 US
(603) 868-1100, *Fax:* (603) 868-7552
www.nhptv.org
themailbox@nhptv.org
License: Littleton, Grafton County, NH held by University of New Hampshire
Washington Law Firm: Schwartz, Woods & Miller
Nat'l Network: PBS *Regional Network:* New Hampshire Public Television
Peter Frid, General Manager
Dennis Malloy, General Sales Mgr
Brian Shepperd, Chief Engineer
Jeff Morris, Advertising Manager

New Jersey

New York (DMA 1)

***WFME-TV** *Digital Channel:* 29 *Virtual Channel:* 66; 200 kw; 548 ft.; N40 47 18 W74 15 19
4135 Northgate Boulevard, Suite 1, Sacramento, CA 95834 US
(973) 736-3600
www.familyradio.com
License: West Milford, Passaic County, NJ held by Family Stations Inc.
Group Owner: Family Stations Inc.
Nat'l Network: ETV
Harold Camping, General Manager
Charles Menut, General Sales Mgr

WMBC-TV *Digital Channel:* 18; 2,190 kw vis, 109 kw aur; 731t; N41 00 36 W74 35 39; *Population Served:* 13,000,000
99 Clinton Rd., West Caldwell, NJ 07849
(973) 852-0300, *Fax:* (973) 808-5516
www.wmbctv.com
info@wmbctv.com
License: Newton, Sussex County, NJ held by Mountain Broadcasting Corp.
Group Owner: Mountain Broadcasting Corp.; *Washington Law Firm:* Fleischman & Walsh
Foreign Language Programming; Size of News Staff: 8; *Hours of Local News Weekly:* news progmg 5 hrs wkly
Victor Joo, General Manager
Hansen Lau, News Director
Joon Joo, Chief Engineer

***WNET** *Digital Channel:* 13 *Virtual Channel:* 13; 9.3 kw; 1329 ft.; N40 44 54 W73 59 10
450 West 33rd Street, Sixth Floor, New York, NY 10001 US
(212) 560-1313, *Fax:* (212) 560-1314
www.thirteen.org
License: Newark, Essex County, NJ held by Educational Broadcasting Corp
(acq 1970); *Washington Law Firm:* Leventhal, Senter & Lerman
Nat'l Network: PBS
Hours of Local News Weekly: News progmg 5 hrs wkly
Neal Shapiro, CEO

***WNJB** *Digital Channel:* 8 *Virtual Channel:* 58; 40.82 kw; 715 ft.; N40 37 17 W74 30 15; *Rebroadcasting:* Satellite of *WNJT(TV) Trenton.
Mailing Address: 1573 Parkside Ave.Cn 777, Trenton, NJ 08625 US
Second Address: 25 S. Stockton St., Trenton, NJ 08608-1832
(609) 777-5000, *Fax:* (609) 633-2920
www.njn.net
audience@njn.org; answers@njn.org
License: New Brunswick, Middlesex County, NJ held by New Jersey Public Broadcasting Authority
Washington Law Firm: Schwartz, Woods & Miller
Nat'l Network: PBS *Regional Network:* New Jersey Network
Hours of Local News Weekly: News progmg 2 hrs wkly
Janice Selinger, Station Manager

***WNJN** *Digital Channel:* 51 *Virtual Channel:* 50; 200 kw; 764 ft.; N40 51 53 W74 12 3; *Rebroadcasting:* Satellite of *WNJT Trenton.
Mailing Address: 1573 Parkside Ave,Cn 777, Trenton, NJ 08625 US
Second Address: 25 S. Stockton St., Trenton, NJ 08608-1832
(609) 777-5000, *Fax:* (609) 633-2920
www.njn.net
audience@njn.org; answers@njn.org
License: Montclair, Essex County, NJ held by New Jersey Public Broadcasting Authority
Washington Law Firm: Schwartz, Woods & Miller
Nat'l Network: PBS *Regional Network:* New Jersey Network
Hours of Local News Weekly: News progmg 3 hrs wkly
Janice Selinger, Station Manager
Howard J. Blumenthal, Interim Executive Director

WNJU *Digital Channel:* 36 *Virtual Channel:* 47; 650 kw; 733 ft.; N40 48 8 W74 14 48
2290 West 8th Avenue, Hialeah, FL 33010 US
(201) 969-4247, *Fax:* (201) 969-4120
www.telemundo47.com
License: Linden, Union County, NJ held by NBC Telemundo License Co.
Group Owner: Telemundo Television Stations; (acq 4-12-2002; grpsl).; *Washington Law Firm:* Hogan & Hartson
Nat'l Network: TELEMUNDO
Foreign Language Programming
Manuel Martinez, General Manager
Sylvia Santiago, Programming Director
Lenny Stole, Chief Engineer

WWOR-TV *Digital Channel:* 38 *Virtual Channel:* 9
9 Broadcast Plaza, Secaucus, NJ 07095 US
(201) 348-0009, *Fax:* (201) 330-3486
www.my9newyork.com
License: Secaucus, Hudson County, NJ held by Fox Television Stations Inc.
Group Owner: Fox Television Stations Inc.; a(cq 7-31-2001; grpsl).
Nat'l Network: MY NETWORK *Wire Services:* Conus
Size of News Staff: 70; *Hours of Local News Weekly:* news progmg 7 hrs wkly
Lew Leone, Operations Dir
Debbie von Ahrens, General Sales Mgr
Dianne Doctor, News Director

Philadelphia (DMA 4)

WACP *Digital Channel:* 4; 10 kw; 256 m; N39 44 05 W74 50 29
400 North Ashley Drive, Suite 3010, Tampa, FL
(813) 579-4491
License: Atlantic City, Atlantic County, NJ held by Western Pacific Broadcast LLC
Dale A. West, Vice President

WGTW-TV *Digital Channel:* 27 *Virtual Channel:* 48; 160 kw; 1161 ft.; N40 2 30 W75 14 11
3900 Main St, Philadelphia, PA 19127 US
(610) 583-1370, *Fax:* (610) 583-1476
www.tbn.org
mrudderow@tbn.org
License: Burlington, Burlington County, NJ held by Trinity Christian Center of Santa Ana Inc.
Group Owner: Trinity Broadcasting Network; (acq 10-1-2004; $7 million plus assumption of $41 million in debt).
Nat'l Network: TRINITY BROADCA
Dennis Pritchett, Operations Dir
Al Box, General Manager
Mark Rudderow, Public Relations

WMCN-TV *Digital Channel:* 44 *Virtual Channel:* 44; 200 kw; 696 ft.; N39 43 41 W74 50 39
19 S. New York Avenue, Atlantic City, NJ 08401 US
(609) 569-7280, *Fax:* (609) 569-7295
www.wmcn.tv
contact@wmcn.tv
License: Atlantic City, Atlantic County, NJ held by Lenfest Broadcasting L.L.C
(acq 7-19-2000; $9 million); *Washington Law Firm:* Wiley, Rein & Fielding
Nat'l Network: IND
H. Chase Lenfest, CEO
Robert Lund, Operations Dir
Steve Cass, General Sales Mgr
Vojislav Radosavljevic, Chief Engineer
Mark Chesterton, Operations Director

WMGM-TV *Digital Channel:* 36 *Virtual Channel:* 40; 205 kw; 415 ft.; N39 7 28 W74 45 56
1601 New Road, Linwood, NJ 08221 US
(609) 927-4440, *Fax:* (609) 926-8875
www.nbc40.net
news@nbc40.net
License: Wildwood, Cape May County, NJ held by Access.1 New Jersey License Co.
Group Owner: Access.1 Communications Corp.; (acq 2004; grpsl)
Nat'l Network: NBC *Wire Services:* AP

Hours of Local News Weekly: News progmg 8 hrs wkly
Arthur Benjamin, CFO
Chesley Maddox-Dorsey, President
Ron Smith, General Manager
Roger Powe, General Sales Mgr

***WNJS** *Digital Channel:* 22 *Virtual Channel:* 23; 197 kw; 866 ft.; N39 43 41 W74 50 39; *Rebroadcasting:* Satellite of *WNJT Trenton.
Mailing Address: 1573 Parkside Ave.Cn 777, Trenton, NJ 08625 US
Second Address: 25 S. Stockton St., Trenton, NJ 08608-1832
(609) 777-5000, *Fax:* (609) 633-2920
www.njn.net
audience@njn.org; answers@njn.org
License: Camden, Camden County, NJ held by New Jersey Public Broadcasting Authority
Washington Law Firm: Schwartz, Woods & Miller
Nat'l Network: PBS *Regional Network:* New Jersey Network
Hours of Local News Weekly: News progmg 2 hrs wkly
Janice Selinger, Station Manager

***WNJT** *Digital Channel:* 43 *Virtual Channel:* 52; 59.4 kw; 873 ft.; N40 16 58 W74 41 11
Mailing Address: 1573 Parkside Ave.Cn 777, Trenton, NJ 08625 US
Second Address: 25 S. Stockton St., Trenton, NJ 08608-1832
(609) 777-5000, *Fax:* (609) 633-2920
www.njn.net
audience@njn.org; answers@njn.org
License: Trenton, Mercer County, NJ held by New Jersey Public Broadcasting Authority
Washington Law Firm: Schwartz, Woods & Miller
Nat'l Network: PBS *Regional Network:* New Jersey Network
Hours of Local News Weekly: News progmg 10 hrs wkly
John Blair, Operations Dir
Andre Butts, Programming Director
Joanne Ruscio, Promotions Manager
Michael Aron, News Director
Janice Selinger, Deputy Executive Director

WWSI *Digital Channel:* 49; 5,000 kw vis, 500 kw aur; ant 972t/970g; N39 37 53 W74 21 12
Mailing Address: 1341 N. Delaware Ave., Suite 408, Philadelphia, PA 19119
Second Address: One S. New York Ave., Atlantic City, NJ 8401
(215) 634-8862,(609) 449-0049, *Fax:* (215) 425-2683,(609) 441-9559
www.holaciudad.com
crivas@zgsgroup.com
License: Atlantic City, Atlantic County, NJ held by ZGS Philadelphia, Inc.
Group Owner: ZGS Communications; (acq 5-14-2002).;
Ownership: ZGS Group
Nat'l Network: Telemundo (Spanish) *Regional Reps:* Telemundo Philadelphia
Foreign Language Programming; Size of News Staff: 4; *Hours of Local News Weekly:* news progmg 3 hrs wkly
Ronald Gordon, Chairman
Peter Housman, CEO/COO
Julissa Marenco, President
Eduardo Zavala, Operations Dir
Clara Rivas, General Manager
Clara Rivas, Station Manager
Clara Rivas, General Sales Mgr
DJ Brown, ProgrammingDirector
Eric Cortes, Promotions Manager
Nikitas Fooskas, Engineering Dir
Frank Polizano, Chief Engineer

New Mexico

Albuquerque-Santa Fe, NM (DMA 44)

KASA-TV *Digital Channel:* 27; 28.2 kw vis, 2.82 kw aur; 1,968t/178g; N35 46 50 W106 31 35; *Population Served:* 1,664,000
13 Broadcast Plaza S.W., Albuquerque, NM 75202
(505) 243-2285, *Fax:* (505) 248-1464
www.kasa.com
newsdesk@krqe.com
License: Santa Fe, Santa Fe County, NM held by LIN License Company LLC
Group Owner: LIN Media; (acq 9-2-99; grpsl).; *Washington Law Firm:* Covington & Burling
Nat'l Network: Fox *Nat'l Reps:* TeleRep
Hours of Local News Weekly: News progmg 7 hrs wkly
Bill Anderson, General Manager
Jim Giudicessi, General Sales Mgr
Pat Gonzales, Programming Director
Parker Harms, Promotions Manager
Ian Munro, News Director
Frank Lilley, Engineering Dir
Yolanda Tyner-Ward, Local SalesManager
Don Pierce, Program Director

KASY-TV *Digital Channel:* 45 *Virtual Channel:* 50; 245 kw; 4222 ft.; N35 12 48 W106 27 0
PO Box 3757, Lubbock, TX 79452 US
(505) 797-1919, *Fax:* (505) 938-4401
www.my50.tv
License: Albuquerque, Bernalillo County, NM held by Acme Television Licenses of New Mexico L.L.C.
Group Owner: ACME Communications Inc.; (acq 6-18-99; $25.4 million); *Washington Law Firm:* Leventhal, Senter & Lerman
Nat'l Network: CW
Stan Gill, General Manager
Rosalie Drake, General Sales Mgr
Chris Iller, Promotions Manager
Scott Stokes, Chief Engineer

***KAZQ** *Digital Channel:* 17 *Virtual Channel:* 32; 65.6 kw; 4091 ft.; N35 12 51 W106 27 1
4501 Montgomery, Ne., Albuquerque, NM 87109 US
(505) 884-8355, *Fax:* (505) 883-1229
www.kazq32.org
info@kazq32.org
License: Albuquerque, Bernalillo County, NM held by Alpha-Omega Broadcasting of Albuquerque Inc
Ownership: Non-Profit Corporation; *Washington Law Firm:* Donald C. Martin
Nat'l Network: ETV
Foreign Language Programming
Raymond Franks, President
Brenton Franks, Operations Dir
Howard Holley, Programming Director
Dale Shamblin, 2nd Vice President
Dan Segura, 3rd Vice President
Ruth Franks, Operations Manager
Steve Minor, Traffic Director

KBIM-TV *Digital Channel:* 10 *Virtual Channel:* 10; 24.32 kw; 2001 ft.; N33 3 20 W103 49 12; *Rebroadcasting:* Rebroadcasts KRQE(TV) Albuquerque 90%.
Mailing Address: Bx 910, Roswell, NM 88202 US
Second Address: 214 N. Main St., Roswell, NM 88202
(575) 622-2120, *Fax:* (505) 623-6606
www.kbimtv.com
License: Roswell, Chaves County, NM held by LIN License Compnay LLC
Group Owner: LIN Media; (acq 11-30-2005; grpsl).; *Washington Law Firm:* Reed, Smith, Shaw & McClay
Nat'l Network: CBS
Size of News Staff: 11; *Hours of Local News Weekly:* news progmg 6 hrs wkly
Marcus Damberger, Operations Dir
Gene Munsey, General Manager
Joshua Pila, Station Manager
Pat Gonzales, Programming Director

KCHF *Digital Channel:* 10 *Virtual Channel:* 11; 30 kw; 1995 ft.; N35 46 49 W106 31 34
Mailing Address: P.O.Box 4338, Albuquerque, NM 87106 US
Second Address: 27556 I 25 &. Frontage Rd., Santa Fe, NM 87508
(505) 345-1991 (radio),(505) 473-1111, *Fax:* (505) 345-5669
www.kchf.com
License: Santa Fe, Santa Fe County, NM held by Son Broadcasting Inc
Washington Law Firm: Gammon & Grange
Nat'l Network: IND
Foreign Language Programming
Belarmino Gonzalez, CEO
Annette Garcia, General Manager
Mary Kay Gonzales, Programming Director
Rob Ramseyer, Chief Engineer

KLUZ-TV *Digital Channel:* 42 *Virtual Channel:* 41; 321 kw; 4140 ft.; N35 12 41 W106 26 56
11900 Olympic Boulevard, Suite 590, Los Angeles, CA 90064 US
(505) 342-4141, *Fax:* (505) 344-8714
www.univision.com
License: Albuquerque, Bernalillo County, NM held by Entravision Holdings L.L.C.
Group Owner: Entravision Communications Corp.; (acq 3-21-99).
Nat'l Network: UNIVISION
Foreign Language Programming; Size of News Staff: 10; *Hours of Local News Weekly:* news progmg 1/2 hr wkly
Walter Ulloa, CEO
Phillip Wilkinson, President
Margarita Wilder, General Manager
Kambiz Victory, Chief Engineer
John DiLorenzo, CFO

KNAT-TV *Digital Channel:* 24 *Virtual Channel:* 23; 320 kw; 4081 ft.; N35 12 54 W106 27 2
1510 Corrs Road, N.W., Albuquerque, NM 87105 US
(505) 836-6585, *Fax:* (505) 831-8725
www.tbn.org
cmansfield@tbn.org
License: Albuquerque, Bernalillo County, NM held by Trinity Broadcasting Network
Group Owner: Trinity Broadcasting Network; (acq 5-8-2000; grpsl).; *Washington Law Firm:* Joseph E. Dunne III
Nat'l Network: TRINITY BROADCA
Foreign Language Programming
Cynthia Mansfield, General Manager

***KNMD-TV** *Digital Channel:* 8 *Virtual Channel:* 9; 5.14 kw; 4180 ft.; N35 12 44 W106 26 57
Of New Mexico, 1130 University Blvd Ne, Albuquerque, NM 87107 US
(505) 277-2121
www.knmetv.org
viewer@knme.org
License: Santa Fe, Santa Fe County, NM held by The Regents of the University of New Mexico.
Washington Law Firm: Dow, Lohnes & Albertson, LLC
Nat'l Network: PBS
Polly Anderson, CEO
Joanne Bachmann, General Manager
Chad Davis, Programming Director
Jim Gale, Engineering Dir
Karen Mann, Director, Finance & Admin

***KNME-TV** *Digital Channel:* 35 *Virtual Channel:* 5; 250 kw; 4222 ft.; N35 12 49 W106 27 1
1130 University Blvd.Ne, Albuquerque, NM 87102 US
(505) 277-2121
www.knmetv.org
License: Albuquerque, Bernalillo County, NM held by Regents of University of New Mexico and Board of Education, Albuquerque
Washington Law Firm: Dow, Lohnes & Albertson
Nat'l Network: PBS
Karen Mann, CFO
Polly Anderson, General Manager
Chad Davis, Programming Director
Jim Gale, Engineering Dir
Joanne Bachmann, Associate General Manager

KOAT-TV *Digital Channel:* 7 *Virtual Channel:* 7; 26.5 kw; 4239 ft.; N35 12 53 W106 27 1
Mailing Address: 888 Seventh Avenue, New York, NY 10106 US
Second Address: 3801 Carlisle N.E., Albuquerque, NM 87107
(505) 884-7777, *Fax:* (505) 884-6282
www.koat.com
koatdesk@hearst.com
License: Albuquerque, Bernalillo County, NM held by KOAT Hearst Television Inc
Group Owner: Hearst-Argyle Television Inc.; (acq 3-18-99; grpsl).; *Washington Law Firm:* Brooks, Pierce, McLendon, Humphrey & Leonard
Nat'l Network: ABC
Mary Lynn Roper, President

KOB *Digital Channel:* 26; 270kW; ant 4,198t/178g; N35 12 42 W106 26 57; *Population Served:* 568,700
Mailing Address: Box 1351, Albuquerque, NM 87103
Second Address: 4 Broadcast Plaza S.W., Albuquerque, NM 87104
(505) 243-4411, *Fax:* (505) 764-2522
www.kob.com
kobtv@kob.com
License: Albuquerque, Bernalillo County, NM held by KOB-TV L.L.C.
Group Owner: Hubbard Broadcasting Inc.; (acq 3-15-57; grpsl;;
Washington Law Firm: Fletcher, Heald & Hildreth
Nat'l Network: NBC *Wire Services:* AP
Hours of Local News Weekly: News progmg 29 hrs wkly
Mike Burgess, Operations Dir
Susan Connor, Station Manager
Jeff Finkel, General Sales Mgr
Juanita Garay, Programming Director
Vince Gasparich, Promotions Manager
Jamie Ioos, News Director
Sean Anker, Engineering Dir
Joan Lucas,Public Affairs Director
Elena Hernandez, Research Director
Jackie Gregory, Traffic Manager

KOBF *Digital Channel:* 12 *Virtual Channel:* 12; 30 kw; 410 ft.; N36 41 43 W108 13 14; *Rebroadcasting:* Satelite of KOB-TV Albuquerque

Mailing Address: 3415 University Avenue, St. Paul, MN 55114 US
Second Address: 825 W. Broadway, Farmington, NM 87401
(505) 326-1141, *Fax:* (505) 327-5196
www.kob.com
License: Farmington, San Juan County, NM held by KOB-TV L.L.C.
Group Owner: Hubbard Broadcasting Inc.; (acq 9-19-83; $2.35 million;; *Washington Law Firm:* Fletcher, Heald & Hildreth
Nat'l Network: NBC
Size of News Staff: 6; *Hours of Local News Weekly:* news progmg 4 hrs wkly
Don Baughan, Operations Dir

KOBR *Digital Channel:* 8 *Virtual Channel:* 8; 40 kw; 1749 ft.; N33 22 31 W103 46 12; *Rebroadcasting:* Rebroadcasts KOB-TV Albuquerque 90%.
3415 University Avenue, St. Paul, MN 55114 US
(505) 625-8888, *Fax:* (505) 625-8866
www.kob.com
kobtv@kob.com
License: Roswell, Chaves County, NM held by Stanley S. Hubbard Revocable Trust.
Group Owner: Hubbard Broadcasting Inc.; (acq 8-10-2001).; *Washington Law Firm:* Fletcher, Heald & Hildreth
Nat'l Network: NBC
Size of News Staff: 4
Stanley Hubbard, President
Charlie Blanco, General Manager
Nora Nieto, Programming Director
Dusty Deane, Promotions Manager
Wayne Koontz, Chief Engineer

KRPV-DT *Digital Channel:* 27; 50 kw vis; ant 399t/269g; N33 23 50 W104 22 34; *Population Served:* 272,826
Mailing Address: Box 61000, Midland, TX 79711
Second Address: Box 967, 2606 S. Main, Roswell, NM 88203-0967
(800) 707-0420, *Fax:* (505) 622-3424
www.godslearningchannel.com
info@ptcbglc.com
License: Roswell, Chaves County, NM held by Prime Time Christian Broadcasting
Foreign Language Programming
Al Cooper, CEO
Tommy Cooper, Operations Dir

KRQE *Digital Channel:* 13 *Virtual Channel:* 13; 21.5 kw; 4222 ft.; N35 12 40 W106 26 57
13 Broadcast Place S.W., Albuquerque, NM 87104 US
(505) 243-2285, *Fax:* (505) 248-1464
www.krqe.com
newsdesk@krqe.com
License: Albuquerque, Bernalillo County, NM held by LIN License Comрnany LLC
Group Owner: LIN Media; (acq 11-30-2005; grpsl).; *Washington Law Firm:* Reed, Smith, Shaw & McClay
Nat'l Network: CBS *Nat'l Reps:* Harrington, Righter & Parsons
Wire Services: CBS
Size of News Staff: 65; *Hours of Local News Weekly:* news progmg 24 hrs wkly
Gina Galindo, Operations Dir
Bill Anderson, General Manager
Dino Damelio, General Sales Mgr
Don Pierce, Programming Director
Parker Harms, Promotions Manager
Ian Munro, News Director
Frank Lilley, Engineering Dir
Frank Montoya,Local Sales Manager
Marilyn Painter, Research Director
Pat Gonzales, Traffic Manager

KRWB-TV *Digital Channel:* 21 *Virtual Channel:* 21; 1000 kw; 420 ft.; N33 6 1 W104 15 15
5925 Cromo, El Paso, TX 79912 US
(505) 797-1919, *Fax:* (505) 938-4401
www.newmexicoscw.tv
License: Roswell, Chaves County, NM held by Acme Television Licenses of New Mexico LLC.
Group Owner: ACME Communications Inc.; (acq 1-7-2004)
Nat'l Network: CW
Stan Gill, General Manager
Rosalie Drake, General Sales Mgr
Chris Iller, Promotions Manager
Larry Oliver, Chief Engineer

KTEL-TV *Digital Channel:* 25 *Virtual Channel:* 25; 50 kw; 394 ft.; N32 26 9 W104 11 14
Mailing Address: P.O. Box 283, Brigham City, UT 84302 US
Second Address: 2400 Monroe St. N. E., Albuquerque, NM 87110
(505) 884-5353, *Fax:* (505) 889-8390
gzavala@kteltv.com
License: Carlsbad, Eddy County, NM held by Ramar Communications II Ltd.
Group Owner: Ramar Communications II Ltd.; (acq 8-10-99; $10,000)
Nat'l Network: TELEMUNDO
Foreign Language Programming
Ray Moran, CEO
Brad Moran, President
Gabriel Zavala, General Manager

KTFQ-TV *Digital Channel:* 22; 5,000 kw vis; ant 1,233t/1,046g; N35 24 44 W106 43 32
2725 Broadbent Pkwy. N.E., Suite E, Albuquerque, NM 87107
(505) 342-4141, *Fax:* (505) 344-8714
www.univision.com
License: Albuquerque, Bernalillo County, NM held by TeleFutura Albuquerque LLC.
Group Owner: Univision Communications Inc.; (acq 5-30-2003; $20 million)
Nat'l Network: TeleFutura (Spanish)
Foreign Language Programming
Margarita Wilder, General Manager
Dudley Bullock, Chief Engineer
Bob Morrison, National Sales Manager

KUPT *Digital Channel:* 29 *Virtual Channel:* 29; 50 kw; 515 ft.; N32 43 28 W103 5 46
Mailing Address: P.O. Box 3757, Lubbock, TX 79452 US
Second Address: 9800 University Ave, Lubbock, TX 79423
(806) 745-3434, *Fax:* (806) 748-1949
License: Hobbs, Lea County, NM held by Ramar Communications, Inc.
Group Owner: Ramar Communications II Ltd.; (acq 6-4-97; $200,000); *Washington Law Firm:* Leventhal, Senter & Lerman
Nat'l Network: MY NETWORK
Brad Moran, General Manager
Chris Torres, Programming Director

KWBQ *Digital Channel:* 29 *Virtual Channel:* 19; 245 kw; 4229 ft.; N35 12 44 W106 26 57
4100 Hawkins, N.E., Albuquerque, NM 87109 US
(505) 797-1919, *Fax:* (505) 344-1145
www.newmexicoscw.tv
License: Santa Fe, Santa Fe County, NM held by Acme TV Licenses of New Mexico L.L.C.
Group Owner: ACME Communications Inc.
Nat'l Network: CW
Stan Gill, General Manager
Dan Marchese, General Sales Mgr
Chris Iller, Promotions Manager
Larry Oliver, Chief Engineer

Amarillo, TX (DMA 131)

***KENW** *Virtual Channel:* 3; 100 kw vis, 20 kw aur; 1,150t/1,085g; N33 33 19 W103 39 03; *Population Served:* 400,000
52 Broadcast Ctr., ENMU, 1500 S. Ave. K, Portales, NM 88130
(505) 562-2112, *Fax:* (505) 562-2590
www.kenw.org
kenwtv@enmu.edu
License: Portales, Roosevelt County, NM held by Regents of Eastern New Mexico University
Washington Law Firm: Dow, Lohnes & Albertson, PLLC
Nat'l Network: PBS; NETA; APT *Wire Services:* AP
Foreign Language Programming; Size of News Staff: 2; *Hours of Local News Weekly:* news progmg 3 hrs wkly
Ronnie Birdsong, Vice President
Steven Gamble, President
Orlando Ortega, Operations Dir
Duane Ryan, General Manager
Rena Garrett, General Sales Mgr
Jenifer Baca, Programming Director
Rena Garrett, Promotions Manager
JanetBresenham, News Director
Jeff Burmeister, Engineering Dir
Don Criss, Public Affairs Director
Richard Rivera, Producer/Director/Sports
Jacob Workman, Producer/Director

KVIH-TV *Digital Channel:* 12 *Virtual Channel:* 12; 5 kw; 669 ft.; N34 11 34 W103 16 44; *Rebroadcasting:* Satellite of KVII-TV Amarillo, TX
1 Broadcast Center, Amarillo, TX 79101 US
(806) 373-1787, *Fax:* (806) 371-7329
www.connectamarillo.com
pronews7@kvii.com
License: Clovis, Curry County, NM held by Barrington Broadcasting Texas Corp.
Group Owner: Barrington Broadcasting Group, LLC.; (acq 8-2-2005; $22.5 million with KVII-TV Amarillo, TX).; *Washington Law Firm:* Wiley, Rein & Fielding
Nat'l Network: CBS
K. James Yager, CEO
Chris Cornelius, President
Marc Gilmour, General Manager
Brenda Holloway, General Sales Mgr
Margaret Burris, Programming Director
Melissa Maeyer, Promotions Manager
Bill Canady, Chief Engineer
Chris Knight,Local Sales Manager

El Paso (Las Cruces, NM), TX (DMA 98)

***KRWG-TV** *Digital Channel:* 23 *Virtual Channel:* 22; 200 kw; 673 ft.; N32 17 33 W106 41 51
Mailing Address: P.O. Box 30001 Msc:Tv22, Las Cruces, NM 88003 US
Second Address: 2915 McFie Cir., Rm. 100, Las Cruces, NM 88003
(575) 646-2222, *Fax:* (575) 646-1924
www.krwg-tv.org
krwgtv@nmsu.edu
License: Las Cruces, Dona Ana County, NM held by Regents of New Mexico State University
Washington Law Firm: Dow, Lohnes & Albertson
Nat'l Network: PBS *Wire Services:* AP
Foreign Language Programming; Hours of Local News Weekly: News progmg 3 hrs wkly
J.D. Jarvis, Operations Dir
Anthony Casaus, General Sales Mgr
William Saggerson, Chief Engineer
Glen Cerny, Director of Broadcasting

KTDO *Digital Channel:* 47 *Virtual Channel:* 48; 200 kw; 1821 ft.; N31 48 19 W106 28 59
400 Putman Building, 215 North Main Street, Davenport, IA 52801 US
(915) 591-9595, *Fax:* (915) 591-9896
www.telemundo.com
License: Las Cruces, Dona Ana County, NM held by ZGS El Paso Televison LP
(acq 9-13-2004; $11.8 million); *Washington Law Firm:* Reed, Smith, Shaw & McClay
Nat'l Network: TELEMUNDO
Foreign Language Programming
Lorena Caltamon, General Manager
Monic Diaz, Programming Director
Phillip Cortez, Promotions Manager
Elios Ventanilla, Chief Engineer

New York

Albany-Schenectady-Troy, NY (DMA 57)

WCDC-TV *Digital Channel:* 36; 538 kw vis, 53 kw aur; 3,688t/248g; N42 38 14 W73 10 07; *Rebroadcasting:* Satellite of WTEN-TV Albany
341 Northern Blvd., Albany, NY 12204
(518) 436-4822, *Fax:* (518) 462-6065
www.wten.com
news@wten.com
License: Adams, Berkshire County, MA held by Young Broadcasting of Albany, Inc., Debtor-in-possession
Group Owner: Young Broadcasting Inc.; (acq 10-11-89; grpsl;; *Washington Law Firm:* Wiley, Rein & Fielding
Nat'l Network: ABC
Size of News Staff: 37; *Hours of Local News Weekly:* news progmg 15 hrs wkly
Michael Sechrist, General Manager

WCWN *Digital Channel:* 43 *Virtual Channel:* 45; 600 kw; 1398 ft.; N42 37 31 W74 0 38
14 Corporate Woods Blvd., Albany, NY 12211 US
(518) 346-6666, *Fax:* (518) 381-3770 (sales)
www.cbs6albany.com
news@cbs6albany.com
License: Schenectady, Schenectady County, NY held by Freedom Broadcasting of New York Licensee L.L.C.
Group Owner: Freedom Communications Inc., Broadcast Division; (acq 12-5-2006; $17 million)
Nat'l Network: CW
Robert Furlong, Operations Dir
Tim Pennings, Promotions Manager
Fred Lass, Chief Engineer

***WMHT** *Digital Channel:* 34 *Virtual Channel:* 17; 325 kw; 1398 ft.; N42 37 31 W74 0 38
P.O Box 17,17 Fern Ave., Schenectady, NY 12301 US
(518) 880-3400, *Fax:* (518) 880-3409
www.wmht.org
email@wmht.org
License: Schenectady, Schenectady County, NY held by WMHT Educational Telecommunications
Washington Law Firm: Schwartz, Woods & Miller
Nat'l Network: PBS
Robert Altman, President

WNYT *Digital Channel:* 12 *Virtual Channel:* 13; 15 kw; 1427 ft.; N42 37 31 W74 0 38
C/O Holland & Knight, Lp, 2100 Pennsylvania Ave NW, Washington, DC 20037 US
(518) 436-4791,(518) 207-4700
www.wnyt.com
License: Albany, Albany County, NY held by WNYT-TV LLC.
Group Owner: Hubbard Broadcasting Inc.; (acq 9-19-96).
Nat'l Network: NBC *Nat'l Reps:* Petry Television Inc.
Hours of Local News Weekly: News progmg 27 hrs wkly
Steve Robbins, Operations Dir
Stephen Baboulis, General Manager
Tony McManus, General Sales Mgr
Maryann Ryan, Programming Director
Paul Lewis, News Director
Richard Klein, Engineering Dir

WRGB *Digital Channel:* 6 *Virtual Channel:* 6; 30.2 kw; 1286 ft.; N42 37 31 W74 0 38
1400 Balltown Road, Schenectady, NY 12309 US
(518) 346-6666, *Fax:* (518) 381-3736 Prog. Mgr.
www.cbs6albany.com,www.wrgb.com
news@wrgb.com
License: Schenectady, Schenectady County, NY held by Freedom Broadcasting of New York Licensee L.L.C.
Group Owner: Freedom Communications Inc., Broadcast Division; acq 3-4-86; *Washington Law Firm:* Latham & Watkins
Nat'l Network: CBS *Nat'l Reps:* TeleRep *Wire Services:* AP
Hours of Local News Weekly: News progmg 31.5 hrs wkly
Scott Flanders, CEO
Doreen Wade, President
Robert Furlong, Operations Dir
Vincent Nelson, General Sales Mgr
Tim Pennings, Promotions Manager
Lisa Jackson, News Director
Fred Lass, Engineering Dir
Robert Hewitt, National SalesManager

WTEN *Digital Channel:* 26 *Virtual Channel:* 10; 700 kw; 1398 ft.; N42 37 31 W74 0 38
341 Northern Blvd., Albany, NY 12204 US
(518) 436-4822, *Fax:* (518) 462-6065
www.wten.com
news@wten.com
License: Albany, Albany County, NY held by Young Broadcasting of Albany, Inc., Debtor-in-possession
Group Owner: Young Broadcasting Inc.; (acq 10-11-89; grpsl).; *Washington Law Firm:* Wiley, Rein & Fielding
Nat'l Network: ABC
Size of News Staff: 50; *Hours of Local News Weekly:* news progmg 22 hrs wkly
Michael Sechrist, General Manager
Ron Romines, General Sales Mgr
Chris Terwilliger, Programming Director
Skeeter Lansing, Chief Engineer

WXXA-TV *Digital Channel:* 7 *Virtual Channel:* 23; 10 kw; 1424 ft.; N42 37 31 W74 0 38
200 Concord Plaza, Suite 600, San Antonio, TX 78216 US
(518) 862-2323,(518) 862-0995, *Fax:* (518) 862-0865,(518) 862-0930
www.fox23news.com
news@fox23news.com
License: Albany, Albany County, NY held by Newport Television License LLC.
Group Owner: Newport Television LLC; (acq 3-14-2008; grpsl); *Washington Law Firm:* Covington & Burling
Nat'l Network: FOX *Nat'l Reps:* Millennium Sales & Marketing
Size of News Staff: 70; *Hours of Local News Weekly:* news progmg 23.5 hrs wkly
Sandy DiPasquale, CEO
Bill Sally, General Manager
Todd Kuhn, General Sales Mgr
Paul Pelliccia, Programming Director
Gene Ross, News Director
Sargent Cathrall, Chief Engineer
Steve Kimatian, Executive Vice President

WYPX-TV *Digital Channel:* 50; 450 kw vis; ant 679t/675g; N42 59 04 W74 10 56
1 Charles Blvd, Guilderland, NY 12084
(518) 464-0143, *Fax:* (518) 464-0633
www.ionmedia.com
License: Amsterdam, Montgomery County, NY held by 10 N Media License, Inc.
Group Owner: ION Media Networks Inc.; (acq 6-1-96; $2.5 million)
Nat'l Network: ION Television
Brandon Burgess, CEO
Chris Iorio, Operations Dir
Renee Osterlitz, Station Manager
Steve Appel, General Sales Mgr
Chris Iorio, Chief Engineer

Binghamton, NY (DMA 157)

WBNG-TV *Digital Channel:* 7; 166 kw vis, 18.2 kw aur; ant 1,210t/785g; N42 02 33 W75 57 06; *Population Served:* 154,400
560 Columbia Dr., Johnson City, NY 13790
(607) 729-8812, *Fax:* (607) 797-6211
www.wbng.com
wbng@wbngtv.com
License: Binghamton, Broome County, NY held by WBNG License Inc.
Group Owner: Granite Broadcasting Corp.; (acq 7-26-2006; $45 million); *Washington Law Firm:* Latham & Watkins
Nat'l Network: CBS; CW *Nat'l Reps:* Continental Television Sales *Wire Services:* AP
Hours of Local News Weekly: News progmg 30 hrs wkly
Greg Catlin, General Manager
Bob Krummunecker, Station Manager
Bob Krummunecker, General Sales Mgr
Kate Garger, Programming Director
Christina Rockhill, Promotions Manager
Candace Chapman, News Director
Chris Ball, ChiefEngineer
Janet Heatherman, Traffic Supervisor

WICZ-TV *Digital Channel:* 8 *Virtual Channel:* 40; 7.9 kw; 1217 ft.; N42 3 22 W75 56 39
2178 Commons Parkway, Okemos, MI 48864 US
(607) 770-4040, *Fax:* (607) 798-7950
www.wicz.com
fox40@wicz.com
License: Binghamton, Broome County, NY held by Stainless Broadcasting L.P.
Group Owner: Northwest Broadcasting Inc.; (acq 7-15-97; $16 million cash-out merger with KTVZ(TV) Bend, OR); *Washington Law Firm:* Leventhal, Senter & Lerman
Nat'l Network: FOX
Size of News Staff: 13; *Hours of Local News Weekly:* news progmg 2 hrs wkly
Brian Brady, CEO
John Leet, General Manager
Bill Quarles, CFO

WIVT *Digital Channel:* 34 *Virtual Channel:* 34; 345 kw; 912 ft.; N42 3 39 W75 56 36
1333 New Hampshire Ave NW, #1000, Washington, DC 20036 US
(607) 771-3434, *Fax:* (607) 723-1034
www.NewsChannel34.com
License: Binghamton, Broome County, NY held by Newport Television License LLC.
Group Owner: Newport Television LLC; (acq 3-14-2008; grpsl)
Nat'l Network: NBC *Nat'l Reps:* Millennium Sales & Marketing
Sandy DiPasquale, President
John Birchall, Operations Dir
Maura Burtis, General Sales Mgr
Vince Spicola, Programming Director
Jim La Vasser, Promotions Manager
Jim Ehmke, News Director
Abiodun Sadik, Chief of Operations
JohnKing, Operations Vice President

***WSKG-TV** *Digital Channel:* 42 *Virtual Channel:* 46; 50 kw; 1339 ft.; N42 3 40 W75 56 45
Mailing Address: 601 Gates Road, Vestal, NY 14850 US
Second Address: 601 Gates Rd., Vestal, NY 13850
(607) 729-0100, *Fax:* (607) 729-7328
www.wskg.org
mail@wskg.org
License: Binghamton, Broome County, NY held by WSKG Public Telecommunications Council
Washington Law Firm: Dow, Lohnes & Albertson
Nat'l Network: PBS
Brian Sickora, CEO
Erik Jensen, Operations Dir

Buffalo, NY (DMA 51)

WBBZ-TV *Digital Channel:* 7; 15.5 kw vis; ant 1,348t/963g; N42 38 15 W78 37 12; *Not on Air/Target Date:* 10/1/2009 ; *Station Currently Dark*; *Population Served:* 500,000
Mailing Address: Box 612066, Dallas, TX 14171
Second Address: 3901 Hwy 121, Bedford, TX 76021
(817) 571-1229, *Fax:* (817) 571-7458
License: Springville, Erie County, NY held by Word of God Fellowship, Inc.
Marcus Lamb, President

WGRZ *Digital Channel:* 33; 100 kw vis, 20 kw aur; ant 941t/899g; N42 43 06 W73 22 48; *Population Served:* 1,325,500
259 Delaware Ave., Buffalo, NY 14202
(716) 849-2222, *Fax:* (716) 849-7602
www.wgrz.com
License: Buffalo, Erie County, NY held by Multimedia Entertainment Inc.
Group Owner: Gannett Broadcasting; (acq 1-27-97; grpsl).
Nat'l Network: NBC *Wire Services:* Newsweek; CNBC; NBC; UPI
Jim Toellner, President

WIVB-TV *Digital Channel:* 39 *Virtual Channel:* 4; 790 kw; 1368 ft.; N42 39 33 W78 37 33
200 Crescent Court, Suite 1600, Dallas, TX 75201 US
(716) 874-4410, *Fax:* (716) 879-4896
www.wivb.com
License: Buffalo, Erie County, NY held by LIN License Company LLC
Group Owner: LIN Media; (acq 12-16-97).; *Washington Law Firm:* Covington & Burling
Nat'l Network: CBS
Chris Musial, CEO
Diane Breen, Programming Director
Dan Meyers, Promotions Manager
Dennis Majewicz, Chief Engineer

WKBW-TV *Digital Channel:* 38 *Virtual Channel:* 7; 358 kw; 1420 ft.; N42 38 14.8 W78 37 11.9
7 Broadcast Plaza, Buffalo, NY 14202 US
(716) 845-6100, *Fax:* (710) 522-1846
www.wkbw.com
License: Buffalo, Erie County, NY held by Granite Broadcasting Corp.
Group Owner: Granite Broadcasting Corp.; (acq 1995; $13.42 million); *Washington Law Firm:* Akin, Gump, Strauss, Haver & Feld
Nat'l Network: ABC *Nat'l Reps:* TeleRep
William Ransom, General Manager
Mike Anger, Chief Engineer

***WNED-TV** *Digital Channel:* 43 *Virtual Channel:* 17; 156 kw; 1076 ft.; N43 1 48 W78 55 15
Mailing Address: 140 Lower Terrace, Buffalo, NY 14202 US
Second Address: Horizons Plaza, 140 Lower Terr., Buffalo, NY 14202
(716) 845-7000, *Fax:* (716) 845-7036
www.wned.org
License: Buffalo, Erie County, NY held by Western New York Public Broadcasting Association
Washington Law Firm: Schwartz, Woods & Miller
Nat'l Network: PBS
Foreign Language Programming
Donald Boswell, CEO
Richard Daly, Operations Dir
Ron Santora, Programming Director
Darwin McPherson, Promotions Manager
Joe Puma, Engineering Dir
Rich Borosky, Traffic Manager
Gordon Bayliss, Underwriting

WNLO *Digital Channel:* 32 *Virtual Channel:* 23; 1000 kw; 994 ft.; N43 1 48 W78 55 15
140 Lower Terrace, Buffalo, NY 14202 US
(716) 874-4410, *Fax:* (716) 879-4896
www.cw23.com
License: Buffalo, Erie County, NY held by LIn License Company LLC
Group Owner: LIN Media; (acq 6-6-2001; $26.2 million); *Washington Law Firm:* Covington & Burling
Nat'l Network: CW
Chris Musial, CEO
Diane Breen, Programming Director
Dan Meyers, Promotions Manager
Dennis Majewicz, Chief Engineer

WNYB *Digital Channel:* 26 *Virtual Channel:* 26; 243 kw; 1519 ft.; N42 23 36 W79 13 44
5775 Big Tree Road, Orchard Park, NY 14217 US

(716) 662-2659, *Fax:* (716) 667-2499
wnyb@tct.tv
License: Jamestown, Chautauqua County, NY held by Faith Broadcasting Network Inc.
Group Owner: Tri-State Christian Television; (acq 5-7-2002).
Nat'l Network: IND
Loren Speery, General Manager

WNYO-TV *Digital Channel:* 49 *Virtual Channel:* 49; 198 kw; 1234 ft.; N42 46 58 W78 27 28
915 Middle River Drive, #409, Forth Lauderdale, FL 33304 US
(716) 447-3200, *Fax:* (716) 875-4919
www.mytvbuffalo.com
wnyo@spgnet.com
License: Buffalo, Erie County, NY held by New York Television Inc.
Group Owner: Sinclair Broadcast Group Inc.; (acq 1-25-2002; $51.5 million for stock).
Nat'l Network: MYTV *Nat'l Reps:* Millennium Sales & Marketing
Nick Magnini, General Manager
Jose Chapa, General Sales Mgr
Candice Zoeller, Promotions Manager
Donald Stewart, Engineering Dir

WPXJ-TV *Digital Channel:* 23 *Virtual Channel:* 51; 455 kw; 906 ft.; N42 53 42 W78 0 56
Mailing Address: 601 Clearwater Park Road, West Palm Beach, FL 33401 US
Second Address: 726 Exchange St., Suite 605, Buffalo, NY 14210
(716) 852-1818, *Fax:* (716) 852-8288
www.iontelevision.com
License: Batavia, Genesee County, NY held by ION Media Buffalo License, Inc.
Group Owner: ION Media Networks Inc.; (acq 7-15-97; $3 million)
Nat'l Network: ION
Barb Lipka, Operations Dir

WUTV *Digital Channel:* 14 *Virtual Channel:* 29; 1000 kw; 983 ft.; N43 1 32 W78 55 43
18 Newbury Street, Boston, MA 02116 US
(716) 477-3200, *Fax:* (716) 875-4919
www.wutv.com
wutv@spgnet.com
License: Buffalo, Erie County, NY held by WUTV Licensee LLC.
Group Owner: Sinclair Broadcast Group Inc.; (acq 12-10-01; grpsl).; *Washington Law Firm:* Arter & Hadden
Nat'l Network: FOX *Nat'l Reps:* Millennium Sales & Marketing
Nick Magnini, General Manager
Jose Chapa, General Sales Mgr
Candice Zoeller, Promotions Manager
Donald Stewart, Engineering Dir

Burlington, VT-Plattsburgh, NY (DMA 93)

***WCFE-TV** *Digital Channel:* 38 *Virtual Channel:* 57; 55 kw; 2418 ft.; N44 41 43 W73 53 0
P. O. Box 617, Plattsburgh, NY 12901 US
(518) 563-9770, *Fax:* (518) 561-1928
www.mountainlake.org
mlpbs@mountainlake.org
License: Plattsburgh, Clinton County, NY held by Mountain Lake Public Telecommunications Council
Washington Law Firm: Dow, Lohnes & Albertson
Nat'l Network: PBS
Hours of Local News Weekly: 30 minutes
Alice Recore, CEO
Zachary Kowalczyk, Operations Dir
Rhonda Santos, Promotions Manager
Charlie Zarbo, Engineering Dir
Sophie Mitsoglou, Director of Fundraising
Colin Powers, Production Director

WNMN *Digital Channel:* 40 *Virtual Channel:* 40
2001 Pennsylvania Ave., N.W., Suite 400, Washington, DC 20006 US
(518) 825-4040, *Fax:* (518) 825-1029
jloper@cecholdings.com
License: Saranac Lake, Franklin County, NY held by Channel 61 Associates LLC.
Nat'l Network: ION
Ben Kulikoulski, General Manager
Kenan Gurino, General Sales Mgr
Mitch Stern, Chief Engineer

WPTZ *Digital Channel:* 14 *Virtual Channel:* 5; 25.1 kw vis, 4.3 kw aur; ant 1,991t/978g; N44 34 26 W73 40 29
Mailing Address: 5 Television Dr., Plattsburgh, NY 10019
Second Address: 553 Roosevelt Highway, Colchester, VT 05446
(518) 561-5555, *Fax:* (518) 561-5940
www.wptz.com
License: North Pole, Lake Placid County, NY held by Hearst Stations Inc.
Group Owner: Hearst Television Inc.; (acq 6-1-98).
Nat'l Network: NBC
Size of News Staff: 31; *Hours of Local News Weekly:* news progmg 23 hrs wkly
Paul Sands, General Manager
Luke Commare, General Sales Mgr
Susan Acklen, Promotions Manager
Sinan Sadar, News Director
William Harp, Chief Engineer
Laura Lareau, Traffic Manager

Elmira (Corning), NY (DMA 175)

WENY-TV *Digital Channel:* 36 *Virtual Channel:* 36; 75 kw; 1122 ft.; N42 8 31 W77 4 40
PO Box 208, Elmira, NY 14902 US
(607) 739-3636, *Fax:* (607) 739-1418
www.weny.com
info@weny.com
License: Elmira, Chemung County, NY held by Lilly Broadcasting L.L.C
(acq 10-17-99; $4.8 million); *Washington Law Firm:* Cordon & Kelly
Nat'l Network: ABC; CW; CBS
Hours of Local News Weekly: News progmg 10 hrs wkly
Kevin Lilly, CEO
Brian Lilly, Operations Dir
Peter Veto, General Manager
Sharon Ewsuk, General Sales Mgr
Dan Beach, Programming Director
Bruce Hauver, Promotions Manager
Scott Cook, News Director

WETM-TV *Digital Channel:* 18 *Virtual Channel:* 18; 45 kw; 1234 ft.; N42 6 22 W76 52 17
Mailing Address: 3839 4th Street, North, Suite 420, St. Petersburg, FL 33703 US
Second Address: 101 E. Water St., Elmira, NY 14901
(607) 733-5518, *Fax:* (607) 734-1176
www.wetmtv.com
info@wetmtv.com
License: Elmira, Chemung County, NY held by Newport Television License LLC.
Group Owner: Newport Television LLC; (acq 3-14-2008; grpsl); *Washington Law Firm:* Covington & Burling
Nat'l Network: NBC
Size of News Staff: 21; *Hours of Local News Weekly:* news progmg 14 hrs wkly
Randy Reid, General Manager
Bob Cibulsky, General Sales Mgr

WFBT *Digital Channel:* 14 *Virtual Channel:* 14; *Not on Air/Target Date:* 10/1/2009 ; *Station Currently Dark*
P.O. Box 1341, Highland, NY 12528 US
(845) 883-7457
License: Bath, Steuben County, NY
William Walker III, General Manager

***WSKA** *Digital Channel:* 30 *Virtual Channel:* 30; 25 kw; 1096 ft.; N42 8 29.73 W77 4 39.11; *Rebroadcasting:* rebroadcast of WSKG(TV) Binghamton
P.O. Box 3000, Binghamton, NY 13902 US
(607) 729-0100, *Fax:* (607) 729-7328
www.wskg.org
mail@wskg.org
License: Corning, Steuben County, NY held by WSKG Public Telecommunications Council
Nat'l Network: PBS
Brian Sickora, General Manager

WYDC *Digital Channel:* 48 *Virtual Channel:* 48; 7.6 kw; 1096 ft.; N42 8 30 W77 4 39
106 Possum Way, Clarks Summit, PA 18411 US
(607) 937-5000, *Fax:* (607) 937-4019
www.wydctv.com
info@wydctv.com
License: Corning, Steuben County, NY held by WYDC Inc (acq 11-19-97; $1.75 million); *Washington Law Firm:* Drinker Biddle & Reath LLP
Nat'l Network: FOX
Bill Christian, CEO
Robin Pickering, Programming Director

New York (DMA 1)

WABC-TV *Digital Channel:* 7; 11.69 kw vis; ant 1,328t/1,322g; N40 44 54 W73 59 10
7 Lincoln Sq., New York, NY 10023
(212) 456-7777, *Fax:* (212) 456-2290
www.7online.com
License: New York, New York County, NY held by ABC Inc.
Group Owner: ABC Inc.; *Ownership:* The Walt Disney Company
Nat'l Network: ABC *Nat'l Reps:* ABC National Television Sales
Dave Davis, President
Evelyn del Cerro, Operations Dir
Scott Simensky, General Sales Mgr
Art Moore, Programming Director
Jim Gorham, Promotions Manager
Kurt Hanson, Engineering Dir
Alyson Rozner, Marketing Manager
SaundraThomas, Public Affairs Director

WCBS-TV *Digital Channel:* 33 *Virtual Channel:* 2; 284 kw; 1302 ft.; N40 44 54 W73 59 10
600 New Hampshire Ave NW, Suite 1200, Washington, DC 20037 US
(212) 975-4321, *Fax:* (212) 975-4677
www.wcbstv.com
cbsnewyork@cbs.com
License: New York, New York County, NY held by CBS Broadcasting Inc.
Group Owner: CBS Television Stations Group
Nat'l Network: CBS *Nat'l Reps:* CBS TV Stations National Sales
Peter Dunn, President
Joel Goldberg, Operations Dir
Vincent McCarthy, General Sales Mgr
David Friend, News Director

WFTY-DT *Digital Channel:* 23; 2,630 kw vis, 263 kw aur; 720t/678g; N40 53 23 W72 57 13; *Population Served:* 3,000,000
3200 Expressway Dr. S., Islandia, NY 11749
(631) 582-6700; (631) 924-4433, *Fax:* (631) 924-7742
www.univision.com
License: Smithtown, Suffolk County, NY held by Univision New York LLC.
Group Owner: Univision Communications Inc.; (acq 5-21-2001; grpsl).; *Washington Law Firm:* Wiley, Rein & Fielding
Nat'l Network: TeleFutura (Spanish)
Foreign Language Programming; Hours of Local News Weekly: News progmg 4 hrs wkly
Cristina Schwarz, Operations Dir
David Marinace, Chief Engineer

WFUT-DT *Digital Channel:* 30; 2,630 kw vis; 1,440t/1,430g; N40 44 54 W73 59 10; *Rebroadcasting:* Rebroadcasts WFTY, Smithtown, NY, 100%.
Univison 41, 500 Frank W. Burr Blvd., 6th Fl., Teaneck, NJ 7666
(201) 287-4042, *Fax:* (201) 287-9422
www.univision.net
noticias41ny@univision.net
License: Newark, Essex County, NJ held by Univision New York LLC
Group Owner: Univision Communications Inc.; (acq 5-21-2001; grpsl).; *Washington Law Firm:* Shaw, Pittman
Foreign Language Programming
Ramon Pineda, Operations Dir
Morris Marotta, Station Manager
John De Simon, General Sales Mgr
Norma Morato, News Director

***WLIW** *Digital Channel:* 21 *Virtual Channel:* 21; 89.9 kw; 364 ft.; N40 47 19 W73 27 9
303 Sunnyside Blvd, PO Box 21, Plainview, NY 11803 US
(516) 367-2100, *Fax:* (516) 692-7629
www.wliw.org
License: Garden City, Nassau County, NY held by Educational Broadcasting Corp
(acq 1-31-2003); *Washington Law Firm:* Schwartz, Woods & Miller
Nat'l Network: PBS *Wire Services:* UPI
Neal Shapiro, President
John Servidio, General Manager

WLNY-TV *Digital Channel:* 47; 425 kw vis; ant 635t/613g; N40 53 50 W72 54 56; *Population Served:* 4,200,000
270 S. Service Rd., Suite 55, Melville, NY 11747
(631) 777-8855, *Fax:* (631) 777-8180
www.wlnytv.com
ny55@wlnytv.com
License: Riverhead, Suffolk County, NY held by WLNY LP
Washington Law Firm: Cohn & Marks
Hours of Local News Weekly: News progmg 2 hrs wkly

Marvin Chauvin, CEO
David Feinblatt, President
Gerald Diorio, Operations Dir
Elliot Simmons, General Sales Mgr
Rosie Miranda, Programming Director
Richard Rose, News Director
Richard Mulliner, Engineering Dir
Andy Starr,National Sales Manager

WNBC *Digital Channel:* 28 *Virtual Channel:* 4; 200.2 kw; 1302 ft.; N40 44 54 W73 59 10
Ms Diane Zipursky, 1299 Pennsylvania Ave, Washington, DC 20004 US
(212) 664-4444, *Fax:* (212) 664-2994 (news)
www.wnbc.com
License: New York, New York County, NY held by NBC Telemundo License Co.
Group Owner: NBC Owned Television Stations; (acq 6-5-86; grpsl).
Nat'l Network: NBC
Karen Seminara, CFO
Thomas O'Brien, President
Mathew Braatz, Operations Dir
Mark Lund, General Sales Mgr
Adele Rifkin, Programming Director
David Hyman, Promotions Manager
Len Berman, News Director
Evan Kutner, ResearchDirector
Laurie Wiseman, Traffic Manager

***WNYE-TV** *Digital Channel:* 24 *Virtual Channel:* 25; 151 kw; 1016 ft.; N40 45 22 W73 59 12
112 Tillary Street, Brooklyn, NY 11201 US
(212) 669-7400, *Fax:* (212) 669-8448
www.nyc.gov/tv
tv@tv.nyc.gov
License: New York, New York County, NY held by New York City Dept. of Info Technology & Telecommunications
Washington Law Firm: Arnold & Porter
Nat'l Network: ETV
Foreign Language Programming
Katherine Oliver, General Manager
Diane Petzke, Programming Director
Chang Kim, Chief Engineer

WNYW *Digital Channel:* 44 *Virtual Channel:* 5; 990 kw; 1204 ft.; N40 44 54 W73 59 10
5151 Wisconsin Ave., Washington, DC 20016 US
(212) 452-5555, *Fax:* (212) 452-5750
www.myfoxny.com
License: New York, New York County, NY held by Fox Television Stations Inc.
Group Owner: Fox Television Stations Inc.; (acq 11-14-86; grpsl).
Nat'l Network: FOX
Al Shjarback, Operations Dir
Lew Leone, General Manager
Dianne Doctor, News Director
Al Shjarback, Engineering Dir
Edward Harris, Engineering Director
Audrey Pass, Public Affairs Director

WPIX *Digital Channel:* 11 *Virtual Channel:* 11; 7.5 kw; 1329 ft.; N40 44 54 W73 59 10
220 East 42nd Street, New York, NY 10017 US
(212) 949-1100, *Fax:* (212) 210-2591
www.wpix.com
License: New York, New York County, NY held by WPIX, Inc., Debtor-in-possession
Group Owner: Tribune Broadcasting Co.; (acq 12-20-2007; grpsl); *Washington Law Firm:* Dow Lohnes PLLC
Nat'l Network: CW *Wire Services:* AP
Hours of Local News Weekly: News progmg 19.5 hrs wkly
Betty Ellen Berlamino, President
Bob Marra, General Sales Mgr
Karen Scott, News Director
John Seminerio, Chief Engineer

WPXN-TV *Digital Channel:* 31 *Virtual Channel:* 31; 180 kw; 1181 ft.; N40 44 54 W73 59 10
601 Clearwater Park Road, West Palm Beach, FL 33401 US
(212) 757-3100, *Fax:* (212) 956-2661
www.ionmedia.tv; www.iontelevision.com
License: New York, New York County, NY held by ION Media License Company, LLC, Debtor-in-possession
Group Owner: ION Media Networks Inc.; (acq 3-4-98; $257.5 million)
Nat'l Network: ION
Mildred Diaz, Operations Dir
Jack Davidson, Chief Engineer

WRNN-TV *Digital Channel:* 48 *Virtual Channel:* 48; 950 kw; 1240 ft.; N41 29 18 W73 56 56
721 Broadway, Kingston, NY 12401 US
(914) 417-2700, *Fax:* (914) 696-0279
www.rnntv.com
comments@rnntv.com
License: Kingston, Ulster County, NY held by WRNN License Co. LLC
(acq 7-31-2001).; *Washington Law Firm:* Baker & Hostetler
Nat'l Network: IND
Size of News Staff: 9; *Hours of Local News Weekly:* news progmg 82 hrs wkly
Richard French, General Manager

WTBY-TV *Digital Channel:* 27 *Virtual Channel:* 54; 1000 kw; 1174 ft.; N41 29 20 W73 56 53
Post Office Box 534, Fishkill, NY 12524 US
(845) 896-4610, *Fax:* (845) 896-4614
www.tbn.org
wtby@tbn.org
License: Poughkeepsie, Dutchess County, NY held by Trinity Broadcasting of N.Y. Inc.
Group Owner: Trinity Broadcasting Network; (acq 7-13-82; $2.97 million;; *Washington Law Firm:* Joseph E. Dunne III
Nat'l Network: TRINITY BROADCA
Paul Crouch, President
Maria Idoni, Operations Dir
Chris Elia, General Manager
Paul Swartzendruber, Chief Engineer

WXTV-DT *Digital Channel:* 40; 2,340 kw vis, 234 kw aur; ant 1,381t; N40 44 54 W73 59 10; *Population Served:* 3,600,000
500 Frank W. Burr Blvd., 6th Fl., Teaneck, NJ 07666-6802
(201) 287-4042, *Fax:* (201) 287-9427
License: Paterson, Passaic County, NJ held by WXTV License Partnership G.P.
Group Owner: Univision Communications Inc.; (acq 1986; grpsl).; *Washington Law Firm:* Shaw, Pittman
Nat'l Network: Univision (Spanish)
Foreign Language Programming; Hours of Local News Weekly: News progmg 17 hrs wkly
Ramon Pineda, Operations Dir
Morris Marotta, Station Manager
John De Simon, General Sales Mgr
Norma Morato, News Director

Rochester, NY (DMA 80)

WHAM-TV *Digital Channel:* 13 *Virtual Channel:* 13; 316 kw vis, 47.9 kw aur; ant 500t/363.5g; N43 08 07 W77 35 03; *Population Served:* 393,630
Mailing Address: 4225 West Henrietta Road, Rochester, NY 20036
Second Address: NY
(585) 334-8700, *Fax:* (585) 359-1570
13wham.com
License: Rochester, Monroe County, NY held by Newport Television License LLC.
Group Owner: Newport Television LLC; (acq 3-14-2008; grpsl); *Washington Law Firm:* Covington & Burling
Nat'l Network: ABC; CW *Nat'l Reps:* Millennium Sales & Marketing *Wire Services:* AP; CNN; Bloomberg News
Size of News Staff: 52; *Hours of Local News Weekly:* news progmg 24 hrs wkly
Craig Heslor, Production Manager
Chuck Samuels, General Manager
David DiProsa, Director of Sales
Kevin Kalvitis, Promotions Manager
Marilynn Garbarino, Local Sales Manager
Mark Zeger, National Sales Manager
Allison Watts,Director of Digital Media

WHEC-TV *Digital Channel:* 10 *Virtual Channel:* 10; 18.1 kw; 502 ft.; N43 8 8 W77 35 2
3415 University Avenue, St. Paul, MN 55114 US
(585) 546-5670
www.10nbc.com
License: Rochester, Monroe County, NY held by WHEC-TV LLC.
Group Owner: Hubbard Broadcasting Inc.; (acq 9-19-96).; *Washington Law Firm:* Arent, Fox, Kintner, Plotkin & Kahn
Nat'l Network: NBC *Nat'l Reps:* Petry Television Inc.
Hours of Local News Weekly: News progmg 22 hrs wkly
Sherron Sheridan, Operations Dir
Arnold Klinsky, General Manager
Lauren Burruto, General Sales Mgr
Lynette Baker, Programming Director

WROC-TV *Digital Channel:* 45 *Virtual Channel:* 8; 1000 kw; 401 ft.; N43 8 8 W77 35 2
3839 - 4th Street, North, Suite 420, St. Petersburg, FL 33703 US
(585) 288-8400, *Fax:* (585) 288-7679
www.wroctv.com
License: Rochester, Monroe County, NY held by Nexstar Broadcasting Inc.
Group Owner: Nexstar Broadcasting Group Inc.; (acq 12-9-99; $46 million)
Nat'l Network: CBS
Size of News Staff: 40; *Hours of Local News Weekly:* news progmg 14 hrs wkly
Tim Busch, President
Don Loy, Station Manager

WUHF *Digital Channel:* 28 *Virtual Channel:* 31; 320 kw; 528 ft.; N43 8 5 W77 35 7
18 Newbury Street, Boston, MA 02116 US
(585) 232-3700, *Fax:* (585) 288-1505
www.rochesterhomepage.net
License: Rochester, Monroe County, NY held by WUHF Licensee LLC.
Group Owner: Sinclair Broadcast Group Inc.; (acq 4-12-2002; for assumption liabilities).; *Washington Law Firm:* Pillsbury, Winthrop & Shaw Pittman
Nat'l Network: FOX
Hours of Local News Weekly: News progmg 3.5 hrs wkly
Louis Gattozzi, General Manager

***WXXI-TV** *Digital Channel:* 16 *Virtual Channel:* 21; 180 kw; 427 ft.; N43 8 7 W77 35 3
Mailing Address: PO Box 21, 280 State St., Rochester, NY 14601 US
Second Address: 280 State St., Rochester, NY 14614
(585) 325-7500, *Fax:* (585) 258-0335
www.wxxi.org
License: Rochester, Monroe County, NY held by WXXI Public Broadcasting Council
Washington Law Firm: Schwartz, Woods & Miller
Nat'l Network: PBS
Foreign Language Programming; Size of News Staff: 4; *Hours of Local News Weekly:* news progmg 2 hrs wkly
Norm Silverstein, CEO
Carole Edelman, Operations Dir
Robert Owens, Programming Director
Kent Hatfield, Engineering Dir
Susan Rogers, COO

Syracuse, NY (DMA 81)

***WCNY-TV** *Digital Channel:* 25 *Virtual Channel:* 24; 97 kw; 1289 ft.; N42 56 42 W76 7 7
Mailing Address: P.O. Box 2400, Syracuse, NY 13220 US
Second Address: 506 Old Liverpool Rd., Liverpool, NY 13088
(315) 453-2424, *Fax:* (315) 451-8824
www.wcny.org
wcny-online@wcny.org
License: Syracuse, Onondaga County, NY held by Public Broadcasting Council of Central New York
Washington Law Firm: Dow, Lohnes & Albertson
Nat'l Network: PBS
Robert Daino, CEO
John Duffy, Operations Dir
Brian Damm, Promotions Manager
Larry Goodsight, Marketing Director
Colleen Edwards, Vice President, Finance & Business

WNYI *Digital Channel:* 20 *Virtual Channel:* 52; 110 kw; 778 ft.; N42 45 30 W76 2 47
Mailing Address: 4811 Jenkins Rd., Vernon, NY 13476 US
Second Address: 401 W. Kirkpatrick St., Syracuse, NY 13204
(501) 219-2400
License: Ithaca, Tompkins County, NY held by EBC Syracuse Inc., debtor in possession
Group Owner: Equity Media Holdings Corp.; (acq 8-6-2004;. $5 million with KWWF(TV) Waterloo, IA)
Nat'l Network: DAYSTAR
Greg Fess, General Manager

WNYS-TV *Digital Channel:* 44 *Virtual Channel:* 43; 680 kw; 1460 ft.; N42 52 50 W76 12 0
137 Spyglass Lane, Fayetteville, NY 13066 US
(315) 472-6800, *Fax:* (315) 471-8889
www.my43.tv
License: Syracuse, Onondaga County, NY held by RKM Media Inc
(acq 7-2-96).; *Washington Law Firm:* Fletcher, Heald & Hildreth
Nat'l Network: MYTV
Mike Asiedu, Operations Dir
Ron Phillips, General Manager
Donald O'Connor, General Sales Mgr
Linda Deeb, Programming Director

Ed Sautter, Promotions Manager
Roy Taylor, Chief Engineer
Ed Kampf, Local Sales Manager
JoanLescenski, Traffic Manager

WSPX-TV *Digital Channel:* 15 *Virtual Channel:* 56; 49 kw; 1243 ft.; N43 18 18 W76 3 0
7320 Market Street, Youngstown, OH 44512 US
(315) 414-0178, *Fax:* (315) 414-0482
www.ionline.tv
License: Syracuse, Onondaga County, NY held by WSPX Syracuse License Inc
Group Owner: ION Media Networks Inc.; (acq 4-29-99).
Nat'l Network: ION
Margo McCaffery, Station Manager
Melissa Dragicevich, Programming Director
Al Szablak, Chief Engineer

WSTM-TV *Digital Channel:* 24 *Virtual Channel:* 3; 210 kw; 1289 ft.; N42 56 41.8 W76 7 7.6
Rsa Tower Suite 710, 201 Monroe Street, Montgomery, AL 36104 US
(315) 477-9400, *Fax:* (315) 474-5082
www.cnycentral.com
License: Syracuse, Onondaga County, NY held by Barrington Syracuse License LLC.
Group Owner: Barrington Broadcasting Group, LLC.; (acq 8-11-2006; grpsl); *Washington Law Firm:* Covington & Burling
Nat'l Network: NBC *Nat'l Reps:* TeleRep
Size of News Staff: 45; *Hours of Local News Weekly:* news progmg 27.5 hrs wkly
Chris Geiger, President
Amy Collins, General Sales Mgr
Rae Fulkerson, News Director
Jim Marco, Chief Engineer
Laura Serway, Local Sales Manager

WSYR-TV *Digital Channel:* 17 *Virtual Channel:* 9; 105 kw; 1319 ft.; N42 56 42 W76 1 28
1333 New Hampshire Ave., N.W., Suite 1000, Washington, DC 20036 US
(315) 446-9999, *Fax:* (315) 446-9283
www.9wsyr.com
newschannel9@9wsyr.com
License: Syracuse, Onondaga County, NY held by Newport Television License LLC.
Group Owner: Newport Television LLC; (acq 3-14-2008; grpsl)
Nat'l Network: ABC *Nat'l Reps:* Millennium Sales & Marketing
Size of News Staff: 55; *Hours of Local News Weekly:* news progmg 22.5 hrs wkly
Sandy DiPasquale, President
Theresa Underwood, Operations Dir
Bill Evans, General Sales Mgr
Vince Spicola, Programming Director
Jim Tortora, News Director
Craig Riker, Chief Engineer
Francis Fasuyi, Engineering Manager
JohnKing, Operations Director

WSYT *Digital Channel:* 19 *Virtual Channel:* 68; 621 kw; 1460 ft.; N42 52 50 W76 12 0
10706 Beaver Dam Road, Cockeysville, MD 21030 US
(315) 472-6800, *Fax:* (315) 471-8889
www.foxsyracuse.com
License: Syracuse, Onondaga County, NY held by WSYT Licensee L.P.
Group Owner: Sinclair Broadcast Group Inc.; (acq 7-7-98; grpsl).
Nat'l Network: FOX
Hours of Local News Weekly: News progmg 3.5 hrs wkly
Mike Asiedu, Operations Dir
Aaron Olander, General Manager
Donald O'Connor, General Sales Mgr
Linda Deeb, Programming Director
Ed Sautter, Promotions Manager
Vinnie Lopez, Chief Engineer
Ed Kampf, Local Sales Manager
JoanLescenski, Traffic Manager

WTVH *Digital Channel:* 47 *Virtual Channel:* 5; 500 kw; 952 ft.; N42 57 18.8 W76 6 34.3
980 James St., Syracuse, NY 13203 US
(315) 477-9400, *Fax:* (315) 477-9429
www.cnycentral.com
License: Syracuse, Onondaga County, NY held by WTVH License Inc.
Group Owner: Granite Broadcasting Corp.; *Washington Law Firm:* Akin, Gump, Strauss, Hauer & Feld
Nat'l Network: CBS *Nat'l Reps:* Harrington, Righter & Parsons
Size of News Staff: 42; *Hours of Local News Weekly:* news progmg 24 hrs wkly
Chris Geiger, President
Tom Stemmler, Operations Dir
Amy Collins, General Sales Mgr
Mary Baker, Programming Director
Dean Walters, Promotions Manager
Rae Fulkerson, News Director
Tom Stemmler, Engineering Dir
Kevin Tubbs, ChiefEngineer
Terri Endries, Local Sales Manager
Pam Sanson, Traffic Manager

Utica, NY
(DMA 169)

WFXV *Digital Channel:* 27 *Virtual Channel:* 33; 1000 kw; 692 ft.; N43 8 43 W75 10 35
18 Newbury Street, Boston, MA 02116 US
(315) 797-5220, *Fax:* (315) 797-5409
www.cnyhomepage.com
License: Utica, Oneida County, NY held by Nexstar Broadcasting, Inc.
Group Owner: Nexstar Broadcasting Group Inc.; (acq 12-31-03; grpsl).; *Washington Law Firm:* Arter & Hadden
Nat'l Network: FOX
Steve Merren, General Manager
Steve Ventura, General Sales Mgr
Rick Lewis, Promotions Manager
Bob Hajec, Chief Engineer

WKTV *Digital Channel:* 29 *Virtual Channel:* 2; 708 kw; 1319 ft.; N43 6 9 W74 56 27
Mailing Address: PO Box 2, Utica, NY 13503 US
Second Address: 5936 Smith Hill Rd., Utica, NY 13503
(315) 733-0404, *Fax:* (315) 793-3498
www.wktv.com
License: Utica, Oneida County, NY held by Smith Media License Holdings LLC.
Group Owner: Smith Media License Holdings LLC; (acq 11-8-2004; grpsl); *Washington Law Firm:* Dow, Lohnes & Albertson, PLLC
Nat'l Network: NBC; CW *Nat'l Reps:* Continental Television Sales
Hours of Local News Weekly: News progmg 31.5 hrs wkly
Vic Vetters, Operations Dir
Ken McCoy, Station Manager
Frank Abbadessa, General Sales Mgr
Dave Streeter, Promotions Manager
Steve McMurray, News Director
Tom McNicholl, Chief Engineer

WUTR *Digital Channel:* 30 *Virtual Channel:* 20; 50 kw; 745 ft.; N43 8 43 W75 10 35
190 Queen Anne Ave., N., Suite 100, Seattle, WA 91809 US
(315) 797-5220, *Fax:* (315) 797-5409
www.cnyhomepage.com
License: Utica, Oneida County, NY held by Mission Broadcasting Inc.
Group Owner: Mission Broadcasting Inc.; (acq 4-1-2004; $3.725 million)
Nat'l Network: ABC
Steve Merren, General Manager
Diane Siembab, Station Manager
Steve Ventura, General Sales Mgr
Delia Jesaitis, Programming Director
Rick Lewis, Promotions Manager
Michael Moran, Chief Engineer

Watertown, NY
(DMA 177)

***WGTV** *Digital Channel:* 41; 59 kw vis; ant 1,212t/914g; N43 51 46 W75 43 39; *Population Served:* 151,000
1056 Arsenal St., Watertown, NY 13601
(315) 782-3142, *Fax:* (315) 782-2491
www.wpbstv.org
License: Watertown, Jefferson County, NY held by St. Lawrence Valley ETV Council
Washington Law Firm: Schwartz, Woods & Miller
Nat'l Network: PBS
Thomas Hanley, President
Lynn Brown, General Sales Mgr

***WNPI** *Digital Channel:* 23; 60.5 kw vis; ant 794t/725g; N44 29 29 W74 51 27; *Rebroadcasting:* Rebroadcasts WPBS-TV Watertown 100%; *Population Served:* 220,000
1056 Arsenal St., Watertown, NY 13601
(315) 782-3142, *Fax:* (315) 782-2491
www.wpbstv.org
License: Norwood, Jefferson County, NY held by St. Lawrence Valley ETV Council
Washington Law Firm: Schwartz, Woods & Miller
Nat'l Network: PBS
Thomas Hanley, President
Lynn Brown, General Sales Mgr
Joline Furgison, Programming Manager

WWNY-TV *Digital Channel:* 7; 316 kw vis, 47 kw aur42kw; ant 718t/572g; N43 57 16 W75 43 45; *Population Served:* 107,406
120 Arcade St., Watertown, NY 13601
(315) 788-3800, *Fax:* (315) 782-7468,(315) 788-3787
www.wwnytv.net
wwny@wwnytv.net
License: Carthage, Jefferson County, NY held by United Communications Corp.
Group Owner: United Communications Corp.; (acq 12-5-81; $8.1 million;; *Washington Law Firm:* Wood, Maines & Brown, Chartered
Nat'l Network: CBS
Size of News Staff: 16; *Hours of Local News Weekly:* news progmg 19 hrs wkly
John Seymour, Operations Dir
Cathy Pircsuk, General Manager
Patrick Powers, General Sales Mgr
Jim Corbin, Programming Director
Jeff Shannon, Promotions Manager
Scott Atkinson, News Director
Jim Felton, Chief Engineer

WWTI *Digital Channel:* 21 *Virtual Channel:* 50; 25 kw; 1086 ft.; N43 52 47 W75 43 12
3839 - 4th Street, North, St. Petersburg, FL 33703 US
(315) 785-8850, *Fax:* (315) 785-0127
www.newswatch50.com
License: Watertown, Jefferson County, NY held by Newport Television License LLC.
Group Owner: Newport Television LLC; (acq 3-14-2008; grpsl)
Nat'l Network: ABC; CW *Nat'l Reps:* Millennium Sales & Marketing *Wire Services:* AP
Size of News Staff: 10; *Hours of Local News Weekly:* news progmg 5 hrs wkly
David Males, General Manager
Keith Rudes, Chief Engineer

North Carolina

Charlotte, NC
(DMA 24)

WAXN-TV *Digital Channel:* 50 *Virtual Channel:* 64; 150 kw; 1194 ft.; N35 15 41 W80 43 38
222 Commerce Street, Kingsport, TN 37660 US
(704) 338-9999, *Fax:* (704) 371-3131
www.action64.com
License: Kannapolis, Cabarrus County, NC held by WSOC-TV Holdings Inc.
Group Owner: Cox Media Group; (acq 1-31-2000); *Washington Law Firm:* Dow, Lohnes & Albertson
Nat'l Network: IND *Nat'l Reps:* TeleRep
Dave Siegler, Operations Dir
Kay Hall, Programming Director
Sally Ganz, Promotions Manager
Robin Whitmeyer, News Director
Ted Hand, Engineering Dir
Patricia Marsden, Research Director
Kierstin Boujlil, Traffic Manager

WBTV *Digital Channel:* 23 *Virtual Channel:* 3; 1000 kw; 1854 ft.; N35 21 51 W81 11 13
One Julian Price Pl, Charlotte, NC 28208 US
(704) 374-3500, *Fax:* (704) 374-3614
www.wbtv.com
assignmentdesk@wbtv.com
License: Charlotte, Mecklenburg County, NC held by WBTV License Subsidiary LLC.
Group Owner: Raycom Media Inc.; (acq 3-31-2008; grpsl); *Washington Law Firm:* Wiley, Rein & Fielding
Nat'l Network: CBS *Nat'l Reps:* Petry Television Inc. *Wire Services:* UPI
Don Shaw, Operations Dir
Nick Simonette, General Manager
Shelly Hill, Promotions Manager
Mike Gurthie, Chief Engineer

WCCB *Digital Channel:* 27 *Virtual Channel:* 18; 1000 kw; 1207 ft.; N35 16 1 W80 44 5
One Television Place, Charlotte, NC 28232 US
(704) 372-1800, *Fax:* (704) 376-3415,(704) 332-7941(sales)
www.foxcharlotte.tv
wccb@foxcharlotte.tv
License: Charlotte, Mecklenburg County, NC held by North Carolina Broadcasting Partners.
Group Owner: Bahakel Communications

Nat'l Network: FOX
Size of News Staff: 1
John Hutchinson, Operations Dir
Jim White, Station Manager
Gaston Bates, General Sales Mgr
Ken White, News Director
Rick Aydlett, Chief Engineer

WCNC-TV *Digital Channel:* 22 *Virtual Channel:* 36; 791 kw; 1893 ft.; N35 20 49 W81 10 15
400 South Record Street, Dallas, TX 75202 US
(704) 329-3636, *Fax:* (704) 357-4980
www.wcnc.com
License: Charlotte, Mecklenburg County, NC held by WCNC-TV Inc.
Group Owner: Belo Corp; (acq 1997; grpsl).; *Washington Law Firm:* Wiley, Rein & Fielding
Nat'l Network: NBC *Nat'l Reps:* Harrington, Righter & Parsons
Timothy J. Morrissey, President
Susan Miller, General Sales Mgr
Steve Kiser, Programming Director
Luanne Stuart, Promotions Manager
Mary Alvarez, News Director

WHKY-TV *Digital Channel:* 40 *Virtual Channel:* 14; 600 kw; 597 ft.; N35 43 59 W81 19 51
Mailing Address: 526 Main Ave., Se, Hickory, NC 28601 US
Second Address: 526 Main Ave. S.E., Hickory, NC 28603
(828) 322-1290, *Fax:* (828) 322-8256
www.whky.com
whky@whky.com
License: Hickory, Catawba County, NC held by Long Communications LLC
(acq 12-31-2001; with WHKY(AM) Hickory).; *Washington Law Firm:* Hardy & Carey
Nat'l Network: IND
Size of News Staff: 4; *Hours of Local News Weekly:* news progmg 5 hrs wkly
Thomas Long, General Manager
Jeff Long, Station Manager
Patty Guthrie, General Sales Mgr
Heather Isenhour, Programming Director
Jim Karas, News Director

WJZY *Digital Channel:* 47 *Virtual Channel:* 46; 1000 kw; 1816 ft.; N35 21 44 W81 9 19
P.O. Box 12800, Charlotte, NC 28266 US
(704) 398-0046, *Fax:* (704) 393-8407
www.wjzy.com
info@wjzy.com
License: Belmont, Gaston County, NC held by WJZY-TV Inc.
Group Owner: Capitol Broadcasting Co. Inc.; (acq 11-87; $1.581 million); *Washington Law Firm:* Fletcher, Heald & Hildreth
Nat'l Network: CW *Nat'l Reps:* Millennium Sales & Marketing
Shawn Harris, General Manager
Don Travis, General Sales Mgr
Chris Wolf, Programming Director
Chris Wolf, Promotions Manager
Robert Costillo, Chief Engineer
Cathy Mozingo, Local Sales Manager
Lori Zannino, Research Director
Sarah Ferris, Traffic Manager
Heather Strfezza, Sales Manager

WSOC-TV *Digital Channel:* 34 *Virtual Channel:* 9; 1000 kw; 1142 ft.; N35 15 41 W80 43 38
Mailing Address: 3773 Howard Hughes Parkway, Suite 300n, Las Vegas, NV 89109 US
Second Address: 1901 N. Tryon St., Charlotte, NC 28206
(704) 338-9999
www.wsoctv.com
License: Charlotte, Mecklenburg County, NC held by WSOC-TV Holdings Inc.
Group Owner: Cox Media Group; (acq 4-13-59; grpsl;;
Washington Law Firm: Dow, Lohnes & Albertson
Nat'l Network: ABC *Nat'l Reps:* TeleRep
Dave Siegler, Operations Dir
Joe Pomilla, General Manager
Kay Hall, Programming Director
Sally Ganz, Promotions Manager

***WTVI** *Digital Channel:* 11 *Virtual Channel:* 42; 2.57 kw; 1191 ft.; N35 17 14 W80 41 45
3242 Commonwealth Avenue, Charlotte, NC 28205 US
(704) 372-2442, *Fax:* (704) 335-1358
www.wtvi.org
License: Charlotte, Mecklenburg County, NC held by Charlotte-Mecklenburg Public Broadcasting Authority
Washington Law Firm: Schwartz, Woods & Miller
Nat'l Network: PBS
Elsie Garner, CEO
Tom Green, Chief Engineer

***WUNE-TV** *Digital Channel:* 17 *Virtual Channel:* 17; 100 kw; 1791 ft.; N36 3 50 W81 50 33
Mailing Address: P.O. Box 14900, Research T'Angle Prk, NC 27709 US
Second Address: 10 TW Alexander Dr., Research Triangle Park, NC 27709
(919) 549-7000, *Fax:* (919) 549-7201
www.unctv.org
viewer@unctv.org
License: Linville, Avery County, NC held by University of North Carolina
Washington Law Firm: Schwartz, Woods & Miller
Nat'l Network: PBS
Tom Howe, General Manager

***WUNG-TV** *Digital Channel:* 44 *Virtual Channel:* 58; 160 kw; 1378 ft.; N35 21 30 W80 36 37
Mailing Address: P.O. Box 14900, Rese'ch Triangle Prk, NC 27709 US
Second Address: 10 TW Alexander Dr, Research Triangle Park, NC 27709
(919) 549-7000, *Fax:* (919) 549-7201
www.unctv.org
viewer@unctv.org
License: Concord, Cabarrus County, NC held by University of North Carolina
Washington Law Firm: Schwartz, Woods & Miller
Nat'l Network: PBS
Tom Howe, General Manager

Greensboro-High Point-Winston Salem, NC (DMA 46)

WCWG *Digital Channel:* 19 *Virtual Channel:* 20; 800 kw; 1890 ft.; N35 52 2 W79 49 26
500 S. Chinowth Rd., Visalia, CA 93277 US
(336) 307-4900, *Fax:* (336) 307-4950
www.wcwg20.com
info@wcwg20.com
License: Lexington, Davidson County, NC held by WCWG License, LLC
Group Owner: Pappas Telecasting Companies; (acq 1995; $4 million); *Washington Law Firm:* Paul, Hastings, Janofsky & Walker LLP
Nat'l Network: CW *Nat'l Reps:* TeleRep
John Bailie, General Manager
Lynn Bailie, General Sales Mgr
Cheronda Jones, Programming Director
Chris Balash, Promotions Manager
Lindsay Bold, Chief Engineer

WFMY-TV *Digital Channel:* 51 *Virtual Channel:* 2; 1000 kw; 1866 ft.; N35 52 13 W79 50 25
Mailing Address: 1615 Phillips Avenue, Greensboro, NC 27405 US
Second Address: 1615 Phillips Ave., Greensboro, NC 27405
(336) 379-9369, *Fax:* (336) 273-3444
www.digtriad.com
news2@wfmy.com
License: Greensboro, Guilford County, NC held by WFMY Television Corp.
Group Owner: Gannett Broadcasting; (acq 2-1-88).
Nat'l Network: CBS *Nat'l Reps:* TeleRep *Wire Services:* CBS; AP
Hours of Local News Weekly: News progmg 32 hrs wkly
Deborah Hooper, President
Bill Lancaster, General Sales Mgr
Jim Walton, Programming Director
David Reeve, Promotions Manager
Jim Platzer, News Director
Eileen Stammett, Multimedia Sales Manager
Kristy Robinson, Traffic Manager

WGHP *Digital Channel:* 35 *Virtual Channel:* 8; 300 kw vis; ant 1,305t/1,217g; N35 48 46 W79 50 29; *Population Served:* 533,300
Mailing Address: HP-8, High Point, NC 20016
Second Address: 2005 Francis St., High Point, NC 27263
(336) 841-8888, *Fax:* (336) 841-8051
www.myfox8wghp.com
License: High Point, Guilford County, NC held by Community Television of North Carolina License LLC.
Group Owner: Local TV LLC; (acq 7-14-2008; grpsl)
Nat'l Network: Fox *Nat'l Reps:* Katz/Millennium *Wire Services:* AP
Size of News Staff: 75; *Hours of Local News Weekly:* 46.5
Bob Ladka, CFO
Karen Adams, Operations Dir
Ramona Alexander, General Sales Mgr
Tim Taylor, Promotions Manager
Karen Koutsky, News Director
Ross Mason, Chief Engineer

WGPX-TV *Digital Channel:* 14; 1,910 kw vis, 191 kw aur; 840t/500g; N36 14 54 W79 39 21
1114 N. O'Henry Blvd., Greensboro, NC 27405
(336) 272-9227, *Fax:* (336) 272-9298
www.ionline.tv
License: Burlington, Alamance County, NC held by Paxson Greensboro License Inc.
Group Owner: ION Media Networks Inc.; (acq 1996; $5.5 million); *Washington Law Firm:* Baraff, Koerner, Olender & Hochberg
Nat'l Network: ION Television *Nat'l Reps:* Roslin
Dana Lambert, Station Manager
Stephanie Black, Programming Director
Steve Hall, Chief Engineer

WLXI *Digital Channel:* 43; 501 kw vis, 50 kw aur; 573t/499g; N36 08 58 W80 03 21; *Population Served:* 2,500,000
2109 Patterson St., Greensboro, NC 27407
(336) 855-5610, *Fax:* (336) 533-6412
www.tct.tv
wlxi@tct.tv
License: Greensboro, Guilford County, NC held by Radiant Life Ministries Inc.
Group Owner: Tri-State Christian Television; (acq 10-7-91; $1.9 million;; *Washington Law Firm:* Joseph E. Dunne III
Larry Patton, General Manager
Gil Couch, Chief Engineer

WMYV *Digital Channel:* 33 *Virtual Channel:* 48; 700 kw; 1886 ft.; N35 52 3 W79 49 26
544 Red Rock, Wadsworth, OH 44281 US
(336) 722-4545, *Fax:* (336) 723-8217
www.my48.tv
info@my48.tv
License: Greensboro, Guilford County, NC held by WUPN Licensee LLC.
Group Owner: Sinclair Broadcast Group Inc.; (acq 1-9-2002; $50,000 and cancellation of debt).; *Washington Law Firm:* Arter & Hadden
Nat'l Network: MYTV *Nat'l Reps:* Millennium Sales & Marketing
Hours of Local News Weekly: News progmg 7 hrs wkly
Ron Inman, General Manager
Fran McRae, General Sales Mgr
Jeanette Pruitt, Programming Director
Eric Gabriel, Promotions Manager
Jim Hartline, Chief Engineer

***WUNL-TV** *Digital Channel:* 32 *Virtual Channel:* 26; 575 kw; 1637 ft.; N36 22 31 W80 22 18
Mailing Address: P. O. Box 14900, Research Triangle Pk, NC 27709 US
Second Address: 10 TW Alexander Dr., Research Triangle Park, NC 27709-4900
(919) 549-7000, *Fax:* (919) 549-7201
www.unctv.org
viewer@unctv.org
License: Winston-Salem, Forsyth County, NC held by University of North Carolina
Washington Law Firm: Schwartz, Woods & Miller
Nat'l Network: PBS
Tom Howe, General Manager

WXII-TV *Digital Channel:* 31 *Virtual Channel:* 12; 815 kw; 1877 ft.; N36 22 31 W80 22 26
888 Seventh Avenue, New York, NY 10106 US
(336) 721-9944, *Fax:* (336) 703-6300
www.wxii12.com
License: Winston-Salem, Forsyth County, NC held by WXII Hearst-Argyle Television Inc.
Group Owner: Hearst-Argyle Television Inc.; (acq 3-18-99; grpsl).; *Washington Law Firm:* Brooks, Pierce, McLendon, Humphrey & Leonard
Nat'l Network: NBC
Henry Price, General Manager
Mark Strand, Promotions Manager
Barry Klaus, News Director
John Norvell, Chief Engineer

WXLV-TV *Digital Channel:* 29 *Virtual Channel:* 45; 990 kw; 1890 ft.; N35 52 3 W79 49 26
18 Newbury Street, Boston, MA 02116 US
(336) 722-4545, *Fax:* (336) 723-8217
www.abc45.com
info@abc45.com
License: Winston-Salem, Forsyth County, NC held by WXLV Licensee LLC.
Group Owner: Sinclair Broadcast Group Inc.; (acq 12-10-01; grpsl).; *Washington Law Firm:* Arter & Hadden
Nat'l Network: ABC
Hours of Local News Weekly: News progmg 2.5 hrs wkly

Ron Inman, General Manager
Fran McRae, General Sales Mgr
Jeanette Pruitt, Programming Director
Eric Gabriel, Promotions Manager
Jim Hartline, Chief Engineer

Greenville-New Bern-Washington, NC (DMA 103)

WCTI-TV *Digital Channel:* 12 *Virtual Channel:* 12; 32.8 kw; 1932 ft.; N35 6 15 W77 20 12
Box 12325, New Bern, NC 28561 US
(252) 638-1212, *Fax:* (252) 637-4141
www.wtci12.com
License: New Bern, Craven County, NC held by Newport License Holdings Inc.
(acq 6-15-2004; $4 million); *Ownership:* Bonten Media Group, LLC; *Washington Law Firm:* Koteen & Naftalin
Nat'l Network: ABC *Nat'l Reps:* Continental Television Sales
Don Fisher, General Manager
Shane Moreland, News Director
Ken Hughes, Chief Engineer

WEPX-TV *Digital Channel:* 51; 5,000 kw vis; 505t; N35 23 52 W77 25 40
1301 S. Glenburnie Rd., New Bern, NC 28562
(252) 636-2550, *Fax:* (252) 633-7851
License: Greenville, Pitt County, NC held by Paxson Greenville License Inc.
Group Owner: ION Media Networks Inc.; (acq 4-13-99; $3.55 million)
Nat'l Network: ION Television
Lisa Stroud, Station Manager
Mileta Smith, General Sales Mgr
Tammy Mason, Programming Director
Joe Clary, Chief Engineer

WFXI *Digital Channel:* 8 *Virtual Channel:* 8; 22.4 kw; 812 ft.; N34 53 1 W76 30 22
7621 Little Avenue, Suite 506, Charlotte, NC 28266 US
(252) 638-1212, *Fax:* (252) 637-4141
www.fox8fox14.com
License: Morehead City, Carteret County, NC held by Esteem Broadcasting of North Carolina LLC.
Group Owner: Esteem Broadcasting; (acq 12-31-2007; $5.885 million wtih WYDO(TV) Greenville); *Washington Law Firm:* Cohn & Marks
Nat'l Network: FOX
Hours of Local News Weekly: News progmg 4 hrs wkly
David Bailey, President
Erick Hardtle, Operations Dir
Lisa Leonard, Station Manager
Joe Carriere, General Sales Mgr
Carolyn Stevens, Programming Director
Walt Young, Promotions Manager
Shane Moreland, News Director
Ken Hughes,Chief Engineer
Charlotte Cohen, General Sales Manager

WITN-TV *Digital Channel:* 32; 795 kW; 605/597 meters; N35 21 55 W77 23 38; *Population Served:* 1,388,000
Mailing Address: Box 468, Washington, NC 27889
Second Address: 3057 Hwy 17S, Chocowinity, NC 27817
(252) 946-3131, *Fax:* (252) 946-0279
www.witn.com
witn@witn.com
License: Washington, Beaufort County, NC held by Gray Television Licensee LLC.
Group Owner: Gray Television Inc.; (acq 8-1-97; $39.4 million).; *Washington Law Firm:* Wiley Rein LLP
Nat'l Network: NBC; MY NET; ME TV *Nat'l Reps:* Self-repped
Wire Services: AP
Size of News Staff: 28; *Hours of Local News Weekly:* news progmg 28.5 hrs wkly
Michael Riddle, Operations Dir
Chris Mossman, General Manager
Mark Gentner, General Sales Mgr
Stephanie Shoop, News Director
Donald Pock, Chief Engineer
Tim Prichard, National Sales Manager
Tom Midyette, Production Manager

WNCT-TV *Digital Channel:* 10 *Virtual Channel:* 9; 35 kw; 1886 ft.; N35 21 55 W77 23 38
333 East Grace Street, Richmond, VA 23219 US
(252) 355-8500, *Fax:* (252) 355-8568
www.wnct.com
newsdesk@wnct.com
License: Greenville, Pitt County, NC held by Media General Broadcasting Inc.
Group Owner: Media General Broadcast Group; (acq 3-21-97; grpsl).; *Washington Law Firm:* Dow, Lohnes & Albertson
Nat'l Network: CBS; CW *Nat'l Reps:* Harrington, Righter & Parsons
Vickie Jones, General Manager
Brad Hargrove, General Sales Mgr
Bertie Cartwright, Chief Engineer

WPXU-TV *Digital Channel:* 34 *Virtual Channel:* 35; 600 kw; 653 ft.; N34 31 10 W77 26 52
7621 Little Avenue, Suite 506, Charlotte, NC 28266 US
(252) 636-2550, *Fax:* (252) 633-7851
License: Jacksonville, Onslow County, NC held by ION Media Jacksonville License, Inc., Debtor-in-possession
Group Owner: ION Media Networks Inc.; (acq 10-1-99; $200,000)
Nat'l Network: ION
Lisa Stroud, Station Manager
Mileta Smith, General Sales Mgr
Tammy Mason, Programming Director
Joe Clary, Chief Engineer

***WUND-TV** *Digital Channel:* 20 *Virtual Channel:* 2; 543 kw; 1601 ft.; N35 54 0 W76 20 45
Mailing Address: 10 T.W. Alexander Drive, P.O. Box 14900, Research Triangle Pk, NC 27709 US
Second Address: 10 TW Alexander Dr., Research Triangle Park, NC 27709
(919) 549-7000, *Fax:* (919) 549-7201
www.unctv.org
viewer@unctv.org
License: Edenton, Tyrrell County, NC held by University of North Carolina
Nat'l Network: PBS
Tom Howe, General Manager

***WUNK-TV** *Digital Channel:* 23 *Virtual Channel:* 25; 1000 kw; 1152 ft.; N35 33 10 W77 36 6
Mailing Address: 10 T.W. Alexander Drive, Rese'ch Triangle Prk, NC 27709 US
Second Address: 10 TW Alexander Dr., Research Triangle Park, NC 27709
(919) 549-7000, *Fax:* (919) 549-7201
www.unctv.org
viewer@unctv.org
License: Greenville, Pitt County, NC held by University of North Carolina
Washington Law Firm: Schwartz, Woods & Miller
Nat'l Network: PBS
Size of News Staff: 15; *Hours of Local News Weekly:* news progmg 3 hrs wkly
Tom Howe, General Manager

***WUNM-TV** *Digital Channel:* 19 *Virtual Channel:* 19; 100 kw; 1841 ft.; N35 6 15 W77 20 12
Mailing Address: 10 T.W. Alexander Drive, Rese'ch Triangle Prk, NC 27709 US
Second Address: 10 TW Alexander Dr, Research Triangle Park, NC 27709
(919) 549-7000, *Fax:* (919) 549-7201
www.unctv.org
viewer@unctv.org
License: Jacksonville, Onslow County, NC held by University of North Carolina
Washington Law Firm: Schwartz, Woods & Miller
Nat'l Network: PBS
Tom Howe, General Manager

WYDO *Digital Channel:* 47 *Virtual Channel:* 14; 200 kw; 1778 ft.; N35 6 15 W77 20 12; *Rebroadcasting:* Satellite of WFXI Morehead City 100%.
7621 Little Avenue, Suite 506, Charlotte, NC 28266 US
(252) 638-1212, *Fax:* (252) 637-4141
www.fox8fox14.com
email@fox8fox14.com
License: Greenville, Pitt County, NC held by Esteem Broadcasting of North Carolina LLC.
Group Owner: Esteem Broadcasting; (acq 12-31-2007; $5.885 million with WFXXI(TV) Morehead City); *Washington Law Firm:* Wilkinson, Barker, Knauer & Quinn
Nat'l Network: FOX
Lisa Leonard, Station Manager
Shane Moreland, News Director
Ken Hughes, Chief Engineer

Greenville-Spartanburg, SC-Asheville, NC-Anderson, SC (DMA 36)

WLOS *Digital Channel:* 13 *Virtual Channel:* 13; 50 kw; 2787 ft.; N35 25 32 W82 45 25
10706 Beaver Dam Road, Cockeysville, MD 21030 US
(828) 684-1340, *Fax:* (828) 651-4618
www.wlos.com
news@wlos.com
License: Asheville, Buncombe County, NC held by WLOS Licensee L.L.C.
Group Owner: Sinclair Broadcast Group Inc.; (acq 6-96).; *Washington Law Firm:* Dow, Lohnes & Albertson
Nat'l Network: ABC *Nat'l Reps:* Harrington, Righter & Parsons
Size of News Staff: 57; *Hours of Local News Weekly:* news progmg 24 hrs wkly
Jack Connors, General Manager
Audra Swain, General Sales Mgr
Scott Bradsher, Programming Director
Guy Chancey, Promotions Manager
Julie Fries, News Director
Rollin Thompkins, Chief Engineer

***WUNF-TV** *Digital Channel:* 25 *Virtual Channel:* 33; 185 kw; 2615 ft.; N35 25 32 W82 45 25
Mailing Address: P.O. Box 14900, 10 T.W. Alexander Drive, Research Triangle Pk, NC 27709 US
Second Address: 10 TW Alexander Dr., Research Triangle Park, NC 27709
(919) 549-7000, *Fax:* (919) 549-7201
www.unctv.org
viewer@unctv.org
License: Asheville, Buncombe County, NC held by University of North Carolina
Washington Law Firm: Schwartz, Woods & Miller
Nat'l Network: PBS
Tom Howe, General Manager

WYCW *Digital Channel:* 45 *Virtual Channel:* 62; 1000 kw; 1821 ft.; N35 13 20 W82 32 58
Mailing Address: 500 South Chinowth Road, Visalia, CA 93277 US
Second Address: 250 International Dr., Spartanburg, NC 29303
(864) 576-7777, *Fax:* (864) 595-4615
www.carolinascw.com
License: Asheville, Buncombe County, NC held by Media General Broadcasting of South Carolina Holdings Inc.
Group Owner: Media General Broadcast Group; (acq 1-15-2002; $4.5 million); *Washington Law Firm:* Dow, Lohnes & Albertson
Nat'l Network: CW
Jim Zimmerman, President
Jim Conschafter, Operations Dir
Phil Lane, General Manager
Randy Ingram, Station Manager
Jimmy Lizer, Operations Manager

Myrtle Beach-Florence, SC (DMA 104)

***WUNU** *Digital Channel:* 31 *Virtual Channel:* 31; 175 kw; 1047 ft.; N34 47 50 W79 2 42
Mailing Address: P.O. Box 2688, Chapel Hill, NC 27514 US
Second Address: 10 TW Alexander Dr., Research Triangle Park, NC 27709
(919) 549-7000, *Fax:* (919) 549-7201
www.unctv.org
viewer@unetv.org
License: Lumberton, Robeson County, NC held by University of North Carolina
Washington Law Firm: Schwartz, Woods & Miller
Nat'l Network: PBS
Tom Howe, General Manager

Norfolk-Portsmouth-Newport News, VA (DMA 43)

WSKY-TV *Digital Channel:* 9; 100 kw vis; ant 1,030t/1,023g; N36 08 08 W75 49 28; *Population Served:* 1,278,000
920 Corporate Ln., Chesapeake, VA 20006
(757) 382-0004, *Fax:* (757) 382-0365
www.4hamptonroads.com
programming@wsky4.com
License: Manteo, Dare County, NC held by Sky Television LLC (acq 8-19-2002).; *Washington Law Firm:* Leventhal, Senter and Lerman
Glenn Holterhaus, CEO
Ed Marlowe, Promotions Manager
Jacquelyn Smullen, CFO
Tom Powers, Operations Vice President

Raleigh-Durham (Fayetteville), NC (DMA 27)

WFPX-TV *Digital Channel:* 36; 337.3 kw vis, 33.7 kw aur; 846t/855g; N34 53 05 W79 04 29; *Population Served:* 275,000

Mailing Address: Drawer 62, Lumber Bridge, NC 28357
Second Address: 19234 NC 71 Hwy N., Lumber Bridge, NC 28357
(910) 843-3884,(910) 843-3885, *Fax:* (910) 843-2873
www.ionmedia.tv
License: Fayetteville, Cumberland County, NC held by ION Media License Company, LLC, Debtor-in-possession
Group Owner: ION Media Networks Inc.; (acq 10-20-97; $4.5 million); *Washington Law Firm:* Baraff, Koerner, Olender & Hochberg
Nat'l Network: ION Television *Nat'l Reps:* Adam Young
Robbie Brock, Operations Dir
Rhonda Schulik Stark, General Sales Mgr
Deborah Howard, Programming Director
Joe Clary, Engineering Dir
Jim Vest, Contract Engineer
Jim McKinney, Production Manager

WLFL *Digital Channel:* 27 *Virtual Channel:* 22; 725 kw; 2001 ft.; N35 40 28 W78 31 40
10706 Beaver Dam Road, Cockeysville, MD 21030 US
(919) 872-9535, *Fax:* (919) 878-3758
www.wlfl22.com
info@wlfl22.com
License: Raleigh, Wake County, NC held by WLFL Licensee L.L.C.
Group Owner: Sinclair Broadcast Group Inc.; *Washington Law Firm:* Shaw, Pittman
Nat'l Network: CW *Nat'l Reps:* Millennium Sales & Marketing
Size of News Staff: 36; *Hours of Local News Weekly:* news progmg 7 hrs wkly
Neal Davis, General Manager
Reggie Smith, General Sales Mgr
Kim Rivenbark, Promotions Manager
Gary Todd, Engineering Dir

WNCN *Digital Channel:* 17 *Virtual Channel:* 17; 291 kw; 2005 ft.; N35 40 29 W78 31 40
C/O Nbc, 1299 Penn. Ave., NW, 11th Floor, Washington, DC 20004 US
(919) 836-1717, *Fax:* (919) 836-1687
www.nbc17.com
License: Goldsboro, Wayne County, NC held by Media General Communications Inc.
Group Owner: Media General Broadcast Group; (acq 6-26-2006; grpsl).
Nat'l Network: NBC *Nat'l Reps:* Harrington, Righter & Parsons
Hours of Local News Weekly: News progmg 30 hrs wkly
Barry Leffler, General Manager
Mike Mougey, General Sales Mgr
Russell Mizelle, Chief Engineer

WRAL-TV *Digital Channel:* 48 *Virtual Channel:* 5; 1000 kw; 2064 ft.; N35 40 29 W78 31 40
Mailing Address: P. O. Box 12000, Raleigh, NC 27605 US
Second Address: 2619 Western Blvd., Raleigh, NC 27606
(919) 821-8555, *Fax:* (919) 821-8541
www.wral.com
License: Raleigh, Wake County, NC held by Capitol Broadcasting Co. Inc.
Group Owner: Capitol Broadcasting Co. Inc.; *Washington Law Firm:* Holland & Knight
Nat'l Network: CBS *Nat'l Reps:* TeleRep *Wire Services:* NWS (National Weather Service); AP
Size of News Staff: 100; *Hours of Local News Weekly:* news progmg 30 hrs wkly
TBA, General Manager
Quinn Koontz, General Sales Mgr
John Harris, Programming Director
Shelly S. Leslie, Promotions Manager
Rick Gall, News Director
Peter Sockett, Chief Engineer
Dave Lyles, Local Sales Manager
Laura Stillman,National Sales Manager

WRAY-TV *Digital Channel:* 42 *Virtual Channel:* 30; 873 kw; 1768 ft.; N35 49 53 W78 8 50
P. O. Box 305249, Nashville, TN 37230 US
(252) 243-0584, *Fax:* (252) 237-6290
License: Wilson, Wilson County, NC held by MTB Raleigh Licensee LLC.
Group Owner: Multicultural Capital Trust; (acq 2-2-2009)
Nat'l Network: IND
Harold Rabinowitz, General Manager
Harold Rabionowitz, Station Manager

WRAZ *Digital Channel:* 49 *Virtual Channel:* 50; 1000 kw; 2015 ft.; N35 40 29 W78 31 40
Mailing Address: P. O. Box 12050, Raleigh, NC 27605 US
Second Address: 512 S. Mangum St., 1st Floor, Durham, NC 27701
(919) 595-5050, *Fax:* (919) 595-5028
www.fox50.com
License: Raleigh, Wake County, NC held by WRAZ-TV Inc.
Group Owner: Capitol Broadcasting Co. Inc.; (acq 2000; $1 million); *Washington Law Firm:* Holland & Knight
Nat'l Network: FOX *Nat'l Reps:* TeleRep
Chris Downey, Operations Dir
Thomas Schenck, General Manager
Evelyn Booker, General Sales Mgr
Joanne Stanley, Programming Director
Kevin Kolbe, Promotions Manager
Jim Gamble, Chief Engineer

WRDC *Digital Channel:* 28 *Virtual Channel:* 28; 725 kw; 1919 ft.; N35 40 35 W78 32 8
3474 William Penn Highway, Pittsburgh, PA 15235 US
(919) 872-2854, *Fax:* (919) 878-3758
www.myrdctv.com
info@myrdctv.com
License: Durham, Durham County, NC held by Raleigh (WRDC-TV) Licensee Inc.
Group Owner: Sinclair Broadcast Group Inc.; (acq 11-15-01; $2.3 million in stock).; *Washington Law Firm:* Fisher, Wayland, Cooper, Leader & Zaragoza
Nat'l Network: MYTV *Nat'l Reps:* Millennium Sales & Marketing
Neal Davis, General Manager
Lon Goldman, General Sales Mgr
Kim Rivenbark, Promotions Manager
Gary Todd, Engineering Dir
Reggie Smith, Local Sales Manager

WRPX-TV *Digital Channel:* 15; 12.3 kw vis; 318t; N35 57 03 W77 55 37; *Population Served:* 352,154
3209 Gresham Lake Rd., Suite 151, Raleigh, NC 27615
(919) 827-4800, *Fax:* (919) 876-1415
www.ionmedia.tv
License: Rocky Mount, Edgecombe County, NC held by Paxson Raleigh License Inc.
Group Owner: ION Media Networks Inc.; (acq 4-5-2000; grpsl).; *Washington Law Firm:* Mitchell, Fielstra & Assoc
Nat'l Network: ION Television *Nat'l Reps:* Roslin
Michelle Barnhill, Operations Dir
Rhonda Schulik, General Sales Mgr
Deborah Howard, Programming Director

WTVD *Digital Channel:* 11 *Virtual Channel:* 11; 45 kw; 2018 ft.; N35 40 5 W78 31 59
411 Liberty Street, Durham, NC 27701 US
(919) 683-1111, *Fax:* (919) 682-7225
www.abc11tv.com
License: Durham, Durham County, NC held by WTVD Television LLC.
Group Owner: ABC Inc.; a(cq 5-24-57; $1,417,800;; *Washington Law Firm:* Wilmer, Cutler & Pickering
Nat'l Network: ABC
John Idler, President

***WUNC-TV** *Digital Channel:* 25 *Virtual Channel:* 4; 1000 kw; 1522 ft.; N35 51 59 W79 10 0
Mailing Address: P. O. Box 14900, Research Triangle Pk, NC 27709 US
Second Address: 10 TW Alexander Dr., Research Triangle Park, NC 27709
(919) 549-7000, *Fax:* (919) 549-7201
www.unctv.org
viewer@unctv.org
License: Chapel Hill, Durham County, NC held by University of North Carolina
Washington Law Firm: Schwartz, Woods & Miller
Nat'l Network: PBS
Tom Howe, General Manager

***WUNP-TV** *Digital Channel:* 36 *Virtual Channel:* 36; 125 kw; 1207 ft.; N36 17 27 W77 50 11
Mailing Address: 10 T.W. Alexander Drive, Rese'ch Triangle Prk, NC 27709 US
Second Address: 10 T W Alexander Dr., Research Triangle Park, NC 27709
(919) 549-7000, *Fax:* (919) 549-7201
www.unctv.org
viewer@unctv.org
License: Roanoke Rapids, Halifax County, NC held by University of North Carolina
Washington Law Firm: Schwartz, Woods & Miller
Nat'l Network: PBS
Tom Howe, General Manager

WUVC-DT *Digital Channel:* 38; 5,000 kw vis, 500 kw aur; ant 1,842t/1,749g; N35 30 45 W75 58 40; *Population Served:* 947,750
Mailing Address: 230 Donaldson St., 3rd Fl., ., Fayetteville, NC 28301
Second Address: Lake Plaza East, 900 Ridgefield Dr., Ste. 100, Raleigh, NC 27609
(910) 323-4040, *Fax:* (910) 323-3924
www.univision.com
License: Fayetteville, Cumberland County, NC held by Capital Broadcasting Partners.
Group Owner: Univision Communications Inc.; (acq 3-31-2003).; *Washington Law Firm:* Brooks, Pierce, McLendon, Humphrey & Leonard
Nat'l Network: Univision (Spanish)
Foreign Language Programming
Mike Munoz, General Manager
Steven Guerra, General Sales Mgr
Maria Tajman, Programming Director
Yvonne Cerna, Promotions Manager
William Acevedo, Chief Engineer
Maria Pinto, Research Director

Wilmington, NC (DMA 134)

WECT *Digital Channel:* 44 *Virtual Channel:* 6; 710 kw; 1936 ft.; N34 7 53 W78 11 17
Rsa Tower, 20th Floor, 201 Monroe Street, Montgomery, AL 36104 US
(910) 791-8070, *Fax:* (910) 392-1509
www.wect.com
wect@wect.com
License: Wilmington, New Hanover County, NC held by Raycom America License Subsidiary LLC.
Group Owner: Raycom Media Inc.; (acq 9-12-96; grpsl)
Nat'l Network: NBC *Nat'l Reps:* Harrington, Righter & Parsons
Regional Reps: Covington & Burling
Gary McNair, General Manager
Mark Mendenhall, General Sales Mgr
Donna Lanier, Programming Director
Dave Toma, Promotions Manager
Raeford Brown, News Director
Dan Ullmer, Chief Engineer
Herschel Howie, Promotions Manager

WSFX-TV *Digital Channel:* 30 *Virtual Channel:* 26; 170.6 kw; 1936 ft.; N34 7 53 W78 11 17
1926 Oleander Drive, Wilmington, NC 28403 US
(910) 791-8070, *Fax:* (910) 202-0493
www.wsfx.com
tpostema@wsfx.com
License: Wilmington, New Hanover County, NC
Group Owner: American Spirit Media; (acq 9-22-2003; $14 million); *Washington Law Firm:* Baraff, Koerner, Olender & Hochberg
Nat'l Network: FOX *Nat'l Reps:* MMT
Size of News Staff: 6; *Hours of Local News Weekly:* news progmg 3 hrs wkly
Tom Postema, General Manager
Kim Herring, Programming Director
Herschel Howie, Promotions Manager
Bob Bonner, News Director
Dan Ullmer, Chief Engineer
Julie Tames, Local Sales Manager
Connie Petway, Sales & Traffic Assistant

***WUNJ-TV** *Digital Channel:* 29 *Virtual Channel:* 39; 1000 kw; 974 ft.; N34 19 16 W78 13 43
Mailing Address: 10 T.W. Alexander Drive, Rese'ch Triangle Prk, NC 27709 US
Second Address: 10 TW Alexander Dr., Research Triangle Park, NC 27709-4900
(919) 549-7000, *Fax:* (919) 549-7201
www.unctv.org
viewer@unctv.org
License: Wilmington, New Hanover County, NC held by University of North Carolina
Washington Law Firm: Schwartz, Woods & Miller
Nat'l Network: PBS
Tom Howe, General Manager

WWAY *Digital Channel:* 46; 1,000 kw vis; and 1,935t/23g; N34 07 53 W78 11 17; *Population Served:* 120,284
615 N. Front St., Wilmington, NC 29615
(910) 762-8581, *Fax:* (910) 762-8367
www.wwaytv3.com
acombs@wwaytv3.com
License: Wilmington, New Hanover County, NC held by WWAY-TV LLC.
Group Owner: Morris Multimedia Inc.; (acq 1-31-2006; grpsl)
Nat'l Network: ABC
Dean Hinson, President
Andy Combs, General Manager
Carolyn Candebat, Local Sales Manager
Brenda Henderson, Traffic Manager

Ashley Hill, Promotions Manager
Scott Pickey, News Director
Billy Stratton, Chief Engineer

North Dakota

Fargo-Valley City, ND (DMA 120)

***KCGE-DT** *Digital Channel:* 16; 105 kw vis; ant 720t/720g; N47 58 38 W96 36 18; *Rebroadcasting:* Satellite of KFME(TV) Fargo, ND
Box 3240, Fargo, ND 58108
(701) 241-6900, *Fax:* (701) 239-7650
www.prairiepublic.org
info@prairiepublic.org
License: Crookston, Polk County, MN held by Prairie Public Broadcasting Inc
Nat'l Network: PBS
John Harris, CEO
Steve Wennblom, Programming Director

KCPM *Digital Channel:* 27 *Virtual Channel:* 27; 11.1 kw; 183 ft.; N47 57 45 W97 3 12
45 Rockefeller Plaza, Suite 3201, New York, NY 10020 US
(701) 364-9900, *Fax:* (605) 334-5575
mail@kcpm.tv
License: Grand Forks, Grand Forks County, ND held by G.I.G. of North Dakota LLC
Nat'l Network: MYTV
Charles Poppen, General Manager

***KFME** *Digital Channel:* 13 *Virtual Channel:* 13; 56.2 kw; 1122 ft.; N47 0 45 W97 11 41
Mailing Address: P.O. Box 3240, Fargo, ND 58108 US
Second Address: 207 N 5th Street, Fargo, ND 58102
(701) 241-6900, *Fax:* (701) 239-7650
www.prairiepublic.org
info@prairiepublic.org
License: Fargo, Cass County, ND held by Prairie Public Broadcasting Inc
Washington Law Firm: Dow, Lohnes & Albertson
Nat'l Network: PBS *Regional Network:* Prairie Public Television
John Harris, CEO
Ann Clark, General Sales Mgr
Steve Wennblom, Programming Director

***KGFE** *Digital Channel:* 15 *Virtual Channel:* 2; 22.6 kw; 611 ft.; N47 58 38 W96 36 18; *Rebroadcasting:* Satellite of *KFME Fargo.
Mailing Address: P.O. Box 3240, Fargo, ND 58108 US
Second Address: 207 N 5th Street, Fargo, ND 58102
(701) 241-6900, *Fax:* (701) 239-7650
www.prairiepublic.org
info@prairiepublic.org
License: Grand Forks, Grand Forks County, ND held by Prairie Public Broadcasting Inc
Washington Law Firm: Dow, Lohnes & Albertson
Nat'l Network: PBS
John Harris, CEO
Steve Wennblom, Programming Director

***KJRE** *Digital Channel:* 20 *Virtual Channel:* 19; 72.3 kw; 533 ft.; N46 17 56 W98 51 56; *Rebroadcasting:* Satellite of *KFME(TV) Fargo.
Mailing Address: Post Office Box 3240, Fargo, ND 58108 US
Second Address: 207 North 5th Street, Fargo, ND 58102
(701) 241-6900, *Fax:* (701) 239-7650
www.prairiepublic.org
info@prairiepublic.org
License: Ellendale, Dickey County, ND held by Prairie Public Broadcasting Inc
Washington Law Firm: Dow, Lohnes & Albertson
Nat'l Network: PBS
John Harris, CEO
Steve Wennblom, Programming Director

KJRR *Digital Channel:* 7 *Virtual Channel:* 7; 21.3 kw; 443 ft.; N46 55 27 W98 46 19; *Rebroadcasting:* Satellite of KVRR(TV) Fargo
P.O. Box 9115, Fargo, ND 58106 US
(701) 277-1515, *Fax:* (701) 277-1830
news@kvrr.com
License: Jamestown, Stutsman County, ND held by Red River Broadcast Co. L.L.C.
Group Owner: Red River Broadcast Co. L.L.C.; *Washington Law Firm:* Crowell & Moring
Nat'l Network: FOX
Kathy Lau, General Manager
Ed Beiswenger, General Sales Mgr
Jim Shaw, News Director
Darren Bjerke, Chief Engineer

***KMDE** *Digital Channel:* 25 *Virtual Channel:* 25; 134 kw; 802 ft.; N48 3 47.8 W99 20 8.7; *Rebroadcasting:* Satellite of KFME Fargo.
US
(701) 241-6900, *Fax:* (701) 239-7650
www.prairiepublic.org
info@prairiepublic.org
License: Devils Lake, Ramsey County, ND held by Prairie Public Broadcasting Inc
Nat'l Network: PBS
John Harris, CEO
Steve Wennblom, Programming Director

KNRR *Digital Channel:* 12 *Virtual Channel:* 12; 4.44 kw; 1401 ft.; N48 59 44 W97 24 28; *Rebroadcasting:* Satellite of KVRR(TV) Fargo
P.O. Box 9115, Fargo, ND 58106 US
(701) 277-1515, *Fax:* (701) 277-1830
news@kvrr.com
License: Pembina, Pembina County, ND held by Red River Broadcast Co. L.L.C.
Group Owner: Red River Broadcast Co. L.L.C.; *Washington Law Firm:* Crowell & Moring
Nat'l Network: FOX
Kathy Lau, General Manager
Ed Beiswenger, General Sales Mgr
Jim Shaw, News Director
Darren Bjerke, Chief Engineer

KVLY-TV *Digital Channel:* 44; 304 kw vis, 45.7 kw aur; 2,000t/2,063g; N47 20 36 W97 17 17; *Population Served:* 577,000
1350 21st Ave. S., Fargo, ND 33703
(701) 237-5211, *Fax:* (701) 237-5396
www.valleynewslive.com
mail@valleynewslive.com
License: Fargo, Cass County, ND held by North Dakota License Sub., LLC
Group Owner: Hoak Media Corporation; (acq 1-3-2007; grpsl);
Washington Law Firm: Wyrick, Robbins, Yates & Pontin
Nat'l Network: NBC *Nat'l Reps:* Blair Television *Wire Services:* AP
Size of News Staff: 36; *Hours of Local News Weekly:* news progmg 16 hrs wkly
Jim Wareham, General Manager
Ron Westrick, General Sales Mgr
Sean Kelly, Programming Director
Vacant, News Director
Doug Jenson, Chief Engineer

KVRR *Digital Channel:* 19 *Virtual Channel:* 15; 1000 kw; 1243 ft.; N46 40 29 W96 13 40
P.O. Box 9115, Fargo, ND 58106 US
(701) 277-1515, *Fax:* (701) 277-1830
news@kvrr.com
License: Fargo, Cass County, ND held by Red River Broadcast Co L.L.C.
Group Owner: Red River Broadcast Co. L.L.C.; *Washington Law Firm:* Crowell & Moring
Nat'l Network: FOX
Kathy Lau, General Manager
Ed Beiswenger, General Sales Mgr
Jim Shaw, News Director
Darren Bjerke, Chief Engineer

KXJB-TV *Digital Channel:* 38 *Virtual Channel:* 4; 382 kw; 1880 ft.; N47 16 45 W97 20 26
Post Office Box 10399, Fargo, ND 58106 US
(701) 282-0444, *Fax:* (701) 232-0493
www.kx4.com
news@kvoytv11.com
License: Valley City, Barnes County, ND held by Parker Broadcasting of Dakota LLC.
Group Owner: Parker Broadcasting Inc.; (acq 1-3-2007);
Washington Law Firm: Cohn & Marks
Nat'l Network: CBS *Nat'l Reps:* Continental Television Sales
Size of News Staff: 20; *Hours of Local News Weekly:* news progmg 10 hrs wkly
Charlie Johnson, General Manager
Mark Von Bank, General Sales Mgr
Jeff Petrik, Programming Director
Wendy Bernier, Promotions Manager
Mike Morken, News Director
Ron Barr, Chief Engineer

WDAY-TV *Digital Channel:* 21 *Virtual Channel:* 6; 100 kw vis, 11.4 kw aur; ant 1,150t/1,206g; N47 00 43 W97 11 58; *Population Served:* 214,200
Mailing Address: Box 2466, Fargo, ND 58103
Second Address: 301 S. 8th St., Fargo, ND 58103
(701) 237-6500, *Fax:* (701) 241-5368
www.wday.com/tv
License: Fargo, Cass County, ND held by Forum Communications Co.
Group Owner: Forum Communications Co.; (acq 7-20-60; $900,000;
Nat'l Network: ABC; CW
Susan Eider, Operations Manager
Mark Prather, General Manager
Carol Anhorn, General Sales Mgr
Susan Eider, Operations Manager
Jeff Nelson, News Director
Dave Johnson, Chief Engineer

WDAZ-TV *Digital Channel:* 8 *Virtual Channel:* 8; 19 kw; 1480 ft.; N48 8 18 W97 59 35; *Rebroadcasting:* Satellite of WDAY-TV Fargo.
Mailing Address: 301 8th St S/PO Box 2466, Fargo, ND 58103 US
Second Address: 2220 S. Washington, Grand Forks, ND 58201
(701) 775-2511, *Fax:* (701) 746-8565
www.wdaz.com
bkerr@wdaz.com
License: Devil's Lake, Ramsey County, ND held by Forum Communications Co.
Group Owner: Forum Communications Co.; *Washington Law Firm:* Holland & Knight
Nat'l Network: ABC
Robert Kerr, General Manager
Rob Horken, General Sales Mgr
Cassie Walder, News Director
Jeff Awes, Chief Engineer

Minot-Bismarck-Dickinson, ND (DMA 158)

***KBME-TV** *Digital Channel:* 22 *Virtual Channel:* 3; 97.3 kw; 1286 ft.; N46 35 23 W100 48 2; *Rebroadcasting:* Satellite of KFME-TV Fargo, ND
Mailing Address: P.O. Box 3240, Fargo, ND 58108 US
Second Address: 207 N. 5th St., Fargo, ND 58102
(701) 241-6900, *Fax:* (701) 239-7650
www.prairiepublic.org
info@prariepublic.org
License: Bismarck, Burleigh County, ND held by Prairie Public Broadcasting Inc
Washington Law Firm: Dow, Lohnes & Albertson
Nat'l Network: PBS
John Harris, CEO
Ann Clark, General Sales Mgr
Steve Wennblom, Programming Director

KBMY *Digital Channel:* 16; 75 kw; 950t/649g; N46 35 11 W100 48 20
1811 N. 15th St., Bismarck, ND 58103
(701) 223-1700, *Fax:* (701) 258-0886
www.abc17.tv
abc@abc17.tv
License: Bismarck, Burleigh County, ND held by KBMY-KMCY LLC.
Group Owner: Forum Communications Co.; *Washington Law Firm:* Marmet & McCombs
Nat'l Network: ABC
Mark Prather, General Manager
Tony Kruckenberg, Chief Engineer

***KDSE** *Digital Channel:* 9 *Virtual Channel:* 9; 30.3 kw; 782 ft.; N46 43 35 W102 54 57; *Rebroadcasting:* Satellite of KFME(TV) Fargo.
P. O. Box 3240, Fargo, ND 58108 US
(701) 241-6900, *Fax:* (701) 239-7650
www.prairiepublic.org
info@prairiepublic.org
License: Dickinson, Stark County, ND held by Prairie Public Broadcasting Inc
Washington Law Firm: Dow, Lohnes & Albertson
Nat'l Network: PBS
John Harris, CEO
Steve Wennblom, Programming Director

KFYR-TV *Digital Channel:* 31 *Virtual Channel:* 5; 500 kw; 1276 ft.; N46 36 20 W100 48 22
Mailing Address: 3839 Fourth Street, North, Suite 420, St. Petersburg, FL 33703 US
Second Address: 200 North 4th Street, Bismarck, ND 58501
(701) 255-5757, *Fax:* (701) 255-8220
www.kfyrtv.com
kfyrtv@kfyrtv.com

License: Bismarck, Burleigh County, ND held by Hoak Media of Dakota License LLC.
Group Owner: Hoak Media Corporation; (acq 1-3-2007; grpsl);
Washington Law Firm: Hogan & Hartson
Nat'l Network: NBC
Size of News Staff: 29; *Hours of Local News Weekly:* news progmg 24 hrs wkly
Dick Heidt, General Manager
Barry Schumaier, General Sales Mgr
Jim Sande, Programming Director
Brian Funk, Chief Engineer

KMCY *Digital Channel:* 14; 40kw; 2,720t/649g; N48 03 13 W101 23 05
1811 N. 15th St., Bismarck, ND 58108
(701) 223-1700
www.abc14.tv
abc@abc17.tv
License: Minot, Ward County, ND held by KBMY-KMCY LLC.
Group Owner: Forum Communications Co.
Nat'l Network: ABC
Mark Prather, General Manager
Anton Kruckenberg, Chief Engineer

KMOT *Digital Channel:* 10 *Virtual Channel:* 10; 7.69 kw; 679 ft.; N48 12 56 W101 19 5; *Rebroadcasting:* Satellite of KFYR-TV Bismarck
Mailing Address: 3839 Fourth Street, North, Suite 420, St. Petersburg, FL 33703 US
Second Address: 1800 S.W. 16th, Minot, ND 58701
(701) 852-4101, *Fax:* (701) 838-8195
www.kmot.com
License: Minot, Ward County, ND held by Hoak Media of Dakota License LLC.
Group Owner: Hoak Media Corporation; (acq 1-3-2007; grpsl);
Washington Law Firm: Hogan & Hartson
Nat'l Network: NBC
Tom Ross, General Manager
Nick Dreyer, News Director
Mike Robinson, Chief Engineer

KNDX *Digital Channel:* 26 *Virtual Channel:* 26; 50 kw; 984 ft.; N46 35 23 W100 47 39
112 High Ridge Avenue, Ridgefield, CT 06877 US
(701) 355-0026, *Fax:* (701) 250-7244
www.fox26.tv
License: Bismarck, Burleigh County, ND held by Prime Cities Broadcasting Inc.
Group Owner: Prime Cities Broadcasting Inc.
Nat'l Network: FOX
Gary O'Halloran, General Manager
Richard Farley, Chief Engineer

KQCD-TV *Digital Channel:* 7 *Virtual Channel:* 7; 11.3 kw; 673 ft.; N46 56 53 W102 59 25; *Rebroadcasting:* Satellite of KFYR-TV Bismarck
3839 Fourth Street, North, Suite 420, St. Petersburg, FL 33703 US
(701) 483-7777, *Fax:* (701) 483-8231
www.kqcd.com
kqcd@kqcd.com
License: Dickinson, Stark County, ND held by Hoak Media of Dakota License LLC.
Group Owner: Hoak Media Corporation; (acq 1-3-2007; grpsl);
Washington Law Firm: Hogan & Hartson
Nat'l Network: NBC
Dick Heidt, General Manager
Barry Schumaier, General Sales Mgr
Jim Sande, Programming Director
LuWanna Lawrence, Promotions Manager
Monica Hannan, News Director
Brian Funk, Chief Engineer

***KSRE** *Digital Channel:* 40 *Virtual Channel:* 6; 146 kw; 818 ft.; N48 3 2 W101 23 25; *Rebroadcasting:* Satellite of KFME Fargo.
P.O. Box 3240, Fargo, ND 58108 US
(701) 241-6900, *Fax:* (701) 239-7650
www.prairiepublic.org
info@prairiepublic.org
License: Minot, Ward County, ND held by Prairie Public Broadcasting
Washington Law Firm: Dow, Lohnes & Albertson
Nat'l Network: PBS
John Harris, CEO
Steve Wennblom, Programming Director

KUMV-TV *Digital Channel:* 8 *Virtual Channel:* 8; 6 kw; 1050 ft.; N48 8 2 W103 51 36; *Rebroadcasting:* Satellite of KFYR-TV Bismarck
Mailing Address: 3839 Fourth Street, North, Suite 420, St. Petersburg, FL 33703 US
Second Address: 602 Main St., Willinston, ND 58801
(701) 572-4676, *Fax:* (701) 572-0118
www.kumv.com
kumv@kumv.com
License: Williston, Williams County, ND held by Hoak Media of Dakota License LLC.
Group Owner: Hoak Media Corporation; (acq 1-3-2007; grpsl)
Nat'l Network: NBC
Size of News Staff: 2; *Hours of Local News Weekly:* news progmg 6 hrs wkly
Deborah Burton, General Manager
Jim Sande, Programming Director
Hawlie Ohe, News Director
Scott Aune, Chief Engineer

***KWSE** *Digital Channel:* 11 *Virtual Channel:* 4; 84.9 kw; 912 ft.; N48 8 30 W103 53 34; *Rebroadcasting:* Satellite of KFME(TV) Fargo.
P.O. Box 3240, Fargo, ND 58108 US
(701) 241-6900, *Fax:* (701) 239-7650
www.prairiepublic.org
info@prairiepublic.org
License: Williston, Williams County, ND held by Prairie Public Broadcasting Inc
Washington Law Firm: Dow, Lohnes & Albertson
Nat'l Network: PBS
John Harris, CEO
Steve Wennblom, Programming Director

KXMA-TV *Digital Channel:* 19 *Virtual Channel:* 2; 150 kw; 712 ft.; N46 43 35 W102 54 57
Drawer B 119 2nd Ave. W, Dickinson, ND 58602 US
(701) 483-1400, *Fax:* (701) 483-1401
www.kxnet.com
treiten@kxnet.com
License: Dickinson, Stark County, ND held by Reiten Television Inc.
Group Owner: Reiten Television Inc.; (acq 12-4-84; $362,500);
Washington Law Firm: Fisher, Wayland, Cooper, Leader & Zaragoza
Nat'l Network: CBS
Mark Enderle, Operations Dir
Tim Reiten, General Manager
Alice Meier, General Sales Mgr
Tom Gerhardt, News Director
Rocky Hefty, Chief Engineer
Julie Bernhardt, National Sales Manager

KXMB-TV *Digital Channel:* 12 *Virtual Channel:* 12; 19.1 kw; 1458 ft.; N46 35 23 W100 48 20
Box 1617 1811 N 15th St., Bismark, ND 58501 US
(701) 223-9197, *Fax:* (701) 223-3320
www.kxnet.com
treiten@kxnet.com
License: Bismarck, Burleigh County, ND held by Reiten Television Inc.
Group Owner: Reiten Television Inc.; (acq 1-27-71; $1.2 million;;
Washington Law Firm: Fisher, Wayland, Cooper, Leader & Zaragoza
Nat'l Network: CBS
Size of News Staff: 11; *Hours of Local News Weekly:* news progmg 9 hrs wkly
Janean Rambaugh, Operations Dir
Tim Reiten, General Manager
Alice Meier, General Sales Mgr
Tom Gerhardt, News Director
Rocky Hefty, Chief Engineer
Julie Bernhardt, National Sales Manager

KXMC-TV *Digital Channel:* 13 *Virtual Channel:* 13; 16.1 kw; 1096 ft.; N48 3 0 W101 20 32
Mailing Address: Box 1686 3425 S Bro/Way, Minot, ND 58702 US
Second Address: 2121 2nd St. SE, Minot, ND 58701
(701) 852-2104, *Fax:* (701) 838-9360
www.kxnet.com
webmasterb@kxnet.com
License: Minot, Ward County, ND held by Reiten Television Inc.
Group Owner: Reiten Television Inc.; (acq 7-31-74;; *Washington Law Firm:* Davis Wright Tremaine
Nat'l Network: CBS *Nat'l Reps:* Continental Television Sales
Size of News Staff: 10; *Hours of Local News Weekly:* news progmg 9 hrs wkly
David Reiten, General Manager
Darren Lenertz, General Sales Mgr
Jim Olson, News Director
Rocky Hefty, Chief Engineer
Kari Rohrich, Office Manager

KXMD-TV *Digital Channel:* 14 *Virtual Channel:* 11; 100 kw; 843 ft.; N48 8 30 W103 53 34
Mailing Address: Box 1802 13th Ave. West, Williston, ND 58801 US
Second Address: 1802 13th Ave. W., Williston, NC 58801
(701) 572-2345, *Fax:* (701) 572-0658
License: Williston, Williams County, ND held by Reiten Television Inc.
Group Owner: Reiten Television Inc.; *Washington Law Firm:* Fisher, Wayland, Cooper, Leader & Zaragoza
Nat'l Network: CBS
Darren Lenertz, General Manager
Amanda Luchsinger, General Sales Mgr
Jim Olson, News Director
Bob Turneau, Chief Engineer
David Reiten, General Manager

KXND *Digital Channel:* 24 *Virtual Channel:* 24; 50 kw; 784 ft.; N48 3 14 W101 26 3; *Rebroadcasting:* Satellite of KNDX-TV Bismarck, ND
Mailing Address: 112 High Ridge Avenue, Ridgefield, CT 06877 US
Second Address: Prime Cities Broadcasting Inc., 3130 E. Broadway, Bismarck, ND 58501
(701) 355-0026, *Fax:* (701) 250-7244
www.fox24.com
License: Minot, Ward County, ND held by Prime Cities Broadcasting Inc
Group Owner: Prime Cities Broadcasting Inc.
Nat'l Network: FOX
Gary O'Halloran, General Manager
Jessie Wald, Programming Director
Richard Farley, Chief Engineer

Ohio

Charleston-Huntington, WV (DMA 65)

***WOUB-TV** *Digital Channel:* 27; 1,000 kw vis, 100 kw aur; 800t/856g; N39 18 50 W82 08 54; *Population Served:* 151,000
9 S. College St., Athens, OH 45701
(740) 593-4555, *Fax:* (740) 593-0240
www.woub.org
woub@woub.org
License: Athens, Athens County, OH held by Ohio University
Washington Law Firm: Dow, Lohnes & Albertson
Nat'l Network: PBS *Regional Network:* Ohio Educ. Telecommunications
Size of News Staff: 3; *Hours of Local News Weekly:* news progmg 3 hrs wkly
Steve Skidmore, Operations Dir
Tom Hodson, General Manager
Loring Lovett, General Sales Mgr
Mark Brewer, Programming Director
Tim Sharp, News Director
Ted Ross, Engineering Dir
Steve Skidmore, Operations Director
JeffreyHarmison, Operations Manager
Joan Butcher, Programming Manager

***WPBO** *Digital Channel:* 43 *Virtual Channel:* 42; 50 kw; 1253 ft.; N38 45 42 W83 3 41; *Rebroadcasting:* Rebroadcasts WOSU-TV Columbus 100%.
2400 Olentangy River Rd, Columbus, OH 43210 US
(614) 292-9678, *Fax:* (614) 688-3399,(614) 688-3343
www.wosu.org
wosu@wosu.org
License: Portsmouth, Scioto County, OH held by The Ohio State University
Washington Law Firm: Dow, Lohnes & Albertson
Nat'l Network: PBS
Foreign Language Programming
Janice Walker, Operations Dir
Thomas Rieland, General Manager
Stacia Hehentz, Station Manager
Doug Partusch, General Sales Mgr
Brent Davis, Programming Director

WQCW *Digital Channel:* 17 *Virtual Channel:* 30; 1000 kw; 1299 ft.; N38 30 21 W82 12 33
Mailing Address: 1732 Dunraven, Knoxville, TN 37922 US
Second Address: 400 Capitol St., Charleston, WV 25301
(740) 353-3391, *Fax:* (740) 353-3372
www.tristatescw.com
License: Portsmouth, Scioto County, OH held by Television Properties Inc
Nat'l Network: CW
Dave Hanna, President
William White, General Manager
Vince Wardell, General Sales Mgr

Cincinnati, OH (DMA 34)

***WCET** *Digital Channel:* 34 *Virtual Channel:* 48; 400 kw; 1070 ft.; N39 7 27 W84 31 18
1223 Central Parkway, Cincinnati, OH 45214 US
(513) 381-4033, *Fax:* (513) 381-7520
www.cetconnect.org
comments@cetconnect.org
License: Cincinnati, Hamilton County, OH held by Greater Cincinnati TV Educational Foundation
Washington Law Firm: Dow, Lohnes & Albertson
Nat'l Network: PBS
Susan Howarth, CEO
Ricardo Ang, Operations Dir
Sherry Sargeant, General Sales Mgr
Brian Snape, Promotions Manager
Neal Schmidt, Chief Engineer
Jack Dominic, COO

WCPO-TV *Digital Channel:* 22 *Virtual Channel:* 9; 880 kw; 984 ft.; N39 7 30 W84 29 56
312 Walnut Street, 28th Floor, Cincinnati, OH 45202 US
(513) 721-9900, *Fax:* (513) 721-7717
www.wcpo.com
bfee@wcpo.com
License: Cincinnati, Hamilton County, OH held by Scripps Howard Broadcasting Co.
Group Owner: The E. W. Scripps Co.; *Washington Law Firm:* Baker & Hostetler
Nat'l Network: ABC *Wire Services:* UPI
Size of News Staff: 70; *Hours of Local News Weekly:* news progmg 24 hrs wkly
Bill Fee, General Manager
Bill Fee, Programming Director
Joe Martinelli, Engineering Dir

WKRC-TV *Digital Channel:* 12 *Virtual Channel:* 12; 15.55 kw; 1001 ft.; N39 6 59 W84 30 7
50 River Center Blvd., Suite 1200, Covington, KY 41011 US
(513) 763-5500, *Fax:* (513) 763-5554
www.wkrc.com
License: Cincinnati, Hamilton County, OH held by Newport Television License LLC.
Group Owner: Newport Television LLC; (acq 3-14-2008; grpsl);
Washington Law Firm: Covington & Burling
Nat'l Network: CBS; CW *Nat'l Reps:* TeleRep *Wire Services:* AP
Les Vann, General Manager
Kurt Thelen, Engineering Dir

WLWT *Digital Channel:* 35 *Virtual Channel:* 5; 1000 kw; 1019 ft.; N39 7 27 W84 31 18
888 Seventh Avenue, New York, NY 10106 US
(513) 412-5000, *Fax:* (513) 412-6121 (news)
www.wlwt.com
newsdesk@wlwt.com
License: Cincinnati, Hamilton County, OH held by Hearst-Argyle Stations Inc.
Group Owner: Hearst-Argyle Television Inc.; (acq 7-16-97; grpsl).; *Washington Law Firm:* Brooks, Pierce, McLendon, Humphrey & Leonard
Nat'l Network: NBC *Nat'l Reps:* Eagle Television Sales
Tracy Ahlers, CFO
Richard J. Dyer, President
Mark Diangela, General Sales Mgr
Pete Salkowski, Promotions Manager
Stacy Owens, News Director
Paul Nowakowski, Chief Engineer

***WPTO** *Digital Channel:* 28 *Virtual Channel:* 14; 400 kw; 881 ft.; N39 7 19 W84 32 52
110 S.Jefferson Street, Dayton, OH 45402 US
(937) 220-1600, *Fax:* (937) 220-1642
www.thinktv.org
License: Oxford, Butler County, OH held by Greater Dayton Public Television Inc
(acq 1975).; *Washington Law Firm:* Dow, Lohnes & Albertson
Nat'l Network: PBS *Regional Network:* Ohio Educ. Telecommunications
Size of News Staff: 1; *Hours of Local News Weekly:* news progmg one hr wkly
Suzanne O'Brien, CFO
David Fogarty, President
Ed Valles, General Sales Mgr
Gloria Skurski, Programming Director
Kitty Lensman, Promotions Manager
H. Stone, Engineering Dir
George Hopstetter, Engineering Manager
Jim Wiener,Programming Manager
Sue Brinson, Promotions Manager

WSTR-TV *Digital Channel:* 33 *Virtual Channel:* 64; 360 kw; 1106 ft.; N39 12 1 W84 31 22
10706 Beaver Dam, Cockeysville, MD 21030 US
(513) 641-4400, *Fax:* (513) 242-2633
www.my64.tv
License: Cincinnati, Hamilton County, OH held by Sinclair Communications Group.
Group Owner: Sinclair Broadcast Group Inc.; (acq 1996; $11 million); *Washington Law Firm:* Cole, Raywid & Braverman
Nat'l Network: MYTV *Nat'l Reps:* Millennium Sales & Marketing
Jon Lawhead, General Manager
Joe Marino, General Sales Mgr
Rick White, Programming Director
Pete Ferraro, Promotions Manager
Terry Roberts, Engineering Dir
Stefan Schellhas, General Sales Manager
Ashly Richards, ResearchDirector
Laurel Adams, Traffic Manager

Cleveland-Akron (Canton), OH (DMA 17)

WBNX-TV *Digital Channel:* 30 *Virtual Channel:* 55; 1000 kw; 1087 ft.; N41 23 2 W81 41 44
2690 State Road, Cuyahoga Falls, OH 44223 US
(330) 922-5500
www.wbnx.com
clevelandswb@wbnx.com
License: Akron, Summit County, OH held by Winston Broadcasting Network Inc
(acq 5-20-87;; *Washington Law Firm:* Irwin, Campbell & Tannenwald
Nat'l Network: CW *Nat'l Reps:* Adam Young
Lou Spangler, President
Dave Armstrong, Operations Dir
Eddie Brown, General Sales Mgr
Colleen Metheney, Programming Director
Duane Sullivan, Promotions Manager
Don Richardson, Chief Engineer

WDLI-TV *Digital Channel:* 49 *Virtual Channel:* 17; 900 kw; 958 ft.; N41 3 20 W81 35 38
P.O. Box C11949, Santa Ana, CA 92711 US
(330) 753-5542, *Fax:* (330) 753-4563
wdli@tbn.org
License: Canton, Stark County, OH held by Trinity Broadcasting Network.
Group Owner: Trinity Broadcasting Network; (acq 4-15-86; $4.5 million;; *Washington Law Firm:* Joseph E. Dunne III
Nat'l Network: TRINITY BROADCA
Joanne Mann, Station Manager

***WEAO** *Digital Channel:* 50; 250 kW; 1,047t/923g; N40 04 58 W81 38 00; *Rebroadcasting:* Rebroadcasts WNEO(TV) Alliance 100%; *Population Served:* 3,920,000
Box 5191, 1750 Campus Center Dr., Kent, OH 44240
(330) 677-4549, *Fax:* (330) 678-0688
www.westernreservepublicmedia.org
questions@westernreservepublicmedia.org
License: Akron, Summit County, OH held by Northeastern Educational TV of Ohio Inc
Washington Law Firm: Dow, Lohnes & Albertson
Nat'l Network: PBS
Hours of Local News Weekly: News progmg one hr wkly
Trina Cutter, President and Chief Executive Officer
Bill O'Neil, Station Manager
Don Freeman, Programming Director
Lisa Martinez, Vice President of Marketing and Development

WEWS-TV *Digital Channel:* 15; 93.3 kw vis, 10 kw aur; 1,020t/851g; N41 22 27 W81 43 06; *Population Served:* 1,463,900
3001 Euclid Ave., Cleveland, OH 44115
(216) 431-5555, *Fax:* (216) 431-3666
www.newsnet5.com
License: Cleveland, Cuyahoga County, OH held by Scripps Howard Broadcasting Co.
Group Owner: The E. W. Scripps Co.; *Washington Law Firm:* Baker & Hostetler
Nat'l Network: ABC *Nat'l Reps:* Eagle Television Sales *Wire Services:* Reuters
Hours of Local News Weekly: News progmg 22 hrs wkly
Victoria Regan, General Manager

WGGN-TV *Digital Channel:* 42 *Virtual Channel:* 52; 450 kw; 928 ft.; N41 4 30 W82 27 5
3809 Maple Ave., Castalia, OH 44824 US
(419) 684-5311, *Fax:* (419) 684-5378
www.cfbroadcast.net
tv52@cfbroadcast.net
License: Sandusky, Erie County, OH held by Christian Faith Broadcasting Inc.
Group Owner: Christian Faith Broadcasting Inc.; *Washington Law Firm:* Joseph E. Dunne III
Nat'l Network: TBN
Shelby Gillam, President
Rusty Yost, General Manager
Roy Billman, Programming Director

WJW *Digital Channel:* 8 *Virtual Channel:* 8; 11 kw; 1122 ft.; N41 21 48 W81 42 58
5151 Wisconsin Ave., NW, Washington, DC 20016 US
(216) 431-8888, *Fax:* (216) 432-4282 (sales)
www.fox8.com
License: Cleveland, Cuyahoga County, OH held by Community Television of Ohio License LLC.
Group Owner: Local TV LLC; (acq 7-14-2008; grpsl)
Nat'l Network: FOX
Greg Easterly, Operations Dir
Paul Perozeni, General Sales Mgr
Kevin Salyer, Promotions Manager
Sonya Thompson, News Director
Paul Bodamer, Local Sales Manager
Barb Toth, National Sales Manager
Sandi Stabb, Traffic Manager

WKYC-DT *Digital Channel:* 17; 100 kw vis, 20 kw aur; 1,000t/906g; N41 23 09 W81 41 23; *Population Served:* 2,800,000
1333 Lakeside Ave., Cleveland, OH 44114
(216) 344-3333, *Fax:* (216) 344-3326
www.wkyc.com
news@wkyc.com
License: Cleveland, Cuyahoga County, OH held by WKYC-TV Inc.
Group Owner: Gannett Broadcasting; (acq 12-4-95; grpsl).
Nat'l Network: NBC
Brooke Spectorsky, President
Mike Szabo, Programming Director
Micki Byrnes, Promotions Manager

WMFD-TV *Digital Channel:* 12 *Virtual Channel:* 68; 14 kw; 591 ft.; N40 45 50 W82 37 4
2900 Park Avenue West, Mansfield, OH 44906 US
(419) 529-5900, *Fax:* (419) 529-2319
www.wmfd.com
comments@wmfd.com
License: Mansfield, Richland County, OH held by Mid-State Television Inc
(acq 5-31-92;; *Washington Law Firm:* Fletcher, Heald & Hildreth
Nat'l Network: IND *Wire Services:* AP; CNN
Size of News Staff: 12; *Hours of Local News Weekly:* news progmg 36 hrs wkly
Gunther Meisse, President
Robert Meisse, Station Manager

WOIO *Digital Channel:* 10 *Virtual Channel:* 19; 3.5 kw; 997 ft.; N41 23 15 W81 41 43
1660 West Second Street, Cleveland, OH 44113 US
(216) 771-1943, *Fax:* (216) 515-7152
www.woio.com
License: Shaker Heights, Cuyahoga County, OH held by WOIO License Subsidiary, LLC
Group Owner: Raycom Media Inc.; (acq 8-13-98).; *Washington Law Firm:* Covington & Burling
Nat'l Network: CBS *Nat'l Reps:* TeleRep
Jim Stunek, Operations Dir
Bill Applegate, General Manager
Renee Morley, General Sales Mgr
Lisa McManus, Programming Director
Rob Boenau, Promotions Manager
Dan Salamone, News Director
Bob Maupin, Chief Engineer
Todd Galloway,Research Director

WQHS-DT *Digital Channel:* 34; 525 kw vis, 200 kw aur; ant 1,160t/1,029g; N41 23 02 W81 42 06; *Population Served:* 3,500,000
2861 W. Ridgewood Dr., Parma, OH 44134
(440) 888-0061, *Fax:* (440) 888-7023
www.univision.com
License: Cleveland, Cuyahoga County, OH held by Univision Partnership of Ohio.
Group Owner: Univision Communications Inc.; (acq 5-21-2001; grpsl).; *Washington Law Firm:* Wiley, Rein & Fielding
Nat'l Network: Univision (Spanish) *Wire Services:* UPI
Foreign Language Programming
Rolo Duartes, General Manager
Jose Godur, General Sales Mgr
Bud Bush, Programming Director
Dave Smith, Chief Engineer

WRLM *Digital Channel:* 47; 5000 kw vis, 500 kw aur; ant 485t/472g; N41 06 33 W81 20 10; *Population Served:* 1,500,000
4385 Sherman Rd., Kent, OH 44240-6847
(330) 677-6760
License: Canton, Stark County, OH held by MTB Cleveland License LLC.
Group Owner: Multicultural Capital Trust; (acq 2-2-2009); *Washington Law Firm:* Sciarrino & Shubert PLLC
Glenn Foldessy, Station Manager
Josh Rule, Chief Engineer

WUAB *Digital Channel:* 28 *Virtual Channel:* 43; 200 kw; 1106 ft.; N41 22 45 W81 43 12
1717 East 12th Street, Cleveland, OH 44114 US
(216) 771-1943, *Fax:* (216) 515-7152
www.wuab.com
License: Lorain, Lorain County, OH held by WOIO License Subsidiary, LLC
Group Owner: Raycom Media Inc.; (acq 3-2-00).; *Washington Law Firm:* Covington & Burling
Nat'l Network: MNT *Nat'l Reps:* TeleRep *Wire Services:* Reuters
Jim Stunek, Operations Dir
Bill Applegate, General Manager
Renee Morley, General Sales Mgr
Lisa McManus, Programming Director
Rob Boenau, Promotions Manager
Dan Salamone, News Director
Bob Maupin, Chief Engineer
Todd Galloway,Research Director

***WVIZ** *Digital Channel:* 26 *Virtual Channel:* 25; 150 kw; 1105 ft.; N41 23 10 W81 41 21
4300 Brookpark Road, Cleveland, OH 44134 US
(216) 916-6100, *Fax:* (216) 916-6123
www.wviz.org
License: Cleveland, Cuyahoga County, OH held by Ideastream
Nat'l Network: PBS
Jerry Wareham, CEO
Bob Stern, Station Manager
Kent Geist, General Sales Mgr
Maureen Paschke, Promotions Manager
Bob Calsin, CFO
Kit Jensen, COO
Jane Temple, Promotions Director
Mark Smukler, Station Manager

WVPX-TV *Digital Channel:* 23; 1,290 kw vis, 175 kw aur; 961t/926g; N41 03 51 W81 34 59; *Population Served:* 1,500,000
1333 Lakeside Ave., East, Cleveland, OH 44114
(216) 344-3333, *Fax:* (216) 344-7430
www.ionmedia.tv
License: Akron, Summit County, OH held by ION Media Akron License, Inc., Debtor-in-possession
Group Owner: ION Media Networks Inc.; (acq 2-29-96; $40 million; with WBPT(TV) Bridgeport, CT).; *Washington Law Firm:* Dow, Lohnes & Albertson
Nat'l Network: ION Television
Amy Sheridan, Operations Dir
LaTonya Pettit, Station Manager
Robert Getze, General Sales Mgr
James Thomas, Chief Engineer

Columbus, OH (DMA 32)

WBNS-TV *Digital Channel:* 21 *Virtual Channel:* 10; 1000 kw; 915 ft.; N39 58 16 W83 1 40
770 Twin Rivers Drive, Columbus, OH 43215 US
(614) 460-3700, *Fax:* (614) 460-2826
www.10tv.com
License: Columbus, Franklin County, OH held by WBNS TV Inc.
Group Owner: Dispatch Broadcast Group; *Washington Law Firm:* Sidley & Austin
Nat'l Network: CBS
Size of News Staff: 80; *Hours of Local News Weekly:* news progmg 31 hrs wkly
Frank Wilson, Operations Dir
Tom Griesdorn, General Manager
Chuck Devendra, General Sales Mgr
John Cardenas, News Director
Pat Wise, National Sales Manager
Mike Berry, Operations Manager
Doug Jones, Promotions Manager
AngelaPace, Public Affairs Director

WCMH-TV *Digital Channel:* 14 *Virtual Channel:* 4; 902 kw; 866 ft.; N39 58 16 W83 1 40
Mailing Address: Ms Diane Zipursky, 1299 Pennsylvania Ave, Washington, DC 20004 US
Second Address: Box 4, Columbus, OH 43216
(614) 263-4444, *Fax:* (614) 447-9107
www.nbc4i.com
License: Columbus, Franklin County, OH held by Media General Communications Inc.
Group Owner: Media General Broadcast Group; (acq 6-26-2006; grpsl).
Nat'l Network: NBC *Nat'l Reps:* MMT
Size of News Staff: 60; *Hours of Local News Weekly:* news progmg 31.5 hrs wkly
Marshall Morton, President
Debra Grivois, Operations Dir
Daniel Bradley, General Manager
Mike Cash, General Sales Mgr
Janna Buckey, Promotions Manager
Robert Golias, National Sales Manager
Ken Lubker, Regional Sales Manager

***WOSU-TV** *Digital Channel:* 38 *Virtual Channel:* 34; 503 kw; 1079 ft.; N40 9 33 W82 55 23
6131 Highland Lake Ave., Columbus, OH 43210 US
(614) 292-9678, *Fax:* (614) 688-3399,(614) 688-3343
www.wosu.org
wosu@wosu.org
License: Columbus, Franklin County, OH held by The Ohio State University
Washington Law Firm: Dow, Lohnes & Albertson
Nat'l Network: PBS
Janice Walker, Operations Dir
Thomas Rieland, General Manager
Stacia Hehentz, Station Manager
Doug Partusch, General Sales Mgr
Brent Davis, Programming Director
Tom Lahr, Chief Engineer

WSFJ-TV *Digital Channel:* 24 *Virtual Channel:* 51; 724 kw vis, 72.4 kw aur; ant 439t/279g; N40 04 44 W82 41 42; *Population Served:* 1,935,300
7790 North Central Drive, Lewis Center, OH 43076
(740) 548-3800, *Fax:* (740) 548-3815
www.tbn.org
lbell@tbn.org
License: Newark, Licking County, OH held by Trinity Christian Center of Santa Ana, Inc.
Group Owner: Trinity Broadcasting Network; 1-Oct-08; *Washington Law Firm:* Colby M. May, Esq., P.C.
Size of News Staff: 1
Art Ratliff, Operations Dir
Linda Bell, Station Manager
Linda Bell, Programming Director
Tim Geist, Chief Engineer

WSYX *Digital Channel:* 48 *Virtual Channel:* 6; 1000 kw; 938 ft.; N39 56 14 W83 1 16
10706 Beaver Dam Road, Cockeysville, MD 21030 US
(614) 481-6666, *Fax:* (614) 481-6624
www.abc6onyourside.com
License: Columbus, Franklin County, OH held by WSYX Licensee Inc.
Group Owner: Sinclair Broadcast Group Inc.; (acq 1998; $228 million)
Nat'l Network: ABC *Nat'l Reps:* Millennium Sales & Marketing
Dan Mellon, General Manager
Tony D'Angelo, General Sales Mgr
Rick White, Programming Director
Mike Hansen, Promotions Manager
Mitch Jacob, News Director
Dan Carpenter, Chief Engineer
Lorie Luthman, General Sales Manager
LindaSiler, Traffic Manager

WTTE *Digital Channel:* 36 *Virtual Channel:* 28; 1000 kw; 889 ft.; N39 56 14 W83 1 16
3474 William Penn Highway, Pittsburgh, PA 15235 US
(614) 481-6666, *Fax:* (614) 485-1458
www.myfox28columbus.com
License: Columbus, Franklin County, OH held by Columbus (WTTE-TV) Licensee Inc.
Group Owner: Cunningham Broadcasting Corporation; (acq 1-9-2002).
Nat'l Network: FOX *Nat'l Reps:* Millennium Sales & Marketing
Zoe Anne Del Borrell, Operations Dir
Dan Mellon, General Manager
Tony D'Angelo, General Sales Mgr
Rick White, Programming Director
Mike Hansen, Promotions Manager
Lyn Tolan, News Director
Dan Carpenter, Chief Engineer

WWHO *Digital Channel:* 46; 1,000 kw; 328 meters; N39 35 20 W83 06 44
1160 Dublin Rd., Suite 400, Columbus, OH 20005
(614) 485-5300, *Fax:* (614) 485-5339
www.wwhotv.com
License: Chillicothe, Ross County, OH held by WWHO Broadcasting LLC.
Group Owner: LIN Television Corporation; (acq 3-31-2005; $85 million with WNDY-TV Marion, IN).; *Washington Law Firm:* Pillsbury Winthrop Shaw Pittman LLP
Nat'l Network: CW
Ellen Daly, Station Manager

Dayton, OH (DMA 64)

WBDT *Digital Channel:* 26 *Virtual Channel:* 26; 770 kw; 1145 ft.; N39 43 28 W84 15 18
10829 Olive Boulevard, Suite 202, St. Louis, MO 63141 US
(937) 384-9226, *Fax:* (937) 384-7392
daytonscw.com
License: Springfield, Clark County, OH held by Acme Television Licenses of Ohio L.L.C.
Group Owner: ACME Communications Inc.; (acq 6-14-99; grpsl)
Nat'l Network: CW *Nat'l Reps:* Harrington, Righter & Parsons
Hours of Local News Weekly: 4
Gregg Abbott, Operations Dir
John Hannon, General Manager
Melanie Simon, General Sales Mgr
Shasta Scarberry, Promotions Manager
Al Schmidt, Chief Engineer
Bonnie Meyers, Business Manager
Billie Sue Adkins, National SalesManager
Brian Mercer, Research & Sales Marketing Director

WDTN *Digital Channel:* 50 *Virtual Channel:* 2; 1000 kw; 1060 ft.; N39 43 7 W84 15 22
3839 - 4th Street, North, Suite 420, St. Petersburg, FL 33703 US
(937) 293-2101, *Fax:* (937) 294-6542
www.wdtn.com
newstips@wdtn.com
License: Dayton, Montgomery County, OH held by LIN License Company LLC
Group Owner: LIN Media; (acq 11-8-2002; grpsl).
Nat'l Network: NBC *Nat'l Reps:* Blair Television
Sharon Howard, Operations Dir
Lisa Barhorst, General Manager
Patrick Donnelly, General Sales Mgr
Jason Doyle, Promotions Manager
Steve Diorio, News Director
Jim Atkinson, Chief Engineer
Shawn MacIntyre, National Sales Manager
Janice Barney, Traffic Manager

WHIO-TV *Digital Channel:* 41 *Virtual Channel:* 7; 1000 kw; 1142 ft.; N39 44 2 W84 14 53
Mailing Address: P.O. Box 1206, Dayton, OH 45401 US
Second Address: Box 1206, Dayton, OH 45402
(937) 259-2111, *Fax:* (937) 259-2005
www.whiotv.com
7online@whiotv.com
License: Dayton, Montgomery County, OH held by Miami Valley Broadcasting Corp.
Group Owner: Cox Television; *Washington Law Firm:* Dow, Lohnes & Albertson
Nat'l Network: CBS *Nat'l Reps:* TeleRep
Harry Delaney, Operations Dir
James Cosby, General Sales Mgr
Fantine Kerckaert, Programming Director
Tony Getts, Promotions Manager
David Bennallack, News Director
Chuck Eastman, Operations Manager

WKEF *Digital Channel:* 51 *Virtual Channel:* 22; 515 kw; 1152 ft.; N39 43 28 W84 15 18
900 Laskin Road, Virginia Beach, VA 23451 US
(937) 263-4500, *Fax:* (937) 268-2332
www.daytonsnewssource.com
License: Dayton, Montgomery County, OH held by WKEF Licensee L.P.
Group Owner: Sinclair Broadcast Group Inc.; (acq 7-7-98; grpsl)
Nat'l Network: NBC
Hours of Local News Weekly: News progmg 17 hrs wkly
Dean Ditmer, General Manager
Julie Gossard, General Sales Mgr
Michelle Steinbrugge, Programming Director
Jason Matlock, Promotions Manager
John Lee, Chief Engineer

***WPTD** *Digital Channel:* 16 *Virtual Channel:* 16; 163 kw; 1129 ft.; N39 43 16 W84 15 0
110 S. Jefferson Street, Dayton, OH 45402 US
(937) 220-1600, *Fax:* (937) 220-1642
www.thinktv.org

License: Dayton, Montgomery County, OH held by Greater Dayton Public TV Inc
Washington Law Firm: Dow, Lohnes & Albertson
Nat'l Network: PBS *Regional Network:* Ohio Educ. Telecommunications
Size of News Staff: 1; *Hours of Local News Weekly:* news progmg one hr wkly
David Fogarty, President
Ed Valles, General Sales Mgr
Gloria Skurski, Programming Director
Kitty Lensman, Promotions Manager
H. Fred Stone, Engineering Dir
George Hopstetter, Engineering Manager
Jim Wiener, ProgrammingManager
Sue Brinson, Promotions Manager

WRGT-TV *Digital Channel:* 30; 5,000 kw vis, 501 kw aur; ant 1,171t/1,158g; N39 43 28 W84 15 18; *Population Served:* 1,773,600
45 Broadcast Plaza, Dayton, OH 02116
(937) 263-4500, *Fax:* (937) 268-5265
www.daytonsnewssource.com
License: Dayton, Montgomery County, OH held by ION Media of Scranton
Group Owner: Cunningham Broadcasting Corporation; (acq 11-15-2001; grpsl).
Nat'l Network: Fox; MyNetworkTV
Hours of Local News Weekly: News progmg 16 hrs wkly
Dean Ditmer, General Manager
Julie Gossard, General Sales Mgr
Michelle Steinbrugge, Programming Director
Jason Matlock, Promotions Manager
Bob Cummings, Chief Engineer

Lima, OH (DMA 186)

WLIO *Digital Channel:* 8 *Virtual Channel:* 35; 27.5 kw; 486 ft.; N40 44 51 W84 7 54.5
Mailing Address: 1424 Rice Avenue, Lima, OH 45802 US
Second Address: 1424 Rice Ave., Lima, OH 45805
(419) 228-8835, *Fax:* (419) 229-7091
www.wlio.com
License: Lima, Allen County, OH held by Lima Communications Corp.
Group Owner: Block Communications Inc.; (acq 2-1-72; $1.5 million); *Washington Law Firm:* Dow, Lohnes & Albertson
Nat'l Network: NBC
Size of News Staff: 17; *Hours of Local News Weekly:* news progmg 24 hrs wkly
Dave Plaugher, CFO
Kevin Creamer, President
Tom Hendrixson, Operations Dir
Kylie Miller, Programming Director
Lon Tegels, News Director
Fred Vobbe, Engineering Dir

WTLW *Digital Channel:* 44 *Virtual Channel:* 44; 165 kw; 679 ft.; N40 45 47 W84 10 59
1844 Baty Rd., Lima, OH 45805 US
(419) 339-4444, *Fax:* (419) 339-1736
www.wtlw.com
kbowers@wtlw.com
License: Lima, Allen County, OH held by American Christian Television Services Inc
Washington Law Firm: Wiley, Rein & Fielding
Nat'l Network: IND
Kevin Bowers, CEO
Jeff Klingler, Chief Engineer

Toledo, OH (DMA 73)

***WBGU-TV** *Digital Channel:* 27 *Virtual Channel:* 27; 153 kw; 1050 ft.; N41 8 12 W83 54 24
245 Troup Street, Bowling Green, OH 43403 US
(419) 372-2700, *Fax:* (419) 372-7048
www.wbgu.org
www@wbgu.bgsu.edu
License: Bowling Green, Wood County, OH held by Bowling Green State University
(acq 11-17-76;; *Washington Law Firm:* Cohn & Marks
Nat'l Network: PBS *Regional Network:* Ohio Educ. Telecommunications
Patrick Fitzgerald, General Manager
Ron Gargasz, Programming Director
Deb Boyce, Promotions Manager
Al Bowe, Chief Engineer
Mike Fitzpatrick, Asst Programming Manager

***WGTE-TV** *Digital Channel:* 29 *Virtual Channel:* 30; 49.5 kw; 1029 ft.; N41 39 26 W83 25 55
Mailing Address: 136 Huron Street, Toledo, OH 43692 US
Second Address: Box 30, Toledo, OH 43614
(419) 380-4600, *Fax:* (419) 380-4710
www.wgte.org
License: Toledo, Lucas County, OH held by Public Broadcasting Foundation of N.W. Ohio
Washington Law Firm: Schwartz, Woods & Miller
Nat'l Network: PBS *Regional Network:* Ohio Educ. Telecommunications
Marlon Kiser, CEO
Barbara Heslop, Operations Dir
Kelly Repka, General Sales Mgr
Darren LaShelle, Programming Director
Jen Homier, Promotions Manager
Ron Harrison, CFO
Lindsey Eberly, Sales Director

WLMB *Digital Channel:* 5 *Virtual Channel:* 40; 10 kw; 509 ft.; N41 44 41 W84 1 6
63 Dixie Highway, Rossford, OH 43460 US
(419) 874-8862, *Fax:* (419) 720-9563
www.wlmb.com
info@wlmb.com
License: Toledo, Lucas County, OH held by Dominion Broadcasting Inc
Washington Law Firm: Wiley, Rein & Fielding
Nat'l Network: IND
Jamey Schmitz, General Manager
Curt MIller, General Sales Mgr
Jeff Millslagle, Programming Director
Eric Jingst, Chief Engineer

WNWO-TV *Digital Channel:* 49 *Virtual Channel:* 24; 118 kw; 1342 ft.; N41 40 3 W83 21 22
1660 West Second Street, Cleveland, OH 44113 US
(419) 535-0024, *Fax:* (419) 535-0202
www.toledonthemove.com
news@nbc24.com
License: Toledo, Lucas County, OH held by Barrington Toledo License LLC.
Group Owner: Barrington Broadcasting Group, LLC.; (acq 8-11-2006; grpsl)
Nat'l Network: NBC *Nat'l Reps:* TeleRep
Hours of Local News Weekly: News progmg 22 hrs wkly
Jon Skorburg, General Manager
Hank Thompson, Chief Engineer

WTOL *Digital Channel:* 11 *Virtual Channel:* 11; 16.9 kw; 1001 ft.; N41 40 22 W83 22 47
730 North Summit, Toledo, OH 43604 US
(419) 248-1111, *Fax:* (419) 248-1177
www.wtol.com
news@wtol.com
License: Toledo, Lucas County, OH held by WTOL License Subsidiary LLC.
Group Owner: Raycom Media Inc.; (acq 1-31-2006; grpsl);
Washington Law Firm: Dow, Lohnes & Albertson
Nat'l Network: CBS *Nat'l Reps:* Harrington, Righter & Parsons
Size of News Staff: 50; *Hours of Local News Weekly:* news progmg 25 hrs wkly
Bob Chirdon, General Manager
Linda Blackburn, General Sales Mgr
Andi Roman, News Director
Steve Crum, Chief Engineer
Nancy Bright, National Sales Manager

WTVG *Digital Channel:* 13 *Virtual Channel:* 13; 16.7 kw; 1002 ft.; N41 41 0 W83 24 49
4247 Dorr Street, Toledo, OH 43607 US
(419) 531-1313, *Fax:* (419) 531-1399
www.13abc.com
License: Toledo, Lucas County, OH held by WTVG Inc.
Group Owner: ABC Inc.; (acq 1995; $155 million with WJRT-TV Flint, MI).; *Washington Law Firm:* Koteen & Naftalin
Nat'l Network: ABC
Size of News Staff: 30; *Hours of Local News Weekly:* news progmg 10 hrs wkly
David Zamichow, President
Ernestine Weathers, Operations Dir
Mary Gerken, General Sales Mgr
Tamara Rost, Programming Director
Brian Trauring, News Director
Barry Gries, Engineering Dir

WUPW *Digital Channel:* 46; 110 kw; 356 meters; N41 39 22 W83 26 41
Four SeaGate, Toledo, OH 33703
(419) 244-3600, *Fax:* (419) 244-8842
www.foxtoledo.com
news@foxtoledo.com
License: Toledo, Lucas County, OH held by WUPW License Sunsidiary LLC
Group Owner: American Spirit Media; (acq 11-8-2002; grpsl).;
Washington Law Firm: Fletcher, Heald & Hildreth PLC
Nat'l Network: Fox *Nat'l Reps:* Blair Television
Size of News Staff: 5; *Hours of Local News Weekly:* news progmg 5 hrs wkly
Gary Yoder, General Manager
Brian Lorenzen, General Sales Mgr
Cathy Stoner, Programming Director
Betsy Russell, Promotions Manager
Steve France, News Director
Steve Pietras, Engineering Dir

Wheeling, WV- Steubenville, OH (DMA 159)

***WOUC-TV** *Digital Channel:* 35; 759 kw vis; ant 1,263t/1,174g; N40 05 32 W81 17 19; *Rebroadcasting:* Rebroadcasts WOUB-TV Athens 100%.
9 S. College St., Athens, OH 45701
(740) 593-4555, *Fax:* (740) 593-0240
www.woub.org
woub@woub.org
License: Cambridge, Guernsey County, OH held by Ohio University
(acq 12-10-75;; *Washington Law Firm:* Cohn & Marks
Nat'l Network: PBS *Regional Network:* Ohio Educ. Telecommunications
Steve Skidmore, Operations Dir
Tom Hodson, General Manager
Loring Lovett, General Sales Mgr
Mark Brewer, Programming Director
Ted Ross, Operations Director
Jeffrey Harmison, Operations Manager
Joan Butcher, Programming Manager

WTOV-TV *Digital Channel:* 9 *Virtual Channel:* 9; 30 kw; 925 ft.; N40 20 33 W80 37 14
Mailing Address: 3839 - 4th Street, North, Suite 420, St. Petersburg, FL 33703 US
Second Address: 9 Red Donelly Plaza (also shipping), Mingo Junction, OH 43938
(740) 282-9999,(304) 232-6933, *Fax:* (740) 282-0350
www.wtov9.com
License: Steubenville, Jefferson County, OH held by WTOV Inc.
Group Owner: Cox Media Group; (acq 9-22-2000; $58 million);
Washington Law Firm: Dow,Lohnes & Albertson
Nat'l Network: NBC *Nat'l Reps:* TeleRep *Wire Services:* AP
Size of News Staff: 28; *Hours of Local News Weekly:* news progmg 22 hrs wkly
Chuck Robinson, CFO
Sandy Schwartz, President
Mike Seachman, Operations Dir
Tim McCoy, General Manager
Tom Pleva, General Sales Mgr
Kristin Murdock, Promotions Manager
Brandon Gobel, News Director
Don Fogle, Chief Engineer
Bruce Baker, Executive Vice President

Youngstown, OH (DMA 109)

WFMJ-TV *Digital Channel:* 20 *Virtual Channel:* 21; 460 kw; 968 ft.; N41 4 48 W80 38 25
101 West Boardman Street, Youngstown, OH 44503 US
(330) 744-8611, *Fax:* (330) 744-3402
www.wfmj.com
information@wfmj.com
License: Youngstown, Mahoning County, OH held by WFMJ Television Inc
(acq 7-14-93;; *Ownership:* NPM Inc.; *Washington Law Firm:* Fisher, Wayland, Cooper, Leader & Zaragoza
Nat'l Network: NBC; CW *Nat'l Reps:* Petry Television Inc.
Regional Reps: OAB *Wire Services:* AP
Size of News Staff: 30; *Hours of Local News Weekly:* news progmg 20 hrs wkly
John Grdic, Operations Dir
Jack Grdic, General Sales Mgr
Jack Stevenson, Promotions Manager
Mona Alexander, News Director
Bob Flis, Chief Engineer
Larry Bell, Chief Photographer
Kathie Brickman, National Sales Manager

WKBN-TV *Digital Channel:* 41 *Virtual Channel:* 27; 650 kw; 1444 ft.; N41 3 23.2 W80 38 43.7

7621 Little Avenue, Suite 506, Charlotte, NC 28266 US
(330) 782-1144
www.wkbn.com
License: Youngstown, Mahoning County, OH held by LIN License Company LLC
Group Owner: LIN Media; (acq 3-2-2007; $47 million);
Washington Law Firm: Wiley Rein LLP
Nat'l Network: CBS *Nat'l Reps:* Continental Television Sales
Size of News Staff: 50; *Hours of Local News Weekly:* news progmg 25 hrs wkly
John Amann, Operations Dir
David Coy, General Manager
Jill Duffy, General Sales Mgr
Phyllis Rappach, Programming Director
Gary Coursen, News Director
Thomas Zocolo, Chief Engineer
Nikki Manuel, Regional Sales Manager
RyanAllison, Sports Director
Don Guthrie, Weather Director

***WNEO** *Digital Channel:* 45; 500 kW; 830t/770g; N40 54 23 W80 54 40; *Population Served:* 450,000
Box 5191, 1750 Campus Center Dr, Kent, OH 44240
(330) 677-4549, *Fax:* (330) 678-0688
www.westernreservepublicmedia.org
questions@westernreservepublicmedia.org
License: Alliance, Stark County, OH held by Northeastern Educational TV of Ohio Inc
Washington Law Firm: Dow, Lohnes & Albertson
Nat'l Network: PBS
Hours of Local News Weekly: News progmg one hr wkly
Trina Cutter, President and Chief Executive Officer
Bill O'Neil, Station Manager
Don Freeman, Programming Director
Lisa Martinez, Vice President of Marketing and Development

WYTV *Digital Channel:* 36 *Virtual Channel:* 33; 1000 kw; 581 ft.; N41 3 43 W80 38 7
3800 Shady Run Road, Youngstown, OH 44502 US
(330) 782-1144, *Fax:* (330) 782-3504
www.wytv.com
License: Youngstown, Mahoning County, OH
Group Owner: Vaughan Media LLC; (acq 8-15-2007);
Washington Law Firm: Drinker Biddle & Reath LLP
Nat'l Network: ABC; MyNetworkTV
Size of News Staff: 26; *Hours of Local News Weekly:* news progmg 20 hrs wkly
Dave Coy, General Manager
Nikki Manuel, General Sales Mgr
Cheryl Huston, Programming Director
John Amann, Promotions Manager
Bill Castrovince, News Director
Tom Zocolo, Chief Engineer
Stan Boney, Weather Director

Zanesville, OH (DMA 203)

WHIZ-TV *Digital Channel:* 40 *Virtual Channel:* 18; 620 kw; 554 ft.; N39 55 42 W81 59 7
629 Downard Road, Zanesville, OH 43701 US
(740) 452-5431, *Fax:* (740) 452-6553
www.whiznews.com
slauka@whiznews.com
License: Zanesville, Muskingum County, OH held by Southeastern Ohio TV System
Washington Law Firm: Leventhal, Senter & Lerman
Nat'l Network: NBC
Size of News Staff: 14; *Hours of Local News Weekly:* news progmg 10 hrs wkly
N.J. Littick, Chairman
H.C. Littick, President
Doug Pickrell, General Sales Mgr
Brian Wagner, Programming Director
George Hiotis, News Director
J. T. Raymond, Sports Commentator
Carolyn Rider, Traffic Manager
Wesley Sass,Weather Director

Oklahoma

Oklahoma City, OK (DMA 45)

KAUT-TV *Digital Channel:* 40 *Virtual Channel:* 43; 1000 kw; 1433 ft.; N35 35 51.89 W97 29 22.06
1501 M Street, N.W., Suite 1100, Washington, DC 20005 US
(405) 478-2239, *Fax:* (405) 478-6205
www.ok43.com
captioning.complaint@ok43.com
License: Oklahoma City, Oklahoma County, OK held by Local TV Oklahoma License LLC.
Group Owner: Local TV LLC; (acq 5-7-2007; grpsl)
Nat'l Network: MYTV
Wes Milbourn, Station Manager
Stacy Johnson, Programming Director
Mitch Morgan, Chief Engineer

***KETA-TV** *Digital Channel:* 13; 50 kw; 1,525t/1,578g; N35 32 58 W97 29 50; *Population Served:* 1,300,000
Box 14190, 7403 N. Kelley Avenue, Oklahoma City, OK 73113
(405) 848-8501, *Fax:* (405) 841-9216
www.keta.tv
programming@keta.com
License: Oklahoma City, Oklahoma County, OK held by Oklahoma Educational TV Authority
Washington Law Firm: DowLohnes
Nat'l Network: PBS
Size of News Staff: 8; *Hours of Local News Weekly:* news progmg 3 hrs wkly
Janette Thornbrue, Operations Dir
Bill Thrash, Station Manager
Mark Norman, Programming Director
Ashley Barcum, Promotions Manager
Bob Sands, News Director
Earle Conners, Engineering Dir
Richard Ladd, Chief Engineer
JohnMcCarroll, Executive Director

KFOR-TV *Digital Channel:* 27; 60 kw; 1,540t/1,602g; N35 34 07 W97 29 20; *Population Served:* 2,177,200
444 E. Britton Rd., Oklahoma City, OK 73113
(405) 424-4444, *Fax:* (405) 478-6228
www.kfor.com
License: Oklahoma City, Oklahoma County, OK held by Local TV Oklahoma License LLC.
Group Owner: Local TV LLC; (acq 5-7-2007; grpsl); *Washington Law Firm:* Dow Lohnes
Nat'l Network: NBC *Nat'l Reps:* Millennium Sales & Marketing
Wire Services: AP
Size of News Staff: 70; *Hours of Local News Weekly:* news progmg 38 hrs wkly
Shannon Gottschalk, Controller
Jim Boyer, General Manager
Wes Milbourn, Station Manager
Wes Milbourn, General Sales Mgr
Joe Kozlowski, Promotions Manager
Mary Ann Eckstein, News Director
Phil Switzer, Technology Director
Mikelsbell, Chief Engineer
Brian White, Interactive Director

KOCB *Digital Channel:* 33 *Virtual Channel:* 34; 900 kw; 1501 ft.; N35 32 58 W97 29 18
10706 Beaver Dam Road, Cockeysville, MD 21030 US
(405) 478-3434, *Fax:* (405) 478-4343, (405) 475-9163(Sales)
www.cwokc.com
License: Oklahoma City, Oklahoma County, OK held by KOCB Licensee L.L.C.
Group Owner: Sinclair Broadcast Group Inc.; (acq 1996; $63 million with WDKY-TV Danville, KY).
Nat'l Network: CW *Nat'l Reps:* Harrington, Righter & Parsons
John Rossi, General Manager
Dan Loving, General Sales Mgr
Joe Spadea, News Director
Steve Bottkol, Engineering Dir
Steve Pennington, Chief Engineer
Gerry Klingbeil, Local Sales Manager
Jimmy Cola, National Sales Manager

KOCM *Digital Channel:* 46 *Virtual Channel:* 46; 50 kw; 1365 ft.; N35 35 52 W97 29 22
2504 Countryside Dr, Silver Spring, MD 20905 US
(817) 571-1229,(405) 292-4600, *Fax:* (817) 571-7458
www.daystartv.net
cpmments@daystar.com
License: Norman, Cleveland County, OK held by Word of God Fellowship Inc.
Nat'l Network: IND
Joni Show, General Manager

KOCO-TV *Digital Channel:* 7 *Virtual Channel:* 5; 100 kw vis, 14.5 kw aur; 1,519t/1,562g; N35 33 45 W97 29 24; *Population Served:* 663,200
1300 E. Britton Rd., Oklahoma City, OK 10106
(405) 478-3000, *Fax:* (405) 475-5242
www.koco.com
License: Oklahoma City, Oklahoma County, OK held by Ohio/Oklahoma Hearst Television
Group Owner: Hearst Television Inc.; (acq 7-16-97; grpsl).;
Washington Law Firm: Brooks, Pierce, McLendon
Nat'l Network: ABC *Nat'l Reps:* HRP Television Sales *Wire Services:* NWS (National Weather Ser; AP
Size of News Staff: 55; *Hours of Local News Weekly:* 30 hrs news progrg wkly
Brent Hensley, President
Christine Toldt, Assistant Chief Engineer
Brent Hensley, General Manager
Joe Meridith, General Sales Mgr
Ashley Johnson, Programming Director
Randal Gage, Promotions Manager
Stephanie Croswait, NewsDirector
David Evans, Engineering Dir

KOKH-TV *Digital Channel:* 24 *Virtual Channel:* 25; 1000 kw; 1561 ft.; N35 32 58 W97 29 18
18 Newbury Street, Boston, MA 02116 US
(405) 843-2525, *Fax:* (405) 478-4343
www.okcfox.com
License: Oklahoma City, Oklahoma County, OK held by Sullivan Broadcasting Co. IV Inc.
Group Owner: Sinclair Broadcast Group Inc.; (acq 1998; grpsl).
Nat'l Network: FOX *Nat'l Reps:* Harrington, Righter & Parsons
John Rossi, General Manager
Dan Loving, General Sales Mgr
Joe Spadea, News Director
Steve Bottkol, Engineering Dir
Steve Pennington, Chief Engineer
Tim Murphy, Local Sales Manager
Jimmy Cola, National Sales Manager

KOPX-TV *Digital Channel:* 50; 2,690 kw vis; 787t; N35 34 24 W97 29 08
13424 Railway Dr., Oklahoma City, OK 73114
(405) 478-9562, *Fax:* (405) 751- 6867
www.ionline.tv
License: Oklahoma City, Oklahoma County, OK held by Paxson Oklahoma City License Inc.
Group Owner: ION Media Networks Inc.; (acq 9-27-96; $6.395 million); *Washington Law Firm:* Dow, Lohnes and Albertson PLLC
Nat'l Network: ION Television
Brandon Burgess, President
Carol Wright-Holzhaver, Operations Dir
Steve Brooks, General Manager
Les Moorman, Programming Director
David Glenn, Engineering Dir
Rod Roberts, Chief Engineer
Steve Appel, President

KSBI *Digital Channel:* 51 *Virtual Channel:* 52; 1000 kw; 1502 ft.; N35 35 52 W97 29 22
P.O. Box 26128, Oklahoma City, OK 73126 US
(405) 631-7335, *Fax:* (405) 631-7367
www.ksbitv.com
info@ksbitv.com
License: Oklahoma City, Oklahoma County, OK held by Family Broadcasting Group Inc
Washington Law Firm: Booth, Freret, Imlay & Tepper
Nat'l Network: IND
Brady Brus, CEO
Cody Blount, Chief Engineer

KTBO-TV *Digital Channel:* 15 *Virtual Channel:* 14; 700 kw; 1175 ft.; N35 34 35 W97 29 9
3705 NW 63rd., Oklahoma City, OK 73116 US
(405) 848-1414
www.tbn.org
comments@tbn.org
License: Oklahoma City, Oklahoma County, OK held by Trinity Broadcasting of Oklahoma City Inc.
Group Owner: Trinity Broadcasting Network; *Washington Law Firm:* Joseph E. Dunne III
Nat'l Network: TRINITY BROADCA
Paul Crouch, President
Liuda Cook, General Manager
Jan Crouch, Promotions Manager
Ken Howerton, Chief Engineer

KTUZ-TV *Digital Channel:* 29 *Virtual Channel:* 30; 1000 kw; 1555 ft.; N35 33 36 W97 29 7
6200 Valeria Ln, El Paso, TX 79912 US
(405) 616-9900, *Fax:* (405) 616-5511
www.ktuztv.com
info@ktuz-tv.com
License: Shawnee, Pottawatomie County, OK held by Oklahoma Land Company LLC.
Group Owner: Tyler Media Broadcasting Corp.; (acq 9-30-2004; $12,375,000).
Nat'l Network: TELEMUNDO
Foreign Language Programming
Armando Rubio, General Manager
Chris Fusselman, General Sales Mgr

KUOK *Digital Channel:* 35 *Virtual Channel:* 35; 8 kw; 646 ft.; N36 16 6 W99 26 56
1 Shackle Ford Dr, Suite 400, Little Rock, AR 72211 US
(405) 616-5500, *Fax:* (405) 616-5511
www.TylerMedia.com
Lee.R@TylerMedia.com
License: Woodward, Woodward County, OK held by Oklahoma Land Company, LLC
7/1/2009; *Ownership:* Tyler Broadcasting Corporation
Foreign Language Programming
Ty Tyler, General Manager
Lee Redick, General Sales Mgr

***KWET** *Digital Channel:* 8; 30 kw; ant 994t/958g; N35 35 36 W99 40 01; *Population Served:* 647,390
Mailing Address: Box 14190, Oklahoma City, OK 73113
Second Address: 7403 N. Kelley Ave., Oklahoma City, OK 73111
(405) 848-8501, *Fax:* (405) 841-9216
www.oeta.tv
License: Cheyenne, Roger Mills County, OK held by Oklahoma Educational TV Authority
Washington Law Firm: DowLohnes
Nat'l Network: PBS
Janette Thorton, Operations Dir
Bill Thrash, Station Manager
Holly Emig, Programming Director
Ashley Barcum, Promotions Manager
Dick Pryor, News Director
Mark Norton, Engineering Dir
Richard Ladd, Chief Engineer
Dan Skiedel,Executive Director

KWTV-DT *Digital Channel:* 39; 316 kw vis, 33.9 kw aur; ant 1,525t/1,537g; N35 32 68 W97 29 50; *Population Served:* 582,000
7401 N. Kelley Ave., Oklahoma City, OK 73111
(405) 843-6641, *Fax:* (405) 841-9926
www.news9.com
License: Oklahoma City, Oklahoma County, OK held by Griffin Television OKC, LLC
Group Owner: Griffin Communications L.L.C.; (acq 7-1-98).;
Washington Law Firm: Holland & Knight
Nat'l Network: CBS *Nat'l Reps:* TeleRep *Wire Services:* CBS; CNN
Size of News Staff: 80; *Hours of Local News Weekly:* news progmg 33 hrs wkly
Rob Krier, COO
Wade Deaver, General Sales Mgr
Kim Eubank, Programming Director
Jenny Monroe, News Director
Julie Cameron, Engineering Dir
Linda Mason, Traffic Manager

Sherman, TX-Ada, OK (DMA 161)

KTEN *Digital Channel:* 26 *Virtual Channel:* 10; 1000 kw; 1398 ft.; N34 21 34 W96 33 34
P.O. Box 549, Hampton, VA 23669 US
(903) 337-4000, *Fax:* (908) 465-1207,(903) 465-1368
www.kten.com
10news@kten.com
License: Ada, Pontotoc County, OK held by Channel 49 Acquisition Corp
Washington Law Firm: Brooks, Pierce, McLendon, Humprey & Leonard
Nat'l Network: NBC; CW *Nat'l Reps:* Continental Television Sales *Wire Services:* AP
Size of News Staff: 25; *Hours of Local News Weekly:* news progmg 36 hrs wkly
Asa Jessee, General Manager
Brian Capaldo, Station Manager
Ken Braswell, General Sales Mgr
TBD, News Director
Kris Anderson, Chief Engineer

Tulsa, OK (DMA 61)

KDOR-TV *Digital Channel:* 17 *Virtual Channel:* 17; 1000 kw; 1043 ft.; N36 30 59 W95 46 10
2120 N. Yellowood Ave., Broken Arrow, OK 74012 US
(918) 250-0777, *Fax:* (918) 461-8817
www.tbn.org
kdor@tbn.org
License: Bartlesville, Washington County, OK held by Trinity Broadcasting Network
Group Owner: Trinity Broadcasting Network; (acq 5-8-2000; grpsl).
Nat'l Network: TRINITY BROADCA
Paul Crouch, CEO
Craig Nelson, General Manager

KGEB *Digital Channel:* 49 *Virtual Channel:* 53; 1,770 kw vis, 177 kw aur; 597t/672g; N36 02 39 W95 57 11
7777 S. Lewis Ave., Tulsa, OK 74101
(918) 488-5300, *Fax:* (918) 495-7388
www.kgeb.net
kgeb@oru.edu
License: Tulsa, Tulsa County, OK held by University Broadcasting Inc
Walter Richardson, General Manager
Amy Calvert, General Sales Mgr
Christi Vanover, Programming Director

KJRH-TV *Digital Channel:* 56 *Virtual Channel:* 2; 100 kw vis, 10 kw aur; ant 1,828t; N36 01 15 W95 40 32; *Population Served:* 1,143,000
3701 S. Peoria Ave., Tulsa, OK 74105-3269
(918) 743-2222, *Fax:* (918) 748-1460
www.kjrh.com
news@kjrh.com
License: Tulsa, Tulsa County, OK held by Scripps Howard Broadcasting Co.
Group Owner: The E. W. Scripps Co.; (acq 1-1-71; $7.8 million);
Washington Law Firm: Baker & Hostetler
Nat'l Network: NBC *Nat'l Reps:* Eagle Television Sales
Size of News Staff: 50; *Hours of Local News Weekly:* news progmg 26.5 hrs wkly
Ken Lowe, CEO
Donna Wilson, VP/General Manager
Joe Brunnhuber, Sales Director
Karen Framel, Research Director
Susan D'Astoli, News Director
Dale Vennes, Chief Engineer
Samantha Knowlton, creative Services/Community RelationsDirector
Al Jerkens, Sports Director
Tracy Hardison, Traffic Manager

KMYT-TV *Digital Channel:* 42 *Virtual Channel:* 41; 900 kw; 1250 ft.; N36 1 36 W95 40 44
115 East Travis, Suite 1427, San Antonio, TX 78205 US
(918) 388-5100, *Fax:* (918) 493-5739
www.my41tulsa.com
License: Tulsa, Tulsa County, OK held by Newport Television License LLC.
Group Owner: Newport Television LLC; (acq 3-14-2008; grpsl);
Washington Law Firm: Covington & Burling
Nat'l Network: MYNETWORK TV *Nat'l Reps:* Millennium Sales & Marketing
Sandy DiPasquale, President
Holly Allen, Operations Dir
Jim Hanning, General Sales Mgr
Chooi Ning, Programming Director
Amber Musselman, Promotions Manager
Brian Egan, Chief Engineer
Stephanie Spry, Local Sales Manager
KariBarrett, National Sales Manager
Joan King, Traffic Manager

***KOED-TV** *Digital Channel:* 11 *Virtual Channel:* 11; 47 kw; 1709 ft.; N36 1 15 W95 40 32
P.O. Box 14190, Oklahoma City, OK 73113 US
405-848-8501, *Fax:* 405-841-9216
www.oeta.tv
License: Tulsa, Tulsa County, OK held by Oklahoma Educational TV Authority
Washington Law Firm: DowLohnes
Nat'l Network: PBS
Size of News Staff: 7; *Hours of Local News Weekly:* 3
Bill Thrash, Station Manager
Mark Norman, Programming Director
Liz Exon, News Director
Roger Newton, Chief Engineer
John McCarroll, Executive Director

***KOET** *Digital Channel:* 31 *Virtual Channel:* 3; 1000 kw; 1195 ft.; N35 11 1 W95 20 19
P.O. Box 14190, Oklahoma City, OK 73113 US
(405) 848-8501, *Fax:* (405) 841-9216
www.oeta.tv
License: Eufaula, Oklahoma County, OK held by Oklahoma Educational Television Authority
Washington Law Firm: DowLohnes
Nat'l Network: PBS
Mike Palmer, Operations Dir
Bill Thrash, Station Manager
Mark Norman, Programming Director
Ashley Barcum, Promotions Manager
Bob Sands, News Director
Earle Connors, Engineering Dir
Richard Ladd, Chief Engineer
John McCarroll,Executive Director

KOKI-TV *Digital Channel:* 22 *Virtual Channel:* 23; 1000 kw; 1312 ft.; N36 1 36 W95 40 44
200 Concord Plaza, Suite 600, San Antonio, TX 78216 US
(918) 491-0023, *Fax:* (918) 491-6650
www.fox23.com
License: Tulsa, Tulsa County, OK held by Newport Television License LLC.
Group Owner: Newport Television LLC; (acq 3-14-2008; grpsl);
Washington Law Firm: Covington & Burling
Nat'l Network: FOX
Size of News Staff: 38; *Hours of Local News Weekly:* news progmg 7 hrs wkly
Sandy DiPasquale, President
Craig Millar, Operations Dir
Holly Allen, General Manager
Chooi Ning, Programming Director
Deedra Determan, Promotions Manager
Melanie Henry, News Director
Brian Egan, Chief Engineer
Jim Hanning,National Sales Manager

KOTV-DT *Digital Channel:* 45; 100 kw vis, 50 kw aur; ant 1,885t/1,849g; N36 01 15 W95 40 32; *Population Served:* 1,893,300
Mailing Address: Box 6, Tulsa, OK 74101
Second Address: 302 S. Frankfort, Tulsa, OK 74120
(918) 732-6000, *Fax:* (918) 732-6016
www.newson6.com
License: Tulsa, Tulsa County, OK held by Griffin Licensing L.L.C.
Group Owner: Griffin Communications L.L.C.; (acq 12-6-2000; $82 million); *Washington Law Firm:* Dow, Lohnes & Albertson
Nat'l Network: CBS *Nat'l Reps:* TeleRep
Size of News Staff: 40
Ted Strickland, CFO
John Quesnel, Operations Dir
John Trook, General Sales Mgr
Christy Sheppler, Programming Director
Ron Harig, News Director
Gerald Weaver, Chief Engineer
Rob Krier, COO
Cheryl Sutton, Business Director
Donita Quesnel, Public Service Director
Travis Meyer, Weather Director

KQCW-DT *Digital Channel:* 20; 5,000 kw vis; ant 823t/777g; N35 45 08 W95 48 15
Mailing Address: Box 6, Tulsa, OK 74101
Second Address: 233 South Detroit Ave., Tulsa, OK 74120
(918) 732-6000, *Fax:* (918) 732-6016
www.tulsacw.com
License: Muskogee, Muskogee County, OK held by Griffin Licensing L.L.C.
Group Owner: Griffin Communications L.L.C.; (acq 12-9-2005; $14.5 million)
Nat'l Network: CW
Rob Krier, COO
John Quesnel, Operations Dir
John Trook, General Sales Mgr
Gerald Weaver, Chief Engineer
Donita Quesnel, Public Affairs Director

***KRSC-TV** *Digital Channel:* 36 *Virtual Channel:* 35; 2,750 kw vis; 840t; N36 24 05 W95 36 33
RSU Public Television, 1701 W. Will Rogers Blvd., Claremore, OK 74017
(800) 823-7210, *Fax:* (918) 343-7952
www.rsupublictv.org
krsc-tv@rsu.edu
License: Claremore, Rogers County, OK held by Board of Regents of Oklahoma Colleges
Washington Law Firm: Schwartz, Woods & Miller
Foreign Language Programming
Dale McKinney, Operations Dir
Dan Schiedel, General Manager
Jennifer Sterling, Programming Director
Jim Mertins, Chief Engineer
OPEN, Traf Coordinator

KTPX-TV *Digital Channel:* 28; 5,000 kw vis, 500 kw aur; 1,770t; N35 50 02 W96 07 28; *Population Served:* 887,000
5800 E. Skelly Dr., Suite 101, Tulsa, OK 74135
(918) 664-1044 (817) 633-6843(Sales), *Fax:* (918) 664-4913
www.ionline.tv
License: Okmulgee, Okmulgee County, OK held by Paxson Tulsa License Inc.
Group Owner: ION Media Networks Inc.; (acq 8-21-98; $404,000 for 51% of stock).
Nat'l Network: ION Television

Peter De Les Dernier, Station Manager
Matthew Pate, General Sales Mgr
Janeen Rode, Programming Director

KTUL *Digital Channel:* 10 *Virtual Channel:* 8; 15 kw; 1896 ft.; N35 58 8 W95 36 55
Mailing Address: P.O. Box 8, Tulsa, OK 74101 US
Second Address: 3333 S. 29th West Ave., Tulsa, OK 74107
(918) 445-8888, *Fax:* (918) 445-9316
www.ktul.com
License: Tulsa, Tulsa County, OK held by KTUL L.L.C.
Group Owner: Allbritton Communications Co.; (acq 4-83; grpsl);
Washington Law Firm: Hogan & Hartson
Nat'l Network: ABC *Wire Services:* AP
Size of News Staff: 50; *Hours of Local News Weekly:* news progmg 17 hrs wkly
Pat Baldwin, President
Roger Herring, Operations Dir
Carol Jones, General Sales Mgr
Amy Miller, Programming Director
Deborah Kurin, Promotions Manager
Sean McLaughlin, News Director
Larry Nitz, Promotions Manager
Randi Carson,Public Affairs Director
Marcia Baker, Regional Sales Manager

KWHB *Digital Channel:* 47 *Virtual Channel:* 47; 50 kw; 1509 ft.; N36 1 15 W95 40 32
11414 East 58th Street, Tulsa, OK 74146 US
(918) 254-4701, *Fax:* (918) 254-5614
www.lesea.com
License: Tulsa, Tulsa County, OK held by LeSea Broadcasting.
Group Owner: Le Sea Broadcasting; (acq 5-14-86; $3.4 million;;
Washington Law Firm: John Fiorini
Nat'l Network: IND
Peter Sumrall, CEO
Royal Aills, General Manager
Keith Krebbs, Station Manager

Wichita Falls, TX & Lawton, OK (DMA 145)

KSWO-TV *Digital Channel:* 11 *Virtual Channel:* 7; 316 kw vis, 63.1 kw aur; 1,050t/1,059g; N34 12 55 W98 43 13;
Population Served: 300,000
Box 708, Hwy. 7, Lawton, OK 23502
(580) 355-7000, *Fax:* (580) 357-3811
www.kswo.com
License: Lawton, Comanche County, OK held by KSWO TV Inc.
Group Owner: R.H. Drewry Group
Nat'l Network: ABC
Larry Patton, General Manager
Cindy Coleman, General Sales Mgr
Todd Young, Promotions Manager
David Bradley, News Director
Nathan Bowers, Chief Engineer

Oregon

Bend, OR (DMA 192)

***KOAB-TV** *Digital Channel:* 11 *Virtual Channel:* 3; 90 kw; 804 ft.; N44 4 41 W121 19 57
7140 Sw Macadam Avenue, Portland, OR 97219 US
(503) 244-9900; (800) 241-8123, *Fax:* (503) 293-1919
www.opb.org
membercenter@opb.org
License: Bend, Deschutes County, OR held by Oregon Public Broadcasting
(acq 9-20-93; grpsl;; *Washington Law Firm:* Schwartz, Woods & Miller
Nat'l Network: PBS
Steve Bass, CEO
Dan Metziga, General Sales Mgr

KOHD *Digital Channel:* 51 *Virtual Channel:* 51; 84.1 kw; 675 ft.; N44 4 40.6 W121 19 56.9
US
(541) 485-5611, *Fax:* (541) 342-1568
www.kohd.com
genmgr@kohd.com
License: Bend, Deschutes County, OR held by Three Sisters Broadcasting LLC.
Group Owner: Chambers Communications Corp.
Nat'l Network: ABC
Jerry Upham, General Manager

KTVZ *Digital Channel:* 21 *Virtual Channel:* 21; 131.8 kw; 646 ft.; N44 4 40 W121 19 49
2178 Commons Parkway, Okemos, MI 48864 US
(541) 383-2121, *Fax:* (541) 382-1616
www.ktvz.com
ktvz@ktvz.com
License: Bend, Deschutes County, OR held by NPG of Oregon Inc.
Group Owner: News-Press & Gazette Co.; (acq 4-17-2002; $18.9 million)
Nat'l Network: NBC; CW; Fox; Telemundo (Spanish) *Nat'l Reps:* Continental Television Sales
Foreign Language Programming; Size of News Staff: 19; *Hours of Local News Weekly:* news progmg 20 hrs wkly
Dan Bauer, CFO
Chris Gallu, General Manager
Eric Bradley, Station Manager
Mike Bothwell, News Director
Amador Velasquez, Chief Engineer
Bob Singer, DOS

Eugene, OR (DMA 119)

KCBY-TV *Digital Channel:* 11 *Virtual Channel:* 11; 5 kw; 630 ft.; N43 23 26 W124 7 46
100 - 4th Avenue, North, Seattle, WA 98109 US
(541) 269-1111, *Fax:* (541) 269-7464
www.kcby.com
kcroes@kcby.com
License: Coos Bay, Coos County, OR held by Fisher Broadcasting - Oregon TV L.L.C.
Group Owner: Fisher Communications Inc.; (acq 12-4-2001; grpsl); *Washington Law Firm:* Dow, Lohnes & Albertson
Nat'l Network: CBS
Size of News Staff: 4
Ken Cross, Station Manager
Paul Greene, Programming Director
Dino Francois, Promotions Manager

***KEPB-TV** *Digital Channel:* 29 *Virtual Channel:* 28; 100 kw; 1322 ft.; N44 0 7 W123 6 53
7140 Sw Macadam Avenue, Portland, OR 97219 US
(503) 244-9900; (800) 241-8123, *Fax:* (503) 293-1919
www.opb.org
membercenter@opb.org
License: Eugene, Lane County, OR held by Oregon Public Broadcasting.
Nat'l Network: PBS
Felipe Olvera, Engineering Dir

KEZI *Digital Channel:* 9; 316 kw vis, 47.4 kw aur; 1,768t/495g; N44 06 57 W122 59 57; *Population Served:* 279,240
Mailing Address: Box 7009, Springfield, OR 97401
Second Address: 2975 Chad Dr., Eugene, OR 97408
(541) 485-5611, *Fax:* (541) 342-1568
www.kezi.com
kezi@kezi.com
License: Eugene, Lane County, OR held by KEZI Inc.
Group Owner: Chambers Communications Corp.; (acq 8-30-83; $18 million)
Nat'l Network: ABC
Size of News Staff: 28; *Hours of Local News Weekly:* news program 22 hrs wkly
Scott Chambers, CEO
Dana Siebert, COO

KLSR-TV *Digital Channel:* 31 *Virtual Channel:* 34; 88 kw; 1220 ft.; N44 0 4 W123 6 45
P. O. Box 1489, Medford, OR 97501 US
(541) 683-2525,(541) 683-3434, *Fax:* (541) 681-3356
klsrtv.com
mark@oregonfox.com
License: Eugene, Lane County, OR held by California Oregon Broadcasting Inc.
Group Owner: California Oregon Broadcasting Inc.; (acq 9-1-94; $2.65 million;; *Washington Law Firm:* Fletcher, Heald & Hildreth
Nat'l Network: FOX
Patricia Smullin, President
Johnathon Johnson, Operations Dir
Mark Metzger, General Manager
Sandra Dornon-Belmont, Programming Director
Tim Hershiser, Engineering Dir
Scott Bonnell, National Sales Manager
Steve Woodward, PublicAffairs Director
Jeannie Crane, Traffic Manager

KMCB *Digital Channel:* 22 *Virtual Channel:* 23; 10 kw; 587 ft.; N43 23 39 W124 7 56; *Rebroadcasting:* Satellite of KMTR(TV) Eugene.
1333 New Hampshire Ave., N.W., Suite 1000, Washington, DC 20036 US
(541) 746-1600, *Fax:* (541) 747-0866
www.kmtr.com
License: Coos Bay, Coos County, OR held by Newport Television License LLC.
Group Owner: Newport Television LLC; (acq 3-14-2008; grpsl);
Washington Law Firm: Covington & Burling
Nat'l Network: NBC *Nat'l Reps:* Millennium Sales & Marketing
Regional Reps: Blair. *Wire Services:* AP
Hours of Local News Weekly: News progmg 22 hrs wkly
Cambra Ward, Operations Dir
Cambra Ward, General Manager
Carl Sundberg, Operations Manager

KMTR *Digital Channel:* 17 *Virtual Channel:* 16; 70 kw; 1552 ft.; N44 6 57 W122 59 57
1333 New Hampshire Ave., N.W., Suite 1000, Washington, DC 20036 US
(541) 746-1600, *Fax:* (541) 747-0866
www.kmtr.com
License: Eugene, Lane County, OR held by Newport Television License LLC.
Group Owner: Newport Television LLC; (acq 3-14-2008; grpsl);
Washington Law Firm: Covington & Burling
Nat'l Network: NBC *Nat'l Reps:* Millennium Sales & Marketing
Regional Reps: Blair. *Wire Services:* AP
Size of News Staff: 22; *Hours of Local News Weekly:* news progmg 15 hrs wkly
Kurt Thelen, Operations Dir

***KOAC-TV** *Digital Channel:* 7 *Virtual Channel:* 7; 18.1 kw; 1171 ft.; N44 38 25 W123 16 25
7140 Sw Macadam Avenue, Portland, OR 97219 US
(503) 244-9900; (800) 241-8123, *Fax:* (503) 293-1919
www.opb.org
membercenter@opb.org
License: Corvallis, Benton County, OR held by Oregon Public Broadcasting
(acq 1993; grpsl;; *Washington Law Firm:* Schwartz, Woods & Miller
Nat'l Network: PBS *Wire Services:* UPI
Steve Bass, CEO
Mary Gardner, Programming Director
Morgan Holm, News Director
Don McKay, Chief Engineer

KPIC *Digital Channel:* 19 *Virtual Channel:* 4; 50 kw; 958 ft.; N43 14 8 W123 19 18; *Rebroadcasting:* Satellite of KVAL-TV Eugene.
12716 Riverside Drive, North Hollywood, CA 91607 US
(541) 672-4481, *Fax:* (541) 672-4482
www.kpic.com
sales@kpic.com
License: Roseburg, Douglas County, OR held by South West Oregon TV Broadcasting Corp.
Group Owner: Fisher Communications Inc.; (acq 1999; grpsl).;
Washington Law Firm: Dow, Lohnes & Albertson
Nat'l Network: CBS
Size of News Staff: 4; *Hours of Local News Weekly:* news progmg 14 hrs wkly
Peter Smith, Operations Dir
Connie Williamson, Station Manager
Paul Greene, Programming Director
Dino Francois, Promotions Manager
Mike Hill, Chief Engineer

KTCW *Digital Channel:* 45 *Virtual Channel:* 46; 12 kw; 358 ft.; N43 12 22 W123 21 56; *Rebroadcasting:* Satellite of KMTR Eugene.
1333 New Hampshire Ave., N.W., Suite 1000, Washington, DC 20036 US
(541) 746-1600, *Fax:* (541) 747-0866
www.kmtr.com
License: Roseburg, Douglas County, OR held by Newport Television License LLC.
Group Owner: Newport Television LLC; (acq 3-14-2008; grpsl);
Washington Law Firm: Covington & Burling
Nat'l Network: NBC *Wire Services:* AP
Hours of Local News Weekly: News progmg 22 hrs wkly
Cambra Ward, Operations Dir
Mike Chisholm, General Sales Mgr
Robert McMichaels, News Director
Carl Sundberg, Operations Manager

KTVC *Digital Channel:* 18 *Virtual Channel:* 36; 50 kw; 698 ft.; N43 14 9 W123 19 16; *Station Currently Dark*
One East Broadway #100, Eugene, OR 97401 US
(541) 474-3089, *Fax:* (541) 474-9409
www.blbn.org
kbln@betterlifetv.tv
License: Roseburg, Douglas County, OR held by Better Life Television, Inc.
Group Owner: Better Life Ministries; (acq 4/16/09)

Nat'l Network: RTN
Ron Davis, General Manager
William Whitt, Chief Engineer

KVAL-TV *Digital Channel:* 13 *Virtual Channel:* 13; 30.64 kw; 1447 ft.; N44 0 7 W123 6 53
Mailing Address: 100 - 4th Avenue, North, Seattle, WA 98109 US
Second Address: 4575 Blanton Rd., Eugene, OR 97405
(541) 342-4961, *Fax:* (541) 342-7252 (sales),(541) 342-2635 (admin),(541
www.kval.com
kval@kval.com
License: Eugene, Lane County, OR held by Fisher Broadcasting - Oregon TV L.L.C.
Group Owner: Fisher Communications Inc.; (acq 12-4-01; grpsl).; *Washington Law Firm:* Pillsbury, Winthrop & Pittman
Nat'l Network: CBS *Regional Reps:* Petry
Hours of Local News Weekly: News progmg 17 hrs wkly
Colleen Brown, CEO
Coleen Brown, President
Greg Raschio, Operations Dir
Paul Greene, Operations Manager

Medford-Klamath Falls, OR (DMA 140)

KBLN *Digital Channel:* 30 *Virtual Channel:* 30; 2 kw; 2146 ft.; N42 22 56 W123 16 29
10255 Sw Arctic Drive, Beaverton, OR 97005 US
(541) 474-3089, *Fax:* (541) 474-9409
www.betterlifetv.tv
kbln@betterlifetv.tv
License: Grants Pass, Josephine County, OR held by Better Life Television Inc
Nat'l Network: 3 ANGLS
Marta Davis, General Manager
Ron Davis, Station Manager

KDKF *Digital Channel:* 29 *Virtual Channel:* 31; 4.87 kw; 2136 ft.; N42 5 50 W121 37 59; *Rebroadcasting:* Satellite of KDRV(TV) Medford, OR.
P.O. Box 7009, Eugene, OR 97401 US
(541) 883-3131, *Fax:* (541) 883-8931
www.kdkf.com
kdkf@kdkf.com
License: Klamath Falls, Klamath County, OR held by Soda Mountain Broadcasting Inc.
Group Owner: Chambers Communications Corp.; (acq 12-5-2001).; *Washington Law Firm:* Fletcher, Heald & Hildreth
Nat'l Network: ABC
Size of News Staff: 20; *Hours of Local News Weekly:* news progmg 12 hrs wkly
Maiwi Renard, General Manager
Rick Carrara, Chief Engineer

KDRV *Digital Channel:* 12 *Virtual Channel:* 12; 16.9 kw; 2700 ft.; N42 41 30 W123 13 44
1090 Knutson Avenue, Medford, OR 97504 US
(541) 773-1212, *Fax:* (541) 779-9261
www.kdrv.com
kdrv@kdrv.com
License: Medford, Jackson County, OR held by Soda Mountain Broadcasting Inc.
Group Owner: Chambers Communications Corp.; (acq 12-5-2001).; *Washington Law Firm:* Fisher, Wayland, Cooper, Leader & Zaragoza
Nat'l Network: ABC *Nat'l Reps:* Millennium Sales & Marketing
Wire Services: AP
Size of News Staff: 12; *Hours of Local News Weekly:* news progmg 20 hrs wkly
Renard Maiuri, General Manager
Rick Carrara, Chief Engineer

***KFTS** *Digital Channel:* 33 *Virtual Channel:* 22; 9.6 kw; 2129 ft.; N42 5 50 W121 37 59; *Rebroadcasting:* Satellite of KSYS(TV) Medford 100%.
Mailing Address: 34 South Fir Street, Medford, OR 97501 US
Second Address: 28 South Fir Street, Suite 200, Medford, OR 97501
(541) 779-0808, *Fax:* (541) 779-2178
www.soptv.org
License: Klamath Falls, Klamath County, OR held by Southern Oregon Public Television Inc
Nat'l Network: PBS
Mark Stanislawski, CEO
Tom Werner, Programming Director

KMVU-DT *Digital Channel:* 26; 110 kw vis; ant 1,444t/113g; N42 17 54 W122 44 53; *Population Served:* 410,000
820 Crater Lake Ave., Suite 105, Medford, OR 97504
(541) 772-2600, *Fax:* (541) 772-7364
www.fox26medford.com
reception@kmvu-tv.com
License: Medford, Jackson County, OR held by Broadcasting Licenses L.P.
Group Owner: Northwest Broadcasting Inc.; *Washington Law Firm:* Leventhal, Senter & Lerman
Nat'l Network: Fox *Nat'l Reps:* Continental Television Sales
Jon Rand, COO
Brian Brady, President
Cary Jones, General Manager
Brian Henning, Chief Engineer

KOBI *Digital Channel:* 5 *Virtual Channel:* 5; 6.35 kw; 2700 ft.; N42 41 49 W123 13 39
Mailing Address: P.O. Box 5m, Medford, OR 97501 US
Second Address: 125 S.Fir, Medford, OR 97501
(541) 779-5555, *Fax:* (541) 779-5564
www.localnewscomesfirst.com
kobi@kobi5.com
License: Medford, Jackson County, OR held by California Oregon Broadcasting Inc.
Group Owner: California Oregon Broadcasting Inc.; *Washington Law Firm:* Wiley, Rein & Fielding
Nat'l Network: NBC *Nat'l Reps:* Blair Television
Patricia Smullin, President
Dan Acklen, News Director

KOTI *Digital Channel:* 13 *Virtual Channel:* 2; 9 kw; 2162 ft.; N42 5 48 W121 37 57; *Rebroadcasting:* Rebroadcasts KOBI Medford 90%.
Box 5m, 125 S. Fir St., Medford, OR 97510 US
(541) 882-2222,(541) 779-5555, *Fax:* (541) 883-7664
www.localnewscomesfirst.com
koti@koti2.com
License: Klamath Falls, Klamath County, OR held by California Oregon Broadcasting Inc.
Group Owner: California Oregon Broadcasting Inc.; *Ownership:* Patricia Smullin; *Washington Law Firm:* Wiley, Rein & Fielding
Nat'l Network: NBC *Wire Services:* NBC
Size of News Staff: 2
Patricia Smallin, President
Bob Wise, General Manager
Chris Krup, General Sales Mgr
Donna Rodriquez, Programming Director
Julie Akins, News Director
Scott McMahon, Chief Engineer
Alicia Lewis, National Sales Manager
DonnaRodriguez, Traffic Manager

***KSYS** *Digital Channel:* 8 *Virtual Channel:* 8; 16.9 kw; 2684 ft.; N42 41 32 W123 13 45
Mailing Address: 34 S. First Street, Medford, OR 97501 US
Second Address: 28 S. Fir St., Suite 200, Medford, OR 97501
(541) 779-0808, *Fax:* (541) 779-2178
www.soptv.org
License: Medford, Jackson County, OR held by Southern Oregon Public Television Inc
Nat'l Network: PBS
Foreign Language Programming
Mark Stanislawski, CEO
Tom Werner, Programming Director

KTVL *Digital Channel:* 35 *Virtual Channel:* 10; 132 kw vis, 26.3 aur; 3,310t/151g; N42 04 55 W122 43 07; *Population Served:* 402,000
Mailing Address: Box 10, Medford, OR 97501
Second Address: 1440 Rossanley Dr., Medford, OR 97501
(541) 773-7373, *Fax:* (541) 779-0451
www.ktvl.com
ktvl@ktvl.com
License: Medford, Jackson County, OR held by Freedom Broadcasting of Oregon Licensee L.L.C.
Group Owner: Freedom Communications Inc., Broadcast Division; (acq 8-28-81; $12.5 million); *Washington Law Firm:* Latham & Watkins
Nat'l Network: CBS; CW *Nat'l Reps:* TeleRep
Hours of Local News Weekly: News progmg 16 hrs wkly
Kingsley Kelley, Operations Dir
Jack Mc Cauley, General Sales Mgr
Sheila Giorgetti, Programming Director
Mike Gantenbein, Promotions Manager
Rick Howard, News Director
Carl Randall, Chief Engineer

Portland, OR (DMA 22)

KATU *Digital Channel:* 43 *Virtual Channel:* 2; 1000 kw; 1719 ft.; N45 30 57 W122 43 59
Mailing Address: 100 Fourth Avenue North, Seattle, WA 98109 US
Second Address: Box 2, Portland, OR 97207
(503) 231-4222, *Fax:* (503) 231-4233
www.katu.com
custserv@katu.com
License: Portland, Multnomah County, OR held by Fisher Broadcasting - Portland TV L.L.C.
Group Owner: Fisher Communications Inc.; (acq 12-4-01; grpsl).; *Washington Law Firm:* Fisher, Wayland, Cooper, Leader & Zaragoza
Nat'l Network: ABC *Nat'l Reps:* TeleRep
Hours of Local News Weekly: News progmg varies hrs wkly
John Tamerlano, General Manager
Jo Anne James, General Sales Mgr
Tami Schell, Programming Director
Steve Denari, Promotions Manager
Don Pratt, News Director
Alan Batdorf, Chief Engineer
Steve Linde, National Sales Manager

KGW *Digital Channel:* 8 *Virtual Channel:* 8; 45 kw; 1719 ft.; N45 31 21 W122 44 45
400 South Record Street, Dallas, TX 75202 US
(503) 226-5000, *Fax:* (503) 226-4448
www.kgw.com
publicfile@kgw.com
License: Portland, Multnomah County, OR held by KGW-TV Inc.
Group Owner: Belo Corp; (acq 1997; grpsl).; *Washington Law Firm:* Wiley, Rein & Fielding
Nat'l Network: NBC *Nat'l Reps:* Blair Television *Wire Services:* UPI
Hours of Local News Weekly: News progmg 35 hrs wkly
Paul Fry, President
Josy Ansley, Operations Dir
DJ Wilson, General Manager
Brenda Buratti, Programming Director
Rod Gramer, News Director

***KNMT** ; 2,690 kw vis, 269 kw aur; 1,519t/2,535g; N45 30 58 W122 43 59
432 N.E. 74th Ave., Portland, OR 97213
(503) 252-0792, *Fax:* (503) 256-4205
www.nmtv.org
License: Portland, Multnomah County, OR held by National Minority TV Inc
Jane Duff, President
Dr. Paul Crouch, Operations Dir
Adolfo Carbajal, Station Manager
Steven Hendrix, Chief Engineer
Bonnie Gaulding, Public Affairs Director

KOIN *Digital Channel:* 40 *Virtual Channel:* 6; 1000 kw; 1717 ft.; N45 30 58 W122 43 58
222 S.W. Columbia Street, Portland, OR 97201 US
(503) 464-0600, *Fax:* (503) 464-0655
www.koin.com
koin@koin.com
License: Portland, Multnomah County, OR held by LIN License Company LLC
Group Owner: LIN Media; (acq 11-1-2007; grpsl)
Nat'l Network: CBS
Hours of Local News Weekly: News progmg 27 hrs wkly
Durwood Werner, CFO
Tim Perry, General Manager
Nicole Meyers, Programming Director
Rodger O'Connor, Promotions Manager
Lynn Heider, News Director
David Bird, Engineering Dir
Carl Gonzales, Traffic Manager

***KOPB-TV** *Digital Channel:* 10 *Virtual Channel:* 10; 46 kw; 1719 ft.; N45 31 21 W122 44 45
7140 Sw Macadam Avenue, Portland, OR 97219 US
(503) 244-9900; (800) 241-8123, *Fax:* (503) 293-1919
www.opb.org
membercenter@opb.org
License: Portland, Multnomah County, OR held by Oregon Public Broadcasting
(acq 9-20-93; grpsl;; *Washington Law Firm:* Schwartz, Woods & Miller
Nat'l Network: PBS
Steve Bass, CEO
Dan Metziga, General Sales Mgr

KPTV *Digital Channel:* 12 *Virtual Channel:* 12; 24.5 kw; 1736 ft.; N45 31 19 W122 44 53
211 Se Caruthers St., Portland, OR 97214 US
(503) 906-1249, *Fax:* (503) 548-6910
www.kptv.com
webstaff@kptv.com

License: Portland, Multnomah County, OR held by Meredith Corp.
Group Owner: Meredith Broadcasting Group, Meredith Corp.; (acq 6-17-2002; swap).; *Washington Law Firm:* Dow, Lohnes & Albertson
Nat'l Network: FOX *Nat'l Reps:* TeleRep *Wire Services:* AP
Hours of Local News Weekly: News progmg 42.5 hrs wkly
Patrick McCreery, General Manager
Andy Delaporte, General Sales Mgr
Ellen Johanson, Programming Director
Corey Hanson, Promotions Manager

KPXG-TV *Digital Channel:* 22; 1,702 kw vis, 170 kw aur; 1,187t/945g; N45 00 00 W122 41 37
811 SW Naito Pkwy, Suite 100, Portland, OR 97204
(503) 222-2221, *Fax:* (503) 222-4613
www.iontelevision.com
License: Salem, Marion County, OR held by Paxson Portland License Inc.
Group Owner: ION Media Networks Inc.; (acq 5-14-98; $30 million)
Linda Massana, Operations Dir
James Kelly, Chief Engineer

KRCW-TV *Digital Channel:* 33 *Virtual Channel:* 32; 750 kw; 1717 ft.; N45 30 58 W122 43 58
10255 Sw Artic Drive, Beaverton, OH 97005 US
(503) 644-3232, *Fax:* (971) 223-0457
portlandscw.trb.com
questions@wb32tv.com
License: Salem, Marion County, OR held by Tribune Broadcast Holdings Inc.
Group Owner: Tribune Broadcasting Co.; (acq 12-20-2007; grpsl); *Washington Law Firm:* Dow Lohnes PLLC
Nat'l Network: CW *Nat'l Reps:* TeleRep
Hours of Local News Weekly: News progmg 3.5 hrs wkly
Pam Pearson, General Manager
Jeremy Berk, General Sales Mgr
Jeff MacDonald, Programming Director
Pat Shearer, Chief Engineer
Steve Martino, Program Coordinator
Trey Yant, Sales Manager
Casey Waage, Sales Manager

***KTVR** *Digital Channel:* 13 *Virtual Channel:* 13; 16.1 kw; 2543 ft.; N45 18 33 W117 43 54
7140 Sw Macadam Avenue, Portland, OR 97219 US
(503) 244-9900, *Fax:* (503) 293-1919
www.opb.org
License: La Grande, Union County, OR held by Oregon Public Broadcasting
(acq 1993; grpsl;; *Washington Law Firm:* Schwartz, Woods & Miller
Nat'l Network: PBS
Steve Bass, CEO
Tom Doggett, Programming Director
Morgan Holm, News Director
Don McKay, Chief Engineer

KUNP *Digital Channel:* 16 *Virtual Channel:* 16; 18.95 kw; 2536 ft.; N45 18 35 W117 43 57
1146 19th St. NW Ste 200, Washington, DC 20036 US
(503) 231-4222, *Fax:* (503) 231-4233
www.kunptv.com
custserv@katu.com
License: La Grande, Union County, OR held by Fisher Radio Regional Group.
Group Owner: Fisher Communications Inc.; (acq 11-1-2006; $19.3 million with KUNP-LP Portland)
Nat'l Network: UNIVISION
Foreign Language Programming
John Tamerlano, General Manager
Tami Schell, Programming Director

Yakima-Pasco-Richland-Kennewick, WA (DMA 126)

KFFX-TV *Digital Channel:* 11 *Virtual Channel:* 11; 60 kw; 1549 ft.; N45 44 51 W118 2 11
Mailing Address: 105 Cedar Green Lane, Berkeley Heights, NJ 07922 US
Second Address: 4600 S Regal Street, Spokane, WA 99223
(509) 735-1700, *Fax:* (509) 735-1004
www.fox11tricities.com
License: Pendleton, Umatilla County, OR held by Mountain Licenses L.P.
Group Owner: Northwest Broadcasting Inc.; (acq 1-14-2003; $239,659 for CP); *Washington Law Firm:* Leventhal, Senter & Lerman
Nat'l Network: FOX *Nat'l Reps:* Millennium Sales & Marketing
Brian Brady, CEO
Rick Andrycha, Operations Dir
Jon Rand, General Manager
Glenn Rousch, Station Manager
Lynn Creager, General Sales Mgr
Robin Lennell, Programming Director
Jennifer Ranney, Promotions Manager
Ron Sweatte, ChiefEngineer
Bill Quarles, CFO
Lonnie Eaton, Regional Sales Manager

Pennsylvania

Erie, PA (DMA 146)

WFXP *Digital Channel:* 22; 882 kw vis, 82 kw aur; 889t/697g; N42 02 31 W80 03 57; *Population Served:* 412,700
8455 Peach St., Erie, PA 16509
(814) 864-2400, *Fax:* (814) 864-5393
www.yourerie.com
actionnews24@wjettv.com
License: Erie, Erie County, PA held by Mission Broadcasting Inc.
Group Owner: Mission Broadcasting Inc.; (acq 10-22-98).;
Washington Law Firm: Arter & Hadden
Nat'l Network: Fox
Hours of Local News Weekly: News progmg 3.5 hrs wkly
Steve Freifeld, General Sales Mgr
Beverly Joyce, Programming Director
Joe Elan, Local Sales Manager

WICU-TV *Digital Channel:* 12 *Virtual Channel:* 12; 5.4 kw; 1006 ft.; N42 3 50 W80 0 21
3514 State Street, Erie, PA 16508 US
(814) 454-5201, *Fax:* (814) 455-0703
www.wicu12.com
info@wicu12.com
License: Erie, Erie County, PA held by SJL of Pennsylvania License Subsidiary LLC
(acq 8-96; $11 million); *Washington Law Firm:* Latham & Watkins
Nat'l Network: NBC
Size of News Staff: 20; *Hours of Local News Weekly:* news progmg 22 hrs wkly
Brian Lilly, General Manager
Doug Beers, General Sales Mgr
Paula Randolph, Programming Director
Julie Eisenman, News Director
John Wilkosz, Chief Engineer

WJET-TV *Digital Channel:* 24 *Virtual Channel:* 24; 523 kw; 997 ft.; N42 2 25 W80 4 9
18 Newbury Street, Boston, MA 02116 US
(814) 864-2400, *Fax:* (814) 868-3041
www.yourerie.com
actionnews24@wjettv.com
License: Erie, Erie County, PA held by Nexstar Broadcasting Group
Group Owner: Nexstar Broadcasting Group Inc.; (acq 12-16-97; $18.5 million); *Washington Law Firm:* Drinker, Riddle & Reath
Nat'l Network: ABC
Hours of Local News Weekly: News progmg 3.5 hrs wkly
Tim Dunst, Operations Dir
Steve Freifeld, General Sales Mgr
Beverly Joyce, Programming Director
Leslie Sadley, Promotions Manager
Lou Baxter, News Director
Chuck Jennings, Chief Engineer

***WQLN** *Digital Channel:* 50 *Virtual Channel:* 54; 39.1 kw; 888 ft.; N42 2 34 W80 3 56
8425 Peach St, Erie, PA 16509 US
(814) 864-3001, *Fax:* (814) 864-4077
www.wqln.org
wqln@wqln.org
License: Erie, Erie County, PA held by Public Broadcasting of Northwest Pennsylvania, Inc
Washington Law Firm: Dow, Lohnes & Albertson
Nat'l Network: PBS *Regional Network:* Pennsylvania Public Television Network
Dwight Miller, President

WSEE-TV *Digital Channel:* 16; 1,170 kw vis, 117 kw aur; 941t/741g; N42 02 20 W80 03 45; *Population Served:* 500,000
3514 State St., Erie, PA 16508
(814) 454-5201, *Fax:* (814) 455-0703
www.wsee.tv
wsee@wsee.tv
License: Erie, Erie County, PA held by Lilly Broadcasting of Pennslvania License Subsidiary LLC
(acq 11-28-02;. $10 million); *Washington Law Firm:* Lathan & Watkins
Nat'l Network: CBS; CW
Size of News Staff: 25; *Hours of Local News Weekly:* news progmg 14 hrs wkly
Kevin Lilly, President
John Christenson, General Manager
Doug Beers, General Sales Mgr
Michael Wolf, Programming Director
Scott Bremner, News Director
John Wilkosz, Chief Engineer

Harrisburg-Lancaster-Lebanon-York, PA (DMA 41)

WGAL *Digital Channel:* 8 *Virtual Channel:* 8; 32.2 kw; 1375 ft.; N40 2 4 W76 37 8
Mailing Address: 888 - 7th Avenue, New York, NY 10106 US
Second Address: 1300 Columbia Ave., Lancaster, PA 17603
(717) 393-5851, *Fax:* (717) 393-9484
www.wgal.com
License: Lancaster, Lancaster County, PA held by WGAL Hearst-Argyle Television Inc.
Group Owner: Hearst-Argyle Television Inc.; (acq 1999; grpsl).;
Washington Law Firm: Brooks, Pierce
Nat'l Network: NBC *Nat'l Reps:* Eagle Television Sales
Size of News Staff: 53; *Hours of Local News Weekly:* news progmg 29 hrs wkly
Paul Quinn, President
Bob Good, Operations Dir
Nancy Tulli, General Sales Mgr
Heather Bruce, Programming Director
John Baldwin, Promotions Manager
Dan O'Donnell, News Director
Paul Ladrow, National Sales Manager

WGCB-TV *Digital Channel:* 30; 617 kw vis, 114 kw aur; 581t/375g; N39 54 18 W76 35 00; *Population Served:* 740,000
Box 88, 2900 Windsor Rd, Red Lion, PA 17356
(717) 246-1681, *Fax:* (717) 244-9316
www.family49.com
lcastriota@wgcbtv.com
License: Red Lion, York County, PA held by Red Lion Broadcasting Co
Ownership: Red Lion Television Inc.; *Washington Law Firm:* Booth, Freret, Imlay and Tepper
Nat'l Network: MeTV
John Peeling, Operations Dir
Lou Castriota, Sr., General Manager
Lou Castriota, Sr., General Sales Mgr
Lou Castriota, Sr., Programming Director
John Sterling, Chief Engineer
George Montgomery, Creative Services Director
BrianGeorge, Satellite Coordinator

WHP-TV *Digital Channel:* 21 *Virtual Channel:* 21; 450 kw; 1211 ft.; N40 20 43 W76 52 9
200 Concord Plaza, Suite 600, San Antonio, TX 78216 US
(717) 238-2100, *Fax:* (717) 238-4903
www.whptv.com
License: Harrisburg, Dauphin County, PA held by Newport Television License LLC.
Group Owner: Newport Television LLC; (acq 3-14-2008; grpsl)
Nat'l Network: CBS
Size of News Staff: 23; *Hours of Local News Weekly:* news progmg 24 hrs wkly
Holly Stuart, General Manager
Stu Brenner, General Sales Mgr
Taylor Miller, Programming Director
Rob Hershey, Engineering Dir
Scott Beaver, Sales Director
Danielle Deritis, Traffic Manager

WHTM-TV *Digital Channel:* 10 *Virtual Channel:* 27; 16.2 kw; 1021 ft.; N40 18 58 W76 57 1
3235 Hoffman Street, Harrisburg, PA 17110 US
(717) 236-2727, *Fax:* (717) 232-5272
www.abc27.com
License: Harrisburg, Dauphin County, PA held by Harrisburg Television Inc.
Group Owner: Allbritton Communications Co.; (acq 1996; $113 million)
Nat'l Network: ABC
Size of News Staff: 46; *Hours of Local News Weekly:* news progmg 27 hrs wkly
Joe Lewin, President
Sharon Chambers, Operations Dir
Rob Saylor, General Sales Mgr
Tishia Falk, Programming Director
Betty Fish, Promotions Manager
Dennis Fisher, News Director
Jan Strock, Chief Engineer

Patti Jarvis, HumanResources
Paul Roda, National Sales Manager

***WITF-TV** *Digital Channel:* 36 *Virtual Channel:* 33; 50 kw; 1348 ft.; N40 20 44 W76 52 7
1982 Locust Lane, P.O. Box 2954, Harrisburg, PA 17109 US 17111
(717) 704-3000, *Fax:* (717) 704-3659
www.witf.org
info@witf.org
License: Harrisburg, Dauphin County, PA held by WITF Inc
Washington Law Firm: Dow, Lohnes & Albertson
Nat'l Network: PBS
Kathleen Pavelko, CEO
Michael Greenwald, Operations Dir
Bob Rich, General Sales Mgr
Craig Cohen, Programming Director
Gregory Poland, CFO
Ron Kain, Senior VP/Technology

WLYH-TV *Digital Channel:* 23 *Virtual Channel:* 15; 500 kw; 1250 ft.; N40 15 45 W76 27 51
12 G/Way Pza.Columbia Dr, Box 12 Johnson City, NY 13790 US
(717) 238-2100, *Fax:* (717) 234-7076
www.cw15.com
License: Lancaster, Lancaster County, PA held by Nexstar Broadcasting Inc.
Group Owner: Nexstar Broadcasting Group Inc.; (acq 12-29-2006; $56 million with WTAJ-TV Altoona)
Nat'l Network: CW
Holly Stuart, General Manager
Scott Beaver, General Sales Mgr
Taylor Miller, Programming Director
Rob Hershey, Engineering Dir
Stuart Brenner, National Sales Manager

WPMT *Digital Channel:* 47 *Virtual Channel:* 43; 933 kw; 1263 ft.; N40 1 41 W76 36 0
2005 South Queen Street, York, PA 17403 US
(717) 843-0043, *Fax:* (717) 843-9741
www.fox43.com
fox43@mail.fox43.com
License: York, York County, PA held by Tribune Television Co.
Group Owner: Tribune Broadcasting Co.; (acq 12-20-2007; grpsl)
Nat'l Network: FOX *Nat'l Reps:* TeleRep
Size of News Staff: 45; *Hours of Local News Weekly:* news progmg 17 hrs wkly
Keith McFarland, Operations Dir
Larry Delia, General Manager
Matthew Uhl, General Sales Mgr
Sandy Hawk, Programming Director
Dave Farish, Promotions Manager
Jim DePury, News Director
Jim Myers, Engineering Dir
Melissa Slatky,Research Director
Cindy Jansky, Traffic Manager

Johnstown-Altoona, PA (DMA 101)

WATM-TV *Digital Channel:* 24 *Virtual Channel:* 23; 1000 kw; 1020 ft.; N40 34 6 W78 26 38
2857 Bedford Street, Johnstown, PA 15904 US
(814) 266-8088,(814) 949-8823(sales), *Fax:* (814) 266-7749
www.abc23.com
License: Altoona, Blair County, PA held by Palm Television LP (acq 8-17-99; $12.5 million); *Washington Law Firm:* Dow, Lohnes & Albertson
Nat'l Network: ABC *Wire Services:* AP
Frank Quitoni, President
Jim Pastore, General Sales Mgr
Dan Owens, Chief Engineer

WJAC-TV *Digital Channel:* 34 *Virtual Channel:* 6; 1000 kw; 1266 ft.; N40 22 17 W78 58 56
2300 N Street, N.W., Washington, DC 20037 US
(814) 255-7600, *Fax:* (814) 255-7675
www.wjactv.com
License: Johnstown, Cambria County, PA held by WPXI, Inc.
Group Owner: Cox Media Group; (acq 9-22-2000); *Washington Law Firm:* Dow, Lohnes & Albertson
Nat'l Network: NBC
Size of News Staff: 38; *Hours of Local News Weekly:* 25 hrs news wkly
Richard Schrott, Operations Dir

WKBS-TV *Virtual Channel:* 47; 1,510 kw vis, 151 kw aur; 1,010t/184g; N40 34 12 W78 26 26
One Signal Hill Dr., Wall, PA 15148
(877) 437-4446, *Fax:* (412) 824-5442
www.ctvn.org
info@ctvn.org
License: Altoona, Blair County, PA held by Cornerstone Television Inc.
Group Owner: Cornerstone TeleVision Inc.; *Washington Law Firm:* Pillsbury, Winthrop & Shaw Pittman
Tom Scott, CFO
Ron Hembree, President
Steve Johnson, Operations Dir
Tom McGough, General Sales Mgr
Tom Hollis, Programming Director

***WPSU-TV** *Digital Channel:* 15 *Virtual Channel:* 3; 810 kw; 1354 ft.; N41 7 20 W78 26 29.8
Wagner Annex, University Park, PA 16802 US
(814) 865-3333, *Fax:* (814) 863-9786
wpsu.org
wpsu@psu.edu
License: Clearfield, Clearfield County, PA held by The Pennsylvania State University
Washington Law Firm: Paul, Hastings, Janofsky & Walker
Nat'l Network: PBS *Regional Network:* Pennsylvania Public Television Network *Wire Services:* AP
Kate Domico, Operations Dir
Ted Krichels, General Manager
Tom Yourchak, General Sales Mgr
Greg Petersen, Promotions Manager
Russ Rockwell, Chief Engineer
Ashear Barr, Advertising Director
Tom Keiter, Creative ServicesDirector
Annie Doncsecz, Finance Director
Amy Kelley, Traffic Manager

WTAJ-TV *Digital Channel:* 32 *Virtual Channel:* 10; 883 kw; 1001 ft.; N40 34 1 W78 26 30
12 G/Way Pza.Columbia Dr, Box 12 Johnson City, NY 13790 US
(814) 942-1010, *Fax:* (814) 946-8746
www.wearecentralpa.com
License: Altoona, Blair County, PA held by Nexstar Broadcasting Inc.
Group Owner: Nexstar Broadcasting Group Inc.; (acq 12-29-2006; $56 million with WLYH-TV Lancaster); *Washington Law Firm:* Latham & Watkins
Nat'l Network: CBS *Wire Services:* AP
Size of News Staff: 39; *Hours of Local News Weekly:* news progmg 29 hrs wkly
Phil Dubrow, Operations Dir
Dave Beeney, Promotions Manager
Dave Kaplar, News Director
Randy Chamberlin, Chief Engineer

WWCP-TV *Digital Channel:* 8 *Virtual Channel:* 8; 9.3 kw; 1207 ft.; N40 10 53 W79 9 5
1450 Scalp Avenue, Johnstown, PA 15904 US
(814) 266-8088, *Fax:* (814) 266-7749
www.fox8tv.com,www.abc23.com
License: Johnstown, Cambria County, PA held by Peak Media of Pennsylvania Licensee LLC
Washington Law Firm: Dow, Lohnes & Albertson
Nat'l Network: FOX *Wire Services:* AP
Frank Quitoni, President

Philadelphia (DMA 4)

KYW-TV *Digital Channel:* 26 *Virtual Channel:* 3; 100 kw vis, 10 kw aur; 1,000t/1,116g; N40 02 39 W75 14 26; *Population Served:* 1,688,210
1555 Hamilton St., Philadelphia, PA 20037
(215) 977-5300, *Fax:* (215) 977-5644
www.cbs3.com
License: Philadelphia, Philadelphia County, PA held by CBS Broadcasting Inc.
Group Owner: CBS Television Stations Group
Nat'l Network: CBS *Nat'l Reps:* CBS TV Stations National Sales
Jon Hitchcock, President
Robert Fein, General Sales Mgr
Perry Casciato, Programming Director
Sara Visomirski, Promotions Manager
Susan Schiller, News Director
Rich Paleski, Chief Engineer
Roy Coddington, National Sales Manager

WBPH-TV *Digital Channel:* 9 *Virtual Channel:* 60; 80.6 kw; 991 ft.; N40 34 1.5 W75 26 4.8
483 Woodland Road, Walnutport, PA 18088 US
(610) 433-4400, *Fax:* (610) 433-8251
www.wbph.org
info@wbph.org
License: Bethlehem, Northampton County, PA held by Sonshine Family TV Inc
Nat'l Network: IND
Pat Huber, CEO

WCAU *Digital Channel:* 34 *Virtual Channel:* 10; 700 kw; 1313 ft.; N40 2 30 W75 14 11
Ms Diane Zipursky, 1299 Pennsylvania Ave, Washington, DC 20004 US
(610) 668-5510, *Fax:* (610) 668-3700
www.nbc10.com
nbc10@nbc.com
License: Philadelphia, Philadelphia County, PA held by NBC Telemundo License Co.
Group Owner: NBC Owned Television Stations; (acq 9-10-95).
Nat'l Network: NBC *Nat'l Reps:* NBC TV Stations Sales *Wire Services:* UPI; AP
Size of News Staff: 110; *Hours of Local News Weekly:* news progmg 21 hrs wkly
Joe Marsini, CFO
Dennis Bianchi, President
Jim Barger, Operations Dir
Joe Collins, General Sales Mgr
Lawana Scales, Programming Director
Lauren Bacigalupi, Promotions Manager
Chris Blackman, News Director
JoAnne Wilder, PublicAffairs Director

WFMZ-TV *Digital Channel:* 46 *Virtual Channel:* 69; 800 kw; 1086 ft.; N40 33 52 W75 26 24
300 East Rock Road, Allentown, PA 18103 US
(610) 797-4530, *Fax:* (610) 791-2288 (sales)
www.WFMZ.com
release@wfmz.com
License: Allentown, Lehigh County, PA held by Maranatha Broadcasting Co
Washington Law Firm: Bentley Law Offices
Nat'l Network: IND *Wire Services:* AP; Accu-Weather; PR Newswire
Size of News Staff: 120; *Hours of Local News Weekly:* news progmg 32 hrs wkly
Richard Dean, Chairman
Mike Kulp, CFO
Barry Fisher, President
Brad Rinehart, General Manager
Kevin Arndt, General Sales Mgr
Charles Gale, News Director

***WLVT-TV** *Digital Channel:* 39 *Virtual Channel:* 39; 52 kw; 968 ft.; N40 33 52 W75 26 24
123 Sesame Street, Bethelem, PA 18015 US
(610) 867-4677, *Fax:* (610) 867-3544
www.wlvt.org
License: Allentown, Lehigh County, PA held by Lehigh Valley Public Telecommunications Corp
Washington Law Firm: Dow, Lohnes
Nat'l Network: PBS *Regional Network:* Pennsylvania Public Television Network
Foreign Language Programming
Patricia Simon, CEO
David Smith, Chief Engineer

WPHL-TV *Digital Channel:* 17 *Virtual Channel:* 17; 645 kw; 1063 ft.; N40 2 30 W75 14 23
5001 Wynnefield Avenue, Philadelphia, PA 19131 US
(215) 878-1700, *Fax:* (215) 879-3665
www.myphl17.com
myphl17@tribune.com
License: Philadelphia, Philadelphia County, PA held by Tribune Broadcasting Co.
Group Owner: Tribune Broadcasting Co.; (acq 12-20-2007; grpsl); *Washington Law Firm:* Dow Lohnes PLLC
Nat'l Network: MYTV *Nat'l Reps:* TeleRep
Vince Giannini, Operations Dir
Kristin Long, General Sales Mgr

WPPX-TV *Digital Channel:* 31; 3,020 kw vis, 302 kw aur; ant 958t/951g; N39 41 43 W75 17 55; *Population Served:* 2,700,000
3901 B. Main St., Suite 301, Philadelphia, PA 19127
(215) 482-4770, *Fax:* (215) 482-4777
www.ionmedia.com
License: Wilmington, New Castle County, DE held by ION Media Philadelphia License Inc., Debtor-in-possession
Group Owner: ION Media Networks Inc.; (acq 1-20-95; $9.635 million;
Nat'l Network: ION Television
Brandon Burgiss, General Manager
Diane Sullivan, General Sales Mgr
Darryl Green, Programming Director
Mark Moss, Chief Engineer
Joanne Levy, Regional Sales Manager

WPSG *Digital Channel:* 32 *Virtual Channel:* 57; 250 kw; 1312 ft.; N40 2 30 W75 14 11
C/O Viacom/D.C., 1501, M St., N.W., Suite 1100, Washington, DC 20005 US
(215) 977- 5700, *Fax:* (215) 977- 5220
www.cwphilly.com
cwphilly@wpsg.com
License: Philadelphia, Philadelphia County, PA held by Philadelphia Television Station WPSG, Inc.
Group Owner: CBS Television Stations Group; (acq 1995); *Washington Law Firm:* Fisher, Wayland, Cooper, Leader & Zaragoza
Nat'l Network: THE CW NETWORK
Jon Hitchcock, President
Bob Fein, General Sales Mgr
Susan Schiller, News Director
Rich Paleski, Chief Engineer

WPVI-TV *Digital Channel:* 6 *Virtual Channel:* 6; 34 kw; 1083 ft.; N40 2 33 W75 14 33
Wpvi Television, 4100 City Line Avenue, Philadelphia, PA 19131 US
(215) 878-9700, *Fax:* (215) 581-4530
www.6abc.com
License: Philadelphia, Philadelphia County, PA held by ABC Inc.
Group Owner: ABC Inc.; (acq 4-27-71; grpsl).; *Washington Law Firm:* Wilmer, Cutler & Pickering
Nat'l Network: ABC
Bernie Prazenica, President
Linda Munich, Operations Dir
James Aronow, General Sales Mgr
Caroline Welch, Programming Director
Paula McDermott, Promotions Manager
Carla Carpenter, News Director
Tim Giannetino, National SalesManager
Dirk Ohley, National Sales Manager
Bob Liga, Regional Sales Manager

WTVE *Digital Channel:* 25 *Virtual Channel:* 51; 126 kw; 1241 ft.; N40 2 29.56 W75 14 12.89
1729 North 11th Street, Reading, PA 19604 US
(610) 921-9181, *Fax:* (610) 921-9139
www.wtve.com
License: Reading, Berks County, PA held by WRNN-TV Associates LP.
(acq 5-12-2008; $13.5 million); *Washington Law Firm:* Covington & Burling
Nat'l Network: IND
George Mattmiller, General Manager
Jack Crumpler, General Sales Mgr
Danny Kischel, Programming Director
Todd Stewart, Chief Engineer

WTXF-TV *Digital Channel:* 42 *Virtual Channel:* 29; 620 kw; 1125 ft.; N40 2 26 W75 14 19
5151 Wisconsin Ave., N.W, Washington, DC 20016 US
(215) 925-2929, *Fax:* (215) 982-5499(sls)
www.myfoxphilly.com
License: Philadelphia, Philadelphia County, PA held by Fox TV Stations Inc.
Group Owner: Fox Television Stations Inc.; (acq 1995; $200 million)
Nat'l Network: FOX
Hours of Local News Weekly: News progmg 36.5 hrs wkly
Michael Renda, General Manager
Pat Loftus, General Sales Mgr

WUVP-DT *Digital Channel:* 29; 4,070 kw vis, 407 kw aur; ant 1,299t/1,220g; N40 02 30 W75 14 11
Mailing Address: 4449 N. Delsea Dr., Newfield, NJ 8344
Second Address: 1608 Walnut St., Philadelphia, PA 19103
(856) 691-6565, *Fax:* (856) 691-2483
www.univision.com
License: Vineland, Cumberland County, NJ held by Univision Philadelphia LLC.
Group Owner: Univision Communications Inc.; (acq 8-21-2001; grpsl)
Nat'l Network: Univision (Spanish)
Foreign Language Programming
Ramon Pineda, General Manager
John Duffin, General Sales Mgr
Josue Duarte, Promotions Manager
John Skelnik, Chief Engineer

***WYBE** *Digital Channel:* 35 *Virtual Channel:* 35; 450 kw; 1234 ft.; N40 2 30 W75 14 11
6070 Ridge Avenue, Phildaelphia, PA 19128 US
(215) 483-3900, *Fax:* (215) 483-6908
www.wybe.org,www.independencemedia.org
License: Philadelphia, Philadelphia County, PA held by Independence Public Media of Philadelphia Inc
Washington Law Firm: Drinker, Biddle & Reath L.L.P.
Nat'l Network: ETV
Foreign Language Programming
Howard Blumenthal, CEO
Joni Helton, Programming Director

Pittsburgh, PA (DMA 23)

KDKA-TV *Digital Channel:* 25 *Virtual Channel:* 2; 1000 kw; 1020 ft.; N40 29 38 W80 1 9
600 New Hampshire Ave NW, Suite 1200, Washington, DC 20037 US
(412) 575-2200, *Fax:* (412) 575-2901
www.kdka.com
License: Pittsburgh, Allegheny County, PA held by CBS Broadcasting Inc.
Group Owner: CBS Television Stations Group; (acq 5-4-2000; grpsl).; *Washington Law Firm:* Wilkes, Artis, Hedrick & Lane
Nat'l Network: CBS *Nat'l Reps:* CBS TV Stations National Sales
Chris Pike, General Manager
Michael Karas, Programming Director

WINP-TV *Digital Channel:* 38; 667 kw vis, 66.1 kw aur; ant 705t/601g; N40 26 46 W79 57 51
4802 Fifth Ave., Pittsburgh, PA 15213
(412) 622-1300, *Fax:* (412) 622-6413
www.wqed.org/wqex
wqexviewers@wqed.org
License: Pittsburgh, Allegheny County, PA held by WQED Multimedia
Washington Law Firm: Schwartz, Woods & Miller
Nat'l Network: ION Television
Deborah Acklin, President
Dorothy Frank, General Sales Mgr
Jill Lykins, Programming Director
Paul Byers, Engineering Dir
George Miles, Jr., President/CEO

WPCB-TV *Digital Channel:* 50 *Virtual Channel:* 40; 326 kw vis; 980t/839g; N40 23 34 W79 46 54; *Rebroadcasting:* To 6 owned and operated affiliated stations nationwide
Signal Hill Dr., Wall, PA 15148
(412) 824-3930, *Fax:* (412) 824-9523
www.ctvn.org
info@ctvn.org
License: Greensburg, Westmoreland County, PA held by Cornerstone Television Inc.
Group Owner: Cornerstone TeleVision Inc.; (acq 7-78).;
Washington Law Firm: Shaw Pittman
Foreign Language Programming
Pastor Gary Mitrick, Chairman of the Board
Paul Bixler, Acting COO
N/A, President
Steve Johnson, Operations Dir
N/A, General Manager
N/A, Station Manager
Tom McGough, General Sales Mgr
Tom Hollis, Programming Director
N/A,Promotions Manager
N/A, News Director
N/A, Engineering Dir
Amanda Roberts, Chief Engineer
Crystal Bynum, Marketing Coordinator

WPCW *Digital Channel:* 11 *Virtual Channel:* 19; 30 kw; 849 ft.; N40 29 38 W80 1 9
1501 M Street, N.W., Suite 1100, Washington, DC 20005 US
(412) 575-2200, *Fax:* (412) 575-2500
www.pittsburghscw.com
License: Jeannette, Westmoreland County, PA held by Pittsburgh Television Station WNPA Inc.
Group Owner: CBS Television Stations Group; (acq 12-9-98; $39 million)
Nat'l Network: THE CW NETWORK
Chris Pike, General Manager

WPGH-TV *Digital Channel:* 43 *Virtual Channel:* 53; 1000 kw; 993 ft.; N40 29 43 W80 0 18
10706 Beaver Dam Road, Cockeysville, MD 21030 US
(412) 931-5300, *Fax:* (412) 931-8135
www.wpgh53.com
License: Pittsburgh, Allegheny County, PA held by WPGH Licensee L.L.C.
Group Owner: Sinclair Broadcast Group Inc.; (acq 8-30-91; $55 million;; *Washington Law Firm:* Pillsbury, Winthrop & Pittman
Nat'l Network: FOX *Nat'l Reps:* Millennium Sales & Marketing
Alan Frank, General Manager
Jim Lapiana, General Sales Mgr
Kerry Check, Engineering Dir

WPMY *Digital Channel:* 42 *Virtual Channel:* 22; 1000 kw; 1033 ft.; N40 29 43 W80 0 17
3474 William Penn Hwy, Pittsburgh, PA 15235 US
(412) 931-5300, *Fax:* (412) 931-8135
www.wpgh53.com
License: Pittsburgh, Allegheny County, PA held by WCWB Licensee LLC.
Group Owner: Sinclair Broadcast Group Inc.; (acq 12-10-2001; $17.808 million); *Washington Law Firm:* Pillsbury, Winthrop & Pittman
Nat'l Network: MYTV *Nat'l Reps:* Millennium Sales & Marketing
Alan Frank, General Manager
Jim Lapiana, General Sales Mgr
Kerry Check, Engineering Dir

WPXI *Digital Channel:* 48 *Virtual Channel:* 11; 1000 kw; 948 ft.; N40 27 48 W80 0 16
3773 Howard Hughes Parkway, Suite 300n, Las Vegas, NV 89109 US
(412) 237-1100, *Fax:* (412) 237-4900
www.wpxi.com
comments@wpxi.com
License: Pittsburgh, Allegheny County, PA held by WPXI-TV Holdings Inc.
Group Owner: Cox Media Group; (acq 1-1-65; $20.5 million;;
Washington Law Firm: Dow, Lohnes & Albertson
Nat'l Network: NBC *Nat'l Reps:* TeleRep
Ann Glausser, CFO
Ray Carter, General Manager
Paul Curran, General Sales Mgr
Mark Barash, Programming Director
Karen Lah, Promotions Manager
Corrie Harding, News Director
Annette Parks, Engineering Dir
Darryl Griffin, NationalSales Manager

***WQED** *Digital Channel:* 13 *Virtual Channel:* 13; 25 kw; 689 ft.; N40 26 46 W79 57 51
4802 Fifth Avenue, Pittsburgh, PA 15213 US
(412) 622-1300, *Fax:* (412) 622-6413
www.wqed.org
viewers@wqed.org
License: Pittsburgh, Allegheny County, PA held by WQED Multimedia
Washington Law Firm: Schwartz, Woods & Miller
Nat'l Network: PBS *Wire Services:* Reuters
George Miles Jr., CEO
Debbie Acklin, General Manager

WTAE-TV *Digital Channel:* 51 *Virtual Channel:* 4; 1000 kw; 896 ft.; N40 16 49 W79 48 11
888 Seventh Avenue, New York, NY 10106 US
(412) 242-4300, *Fax:* (412) 244-4595
www.thepittsburghchannel.com
License: Pittsburgh, Allegheny County, PA held by WTAE Hearst-Argyle Television Inc.
Group Owner: Hearst-Argyle Television Inc.; (acq 7-16-97; grpsl).; *Washington Law Firm:* Brooks, Pierce, McLendon, Humphrey & Leonard
Nat'l Network: ABC *Nat'l Reps:* Eagle Television Sales
Size of News Staff: 70; *Hours of Local News Weekly:* news progmg 32 hrs wkly
Bob Bee, General Sales Mgr
Luanne Russell, Programming Director
Leslie Wojdowski, Promotions Manager

Wilkes Barre-Scranton, PA (DMA 54)

WBRE-TV *Digital Channel:* 11 *Virtual Channel:* 28; 30 kw; 1545 ft.; N41 10 58 W75 52 26
200 Abington Executive Park, Suite 201, Clarks Summit, PA 18411 US
(570) 823-2828, *Fax:* (570) 823-4523
www.pahomepage.com
wbrenews@pahomepage.com
License: Wilkes-Barre, Luzerne County, PA held by Nexstar Broadcasting Inc.
Group Owner: Nexstar Broadcasting Group Inc.; (acq 11-14-97; $47 million); *Washington Law Firm:* Drinker, Biddle & Reath, LLP
Nat'l Network: NBC *Nat'l Reps:* Continental Television Sales
Size of News Staff: 68; *Hours of Local News Weekly:* news progmg 24 hrs wkly
Louis J. Abitabilo, General Manager
Randy Williams, Station Manager
Michael Draman, General Sales Mgr
Ron Krisulevicz, News Director

WNEP-TV *Digital Channel:* 50 *Virtual Channel:* 16; 500 kw; 1696 ft.; N41 10 57 W75 52 15
16 Montage Mountain Road, Moosic, PA 18507 US

(570) 346-7474, *Fax:* (570) 347-0359
www.wnep.com
newstip@wnep.com
License: Scranton, Lackawanna County, PA held by Local TV Pennsylvania License LLC.
Group Owner: Local TV LLC; (acq 5-7-2007; grpsl); *Washington Law Firm:* Covington & Burling
Nat'l Network: ABC *Nat'l Reps:* Millennium Sales & Marketing
Wire Services: AP; PR Newswire
Size of News Staff: 64; *Hours of Local News Weekly:* news progmg 36 hrs wkly
Frank Gerardi, Operations Dir
Chuck Morgan, General Manager
Mike Last, General Sales Mgr
Debbie Drechin, Programming Director
Laurie LaMaster, Promotions Manager
Mike Morkavage, Chief Engineer
David Lewandoski, ProductionManager

WOLF-TV *Digital Channel:* 45 *Virtual Channel:* 56; 420 kw; 1601 ft.; N41 11 0 W75 52 10
Pegasus Corp. Office, 225 Cty Lne Ave., Ste200, Bala Cynwyd, PA 19004 US
(570) 970-5600, *Fax:* (570) 970-5601
www.myfoxnepa.com
myfoxnepa@fox56.com
License: Hazleton, Luzerne County, PA held by New Age Media of Pennsylvania License LLC.
Group Owner: CP Media LLC; (acq 3-31-2007; grpsl);
Washington Law Firm: Leventhal Senter & Lerman PLLC
Nat'l Network: FOX *Regional Reps:* Petry
Hours of Local News Weekly: News progmg 6.5 hrs wkly
Michael Yanuzzi, President
Jon Cadman, General Manager
Maria Hayduk, General Sales Mgr
Bob Spager, Regional Sales Manager

WQMY *Digital Channel:* 29 *Virtual Channel:* 53; 50 kw; 797 ft.; N41 12 1 W77 7 13
Pegasus Corp. Office, 225 Cty Lne Ave., Ste200, Bala Cynwyd, PA 19004 US
(570) 970-5600, *Fax:* (570) 970-5601
www.myfoxnepa.com
myfoxnepa@fox56.com
License: Williamsport, Lycoming County, PA held by New Age Media of Pennsylvania License LLC.
Group Owner: CP Media LLC; (acq 3-31-2007; grpsl);
Washington Law Firm: Leventhal Senter & Lerman PLLC
Nat'l Network: MYTV
Jon Cadmon, General Manager
Maria Hayduk, General Sales Mgr
Bob Spager, Regional Sales Manager

WQPX-TV *Digital Channel:* 32; 3,090 kw vis; ant 1,220t/377g; N41 26 06 W75 43 35
409 Lackawanna Ave., Suite 700, Scranton, PA 18503
(570) 344-6400, *Fax:* (570) 344-3303
www.ionmedia.tv
reginalanzo@ionmedia.tv
License: Scranton, Lackawanna County, PA held by Paxson Scranton License Inc.
Group Owner: ION Media Networks Inc.; (acq 7-31-98; $6 million); *Washington Law Firm:* Schwartz, Woods & Miller
Nat'l Network: ION Television
Regina Lanzo, Operations Dir
Jean Biondollo, Programming Director
Robert Andrade, Chief Engineer

WSWB *Digital Channel:* 31 *Virtual Channel:* 38; 100 kw; 1155 ft.; N41 26 9 W75 43 46
2130 Greenbrier Drive, Villanova, PA 19085 US
(570) 970-5600, *Fax:* (570) 970-5601
www.myfoxnepa.com
myfoxnepa@fox56.com
License: Scranton, Lackawanna County, PA held by MPS Media of Scranton License LLC.
(acq 3-31-2007; $3.044 million with WTLF(TV) Tallahassee, FL);
Ownership: Eugene J. Brown, 100% votes
Nat'l Network: CW
Michael Yanuzzi, President
Aldo Cardoni, Operations Dir
Jon Cadman, General Manager
Maria Hayduk, General Sales Mgr
Linda Greenwald, Programming Director
Steve Phillips, Promotions Manager
Rich Chofey, Chief Engineer
BobSpager, Regional Sales Manager
Lisa Miller, Traffic Manager

***WVIA-TV** *Digital Channel:* 41 *Virtual Channel:* 44; 365 kw; 1673 ft.; N41 10 55.3 W75 52 16.3
The Public Bc'ing Ctr., Pittston, PA 18640 US
(570) 826-6144,(570) 344-1244, *Fax:* (570) 655-1180
www.wvia.org
License: Scranton, Lackawanna County, PA held by Northeastern Pennsylvania Educational TV Association
Washington Law Firm: Dow, Lohnes & Albertson
Nat'l Network: PBS
A. William Kelly, President
Thomas Curra, Operations Dir
Joseph Glynn, Engineering Dir

WYOU *Digital Channel:* 13 *Virtual Channel:* 22; 30 kw; 1545 ft.; N41 10 58 W75 52 26
544 Red Rock, Wadsworth, OH 44281 US
(570) 961-2222, *Fax:* (570) 344-4484
www.pahomepage.com
newsdesk@pahomepage.com
License: Scranton, Lackawanna County, PA held by Mission Broadcasting Inc.
Group Owner: Mission Broadcasting Inc.; (acq 1-5-98; $21 million); *Washington Law Firm:* Drinker, Biddle & Reath LLP
Nat'l Network: CBS *Nat'l Reps:* Blair Television
Hours of Local News Weekly: News progmg 19.5 hrs wkly
Randy Williams, Operations Dir
Louis Abitabilo, General Manager
Gina Schreiber, Station Manager
Michael Draman, General Sales Mgr
Susan Kalinowski, Programming Director
Gary Talkiewicz, Chief Engineer
Robyn Ziska, National SalesManager
Nicole Fitch, Regional Sales Manager

Puerto Rico

Aguada

WQHA *Digital Channel:* 50 *Virtual Channel:* 50; 50 kw; 1125 ft.; N18 19 7 W67 10 48
Post Office Box 847, Mayaguez, PR 0681 US
(787) 750-4090, *Fax:* (787) 701-4245
www.ncntelevision.com
conciliofav@hotmail.com
License: Aguada, Aguada County, PR held by Concilio Mision Cristiana Fuente de Agua Viva
Nat'l Network: IND
Otoniel Font, General Manager
Edwin Rodriguez, General Sales Mgr
Josue Salgado, Programming Director

Aguadilla

***WELU** *Digital Channel:* 34; 9.33 kw vis, 933 kw aur; ant 971t/121g; N18 18 46 W67 11 09; *Population Served:* 1,500,000
Box 1093, Hormigueros, PR 0680
(787) 849-4020, *Fax:* (787) 849-2092
victoriavisioncanal32@gmail.com
License: Aguadilla, Aguadilla County, PR held by Pabellon Educational Broadcasting Inc
Hector Perez, President
Angel Martinez, General Manager
Angel Martinez, Station Manager
Yesica Acosta, General Sales Mgr
Laura Pena, Programming Director
Yesica Acosta, Promotions Manager
Jose Delgado, News Director
RamonRivera, Engineering Dir

WOLE-DT ; 275 kw vis, 27.5 kw aur; 2,181t; N18 09 00 W66 59 00; *Rebroadcasting:* Rebroadcasts WKAQ-TV San Juan.
Mailing Address: Box 1200, Mayaguez, PR 00681-1200
Second Address: Mckinley Edif. Westerbank Piso 7, Mayaguez, PR 00681-1200
(787) 833-1200,(787) 891-8100, *Fax:* (787) 891-3380
License: Aguadilla, Aguadilla County, PR held by Western Broadcasting Corp. of Puerto Rico
Foreign Language Programming
Wilson Lugo, General Manager
Santiago Hernandez, Programming Director
Doel Oriol, Chief Engineer

WVEO *Digital Channel:* 17 *Virtual Channel:* 44; 42 kw; 1220 ft.; N18 19 6 W67 10 42
Ph Darlington Building, Rio Piedras, PR 0925 US
(787) 274-1800, *Fax:* (787) 281-9758
License: Aguadilla, Aguadilla County, PR held by International Broadcasting Corp.
Group Owner: International Broadcasting Corp.; (acq 10-7-2004; $1,382,961 with WXRF(AM) Guayama).
Nat'l Network: IND
Foreign Language Programming
Pedro Roman Collazo, General Manager
Margarita Nazario, Programming Director

Arecibo

WCCV-TV *Digital Channel:* 46 *Virtual Channel:* 54; 50 kw; 1969 ft.; N18 14 6 W66 45 36
P.O. Box 949, Camuy, PR 0627 US
(787) 262-5400,(787) 898-5120, *Fax:* (787) 262-0541
www.cdminternational.com
plaud@cdminternational.com,plaud@yiyeavila.org
License: Arecibo, Arecibo County, PR held by Asociacion Evan. Cristo Viene Inc
Washington Law Firm: Fletcher, Heald & Hildreth, P.L.C.
Nat'l Network: IND
Marcos Plaud, General Manager

WMEI *Digital Channel:* 14 *Virtual Channel:* 14; 315 kw; 2733 ft.; N18 9 17.1 W66 33 16.4; *Not on Air/Target Date:* unknown
Gpo 7017, Caguas, PR 0626 US
(757) 437-9800, *Fax:* (757) 437-0034
www.maxmediallc.com
License: Arecibo, Arecibo County, PR held by CMCG Puerto Rico License LLC.
Group Owner: MAX Media L.L.C.; (acq 7-17-2006; $4.25 million)
Nat'l Network: IND
A. Eugene Loving Jr., Chairman
John A. Trinder, President

Bayamon

WDWL *Digital Channel:* 30 *Virtual Channel:* 36; 100 kw; 1027 ft.; N18 16 49 W66 6 35
P.O. Box 50615, Levitown Station, PR 0950 US
(787) 795-8113, *Fax:* (787) 795-8140
www.teleadoracion.com
jbenle@prtc.net
License: Bayamon, Bayamon County, PR held by Bayamon Christian Network.
Nat'l Network: TBN ENLACE
Jesus Velez, President
Zoraida Jostinano, General Manager
David Baez, Chief Engineer

Caguas

WLII *Digital Channel:* 56; 316 kw vis; ant 1,164t/207g; N18 16 54 W66 06 46; *Population Served:* 3,900,000
Mailing Address: Box 7888, Guaynabo, PR 970
Second Address: 64 Calle Carazo, Guaynabo, PR 969
(787) 300-5000, *Fax:* (787) 300-5003
License: Caguas, Caguas County, PR held by WLII/WSUR License Partnership G.P.
Group Owner: Univision Communications Inc.; (acq 6-30-2005; with WSUR-TV Ponce).; *Washington Law Firm:* Pillsbury
Foreign Language Programming; Size of News Staff: 31
Larry Sands, General Manager
Carlos Pagan, General Sales Mgr
Jessica Rodriguez, Programming Director
Susanne Ramirez de Arellano, News Director
Andres Diaz, Chief Engineer

***WUJA** *Digital Channel:* 48 *Virtual Channel:* 58; 50 kw; 1024 ft.; N18 16 48 W66 6 33
Post Office Box 4039, Carolina, PR 0628 US
(787) 625-5858, *Fax:* (787) 701-4245
License: Caguas, Caguas County, PR held by Caguas Educational TV Inc
Nat'l Network: ETV
Otoniel Font, General Manager

Carolina

WRFB *Digital Channel:* 51 *Virtual Channel:* 52; 16 kw; 1847 ft.; N18 16 44 W65 51 12
No. 21 B Street Sabana, Carolina, PR 0984 US
(787) 762-5500, *Fax:* (787) 752-1825
videomaxpr.tv
License: Carolina, San Juan County, PR held by R &F Broadcasting Inc
Washington Law Firm: Fletcher, Heald & Hildeth, P.L.C.
Nat'l Network: IND
Rickin Sanchez, General Manager

Fajardo

***WMTJ** *Digital Channel:* 16 *Virtual Channel:* 40; 140 kw; 2796 ft.; N18 18 35 W65 47 43
Mailing Address: P. O. Box 21345, Rio Piedras, PR 0928 US
Second Address: 1395 Isidoro Colon St., San Juan, PR 928
(787) 766-2600, *Fax:* (787) 250-8546
www.suagm.edu/sitv
License: Fajardo, Fajardo County, PR held by Sistema Universitario Ana G. Mendez, Inc.
Washington Law Firm: Dow, Lohnes & Albertson

Nat'l Network: PBS
Foreign Language Programming
Margarita Millan, Operations Dir

WRUA *Digital Channel:* 33 *Virtual Channel:* 34; 50 kw; 2782 ft.; N18 18 36 W65 47 41
331 Camino Del Prado, Saberna, Cedra, PR 0739 US
(787) 279-3434, *Fax:* (787) 279-5549
License: Fajardo, Fajardo County, PR held by Eastern Television Corp
Nat'l Network: IND
Rafael Padilla, General Manager

Guayama

WIDP *Digital Channel:* 45 *Virtual Channel:* 46; 50.1 kw; 2070 ft.; N18 16 44 W65 51 10
P.O. Box 21065, San Juan, PR 0928 US
(787) 999-0360, *Fax:* (787) 999-1560
www.teletriunso.com
info@teletriunfo.com
License: Guayama, Guayama County, PR held by Ebenezer Broadcasting Group Inc
Washington Law Firm: Shaw Pittman LLP
Nat'l Network: TBN
Alcardo Aponte, General Manager

Hagatna

***KGTF** *Digital Channel:* 5; 27.5 kw vis, 5.47 kw aur; ant 297t/196g; N13 26 13 E144 48 17; *Population Served:* 160,000
Mailing Address: Box 21449 GMF, Barrigada, GU 96921
Second Address: 194 Sesame St, Washington Dr., Mangilao, GU 96921
(671) 734-2207,(671) 734-5788, *Fax:* (671) 734-3476
www.kgtf.org
kgtf12@kgtf.org
License: Hagatna, Guam County, GU held by Guam Educational Telecommunications Corp
Washington Law Firm: Cohn & Marks
Nat'l Network: PBS
Benny Flores, Operations Dir
Sam Soza, General Manager
Vickey Manglona, Programming Director

Mayaguez

***WIPM-TV** *Digital Channel:* 35 *Virtual Channel:* 3; 620 kw; 2211 ft.; N18 9 0 W66 59 0; *Rebroadcasting:* WIPR (San Juan) 100%
P. O. Box 190909, Hato Rey, PR 0919 US
(787) 834-0164, *Fax:* (787) 832-9139
www.tutv.puertorico.pr
tutvwebmaster@tutv.puertorico.pr
License: Mayaguez, Mayaguez County, PR held by Puerto Rico Public Broadcasting Corp
Washington Law Firm: Steptoe & Johnson
Nat'l Network: ETV
Victor Morales, Operations Dir
E. Feliciano, General Manager
Diane Ramos, General Sales Mgr
Jorge Gonzalez, Chief Engineer

WNJX-TV *Digital Channel:* 23 *Virtual Channel:* 4; 400 kw; 2274 ft.; N18 9 0 W66 59 0; *Rebroadcasting:* Rebroadcasts WAPA-TV San Juan 100%
Carribean Plaza, Mendez, Viga #69, Suite 303, Mayaguez, PR 0680 US
(787) 792-4444, *Fax:* (787) 782-4420
www.wapa.tv
License: Mayaguez, Mayaguez County, PR held by Televicentro of Puerto Rico, L.L.C.
Group Owner: InterMedia Partners L.P.; (acq 3-1-2001; up to $1.075 million for stock).
Nat'l Network: IND
Foreign Language Programming
Joe Ramos, General Manager
Jonathan Garcia, General Sales Mgr
Jimmy Artega, Programming Director
Enrique Cruz, News Director
Jose Guerra, Chief Engineer
Aurora Tirado, Traffic Manager

WORA-TV *Digital Channel:* 29; 100 kw vis, 20 kw aur; 2,001t/241g; N18 09 02 W66 59 20
Box 43, Mayaguez, PR 0708
(787) 831-5555/(787) 721-4054, *Fax:* (787) 833-0075/(787) 724-1554
www.woratv.com
gvega@woratv.com
License: Mayaguez, Mayaguez County, PR held by Telecinco Inc
Washington Law Firm: Drinker Biddle & Reath LLP
Foreign Language Programming
Jose Vizcarronda, President
Alejandro Luciano, Engineering Director
Lilliam Rodriguez, Sales Department
Fred Toledo, Chief Engineer
Aixa Benejan, Traffic Manager

WOST *Digital Channel:* 22 *Virtual Channel:* 14; 50 kw; 1073 ft.; N18 18 51 W67 11 24; *Not on Air/Target Date:* unknown
Mailing Address: P.O. Box 980, Quebradillas, PR 0678 US
Second Address: 1095 Avenida Wilson Edificio Puerta, del Condado, Suite 2, San Juan, PR 907
(757) 437-9800, (787) 723-6060, *Fax:* (787) 723-0087
License: Mayaguez, Mayaguez County, PR held by CMCG Puerto Rico License LLC.
(acq 2-17-2006; $4.25 million with WMEI(TV) Arecibo);
Ownership: Power Television International LLC, 51%; and Max Media IV LLC, 49%
Nat'l Network: IND
Foreign Language Programming
A. Eugene Loving Jr., Chairman
John A. Trinder, President

Naranjito

WECN *Digital Channel:* 18 *Virtual Channel:* 64; 50 kw; 466 ft.; N18 17 34 W66 16 2
Mailing Address: P. O. Box 310, Bayamon, PR 0960 US
Second Address: Hwy. 167, Naranjito, PR 960
(787) 799-1480
evn@centennialpr.net
License: Naranjito, Naranjito County, PR held by Encuentro Christian Network
(acq 9-87; $175,000;; *Washington Law Firm:* Irwin, Campbell & Tannenwald
Nat'l Network: IND
Foreign Language Programming
Rafael Padilla, General Manager

Ponce

WKPV *Digital Channel:* 19 *Virtual Channel:* 20; 700 kw; 883 ft.; N18 4 49 W66 44 53; *Rebroadcasting:* Satellite of WJPX(TV) San Juan
601clearwater Park Rd, West Palm Beach, FL 33401 US
(787) 792-4760,(787) 705-4153, *Fax:* (787) 782-7825
www.caribevision.com
edwn.pujols@wapa-tv.com
License: Ponce, Ponce County, PR held by S & E Network Inc.
Group Owner: CaribeVision Station Group LLC; (acq 9-20-2007; grpsl)
Nat'l Network: Cablevision
Joe Ramos, General Manager

***WQTO** *Digital Channel:* 25 *Virtual Channel:* 26; 800 kw; 1017 ft.; N18 4 48 W66 44 56; *Rebroadcasting:* Satellite of WMTJ Fajardo
Mailing Address: P.O. Box E, Rio Piedras, PR 0928 US
Second Address: 1395 Isidoro Colon St., San Juan, PR 928
(787) 766-2600, *Fax:* (787) 250-8546
www.suagm.edu/sitv
License: Ponce, Ponce County, PR held by Sistema Universitario Ana G. Mendez, Inc
Washington Law Firm: Dow, Lohnes & Albertson
Nat'l Network: PBS
Margarita Millan, Operations Dir

WSTE-DT *Digital Channel:* 7; 3.2 kw vis; ant 289t/220g; N18 02 52 W66 39 16
Mailing Address: Box 7888, Guaynavo, PR 970
Second Address: Calle Carazo #64, Guaynavo, PR 969
(787) 724-7777
www.univision.com
License: Ponce, Ponce County, PR held by WLII/WSUR License Partnership G.P.
Group Owner: Univision Communications Inc.; (acq 11-30-2007; $15.5 million)
Foreign Language Programming
Larry Sands, General Manager
Carlos Pagan, General Sales Mgr
Jessica Rodriguez, Programming Director
Andres Diaz, Chief Engineer

WSUR-DT *Digital Channel:* 43; 178 kw vis; ant 2,811t/266g; N18 10 09 W66 34 36
Mailing Address: Box 7888, Guaynabo, PR 00970-7888
Second Address: One 3rd St., San Juan, PR 908
(787) 724-1111
License: Ponce, Ponce County, PR held by WLII/WSUR License Partnership G.P.
Group Owner: Univision Communications Inc.; (acq 6-30-2005; with WLII(TV) Caguas).; *Washington Law Firm:* Hamel & Park
Nat'l Network: Univision (Spanish)
Foreign Language Programming
Larry Sands, Operations Dir
Carlos Pagan, General Sales Mgr
Jessica Rodriguez, Programming Director
Manuel Santiago, Promotions Manager
Jose Morales, News Director
Andres Diaz, Chief Engineer

WTIN-TV *Digital Channel:* 15; 1070 kw vis, 10 kw aur; ant 2,824t/53g; N18 10 11 W66 34 38; *Rebroadcasting:* Rebroadcasts WAPA-TV San Juan 100%
Box 362050, San Juan, PR 00936-2050
(787) 792-4444, *Fax:* (787) 782-4420
www.wapa.tv
License: Ponce, Ponce County, PR held by Televicentro of Puerto Rico LLC.
Group Owner: InterMedia Partners L.P.; (acq 5-6-2004; $5 million); *Washington Law Firm:* Baraff, Koerner, Olender & Hochberg
Jimmy Artega, Programming Director
Jose Guerra, Chief Engineer

WVOZ-TV *Digital Channel:* 47 *Virtual Channel:* 48; 50.1 kw; 810 ft.; N18 4 50 W66 44 50
7425 Sw 42nd Street, Miami, FL 33155 US
(787) 274-1800, *Fax:* (787) 281-9758
License: Ponce, Ponce County, PR held by International Broadcasting Corp.
Group Owner: International Broadcasting Corp.; (acq 10-9-2001; grpsl).
Nat'l Network: IND
Margarita Nazario, General Manager
Pedro Roman Callazo, Programming Director
Rudi Rivas, Chief Engineer

San Juan

WAPA-TV *Digital Channel:* 27 *Virtual Channel:* 4; 1000 kw; 2605 ft.; N18 6 42 W66 3 5
300 Crescent Court, Suite 600, Dallas, TX 75201 US
(787) 792-4444, *Fax:* (787) 782-4420
www.wapa.tv
info@wapa.tv
License: San Juan, San Juan County, PR held by Televicentro of Puerto Rico L.L.C.
Group Owner: InterMedia Partners L.P.; (acq 7-12-2000; grpsl).;
Washington Law Firm: Fletcher, Heald & Hildreth
Nat'l Network: IND
Foreign Language Programming; Size of News Staff: 29; *Hours of Local News Weekly:* news progmg 20 hrs wkly
Joe Ramos, General Manager
Jonathan Garcia, General Sales Mgr
Jimmy Artega, Programming Director
Enrique Cruz, News Director
Jose Guerra, Chief Engineer
Aurora Tirado, Traffic Manager

***WIPR-TV** *Digital Channel:* 43 *Virtual Channel:* 6; 791 kw; 2546 ft.; N18 6 42 W66 3 5
P. O. Box 190909, Hato Rey, PR 0919 US
(787) 766-0505, *Fax:* (787) 753-9846
www.tutv.puertorico.pr
tutvwebmaster@tutv.puertorico.pr
License: San Juan, San Juan County, PR held by Puerto Rico Public Broadcasting Corp
Washington Law Firm: Steven Huffines
Nat'l Network: PBS
Foreign Language Programming
Pedro Rua, Operations Dir
Ray Cruz, General Manager
Jocelyn Lamas, General Sales Mgr
Evangeline Vazquez, Programming Director
Jorge Gonzalez, Chief Engineer
Victor Morales, Operations Vice President

WJPX *Digital Channel:* 21 *Virtual Channel:* 24; 1000 kw; 1850 ft.; N18 16 45 W65 51 14
601 Clearwater Park Rd, West Palm Beach, FL 33401 US
(787) 792-4444,(787) 706-4153, *Fax:* (787) 782-7825
www.caribevision.com
edwin.pujols@wapa-tv.com
License: San Juan, San Juan County, PR held by S&E Network Inc.
Group Owner: CaribeVision Station Group LLC; (acq 9-20-2007; grpsl); *Washington Law Firm:* Dow, Lohnes & Albertson
Nat'l Network: Cablevision
Joe Ramos, General Manager
Edwin Pujols, Station Manager
Jonathan Garcia, General Sales Mgr
Margarita Millan, Programming Director

Enrique Cruz, News Director
Jose Guerra, Chief Engineer
Aurora Tirado, Traffic Manager

WKAQ-TV *Digital Channel:* 28 *Virtual Channel:* 2; 925 kw; 2802 ft.; N18 6 55 W66 3 11
Mailing Address: 2290 West 8th Avenue, Hialeah, FL 33010 US
Second Address: 383 Roosevelt Ave., Hato Rey, PR 919
(787) 758-2222,(787) 641-2222
www.telemundopr.com
License: San Juan, San Juan County, PR held by NBC Telemundo License Co.
Group Owner: Telemundo Television Stations; (acq 4-10-2002; grpsl).; *Washington Law Firm:* Hogan & Hartson
Nat'l Network: NBC
Foreign Language Programming; Size of News Staff: 40; *Hours of Local News Weekly:* news progmg 10 hrs wkly
Sonia Melendez, CFO
Jose Medina, Operations Dir
Hilary Hattler, General Manager
Raymond Totti, General Sales Mgr
Ileana Santiago, Programming Director
Juan Miguel Muniz, News Director

WSJU-TV *Digital Channel:* 31 *Virtual Channel:* 30; 66 kw; 876 ft.; N18 16 30 W66 5 36
1508 Calle Bori, Urb Antonsanti, San Juan, PR 0927 US
(787) 767-6200, *Fax:* (787) 767-6200
www.canal30.net
angel@aercobroadcasting.com
License: San Juan, San Juan County, PR held by Aerco Broadcasting Corp
(acq 1-11-2005).; *Washington Law Firm:* Borsari & Assoc.
Nat'l Network: SBS/MEGA
Angel Roman Lopez, General Manager
Sergio Ballesteros, General Sales Mgr
Rudi Rivas, Chief Engineer

WTCV *Digital Channel:* 32 *Virtual Channel:* 18; 3.9 kw; 951 ft.; N18 16 30 W66 5 36
Bori 1554 St. Urb Point, Antonsanti, PR 0927 US
(787) 274-1800,(787) 203-9178, *Fax:* (787) 281-9758
License: San Juan, San Juan County, PR held by International Broadcasting Corp.
Group Owner: International Broadcasting Corp.; (acq 10-9-2001; grpsl).; *Washington Law Firm:* Marmet & McCombs
Nat'l Network: IND
Pedro Roman Collazo, President
Margarita Nazario, General Sales Mgr

San Sebastian

WJWN-TV *Digital Channel:* 39 *Virtual Channel:* 38; 700 kw; 2057 ft.; N18 9 0 W66 59 0; *Rebroadcasting:* Satellite of WJPX(TV) San Juan
P. O. Box 10001, El Commandate, Canovanas, PR 0729 US
(787) 792-4444, *Fax:* (787) 782-7825
www.caribevision.com
edwin.pujols@wapa-tv.com
License: San Sebastian, San Sebastian County, PR held by S&E Network Inc.
Group Owner: CaribeVision Station Group LLC; (acq 9-20-2007; grpsl)
Nat'l Network: Cablevision
Joe Ramos, General Manager

Yauco

WIRS *Digital Channel:* 41 *Virtual Channel:* 42; 185 kw; 2730 ft.; N18 10 10 W66 34 36; *Rebroadcasting:* Satellite of WJPX(TV) San Juan
Post Office Box 635, Bayamon, PR 0621 US
(787) 799-1480
License: Yauco, Yauco County, PR held by CaribeVision Station Group LLC.
Group Owner: CaribeVision Station Group LLC; (acq 9-20-2007; grpsl)
Nat'l Network: Cablevision
Myriam Rodriguez, General Manager

Rhode Island

Providence, RI-New Bedford, MA (DMA 52)

WDPX-TV *Digital Channel:* 40; 1,191 kw vis, 119.1 kw aur; 470t/350g; N41 41 19 W70 20 49; *Rebroadcasting:* Satellite of WBPX Boston.
1120 Soldiers Field Rd., Boston, MA 2134
(617) 787-6868, *Fax:* (617) 787-4114
www.ionline.tv
License: Vineyard Haven, Dukes County, MA held by ION Media Boston License, Inc., Debtor-in-possession
Group Owner: ION Media Networks Inc.; (acq 5-2-2000; grpsl).; *Washington Law Firm:* Arter & Hadden
Dianne McLaughlin, General Manager

WJAR *Digital Channel:* 51 *Virtual Channel:* 10; 1000 kw; 1004 ft.; N41 51 54 W71 17 15
Ms Diane Zipursky, 1299 Pennsylvania Ave, Washington, DC 20004 US
(401) 455-9100, *Fax:* (401) 455-9140
www.turnto10.com
License: Providence, Providence County, RI held by Media General Communications Inc.
Group Owner: Media General Broadcast Group; (acq 6-26-2006; grpsl).
Nat'l Network: NBC *Nat'l Reps:* Harrington, Righter & Parsons
Foreign Language Programming
Lisa Churchville, General Manager
Valerie McCain, General Sales Mgr
Chris Lanni, Promotions Manager
Mark McMillen, Chief Engineer
Stephen Delpico, Sales Manager

WLNE-TV *Digital Channel:* 49; 100 kw vis, 22.4 kw aur; ant 940t/996g; N41 46 39 W70 55 41; *Population Served:* 1,437,000
10 Orms St., Providence, RI 2904
(401) 453-8000, *Fax:* (401) 331-4399
www.abc6.com
License: New Bedford, Bristol County, MA held by Global Broadcasting of Southern New England LLC.
(acq 10-9-2007; $14 million); *Ownership:* Global Broadcasting LLC, 100%; *Washington Law Firm:* Latham & Watkins
Nat'l Network: ABC *Nat'l Reps:* TeleRep
Stephen Doerr, Operations Dir
Michael Brostek, General Sales Mgr
Bill Mushrush, Promotions Manager
BJ Finnell, News Director
Jim Brown, Operations Manager

WNAC-TV *Digital Channel:* 12 *Virtual Channel:* 64; 30 kw; 1001 ft.; N41 52 36 W71 16 57
3839 - 4th Street, North, Suite 420, St. Petersburg, FL 33703 US
(401) 438-7200, *Fax:* (401) 434-3761
www.foxprovidence.com
License: Providence, Providence County, RI held by WNAC LLC
Nat'l Network: FOX *Nat'l Reps:* Blair Television
Jay Howell, President
Patrick Wholey, General Sales Mgr
Pam Brennan, Programming Director
Susan Tracy-Durant, Promotions Manager
Joe Abouzeid, News Director
William Hague, Chief Engineer
John Macek, Local Sales Manager
RyanMachado, Regional Sales Manager

WPRI-TV *Digital Channel:* 13 *Virtual Channel:* 12; 30 kw; 1001 ft.; N41 52 36 W71 16 57
200 Concord Plaza, Suite 600, San Antonio, TX 78216 US
(401) 438-7200, *Fax:* (401) 434-3761
www.wpri.com
License: Providence, Providence County, RI held by LIN License Company LLC
Group Owner: LIN Media; (acq 11-8-2002; grpsl).
Nat'l Network: CBS *Nat'l Reps:* Blair Television
Jay Howell, President
Patrick Wholey, General Sales Mgr
Pam Brennan, Programming Director
Susan Tracy-Durant, Promotions Manager
William Hague, Chief Engineer
Patti St. Pierre, National Sales Manager

WPXQ-TV *Digital Channel:* 17; 3470 kw vis; ant 272t; N41 29 41 W71 47 05
3 Shaws CV, Ste 226, New London, CT 06320-4943
(401) 455-9263, *Fax:* (401) 455-9156
www.ionline.tv
Robert.melfi@nbc.com
License: Block Island, Washington County, RI held by Ocean State Television L.L.C.
Group Owner: ION Media Networks Inc.; (acq 8-2-96).; *Ownership:* A joint venture of Paxson Communications Corp. and Offshore Broadcasting Corp. (Raymond Yorke, 100%).; *Washington Law Firm:* Cohn & Marks
Nat'l Network: ION Television
Hours of Local News Weekly: News progmg 5 hrs wkly
Robert Melfi, General Sales Mgr

***WSBE-TV** *Digital Channel:* 21 *Virtual Channel:* 36; 50 kw; 879 ft.; N41 51 54 W71 17 15
50 Park Lane, Providence, RI 02907 US
(401) 222-3636, *Fax:* (401) 222-3407
www.ripbs.org
info@ripbs.org
License: Providence, Providence County, RI held by Rhode Island Public Telecommunications Authority
Washington Law Firm: Schwartz, Woods & Miller
Nat'l Network: PBS
David Piccerelli, CFO
Robert Fish, President
Janet Zwolinski, General Sales Mgr
Kathryn Larsen, Programming Director
Gunnar Rieger, Chief Engineer

South Carolina

Augusta, GA (DMA 115)

***WEBA-TV** *Digital Channel:* 33 *Virtual Channel:* 14; 427 kw; 792 ft.; N33 11 15 W81 23 50
1101g.R.Blvd.PO Bx 11000, Columbia, SC 29211 US
(803) 737-3545, *Fax:* (803) 737-3495
www.scetv.org
mail@myetv.org
License: Allendale, Allendale County, SC held by South Carolina ETV Commission
Nat'l Network: PBS
David Crouch, CEO
L.W. Griffin Jr., Engineering Dir

Charleston, SC (DMA 99)

WCBD-TV *Digital Channel:* 50 *Virtual Channel:* 2; 1000 kw; 1906 ft.; N32 56 24 W79 41 45
333 East Grace Street, Richmond, VA 23219 US
(843) 884-2222, *Fax:* (843) 881-3410
www.wcbd.com
License: Charleston, Charleston County, SC held by Media General Broadcasting Inc.
Group Owner: Media General Broadcast Group; (acq 3-1-83; $8 million;; *Washington Law Firm:* Cohn & Marks
Nat'l Network: NBC; CW *Nat'l Reps:* Harrington, Righter & Parsons
Size of News Staff: 29; *Hours of Local News Weekly:* news progmg 17 hrs wkly
Rick Lipps, General Manager
Patrick J. Ryal, General Sales Mgr
Lowell Beckner, Chief Engineer

WCIV *Digital Channel:* 34 *Virtual Channel:* 4; 630 kw; 1713 ft.; N32 55 28 W79 41 58
Mailing Address: 888 Allbritton Boulevard, Mount Pleasant, SC 29464 US
Second Address: 888 Allbritton Blvd., Mt. Pleasant, SC 29464
(843) 881-4444, *Fax:* (843) 849-2519
www.abcnews4.com
License: Charleston, Charleston County, SC held by WCIV Inc.
Group Owner: Allbritton Communications Co.; (acq 1-26-76; grpsl); *Washington Law Firm:* Hogan & Hartson
Nat'l Network: ABC *Wire Services:* Conus
Size of News Staff: 32; *Hours of Local News Weekly:* news progmg 12 hrs wkly
Terry Wright, Operations Dir
Suzanne Teagle, General Manager
Octavia Walker, General Sales Mgr
Deborah Jackson, Programming Director
Tim Greeney, Promotions Manager
Perry Boxx, News Director
Chuck Groome, Regional SalesManager
Sybil Blanton, Traffic Manager

WCSC-TV *Digital Channel:* 47 *Virtual Channel:* 5; 1000 kw; 1709 ft.; N32 55 28 W79 41 58
PO Box 160005, Charleston, SC 29416 US
(843) 402-5555, *Fax:* (843) 402-5744
www.wcsc.com
License: Charleston, Charleston County, SC held by WCSC License Subsidiary LLC.
Group Owner: Raycom Media Inc.; (acq 3-31-2008; grpsl)
Nat'l Network: CBS
Size of News Staff: 44; *Hours of Local News Weekly:* news progmg 21 hrs wkly
Rita O'Neill, General Manager
Sandy Smith, General Sales Mgr
Amanda Curry, Promotions Manager
James Warner, News Director
Mike Miller, Chief Engineer

***WITV** *Digital Channel:* 7 *Virtual Channel:* 7; 20 kw; 1844 ft.; N32 55 28 W79 41 58

Mailing Address: 1101g.R.Blvd.PO Bx 11000, Columbia, SC 29211 US
Second Address: 1101 George Rogers Blvd., Columbia, SC 29201
(803) 737-3200; (803) 737-3545, *Fax:* (803) 737-3417
www.myetv.org
mail@myetv.org
License: Charleston, Charleston County, SC held by South Carolina Educational TV Commission
Washington Law Firm: Dow, Lohnes & Albertson
Nat'l Network: PBS
David Crouch, CEO
L. W. Griffin, Jr., Engineering Dir

WMMP *Digital Channel:* 36 *Virtual Channel:* 36; 1000 kw; 1914 ft.; N32 56 24 W79 41 45
10706 Beaver Dam Road, Cockeysville, MD 21030 US
(843) 744-2424, *Fax:* (843) 554-9649
www.wmmp36.com
comments@wmmp36.com
License: Charleston, Charleston County, SC held by WMMP Licensee L.P.
Group Owner: Sinclair Broadcast Group Inc.; (acq 1998; grpsl).
Nat'l Network: MYTV
Allison Taylor, General Manager
Mary Margaret Johnson, General Sales Mgr
Bill Littleton, Programming Director
Jason Lewis, Promotions Manager
Sallie Moultrie, Traffic Manager

WTAT-TV *Digital Channel:* 24 *Virtual Channel:* 24; 1000 kw; 1914 ft.; N32 56 24 W79 41 45
18 Newbury Street, Boston, MA 02116 US
(843) 744-2424, *Fax:* (843) 554-9649
www.wtat24.com
comments@wmmp36.com
License: Charleston, Charleston County, SC held by WTAT Licensee LLC.
Group Owner: Cunningham Broadcasting Corporation; (acq 11-15-2001; grpsl).; *Washington Law Firm:* Arter & Hadden
Nat'l Network: FOX
Hours of Local News Weekly: News progmg 3.5 hrs wkly
Allison Taylor, General Manager
Mary Margaret Johnson, General Sales Mgr
Bill Littleton, Programming Director
Jason Lewis, Promotions Manager
Sallie Moultrie, Traffic Manager

Charlotte, NC (DMA 24)

WMYT-TV *Digital Channel:* 39 *Virtual Channel:* 55; 225 kw; 1873 ft.; N35 21 44 W81 9 19
201a Hillside Avenue, Charlotte, NC 28209 US
(704) 398-0046, *Fax:* (704) 393-8407
www.wmyt12.com
info@wmyt12.com
License: Rock Hill, York County, SC held by WMYT-TV Inc.
Group Owner: Capitol Broadcasting Co. Inc.; (acq 2—2000; $4.5 million)
Nat'l Network: MNT *Nat'l Reps:* Millennium Sales & Marketing
Shawn Harris, General Manager
Don Travis, General Sales Mgr
Chris Wolf, Programming Director
Chris Wolf, Promotions Manager
Robert Castillo, Chief Engineer
Cathy Mozingo, Local Sales Manager
Lori Zannino, Research Director
Sarah Ferris, Traffic Manager

***WNSC-TV** *Digital Channel:* 15 *Virtual Channel:* 30; 403 kw; 694 ft.; N34 50 23 W81 1 7
Mailing Address: 1101g.R.Blvd.PO Bx 11000, Columbia, SC 29211 US
Second Address: 452 S. Anderson Rd., Rock Hill, SC 29730
(803) 324-3184, *Fax:* (803) 324-0580
www.myetv.org
mail@myetv.org
License: Rock Hill, York County, SC held by S.C. Educ TV Commission
Nat'l Network: PBS
David Crouch, President
Tim Coghill, Operations Dir
Gary Stevens, Chief Engineer

Columbia, SC (DMA 79)

WACH *Digital Channel:* 48 *Virtual Channel:* 57; 520 kw; 1522 ft.; N34 6 58 W80 45 51
Rsa Tower, 20th Floor, 201 Monroe Street, Montgomery, AL 36104 US
(803) 252-5757, *Fax:* (803) 212-7270
www.wach.com
webmaster@wach.com
License: Columbia, Richland County, SC held by Barrington Columbia License LLC.
Group Owner: Barrington Broadcasting Group, LLC.; (acq 8-11-2006; grpsl); *Washington Law Firm:* Covington & Burling
Nat'l Network: FOX *Nat'l Reps:* TeleRep
Scott McBride, Operations Dir
Cheri Spets, General Sales Mgr
Nina Gibson, Programming Director
Ernest Robinson, News Director
Phil Shreves, Operations Manager
Reese Barkley, Public Affairs Director

WIS *Digital Channel:* 10 *Virtual Channel:* 10; 57 kw; 1578 ft.; N34 7 29 W80 45 23
Mailing Address: 1111 Bull Street, Columbia, SC 29201 US
Second Address: Box 367, Columbia, SC 29202
(803) 799-1010, *Fax:* (803) 758-1171
www.wistv.com
dtodd@wistv.com
License: Columbia, Richland County, SC held by WIS License Subsidiary LLC.
Group Owner: Raycom Media Inc.; (acq 1-31-2006; grpsl); *Washington Law Firm:* Covington & Burling LLP
Nat'l Network: NBC *Nat'l Reps:* Harrington, Righter & Parsons
Hours of Local News Weekly: News progmg 26.5 hrs wkly
Donita Todd, Operations Dir
Scott Sanders, General Sales Mgr
Barry Ahrendt, Promotions Manager
Brad Neuhoff, News Director
Emir Hadziahmetovic, Chief Engineer
Quentin Kenney, Regional Business Manager

WKTC *Digital Channel:* 39 *Virtual Channel:* 63; 500 kw; 1283 ft.; N34 6 58 W80 45 51
15 South Main Street, Sumter, SC 29150 US
(803) 419-6363, *Fax:* (803) 419-6399
www.wktctv.com
mail@wktctv.com
License: Sumter, Sumter County, SC held by WBHQ Columbia LLC.
Washington Law Firm: Pillsbury, Withrop, Shaw Pittman
Nat'l Network: MYTV
Stefanie Rein, General Manager

WLTX *Digital Channel:* 17 *Virtual Channel:* 19; 5,000 kw vis, 500 kw aur; ant 1,749t/1,706g; N34 05 49 W80 45 51; *Population Served:* 1,013,410
6027 Garners Ferry Rd., Columbia, SC 29209
(803) 776-3600, *Fax:* (803) 695-3714
www.wltx.com
License: Columbia, Richland County, SC held by Pacific and Southern Co. Inc.
Group Owner: Gannett Broadcasting; (acq 4-29-98; $87.5 million)
Nat'l Network: CBS *Nat'l Reps:* TeleRep *Wire Services:* AP
Hours of Local News Weekly: News progmg 27 hrs wkly
Rich O'Dell, General Manager
Position open, General Sales Mgr
Terry Wright, Programming Director
Michael Penix, Promotions Manager
Marybeth Jacoby, News Director
Andy Peeler, Engineering Dir
Deborah Kehoe, National SalesManager
Steve Conway, Local Sales Manager
Mandi Gilbert, Digital Sales Manager
Rich O'Dell, Program Director
Keely Richardson, Business Manager

WOLO-TV *Digital Channel:* 8 *Virtual Channel:* 25; 43.7 kw; 1736 ft.; N34 6 58 W80 45 51
5807 Shakespeare Rd., Columbia, SC 29223 US
(803) 754-7525, *Fax:* (803) 754-6147
www.wolo.com
License: Columbia, Richland County, SC held by South Carolina Broadcasting Partners.
Group Owner: Bahakel Communications; (acq 7-20-92)
Nat'l Network: ABC *Wire Services:* AP
Chris Bailey, General Manager
Dave Aiken, Station Manager

***WRJA-TV** *Digital Channel:* 28 *Virtual Channel:* 27; 98.4 kw; 1194 ft.; N33 52 51 W80 16 15
1101g.R.Blvd.PO Bx 11000, Columbia, SC 29211 US
(803) 773-5546, *Fax:* (803) 775-1059
www.wrja.org; www.myetv.org
mail@myetv.org
License: Sumter, Sumter County, SC held by South Carolina Educational TV Commission
Nat'l Network: PBS
Foreign Language Programming
Victor Miller, General Manager
Kevin Jordan, Engineering Dir

***WRLK-TV** *Digital Channel:* 32 *Virtual Channel:* 35; 250 kw; 1035 ft.; N34 7 6 W80 56 13
Mailing Address: 1101g.R.Blvd.PO Bx 11000, Columbia, SC 29211 US
Second Address: 1101 George Rogers Blvd., Columbia, SC 29201
(803) 737-3200, *Fax:* (803) 737-3417
www.myetv.org
mail@myetv.org
License: Columbia, Richland County, SC held by South Carolina Educational TV Commission
Washington Law Firm: Dow, Lohnes & Albertson
Nat'l Network: PBS
David Crouch, CEO
L.W. Griffin Jr., Engineering Dir

WZRB *Digital Channel:* 47 *Virtual Channel:* 47; 240 kw; 630 ft.; N34 2 38 W80 59 51
US
(803) 714-2347, *Fax:* (803) 691-3848
www.cw47columbia.com
License: Columbia, Richland County, SC held by Roberts Broadcasting Co. of Columbia, SC LLC.
Group Owner: Roberts Broadcasting Co.; *Washington Law Firm:* Dow, Lohnes & Albertson
Nat'l Network: CW
Dody Yarborough, General Manager

Greenville-Spartanburg, SC-Asheville, NC-Anderson, SC (DMA 36)

WGGS-TV *Digital Channel:* 16 *Virtual Channel:* 16; 175 kw; 1181 ft.; N34 56 26 W82 24 41
Mailing Address: 3409 Rutherford Road, Taylors, SC 29687 US
Second Address: 3409 Rutherford Rd., Taylors, SC 29687
(864) 244-1616, *Fax:* (864) 292-8481
www.dovebroadcasting.com
ccbtv16@aol.com
License: Greenville, Greenville County, SC held by Carolina Christian Broadcasting Inc
Washington Law Firm: Hardy & Chautin
Nat'l Network: IND
James Thompson, President
Joanne Thompson, Operations Dir
Billy Rainey, General Sales Mgr
Derek Myers, Programming Director
Pete Littlefield, Chief Engineer
Dante Thompson, National Sales Manager
Kym MacKinnon, ProgrammingDirector

WHNS *Digital Channel:* 21 *Virtual Channel:* 21; 400 kw; 2500 ft.; N35 10 56 W82 40 56
1716 Locust Street, Des Moines, IA 50309 US
(864) 288-2100, *Fax:* (864) 297-0728
www.foxcarolina.com
foxcarolinanews@foxcarolina.com
License: Greenville, Greenville County, SC held by Meredith Corp.
Group Owner: Meredith Broadcasting Group, Meredith Corp.; (acq 7-1-97; grpsl); *Washington Law Firm:* Dow, Lohnes & Albertson
Nat'l Network: FOX *Nat'l Reps:* TeleRep
Size of News Staff: 45; *Hours of Local News Weekly:* news progmg 27 hrs wkly
William Kerr, Chairman
Steve Lacy, CEO
Paul Karpowicz, President
Guy Hempel, Operations Dir
Brent Lane, General Sales Mgr
April Osborne, Promotions Manager
Dalton Lee, CFO
Douglas Lowe, Executive Vice President
Alan DeFlorio,Regional Sales Manager

WMYA-TV *Digital Channel:* 14 *Virtual Channel:* 40; 360 kw; 940 ft.; N34 38 51 W82 16 13
Mailing Address: 3474 William Penn Highway, Pittsburgh, PA 15235 US
Second Address: 110 Technology Dr., Asheville, NC 28803
(828) 684-1340, *Fax:* (828) 651-4601
www.my40.tv
License: Anderson, Anderson County, SC held by Anderson (WFBC-TV) Licensee Inc.

Group Owner: Cunningham Broadcasting Corporation; (acq 1-7-2002).
Nat'l Network: MYTV
Jack Connors, General Manager
Audra Swain, General Sales Mgr
Rollins Thompkins, Chief Engineer

***WNEH** *Digital Channel:* 18 *Virtual Channel:* 38; 106.7 kw; 754 ft.; N34 22 19 W82 10 5
Mailing Address: 1101g.R.Blvd.PO Bx 11000, Columbia, SC 29211 US
Second Address: 1101 George Rogers Blvd., Columbia, SC 29201
(803) 737-3200; (803) 737-3545, *Fax:* (803) 737-3417
www.myetv.org
mail@myetv.org
License: Greenwood, Greenwood County, SC held by South Carolina Educational TV Commission
Nat'l Network: PBS
David Crouch, CEO
L. W. Griffin, Jr., Engineering Dir

***WNTV** *Digital Channel:* 9 *Virtual Channel:* 29; 102.3 kw; 1239 ft.; N34 56 29 W82 24 38
1101g.R.Blvd.PO Bx 11000, Columbia, SC 29211 US
(803) 737-3545, *Fax:* (803) 737-3495
www.scetv.org
mail@myetv.org
License: Greenville, Greenville County, SC held by South Carolina ETV Commission
Nat'l Network: PBS
David Crouch, CEO
L.W. Griffin Jr., Engineering Dir

***WRET-TV** *Digital Channel:* 43 *Virtual Channel:* 49; 106.2 kw; 991 ft.; N34 53 11 W81 49 16; *Rebroadcasting:* Satellite of WNTV Greenville.
1101g.R.Blvd.PO Bx 11000, Columbia, SC 29211 US
(864) 503-9371, *Fax:* (864) 503-3615
www.wret.org
License: Spartanburg, Spartanburg County, SC held by South Carolina Educational TV Commission
Washington Law Firm: Dow, Lohnes & Albertson
Nat'l Network: PBS
William Richardson, Operations Dir
Gary Stevens, Chief Engineer

WSPA-TV *Digital Channel:* 7 *Virtual Channel:* 7; 25.7 kw; 2188 ft/667m HAAT; N35 10 12 W82 17 27; *Population Served:* 784,300
250 International Drive, Spartanburg, SC 29304
(864) 576-7777, *Fax:* (864) 587-4480
www.wspa.com
License: Spartanburg, Spartanburg County, SC held by Media General Communications Holdings, LLC
Group Owner: Media General Broadcast Group; (acq 3-27-2000; grpsl).; *Washington Law Firm:* Dow, Lohnes
Nat'l Network: CBS *Wire Services:* UPI
Size of News Staff: 51; *Hours of Local News Weekly:* news progmg 26.5 hrs wkly
Bob Romine, General Manager
Beth Worsham, General Sales Mgr
Ross Lytle, Promotions Manager
Dan Cates, News Director
Bob Richardson, Chief Engineer
Jimmy Lizer, Operations Manager

WYFF *Digital Channel:* 36 *Virtual Channel:* 4; 1000 kw; 1955 ft.; N35 6 43 W82 36 24
Mailing Address: 888 Seventh Avenue, New York, NY 10106 US
Second Address: 505 Rutherford St., Greenville, SC 29609
(864) 242-4404, *Fax:* (864) 240-5329
www.wyff4.com
news4@wyff.com
License: Greenville, Greenville County, SC held by WYFF Hearst-Argyle Television Inc
Group Owner: Hearst-Argyle Television Inc.; (acq 3-18-99; grpsl).; *Washington Law Firm:* Brooks, Pierce, McLendon, Humphrey & Leonard
Nat'l Network: NBC *Nat'l Reps:* Eagle Television Sales *Wire Services:* AP
Size of News Staff: 55; *Hours of Local News Weekly:* news progmg 30 hrs wkly
Michael Hayes, President
Doug Durkee, Operations Dir
John Humphries, General Sales Mgr
Cathy Petroupoulos, Programming Director
Marsa Jarrett, Promotions Manager
Justin Antoniotte, News Director
Steve Eaton, Local SalesManager
Blake Bridges, National Sales Manager
Danny Ross, Program/Production Manager

Myrtle Beach-Florence, SC (DMA 104)

WBTW *Digital Channel:* 13 *Virtual Channel:* 13; 31.6 kw; 1962 ft.; N34 22 4 W79 19 21
Mailing Address: 250 International Drive, Spartanburg, SC 29304 US
Second Address: 101 McDonald Ct., Myrtle Beach, SC 29588
(843) 317-1313, *Fax:* (843) 317-1410
www.scnow.com
License: Florence, Florence County, SC held by Media General Communications Inc.
Group Owner: Media General Broadcast Group; (acq 3-27-2000; grpsl).
Nat'l Network: CBS *Nat'l Reps:* Harrington, Righter & Parsons
Size of News Staff: 14; *Hours of Local News Weekly:* news progmg 78 hrs wkly
Michael Caplan, Operations Dir
Brian Lang, General Sales Mgr
Sandra Sellers, Programming Director
Chuck Spruill, Promotions Manager
David Halt, News Director
Scott Johnson, Chief Engineer
Don Luehrs, Chief Meteorologist

WFXB *Digital Channel:* 18 *Virtual Channel:* 43; 1000 kw; 1506 ft.; N34 11 19 W79 11 0
P. O. Box 586, Durham, NC 27702 US
(843) 828-4300, *Fax:* (843) 828-4343
www.wfxb.com
License: Myrtle Beach, Horry County, SC held by Springfield Broadcasting Partners.
Group Owner: Bahakel Communications; (acq 8-18-2006; $19.5 million); *Washington Law Firm:* Fisher, Wayland, Cooper, Leader & Zaragoza
Nat'l Network: FOX *Nat'l Reps:* Millennium Sales & Marketing
Size of News Staff: 50; *Hours of Local News Weekly:* 2.5 hrs news progmg wkly
Dave Milligan, Operations Dir
Rigby Wilson, General Manager

***WHMC** *Digital Channel:* 9 *Virtual Channel:* 23; 31.8 kw; 753 ft.; N33 56 58 W79 6 31
1101g.R.Blvd.PO Bx 11000, Columbia, SC 29211 US
(803) 737-3545, *Fax:* (803) 737-3495
www.scetv.org
mail@myetv.org
License: Conway, Horry County, SC held by South Carolina Educational TV Commission.
Nat'l Network: PBS
David Crouch, CEO
L.W. Griffin Jr., Engineering Dir

***WJPM-TV** *Digital Channel:* 45 *Virtual Channel:* 33; 108.9 kw; 795 ft.; N34 16 48 W79 44 35
1101g.R.Blvd.PO Bx 11000, Columbia, SC 29211 US
(803) 737-3545, *Fax:* (803) 737-3495
www.scetv.org
mail@myetv.org
License: Florence, Florence County, SC held by South Carolina ETV Commission
Nat'l Network: PBS
David Crouch, CEO

WMBF-TV *Digital Channel:* 32 *Virtual Channel:* 32; 530 kw; 600 ft.; N33 43 50 W79 4 32
PO Box 19023, Greenville, SC 29602 US
(843) 839-9623, *Fax:* (843) 839-9625
www.wmbfnews.com
License: Myrtle Beach, Horry County, SC held by Raycom TV Broadcasting Inc.
Group Owner: Raycom Media Inc.; (acq 1-31-2006; grpsl); *Washington Law Firm:* Covington & Burling
Nat'l Network: N/A *Nat'l Reps:* TeleRep *Wire Services:* AP
Size of News Staff: 52; *Hours of Local News Weekly:* news progmg 30.5 hrs wkly
Ted Fortenberry, Operations Dir
Eileen Russo, General Sales Mgr
Matt Miller, News Director

WPDE-TV *Digital Channel:* 16 *Virtual Channel:* 15; 421 kw; 1969 ft.; N34 22 2 W79 19 49
3215 South Cashua Drive, Florence, SC 29501 US
(843) 234-9733, *Fax:* (843) 234-9739
www.wpdetv.com
feedback@wpde.com
License: Florence, Florence County, SC held by Barrington Broadcasting of South Carolina Corp.
Group Owner: Barrington Broadcasting Group, LLC.; (acq 2-6-2006; $24.1 million); *Washington Law Firm:* Covington & Burling LLP

Nat'l Network: ABC
William Huggins, Operations Dir

WWMB *Digital Channel:* 21 *Virtual Channel:* 21; 400 kw; 1906 ft.; N34 22 2 W79 19 49
2920 Midiron Court, Myrtle Beach, SC 29577 US
(843) 234-9733, *Fax:* (843) 234-9739
www.cwtv21.com
License: Florence, Florence County, SC held by SagamoreHill of Carolina Licenses LLC.
Group Owner: SagamoreHill Midwest LLC; (acq 2-6-2006; $2.4 million)
Nat'l Network: CW
Louis Wall, CEO
William Huggins, General Manager
Leigh Vaters, General Sales Mgr
Debbie Yost, Programming Director
Marty Shelley, Promotions Manager
Mark Olson, Chief Engineer

Savannah, GA (DMA 96)

***WJWJ-TV** *Digital Channel:* 44 *Virtual Channel:* 16; 440 kw; 1196 ft.; N32 42 42 W80 40 54
Mailing Address: 1101g.R.Blvd.PO Bx 11000, Columbia, SC 29211 US
Second Address: 925 Ribaut Rd., Beaufort, SC 29902
(843) 524-0808, *Fax:* (843) 524-1016
www.myetv.org
mail@myetv.org
License: Beaufort, Beaufort County, SC held by South Carolina ETV Commission
Nat'l Network: PBS
Scott Johnson, Operations Dir
Mike Milburn, Chief Engineer

WTGS *Digital Channel:* 28 *Virtual Channel:* 28; 1000 kw; 1493 ft.; N32 2 45 W81 20 27
4101 Lake Boone Trail, Suite 300, Raleigh, NC 27607 US
(912) 925-2287, *Fax:* (912) 925-7026
www.fox28tv.com
comments@wjcl.com
License: Hardeeville, Jasper County, SC
Group Owner: Vaughan Media LLC; (acq 9-19-2007; $17.5 million); *Washington Law Firm:* Drinker Biddle & Reath LLP
Nat'l Network: FOX
Hours of Local News Weekly: News progmg 5 hrs wkly
Todd Parkin, CEO
Chris Hays, Operations Dir
Lynn Fairbanks, General Manager
Morgan Sladick, General Sales Mgr
Karon Johnson, Programming Director
Jason Usry, Promotions Manager
Michael Sullivan, News Director
Ed Youmans, ChiefEngineer
Frank Sulkowski, Sports Commentator

South Dakota

Minot-Bismarck-Dickinson, ND (DMA 158)

***KPSD-TV** *Digital Channel:* 13 *Virtual Channel:* 13; 27 kw; 1693 ft.; N45 3 14 W102 15 47
Mailing Address: Cherry & Dakota Streets, Box 5000, Vermillion, SD 57069 US
Second Address: 555 N. Dakota St., Vermillion, SD 57069
(605) 677-5861,(800) 456-0766, *Fax:* (605) 677-5010
www.sdpd.org
programming@sdpb.org
License: Eagle Butte, Roberts County, SD held by South Dakota Board of Directors for Educational Telecommunications
Washington Law Firm: Cohn & Marks
Nat'l Network: PBS
Julie Andersen, President
Terry Spencer, General Sales Mgr
Bob Bosse, Programming Director

***KQSD-TV** *Digital Channel:* 11 *Virtual Channel:* 11; 33.72 kw; 1026 ft.; N45 16 38 W99 59 10
Mailing Address: Cherry & Dakota Streets, Box5000, Vermillion, SD 57069 US
Second Address: 555 N. Dakota St., Vermillion, SD 57069
(605) 677-5861,(800) 456-0766, *Fax:* (605) 677-5010
www.sdpd.org
programming@sdpb.org
License: Lowry, Walworth County, SD held by South Dakota Board of Directors for Educational Telecommunications
Washington Law Firm: Cohn & Marks
Nat'l Network: PBS

Julie Andersen, President
Craig Jensen, Operations Dir
Terry Spencer, General Sales Mgr
Bob Bosse, Programming Director
Fritz Miller, Promotions Manager

Rapid City, SD (DMA 174)

***KBHE-TV** *Digital Channel:* 26 *Virtual Channel:* 9; 79.06 kw; 629 ft.; N44 3 8 W103 14 34
Cherry & Dakota Streets, Box 5000, Vermillion, SD 57069 US
(605) 394-2551, *Fax:* (605) 394-5384
www.sdpb.org
admin@sdpb.org
License: Rapid City, Pennington County, SD held by South Dakota Board of Directors for Educational Telecommunications
Nat'l Network: PBS
Julie Andersen, Station Manager
Terry Spencer, General Sales Mgr
Severn Ashes, Chief Engineer

KCLO-TV *Digital Channel:* 16 *Virtual Channel:* 15; 150 kw; 505 ft.; N44 4 13 W103 15 1; *Rebroadcasting:* Satellite of KELO-TV Sioux Falls 99%
599 Lexington Avenue, 47th Floor, New York, NY 10022 US
(605) 336-1100, *Fax:* (605) 334-3447
www.keloland.com
kelotv@keloland.com
License: Rapid City, Pennington County, SD held by Young Broadcasting of Rapid City Inc.
Group Owner: Young Broadcasting Inc.; (acq 1996; grpsl).; *Washington Law Firm:* Brooks, Pierce, McLendon, Humphrey & Leonard
Nat'l Network: CBS *Nat'l Reps:* Adam Young
Karen Floyd, Programming Director
Paul Farmer, Promotions Manager
Beth Jensen, News Director
Paul Myrick, Chief Engineer

KEVN-TV *Digital Channel:* 7 *Virtual Channel:* 7; 43.5 kw; 669 ft.; N44 4 0 W103 15 1
Mailing Address: 152 West 57th Street, 42nd Floor, New York, NY 10019 US
Second Address: 2000 Skyline Drive, Rapid City, SD 57701
(605) 394-7777, *Fax:* (605) 348-9128,(605) 394-3652
www.blackhillsfox.com
news@blackhillsfox.com
License: Rapid City, Pennington County, SD held by KEVN Inc.
Group Owner: KEVN Inc.; 10/29/1998; *Washington Law Firm:* Law Offices of Covington & Burling
Nat'l Network: FOX *Nat'l Reps:* Millennium Sales & Marketing
Wire Services: AP
Size of News Staff: 14; *Hours of Local News Weekly:* news progmg 9 hrs wkly
Bob Slocum, CFO
Cindy McNeil, Operations Dir
Nancy Reber, General Sales Mgr
Jack Caudill, News Director
Lance Cratty, Chief Engineer

KHSD-TV *Digital Channel:* 10 *Virtual Channel:* 11; 34.8 kw; 1890 ft.; N44 19 36 W103 50 12; *Rebroadcasting:* Satellite of KOTA-TV Rapid City.
Mailing Address: P. O. Box 1760, Rapid City, SD 57709 US
Second Address: 518 Saint Joseph Street, Rapid City, SD 57701
(605) 342-2000, *Fax:* (605) 342-7305
www.kotatv.com
License: Lead, Lawrence County, SD held by Duhamel Broadcasting Enterprises.
Group Owner: Duhamel Broadcasting Enterprises; *Washington Law Firm:* Pillsbury Law
Nat'l Network: ABC *Nat'l Reps:* Continental Television Sales
William Duhamel, President
Monte Loos, Operations Dir
Steve Duffy, General Sales Mgr
Doug Loos, Programming Director
John Petersen, News Director
Dan Black, Engineering Dir
Gerry Fenske, Regional Sales Manager

KIVV-TV *Digital Channel:* 5 *Virtual Channel:* 5; 9.2 kw; 1841 ft.; N44 19 30 W103 50 14; *Rebroadcasting:* Satellite of KEVN-TV Rapid City.
Mailing Address: 152 West 57th Street, 42nd Floor, New York, NY 10019 US
Second Address: 2000 Skyline Dr., Rapid City, SD 57709
(605) 394-7777, *Fax:* (605) 348-9128
www.blackhillsfox.com
news@blackhillsfox.com
License: Lead, Lawrence County, SD held by KEVN Inc.
Group Owner: KEVN Inc.; 10/29/1998; *Washington Law Firm:* Law Offices of Covington & Burling
Nat'l Network: FOX *Nat'l Reps:* Millennium Sales & Marketing
Wire Services: AP
Size of News Staff: 14; *Hours of Local News Weekly:* news progmg 9 hrs wkly
Bob Slocum, CFO
Cindy McNeil, Operations Dir
Nancy Reber, General Sales Mgr
Jack Caudill, News Director
Lance Cratty, Chief Engineer

KNBN *Digital Channel:* 21 *Virtual Channel:* 21; 50 kw; 692 ft.; N44 5 33 W103 14 53
Mailing Address: P.O. Box 2860, 2504 West Main Street, Rapid City, SD 57709 US
Second Address: 2424 S. Plaza Dr., Rapid City, SD 57709
(605) 355-0024, *Fax:* (605) 355-9274
www.newscenter1.tv
License: Rapid City, Pennington County, SD held by Rapid Broadcasting Co.
Ownership: James F. Simpson, 10.5%; Scott Barbour, 9.1%; Leeann Rieman, 9.1%; Frank Simpson, 8.3%; Clark D. Moyle, 8.1%;; Gilbert D. Moyle III, 8.1%; W.R. Barbour, 6.1%; William F. Turner, 3.2%; Suzanne M. Gabrielson, 2.4%;Charles H. Lien, 2.4%; and David M. Simpson, 1.3%
Nat'l Network: NBC
Hours of Local News Weekly: News progmg 11 hrs wkly
Jim Simpson, Operations Dir
Mark Walter, Operations Manager

KOTA-TV *Digital Channel:* 2 *Virtual Channel:* 3; 18.2 kw; 673 ft.; N44 4 8 W103 15 3
Mailing Address: P. O. Box 1760, Rapid City, SD 57709 US
Second Address: 518 St. Joseph St., Rapid City, SD 57701
(605) 342-2000, *Fax:* (605) 342-7305
www.kotatv.com
License: Rapid City, Pennington County, SD held by Duhamel Broadcasting Enterprises.
Group Owner: Duhamel Broadcasting Enterprises; *Washington Law Firm:* Pillsbury Law
Nat'l Network: ABC *Nat'l Reps:* Continental Television Sales
Wire Services: AP
Hours of Local News Weekly: News progmg 9 hrs wkly
William Duhamel, President
Monte Loos, Operations Dir
Steve Duffy, General Sales Mgr
Doug Loos, Programming Director
John Peterson, News Director
Dan Black, Engineering Dir
Gerry Fenske, Regional Sales Manager

***KZSD-TV** *Digital Channel:* 8 *Virtual Channel:* 8; 44.7 kw; 873 ft.; N43 25 59 W101 33 16
Mailing Address: Cherry & Dakota Streets, Box 5000, Vermillion, SD 57069 US
Second Address: 555 N. Dakota St., Vermillion, SD 57069-5000
(605) 677-5861, *Fax:* (605) 677-5010
www.sdpb.org
programming@sdpb.org
License: Martin, Bennett County, SD held by South Dakota Board of Directors for Educational Telecommunications
Washington Law Firm: Cohn & Marks
Nat'l Network: PBS
Julie Andersen, President
Craig Jensen, Operations Dir
Terry Spencer, General Sales Mgr
Bob Bosse, Programming Director
Carol Robertson, Promotions Manager
Severn Ashes, Engineering Dir
Steve Thum, Traffic Manager

Sioux Falls (Mitchell), SD (DMA 113)

***KCSD-TV** *Digital Channel:* 24 *Virtual Channel:* 23; 80.9 kw; 246 ft.; N43 34 28 W96 39 19
Mailing Address: Cherry & Dakota Streets, Box 5000, Vermillion, SD 57069 US
Second Address: 555 N. Dakota St., Vermillion, SD 57069-5000
(605) 677-5861, *Fax:* (605) 677-5010
www.sdpb.org
programming@sdpb.org
License: Sioux Falls, Minnehaha County, SD held by South Dakota Board of Directors for Educational Telecommunications
Washington Law Firm: Cohn & Marks
Nat'l Network: PBS
Julie Andersen, President
Craig Jensen, Operations Dir
Terry Spencer, General Sales Mgr
Bob Bosse, Programming Director
Fritz Miller, Promotions Manager

KDLO-TV *Digital Channel:* 3 *Virtual Channel:* 3; 14.4 kw; 1684 ft.; N44 57 56 W97 35 22; *Rebroadcasting:* Satellite of KELO-TV Sioux Falls 100%.
599 Lexington Avenue, 47th Floor, New York, NY 10022 US
(605) 336-1100, *Fax:* (605) 334-3447
www.keloland.com
kelotv@keloland.com
License: Florence, Clark County, SD held by Young Broadcasting of Sioux Falls Inc.
Group Owner: Young Broadcasting Inc.; (acq 6-1-96; grpsl).; *Washington Law Firm:* Brooks, Pierce, McLendon, Humphrey & Leonard
Nat'l Network: CBS *Nat'l Reps:* Adam Young
Karen Floyd, Programming Director
Paul Farmer, Promotions Manager
Beth Jensen, News Director
Paul Myrick, Chief Engineer

KDLT-TV *Digital Channel:* 47 *Virtual Channel:* 46; 1000 kw; 1995 ft.; N43 30 18 W96 33 22
P.O. Box 9115, Fargo, ND 58106 US
(605) 361-5555, *Fax:* (605) 361-7017,(605) 361-3982
www.kdlt.com
info@kdlt.com
License: Sioux Falls, Minnehaha County, SD held by Red River Broadcast Co. L.L.C.
Group Owner: Red River Broadcast Co. L.L.C.; *Washington Law Firm:* Holland and Knight
Nat'l Network: NBC *Nat'l Reps:* Harrington, Righter & Parsons
Wire Services: AP
Size of News Staff: 25; *Hours of Local News Weekly:* news progmg 19 hrs wkly
Myron Kunin, CEO
Ro Grignon, President
Kathy Lau, Operations Dir
Mari Ossenfort, General Manager
Stacey Torvik, Programming Director
Amanda Sievert, Promotions Manager
Jen Wahle, News Director
Donald Sturzenbecher, ChiefEngineer
Susan Endres, Operations Manager

KDLV-TV *Digital Channel:* 26 *Virtual Channel:* 5; 1000 kw; 1033 ft.; N43 45 33 W98 24 44; *Rebroadcasting:* Satellite of KDLT-TV Sioux Falls.
P.O. Box 9115, Fargo, ND 58106 US
(605) 361-5555, *Fax:* (605) 361-3982/(605) 361-7017
www.kdlt.com
License: Mitchell, Davison County, SD held by Red River Broadcast Co. L.L.C.
Group Owner: Red River Broadcast Co. L.L.C.; (acq 8-26-94; $4 million;; *Washington Law Firm:* Holland & Knight
Nat'l Network: NBC *Nat'l Reps:* Harrington, Righter & Parsons
Foreign Language Programming; Size of News Staff: 25; *Hours of Local News Weekly:* news progmg 20 hrs wkly
Ro Grignon, President
Susan Endres, Operations Dir
Mari Ossenfort, General Manager
Emily Dimock, Promotions Manager
Bobbi Lauer, News Director
Don Sturzenbecher, Chief Engineer

***KDSD-TV** *Digital Channel:* 17 *Virtual Channel:* 16; 37.82 kw; 1145 ft.; N45 29 54 W97 40 28
Mailing Address: Cherry & Dakota Streets, Box 5000, Vermillion, SD 57069 US
Second Address: 555 North Dakota Street, Vermillion, SD 57069-5000
(605) 677-5861, *Fax:* (605) 677-5010
www.sdpb.org
programming@sdpb.org
License: Aberdeen, Brown County, SD held by South Dakota Board of Directors for Educational Telecommunications
Washington Law Firm: Cohn & Marks
Nat'l Network: PBS
Julie Andersen, President
Craig Jensen, Operations Dir
Terry Spencer, General Sales Mgr
Bob Bosse, Programming Director
Fritz Miller, Promotions Manager

KELO-TV *Digital Channel:* 11 *Virtual Channel:* 11; 30 kw; 2001 ft.; N43 31 7 W96 32 5
501 South Phillips Avenu, Sioux Falls, SD 57104 US
(605) 336-1100, *Fax:* (605) 334-3447(sales),(605) 357-5530
www.keloland.com
kelotv@keloland.com
License: Sioux Falls, Minnehaha County, SD held by Young Broadcasting of Sioux Falls Inc.

Group Owner: Young Broadcasting Inc.; (acq 6-1-96; grpsl).;
Washington Law Firm: Brooks, Pierce, McLendon, Humphrey & Leonard
Nat'l Network: CBS; MyNetworkTV *Nat'l Reps:* Adam Young
Jay Huizenga, General Manager
Karen Floyd, Programming Director
Paul Farmer, Promotions Manager
Beth Jensen, News Director
Paul Myrick, Chief Engineer

***KESD-TV** *Digital Channel:* 8 *Virtual Channel:* 8; 15 kw; 751 ft.; N44 20 16 W97 13 42
Mailing Address: Cherry & Dakota Streets, Box 5000, Vermittion, SD 57069 US
Second Address: 555 North Dakota Street, Vermillion, SD 57069-5000
(605) 677-5861, *Fax:* (605) 677-5010
www.sdpb.org
programming@sdpb.org
License: Brookings, Brookings County, SD held by South Dakota Board of Directors for Educational Telecommunications
Washington Law Firm: Cohn & Marks
Nat'l Network: PBS
Julie Andersen, President
Terry Spencer, General Sales Mgr

KPLO-TV *Digital Channel:* 13 *Virtual Channel:* 6; 40 kw; 1043 ft.; N43 57 57 W99 36 11; *Rebroadcasting:* Satellite of KELO-TV Sioux Falls 100%.
599 Lexington Avenue, 47th Floor, New York, NY 10022 US
(605) 336-1100, *Fax:* (605) 334-3447
www.keloland.com
kelotv@keloland.com
License: Reliance, Lyman County, SD held by Young Broadcasting of Sioux Falls Inc.
Group Owner: Young Broadcasting Inc.; (acq 6-1-96; grpsl).;
Washington Law Firm: Brooks, Pierce, McLendon, Humphrey & Leonard
Nat'l Network: CBS *Nat'l Reps:* Adam Young
Karen Floyd, Programming Director
Paul Farmer, Promotions Manager
Beth Jensen, News Director
Paul Myrick, Chief Engineer

KPRY-TV *Digital Channel:* 19 *Virtual Channel:* 4; 311 kw; 1138 ft.; N44 3 7 W100 5 3; *Rebroadcasting:* Rebroadcasts KSFY-TV Sioux Falls
Rsa Tower, 20th Floor, 201 Monroe Street, Montgomery, AL 36104 US
(605) 336-1300, *Fax:* (605) 336-7936, (605) 336-3468 (sales)
www.ksfy.com
License: Pierre, Hughes County, SD held by Hoak Media of Dakota License LLC.
Group Owner: Hoak Media Corporation; (acq 1-3-2007; grpsl);
Washington Law Firm: Arent, Fox, Kintner, Plotkin & Kahn
Nat'l Network: ABC
Size of News Staff: 45; *Hours of Local News Weekly:* news progmg 15 hrs wkly
Kelly Manning, General Manager
Darrel Nelson, Chief Engineer

KSFY-TV *Digital Channel:* 13 *Virtual Channel:* 13; 22.7 kw; 2001 ft.; N43 31 7 W96 32 5
Rsa Tower, 20th Floor, 201 Monroe Street, Montgomery, AL 36104 US
(605) 336-1300, *Fax:* (605) 336-7936
www.ksfy.com
License: Sioux Falls, Minnehaha County, SD held by Hoak Media of Dakota License LLC.
Group Owner: Hoak Media Corporation; (acq 1-3-2007; grpsl)
Nat'l Network: ABC *Nat'l Reps:* TeleRep
Size of News Staff: 30; *Hours of Local News Weekly:* news progmg 15 hrs wkly
Kelly Manning, General Manager
Ryan Welsh, General Sales Mgr
Jeff Morlan, Programming Director
Jeff Bonk, Promotions Manager
Darrel Nelson, Chief Engineer

***KTSD-TV** *Digital Channel:* 10 *Virtual Channel:* 10; 54.7 kw; 1600 ft.; N43 58 5 W99 35 40
Mailing Address: Cherry & Dakota Streets, Box 5000, Vermillion, SD 57069 US
Second Address: 555 N. Dakota St., Vermillion, SD 57069-5000
(605) 677-5861,(800) 456-0766, *Fax:* (605) 677-5010
www.sdpb.org
programming@sdpb.org
License: Pierre, Hughes County, SD held by South Dakota Board of Directors for Educational Telecommunications
Washington Law Firm: Cohn & Marks
Nat'l Network: PBS
Julie Andersen, President
Craig Jensen, Operations Dir
Terry Spencer, General Sales Mgr
Bob Bosse, Programming Director

KTTM *Digital Channel:* 12 *Virtual Channel:* 12; 12.6 kw; 843 ft.; N44 11 39 W98 19 5; *Rebroadcasting:* Satellite of KTTW(TV) Sioux Falls 100%
Mailing Address: P.O. Box 5103, Sioux Falls, SD 57117 US
Second Address: 2817 W. 11th St., Sioux Falls, SD 57104
(605) 338-0017, *Fax:* (605) 338-7173
www.kttw.com
yourcomments@foxnews.com
License: Huron, Beadle County, SD held by Independent Communications Inc
Group Owner: Independent Communications Inc.
Nat'l Network: FOX *Nat'l Reps:* Continental Television Sales
Ed Hoffman, General Manager
Stacey Sieverding, General Sales Mgr
Judy Buie, Programming Director

KTTW *Digital Channel:* 7 *Virtual Channel:* 17; 7.5 kw; 714 ft.; N43 30 19 W96 34 19
Mailing Address: P. O. Box 5103, Sioux Falls, SD 57117 US
Second Address: 2817 W. 11th St., Sioux Falls, SD 57104
(605) 338-0017, *Fax:* (605) 338-7173
www.kttw.com
yourcomments@foxnews.com
License: Sioux Falls, Minnehaha County, SD held by Independent Communications Inc
Group Owner: Independent Communications Inc.; (acq 3-9-88).;
Washington Law Firm: Reddy, Begley & McCormick
Nat'l Network: FOX *Nat'l Reps:* Continental Television Sales
Ed Hoffman, General Manager
Stacey Sieverding, General Sales Mgr
Judy Buie, Programming Director

***KUSD-TV** *Digital Channel:* 34 *Virtual Channel:* 2; 277 kw; 768 ft.; N43 3 1 W96 47 1
Mailing Address: Cherry & Dakota Streets, Box 5000, Vermillion, SD 57069 US
Second Address: 555 N. Dakota St., Vermillion, SD 57069
(605) 677-5861, *Fax:* (605) 677-5010
www.sdpb.org
programming@sdpb.org
License: Vermillion, Clay County, SD held by South Dakota Board of Directors for Educational Telecommunications
Washington Law Firm: Cohn & Marks
Nat'l Network: PBS
Julie Andersen, President
Craig Jensen, Operations Dir
Terry Spencer, General Sales Mgr
Bob Bosse, Programming Director
Fritz Miller, Promotions Manager

KWSD *Digital Channel:* 36 *Virtual Channel:* 36; 36.9 kw; 754 ft.; N43 30 19 W96 34 19
Mailing Address: 2504 West Main Street, Rapid City, SD 57702 US
Second Address: 6809 S. Minnesota Ave., Suite 203, Sioux Falls, SD 57108
(605) 336-3100, *Fax:* (605) 338-5484
www.siouxfallscw.com
jsimpson@siouxfallscw.com
License: Sioux Falls, Minnehaha County, SD held by J.F. Broadcasting LLC
(acq 3-2-2007; $300,000); *Ownership:* James F. Simpson, 100%
Nat'l Network: CW
James Simpson, General Manager
John Bennet, Chief Engineer

Tennessee

Chattanooga, TN (DMA 86)

WDEF-TV *Digital Channel:* 12 *Virtual Channel:* 12; 26 kw vis; ant 1,260t/16g; N35 08 06 W85 19 25; *Population Served:* 884,000
3300 Broad St., Chattanooga, TN 23219
(423) 785-1200, *Fax:* (423) 785-1271
www.wdef.com
news@wdef.com
License: Chattanooga, Hamilton County, TN held by WDEF-TV Inc.
Group Owner: Morris Multimedia Inc.; (acq 10-13-2006; $23 million); *Washington Law Firm:* Fletcher, Heald & Hildreth, P.L.C.
Nat'l Network: CBS; Bounce TV *Nat'l Reps:* Millennium
Size of News Staff: 23; *Hours of Local News Weekly:* news progmg 26 hrs wkly
Dean Hinson, President
Phillip D. Cox, General Manager
Bill Downs, General Sales Mgr
Doris Ellis, Community Service Director
Todd Buccelli, Marketing/News Media
Dutch Terry, News Director
Rick McClain, Chief Engineer
ChrisHull, Production Manager

WDSI-TV *Digital Channel:* 40 *Virtual Channel:* 61; 84 kw; 1148 ft.; N35 12 34 W85 16 39
Pegasus Corp. Office, 225 Cty Lne Ave., Ste200, Bala Cynwyd, PA 19004 US
(423) 265-0061, *Fax:* (423) 265-3636
www.myfoxchattanooga.com
info@myfoxchattanooga.com
License: Chattanooga, Hamilton County, TN held by New Age Media of Tennessee License LLC.
(acq 3-31-2007;; *Ownership:* Sedgwick Media LLC, 65%; Dallas Media LLC, 33.64%; Michael Yanuzzi, 1.36%; *Washington Law Firm:* Leventhal Senter & Lerman PLLC
Nat'l Network: FOX; MyNetworkTV
Hours of Local News Weekly: 3.5
Patrick Notley, Operations Dir
Tracye McCarthy, General Manager
Nathan Mears, General Sales Mgr
Jenny Giddens, Programming Director
Rebecca Sims, Promotions Manager
Latricia Thomas, News Director
Patrick Motley, ChiefEngineer
Tonetta Jones, Traffic Manager

WFLI-TV *Digital Channel:* 42 *Virtual Channel:* 53; 500 kw; 1093 ft.; N35 12 34 W85 16 39
1999 Avenue of the Stars, Suite 500, Los Angeles, CA 90067 US
(423) 265-0061, *Fax:* (423) 265-3636
www.thecwchattanooga.com
License: Cleveland, Bradley County, TN held by MPS Media of Tennessee License LLC
(acq 4-1-2008; $6.8 million); *Ownership:* Eugene J. Brown, 100%; *Washington Law Firm:* Fletcher, Heald & Hildreth
Nat'l Network: CW *Nat'l Reps:* MMT
Tracye McCarthy, General Manager

WRCB-DT *Digital Channel:* 13; 111 kw; DCBR-C3SP-4H/10H-1; N35 09 40 W85 18 52; *Population Served:* 900,000
900 Whitehall Rd., Chattanooga, TN 37405
(423) 267-5412, *Fax:* (423) 267-6840,(423) 756-3148
www.wrcbtv.com
ttolar@wrcbtv.com
License: Chattanooga, Hamilton County, TN held by Sarkes Tarzian Inc.
Group Owner: Sarkes Tarzian Inc.; (acq 10-82; $16 million;;
Washington Law Firm: Lerman, Senter
Nat'l Network: NBC (3.1); Antenna TV (3.2) *Nat'l Reps:* Continental Television Sales *Wire Services:* AP
Hours of Local News Weekly: News progmg 24.5 hrs wkly
Tom Tarzian, Chairman
Bob Davis, CFO
Tom Tolar, President
Doug Loveridge, Operations Dir
Tom Tolar, General Manager
Ralph Flynn, General Sales Mgr
Pam Teaque, Programming Director
Ronnie Minton, Promotions Manager
DerrallStalvey, News Director
Dan Sommers, Chief Engineer
Pam Teague, Controller/Program Director

***WTCI** *Digital Channel:* 29 *Virtual Channel:* 45; 200 kw; 1102 ft.; N35 12 26 W85 16 52
4411 Amnicola Highway, Chattanooga, TN 37406 US
(423) 702-7800, *Fax:* (423) 702-7823
www.wtcitv.org
License: Chattanooga, Hamilton County, TN held by The Greater Chattanooga Public Television Corporation
(acq 7-84).; *Washington Law Firm:* Dow, Lohnes & Albertson
Nat'l Network: PBS
Paul Grove, President
Jennifer Hoff, Operations Dir
Ann Cater, General Sales Mgr
Bryan Fuqua, Programming Director
Pam Carpenter, News Director
Julie Taylor, Director Major Giving
Sara Maloney, Membership Director
Susan Cates,Office & Business Manager
Peter DeLynn, VP Production & Operations

WTVC *Digital Channel:* 9; 316 kw vis, 31.6 kw aur; ant 1,056t/246g; N35 09 38 W85 19 06; *Population Served:* 350,000
4279 Benton Drive, Chattanooga, TN 37401
(423) 756-5500, *Fax:* (423) 757-7400
www.newschannel9.com
producers@newschannel9.com
License: Chattanooga, Hamilton County, TN held by Sinclair Broadcast Group
Group Owner: Freedom Communications Inc., Broadcast Division; acq 12-13-83; grpsl;; *Washington Law Firm:* Latham & Watkins
Nat'l Network: ABC *Nat'l Reps:* TeleRep *Wire Services:* AP; CNN; ABC
Size of News Staff: 40; *Hours of Local News Weekly:* news progmg 32 hrs wkly
Mike Costa, General Manager
Mike Costa, Station Manager
Ted Rudolph, General Sales Mgr
Margie Scott, Programming Director
Sheldon Harrell, Promotions Manager
Tom Henderson, News Director
Dennis Brown, Engineering Dir
DennisBrown, Chief Engineer

Jackson, TN (DMA 173)

WBBJ-TV *Digital Channel:* 43 *Virtual Channel:* 7; 316 kw vis, 31.6 kw aur; ant 1,060t/1,065g; N35 38 15 W88 41 32; *Population Served:* 198,150
346 Muse St., Jackson, TN 38301
(731) 424-4515, *Fax:* (731) 424-9299
www.wbbjtv.com
License: Jackson, Madison County, TN held by Tennessee Broadcasting Partners
Group Owner: Bahakel Communications; (acq 7-20-92)
Nat'l Network: ABC; CBS
Jerry Moore, General Manager
Robert Fay, General Sales Mgr
Anthony Matrisciano, Programming Director
Ken Galey, News Director
Randy McCaskill, Chief Engineer

WJKT *Digital Channel:* 39 *Virtual Channel:* 16; 392 kw; 971 ft.; N35 47 22 W89 6 14
2701 Union Ext., Memphis, TN 38812 US
(901) 323-2430, *Fax:* (901) 323-9503
www.myeyewitnessnews.com
newsdesk@myeyewitnessnews.com
License: Jackson, Madison County, TN held by Newport Television License LLC.
Group Owner: Newport Television LLC; (acq 3-14-2008;. grpsl)
Nat'l Network: FOX
Rene LaSpina, General Manager

***WLJT-DT** ; 316 kw vis, 63.1 kw aur; 640t/496g; N35 45 12 W88 36 10; *Population Served:* 211,000
Mailing Address: Box 966, Martin, TN 38237-0966
Second Address: Clement Hall, U.T.-Martin, Martin, TN 38238
(731) 881-7561, *Fax:* (731) 881-7566
www.wljt.org
wljt@wljt.org
License: Lexington, Henderson County, TN held by West Tennessee Public Television Council Inc
Nat'l Network: PBS
Dave Hinman, CEO
Bud Grimes, President
Emily Elliston, Operations Dir
Shorri Puckett, General Sales Mgr
Robbie Green, Promotions Manager
Monica Shumake, CFO
Katrina Cobb, Operations Director

Knoxville, TN (DMA 59)

WATE-TV *Digital Channel:* 26 *Virtual Channel:* 6; 930 kw; 1736 ft.; N36 0 13 W83 56 34
Mailing Address: 599 Lexington Avenue, 47th Floor, New York, NY 10022 US
Second Address: 1306 N.E. Broadway, Knoxville, TN 37917
(865) 637-6666, *Fax:* (865) 525-4091
www.wate.com
License: Knoxville, Knox County, TN held by Young Broadcasting of Knoxville
Group Owner: Young Broadcasting Inc.; (acq 11-14-94; grpsl;
Nat'l Network: ABC; Live Well *Nat'l Reps:* Cox Reps g
Size of News Staff: 50; *Hours of Local News Weekly:* news progmg 24 hrs wkly
Tom McCoy, Operations Dir
Dan Phillips, General Manager
Tony Kahl, General Sales Mgr
Melanie Morris, Programming Director
Jamie Foster, News Director
Steve Martin, Chief Engineer
Sarah Burton, Sales Manager

WBIR-TV *Digital Channel:* 10 *Virtual Channel:* 10; 40.9 kw; 1791 ft.; N36 0 19 W83 56 23
1100 Wilson Boulevard, Arlington, VA 22234 US
(865) 637-1010, *Fax:* (865) 637-6280(sales),(865) 637-6380
www.wbir.com
manager@wbir.com
License: Knoxville, Knox County, TN held by Gannett Pacific Corp.
Group Owner: Gannett Broadcasting; (acq 12-4-95; grpsl).;
Washington Law Firm: Wiley, Rein & Fielding
Nat'l Network: NBC
Size of News Staff: 50; *Hours of Local News Weekly:* news progmg 24 hrs wkly
Jeff Lee, President
Debbie Brizendine, General Sales Mgr
Tonja Bolander, Programming Director
Julie Morris, Promotions Manager
Bill Shory, News Director
Gary Davis, Chief Engineer
Joy Davidson, Traffic Manager

WBXX-TV/DT *Digital Channel:* 20; 562kw; ant 157t; N35 56 12 W85 00 46; *Population Served:* 1,000,000
10427 Cogdill Rd., Suite 100, Knoxville, TN 37932
(865) 777-9220, *Fax:* (865) 777-9221
www.wbxx.tv
promotions@wbxx.tv
License: Crossville, Cumberland County, TN held by Acme Television Licenses of Tennessee L.L.C.
Group Owner: ACME Communications Inc.; (acq 8-28-97; $13.2 million); *Washington Law Firm:* Dickstein Shapiro Morin & Oshinsky L.L.P.
Nat'l Network: CW *Nat'l Reps:* Harrington, Righter & Parsons
Dan Phillippi, Operations Dir
Joanne Marcenkus, General Sales Mgr
Anna Robins, Programming Director
Ferdy Guidry, Chief Engineer

***WETP-TV** *Digital Channel:* 41 *Virtual Channel:* 2; 445 kw; 1859 ft.; N36 22 52 W83 10 49
1611 E. Magnolia Avenue, Knoxville, TN 37917 US
(865) 595-0220, *Fax:* (865) 595-0300
www.etptv.org
etptv.mail@etptv.org
License: Sneedville, Knox County, TN held by East Tennessee Public Communications Corp
Nat'l Network: PBS
Teresa James, President
Frank Miller, Operations Dir
Kelly Hodges, General Sales Mgr
Bob Hutchinson, Programming Director
Katharine Seaton, Promotions Manager
Curtis Allin, Chief Engineer
Russ Manning, Public Affairs Director

***WKOP-TV** *Digital Channel:* 17 *Virtual Channel:* 15; 100 kw; 1809 ft.; N35 59 44 W83 57 23
1611 E. Magnolia Avenue, Knoxville, TN 37917 US
(865) 595-0220, *Fax:* (865) 595-0300
www.etptv.org
etptvmail@etptv.org
License: Knoxville, Knox County, TN held by East Tennessee Public Communications Corp
Nat'l Network: PBS
Teresa James, President
Frank Miller, Operations Dir
Kelly Hodges, General Sales Mgr
Bob Hutchinson, Programming Director
Katharine Seaton, Promotions Manager
Curtis Allin, Chief Engineer
Russ Manning, Public Affairs Director

WMAK *Digital Channel:* 7 *Virtual Channel:* 7; 55 kw; 1253 ft.; N36 0 36 W83 55 57
6215 Kingston Pike, Suite A, Knoxville, TN 37919 US
(865) 329-8777, *Fax:* (817) 571-0239
www.wmaktv.com
License: Knoxville, Knox County, TN held by Knoxville Channel 7 LLC.
Group Owner: South Central Communications Corp.;
Washington Law Firm: Fletcher, Heald & Hildreth
Nat'l Network: IND
J.P. Engelbrecht, President

WPXK-TV *Digital Channel:* 23; 28.8 kw vis, 3.9 kw aur; ant 1,007t; N36 30 26 W84 02 36; *Population Served:* 490,000
Bldg. D, 9000 Executive Park Dr., Suite 210, Knoxville, TN 37923
(865) 531-4037, *Fax:* (865) 531-4760
www.ionmedia.tv
License: Jellico, Campbell County, TN held by ION Media Knoxville License, Inc., Debtor-in-possession
Group Owner: ION Media Networks Inc.; (acq 9-23-98).
Nat'l Network: ION Television
Holly Jones, Operations Dir
Brad Cope, Chief Engineer

WTNZ *Digital Channel:* 34 *Virtual Channel:* 43; 460 kw; 1736 ft.; N36 0 13 W83 56 34
Rsa Tower, 20th Floor, 201 Monroe Street, Montgomer, AL 36104 US
(865) 693-4343, *Fax:* (865) 691-6904
wtnzfox43.com
License: Knoxville, Knox County, TN held by Raycom America License Subsidiary LLC.
Group Owner: Raycom Media Inc.; (acq 1996; grpsl).;
Washington Law Firm: Covington & Burling
Nat'l Network: FOX *Nat'l Reps:* TeleRep
Hours of Local News Weekly: 7 hrs weekly
Paul McTear, CEO
John Hayes, Operations Dir
Wayne Daugherty, COO

WVLR *Digital Channel:* 48 *Virtual Channel:* 48; 1000 kw; 1411 ft.; N36 15 30 W83 37 43
1724 South Hills Dr., Knoxville, TN 37920 US
(865) 932-4803, *Fax:* (865) 932-4102
www.tv48.org
MariaTV48@comcast.net
License: Tazewell, Claiborne County, TN held by Volunteer Christian Television Inc.
Nat'l Network: REL
Theron Woodward, General Manager
Tom Evenson, Chief Engineer

WVLT-TV *Digital Channel:* 30 *Virtual Channel:* 8; 870 kw; 1809 ft.; N35 59 44 W83 57 23
Mailing Address: 1201 New York Avenue, NW, Suite 1000, Washington, DC 20005 US
Second Address: 6450 Papermill Rd., Knoxville, TN 37919
(865) 450-8888, *Fax:* (865) 450-9663
www.volunteertv.com
License: Knoxville, Knox County, TN held by Gray Television Licensee Inc.
Group Owner: Gray Television Inc.; (acq 1996; $165 million with WCTV(TV) Thomasville, GA).
Nat'l Network: CBS; MyNetworkTV *Nat'l Reps:* Continental Television Sales
Size of News Staff: 38; *Hours of Local News Weekly:* news progmg 24.5 hrs wkly
Chris Baker, President
Les Phillips, Operations Dir
Marty Parham, Programming Director
Dino Cartwright, Promotions Manager
Steve Crabtree, News Director
Doug Stallard, Engineering Dir

Memphis, TN (DMA 48)

WHBQ-TV *Digital Channel:* 13 *Virtual Channel:* 13; 95 kw; 1001 ft.; N35 10 29 W89 50 43
5151 Wisconsin Ave., NW, Washington, DC 20016 US
(901) 320-1313
www.myfoxmemphis.com
License: Memphis, Shelby County, TN held by Fox Television Stations Inc.
Group Owner: Fox Television Stations Inc.; (acq 7-5-95; $80 million)
Nat'l Network: FOX *Nat'l Reps:* Fox Stations Sales
Size of News Staff: 55; *Hours of Local News Weekly:* news progmg 27 hrs wkly
Rupert Murdoch, Chairman
Betsy Swanson, CFO
Paul Sloan, Operations Dir
John Koski, General Manager
Bill Lane, General Sales Mgr
Ken Jobe, News Director
David Brant, Chief Engineer
Kim Moore, National Sales Manager

***WKNO** *Digital Channel:* 29; 316 kw vis, 56.2 kw aur; ant 1,079t/1,113g; N35 09 17 W89 49 20; *Population Served:* 1,600,000
Mailing Address: Box 241880, Memphis, TN 38124-1880
Second Address: 900 Getwell Rd., Memphis, TN 38111

(901) 458-2521, *Fax:* (901) 325-6505
www.wkno.org
wknopi@wkno.org
License: Memphis, Shelby County, TN held by Mid-South Public Communications Foundation
Washington Law Firm: Schwartz, Woods & Miller
Nat'l Network: PBS
Michael LaBonia, CEO
Russ Abernathy, Station Manager
Charles McLarty, General Sales Mgr

WLMT *Digital Channel:* 31 *Virtual Channel:* 30; 871 kw; 1115 ft.; N35 16 33 W89 46 38
2701 Union Ext., Memphis, TN 38812 US
(901) 323-2430, *Fax:* (901) 323-9503
www.myeyewitnessnews.com
newsdesk@myeyewitnessnews.com
License: Memphis, Shelby County, TN held by Newport Television License LLC.
Group Owner: Newport Television LLC; (acq 3-14-2008; grpsl);
Washington Law Firm: Covington & Burling
Nat'l Network: CW
Rene LaSpina, General Manager
Robyn Callaway, General Sales Mgr
Pete Jacobus, News Director

WMC-TV *Digital Channel:* 5 *Virtual Channel:* 5; 34.5 kw; 1010 ft.; N35 10 9 W89 53 10
Rsa Tower, 20th Floor, 201 Monroe Street, Montgomery, AL 36104 US
(901) 726-0555, *Fax:* (901) 278-7633
www.wmctv.com
License: Memphis, Shelby County, TN held by WMC License Subsidiary, LLC.
Group Owner: Raycom Media Inc.; (acq 1997; grpsl).;
Washington Law Firm: Goldberg, Godles, Wiener & Wright
Nat'l Network: NBC *Nat'l Reps:* TeleRep
Lee Meredith, Operations Dir
Gary Macko, General Sales Mgr
Chris Conroy, Promotions Manager
Tracey Rogersw, News Director
Tim Seymour, Local Sales Manager

WPTY-TV *Digital Channel:* 25 *Virtual Channel:* 24; 1000 kw; 1115 ft.; N35 16 33 W89 46 38
200 Concord Plaza, Suite 600, San Antonio, TX 78216 US
(901) 323-2430, *Fax:* (901) 323-9503
www.myeyewitnessnews.com
newsdesk@myeyewitnessnews.com
License: Memphis, Shelby County, TN held by Newport Television License LLC.
Group Owner: Newport Television LLC; (acq 3-14-2008; grpsl);
Washington Law Firm: Covington & Burling
Nat'l Network: ABC
Size of News Staff: 50; *Hours of Local News Weekly:* news progmg 7 hrs wkly
Rene LaSpina, General Manager

WPXX-TV *Digital Channel:* 51 *Virtual Channel:* 50; 1000 kw; 978 ft.; N35 12 41 W89 48 54
Mailing Address: 188 South Bellevue #222, Memphis, TN 38104 US
Second Address: 3145 Bartlett Corp. Dr., Memphis, TN 38133
(901) 821-8593, *Fax:* (901) 821-8331
www.ionmediatv.com
License: Memphis, Shelby County, TN held by ION Media Memphis License, Inc., Debtor-in-possession
Group Owner: ION Media Networks Inc.
Nat'l Network: ION
Terry Digel, Station Manager

WREG-TV *Digital Channel:* 28 *Virtual Channel:* 3; 906 kw; 1027 ft.; N35 10 52 W89 49 56
803 Channel 3 Drive, Memphis, TN 38103 US
(901) 543-2333, *Fax:* (901) 543-2198,(901) 543-2167 (news)
www.wreg.com
news@wreg.com
License: Memphis, Shelby County, TN held by Local TV Tennessee License LLC.
Group Owner: Local TV LLC; (acq 5-7-2007; grpsl); *Washington Law Firm:* Koteen & Naftalin
Nat'l Network: CBS *Nat'l Reps:* Eagle Television Sales *Wire Services:* New York Times News Service
Size of News Staff: 50
Robert Lawrence, President
Ronald Walter, General Manager
Leatha Moore, Programming Director
Wes Pollard, Promotions Manager
Bruce Moore, News Director
Norm Brewer, News Commentator
Jim Jaggers, Reporter
Tim Simpson, WeatherDirector

Mobile, AL-Pensacola (Ft. Walton Beach), FL (DMA 60)

DKB-97071 *Digital Channel:* 28; *Not on Air/Target Date:* unknown
P.O. Box Wkpt, Kingsport, TN 37662 US
(817) 571-1229, *Fax:* (817) 571-7458
www.daystar.com
contactus@daystar.com
License: Kingsport, Mobile County, TN
Marcus Lamb, President

Nashville, TN (DMA 29)

***WCTE** *Digital Channel:* 22 *Virtual Channel:* 22; 200 kw; 1394 ft.; N36 10 26 W85 20 37
Mailing Address: P.O. Box 2040, Cookeville, TN 38502 US
Second Address: 1151 Stadium Dr.,Ste 104, Cookeville, TN 38501
(931) 528-2222, *Fax:* (931) 372-6284
www.wcte.org
info@wcte.org
License: Cookeville, Putnam County, TN held by Upper Cumberland Broadcast Council
Nat'l Network: PBS
Becky Magura, President
Lindsey Sasser, Programming Director

WHTN *Digital Channel:* 38 *Virtual Channel:* 39; 1000 kw; 820 ft.; N36 4 58 W86 25 52
14346 Lebanon Road, Old Hickory, TN 37138 US
(615) 754-0039, *Fax:* (615) 754-0047
www.ctnonline.com
License: Murfreesboro, Rutherford County, TN held by Christian Television Network Inc
Washington Law Firm: Gammon & Grange
Nat'l Network: IND
Foreign Language Programming; Size of News Staff: 1; *Hours of Local News Weekly:* news progmg 2 hrs wkly
Monica Schmelter, Station Manager

WJFB *Digital Channel:* 44 *Virtual Channel:* 66; 1000 kw; 528 ft.; N36 9 13 W86 22 46
200 East Spring St., Lebanon, TN 37087 US
(615) 444-8206, *Fax:* (615) 444-7592
bclinic@bellsouth.net
License: Lebanon, Wilson County, TN held by Bryant Broadcasting Inc
Nat'l Network: IND
Size of News Staff: 2; *Hours of Local News Weekly:* news progmg 4 hrs wklyd
Dr. Joe Bryant, President
Pat Bryant, General Manager

WKRN-TV *Digital Channel:* 27 *Virtual Channel:* 2; 1,000 kw; 1,350t/942g; N36 02 50 W86 49 48; *Population Served:* 1,844,000
441 Murfreesboro Rd., Nashville, TN 10022
(615) 369-7222, *Fax:* (615) 369-7388
www.wkrn.com
License: Nashville, Davidson County, TN held by WKRN G.P.
Group Owner: Young Broadcasting LLC; (acq 7-1-89; $42 million;; *Washington Law Firm:* Brooks Pierce
Nat'l Network: ABC *Nat'l Reps:* Cox Reps
Size of News Staff: 65; *Hours of Local News Weekly:* news progmg 33 hrs wkly
Stan Knott, General Manager
Steve Watt, General Sales Mgr
Michelle Dube', Programming Director
Mike Tarrolly, Promotions Manager
Matthew Zelkind, News Director
Dave Parker, Chief Engineer
Traffic Manager, Barry Cunningham
Business Manager

WNAB *Digital Channel:* 23 *Virtual Channel:* 58; 350 kw; 1204 ft.; N36 15 50 W86 47 39
1999 Avenue of the Stars, Suite 500, Los Angeles, CA 90067 US
(410) 568-1500, *Fax:* (410) 568-1537
www.cw58.net
License: Nashville, Davidson County, TN held by Nashville License Holdings LLC
Nat'l Network: CW
Michael Jones, CFO
Michael Lambert, President
Mark Dillion, Station Manager
DeJuan Buford, General Sales Mgr
Michael Hook, Programming Director
Lee Scott, Promotions Manager
Dale Bukowski, National Sales Manager
PattyDaugherty, Traffic Manager

***WNPT** *Digital Channel:* 8 *Virtual Channel:* 8; 17.65 kw; 1280 ft.; N36 2 49 W86 49 49
161 Rains Avenue, Nashville, TN 37203 US
(615) 259-9325, *Fax:* (615) 248-6120
www.wnpt.org
tv8@wnpt.net
License: Nashville, Davidson County, TN held by Nashville Public Television Inc
Washington Law Firm: Schwartz, Woods & Miller
Nat'l Network: PBS
Beth Curley, CEO
Kevin Crane, Operations Dir
Justin Harvey, Programming Director

WNPX-TV *Digital Channel:* 20; 229 kw vis, 22.9 kw aur; 869t/623g; N36 07 33 W85 17 33; *Population Served:* 2,474,000
1281 N. Mt. Juliet Rd., Suite K, Mt. Juliet, TN 37122
(615) 773-6100
www.iontelevision.com
License: Cookeville, Putnam County, TN held by ION Media LPTV, Inc., Debtor-in-possession
Group Owner: ION Media Networks Inc.; (acq 9-4-97; $4.3 million)
Nat'l Network: ION Television
Tim Cooke, Engineering Dir

WPGD-TV *Digital Channel:* 33 *Virtual Channel:* 50; 1000 kw; 1352 ft.; N36 16 5 W86 47 45
250 West Arrow Highway, San Dimas, CA 91773 US
(615) 822-1243, *Fax:* (615) 822-1642
www.tbn.org
License: Hendersonville, Sumner County, TN held by Trinity Broadcasting Network
Group Owner: Trinity Broadcasting Network; (acq 7-2000; grpsl)
Nat'l Network: TRINITY BROADCA
Russell Hall, General Manager
Allen Partlow, Chief Engineer

WSMV-TV *Digital Channel:* 10 *Virtual Channel:* 4; 42.4 kw; 1362 ft.; N36 8 27 W86 51 56
5700 Knob Road, Nashville, TN 37209 US
(615) 353-4444, *Fax:* (615) 353-2375
www.wsmv.com
news@wsmv.com
License: Nashville, Davidson County, TN held by Meredith Corp.
Group Owner: Meredith Broadcasting Group, Meredith Corp.; (acq 11-1-94; $159 million;; *Washington Law Firm:* Wilmer, Cutler & Pickering
Nat'l Network: NBC *Nat'l Reps:* TeleRep
Elden Hale, General Manager
Paul Scott, General Sales Mgr
Wendy Reid, Chief Engineer

WTVF *Digital Channel:* 25 *Virtual Channel:* 5; 1000 kw; 428 meters; N36 16 05 W86 47 16; *Population Served:* 2,268,000
474 James Robertson Pkwy., Nashville, TN 37219
(615) 244-5000, *Fax:* (615) 248-5353,TWX: 810-371-1168
www.newschannel5.com
news@newschannel5.com
License: Nashville, Davidson County, TN held by NewsChannel 5 Network LP.
Group Owner: Landmark Communications Inc.; (acq 9-12-91; $46 million;; *Washington Law Firm:* Hogan & Hartson
Nat'l Network: CBS
Hours of Local News Weekly: News progmg 24 hrs wkly
Debbie Turner, General Manager
Mark Binda, Programming Director
Mike Cutler, News Director

WUXP-TV *Digital Channel:* 21 *Virtual Channel:* 30; 1000 kw; 1355 ft.; N36 15 50 W86 47 39
544 Red Rock, Wadsworth, OH 44281 US
(615) 259-5617, *Fax:* (615) 259-3962
www.mytv30web.com
License: Nashville, Davidson County, TN held by WUXP Licensee LLC.
Group Owner: Sinclair Broadcast Group Inc.; (acq 12-10-2001; $2.829 million); *Washington Law Firm:* Arter & Hadden
Nat'l Network: MYTV
Steven Mann, General Manager
Mark Dillon, Station Manager
Pam Sullivan, General Sales Mgr
Lee Scott, Promotions Manager
David Birdsong, Chief Engineer
Dale Bukowski, Local Sales Manager
Deborah Williams, Promotions Manager

WZTV *Digital Channel:* 15 *Virtual Channel:* 17; 1000 kw; 1348 ft.; N36 15 50 W86 47 39

18 Newbury Street, Boston, MA 02116 US
(615) 259-5617, *Fax:* (615) 259-3962
www.wztv.com
comments@wztv.com
License: Nashville, Davidson County, TN held by WZTV Licensee LLC.
Group Owner: Sinclair Broadcast Group Inc.; (acq 12-10-01; grpsl).; *Washington Law Firm:* Arter & Hadden
Nat'l Network: FOX
Size of News Staff: 9; *Hours of Local News Weekly:* news progmg 7 hrs wkly
Steven Mann, General Manager
Mark Dillon, Station Manager
Greg Carr, General Sales Mgr
Patty Daugherty, Programming Director
Lee Scott, Promotions Manager
David Birdsong, Chief Engineer
Randy Keys, Program Services

Tri-Cities, TN-VA (DMA 92)

WEMT *Digital Channel:* 38 *Virtual Channel:* 39; 1000 kw; 2365 ft.; N36 26 58 W82 6 29
Mailing Address: 900 Laskin Road, Virginia Beach, VA 23451 US
Second Address: 3206 Hanover Rd., Johnson City, TN 37602-3489
(423) 283-3900, *Fax:* (423) 283-4938
www.wemt39.com
License: Greeneville, Greene County, TN held by Esteem License Holdings Inc.
Group Owner: Esteem Broadcasting; (acq 5-31-2007; for stock); *Washington Law Firm:* Shaw, Pittman
Nat'l Network: FOX
Leesa Wilcher, General Manager
Rebecca Berry, Programming Director
Jim Hartline, Chief Engineer
Amy McClary, Regional Sales Manager

WJHL-TV *Digital Channel:* 11 *Virtual Channel:* 11; 34.5 kw; 2323 ft.; N36 25 55 W82 8 15
Mailing Address: 333 East Grace Street, Richmond, VA 23219 US
Second Address: 338 E. Main St., Johnson City, TN 37601
(423) 926-2151, *Fax:* (423) 434-4537
www.tricities.com
jdempsey@11connects.com
License: Johnson City, Washington County, TN held by Media General Communications Holdings, LLC
Group Owner: Media General Broadcast Group; (acq 3-21-97; grpsl).; *Washington Law Firm:* Dow, Lohnes and Albertson
Nat'l Network: CBS *Nat'l Reps:* Harrington, Righter & Parsons
Jack Dempsey, General Manager
Lisa Wilcher, General Sales Mgr
Amanda Adams, Promotions Manager
Neal Boling, News Director
Mike Moore, Chief Engineer
Kenny Hawkins, Sports Commentator
Mark Reynolds, Weather Director

WKPT-TV *Digital Channel:* 27 *Virtual Channel:* 19; 200 kw; ant 2,320t/225g; N36 25 54 W82 08 15; *Population Served:* 1,000,000
222 Commerce St., Kingsport, TN 37662
(423) 246-9578, *Fax:* (423) 246-6261/(423) 246-1863
www.wkpttv.com
gdevault@hvbc.com
License: Kingsport, Sullivan County, TN held by Holston Valley Broadcasting Corp.
Group Owner: Glenwood Communications Corp.; *Ownership:* Glenwood Communications Corp, 100%.; *Washington Law Firm:* Dennis J. Kelly
Nat'l Network: ABC *Nat'l Reps:* Harrington, Righter & Parsons
George DeVault Jr, President
Bobby Flowers, Operations Dir
George Devault Jr, General Manager
Lamar Reid, General Sales Mgr
Fred Falin, Programming Director
Jerreese Rockwell, Promotions Manager
Jim Bailey, News Director
GeorgeDevault, Engineering Dir
Bob Haywood, VP/Local Sales Manager
Bette Lawson, VP/Treasurer

Texas

Abilene-Sweetwater, TX (DMA 165)

KPCB-DT ; 464 kw vis; 443t; N32 46 52 W100 53 52
Mailing Address: Box 61000, Midland, TX 79711-1000
Second Address: 88 E. County Rd. 112, Snyder, TX 79549
(800) 707-0420, *Fax:* (325) 573-9417
www.godslearningchannel.com
info@ptcbglc.com
License: Snyder, Scurry County, TX held by Prime Time Christian Broadcasting Inc
Jeff Tveit, General Manager

KRBC-TV *Digital Channel:* 29 *Virtual Channel:* 9; 1000 kw; 846 ft.; N32 16 38 W99 35 51
3849 4th St N, Suite 420, St. Petersburg, FL 33703 US
(325) 692-4242, *Fax:* (325) 695-9922
www.krbc.tv
ksbcnews@krbc.tv
License: Abilene, Taylor County, TX held by Mission Broadcasting Inc.
Group Owner: Mission Broadcasting Inc.; (acq 6-13-2003; $10 million with KSAN-TV San Angelo); *Washington Law Firm:* Hogan & Hartson
Nat'l Network: NBC
Dennis Thatcher, CEO
Eric Thomas, General Manager
Justin Riggar, General Sales Mgr
Tom Vodak, News Director
David Smith, CFO

KTAB-TV *Digital Channel:* 24 *Virtual Channel:* 32; 1,000 ERP; 261 m HAAT; N32 16 35 W99 35 39; *Population Served:* 330,000
4510 S. 14th St., Abilene, TX 18411
(915) 695-2777, *Fax:* (915) 691-5822
bigcountryhomepage.com
news@ktab.tv
License: Abilene, Taylor County, TX held by Nexstar Finance Inc.
Group Owner: Nexstar Broadcasting Group Inc.; (acq 8-15-99; $16.7 million)
Nat'l Network: CBS
Size of News Staff: 32; *Hours of Local News Weekly:* news progmg 21.5 hr wkly
Eric Thomas, General Manager
Saundra Carriker, General Sales Mgr
Karen Yarbrough, Promotions Manager
Kevin Osgood, News Director
James Lester, Engineering Dir

KTXS-TV *Digital Channel:* 20 *Virtual Channel:* 12; 530 kw; 1319 ft.; N32 24 48 W100 6 25
Mailing Address: Box 2997, Abilene, TX 79604 US
Second Address: 4420 N. Clack, Abilene, TX 79601
(325) 677-2281, *Fax:* (325) 676-9231
www.ktxs.com
License: Sweetwater, Nolan County, TX held by BlueStone License Holdings Inc.
Group Owner: Bonten Media Group LLC; (acq 5-31-2007; grpsl)
Nat'l Network: ABC & CW (DIGIT; CW
Jackie Rutledge, Operations Dir
Jorge Montoya, General Sales Mgr
Sylvia Holmes, Programming Director
David Caldwell, Promotions Manager
Iain Munro, News Director
Leland Ohlhausen, Chief Engineer

KXVA *Virtual Channel:* 15; 3,947 kw vis; ant 978t/769g; N32 16 31 W99 35 23; *Rebroadcasting:* Rebroadcasts KIDY(TV) San Angelo 98%.; *Population Served:* 364,000
500 Chestnut Street, Suite 804, Abilene, TX 77057
(325) 672-5606, *Fax:* (325) 676-2437
www.kxvafox.com
License: Abilene, Taylor County, TX held by Sage Broadcasting Corp.
Group Owner: Sage Broadcasting Corp.; (acq 12-28-2004).; *Washington Law Firm:* Fletcher, Heard and Hildreth0
Nat'l Network: Fox *Nat'l Reps:* Millennium Sales & Marketing
Dujvan McCoy, President
Tednye Read, General Manager
Glenn Edwards, Chief Engineer

Amarillo, TX (DMA 131)

***KACV-TV** *Digital Channel:* 9; 5 kw; 481.7 meters AGL; 35Â° 22' 30.00"" N 101Â° 52' 56.00"" W (NAD 27); *Population Served:* 400,000
Mailing Address: Box 447, Amarillo, TX 79178
Second Address: 2408 S. Jackson, Amarillo, TX 79178
(806) 371-5222, *Fax:* (806) 371-5258
www.kacvtv.org
kacvtv@actx.edu
License: Amarillo, Potter County, TX held by Amarillo Junior College District.
Washington Law Firm: Cohn & Marks LLP
Nat'l Network: PBS
Jackie Smith, Operations Dir
Linda Pitner, General Manager
Lynne Groom, General Sales Mgr
Lee Proctor, Engineering Dir
Melissa Treiber, Outreach Coordinator

KAMR-TV *Digital Channel:* 19 *Virtual Channel:* 4; 400 kw; 1493 ft.; N35 20 33 W101 49 21
18 Newbury Street, Boston, MA 02116 US
(806) 383-3321, *Fax:* (806) 381-2943
www.kamr.com
nbc4@kamr.com
License: Amarillo, Potter County, TX held by Nexstar Finance Inc.
Group Owner: Nexstar Broadcasting Group Inc.; (acq 12-31-03; grpsl).; *Washington Law Firm:* Arter & Hadden
Nat'l Network: NBC
Cindy Perez, Operations Dir
Mark McKay, General Manager
Sherry Avara, General Sales Mgr
Amanda Bustamane, Promotions Manager
NyLynn Nichols, News Director
Ken High, Chief Engineer
Heather Brunson, Regional Sales Manager
Dennisde la Pena, Sports Commentator
Lori Kimber, Traffic Manager

KCIT *Digital Channel:* 15 *Virtual Channel:* 14; 925 kw; 1522 ft.; N35 20 33 W101 49 21
Mailing Address: 544 Red Rock, Wadsworth, OH 44281 US
Second Address: 1015 South Fillmore, Amarillo, TX 79101
(806) 374-1414, *Fax:* (806) 349-9083
fox14.tv
tgarcia@fox14.tv
License: Amarillo, Potter County, TX held by Mission Broadcasting Inc.
Group Owner: Mission Broadcasting Inc.; (acq 1999; $28.5 million with KJTL(TV) Wichita Falls).; *Washington Law Firm:* Drinker Biddle & Reath L.L.P.
Nat'l Network: FOX *Nat'l Reps:* Blair Television
Hours of Local News Weekly: News progmg 3 hrs wkly
Tom Garcia, Station Manager
Deb York, General Sales Mgr
Jim O'Malley, Programming Director
Mike Crowell, Promotions Manager
Wesley Willson, Chief Engineer

KEYU *Digital Channel:* 31 *Virtual Channel:* 31; 700 kw; 1002 ft.; N35 20 33 W101 49 20
Mailing Address: #1 Shackleford Drive, Suite 400, Little Rock, AR 72211 US
Second Address: PO Box 10, Amarillo, TX 79105
(806) 359-8900, *Fax:* (806) 352-8912
www.univision-amarillo.com
License: Borger, Hutchinson County, TX held by Borger Broadcasting Inc., debtor in possession.
Group Owner: Equity Media Holdings Corp.
Nat'l Network: UNIVISION
Foreign Language Programming
Brent McClure, General Manager

KFDA-TV *Digital Channel:* 10 *Virtual Channel:* 10; 62 kw; 1529 ft.; N35 17 34 W101 50 42
Mailing Address: P.O. Box 10, Amarillo, TX 79105 US
Second Address: 7900 Broadway, Amarillo, TX 79108
(806) 383-1010,(806) 383-6397, *Fax:* (806) 381-9859
www.newschannel10.com
License: Amarillo, Potter County, TX held by Panhandle Telecasting Co.
Group Owner: R.H. Drewry Group; (acq 10-4-76; $3 million;; *Washington Law Firm:* Shaw Pittman
Nat'l Network: CBS *Wire Services:* AP
Size of News Staff: 32; *Hours of Local News Weekly:* news progmg 19.5 hrs wkly
Bill Drewry, President
Larry Patton, Operations Dir
Brent McClure, General Manager
Joyce Austin, General Sales Mgr
Tony Smitherman, Promotions Manager
Richard Fulkerson, Operations Manager
Robert Drewry, President
BrentMcClure, Vice President

KPTF-DT *Digital Channel:* 18; 5,000 kw vis; ant 331t; N34 21 48 W103 13 05
Box 61000, Midland, TX 79711-1000
(432) 563-0420, *Fax:* (432) 563-1736
www.GLC.US.com
info@glc.us.com

License: Farwell, Parmer County, TX held by Prime Time Christian Broadcasting Inc
Al Cooper, President
Al Cooper, General Manager

KVII-TV *Digital Channel:* 7 *Virtual Channel:* 7; 21.9 kw; 1703 ft.; N35 22 30 W101 52 56
One Broadcast Center, Amarillo, TX 79101 US
(806) 373-1787, *Fax:* (806) 371-7329
www.connectamarillo.com
pronews7@kvii.com
License: Amarillo, Potter County, TX held by Barrington Broadcasting Texas Corp.
Group Owner: Barrington Broadcasting Group, LLC.; (acq 8-2-2005; $22.5 million with KVIH-TV Clovis, NM).; *Washington Law Firm:* Wiley, Rein & Fielding
Nat'l Network: CBS
Foreign Language Programming; Hours of Local News Weekly: News progmg 36 hrs wkly
K. James Yager, CEO
Chris Cornelius, President
Lane Philley, Operations Dir
Marc Gilmour, General Manager
Chris Knight, General Sales Mgr
Steve Pair, News Director
Bill Canady, Chief Engineer
Brenda Holloway, General SalesManager

Austin, TX (DMA 49)

KBVO *Digital Channel:* 27; 700 kw; 1297 ft.; N30 19 33 W97 47 58
200 Crescent Court, Suite 1600, Dallas, TX 75201 US
(512) 476-3636, *Fax:* (512) 476-1520
www.kxan.com
License: Llano, Travis County, TX held by LIN License Company LLC
Group Owner: LIN Media; (acq 11-14-94;; *Washington Law Firm:* Covington & Burling
Nat'l Network: NBC
Size of News Staff: 60; *Hours of Local News Weekly:* news progmg 22 hrs wkly
Eric Lassberg, General Manager

KEYE-TV *Digital Channel:* 43 *Virtual Channel:* 42; 1000 kw; 1296 ft.; N30 19 18 W97 48 11
2000 K Street N.W., Suite 725, Washington, DC 20006 US
(512) 835-0042, *Fax:* (512) 837-6753
www.keyetv.com
programming@kevtv.com
License: Austin, Travis County, TX held by Austin TV Licensee Corp.
Group Owner: Four Points Media Group; (acq 11-21-2007; grpsl); *Washington Law Firm:* Wiley Rein LLP
Nat'l Network: CBS *Nat'l Reps:* TeleRep
Size of News Staff: 50; *Hours of Local News Weekly:* news progmg 20 hrs wkly
Amy Villarreal, Operations Dir
Jeff Stern, General Sales Mgr
Stan Teater, Promotions Manager
Fred Undstrom, National Sales Manager
Dusty Granberry, Operations Manager
Lee Maaz, Regional Sales Manager
Steve Colkins, Regional SalesManager
Ira Poole, Regional Sales Manager

***KLRU** *Digital Channel:* 22 *Virtual Channel:* 18; 700 kw; 1173 ft.; N30 19 19 W97 48 12
PO Box 7158, Austin, TX 78713 US
(512) 471-4811, *Fax:* (512) 475-9090
www.klru.org
info@klru.org
License: Austin, Travis County, TX held by Capital of Texas Public Telecomm
Washington Law Firm: Cohn & Marks
Nat'l Network: PBS
Bill Stotesbery, CEO
Karin Morrison, Operations Dir
Bill Statesbury, General Manager
Lori Holliday, General Sales Mgr
Maury Sullivan, Promotions Manager
David Kuipers, Chief Engineer
Pat Wertz, CFO
Dick Peterson, Executive VicePresident
Ed Bailey, VP, Sales

KNVA *Digital Channel:* 49 *Virtual Channel:* 54; 500 kw; 1299 ft.; N30 19 33 W97 47 58
Mailing Address: P.O. Box 684647, Austin, TX 78768 US
Second Address: 908 W. Martin Luther King Blvd., Austin, TX 78701
(512) 478-5400, *Fax:* (512) 476-1520
www.thecwaustin.com
License: Austin, Travis County, TX held by 54 Broadcasting Inc
Nat'l Network: CW
Eric Lassberg, General Manager
Denise Daniels, General Sales Mgr
Jamie Aragon, Programming Director
Tish Saliani, Promotions Manager
Michael Fabac, News Director
Mark Dunham, Engineering Dir
Tom Michel, Local Sales Manager
Bryan Hastings, National Sales Manager
Amy Coplen, Regional Sales Manager

KTBC *Digital Channel:* 7 *Virtual Channel:* 7; 98.6 kw; 1257 ft.; N30 18 35 W97 47 34
5151 Wisconsin Ave., NW, Washington, DC 20016 US
(512) 476-7777, *Fax:* (512) 495-7060
www.myfoxaustin.com
management@fox7.com
License: Austin, Travis County, TX held by KTBC License Inc.
Group Owner: Fox Television Stations Inc.; (acq 1-97)
Nat'l Network: FOX
Size of News Staff: 54; *Hours of Local News Weekly:* news progmg 24 hrs wkly
Mark Rodman, Operations Dir
Scott Moore, General Sales Mgr
Holly Morrison-Breaux, Programming Director
Kathie Smith, Promotions Manager
Pam Vaught, News Director
Ken Smith, Chief Engineer
Rob Cunningham, Public AffairsDirector
Karen McCarty, Research Director

KVUE *Digital Channel:* 33 *Virtual Channel:* 24; 1000 kw; 1234 ft.; N30 19 18 W97 48 11
Mailing Address: 400 South Record Street, Dallas, TX 75202 US
Second Address: 3201 Steck Ave., Austin, TX 78757
(512) 459-6521, *Fax:* (512) 533-2215
www.kvue.com
listens@kvue.com
License: Austin, Travis County, TX held by KVUE Television Inc.
Group Owner: Belo Corp; (acq 6-1-99; swap with KXTV(TV) Sacramento, CA).
Nat'l Network: ABC *Nat'l Reps:* Harrington, Righter & Parsons
Hours of Local News Weekly: News progmg 29.5
Patti C. Smith, President

KXAN-TV *Digital Channel:* 21 *Virtual Channel:* 36; 700 kw; 1297 ft.; N30 19 33 W97 47 58
Mailing Address: 200 Crescent Court, Suite 1600, Dallas, TX 75201 US
Second Address: 908 W. Martin Luther King Blvd., Austin, TX 78701
(512) 476-3636, *Fax:* (512) 476-1520
www.kxan.com
License: Austin, Travis County, TX held by LIN License Company LLC
Group Owner: LIN Media; (acq 11-14-94;; *Washington Law Firm:* Covington & Burling
Nat'l Network: NBC
Size of News Staff: 60; *Hours of Local News Weekly:* news progmg 22 hrs wkly
Eric Lassberg, General Manager
Denise Daniels, General Sales Mgr
Laura Franklin, Programming Director
Tish Saliani, Promotions Manager
Michael Fabac, News Director
Mark Dunham, Engineering Dir
Todd Krauss, Local Sales Manager
Amy Coplen, Regional Sales Manager
Jamie Aragon, Traffic and Program Director
Jim Spencer, Weather Director

Beaumont-Port Arthur, TX (DMA 141)

KBMT *Digital Channel:* 12 *Virtual Channel:* 12; 18.2 kw; 1001 ft.; N30 11 26 W93 53 8
P.O. Box 1550, Beaumont, TX 77704 US
(409) 833-7512,(409) 838-1212, *Fax:* (409) 835-1617
www.12newsnow.com
License: Beaumont, Jefferson County, TX held by Texas Telecasting Inc.
Group Owner: McKinnon Broadcasting Co.; (acq 11-1-76; $2.4 million;; *Washington Law Firm:* Cohn & Marks
Nat'l Network: ABC; NBC
Size of News Staff: 26; *Hours of Local News Weekly:* news progmg 13 hrs wkly
Michael McKinnon, President
Mark McKinnon, Operations Dir
David King, General Sales Mgr
Elizabeth West, Programming Director
Don Haener, Promotions Manager
Mark Cormier, Chief Engineer
Mike Elord, General Manager
Don Williams,Operations Director
Elda Gaudet, Regional Sales Manager

KBTV-TV *Digital Channel:* 40 *Virtual Channel:* 4; 1000 kw; 829 ft.; N30 9 20 W93 59 10
200 Abington Executive Park, Suite 201, Clarks Summit, PA 18411 US
(409) 840-4444, *Fax:* (409) 985-4927,(409) 899-4639 (news)
www.kbtv4.tv
License: Port Arthur, Jefferson County, TX held by Nexstar Broadcasting Inc.
Group Owner: Nexstar Broadcasting Group Inc.; (acq 11-6-97; grpsl).; *Washington Law Firm:* Drinker, Biddle & Roth
Nat'l Network: NBC *Nat'l Reps:* Blair Television *Wire Services:* AP
Perry Sook, CEO
Ed Stowell, Operations Dir
Chris Puritt, General Manager
Margie Redkey, Programming Director
Paul Bergen, News Director
Charlie Ravell, Chief Engineer
Duane Lammers, COO
Dawn Stout, Public Affairs Director
James Ware, Sports Commentator

KFDM-TV *Digital Channel:* 21; 100 kw vis, 20 kw aur; 960t/1,031g; N30 08 24 W93 58 44; *Population Served:* 163,500
Box 7128, 2955 I-10 E., Beaumont, TX 77726-7128
(409) 892-6622, *Fax:* (409) 892-6665
www.kfdm.com
License: Beaumont, Jefferson County, TX held by Freedom Broadcasting of Texas Licensee L.L.C
Group Owner: Freedom Communications Inc., Broadcast Division; (acq 1-4-84; grpsl;; *Washington Law Firm:* Latham & Watkins
Nat'l Network: CBS; CW *Nat'l Reps:* TeleRep
Larry Beaulieu, General Manager

***KITU-TV** *Digital Channel:* 33 *Virtual Channel:* 34; 1,000 kw vis; ant 1,023t/1,027g; N30 10 41 W93 54 26
11221 IH 10, Orange, TX 77272
(409) 745-3434, *Fax:* (409) 745-4752
www.communityedtv.org
License: Beaumont, Jefferson County, TX held by Community Educational Television Inc
Dr. Reginald Cherry, President
Sandy Aulquist, Operations Dir
Wayne Ozio, Station Manager
Wayne Ozio, Chief Engineer

Corpus Christi, TX (DMA 129)

***KEDT** *Digital Channel:* 23 *Virtual Channel:* 16; 50 kw; 896 ft.; N27 39 20 W97 33 55
4455 S.Padre Isl.Dr.St38, Corpus Christi, TX 78411 US
(361) 855-2213, *Fax:* (361) 855-3877
www.kedt.org
License: Corpus Christi, Nueces County, TX held by South Texas Public Broadcasting System
Washington Law Firm: Schwartz, Woods & Miller
Nat'l Network: PBS
Trey McCampbell, Chairman
Norma Camarillo, CFO
Don Dunlap, President
Myra Lombardo, Operations Dir
Don Dunlap, General Manager
Molly Goodwin, General Sales Mgr
Sylvia Coronado, Programming Director
Johanna Zwernemann, AsstMusic Director
Robert Chabot, Music Director
Cody Blount, Operations Director

KIII *Digital Channel:* 8 *Virtual Channel:* 3; 160 kw; 883 ft.; N27 39 30 W97 36 4
Mailing Address: P.O. Box 6669, Corpus Christi, TX 78411 US
Second Address: Box 6669, Corpus Christi, TX 78466
(361) 986-8300, *Fax:* (361) 986-8311
www.kiiitv.com
news@kiiitv.com
License: Corpus Christi, Nueces County, TX held by Channel 3 of Corpus Christi Inc.

Group Owner: McKinnon Broadcasting Co.; (acq 7-79; $171,720); *Washington Law Firm:* Cohn & Marks
Nat'l Network: ABC *Nat'l Reps:* Continental Television Sales
Foreign Language Programming; Size of News Staff: 30; *Hours of Local News Weekly:* news progmg 17.5 hrs wkly
Michael McKinnon, President
Dick Drilling, Operations Dir
Bill Beck, General Sales Mgr
Richard Longoria, News Director
Ralph Quiroz, Chief Engineer
Larry Hogue, National Sales Manager
Scott Jones, Operations Director
PaulaTilton, Traffic Manager

KORO *Digital Channel:* 27 *Virtual Channel:* 28; 1000 kw; 943 ft.; N27 42 27.9 W97 37 59
Mailing Address: 11900 Olympic Boulevard, Suite 590, Los Angeles, CA 90064 US
Second Address: 102 N. Mesquite, Corpus Christi, TX 78403
(361) 883-2823, *Fax:* (361) 883-2931
License: Corpus Christi, Nueces County, TX held by Entravision Holdings L.L.C.
Group Owner: Entravision Communications Corp.; (acq 3-17-98; $1.336 million); *Washington Law Firm:* Mullin, Rhyne, Emmons & Topel
Nat'l Network: UNIVISION
Foreign Language Programming; Size of News Staff: 5; *Hours of Local News Weekly:* news progmg 5 hrs wkly
Anita Saenz-Carvalho, General Manager

KRIS-TV *Digital Channel:* 13 *Virtual Channel:* 6; 46.1 kw; 786 ft.; N27 44 29 W97 36 9
Mailing Address: 134 Columbus Street, Charleston, SC 29403 US
Second Address: 409 S. Staples, Corpus Christi, TX 78403
(361) 886-6100, *Fax:* (361) 887-6666
www.kristv.com
License: Corpus Christi, Nueces County, TX held by KVOA Communications Inc.
Group Owner: Cordillera Communications Inc.; *Washington Law Firm:* Nixon, Hargrave, Devans & Doyle
Nat'l Network: NBC/CW; CW
Size of News Staff: 31; *Hours of Local News Weekly:* news progmg 14 hrs wkly
Tim Noble, President
Bob Webb, Operations Dir
Don Grubaugh, General Sales Mgr
James Smith, Programming Director
Jay Sanchez, Promotions Manager
Sandra Richards, News Director
Steve West, Chief Engineer
Roger Brandt, GeneralSales Manager
Heidi Garcia, Public Service Director

KUQI *Digital Channel:* 38 *Virtual Channel:* 38; 50 kw; 810 ft.; N27 45 31.8 W97 36 26.3; *Not on Air/Target Date:* unknown
7228 Canyon Run, El Paso, TX 79912 US
(202) 625-3695, *Fax:* (202) 295-1122
lee.shubert@kattenlaw.com
License: Corpus Christi, Nueces County, TX
Nat'l Network: FOX
Lee W. Shubert, Court-Appointed Rece

KZTV *Digital Channel:* 10 *Virtual Channel:* 10; 39 kw; 951 ft.; N27 42 27.9 W97 37 59
P.O. Box Tv-10, Corpus Christi, TX 78403 US
(361) 883-7070, *Fax:* (361) 882-8553
www.kztv10.com
contactus@kztv10.com
License: Corpus Christi, Nueces County, TX held by Eagle Creek of Corpus Christi LLC.
Group Owner: Eagle Creek Broadcasting LLC; (acq 6-13-2002; grpsl)
Nat'l Network: CBS
Size of News Staff: 18
Billy Brotherton, General Manager
Norman Barron, General Sales Mgr
Hollis Grizzard, News Director
Russell Vaughan, Chief Engineer

Dallas-Ft. Worth (DMA 5)

KAZD *Digital Channel:* 54; 1,039 kw vis; ant 341t; N32 59 56 W96 55 02
2450 Rockbrook, Louisville, TX 77063
(972) 316-2115, *Fax:* (972) 316-1112
License: Lake Dallas, Denton County, TX held by Johnson Broadcasting of Dallas Inc
Nat'l Network: Azteca America
Jason Clegg, Operations Dir

KDAF *Digital Channel:* 32 *Virtual Channel:* 33; 780 kw; 1762 ft.; N32 32 35 W96 57 32
8001 John Carpenter Freeway, Dallas, TX 75247 US
(214) 252-9233, *Fax:* (214) 252-3379
cw33.trb.com
cw33news@tribune.com
License: Dallas, Dallas County, TX held by Tribune Broadcasting Co.
Group Owner: Tribune Broadcasting Co.; (acq 12-20-2007; grpsl); *Washington Law Firm:* Dow Lohnes PLLC
Nat'l Network: CW *Nat'l Reps:* TeleRep
Size of News Staff: 40; *Hours of Local News Weekly:* news progmg 6 hrs wkly
Joe Young, Operations Dir
Steve McDonald, General Sales Mgr
Wendy Logsdon, Programming Director
David Duitch, News Director
Rick Anderson, Chief Engineer

KDFI *Digital Channel:* 36 *Virtual Channel:* 27; 1000 kw; 1624 ft.; N32 32 36 W96 57 32
400 North Griffin Street, Dallas, TX 75202 US
(214) 720-4444, *Fax:* (214) 720-3207
www.myfoxdfw.com
kdfi27@foxinc.com
License: Dallas, Dallas County, TX held by New DMIC Inc.
Group Owner: Fox Television Stations Inc.; (acq 2-18-00; $6.2 million)
Nat'l Network: MY NETWORK *Nat'l Reps:* Fox Stations Sales
Kathy Saunders, Operations Dir
Andy Alexander, Engineering Dir

KDFW *Digital Channel:* 35 *Virtual Channel:* 4; 1000 kw; 1673 ft.; N32 35 6 W96 58 41
5151 Wisconsin Ave NW, Washington, DC 20016 US
(214) 720-4444, *Fax:* (214) 720-3177 (gen.mgr.),(214) 720-3263 (news)
www.myfoxdfw.com
kdfw@foxtv.com
License: Dallas, Dallas County, TX held by KDFW License Inc.
Group Owner: Fox Television Stations Inc.; (acq 1-97; grpsl).
Nat'l Network: FOX
Hours of Local News Weekly: News progmg 50 hrs wkly
Kathy Saunders, Operations Dir
Dennis Welsh, General Sales Mgr
Andy Alexander, Programming Director
John Kukla, Promotions Manager
Maria Barrs, News Director
Jeff Gurley, General Sales Manager
Stacy Garland, National SalesManager
Jennifer Owen, National Sales Manager
TBA, Promotions Manager

***KDTN** *Digital Channel:* 43 *Virtual Channel:* 2; 1000 kw; 1621 ft.; N32 32 35 W96 57 32
3000 Harry Hines Blvd, Dallas, TX 75201 US
(817) 799-2138, *Fax:* (817) 571-0239
www.daystar.com
License: Denton, Denton County, TX held by Community Television Educators of DFW Inc
Nat'l Network: IND
Marcus Lamb, CEO
Arnold Torres, General Manager
Jennette Hawkins, Programming Director

KDTX-TV *Digital Channel:* 45 *Virtual Channel:* 58; 1000 kw; 1621 ft.; N32 32 36 W96 57 32
2823 W. Irving Blvd., Irving, TX 75061 US
(972) 313-1333, *Fax:* (972) 790-5853
www.tbn.org
License: Dallas, Dallas County, TX held by Trinity Broadcasting of Texas Inc.
Group Owner: Trinity Broadcasting Network; (acq 7-86; $1.6 million;
Nat'l Network: TRINITY BROADCA
Paul Crouch, President
Jennye Gardner, Operations Dir
Steve Fjordbak, General Manager
Corrie Hickey, Public Affairs Director
Jim Forman, Chief Engineer

***KERA-TV** *Digital Channel:* 14 *Virtual Channel:* 13; 474 kw; 1640 ft.; N32 34 43 W96 57 12
3000 Harry Hines Blvd., Dallas, TX 75201 US
(214) 871-1390, *Fax:* (214) 754-0635
www.kera.org
License: Dallas, Dallas County, TX held by North Texas Public Broadcasting Inc
Washington Law Firm: Schwartz, Woods & Miller
Nat'l Network: PBS
Daniel Slentz, Operations Dir
Mary Anne Alhadeff, General Manager

KFWD *Digital Channel:* 9 *Virtual Channel:* 52; 13 kw; 1791 ft.; N32 35 19 W96 58 5
3000 West Story Road, Irving, TX 75038 US
(214) 977-6780, *Fax:* (214) 977-6544
www.kfwd.tv
wayne.casa@mundofox52.com
License: Fort Worth, Tarrant County, TX held by HIC Broadcast Inc
Washington Law Firm: Dow, Lohnes & Albertson
Nat'l Network: IND
Wayne Casa, General Manager
Tony Montes, Station Manager
Steve Brooks, General Sales Mgr
Sandra Ventura, Programming Director
Don Guemmer, Chief Engineer

KMPX *Digital Channel:* 30 *Virtual Channel:* 29; 1000 kw; 1785 ft.; N32 35 19 W96 58 5
Mailing Address: 5000 Westgrove Lane, Colleyville, TX 76034 US
Second Address: 4201 Pool Rd., Colleyville, TX 76034-5017
(817) 868-7776, *Fax:* (817) 571-7458
www.daystar.tv
comments@daystar.com
License: Decatur, Wise County, TX held by Liberman Television of Dallas License LLC.
Group Owner: Liberman Broadcasting Inc.; (acq 1-12-2004; $37 million)
Nat'l Network: IND
Joni Snow, General Manager

KPXD ; 5,000 kw vis; 1,181t; N32 35 24 W96 58 21
600 Six Flags Dr. Ste 652, Arlington, TX 76011-6353
(817) 654-6467
www.ionline.tv
License: Arlington, Tarrant County, TX held by Paxson Dallas License Inc.
Group Owner: ION Media Networks Inc.; (acq 4-4-97; $2.5 million for 51%).
Nat'l Network: ION Television
Rick Fetter, Station Manager

KTVT *Digital Channel:* 11 *Virtual Channel:* 11; 23 kw; 1708 ft.; N32 34 43 W96 57 12
Mailing Address: One Gaylord Drive, Nashville, TN 37214 US
Second Address: 5233 Bridge St., Fort Worth, TX 76103
(817) 451-1111/654-1100, *Fax:* (817) 457-1897
www.cbs11tv.com
news@ktvt.com
License: Fort Worth, Tarrant County, TX held by CBS Stations Group of Texas L.P.
Group Owner: CBS Television Stations Group; (acq 8-3-99; $485 million in stock).; *Washington Law Firm:* Leventhal, Senter & Lerman
Nat'l Network: CBS
Size of News Staff: 100; *Hours of Local News Weekly:* news progmg 27 hrs wkly
Steve Mauldin, President
Gary Schneider, Operations Dir
Adam Levy, General Sales Mgr
Ken Foote, Programming Director
David Hershey, Promotions Manager
Scott Diener, News Director
Steve Williams, Operations Manager

KTXA *Digital Channel:* 29 *Virtual Channel:* 21; 1000 kw; 1752 ft.; N32 32 36 W96 57 32
Mailing Address: 1501 M Street, N.W., Suite 1100, Washington, DC 20005 US
Second Address: 5233 Bridge St., Fort Worth, TX 76103
(214) 743-2100, *Fax:* (214) 743-2121,(214) 743-2150
ktxa.com
news@ktvt.com
License: Fort Worth, Tarrant County, TX held by Viacom Television Stations Group of Dallas/Fort Worth L.P.
Group Owner: CBS Television Stations Group; (acq 2-28-91).; *Washington Law Firm:* Leventhal, Senter & Lerman
Nat'l Network: INDEPENDENT
Steve Mauldin, President
Gary Schneider, Operations Dir
Julia O'Hickey, General Sales Mgr
Ken Foote, Programming Director
David Hershey, Promotions Manager
Kyle Brawner, National Sales Manager
Steve Williams, OperationsManager

KTXD-TV *Digital Channel:* 46 *Virtual Channel:* 47; 600 kw; 1627 ft.; N32 32 36 W96 57 32

Mailing Address: C/O Gammon & Grange, 8280 Greensboro Dr, 7th, McLean, VA 22102 US
Second Address: 1058 Country Rd., Greenville, TX 75404
(903) 455-8847, *Fax:* (903) 455-8891
License: Greenville, Hunt County, TX held by Simons Broadcasting LP
Nat'l Network: IND
Mike Simons, General Manager

KUVN-DT ; 5,000 kw vis, 1,000 kw aur; 1,142t; N32 54 04 W96 41 14
2323 Bryan St., Suite 1900, Dallas, TX 75201-2646
(214) 758-2300, *Fax:* (214) 758-2324
www.univision.com
License: Garland, Dallas County, TX held by KUVN License Partnership L.P.
Group Owner: Univision Communications Inc.; (acq 5-88; $5.2 million)
Nat'l Network: Univision (Spanish)
Foreign Language Programming; Size of News Staff: 22; *Hours of Local News Weekly:* news progmg 10 hrs wkly
Becky Munoz-Diaz, General Manager

KXAS-TV *Digital Channel:* 41 *Virtual Channel:* 5; 891 kw; 1660 ft.; N32 35 7 W96 58 6
Mailing Address: C/O Nbc, Inc., 11th Flr., 1299 Pennsylvania Ave., N.W., Washington, DC 20004 US
Second Address: 3900 Barnett, Fort Worth, TX 76103
(817) 429-5555,(214) 745-5555, *Fax:* (817) 654-6362
www.nbc5i.com
nbc5i@nbc.com
License: Fort Worth, Tarrant County, TX held by Station Venture Operations LP
Nat'l Network: NBC *Nat'l Reps:* NBC TV Stations Sales
Hours of Local News Weekly: News progmg 37 hrs wkly
Jim Borden, Operations Dir

KXTX-TV *Digital Channel:* 40 *Virtual Channel:* 39; 1000 kw; 1621 ft.; N32 35 7 W96 58 6
P. O. Box 36107, Dallas, TX 75235 US
(214) 521-3900, *Fax:* (214) 303-5156
www.telemundodallas.com
License: Dallas, Dallas County, TX held by NBC Telemundo License Co.
Group Owner: NBC Owned Television Stations; (acq 4-12-2002; grpsl).; *Washington Law Firm:* Fisher, Wayland, Cooper, Leader & Zaragoza
Nat'l Network: TELEMUNDO *Nat'l Reps:* Harrington, Righter & Parsons
Foreign Language Programming
Brian McCall, Operations Dir
Jose Valle, General Manager

WFAA *Digital Channel:* 9; 316 kw vis, 31.6 kw aur; 1,680t/1,521g; N32 35 06 W96 58 41; *Population Served:* 3,591,600
Communications Ctr., 606 Young St., Dallas, TX 75202-4870
(214) 748-9631, *Fax:* (214) 977-6268
wfaa.com
License: Dallas, Dallas County, TX held by WFAA-TV Inc.
Group Owner: Belo Corp; (acq 2-1950); *Washington Law Firm:* Wiley, Rein & Fielding
Nat'l Network: ABC *Nat'l Reps:* TeleRep *Wire Services:* Reuters; NWS (National Weather Service)
Size of News Staff: 85; *Hours of Local News Weekly:* news progmg 28 hrs wkly
Robert Iecherd, CEO
Mike Devlin, President
Angela Betasso, General Sales Mgr
David Walther, Programming Director
Nick Nicholson, Promotions Manager
Linda Ross, National Sales Manager
Eric Nelson, National Sales Manager
JimGlass, Promotions Director
Cathy Helean, Promotions Manager

El Paso (Las Cruces, NM), TX (DMA 98)

***KCOS** *Digital Channel:* 13 *Virtual Channel:* 13; 42 kw; 850 ft.; N31 47 15 W106 28 47
P.O. Box 650, El Paso, TX 79968 US
(915) 590-1313, *Fax:* (915) 594-5394
www.kcostv.org
cbrush@kcostv.org
License: El Paso, El Paso County, TX held by El Paso Public Television Foundation
Washington Law Firm: Cohn & Marks
Nat'l Network: PBS
Craig Brush, CEO
David Echaniz, Engineering Dir

KDBC-TV *Digital Channel:* 18 *Virtual Channel:* 4; 413.9 kw; 1532 ft.; N31 47 46 W106 28 57
Mailing Address: 2201 Wyoming Avenue, El Paso, TX 77903 US
Second Address: 2201 East Wyoming Avenue, El Paso, TX 79903
(915) 496-4444, *Fax:* (915) 496-4591 (sls),(915) 496-4593 (news)
www.kdbc4.com
news@kdbc4.com
License: El Paso, TX held by KDBC License Sub, LLC
Group Owner: Pappas Telecasting Companies; (acq 3-29-2004; $20 million); *Washington Law Firm:* Fletcher, Heald & Hildreth, P.L.C.
Nat'l Network: CBS; MyNetworkTV *Nat'l Reps:* Harrington, Righter & Parsons
Size of News Staff: 22; *Hours of Local News Weekly:* news progmg 7 hrs wkly
Margafet Carrillo, Operations Dir
Steve Scollard, General Manager
John Burton, General Sales Mgr
Yolonda Garcia, Programming Director
Aaron Barnes, Promotions Manager
Scott Pickey, News Director
Jaime Martinez, Chief Engineer
Dawn Alexander, Production Supervisor
Cheri Dorsey, Regional Sales Manager

KFOX-TV *Digital Channel:* 15 *Virtual Channel:* 14; 1000 kw; 1975 ft.; N31 48 55 W106 29 20
6004 North Mesa St., El Paso, TX 79912 US
(915) 833-8585, *Fax:* (915) 833-1358
www.kfoxtv.com
License: El Paso, El Paso County, TX held by KTVU Partnership.
Group Owner: Cox Media Group; (acq 1996; $20.855 million); *Washington Law Firm:* Dow, Lohnes & Albertson
Nat'l Network: FOX *Nat'l Reps:* TeleRep
Size of News Staff: 23; *Hours of Local News Weekly:* news progmg 6 hrs wkly
John Witte, General Manager
Nichole Villalobos, Site Services Manager

KINT-TV *Digital Channel:* 25 *Virtual Channel:* 26; 1000 kw; 1441 ft.; N31 47 46 W106 28 57
11900 Olympic Boulevard, Los Angeles, CA 90064 US
(915) 581-1126, *Fax:* (915) 581-1393
www.univision26.com
info@univision26.com
License: El Paso, El Paso County, TX held by Entravision Communications Co. L.L.C.
Group Owner: Entravision Communications Corp.; (acq 6-4-97; grpsl).; *Washington Law Firm:* Thompson, Hine & Flory L
Nat'l Network: UNIVISION
Foreign Language Programming; Size of News Staff: 14; *Hours of Local News Weekly:* news progmg 10 hrs wkly
David Candelaria, General Manager
Diana DeLara, General Sales Mgr
Nidia Holguin, Programming Director
Abel Rodriguez, Promotions Manager
Zoltan Csanyi, News Director
Alfredo Durand, Chief Engineer

***KSCE** *Digital Channel:* 39 *Virtual Channel:* 38; 150 kw; 1827 ft.; N31 48 19 W106 28 59
6400 Escondido Drive, El Paso, TX 79912 US
(915) 585-8838, *Fax:* (915) 585-8841
www.kscetv.com
ksce@aol.com
License: El Paso, El Paso County, TX held by Channel 38 Christian Television
Ownership: Channel 38 Christian Television; *Washington Law Firm:* James L. Oyster
Nat'l Network: ETV
Foreign Language Programming
Grace Rendall, Operations Dir
Angel Conger, General Sales Mgr
Mark Stephenson, Operations Manager

KTFN *Digital Channel:* 51 *Virtual Channel:* 65; 250 kw; 1722 ft.; N31 48 19 W106 28 59
1116-G Coolidge Drive, Lafayette, LA 70503 US
(915) 581-1126, *Fax:* (915) 581-1393
info@univision26.com
License: El Paso, El Paso County, TX held by Entravision Holdings LLC.
Group Owner: Entravision Communications Corp.; (acq 12-10-01; $18 million)
Nat'l Network: TELEFUTURA
Foreign Language Programming
David Candelaria, General Manager
Diana DeLara, General Sales Mgr
Abel Rodriguez, Promotions Manager
Alfredo Durand, Chief Engineer

KTSM-TV *Digital Channel:* 9 *Virtual Channel:* 9; 34 kw; 1893 ft.; N31 48 18 W106 28 57.6
P.O. Box 53708, Lafayette, LA 70505 US
(915) 532-5421, *Fax:* (915) 532-6793
www.ktsm.com
ktsmtv@whc.net
License: El Paso, El Paso County, TX held by ComCorp of El Paso License Corp.
Group Owner: Communications Corp. of America; (acq 7-25-97; $30.5 million for stock with KTSM-AM-FM).; *Washington Law Firm:* Fletcher, Heald & Hildreth
Nat'l Network: NBC *Nat'l Reps:* Millennium Sales & Marketing
Wire Services: AP
Size of News Staff: 33; *Hours of Local News Weekly:* news progmg 19.5 hrs wkly
Courtney Elam, Operations Dir
Gary Sotir, General Manager
Danny Aguilar, General Sales Mgr
Victor Veuegus, News Director
Ernie Hartt, Engineering Dir
Debra Hastings, National Sales Manager

KVIA-TV *Digital Channel:* 7 *Virtual Channel:* 7; 32.4 kw; 1942 ft.; N31 48 18 W106 28 58
PO Box 12277, El Paso, TX 79902 US
(915) 496-7777, *Fax:* (915) 532-0070
www.kvia.com
kvia@kvia.com
License: El Paso, El Paso County, TX held by NPG of Texas L.P.
Group Owner: News-Press & Gazette Co.; (acq 12-9-94; $19.9 million;; *Washington Law Firm:* Robert Thompson
Nat'l Network: ABC; CW
Size of News Staff: 30; *Hours of Local News Weekly:* news progmg 31.5 hrs wkly
David Bradley, CEO
John Kueneke, President
Chris Swann, Operations Dir
Kevin Lovell, General Manager
Nathan Price, General Sales Mgr
Karla Huelga, Programming Director
David Gonzalez, Promotions Manager
Eric Huseby, NewsDirector
Dan Overstreet, National Sales Manager

XHIJ-DT *Digital Channel:* 45; 240 kw vis, 60 kw aur; 1,200t/150g
5925 Cromo Dr., El Paso, TX 79912
(915) 585-6344, *Fax:* (915) 585-6333
www.canal44.com
License: Ciudad Juarez, MX held by Arnoldo Cabada De la O
Nat'l Network: Telemundo (Spanish)
Foreign Language Programming; Size of News Staff: 20; *Hours of Local News Weekly:* news progmg 15 hrs wkly
Sergio Cavada, General Manager

Harlingen-Weslaco-Brownsville-McAllen, TX (DMA 87)

KGBT-TV *Digital Channel:* 31 *Virtual Channel:* 4; 1000 kw; 1207 ft.; N26 8 56 W97 49 18
2000 Wade Hampton Blvd., Greenville, SC 29615 US
(956) 366-4444, *Fax:* (956) 366-4494
www.kgbt4.com
listens@kgbt4.com
License: Harlingen, Cameron County, TX held by Barrington Harlingen License LLC
Group Owner: Barrington Broadcasting Group, LLC.; (acq 8-11-2006; grpsl); *Washington Law Firm:* Dow, Lohnes & Albertson
Nat'l Network: CBS
Foreign Language Programming; Size of News Staff: 29; *Hours of Local News Weekly:* news progmg 22 hrs wkly
Phil Rich, Operations Dir
Teresa Burgess, General Manager
Randy Roberts, General Sales Mgr
Monica Ortiz, Programming Director
Linda Guerro Deicia, Promotions Manager
Kimberly Wyatt, News Director

***KLUJ-TV** *Digital Channel:* 34 *Virtual Channel:* 44; 45 kw; 928 ft.; N26 13 0 W97 46 48
PO Box 721582, Houston, TX 77272 US
(956) 425-4225, *Fax:* (956) 412-1740
www.communityedtv.org
klujtv@asbglobal.net
License: Harlingen, Cameron County, TX held by Community Educational TV Inc
(acq 4-84).; *Washington Law Firm:* Joseph E. Dunne III

Nat'l Network: TRINITY BROADCA
Foreign Language Programming
Margie Gonzales, General Manager
Corrie Hickey, Public Affairs Director

***KMBH** *Digital Channel:* 38 *Virtual Channel:* 60; 1000 kw; 1134 ft.; N26 7 14 W97 49 18
Mailing Address: P.O. Box 2147, Harlingen, TX 78550 US
Second Address: 1701 Tennessee St., Harlingen, TX 78551
(956) 421-4111, *Fax:* (956) 421-4150
www.kmbh.org
rgveduca@aol.com
License: Harlingen, Cameron County, TX held by RGV Educational Broadcasting Inc
Washington Law Firm: Thelen Reid & Priest LLP
Nat'l Network: PBS
Foreign Language Programming
Father Pedro Briseno, CEO
John Ross, Chief Engineer

KNVO *Digital Channel:* 49 *Virtual Channel:* 48; 1000 kw; 937 ft.; N26 5 18 W98 3 44
801 North Jackson, McAllen, TX 78504 US
(956) 687-4848, *Fax:* (956) 687-7784
License: McAllen, Hidalgo County, TX held by Entravision Holdings L.L.C.
Group Owner: Entravision Communications Corp.; (acq 4-25-97);
Washington Law Firm: Schwartz, Woods & Miller
Nat'l Network: UNIVISION
Foreign Language Programming
Larry Safir, General Manager
Joe Medrano, News Director

KRGV-TV *Digital Channel:* 13 *Virtual Channel:* 5; 57 kw; 1460 ft.; N26 6 2 W97 50 21
Mailing Address: P.O. Box 5, Weslaco, TX 78599 US
Second Address: 900 E. Expwy. 83, Weslaco, TX 78596
(956) 968-5555, *Fax:* (956) 973-5016
www.krgv.com
License: Weslaco, Hidalgo County, TX held by Mobile Video Tapes Inc.
Group Owner: Manship Stations; (acq 1-28-64; grpsl;;
Washington Law Firm: Pillsbury
Nat'l Network: ABC *Nat'l Reps:* Blair Television *Wire Services:* AP
Size of News Staff: 40; *Hours of Local News Weekly:* news progmg 24.5 hrs wkly
Richard Manship, Chairman
John Kittleman, General Manager
Danny Aguilar, General Sales Mgr
Michelle Martone, Programming Director
Jerry Berg, Promotions Manager
Jenny Martinez, News Director
Chuck Salge, Chief Engineer
GingerWalker, Traffic Manager

KTLM *Digital Channel:* 40 *Virtual Channel:* 40; 355 kw; 1893 ft.; N26 31 1 W98 39 7
Post Office Box 502, Rio Grande City, TX 78582 US
(956) 686-0040, *Fax:* (956) 686-0770
www.telemundo40.com
License: Rio Grande City, Starr County, TX held by Sunbelt Multimedia Co
Nat'l Network: TELEMUNDO
Foreign Language Programming; Size of News Staff: 12; *Hours of Local News Weekly:* news progmg 8 hrs wkly
Emmett Wells, General Manager

KVEO-TV *Digital Channel:* 24; 2,570 kw vis, 1,000 kw aur; ant 1,460t/1,454g; N26 05 59 W97 50 16; *Population Served:* 700,000
Mailing Address: 394 N. Expressway, Brownsville, TX 78521
Second Address: Box 4314, Brownsville, TX 78521
(956) 544-2323, *Fax:* (956) 544-4636
www.kveo.com
License: Brownsville, Cameron County, TX held by Communications Corp. of America.
Group Owner: Communications Corp. of America; (acq 2-13-95;;
Washington Law Firm: Dow, Lohnes
Nat'l Network: NBC *Wire Services:* AP
Greg Boulanger, CFO
Steve Pruett, President
Bill Jorn, General Manager
Sheldon Galloway, General Sales Mgr

Houston (DMA 10)

***KETH-TV** *Digital Channel:* 24 *Virtual Channel:* 14; 1000 kw; 1903 ft.; N29 34 15 W95 30 37
PO Box 721582, Houston, TX 77059 US
(281) 561-5828, *Fax:* (281) 561-9793
www.communityedtv.org
License: Houston, Harris County, TX held by Community Educational Television Inc
Nat'l Network: TRINITY BROADCA
Hours of Local News Weekly: News progmg 3 hrs wkly
Laura Hanks, Operations Dir
Rod Harty, Chief Engineer

KFTH-DT *Digital Channel:* 36; 5,000 kw vis, 500 kw aur; ant 1,781t/1,155g; N29 34 06 W95 29 57
5100 SW Freeway, Houston, TX 77056
(713) 662-4545, *Fax:* (713) 965-2610
www.univision.com
info@univision.net
License: Alvin, Brazoria County, TX held by TeleFutura Houston LLC.
Group Owner: Univision Communications Inc.; (acq 5-21-2001; grpsl).
Nat'l Network: TeleFutura (Spanish)
Foreign Language Programming
Craig Bland, Operations Dir
Chas Wilson, General Sales Mgr
Arlene Kelsch, Promotions Manager
Tom Daniels, Chief Engineer
Melissa Covarrubias, Local Sales Manager
Grace Olivares-Hernandez, Public Affairs Director

KHOU *Digital Channel:* 31; 316 kw vis, 31.6 kw aur; 1,870t/1,473g; N29 33 40 W95 30 04; *Population Served:* 5,000,000
1945 Allen Parkway, Houston, TX 77019
(713) 526-1111, *Fax:* (713) 521-4326
www.khou.com
11listens@khou.com
License: Houston, Harris County, TX held by KHOU-TV Inc.
Group Owner: Belo Corp; (acq 1984; grpsl;
Nat'l Network: CBS *Nat'l Reps:* TeleRep *Wire Services:* Reuters
Rudy Gonzalez, Operations Dir
Dan Lyons, General Sales Mgr
Keith Connors, News Director

KIAH *Digital Channel:* 38 *Virtual Channel:* 39; 1000 kw; 1909 ft.; N29 34 6 W95 29 57
7700 Westpark Drive, Houston, TX 77063 US
(713) 781-3939, *Fax:* (713) 781-3441
khcw.trb.com
pasmith@39online.com
License: Houston, Harris County, TX held by KHCW Inc.
Group Owner: Tribune Broadcasting Co.; (acq 12-20-2007; grpsl); *Washington Law Firm:* Dow Lohnes PLLC
Nat'l Network: CW *Nat'l Reps:* Harrington, Righter & Parsons
Size of News Staff: 34; *Hours of Local News Weekly:* news progmg 4 hrs wkly
Roger Bare, Operations Dir
Peggy Nan Moore, Engineering Dir

***KLTJ** *Digital Channel:* 23 *Virtual Channel:* 22; 350 kw; 1900 ft.; N29 34 15 W95 30 37
1050 Gemini Road, Houston, TX 77058 US
(281) 212-1022, *Fax:* (281) 212-1031
www.daystar.com
comments@daystar.com
License: Galveston, Galveston County, TX held by Word of God Fellowship Inc. aka Community TV Educators
Nat'l Network: IND
Foreign Language Programming
Nathan Williams, General Manager
Arnold Torres, Chief Regulatory Officer

KPRC-TV *Digital Channel:* 35 *Virtual Channel:* 2; 1000 kw; 1919 ft.; N29 34 6 W95 29 57
Mailing Address: Kprc-Tv, 8181 Southwest Freeway, Houston, TX 77074 US
Second Address: 8181 Southwest Fwy., Houston, TX 77074
(713) 222-2222, *Fax:* (713) 270-9334
www.click2houston.com
License: Houston, Harris County, TX held by Post-Newsweek Stations Inc.
Group Owner: Post-Newsweek Stations Inc.; (acq 4-22-94;;
Washington Law Firm: Covington & Burling
Nat'l Network: NBC *Nat'l Reps:* MMT *Wire Services:* AP
Size of News Staff: 80; *Hours of Local News Weekly:* news progmg 34 hrs wkly
Tammy Dean, Operations Dir
Larry Blackerby, General Manager
Ben Oldham, General Sales Mgr
Mr. Skip Valet, News Director
Dale Werner, Chief Engineer

KPXB-TV *Digital Channel:* 5; 4,100 kw vis, 410 kw aur; 1,775t/1,200g; N30 15 45 W95 14 50; *Population Served:* 3,050,000
256 N. Sam Houston Pkwy. E., Suite 49, Houston, TX 77060
(281) 820-4900, *Fax:* (281) 820-3916
www.ionline.tv
License: Conroe, Montgomery County, TX held by Paxson Houston License Inc.
Group Owner: ION Media Networks Inc.; (acq 1995; $7.9 million);
Washington Law Firm: Pepper & Corazzini
Nat'l Network: ION Television
Alex Stroot, Station Manager
Wendy Wiesinger, Engineering Dir

KRIV *Digital Channel:* 26 *Virtual Channel:* 26; 800 kw; 1962 ft.; N29 34 28 W95 29 37
Mailing Address: 5151 Wisconsin Ave.,N.W., Washington, DC 20015 US
Second Address: 4261 Southwest Fwy., Houston, TX 77027
(713) 479-2600, *Fax:* (713) 479-2604
www.myfoxhouston.com
License: Houston, Harris County, TX held by Fox Television Stations Inc.
Group Owner: Fox Television Stations Inc.; *Washington Law Firm:* Molly Pauker
Nat'l Network: FOX *Nat'l Reps:* Fox Stations Sales *Wire Services:* AP
Charles Hughes, Operations Dir
D'Artagnan Bebel, General Manager
Du Juan McCoy, General Sales Mgr
Stan Wasilik, Programming Director
Larry Parker, Promotions Manager
Kathy Williams, News Director
Sheila Birenbaun, OperationsDirector
Lisa Whitlock, Public Affairs Director
Geri Fieler, Traffic Manager

KTBU *Digital Channel:* 42 *Virtual Channel:* 55; 1000 kw; 1959 ft.; N29 33 44 W95 30 35
23 Deep Water, Montgomery, TX 77356 US
(713) 864-1999, *Fax:* (713) 864-1993
www.thetube.net
License: Conroe, Montgomery County, TX held by Humanity Interested Media L.P
Nat'l Network: IND
Lara Bell, Operations Dir
Matt Reiss, General Manager
Bruce Dinehart, Station Manager
Phil Lonsway, General Sales Mgr
Eric Peterson, Chief Engineer

KTMD *Digital Channel:* 48 *Virtual Channel:* 47; 1000 kw; 1959 ft.; N29 34 15 W95 30 37
2290 West 8th Avenue, Hialeah, FL 33010 US
(713) 974-4848, *Fax:* (713) 782-5575
www.ktmd.com
License: Galveston, Galveston County, TX held by NBC Telemundo License Co.
Group Owner: Telemundo Television Stations; (acq 4-12-2002; grpsl).; *Washington Law Firm:* Hogan & Hartson
Nat'l Network: TELEMUNDO
Foreign Language Programming; Size of News Staff: 14; *Hours of Local News Weekly:* news progmg 7 hrs wkly
Roel Medina, General Manager
Dominic Fails, General Sales Mgr
Gregorio Cervantes, National Sales Manager

KTRK-TV *Digital Channel:* 13 *Virtual Channel:* 13; 32.4 kw; 1929 ft.; N29 34 27 W95 29 37
Mailing Address: 3310 Bissonnet Street, Houston, TX 77001 US
Second Address: 3310 Bissonnet St., Houston, TX 77005
(713) 666-0713, *Fax:* (713) 663-0013
www.ABC13.com,www.ktrk.com
License: Houston, Harris County, TX held by ABC Inc.
Group Owner: ABC Inc.; (acq 7-17-67).
Nat'l Network: ABC *Wire Services:* TWX
Henry Florsheim, President

KTXH *Digital Channel:* 19 *Virtual Channel:* 20; 1000 kw; 1955 ft.; N29 33 44 W95 30 35
1501 M Street, N.W., Suite 1100, Washington, DC 20005 US
(713) 479-2600, *Fax:* (713) 479-2859
License: Houston, Harris County, TX held by Fox Television Stations Inc.
Group Owner: Fox Television Stations Inc.; (acq 11-6-2001; with WDCA(TV) Washington, DC in swap for KBHK-TV San Francisco, CA).
Nat'l Network: MY NETWORK
Charles Hughes, Operations Dir
D'Artagnan Bebel, General Manager

KUBE-TV *Digital Channel:* 53 *Virtual Channel:* 57; 5,000 kw vis, 500 kw aur; ant 1,958t/1,944g; N29 34 15 W95 30 37
2620 Fountain View, Ste.322, Houston, TX 55344
(713) 467-5757, *Fax:* (713) 783-4157
www.kube57.com
License: Baytown, Liberty County, TX held by KAZH License LLC.
Group Owner: Pappas Telecasting Companies; (acq 7-7-99; $28 million)
Foreign Language Programming
Harry Pappas, CEO
Emilio Nicolas Jr., General Manager
Emilio Nicolas, Station Manager

***KUHT** *Digital Channel:* 8 *Virtual Channel:* 8; 64.6 kw; 1857 ft.; N29 34 28 W95 29 37
4513 Cullen Blvd., Houston, TX 77004 US
(713) 748-8888,(800) 364-8300, *Fax:* (713) 743-8867
www.houstonpbs.org
License: Houston, Harris County, TX held by University of Houston System, Board of Regents
Washington Law Firm: Dow, Lohnes & Albertson
Nat'l Network: PBS
Foreign Language Programming
Steve Pyndus, Operations Dir
John Hesse, General Manager
Jack Neal, Station Manager

KYAZ *Digital Channel:* 52 *Virtual Channel:* 51; 2,290 kw vis; ant 1,640t/1,624g; N29 33 40 W95 30 04
8440 Westpark, Houston, TX 77063
(713) 974-5151, *Fax:* (713) 974-5188
www.knws51.com
License: Katy, Harris County, TX held by Johnson Broadcasting Inc
Washington Law Firm: Smithwick & Belendiuk
Nat'l Network: Azteca America
Douglas Johnson, President
Chris Bourne, Operations Dir
Jack Dabbah, General Manager

KZJL *Digital Channel:* 44 *Virtual Channel:* 61; 1000 kw; 1513 ft.; N29 33 44 W95 30 35
P.O. Box 305249, Nashville, TN 37230 US
(818) 563-5722
License: Houston, Harris County, TX held by KZJL License LLC.
Group Owner: Liberman Broadcasting Inc.; (acq 1-10-2001; $57 million)
Nat'l Network: IND
Winter Horton, General Manager

Laredo, TX (DMA 188)

KGNS-TV *Digital Channel:* 8 *Virtual Channel:* 8; 20 kw; 1024 ft.; N27 40 21 W99 39 51
120 West Del Mar Blvd., Laredo, TX 78041 US
(956) 727-8888, *Fax:* (956) 727-5336
pro8news.com
email8@pro8news.com
License: Laredo, Webb County, TX held by SagamoreHill Broadcasting of Texas LLC.
Group Owner: SagamoreHill Broadcasting LLC; (acq 9-28-2004; $14.4 million); *Washington Law Firm:* Wiley, Rein & Fielding, LLP
Nat'l Network: NBC; NBC; Telemundo (Spanish) *Nat'l Reps:* Continental Television Sales
Foreign Language Programming; Size of News Staff: 26; *Hours of Local News Weekly:* news progmg 17 hrs wkly
Jose Luis Salinas, Operations Dir
Carlos Salinas, General Manager
Olga Ramirez, Programming Director
Ramiro Saucedo, Promotions Manager
Ray Gomez, News Director
David York, Chief Engineer
Priscilla A. Flores, Business Manager

KLDO-TV *Digital Channel:* 19 *Virtual Channel:* 27; 150 kw; 443 ft.; N27 39 54 W99 36 30
11900 Olymp0ic Boulevard, Suite 590, Los Angeles, CA 90064 US
(956) 727-0027, *Fax:* (956) 727-2673
www.entravision.com
License: Laredo, Webb County, TX held by Entravision Holdings L.L.C.
Group Owner: Entravision Communications Corp.; (acq 7-30-97; $6.2 million); *Washington Law Firm:* Martin E. Firestone
Nat'l Network: UNIVISION
Foreign Language Programming
Terry Elena Ordaz, General Manager
Elia Solis, General Sales Mgr
Jose Salinas, Promotions Manager
Marisa Limon, News Director
Merlin Miller, Chief Engineer
Jose Gomez, Regional Sales Manager

KVTV *Digital Channel:* 13 *Virtual Channel:* 13; 3 kw; 932 ft.; N27 31 12 W99 31 19
P.O. Box 2039, Laredo, TX 78044 US
(956) 727-1300, *Fax:* (956) 712-0185
www.cbs13kvtv.com
License: Laredo, Webb County, TX held by Eagle Creek of Laredo LLC.
Group Owner: Eagle Creek Broadcasting LLC; (acq 6-13-2002; grpsl).
Nat'l Network: FOX
Dale Remy, General Manager
Joe Herrera, General Sales Mgr
Carol Rostohar, Promotions Manager
Kent Harrell, News Director
George Sanders, Chief Engineer

Lubbock, TX (DMA 143)

KAMC *Digital Channel:* 27 *Virtual Channel:* 28; 1000 kw; 720 ft.; N33 31 33 W101 52 7
1201 - 8th Avenue, South, Nashville, TN 37203 US
(806) 745-2828, *Fax:* (806) 748-2214
www.everythinglubbock.com
jsherwood@klbk13.tv
License: Lubbock, Lubbock County, TX held by Mission Broadcasting Inc.
Group Owner: Mission Broadcasting Inc.; (acq 12-17-2003).; *Washington Law Firm:* Bryan Cave
Nat'l Network: ABC
Size of News Staff: 26; *Hours of Local News Weekly:* news progmg 39 hrs wkly
Chuck Spaugh, Operations Dir
Greg McAlister, General Manager
Gary Melton, General Sales Mgr
Shanna Smith, Programming Director
Jeff Pitner, Promotions Manager
Russ Protect, News Director
Eric Hosch, Chief Engineer
Rosie Duran,Traffic Manager
Ron Roberts, Weather Director

KCBD *Digital Channel:* 11 *Virtual Channel:* 11; 41 kw; 761 ft.; N33 32 32 W101 50 14
5600 Ave. A, Lubbock, TX 79404 US
(806) 744-1414, *Fax:* (806) 744-0449
www.kcbd.com
kcbd@kcbd.com
License: Lubbock, Lubbock County, TX held by KCBD License Subsidiary LLC.
Group Owner: Raycom Media Inc.; (acq 1-31-2006; grpsl); *Washington Law Firm:* Dow, Lohnes & Albertson
Nat'l Network: NBC
Brent McClure, Operations Dir
Dan Jackson, General Manager
Beverly McBeth, General Sales Mgr
Peggy Sullivan, Programming Director
Benji Snead, News Director
Ricky Price, Chief Engineer
Josh Young, Public Service Director
Michele Doggett, Traffic Manager

KJTV-TV *Digital Channel:* 35 *Virtual Channel:* 34; 1000 kw; 899 ft.; N33 30 8 W101 52 20
Mailing Address: PO Box 3757, Lubbock, TX 79452 US
Second Address: 9800 University Ave., Lubbock, TX 79423
(806) 745-3434, *Fax:* (806) 748-1949
www.myfoxlubbock.com
License: Lubbock, Lubbock County, TX held by Ramar Communications, Inc.
Group Owner: Ramar Communications II Ltd.; *Washington Law Firm:* Leventhal, Senter & Lerman
Nat'l Network: FOX *Nat'l Reps:* Millennium Sales & Marketing
Size of News Staff: 20; *Hours of Local News Weekly:* news progmg 7 hrs wkly
Brad Moran, General Manager
Sherry Saffle, General Sales Mgr
Chris Torres, Programming Director
Branden Waits, Promotions Manager
Tee Thomas, Chief Engineer
Amy Stephens, Traffic Manager

KLBK-TV *Digital Channel:* 40 *Virtual Channel:* 13; 1000 kw; 720 ft.; N33 31 33 W101 52 7
18 Newbury Street, Boston, MA 02116 US
(806) 745-2345, *Fax:* (806) 748-2214
www.everythinglubbock.com
License: Lubbock, Lubbock County, TX held by Nexstar Finance Inc.
Group Owner: Nexstar Broadcasting Group Inc.; (acq 12-31-03; grpsl).; *Washington Law Firm:* Arter & Hadden
Nat'l Network: CBS
Size of News Staff: 47; *Hours of Local News Weekly:* news progmg 27 hrs wkly
Chuck Spaugh, Operations Dir
Greg McAlister, General Manager
Gary Melton, General Sales Mgr
Shanna Smith, Programming Director
Russ Poteet, News Director
Eric Hosch, Chief Engineer
Joyce Kelly, Business Manager

KLCW-TV *Digital Channel:* 43 *Virtual Channel:* 22; 179 kw vis; ant 923t; N33 30 08 W101 52 20
Mailing Address: 9800 University Ave., Lubbock, TX 36111
Second Address: PO Box 3757, Lubbock, TX 79423
(806) 745-3434, *Fax:* (806) 748-9387
www.fox34.com
bmoran@ramarcom.com
License: Wolfforth, Lubbock County, TX held by Woods Communications Corp.
Group Owner: Woods Communications Corp.
Nat'l Network: CW *Nat'l Reps:* Millennium
David Woods, CEO/COO
Brad Moran, (GM of JSA)
Paula Poole, Station Manager
Sherry Saffle, General Sales Mgr

KPTB-DT ; 214 kw vis; 272t; N33 33 12 W101 49 13
Mailing Address: Box 61000, Midland, TX 79711
Second Address: 5604 Martin Luther King Blvd., Lubbock, TX 79404
(800) 707-0420 (806) 846-5200, *Fax:* (806) 749-7732
www.godslearningchannel.com
info@ptcbglc.com
License: Lubbock, Lubbock County, TX held by Prime Time Christian Broadcasting Inc
Jeff Tveit, General Manager
Jeff Cooper, Station Manager

***KTTZ-TV** *Digital Channel:* 39 *Virtual Channel:* 5; 100 kw vis, 25 kw aur; 440t/817g; N33 34 55 W101 53 25; *Population Served:* 375,000
Mailing Address: Box 42161, Lubbock, TX 79409
Second Address: 17th St. & Indiana Ave., Lubbock, TX 79409-2161
(806) 742-2209, *Fax:* (806) 742-1274
www.ktxt.org
License: Lubbock, Lubbock County, TX held by Texas Tech University
Washington Law Firm: Cohn & Marks
Nat'l Network: PBS
Pat Cates, General Manager

Odessa-Midland, TX (DMA 156)

KMID *Digital Channel:* 26 *Virtual Channel:* 2; 1000 kw; 902 ft.; N32 5 51 W102 17 21
7621 Little Avenue, Suite 506, Charlotte, NC 28266 US
(432) 563-2222, *Fax:* (432) 563-5819
www.kmid.tv
news@kmid.tv
License: Midland, Midland County, TX held by Nexstar Finance Inc.
Group Owner: Nexstar Broadcasting Group Inc.; (acq 7-31-2000; $10 million); *Washington Law Firm:* Cohn & Marks
Nat'l Network: ABC *Regional Network:* Alabama Public Television *Nat'l Reps:* Blair Television
Size of News Staff: 23; *Hours of Local News Weekly:* news progmg 17 hrs wkly
Chris Pruitt, General Manager
Kirk Keller, Station Manager

KMLM-DT *Digital Channel:* 42; 1,120 kw vis, 112 kw aur; ant 479t/473g; N32 02 53 W102 17 44; *Population Served:* 245,000
Mailing Address: Box 61000, Midland, TX 79711-1000
Second Address: 12706 W. Highway 80 E., Odessa, TX 79765
(800) 707-0420 (432) 563-0420, *Fax:* (432) 563-1736
www.GLC.US.com
info@glc.us.com
License: Odessa, Ector County, TX held by Prime Time Christian Broadcasting Inc
Foreign Language Programming
Al Cooper, General Manager
Matt Montgomery, Chief Engineer

KOSA-TV *Digital Channel:* 7 *Virtual Channel:* 7; 48 kw; 741 ft.; N31 51 50 W102 34 41
P.O. Box 4186, Odessa, TX 76763 US
(432) 580-5672, *Fax:* (432) 580-8010
www.cbs7.com
news@cbs7.com
License: Odessa, Ector County, TX held by ICA Broadcasting I Ltd
(acq 3-10-00; $8 million); *Washington Law Firm:* Covington Burling
Nat'l Network: CBS; MyNetworkTV *Nat'l Reps:* Continental Television Sales
Size of News Staff: 22; *Hours of Local News Weekly:* news progmg 22 hrs wkly
John Bushman, Chairman
John Nichols, CFO
Barry Marks, President
Rick McGee, Operations Dir
Randy Roberts, Station Manager

***KPBT-TV** *Digital Channel:* 38 *Virtual Channel:* 36; 513 kw vis, 51.3 kw aur; ant 289t/306g; N31 51 59 W102 22 50;
Population Served: 350,000
Mailing Address: Box 8940, Midland, TX 79764
Second Address: 201 West University, Odessa, TX 79764
(432) 563-5728, *Fax:* (432) 563-5731
www.kpbt.org
kpbt@basinpbs.org
License: Odessa, Ector County, TX held by Permian Basin Public Telecommunications Inc
Nat'l Network: PBS
John James, Chairman
Daphne Dowdy, General Manager
Amy Lynch, Programming Director
Domingo Machuca, Chief Engineer

KPEJ-TV *Digital Channel:* 23; 2,880 kw vis; ant 1,099t/1,102g; N32 05 51 W102 17 21; *Population Served:* 133,600
Box 11009, 1550 W. I-20, Odessa, TX 79763
(432) 580-0024, *Fax:* (432) 337-3707
www.kpejtv.com
lwolf@kpejtv.com
License: Odessa, Ector County, TX held by Comcorp of Texas License Corp.
Group Owner: Communications Corp. of America; (acq 10-31-90; grpsl;; *Washington Law Firm:* Dow Lohnes PLLC
Nat'l Network: Fox *Nat'l Reps:* Millennium Sales & Marketing
Laura Wolf, General Manager

KUPB *Digital Channel:* 18 *Virtual Channel:* 18; 1000 kw; 922 ft.; N31 50 19 W102 31 59
Mailing Address: 11900 Olympic Boulevard, Suite 590, Los Angeles, CA 90064 US
Second Address: 10313 West County Road 117, Midland, TX 79706
(432) 563-1826, *Fax:* (432) 563-0215
www.entravision.com
License: Midland, Midland County, TX held by Entravision Holdings LLC.
Group Owner: Entravision Communications Corp.; *Washington Law Firm:* Thompson, Hine & Flory L
Nat'l Network: UNIVISION
Foreign Language Programming
Walter Ulloa, CEO
Philip Wilkinson, President
Leticia Martinez, General Manager
John DeLorenzo, CFO
Larry Safir, Executive Vice President

KWAB-TV *Digital Channel:* 33 *Virtual Channel:* 4; 33.5 kw; 273 ft.; N32 16 55 W101 29 34
P.O. Box 708, Lawton, OK 73502 US
(432) 567-9999, *Fax:* (432) 567-9994
www.kwes.com
License: Big Spring, Howard County, TX held by Midessa Television Co
Group Owner: R.H. Drewry Group; (acq 9-9-91; $4.85 million with KWES-TV Odessa;
Nat'l Network: NBC
Mac Douglas, General Manager

KWES-TV *Digital Channel:* 9 *Virtual Channel:* 9
Mailing Address: P.O. Box 708, Lawton, OK 73502 US
Second Address: 11320 County Rd. 127 W., Midland, TX 79711
(432) 567-9999, *Fax:* (432) 567-9992
www.kwes.com
info@kwestv.com
License: Odessa, Ector County, TX held by Midessa Television Co.
Group Owner: R.H. Drewry Group; (acq 10-31-91; $4.85 million with KWAB(TV) Big Spring;
Nat'l Network: NBC
Mac Douglas, General Manager
Carlos Fernandez, News Director

KWWT *Digital Channel:* 30 *Virtual Channel:* 30; 50 kw; 482 ft.; N32 2 52.5 W102 17 44
1146 19th St NW, Suite 200, Washington, DC 20036 US
(432) 272-7514, *Fax:* (432) 614-4054
www.cwtv.com
License: Odessa, Ector County, TX held by WinStar Odessa Inc.
Nat'l Network: CW
James Primm, General Manager
Jayne Faltus, Station Manager
Doug Faltus, Chief Engineer

San Angelo, TX (DMA 196)

KIDY *Digital Channel:* 19 *Virtual Channel:* 6; 3.7 kw; 433 ft.; N31 35 21 W100 31 0
406 South Irving, San Angelo, TX 76901 US
(325) 655-6006, *Fax:* (325) 655-8461
foxsanangelo.com
kidy@foxsanangelo.com
License: San Angelo, Tom Green County, TX held by Sage Broadcasting Corp.
Group Owner: Sage Broadcasting Corp.; *Washington Law Firm:* Fletcher, Heeald & Hildreth
Nat'l Network: FOX *Nat'l Reps:* Millennium Sales & Marketing
Size of News Staff: 2
Paris Schindler, CEO
Bill Carter, President
Teddye Read, General Sales Mgr

KLST *Digital Channel:* 11 *Virtual Channel:* 8; 18.8 kw; 1425 ft.; N31 22 1 W100 2 48
Box 1941, San Angelo, TX 76902 US
(325) 949-8800, *Fax:* (325) 658-1118
www.klst.tv
klst@klst.net
License: San Angelo, Tom Green County, TX held by Nexstar Broadcasting Inc.
Group Owner: Nexstar Broadcasting Group Inc.; (acq 9-2-2004; $12 million); *Washington Law Firm:* Skadden, Arps, Slate, Meagher & Flom
Nat'l Network: CBS
Size of News Staff: 12; *Hours of Local News Weekly:* news progmg 17 hrs wkly
Mark McCain, Operations Dir
Tom Stovall, General Manager
Lanny Kiest, General Sales Mgr
Gordon Hay, Programming Director
Don Plachno, Promotions Manager
Kathy Munoz, News Director
Len Martinez, Chief Engineer
Joy Kimbell, Executive Vice President
Teresa Gill, Traffic Manager

KSAN-TV *Virtual Channel:* 3; 17.8 kw vis, 3.5 kw aur; 600t/469g; N31 37 22 W100 26 14
2800 Armstrong St., San Angelo, TX 33703
(325) 949-8800, *Fax:* (325) 655-1118
www.ksan.tv
nbc3@wcc.com
License: San Angelo, Tom Green County, TX held by Mission Broadcasting Inc.
Group Owner: Mission Broadcasting Inc.; (acq 6-13-2003; $10 million with KRBC-TV Abilene).; *Washington Law Firm:* Kenkel, Barnard & Edmundson
Nat'l Network: NBC *Nat'l Reps:* Blair Television
Tom Stovall, Station Manager
Albert Gutierrez, General Sales Mgr
Kathy Munoz, News Director
Len Martinez, Chief Engineer

San Antonio, TX (DMA 37)

KABB *Digital Channel:* 30 *Virtual Channel:* 29; 1000 kw; 1447 ft.; N29 17 28 W98 16 12
10706 Beaver Dam Road, Cockeysville, MD 21030 US
(210) 366-1129, *Fax:* (210) 377-4758
www.kabb.com
kabbtv@kabb.com
License: San Antonio, Bexar County, TX held by KABB Licensee L.L.C.
Group Owner: Sinclair Broadcast Group Inc.; *Washington Law Firm:* Shaw, Pittman
Nat'l Network: FOX *Nat'l Reps:* Millennium Sales & Marketing
Size of News Staff: 35; *Hours of Local News Weekly:* news progmg 7 hrs wkly
Dean Radia, General Manager
David Ostmo, Operations Director
Dean Radla, General Sales Mgr
Azalia Hoelting, Promotions Manager
Keith McMahan, News Director
John Seabers, General Sales Manager
Yesenia Riva, Local Sales Manager
Jimmy Cola, National Sales Manager

KCWX *Digital Channel:* 5 *Virtual Channel:* 2; 100 kw vis, 10 kw aur; 1,355t/1,017g; N30 08 13 W98 36 35
5400 Fredericksburg Rd., San Antonio, TX 78701
(210) 366-5000, *Fax:* (210) 348-9142,(210) 377-8779
www.kens5.com
License: Fredericksburg, Gillespie County, TX held by Corridor Television L.L.P
Nat'l Network: MyNetworkTV *Nat'l Reps:* TeleRep
Robert McGann, General Manager
Boots Walker, General Sales Mgr
Rich Barton, Engineering Dir

KENS *Digital Channel:* 55; 100 kw vis, 10 kw aur; ant 1,390t/1,531g; N29 16 10 W98 15 55; *Population Served:* 700,000
Mailing Address: Box TV5, San Antonio, TX 78299
Second Address: 5400 Fredericksburg Road, San Antonio, TX 78229
(210) 366-5000, *Fax:* (210) 377-0740
www.mysanantonio.com
License: San Antonio, Bexar County, TX held by KENS-TV Inc.
Group Owner: Belo Corp; (acq 1997; $75 million with co-located AM plus interest in Television Food Network).; *Washington Law Firm:* Wiley, Rein & Fielding
Nat'l Network: CBS *Nat'l Reps:* TeleRep *Wire Services:* NWS (National Weather Service)
Size of News Staff: 55; *Hours of Local News Weekly:* news progmg 24 hrs wkly
Bob McGann, General Manager
Boots Walker, General Sales Mgr
Mandy Liles, Programming Director
Allen Lansing, Promotions Manager
Kurt Davis, News Director
Frank Peterman, Engineering Dir

***KHCE-TV** *Digital Channel:* 16 *Virtual Channel:* 23; 850 kw; 1076 ft.; N29 17 24 W98 15 20
Mailing Address: P.O. Box 691246, San Antonio, TX 78269 US
Second Address: Box 691246, San Antonio, TX 78249
(210) 479-0123, *Fax:* (210) 492-5679
www.khce.org
License: San Antonio, Bexar County, TX held by San Antonio Community Educational TV Inc
Nat'l Network: TRINITY BROADCA
Paul Crouch, President
Dr. Cherry, Operations Dir
Laura Hanks, General Manager
Dorcas Rogers, Station Manager
Jessica Mathews, Programming Director
Mike Bundrant, Engineering Dir
Corrie Hickey, Public Affairs Director

***KLRN** *Digital Channel:* 9 *Virtual Channel:* 9; 28 kw; 938 ft.; N29 19 38 W98 21 17
PO Box 9, San Antonio, TX 78291 US
(210) 270-9000, *Fax:* (210) 270-9078
www.klrn.org
info@klrn.org
License: San Antonio, Bexar County, TX held by Alamo Public Telecommunications Council
(acq 8-11-89).; *Washington Law Firm:* Cohn & Marks
Nat'l Network: PBS
Mike Novak, Chairman
Charles Vaughn, COO
Patrick Lopez, Operations Dir
Joanne Winik, General Manager
Cynthia Shields, General Sales Mgr
Charles Vaughn, Senior Vice President

KMYS *Digital Channel:* 32; 5,000 kw vis, 500 kw aur; ant 1,758t; N29 36 37 W98 53 35; *Population Served:* 1,500,000
4335 N.W. Loop 410, San Antonio, TX 15235
(210) 366-1129, *Fax:* (210) 377-4758
www.kmys.tv
kmys@kmys.tv
License: Kerrville, Kerr County, TX held by San Antonio (KRRT-TV) Licensee Inc.
Group Owner: Sinclair Broadcast Group Inc.; (acq 12-10-01; grpsl).; *Washington Law Firm:* Shaw, Pittman
Nat'l Network: CW

Dean Radla, General Sales Mgr
Jessica Aguilar, Promotions Manager
Gwen Frames, Local Sales Manager
Jimmy Cola, National Sales Manager

KPXL-TV ; 5,000 kw vis; 1,837t; N29 37 11 W99 02 55
6100 Bandera Rd., Suite 304, San Antonio, TX 78238
(210) 682-2626, *Fax:* (210) 682-3155
www.ionline.tv
License: Uvalde, Uvalde County, TX held by Paxson San Antonio License Inc.
Group Owner: ION Media Networks Inc.; (acq 6-24-99; $5 million for remaining 51%).
Nat'l Network: ION Television
Kathy Williams, Station Manager

KSAT-TV *Digital Channel:* 12 *Virtual Channel:* 12; 22.2 kw; 1493 ft.; N29 16 11 W98 15 31
1408 N. St Mary's Street, San Antonio, TX 78215 US
(210) 351-1200, *Fax:* (210) 351-1310
www.ksat.com
License: San Antonio, Bexar County, TX held by Post-Newsweek Stations Inc.
Group Owner: Post-Newsweek Stations Inc.; (acq 2-28-94;;
Washington Law Firm: Covington & Burling
Nat'l Network: ABC *Nat'l Reps:* MMT
Hours of Local News Weekly: News progmg 21 hrs wkly
James Joslyn, Operations Dir

KWEX-DT *Digital Channel:* 39; 832 kw vis, 83.2 kw aur; ant 500t/604g; N29 25 03 W98 29 26; *Population Served:* 2,478,680
411 E. Durango Blvd., San Antonio, TX 78204
(210) 227-4141/(210) 242-7451 (news), *Fax:* (210) 227-0469
www.univision.com
License: San Antonio, Bexar County, TX held by KWEX L.P., G.P.
Group Owner: Univision Communications Inc.; (acq 7-86; grpsl).;
Washington Law Firm: Fisher, Wayland, Cooper, Leader & Zaragoza
Nat'l Network: Univision (Spanish)
Foreign Language Programming; Hours of Local News Weekly: News progmg 5 hrs wkly
David Loving, Operations Dir

KYVV-TV *Virtual Channel:* 10; 316 kw vis; ant 328t/285g; N29 20 39 W100 51 39; *Population Served:* 500,000
Box 530391, Harlingen, TX 78552
(956) 421-2635, *Fax:* (956) 428-7556
License: Del Rio, Val Verde County, TX held by SATV 10 LLC.
Foreign Language Programming
Paul McTear, CEO
Artie Bedard, Operations Dir
Melissa Thurber, CFO
Wayne Dougherty, Executive Vice President

WOAI-TV *Digital Channel:* 48 *Virtual Channel:* 4; 905 kw; 1499 ft.; N29 16 11 W98 15 55
Mailing Address: 1031 Navarro, San Antonio, TX 78205 US
Second Address: 1031 Navarro St., San Antonio, TX 78205
(210) 226-4444, *Fax:* (210) 224-9898
www.woai.com
License: San Antonio, Bexar County, TX held by High Plains Broadcasting License Co. LLC.
Group Owner: High Plains Broadcasting Inc.; (acq 9-15-2008; grpsl); *Washington Law Firm:* Pillsbury Winthrop Shaw Pittman LLP
Nat'l Network: NBC
Size of News Staff: 68; *Hours of Local News Weekly:* news progmg 19.5 hrs wkly
Donita Todd, Operations Dir
Greg Derkowski, General Sales Mgr
Carolyn Mastin, Programming Director
Mark Pipitone, News Director
Harold Friesenhahn, Chief Engineer
Liz Quinones, Public Affairs Director

Sherman, TX-Ada, OK (DMA 161)

KXII *Digital Channel:* 12 *Virtual Channel:* 12; 36 kw; 1790 ft.; N34 1 58 W96 48 0
4201 Texoma Parkway, Sherman, TX 75090 US
(903) 892-8123, *Fax:* (903) 893-7858
www.kxii.com
comments @kxii.com
License: Sherman, Grayson County, TX held by Gray Television Licensee Inc.
Group Owner: Gray Television Inc.; (acq 6-29-99; $41.5 million);
Washington Law Firm: Wiley Rein, LLP
Nat'l Network: CBS; Fox; MyNetworkTV *Nat'l Reps:* Millennium Sales & Marketing *Wire Services:* AP; CNN; CBS
Hours of Local News Weekly: News progmg 20 hrs wkly
Rick Dean, Operations Dir
Todd Bates, General Sales Mgr
Nancy Alley, Programming Director
Craig Luthe, Promotions Manager
Charlie Haldeman, News Director
Randy Wells, Chief Engineer
Richard Flaker, Public Service Director

Shreveport, LA (DMA 84)

KTAL-TV *Digital Channel:* 15 *Virtual Channel:* 6; 1000 kw; 1490 ft.; N32 54 11 W94 0 20
Mailing Address: 3150 North Market Street, Shreveport, LA 71107 US
Second Address: Box 7428, Shreveport, LA 71107
(318) 629-6000, *Fax:* (318) 629-6001
www.arklatexhomepage.com
License: Texarkana, Bowie County, TX held by Nexstar Finance Inc.
Group Owner: Nexstar Broadcasting Group Inc.; (acq 9-11-2000; $35.25 million); *Washington Law Firm:* Covington & Burling
Nat'l Network: NBC
Scott Thomas, General Manager
Chaunte Robinson, Programming Director
Joel Lynch, Promotions Manager
Andrew Pontz, News Director
Kevin Southernland, Chief Engineer
Jay Barton, New Media Director

Tyler-Longview (Lufkin & Nacogdoches), TX (DMA 110)

KCEB *Digital Channel:* 51 *Virtual Channel:* 54; 500 kw; 1243 ft.; N32 15 36 W94 57 2
14141 Sw Freeway, Suite 6200, Sugar Land, TX 77478 US
(337) 896-1600, *Fax:* (337) 896-2695
License: Longview, Gregg County, TX held by Estes Broadcasting Inc
(acq 11-24-2003).; *Washington Law Firm:* Fletcher, Heald & Hildreth
Nat'l Network: CW
Eddie Blanchard, General Manager

KETK-TV *Digital Channel:* 22 *Virtual Channel:* 56; 1000 kw; 1505 ft.; N32 3 40 W95 18 50
10706 Beaver Dam Road, Cockeysville, MD 21030 US
(903) 581-5656, *Fax:* (903) 561-1648
www.ketknbc.com
yclater@ketknbc.com
License: Jacksonville, Cherokee County, TX held by Comcorp of Tyler License Corp.
Group Owner: Communications Corp. of America; (acq 11-12-2004; $38 million); *Washington Law Firm:* Dow, Lohnes
Nat'l Network: NBC *Nat'l Reps:* Millennium Sales & Marketing
Size of News Staff: 37; *Hours of Local News Weekly:* news progmg 25 hrs wkly
Chris Dudley, Operations Dir
Dave Tillery, General Manager
Suzanne Calhoun, General Sales Mgr
Yolanda Clater, Programming Director
Neal Barton, News Director
John Cummings, Chief Engineer
Connie Jobe, Traffic Manager

KFXK-TV *Digital Channel:* 31; 4,680 kw vis, 36.70 kw au; ant 1,249t/1,199g; N32 15 35 W94 57 02
Mailing Address: 4300 Richmond Rd., Tyler, TX 75703
Second Address: 320 E. Methvin, 2nd Floor, Longview, TX 75601
(903) 581-5656, *Fax:* (903) 561-1648
www.fox51.com
drew@fox51.com
License: Longview, Gregg County, TX held by Warwick Communications Inc.
Group Owner: White Knight Broadcasting of Longview, Inc.; (acq 9-1-99; $11.5 million for stock plus 3 low-power stns)
Nat'l Network: Fox
Sheldon Galloway, President
Drew Balch, Operations Dir
Dave Tillery, General Manager
Suzanne Calhoun, General Sales Mgr
Drew Balch, Programming Director
K. J. Lambein, Promotions Manager
Neal Barton, News Director
JohnCummings, Chief Engineer
Lori McBride, Traffic Manager
Cindy Terry, Local Sales Manager
David Bailey, Regional Sales Manager
Dave Tillery, General Sales Manager

KLTV *Digital Channel:* 7 *Virtual Channel:* 7; 66 kw; 984 ft.; N32 32 23 W95 13 11
715 South Jefferson Street, Jackson, MD 39205 US
(903) 597-5588, *Fax:* (903) 510-7847
www.kltv.com
License: Tyler, Smith County, TX held by Civco Inc.
Group Owner: Raycom Media Inc.; (acq 1-13-2006; grpsl).;
Washington Law Firm: Covington & Burling
Nat'l Network: ABC
Pat Stacey, General Manager
Cory Bowler, General Sales Mgr
Cathy Carmichael, Programming Director
Kenny Boles, News Director
Butch Adair, Chief Engineer
Mary Ryan, National Sales Manager
Hazel Kennedy, Traffic Manager
MarkScirto, Weather Director

KTRE *Digital Channel:* 9 *Virtual Channel:* 9; 23.5 kw; 669 ft.; N31 25 9 W94 48 3
Mailing Address: 715 South Jefferson Street, Jackson, MD 39205 US
Second Address: 358 TV Rd., Pollok, TX 75969
(936) 853-5873, *Fax:* (936) 853-3084
www.ktre.com
dlorenz@ktre.com
License: Lufkin, Angelina County, TX held by Raycom Media, Inc.
Group Owner: Raycom Media Inc.; (acq 1-13-2006; grpsl).;
Washington Law Firm: Covington & Burling
Nat'l Network: ABC
Foreign Language Programming; Size of News Staff: 15; *Hours of Local News Weekly:* news progmg 20 hrs wkly
Paul McTear, CEO
Artie Bedard, Operations Dir
Melissa Thurber, CFO
Wayne Dougherty, Executive Vice President

KYTX *Digital Channel:* 18 *Virtual Channel:* 19; 640 kw; 1499 ft.; N31 54 20 W95 5 5
Mailing Address: 200 College Place, Suite 118, Norfolk, VA 23510 US
Second Address: 911 W Loop 281, Suite 112, Longview, TX 75604
(903) 581-2211, *Fax:* (903) 581-5769
www.cbs19.tv
closedcaptioning@cbs19.tv
License: Nacogdoches, Nacogdoches County, TX held by KYTX License Co. LLC
(acq 12-21-2007; $25 million); *Ownership:* London Broadcasting Co. Inc., 100%; *Washington Law Firm:* William Mullen
Nat'l Network: CBS *Nat'l Reps:* Blair Television *Wire Services:* AP
Size of News Staff: 25; *Hours of Local News Weekly:* news progmg 19.5 hrs wkly
John Gaston, General Manager
Chesley Bryan, General Sales Mgr
Margaret Strout, Programming Director
Kent Domingue, Director
Dan Delgado, News Director
Moe Strout, Chief Engineer
Holly Austin, Local Sales Manager

Victoria, TX (DMA 205)

KAVU-TV *Digital Channel:* 15 *Virtual Channel:* 25; 900 kw; 1024 ft.; N28 50 42 W97 7 33
73 Kercheval Avenue, Grosse Pointe Farms, MI 48236 US
(361) 575-2500, *Fax:* (361) 575-2255
www.myvictoriaonline.com
License: Victoria, Victoria County, TX held by Saga Broadcasting LLC.
Group Owner: Saga Communications Inc.; (acq 10-20-98; $11.875 million; with KNAL(AM) Victoria).; *Washington Law Firm:* Smithwick & Belendiuk, P.C
Nat'l Network: ABC *Nat'l Reps:* Continental Television Sales
Regional Reps: Katz Continental *Wire Services:* AP
Size of News Staff: 15; *Hours of Local News Weekly:* news progmg 29 hrs wkly
Jeff Pryor, General Manager
Rebecca Sarlls, Programming Director
Todd Long, Promotions Manager
Don Bradley, News Director
Kevin John, Engineering Dir
Phil Stevens, Interactive Media
Jennifer Rosales, Traffic Manager

KVCT *Digital Channel:* 11 *Virtual Channel:* 19; 11.35 kw; 951 ft.; N28 50 42 W97 7 33
943 Lincoln Road, Grosse Pointe, MI 48230 US

(361) 575-2500, *Fax:* (361) 575-2255
www.myvictoriaonline.com
License: Victoria, Victoria County, TX held by Surtsey Media LLC
Group Owner: Surtsey Media LLC; (acq 4-26-99).; *Washington Law Firm:* Fletcher, Heald & Hildreth, P.L.C.
Nat'l Network: FOX *Nat'l Reps:* Continental Television Sales
Wire Services: AP
Hours of Local News Weekly: News progmg 2.5 hrs wkly
John Garcia, Operations Dir
Jeff Pryor, General Manager
Rebecca Sarlls, Programming Director
Don Bradley, News Director
Kevin John, Chief Engineer
Phil Stevens, Interactive Media
Todd Long, Public Affairs Director
JenniferRosales, Traffic Manager

Waco-Temple-Bryan, TX (DMA 94)

***KAMU-TV** *Digital Channel:* 12 *Virtual Channel:* 15; 3.2 kw; 344 ft.; N30 37 47 W96 20 33
Corner Houston & Russel, College Station, TX 77843 US
(979) 845-5611, *Fax:* (979) 845-1643
www.kamu.tamu.edu
License: College Station, Brazos County, TX held by Texas A&M University
Nat'l Network: PBS
John Prihoda, Operations Dir
Rodney Zent, General Manager
Penny Zent, Station Manager
Elaine Hoyak, General Sales Mgr
Jon Bennett, Programming Director
Wayne Pecena, Engineering Dir
Ken Nelson, Chief Engineer
Sherill Simpson,Traffic Manager

KBTX-TV *Digital Channel:* 50 *Virtual Channel:* 3; 1000 kw; 1664 ft.; N30 33 16 W96 1 51
4141 E 29th St. Box 3730, Bryan, TX 77801 US
(979) 846-7777, *Fax:* (979) 846-1490 (sls),(979) 846-1888 (news)
www.kbtx.com
closedcaptioning@kbtx.com
License: Bryan, Brazos County, TX held by Gray Television Licensee Inc.
Group Owner: Gray Television Inc.; (acq 6-29-99; $97.5 million cash and shares with KWTX-TV Waco).
Nat'l Network: CBS; CW *Nat'l Reps:* Millennium Sales & Marketing *Wire Services:* AP
Size of News Staff: 30; *Hours of Local News Weekly:* news progmg 19 hrs. wkly
Mike Wright, Operations Dir
Jon Boaz, General Sales Mgr
Mike George, News Director
Mandy Riske, Operations Manager

KCEN-TV *Digital Channel:* 9 *Virtual Channel:* 6; 25 kw; 1729 ft.; N31 16 24 W97 13 14
17 S. 3th St/PO Box 6103, Temple, TX 76503 US
(254) 859-5481, *Fax:* (254) 859-4004
www.kcendt.com
news@kcendt.com
License: Temple, Bell County, TX held by KCEN Channel 9 5/1/2009; *Ownership:* London Broadcasting Company; *Washington Law Firm:* Wiley Rein LLP
Nat'l Network: NBC *Nat'l Reps:* Petry Television Inc. *Wire Services:* AP
Size of News Staff: 33; *Hours of Local News Weekly:* news progmg 17 hrs wkly
Terry London, President
Philip Hurley, Operations Dir
Gayle Kiger, General Manager
Mike Stanford, Brand Marketing Director

***KDYW** *Digital Channel:* 20 *Virtual Channel:* 34; 79.4 kw vis, 7.9 kw aur; 508t/446g; N31 30 31 W97 10 03; *Population Served:* 100,000
Mailing Address: One Bear Pl. #97296, Waco, TX 76703
Second Address: 2100 River Street, Waco, TX 76706
(254) 710-3472, *Fax:* (254) 710-3874
www.kwbu.org
comments@kwbu.org
License: Waco, McLennan County, TX held by Brazos Valley Public Broadcasting Foundation
(acq 12-6-93; $80,000;; *Washington Law Firm:* Cohn & Marks
Nat'l Network: PBS *Regional Network:* National Educational Telecommunications Associatio
Phil Adkins, Chairman
Joe Riley, CEO
Ashley Kortis, General Sales Mgr
Clare Paul, Promotions Manager
Derek Smith, News Director
Tony Poole, Chief Engineer

***KNCT** *Digital Channel:* 46; 479 kw vis, 67.6 kw aur; 1,261t/1,126g; N30 59 12 W97 37 47
Mailing Address: Box 1800, Killeen, TX 76540
Second Address: KNCT/ Central Texas College, 6200 W. Centex Expwy., Killeen, TX 76549-4199
(254) 526-1176, *Fax:* (254) 526-1850
www.knct.org
knct@knct.org
License: Belton, Bell County, TX held by Central Texas College
Nat'l Network: PBS; Create
Size of News Staff: 1; *Hours of Local News Weekly:* news progmg one hr wkly
Max Rudolph, General Manager
Steve Benger, Programming Director
Sean Greenthaner, Promotions Manager
Steve Sulzer, Engineering Dir

KWKT-TV *Digital Channel:* 57; 4,170 kw vis, 417 kw aur; ant 1,811t/1,673g; N31 18 52 W97 19 37
Mailing Address: Box 2544, Waco, TX 76702-2544
Second Address: 8803 Woodway Dr., Waco, TX 76712
(254) 776-3844, *Fax:* (254) 388-5958
kwkt.com
info@kwkt.com
License: Waco, McLennan County, TX held by Comcorp of Texas License Corp.
Group Owner: Communications Corp. of America; (acq 10-31-90; grpsl;; *Washington Law Firm:* Fletcher, Heald & Hildreth
Nat'l Network: Fox; MyNetworkTV *Nat'l Reps:* Millennium Sales & Marketing
Duane Sartor, Station Manager
Bill Knobler, General Sales Mgr
Lou Strowger, Chief Engineer
Robin Rice, National Sales Manager
Amy Bishop, Public Affairs Director

KWTX-TV *Digital Channel:* 10 *Virtual Channel:* 10; 39 kw; 1821 ft.; N31 19 19 W97 19 2
200 West Highway 6, Suite 210, Waco, TX 76712 US
(254) 776-1330, *Fax:* (254) 751-1088
www.kwtx.com
mail@kwtx.com
License: Waco, McLennan County, TX held by Gray Television Licensee Inc.
Group Owner: Gray Television Inc.; (acq 6-29-99; $97.5 million cash and shares with KBTX-TV Bryan).; *Washington Law Firm:* Wiley Rein
Nat'l Network: CBS; CW *Nat'l Reps:* Millennium Sales & Marketing
Size of News Staff: 30; *Hours of Local News Weekly:* news progmg 20 hrs wkly
Ken Musgrave, Operations Dir
Bob Bunch, General Manager
Robert Lepping, General Sales Mgr

KXXV *Digital Channel:* 26 *Virtual Channel:* 25; 1000 kw; 1842 ft.; N31 20 16 W97 18 36; *Rebroadcasting:* ABC, Telemundo, Weather Now(Local Weather)
Mailing Address: P.O. Box 2522, Waco, TX 76702 US
Second Address: 1909 S. New Rd., Waco, TX 76711
(254) 754-2525, *Fax:* (254) 752-1002
www.kxxv.com
news25@kxxv.com
License: Waco, McLennan County, TX held by Centex Television L.P.
Group Owner: R.H. Drewry Group; (acq 1994).
Nat'l Network: ABC; Telemundo (Spanish)
Size of News Staff: 18; *Hours of Local News Weekly:* news progmg 14.5 hrs wkly
Mike Lee, Operations Dir
Jeff Armstrong, General Sales Mgr
Dani Fox, Programming Director
Dennis Kinney, News Director
Randy Lee, Chief Engineer
Darlene Mahler, National Sales Manager

KYLE-TV *Digital Channel:* 28 *Virtual Channel:* 28; 50 kw vis; ant 722t/640g; N30 41 18 W96 25 35; *Rebroadcasting:* Satellite of KWKT(TV) Waco.; *Population Served:* 200,000
2402 Broadmoor Dr., Suite B-101, Bryan, TX 77805
(979) 774-1800, *Fax:* (979) 774-1901
www.kyle28.com
License: Bryan, Brazos County, TX held by Comcorp of Bryan License Corp.
Group Owner: Communications Corp. of America; (acq 1996; $1.1 million); *Washington Law Firm:* Gardner, Carton & Douglas
Nat'l Network: Fox; MyNetworkTV
Duane Sartor, Station Manager
Donna Fowler, General Sales Mgr
Lou Stranger, Chief Engineer

Wichita Falls, TX & Lawton, OK (DMA 145)

KAUZ-TV *Digital Channel:* 22 *Virtual Channel:* 6; 433 kw; 1020 ft.; N33 54 4 W98 32 21
P.O. Box 2130, Wichita Falls, TX 76307 US
(940) 322-6957, *Fax:* (940) 761-3331,TWX: 910-890-5836
www.kauz.com
email@kauz.com
License: Wichita Falls, Wichita County, TX held by Hoak Media of Wichita Falls L.P.
Group Owner: Hoak Media Corporation; (acq 11-5-2003; $8.2 million); *Washington Law Firm:* Covington & Burling
Nat'l Network: CBS; CW *Nat'l Reps:* Harrington, Righter & Parsons *Wire Services:* CBS
Size of News Staff: 20; *Hours of Local News Weekly:* news progmg 15 hrs wkly
Mike Taylor, General Manager
Randy Blake, General Sales Mgr
Elayne Thompson, Programming Director
Jackie McCartney, Promotions Manager
Drew Hadwall, News Director
Tony Guess, Chief Engineer
Kyle Williams, National SalesManager
Mark Walker, Regional Sales Manager

KFDX-TV *Digital Channel:* 28 *Virtual Channel:* 3; 1000 kw; 884 ft.; N33 53 23 W98 33 30
Mailing Address: 200 Abington Executive Park, Suite 201, Clarks Summit, PA 18411 US
Second Address: Box 4888, Wichita Falls, TX 76309
(940) 691-0003, *Fax:* (940) 691-0330
www.kfdx.com
kfdx@kfdx.com
License: Wichita Falls, Wichita County, TX held by Nexstar Broadcasting Inc.
Group Owner: Nexstar Broadcasting Group Inc.; (acq 11-6-97; grpsl).; *Washington Law Firm:* Arter & Hadden
Nat'l Network: NBC
Size of News Staff: 24; *Hours of Local News Weekly:* news progmg 19.5 hrs wkly
Greg Collier, Operations Dir
Julie Pruett, General Manager
Wayne Reed, General Sales Mgr
Troy Short, Promotions Manager
Terry Porter, Chief Engineer

KJTL *Digital Channel:* 15 *Virtual Channel:* 18; 1000 kw; 863 ft.; N34 12 5 W98 43 45
US
(940) 691-1808, *Fax:* (940) 691-4856
www.texomashomepage.com
kjtl@fox18.com
License: Wichita Falls, Wichita County, TX held by Mission Broadcasting of Wichita Falls License Inc.
Group Owner: Mission Broadcasting Inc.; (acq 1999; $28.5 million with KCIT(TV) Amarillo); *Washington Law Firm:* Spector & Goldberg
Nat'l Network: FOX
Stephanie Reed, General Manager

Utah

Salt Lake City, UT (DMA 33)

***KBYU-TV** *Digital Channel:* 44 *Virtual Channel:* 11; 346 kw; 4124 ft.; N40 39 33 W112 12 7
C-302 Hfac, Provo, UT 84602 US
(801) 422-8450, *Fax:* (801) 422-8478
www.kbyu.org
kbyu@byu.edu
License: Provo, Utah County, UT held by Brigham Young University
Washington Law Firm: Wilkinson, Barker, Knauer & Quinn
Nat'l Network: PBS
Foreign Language Programming; Size of News Staff: 3; *Hours of Local News Weekly:* news progmg 3 hrs wkly
Derek Marquis, General Manager
Bart Chidester, Production Supervisor
Wendy Thomas, Programming Director
Jim Bell, Promotions Manager
Wesley Sims, News Director
Brian Leifson, Chief Engineer

KCBU-DT *Digital Channel:* 3; 70 kw vis; ant 2,158t/167g; N39 45 22 W110 59 22

Equity Media Holdings Corp., 1 Shackleford Dr., Little Rock, AR 72211
(501) 219-2400, *Fax:* (501) 716-3502
License: Price, Utah County, UT held by Price Broadcasting Inc., debtor in possession
Nat'l Network: TeleFutura (Spanish)
Doug Cryle, General Manager

KCSG *Digital Channel:* 14 *Virtual Channel:* 4; 25 kw; 1263 ft.; N37 38 22 W113 2 0
PO Box 1160, Salt Lake City, UT 84110 US
(435) 634-7500, *Fax:* (435) 674-2774
www.kcsg.com
info@kcsg.com
License: Cedar City, Iron County, UT held by Southwest Media LLC
(acq 7-30-2002; $450,000); *Washington Law Firm:* Garvey, Schubert & Barer
Nat'l Network: IND
Ed Merrifield, General Manager

KENV-DT ; 3.09 kw vis; 1,850t; N40 41 52; *Rebroadcasting:* Rebroadcasts KRNV(TV) Reno.; *Population Served:* 37,000
1025 Chilton Circle, Elko, NV 89801
(775) 777-8500, *Fax:* (775) 777-7758
www.kenvtv.com
License: Elko, Elko County, NV held by Ruby Mountain Broadcasting Co.
Group Owner: Sunbelt Communications Co.; (acq 11-8-96).
Nat'l Network: NBC
John Finkbohner, Operations Dir
Terry Hritz, Station Manager/Operations Manager

KJZZ-TV *Digital Channel:* 46 *Virtual Channel:* 14; 200 kw; 4154 ft.; N40 39 33 W112 12 7
Mailing Address: 5181 Amelia Earhart Dr., Salt Lake City, UT 84123 US
Second Address: UT
(801) 537-1414, *Fax:* (801) 238-6414
www.kjzz.com
bquigley@kjzz.com
License: Salt Lake City, Salt Lake County, UT held by Larry H. Miller Communications Corp
(acq 2-12-93;; *Washington Law Firm:* Fleischman & Walsh
Nat'l Network: MYTV *Nat'l Reps:* Blair Television
Randy Wright, Operations Dir
Chris Baum, General Manager
Marc Lowry, General Sales Mgr
Robert Quigley, Programming Director
Eric Schulz, Promotions Manager
Mike Grover, Chief Engineer
Bob Gauld, National Sales Manager
DeanPaynter, Production Director
Charla Hastings, Traffic Manager

KMYU *Digital Channel:* 9 *Virtual Channel:* 12; 9.8 kw vis; ant 138t; N37 03 49 W113 34 20; *Rebroadcasting:* Rebroadcasts KUTV Salt Lake City 10
299 S. Main, Ste 156, Salt Lake City, UT 20037
(801) 973-3000, *Fax:* (801) 973-3002
www.kutv.com
License: Saint George, Washington County, UT held by SLC TV Licensee Corp.
Group Owner: Four Points Media Group; (acq 11-21-2007; grpsl)
Nat'l Network: MyNetworkTV *Nat'l Reps:* TeleRep
David Phillips, Operations Dir
Kipp Greene, Engineering Dir
Scott Jones, Operations Director

KPNZ *Digital Channel:* 24 *Virtual Channel:* 24; 450 kw; 4032 ft.; N40 39 33 W112 12 7
1077 West Morton Ave, Porterville, CA 93257 US
(801) 519-2424, *Fax:* (801) 359-1272
www.utahs24tv.com
info@utahs24tv.com
License: Ogden, Weber County, UT held by KRCA License LLC.
Group Owner: Liberman Broadcasting Inc.; (acq 11-30-2007; $10 million)
Nat'l Network: IND
Wayne Casa, General Manager
Winter Horton, Chief Engineer

KSL-TV *Digital Channel:* 38 *Virtual Channel:* 5; 546 kw; 4157 ft.; N40 39 33 W112 12 7
P.O. Box 1160, Salt Lake City, UT 84110 US
(801) 575-5555, *Fax:* (801) 575-5561
www.ksl.com
License: Salt Lake City, Salt Lake County, UT held by Bonneville International Corp.
Group Owner: Bonneville International Corporation; *Washington Law Firm:* Wilkinson, Barker, Knauer & Quinn
Nat'l Network: NBC *Nat'l Reps:* Eagle Television Sales *Wire Services:* UPI
Foreign Language Programming; Size of News Staff: 65; *Hours of Local News Weekly:* news progmg 21 hrs wkly
Bruce Christensen, General Manager

KSTU *Digital Channel:* 28 *Virtual Channel:* 13; 350 kw; 3970 ft.; N40 39 33 W112 12 8
5151 Wisconsin Ave, N.W., Washington, DC 20016 US
(801) 532-1300
www.myfoxutah.com
news@fox13.com
License: Salt Lake City, Salt Lake County, UT held by Community Television of Utah License LLC.
Group Owner: Local TV LLC; (acq 7-14-2008; grpsl)
Nat'l Network: FOX *Nat'l Reps:* Fox Stations Sales
Hours of Local News Weekly: News progmg 34 hrs wkly
Mari Chambers, CFO
Tim Ermish, Operations Dir
Ken Freedman, General Sales Mgr
Melanie Say, Promotions Manager
Renai Bodley, News Director
Al Schultz, Engineering Dir
Kent Carlton, National Sales Manager
Kirt Burton, RegionalSales Manager

KTMW *Digital Channel:* 20 *Virtual Channel:* 20
Company, Llc, 530 East First S, #204, Salt Lake City, UT 84102 US
(801) 973-8820, *Fax:* (801) 973-7145
www.tv20.org
License: Salt Lake City, Salt Lake County, UT held by Alpha & Omega Communications LLC
(acq 7-31-2003; $1.5 million); *Washington Law Firm:* Wood, Maines & Nolan, Chartered
Nat'l Network: IND *Nat'l Reps:* Apex Media Sales Inc.
Pat Openhaw, President
Anthon Jeppesan, Operations Dir
Dennis Ermel, General Manager
Michelle Ermel, Promotions Manager
Dennis Silver, Chief Engineer

KTVX *Digital Channel:* 40 *Virtual Channel:* 4; 475.7 kw; 4121 ft.; N40 39 33 W112 12 7
1760 Fremont Dr., Salt Lake City, UT 84104 US
(801) 975-4444, *Fax:* (801) 975-4440
www.abc4.com
news@abc4.com
License: Salt Lake City, Salt Lake County, UT held by Newport Television License LLC.
Group Owner: Newport Television LLC; (acq 3-14-2008; grpsl)
Nat'l Network: ABC
Size of News Staff: 50; *Hours of Local News Weekly:* news progmg 14 hrs wkly
Matt Jaquint, General Manager
John Cronan, Programming Director
Roland Steadham, News Director
Bob Lyon, Chief Engineer
Shara Meredith, Traffic Manager

KUCW *Digital Channel:* 48 *Virtual Channel:* 30; 200 kw; 4124 ft.; N40 39 33 W112 12 7
1408 North Kingshighway, Suite 300, St. Louis, MO 63113 US
(801) 975-4444, *Fax:* (801) 975-4442
www.cw30.com
info@cw30.com
License: Ogden, Weber County, UT held by High Plains Broadcasting License Co. LLC.
Group Owner: High Plains Broadcasting Inc.; (acq 9-15-2008; grpsl)
Nat'l Network: CW *Nat'l Reps:* MMT
Matt Jaquint, General Manager

***KUED** *Digital Channel:* 42 *Virtual Channel:* 7; 239 kw; 4154 ft.; N40 39 33 W112 12 7
101 Wasatch Drive, Room 118, Salt Lake City, UT 84112 US
(801) 581-7777, *Fax:* (801) 585-5096
www.kued.org
License: Salt Lake City, Salt Lake County, UT held by University of Utah
Nat'l Network: PBS
Foreign Language Programming
Larry Smith, General Manager

***KUEN** *Digital Channel:* 36 *Virtual Channel:* 9; 200 kw; 4121 ft.; N40 39 33 W112 12 7
101 Wasatch Drive, Salt Lake City, UT 84112 US
(801) 581-2999, *Fax:* (801) 585-6105
www.uen.org
resources@uen.org
License: Ogden, Weber County, UT held by Utah State Board of Regents
Nat'l Network: PBS
Foreign Language Programming
Mike Petersen, General Manager
Phil Titus, Chief Engineer

***KUES** *Digital Channel:* 19 *Virtual Channel:* 19; 0.33 kw; 1447 ft.; N38 38 4 W112 3 33
Philip Titus, 101 Wasatch Drive, Salt Lake City, UT 84112 US
(801) 581-2999, *Fax:* (801) 581-3576
License: Richfield, Sevier County, UT held by University of Utah.
Nat'l Network: PBS
Philip Titus, Engineering Dir

***KUEW** *Digital Channel:* 18 *Virtual Channel:* 18; 1.62 kw; 218 ft.; N37 3 50 W113 34 20; *Rebroadcasting:* Rebroadcasts KUED-TV Salt Lake City 100%
Philip Titus, 101 Wasatch Blvd, Salt Lake City, UT 84112 US
(801) 581-2999, *Fax:* (801) 585-6105
www.kued.com
License: St. George, Washington County, UT held by University of Utah.
Nat'l Network: PBS
Larry Smith, General Manager
Phil Titus, Chief Engineer

KUPX-TV *Digital Channel:* 29; 3,890 kw vis; 2,308t; N39 51 54 W111 53 39; *Rebroadcasting:* Pax Network; *Population Served:* 800,000
466 C Lawndale Dr., Salt Lake City, UT 84115
(801) 474-0016, *Fax:* (801) 463-9667
www.ionline.tv
License: Provo, Utah County, UT held by Paxson Salt Lake City License Inc.
Group Owner: ION Media Networks Inc.
Nat'l Network: ION Television
Jim Powell, General Sales Mgr

KUTF *Digital Channel:* 12 *Virtual Channel:* 12; 22.3 kw; 2264 ft.; N41 47 3 W112 13 55
1772 North 600 West, Logan, UT 84341 US
(501) 219-2400, *Fax:* (501) 716-3502
License: Logan, Cache County, UT held by Logan 12 Inc., debtor in possession.
Group Owner: Equity Media Holdings Corp.; (acq 2-1-2001; $4 million)
Nat'l Network: DAYSTAR
Doug Cryle, Operations Dir

KUTH-DT *Digital Channel:* 32; 3,072 kw vis; ant 2,663t/125g; N40 16 45 W111 56 00
215 S. State ST., Ste. 100-A, Salt Lake City, UT 84111-2348
(801) 519-9784, *Fax:* (801) 519-9785
www.univision-utah.com
aurias@ebcorp.net
License: Provo, Utah County, UT held by Univision Television Group Inc.
Group Owner: Equity Media Holdings Corp.; (acq 10-20-2004; $9.5 million)
Nat'l Network: Univision (Spanish)
Foreign Language Programming; Hours of Local News Weekly: News progmg 5 hrs wkly
Arlene Urias, General Manager

KUTV *Digital Channel:* 34 *Virtual Channel:* 2; 423 kw; 4157 ft.; N40 39 33 W112 12 7
C/O Cbs Inc. 600 New, Hampshire Ave NW # 1200, Washington, DC 20037 US
(801) 973-3000, *Fax:* (801) 973-3387
www.kutv2.com
License: Salt Lake City, Salt Lake County, UT held by SLC TV Licensee Corp.
Group Owner: Four Points Media Group; (acq 11-21-2007; grpsl); *Washington Law Firm:* Wiley Rein LLP
Nat'l Network: CBS *Nat'l Reps:* TeleRep
Size of News Staff: 73; *Hours of Local News Weekly:* news progmg 34.5 hrs wkly
Scott Jones, Operations Dir
Dave Phillips, General Manager

Vermont

Burlington, VT-Plattsburgh, NY (DMA 93)

WCAX-TV *Digital Channel:* 22; 38 kw vis, 7.25 kw aur; ant 2,739t; N44 31 36 W72 48 57; *Population Served:* 550,000
Mailing Address: Box 4508, Burlington, VT 05402
Second Address: 30 Joy Dr, S. Burlington, VT 5403
(802) 652-6300, *Fax:* (802) 652-6319
www.wcax.com

License: Burlington, Chittenden County, VT held by Mount Mansfield TV Inc
Washington Law Firm: Wilmer/Hace
Nat'l Network: CBS *Nat'l Reps:* Harrington, Righter & Parsons
Size of News Staff: 35; *Hours of Local News Weekly:* news progmg 15 hrs wkly
Peter Martin, President
Phil Scharf, Operations Dir
Peter Martin, General Manager
Bruce Grindle, General Sales Mgr
Peter Martin, Programming Director
Anson Tebbits, News Director
Tim Thayer, Chief Engineer
Alex Martin, NewMedia Director
Meredith Neary, Public Service Director
Mike McCune, Sports Director
Brenda Bouvier, Traffic Manager
Sharon Myer, Weather Director

***WETK** *Digital Channel:* 32 *Virtual Channel:* 33; 90 kw; 2723 ft.; N44 31 32 W72 48 51
88 Ethan Allen Avenue, Colchester, VT 05446 US
(802) 655-4800
www.vpt.org
view@vpt.org
License: Burlington, Chittenden County, VT held by Vermont ETV Inc
(acq 11-6-89).; *Washington Law Firm:* Covington & Burling
Nat'l Network: PBS *Regional Network:* Vermont Public Television
John King, CEO
Lee Ann Lee, General Sales Mgr

WFFF-TV *Digital Channel:* 43 *Virtual Channel:* 44; 5,000 kw vis; ant 1,738t; N44 31 32 W72 48 54
298 Mountain View Dr., Colchester, VT 33703
(802) 660-9333, *Fax:* (802) 660-8673
www.fox44.net
License: Burlington, Chittenden County, VT held by Smith Media License Holdings LLC.
Group Owner: Nexstar Broadcasting; (acq 11-15-2004; grpsl).
Nat'l Network: Fox; CW *Nat'l Reps:* Continental Television Sales
Wire Services: AP; CNN
Size of News Staff: 30; *Hours of Local News Weekly:* 24.5
Vic Vetters, Operations Dir
Dave Rawson, Promotions Manager
Vacant, News Director
Matt Servis, Chief Engineer

WNNE *Digital Channel:* 25; 2,240 kw vis, 2.24 kw aur; ant 2,220t/149g; N43 26 38 W72 27 17; *Population Served:* 133,000
Box 1310, White River Junction, VT 5001
(802) 295-3100, *Fax:* (802) 655-5451
www.wnne.com
License: Hartford, Windsor County, VT held by Hearst-Argyle Stations Inc.
Group Owner: Hearst-Argyle Television Inc.
Nat'l Network: NBC
Paul Sands, General Manager

***WVER** *Digital Channel:* 9 *Virtual Channel:* 28; 15 kw; 1263 ft.; N43 39 31 W73 6 25; *Rebroadcasting:* Satellite of WETK(TV) Burlington.
88 Ethan Allen Avenue, Colchester, VT 05446 US
(802) 655-4800
www.vpt.org
veiw@vpt.org
License: Rutland, Rutland County, VT held by Vermont ETV Inc
Washington Law Firm: Covington & Burling
Nat'l Network: PBS *Regional Network:* Vermont Public Television
Jim Wyant, Chairman
John King, CEO
Lee Ann Lee, General Sales Mgr
Kelly Luoma, Programming Director
Jeff Vande Griek, Promotions Manager
Rob Belle-Isle, Engineering Dir
Andrea Bergeron, CFO
Peter Shea, Sales Director

WVNY *Digital Channel:* 22 *Virtual Channel:* 22; 1,000 kw vis, 100 kw aur; 2,739t/310g; N44 31 40 W72 48 58
298 Mountain View Dr., Colchester, VT 10111
(802) 660-9333, *Fax:* (802) 660-8673
www.abc22.com
abc22@abc22.com
License: Burlington, Chittenden County, VT held by Lambert Broadcasting of Burlington LLC
Group Owner: Nexstar Broadcasting; (acq 5-21-2005; $10.2 million plus assumption of liabilities).
Nat'l Network: ABC *Nat'l Reps:* Continental Television Sales
Ken Kasz, Operations Dir
Steve Doerr, General Manager
JoAnn Cyr, General Sales Mgr
Sara Carpenter, Programming Director
Dave Rawson, Promotions Manager
Tracy Davis, News Director
Dana Nahumck, Chief Engineer

***WVTA** *Digital Channel:* 24 *Virtual Channel:* 41; 55.7 kw; 2270 ft.; N43 26 14.7 W72 27 7.7; *Rebroadcasting:* Satellite of *WETK Burlington.
88 Ethan Allen Avenue, Colchester, VT 05446 US
(802) 655-4800
www.vpt.org
view@vpt.org
License: Windsor, Windsor County, VT held by Vermont ETV Inc
Washington Law Firm: Covington & Burling
Nat'l Network: PBS *Regional Network:* Vermont Public Television
John King, CEO
Joseph Merone, Operations Dir
Lee Ann Lee, General Sales Mgr
Kelly Luoma, Programming Director
Jeff Vande Griek, Promotions Manager
Rob Belle-Isle, Engineering Dir
Peter Shea, Sales Director

***WVTB** *Digital Channel:* 18 *Virtual Channel:* 20; 67 kw; 1936 ft.; N44 34 16 W71 53 39; *Rebroadcasting:* Satellite of WETK(TV) Burlington
88 Ethan Allen Avenue, Colchester, VT 05446 US
(802) 655-4800
www.vpt.org
view@vpt.org
License: St. Johnsbury, Caledonia County, VT held by Vermont ETV Inc
Washington Law Firm: Covington & Burling
Nat'l Network: PBS *Regional Network:* Vermont Public Television
John King, CEO
Lee Ann Lee, General Sales Mgr

Virgin Islands

Charlotte Amalie

***WTJX-TV** *Digital Channel:* 44; 28.8 kw vis, 2.9 kw aur; ant 1,479t; N18 21 26 W64 56 50; *Population Served:* 110,000
Box 7879, St. Thomas, VI 0801
(340) 774-6255, *Fax:* (340) 774-7092
www.wtjx.org
opotter@wtjx.org
License: Charlotte Amalie, VI held by Virgin Islands Public Television System
Washington Law Firm: Schwartz, Woods & Miller
Nat'l Network: PBS
Osbert E Potter, CEO
Tanya Marie Singh, COO
Yvette Delaubanque, Director, Development/Funding
Jose Raul Carrillo, Board Chair
Robert Dickinson, Chief Engineer

WVXF *Digital Channel:* 17 *Virtual Channel:* 17; 4.2 kw; 1490 ft.; N18 21 26 W64 56 50
Post Office Box 1605, Milwaukee, WI 53201 US
(323) 934-8283/ (800) 275-6437
www.lkkgroup.com
info@wvxftv.com
License: Charlotte Amalie, VI held by Storefront Television (acq 9-30-2004; $600,000); *Washington Law Firm:* Dow, Lohnes & Albertson
Nat'l Network: CBS
Keith Bass, General Manager

WZVI *Digital Channel:* 43 *Virtual Channel:* 43; 1.4 kw; 92 ft.; N18 20 43 W64 55 45; *Rebroadcasting:* WSVI (Christiansted) 100%
Mailing Address: C/O Thomas J. Dougherty, Jr., 1301 K St., NW Ste.900 East, Washington, DC 20005 US
Second Address: Barren Spot, Village Mall, downstairs, Kingshill, VI 851
(340) 778-5008, *Fax:* (340) 778-5011
www.wsvi.tv
channel8@wsvitv.com
License: Charlotte Amalie, VI held by Marri Broadcasting LP.
Nat'l Network: ABC
David Lampel, President
Glen Dratte, General Manager
Chester Benjamin, Chief Engineer

Christiansted

WCVI-TV *Digital Channel:* 23 *Virtual Channel:* 39; 0.659 kw; 407 ft.; N17 44 53 W64 43 40
PO B. 24027 Gallows Bay, Christiansted, VI 0824 US
(340) 718-9927, *Fax:* (340) 718-0712
www.wcvi.tv
mbox@wcvi.tv
License: Christiansted, Saint Croix County, VI held by Virgin Blue Inc.
Nat'l Network: CW
Victor Gold, General Manager
Marty Adamshick, Programming Director

WSVI *Digital Channel:* 20 *Virtual Channel:* 8; 1.1 kw; 951 ft.; N17 45 21 W64 47 56
Mailing Address: PO Box 8, Abc, Christiansted, VI 0823 US
Second Address: Barren Spot, Village Mall, downstairs, Kingshill, VI 851
(340) 778-5008, *Fax:* (340) 778-5011
www.wsvi.tv
channel8@wsvitv.com
License: Christiansted, Saint Croix County, VI held by Alpha Broadcasting Corp.
Washington Law Firm: Marmet & McCombs
Nat'l Network: ABC *Nat'l Reps:* Roslin
Foreign Language Programming
David Lampel, CEO
Glen Dratte, General Manager
Chester Benjamin, Chief Engineer

Virginia

Charlottesville, VA (DMA 183)

WCAV *Digital Channel:* 19 *Virtual Channel:* 19; 155 kw; 1068 ft.; N37 59 3 W78 28 52
1532 Sixteenth St. N.W., Washington, DC 20036 US
(434) 242-1919, *Fax:* (434) 220-0398
www.charlottesvillenewsplex.tv
License: Charlottesville, Albemarle County, VA held by Gray Television Licensee Inc.
Group Owner: Gray Television Inc.; (acq 5-28-2004; $1 million for CP).
Nat'l Network: CBS
Brad Ramsey, General Manager
Megan Huffman, General Sales Mgr
Jim Hanchett, News Director

***WHTJ** *Digital Channel:* 46 *Virtual Channel:* 41; 165 kw; 1088 ft.; N37 58 59 W78 29 2; *Rebroadcasting:* Rebroadcasts WCVE-TV Richmond.
23 Sesame Street, Richmond, VA 23235 US
(434) 295-7671; (804) 320-1301, *Fax:* (804) 320-8729
www.ideastations.org
License: Charlottesville, Charlottesville City County, VA held by Commonwealth Public Broadcsting Corp
Washington Law Firm: Wiley, Rein & Fielding
Nat'l Network: PBS
John Felton, General Manager
Lisa Tait, General Sales Mgr

WVIR-TV *Digital Channel:* 32 *Virtual Channel:* 29; 1000 kw; 1207 ft.; N37 59 2 W78 28 53
P.O. Box 769, Charlottesville, VA 22902 US
(434) 220-2900, *Fax:* (434) 220-2904
www.nbc29.com
newsdesk@nbc29.com
License: Charlottesville, Charlottesville City County, VA held by Virginia Broadcasting Corp.
Group Owner: Waterman Broadcasting Corp.; *Washington Law Firm:* Fletcher, Heald, & Hildreth
Nat'l Network: NBC/CW; CW *Nat'l Reps:* Continental Television Sales *Wire Services:* AP
Size of News Staff: 50; *Hours of Local News Weekly:* news progmg 32 hrs wkly
Harold Wright, Operations Dir
Jim Fernald, General Sales Mgr
Ralph Tobias, Promotions Manager
Neal Bennett, News Director
Bob Jenkins, Chief Engineer

Harrisonburg, VA (DMA 178)

WHSV-TV *Digital Channel:* 49; 832 kw vis, 432 kw aur; ant 2,130t/337g; N38 36 05 W78 37 57; *Population Served:* 350,000
50 N. Main St., Harrisonburg, VA 22802
(540) 433-9191, *Fax:* (540) 433-4028; (540)433-2700
www.whsv.com
whsv@whsv.com
License: Harrisonburg, Rockingham County, VA held by Gray Television Licensee, LLC
Group Owner: Gray Television Inc.; (acq 8-29-2002; grpsl).;
Washington Law Firm: Wiley, Rein LLP

Nat'l Network: ABC; Fox; MyNetworkTV
Size of News Staff: 18; *Hours of Local News Weekly:* news progmg 16 hrs wkly
Tracey Jones, General Manager
Tim Merritt, General Sales Mgr
Jeremy Harman, Promotions Manager
Kay Norred, News Director
Ed Morano, Chief Engineer
Tina Wood, Operations Manager

***WVPT** *Digital Channel:* 11 *Virtual Channel:* 51; 10 kw; 2231 ft.; N38 9 54 W79 18 51
Port Republic Road, Harrisonburg, VA 22801 US
(540) 434-5391, *Fax:* (540) 434-7084
www.wvpt.net
wvptcomments@wvpt.net
License: Staunton, Staunton City County, VA held by Shenandoah Valley ETV Corp
Washington Law Firm: Covington & Burling
Nat'l Network: PBS
Tony Mancari, COO
David Mullins, President

Norfolk-Portsmouth-Newport News, VA (DMA 43)

WAVY-TV *Digital Channel:* 31 *Virtual Channel:* 10; 1000 kw; 919 ft.; N36 49 14 W76 30 41
200 Crescent Court, Suite 200, Dallas, TX 75201 US
(757) 393-1010, *Fax:* (757) 399-7628
www.wavy.com
doug.davis@wavy.com
License: Portsmouth, Portsmouth City County, VA held by LIN License Company LLC
Group Owner: LIN Media; (acq 12-16-97; grpsl).; *Washington Law Firm:* Covington & Burling
Nat'l Network: NBC *Nat'l Reps:* Petry Television Inc. *Wire Services:* AP
Size of News Staff: 80; *Hours of Local News Weekly:* news progmg 31 hrs wkly
Doug Davis, President
John Cochran, General Sales Mgr
Eather White, Programming Director
Judy Triska, Promotions Manager
Mark Johnson, Engineering Dir

WGNT *Digital Channel:* 50 *Virtual Channel:* 27; 800 kw; 866 ft.; N36 48 43 W76 27 45
1501 M Street, N.W., Suite 1100, Washington, DC 20005 US
(757) 393-2501, *Fax:* (757) 399-3303
www.cw.27.com
cw27@wgnttv.com
License: Portsmouth, Portsmouth City County, VA held by CBS Television Stations Inc.
Group Owner: CBS Television Stations Group; (acq 10-31-97; $42.5 million)
Nat'l Network: THE CW NETWORK *Nat'l Reps:* Harrington, Righter & Parsons
Steven Soldinger, Operations Dir
Jon Erkenbrack, General Sales Mgr
Chris Wolf, Promotions Manager
George Randell, Chief Engineer
Chuck Martin, National Sales Manager
Kafi Rouse, Public Affairs Director
Diane Hall, TrafficManager

***WHRO-TV** *Digital Channel:* 16 *Virtual Channel:* 15; 2,630 kw vis, 263 kw aur; 964t/964g; N36 48 32 W76 30 13; *Not on Air/Target Date:* DTV on Air 2/5/2001 ; *Population Served:* 707,750
5200 Hampton Blvd., Norfolk, VA 23508
(757) 889-9400, *Fax:* (757) 489-0007
www.whro.org
info@whro.org
License: Hampton-Norfolk, Hampton City County, VA held by Hampton Roads Educ. Telecommunications Association Inc
Washington Law Firm: Dow-Lohnes
Nat'l Network: PBS
Size of News Staff: 2; *Hours of Local News Weekly:* news progmg 1 hr wkly
Bert Schmidt, CEO
Doug Weiss, VP/Operations
Chris Gunnufsen, Engineering/IT Officer
Virginia Thumm, VP/Development
Bobbie Fisher, Promotions Manager
Tom Morehouse, CFO
Heather Mazzoni, Content Officer
Brian Callahan, ChiefEducation Officer

WPXV-TV *Digital Channel:* 46; 501 kw vis, 50.1 kw aur; ant 508t; N36 48 32 W76 30 13
230 Clearfield Ave. #104, Virginia Beach, VA 23462
(757) 499-1261, *Fax:* (757) 499-1679
www.ionmedia.tv
License: Norfolk, Norfolk City County, VA held by ION Media License Company, LLC, Debtor-in-possession
Group Owner: ION Media Networks Inc.; (acq 12-18-97; $14.75 million)
Nat'l Network: ION Television
Rhonda Nelson, Operations Dir
Cindy Arthur, Programming Director

WTKR *Digital Channel:* 40 *Virtual Channel:* 3; 950 kw; 1237 ft.; N36 48 31 W76 30 13
720 Boush St ., Norfolk, VA 23510 US
(757) 446-1000, *Fax:* (757) 446-1376
www.wtkr.com
License: Norfolk, Norfolk City County, VA held by Local TV Virginia License LLC.
Group Owner: Local TV LLC; (acq 5-7-2007; grpsl); *Washington Law Firm:* Reed, Smith, Shaw & McClay
Nat'l Network: CBS
Jeff Hoffman, General Manager
Jeff McCallister, Station Manager
Tina Blacklocke, News Director

WTPC-TV *Digital Channel:* 7; 5,000 kw vis; ant 1,017t/1,014g; N36 48 31 W76 30 12
1333 Regent University Dr., Suite 202, Virginia Beach, VA 23462
(757) 605-2601
www.tbn.org
whrepa@tbn.org
License: Virginia Beach, Virginia Beach County, VA held by Copeland Channel 21 LLC
J. R. Brestin, Station Manager
Mike Cochran, Engineering Dir

WTVZ-TV *Digital Channel:* 33 *Virtual Channel:* 33; 960 kw; 1232 ft.; N36 48 31 W76 30 13
10706 Beaver Dam Road, Cockeysville, MD 21030 US
(757) 622-3333, *Fax:* (757) 623-1541
www.mytvz.com
License: Norfolk, Norfolk City County, VA held by WTVZ Licensee L.L.C.
Group Owner: Sinclair Broadcast Group Inc.; (acq 2-9-95; $47 million;; *Washington Law Firm:* Gardner, Carton & Douglas
Nat'l Network: MYTV
Bill Scaffide, General Manager
Bill Barber, Chief Engineer

WVBT *Digital Channel:* 29 *Virtual Channel:* 43; 1000 kw; 791 ft.; N36 49 14 W76 30 41
15304 Sunset Boulevard, Suite 204, Pacific Palisades, CA 90272 US
(757) 393-4343, *Fax:* (757) 673-5300
www.fox43tv.com
doug.davis@wavy.com
License: Virginia Beach, Virginia Beach County, VA held by WAVY Broadcasting LLC.
Group Owner: LIN Television Corporation; (acq 1-9-2002; $4.25 million)
Nat'l Network: FOX *Nat'l Reps:* Petry Television Inc.
Doug Davis, General Manager
John Cochrane, General Sales Mgr
Nick Hasenecz, Local Sales Director
Jane Plante, Local Sales Director
Andrew Hilton, National Sales Director
Eileen Baggett, National Sales Director

WVEC *Digital Channel:* 13; 316 kw vis, 31.6 kw aur; 980t/1,028g; N36 49 00 W76 28 05; *Population Served:* 1,253,200
613 Woodis Ave., Norfolk, VA 23510
(757) 625-1313, *Fax:* (757) 628-5855
www.wvec.com
License: Hampton, Hampton City County, VA held by WVEC Television Inc.
Group Owner: Belo Corp; (acq 11-28-83; grpsl;
Nat'l Network: ABC *Nat'l Reps:* TeleRep *Wire Services:* Reuters
Size of News Staff: 65; *Hours of Local News Weekly:* news progmg 24 hrs wkly
Tod A. Smith, President
Amy Warren, General Sales Mgr
Deborah Shollenberger, Programming Director
Rich Lebenson, News Director
John Dolive, Chief Engineer
Sandra Johnson, Asst Traffic Manager
Kari Jacobs, Local Sales Manager
Greg Watkins, National Sales Manager
Jeff Lawson, Weather Director

Richmond-Petersburg, VA (DMA 58)

***WCVE-TV** *Digital Channel:* 42 *Virtual Channel:* 23; 160 kw; 1136 ft.; N37 30 44 W77 36 4
23 Sesame Street, Richmond, VA 23235 US
(804) 320-1301, *Fax:* (804) 320-8729
www.ideastations.org
info@ideastations.org
License: Richmond, Richmond City County, VA held by Commonwealth Public Broadcasting Corp
Washington Law Firm: Wiley, Rein & Fielding
Nat'l Network: PBS
Curtis Monk, President
Lisa Tait, General Sales Mgr
John Felton, Programming Director

***WCVW** *Digital Channel:* 44 *Virtual Channel:* 57; 112 kw; 1076 ft.; N37 30 45 W77 36 5
23 Sesame Street, Richmond, VA 23235 US
(804) 320-1301, *Fax:* (804) 320-8729
www.ideastations.org
info@ideastations.org
License: Richmond, Richmond City County, VA held by Commonwealth Public Broadcasting Corporation
Washington Law Firm: Wiley, Rein & Fielding
Nat'l Network: PBS
Curtis Monk, President
Lisa Tait, General Sales Mgr
John Felton, Programming Director

WRIC-TV *Digital Channel:* 22 *Virtual Channel:* 8; 850 kw; 1077 ft.; N37 30 45 W77 36 6
Arboretum Place, Richmond, VA 23236 US
(804) 330-8888, *Fax:* (804) 330-8882
www.wric.com
news@wric.com
License: Petersburg, Chesterfield County, VA held by Young Broadcasting of Richmond Inc.
Group Owner: Young Broadcasting Inc.; (acq 11-14-94; grpsl;;
Washington Law Firm: Brooks, Pierce, McLendon, Humphrey & Leonard
Nat'l Network: ABC *Nat'l Reps:* Adam Young
Robert Peterson, General Manager
Matthew Zelkird, Station Manager

WRLH-TV *Digital Channel:* 26 *Virtual Channel:* 35; 800 kw; 1075 ft.; N37 30 45 W77 36 5
18 Newbury Street, Boston, MA 02116 US
(410) 568-1500, *Fax:* (410) 568-1537
www.foxrichmond.com,www.mytvrichmond.com
License: Richmond, Richmond City County, VA held by WRLH Licensee LLC.
Group Owner: Sinclair Broadcast Group Inc.; (acq 12-10-01; grpsl).; *Washington Law Firm:* Arter & Hadden
Nat'l Network: FOX; MyNetworkTV
Size of News Staff: 15; *Hours of Local News Weekly:* news progmg 3 hrs wkly
Steve Genett, General Manager
Michael Dunlap, General Sales Mgr
Mark Bartholomew, Promotions Manager
Paul Glover, Chief Engineer

WTVR-TV *Digital Channel:* 25 *Virtual Channel:* 6; 410 kw; 1138 ft.; N37 30 45 W77 36 5
Rsa Tower, 20th Floor, 201 Monroe Street, Montgomery, AL 36104 US
(804) 254-3600, *Fax:* (804) 254-3697
www.wtvr.com
License: Richmond, Richmond City County, VA held by Community Television of Alabama License LLC.
Group Owner: Local TV LLC; (acq 3-31-2009; exchange for WBRC(TV) Birmingham, AL); *Washington Law Firm:* Dow Lohnes PLLC
Nat'l Network: CBS *Nat'l Reps:* TeleRep *Wire Services:* AP
Peter Maroney, Operations Dir
Stephen Hayes, General Sales Mgr
Bill Anderson, Promotions Manager
Roger Katchen, Chief Engineer
Steve Young, Local Sales Manager
James Taguchi, National Sales Manager
Don Cox, OperationsDirector
Tina Woody, Operations Manager

WUPV *Digital Channel:* 47 *Virtual Channel:* 65; 1,000 kw ERP; 219m/153m AGL; N37 44 31 W77 15 15; *Population Served:* 1,362,000
5710 Midlothian Turnpike, Richmond, VA 23228
804-230-1212, *Fax:* 804-230-7059
www.cwrichmond.tv
programming@cwrichmond.tv

License: Ashland, Hanover County, VA held by WUPV License Subsidiary LLC
Group Owner: American Spirit Media; April 2011
Nat'l Network: CW (Ch 65.1); Bounce TV (Ch 65.2) *Nat'l Reps:* TeleRep
Size of News Staff: 30; *Hours of Local News Weekly:* 2.5
Rosalie Drake, General Manager
Rosalie Drake, General Sales Mgr
Blake Peddicord, Program Coordinator
Nancy Kent Smith, News Director
Bruce Tinoco, Engineering Dir
Rob Whitley, Chief Engineer

WWBT *Digital Channel:* 12 *Virtual Channel:* 12; 26 kw; 794 ft.; N37 30 23 W77 30 12
Mailing Address: 5710 Midlothian Turnpike, Richmond, VA 23225 US
Second Address: 5710 Midlothian Tpke., Richmond, VA 23225
(804) 230-1212, *Fax:* (804) 230-2793
www.nbc12.com
newsroom@nbc12.com
License: Richmond, Richmond City County, VA held by WWBT License Subsidiary LLC.
Group Owner: Raycom Media Inc.; (acq 3-31-2008; grpsl);
Washington Law Firm: Covington & Burling
Nat'l Network: NBC
Donald S. Richards, Operations Dir
M. Kym Grinnage, General Sales Mgr
Nancy Kent, News Director

Roanoke-Lynchburg, VA (DMA 67)

***WBRA-TV** *Digital Channel:* 3 *Virtual Channel:* 15; 7.25 kw; 2028 ft.; N37 11 46 W80 9 17
Mailing Address: P.O. Box 13246, Roanoke, VA 24032 US
Second Address: Blue Ridge PBS, 1215 McNeil Dr. S.W., Roanoke, VA 24015
(540) 344-0991, *Fax:* (540) 344-2148
www.blueridgepbs.org
License: Roanoke, Roanoke City County, VA held by Blue Ridge Public Television Inc
Nat'l Network: PBS
Greg Feldman, Chairman
Anita Sims, CFO
James Baum, President
Will Anderson, Operations Dir
Sherry Spradlin, Programming Director
Erwin Roman, Chief Engineer
Kate Foreman, VP of Advancement

WDBJ *Digital Channel:* 18 *Virtual Channel:* 7; 675 kw; 1988 ft.; N37 11 42 W80 9 23
Mailing Address: 2001 Colonial Avenue, Roanoke, VA 24015 US
Second Address: VA
(540) 344-7000, *Fax:* (540) 344-5097
www.wdbj7.com
firstinitiallastname@wdbj7.com
License: Roanoke, Roanoke City County, VA held by WDBJ Television Inc.
Group Owner: Schurz Communications Inc.; (acq 11-1-69; $8.2 million;; *Washington Law Firm:* Wilmer Cutler Pickering Hale and Dorr
Nat'l Network: CBS; MyNetworkTV *Nat'l Reps:* Harrington, Righter & Parsons *Wire Services:* UPI; AP
Size of News Staff: 48; *Hours of Local News Weekly:* news progmg 18 hrs wkly
Jeffrey Marks, President
Kelly Zuber, Operations Dir
Lolly Quigley, General Sales Mgr
Mike Bell, Programming Director
Amy Morris, News Director
Alan Novitsky, Engineering Dir
Brian Boush, National Sales Manager
Marilyn Brock,Treasurer/Business Manager

WEFC-TV *Digital Channel:* 41; 5,000 kw vis, 1,000 kw au; ant 522t; *Rebroadcasting:* Rebroadcasts W54BT(TV) Roanoke 100%
5002 Airport Rd., Roanoke, VA 24540
(540) 366-2424, *Fax:* (540) 366-7530
www.wdrl-tv.com
manager@wdrl-tv.com
License: Danville, Pittsylvania County, VA held by MNE Broadcasting L.L.C.
Amy Ragsdale, Operations Dir
Mel Eleazer, General Manager
Dave Ross, General Sales Mgr
Rob Ruthenberg, Programming Director
Nel Kirt, Public Affairs Director

WFXR *Digital Channel:* 17; 2,690 kw vis, 269 kw aur; ant 1,991t/200g; N37 11 46 W80 09 16; *Population Served:* 206,000
Mailing Address: Box 2127, Roanoke, VA 24009-2127
Second Address: 2618 Colonial Ave. S.W., Roanoke, VA 24015
(540) 344-2127, *Fax:* (540) 345-1912,(540) 342-2753
www.fox2127.com
info@fox2127.com
License: Roanoke, Roanoke City County, VA held by Grant Broadcasting System II Inc.
Group Owner: Grant Communications Inc.; (acq 9-93; $5.5 million with WWCW(TV) Lynchburg;; *Washington Law Firm:* Birch, Horton, Bittner & Cherot
Nat'l Network: Fox; CW
Size of News Staff: 2; *Hours of Local News Weekly:* news progmg 2 hrs wkly
Dave Bunnell, General Manager
Ralph C, Station Manager

WPXR-TV *Digital Channel:* 36; 1,350 kw vis, 135 kw aur; ant 2,043t/180g; N37 11 37 W80 09 25; *Population Served:* 369,000
401 3rd St. S.W., Roanoke, VA 24011
(540) 857-0038, *Fax:* (540) 345-8568
www.ionmedia.tv
shirleybundy@ionmedia.tv
License: Roanoke, Roanoke City County, VA held by ION Media License Company, LLC, Debtor-in-possession
Group Owner: ION Media Networks Inc.; (acq 10-28-97).
Nat'l Network: ION Television
Shirley Bundy, Station Manager
Genia Wright, Programming Director
George Stein, Chief Engineer

WSET-TV *Digital Channel:* 34 *Virtual Channel:* 13; 302 kw vis, 50 kw aur; 2,050t/1,240g; N37 18 54 W79 38 06; *Population Served:* 1,023,000
Mailing Address: Box 11588, Lynchburg, VA 24506
Second Address: 2320 Langhorne Rd., Lynchburg, VA 24501
(434) 528-1313, *Fax:* (434) 847-0458
www.wset.com
wset@wset.com
License: Lynchburg, Lynchburg City County, VA held by WSET, Incorporated.
Group Owner: Allbritton Communications Co.; (acq 10-76; grpsl).; *Washington Law Firm:* Sidley, Austin, LLP
Nat'l Network: ABC; RTV; WeatherNation *Nat'l Reps:* Continental Television Sales *Wire Services:* AP; ABC
Size of News Staff: 41; *Hours of Local News Weekly:* news progmg 17 hrs wkly
Randall Smith, President
K.C. Spiron, Director of Operations and Engineering
Randall Smith, General Manager
George Kayes, General Sales Mgr
Randall Smith, Programming Director
John Crumpler, Promotions Coordinator
Bill Foy, NewsDirector
K.C. Spiron, Director of Operations and Engineering
Willis=Little, Chief Engineer
Russ Griffin, Business Manager
Jenny Marshall, HR Director
Deb Coleman, Director of Administration

WSLS-TV *Digital Channel:* 30 *Virtual Channel:* 10; 1000 kw; 1942 ft.; N37 12 3 W80 8 54
Mailing Address: 333 East Grace Street, Richmond, VA 23219 US
Second Address: 401 3rd St. S.W., Roanoke, VA 24011
(540) 981-9110,540-981-9126, *Fax:* (540) 343-3157/(540)343-2059
www.wsls.com
news@wsls.com
License: Roanoke, Roanoke City County, VA held by Media General Broadcasting Inc.
Group Owner: Media General Broadcast Group; (acq 3-21-97; grpsl).; *Washington Law Firm:* Wiley, Rein & Fielding
Nat'l Network: NBC
Size of News Staff: 33; *Hours of Local News Weekly:* news progmg 15 hrs wkly
Kathy Mohn, Operations Dir
Candy Crigger, General Sales Mgr
Daniel Coyle, Promotions Manager
Scott Martin, National Sales Manager
Robert Kerry, Operations Vice President

WWCW *Digital Channel:* 20 *Virtual Channel:* 21; 916 kw; 1641 ft.; N37 19 14 W79 37 58
Mailing Address: 915 Middle River Drive, Ft. Lauderdale, FL 33304 US
Second Address: 2618 Colonial Ave. S.W., Roanoke, VA 24015
(540) 344-2127, *Fax:* (540) 345-1912/(540) 342-2753
www.fox2127.com
info@fox2127.com
License: Lynchburg, Lynchburg City County, VA held by Grant Broadcasting System II Inc.
Group Owner: Grant Communications Inc.; (acq 9-15-93; $5.5 million with satellite stn WFXR-TV Roanoke;; *Washington Law Firm:* Birch, Horton, Bittner & Cherot
Nat'l Network: FOX; CW
Size of News Staff: 2; *Hours of Local News Weekly:* news progmg one hr wkly
Frank Quitoni, President
Jim Penna, News Director

Tri-Cities, TN-VA (DMA 92)

WCYB-TV *Digital Channel:* 5 *Virtual Channel:* 5; 29.9 kw; 2438 ft.; N36 26 58 W82 6 29
101 Lee Street, Bristol, VA 24201 US
(276)-645-1555, *Fax:* (276) 645-1513
www.wcyb.com
news@wcyb.com
License: Bristol, Washington County, VA held by BlueStone License Holdings Inc.
Group Owner: Bonten Media Group LLC; (acq 5-31-2007; grpsl);
Washington Law Firm: Covington & Burling LLP
Nat'l Network: NBC & CW (DIGIT; CW; Fox
Conie McCully, CFO
Jim McKerman, General Manager
Matt Bowman, General Sales Mgr
Tony Venable, Promotions Manager
Steve Hawkins, News Director
Tom Cupp, Chief Engineer

WLFG *Digital Channel:* 49 *Virtual Channel:* 68; 1000 kw; 2172 ft.; N36 49 47 W82 4 45
Mailing Address: Route 460, Vansant, VA 24556 US
Second Address: 8594 Hidden Valley Rd, Abingdon, VA 24210
(276) 676-3806, *Fax:* (276) 676-3572
www.livingfaithtv.com
lisa@livingfaithtv.com
License: Grundy, Buchanan County, VA held by Living Faith Ministries Inc
Nat'l Network: REL
Michael Smith, CEO
Lisa Smith, Operations Dir
Wayne Price, Engineering Dir
Sue Howington, Traffic Manager

***WMSY-TV** *Digital Channel:* 42 *Virtual Channel:* 52; 100 kw; 1470 ft.; N36 54 7 W81 32 32
Mailing Address: P. O. Box 13246, Roanoke, VA 24032 US
Second Address: Blue Ridge PBS, 1215 McNeil Dr. S. W., Roanoke, VA 24015
(540) 344-0991, *Fax:* (540) 344-2148
www.blueridgepbs.com
License: Marion, Smyth County, VA held by Blue Ridge Public Television Inc
Nat'l Network: PBS
Greg Feldman, Chairman
James Baum, CEO
William Anderson, Operations Dir
Kate Foreman, General Sales Mgr
Anita Sims, CFO

***WSBN-TV** *Digital Channel:* 32 *Virtual Channel:* 47; 100 kw; 1939 ft.; N36 53 53 W82 37 21
Mailing Address: PO Box 13246, Roanoke, VA 24032 US
Second Address: Blue Ridge PBS, 1215 McNeil Dr. S.W., Roanoke, VA 24015
(540) 344-0991, *Fax:* (540) 344-2148
www.blueridgepbs.org
License: Norton, Wise County, VA held by Blue Ridge Public Television Inc
Nat'l Network: PBS
Barbara Spencer, Operations Dir
Kate Foreman, General Sales Mgr
Erwin Roman, Chief Engineer

Washington, DC (Hagerstown, MD) (DMA 9)

***WNVC** *Digital Channel:* 24 *Virtual Channel:* 30; 160 kw; 725 ft.; N38 52 28 W77 13 24
8101a Lee Highway, Falls Church, VA 22042 US
(703) 770-7100
www.mhznetworks.org
viewerservices@mhznetworks.org
License: Fairfax, Fairfax County, VA held by Commonwealth Public Broadcasting Corp.

(acq 6-4-2004); *Washington Law Firm:* Wiley, Rein & Fielding
Nat'l Network: ETV
Fred Thomas, General Manager

***WNVT** *Digital Channel:* 30 *Virtual Channel:* 53; 160 kw; 751 ft.; N38 37 43 W77 26 21
8101a Lee Highway, Falls Church, VA 22042 US
(703) 770-7100
www.mhznetworks.org
License: Goldvein, Fairfax County, VA held by Commonweath Public Broadcasting Corp
(acq 6-4-2004); *Washington Law Firm:* Wiley, Rein & Fielding
Nat'l Network: ETV
Fred Thomas, General Manager

***WVPY** *Digital Channel:* 21; 50 KW; ant 1,309t/89g; N38 57 36 W78 19 52; *Rebroadcasting:* Rebroadcasts WVPT Staunton 100%.; *Population Served:* 345,000
c/o WVPT, 298 Port Republic Rd., Harrisonburg, VA 22801
(540) 434-5391, *Fax:* (540) 434-7084
www.wvpt.net
License: Front Royal, Warren County, VA held by Shenandoah Valley Educational TV Corp
Washington Law Firm: Covington & Burling
Nat'l Network: PBS
Tony Mancari, COO
David Mullins, President
David Mullins, General Manager
George Lilly, Promotions Manager
John Harper, Engineering Dir

Washington

Portland, OR (DMA 22)

KPDX *Digital Channel:* 30 *Virtual Channel:* 49; 741 kw; 1732 ft.; N45 31 19 W122 44 53
1716 Locust Street, Des Moines, IA 50309 US
(503) 906-1249, *Fax:* (503) 548-6910
www.kpdx.com
webstaff@kptv.com
License: Vancouver, Clark County, WA held by Meredith Corp.
Group Owner: Meredith Broadcasting Group, Meredith Corp.; (acq 7-1-97; grpsl); *Washington Law Firm:* Dow, Lohnes & Albertson
Nat'l Network: MYNETWORKTV *Nat'l Reps:* TeleRep *Wire Services:* AP
Patrick McCreery, General Manager
Andy Delaporte, General Sales Mgr
Ellen Johanson, Programming Director
Kelly Martin, Internet Advertising

Seattle-Tacoma, WA (DMA 14)

KBCB *Digital Channel:* 19 *Virtual Channel:* 24; 165 kw; 2484 ft.; N48 40 46 W122 50 31; *Rebroadcasting:* ShopNBC
Mailing Address: 5670 Wilshire Blvd., Suite 1300, Los Angeles, CA 90036 US
Second Address: WA
(360) 647-8842, *Fax:* (360) 647-9204
www.kbcbtv.com
kbcb@kbcbtv.com
License: Bellingham, Whatcom County, WA held by World Television of Washington LLC
Washington Law Firm: Wiley, Rein & Fielding
Nat'l Network: IND
Hours of Local News Weekly: News progmg 4 hrs wkly
Garry Spire, CEO
Paul Koplin, President
Brian Holton, Operations Dir
Andy Wilcoxson, Station Manager
Dewi Cashion, CFO

***KBTC-TV** *Digital Channel:* 27 *Virtual Channel:* 28; 100 kw; 771 ft.; N47 16 44 W122 30 42
1101 South Yakima Avenue, Tacoma, WA 98405 US
(253) 680-7700, *Fax:* (253) 680-7725
www.kbtc.org
bwelch@bates.ctc.edu
License: Tacoma, Pierce County, WA held by Bates Technical College
Nat'l Network: PBS
Darin Gerchak, Operations Dir
David Hinman, General Manager
Phil Kane, Programming Director
Ed Ulman, Promotions Manager
Sherri Stanton, Membership Manager

***KCKA** *Digital Channel:* 19 *Virtual Channel:* 15; 187 kw; 1138 ft.; N46 33 16 W123 3 26; *Rebroadcasting:* Rebroadcasts KBTC(TV) Tacoma.
1101 South Yakima Avenue, Tacoma, WA 98405 US
(253) 680-7700, *Fax:* (253) 680-7725
www.kbtc.org
bwelch@bates.ctc.edu
License: Centralia, Lewis County, WA held by Bates Technical College
(acq 11-29-91;; *Washington Law Firm:* Akin, Gump, Strauss, Hauer & Feld
Nat'l Network: PBS
David Hinman, General Manager
Phil Kane, Programming Director
Darin Gerchak, Chief Engineer

KCPQ *Digital Channel:* 13 *Virtual Channel:* 13; 30 kw; 2001 ft.; N47 32 53 W122 48 22
C/O Charles J. Sennet, 435 N. Michigan Avenue, Chicago, IL 60611 US
(206) 674-1313, *Fax:* (206) 674-1777
www.q13.trb.com
askus@q13.com
License: Tacoma, Pierce County, WA held by Tribune Television Northwest Inc.
Group Owner: Tribune Broadcasting Co.; (acq 12-20-2007; grpsl).; *Ownership:* Tribune; *Washington Law Firm:* Sidley & Austin
Nat'l Network: FOX *Nat'l Reps:* TeleRep *Wire Services:* SportsTicker
Size of News Staff: 44; *Hours of Local News Weekly:* news progmg 21 hrs wkly
Marty Gustafson, Operations Dir
Pamela Pearson, General Manager
Mark Boe, Station Manager
Paul Rennie, General Sales Mgr
Sheri Liguori, Programming Director
Steve Kraycik, News Director
Michael Goodman, Engineering Dir
RobKinsey, National Sales Manager
Jeremy Dietz, Research Director
Wendy Anderson, Traffic Manager

***KCTS-TV** *Digital Channel:* 9 *Virtual Channel:* 9; 21.7 kw; 817 ft.; N47 36 58 W122 18 28
401 Mercer Street, Seattle, WA 98109 US
(206) 728-6463, *Fax:* (206) 443-6691
www.kcts.org
viewer@kcts.org
License: Seattle, King County, WA held by KCTS Television
(acq 7-15-87).; *Washington Law Firm:* Dow, Lohnes & Albertson
Nat'l Network: PBS
William Mohler, CEO
Randy Brinson, General Manager
Cliff Anderson, Engineering Dir

KFFV *Digital Channel:* 44; 2,000 kw vis; ant 2,283t; N47 30 17 W121 58 06; *Population Served:* 3,000,000
9825 Willows Rd. NE., Suite 140, Redmond, WA 98032
(425) 497-1515, *Fax:* (425) 497-1616
www.npitv.com
media@npitv.com
License: Seattle, King County, WA
Group Owner: OTA Broadcasting; acq 12-24-92; *Ownership:* Dr Kenneth & Charlene Casey
Nat'l Network: Azteca America (Spanish)
Foreign Language Programming
Charlene Casey, CFO
Dr. Kenneth Casey, President

KING-TV *Digital Channel:* 48 *Virtual Channel:* 5; 960 kw; 820t/570g; N47 37 55 W122 20 59; *Population Served:* 3,848,400
333 Dexter Ave. N., Seattle, WA 75202
(206) 448-5555, *Fax:* (206) 448-3195
www.king5.com
License: Seattle, King County, WA held by KING-TV Inc.
Group Owner: Belo Corp; (acq 1997; grpsl).; *Washington Law Firm:* Wiley Rein
Nat'l Network: NBC *Nat'l Reps:* TeleRep
Ray Heacox, President
Pat Costello, Station Manager
Ann Sobil, Executive Director of Sales
Rick Swanson, Programming Director
Cherylynne Crowther, Promotions Manager
Mark Ginther, News Director
Kathy Palmer, Chief Engineer

KIRO-TV *Digital Channel:* 39 *Virtual Channel:* 7; 1000 kw; 843 ft.; N47 38 1 W122 21 20
3773 Howard Hughes Parkway, Suite 300n, Las Vegas, NV 89109 US
(206) 728-7777, *Fax:* (206) 728-8230
www.kirotv.com
License: Seattle, King County, WA held by KIRO-TV Inc.
Group Owner: Cox Media Group; (acq 4-16-97); *Washington Law Firm:* Dow, Lohnes & Alberterson, PLLC
Nat'l Network: CBS *Nat'l Reps:* Harrington, Righter & Parsons
Size of News Staff: 115; *Hours of Local News Weekly:* news progmg 46 hrs wkly
Eric Lerner, General Manager
Kristin Reese, General Sales Mgr
Therese Weiler, Programming Director
Todd Mokhtari, News Director
John Walters, Engineering Dir
Pat Otis, Chief Engineer
Sandy Zogg, General Sales Manager
DaveBlakely, National Sales Manager
Holly Grambihler, Regional Sales Manager
Pat Norris, Regional Sales Manager

KOMO-TV *Digital Channel:* 38 *Virtual Channel:* 4; 1000 kw; 850 ft.; N47 37 55 W122 21 9
C/O Fisher Wayland, 2001 Pennsylvania Ave., Washington, DC 20006 US
(206) 404-4000, *Fax:* (206) 404-4034
www.komotv.com
License: Seattle, King County, WA held by Fisher Broadcasting - Seattle TV L.L.C.
Group Owner: Fisher Communications Inc.; (acq 12-4-01; grpsl).; *Washington Law Firm:* Shaw Pittman
Nat'l Network: ABC *Nat'l Reps:* Blair Television
James Clayton, General Manager
Ted Davis, General Sales Mgr
Doreen Kaylor, Programming Director
Scott Altus, Promotions Manager
Holly Gauntt, News Director
Lloyd Low, National Sales Manager

KONG ; 5,000 kw vis, 500 kw aur; 1,079t/299g; N47 32 34 W122 06 25
333 Dexter Ave. N., Seattle, WA 98109
(206) 448-3166,(206) 448-5555, *Fax:* (206) 448-3167
www.kongtv.com
License: Everett, Snohomish County, WA held by KONG-TV Inc.
Group Owner: Belo Corp; (acq 2-18-00).; *Washington Law Firm:* Thompson, Hine & Flory L
Ray Heacox, General Manager

KSTW *Digital Channel:* 11 *Virtual Channel:* 11; 100 kw; 905 ft.; N47 36 56 W122 18 29
1501 M Street, N.W., Suite 1100, Washington, DC 20005 US
(206) 441-1111, *Fax:* (206) 861-8915
kstw.com
License: Tacoma, Pierce County, WA held by CW Television Stations Inc.
Group Owner: CBS Television Stations Group; (acq 4-16-97)
Nat'l Network: THE CW NETWORK
Steve Gahler, Operations Dir
Tom Spitz, Programming Director
Megan Temple, Promotions Manager
Ron Diotte, Chief Engineer
Amber Stelzer, National Sales Manager
D. Poor, Promotions Manager
Florence Higa, Traffic Manager

KTBW-TV *Digital Channel:* 14 *Virtual Channel:* 20; 90 kw; 1552 ft.; N47 32 50 W122 47 40
1909 So. 341st Place, Federal Way, WA 98003 US
(253) 927-7720,(253) 874-7420, *Fax:* (253) 874-7432
ktbw@tbn.org
License: Tacoma, Pierce County, WA held by Trinity Broadcasting of Washington.
Group Owner: Trinity Broadcasting Network
Nat'l Network: TRINITY BROADCA
Paul Crouch, President
Mary Jane Allen, Station Manager

KUNS-TV *Digital Channel:* 50 *Virtual Channel:* 51; 240 kw; 2359 ft.; N47 30 17 W121 58 4
203 Bellevue Way, N.E., Suite 487, Bellevue, WA 98004 US
(206) 404-5867, *Fax:* (206) 248-6818
www.kunstv.com
info@kunstv.com
License: Bellevue, King County, WA held by Fisher Broadcasting - Bellevue TV L.L.C.
Group Owner: Fisher Communications Inc.; (acq 9-26-2006; $16 million)
Nat'l Network: UNIVISION
Foreign Language Programming
John Tamerlano, General Manager
Tami Schell, Programming Director

KVOS-TV *Digital Channel:* 35 *Virtual Channel:* 12; 580 kw; 2621 ft.; N48 40 50 W122 50 22
1333 New Hampshire, N.W., Suite 100, Washington, DC 20036 US
(360) 671-1212,(604) 681-1212 (sales), *Fax:* (360) 647-0824
www.kvos.com
License: Bellingham, Whatcom County, WA
Group Owner: OTA Broadcasting; (acq 3-14-2008; grpsl);
Washington Law Firm: Covington & Burling
Nat'l Network: IND *Nat'l Reps:* Airtime TV
Size of News Staff: 10; *Hours of Local News Weekly:* news progmg one hr wkly
Gary Nielsen, President
Dave Kerrigan, Operations Dir
Yvette Perez, Promotions Manager
Kathleen Choal, News Director

***KWDK** *Digital Channel:* 42 *Virtual Channel:* 56; 144 kw; 2280 ft.; N47 30 17 W121 58 6
P.O. Box 8969, Waikiki, HI 96830 US
(425) 251-4313
www.daystar.com
License: Tacoma, Pierce County, WA held by Puget Sound Educational TV Inc
Nat'l Network: REL
Les Heen, President
Janet Suckow, Operations Dir
Jon Panzer, Station Manager
Shirley Schwarz, Programming Director

KWPX-TV *Digital Channel:* 32; 14.8 kw vis, 1.5 kw aur; 938t; N47 36 17 W122 19 46
Mailing Address: Box 426, Preston, WA 98050
Second Address: 8112-C 304th Ave. SE, Preston, WA 98050
(425) 222-6010, *Fax:* (425 222-6032
www.ionline.tv
License: Bellevue, King County, WA held by ION Media License Co. L.L.C.
Group Owner: ION Media Networks Inc.; (acq 2-2-98; $35 million)
Nat'l Network: ION Television
Marcus Lamb, President
Harvey Rogers, Chief Engineer

KZJO *Digital Channel:* 22 *Virtual Channel:* 22; 5,000 kw vis, 501 kw aur; ant 890t/639g; N47 36 57 W122 18 26; *Population Served:* 3,516,000
1813 Westlake Ave., Seattle, WA 54402
(206) 674-1313, *Fax:* (206) 674-1777
www.joeswall.com
askus@ktwbtv.com
License: Seattle, King County, WA held by Tribune Television Holdings Inc.
Group Owner: Tribune Broadcasting Co.; (acq 12-20-2007; grpsl); *Washington Law Firm:* Dow Lohnes PLLC
Nat'l Network: MyNetworkTV *Nat'l Reps:* TeleRep
Marty Gustafson, Operations Dir
Pamela Pearson, General Manager
Mark Boe, Station Manager
Paul Rennie, General Sales Mgr
Natalie Grant, Programming Director
Jamie McDowell, Promotions Manager
Michael Goodman, Engineering Dir
Adam Bischoff, Local Sales Manager
Jeremy Dietz, Research Director
Wendy Anderson, Traffic Manager

Spokane, WA (DMA 75)

KAYU-TV *Digital Channel:* 28 *Virtual Channel:* 28; 445 kw; 1972 ft.; N47 34 44 W117 17 46
P. O. Box 30028, Spokane, WA 99223 US
(509) 448-2828, *Fax:* (509) 448-0926
www.myfoxspokane.com
ron.sweatte@northwestbroadcasting.com
License: Spokane, Spokane County, WA held by Mountain Licenses L.P.
Group Owner: Northwest Broadcasting Inc.; (acq 1996; $6.44 million); *Washington Law Firm:* Leventhal, Senter and Lerman
Nat'l Network: FOX *Nat'l Reps:* Millennium Sales & Marketing
Wire Services: AP
Hours of Local News Weekly: News progmg 8 hrs wkly
Rick Andrycha, Operations Dir
Jon Rand, General Manager
David Lockhert, General Sales Mgr
Kim Rogge, Promotions Manager
Ron Sweatte, Chief Engineer
Lowell Pederson, Business Manager
Bill Quarles, CFO
Becky Martin, NationalSales Manager

***KCDT** *Virtual Channel:* 26; 12.3 kw vis, 1.2 kw aur; 1,525t; N47 43 54 W116 43 47; *Rebroadcasting:* Rebroadcasts KUID Moscow 100%.
Mailing Address: c/o KAID, 1455 N. Orchard St., Boise, ID 83706
Second Address: Box 443101, University of Idaho, Moscow, ID 83844-3101
(208) 885-1226
www.idahoptv.org
idptv@idahoptv.org
License: Coeur d'Alene, Kootenai County, ID held by State Board of Education, State of Idaho
Washington Law Firm: Fletcher, Heald & Hildreth
Nat'l Network: PBS
Peter Morrill, General Manager
Kris Freeland, Station Manager
Megan Griffin, General Sales Mgr
Ron Pisaneschi, Programming Director
Rich Van Genderen, Engineering Dir
Ken Segota, Chief Engineer

KGPX-TV *Digital Channel:* 34; 2,820 kw vis; ant 1,476t/535g; N47 36 04 W117 17 53
8112-C 304th Avenue SE, Preston, WA 98050
(509) 340-3400, *Fax:* (509) 340-3417
www.ionline.tv/stations/list.cfm
License: Spokane, Spokane County, WA held by Paxson Spokane License Inc.
Group Owner: ION Media Networks Inc.
William Watson, Vice President
Amber Morales, Operations Dir
Jennifer Perry, Programming Director
Mitch Wasson, Chief Engineer

KHQ-TV *Digital Channel:* 15 *Virtual Channel:* 6; 1000 kw; 2142 ft.; N47 34 52 W117 17 47
Mailing Address: P.O. Box 8088, Spokane, WA 99203 US
Second Address: 1201 W Sprague Ave, Spokane, WA 99201-4102
(509) 448-6000, *Fax:* (509) 448-4694
www.khq.com
q6news@khq.com
License: Spokane, Spokane County, WA held by KHQ Inc.
Group Owner: KHQ Inc.; *Washington Law Firm:* Skadden, Arps
Nat'l Network: NBC *Nat'l Reps:* Blair Television
Size of News Staff: 52; *Hours of Local News Weekly:* news progmg 26 hrs wkly
Betsy Cowles, Chairman
Paula Bauer, CFO
Patricia McRae, President
Doug Miles, Operations Dir
Bill Storms, General Manager
Brian Sullivan, General Sales Mgr
Mike Dugger, Programming Director
Jonathan Mitchell, PromotionsManager
Jonathan Michell, News Director
Jennifer Petruso, Local Sales Manager

KQUP *Digital Channel:* 24 *Virtual Channel:* 24
1146 - 19th Street, N.W., Suite 200, Washington, DC 20036 US
(509) 924-5787, *Fax:* (509) 924-5789
www.kqup.com
rhall@kqup.com
License: Pullman, Whitman County, WA held by Pullman Broadcasting Inc., debtor in possession.
Group Owner: Equity Media Holdings Corp.; (acq 8-23-99)
Nat'l Network: DAYSTAR
Rod Hall, General Manager

KREM *Digital Channel:* 20; 84.7 kw vis, 15.5 kw aur; ant 2,200t/969g; N47 35 42 W117 17 53; *Population Served:* 174,500
Mailing Address: Box 8037, Spokane, WA 99203
Second Address: 4103 S. Regal, Spokane, WA 99223
(509) 448-2000, *Fax:* (509) 448-6397
www.krem.com
License: Spokane, Spokane County, WA held by KREM-TV Inc.
Group Owner: Belo Corp; (acq 9-92; grpsl;; *Washington Law Firm:* Covington & Burling
Nat'l Network: CBS
Size of News Staff: 36; *Hours of Local News Weekly:* news progmg 17 hrs wkly
Robert Decherd, CEO
Jim Maroney, President
Jamie Aitken, General Manager
Amy Warren, General Sales Mgr
Christine Werfelmann, Programming Director
Bruce Felt, Promotions Manager
Boyd Lundberg, Chief Engineer
Deannie Armstrong,Traffic Manager

KSKN *Digital Channel:* 36 *Virtual Channel:* 22; 250 kw; 2041 ft.; N47 35 41 W117 17 53
4103 S. Regal Street, Spokane, WA 99223 US
(509) 448-2000, *Fax:* (509) 448-2090
www.krem.com
License: Spokane, Spokane County, WA held by KSKN Television Inc.
Group Owner: Belo Corp; (acq 8-24-01; $5 million)
Nat'l Network: CW
Size of News Staff: 5; *Hours of Local News Weekly:* news progmg 6 hrs wkly
D.J. Wilson, Operations Dir
Jamie Aitken, General Manager
Susan Miller, General Sales Mgr
Terry Cocker, Programming Director
Ron Keller, Promotions Manager
Noah Cooper, News Director
John Souza, Engineering Dir
Boyd Lundberg,Chief Engineer
Dan Lamphere, Operations Manager
Tom Hudson, Sports Commentator

***KSPS-TV** *Digital Channel:* 7 *Virtual Channel:* 7; 45.1 kw; 1831 ft.; N47 34 34 W117 17 58
N. 200 Bernard St., Spokane, WA 99201 US
(509) 354-7800, *Fax:* (509) 354-7757
www.ksps.org
License: Spokane, Spokane County, WA held by Spokane School District No. 81
Washington Law Firm: Garvey, Schubert & Barer
Nat'l Network: PBS
Claude Kistler, General Manager
Patty Starkey, General Sales Mgr
Cary Balzer, Programming Director
Kerry Faggiano, Promotions Manager

***KWSU-TV** *Digital Channel:* 10 *Virtual Channel:* 10; 6.2 kw; 1339 ft.; N46 51 43 W117 10 26
P.O. Box 642530, 382 Murrow Center, Pullman, WA 99164 US
(509) 335-6511, *Fax:* (509) 335-3772
www.kwsu.org
kwsu@wsu.edu
License: Pullman, Whitman County, WA held by Washington State University
Washington Law Firm: Dow, Lohnes & Albertson
Nat'l Network: PBS
Sarah McDaniel, Operations Dir
Kari Watkins, Interim Program Manager

KXLY-TV *Digital Channel:* 13 *Virtual Channel:* 4; 23.3 kw; 3071 ft.; N47 55 18 W117 6 48
500 West Boone Avenue, Spokane, WA 99201 US
(509) 324-4000, *Fax:* (509) 328-5274
www.kxly.com
License: Spokane, Spokane County, WA held by Spokane TV Inc.
Group Owner: Morgan Murphy Media (Evening Telegram Co); (acq 1-17-63; grpsl;; *Washington Law Firm:* Rini, Coran, PC
Nat'l Network: ABC; MyNetworkTV *Nat'l Reps:* Continental Television Sales *Wire Services:* AP
Hours of Local News Weekly: News progmg 19 hrs wkly
Elizabeth Burns, President
Steve Herling, General Manager

Yakima-Pasco-Richland-Kennewick, WA (DMA 126)

KAPP *Digital Channel:* 14 *Virtual Channel:* 35; 160 kw; 961 ft.; N46 31 57 W120 30 37
Mailing Address: 1610 24th Ave., Yakima, WA 98902 US
Second Address: 114 North 4th Street, Yakima, WA 98902
(509) 453-0351, *Fax:* (509) 453-3623
www.kapptv.com
comments@kapptv.com
License: Yakima, Yakima County, WA held by Apple Valley Broadcasting Inc.
Group Owner: Morgan Murphy Media (Evening Telegram Co);
Washington Law Firm: Manatt, Phelps & Phillips
Nat'l Network: ABC; MyNetworkTV
Size of News Staff: 11; *Hours of Local News Weekly:* 3
Elizabeth Burns, President
Cheryl Sentel, Operations Dir
Brian Paul, General Manager
Kevin Uretsky, Station Manager
Bob Powers, General Sales Mgr
John Wilkerson, Programming Director
Neil Bennett, Chief Engineer

KEPR-TV *Digital Channel:* 18 *Virtual Channel:* 19; 32.43 kw; 1166 ft.; N46 5 51 W119 11 29

Mailing Address: 100 - 4th Avenue, North, Seattle, WA 98109 US
Second Address: 2807 West Lewis, Pasco, WA 99301
(509) 547-0547, *Fax:* (509) 547-2845
www.keprtv.com
License: Pasco, Franklin County, WA held by Fisher Broadcasting - Washington TV L.L.C.
Group Owner: Fisher Communications Inc.; (acq 12-4-2001; grpsl).; *Washington Law Firm:* Winthrope, Shaw, Pittman, LLP
Nat'l Network: CBS *Wire Services:* CBS; Pacifica News Network
Size of News Staff: 12; *Hours of Local News Weekly:* news progmg 17 hrs wkly
Ben Tucker, President
Brad Gayken, Operations Dir
Ken Messer, General Manager
David Praga, Station Manager
Steve Crow, General Sales Mgr
Stu Seibel, Programming Director
Randy Irwin, Promotions Manager
John Housholder, ChiefEngineer
Cris Headley, Public Affairs Director

KIMA-TV *Digital Channel:* 33 *Virtual Channel:* 29; 100 kw; 958 ft.; N46 31 58 W120 30 33
Mailing Address: 100 - 4th Avenue, North, Seattle, WA 98109 US
Second Address: 2801 Terrace Heights Dr, Yakima, WA 98901
(509) 575-0029, *Fax:* (509) 248-1218
www.kimatv.com
information@kimatv.com
License: Yakima, Yakima County, WA held by Fisher Broadcasting - Washington TV L.L.C.
Group Owner: Fisher Communications Inc.; (acq 12-4-2001; grpsl); *Washington Law Firm:* Shaw Pittman
Nat'l Network: CBS *Nat'l Reps:* Petry Television Inc. *Wire Services:* CBS; CNN; AP
Size of News Staff: 24; *Hours of Local News Weekly:* news progmg 15 hrs wkly
Ken Messer, Operations Dir
Bob Berry, Station Manager
Steve Crow, General Sales Mgr
Stu Seibel, Programming Director
Robin Wojtanik, News Director
Cliff Grady, Chief Engineer
Karla Griffin, Operations Manager

KNDO *Digital Channel:* 16 *Virtual Channel:* 23; 150 kw; 873 ft.; N46 31 59 W120 30 26
P.O. Box 8088, Spokane, WA 99203 US
(509) 225-2323, *Fax:* (509) 225-2330
www.kndo.com
news@kndo.com
License: Yakima, Yakima County, WA held by KHQ Inc.
Group Owner: KHQ Inc.; (acq 6-17-99; $22.25 million with KNDU(TV) Richland).
Nat'l Network: NBC
Size of News Staff: 9; *Hours of Local News Weekly:* news progmg 27 hrs wkly
Lon Lee, President
Paul Dughi, General Manager
Larry Forsgren, General Sales Mgr
Susan Martinez, Programming Director
Scott Morgan, Promotions Manager
Christine Brown, News Director
Mark Kennedy, Chief Engineer

KNDU *Digital Channel:* 26 *Virtual Channel:* 25; 150 kw; 1319 ft.; N46 6 12 W119 7 49; *Rebroadcasting:* Satellite of KNDO(TV) Yakima 94%.
P.O. Box 8088, Spokane, WA 99203 US
(509) 737-6700,(509)737-6725, *Fax:* (509) 737-6749
www.kndu.com
news@kndu.com
License: Richland, Benton County, WA held by KHQ Inc.
Group Owner: KHQ Inc.; (acq 6-17-99; $22.25 million with KNDO(TV) Yakima).; *Washington Law Firm:* Hogan & Hartson
Nat'l Network: NBC
Size of News Staff: 20; *Hours of Local News Weekly:* news progmg 22.5 hrs wkly
Larry Forsgren, General Manager
Susan Martinez, Programming Director
Christine Brown, News Director
Sheri Bissell, Local Manager

***KTNW** *Digital Channel:* 38 *Virtual Channel:* 31; 47.6 kw; 1184 ft.; N46 6 12 W119 7 40
P.O. Box 642530, 382 Murrow Center, Pullman, WA 99164 US
(509) 335-6588, *Fax:* (509) 335-3772
www.kwsu.org
nwptv@wsu.edu
License: Richland, Benton County, WA held by Washington State University
Washington Law Firm: Dow, Lohnes & Albertson
Nat'l Network: PBS
Sarah McDaniel, Operations Dir
Kari Watkins, Programming Director

KVEW *Digital Channel:* 44 *Virtual Channel:* 42; 160 kw; 1325 ft.; N46 6 12 W119 7 57; *Rebroadcasting:* Satellite of KAPP Yakima.
601 N. Edison, Kennewick, WA 99336 US
(509) 735-8369, *Fax:* (509) 735-7889
www.kvewtv.com
License: Kennewick, Benton County, WA held by Apple Valley Broadcasting Inc.
Group Owner: Morgan Murphy Media (Evening Telegram Co)
Nat'l Network: ABC; MyNetworkTV
Brian Paul, General Manager
Mike Balmelli, News Director

***KYVE** *Digital Channel:* 21 *Virtual Channel:* 47; 50 kw; 919 ft.; N46 31 58 W120 30 33
1105 South 15th Avenue, Yakima, WA 98902 US
(509) 452-4700, *Fax:* (509) 452-4704
www.kyve.org
License: Yakima, Yakima County, WA held by KCTS Television (acq 8-1-94;; *Washington Law Firm:* Schwartz, Woods & Miller
Nat'l Network: PBS
Bill Mohler, CEO
Mark Leonard, General Manager
Rod Venable, Station Manager
Brenda Setterlund, General Sales Mgr
Chris Splawn, Programming Director
Ken Messer, Station Manager

West Virginia

Bluefield-Beckley-Oak Hill, WV (DMA 155)

WLFB *Digital Channel:* 40 *Virtual Channel:* 40; 1000 kw; 1309 ft.; N37 13 12 W81 15 20; *Rebroadcasting:* Satellite of WLFG(TV) Grundy, VA.
Mailing Address: Post Office Box 151, Vansant, VA 24656 US
Second Address: 8594 Hidden Valley Rd., Abingdon, VA 24210
(276) 676-3806, *Fax:* (276) 676-3572
www.livingfaithtv.com
lisa@livingfaithtv.com
License: Bluefield, Mercer County, WV held by Living Faith Ministries Inc
Nat'l Network: IND
Michael Smith, CEO

WOAY-TV *Digital Channel:* 50 *Virtual Channel:* 4; 600 kw; 656 ft.; N37 57 26 W81 9 3
PO Box 251, Oak Hill, WV 25901 US
(304) 469-3361, *Fax:* (304) 465-1420
www.woay.com
amarra@woay.com
License: Oak Hill, Fayette County, WV held by Thomas Broadcasting Co
Washington Law Firm: Fletcher, Heald & Hildreth
Nat'l Network: ABC *Nat'l Reps:* Continental Television Sales
Robert Thomas III, President
Al Marra, General Manager
Joetta Kelly-Oliver, General Sales Mgr
Keith Conner, News Director
Joe Wynne, Traffic Manager

***WSWP-TV** *Digital Channel:* 10 *Virtual Channel:* 9; 24 kw; 1043 ft.; N37 53 46 W80 59 21
Mailing Address: 600 Capitol Street, Charleston, WV 25301 US
Second Address: 124 Industrial Dr., Beaver, WV 25813
(304) 254-7840, *Fax:* (304) 254-7879
www.wvpubcast.org
audienceservices@wvpubcast.org
License: Grandview, Raleigh County, WV held by West Virginia Educational Broadcasting Authority
Nat'l Network: PBS
Hours of Local News Weekly: News progmg 5 hrs wkly
Dennis Atkins, CEO
Bill Acker, Operations Dir
Mike Meador, Station Manager
Marilyn DiVita, General Sales Mgr

WVNS-TV *Digital Channel:* 8 *Virtual Channel:* 59; 3.68 kw; 1893 ft.; N37 46 22 W80 42 25
Mailing Address: 112 High Ridge Avenue, Ridgefield, CT 06877 US
Second Address: 141 Old Cline Rd., Ghent, WV 25843
(304) 929-6400, *Fax:* (304) 787-2440
www.cbs59.com
cleister@wvnstv.com
License: Lewisburg, Greenbrier County, WV held by West Virginia Media Holdings LLC
Group Owner: West Virginia Media Holdings LLC; (acq 1-9-2003).; *Washington Law Firm:* Borsari & Paxson
Nat'l Network: CBS; Fox *Nat'l Reps:* Petry Television Inc.
Marstow Becker, Chairman
Bray Cary, CEO
Chris Leister, Operations Dir
Mark Ford, General Sales Mgr
Christy Buckland, News Director
Garth Kirk, Chief Engineer
Charlie Dusic, CFO

WVVA *Digital Channel:* 46 *Virtual Channel:* 6; 1000 kw; 1220 ft.; N37 15 20.7 W81 10 54
P.O. Box 1930, Bluefield, WV 24701 US
(304) 325-5487, *Fax:* (304) 327-5586
www.wvva.com
License: Bluefield, Mercer County, WV held by WVVA TV Inc.
Group Owner: Quincy Newspapers Inc.; (acq 5-1-79; $8 million;; *Washington Law Firm:* Wilkinson, Barker, Knauer & Quinn
Nat'l Network: NBC; CW *Nat'l Reps:* Blair Television
Size of News Staff: 20; *Hours of Local News Weekly:* news progmg 27 hrs wkly
Ralph Oakley, CEO
Frank Brady, Operations Dir
Charity Holman, General Sales Mgr
Danny Via, Engineering Dir
Yvonne Moses, Regional Sales Manager

Charleston-Huntington, WV (DMA 65)

WCHS-TV *Digital Channel:* 41 *Virtual Channel:* 8; 475 kw; 1687 ft.; N38 24 28 W81 54 13
10706 Beaver Dam Road, Cockeysville, MD 21030 US
(304) 346-5358, *Fax:* (304) 346-4765(sales)
www.wchstv.com
info@wchstv.com
License: Charleston, Kanawha County, WV held by WCHS Licensee L.L.C.
Group Owner: Sinclair Broadcast Group Inc.; (acq 10-8-97).; *Washington Law Firm:* Fisher, Wayland, Cooper, Leader & Zaragoza
Nat'l Network: ABC
Size of News Staff: 37; *Hours of Local News Weekly:* 19.5 hrs news progmg wkly
Harold Cooper, General Manager
Lori Marquette, Programming Director
Paul Fox, Promotions Manager
Matt Snyder, News Director
Raymond Beckner, Chief Engineer
Sherry Allen, Traffic Manager

***WKPI-TV** *Digital Channel:* 24; 468 kw vis, 93.3 kw aur; 1,410t/153g; N37 17 06 W82 31 29
600 Cooper Dr., Lexington, KY 40502
(859) 233-3000, *Fax:* (859) 258-7399
www.ket.org
License: Pikeville, Pike County, KY held by Kentucky Authority for Educational TV
Nat'l Network: PBS *Regional Network:* Kentucky Educational Television
Mike Brower, Operations Dir
Malcolm Wall, Station Manager
Craig Cornwell, Programming Director
Tim Bischoff, Promotions Manager

WLPX-TV *Digital Channel:* 39; 1,000 kw; ant 1,207t/968g; N38 28 12 W81 46 35
600 C Prestige Dr., Hurricane, WV 06877
(304) 760-1029, *Fax:* (304) 760-1036
http://www.iontelevision.com/
License: Charleston, Kanawha County, WV held by ION Charleston License Inc.
Group Owner: ION Media Networks Inc.; (acq 10-28-98; $8.25 million); *Washington Law Firm:* Dow Lohnes
Nat'l Network: ION Television
Brandon Burgess, CEO
Joseph Koker, President
Tony Polcaro, Operations Dir
Steven Stanley, Station Manager
Marc Zand, Programming Director
Gene Monday, Chief Engineer

WOWK-TV *Digital Channel:* 13 *Virtual Channel:* 13; 12.5 kw; 1358 ft.; N38 30 20 W82 12 32

12 G/Way Pza.Columbia Dr, Box 12 Johnson City, NY 13790 US
(304) 525-1313, *Fax:* (304) 529-4910
wowktv.com
License: Huntington, Cabell County, WV held by West Virginia Media Holdings LLC
Group Owner: West Virginia Media Holdings LLC; (acq 4-8-2002; $40.5 million); *Washington Law Firm:* Cohn & Marks LLP
Nat'l Network: CBS *Nat'l Reps:* Petry Television Inc.
Bray Cary, President
John Fawcett, General Manager
Sean Banks, General Sales Mgr
M.J. Coss, Programming Director
Leeza Glazier, News Director
Bill Gallaway, Chief Engineer
Sabrina Moore, Traffic Manager

***WPBY-TV** *Digital Channel:* 34 *Virtual Channel:* 33; 2,371 kw vis, 105 kw aur; 1,243t; N38 29 41 W82 12 03; *Population Served:* 300,000
600 Capitol St., Charleston, WV 25301
(304) 556-4900 / (304) 556-4903, *Fax:* (304) 556-4980
www.wvpubcast.org
License: Charleston, Kanawha County, WV held by West Virginia Educational Broadcasting Authority
Nat'l Network: PBS
Willima File III, Chairman
Tammy Threadley, CEO
Dennis Adkins, General Manager
Jane Siers Wright, General Sales Mgr
Craig Lanburg, Programming Director
Shawn Patterson, Promotions Manager
Beth Vorhees, News Director
CraigLanham, Programming Director

WSAZ-TV *Digital Channel:* 23 *Virtual Channel:* 3; 724 kw; 1203 ft.; N38 30 36 W82 13 10
645 Fifth Avenue, Huntington, WV 25701 US
(304) 697-4780, *Fax:* (304) 690-3065 (news)
www.wsaz.com
news@wsaz.com
License: Huntington, Cabell County, WV held by Gray Television Licensee, LLC
Group Owner: Gray Television Inc.; (acq 11-30-2005; $186 million)
Nat'l Network: NBC; MyNetworkTV
Aaron Withrow, Operations Dir
Don Ray, General Manager

WVAH-TV *Digital Channel:* 19 *Virtual Channel:* 11; 475 kw; 1687 ft.; N38 24 28 W81 54 13
18 Newbury Street, Boston, MA 02116 US
(304) 346-5358, *Fax:* (304) 346-4765(sales)
www.wvah.com
info@wvah.com,news@wvah.com,programming@wvah.com
License: Charleston, Kanawha County, WV held by WVAH Licensee LLC.
Group Owner: Sinclair Broadcast Group Inc.; (acq 11-15-2001; grpsl).; *Washington Law Firm:* Arter & Hadden
Nat'l Network: FOX
Size of News Staff: 38; *Hours of Local News Weekly:* news progmg 7 hrs wkly
Harold Cooper, General Manager
Lori Marquette, Programming Director
Paul Fox, Promotions Manager
Matt Snyder, News Director
Raymond Beckner, Chief Engineer
Sherry Allen, Traffic Manager

Clarksburg-Weston, WV (DMA 168)

WBOY-TV *Digital Channel:* 12 *Virtual Channel:* 12; 12.25 kw; 860 ft.; N39 17 6 W80 19 46
Mailing Address: 912 West Pike Street, Clarksburg, WV 26301 US
Second Address: 912 W. Pike St., Clarksburg, WV 26301
(304) 623-3311, *Fax:* (304) 624-6152
www.wboy.com
License: Clarksburg, Harrison County, WV held by West Virginia Media Holdings LLC
Group Owner: West Virginia Media Holdings LLC; (acq 10-25-2001; $20 million); *Washington Law Firm:* Cohn & Marks LLP
Nat'l Network: NBC; ABC *Nat'l Reps:* Petry Television Inc. *Wire Services:* AP
Size of News Staff: 24; *Hours of Local News Weekly:* news progmg 24 hrs wkly
Marty Becker, Chairman
Bray Cary, CEO
James F. Matuga, General Manager
Dave Stingo, General Sales Mgr
Gary McNair, Programming Director
Jim Platzer, News Director
Bob Hardman, Chief Engineer
Charlie Dusic, CFO
VirginiaRichison, Traffic Manager

WDTV *Digital Channel:* 5 *Virtual Channel:* 5; 10 kw; 787 ft.; N39 18 2 W80 20 37
Mailing Address: P. O. Box 1508, Mount Vernon, IL 62864 US
Second Address: 5 Television Dr., Bridgeport, WV 26330
(304) 848-5000, *Fax:* (304) 842-7501
www.wdtv.com
wdtv@wdtv.com
License: Weston, Lewis County, WV held by Withers Broadcasting Company of West Virginia
Group Owner: Withers Broadcasting Co.; (acq 5-8-73; $600,000;; *Washington Law Firm:* Gardner, Carton & Douglas
Nat'l Network: CBS
Size of News Staff: 21; *Hours of Local News Weekly:* news progmg 18.5 hrs wkly
W. Russell Withers Jr., President
John Breen, Operations Dir
Tim DeFazio, General Manager

WVFX *Digital Channel:* 10 *Virtual Channel:* 46; 30 kw; 771 ft.; N39 18 2 W80 20 37
Mailing Address: 2121 Avenue of the Stars, Suite 2800, Los Angeles, CA 90067 US
Second Address: 5 Television Dr., Bridgeport, WV 26330
(304) 848-5000, *Fax:* (304) 842-7501
www.wdtv.com
wdtv@wdtv.com
License: Clarksburg, Harrison County, WV held by Withers Broadcasting Co. of Clarksburg LLC
Group Owner: Withers Broadcasting Co.; (acq 5-6-2008; $5 million); *Washington Law Firm:* Law Office of Dennis J. Kelly
Nat'l Network: FOX; CW
W. Russell Withers Jr., President
John Breen, Operations Dir
Tim DeFazio, General Manager

Parkersburg, WV (DMA 193)

WTAP-TV *Digital Channel:* 49 *Virtual Channel:* 15; 315 kw; 645 ft.; N39 21 0 W81 33 56
One Tv Plaza, Parkersburg, WV 26101 US
(304) 485-4588, *Fax:* (304) 422-3920
www.wtap.com
gm@wtap.com
License: Parkersburg, Wood County, WV held by Gray Television Group, Inc.
Group Owner: Gray Television Inc.; (acq 8-29-2002; grpsl).; *Washington Law Firm:* Covington & Burling
Nat'l Network: NBC; Fox; MyNetworkTV *Nat'l Reps:* Continental Television Sales *Wire Services:* AP; CNN
Size of News Staff: 15; *Hours of Local News Weekly:* news progmg 24 hrs wkly
Roger Sheppard, Operations Dir
Ken Long, General Sales Mgr
Dirk Kreiss, Promotions Manager
Bruce Layman, News Director
Kevin Buskirk, Engineering Dir
Jeff Nutter, Creative Director
Charlie Boush, National Sales Coordinator

Pittsburgh, PA (DMA 23)

***WNPB-TV** *Digital Channel:* 33 *Virtual Channel:* 24; 92 kw; 1498 ft.; N39 41 44.7 W79 45 44.8
600 Capitol Street, Charleston, WV 26301 US
(304) 284-1440, *Fax:* (304) 284-1454
www.wvpubcast.org
audienceservices@wvpubcast.org
License: Morgantown, Monongalia County, WV held by West Virginia Educational Broadcasting Authority
(acq 7-1-83).; *Washington Law Firm:* Wilkinson, Barker, Knauer & Quinn
Nat'l Network: PBS
Size of News Staff: 2; *Hours of Local News Weekly:* news progmg one hr wkly
Dennis Atkins, CEO
Bill Acker, Operations Dir
Jack Wells, Station Manager
Marilyn DiVita, General Sales Mgr
Jack Wells, Engineering Dir
Mike Meador, CFO

Wheeling, WV- Steubenville, OH (DMA 159)

WTRF-TV *Digital Channel:* 7 *Virtual Channel:* 7; 25.4 kw; 961 ft.; N40 3 41 W80 45 8
P.O. Box 7004, Wheeling, WV 26003 US
(304) 232-7777, *Fax:* (304) 232-4975
www.wtrf.com
License: Wheeling, Ohio County, WV held by West Virginia Media Holdings LLC
Group Owner: West Virginia Media Holdings LLC; (acq 3-12-2002; grpsl).; *Washington Law Firm:* Edmundson & Edmundson
Nat'l Network: CBS; Fox; ABC *Nat'l Reps:* Petry Television Inc.
Size of News Staff: 25; *Hours of Local News Weekly:* news progmg 28 hrs wkly
Roger Lyons, General Manager
Mike Allodi, General Sales Mgr
M.J. Coss, Programming Director
Jessica Nixon, Promotions Manager
Brenda Danehart, News Director
Brad Stanford, Chief Engineer

Wisconsin

Duluth, MN-Superior, WI (DMA 139)

KBJR-TV *Digital Channel:* 19 *Virtual Channel:* 6; 384 kw; 1023 ft.; N46 47 21.3 W92 6 50.7
230 East Superior Street, Duluth, MN 55802 US
(218) 720-9600, *Fax:* (218) 720-9699
www.northlandnewscenter.com
news6@kbjr.com
License: Superior, Douglas County, WI held by KBJR License Inc.
Group Owner: Granite Broadcasting Corp.; (acq 11-1-88; $12.8 million;; *Washington Law Firm:* Akin, Gump, Strauss, Hauer & Feld
Nat'l Network: NBC; MyNetworkTV
Size of News Staff: 80; *Hours of Local News Weekly:* news progmg 10 hrs wkly
Robert Wilmers, General Manager
David Jensch, Station Manager

Green Bay-Appleton, WI (DMA 70)

WACY-TV *Digital Channel:* 27; 1,070 kw vis, 107 kw aur; 1,220t/1,026g; N44 21 32 W87 58 58
1391 North Rd., Green Bay, WI 54313
(920) 494-2626, *Fax:* (920) 490-7071
www.mynew32.com
wglover@journalbroadcastgroup.com
License: Appleton, Outagamie County, WI held by Journal Broadcast Corp
Group Owner: Journal Communications; *Washington Law Firm:* Lerman Senter PLLC
Nat'l Network: MyNetworkTV
Warren Glover, General Manager
Joe Poss, General Sales Mgr

WBAY-TV *Digital Channel:* 23 *Virtual Channel:* 2; 1000 kw; 1220 ft.; N44 24 35 W88 0 6
115 S.Jefferson St., Green Bay, WI 54301 US
(920) 432-3331,(800) 242-8090, *Fax:* (920) 432-1190 (news)
www.wbay.com
wbay@wbay.com
License: Green Bay, Brown County, WI held by Young Broadcasting of Green Bay Inc., Debtor-in-possession
Group Owner: Young Broadcasting Inc.; (acq 8-24-94; grpsl;; *Washington Law Firm:* Brooks, Pierce, McClendon & Humphry
Nat'l Network: ABC *Nat'l Reps:* Adam Young
Size of News Staff: 100; *Hours of Local News Weekly:* news progmg 19 hrs wkly
Richard Millhiser, Operations Dir
Don Carmichael, General Manager
Steve Lavin, Station Manager

WCWF *Digital Channel:* 14; 1000 kw vis, 100 kw aur; 613t/544g; N44 59 30 W88 23 55; *Population Served:* 1,035,000
975 Parkview Rd., Suite 4, Green Bay, WI 63141
(920) 983-9014, *Fax:* (920) 983-9424
www.wisconsinscw.com
promotions@wisconsinscw.com
License: Suring, Oconto County, WI held by LIN License Company LLC
Group Owner: LIN Media; (acq 6-1-99; grpsl).; *Washington Law Firm:* Dickstein, Shapiro, Morin & Oshinsky LLP
Nat'l Network: CW *Nat'l Reps:* Millennium Sales & Marketing

Jim Parfitt, Operations Dir
Stephen Shanks, General Manager
Todd Ziegler, General Sales Mgr
Heidi Gillis, Programming Director
Jeff Bartel, Promotions Manager
Tim Brusky, Chief Engineer
Peter Marquardt, National Sales Manager

WFRV-TV *Digital Channel:* 39 *Virtual Channel:* 5; 1000 kw; 1194 ft.; N44 20 1 W87 58 56
Mailing Address: 600 New Hampshire Ave., NW, Suite 1200, Washington, DC 20037 US
Second Address: Box 19055, Green Bay, WI 54307
(920) 437-5411, *Fax:* (920) 437-4576
www.wfrv.com
tips@wfrv.com
License: Green Bay, Brown County, WI held by WFRV and WJMN Television Station Inc.
Group Owner: Liberty Media Corp.; (acq 4-16-2007; with WJMN-TV Escanaba, MI)
Nat'l Network: CBS *Nat'l Reps:* TeleRep
Hours of Local News Weekly: News progmg 24.5 hrs wkly
Perry Kidder, President
Jackie Stewart, General Sales Mgr
Kristen Kent, Promotions Manager
Lee Hitter, News Director
Dale Mitchell, Chief Engineer

WGBA-TV *Digital Channel:* 41; 5,000 kw vis, 500 kw aur; ant 1,181t/982g; N44 21 30 W87 58 48; *Population Served:* 1,930,100
1391 North Rd., Green Bay, WI 54313
(920) 494-2626, *Fax:* (920) 490-2500
www.nbc26.com
License: Green Bay, Brown County, WI held by Journal Broadcast Corp.
Group Owner: Journal Communications Inc.; (acq 10-7-2004; $43.25 million); *Washington Law Firm:* Shaw Pittman
Nat'l Network: NBC *Nat'l Reps:* Petry Television Inc. *Wire Services:* AP
Size of News Staff: 33; *Hours of Local News Weekly:* news progmg 16 hrs wkly
Guyanne Taylor, General Manager
Joe Poss, General Sales Mgr
Dave Driessen, Chief Engineer

WLUK-TV *Digital Channel:* 11 *Virtual Channel:* 11; 316 kw vis, 47.4 kw aur; ant 1,260t/1,159g; N44 24 31 W87 59 29; *Population Served:* 1,049,000
Box 19011, 787 Lombardi Ave., Green Bay, WI 46204
(920) 494-8711, *Fax:* (920) 494-8782
www.wluk.com
jlynch@wluk.com
License: Green Bay, Brown County, WI held by LIN License Company LLC
Group Owner: LIN Media; (acq 11-30-2005; grpsl).
Nat'l Network: Fox *Nat'l Reps:* Petry Television *Wire Services:* AP
Size of News Staff: 55; *Hours of Local News Weekly:* news progmg 37.5 hrs wkly
Jay Zollar, General Manager
Jay Zollar, Programming Director
Dan Spangler, Promotions Manager
Juli Buehler, News Director
Mike Nipps, Chief Engineer

***WPNE** *Digital Channel:* 42; 97 kw; 938 ft.; N44 24 35 W88 0 6; *Rebroadcasting:* Rebroadcasts WHA-TV Madison 100%
3319 W. Beltline Hwy., Madison, WI 53713 US
(608) 263-2121, *Fax:* (608) 263-9763
www.wpt.org
comments@wpt.org
License: Green Bay, Brown County, WI held by State of Wisconsin-Educational Communications Board
Washington Law Firm: Dow, Lohnes & Albertson
Nat'l Network: PBS
James Steinbach, Operations Dir
Jon Miskowski, General Sales Mgr
Mike Edgette, Operations Manager

La Crosse-Eau Claire, WI (DMA 127)

WEAU-TV *Digital Channel:* 38 *Virtual Channel:* 13; 316 kw vis, 37 kw aur; ant 1,990t/2,000g; N44 39 51 W90 57 41; *Population Served:* 224,000
Mailing Address: Box 47, Eau Claire, WI 31707
Second Address: 1907 S. Hastings Way, Eau Claire, WI 54701
(715) 835-1313, *Fax:* (715) 832-0246
www.weau.com
info@weau.com,weau@weau.com
License: Eau Claire, Eau Claire County, WI held by WEAU Licensee Corp.
Group Owner: Gray Television Inc.; (acq 8-1-98; grpsl).;
Washington Law Firm: Pepper & Corazzini
Nat'l Network: NBC *Nat'l Reps:* Continental Television Sales
Wire Services: Medialink
Hours of Local News Weekly: News progmg 34 hrs wkly
Tom Benson, Operations Dir
Terry McHugh, General Manager
Andrew Felix, Promotions Manager
TBA, News Director
Ron Wiedemeier, Chief Engineer

WEUX *Digital Channel:* 49 *Virtual Channel:* 48; 1000 kw; 732 ft.; N44 57 24 W91 40 3
915 Middle River Drive, Suite 409, Fort Lauderdale, FL 33304 US
(715) 831-2548, *Fax:* (715) 831-2550
www.fox25fox48.com
info@fox25fox48.com
License: Chippewa Falls, Chippewa County, WI held by Grant Media LLC.
Group Owner: Grant Communications Inc.; (acq 1996; $6.25 million with WLAX(TV) La Crosse)
Nat'l Network: FOX *Nat'l Reps:* TeleRep
Steve Roth, General Sales Mgr
Eric Barczak, Programming Director
Barb Quillin, Promotions Manager
Mark Burg, Chief Engineer
Pat Stiphout, Promotions Director

***WHLA-TV** *Digital Channel:* 30 *Virtual Channel:* 31; 307.5 kw; 1131 ft.; N43 48 17 W91 22 6
3319 W.Beltline Hwy., Madison, WI 53713 US
(608) 264-9600 / (507) 895-2026, *Fax:* (608) 264-9664
www.ecb.org
License: La Crosse, La Crosse County, WI held by State of Wisconsin-Educational Communications Board
Washington Law Firm: Dow, Lohnes & Albertson
Nat'l Network: PBS
Mike Edgette, Operations Dir
James Steinbach, General Manager
Jon Miskowski, General Sales Mgr
Irene Ekleberry, Programming Director
Michael Bridgeman, Promotions Manager
Kathy Bissen, News Director
Terry Baun, Chief Engineer
Mary Clare Sorenson, Advertising Director

WKBT *Digital Channel:* 8; 316 kw vis, 57.5 kw aur; ant 1,625t/1,540g; N44 05 28 W91 20 15
141 S. 6th St., La Crosse, WI 54601
(608) 782-4678, *Fax:* (608) 782-4674
www.wkbt.com
news8@wkbt.com
License: La Crosse, La Crosse County, WI held by QueenB Television L.L.C.
Group Owner: Morgan Murphy Media (Evening Telegram Co); (acq 3-31-2000; $22 million).
Nat'l Network: CBS; MyNetworkTV *Nat'l Reps:* Harrington, Righter & Parsons
Scott Chorski, Operations Dir
Barb Pervisky, General Sales Mgr
Maria Roswall, Programming Director
Dennis Corcoran, Promotions Manager
Anne Paape, News Director
Dennis McSorley, Chief Engineer
Lynn St. Jacque, Traffic Manager

WLAX *Digital Channel:* 17 *Virtual Channel:* 25; 852 kw; 975 ft.; N43 48 16.14 W91 22 19.29
1305 Interchange Place, Lacrosse, WI 54603 US 54603
(608) 781-0025, *Fax:* (608) 783-2520
www.fox2548.com
news@fox25fox48.com
License: La Crosse, La Crosse County, WI held by GM La Cross Licensing LLC
Group Owner: Grant Communications Inc.; (acq 5-15-96; $6.25 million with WEUX(TV) Chippewa Falls)
Nat'l Network: FOX *Nat'l Reps:* TeleRep
Hours of Local News Weekly: News progmg 3.5 hrs wkly
Penny Ammerman, Station Manager
Steve Roth, General Sales Mgr
Mark Burg, Chief Engineer

WQOW-DT *Digital Channel:* 15; 407 kw vis, 40.7 kw aur; 741t/507g; N44 57 49 W91 40 05; *Population Served:* 214,000
5545 Hwy. 93 S., Eau Claire, WI 54701
(715) 835-1881, *Fax:* (715) 835-8009
www.wqow.com
info@wqow.com
License: Eau Claire, Eau Claire County, WI held by WXOW-WQOW Television Inc.
Group Owner: Quincy Newspapers Inc.; (acq 6-1-2001; grpsl).;
Washington Law Firm: Wilkinson, Barker, Knauer LLP
Nat'l Network: ABC; CW *Nat'l Reps:* Petry Television Inc.
Size of News Staff: 16; *Hours of Local News Weekly:* news progmg 18 hrs wkly
Ralph Oakley, President
Dave Booth, General Manager
Mark Golden, General Sales Mgr
Todd Zschernitz, Engineering Dir

WXOW *Digital Channel:* 48 *Virtual Channel:* 19; 631 kw vis, 63 kw aur; ant 1,138t/790g; N43 48 23 W91 22 02; *Population Served:* 1,542,600
Mailing Address: Box C-4019, La Crosse, WI 54602-4019
Second Address: 3705 County Hwy. 25, La Crescent, MN 55947
(507) 895-9969, *Fax:* (507) 895-8124
www.wxow.com
License: La Crosse, La Crosse County, WI held by WXOW-WQOW Television Inc.
Group Owner: Quincy Newspapers Inc.; (acq 6-1-2001).;
Washington Law Firm: Wilkinson, Barker & Knauer, L.L.P.
Nat'l Network: ABC; CW; This TV *Nat'l Reps:* Millenium *Wire Services:* AP
Size of News Staff: 24; *Hours of Local News Weekly:* news progmg 19 hrs wkly
David Booth, General Manager
Brian Schumacher, General Sales Mgr
Deb Simonis, Programming Director
Jake Anderson, Promotions Manager
Sean Dwyer, News Director
Dan Rasmussen, Chief Engineer

Madison, WI (DMA 85)

WBUW *Digital Channel:* 32 *Virtual Channel:* 57; 200 kw; 1270 ft.; N43 3 3 W89 29 13
P.O. Box 5726, Rockford, IL 61125 US
(608) 270-5700, *Fax:* (608) 270-5717
www.madisonscw.com
License: Janesville, Rock County, WI held by Acme Television Licenses of Madison LLC.
Group Owner: ACME Communications Inc.; (acq 1-1-2003).;
Washington Law Firm: Dickstein, Shapiro, Morin & Oshinsky LLP
Nat'l Network: CW *Nat'l Reps:* MMT
Jamie Kellner, CEO
Tom Keeler, General Manager
Sharon Weiler, General Sales Mgr
Christopher Hawbaker, Promotions Manager
Emmy Fink, News Director
Tom Allen, CFO
Doug Gealy, COO
Eric Krieghoff, National Sales Manager

***WHA-TV** *Digital Channel:* 20 *Virtual Channel:* 21; 140 kw; 1486 ft.; N43 3 21 W89 32 6
1866 Van Hise Hall, Madison, WI 53706 US
(608) 263-2121, *Fax:* (608) 263-9763
www.wpt.org
comments@wpt.org
License: Madison, Dane County, WI held by University of Wisconsin Board of Regents
Washington Law Firm: Dow, Lohnes & Albertson
Nat'l Network: PBS
James Steinbach, Operations Dir
Jon Miskowski, General Sales Mgr
Mike Edgette, Operations Manager

WISC-TV *Digital Channel:* 50; 603 KW ERP; 466 Meters HAAT; N43 03 21 W89 32 06; *Population Served:* 385,000
7025 Raymaond Rd., Madison, WI 53719
(608) 271-4321, *Fax:* (608) 271-6111
www.channel3000.com
License: Madison, Dane County, WI held by TV Wisconsin Inc.
Group Owner: Morgan Murphy Media (Evening Telegram Co);
Washington Law Firm: Rini Coran, PC
Nat'l Network: CBS; MyNetworkTV *Nat'l Reps:* Harrington, Righter & Parsons
Size of News Staff: 34; *Hours of Local News Weekly:* news progmg 22 hrs wkly
Brian Burns, COO
Elizabeth Murphy Burns, President
Tom Bier, General Manager
Steve Scadden, General Sales Mgr
Jill Sammers, Programming Director
Nan Blum Roach, Promotions Manager
Colin Bendict, News Director
Leonard Charles,Chief Engineer
Tom Bier, Executive Vice President/General Manager

WKOW *Digital Channel:* 27; 1,000 kw vis, 100 kw aur; 1,250t/1,182g; N43 03 09 W89 28 42; *Population Served:* 214,800
5727 Tokay Blvd., Madison, WI 53719
(608) 274-1234, *Fax:* (608) 274-9514
www.wkowtv.com
License: Madison, Dane County, WI held by WKOW Television Inc.
Group Owner: Quincy Newspapers Inc.; (acq 5-22-2001; grpsl).; *Washington Law Firm:* Rosenman & Colin
Nat'l Network: ABC
Size of News Staff: 28; *Hours of Local News Weekly:* news progmg 22 hrs wkly
Tom Allen, General Manager

WMSN-TV *Digital Channel:* 49 *Virtual Channel:* 47; 310 kw; 1476 ft.; N43 3 21 W89 32 6
18 Newbury Street, Boston, MA 02116 US
(608) 833-0047, *Fax:* (608) 833-5055,(608) 833-0665 (Natl Sls)
www.fox47.com
comments@fox47.com
License: Madison, Dane County, WI held by WMSN Licensee LLC.
Group Owner: Sinclair Broadcast Group Inc.; (acq 12-10-01; grpsl).
Nat'l Network: FOX
Kerry Johnson, General Manager
Ed Woloszyn, General Sales Mgr
Collin Campbell, Programming Director
Audra Johnson, Promotions Manager
Al Zobel, News Director
Kerry Maki, Chief Engineer
Joel Helzer, Local Sales Manager
CarolPoole, Traffic Manager

WMTV *Digital Channel:* 19 *Virtual Channel:* 15; 155 kw; 1361 ft.; N43 3 3 W89 29 13
2730 Verona Terrace, Mission Hills, KS 66208 US
(608) 274-1515/(608) 274-1500 (news), *Fax:* (608) 271-5193/(608) 271-5194 (news)
www.nbc15.com
feedback@nbc15.com
License: Madison, Dane County, WI held by Gray Television Licensee, LLC
Group Owner: Gray Television Inc.; (acq 8-29-2002; grpsl).; *Washington Law Firm:* Covington & Burling
Nat'l Network: NBC *Wire Services:* AP; CNN
Size of News Staff: 36; *Hours of Local News Weekly:* news progmg 19 hrs wkly
Jim Ryan, CFO
J. Mack Robinson, President
Bob Smith, General Manager
Don Vesely, General Sales Mgr
Ellen Buss, Programming Director
Chris Gegg, News Director
Tom Weeden, Chief Engineer
Robert Prather, Executive VicePresident

Milwaukee, WI (DMA 35)

WCGV-TV *Digital Channel:* 25 *Virtual Channel:* 24; 1000 kw; 1116 ft.; N43 5 46 W87 54 15
0706 Beaver Dam Road, Cockeysville, MD 21030 US
(414) 442-7050, *Fax:* (414) 874-1899
www.My24Milwaukee.com
comments@wcgv24.com
License: Milwaukee, Milwaukee County, WI held by WCGV Licensee L.L.C.
Group Owner: Sinclair Broadcast Group Inc.; (acq 5-23-94; grpsl; *Nat'l Network:* MYTV *Nat'l Reps:* Millennium Sales & Marketing
Milan Macksimovic, Operations Dir
David Ford, General Manager
Rob Krieghoff, General Sales Mgr
Kay Mazurkiewicz, Programming Director
Jason Van Acker, Promotions Manager
Dennis Brechlin, Chief Engineer
Julie Ford-Moody, BusinessManager
Paul Rudolph, Chief of Operations

WDJT-TV *Digital Channel:* 46 *Virtual Channel:* 58; 1000 kw; 1056 ft.; N43 6 42 W87 55 50
Suite 2500, 509 W. Wisconsin Ave., Milwaukee, WI 53203 US
(414) 777-5800, *Fax:* (414) 777-5814
www.cbs58.com
newsdesk@cbs58.com
License: Milwaukee, Milwaukee County, WI held by WDJT-TV L.P.
Group Owner: Weigel Broadcasting Co.; *Washington Law Firm:* Cohn & Marks
Nat'l Network: CBS *Nat'l Reps:* Harrington, Righter & Parsons
Norman Shapiro, President
Jim Hall, General Manager
Marty Schack, General Sales Mgr
Grant Uitti, News Director
Dan Dyer, Chief Engineer

WISN-TV *Digital Channel:* 34 *Virtual Channel:* 12; 1000 kw; 993 ft.; N43 6 42 W87 55 42
C/O Brooks, Pierce, Et. Al., P.O. Box 1800, Raleigh, NC 27602 US
(414) 342-8812, *Fax:* (414) 342-4486
www.wisn.com
License: Milwaukee, Milwaukee County, WI held by WISN Hearst-Argyle Television Inc., a California corp.
Group Owner: Hearst-Argyle Television Inc.; (acq 7-16-97; grpsl).; *Washington Law Firm:* Peper, Martin, Jensen, Maichel & Hetlage
Nat'l Network: ABC *Nat'l Reps:* Continental Television Sales
Wire Services: News 1
Jan Wade, General Manager
Pete Monfre, General Sales Mgr
Dean Maytag, Programming Director
Lori Waldon, News Director
Tony Coleman, Chief Engineer
Sue Samuelson, Traffic Manager

WITI *Digital Channel:* 33 *Virtual Channel:* 6; 1000 kw; 997 ft.; N43 5 26 W87 53 50
9001 N. Green Bay Road, Box 17600, Milwaukee, WI 53209 US
(414) 355-6666, *Fax:* (414) 586-2141
www.myfox.com
fox6news@foxtv.com
License: Milwaukee, Milwaukee County, WI held by Community Television of Wisconsin License LLC.
Group Owner: Local TV LLC; (acq 7-14-2008; grpsl); *Washington Law Firm:* Dow Lohnes PLLC
Nat'l Network: FOX *Nat'l Reps:* Millennium Sales & Marketing
Wire Services: CNN
Hours of Local News Weekly: 43
Parveen Hughes, CFO
Chuck Steinmetz, Operations Dir
Mike Neale, General Sales Mgr
Eric Steele, Programming Director
Lori Wucherer, Promotions Manager
John Workman, Engineering Dir
Anne Brown, Community Affairs
Bob O'Neil, LocalSales Manager
Stu Swaziek, National Sales Manager
Jim Lemon, Vice President

WMLW-TV *Digital Channel:* 48; 500 kw; 300 m; N43 06 42 W87 55 50
809 S. 60th St., Milwaukee, WI 53154
(414) 777-5800, *Fax:* (414) 777-5802
www.wmlw.com
License: Racine, Racine County, WI held by TV-49 Inc
Group Owner: Weigel Broadcasting Co.; (acq 4-21-2008; $6.5 million); *Washington Law Firm:* Cohn & Marks
Nat'l Reps: Harrington, Righter & Parsons
Norman Shapiro, President
Jim Hall, General Manager
Marty Schack, General Sales Mgr
Dan Dyer, Chief Engineer

***WMVS** *Digital Channel:* 8 *Virtual Channel:* 10; 25 kw; 1161 ft.; N43 5 46 W87 54 15
1036 North 8th Street, Milwaukee, WI 53233 US
(414) 271-1036, *Fax:* (414) 297-7536
www.mptv.org
info@mptv.org
License: Milwaukee, Milwaukee County, WI held by Milwaukee Area Technical College District Board
Washington Law Firm: Dow, Lohnes & Albertson
Nat'l Network: PBS
Tom Dvorak, Operations Dir
Ellis Bromberg, General Manager
David Felland, Chief Engineer
Dan Jones, Producer
Debbie O'Connor-Callahan, Publicist

***WMVT** *Digital Channel:* 35 *Virtual Channel:* 36; 500 kw; 1164 ft.; N43 5 46 W87 54 15
1036 North 8th Street, Milwaukee, WI 53233 US
(414) 271-1036, *Fax:* (414) 297-7536
www.mptv.org
info@mptv.org
License: Milwaukee, Milwaukee County, WI held by Milwaukee Area Technical College District Board
Washington Law Firm: Dow, Lohnes & Albertson
Nat'l Network: PBS
Foreign Language Programming
Tom Dvorak, Operations Dir
Ellis Bromberg, General Manager
David Felland, Chief Engineer
Dan Jones, Producer
Debbie O'Connor-Callahan, Publicist

WPXE-TV *Digital Channel:* 40; 741 kw vis, 74.1 kw aur; ant 449t/349g; N42 30 36 W87 53 11
6161 N. Flint Rd., Suite F, Glendale, WI 53209
(414) 247-0117, *Fax:* (414) 247-1302
www.ionline.tv
License: Kenosha, Kenosha County, WI held by Paxson Milwaukee License Inc.
Group Owner: ION Media Networks Inc.; (acq 2-18-00; grpsl).; *Washington Law Firm:* Gardner, Carton & Douglas
Nat'l Network: ION Television *Wire Services:* CNN
Laurie Lau, Operations Dir
Joanne Levy, General Sales Mgr

WTMJ-TV *Digital Channel:* 28 *Virtual Channel:* 4; 1000 kw; 894 ft.; N43 5 29 W87 54 7
P.O. Box 693, 720 East Capitol Dr., Milwaukee, WI 53212 US
(414) 332-9611, *Fax:* (414) 967-5378
www.todaystmj4.com
tmj4feedback@todaystmj4.com
License: Milwaukee, Milwaukee County, WI held by Journal Broadcast Corp.
Group Owner: Journal Communications Inc.; *Washington Law Firm:* Hogan & Hartson
Nat'l Network: NBC
Steve Wexler, General Manager
Mark LeGrand, General Sales Mgr
Brenda Serio, Programming Director
Sean O'Flaherty, News Director
Ron Adair, Chief Engineer
Mike O'Brien, Local Sales Manager
Tim McCormack, Traffic Manager

WVCY-TV *Digital Channel:* 22; 1070 kw, 30.3 DBK; 301.4 meters agl; N43 05 15 W87 54 12
3434 W. Kilbourn Ave., Milwaukee, WI 53208
(414) 935-3000, *Fax:* (414) 935-3015
www.vcyamerica.org
tv30@vcyamerica.org
License: Milwaukee, Milwaukee County, WI held by VCY America Inc.
Group Owner: VCY America Inc.; *Ownership:* VCY America, Inc.; *Washington Law Firm:* Wiley Rein LLP
Dr. Randall Melchert, President
Vic Eliason, General Manager
Jim Schneider, Programming Director
Andy Eliason, Chief Engineer
Jim Cronin, Operations Manager

WVTV *Digital Channel:* 18; 5,000 kw vis, 500 kw aur; ant 1,008t/1,101g; N43 05 48 W87 54 19; *Population Served:* 1,826,000
4041 N. 35th St., Milwaukee, WI 15235
(414) 442-7050, *Fax:* (414) 874-1899
www.my24milwaukee.com
License: Milwaukee, Milwaukee County, WI held by WVTV Licensee Inc.
Group Owner: Sinclair Broadcast Group Inc.; (acq 2-1-2002).
Nat'l Network: CW *Nat'l Reps:* Millennium Sales & Marketing
David Smith, CEO
Milan Macksimovic, Operations Dir
David Ford, General Manager
Mark Martin, DOS
Jamie Czarnezki, Programming Director
Paul Fix, Promotions Manager
N/A, News Director
Dennis Brechlin, Engineering Dir
DennisBrechlin, Chief Engineer
Paul Rudulph, Chief of Operations
Carol=Poole, Traffic Manager

WWRS-TV *Digital Channel:* 43 *Virtual Channel:* 52; 300 kw; 610 ft.; N43 26 11 W88 31 34
5405 Alton Parkway, Suite 5a-648, Irvine, CA 92604 US
(920) 387-9052, *Fax:* (920) 387-9053
www.tbn.org
dcalhoun@tbn.org
License: Mayville, Dodge County, WI held by National Minority T.V. Inc
(acq 2-16-99; $3,300,000); *Washington Law Firm:* Shaw Pittman
Nat'l Network: TRINITY BROADCA
Dinah Calhoun, General Manager

Minneapolis-St. Paul, MN (DMA 15)

***WHWC-TV** *Digital Channel:* 27 *Virtual Channel:* 28; 291 kw; 1148 ft.; N45 2 49 W91 51 47; *Rebroadcasting:* Rebroadcasts WHA-TV Madison 100%
3319 W.Beltline Hwy., Madison, WI 53713 US
(608) 263-2121, *Fax:* (608) 263-9763
www.wpt.org
comments@wpt.org
License: Menomonie, Dunn County, WI held by State of Wisconsin-Educational Communications Board
Washington Law Firm: Dow, Lohnes & Albertson
Nat'l Network: PBS
Mike Edgette, Operations Dir
Jon Miskowski, General Sales Mgr
Michael Bridgeman, Promotions Manager
Kathy Bissen, Director of Production

Wausau-Rhinelander, WI (DMA 135)

WAOW *Digital Channel:* 9; 316 kw vis, 31.6 kw aur; ant 1,210t/647g; N44 55 14 W89 41 31; *Population Served:* 533,000
1908 Grand Ave., Wausau, WI 53719
(715) 842-2251, *Fax:* (715) 848-0195,(715) 842-7808
www.waow.com
info@waow.com
License: Wausau, Marathon County, WI held by WAOW-WYOW Television Inc.
Group Owner: Quincy Newspapers Inc.; (acq 5-22-2001; grpsl).; *Washington Law Firm:* Wilkinson, Baker & Knauer, LLP
Nat'l Network: ABC; CW *Nat'l Reps:* Petry Television Inc. *Wire Services:* AP; CNN
Size of News Staff: 26; *Hours of Local News Weekly:* news progmg 15.5 hrs wkl
Ralph Oakley, CEO
Laurin Jorstad, Operations Dir
Randy Winters, Station Manager
Tricia Schairer, Programming Director
Mark Oliver, Promotions Manager
Randy Winter, News Director
Russ Crass, Chief Engineer

***WHRM-TV** *Digital Channel:* 24 *Virtual Channel:* 20; 172 kw; 1270 ft.; N44 55 14 W89 41 28
3319 W. Beltline Hwy., Madison, WI 53713 US
(608) 264-9600, *Fax:* (608) 264-9664
www.ecb.org
License: Wausau, Marathon County, WI held by State of Wisconsin-Educational Communications Board
Washington Law Firm: Dow, Lohnes & Albertson
Nat'l Network: PBS
Mike Edgette, Operations Dir
James Steinbach, General Manager
Jon Miskowski, General Sales Mgr
Irene Ekleberry, Programming Director
Michael Bridgeman, Promotions Manager
Kathy Bissen, News Director
Terry Baun, Chief Engineer
Mary Clare Sorenson, Advertising Director

WJFW-TV *Digital Channel:* 16 *Virtual Channel:* 12; 269 kw; 1188 ft.; N45 40 3 W89 12 29
P. O. Box 558, Rhinelander, WI 54501 US
(715) 365-8812, *Fax:* (715) 365-8810
www.wjfw.com
e-mail@wjfw.com
License: Rhinelander, Oneida County, WI held by Northland Television LLC.
Group Owner: Rockfleet Broadcasting Inc.; *Washington Law Firm:* Wiley, Rein & Fielding
Nat'l Network: NBC *Nat'l Reps:* Blair Television
Size of News Staff: 13; *Hours of Local News Weekly:* news progmg 18.5 hrs wkly
Gil Buettner, General Manager
Charlotte Berens, General Sales Mgr
Heather Schellock, News Director
Greg Buzzell, Chief Engineer
Angela Barr, Traffic Manager

***WLEF-TV** *Digital Channel:* 36 *Virtual Channel:* 36; 277 kw; 1460 ft.; N45 56 43 W90 16 22; *Rebroadcasting:* Rebroadcasts WHA-TV Madison 100%
3319 W.Beltline Hwy., Madison, WI 53713 US
(608) 263-2121, *Fax:* (608) 263-9763
www.wpt.org
comments@wpt.org
License: Park Falls, Price County, WI held by State of Wisconsin-Educational Communications Board
Washington Law Firm: Dow, Lohnes & Albertson
Nat'l Network: PBS
Mike Edgette, Operations Dir
Jon Miskowski, General Sales Mgr
Michael Bridgeman, Promotions Manager
Kathy Bissen, Director of Production

WMOW *Digital Channel:* 12; 1.7 kw vis; ant 403t/255g; N45 34 23 W88 52 57; *Station Currently Dark*
210 S. Lake St., Crandon, WI 54904
License: Crandon, Forest County, WI held by Selenka Communications LLC
Nat'l Network: ABC; CW
Dennis Selenka, General Manager

WSAW-TV *Digital Channel:* 7 *Virtual Channel:* 7; 72 kw; 1224 ft.; N44 55 14 W89 41 28
1114 Grand Avenue, Wausau, WI 54401 US
(715) 845-4211, *Fax:* (715) 845-2649
www.wsaw.com
License: Wausau, Marathon County, WI held by WEAU Licensee Corp.
Group Owner: Gray Television Inc.; (acq 8-29-2002; grpsl).
Nat'l Network: CBS; MyNetworkTV *Nat'l Reps:* Continental Television Sales *Wire Services:* AP
Size of News Staff: 21; *Hours of Local News Weekly:* news progmg 15 hrs wkly
Al Lancaster, Operations Dir
Judy Stark, General Sales Mgr
Dan Froelich, Promotions Manager
Susan Ramsett, News Director
Chad Myers, Chief Engineer
Patti Shook, Operations Manager

WTPX-TV *Digital Channel:* 46; 3,090 kw vis; ant 918t; N45 03 33 W89 26 10
720 E. Capitol Dr., Milwaukee, WI 53212-1308
(561) 659-4122, *Fax:* (561) 659-4754
License: Antigo, Langlade County, WI held by Paxson Wausau License Inc.
Group Owner: ION Media Networks Inc.; (acq 4-18-2000; $887,500 for CP).
Nat'l Network: ION Television
Chuck Robinson, CFO
Andrew Fisher, President
Mike Seachman, Operations Dir
Tim McCoy, General Manager
Tom Pleva, General Sales Mgr
Bill Seifert, Promotions Manager
Melissa Knollinger, News Director
Leonard Smith, ChiefEngineer
Bruce Baker, Executive Vice President

WYOW *Digital Channel:* 28 *Virtual Channel:* 34; 70 kw; 472 ft.; N45 46 30 W89 14 55; *Rebroadcasting:* Rebroadcasts WAOW-TV Wausau 100%
5727 Tokay Boulevard, Madison, WI 53719 US 54521
(715) 842-2251, *Fax:* (715) 848-0195, (715) 842-7808
www.waow.com
info@waow.com
License: Eagle River, Vilas County, WI held by WAOW-WYOW Television Inc.
Group Owner: Quincy Newspapers Inc.; (acq 5-22-2001; grpsl).; *Washington Law Firm:* Wilkinson, Barker & Knauer, LLP.
Nat'l Network: ABC; CW *Nat'l Reps:* Petry Television Inc. *Wire Services:* AP; CNN
Ralph Oakley, CEO
Laurin Jorstad, General Manager
Carol Kellum, General Sales Mgr
Tricia Schairer, Programming Director
Mark Oliver, Promotions Manager
Randy Winter, News Director
Russ Crass, Chief Engineer
Tim Atterberg,Regional Sales Manager

Wyoming

Casper-Riverton, WY (DMA 197)

KFNB *Digital Channel:* 20; 58.9 kw vis; 1,909t; N42 44 37 W106 18 31; *Population Served:* 32,000
1856 Skyview Drive, Casper, WY 82601
(307) 577-5923, *Fax:* (307) 234-4005
kfnb@wyoming.com
License: Casper, Natrona County, WY held by WyoMedia Corp
Group Owner: Wyomedia Corp.; *Washington Law Firm:* Irwin, Campbell & Tannenwald
Nat'l Network: Fox
Mark Nalbone, General Manager
Judie Lewis, General Sales Mgr
Amy Anderson, Programming Director
Joe Lowndes, Promotions Manager
Jim Nagy, News Director
Terry Lane, Chief Engineer
Tony Lattea, Traffic Manager

KFNE *Digital Channel:* 10 *Virtual Channel:* 10; 11.3 kw; 1726 ft.; N43 27 26 W108 12 2
7075 Salt Creek Hwy. #1, Casper, WY 82601 US
(307) 577-5923, *Fax:* (307) 234-4005
kfnb@wyoming.com
License: Riverton, Fremont County, WY held by Wyomedia Corp.
Group Owner: Wyomedia Corp.; (acq 2-28-2009; with KFNR(TV) Rawlins)
Nat'l Network: FOX
Mark Nalbone, General Manager
Judie Lewis, General Sales Mgr
Amy Anderson, Programming Director
Joe Lowndes, Promotions Manager
Terry Lane, Chief Engineer
Tony Lattea, Traffic Manager

KGWC-TV *Digital Channel:* 14 *Virtual Channel:* 14; 53.3 kw; 1844 ft.; N42 44 26 W106 21 34
Kgwc-Tv, PO Box 170, Casper, WY 82602 US
(307) 577-5923 / 5924, *Fax:* (307) 634-7511
kfnb@wyoming.com
License: Casper, Natrona County, WY held by Mark III Media Inc.
Group Owner: Mark III Media Inc.; (acq 5-31-2006; grpsl);
Washington Law Firm: Dow, Lohnes & Albertson
Nat'l Network: CBS; Fox
Terry Lane, Operations Dir
Mark Nalbone, General Manager
Tina Nalbone, General Sales Mgr
Joe Lownden, Promotions Manager
Greg Flabager, News Director
Dave Ericson, Chief Engineer
Tony Lattea, Traffic Manager

KGWL-TV *Digital Channel:* 7 *Virtual Channel:* 5; 14.3 kw; 371 ft.; N42 53 43 W108 43 34; *Rebroadcasting:* Satellite of KGWC-TV Casper.
Kgwc-Tv, PO Box 170, Casper, WY 82602 US
(307) 234-1111, *Fax:* (307) 234-4005
kfnb@wyoming.com
License: Lander, Fremont County, WY held by Mark III Media Inc.
Group Owner: Mark III Media Inc.; (acq 5-31-2006; grpsl).;
Washington Law Firm: Covington & Burling
Nat'l Network: CBS
Mark Nalbone, General Manager
Terry Lane, Chief Engineer

***KPTW** *Digital Channel:* 8 *Virtual Channel:* 6; 2.3 kw; 1864 ft.; N42 44 26 W106 21 34; *Rebroadcasting:* Satellite of KCWC-TV Lander 100%
Gregory T. Ray, 2660 Peck Avenue, Riverton, WY 82501 US
(307) 856-6944, *Fax:* (307) 856-3893
wyoptv.org
License: Casper, Natrona County, WY held by Central Wyoming College.
Nat'l Network: PBS *Regional Network:* Wyoming Public Television
Ruby Calvert, General Manager
Suze Kanack, Programming Director
Bob Spain, Chief Engineer

KTWO-TV *Digital Channel:* 17 *Virtual Channel:* 2; 52.9 kw; 1837 ft.; N42 44 26 W106 21 34
The Pinnacle, Suite 875, 3455 Peachtree Rd., N.E., Atlanta, GA 30326 US
(307) 237-3711, *Fax:* (307) 237-4458
www.k2tv.com
k2@k2tv.com
License: Casper, Natrona County, WY held by Silverton Broadcasting Co. LLC
(acq 5-31-2006; $1.2 million); *Ownership:* Barry Silverton, 100%
Nat'l Network: ABC *Nat'l Reps:* Millennium Sales & Marketing
Size of News Staff: 23; *Hours of Local News Weekly:* news progmg 19.5 hrs wkly
Kristi Lockard, General Manager
Mick Birge, Station Manager
Tina Nalbone, General Sales Mgr
Amie Miller, News Director

Cheyenne, WY-Scottsbluff, NE (DMA 198)

KGWN-TV *Digital Channel:* 30 *Virtual Channel:* 5; 459 kw; 531 ft.; N41 6 1 W105 0 23
2923 East Lincolnway, Cheyenne, WY 82001 US

(307) 634-7755, *Fax:* (307) 638-0182
www.kgwn.tv
news@kgwn.tv
License: Cheyenne, Laramie County, WY held by SagamoreHill Broadcasting Co. of Wyoming/Northern Colorado LLC.
Group Owner: SagamoreHill Broadcasting LLC; (acq 3-19-2004; $6.5 million with KSTF(TV) Scottsbluff, NE).; *Washington Law Firm:* Dow, Lohnes & Albertson
Nat'l Network: CBS; CW *Nat'l Reps:* Continental Television Sales
Size of News Staff: 16; *Hours of Local News Weekly:* news progmg 15 hrs wkly

Louis Wall, President
Joan Turner, General Manager
Dusty Thein, General Sales Mgr
Barbara Parenti, Programming Director
Tregg White, News Director
Tony Schaefer, Engineering Dir
Keith Yosten, Chief Engineer
Keith Lindstrom,Regional Sales Manager

KLWY *Digital Channel:* 27 *Virtual Channel:* 27; 169 kw; 761 ft.; N41 2 55 W104 53 28
1856 Skyview Drive, Casper, WY 82601 US
(307) 577-5923, *Fax:* (307) 234-4005
kfnb@wyoming.com
License: Cheyenne, Laramie County, WY held by Wyomedia Corp
Group Owner: Wyomedia Corp.; (acq 12-4-91; $100,000;
Nat'l Network: FOX

T. J. Corson, Operations Dir
Mark Nalbone, General Manager
Judie Lewis, General Sales Mgr
Amy Anderson, Programming Director
Joe Lowndes, Promotions Manager
Jim Nagy, News Director
Terry Lane, Chief Engineer
Tony Lattea,Traffic Manager

KQCK *Digital Channel:* 11 *Virtual Channel:* 33; 16 kw; 2133 ft.; N40 32 47 W105 11 50
The Pinnacle, Suite 875, 3455 Peachtree Rd., N.E., Atlanta, GA 30326 US
(501) 219-2400
www.katv.com
License: Cheyenne, Laramie County, WY held by Denver Broadcasting Inc., debtor in possession
Group Owner: Equity Media Holdings Corp.; (acq 3-26-2001; $3.5 million with KTWO-TV Casper)

Nat'l Network: ABC *Nat'l Reps:* Millennium Sales & Marketing
Size of News Staff: 17; *Hours of Local News Weekly:* news progmg 15 hrs wkly

Barbara Laurence, Director
Barry Schumaier, General Sales Mgr
Jim Sande, Programming Director
LuWanna Lawrence, Promotions Manager
Monica Hannan, News Director
Brian Funk, Chief Engineer

Denver, CO (DMA 18)

KFNR *Digital Channel:* 9 *Virtual Channel:* 11; 0.978 kw; 168 ft.; N41 46 16 W107 14 15
7075 Salt Creek Hwy #1, Casper, WY 82601 US
(307) 577-5923, *Fax:* (307) 234-4005
kfnb@wyoming.com
License: Rawlins, Carbon County, WY held by Wyomedia Corp
Group Owner: Wyomedia Corp.; (acq 2-28-2009; with KFNE(TV) Riverton); *Washington Law Firm:* Drinker Biddle & Reath LLP
Nat'l Network: FOX

Mark Nalbone, General Manager
Judie Lewis, General Sales Mgr
Amy Anderson, Programming Director
Joe Lowndes, Promotions Manager
Terry Lane, Chief Engineer
Tony Lattea, Traffic Manager

Idaho Falls-Pocatello, ID (DMA 162)

KJWY *Digital Channel:* 2 *Virtual Channel:* 2; 0.27 kw; 1097 ft.; N43 29 25 W110 57 20
1500 Foremaster Lane, Las Vegas, NV 89101 US
(307) 733-2066, *Fax:* (307) 733-4834
www.kjwy2.com
License: Jackson, Teton County, WY held by Two Ocean Broadcasting Co.
Group Owner: Sunbelt Communications Co.; (acq 11-95; grpsl).
Nat'l Network: NBC
Size of News Staff: 1; *Hours of Local News Weekly:* news progmg 5 hrs wkly

James Rogers, CEO
Ralph Toddre, President
Christel Rahme, Station Manager
Robin Estopinal, Engineering Dir
Carl Shuptrine, News Commentator

Rapid City, SD (DMA 174)

KSGW-TV *Digital Channel:* 13; 50.0 kW; 16.99 DBK; ant 1,220t; N44 37 20 W107 06 57; *Population Served:* 241,224
Box 1760, Rapid City, SD 57709
(605) 342-2000, *Fax:* (605) 342-7305
www.kotatv.com
License: Sheridan, Sheridan County, WY held by Duhamel Broadcasting Enterprises.
Group Owner: Duhamel Broadcasting Enterprises; *Washington Law Firm:* Pillsbury Law
Nat'l Network: ABC *Nat'l Reps:* Continental Television Sales
Wire Services: AP
Hours of Local News Weekly: News progmg 8 hrs wkly

William Duhamel, President
Monte Loos, Operations Dir
Steve Duffy, General Sales Mgr
Doug Loos, Programming Director
John Petersen, News Director
Dan Black, Engineering Dir
Dan Duff, Chief Engineer
Gerry Fenske, Regional SalesManager

Salt Lake City, UT (DMA 33)

KGWR-TV *Digital Channel:* 13 *Virtual Channel:* 13; 14.2 kw; 1624 ft.; N41 26 21 W109 6 42; *Rebroadcasting:* Satellite of KGWC-TV Casper.
Kgwc-Tv, 2500 C Y Avenue, Casper, WY 82604 US
(307) 234-1111, *Fax:* (307) 234-4005
kfnb@wyoming.com
License: Rock Springs, Sweetwater County, WY held by Mark III Media Inc.
Group Owner: Mark III Media Inc.; (acq 5-31-2006; grpsl).;
Washington Law Firm: Covington & Burling
Nat'l Network: CBS

Mark Nalbone, General Manager
Terry Lane, Chief Engineer

US Television Stations by Call Letters

DKB-97071 Kingsport, Tennessee
DKBTZ Butte, Montana
DKSQA Topeka, Idaho
DWMDE Seaford, Georgia
DWUNW Canton, Florida
KAAH-TV Honolulu, Hawaii
KAAL Austin, Minnesota
KAAS-TV Salina, Kansas
KABB San Antonio, Texas
KABC-TV Los Angeles, California
KACV-TV Amarillo, Texas
KADN-TV Lafayette, Louisiana
KAEF-TV Arcata, California
KAET Phoenix, Arizona
KAFT Fayetteville, Arkansas
KAID Boise, Idaho
KAII-TV Wailuku, Hawaii
KAIL Fresno, California
KAIT Jonesboro, Arkansas
KAKE Wichita, Kansas
KAKM Anchorage, Alaska
KALB-TV Alexandria, Louisiana
KALO Honolulu, Hawaii
KAMC Lubbock, Texas
KAME-TV Reno, Nevada
KAMR-TV Amarillo, Texas
KAMU-TV College Station, Texas
KAPP Yakima, Washington
KAQY Columbia, Louisiana
KARD West Monroe, Louisiana
KARE Minneapolis, Minnesota
KARK-TV Little Rock, Arkansas
KARZ-TV Little Rock, Arkansas
KASA-TV Santa Fe, New Mexico
KASN Pine Bluff, Arkansas
KASW Phoenix, Arizona
KASY-TV Albuquerque, New Mexico
KATC Lafayette, Louisiana
KATN Fairbanks, Alaska
KATU Portland, Oregon
KATV Little Rock, Arkansas
KAUT-TV Oklahoma City, Oklahoma
KAUZ-TV Wichita Falls, Texas
KAVU-TV Victoria, Texas
KAWB Brainerd, Minnesota
KAWE Bemidji, Minnesota
KAYU-TV Spokane, Washington
KAZA-TV Avalon, California
KAZD Lake Dallas, Texas
KAZQ Albuquerque, New Mexico
KAZT-TV Prescott, Arizona
KBAK-TV Bakersfield, California
KBCA Alexandria, Louisiana
KBCB Bellingham, Washington
KBCW San Francisco, California
KBDI-TV Broomfield, Colorado
KBEH Oxnard, California
KBFD-DT Honolulu, Hawaii
KBHE-TV Rapid City, South Dakota
KBIM-TV Roswell, New Mexico
KBIN-TV Council Bluffs, Nebraska
KBJR-TV Superior, Wisconsin
KBLN Grants Pass, Oregon
KBLR Paradise, Nevada
KBME-TV Bismarck, North Dakota
KBMT Beaumont, Texas
KBMY Bismarck, North Dakota
KBOI-TV Boise, Idaho
KBRR Thief River Falls, Minnesota
KBSI Cape Girardeau, Missouri
KBSV Ceres, California
KBTC-TV Tacoma, Washington
KBTV-TV Port Arthur, Texas
KBTX-TV Bryan, Texas
KBVO Llano, Texas
KBVU Eureka, California
KBYU-TV Provo, Utah
KBZK Bozeman, Montana
KCAL Redlands, California
KCAU-TV Sioux City, Iowa
KCBA Salinas, California
KCBD Lubbock, Texas
KCBS-TV Los Angeles, California
KCBU-DT Price, Utah
KCBY-TV Coos Bay, Oregon
KCCI Des Moines, Iowa
KCCO-TV Alexandria, Minnesota
KCCW-TV Walker, Minnesota
KCDO-TV Sterling, Colorado
KCDT Coeur d'Alene, Washington
KCEB Longview, Texas
KCEC Denver, Colorado
KCEN-TV Temple, Texas
KCET Los Angeles, California
KCFG Flagstaff, Arizona
KCFW-TV Kalispell, Montana
KCGE-DT Crookston, North Dakota
KCHF Santa Fe, New Mexico
KCIT Amarillo, Texas
KCKA Centralia, Washington
KCLO-TV Rapid City, South Dakota
KCNC-TV Denver, Colorado
KCNS San Francisco, California
KCOP-TV Los Angeles, California
KCOS El Paso, Texas
KCOY-TV Santa Maria, California
KCPM Grand Forks, North Dakota
KCPQ Tacoma, Washington
KCPT Kansas City, Missouri
KCRA-TV Sacramento, California
KCRG-TV Cedar Rapids, Iowa
KCSD-TV Sioux Falls, South Dakota
KCSG Cedar City, Utah
KCSM-TV San Mateo, California
KCTS-TV Seattle, Washington
KCTV Kansas City, Missouri
KCVU Paradise, California
KCWE Kansas City, Missouri
KCWI-TV Ames, Iowa
KCWK North Las Vegas, Nevada
KCWV Duluth, Minnesota
KCWX Fredericksburg, Texas
KDAF Dallas, Texas
KDBC-TV El Paso, Texas
KDCK Dodge City, Kansas
KDCU-DT Derby, Kansas
KDEN-TV Longmont, Colorado
KDFI Dallas, Texas
KDFW Dallas, Texas
KDIN-TV Des Moines, Iowa
KDKA-TV Pittsburgh, Pennsylvania
KDKF Klamath Falls, Oregon
KDLH Duluth, Minnesota
KDLO-TV Florence, South Dakota
KDLT-TV Sioux Falls, South Dakota
KDLV-TV Mitchell, South Dakota
KDMD Anchorage, Alaska
KDMI Des Moines, Iowa
KDNL-TV St. Louis, Missouri
KDOC-TV Anaheim, California
KDOR-TV Bartlesville, Oklahoma
KDRV Medford, Oregon
KDSD-TV Aberdeen, South Dakota
KDSE Dickinson, North Dakota
KDSM-TV Des Moines, Iowa
KDTN Denton, Texas
KDTP Holbrook, Arizona
KDTV-DT San Francisco, California
KDTX-TV Dallas, Texas
KDUH-TV Scottsbluff, Nebraska
KDVR Denver, Colorado
KDYW Waco, Texas
KECI-TV Missoula, Montana
KECY-TV El Centro, California
KEDT Corpus Christi, Texas
KEET Eureka, California
KEFB Ames, Iowa
KELO-TV Sioux Falls, South Dakota
KEMO-TV Santa Rosa, California
KEMV Mountain View, Arkansas
KENS San Antonio, Texas
KENV-DT Elko, Utah
KENW Portales, New Mexico
KEPB-TV Eugene, Oregon
KEPR-TV Pasco, Washington
KERA-TV Dallas, Texas
KERO-TV Bakersfield, California
KESD-TV Brookings, South Dakota
KESQ-TV Palm Springs, California
KETA-TV Oklahoma City, Oklahoma
KETC St. Louis, Missouri
KETD Castle Rock, Colorado
KETG Arkadelphia, Arkansas
KETH-TV Houston, Texas
KETK-TV Jacksonville, Texas
KETS Little Rock, Arkansas
KETV Omaha, Nebraska
KETZ El Dorado, Arkansas
KEVN-TV Rapid City, South Dakota
KEYC-TV CBS & NEYC FOX Mankato, Minnesota
KEYE-TV Austin, Texas
KEYT-TV Santa Barbara, California
KEYU Borger, Texas
KEZI Eugene, Oregon
KFBB-TV Great Falls, Montana
KFCT Fort Collins, Colorado
KFCT Fort Collins, Colorado
KFDA-TV Amarillo, Texas
KFDM-TV Beaumont, Texas
KFDX-TV Wichita Falls, Texas
KFFV Seattle, Washington
KFFX-TV Pendleton, Oregon
KFJX-DT Pittsburg, Missouri
KFMB-TV San Diego, California
KFME Fargo, North Dakota
KFNB Casper, Wyoming
KFNE Riverton, Wyoming
KFNR Rawlins, Wyoming
KFOR-TV Oklahoma City, Oklahoma
KFOX-TV El Paso, Texas
KFPH-DT Flagstaff, Arizona
KFQX Grand Junction, Colorado
KFRE-TV Sanger, California
KFSF-DT Vallejo, California
KFSM-TV Fort Smith, Arkansas
KFSN-TV Fresno, California
KFTA-TV Fort Smith, Arkansas
KFTC Bemidji, Minnesota
KFTH-DT Alvin, Texas
KFTR-DT Ontario, California
KFTS Klamath Falls, Oregon
KFTU-DT Douglas, Arizona
KFTV-DT Hanford, California
KFVE Honolulu, Hawaii
KFVS-TV Cape Girardeau, Missouri
KFWD Fort Worth, Texas
KFXA Cedar Rapids, Iowa
KFXB-TV Dubuque, Missouri
KFXF Fairbanks, Alaska
KFXK-TV Longview, Texas
KFXP Pocatello, Idaho
KFYR-TV Bismarck, North Dakota
KGAN Cedar Rapids, Missouri
KGBT-TV Harlingen, Texas
KGCW Burlington, Missouri
KGEB Tulsa, Oklahoma
KGET-TV Bakersfield, California
KGFE Grand Forks, North Dakota
KGIN Grand Island, Nebraska
KGLA-AM Hammond, Louisiana
KGMB Honolulu, Hawaii
KGMC Clovis, California
KGMD-TV Hilo, Hawaii
KGMV Wailuku, Hawaii
KGNS-TV Laredo, Texas
KGO-TV San Francisco, California
KGPE Fresno, California
KGPX-TV Spokane, Washington
KGTF Hagatna, Puerto Rico
KGTV San Diego, California
KGUN-TV Tucson, Arizona
KGW Portland, Oregon
KGWC-TV Casper, Wyoming
KGWL-TV Lander, Wyoming
KGWN-TV Cheyenne, Wyoming
KGWR-TV Rock Springs, Wyoming
KHAS-TV Hastings, Nebraska
KHAW-TV Hilo, Hawaii
KHBC-TV Hilo, Hawaii
KHBS Fort Smith, Arkansas
KHCE-TV San Antonio, Texas
KHET Honolulu, Hawaii
KHGI-TV Kearney, Nebraska
KHIN Red Oak, Iowa
KHMT Hardin, Montana
KHNE-TV Hastings, Nebraska
KHNL Honolulu, Hawaii
KHOG-TV Fayetteville, Arkansas
KHON-TV Honolulu, Hawaii
KHOU Houston, Texas
KHQ-TV Spokane, Washington
KHQA-TV Hannibal, Missouri
KHRR Tucson, Arizona
KHSD-TV Lead, South Dakota

KHSL-TV Chico, California
KHVO Hilo, Hawaii
KIAH Houston, Texas
KICU-TV San Jose, California
KIDK Idaho Falls, Idaho
KIDY San Angelo, Texas
KIEM-TV Eureka, California
KIFI-TV Idaho Falls, Idaho
KIII Corpus Christi, Texas
KIIN Iowa City, Missouri
KIKU Honolulu, Hawaii
KILM Barstow, California
KIMA-TV Yakima, Washington
KIMT Mason City, Iowa
KINC Las Vegas, Nevada
KING-TV Seattle, Washington
KINT-TV El Paso, Texas
KION-TV Monterey, California
KIPT Twin Falls, Idaho
KIRO-TV Seattle, Washington
KISU-TV Pocatello, Idaho
KITU-TV Beaumont, Texas
KITV Honolulu, Hawaii
KIVI-TV Nampa, Idaho
KIVV-TV Lead, South Dakota
KIXE-TV Redding, California
KJCT Grand Junction, Colorado
KJLA Ventura, California
KJNP-TV North Pole, Alaska
KJRE Ellendale, North Dakota
KJRH-TV Tulsa, Oklahoma
KJRR Jamestown, North Dakota
KJTL Wichita Falls, Texas
KJTV-TV Lubbock, Texas
KJUD Juneau, Alaska
KJWY Jackson, Wyoming
KJZZ-TV Salt Lake City, Utah
KKAI Kailua, Hawaii
KKAP Little Rock, Arkansas
KKCO Grand Junction, Colorado
KKJB Boise, Idaho
KKPX-TV San Jose, California
KKTV Colorado Springs, Colorado
KLAS-TV Las Vegas, Nevada
KLAX-TV Alexandria, Louisiana
KLBK-TV Lubbock, Texas
KLBY Colby, Kansas
KLCS Los Angeles, California
KLCW-TV Wolfforth, Texas
KLDO-TV Laredo, Texas
KLEI-TV Kailua-Kona, Hawaii
KLEW-TV Lewiston, Idaho
KLFY-TV Lafayette, Louisiana
KLJB Davenport, Missouri
KLKN Lincoln, Nebraska
KLNE-TV Lexington, Nebraska
KLPA-TV Alexandria, Louisiana
KLPB-TV Lafayette, Louisiana
KLRN San Antonio, Texas
KLRT-TV Little Rock, Arkansas
KLRU Austin, Texas
KLSR-TV Eugene, Oregon
KLST San Angelo, Texas
KLTJ Galveston, Texas
KLTL-TV Lake Charles, Louisiana
KLTM-TV Monroe, Louisiana
KLTS-TV Shreveport, Louisiana
KLTV Tyler, Texas
KLUJ-TV Harlingen, Texas
KLUZ-TV Albuquerque, New Mexico
KLVX Las Vegas, Nevada
KLWB New Iberia, Louisiana
KLWY Cheyenne, Wyoming
KMAU Wailuku, Hawaii
KMAX-TV Sacramento, California
KMBC-TV Kansas City, Missouri
KMBH Harlingen, Texas
KMCB Coos Bay, Oregon
KMCC Laughlin, Nevada
KMCI-TV Lawrence, Missouri
KMCT-TV West Monroe, Louisiana
KMCY Minot, North Dakota
KMDE Devils Lake, North Dakota
KMEB Wailuku, Hawaii
KMEG Sioux City, Iowa
KMEX-DT Los Angeles, California
KMGH-TV Denver, Colorado
KMID Midland, Texas
KMIR-TV Palm Springs, California
KMIZ Columbia, Missouri
KMLM-DT Odessa, Texas
KMNE-TV Bassett, Nebraska
KMOH-TV Kingman, Arizona
KMOS-TV Sedalia, Missouri
KMOT Minot, North Dakota
KMOV St. Louis, Missouri
KMPH-TV Visalia, California
KMPX Decatur, Texas
KMSB Tucson, Arizona
KMSP-TV Minneapolis, Minnesota
KMSS-TV Shreveport, Louisiana
KMTF Helena, Montana
KMTP-TV San Francisco, California
KMTR Eugene, Oregon
KMTV-TV Omaha, Nebraska
KMTW Hutchinson, Kansas
KMVT Twin Falls, Idaho
KMVU-DT Medford, Oregon
KMYA-DT Camden, Arkansas
KMYS Kerrville, Texas
KMYT-TV Tulsa, Oklahoma
KMYU Saint George, Utah
KNAT-TV Albuquerque, New Mexico
KNAZ-TV Flagstaff, Arizona
KNBC Los Angeles, California
KNBN Rapid City, South Dakota
KNCT Belton, Texas
KNDO Yakima, Washington
KNDU Richland, Washington
KNDX Bismarck, North Dakota
KNIN-TV Caldwell, Idaho
KNLC St. Louis, Missouri
KNLJ Jefferson City, Missouri
KNMD-TV Santa Fe, New Mexico
KNME-TV Albuquerque, New Mexico
KNMT Portland, Oregon
KNOE-TV Monroe, Louisiana
KNOP-TV North Platte, Nebraska
KNPB Reno, Nevada
KNRR Pembina, North Dakota
KNSD San Diego, California
KNSO Merced, California
KNTV San Jose, California
KNVA Austin, Texas
KNVN Chico, California
KNVO McAllen, Texas
KNWA-TV Rogers, Arkansas
KNXT Visalia, California
KNXV-TV Phoenix, Arizona
KOAA-TV Pueblo, Colorado
KOAB-TV Bend, Oregon
KOAC-TV Corvallis, Oregon
KOAM-TV Pittsburg, Kansas
KOAT-TV Albuquerque, New Mexico
KOB Albuquerque, New Mexico
KOBF Farmington, New Mexico
KOBI Medford, Oregon
KOBR Roswell, New Mexico
KOCB Oklahoma City, Oklahoma
KOCE-TV Huntington Beach, California
KOCM Norman, Oklahoma
KOCO-TV Oklahoma City, Oklahoma
KOCW Hoisington, Kansas
KODE-TV Joplin, Missouri
KOED-TV Tulsa, Oklahoma
KOET Eufaula, Oklahoma
KOFY-TV San Francisco, California
KOGG Wailuku, Hawaii
KOHD Bend, Oregon
KOIN Portland, Oregon
KOKH-TV Oklahoma City, Oklahoma
KOKI-TV Tulsa, Oklahoma
KOLD-TV Tucson, Arizona
KOLN Lincoln, Nebraska
KOLO-TV Reno, Nevada
KOLR Springfield, Missouri
KOMO-TV Seattle, Washington
KOMU-TV Columbia, Missouri
KONG Everett, Washington
KOOD Hays, Kansas
KOPB-TV Portland, Oregon
KOPX-TV Oklahoma City, Oklahoma
KORO Corpus Christi, Texas
KOSA-TV Odessa, Texas
KOTA-TV Rapid City, South Dakota
KOTI Klamath Falls, Oregon
KOTV-DT Tulsa, Oklahoma
KOVR Stockton, California
KOZJ Joplin, Missouri
KOZK Springfield, Missouri
KOZL-TV Springfield, Missouri
KPAX-TV Missoula, Montana
KPAZ-TV Phoenix, Arizona
KPBS San Diego, California
KPBT-TV Odessa, Texas
KPCB-DT Snyder, Texas
KPDX Vancouver, Washington
KPEJ-TV Odessa, Texas
KPHO-TV Phoenix, Arizona
KPIC Roseburg, Oregon
KPIX-TV San Francisco, California
KPJR-DT Greeley, Colorado
KPLC Lake Charles, Louisiana
KPLO-TV Reliance, South Dakota
KPLR-TV St. Louis, Missouri
KPMR Santa Barbara, California
KPNE-TV North Platte, Nebraska
KPNX Mesa, Arizona
KPNZ Ogden, Utah
KPOB-TV Poplar Bluff, Missouri
KPPX-TV Tolleson, Arizona
KPRC-TV Houston, Texas
KPRY-TV Pierre, South Dakota
KPSD-TV Eagle Butte, South Dakota
KPTB-DT Lubbock, Texas
KPTF-DT Farwell, Texas
KPTH Sioux City, Iowa
KPTM Omaha, Nebraska
KPTS Hutchinson, Kansas
KPTV Portland, Oregon
KPTW Casper, Wyoming
KPVI-DT Pocatello, Idaho
KPXB-TV Conroe, Texas
KPXC-TV Denver, Colorado
KPXD Arlington, Texas
KPXE-TV Kansas City, Missouri
KPXG-TV Salem, Oregon
KPXJ Minden, Louisiana
KPXL-TV Uvalde, Texas
KPXM-TV Saint Cloud, Minnesota
KPXN-TV San Bernardino, California
KPXO-TV Kaneohe, Hawaii
KPXR-TV Cedar Rapids, Missouri
KQCA Stockton, California
KQCD-TV Dickinson, North Dakota
KQCK Cheyenne, Wyoming
KQCW-DT Muskogee, Oklahoma
KQDS-TV Duluth, Minnesota
KQED San Francisco, California
KQEH San Jose, California
KQET Watsonville, California
KQIN Davenport, Missouri
KQSD-TV Lowry, South Dakota
KQSL Fort Bragg, California
KQTV St. Joseph, Missouri
KQUP Pullman, Washington
KRBC-TV Abilene, Texas
KRBK Osage Beach, Missouri
KRCA Riverside, California
KRCB Cotati, California
KRCG Jefferson City, Missouri
KRCR-TV Redding, California
KRCW-TV Salem, Oregon
KRDO-TV Colorado Springs, Colorado
KREG-TV Glenwood Springs, Colorado
KREM Spokane, Washington
KREN-TV Reno, Nevada
KREX-TV Grand Junction, Colorado
KREY-TV Montrose, Colorado
KREZ-TV Durango, Colorado
KRGV-TV Weslaco, Texas
KRII Chisholm, Minnesota
KRIN Waterloo, Iowa
KRIS-TV Corpus Christi, Texas
KRIV Houston, Texas
KRMA-TV Denver, Colorado
KRMJ Grand Junction, Colorado
KRMT Denver, Colorado
KRMU Durango, Colorado
KRMZ Steamboat Springs, Colorado
KRNE-TV Merriman, Nebraska
KRNV-DT Reno, Nevada
KRON-TV San Francisco, California
KRPV-DT Roswell, New Mexico
KRQE Albuquerque, New Mexico
KRSC-TV Claremore, Oklahoma
KRTN-TV Durango, Colorado
KRTV Great Falls, Montana
KRWB-TV Roswell, New Mexico
KRWF Redwood Falls, Minnesota
KRWG-TV Las Cruces, New Mexico
KRXI-TV Reno, Nevada
KSAN-TV San Angelo, Texas

KSAS-TV Wichita, Kansas
KSAT-TV San Antonio, Texas
KSAX Alexandria, Minnesota
KSBI Oklahoma City, Oklahoma
KSBW Salinas, California
KSBY San Luis Obispo, California
KSCE El Paso, Texas
KSCI Long Beach, California
KSCW-DT Wichita, Kansas
KSDK St. Louis, Missouri
KSEE Fresno, California
KSFY-TV Sioux Falls, South Dakota
KSGW-TV Sheridan, Wyoming
KSHB-TV Kansas City, Missouri
KSHV-TV Shreveport, Louisiana
KSIN-TV Sioux City, Missouri
KSKN Spokane, Washington
KSL-TV Salt Lake City, Utah
KSLA Shreveport, Louisiana
KSMN Worthington, Minnesota
KSMO-TV Kansas City, Missouri
KSMQ-TV Austin, Minnesota
KSMS-TV Monterey, California
KSNC Great Bend, Kansas
KSNF Joplin, Missouri
KSNG Garden City, Kansas
KSNK McCook, Nebraska
KSNT Topeka, Kansas
KSNV-DT Las Vegas, Nevada
KSNW Wichita, Kansas
KSPR Springfield, Missouri
KSPS-TV Spokane, Washington
KSPX-TV Sacramento, California
KSRE Minot, North Dakota
KSTC-TV Minneapolis, Minnesota
KSTF Scottsbluff, Nebraska
KSTP-TV St. Paul, Minnesota
KSTS San Jose, California
KSTU Salt Lake City, Utah
KSTW Tacoma, Washington
KSVI Billings, Montana
KSWB-TV San Diego, California
KSWK Lakin, Kansas
KSWO-TV Lawton, Oklahoma
KSWT Yuma, Arizona
KSYS Medford, Oregon
KTAB-TV Abilene, Texas
KTAJ-TV St. Joseph, Missouri
KTAL-TV Texarkana, Texas
KTAS San Luis Obispo, California
KTBC Austin, Texas
KTBN-TV Santa Ana, California
KTBO-TV Oklahoma City, Oklahoma
KTBS-TV Shreveport, Louisiana
KTBU Conroe, Texas
KTBW-TV Tacoma, Washington
KTBY Anchorage, Alaska
KTCA-TV St. Paul, Minnesota
KTCI-TV St. Paul, Minnesota
KTCW Roseburg, Oregon
KTDO Las Cruces, New Mexico
KTEJ Jonesboro, Arkansas
KTEL-TV Carlsbad, New Mexico
KTEN Ada, Oklahoma
KTFF-DT Porterville, California
KTFN El Paso, Texas
KTFQ-TV Albuquerque, New Mexico
KTGF Great Falls, Montana
KTGM Tamuning, Guam
KTHV Little Rock, Arkansas
KTIN Fort Dodge, Iowa
KTIV Sioux City, Iowa
KTKA-TV Topeka, Kansas
KTLA Los Angeles, California
KTLM Rio Grande City, Texas
KTLN-TV Novato, California
KTMD Galveston, Texas
KTMF Missoula, Montana
KTMW Salt Lake City, Utah
KTNC-TV Concord, California
KTNE-TV Alliance, Nebraska
KTNL-TV Sitka, Alaska
KTNV-TV Las Vegas, Nevada
KTNW Richland, Washington
KTOO-TV Juneau, Alaska
KTPX-TV Okmulgee, Oklahoma
KTRE Lufkin, Texas
KTRK-TV Houston, Texas
KTRV-TV Nampa, Idaho
KTSC Pueblo, Colorado
KTSD-TV Pierre, South Dakota
KTSF San Francisco, California
KTSM-TV El Paso, Texas
KTTC Rochester, Minnesota
KTTM Huron, South Dakota
KTTU Tucson, Arizona
KTTV Los Angeles, California
KTTW Sioux Falls, South Dakota
KTTZ-TV Lubbock, Texas
KTUL Tulsa, Oklahoma
KTUU-TV Anchorage, Alaska
KTUZ-TV Shawnee, Oklahoma
KTVA Anchorage, Alaska
KTVB Boise, Idaho
KTVC Roseburg, Oregon
KTVD Denver, Colorado
KTVE El Dorado, Arkansas
KTVF Fairbanks, Alaska
KTVG-TV Grand Island, Nebraska
KTVH-DT Helena, Montana
KTVI St. Louis, Missouri
KTVK Phoenix, Arizona
KTVL Medford, Oregon
KTVM-TV Butte, Montana
KTVN Reno, Nevada
KTVO Kirksville, Missouri
KTVQ Billings, Montana
KTVR La Grande, Oregon
KTVT Fort Worth, Texas
KTVU Oakland, California
KTVX Salt Lake City, Utah
KTVZ Bend, Oregon
KTWO-TV Casper, Wyoming
KTWU Topeka, Kansas
KTXA Fort Worth, Texas
KTXD-TV Greenville, Texas
KTXH Houston, Texas
KTXL Sacramento, California
KTXS-TV Sweetwater, Texas
KUAC-TV Fairbanks, Alaska
KUAS-TV Tucson, Arizona
KUAT-TV Tucson, Arizona
KUBD Ketchikan, Alaska
KUBE-TV Baytown, Texas
KUCW Ogden, Utah
KUED Salt Lake City, Utah
KUEN Ogden, Utah
KUES Richfield, Utah
KUEW St. George, Utah
KUFM-TV Missoula, Montana
KUGF Great Falls, Montana
KUHT Houston, Texas
KUID-TV Moscow, Idaho
KUKL-TV Kalispell, Montana
KULR-TV Billings, Montana
KUMV-TV Williston, North Dakota
KUNP La Grande, Oregon
KUNS-TV Bellevue, Washington
KUOK Woodward, Oklahoma
KUON-TV Lincoln, Nebraska
KUPB Midland, Texas
KUPK Garden City, Kansas
KUPT Hobbs, New Mexico
KUPU Waimanalo, Hawaii
KUPX-TV Provo, Utah
KUQI Corpus Christi, Texas
KUSA Denver, Colorado
KUSD-TV Vermillion, South Dakota
KUSI-TV San Diego, California
KUSM-TV Bozeman, Montana
KUTF Logan, Utah
KUTH-DT Provo, Utah
KUTP Phoenix, Arizona
KUTV Salt Lake City, Utah
KUVI-DT Bakersfield, California
KUVN-DT Garland, Texas
KUVS-DT Modesto, California
KVAL-TV Eugene, Oregon
KVCR-DT San Bernardino, California
KVCT Victoria, Texas
KVCW Las Vegas, Nevada
KVEA Corona, California
KVEO-TV Brownsville, Texas
KVEW Kennewick, Washington
KVHP Lake Charles, Louisiana
KVIA-TV El Paso, Texas
KVIE Sacramento, California
KVIH-TV Clovis, New Mexico
KVII-TV Amarillo, Texas
KVIQ Eureka, California
KVLY-TV Fargo, North Dakota
KVMD Twentynine Palms, California
KVME-TV Bishop, California
KVMY Las Vegas, Nevada
KVNV Ely, Nevada
KVOA Tucson, Arizona
KVOS-TV Bellingham, Washington
KVPT Fresno, California
KVRR Fargo, North Dakota
KVSN-DT Pueblo, Colorado
KVTH-DT Hot Springs, Arkansas
KVTJ-DT Jonesboro, Arkansas
KVTN-DT Pine Bluff, Arkansas
KVTV Laredo, Texas
KVUE Austin, Texas
KVVU-TV Henderson, Nevada
KVYE El Centro, California
KVZK-2 Pago Pago, American Samoa
KVZK-4 Pago Pago, American Samoa
KVZK-5 Pago Pago, American Samoa
KWAB-TV Big Spring, Texas
KWBA-TV Sierra Vista, Arizona
KWBM Harrison, Arkansas
KWBN Honolulu, Hawaii
KWBQ Santa Fe, New Mexico
KWCM-TV Appleton, Minnesota
KWDK Tacoma, Washington
KWES-TV Odessa, Texas
KWET Cheyenne, Oklahoma
KWEX-DT San Antonio, Texas
KWGN-TV Denver, Colorado
KWHB Tulsa, Oklahoma
KWHD Hilo, Hawaii
KWHE Honolulu, Hawaii
KWHM Wailuku, Hawaii
KWHY-TV Los Angeles, California
KWKB Iowa City, Iowa
KWKS Colby, Kansas
KWKT-TV Waco, Texas
KWNB-TV Hayes Center, Nebraska
KWOG Springdale, Arkansas
KWPX-TV Bellevue, Washington
KWQC-TV Davenport, Iowa
KWSD Sioux Falls, South Dakota
KWSE Williston, North Dakota
KWSU-TV Pullman, Washington
KWTV-DT Oklahoma City, Oklahoma
KWTX-TV Waco, Texas
KWWF Waterloo, Iowa
KWWL Waterloo, Iowa
KWWT Odessa, Texas
KWYB Butte, Montana
KXAN-TV Austin, Texas
KXAS-TV Fort Worth, Texas
KXGN-TV Glendive, Montana
KXII Sherman, Texas
KXJB-TV Valley City, North Dakota
KXLA Rancho Palos Verdes, California
KXLF-TV Butte, Montana
KXLT-TV Rochester, Minnesota
KXLY-TV Spokane, Washington
KXMA-TV Dickinson, North Dakota
KXMB-TV Bismarck, North Dakota
KXMC-TV Minot, North Dakota
KXMD-TV Williston, North Dakota
KXND Minot, North Dakota
KXNE-TV Norfolk, Nebraska
KXNW Eureka Springs, Arkansas
KXRM-TV Colorado Springs, Colorado
KXTF Twin Falls, Idaho
KXTV Sacramento, California
KXTX-TV Dallas, Texas
KXVA Abilene, Texas
KXVO Omaha, Nebraska
KXXV Waco, Texas
KYAZ Katy, Texas
KYES-TV Anchorage, Alaska
KYIN Mason City, Iowa
KYLE-TV Bryan, Texas
KYMA-DT Yuma, Arizona
KYNE-TV Omaha, Nebraska
KYOU-TV Ottumwa, Iowa
KYTV Springfield, Missouri
KYTX Nacogdoches, Texas
KYUR Anchorage, Alaska
KYUS-TV Miles City, Montana
KYVE Yakima, Washington
KYVV-TV Del Rio, Texas
KYW-TV Philadelphia, Pennsylvania
KZJL Houston, Texas
KZJO Seattle, Washington
KZSD-TV Martin, South Dakota
KZTV Corpus Christi, Texas

WAAY-TV Huntsville, Alabama
WABC-TV New York, New York
WABG-TV Greenwood, Mississippi
WABI-TV Bangor, Maine
WABM Birmingham, Alabama
WABW-TV Pelham, Georgia
WACH Columbia, South Carolina
WACP Atlantic City, New Jersey
WACS-TV Dawson, Georgia
WACX-DT Leesburg, Florida
WACY-TV Appleton, Wisconsin
WADL Mount Clemens, Michigan
WAFB Baton Rouge, Louisiana
WAFF Huntsville, Alabama
WAGA-TV Atlanta, Georgia
WAGM-TV Presque Isle, Maine
WAGT Augusta, Georgia
WAGV Harlan, Kentucky
WAIQ Montgomery, Alabama
WAKA Selma, Alabama
WALA-TV Mobile, Alabama
WALB Albany, Georgia
WAND Decatur, Illinois
WANE-TV Fort Wayne, Indiana
WAOE Peoria, Illinois
WAOW Wausau, Wisconsin
WAPA-TV San Juan, Puerto Rico
WAPT Jackson, Mississippi
WAQP Saginaw, Michigan
WATC-DT Atlanta, Georgia
WATE-TV Knoxville, Tennessee
WATL Atlanta, Georgia
WATM-TV Altoona, Pennsylvania
WAVE Louisville, Kentucky
WAVY-TV Portsmouth, Virginia
WAWD Fort Walton Beach, Florida
WAWS Jacksonville, Florida
WAWV-TV Terre Haute, Indiana
WAXN-TV Kannapolis, North Carolina
WBAL-TV Baltimore, Maryland
WBAY-TV Green Bay, Wisconsin
WBBH-TV Fort Myers, Florida
WBBJ-TV Jackson, Tennessee
WBBM-TV Chicago, Illinois
WBBZ-TV Springville, New York
WBCC Cocoa, Florida
WBDT Springfield, Ohio
WBEC-TV Boca Raton, Florida
WBFF Baltimore, Maryland
WBFS-TV Miami, Florida
WBGU-TV Bowling Green, Ohio
WBIF Marianna, Florida
WBIH Selma, Alabama
WBIN-TV Derry, New Hampshire
WBIQ Birmingham, Alabama
WBIR-TV Knoxville, Tennessee
WBKB-TV Alpena, Michigan
WBKI-TV Campbellsville, Kentucky
WBKO Bowling Green, Kentucky
WBKP Calumet, Michigan
WBMM Tuskegee, Alabama
WBNA Louisville, Kentucky
WBNG-TV Binghamton, New York
WBNS-TV Columbus, Ohio
WBNX-TV Akron, Ohio
WBOC-TV Salisbury, Maryland
WBOY-TV Clarksburg, West Virginia
WBPH-TV Bethlehem, Pennsylvania
WBPX-TV Boston, Massachusetts
WBRA-TV Roanoke, Virginia
WBRC Birmingham, Alabama
WBRE-TV Wilkes-Barre, Pennsylvania
WBRZ-TV Baton Rouge, Louisiana
WBSF Bay City, Michigan
WBTV Charlotte, North Carolina
WBTW Florence, South Carolina
WBUI Decatur, Illinois
WBUP Ishpeming, Michigan
WBUW Janesville, Wisconsin
WBUY-TV Holly Springs, Mississippi
WBXX-TV/DT Crossville, Tennessee
WBZ-TV Boston, Massachusetts
WCAU Philadelphia, Pennsylvania
WCAV Charlottesville, Virginia
WCAX-TV Burlington, Vermont
WCBB Augusta, Maine
WCBD-TV Charleston, South Carolina
WCBI-TV Columbus, Mississippi
WCBS-TV New York, New York
WCCB Charlotte, North Carolina
WCCO-TV Minneapolis, Minnesota
WCCT-TV Waterbury, Connecticut
WCCU Urbana, Illinois
WCCV-TV Arecibo, Puerto Rico
WCDC-TV Adams, New York
WCES-TV Wrens, Georgia
WCET Cincinnati, Ohio
WCFE-TV Plattsburgh, New York
WCFT-TV Tuscaloosa, Alabama
WCGV-TV Milwaukee, Wisconsin
WCHS-TV Charleston, West Virginia
WCIA Champaign, Illinois
WCIQ Mount Cheaha, Alabama
WCIU-TV Chicago, Illinois
WCIV Charleston, South Carolina
WCIX Springfield, Illinois
WCJB-TV Gainesville, Florida
WCLF Clearwater, Florida
WCLJ-TV Bloomington, Indiana
WCMH-TV Columbus, Ohio
WCML Alpena, Michigan
WCMU-TV Mount Pleasant, Michigan
WCMV Cadillac, Michigan
WCMW Manistee, Michigan
WCNC-TV Charlotte, North Carolina
WCNY-TV Syracuse, New York
WCOV-TV Montgomery, Alabama
WCPB Salisbury, Maryland
WCPO-TV Cincinnati, Ohio
WCPX-TV Chicago, Illinois
WCSC-TV Charleston, South Carolina
WCSH Portland, Maine
WCTE Cookeville, Tennessee
WCTI-TV New Bern, North Carolina
WCTV Thomasville, Georgia
WCTX New Haven, Connecticut
WCVB-TV Boston, Massachusetts
WCVE-TV Richmond, Virginia
WCVI-TV Christiansted, Virgin Islands
WCVN-TV Covington, Kentucky
WCVW Richmond, Virginia
WCWF Suring, Wisconsin
WCWG Lexington, North Carolina
WCWJ Jacksonville, Florida
WCWN Schenectady, New York
WCYB-TV Bristol, Virginia
WDAF-TV Kansas City, Missouri
WDAM-TV Laurel, Mississippi
WDAY-TV Fargo, North Dakota
WDAZ-TV Devil's Lake, North Dakota
WDBB Bessemer, Alabama
WDBD Jackson, Mississippi
WDBJ Roanoke, Virginia
WDCA Washington, District of Columbia
WDCQ-TV Bad Axe, Michigan
WDCW Washington, District of Columbia
WDEF-TV Chattanooga, Tennessee
WDFX-TV Ozark, Alabama
WDHN Dothan, Alabama
WDHS Iron Mountain, Michigan
WDIO-DT Duluth, Minnesota
WDIQ Dozier, Alabama
WDJT-TV Milwaukee, Wisconsin
WDKA Paducah, Kentucky
WDKY-TV Danville, Kentucky
WDLI-TV Canton, Ohio
WDPB Seaford, Delaware
WDPX-TV Vineyard Haven, Rhode Island
WDRB Louisville, Kentucky
WDSC-TV New Smyrna Beach, Florida
WDSE Duluth, Minnesota
WDSI-TV Chattanooga, Tennessee
WDSU New Orleans, Louisiana
WDTI Indianapolis, Indiana
WDTN Dayton, Ohio
WDTV Weston, West Virginia
WDWL Bayamon, Puerto Rico
WEAO Akron, Ohio
WEAR-TV Pensacola, Florida
WEAU-TV Eau Claire, Wisconsin
WEBA-TV Allendale, South Carolina
WECN Naranjito, Puerto Rico
WECT Wilmington, North Carolina
WEDH Hartford, Connecticut
WEDN Norwich, Connecticut
WEDU Tampa, Florida
WEDW Bridgeport, Connecticut
WEDY New Haven, Connecticut
WEEK-TV Peoria, Illinois
WEFC-TV Danville, Virginia
WEHT Evansville, Indiana
WEIQ Mobile, Alabama
WEIU-TV Charleston, Illinois
WEKW-TV Keene, New Hampshire
WELF-TV Dalton, Georgia
WELU Aguadilla, Puerto Rico
WEMT Greeneville, Tennessee
WENH-TV Durham, New Hampshire
WENY-TV Elmira, New York
WEPX-TV Greenville, North Carolina
WESH Daytona Beach, Florida
WETA-TV Washington, District of Columbia
WETK Burlington, Vermont
WETM-TV Elmira, New York
WETP-TV Sneedville, Tennessee
WEUX Chippewa Falls, Wisconsin
WEVV-TV Evansville, Indiana
WEWS-TV Cleveland, Ohio
WEYI-TV Saginaw, Michigan
WFAA Dallas, Texas
WFBD Destin, Florida
WFBT Bath, New York
WFDC-DT Arlington, District of Columbia
WFFF-TV Burlington, Vermont
WFFT-TV Fort Wayne, Indiana
WFGC Palm Beach, Florida
WFGX Fort Walton Beach, Florida
WFIE Evansville, Indiana
WFIQ Florence, Alabama
WFLA-TV Tampa, Florida
WFLD Chicago, Illinois
WFLI-TV Cleveland, Tennessee
WFLX West Palm Beach, Florida
WFME-TV West Milford, New Jersey
WFMJ-TV Youngstown, Ohio
WFMY-TV Greensboro, North Carolina
WFMZ-TV Allentown, Pennsylvania
WFNA Gulf Shores, Alabama
WFOR-TV Miami, Florida
WFPT Frederick, Maryland
WFPX-TV Fayetteville, North Carolina
WFQX-TV Cadillac, Michigan
WFRV-TV Green Bay, Wisconsin
WFSB Hartford, Connecticut
WFSG Panama City, Florida
WFSU-TV Tallahassee, Florida
WFTC Minneapolis, Minnesota
WFTS-TV Tampa, Florida
WFTT-DT Tampa, Florida
WFTV Orlando, Florida
WFTX-TV Cape Coral, Florida
WFTY-DT Smithtown, New York
WFUM Flint, Michigan
WFUP Vanderbilt, Michigan
WFUT-DT Newark, New York
WFWA Fort Wayne, Indiana
WFXB Myrtle Beach, South Carolina
WFXG Augusta, Georgia
WFXI Morehead City, North Carolina
WFXL Albany, Georgia
WFXP Erie, Pennsylvania
WFXR Roanoke, Virginia
WFXT Boston, Massachusetts
WFXU Live Oak, Florida
WFXV Utica, New York
WFYI Indianapolis, Indiana
WGAL Lancaster, Pennsylvania
WGBA-TV Green Bay, Wisconsin
WGBC Meridian, Mississippi
WGBH Boston, Massachusetts
WGBH-TV Boston, Massachusetts
WGBY-TV Springfield, Massachusetts
WGCB-TV Red Lion, Pennsylvania
WGCL-TV Atlanta, Georgia
WGCU Fort Myers, Florida
WGEM-TV Quincy, Illinois
WGEN-TV Key West, Florida
WGFL High Springs, Florida
WGGB-TV Springfield, Massachusetts
WGGN-TV Sandusky, Ohio
WGGS-TV Greenville, South Carolina
WGHP High Point, North Carolina
WGIQ Louisville, Alabama
WGMB-TV Baton Rouge, Louisiana
WGME-TV Portland, Maine
WGN Chicago, Illinois
WGNM Macon, Georgia
WGNO New Orleans, Louisiana
WGNT Portsmouth, Virginia
WGPT Oakland, Maryland
WGPX-TV Burlington, North Carolina
WGRZ Buffalo, New York
WGSA Baxley, Georgia

WGTE-TV Toledo, Ohio
WGTQ Sault Ste. Marie, Michigan
WGTU Traverse City, Michigan
WGTV Athens, Georgia
WGTV Watertown, New York
WGTW-TV Burlington, New Jersey
WGVK Kalamazoo, Michigan
WGVU-TV Grand Rapids, Michigan
WGXA Macon, Georgia
WHA-TV Madison, Wisconsin
WHAG-TV Hagerstown, Maryland
WHAM-TV Rochester, New York
WHAS-TV Louisville, Kentucky
WHBF-TV Rock Island, Illinois
WHBQ-TV Memphis, Tennessee
WHBR Pensacola, Florida
WHDF Florence, Alabama
WHDH Boston, Massachusetts
WHEC-TV Rochester, New York
WHFT-TV Miami, Florida
WHIO-TV Dayton, Ohio
WHIQ Huntsville, Alabama
WHIZ-TV Zanesville, Ohio
WHKY-TV Hickory, North Carolina
WHLA-TV La Crosse, Wisconsin
WHLT Hattiesburg, Mississippi
WHMB-TV Indianapolis, Indiana
WHMC Conway, South Carolina
WHME-TV South Bend, Indiana
WHNO New Orleans, Louisiana
WHNS Greenville, South Carolina
WHNT-TV Huntsville, Alabama
WHO-DT Des Moines, Missouri
WHOI Peoria, Illinois
WHP-TV Harrisburg, Pennsylvania
WHPX-TV New London, Connecticut
WHRM-TV Wausau, Wisconsin
WHRO-TV Hampton-Norfolk, Virginia
WHSG-TV Monroe, Georgia
WHSV-TV Harrisonburg, Virginia
WHTJ Charlottesville, Virginia
WHTM-TV Harrisburg, Pennsylvania
WHTN Murfreesboro, Tennessee
WHTV Jackson, Michigan
WHUT-TV Washington, District of Columbia
WHWC-TV Menomonie, Wisconsin
WHYY-TV Wilmington, Delaware
WIAT Birmingham, Alabama
WIBW-TV Topeka, Kansas
WICD Champaign, Illinois
WICU-TV Erie, Pennsylvania
WICZ-TV Binghamton, New York
WIDP Guayama, Puerto Rico
WIFR Freeport, Illinois
WIIQ Demopolis, Alabama
WILL-TV Urbana, Illinois
WILX-TV Onondaga, Michigan
WINK-TV Fort Myers, Florida
WINM Angola, Indiana
WINP-TV Pittsburgh, Pennsylvania
WIPB Muncie, Indiana
WIPM-TV Mayaguez, Puerto Rico
WIPR-TV San Juan, Puerto Rico
WIPX-TV Bloomington, Indiana
WIRS Yauco, Puerto Rico
WIRT Hibbing, Minnesota
WIS Columbia, South Carolina
WISC-TV Madison, Wisconsin
WISE-TV Fort Wayne, Indiana
WISH-TV Indianapolis, Indiana
WISN-TV Milwaukee, Wisconsin
WITF-TV Harrisburg, Pennsylvania
WITI Milwaukee, Wisconsin
WITN-TV Washington, North Carolina
WITV Charleston, South Carolina
WIVB-TV Buffalo, New York
WIVT Binghamton, New York
WJAC-TV Johnstown, Pennsylvania
WJAL Hagerstown, Maryland
WJAR Providence, Rhode Island
WJBF Augusta, Georgia
WJBK Detroit, Michigan
WJCL Savannah, Georgia
WJCT Jacksonville, Florida
WJEB-TV Jacksonville, Florida
WJET-TV Erie, Pennsylvania
WJFB Lebanon, Tennessee
WJFW-TV Rhinelander, Wisconsin
WJHG-TV Panama City, Florida
WJHL-TV Johnson City, Tennessee
WJKT Jackson, Tennessee

WJLA-TV Washington, District of Columbia
WJMN-TV Escanaba, Michigan
WJPM-TV Florence, South Carolina
WJPX San Juan, Puerto Rico
WJRT-TV Flint, Michigan
WJSP-TV Columbus, Georgia
WJSU-TV Anniston, Alabama
WJTC Pensacola, Florida
WJTV Jackson, Mississippi
WJW Cleveland, Ohio
WJWJ-TV Beaufort, South Carolina
WJWN-TV San Sebastian, Puerto Rico
WJXT Jacksonville, Florida
WJXX Orange Park, Florida
WJYS Hammond, Illinois
WJZ-TV Baltimore, Maryland
WJZY Belmont, North Carolina
WKAQ-TV San Juan, Puerto Rico
WKAR-TV East Lansing, Michigan
WKAS Ashland, Kentucky
WKBD-TV Detroit, Michigan
WKBN-TV Youngstown, Ohio
WKBS-TV Altoona, Pennsylvania
WKBT La Crosse, Wisconsin
WKBW-TV Buffalo, New York
WKCF Clermont, Florida
WKDH Houston, Mississippi
WKEF Dayton, Ohio
WKGB-TV Bowling Green, Kentucky
WKHA Hazard, Kentucky
WKLE Lexington, Kentucky
WKMA-TV Madisonville, Indiana
WKMG-TV Orlando, Florida
WKMJ-TV Louisville, Kentucky
WKMR Morehead, Kentucky
WKMU Murray, Kentucky
WKNO Memphis, Tennessee
WKOH Owensboro, Kentucky
WKOI-TV Richmond, Indiana
WKON Owenton, Kentucky
WKOP-TV Knoxville, Tennessee
WKOW Madison, Wisconsin
WKPC-TV Louisville, Kentucky
WKPD Paducah, Kentucky
WKPI-TV Pikeville, West Virginia
WKPT-TV Kingsport, Tennessee
WKPV Ponce, Puerto Rico
WKRC-TV Cincinnati, Ohio
WKRG-TV Mobile, Alabama
WKRN-TV Nashville, Tennessee
WKSO-TV Somerset, Kentucky
WKTC Sumter, South Carolina
WKTV Utica, New York
WKYC-DT Cleveland, Ohio
WKYT-TV Lexington, Kentucky
WKYU-TV Bowling Green, Kentucky
WKZT-TV Elizabethtown, Kentucky
WLAE-TV New Orleans, Louisiana
WLAJ Lansing, Michigan
WLAX La Crosse, Wisconsin
WLBT Jackson, Mississippi
WLBZ Bangor, Maine
WLED-TV Littleton, New Hampshire
WLEF-TV Park Falls, Wisconsin
WLEX-TV Lexington, Kentucky
WLFB Bluefield, West Virginia
WLFG Grundy, Virginia
WLFI-TV Lafayette, Indiana
WLFL Raleigh, North Carolina
WLGA Opelika, Alabama
WLII Caguas, Puerto Rico
WLIO Lima, Ohio
WLIW Garden City, New York
WLJC-TV Beattyville, Kentucky
WLJT-DT Lexington, Tennessee
WLKY-TV Louisville, Kentucky
WLLA Kalamazoo, Michigan
WLMB Toledo, Ohio
WLMT Memphis, Tennessee
WLNE-TV New Bedford, Rhode Island
WLNS-TV Lansing, Michigan
WLNY-TV Riverhead, New York
WLOS Asheville, North Carolina
WLOV-TV West Point, Mississippi
WLOX Biloxi, Mississippi
WLPB-TV Baton Rouge, Louisiana
WLPX-TV Charleston, West Virginia
WLRN-TV Miami, Florida
WLS-TV Chicago, Illinois
WLTV-DT Miami, Florida
WLTX Columbia, South Carolina

WLTZ Columbus, Georgia
WLUC-TV Marquette, Michigan
WLUK-TV Green Bay, Wisconsin
WLVI Cambridge, Massachusetts
WLVT-TV Allentown, Pennsylvania
WLWC New Bedford, Massachusetts
WLWT Cincinnati, Ohio
WLXI Greensboro, North Carolina
WLYH-TV Lancaster, Pennsylvania
WMAB-TV Mississippi State, Mississippi
WMAE-TV Booneville, Mississippi
WMAH-TV Biloxi, Mississippi
WMAI Cleveland, Mississippi
WMAK Knoxville, Tennessee
WMAO-TV Greenwood, Mississippi
WMAQ-TV Chicago, Illinois
WMAR-TV Baltimore, Maryland
WMAU-TV Bude, Mississippi
WMAV-TV Oxford, Mississippi
WMAW-TV Meridian, Mississippi
WMAZ-TV Macon, Georgia
WMBB Panama City, Florida
WMBC-TV Newton, New Jersey
WMBD-TV Peoria, Illinois
WMBF-TV Myrtle Beach, South Carolina
WMC-TV Memphis, Tennessee
WMCF-TV Montgomery, Alabama
WMCN-TV Atlantic City, New Jersey
WMDN Meridian, Mississippi
WMDT Salisbury, Maryland
WMEA-TV Biddeford, Maine
WMEB-TV Orono, Maine
WMEC Macomb, Illinois
WMED-TV Calais, Maine
WMEI Arecibo, Puerto Rico
WMEM-TV Presque Isle, Maine
WMFD-TV Mansfield, Ohio
WMFE-TV Orlando, Florida
WMFP Lawrence, Massachusetts
WMGM-TV Wildwood, New Jersey
WMGT-TV Macon, Georgia
WMHT Schenectady, New York
WMLW-TV Racine, Wisconsin
WMMP Charleston, South Carolina
WMOW Crandon, Wisconsin
WMPB Baltimore, Maryland
WMPN-TV Jackson, Mississippi
WMPT Annapolis, Maryland
WMPV-TV Mobile, Alabama
WMSN-TV Madison, Wisconsin
WMSY-TV Marion, Virginia
WMTJ Fajardo, Puerto Rico
WMTV Madison, Wisconsin
WMTW Poland Spring, Maine
WMUM-TV Cochran, Georgia
WMUR-TV Manchester, New Hampshire
WMVS Milwaukee, Wisconsin
WMVT Milwaukee, Wisconsin
WMYA-TV Anderson, South Carolina
WMYD Detroit, Michigan
WMYO Salem, Indiana
WMYT-TV Rock Hill, South Carolina
WMYV Greensboro, North Carolina
WNAB Nashville, Tennessee
WNAC-TV Providence, Rhode Island
WNBC New York, New York
WNBW-DT Gainesville, Florida
WNCF Montgomery, Alabama
WNCN Goldsboro, North Carolina
WNCT-TV Greenville, North Carolina
WNDU-TV South Bend, Indiana
WNDY-TV Marion, Indiana
WNED-TV Buffalo, New York
WNEH Greenwood, South Carolina
WNEM-TV Bay City, Michigan
WNEO Alliance, Ohio
WNEP-TV Scranton, Pennsylvania
WNET Newark, New Jersey
WNEU Merrimack, New Hampshire
WNGH-TV Chatsworth, Georgia
WNIN Evansville, Indiana
WNIT South Bend, Indiana
WNJB New Brunswick, New Jersey
WNJN Montclair, New Jersey
WNJS Camden, New Jersey
WNJT Trenton, New Jersey
WNJU Linden, New Jersey
WNJX-TV Mayaguez, Puerto Rico
WNKY Bowling Green, Kentucky
WNLO Buffalo, New York
WNMN Saranac Lake, New York

WNMU Marquette, Michigan
WNNE Hartford, Vermont
WNOL-TV New Orleans, Louisiana
WNPB-TV Morgantown, West Virginia
WNPI Norwood, New York
WNPT Nashville, Tennessee
WNPX-TV Cookeville, Tennessee
WNSC-TV Rock Hill, South Carolina
WNTV Greenville, South Carolina
WNTZ-TV Natchez, Mississippi
WNUV Baltimore, Maryland
WNVC Fairfax, Virginia
WNVT Goldvein, Virginia
WNWO-TV Toledo, Ohio
WNYA Pittsfield, Massachusetts
WNYB Jamestown, New York
WNYE-TV New York, New York
WNYI Ithaca, New York
WNYO-TV Buffalo, New York
WNYS-TV Syracuse, New York
WNYT Albany, New York
WNYW New York, New York
WOAI-TV San Antonio, Texas
WOAY-TV Oak Hill, West Virginia
WOFL Orlando, Florida
WOGX Ocala, Florida
WOI-TV Ames, Missouri
WOIO Shaker Heights, Ohio
WOLE-DT Aguadilla, Puerto Rico
WOLF-TV Hazleton, Pennsylvania
WOLO-TV Columbia, South Carolina
WOOD-TV Grand Rapids, Michigan
WOPX-TV Melbourne, Florida
WORA-TV Mayaguez, Puerto Rico
WOST Mayaguez, Puerto Rico
WOSU-TV Columbus, Ohio
WOTF-DT Melbourne, Florida
WOTV Battle Creek, Michigan
WOUB-TV Athens, Ohio
WOUC-TV Cambridge, Ohio
WOWK-TV Huntington, West Virginia
WOWT Omaha, Nebraska
WPAN Fort Walton Beach, Florida
WPBA Atlanta, Georgia
WPBF Tequesta, Florida
WPBN-TV Traverse City, Michigan
WPBO Portsmouth, Ohio
WPBT Miami, Florida
WPBY-TV Charleston, West Virginia
WPCB-TV Greensburg, Pennsylvania
WPCH-TV Atlanta, Georgia
WPCT Panama City Beach, Florida
WPCW Jeannette, Pennsylvania
WPDE-TV Florence, South Carolina
WPEC West Palm Beach, Florida
WPFO Waterville, Maine
WPGA-TV Perry, Georgia
WPGD-TV Hendersonville, Tennessee
WPGH-TV Pittsburgh, Pennsylvania
WPGX Panama City, Florida
WPHL-TV Philadelphia, Pennsylvania
WPIX New York, New York
WPLG Miami, Florida
WPME Lewiston, Maine
WPMI-TV Mobile, Alabama
WPMT York, Pennsylvania
WPMY Pittsburgh, Pennsylvania
WPNE Green Bay, Wisconsin
WPPX-TV Wilmington, Pennsylvania
WPRI-TV Providence, Rhode Island
WPSD-TV Paducah, Kentucky
WPSG Philadelphia, Pennsylvania
WPSU-TV Clearfield, Pennsylvania
WPTA Fort Wayne, Indiana
WPTD Dayton, Ohio
WPTO Oxford, Ohio
WPTV-TV West Palm Beach, Florida
WPTY-TV Memphis, Tennessee
WPTZ North Pole, New York
WPVI-TV Philadelphia, Pennsylvania
WPWR-TV Gary, Indiana
WPXA-TV Rome, Georgia
WPXC-TV Brunswick, Georgia
WPXD-TV Ann Arbor, Michigan
WPXE-TV Kenosha, Wisconsin
WPXG-TV Concord, Massachusetts
WPXH-TV Gadsden, Alabama
WPXI Pittsburgh, Pennsylvania
WPXJ-TV Batavia, New York
WPXK-TV Jellico, Tennessee
WPXL-TV New Orleans, Louisiana
WPXM-TV Miami, Florida
WPXN-TV New York, New York
WPXP-TV Lake Worth, Florida
WPXQ-TV Block Island, Rhode Island
WPXR-TV Roanoke, Virginia
WPXS Mount Vernon, Illinois
WPXT Portland, Maine
WPXU-TV Jacksonville, North Carolina
WPXV-TV Norfolk, Virginia
WPXW-TV Manassas, District of Columbia
WPXX-TV Memphis, Tennessee
WQAD-TV Moline, Illinois
WQCW Portsmouth, Ohio
WQEC Quincy, Illinois
WQED Pittsburgh, Pennsylvania
WQHA Aguada, Puerto Rico
WQHS-DT Cleveland, Ohio
WQLN Erie, Pennsylvania
WQMY Williamsport, Pennsylvania
WQOW-DT Eau Claire, Wisconsin
WQPT-TV Moline, Illinois
WQPX-TV Scranton, Pennsylvania
WQRF-TV Rockford, Illinois
WQTO Ponce, Puerto Rico
WRAL-TV Raleigh, North Carolina
WRAY-TV Wilson, North Carolina
WRAZ Raleigh, North Carolina
WRBJ Magee, Mississippi
WRBL Columbus, Georgia
WRBU East St. Louis, Illinois
WRBW Orlando, Florida
WRC-TV Washington, District of Columbia
WRCB-DT Chattanooga, Tennessee
WRDC Durham, North Carolina
WRDQ Orlando, Florida
WRDW-TV Augusta, Georgia
WREG-TV Memphis, Tennessee
WRET-TV Spartanburg, South Carolina
WREX-TV Rockford, Illinois
WRFB Carolina, Puerto Rico
WRGB Schenectady, New York
WRGT-TV Dayton, Ohio
WRIC-TV Petersburg, Virginia
WRJA-TV Sumter, South Carolina
WRJM Troy, Alabama
WRLH-TV Richmond, Virginia
WRLK-TV Columbia, South Carolina
WRLM Canton, Ohio
WRNN-TV Kingston, New York
WROC-TV Rochester, New York
WRPX-TV Rocky Mount, North Carolina
WRSP-TV Springfield, Illinois
WRTV Indianapolis, Indiana
WRUA Fajardo, Puerto Rico
WRXY-TV Tice, Florida
WSAV-TV Savannah, Georgia
WSAW-TV Wausau, Wisconsin
WSAZ-TV Huntington, West Virginia
WSB-TV Atlanta, Georgia
WSBE-TV Providence, Rhode Island
WSBK-TV Boston, Massachusetts
WSBN-TV Norton, Virginia
WSBS-TV Key West, Florida
WSBT-TV South Bend, Indiana
WSCV Fort Lauderdale, Florida
WSEC Jacksonville, Illinois
WSEE-TV Erie, Pennsylvania
WSET-TV Lynchburg, Virginia
WSFA Montgomery, Alabama
WSFJ-TV Newark, Ohio
WSFL-TV Miami, Florida
WSFX-TV Wilmington, North Carolina
WSIL-TV Harrisburg, Illinois
WSIU-TV Carbondale, Illinois
WSJU-TV San Juan, Puerto Rico
WSJV Elkhart, Indiana
WSKA Corning, New York
WSKG-TV Binghamton, New York
WSKY-TV Manteo, North Carolina
WSLS-TV Roanoke, Virginia
WSMH Flint, Michigan
WSMV-TV Nashville, Tennessee
WSNS-TV Chicago, Illinois
WSOC-TV Charlotte, North Carolina
WSPA-TV Spartanburg, South Carolina
WSPX-TV Syracuse, New York
WSRE Pensacola, Florida
WSST-TV Cordele, Georgia
WSTE-DT Ponce, Puerto Rico
WSTM-TV Syracuse, New York
WSTR-TV Cincinnati, Ohio
WSUR-DT Ponce, Puerto Rico
WSVI Christiansted, Virgin Islands
WSVN Miami, Florida
WSWB Scranton, Pennsylvania
WSWG Valdosta, Georgia
WSWP-TV Grandview, West Virginia
WSYM-TV Lansing, Michigan
WSYR-TV Syracuse, New York
WSYT Syracuse, New York
WSYX Columbus, Ohio
WTAE-TV Pittsburgh, Pennsylvania
WTAJ-TV Altoona, Pennsylvania
WTAP-TV Parkersburg, West Virginia
WTAT-TV Charleston, South Carolina
WTBY-TV Poughkeepsie, New York
WTCE-TV Fort Pierce, Florida
WTCI Chattanooga, Tennessee
WTCT Marion, Illinois
WTCV San Juan, Puerto Rico
WTEN Albany, New York
WTEV-TV Jacksonville, Florida
WTGL Cocoa, Florida
WTGS Hardeeville, South Carolina
WTHI-TV Terre Haute, Indiana
WTHR Indianapolis, Indiana
WTIC-TV Hartford, Connecticut
WTIN-TV Ponce, Puerto Rico
WTIU Bloomington, Indiana
WTJP-TV Gadsden, Alabama
WTJR Quincy, Illinois
WTJX-TV Charlotte Amalie, Virgin Islands
WTKR Norfolk, Virginia
WTLF Tallahassee, Florida
WTLH Bainbridge, Georgia
WTLJ Muskegon, Michigan
WTLV Jacksonville, Florida
WTLW Lima, Ohio
WTMJ-TV Milwaukee, Wisconsin
WTNH New Haven, Connecticut
WTNZ Knoxville, Tennessee
WTOC-TV Savannah, Georgia
WTOG St. Petersburg, Florida
WTOK-TV Meridian, Mississippi
WTOL Toledo, Ohio
WTOM-TV Cheboygan, Michigan
WTOV-TV Steubenville, Ohio
WTPC-TV Virginia Beach, Virginia
WTPX-TV Antigo, Wisconsin
WTRF-TV Wheeling, West Virginia
WTSF Ashland, Kentucky
WTSP St. Petersburg, Florida
WTTA St. Petersburg, Florida
WTTE Columbus, Ohio
WTTG Washington, District of Columbia
WTTK Kokomo, Indiana
WTTO Homewood, Alabama
WTTV Bloomington, Indiana
WTTW Chicago, Illinois
WTVA Tupelo, Mississippi
WTVC Chattanooga, Tennessee
WTVD Durham, North Carolina
WTVE Reading, Pennsylvania
WTVF Nashville, Tennessee
WTVG Toledo, Ohio
WTVH Syracuse, New York
WTVI Charlotte, North Carolina
WTVJ Miami, Florida
WTVM Columbus, Georgia
WTVO Rockford, Illinois
WTVP Peoria, Illinois
WTVQ-DT Lexington, Kentucky
WTVR-TV Richmond, Virginia
WTVS Detroit, Michigan
WTVT Tampa, Florida
WTVW Evansville, Indiana
WTVX Fort Pierce, Florida
WTVY Dothan, Alabama
WTVZ-TV Norfolk, Virginia
WTWC-TV Tallahassee, Florida
WTWO Terre Haute, Indiana
WTXF-TV Philadelphia, Pennsylvania
WTXL-TV Tallahassee, Florida
WUAB Lorain, Ohio
WUCW Minneapolis, Minnesota
WUFT Gainesville, Florida
WUFX Vicksburg, Mississippi
WUGA-TV Toccoa, Georgia
WUHF Rochester, New York
WUJA Caguas, Puerto Rico
WUNC-TV Chapel Hill, North Carolina
WUND-TV Edenton, North Carolina

WUNE-TV Linville, North Carolina
WUNF-TV Asheville, North Carolina
WUNG-TV Concord, North Carolina
WUNI Worcester, Massachusetts
WUNJ-TV Wilmington, North Carolina
WUNK-TV Greenville, North Carolina
WUNL-TV Winston-Salem, North Carolina
WUNM-TV Jacksonville, North Carolina
WUNP-TV Roanoke Rapids, North Carolina
WUNU Lumberton, North Carolina
WUOA Tuscaloosa, Alabama
WUPA Atlanta, Georgia
WUPL Slidell, Louisiana
WUPV Ashland, Virginia
WUPW Toledo, Ohio
WUPX-TV Morehead, Kentucky
WUSA Washington, District of Columbia
WUSF-TV Tampa, Florida
WUSI-TV Olney, Illinois
WUTB Baltimore, Maryland
WUTF-DT Marlborough, Massachusetts
WUTR Utica, New York
WUTV Buffalo, New York
WUVC-DT Fayetteville, North Carolina
WUVG-DT Athens, Georgia
WUVN Hartford, Connecticut
WUVP-DT Vineland, Pennsylvania
WUXP-TV Nashville, Tennessee
WVAH-TV Charleston, West Virginia
WVAN-TV Savannah, Georgia
WVBT Virginia Beach, Virginia
WVCY-TV Milwaukee, Wisconsin
WVEA-TV Venice, Florida
WVEC Hampton, Virginia
WVEN-TV Daytona Beach, Florida
WVEO Aguadilla, Puerto Rico
WVER Rutland, Vermont
WVFX Clarksburg, West Virginia
WVIA-TV Scranton, Pennsylvania
WVII-TV Bangor, Maine
WVIR-TV Charlottesville, Virginia
WVIT New Britain, Connecticut
WVIZ Cleveland, Ohio
WVLA-TV Baton Rouge, Louisiana
WVLR Tazewell, Tennessee
WVLT-TV Knoxville, Tennessee
WVNS-TV Lewisburg, West Virginia
WVNY Burlington, Vermont
WVOZ-TV Ponce, Puerto Rico
WVPT Staunton, Virginia
WVPX-TV Akron, Ohio
WVPY Front Royal, Virginia
WVTA Windsor, Vermont
WVTB St. Johnsbury, Vermont
WVTM-TV Birmingham, Alabama
WVTV Milwaukee, Wisconsin
WVUE-DT New Orleans, Louisiana
WVUT Vincennes, Indiana
WVVA Bluefield, West Virginia
WVXF Charlotte Amalie, Virgin Islands
WWAY Wilmington, North Carolina
WWBT Richmond, Virginia
WWCP-TV Johnstown, Pennsylvania
WWCW Lynchburg, Virginia
WWDP Norwell, Massachusetts
WWHO Chillicothe, Ohio
WWJ-TV Detroit, Michigan
WWJX Jackson, Mississippi
WWL-TV New Orleans, Louisiana
WWLP Springfield, Massachusetts
WWMB Florence, South Carolina
WWMT Kalamazoo, Michigan
WWNY-TV Carthage, New York
WWOR-TV Secaucus, New Jersey
WWPB Hagerstown, Maryland
WWPX-TV Martinsburg, District of Columbia
WWRS-TV Mayville, Wisconsin
WWSB Sarasota, Florida
WWSI Atlantic City, New Jersey
WWTI Watertown, New York
WWTO-TV La Salle, Illinois
WWTV Cadillac, Michigan
WWUP-TV Sault Ste. Marie, Michigan
WXCW Naples, Florida
WXEL-TV West Palm Beach, Florida
WXFT-DT Aurora, Illinois
WXGA-TV Waycross, Georgia
WXIA-TV Atlanta, Georgia
WXII-TV Winston-Salem, North Carolina
WXIN Indianapolis, Indiana
WXIX-TV Newport, Kentucky
WXLV-TV Winston-Salem, North Carolina
WXMI Grand Rapids, Michigan
WXOW La Crosse, Wisconsin
WXPX-TV Bradenton, Florida
WXTV-DT Paterson, New York
WXTX Columbus, Georgia
WXVT Greenville, Mississippi
WXXA-TV Albany, New York
WXXI-TV Rochester, New York
WXXV-TV Gulfport, Mississippi
WXYZ-TV Detroit, Michigan
WYBE Philadelphia, Pennsylvania
WYCC Chicago, Illinois
WYCW Asheville, North Carolina
WYDC Corning, New York
WYDN Worcester, Massachusetts
WYDO Greenville, North Carolina
WYES-TV New Orleans, Louisiana
WYFF Greenville, South Carolina
WYIN Gary, Indiana
WYMT-TV Hazard, Kentucky
WYOU Scranton, Pennsylvania
WYOW Eagle River, Wisconsin
WYPX-TV Amsterdam, New York
WYTV Youngstown, Ohio
WYZZ-TV Bloomington, Illinois
WZDX Huntsville, Alabama
WZME Bridgeport, Connecticut
WZMQ Marquette, Michigan
WZPX-TV Battle Creek, Michigan
WZRB Columbia, South Carolina
WZTV Nashville, Tennessee
WZVI Charlotte Amalie, Virgin Islands
WZVN-TV Naples, Florida
WZZM Grand Rapids, Michigan
XETV-DT Tijuana, California
XEWT-DT Tijuana, California
XHIJ-DT Ciudad Juarez, Texas

US Television Stations by Digital Channel

Channel 2

KJWY Jackson, Wyoming
KNOP-TV North Platte, Nebraska
KOTA-TV Rapid City, South Dakota
KREX-TV Grand Junction, Colorado
KSNV-DT Las Vegas, Nevada
WLBZ Bangor, Maine

Channel 3

KVNV Ely, Nevada
KDLO-TV Florence, South Dakota
KIEM-TV Eureka, California
KYUS-TV Miles City, Montana
WBRA-TV Roanoke, Virginia
WSBS-TV Key West, Florida
KCBU-DT Price, Utah

Channel 4

WHBF-TV Rock Island, Illinois
WACP Atlantic City, New Jersey

Channel 5

KCWX Fredericksburg, Texas
KGTF Hagatna, Puerto Rico
KHAS-TV Hastings, Nebraska
KIVV-TV Lead, South Dakota
KOBI Medford, Oregon
KPXB-TV Conroe, Texas
KVZK-5 Pago Pago, American Samoa
KXGN-TV Glendive, Montana
KXLF-TV Butte, Montana
WBKP Calumet, Michigan
WCYB-TV Bristol, Virginia
WDTV Weston, West Virginia
WGVK Kalamazoo, Michigan
WLMB Toledo, Ohio
WMC-TV Memphis, Tennessee
WOI-TV Ames, Missouri
DWMDE Seaford, Georgia

Channel 6

KWNB-TV Hayes Center, Nebraska
KYES-TV Anchorage, Alaska
WABW-TV Pelham, Georgia
WCES-TV Wrens, Georgia
WEDY New Haven, Connecticut
WUOA Tuscaloosa, Alabama
WPVI-TV Philadelphia, Pennsylvania
WRGB Schenectady, New York

Channel 7

KABC-TV Los Angeles, California
KAII-TV Wailuku, Hawaii
KAIL Fresno, California
KCCO-TV Alexandria, Minnesota
KDUH-TV Scottsbluff, Nebraska
KETS Little Rock, Arkansas
KEVN-TV Rapid City, South Dakota
KFXF Fairbanks, Alaska
KGO-TV San Francisco, California
KGWL-TV Lander, Wyoming
KHQA-TV Hannibal, Missouri
KJCT Grand Junction, Colorado
KJRR Jamestown, North Dakota
KLAS-TV Las Vegas, Nevada
KLTV Tyler, Texas
KMGH-TV Denver, Colorado
KMNE-TV Bassett, Nebraska
KOAC-TV Corvallis, Oregon
KOAM-TV Pittsburg, Kansas
KOAT-TV Albuquerque, New Mexico
KOCO-TV Oklahoma City, Oklahoma
KOSA-TV Odessa, Texas
KPAX-TV Missoula, Montana
KPLC Lake Charles, Louisiana
KQCD-TV Dickinson, North Dakota
KQTV St. Joseph, Missouri
KRCR-TV Redding, California
KRNV-DT Reno, Nevada
KRTV Great Falls, Montana
KSPS-TV Spokane, Washington
KTBC Austin, Texas
KTNL-TV Sitka, Alaska
KTTW Sioux Falls, South Dakota
KTVB Boise, Idaho
KAZT-TV Prescott, Arizona
KVIA-TV El Paso, Texas
KVII-TV Amarillo, Texas
KWWL Waterloo, Iowa
WABC-TV New York, New York
WBNG-TV Binghamton, New York
WCIQ Mount Cheaha, Alabama
WDAM-TV Laurel, Mississippi
WMUM-TV Cochran, Georgia
WEHT Evansville, Indiana
WFLA-TV Tampa, Florida
WITV Charleston, South Carolina
WJBK Detroit, Michigan
WJCT Jacksonville, Florida
WJHG-TV Panama City, Florida
WJLA-TV Washington, District of Columbia
WLJC-TV Beattyville, Kentucky
WLS-TV Chicago, Illinois
WBBZ-TV Springville, New York
WOOD-TV Grand Rapids, Michigan
WSAW-TV Wausau, Wisconsin
WSPA-TV Spartanburg, South Carolina
WSTE-DT Ponce, Puerto Rico
WSVN Miami, Florida
WTRF-TV Wheeling, West Virginia
WVII-TV Bangor, Maine
WWNY-TV Carthage, New York
WXXA-TV Albany, New York
WMAK Knoxville, Tennessee
WTPC-TV Virginia Beach, Virginia

Channel 8

KAET Phoenix, Arizona
KAIT Jonesboro, Arkansas
KAKM Anchorage, Alaska
KCCI Des Moines, Iowa
KESD-TV Brookings, South Dakota
KFBB-TV Great Falls, Montana
KFMB-TV San Diego, California
KGNS-TV Laredo, Texas
KGW Portland, Oregon
KHON-TV Honolulu, Hawaii
KIFI-TV Idaho Falls, Idaho
KIII Corpus Christi, Texas
KLKN Lincoln, Nebraska
KNOE-TV Monroe, Louisiana
KOBR Roswell, New Mexico
KOLO-TV Reno, Nevada
KOMU-TV Columbia, Missouri
KSBW Salinas, California
KSWK Lakin, Kansas
KSYS Medford, Oregon
KTSC Pueblo, Colorado
KUHT Houston, Texas
KUMV-TV Williston, North Dakota
KUSM-TV Bozeman, Montana
KWET Cheyenne, Oklahoma
KZSD-TV Martin, South Dakota
WACS-TV Dawson, Georgia
WAGM-TV Presque Isle, Maine
WBNA Louisville, Kentucky
WDAZ-TV Devil's Lake, North Dakota
WNPT Nashville, Tennessee
WDHS Iron Mountain, Michigan
WDSE Duluth, Minnesota
WFXI Morehead City, North Carolina
WGAL Lancaster, Pennsylvania
WGTQ Sault Ste. Marie, Michigan
WGTV Athens, Georgia
WICZ-TV Binghamton, New York
WJW Cleveland, Ohio
WKBT La Crosse, Wisconsin
WLIO Lima, Ohio
WMTW Poland Spring, Maine
WMVS Milwaukee, Wisconsin
WNJB New Brunswick, New Jersey
WOLO-TV Columbia, South Carolina
WSIU-TV Carbondale, Illinois
WTVA Tupelo, Mississippi
WVNS-TV Lewisburg, West Virginia
WWCP-TV Johnstown, Pennsylvania
WGEN-TV Key West, Florida
WWMT Kalamazoo, Michigan
WXGA-TV Waycross, Georgia
KNMD-TV Santa Fe, New Mexico
KPTW Casper, Wyoming

Channel 9

KACV-TV Amarillo, Texas
KAFT Fayetteville, Arkansas
KAWE Bemidji, Minnesota
KCWK North Las Vegas, Nevada
KCEN-TV Temple, Texas
KCFW-TV Kalispell, Montana
KCRG-TV Cedar Rapids, Iowa
KCTS-TV Seattle, Washington
KDSE Dickinson, North Dakota
KECY-TV El Centro, California
KEZI Eugene, Oregon
KFNR Rawlins, Wyoming
KFWD Fort Worth, Texas
KGMD-TV Hilo, Hawaii
KIXE-TV Redding, California
KLRN San Antonio, Texas
KMSP-TV Minneapolis, Minnesota
KPNE-TV North Platte, Nebraska
KTRE Lufkin, Texas
KTSM-TV El Paso, Texas
KUAC-TV Fairbanks, Alaska
KMYU Saint George, Utah
KVIE Sacramento, California
KVVU-TV Henderson, Nevada
KWES-TV Odessa, Texas
WAFB Baton Rouge, Louisiana
WALA-TV Mobile, Alabama
WAOW Wausau, Wisconsin
WBPH-TV Bethlehem, Pennsylvania
WEDN Norwich, Connecticut
WFAA Dallas, Texas
WHMC Conway, South Carolina
WILL-TV Urbana, Illinois
WISH-TV Indianapolis, Indiana
WJSU-TV Anniston, Alabama
WMEB-TV Orono, Maine
WNIN Evansville, Indiana
WNTV Greenville, South Carolina
WPGX Panama City, Florida
WTOV-TV Steubenville, Ohio
WTVC Chattanooga, Tennessee
WUSA Washington, District of Columbia
WVAN-TV Savannah, Georgia
WVER Rutland, Vermont
WWTV Cadillac, Michigan
WSKY-TV Manteo, North Carolina
WNBW-DT Gainesville, Florida

Channel 10

KBIM-TV Roswell, New Mexico
KBRR Thief River Falls, Minnesota
KCHF Santa Fe, New Mexico
KERO-TV Bakersfield, California
KFDA-TV Amarillo, Texas
KFNE Riverton, Wyoming
KGTV San Diego, California
KHSD-TV Lead, South Dakota
KLFY-TV Lafayette, Louisiana
KMEB Wailuku, Hawaii
KMOT Minot, North Dakota
KNIN-TV Caldwell, Idaho
KOLN Lincoln, Nebraska
KOPB-TV Portland, Oregon
KRMZ Steamboat Springs, Colorado
KTOO-TV Juneau, Alaska
KTSD-TV Pierre, South Dakota
KTTC Rochester, Minnesota
KTUL Tulsa, Oklahoma
KTUU-TV Anchorage, Alaska
KTVQ Billings, Montana
KWCM-TV Appleton, Minnesota
KWSU-TV Pullman, Washington
KWTX-TV Waco, Texas
KXTV Sacramento, California
KZTV Corpus Christi, Texas
WALB Albany, Georgia
WBIQ Birmingham, Alabama
WBIR-TV Knoxville, Tennessee
WCBB Augusta, Maine
WDIO-DT Duluth, Minnesota
WDIQ Dozier, Alabama
WGEM-TV Quincy, Illinois
WHEC-TV Rochester, New York
WHTM-TV Harrisburg, Pennsylvania
WILX-TV Onondaga, Michigan
WIS Columbia, South Carolina
WJXX Orange Park, Florida
WMAB-TV Mississippi State, Mississippi
WMED-TV Calais, Maine
WMEM-TV Presque Isle, Maine

WNCT-TV Greenville, North Carolina
WOIO Shaker Heights, Ohio
WPLG Miami, Florida
WSMV-TV Nashville, Tennessee
WSWP-TV Grandview, West Virginia
WTHI-TV Terre Haute, Indiana
WTNH New Haven, Connecticut
WTSP St. Petersburg, Florida
WVFX Clarksburg, West Virginia
WWDP Norwell, Massachusetts
WWTO-TV La Salle, Illinois
WWUP-TV Sault Ste. Marie, Michigan
WXIA-TV Atlanta, Georgia
WBUP Ishpeming, Michigan
KETZ El Dorado, Arkansas

Channel 11

KAQY Columbia, Louisiana
KARE Minneapolis, Minnesota
KCBD Lubbock, Texas
KCBY-TV Coos Bay, Oregon
KDIN-TV Des Moines, Iowa
KEET Eureka, California
KELO-TV Sioux Falls, South Dakota
KFFX-TV Pendleton, Oregon
KGIN Grand Island, Nebraska
KHAW-TV Hilo, Hawaii
KHET Honolulu, Hawaii
KJUD Juneau, Alaska
KQCK Cheyenne, Wyoming
KLST San Angelo, Texas
KLVX Las Vegas, Nevada
KMVT Twin Falls, Idaho
KNSO Merced, California
KOAB-TV Bend, Oregon
KOED-TV Tulsa, Oklahoma
KQSD-TV Lowry, South Dakota
KSNG Garden City, Kansas
KSTW Tacoma, Washington
KSWO-TV Lawton, Oklahoma
KTTV Los Angeles, California
KTVT Fort Worth, Texas
KTWU Topeka, Kansas
KUFM-TV Missoula, Montana
KULR-TV Billings, Montana
KVCT Victoria, Texas
KWSE Williston, North Dakota
WBKB-TV Alpena, Michigan
WBRE-TV Wilkes-Barre, Pennsylvania
WENH-TV Durham, New Hampshire
WESH Daytona Beach, Florida
WGVU-TV Grand Rapids, Michigan
WHAS-TV Louisville, Kentucky
WJHL-TV Johnson City, Tennessee
WLFI-TV Lafayette, Indiana
WLUK-TV Green Bay, Wisconsin
WPCW Jeannette, Pennsylvania
WPIX New York, New York
WTOC-TV Savannah, Georgia
WTOK-TV Meridian, Mississippi
WTOL Toledo, Ohio
WTVD Durham, North Carolina
WTVI Charlotte, North Carolina
WTVM Columbus, Georgia
WVPT Staunton, Virginia
WWLP Springfield, Massachusetts
WYES-TV New Orleans, Louisiana
KDTP Holbrook, Arizona
KRII Chisholm, Minnesota

Channel 12

KAMU-TV College Station, Texas
KBMT Beaumont, Texas
KCCW-TV Walker, Minnesota
KDRV Medford, Oregon
KEYC-TV CBS & NEYC FOX Mankato, Minnesota
KFVS-TV Cape Girardeau, Missouri
KIIN Iowa City, Missouri
KYUR Anchorage, Alaska
KKCO Grand Junction, Colorado
KMAU Wailuku, Hawaii
KNRR Pembina, North Dakota
KNTV San Jose, California
KOBF Farmington, New Mexico
KPNX Mesa, Arizona
KPTV Portland, Oregon
KRCG Jefferson City, Missouri
KRNE-TV Merriman, Nebraska
KSAT-TV San Antonio, Texas
KSNK McCook, Nebraska
KTHV Little Rock, Arkansas
KTNV-TV Las Vegas, Nevada
KTTM Huron, South Dakota
KTVH-DT Helena, Montana
KUID-TV Moscow, Idaho
KUON-TV Lincoln, Nebraska
KVIH-TV Clovis, New Mexico
KXII Sherman, Texas
KXMB-TV Bismarck, North Dakota
WBBM-TV Chicago, Illinois
WMOW Crandon, Wisconsin
WBOY-TV Clarksburg, West Virginia
WCTI-TV New Bern, North Carolina
WDEF-TV Chattanooga, Tennessee
WFXL Albany, Georgia
WHYY-TV Wilmington, Delaware
WICU-TV Erie, Pennsylvania
WINM Angola, Indiana
WJRT-TV Flint, Michigan
WJTV Jackson, Mississippi
WKRC-TV Cincinnati, Ohio
WMAE-TV Booneville, Mississippi
WMFD-TV Mansfield, Ohio
WNAC-TV Providence, Rhode Island
WNYT Albany, New York
WPTV-TV West Palm Beach, Florida
WRDW-TV Augusta, Georgia
WSFA Montgomery, Alabama
WTVT Tampa, Florida
WWBT Richmond, Virginia
WWPX-TV Martinsburg, District of Columbia
WYMT-TV Hazard, Kentucky
KUTF Logan, Utah
DKSQA Topeka, Idaho

Channel 13

KBDI-TV Broomfield, Colorado
KCBA Salinas, California
KCOP-TV Los Angeles, California
KCOS El Paso, Texas
KCPQ Tacoma, Washington
KBZK Bozeman, Montana
KECI-TV Missoula, Montana
KEMV Mountain View, Arkansas
KETA-TV Oklahoma City, Oklahoma
KETG Arkadelphia, Arkansas
KFME Fargo, North Dakota
KGWR-TV Rock Springs, Wyoming
KHGI-TV Kearney, Nebraska
KHVO Hilo, Hawaii
KLTM-TV Monroe, Louisiana
KOTI Klamath Falls, Oregon
KPLO-TV Reliance, South Dakota
KPSD-TV Eagle Butte, South Dakota
KREY-TV Montrose, Colorado
KRGV-TV Weslaco, Texas
KRIS-TV Corpus Christi, Texas
KRQE Albuquerque, New Mexico
KSFY-TV Sioux Falls, South Dakota
KSGW-TV Sheridan, Wyoming
KSWT Yuma, Arizona
KTNE-TV Alliance, Nebraska
KTRK-TV Houston, Texas
KTRV-TV Nampa, Idaho
KTVN Reno, Nevada
KTVR La Grande, Oregon
KUBD Ketchikan, Alaska
KVAL-TV Eugene, Oregon
KVTV Laredo, Texas
KXLY-TV Spokane, Washington
KXMC-TV Minot, North Dakota
WABI-TV Bangor, Maine
WBKO Bowling Green, Kentucky
WBRZ-TV Baton Rouge, Louisiana
WBTW Florence, South Carolina
WCIX Springfield, Illinois
WEDU Tampa, Florida
WHBQ-TV Memphis, Tennessee
WHO-DT Des Moines, Missouri
WIBW-TV Topeka, Kansas
WIRT Hibbing, Minnesota
WJZ-TV Baltimore, Maryland
WKYT-TV Lexington, Kentucky
WLOS Asheville, North Carolina
WMAZ-TV Macon, Georgia
WMBB Panama City, Florida
WNET Newark, New Jersey
WHAM-TV Rochester, New York
WOWK-TV Huntington, West Virginia
WPEC West Palm Beach, Florida
WPRI-TV Providence, Rhode Island
WQED Pittsburgh, Pennsylvania
WRCB-DT Chattanooga, Tennessee
WREX-TV Rockford, Illinois
WTHR Indianapolis, Indiana
WTLV Jacksonville, Florida
WTVG Toledo, Ohio
WVEC Hampton, Virginia
WVTM-TV Birmingham, Alabama
WYOU Scranton, Pennsylvania
WZZM Grand Rapids, Michigan
WNYA Pittsfield, Massachusetts

Channel 14

KAPP Yakima, Washington
KOCW Hoisington, Kansas
KCSG Cedar City, Utah
KERA-TV Dallas, Texas
KGWC-TV Casper, Wyoming
KMCY Minot, North Dakota
KNLC St. Louis, Missouri
KTBW-TV Tacoma, Washington
KTGM Tamuning, Guam
KTNC-TV Concord, California
KXMD-TV Williston, North Dakota
WMYA-TV Anderson, South Carolina
WCMH-TV Columbus, Ohio
WGPX-TV Burlington, North Carolina
WHDF Florence, Alabama
WCWF Suring, Wisconsin
WKBD-TV Detroit, Michigan
WKSO-TV Somerset, Kentucky
WMEI Arecibo, Puerto Rico
WPTZ North Pole, New York
WTIU Bloomington, Indiana
WUTV Buffalo, New York
WFBT Bath, New York

Channel 15

KAVU-TV Victoria, Texas
KBSV Ceres, California
KCIT Amarillo, Texas
KFOX-TV El Paso, Texas
KFQX Grand Junction, Colorado
KQSL Fort Bragg, California
KGFE Grand Forks, North Dakota
KHOG-TV Fayetteville, Arkansas
KHQ-TV Spokane, Washington
KJTL Wichita Falls, Texas
KMOS-TV Sedalia, Missouri
KNPB Reno, Nevada
KNXV-TV Phoenix, Arizona
KPOB-TV Poplar Bluff, Missouri
KREZ-TV Durango, Colorado
KSBY San Luis Obispo, California
KSMN Worthington, Minnesota
KTAL-TV Texarkana, Texas
KTBO-TV Oklahoma City, Oklahoma
KYOU-TV Ottumwa, Iowa
WBBH-TV Fort Myers, Florida
WDCQ-TV Bad Axe, Michigan
WEWS-TV Cleveland, Ohio
WKMR Morehead, Kentucky
WNOL-TV New Orleans, Louisiana
WNSC-TV Rock Hill, South Carolina
WPMI-TV Mobile, Alabama
WPSU-TV Clearfield, Pennsylvania
WQOW-DT Eau Claire, Wisconsin
WRBL Columbus, Georgia
WRPX-TV Rocky Mount, North Carolina
WSEC Jacksonville, Illinois
WSPX-TV Syracuse, New York
WTIN-TV Ponce, Puerto Rico
WFDC-DT Arlington, District of Columbia
WXVT Greenville, Mississippi
WZTV Nashville, Tennessee
KUPU Waimanalo, Hawaii

Channel 16

KADN-TV Lafayette, Louisiana
KBMY Bismarck, North Dakota
KUNP La Grande, Oregon
KCLO-TV Rapid City, South Dakota
KDSM-TV Des Moines, Iowa
KHCE-TV San Antonio, Texas
KINC Las Vegas, Nevada
KNDO Yakima, Washington
KOGG Wailuku, Hawaii
KOOD Hays, Kansas
KUSA Denver, Colorado
WCJB-TV Gainesville, Florida
WELF-TV Dalton, Georgia

WGGS-TV Greenville, South Carolina
WGXA Macon, Georgia
WHRO-TV Hampton-Norfolk, Virginia
WJFW-TV Rhinelander, Wisconsin
WKHA Hazard, Kentucky
WNKY Bowling Green, Kentucky
WLOV-TV West Point, Mississippi
WMAH-TV Biloxi, Mississippi
WMTJ Fajardo, Puerto Rico
WPBF Tequesta, Florida
WPDE-TV Florence, South Carolina
WPTD Dayton, Ohio
WSEE-TV Erie, Pennsylvania
WSMH Flint, Michigan
WTVO Rockford, Illinois
WXXI-TV Rochester, New York
KCGE-DT Crookston, North Dakota

Channel 17

KAAS-TV Salina, Kansas
KAZQ Albuquerque, New Mexico
KDOR-TV Bartlesville, Oklahoma
KDSD-TV Aberdeen, South Dakota
KLBY Colby, Kansas
KMIZ Columbia, Missouri
KMTR Eugene, Oregon
KPHO-TV Phoenix, Arizona
KQDS-TV Duluth, Minnesota
KSLA Shreveport, Louisiana
KTWO-TV Casper, Wyoming
KVIQ Eureka, California
KYNE-TV Omaha, Nebraska
WAND Decatur, Illinois
WCMV Cadillac, Michigan
WEAR-TV Pensacola, Florida
WFXR Roanoke, Virginia
WQCW Portsmouth, Ohio
WSYR-TV Syracuse, New York
WKCF Clermont, Florida
WKOP-TV Knoxville, Tennessee
WKPC-TV Louisville, Kentucky
WKYC-DT Cleveland, Ohio
WLAX La Crosse, Wisconsin
WLTX Columbia, South Carolina
WNCN Goldsboro, North Carolina
WPHL-TV Philadelphia, Pennsylvania
WPXQ-TV Block Island, Rhode Island
WTCT Marion, Illinois
WUNE-TV Linville, North Carolina
WVEO Aguadilla, Puerto Rico
WVXF Charlotte Amalie, Virgin Islands
WYIN Gary, Indiana

Channel 18

KATN Fairbanks, Alaska
KPTF-DT Farwell, Texas
KCPT Kansas City, Missouri
KDBC-TV El Paso, Texas
KEPR-TV Pasco, Washington
KFSM-TV Fort Smith, Arkansas
KYTX Nacogdoches, Texas
KRMA-TV Denver, Colorado
KRMJ Grand Junction, Colorado
KSCI Long Beach, California
KSVI Billings, Montana
KTVC Roseburg, Oregon
KUEW St. George, Utah
KUPB Midland, Texas
KUPK Garden City, Kansas
KUSI-TV San Diego, California
KUVS-DT Modesto, California
KYIN Mason City, Iowa
WDBB Bessemer, Alabama
WDBJ Roanoke, Virginia
WECN Naranjito, Puerto Rico
WETM-TV Elmira, New York
WFXB Myrtle Beach, South Carolina
WKYU-TV Bowling Green, Kentucky
WMAU-TV Bude, Mississippi
WMBC-TV Newton, New Jersey
WMFP Lawrence, Massachusetts
WNEH Greenwood, South Carolina
WPBT Miami, Florida
WVTB St. Johnsbury, Vermont
WVTV Milwaukee, Wisconsin

Channel 19

KAMR-TV Amarillo, Texas
KBCB Bellingham, Washington
KBJR-TV Superior, Wisconsin
KOFY-TV San Francisco, California
KCKA Centralia, Washington
KCOY-TV Santa Maria, California
KIDY San Angelo, Texas
KIKU Honolulu, Hawaii
KLDO-TV Laredo, Texas
KMOH-TV Kingman, Arizona
KPIC Roseburg, Oregon
KPRY-TV Pierre, South Dakota
KSPR Springfield, Missouri
KSWB-TV San Diego, California
KTTU Tucson, Arizona
KTVD Denver, Colorado
KTVG-TV Grand Island, Nebraska
KTXH Houston, Texas
KUES Richfield, Utah
KVRR Fargo, North Dakota
KSCW-DT Wichita, Kansas
KWYB Butte, Montana
KXMA-TV Dickinson, North Dakota
KXNE-TV Norfolk, Nebraska
WCWG Lexington, North Carolina
WSFL-TV Miami, Florida
WGBH-TV Boston, Massachusetts
WGBH Boston, Massachusetts
WGN Chicago, Illinois
WGCL-TV Atlanta, Georgia
WBKI-TV Campbellsville, Kentucky
WHNT-TV Huntsville, Alabama
WHOI Peoria, Illinois
WIIQ Demopolis, Alabama
WISE-TV Fort Wayne, Indiana
WKPV Ponce, Puerto Rico
WMTV Madison, Wisconsin
WSYT Syracuse, New York
WTEV-TV Jacksonville, Florida
WUNM-TV Jacksonville, North Carolina
WUSI-TV Olney, Illinois
WVAH-TV Charleston, West Virginia
WXMI Grand Rapids, Michigan
WZMQ Marquette, Michigan
KDMI Des Moines, Iowa
WCAV Charlottesville, Virginia
KWKS Colby, Kansas

Channel 20

KAME-TV Reno, Nevada
KDYW Waco, Texas
KCVU Paradise, California
KETV Omaha, Nebraska
KFNB Casper, Wyoming
KFTV-DT Hanford, California
KJNP-TV North Pole, Alaska
KJRE Ellendale, North Dakota
KLTL-TV Lake Charles, Louisiana
KNLJ Jefferson City, Missouri
KPAZ-TV Phoenix, Arizona
KREM Spokane, Washington
KSMQ-TV Austin, Minnesota
KTBY Anchorage, Alaska
KTEJ Jonesboro, Arkansas
KTMW Salt Lake City, Utah
KTXS-TV Sweetwater, Texas
KQCW-DT Muskogee, Oklahoma
WBXX-TV/DT Crossville, Tennessee
WCOV-TV Montgomery, Alabama
WCVB-TV Boston, Massachusetts
WFMJ-TV Youngstown, Ohio
WHA-TV Madison, Wisconsin
WHMB-TV Indianapolis, Indiana
WWCW Lynchburg, Virginia
WLRN-TV Miami, Florida
WMPN-TV Jackson, Mississippi
WMPV-TV Mobile, Alabama
WNPX-TV Cookeville, Tennessee
WOTV Battle Creek, Michigan
WSVI Christiansted, Virgin Islands
WPCH-TV Atlanta, Georgia
WCCT-TV Waterbury, Connecticut
WUND-TV Edenton, North Carolina
KRMU Durango, Colorado
WNYI Ithaca, New York
KVME-TV Bishop, California

Channel 21

KAID Boise, Idaho
KAKE Wichita, Kansas
KDCK Dodge City, Kansas
KFCT Fort Collins, Colorado
KFDM-TV Beaumont, Texas
KHBS Fort Smith, Arkansas
KMAX-TV Sacramento, California
KPMR Santa Barbara, California
KPXJ Minden, Louisiana
KTAJ-TV St. Joseph, Missouri
KTVZ Bend, Oregon
KWHM Wailuku, Hawaii
KXAN-TV Austin, Texas
KYVE Yakima, Washington
WUPX-TV Morehead, Kentucky
WAPT Jackson, Mississippi
WBNS-TV Columbus, Ohio
WBOC-TV Salisbury, Maryland
WCLF Clearwater, Florida
WCMW Manistee, Michigan
WDAY-TV Fargo, North Dakota
WDHN Dothan, Alabama
WMYD Detroit, Michigan
WFYI Indianapolis, Indiana
WHNO New Orleans, Louisiana
WHNS Greenville, South Carolina
WHP-TV Harrisburg, Pennsylvania
WJPX San Juan, Puerto Rico
WLIW Garden City, New York
WMEC Macomb, Illinois
WPBA Atlanta, Georgia
WPXS Mount Vernon, Illinois
WSBE-TV Providence, Rhode Island
WUXP-TV Nashville, Tennessee
WVPY Front Royal, Virginia
WWMB Florence, South Carolina
WWTI Watertown, New York
KNBN Rapid City, South Dakota
KRWB-TV Roswell, New Mexico
KUGF Great Falls, Montana
KFCT Fort Collins, Colorado

Channel 22

KTFQ-TV Albuquerque, New Mexico
KATV Little Rock, Arkansas
KAUZ-TV Wichita Falls, Texas
KBME-TV Bismarck, North Dakota
WBMM Tuskegee, Alabama
KBSI Cape Girardeau, Missouri
KETK-TV Jacksonville, Texas
KFVE Honolulu, Hawaii
KHBC-TV Hilo, Hawaii
KHMT Hardin, Montana
KIPT Twin Falls, Idaho
KLRU Austin, Texas
KMCB Coos Bay, Oregon
WUCW Minneapolis, Minnesota
KNAZ-TV Flagstaff, Arizona
KOKI-TV Tulsa, Oklahoma
KPXG-TV Salem, Oregon
KSNC Great Bend, Kansas
KZJO Seattle, Washington
KVMY Las Vegas, Nevada
KVYE El Centro, California
KXRM-TV Colorado Springs, Colorado
WBUI Decatur, Illinois
WCAX-TV Burlington, Vermont
WCNC-TV Charlotte, North Carolina
WCPO-TV Cincinnati, Ohio
WCTE Cookeville, Tennessee
WFIQ Florence, Alabama
WFOR-TV Miami, Florida
WFXP Erie, Pennsylvania
WGBY-TV Springfield, Massachusetts
WHLT Hattiesburg, Mississippi
WJCL Savannah, Georgia
WLWC New Bedford, Massachusetts
WNEM-TV Bay City, Michigan
WNJS Camden, New Jersey
WOFL Orlando, Florida
WOWT Omaha, Nebraska
WRIC-TV Petersburg, Virginia
WSBT-TV South Bend, Indiana
WVCY-TV Milwaukee, Wisconsin
WVNY Burlington, Vermont
WVUT Vincennes, Indiana
KWWF Waterloo, Iowa
WOST Mayaguez, Puerto Rico

Channel 23

KEDT Corpus Christi, Texas
KGMB Honolulu, Hawaii
KLPB-TV Lafayette, Louisiana
KLTJ Galveston, Texas
KOZK Springfield, Missouri
KPEJ-TV Odessa, Texas
KCWI-TV Ames, Iowa

KRCB Cotati, California
KREG-TV Glenwood Springs, Colorado
KRWG-TV Las Cruces, New Mexico
KTCI-TV St. Paul, Minnesota
KTMF Missoula, Montana
KCDO-TV Sterling, Colorado
KVMD Twentynine Palms, California
KVOA Tucson, Arizona
KWHD Hilo, Hawaii
WBAY-TV Green Bay, Wisconsin
WBTV Charlotte, North Carolina
WCVI-TV Christiansted, Virgin Islands
WFTY-DT Smithtown, New York
WIPB Muncie, Indiana
WJSP-TV Columbus, Georgia
WLYH-TV Lancaster, Pennsylvania
WPFO Waterville, Maine
WNAB Nashville, Tennessee
WNJX-TV Mayaguez, Puerto Rico
WNPI Norwood, New York
WPXJ-TV Batavia, New York
WPXK-TV Jellico, Tennessee
WQPT-TV Moline, Illinois
WSAZ-TV Huntington, West Virginia
WUNK-TV Greenville, North Carolina
WVPX-TV Akron, Ohio
XETV-DT Tijuana, California
WWJX Jackson, Mississippi

Channel 24

KBEH Oxnard, California
KPNZ Ogden, Utah
KQUP Pullman, Washington
KCSD-TV Sioux Falls, South Dakota
KCTV Kansas City, Missouri
KETH-TV Houston, Texas
KGMV Wailuku, Hawaii
KLTS-TV Shreveport, Louisiana
KMOV St. Louis, Missouri
KNAT-TV Albuquerque, New Mexico
KNVN Chico, California
KOKH-TV Oklahoma City, Oklahoma
KRDO-TV Colorado Springs, Colorado
KTAB-TV Abilene, Texas
KTVK Phoenix, Arizona
KVEO-TV Brownsville, Texas
KVTN-DT Pine Bluff, Arkansas
KXND Minot, North Dakota
WATM-TV Altoona, Pennsylvania
WPXC-TV Brunswick, Georgia
WCML Alpena, Michigan
WCVN-TV Covington, Kentucky
WHIQ Huntsville, Alabama
WHRM-TV Wausau, Wisconsin
WJET-TV Erie, Pennsylvania
WKPI-TV Pikeville, West Virginia
WMDN Meridian, Mississippi
WMFE-TV Orlando, Florida
WUGA-TV Toccoa, Georgia
WNVC Fairfax, Virginia
WNYE-TV New York, New York
WPTA Fort Wayne, Indiana
WSFJ-TV Newark, Ohio
WSTM-TV Syracuse, New York
WTAT-TV Charleston, South Carolina
WTLJ Muskegon, Michigan
WUPL Slidell, Louisiana
WVTA Windsor, Vermont
WWSB Sarasota, Florida
DKBTZ Butte, Montana
WTLF Tallahassee, Florida

Channel 25

KQET Watsonville, California
KDKA-TV Pittsburgh, Pennsylvania
KGET-TV Bakersfield, California
KINT-TV El Paso, Texas
KLEI-TV Kailua-Kona, Hawaii
KMSB Tucson, Arizona
KOVR Stockton, California
KOZJ Joplin, Missouri
KTIN Fort Dodge, Iowa
KTEL-TV Carlsbad, New Mexico
KWKB Iowa City, Iowa
WATL Atlanta, Georgia
WVEA-TV Venice, Florida
WCGV-TV Milwaukee, Wisconsin
WCNY-TV Syracuse, New York
WEEK-TV Peoria, Illinois
WLPB-TV Baton Rouge, Louisiana
WMAO-TV Greenwood, Mississippi
WNNE Hartford, Vermont
WPTY-TV Memphis, Tennessee
WQTO Ponce, Puerto Rico
WRTV Indianapolis, Indiana
WTVE Reading, Pennsylvania
WTVF Nashville, Tennessee
WTVR-TV Richmond, Virginia
WUNC-TV Chapel Hill, North Carolina
WUNF-TV Asheville, North Carolina
WFNA Gulf Shores, Alabama
KMDE Devils Lake, North Dakota

Channel 26

KBHE-TV Rapid City, South Dakota
KDLV-TV Mitchell, South Dakota
KFTC Bemidji, Minnesota
KLNE-TV Lexington, Nebraska
KLPA-TV Alexandria, Louisiana
KMID Midland, Texas
KMVU-DT Medford, Oregon
KNDU Richland, Washington
KNDX Bismarck, North Dakota
KOB Albuquerque, New Mexico
KPLR-TV St. Louis, Missouri
KREN-TV Reno, Nevada
KRIV Houston, Texas
KSAS-TV Wichita, Kansas
KTEN Ada, Oklahoma
KTVF Fairbanks, Alaska
KUTP Phoenix, Arizona
KVCR-DT San Bernardino, California
KVTH-DT Hot Springs, Arkansas
KXXV Waco, Texas
KYW-TV Philadelphia, Pennsylvania
WATE-TV Knoxville, Tennessee
WBDT Springfield, Ohio
WCCU Urbana, Illinois
WCMU-TV Mount Pleasant, Michigan
WGNO New Orleans, Louisiana
WHAG-TV Hagerstown, Maryland
WHPX-TV New London, Connecticut
WKAS Ashland, Kentucky
WKMG-TV Orlando, Florida
WLKY-TV Louisville, Kentucky
WNYB Jamestown, New York
WRLH-TV Richmond, Virginia
WTEN Albany, New York
WTJP-TV Gadsden, Alabama
WVIZ Cleveland, Ohio

Channel 27

KAAH-TV Honolulu, Hawaii
KAMC Lubbock, Texas
KASA-TV Santa Fe, New Mexico
KFPH-DT Flagstaff, Arizona
KBTC-TV Tacoma, Washington
KEYT-TV Santa Barbara, California
KFOR-TV Oklahoma City, Oklahoma
KFXA Cedar Rapids, Iowa
KLWY Cheyenne, Wyoming
KORO Corpus Christi, Texas
KFTA-TV Fort Smith, Arkansas
KRPV-DT Roswell, New Mexico
KRWF Redwood Falls, Minnesota
KSNT Topeka, Kansas
KTSF San Francisco, California
KTVE El Dorado, Arkansas
WACY-TV Appleton, Wisconsin
WAGA-TV Atlanta, Georgia
WAIQ Montgomery, Alabama
WAPA-TV San Juan, Puerto Rico
WBGU-TV Bowling Green, Ohio
WCCB Charlotte, North Carolina
WCIU-TV Chicago, Illinois
WETA-TV Washington, District of Columbia
WFXV Utica, New York
WGTW-TV Burlington, New Jersey
WUTF-DT Marlborough, Massachusetts
WHWC-TV Menomonie, Wisconsin
WIPX-TV Bloomington, Indiana
WKOW Madison, Wisconsin
WKPT-TV Kingsport, Tennessee
WKRG-TV Mobile, Alabama
WKRN-TV Nashville, Tennessee
WLFL Raleigh, North Carolina
WOUB-TV Athens, Ohio
WRDQ Orlando, Florida
WTBY-TV Poughkeepsie, New York
WTXL-TV Tallahassee, Florida
WXEL-TV West Palm Beach, Florida
KCPM Grand Forks, North Dakota
KCWV Duluth, Minnesota
DWUNW Canton, Florida
KBVO Llano, Texas

Channel 28

KATC Lafayette, Louisiana
KAWB Brainerd, Minnesota
KAYU-TV Spokane, Washington
KBOI-TV Boise, Idaho
KBVU Eureka, California
KOZL-TV Springfield, Missouri
KFDX-TV Wichita Falls, Texas
KHNE-TV Hastings, Nebraska
KMPH-TV Visalia, California
KSIN-TV Sioux City, Missouri
KSTU Salt Lake City, Utah
KTBS-TV Shreveport, Louisiana
KTPX-TV Okmulgee, Oklahoma
KTVA Anchorage, Alaska
KUAS-TV Tucson, Arizona
KYLE-TV Bryan, Texas
WCPB Salisbury, Maryland
WFLX West Palm Beach, Florida
WFPT Frederick, Maryland
WFUM Flint, Michigan
WGFL High Springs, Florida
WKAQ-TV San Juan, Puerto Rico
WNBC New York, New York
WPTO Oxford, Ohio
WRDC Durham, North Carolina
WREG-TV Memphis, Tennessee
WRJA-TV Sumter, South Carolina
WSJV Elkhart, Indiana
WTGS Hardeeville, South Carolina
WTMJ-TV Milwaukee, Wisconsin
WTTO Homewood, Alabama
WTVW Evansville, Indiana
WUAB Lorain, Ohio
WUHF Rochester, New York
WYOW Eagle River, Wisconsin
WYZZ-TV Bloomington, Illinois
DKB-97071 Kingsport, Tennessee

Channel 29

KTUZ-TV Shawnee, Oklahoma
KDEN-TV Longmont, Colorado
KDKF Klamath Falls, Oregon
KEPB-TV Eugene, Oregon
KVCW Las Vegas, Nevada
KUPT Hobbs, New Mexico
KMBC-TV Kansas City, Missouri
KMTF Helena, Montana
KPIX-TV San Francisco, California
KPTS Hutchinson, Kansas
KRBC-TV Abilene, Texas
KSTF Scottsbluff, Nebraska
KTXA Fort Worth, Texas
KUPX-TV Provo, Utah
KWBQ Santa Fe, New Mexico
WBIH Selma, Alabama
WFME-TV West Milford, New Jersey
WFTC Minneapolis, Minnesota
WFTS-TV Tampa, Florida
WGTE-TV Toledo, Ohio
WGTU Traverse City, Michigan
WUVP-DT Vineland, Pennsylvania
WQMY Williamsport, Pennsylvania
WKNO Memphis, Tennessee
WKTV Utica, New York
WMAQ-TV Chicago, Illinois
WMPB Baltimore, Maryland
WORA-TV Mayaguez, Puerto Rico
WTCI Chattanooga, Tennessee
WTTK Kokomo, Indiana
WUNI Worcester, Massachusetts
WUNJ-TV Wilmington, North Carolina
WVBT Virginia Beach, Virginia
WVUE-DT New Orleans, Louisiana
WXIX-TV Newport, Kentucky
WXLV-TV Winston-Salem, North Carolina

Channel 30

KABB San Antonio, Texas
KFSN-TV Fresno, California
KGWN-TV Cheyenne, Wyoming
KLRT-TV Little Rock, Arkansas
KMPX Decatur, Texas
KPBS San Diego, California
KPDX Vancouver, Washington
KWWT Odessa, Texas

KQED San Francisco, California
KUAT-TV Tucson, Arizona
KVHP Lake Charles, Louisiana
WAGT Augusta, Georgia
WBCC Cocoa, Florida
WBNX-TV Akron, Ohio
WBZ-TV Boston, Massachusetts
WDWL Bayamon, Puerto Rico
WEYI-TV Saginaw, Michigan
WGCB-TV Red Lion, Pennsylvania
WGCU Fort Myers, Florida
WHLA-TV La Crosse, Wisconsin
WFUT-DT Newark, New York
WIAT Birmingham, Alabama
WKOH Owensboro, Kentucky
WLBT Jackson, Mississippi
WMBD-TV Peoria, Illinois
WNVT Goldvein, Virginia
WRGT-TV Dayton, Ohio
WSCV Fort Lauderdale, Florida
WSFX-TV Wilmington, North Carolina
WSLS-TV Roanoke, Virginia
WUTR Utica, New York
WVLT-TV Knoxville, Tennessee
KBLN Grants Pass, Oregon
WSKA Corning, New York

Channel 31

KEYU Borger, Texas
KCWE Kansas City, Missouri
KDNL-TV St. Louis, Missouri
KFXK-TV Longview, Texas
KFXP Pocatello, Idaho
KFYR-TV Bismarck, North Dakota
KGBT-TV Harlingen, Texas
KHOU Houston, Texas
KLAX-TV Alexandria, Louisiana
KLSR-TV Eugene, Oregon
KOET Eufaula, Oklahoma
KSMS-TV Monterey, California
KTLA Los Angeles, California
KWBM Harrison, Arkansas
KWHE Honolulu, Hawaii
WANE-TV Fort Wayne, Indiana
WAVY-TV Portsmouth, Virginia
WDKY-TV Danville, Kentucky
WFLD Chicago, Illinois
WFXT Boston, Massachusetts
WGBC Meridian, Mississippi
WLAE-TV New Orleans, Louisiana
WLMT Memphis, Tennessee
WMAI Cleveland, Mississippi
WOGX Ocala, Florida
WPPX-TV Wilmington, Pennsylvania
WPXD-TV Ann Arbor, Michigan
WPXN-TV New York, New York
WSJU-TV San Juan, Puerto Rico
WSRE Pensacola, Florida
WSWB Scranton, Pennsylvania
WTIC-TV Hartford, Connecticut
WTVJ Miami, Florida
WUNU Lumberton, North Carolina
WXII-TV Winston-Salem, North Carolina
KDCU-DT Derby, Kansas

Channel 32

KARK-TV Little Rock, Arkansas
KCFG Flagstaff, Arizona
KDAF Dallas, Texas
KDOC-TV Anaheim, California
KDVR Denver, Colorado
KEMO-TV Santa Rosa, California
KION-TV Monterey, California
KLEW-TV Lewiston, Idaho
KMCC Laughlin, Nevada
KOLD-TV Tucson, Arizona
KMYS Kerrville, Texas
KWPX-TV Bellevue, Washington
WAAY-TV Huntsville, Alabama
WABG-TV Greenwood, Mississippi
WAWS Jacksonville, Florida
WBFS-TV Miami, Florida
WBPX-TV Boston, Massachusetts
WCCO-TV Minneapolis, Minnesota
WETK Burlington, Vermont
WFSU-TV Tallahassee, Florida
WFQX-TV Cadillac, Michigan
WBUW Janesville, Wisconsin
WITN-TV Washington, North Carolina
WNCF Montgomery, Alabama
WNDY-TV Marion, Indiana
WNLO Buffalo, New York
WPGA-TV Perry, Georgia
WPSD-TV Paducah, Kentucky
WPSG Philadelphia, Pennsylvania
WQPX-TV Scranton, Pennsylvania
WRLK-TV Columbia, South Carolina
WSBN-TV Norton, Virginia
WTAJ-TV Altoona, Pennsylvania
WTCV San Juan, Puerto Rico
WTJR Quincy, Illinois
WTTA St. Petersburg, Florida
WUNL-TV Winston-Salem, North Carolina
WVIR-TV Charlottesville, Virginia
XEWT-DT Tijuana, California
KUTH-DT Provo, Utah
WMBF-TV Myrtle Beach, South Carolina

Channel 33

KBAK-TV Bakersfield, California
KRTN-TV Durango, Colorado
KBFD-DT Honolulu, Hawaii
KBIN-TV Council Bluffs, Nebraska
KDLH Duluth, Minnesota
KDMD Anchorage, Alaska
KFTS Klamath Falls, Oregon
KIMA-TV Yakima, Washington
KITU-TV Beaumont, Texas
KMTP-TV San Francisco, California
KOCB Oklahoma City, Oklahoma
KTBN-TV Santa Ana, California
KTVM-TV Butte, Montana
KTVO Kirksville, Missouri
KVUE Austin, Texas
KWAB-TV Big Spring, Texas
KRCW-TV Salem, Oregon
WCBS-TV New York, New York
WDSC-TV New Smyrna Beach, Florida
WCFT-TV Tuscaloosa, Alabama
WNGH-TV Chatsworth, Georgia
WDFX-TV Ozark, Alabama
WEBA-TV Allendale, South Carolina
WFSB Hartford, Connecticut
WGRZ Buffalo, New York
WHUT-TV Washington, District of Columbia
WITI Milwaukee, Wisconsin
WNMU Marquette, Michigan
WNPB-TV Morgantown, West Virginia
WPGD-TV Hendersonville, Tennessee
WPXG-TV Concord, Massachusetts
WRUA Fajardo, Puerto Rico
WRXY-TV Tice, Florida
WSTR-TV Cincinnati, Ohio
WTVZ-TV Norfolk, Virginia
WMYV Greensboro, North Carolina

Channel 34

KGPX-TV Spokane, Washington
KGPE Fresno, California
KLUJ-TV Harlingen, Texas
KMSS-TV Shreveport, Louisiana
KFSF-DT Vallejo, California
KTAS San Luis Obispo, California
KTCA-TV St. Paul, Minnesota
KUSD-TV Vermillion, South Dakota
KUTV Salt Lake City, Utah
KXNW Eureka Springs, Arkansas
KWGN-TV Denver, Colorado
KXTF Twin Falls, Idaho
WCAU Philadelphia, Pennsylvania
WCET Cincinnati, Ohio
WCIV Charleston, South Carolina
WDAF-TV Kansas City, Missouri
WELU Aguadilla, Puerto Rico
WPXU-TV Jacksonville, North Carolina
WHBR Pensacola, Florida
WHTV Jackson, Michigan
WISN-TV Milwaukee, Wisconsin
WIVT Binghamton, New York
WJAC-TV Johnstown, Pennsylvania
WCWJ Jacksonville, Florida
WMHT Schenectady, New York
WPBY-TV Charleston, West Virginia
WNEU Merrimack, New Hampshire
WPXW-TV Manassas, District of Columbia
WQEC Quincy, Illinois
WQHS-DT Cleveland, Ohio
WSET-TV Lynchburg, Virginia
WSIL-TV Harrisburg, Illinois
WSOC-TV Charlotte, North Carolina
WTNZ Knoxville, Tennessee
WTVX Fort Pierce, Florida
WUSF-TV Tampa, Florida
WVLA-TV Baton Rouge, Louisiana
KEFB Ames, Iowa

Channel 35

KALB-TV Alexandria, Louisiana
KCNC-TV Denver, Colorado
KCRA-TV Sacramento, California
KDFW Dallas, Texas
KGUN-TV Tucson, Arizona
KHIN Red Oak, Iowa
KHNL Honolulu, Hawaii
KJTV-TV Lubbock, Texas
KMEX-DT Los Angeles, California
KNME-TV Albuquerque, New Mexico
KPRC-TV Houston, Texas
KRCA Riverside, California
KRIN Waterloo, Iowa
KMTW Hutchinson, Kansas
KSDK St. Louis, Missouri
KSTP-TV St. Paul, Minnesota
KTVL Medford, Oregon
KVOS-TV Bellingham, Washington
WCBI-TV Columbus, Mississippi
WDCA Washington, District of Columbia
WFTX-TV Cape Coral, Florida
WGHP High Point, North Carolina
WGSA Baxley, Georgia
WIPM-TV Mayaguez, Puerto Rico
WLTZ Columbus, Georgia
WLUC-TV Marquette, Michigan
WLWT Cincinnati, Ohio
WMVT Milwaukee, Wisconsin
WNIT South Bend, Indiana
WOUC-TV Cambridge, Ohio
WPME Lewiston, Maine
WPXM-TV Miami, Florida
WTOM-TV Cheboygan, Michigan
WVIT New Britain, Connecticut
WYBE Philadelphia, Pennsylvania
KUOK Woodward, Oklahoma

Channel 36

KAAL Austin, Minnesota
KARD West Monroe, Louisiana
KWSD Sioux Falls, South Dakota
KDFI Dallas, Texas
KFTH-DT Alvin, Texas
KICU-TV San Jose, California
KKAP Little Rock, Arkansas
KMCI-TV Lawrence, Missouri
KFRE-TV Sanger, California
KNBC Los Angeles, California
KRSC-TV Claremore, Oklahoma
KSKN Spokane, Washington
KUEN Ogden, Utah
KWQC-TV Davenport, Iowa
WABM Birmingham, Alabama
WCDC-TV Adams, New York
WENY-TV Elmira, New York
WFFT-TV Fort Wayne, Indiana
WFPX-TV Fayetteville, North Carolina
WGPT Oakland, Maryland
WITF-TV Harrisburg, Pennsylvania
WJYS Hammond, Illinois
WKMU Murray, Kentucky
WLEF-TV Park Falls, Wisconsin
WLNS-TV Lansing, Michigan
WMAV-TV Oxford, Mississippi
WMGM-TV Wildwood, New Jersey
WMMP Charleston, South Carolina
WNJU Linden, New Jersey
WPXP-TV Lake Worth, Florida
WPXR-TV Roanoke, Virginia
WTTE Columbus, Ohio
WTTG Washington, District of Columbia
WTVY Dothan, Alabama
WTWO Terre Haute, Indiana
WUFT Gainesville, Florida
WUNP-TV Roanoke Rapids, North Carolina
WWL-TV New Orleans, Louisiana
WYFF Greenville, South Carolina
WYTV Youngstown, Ohio

Channel 38

KALO Honolulu, Hawaii
KIAH Houston, Texas
KMBH Harlingen, Texas
KMCT-TV West Monroe, Louisiana
KPBT-TV Odessa, Texas

KOMO-TV Seattle, Washington
KPXN-TV San Bernardino, California
KRON-TV San Francisco, California
KSEE Fresno, California
KSL-TV Salt Lake City, Utah
KTNW Richland, Washington
KXJB-TV Valley City, North Dakota
KXVO Omaha, Nebraska
WCFE-TV Plattsburgh, New York
WEAU-TV Eau Claire, Wisconsin
WEMT Greeneville, Tennessee
WFSG Panama City, Florida
WGME-TV Portland, Maine
WHTN Murfreesboro, Tennessee
WKBW-TV Buffalo, New York
WUVC-DT Fayetteville, North Carolina
WKMJ-TV Louisville, Kentucky
WMAR-TV Baltimore, Maryland
WOSU-TV Columbus, Ohio
WQAD-TV Moline, Illinois
WINP-TV Pittsburgh, Pennsylvania
WSYM-TV Lansing, Michigan
WTCE-TV Fort Pierce, Florida
WWOR-TV Secaucus, New Jersey
KUQI Corpus Christi, Texas
KPJR-DT Greeley, Colorado

Channel 39

KASN Pine Bluff, Arkansas
KCNS San Francisco, California
KETC St. Louis, Missouri
KIRO-TV Seattle, Washington
KMEG Sioux City, Iowa
KWOG Springdale, Arkansas
KSCE El Paso, Texas
KTTZ-TV Lubbock, Texas
KVEA Corona, California
KWEX-DT San Antonio, Texas
KWTV-DT Oklahoma City, Oklahoma
WADL Mount Clemens, Michigan
WAOE Peoria, Illinois
WAWV-TV Terre Haute, Indiana
WCTX New Haven, Connecticut
WFRV-TV Green Bay, Wisconsin
WFTV Orlando, Florida
WMYT-TV Rock Hill, South Carolina
WIVB-TV Buffalo, New York
WJAL Hagerstown, Maryland
WJWN-TV San Sebastian, Puerto Rico
WKOI-TV Richmond, Indiana
WLEX-TV Lexington, Kentucky
WLOX Biloxi, Mississippi
WLPX-TV Charleston, West Virginia
WLVT-TV Allentown, Pennsylvania
WJKT Jackson, Tennessee
WKTC Sumter, South Carolina
WSAV-TV Savannah, Georgia
WSB-TV Atlanta, Georgia
WSBK-TV Boston, Massachusetts
KKJB Boise, Idaho

Channel 40

KAUT-TV Oklahoma City, Oklahoma
KBLR Paradise, Nevada
KBTV-TV Port Arthur, Texas
KHRR Tucson, Arizona
KITV Honolulu, Hawaii
KLBK-TV Lubbock, Texas
KNSD San Diego, California
KOIN Portland, Oregon
KPXM-TV Saint Cloud, Minnesota
KRMT Denver, Colorado
KSRE Minot, North Dakota
KTLM Rio Grande City, Texas
KTVX Salt Lake City, Utah
KTXL Sacramento, California
KVPT Fresno, California
KXTX-TV Dallas, Texas
WACX-DT Leesburg, Florida
WDBD Jackson, Mississippi
WDPX-TV Vineyard Haven, Rhode Island
WDSI-TV Chattanooga, Tennessee
WFWA Fort Wayne, Indiana
WGGB-TV Springfield, Massachusetts
WHIZ-TV Zanesville, Ohio
WHKY-TV Hickory, North Carolina
WKAR-TV East Lansing, Michigan
WLFB Bluefield, West Virginia
WMGT-TV Macon, Georgia
WNUV Baltimore, Maryland
WPAN Fort Walton Beach, Florida
WBEC-TV Boca Raton, Florida
WPXE-TV Kenosha, Wisconsin
WTKR Norfolk, Virginia
WTVQ-DT Lexington, Kentucky
WTWC-TV Tallahassee, Florida
WXTV-DT Paterson, New York
WNMN Saranac Lake, New York

Channel 41

KGCW Burlington, Missouri
KLCS Los Angeles, California
KPXO-TV Kaneohe, Hawaii
KTIV Sioux City, Iowa
KXAS-TV Fort Worth, Texas
WATC-DT Atlanta, Georgia
WBUY-TV Holly Springs, Mississippi
WCHS-TV Charleston, West Virginia
WEFC-TV Danville, Virginia
WEIQ Mobile, Alabama
WGBA-TV Green Bay, Wisconsin
WHIO-TV Dayton, Ohio
WICD Champaign, Illinois
WIFR Freeport, Illinois
WIRS Yauco, Puerto Rico
WKBN-TV Youngstown, Ohio
WKPD Paducah, Kentucky
WLVI Cambridge, Massachusetts
WGTV Watertown, New York
WRBW Orlando, Florida
WETP-TV Sneedville, Tennessee
WUTB Baltimore, Maryland
WVIA-TV Scranton, Pennsylvania
WXYZ-TV Detroit, Michigan
WZDX Huntsville, Alabama
WZVN-TV Naples, Florida
KBCA Alexandria, Louisiana
WUFX Vicksburg, Mississippi

Channel 42

KESQ-TV Palm Springs, California
KIMT Mason City, Iowa
KLUZ-TV Albuquerque, New Mexico
KMLM-DT Odessa, Texas
KOAA-TV Pueblo, Colorado
KSAX Alexandria, Minnesota
KSHB-TV Kansas City, Missouri
KTBU Conroe, Texas
KMYT-TV Tulsa, Oklahoma
KUED Salt Lake City, Utah
KWDK Tacoma, Washington
KWHY-TV Los Angeles, California
WAKA Selma, Alabama
WCLJ-TV Bloomington, Indiana
WCVE-TV Richmond, Virginia
WPMY Pittsburgh, Pennsylvania
WFLI-TV Cleveland, Tennessee
WGGN-TV Sandusky, Ohio
WHDH Boston, Massachusetts
WJBF Augusta, Georgia
WJXT Jacksonville, Florida
WKLE Lexington, Kentucky
WKMA-TV Madisonville, Indiana
WMPT Annapolis, Maryland
WMSY-TV Marion, Virginia
WNDU-TV South Bend, Indiana
WPNE Green Bay, Wisconsin
WQRF-TV Rockford, Illinois
WRAY-TV Wilson, North Carolina
WZME Bridgeport, Connecticut
WSKG-TV Binghamton, New York
WTXF-TV Philadelphia, Pennsylvania
WXPX-TV Bradenton, Florida
KGLA-AM Hammond, Louisiana

Channel 43

KATU Portland, Oregon
KLCW-TV Wolfforth, Texas
KCAL Redlands, California
KCBS-TV Los Angeles, California
KCSM-TV San Mateo, California
KDTN Denton, Texas
KEYE-TV Austin, Texas
KFXB-TV Dubuque, Missouri
KGMC Clovis, California
KHSL-TV Chico, California
KODE-TV Joplin, Missouri
KPTM Omaha, Nebraska
KPXC-TV Denver, Colorado
KTVI St. Louis, Missouri
KWBN Honolulu, Hawaii
WBBJ-TV Jackson, Tennessee
WOTF-DT Melbourne, Florida
WCPX-TV Chicago, Illinois
WDSU New Orleans, Louisiana
WFFF-TV Burlington, Vermont
WSWG Valdosta, Georgia
WIPR-TV San Juan, Puerto Rico
WKZT-TV Elizabethtown, Kentucky
WLXI Greensboro, North Carolina
WCWN Schenectady, New York
WNED-TV Buffalo, New York
WNJT Trenton, New Jersey
WPBO Portsmouth, Ohio
WPGH-TV Pittsburgh, Pennsylvania
WPXT Portland, Maine
WRET-TV Spartanburg, South Carolina
WSUR-DT Ponce, Puerto Rico
WTVS Detroit, Michigan
WUPA Atlanta, Georgia
WWRS-TV Mayville, Wisconsin
WZVI Charlotte Amalie, Virgin Islands

Channel 44

KBYU-TV Provo, Utah
KFFV Seattle, Washington
KILM Barstow, California
KRXI-TV Reno, Nevada
KSHV-TV Shreveport, Louisiana
KTVU Oakland, California
KVEW Kennewick, Washington
KVLY-TV Fargo, North Dakota
KWBA-TV Sierra Vista, Arizona
KARZ-TV Little Rock, Arkansas
KYTV Springfield, Missouri
KZJL Houston, Texas
WCSH Portland, Maine
WCVW Richmond, Virginia
WDPB Seaford, Delaware
WECT Wilmington, North Carolina
WGIQ Louisville, Alabama
WHSG-TV Monroe, Georgia
WJEB-TV Jacksonville, Florida
WJFB Lebanon, Tennessee
WJWJ-TV Beaufort, South Carolina
WKON Owenton, Kentucky
WMAW-TV Meridian, Mississippi
WNYS-TV Syracuse, New York
WNYW New York, New York
WRSP-TV Springfield, Illinois
WDTI Indianapolis, Indiana
WTJX-TV Charlotte Amalie, Virgin Islands
WTLW Lima, Ohio
WTOG St. Petersburg, Florida
WTSF Ashland, Kentucky
WUNG-TV Concord, North Carolina
WMCN-TV Atlantic City, New Jersey
WWJ-TV Detroit, Michigan
WWPB Hagerstown, Maryland
WZPX-TV Battle Creek, Michigan

Channel 45

KASY-TV Albuquerque, New Mexico
KBCW San Francisco, California
KDTX-TV Dallas, Texas
KMTV-TV Omaha, Nebraska
KTCW Roseburg, Oregon
KOTV-DT Tulsa, Oklahoma
KSNW Wichita, Kansas
KTGF Great Falls, Montana
KSTC-TV Minneapolis, Minnesota
WYCW Asheville, North Carolina
WEDH Hartford, Connecticut
WEVV-TV Evansville, Indiana
WFUP Vanderbilt, Michigan
WGMB-TV Baton Rouge, Louisiana
WGNM Macon, Georgia
WIDP Guayama, Puerto Rico
WJPM-TV Florence, South Carolina
WJTC Pensacola, Florida
WKDH Houston, Mississippi
WLLA Kalamazoo, Michigan
WMEA-TV Biddeford, Maine
WNEO Alliance, Ohio
WOLF-TV Hazleton, Pennsylvania
WPXH-TV Gadsden, Alabama
WROC-TV Rochester, New York
WTGL Cocoa, Florida
WXCW Naples, Florida
WXIN Indianapolis, Indiana
XHIJ-DT Ciudad Juarez, Texas

Channel 46

KJZZ-TV Salt Lake City, Utah
KMIR-TV Palm Springs, California
KNCT Belton, Texas
KQCA Stockton, California
KSNF Joplin, Missouri
KTXD-TV Greenville, Texas
KETD Castle Rock, Colorado
KXLT-TV Rochester, Minnesota
WBFF Baltimore, Maryland
WCCV-TV Arecibo, Puerto Rico
WCTV Thomasville, Georgia
WDJT-TV Milwaukee, Wisconsin
WFIE Evansville, Indiana
WFMZ-TV Allentown, Pennsylvania
WUVN Hartford, Connecticut
WHFT-TV Miami, Florida
WHTJ Charlottesville, Virginia
WMCF-TV Montgomery, Alabama
WPXV-TV Norfolk, Virginia
WTPX-TV Antigo, Wisconsin
WTVP Peoria, Illinois
WUPW Toledo, Ohio
WVVA Bluefield, West Virginia
WWAY Wilmington, North Carolina
WWHO Chillicothe, Ohio
KOCM Norman, Oklahoma
KUKL-TV Kalispell, Montana

Channel 47

KDLT-TV Sioux Falls, South Dakota
KAZA-TV Avalon, California
KTDO Las Cruces, New Mexico
KSMO-TV Kansas City, Missouri
KTLN-TV Novato, California
KWHB Tulsa, Oklahoma
WAVE Louisville, Kentucky
WFTT-DT Tampa, Florida
WCSC-TV Charleston, South Carolina
WRBU East St. Louis, Illinois
WJZY Belmont, North Carolina
WLNY-TV Riverhead, New York
WRLM Canton, Ohio
WPBN-TV Traverse City, Michigan
WPCT Panama City Beach, Florida
WPMT York, Pennsylvania
WLGA Opelika, Alabama
WTTW Chicago, Illinois
WTVH Syracuse, New York
WUPV Ashland, Virginia
WVOZ-TV Ponce, Puerto Rico
WYDN Worcester, Massachusetts
WYDO Greenville, North Carolina
WZRB Columbia, South Carolina

Channel 48

KING-TV Seattle, Washington
WOAI-TV San Antonio, Texas
KOCE-TV Huntington Beach, California
KTFF-DT Porterville, California
KSPX-TV Sacramento, California
KTMD Galveston, Texas
KUCW Ogden, Utah
KVTJ-DT Jonesboro, Arkansas
WACH Columbia, South Carolina
WAFF Huntsville, Alabama
WAQP Saginaw, Michigan
WCIA Champaign, Illinois
WFXU Live Oak, Florida
WHME-TV South Bend, Indiana
WUVG-DT Athens, Georgia
WMLW-TV Racine, Wisconsin
WJMN-TV Escanaba, Michigan
WKGB-TV Bowling Green, Kentucky
WLED-TV Littleton, New Hampshire
WOPX-TV Melbourne, Florida
WPXI Pittsburgh, Pennsylvania
WRAL-TV Raleigh, North Carolina
WRC-TV Washington, District of Columbia
WRJM Troy, Alabama
WRNN-TV Kingston, New York
WSYX Columbus, Ohio
WTTV Bloomington, Indiana
WUJA Caguas, Puerto Rico
WXOW La Crosse, Wisconsin
WXXV-TV Gulfport, Mississippi
WYDC Corning, New York
WVLR Tazewell, Tennessee
WFBD Destin, Florida
KVSN-DT Pueblo, Colorado

Channel 49

KASW Phoenix, Arizona
KJLA Ventura, California
KKTV Colorado Springs, Colorado
KMYA-DT Camden, Arkansas
KLJB Davenport, Missouri
KNVA Austin, Texas
KNVO McAllen, Texas
KPTH Sioux City, Iowa
KSTS San Jose, California
KTKA-TV Topeka, Kansas
KGEB Tulsa, Oklahoma
WWSI Atlantic City, New Jersey
WAWD Fort Walton Beach, Florida
WDKA Paducah, Kentucky
WDLI-TV Canton, Ohio
WDRB Louisville, Kentucky
WEDW Bridgeport, Connecticut
WEKW-TV Keene, New Hampshire
WEUX Chippewa Falls, Wisconsin
WFGC Palm Beach, Florida
WHSV-TV Harrisonburg, Virginia
WLFG Grundy, Virginia
WLNE-TV New Bedford, Rhode Island
WMSN-TV Madison, Wisconsin
WNTZ-TV Natchez, Mississippi
WNWO-TV Toledo, Ohio
WNYO-TV Buffalo, New York
WRAZ Raleigh, North Carolina
WTAP-TV Parkersburg, West Virginia
WXTX Columbus, Georgia

Channel 50

KUNS-TV Bellevue, Washington
KBTX-TV Bryan, Texas
KNWA-TV Rogers, Arkansas
KNXT Visalia, California
KOPX-TV Oklahoma City, Oklahoma
KQEH San Jose, California
WAXN-TV Kannapolis, North Carolina
WDCW Washington, District of Columbia
WBRC Birmingham, Alabama
WCBD-TV Charleston, South Carolina
WDTN Dayton, Ohio
WEAO Akron, Ohio
WEIU-TV Charleston, Illinois
WFGX Fort Walton Beach, Florida
WGNT Portsmouth, Virginia
WINK-TV Fort Myers, Florida
WISC-TV Madison, Wisconsin
WBIN-TV Derry, New Hampshire
WNEP-TV Scranton, Pennsylvania
WOAY-TV Oak Hill, West Virginia
WPCB-TV Greensburg, Pennsylvania
WPXL-TV New Orleans, Louisiana
WQHA Aguada, Puerto Rico
WQLN Erie, Pennsylvania
WTLH Bainbridge, Georgia
WYPX-TV Amsterdam, New York
KKAI Kailua, Hawaii
KLWB New Iberia, Louisiana

Channel 51

KCEC Denver, Colorado
KDTV-DT San Francisco, California
KGAN Cedar Rapids, Missouri
KTFN El Paso, Texas
KPXE-TV Kansas City, Missouri
KXLA Rancho Palos Verdes, California
KSBI Oklahoma City, Oklahoma
WAGV Harlan, Kentucky
WBIF Marianna, Florida
WEPX-TV Greenville, North Carolina
WFMY-TV Greensboro, North Carolina
WMYO Salem, Indiana
WFXG Augusta, Georgia
WJAR Providence, Rhode Island
WKEF Dayton, Ohio
WLAJ Lansing, Michigan
WNJN Montclair, New Jersey
WPWR-TV Gary, Indiana
WPXA-TV Rome, Georgia
WPXX-TV Memphis, Tennessee
WSST-TV Cordele, Georgia
WTAE-TV Pittsburgh, Pennsylvania
WRFB Carolina, Puerto Rico
KCEB Longview, Texas
KOHD Bend, Oregon

Channel 52

KYAZ Katy, Texas
KOLR Springfield, Missouri

Channel 53

KUBE-TV Baytown, Texas
WMDT Salisbury, Maryland

Channel 54

KAZD Lake Dallas, Texas

Channel 55

KENS San Antonio, Texas
KUVI-DT Bakersfield, California

Channel 56

KJRH-TV Tulsa, Oklahoma
WLII Caguas, Puerto Rico

Channel 57

KWKT-TV Waco, Texas

Channel 59

KCET Los Angeles, California
WBAL-TV Baltimore, Maryland
WMUR-TV Manchester, New Hampshire

US Television Stations by Virtual Channel

Channel 2

KATN Fairbanks, Alaska
KATU Portland, Oregon
KBOI-TV Boise, Idaho
KCBS-TV Los Angeles, California
KCWX Fredericksburg, Texas
KDKA-TV Pittsburgh, Pennsylvania
KDTN Denton, Texas
KETS Little Rock, Arkansas
KGFE Grand Forks, North Dakota
KHBC-TV Hilo, Hawaii
KHON-TV Honolulu, Hawaii
KJRH-TV Tulsa, Oklahoma
KJWY Jackson, Wyoming
KMID Midland, Texas
KNAZ-TV Flagstaff, Arizona
KNOP-TV North Platte, Nebraska
KOTI Klamath Falls, Oregon
KPRC-TV Houston, Texas
KQTV St. Joseph, Missouri
KSNC Great Bend, Kansas
KTCA-TV St. Paul, Minnesota
KTUU-TV Anchorage, Alaska
KTVI St. Louis, Missouri
KTVN Reno, Nevada
KTVQ Billings, Montana
KTVU Oakland, California
KTWO-TV Casper, Wyoming
KUSD-TV Vermillion, South Dakota
KUTV Salt Lake City, Utah
KWGN-TV Denver, Colorado
KXMA-TV Dickinson, North Dakota
WBAY-TV Green Bay, Wisconsin
WBBM-TV Chicago, Illinois
WCBD-TV Charleston, South Carolina
WCBS-TV New York, New York
WDIQ Dozier, Alabama
WDTN Dayton, Ohio
WESH Daytona Beach, Florida
WETP-TV Sneedville, Tennessee
WFMY-TV Greensboro, North Carolina
WGBH-TV Boston, Massachusetts
WJBK Detroit, Michigan
WKAQ-TV San Juan, Puerto Rico
WKRN-TV Nashville, Tennessee
WKTV Utica, New York
WLBZ Bangor, Maine
WMAB-TV Mississippi State, Mississippi
WMAR-TV Baltimore, Maryland
WPBT Miami, Florida
WSB-TV Atlanta, Georgia
WUND-TV Edenton, North Carolina

Channel 3

KATC Lafayette, Louisiana
KBME-TV Bismarck, North Dakota
KBTX-TV Bryan, Texas
KCRA-TV Sacramento, California
KDLH Duluth, Minnesota
KDLO-TV Florence, South Dakota
KENW Portales, New Mexico
KEYT-TV Santa Barbara, California
KFDX-TV Wichita Falls, Texas
KGMV Wailuku, Hawaii
KIEM-TV Eureka, California
KIII Corpus Christi, Texas
KIMT Mason City, Iowa
KLEW-TV Lewiston, Idaho
KLNE-TV Lexington, Nebraska
KOAB-TV Bend, Oregon
KOET Eufaula, Oklahoma
KOTA-TV Rapid City, South Dakota
KREG-TV Glenwood Springs, Colorado
KRTV Great Falls, Montana
KSAN-TV San Angelo, Texas
KSNV-DT Las Vegas, Nevada
KSNW Wichita, Kansas
KSWK Lakin, Kansas
KTBS-TV Shreveport, Louisiana
KTOO-TV Juneau, Alaska
KTVK Phoenix, Arizona
KTVO Kirksville, Missouri
KVNV Ely, Nevada
KYTV Springfield, Missouri
KYUS-TV Miles City, Montana
KYW-TV Philadelphia, Pennsylvania
WAVE Louisville, Kentucky
WBTV Charlotte, North Carolina
WEAR-TV Pensacola, Florida
WEDU Tampa, Florida
WFSB Hartford, Connecticut
WIPM-TV Mayaguez, Puerto Rico
WJMN-TV Escanaba, Michigan
WLBT Jackson, Mississippi
WPSU-TV Clearfield, Pennsylvania
WRBL Columbus, Georgia
WREG-TV Memphis, Tennessee
WSAV-TV Savannah, Georgia
WSAZ-TV Huntington, West Virginia
WSIL-TV Harrisburg, Illinois
WSTM-TV Syracuse, New York
WTKR Norfolk, Virginia
WWMT Kalamazoo, Michigan

Channel 4

KAMR-TV Amarillo, Texas
KARK-TV Little Rock, Arkansas
KBTV-TV Port Arthur, Texas
KCNC-TV Denver, Colorado
KCSG Cedar City, Utah
KDBC-TV El Paso, Texas
KDFW Dallas, Texas
KDUH-TV Scottsbluff, Nebraska
KFQX Grand Junction, Colorado
KGBT-TV Harlingen, Texas
KITV Honolulu, Hawaii
KLBY Colby, Kansas
KMOV St. Louis, Missouri
KNBC Los Angeles, California
KOMO-TV Seattle, Washington
KPIC Roseburg, Oregon
KPRY-TV Pierre, South Dakota
KRON-TV San Francisco, California
KTBY Anchorage, Alaska
KTIV Sioux City, Iowa
KTVX Salt Lake City, Utah
KUBD Ketchikan, Alaska
KVOA Tucson, Arizona
KWAB-TV Big Spring, Texas
KWSE Williston, North Dakota
KXJB-TV Valley City, North Dakota
KXLY-TV Spokane, Washington
WAPA-TV San Juan, Puerto Rico
WBZ-TV Boston, Massachusetts
WCCO-TV Minneapolis, Minnesota
WCIV Charleston, South Carolina
WCMH-TV Columbus, Ohio
WDAF-TV Kansas City, Missouri
WFOR-TV Miami, Florida
WHBF-TV Rock Island, Illinois
WIVB-TV Buffalo, New York
WJXT Jacksonville, Florida
WNBC New York, New York
WNJX-TV Mayaguez, Puerto Rico
WOAI-TV San Antonio, Texas
WOAY-TV Oak Hill, West Virginia
WRC-TV Washington, District of Columbia
WSMV-TV Nashville, Tennessee
WTAE-TV Pittsburgh, Pennsylvania
WTMJ-TV Milwaukee, Wisconsin
WTOM-TV Cheboygan, Michigan
WTTV Bloomington, Indiana
WTVY Dothan, Alabama
WUNC-TV Chapel Hill, North Carolina
WWL-TV New Orleans, Louisiana
WYFF Greenville, South Carolina

Channel 5

KALB-TV Alexandria, Louisiana
KCTV Kansas City, Missouri
KDLV-TV Mitchell, South Dakota
KFBB-TV Great Falls, Montana
KFSM-TV Fort Smith, Arkansas
KFYR-TV Bismarck, North Dakota
KGWL-TV Lander, Wyoming
KGWN-TV Cheyenne, Wyoming
KHAS-TV Hastings, Nebraska
KING-TV Seattle, Washington
KIVV-TV Lead, South Dakota
KNME-TV Albuquerque, New Mexico
KNPB Reno, Nevada
KOAA-TV Pueblo, Colorado
KOBI Medford, Oregon
KOCO-TV Oklahoma City, Oklahoma
KPHO-TV Phoenix, Arizona
KPIX-TV San Francisco, California
KREX-TV Grand Junction, Colorado
KRGV-TV Weslaco, Texas
KSDK St. Louis, Missouri
KSL-TV Salt Lake City, Utah
KSTP-TV St. Paul, Minnesota
KTLA Los Angeles, California
KTTZ-TV Lubbock, Texas
KVVU-TV Henderson, Nevada
KXAS-TV Fort Worth, Texas
KXGN-TV Glendive, Montana
WABI-TV Bangor, Maine
WBKP Calumet, Michigan
WCSC-TV Charleston, South Carolina
WCVB-TV Boston, Massachusetts
WCYB-TV Bristol, Virginia
WDTV Weston, West Virginia
WFRV-TV Green Bay, Wisconsin
WKRG-TV Mobile, Alabama
WLWT Cincinnati, Ohio
WMAQ-TV Chicago, Illinois
WMC-TV Memphis, Tennessee
WNEM-TV Bay City, Michigan
WNYW New York, New York
WPTZ North Pole, New York
WRAL-TV Raleigh, North Carolina
WTTG Washington, District of Columbia
WTVF Nashville, Tennessee
WTVH Syracuse, New York
WUFT Gainesville, Florida

Channel 6

KAAL Austin, Minnesota
KAUZ-TV Wichita Falls, Texas
KBJR-TV Superior, Wisconsin
KCEN-TV Temple, Texas
KEMV Mountain View, Arkansas
KHQ-TV Spokane, Washington
KIDY San Angelo, Texas
KLEI-TV Kailua-Kona, Hawaii
KMOH-TV Kingman, Arizona
KMOS-TV Sedalia, Missouri
KOIN Portland, Oregon
KPLO-TV Reliance, South Dakota
KPTW Casper, Wyoming
KREZ-TV Durango, Colorado
KRIS-TV Corpus Christi, Texas
KRMA-TV Denver, Colorado
KSBY San Luis Obispo, California
KSRE Minot, North Dakota
KSVI Billings, Montana
KTAL-TV Texarkana, Texas
KUAT-TV Tucson, Arizona
KVIE Sacramento, California
KVIQ Eureka, California
KWNB-TV Hayes Center, Nebraska
KWQC-TV Davenport, Iowa
WABG-TV Greenwood, Mississippi
WATE-TV Knoxville, Tennessee
WBRC Birmingham, Alabama
WCML Alpena, Michigan
WCSH Portland, Maine
WCTV Thomasville, Georgia
WDAY-TV Fargo, North Dakota
WDSU New Orleans, Louisiana
WECT Wilmington, North Carolina
WIPR-TV San Juan, Puerto Rico
WITI Milwaukee, Wisconsin
WJAC-TV Johnstown, Pennsylvania
WJBF Augusta, Georgia
WKMG-TV Orlando, Florida
WLNS-TV Lansing, Michigan
WLUC-TV Marquette, Michigan
WOWT Omaha, Nebraska
WPSD-TV Paducah, Kentucky
WPVI-TV Philadelphia, Pennsylvania
WRGB Schenectady, New York
WRTV Indianapolis, Indiana
WSYX Columbus, Ohio
WTVJ Miami, Florida
WTVR-TV Richmond, Virginia
WVVA Bluefield, West Virginia

Channel 7

KABC-TV Los Angeles, California
KAII-TV Wailuku, Hawaii
KAKM Anchorage, Alaska
KATV Little Rock, Arkansas
KAZT-TV Prescott, Arizona

KBZK Bozeman, Montana
KCCO-TV Alexandria, Minnesota
KETV Omaha, Nebraska
KEVN-TV Rapid City, South Dakota
KFXF Fairbanks, Alaska
KGO-TV San Francisco, California
KHQA-TV Hannibal, Missouri
KIRO-TV Seattle, Washington
KJRR Jamestown, North Dakota
KLTV Tyler, Texas
KMGH-TV Denver, Colorado
KMNE-TV Bassett, Nebraska
KOAC-TV Corvallis, Oregon
KOAM-TV Pittsburg, Kansas
KOAT-TV Albuquerque, New Mexico
KOSA-TV Odessa, Texas
KPLC Lake Charles, Louisiana
KQCD-TV Dickinson, North Dakota
KRCR-TV Redding, California
KSPS-TV Spokane, Washington
KSWO-TV Lawton, Oklahoma
KTBC Austin, Texas
KTVB Boise, Idaho
KUED Salt Lake City, Utah
KVIA-TV El Paso, Texas
KVII-TV Amarillo, Texas
KVYE El Centro, California
KWWL Waterloo, Iowa
WBBJ-TV Jackson, Tennessee
WCIQ Mount Cheaha, Alabama
WDAM-TV Laurel, Mississippi
WDBJ Roanoke, Virginia
WHIO-TV Dayton, Ohio
WITV Charleston, South Carolina
WJCT Jacksonville, Florida
WJHG-TV Panama City, Florida
WJLA-TV Washington, District of Columbia
WKBW-TV Buffalo, New York
WLS-TV Chicago, Illinois
WMAK Knoxville, Tennessee
WPBN-TV Traverse City, Michigan
WSAW-TV Wausau, Wisconsin
WSPA-TV Spartanburg, South Carolina
WSVN Miami, Florida
WTRF-TV Wheeling, West Virginia
WVII-TV Bangor, Maine
WXYZ-TV Detroit, Michigan

Channel 8

KAET Phoenix, Arizona
KAIT Jonesboro, Arkansas
KCCI Des Moines, Iowa
KESD-TV Brookings, South Dakota
KGNS-TV Laredo, Texas
KGW Portland, Oregon
KIFI-TV Idaho Falls, Idaho
KJCT Grand Junction, Colorado
KJUD Juneau, Alaska
KLAS-TV Las Vegas, Nevada
KLKN Lincoln, Nebraska
KLST San Angelo, Texas
KNOE-TV Monroe, Louisiana
KOBR Roswell, New Mexico
KOMU-TV Columbia, Missouri
KPAX-TV Missoula, Montana
KQSL Fort Bragg, California
KSBW Salinas, California
KSNK McCook, Nebraska
KSYS Medford, Oregon
KTSC Pueblo, Colorado
KTUL Tulsa, Oklahoma
KUHT Houston, Texas
KULR-TV Billings, Montana
KUMV-TV Williston, North Dakota
KZSD-TV Martin, South Dakota
WAGM-TV Presque Isle, Maine
WAKA Selma, Alabama
WCHS-TV Charleston, West Virginia
WDAZ-TV Devil's Lake, North Dakota
WDHS Iron Mountain, Michigan
WDSE Duluth, Minnesota
WFLA-TV Tampa, Florida
WFXI Morehead City, North Carolina
WGAL Lancaster, Pennsylvania
WGEN-TV Key West, Florida
WGHP High Point, North Carolina
WGTQ Sault Ste. Marie, Michigan
WGTV Athens, Georgia
WISH-TV Indianapolis, Indiana
WJW Cleveland, Ohio
WNPT Nashville, Tennessee
WOOD-TV Grand Rapids, Michigan
WQAD-TV Moline, Illinois
WRIC-TV Petersburg, Virginia
WROC-TV Rochester, New York
WSIU-TV Carbondale, Illinois
WSVI Christiansted, Virgin Islands
WVLT-TV Knoxville, Tennessee
WWCP-TV Johnstown, Pennsylvania
WXGA-TV Waycross, Georgia

Channel 9

KAWE Bemidji, Minnesota
KBHE-TV Rapid City, South Dakota
KCAU-TV Sioux City, Iowa
KCFG Flagstaff, Arizona
KCFW-TV Kalispell, Montana
KCRG-TV Cedar Rapids, Iowa
KCTS-TV Seattle, Washington
KDSE Dickinson, North Dakota
KECY-TV El Centro, California
KETC St. Louis, Missouri
KETG Arkadelphia, Arkansas
KGMD-TV Hilo, Hawaii
KIXE-TV Redding, California
KLRN San Antonio, Texas
KMBC-TV Kansas City, Missouri
KMSP-TV Minneapolis, Minnesota
KNIN-TV Caldwell, Idaho
KNMD-TV Santa Fe, New Mexico
KOOD Hays, Kansas
KPNE-TV North Platte, Nebraska
KQED San Francisco, California
KRBC-TV Abilene, Texas
KTRE Lufkin, Texas
KTSM-TV El Paso, Texas
KUAC-TV Fairbanks, Alaska
KUEN Ogden, Utah
KWES-TV Odessa, Texas
WAFB Baton Rouge, Louisiana
WCPO-TV Cincinnati, Ohio
WFTV Orlando, Florida
WNBW-DT Gainesville, Florida
WNCT-TV Greenville, North Carolina
WSOC-TV Charlotte, North Carolina
WSWP-TV Grandview, West Virginia
WSYR-TV Syracuse, New York
WTOV-TV Steubenville, Ohio
WTVM Columbus, Georgia
WUSA Washington, District of Columbia
WVAN-TV Savannah, Georgia
WWOR-TV Secaucus, New Jersey
WWTV Cadillac, Michigan

Channel 10

KBIM-TV Roswell, New Mexico
KBRR Thief River Falls, Minnesota
KFDA-TV Amarillo, Texas
KFNE Riverton, Wyoming
KGTV San Diego, California
KISU-TV Pocatello, Idaho
KLFY-TV Lafayette, Louisiana
KLVX Las Vegas, Nevada
KMEB Wailuku, Hawaii
KMOT Minot, North Dakota
KMTF Helena, Montana
KOLN Lincoln, Nebraska
KOPB-TV Portland, Oregon
KREY-TV Montrose, Colorado
KSTF Scottsbluff, Nebraska
KTEN Ada, Oklahoma
KTSD-TV Pierre, South Dakota
KTTC Rochester, Minnesota
KTVE El Dorado, Arkansas
KTVL Medford, Oregon
KWCM-TV Appleton, Minnesota
KWSU-TV Pullman, Washington
KWTX-TV Waco, Texas
KXTV Sacramento, California
KYVV-TV Del Rio, Texas
KZTV Corpus Christi, Texas
WALA-TV Mobile, Alabama
WALB Albany, Georgia
WAVY-TV Portsmouth, Virginia
WBIQ Birmingham, Alabama
WBIR-TV Knoxville, Tennessee
WBNS-TV Columbus, Ohio
WBUP Ishpeming, Michigan
WCAU Philadelphia, Pennsylvania
WCBB Augusta, Maine
WGEM-TV Quincy, Illinois
WHEC-TV Rochester, New York
WILX-TV Onondaga, Michigan
WIS Columbia, South Carolina
WJAR Providence, Rhode Island
WMEM-TV Presque Isle, Maine
WMVS Milwaukee, Wisconsin
WPLG Miami, Florida
WSLS-TV Roanoke, Virginia
WTAJ-TV Altoona, Pennsylvania
WTEN Albany, New York
WTSP St. Petersburg, Florida
WWUP-TV Sault Ste. Marie, Michigan

Channel 11

KAQY Columbia, Louisiana
KBYU-TV Provo, Utah
KCBD Lubbock, Texas
KCBY-TV Coos Bay, Oregon
KCHF Santa Fe, New Mexico
KDIN-TV Des Moines, Iowa
KDTP Holbrook, Arizona
KELO-TV Sioux Falls, South Dakota
KFFX-TV Pendleton, Oregon
KFNR Rawlins, Wyoming
KGIN Grand Island, Nebraska
KHAW-TV Hilo, Hawaii
KHET Honolulu, Hawaii
KHSD-TV Lead, South Dakota
KKCO Grand Junction, Colorado
KKTV Colorado Springs, Colorado
KMVT Twin Falls, Idaho
KNTV San Jose, California
KOED-TV Tulsa, Oklahoma
KPLR-TV St. Louis, Missouri
KQSD-TV Lowry, South Dakota
KRII Chisholm, Minnesota
KRXI-TV Reno, Nevada
KSNG Garden City, Kansas
KSTW Tacoma, Washington
KTHV Little Rock, Arkansas
KTTV Los Angeles, California
KTVA Anchorage, Alaska
KTVF Fairbanks, Alaska
KTVT Fort Worth, Texas
KTWU Topeka, Kansas
KUFM-TV Missoula, Montana
KXMD-TV Williston, North Dakota
WBAL-TV Baltimore, Maryland
WBKB-TV Alpena, Michigan
WENH-TV Durham, New Hampshire
WFSU-TV Tallahassee, Florida
WHAS-TV Louisville, Kentucky
WINK-TV Fort Myers, Florida
WJHL-TV Johnson City, Tennessee
WLUK-TV Green Bay, Wisconsin
WPIX New York, New York
WPXI Pittsburgh, Pennsylvania
WTOC-TV Savannah, Georgia
WTOK-TV Meridian, Mississippi
WTOL Toledo, Ohio
WTVD Durham, North Carolina
WVAH-TV Charleston, West Virginia
WXIA-TV Atlanta, Georgia

Channel 12

KBDI-TV Broomfield, Colorado
KBMT Beaumont, Texas
KCCW-TV Walker, Minnesota
KCOY-TV Santa Maria, California
KDRV Medford, Oregon
KETZ El Dorado, Arkansas
KEYC-TV CBS & NEYC FOX Mankato, Minnesota
KFVS-TV Cape Girardeau, Missouri
KHSL-TV Chico, California
KMAU Wailuku, Hawaii
KMYU Saint George, Utah
KNRR Pembina, North Dakota
KOBF Farmington, New Mexico
KODE-TV Joplin, Missouri
KPNX Mesa, Arizona
KPTV Portland, Oregon
KRNE-TV Merriman, Nebraska
KSAT-TV San Antonio, Texas
KTRV-TV Nampa, Idaho
KTTM Huron, South Dakota
KTXS-TV Sweetwater, Texas
KUON-TV Lincoln, Nebraska
KUTF Logan, Utah
KVIH-TV Clovis, New Mexico
KVOS-TV Bellingham, Washington
KXII Sherman, Texas
KXMB-TV Bismarck, North Dakota

WBOY-TV Clarksburg, West Virginia
WCTI-TV New Bern, North Carolina
WDEF-TV Chattanooga, Tennessee
WICU-TV Erie, Pennsylvania
WILL-TV Urbana, Illinois
WISN-TV Milwaukee, Wisconsin
WJFW-TV Rhinelander, Wisconsin
WJRT-TV Flint, Michigan
WJTV Jackson, Mississippi
WKRC-TV Cincinnati, Ohio
WMAE-TV Booneville, Mississippi
WMEB-TV Orono, Maine
WPEC West Palm Beach, Florida
WPRI-TV Providence, Rhode Island
WRDW-TV Augusta, Georgia
WSFA Montgomery, Alabama
WTLV Jacksonville, Florida
WWBT Richmond, Virginia
WXII-TV Winston-Salem, North Carolina
WYES-TV New Orleans, Louisiana

Channel 13

KAFT Fayetteville, Arkansas
KCOS El Paso, Texas
KCPQ Tacoma, Washington
KECI-TV Missoula, Montana
KEET Eureka, California
KERA-TV Dallas, Texas
KFME Fargo, North Dakota
KGWR-TV Rock Springs, Wyoming
KHGI-TV Kearney, Nebraska
KHNL Honolulu, Hawaii
KHVO Hilo, Hawaii
KLBK-TV Lubbock, Texas
KLTM-TV Monroe, Louisiana
KOLD-TV Tucson, Arizona
KOVR Stockton, California
KPSD-TV Eagle Butte, South Dakota
KRCG Jefferson City, Missouri
KRDO-TV Colorado Springs, Colorado
KRQE Albuquerque, New Mexico
KSFY-TV Sioux Falls, South Dakota
KSTU Salt Lake City, Utah
KSWT Yuma, Arizona
KTNE-TV Alliance, Nebraska
KTNL-TV Sitka, Alaska
KTRK-TV Houston, Texas
KTVR La Grande, Oregon
KVAL-TV Eugene, Oregon
KVTV Laredo, Texas
KXMC-TV Minot, North Dakota
KYUR Anchorage, Alaska
WBTW Florence, South Carolina
WEAU-TV Eau Claire, Wisconsin
WGME-TV Portland, Maine
WHAM-TV Rochester, New York
WHBQ-TV Memphis, Tennessee
WIBW-TV Topeka, Kansas
WJZ-TV Baltimore, Maryland
WLOS Asheville, North Carolina
WLOX Biloxi, Mississippi
WMAZ-TV Macon, Georgia
WMBB Panama City, Florida
WMED-TV Calais, Maine
WNET Newark, New Jersey
WNYT Albany, New York
WOWK-TV Huntington, West Virginia
WPXS Mount Vernon, Illinois
WQED Pittsburgh, Pennsylvania
WSET-TV Lynchburg, Virginia
WTHR Indianapolis, Indiana
WTVG Toledo, Ohio
WTVT Tampa, Florida
WVTM-TV Birmingham, Alabama

Channel 14

KARD West Monroe, Louisiana
KCIT Amarillo, Texas
KETH-TV Houston, Texas
KFOX-TV El Paso, Texas
KGWC-TV Casper, Wyoming
KJZZ-TV Salt Lake City, Utah
KMEG Sioux City, Iowa
KOCW Hoisington, Kansas
KTBO-TV Oklahoma City, Oklahoma
KTGM Tamuning, Guam
KWHD Hilo, Hawaii
KWHE Honolulu, Hawaii
WABW-TV Pelham, Georgia
WCMU-TV Mount Pleasant, Michigan
WEBA-TV Allendale, South Carolina
WFBT Bath, New York
WHKY-TV Hickory, North Carolina
WMAW-TV Meridian, Mississippi
WMEI Arecibo, Puerto Rico
WOST Mayaguez, Puerto Rico
WPTO Oxford, Ohio
WSEC Jacksonville, Illinois
WYDO Greenville, North Carolina

Channel 15

KAMU-TV College Station, Texas
KCKA Centralia, Washington
KCLO-TV Rapid City, South Dakota
KINC Las Vegas, Nevada
KNXV-TV Phoenix, Arizona
KOGG Wailuku, Hawaii
KPBS San Diego, California
KPOB-TV Poplar Bluff, Missouri
KSMQ-TV Austin, Minnesota
KVRR Fargo, North Dakota
KXVA Abilene, Texas
KXVO Omaha, Nebraska
KYOU-TV Ottumwa, Iowa
WANE-TV Fort Wayne, Indiana
WBRA-TV Roanoke, Virginia
WDSC-TV New Smyrna Beach, Florida
WHDF Florence, Alabama
WHRO-TV Hampton-Norfolk, Virginia
WKOP-TV Knoxville, Tennessee
WKPC-TV Louisville, Kentucky
WLYH-TV Lancaster, Pennsylvania
WMTV Madison, Wisconsin
WPDE-TV Florence, South Carolina
WPMI-TV Mobile, Alabama
WTAP-TV Parkersburg, West Virginia
WXVT Greenville, Mississippi

Channel 16

KDSD-TV Aberdeen, South Dakota
KEDT Corpus Christi, Texas
KLRT-TV Little Rock, Arkansas
KMTR Eugene, Oregon
KSNF Joplin, Missouri
KTAJ-TV St. Joseph, Missouri
KTGF Great Falls, Montana
KUNP La Grande, Oregon
WAPT Jackson, Mississippi
WBOC-TV Salisbury, Maryland
WGGS-TV Greenville, South Carolina
WJKT Jackson, Tennessee
WJWJ-TV Beaufort, South Carolina
WNDU-TV South Bend, Indiana
WNEP-TV Scranton, Pennsylvania
WPTD Dayton, Ohio
WTJR Quincy, Illinois
WUSF-TV Tampa, Florida
WUSI-TV Olney, Illinois

Channel 17

KDOR-TV Bartlesville, Oklahoma
KDSM-TV Des Moines, Iowa
KGET-TV Bakersfield, California
KMIZ Columbia, Missouri
KTCI-TV St. Paul, Minnesota
KTTW Sioux Falls, South Dakota
WAND Decatur, Illinois
WCWJ Jacksonville, Florida
WDBB Bessemer, Alabama
WDLI-TV Canton, Ohio
WLRN-TV Miami, Florida
WMAU-TV Bude, Mississippi
WMHT Schenectady, New York
WNCN Goldsboro, North Carolina
WNED-TV Buffalo, New York
WPCH-TV Atlanta, Georgia
WPHL-TV Philadelphia, Pennsylvania
WTVO Rockford, Illinois
WUNE-TV Linville, North Carolina
WVXF Charlotte Amalie, Virgin Islands
WXMI Grand Rapids, Michigan
WZTV Nashville, Tennessee

Channel 18

KAAS-TV Salina, Kansas
KJTL Wichita Falls, Texas
KLRU Austin, Texas
KLTL-TV Lake Charles, Louisiana
KRMJ Grand Junction, Colorado
KSCI Long Beach, California
KUEW St. George, Utah
KUPB Midland, Texas
KVPT Fresno, California
KWYB Butte, Montana
WCCB Charlotte, North Carolina
WDHN Dothan, Alabama
WETM-TV Elmira, New York
WHIZ-TV Zanesville, Ohio
WHTV Jackson, Michigan
WKCF Clermont, Florida
WLEX-TV Lexington, Kentucky
WLFI-TV Lafayette, Indiana
WMAV-TV Oxford, Mississippi
WNGH-TV Chatsworth, Georgia
WTCV San Juan, Puerto Rico
WUVN Hartford, Connecticut

Channel 19

KCPT Kansas City, Missouri
KEPR-TV Pasco, Washington
KJRE Ellendale, North Dakota
KTEJ Jonesboro, Arkansas
KUES Richfield, Utah
KVCT Victoria, Texas
KWBQ Santa Fe, New Mexico
KWKS Colby, Kansas
KXNE-TV Norfolk, Nebraska
KYTX Nacogdoches, Texas
WCAV Charlottesville, Virginia
WHNT-TV Huntsville, Alabama
WHOI Peoria, Illinois
WKPT-TV Kingsport, Tennessee
WLTX Columbia, South Carolina
WMAH-TV Biloxi, Mississippi
WOIO Shaker Heights, Ohio
WPCW Jeannette, Pennsylvania
WUNM-TV Jacksonville, North Carolina
WXOW La Crosse, Wisconsin
WZMQ Marquette, Michigan

Channel 20

KOFY-TV San Francisco, California
KRMU Durango, Colorado
KSMN Worthington, Minnesota
KTBW-TV Tacoma, Washington
KTMW Salt Lake City, Utah
KTXH Houston, Texas
KVME-TV Bishop, California
KWKB Iowa City, Iowa
WBBH-TV Fort Myers, Florida
WCES-TV Wrens, Georgia
WCOV-TV Montgomery, Alabama
WCWG Lexington, North Carolina
WDCA Washington, District of Columbia
WHNO New Orleans, Louisiana
WHRM-TV Wausau, Wisconsin
WKPV Ponce, Puerto Rico
WMYD Detroit, Michigan
WUTR Utica, New York
WVTB St. Johnsbury, Vermont
WYCC Chicago, Illinois

Channel 21

KAME-TV Reno, Nevada
KDCK Dodge City, Kansas
KNBN Rapid City, South Dakota
KOZK Springfield, Missouri
KPAZ-TV Phoenix, Arizona
KPXJ Minden, Louisiana
KQDS-TV Duluth, Minnesota
KRWB-TV Roswell, New Mexico
KTIN Fort Dodge, Iowa
KTVZ Bend, Oregon
KTXA Fort Worth, Texas
KUGF Great Falls, Montana
KVMY Las Vegas, Nevada
KWHM Wailuku, Hawaii
KXRM-TV Colorado Springs, Colorado
WBNA Louisville, Kentucky
WCMW Manistee, Michigan
WFMJ-TV Youngstown, Ohio
WHA-TV Madison, Wisconsin
WHNS Greenville, South Carolina
WHP-TV Harrisburg, Pennsylvania
WKMU Murray, Kentucky
WLIW Garden City, New York
WMPV-TV Mobile, Alabama
WPTA Fort Wayne, Indiana
WPXC-TV Brunswick, Georgia
WTCE-TV Fort Pierce, Florida
WTTO Homewood, Alabama

WWCW Lynchburg, Virginia
WWMB Florence, South Carolina
WXXI-TV Rochester, New York

Channel 22

KAWB Brainerd, Minnesota
KFCT Fort Collins, Colorado
KFTS Klamath Falls, Oregon
KLCW-TV Wolfforth, Texas
KLTJ Galveston, Texas
KRCB Cotati, California
KRWG-TV Las Cruces, New Mexico
KSKN Spokane, Washington
KWHY-TV Los Angeles, California
KWWF Waterloo, Iowa
KZJO Seattle, Washington
WBMM Tuskegee, Alabama
WCLF Clearwater, Florida
WCTE Cookeville, Tennessee
WHLT Hattiesburg, Mississippi
WJCL Savannah, Georgia
WKEF Dayton, Ohio
WLFL Raleigh, North Carolina
WMPT Annapolis, Maryland
WPMY Pittsburgh, Pennsylvania
WSBS-TV Key West, Florida
WSBT-TV South Bend, Indiana
WVNY Burlington, Vermont
WVUT Vincennes, Indiana
WWLP Springfield, Massachusetts
WYOU Scranton, Pennsylvania

Channel 23

KBSI Cape Girardeau, Missouri
KBSV Ceres, California
KCSD-TV Sioux Falls, South Dakota
KERO-TV Bakersfield, California
KHCE-TV San Antonio, Texas
KMCB Coos Bay, Oregon
KNAT-TV Albuquerque, New Mexico
KNDO Yakima, Washington
KOKI-TV Tulsa, Oklahoma
KTMF Missoula, Montana
WATM-TV Altoona, Pennsylvania
WBUI Decatur, Illinois
WCVE-TV Richmond, Virginia
WELF-TV Dalton, Georgia
WHMC Conway, South Carolina
WIFR Freeport, Illinois
WKAR-TV East Lansing, Michigan
WKZT-TV Elizabethtown, Kentucky
WMAO-TV Greenwood, Mississippi
WNDY-TV Marion, Indiana
WNJS Camden, New Jersey
WNLO Buffalo, New York
WPFO Waterville, Maine
WSRE Pensacola, Florida
WUCW Minneapolis, Minnesota
WUOA Tuscaloosa, Alabama
WXXA-TV Albany, New York

Channel 24

DKBTZ Butte, Montana
KBCB Bellingham, Washington
KFTA-TV Fort Smith, Arkansas
KLPB-TV Lafayette, Louisiana
KLTS-TV Shreveport, Louisiana
KNLC St. Louis, Missouri
KNVN Chico, California
KPNZ Ogden, Utah
KQUP Pullman, Washington
KRMZ Steamboat Springs, Colorado
KSAS-TV Wichita, Kansas
KSEE Fresno, California
KVUE Austin, Texas
KXND Minot, North Dakota
KYIN Mason City, Iowa
WCGV-TV Milwaukee, Wisconsin
WCNY-TV Syracuse, New York
WEDH Hartford, Connecticut
WGXA Macon, Georgia
WJET-TV Erie, Pennsylvania
WJPX San Juan, Puerto Rico
WKYU-TV Bowling Green, Kentucky
WMDN Meridian, Mississippi
WNPB-TV Morgantown, West Virginia
WNWO-TV Toledo, Ohio
WPTY-TV Memphis, Tennessee
WQPT-TV Moline, Illinois
WTAT-TV Charleston, South Carolina
WTLF Tallahassee, Florida
WUTB Baltimore, Maryland

Channel 25

KAVU-TV Victoria, Texas
KLPA-TV Alexandria, Louisiana
KMDE Devils Lake, North Dakota
KNDU Richland, Washington
KNLJ Jefferson City, Missouri
KOKH-TV Oklahoma City, Oklahoma
KTEL-TV Carlsbad, New Mexico
KXXV Waco, Texas
WACS-TV Dawson, Georgia
WEEK-TV Peoria, Illinois
WEHT Evansville, Indiana
WEYI-TV Saginaw, Michigan
WFXT Boston, Massachusetts
WHAG-TV Hagerstown, Maryland
WHIQ Huntsville, Alabama
WJXX Orange Park, Florida
WKAS Ashland, Kentucky
WLAX La Crosse, Wisconsin
WNYE-TV New York, New York
WOLO-TV Columbia, South Carolina
WPBF Tequesta, Florida
WUNK-TV Greenville, North Carolina
WVIZ Cleveland, Ohio
WXXV-TV Gulfport, Mississippi

Channel 26

KAAH-TV Honolulu, Hawaii
KCDT Coeur d'Alene, Washington
KFTC Bemidji, Minnesota
KINT-TV El Paso, Texas
KMPH-TV Visalia, California
KNDX Bismarck, North Dakota
KOZJ Joplin, Missouri
KRIV Houston, Texas
KTSF San Francisco, California
KYNE-TV Omaha, Nebraska
WAGT Augusta, Georgia
WAIQ Montgomery, Alabama
WBDT Springfield, Ohio
WCIU-TV Chicago, Illinois
WETA-TV Washington, District of Columbia
WGNO New Orleans, Louisiana
WMEA-TV Biddeford, Maine
WNYB Jamestown, New York
WQTO Ponce, Puerto Rico
WSFX-TV Wilmington, North Carolina
WUNL-TV Winston-Salem, North Carolina
WVEN-TV Daytona Beach, Florida
WZVN-TV Naples, Florida

Channel 27

KCPM Grand Forks, North Dakota
KCWV Duluth, Minnesota
KDFI Dallas, Texas
KLDO-TV Laredo, Texas
KLWY Cheyenne, Wyoming
KOZL-TV Springfield, Missouri
KREN-TV Reno, Nevada
KSNT Topeka, Kansas
KUAS-TV Tucson, Arizona
WBGU-TV Bowling Green, Ohio
WCCU Urbana, Illinois
WCMV Cadillac, Michigan
WGNT Portsmouth, Virginia
WHTM-TV Harrisburg, Pennsylvania
WKBN-TV Youngstown, Ohio
WLOV-TV West Point, Mississippi
WLPB-TV Baton Rouge, Louisiana
WQEC Quincy, Illinois
WRDQ Orlando, Florida
WRJA-TV Sumter, South Carolina
WTCT Marion, Illinois
WTXL-TV Tallahassee, Florida
WUNI Worcester, Massachusetts

Channel 28

KAMC Lubbock, Texas
KAYU-TV Spokane, Washington
KBTC-TV Tacoma, Washington
KCET Los Angeles, California
KEPB-TV Eugene, Oregon
KFXA Cedar Rapids, Iowa
KORO Corpus Christi, Texas
KYLE-TV Bryan, Texas
WBRE-TV Wilkes-Barre, Pennsylvania
WCPB Salisbury, Maryland
WHWC-TV Menomonie, Wisconsin
WJSP-TV Columbus, Georgia
WLWC New Bedford, Massachusetts
WPGX Panama City, Florida
WRDC Durham, North Carolina
WSJV Elkhart, Indiana
WTGS Hardeeville, South Carolina
WTTE Columbus, Ohio
WVER Rutland, Vermont

Channel 29

KABB San Antonio, Texas
KBAK-TV Bakersfield, California
KBVU Eureka, California
KCWE Kansas City, Missouri
KHNE-TV Hastings, Nebraska
KHOG-TV Fayetteville, Arkansas
KIMA-TV Yakima, Washington
KMPX Decatur, Texas
KUPT Hobbs, New Mexico
KVHP Lake Charles, Louisiana
WBIH Selma, Alabama
WFLX West Palm Beach, Florida
WFTC Minneapolis, Minnesota
WGTU Traverse City, Michigan
WKPD Paducah, Kentucky
WKSO-TV Somerset, Kentucky
WMPN-TV Jackson, Mississippi
WMUM-TV Cochran, Georgia
WNTV Greenville, South Carolina
WTTK Kokomo, Indiana
WTXF-TV Philadelphia, Pennsylvania
WUTV Buffalo, New York
WVIR-TV Charlottesville, Virginia

Channel 30

KBLN Grants Pass, Oregon
KCVU Paradise, California
KDNL-TV St. Louis, Missouri
KFSN-TV Fresno, California
KTUZ-TV Shawnee, Oklahoma
KUCW Ogden, Utah
KWWT Odessa, Texas
WAWS Jacksonville, Florida
WGBC Meridian, Mississippi
WGTE-TV Toledo, Ohio
WLMT Memphis, Tennessee
WNSC-TV Rock Hill, South Carolina
WNVC Fairfax, Virginia
WPBA Atlanta, Georgia
WQCW Portsmouth, Ohio
WRAY-TV Wilson, North Carolina
WSJU-TV San Juan, Puerto Rico
WSKA Corning, New York
WTIU Bloomington, Indiana
WUXP-TV Nashville, Tennessee
WVIT New Britain, Connecticut

Channel 31

KDKF Klamath Falls, Oregon
KDVR Denver, Colorado
KEYU Borger, Texas
KFXP Pocatello, Idaho
KLAX-TV Alexandria, Louisiana
KTNW Richland, Washington
KVMD Twentynine Palms, California
KWBM Harrison, Arkansas
WAAY-TV Huntsville, Alabama
WHLA-TV La Crosse, Wisconsin
WKOH Owensboro, Kentucky
WMBD-TV Peoria, Illinois
WPXN-TV New York, New York
WUHF Rochester, New York
WUNU Lumberton, North Carolina
WWPB Hagerstown, Maryland

Channel 32

KAZQ Albuquerque, New Mexico
KMTP-TV San Francisco, California
KRCW-TV Salem, Oregon
KRIN Waterloo, Iowa
KTAB-TV Abilene, Texas
WFLD Chicago, Illinois
WHUT-TV Washington, District of Columbia
WLAE-TV New Orleans, Louisiana
WLKY-TV Louisville, Kentucky
WMBF-TV Myrtle Beach, South Carolina
WNCF Montgomery, Alabama

Channel 33

KDAF Dallas, Texas
KDMD Anchorage, Alaska
KMSS-TV Shreveport, Louisiana
KQCK Cheyenne, Wyoming
KSPR Springfield, Missouri
KTAS San Luis Obispo, California
KVCW Las Vegas, Nevada
WBFS-TV Miami, Florida
WCFT-TV Tuscaloosa, Alabama
WETK Burlington, Vermont
WFQX-TV Cadillac, Michigan
WFXV Utica, New York
WHBR Pensacola, Florida
WITF-TV Harrisburg, Pennsylvania
WJPM-TV Florence, South Carolina
WPBY-TV Charleston, West Virginia
WTVZ-TV Norfolk, Virginia
WUNF-TV Asheville, North Carolina
WYTV Youngstown, Ohio

Channel 34

KDYW Waco, Texas
KEFB Ames, Iowa
KITU-TV Beaumont, Texas
KJTV-TV Lubbock, Texas
KLSR-TV Eugene, Oregon
KMCC Laughlin, Nevada
KOCB Oklahoma City, Oklahoma
KXNW Eureka Springs, Arkansas
WBKI-TV Campbellsville, Kentucky
WDFX-TV Ozark, Alabama
WGSA Baxley, Georgia
WIVT Binghamton, New York
WOSU-TV Columbus, Ohio
WRBJ Magee, Mississippi
WRUA Fajardo, Puerto Rico
WTVX Fort Pierce, Florida
WYOW Eagle River, Wisconsin

Channel 35

KAPP Yakima, Washington
KCBA Salinas, California
KRSC-TV Claremore, Oklahoma
KUID-TV Moscow, Idaho
KUOK Woodward, Oklahoma
KXTF Twin Falls, Idaho
WDCQ-TV Bad Axe, Michigan
WFGX Fort Walton Beach, Florida
WGVU-TV Grand Rapids, Michigan
WKHA Hazard, Kentucky
WLIO Lima, Ohio
WOFL Orlando, Florida
WPME Lewiston, Maine
WPXU-TV Jacksonville, North Carolina
WRLH-TV Richmond, Virginia
WRLK-TV Columbia, South Carolina
WUFX Vicksburg, Mississippi
WWTO-TV La Salle, Illinois
WYBE Philadelphia, Pennsylvania

Channel 36

KHIN Red Oak, Iowa
KICU-TV San Jose, California
KKAP Little Rock, Arkansas
KMIR-TV Palm Springs, California
KMTW Hutchinson, Kansas
KPBT-TV Odessa, Texas
KTVC Roseburg, Oregon
KWSD Sioux Falls, South Dakota
KXAN-TV Austin, Texas
WATL Atlanta, Georgia
WCNC-TV Charlotte, North Carolina
WDWL Bayamon, Puerto Rico
WENY-TV Elmira, New York
WFIQ Florence, Alabama
WGPT Oakland, Maryland
WLEF-TV Park Falls, Wisconsin
WMMP Charleston, South Carolina
WMVT Milwaukee, Wisconsin
WSBE-TV Providence, Rhode Island
WTVQ-DT Lexington, Kentucky
WUNP-TV Roanoke Rapids, North Carolina

Channel 38

KALO Honolulu, Hawaii
KCNS San Francisco, California
KPMR Santa Barbara, California
KSCE El Paso, Texas
KUQI Corpus Christi, Texas
WADL Mount Clemens, Michigan
WJWN-TV San Sebastian, Puerto Rico
WKMR Morehead, Kentucky
WLTZ Columbus, Georgia
WNEH Greenwood, South Carolina
WNOL-TV New Orleans, Louisiana
WSWB Scranton, Pennsylvania
WTTA St. Petersburg, Florida

Channel 39

KBLR Paradise, Nevada
KIAH Houston, Texas
KKJB Boise, Idaho
KMCT-TV West Monroe, Louisiana
KNSD San Diego, California
KXTX-TV Dallas, Texas
WCVI-TV Christiansted, Virgin Islands
WEMT Greeneville, Tennessee
WFWA Fort Wayne, Indiana
WHTN Murfreesboro, Tennessee
WLVT-TV Allentown, Pennsylvania
WQRF-TV Rockford, Illinois
WSFL-TV Miami, Florida
WUNJ-TV Wilmington, North Carolina

Channel 40

KHBS Fort Smith, Arkansas
KHRR Tucson, Arizona
KTBN-TV Santa Ana, California
KTLM Rio Grande City, Texas
KTXL Sacramento, California
WBUY-TV Holly Springs, Mississippi
WDBD Jackson, Mississippi
WGGB-TV Springfield, Massachusetts
WICZ-TV Binghamton, New York
WJSU-TV Anniston, Alabama
WLFB Bluefield, West Virginia
WLMB Toledo, Ohio
WMGM-TV Wildwood, New Jersey
WMTJ Fajardo, Puerto Rico
WMYA-TV Anderson, South Carolina
WNKY Bowling Green, Kentucky
WNMN Saranac Lake, New York
WPCB-TV Greensburg, Pennsylvania
WTWC-TV Tallahassee, Florida
WWSB Sarasota, Florida

Channel 41

KBCA Alexandria, Louisiana
KLUZ-TV Albuquerque, New Mexico
KMYT-TV Tulsa, Oklahoma
KRMT Denver, Colorado
KSHB-TV Kansas City, Missouri
WDRB Louisville, Kentucky
WHTJ Charlottesville, Virginia
WIIQ Demopolis, Alabama
WMGT-TV Macon, Georgia
WOTV Battle Creek, Michigan
WVTA Windsor, Vermont

Channel 42

KARZ-TV Little Rock, Arkansas
KESQ-TV Palm Springs, California
KEYE-TV Austin, Texas
KPTM Omaha, Nebraska
KSAX Alexandria, Minnesota
KTNC-TV Concord, California
KVEW Kennewick, Washington
WCLJ-TV Bloomington, Indiana
WEIQ Mobile, Alabama
WIAT Birmingham, Alabama
WIRS Yauco, Puerto Rico
WPBO Portsmouth, Ohio
WTVI Charlotte, North Carolina
WXEL-TV West Palm Beach, Florida

Channel 43

KAUT-TV Oklahoma City, Oklahoma
KGMC Clovis, California
KRWF Redwood Falls, Minnesota
WFXB Myrtle Beach, South Carolina
WGIQ Louisville, Alabama
WKOI-TV Richmond, Indiana
WNYS-TV Syracuse, New York
WPMT York, Pennsylvania
WTNZ Knoxville, Tennessee
WUAB Lorain, Ohio
WVBT Virginia Beach, Virginia
WYZZ-TV Bloomington, Illinois
WZVI Charlotte Amalie, Virgin Islands

Channel 44

KBCW San Francisco, California
KLUJ-TV Harlingen, Texas
KPTH Sioux City, Iowa
KWBN Honolulu, Hawaii
KXLA Rancho Palos Verdes, California
WAGV Harlan, Kentucky
WEVV-TV Evansville, Indiana
WFFF-TV Burlington, Vermont
WJTC Pensacola, Florida
WMCN-TV Atlantic City, New Jersey
WSWG Valdosta, Georgia
WTLW Lima, Ohio
WTOG St. Petersburg, Florida
WVEO Aguadilla, Puerto Rico
WVIA-TV Scranton, Pennsylvania

Channel 45

KSTC-TV Minneapolis, Minnesota
KUTP Phoenix, Arizona
WBFF Baltimore, Maryland
WCWN Schenectady, New York
WFUP Vanderbilt, Michigan
WHFT-TV Miami, Florida
WKDH Houston, Mississippi
WMCF-TV Montgomery, Alabama
WTCI Chattanooga, Tennessee
WXLV-TV Winston-Salem, North Carolina

Channel 46

KDLT-TV Sioux Falls, South Dakota
KION-TV Monterey, California
KOCM Norman, Oklahoma
KTCW Roseburg, Oregon
WBSF Bay City, Michigan
WHME-TV South Bend, Indiana
WIDP Guayama, Puerto Rico
WJZY Belmont, North Carolina
WKLE Lexington, Kentucky
WPCT Panama City Beach, Florida
WRBU East St. Louis, Illinois
WSKG-TV Binghamton, New York
WVFX Clarksburg, West Virginia
WWDP Norwell, Massachusetts
WXCW Naples, Florida

Channel 47

KGPE Fresno, California
KTMD Galveston, Texas
KTXD-TV Greenville, Texas
KWHB Tulsa, Oklahoma
KXLT-TV Rochester, Minnesota
KYVE Yakima, Washington
WKBS-TV Altoona, Pennsylvania
WMDT Salisbury, Maryland
WMSN-TV Madison, Wisconsin
WNJU Linden, New Jersey
WSBN-TV Norton, Virginia
WSYM-TV Lansing, Michigan
WTEV-TV Jacksonville, Florida
WTVP Peoria, Illinois
WZRB Columbia, South Carolina

Channel 48

KNVO McAllen, Texas
KSTS San Jose, California
KTDO Las Cruces, New Mexico
WAFF Huntsville, Alabama
WCET Cincinnati, Ohio
WEUX Chippewa Falls, Wisconsin
WFBD Destin, Florida
WGTW-TV Burlington, New Jersey
WMYV Greensboro, North Carolina
WRNN-TV Kingston, New York
WVLR Tazewell, Tennessee
WVOZ-TV Ponce, Puerto Rico
WYDC Corning, New York
WYDN Worcester, Massachusetts

Channel 49

KMYA-DT Camden, Arkansas
KNXT Visalia, California
KPDX Vancouver, Washington
KRBK Osage Beach, Missouri
KTKA-TV Topeka, Kansas
WAQP Saginaw, Michigan
WDKA Paducah, Kentucky
WEDW Bridgeport, Connecticut
WIPB Muncie, Indiana
WLED-TV Littleton, New Hampshire

WNYO-TV Buffalo, New York
WRET-TV Spartanburg, South Carolina
WRXY-TV Tice, Florida
WTLH Bainbridge, Georgia

Channel 50

KASY-TV Albuquerque, New Mexico
KCEC Denver, Colorado
KKAI Kailua, Hawaii
KLWB New Iberia, Louisiana
KOCE-TV Huntington Beach, California
WDCW Washington, District of Columbia
WNJN Montclair, New Jersey
WPGD-TV Hendersonville, Tennessee
WPWR-TV Gary, Indiana
WPXX-TV Memphis, Tennessee
WQHA Aguada, Puerto Rico
WRAZ Raleigh, North Carolina
WWTI Watertown, New York

Channel 51

KNSO Merced, California
KNWA-TV Rogers, Arkansas
KOHD Bend, Oregon
KUNS-TV Bellevue, Washington
KUSI-TV San Diego, California
KYAZ Katy, Texas
WBIF Marianna, Florida
WEIU-TV Charleston, Illinois
WNYA Pittsfield, Massachusetts
WOGX Ocala, Florida
WPXJ-TV Batavia, New York
WPXT Portland, Maine
WSCV Fort Lauderdale, Florida
WSFJ-TV Newark, Ohio
WTVE Reading, Pennsylvania
WVPT Staunton, Virginia
WWJX Jackson, Mississippi

Channel 52

KFWD Fort Worth, Texas
KSBI Oklahoma City, Oklahoma
KVEA Corona, California
WEKW-TV Keene, New Hampshire
WGGN-TV Sandusky, Ohio
WGVK Kalamazoo, Michigan
WKON Owenton, Kentucky
WMSY-TV Marion, Virginia
WNJT Trenton, New Jersey
WNYI Ithaca, New York
WRFB Carolina, Puerto Rico
WWRS-TV Mayville, Wisconsin

Channel 53

KETD Castle Rock, Colorado
KGEB Tulsa, Oklahoma
WEDN Norwich, Connecticut
WFLI-TV Cleveland, Tennessee
WKGB-TV Bowling Green, Kentucky
WLAJ Lansing, Michigan
WNVT Goldvein, Virginia
WPAN Fort Walton Beach, Florida
WPGH-TV Pittsburgh, Pennsylvania
WQMY Williamsport, Pennsylvania

Channel 54

KAZA-TV Avalon, California
KCEB Longview, Texas
KNVA Austin, Texas
WCCV-TV Arecibo, Puerto Rico
WCVN-TV Covington, Kentucky
WFXG Augusta, Georgia
WNUV Baltimore, Maryland
WQLN Erie, Pennsylvania
WTBY-TV Poughkeepsie, New York
WTLJ Muskegon, Michigan
WUPL Slidell, Louisiana
WXTX Columbus, Georgia
WZDX Huntsville, Alabama

Channel 55

KTBU Conroe, Texas
WBNX-TV Akron, Ohio
WFFT-TV Fort Wayne, Indiana
WMYT-TV Rock Hill, South Carolina
WRSP-TV Springfield, Illinois

Channel 56

KDMI Des Moines, Iowa
KDOC-TV Anaheim, California
KETK-TV Jacksonville, Texas
KUPU Waimanalo, Hawaii
KWDK Tacoma, Washington
WDKY-TV Danville, Kentucky
WFSG Panama City, Florida
WOLF-TV Hazleton, Pennsylvania
WSPX-TV Syracuse, New York
WYIN Gary, Indiana

Channel 57

KJLA Ventura, California
KUBE-TV Baytown, Texas
KWOG Springdale, Arkansas
WACH Columbia, South Carolina
WBUW Janesville, Wisconsin
WCFE-TV Plattsburgh, New York
WCVW Richmond, Virginia
WFXU Live Oak, Florida
WGBY-TV Springfield, Massachusetts
WPSG Philadelphia, Pennsylvania
WYMT-TV Hazard, Kentucky

Channel 58

KDTX-TV Dallas, Texas
KLCS Los Angeles, California
KQCA Stockton, California
WAWD Fort Walton Beach, Florida
WDJT-TV Milwaukee, Wisconsin
WMYO Salem, Indiana
WNAB Nashville, Tennessee
WNJB New Brunswick, New Jersey
WPGA-TV Perry, Georgia
WUJA Caguas, Puerto Rico
WUNG-TV Concord, North Carolina

Channel 59

KFRE-TV Sanger, California
KPXC-TV Denver, Colorado
WAOE Peoria, Illinois
WCTX New Haven, Connecticut
WJEB-TV Jacksonville, Florida
WVNS-TV Lewisburg, West Virginia
WXIN Indianapolis, Indiana

Channel 60

KCSM-TV San Mateo, California
KMBH Harlingen, Texas
WBPH-TV Bethlehem, Pennsylvania
WNEU Merrimack, New Hampshire
WTJP-TV Gadsden, Alabama

Channel 61

KASW Phoenix, Arizona
KZJL Houston, Texas
WDSI-TV Chattanooga, Tennessee
WFGC Palm Beach, Florida
WTIC-TV Hartford, Connecticut
WTSF Ashland, Kentucky

Channel 62

KRCA Riverside, California
KSMO-TV Kansas City, Missouri
WFPT Frederick, Maryland
WMFP Lawrence, Massachusetts
WVEA-TV Venice, Florida
WWJ-TV Detroit, Michigan
WYCW Asheville, North Carolina

Channel 63

KBEH Oxnard, California
WBEC-TV Boca Raton, Florida
WHSG-TV Monroe, Georgia
WINM Angola, Indiana
WKTC Sumter, South Carolina

Channel 64

KILM Barstow, California
WAXN-TV Kannapolis, North Carolina
WDPB Seaford, Delaware
WECN Naranjito, Puerto Rico
WGNM Macon, Georgia
WLLA Kalamazoo, Michigan
WNAC-TV Providence, Rhode Island
WSTR-TV Cincinnati, Ohio

Channel 65

KTFN El Paso, Texas
WEDY New Haven, Connecticut
WLJC-TV Beattyville, Kentucky
WRBW Orlando, Florida
WUPV Ashland, Virginia

Channel 66

WFME-TV West Milford, New Jersey
WJFB Lebanon, Tennessee
WSMH Flint, Michigan

Channel 67

KSMS-TV Monterey, California
WMPB Baltimore, Maryland
WUPX-TV Morehead, Kentucky

Channel 68

KTLN-TV Novato, California
WABM Birmingham, Alabama
WBCC Cocoa, Florida
WJAL Hagerstown, Maryland
WLFG Grundy, Virginia
WMFD-TV Mansfield, Ohio
WSYT Syracuse, New York

Channel 69

KSWB-TV San Diego, California
WDTI Indianapolis, Indiana
WFMZ-TV Allentown, Pennsylvania
WUPA Atlanta, Georgia

US Spanish-Language Television Stations

Arizona

Phoenix (Prescott), AZ
KAET Phoenix (ch 88)
KFPH-DT Flagstaff (ch 27)

Tucson (Sierra Vista), AZ
KFTU-DT Douglas (ch 0)
KHRR Tucson (ch 4040)
KTTU Tucson (ch 19)
KUAS-TV Tucson (ch 2728)
KUAT-TV Tucson (ch 630)

California

Fresno-Visalia, CA
KFTV-DT Hanford (ch 20)
KNSO Merced (ch 5111)
KNXT Visalia (ch 4950)
KVPT Fresno (ch 1840)

Los Angeles
KAZA-TV Avalon (ch 5447)
KFTR-DT Ontario (ch 0)
KJLA Ventura (ch 5749)
KMEX-DT Los Angeles (ch 35)
KRCA Riverside (ch 6235)
KVEA Corona (ch 5239)
KWHY-TV Los Angeles (ch 2242)

Monterey-Salinas, CA
KSMS-TV Monterey (ch 6731)

Sacramento-Stockton-Modest
KMAX-TV Sacramento (ch 21)
KUVS-DT Modesto (ch 18)

San Diego, CA
KNSD San Diego (ch 3940)
XEWT-DT Tijuana (ch 32)

San Francisco-Oakland-San
KCSM-TV San Mateo (ch 6043)
KDTV-DT San Francisco (ch 51)
KFSF-DT Vallejo (ch 34)
KRCB Cotati (ch 2223)
KSTS San Jose (ch 4849)
KTNC-TV Concord (ch 4214)

Santa Barbara-Santa Maria-
KPMR Santa Barbara (ch 3821)
KTAS San Luis Obispo (ch 3334)

Yuma, AZ-El Centro, CA
KVYE El Centro (ch 722)

Colorado

Albuquerque-Santa Fe, NM
KRTN-TV Durango (ch 33)

Denver, CO
KCEC Denver (ch 5051)
KDEN-TV Longmont (ch 29)
KETD Castle Rock (ch 5346)
KRMT Denver (ch 4140)

District of Columbia

Washington, DC (Hagerstown
WFDC-DT Arlington (ch 15)

Florida

Miami-Ft. Lauderdale, FL
WHFT-TV Miami (ch 4546), WLTV-DT Miami (ch 0)
WSBS-TV Key West (ch 223), WSCV Fort Lauderdale (ch 5130)

Orlando-Daytona Beach-Melb
WACX-DT Leesburg (ch 40), WOTF-DT Melbourne (ch 43)
WVEN-TV Daytona Beach (ch 260)

Tampa-St Petersburg (Saras
WCLF Clearwater (ch 2221), WFTT-DT Tampa (ch 47)
WVEA-TV Venice (ch 6225)

Georgia

Atlanta
WUVG-DT Athens (ch 48)

Hawaii

Honolulu, HI
KKAI Kailua (ch 5050)
KLEI-TV Kailua-Kona (ch 625)

Illinois

Chicago
WSNS-TV Chicago (ch 0)
WYCC Chicago (ch 200)

Kansas

Wichita-Hutchinson Plus, K
KOOD Hays (ch 916)

Louisiana

New Orleans, LA
KGLA-AM Hammond (ch 42)
WLAE-TV New Orleans (ch 3231)

Maine

Bangor, ME
WMEB-TV Orono (ch 129)
WMED-TV Calais (ch 1310)

Portland-Auburn, ME
WCBB Augusta (ch 1010)

Presque Isle, ME
WMEM-TV Presque Isle (ch 1010)

Massachusetts

Boston (Manchester, NH)
WBZ-TV Boston (ch 430)
WCVB-TV Boston (ch 520)
WUNI Worcester (ch 2729)
WUTF-DT Marlborough (ch 27)

Missouri

Kansas City, MO
KPXE-TV Kansas City (ch 51)

Nevada

Las Vegas, NV
KBLR Paradise (ch 3940)
KINC Las Vegas (ch 1516)

New Hampshire

Boston (Manchester, NH)
WNEU Merrimack (ch 6034)

New Jersey

New York
WMBC-TV Newton (ch 18)
WNJU Linden (ch 4736)

Philadelphia
WWSI Atlantic City (ch 49)

New Mexico

Albuquerque-Santa Fe, NM
KAZQ Albuquerque (ch 3217)
KCHF Santa Fe (ch 1110)
KLUZ-TV Albuquerque (ch 4142)
KNAT-TV Albuquerque (ch 2324)
KRPV-DT Roswell (ch 27)
KTEL-TV Carlsbad (ch 2525)
KTFQ-TV Albuquerque (ch 22)

Amarillo, TX
KENW Portales (ch 30)

El Paso (Las Cruces, NM),
KRWG-TV Las Cruces (ch 2223)
KTDO Las Cruces (ch 4847)

New York

New York
WFTY-DT Smithtown (ch 23)
WFUT-DT Newark (ch 30)
WXTV-DT Paterson (ch 40)

North Carolina

Raleigh-Durham (Fayettevil
WUVC-DT Fayetteville (ch 38)

Ohio

Cleveland-Akron (Canton),
WQHS-DT Cleveland (ch 34)

Oklahoma

Oklahoma City, OK
KTUZ-TV Shawnee (ch 3029), KUOK Woodward (ch 3535)

Tulsa, OK
KRSC-TV Claremore (ch 3536)

Oregon

Portland, OR
KUNP La Grande (ch 1616)

Pennsylvania

Philadelphia
WLVT-TV Allentown (ch 3939)
WUVP-DT Vineland (ch 29)
WYBE Philadelphia (ch 3535)

Rhode Island

Providence, RI-New Bedford
WJAR Providence (ch 1051)

South Dakota

Sioux Falls (Mitchell), SD
KDLV-TV Mitchell (ch 526)

Tennessee

Nashville, TN
WHTN Murfreesboro (ch 3938)

Texas

Amarillo, TX
KEYU Borger (ch 3131)
KVII-TV Amarillo (ch 77)

Corpus Christi, TX
KIII Corpus Christi (ch 38)
KORO Corpus Christi (ch 2827)

Dallas-Ft. Worth
KUVN-DT Garland (ch 0)
KXTX-TV Dallas (ch 3940)

El Paso (Las Cruces, NM),
KINT-TV El Paso (ch 2625)
KSCE El Paso (ch 3839)
KTFN El Paso (ch 6551)
XHIJ-DT Ciudad Juarez (ch 45)

Harlingen-Weslaco-Brownsvi
KGBT-TV Harlingen (ch 431)
KLUJ-TV Harlingen (ch 4434)
KMBH Harlingen (ch 6038)
KNVO McAllen (ch 4849)
KTLM Rio Grande City (ch 4040)

Houston
KFTH-DT Alvin (ch 36)
KLTJ Galveston (ch 2223)
KTMD Galveston (ch 4748)
KUBE-TV Baytown (ch 5753)
KUHT Houston (ch 88)

Laredo, TX
KGNS-TV Laredo (ch 88)
KLDO-TV Laredo (ch 2719)

Odessa-Midland, TX
KMLM-DT Odessa (ch 42)
KUPB Midland (ch 1818)

San Antonio, TX
KWEX-DT San Antonio (ch 39)
KYVV-TV Del Rio (ch 100)

Tyler-Longview (Lufkin & N
KTRE Lufkin (ch 99)

Utah

Salt Lake City, UT
KBYU-TV Provo (ch 1144)
KSL-TV Salt Lake City (ch 538)
KUEN Ogden (ch 936)
KUTH-DT Provo (ch 32)

Washington

Seattle-Tacoma, WA
KFFV Seattle (ch 44)
KUNS-TV Bellevue (ch 5150)

Wisconsin

Milwaukee, WI
WMVT Milwaukee (ch 3635)

Puerto Rico

Aguadilla
WOLE-DT Aguadilla (ch 0), WVEO Aguadilla (ch 4417)

Caguas
WLII Caguas (ch 56)

Fajardo
WMTJ Fajardo (ch 4016)

Mayaguez
WNJX-TV Mayaguez (ch 423), WORA-TV Mayaguez (ch 29)
WOST Mayaguez (ch 1422)

Ponce
WSTE-DT Ponce (ch 7), WSUR-DT Ponce (ch 43)

San Juan
WAPA-TV San Juan (ch 427), WIPR-TV San Juan (ch 643)
WKAQ-TV San Juan (ch 228)

Virgin Islands

Christiansted
WSVI Christiansted (ch 820)

Top Canadian TV Programs

Measuring Audiences. Delivering Intelligence.

Auditoires mesurés. Décisions éclairées.

Top Programs – Total Canada (English)

October 22 - October 28, 2012

Based on confirmed program schedules and preliminary audience data, Demographic: All Persons 2+

Rank	Program	Broadcast Outlet	Weekday	Start	End	Total 2+ AMA(000)
1	BIG BANG THEORY	CTV Total	...T...	20:00	20:31	**4357**
2	TWO AND A HALF MEN	CTV Total	...T...	20:31	21:00	**2863**
3	AMAZING RACE 21	CTV Total	......S	20:00	21:00	**2726**
4	NCIS	Global Total	.T.....	20:00	21:00	**2418**
5	NCIS: LOS ANGELES	Global Total	.T.....	21:00	22:00	**2399**
6	SURVIVOR:PHILIPPINES	Global Total	..W....	20:00	21:00	**2358**
7	CRIMINAL MINDS	CTV Total	..W....	21:00	22:00	**2308**
8	GREY'S ANATOMY	CTV Total	...T...	21:00	22:02	**2105**
9	DANCING/STARS 15 PRF	CTV Total	M......	20:00	21:00	**1987**
10	C.S.I.	CTV Total	..W....	22:00	23:00	**1913**
11	ARROW	CTV Total	..W....	20:00	21:00	**1775**
12	FLASHPOINT	CTV Total	...T...	22:02	23:00	**1660**
13	CTV EVENING NEWS	CTV Total	MTWTF..	18:00	19:00	**1609**
14	BLUE BLOODS	CTV Total	....F..	22:00	23:00	**1604**
15	VEGAS	Global Total	.T.....	22:00	23:00	**1589**
16	THE MENTALIST	CTV Total	......S	22:00	23:00	**1560**
17	ELEMENTARY	Global Total	...T...	22:01	23:00	**1511**
18	BIG BANG THEORY	CTV Total	M......	21:00	21:30	**1477**
19	ONCE UPON A TIME	CTV Total	......S	19:00	20:00	**1453**
20	DANCING/STARS 15 RES	CTV Two Total	.T.....	20:00	21:01	**1437**
21	BIG BANG THEORY	CTV Total	MTWTF..	19:30	20:00	**1416**
22	CTV EVENING NEWS WKD	CTV Total	.....SS	18:00	19:00	**1334**
23	THE VOICE	CTV Total	.T.....	20:00	21:01	**1292**
24	ANGER MANAGEMENT	CTV Total	.T.....	21:01	21:31	**1170**
25	MODERN FAMILY	Citytv Total	..W....	21:00	21:30	**1168**
26	GRIMM	CTV Total	....F..	21:00	22:00	**1153**
27	C.S.I. NEW YORK	CTV Total	....F..	20:00	21:00	**1152**
28	CASTLE	CTV Total	M......	22:00	23:00	**1129**
29	CTV NATIONAL NEWS	CTV Total	MTWTFSS	23:00	23:30	**1113**
30	CHICAGO FIRE	Global Total	..W....	22:00	23:00	**1086**

Understanding this report ...

This chart shows the Top 30 TV programs for all national networks and Canadian English specialty networks for the week indicated. Programs are ranked based on their AMA(000). AMA(000) is the average minute audience in thousands. The chart also indicates the broadcast outlet on which the program aired and the program's start and end time (shown in Eastern Time).

"Weekly Top 30 TV Programs," October 22-October 28, 2012, *BBM Canada*, accessed November 9, 2012, http://www.bbm.ca/en/weekly-top-30-tv-programs.

Financial indicators: Television broadcasting industries[1]

	2010	2011	2010 to 2011
	$ millions		% change
Total operating revenues by type of broadcaster	**7,082.6**	**7,466.0**	**5.4**
Conventional television	3,623.2	3,733.8	3.1
Private conventional television	2,156.8	2,163.0	0.3
Public and non-commercial television	1,466.4	1,570.8	7.1
Pay and speciality television[2]	3,459.4	3,732.1	7.9
Speciality television[2]	2,660.8	2,876.5	8.1
Pay television[2]	798.6	855.6	7.1
Total operating revenues by source	**7,082.6**	**7,466.0**	**5.4**
Air time	3,416.4	3,577.8	4.7
Subscription	2,246.5	2,403.5	7.0
Grants	937.8	972.5	3.7
Other revenues	481.9	512.1	6.3
Sale of airtime by type of broadcaster	**3,416.4**	**3,577.8**	**4.7**
Conventional television	2,303.5	2,343.6	1.7
Private conventional television	1,949.7	1,959.0	0.5
Public and non-commercial television	353.8	384.6	8.7
Pay and speciality television[2]	1,112.9	1,234.3	10.9
Speciality television[2]	1,112.1	1,232.7	10.8
Pay television[2]	0.8	1.6	107.3

1. North American Industry Classification System 2007 (51512 – Television Broadcasting and 51521 – Pay and Speciality Television)
2. Statistics published by the Canadian Radio-television and Telecommunications Commission, Industry Statistics and Analysis, Broadcast Analysis Branch.

Financial indicators: Television broadcasting industries[1]

	2010	2011
	%	
Profit margin (before interest and taxes) by type of broadcaster, total	**15.7**	**18.4**
Private conventional television	0.2	7.2
Pay and speciality television[2]	25.3	24.9
Market share by type of broadcaster (revenue)		
Conventional television	51.2	50.0
Private conventional television	30.5	29.0
Public and non-commercial television	20.7	21.0
Pay and speciality television[2]	48.8	50.0
Speciality television[2]	37.6	38.5
Pay television[2]	11.3	11.5
Market share by type of broadcaster (air time)		
Conventional television	67.4	65.5
Private conventional television	57.1	54.8
Public and non-commercial television	10.4	10.7
Pay and speciality television[2]	32.6	34.5
Speciality television[2]	32.6	34.5
Pay television[2]	0.0	0.0

1. North American Industry Classification System 2007 (51512 – Television Broadcasting and 51521 – Pay and Speciality Television)
2. Statistics published by the Canadian Radio-television and Telecommunications Commission, Industry Statistics and Analysis, Broadcast Analysis Branch.

Source: *Statistics Canada*, "Table 357-0001, Television broadcasting industry, by North American Industry Classification System (NAICS), CANSIM," accessed November 9, 2012, http://www.statcan.gc.ca/daily-quotidien/120712/dq120712c-eng.htm.

TV Basics

TV FACILITIES IN CANADA

Year	Total Conv. Pay, Spec. Stations	Conventional Stations^	Pay & Specialty^	Commercial Specialty^	Pop'n (000)+	Households With TV (%)+	Multi-Set Hhlds (%)+
2011				179*	34.605	99	74.0*
2010	327	135	192	164*	34,108	99	74.0*
2009	310	141	169	139*	33,873	99	67.0*
2008	312	146	166	122*	33,091	99	65.0
2007	311	148	163	126*	32,730	99	65.0
2006	302	143	159	121*	32,623	99	65.6
2005	287	146	141	109*	32,299	99	65.0
2004	267	152	115	101*	31,989	99	62.9
2000	214	155	59	42	30,790	99	57.9
1995	166	137	29	18	29,530	99	56.1
1990	146	129	17	10	26,428	99	53.5

Source: ^CRTC – Communications Monitoring Report, +Statistics Canada, *BBM Canada

CONNECTED TV IN CANADA

Year	Operating Systems	Subscribers (000)	Digital (000)	HDTV Subs (000)	DTH (000)	Telco (000)	*Cable Penetration
2011^	2,160	8,430	5,826	1,783	2,942	440	
2010^	2,145	8,465	5,359	1,291	2,884	358	63%
2009^	1,940	8,352	4,779		2,774	306	66%
2008^	1,941	8,316	3,783		2,647	201	65%
2007^	1,943	8,167	3,348		2,701	170	65%
2006^	1,955	8,033	2,973		2,658	134	64%
2005^	2,097	7,984	2,784		2,597	105	64%
2000	2,001	8,285	500		1,167		73%
1995	1,915	8,102					76%

Source: Canadian Cable and Television Association, *BBM Fall Surveys, ^Media Stats
***** All cable TV subscribers (including residential and commercial)**

WEEKLY TELEVISION REACH

Demographic	1995	2000	2005	2008	2009	2010	2011
All Persons 2+	96%	96%	97%	94%	95%	94%	93%
Adults 18+	96%	96%	98%	95%	95%	95%	93%
Women 18+	97%	97%	98%	96%	96%	96%	94%
Men 18+	96%	95%	97%	93%	94%	93%	92%
Teens 12-17	93%	95%	95%	91%	90%	91%	89%
Children 2-11	96%	96%	98%	95%	97%	93%	94%

Source: BBM Fall Surveys - diary

AVERAGE WEEKLY HOURS TUNED PER CAPITA

Demographic	1995	2000	2005	2008	2009	2010	2011
All Persons 2+	24:36	21:30	24:12	20:30	20:48	20:24	20:12
Adults 18+	26:06	23:15	26:15	22:24	22.42	22:18	22:06
Women 18+	28:24	25:28	28:54	24:36	25.06	24:24	23:48
Men 18+	23:48	20:56	23:36	20:12	20.18	20:12	20:24
Teens 12-17	18:55	14:04	13:42	11:00	11.24	10:54	10:12
Children 2-11	19:36	15:27	13:48	12:30	12.54	12:12	12:18

Source: BBM Fall Surveys - diary markets

"TV Basics, 2012-2013," *Television Bureau of Canada*, accessed November 9, 2012, http://www.tvb.ca/page_files/pdf/InfoCentre/TVBasics.pdf.

Major Broadcast Networks

Alberta

Bear Creek Broadcasting
81716-108 Street, Suite 104, Grande Prarie, AB T8V 4C7 Canada
(780) 882-6612, *Fax:* (780) 882-6708
www.q99live.com
qbreak@q99live.com
Ken Trulen, General Manager
Barb Shannon, General Sales Mgr
Paul Oulette, Programming Director
Cristy Ellen, Promotions Manager
Shannon Wallace, Traffic Manager
Justin Alloway, Creative Director

The Miracle Channel Association
450-31 Street North, Lethbridge, AB T1H 3Z3 Canada
(403) 380-3399, *Fax:* (403) 380-3322
www.miraclechannel.ca
info@miraclechannel.ca
Services Offered: Miracle Channel reaches people with the hope of Christ through contemporary, life-giving and life-changing programs from leading ministries as well as documentaries, talk shows, music videos, movies, Canadian news,and live programs.
Leon Fontaine, CEO/COO

Aboriginal Multi-Media Society
13425-146 Street, Edmonton, AB T5L 4S8 Canada
(780) 455-2700, *Fax:* (780) 455-7639
www.ammsa.com
letters@ammsa.com
Services Offered: The Aboriginal Multi-Media Society is an independent Aboriginal communications organization committed to facilitating the exchange of information reflecting Aboriginal culture to a growing and diverse audience. AMMSA is dedicated to providing objective, mature and balanced coverage of news, information and entertainment relevant to Aboriginal issues and peoples while maintaining profound respect for the values, principles and traditions of Aboriginal people.
Paul Macedo, CEO/Publisher/Founder
Bert Crowfoot, General Manager
Paul Macedo, Marketing Director
Deborah Steel, News Director

British Columbia

The Jim Pattison Broadcast Group
460 Pemberton Terrace, Kamloops, BC V2C 1T5 Canada
(250) 372-3322, *Fax:* (250) 370-0445
http://www.jimpattison.com/media/broadcast-group
info@jpbroadcast.com
Rick Arnish, Chairman
Rod Schween, President
Bill Dinicol, VP/Finance
Bruce Davis, VP/Sales
Richard Davis, Technical Director

Mainstream Broadcasting Corporation
100-1200 West 73rd Street, Vancouver, BC V5B 2S2 Canada
(604) 263-1320, *Fax:* (604) 261-0310
www.am1320.com
adm@am1320.com
Services Offered: Mainstream Broadcasting Corporation is a British Columbia media company owned and operated by local Vancouver resident and businessman, James Ho. Mainstream began its broadcasting service in 1973 as Overseas Chinese Voice (OCV). In 1993, OCV programming was incorporated into the multicultural AM radio station of CHMB AM1320, serving the needs of Vancouver's multicultural community.
Kat Lai Li Jiayu, General Sales Mgr
Harry Lee Shaoming, Programming Director
Andy Cheung Zhang Yi Liang, News Director

New Brunswick

Radio Beausejour Inc
51 Cornwall, Shediac, NB E4P 8T8 Canada
(506) 532-0080, *Fax:* (506) 532-0120
www.cjse.ca
cjse@cjse.ca
Services Offered: After eight years in development, Radio Beausejour began broadcasting July 26, 1994. Located in southeastern New Brunswick, at the heart of the seaside town of Shediac and near the Greater Moncton Radio Beausejour serves a large Acadian community.
Gilles Arsenault, CEO/COO
Founder, President
John Richard, Advertising Representative
Diane Richard, Host
Roger Boudreau, Host

Newfoundland

Okalakatiget Society
PO Box 160, Nail, NL A0P 1L0 Canada
(709) 922-2187, *Fax:* (709) 922-2293
www.oksociety.com
okradio@oksociety.com
Services Offered: The OKalaKatiget Society provides Inuktitut and English language programming to Inuit in the Northern Labrador and Lake Melville region. This aboriginal language programming is designed to strengthen our culturethrough language retention.
Morris Prokop, President
Joanna Dicker, Sr Radio Producer
Sarah Abel, Sr Television Producer

VOWR 800 Radio Broadcasting
Patrick Street, PO Box 7430, St John's, NL A1E 3Y5 Canada
(709) 579-9233
vowr.org
vowr@vowr.org
Services Offered: VOWR is the only radio station owned by The United Church of Canada and has been broadcasting from the same location (Patrick Street and Hamilton Avenue) since 1924. The station began as an outreach ministry ofWesley United Church and was the 'child' of Rev. Dr. J.G. Joyce. Operated solely by volunteers, our station broadcasts 24 hours a day, 365 days a year - They are never off the air!
Marvin Barnes, Chairman
Glenn Tilley, Vice Chairperson
Doreen Whalen, Secretary
John Tessier, Station Manager
Trevor Pike, Technical Advisor

Ontario

Rogers Communications Inc (RCI)
Div/DOB: Rogers Media
One Mountain Pleasant Road, Toronto, ON M4Y 2Y5 Canada
(416) 935-8294, *Fax:* (416) 764-2098
www.rci.rogers.com
rogersdigitalmedia@rci.rogers.com
Services Offered: Roger's Communications Inc. is one of Canada's largest communications companies, particularly in the field of wireless communications, cable television, radio and broadcasting, telecommunications, and mass mediaassets.
Nadir Mohamed, President/CEO
Rob Bruce, President/CEO/Communications
Keith Pelley, President/Communications
Anthony Staffieri, President/CEO/Media
Bob Berner, EVP/CFO
Edward Rogers, EVP/Network and Chief Technology Officer
LindaJojo, Deputy Chairman/EVP Emerging Business
Phillip Lind, EVP/Chief Information Officer
David Miller, EVP Regulatory/Vice Chairman
Jim Reid, SVP Legeal/General Counsel

Inuit Broadcasting Corporation
331 Cooper Street, Suite 301, Ottawa, ON K2P 0G5 Canada
(613) 235-1892, *Fax:* (613) 230-8824
www.inuitbroadcasting.ca
info@nuitbroadcasting.ca
Services Offered: The Inuit Broadcasting Corporation provides a window to the Arctic by producing award winning television programming by Inuit, for Inuit. IBC is indeed, Nunavut's public producer. IBC does not produce the regularfare of TV sitcoms and talk shows. Instead, IBC producers make programming about one of the richest and enduring cultures in our nation, the Inuit of Canada, in the language Inuit speak.Inuktitut. We produce shows about our kids, our musicians, ourpoliticians, our humour, our issues, etc. No one else can make these shows for us!
Debbie Brisebois, Executive Director
Malakie Kilabuk, Director/Operations
Monica Eli, Director/Programming

Shaw Media
121 Bloor Street East, 15th Floor, Toronto, ON M4W 3M5 Canada
(416) 967-1164 (877) 345-9195, *Fax:* (416) 967-2854
shawmedia.ca
corporateinquiries@shawmedia.ca
Services Offered: Shaw Media operates Global Television and 18 of the country's most popular specialty channels, including HGTV Canada, Mystery TV, National Geographic Channel, Showcase, History, Food Network Canada and TVtropolis,plus more than 20 online properties.
Paul Robertson, Group VP/Brodcasting/President Shaw Media
Paul Burns, VP/Online Experience
Carol Darling, VP/Engineering and Broadcast Systems
Michael French, VP/Finance
Errol Da Re, SVP/Sales
Dervia Kelly, SRDirector/Communications
Barb Williams, SVP/Content

Bay Shore Broadcasting Inc
270 9th East Street, Owen Sound, ON N4K 5P5 Canada
(519) 376-2030, *Fax:* (519) 371-4242
bayshorebroadcasting.ca
info@bayshorebroadcasting.ca
Services Offered: Bayshore Broadcasting Corporation, which began in Owen Sound, Ontario, is an independent private broadcaster operating seven radio stations in Grey, Bruce, Huron and Simcoe Counties in Southern Ontario.
Jim Bichard, News Director
Peter Jackson, Assistant Nes Director
Marianne McLeod, Assistant Nes Director
Manny Paiva, News Manager
Fred Wallace, Sports Director

Blackburn Radio Inc
700 Richmond Street, Unit 102, London, ON N6A 5C7 Canada
(519) 679-8680, *Fax:* (519) 679-5321
www.blacburnradio.com
info@blackburnradio.com
Services Offered: Blackburn Radio Inc. is a family-owned broadcasting company with 13 radio stations serving Southwestern and Midwestern Ontario. The company operates 14 radio stations in Wingham, Sarnia, London, Chatham, Leamingtonand Windsor.
Richard Costley, CEO
Doug Caldwell, President

Ontario Educational Communications Authority
Mailing Address: Box 200, Station Q, Toronto, ON M4T 2T1 Canada
Second Address: 2180 Yonge Street, Toronto, ON M4S 2B9
(416) 484-2665, *Fax:* (416) 484-2600
ww3.tvo.org
asktvo@tvo.org
Services Offered: TVO's vision is to empower people to be engaged citizens of Ontario through educational media.
Lisa De Wilde, CEO
Jim Marchbank, Board of Directors
Toby Jenkins, Board of Directors
Paul Ginis, Director/Sales/Media

Corus Entertainment Inc
Mailing Address: 25 Dockside Drive, Toronto, ON M5A 0B5 Canada
Second Address: 630 3rd Ave SW, Suite 300, Calgary, AB T2P 4L4
(416) 479-7000, *Fax:* (416) 479-7006
www.corusent.com
Services Offered: Corus Entertainment is one of Canada's most successful integrated media and entertainment companies. Founded by JR Shaw, the company was built from the media assets originally owned by Shaw Communications, and spunoff as a separate, publicly-traded company in 1999. Since then, the Company's asset base has grown substantially through strategic acquisitions and a strong operating discipline.
Heather Shaw, Executive Chair
John Cassaday, President/CEO
Scott Dyer, EVP/Shared Services
Gary Maavara, EVP/General Counsel
Tom Peddie, EVP/CFO

Wawatay Native Communications Society
16 Fifth Avenue, Box 1180, Sioux Lookout, ON P8T 1B7 Canada
(807) 737-2951, *Fax:* (807) 737-3224
www.wawatay.on.ca
reception@wawatay.on.ca
Services Offered: Wawatay Native Communications Society serves the communication needs of First Nations people and communities of Nishnawbe Aski Nation. It does this through the distribution of a bi-weekly newspaper, daily radioprogramming, television production services and a multimedia website that seeks to preserve and enhance indigenous languages and cultures of Aboriginal people in northern Ontario.
David Neegan, CEO
Tabatha Jourdon, Chief Financial Officer
Shawn Bell, Interim Editor

James Brohm, General Sales Mgr
Vacant, News Director

Distribution Access (Access Learning)
2 Pardee Avenue, Suite 102, Toronto, ON M6K 3H5 Canada
(416) 363-6765, *Fax:* (416) 363-7834
www.accesslearning.com
ontariosales@accesslearning.com
Services Offered: DISTRIBUTION ACCESS is Canada's leading provider of the world's best educational video programs and multi media content. With a library of over 15,000 titles, DISTRIBUTION ACCESS serves over 16,000 Canadianeducational institutions - elementary, secondary, post-secondary, libraries - Canadian learners of all ages in their homes and educational and broadcasting organizations around the world.
Doug Connolly, Operations Dir
Marijke Daye, Director Sales/Marketing

Pineridge Broadcasting
PO Box 520, Cobourg, ON K9A 4L3 Canada
(905) 372-5401, *Fax:* (905) 372-6280
www.pineridgebroadcasting.com
Don Conway, President
Dave Hughes, General Sales Mgr
Jennifer Daignault, Peterborough Sales Manager

CTV
Box 9, Station O, Toronto, ON M4A 2M9 Canada
(416) 384-5000, *Fax:* (416) 332-5022
www.ctv.ca
Rick Brace, President/Specialty Channels
Wendy Freeman, President/CTV News
Phil King, President/CTV Programming/Sports
Mike Cosentino, SVP Programming/CTV Networks

Canadian Broadcasting Corp (CBC)
Box 3220, Station C, Ottawa, ON K1Y 1E4 Canada
(613) 288-6455
www.cbc.ca
liason@cbc.ca
Services Offered: The Canadian Broadcasting Corp. (CBC) is a publicly owned corporation established by the Broadcasting Act (1936) of the Canadian Parliament to provide the natl bcstg svc in Canada in the two official languagesEnglish and French. Under this legislation, the CBC is subject to regulations of the Canadian Radio-Television & Telecommunications Commission (CRTC).
Hubert Lacroix, President/CEO
Kristine Stewart, EVP English Services

Global Television Network/Shaw Media
121 Bloor Street, Toronto, ON M4W 3M5 Canada
(877) 307-1999
www.globaltv.com
Services Offered: Shaw Media operates Global Television and 18 of the country's most popular specialty channels, including HGTV Canada, Mystery TV, National Geographic Channel, Showcase, History, Food Network Canada and TVtropolis,plus more than 20 online properties.
Paul Robertson, President/Group VP
Paul Burns, VP Online Experience
Carol Darling, Vice President
Michael French, VP/Finance
Errol Da Re, VP/Sales

TVA Group Inc
1600 de Maisonneuve Boulevard, Montreal, QC H2L 4P2 Canada
(514) 526-9251, *Fax:* (514) 598-6086
www.tva.ca
Pierre Dion, President

Quebec

Groupe TVA Incorporated
1600 Bool De Maisonneuve East, Montreal, QC H2L 4P2 Canada
(514) 526-9251
groupetva.ca
Services Offered: TVA., A subsidiary of Quebecor Media inc., Is a communications company that operates in two business segments: television and publishing. In television, the company is active in the creation, production anddistribution of entertainment, information and public affairs, distribution of audiovisual products, commercial production and teleshopping. It operates largest private network of French-language television in North America, in addition to operatingeleven specialized services.
Pierre Dion, President/CEO
Jocelyn Poirier, President
Denis Rozon, VP/CFO
Daniel Boudreau, VP/Operations
Frances Lauziere, VP/Programming
Edith Perreault, VP/Sales/Marketing

RNC Media
1 Place Villa Marie, Suite 1523, Montreal, QC H3B 2B5 Canada
(514) 866-8686, *Fax:* (514) 866-8056
www.rncmedia.ca
info@rncmedia.ca
Services Offered: Since 1948, RNC MEDIA offers guests advertisers, listeners and viewers, advertising, production and quality programming. Faithful to its origins which is now one of the largest broadcasting companies in Quebec, RNCMEDIA continues to invest in its mission with a passion to communicate. Today the company has 16 radio stations, five television stations in major regions of Quebec.
Pierre Brosseau, Chairman/CEO
Jean-Yves Gourd, Board Member
Pierre Parent, Board Member
Claude Beaudoin, Board Member

Radio Canada International
1400 Rene-Levesque Blvd East, Montreal, QC H2L 2M2 Canada
(514) 597-7500, *Fax:* (514) 597-7621
www.rcinet.ca
info@rcinet.ca
Services Offered: RCI is CBC/Radio-Canada's multilingual service, providing audiences with an opportunity to discover and, above all, to understand and gain insight into the reality of Canadian society, along with its cultural anddemocratic values.
Helene Parent, Director
Soleiman, Editor-in-Chief
Lynn Desjardins, Producer

Saskatchewan

Harvard Broadcasting
2060 Halifax Street, Regina, SK S4P 1T7 Canada
(403) 670-0210, *Fax:* (403) 670-0518
www.harvardbroadcasting.com
ccowie@harvardbroadcasting.com
Services Offered: Originally opening its doors in 1926, 620 CKRM has almost as long a history as The Hill Companies in Saskatchewan. Currently, 620 CKRM the Source has been the official Saskatchewan Roughrider broadcast rights holdersince 1983. Under their current agreement, Harvard Broadcasting will have 620 CKRM as the Rider Play-by Play voice until the year 2015.
Cam Cowie, General Manager
Gary Brasil, National Sales Manager
Bonnie Day, Interactive Producer
Christian Hall, National Program Manager

Missinipi Broadcasting
Mailing Address: PO Box 1526, La Ronge, SK S0J 1L0 Canada
Second Address: 27-11th Street West, 2nd Floor, Prince Albert, SK S6V 3A8
(306) 425-4003 (306) 922-4566, *Fax:* (306) 425-3123 306) 922-6969
www.mbcradio.com
mcbradio@mcbradio.com
Services Offered: MBC Network Radio currently airs 24 hours of programming daily, 7 days a week, from studios located in La Ronge Saskatchewan. It reaches an ever expanding listening audience of over 100,000 people in dozens ofcommunities and offers programming featuring interviews, information, education, (and music) in the Cree, Dene and English languages. MBC maintains a grass roots connection in it's programming via phone-in shows and on-location broadcasts.
William Dumais, Chairman
Mike Bouvier, Vice Chairperson
Deborah Charles, President/CEO
Darrell Prokopie, General Sales Mgr

Rawlco Radio Broadcasting
Mailing Address: 715 Saskatchewan Crescent West, Saskatoon, SK S7M 5V7 Canada
Second Address: 210-2401 Saskatchewan Drive, Regina, SK S4P 4HB
(306) 525-0000
www.rawlco.com
kwerner@rawlco.com
Services Offered: No one loves being in radio more than we do at Rawlco Radio! We're a private, family owned radio company and we're debt free - something that's increasingly rare.. We work really hard every day to provide trulygreat radio stations to our listeners and clients in the communities we serve. Rawlco has 15 stations - 12 in Saskatchewan and 3 in Alberta. You'll find links on this site to all of them. Check us out! If you're interested in working for, or with, apassionate, fun-loving, enthusiastic bunch of radio people, you're at the right place.
Tom Newton, VP/General Manager
Kurt Leavine, VP/General Manager
Kristey Werner, Station Manager
Janelle Cignac, Promotions Coordinator
Vanessa Thomas, Promotions Coordinator

Yukon Territory

Northern Native Broadcasting, Yukon
Suite 6 4230A, 4th Avenue, Whitehorse, YT Y1A 1K1 Canada
(867) 668-6629, *Fax:* (867) 668-6612
www.nnby.net
nnby@nnby.net
Services Offered: NNBY reaffirms and maintains First Nation culture, spiritual beliefs, language, traditional values, land and animals. NNBY works for present and future generations, looking seven generations into the future. Whilewe focus on First Nations, NNBY is for all people. NNBY protects traditional knowledge, empowers First Nations people, supports self determination of First Nations, and facilitates the development of a respectful relationship between First Nationsand other people. Culture also includes stories and customs, improving quality of life, and fosters the development of positive social and economic partnerships.
Stanley James Jr, Chairman
Jessie Peter, Vice Chairman
Dennis Gerard, General Manager
Marion Telep, Director/Finance
Dennis Gerard, Engineering Dir

TV Group Ownership

Astral Media Inc.
1800 avenue McGill College, Bureau 2700, Montreal PQ H3A 3J6
(514) 939-5000; *Fax:*(514) 939-1515
www.astral.com
Ownership: Abgreen Holdings Ltd., 55.71% vote; 654625 Ontario Inc., 13.63% vote.

Bell Media Inc.
299 Queen Street West, Toronto ON M5V 2Z5
(416) 384-8000
www.bellmedia.ca
bellmediacommunications@bellmedia.ca

CanWest Global Communications Corp.
201 Portage Ave., 31st Fl., Winnipeg MB R3B 3L7
(204) 956-2025; *Fax:*(204) 947-9841
www.canwestglobal.com
bleslie@canwest.com

Corus Entertainment Inc.
630 3rd Ave. S.W., Suite 105, Calgary AB T2P 4L4
(403) 444-4244; *Fax:*(403) 444-4242
www.corusent.com
Ownership: J.R. Shaw controls an aggregate of 80% of the voting rights.

Crossroads Television System
1295 N. Service Rd., Burlington ON L7R 4X5
(905) 331-7333; *Fax:*(905) 332-6005
www.ctstv.com
cts@ctstv.com

NewCap Inc.
745 Windmill Rd., Dartmouth NS B3B1C2
(902) 468-7557; *Fax:*(902) 468-7558
www.ncc.ca
Ownership: H.R. Steele, Blavin & Company.

Newfoundland Broadcasting Co.
Box 2020, St. John's NF A1C 5S2
(709) 722-5015; *Fax:*(709) 726-5107
www.ntv.ca
ozfm@ozfm.com,ntv@ntv.com
Ownership: Geoffrey W. Stirling, 89.95%; G. Scott Stirling, 10%; and others, 0.05%.

Remstar Broadcasting Inc.
85 rue Saint-Paul Ouest, Bureau 300, Montreal QC H2Y 3V4
(514) 847-1136; *Fax:*(514) 847-0019
www.remstarcorp.com
remstar@remstarcorp.com

RNC MEDIA Inc.
380 av Murdoch, Rouyn-Noranda PQ J9X 1G5
(819) 762-0741; *Fax:*(819) 762-6331;

Rogers Broadcasting Ltd.
One Ted Rogers Way, Toronto ON M4Y 3B7
(416) 935-8200; *Fax:*(416) 935-8288
www.rogersmedia.com
Ownership: Rogers Media Inc., 100%. Note: Rogers Media Inc. is 100% owned by Rogers Communications Inc.

S-VOX
171 E. Liberty St., Suite 230, Toronto ON M6K 3P6
(416) 368-3194; *Fax:*(416) 368-9774
www.s-vox.com

Shaw Communications
2055 Flavelle Boulevard, Mississauga ON L5K 1Z8
(800) 268-2943; *Fax:*(905) 403-2022
www.shawbroadcast.com
support@shawbroadcast.com

Shaw Media Inc.
121 Bloor St. E., 15th Fl., Toronto ON M4W 3M5
(416) 967-1174
shawmedia.ca
Ownership: Shaw Communications Inc., 100%. Shaw Communications Inc. also owns CJBN-TV Kenora, ON.

Tele Inter-Rives Ltee.
298 Boulevard Theriault, Riviere-du-Loup QC G5R 4C2
(418) 867-1341; *Fax:*(418) 867-4710
www.cimt.ca

Tele-Quebec
1000 rue Fullum, Montreal PQ H2K 3L7
(514) 521-2424; *Fax:*(514) 873-4413
www.telequebec.tv
info@telequebec.qc.ca
Ownership: La Societe de radio-television du Quebec is a para-governmental organization. Its mandate is to manage an educ TV net throughout theprovince of Quebec.

The Jim Pattison Broadcast Group
460 Pemberton Terrace, Kamloops BC V2C 1T5
(250) 372-3322; *Fax:*(250) 374-0445
www.jpbroadcast.com
Ownership: Jim Pattison Group.

TVA Group Inc.
1600 de Maisonneuve Blvd. East, Montreal QC H2L 4P2
(514) 526-9251
tva.canoe.ca
Ownership: Quebecor Media Inc., 99.95%; and others, 0.05%.

TV Stations in Canada

Alberta

Calgary

CBRT
Digital Channel: 21; 253.5 kw; 350.8 m
1724 Westmount Blvd. N.W., Calgary, AB Canada
(403) 521-6000, *Fax:* (403) 521-6007
cbc.ca
del_simon@cbc.ca
License: Calgary, AB held by CBC
Nat'l Network: CBC
Carole Taylor, Chairman
Robert Rabinovich, President
Don Orchard, General Manager
Wendy Ell, General Sales Mgr
Fred Youngs, Programming Director
Irene Karras, Promotions Manager
Harold Redekopp, Executive Vice President
DelSimon, Promotions Manager
Pat Paproski, Regional Sales Manager

CFCN-DT
Analog Hrs: 24*Digital Channel:* 36*Digital Hrs:* 24; 120 kw; ant 623t/380g; N52 03 37 W114 10 13
Broadcast House, 80 Patina Rise S.W., Calgary, AB T3H 2W4 Canada
(403) 240-5600, *Fax:* (403) 240-5759
www.calgary.ctv.ca
cfcnnews@ctv.ca
License: Calgary, AB held by Bell Media Inc.
Group Owner: CTV Inc.
Nat'l Network: CTV
Len Perry, General Manager

CIANTV
Analog Hrs: 22; 9.9 kw vis; ant 807t; N51 03 54 W114 12 47
18520 Stony Plain Rd., Edmonton, AB Canada
(780) 483-3311, *Fax:* (780) 484-4426
www.accesstv.ca
info@accesstv.ca
License: Calgary, AB held by Learning and Skills Television of Alberta Ltd
Group Owner: Bell Media Inc.; (acq 1995).
Lloyd Lewis, Operations Dir
Brad Hooper, Engineering Dir

CICT-DT
Analog Hrs: 24*Digital Channel:* 41; 100 kw vis, 20 kw aur; ant 989t/633g;*Rebroadcasting:* Rebroadcast CISA-TV Lethbridge 90%.
222 23rd St. N.E., Calgary, AB T2E 7N2 Canada
(403) 235-7777, *Fax:* (403) 248-0252
www.canada.com
License: Calgary, AB held by Canwest Television GP Inc. (the general partner) and Canwest Media Inc. (the limited partner), carrying on business as Canwest Television L.P.
Group Owner: Shaw Media Inc.
Size of News Staff: 50; *Hours of Local News Weekly:* news progmg 13 hrs wkly
C. McGinley, Operations Dir
Greg Campbell, General Sales Mgr
Dawna Docherty, Programming Director
J. Eisler, Promotions Manager
Dave Budge, News Director
Dan Gold, Engineering Dir
Norm Michaelis, Operations Director
Lynda Ritz,Promotions Manager
Jeff Eisler, Public Affairs Director

CJCO-TV
Digital Channel: 38; 84 kw; 325.1 meters; N51 03 54 W114 12 51
10212 Jasper Ave., Edmonton, AB Canada
(780) 424-2222, *Fax:* (780) 440-7793
www.omniab.ca
info@omniab.ca
License: Calgary, AB held by Rogers Broadcasting Ltd.
Group Owner: Rogers Broadcasting Ltd.
Arjuna Ranawana, News Director

CKAL-DT
Digital Channel: 49; 100 kw; 378 m
535 7th Ave. S.W., Calgary, AB T2P 0Y4 Canada
(403) 508-2222, *Fax:* (403) 508-2224
www.a-channel.com
License: Calgary, AB held by Rogers Broadcasting Ltd.
Group Owner: Rogers Broadcasting Ltd.; (acq 10-31-2007; grpsl)
Andy Pernal, CFO
Al Thorgeikson, General Manager
Mike Pietrus, News Director

CKCS-TV
Analog Channel: 32; 75 kw vis; N51 03 00 W114 05 00
839 5 Ave. S.W., Suite 100 B, Calgary, AB Canada
(403) 263-3191, *Fax:* (403) 263-3705
www.ctstv.com
License: Calgary, AB held by Crossroads Television System
Group Owner: Crossroads Television System
Nat'l Reps: Airtime TV
Byron Winsor, COO
Natalie Faith, Station Manager
Glenn Stewart, General Sales Mgr
Rob Sheppard, Programming Director
Carolyn Ennis, Director, Communications
David Storey, Engineering Dir
Matt Hillier, CFO

Cardston

CFSO-TV
20 w; N49 10 40 W113 19 36
Box 1238, Cardston, AB T0K 0K0 Canada
(403) 653-3792, *Fax:* (403) 653-3792
www.channel32.ca
channel32@mac.com
License: Cardston, AB held by Logan McCarthy
Logan McCarthy, Station Manager

Coronation

CHCA-TV-1
Analog Channel: 10*Analog Hrs:* 6 AM-2 AM; 190 kw vis, 19 kw aur; ant 697t/240g; N50 09 15 W111 09 30;*Rebroadcasting:* Rebroadcasts CHCA-TV Red Deer.
2840 Bremner Ave., 2nd Fl., Red Deer, AB T4R 1M9 Canada
(403) 346-2573, *Fax:* (403) 346-9980
www.canada.com
chcanews@chcanews.ca
License: Coronation, AB held by Canwest Television L.P.
Group Owner: CanWest Global Communications Corp.
Size of News Staff: 12; *Hours of Local News Weekly:* news progmg 5 hrs wkly
Stan Schmidt, General Manager

Edmonton

CBXFT-DT
Digital Channel: 47
Mailing Address: Box 555, Edmonton, AB T5J 2P4 Canada
Second Address: Edmonton City Centre, 10062-102 Ave., Edmonton, AB T5J 2Y8
(780) 468-7500, *Fax:* (780) 468-7868
www.cbc.ca
License: Edmonton, AB held by CBC
Nat'l Network: CBC
Foreign Language Programming; Size of News Staff: 15; *Hours of Local News Weekly:* news progmg 2 hrs wkly
Don Orchard, CFO
Carol Nielsen, Chief Engineer

CBXT-DT
Analog Hrs: 24*Digital Channel:* 42; 94.11 kw; 233.1 m
Mailing Address: Box 555, Edmonton, AB T5J 2P4 Canada
Second Address: 123 Edmonton City Centre, 10062-102 Ave., Edmonton, AB T5J 2Y8
(780) 468-7500, *Fax:* (780) 468-7792
www.cbc.ca/edmonton
License: Edmonton, AB held by CBC
Nat'l Network: CBC
Mike Linder, General Manager

CFRN-DT
Digital Channel: 12; 16 kw; 228.1 m; N53 23 06 W113 12 48*Population Served:* 1,200,000
18520 Stony Plain Rd., Edmonton, AB T5S 1A8 Canada
(780) 483-3311, *Fax:* (780) 484-4426
www.ctvedmonton.ca
cfrn@ctv.ca
License: Edmonton, AB held by Bell Media Inc.
Group Owner: CTV Inc.; (acq 1998).
Nat'l Network: CTV
Hours of Local News Weekly: News progmg 12 hrs wkly
Lloyd Lewis, Operations Dir
David Fisher, Promotions Manager

CITV-DT
Digital Channel: 47; 325 kw vis, 32.5 kw aur; ant 900t; N53 23 06 W113 12 48
5325 Allard Way, Edmonton, AB T6H 5B8 Canada
(780) 436-1250, *Fax:* (780) 989-4613
www.canada.com
edmonton@globaltv.ca
License: Edmonton, Canada County, AB held by Canwest Television GP Inc. (the general partner) and Canwest Media Inc. (the limited partner), carrying on business as Canwest Television L.P.
Group Owner: Shaw Media Inc.; (acq 2-6-91)
Size of News Staff: 33; *Hours of Local News Weekly:* news progmg 11 hrs wkly
Tim Spelliscy, General Manager
Neill Fitzpatrick, News Director

CJEO-DT
340 kw vis; ant 705g; N53 27 49 W113 20 11
10212 Jasper Ave., Edmonton, AB T5J 5A3 Canada
(780) 424-2222, *Fax:* (780) 440-7793
www.omniab.ca
info@omniab.ca
License: Edmonton, AB held by Rogers Broadcasting Ltd.
Group Owner: Rogers Broadcasting Ltd.
Stanley Papulkas, Operations Dir
Richard Hiron, General Manager

CKEM-DT
Digital Channel: 17; 704 kw vis
10212 Jasper Ave., Edmonton, AB T5J 5A3 Canada
(780) 424-2222, *Fax:* (780) 424-0357
www.a-channel.com
webmaster@appliedthemalsciences.com
License: Edmonton, AB held by 4384903 Canada Inc.
Group Owner: Rogers Broadcasting Ltd.; (acq 10-31-2007; grpsl)
John Cuccaro, Operations Dir
Jim Haskins, General Manager
Art Eden, General Sales Mgr
Tania Nease, Programming Director
Barry Close, Promotions Manager
Chris Duncan, News Director
Peter Nobel, Engineering Dir

CKES-TV
34 kw vis
5330 Calgary Tr., Edmonton, AB T6H 4J8 Canada
(780) 433-3118, *Fax:* (780) 433-3248
www.ctstv.com
License: Edmonton, AB held by Crossroads Television System
Group Owner: Crossroads Television System
Nat'l Reps: Airtime TV
Byron Winsor, COO
Richard Landau, Station Manager
Glenn Stewart, General Sales Mgr
Rob Sheppard, Programming Director
Matt Hillier, CFO

Lethbridge

CFCN-DT-5
Analog Hrs: 24*Digital Channel:* 13; 47 kw vis, 7.34 kw aur; ant 564t; N49 43 59 W112 57 36
c/o CFCN-TV, 80 Patina Rise S.W., Calgary, AB T3H 2W4 Canada
(403) 240-5600, *Fax:* (403) 240-5759
www.calgary.ctv.ca
cfcnnews@ctv.ca
License: Lethbridge, AB held by Bell Media Inc.
Group Owner: CTV Inc.
Nat'l Network: CTV
Len Perry, General Manager

CISA-DT
Digital Channel: 7; 167 kw vis, 33.4 kw aur; 662t/600g; N49 47 01 W112 52 01
1401-28 Street N., Lethbridge, AB T1H 6H9 Canada
(403) 327-1521, *Fax:* (403) 320-2620
www.canada.com/lethbridge
cisa@globaltv.ca
License: Lethbridge, AB held by Canwest Television L.P.
Group Owner: Shaw Media Inc.; (acq 9-1-2000; grpsl)
Size of News Staff: 19; *Hours of Local News Weekly:* news progmg 12 hrs wkly
Peter Deys, General Manager

CJIL
31.6 kw vis
Box 1566, 450 31st St. N., Lethbridge, AB Canada
(403) 380-3399, *Fax:* (403) 380-3322
www.miraclechannel.ca
info@mireaclechannel.ca
License: Lethbridge, AB held by Miracle Channel
Leon Fontaine, CEO
Gord Klussen, General Manager
Len Whyte, Chief Engineer

Lloydminster

CITL-TV
Digital Channel: 4; 9.1 kw; 220.6 m
5026 50th St., Lloydminster, AB T9V 1P3 Canada
(780) 875-3321, *Fax:* (780) 875-4704
www.newcaptv.com
tvnews@newcap.ca
License: Lloydminster, AB held by NewCap Inc.
Group Owner: NewCap Inc.; (acq 12-22-2004; C$6,304,000 with CKSA-TV Lloydminster).
Nat'l Network: CTV
R.G. Steele, President
Chad Tabish, General Sales Mgr
Raymond Green, Chief Engineer

CKSA-TV
Digital Channel: 2; 8.1 kw; 220.6 m
5026 50th St., Lloydminster, AB T9V 1P3 Canada
(780) 875-3321, *Fax:* (780) 875-4704
www.newcaptv.com
tvnews@newcap.ca
License: Lloydminster, AB held by NewCap Inc.
Group Owner: NewCap Inc.; (acq 12-22-2004; C$6,304,000 with CITL-TV Lloydminster).
Nat'l Network: CBC
R.G. Steele, President
Chad Tabish, General Sales Mgr
Raymond Green, Chief Engineer

Meander River

CJTG-TV
10 w vis
Box 1377, High Level, AB T0H 1Z0 Canada

www.tachegondihesociety.com
License: Meander River, AB held by Tache Gondihe Society
Camille Piche, General Manager

Medicine Hat

CHATTV
Analog Channel: 6; 58 kw vis, 5.8 kw aur; 700t/559g
10 Boundary Road S E, Red Cliff, AB Canada
(403) 548-8282, *Fax:* (403) 548-8270
www.chattelevision.ca
chatnews@jpbg.com
License: Medicine Hat, AB held by Jim Pattison Broadcast Group Ltd. (the general partner) and Jim Pattison Industries Ltd. (the limited partner) carrying on business as Jim Pattison Broadcast Group L.P.
Group Owner: The Jim Pattison Broadcast Group; (acq 12-21-2000; grpsl).
Nat'l Reps: Airtime TV
Curtis Cruickshank, Creative Supervisor

Red Deer

CFRN-TV-6
Analog Channel: 8; 22 kw vis, 2.2 kw aur; ant 882t/588g; N52 19 10 W113 40 37
c/o CTV Edmonton, 18520 Stony Plain Rd., Edmonton, AB T5S 1A8 Canada
(780) 483-3311, *Fax:* (780) 484-4426
www.ctvedmonton.ca
cfrn@ctv.ca
License: Red Deer, AB held by CFRN-TV, a div. of CTV Television Inc
Nat'l Network: CTV
Lloyd Lewis, Operations Dir

British Columbia

Abbotsford

CFEG-TV
50 w vis; N49 03 07 W122 20 29
2719 Clearbrook Rd., Abbotsford, BC V2T 2Y9 Canada
(604) 850-6607, *Fax:* (604) 850-5717
clearbrookmbchurch@telus.net
License: Abbotsford, BC held by Clearbrook Mennonite Brethren Church.
Len Perry, General Manager

Dawson Creek

CJDC-TV
10 kw vis, 5 kw aur; ant 1,500t/500g
CJDC-TV Astral Media GP, 901 102nd Ave., Dawson Creek, BC V1G 2B6 Canada
(250) 782-3341, *Fax:* (250) 782-3154
www.cjdctv.com
License: Dawson Creek, BC held by Astral Media Radio G.P.
Group Owner: Astral Media Inc.; (acq 10-29-2007; grpsl)
Nat'l Network: CBC
Size of News Staff: 4; *Hours of Local News Weekly:* news progmg 10 hrs wkly
Terry Shepherd, General Manager
Dave Mc Connell, Operations Manager
Andre Da Costa, News Director

Fraser Valley

CHNU-DT
Analog Hrs: 6 AM-2 AM*Digital Channel:* 47; 17 kw vis*Population Served:* 2,200,000
5668 192 St., Suite 201, Surrey, BC V3S 2V7 Canada
(604) 575-4112, *Fax:* (604) 576-6895
www.joytv10.ca
License: Fraser Valley, BC held by Christian Channel Inc.
Group Owner: S-VOX; (acq 5-26-2008; C$6,247,908 with CIIT-TV Winnipeg, MB)
Terry Mahoney, General Manager
Gary Milne, General Sales Mgr
Karen Corbeil, Promotions Manager

Kamloops

CFJCTV
Analog Channel: 4*Digital Channel:* 7; 4.4 kw vis, 2.4 kw aur; 501t/114g*Population Served:* 200,000
460 Pemberton Terrace, Kamloops, BC Canada
(250) 372-3322, *Fax:* (250) 374-0445
www.cfjctv.com
info@cfjctv.com
License: Kamloops, BC held by Jim Pattison Broadcast Group Ltd. (the general partner) and Jim Pattison Industries Ltd. (the limited partner) carrying on business as Jim Pattison Broadcast Group L.P.
Group Owner: The Jim Pattison Broadcast Group; (acq 1987).
Size of News Staff: 8; *Hours of Local News Weekly:* news progmg 14 hrs wkly
Richard Arnish, President
Dave Somerton, Operations Dir

Kelowna

CHBC-DT
Digital Channel: 27; 23.3 kw; 509.6 m; N49 58 00 W119 31 40*Population Served:* 360,000
342 Leon Ave., Kelowna, BC V1Y 6J2 Canada
(250) 762-4535, *Fax:* (250) 860-2422,(250) 868-0662
www.chbc.com
comments@chbc.com
License: Kelowna, Yale County, BC held by Shaw Television L.P.
Group Owner: CanWest Global Communications Corp.
Size of News Staff: 31; *Hours of Local News Weekly:* news progmg 20 hrs wkly
Rob Weller, Operations Dir
Keith Williams, General Manager

Prince George

CKPG-TV
778 w vis, 389 w aur
1810 Third Avenue, 2ns Floor, Prince George, BC V2M 164 Canada
(250) 564-8861, *Fax:* (250) 562-8768
www.ckpgtv.com
ckpgmail@ckpg.bc.ca
License: Prince George, BC held by Jim Pattison Broadcast Group LP. (the general partner) and Jim Pattison Industries Ltd. (the limited partner) carrying on business as Jim Pattison Broadcast Group L.P.
Group Owner: The Jim Pattison Broadcast Group; (acq 12-21-2000; grpsl).
Nat'l Reps: Airtime TV
Ken Kilcullen, General Manager
Ron Polillo, General Sales Mgr
Mike Clotildes, Programming Director
Dave Barry, News Director

Valemount

CHVC-TV
10 kw vis
Box 922, Valemount, BC V0E 2Z0 Canada
(250) 566-8288, *Fax:* (250) 566-4645
License: Valemount, BC held by The Valemount Entertainment Society
Penni Osadchuk, General Manager

Vancouver

CBUBT-7
Analog Channel: 10; 900 w vis, 90 w aur;*Rebroadcasting:* Rebroadcasts CBUT-TV Vancouver 100%
Box 4600, c/o CBUT-TV, Vancouver, BC V6B 4A2 Canada
(604) 662-6000, *Fax:* (604) 662-6335
www.cbc.ca
cbc.vancouver.communications@cbc.ca
License: Vancouver, BC held by CBC
Nat'l Network: CBC
Hubert LaCroix, President
Ken Golemra, Operations Dir
Johnny Michel, Managing Director
Jennifer Smith, General Sales Mgr
Lorna Haeber, Programming Director
Wayne Williams, News Director

CBUFT-DT
Digital Channel: 26; 256 kw vis; ant 2,011t; N49 21 12 W122 57 18
Box 4600, Vancouver, BC V6B 4A2 Canada
(604) 662-6000, *Fax:* (604) 662-6161
www.radio-canada.ca/c-b
License: Vancouver, BC held by Societe Radio-Canada
Nat'l Network: Radio Canada
Mario Deschamp, General Sales Mgr
Michele Smolkin, Programming Director
Dave Newbury, Engineering Dir

CBUT-DT
Digital Channel: 43; 47.6 kw vis, 7.6 kw aur; ant 2,400t/190g
Box 4600, 700 Hamilton St., Vancouver, BC V6B 4A2 Canada
(604) 662-6000, *Fax:* (604) 662-6414
www.cbc.ca
License: Vancouver, BC held by CBC
Nat'l Network: CBC
Luz Hughes, Operations Dir

CHAN-DT
Analog Hrs: 24*Digital Hrs:* 24; 193.6 kw vis, 19.4 kw aur; ant 2,315t/250g; N49 21 29 W122 57 09
Global BC, 7850 Enterprise St., Burnaby, BC V5A 1V7 Canada
(604) 420-2288, *Fax:* (604) 422-6427
www.globaltvbc.com
License: Vancouver, BC held by Canwest Television L.P.
Group Owner: CanWest Global Communications Corp.
Nat'l Network: Global
Brett Manlove, General Manager

CHNM-TV
Digital Channel: 20; 76 kw vis*Population Served:* 3,000,000
channel m, 88 E. Pender St., Vancouver, BC Canada
(604) 678-3800, *Fax:* (604) 678-3810
www.channelm.ca
License: Vancouver, BC held by Rogers Broadcasting Ltd.
Group Owner: Rogers Broadcasting Ltd.; (acq 4-30-2008; C$61,291,913)
Rael Merson, President
Marisa Doolan, Operations Dir
Geoff Poulton, General Manager
Bruce Hamlin, General Sales Mgr
Mike Maslenki, Promotions Manager
Dianne Collins, News Director

CIVT-DT
710 kw vis; N49 21 29 W122 57 09*Population Served:* 2,500,000
750 Burrard St., Suite 300, Vancouver, BC V6Z 1X5 Canada
(604) 608-2868, *Fax:* (604) 608-2698
www.ctv.ca
bccomments@ctv.ca
License: Vancouver, BC held by Bell Media Inc.
Group Owner: Bell Media Inc.; Baton, Bell Globemedia, CTVglobemedia, Bell Media; *Ownership:* Bell Media
Nat'l Network: CTV *Regional Network:* CTV Two Vancouver Island
Hours of Local News Weekly: 24/7
Kevin Crull, CEO
Rick Brace, Specialty Channels & CTV Productions
James Stuart, Regional Vice President
Tom Haberstroh, General Manager
Lynne Forbes, General Sales Mgr
Roger Lemire, Community Relations Manager
Jim Olsen,Promotions Manager
Margo Harper, News Director
Rob Chambers, Engineering Dir
Jennifer Cheung, Finance Manager
Lily Dong, Traffic Manager
Allison Wolfe, Human Resources Manager
Dave Aleaxander, Technical Operations Manager
David Seemann,News Operations Manager
Perry Solkowski, Sports Director

CKVU-DT
Digital Channel: 33; 4.3 kw; 2198t; N48 45 13 W123 29 25
180 W. Second Ave., Vancouver, BC V5Y 3T9 Canada
(604) 876-1344, *Fax:* (604) 876-3100
www.citytv.com
License: Vancouver, BC held by Rogers Broadcasting Ltd.
Group Owner: Rogers Broadcasting Ltd.; (acq 10-31-2007; grpsl)
Geoff Poulton, Operations Dir
Bruce Hamlin, General Sales Mgr
Manuel Ponseca, Programming Director
Steve Scarrow, Promotions Manager
Tamara Poirier, Engineering Dir

Victoria

CHEKTV
Analog Channel: 6*Analog Hrs:* 24; 100 kw vis, 10 kw aur; 1,628t/380g
780 Kings Road, Victoria, BC Canada
(250) 383-2435, *Fax:* (250) 384-7766
www.cheknews.ca
info@cheknews.ca
License: Victoria, BC held by CHEK Media Group
Ownership: CHEK Media Group
John Pollard, President
John Pollard, General Manager
Bill Pollock, Programming Director
Tanya Smith, Promotions Manager
Rob Germain, News Director
Bill Pollock, Engineering Dir

CIVI-DT
Analog Hrs: 24*Digital Channel:* 23; 12 kw vis
1420 Broad St., Victoria, BC V8W 2B1 Canada
(250) 381-2484, *Fax:* (250) 381-2485
www.atv.ca/victoria
islandcontactus@achannel.ca
License: Victoria, Canada County, BC held by Bell Media Inc.
Group Owner: Bell Media Inc.
Nat'l Network: CTV
Jim Blundell, Operations Dir
Stephen Olafson, Promotions Manager
Hudson Mack, News Director
Brian Gatensby, Engineering Dir

Manitoba

Brandon

CKX-TV
Analog Channel: 5*Analog Hrs:* 6 AM-2 AM; 44 kw vis, 27 kw aur; ant 511t/525g
2940 Victoria Ave., Brandon, MB R7B 3Y3 Canada
(204) 728-1150, *Fax:* (204) 727-2505
www.cktv.com
feedbackbrandon@chumtv.com
License: Brandon, MB
Group Owner: Bell Media Inc.; (acq 11-19-2004; grpsl)
Nat'l Network: CBC
Size of News Staff: 20; *Hours of Local News Weekly:* news progmg 15 hrs wkly
Alan Cruise, General Manager
Brian Atkinson, Station Manager

Fisher Branch

CBWGT
Analog Channel: 10*Analog Hrs:* 24; 27.4 kw vis, 5.48 kw aur; 559t/548g;*Rebroadcasting:* CBWT
Mailing Address: 541 Portage Avenue, Winnipeg, MB R3C 2H1 Canada
Second Address: c/o CBWT, 541 Portage Ave., Winnipeg, MB R3B 2G1
(204) 788-3222, *Fax:* (204) 788-3635
www.cbc.ca/manitoba
License: Fisher Branch, MB held by CBC
Nat'l Network: CBC
John Bertrand, Director
Cecil Rosner, Managing Editor
Leona Johnson, Promotions Manager

Flin Flon

CBWBT
Analog Channel: 10*Analog Hrs:* 24; 7.8 kw vis, 1.6 kw aur;*Rebroadcasting:* CBWT
Mailing Address: Box 160, c/o CBWT, Winnipeg, MB R3C 2H1 Canada
Second Address: c/o CBWT, 541 Portage Ave., Winnipeg, MB R3B 2G1
(204) 788-3222, *Fax:* (204) 788-3635
www.cbc.ca/manitoba
License: Flin Flon, MB held by CBC
Nat'l Network: CBC
Sabrina Seepaul, Operations Dir
John Bertrand, General Manager
Leona Johnson, Promotions Manager

Mafeking

CBWYT
Analog Channel: 2*Analog Hrs:* 24; 4 kw vis; 370g
Mailing Address: 541 Portage Avenue, c/o CBWT, Winnipeg, MB R3C 2H1 Canada
Second Address: c/o CBC, 541 Portage Ave., Winnipeg, MB R3B 2G1
(204) 788-3222, *Fax:* (204) 788-3635
www.cbc.ca/manitoba
License: Mafeking, MB held by CBC
Nat'l Network: CBC
John Bertrand, Director
Managing Editor, General Sales Mgr
Leona Johnson, Promotions Manager

Portage la Prarie

CHMI-DT
Digital Channel: 13; 325 kw vis, 32.5 kw aur; 1,029t/1,100g*Population Served:* 813,000
#8 Forks Market Rd., Winnipeg, MB R3C 4Y3 Canada
(204) 947-9613, *Fax:* (204) 956-0811
www.citytv.com
winnipeginteractive@chumtv.com
License: Portage la Prarie, MB held by Portage la Prarie
Group Owner: Rogers Broadcasting Ltd.; (acq 10-31-2007; grpsl)
Size of News Staff: 35; *Hours of Local News Weekly:* news progmg 34 hrs wkly
Cam Cowie, Operations Dir
Glen Cassie, Programming Director
Christine Ljungberg, Operations Manager

Winnipeg

CBWFT-DT
Digital Channel: 51; 7.6 kw; 138.9 m
Mailing Address: Box 160, Winnipeg, MB R3C 2H1 Canada
Second Address: 541 Portage Ave., Winnipeg, MB R3B 2G1
(204) 788-3222, *Fax:* (204) 788-3639
www.radio-canada.ca
License: Winnipeg, MB held by Societe Radio-Canada
Nat'l Network: Radio Canada
Philippe Vrignon, Operations Dir
Richard Augert, General Manager
Martine Bordeleau, Promotions Manager

CBWT-DT
Digital Channel: 27; 42 kw; 138.6 m; N49 46 15 W97 30 35
Mailing Address: Box 160, Winnipeg, MB R3C 2H1 Canada
Second Address: 541 Portage Ave., Winnipeg, MB R3B 2G1
(204) 788-3222, *Fax:* (204) 788-3167
www.winnipeg.cbc.ca
communications@winnipeg.cbc.ca
License: Winnipeg, MB held by CBC
Nat'l Network: CBC
John Mang, Operations Dir
John Bertrand, General Manager

CIIT-DT
Digital Channel: 35
171 E. Liberty St., Suite 230, Toronto, ON M6K 3P6 Canada
(416) 368-3194, *Fax:* (416) 368-9774
www.joytv11.ca
License: Winnipeg, MB held by Christian Channel Inc.
Group Owner: S-VOX; (acq 6-30-2008; C$6,247,908 with CHNU-TV Fraser Valley, BC)
David Garby, General Manager
Jennifer Craig, Programming Director
Mark Prasuhn, Chief Content Officer

CKND-DT
Analog Hrs: 24*Digital Channel:* 40; 14.9 kw; 131.2 m
603 St. Mary's Rd., Winnipeg, MB R2M 3L8 Canada
(204) 233-3304, *Fax:* (204) 233-5615
www.globaltv.com
License: Winnipeg, MB held by Canwest Television L.P.
Group Owner: CanWest Global Communications Corp.
Size of News Staff: 19; *Hours of Local News Weekly:* news progmg 12 hrs wkly
Tim Schellenberg, General Manager
Heather McIntyre, Promotions Manager
Jon Lovlin, News Director
Len Virog, Engineering Dir

CKY-DT
Analog Hrs: 24*Digital Channel:* 7; 325 kw vis, 65 kw aur; ant 1,000g
400-345 Grahm Ave., Winnipeg, MB R3C 5S6 Canada
(204) 788-3300, *Fax:* (204) 788-3399
www.ctvwinnipeg.ca
winnipegnews@ctv.ca
License: Winnipeg, MB held by Bell Media Inc.
Group Owner: CTV Inc.
Nat'l Network: CTV
Bill Hanson, Operations Dir
Wally Comrie, General Sales Mgr
Winnie Navarro, Programming Director
Diane Kashton, Promotions Manager
Karen Mitchell, News Director
Kenneth Peron, Operations Manager

New Brunswick

Campbellton

CKCDTV
Analog Channel: 7; 920 w vis, 180 w aur; 75t;*Rebroadcasting:* Rebroadcasts CKCW-TV Moncton 100%.
191 Halifax St., Moncton, NB Canada
(506) 857-2600, *Fax:* (506) 857-2617
www.ctv.ca
ckcw@ctv.ca
License: Campbellton, NB held by CTV Television Inc.
Group Owner: CTV Inc.; (acq 11-1-97).
Nat'l Network: CTV
Ivan Fecan, CEO
Rick Brace, President
Mike Elgie, Operations Dir
Brian Lewis, Station Manager
Robin Fillingham, CFO
Elaine Ali, Executive Vice President
John Silver, Operations Manager
Renee Fournier, Program Manager

Fredericton-Saint John

CBAT
Digital Channel: 31; 4.2 kw; 102.8 m; N45 28 39 W66 13 59
1160 Regent Street, Fredericton, NB E3B 5G4 Canada
(506) 451-4000
www.cbc.radio-canada.ca
License: Fredericton-Saint John, NB
Group Owner: Canadian Broadcasting Company
Remi Racine, Chairman of the Board
Hubert T. Lacroix, President/CEO

Moncton

CBAFT-DT
Digital Channel: 11; 17.65 kw; 227.5 m; N46 8 37 W64 54 8
250 University Avenue, Moncton, NB E1C 5K3 Canada
(506) 853-6666
www.cbc.radio-canada.ca
License: Moncton, NB held by Canadian Broadcasting Corporation
Hubert T. Lacroix, President/CEO

CKCW-DT
Digital Channel: 29; 56 kw vis, 9.2 kw aur
191 Halifax St., Moncton, NB E1C 9R7 Canada
(506) 857-2600, *Fax:* (506) 857-2617
www.ctv.ca
ckcw@ctv.ca
License: Moncton, NB held by Bell Media Inc.
Group Owner: CTV Inc.; (acq 11-1-97).
Nat'l Network: CTV
Ivan Fecan, CEO
Rick Brace, President
Mike Elgie, Operations Dir
Brian Lewis, Station Manager
Robin Fillingham, CFO
Elaine Ali, Executive Vice President
John Silver, Operations Manager
Renee Fournier, Program Manager

Saint John

CKLT-DT
Digital Channel: 9; 162 kw vis, 32 kw aur; 1,361t/241g
12 Smythe St., Suite 126, Saint John, NB E2L 5G5 Canada
(506) 658-1010, *Fax:* (506) 658-1208
www.ctv.ca
cklt@ctv.ca
License: Saint John, NB held by Bell Media Inc.
Group Owner: CTV Inc.; (acq 11-1-97).

Nat'l Network: CTV
Mike Elgie, General Manager

St. Andrews

CHCT-TV
480 w vis; N45 04 54 W67 03 34*Population Served:* 20,000
24 Reed Ave., Unit 2, St. Andrews, NB E5B 1A1 Canada
(506) 529-8826, *Fax:* (506) 529-2601
www.chct.ca
general.mail@chct.ca
License: St. Andrews, Charlotte County, NB held by St. Andrews Community Channel
Size of News Staff: 2; *Hours of Local News Weekly:* 5
David Welch, Chairman
Patrick Watt, Operations Dir

Upsalquitch Lake

CKAMTV
280 kw vis, 141 kw aur;*Rebroadcasting:* Rebroadcasts CKCW-TV Moncton 100%.
c/o CKCW-TV, 191 Halifax St., Moncton, NB Canada
(506) 857-2600, *Fax:* (506) 857-2617
www.ctv.ca
ckcw@ctv.ca
License: Upsalquitch Lake, NB held by CTV Television Inc.
Group Owner: CTV Inc.; (acq 11-1-97).; *Washington Law Firm:* Alexander, Pearson & Dawson
Nat'l Network: CTV
Ivan Fecan, CEO
Rick Brace, President
Mike Elgie, Operations Dir
Brian Lewis, Station Manager
Robin Fillingham, CFO
Elaine Ali, Executive Vice President
John Silver, Operations Manager
Renee Fournier, Program Manager

Newfoundland

Grand Falls

CJCN-TV
Digital Channel: 21; 128.4 kw; 254.6 m; N49 04 12 W55 16 54;*Rebroadcasting:* Rebroadcasts CJON-TV St. John's 100%*Population Served:* 575,000
Box 2020, 446 Logy Bay Rd., St. John's, NF A1C 5S2 Canada
(709) 722-5015, *Fax:* (709) 726-5107
www.ntv.ca
ntv@ntv.ca
License: Grand Falls, NL held by Newfoundland Broadcasting Co. Ltd.
Group Owner: Newfoundland Broadcasting Co.
Nat'l Network: CTV
Size of News Staff: 12; *Hours of Local News Weekly:* news progmg 11 hrs wkly
Scott Stirling, President
Fred Hutton, News Director

Saint John's

CBNT-DT
Digital Channel: 8; 3 kw vis, 300 w aur; N48 26 27 W53 21 25
Mailing Address: Box 12010, Stn A, Saint John's, NF A1B 3T8 Canada
Second Address: 95 University Ave., Saint John's, NF A1B 1Z4
(709) 576-5000, *Fax:* (709) 576-5011
www.cbc.ca/nl
License: Saint John's, NL held by CBC
Nat'l Network: CBC
Denise Wilson, General Sales Mgr
Keith Durnford, Chief Engineer

St John's

CJON-DT
Digital Channel: 21; 128.4 kw; 254.6 m; N47 31 36 W52 42 50*Population Served:* 575,000
Box 2020, 446 Logy Bay Rd., St John's, NF A1C 5S2 Canada
(709) 722-5015, *Fax:* (709) 726-5107
www.ntv.ca
ntv@ntv.ca
License: St John's, NL held by Newfoundland Broadcasting Co. Ltd
Washington Law Firm: Johnston & Buchan
Nat'l Network: CTV *Wire Services:* BN Wire
Size of News Staff: 12; *Hours of Local News Weekly:* news progmg 11 hrs wkly
Scott Stirling, President
Doug Neal, General Manager
Fred Hutton, News Director

Northwest Territorie

Inuvik

CHAKTV
Analog Channel: 8*Analog Hrs:* 24; 3 kw vis, 300 w aur; 443t/360g;*Rebroadcasting:* Rebroadcast of CFYK-TV Yellowknife
Mailing Address: Box 160, Yellowknife, NT Canada
Second Address: 5002 Forest Dr., Yellowknife, NT X1A 2N2
(867) 920-5400, *Fax:* (867) 920-5489
www.cbc.ca/north
cbcnorth@cbc.ca
License: Inuvik, NT held by CBC
Nat'l Network: CBC
Size of News Staff: 2
Joe Hill, Operations Dir
John Agnew, General Sales Mgr

Yellowknife

CFYK-DT
Digital Channel: 8; 2.4 kw; 62.48 m
Mailing Address: Box 160, Yellowknife, NT X1A2N2 Canada
Second Address: 5002 Forest Dr., Yellowknife, NT X1A2N2
(867) 920-5400, *Fax:* (867) 920-5489
www.cbc.ca/north
cbcnorth@cbc.ca
License: Yellowknife, NT held by CBC
Nat'l Network: CBC
Joe Hill, Operations Dir
John Agnew, General Sales Mgr

Nova Scotia

Halifax

CBHT
Digital Channel: 39; 92.59 kw; 266.47 m; N44 38 3 W63 39 26
1840 Bell Roaad, Halifax, NS B3H 2Z5 Canada
(902) 420-8311
www.cbc.ca
License: Halifax, NS
Group Owner: Canadian Broadcasting Corporation
Hubert T. Lacroix, President/CEO

CIHF-DT
Digital Channel: 8; 410 kw; 241 m; N44 39 03 W63 39 28*Population Served:* 1,500,000
14 Akerley Blvd, Dartmouth, NS B3B 1J8 Canada
(902) 481-7400,(506) 632-3400, *Fax:* (902) 468-2154
www.globalmaritimes.com
news@globaltv.com
License: Halifax, NS held by Canwest Television L.P.
Group Owner: CanWest Global Communications Corp.; (acq 8-29-94; $11 million)
Size of News Staff: 15; *Hours of Local News Weekly:* news progmg 17 hrs wkly
Leonard Asper, CEO
Bill Albert, General Manager

CJCH-DT
Digital Channel: 48; 100 kw vis, 10 kw aur; ant 821t/575g; N44 39 03 W63 39 28
Mailing Address: Box 1653, Halifax, NS B3J 2Z4 Canada
Second Address: 2885 Robie St., Halifax, NS B3K 5Z4
(902) 453-4000, *Fax:* (902) 454-3302
www.ctv.ca
cjch@ctv.ca
License: Halifax, NS held by Bell Media Inc.
Group Owner: CTV Inc.
Nat'l Network: CTV
Michael Elgie, Operations Dir
Ian MacArthur, General Sales Mgr
Renee Fournier, Promotions Manager
Jay Witherbee, News Director
Gary Robertson, Chief Engineer

Isle Madame

CIMC-TV
Analog Hrs: 24; 450 w vis
Mailing Address: Box 87, Arichat, NS B0E 1A0 Canada
Second Address: 705 Lower Rd., Arichat, NS B0E 1A0
(902) 226-1928, *Fax:* (902) 226-1331
www.telile.tv
telile@telile.tv
License: Isle Madame, NS held by Telile:Isle Madame Community Television Association/Association Television Communautaire de l'Ile Madame
Gloria Hill, General Manager

Sydney

CJCB-TV
Analog Channel: 4*Analog Hrs:* 24; 100 kw vis, 60 kw aur
1283 George St., Sydney, NS B1P 1N7 Canada
(902) 562-5511, *Fax:* (902) 562-9714
www.ctv.ca
cjcb@ctv.ca
License: Sydney, NS held by Bell Media Inc.
Group Owner: CTV Inc.
Nat'l Network: CTV
Glenn McLanders, Station Manager
Renee Fournier, Promotions Manager
Jay Witherbee, News Director
Edgar Bennett, Engineering Dir
Gary Robertson, Chief Engineer

Ontario

Barrie

CKVR-DT
Digital Channel: 10; 8.9 kw; 332.3 m; N44 21 05 W79 41 55*Population Served:* 6,000,000
Mailing Address: Box 519, 33 Beacon Road, Barrie, ON L4M 4T9 Canada
Second Address: ON
(705) 734-3300, *Fax:* (705) 733-0302,(705) 734-2061
www.atv.ca
news@atv.ca
License: Barrie, ON held by Bell Media Inc.
Group Owner: Bell Media Inc.
Size of News Staff: 30; *Hours of Local News Weekly:* news progmg 10 hrs wkly
Brian Cathline, Operations Dir
Peggy Hebden, Station Manager
Paul Woodhouse, General Sales Mgr
Sandra Bryson, Programming Director
Ruth Anderson, News Director
Michelle Wilson, Business/HR Manager

Hamilton

CHCH-DT
Digital Channel: 15; 59 kw; 355 m
Box 2230, Stn. A, 163 Jackson St. W., Hamilton, ON L8N 3A6 Canada
(905) 522-1101, *Fax:* (905) 523-8778
www.chtv.ca
newstips@chtv.ca
License: Hamilton, ON held by Canwest Television L.P.
Group Owner: CanWest Global Communications Corp.; (acq 7-6-2000)
Nat'l Network: Global
Patrick O'Hara, General Manager

CITS-TV
Digital Channel: 36; 9.5 kw; 335 m
1295 N. Service Rd., Burlington, ON L7R 4X5 Canada
(905) 331-7333, *Fax:* (905) 332-6005
www.ctstv.com
cts@ctstv.com
License: Hamilton, ON held by Crossroads Television System
Group Owner: Crossroads Television System
Fred Vanstone, President
Terry Maskel, Operations Dir
Glenn Stewart, General Sales Mgr
Rob Sheppard, Programming Director
Chris Somerville, Promotions Manager
David Storey, Engineering Dir

Kenora

CBWAT
Analog Channel: 8; 2 kw vis, 200 w aur; 433t/371g
c/o CBC, Box 160, Winnipeg, MB R3C 2H1 Canada
(204) 788-3222, *Fax:* (204) 788-3643
www.winnipeg.cbc.ca
License: Kenora, ON held by CBC
Nat'l Network: CBC
Louise Cordeau, General Manager

CJBNTV
177 kw vis, 35 kw aur; 200g
Mailing Address: 102 10th Street, Keewatin, ON Canada
Second Address: 104 Tenth St., Keewatin, ON P9N 3X8

(807) 547-2852, *Fax:* (807) 547-2348
www.norcomcable.ca
darrylm@norcomcable.ca
License: Kenora, ON held by Shaw Cablesystems G.P.
Nat'l Network: CTV
Size of News Staff: 2; *Hours of Local News Weekly:* news progmg one hr wkly
Darryl Michaluk, Station Manager

Kingston

CKWSTV
Analog Hrs: 24; 325 kw vis, 32.5 kw aur; ant 830t/785g; N44 10 02 W76 25 40
170 Queen Street, Kingston, ON Canada
(613) 544-2340, *Fax:* (613) 544-5508
www.ckwstv.com
newswatch@corusent.com
License: Kingston, Canada County, ON held by 591987 B.C. Ltd.
Group Owner: Corus Entertainment Inc.; (acq 3-24-2000; grpsl).
Nat'l Network: CBC
Hours of Local News Weekly: News progmg 12 hrs wkly
Mike Ferguson, General Manager
Tim Wieczorek, General Sales Mgr
Jackie Calverley, Promotions Manager
Jay Westman, News Director
Roger Cole, Chief Engineer

Kitchener

CKCO-DT
Digital Channel: 13; 325 kw vis, 32.5 kw aur; 954t/653g; N43 24 15 W80 38 05*Population Served:* 2,000,000
CTV Southwestern Ontario, Box 91026, Kitchener, ON N2G 4E9 Canada
(519) 578-1313, *Fax:* (519) 743-0730 (news)
www.swo.ctv.ca
viewermail@swo.ctv.ca
License: Kitchener, ON held by Bell Media Inc.
Group Owner: CTV Inc.; (acq 8-31-97).
Nat'l Network: CTV
Foreign Language Programming
Ivan Fecan, CEO
Dennis Watson, Operations Dir
Cameron Crassweller, General Sales Mgr
Janet Taylor, Promotions Manager
Andy LeBlanc, News Director
Dave Melse, Chief Engineer
Dave MacNeill, Operations Director

Leamington

CFTV-DT
Digital Channel: 34; 356 w; 56 m
223 Talbot St. W., Leamington, ON N8H 1N8 Canada
(519) 326-4000
www.cftv.ca
info@cftv.ca
License: Leamington, ON held by Southshore Broadcasting Inc
Tony Vidal, President
Ted Mastronardi, Operations Dir

London

CFPL-DT
Digital Channel: 10; 325 kw vis, 43.2 kw aur; 1,000t/975g*Population Served:* 500,000
1 Communications Road, London, ON N6J 4Z1 Canada
(519) 686-8810, *Fax:* (519) 668-3288
www.achannel.ca
License: London, Middlesex County, ON held by Bell Media Inc.
Group Owner: Bell Media Inc.; (acq 1997)
Don Mumford, Station Manager
Jim Kippen, Chief Engineer

Marathon

CBLAT-4
Analog Channel: 11*Analog Hrs:* 17; 7.5 kw vis, 1.532 kw aur; 599t; N48 44 50 W86 34 00;*Rebroadcasting:* Rebroadcast of CBLT Toronto 100%.
Box 500, Stn A, c/o CBLT, Toronto, ON M5W 1E6 Canada
(416) 205-3311, *Fax:* (416) 205-2552
www.cbc.ca
License: Marathon, ON held by Canadian Broadcasting Corp
Nat'l Network: CBC
David Kyle, General Manager
Nigel Sims, Programming Director
Bob Rankin, News Director
Jon Anderson, Chief Engineer

North Bay

CKNYTV
Analog Channel: 10*Analog Hrs:* 20; 70.5 kw vis, 7.1 kw aur; 607t/1,165g*Population Served:* 156,000
245 Oak St. E., North Bay, ON Canada
(705) 476-3111, *Fax:* (705) 495-4474,(705) 495-0922 (news)
www.ctv.ca
northbaynews@ctv.ca
License: North Bay, Nipissing County, ON held by Bell Media Inc.
Group Owner: CTV Inc.; (acq 1991).
Nat'l Network: CTV
Hours of Local News Weekly: News progmg 10 hrs wkly
Scott Lund, General Manager
Ron Driscoll, General Sales Mgr

Oshawa

CHEX-TV-2
Analog Hrs: 20; 550 kw vis; ant 440t; N43 57 15 W78 48 24
500 Wentworth St. E., Unit 7, Oshawa, ON L1H 3V9 Canada
(905) 434-2421, *Fax:* (905) 432-2315
www.channel12.ca
License: Oshawa, ON held by 591987 B.C. Ltd.
Group Owner: Corus Entertainment Inc.; (acq 3-24-2000; grpsl).
Nat'l Network: CBC
Kathleen McNair, Operations Dir

Ottawa

CBOFT-DT
Digital Channel: 33; 282 kw; ant 1,394t/702g
Mailing Address: Box 3220, Stn C, Ottawa, ON K1Y 1E4 Canada
Second Address: Ottawa Broadcast Centre, 181 Queen St., Ottawa, ON K1P 1K9
(613) 288-6000,(613) 288-6750 (news), *Fax:* (613) 288-6770
www.radio-canada.ca
tjottawa-gatincau@radio-canada.ca
License: Ottawa, ON held by CBC
Nat'l Network: Radio Canada
Richard Simoens, General Manager

CBOT-DT
Digital Channel: 25; 214.8 kw; 426.4 meters
Mailing Address: Box 3220, Stn C, Ottawa, ON K1Y 1E4 Canada
Second Address: Ottawa Broadcast Centre, 181 Queen St., Ottawa, ON K1P 1K9
(613) 288-6000, *Fax:* (613) 288-6423
www.cbc.ca
newsatsixottawa@cbc.ca
License: Ottawa, ON held by CBC
Nat'l Network: CBC
Rob Renaud, General Sales Mgr

CHRO-DT-43
Digital Channel: 43; 282 kw vis; N45 13 01 W75 33 51
'A' Ottawa, 87 George St., Ottawa, ON K1N 9H7 Canada
(613) 789-0606, *Fax:* (613) 789-7310
www.Atv.ca
Amorning@Atv.ca
License: Ottawa, ON held by Bell Media Inc.
Group Owner: Bell Media Inc.
Richard Gray, Operations Dir
Peter Angione, News Director

CJOH-DT
10 kw; 373.4 m; N45 30 11 W75 51 02*Population Served:* 2,000,000
Mailing Address: CTV Ottawa, Box 5813, Merivale Depot, Ottawa, ON K2C 3G6 Canada
Second Address: 1500 Merivale Rd., Nepean, ON K2E 6Z5
(613) 224-1313, *Fax:* (613) 274-4215
www.ottawa.ctv.ca
ctvottawa@ctv.ca
License: Ottawa, ON held by Bell Media Inc.
Group Owner: CTV Inc.
Nat'l Network: CTV *Nat'l Reps:* Canadian Broadcast Sales
Louis Douville, Operations Dir
Dan Champagne, General Sales Mgr
Kim Closs, Programming Director
Brent Corbeil, Promotions Manager
Scott Hannant, News Director
Art Clarke, Operations Manager

Pembroke

CHROTV
Analog Channel: 5*Analog Hrs:* 24; 100 kw vis, 10 kw aur; 496t/520g; N45 50 02 W77 09 50*Population Served:* 1,000,000
87 George St., Ottawa, ON Canada
(613) 789-0606, *Fax:* (613) 789-7310
www.Atv.ca
Amorning@Atv.ca
License: Pembroke, ON held by Bell Media Inc.
Group Owner: Bell Media Inc.; (acq 1997)
Hours of Local News Weekly: News progmg 30 hrs wkly
Richard Gray, Operations Dir
Peter Angione, News Director
Robert Edgley, Chief Engineer

Peterborough

CHEXTV
Analog Channel: 12*Analog Hrs:* 20; 185 kw vis, 18.5 kw aur; ant 772t/753g; N44 19 45 W78 18 03
743 Monaghan Rd., Peterborough, ON Canada
(705) 742-0451, *Fax:* (705) 742-7274
www.chextv.com
newswatch@chextv.com
License: Peterborough, ON held by 5191987 B.C. Ltd.
Group Owner: Corus Entertainment Inc.; (acq 3-24-2000; grpsl).
Nat'l Network: CBC *Nat'l Reps:* TeleRep
Michael Harris, General Manager/Vice President
Brenda O'Brien, General Sales Mgr
Paul Burke, Broadcast Operations Manager
Judy Carswell, Program Manager
Dave Patterson, News Director
Paul Ward, Chief Engineer

Sault Ste. Marie

CHBXTV
Analog Channel: 2*Analog Hrs:* 6 AM-2 AM; 100 kw vis, 10 kw aur; 600t/500g*Population Served:* 104,000
119 East St., Sault Ste. Marie, ON Canada
(705) 759-8232, *Fax:* (705) 759-7783
www.ctv.ca
saultnews@ctv.ca
License: Sault Ste. Marie, ON held by Bell Media Inc.
Group Owner: CTV Inc.
Nat'l Network: CTV *Nat'l Reps:* Canadian Broadcast Sales
Scott Lund, General Manager
Brett Lund, General Sales Mgr
John Corbett, Programming Director

Sudbury

CICITV
Analog Channel: 5; 100 kw vis, 10 kw aur; 1,057t/975g
699 Frood Rd., Sudbury, ON Canada
(705) 674-8301, *Fax:* (705) 674-2706
www.ctv.ca
newsforthenorth@ctv.ca
License: Sudbury, ON held by Bell Media Inc.
Group Owner: CTV Inc.; (acq 4-1-80).
Nat'l Network: CTV
Size of News Staff: 15; *Hours of Local News Weekly:* news progmg 10 hrs wkly
Scott Lund, Operations Dir
John Eddy, Operations Manager

Thunder Bay

CHFD-DT
Digital Channel: 4; 1.2 kw; 366.2 m; N48 31 30 W89 06 50*Population Served:* 160,000
87 Hill St. N., Thunder Bay, ON P7A 5V6 Canada
(807) 346-2600, *Fax:* (807) 345-9923
tbtv.com
tbtv@tbtv.com
License: Thunder Bay, Thunder Bay County, ON held by Thunder Bay Electronics Ltd
Nat'l Network: Global *Nat'l Reps:* CanWest Media Sales *Wire Services:* CNW Broadcast
D. Caron, CFO
H.F. Dougall, President
A. Snell, Operations Dir
K. Harris, General Sales Mgr
P. Bentz, Programming Director
S. Lockwood, National Sales Director

CKPR-DT
Digital Channel: 2; 1.2 kw; 366.2 m; N48 31 30 W89 06 50*Population Served:* 160,000
87 N. Hill St., Thunder Bay, ON P7A 5V6 Canada
(807) 346-2600, *Fax:* (807) 345-9923
www.tbtv.com
tbt@tbtv.com
License: Thunder Bay, Thunder Bay County, ON held by Thunder Bay Electronics Ltd
Nat'l Network: CBC *Nat'l Reps:* CanWest Media Sales
Hours of Local News Weekly: News progmg 11 hrs wkly

H.F. Dougall, President
D. Caron, Operations Dir
K. Harris, General Sales Mgr
P. Bentz, Programming Director
S. Lockwood, National Sales Director
A. Snell, Operations Director

Timmins

CITOTV
Analog Channel: 3*Analog Hrs:* 6am - 2am; 100 kw vis, 10 kw aur; 544t/499g*Population Served:* 132,900
681 Pine St. North, Timmins, ON Canada
(705) 264-4211, *Fax:* (705) 264-3266
www.ctv.ca
newsforthenorth@ctv.ca
License: Timmins, Cochrane County, ON held by Bell Media Inc.
Group Owner: CTV Inc.
Nat'l Network: CTV
Jason Laneville, General Sales Mgr

Toronto

CBLFT-DT
Digital Channel: 25
250 Front St. W, Toronto, ON M5V 3G5 Canada
(416) 205-3311
License: Toronto, ON

CBLT-DT
Digital Channel: 20; 77 kw vis, 7 kw aur; ant 444t/541g
Mailing Address: Box 500, Stn A, Toronto, ON M5W 1E6 Canada
Second Address: 205 Wellington St. W., Toronto, ON M5V 3G7
(416) 205-3311, *Fax:* (416) 205-7166
www.cbc.ca
License: Toronto, ON held by CBC
Nat'l Network: CBC
Size of News Staff: 45; *Hours of Local News Weekly:* news progmg 10 hrs wkly
Richard Stursberg, President

CFMT-DT
Digital Channel: 47*Digital Hrs:* 24; 807 kw vis, 80.7 kw aur; ant 1,600t/1,427g
Mailing Address: Omni Television, 33 Dundas St., Toronto, ON M5B 1B8 Canada
Second Address: 545 Lake Shore Blvd. W., Toronto, ON M5V 1A3
(416) 260-0047, *Fax:* (416) 260-3621
www.omnitv.ca
info@omnitv.ca
License: Toronto, ON held by Rogers Broadcasting Ltd.
Group Owner: Rogers Broadcasting Ltd.
Foreign Language Programming
Madeline Ziniak, Operations Dir
Jamie Haggarty, Executive Vice Presiden/TV Operations
Alain Strati, VP-Omni Station

CFTO-DT
Analog Hrs: 24*Digital Channel:* 9; 325 kw vis, 162 kw aur; ant 1815t/1614g; N43 38 33 W79 23 15
9 Channel 9 Ct., Scarborough, ON M1S 4B5 Canada
(416) 332-5000, *Fax:* (416) 332-5022
www.ctv.ca
cftonews@ctv.ca
License: Toronto, ON held by Bell Media Inc.
Group Owner: CTV Inc.
Nat'l Network: CTV
Paul Rogers, Operations Dir

CICATV
Digital Channel: 18; 2.4 kw; 316 m
Mailing Address: Box 200, Stn Q, c/o TV Ontario, Toronto, ON Canada
Second Address: 2180 Yonge St., Toronto, ON M4S 2B9
(416) 484-2600, *Fax:* (416) 484-4234
www.tvo.org
asktvo@tvo.org
License: Toronto, ON held by Ontario Educational Communications Authority
Lisa de Wilde, CEO

CIII-DT-41
Digital Channel: 41; 100 kw; 503 m; N43 38 33 W79 23 15
81 Barber Greene Rd., Toronto, ON M3C 2A2 Canada
(416) 446-5311, *Fax:* (416) 446-5447
www.canada.com
newstips@globaltv.com
License: Toronto, ON held by Canwest Television L.P.
Group Owner: Shaw Media Inc.

Patrick O'Hara, General Manager
Paul Thomas, Engineering Dir

CITY-DT
Digital Channel: 53; 280 kw vis, 28 kw aur; 1,690t/1,780g*Population Served:* 4,000,000
299 Queen St. W., Toronto, ON M5V 2Z5 Canada
(416) 591-5757, *Fax:* (416) 340-7005
www.citytv.com
License: Toronto, Canada County, ON held by Rogers Broadcasting Ltd.
Group Owner: Rogers Broadcasting Ltd.; (acq 10-31-2007; grpsl)
Hours of Local News Weekly: News progmg 25 hrs wkly
Maria Hale, Operations Dir
Dan Hamilton, General Sales Mgr
Ellen Baine, Programming Director
Susan Arthur, Promotions Manager
Stephen Hurlbut, News Director
Jenny Norush, Advertising Director
John Morrison, Operations Manager
Bev Nenson, Promotions Director
Sarah Crawford, Public Affairs Director

CJMT-DT
Digital Channel: 40*Digital Hrs:* 24; 500 kw vis
Mailing Address: 33 Dundas St. E., Toronto, ON M5B 1B8 Canada
Second Address: 545 Lake Shore Blvd. W., Toronto, ON M5V 1A3
(416) 260-0060, *Fax:* (416) 260-3621
www.omnitv.ca
info@omnitv.ca
License: Toronto, ON held by Rogers Broadcasting Ltd.
Group Owner: Rogers Broadcasting Ltd.
Leslie Sole, CEO
Madeline Ziniak, Operations Dir
Mitch Dent, General Sales Mgr
Malcolm Dunlop, Programming Director
Kelly Colasanti, Chief Engineer

Wheatley

CHWI-DT
Digital Channel: 16; 183 kw vis*Station Currently Dark*
300 Oullette Ave., Suite 200, Windsor, ON N9A 7B4 Canada
(519) 977-7432, *Fax:* (519) 977-0564
License: Wheatley, Middlesex County, ON
Group Owner: Bell Media Inc.; (acq 1997)
Don Mumford, General Manager

Windsor

CBET-DT
Digital Channel: 9; 13.03 kw; 186.1 m
825 Riverside Drive W, Windsor, ON N9A 5K9 Canada
(519) 255-3411
www.cbc.ca/windsor
License: Windsor, ON

Prince Edward Island

Charlottetown

CBCT-DT
Digital Channel: 13; 13.03 kw; 268.8 m; N46 12 44 W63 20 30
430 University Ave., Charlottetown, PE C1A 4N6 Canada
(902) 629-6400
www.cbc.ca
License: Charlottetown, PE
Group Owner: Canadian Broadcasting Corporation

Quebec

Baie-Trinite

CIVFTV
Analog Channel: 12*Analog Hrs:* 24; 62 kw vis; 2,001t; N49 23 28 W67 28 18
1000 Fullum, Montreal, QC Canada
(514) 521-2424, *Fax:* (514) 873-2601,(514) 873-4413
www.telequebec.tv
info@telequebec.tv
License: Baie-Trinite, QC held by Societe de telediffusion du Quebec.
Group Owner: Tele-Quebec
Michele Fortin, President
Luc Chartier, General Manager

Carleton

CHAUTV
Analog Hrs: 5:15am -3:00am*Digital Channel:* 5; 482.8 meters; 2,180t/475g
349 Blvd. Peron, Carleton, QC Canada
(418) 364-3344, *Fax:* (418) 364-7168
License: Carleton, QC held by CHAU-TV Communications Ltee.
Group Owner: Tele Inter-Rives Ltee.; (acq 1-5-01).
Nat'l Network: TVA
Pierre Harvey, General Manager

Chapeau

CIVPTV
Analog Channel: 23*Analog Hrs:* 24; 8.65 kw vis; N45 55 29 W77 04 23
1000, rue Fullum, Montreal, QC Canada
(514) 521-2424, *Fax:* (514) 873-2601,(514) 864-4222
www.telequebec.tv
info@telequebec.tv
License: Chapeau, QC held by Societe de telediffusion du Quebec.
Group Owner: Tele-Quebec
Michele Fortin, President
Luc Chartier, General Manager

Gatineau

CFGS-DT
Digital Channel: 34; 54.9 kw; 358 m
171 A Jean-Proulx St., Gatineau, QC J8Z 1W5 Canada
(819) 770-1040, *Fax:* (819) 770-0272
www.rncmedia.ca
tqs@rncmedia.ca
License: Gatineau, QC held by RNC MEDIA Inc.
Group Owner: RNC MEDIA Inc.
Nat'l Network: Quatre Saisons *Nat'l Reps:* Canadian Broadcast Sales
Pierre Brosseau, CEO
Justine Lefbvre, Operations Dir
Sylvie Charrette, General Manager

CHOT-DT
Digital Channel: 40; 46.5 kw; 358 m
171 A Jean-Proulx St., Gatineau, QC J8Z 1W5 Canada
(819) 770-1040, *Fax:* (819) 770-1490 (news)
www.radionord.com
chot@radionord.com
License: Gatineau, QC held by RNC MEDIA Inc.
Group Owner: RNC MEDIA Inc.
Nat'l Network: TVA
Pierre Brosseau, CEO
Michel Noiseux, Operations Dir
Robert Parent, General Manager
Benoit Pilote, General Sales Mgr
Eric Brousseau, Promotions Manager
Daniele Young, News Director

Montreal

CBFT-DT
Digital Channel: 19; 250 kw; 300 m; N45 30 19 W73 35 29
1400 Rene-Levesque Blvd E., Montreal, QC H2L 2M2 Canada
(514) 597-6000
www.radio-canada.ca
License: Montreal, QC
Group Owner: Canadian Broadcasting Corporation

CBMT-DT
Digital Channel: 21; 100 kw vis, 15 kw aur; ant 820t/167g
Box 6000, Montreal, ON H3C 3A8 Canada
(514) 597-6000, *Fax:* (514) 597-4537
www.cbc.ca/montreal
License: Montreal, QC held by CBC
Nat'l Network: CBC
Richard Stursberg, President
Rob Renaud, General Manager
Kenny King, General Sales Mgr
Hugh Brodie, Promotions Manager

CFCF-DT
Digital Channel: 12; 10.6 kw; 299.6 m
CTV Television Inc., 1205 Papineau Ave., Montreal, QC H2K 4R2 Canada
(514) 273-6311, *Fax:* (514) 276-9399
www.cfcf.ca
cfcfpromo@ctv.ca
License: Montreal, QC held by Bell Media Inc.
Group Owner: CTV Inc.; (acq 9-21-01; C$141.5 million).
Nat'l Network: CTV

Donald Bastien, Operations Dir
George Goulakos, General Sales Mgr
Mary Anne Gyba, Programming Director
Michael Curran, Promotions Manager
Mike Piperni, News Director

CFJPTV
Analog Channel: 35*Digital Channel:* 42; 697 kw vis, 70 kw aur; ant 900t/335g; N45 35 20 W73 35 32
612 Rue St-Jacques Bur 100, Montreal, QC Canada
(514) 390-6035, *Fax:* (514) 390-0773
www.tqs.ca
tvpublic@tqs.ca
License: Montreal, QC held by TQS Inc
Group Owner: Remstar Broadcasting Inc.; (acq 6-26-2008; grpsl)
Size of News Staff: 51; *Hours of Local News Weekly:* news progmg 12 hrs wkly
Francois Birtz, Operations Dir
Annie Villeneuve, General Sales Mgr
Louis Trepanier, Programming Director

CFTMTV
Analog Channel: 10*Digital Channel:* 59; 365 kw vis, 65 kw aur; ant 325t/1,068g
Box 170, Stn C, Montreal, QC Canada
(514) 790-0461,(514) 526-9251, *Fax:* (514) 598-6082
www.tva.canoe.com
License: Montreal, QC held by Groupe TVA Inc.
Group Owner: Groupe TVA Inc.
Nat'l Network: TVA
Pierre Viem, General Manager

CFTUTV
Analog Hrs: 24*Digital Channel:* 29; 910w; 196.4 meters
4750 Ave. Henri-Julien, Bureau 100, local 0058, Montreal, QC Canada
(514) 841-2626, *Fax:* (514) 284-9363
www.canal.qc.ca
info@canal.qc.ca
License: Montreal, QC held by Canal Savoir
Michel Umbriaco, President
Guy Massicotte, Operations Dir
Sylvie Godbout, General Manager

CIVMTV
Digital Channel: 45; 126.6 kw; 398.1 m*Population Served:* 7,000,000
1000, rue Fullum, Montreal, QC Canada
(514) 521-2424, *Fax:* (514) 873-2601,(514) 873-4413
www.telequebec.tv
info@telequebec.tv
License: Montreal, QC held by Societe de telediffusion du Quebec.
Group Owner: Tele-Quebec
Size of News Staff: 25; *Hours of Local News Weekly:* news progmg 5 hrs wkly
Michele Fortin, President
Luc Chartier, General Manager

CJNT-DT
Digital Channel: 49; 11 kw vis
1751 Richardson Street, Suite 2106, Montreal, QC H3K 1G6 Canada
(514) 522-4150, *Fax:* (514) 522-9579
www.metro14.ca
info@metro14.ca
License: Montreal, QC held by 2209005 Ontario Inc.
Group Owner: CanWest Global Communications Corp.; (acq 11-29-2000).
Isabella Federigi, General Manager

CKMI-DT-1
Digital Channel: 15; 8 kw; 298 m
Mailing Address: 1000 Myrand Ave., Ste.-Foy, QC G1V 2W3 Canada
Second Address: 1600 Boul.de Maisonneuve East, Montreal, PQ H2L 4P2
(418) 682-2020,(514) 521-4323, *Fax:* (418) 682-2620,(514) 521-2829,(514) 590-4060
www.globaltv.ca
globalnews.que@globaltv.ca
License: Montreal, QC held by Canwest Television GP Inc. (the general partner) and Canwest Media Inc. (the limited partner), carrying on business as Canwest Television L.P.
Group Owner: CanWest Global Communications Corp.; (acq 1997)
Michel Yeos, Operations Dir
Marven Rogers, General Manager
Suzanne Lapalme, General Sales Mgr
Masikc Vergcilles, Promotions Manager
Karen Macdonald, News Director
Michel Paquet, Engineering Dir

Quebec City

CBVT-DT
Digital Channel: 25; 126.1 kw; 515.4 m
888 Saint-Jean St., Quebec, QC G1R 5H6 Canada
(418) 656-8500, *Fax:* (418) 656-8505
www.cbc.ca
License: Quebec City, QC held by CBC
Nat'l Network: Radio Canada
Louise Cordeau, General Manager

CFAPTV
Digital Channel: 39; 12.7 kw; 551t/501g; N46 48 27 W71 13 02;*Rebroadcasting:* Rebroadcasts CFJP-TV Montreal.
330 St.-Vallier St. East, Quebec City, QC Canada
(418) 624-2222, *Fax:* (418) 624-3099,(418) 624-0162
www.tqs.ca
www@tqs.ca
License: Quebec City, QC held by TQS Inc.
Group Owner: Remstar Broadcasting Inc.; (acq 6-26-2008; grpsl)
Nat'l Network: Quatre Saisons
Foreign Language Programming; Size of News Staff: 29; *Hours of Local News Weekly:* news progmg 10 hrs wkly
Jean Simard, Operations Dir
Renaud Francoeur, General Manager
Joel Godin, General Sales Mgr
Denise Delisle, Engineering Manager
Pierre Martineau, Public Affairs Director

CFCMTV
Digital Channel: 17; 12.5 kw; 384t
1000 Ave. Myrand, Quebec City, QC Canada
(418) 688-9330, *Fax:* (418) 681-4239
www.tva.ca
License: Quebec City, QC held by Tele-Metropole Inc.
Group Owner: Groupe TVA Inc.
Richard Renaud, General Manager

CIVQTV
Analog Channel: 15; 1,298 kw vis, 259 kw aur; 628t/576g; N46 48 27 W71 13 02
1000 Fullum, Montreal, QC Canada
(514) 521-2424, *Fax:* (514) 873-2601,(514) 873-4413
www.telequebec.tv
info@telequebec.tv
License: Quebec City, QC held by Societe de telediffusion du Quebec.
Group Owner: Tele-Quebec
Michele Fortin, President
Luc Chartier, General Manager

Rimouski

CFERTV
Analog Channel: 11; 325 kw vis, 32.5 kw aur; 1,420t/289g
465 boul. Ste.-Anne, Rimouski, QC Canada
(418) 722-6011, *Fax:* (418) 724-7810,(418) 723-0857
www.tva.canoe.com
License: Rimouski, QC held by Tele-Metropole Inc.
Group Owner: Groupe TVA Inc.
Nat'l Network: TVA
Claude Auger, General Manager

CIVBTV
Analog Channel: 22*Analog Hrs:* 24; 55 kw vis; 300t; N48 28 02 W68 12 53
1000 Fullum, Montreal, QC Canada
(514) 521-2424, *Fax:* (514) 873-2601,(514) 873-4413
www.telequebec.tv
info@telequebec.tv
License: Rimouski, QC held by Societe de telediffusion du Quebec.
Group Owner: Tele-Quebec
Michele Fortin, President
Luc Chartier, General Manager

CJBR-DT
Digital Channel: 45; 110.22 kw; 283.4 m
273 St. Jeans Baptiste W., Rimouski, QC G5L 4J8 Canada
(418) 723-2217,(418) 723-4730, *Fax:* (418) 743-6126
License: Rimouski, QC held by CBC
Nat'l Network: CBC
Bernard Lepage, General Manager

Riviere-du-Loup

CFTFTV
50 kw vis; ant 1,086t; N47 35 03 W69 22 10*Population Served:* 600,000
Mailing Address: 103 des Equipements Parc Industriel, Rivieres-du-Loup, QC Canada
Second Address: 298 Boulevard Armand-Theriault, Bureau 100, Riviere-du-Loup, PQ G5R 4C2
(418) 862-2909, *Fax:* (418) 862-8147
cftf@qc.aira.com
License: Riviere-du-Loup, QC held by Television MBS Inc.
Group Owner: Tele Inter-Rives Ltee.
Marc Simard, President
Michel Belanger, Operations Dir
Catherine Simard, General Manager
Nancy Fortin, Promotions Vice President
Yves Belanger, Sales Director
Ginette Dumant, VP, Sales

CIMTTV
Analog Channel: 9*Analog Hrs:* 24; 275.6 kw vis, 2.7 kw aur; ant 1,178t/200g; N47 35 03 W69 22 10
15 Rue de la Chute, Riviere-du-Loup, QC Canada
(418) 867-1341, *Fax:* (418) 867-4710
www.cimt.ca
License: Riviere-du-Loup, QC held by Tele Inter-Rives Ltee.
Group Owner: Tele Inter-Rives Ltee.
Nat'l Network: TVA
Marc Simard, General Manager

CKRTTV
Digital Channel: 7; 7 kw; ant 1,156t/200g; N47 35 03 W69 22 10
15 Rue de la Chute, Riviere-du-Loup, QC Canada
(418) 867-1341, *Fax:* (418) 867-4710
License: Riviere-du-Loup, QC held by CKRT-TV Ltee.
Group Owner: Tele Inter-Rives Ltee.
Nat'l Network: Radio Canada
Marc Simard, General Manager

Rouyn-Noranda

CKRN-DT
Digital Channel: 9; 9.096 kw; 219.6 m
380 Murdoch, Rouyn-Noranda, QC J9X 1G5 Canada
(819) 762-0741, *Fax:* (819) 762-2466
www.radionord.com
License: Rouyn-Noranda, QC held by RNC MEDIA Inc.
Group Owner: RNC MEDIA Inc.
Nat'l Network: Radio Canada
Pierre Brosseau, President
Denis Chenier, Operations Dir
Andre Houle, General Manager
Nancy Desches, General Sales Mgr
Robert Ashby, News Director
Gerald Landry, Chief Engineer

Saguenay

CFRS-DT
Digital Channel: 13; 1.824 kw; 593.8 m*Population Served:* 300,000
2303 rue Sir Wilfred Laurier, Jonquiere, QC G7X 5Z2 Canada
(418) 542-4551, *Fax:* (418) 542-7217,(418) 542-8319
www.cgotv.ca
License: Saguenay, QC held by TQS Inc.
Group Owner: Remstar Broadcasting Inc.; (acq 6-26-2008; grpsl)
Nat'l Network: Quatre Saisons
Michel Goulet, Operations Dir
Martin Gagnon, General Manager
Ammie Tremblay, General Sales Mgr
Annie Tremblay, Promotions Manager

CIVV-TV
Analog Hrs: 24*Digital Channel:* 8; 278.1 kw vis, 27.8 kw aur; 1,948t/570g; N48 36 04 W70 49 46
3788 rue de la Fabrique, Pavillon Joseph-Angers, Jonquiere, QC G7X 3P4 Canada
(418) 695-8152, *Fax:* (418) 695-8155
www.telequebec.tv
info@telequebec.tv
License: Saguenay, QC held by Societe de telediffusion du Quebec.
Group Owner: Tele-Quebec
Nat'l Network: TeleFutura (Spanish)
Michele Fortin, President
Luc Chartier, General Manager

CJPM-DT
Digital Channel: 46; 89.3 kw; 107.4 m
One Mont Ste-Claire St, Saguenay, QC G7H 5G3 Canada
(418) 549-2576, *Fax:* (418) 549-1130
tva.canoe.ca/stations/cjpm
cjpm@saglac.qc.ca
License: Saguenay, QC held by Groupe TVA Inc.
Group Owner: Groupe TVA Inc.
Nat'l Network: TVA
Hours of Local News Weekly: News progmg 6 hrs wkly

Pierre Dion, President
Roger Jobin, General Manager
Michel Roberge, Promotions Manager
Myriam Donaldson, News Director

CKTV-DT
Digital Channel: 12; 3.1 kw; 581.1 m
500 rue des Sagueneens, Chicoutimi, QC G7H 6N4 Canada
(418) 696-6600, *Fax:* (418) 696-6689
www.radio-canada.ca/saguenay-lac-saint-jean
License: Saguenay, QC
Nat'l Network: Radio Canada

Sept-Iles

CIVGTV
Analog Channel: 9*Analog Hrs:* 16; 246 kw vis, 49.2 kw aur; 943t/500g
c/o Tele-Quebec, 1000 Fullum, Montreal, QC Canada
(514) 521-2424, *Fax:* (514) 873-2601,(514) 873-7464
www.telequebec.tv
info@telequebec.tv
License: Sept-Iles, QC held by Societe de telediffusion du Quebec.
Group Owner: Tele-Quebec
Michele Fortin, President
Luc Chartier, General Manager

Sherbrooke

CFKSTV
Analog Hrs: 24*Digital Channel:* 30; 2.62 kw; 591.19 m; N45 18 43 W72 14 32
3720 Boul. Industrial, Sherbrooke, QC Canada
(819) 565-9999, *Fax:* (819) 822-4205
www.vtele.ca
License: Sherbrooke, QC held by TQS Inc.
(acq 6-26-2008; grpsl); *Ownership:* V Interactions Inc.
Foreign Language Programming
Maxime Ramillard, Operations Dir
Julien Ramillard, Co-President
Sami Chaouch, Vice President

CHLTTV
Digital Channel: 7; 2.369 kw; 588.1 m
3330 Ouest Rue King, Sherbrooke, QC Canada
(819) 565-7777, *Fax:* (819) 565-4650,(819) 563-0141
License: Sherbrooke, QC held by Tele-Metropole Inc.
Group Owner: Groupe TVA Inc.; (acq 7-9-90).
Nat'l Network: TVA
Serge Matte, General Manager

CIVSTV
Analog Channel: 24*Analog Hrs:* 24; 475 kw vis, 47.5 kw aur; 2,000t/90g
1000 Fullum, Montreal, QC Canada
(514) 521-2424, *Fax:* (514) 873-2601,(514) 864-4222
www.telequebec.tv
info@telequebec.tv
License: Sherbrooke, QC held by Societe de telediffusion du Quebec.
Group Owner: Tele-Quebec
Michele Fortin, President
Luc Chartier, General Manager

CKSH-DT
Digital Channel: 9; 11.16 kw
1335 King St. W., Sherbrooke, QC J1J 2B8 Canada
(819) 620-0000, *Fax:* (819) 348-1326
www.radio-canada.ca
License: Sherbrooke, QC held by Canadian Broadcasting Corp.
Nat'l Network: Radio Canada
Stephane Laberge, General Manager
Vincent Vesmarais, Chief Engineer

Trois-Rivieres

CFKMTV
Analog Channel: 16; 169.5 kw vis,; ant 1,073t/1,071g; N46 29 27 W72 39 00
Box 277, Trois-Rivieres, QC Canada
(819) 377-6053, *Fax:* (819) 377-5442
License: Trois-Rivieres, QC held by TQS Inc.
Group Owner: Remstar Broadcasting Inc.; (acq 6-26-2008; grpsl)
Nat'l Network: Quatre Saisons
Michel Cloutier, General Sales Mgr

CHEMTV
Analog Channel: 8; 325 kw vis, 32.5 kw aur; 946t/698g
3625 boul. Chanoine-Moreau, Trois-Rivieres, QC Canada
(819) 376-8880, *Fax:* (819) 376-2906
License: Trois-Rivieres, QC held by Tele-Metropole Inc.
Group Owner: Groupe TVA Inc.; (acq 7-9-90).
Nat'l Network: TVA
Richard Renault, Station Manager
Gerald Trives, Chief Engineer

CIVCTV
Analog Channel: 45*Analog Hrs:* 16; 651.8 kw vis; ant 1,575t/1,000g; N46 29 27 W72 39 00
c/o Tele-Quebec, 1000 Fullum, Montreal, QC Canada
(514) 521-2424, *Fax:* (514) 873-2601,(514) 864-4222
www.telequebec.tv
info@telequebec.tv
License: Trois-Rivieres, QC held by Societe de telediffusion du Quebec.
Group Owner: Tele-Quebec
Michele Fortin, President
Luc Chartier, General Manager

CKTM-DT
Analog Hrs: 6:00am - 2:00am*Digital Channel:* 28; 164.4 kw vis, 65 kw aur; ant 1,660t/1,085g; N46 29 27 W72 39 00
4141 boul.St-Jean, Trois-Rivieres, QC G9B 2M8 Canada
(819) 377-4413, *Fax:* (819) 377-5239
paul_rousseau@radiocanada.ca
License: Trois-Rivieres, QC held by Canadian Broadcasting Corp.
Nat'l Network: CBC
Hubert Lacroix, President

Val-d'Or

CFVS-DT
Digital Channel: 25; 133.3 kw; 182.9 m
1729 3ieme Ave., Val d'Or, QC J9P 1W3 Canada
(819) 825-0010, *Fax:* (819) 825-7313
www.rncmedia.ca
License: Val-d'Or, Canada County, QC held by RNC MEDIA INC.
Group Owner: RNC MEDIA Inc.
Pierre Brosseau, President
Andre Houle, General Manager
Nancy Deschenes, General Sales Mgr
David Chabot, News Director
Gerald Landry, Chief Engineer

Saskatchewan

Prince Albert

CIPA-TV
Analog Channel: 9*Analog Hrs:* 24; 325 kw vis, 32.5 kw aur; 711t/460g
22 10th St. W., Prince Albert, SK S6V 3A5 Canada
(306) 922-6066, *Fax:* (306) 763-3041
www.ctv.ca
cipa@ctv.ca
License: Prince Albert, SK held by Bell Media Inc.
Group Owner: CTV Inc.; (acq 8-1-86).
Nat'l Network: CTV
Size of News Staff: 5
Dennis Dunlop, General Manager

Regina

CBKFT-DT
Digital Channel: 13; 27.1 kw; 183.7 m; N50 28 58 W104 30 20
2440 rue Broad, Regina, SK S4P 0A4 Canada
(306) 347-9540, *Fax:* (306) 347-9493
www.cbc.radio-canada.ca
License: Regina, SK held by Canadian Broadcasting Corporation
Group Owner: Canadian Broadcasting Corporaton

CBKT-DT
Analog Hrs: 24*Digital Channel:* 9; 33.6 kw; 207.2 m
Box 540, Regina, SK S4P 4A1 Canada
(306) 347-9540, *Fax:* (306) 347-9616
www.cbc.ca/sask/
License: Regina, SK held by CBC
Nat'l Network: CBC
Jill Spelliscy, General Manager
Jason Perring, General Sales Mgr
Shawna Kelly, Promotions Manager
Bob Rankin, News Director

CFRE-DT
Analog Channel: 11*Analog Hrs:* 24; 146 kw vis; 984t*Population Served:* 320,000
370 Hoffer Dr., Regina, SK S4N 7A4 Canada
(306) 775-4000, *Fax:* (306) 721-4817
www.canada.com
License: Regina, SK held by Shaw Television L.P.
Group Owner: Shaw Communications
Mitch Bozak, Station Manager & Sales Manager
Lyndon Bray, Marketing Manager - Saskatchewan
Ryan Ellis, News Director
Paul=Godfrey, Manager Technical Services
Len Virog, Chief Engineer
Doug Hoover, Film Buyer

CKCK-DT
Digital Channel: 8; 100 kw vis, 10 kw aur; 588t/670g; N50 26 52 W104 30 00
Mailing Address: Box 2000, Regina, SK S4P 3E5 Canada
Second Address: One Hwy. 1 East, Regina, SK S4P 3E5
(306) 569-2000, *Fax:* (306) 522-0991
www.ctv.ca
ckcknews@ctv.ca
License: Regina, SK held by Bell Media Inc.
Group Owner: CTV Inc.
Nat'l Network: CTV
Hours of Local News Weekly: 15.5 hrs local news wkly
Dennis Dunlop, General Manager

Saskatoon

CBKST
Analog Channel: 11*Analog Hrs:* 20; 325 kw vis, 32 kw aur; ant 559t/595g
144 Second Ave. South, Saskatoon, SK S7K 1K5 Canada
(306) 956-7400, *Fax:* (306) 347-9650 (admin)
www.cbc.ca/sask
License: Saskatoon, SK held by CBC
Nat'l Network: CBC
David Kyle, General Manager

CFQC-DT
Analog Hrs: 24*Digital Channel:* 8; 13 kw; 267.9 m; N52 07 51 W106 39 49*Population Served:* 333,400
216 First Ave. N., Saskatoon, SK S7K 3W3 Canada
(306) 665-8600, *Fax:* (306) 665-0450
www.ctv.ca
cfqcnews@ctv.ca
License: Saskatoon, SK held by Bell Media Inc.
Group Owner: CTV Inc.; (acq 1972).
Nat'l Network: CTV
Denis Gibertson, Operations Dir
Wade Moffatt, General Manager
Barry Berglund, General Sales Mgr
Bonnie Mackenzie, Programming Director
Chris Ransom, Promotions Manager
Doug Lett, News Director
Dale Leibrecht, Chief Engineer
Geoff Bradley, Promotions Manager

CFSK-DT
Digital Channel: 42; 54 kw vis, 5.4 kw aur; 455t/219g*Population Served:* 290,000
218 Robin Crescent, Saskatoon, SK S7L 7C3 Canada
(306) 665-6969, *Fax:* (306) 665-6069
License: Saskatoon, SK held by Shaw Television L.P.
Group Owner: CanWest Global Communications Corp.
Nat'l Network: Global
Size of News Staff: 17; *Hours of Local News Weekly:* news progmg 10 hrs wkly
Wayne Rorke, Station Manager

Yorkton

CICCTV
Analog Channel: 10*Analog Hrs:* 24; 56 kw vis, 18 kw aur
95 E. Broadway St., Yorkton, SK Canada
(306) 786-8400, *Fax:* (306) 782-7212
www.ctv.ca
ctvyorktonnews@ctv.ca
License: Yorkton, SK held by Bell Media Inc.
Group Owner: CTV Inc.
Nat'l Network: CTV
Wade Moffatt, General Manager
Barry Berglund, General Sales Mgr
Bob Maloney, Programming Director
Peter Whitehead, Chief Engineer

Canadian Television Stations by Call Letters

CBAFT-DT Moncton, New Brunswick
CBAT Fredericton-Saint John, New Brunswick
CBCT-DT Charlottetown, Prince Edward Island
CBET-DT Windsor, Ontario
CBFT-DT Montreal, Quebec
CBHT Halifax, Nova Scotia
CBKFT-DT Regina, Saskatchewan
CBKST Saskatoon, Saskatchewan
CBKT-DT Regina, Saskatchewan
CBLAT-4 Marathon, Ontario
CBLFT-DT Toronto, Ontario
CBLT-DT Toronto, Ontario
CBMT-DT Montreal, Quebec
CBNT-DT Saint John's, Newfoundland
CBOFT-DT Ottawa, Ontario
CBOT-DT Ottawa, Ontario
CBRT Calgary, Alberta
CBUBT-7 Vancouver, British Columbia
CBUFT-DT Vancouver, British Columbia
CBUT-DT Vancouver, British Columbia
CBVT-DT Quebec City, Quebec
CBWAT Kenora, Ontario
CBWBT Flin Flon, Manitoba
CBWFT-DT Winnipeg, Manitoba
CBWGT Fisher Branch, Manitoba
CBWT-DT Winnipeg, Manitoba
CBWYT Mafeking, Manitoba
CBXFT-DT Edmonton, Alberta
CBXT-DT Edmonton, Alberta
CFAPTV Quebec City, Quebec
CFCF-DT Montreal, Quebec
CFCMTV Quebec City, Quebec
CFCN-DT Calgary, Alberta
CFCN-DT-5 Lethbridge, Alberta
CFEG-TV Abbotsford, British Columbia
CFERTV Rimouski, Quebec
CFGS-DT Gatineau, Quebec
CFJCTV Kamloops, British Columbia
CFJPTV Montreal, Quebec
CFKMTV Trois-Rivieres, Quebec
CFKSTV Sherbrooke, Quebec
CFMT-DT Toronto, Ontario
CFPL-DT London, Ontario
CFQC-DT Saskatoon, Saskatchewan
CFRE-DT Regina, Saskatchewan
CFRN-DT Edmonton, Alberta
CFRN-TV-6 Red Deer, Alberta
CFRS-DT Saguenay, Quebec
CFSK-DT Saskatoon, Saskatchewan
CFSO-TV Cardston, Alberta
CFTFTV Riviere-du-Loup, Quebec
CFTMTV Montreal, Quebec
CFTO-DT Toronto, Ontario
CFTUTV Montreal, Quebec
CFTV-DT Leamington, Ontario
CFVS-DT Val-d'Or, Quebec
CFYK-DT Yellowknife, Northwest Territories
CHAKTV Inuvik, Northwest Territories
CHAN-DT Vancouver, British Columbia
CHATTV Medicine Hat, Alberta
CHAUTV Carleton, Quebec
CHBC-DT Kelowna, British Columbia
CHBXTV Sault Ste. Marie, Ontario
CHCA-TV-1 Coronation, Alberta
CHCH-DT Hamilton, Ontario
CHCT-TV St. Andrews, New Brunswick
CHEKTV Victoria, British Columbia
CHEMTV Trois-Rivieres, Quebec
CHEX-TV-2 Oshawa, Ontario
CHEXTV Peterborough, Ontario
CHFD-DT Thunder Bay, Ontario
CHLTTV Sherbrooke, Quebec
CHMI-DT Portage la Prarie, Manitoba
CHNM-TV Vancouver, British Columbia
CHNU-DT Fraser Valley, British Columbia
CHOT-DT Gatineau, Quebec
CHRO-DT-43 Ottawa, Ontario
CHROTV Pembroke, Ontario
CHVC-TV Valemount, British Columbia
CHWI-DT Wheatley, Ontario
CIANTV Calgary, Alberta
CICATV Toronto, Ontario
CICCTV Yorkton, Saskatchewan
CICITV Sudbury, Ontario
CICT-DT Calgary, Alberta
CIHF-DT Halifax, Nova Scotia
CIII-DT-41 Toronto, Ontario
CIIT-DT Winnipeg, Manitoba
CIMC-TV Isle Madame, Nova Scotia
CIMTTV Riviere-du-Loup, Quebec
CIPA-TV Prince Albert, Saskatchewan
CISA-DT Lethbridge, Alberta
CITL-TV Lloydminster, Alberta
CITOTV Timmins, Ontario
CITS-TV Hamilton, Ontario
CITV-DT Edmonton, Alberta
CITY-DT Toronto, Ontario
CIVBTV Rimouski, Quebec
CIVCTV Trois-Rivieres, Quebec
CIVFTV Baie-Trinite, Quebec
CIVGTV Sept-Iles, Quebec
CIVI-DT Victoria, British Columbia
CIVMTV Montreal, Quebec
CIVPTV Chapeau, Quebec
CIVQTV Quebec City, Quebec
CIVSTV Sherbrooke, Quebec
CIVT-DT Vancouver, British Columbia
CIVV-TV Saguenay, Quebec
CJBNTV Kenora, Ontario
CJBR-DT Rimouski, Quebec
CJCB-TV Sydney, Nova Scotia
CJCH-DT Halifax, Nova Scotia
CJCN-TV Grand Falls, Newfoundland
CJCO-TV Calgary, Alberta
CJDC-TV Dawson Creek, British Columbia
CJEO-DT Edmonton, Alberta
CJIL Lethbridge, Alberta
CJMT-DT Toronto, Ontario
CJNT-DT Montreal, Quebec
CJOH-DT Ottawa, Ontario
CJON-DT St John's, Newfoundland
CJPM-DT Saguenay, Quebec
CJTG-TV Meander River, Alberta
CKAL-DT Calgary, Alberta
CKAMTV Upsalquitch Lake, New Brunswick
CKCDTV Campbellton, New Brunswick
CKCK-DT Regina, Saskatchewan
CKCO-DT Kitchener, Ontario
CKCS-TV Calgary, Alberta
CKCW-DT Moncton, New Brunswick
CKEM-DT Edmonton, Alberta
CKES-TV Edmonton, Alberta
CKLT-DT Saint John, New Brunswick
CKMI-DT-1 Montreal, Quebec
CKND-DT Winnipeg, Manitoba
CKNYTV North Bay, Ontario
CKPG-TV Prince George, British Columbia
CKPR-DT Thunder Bay, Ontario
CKRN-DT Rouyn-Noranda, Quebec
CKRTTV Riviere-du-Loup, Quebec
CKSA-TV Lloydminster, Alberta
CKSH-DT Sherbrooke, Quebec
CKTM-DT Trois-Rivieres, Quebec
CKTV-DT Saguenay, Quebec
CKVR-DT Barrie, Ontario
CKVU-DT Vancouver, British Columbia
CKWSTV Kingston, Ontario
CKX-TV Brandon, Manitoba
CKY-DT Winnipeg, Manitoba

Canadian Television Stations by Analog Channel

Channel 2
CBWYT Mafeking, Manitoba
CHBXTV Sault Ste. Marie, Ontario

Channel 3
CITOTV Timmins, Ontario

Channel 4
CFJCTV Kamloops, British Columbia
CJCB-TV Sydney, Nova Scotia

Channel 5
CHROTV Pembroke, Ontario
CICITV Sudbury, Ontario
CKX-TV Brandon, Manitoba

Channel 6
CHATTV Medicine Hat, Alberta
CHEKTV Victoria, British Columbia

Channel 7
CKCDTV Campbellton, New Brunswick

Channel 8
CBWAT Kenora, Ontario
CFRN-TV-6 Red Deer, Alberta
CHAKTV Inuvik, Northwest Territories
CHEMTV Trois-Rivieres, Quebec

Channel 9
CIMTTV Riviere-du-Loup, Quebec
CIPA-TV Prince Albert, Saskatchewan
CIVGTV Sept-Iles, Quebec

Channel 10
CBUBT-7 Vancouver, British Columbia
CBWBT Flin Flon, Manitoba
CBWGT Fisher Branch, Manitoba
CFTMTV Montreal, Quebec
CHCA-TV-1 Coronation, Alberta
CICCTV Yorkton, Saskatchewan
CKNYTV North Bay, Ontario

Channel 11
CBKST Saskatoon, Saskatchewan
CBLAT-4 Marathon, Ontario
CFERTV Rimouski, Quebec
CFRE-DT Regina, Saskatchewan

Channel 12
CHEXTV Peterborough, Ontario
CIVFTV Baie-Trinite, Quebec

Channel 15
CIVQTV Quebec City, Quebec

Channel 16
CFKMTV Trois-Rivieres, Quebec

Channel 22
CIVBTV Rimouski, Quebec

Channel 23
CIVPTV Chapeau, Quebec

Channel 24
CIVSTV Sherbrooke, Quebec

Channel 32
CKCS-TV Calgary, Alberta

Channel 35
CFJPTV Montreal, Quebec

Channel 45
CIVCTV Trois-Rivieres, Quebec

Canadian Television Stations by Digital Channel

Channel 2
CKPR-DT Thunder Bay, Ontario
CKSA-TV Lloydminster, Alberta

Channel 4
CHFD-DT Thunder Bay, Ontario
CITL-TV Lloydminster, Alberta

Channel 5
CHAUTV Carleton, Quebec

Channel 7
CFJCTV Kamloops, British Columbia
CHLTTV Sherbrooke, Quebec
CISA-DT Lethbridge, Alberta
CKRTTV Riviere-du-Loup, Quebec
CKY-DT Winnipeg, Manitoba

Channel 8
CBNT-DT Saint John's, Newfoundland
CFQC-DT Saskatoon, Saskatchewan
CFYK-DT Yellowknife, Northwest Territories
CIHF-DT Halifax, Nova Scotia
CIVV-TV Saguenay, Quebec
CKCK-DT Regina, Saskatchewan

Channel 9
CBKT-DT Regina, Saskatchewan
CFTO-DT Toronto, Ontario
CKLT-DT Saint John, New Brunswick
CKRN-DT Rouyn-Noranda, Quebec
CKSH-DT Sherbrooke, Quebec
CBET-DT Windsor, Ontario

Channel 10
CFPL-DT London, Ontario
CKVR-DT Barrie, Ontario

Channel 11
CBAFT-DT Moncton, New Brunswick

Channel 12
CFCF-DT Montreal, Quebec
CFRN-DT Edmonton, Alberta
CKTV-DT Saguenay, Quebec

Channel 13
CFCN-DT-5 Lethbridge, Alberta
CFRS-DT Saguenay, Quebec
CHMI-DT Portage la Prarie, Manitoba
CKCO-DT Kitchener, Ontario
CBCT-DT Charlottetown, Prince Edward Island
CBKFT-DT Regina, Saskatchewan

Channel 15
CHCH-DT Hamilton, Ontario
CKMI-DT-1 Montreal, Quebec

Channel 16
CHWI-DT Wheatley, Ontario

Channel 17
CFCMTV Quebec City, Quebec
CKEM-DT Edmonton, Alberta

Channel 18
CICATV Toronto, Ontario

Channel 19
CBFT-DT Montreal, Quebec

Channel 20
CBLT-DT Toronto, Ontario
CHNM-TV Vancouver, British Columbia

Channel 21
CBMT-DT Montreal, Quebec
CBRT Calgary, Alberta
CJCN-TV Grand Falls, Newfoundland
CJON-DT St John's, Newfoundland

Channel 23
CIVI-DT Victoria, British Columbia

Channel 25
CBOT-DT Ottawa, Ontario
CBVT-DT Quebec City, Quebec
CFVS-DT Val-d'Or, Quebec
CBLFT-DT Toronto, Ontario

Channel 26
CBUFT-DT Vancouver, British Columbia

Channel 27
CBWT-DT Winnipeg, Manitoba
CHBC-DT Kelowna, British Columbia

Channel 28
CKTM-DT Trois-Rivieres, Quebec

Channel 29
CFTUTV Montreal, Quebec
CKCW-DT Moncton, New Brunswick

Channel 30
CFKSTV Sherbrooke, Quebec

Channel 31
CBAT Fredericton-Saint John, New Brunswick

Channel 33
CBOFT-DT Ottawa, Ontario
CKVU-DT Vancouver, British Columbia

Channel 34
CFGS-DT Gatineau, Quebec
CFTV-DT Leamington, Ontario

Channel 35
CIIT-DT Winnipeg, Manitoba

Channel 36
CFCN-DT Calgary, Alberta
CITS-TV Hamilton, Ontario

Channel 38
CJCO-TV Calgary, Alberta

Channel 39
CFAPTV Quebec City, Quebec
CBHT Halifax, Nova Scotia

Channel 40
CHOT-DT Gatineau, Quebec
CKND-DT Winnipeg, Manitoba
CJMT-DT Toronto, Ontario

Channel 41
CICT-DT Calgary, Alberta
CIII-DT-41 Toronto, Ontario

Channel 42
CBXT-DT Edmonton, Alberta
CFJPTV Montreal, Quebec
CFSK-DT Saskatoon, Saskatchewan

Channel 43
CBUT-DT Vancouver, British Columbia
CHRO-DT-43 Ottawa, Ontario

Channel 45
CIVMTV Montreal, Quebec
CJBR-DT Rimouski, Quebec

Channel 46
CJPM-DT Saguenay, Quebec

Channel 47
CBXFT-DT Edmonton, Alberta
CFMT-DT Toronto, Ontario
CITV-DT Edmonton, Alberta
CHNU-DT Fraser Valley, British Columbia

Channel 48
CJCH-DT Halifax, Nova Scotia

Channel 49
CJNT-DT Montreal, Quebec
CKAL-DT Calgary, Alberta

Channel 51
CBWFT-DT Winnipeg, Manitoba

Channel 53
CITY-DT Toronto, Ontario

Channel 59
CFTMTV Montreal, Quebec

Arbitron Metro Survey Area Ranking

METRO 12+ RANK	MARKET	METRO PERSONS 12+ ESTIMATED POPULATION
1	New York	15,867,400
2	Los Angeles	11,044,200
3	Chicago	7,878,800
4	San Francisco	6,264,600
5	Dallas-Ft. Worth	5,431,900
6	Houston-Galveston	5,126,200
7	Washington, DC	4,635,000
8	Philadelphia	4,517,800
9	Atlanta	4,385,000
10	Boston	4,082,100
11	Miami-Ft. Lauderdale-Hollywood	3,781,100
12	Detroit	3,760,200
13	Seattle-Tacoma	3,538,100
14	Phoenix	3,255,500
15	Puerto Rico	3,152,100
16	Minneapolis-St. Paul	2,793,800
17	San Diego	2,700,300
18	Tampa-St. Petersburg-Clearwater	2,475,100
19	Nassau-Suffolk (Long Island)[1]	(2,448,100)
20	Denver-Boulder	2,429,700
21	Baltimore	2,341,300
22	St. Louis	2,308,100
23	Portland, OR	2,152,300
24	Charlotte-Gastonia-Rock Hill	2,071,600
25	Pittsburgh, PA	2,004,900
26	Riverside-San Bernardino	1,986,600
27	Sacramento	1,887,800
28	San Antonio	1,858,500
29	Cincinnati	1,768,600
30	Cleveland	1,760,100
31	Salt Lake City-Ogden-Provo	1,745,000
32	Las Vegas	1,656,200
33	Kansas City	1,649,000
34	Orlando	1,622,000
35	Columbus, OH	1,542,700
36	San Jose[2]	(1,541,800)
37	Austin	1,537,600
38	Milwaukee-Racine	1,481,300
39	Hudson Valley[3]	(1,478,400)
40	Indianapolis	1,443,700
41	Middlesex-Somerset-Union[4]	(1,431,200)
42	Raleigh-Durham	1,402,100
43	Providence-Warwick-Pawtucket	1,382,200

[1] The Nassau-Suffolk (Long Island), NY Metro is embedded in the New York Metro.

[2] The San Jose Metro is embedded in the San Francisco Metro.

[3] Putnam, NY (population 86,700), Rockland, NY (population 260,500) and Westchester, NY (population 819,300) are included in the Hudson Valley and the New York Metro definitions.

[4] The Middlesex-Somerset-Union Metro is embedded in the New York Metro.

The population estimates for footnoted markets are not duplicated in the cumulative population totals.
Courtesy: Arbitron Inc.

Arbitron Metro Survey Area Ranking

METRO 12+ RANK	MARKET	METRO PERSONS 12+ ESTIMATED POPULATION
44	Norfolk-Virginia Beach-Newport News	1,367,100
45	Nashville	1,303,800
46	Greensboro-Winston-Salem-High Point	1,226,900
47	New Orleans	1,213,400
48	West Palm Beach-Boca Raton	1,176,600
49	Oklahoma City	1,174,300
50	Jacksonville	1,162,300
51	Memphis	1,112,400
52	Hartford-New Britain-Middletown	1,072,900
53	Monmouth-Ocean[5]	(1,031,400)
54	Louisville	1,001,200
55	Richmond	988,500
56	Buffalo-Niagara Falls	980,900
57	McAllen-Brownsville-Harlingen	965,300
58	Rochester, NY	959,500
59	Greenville-Spartanburg	904,200
60	Birmingham	901,200
61	Ft. Myers-Naples-Marco Island	854,000
62	Tucson	847,200
63	Dayton	839,000
64	Honolulu	828,800
65	Albany-Schenectady-Troy	797,800
66	Tulsa	781,400
67	Fresno	771,100
68	Albuquerque	748,700
69	Grand Rapids	732,700
70	Allentown-Bethlehem	710,800
71	Wilkes Barre-Scranton	697,600
72	Knoxville	690,000
73	El Paso	680,100
74	Des Moines	669,700
75	Omaha-Council Bluffs	667,800
76	Sarasota-Bradenton	638,600
77	Bakersfield	624,600
78	Wilmington, DE	607,100
79	Akron	601,500
80	Baton Rouge	593,800
81	Harrisburg-lebanon-Carlisle	592,500
82	Charleston, SC	589,800
83	Monterey-Salinas-Santa Cruz	582,200
84	Little Rock	578,800
85	Stockton	574,000
86	Greenville-New Bern-Jacksonville	573,100
87	Syracuse	567,700
88	Columbia, SC	564,000
89	Gainesville-Ocala	563,900

[5] Monmouth County (population 541,900) is included in the Monmouth-Ocean and the New York Metro definitions.

The population estimates for footnoted markets are not duplicated in the cumulative population totals.
Courtesy: Arbitron Inc.

METRO 12+ RANK	MARKET	METRO PERSONS 12+ ESTIMATED POPULATION
90	Portland, ME	541,100
91	Colorado Springs	541,000
92	Springfield, MA	537,400
93	Spokane	527,300
94	Daytona Beach	526,100
95	Lakeland-Winter Haven	521,500
96	Toledo	513,700
97	Mobile	508,100
98	Ft. Pierce-Stuart-Vero Beach	501,500
99	Madison	499,100
100	Wichita	494,500
101	Boise	491,700
102	Lexington-Fayette	485,000
103	Visalia-Tulare-Hanford	484,800
104	Melbourne-Titusville-Cocoa	482,400
105	Huntsville	470,600
106	Johnson City-Kingsport-Bristol	469,500
107	Lafayette, IA	462,300
108	York	460,800
109	Chattanooga	460,400
110	Augusta, GA	455,800
111	Corpus Christi	455,200
112	Ft. Wayne	443,200
113	Lancaster	441,500
114	Roanoke-lynchburg	435,000
115	Victor Valley	434,500
116	Worcester	433,700
117	New Haven	428,000
118	Oxnard-Ventura	428,000
119	Modesto	427,900
120	Ft. Collins-Greeley, CO	426,400
121	Morristown, NJ[6]	(426,300)
122	Santa Rosa[7]	(423,000)
123	Portsmouth-Dover-Rochester	416,100
124	Bridgeport	411,700
125	Jackson, MS	410,800
126	Reno	408,100
127	Lansing-East Lansing	400,700
128	Pensacola	395,200
129	Youngstown-Warren	383,100
130	Fayetteville, NC	382,500
131	Fayetteville (North West Arkansas)	378,600
132	Macon	370,000
133	Shreveport	352,900
134	Reading, PA	351,700
135	Flint	351,400
136	Canton	345,000
137	Appleton-Oshkosh	336,400
138	Palm Springs	334,400
139	Springfield, MO	334,300
140	Salisbury-Ocean City	329,700

[6] The Morristown Metro is embedded in the New York Metro.

[7] The Santa Rosa Metro is embedded in the San Francisco Metro.

The population estimates for footnoted markets are not duplicated in the cumulative population totals.
Courtesy: Arbitron Inc.

METRO 12+ RANK	MARKET	METRO PERSONS 12+ ESTIMATED POPULATION
141	Beaumont-Port Arthur, TX	329,300
142	Tyler-Longview	325,700
143	Burlington-Plattsburgh	324,500
144	Killeen-Temple, TX	319,700
145	Atlantic City-Cape May	318,800
146	Biloxi-Gulfport-Pascagoula	318,000
147	Stamford-Norwalk, CT[8]	(315,100)
148	Trenton	314,700
149	Fredericksburg[9]	(312,600)
150	Montgomery	312,200
151	Eugene-Springfield	310,900
152	Quad Cities (Davenport-Rock Island-Moline)	309,400
153	Savannah	304,900
154	Peoria	304,600
155	Flagstaff-Prescott, AZ	300,200
156	Myrtle Beach, SC	297,500
157	Rockford	289,900
158	Ft. Smith, AR	284,100
159	Asheville	281,300
160	Tallahassee	271,000
161	Huntington-Ashland	269,900
162	Evansville	265,200
163	Poughkeepsie, NY	259,600
164	Utica-Rome	256,200
165	Hagerstown-Chambersburg-Waynesboro, MD-PA	254,900
166	Amarillo, TX	249,700
167	Anchorage	248,300
168	Lincoln	246,400
169	Morgantown-Clarksburg-Fairmont, WV	243,700
170	San luis Obispo, CA	241,100
171	Erie	240,700
172	Lubbock	240,600
173	Wausau-Stevens Point, WI (Central WI)	238,200
174	Concord (lakes Region)	236,600
175	New london, CT	235,800
176	Odessa-Midland, TX	232,300
177	New Bedford-Fall River, MA[10]	(226,200)
178	Merced, CA	226,000
179	South Bend	223,100
180	Columbus, GA	221,100
181	Tri-Cities, WA (Richland-Kennewick-Pasco)	220,000
182	Kalamazoo	215,700
183	Binghamton	215,200
184	Charleston, WV	213,400
185	Green Bay	213,400

8 The Stamford-Norwalk Metro is embedded in the New York Metro.

9 Stafford County (population 111,700) is included in the Fredericksburg and Washington, DC, Metro definitions .

10 The New Bedford-Fall River Metro is embedded in the Providence-Warwick-Pawtucket Metro.

The population estimates for footnoted markets are not duplicated in the cumulative population totals.

Courtesy: Arbitron Inc.

METRO 12+ RANK	MARKET	METRO PERSONS 12+ ESTIMATED POPULATION
186	Lebanon-Rutland-White River Junction	210,600
187	Dothan, AL	209,000
188	Ft. Walton Beach-Destin, FL	207,100
189	Tupelo, MS	203,500
190	Frederick, MD[11]	(202,900)
191	Laredo, TX	202,200
192	Waco, TX	201,600
193	Salina-Manhattan, KS	201,400
194	Bryan-College Station, TX	200,200
195	Yakima, WA	200,100
196	Manchester[12]	(196,900)
197	Traverse City-Petoskey, MI	196,600
198	Topeka	196,500
199	Danbury, CT	195,700
200	Cape Cod, MA	193,200
201	Chico, CA	191,400
202	Santa Maria-lompoc, CA	189,300
203	Fargo-Moorhead	182,200
204	Cedar Rapids	181,700
205	Las Cruces, NM	180,000
206	Duluth-Superior	178,500
207	Terre Haute	177,300
208	Medford-Ashland, OR	177,200
209	Santa Barbara, CA	175,500
210	Champaign, IL	175,100
211	Bend, OR	174,400
212	Florence, SC	173,600
213	Muncie-Marion, IN	172,500
214	Tuscaloosa, Al	171,500
215	Winchester, VA	171,300
216	Laurel-Hattiesburg, MS	169,500
217	Wenatchee-Moses lake, WA	169,200
218	Bangor	167,900
219	St. Cloud, MN	166,200
220	Alexandria, IA	163,900
221	La Crosse, WI	162,500
222	Lake Charles, IA	162,200
223	Olean, NY	161,600
224	Elmira-Corning, NY	160,500
225	Rochester, MN	156,600
226	Lima, OH	155,500
227	Jonesboro, AR	154,400
228	Redding, CA	153,400
229	Twin Falls (Sun Valley), ID	151,400
230	Lafayette, IN	151,200
231	Joplin, MO	147,200
232	Panama City, FL	146,400
233	Bloomington	145,800
234	Columbia, MO	144,500
235	Muskegon, MI	143,000

11 The Frederick Metro is embedded in the Washington, DC, Metro.

12 The M-Split portionof Rockingham Counmty (population 49,900) is included in the Manchester and Portsmouth-Dover-Rochester metro definitions.

The population estimates for footnoted markets are not duplicated in the cumulative population totals.
Courtesy: Arbitron Inc.

METRO 12+ RANK	MARKET	METRO PERSONS 12+ ESTIMATED POPULATION
236	Abilene, TX	140,300
237	Eau Claire, WI	140,300
238	Albany, GA	137,300
239	Lufkin-Nacogdoches, TX	136,500
240	Pueblo	135,900
241	LaSalle-Peru, IL	130,800
242	Monroe, IA	129,000
243	Parkersburg-Marietta, WV-OH	128,600
244	Wheeling	128,000
245	Billings, MT	127,900
246	Sussex, NJ	127,300
247	2A Florence-Muscle Shoals, AL	127,000
248	Grand Junction, CO	123,700
249	Valdosta, GA	120,300
250	Wichita Falls, TX	116,400
251	Texarkana, TX-AR	115,000
252	Grand Island-Kearney, NE	114,400
253	Battle Creek, MI	113,500
254	Harrisonburg, VA	111,300
255	Altoona	109,500
256	Rapid City, SD	108,200
257	Montpelier-Barre-St. Johnsbury	108,000
258	Augusta-Waterville, ME	105,900
259	Mankato-New Ulm-St. Peter, MN	105,400
260	Lawton, OK	105,300
261	Williamsport, PA	101,600
262	Sioux City, IA	100,800
263	Watertown, NY	98,200
264	Sheboygan, WI	97,200
265	Bismarck, ND	95,700
266	San Angelo, TX	94,900
267	Decatur, IL	93,900
268	Bluefield, WV	93,500
269	Hot Springs, AR	85,000
270	Grand Forks, ND-MN	83,300
271	Jackson, TN	82,500
272	Cheyenne, WY	77,800
273	Brunswick, GA	68,300
274	Beckley, WV	68,200
275	Casper, WY	64,600
	Total	216,426,500

The population estimates for footnoted markets are not duplicated in the cumulative population totals.
Courtesy: Arbitron Inc.

National Radio Networks

ABC Radio Networks
444 Madison Avenue, New York, NY 10022
(212) 735-1700
www.abcradio.com
Lewis Dickey, Chairman
Jonathan Pinch, Co-COO/EVP
John Dickey, Co-COO/EVP
Richard Denning, SVP/Secretary/General Counsel
Joseph Hannan, SVP/Treasurer/CFO
Linda Hill, Corporate Controller/Chief Accounting Officer
East Region, ABC Inc
47 West 66th Street, New York, NY 10023; Tel: (212) 456-7777; Departments: ABC News Radio, Engineering, Network Programming, International; Executives: John Mohoney, EVP/Programming; Chris Berry, VP News Radio.
West Region, ABC Inc
13725 Montfort Drive, Dallas, TX 75240; Tel: (972) 991-9200; Departments: Affiliate marketing West, Entertainment Programming, Marketing and Promotion, 24 Hour Formats, Advertising/Sales, Engineering, Finance, MIS, Research; Executives: JamesRobinson, President; Michael Connolly, SVP/Advertising; Kevin Miller, SVP/Business Development.

American Urban Radio Networks
432 Park Avenue, South, 14th Floor, New York, NY 10016
(212) 883-2100
www.aurn.com
Howard Elsen, President
Andy Anderson, VP Sales/Eastern Region
Michelle Pearson, Executive Sales
Basil Murrain, VP Promotions
Barry Feldman, VP Research
Sharita Manickham, Marketing Manager
Programming Headquarters
960 Penn Ave., 4th Floor, Pittsburgh, PA 15222; Tel: (412) 456-4000
Atlanta Office
2424 Old Rex Morrow Road, Ellenwood, GA 30294; Tel: (732) 309-0301; Contact: Tanya Forret Hall, Executive Sales Director.
Chicago Office
180 North Stetson, Suite 3500, Chicago, IL 60601; Tel: (312) 558-9090; Contact: Stephen Bates, Executive Sales Director.
Detroit Office
1133 Whittier Road, Grosse Pointe, MI 48230; Tel: (313) 885-4243; Contact: J.D. Mackay, Executive Sales Director.

AP Broadcast
1100 13th Street, Suite 700, Washington, DC 20005
(800) 527-7234
www.apbroadcast.com
James Williams, VP/Director Global Broadcast
Greg Groce, Director Business Operations
Brad Kalbfeld, Managing Editor
Roger Lockhart, Director Marketing Communications
Lee Perryman, Deputy Director
John Phillips, Director FinancialPlanning

CBS Radio
1515 Broadway Avenue, New York, NY 10036
(212) 846-3939
www.cbsradio.com
Anton Guitano, COO
Dan Mason, President/CEO
Scott Herman, EVP Operations
Micheal Weiss, President of Sales
Ezra Kucharz, President of Digital Media
Jo Ann Haller, VP/General Counsel

CNN Radio Networks
One CNN Center NW, Atlanta, GA 30303
(404) 827-1700
www.cnnradio.cnn.com
Robert Garcia, Principle Executive
Harley Hotchkiss, Director Operations
Richard Benson, Executive Producer
Bureaus
Atlanta, Boston, Chicago, Denver, Dallas, Los Angeles, Miami, New York, San Francisco, Seattle, Washington DC, Baghdad, Buenos Aires, Dubai, Frankfurt, Hong Kong, Istanbul, Jakarta, Jerusalem, Lagos, London, Madrid, Mexico City, Moscow,Nairobi, New Delhi, Paris, Rome, Tokyo, Seoul, Sidney.

Eastern Region Public Radio
PO Box 615, Kensington, MD 20895
(301) 961-0252
www.erpm.com
Glenn Gleixner, Chairman
James Muhammad, Vice Chairman
Georgette Bronfman, Executive Director
Lafontaine Oliver, General Manager

Jones Radio Network
8200 South Akron Street, Suite 103, Centennial, CO 80112
(800) 609-5663
www.jonesradio.com
Glenn Jones, Chairman
Phil Barry, General Manager/VP
Frank De Santis, General Manager/VP
James LaMarca, EVP/COO
Amy Bolton, VP/General Manager News
Patrick Crocker, Sales/Marketing

Moody Broadcasting
820 North Lasalle Blvd, Chicago, IL 60610
(312) 329-4271, *Fax:* (312) 329-4368
www.moodyradio.org
mbn@moody.edu
Dr Paul Nyquist, President
Collin Lambert, Vicep President
Doug Hastings, General Manager
Denny Nugent, National Program Director
Don Craig, Programming Manager
Chris Segard, Production Services Manager

National Public Radio
635 Massachusetts Avenue NW, Washington, DC 20001
(202) 513-2000, *Fax:* (202) 513-3329
www.npr.org
Gary Knell, President
Antoine Van Agtmael, Chief Investment Officer
Zach Brand, VP Digital Media
Jeff Perkins, Chief People Officer
Margaret Smith, SVP/News
Mike Starling, Executive Director

Public Radio International
401 Second Avenue, Minneapolis, MN 55401
(612) 338-5000
www.pri.org
Peter Darrow, Chairman
Linda Larson, Vice Chair
Alisa Miller, President
Stewart Vanderwilt, Secretary
Lawrence Wilkinson, Treasurer
Sharon Ferraro, VP/Resource Development
Michael Skoler, VP Interactive Media
Julie Yager, VPBrand Management

Super Radio Network
24 Boston Post Road West, Marlborough, MA 01752
(508) 620-0006, *Fax:* (952) 556-9375
www.superadio.com
mixes@superadio.com
Rich O'Brien, SVP/Programming
Joan Brooks, Business Manager
Dianne Cook, Business Manager
Headquarters New York
112 West 34th Street, Suite 1401, New York, NY 10120; Tel: (212) 714-1000; Executives: Jack Bryant, COO; Eric Faison, VP; Barbara DeLaleu, Affiliation Rep.

United Press International
1133 19th Street NW, Washington, DC 20036
(202) 898-8000, *Fax:* (202) 898-8048
www.upi.com
support@upi.com
Sayla Seng, COO
Nicholas Chiaia, President
John Hendel, Executive Editor

The Wall Street Network
1155 Avenue of the Americas, 8th Floor, New York, NY 10036
(212) 659-1208, *Fax:* (212) 659-1908
www.wsjradio.com
wsjradio@dowjones.com
Nancy Abramson, Executive Director
Susan O'Connell, Senior Director
Susan Moran, Sales Director
Jean Rodier, New Media Manager

Westwood One
1166 Avenue of the Americas, 10th Floor, New York, NY 10036
(212) 641-2000
www.westwood-backup.com
Rod Sherwood, President
David Hillman, EVP/Business Affairs
Stephen Chessare, SVP/Network Radio Sales
Max Krasney, General Manager
Howard Dennerоff, VP/Sports
Bert Tessler, VP/Network News
Ezra Palmer, SVP/Digital Content
GaryWilliams, VP/Production
Programming
CBS Radio News, CNBC Business Radio, Marketwatch, NBC News Radio, The Insider, Ask Dr Phil, Daily Dose With Dr Oz, ET Radio Minute, Inside Edition, Late Show with David Letterman, Late Night with Jimmy Fallon, Meet the Press, Dennis Miller,America in the Morning, Adam Carolla Show, First Light, The Radio Factor, This Week in Review.

WFMT Radio Network
5400 North St Louis Avenue, Chicago, IL 60625
(773) 279-2000
www.wfmt.com
Daniel Schmidt, President/CEO
Greg Cameron, COO
Reese Marcusson, EVP/CFO
Steve Robinson, EVP Radio
Anne Gleason, VP Marketing

Regional Radio Networks

Alaska Public Radio Network
3877 University Dr., Anchorage, AK 99508
(907) 550-8400, *Fax:* (907) 550-8401
www.aprn.org
aprn@alaska.net
Bede Trantina, Station Manager
Duncan Moon, News Director
Satellite-delivered news/info programs to 26 member stn across Alaska from state-of-the-art studios, hqtr in Anchorage.
Washington, DC News Bureau
2801 Quebec St. N.W., Suite 505, Washington, DC 20008-1227
(202) 488-1961;
Joel Southern, Capitol Bureau Chief
Washington, DC News Bureau
2801 Quebec St. N.W., Suite 505, Washington, DC 20008-1227
(202) 488-1961;
Joel Southern, Capitol Bureau Chief
Juneau Alaska News Bureau
530 Park St, Juneau, AK 99801-1065
(907) 586-6948;
Dave Donaldson, State Capitol Bureau Chief
Juneau Alaska News Bureau
530 Park St, Juneau, AK 99801-1065
(907) 586-6948;
Dave Donaldson, State Capitol Bureau Chief

Allegheny Mountain Network
Box 247, Tyrone, PA 16686
(814) 684-3200, *Fax:* (814) 684-1220
amnnet@aol.com
Cary Simpson, President
Alfred Haper, Operations Dir
Comprises 9 stns in Pennsylvania. Represented by Dome & Associates.
Box 98, Wellsboro, PA 16901-0098
(570) 724-1490;
Albert Harper, Vp Sls

American Ag Network
214 W. Pleasant Dr., Pierre, SD 57501-2472
(605) 224-9911, *Fax:* (605) 224-8984
americanagnetwork.com
markswendsen@amfmradio.biz
Mark Swendsen, President
Comprises 40 stns: 16 in South Dakota, 22 in North Dakota & 2 in Montana.
2501 13th Ave., Suite 201, Fargo, ND 58103-3601
(701) 237-5000; *Fax:* (701) 280-0816
Steve Carlson, Opns Mgr
Box 13919, Grand Forks, ND 58208-3919
(701) 775-3910; *Fax:* (701) 775-3932
Lance Knudson, Sls Mgr

Arkansas Radio Network
700 Wellington Hills Rd., Little Rock, AR 72211
(501) 401-0228, (800) 839.4610, *Fax:* (501) 401-0367
www.arkansasradionetwork.com
gordon.stephan@citcomm.com
Ross McKenney, Programming Director
Comprises 55 interconnected stns, all in Arkansas, Texas & Mississippi. Represented by StateNets & McGauren Guild.

Beasley Broadcast Group
3033 Riviera Dr., Suite 200, Naples, FL 34103
(239) 263-5000, *Fax:* (239) 263-8191
www.bbgi.com
email@bbgi.com
George G. Beasley, Chairman
Radio stns 44: 27 FMs & 17 AMs in 11 large, mid-sized markets.

RADIO - U.S.

Brownfield Network
Div/DBA: (A division of Learfield Communications Inc.)
505 Hobbs Rd., Jefferson City, MO 65109-6829
(573) 893-5700, *Fax:* (573) 893-8094
www.brownfieldnetwork.com
jsteinman@learfield.com
Bruce Beasley, President
Joyce Steinman, General Sales Mgr
Comprises 280 stns in Illinois, Iowa, Missouri, Nebraska, Indiana, South Dakota & Wisconsin. Represented by In-House.

California News Radio
14605 N. Airport Dr., Suite 370, Scottsdale, AZ 85260
(480) 503-8700, *Fax:* (480) 998-5751
www.skyviewsatellite.com
Ken Thiele, President
Jeanne-Marie Condo, General Manager
Comprises 26 stns in California.

Compu-Weather Inc.
2566 Rt. 52, Hopewell Junction, NY 12533
(800) 284-7246, *Fax:* (845) 226-1918
www.compuweather.com
sales@compuweather.com
Jeff Wimmer, President

CRN International, Inc.
One Circular Ave., Hamden, CT 06514
(203) 288-2002, *Fax:* (203) 281-3291
www.crnradio.com
info@crnradio.com
S. Richard Kalt, President
Steve Wakeen, Operations Dir
Stragtegy & execution, retail mktg, lifestyle progmg, promotions, digital media & other non-traditional communication tactics, small business, collaborative mktg, weather-triggered media placement, Ethnic, Just -In-Time Marketing.
Branch Office: Minneapolis, MN,

Florida News Network
2500 Maitland Ctr. Pkwy., Suite 407, Maitland, FL 32751
(407) 916-7810, (407) 916-7800, *Fax:* (407) 916-7425
www.fnnonline.net
jimpoling@fnnonline.net
Jim Poling, Operations Dir
Rick Green, General Manager
Jim Underwood, General Sales Mgr
Comprises 58 stns in Florida. Represented by StateNets Inc.

Florida Public Radio Network
1600 Red Barber Plaza, Tallahassee, FL 32310
(850) 487-3194, *Fax:* (850) 487-3293
www.wfsu.org
fpr@wfsu.org
Carolina Austin, Operations Dir
Tom Flanigan, News Director
Serves 13 FM public radio stns in Florida.

Georgia News Network
1819 Peachtree Rd., Suite 700, Atlanta, GA 30309
(404) 607-9045, (800) 776-4638, *Fax:* (404) 367-6404
www.georgianewsnetwork.com
robmaynard@clearchannel.com
Linda Kent, General Sales Mgr
Rob Maynard, Programming Director
Comprises 108 stns in Georgia. Represented by StateNts.

Hawkeye Network
505 Hobbs Rd., Jefferson City, MO 65109
(573) 893-7200, *Fax:* (573) 893-8076
www.learfield.com
Clyde G. Lear, President
Greg Brown, Operations Dir
Bob Agramonte, General Manager
Keith Sampson, Programming Director
Comprises 50 stns in Iowa. Sports Network.

Hispanic Communications Network
1126 16th St. N.W., Suite 350, Washington, DC 20036
(202) 637-8800, *Fax:* (202) 637-8801
www.hcnmedia.com
info@hcnmedia.com
Carlos Alcazar, President
National-All 50 states & Puerto Rico: 200 radio stns.

Hometown Radio Network
1100 Chester Ave., Suite 100, Cleveland, OH 44115
(216) 781-0035, *Fax:* (216) 781-7508
www.regionalreps.com
sjsharpe@regionalreps.com
Stuart J. Sharpe, President
Comprises over 1000 affils in Delaware, Florida, Georgia, Iowa, Illinois, Indiana, Kansas, Kentucky, Maryland, Nebraska, North Carolina, Ohio, Oklahoma, Pennsylvania, South Carolina, Virginia, & West Virginia. Represented by: Rgnl Reps Corp.

Illinois Radio Network
430 W. Erie, Suite 505, Chicago, IL 60610
(312) 943-6363, *Fax:* (312) 943-5109
www.illinoisradionetwork.com
Dennis Mellott, President
A statewide satellite-delivered net providing news, sports, business & special progmg. IRN 67 affils. Representative: StateNets.

ION Radio Network
Box 1223, Airport Rd., Morristown, NJ 07960
(973) 983-8222, *Fax:* (973) 983-1390
www.ionweather.com
steve@ionweather.com
Stephen Pellettiere, President
Comprises 10 stns, four in New Jersey, four in New York, one in Pennsylvania & one in Connecticut.

Kansas Agriculture Network
Box 1818, Topeka, KS 66601-1818
(785) 272-3456, *Fax:* (785) 272-7282
www.radionetworks.com
dan.johnson@morris.com
Comprises 30 stns in Kansas. Represented by Learfield Radio.

Kansas Information Network
Box 1818, Topeka, KS 66601-1818
(785) 272-3456, *Fax:* (785) 228-7282
www.radionetworks.com
dan.johnson@morris.com
Comprises 32 stns in Kansas. Represented by StateNets.

Kansas State Sports Network
1632 S. Maze Rd., Wichita, KS 67209
(316) 721-8484

KEDA Radio
510 S. Flores, San Antonio, TX 78204
(210) 226-5254
www.star-tv.com
info@star-tv.com
Canada's only 24-hour national specialty service dedicated to the world of showbiz news and information. Programming includes in-depth specials and events, detailed behind-the scene features on major movies, exclusive interviews with theworld's biggest celebrities and extensive live coverage of award shows, premieres and galas.

Kentucky News Network
Div/DBA: (A subsidiary of Clear Channel Radio Inc.)
4000 # 1 Radio Dr., Louisville, KY 40218
(502) 479-2248, *Fax:* (502) 479-2231
www.kentuckynewsnetwork.com
nathanbutler@clearchannel.com
Comprises 87 stns in Kentucky. Represented by StatesNets. Live via satellite.

Linder Farm Network
255 Cedardale Dr., Owatonna, MN 55060
(507) 444-9224, *Fax:* (507) 444-9080
www.linderfarmnetwork.com
farm@linderradio.com
Lynn Ketelsen, General Manager
Jeff Stewart, General Sales Mgr
Comprises 22 stns in Minnesota. Represented by Katz Radio.

Louisiana Agri-News Network
10500 Coursey Blvd., Ste. 104, Baton Rouge, LA 70816
(225) 291-2727, *Fax:* (225) 297-7539
www.la-net.net
jim@la-net.net
Bill Rigell, President
Jim Engster, General Manager
Comprises 46 stns in Louisiana & Mississippi. Represented by McGavren Guild.

Louisiana Network Inc.
10500 Coursey Blvd., Suite 104, Baton Rouge, LA 70816
(225) 291-2727, *Fax:* (225) 297-7539
www.la-net.net
jim@la-net.net
Comprises 84 stns in Louisiana. Represented by news net: State Nets, Agri-News Network: McGavren Guild.

Michigan Farm Radio Network
325 South Walnut, Lansing, MI 48933
(517) 484-4888, *Fax:* (517) 484-5015
www.mfrn.com
rhermes@irnradionet.com
Dennis Mellott, President
Janelle Brose, General Manager
Comprises 21 Michigan, affils. Represented by J.L. Farmakis.

Michigan Radio Network
325 S. Walnut, Lansing, MI 48933
(517) 484-4888, *Fax:* (517) 484-9404
www.michiganradionetwork.com
news@mrnradionet.com
Dennis Mellott, President
Kirsten Buys, General Manager
Rob Baykian, News Director
A statewide satellite-delivered net providing news, sports, business & special progmg. MRN 55 affils. Representative: StateNets.

Mid-America Ag Network
1632 S. Maize Rd., Wichita, KS 67209
(316) 721-8484, *Fax:* (316) 721-8276
www.maanradio.com
Greg Steckline, President
Rick Betzen, General Manager
Comprises 33 stns in Colorado, Kansas & Nebraska.. Represented by Torbet Radio.

Midwestern Broadcsting Company
Div/DBA: (Formerly Paul Bunyan Network)
Paul Bunyan Bldg., 314 E. Front, Traverse City, MI 49684
(231) 947-7675, *Fax:* (231) 929-3988
www.wtcmradio.com
chrisw@wtcmradio.com
Ross Biederman, President
Chris Warren, General Manager
Comprises 10 stns in Michigan. Represented by Katz Radio.

Mississippi Agri Network
6311 Ridgewood Rd., Jackson, MS 39211
(601) 957-1700, *Fax:* (601) 956-5228
www.supertalkms.com
lsheldon@telesouth.com
Stacy Long, General Sales Mgr
Comprises 35 affils in Mississippi. Represented by McGavren/Guild.

Mississippi News Network
6311 Ridgewood Rd., Jackson, MS 39211
(601) 957-1700, *Fax:* (601) 956-5228
www.supertalkms.com
lsheldon@telesouth.com
Stacy Long, General Sales Mgr
Comprises 82 affils in Mississippi. Represented by StateNets.

Mississippi State Basketball Network
6311 Ridgewood Rd., Jackson, MS 39211
(601) 957-1700, *Fax:* (601) 956-5228
www.supertalkms.com
kdillon@telesouth.com
Kim Dillon, Promotions Manager
Comprises 28 affils in Mississippi & one in Tennessee.

Mississippi State Football Network
6311 Ridgewood Rd., Jackson, MS 39211
(601) 957-1700, *Fax:* (601) 956-5228
www.supertalkms.com
kdillon@telesouth.com
Steve Davenport, President
Comprises 30 affils in Mississippi & one in Alabama. Represented by Kim Dillon.

Missourinet
Div/DBA: (A division of Learfield Communications Inc.)
505 Hobbs Rd., Jefferson City, MO 65109
(573) 893-2829, *Fax:* (573) 893-8094
www.missourinet.com
info@missourinet.com
Serves Missouri, 50-60 affils.

Mountain News Network
50 Vashell Way, Suite 200, Orinda, CA 94563
(925) 254-4456, (800) 736-0370 Eastern Bureau, *Fax:* (925) 254-6135
www.mnn.net
news@mnn.net
Comprises 1,537 stns nationwide.

National Educational Telecommunications Association
Box 50008, Columbia, SC 29250

(803) 799-5517, *Fax:* (803) 771-4831
www.netaonline.org
skip@netaonline.org
Skip Hinton, President
Ninety-five members in 45 states & the U.S. Virgin Islands.

New South Communications Inc.
Box 5797, Meridian, MS 39302
(601) 693-2661, *Fax:* (601) 483-0826
Ed Holladau, President
Comprises 18 stns: five in Louisiana, ten in Mississippi & three in Alabama. Represented by McGavren Guild.

North Carolina News Network
711 Hillsborough St., Raleigh, NC 27603
(919) 890-6128, *Fax:* (919) 890-6146
www.ncnn.com
rhankin@ncnn.com
Ardie Gregory, General Manager
Comprises 75 stns in North Carolina. Represented by StateNets.

North Dakota News Network
Box 1197, Pierre, SD 57501
(605) 224-9911, *Fax:* (605) 224-8984
markswendsen@amfmradio.biz
Mark Swendsen, President
Comprises 24 stns in North Dakota. Represented by StateNets.

NRG Media, LLC
Box 94, Fort Atkinson, WI 53538
(920) 563-2667, *Fax:* (920) 563-0315
www.lite1073.com
jvriezen@nrgmedia.com
Jim Vriezen, General Manager
Comprises 55 radio stns in Illinois, Iowa, Nebraska & Wisconsin.

Ohio Educational Telecommunications Network Commission
2470 North Star Rd., Columbus, OH 43221
(614) 228-4526, *Fax:* (614) 644-3112

Oklahoma News Network
Div/DBA: (Oklahoma Agrinet)
Box 1000, Oklahoma City, OK 73101
(405) 840-5271 Ext. 278, *Fax:* (405) 840-5808
Jerry Bohnen, News Director
Comprises 55 stns in Oklahoma.

Pittsburgh Country Network
1439 Denniston St., Pittsburgh, PA 15217
(412) 421-2600, *Fax:* (412) 421-6001
www.cmsradio.com
rafson@cmsradio.com
Roger Rafson, President
Comprises three stns in Pennsylvania. Represented by Commercial Media Sales.

Radio Iowa
Div/DBA: (A division of Learfield Communications Inc.)
2700 Grand Ave., Suite 103, Des Moines, IA 50312
(515) 282-1984, *Fax:* (515) 282-1879
www.radioiowa.com
radioiowa@learfield.com
Clyde G. Lear, President
Jennifer Shaefer, General Sales Mgr
O. Kay Henderson, News Director
Comprises 66 affils in Iowa.

Radio Pennsylvania Network
Div/DBA: (A Division of WITF Inc.)
4801 Lindle Rd., Harrisburg, PA 17111
(717) 704-3000, *Fax:* (717) 704-3659
www.radiopa.com, craig_rhodes@radiopa.org
Brad Christman, Operations Dir
Bcsts state news, sports & features to affils in Pennsylvania. Comprises 80 stns. Represented by NASRN.

Saga Communications, Inc,
73 Kercheval Ave., Suite 201, Grosse Pointe Farms, MI 48236
(313) 886-7070, *Fax:* (313) 886-7150
Edward hrstian, President

South Carolina News Network
Div/DBA: (A division of Learfield Communications)
3710 Landmark Dr., Suite 100, Columbia, SC 29204
(803) 790-4300, *Fax:* (803) 790-4309
Scott Brandon
Comprises 45 affils in South Carolina.

South Dakota News Network
Box 1197, Pierre, SD 57501
(605) 224-9911, *Fax:* (605) 224-8984
markswendsen@amfmradio.biz
Mark Swendsen, President
Comprises 20 stns in South Dakota. Represented by StateNets.

Southeast AgNet
5053 N.W. Hwy. 225 A, Ocala, FL 34482
(352) 671-1909, *Fax:* (352) 671-1364
www.southeastagnet.com
gary@southeastagnet.com
Gary Cooper, President
Robin Loftin, Operations Dir
Stns interconnected via Internet. Comprises 65 affils in Florida, Georgia & the Alabama rgn.

Southern Farm Network
3012 Highwoods Blvd., Suite 200, Raleigh, NC 27604
(919) 876-0674, *Fax:* (919) 790-8369
www.southernfarmnetwork.com
bprice@southernfarmnetwork.com
Barbara G. Price, General Sales Mgr
Comprises 20 affils in North Carolina & South Carolina.

Tennessee Agri-Net
Div/DBA: (Subsidiary of Clear Channel Communications Inc.)
55 Music Square West, Nashville, TN 37203
(615) 664-2400, *Fax:* (615) 687-9797
www.tennesseeradionetwork.com
craighahn@clearchannel.com
Tom English
Comprises 48 stns in Tennessee.

Tennessee Radio Network
Div/DBA: (A subsidiary of Clear Channel Broadcasting Inc.)
55 Music Sq. W., Nashville, TN 37203
(615) 664-2400, *Fax:* (615) 687-9797
www.tennesseeradionetwork.com
craighahn@clearchannel.com
Tom English, Promotions Manager
Comprises 74 stns in Tennessee. Representative Nathan Butler (Loisville, KY location) affil rel dir.

Texas State Network
4131 N. Central Expwy., Suite 500, Dallas, TX 75204
(214) 525-7400, *Fax:* (214) 525-7371
www.tsnradio.com
dbell@cbs.com
Brian Purdy, Operations Dir
Jerry Bobo, General Manager
Dan Bell, General Sales Mgr
Julis Graw, News Director
Provides newscasts, sportscasts, agriculture reports, longform programs to 165 stns in Texas & the Texas Rangers Radio Network. The oldest & largest state radio net owned by CBS Radio. Represented by StateNets.
502 E. 11th St, Suite 320, Austin, TX 78701-2658
(512) 474-5275; *Fax:* 512 476 9232
Candy Schmidt, Regional Sales Director

Tiger Network
Div/DBA: (A division of Learfield Communications Inc.)
505 Hobbs Rd., Jefferson City, MO 65109
(573) 893-7200, *Fax:* (573) 893-2321
www.learfield.com
Clyde G. Lear, President
Aaron Worsham, Operations Dir
Bob Agramonte, General Manager
Keith Sampson, Programming Director
Comprises 55 stns in Missouri.

Tribune Radio Networks
435 N. Michigan Ave., Chicago, IL 60611
(312) 222-3342
tkbrady@earthlink.net

University of Mississippi Baseball Network
6311 Ridgewood Rd., Jackson, MS 39211
(601) 957-1700, *Fax:* (601) 956-5228
www.supertalkms.com, kdillon@telesouth.com
Comprises 30 affils in Mississippi & one in Tennessee. Represented by Kim Dillon.

University of Mississippi Basketball Network
6311 Ridgewood Rd., Jackson, MS 39211
(601) 957-1700, *Fax:* (601) 956-5228
www.telesouth.com
Steve Davenport, President
Stacy Long, General Sales Mgr
Comprises 30 affils in Mississippi & one in Tennessee. Represented by Kim Dillon.

University of Mississippi Football Network
6311 Ridgewood Rd., Jackson, MS 39211
(601) 957-1700, *Fax:* (601) 956-5228
www.supertalkms.com
kdillon@telesouth.com
Steve Davenport, President
Comprises 30 affils in Mississippi & one in Tennessee. Represented by Tim Fritts.

Univision Radio
3102 Oak Lawn Ave., Suite 215, Dallas, TX 75219
(214) 525-7700, *Fax:* (214) 525-7750
www.univision.com
Alan F. Horn, President
Comprises 72 stns, 18 in California, four in Florida, five in Illinois, three in Nevada, three in New York, 26 in Texas & five in Arizona, four in New Mexico, four in Puerto Rico.

Vox Communications
Div/DBA: (formerly Berkshire Broadcasting Co. Inc.)
211 Jason St., Pittsfield, MA 01201
(413) 499-3333, *Fax:* (413) 442-1590
www.wnaw.com
wnaw@wnaw.com
Comprises 6 stns in Berkshire County, MA.

The Weather Center
Div/DBA: (A broadcast service of Aviation Weather Inc.)
701 Gervais St., Suite 224, Columbia, SC 29201
(803) 422-4823
jim@condo-lawyers.com

Western Agri-Radio Networks Inc.
Div/DBA: (dba California Agri-Radio Network & Southwest Agr
1700 S. 1st Ave., Suite 214, Yuma, AZ 85364
(928) 782-1440, *Fax:* (928) 782-1474
www.farmnewswest.com
ggatley@sprynet.com
George G. Gatley, President
Fifteen radio stns in California, two in Arizona & one in Texas. Represented by J.L. Famakis.
Southwest Agri-Radio Network
1700 S. 1st Ave, Suite 214, Yuma, AZ 85364-5745
(800) 944-6077; *Fax:* (520) 782-1474
www.home.com/sprynet/ggatley
ggatley@sprynet.com
California Agri-Radio Network
1700 S. 1st Ave, Suite 214, Yuma, AZ 85364-5745
(800) 944-6077, (520) 782-1440; *Fax:* (520) 782-1474
www.home.com/sprynet/ggatley
ggatley@sprynet.com

Wisconsin Radio Network
222 State St., Suite 401, Madison, WI 53703
(608) 251-3900, *Fax:* (608) 251-7233
www.wrn.com
info@wrn.com
Joyce Steinman, General Sales Mgr
Bob Hague, News Director
Statewide satellite-delivered net providing Wisconsin news & sports.

WRTI-FM
1509 Cecil B. Moore, 3rd Fl., Philadelphia, PA 19121-3410
(215) 204-8405, *Fax:* (215) 204-7027
www.wrti.org
Tobias Poole, Operations Dir
David S. Conant, General Manager
Patty Prevost, General Sales Mgr
Comprises four stns in Pennsylvania, one in New Jersey & one in Delaware.

WV Radio Corp. and Metronews Radio Network
Greer Bldg., 1251 Earl L. Core Rd., Morgantown, WV 26505
(304) 296-0029, *Fax:* (304) 296-3876
www.wvmetronews.com, dmiller@wvradio.com
Dale B. Miller, President
Hoppy Kercheval, Operations Dir
Comprises West Virginia News, 58 stns in West Virginia & Mountaineer Sports Network, 72 stns in West Virginia.
1111 Virginia St. E., Charleston, WV 25301-2406
(304) 342-8131;

Yancey AG Network
Box 1000, Oklahoma City, OK 73101
(405) 858-10297
www.oklahomaagrinet.net
ashliacker@clearchannel.com
Ben Buckland, Station Manager
Ron Hays, Programming Director
A satellite delivered Agsource providing affil radio stns with agricultural markets, news & weather. Represents 17 stns.

Radio Group Ownership

ABC Inc.
2300 Riverside Dr., Burbank CA 91521
(818) 249-9999
www.abc.go.com
Ownership: ABC Enterprises Inc., 100%. Note: ABC Enterprises Inc. is 100% owned by Disney Enterprises Inc.
Radio Stns: 41 AM. 3 FM.
KWDZ Salt Lake City, UT; KDDZ Arvada, CO; KSPN Los Angeles, CA; KDIZ Golden Valley, MN; KRDY San Antonio, TX; KKDZ Seattle, WA; KDZR Lake Oswego, OR; KMIK Tempe, AZ; KMKI Plano, TX; KMKY Oakland, CA; KPHN Kansas City, MO; KQAM Wichita, KS; KIID Sacramento, CA; KDIS Pasadena, CA; KMIC Houston, TX; WBOB(AM) Jacksonville, FL; WCOG Greensboro, NC; WDWD Atlanta, GA; WSDK Bloomfield, CT; WDZY Colonial Heights, VA; WEPN New York, NY; WMYM Miami, FL; WFDF Farmington Hills, MI; WGFY Charlotte, NC; WDDY Albany, NY; WHKT Portsmouth, VA; WDYZ Orlando, FL; WKSH Sussex, WI; WDDZ Pittsburgh, PA; WMVP Chicago, IL; WHBE Newburg, KY; WNTT Tazewell, TN; WPMH Portsmouth, VA; WHTY(AM) Riviera Beach, FL; WMKI Boston, MA; WQEW New York, NY; WRDZ La Grange, IL; WSDZ Belleville, IL; WWJZ Mount Holly, NJ; WWMI St. Petersburg, FL; WWMK Cleveland, OH; KESN Allen, TX; KDIS-FM Little Rock, AR; WRDZ-FM Plainfield, IN;
TV Stns: 10 TV.
KABC-TV Los Angeles, CA; KFSN-TV Fresno, CA; KGO-TV San Francisco, CA; KTRK-TV Houston, TX; WABC-TV New York, NY; WJRT-TV Flint, MI; WLS-TV Chicago, IL; WPVI-TV Philadelphia, PA; WTVD Durham, NC; WTVG Toledo, OH;
Phillip J. Meek, President
Robert A. Iger, Vice President
Lawrence J. Pollock, Chairman/Owner

Absolute Broadcasting LLC
30 Temple Dr., Litchfield NH 3052
(603) 883-9900
Radio Stns: 3 AM.
WGAM Manchester, NH; WGHM Nashua, NH; WSMN Nashua, NH;

Access.1 Communications Corp.
11 Penn Plaza,16th Fl., New York NY 10001
(212) 714-1000; *Fax:*(212) 714-1563;
Radio Stns: 5 AM. 10 FM.
KCUL Marshall, TX; KFRO Longview, TX; KOKA Shreveport, LA; WGYM Hammonton, NJ; WWRL New York, NY; KCUL-FM Marshall, TX; KBTT Haughton, LA; KKUS Tyler, TX; KOYE Frankston, TX; KSYR Benton, LA; KOOI Jacksonville, TX; KDKS-FM Blanchard, LA; KLKL Minden, LA; KTAL-FM Texarkana, TX; KYKX Longview, TX;
TV Stns: 1 TV.
WMGM-TV Wildwood, NJ;
Sydney Small, CEO

Ace Radio Corp.
2801 Via Fortuna Dr.,Suite 675, Austin TX 78746
Radio Stns: 7 FM.
KQLP Leupp, AZ; KQNO Coalinga, CA; KCOO Dunkerton, IA; WTPO New Albany, MS; KQMX Lost Hills, CA; WZHL New Augusta, MS; KRPH Morristown, AZ;

Ad Astra Per Aspera Broadcasting Inc.
106 N. Main St., Hutchinson KS 67501-5219
(620) 665-5758; *Fax:*(620) 665-6655
cliffcshank@yahoo.com
Radio Stns: 4 FM.
KSKU Sterling, KS; KNZS Arlington, KS; KXKU Lyons, KS; KWHK Hutchinson, KS;
Cliff Shank, President
Michael Hill, Operations Dir

Adelante Media Group LLC
500 Media Place, Sacramento CA 95815
(916) 368-6300; *Fax:*(916) 473-0143
www.adelantemediagroup.com
Ownership: ACM Bustos Inc., 33% of total assets; Terry S. Jacobs, 33% votes; Jack Patrick Edwards, 33% votes; Michael E. Bogdan, 33% votes.
Radio Stns: 4 AM. 15 FM.
KMIA Auburn-Federal Way, WA; KTUB Centerville, UT; KULE Ephrata, WA; KDYK Union Gap, WA; KDUT Randolph, UT; KDDS-FM Elma, WA; KQTA Homedale, ID; KBBU Modesto, CA; KZML Quincy, WA; KDBI Emmett, ID; KBMG Evanston, WY; KZTB Milton-Freewater, OR; KLMG Esparto, CA; KULE-FM Ephrata, WA; KZTA Naches, WA; KMMG Benton City, WA; WDDW Sturtevant, WI; KBAA Grass Valley, CA; KGRB(FM) Jackson, CA;
Jay Meyers, CEO
Ed Krampf, COO

Adelman Broadcasting Inc.
731 N. Balsam, Ridgecrest CA 93555
(760) 371-1700; *Fax:*(760) 371-1824
adelmanbroadcasting.com
Radio Stns: 1 AM. 3 FM.
KLOA Ridgecrest, CA; KGBB Edwards, CA; KLOA(FM) Ridgecrest, CA; KRAJ Johannesburg, CA;
Robert Adelman, President

Adonai Radio Group
2448 E. 81st St.,Suite 5500, Tulsa OK 74137
(918) 492-2660; *Fax:*(918) 492-8840
www.kxoj.com
mail@kxoj.com
Radio Stns: 2 AM. 6 FM.
KBIX Muskogee, OK; KYAL Sapulpa, OK; KEMX Locust Grove, OK; KEOJ Caney, KS; KCXR Taft, OK; KYAL-FM Muskogee, OK; KTFR Chelsea, OK; KXOJ-FM Sapulpa, OK;
Michael Stephens, President

Air South Radio Inc.
Box 2116, Tupelo MS 38803
(662) 842-9595; *Fax:*(662) 842-9568
Ownership: Olvie E. Sisk; Kathern Sisk.
Radio Stns: 3 FM.
WCNA Potts Camp, MS; WFTA Fulton, MS; WLZA Eupora, MS;
Olvie E. Sisk, President
Kathern Sisk, Secretary

Alaska Broadcast Communications Inc.
3161 Channel Dr.,Suite 2, Juneau AK 99801
(907) 586-3630; *Fax:*(907) 463-3685
www.kjno.com,www.taku105.com
Radio Stns: 3 AM. 3 FM.
KIFW Sitka, AK; KJNO Juneau, AK; KTKN Ketchikan, AK; KGTW Ketchikan, AK; KSBZ Sitka, AK; KTKU Juneau, AK;
Richard Burns, CEO

Aleluya Christian Broadcasting Inc.
912 Curtis Ave., Pasadena TX 77502-2402
(713) 589-1336; *Fax:*(713) 589-1335;
Radio Stns: 2 AM. 2 FM.
KBRZ Missouri City, TX; KRTX Rosenburg-Richmond, TX; KUZN Centerville, TX; KFTG Pasadena, TX;

Alex Media Inc.
25 E. 86th St.,Apt 13B, New York NY 10028
(917) 535-0419
Ownership: Alexander Berger, 51%; Darryl Delawder, 24.5%; Evan Carb, 24.5%.
Radio Stns: 2 FM.
WURB Cross City, FL; WTCF(FM) Wardenville, WV;
Alexander Berger, Chairman

Alexandra Communications Inc.
1600 Gray Lynn Dr., Walla Walla WA 99362
(509) 527-1000; *Fax:*(509) 529-5534;
Radio Stns: 1 AM. 4 FM.
KUJ Walla Walla, WA; KDEP Garibaldi, OR; KZIU-FM Weston, OR; KLKY Stanfield, OR; KIXT(FM) Bay City, OR;

Allegheny Mountain Network Stations
Box 247, Tyrone PA 16686
(814) 684-3200; *Fax:*(814) 684-1220
amnet@aol.com
Ownership: Cary H. Simpson.
Radio Stns: 4 AM. 4 FM.
WFRM Coudersport, PA; WKBI St. Marys, PA; WNBT Wellsboro, PA; WTRN Tyrone, PA; WEEO-FM McConnellsburg, PA; WKBI-FM St. Marys, PA; WNBQ Mansfield, PA; WNBT-FM Wellsboro, PA;
Cary Simpson, President
John Simpson, VP

Altus FM Inc.
Box 1077, Altus OK 73522
(580) 482-1555; *Fax:*(580) 482-8353
Ownership: Paul Wilmes, 46%; Scott Wilmes, 44%; Gayle Ledbetter, 10%.
Radio Stns: 3 FM.
KEYB Altus, OK; KKRE Hollis, OK; KJOK Hollis, OK;
Gayle Ledbetter, CEO
Paul Wilmes, President

Amaturo Groups
3101 N. Federal Hwy.,6th Fl., Fort Lauderdale FL 33306-1018
(954) 565-1411; *Fax:*(954) 565-1311
jca@amaturogroups.com
Ownership: Amaturo Group of L.A. Inc. (Joseph C. Amaturo, gen ptnr): KAJL(FM), KJLL-FM and KHJL(FM).
Radio Stns: 2 FM.
KJLL(FM) Fountain Valley, CA; KHJL(FM) Thousand Oaks, CA;
Joseph Amaturo, General Partner

American Family Radio
Box 3206, Tupelo MS 38803
(662) 844-8888; *Fax:*(662) 842-6791
www.afr.net
comments@afr.net
Ownership: American Family Association, a nonprofit organization.
Radio Stns: 158 FM.
KAKA Salina, KS; KANX Sheridan, AR; KAOG Jonesboro, AR; KAOW Fort Smith, AR; KAPI Ruston, LA; KAPK Grants Pass, OR; KAPM Alexandria, LA; KAQD Abilene, TX; KSJY St. Martinville, LA; KAQF Clovis, NM; KARG Poteau, OK; KARH Forrest City, AR; KAUF Kennett, MO; KAVK Many, LA; KAVW Amarillo, TX; KAFR Conroe, TX; KAVO Pampa, TX; KAXR Arkansas City, KS; KAXV Bastrop, LA; KAYA Hubbard, NE; KAYB Sunnyside, WA; KAYC Durant, OK; KAYK Victoria, TX; KAYM Weatherford, OK; KAYP Burlington, IA; KBAH Plainview, TX; KBAN De Ridder, LA; KBCM Blytheville, AR; KBCX Big Spring, TX; KBDA Great Bend, KS; KBDC Mason City, IA; KBDE Temple, TX; KBDO Des Arc, AR; KBGM Park Hills, MO; KBJQ Bronson, KS; KBMH Holbrook, AZ; KBMJ Heber Springs, AR; KBMM Odessa, TX; KBNV Fayetteville, AR; KBPG Montevideo, MN; KBUZ Topeka, KS; KCFN Wichita, KS; KRBW Ottawa, KS; KVRS Lawton, OK; WAAE New Bern, NC; WAEF Cordele, GA; WAII Hattiesburg, MS; WAJS Tupelo, MS; WAKD Sheffield, AL; WALN Carrollton, AL; WAMP Jackson, TN; WAOY Gulfport, MS; WAPD Campbellsville, KY; WAPO Mount Vernon, IL; WAQB Tupelo, MS; WAQG Ozark, AL; WAQL McComb, MS; WAQU Selma, AL; WARN Culpeper, VA; WASM Natchez, MS; WASW Waycross, GA; WATI Vincennes, IN; WATP Laurel, MS; WATU Port Gibson, MS; WAUI Shelby, OH; WAUM Duck Hill, MS; WAUO Hohenwald, TN; WAUQ Charles City, VA; WYLJ(FM) Tullahoma, TN; WAUV Ripley, TN; WAVI Oxford, MS; WAWF Kankakee, IL; WAWH Dublin, GA; WAWI Lawrenceburg, TN; WAWJ Marion, IL; WAWN Franklin, PA; WAXG Mount Sterling, KY; WAXR Geneseo, IL; WAXU Troy, AL; WAZD Savannah, TN; WBEL Cairo, IL; WBFY Pinehurst, NC; WBHZ Elkins, WV; WBIA Shelbyville, TN; WBIE Delphos, OH; WBJV Steubenville, OH; WBJY Americus, GA; WBKG Macon, GA; WBKU Ahoskie, NC; WBMF Crete, IL; WBMK Morehead, KY; WGCF Paducah, KY; WIGH Jackson, TN; WJZB Starkville, MS; WMSB Byhalia, MS; WQST-FM Forest, MS; WTLG Starke, FL; WWGN Ottawa, IL; KBPW Hampton, AR; KBQC Independence, KS; KQPD Ardmore, OK; KXRT Idabel, OK; KCKT Crockett, TX; KQRB Windom, MN; WMCQ Muskegon, MI; KYLC Lake Charles, LA; WZKM Waynesboro, MS; WPRG Columbia, MS; WPAS Pascagoula, MS; KAPG Bentonville, AR; WPWV Princeton, WV; KANL Baker, OR; KZFT Fannett, TX; WXBE Beaufort, NC; WQVI Madison, MS; KSUL Port Sulphur, LA; WJJE Delaware, OH; WQSG Lafayette, IN; WSLE Salem, IL; WYTF Indianola, MS; WYAZ Yazoo City, MS; WCSO Columbus, MS; WRAE Raeford, NC; KPAQ Plaquemine, LA; KASD Rapid City, SD; KTXG Greenville, TX; KIAD Dubuque, IA; WRIH Richmond, VA; KAKO Ada, OK; KAFH Great Falls, MT; KMEO Mertzon, TX; KWVI Waverly, IA; WJKA Jacksonville, NC; KSUR Mart, TX; KATG Elkhart, TX; WEFI Effingham, IL; KLGS College Station, TX; KNLL Nashville, AR; KDVI Devils Lake, ND; KTDA Dalhart, TX; KHYS Hays, KS; KDLI Del Rio, TX; WDLL Dillon, SC; WPRH Paris, TN; KLKI Dolan Springs, AZ; KJTW Jamestown, ND; KOBH Hobbs, NM; WRYN Hickory, NC; WWGV Grove City, OH; KVHR Van Horn, TX; KEEA Aberdeen, SD; WWEN Wentworth, WI; KKNL Valentine, NE; KAWN Winslow, AZ; WWVY Waverly, OH; KMLL Marysville, KS; KSNB Norton, KS; KPKO Pecos, TX;
Tim Wildmon, President/CEO

American General Media
Box 2700, Bakersfield CA 93303
(661) 328-0118; *Fax:*(661) 328-1648;
Radio Stns: 5 AM. 17 FM.
KARS Belen, NM; KERN Wasco-Greenacres, CA; KERI Bakersfield, CA; KGEO Bakersfield, CA; KKIM Albuquerque, NM; KABG Los Alamos, NM; KDLW Los Alamos, NM; KBOX Lompoc, CA; KKXX-FM Shafter, CA; KKAL Paso Robles, CA; KGFM Bakersfield, CA; KIQO Atascadero, CA; KISV Bakersfield, CA; KKJG San Luis Obispo, CA; KLVO Belen, NM; KHFM Santa Fe, NM; KPAT Orcutt, CA; KRQK Lompoc, CA; KEBT Lost Hills, CA; KAGM Los Lunas, NM; KZOZ San Luis Obispo, CA; KKIM-FM Santa Fe, NM;
L. Rogers Brandon, Operations Dir

American Media Investments Inc.
1162 E. Hwy. 126, Pittsburg KS 66762

(620) 231-7200;
Radio Stns: 4 AM. 7 FM.
KBTN Neosho, MO; KCAR Clarksville, TX; KKTK Texarkana, TX; KQYX Galena, KS; KCAR-FM Baxter Springs, KS; KBTN-FM Neosho, MO; KEWL-FM New Boston, TX; KGAP Clarksville, TX; KPGG Ashdown, AR; KMOQ Columbus, KS; KJML(FM) Columbus, KS;
O. Gene Bicknell, CEO

Americom
11400 W. Olympic Blvd,Suite 780, Los Angeles CA 90064
(310) 481-0440; *Fax:*(310) 481-0445;
Radio Stns: 2 AM. 3 FM.
KJFK Reno, NV; KBZZ Sparks, NV; KLCA Tahoe City, CA; KRNO Incline Village, NV; KSGG Carson City, NV;
Tom Quinn, President/CEO

Amistad Communications Inc.
7480 Greenwood Rd., Shreveport LA 71119
(318) 938-1885; *Fax:*(318) 425-7507;
Radio Stns: 2 AM. 1 FM.
KASO Minden, LA; KSYB Shreveport, LA; KBEF Gibsland, LA;

Anaheim Broadcasting Corp.
Box 2668, Del Mar CA 92014-5668
(858) 794-1626; *Fax:*(858) 794-4068
Ownership: Tim Sullivan.
Radio Stns: 2 FM.
KCAL-FM Redlands, CA; KOLA San Bernardino, CA;
Tim Sullivan, President
Doug Lida, CFO

Anastos Media Group Inc.
21 Malta Commons,100 Saratoga Village Blvd, Malta NY 12020
(518) 899-3000; *Fax:*(518) 899-3057
www.star1013.com
star1013fm@aol.com
Radio Stns: 3 AM. 1 FM.
WUAM Watervliet, NY; WABY Mechanicville, NY; WPTR(AM) Schenectady, NY; WJKE(FM) Stillwater, NY;
Scott Collins, President

Anderson Radio Broadcasting Inc.
581 N. Reservoir Rd., Polson MT 59860
(406) 883-5255; *Fax:*(406) 883-4441;
Radio Stns: 2 AM. 5 FM.
KERR Polson, MT; KQJZ Evergreen, MT; KQRK Ronan, MT; KIBG Bigfork, MT; KZXT Eureka, MT; KZJZ St. Regis, MT; KKMT Pablo, MT;

Apex Broadcasting Inc.
Box 61091, N Charleston SC 29419-1091
(843) 852-9003; *Fax:*(843) 852-9041;
Radio Stns: 1 AM. 3 FM.
WSPO Charleston, SC; WXST Hollywood, SC; WAVF Hanahan, SC; WXTC Greenville, PA;
Houston Pearce, Chairman
G. Dean Pearce, President

Arkansas County Broadcasters Inc.
Box 789, Wynne AR 72396-0789
(870) 238-8141; *Fax:*(870) 238-5997;
Radio Stns: 1 AM. 3 FM.
KWAK Stuttgart, AR; KOTN(FM) Gould, AR; KDEW-FM De Witt, AR; KWAK-FM Stuttgart, AR;

Arklatex LLC
615 W. Olive, Texarkana TX 75501
(903) 793-4671; *Fax:*(903) 792-4261
alex@101jams.com
Radio Stns: 2 AM. 3 FM.
KCMC Texarkana, TX; KTFS Texarkana, TX; KFYX(FM) Texarkana, AR; KBYB Hope, AR; KTOY Texarkana, AR;
Alex Rain, Operations Dir
Mike Simpson, General Manager

ARKLATEX Radio Inc.
111 Westwood Dr., De Queen AR 71832
(870) 642-2446; *Fax:*(870) 642-2442;
Radio Stns: 1 AM. 2 FM.
KBHC Nashville, AR; KMTB Murfreesboro, AR; KNAS Nashville, AR;
Bonita Smith, CFO
Jay Bunyard, President

Armada Media Corp.
1 W. Second St., 2nd Fl., Fond du Lac WI 54935-4908
(920) 906-9900; *Fax:*(920) 906-9800
www.armadamedia.com
Radio Stns: 9 AM. 18 FM.
KBRL McCook, NE; KDIO Ortonville, MN; KGIM Aberdeen, SD; KMSD Mibank, SD; KODY North Platte, NE; KSDN Aberdeen, SD; KUVR Holdrege, NE; WAGN Menominee, MI; WMAM Marinette, WI; KBFO Aberdeen, SD; KBWS-FM Sisseton, SD; KFNF Oberlin, KS; KGIM-FM Redfield, SD; KICX-FM McCook, NE; KSTH Holyoke, CO; KMTY Gibbon, NE; KNBZ Redfield, SD; KPHR Ortonville, MN; KSDN-FM Aberdeen, SD; KXNP North Platte, NE; WHYB Menominee, MI; WLST Marinette, WI; WSFQ Peshtigo, WI; KHAQ Maxwell, NE; KADL Imperial, NE; KJBL Julesburg, CO; KQHK McCook, NE;
Terry Shockley, Chairman
Chris Bernier, CEO
John Larson, Operations Dir

Arnold Broadcasting Inc.
Box 753, Lamar CO 81052
(719) 336-4227;
Radio Stns: 1 AM. 3 FM.
KSTC Sterling, CO; KNEC Yuma, CO; KNNG Sterling, CO; KECK Eckley, CO;
Bill Arnold, President

Artistic Media Partners Inc.
5520 E. 75th St., Indianapolis IN 46250
(317) 594-0600; *Fax:*(317) 594-9567
www.artisticradio.com
artradio@aol.com
Ownership: Arthur A. Angotti.
Radio Stns: 2 AM. 8 FM.
WSHY Lafayette, IN; WDND South Bend, IN; WAZY-FM Lafayette, IN; WBWB Bloomington, IN; WSHP Attica, IN; WHCC Ellettsville, IN; WSMM New Carlisle, IN; WBPE Brookston, IN; WNDV-FM South Bend, IN; WSSM(FM) Goshen, IN;
Arthur Angotti, CEO

Asterisk Inc.
2848 E. Oakland Park Blvd., Fort Lauderdale FL 33306
(954) 566-7559; *Fax:*(954) 564-6753
Ownership: Richard S. Ingham, 100%.
Radio Stns: 3 FM.
WMFQ Ocala, FL; WYGC High Springs, FL; WXJZ Gainesville, FL;
Frederick Ingham, President

Astor Broadcast Group
1835 Aston Ave., Carlsbad CA 92008
(760) 729-1000; *Fax:*(760) 476-9604;
Radio Stns: 3 AM.
KCEO Vista, CA; KSPA Ontario, CA; KFSD Escondido, CA;
Peri Corso, General Manager

Astro Tele-Communications Corp. Rhode Island
Box 920365, Needham MA 2492
(781) 444-4754; *Fax:*(781) 444-8630
www.wadk.com
addelco@gis.net
Radio Stns: 1 AM. 1 FM.
WADK Newport, RI; WJZS Block Island, RI;
Maurice Polayes, President

Atlantic Broadcasting
1601 New Rd., Linwood NJ 08221-1116
(609) 653-1400; *Fax:*(609) 601-0450;
Radio Stns: 2 AM. 3 FM.
WBSS(AM) Pleasantville, NJ; WOND Pleasantville, NJ; WWAC Ocean City, NJ; WMGM Atlantic City, NJ; WTKU-FM Petersburg, NJ;
Brett DeNafo, CEO

Atlantic Coast Radio L.L.C.
779 Warren Avenue, Portland ME 4103
(207) 773-9695; *Fax:*(207) 761-4406
www.redhot95.com
Radio Stns: 2 AM. 3 FM.
WRED Westbrook, ME; WLOB Portland, ME; WJJB-FM Gray, ME; WPEI Saco, ME; WPPI Topsham, ME;
J.J. Jeffrey, President

AVC Communications Inc.
Box 338, Cambridge OH 43725
(740) 432-5605; *Fax:*(740) 432-1991
www.yourradioplace.com
Radio Stns: 2 FM.
WCMJ Cambridge, OH; WILE-FM Byesville, OH;
Grant Hafley, President
David Wilson, Operations Dir
Joel Losego, General Manager

Azteca Broadcasting Corp.
323 E. San Joaquin St., Tulare CA 93274
(559) 686-1370; *Fax:*(559) 685-1394
wwwkgen@sbcglobal.net
Radio Stns: 3 AM. 1 FM.
KGEN Tulare, CA; KSVN Ogden, UT; KXEQ Reno, NV; KGEN-FM Hanford, CA;
Margarita Hernandez, General Manager

Backyard Broadcasting LLC
4237 Salisbury Rd.,Suite 225, Jacksonville FL 32216
(904) 674-0260; *Fax:*(904) 854-4596
www.bybradio.com
Radio Stns: 10 AM. 19 FM.
KELO Sioux Falls, SD; KSQB(AM) Sioux Falls, SD; KWSN Sioux Falls, SD; WRCE Watkins Glen, NY; WHBU Anderson, IN; WHDL Olean, NY; WHTY Riviera Beach, FL; WWLZ Horseheads, NY; WWPA Williamsport, PA; WXFN Muncie, IN; KELO-FM Sioux Falls, SD; KRRO Sioux Falls, SD; KSQB-FM Dell Rapids, SD; KXQL Flandreau, SD; KTWB Sioux Falls, SD; WCXR Lewisburg, PA; WERK Muncie, IN; WBZD-FM Muncy, PA; WILQ Williamsport, PA; WLBC-FM Muncie, IN; WNGZ Montour Falls, NY; WNKI Corning, NY; WPGI Horseheads, NY; WPIG Olean, NY; WRVH Clayton, NY; WJLV Jackson, MS; WIKL(FM) Elwood, IN; WJAI Pearl, MS; WZXR South Williamsport, PA;
Barry Drake, CEO
Robin Smith, Operations Dir
Tom Atkins, VP/Engineering Director

Bahakel Communications
Box 32488, Charlotte NC 28232
(704) 372-4434; *Fax:*(704) 335-9904
Ownership: Bahakel Communications
Radio Stns: 3 AM. 5 FM.
KWLO Waterloo, IA; KXEL Waterloo, IA; WDEF Chattanooga, TN; KFMW Waterloo, IA; KILO Colorado Springs, CO; KOKZ Waterloo, IA; KRXP Pueblo West, CO; WDEF-FM Chattanooga, TN;
TV Stns: 7 TV.
WAKA Selma, AL; WBBJ-TV Jackson, TN; WCCB Charlotte, NC; WCCU Urbana, IL; WFXB Myrtle Beach, SC; WOLO-TV Columbia, SC; WRSP-TV Springfield, IL;
Beverly B. Poston, President
Russell Schwartz, General Counsel
John Hutchinson, SVP/Television
Jim Babb, Executive Vice President

Baker Family Stations
Box 889, Blacksburg VA 24063
(540) 552-4252; *Fax:*(540) 951-5282
Ownership: Principal owners: Vernon H. Baker, Edward A. Baker, Virginia L. Baker.
Radio Stns: 12 AM. 5 FM.
WAMN Green Valley, WV; WBGS Point Pleasant, WV; WFIC Collinsville, VA; WKEX Blacksburg, VA; WKGM Smithfield, VA; WKNV Fairlawn, VA; WKTR Earlysville, VA; WLGN Logan, OH; WMPO Middleport-Pomeroy, OH; WODY Fieldale, VA; WYHY Cannonsburg, KY; WMUX Hurricane, WV; WBNN-FM Dillwyn, VA; WCEF Ripley, WV; WKNA Logan, OH; WTGR Union City, OH; WZFM Narrows, VA;
Vernon H. Baker, CEO
Edward A. Baker, President
Virginia L. Baker, Treasurer

Baldridge-Dumas Communications Inc.
605 San Antonio Ave., Many LA 71449
(318) 256-5924; *Fax:*(318) 256-0950
www.bdcradio.com
Radio Stns: 6 FM.
KDBH-FM Natchitoches, LA; KTEZ Zwolle, LA; KVCL-FM Winnfield, LA; KZBL Natchitoches, LA; KTHP Hemphill, TX; KBDV Leesville, LA;
Tedd Dumas, President
Rhonda Benson, General Manager

Barry P. Lunderville Stns
195 Main St., Lancaster NH 3584
(603) 788-3636; *Fax:*(603) 788-3536;
Radio Stns: 4 AM. 2 FM.
WLTN Littleton, NH; WMOU Berlin, NH; WKDR Berlin, NH; WGAM(AM) Manchester, NH; WLTN-FM Lisbon, NH; WXXS Lancaster, NH;

BAS Broadcasting Inc.
1281 N. River Rd., Fremont OH 43420
(419) 332-8218; *Fax:*(419) 333-8226
www.basohio.com
Ownership: James A. Lorenzen, 42.5%; Thomas W. Klein, 23.5%; BAS Broadcasting Inc. Retirement Savings Plan, 19%.

Radio Stns: 3 AM. 6 FM.
WLEC Sandusky, OH; WMVO Mount Vernon, OH; WTTF Tiffin, OH; WMJK Clyde, OH; WFRO-FM Fremont, OH; WPFX-FM Luckey, OH; WCPZ Sandusky, OH; WOHF Bellevue, OH; WQIO Mount Vernon, OH;
James A. Lorenzen, President

Basin Mediactive LLC
404 Main St., Suite 4, Klamath Falls OR 97601
(541) 882-8833
www.mybasin.com
Ownership: Robert J. Ingstad, 50%;Tor H. Ingstad, 50%.
Radio Stns: 2 AM. 1 FM.
KAGO Klamath Falls, OR; KLAD Klamath Falls, OR; KLAD-FM Klamath Falls, OR;

Beacon Broadcasting Inc.
Box 1789, Warren OH 44482-1790
(330) 394-7700; *Fax:*(330) 394-7701;
Radio Stns: 3 AM. 2 FM.
WHTX Warren, OH; WGRP Greenville, PA; WLOA Farrell, PA; WLVX(FM) Greenville, PA; WRTK Paxton, IL;

Beasley Broadcast Group Inc.
3033 Riviera Dr.,Suite 200, Naples FL 34103
(239) 263-5000; *Fax:*(239) 263-8191
www.bbgi.com
email@bbgi.com
Ownership: George G. Beasley.
Radio Stns: 17 AM. 26 FM.
KDWN Las Vegas, NV; WAEC Atlanta, GA; WRDW Augusta, GA; WAZZ Fayetteville, NC; WGAC Augusta, GA; WHSR Pompano Beach, FL; WNCT Greenville, NC; WQAM Miami, FL; WRCA Watertown, MA; WCHZ Augusta, GA; WSBR Boca Raton, FL; WTEL Red Springs, NC; WTMR Camden, NJ; WWCN North Fort Myers, FL; WWDB Philadelphia, PA; WWNN Pompano Beach, FL; WWWE Hapeville, GA; KCYE Boulder City, NV; KKLZ Las Vegas, NV; KFRH North Las Vegas, NV; WGUS-FM New Ellenton, SC; WGAC-FM Harlem, GA; WFLB Laurinburg, NC; WDRR Martinez, GA; WIKS New Bern, NC; WJBX Fort Myers Beach, FL; WJPT Fort Myers Villas, FL; WKIS Boca Raton, FL; WKML Lumberton, NC; WKXC-FM Aiken, SC; WMGV Newport, NC; WNCT-FM Greenville, NC; WPOW Miami, FL; WCHZ-FM Warrenton, GA; WRXK-FM Bonita Springs, FL; WSFL-FM New Bern, NC; WHHD Clearwater, SC; WUKS St. Pauls, NC; WRDW-FM Philadelphia, PA; WXKB Cape Coral, FL; WXNR Grifton, NC; WXTU Philadelphia, PA; WZFX Whiteville, NC;
George Beasley, Chairman/CEO
Bruce Beasley, President/COO
Caroline Beasley, EVP/CFO

Bee Broadcasting Inc.
Box 5409, Kalispell MT 59903
(406) 755-8700; *Fax:*(406) 755-8770
www.kbbz.com
Radio Stns: 2 AM. 3 FM.
KJJR Whitefish, MT; KSAM Whitefish, MT; KBBZ Kalispell, MT; KDBR Kalispell, MT; KHNK Columbia Falls, MT;
Benny Bee, President

Benedetti Media Group LLC
222 N. 32nd St., 10th Fl., Billings MT 59101
(406) 238-1000; *Fax:*(406) 238-1038
benedettimedia.com
Ownership: Peter J. Benedetti, 85.1% votes, 58.8% equity; Richard G. Maynard, 10.6% votes, 29.4% equity; Paul C. Benedetti, 2.6% votes, 7.1% equity; Barry R. Remington,1.7% votes, 4.7% equity.
Radio Stns: 4 FM.
KYSX(FM) Billings, MT; KRSQ Laurel, MT; KRPM Billings, MT; KEWF(FM) Billings, MT;
Pete Benedetti, Chairman

Bennie E. Hewett Stns
Box 907670, Gainesville GA 30501-0911
(770) 519-0082; *Fax:*(770) 536-4103
Ownership: Bennie Hewett.
Radio Stns: 1 AM. 2 FM.
WRJX Jackson, AL; WBMH Grove Hill, AL; WHOD Jackson, AL;
Bennie E. Hewett, President

Benton-Weatherford Broadcasting Inc. of Tennessee
110 India Rd., Paris TN 38242
(731) 644-9455; *Fax:*(731) 644-9421
wmuf@bellsouth.net
Radio Stns: 2 AM. 2 FM.
WHDM McKenzie, TN; WRQR(AM) Paris, TN; WLZK Paris, TN; WMUF Henry, TN;
Gary Benton, President

Berkshire Broadcasting Corp.
WLAD(AM)/WDAQ(FM)/WREF(AM),198 Main St., Danbury CT 6810
(203) 744-4800; *Fax:*(203) 778-4655
www.98q.com,www.wlad.com,www.850wref.com
Radio Stns: 2 AM. 1 FM.
WLAD Danbury, CT; WAXB Ridgefield, CT; WDAQ Danbury, CT;
Irv Goldstein, President

Bernard Radio LLC
745 Fifth Ave., 18th Fl., New York NY 10151
(646) 720-9100;
Radio Stns: 5 AM. 2 FM.
KFCD Farmersville, TX; WGFT Campbell, OH; WASN Youngstown, OH; WVKO Columbus, OH; KHSE Wylie, TX; WRBP Hubbard, OH; WVKO-FM Johnstown, OH;

Best Broadcast Group
107 S. Main St., Brookfield MO 64628
(660) 258-3383; *Fax:*(660) 258-7307
www.bestbroadcastgroup.com
corporate@bestbroadcastgroup.com
Radio Stns: 3 AM. 3 FM.
KLTI Macon, MO; KFMZ Brookfield, MO; KFMZ(AM) Brookfield, MO; KMCR Montgomery City, MO; KZBK Brookfield, MO; KZZT Moberly, MO;
Phil Chirillo, President
Dale Palmer, Operations Dir

Bethesda Christian Broadcasting
Box 168, Rapid City SD 57709
(719) 481-0100; *Fax:*(719) 481-4649
www.klmp.com
bcbpres@aol.com
Ownership: Nonprofit bd of directors.
Radio Stns: 5 FM.
KTPT Rapid City, SD; KSLT Spearfish, SD; WPFF Sturgeon Bay, WI; WNLI Sturgeon Bay, WI; KLMP Rapid City, SD;
Mark Pluimer, President

Bible Broadcasting Network
11530 Carmel Commons Blvd., Charlotte NC 28226
(704) 523-5555; *Fax:*(704) 522-1967
www.bbnradio.org
Ownership: Nonprofit, non-stock corporation.
Radio Stns: 4 AM. 29 FM.
WYBY Cortland, NY; WYFN Nashville, TN; WYFQ Charlotte, NC; WKAL Rome, NY; KVSS Omaha, NE; KYFL Monroe, LA; KYFO-FM Ogden, UT; KYFP Palestine, TX; KYFS San Antonio, TX; KYFW Wichita, KS; WYFZ Belleview, FL; WYFA Waynesboro, GA; WYFB Gainesville, FL; WYFC Clinton, TN; WYFD Decatur, AL; WYFE Tarpon Springs, FL; WYFG Gaffney, SC; WYFH North Charleston, SC; WYFI Norfolk, VA; WYFJ Ashland, VA; WYFK Columbus, GA; WYFL Henderson, NC; WYFO Lakeland, FL; WYFP Harpswell, ME; WYFQ-FM Wadesboro, NC; WYFS Savannah, GA; WYFT Luray, VA; WYFU Masontown, PA; WYFV Cayce, SC; WYFW Winder, GA; WYBV Wakarusa, IN; KYFB Denison, TX; WYBH Fayetteville, NC;
Lowell Davey, President
Leo Galletta, Operations Manager

Bick Broadcasting Co.
Box 711,119 N. Third St., Hannibal MO 63401
(573) 221-3450; *Fax:*(573) 221-5331
www.979kickfm.com
kickfm@bickbroadcasting.com,979kickfm@nemonet.com
Ownership: Frank C. Bick, 46%; James P. Bick, 46%; James E. Janes, 8%.
Radio Stns: 3 AM. 3 FM.
KHMO Hannibal, MO; WLIQ Quincy, IL; KSIS Sedalia, MO; KICK-FM Palmyra, MO; KSDL Sedalia, MO; KXKX Knob Noster, MO;
James E. Janes, President

Bicoastal Media L.L.C.
140 N. Main St., Lake Port CA 94953
(707) 263-6113; *Fax:*(707) 263-0939
www.bicoastalmedia.com
Radio Stns: 19 AM. 28 FM.
KACI The Dalles, OR; KATA Arcata, CA; KBAM Longview, WA; KBBR North Bend, OR; KDAC Fort Bragg, CA; KEDO Longview, WA; KEJO Corvallis, OR; KELA Centralia-Chehalis, WA; KGOE Eureka, CA; KIHR Hood River, OR; KLLK Willits, CA; KLOO Corvallis, OR; KMED Medford, OR; KPNW Eugene, OR; KPOD Crescent City, CA; KTHH Albany, OR; KUKI Ukiah, CA; KWRO Coquille, OR; KXBX Lakeport, CA; KACI-FM The Dalles, OR; KOOS North Bend, OR; KBDN Bandon, OR; KCGB-FM Hood River, OR; KDUK-FM Florence, OR; KFLY Corvallis, OR; KFMI Eureka, CA; KKHB Eureka, CA; KIFS Ashland, OR; KLDZ Medford, OR; KLOO-FM Corvallis, OR; KNTI Lakeport, CA; KODZ Eugene, OR; KTEE North Bend, OR; KPOD-FM Crescent City, CA; KQPM Ukiah, CA; KJMX Reedsport, OR; KRED-FM Eureka, CA; KRKT-FM Albany, OR; KRQT Castle Rock, WA; KRWQ Gold Hill, OR; KSHR-FM Coquille, OR; KUKI-FM Ukiah, CA; KLYK Kelso, WA; KZZE Eagle Point, OR; KMSW The Dalles, OR; KPPK Rainier, OR; KMNT Chehalis, WA;
Ken Dennis, CEO
Mike Wilson, President

Big League Broadcasting LLC
3350 Peachtree Rd.,Suite 1610, Atlanta GA 30326-1040
(404) 467-1877; *Fax:*(404) 231-5923;
Radio Stns: 2 AM. 1 FM.
KFNS Wood River, IL; KQQZ Fairview Heights, IL; KFNS-FM Troy, MO;

Big River Broadcasting Corp.
624 Sam Phillips St., Florence AL 35630
(256) 764-8121; *Fax:*(256) 764-8169
www.wqlt.com,www.kix96country.com,www.wsbm.com
nmartin@bigriverbroadcasting.com
Radio Stns: 1 AM. 2 FM.
WSBM Florence, AL; WQLT-FM Florence, AL; WXFL Florence, AL;
Jerry Phillips, President
Knox Phillips, Operations Dir

Birach Broadcasting Corp.
21700 Northwestern Hwy.,Suite 1190, Southfield MI 48075
(248) 557-3500; *Fax:*(248) 557-3241
www.birach.com
sima@birach.com
Ownership: Sima Birach, 100%.
Radio Stns: 19 AM.
KTUV Little Rock, AR; KOLE Port Arthur, TX; KJMU Sand Springs, OK; WCND Shelbyville, KY; WCXN Claremont, NC; WGOP Pocomoke City, MD; WEW St. Louis, MO; WIJR Highland, IL; WKGE Johnstown, PA; WMFN Zeeland, MI; WMJH Rockford, MI; WNWI Oak Lawn, IL; WNZK Dearborn Heights, MI; WPON Walled Lake, MI; WSDS Salem Township, MI; WTOR Youngstown, NY; WWCS Canonsburg, PA; WCXI Fenton, MI; WDMV Walkersville, MD;
Sima Birach, President

Birch Broadcasting Corp.
11971 Glenmore Dr., Coral Springs FL 33071-7806
(954) 323-8531;
Radio Stns: 2 AM. 2 FM.
KXLQ Indianola, IA; WSHV South Hill, VA; WLUS-FM Clarksville, VA; WKSK-FM South Hill, VA;

Black Crow Media Group LLC
126 W. International Speedway Blvd., Daytona Beach FL 32114
(386) 255-9300;
Radio Stns: 5 AM. 17 FM.
WJAK Jackson, TN; WLOR Huntsville, AL; WNDB Daytona Beach, FL; WQHL Live Oak, FL; WVLD Valdosta, GA; WAHR Huntsville, AL; WCJX Five Points, FL; WKAA Willacoochee, GA; WFKX Henderson, TN; WVGA Lakeland, GA; WHHM-FM Henderson, TN; WHOG-FM Ormond-By-The-Sea, FL; WKRO-FM Port Orange, FL; WRTT-FM Huntsville, AL; WQHL-FM Live Oak, FL; WQPW Valdosta, GA; WSTI-FM Quitman, GA; WVYB Holly Hill, FL; WWRQ-FM Valdosta, GA; WWYN McKenzie, TN; WZDQ Humboldt, TN; WXHT Madison, FL;
Mike Linn, CEO

Black Media Works Inc.
1150 W. King St., Cocoa FL 32922
(321) 632-1000; *Fax:*(321) 636-0000;
Radio Stns: 3 FM.
KAYT Jena, LA; WJFP Fort Pierce, FL; WJCB Clewiston, FL;
Kimberly Holman Kassis, President

Blakeney Communications Inc.
Box 6408, Laurel MS 39441
(601) 649-0095; *Fax:*(601) 649-8199
www.b95country.com
b95@b95country.com
Radio Stns: 4 FM.
WBBN Taylorsville, MS; WKZW Sandersville, MS; WXHB Richton, MS; WXRR Hattiesburg, MS;
Larry Blakeney, CEO

Bliss Communications Inc.
Box 5001,One S. Parker Dr., Janesville WI 53547-5001
(608) 754-3311; *Fax:*(608) 754-8038
www.wclo.com; www.wjvl.com

sbliss@gazetteextra.com
Ownership: Bliss Communications, Inc

Radio Stns: 3 AM. 1 FM.
WBKV West Bend, WI; WCLO Janesville, WI; WRJN Racine, WI; WBWI-FM West Bend, WI;
Sidney Bliss, President/CEO

Blount Communications Group
8 Lawrence Rd., Derry NH 03038
(603) 437-9337; *Fax:*(603) 434-1035
www.lifechangingradio.com
warv@aol.com
Ownership: William A. Blount, Deborah C. Blount.

Radio Stns: 5 AM. 1 FM.
WARV Warwick, RI; WDER Derry, NH; WFIF Milford, CT; WNEB Worcester, MA; WVNE Leicester, MA; WBCI Bath, ME;
William Blount, President
Deborah Blount, EVP
David Young, VP

Blue Ridge Radio Inc.
312 Robin Rd., Mount Airy NC 27030
(336) 786-4498; *Fax:*(336) 789-7792;

Radio Stns: 3 AM. 1 FM.
WPAQ Mount Airy, NC; WSYD Mount Airy, NC; WWWJ Galax, VA; WBRF Galax, VA;
Earlene Epperson, President
Ralph Epperson, Operations Dir
John Mullins, Chief Engineer

Blueberry Broadcasting LLC
Box 2600, Kennebunkport ME 4046
(207) 967-8094;

Radio Stns: 3 AM. 11 FM.
WAEI Bangor, ME; WFAU Gardiner, ME; WRKD Rockland, ME; WABK-FM Gardiner, ME; WBAK Belfast, ME; WTQX Boothbay Harbor, ME; WIGY Madison, ME; WVQM Augusta, ME; WKSQ Ellsworth, ME; WLKE Bar Harbor, ME; WQSS Camden, ME; WTOS-FM Skowhegan, ME; WVOM Howland, ME; WBFB Bangor, ME;
Louis Vitali, CEO

Bold Gold Media Group LP
575 Grove St., Honesdale PA 18431
(570) 253-1616; *Fax:*(570) 253-6297
www.boldgoldmedia.com
vbenedetto@boldgoldmedia.com

Radio Stns: 4 AM. 4 FM.
WICK Scranton, PA; WBWX(AM) Berwick, PA; WPSN Honesdale, PA; WYCK Plains, PA; WDNH-FM Honesdale, PA; WWRR Scranton, PA; WDNB Jeffersonville, NY; WYCY Hawley, PA;
Robert VanDerneyden, COO
Vince Benedetto, President

Bolland Enterprises LLC
403 Capital St., Lewiston ID 83501
(208) 743-6564; *Fax:*(208) 798-0110;

Radio Stns: 1 FM.
KVAB Clarkston, WA;

Bonneville International Corporation
Broadcast House,Box 1160, Salt Lake City UT 84110-1160
(801) 575-7500; *Fax:*(801) 575-7521
www.bonnint.com
Ownership: Deseret Management Corp. Deseret Management Corp. owns The Deseret Morning News, a Salt Lake City, UT, daily.

Radio Stns: 8 AM. 21 FM.
KIRO Seattle, WA; KMVP Phoenix, AZ; KTTH Seattle, WA; KSL Salt Lake City, UT; KTAR Phoenix, AZ; WBQH(AM) Silver Spring, MD; WFED Washington, DC; WWFD Frederick, MD; KIRO-FM Tacoma, WA; KSWD Los Angeles, CA; KTAR-FM Glendale, AZ; KPKX Phoenix, AZ; KSL-FM Midvale, UT; KRSP-FM Salt Lake City, UT; KSFI Salt Lake City, UT; WTOP-FM Washington, DC; WIL-FM St. Louis, MO; WARH Granite City, IL; WKRQ Cincinnati, OH; WYGY Fort Thomas, KY; WDRV Chicago, IL; WWDV Zion, IL; WILV Chicago, IL; WTMX Skokie, IL; WWWT-FM Manassas, VA; WUBE-FM Cincinnati, OH; WXOS East St. Louis, IL; WTLP Braddock Heights, MD; WYGY(FM) Fort Thomas, KY;

TV Stns: 1 TV.
KSL-TV Salt Lake City, UT;
Robert Johnson, COO
Bruce Reese, President

Border Media Partners LLC
201 Main St.,Suite 2001, Fort Worth TX 76102
(817) 335-5999; *Fax:*(817) 335-1197
www.bmpradio.com

Radio Stns: 8 AM. 14 FM.
KLGO Austin, TX; KLNT Laredo, TX; KSAH Universal City, TX; KSOX Raymondville, TX; KTSA San Antonio, TX; KURV Edinburg, TX; KVJY Pharr, TX; KZDC San Antonio, TX; KTXX-FM Dripping Springs, TX; KBDR Mirando City, TX; KLEY-FM Jourdanton, TX; KESO South Padre Island, TX; KBUC Raymondville, TX; KJAV Alamo, TX; KXBT Leander, TX; KVLR Elgin, TX; KTFM Floresville, TX; KNEX Laredo, TX; KJXK San Antonio, TX; KWOW Clifton, TX; KZSP South Padre Island, TX; KSAH-FM Pearsall, TX;

Bott Radio Network
10550 Barkley St.,Suite 100, Overland Park KS 66212
(913) 642-7770; *Fax:*(913) 642-1319
www.bottradionetwork.com
comments@bottradionetwork.com
Ownership: Richard P. Bott Sr.

Radio Stns: 12 AM. 22 FM.
KAMI Cozad, NE; KCCV Overland Park, KS; KJRG Newton, KS; KLEX Lexington, MO; KMOZ Rolla, MO; KOFC Fayetteville, AR; KQCV Oklahoma City, OK; KSIV Clayton, MO; WCRT Donelson, TN; WCRV Collierville, TN; WFCV Fort Wayne, IN; KBCV Hollister, MO; KSCV Springfield, MO; KCVN Cozad, NE; KARF Independence, KS; KAYH Fayetteville, AR; KAYX Richmond, MO; KTAA Big Sandy, TX; KMCV High Point, MO; KBMP Enterprise, KS; KCCV-FM Olathe, KS; KCIV Mount Bullion, CA; KCRL Sunrise Beach, MO; KCVT Silver Lake, KS; KCVW Kingman, KS; KLCV Lincoln, NE; KLTE Kirksville, MO; KQCV-FM Shawnee, OK; KSIV-FM St. Louis, MO; KTFC Sioux City, IA; KTFG Sioux Rapids, IA; KJCV-FM Country Club, MO; KKCV Rozel, KS; KCGR Oran, MO;
Trace Thurlby, COO
Richard Bott Sr., President
Tom Holdeman, CFO
Richard Bott II, EVP

Bravo Mic Communications LLC
101 Perkins Dr., Las Cruces NM 88005
(505) 527-1111; *Fax:*(505) 527-1100;

Radio Stns: 1 AM. 3 FM.
KOBE Las Cruces, NM; KMVR Mesilla Park, NM; KXPZ Las Cruces, NM; KVLC Hatch, NM;

Brazos Communications West LLC
1240 E. Villa Maria Rd., Bryan TX 77802
(432) 520-9912; *Fax:*(432) 520-0112
Ownership: C & J Woodcock LP, 60%; Tommy R. Vascocu, 40%.

Radio Stns: 3 FM.
KHKX Odessa, TX; KMCM Odessa, TX; KQRX Midland, TX;
John Moesch, General Manager

Brazos Valley Communications Ltd.
1240 E. Villa Maria Rd., Bryan TX 77802
(979) 776-1240; *Fax:*(979) 776-0123
brazosradio.com
Ownership: Brazos Valley Communications GP LLC, 100% votes, 10% equity; Tommy R. Vascocu, 24% equity.

Radio Stns: 1 AM. 4 FM.
KTAM Bryan, TX; KJXJ Franklin, TX; KAPN Caldwell, TX; KORA-FM Bryan, TX; KBXT Wixon Valley, TX;
Chris Kiske, VP/gen mgr

Brewer Broadcasting Corp.
1305 Carter St., Chattanooga TN 37402
(423) 265-9494; *Fax:*(423) 266-2335
www.BrewerMediaGroup.com
jlb@brewerradio.com

Radio Stns: 1 AM. 5 FM.
WHON Centerville, IN; WPLZ Ooltewah, TN; WALV-FM Lakesite, TN; WJTT Red Bank, TN; WMPZ Harrison, TN; WQLK Richmond, IN;
James Brewer Sr., President

Bristol Broadcasting Co. Inc.
Box 1389, Bristol VA 24203
(276) 669-8112; *Fax:*(276) 669-0541
Ownership: Lisa Nininger Hale, 100%.

Radio Stns: 8 AM. 11 FM.
WDXR Paducah, KY; WNGO Mayfield, KY; WKYX Paducah, KY; WPAD Paducah, KY; WBES Charleston, WV; WVTS Dunbar, WV; WFHG Bristol, VA; WVTS(AM) Charleston, WV; WFHG-FM Bluff City, TN; WTZR Elizabethton, TN; WVTS-FM Dunbar, WV; WLLE Mayfield, KY; WDDJ Paducah, KY; WKYX-FM Golconda, IL; WAEZ Greeneville, TN; WQQR Clinton, KY; WKYQ Paducah, KY; WLNQ-FM Newport, TN; WXBQ-FM Bristol, VA;
W.L. Nininger, President

Broadcast Communications Inc.
Box 990, Greensburg PA 15601
(724) 853-7000;

Radio Stns: 4 AM. 1 FM.
WANB Waynesburg, PA; WKFB Jeannette, PA; WKHB Irwin, PA; WCMD Cumberland, MD; WKVE Mount Pleasant, PA;
Robert Stevens, President
Ashley Stevens, Operations Dir

Broadcast South LLC
1931 Ga. Hwy. 32 East, Douglas GA 31533
(912) 389-0995; *Fax:*(912) 383-8552;

Radio Stns: 3 AM. 4 FM.
WBHB Fitzgerald, GA; WDMG Douglas, GA; WHJD Hazlehurst, GA; WDMG-FM Ambrose, GA; WKZZ Tifton, GA; WRDO Fitzgerald, GA; WVOH-FM Nicholls, GA;
John Higgs, President

Brooke Communications Inc.
1445 W. Harvard Ave., Roseburg OR 97470
(541) 672-6641; *Fax:*(541) 673-7598;

Radio Stns: 2 AM. 3 FM.
KQEN Roseburg, OR; KSKR Roseburg, OR; KSKR-FM Sutherlin, OR; KKMX Tri City, OR; KRSB-FM Roseburg, OR;
Mike Carter, Operations Dir
Patrick Markham, General Manager
David Hansen, General Sales Mgr

Brothers Broadcasting Corp.
Box D, Rensselaer IN 47978
(219) 866-4104; *Fax:*(219) 866-5106
wirn@ffni.com

Radio Stns: 1 FM.
WIBN Earl Park, IN;
John Balvich, General Manager

Bryan Broadcasting Corp.
Box 3248, Bryan TX 77805-3248
(979) 695-9595; *Fax:*(979) 695-1933
bryanbroadcasting.com
Ownership: William R. Hicks, 89%; Ben D. Downs, 11%.

Radio Stns: 4 AM. 2 FM.
KAGC Bryan, TX; WTAW College Station, TX; KWBC Navasota, TX; KZNE College Station, TX; KNDE College Station, TX; KPWJ(FM) Madisonville, TX;
William R. Hicks, President
Ben D. Downs, VP

Buck Owens Productions Inc.
3223 Sillect, Bakersfield CA 93308
(661) 326-1011; *Fax:*(661) 328-7503
Ownership: Buck Owens Revocable Trust II (Michael Owens and Melvin L. Owens Jr., co-trustees), 100%.

Radio Stns: 1 AM. 2 FM.
KUZZ Bakersfield, CA; KCWR Bakersfield, CA; KUZZ-FM Bakersfield, CA;

Buckley Broadcasting Corp.
166 West Putnam Ave., Greenwich CT 06830
(203) 661-4307; *Fax:*(203) 622-7341
www.buckleyradio.com
rbuckley@buckleyradio.com
Ownership: Steven Buckley; Dana Buckley; Constance Buckley; Martha Fahnoe

Radio Stns: 9 AM. 10 FM.
KIDD Monterey, CA; KNZR Bakersfield, CA; WFBL Syracuse, NY; WDRC Hartford, CT; WSEN Baldwinsville, NY; WMMW Meriden, CT; WOR New York, NY; WSNG Torrington, CT; WWCO Waterbury, CT; KHTN Planada, CA; KIOO Porterville, CA; KKBB Bakersfield, CA; KLLY Oildale, CA; KYZZ Salinas, CA; KSMJ Shafter, CA; KSEQ Visalia, CA; KUBB Mariposa, CA; KWAV Monterey, CA; WDRC-FM Hartford, CT;
Joseph Bilotta, COO
Richard Buckley, President

Buddy Tucker Association Inc.
Box 63, Mobile AL 36601
(386) 738-1348; *Fax:*(251) 432-1396;

Radio Stns: 3 AM.
WTOF Bay Minette, AL; WMOB Mobile, AL; WYND Deland, FL;

Burbach Broadcasting Group
100 Ryan Ct.,Suite 98, Pittsburgh PA 15205
(412) 489-1001; *Fax:*(412) 278-1002
Ownership: Estate of John L. Laubach Jr., Nicholas A. Galli, chmn/pres.

Radio Stns: 3 AM. 7 FM.
WADC Parkersburg, WV; WXKX Clarksburg, WV; WVNT Parkersburg, WV; WHBR-FM Parkersburg, WV; WOBG-FM Salem, WV; WRZZ Parkersburg, WV; WGYE Mannington, WV; WGIE Clarksburg, WV; WXIL Elizabeth, WV; WGGE Parkersburg, WV;

Nicholas Galli, President
Nicholas Galli, General Manager
Thomas Bayer, VP Finance

Burt Broadcasting Inc.
Box 1848, Alamogordo NM 88311
(505) 434-1414; *Fax:*(505) 434-2213
burtbroadcasting@charter.net
Radio Stns: 1 AM. 3 FM.
KINN Alamogordo, NM; KYEE Alamogordo, NM; KZZX Alamogordo, NM; KQEL Alamogordo, NM;
Bill Burt, General Manager

BusinessTalkRadio.Net Inc.
Box 4826, Greenwich CT 06831-9998
(203) 323-7300; *Fax:*(203) 323-7302
businesstalkradio.net
Radio Stns: 4 AM.
KNUU Paradise, NV; WXBR Brockton, MA; WLFP Braddock, PA; WGCH Greenwich, CT;
Michael Metter, CEO

Bustos Media Holdings L.L.C.
5110 S.E. Stark St., Portland OR 97215
(503) 234-5550; *Fax:*(503) 234-5550
www.bustosmedia.com
contact@bustosmedia.com
Ownership: Bustos Asset Management LLC, 100%. Note: Group also owns translator stn K228EU Portland, OR rebroadcasting KXET(AM) Portland, OR.
Radio Stns: 11 AM. 3 FM.
KGDD Oregon City, OR; KSZN(AM) Gresham, OR; KREH Pecan Grove, TX; KDYM Sunnyside, WA; KOOR Milwaukie, OR; KZSJ San Martin, CA; KTXV Mabank, TX; KTXW Manor, TX; KRYN(AM) Gresham, OR; KQRR(AM) Mount Angel, OR; KXET(AM) Portland, OR; KKHI Kihei, HI; KTTA(FM) Jackson, CA; KZZR Government Camp, OR;
Amador S. Bustos, Chairman

Butler County Radio Network Inc.
112 Hollywood Dr.,Suite 203, Butler PA 16001
(724) 287-5778; *Fax:*(724) 282-9188
www.insidebutlercountry.com
Radio Stns: 2 AM. 1 FM.
WBUT Butler, PA; WISR Butler, PA; WLER-FM Butler, PA;
Scott Briggs, Operations Dir
Vicki Hinterberger, General Manager
Ron Willison, Programming Director
Bill Davis, News Director

Calvary Evangelistic Mission Inc.
Box 367000, San Juan PR 00936-7000
(787) 724-1190; *Fax:*(787) 722-5395
www.therockradio.org
radio@therockradio.org
Radio Stns: 3 AM.
WBMJ San Juan, PR; WCGB Juana Diaz, PR; WIVV Island of Vieques, PR;
Nila Luttrell, CFO
Ruth Lutterall, President
Janet Luttrell, General Manager

Cameron Broadcasting Inc.
1615 Orange Tree Ln.,Suite 102, Redlands CA 92374
(909) 793-2233; *Fax:*(909) 798-6984
""kflg947.com; lucky98fm.com; theknack107.com""
Radio Stns: 3 AM. 3 FM.
KAAA Kingman, AZ; KZZZ Bullhead City, AZ; KFLG Bullhead City, AZ; KLUK Needles, CA; KFLG-FM Big River, CA; KNKK Needles, CA;
William Jaeger, CEO
Don Jaeger, Operations Dir

Canfin Enterprises Inc.
Box 3498, Abilene TX 79604
(325) 672-5442; *Fax:*(325) 672-6128
radioabilene.com
info@radioabilene.com
Radio Stns: 2 AM. 1 FM.
KZQQ Abilene, TX; KWKC Abilene, TX; KKHR Abilene, TX;

Canxus Broadcasting Corp.
152 E. Green Ridge Rd., Caribou ME 04736-3737
(207) 473-7513; *Fax:*(207) 472-3221
www.channelxradio.com
Radio Stns: 3 FM.
WCXU Caribou, ME; WCXX Madawaska, ME; WCXV Van Buren, ME;

Capital Community Broadcasting Inc.
360 Egan Dr., Juneau AK 99801-1748
(907) 586-1670; *Fax:*(907) 586-3612;
Radio Stns: 3 FM.
KRNN Juneau, AK; KXLL Juneau, AK; KTOO Juneau, AK;
TV Stns: 1 TV.
KTOO-TV Juneau, AK;

Capital Media Corp.
30 Park Ave., Cohoes NY 12047-3330
(518) 237-1330; *Fax:*(518) 235-4468
www.whaz.com
info@whaz.com
Radio Stns: 1 AM. 4 FM.
WHAZ Troy, NY; WBAR-FM Lake Luzerne, NY; WMNV Rupert, VT; WMYY Schoharie, NY; WHAZ-FM Hoosick Falls, NY;
Steve Klob, Operations Dir
Paul Lotters, General Manager

Capitol Broadcasting Co. Inc.
Box 12000, Raleigh NC 27605
(919) 821-8555; *Fax:*(919) 821-8733
www.cbc-raleigh.com
Ownership: Capitol Holding Co. Inc.
Radio Stns: 1 AM. 8 FM.
WMFD Wilmington, NC; WUIN Oak Island, NC; WCMC-FM Holly Springs, NC; WRMR(FM) Jacksonville, NC; WKXB Boiling Spring Lakes, NC; WRAL Raleigh, NC; WILT Wilmington, NC; WAZO Southport, NC; WLQC Sharpsburg, NC;
TV Stns: 4 TV.
WMYT-TV Rock Hill, SC; WJZY Belmont, NC; WRAL-TV Raleigh, NC; WRAZ Raleigh, NC;
James R. Hefner, III, VP, TV
Michael D. Hill, VP/General Counsel
Daniel P. McGrath, Vp/CFO
James Goodmon, President
Vicke S. Murray, Secretary

Capps Broadcast Group
2003 N.W. 56th Dr., Pendleton OR 97801
(541) 276-1511; *Fax:*(541) 276-1480;
Radio Stns: 3 AM. 3 FM.
KTEL Walla Walla, WA; KTIX Pendleton, OR; KUMA Pendleton, OR; KUMA-FM Pilot Rock, OR; KWHT Pendleton, OR; KWRL La Grande, OR;
Randy McKone, General Manager

CapSan Media LLC
277 Bendix Rd.,Suite 411, Virginia Beach VA 23452
(757) 497-1415; *Fax:*(757) 497-2560
www.capsanmedia.com
Radio Stns: 4 FM.
WFMZ Hertford, NC; WZPR Nags Head, NC; WVOD Manteo, NC; WYND-FM Hatteras, NC;

Carlson Communications International
3606 S. 500 W., Salt Lake City UT 84115
(801) 262-5624; *Fax:*(801) 266-1510;
Radio Stns: 3 AM. 2 FM.
KDYL South Salt Lake, UT; KTSN Elko, NV; KCPX Spanish Valley, UT; KCYN Moab, UT; KRJC Elko, NV;
Ralph J. Carlson, President

Carolina Christian Radio
Box 957, Wilmington NC 28402
(910) 763-2452; *Fax:*(910) 763-6578
www.life905.com
life@life905.com
Radio Stns: 3 AM. 3 FM.
WLSG Wilmington, NC; WSFM Carolina Beach, NC; WWIL Wilmington, NC; WDVV Wilmington, NC; WWIL-FM Wilmington, NC; WZDG Scotts Hill, NC;
Jim Stephens, President

Carroll Broadcasting Co.
1119 E. Plaza Dr., Carroll IA 51401
(712) 792-4321; *Fax:*(712) 792-6667
www.carrollbroadcasting.com
Radio Stns: 1 AM. 2 FM.
KCIM Carroll, IA; KIKD Lake City, IA; KKRL Carroll, IA;
Mary Collison, President

Carroll Enterprises Inc.
Box 549, Tawas City MI 48764
(989) 362-3417; *Fax:*(989) 362-4544
www.wkjc.com
wkjc@wkjc.com
Radio Stns: 1 AM. 2 FM.
WIOS Tawas City-East Tawa, MI; WKJC Tawas City, MI; WKJZ Hillman, MI;
John Carroll Jr., General Manager

Carroll Stations
Box 271, Kemmerer WY 83101
(307) 877-0000; *Fax:*(307) 877-5524;
Radio Stns: 3 AM. 3 FM.
KEVA Evanston, WY; KTHE Thermopolis, WY; KWUD Woodville, TX; KDNO Thermopolis, WY; KTRZ Riverton, WY; KWYW Lost Cabin, WY;
Jimmy Carroll, President

Carter Broadcast Group Inc.
11131 Colorado Ave., Kansas City MO 64137
(816) 763-2040; *Fax:*(816) 966-1055;
Radio Stns: 1 AM. 1 FM.
KPRT Kansas City, MO; KPRS Kansas City, MO;
Michael Carter, President

Catholic Radio Network Inc.
201 N. Industrial Park Rd., Excelsior Springs MO 64024-1736
(816) 630-1090;
Radio Stns: 4 AM. 1 FM.
KEXS Excelsior Springs, MO; KFEL Pueblo, CO; KPIO Loveland, CO; KAHS El Dorado, KS; KEXS-FM Ravenwood, MO;
James O'Laughlin, President

CBS Radio
1515 Broadway, 46th Fl., New York NY 10036
(212) 846-3939
www.cbsradio.com
Ownership: Viacom Inc., 100%. Note: Viacom Inc. also owns the CBS Television Stations Group (see listing under TV Group Ownership, Section B).
Radio Stns: 34 AM. 97 FM.
KCBS San Francisco, CA; KDKA Pittsburgh, PA; KFWB Los Angeles, CA; KHTK Sacramento, CA; KIKK Pasadena, TX; KILT Houston, TX; KMOX St. Louis, MO; KPTK Seattle, WA; KNX Los Angeles, CA; KRLD Dallas, TX; KYDZ North Las Vegas, NV; KRAK Hesperia, CA; KXNT North Las Vegas, NV; KZDG(AM) San Francisco, CA; KYW Philadelphia, PA; WAOK Atlanta, GA; WBBM Chicago, IL; WBCN Charlotte, NC; WBCN(AM) Charlotte, NC; WBZ Boston, MA; WCBS New York, NY; WCCO Minneapolis, MN; WFAN New York, NY; WFNZ Charlotte, NC; WINS New York, NY; WIP Philadelphia, PA; WJZ Baltimore, MD; WSCR Chicago, IL; WNEW Morningside, MD; WPHT Philadelphia, PA; WHFS(AM) Seffner, FL; WTIC Hartford, CT; WWJ Detroit, MI; WXYT Detroit, MI; KFRC-FM San Francisco, CA; KEZK-FM St. Louis, MO; KEZN Palm Desert, CA; KMVQ-FM San Francisco, CA; KFRG San Bernardino, CA; KVFG Victorville, CA; KHMX Houston, TX; KKHH Houston, TX; KILT-FM Houston, TX; KINK Portland, OR; KITS San Francisco, CA; KLLC San Francisco, CA; KLOL Houston, TX; KLSX Rozet, WY; KLUC-FM Las Vegas, NV; KLUV Dallas, TX; KMLE Chandler, AZ; KMPS-FM Seattle, WA; KMXB Henderson, NV; KXNT-FM Henderson, NV; KNCI Sacramento, CA; KMVK Fort Worth, TX; KOOL-FM Phoenix, AZ; KEGY(FM) San Diego, CA; KJKK Dallas, TX; KROQ-FM Pasadena, CA; KRTH Los Angeles, CA; KSFM Woodland, CA; KTWV Los Angeles, CA; KUFO-FM Portland, OR; KCMD Grants Pass, OR; KUPL Portland, OR; KVIL Highland Park-Dallas, TX; KXFG Sun City, CA; KXTE Pahrump, NV; KJAQ Seattle, WA; KYKY St. Louis, MO; KYMX Sacramento, CA; KRLD-FM Dallas, TX; KYXY San Diego, CA; KZOK-FM Seattle, WA; KZON Phoenix, AZ; KZZO Sacramento, CA; WIAD Bethesda, MD; WBAV-FM Gastonia, NC; WBBM-FM Chicago, IL; WBMX Boston, MA; WXXF(FM) Pittsburgh, PA; WCBS-FM New York, NY; WCFS-FM Elmwood Park, IL; WDOK Cleveland, OH; WDSY-FM Pittsburgh, PA; WEAT West Palm Beach, FL; WNEW(FM) Bowie, MD; WIRK Indiantown, FL; WJFK-FM Manassas, VA; WJHM Daytona Beach, FL; WJMK Chicago, IL; WXYT-FM Detroit, MI; WLIF Baltimore, MD; WLLD Lakeland, FL; WMBX Jensen Beach, FL; WNCX Cleveland, OH; WWFS New York, NY; WNKS Charlotte, NC; WOCL Deland, FL; WODS Boston, MA; WOGL Philadelphia, PA; WOMC Detroit, MI; WOMX-FM Orlando, FL; WIRK(FM) Indiantown, FL; WPEG Concord, NC; WPGC-FM Morningside, MD; WQAL Cleveland, OH; WJZ-FM Catonsville, MD; WQYK-FM St. Petersburg, FL; WRBQ-FM Tampa, FL; WRCH New Britain, CT; WLLD(FM) Lakeland, FL; WSOC-FM Charlotte, NC; WKQC Charlotte, NC; WUSN Chicago, IL; WDZH Detroit, MI; WWMX Baltimore, MD; KZJK St. Louis Park, MN; WXRK New York, NY; WXRT Chicago, IL; WYCD Detroit, MI; WYSP Dushore, PA; WYUU Safety Harbor, FL; WZGC Atlanta, GA; WKRK-FM Cleveland Heights, OH; WZLX Boston, MA; WZMX Hartford, CT; WBZZ(FM) New Kensington, PA; WUUB Jupiter, FL; WAXY-FM West Palm Beach, FL;
Ken O'Keefe, EVP
Clancy Woods, SVP
Brian Ongaro, SVP

CBS Television Stations Group
524 W. 57th St., 3rd Fl., New York NY 10019

(212) 975-4321
cbslocal.com
Ownership: Viacom Inc., 100%.

Radio Stns: 1 AM.
KCAL Redlands, CA;

TV Stns: 30 TV.
KBCW San Francisco, CA; KCAL Redlands, CA; KCBS-TV Los Angeles, CA; KCCO-TV Alexandria, MN; KCCW-TV Walker, MN; KCNC-TV Denver, CO; KDKA-TV Pittsburgh, PA; KMAX-TV Sacramento, CA; KOVR Stockton, CA; KPIX-TV San Francisco, CA; KSTW Tacoma, WA; KTVT Fort Worth, TX; KTXA Fort Worth, TX; KYW-TV Philadelphia, PA; WBBM-TV Chicago, IL; WBFS-TV Miami, FL; WBZ-TV Boston, MA; WCBS-TV New York, NY; WCCO-TV Minneapolis, MN; WFOR-TV Miami, FL; WGNT Portsmouth, VA; WJZ-TV Baltimore, MD; WKBD-TV Detroit, MI; WPCW Jeannette, PA; WPSG Philadelphia, PA; WSBK-TV Boston, MA; WTOG St. Petersburg, FL; WUPA Atlanta, GA; WUPL Slidell, LA; WWJ-TV Detroit, MI;
Tom Kane, President

Cenla Broadcasting Co. Inc.
1115 Texas Ave., Alexandria LA 71301
(318) 445-1234; *Fax:*(318) 473-1960
www.cenlabroadcasting.com

Radio Stns: 2 AM. 4 FM.
KDBS Alexandria, LA; KSYL Alexandria, LA; KKST Oakdale, LA; KQID-FM Alexandria, LA; KRRV-FM Alexandria, LA; KZMZ Alexandria, LA;
Taylor Thompson, President

Centennial Broadcasting LLC
3443 Robinhood Rd.,Suite H, Winston-Salem NC 27106
(336) 794-7971;

Radio Stns: 4 FM.
WLNI Lynchburg, VA; WZZK(FM) Bedford, VA; WZZU Lynchburg, VA; WVMP Vinton, VA;

Center Broadcasting Co. Inc.
307 San Augustine St., Center TX 75935
(936) 598-3304; *Fax:*(936) 598-9537;

Radio Stns: 1 AM. 2 FM.
KDET Center, TX; KDET-FM San Augustine, TX; KQBB Center, TX;
Lori Alvis, General Manager

Central Wisconsin Broadcasting Inc.
Box 387,1201 E. Division St., Neillsville WI 54456
(715) 743-3333; *Fax:*(715) 743-2288
1075therock.com
1075therock@tds.net

Radio Stns: 1 AM. 2 FM.
WCCN Neillsville, WI; WCCN-FM Neillsville, WI; WPKG Neillsville, WI;
J. Kevin Grap, General Manager

Cessna Communications Inc.
Box 1, Bedford PA 15522
(814) 623-1000; *Fax:*(814) 623-9692
cesscomm@earthlink.net

Radio Stns: 2 AM. 2 FM.
WHJB Bedford, PA; WBFD Bedford, PA; WAYC-FM Bedford, PA; WBVE Bedford, PA;
Jay Cessna, President
John H. Cessna, Operations Dir

Chaparral Communications
Box 100, Jackson WY 83001
(307) 733-2120; *Fax:*(307) 733-4760
www.jacksonholeradio.com
jacksonholeradio@onewest.net
Ownership: Jerrold Lundquist.

Radio Stns: 3 AM. 8 FM.
KPOW Powell, WY; KSGT Jackson, WY; KWYS West Yellowstone, MT; KJAX Jackson, WY; KECH-FM Sun Valley, ID; KWMY Joliet, MT; KMTN Jackson, WY; KSKI-FM Sun Valley, ID; KZJH Jackson, WY; KYZK Sun Valley, ID; KLZY Honokaa, HI;
Scott Anderson, General Manager

Charles A. Hecht and Alfredo Alonso Stns
16 Doe Run, Pittstown NJ 8867
(908) 730-7959; *Fax:*(908) 730-7408
hechtassoc@sprintmail.com

Radio Stns: 1 AM.
WRME Hampden, ME;

Cherry Creek Radio LLC
501 S. Cherry St.,Suite 480, Denver CO 80246
(303) 468-6500; *Fax:*(303) 468-6555
www.cherrycreekradio.com
jschwartz@cherrycreekradio.com

Radio Stns: 21 AM. 40 FM.
KBLG Billings, MT; KBLL Helena, MT; KBLJ La Junta, CO; KCAP Helena, MT; KCOM Comanche, TX; KDXU St. George, UT; KEYZ Williston, ND; KGRZ Missoula, MT; KROP Brawley, CA; KLMR Lamar, CO; KMON Great Falls, MT; KONA Kennewick-Richland-P, WA; KUNF Washington, UT; KSTV Stephenville, TX; KSUB Cedar City, UT; KTAN Sierra Vista, AZ; KUBC Montrose, CO; KZNW Wenatchee, WA; KXTL Butte, MT; KYLT Missoula, MT; KOWL South Lake Tahoe, CA; KAAK Great Falls, MT; KAAR Butte, MT; KTHN La Junta, CO; KBLL-FM Helena, MT; KSNN-FM Ridgway, CO; KCIN Cedar City, UT; KXFF Colorado City, AZ; KRZN Billings, MT; KGGL Missoula, MT; KHKR-FM East Helena, MT; KKXK Montrose, CO; KLFM Great Falls, MT; KVVR Dutton, MT; KMBR Butte, MT; KMON-FM Great Falls, MT; KONA-FM Kennewick, WA; KREC Brian Head, UT; KRKX Billings, MT; KRLT South Lake Tahoe, CA; KLMR-FM Lamar, CO; KIYK Saint George, UT; KXBN Cedar City, UT; KSTV-FM Dublin, TX; KTHC Sidney, MT; KWCD Bisbee, AZ; KWWW-FM Quincy, WA; KAAP Rock Island, WA; KXDR Pinesdale, MT; KYOX Comanche, TX; KYSN East Wenatchee, WA; KURL(FM) Billings, MT; KYYZ Williston, ND; KZHR Dayton, WA; KZMK Sierra Vista, AZ; KZMT Helena, MT; KZOQ-FM Missoula, MT; KWWX Cashmere, WA; KXDR(FM) Pinesdale, MT; KOYT(FM) Alberton, MT; KOYT(FM) Montana City, MT;
Joe Schwartz, CEO
Dennis Goodman, Operations Dir
Dan Gittings, General Sales Mgr

Chesapeake-Portsmouth Broadcasting Corp.
2202 Jolliff Rd., Chesapeake VA 23321
(757) 488-1010;

Radio Stns: 5 AM.
WBOB Jacksonville, FL; WLES Bon Air, VA; WLVA Lynchburg, VA; WTJZ Newport News, VA; WRJR Claremont, VA;

Christian Broadcasting System Ltd.
29200 Vassar Dr. Ste.150, Livonia MI 48152
(248) 477-4600; *Fax:*(248) 477-6911;

Radio Stns: 5 AM. 3 FM.
WDJO(AM) Florence, KY; WCGW Nicholasville, KY; WLCM Holt, MI; WSNL Flint, MI; WCVX Cincinnati, OH; WJIV Cherry Valley, NY; WJMM-FM Keene, KY; WVKY Shelbyville, KY;
Jon Yinger, CEO
Ralph Van Luven, Operations Dir
Sally Van Luven, Secretary
Vicky Yinger, Treasurer

Christian Listening Network Inc.
996 Helen St., Fayetteville NC 28303
(910) 864-5028; *Fax:*(910) 864-6270;

Radio Stns: 2 FM.
WCLN-FM Clinton, NC; WZKB Wallace, NC;

Christian Ministries of the Valley
2720 West Business Highway 83, Weslaco TX 78596
(956) 968-7777;

Radio Stns: 1 FM.
KMRV San Isidro, TX;
Enrique Garza, General Manager

Christian Voice of Central Ohio Inc.
Box 793, New Albany OH 43054
(614) 855-9171; *Fax:*(614) 855-9280;

Radio Stns: 1 AM. 3 FM.
WTKI Huntsville, AL; WCVO Gahanna, OH; WZCP Chillicothe, OH; WZWP West Union, OH;
Drenda Keesee, Chairman
Dan Baughman, President

Churchill Communications LLC
871 Country Club Rd., Eugene OR 97401
(541) 344-5500; *Fax:*(541) 485-2550;

Radio Stns: 3 AM.
KLZS Eugene, OR; KXPD Tigard, OR; KXOR Junction City, OR;

Clancy-Mance Communications
199 Wealtha Ave., Watertown NY 13601
(315) 782-1240; *Fax:*(315) 782-0312
Ownership: Jack Clancy, David Mance.

Radio Stns: 1 AM. 2 FM.
WCDO Sidney, NY; WLYK Cape Vincent, NY; WCDO-FM Sidney, NY;
David Mance, President
John Clancy, Treasurer

Clarion County Broadcasting Corp.
1168 Greenville Pike, Clarion PA 16214-0688
(814) 226-4500; *Fax:*(814) 226-5898
www.clarioncountydailynews.com
clarionradio@comcast.net

Radio Stns: 2 AM. 2 FM.
WKQW Oil City, PA; WWCH Clarion, PA; WCCR Clarion, PA; WKQW-FM Oil City, PA;
William S. Hearst, President

Clarke Broadcasting Corp.
1175 Fairview Dr.,Suite N, Carson City NV 89701
(775) 887-0588; *Fax:*(775) 887-1752;

Radio Stns: 1 AM. 2 FM.
KVML Sonora, CA; KKBN Twain Harte, CA; KZSQ-FM Sonora, CA;
H. Randolph Holder, President
Larry England, General Manager

Claro Communications Ltd.
11737 Nelon Dr., Corpus Christi TX 78410
(361) 774-4354; *Fax:*(361) 241-7945;

Radio Stns: 3 AM. 4 FM.
KBRN Boerne, TX; KROB Robstown, TX; KOPY Alice, TX; KMZZ Bishop, TX; KOPY-FM Alice, TX; KUKA San Diego, TX; KGGB Yorktown, TX;

Classic Communications Inc.
Box 1600, Woodward OK 73802-1600
(580) 256-1450; *Fax:*(580) 254-9102;

Radio Stns: 1 AM. 2 FM.
KSIW Woodward, OK; KWDQ Woodward, OK; KWFX Woodward, OK;
Sherre House, President
Bret Brewer, Operations Dir

Clear Channel Communications Inc.
200 E. Basse Rd., San Antonio TX 78209
(210) 822-2828; *Fax:*(210) 822-2299
www.clearchannel.com
Ownership: CC Media Holdings Inc., 100%.

Radio Stns: 259 AM. 576 FM.
KNEW(AM) Oakland, CA; KABQ Albuquerque, NM; KHTY Bakersfield, CA; KAKC Tulsa, OK; KQNT Spokane, WA; KASI Ames, IA; KATZ St. Louis, MO; KTPI Mojave, CA; KBME Houston, TX; KBMR Bismarck, ND; KBTM Jonesboro, AR; KCBL Fresno, CA; KCJB Minot, ND; KTDD San Bernardino, CA; KIIX Fort Collins, CO; KCQL Aztec, NM; KCSJ Pueblo, CO; KXNO Des Moines, IA; KENI Anchorage, AK; KPOJ Portland, OR; KEX Portland, OR; KFAB Omaha, NE; KTCN Minneapolis, MN; KFBK Sacramento, CA; KFI Los Angeles, CA; KFIV Modesto, CA; KFXN Minneapolis, MN; KGME Phoenix, AZ; KFYR Bismarck, ND; KCCY(AM) Pueblo, CO; KFYI Phoenix, AZ; KGMY Springfield, MO; KTSM El Paso, TX; KYHN Ft. Smith, AR; KHHO Tacoma, WA; KBFP Bakersfield, CA; KHOW Denver, CO; KHVH Honolulu, HI; KFBX Fairbanks, AK; KCOL Wellington, CO; KIKI(AM) Honolulu, HI; KWSX Stockton, CA; KJR Seattle, WA; KKDD San Bernardino, CA; KKSF Oakland, CA; KKXL Grand Forks, ND; KLAC Los Angeles, CA; KLTC Dickinson, ND; KFXR Dallas, TX; KLVI Beaumont, TX; WBHA Wabasha, MN; KMNS Sioux City, IA; KNEA Jonesboro, AR; KNEW Oakland, CA; KNRS Salt Lake City, UT; KNST Tucson, AZ; KOA Denver, CO; KOGA Ogallala, NE; KOGO San Diego, CA; KOY Phoenix, AZ; KLSD San Diego, CA; KPRC Houston, TX; KTBZ Tulsa, OK; KVNS Brownsville, TX; KRDU Dinuba, CA; KRRZ Minot, ND; KKTX Corpus Christi, TX; KRZR Visalia, CA; KSEN Shelby, MT; KSSK Honolulu, HI; KSTE Rancho Cordova, CA; KTKR San Antonio, TX; KKZN Thornton, CO; KMJM Cedar Rapids, IA; KTOK Oklahoma City, OK; KTRH Houston, TX; KHEY El Paso, TX; KION Salinas, CA; KTZN Anchorage, AK; KTZR Tucson, AZ; KPTQ Spokane, WA; KUNO Corpus Christi, TX; KEZL(AM) Visalia, CA; KVET Austin, TX; KFAN Rochester, MN; KWHN Fort Smith, AR; KWSL Sioux City, IA; KWTX Waco, TX; KXEW South Tucson, AZ; KXIC Iowa City, IA; KXMR Bismarck, ND; KTLK Los Angeles, CA; WAAX Gadsden, AL; WACT Tuscaloosa, AL; WAEB Allentown, PA; WALK Patchogue, NY; WDDV Venice, FL; WAVZ New Haven, CT; WZTA Vero Beach, FL; WBBD Wheeling, WV; WYNF Augusta, GA; WBEX Chillicothe, OH; WBHP Huntsville, AL; WBIZ Eau Claire, WI; WJNO West Palm Beach, FL; WCAO Baltimore, MD; WCCF Punta Gorda, FL; WCHI Chillicothe, OH; WCHO Washington Ct House, OH; WTKS Savannah, GA; WSAI Cincinnati, OH; WCOH Newnan, GA; WCOS Columbia, SC; WCWA Toledo, OH; WHNZ Tampa, FL; WDAK Columbus, GA; WLBY Saline, MI; WDFN Detroit, MI; WDIA Memphis, TN; WDIZ Panama City, FL; WDOV Dover, DE; WDUZ Green Bay, WI; WHJA Laurel, MS; WELI New Haven, CT; WJIP Ellenville, NY; WENE Endicott, NY; WERC Birmingham, AL; WLFJ Greenville, SC; WYHL Meridian, MS; WYTS Columbus, OH; WFLA Tampa, FL; WFOR Hattiesburg, MS; WGRB Chicago, IL; WPKX(AM) Rochester, NH; WGIR Manchester, NH; WGST Atlanta, GA; WNRR North Augusta, SC; WGVL Greenville, SC; WGY Schenectady, NY; WHAM Rochester, NY; WHAS Louisville, KY; WMXF Waynesville, NC; WHEN Syracuse, NY; WHJJ Providence, RI; WHLO Akron, OH; WHO Des Moines, IA; WHOS Decatur, AL; WHP Harrisburg, PA;

RADIO - U.S.

WVON Berwyn, IL; WHTK Rochester, NY; WHUC Hudson, NY; WHYN Springfield, MA; WIBA Madison, WI; WILM Wilmington, DE; WIMA Lima, OH; WKCI Waynesboro, VA; WINR Binghamton, NY; WINZ Miami, FL; WIOD Miami, FL; WISN Milwaukee, WI; WIZE Springfield, OH; WJBO Baton Rouge, LA; WWTX Wilmington, DE; WJDX Jackson, MS; WJDY Salisbury, MD; WBZT West Palm Beach, FL; WJYZ Albany, GA; WSAN Allentown, PA; WKBN Youngstown, OH; WKBO Harrisburg, PA; WKCY Harrisonburg, VA; WKDW Staunton, VA; WVHU Huntington, WV; WSFE Burnside, KY; WKII Solana, FL; WKIP Poughkeepsie, NY; WKJK Louisville, KY; WXKS Newton, MA; WKRC Cincinnati, OH; WLAC Nashville, TN; WLAN Lancaster, PA; WLAP Lexington, KY; WIBB Macon, GA; WFXN Moline, IL; WHNK Parkersburg, WV; WLW Cincinnati, OH; WMAN Mansfield, OH; WMEQ Menomonie, WI; WSHE Columbus, GA; WMMB Melbourne, FL; WMMV Cocoa, FL; WMRE Charlestown, WV; WMRN Marion, OH; WMT Cedar Rapids, IA; WKBZ Muskegon, MI; WVCC Hogansville, GA; WMYF Portsmouth, NH; WNCO Ashland, OH; WNDE Indianapolis, IN; WNLS Tallahassee, FL; WTOC Newton, NJ; WNNZ Westfield, MA; WKMQ Tupelo, MS; WNTM Mobile, AL; WXVA Winchester, VA; WFXJ Jacksonville, FL; WOAI San Antonio, TX; WOC Davenport, IA; WODT New Orleans, LA; WOKY Milwaukee, WI; WONE Dayton, OH; WONW Defiance, OH; WOOD Grand Rapids, MI; WHAL Phenix City/Columbus, AL; WPOP Hartford, CT; WFLF Pine Hills, FL; WRAK Williamsport, PA; WRAW Reading, PA; WREC Memphis, TN; WRKK Hughesville, PA; WPLA(AM) Dry Branch, GA; WRNL Richmond, VA; WPLA Dry Branch, GA; WNIO Youngstown, OH; WRVA Richmond, VA; WCKY Cincinnati, OH; WXBT Columbia, SC; WSFC Somerset, KY; WLRO Denham Springs, LA; WSOK Savannah, GA; WSDV Sarasota, FL; WSPD Toledo, OH; WQLX Chillicothe, OH; WSYR Syracuse, NY; WTAG Worcester, MA; WTAM Cleveland, OH; WTCR Kenova, WV; WTGM Salisbury, MD; WTKA Ann Arbor, MI; WTKG Grand Rapids, MI; WWTF Georgetown, KY; WARF Akron, OH; WOFX Troy, NY; WTSO Madison, WI; WTUP Tupelo, MS; WTVN Columbus, OH; WPEK Fairview, NC; WXBT(AM) Columbia, SC; WTKT Harrisburg, PA; WKRD Louisville, KY; WWNC Asheville, NC; WYGM Orlando, FL; WBGG Pittsburgh, PA; WWVA Wheeling, WV; WKOX Everett, MA; WYCL Niles, OH; WYLD New Orleans, LA; WLTP Marietta, OH; WDTW Dearborn, MI; KAGG Madisonville, TX; KAJA San Antonio, TX; KAKQ-FM Fairbanks, AK; KHGE Fresno, CA; KASE-FM Austin, TX; KASH-FM Anchorage, AK; KAZX Kirtland, NM; KXJM Banks, OR; KBCO Boulder, CO; KBFM Edinburg, TX; KBFX Anchorage, AK; KBIG-FM Los Angeles, CA; KBKS-FM Tacoma, WA; KNFX-FM Bryan, TX; KBOS-FM Tulare, CA; KBPI Denver, CO; KCAD Dickinson, ND; KCCQ Ames, IA; KCCY-FM Pueblo, CO; KCDA Post Falls, ID; KBGO Waco, TX; KXSC(FM) Sunnyvale, CA; KCQQ Davenport, IA; KDAG Farmington, NM; KHKN Maumelle, AR; KDMX Dallas, TX; KDON-FM Salinas, CA; KDWB-FM Richfield, MN; KDZA-FM Pueblo, CO; KEEY-FM St. Paul, MN; KISO Omaha, NE; KEGL Fort Worth, TX; KESZ Phoenix, AZ; KEZA Fayetteville, AR; KALZ Fowler, CA; KFIN Jonesboro, AR; KFMQ Gallup, NM; KFSO-FM Visalia, CA; KFXR-FM Chinle, AZ; KGB-FM San Diego, CA; KGBX-FM Nixa, MO; KFBK-FM Sacramento, CA; KGGI Riverside, CA; KGLI Sioux City, IA; KSME Greeley, CO; KGLX Gallup, NM; KNST-FM Green Valley, AZ; KSWF Aurora, MO; KGOR Omaha, NE; KGOT Anchorage, AK; KHFI-FM Georgetown, TX; KPTT Denver, CO; KHKS Denton, TX; KHTS-FM El Cajon, CA; KHYL Auburn, CA; KIAK-FM Fairbanks, AK; KXBG Cheyenne, WY; KIIS-FM Los Angeles, CA; KIIZ-FM Killeen, TX; KIOC Orange, TX; KIOI San Francisco, CA; KIOZ San Diego, CA; KZHT Salt Lake City, UT; KISQ San Francisco, CA; KIYS Walnut Ridge, AR; KIZZ Minot, ND; KHLX Pollock Pines, CA; KIGL Seligman, MO; KJKJ Grand Forks, ND; KJMS Olive Branch, MS; KMYI San Diego, CA; KJR-FM Seattle, WA; KJSN Modesto, CA; KHHT Los Angeles, CA; KKBW Eatonville, WA; KKCW Beaverton, OR; KBFP-FM Delano, CA; KKDM Des Moines, IA; KKED Fairbanks, AK; KWHF Harrisburg, AR; KKFG Bloomfield, NM; KKIX Fayetteville, AR; KLTH Lake Oswego, OR; KKLI Widefield, CO; KQOL Sleepy Hollow, WY; KDNN Honolulu, HI; KMRQ Riverbank, CA; KKMY Orange, TX; KTHR Wichita, KS; KKRQ Iowa City, IA; KKRW Houston, TX; KKRZ Portland, OR; KKYS Bryan, TX; KKZX Spokane, WA; KTBZ-FM Houston, TX; KLFX Nolanville, TX; KLOU St. Louis, MO; KTEG Santa Fe, NM; KMAG Fort Smith, AR; KMCX-FM Ogallala, NE; KMEL San Francisco, CA; KMFX-FM Lake City, MN; KMJM-FM Columbia, IL; KMJX Conway, AR; KNBQ Centralia, WA; KMOD-FM Tulsa, OK; KIZS Collinsville, OK; KUSS(FM) Carlsbad, CA; KMXA-FM Minot, ND; KDRB Des Moines, IA; KMXF Lowell, AR; KMXG Clinton, IA; KKBD Sallisaw, OK; KMXP Phoenix, AZ; KMXR Corpus Christi, TX; KNCN Sinton, TX; KIXZ-FM Opportunity, WA; KNIX-FM Phoenix, AZ; KTBT Broken Arrow, OK; KOCN Pacific Grove, CA; KODA Houston, TX; KODJ Salt Lake City, UT; KOGA-FM Ogallala, NE; KOHT Marana, AZ; KHLR Benton, AR; KOLZ Cheyenne, WY; KPHT Rocky Ford, CO; KOSO Patterson, CA; KVVS Rosamond, CA; KOST Los Angeles, CA; KOSY-FM Spanish Fork, UT; KPAW Fort Collins, CO; KPEK Albuquerque, NM; KPEZ Austin, TX; KPRR El Paso, TX; KIBT Fountain, CO; KDJE Jacksonville, AR; KQDY Bismarck, ND; KQHT Crookston, MN; KTGX Owasso, OK; KQOD Stockton, CA; KPLV Las Vegas, NV; KQQL Anoka, MN; KBRU Oklahoma City, OK; KQXT-FM San Antonio, TX; KRAB Greenacres, CA; KRBB Wichita, KS; KRCH Rochester, MN; KRFX Denver, CO; KTOM-FM Marina, CA; KRQQ Tucson, AZ; KRVE Brusly, LA; KRYS-FM Corpus Christi, TX; KZCH Derby, KS; KSAB Robstown, TX; KSD St. Louis, MO; KSEZ Sioux City, IA; KSFT-FM South Sioux City, NE; KRPT Devine, TX; KSLZ St. Louis, MO; KDFO Delano, CA; KSNE-FM Las Vegas, NV; KSNR Fisher, MN; KSOF Dinuba, CA; KSSK-FM Waipahu, HI; KSSN Little Rock, AR; KSSS Bismarck, ND; KLQT Corrales, NM; KTCL Wheat Ridge, CO; KTCZ-FM Minneapolis, MN; KBQI Albuquerque, NM; KTEX Mercedes, TX; KCOL-FM Groves, TX; KHKZ San Benito, TX; KQXX-FM Mission, TX; KFFF Bennington, NE; KPRC-FM Salinas, CA; KTOZ-FM Pleasant Hope, MO; KSRY Tehachapi, CA; KTRA-FM Farmington, NM; KTSM-FM El Paso, TX; KTST Oklahoma City, OK; KDGE Fort Worth-Dallas, TX; KUBE Seattle, WA; KUCD Pearl City, HI; KTMY Coon Rapids, MN; KVDU Houma, LA; KJMY Bountiful, UT; KUUL East Moline, IL; KVET-FM Austin, TX; KVUU Pueblo, CO; KMIY Tucson, AZ; KWNR Henderson, NV; KWTX-FM Waco, TX; KXKT Glenwood, IA; KQJK Roseville, CA; KXTC Thoreau, NM; KXUS Springfield, MO; KXXM San Antonio, TX; KXXY-FM Oklahoma City, OK; KYKR Beaumont, TX; KYLD San Francisco, CA; KYMG Anchorage, AK; KYOT-FM Phoenix, AZ; KYSR Los Angeles, CA; KPTL Ankeny, IA; KYYX Minot, ND; KYYY Bismarck, ND; KZBB Poteau, OK; KZEP-FM San Antonio, TX; KZIN-FM Shelby, MT; KZPR Minot, ND; KZPS Dallas, TX; KZRR Albuquerque, NM; KZRX Dickinson, ND; KZSN Hutchinson, KS; KZZP Mesa, AZ; WACL Elkton, VA; WACO-FM Waco, TX; WWKZ Okolona, MS; WAEV Savannah, GA; WBFA Fort Mitchell, AL; WAIL Key West, FL; WMTX Tampa, FL; WAMX Milton, WV; WAMZ Louisville, KY; WASH Washington, DC; WATQ Chetek, WI; WAXQ New York, NY; WAZR Woodstock, VA; WNCD Youngstown, OH; WBBI Endwell, NY; WBBQ-FM Augusta, GA; WBBS Fulton, NY; WBCT Grand Rapids, MI; WAGH Smiths, AL; WBGG-FM Fort Lauderdale, FL; WBIG-FM Washington, DC; WBVV Guntown, MS; WBIZ-FM Eau Claire, WI; WZRX-FM Fort Shawnee, OH; WBUL-FM Lexington, KY; WBVB Coal Grove, OH; WFKS(FM) Melbourne, FL; WBWZ New Paltz, NY; WBCK-FM Battle Creek, MI; WXXF Loudonville, OH; WCKT Lehigh Acres, FL; WCKY-FM Pemberville, OH; WCOL-FM Columbus, OH; WCTH Plantation Key, FL; WCTQ Sarasota, FL; WCTW Catskill, NY; WBFX Grand Rapids, MI; WCVU Solana, FL; WUBA High Springs, FL; WDAS-FM Philadelphia, PA; WDCG Durham, NC; WLTQ-FM Venice, FL; WDFM Defiance, OH; WMRN-FM Marion, OH; WDMX Vienna, WV; WDRM Decatur, AL; WRDX Smyrna, DE; WDVE Pittsburgh, PA; WBUV Moss Point, MS; WEBN Cincinnati, OH; WVKF Shadyside, OH; WEGR Arlington, TN; WEGW Wheeling, WV; WEND Salisbury, NC; WEOW Key West, FL; WERZ Exeter, NH; WESC-FM Greenville, SC; WESE Baldwyn, MS; WEZL Charleston, SC; WFBQ Indianapolis, IN; WKKJ Chillicothe, OH; WFKZ Plantation Key, FL; WMKS Clemmons, NC; WFQX Front Royal, VA; WFKS Melbourne, FL; WFSY Panama City, FL; WGAR-FM Cleveland, OH; WGCI-FM Chicago, IL; WGIR-FM Manchester, NH; WFXN-FM Galion, OH; WGMZ Glencoe, AL; WWVA-FM Canton, GA; WGSY Phenix City, AL; WHCN Hartford, CT; WHCY Blairstown, NJ; WHEB Portsmouth, NH; WLAU Heidelberg, MS; WHJY Providence, RI; WKDD Munroe Falls, OH; WNRW(FM) Salem, IN; WHRK Memphis, TN; WGY-FM Albany, NY; WVBZ High Point, NC; WHTZ Newark, NJ; WHYI-FM Fort Lauderdale, FL; WHYN-FM Springfield, MA; WIBA-FM Sauk City, WI; WIBB-FM Fort Valley, GA; WIMT Lima, OH; WIOQ Philadelphia, PA; WIOT Toledo, OH; WWWW-FM Ann Arbor, MI; WBLJ-FM Shamokin, PA; WVOR Canandaigua, NY; WVMA(FM) Norfolk, VA; WJDQ Meridian, MS; WHOF North Canton, OH; WJIZ-FM Albany, GA; WPGB Pittsburgh, PA; WISX Philadelphia, PA; WJKX Ellisville, MS; WJLB Detroit, MI; WJMN Boston, MA; WIHT Washington, DC; WJRR Cocoa Beach, FL; WUBT Russellville, KY; WFLA-FM Midway, FL; WMXY Youngstown, OH; WKCI-FM Hamden, CT; WKCY-FM Harrisonburg, VA; WKEE-FM Huntington, WV; WKFS Milford, OH; WKGB-FM Conklin, NY; WKGR Wellington, FL; WKGS Irondequoit, NY; WODC Ashville, OH; WKKT Statesville, NC; WKKV-FM Racine, WI; WWPW(FM) Atlanta, GA; WKNN-FM Pascagoula, MS; WKQI Detroit, MI; WKQQ Winchester, KY; WKSJ-FM Mobile, AL; WKSS Hartford-Meriden, CT; WHLH Jackson, MS; WKTU Lake Success, NY; WKWK-FM Wheeling, WV; WLAN-FM Lancaster, PA; WLDI Juno Beach, FL; WJJX Appomattox, VA; WLIT-FM Chicago, IL; WLKT Lexington-Fayette, KY; WLLK-FM Somerset, KY; WLLR-FM Davenport, IA; WRXR-FM Rossville, GA; WLND Signal Mountain, TN; WLQT Englewood, OH; WFMF Baton Rouge, LA; WRNW Milwaukee, WI; WLTW New York, NY; WLTY Cayce, SC; WMIA-FM Miami Beach, FL; WLVH Hardeeville, SC; WLKO Hickory, NC; WXXM Sun Prairie, WI; WMAG High Point, NC; WODX South Bristol Township, NY; WWMG Millbrook, AL; WMEQ-FM Menomonie, WI; WZLD Petal, MS; WMGF Mount Dora, FL; WGEX Bainbridge, GA; WMIL-FM Waukesha, WI; WMJI Cleveland, OH; WMJJ Birmingham, AL; WMJY Biloxi, MS; WWLG Peachtree City, GA; WMAD Cross Plains, WI; WMLX St. Marys, OH; WMMS Cleveland, OH; WMMX Dayton, OH; WCGX Dublin, OH; WMRR Muskegon Heights, MI; WMRV-FM Endicott, NY; WMSI-FM Jackson, MS; WOOD-FM Muskegon, MI; WHLK Cleveland, OH; WMXC Mobile, AL; WMXD Detroit, MI; WQNQ Fletcher, NC; WMXL Lexington, KY; WMXW Vestal, NY; WMYI Hendersonville, NC; WBYL Salladasburg, PA; WUCL Newton, MS; WMZQ-FM Washington, DC; WBBG Niles, OH; WNCI Columbus, OH; WNCO-FM Ashland, OH; WNDH Napoleon, OH; WNIC Dearborn, MI; WNNJ Newton, NJ; WNOE-FM New Orleans, LA; WNOK Columbia, SC; WNSL Laurel, MS; WNUA Chicago, IL; WNUS Belpre, OH; WQBW Honeoye Falls, NY; WOBB Tifton, GA; WZFT Baltimore, MD; WOGB Kaukauna, WI; WGMI(FM) Thomasville, GA; WOLZ Fort Myers, FL; WSRW-FM Grand Rapids, MI; WKZP Bethany Beach, DE; WZJZ Port Charlotte, FL; WHAL-FM Horn Lake, MS; WDXB Jasper, AL; WOWI Norfolk, VA; WPAP-FM Panama City, FL; WFLF-FM Parker, FL; WUBL Atlanta, GA; WPCK Denmark, WI; WKST-FM Pittsburgh, PA; WUCS Windsor Locks, CT; WJBT Callahan, FL; WSHE-FM Fort Lauderdale, FL; WPOC Baltimore, MD; WPYX Albany, NY; WQBZ Fort Valley, GA; WQEN Trussville, AL; WQIK-FM Jacksonville, FL; WJDX-FM Kosciusko, MS; WHLW Luverne, AL; WQLH Green Bay, WI; WQMF Jeffersonville, IN; WQNS Waynesville, NC; WBTT Naples Park, FL; WQOL Vero Beach, FL; WQRB Bloomer, WI; WTFX-FM Clarksville, IN; WQSO Rochester, NH; WQUE-FM New Orleans, LA; WQYZ Ocean Springs, MS; WRBT Harrisburg, PA; WRBV Warner Robins, GA; WRBTJ Richmond, VA; WJJS Roanoke, VA; WRDU Knightdale, NC; WDSD Dover, DE; WRFQ Mount Pleasant, SC; WRFX Kannapolis, NC; WRFY-FM Reading, PA; WRKH Mobile, AL; WRLX West Palm Beach, FL; WPCH Gray, GA; WRNO-FM New Orleans, LA; WRNQ Poughkeepsie, NY; WRNX Amherst, MA; WROV-FM Martinsville, VA; KFXN-FM Minneapolis, MN; WRQK-FM Canton, OH; WKSL Cary, NC; WRTR Brookwood, AL; WRVB Marietta, OH; WRVE Schenectady, NY; WRVF Toledo, OH; WRVQ Richmond, VA; WRVV Harrisburg, PA; WRVW Lebanon, TN; WRWD-FM Highland, NY; WRXL Richmond, VA; WKSP Aiken, SC; WRZX Indianapolis, IN; WSBY-FM Salisbury, MD; WKEQ Somerset, KY; WRUM Orlando, FL; WEBZ Mexico Beach, FL; WMUS Muskegon, MI; WSIX-FM Nashville, TN; WUMX Rome, NY; WSNE-FM Taunton, MA; WSNX-FM Muskegon, MI; WSOL-FM Brunswick, GA; WVRZ Mount Carmel, PA; WSRS Worcester, MA; WSRZ-FM Coral Cove, FL; WSSL-FM Gray Court, SC; WSCC-FM Goose Creek, SC; WBTP Clearwater, FL; WSTH-FM Alexander City, AL; WSTZ-FM Vicksburg, MS; WSUS Franklin, NJ; WSVO Staunton, VA; WCDG(FM) Moyock, NC; WSWR Shelby, OH; WTAK-FM Hartselle, AL; WFUS Gulfport, FL; WTCR-FM Huntington, WV; WLGX Louisville, KY; WZCR Hudson, NY; WRWB-FM Ellenville, NY; WVKY(FM) Shelbyville, KY; WWPR-FM New York, NY; WTKS-FM Cocoa Beach, FL; WTKX-FM Pensacola, FL; WPKF Poughkeepsie, NY; WTNT-FM Tallahassee, FL; WAKZ Sharpsville, PA; WTQR Winston-Salem, NC; WRVA-FM Wake Forest, NC; WTRY-FM Rotterdam, NY; WTUE Dayton, OH; WTVR-FM Richmond, VA; WTXT Fayette, AL; WSKX York Center, ME; WKSC-FM Chicago, IL; WUSL Philadelphia, PA; WFFX Hattiesburg, MS; WUSY Cleveland, TN; WPRW-FM Martinez, GA; WVAZ Oak Park, IL; WVKS Toledo, OH; WQRV Meridianville, AL; WOLF-FM DeRuyter, NY; WDVI Rochester, NY; WVRK Columbus, GA; WVRT Mill Hall, PA; WMAX-FM Holland, MI; WWBB Providence, RI; WMAN-FM Fredericktown, OH; WWDC Washington, DC; WWFG Ocean City, MD; WWHT Syracuse, NY; WBXX Marshall, MI; WZZR Riviera Beach, FL; WHQC Shelby, NC; WWSW-FM Pittsburgh, PA; WWYZ Waterbury, CT; WSEK Burnside, KY; WWZD-FM New Albany, MS; WKKF Ballston Spa, NY; WXDX-FM Pittsburgh, PA; WXEG Beavercreek, OH; WXKS-FM Medford, MA; WXLY North Charleston, SC; WPTI Eden, NC; WXSR Quincy, FL; WXTB Clearwater, FL; WKSI-FM Stephens City, VA; WDUZ-FM Brillion, WI; WXXL Tavares, FL; WQSR Baltimore, MD; WBZY Bowdon, GA; WYLD-FM New Orleans, LA; WTZB Englewood, FL; WYNK-FM Baton Rouge, LA; WYNT Caledonia, OH; WRFF Philadelphia, PA; WYYD Amherst, VA; WKZB Marion, MS; WYYY Syracuse, NY; WBWR Hilliard, OH; WZBQ Carrollton, AL; WZHT Troy, AL; WZKS Union, MS; WMGP Hogansville, GA; WEKL Augusta, GA; WZOM Defiance, OH; WMGE Miami Beach, FL; WRIT-FM Milwaukee, WI; WZZO Bethlehem, PA; WAVW Stuart, FL; KMYT Temecula, CA; WDTW-FM Detroit, MI; KTMQ Temecula, CA; WBKS Columbus Grove, OH; WMRZ Dawson, GA; KKSY-FM Cedar Rapids, IA;

Bob Pittman, CEO
John Hogan, CEO, Clear Channel Media and Entertainment
Herbert W. Hill, Senior VP
Kenneth E. Wyker, Senior VP

Coast Radio Company Inc.
600 E. Main St., Vacaville CA 95688
(707) 446-0200; *Fax:*(707) 446-0122;

Radio Stns: 3 FM.

KKDV Walnut Creek, CA; KKIQ Livermore, CA; KUIC Vacaville, CA;

Coastal Broadcasting Systems Inc.
3208 Pacific Ave., Wildwood NJ 8260
(609) 522-1987; *Fax:*(609) 522-3666;

Radio Stns: 3 FM.
WIBG-FM Avalon, NJ; WJSE North Cape May, NJ; WCZT Villas, NJ;
Bill Huf, President

Cochise Broadcasting LLC
Box 11060, Jackson WY 83002
(703) 812-0482;

Radio Stns: 2 AM. 7 FM.
KCUZ Clifton, AZ; KOMJ Omaha, NE; KCDQ Douglas, AZ; KFMM Thatcher, AZ; KKYZ Sierra Vista, AZ; KWYX Casper, WY; KWXR Reliance, WY; KXZK Vail, AZ; KZXK Doney Park, AZ;

Codcomm Inc.
24 Fairview Dr., Southborough MA 01772
(617) 261-6000
Ownership: John H. Garabedian, 100% votes.

Radio Stns: 2 FM.
WPXC Hyannis, MA; WHYA(FM) Mashpee, MA;
John H. Garabedian, Chairman

Cohan Radio Group Inc.
3750 US 27N,Suite 1, Sebring FL 33870
(863) 382-9999; *Fax:*(863) 382-1982
www.cohanradiogroup.com
cohanradiogroup@htn.net

Radio Stns: 3 AM. 2 FM.
WITS Sebring, FL; WJCM Sebring, FL; WWTK Lake Placid, FL; WWLL Sebring, FL; WWOJ Avon Park, FL;
Peter Coughlin, President

College Creek Media LLC
980 N. Michigan Ave.,Suite 1875, Chicago IL 60611
(312) 204-9900;

Radio Stns: 20 FM.
KCLS Leeds, UT; KLWA Westport, WA; KRPX Wellington, UT; KADQ-FM Evanston, WY; KPHD Elko, NV; KMXM(FM) Helena Valley N, MT; KQPI Aberdeen, ID; DKEAU Hilo, HI; KYLI Bunkerville, NV; KYEN Severance, CO; KXNC Ness City, KS; KXJO St. Maries, ID; KKDT Burdett, KS; KHUN Huntington, UT; KHSK Allen, NE; KEMR Castle Dale, UT; KDVC Loma, CO; KRPW(FM) Coarsegold, CA; KAYF Bayfield, CO; KPAU Center, CO;

Combined Communications
Box 5037, Bend OR 97708
(541) 382-5263; *Fax:*(541) 388-0456
www.klrr.com,www.thetwins.com
mcheney@bendradio.com

Radio Stns: 1 AM. 3 FM.
KBND Bend, OR; KLRR Redmond, OR; KTWS Bend, OR; KMTK Bend, OR;
Chuck Chackel, President

Combined Media Group Inc.
Box 789, Wynne AR 72396
(870) 238-8141; *Fax:*(870) 238-5997;

Radio Stns: 2 AM.
KPOC Pocahontas, AR; KRLW Walnut Ridge, AR;
Tim Scott, General Manager

Commonwealth Broadcasting Corp.
113 W. Public Sq.,Suite 400, Glasgow KY 42141
(270) 659-2002; *Fax:*(270) 651-1771;

Radio Stns: 8 AM. 13 FM.
WGRK Jeffersontown, KY; WWKU Plum Springs, KY; WIEL Elizabethtown, KY; WLUE Eminence, KY; WLBN Lebanon, KY; WPKY Princeton, KY; WTCO Campbellsville, KY; WTTL Madisonville, KY; WYSB Springfield, KY; WAVJ Princeton, KY; WCKQ Campbellsville, KY; WGRK-FM Greensburg, KY; WHHT Horse Cave, KY; WWKY Providence, KY; WRZI Hodgenville, KY; WLSK Lebanon, KY; WKMO Lebanon Junction, KY; WOVO Glasgow, KY; WHHT(FM) Cave City, KY; WTHX Vine Grove, KY; WTTL-FM Madisonville, KY;

TV Stns: 1 TV.
WABG-TV Greenwood, MS;
Steven Newberry, CEO
W. Dale Thornhill, President

Communications Capital Managers LLC
1111 Michigan Ave.,Suite 301, East Lansing MI 48823-1096
(517) 351-3333; *Fax:*(517) 351-4481;

Radio Stns: 2 AM. 3 FM.
KRUS Ruston, LA; WUBR Baton Rouge, LA; KPCH Ruston, LA; KNBB Dubach, LA; KXKZ Ruston, LA;
Deb Grugen, CFO
Michael Oesterle, CEO

Communications Corp. of the Americas Inc.
Box 2128, Rock Springs WY 82902
(307) 362-3793; *Fax:*(307) 362-8727
www.wyoradio.com

Radio Stns: 1 AM. 3 FM.
KRKK Rock Springs, WY; KSIT Rock Springs, WY; KQSW Rock Springs, WY; KMRZ-FM Superior, WY;

Communicom Broadcasting LLC
220 Josephine St.,Suite 200, Denver CO 80206
(303) 759-8481;

Radio Stns: 3 AM.
KXEG Phoenix, AZ; KXXT Tolleson, AZ; WLVJ Boynton Beach, FL;

Community Broadcasters LLC
199 Wealtha Ave., Watertown NY 13601
(315) 782-1240;

Radio Stns: 2 AM. 7 FM.
WATN Watertown, NY; WSLB Ogdensburg, NY; WLFK Gouverneur, NY; WEFX Henderson, NY; WQTK Ogdensburg, NY; WTOJ Carthage, NY; WBDR Copenhagen, NY; WOTT Calcium, NY; KYLF Adrian, MO;

Conner Media Corp.
702 Hartness Rd., Statesville NC 28677
(704) 878-9004;

Radio Stns: 3 AM. 2 FM.
WEGG Rose Hill, NC; WJNC Jacksonville, NC; WAVQ Jacksonville, NC; WZUP La Grange, NC; WSTK Aurora, NC;
Ronald Benfield, President

Connoisseur Media LLC
136 Main St.,Suite 202, Westport CT 06880-3304
(203) 227-1978; *Fax:*(203) 227-2373
www.connoisseurmedia.com

Radio Stns: 2 AM. 16 FM.
WFNN Erie, PA; WJET Erie, PA; KBBX-FM Nebraska City, NE; KIBB Haven, KS; WXBB Erie, PA; WIHN Normal, IL; WRKT North East, PA; WRTS Erie, PA; WXBW Gallipolis, OH; WTWF Fairview, PA; WBBE Heyworth, IL; WMGA Kenova, WV; KVWF Augusta, KS; KPLN Lockwood, MT; KPBR Poplar Bluff, MO; KICL(FM) Pleasantville, IA; KXMZ Box Elder, SD; KKBO Flasher, ND;
Jeffrey Warshaw, CEO
Michael Driscoll, President

Contemporary Communications
9408 Grand Gate St., Las Vegas NV 89143
(702) 898-4669; *Fax:*(208) 567-6865
www.radioguys.net
contemporary@cox.net

Radio Stns: 1 AM. 2 FM.
WROX Clarksdale, MS; KKHJ-FM Pago Pago, AS; WKXY Merigold, MS;
Larry Fuss, President

Convergent Broadcasting LP
826 S. Padre Island Drive, Corpus Christi TX 78416
(361) 814-3800; *Fax:*(361) 855-3770;

Radio Stns: 2 FM.
KKPN Rockport, TX; KPUS Gregory, TX;
Bruce Danziger, President
John Hiatt, Operations Dir

Coon Valley Communications Inc.
2260 141st Dr., Perry IA 50220
(507) 643-0065;

Radio Stns: 1 AM. 2 FM.
KDLS Perry, IA; KGRA Jefferson, IA; KKRF Stuart, IA;

Coshocton Broadcasting Co.
114 N. Sixth St., Coshocton OH 43812
(740) 622-1560; *Fax:*(740) 622-7940
Ownership: Bruce Wallace, 100%.

Radio Stns: 1 AM. 1 FM.
WTNS Coshocton, OH; WKLM Millersburg, OH;
Bruce Wallace, President
Randy Wallace, General Manager

Costa-Eagle Radio Ventures L.P.
462 Merrimack St., Methuen MA 1844
(978) 686-9966; *Fax:*(978) 687-1180
pcosta@ceradio.com

Radio Stns: 3 AM.
WNNW Lawrence, MA; WCEC Haverhill, MA; WCCM Salem, NH;

Country Mountain Airwaves LLC
1491 W. Thatcher Blvd., Safford AZ 85546-3306
(928) 428-2217;

Radio Stns: 1 AM. 3 FM.
KRVZ Springerville, AZ; KQAZ Springerville, AZ; KTHQ Eagar, AZ; KJIK Duncan, AZ;

Covenant Network
4424 Hampton Ave., St. Louis MO 63109
(314) 752-7000; *Fax:*(314) 752-7702
www.covenantnet.net

Radio Stns: 5 AM. 3 FM.
KHOJ St. Charles, MO; WCKW Garyville, LA; WIHM Taylorville, IL; WRMS Beardstown, IL; WRYT Edwardsville, IL; KBKC Moberly, MO; WHOJ Terre Haute, IN; WOLG Carlinville, IL;
John Anthony Holman, President

Cox Media Group
6205 Peachtree Dunwoody Rd., Atlanta GA 30328
(678) 645-0000; *Fax:*(678) 645-5002
www.coxmediagroup.com
Ownership: Cox Enterprises Inc., 100%.

Radio Stns: 1 FM.
WHIO-FM Pleasant Hill, OH;

TV Stns: 13 TV.
KFOX-TV El Paso, TX; KICU-TV San Jose, CA; KIRO-TV Seattle, WA; KRXI-TV Reno, NV; KTVU Oakland, CA; WAXN-TV Kannapolis, NC; WFTV Orlando, FL; WJAC-TV Johnstown, PA; WPXI Pittsburgh, PA; WRDQ Orlando, FL; WSB-TV Atlanta, GA; WSOC-TV Charlotte, NC; WTOV-TV Steubenville, OH;
Doug Franklin, Chairman
Bill Hoffman, EVP
Jane Williams, SVP

Cox Radio Inc.
6205 Peachtree Dunwoody Rd., Atlanta GA 30328
(678) 645-0000; *Fax:*(678) 645-5002
www.coxmediagroup.com
Ownership: Cox Enterprises Inc., 100%. Note: Cox Enterprises Inc. also owns 100% of Cox Media Group (see listing).

Radio Stns: 16 AM. 67 FM.
KRTR Honolulu, HI; KKNE Waipahu, HI; KKYX San Antonio, TX; KONO San Antonio, TX; KRMG Tulsa, OK; WAGG Birmingham, AL; WDBO Orlando, FL; WENN Birmingham, AL; WGAU Athens, GA; WGBB Freeport, NY; WHIO Dayton, OH; WNLK Norwalk, CT; CFVM-1 Causapscal, QC; WRFC Athens, GA; WSB Atlanta, GA; WSTC Stamford, CT; KCCN-FM Honolulu, HI; KTKX Terrell Hills, TX; KCYY San Antonio, TX; KINE-FM Honolulu, HI; KISS-FM San Antonio, TX; KJSR Tulsa, OK; KKBQ-FM Pasadena, TX; KHPT Conroe, TX; KTHT Cleveland, TX; KONO-FM Helotes, TX; KRAV-FM Tulsa, OK; KRMG-FM Sand Springs, OK; KRTR-FM Kailua, HI; KSMG Seguin, TX; KHTC(FM) Lake Jackson, TX; KWEN Tulsa, OK; KPHW Kaneohe, HI; WAPE-FM Jacksonville, FL; WBAB Babylon, NY; WOKV-FM Ponte Vedra Beach, FL; WBHJ Midfield, AL; WBHK Warrior, AL; WBLI Patchogue, NY; WCFB Daytona Beach, FL; WXGL St. Petersburg, FL; WDUV New Port Richey, FL; WHTI(FM) Lakeside, VA; WEDR Miami, FL; WFOX Norwalk, CT; WEZN-FM Bridgeport, CT; WPOI St. Petersburg, FL; WFLC Miami, FL; WSRV Gainesville, GA; WFYV-FM Atlantic Beach, FL; WGMG Crawford, GA; WHFM Southampton, NY; WHKO Dayton, OH; WHPT Sarasota, FL; WHQT Coral Gables, FL; WHTQ(FM) Orlando, FL; WJMZ-FM Anderson, SC; WALR-FM Palmetto, GA; WKHK Colonial Heights, VA; WKLV-FM Port Chester, NY; WKLR Fort Lee, VA; WJGL Jacksonville, FL; WRKA Louisville, KY; WMMO Orlando, FL; WURV(FM) Richmond, VA; WXXJ Jacksonville, FL; WSSB(FM) Doraville, GA; WBPT Homewood, AL; WHZT Williamston, SC; WPLR New Haven, CT; WXKT Maysville, GA; WPYO Maitland, FL; WQNU Lyndon, KY; WSB-FM Atlanta, GA; WSFR Corydon, IN; WNGC Arcade, GA; WSUN-FM Holiday, FL; WFEZ(FM) Miami, FL; WVEZ St. Matthews, KY; WWRM Tampa, FL; WPUP Watkinsville, GA; WZLR Xenia, OH; WZZK-FM Birmingham, AL;
Doug Franklin, President
Bill Hoffman, EVP
Kim Guthrie, SVP
Neil Johnston, CFO

Crain Media Group LLC
200 S. Commerce,Suite 702, Little Rock AR 72201
(501) 537-0720; *Fax:*(501) 537-0722;

Radio Stns: 2 AM. 7 FM.
KAWW Heber Springs, AR; KWCK Searcy, AR; KEAZ Heber Springs, AR; KOLL Lonoke, AR; KCNY Greenbrier, AR; KHTE-FM England, AR; KKSP Bryant, AR; KWCK-FM Searcy, AR; KSMD Pangburn, AR;

Paul Coates, General Manager
Phil Weaver, General Manager

Cram Communications LLC
401 W. Kirkpatrick St., Syracuse NY 13204
(315) 468-0908;

Radio Stns: 2 AM.
WSIV E. Syracuse, NY; WOSW Fulton, NY;
Craig Fox, President

Crawford Broadcasting Co.
Box 3003, Blue Bell PA 19422
(215) 628-3500; *Fax:*(215) 628-0818
www.crawfordbroadcasting.com
Ownership: Donald B. Crawford is sole owner of all the stns except WMUZ(FM), WRDT(AM), WEXL(AM), KJSL(AM) and KSTL(AM). WMUZ(FM), WRDT(AM), WEXL(AM), KJSL(AM)and KSTL(AM) are owned by Donald B. Crawford and Dean A. Crawford.

Radio Stns: 15 AM. 11 FM.
KLDC Denver, CO; KBRT Avalon, CA; KCBC Manteca, CA; KJSL St. Louis, MO; KKPZ Portland, OR; KLVZ Brighton, CO; KLTT Commerce City, CO; KLZ Denver, CO; KAAM Garland, TX; KSTL St. Louis, MO; WDCX Rochester, NY; WYDE Birmingham, AL; WEXL Royal Oak, MI; WRDT Monroe, MI; WXJC Birmingham, AL; WDCD-FM Clifton Park, NY; WDCX-FM Buffalo, NY; WLGZ-FM Webster, NY; WDJC-FM Birmingham, AL; WMUZ Detroit, MI; WYRB Genoa, IL; WYDE-FM Cullman, AL; WYCA Crete, IL; WSRB Lansing, IL; WPWX Hammond, IN; WXJC-FM Cordova, AL;
Donald Crawford, President/CEO

CRISTA Broadcasting
19303 Fremont Ave. N., Seattle WA 98133
(206) 546-7350; *Fax:*(206) 289-7792
www.spirit1053.com
comments@spirit1053.com
Ownership: CRISTA Ministries.

Radio Stns: 1 AM. 2 FM.
KCIS Edmonds, WA; KCMS Edmonds, WA; KWPZ Lynden, WA;
Bob Lonac, CEO & President
Rick Carter, Senior VP
Stan Mak, VP/Gen Mgr

Criswell Communications
Box 619000, Dallas TX 75261-9000
(817) 792-3800; *Fax:*(817) 277-9929
www.kcbi.org
kcbi@kcbi.org

Radio Stns: 1 AM. 3 FM.
KCRN San Angelo, TX; KCBI Dallas, TX; KCRN-FM San Angelo, TX; KSYE Frederick, OK;
Dr. Jerry Johnson, President
Ronald Harris, EVP

Crossroads Communications Inc.
1301 Ohio St., Terre Haute IN 47807
(812) 234-9770; *Fax:*(812) 238-1576
www.radioworksforme.com
mike@radioworksforme.com

Radio Stns: 2 AM. 2 FM.
WBOW Terre Haute, IN; WSDX Brazil, IN; WAXI Rockville, IN; WSDM-FM Brazil, IN;
Dan Lacy, CFO
Michael Petersen, President

CSN International
3232 W. MacArthur Blvd., Santa Ana CA 92704
(714) 825-9663; *Fax:*(714) 825-9660
www.csnradio.com

Radio Stns: 1 AM. 65 FM.
WFGL Fitchburg, MA; KBLD Kennewick, WA; KDKR Decatur, TX; KEFX Twin Falls, ID; KKRS Davenport, WA; KLWD Gillette, WY; KTWD Wallace, ID; KRSS Tarkio, MO; KSGR Portland, TX; KTBJ Festus, MO; WVRD Zebulon, NC; WVRH Norlina, NC; WCVM Bronson, MI; WJCX Pittsfield, ME; WIFF Windsor, NY; WQKO Howe, IN; WZKN(FM) Ridgebury, PA; WWUN-FM Friar's Point, MS; WVRP Roanoke Rapids, NC; WPJC Pontiac, IL; KHJC Lihue, HI; WHLP Hanna, IN; WJWD Marshall, WI; KIHS Adel, IA; WVRL Elizabeth City, NC; KWYC Cheyenne, WY; KAJC Salem, OR; KZJB Pocatello, ID; KDJC Baker, OR; KJCC Carnegie, OK; KJCH Coos Bay, OR; KJCU Fort Bragg, CA; KTJC Kelso, WA; KVJC Globe, AZ; WJCO Montpelier, IN; WJCY Cicero, IN; WJCZ Milford, IL; WOJC Crothersville, IN; WUJC St. Marks, FL; WYJC Greenville, FL; KWCF Sheridan, WY; WTMK Wanatah, IN; WCJL Morgantown, IN; KYJC Commerce, TX; WSMA Scituate, MA; WWFP Brigantine, NJ; KYWH Lockwood, MT; KYMS Rathdrum, ID; WJWT Gardner, MA; KJCQ Westwood, CA; KKCJ Cannon Afb, NM; KJFT Arlee, MT; KWRC Hermosa, SD; KEFS North Powder, OR; KPIJ Junction City, OR; KNMA Tularosa, NM; KGSF Green Forest, AR; KPKJ Mentmore, NM; KKJA Redmond, OR; KJCF Asotin, WA; KVIR Bullhead City, AZ; WJIK Fulton, AL; WKJA Brunswick, OH; KGFJ Belt, MT; WTPG Whitehouse, OH; WIGW Eustis, FL;
Charles W. Smith, President
Mike Stocklin, Operations Dir

CTC Media Group Inc.
Box 353, Royal Oak MD 21662
(410) 745-5958
www.ctc-media.com
mail@ctc-media.com

Radio Stns: 4 AM.
WNOS New Bern, NC; WSME Camp Lejeune, NC; WWNB New Bern, NC; WECU Winterville, NC;
Lee Afflerbach, CEO
Mike Afflerbach, Operations Dir

Cumulus Media Inc.
3280 Peachtree Road N.E.,Suite 2300, Atlanta GA 30305
(404) 949-0700; *Fax:*(404) 949-0740
www.cumulus.com

Radio Stns: 71 AM. 181 FM.
KAAY Little Rock, AR; KABC Los Angeles, CA; KESP Modesto, CA; KARN Little Rock, AR; KKAT(AM) Salt Lake City, UT; KBGG Des Moines, IA; KBOI Boise, ID; KCMO Kansas City, MO; KCUB Tucson, AZ; KFNZ Salt Lake City, UT; KGO San Francisco, CA; KNML Albuquerque, NM; KKOB Albuquerque, NM; KKOH Reno, NV; KLIF Dallas, TX; KPZK Little Rock, AR; KNBR San Francisco, CA; KNEK Washington, LA; KTBL Los Ranchos, NM; KSFO San Francisco, CA; KKLF Richardson, TX; KTCK Dallas, TX; KTCT San Mateo, CA; KTIK Nampa, ID; KTUC Tucson, AZ; KCSF Colorado Springs, CO; KVOR Colorado Springs, CO; KJQS Murray, UT; WABC New York, NY; WAPI Birmingham, AL; WARM Scranton, PA; WQKC Jeffersonville, IN; WBAP Fort Worth, TX; WBSM New Bedford, MA; WJZN Augusta, ME; WXSM Blountville, TN; WGOW Chattanooga, TN; WHLD Niagara Falls, NY; WIBR Baton Rouge, LA; WIOV Reading, PA; WISW Columbia, SC; WJCW Johnson City, TN; WJIM Lansing, MI; WSPZ(AM) Birmingham, AL; WJR Detroit, MI; WGOC Kingsport, TN; WYOS Binghamton, NY; WKY Oklahoma City, OK; WLS Chicago, IL; WMAL Washington, DC; WHLL Springfield, MA; WLTI(AM) New Castle, IN; WBBF Buffalo, NY; WNBF Binghamton, NY; WNML Knoxville, TN; WSKO Syracuse, NY; WKLQ Whitehall, MI; WPRO Providence, RI; WRIE Erie, PA; WSBA York, PA; WPRV Providence, RI; WXLM Groton, CT; WGLD Manchester Township, PA; WTMA Charleston, SC; WTRX Flint, MI; WTVL Waterville, ME; WODJ Big Rapids, MI; WVFN East Lansing, MI; WVNN Athens, AL; KWPN(AM) Moore, OK; WXOK Port Allen, LA; KATM Modesto, CA; KATT-FM Oklahoma City, OK; KFNC Mont Belvieu, TX; KBEE Salt Lake City, UT; KBER Ogden, UT; KBUL-FM Carson City, NV; KCFX Harrisonville, MO; KCHZ Ottawa, KS; KCMO-FM Shawnee, KS; KDJK Mariposa, CA; KKAT Orem, UT; KFFG Los Altos, CA; KFOG San Francisco, CA; KCJK Garden City, MO; KGGO Des Moines, IA; KHKI Des Moines, IA; KHKK Modesto, CA; KHOP Oakdale, CA; KHYT Tucson, AZ; KIIM-FM Tucson, AZ; KIPR Pine Bluff, AR; KIZN Boise, ID; KJJY West Des Moines, IA; KJOY Stockton, CA; KENZ Ogden, UT; KKFM Colorado Springs, CO; KKGL Nampa, ID; KKMG Pueblo, CO; KMEZ Port Sulphur, LA; KKOB-FM Albuquerque, NM; KLIF-FM Haltom City, TX; KLAL Wrightsville, AR; KLOS Los Angeles, CA; WBAP-FM Flower Mound, TX; KKND Belle Chasse, LA; KNEK-FM Washington, LA; KNEV Reno, NV; KMJK North Kansas City, MO; KSZR Oro Valley, AZ; KOKY Sherwood, AR; KRDJ New Iberia, LA; KPLX Fort Worth, TX; KQFC Boise, ID; KQRS-FM Golden Valley, MN; KQXL-FM New Roads, LA; KRBE Houston, TX; KATC-FM Colorado Springs, CO; KWQW Boone, IA; KRRQ Lafayette, LA; KRST Albuquerque, NM; KSAN San Mateo, CA; KSCS Fort Worth, TX; KSMB Lafayette, LA; KKPK Colorado Springs, CO; KDRF Albuquerque, NM; WKIM Munford, TN; KURB Little Rock, AR; KHJK La Porte, TX; KWIN Lodi, CA; KWNN Turlock, CA; KXKC New Iberia, LA; KXXR Minneapolis, MN; KTDK Sanger, TX; KYIS Oklahoma City, OK; KHTB Provo, UT; WGVX Lakeville, MN; WGVY Cambridge, MN; WGVZ Eden Prarie, MN; KWYL South Lake Tahoe, CA; WLVM(FM) Mobile, AL; WAQX-FM Manlius, NY; WARM-FM York, PA; WELJ Montauk, NY; WBHT Mountain Top, PA; WBLM Portland, ME; WBPW Presque Isle, ME; WRQQ(FM) Hammond, LA; WDVW(FM) LaPlace, LA; WSJR Dallas, PA; WCTO Easton, PA; WHTS Coopersville, MI; WCYY Biddeford, ME; WDRQ Detroit, MI; WEBB Waterville, ME; WEDG Buffalo, NY; WEMX Kentwood, LA; WNRX Jefferson City, TN; WFBE Flint, MI; WFHN Fairhaven, MA; WFMK East Lansing, MI; WFMS Fishers, IN; WGFX Gallatin, TN; WGKX Memphis, TN; WJJK Noblesville, IN; WGOW-FM Soddy-Daisy, TN; WGRF Buffalo, NY; WRWM(FM) Lawrence, IN; WGRR Hamilton, OH; WNNX College Park, GA; WHNN Bay City, MI; WHOM Mount Washington, NH; WHTT-FM Buffalo, NY; WHWK Binghamton, NY; WCAT-FM Carlisle, PA; WILZ Saginaw, MI; WIOG Bay City, MI; WIOV-FM Ephrata, PA; WITL-FM Lansing, MI; WIVK-FM Knoxville, TN; WJBQ Portland, ME; WQHZ Erie, PA; WJIM-FM Lansing, MI; WMAL-FM Woodbridge, VA; WKDF Nashville, TN; WKHX-FM Marietta, GA; WTNR Holland, MI; WKOS Kingsport, TN; WKQZ Midland, MI; WMTI Picayune, MS; WLAV-FM Grand Rapids, MI; WLCS North Muskegon, MI; WLEV Allentown, PA; WXTL Syracuse, NY; WOMG Lexington, SC; WAPI-FM Northport, AL; WMAS-FM Enfield, CT; WMDH-FM New Castle, IN; WMGS Wilkes-Barre, PA; WMME-FM Augusta, ME; WMMQ East Lansing, MI; WMXS Montgomery, AL; WNKT Eastover, SC; WWWQ Atlanta, GA; WNML-FM Friendsville, TN; WNTQ Syracuse, NY; WOGT East Ridge, TN; WOKQ Dover, NH; WLXC Columbia, SC; WORC-FM Webster, MA; WOZI Presque Isle, ME; WPKQ North Conway, NH; WPLJ New York, NY; WDVD Detroit, MI; WQHR Presque Isle, ME; WAYI(FM) Sellersville, IN; WQUT Johnson City, TN; WQXA-FM York, PA; WUHT Birmingham, AL; WRBO Como, MS; WMHX(FM) Hershey, PA; WRQX Washington, DC; WRRM Cincinnati, OH; WVIB Holton, MI; WOKI Oliver Springs, TN; WSOX Red Lion, PA; WXMX Millington, TN; WSSX-FM Charleston, SC; WIWF Charleston, SC; WTCB Orangeburg, SC; WMOS Stonington, CT; WWFX Southbridge, MA; WWKI Kokomo, IN; WWKX Woonsocket, RI; WWLI Providence, RI; WWWZ Summerville, SC; WBHD Olyphant, PA; WSHK Kittery, ME; WBSX Hazleton, PA; WSAK Hampton, NH; WLS-FM Chicago, IL; WEAN-FM Wakefield-Peacedale, RI; WXLO Fitchburg, MA; WXTA Edinboro, PA; WYAY Gainesville, GA; WFTK Lebanon, OH; WWYL Chenango Bridge, NY; WJOX-FM Birmingham, AL; WZRR Birmingham, AL; WZYP Athens, AL; KRQN Vinton, IA; WLAW Newaygo, MI;
Lewis W. Dickey Jr., President

Curtis Media Group
3012 Highwoods Blvd., Raleigh NC 27604
(919) 876-0674; *Fax:*(919) 790-8369
www.curtismedia.com
Ownership: Donald W. Curtis.

Radio Stns: 14 AM. 11 FM.
WATA Boone, NC; WCLY Raleigh, NC; WDNC Durham, NC; WECR Newland, NC; WFMC Goldsboro, NC; WGBR Goldsboro, NC; WMFR High Point, NC; WPCM Burlington-Graham, NC; WPTF Raleigh, NC; WFNL Raleigh, NC; WSJS Winston-Salem, NC; WSML Graham, NC; WXIT Blowing Rock, NC; WYRN Louisburg, NC; WMMY Jefferson, NC; WBBB Raleigh, NC; WECR-FM Beech Mountain, NC; WWPL Smithfield, NC; WPLW Hillsborough, NC; WYMY Goldsboro, NC; WZTK Burlington, NC; WQDR-FM Raleigh, NC; WKIX-FM Raleigh, NC; WEQR Walnut Creek, NC; WZJS Banner Elk, NC;
Donald Curtis, Chairman
Phillip Zachary, CEO/COO
Allen Sherrill, Engineering Dir

Dailey Corp.
Box 10, New Martinsviille WV 26155
(304) 455-1111; *Fax:*(304) 455-1170
www.powercountry104.com

Radio Stns: 1 AM. 1 FM.
WETZ New Martinsville, WV; WYMJ New Martinsville, WV;
Calvin Dailey Jr., President

Dakota Communications Ltd.
Box 364, Pierre SD 57501
(605) 224-5434; *Fax:*(605) 224-5444
performanceradio.com
ddb@eaglecarver.com

Radio Stns: 2 AM. 3 FM.
KIJV Huron, SD; KOKK Huron, SD; KZKK Huron, SD; KXLG Milbank, SD; KJRV Wessington Springs, SD;
Linda Marcus, General Manager

Darby Advertising Inc.
Box 1766, Gaylord MI 49734
(989) 732-2341; *Fax:*(989) 732-6202;

Radio Stns: 3 FM.
WMJZ-FM Gaylord, MI; WUPN Paradise, MI; WWSS Tuscarora Township, MI;
Kent Smith, President

Davidson Media Group LLC
709 Peninsula Dr., Davidson NC 28036-7200
(704) 987-3585; *Fax:*(704) 987-3586
www.davidsonmediagroup.com

Radio Stns: 31 AM. 7 FM.
KDTD Kansas City, KS; KMNV St. Paul, MN; KCZZ Mission, KS; WACM West Springfield, MA; WVXX Norfolk, VA; WCVG Covington, KY; WZZQ(AM) Gaffney, SC; WPYR Baton Rouge, LA; WFNO Norco, LA; WVNZ Richmond, VA; WLLV Louisville, KY; KMNQ Brooklyn Park, MN; WLOU Louisville, KY; WMDB Nashville, TN; WDRJ Inkster, MI; WNOW Mint Hill, NC; WNVL Nashville, TN; WNTS Beech Grove, IN; WXCT Southington, CT; WOLI Spartanburg, SC; WREJ Richmond, VA; WSGH Lewisville,

NC; WSPR Springfield, MA; WRJD Durham, NC; WEMG Camden, NJ; WTIK Durham, NC; WTUV Louisville, KY; WTOB Winston-Salem, NC; WLEE Richmond, VA; WWBG Greensboro, NC; WTOX Glen Allen, VA; KAKS Huntsville, AR; WNOW-FM Gaffney, SC; WKKB Middletown, RI; WOLI-FM Easley, SC; WOLT Greer, SC; WSTS Fairmont, NC; WTUV-FM Eminence, KY
Russ Jones, Operations Dir

Davis Broadcasting Inc.
2203 Wynnton Rd., Columbus GA 31906
(706) 576-3565; *Fax:*(706) 576-3683
www.foxie105.com
Ownership: Gregory A. Davis, 76%.
Radio Stns: 3 AM. 5 FM.
WCHK Canton, GA; WIOL Columbus, GA; WOKS Columbus, GA; WKZJ Eufaula, AL; WIOL-FM Waverly Hall, GA; WLKQ-FM Buford, GA; WEAM-FM Buena Vista, GA; WNSY Talking Rock, GA;
Gregory Davis, President/CEO

DCBroadcasting Inc.
511 Newton Street, Suite 202,P O Box 1009, Jasper IN 47546-1009
(812) 634-9232; *Fax:*(812) 482-3696
www.dcbroadcasting.com
pknies@dcbroadcasting.com
Radio Stns: 1 AM. 3 FM.
WXGO Madison, IN; WAXL Santa Claus, IN; WBDC Huntingburg, IN; WORX-FM Madison, IN;
Paul Knies, President
Caroline Knies, Operations Dir
Giesla Knies Schepers, Secretary

Debut Broadcasting Corp. Inc.
1209 16th Ave. S.,Suite 200, Nashville TN 37212
(615) 301-0001; *Fax:*(615) 301-0002;
Radio Stns: 2 AM. 4 FM.
WNIX Greenville, MS; WNLA Indianola, MS; WLTM Greenville, MS; WBBV Vicksburg, MS; WIQQ Leland, MS; WIBT Indianola, MS;

Dee Rivers Radio Group
GRAM Corp.,43 Sherman Hill Rd. #204, Woodbury CT 6798
(203) 263-1900; *Fax:*(203) 263-1969;
Radio Stns: 1 AM. 2 FM.
WGOV Valdosta, GA; WAAC Valdosta, GA; WGOV-FM Valdosta, GA;
Georgia Salva, CEO

Deer Creek Broadcasting LLC
2225 First Ave., Napa CA 94558
(707) 226-2309;
Radio Stns: 2 AM. 3 FM.
KEWE Oroville, CA; KPAY Chico, CA; KHSL-FM Paradise, CA; KMXI Chico, CA; KHHZ Gridley, CA;

Delmarva Broadcasting Co.
Box 7492,2727 Shipley Rd., Wilmington DE 19803
(302) 478-2700; *Fax:*(302) 478-0100
www.delmarvabroadcasting.com
Ownership: Steinman
Radio Stns: 3 AM. 8 FM.
WDEL Wilmington, DE; WICO Salisbury, MD; WYUS Milford, DE; WAFL Milford, DE; WKTT Salisbury, MD; WAVD Ocean Pines, MD; WSTW Wilmington, DE; WXCY Havre De Grace, MD; WXDE Lewes, DE; WNCL Milford, DE; WICO-FM Pocomoke City, MD;
Julian Booker, President

Delmarva Educational Association
4190 Belfort Road, Jacksonville FL 32216
(904) 642-3688; *Fax:*(904) 641-9626
www.fm88.org
contact@fm88.org
Radio Stns: 1 AM.
WGGM Chester, VA;
Henry Hoot, Regional Vice President
Calvin Grabau, General Manager
Christina Bruno, General Sales Mgr

Delta Media Corp.
3501 N.W. Evangeline Thruway, Carencro LA 70520
(337) 896-1600; *Fax:*(337) 896-2681
www.deltamediacorp.com
Ownership: Charles Chatelain, 100%.
Radio Stns: 1 AM. 1 FM.
KSLO Opelousas, LA; KOGM Opelousas, LA;
Eddie Blanchard, VP

Dickey Broadcasting Co.
3535 Piedmont Rd.,Bldg. 14, Suite 1200, Atlanta GA 30305
(404) 688-0068; *Fax:*(404) 995-4045
www.680thefan.com
Radio Stns: 3 AM.
WIFN Atlanta, GA; WCNN North Atlanta, GA; WFOM Marietta, GA
David Dickey, CEO

Dierking Communications Inc.
937 Jayhawk Rd., Marysville KS 66508
(785) 562-2361; *Fax:*(785) 562-2188
kndy@bluevalley.net
Radio Stns: 2 AM. 4 FM.
KNDY Marysville, KS; KQNK Norton, KS; KDNS Downs, KS; KNDY-FM Marysville, KS; KQNK-FM Norton, KS; KZDY Cawker City, KS;
Bruce Dierking, General Manager

Digital Radio Broadcasting Inc.
135 White Bridge Rd., Middletown NY 10940
(845) 355-4001; *Fax:*(845) 355-4002;
Radio Stns: 3 AM.
WYNY(AM) Ontario, NY; WYNY(AM) Milford, PA; WYNY(AM) Milford, PA;
Charles Williamson, President

Dispatch Broadcast Group
770 Twin Rivers Dr., Columbus OH 43215
(614) 460-3700; *Fax:*(614) 460-2809
www.10tv.com
Ownership: Dispatch Printing Company
Radio Stns: 1 AM. 1 FM.
WBNS Columbus, OH; WBNS-FM Columbus, OH;
TV Stns: 2 TV.
WBNS-TV Columbus, OH; WTHR Indianapolis, IN;
Michael Fiorile, President
Tamara Clapsaddle, Controller

DMC Broadcasting Inc.
5542 NDCBU, Taos NM 87571-6122
(505) 758-4491; *Fax:*(505) 758-4452;
Radio Stns: 1 AM. 3 FM.
KVOT Taos, NM; KXMT Taos, NM; KKTC Angel Fire, NM; KKIT Taos, NM;

Donald Venita Bawles
334 Recreation Park Rd., Flemingsburg KY 41041
(606) 849-4433; *Fax:*(606) 845-9353;
Radio Stns: 1 FM.
WFLE-FM Flemingsburg, KY;
Donald Bawles, President
Kim Hester, General Sales Mgr
Eddie Plummer, News Director
Tyrone Henry, Chief Engineer

Dos Costas Communications Corp.
1818 S. Australian Ave.,Suite 102, West Palm Beach FL 33409
(561) 655-6615;
Radio Stns: 3 FM.
KDUC Barstow, CA; KDUQ Ludlow, CA; KXXZ Barstow, CA;
Roland Ulloa, President
Jime Garza, Operations Dir

Dr. Pepper Pepsi-Cola Bottling Co. of Dyersburg
35 Radio Rd., Dyersburg TN 38025-0100
(731) 285-1339; *Fax:*(731) 287-0100
sl100@wasl.net
Radio Stns: 1 AM. 2 FM.
WTRO Dyersburg, TN; WASL Dyersburg, TN; WTNV Tiptonville, TN;

DreamCatcher Communications Inc.
114 S. Manchester Ave., West Union OH 45693
(937) 544-9722; *Fax:*(937) 544-5523
c103@lycos.com
Radio Stns: 1 AM. 1 FM.
WFLE Flemingsburg, KY; WRAC Georgetown, OH;
Don Bowles, CEO
Ted Foster, Station Manager

Duhamel Broadcasting Enterprises
Box 1760, Rapid City SD 57709
(605) 342-2000; *Fax:*(605) 342-7305
www.kotatv.com
Ownership: William F. Duhamel, 63%; Peter A. and Lois G. Duhamel, 37%.
Radio Stns: 1 AM. 1 FM.
KOTA Rapid City, SD; KDDX Spearfish, SD;
TV Stns: 4 TV.
KDUH-TV Scottsbluff, NE; KHSD-TV Lead, SD; KOTA-TV Rapid City, SD; KSGW-TV Sheridan, WY;
William Duhamel, President

Eagle Bluff Enterprises
932 County Rd. 448, Poplar Bluff MO 63901
(573) 686-3700;
Radio Stns: 1 AM. 2 FM.
KDFN Doniphan, MO; KFEB Campbell, MO; KOEA Doniphan, MO;
Steven Fuch, President

Eagle Communications Group
2703 Hall St.,Suite 15, Hays KS 67601
(785) 625-4000; *Fax:*(785) 625-8030
www.eaglecom.net
Ownership: Eagle Communications Inc. Employee Stock Ownership Trust. Cable TV.
Radio Stns: 8 AM. 14 FM.
KAYS Hays, KS; KCOW Alliance, NE; KFEQ St. Joseph, MO; KINA Salina, KS; KOOQ North Platte, NE; KSFT(AM) Saint Joseph, MO; KVGB Great Bend, KS; KWBW Hutchinson, KS; KAAQ Alliance, NE; KHMY Pratt, KS; KELN North Platte, NE; KHAZ Hays, KS; KHOK Hoisington, KS; KHUT Hutchinson, KS; KJLS Hays, KS; KKQY Hill City, KS; KQSK Chadron, NE; KSJQ Savannah, MO; KSKG Salina, KS; KVGB-FM Great Bend, KS; KNPQ Hershey, NE; KCNB Chadron, NE;
Gary Shorman, President/CEO

Eagle's Nest Inc.
Box 710, Roanoke AL 36274
(334) 863-4139; *Fax:*(334) 863-2540
www.eagle1023.com
Ownership: Jim Vice, 51%; Kay Vice, 49%.
Radio Stns: 2 AM. 1 FM.
WELR Roanoke, AL; WLAG La Grange, GA; WELR-FM Roanoke, AL;
Jim Vice, President

Earls Broadcasting Co.
202 Courtney St., Branson MO 65616
(417) 334-6003; *Fax:*(417) 334-7141
www.komc.com,www.krzk.com
Ownership: Charles Earls, Scottie Earls, Scott Earls.
Radio Stns: 2 AM. 3 FM.
KHOZ Harrison, AR; KOMC Branson, MO; KHOZ-FM Harrison, AR; KOMC-FM Kimberling City, MO; KRZK Branson, MO;
Charles Earls, CEO
Scott Earls, President

East Arkansas Broadcasters Inc.
Box 789, Wynne AR 72396
(870) 238-8141; *Fax:*(870) 238-5997;
Radio Stns: 2 AM. 2 FM.
KBRI Brinkley, AR; KWYN Wynne, AR; KTRQ Colt, AR; KWYN-FM Wynne, AR;

East Carolina Radio Group
2422 S. Wrightsville Ave., Nags Head NC 27959
(252) 449-8331; *Fax:*(252) 449-8354
www.ecri.net
Radio Stns: 3 AM. 4 FM.
WCNC Elizabeth City, NC; WOBX Wanchese, NC; WZBO Edenton, NC; WERX-FM Columbia, NC; WKJX Elizabeth City, NC; WOBR-FM Wanchese, NC; WRSF Columbia, NC;
Rick Loesch, President

East Kentucky Broadcasting Corp.
Box 2200, Pikeville KY 41502
(606) 437-4051; *Fax:*(606) 432-2809
www.ekbradio.com
wpke@wpke.com,wdhr@wdhr.com
Radio Stns: 3 AM. 3 FM.
WEKB Elkhorn City, KY; WLSI Pikeville, KY; WPKE Pikeville, KY; WDHR Pikeville, KY; WPKE-FM Coal Run, KY; WZLK Virgie, KY;
Walter May, President
Keith Casebolt, General Manager

East Kentucky Radio Network Inc.
Box 2200, Pikeville KY 41502
(606) 437-4051; *Fax:*(606) 432-2809
www.ekbradio.com
Radio Stns: 2 AM.
WBTH Williamson, WV; WPRT Prestonsburg, KY;
Walter May, President
Keith Casebolt, Operations Dir
Pamela May, Sec/Treasurer

RADIO - U.S.

East Tennessee Radio Group III L.P.
112 Jordan Dr., Chattanooga TN 47421
(423) 485-8987;
Radio Stns: 3 AM. 1 FM.
WBAC Cleveland, TN; WDNT Dayton, TN; WRHA(AM) Spring City, TN; WAYA-FM Ridgeville, SC;

East Tennessee Radio Group L.P.
112 Jordan Dr., Chattanooga TN 37421
(423) 485-8987;
Radio Stns: 2 FM.
WSEV-FM Gatlinburg, TN; WPFT Pigeon Forge, TN;

East Texas Broadcasting Inc.
Box 990, Mount Pleasant TX 75456
(903) 572-8726; *Fax:*(903) 572-7232
www.eastexasradio.com
Radio Stns: 2 AM. 5 FM.
KIMP Mount Pleasant, TX; KPLT Paris, TX; KALK Winfield, TX; KBUS Paris, TX; KOYN Paris, TX; KSCH Sulphur Springs, TX; KSCN Pittsburg, TX;
John Mitchell, Chairman
Bud Kitchens, President
Bob Gibson, Operations Dir

Edwards Communications L.C.
125 Eagles Nest Dr., Seneca SC 29678
(864) 882-3272; *Fax:*(864) 882-3718
www.edwgroupinc.com
Radio Stns: 3 AM. 5 FM.
KVOW Riverton, WY; WHAK Rogers City, MI; WKYO Caro, MI; KTAK Riverton, WY; WWTH Oscoda, MI; WHAK-FM Rogers City, MI; WHSB Alpena, MI; WIDL Caro, MI;
Jerry Edwards, President
Steve Edwards Jr., Operations Dir

Electronic Applications Radio Service Inc.
15 Wood St., Greenfield IN 46140
(317) 467-1062;
Radio Stns: 1 AM. 3 FM.
WRFM Muncie, IN; WYJZ Fearsville, KY; WBOO Morganfield, KY; WHUZ(FM) Cole, IN;
Patrick Diemer, President

Elkhorn Media Group
PO Box 1426, Pikeville KY 41651
(606) 226-1476
www.elkhornmedia.com
elkhornmedia@gmail.com
Radio Stns: 1 FM.
KCMB Baker City, OR;
Adam Justice, President

Ely Radio LLC
5010 Spencer, Las Vegas NV 89119
(702) 740-5588;
Radio Stns: 2 AM. 1 FM.
KELY Ely, NV; KWNA Winnemucca, NV; KWNA-FM Winnemucca, NV;

Elyria-Lorain Broadcasting Co.
Box 4006, Elyria OH 44036
(440) 322-3761; *Fax:*(440) 284-3189;
Radio Stns: 2 AM. 3 FM.
WEOL Elyria, OH; WLKR Norwalk, OH; WKFM Huron, OH; WLKR-FM Norwalk, OH; WNWV Elyria, OH;
Lonnie Gronek, Operations Dir

Emerald Wave Media
718 E. Chapel St., Santa Maria CA 93454
(805) 928-4334; *Fax:*(805) 349-2765;
Radio Stns: 1 AM. 2 FM.
KTAP Santa Maria, CA; KIDI-FM Lompoc, CA; KRTO Guadalupe, CA;

EMF Broadcasting
2351 Sunset Blvd.,Suite 170-218, Rocklin CA 95765
(916) 251-1600; *Fax:*(916) 251-1650
www.emfbroadcasting.com
Radio Stns: 2 AM. 256 FM.
WNWT Rossford, OH; DWKEL Myrtle Beach, SC; KKLV Orem, UT; KALR Hot Springs, AR; KDKL Coalinga, CA; KDRH King City, CA; KLVK Fountain Hills, AZ; KWLU Chester, CA; KKRD Enid, OK; KMLR Gonzales, TX; KLXV Glenwood Springs, CO; KLVB Citrus Heights, CA; KKLM Corpus Christi, TX; KFLV Wilber, NE; KARO Nyssa, OR; KJBR Marked Tree, AR; KLFV Grand Junction, CO; KKVO Altus, OK; KXLV Amarillo, TX; KPOS Fouke, AR; KLOV Winchester, OR; KLRD Yucaipa, CA; KSBC Nile, WA; KLRQ Clinton, MO; KSRI Santa Cruz, CA; KLVA Maricopa, AZ; KLVH San Luis Obispo, CA; KLVC Magalia, CA; KLVG Garberville, CA; KLVJ Julian, CA; KLVN Livingston, CA; KLVP Sandy, OR; KLVR Middletown, CA; KLVS Livermore, CA; KLVU Sweet Home, OR; KLVY Fairmead, CA; KILV Castana, IA; KKLC Fall River Mills, CA; KMLV Ralston, NE; KOBC Joplin, MO; KJLV Hoxie, AR; KSSL Post, TX; KOKF Edmond, OK; KLXA Alexandria, LA; KOAR Beebe, AR; KLRJ Aberdeen, SD; KYKV Selah, WA; KQLV(FM) Bosque Farms, NM; KYLR Hutto, TX; KKLQ Harwood, ND; KYAR Lorena, TX; KLRO Hot Springs, AR; KIKL Lafayette, LA; KZKL Wichita Falls, TX; KTLI El Dorado, KS; KZLO Kilgore, TX; KTSL Medical Lake, WA; KRKL Walla Walla, WA; KLMK Marvell, AR; KLDV Morrison, CO; KKLY El Paso, TX; KZLV Lytle, TX; KXRD Victorville, CA; KXRI Amarillo, TX; KKLU Lubbock, TX; KYLA Homer, LA; KYLV Oklahoma City, OK; WYKV Ravena, NY; WKIV Westerly, RI; WKVV Searsport, ME; WCVJ Jefferson, OH; WARX Lewiston, ME; WKHL West Lafayette, IN; WAKL Flint, MI; WKVZ Dexter, ME; WLAI Wilmore, KY; WLKU Rock Island, IL; WJKL Glendale Heights, IL; WJLR Seymour, IN; WORI Harrison, OH; WVKV Nashville, GA; WZKV Dyersburg, TN; WLVZ Collins, MS; WLKP Belpre, OH; WHKU Proctorville, OH; WKVC North Myrtle Beach, SC; WKVN Morganfield, KY; WMXK Morristown, TN; WKVK Semora, NC; WBKL Clinton, LA; WQRP Dayton, OH; WKVU Utica, NY; WOKR Remsen, NY; WBGI-FM Moundsville, WV; WOKL Troy, OH; WKDL-FM Brockport, NY; WXKY-FM Stanford, KY; WKVO Georgetown, KY; WHKV Sylvester, GA; WGKV Pulaski, NY; WKVP Cherry Hill, NJ; WTKL North Dartmouth, MA; WARA New Washington, IN; WDKL Grafton, WV; WGCQ Hayti, MO; WLKB Bay City, MI; WLKV Ripley, WV; WUTQ-FM Utica, NY; WMSO Quitman, MS; WKVF Bartlett, TN; WYKL Crestline, OH; WNHI Farmington, NH; WEKV South Webster, OH; WKVW Marmet, WV; WKGV Swansboro, NC; WYAI Scotia, NY; WKWV Watertown, NY; KLVW Odessa, TX; WLKA Tafton, PA; WNKL Wauseon, OH; KHRI Hollister, CA; WCLR Arlington Heights, IL; KZRI Welches, OR; KWBI Great Bend, KS; KMKL North Branch, MN; KWKL Grandfield, OK; KAIS(FM) Tracy, CA; KAKV El Dorado, AR; KKRI Pocola, OK; WTRK Freeland, MI; KWRI Bartlesville, OK; WLVE Mukwonago, WI; KGBM Randsburg, CA; KHKL Laytonville, CA; WSRI Sugar Grove, IL; WKVH Monticello, FL; KLFS Van Buren, AR; KLWV Chugwater, WY; KARQ San Andreas, CA; KJKL Selma, OR; KQKL Selma, CA; KBIL Park City, MT; KLRV Billings, MT; KTKL Stigler, OK; KGCL Jordan Valley, OR; KLWC Casper, WY; KGCO Fort Collins, CO; KARA Williams, CA; KKLP La Pine, OR; KULV Ukiah, CA; KAIZ Mesquite, NV; KKRO Red Bluff, CA; KVLB Bend, OR; KARU Cache, OK; KKLW Willmar, MN; KLRI Rigby, ID; KAKL Anchorage, AK; KNKL North Ogden, UT; KHCO Hayden, CO; KLBV Steamboat Springs, CO; KKLT Texarkana, AR; WTAI Union City, TN; KLNB Grand Island, NE; KARJ Kuna, ID; KAIP Wapello, IA; KLJV Scottsbluff, NE; KKLJ Klamath Falls, OR; WVDA Valdosta, GA; KKLG Newton, IA; WIKV Plymouth, IN; KAGT Abilene, TX; KGRI Lebanon, OR; KAIA Bloomfield, MO; KFRI West Odessa, TX; KHLV Helena, MT; WDKV Fond Du Lac, WI; WKVY Somerset, KY; WZRI Spring Lake, NC; KLZV Brush, CO; KLRW Byrne, TX; KBMK Bismarck, ND; WQRA Greencastle, IN; WGCN Nashville, GA; WLRK Greenville, MS; KNRI Bismarck, ND; KQRI Bosque Farms, NM; KGCD Wray, CO; WARW Dorsey, IL; KDRE Sterling, CO; KAER Mesquite, NV; KLKM Kalispell, MT; KZAI Superior, AZ; KLRH Sparks, NV; KAIK Tillamook, OR; KLON Rockaway Beach, OR; KWAO Ocean Park, WA; WQKV Rochester, IN; KRLU Roswell, NM; KELU Clovis, NM; KLRY Gypsum, CO; KLOY Astoria, OR; KAIB Shafter, CA; KAIH Lake Havasu City, AZ; KQAI Roswell, NM; KVLK Milan, NM; KNAR San Angelo, TX; KGFA Great Falls, MT; KAIC Tucson, AZ; KAIX Cheyenne, WY; KITA Iota, LA; WNKV Norco, LA; KYAI McKee, KY; KDRI Grants, NM; KLBZ Bozeman, MT; KLLR Dripping Springs, TX; WOAR South Vienna, OH; WXKV Selmer, TN; WPAI Nanty Glo, PA; KMLT Jackson, WY; KRLR Sulphur, LA; WKMY Winchendon, MA; KAIW Laramie, WY; KRNZ Gonzales, TX; KQLR Whitehall, MT; KBLV Tehachapi, CA; KLUW East Wenatchee, WA; KLRM Melbourne, AR; KZLU Inyokern, CA; KDAI Scottsbluff, NE; KGCM Belgrade, MT; KAIO Idaho Falls, ID; KAIG Dodge City, KS; WKMV Muncie, IN; KGGA Gallup, NM; KLLU Gallup, NM; WKIW Ironwood, MI; KLUU Jamestown, ND; KSFS Sioux Falls, SD; WLVU Belle Meade, TN; KHAI Wahiawa, HI; KKWV Aransas Pass, TX; WQAI Thomson, GA; KVRA Sisters, OR; WPRZ-FM Brandy Station, VA; KRLP Fairmont, MN; KGLV Manhattan, KS; KVLP Tucumcari, NM; KVLZ Sheridan, WY; KRLE Oberlin, KS; KRLH Hereford, TX; KCAI Lodi, CA; KLOF Gillette, WY; KGCN Roswell, NM; KPGA Morton, TX; WCKU Clarksburg, WV; WZKL Woodstock, IL; KAKI Juneau, AK; WKYV Colonial Heights, VA;
Richard Jenkins, President
Devona R. Porter, Operations Dir
Keith Whipple, General Sales Mgr
David Pierce, Programming Director
Mike Novak, Operations VP

Emmis Communications Corp.
40 Monument Cir Ste 700, Indianapolis IN 46204-3011
317-266-0100; *Fax:*317-631-3750
www.emmis.com
Ownership: Jeffrey H. Smulyan, approximately 61% votes.
Radio Stns: 2 AM. 17 FM.
KLBJ Austin, TX; WFNI Indianapolis, IN; KBPA San Marcos, TX; KIHT St. Louis, MO; KGSR Cedar Park, TX; KPNT Collinsville, IL; KPWR Los Angeles, CA; KROX-FM Buda, TX; KSHE Crestwood, MO; KFTK Florissant, MO; KMVN Palmer, AK; WLHK Shelbyville, IN; WKQX Watseka, IL; WIBC Indianapolis, IN; WQHT New York, NY; WEPN-FM New York, NY; WTHI-FM Terre Haute, IN; WYXB Indianapolis, IN; WWVR West Terre Haute, IN;
Jeffrey Smulyan, Chairman/CEO
Patrick Walsh, COO/CFO
Rick Cummings, President, Programming

Empire Broadcasting Corp.
750 Story Rd., San Jose CA 95122
(408) 293-8030; *Fax:*(408) 293-6124
www.kliv.com
Radio Stns: 1 AM. 1 FM.
KLIV San Jose, CA; KRTY Los Gatos, CA;
Robert Kieve, President
John McLeod, Programming Director

Emporia's Radio Stations Inc.
Box 968, Emporia KS 66801
(620) 342-1400; *Fax:*(620) 342-0804
Ownership: Steve Sauder, 100%.
Radio Stns: 1 AM. 2 FM.
KVOE Emporia, KS; KFFX Emporia, KS; KVOE-FM Emporia, KS;
Lee Schroeder, General Manager
Susan Grother, Business Manager

Encino Broadcasting LLC
9434 Parkfield Dr., Austin TX 78758
(512) 453-1491; *Fax:*(512) 834-1491
spots@austintejas.com
Radio Stns: 3 AM.
KELG Manor, TX; KOKE Pflugerville, TX; KTXZ West Lake Hills, TX;
Alma Kyle, General Manager
Jose Garcia, General Manager

Entercom Communications Corp.
401 City Ave.,Suite 809, Bala-Cynwyd PA 19004
(610) 660-5610; *Fax:*(610) 660-5620
www.entercom.com
Ownership: Joseph M. Field.
Radio Stns: 31 AM. 80 FM.
KUDL Kansas City, KS; KCTC West Sacramento, CA; KEZW Aurora, CO; KNSS Wichita, KS; KKSN Vancouver, WA; KJCE Rollingwood, TX; KMBZ Kansas City, MO; KFH Wichita, KS; KFXX Portland, OR; WBEN Buffalo, NY; KCSP Kansas City, MO; WEAL Greensboro, NC; WEEI Boston, MA; WSSP Milwaukee, WI; WROC Rochester, NY; WBZU Scranton, PA; WGR Buffalo, NY; WILK Wilkes-Barre, PA; WKZN West Hazleton, PA; WMC Memphis, TN; WXNT Indianapolis, IN; WPET Greensboro, NC; KYYS Kansas City, KS; WRKO Boston, MA; WWWL New Orleans, LA; WORD Spartanburg, SC; WWKB Buffalo, NY; WWL New Orleans, LA; WVEI Worcester, MA; WWWS Buffalo, NY; WYRD Greenville, SC; KALC Denver, CO; KAMX Luling, TX; KFH-FM Clearwater, KS; WDAF-FM Liberty, MO; KDFC Angwin, CA; KDGS Andover, KS; KDND Sacramento, CA; KEYN-FM Wichita, KS; KGON Portland, OR; KISW Seattle, WA; KQMT Denver, CO; KKMJ-FM Austin, TX; KYCH-FM Portland, OR; KMTT Tacoma, WA; KNDD Seattle, WA; KNRK Camas, WA; KOIT San Francisco, CA; KOSI Denver, CO; KLQB Taylor, TX; KKWF Seattle, WA; KQRC-FM Leavenworth, KS; KRSK Molalla, OR; KRXQ Sacramento, CA; KSEG Sacramento, CA; KVXX Quincy, CA; KSSJ(FM) Fair Oaks, CA; KMBZ-FM Kansas City, KS; KWJJ-FM Portland, OR; KBZC Sacramento, CA; KFBZ Haysville, KS; KRBZ Kansas City, MO; KZPT Kansas City, MO; KGMZ(FM) San Francisco, CA; WAAF Westborough, MA; WBZA Rochester, NY; WWEI Easthampton, MA; WBEE-FM Rochester, NY; WKAF Brockton, MA; WCMF-FM Rochester, NY; WYRD-FM Simpsonville, SC; WEZB New Orleans, LA; WGGI Benton, PA; WGGY Scranton, PA; WSMB Harbor Beach, MI; WJMH Reidsville, NC; WKRF Tobyhanna, PA; WKRZ Freeland, PA; WKSE Niagara Falls, NY; WSMW Greensboro, NC; WKTK Crystal River, FL; WLMG New Orleans, LA; WWL-FM Kenner, LA; WMC-FM Memphis, TN; WMFS-FM Bartlett, TN; WMMM-FM Verona, WI; WPAW Winston-Salem, NC; WMYX-FM Milwaukee, WI; WLKK Wethersfield Twnshp, NY; WNVZ Norfolk, VA; WKQK Germantown, TN; WOLX-FM Baraboo, WI; WPTE Virginia Beach, VA; WPXY-FM Rochester, NY; WQMG Greensboro, NC; WEEI(FM) Lawrence, MA; WROQ Anderson, SC; WRVR Memphis, TN; WDMT Pittston, PA; WSKY-FM Micanopy, FL;

WSPA-FM Spartanburg, SC; WKBU New Orleans, LA; WNTR Indianapolis, IN; WTPT Forest City, NC; WVKL Norfolk, VA; WWDE-FM Hampton, VA; WILK-FM Avoca, PA; WEEI-FM Lawrence, MA; WXSS Wauwatosa, WI; WCHY Waunakee, WI; WZPL Greenfield, IN;

John Donlevle, EVP
Steve Fisher, SVP
Eugene Levin, Treasurer
Martin Hadfield, VP Engineering
Deborah Kane, VP Sales

Entravision Communications Corp.

2425 Olympic Blvd.,Suite 6000W, Santa Monica CA 90404
(310) 447-3872; *Fax:*(310) 447-3899
www.entravision.com
kthompson@entravision.com

Radio Stns: 12 AM. 36 FM.
KWST El Centro, CA; KSVE El Paso, TX; KBZO Lubbock, TX; KCVR Lodi, CA; KGOL Humble, TX; KMXA Aurora, CO; KRZY Albuquerque, NM; KHRO El Paso, TX; KBMB Black Canyon City, AZ; KMBX Soledad, CA; WACA Wheaton, MD; WLQY Hollywood, FL; KDLD Santa Monica, CA; KYSE El Paso, TX; KDLE Newport Beach, CA; KBMB(FM) Sacramento, CA; KFRQ Harlingen, TX; KXSE Davis, CA; KINT-FM El Paso, TX; KJMN Castle Rock, CO; KKPS Brownsville, TX; KLNZ Glendale, AZ; KLOB Thousand Palms, CA; KLOK-FM Greenfield, CA; KSSE Arcadia, CA; KMIX Tracy, CA; KDVA Buckeye, AZ; KMXX Imperial, CA; KOFX El Paso, TX; KRCX-FM Marysville, CA; KRRN Moapa Valley, NV; KRNV-FM Reno, NV; KNTY Shingle Springs, CA; KLYY Riverside, CA; KSSD Fallbrook, CA; KCVR-FM Columbia, CA; KQRT Las Vegas, NV; KVLY Edinburg, TX; KNVO-FM Port Isabel, TX; KSES-FM Seaside, CA; KVVA-FM Apache Junction, AZ; KSSC Ventura, CA; KSEH Brawley, CA; KXPK Evergreen, CO; KTSE-FM Patterson, CA; WNUE-FM Deltona, FL; KAIQ Wolfforth, TX; KPVW Aspen, CO;

TV Stns: 20 TV.
KCEC Denver, CO; KINC Las Vegas, NV; KINT-TV El Paso, TX; KTFN El Paso, TX; KLDO-TV Laredo, TX; KLUZ-TV Albuquerque, NM; KNVO McAllen, TX; KORO Corpus Christi, TX; KPMR Santa Barbara, CA; KREN-TV Reno, NV; KSMS-TV Monterey, CA; KUPB Midland, TX; KVYE El Centro, CA; WVEA-TV Venice, FL; WUVN Hartford, CT; WJAL Hagerstown, MD; WVEN-TV Daytona Beach, FL; WUNI Worcester, MA; KVSN-DT Pueblo, CO; KDCU-DT Derby, KS;

Philip Wilkinson, President
Walter Ulloa, Chairman/CEO

Equity Communications LP

8025 Black Horse Pike,Bayport One, Suite 100-102, West Atlantic City NJ 8232
(609) 484-8444; *Fax:*(609) 646-6331
951wayv.com
gfequity@aol.com

Radio Stns: 2 AM. 7 FM.
WCMC Wildwood, NJ; WMID Atlantic City, NJ; WAYV Atlantic City, NJ; WEZW Wildwood Crest, NJ; WAIV Cape May, NJ; WZBZ Pleasantville, NJ; WTTH Margate City, NJ; WSNQ Cape May Court House, NJ; WZXL Wildwood, NJ;

Gary Fisher, President

Eureka Broadcasting Co.

1101 Marsh Rd., Eureka CA 95501
(707) 442-5744

Ownership: Barbara Papstein, 50%; Hugo Papstein, 28%; and Brian Papstein, 22%.

Radio Stns: 4 AM. 2 FM.
KWSW(AM) Eureka, CA; KURY Brookings, OR; KWSW Eureka, CA; KEJY Eureka, CA; KEKA-FM Eureka, CA; KURY-FM Brookings, OR;

Hugo Papstein, General Manager

Evangel Ministries Inc.

1909 W. 2nd, Appleton WI 54914
(920) 749-9456; *Fax:*(920) 749-0474
www.christianfamilyradio.net

Radio Stns: 3 FM.
WEMI Appleton, WI; WEMY Green Bay, WI; WGNV Milladore, WI;

Paul Comeron, Executive Director

F W Robbert Broadcasting Co. Inc.

2730 Loumor Ave., Metairie LA 70001
(504) 831-6941
www.wwcr.com

Ownership: Fred P. Westenberger, 51%; Chris P. Westenberger, 9.75%; Fritz N. Westenberger, 9.75%; Lisa M. Westenberger, 9.75%; Eric M. Westenberger, 9.75%; George McClintock, 10%.

Radio Stns: 3 AM.
WMQM Lakeland, TN; WNQM Nashville, TN; WVOG New Orleans, LA;

Fred P. Westenberger, President
Eric Westenberger, General Manager

Faith Communications Corp.

2201 S. 6th St., Las Vegas NV 89104
(702) 731-5452; *Fax:*(702) 731-1992
www.sosradio.net

Radio Stns: 1 AM. 6 FM.
KANN Roy, UT; KCIR Twin Falls, ID; KHMS Victorville, CA; KSOS Las Vegas, NV; KMZL Missoula, MT; KMZO Hamilton, MT; KSQS Ririe, ID;

Brad Staley, President

Family Life Communications Inc.

Box 35300, Tucson AZ 85740
(520) 742-6976; *Fax:*(520) 742-6979
www.flc.org

Ownership: All stns are owned by Family Life Communications Inc. A nonprofit, noncommercial Christian organization. No individual stockholders.

Radio Stns: 4 AM. 15 FM.
KFLB Odessa, TX; KFLT Tucson, AZ; WUFL Sterling Heights, MI; WUNN Mason, MI; KAMY Lubbock, TX; KFLB-FM Stanton, TX; KFLQ Albuquerque, NM; KFLR-FM Phoenix, AZ; KJTA Flagstaff, AZ; KJTY Topeka, KS; KRGN Amarillo, TX; KWFL Roswell, NM; WJBP Red Bank, TN; WJTF Panama City, FL; WJTG Fort Valley, GA; WJTY Lancaster, WI; WUFN Albion, MI; WUGN Midland, MI; KFLT-FM Tucson, AZ;

Randy Carlson, President

Family Life Network

Box 506, Bath NY 14810
(607) 776-4151; *Fax:*(607) 776-6929
www.fln.org
mail@fln.org

Radio Stns: 13 FM.
WCID Friendship, NY; WCIH Elmira, NY; WCII Spencer, NY; WCIY Canandaigua, NY; WCOG-FM Galeton, PA; WCOT Jamestown, NY; WCOU Attica, NY; WCOV-FM Clyde, NY; WCIT-FM Trout Run, PA; WCOF Arcade, NY; WCIG Dallas, PA; WCIM Shenandoah, PA; WCIJ Unadilla, NY;

Dick Snavely, CFO
Rick Snavely, President
Cecil VanHouten, Programming Director
Jim Travis, Chief Engineer

Family Stations Inc.

290 Hegenberger Rd., Oakland CA 94621
(510) 568-6200; *Fax:*(510) 568-6190

Ownership: Nonprofit corporation.

Radio Stns: 12 AM. 54 FM.
KARR Kirkland, WA; KEBR Rocklin, CA; KECR El Cajon, CA; KEAR San Francisco, CA; KFRN Long Beach, CA; KKAA Aberdeen, SD; KQKD Redfield, SD; KYFR Shenandoah, IA; WFSI Baltimore, MD; WBMD Baltimore, MD; WCTF Vernon, CT; WCUE Cuyahoga Falls, OH; KDFR Des Moines, IA; KEAR-FM Sacramento, CA; KEFR Le Grand, CA; KFNO Fresno, CA; KFRB Bakersfield, CA; KFRS Soledad, CA; KHAP Chico, CA; KJVH Longview, WA; KPHF Phoenix, AZ; KPOR Emporia, KS; KPRA Ukiah, CA; KQFE Springfield, OR; KTXB Beaumont, TX; KUFR Salt Lake City, UT; WBFR Birmingham, AL; WEFR Erie, PA; WFBF Buffalo, NY; WFCH Charleston, SC; WFME Newark, NJ; WFRC Columbus, GA; WFRH Kingston, NY; WFRJ Johnstown, PA; WFRS Smithtown, NY; WFRW Webster, NY; WLZL Annapolis, MD; WFTI-FM St. Petersburg, FL; WJCH Joliet, IL; WMFL Florida City, FL; WMWK Milwaukee, WI; WOTL Toledo, OH; WQLZ Taylorville, IL; WWFR Stuart, FL; WYTN Youngstown, OH; WOFR Schoolcraft, MI; KBFR Bismarck, ND; KEDR(FM) Butte, MT; KEGR Fort Dodge, IA; KPFR Pine Grove, OR; KFRJ China Lake, CA; KHFR Santa Maria, CA; WFRP Americus, GA; KQFR Rapid City, SD; KFRP Coalinga, CA; KEDR Bay City, TX; KFRW Great Falls, MT; KFRY Pueblo, CO; KFRD Butte, MT; KYOR Newport, OR; WUFR Bedford, PA; WKDN(FM) State College, PA; KXFR Socorro, NM; KEAF Fort Smith, AR; KXBC Garberville, CA; KIFR Alice, TX;

TV Stns: 1 TV.
WFME-TV West Milford, NJ;

Harold Camping, President

Family Worship Center Church Inc.

Box 262550, Baton Rouge LA 70826
(225) 768-3224
www.jsm.org

Radio Stns: 3 AM. 20 FM.
KNHD Camden, AR; KMFS Guthrie, OK; WJYM Bowling Green, OH; KJSM-FM Augusta, AR; KBDD Winfield, KS; KDJR De Soto, MO; KNRB Atlanta, TX; KTOC-FM Jonesboro, LA; KUUZ Lake Village, AR; WAYB-FM Graysville, TN; WJCA Albion, NY; WJFM Baton Rouge, LA; WJNS-FM Bentonia, MS; WQUA Citronelle, AL; WTGY Charleston, MS; KSSW Nashville, AR; KPSH Coachella, CA; KAJT Ada, OK; KNFA Grand Island, NE; KSSO Norman, OK; WFFL Panama City, FL; KCKR Church Point, LA; KNBE Beatrice, NE;

Jimmy Swaggart, President
David Whitelaw, Operations Dir

Fantasia Broadcasting Inc.

450 Leonard Ave., Fairmont WV 26554
(304) 366-3700; *Fax:*(304) 366-3706;

Radio Stns: 2 AM. 2 FM.
WMMN Fairmont, WV; WTCS Fairmont, WV; WRLF Fairmont, WV; WZST Westover, WV;

Nick Fantasia, President

Federated Media

Box 2500, Elkhart IN 46515
(574) 295-2500; *Fax:*(574) 294-4014
www.federatedmedia.com

Radio Stns: 4 AM. 7 FM.
WKJG Fort Wayne, IN; WNIL Niles, MI; WOWO Fort Wayne, IN; WTRC Elkhart, IN; WTRC-FM Niles, MI; WBYR Woodburn, IN; WBYT Elkhart, IN; WOWO-FM Fort Wayne, IN; WLEG Ligonier, IN; WMEE Fort Wayne, IN; WQHK-FM Huntertown, IN;

John F. Dille, President
Jeffrey P. Laderer, Secretary

Finger Lakes Radio Group

3568 Lenox Rd., Geneva NY 14456
(315) 781-7000; *Fax:*(315) 781-7700
www.fingerlakes1.com

Radio Stns: 4 AM. 1 FM.
WAUB Auburn, NY; WCGR Canandaigua, NY; WFLR Dundee, NY; WSFW Seneca Falls, NY; WFIZ Odessa, NY;

George Kimble, President
Alan Bishop, Operations Dir

First Broadcasting Operating Inc.

8300 Douglas Ave.,Suite 730, Dallas TX 75225
(214) 855-0002; *Fax:*(214) 855-5145
www.firstbroadcasting.com
info@firstbroadcasting.com

Radio Stns: 3 AM. 4 FM.
KRKZ Forks, WA; KREL Colorado Springs, CO; WAMD Aberdeen, MD; KBDB-FM Forks, WA; KMCQ Covington, WA; WAOL Ripley, OH; WOXY Mason, OH;

Hal Rose, COO
Gary Lawrence, President
Neil Read, CFO

First Media Radio LLC

306 Port St., Easton MD 21601
(410) 822-3301; *Fax:*(410) 822-0576;

Radio Stns: 9 AM. 17 FM.
WCBT Roanoke Rapids, NC; WKHZ Easton, MD; WCPA Clearfield, PA; WIEZ Lewistown, PA; WJLS Beckley, WV; WREL Lexington, VA; WRMT Rocky Mount, NC; WSMY Weldon, NC; WWDR Murfreesboro, NC; WWDW Alberta, VA; WCEI-FM Easton, MD; WDLZ Murfreesboro, NC; WJLS-FM Beckley, WV; WPWZ Pinetops, NC; WLAK Huntingdon, PA; WTRG Gaston, NC; WMRF-FM Lewistown, PA; WOWQ Du Bois, PA; WPTM Roanoke Rapids, NC; WQYX Clearfield, PA; WWZW Buena Vista, VA; WDWG Rocky Mount, NC; WZAX Nashville, NC; WZWW Bellefonte, PA; WYTT Emporia, VA; WZDB Sykesville, PA;

Alex Kolobielski, CEO

First Natchez Radio Group

Box 768, Natchez MS 39121
(601) 442-4895; *Fax:*(601) 446-8260
95country.com

Radio Stns: 1 AM. 3 FM.
WNAT Natchez, MS; KZKR Jonesville, LA; WQNZ Natchez, MS; WKSO Natchez, MS;

Stephen Perkins, Operations Dir
Margaret Perkins, General Manager

Fisher Communications Inc.

100 4th Ave. N., Suite 440,Suite 1525, Seattle WA 98109
(206) 404-7000; *Fax:*(206) 404-7050
www.fsci.com

Radio Stns: 3 AM. 4 FM.
KOMO Seattle, WA; KQDI Great Falls, MT; KVI Seattle, WA; KPLZ-FM Seattle, WA; KQDI-FM Great Falls, MT; KINX Fairfield, MT; KIKF Cascade, MT;

TV Stns: 12 TV.
KATU Portland, OR; KBOI-TV Boise, ID; KUNS-TV Bellevue, WA; KUNP La Grande, OR; KCBY-TV Coos Bay, OR; KEPR-TV Pasco, WA; KIDK Idaho Falls, ID; KIMA-TV Yakima, WA;

KLEW-TV Lewiston, ID; KOMO-TV Seattle, WA; KPIC Roseburg, OR; KVAL-TV Eugene, OR;
Collen Brown, President/CEO

Flint Media Inc.
Box 7425, Bainbridge GA 39818-7425
(229) 416-6021; *Fax:*(229) 246-9995;
Radio Stns: 1 AM. 2 FM.
WSEM Donalsonville, GA; WGMK Donalsonville, GA; WBGE Bainbridge, GA;

FM Idaho Co. LLC dba Impact Radio Group
5660 Franklin Road,Suite 200, Nampa ID 83687
(208) 465-9966; *Fax:*208-465-2922
www.impactradiogroup.com
darrell@impactradiogroup.com
Radio Stns: 2 AM. 3 FM.
KMHI Mountain Home, ID; KSRV Ontario, OR; KWYD Parma, ID; KPDA-FM Gooding, ID; KSRV-FM Ontario, OR;
Darrell Calton, General Manager
Mark Broz, General Sales Mgr

Foothills Radio Group LLC
Box 1678, Lenoir NC 28645
(828) 758-1033; *Fax:*(828) 757-3300
foothillsradio.com
abunch@kicksradio.com
Radio Stns: 2 AM. 1 FM.
WJRI Lenoir, NC; WKGX Lenoir, NC; WKVS Lenoir, NC;
Al Bunch, President

Forever Broadcasting
One Forever Dr., Hollidaysburg PA 16648
(814) 941-9800; *Fax:*(814) 943-2754
www.foreverradio.com
Ownership: Kerby Confer, Donald Alt, Carol Logan, Lynn Deppen.
Radio Stns: 12 AM. 16 FM.
WKST New Castle, PA; WFBG Altoona, PA; WFRA Franklin, PA; WLLI(AM) Huntingdon, PA; WJST New Castle, PA; WQWK(AM) State College, PA; WMGW Meadville, PA; WBSS Pleasantville, NJ; WRSC State College, PA; WTIV Titusville, PA; WVAM Altoona, PA; WNTW Somerset, PA; WALY Bellwood, PA; WXMJ Cambridge Springs, PA; WBUS Boalsburg, PA; WHMJ Franklin, PA; WJHT Johnstown, PA; WFGE Tyrone, PA; WWGY Grove City, PA; WFGI-FM Johnstown, PA; WUZZ Saegertown, PA; WKYE Johnstown, PA; WRKY-FM Hollidaysburg, PA; WWOT Altoona, PA; WRKW Ebensburg, PA; WMAJ-FM Centre Hall, PA; WGYY Meadville, PA; WUUZ Cooperstown, PA;
Carol Logan, President

Forever Communications Inc.
1919 Scottsville Rd., Bowling Green KY 42104-3303
(270) 843-3333; *Fax:*(270) 843-0454
chris@forevercomm.com
Radio Stns: 6 AM. 10 FM.
WBGN Bowling Green, KY; WKYW Frankfort, KY; WLLI Huntingdon, PA; WNBS Murray, KY; WOFC Murray, KY; WTJS Jackson, TN; WUHU Smiths Grove, KY; WBVR-FM Auburn, KY; WFGS Murray, KY; WLYE-FM Glasgow, KY; WSTV-FM Frankfort, KY; WFKY Frankfort, KY; WTJJ Dyer, TN; WDVW(FM) Humboldt, TN; WOGY Jackson, TN; WYNU Milan, TN;
Christine Hillard, COO

Fort Bend Broadcasting Co.
1610 Woodstead Ct.,Suite 350, Spring TX 77380-3414
(281) 298-6797; *Fax:*(281) 298-8707;
Radio Stns: 1 AM. 8 FM.
WARD Petoskey, MI; KJAZ Point Comfort, TX; KROY Palacios, TX; KLTR Brenham, TX; KULM-FM Columbus, TX; KHTZ Ganado, TX; WOUF Beulah, MI; WLDR-FM Traverse City, MI; WCUZ Bear Lake, MI;
Roy Henderson, President

Fort Myers Broadcasting Co.
2824 Palm Beach Blvd., Fort Myers FL 33916
(239) 334-1111; *Fax:*(239) 334-0744
winktv.com
manaager@winktv.com
Radio Stns: 1 AM. 2 FM.
WNPL Golden Gate, FL; WTLQ-FM Punta Rassa, FL; WINK-FM Fort Myers, FL;
TV Stns: 1 TV.
WINK-TV Fort Myers, FL;
Brian McBride, CEO
Gary Gardner, Operations Dir

Forum Communications Co.
Box 2020, Fargo ND 58107
(701) 235-7311; *Fax:*(701) 241-5406
www.in-forum.com
Radio Stns: 1 AM. 1 FM.
WDAY Fargo, ND; WZUU Mattawan, MI;
TV Stns: 4 TV.
KBMY Bismarck, ND; KMCY Minot, ND; WDAY-TV Fargo, ND; WDAZ-TV Devil's Lake, ND;
William Marcil, President

Foster Communications Co. Inc.
Box 2191, San Angelo TX 76902-2191
(325) 949-2112; *Fax:*(325) 944-0851
www.fostercommunications.us
Radio Stns: 1 AM. 3 FM.
KKSA San Angelo, TX; KIXY-FM San Angelo, TX; KWFR San Angelo, TX; KCLL San Angelo, TX;
Fred Key, President
Jay Michaels, Operations Dir
Doug Smith, General Sales Mgr

Four Corners Broadcasting L.L.C.
Drawer P, Durango CO 81302
(970) 259-4444; *Fax:*(970) 247-1005
www.radiodurango.com
fcb@frontier.net
Radio Stns: 1 AM. 3 FM.
KIUP Durango, CO; KIQX Durango, CO; KRSJ Durango, CO; KKDC Dolores, CO;
Allen Brill, CEO
Ward Holmes, General Manager

4-K Radio Inc.
Box 936, Lewiston ID 83501
(208) 743-2502; *Fax:*(208) 743-1995
www.koze.com
radiorip@aol.com
Ownership: Eugene Hamblin Trust; Michael R. Ripley.
Radio Stns: 2 AM. 2 FM.
KORT(AM/FM) Grangeville, ID; KOZE Lewiston, ID; KORT-FM Grangeville, ID; KOZE-FM Lewiston, ID;
Michael Ripley, President

Freedom Communications of Connecticut Inc.
330 Main St., Hartford CT 6106
(860) 524-0001; *Fax:*(860) 548-1922
mssm2115@msn.com
Radio Stns: 3 AM.
WKND Windsor, CT; WNEZ Manchester, CT; WLAT New Britain, CT;
Stephen Brisker, Chairman

Freeland Broadcasting Stations
Box 387, Benton KY 42025
(270) 527-3102; *Fax:*(270) 527-5606;
Radio Stns: 2 AM. 3 FM.
WCBL Benton, KY; WWDX Huntingdon, TN; WCBL-FM Grand Rivers, KY; WCCK Calvert City, KY; WEIO(FM) Huntingdon, TN;

Friends Communications Inc.
121 W. Maumee St., Adrian MI 49221-2019
(517) 265-1500; *Fax:*(517) 263-4525
friends@tc3net.com,wabj@dmci.net,q95@dmci.net,q95@frontiernet.net
Ownership: Bob Elliot, 100%.
Radio Stns: 1 AM. 2 FM.
WABJ Adrian, MI; WBZV Hudson, MI; WQTE Adrian, MI;
Bob Elliot, President
Moneca Morton, General Sales Manager

Fritz Communications Inc.
1355 N. Dutton Ave. #225, Santa Rosa CA 95401-7107
(707) 546-9185; *Fax:*(707) 546-9188;
Radio Stns: 12 FM.
KHRD Weaverville, CA; KKXS Shingletown, CA; KTHU Corning, CA; KEWB Anderson, CA; KESR Shasta Lake City, CA; KKCY Colusa, CA; KBQB Chico, CA; KMJE Woodland, CA; KNCQ Redding, CA; KRQR Orland, CA; KCEZ Los Molinos, CA; KCCL Placerville, CA;
Jack Fritz, CEO

Frontier Radio Management Inc.
4311 Wilshire Blvd.,Suite 412, Los Angeles CA 90010
(323) 931-1745; *Fax:*(323) 931-0925;
Radio Stns: 4 AM. 12 FM.
KBLU Yuma, AZ; KIXW Apple Valley, CA; KSMX Santa Maria, CA; KVEC San Luis Obispo, CA; KSMY Lompoc, CA; KATJ-FM George, CA; KIXA Lucerne Valley, CA; KURQ Grover Beach, CA; KSLY-FM San Luis Obispo, CA; KSNI-FM Santa Maria, CA; KSTT-FM Los Osos-Baywood Par, CA; KTTI Yuma, AZ; KXFM Santa Maria, CA; KRSX-FM Twentynine Palms, CA; KQSR Yuma, AZ; KZXY-FM Apple Valley, CA;
Jason Wolff, President

Fuchs Radio L.L.C.
Box 311, Hobart OK 73651
(580) 726-5656; *Fax:*(580) 726-2222;
Radio Stns: 1 AM. 3 FM.
KTJS Hobart, OK; KHIM Mangum, OK; KJCM Snyder, OK; KTIJ Elk City, OK;

Galaxy Communications L.P.
235 Walton St., Syracuse NY 13202
(315) 472-9111; *Fax:*(315) 472-1888
www.galaxycommunications.com
Radio Stns: 6 AM. 7 FM.
WIXT Little Falls, NY; WRNY Rome, NY; WSCP Sandy Creek-Pulaski, NY; WSGO Oswego, NY; WTLA North Syracuse, NY; WTLB Utica, NY; WKLL Frankfort, NY; WKRH Minetto, NY; WKRL-FM North Syracuse, NY; WOUR Utica, NY; WZUN Phoenix, NY; WTKV Oswego, NY; WTKW Bridgeport, NY;
Michael Lucarelli, CFO
Ed Levine, President
Mimi Griswold, Operations Dir
Lisa Morrow, General Sales Mgr

Galesburg Broadcasting Co.
154 E. Simmons St., Galesburg IL 61401
(309) 342-5131; *Fax:*(309) 342-0840
www.galesburgradio.com
results@galesburgradio.com
Radio Stns: 1 AM. 3 FM.
WGIL Galesburg, IL; WAAG Galesburg, IL; WKAY Knoxville, IL; WLSR Galesburg, IL;
John Pritchard, President
Roger Lundeen, General Manager

Gateway Radio Works Inc.
22 West Main Street, Mount Sterling KY 40353
(859)-498-1077; *Fax:*(859)-498-7930;
Radio Stns: 1 AM. 3 FM.
WMST Mt. Sterling, KY; WKCA Salt Lick, KY; WIVY Morehead, KY; WKYN Owingsville, KY;
Hays McMakin, President
Jeff Ray, Operations Dir

GCC Bend LLC
969 S. W. Colorado, Bend OR 97702
(541) 388-3300; *Fax:*(541) 389-7885
www.ksjj.com,www.magic100fm.com,www.power94.fm
Radio Stns: 1 AM. 3 FM.
KICE Bend, OR; KMGX Bend, OR; KSJJ Redmond, OR; KXIX Sunriver, OR;
Dana Horner, COO

Genesis Communications Inc.
2110 Powers Ferry Rd.,Suite 198, Atlanta GA 30339
(678) 324-0170; *Fax:*(678) 324-0174
www.radiogenesis.com
ceo@radiogenesis.com
Ownership: Bruce C. Maduri, J. Donald Childress.
Radio Stns: 6 AM.
WAMT Pine Castle Sky Lake, FL; WIXC Titusville, FL; WHOO Kissimmee, FL; WMGG Egypt Lake, FL; WHBO Pinellas Park, FL; WWBA Largo, FL;
Bruce C. Maduri, President/CEO
J Donald Childress, VP

Georgia Eagle Broadcasting Inc.
1350 Radio Loop Rd., Warner Robins GA 31088
(478) 923-3416; *Fax:*(478) 923-3236
www.georgiaeagleradio.com
Radio Stns: 6 AM. 8 FM.
WCEH Hawkinsville, GA; WRWR Warner Robins, GA; WPTB Statesboro, GA; WSYL Sylvania, GA; WDXQ Cochran, GA; WWNS Statesboro, GA; WNNG-FM Unadilla, GA; WMCD Claxton, GA; WHKN Millen, GA; WSSY Pinehurst, GA; WPMX Statesboro, GA; WQXZ Hawkinsville, GA; WRWR-FM Cochran, GA; WZBX Rocky Ford, GA;

Georgia-Carolina Radiocasting Companies
Drawer E, Toccoa GA 30577
(706) 297-7264; *Fax:*(706) 297-7266
www.gacaradio.com
sutton@gacaradio.com
Radio Stns: 8 AM. 6 FM.
WALH Mountain City, GA; WFSC Franklin, NC; WGHC(AM) Clayton, GA; WNEG Toccoa, GA; WRGC Sylva, NC; WSNW Seneca, SC; WSGC Elberton, GA; WGHC Clayton, GA; WSGC-FM Elberton, GA; WGOG Walhalla, SC; WNGA

Clermont, GA; WRBN Clayton, GA; WNCC-FM Franklin, NC; WLHR-FM Lavonia, GA;
Douglas M. (Art) Sutton Jr., Chairman
M. Terry Carter, President
Tonya Burgess, Operations Dir

Geos Communications
Box 701, Tunkhannock PA 18657
(570) 836-4200; *Fax:*(570) 928-2100;
Radio Stns: 2 FM.
WEMR Pleasant Gap, PA; WNKZ Dushore, PA;
Kevin Fitzgerald, President

GHB Radio Group
1776 Briarcliff Rd. N.E.,Suite A, Atlanta GA 30306-2106
(404) 875-1110; *Fax:*(404) 875-1186
Ownership: George H. Buck Jr.
Radio Stns: 11 AM. 1 FM.
WEGO(AM) Winston-Salem, NC; WAVO Rock Hill, SC; WCGC Belmont, NC; WHVN Charlotte, NC; WAME Statesville, NC; WMGY Montgomery, AL; WNAP Norristown, PA; WSVM Valdese, NC; WIST New Orleans, LA; WBLO Thomasville, NC; WYZE Atlanta, GA; WOLS Waxhaw, NC;
Jacob Bogan, COO
George Buck Jr., President

Gleason Radio Group
555 Center St., Auburn ME 04210
(207) 748-5868; *Fax:*(207) 784-4700
www.gleasonmedia.com
dick@gleasonmedia.com
Ownership: Richard D. Gleason, 100%.
Radio Stns: 3 AM. 2 FM.
WKTQ South Paris, ME; WTME Rumford, ME; WEZR Lewiston, ME; WOXO-FM Norway, ME; WTBM Mexico, ME;
Richard Gleason, President

Gleiser Communications LLC
1001 E. Southeast Loop 323,Suite 455, Tyler TX 75701
(903) 593-2519; *Fax:*(903) 597-4141
www.gleisercom.com,www.kdok.com
info@ktbb.com
Radio Stns: 3 AM. 1 FM.
KEES Gladewater, TX; KTBB Tyler, TX; KYZS Tyler, TX; KTBB-FM Tyler, TX;
Paul Gleiser, CEO

Glory Communications Inc.
Box 2355, West Columbia SC 29171
(803) 939-9530; *Fax:*(803) 939-9469;
Radio Stns: 4 AM. 5 FM.
WEAF Saint Stephen, SC; WQXL Columbia, SC; WGCV Cayce, SC; WTQS Cameron, SC; WFMV South Congaree, SC; WLJI Summerton, SC; WPDT Coward, SC; WSPX Bowman, SC; WTUA Pinopolis, SC;
Alex Snipe, CEO

Goforth Media Inc.
Box 1328, Mobile AL 36633
(251) 473-8488; *Fax:*(251) 473-8854
www.goforth.org
wgoforth@goforth.org
Radio Stns: 1 AM. 1 FM.
WBHY Mobile, AL; WBHY-FM Mobile, AL;
Wilbur Goforth, President
Stephen Goforth, Operations Dir
Steve Riggs, Vice President

Gold Coast Broadcasting LLC
2284 S. Victoria,Suite 2M, Ventura CA 93003
(805) 289-1400,; *Fax:*(805) 644-4257;
Radio Stns: 3 AM. 3 FM.
KKZZ Santa Paula, CA; KUNX Ventura, CA; KVTA Port Hueneme, CA; KCAQ Oxnard, CA; KFYV Ojai, CA; KOCP Camarillo, CA;
John Hearne, Chairman
Miles Sexton, President

Good Karma Broadcasting L.L.C.
Box 902, Beaver Dam WI 53916
(920) 885-4442; *Fax:*(920) 885-2152;
Radio Stns: 8 AM. 3 FM.
WWGK Cleveland, OH; WRRD Waukesha, WI; WEFL Tequesta, FL; WBEV Beaver Dam, WI; WKNR Cleveland, OH; WTJK South Beloit, IL; WTTN Columbus, WI; WAUK Jackson, WI; WWHG Evansville, WI; WTLX Monona, WI; WXRO Beaver Dam, WI;
Chris Hartl, Operations Dir
Craig Karmazin, General Manager
Rick Armon, Operations Director

Good News Communications Inc.
3222 S. Richey Ave., Tucson AZ 85713
(520) 790-2440; *Fax:*(520) 790-2937;
Radio Stns: 4 AM.
KAPR Douglas, AZ; KGMS Tucson, AZ; KNXN Sierra Vista, AZ; KVOI Cortaro, AZ;
Douglas Martin, President
Mary Martin, Operations Dir

Good News Media Inc.
Box 1400, Traverse City MI 49685-1400
(231) 946-1400; *Fax:*(231) 946-3959
www.wljn.com
Radio Stns: 2 AM. 1 FM.
WLJW Cadillac, MI; WLJN Elmwood Township, MI; WLJN-FM Traverse City, MI;
Doug Knorr, President

Good News Network
2278 Wortham Lane, Grovetown GA 30813-5103
(706) 309-9610; *Fax:*(706) 309-9669
www.gnnradio.org
ctbarinowski@comcast.net
Radio Stns: 1 AM. 8 FM.
WQRX Valley Head, AL; WGPH Vidalia, GA; WLGP Harkers Island, NC; WLPF Ocilla, GA; WPMA Buckhead, GA; WPWB Byron, GA; WWGF Donalsonville, GA; WZIQ Smithville, GA; WTHP Gibson, GA;
Clarence Barinowski, CEO

GoodRadio.TV
777 S. Flagler Dr.,Suite 800, West Palm Beach FL 33401
(561) 515-6142
goodradio.tv
info@goodradio.tv
Radio Stns: 12 AM. 13 FM.
KAAN Bethany, MO; KBNN Lebanon, MO; KCOB Newton, IA; KDKD Clinton, MO; KGRN Grinnell, IA; KJFF Festus, MO; KJPW Waynesville, MO; KMCD Fairfield, IA; KMRN Cameron, MO; KIIK Waynesville, MO; KREI Farmington, MO; KWIX Moberly, MO; KAAN-FM Bethany, MO; KCOB-FM Newton, IA; KDKD-FM Clinton, MO; KFBD-FM Waynesville, MO; KKFD-FM Fairfield, IA; KIRK Macon, MO; KJEL Lebanon, MO; KOZQ-FM Waynesville, MO; KKWK Cameron, MO; KRES Moberly, MO; KRTI Grinnell, IA; KTJJ Farmington, MO; KTCM Madison, MO;
Dean Goodman, CEO

Gordon Ackley Stns
Box 302179, St. Thomas VI 00803-2179
(340) 776-3291; *Fax:*(340) 776-7060;
Radio Stns: 1 AM. 2 FM.
WVWI Charlotte Amalie, VI; WVJZ Charlotte Amalie, VI; WWKS Cruz Bay, VI;

Gore-Overgaard Broadcasting Inc.
11310 E. Arabian Park Dr., Scottsdale AZ 85259
(480) 314-0144; *Fax:*(480) 314-4942;
Radio Stns: 3 AM.
KLHC Bakersfield, CA; KBIF Fresno, CA; KIRV Fresno, CA;
Harold Gore, CEO
Cordell J. Overgaard, President

Grace Broadcasting Services Inc.
25 Stonebrook Pl.,Suite G, #322, Jackson TN 38305
(731) 663-3931; *Fax:*(731) 663-9804
www.gracebroadcasting.com
Radio Stns: 3 AM. 4 FM.
WDTM Selmer, TN; WNKX Lobelville, TN; WTNE Trenton, TN; WHPY-FM Lobelville, TN; WSIB Selmer, TN; WTKB-FM Atwood, TN; WWGM Alamo, TN;

Graham Newspapers Inc.
620 Oak St., Graham TX 76450
(940) 549-1330; *Fax:*(940) 549-8628
gm@kwkq-kswa.com
Radio Stns: 2 AM. 2 FM.
KROO Breckenridge, TX; KSWA Graham, TX; KLXK Breckenridge, TX; KWKQ Graham, TX;
Joe Graham, General Manager

Great Eastern Radio LLC
35 S. Main St.,Suite 300, Hanover NH 3755
(603) 643-4007;
Radio Stns: 1 AM. 6 FM.
WTSL Hanover, NH; WEEY Swanzey, NH; WGXL Hanover, NH; WMXR Woodstock, VT; WTPL Hillsboro, NH; WKKN Westminster, VT; WXXK Lebanon, NH;

Great Lakes Radio Inc.
2025 US 41 W., Marquette MI 49855
(906) 227-7777,; *Fax:*(906) 475-8888,
www.greatlakesradio.org
todd@greatlakesradio.org
Radio Stns: 1 AM. 4 FM.
WQXO Munising, MI; WFXD Marquette, MI; WRUP Palmer, MI; WKQS-FM Negaunee, MI; WPIQ Manistique, MI;
Todd Noordyk, President

Great Plains Media Inc.
Box 1628, Cape Girardeau MO 63702-1628
(573) 651-0707;
Radio Stns: 3 AM. 7 FM.
KLWN Lawrence, KS; WHUB Cookeville, TN; WPTN Cookeville, TN; KMXN Osage City, KS; KKSW Lawrence, KS; WGIC Cookeville, TN; WGSQ Cookeville, TN; WRPW Colfax, IL; WZIM(FM) Lexington, IL; WIBL(FM) Fairbury, IL;
Jerome Zimmer, President

Great Scott Broadcasting
224 Maugers Mill Rd., Pottstown PA 19464
(610) 326-4000; *Fax:*(610) 326-7984
www.1370wpaz.com
jay.warren@1370wpaz.com
Ownership: Faye Scott, special trustee, Charles Mott & James Worthington, co-trustees, Family Trust U/D/T dated 11/6/81, 86.72% of total assets;Faye Scott Annuity Trust U/D/T dated 3/6/02, Charles Mott & James Worthington, co-trustees, 6.64% of total assets; Faye Scott & James Worthington, co-trustees, Marita
Radio Stns: 2 AM. 9 FM.
WJWK Seaford, DE; WJWL Georgetown, DE; WGBG Seaford, DE; WKDB Laurel, DE; WJKI Bethany Beach, DE; WKHI Fruitland, MD; WXSH Pocomoke City, MD; WOCQ Berlin, MD; WPAZ Pottstown, PA; WZEB Ocean View, DE; WZBH Georgetown, DE;
Faye Scott, CEO
Jay Warren, General Manager

Greater Media Inc.
35 Braintree Hill Office Park,Suite 300, Braintree MA 02184
(781) 348-8600; *Fax:*(781) 348-8680
www.greatermedia.com
Ownership: Bordes family, 100%.
Radio Stns: 5 AM. 17 FM.
WBT Charlotte, NC; WCTC New Brunswick, NJ; WMTR Morristown, NJ; WPEN Philadelphia, PA; WWTR Bridgewater, NJ; WBOS Brookline, MA; WBT-FM Chester, SC; WKLB-FM Waltham, MA; WCSX Birmingham, MI; WDHA-FM Dover, NJ; WJRZ-FM Manahawkin, NJ; WLNK Charlotte, NC; WMGQ New Brunswick, NJ; WMJX Boston, MA; WMMR Philadelphia, PA; WPEN-FM Burlington, NJ; WRAT Point Pleasant, NJ; WRIF Detroit, MI; WROR-FM Framingham, MA; WTKK Boston, MA; WMGC-FM Detroit, MI; WBEN-FM Philadelphia, PA;
Peter Smyth, Chairman

Greeley Broadcasting Corp.
1020 9th St.,Suite 201, Greeley CO 80631
(970) 356-1452; *Fax:*(970) 356-8522;
Radio Stns: 1 AM. 2 FM.
KGRE Greeley, CO; KFVR-FM Beulah, CO; KLMI Rock River, WY;
Ricardo Salazar, President

Grenax Broadcasting LLC
10337 Carriage Club Dr., Lone Tree CO 80124
(303) 790-4015;
Radio Stns: 4 FM.
KBTK(FM) Kachina Village, AZ; KSED Sedona, AZ; KWMX Williams, AZ; WCFX Clare, MI;
Greg Dinetz, President

Guaranty Broadcasting Co. of Baton Rouge LLC
929 Government St.,Suite B, Baton Rouge LA 70802-6034
(225) 388-9898; *Fax:*(225) 344-3077
www.gbcradio.com
owen.weber@gbcradio.com
Ownership: Guaranty Broadcasting Company LLC, 100%.
Radio Stns: 5 FM.
KYPY Donaldsonville, LA; WNXX Jackson, LA; WDGL Baton Rouge, LA; WBRP Baker, LA; WTGE Baton Rouge, LA;
Owen Weber, VP

Guyann Corp.
Box 1930, Flagstaff AZ 86002
(928) 774-5231; *Fax:*(928) 779-2988
www.kaff.com
Ownership: Richard D. Guest, 50%; Pamela Flaherty, 50%. Note: Richard D. Guest and Pamela Flaherty are co-special administrators.
Radio Stns: 2 AM. 3 FM.

KAFF Flagstaff, AZ; KNOT Prescott, AZ; KAFF-FM Flagstaff, AZ; KMGN Flagstaff, AZ; KTMG Prescott, AZ;

Hall Communications Inc.
Box 2038,404 W. Lime St., Lakeland FL 33806
(863) 682-8184; *Fax:*(863) 683-2409
www.hallradio.com
Ownership: Bonnie Hall Rowbotham.
Radio Stns: 8 AM. 12 FM.
WLKW West Warwick, RI; WICH Norwich, CT; WILI Willimantic, CT; WJOY Burlington, VT; WLKF Lakeland, FL; WLPA Lancaster, PA; WNBH New Bedford, MA; WONN Lakeland, FL; WBTZ Plattsburgh, NY; WCTK New Bedford, MA; WCTY Norwich, CT; WILI-FM Willimantic, CT; WIZN Vergennes, VT; WKOL Plattsburgh, NY; WNLC East Lyme, CT; WOKO Burlington, VT; WPCV Winter Haven, FL; WROZ Lancaster, PA; WKNL New London, CT; WWRZ Fort Meade, FL;
Bonnie Rowbotham, Chairman
Arthur Rowbotham, President
Bill Baldwin, EVP

Haugo Broadcasting Inc.
Box 1680, Rapid City SD 57709
(605) 343-0888; *Fax:*(605) 342-3075;
Radio Stns: 1 AM. 1 FM.
KTOQ Rapid City, SD; KSQY Deadwood, SD;
Chris Haugo, President

He's Alive Inc.
Box 540, Grantsville MD 21536
(301) 895-3292; *Fax:*(301) 895-3293
www.hesalive.net
hesalive@hesalive.net
Ownership: Non-stock, nonprofit organization.
Radio Stns: 4 FM.
WAIJ Grantsville, MD; WLIC Frostburg, MD; WPCL Northern Cambria, PA; WRIJ Masontown, PA;
Dewayne Johnson, President

Heartland Christian Broadcasters Inc.
Box 433, International Falls MN 56649
(218) 285-7398; *Fax:*(218) 285-7419;
Radio Stns: 3 FM.
KBHW International Falls, MN; KXBR International Falls, MN; KADU Hibbing, MN;

Heartland Communications Group LLC
4650 W. Spencer St., Appleton WI 54914
(920) 882-4750; *Fax:*(920) 882-4751
www.heartlandcomm.com
Radio Stns: 5 AM. 8 FM.
WATW Ashland, WI; WCCY Houghton, MI; WERL Eagle River, WI; WFER Iron River, MI; WPFP Park Falls, WI; WBSZ Ashland, WI; WCQM Park Falls, WI; WHKB Houghton, MI; WIKB-FM Iron River, MI; WJJH Ashland, WI; WNXR Iron River, WI; WOLV Houghton, MI; WRJO Eagle River, WI;
Tom Bookey, CEO
James Gregori, President

Hi-Favor Broadcasting LLC
136 S. Oak Knoll Ave., Pasadena CA 91101
(626) 356-4230; *Fax:*(626) 795-9185;
Radio Stns: 3 AM.
KEZY San Bernardino, CA; KLTX Long Beach, CA; KSDO San Diego, CA;

High Desert Broadcasting LLC
570 East Ave. Q9, Palmdale CA 93550
(661) 947-3107; *Fax:*(661) 272-5688;
Radio Stns: 2 AM. 3 FM.
KOSS Lancaster, CA; KUTY Palmdale, CA; KGMX Lancaster, CA; KKZQ Tehachapi, CA; KLKX(FM) Rosamond, CA;
Miles Sexton, President

Hispanic Target Media Inc.
c/o Leventhal Senter & Lerman PLLC,2000 K St. N.W., Suite 600, Washington DC 20006-1809
(202) 429-8970; *Fax:*(202) 293-7783;
Radio Stns: 4 FM.
KJJS Zapata, TX; KGWT George West, TX; KAJP Carrizo Springs, TX; KALN Dexter, NM;
Francisco San Millan, President

Holladay Broadcasting of Louisiana LLC
Box 4808, Monroe LA 71211
(318) 398-1618;
Radio Stns: 3 AM. 5 FM.
KRJO Monroe, LA; KBYO Tallulah, LA; KMLB Monroe, LA; KLSM Tallulah, LA; KJLO-FM Monroe, LA; KJMG Bastrop, LA; KLIP Monroe, LA; KRVV Bastrop, LA;
Robert Holladay, Member

Holston Valley Broadcasting Corp.
222 Commerce St., Kingsport TN 37660
(423) 246-9578; *Fax:*(423) 247-9836
hvbcgroup.com
Ownership: Glenwood Communications Corp., 100%.
Radio Stns: 4 AM. 4 FM.
WKPT Kingsport, TN; WKTP Jonesborough, TN; WUKZ(AM) Marion, VA; WOPI Bristol, TN; WMEV-FM Marion, VA; WRZK Colonial Heights, TN; WVEK-FM Weber City, VA; WTFM Kingsport, TN;
TV Stns: 1 TV.
WKPT-TV Kingsport, TN;
George DeVault Jr., President

Holy Family Communications
6325 Sheridan Dr., Williamsville NY 14221
(716) 839-6117; *Fax:*(716) 839-0400
www.wlof.net
Radio Stns: 2 AM. 1 FM.
WQOR Olyphant, PA; WHIC Rochester, NY; WLOF Elma, NY;
James Wright, President

Hoosier Broadcasting Corp.
3500 DePauw Blvd.,Suite 2085, Indianapolis IN 46268-6103
(317) 870-8400; *Fax:*(317) 870-8404;
Radio Stns: 3 FM.
WIRE Lebanon, IN; WSPM Cloverdale, IN; WCNB Dayton, IN;
William Poorman, President

Horizon Broadcasting Group, LLC
854 N.E. 4th Street, Bend OR 97701
(541) 383-3825; *Fax:*(541) 383-3403
www.horizonbroadcasting.com
Radio Stns: 1 AM. 4 FM.
KRCO Prineville, OR; KLTW-FM Prineville, OR; KWPK-FM Sisters, OR; KQAK Bend, OR; KWLZ-FM West Linn, OR;
Keith Shipman, CEO

Horizon Christian Fellowship
5331 Mt. Alifan Dr., San Diego CA 92111
(858) 277-4991; *Fax:*(858) 277-1365
www.horizonsd.org/radio.asp
Radio Stns: 19 FM.
KSRD St. Joseph, MO; WRYP Wellfleet, MA; KRBG Umbarger, TX; WMJC Richland, MI; KWDS Kettleman City, CA; WHZN New Whiteland, IN; WWDL Plainfield, IN; KWDI Idalia, CO; KXCS(FM) Coahoma, TX; KHZZ Sargent, NE; KHZY Overton, NE; KHZK Kotzebue, AK; WVUV-FM Fagaitua, AS; KLTQ New England, ND; KHRW Ranchester, WY; KWDR Royal City, WA; WTPN Westby, WI; WSRC(FM) Waynetown, IN; KLED Antelope Valley Crestview, WY;
Tom Phillips, COO

Horne Radio Group
517 Watt Rd., Knoxville TN 37922
(865) 675-4105; *Fax:*(865) 675-4859
www.wkvl.com
knoxvilletalk@aol.com
Radio Stns: 5 AM. 1 FM.
WDEH Sweetwater, TN; WGAP Maryville, TN; WKVL Knoxville, TN; WMTY Farragut, TN; WLOD Loudon, TN; WFIV-FM Loudon, TN;
Douglas A. Horne, President

Houston Christian Broadcasters Inc.
KHCB Network,2424 South Blvd., Houston TX 77098-5110
(713) 520-5200
www.khcb.org
email@khcb.org
Radio Stns: 3 AM. 15 FM.
KHCB League City, TX; KHCH Huntsville, TX; DKCPC Rancho Mirage, CA; KANJ Giddings, TX; KKER Kerrville, TX; KHCP Paris, TX; KHTA Wake Village, TX; KHCB-FM Houston, TX; KHBW(FM) Brownwood, TX; KHKV Kerrville, TX; KHMD Mansfield, LA; KHIB Bastrop, TX; KHCL Arcadia, LA; KHCJ Jefferson, TX; KHVT Bloomington, TX; KHML Madisonville, TX; KBLC Fredericksburg, TX; KHPO Port O'Connor, TX;
Bruce E. Munsterman, President
Bonnie BeMent, General Manager

HRN Broadcasting Inc.
Box 430, Lincolnton NC 28093
(704) 735-8071; *Fax:*(704) 732-9567
www.hrnb.com
Radio Stns: 6 AM.
WOHS Shelby, NC; WCSL Cherryville, NC; WGNC Gastonia, NC; WLON Lincolnton, NC; WZGV Cramerton, NC; WZGM Black Mountain, NC;

Hubbard Broadcasting Inc.
3415 University Ave., St. Paul MN 55114
(651) 646-5555; *Fax:*(651) 642-4103
jmahoney@hbi.com
Radio Stns: 3 AM. 2 FM.
KSTP St. Paul, MN; WIXK New Richmond, WI; WBQH Silver Spring, MD; KSTP-FM St. Paul, MN; WTMY(FM) Coon Rapids, MN;
TV Stns: 12 TV.
KAAL Austin, MN; KOB Albuquerque, NM; KOBF Farmington, NM; KOBR Roswell, NM; KRWF Redwood Falls, MN; KSAX Alexandria, MN; KSTP-TV St. Paul, MN; KSTC-TV Minneapolis, MN; WDIO-DT Duluth, MN; WHEC-TV Rochester, NY; WIRT Hibbing, MN; WNYT Albany, NY;
Gerald Deeney, SVP/CFO
Edward Aiken, Vice President
Harold Crump, Vice President
Julia Coyte, Vice President
Linda Tremere, Vice President
Robert Hubbard, Vice President
Stanley Hubbard II, Vice President

Hunt County Radio LLC
1517 Wolfe City Drive, Greenville TX 75401
(903) 455-1400; *Fax:*(903) 455-1485
www.biggvl14.com
hrbeavers@yahoo.com
Radio Stns: 1 AM. 1 FM.
KGVL Greenville, TX; KIKT Greenville, TX;
Jean McCoy, Programming Director

Huth Broadcasting
Box 669, Marysville CA 95901
(530) 742-5555; *Fax:*(530) 741-3758;
Radio Stns: 4 AM.
KBLF Red Bluff, CA; KMYC Marysville, CA; KOBO Yuba City, CA; KRAC Quincy, CA;

Hutton Broadcasting LLC
915 Orchid Point Way, Vero Beach FL 32963-9518
(772) 559-3790;
Radio Stns: 2 AM. 4 FM.
KVSF Santa Fe, NM; KTRC Santa Fe, NM; KBAC Las Vegas, NM; KQBA Los Alamos, NM; KLBU Pecos, NM; KVSF-FM Pecos, NM;
Jennifer Owens Hutton, President
Scott Hutton, General Manager

ICA Radio Ltd.
700 N. Grant St., 6th Fl., Odessa TX 79761
(432) 580-5672; *Fax:*(432) 580-9102
Ownership: ICA Broadcasting L.L.C., sole gen ptnr, 100% votes. Note: ICA Broadcasting L.L.C. also owns KOSA-TV Odessa, TX.
Radio Stns: 1 AM. 4 FM.
KCRS Midland, TX; KCHX Midland, TX; KCRS-FM Midland, TX; KFZX Gardendale, TX; KMRK-FM Odessa, TX;
Barry Marks, President

Icicle Broadcasting Inc.
7475 KOHO Pl., Leavenworth WA 98826
(509) 548-1011; *Fax:*(509) 548-3222
www.kohoradio.com,www.kozi.com
Radio Stns: 1 AM. 3 FM.
KOZI Chelan, WA; KOHO-FM Leavenworth, WA; KOZI-FM Chelan, WA; KZAL Manson, WA;
Gary Mathews, General Manager

Idaho Wireless Corp.
Box 97, Pocatello ID 83204
(208) 234-1290; *Fax:*(208) 234-9451;
Radio Stns: 1 AM. 2 FM.
KOUU Pocatello, ID; KORR American Falls, ID; KZBQ Pocatello, ID;
Paul Anderson, General Manager

IdaVend Broadcasting Inc.
805 Stewart Ave., Lewiston ID 83501
(208) 743-1551; *Fax:*(208) 743-4440
rprasil@idavend.com
Radio Stns: 1 AM. 2 FM.
KRLC Lewiston-Clarkston, ID; KMOK Lewiston, ID; KVTY Lewiston, ID;
Michelle King, Operations Dir
Robert Prasil, General Manager
Melva Prasil, Station Manager
Kevin Keenan, General Sales Mgr
Zoanne Davis, Programming Director

IHR Educational Broadcasting
Box 180, Tahoma CA 96142

(530) 584-5700; *Fax:*(530) 584-5705
www.ihradio.org
info@ihradio.org

Radio Stns: 8 AM. 2 FM.
KAHI Auburn, CA; KIHM Reno, NV; KJOP Lemoore, CA; KSFB San Francisco, CA; KSMH West Sacramento, CA; KJPG Frazier Park, CA; KWG Stockton, CA; KIHH Eureka, CA; KXXQ Milan, NM; KPJP Greenville, CA;

Illinois Bible Institute Inc.
Box 140, Carlinville IL 62626
(217) 854-4600; *Fax:*(217) 854-4610
www.wibi.org
rwhitworth@idcag.org

Radio Stns: 8 FM.
WBGL Champaign, IL; WBMV Mount Vernon, IL; WCIC Pekin, IL; WCRT-FM Terre Haute, IN; WIBI Carlinville, IL; WTSG Carlinville, IL; WPRC Sheffield, IL; WZGL Charleston, IL;
Richard Whitworth, Director

Impact Radio LLC
59750 Constantine Rd., Three Rivers MI 49093-9303
(269) 278-1815; *Fax:*(269) 273-7975
drumsey@wlkm.com

Radio Stns: 2 AM. 3 FM.
WRCI Three Rivers, MI; WQCT Bryan, OH; KQLZ(FM) Mt Home, ID; WBNO-FM Bryan, OH; WLKM-FM Three Rivers, MI;
Dennis Rumsey, President

Independence Media Holdings LLC
8226 Douglas Ave.,Suite 627, Dallas TX 75225
(469) 619-1001;

Radio Stns: 1 AM. 5 FM.
WOCN Miami, FL; WHPI Glasford, IL; WPIA Eureka, IL; WWCT Bartonville, IL; WZPN Farmington, IL; WWKN Morgantown, KY;

Information Communications Corp.
Box 2061, Bristol TN 37621-2061
(423) 878-6279; *Fax:*(423) 878-6520;

Radio Stns: 3 AM.
WABN Abingdon, VA; WHGG Kingsport, TN; WPWT Colonial Heights, TN;
Dr. Kenneth C. Hill, CEO

Ingstad Brothers Broadcasting LLC
Box 1248, Minnetonka MN 55345
(952) 938-0575; *Fax:*(952) 938-2295;

Radio Stns: 2 AM. 2 FM.
KCHK New Prague, MN; KNUJ New Ulm, MN; KRDS-FM New Prague, MN; KNUJ-FM Sleepy Eye, MN;

Inland Northwest Broadcasting LLC
805 Stewart Ave., Lewiston ID 83501
(208) 791-2605; *Fax:*(208) 743-4440
rprasil@idavend.com

Radio Stns: 2 AM. 2 FM.
KCLX Colfax, WA; KMAX Colfax, WA; KRAO-FM Colfax, WA; KZZL-FM Pullman, WA;
Robert Prasil, President
Gary Cummings, Operations Dir
Steve Franko, Chief Engineer
Michelle King, Director, Operations

Inner Banks Media LLC
408 W. Arlington Blvd.,Suite 101-B, Greenville NC 27834
(252) 355-8822;

Radio Stns: 4 FM.
WTIB Williamston, NC; WRHD Farmville, NC; WNBU(FM) Oriental, NC; WRHT Morehead City, NC;

Inner City Broadcasting
3 Park Ave., 41st Fl., New York NY 10016
(212) 447-1000; *Fax:*(212) 447-5197
www.wbls.com
info@wbls.com

Radio Stns: 7 AM. 9 FM.
KVTO Berkeley, CA; KVVN Santa Clara, CA; WJNT Pearl, MS; WJQS Jackson, MS; WLIB New York, NY; WOAD Jackson, MS; WOIC Columbia, SC; KBLX-FM Berkeley, CA; WARQ Columbia, SC; WBLS New York, NY; WHXT Orangeburg, SC; WJMI Jackson, MS; WKXI-FM Magee, MS; WMFX St. Andrews, SC; WWDM Sumter, SC; WZMJ Batesburg, SC;
Pierre Sutton, Chairman

Inter-Island Communications Inc.
1868 Halsey Dr., Piti GU 96915
(671) 477-7108; *Fax:*(671) 477-6411;

Radio Stns: 2 AM. 4 FM.
KCNM Saipan, MP; KTWG Agana, GU; KNUT Tamuning, GU; KSTO Agana, GU; KZMI Garapan-Saipan, MP; KISH Agana, GU;
Edward Poppe Jr., President

International Broadcasting Corp.
1554 Bori St., San Juan PR 00927-6113
(787) 274-1800; *Fax:*(787) 281-9758;

Radio Stns: 7 AM. 1 FM.
WIBS Guayama, PR; WDNO Quebradillas, PR; WEKO Morovis, PR; WRSJ Bayamon, PR; WTIL Mayaguez, PR; WXRF Guayama, PR; WGIT Canovanas, PR; WVOZ-FM Carolina, PR;

TV Stns: 3 TV.
WTCV San Juan, PR; WVEO Aguadilla, PR; WVOZ-TV Ponce, PR;
Pedro Callazo, President
Margarita Nazario, General Manager

Iorio Broadcasting Inc.
1316 7th Ave., Beaver Falls PA 15010
(724) 846-4100; *Fax:*(724) 843-7771;

Radio Stns: 2 AM.
WBVP Beaver Falls, PA; WMBA Ambridge, PA;
Frank Iorio, President

J&V Communications Inc.
222 Hazard St., Orlando FL 32804
(407) 841-8282; *Fax:*(407) 841-8250
WWW.WPRD.COM
WPRD1440@GMAIL.COM

Radio Stns: 4 AM.
WOTS Kissimmee, FL; WPRD Winter Park, FL; WSDO Sanford, FL; WTJV Deland, FL;
JOHN TORRADO, President
JOCELYN TORRADO, Operations Dir
HECTOR L. REYES, General Manager

J-Systems Franchising Corp.
Hotel Traylor,1444 Hamilton St., Allentown PA 18102
(610) 435-5913; *Fax:*(610) 435-8918
www.wmgh.com
wmgh@ptd.net
Ownership: Harold G. Fulmer III, 100%.

Radio Stns: 1 AM. 1 FM.
WLSH Lansford, PA; WMGH-FM Tamaqua, PA;
Harold Fulmer III, President

J. & J. Fritz Media Ltd.
Box 311, Fredericksburg TX 78624
(830) 997-2197; *Fax:*(830) 997-2198
www.texasrebelradio.com
txradio@ktc.com

Radio Stns: 1 AM. 3 FM.
KNAF Fredericksburg, TX; KEEP Bandera, TX; KFAN-FM Johnson City, TX; KNAF-FM Fredericksburg, TX;
Jayson Fritz, General Manager
Jan Fritz, General Sales Mgr

J.R. Livesay Group
Box 322, Mattoon IL 61938-0322
(217) 234-6464; *Fax:*(217) 234-6019
wlbh@wlbh.com
Ownership: J.R. Livesay II owns 50% of WLBH-AM-FM. Shirley L. Herrington owns 35% of WLBH-AM-FM.

Radio Stns: 1 AM. 1 FM.
WLBH Mattoon, IL; WLBH-FM Mattoon, IL;
J.R. Livesay, Chairman
Shirley Herrington, CFO

Jabar Communications Inc.
5081 Rivers Ave., North Charleston SC 29406
(843) 554-1063; *Fax:*(843) 554-1088
jabarcommunications.com
traffic@jabarcommunications.com

Radio Stns: 2 AM. 1 FM.
WAZS Summerville, SC; WZJY Mount Pleasant, SC; WJNI Ladson, SC;
Thomas Daniel, President

Jackson County Broadcasting Inc.
Box 667,295 E. Main St., Jackson OH 45640
(740) 286-3023; *Fax:*(740) 286-6679
jmossbarger@jbiradio.com
Ownership: Alan Stockmeister

Radio Stns: 1 AM. 2 FM.
WYPC Wellston, OH; WCJO Jackson, OH; WKOV-FM Wellston, OH;
Jerry Mossbarger, General Manager

Jackson Radio Works Inc.
1700 Glenshire Dr., Jackson MI 49201
(517) 787-9546; *Fax:*(517) 787-7517
www.wkhm.com
bgoldsen@wkhm.com

Radio Stns: 2 AM. 1 FM.
WIBM Jackson, MI; WKHM Jackson, MI; WKHM-FM Brooklyn, MI;
Bruce Goldsen, President

Jacobs Media Corp.
PO Box 10, Gainesville GA 30503
(770) 532-9921; *Fax:*(770) 532-0506
www.jacobsmedia.net
jay.jacobs@jacobsmedia.net
Ownership: John W. Jacobs, III

Radio Stns: 2 AM. 1 FM.
WDUN Gainesville, GA; WGGA Gainesville, GA; WDUN-FM Clarkesville, GA;
John W. Jacobs III, President & CEO
Elizabeth J. Carswell, Secretary

James Crystal Inc.
6600 N. Andrews Ave.,Suite 160, Fort Lauderdale FL 33309
(954) 315-1515; *Fax:*(954) 315-1555;

Radio Stns: 5 AM.
KCKN Roswell, NM; KBXD Dallas, TX; WFTL West Palm Beach, FL; WFLL Fort Lauderdale, FL; WMEN Royal Palm Beach, FL;
James Hilliard, President

James D. Ingstad Stns
1020 25th St. South, Fargo ND 58103
(701) 277-4200
Ownership: James D. Ingstad, 100%.

Radio Stns: 4 AM. 8 FM.
KALE Richland, WA; KTCR Yakima, WA; KBBO Selah, WA; KJOX Kennewick, WA; KARY-FM Grandview, WA; KEGX Richland, WA; KHHK Yakima, WA; KIOK Richland, WA; KKSR Walla Walla, WA; KRSE Yakima, WA; KUJ-FM Burbank, WA; KXDD Yakima, WA;

JER Licenses LLC
194 McGee Rd., Versailles KY 40383
(859) 879-0818;

Radio Stns: 3 FM.
WDTX Rothschild, WI; KXZT Newell, SD; KXZS Wall, SD;

Jodesha Broadcasting Inc.
Box 1198, Aberdeen WA 98520
(360) 533-3000; *Fax:*(360) 532-1456
www.jodesha.com
bossbill@jodesha.com

Radio Stns: 1 AM. 3 FM.
KBKW Aberdeen, WA; KJET Raymond, WA; KSWW Ocean Shores, WA; KANY Montesano, WA;
William J. Wolfenbarger, President
Susan Wolfenbarger, Operations Dir

Johnson Enterprises Inc.
338 S. KLEY Dr., Wellington KS 67152
(620) 326-3341; *Fax:*(620) 326-8512
www.kleyam.com
kley@sutv.com
Ownership: E. Gordon Johnson, Susan G. Johnson.

Radio Stns: 2 AM. 1 FM.
KKLE Winfield, KS; KLEY Wellington, KS; KWME Wellington, KS;
E. Gordon Johnson, President

Journal Communications Inc.
333 W. State St., Milwaukee WI 53203
(414) 224-2616; *Fax:*(414) 224-2469
www.jc.com

Radio Stns: 9 AM. 26 FM.
KCID Caldwell, ID; KLIO Wichita, KS; KFFN Tucson, AZ; KGEM Boise, ID; KSGF Springfield, MO; KFAQ Tulsa, OK; KXSP Omaha, NE; WKTI Powell, TN; WTMJ Milwaukee, WI; KTHI Caldwell, ID; KXBL Henryetta, OK; KEZO-FM Omaha, NE; KFDI-FM Wichita, KS; KRVB Nampa, ID; KTGV Oracle, AZ; KRVI Mount Vernon, MO; KICT-FM Wichita, KS; KJOT Boise, ID; KKCD Omaha, NE; KFXJ Augusta, KS; KSPW Sparta, MO; KMXZ-FM Tucson, AZ; KFTI-FM Newton, KS; KQXR Payette, ID; KSRZ Omaha, NE; KTTS-FM Springfield, MO; KVOO-FM Tulsa, OK; KYQQ Arkansas City, KS; KQTH Tucson, AZ; KSGF-FM Ash Grove, MO; WLWK-FM Milwaukee, WI; WWST Sevierville, TN; KQCH Omaha, NE; WKHT Knoxville, TN; WCYQ Karns, TN;

TV Stns: 12 TV.

KGUN-TV Tucson, AZ; KIVI-TV Nampa, ID; KMIR-TV Palm Springs, CA; KMTV-TV Omaha, NE; KNIN-TV Caldwell, ID; KTNV-TV Las Vegas, NV; KWBA-TV Sierra Vista, AZ; WACY-TV Appleton, WI; WFTX-TV Cape Coral, FL; WGBA-TV Green Bay, WI; WSYM-TV Lansing, MI; WTMJ-TV Milwaukee, WI;
Douglas Kiel, President

JVC Broadcasting
3075 Veterans Memorial Hwy.,Suite 201, Ronkonkoma NY 11779
(631) 648-2500; *Fax:*(631) 648-2510
www.jvcbroadcasting.com
Ownership: Northwood Ventures LLC.
Radio Stns: 1 AM. 6 FM.
WHLI Hempstead, NY; WBZO Bay Shore, NY; WKJY Hempstead, NY; WJVC Center Moriches, NY; WIGX Smithtown, NY; WRCN-FM Riverhead, NY; WPTY Calverton-Roanoke, NY;
John Caracciolo, President

JWC Broadcasting
259 S. Willow Ave., Cookeville TN 38501
(931) 528-6064; *Fax:*(931) 520-1590;
Radio Stns: 1 AM. 3 FM.
WATX Algood, TN; WBXE Baxter, TN; WKXD-FM Monterey, TN; WLQK Livingston, TN;
Joel Wilmoth, President

K95.5 Inc.
24189 E. 865 Rd., Welling OK 74471-2245
(918) 230-2165; *Fax:*(918) 457-3512
www.k955.com
Paynewh@aol.com
Radio Stns: 3 FM.
KTFX-FM Warner, OK; KTNT Eufaula, OK; KITX Hugo, OK;
William Payne, President

Kaspar Broadcasting Group
1401 W. Barner St., Frankfort IN 46041
(765) 659-3338; *Fax:*(765) 659-3338
www.kasparradio.com,www.wshw.com,www.wilc.com
Radio Stns: 2 AM. 2 FM.
KWRE Warrenton, MO; WILO Frankfort, IN; KFAV Warrenton, MO; WSHW Frankfort, IN;
Vern Kaspar, CEO
Russ Kaspar, Operations Dir

KCD Enterprises Inc.
Box 1100, Bartlesville OK 74005
(918) 336-1001; *Fax:*(918) 336-3939
www.bartlesvilleradio.com
radio@bartlesvilleradio.com
Radio Stns: 2 AM. 2 FM.
KPGM Pawhuska, OK; KWON Bartlesville, OK; KRIG-FM Nowata, OK; KYFM Bartlesville, OK;
Kevin Potter, President

KD Radio Inc.
733 E. Roosevelt Ave., Grants NM 87020
(505) 285-5598; *Fax:*(505) 285-5575
Ownership: Derek Underhill, 100%.
Radio Stns: 2 AM. 1 FM.
KALY Los Ranchos De Albuquerque, NM; KMIN Grants, NM; KDSK Grants, NM;
Derek Underhill, Chairman

KEA Radio Inc.
Box 966, Scottsboro AL 35768
(256) 259-2341; *Fax:*(256) 574-2156
www.wkeafm.com
Radio Stns: 2 FM.
WKEA-FM Scottsboro, AL; WMXN-FM Stevenson, AL;
Ronald Livengood, President
Diane Livengood, Operations Dir
Ivous Sisk, Treasurer
Gene Sisk, Vice President

Kemp Communications Inc.
3800 Howard Hughes Pkwy.,Wells Fargo Tower, 17th Fl., Las Vegas NV 89169
(702) 385-6000; *Fax:*(702) 385-6001;
Radio Stns: 1 AM. 4 FM.
KMZQ Las Vegas, NV; KVEG Mesquite, NV; KMZQ-FM Payson, AZ; KVGQ Overton, NV; KVGG Salome, AZ;
Will Kemp, President

KERM Inc.
201 W. 2nd, Russellville AR 72801
(479) 968-1184; *Fax:*(479) 967-5278
karv610@cei.net
Radio Stns: 2 AM. 2 FM.
KARV Russellville, AR; KURM Rogers, AR; KARV-FM Ola, AR; KURM-FM Gravette, AR;
James Womack, President
Chris Womack, General Manager

Key Broadcasting Inc.
Box 1227, Corbin KY 40702
(606) 528-8787; *Fax:*(606) 528-9928
Ownership: Terry E. Forcht.
Radio Stns: 8 AM. 11 FM.
WAIN Columbia, KY; WCVL Crawfordsville, IN; WFTG London, KY; WHOP Hopkinsville, KY; WSIP Paintsville, KY; WTCW Whitesburg, KY; WTLO Somerset, KY; WVLN Olney, IL; WAIN-FM Columbia, KY; WHOP-FM Hopkinsville, KY; WIKK Newton, IL; WIMC Crawfordsville, IN; WSEI Olney, IL; WSIP-FM Paintsville, KY; WCDQ Crawfordsville, IN; WWEL London, KY; WXKQ-FM Whitesburg, KY; WANV Annville, KY; WYKY Science Hill, KY;
Terry Forcht, President/CEO

Keymarket Communications LLC
100 Ryan Ct.,Suite 98, Pittsburgh PA 15205
(412) 489-1001; *Fax:*(412) 279-5500
www.froggyland.com
Radio Stns: 3 AM. 6 FM.
WOHI East Liverpool, OH; WOMP Bellaire, OH; WSTV Steubenville, OH; WOGG Oliver, PA; WOGI(FM) Moon Township, PA; WKPL Ellwood City, PA; WYJK-FM Bellaire, OH; WPKL Uniontown, PA; WUKL Bethlehem, WV;
Gerald Getz, CEO

KHWY Inc.
12381 Wilshire Blvd. #105, Los Angeles CA 90025
(310) 820-4628; *Fax:*(310) 826-7866
www.thehighwaystations.com
khwyha@earthlink.net
Radio Stns: 8 FM.
KHWY Essex, CA; KHWZ Ludlow, CA; KHYZ Mountain Pass, CA; KIXF Baker, CA; KIXW-FM Lenwood, CA; KRXV Yermo, CA; KHDR Lenwood, CA; KHRQ Baker, CA;
Howard Anderson, CEO
Kirk Anderson, President
Jean Sheranian, Operations Dir

Kindred Communications Inc.
401 11th St.,Suite 200, Huntington WV 25701
(304) 523-8401; *Fax:*(304) 523-4848
www.kindredcom.net
Radio Stns: 2 AM. 2 FM.
WCMI Ashland, KY; WRVC Huntington, WV; WDGG Ashland, KY; WCMI-FM Catlettsburg, KY;
Mike Kirtner, General Manager

Kirkman Broadcasting Inc.
Indigo Executive Park,60 Markfield Dr., Suite 4, Charleston SC 29407
(843) 763-6631
www.kirkmanbroadcasting.com
Radio Stns: 4 AM. 1 FM.
WJKB Moncks Corner, SC; WQNT Charleston, SC; WQSC Charleston, SC; WTMZ Dorchester Terrace-Brentwood, SC; WAZS(FM) McClellanville, SC;
Gil Kirkman, CEO

KM Communications Inc.
3654 Jarvis Ave., Skokie IL 60076
(847) 674-0864; *Fax:*(847) 674-9188
www.kmcommunications.com
Radio Stns: 1 AM. 7 FM.
KQMG Independence, IA; KQMG-FM Independence, IA; KWKM St. Johns, AZ; WLCN Atlanta, IL; WPNG Pearson, GA; WMKB Earlville, IL; KHMR Lovelady, TX; KBDK Leakey, TX;
TV Stns: 1 TV.
KWKB Iowa City, IA;
Myoung Hwa Bae, President
Kevin Bae, Operations Dir

Knight Broadcasting Inc.
1693 Mission Dr., Solvang CA 93463
(805) 688-8386; *Fax:*(805) 688-2271;
Radio Stns: 2 AM. 2 FM.
KSMA Lompoc, CA; KUHL Santa Maria, CA; KRAZ Santa Ynez, CA; KSYV Solvang, CA;

KNZA Inc.
Box 104, Hiawatha KS 66434-0104
(785) 547-3461; *Fax:*(785) 547-9900
www.knzafm.com
knza@rainbowtel.net
Radio Stns: 2 AM. 4 FM.
KAIR Atchison, KS; KTNC Falls City, NE; KAIR-FM Horton, KS; KLZA Falls City, NE; KMZA Seneca, KS; KNZA Hiawatha, KS;
Greg Buser, President
Robert Hilton, Operations Dir

Kona Coast Radio LLC
87 Jasper Lake Rd., Loveland CO 80537
(970) 669-9200
vicmichael@aol.com
Radio Stns: 1 AM. 2 FM.
KLIM Black Forest, CO; KHIH Estes Park, CO; KMAP Fleming, CO;

KOOR Communications Inc.
Box 2295, New London NH 3257
(603) 448-0500; *Fax:*(603) 448-6601
www.wntk.com
bob@wntk.com
Radio Stns: 3 AM. 1 FM.
WCFR Springfield, VT; WCNL Newport, NH; WUVR Lebanon, NH; WNTK-FM New London, NH;
Sheila E. Vinikoor, Operations Dir
Robert Vinikoor, General Manager

Koser Radio Group
P.O. Box 352, Rice Lake WI 54868
(715) 234-2131; *Fax:*(715) 234-6942;
Radio Stns: 2 AM. 1 FM.
WAQE Rice Lake, WI; WJMC Rice Lake, WI; WJMC-FM Rice Lake, WI;
Thomas A. Koser, President

KSPD Inc.
1440 S. Weideman Ave., Boise ID 83709
(208) 377-3790; *Fax:*(208) 377-3792
www.myfamilyradio.com
info@myfamilyradio.com
Radio Stns: 1 AM. 2 FM.
KSPD Boise, ID; KBXL Caldwell, ID; KDZY McCall, ID;
David Schafer, General Manager
Lee Schafer, General Manager

KSRM Inc.
40960 K. Beach Rd., Kenai AK 99611
(907) 283-5811; *Fax:*(907) 283-9177
www.radiokenai.com
info@radiokenai.com
Radio Stns: 2 AM. 3 FM.
KSLD Soldotna, AK; KSRM Soldotna, AK; KKIS-FM Soldotna, AK; KWHQ-FM Kenai, AK; KFSE Kasilof, AK;
John Davis, President
Cherie Curry, General Manager

KTLO LLC
Box 2010, Mountain Home AR 72654-2010
(870) 425-3101; *Fax:*(870) 424-4314
Ownership: Mountain Lakes Broadcasting Corp., 92%.
Radio Stns: 1 AM. 3 FM.
KTLO Mountain Home, AR; KCTT-FM Yellville, AR; KMAC Gainesville, MO; KTLO-FM Mountain Home, AR;
Bobby Dean Knight, President

Kuiper Stns
Box 1808, Grand Rapids MI 49501
(616) 451-9387; *Fax:*(616) 451-8460
Ownership: William E. Kuiper Sr.
Radio Stns: 2 AM.
WFUR Grand Rapids, MI; WKPR Kalamazoo, MI;
William Kuiper Sr., President

KUTE Inc.
Box 737, Ignacio CO 81137-0737
(970) 563-0255; *Fax:*(970) 563-0399;
Radio Stns: 6 FM.
KSUT Ignacio, CO; KUTE Ignacio, CO; KUUT Farmington, NM; KPGS Pagosa Springs, CO; KUSW Flora Vista, NM; KDNG Durango, CO;

KZLZ LLC
204 E. 4th St., North Little Rock AR 72114
(501) 375-9131; *Fax:*(520) 325-3495;
Radio Stns: 1 AM. 2 FM.
KHIL Willcox, AZ; KWCX-FM Tanque Verde, AZ; KZLZ Casas Adobes, AZ;

L M Communications Inc.
401 W. Main St.,Suite 301, Lexington KY 40507
(859) 233-1515; *Fax:*(859) 233-1517
www.lmcomm.com
jmac@lmcomm.com

Radio Stns: 4 AM. 8 FM.
WJYP St. Albans, WV; WLXG Lexington, KY; WMON Montgomery, WV; WSCW South Charleston, WV; WBTF Midway, KY; WCDA Versailles, KY; WCOO Kiawah Island, SC; WGKS Paris, KY; WMXE South Charleston, WV; WKLC-FM St. Albans, WV; WBVX Carlisle, KY; WYBB Folly Beach, SC;
Lynn Martin, President
James MacFarlane, General Manager

La Crosse Radio Group
Box 2017, La Crosse WI 54602
(608) 782-8335; *Fax:*(608) 782-8340
www.lacrosseradiogroup.net
Ownership: Howard G. Bill, 45%; TCOM Inc., 45%; and Patrick H. Smith, 10%.
Radio Stns: 1 AM. 4 FM.
WLFN La Crosse, WI; KQEG La Crescent, MN; WKBH-FM West Salem, WI; WLXR-FM La Crosse, WI; WQCC La Crosse, WI;
Patrick Smith, General Manager

La Favorita Inc.
Box 746, Austell GA 30106
(770) 944-0900; *Fax:*(770) 944-9794
www.radiolafavorita.com
Radio Stns: 3 AM.
WAOS Austell, GA; WLBA Gainesville, GA; WXEM Buford, GA;
Samuel Zamarron, CEO
Graciela Zamarron, Operations Dir

La Promesa Foundation
1406 E. Garden Ln., Midland TX 79702
(432) 682-1485; *Fax:*(432) 682-5230
www.grnonline.com
Radio Stns: 2 AM. 4 FM.
KWMF Pleasanton, TX; KLPF Midland, TX; KBKN Lamesa, TX; KBMD Marble Falls, TX; KJMA Floresville, TX; KVDG Midland, TX;

La Salle County Broadcasting Corp.
1 Broadcast Lane, Oglesby IL 61348
(815) 223-3100; *Fax:*(815) 223-3095
www.wlpo.net
joyce@wlpo.net
Radio Stns: 1 AM. 2 FM.
WLPO Lasalle, IL; WAJK La Salle, IL; WLWF(FM) Marseilles, IL;
Peter Miller, President
Joyce McCullough, Operations Dir
Mark Lippert, General Sales Mgr
John Spencer, Programming Director

Lake Michigan Broadcasting Inc.
5941 W. U.S. 10, Ludington MI 49431
(231) 843-3438; *Fax:*(231) 843-1886
www.wkla.com ,www.oldies1015.com
Radio Stns: 2 AM. 3 FM.
WKLA Ludington, MI; WMTE Manistee, MI; WKLA-FM Ludington, MI; WKZC Scottville, MI; WMTE-FM Manistee, MI;
Lynn Barewolf, President

Lake Region Radio Works
Box 882, Devils Lake ND 58301
(701) 662-7563; *Fax:*(701) 662-2222
www.lrradioworks.com
kzzyfm@gondtc.com
Radio Stns: 1 AM. 2 FM.
KDLR Devils Lake, ND; KDVL Devils Lake, ND; KZZY Devils Lake, ND;
Curtis Teigen, Operations Dir

Lakes Radio Inc.
524 Ludington,Suite 300, Escanaba MI 49829
(906) 789-9700; *Fax:*(906) 789-9700
www.radioresultsnetwork.com
Radio Stns: 2 AM. 2 FM.
WCHT Escanaba, MI; WTIQ Manistique, MI; WCMM Gulliver, MI; WGKL Gladstone, MI;
Rick Duerson, President

Langer Broadcasting Group LLC
94 St. Rose St., Boston MA 02130
(617) 522-4889;
Radio Stns: 4 AM.
WQOM Natick, MA; WFYL King of Prussia, PA; WSRO Ashland, MA; WFNX Coral Springs, FL;
Alexander G. Langer, Managing Member

Last Frontier Mediactive LLC
819 1st Ave., Suite A, Fairbanks AK 99701-4449
(907) 451-5910; *Fax:*(907) 451-5999
Ownership: Robert J. Ingstad, 50%; Tor H. Ingstad, 50%.
Radio Stns: 2 AM. 4 FM.
KCBF Fairbanks, AK; KFAR Fairbanks, AK; KTDZ College, AK; KWLF Fairbanks, AK; KXLR Fairbanks, AK; KWDD(FM) Fairbanks, AK;
Perry Walley, Chairman

Latino Communications LLC
600 Grant St.,Suite 600, Denver CO 80203
(303) 733-5266; *Fax:*(303) 733-5242
www.kbno.net
kbno@kbno.net
Radio Stns: 3 AM.
KAVA Pueblo, CO; KBNO Denver, CO; KXRE Manitou Springs, CO;
Zee Ferrufino, CEO

Lazer Broadcasting Corp.
200 S. A St., 4th Fl., Oxnard CA 93030
(805) 240-2070; *Fax:*(805) 240-5960;
Radio Stns: 4 AM. 14 FM.
KCAL(AM) Redlands, CA; KZER Santa Barbara, CA; KOXR Oxnard, CA; KSBQ Santa Maria, CA; KSRT Cloverdale, CA; KBTW Lenwood, CA; KLMM Oceano, CA; KLUN Paso Robles, CA; KXSM Hollister, CA; KLJR-FM Santa Paula, CA; KXZM Felton, CA; KSRN Kings Beach, CA; KJOR Windsor, CA; KSSB Calipatria, CA; KXRS Hemet, CA; KXSB Big Bear Lake, CA; KXTT Maricopa, CA; KEAL Taft, CA;
Alfredo Plascencia, CEO
Terry Janisch, General Manager

Le Sea Broadcasting
Box 12, South Bend IN 46624
(574) 291-8200; *Fax:*(574) 291-9043
www.lesea.com
leseabroadcasting@lesea.com
Radio Stns: 3 FM.
WHME South Bend, IN; WHPZ Bremen, IN; WHPD Dowagiac, MI;
TV Stns: 8 TV.
KWHB Tulsa, OK; KETD Castle Rock, CO; KWHE Honolulu, HI; KWHD Hilo, HI; KWHM Wailuku, HI; WHMB-TV Indianapolis, IN; WHME-TV South Bend, IN; WHNO New Orleans, LA;
Peter Sumrall, President

Lee Family Broadcasting Inc
3219 Laurelwood Drive, Twin Falls ID 83301
(208) 733-2974; *Fax:*(208) 733-4571
www.leeradio.net
kimlee@leeradio.net
Radio Stns: 1 FM.
KZNO (FM) Jerome, ID;
Kim Lee, President

Legacy Communications LLC
3205 W. North Front St., Grand Island NE 68803-4024
(308) 381-0206;
Radio Stns: 3 AM. 11 FM.
KOAQ Terrytown, NE; KOLT Scottsbluff, NE; KRGI Grand Island, NE; KOZY-FM Bridgeport, NE; KIOD McCook, NE; KRGY Aurora, NE; KMOR Gering, NE; KRGI-FM Grand Island, NE; KSWN McCook, NE; KHYY Minatare, NE; KETT Mitchell, NE; KZMC McCook, NE; KRNP Sutherland, NE; KZTL Paxton, NE;

Legacy Media Corporation
210 North 1000 E.,Box 1450, St. George UT 84771-1450
(435) 628-1000; *Fax:*(435) 628-6636
www.legacy.cc
legacy1@infowest.com
Radio Stns: 4 AM. 1 FM.
KOBY Cedar City, UT; KOGN Ogden, UT; KNFL Tremonton, UT; KPTO Pocatello, ID; KITT Soda Springs, ID;
E. Morgan Skinner, CEO
R. Michael Bull, President
Lavon Randall, Operations Dir
Jeffrey B. Bate, General Manager

Legend Communications L.L.C.
6805 Douglas Legum Dr.,Suite 100, Elkridge MD 21075
(410) 799-1740; *Fax:*(410) 799-1705
www.patcomm.com
larry@patcomm.com
Radio Stns: 5 AM. 10 FM.
KBBS Buffalo, WY; KIML Gillette, WY; KODI Cody, WY; KWOR Worland, WY; KZMQ Ten Sleep, WY; KAML-FM Gillette, WY; KGWY Gillette, WY; KKLX Worland, WY; KLGT Buffalo, WY; KTAG Cody, WY; KZMQ-FM Greybull, WY; KCGL Powell, WY; KZZS Story, WY; KYTS Manderson, WY; KDDV-FM Wright, WY;
Larry Patrick, President
Susan Patrick, Managing Partner

Leighton Enterprises Inc.
Box 1458, St. Cloud MN 56302
(320) 251-1450; *Fax:*(320) 251-8952
www.1047kcld.com
Ownership: Thomas H. Graham, trustee, Leighton Children's LP Trust, 27.3%; Thomas H. Graham, trustee, Leighton Grandchildren's LP Trust, 25.7%.
Radio Stns: 4 AM. 7 FM.
KGFK East Grand Forks, MN; KDLM Detroit Lakes, MN; KNOX Grand Forks, ND; KNSI St. Cloud, MN; KBOT Pelican Rapids, MN; KCLD-FM St. Cloud, MN; KCML St. Joseph, MN; KZGF Grand Forks, ND; KYCK Crookston, MN; KZLT-FM East Grand Forks, MN; KZPK Paynesville, MN;
John Sowada, President
Dennis Niess, VP
Al Leighton, Chairman

RADIO - U.S.

Lew Latto Group of Northland Radio Stations
5732 Eagle View Dr., Duluth MN 55803-9498
(218) 729-9888; *Fax:*(218) 729-9888
LewLatto@aol.com
Ownership: Lew Latto, 100%.
Radio Stns: 1 AM. 2 FM.
KRBT Eveleth, MN; KGPZ Coleraine, MN; WEVE-FM Eveleth, MN;
Lew Latto, President

Liberman Broadcasting Inc.
1845 Empire Ave., Burbank CA 91504
(818) 729-5300; *Fax:*(818) 729-5678
www.lbimedia.com
LBIinfo@lbimedia.com
Radio Stns: 7 AM. 15 FM.
KEYH Houston, TX; KJOZ Conroe, TX; KHJ Los Angeles, CA; KQUE Houston, TX; KSEV Tomball, TX; KVNR Santa Ana, CA; KZMP University Park, TX; KBOC Bridgeport, TX; KBUA San Fernando, CA; KBUE Long Beach, CA; KNOR Krum, TX; KEBN Garden Grove, CA; KXBJ El Campo, TX; KJOJ-FM Freeport, TX; KZMP-FM Pilot Point, TX; KTJM Port Arthur, TX; KWIZ Santa Ana, CA; KRQB San Jacinto, CA; KNTE Bay City, TX; KZZA Muenster, TX; KQQK Beaumont, TX; KTCY Azle, TX;
TV Stns: 4 TV.
KPNZ Ogden, UT; KMPX Decatur, TX; KRCA Riverside, CA; KZJL Houston, TX;
Brett Zane, CEO
Lenard Liberman, President

Liggett Communications L.L.C.
808 Huron Ave., Port Huron MI 48060
(810) 982-9000; *Fax:*(810) 987-9380;
Radio Stns: 2 AM. 1 FM.
WHLX Marine City, MI; WPHM Port Huron, MI; WBTI Lexington, MI;
Robert Liggett, President
Larry Smith, Operations Dir

Lincoln Financial Media
100 N. Greene St., Greensboro NC 27420
(336) 691-3000; *Fax:*(336) 691-3222
www.lincolnfinancialmedia.com
Ownership: The Lincoln National Life Insurance Company 100%.
Radio Stns: 4 AM. 10 FM.
KEPN Lakewood, CO; KRWZ Parker, CO; WAXY South Miami, FL; WQXI Atlanta, GA; KBZT San Diego, CA; KKFN Longmont, CO; KSOQ-FM Escondido, CA; KIFM San Diego, CA; KQKS Lakewood, CO; KSON San Diego, CA; KYGO-FM Denver, CO; WLYF Miami, FL; WMXJ Pompano Beach, FL; WSTR Smyrna, GA;
Don Benson, CEO/Pres, Lincoln Financial Media Company
Laura James, CFO/SVP, Lincoln Financial Media Company

Linder Broadcasting Group
Box 1420, Mankato MN 56002
(507) 345-4537; *Fax:*(507) 345-5364
www.katoinfo.com
Ownership: Donald Linder, John Linder.
Radio Stns: 4 AM. 9 FM.
KMHL Marshall, MN; KRUE Waseca, MN; KTOE Mankato, MN; KYSM Mankato, MN; KARL Tracy, MN; KARZ Marshall, MN; KDOG North Mankato, MN; KOLV Olivia, MN; KOWZ-FM Blooming Prairie, MN; KRRW St. James, MN; KKOR Waseca, MN; KXAC St. James, MN; KATO-FM New Ulm, MN;
John Linder, President

Little Falls Radio Corp.
25801 Nacre St. N.W., St. Francis MN 55070
(763) 862-9909
www.fallsradio.com
rod.grams@att.net

Radio Stns: 1 AM. 2 FM.
KLTF Little Falls, MN; KFML Little Falls, MN; WYRQ-FM Little Falls, MN;

LKCM Radio Group L.P.
115 W. 3rd St., Fort Worth TX 76102
(817) 332-0959; *Fax:*(817) 332-4630
gerry@lkcmradio.com
Radio Stns: 1 AM. 10 FM.
KVSO Ardmore, OK; KKAJ-FM Davis, OK; KTFW-FM Glen Rose, TX; KYBE Frederick, OK; KYNZ Lone Grove, OK; KFWR Jacksboro, TX; KRVA-FM Campbell, TX; KRVF Kerens, TX; KTRX Dickson, OK; KFSZ Munds Park, AZ; KOME-FM Meridian, TX;
Gerry Schlegel, President

Locally Owned Radio LLC
21361 Hwy. 30, Twin Falls ID 83301
(208) 735-8300; *Fax:*(208) 733-4196
www.locallyownedradio.com
Radio Stns: 1 AM. 4 FM.
KTFI Wendell, ID; KIKX Ketchum, ID; KTPZ Hazelton, ID; KIRQ Twin Falls, ID; KYUN Hailey, ID;
Stephanie Johnson, President
Jerry Fender, Operations Dir
Larry Johnson, General Manager

Long Island Radio Broadcasting LLC
Box 157, Water Mill NY 11976
(631) 267-7800; *Fax:*(631) 267-1018
Ownership: Cherry Creek Radio LLC, 98.26% votes, 95.44% of total assets (see listing).
Radio Stns: 4 FM.
WBEA Southold, NY; WBAZ Bridgehampton, NY; WEHN East Hampton, NY; WEHM Manorville, NY;
Barbara King, Business Manager

Lost Coast Communications Inc.
Box 25, Ferndale CA 95536
(707) 786-5104; *Fax:*(707) 786-5100
www.khum.com www.kslg.com
Radio Stns: 4 FM.
KSLG-FM Hydesville, CA; KHUM Cutten, CA; KWPT Fortuna, CA; KXGO Arcata, CA;
Patrick Cleary, President

Lotus Communications Corp.
3301 Barham Blvd.,Suite 200, Los Angeles CA 90068
(323) 512-2225; *Fax:*(323) 512-2224
www.lotuscorp.com
hq@lotuscorp.com
Radio Stns: 12 AM. 15 FM.
KBAD Las Vegas, NV; KCHJ Delano, CA; KENO Las Vegas, NV; KGST Fresno, CA; KHIT Reno, NV; KPLY Reno, NV; KTKT Tucson, AZ; KIRN Simi Valley, CA; KWAC Bakersfield, CA; KWKW Los Angeles, CA; KWKU Pomona, CA; KWWN Las Vegas, NV; KDOT Reno, NV; KFMA Green Valley, AZ; KWID Las Vegas, NV; KUUB Sun Valley, NV; KPSL-FM Bakersfield, CA; KVMX Bakersfield, CA; KKBZ Auberry, CA; KLPX Tucson, AZ; KHIT-FM Madera, CA; KOMP Las Vegas, NV; KLBN Fresno, CA; KOZZ-FM Reno, NV; KIWI McFarland, CA; KXPT Las Vegas, NV; KCMT Oro Valley, AZ;
Howard Kalmenson, President
Jerry Roy, SVP
Bill Shriftman, SVP

Lovcom Inc.
Box 5086, Sheridan WY 82801
(307) 672-7421; *Fax:*(307) 672-2933
www.sheridanmedia.com
info@sheridanmedia.com
Ownership: W.K. Love and family.
Radio Stns: 2 AM. 3 FM.
KROE Sheridan, WY; KWYO Sheridan, WY; KYTI Sheridan, WY; KZWY Sheridan, WY; KLQQ Clearmont, WY;
Bob Grammens, General Manager
Kim Love, Owner

M.B. Communications
481 Hamilton St., Geneva NY 14456
(315) 781-1101,; *Fax:*(315) 781-6666,
www.k1017.com
k1017@fltg.net
Ownership: Russ Kimble, 100%.
Radio Stns: 1 AM. 1 FM.
WYLF Penn Yan, NY; WFLK Geneva, NY;
Russell Kimble, President
Deborah Kimble, VP

M.R.S. Ventures Inc.
100 E. Ferguson,Suite 614, Tyler TX 75702
(903) 595-4795; *Fax:*(903) 593-2666
jdonrussell@aol.com
Radio Stns: 2 FM.
KOTN Gould, AR; KPBQ-FM Pine Bluff, AR;

MacDonald Broadcasting Co.
Box 1776, Saginaw MI 48605
(989) 752-8161; *Fax:*(989) 752-8102
www.98fmkcq.com
wkcq@chartermi.net
Ownership: Ken MacDonald Jr. Note: Group also owns and operates a Muzak franchise in a six-county area in mid-Michigan.
Radio Stns: 3 AM. 5 FM.
WILS Lansing, MI; WSAM Saginaw, MI; WXLA Dimondale, MI; WMJO Essexville, MI; WHZZ Lansing, MI; WKCQ Saginaw, MI; WQHH Dewitt, MI; WSAG Linwood, MI;
Kenneth MacDonald Jr., CEO
Duane Alverson, President

MacDonald Garber Broadcasting Co.
Box 286, Petoskey MI 49770
(231) 347-8713; *Fax:*(231) 347-8782
www.lite96.com,www.106khq.com
Radio Stns: 3 AM. 3 FM.
WATT Cadillac, MI; WMBN Petoskey, MI; WMKT Charlevoix, MI; WKHQ-FM Charlevoix, MI; WLXT Petoskey, MI; WLXV Cadillac, MI;
Trish Garber, President

Magic Broadcasting LLC
7106 Laird St.,Suite 102, Panama City Beach FL 32408
(850) 234-8388; *Fax:*(850) 230-6988
magicbroadcasting.net
Radio Stns: 1 AM. 11 FM.
WPCF Panama City Beach, FL; KDAY Redondo Beach, CA; KDEY(FM) Ontario, CA; WBBK-FM Blakely, GA; WILN Panama City, FL; WKMX Enterprise, AL; WVVE Panama City Beach, FL; WJRL-FM Fort Rucker, AL; WTVY-FM Dothan, AL; WLDA Slocomb, AL; WYOO Springfield, FL; WYYX Bonifay, FL;
Thomas DiBacco, President
Kim Styles, General Manager

Magnum Broadcasting Inc.
Box 436, State College PA 16804
(814) 272-1320; *Fax:*(814) 272-3291
www.1059joefm.com
Radio Stns: 2 AM. 2 FM.
WBLF Bellefonte, PA; WPHB Philipsburg, PA; WQCK(FM) Philipsburg, PA; WQKK(FM) Renovo, PA;
Diana Albright, General Manager

Magnum Communications Inc.
1021 N. Superior Ave.,Suite 5, Tomah WI 54660
(608) 742-2544;
Radio Stns: 2 AM. 4 FM.
WDLS Wisconsin Dells, WI; WRDB Reedsburg, WI; WBDL Reedsburg, WI; WBKY Portage, WI; WNFM Reedsburg, WI; WNNO-FM Wisconsin Dells, WI;
David R. Magnum, President

Magnum Radio Inc.
1021 N. Superior Ave.,Suite 5, Tomah WI 54660
(608) 372-9600; *Fax:*(608) 372-7566
magnumradio@charter.net
Radio Stns: 1 AM. 2 FM.
WBOG Tomah, WI; WTMB Tomah, WI; WXYM Tomah, WI;
Dave Magnum, President

Mahaffey Enterprises Inc.
Box 4584, Springfield MO 65808
(417) 883-9180; *Fax:*(417) 883-9096
Ownership: John B. Mahaffey, Fredna B. Mahaffey, Robert B. Mahaffey.
Radio Stns: 3 AM. 9 FM.
KGGF Coffeyville, KS; KSPI Stillwater, OK; KTTR Rolla, MO; KDAA Rolla, MO; KGFY Stillwater, OK; KGGF-FM Fredonia, KS; KUSN Dearing, KS; KSPI-FM Stillwater, OK; KTTR-FM St. James, MO; KKRK Coffeyville, KS; KVRO Stillwater, OK; KZNN Rolla, MO;
John Mahaffey, Chairman
Robert Mahaffey, CEO

Mahalo Broadcasting L.L.C.
6890 E. Sunrise Dr.,Box 120-40, Tucson AZ 85750
(407) 488-2098;
Radio Stns: 2 AM. 2 FM.
KHNU Hilo, HI; KHNU(AM) Hilo, HI; KKOA Volcano, HI; KBGX Keaau, HI;

Main Line Broadcasting LLC
300 Conshohocken State Rd.,Suite 380, West Conshohocken PA 19428-3801
(610) 825-8101; *Fax:*(610) 825-8106;
Radio Stns: 3 AM. 16 FM.
WCHA Chambersburg, PA; WHAG Halfway, MD; WING Dayton, OH; WQCM Greencastle, PA; WDJX Louisville, KY; WGTZ Eaton, OH; WGZB-FM Lanesville, IN; WIKZ Chambersburg, PA; WDHT Urbana, OH; WWLB Midlothian, VA; WCLI-FM Enon, OH; WXMA Louisville, KY; WMJM Jeffersontown, KY; WDLD Halfway, MD; WROU-FM West Carrollton, OH; WARV-FM Petersburg, VA; WLRS Shepherdsville, KY; WBBT-FM Powhatan, VA; WLFV Ettrick, VA;
Daniel Savadove, CEO
J. Edwin Conrad, President
Marc Guralnick, General Sales Mgr

Malkan Broadcast Associates
2117 Leopard St., Corpus Christi TX 78408-3925
(361) 883-3516; *Fax:*(361) 882-9767
thechief@star94.net
Ownership: Malkan Broadcasting Management L.L.C, gen ptnr; Matthew Malkan; Hope Malkan; Glen Powers.
Radio Stns: 1 AM. 2 FM.
KEYS Corpus Christi, TX; KKBA Kingsville, TX; KZFM Corpus Christi, TX;
Glen Powers, President

Manhattan Broadcasting Inc
Manhattan Broadcasting Inc.,2414 Casement Rd., Manhattan KS 66502
(785) 776-1350; *Fax:*(785) 539-1000;
Radio Stns: 1 AM. 2 FM.
KMAN Manhattan, KS; KXBZ Manhattan, KS; KACZ Riley, KS;
Richard Wartell, General Manager

Mapleton Communications LLC
10900 Wilshire Blvd.,Suite 1500, Los Angeles CA 90024
(310) 209-7221; *Fax:*(310) 209-7239
www.mapletoncomm.com
Radio Stns: 10 AM. 30 FM.
KTIQ Merced, CA; KNRO Redding, CA; KCMX Phoenix, OR; KEYF Dishman, WA; KGA Spokane, WA; KYNS San Luis Obispo, CA; KSFN(AM) Piedmont, CA; KJRB Spokane, WA; KQMS Redding, CA; KYOS Merced, CA; KABX-FM Merced, CA; KZBD Spokane, WA; KAKT Phoenix, OR; KALF Red Bluff, CA; KKHK Carmel, CA; KBOY-FM Medford, OR; KCDU Carmel, CA; KCMX-FM Ashland, OR; KDRK-FM Spokane, WA; KEYF-FM Cheney, WA; KFMF Chico, CA; KGAM(FM) Merced, CA; KBOQ Seaside, CA; KBRE Atwater, CA; KWWV Santa Margarita, CA; KLOQ-FM Winton, CA; KHIP Gonzales, CA; KNNN(FM) Shasta Lake City, CA; KPYG Cayucos, CA; KPIG-FM Freedom, CA; KQPT Colusa, CA; KRDG Shingletown, CA; KRRX Burney, CA; KSHA Redding, CA; KTMT-FM Medford, OR; KBBD Spokane, WA; KXTZ Pismo Beach, CA; KZAP Paradise, CA; KXDZ Templeton, CA; KBLO Corcoran, CA;
Adam Nathanson, CEO
Raul Salvador, Operations Dir
Mike Anthony, Programming Director
Rich Elmendorf, CFO

Marion R. Williams Stns
925 N. 5th St., Niles MI 49120
(269) 683-4343; *Fax:*(269) 683-7759
www.wsmkradio.com
Radio Stns: 2 AM. 1 FM.
WONG Canton, MS; WSTT Thomasville, GA; WSMK Buchanan, MI;
Marion Williams, President

Mark Media Group
Box 607, Burnsville NC 28714
(828) 682-6221; *Fax:*(828) 682-0998
www.wkyk.com
mmg@wkyk.com
Radio Stns: 3 AM.
WKYK Burnsville, NC; WTOE Spruce Pine, NC; WTZQ Hendersonville, NC;
J. Ardell Sink, Chairman
Remelle Sink, CFO
Michael Sink, President

MarMac Communications LLC
7515 Blythe Island Hwy., Brunswick GA 31523
(912) 264-6251; *Fax:*(912) 264-9991;
Radio Stns: 4 AM.
WFNS Blackshear, GA; WSFN Brunswick, GA; WSEG Savannah, GA; WWGA(AM) Waycross, GA;

Mars Hill Network
4044 Makyes Rd., Syracuse NY 13215
(315) 469-5051; *Fax:*(315) 469-4066
www.marshillnetwork.org
mhn@marshillnetwork.org
Ownership: Not-for-profit corporation. Note: Group also has a radio net, 14 translators.
Radio Stns: 5 FM.
WMHI Cape Vincent, NY; WMHN Webster, NY; WMHR Syracuse, NY; WMHQ Malone, NY; WMHU(FM) Cold Brook, NY;
Clayton R. Roberts, President
Wayne Taylor, General Manager
John Seeland, Treasurer
Michael Gettman, Vice President

Martin Broadcasting Inc.
4638 Decker Dr., Baytown TX 77520
(210) 333-0050; *Fax:*(210) 333-0081
kchl1480@yahoo.com
Radio Stns: 6 AM.
KANI Wharton, TX; KYOK Conroe, TX; KCHL San Antonio, TX; KRMY Killeen, TX; KZZB Beaumont, TX; WNGL Mobile, AL;
Darrell E. Martin, President

Martz Communications Group
86 Porter Rd., Malone NY 12953
(518) 483-1100; *Fax:*(518) 483-1382
radioworksbest.com
Ownership: Timothy D. Martz, 100%.
Radio Stns: 1 AM. 2 FM.
WICY Malone, NY; WVNV Malone, NY; WYUL Chateaugay, NY;
Timothy Martz, President/CEO

Matinee Radio LLC
2801 Via Fortuna,Suite 675, Austin TX 78746
(512) 329-5843; *Fax:*(512) 329-5847;
Radio Stns: 2 FM.
KTXO Goldsmith, TX; KRTS Marfa, TX;

Maverick Media LLC
136 Main St.,Suite 202, Westport CT 6880
(203) 227-2800; *Fax:*(203) 227-4819;
Radio Stns: 5 AM. 14 FM.
KSRO Santa Rosa, CA; WAYY Eau Claire, WI; WEAQ Chippewa Falls, WI; WCIT(AM) Lima, OH; WNTA Rockford, IL; KFGY Healdsburg, CA; KVRV Monte Rio, CA; KMHX Rohnert Park, CA; WEGE Lima, OH; WAXX Eau Claire, WI; WDOH Delphos, OH; WECL Elk Mound, WI; WFGF Wapakoneta, OH; WIAL Eau Claire, WI; WRTB Winnebago, IL; WGFB Rockton, IL; WXRX Belvidere, IL; WWSR Lima, OH; WDRK Cornell, WI;
Gary Rozynek, CEO

MAX Media L.L.C.
900 Laskin Rd., Virginia Beach VA 23451
(757) 437-9800; *Fax:*(757) 437-0034
www.maxmediallc.com
Ownership: MBG-GG LLC, 42.0345%; MBG Quad-C Investors I Inc., 41.4124%; Aardvarks Also LLC, 6.1967%; Colonnade Max Investors Inc., 4.8671%; Quad-C Max Investors Inc., 4.6799%; MBG Quad-C Investors II Inc., 0.6221%; and Quad-C Max Investors II Inc., 0.1872%.
Radio Stns: 12 AM. 25 FM.
KCAB Dardanelle, AR; KGIR Cape Girardeau, MO; KSIM Sikeston, MO; KMAL Malden, MO; KVOM Morrilton, AR; KWOC Poplar Bluff, MO; KZIM Cape Girardeau, MO; WCIL Carbondale, IL; WGAI Elizabeth City, NC; WGH Newport News, VA; WJPF Herrin, IL; WVSL(AM) Selinsgrove, PA; KCGQ-FM Gordonville, MO; KCJC Dardanelle, AR; KEZS-FM Cape Girardeau, MO; KGKS Scott City, MO; KJEZ Poplar Bluff, MO; KKLR-FM Poplar Bluff, MO; KLSC Malden, MO; KVLD Atkins, AR; KONN-FM Bennett, CO; KVOM-FM Morrilton, AR; KWKK Russellville, AR; WVHT Norfolk, VA; WCXL Kill Devil Hills, NC; WVBW Suffolk, VA; WGH-FM Newport News, VA; WFYY Bloomsburg, PA; WVSL-FM Riverside, PA; WOOZ-FM Harrisburg, IL; WQDK Gatesville, NC; WXLT Christopher, IL; WWBE Mifflinburg, PA; WCMS-FM Hatteras, NC; WVSP-FM Yorktown, VA; WUEZ Carterville, IL; WYGL-FM Elizabethville, PA;
TV Stns: 6 TV.
KTMF Missoula, MT; KULR-TV Billings, MT; KWYB Butte, MT; WNKY Bowling Green, KY; WMEI Arecibo, PR; WPFO Waterville, ME;
John A. Trinder, President

MBC Grand Broadcasting Inc.
1360 E. Sherwood Dr., Grand Junction CO 81501
(970) 254-2100; *Fax:*(970) 245-7551
www.gjradio.com
Radio Stns: 3 AM. 4 FM.
KGLN Glenwood Springs, CO; KNZZ Grand Junction, CO; KTMM Grand Junction, CO; KKVT(FM) Grand Junction, CO; KMGJ Grand Junction, CO; KMOZ-FM Grand Junction, CO; KSTR-FM Montrose, CO;
Richard C. Dean, CEO

McKenzie River Broadcasting Company, Inc.
925 Country Club Rd.,Suite 200, Eugene OR 97401
(541) 484-9400; *Fax:*(541) 344-9424;
Radio Stns: 3 FM.
KEUG Veneta, OR; KKNU Springfield-Eugene, OR; KMGE Eugene, OR;
John Q. Tilson III, President
Renate R. Tilson, Operations Dir

McMurray Communications Inc.
3335 W. 8th St., Safford AZ 85546
(928) 428-1230; *Fax:*(928) 428-1311
www.mysouthernaz.com
traffic@eaznet.com
Radio Stns: 1 AM. 2 FM.
KATO Safford, AZ; KWRQ Clifton, AZ; KXKQ Safford, AZ;
Harry McMurray, CEO
David Nathan, General Manager

McNaughton-Jakle Stations
14 Douglas Avenue, Elgin IL 60120
(847) 741-7700; *Fax:*(847) 468-0000
www.wrmn1410.com
mail@wrmn.com
Ownership: Bradley L. Beesley, K. Richard Jakle
Radio Stns: 3 AM.
KSHP North Las Vegas, NV; WBIG Aurora, IL; WRMN Elgin, IL;
K. Richard Jakle, Chairman

Media Logic LLC
Box 430, Fort Morgan CO 80701-0430
(970) 867-5674; *Fax:*(970) 542-1023;
Radio Stns: 2 AM. 2 FM.
KFTM Fort Morgan, CO; KRDZ Wray, CO; KATR-FM Wray, CO; KSRX Sterling, CO;
Wayne Johnson, General Manager

Media One Group
147 Bell St.,Suite 200, Chagrin Falls OH 44022
(440) 893-8114;
Radio Stns: 2 AM. 3 FM.
WJTN Jamestown, NY; WKSN Jamestown, NY; WHUG Jamestown, NY; WQFX-FM Russell, PA; WWSE Jamestown, NY;

Media Power Group Inc.
100 Gran Bulevar Paseos,Suite 403A, San Juan PR 926
(787) 292-1700; *Fax:*(787) 292-1717
wskn1320@yahoo.com
Radio Stns: 4 AM.
WKFE Yauco, PR; WDEP Ponce, PR; WLEY Cayey, PR; WSKN San Juan, PR;
Eduardo Albino Rivero, President
Ismael Nieves, Operations Dir

Mel Wheeler Inc.
3934 Electric Rd., Roanoke VA 24018-4513
(540) 989-4591; *Fax:*(540) 774-5667
melwheelerinc.com
Ownership: Leonard E. Wheeler, 35%; Steve Wheeler, 34%; and Clark Wheeler, 31%.
Radio Stns: 2 AM. 4 FM.
WFIR Roanoke, VA; WVBE Roanoke, VA; WVBE-FM Lynchburg, VA; WSLC-FM Roanoke, VA; WSLQ Roanoke, VA; WXLK Roanoke, VA;
TV Stns: 2 TV.
KPOB-TV Poplar Bluff, MO; WSIL-TV Harrisburg, IL;
Leonard Wheeler, President
Gretchen Cummings, Sec/Treasurer

Melia Communications Inc.
Box 569, Goodland KS 67735
(785) 899-2309; *Fax:*(785) 899-3062
www.kloe.com
kloe@eaglecom.net
Radio Stns: 1 AM. 1 FM.
KLOE Goodland, KS; KWGB Colby, KS;
Kathleen Melia, Operations Dir
Martin Melia, General Manager

Mentor Partners Inc.
18720 16 Mile Rd., Big Rapids MI 49307
(231) 796-7000; *Fax:*(231) 796-7951;
Radio Stns: 1 AM. 2 FM.
WBRN Big Rapids, MI; WWBR Big Rapids, MI; WYBR Big Rapids, MI;

Meredith Broadcasting Group, Meredith Corp.
1716 Locust St., Des Moines IA 50309-3023
(515) 284-2159; *Fax:*(515) 284-2514
www.meredith.com
Ownership: Meredith Broadcasting is an operating group of Meredith Corp., Des Moines, IA.
Radio Stns: 1 AM.
WNEM Bridgeport, MI;
TV Stns: 11 TV.
KCTV Kansas City, MO; KPDX Vancouver, WA; KPHO-TV Phoenix, AZ; KPTV Portland, OR; KSMO-TV Kansas City, MO; KVVU-TV Henderson, NV; WFSB Hartford, CT; WGCL-TV Atlanta, GA; WHNS Greenville, SC; WNEM-TV Bay City, MI; WSMV-TV Nashville, TN;
Paul Karpowic, President
Douglas Lowe, EVP

Meridian Broadcasting Inc.
2824 Palm Beach Blvd., Fort Myers FL 33916
(239) 337-2346; *Fax:*(239) 332-0767;
Radio Stns: 2 AM. 3 FM.
WINK Pine Island Center, FL; WNOG Naples, FL; WARO Naples, FL; WTLT Sanibel, FL; WFSX-FM Estero, FL;
Joseph Schwartzel, President

Merlin Media LLC
222 Merchandise Mart Plaza,Suite 230, Chicago IL 60654
(312) 245-1230; *Fax:*(312) 527-3620
www.merlinmediallc.com
Ownership: GTCR Merlin Holdings LLC, 60% votes, 74% equity.
Radio Stns: 3 FM.
WWIQ Camden, NJ; WLUP-FM Chicago, IL; WFAN-FM New York, NY;
Randy Michaels, CEO

Metro Radio Inc.
2251 Hunter Mill Rd., Vienna VA 22181
(703) 938-1016; *Fax:*(703) 331-4706
www.metroradioinc.com
Radio Stns: 3 AM.
WKCW Warrenton, VA; WKDV Manassas, VA; WKDL Warrenton, VA;
Bruce Houston, President

Metropolitan Radio Group Inc.
318 E. Pershing St., Springfield MO 65806
(417) 862-0852; *Fax:*(417) 862-9079;
Radio Stns: 6 AM. 5 FM.
KBTC Houston, MO; KIJN Farwell, TX; KIOU Shreveport, LA; WBRD Palmetto, FL; WRXB St. Petersburg Beach, FL; WTMY Sarasota, FL; KGHT El Jebel, CO; KIJN-FM Farwell, TX; KJVC Mansfield, LA; KTKC-FM Springhill, LA; KUNQ Houston, MO;
Mark Acker, President

Meyer Communications Inc.
Box 3676, Springfield MO 65808
(417) 862-3990; *Fax:*(417) 869-7675
www.ktxrfm.com
manager@radiospringfield.com
Ownership: Kenneth E. Meyer, 100%.
Radio Stns: 2 AM. 3 FM.
KBFL Springfield, MO; KWTO Springfield, MO; KBFL-FM Buffalo, MO; KTXR Springfield, MO; KWTO-FM Springfield, MO;
Kenneth Meyer, President

Michael Radio Group
1063 W Hwy. 34,Apt. F, Loveland CO 80537-9424
(307) 778-9318;
Radio Stns: 3 FM.
KYOY Hillsdale, WY; KRKI Keystone, SD; KGRK Glenrock, WY;

Mid-America Radio Group Inc.
Box 1970, Martinsville IN 46151
(765) 349-1485; *Fax:*(765) 342-3569
mid-americaradio@scican.net
Ownership: David Keister, principal owner.
Radio Stns: 6 AM. 10 FM.
WARU Peru, IN; WBAT Marion, IN; WMRI Marion, IN; WIOU Kokomo, IN; WJOT Wabash, IN; WMYJ Martinsville, IN; WMYK Peru, IN; WARU-FM Roann, IN; WCBK-FM Martinsville, IN; WCJC Van Buren, IN; WHZR Royal Center, IN; WJOT-FM Wabash, IN; WXXC Marion, IN; WCLS Spencer, IN; WVNI Nashville, IN; WZWZ Kokomo, IN;
David C. Keister, President

Midwest Communications Inc.
904 Grand Ave., Wausau WI 54403
(715) 842-1437; *Fax:*(715) 842-7061
www.mwcradio.com
Ownership: Duey E. Wright, 100% votes, 10% equity; Wright Family Irrevocable Trust of 2010, 90% equity.
Radio Stns: 15 AM. 28 FM.
KDAL Duluth, MN; WGEE Superior, WI; WDSM Superior, WI; WTAQ Green Bay, WI; WHBL Sheboygan, WI; WHTC Holland, MI; WKZO Kalamazoo, MI; WMFG Hibbing, MN; WNFL Green Bay, WI; WNMT Nashwauk, MN; WNWN Portage, MI; WPRS Paris, IL; WRIG Schofield, WI; WSAU Wausau, WI; WTVB Coldwater, MI; KDAL-FM Duluth, MN; KDWZ Superior, WI; KTCO Duluth, MN; WIBQ Paris, IL; WBFM Sheboygan, WI; WDEZ Wausau, WI; WYVN Saugatuck, MI; WKZO-FM Portage, MI; WIFC Wausau, WI; WIXX Green Bay, WI; WSAU-FM Rudolph, WI; WZDR(FM) Sturgeon Bay, WI; WMFG-FM Hibbing, MN; WMGI Terre Haute, IN; WNCY-FM Neenah-Menasha, WI; WNWN-FM Coldwater, MI; WOZZ Mosinee, WI; WRQE New London, WI; WVFM Kalamazoo, MI; WYZO-FM Portage, MI; WYDR Neenah-Menasha, WI; WTBX Hibbing, MN; WXXR(FM) Seelyville, IN; WUSZ Virginia, MN; WHBZ Sheboygan Falls, WI; WXER Plymouth, WI; KMFG Nashwauk, MN; WTRW Carbondale, PA;
Duke Wright, President/CEO

Midwestern Broadcasting Co.
314 E. Front St., Traverse City MI 49684
(231) 947-7675; *Fax:*(231) 929-3988
www.wtcmi.com
Ownership: Ross Biederman, 52.5%; William Kiker Estate, 16.25%; William McClay, 15%.
Radio Stns: 3 AM. 5 FM.
WATZ Alpena, MI; WCCW Traverse City, MI; WTCM Traverse City, MI; WATZ-FM Alpena, MI; WBCM Boyne City, MI; WJZQ Cadillac, MI; WRGZ Rogers City, MI; WCZW Charlevoix, MI;
Ross Biederman, President

Mildred R Porter
4400 Clear Creek Parkway, Northport AL 35475
(205)345-4787; *Fax:*(205)345-4790;
Radio Stns: 1 FM.
WQZZ Boligee, AL;
Mildred R. Porter, President

Millcreek Broadcasting L.L.C.
980 N. Michigan Ave.,Suite 1880, Chicago IL 60611
(312) 204-9900; *Fax:*(312) 587-9466;
Radio Stns: 4 FM.
KAUU Manti, UT; KUDD Roy, UT; KUUU South Jordan, UT; KUDE Nephi, UT;
Bruce Buzil, President
Christopher Devine, President

Miller Communications Inc.
Box 1269, Sumter SC 29151
(803) 775-2321; *Fax:*(803) 773-4856
www.miller.fm
Radio Stns: 5 AM. 7 FM.
WDKD Kingstree, SC; WDXY Sumter, SC; WHYM Lake City, SC; WOLH Florence, SC; WWHM Sumter, SC; WGFG Branchville, SC; WIBZ Wedgefield, SC; WWBD Sumter, SC; WQKI-FM Orangeburg, SC; WSIM Lamar, SC; WSCZ(FM) Saint Matthews, SC; WWKT-FM Kingstree, SC;
Harold Miller Jr., CEO
Dave Baker, Operations Dir
Theresa Miller, General Manager

Miller Media Group
Box 169,918 East Park, Taylorville IL 62568-0169
(217) 824-3395; *Fax:*(217) 824-3301
www.randyradio.com
Radio Stns: 2 AM. 6 FM.
WHOW Clinton, IL; WKEI Kewanee, IL; WJRE Galva, IL; WEZC Clinton, IL; WYEC Cambridge, IL; WMKR Pana, IL; WRAN Tower Hill, IL; WTIM-FM Taylorville, IL;
Randal Miller, President
Cathaleen R. Miller, Operations Dir

Milner Broadcasting
292 N. Convent, Bourbonnais IL 60914
(815) 933-9287; *Fax:*(815) 933-8696;
Radio Stns: 3 FM.
WVLI Kankakee, IL; WIVR Kentland, IN; WFAV Gilman, IL;

Milwaukee Radio Alliance L.L.C.
N72 W12922 Good Hope Rd., Menomonee Falls WI 53051-4441
(414) 771-1021; *Fax:*(414) 771-3036
www.milwaukeeradio.com
bhurwitz@milwaukeeradio.com
Radio Stns: 1 AM. 2 FM.
WMCS Greenfield, WI; WLDB Milwaukee, WI; WLUM-FM Milwaukee, WI;
Willie Davis, Chairman
William Lynette, President

Minn-Iowa Christian Broadcasting Inc.
Box 72, Blue Earth MN 56013
(507) 526-3233; *Fax:*(507) 526-3235
www.kjly.com
kjly@kjly.com
Radio Stns: 5 FM.
KJCY St. Ansgar, IA; KJLY Blue Earth, MN; KJYL Eagle Grove, IA; KJIA Spirit Lake, IA; KJWR Windom, MN;
Matt Dorfner, Station Manager

Miriam Media Inc.
6117 Lemon Thyme Dr., Alexandria VA 22310
(571) 228-1258; *Fax:*(703) 299-6626;
Radio Stns: 1 FM.
KCHT Childress, TX;
Darryl Delawder, President

Mission Nebraska Inc.
Box 30345, Lincoln NE 68503-0345
(402) 477-1090
www.missionnebraska.org
Radio Stns: 1 AM. 3 FM.
KMMJ Grand Island, NE; KPNY Alliance, NE; KROA Grand Island, NE; KMBV Valentine, NE;

Mississippi Broadcasters L.L.C.
Box 1699, Meridian MS 39302
(601) 693-2661; *Fax:*(601) 483-0826;
Radio Stns: 4 FM.
WJXM De Kalb, MS; WMLV Butler, AL; WEXR Stonewall, MS; WALT-FM Meridian, MS;
Clay Holladay, General Manager

Missouri River Christian Broadcasting Inc.
Box 187, Washington MO 63090
(636) 239-0400; *Fax:*(636) 293-4448
www.goodnewsvoice.org
Radio Stns: 3 FM.
KGNA-FM Arnold, MO; KGNN-FM Cuba, MO; KGNV Washington, MO;
J.C. Goggan, General Manager

Monarch Broadcasting Inc.
212 W. Cypress St., Altus OK 73521
(580) 482-1450; *Fax:*(580) 482-3420
www.kwhw.com
Radio Stns: 1 AM. 1 FM.
KWHW Altus, OK; KQTZ Hobart, OK;
Matthew Ward, President

Monticello Media LLC
3948 S. Third St.,Suite 191, Jacksonville Beach FL 32250
(904) 285-3239;
Radio Stns: 2 AM. 4 FM.
WCHV Charlottesville, VA; WKAV Charlottesville, VA; WCYK-FM Staunton, VA; WCHV-FM Charlottesville, VA; WZGN Crozet, VA; WHTE-FM Ruckersville, VA;
George Reed, President

Montrose Broadcasting Corp.
Box 248,9 Locust St., Montrose PA 18801
(570) 278-2811; *Fax:*(570) 278-1442
www.wpel.org,www.wpgm.org
mail@wpel.org
Ownership: Non Profit Non Stock Corporation.
Radio Stns: 2 AM. 3 FM.
WPEL Montrose, PA; WPGM Danville, PA; WBGM New Berlin, PA; WPEL-FM Montrose, PA; WPGM-FM Danville, PA;
Larry Souder, President
John Hagenboch, VP
Barbara Snyder, Secretary
Charles Scott, Treasurer

Moon Broadcasting
1200 W. Venice Blvd., Los Angeles CA 90006
(213) 745-6224; *Fax:*(213) 745-7577;
Radio Stns: 5 AM. 7 FM.
KIQQ Barstow, CA; KRRS Santa Rosa, CA; KTNS Oakhurst, CA; KTOB Petaluma, CA; KZXR Prosser, WA; KAAT Oakhurst, CA; KAEH Beaumont, CA; KIQQ-FM Newberry Springs, CA; KMNA Mabton, WA; KMQA East Porterville, CA; KLES Prosser, WA; KMEN Mendota, CA;
Abel DeLuna, President

Morgan County Industries Inc.
129 College St., West Liberty KY 41472
(606) 743-3145; *Fax:*(606) 743-9557
radio41472@yahoo.com
Radio Stns: 3 AM. 4 FM.
WLKS West Liberty, KY; WMOR Morehead, KY; WRLV Salyersville, KY; WCBJ Campton, KY; WLKS-FM West Liberty, KY; WMOR-FM Morehead, KY; WRLV-FM Salyersville, KY;
Paul Lyons, COO

Morgan Murphy Media (Evening Telegram Co)
7025 Raymond Rd., Madison WI 53719
(608) 271-4321; *Fax:*(608) 271-6111
www.channel3000.com
talkback@wisctv.com
Ownership: Evening Telegram Co. owns 100% of KVEW(TV), KXLY-AM-FM-TV, KXLY-DT and KAPP(TV). Evening Telegram Co. owns 84.4% of TelevisionWisconsin Inc., with an additional 15.2% of the stn held by Evening Telegram stockholders.
Radio Stns: 4 AM. 4 FM.
KXLX Airway Heights, WA; KXLY Spokane, WA; WGLR Lancaster, WI; WPVL Platteville, WI; KEZE Spokane, WA; KZZU-FM Spokane, WA; WGLR-FM Lancaster, WI; WPVL-FM Platteville, WI;
TV Stns: 5 TV.
KAPP Yakima, WA; KVEW Kennewick, WA; KXLY-TV Spokane, WA; WISC-TV Madison, WI; WKBT La Crosse, WI;
Brian Lubanski, Gen Mgr
George Nelson, Executive Vice President
Steve Herling, Executive Vice President
Elizabeth Murphy Burns, President

Morris Radio LLC
725 Broad St., Augusta GA 30903-0936
(706) 823-3331; *Fax:*(706) 823-3212
www.morris.com
Ownership: Owned by Morris Communications Company LLC. Group also owns the Kansas Agriculture Network, Topeka, KS; Kansas Information Network, Topeka, KS; and the WildcatSports Network, Topeka, KS.
Radio Stns: 15 AM. 16 FM.
KABI Abilene, KS; KNWZ Coachella, CA; KNWQ Palm Springs, CA; KFQD Anchorage, AK; KWOK Hoquiam, WA; KGNC Amarillo, TX; KHAR Anchorage, AK; KKRT Wenatchee, WA; KXPS Thousand Palms, CA; KNWH Yucca Valley, CA; KSAL Salina, KS; KWIQ Moses Lake North, WA; KFUT Thousand Palms, CA; KXRO Aberdeen, WA; WIBW Topeka, KS; KBLS North Fort Riley, KS; KBRJ Anchorage, AK; KEAG Anchorage, AK; KXXK Hoquiam, WA; KGNC-FM Amarillo, TX; KKUU Indio, CA; KMXS Anchorage, AK; KSAJ-FM Abilene, KS; KWLN Wilson Creek, WA; KWHL Anchorage, AK; KWIQ-FM Moses Lake, WA; KYEZ Salina, KS; KDGL Yucca Valley, CA; KSAL-FM Salina, KS; WIBW-FM Topeka, KS; KAYO Wasilla, AK;
Michael D. Osterhout, COO

Mortenson Broadcasting Co.
3270 Blazer Pkwy. #101, Lexington KY 40509-1847
(859) 245-1000; *Fax:*(859) 245-1600
Ownership: Jack Mortenson, 100%.
Radio Stns: 7 AM. 1 FM.
KGGN Gladstone, MO; KGGR Dallas, TX; KHVN Fort Worth, TX; KKGM Fort Worth, TX; KRVA Cockrell Hill, TX; KTNO University Park, TX; WEMM Huntington, WV; WEMM-FM Huntington, WV;
Jack Mortenson, President

Mountain Broadcasting Corp.
99 Clinton Rd., West Caldwell NJ 7006
(973) 852-0300; *Fax:*(973) 808-5516;
Radio Stns: 3 AM.
WPWA Chester, PA; WBTK Richmond, VA; WWGB Indian Head, MD;
TV Stns: 1 TV.
WMBC-TV Newton, NJ;
Sun Young Joo, President

Mountain Communications
Box 211, Saranac Lake NY 12983-0211
(518) 891-1544; *Fax:*(518) 891-1545;
Radio Stns: 2 AM. 3 FM.
WIRD Lake Placid, NY; WNBZ Saranac Lake, NY; WLPW Lake Placid, NY; WRGR Tupper Lake, NY; WYZY Saranac, NY;
Ted Morgan, President

Mountain Dog Media
254 Winnebago Dr., Fond du Lac WI 54935
(920) 921-1071; *Fax:*(920) 921-0757;
Radio Stns: 2 AM. 1 FM.
KFIZ Fond Du Lac, WI; WCLB Sheboygan, WI; WFON Fond Du Lac, WI;

Randy Hopper, President

Mountain Wireless Inc.
Box 159, Skowhegan ME 4976
(207) 474-5171; *Fax:*(207) 474-3299;
Radio Stns: 1 AM. 2 FM.
WSKW Skowhegan, ME; WCTB Fairfield, ME; WFMX Skowhegan, ME;
Alan W. Anderson, President

Mt. Rushmore Broadcasting Inc.
218 N. Wolcott, Casper WY 82602
(307) 265-1984; *Fax:*(307) 266-3295
www.wyomingradio.com
mtrushmore@wyoming.com
Radio Stns: 5 AM. 8 FM.
KFCR Custer, SD; KGOS Torrington, WY; KRAL Rawlins, WY; KVOC Casper, WY; KZMX Hot Springs, SD; KASS Casper, WY; KAWK Custer, SD; KERM Torrington, WY; KHOC Casper, WY; KIQZ Rawlins, WY; KMLD Casper, WY; KQLT Casper, WY; KZMX-FM Hot Springs, SD;
Jan Gray, CEO

Mt. Washington Radio & Gramophone L.L.C.
Box 2008, Conway NH 03818
(603) 356-8870; *Fax:*(603) 356-8875
Ownership: Greg Frizzell, 51%; Frizzell Family Revocable Trust, 49%.
Radio Stns: 1 AM. 2 FM.
WBNC Conway, NH; WVMJ Conway, NH; WMWV Conway, NH;
Greg Frizzell, General Manager

MTD Inc.
Box 2010, Ruidoso Downs NM 88346
(505) 258-9922; *Fax:*(505) 258-2363
www.ruidoso.net/krui
kruikwmw@trailnet.com
Radio Stns: 1 AM. 4 FM.
KRUI Ruidoso Downs, NM; KWMW Maljamar, NM; KIDX Ruidoso, NM; KNMB Cloudcroft, NM; KTUM Tatum, NM;
Bruce Rimbo, President
Timothy Keithley, General Manager

MTS Broadcasting
Box 237, Cambridge MD 21613
(410) 228-4800; *Fax:*(410) 228-0130
www.mtslive.com
theheat@intercom.net,waai@intercom.net,theduck@intercom.net
Radio Stns: 1 AM. 2 FM.
WCEM Cambridge, MD; WAAI Hurlock, MD; WTDK Federalsburg, MD;
Thomas C. Mulitz, CEO

Muirfield Broadcasting Inc.
200 Short Rd., Southern Pines NC 28387
(910) 692-2107; *Fax:*(910) 692-6849
www.star1025fm.com
Radio Stns: 1 AM. 1 FM.
WIOZ Pinehurst, NC; WIOZ-FM Southern Pines, NC;
Walker Morris, President

Multicultural Radio Broadcasting Inc.
449 Broadway, New York NY 10013
(212) 966-1059; *Fax:*(212) 966-9580
www.mrbi.net
Radio Stns: 31 AM.
KMNY Hurst, TX; KALI West Covina, CA; KATD Pittsburg, CA; KAZN Pasadena, CA; KBLA Santa Monica, CA; KDFT Ferris, TX; KEST San Francisco, CA; KWRU Fresno, CA; KIQI San Francisco, CA; KAHZ Pomona, CA; KSJX San Jose, CA; KNSN San Diego, CA; KXPA Bellevue, WA; KXYZ Houston, TX; KYPA Los Angeles, CA; WEXY Wilton Manors, FL; WGFS Covington, GA; WHWH Princeton, NJ; WLXE Rockville, MD; WJDM Elizabeth, NJ; WKDM New York, NY; WLYN Lynn, MA; WNMA Miami Springs, FL; WNSW Newark, NJ; WNYG Medford, NY; WPAT Paterson, NJ; WAZN Watertown, MA; WTTM Lindenwold, NJ; WWRU Jersey City, NJ; WZHF Arlington, VA; WZRC New York, NY;
Arthur Liu, CEO

Munbilla Broadcasting Properties Ltd.
5526 Hwy. 281 N., Marble Falls TX 78654
(830) 693-5551; *Fax:*(830) 693-5107;
Radio Stns: 5 FM.
KBEY Burnet, TX; KHLE Kempner, TX; KHLB Mason, TX; KRZS Hunt, TX; KYRT Hunt, TX;
Duane Fox, General Manager
Sabrina Preiss, Programming Director
Bill Woleben, Chief Engineer

Muzzy Broadcasting L.L.C.
500 Division St., Stevens Point WI 54481
(715) 341-9800; *Fax:*(715) 341-0000
www.979wspt.com
Ownership: Richard L. Muzzy.
Radio Stns: 1 AM. 2 FM.
WPCN Stevens Point, WI; WKQH Marathon, WI; WSPT Stevens Point, WI;
Richard Muzzy, President

My Town Media, Inc.
250 N. Water, Suite 300, Wichita KS 67202
(620) 431-1333; *Fax:*(620) 431-4643
www.kkoyfm.com
dave@mytown-media.com
Radio Stns: 1 AM. 4 FM.
KKOY Chanute, KS; KHST Lamar, MO; KKOY-FM Chanute, KS; KSNP Burlington, KS; KWXD Asbury, MO;
William Wachter, President

Nassau Broadcasting Partners L.P.
619 Alexander Rd.,3rd Fl., Princeton NJ 8540
(609) 452-9696; *Fax:*609) 419-0143
www.nassaubroadcasting.com
Radio Stns: 14 AM. 32 FM.
WARK Hagerstown, MD; WCHR Trenton, NJ; WEEX Easton, PA; WEMJ Laconia, NH; WIKE Newport, VT; WPLY Mount Pocono, PA; WNJE Flemington, NJ; WLVP Gorham, ME; WSNO Barre, VT; WTKZ Allentown, PA; WTSV Claremont, NH; WVPO Stroudsburg, PA; WBYN Lehighton, PA; WLAM Lewiston, ME; WAFY Middletown, MD; WWEG Myersville, MD; WBYA Islesboro, ME; WWHQ Meredith, NH; WBQQ Kennebunk, ME; WHXR Scarborough, ME; WBQX Thomaston, ME; WEXP Brandon, VT; WWOD Hartford, VT; WHDQ Claremont, NH; WFNQ Nashua, NH; WJYY Concord, NH; WCRB Lowell, MA; WXTP North Windham, ME; WLKZ Wolfeboro, NH; WLNH-FM Laconia, NH; WBQI Bar Harbor, ME; WMOO Derby Center, VT; WTHK Wilmington, VT; WTHT Auburn, ME; WNHW Belmont, NH; WPST Trenton, NJ; WNNH Henniker, NH; WODE-FM Easton, PA; WORK Barre, VT; WBQW Kennebunkport, ME; WFNK Lewiston, ME; WWFY Berlin, VT; WXLF Hartford, VT; WWYY Belvidere, NJ; WZLF Bellows Falls, VT; WFYX Walpole, NH;
Louis Mercatani, President

Nebraska Rural Radio Association
Box 880, Lexington NE 68850
(308) 324-2371; *Fax:*(308) 324-5786
www.krvn.com
krvnam@krvn.com
Ownership: Nebraska Rural Radio Association, 100%
Radio Stns: 3 AM. 3 FM.
KNEB Scottsbluff, NE; KRVN Lexington, NE; KTIC West Point, NE; KNEB-FM Scottsbluff, NE; KRVN-FM Lexington, NE; KTIC-FM West Point, NE;
Larry Hudkins, President
Kevin Cooksley, VP
Eric Brown, Secretary

Neuhoff Family L.P.
1501 N. Washington, Danville IL 61832
(217) 442-1700,; *Fax:*(217) 431-1489
neuhoffmedia.com
mhulvey@cooketech.net
Ownership: Neuhoff Corp., North Palm Beach, FL, 100% of votes.
Radio Stns: 4 AM. 8 FM.
WDAN Danville, IL; WDZ Decatur, IL; WFMB Springfield, IL; WSOY Decatur, IL; WCVS-FM Virden, IL; WCZQ Monticello, IL; WDNL Danville, IL; WDZQ Decatur, IL; WFMB-FM Springfield, IL; WRHK Danville, IL; WSOY-FM Decatur, IL; WXAJ Hillsboro, IL;
TV Stns: 1 TV.
KMVT Twin Falls, ID;
Geoff Neuhoff, President
Mike Hulvey, General Manager

Nevada County Broadcasters Inc.
1255 E. Main St.,Suite A, Grass Valley CA 95945
(530) 272-3424; *Fax:*(530) 272-2872
www.knco.com
knco@nccn.com
Radio Stns: 2 AM. 1 FM.
KNCO Grass Valley, CA; KUBA Yuba City, CA; KNCO-FM Grass Valley, CA;
Bob Breck, CEO

New Media Broadcasters Inc.
2210 31st St. N., Havre MT 59501-8003
(406) 265-7841; *Fax:*(406) 265-8855
www.nmbi.com
nmb@nmbi.com
Radio Stns: 1 AM. 2 FM.
KOJM Havre, MT; KPQX Havre, MT; KRYK Chinook, MT;
C. David Leeds, President
Cynthia H. Leeds, Operations Dir

New South Communications Inc.
Box 5797, Meridian MS 39302
(601) 693-2661; *Fax:*(601) 483-0826
Ownership: F.E. Holladay, 100%.
Radio Stns: 2 AM. 3 FM.
WALT Meridian, MS; WIIN Ridgeland, MS; WJKK Vicksburg, MS; WUSJ Madison, MS; WYOY Gluckstadt, MS;
F.E. Holladay, President

New West Broadcasting Corp.
1145 Kilauea Ave., Hilo HI 96720
(808) 935-5461; *Fax:*(808) 935-7761;
Radio Stns: 1 AM. 2 FM.
KPUA Hilo, HI; KAOY Kealakekua, HI; KNWB Hilo, HI;

News-Press & Gazette Co.
Box 29, St. Joseph MO 64502
(816) 271-8500; *Fax:*(816) 271-8695;
Radio Stns: 2 AM. 1 FM.
KESQ Indio, CA; KRDO Colorado Springs, CO; KUNA-FM La Quinta, CA;
TV Stns: 7 TV.
KECY-TV El Centro, CA; KESQ-TV Palm Springs, CA; KIFI-TV Idaho Falls, ID; KJCT Grand Junction, CO; KRDO-TV Colorado Springs, CO; KTVZ Bend, OR; KVIA-TV El Paso, TX;
John Kueneke, President

Newsweb Corp.
1645 W. Fullerton Ave., Chicago IL 60614
(773) 975-0401; *Fax:*(773) 975-1301
Ownership: Fred Eychaner, 100%.
Radio Stns: 5 AM. 4 FM.
WAIT Crystal Lake, IL; WCFJ Chicago Heights, IL; WNDZ Portage, IN; WSBC Chicago, IL; WCPT Willow Springs, IL; WCPY Dekalb, IL; WCPT-FM Arlington Heights, IL; WKIF Kankakee, IL; WCPQ Park Forest, IL;
TV Stns: 1 TV.
KCDO-TV Sterling, CO;
Fred Eychaner, CEO
Charley Gross, COO

NextMedia Group Inc.
6312 S. Fiddler's Green Cir.,Suite 360E, Englewood CO 80111
(303) 694-9118; *Fax:*(303) 694-4940
www.nextmediagroup.com
Ownership: NextMedia Investors LLC, 100% of votes.
Radio Stns: 8 AM. 26 FM.
WANG Havelock, NC; WHBC Canton, OH; WJOL Joliet, IL; WKRS Waukegan, IL; WRNN Myrtle Beach, SC; WLIP Kenosha, WI; WRNS Kinston, NC; WSGW Saginaw, MI; KBAY Gilroy, CA; KEZR San Jose, CA; KLAK Tom Bean, TX; KMAD-FM Whitesboro, TX; KMKT Bells, TX; WLVG Havelock, NC; WQZL Belhaven, NC; WKZQ-FM Forestbrook, SC; WRXQ Coal City, IL; WCEN-FM Hemlock, MI; WERO Washington, NC; WHBC-FM Canton, OH; WJBR-FM Wilmington, DE; WMYB Myrtle Beach, SC; WERV-FM Aurora, IL; WSSR Joliet, IL; WRNN-FM Socastee, SC; WQSL Jacksonville, NC; WRNS-FM Kinston, NC; WSGW-FM Carrollton, MI; WTLZ Saginaw, MI; WXLC Waukegan, IL; WXQR-FM Jacksonville, NC; WYAV Myrtle Beach, SC; WWYW Dundee, IL; WZSR Woodstock, IL;
Steven Dinetz, CEO
Skip Weller, President

Nicolet Broadcasting Inc.
3030 Park Drive,Suite 3, Sturgeon Bay WI 54235
(920) 746-9430; *Fax:*(920) 746-9433
www.doorcountydailynews.com
wbbk@doorcoundtydailynews.com
Ownership: Roger Utnehmer.
Radio Stns: 4 FM.
WBDK Algoma, WI; WRKU Forestville, WI; WRLU Algoma, WI; WSBW Sister Bay, WI;
Roger Utnehmer, President

Noalmark Broadcasting Corp.
202 W. 19th St., El Dorado AR 71730
(870) 862-7777; *Fax:*(870) 862-0203
Ownership: William C. Nolan Jr., 65%; Edwin B. Alderson Jr., 35%.
Radio Stns: 8 AM. 14 FM.

RADIO - U.S.

KZHS Hot Springs, AR; KBIM Roswell, NM; KBOK Malvern, AR; KELD El Dorado, AR; KVMA Magnolia, AR; KVRC Arkadelphia, AR; KBHS Hot Springs, AR; KYKK Humble City, NM; KAGL El Dorado, AR; KBIM-FM Roswell, NM; KMRX El Dorado, AR; KDEL-FM Arkadelphia, AR; KMLK El Dorado, AR; KIXV(FM) Malvern, AR; KIXB El Dorado, AR; KIXN Hobbs, NM; KELD-FM Hampton, AR; KLAZ Hot Springs, AR; KPER Hobbs, NM; KPZA-FM Jal, NM; KYXK Gurdon, AR; KVMZ Waldo, AR;
William Nolan, President
Paul Starr, Vice President

Norsan Consulting and Management Inc.
Box 2148, Tucker GA 30085
(770) 414-5026;
Radio Stns: 9 AM. 1 FM.
WCEO Columbia, SC; WEWC Callahan, FL; WFAY Fayetteville, NC; WGSP Charlotte, NC; WVOJ Fernandina Beach, FL; WKGN Knoxville, TN; WSOS St. Augustine Beach, FL; WXNC Monroe, NC; WNNR Jacksonville, FL; WGSP-FM Pageland, SC;

North American Broadcasting Co. Inc.
1458 Dublin Rd., Columbus OH 43215
(614) 481-7800; *Fax:*(614) 481-8070
www.nabco-inc.com
Radio Stns: 1 AM. 2 FM.
WMNI Columbus, OH; WRKZ Columbus, OH; WMNI-FM Westerville, OH;
Norma Mnich, Chairman
Matthew Mnich, CEO
Mark Jividen, Operations Dir
Nick Reed, VP/Sec/Treas

North Cascades Broadcasting Inc.
Box 151, Omak WA 98841
(509) 826-0100; *Fax:*(509) 826-3929
www.komw.net
Radio Stns: 1 AM. 1 FM.
KOMW Omak, WA; KZBE Omak, WA;
John Andrist, President

North Georgia Radio Group L.P.
112 Jordan Dr., Chattanooga TN 37421
(423) 425-8987;
Radio Stns: 2 AM. 2 FM.
WBLJ Dalton, GA; WDAL Dalton, GA; WOCE Ringgold, GA; WYYU Dalton, GA;

Northeast Broadcasting Company Inc.
288 S. River Rd., Bedford NH 03110
(603) 668-9999; *Fax:*(603) 668-6470
www.nebcast.com
Ownership: Steven A. Silberberg, Ed Flanagan.
Radio Stns: 10 AM. 28 FM.
KHAT Laramie, WY; KRAE Cheyenne, WY; WJOE Lake City, FL; WTWK Plattsburgh, NY; WFAD Middlebury, VT; WGAW Gardner, MA; WCAT Burlington, VT; WSKI Montpelier, VT; WRSA St. Albans, VT; KJMP Pierce, CO; KIMX Nunn, CO; WXRG Athol, MA; WWMP Waterbury, VT; WNCS Montpelier, VT; WRJT Royalton, VT; WIFY Addison, VT; WDOT Danville, VT; WXRV Andover, MA; KVUW Wendover, NV; KFMH Belle Fourche, SD; KVRG Victor, ID; KRVQ-FM Lake Isabella, CA; KRQU Medicine Bow, WY; KTED Evansville, WY; KDAD Bar Nunn, WY; KZQL Mills, WY; KWHO Lovell, WY; KAAZ Laramie, WY; KANT Guernsey, WY; KAZY Cheyenne, WY; KPAD Rawlins, WY; KRAN Warren Afb, WY; KROW Cody, WY; WNYN-FM Whitefield, NH; KTUG Hudson, WY; KHAD Upton, WY; KHNA Wamsutter, WY; KBEN-FM Cowley, WY;
Steven Silberberg, CEO
Edward Flanagan, VP

Northeast Colorado Broadcasting LLC
220 State St.,Suite 106, Fort Morgan CO 80701
(970) 867-7271; *Fax:*(970) 867-2676;
Radio Stns: 1 AM. 2 FM.
KSIR Brush, CO; KPMX Sterling, CO; KPRB Brush, CO;
Alec Creighton, General Manager

Northeast Communications Corp.
110 Babbit Rd., Franklin NH 03235
(603) 934-2500; *Fax:*(603) 934-2933
www.mix941fm.com
onair@mix941fm.com
Ownership: Jeff Fisher, 44.5%; Chris Fisher, 17.5%; and Phil Fisher, 16.5%.
Radio Stns: 2 AM. 1 FM.
WFTN Franklin, NH; WPNH Plymouth, NH; WSCY Moultonborough, NH;
Jeff Fisher, President
Cathy Keyser, Operations Manager
Fred Caruso, Programming
Rick Ganley, Programming Director

Northeast Oklahoma Broadcast Network Inc.
1 W. 3rd St., Grove OK 74344
(918) 786-2211; *Fax:*(918) 786-2284;
Radio Stns: 1 AM. 2 FM.
KVIS Miami, OK; KGLC Miami, OK; KESA Eureka Springs, AR;
Larry Hestand, President

Northern Christian Radio Inc.
Box 695, Gaylord MI 49734-0695
(800) 545-8857,; *Fax:*(989) 732-8171
www.ncradio.org
ncr@ncradio.org
Radio Stns: 5 FM.
WHST Tawas City, MI; WOLW Cadillac, MI; WPHN Gaylord, MI; WTHN Sault Ste. Marie, MI; WRQC(FM) East Tawas, MI;
Joe Sereno, Chairman
George Lake, Operations Dir
Patrick Green, Programming Director

Northern Star Broadcasting L.L.C.
1356 Mackinaw Ave., Cheboygan MI 49721
(231) 627-2341; *Fax:*(231) 627-7000
www.nsbroadcasting.com
cmonk@nsbroadcasting.com
Radio Stns: 5 AM. 15 FM.
WCBY Cheboygan, MI; WDMJ Marquette, MI; WIAN Ishpeming, MI; WKNW Sault Sainte Marie, MI; WMIQ Iron Mountain, MI; WAVC Mio, MI; WCKC Cadillac, MI; WGFM Cheboygan, MI; WGFN Glen Arbor, MI; WIHC Newberry, MI; WIMK Iron Mountain, MI; WJPD Ishpeming, MI; WJZJ Glen Arbor, MI; WLJZ Mackinaw City, MI; WMKC Indian River, MI; WNGE Negaunee, MI; WUPK Marquette, MI; WYSS Sault Ste. Marie, MI; WZNL Norway, MI; WMKD Pickford, MI;
Palmer Pyle, President
Chris Monk, Operations Dir

Northwestern College & Radio
3003 Snelling Ave. N., St. Paul MN 55113-1598
(651) 631-5000; *Fax:*(651) 631-5086
www.nwc.edu
phvirts@nwc.edu
Ownership: Non-profit organization. Northwestern College, St. Paul, is the owner and operator of the 15 radio licenses.
Radio Stns: 5 AM. 9 FM.
KFNW West Fargo, ND; KNWC Sioux Falls, SD; KNWS Waterloo, IA; KTIS Minneapolis, MN; WNWC Sun Prairie, WI; KDNI Duluth, MN; KDNW Duluth, MN; KFNW-FM Fargo, ND; KNWI Osceola, IA; KNWM Madrid, IA; KFNL Kindred, ND; KTIS-FM Minneapolis, MN; WNWC-FM Madison, WI; WSMR Sarasota, FL;
Dr. Alan Cureton, President
Dr. Paul Virts, SVP

NRC Broadcasting Inc.
1201 Eighteenth St.,Suite 250, Denver CO 80202
(303) 675-4698; *Fax:*(303) 296-7030
www.nrcbroadcasting.com
Radio Stns: 1 AM. 10 FM.
KCKK Littleton, CO; KDSP(FM) Greenwood Village, CO; KQZR Hayden, CO; KFMU-FM Oak Creek, CO; KIDN-FM Burns, CO; KJAC Timnath, CO; KKCH Glenwood Springs, CO; KNFO Basalt, CO; KSMT Breckenridge, CO; KSPN-FM Aspen, CO; KTUN New Castle, CO;
Tim Brown, Chairman
Dave Rogers, CFO
Ray Skibitsky, President

NRG Media LLC
2875 Mount Vernon Rd. S.E., Cedar Rapids IA 52403
(319) 862-0300; *Fax:*(319) 286-9383
www.nrgmedia.com
jlink@nrgmedia.com
Radio Stns: 14 AM. 26 FM.
KAYL Storm Lake, IA; KGFW Kearney, NE; KHUB Fremont, NE; KLGA Algona, IA; KLIN Lincoln, NE; KQWC Webster City, IA; KWBE Beatrice, NE; KWBG Boone, IA; WCMY Ottawa, IL; WFAW Fort Atkinson, WI; WIXN Dixon, IL; WJBD Salem, IL; WLKD Minocqua, WI; WOBT Rhinelander, WI; KAYL-FM Storm Lake, IA; KBBK Lincoln, NE; KFGE Milford, NE; KFMT-FM Fremont, NE; KHBT Humboldt, IA; KKIA Ida Grove, IA; KLNC Lincoln, NE; KLGA-FM Algona, IA; KQKY Kearney, NE; KQWC-FM Webster City, IA; KRNY Kearney, NE; KROR Hastings, NE; KSYZ-FM Grand Island, NE; WGLX-FM Wisconsin Rapids, WI; WHDG Rhinelander, WI; WRCV Dixon, IL; WJBD-FM Salem, IL; WKCH Whitewater, WI; WYTE Marshfield, WI; WMQA-FM Minocqua, WI; WRHN Rhinelander, WI; WRKX Ottawa, IL; WRLO-FM Antigo, WI; WSEY Oregon, IL; WSJY Fort Atkinson, WI; WBCV Wausau, WI;
Norman W. Waitt Jr., Chairman
Mary Quass, CEO

O-Town Communications Inc.
416 E. Main St., Ottumwa IA 52501
(641) 684-5563; *Fax:*(641) 684-5832
www.ottumwaradio.com
mail@ottumwaradio.com
Radio Stns: 1 AM. 3 FM.
KBIZ Ottumwa, IA; KKSI Eddyville, IA; KRKN Eldon, IA; KTWA Ottumwa, IA;

Ohana Media Group LLC
Box 99827, Seattle WA 98139-0827
(425) 891-1200
www.ohanamediagroup.com
info@ohanamediagroup.com
Ownership: Trila Bumstead, 100%.
Radio Stns: 6 FM.
KVAS-FM Ilwaco, WA; KFAT Anchorage, AK; KDBZ Anchorage, AK; KBBO-FM Houston, AK; KCRX-FM Seaside, OR; KXLW Houston, AK;
Trila Bumstead, CEO
Bill Sigmar, COO
Tom Oakes, VP of Programming

Omni Broadcasting Co.
502 Beltrami Ave. N.W., Bemidji MN 56601-3010
(218) 444-1500; *Fax:*(218) 759-0345
Ownership: Louis H. Buron Jr., Mary Campbell, G. Michael Boen.
Radio Stns: 5 AM. 11 FM.
KBUN Bemidji, MN; KLIZ Brainerd, MN; KNSP Staples, MN; KVBR Brainerd, MN; KWAD Wadena, MN; KBHP Bemidji, MN; KBLB Nisswa, MN; KUAL-FM Brainerd, MN; KIKV-FM Sauk Centre, MN; KKWS Wadena, MN; KKZY Bemidji, MN; KLIZ-FM Brainerd, MN; KLLZ-FM Walker, MN; KULO Alexandria, MN; WJJY-FM Brainerd, MN; WQXJ Blackduck, MN;
Mary Campbell, VP/CFO
Louis Buron Jr., President

One Ten Broadcast Group Inc.
2 E. Main St., Shawnee OK 74801-6906
(405) 878-1803
kirc1059@aol.com
Radio Stns: 1 AM. 2 FM.
KWSH Wewoka, OK; KIRC Seminole, OK; KSLE Wewoka, OK;
Linda Jones, President

1TV.Com Inc.
Box 1416, Los Altos CA 94023
(650) 520-6002;
Radio Stns: 3 AM. 1 FM.
KBSZ Apache Junction, AZ; KIKO Miami, AZ; KJAA Globe, AZ; KIKO-FM Claypool, AZ;
John Low, President

Opus Broadcasting Systems Inc.
511 Rossanley Dr., Medford OR 97501
(541) 772-0322; *Fax:*(541) 772-4233;
Radio Stns: 2 AM. 3 FM.
KEZX Medford, OR; KRTA Medford, OR; KCNA Cave Junction, OR; KROG Grants Pass, OR; KRVC Hornbrook, CA;
Dean Flock, General Manager
Brian Fraser, General Sales Mgr

Opus Media Holdings LLC
950 Third Ave.,19th Fl., New York NY 10022
(212) 634-3376;
Radio Stns: 10 FM.
KQLQ Columbia, LA; KEZP Bunkie, LA; KBKK Ball, LA; KLAA-FM Tioga, LA; KXRR Monroe, LA; KMYY Rayville, LA; KZRZ West Monroe, LA; WWOF(FM) Tallahassee, FL; WHTF Havana, FL; WQTL Tallahassee, FL;
Richard Linhart, Chairman
James Shea, CEO

Ouachita Broadcasting Inc.
Box 1450, Mena AR 71953
(479) 394-1450;
Radio Stns: 1 AM. 3 FM.
KENA Fort Smith, AR; KILX Hatfield, AR; KQOR Mena, AR; KENA-FM Mena, AR;
Jay Bunyard, President
Teresa Bunyard, Operations Dir

Our Three Sons Broadcasting L.L.P.
Box 307, Rock Hill SC 29731
(803) 324-1340; *Fax:*(803) 324-2860
www.wrhi.com,www.fm107.com

Radio Stns: 1 AM. 1 FM.
WRHI Rock Hill, SC; WVSZ Chesterfield, SC;
Allan Miller, President

Ozark Media Inc.
555 Marshall Dr., St. Robert MO 65584
(573) 336-5535; *Fax:*(573) 336-7619;

Radio Stns: 3 FM.
KELE-FM Mountain Grove, MO; KFLW St. Robert, MO; KOZX Cabool, MO;
Dalton Wright, President

Pacific Cascade Communications Corp.
1139 Hartnell Ave., Redding CA 96002-2113
(530) 222-4455; *Fax:*(530) 222-4484;

Radio Stns: 2 AM. 3 FM.
KGRV Winston, OR; KVIP Redding, CA; KVIP-FM Redding, CA; KMWR Brookings, OR; KNDZ McKinleyville, CA;
David Morrow, Operations Dir

Pacific Empire Radio Corp.
111 Main St., Lewiston ID 83501
(208) 799-9056
pacempire.com
Ownership: Mary E. Bolland, 26%; Mark Bolland, 26%; AIA Services Corp., 19%; Connie Taylor, 13%; R. John Taylor, 13%.

Radio Stns: 4 AM. 7 FM.
KBKR Baker, OR; KCLK Asotin, WA; KLBM La Grande, OR; KSEI Pocatello, ID; KATW Lewiston, ID; KCLK-FM Clarkston, WA; KKBC-FM Baker, OR; KMGI Pocatello, ID; KUBQ La Grande, OR; KRJT Elgin, OR; KQZB Troy, ID;
Kurt Luchs, President

Pacific Radio Group Inc.
311 Ano St., Kahului HI 96732
(808) 877-5566; *Fax:*(808) 871-0666
www.pacificradiogroup.com
bergson@pacificradiogroup.com

Radio Stns: 4 AM. 10 FM.
KHLO Hilo, HI; KKON Kealakekua, HI; KMVI Wailuku, HI; KNUI Kahului, HI; KAGB Waimea, HI; KAPA Hilo, HI; KKBG Hilo, HI; KLEO Kahaluu, HI; KLUA Kailua Kona, HI; KJMD Pukalani, HI; KJKS Kahului, HI; KPOA Lahaina, HI; KPVS Hilo, HI; KLHI-FM Kahului, HI;
Chuck Bergson, CEO
Robert Van Dine, General Manager
L.E. Johnson, CFO

Pacific West Broadcasting Inc.
Box 1430, Newport OR 97365
(541) 265-2266; *Fax:*(541) 265-6397
ybcradio.com
info@ybcradio.com

Radio Stns: 1 AM. 2 FM.
KBCH Lincoln City, OR; KNCU Newport, OR; KCRF-FM Lincoln City, OR;
David Miller, President

Pacifica Foundation Inc.
1925 Martin Luther King Jr. Way, Berkeley CA 94704
(510) 849-2590
www.pacifica.org
Ownership: (dba Pacific Radio).

Radio Stns: 6 FM.
KPFA Berkeley, CA; KPFB Berkeley, CA; KPFK Los Angeles, CA; KPFT Houston, TX; WBAI New York, NY; WPFW Washington, DC;
Dan Cougjhlin, Executive Director

Pamal Broadcasting Ltd.
6 Johnson Rd., Latham NY 12110
(518) 786-6600; *Fax:*(518) 786-6610
www.pamal.com
Ownership: James Morrell, owner.

Radio Stns: 11 AM. 22 FM.
WBNR Beacon, NY; WENU South Glen Falls, NY; WGHQ Kingston, NY; WIZR Johnstown, NY; WDVH Gainesville, FL; WMML Glens Falls, NY; WROW Albany, NY; WRZN Hernando, FL; WSYB Rutland, VT; WPNI Amherst, MA; WTMN Gainesville, FL; WAJZ Voorheesville, NY; WLVW(FM) Trenton, FL; WJEN Killington, VT; WNYQ Hudson Falls, NY; WFLY Troy, NY; WFFG-FM Corinth, NY; WHUD Peekskill, NY; WDVT Rutland, VT; WJJR Rutland, VT; WKBE Warrensburg, NY; WKLI-FM Albany, NY; WKZY Cross City, FL; WMEZ Pensacola, FL; WHHZ Newberry, FL; WBPM Saugerties, NY; WSPK Poughkeepsie, NY; WTMG Williston, FL; WXBM-FM Milton, FL; WYJB Albany, NY; WXPK Briarcliff Manor, NY; WZMR Altamont, NY; WZRT Rutland, VT;
Michael Dufort, CFO
Debbie Grembowicz, General Manager

Dan Austin, Market Manager
Jason Finkelberg, Market Manager

Pamplin Broadcasting
888 S.W. Fifth Ave.,Suite 790, Portland OR 97204
(503) 223-4321; *Fax:*(503) 222-2850
kpam@kpam.com

Radio Stns: 2 AM.
KPAM Troutdale, OR; KKOV Vancouver, WA;
Andrea Marek, President
Paul Clithero, General Manager

Pappas Telecasting Companies
500 S. Chinowth Rd., Visalia CA 93277
(559) 733-7800; *Fax:*(559) 733-7878
www.pappastv.com
Ownership: Harry J. Pappas.

Radio Stns: 3 AM.
KTRB San Francisco, CA; KCWK North Las Vegas, NV; KMPH Modesto, CA;

TV Stns: 14 TV.
KCWK North Las Vegas, NV; KDBC-TV El Paso, TX; KQSL Fort Bragg, CA; KHGI-TV Kearney, NE; KAZA-TV Avalon, CA; KPTH Sioux City, IA; KCWI-TV Ames, IA; KSWT Yuma, AZ; KTNC-TV Concord, CA; KUBE-TV Baytown, TX; KWNB-TV Hayes Center, NE; WCWG Lexington, NC; WLGA Opelika, AL; KDMI Des Moines, IA;
Bruce Yeager, EVP/CFO
Harry J. Pappas, CEO
Dennis J. Davis, COO

Paradis Broadcasting of Alexandria Inc.
1312 Broadway, Alexandria MN 56308
(320) 763-3131; *Fax:*(320) 763-5641
www.kxra.com
thefolks@kxra.com

Radio Stns: 1 AM. 2 FM.
KXRA Alexandria, MN; KXRZ Alexandria, MN; KXRA-FM Alexandria, MN;
Mel Paradis, CEO
Brett Paradis, General Manager

Paragon Communications Inc.
Box 945, Elk City OK 73648
(580) 225-9696; *Fax:*(580) 225-9699
www.kecofm.com
keco@io2online.com

Radio Stns: 1 AM. 2 FM.
KADS Elk City, OK; KECO Elk City, OK; KXOO Elk City, OK;
Blake Brewer, General Manager

Peak Broadcasting LLC
1071 W. Shaw Ave., Fresno CA 93711
(559) 490-5800; *Fax:*(559) 490-5843;

Radio Stns: 4 AM. 8 FM.
KIDO Nampa, ID; KFXD Boise, ID; KMJ Fresno, CA; KFPT Clovis, CA; KSAS-FM Caldwell, ID; KCIX Garden City, ID; KAWO Boise, ID; KMGV Fresno, CA; KMJ-FM Fresno, CA; KSKS Fresno, CA; KWYE Fresno, CA; KXLT-FM Eagle, ID;
Tim Lyons, CFO
Todd Lawley, CEO

Pearson Broadcasting
9530 Miolothian Pike, Richmond VA 23235
(804) 521-0603; *Fax:*(804) 674-8938
Ownership: Max H. Pearson, 100%.

Radio Stns: 3 FM.
KBCN-FM Marshall, AR; KERX Paris, AR; KTTG Mena, AR;
Max Pearson, President
Bruce Hale, VP

Pecos Valley Broadcasting Co.
317 W. Quay Ave., Artesia NM 88210
(505) 746-2751; *Fax:*(505) 748-3748;

Radio Stns: 1 AM. 3 FM.
KSVP Artesia, NM; KPZE-FM Carlsbad, NM; KEND Roswell, NM; KTZA Artesia, NM;
Sam Beard, President
David Ruckman, Operations Dir
Gene Dow, General Manager

Peg Broadcasting Crossville LLC
961 Miller Ave., Crossville TN 38555
(931) 707-1102; *Fax:*(931) 707-1220;

Radio Stns: 6 AM. 4 FM.
WAEW Crossville, TN; WAKI McMinnville, TN; WBMC McMinnville, TN; WCSV Crossville, TN; WSMT Sparta, TN; WTZX Sparta, TN; WOWF Crossville, TN; WOWC Morrison, TN; WTRZ Spencer, TN; WPBX Crossville, TN;

Peggy Sue Broadcasting Corp.
Box 838, Richlands VA 24641
(276) 964-4066; *Fax:*(276) 963-4927;

Radio Stns: 1 AM. 2 FM.
WNRG Grundy, VA; WMJD Grundy, VA; WRIC-FM Richlands, VA;

Pembrook Pines Media Group
1705 Lake St., Elmira NY 14901
(607) 733-5626; *Fax:*(607) 733-5627
www.pembrookpines.com
ppinesmedia1@stny.rr.com
Ownership: Robert J. Pfuntner, 100%. Company also owns Pembrook Pines Media agency.

Radio Stns: 6 AM. 7 FM.
WABH Bath, NY; WEHH Elmira Hts-Horsehds, NY; WELM Elmira, NY; WGGO Salamanca, NY; WOEN Olean, NY; WPIE Trumansburg, NY; WLVY Elmira, NY; WMXO Olean, NY; WOKN Southport, NY; WQRS Salamanca, NY; WZKZ Alfred, NY; WQRW Wellsville, NY; WZKZ(FM) Alfred, NY;
Robert Pfuntner, President/CEO

Peninsula Communications Inc.
Box 109, Homer AK 99603
(907) 235-6000; *Fax:*(907) 235-6683
kwavefm@xyz.net
Ownership: David F. Becker, 50%; Eileen L. Becker, 50%.

Radio Stns: 2 AM. 3 FM.
KGTL Homer, AK; KGTL(AM) Homer, AK; KPEN-FM Soldotna, AK; KWVV-FM Homer, AK; KXBA Nikiski, AK;
David Becker, General Manager
Tim White, Operations
Dave Webb, Production Manager

Perry Publishing & Broadcasting Co.
1457 N.E. 23rd St., Oklahoma City OK 73111
(405) 425-4100; *Fax:*(405) 424-8811
www.perry-pub-broadcasting.com

Radio Stns: 6 AM. 9 FM.
KGTO Tulsa, OK; KPNS Duncan, OK; KKRX Lawton, OK; KRMP Oklahoma City, OK; KXCA Lawton, OK; WTHB Augusta, GA; KACO Apache, OK; KDDQ Comanche, OK; KJMM Bixby, OK; KJMZ Cache, OK; KVSP Anadarko, OK; WAEG Evans, GA; WAKB Hephzibah, GA; WTHB-FM Wrens, GA; WFXA-FM Augusta, GA;
Russell Perry, CEO

Pharis Broadcasting Inc.
Box 908, Fort Smith AR 72902
(479) 288-1047; *Fax:*(479) 785-2638
www.fortsmithradiogroup.com
ssrg@sbcglobal.net

Radio Stns: 2 AM. 3 FM.
KHGG Van Buren, AR; KFPW Fort Smith, AR; KQBK Booneville, AR; KFPW-FM Barling, AR; KHGG-FM Waldron, AR;
William Pharis, CEO
Karen Pharis, General Manager

Phillips Broadcasting Inc.
100 Fisher Dr., Trinidad CO 81082
(719) 846-3355; *Fax:*(719) 846-4711
kcrt@adelphia.net

Radio Stns: 1 AM. 2 FM.
KCRT Trinidad, CO; KBKZ Raton, NM; KCRT-FM Trinidad, CO;
David Phillips, President

Phoenix Media Communications Group
126 Brookline Ave., Boston MA 2215
(617) 536-5390; *Fax:*(617) 859-8201
www.thephoenix.com

Radio Stns: 1 AM. 3 FM.
WWSF Sanford, ME; WXEX-FM Sanford, ME; WHBA Lynn, MA; WDER-FM Peterborough, NH;
Stephen Mindich, CEO
Barry Morris, President

Piedmont Communications Inc.
Box 271, Orange VA 22960
(540) 672-1000; *Fax:*(540) 672-0282;

Radio Stns: 2 AM. 2 FM.
WCVA Culpeper, VA; WVCV Orange, VA; WJMA Culpeper, VA; WOJL Louisa, VA;

Pilgrim Communications Inc.
Box 90, New Palestine IN 46163
(317) 894-2000;

Radio Stns: 3 AM. 2 FM.
KSKE Buena Vista, CO; KRCN Longmont, CO; KVLE Vail, CO; KVLE-FM Gunnison, CO; WFDM-FM Franklin, IN;

Bill Fielder, CFO
Paul Brissette, President

Pillar of Fire Inc.
Box 9058,Weston Canal Rd., Zarephath NJ 08890
(732) 469-0991; *Fax:*(732) 469-2115
www.star991fm.com
info@star991fm.com
Ownership: No stockholders; non-profit corporation.
Radio Stns: 1 AM. 2 FM.
KPOF Denver, CO; WAKW Cincinnati, OH; WAWZ Zarephath, NJ;
Robert Dallenbach, Network President
Scott Taylor, Station Manager

Pines Broadcasting Inc.
1255 N. Myrtle St., Warren AR 71671
(870) 226-2653; *Fax:*(870) 226-3039;
Radio Stns: 1 AM. 3 FM.
KHBM Monticello, AR; KGPQ Monticello, AR; KHBM-FM Monticello, AR; KXSA-FM Dermott, AR;
Jimmy Sledge, President

Pittman Broadcasting Services LLC
307 S. Jefferson Ave., Covington LA 70433
(985) 892-3661
www.pittmanbroadcasting.com
Radio Stns: 3 AM. 3 FM.
KFXZ Lafayette, LA; KVOL Lafayette, LA; WOMN Franklinton, LA; KYMK-FM Maurice, LA; KFXZ-FM Opelousas, LA; WUUU Franklinton, LA;
Marcus Pittman, President

Plant Broadcasting
601 West 2nd Street, Tifton GA 31794
(229) 382-1340; *Fax:*(229) 386-8658
www.plantbroadcasting.com
nettie@plantbroadcasting.com
Radio Stns: 1 AM.
WTIF Tifton, GA;
Nettie Hatcher, General Manager

Platinum Broadcasting Co.
Box 789, Junction City KS 66441
(785) 762-5525; *Fax:*(785) 762-5387
www.kjck.com
platinum@kjck.com
Radio Stns: 1 AM. 2 FM.
KJCK Junction City, KS; KJCK-FM Junction City, KS; KQLA Ogden, KS;
Mark Ediger, General Manager
Ed Klimek, General Sales Mgr

Platte River Radio Inc.
Box 130, Kearney NE 68848
(308) 236-9900; *Fax:*(308) 234-6781;
Radio Stns: 3 AM. 2 FM.
KHAS Hastings, NE; KICS Hastings, NE; KXPN Kearney, NE; KLIQ Hastings, NE; KKPR-FM Kearney, NE;

PMB Broadcasting LLC
c/o Bradley & Hatcher,33 W. 11th St., Suite 100, Columbus GA 31901
(706) 660-9988;
Radio Stns: 1 AM. 3 FM.
WRCG Columbus, GA; WCGQ Columbus, GA; WKCN Fort Benning South, GA; WRLD Valley, AL;

Point Broadcasting Company
715 Broadway,Suite 320, Santa Monica CA 90401
(310) 451-4430; *Fax:*(310) 451-1423;
Radio Stns: 2 FM.
KMVE California City, CA; KSPE-FM Ellwood, CA;
John Hearne, Chairman

Pollack Broadcasting Co.
5500 Poplar Ave. #1, Memphis TN 38119
(901) 685-3993; *Fax:*(901) 685-3995
wpollack@midsouth.rr.com
Radio Stns: 4 AM. 3 FM.
KBOA Kennett, MO; KCRV Caruthersville, MO; KMIS Portageville, MO; KXIQ(AM) Turrell, AR; KBOA-FM Piggott, AR; KCRV-FM Caruthersville, MO; KTMO New Madrid, MO;
TV Stns: 2 TV.
KIEM-TV Eureka, CA; KLAX-TV Alexandria, LA;
William Pollack, President

Polnet Communications Ltd.
3656 W. Belmont Ave., Chicago IL 60618
(773) 588-6300; *Fax:*(773) 588-0834
www.pclradio.com
Radio Stns: 6 AM.
WPJX Zion, IL; WEEF Deerfield, IL; WKTA Evanston, IL; WLIM Patchogue, NY; WNVR Vernon Hills, IL; WRKL New City, NY;
Kent Gustafson, CEO
Walter Kotaby, President

Porter County Broadcasting Corp.
2755 Sager Rd., Valparaiso IN 46383
(219) 462-8125;
Radio Stns: 1 AM. 3 FM.
WAKE Valparaiso, IN; WLJE Valparaiso, IN; WXRD Crown Point, IN; WZVN Lowell, IN;

Positive Alternative Radio Inc.
Box 889, Blacksburg VA 24063
(540) 552-4282; *Fax:*(540) 951-5282
www.parfm.com
Radio Stns: 22 FM.
WCQR-FM Kingsport, TN; WJYA Emporia, VA; WJYJ Fredericksburg, VA; WOKD-FM Danville, VA; WPAR Salem, VA; WPCN(FM) Point Pleasant, WV; WPER Culpeper, VA; WPIB Bluefield, WV; WPIM Martinsville, VA; WPIN-FM Dublin, VA; WPIR Hickory, NC; WPVA Waynesboro, VA; WRXT Roanoke, VA; WTJY Asheboro, NC; WTTX-FM Appomattox, VA; WXRI Winston-Salem, NC; WOKG Galax, VA; WHRX Nassawadox, VA; WRFE Chesterfield, SC; WPJY Blennerhassett, WV; WPJW Hurricane, WV; WKAO Ashland, KY;
Edward Baker, President

Powell Broadcasting Co. L.L.C.
Box 788, Baton Rouge LA 70821-0788
(225) 922-4662; *Fax:*(225) 922-4544
Ownership: The Powell Group L.L.C., 100%.
Radio Stns: 2 AM. 8 FM.
KLEM Le Mars, IA; KSCJ Sioux City, IA; KKYY Whiting, IA; KKMA Le Mars, IA; KSUX Winnebago, NE; KQNU(FM) Onawa, IA; WASJ Panama City Beach, FL; WPFM-FM Panama City, FL; WRBA Springfield, FL; WKNK(FM) Callaway, FL;
Thomas J. Spies, COO
Nanette Noland, President

Prairie Radio Communications
2410 Sycamore Rd.,Suite C, De Kalb IL 60115
(815) 758-8686; *Fax:*(815) 756-9723
www.radiomacomb.com
Radio Stns: 7 AM. 10 FM.
KCLN Clinton, IA; KWPC Muscatine, IA; WAIK Galesburg, IL; WBYS Canton, IL; WLBK Dekalb, IL; WLRB Macomb, IL; WRAM Monmouth, IL; KWBZ Monroe City, MO; KMCS Muscatine, IA; KMCN Clinton, IA; WCDD Canton, IL; WKAI Macomb, IL; WKXQ Rushville, IL; WLMD Bushnell, IL; WPWQ Mount Sterling, IL; WMOI Monmouth, IL; WSLD Whitewater, WI;
Don Davis, CEO

Premier Broadcasters
1133 Kresky, Centralia WA 98531
(360) 736-1355; *Fax:*(360) 736-4761
www.live95.com
live95@live95.com
Ownership: Rod Etherton.
Radio Stns: 1 AM. 3 FM.
KITI Chehalis-Centralia, WA; KITI-FM Winlock, WA; KRXY Shelton, WA; KRZY-FM Santa Fe, NM;
Rod Etherton, President

Prescott Valley Broadcasting Co. Inc.
Box 26523, Prescott Valley AZ 86312
(928) 445-8289; *Fax:*(928) 442-0448;
Radio Stns: 1 AM. 3 FM.
KQNA Prescott Valley, AZ; KDDL Chino Valley, AZ; KPPV Prescott Valley, AZ; KPKR Parker, AZ;

Press Communications L.L.C.
1329 Campus Pkwy.,Suite 106, Wall NJ 07753-6815
(732) 751-1119; *Fax:*(732) 751-1726;
Radio Stns: 1 AM. 4 FM.
WHTG Eatontown, NJ; WBBO(FM) Ocean Acres, NJ; WBHX Tuckerton, NJ; WKMK Eatontown, NJ; WWZY Long Branch, NJ;

Prettyman Broadcasting Co.
1606 W. King St., Martinsburg WV 25401
(304) 263-8868; *Fax:*(304) 263-8906
www.wepm.com
Radio Stns: 1 AM. 2 FM.
WEPM Martinsburg, WV; WLTF Martinsburg, WV; WICL Williamsport, MD;
William Prettyman, CEO
Norm Slemenda, General Manager

Prieto Broadcasting Inc.
Box 48122, Doraville GA 30362
(770) 825-0095; *Fax:*(770) 246-0054
www.prietobroadcasting.com
Radio Stns: 3 AM.
WDUR Durham, NC; WETC Wendell-Zebulon, NC; WFTD Marietta, GA;
Filiberto Prieto, CEO
Franco Vera, General Sales Mgr

Priority Communications
12 W. Long Ave., DuBois PA 15801-2100
(814) 375-5260; *Fax:*(814) 375-5263;
Radio Stns: 2 AM. 2 FM.
WCED Du Bois, PA; WEIR Weirton, WV; WCDK Cadiz, OH; WDSN Reynoldsville, PA;
Jay Philippone, President

Priority Radio Inc.
Box 5204, Wilmington DE 19808-5204
(302) 731-7270; *Fax:*(302) 738-3090
www.thereachfm.com
Radio Stns: 1 AM. 4 FM.
WSRY Elkton, MD; WXHL-FM Christiana, DE; WVBH Beach Haven West, NJ; KXRL Cherry Valley, AR; WXHM Middletown, DE;

Pritchard Broadcasting Corp.
610 N. 4th Street, Suite 300, Burlington IA 52601
(319) 752-5402; *Fax:*(319) 752-4715
johnp@ burlingtonradio.com
Radio Stns: 2 AM. 4 FM.
KBKB Fort Madison, IA; KBUR Burlington, IA; KDMG Burlington, IA; KKMI Burlington, IA; WQKQ Carthage, IL; KHDK New London, IA;
John Pritchard, President

Programmers Broadcasting Inc.
Box 28, Bottineau ND 58318-0028
(701) 228-5151; *Fax:*(701) 228-2483;
Radio Stns: 3 FM.
KBTO Bottineau, ND; KWGO Burlington, ND; KTZU Velva, ND;

Progressive Broadcasting System Inc.
Box 307, Elkhart IN 46515
(574) 875-5166; *Fax:*(574) 875-6662
www.wfrn.com
Radio Stns: 1 AM. 2 FM.
WCMR Elkhart, IN; WFRI Winamac, IN; WFRN-FM Elkhart, IN;
Edwin Moore, President

Qantum Communications Corp.
1266 E. Main St.,6th Fl., Stamford CT 6902
(203) 388-0048;
Radio Stns: 8 AM. 24 FM.
WDSC Dillon, SC; WGIG Brunswick, GA; WJMX Florence, SC; WMOG Brunswick, GA; WWRK Darlington, SC; WPLV West Point, GA; WTLM Opelika, AL; WZMG Pepperell, AL; WYNR Waycross, GA; WCIB Falmouth, MA; WCJM-FM West Point, GA; WCOD-FM Hyannis, MA; WDAR-FM Darlington, SC; WLQB Ocean Isle Beach, NC; WEGX Dillon, SC; WRZE Kingstree, SC; WGTR Bucksport, SC; WBGA St. Simons Island, GA; WJMX-FM Cheraw, SC; WKKR Auburn, AL; WECQ(FM) Destin, FL; WMXA Opelika, AL; WMXZ Isle of Palms, SC; WEII Dennis, MA; WZTF Scranton, SC; WWAV Santa Rosa Beach, FL; WRXZ Briarcliff Acres, SC; WQGA Waycross, GA; WWXM Garden City, SC; WXTK West Yarmouth, MA; WYNA Calabash, NC; WHFX Darien, GA;
Michael Mangan, CFO
Frank Osborn, President

Quarnstrom Media Group LLC
1104 Cloquet Ave., Cloquet MN 55720
(218) 879-4534; *Fax:*(218) 879-1962
Ownership: Alan & Linda Quarnstrom, 100%.
Radio Stns: 3 AM. 4 FM.
KCUE Red Wing, MN; WCMP Pine City, MN; WKLK Cloquet, MN; WMOZ Moose Lake, MN; KWNG Red Wing, MN; WCMP-FM Pine City, MN; WKLK-FM Cloquet, MN;
Aian Quarnstrom, President
Don Welch, VP

Quincy Newspapers Inc.
130 S. Fifth St., Quincy IL 62301
(217) 223-5100; *Fax:*(217) 223-5019
www.qni.biz
Radio Stns: 1 AM. 1 FM.
WGEM Quincy, IL; WGEM-FM Quincy, IL;
TV Stns: 12 TV.

KTIV Sioux City, IA; KTTC Rochester, MN; KWWL Waterloo, IA; WAOW Wausau, WI; WGEM-TV Quincy, IL; WKOW Madison, WI; WQOW-DT Eau Claire, WI; WREX-TV Rockford, IL; WSJV Elkhart, IN; WVVA Bluefield, WV; WXOW La Crosse, WI; WYOW Eagle River, WI;
Thomas Oakley, President

Quorum Radio Partners of Virginia Inc.
8512 Beech Ln., McKinney TX 75070
(972) 529-1192; *Fax:*(972) 540-2454;
Radio Stns: 2 AM. 1 FM.
WKEY Covington, VA; WSLW White Sulphur Spring, WV; WIQO-FM Forest, VA;
Todd Fowler, CEO

RAAD Broadcasting Corp
Bambbo Drive K-8, Guaynabo PR 00657
(787) 785-9390; *Fax:*(787) 785-9377
www.lax.fm
Radio Stns: 1 FM.
WXLX Lajas, PR;
Carlos Alvarez, Programming Director

Radio Cleveland Inc.
Drawer 780, Cleveland MS 38732
(662) 843-4091; *Fax:*(662) 843-9805
www.radiomiss.com
wcld@tecinfo.com
Ownership: Homer Sledge Jr., pres, 37.1/5%; Kevin W. Cox, treas, 37.1/2%; Clint L. Webster, gen mgr, 37.1/2%.
Radio Stns: 1 AM. 2 FM.
WCLD Cleveland, MS; WAID Clarksdale, MS; WMJW Rosedale, MS;
Clint Webster, General Manager

Radio Dubuque Inc.
Box 659, Dubuque IA 52004
(563) 690-0800; *Fax:*(563) 588-5688;
Radio Stns: 1 AM. 3 FM.
KDTH Dubuque, IA; KATF Dubuque, IA; KGRR Epworth, IA; WVRE Dickeyville, WI;
Thomas Parsley, General Manager

Radio Fargo-Moorhead Inc.
1020 25th St. S., Fargo ND 58103
(701) 277-4200;
Radio Stns: 2 AM. 4 FM.
KFGO Fargo, ND; KVOX Fargo, ND; KRWK Fargo, ND; KBVB Barnesville, MN; WDAY-FM Fargo, ND; KMJO Hope, ND;

Radio Greeneville Inc.
Box 278, Greeneville TN 37744
(423) 638-4147; *Fax:*(423) 638-1979
www.greeneville.com\wgrv
wgrv@greeneville.com
Radio Stns: 2 AM. 1 FM.
WGRV Greeneville, TN; WSMG Greeneville, TN; WIKQ Tusculum, TN;
Ronnnie Metcalfe, President

Radio La Grande
1010 Vermont Ave. N.W.,Suite 100, Washington DC 20005
(202) 638-1959; *Fax:*(202) 393-7464
radiolagrande.net
VALTRAVEL@RCN.com,EsturadoValdemar@Hotmail.com
Radio Stns: 7 AM.
WGSB Mebane, NC; WLLY Wilson, NC; WLNR Kinston, NC; WREV Reidsville, NC; WRTG Garner, NC; WLLQ Chapel Hill, NC; WSRP Jacksonville, NC;
Ronald Metcalfe, President

Radio Maria Inc.
601 Washington St., Alexandria LA 71301
(318) 561-6145; *Fax:*(318) 449-9954
www.radiomaria.us
info.usa@radiomaria.org
Radio Stns: 4 AM. 3 FM.
KDEI Port Arthur, TX; KJMJ Alexandria, LA; KNIR New Iberia, LA; WULM Springfield, OH; KBIO Natchitoches, LA; KOJO Lake Charles, LA; WHJM Anna, OH;

Radio One Inc.
5900 Princess Garden Pkwy., Lanham MD 20706
(301) 306-1111; *Fax:*(301) 306-9426
www.radio-one.com
Radio Stns: 11 AM. 41 FM.
WCHB Taylor, MI; WJMO Cleveland, OH; WTPS Petersburg, VA; WILD Boston, MA; WERE Cleveland Heights, OH; WOL Washington, DC; WOLB Baltimore, MD; WTLC Indianapolis, IN; WDBZ Cincinnati, OH; WWIN Baltimore, MD; WYCB Washington, DC; KBFB Dallas, TX; KBXX Houston, TX; KSOC Gainesville, TX; KMJQ Houston, TX; KROI Seabrook, TX; WQNC Indian Trail, NC; WAMJ Roswell, GA; WPZE Mableton, GA; WTLC-FM Greenwood, IN; WPZS Harrisburg, NC; WCDX Mechanicsville, VA; WCKX Columbus, OH; WXMG London, OH; WPZR Mount Clemens, MI; WDMK Detroit, MI; WENZ Cleveland, OH; WERQ-FM Baltimore, MD; WFUN-FM Bethalto, IL; WFXC Durham, NC; WFXK Bunn, NC; WHHH Indianapolis, IN; WUMJ Fayetteville, GA; WMOJ-FM Norwood, OH; WIZF Erlanger, KY; WKJS Richmond, VA; WPZZ Crewe, VA; WKYS Washington, DC; WMMJ Bethesda, MD; WNNL Fuquay-Varina, NC; WHTA Hampton, GA; WPPZ-FM Jenkintown, PA; WPHI-FM Pennsauken, NJ; WKJM Petersburg, VA; WQOK Carrboro, NC; WRNB Media, PA; WWIN-FM Glen Burnie, MD; WPRS-FM Waldorf, MD; WJKR Upper Arlington, OH; WHHL Hazelwood, MO; WNOU Speedway, IN; WZAK Cleveland, OH;
Catherine Hughes, Chairman
Scott Royster, CFO
Alfred Liggins, President
Tony Washington, General Sales Mgr
Darrell Huckaby, Programming Director
Charles Kinney, Chief Engineer

Radio Palouse Inc.
Box 1, Pullman WA 99163
(509) 332-6551; *Fax:*(509) 332-5151
www.border104.com
khtr@aol.com
Radio Stns: 1 AM.
KQQQ Pullman, WA;
Bill Weed, General Manager

Radio Partners LLC
Box 719, Beaver Falls PA 15010
(724) 846-4100; *Fax:*(724) 843-7771
kibcoradio.com
iorio@wbvp-wmba.com
Radio Stns: 1 AM. 2 FM.
WNAE Warren, PA; WKNB Clarendon, PA; WRRN Warren, PA;
Dave Whipple, General Sales Mgr

Radio Stations WPAY/WPFB Inc.
4505 Central Ave., Middletown OH 45044
(513) 422-3625; *Fax:*(513) 424-9732
www.rebel1059.com
Ownership: Douglas L. Braden, 100%.
Radio Stns: 1 AM. 2 FM.
WPFB Middletown, OH; WNKE New Boston, OH; WNKN Middletown, OH;
Douglas Branden, President

Radio Vermont Group Inc.
Box 550, Waterbury VT 5676
(802) 244-7321; *Fax:*(802) 244-1771;
Radio Stns: 1 AM. 3 FM.
WDEV Waterbury, VT; WCVT Stowe, VT; WDEV-FM Warren, VT; WLVB Morrisville, VT;
Ken Squier, President
Eric Michaels, Operations Dir

Radio Works Inc.
111 Westwood Dr., De Queen AR 71832
(870) 642-3637;
Radio Stns: 3 FM.
KAMD-FM Camden, AR; KCXY East Camden, AR; KMGC Camden, AR;

Radioactive LLC
1717 Dixie Hwy.,Suite 650, Fort Wright KY 41011
(859) 331-9100;
Radio Stns: 19 FM.
WDYK Ridgeley, WV; WUPF Powers, MI; WUPG Republic, MI; WUPZ Chocolay Township, MI; WUPT Gwinn, MI; WKFC North Corbin, KY; WPBK Crab Orchard, KY; KSYY Ingram, TX; KXLP Eagle Lake, MN; KMML Cimarron, KS; KRMR Hays, KS; KDJM Lindsborg, KS; WZXP Au Sable, NY; WRAX Lake Isabella, MI; KYME Rockford, IA; KEWS(FM) Sac City, IA; WNMR Dannemora, NY; WBLH Black River, NY; WPLB Plattsburgh West, NY;

RadioJones LLC
Box 5356, Atlanta GA 31107-5356
(404) 432-1450
www.radiojones.com
dj@radiojones.com
Radio Stns: 2 AM. 2 FM.
WJAT Swainsboro, GA; WXRS Swainsboro, GA; WEDB East Dublin, GA; WXRS-FM Portal, GA;
Dennis Jones, President

RadioStar Inc.
781 Bolsana Dr., Laguna Beach CA 92651-4124
(915) 715-9770;
Radio Stns: 4 FM.
WSJK(FM) Tuscola, IL; WGKC Mahomet, IL; WQQB Rantoul, IL; WJEK(FM) Rantoul, IL;
Jim Glassman, President

Rama Communications Inc.
3765 N. John Young Pkwy., Orlando FL 32804
(407) 523-2770; *Fax:*(407) 523-2888
www.gospelrama.com
Radio Stns: 7 AM.
WRFV Valdosta, GA; WKIQ Eustis, FL; WNTF Bithlo, FL; WLAA Winter Garden, FL; WQBQ Leesburg, FL; WOKB Winter Garden, FL; WMEL Cocoa Beach, FL;
Sabita Persaud, President

Ramar Communications II Ltd.
Box 3757, Lubbock TX 79452
(806) 745-3434; *Fax:*(806) 748-1949
www.ramarcom.com
bmoran@ramarcom.com
Radio Stns: 1 AM. 3 FM.
KJTV Lubbock, TX; KLZK New Deal, TX; KSTQ(FM) Brownfield, TX; KXTQ-FM Lubbock, TX;
TV Stns: 4 TV.
KRTN-TV Durango, CO; KUPT Hobbs, NM; KJTV-TV Lubbock, TX; KTEL-TV Carlsbad, NM;
Ray Moran, Chairman
Brad Moran, President

Randy Sheffield-Wayne Bishop
Box 27272, Panama City Beach FL 32411
(850) 235-2195; *Fax:*(850) 235-2795
www.beach951.com
Radio Stns: 1 FM.
WBPC Ebro, FL;
David Nolan, Operations Dir
Randy Sheffield, General Manager
Wayne Bishop, General Sales Mgr

Red River Broadcast Co. L.L.C.
Box 9115, Fargo ND 58106
(701) 277-1515; *Fax:*(701) 277-1830
Ownership: Curtis Squire Inc., 100%. Myron Kunin owns 100% of Curtis Squire Inc.
Radio Stns: 1 AM.
KQDS Duluth, MN;
TV Stns: 7 TV.
KBRR Thief River Falls, MN; KDLT-TV Sioux Falls, SD; KDLV-TV Mitchell, SD; KJRR Jamestown, ND; KNRR Pembina, ND; KQDS-TV Duluth, MN; KVRR Fargo, ND;
Ro Grignon, President
Kathy Lau, VP

Red Rock Radio Corp.
501 Lake Ave. S., Duluth MN 55802
(218) 728-9500; *Fax:*(218) 723-1499;
Radio Stns: 3 AM. 12 FM.
KGHS International Falls, MN; KKIN Aitkin, MN; WHSM Hayward, WI; KAOD Babbitt, MN; KBAJ Deer River, MN; KKIN-FM Aitkin, MN; KQDS-FM Duluth, MN; KSDM International Falls, MN; KFGI Crosby, MN; KZIO Two Harbors, MN; WXCX Siren, WI; WHSM-FM Hayward, WI; WWAX Hermantown, MN; WLMX-FM Balsam Lake, WI; WXXZ Grand Marais, MN;
Ro Grignon, President

Red Zebra Holdings LLC
21300 Redskin Park Dr., Ashburn VA 20147
(703) 726-7015
www.espn980.com
Radio Stns: 5 AM. 3 FM.
WXTG Hampton, VA; WTNT Alexandria, VA; WWRC Washington, DC; WTEM Washington, DC; WXGI Richmond, VA; WXTG-FM Virginia Beach, VA; WWXT Prince Frederick, MD; WWXX Warrenton, VA;

Redwood Empire Broadcasters
Box 100, Santa Rosa CA 95402
(707) 528-4434; *Fax:*(707) 284-9114
Ownership: Gordon D. Zlot Revocable Trust, 98% of assets; Gordon D. Zlot trustee, 98% votes.
Radio Stns: 4 FM.
KJZY Sebastopol, CA; KZST Santa Rosa, CA; KGRP Grand Rapids, MN; KTRY(FM) Cazadero, CA;
Gordon D. Zlot, President

RADIO - U.S.

Regional Radio Group LLC
128 Glen St., Glens Falls NY 12801
(518) 761-9890; *Fax:*(518) 761-9893
www.radiowins.com

Radio Stns: 1 AM. 2 FM.
WWSC Glens Falls, NY; WCKM-FM Lake George, NY; WCQL Queensbury, NY;
Clay Ashworth, General Manager

Reier Broadcasting Co. Inc.
Box 20, Bozeman MT 59718
(406) 587-9999; *Fax:*(406) 587-5855;

Radio Stns: 2 AM. 3 FM.
KBOZ Bozeman, MT; KOBB Bozeman, MT; KOBB-FM Bozeman, MT; KOZB Livingston, MT; KBOZ-FM Bozeman, MT;

Relevant Radio
3200 Riverside Dr., Green Bay WI 54307
(800) 342-0306; *Fax:*(920) 469-3023
www.relevantradio.com
info@relevantradio.com

Radio Stns: 10 AM. 4 FM.
KIXL Del Valle, TX; WAUR Sandwich, IL; WDVM Eau Claire, WI; WHFA Poynette, WI; WJOK Kaukauna, WI; WKBH Holmen, WI; WLOL Minneapolis, MN; WNTD Chicago, IL; WWCA Gary, IN; WZUM Carnegie, PA; WPJP Port Washington, WI; WOVM Appleton, WI; WMMA Nekoosa, WI; WYNW Birnamwood, WI;
Mark Follett, Chairman
Mark Follett, CEO

Renda Broadcasting Corp.
900 Parish Street, 4th Fl, Pittsburgh PA 15220
(412) 875-1800; *Fax:*(412) 875-1801
Ownership: S.F. Renda, 100%.

Radio Stns: 5 AM. 17 FM.
KOKC Oklahoma City, OK; WCCS Homer City, PA; WDAD Indiana, PA; WECZ Punxsutawney, PA; WJAS Pittsburgh, PA; KBEZ Tulsa, OK; KHTT Muskogee, OK; KMGL Oklahoma City, OK; KOMA Oklahoma City, OK; KRXO Oklahoma City, OK; WJGO Tice, FL; WKQL Brookville, PA; WEJZ Jacksonville, FL; WGNE-FM Middleburg, FL; WGUF Marco, FL; WLCY Blairsville, PA; WQMU Indiana, PA; WSGL Naples, FL; WSHH Pittsburgh, PA; WSOS-FM Fruit Cove, FL; WWGR Fort Myers, FL; WMUV Brunswick, GA;
Anthony Renda, President
Maryann Kelly, VP
Alan Serena, VP Operations
Judy Reich, VP Sales

Results Broadcasting
1456 E. Green Bay St., Shawano WI 54166
(715) 524-2194; *Fax:*(715) 524-9980;

Radio Stns: 3 AM. 7 FM.
WATK Antigo, WI; WOTE Clintonville, WI; WTCH Shawano, WI; WACD Antigo, WI; WCYE Three Lakes, WI; WJMQ Clintonville, WI; WJNR-FM Iron Mountain, MI; WOBE Crystal Falls, MI; WOWN Shawano, WI; WHTO Iron Mountain, MI;
Bruce Grassman, President

Revolution Broadcast Company of the West
2125 Sidney Baker North, Kerrville TX 78028
(830) 896-1230; *Fax:*(830) 792-4142;

Radio Stns: 2 AM. 4 FM.
KERV Kerrville, TX; KMBL Junction, TX; KHOS-FM Sonora, TX; KOOK Junction, TX; KRVL Kerrville, TX; KYXX Ozona, TX;
David Greenwald, President

Reynolds Radio Inc.
Box 11196, College Station TX 77842
(979) 696-1196
www.theblaze.cc
rusty@reynoldsradio.com

Radio Stns: 3 FM.
KBLZ Winona, TX; KZTK White Oak, TX; KAZE Ore City, TX;
Kenneth Reynolds, President

Rhattigan Broadcasting (Texas) LP
Box 1420, Plainview TX 79073
(806) 853-9147; *Fax:*(815) 346-2084;

Radio Stns: 5 AM. 7 FM.
KBST Big Spring, TX; KEPS Eagle Pass, TX; KVOP Plainview, TX; KREW Plainview, TX; KGWU Uvalde, TX; KBST-FM Big Spring, TX; KBTS Big Spring, TX; KINL Eagle Pass, TX; KKYN-FM Plainview, TX; KUVA Uvalde, TX; KRIA Plainview, TX; KVOU-FM Uvalde, TX;

Rich Broadcasting LLC
1401 E. Stillwood Dr., Salt Lake City UT 84117
(801) 277-6139; *Fax:*(801) 294-5145
richbroadcasting.com
Ownership: Richard O. Mecham, 38.4%; Trevor Larsen, 9.6%; Mark Nelson, 8%.

Radio Stns: 3 AM. 8 FM.
KID Idaho Falls, ID; KRXK Rexburg, ID; KWIK Pocatello, ID; KQEZ(FM) Shelley, ID; KGTM Rexburg, ID; KID-FM Idaho Falls, ID; KLLP Chubbuck, ID; KPKY Pocatello, ID; KCHQ Driggs, ID; KEGE Pocatello, ID; KZKY(FM) Ucon, ID;
Richard O. Mecham, Manager

Rincon Broadcasting LLC
414 E. Cota St., Santa Barbara CA 93101
(805) 879-8300; *Fax:*(805) 879-8430
www.rinconbroadcasting.com
Ownership: Point Broadcasting Co., 95%.

Radio Stns: 1 AM. 3 FM.
KTMS Santa Barbara, CA; KIST-FM Carpinteria, CA; KSBL Isla Vista, CA; KTYD Santa Barbara, CA;

Riverbend Communications LLC
2880 N. 55th W., Idaho Falls ID 83402
(208) 528-6635;

Radio Stns: 2 AM. 4 FM.
KBLI Blackfoot, ID; KBLY Idaho Falls, ID; KCVI Blackfoot, ID; KFTZ Idaho Falls, ID; KLCE Blackfoot, ID; KTHK Idaho Falls, ID;

Riviera Broadcast Group LLC
3333 Sierra Oaks Dr., Sacramento CA 95864-5738
(916) 768-8049; *Fax:*(480) 247-5123
www.rivierabroadcast.com

Radio Stns: 4 FM.
KOAS Dolan Springs, AZ; KKFR Mayer, AZ; KVGS Meadview, AZ; KEXX(FM) Gilbert, AZ;
Chris Maguire, CFO
Tim Pohlman, President

Robert Ingstad Broadcast Properties
Box 994, Valley City ND 58072
(701) 845-1490; *Fax:*(701) 845-1245
Ownership: the estate of Robert E. Ingstad, Janice M. Ingstad, Robert J. Ingstad and Todd M. Ingstad.

Radio Stns: 8 AM. 14 FM.
KBUF Holcomb, KS; KDAK Carrington, ND; KDDR Oakes, ND; KGFX Pierre, SD; KOLY Mobridge, SD; KOVC Valley City, ND; KQDJ Jamestown, ND; KULY Ulysses, KS; KFXX-FM Hugoton, KS; KGFX-FM Pierre, SD; KKJQ Garden City, KS; KMLO Lowry, SD; KPLO-FM Reliance, SD; KQZZ Devils Lake, ND; KSKL Scott City, KS; KWKR Leoti, KS; KSSA Ingalls, KS; KYNU Jamestown, ND; KSKZ Copeland, KS; KXGT Carrington, ND; KRVX Wimbledon, ND; KJBI Fort Pierre, SD;

Robinson Corporation
E7601A County Rd. SS, Viroqua WI 54665
(608) 637-7200; *Fax:*(608) 637-7299
www.wqpcradio.com
wvrq@mwt.net

Radio Stns: 2 AM. 3 FM.
WPRE Prairie Du Chien, WI; WVRQ Viroqua, WI; WQPC Prairie Du Chien, WI; WVRQ-FM Viroqua, WI; WKPO Soldiers Grove, WI;
David Robinson, President
Jeff Robinson, General Manager

Rocking M Radio Inc.
4806 Vue du Lac Place,Suite B, Manhattan KS 66503
(785) 565-0406; *Fax:*(785) 565-0437
www.rockingmradio.com

Radio Stns: 5 AM. 9 FM.
KGNO Dodge City, KS; KNNS Larned, KS; KMMM Pratt, KS; KXXX Colby, KS; KSMM Liberal, KS; KERP Ingalls, KS; KSOB Larned, KS; KZUH Minneapolis, KS; KAHE Dodge City, KS; KRDQ Colby, KS; KVOB Lindsborg, KS; KZRD Dodge City, KS; KSMM-FM Liberal, KS; KZRS Great Bend, KS;
Monte Miller, President
Christopher Miller, Operations Dir
Doris Miller, Tresurer/Secretary

Rodgers Broadcasting Corp.
Box 1646, Richmond IN 47374
(765) 962-6533; *Fax:*(765) 966-1499
Ownership: David Rodgers, 100%.

Radio Stns: 3 AM. 3 FM.
WBML Macon, GA; WIFE Connersville, IN; WKBV Richmond, IN; WFMG Richmond, IN; WIFE-FM Rushville, IN; WZZY Winchester, IN;
David Rodgers, President

Rooney Moon Broadcasting Inc.
208 E. Grand Ave., Clovis NM 88101
(505) 763-4649; *Fax:*(505) 763-1693
www.bettermix.com
info.rmb@yucca.net

Radio Stns: 1 AM. 3 FM.
KSEL Portales, NM; KSEL-FM Portales, NM; KSMX-FM Clovis, NM; KRMQ-FM Clovis, NM;
Steve Rooney, President

Roser Communications Network Inc.
185 Genessee St.,Suite 1600, Utica NY 13501
(315) 734-9245; *Fax:*(315) 624-9245
Ownership: Kenneth F. Roser, 100%.

Radio Stns: 3 AM. 4 FM.
WRCK Remsen, NY; WVTL Amsterdam, NY; WUSP Utica, NY; WBGK Newport Village, NY; WBUG-FM Fort Plain, NY; WSKU Little Falls, NY; WSKS Whitesboro, NY;
Ken Roser, Chairman

Roswell Radio Inc./Quay Broadcasters Inc.
Box 670, Roswell NM 88202
(505) 622-6450; *Fax:*(505) 622-9041;

Radio Stns: 2 AM. 4 FM.
KBCQ Roswell, NM; KTNM Tucumcari, NM; KBCQ-FM Roswell, NM; KMOU Roswell, NM; KQAY-FM Tucumcari, NM; KSFX Roswell, NM;
John Dunn, President

RR Broadcasting
2100 E. Tahquitz Canyon Way, Palm Springs CA 92262
(760) 325-2582; *Fax:*(760) 322-3562
www.rrbroadcasting.com

Radio Stns: 2 AM. 3 FM.
KPSI Palm Springs, CA; KPTR Palm Springs, CA; KDES-FM Cathedral City, CA; KGAM Merced, CA; KPSI-FM Palm Springs, CA;
Mike Keane, General Manager

Rubber City Radio Group Inc.
1795 W. Market St., Akron OH 44313
(330) 869-9800; *Fax:*(330) 864-6799
www.wqmx.com,www.921theedge.com
mail@wakr.net
Ownership: Morton L. Mandel, 52%; Barbara A. Mandel, trustee under The Living Trust Between Thomas Mandel and Barbara Mandel FTB ThomasMandel, 48%.

Radio Stns: 1 AM. 5 FM.
WAKR Akron, OH; WJXQ Charlotte, MI; WONE-FM Akron, OH; WQMX Medina, OH; WQTX Saint Johns, MI; WVIC Jackson, MI;
Thomas A. Mandel, President
Nick Anthony, Vice President

Ruby Radio Corp.
1750 Manzanita,Suite 1, Elko NV 89801
(775) 777-1196; *Fax:*(775) 777-9587;

Radio Stns: 3 FM.
KHIX Carlin, NV; KZBI Elko, NV; KBGZ Spring Creek, NV;
Ken Sutherland, President

Saga Communications Inc.
73 Kercheval Ave.,Suite 201, Grosse Pointe Farms MI 48236
(313) 886-7070; *Fax:*(313) 886-7150
www.sagacommunications.com
chapsburg@sagacom.com
Ownership: Edward K. Christian, 56.5% of the voting stock.
Other Interests: Illinois Radio Network, Michigan Radio Network, Michigan FarmRadio Network.

Radio Stns: 28 AM. 59 FM.
KGMI Bellingham, WA; KICD Spencer, IA; KBAI Bellingham, WA; KPUG Bellingham, WA; KRNT Des Moines, IA; KPSZ Des Moines, IA; WEGI Fort Campbell, KY; WBAE Portland, ME; WBCO Bucyrus, OH; WKFN Clarksville, TN; WFEA Manchester, NH; WGAN Portland, ME; WHMQ Greenfield, MA; WHCU Ithaca, NY; WHMP Northampton, MA; WVAE Biddeford, ME; WINA Charlottesville, VA; WJOI Norfolk, VA; WJYI Milwaukee, WI; WZBK Keene, NH; WKBK Keene, NH; WKVT Brattleboro, VT; WHNP East Longmeadow, MA; WTAX Springfield, IL; WNYY Ithaca, NY; WYSE Canton, NC; WZAN Portland, ME; WVAX Charlottesville, VA; KAZR Pella, IA; KEGI Jonesboro, AR; KDXY Lake City, AR; KUQL Ethan, SD; KICD-FM Spencer, IA; KLLT Spencer, IA; KIOA Des Moines, IA; KISM Bellingham, WA; KJBX Cash, AR; KLTI-FM Ames, IA; KMIT Mitchell, SD; KSTZ Des Moines, IA; WAFX Suffolk, VA; WAQY Springfield, MA; WCNR Keswick, VA; WCLZ North Yarmouth, ME; WTMT Weaverville, NC; WCVQ Fort Campbell, KY; WEGI-FM Oak Grove, KY; WDBR Springfield, IL; WJMR-FM Menomonee Falls, WI; WHAI Greenfield, MA; WLZX Northampton, MA; WYXY(FM) Danville, IL; WIII Cortland, NY; WSNI Keene, NH; WIXY Champaign, IL; WJZX(FM) Brookfield, WI; WNND Pickerington, OH; WCFF Urbana, IL; WKLH Milwaukee, WI; WKNE Keene, NH; WKVT-FM Brattleboro, VT; WLRW Champaign, IL; WHQG

Milwaukee, WI; WMGX Portland, ME; WNOR Norfolk, VA; WPOR Portland, ME; WRSI Turners Falls, MA; WQEL Bucyrus, OH; WMLL Bedford, NH; WQMZ Charlottesville, VA; WQNY Ithaca, NY; WQQL Springfield, IL; WPVQ Greenfield, MA; WSNY Columbus, OH; WRSY Marlboro, VT; WVVR Hopkinsville, KY; WWWV Charlottesville, VA; WINQ Winchester, NH; WVMX Westerville, OH; WYMG Chatham, IL; WYNZ South Portland, ME; WYXL Ithaca, NY; WABZ Sherman, IL; WZID Manchester, NH; WNNP Richwood, OH; WZZP Hopkinsville, KY; WOXL-FM Biltmore Forest, NC;

TV Stns: 3 TV.
KAVU-TV Victoria, TX; KOAM-TV Pittsburg, KS; WXVT Greenville, MS;
Sam Bush, CFO
Edward Christian, CEO
Marcia Lobaito, VP
Warren Lada, VP Operations

Salem Communications Corp.
4880 Santa Rosa Rd., Suite 100, Camarillo CA 93012
(805) 987-0400; *Fax:*(805) 384-4511
www.salem.cc

Radio Stns: 63 AM. 30 FM.
KHCM Honolulu, HI; KNTS Seattle, WA; KOTK Omaha, NE; KBJD Denver, CO; KDOW Palo Alto, CA; KCBQ San Diego, CA; KCRO Omaha, NE; KNTH Houston, TX; KFAX San Francisco, CA; KPXQ Glendale, AZ; KFIA Carmichael, CA; KGNW Burien-Seattle, WA; KGU Honolulu, HI; KRLA Glendale, CA; KZNT Colorado Springs, CO; KKMO Tacoma, WA; KKMS Richfield, MN; KKOL Seattle, WA; KLFE Seattle, WA; KLUP Terrell Hills, TX; KNUS Denver, CO; KPDQ Portland, OR; KPRZ San Marcos-Poway, CA; KKNT Phoenix, AZ; KRKS Denver, CO; KSKY Balch Springs, TX; KSLR San Antonio, TX; KTIE San Bernardino, CA; KTKZ Sacramento, CA; KYCR Golden Valley, MN; WAVA Arlington, VA; WGKA Atlanta, GA; WEZE Boston, MA; WFIA Louisville, KY; WFIL Philadelphia, PA; WAFS Atlanta, GA; WGUL Dunedin, FL; WHIM Coral Gables, FL; WHK Cleveland, OH; WTBN Pinellas Park, FL; WIND Chicago, IL; WKAT North Miami, FL; WHKW Cleveland, OH; WLSS Sarasota, FL; WGTK Louisville, KY; WLQV Detroit, MI; WLTA Alpharetta, GA; WMCA New York, NY; WWDJ Boston, MA; WNIV Atlanta, GA; WORL Altamonte Springs, FL; WPIT Pittsburgh, PA; WDTK Detroit, MI; WRFD Columbus-Worthington, OH; WROL Boston, MA; WYLL Chicago, IL; WTWD Plant City, FL; WTLN Orlando, FL; WHIM(AM) Coral Gables, FL; WNYM Hackensack, NJ; WWTC Minneapolis, MN; WZAZ Jacksonville, FL; WNTP Philadelphia, PA; KAIM-FM Honolulu, HI; KRYP Gladstone, OR; KBIQ Manitou Springs, CO; KDAR Oxnard, CA; KXMX Muldrow, OK; KGBI-FM Omaha, NE; KGFT Pueblo, CO; KKOL-FM Aiea, HI; KFIS Scappoose, OR; KKLA-FM Los Angeles, CA; KSAC-FM Dunnigan, CA; KHUI Alamosa, CO; KPDQ-FM Portland, OR; KHCM-FM Honolulu, HI; KPXI Overton, TX; KWRD-FM Highland Village, TX; KRKS-FM Lafayette, CO; KKHT-FM Lumberton, TX; KLTY Arlington, TX; KKFS Lincoln, CA; KFSH-FM La Mirada, CA; WFSH-FM Athens, GA; WAVA-FM Arlington, VA; WBOZ Woodbury, TN; WFHM-FM Cleveland, OH; WFIA-FM New Albany, IN; WORD-FM Pittsburgh, PA; WFFH Smyrna, TN; WVRY Waverly, TN; WFFI Kingston Springs, TN;
Stuart Epperson, Chairman
Eric Halvorson, VP
Edward Atsinger, CEO

San Luis Valley Broadcasting Inc.
Box 631, Monte Vista CO 81144
(719) 852-3581; *Fax:*(719) 852-3583;

Radio Stns: 1 AM. 2 FM.
KSLV Monte Vista, CO; KYDN Monte Vista, CO; KSLV-FM Del Norte, CO;

Sand Hill Media Corp.
Box 570, Logan UT 84323
(435) 752-1390;

Radio Stns: 1 AM. 3 FM.
KSPZ Ammon, ID; KSNA Idaho Falls, ID; KUPI-FM Rexburg, ID; KQEO Idaho Falls, ID;

Sandab Communications L.P. II
2201 Old Court Rd., Baltimore MD 21208
(508) 771-1224
www.capecodbroadcasting.com

Radio Stns: 4 FM.
WFCC-FM Chatham, MA; WOCN-FM Orleans, MA; WKPE-FM South Yarmouth, MA; WQRC Barnstable, MA;
Stephen Seymour, President
Scott Frothinghan, Operations Dir
Gregory Bone, General Manager

Sandusky Radio
515 Park Ave.,Apt. 4A, New York NY 10022
(212) 355-3074; *Fax:*(212) 355-3075
Ownership: Alice S. White trust. All 100% owned by the White and Rau families

Radio Stns: 4 AM. 6 FM.
KDUS Tempe, AZ; KIXI Mercer Island/Seattl, WA; KAZG Scottsdale, AZ; KKNW Seattle, WA; KDKB Mesa, AZ; KQMV Bellevue, WA; KRWM Bremerton, WA; KSLX-FM Scottsdale, AZ; KUPD Tempe, AZ; KLCK-FM Seattle, WA;
Norman Rau, President
Peter Vogt, CFO
David Rau, General Manager

Sanpete County Broadcasting Co.
Box 40, Manti UT 84642
(435) 835-7301; *Fax:*(435) 835-2250;

Radio Stns: 1 AM. 2 FM.
KMTI Manti, UT; KLGL Richfield, UT; KMXD Monroe, UT;

Sarkes Tarzian Inc.
Box 62, Bloomington IN 47402
(812) 332-7251; *Fax:*(812) 331-4575
Ownership: Tom Tarzian; Gray Television Inc.

Radio Stns: 1 AM. 3 FM.
WGCL Bloomington, IN; WAJI Fort Wayne, IN; WLDE Fort Wayne, IN; WTTS Bloomington, IN;

TV Stns: 2 TV.
KTVN Reno, NV; WRCB-DT Chattanooga, TN;
Tom Tarzian, Chairman
Bob Davis, CFO
Geoff Vargo, Pres, Radio
Tom Tolar, Pres, TV

Schurz Communications Inc.
225 W. Colfax Ave., South Bend IN 46626
(574) 287-1001; *Fax:*(574) 287-2257
www.schurz.com
mburdick@schurz.com
Ownership: Franklin D. Schurz Jr., James M. Schurz, Scott C. Schurz and Mary Schurz, trustees.

Radio Stns: 4 AM. 8 FM.
KBHB Sturgis, SD; KKLS Rapid City, SD; WASK Lafayette, IN; WSBT South Bend, IN; KFXS Rapid City, SD; KKMK Rapid City, SD; KOUT Rapid City, SD; KRCS Sturgis, SD; WASK-FM Battle Ground, IN; WKOA Lafayette, IN; WXXB Delphi, IN; WNSN South Bend, IN;

TV Stns: 6 TV.
KTUU-TV Anchorage, AK; KSCW-DT Wichita, KS; KYTV Springfield, MO; WAGT Augusta, GA; WDBJ Roanoke, VA; WSBT-TV South Bend, IN;
Franklin Schurz Jr., Chairman
Todd Schurz, President
Marcia Burdick, SVP

Scott Communications Inc.
Box 1150, Selma AL 36702-1150
(334) 875-9360; *Fax:*(334) 875-1340;

Radio Stns: 1 AM. 2 FM.
WJAM Selma, AL; WALX Orrville, AL; WMRK-FM Shorter, AL;

Sea-Comm Inc.
122 Cinema Dr., Wilmington NC 28403
(910) 772-6300; *Fax:*(910) 772-6310
www.sea-comm.com

Radio Stns: 3 FM.
WLTT Bolivia, NC; WBNE Wrightsville Beach, NC; WNTB Topsail Beach, NC;
Rick Jorgenson, CEO
Paul Knight, General Manager

Seattle Streaming Radio LLC
Box 1471, Evergreen CO 80437
(303) 688-5162; *Fax:*(303) 660-4930;

Radio Stns: 5 AM.
KBRO Bremerton, WA; KLDY Lacey, WA; KNTB Lakewood, WA; WKIZ Key West, FL; KXXJ Juneau, AK;

Seehafer Broadcasting Corp.
Box 1385, Manitowoc WI 54221-1385
(920) 682-0351; *Fax:*(920) 682-1008;

Radio Stns: 4 AM. 3 FM.
WDLB Marshfield, WI; WFHR Wisconsin Rapids, WI; WOMT Manitowoc, WI; WXCO Wausau, WI; WOSQ Spencer, WI; WQTC-FM Manitowoc, WI; WRCW Nekoosa, WI;
Don Seehafer, President
Mark Seehafer, Operations Dir

Service Broadcasting Group LLC
621 N.W. 6th St., Grand Prairie TX 75050-5555
(972) 263-9911; *Fax:*(972) 558-0010
www.k104fm.com

Radio Stns: 1 AM. 2 FM.
KKDA Grand Prairie, TX; KKDA-FM Dallas, TX; KRNB Decatur, TX;
Hymen Childs, President
Chuck Smith, General Manager

Seward County Broadcasting Co.
1410 N. Western, Liberal KS 67901
(620) 624-3891; *Fax:*(620) 624-7885
www.kscb.net
sales@kscb.net
Ownership: Jack Landon, Robert Larrabee, Stuart Melchert.

Radio Stns: 1 AM. 2 FM.
KSCB Liberal, KS; KLDG Liberal, KS; KSCB-FM Liberal, KS;
Stuart Melchert, General Manager

Shamrock Communications Inc.
149 Penn Ave., Scranton PA 18503
(570) 348-9108; *Fax:*(570) 348-9109
www.nepanews.com
Ownership: Principal owners: William R. Lynett, James J. Haggerty, Edward J. Lynett, George V. Lynett. Shamrock Communications owns 50% of the Milwaukee Radio Alliance LLC(see listing).

Radio Stns: 3 AM. 8 FM.
WBAX Wilkes-Barre, PA; WEJL Scranton, PA; WJZI Decatur, IN; KTSO Glenpool, OK; KMYZ-FM Pryor, OK; WEZX Scranton, PA; WZBA Westminster, MD; WQFM Forest City, PA; WQFN(FM) Forest City, PA; WPZX Pocono Pines, PA; KWNZ Lovelock, NV;
Jim Loftus, COO
William Lynett, President

Sheila Callahan and Friends Inc.
Box 309, Missoula MT 59806-0309
(406) 542-1025; *Fax:*(406) 721-1036;

Radio Stns: 4 FM.
KMSO Missoula, MT; KMTZ Three Forks, MT; KDXT Lolo, MT; KHDV Darby, MT;
Max Murphy, CFO
Sheila Callahan, President

Sheridan Broadcasting Corp.
960 Penn Ave.,Suite 200, Pittsburgh PA 15222
(412) 456-4000; *Fax:*(412) 456-4022
www.wamo.com

Radio Stns: 5 AM. 1 FM.
WAMO Wilkinsburg, PA; WATV Birmingham, AL; WIGO Morrow, GA; WUFO Amherst, NY; WPGR Monroeville, PA; WAOB-FM Beaver Falls, PA;
Ronald Davenport Sr., Chairman

SIGA Broadcasting Corp.
1302 N. Shepherd Dr., Houston TX 77008
(713) 868-5559; *Fax:*(713) 868-9631
www.sigabroadcasting.com
sigabroadcasting@gmail.com

Radio Stns: 6 AM.
KAML Kenedy-Karnes City, TX; KHFX Cleburne, TX; KFJZ Fort Worth, TX; KGBC Galveston, TX; KLVL Pasadena, TX; KTMR Converse, TX;

Simmons Broadcasting Inc.
1403 Third St., Langdon ND 58249
(701) 256-1080; *Fax:*(701) 256-1081
kndkkicksbs@utma.com

Radio Stns: 1 AM. 3 FM.
KNDK Langdon, ND; KAOC Cavalier, ND; KYTZ Walhalla, ND; KNDK-FM Langdon, ND;

Simmons Media Group
515 South 700 East, Salt Lake City UT 84102
(801) 524-2600; *Fax:*(801) 524-6002
www.simmonsmedia.com

Radio Stns: 12 AM. 10 FM.
KRZI Waco, TX; KZNS Salt Lake City, UT; KMER Kemmerer, WY; KOVO Provo, UT; KZNX Creedmoor, TX; KDXE North Little Rock, AR; KLRK Mexia, TX; KQPN West Memphis, AR; KWNX Taylor, TX; KXOL Brigham City, UT; KXFN Saint Louis, MO; WFFX(AM) East St. Louis, IL; KAOX Kemmerer, WY; KDWY Diamondville, WY; KRMX(FM) Marlin, TX; KEGH Brigham City, UT; KXRK Provo, UT; KWBT Mexia, TX; KEGA Oakley, UT; KYMV Woodruff, UT; KLO-FM Coalville, UT; KURR Indian Springs, NV;
David Simmons, Chairman
Bruce Thomas, CFO
Craig Hanson, President
Alan Hague, Operations Dir
Bret Leifson, Controller

Sinclair Communications Inc.
999 Waterside Dr.,Suite 500, Norfolk VA 23510
(757) 640-8500; *Fax:*(757) 640-8552
www.sinclairstations.com
Ownership: John L. Sinclair, chmn; Robert Sinclair, J. David Sinclair, Ann Adams. Note: Group also manages KNOB(FM) Healdsburg, CA.
Radio Stns: 2 AM. 6 FM.
WNIS Norfolk, VA; WTAR Norfolk, VA; KSXY Forestville, CA; KXTS Geyserville, CA; KRSH Healdsburg, CA; WNOB Chesapeake, VA; WROX-FM Exmore, VA; WUSH Poquoson, VA;
John Sinclair, Chairman
J. David Sinclair, President
Robert L. Sinclair, Secretary

SkyWest Media L.L.C.
Box 36148, Tucson AZ 85740
(520) 797-4434;
Radio Stns: 1 AM. 6 FM.
KNFT Bayard, NM; KNFT-FM Bayard, NM; KPSA-FM Lordsburg, NM; KSCQ Silver City, NM; KFMR Ballard, UT; KRZX Redlands, CO; KXML Fairfield, ID;

Smoke and Mirrors LLC
Number 10 Media Center Dr., Lake Havasu City AZ 86403
(928) 855-1051; *Fax:*(928) 855-7996;
Radio Stns: 4 FM.
KFTT Bagdad, AZ; KRRK Desert Hills, AZ; KVAL Cal-Nev-Ari, NV; KVYL Mohave Valley, AZ;

Somar Communications Inc.
28095 Three Notch Rd.,Suite 2-B, Mechanicsville MD 20659
(301) 870-5550; *Fax:*(301) 884-0280;
Radio Stns: 2 AM. 3 FM.
WKIK La Plata, MD; WPTX Lexington Park, MD; WKIK-FM California, MD; WMDM Lexington Park, MD; WSMD-FM Mechanicsville, MD;
Roy Robertson, CEO

Sorensen Pacific Broadcasting Inc.
111 W. Chanlan Santo Papa,Suite 800, Hagatna GU 96910
(671) 477-5700; *Fax:*(671) 477-3982
www.radiopacific.com
comments@radiopacific.com
Ownership: Rex W. Sorensen, 97.6%.
Radio Stns: 1 AM. 4 FM.
KGUM Hagatna, GU; KGUM-FM Dededo, GU; KPXP Garapan-Saipan, MP; KRSI Garapan-Saipan, MP; KZGZ Hagatna, GU;
Jon Anderson, President
Rex Sorensen, CEO

Sorenson Broadcasting Corp.
2804 S. Ridgeview Way, Sioux Falls SD 57105
(605) 334-1117; *Fax:*(605) 338-0326
sorenson@sbcradio.com
Ownership: Dean P. Sorenson, 100%. Note: WZGA(FM) Helen, GA is licensed to Sorenson Southeast Radio LLC, a separate entity also owned 100% by Dean Sorenson.
Radio Stns: 4 AM. 7 FM.
KCCR Pierre, SD; KORN Mitchell, SD; KSOU Sioux Center, IA; KYNT Yankton, SD; KIHK Rock Valley, IA; KKYA Yankton, SD; KLXS-FM Pierre, SD; KQRN Mitchell, SD; KSOU-FM Sioux Center, IA; KUOO Spirit Lake, IA; KUQQ Milford, IA;
Dean Sorenson, President

South Central Communications Corp.
Box 3848, Evansville IN 47736
(812) 463-7950; *Fax:*(812) 463-7915
www.southcentralcommunications.net
Ownership: John D. Engelbrecht, 80%, J.P. Engelbrecht, 20%.
Radio Stns: 1 AM. 11 FM.
WEOA Evansville, IN; WABX Evansville, IN; WLYT(FM) Norris, TN; WEJK Boonville, IN; WIKY-FM Evansville, IN; WIMZ-FM Knoxville, TN; WLFW Chandler, IN; WJXA Nashville, TN; WJXB-FM Knoxville, TN; WCJK Murfreesboro, TN; WSTO Owensboro, KY; WQJK Maryville, TN;
TV Stns: 1 TV.
WMAK Knoxville, TN;
John D. Engelbrecht, President
J.P. Engelbrecht, VP

South Texas FM Investments LLC
Box 880, Roma TX 78584
(956) 487-8015;
Radio Stns: 1 FM.
KZAM Pleasant Valley, TX;

Southeast Kansas Independent Living Resource Center Inc.
202 E. Centennial Ave.,Suite 2B, Pittsburg KS 66762
(620) 232-9912; *Fax:*(620) 232-9915;
Radio Stns: 2 AM. 1 FM.
KLKC Parsons, KS; KSEK Pittsburg, KS; KSEK-FM Girard, KS;
Shari Coatney, President

Southeastern Oklahoma Radio LLC
Box 1011, Hartshorne OK 74547
(918) 297-2501;
Radio Stns: 2 AM. 2 FM.
KNED McAlester, OK; KTMC McAlester, OK; KMCO Wilburton, OK; KTMC-FM McAlester, OK;

Southern Broadcasting Companies Inc.
1010 Tower Pl., Bogart GA 30622
(706) 369-7301; *Fax:*(706) 353-1967
www.magic1021.com,www.rock1037.com
Ownership: Paul C. Stone.
Radio Stns: 2 AM. 3 FM.
WLOV Washington, GA; WRGA Rome, GA; WMGZ Eatonton, GA; WQTU Rome, GA; WSRM Coosa, GA;
Paul Stone, President
Traci Long, General Manager

Southern Communications Corp.
306 S. Kanawaha St., Beckley WV 25801
(304) 253-7000; *Fax:*(304) 255-1044
www.103cir.com
Ownership: R. Shane Southern, 50.4%; Karen L. Martin, 24.8%; and Kristin E. Wallace, 24.8%.
Radio Stns: 3 AM. 4 FM.
WBKW(AM) Beckley, WV; WMTD Hinton, WV; WWNR Beckley, WV; WAXS Oak Hill, WV; WCIR-FM Beckley, WV; WMTD-FM Hinton, WV; WTNJ Mount Hope, WV;
R. Shane Southern, President
Jay Quesenberry, General Manager

Southern Wabash Communications Corp.
435 37th Ave. N., Nashville TN 37209
(615) 844-1039; *Fax:*(615) 777-2284
www.wnsr.com
Radio Stns: 2 AM. 2 FM.
WMGC Murfreesboro, TN; WNSR Brentwood, TN; WNTC Drakesboro, KY; WSJD Princeton, IN;
Randy Bell, President
Ted Johnson, General Manager

Southwest Broadcasting Inc.
206 N. Front, McComb MS 39648
(601) 684-4116; *Fax:*(601) 684-4654
spots@k106.net
Radio Stns: 2 AM. 6 FM.
WAPF McComb, MS; WAKK McComb, MS; WAKH McComb, MS; WAZA Liberty, MS; WTGG Amite, LA; WJSH Folsom, LA; WKJN Centreville, MS; WFCG Tylertown, MS;
C. Wayne Dowdy, President

Spanish Broadcasting System Inc.
2601 South Bayshore Dr.,PH 2, Coconut Grove FL 33133
(305) 441-6901; *Fax:*(305) 446-5148
www.spanishbroadcasting.com
Ownership: Raul Alarcon Jr., Jose Grimalt.
Radio Stns: 20 FM.
KXOL-FM Los Angeles, CA; KLAX-FM East Los Angeles, CA; KRZZ San Francisco, CA; WCMQ-FM Hialeah, FL; WODA Bayamon, PR; WEGM San German, PR; WRXD Fajardo, PR; WZET Hormigueros, PR; WIOA San Juan, PR; WIOB Mayaguez, PR; WIOC Ponce, PR; WLEY-FM Aurora, IL; WMEG Guayama, PR; WNOD Mayaguez, PR; WPAT-FM Paterson, NJ; WRMA Fort Lauderdale, FL; WSKQ-FM New York, NY; WXDJ North Miami Beach, FL; WZMT Ponce, PR; WZNT San Juan, PR;
TV Stns: 1 TV.
WSBS-TV Key West, FL;
Jose Grimalt, EVP
Raul Alarcon, CEO

Spanish Peaks Broadcasting Inc.
3702 Sunridge Dr., Park City UT 84098-4618
(801) 560-9595;
Radio Stns: 3 FM.
KKVU Stevensville, MT; KYJK Missoula, MT; KDTR Florence, MT;

Sparta-Tomah Broadcasting Co. Inc.
113 W. Oak St., Sparta WI 54656
(608) 269-3307; *Fax:*(608) 269-5170;
Radio Stns: 1 AM. 2 FM.
WKLJ Sparta, WI; WCOW-FM Sparta, WI; WFBZ Trempealeau, WI;
William R. Hoffman, General Manager

Spotlight Broadcasting LLC
Box 8888, Metairie LA 70011
(504) 309-7260; *Fax:*(504) 309-7262
www.kmrc1430.com
kmrc@kmrc1430.com
Radio Stns: 3 AM.
KAGY Port Sulphur, LA; KMRC Morgan City, LA; WABL Amite, LA;
Patrick Andras, President

Stanford Communications Inc.
Box 458, Amory MS 38821
(662) 256-9726; *Fax:*(662) 256-9725
www.fm95radio.com
wamywafm@traceroad.net
Radio Stns: 2 AM. 1 FM.
WAMY Amory, MS; WWZQ Aberdeen, MS; WAFM Amory, MS;
Ed Stanford, President
Teresa Stanford, Operations Dir

Star Broadcasting Inc.
21 Miracle Strip Pkwy., Fort Walton Beach FL 32548
(850) 244-1400; *Fax:*(850) 243-1471;
Radio Stns: 2 AM. 1 FM.
WEDM(AM) Fort Walton Beach, FL; WEVG Evergreen, AL; WTKE-FM Niceville, FL;

STARadio Corp.
329 Maine St., Quincy IL 62301-3928
(217) 224-4102; *Fax:*(217) 224-4133
reception@staradio.com
Ownership: Howard A. Doss, Derek Parrish and Jack Whitley.
Radio Stns: 3 AM. 7 FM.
KXGF Great Falls, MT; WKAN Kankakee, IL; WTAD Quincy, IL; KGRC Hannibal, MO; KZZK New London, MO; WQCY Quincy, IL; WCOY Quincy, IL; WYKT Wilmington, IL; WYKZ Beaufort, SC; WXNU St. Anne, IL;
Mike Moyers, General Manager

Starlight Broadcasting Co.
Box 106,314 Main, Hartford KY 42347
(270) 298-3268; *Fax:*(270) 298-9326
www.wxmz.com
Radio Stns: 1 FM.
WKYA Greenville, KY;
Andy Anderson, President

Steckline Communications Inc.
1632 S. Maize Rd., Wichita KS 67209
(316) 721-8484; *Fax:*(316) 721-8276
www.maanradio.com
Radio Stns: 3 AM.
KYUL Scott City, KS; KIUL Garden City, KS; KGSO Wichita, KS;
Greg Steckline, President

Stephens Family L.P.
Box 1250, Sapulpa OK 74067
(918) 492-2660;
Radio Stns: 4 AM. 11 FM.
KGND Vinita, OK; WMSA Massena, NY; WTNY Watertown, NY; WNER Watertown, NY; KITO-FM Vinita, OK; WVLF Norwood, NY; WCIZ-FM Watertown, NY; WFRY-FM Watertown, NY; WYSX Morristown, NY; WFKL Fairport, NY; WRCD Canton, NY; WRMM-FM Rochester, NY; WNCQ-FM Canton, NY; WPAC Ogdensburg, NY; WZNE Brighton, NY;
Michael Stephens, President

Studstill Broadcasting
3905 Progress Blvd., Peru IL 61354
(815) 224-2100,; *Fax:*(815) 224-2066;
Radio Stns: 1 AM. 6 FM.
WSPL Streator, IL; WIVQ Spring Valley, IL; WALS Oglesby, IL; WGLC-FM Mendota, IL; WBZG Peru, IL; WSTQ Streator, IL; WYYS Streator, IL;
Lamar Studstill, Chairman
Owen Studstill, President
Cole Studstill, Operations Dir

Sudbury Services Inc.
Box 989, Blytheville AR 72316
(870) 762-2093; *Fax:*(870) 763-8459
www.thundercountry963.com
Ownership: Harold L. Sudbury Jr., Lydia Sudbury Langston, LaNeal Sudbury Salter. Cable TV: Blytheville TV Cable Co., Blytheville, AR.
Radio Stns: 5 AM. 5 FM.

KLCN Blytheville, AR; KNBY Newport, AR; KOSE Wilson, AR; KTPA Prescott, AR; KXAR Hope, AR; KAMJ Gosnell, AR; KHLS Blytheville, AR; KHPA Hope, AR; KOKR Newport, AR; KQMJ(FM) Osceola, AR;
Harold Sudbury, Chairman

Summit City Radio Group
2000 Lower Huntington Rd., Fort Wayne IN 46819
(260) 747-1511; *Fax:*(260) 747-3999
www.summitcityradio.com
lloyd@summitcityradio.com
Radio Stns: 1 AM. 3 FM.
WGL Fort Wayne, IN; WNHT Churubusco, IN; WGL-FM Huntington, IN; WXKE Fort Wayne, IN;
Lloyd B. Roach, President

Summit Media Broadcasting LLC
180 Main St., Sutton WV 26601
(304) 765-7373; *Fax:*(304) 765-7836
www.theboss97fm.com
info@theboss97fm.com
Radio Stns: 2 AM. 3 FM.
WSGB Sutton, WV; WVAR Richwood, WV; WAFD Webster Springs, WV; WDBS Sutton, WV; WKQV Cowen, WV;
Al Sergi, General Manager

Sumter Broadcasting Co. Inc.
Box 727, Americus GA 31709
(229) 924-1390; *Fax:*(229) 928-2337
www.americusradio.com
Radio Stns: 1 AM. 2 FM.
WISK Lawrenceville, GA; WDEC-FM Americus, GA; WISK-FM Americus, GA;
Steve Lashley, President

Sun Mountain Inc.
9045 Hobble Creek, Billings MT 59101
(406) 665-2828; *Fax:*(406) 665-2131
www.bigskyradio.net
Radio Stns: 3 AM.
KBSR Laurel, MT; KHDN Hardin, MT; KYLW Lockwood, MT;

Sun Valley Radio Inc.
810 W. 200 North, Logan UT 84321
(435) 752-1390; *Fax:*(435) 752-1392
Ownership: M. Kent Frandsen, owner.
Radio Stns: 2 AM. 4 FM.
KLGN Logan, UT; KVNU Logan, UT; KGNT Smithfield, UT; KKEX Preston, ID; KZHK St. George, UT; KLZX Weston, ID;
M. Kent Frandsen, President

Sunbelt Broadcasting Corp.
Box 351, Columbia MS 39429
(601) 731-2298
wjdr@zzip.cc
Radio Stns: 2 FM.
WCJU-FM Prentiss, MS; WJDR Prentiss, MS;
Thomas McDaniel, President

Sunburst Media-Louisiana LLC
300 Crescent Ct.,Suite 850, Dallas TX 75201
(214) 661-3100;
Radio Stns: 1 AM. 3 FM.
KJIN Houma, LA; KXMG Jean Lafitte, LA; KCIL Gray, LA; KXOR-FM Thibodaux, LA;

Sunbury Broadcasting Corp.
Box 1070, Sunbury PA 17801
(570) 286-5838; *Fax:*(570) 743-7837
www.wqkx.com
wqkx@wqkx.com
Radio Stns: 2 AM. 3 FM.
WKOK Sunbury, PA; WMLP Milton, PA; WEGH Northumberland, PA; WQKX Sunbury, PA; WVLY-FM Milton, PA;
Roger Haddon Jr., CEO

Sunrise Broadcasting Corp.
Box 2307, Newburgh NY 12550
(845) 561-2131; *Fax:*(845) 561-2138
www.wgnyfm.com
Ownership: CVC Capital Corp.
Radio Stns: 2 AM. 2 FM.
KSNM Las Cruces, NM; WGNY Newburgh, NY; KGRT-FM Las Cruces, NM; WJGK(FM) Newburgh, NY;
J. Klebe, President

Superior Communications
3302 N. Van Dyke, Imlay City MI 48444
(810) 724-2638; *Fax:*(877) 850-0881
www.positivehits.com
Radio Stns: 8 FM.
WEJC White Star, MI; WLGH Leroy Township, MI; WTLI Bear Creek Township, MI; WAIR Lake City, MI; WHYT Goodland Township, MI; WSLI Belding, MI; WTAC Burton, MI; WSIS Riverside, MI;
Edward Czelada, President

Sweet Home Ashtabula LLC
Second Generation Place,3209 Prospect, Cleveland OH 44115
(216) 426-1500; *Fax:*(216) 588-1558;
Radio Stns: 1 AM. 4 FM.
WFUN Ashtabula, OH; WREO-FM Ashtabula, OH; WZOO-FM Edgewood, OH; WFXJ-FM North Kingsville, OH; WYBL Ashtabula, OH;
James Embrescia, President

Tackett-Boazman Broadcasting LP
600 Fisk Ave., Brownwood TX 76801
(325) 646-3535; *Fax:*(325) 646-3535
Wendleebroadcasting.com
rextackett@wendlee.com
Radio Stns: 2 AM. 1 FM.
KSTA Coleman, TX; KQBZ Brownwood, TX; KXYL-FM Coleman, TX;
Rex Tackett, President

Talking Stick Communications LLC
421 S. Second St., Elkhart IN 46514
(574) 258-5483;
Radio Stns: 1 AM. 4 FM.
WRSW Warsaw, IN; WAWC Syracuse, IN; WAOR(FM) Nappanee, IN; WRBR-FM South Bend, IN; WRSW-FM Warsaw, IN;
Alec Dille, President

Talley Radio Stations
Box 10, Litchfield IL 62056
(217) 324-5921; *Fax:*(217) 532-2431
wsmiradio.com
wsmi@wsmiradio.com
Ownership: Hayward L. Talley, Emma C. Talley.
Radio Stns: 1 AM. 2 FM.
WSMI Litchfield, IL; WAOX Staunton, IL; WSMI-FM Litchfield, IL;
Hayward Talley, President
Brian Talley, SVP

Tallgrass Broadcasting LLC
1174 Hunters Ridge East, Hoffman Estates IL 60192-4540
(847) 289-8018; *Fax:*(847) 289-1423;
Radio Stns: 3 AM. 6 FM.
KICA Clovis, NM; KIND Independence, KS; KMUL Farwell, TX; KOSG Pawhuska, OK; KICA-FM Farwell, TX; KBIK Independence, KS; KKYC Clovis, NM; KMUL-FM Muleshoe, TX; KIND-FM Elk City, KS;

Tama Broadcasting Inc.
5207 Washington Blvd., Tampa FL 33619
(813) 620-1300; *Fax:*(813) 628-0713
www.wtmp.com
Radio Stns: 1 AM. 8 FM.
WTMP Egypt Lake, FL; WTHG Hinesville, GA; WYRE-FM Saint Augustine Beach, FL; WSSJ Rincon, GA; WTMP-FM Dade City, FL; WFJO Jacksonville Beach, FL; WSGA Hinesville, GA; WJGM(FM) Baldwin, FL; WJSJ Fernandina Beach, FL;
Glenn Cherry, CEO

Tanana Valley Television Co.
3650 Braddock St., Suite 2, Fairbanks AK 99701
(907) 452-3697; *Fax:*(907) 456-3428
Ownership: William St. Pierre, 85%.
Radio Stns: 3 FM.
KYSC Fairbanks, AK; KDJF Ester, AK; KNLT(FM) Palmer, AK;
TV Stns: 2 TV.
KFXF Fairbanks, AK; KNLT(FM) Palmer, AK;

TCU
Box 298020,Moudy Bldg., Fort Worth TX 76129
(817) 257-7631,; *Fax:*(817) 257-7637
www.ktcu.net
ktcu@tcu.edu
Radio Stns: 1 FM.
KTCU-FM Fort Worth, TX;
Russell Scott, General Manager
Janice McCall, Assistant Manager

Team Radio LLC
Box 2509, Ponca City OK 74602
(580) 765-2485; *Fax:*(580) 767-1103
www.eteamradio.com
Radio Stns: 2 AM. 3 FM.
KOKB Blackwell, OK; KOKP Perry, OK; KLOR-FM Ponca City, OK; KOSB Perry, OK; KPNC Ponca City, OK;
Bill Coleman, General Manager

Tejas Broadcasting Ltd. LLP
1227 W. Magnolia Ave.,Suite 300, Fort Worth TX 76104-4400
(817) 920-7599;
Radio Stns: 1 AM. 8 FM.
KTNZ Amarillo, TX; KBZD Amarillo, TX; KGRW Friona, TX; KMJR Odem, TX; KLTG Corpus Christi, TX; KOUL Refugio, TX; KQFX Borger, TX; KLHB Portland, TX; KKNM Bovina, TX;
Jim Anderson, CEO

TeleSouth Communications Inc.
6311 Ridgewood Rd., Jackson MS 39211
(601) 957-1700; *Fax:*(601) 957-2389
www.supertalkms.com
Radio Stns: 3 AM. 10 FM.
WKCU Corinth, MS; WKXG Greenwood, MS; WOEG Hazlehurst, MS; WDXO Hazlehurst, MS; WFMM Sumrall, MS; WFMN Flora, MS; WTNM Water Valley, MS; WQLJ Oxford, MS; WRQO Monticello, MS; WTCD Indianola, MS; WXRZ Corinth, MS; WYMX Greenwood, MS; WBZL(FM) Greenwood, MS;
Stephen Davenport, CEO

Texoma Broadcasting Inc.
1418 N. 1st Ave., Durant OK 74701
(580) 924-3100
Ownership: Allen Wheeler, 50%; Gerald Todd Tidwell, 40%; Gerald Winston Tidwell, 10%.
Radio Stns: 1 AM. 2 FM.
KSEO Durant, OK; KLBC Durant, OK; KBBC Tishomingo, OK;
Gerald Todd Tidwell, President

The Chickasaw Nation
Box 609, Ada OK 74821-0609
(580) 332-1212; *Fax:*(580) 332-0128
www.chickasaw.net
Radio Stns: 1 AM. 5 FM.
KADA Ada, OK; KADA-FM Ada, OK; KXFC Coalgate, OK; KCNP Ada, OK; KTLS-FM Holdenville, OK; KYKC Byng, OK;

The Cromwell Group Inc.
Box 150846, Nashville TN 37215
(615) 361-7560; *Fax:*(615) 366-4313
www.cromwellradio.com
bwalters@comwellradio.com
Ownership: Bayard H. Walters, 100%.
Radio Stns: 6 AM. 16 FM.
WCRA Effingham, IL; WQZQ Goodlettsville, TN; WKCM Hawesville, KY; WPMB Vandalia, IL; WTCJ Tell City, IN; WVJS Owensboro, KY; WBIO Philpot, KY; WCBH Casey, IL; WCRC Effingham, IL; WEJT Shelbyville, IL; WHQQ Neoga, IL; WKRV Vandalia, IL; WLME Lewisport, KY; WMCI Neoga B, IL; WPRT-FM Pegram, TN; WWGO Charleston, IL; WXCM Whitesville, KY; WZUS Macon, IL; WYDS Decatur, IL; WZNX Sullivan, IL; WBUZ La Vergne, TN; WTCJ-FM Cannelton, IN;
Bayard Walters, President
Thomas Crocker, CFO

The Curators of the University of Missouri
University of Missouri,316 University Hall, Columbia MO 65211
(573) 882-2388; *Fax:*(573) 882-0010
www.umsystem.edu
Ownership: (Business Services Division).
Radio Stns: 6 FM.
KBIA Columbia, MO; KCUR-FM Kansas City, MO; KMNR Rolla, MO; KMST Rolla, MO; KWMU St. Louis, MO; KAUD Mexico, MO;
TV Stns: 1 TV.
KOMU-TV Columbia, MO;
Michael Dunn, General Manager

The Findlay Publishing Co.
701 W. Sandusky St., Findlay OH 45840
(419) 422-5151; *Fax:*(419) 422-2937
daveglass@findlayoh.com
Radio Stns: 2 AM. 6 FM.
WCSI Columbus, IN; WFIN Findlay, OH; WWWY North Vernon, IN; WKKG Columbus, IN; WKXA-FM Findlay, OH; WBUK Ottawa, OH; WRBI Batesville, IN; WINN Columbus, IN;
Karl Heminger, President

The Free Lance-Star Publishing Co.
616 Amelia St., Fredericksburg VA 22401
(540) 373-1500; *Fax:*(540) 374-5525;
Radio Stns: 1 AM. 2 FM.
WNTX Fredericksburg, VA; WFLS-FM Fredericksburg, VA; WWUZ Bowling Green, VA;
Josiah P. Rowe III, President

Florence Barnick, Operations Dir
John Moen, General Manager
Nicholas Cadwallender, Associate Publisher

The Mid-West Family Broadcast Group
Box 44408, Madison WI 53744
(608) 273-1000; *Fax:*(608) 273-3588
www.midwestfamilybroadcasting.com
tom.walker@mwfbg.net
Ownership: Philip Fisher, Richard T. Record, Thomas A. Walker.
Radio Stns: 7 AM. 20 FM.
WHIT Madison, WI; WIZM La Crosse, WI; WKTY La Crosse, WI; WMAY Springfield, IL; WSJM St. Joseph, MI; WLMV Madison, WI; WTDY Madison, WI; KOSP Ozark, MO; KKLH Marshfield, MO; KOMG Willard, MO; KQYB Spring Grove, MN; KCLH Caledonia, MN; WSJM-FM Benton Harbor, MI; WCXT Hartford, MI; WIRX St. Joseph, MI; WIZM-FM La Crosse, WI; WJJO Watertown, WI; WLCE Petersburg, IL; WMGN Madison, WI; WNNS Springfield, IL; WRQT La Crosse, WI; WWQM-FM Middleton, WI; WYTZ Bridgman, MI; WCSY-FM South Haven, MI; WJQM De Forest, WI; KQRA Brookline, MO; WTDY-FM Mount Horeb, WI;
Thomas Walker, President
Jason McCutchin, CFO
Richard Record, Director

The Moody Bible Institute of Chicago
820 N. LaSalle Blvd., Chicago IL 60610
(312) 329-4300; *Fax:*(312) 329-8980
www.mbn.org
mbn@moody.edu
Radio Stns: 5 AM. 26 FM.
KMBI Spokane, WA; WDLM East Moline, IL; WFCM Smyrna, TN; WGNR Anderson, IN; WMBI Chicago, IL; KMBN Las Cruces, NM; KMBI-FM Spokane, WA; KMLW Moses Lake, WA; KSPL Kalispell, MT; WCRF-FM Cleveland, OH; WGNB Zeeland, MI; WGNR-FM Anderson, IN; WHPL West Lafayette, IN; WIWC Kokomo, IN; WJSO Pikeville, KY; WKES Lakeland, FL; WKZM Sarasota, FL; WMBI-FM Chicago, IL; WMBU Forest, MS; WMBV Dixons Mills, AL; WMBW Chattanooga, TN; WRMB Boynton Beach, FL; WVMN New Castle, PA; WVMS Sandusky, OH; WHGN Crystal River, FL; WVME Meadville, PA; WMBL Mitchell, IN; WVML Millersburg, OH; WMFT Tuscaloosa, AL; KJCG Missoula, MT; KMWY Jackson, WY;
Joseph Stowell, President
Wayne Pederson, VP broadcasting

The Original Company Inc.
Box 242, Vincennes IN 47591
(812) 882-6060; *Fax:*(812) 885-2604
www.originalcompany.com
marklange@originalcompany.com
Ownership: Mark R. Lange, 50%; Saundra K. Lange, 50%.
Radio Stns: 2 AM. 7 FM.
WAOV Vincennes, IN; WRCY Mt. Vernon, IN; WYFX Mount Vernon, IN; WBTO-FM Petersburg, IN; WQTY Linton, IN; WREB Greencastle, IN; WUZR Bicknell, IN; WWBL Washington, IN; WZDM Vincennes, IN;
Mark Lange, President

The Presence Radio Network
PO Box 10660,4 Washington Street, Portland ME 04104
(207) 689-9939
www.thepresence.fm
info@thepresence.fm
Radio Stns: 1 FM.
WXBP Corinth, ME;
Cynthia Nickless, Executive Director
Josh Houde, Production Assistant

The Radio Group
Box 1319, Columbia LA 71418
(318) 649-7959; *Fax:*(318) 649-5874
radiotom1@yahoo.com
Ownership: Tom D. Gay, 100%.
Radio Stns: 5 FM.
KAPB-FM Marksville, LA; KFNV-FM Ferriday, LA; KJNA-FM Jena, LA; KMAR-FM Winnsboro, LA; KWTG Vidalia, LA;
Tom Gay, General Manager

The Result Radio Group
Box 767, Winona MN 55987-0767
(507) 452-4000; *Fax:*(507) 452-9494
winonaradio.com
jpapenfuss@winonaradio.com
Ownership: Jerry Papenfuss.
Radio Stns: 6 AM. 8 FM.
KAGE Winona, MN; KBEW Blue Earth, MN; KBRF Fergus Falls, MN; KDOM Windom, MN; KJJK Fergus Falls, MN; KWNO Winona, MN; KAGE-FM Winona, MN; KBEW-FM Blue Earth, MN; KDOM-FM Windom, MN; KHME Winona, MN; KJJK-FM Fergus Falls, MN; KPRW Perham, MN; KWNO-FM Rushford, MN; KZCR Fergus Falls, MN;
Jerry Papenfuss, Owner

The Wireless Group Inc.
Box 198, Brownsville TN 38012
(731) 772-3700
Ownership: Carlton Veirs, pres, 50%; Lyle Reid, 50%. (See also Cross-Ownership, Sect. A.)
Radio Stns: 1 AM. 1 FM.
WNWS Brownsville, TN; WNWS-FM Jackson, TN;
Carlton Veirs, President

The Zone Corp.
Box 1929, Bangor ME 4402
(207) 990-2800; *Fax:*(207) 990-2444
www.zoneradio.com
Radio Stns: 1 AM. 1 FM.
WZON Bangor, ME; WKIT-FM Brewer, ME;
Stephen King, President
Arthur Greene, Operations Dir
Bobby Russell, General Manager
Tabitha King, Vice President

3 Daughters Media Inc.
c/o Brooks, Pierce, et al,Box 1800, Raleigh NC 27602
(919) 839-0300;
Radio Stns: 6 AM. 2 FM.
KSOP South Salt Lake, UT; WGMN Roanoke, VA; WDYN Rossville, GA; WMNA Gretna, VA; WVGM Lynchburg, VA; WBLT Bedford, VA; WUUQ South Pittsburg, TN; WMNA-FM Gretna, VA;

Three Eagles Communications
3800 Cornhusker Hwy., Lincoln NE 68504
(402) 466-1234; *Fax:*(402) 467-4095
www.threeeagles.com
gbuchanan@threeeagles.com
Radio Stns: 18 AM. 30 FM.
KATE Albert Lea, MN; KAUS Austin, MN; KBRK Brookings, SD; KFOR Lincoln, NE; KGLO Mason City, IA; KJAM Madison, SD; KJJQ Volga, SD; KJSK Columbus, NE; KLGR Redwood Falls, MN; KLMS Lincoln, NE; KQAD Luverne, MN; KRIB Mason City, IA; KSDR Watertown, SD; KTTT Columbus, NE; KVFD Fort Dodge, IA; KWAT Watertown, SD; KWMT Fort Dodge, IA; KWOA Worthington, MN; KAUS-FM Austin, MN; KDBX Clear Lake, SD; KCPI Albert Lea, MN; KDLO-FM Watertown, SD; KEEZ-FM Mankato, MN; KIAI Mason City, IA; KIAQ Clarion, IA; KFRX Lincoln, NE; KITN Worthington, MN; KIXX Watertown, SD; KJAM-FM Madison, SD; KKEZ Fort Dodge, IA; KIBZ Crete, NE; KKQQ Volga, SD; KKSD Milbank, SD; KLIR Columbus, NE; KLKK Clear Lake, IA; KRBI-FM St. Peter, MN; KTGL Beatrice, NE; KTLB Twin Lakes, IA; KUEL(FM) Fort Dodge, IA; KSMA-FM Osage, IA; KUSQ-FM Worthington, MN; KYSM-FM Mankato, MN; KYTC Northwood, IA; KZEN Central City, NE; KZKX Seward, NE; WCCQ Crest Hill, IL; KMKO-FM Lake Crystal, MN; KXFT Manson, IA;
Gary Buchanan, COO

3 Point Media
980 N. Michigan Ave.,Suite 1880, Chicago IL 60611
(312) 204-9900; *Fax:*(312) 587-9466;
Radio Stns: 4 FM.
KCUA Naples, UT; KNIV Lyman, WY; KMGR Delta, UT; KZNSFM) Coalville, UT;

Three Rivers Media Corp.
Box 1247, Wytheville VA 24382
(276) 228-3185; *Fax:*(276) 228-9261
3 Rivers Media.net
wyve.wxbx@wiredog.com
Radio Stns: 2 AM. 1 FM.
WLOY Rural Retreat, VA; WYVE Wytheville, VA; WXBX Rural Retreat, VA;
Gary W. Hagerich, COO

Three Trees Communications Inc.
113 E. College Ave., Ashburn GA 31714
(229) 567-9038;
Radio Stns: 2 FM.
WFFM Ashburn, GA; WTIF-FM Omega, GA;

Thunderbolt Broadcasting Co.
Box 318,1410 N. Lindell St., Martin TN 38237
(731) 587-9526; *Fax:*(731) 587-5079;
Radio Stns: 1 AM. 4 FM.
WCMT Martin, TN; WCDZ Dresden, TN; WCMT-FM Martin, TN; WQAK Union City, TN; KYTN(FM) Union City, TN;
Paul Tinkle, President

Tiger Communications Inc.
1695 E. University Dr., Auburn AL 36830
(334) 821-8624; *Fax:*(334) 821-8630
Ownership: Thomas Hayley, 100%.
Radio Stns: 4 AM. 3 FM.
WAUD Auburn, AL; WACQ(AM) Tuskegee, AL; WRLA West Point, GA; WTRP La Grange, GA; WQNR Tallassee, AL; WTGZ Union Springs, AL; WQSI Tuskegee, AL;
Thomas Hayley, Chairman

Tom Ingstad Broadcasting Group
Box 1248, Minnetonka MN 55345
(952) 938-0575; *Fax:*(952) 938-2295;
Radio Stns: 4 AM. 4 FM.
KDMA Montevideo, MN; KDUZ Hutchinson, MN; KKAQ Thief River Falls, MN; KMRS Morris, MN; KRVY-FM Starbuck, MN; KARP-FM Dassel, MN; KKRC Granite Falls, MN; KMGM Montevideo, MN;
Tom Ingstad, President/CEO

Tomlinson-Leis Communications LP
Box 3649, Palestine TX 75802
(903) 729-6077; *Fax:*(903) 729-4742
www.youreasttexas.com
Radio Stns: 1 FM.
KYYK Palestine, TX;
Edward Tomlinson II, Chairman
Kent Burkhart, CEO/COO
Alex Ward, Operations Dir
Lee Parkinson, General Manager
Michael McCulloch, Programming Director
Gary Richards, News Director

Tower Investment Trust Inc.
819 S. Federal Hwy.,Suite 106, Stuart FL 34994-2952
(772) 215-1634
www.toweritrust.com
Radio Stns: 4 FM.
KTTY New Boston, TX; KLOW Reno, TX; KXXN Iowa Park, TX; WBNK Pine Knoll Shores, NC;
Bill Brothers, President
Gary Hess, Operations Dir

Town and Country Broadcasting Inc.
486 W. 2nd St., Xenia OH 45385-3610
(937) 372-3531; *Fax:*(937) 372-3508;
Radio Stns: 3 AM.
WBZI Xenia, OH; WEDI Eaton, OH; WKFI Wilmington, OH;

Townsend Broadcasting Enterprise
100 Water Street, Camden AL 36726-1755
(866) 270-8849; *Fax:*(334) 682-9992
www.wqls905.com
info@wqls905.com
Radio Stns: 1 FM.
WVPL Dozier, AL;
Tom Love, Station Manager

Townsquare Media
,240 Greenwood Ave., Greenwich CT 06830
(203) 861-0900
townsquaremedia.com
Radio Stns: 14 AM. 49 FM.
KPEL Lafayette, LA; KROD El Paso, TX; KROF Abbeville, LA; KXSS Waite Park, MN; WFNT Flint, MI; WGBF Evansville, IN; WIBX Utica, NY; WJBC Bloomington, IL; WJON St. Cloud, MN; WLCO Lapeer, MI; WNWZ Grand Rapids, MI; WOMI Owensboro, KY; WTSK Tuscaloosa, AL; WVEL Pekin, IL; KPEL-FM Breaux Bridge, LA; KZRV Sartell, MN; KLZZ Waite Park, MN; KMDL Kaplan, LA; KMXK Cold Spring, MN; KFTE Abbeville, LA; KARS-FM Laramie, WY; KKPL Cheyenne, WY; KHXT Erath, LA; KSII El Paso, TX; KTDY Lafayette, LA; KTRR Loveland, CO; KUAD-FM Windsor, CO; WTMM-FM Mechanicville, NY; WZPW Peoria, IL; WBKR Owensboro, KY; WBLK Depew, NY; WBNQ Bloomington, IL; WBWN Le Roy, IL; WDKS Newburgh, IN; WFFN Coaling, AL; WFGR Grand Rapids, MI; WFRG-FM Utica, NY; WFYR Elmwood, IL; WGBF-FM Henderson, KY; WGLO Pekin, IL; WGNA-FM Albany, NY; WGRD-FM Grand Rapids, MI; WJYE Buffalo, NY; WKDQ Henderson, KY; WBUF Buffalo, NY; WJEZ Dwight, IL; WLZW Utica, NY; WQSH Malta, NY; WODZ-FM Rome, NY; WQBJ Cobleskill, NY; WQBK-FM Rensselaer, NY; WQUS Lapeer, MI; WBEI Reform, AL; WTRV Walker, MI; WTUG-FM Northport, AL; WWBN Tuscola, MI; WIXO Peoria, IL; WWJO St. Cloud, MN; WJLT Evansville, IN; WYRK Buffalo, NY; WRCL Frankenmuth, MI; WDGM Greensboro, AL; KMAX-FM Wellington, CO;
Steven Price, Chairman

Tri-County Broadcasting Inc.
Box 366, Sauk Rapids MN 56379
(320) 252-6200; *Fax:*(320) 252-9367;

Radio Stns: 2 AM. 1 FM.
WBHR Sauk Rapids, MN; WVAL Sauk Rapids, MN; WHMH-FM Sauk Rapids, MN;

Tri-Market Radio Broadcasters Inc. & Eagle Rock Broadcasting Inc.
120 South 300 W., Rupert ID 83350
(208) 436-4757; *Fax:*(208) 436-3050;

Radio Stns: 2 AM. 2 FM.
KBAR Burley, ID; KFTA Rupert, ID; KKMV Rupert, ID; KZDX Burley, ID;
Kim Lee, General Manager

Triad Broadcasting Co. L.L.C.
2511 Garden Rd.,Bldg. A, Suite 104, Monterey CA 93940
(831) 655-6350; *Fax:*(831) 655-6355
www.triadbroadcasting.com

Radio Stns: 10 AM. 18 FM.
KBMW Breckenridge, MN; KQWB West Fargo, ND; WFXH(AM) Hilton Head Island, SC; WHIS Bluefield, WV; WIRL Peoria, IL; WKEZ Bluefield, WV; WMBD Peoria, IL; WTZE Tazewell, VA; WXBD Biloxi, MS; WTNI Biloxi, MS; KLTA Breckenridge, MN; KPFX Fargo, ND; KQWB-FM Moorhead, MN; KVOX-FM Moorhead, MN; WCPR-FM Wiggins, MS; WGCO Midway, GA; WHAJ Bluefield, WV; WHQX Gary, WV; WKOY-FM Princeton, WV; WXYY(FM) Port Royal, SC; WUJM Gulfport, MS; WPBG Peoria, IL; WSWT Peoria, IL; WDQX Morton, IL; WGZR Bluffton, SC; WXCL Pekin, IL; WHGO Hertford, NC; WXYK Gulfport, MS;
James E Graber, CFO
David J Benjamin, President

Tribune Broadcasting Co.
435 N. Michigan Ave.,Suite 1800, Chicago IL 60611
(312) 222-3333; *Fax:*(312) 329-0611
www.tribune.com
Ownership: The Tribune Employee Stock Ownership Plan as implemented through the Tribune Employee Stock Ownership Trust, Oak Brook, IL, 100%.

Radio Stns: 2 AM.
WGN(AM) Chicago, IL; WGN Chicago, IL;

TV Stns: 24 TV.
KCPQ Tacoma, WA; KDAF Dallas, TX; KIAH Houston, TX; KPLR-TV St. Louis, MO; KSWB-TV San Diego, CA; KTLA Los Angeles, CA; KZJO Seattle, WA; KTXL Sacramento, CA; KRCW-TV Salem, OR; KWGN-TV Denver, CO; WDCW Washington, DC; WSFL-TV Miami, FL; WGN Chicago, IL; WGNO New Orleans, LA; WNOL-TV New Orleans, LA; WPHL-TV Philadelphia, PA; WPIX New York, NY; WPMT York, PA; WTIC-TV Hartford, CT; WTTK Kokomo, IN; WTTV Bloomington, IN; WCCT-TV Waterbury, CT; WXIN Indianapolis, IN; WXMI Grand Rapids, MI;
Ed Wilson, President
Nils Larsen, CEO

Truth Broadcasting Corp.
4405 Providence Ln.,Suite D, Winston-Salem NC 27106
(336) 759-0363; *Fax:*(336) 759-0366
www.wtru.com
tbooth@830wtru.com

Radio Stns: 5 AM.
WCRU Dallas, NC; WDRU Creedmore, NC; WKEW Greensboro, NC; WPOL Winston-Salem, NC; WTRU Kernersville, NC;
Stuart Epperson, President

2510 Licenses LLC
100 Ryan Ct.,Suite 98, Pittsburgh PA 15205
(412) 489-1001; *Fax:*(412) 489-1002;

Radio Stns: 1 AM. 7 FM.
WNTJ Johnstown, PA; KFFB Fairfield Bay, AR; WBHV-FM State College, PA; WLKJ Portage, PA; WKVB Port Matilda, PA; WOWY University Park, PA; WLKH Somerset, PA; WCCL Central City, PA;

Tyler Media Broadcasting Corp.
5101 S. Shields Blvd., Oklahoma City OK 73129
(405) 616-5500; *Fax:*(405) 616-5505
www.kkng.com

Radio Stns: 2 AM. 3 FM.
KTLR Oklahoma City, OK; KEBC Del City, OK; KTUZ-FM Okarche, OK; KJKE Newcastle, OK; KKNG-FM Blanchard, OK;

TV Stns: 1 TV.
KTUZ-TV Shawnee, OK;
Robert De Negri, CFO
Skip Stow, Promotions Manager

United Ministries
300 E. Rock Rd., Allentown PA 18103
(970) 254-5565; *Fax:*(970) 254-5550;

Radio Stns: 2 AM. 1 FM.
KDTA Delta, CO; KJOL Grand Junction, CO; WBMR Telford, PA;

United States CP LLC
1311 Swanner Court, High Point NC 27262
(336) 307-3828
Ownership: W. Philip Robinson, 100% voting interest, 9.9% ownership interest.

Radio Stns: 1 AM. 7 FM.
KCBR Monument, CO; KNKN(FM) Pueblo, CO; KRKY-FM Estes Park, CO; KRMX Marlin, TX; KRYE Olney Springs, CO; KXCL Westcliffe, CO; KIQN-FM Pueblo, CO; WKHF(FM) Lynchburg, VA;

Universal Broadcasting of New York Inc.
Corporate Offices,WTHE Radio 260 E. 2nd St., Mineola NY 11501
(516) 742-1520; *Fax:*(516) 742-2878
www.wthe1520am.com
nygospelradio@aol.com
Ownership: Howard Warshaw and Miriam Warshaw.

Radio Stns: 2 AM.
WTHE Mineola, NY; WVNJ Oakland, NJ;
Miriam Warshaw, President
Howard Warshaw, VP

Univision Radio
3102 Oak Lawn,Suite 215, Dallas TX 75219
(214) 525-7700; *Fax:*(214) 525-7750
www.univision.net/corp/en/urg.jsp
Ownership: Univision Communications Inc., 100% (see listing under TV Group Ownership, Section B).

Radio Stns: 16 AM. 53 FM.
KAMA El Paso, TX; KQBU El Paso, TX; KCOR San Antonio, TX; KFLC Fort Worth, TX; KGBT Harlingen, TX; KLAT Houston, TX; KLOK San Jose, CA; KLSQ Whitney, NV; KTNQ Los Angeles, CA; WADO New York, NY; WYEL Mayaguez, PR; WAQI Miami, FL; WUKQ Ponce, PR; WKAQ San Juan, PR; WRTO Chicago, IL; WQBA Miami, FL; KRCD Inglewood, CA; KLJA(FM) Georgetown, TX; KLLE North Fork, CA; KVVF Santa Clara, CA; KBNA-FM El Paso, TX; KBRG San Jose, CA; KBBT Schertz, TX; KKMR Arizona City, AZ; KJFA Santa Fe, NM; KQMR Globe, AZ; KESS-FM Lewisville, TX; KZFO(FM) Benbrook, TX; KWPW Robinson, TX; KOMR Sun City, AZ; KGBT-FM McAllen, TX; KDXX Denton, TX; KHOT-FM Paradise Valley, AZ; KISF Las Vegas, NV; KBTQ Harlingen, TX; KVVZ San Rafael, CA; KKSS Santa Fe, NM; KLNV San Diego, CA; KLQV San Diego, CA; KLTN Houston, TX; KPTY Winnie, TX; KLNO Fort Worth, TX; KLVE Los Angeles, CA; KRDA Hanford, CA; KHOV-FM Wickenburg, AZ; KAMA-FM Deer Park, TX; KQBU-FM Port Arthur, TX; KRGT Indian Springs, NV; KOVE-FM Galveston, TX; KGSX Comfort, TX; KROM San Antonio, TX; KKRG Albuquerque, NM; KRCV West Covina, CA; KSCA Glendale, CA; KSOL San Francisco, CA; KZAR McQueeney, TX; KXTN-FM San Antonio, TX; KOND Clovis, CA; KSQL Santa Cruz, CA; WAMR-FM Miami, FL; WQXR-FM Newark, NJ; WVIX Lemont, IL; WQBU-FM Garden City, NY; WOJO Evanston, IL; WRTO-FM Goulds, FL; WUKQ-FM Mayaguez, PR; WVIV-FM Highland Park, IL; WPPN Des Plaines, IL; KAJZ Llano, TX;
McHenry Tichenor, CEO

Uno Radio Group
Box 363222, San Juan PR 00936-3222
(787) 758-1300; *Fax:*(787) 282-6060
www.unoradio.com
lsoto@unoradio.com
Ownership: Jesus M. Soto.

Radio Stns: 6 AM. 7 FM.
WCMN Arecibo, PR; WNEL Caguas, PR; WORA Mayaguez, PR; WPRP Ponce, PR; WUNO San Juan, PR; WLEO Ponce, PR; WCMN-FM Arecibo, PR; WFID Rio Piedras, PR; WIVA-FM Aguadilla, PR; WMIO Cabo Rojo, PR; WFDT Aguada, PR; WPRM-FM San Juan, PR; WRIO Ponce, PR;
Jesus Soto, CEO
Luis Soto, President
Elba Esmurria, VP/Sales
Alberte Pereira, VP
Luis Gonzalez, VP/Finance
Ray Cruz, VP/Programming

Urban Radio Licenses LLC
273 Azalea Rd.,Suite 1-308, Mobile AL 36609
(251) 343-4900; *Fax:*(251) 343-4905
www.urbanradio.fm
info@urbanradio.fm

Radio Stns: 2 AM. 8 FM.
WLAY Muscle Shoals, AL; WVNA Tuscumbia, AL; WAJV Brooksville, MS; WIMX Gibsonburg, OH; WMXV St. Joseph, TN; WJZE Oak Harbor, OH; WLAY-FM Littleville, AL; WVNA-FM Muscle Shoals, AL; WMSU Starkville, MS; WACR-FM Columbus Afb, MS;

US Capital Inc
2975 Valmont Road,#230, Boulder CO 80301
(435) 477-2000; *Fax:*(435) 477-1400
legacy1@infowest.com

Radio Stns: 1 AM.
KENT Parowan, UT;
Lee Weinstein Esq., President

US Stations LLC
125 Corporate Terr., Hot Springs AR 71913
(501) 525-9700; *Fax:*(501) 525-9739
www.usstations.com

Radio Stns: 2 AM. 4 FM.
KWXI Glenwood, AR; KZNG Hot Springs, AR; KYDL(FM) Hot Springs, AR; KQUS-FM Hot Springs, AR; KLBL Pearcy, AR; KLXQ Mountain Pine, AR;
Charles Shinn,
Craig Dale,
Gary Terrell,

VCY America Inc.
3434 W. Kilbourn Ave., Milwaukee WI 53208
(414) 935-3000; *Fax:*(414) 935-3015
www.vcyamerica.org
vcy@vcyamerica.org
Ownership: VCY America, Inc.

Radio Stns: 1 AM. 18 FM.
WVCY Oshkosh, WI; KCVS Salina, KS; KVCX Gregory, SD; KVCY Fort Scott, KS; WVCN Baraga, MI; WEGZ Washburn, WI; WJIC Zanesville, OH; WVCF Eau Claire, WI; WVCX Tomah, WI; WVCY-FM Milwaukee, WI; WVCM Iron Mountain, MI; WVFL Fond Du Lac, WI; KVCF Freeman, SD; WVRN Wittenberg, WI; KVFL Pierre, SD; KVCS Spring Valley, MN; KVCH Huron, SD; WQRN Cook, MN; WVCS Owen, WI;

TV Stns: 1 TV.
WVCY-TV Milwaukee, WI;
Vic Eliason, VP/Gen Mgr
Jim Schneider, Programming Director

Vermont Broadcast Associates Inc.
Box 97, Lyndonville VT 05851
(802) 626-9800; *Fax:*(802) 626-8500
Ownership: Bruce A. James, 100%.

Radio Stns: 1 AM. 5 FM.
WSTJ St. Johnsbury, VT; WGMT Lyndon, VT; WKXH St. Johnsbury, VT; WMTK Littleton, NH; WQJQ Barton, VT; WJJZ Irasberg, VT;
Bruce A. James, President

Vernal Enterprises Inc.
Box 1032, Indiana PA 15701-1032
(724) 543-1380; *Fax:*(724) 543-1140;

Radio Stns: 3 AM.
WNCC Barnesboro, PA; WRDD Ebensburg, PA; WTYM Kittanning, PA;

Vernon R Baldwin Inc.
8686 Michael Ln., Fairfield OH 45014-3015
(513) 829-7700
Ownership: Estate of Vernon R. Baldwin, 100%.

Radio Stns: 2 AM. 5 FM.
WCNW Fairfield, OH; WMOH Hamilton, OH; WNLT Delhi Hills, OH; WKLN Wilmington, OH; WVRB Wilmore, KY; WWLT Manchester, KY; WKYB Burgin, KY;
Marcella Baldwin, President

Vero Beach Broadcasters LLC
1235 16th St., Vero Beach FL 32960
(772) 567-0937; *Fax:*(772) 562-4747
wosnfm.com

Radio Stns: 1 AM. 3 FM.
WTTB Vero Beach, FL; WGYL Vero Beach, FL; WOSN Indian River Shores, FL; WJKD Vero Beach, FL;
Jim Davis, General Manager

VerStandig Broadcasting
4850 Connecticut Ave. N.W.,Suite 103, Washington DC 20008
(202) 244-1422; *Fax:*(202) 362-4149
Ownership: John VerStandig, 1996 VerStandig Children's Trust, M. Belmont VerStandig Trust.

Radio Stns: 3 AM. 5 FM.
WHBG Harrisonburg, VA; WCBG Waynesboro, PA; WSVA Harrisonburg, VA; WTGD Bridgewater, VA; WBHB-FM Waynesboro, PA; WJDV Broadway, VA; WQPO Harrisonburg, VA; WAYZ Hagerstown, MD;
John VerStandig, CEO

Victoria RadioWorks Ltd.
8023 Vantage Dr.,Suite 840, San Antonio TX 78230
(210) 340-7080; *Fax*:(210) 341-1777;
Radio Stns: 2 AM. 3 FM.
KVNN Victoria, TX; KNAL Victoria, TX; KBAR-FM Victoria, TX; KITE Port Lavaca, TX; KVIC Victoria, TX;
John Barger, President
Cindy Cox, General Manager

Vidalia Communications Corp.
Box 900, Vidalia GA 30475
(912) 537-9202; *Fax*:(912) 537-4477
www.vidaliacommunications.com
wtcq@vidaliacommunications.com
Radio Stns: 1 AM. 1 FM.
WVOP Vidalia, GA; WYUM Mount Vernon, GA;
John Ladson, President
Zack Fowler, General Manager

Viper Communications Broadcast Group
Box 225, Osage Beach MO 65065
(573) 348-2772; *Fax*:(573) 348-2779
www.krmsradio.com
Radio Stns: 2 AM. 1 FM.
KRMS Osage Beach, MO; WENG Englewood, FL; KMYK Osage Beach, MO;
Dennis Klautzer, Operations Dir

Visionary Related Entertainment L.L.C.
Box 1437, Wailuku HI 96793
(808) 244-9145; *Fax*:(808) 244-8247
www.kaoi.net
kaoi@kaoi.net
Ownership: Visionary Related Entertainment Inc., 50.1% of votes, 40.58% of total assets; Frontier Radio Investors L.L.C., 49.9% of votes, 59.42% of totalassets.
Radio Stns: 4 AM. 12 FM.
KAOI Kihei, HI; KQNG Lihue, HI; KUAI Eleele, HI; KUMU(AM) Honolulu, HI; KAOI-FM Wailuku, HI; KDLX Makawao, HI; KDDB Waipahu, HI; KPOI-FM Honolulu, HI; KNUQ Paauilo, HI; KQMQ-FM Honolulu, HI; KSHK Kekaha, HI; KSRF Poipu, HI; KUMU-FM Honolulu, HI; KTBH-FM Kurtistown, HI; KMKK-FM Kaunakakai, HI; KHEI-FM Kihei, HI;
John Detz, President
James McKeon, VP

Vox AM/FM LLC
70 Walnut St.,Suite 411, Wellesley MA 2481
(781) 239-8018; *Fax*:(781) 239-8007
voxmedia@aol.com
Radio Stns: 2 AM. 5 FM.
WEAV Plattsburgh, NY; WCVR(AM) Randolph, VT; WCPV Essex, NY; WVXR Randolph, VT; WEZF Burlington, VT; WVTK Port Henry, NY; WXZO Willsboro, NY;

Vox Communications
70 Walnut St., Wellesley MA 02481
(781) 239-8018; *Fax*:(781) 239-8007
www.voxcommunicationsllc.com
voxmedia@aol.com
Radio Stns: 4 AM. 8 FM.
WBEC Pittsfield, MA; WNAW North Adams, MA; WSBS Great Barrington, MA; WUPE Pittsfield, MA; WCNK Key West, FL; WAVK Marathon, FL; WWHK Concord, NH; WUPE-FM North Adams, MA; WSIG Mount Jackson, VA; WBEC-FM Pittsfield, MA; WWUS Big Pine Key, FL; WBOP Buffalo Gap, VA;
Bruce Danziger, CEO
Ken Barlow, COO

W&B Broadcasting Inc
519 North Miles Street,Suite 3, Elizabethtown KY 42701
(270) 351-1188; *Fax*:(270) 351-1275;
Radio Stns: 1 FM.
WAKY Radcliff, KY;
Bill Walters, President

Wagenvoord Advertising Group Inc.
2360 N.E. Coachman Rd., Clearwater FL 33765
(727) 726-8247; *Fax*:(727) 799-8866
www.tantalk1340.com
Radio Stns: 3 AM.
WDCF Dade City, FL; WTAN Clearwater, FL; WZHR Zephyrhills, FL;
Lola Wagenvoord, General Manager

Wagon Wheel Broadcasting LLC
201 N. Union St.,Suite 340, Alexandria VA 22314
(703) 519-3703; *Fax*:(703) 519-9756;
Radio Stns: 3 FM.
WIKI Carrollton, KY; WSCH Aurora, IN; WXCH Columbus, IN;

Wagonwheel Communications Corp.
40 Shoshone Ave., Green River WY 82935
(307) 875-6666; *Fax*:(303) 875-5847
www.theradionetwork.net
kugr@sweetwater.net
Radio Stns: 1 AM. 3 FM.
KUGR Green River, WY; KFRZ Green River, WY; KYCS Rock Springs, WY; KZWB Green River, WY;

Walking by Faith Ministries Inc.
336 Rodenberg Ave., Biloxi MS 39531-3444
(228) 374-9739;
Radio Stns: 3 AM.
WAML Laurel, MS; WQFX Gulfport, MS; WMLC Monticello, MS;
James Black, President

Waller Broadcasting
Box 1648, Jacksonville TX 75766
(903) 586-2527; *Fax*:(903) 586-1394
www.wallerbroadcasting.com
jacksonville@wallerbroadcasting.com
Radio Stns: 1 AM. 4 FM.
KEBE Jacksonville, TX; KZQX Tatum, TX; KFRO-FM Gilmer, TX; KLJT Jacksonville, TX; KMPA Pittsburg, TX;
Dudley Waller, CEO
Dave Moreland, Operations Dir

Wallingford Broadcasting Co.
128 Big Hill Ave., Richmond KY 40475
(859) 623-1340; *Fax*:(859) 623-1341
www.wcyo.com
coyote@chpl.net
Radio Stns: 3 AM. 2 FM.
WEKY Richmond, KY; WIRV Irvine, KY; WKXO Berea, KY; WCYO Irvine, KY; WLFX Berea, KY;
Kelly Wallingford, CEO
Kendra Steele, Operations Dir

Walton Stns
Box 776, Kermit TX 79745
(432) 586-3366; *Fax*:(432) 586-3958
Ownership: John B. Walton, 100%.
Radio Stns: 2 AM. 1 FM.
KBUY Ruidoso, NM; KWES Ruidoso, NM; KWES-FM Ruidoso, NM;
John Walton, President
Harold Oakes, General Manager

WAMC/Northeast Public Radio
318 Central Ave., Albany NY 12206
(518) 465-5233; *Fax*:(518) 432-6974
www.wamc.org
mail@wamc.org
Ownership: Non-stock educ corporation.
Radio Stns: 2 AM. 9 FM.
WAMC Albany, NY; WUTI Utica, NY; WAMC-FM Albany, NY; WAMK Kingston, NY; WAMQ Great Barrington, MA; WANC Ticonderoga, NY; WCAN Canajoharie, NY; WCEL Plattsburgh, NY; WOSR Middletown, NY; WRUN Remsen, NY; WWES Mount Kisco, NY;
Alan Chartock, CEO
David Galletly, SVP/CFO

WAY Media Inc.
Box 64500, Colorado Springs CO 80962
(719) 533-0300
www.wayfm.com
Ownership: Robert D. Augsburg, 12.5%; Joe Battaglia, 12.5%; John Scaggs, 12.5%; Felice Augsburg, 12.5%; Kurt Leander, 12.5%; Dusty Black, 12.5%; Neal Joseph, 12.5%; Nancy Overfield-Delmar, 12.5%.
Radio Stns: 19 FM.
KLWO Longview, WA; KYWA Wichita, KS; WAYF West Palm Beach, FL; WAYJ Naples, FL; WAYM Spring Hill, TN; WAYI Charlestown, IN; WAYP Marianna, FL; WSYI Valley Station, KY; WAYW New Johnsonville, TN; WAYQ Clarksville, TN; WAYH Harvest, AL; WAYT Thomasville, GA; WAYD Auburn, KY; KXWA Centennial, CO; KBWA Brush, CO; KJWA Trinidad, CO; KRWA Rye, CO; WAYU Steele, AL; KFWA(FM) Weldona, CO;
Robert D. Augsburg, President
Lloyd Parker, COO

Wayne County Broadcasting Co.
Box 310, Fairfield IL 62837
(618) 842-2159; *Fax*:(618) 847-5907;
Radio Stns: 1 AM. 2 FM.
WFIW Fairfield, IL; WFIW-FM Fairfield, IL; WOKZ Fairfield, IL;
Thomas Land, Chairman

WENK of Union City Inc.
1729 Nailling Dr., Union City TN 38261
(731) 885-1240; *Fax*:(731) 885-3405
thailey@wenkwtpr.com
Ownership: Bill Latimer; Robert Kirkland; Robert Terrell Jr.
Radio Stns: 2 AM. 3 FM.
WENK Union City, TN; WTPR Paris, TN; WAKQ Paris, TN; WTPR-FM McKinnon, TN; WWKF Fulton, KY;
Bill Latimer, Chairman
Terry Hailey, President

West Alabama Radio Inc.
Box 938, Demopolis AL 36732
(334) 289-9850; *Fax*:(334) 289-9811;
Radio Stns: 1 AM. 2 FM.
WXAL Demopolis, AL; WINL Linden, AL; WZNJ Demopolis, AL;

West Virginia Radio Corp.
1251 Earl L. Core Rd., Morgantown WV 26505
(304) 296-0029; *Fax*:(304) 296-3876
wvmetronews.com
Ownership: John R. Raese, David A. Raese, Dale B. Miller.
Radio Stns: 7 AM. 16 FM.
WAJR Morgantown, WV; WBUC Buckhannon, WV; WKAZ Charleston, WV; WCHS Charleston, WV; WDNE Elkins, WV; WKLP Keyser, WV; WSWW Charleston, WV; WBRB Buckhannon, WV; WBTQ Buckhannon, WV; WDNE-FM Elkins, WV; WDZN Midland, MD; WELK Elkins, WV; WWLW Clarksburg, WV; WKAZ-FM Miami, WV; WKWS Charleston, WV; WQZK-FM Keyser, WV; WRVZ Pocatalico, WV; WFBY Weston, WV; WVAF Charleston, WV; WVAQ Morgantown, WV; WAJR-FM Salem, WV; WVMD Romney, WV; WSWW-FM Craigsville, WV;
Harvey Kercheval, Operations
Joe Parsons, VP/Sales
Dale Miller, President

Westburg Media Capital LP
530 9th Ave., Kirkland WA 98033
(425) 893-9230;
Radio Stns: 2 AM. 2 FM.
KDEB(AM) Estes Park, CO; KRSY Alamogordo, NM; KNMZ Alamogordo, NM; KRSY-FM La Luz, NM;

Western Inspirational Broadcasters Inc
PO Box 21888, Carson City NV 89721
(800) 541-5647
www.pilgrimradio.com
info@pilgrimradio.com
Radio Stns: 2 FM.
KCSP-FM Casper, WY; KCWW Battle Mountain, NV;

Western Slope Communications LLC
751 Horizon Court,Suite 225, Grand Junction CO 81506
(970) 241-6460; *Fax*:(970) 241-6452
www.kissradio.com
kiss@kissradio.com
Radio Stns: 2 AM. 3 FM.
KAVP Colona, CO; KRGS Rifle, CO; KAYW Meeker, CO; KZKS Rifle, CO; KRVG Glenwood Springs, CO;
Steve Wennerstrom, President
John Monroe, General Manager

Weston Entertainment L.P.
112 E. Pecan St.,Suite 1212, San Antonio TX 78205
(386) 423-3289
www.westonentertainment.net
dennis1@ucnsb.net
Radio Stns: 1 AM. 2 FM.
KVRP Stamford, TX; KBHT Crockett, TX; KVRP-FM Haskell, TX;
Dennis W. Goodman, Station Manager

Wheeler Broadcasting Inc.
Box K, Grand Coulee WA 99133-0841
(509) 633-2020; *Fax*:(509) 633-1014
keygfm@nwi.net
Radio Stns: 1 AM. 2 FM.
KEYG Grand Coulee, WA; KEYG-FM Grand Coulee, WA; KXAA Cle Elum, WA;
Verl Wheeler, CEO
Mark Wheeler, Operations Dir

White Mountain Radio
1838 W. Commerce Dr.,Suite A, Lakeside AZ 85929
(928) 368-8100; *Fax*:(928) 368-8108;
Radio Stns: 3 AM. 3 FM.
KDJI Holbrook, AZ; KVSL Show Low, AZ; KVWM Show Low, AZ; KRFM Show Low, AZ; KSNX(FM) Show Low, AZ; KZUA Holbrook, AZ;

F. Lewis Robertson, COO
Henry Ash, President
Joseph Fry, CFO

Wilderness Communications LLC
3501 Northwest Evangeline Thruway, Carencro LA 70520
(337) 896-1600; *Fax:*(337) 896-2695;
Radio Stns: 1 AM.
WROD Daytona Beach, FL;
TV Stns: 2 TV.
KBCA Alexandria, LA; KLWB New Iberia, LA;

Wilkins Communications Network Inc.
Box 444, Spartanburg SC 29304
(864) 585-1885; *Fax:*(864) 597-0687
www.wilkinsradio.com
info@wilkinsradio.com
Ownership: Robert Wilkins; LuAnn Wilkins
Radio Stns: 16 AM.
KCNW Fairway, KS; KLNG Council Bluffs, IA; KXKS Albuquerque, NM; WBRI Indianapolis, IN; WBXR Hazel Green, AL; WCPC Houston, MS; WELP Easley, SC; WFAM Augusta, GA; WITK Pittston, PA; WIJD Prichard, AL; WLMR Chattanooga, TN; WNVY Cantonment, FL; WWNL Pittsburgh, PA; WYYC York, PA; WSKY Asheville, NC; WVTJ Pensacola, FL;
Robert Wilkins, CEO
Mitchell Mathis, President/COO
LuAnn Wilkins, Exec VP

Wilks Broadcast Group LLC
100 North Point Center East,Suite 310, Alpharetta GA 30022
(770) 754-3211; *Fax:*(678) 893-0123
wilksbroadcasting.com
info@wilksbroadcasting.com
Radio Stns: 21 FM.
KBEQ-FM Kansas City, MO; KWOF Broomfield, CO; KFKF-FM Kansas City, KS; KFRR Woodlake, CA; KIMN Denver, CO; KJFX Fresno, CA; KBTE Tulia, TX; KLLL-FM Lubbock, TX; KMMX Tahoka, TX; KMXV Kansas City, MO; KURK Reno, NV; KONE Lubbock, TX; KMXW Sparks, NV; KCKC Kansas City, MO; KWFP Sparks, NV; KTHX-FM Dayton, NV; KJZN San Joaquin, CA; KXKL-FM Denver, CO; WNKK Circleville, OH; WHOK-FM Lancaster, OH; WLVQ Columbus, OH;
Jeff Wilks, CEO
Jeff Sanders, President
Stephen Bradshaw, CFO
Lee Killian, Executive Vice President

William W. McCutchen III Stns
1551 Queens Rd., Los Angeles CA 90069
(323) 656-0796;
Radio Stns: 2 FM.
KQDR Savoy, TX; KMDR McKinleyville, CA;

Williams Communications Inc.
801 Noble St,8th Fl., Suite 30, Anniston AL 36201
(256) 236-1880; *Fax:*(256) 236-4480
whmabig95.com
whmabig95@cableone.net
Radio Stns: 3 AM. 5 FM.
WHMA Anniston, AL; WLTG Panama City, FL; WZZX Lineville, AL; WHMA-FM Hobson City, AL; WTXO Ashland, AL; WFMH-FM Hackleburg, AL; WFXO Southside, AL; WFCT Apalachicola, FL;
Walton Williams Jr., President

Willis Broadcasting Corp.
645 Church St.,Suite 400, Norfolk VA 23510
(757) 622-4600; *Fax:*(757) 624-6515;
Radio Stns: 7 AM. 3 FM.
KDLA De Ridder, LA; KLPL(AM) Lake Providence, LA; WCPK Chesapeake, VA; WGPL Portsmouth, VA; WGRM Greenwood, MS; WPCE Portsmouth, VA; WTJH East Point, GA; WBXB Edenton, NC; WGRM-FM Greenwood, MS; WHLQ Lawrenceville, VA;
Levi Willis, President

Wilson Broadcasting Inc.
805 N. Lena St.,Suite 13, Dothan AL 36303
(334) 671-1753; *Fax:*(334) 677-6923
www.wjjn.greatnow.com
Radio Stns: 1 AM. 2 FM.
WAGF Dothan, AL; WAGF-FM Dothan, AL; WJJN Columbia, AL;
James Wilson III, General Manager

Winton Road Broadcasting Co. LLC
Box 2700, Bakersfield CA 93303
(661) 328-0118; *Fax:*(661) 328-1648;
Radio Stns: 3 AM. 3 FM.
KDGO Durango, CO; KENN Farmington, NM; KVFC Cortez, CO; KISZ-FM Cortez, CO; KPTE Durango, CO; KRWN Farmington, NM;
Rogers Brandon, President

Withers Broadcasting Co.
Box 1508, Mount Vernon IL 62864
(618) 242-3500; *Fax:*(618) 242-4444
Ownership: W. Russell Withers Jr., 100%.
Radio Stns: 13 AM. 20 FM.
KAPE Cape Girardeau, MO; KOKX Keokuk, IA; KRHW Sikeston, MO; KJXX Jackson, MO; WAYE Birmingham, AL; WEBQ Harrisburg, IL; WFRX West Frankfort, IL; WILY Centralia, IL; WMIX Mount Vernon, IL; WMOK Metropolis, IL; WQUL Woodruff, SC; WROY Carmi, IL; WSDR Sterling, IL; KBXB Sikeston, MO; KGMO Cape Girardeau, MO; KOKX-FM Keokuk, IA; KRNQ Keokuk, IA; WDDD-FM Johnston City, IL; WEBQ-FM Eldorado, IL; WGKY Wickliffe, KY; WKIB Anna, IL; WMIX-FM Mount Vernon, IL; WREZ Metropolis, IL; WRUL Carmi, IL; WRXX Centralia, IL; WSSQ Sterling, IL; WTAO-FM Herrin, IL; WYNG Mount Carmel, IL; WVZA Murphysboro, IL; WZZL Reidland, KY; WZZT Morrison, IL; WISH-FM Galatia, IL; WCEZ Carthage, IL;
TV Stns: 3 TV.
WDHS Iron Mountain, MI; WDTV Weston, WV; WVFX Clarksburg, WV;
W. Russell Withers, President

WJAG Inc.
Box 789, Norfolk NE 68702-0789
(402) 371-0780; *Fax:*(402) 371-6303
Ownership: E.F. Huse Jr., 51%; Mary E. Olsen Revocable Trust, Doug Oldaker, trustee, 45%.
Radio Stns: 1 AM. 2 FM.
WJAG Norfolk, NE; KQKX Norfolk, NE; KEXL Pierce, NE;
Bradley S. Hughes, EVP

Wolf Creek Broadcasting Inc.
Box 490, Mineral Bluff GA 30559-0490
(706) 379-9770;
Radio Stns: 1 AM. 1 FM.
WLSB Copper Hill, TN; WACF Young Harris, GA;

WOLF Radio Inc.
401 W. Kirkpatrick St., Syracuse NY 13204
(315) 472-0222; *Fax:*(315) 478-7745;
Radio Stns: 2 AM. 2 FM.
WWLF Auburn, NY; WOLF Syracuse, NY; WMVN Sylvan Beach, NY; WWLF-FM Oswego, NY;
Craig Fox, President

Wolfhouse Radio Group Inc.
548 E. Alisal St., Salinas CA 93905
(831) 757-1910; *Fax:*(831) 757-8015;
Radio Stns: 1 AM. 3 FM.
KTGE Salinas, CA; KMJV Soledad, CA; KRAY-FM Salinas, CA; KEXA King City, CA;
Hector Villalobos, President

Woodrow Michael Warren Stns
Box 106, Alturas CA 96101
(530) 233-4842; *Fax:*(530) 233-4173;
Radio Stns: 2 FM.
KALT-FM Alturas, CA; KLCR Lakeview, OR;
Woodrow Warren, President
Matt Warren, Operations Dir

Woodward Communications Inc.
Box 688, Dubuque IA 52004-0688
(563) 588-5687; *Fax:*(563) 588-5739
www.wcinet.com
Ownership: M. Jeanne Woodward, F. Robert Woodward.
Radio Stns: 2 AM. 5 FM.
WHBY Kimberly, WI; WSCO Appleton, WI; WAPL Appleton, WI; WECB Headland, AL; WCHK-FM Seymour, WI; WZOR Mishicot, WI; WKSZ De Pere, WI;
Tom Yunt, President

Wooster Republican Printing Co.
212 E. Liberty St., Wooster OH 44691
(330) 264-3511; *Fax:*(330) 263-5013
www.dixcom.com
Ownership: (dba Dix Communications).
Radio Stns: 3 AM. 6 FM.
WFRB Frostburg, MD; WKVX Wooster, OH; WTBO Cumberland, MD; WFRB-FM Frostburg, MD; WKGO Cumberland, MD; WNDD Silver Springs, FL; WNDT Alachua, FL; WOGK Ocala, FL; WQKT Wooster, OH;
TV Stns: 1 TV.
KFBB-TV Great Falls, MT;
Dale Gerber, CFO
G. Charles Dix, VP
Robert Dix, TV Division Chairman

Word Broadcasting Network Inc.
Box 19229, Louisville KY 40259
(502) 964-3304; *Fax:*(502) 966-9692
www.wbna21.com
Radio Stns: 3 AM.
WYRM Norfolk, VA; WYMM Jacksonville, FL; WVHI Evansville, IN;
TV Stns: 1 TV.
WBNA Louisville, KY;
Bob Rogers, President
Greg Holt, Operations Dir

World Radio Link Inc.
Box 5429, Twin Falls ID 83303-5429
(208) 733-3551;
Radio Stns: 4 FM.
KMVV Meadow Lakes, AK; WSIZ-FM Jacksonville, GA; WCOP Farmington Township, PA; KXRV Cannon Ball, ND;
Earl Williamson, President

World Radio Network Inc.
Box 3765, McAllen TX 78502-3765
(956) 787-9788; *Fax:*(956) 787-9783
www.wrn-rcm.org
wrn@hcjb.org
Ownership: Non-profit corporation. Note: World Radio Network Inc. is affiliated with World Radio Missionary Fellowship Inc., which operates international swmissionary stn HCJB in Quito, Ecuador.
Radio Stns: 8 FM.
KBNJ Corpus Christi, TX; KBNL Laredo, TX; KBNR Brownsville, TX; KRMB Bisbee, AZ; KRUC Las Cruces, NM; KVER El Paso, TX; KVMV Mc Allen, TX; KYRM Yuma, AZ;
Ted Haney, President
Glenn Lafitte, Director

WRD Entertainment Inc.
Box 2077, Batesville AR 72503
(870) 793-4196; *Fax:*(870) 793-5222
maxfm.com,arkansas103.com
rob@maxfm.com
Radio Stns: 2 AM. 4 FM.
KAAB Batesville, AR; KBTA Batesville, AR; KBTA-FM Batesville, AR; KWOZ Mountain View, AR; KZLE Batesville, AR; KKIK Horseshoe Bend, AR;
John Grace, President
Gary Bridgman, General Manager

Wright Broadcasting Systems
Box 587, Weatherford OK 73096
(580) 772-5939; *Fax:*(580) 772-1590
www.wrightwradio.com
traffic@wrightradio.com
Ownership: G. Harold Wright, 100%.
Radio Stns: 2 AM. 2 FM.
KCLI Clinton, OK; KWEY Weatherford, OK; KCLI-FM Cordell, OK; KWEY-FM Clinton, OK;
G. Harold Wright, President

WS2K Radio LLC dba WS Media
770 E Market St.,Suite 110, West Chester PA 19382
(610) 696-5472; *Fax:*(610) 696-5072
www.ws2kmedia.com
ken@ws2kmedia.com
Radio Stns: 7 AM. 4 FM.
WAZL Hazleton, PA; WCBA Corning, NY; WENI Corning, NY; WENY Elmira, NY; WHYL Carlisle, PA; WCDL Carbondale, PA; WZMF(AM) Nanticoke, PA; WGMM Corning, NY; WTRW(FM) Carbondale, PA; WENY-FM Elmira, NY; WENI-FM Big Flats, NY;
Ira Rosenblatt, CEO
Ken Karaszkiewicz, CFO

Wynne Enterprises LLC
1338 Oregon Ave., Klamath Falls OR 97601
(541) 882-4656; *Fax:*(541) 884-2845
www.klamathradio.com
kflskkrb@aol.com
Ownership: Robert Wynne, Floyd Wynne, Barbara Wynne.
Radio Stns: 1 AM. 2 FM.
KFLS Klamath Falls, OR; KFLS-FM Tulelake, CA; KKRB Klamath Falls, OR;
Floyd Wynne, VP
Robert Wynne, CEO

WZOE Inc.
Box 69, Princeton IL 61356

(815) 875-8014
www.wzoeradio.com
Radio Stns: 1 AM. 2 FM.
WZOE Princeton, IL; WRVY-FM Henry, IL; WZOE-FM Princeton, IL;
Steve Samet, President

Yavapai Broadcasting Corp.
3405 E. Hwy. 89-A,Suite A, Cottonwood AZ 86326
(928) 634-2286; *Fax:*(928) 634-2295
www.myradioplace.com
Radio Stns: 2 AM. 4 FM.
KVNA Flagstaff, AZ; KYBC Cottonwood, AZ; KVNA-FM Flagstaff, AZ; KQST Sedona, AZ; KVRD-FM Cottonwood, AZ; KKLD Cottonwood, AZ;
Grant Hafley, President
David Kessel, General Manager

Zia Broadcasting Co.
Box 1907, Clovis NM 88102-1907
(505) 763-4401; *Fax:*(505) 769-2564
kclv@allsups.com
Ownership: Allsup's Convenience Stores Inc., 100%.
Radio Stns: 3 AM. 3 FM.
KACT Andrews, TX; KCLV Clovis, NM; KQTY Borger, TX; KACT-FM Andrews, TX; KCLV-FM Clovis, NM; KQTY-FM Borger, TX;
Lonnie Alsup, President
Rick Keefer, General Manager

Zimmer Radio Inc.
2702 E. 32nd St., Joplin MO 64804
(417) 624-1025; *Fax:*(417) 781-6842
www.joplinradio.com
Radio Stns: 2 AM. 5 FM.
KZRG Joplin, MO; KZYM Joplin, MO; KCLR-FM Boonville, MO; KIXQ Joplin, MO; KJMK Webb City, MO; KSYN Joplin, MO; KXDG Webb City, MO;
James Zimmer, President
Larry Boyd, General Manager

Zoe Communications Inc.
Box 190, Shell Lake WI 54871
(715) 468-9500; *Fax:*(715) 468-9505
www.zoestations.com
Radio Stns: 3 AM. 2 FM.
WCSW Shell Lake, WI; WPDR Portage, WI; WRDN Durand, WI; WDMO Baldwin, WI; WPLT Sarona, WI;
Wendy Oberg, General Manager

Key to Radio Listings

Radio listings include Radio stations in the United States, its territories and Canada. All collected data for these listings include information current to fall 2012. To use the radio key, see boldface numbers and corresponding explanations.

(1) KSDS-FM (2) On air date: n/a **(3)** Frequency: 88.3 mhz (3a) KSDS broadcasts in stereo. (3b) KSDS broadcasts 24 hours a day. **(4)** 1313 Park Blvd., San Diego, CA 92108; Phone: (619) 292-2000 FAX: (619) 388-3928. Web Site: www.jazz88.org. **(5)** Licensee: San Diego, San Diego County, CA held by San Diego Community College District. **(6)** Population served: 696,679. **(7)** Network: NPR; Arbitron Metro Market: San Diego, CA; Hrs of News Programming: 7 hrs weekly; Number of News Employees: 1; Target Audience: 25-65 plus, affluent professional adults. **(8)** Key Personnel:
Joseph Kocherhams . . . . Executive Director
Mark DeBoskey . . . . Station Manager
Ann Bauer . . . . General Sales Manger
Claudia Russell . . . . Programming Director
(9) KSDS frequency is 88.3 mhz, with 22 kilowatts of radiated power and an antenna height of 246 ft above average terrain, KSDS broadcasts in stereo (see (3a)). **(10)** Programming: Jazz format. **(11)** Co-Ownership: No.

(1) Station call letters as assigned by the Federal Communications Commission (FCC) or Canadian Radio-television and Telecommunications Commission (CRTC)

(2) Date station first went on the air (regardless of subsequent owner changes).

(3) Frequency in kilohertz.

(4) Address and zip code, telephone, fax, web site and email address.

(5) Licensee name and date of acquisition (if not original owner). If the licensee is a group owner-company with several broadcast properties is so identified, as a group owner of which the licensee is a subsidiary. Details on group owners are listed in the Group Owner section. If the station has been sold and the sale information is available, it is recorded after the acquisition date.

(6) Population served refers to the station's potential market.

(7) Network, representative and programming.

(8) Key personnel.

(9) Frequency, kilowatts of effective radiated power, antenna height, and broadcasting.

(10) Programming and format.

(11) Co-ownership.

An asterisk (*) preceding station call letters indicates noncommercial stations

Radio Stations in the United States

Alabama

Abbeville

***WIZB**
02-02-1968; 94.3 mhz FM *Hrs Open:* 24; 19.5 kw; 371 ft.; N31 26 19 W85 17 22
Mailing Address: Post Ofc Box 126, Headland, AL 36345 US
Second Address: 2563 Montgomery Hwy., Dothan, AL 36303
(334) 699-5672, *Fax:* (334) 699-5034
www.hisradio943.com
ekelley@hisradio943.com
License: Abbeville, Henry County, AL held by Radio Training Network, Inc.
Arbitron Metro Market: Dothan, AL *Format:* Christian *Hrs. of News Programming:* News progmg 3 hrs wkly *Target Audience:* 25-49; women *Adv. Rates:* 28; 26; 25; 18
Jim Campbell, CEO
Earl Kelley, General Manager
Russell Brooks, Programming Director
K.W. Keene, Promotions Manager
Melinda McKenna, News Director
Neal Riddle, Engineering Dir

Addison

WQAH-FM
01-01-1996; 105.7 mhz FM *Hrs Open:* 24; 6 kw; 328 ft.; N34 18 19 W87 4 24
Mailing Address: 2231 Burningtree Drive, Decatur, AL 35603 US
Second Address: 219 Chestnut St, Hartelle, AL 35640
(256) 773-2563, *Fax:* (256) 773-6915
www.wqah.com
info@WQAH.com
License: Addison, Winston County, AL held by Abercrombie Broadcasting FM Inc.
Arbitron Metro Market: Addison, FL *Format:* Country
Alvin Abercrombie, President
Carol Lynn, General Manager
Keith Abercrombie, Engineering Dir
Mark Donovan, Disc Jockey

Alabaster

WQCR
09-28-1981; 1500 khz AM *Hrs Open:* Sunrise-sunset
PO Box X 584, Alabaster, AL 35007 US
(508) 771-1224, *Fax:* (508) 775-2605
www.wqrc.com
joelrivera1500am@yahoo.com
License: Alabaster, AL held by Rivera Communications LLC
Arbitron Metro Market: Birmingham, AL
Maria Esparza, Operations Dir
Joel Rivera, General Manager
Israel deJesus, Programming Director

Albertville

WAVU
01-01-1947; 630 khz AM *Hrs Open:* 24; 1 kw-D, 28 w-N; N34 14 19 W86 09 59
Mailing Address: Box 190, Albertville, AL 35950
Second Address: 3770 US Hwy. 431, Albertville, AL 35951
(256) 878-8575, *Fax:* (256) 878-1051
tommylee@wqsb.com
License: Albertville, Marshall County, AL held by Sand Mountain Broadcasting Service Inc.
Nat'l Network: AP Radio *Wire Services:* AP
Population Served: 25,000*No. News Employees:* 1 *Target Audience:* 35 plus. *Adv. Rates:* 10; 8; 9; 3
Pat Courington Jr., President
Tommy Lee, General Manager
Ted McCreless, General Sales Mgr
Dale Stallings, Programming Director
Al Taylor, News Director

WQSB
01-01-1948; 105.1 mhz FM *Hrs Open:* 24; 2.7 kw; 1001 ft.; N34 9 27 W86 2 44
Mailing Address: P.O Box 190, Albertville, AL 35950 US
Second Address: 3770 US Hwy. 431, Albertville, AL 35951
(256) 878-8575, *Fax:* (256) 878-1051
www.wqsb.com
wqsb@aol.com
License: Albertville, Marshall County, AL held by Sand Mountain Broadcasting Service Inc.
Wire Services: AP
Format: Country *No. News Employees:* 1 *Target Audience:* 25-54. *Adv. Rates:* 68; 58; 63; 20
Tommy Lee, General Manager
Ted McCreless, General Sales Mgr
Barry Galloway, Programming Director
Dale Stallings, Music Director
Al Taylor, News Director

WWGC
04-01-1982; 1090 khz AM *Hrs Open:* 6 AM-7:15 PM
P.O. Box 889, Albertville, AL 35950 US
(256) 894-6294, *Fax:* (256) 894-6495
wwgc1090@yahoo.com
License: Albertville, AL held by Quality Properties LLC
Arbitron Metro Market: Albertville, AL *Format:* Spanish
Jeff Beck, General Manager
Joel Arriga, Programming Director

Alexander City

WBNM
05-31-1947; 1050 khz AM *Hrs Open:* 24
908 Opelika Road, Auburn, AL 36830 US
(256) 215-7296
License: Alexander City, AL held by William and Margaret Neeck, Co-Trustees
Nat'l Network: ABC *Regional Network:* Alabama Radio Net.
Format: Gospel, Sports *Adv. Rates:* 7; 5; 7; 5
Ralph Turpen, President

WSTH-FM
09-30-1949; 106.1 mhz FM *Hrs Open:* 24; 86 kw; 1047 ft.; N32 45 30 W85 28 20
Mailing Address: P.O. Box 1640, Columbus, GA 31994 US
Second Address: 1501 13th Ave., Columbus, GA 31901
(706) 576-3000, *Fax:* (706) 576-3010
www.rooster106online.com
info@rooster106online.com
License: Alexander City, Tallapoosa County, AL held by CC Licenses LLC.
Group Owner: Clear Channel Communications Inc.; (acq 5-9-2003; $2.73 million with WDAK(AM) Columbus, GA).
Nat'l Network: ABC
Arbitron Metro Market: Columbus, GA *Format:* Country *No. News Employees:* 1 *Target Audience:* General.
Brian Waters, Operations Dir
Jim Martin, General Manager

***WJHO**
01-01-2008; 89.7 mhz FM; 10.5 kw vert; 492 ft.; N33 12 30 W85 59 31
US
(334) 705-8004, *Fax:* (334) 705-8006
www.wjhofm.com
webmaster@wjhofm.com
License: Alexander City, Tallapoosa County, AL held by Jimmy Jarrell Communications Foundation Inc.
Arbitron Metro Market: Alexander City, AL *Format:* Gospel
Jimmy Jarrell, President

Andalusia

WAAO-FM
08-24-1987; 103.7 mhz FM *Hrs Open:* 24; 3 kw; 328 ft.; N31 20 27 W86 28 2
PO Bx 987 2121 E Bypass, Andalusia, AL 36420 US
(800) 877-5600, *Fax:* (916) 251-1650
www.air1.com, info@air1.com
License: Andalusia, Covington County, AL held by Companion Broadcasting Service Inc.
Arbitron Metro Market: McAllen-Brownsville-Harlingen TX
Format: Alternative, Christian
Mike Novak, President

***WSTF**
03-01-1996; 91.5 mhz FM; 20.5 kw; 361 ft.; N31 26 20 W86 30 48
P.O. Box 210789, Montgomery, AL 36121 US
(334) 271-8900, *Fax:* (334) 260-8962
www.faithradio.org
mail@faithradio.org
License: Andalusia, Covington County, AL held by Faith Broadcasting Inc.
Format: Adult Contemp, Religious
Russell Dean, General Manager
Gary Hundley, General Sales Mgr

***WDWZ**
89.3 mhz FM; 700 w; 108 m; N31 17 47.9 W86 30 09.6
828 20th St. SW, Lanett, AL
(706)518-3911
License: Andalusia, Covington County, AL held by B. Jordan Communications Corp.
Ben Jordan, President

Anniston

WSYA(AM)
08-01-1954; 1490 khz AM *Hrs Open:* 24; 1 kw-U; N33 41 15 W85 49 49
Box 7785, 1913 Barry St., Suite B, Oxford, AL 36203
(256) 741-6088, *Fax:* (256) 741-6080
www.wtdrthunder.com
jimj@wtdrthunder.com
License: Anniston, Calhoun County, AL held by Jacobs Broadcast Group Inc.
Wire Services: AP
Population Served: 22,959 *Arbitron Metro Market:* Anniston, Al *Format:* Country *No. News Employees:* 1 *Adv. Rates:* 18; 16; 17; 14
Jim Jacobs, President
Laura Jacobs, Operations Dir

WDNG
07-01-1957; 1450 khz AM *Hrs Open:* 24; 1 kw-U, ND1; N33 40 1 W85 50 56
1115 Leighton Avenue, Anniston, AL 36201 US
(256) 236-8291, *Fax:* (256) 236-8292
www.wdng.net
jj@wdng.net
License: Anniston, AL held by WDNG Inc.
Nat'l Network: CBS
Arbitron Metro Market: Anniston, AL *Format:* News, News/Talk, 86 *Target Audience:* General.
J.J. Dark, President
Pamela, Operations Dir
Jim, General Manager

***WGRW**
07-01-1999; 90.7 mhz FM *Hrs Open:* 24; 3 kw vert; 328 ft.; N33 46 41 W85 56 38
Mailing Address: P.O. Box 2555, Anniston, AL 36202 US
Second Address: 4265 Hill St., Anniston, AL 36206
(256) 238-9990, *Fax:* (256) 237-1102
www.graceradio.com
jon@graceradio.com
License: Anniston, Calhoun County, AL held by Word Works Inc.
Nat'l Network: Moody
Format: Christian
Aaron Acker, President
Jon Holder, General Manager

WHMA
01-01-1938; 1390 khz AM *Hrs Open:* 24; 5 kw-D, DAN; 1 kw-N, DAN; N33 42 31 W85 51 14
140 East Market Street, York, PA 17401 US
(256) 237-8741, *Fax:* (256) 231-9414
www.whmabig95.com
texbig95@cableone.net
License: Anniston, AL held by Williams Communications Inc.
Group Owner: Williams Communications Inc.; acq 8-12-2003; $275,000).
Format: Gospel *Hrs. of News Programming:* news progmg 12 hrs wkly *No. News Employees:* 1 *Target Audience:* 25-54; those with upscale, mobile, discretionary incomes
Walt Williams, General Manager
John Goodbread, Programming Director

Arab

WAFN-FM
11-05-1979; 92.7 mhz FM *Hrs Open:* 24; 1.15 kw; 663 ft.; N34 20 40.6 W86 26 23.3
6121 Marwinette Avenue, St. Louis, MO 63116 US
(256) 586-9300, *Fax:* (256) 586-9301
www.fun927.com
funhouse@fun927.com
License: Arab, Marshall County, AL held by Fun Media Group Inc.
Nat'l Network: CNN Radio
Arbitron Metro Market: Arab, AL *Format:* Oldies *Hrs. of News Programming:* news progmg 3 hrs wkly *No. News Employees:* 1 *Target Audience:* 18-54.
Susan McKenney, President
Michael St. John, Operations Dir
Suan McKenney, General Sales Mgr

WRAB
10-25-1961; 1380 khz AM *Hrs Open:* 6am-6pm; 1 kw-D, ND1; 0.049 kw-N, ND1; N34 20 6 W86 28 7
Mailing Address: P.O. Box 625, Arab, AL 35016 US
Second Address: 619 S. Brindlee Mountain Pkwy., Arab, AL 35016
(256) 586-4123, *Fax:* (256) 586-4124
www.wrab.net
wrab@otclco.net
License: Arab, AL held by Reed Broadcasting LLC

Wire Services: AP
Format: Country, Gospel, 74 *Hrs. of News Programming:* news progmg 12 hrs. wkly *No. News Employees:* 1 *Adv. Rates:* 8; 6.50; 6.50; na
Ed Reed, President
Archie Anderson, General Manager

Ashland

WTXO
12-20-1959; 98.3 mhz FM *Hrs Open:* 24; 1.7 kw; Ant 617 ft; N33 18 30 W85 50 58
801 Noble St. 8th Fl., Suite 30, Anniston, AL 35150
(256) 236-1880, *Fax:* (256) 231-9414
www.rock983.net
License: Ashland, Clay County, AL held by Williams Communications Inc.
Group Owner: Williams Communications Inc.; (acq 8-16-2001)
Nat'l Network: ABC
No. News Employees: 1 *Target Audience:* 25-54.
Eva Gibson, General Manager

WCKF
12-17-2007; 100.7 mhz FM; 1.9 kw; Ant 590 ft; N33 19 14.2 W85 51 39.2
PO Box 10, Ashland, AL
(256) 354-1444, *Fax:* (256) 254-1445
License: Ashland, Clay County, AL held by Alabama 810 LLC.
Nat'l Network: Fox *Regional Network:* Alabama Radio Net.
Hrs. of News Programming: news progmg 5 hrs wkly *No. News Employees:* 1
Teresa Goodman, CEO/COO
E. Gradick, Engineer/Owner
Leslie Gradick, General Manager
Teresa Goodman, Station Manager
Alicia Hamburger, General Sales Mgr
Teresa Goodman, Programming Director
Andy Evans, Promotions Manager
MikeMitchell, News Director

Athens

WKAC
09-01-1964; 1080 khz AM *Hrs Open:* Sunrise-sunset; 2.5 kw-C, NDD; 5 kw-D, NDD; N34 50 13 W86 58 28
Mailing Address: P.O. Box 1083, Athens, AL 35612 US
Second Address: 19245 Hwy. 127, Athens, AL 35614
(256) 232-6827, *Fax:* (256) 232-6828
www.wkac1080.com
wkac@companet.net
License: Athens, AL held by Limestone Broadcasting Co.
Nat'l Network: CNN Radio
Arbitron Metro Market: Huntsville, AL *Format:* Oldies *Special Programming:* Farm 5 hrs *Hrs. of News Programming:* News progmg 6 hrs wkly *Target Audience:* 25-54; adults mid/upper income, blue/white collar *Adv.Rates:* 10; 8; 10; n/a
Kenneth Casey, President
Keith Casey, General Manager
Kirk Harvey, Programming Director
Joyce Casey, News Director

WVNN
11-08-1948; 770 khz AM *Hrs Open:* 24
P.O. Box 389, Athens, AL 35611 US
(256) 830-8300, *Fax:* (256) 232-6842
www.wvnn.com
dale@wvnn.com
License: Athens, AL held by Cumulus Licensing LLC.
Group Owner: Cumulus Media Inc.; (acq 7-21-2003; grpsl)
Nat'l Network: ABC *Nat'l Reps:* Katz Radio
Arbitron Metro Market: Huntsville, AL *Format:* News, News/Talk, 86 *Hrs. of News Programming:* news progmg 60 hrs wkly *Target Audience:* 25-64.
Brian Zabomy, Operations Dir
Bill West, General Manager
Tracy Flesch, General Sales Mgr
Dale Jackson, Programming Director
Aaron Hurd, Promotions Manager
Audrey Raines, News Director
Chuck Miller, Chief Engineer

WZYP
10-01-1958; 104.3 mhz FM *Hrs Open:* 24; 100 kw; 1115 ft.; N34 49 6 W86 44 16
P.O. Box 389, Athens, AL 35611 US
(256) 830-8300, *Fax:* (256) 232-6842
www.wzyp.com
steve.smith@cumulus.com
License: Athens, Limestone County, AL
Group Owner: Cumulus Media Inc.
Nat'l Reps: Katz Radio
Arbitron Metro Market: Athens, AL *Format:* Contemporary Hits/Top 40 *Hrs. of News Programming:* news progmg 3 hrs wkly *Target Audience:* 18-49.
Brian Zaborny, Operations Dir
Bill West, General Manager
Tracy Flesch, General Sales Mgr
Steve Smith, Programming Director
Aaron Hurd, Promotions Manager
Audrey Raines, News Director
Chuck Miller, Engineering Dir

Atmore

WDLT-FM
05-19-1966; 104.1 mhz FM *Hrs Open:* 24; 100 kw; Ant 1,555 ft; N30 37 35 W87 38 50
2800 Dauphin St., #104, Mobile, AL 36606-2400
(251) 652-2000, *Fax:* (251) 652-2001
www.jack104online.com
mobile.prog@cumulus.com
License: Atmore, Escambia County, AL held by Cumulus Licensing Corp.
Group Owner: Cumulus Media Inc.; (acq 10-18-99; grpsl)
Population Served: 954,300 *Arbitron Metro Market:* Mobile, AL *Format:* Adult Contemp *Hrs. of News Programming:* news progmg 5 hrs wkly *No. News Employees:* 1 *Target Audience:* 25-40.
Steve Crumbely, Operations Dir
Gary Pizzati, General Manager

Attalla

WKXX
08-31-1991; 102.9 mhz FM *Hrs Open:* 24; 1.1 kw; 702 ft.; N33 58 28 W86 12 24
Mailing Address: Post Office Box 190, Albertville, AL 35950 US
Second Address: Box 8405, Gadsden, AL 35902
(256) 442-3944, *Fax:* (256) 442-7287
www.wkxx.com
tommylee@wasc.com
License: Attalla, Etowah County, AL held by Broadcast Media L.L.C.
Wire Services: AP
Format: Adult Contemp *Hrs. of News Programming:* news progmg 2 hrs wkly *No. News Employees:* 1 *Target Audience:* 18-49. *Adv. Rates:* 35; 20; 25; 18
Pat Courington, CEO
Tommy Lee, General Manager
Ted McReless, General Sales Mgr
Brandon Murray, Programming Director
Dave Fitz, News Director

Auburn

WAUD
12-22-1947; 1230 khz AM *Hrs Open:* 24
320 Barnett Blvd, Tallassee, AL 30678 US
(334) 887-3401, *Fax:* (334) 826-9599
info@thetiger.fm
License: Auburn, AL held by Tiger Communications Inc.
Group Owner: Tiger Communications Inc.; (acq 2-26-98)
Nat'l Network: CBS Radio *Regional Network:* Alabama Radio Net. *Nat'l Reps:* Rgnl Reps
Arbitron Metro Market: Dubuque, IA *Format:* Big Band, Jazz, 84 *Hrs. of News Programming:* news progmg 7 hrs wkly *No. News Employees:* 1 *Target Audience:* 25 plus. *Adv. Rates:* 12; 10; 10; 8
Chris Bailey, General Manager

*WEGL
04-25-1971; 91.1 mhz FM *Hrs Open:* 24; 3 kw; 213 ft.; N32 36 11 W85 29 12
Samford Hall, Auburn, AL 36849 US
(334) 844-4114, *Fax:* (334) 844-4118
wegl.auburn.edu
greendm@auburn.edu
License: Auburn, Lee County, AL held by Board of Trustees Auburn University.
Arbitron Metro Market: Auburn, AL *Format:* Alternative *Special Programming:* Various specialty shows *Hrs. of News Programming:* news progmg 6 hrs wkly *No. News Employees:* 1 *Target Audience:* Collegestudents.
Elizabeth Kent, General Manager
Natalie Stevenson, Station Manager
Rachel Warfield, Programming Director
Kasey Langley, Promotions Manager
Chandler White, Music Director

WKKR
07-08-1968; 97.7 mhz FM *Hrs Open:* 24; 3.1 kw; 453 ft.; N32 33 54 W85 22 13
Mailing Address: 139 Executive Circle, Suite 203, Daytona Beach, FL 32114 US
Second Address: 915 Veterans Pkwy., Opelika, AL 36801
(334) 745-4657, *Fax:* (334) 749-1520
www.kickerfm.com
genmorj@charter.net
License: Auburn, Lee County, AL held by Qantum of Auburn License Co. LLC.
Group Owner: Qantum Communications Corp.; (acq 7-2-2003; grpsl)
Format: Country *Hrs. of News Programming:* news progmg 7 hrs wkly *No. News Employees:* 2 *Target Audience:* 25-54.
Frank Osborn, President
Sandy Mathews, General Sales Mgr
Bill Morgan, Programming Director
Ruth Law, Promotions Manager

Bay Minette

WTOF
01-01-1958; 1110 khz AM; 2.5 kw-C, ND2; 10 kw-D, ND2; N30 52 10 W87 46 9
720 South White Avenue, Bay Minette, AL 36507 US
(435) 649-9004, *Fax:* (435) 645-9063
License: Bay Minette, AL held by Buddy Tucker Association Inc.
Group Owner: Buddy Tucker Association Inc.; (acq 1-16-2007; $300,000)
Arbitron Metro Market: Sioux Falls SD
Blair Feulner, General Manager

WNSP
10-01-1964; 105.5 mhz FM *Hrs Open:* 24; 5.3 kw; 348 ft.; N30 49 34 W87 51 52
2163 Venetia Road, Mobile, AL 36605 US
(251) 438-5460, *Fax:* (251) 438-5462
www.wnsp.com
wnsp@wnsp.com
License: Bay Minette, Baldwin County, AL held by Dot Com+ L.L.C.
Arbitron Metro Market: Mobile, AL *Format:* Sports *Target Audience:* 18-49.
Ken Johnson, President
Clint Crouch, Operations Dir
Ken Johnson, General Manager
Kenny Johnson, General Sales Mgr
Chip Ramsey, Programming Director
Ryan Foster, Promotions Manager

Bessemer

WZGX
06-01-1950; 1450 khz AM; 1 kw-U, ND1; N33 25 23 W86 57 17
P.O. Box 368, Bessemer, AL 35020 US
(205) 428-0146, *Fax:* (205) 426-3178
www.doblex1450.com
License: Bessemer, AL held by Bessemer Radio Inc.
Arbitron Metro Market: Birmingham, AL
Joel Garcia, General Manager
Jerry Lopez, Programming Director

*WSJL
01-01-2008; 88.1 mhz FM; 0.01 kw horiz, 15 kw vert; 492 ft.; N33 28 51 W87 24 3
516 S Fourth Street, Las Vegas, NV 89101 US
(817) 641-3495
License: Bessemer, Tuscaloosa County, AL held by Mary V. Harris Foundation.
Arbitron Metro Market: Tuscaloosa, AL
Linda De Romanett, President

Birmingham

WAGG
01-01-1927; 610 khz AM; 5 kw-D, DAN; 1 kw-N, DAN; N33 29 40 W86 52 30
3773 Howard Hughes Pwy, Suite 300n, Las Vegas, NV 89109 US
(205) 322-2987, *Fax:* (205) 322-2390
www.wagg610.com,www.987.q.com
david.dubose@coxradio.com
License: Birmingham, AL held by Cox Radio Inc.
Group Owner: Cox Radio Inc.; (acq 9-9-97)
Nat'l Network: ABC *Nat'l Reps:* Christal *Wire Services:* AP
Arbitron Metro Market: Birmingham, AL *Format:* Gospel *Hrs. of News Programming:* news progmg 5 hrs wkly *No. News Employees:* 2 *Target Audience:* 45 plus. *Adv. Rates:* 200; 75; 100; 25
David DuBose, General Manager
David Ellis, General Sales Mgr
Darryl Johnson, Programming Director
Kori White, Promotions Manager

WAPI
01-01-1922; 1070 khz AM *Hrs Open:* 24; 50 kw-D, DAN; 5 kw-N, DAN; N33 33 7 W86 54 40
244 Goodwin Crest Drive, Suite 300, Birmingham, AL 35209 US
(205) 945-4646, *Fax:* (205) 945-3999
www.100wapi.com
License: Birmingham, AL held by Citadel Broadcasting Co.
Group Owner: Cumulus Media Inc
Nat'l Reps: Christal
Arbitron Metro Market: Birmingham, AL *Format:* News, News/Talk, 86 *Target Audience:* 35 plus.
Dale Daniels, General Manager
Hertisene Riley, General Sales Mgr
Jacob Allison, Programming Director
Laurence Salvary, Promotions Manager

WATV
05-20-1946; 900 khz AM *Hrs Open:* 24 hrs
3025 Ensley Ave, Birmingham, AL 35208 US
(205) 780-2014, *Fax:* (205) 780-4034
www.900goldwatv.com/
rjanuary@watv900.com
License: Birmingham, AL held by McL/McM Alabama LLC.
Group Owner: Sheridan Broadcasting Corp.; (acq 10-12-2004; $1.5 million)
Nat'l Network: American Urban *Nat'l Reps:* Interep
Arbitron Metro Market: Birmingham, AL *Format:* Black, Oldies, 74 *Target Audience:* 18 plus.
Ron Davenport, President
Ron January, Operations Dir

WAYE
08-01-1972; 1220 khz AM *Hrs Open:* 24 hours; 1 kw-D, ND1; 0.075 kw-N, ND1; N33 28 39 W86 50 57
C/O Putbrese Hunsaker Et, PO Box 217, Sterling, VA 20167 US
(360) 425-1500, *Fax:* (360) 423-1554
grodman@biocoastalmedia.com
License: Birmingham, AL held by Birmingham Christian Radio, Inc
Group Owner: Withers Broadcasting Co.; unk.
Arbitron Metro Market: Rainier OR *Format:* Adult Contemp
Kevin Mostyn, Operations Dir

***WBFR**
01-01-1988; 89.5 mhz FM; 0.1 kw vert; 673 ft.; N33 29 2 W86 48 35
Mailing Address: 4135 Northgate Blvd, Suite 1, Sacramento, CA 95834 US
Second Address: 290 Hegenberger Rd., Oakland, CA 94621
1-(800)-543-1495, *Fax:* (916) 641-8238 (510) 633-7983
www.familyradio.com
familyradio@familyradio.org
License: Birmingham, Jefferson County, AL held by Family Stations Inc.
Group Owner: Family Stations Inc.
Arbitron Metro Market: Oakland, CA *Format:* Christian, Religious
Stanley Jackson, Operations Dir

***WBHM**
12-01-1976; 90.3 mhz FM *Hrs Open:* 24; 32 kw; 1214 ft.; N33 29 19 W86 47 58 *Rebroadcasts:* Rebroadcasts WSGN(FM) Gadsden 100%
1028 7th Avenue South, Birmingham, AL 35294 US
(205) 934-2606, *Fax:* (205) 934-5075
www.wbhm.org
info@wbhm.org
License: Birmingham, Jefferson County, AL held by Board of Trustees, University of Alabama.
Nat'l Network: NPR; PRI *Wire Services:* AP
Arbitron Metro Market: Birmingham, AL *Format:* News *Special Programming:* New age 6 hrs wkly *Hrs. of News Programming:* news progmg 74 hrs wkly *No. News Employees:* 3 *Target Audience:* General.
Scott E. Hanley, General Manager
Mary Hendley, General Sales Mgr
Michael Krall, Programming Director
Tanya Ott, News Director
Dave Shy, Underwriting Manager
Audrey Atkins, Marketing Manager
Mary Hendley, Development Director
Ernest Williams, Financial and Business Manager

WYDE
03-25-1953; 1260 khz AM; 5 kw-D, ND2; 0.041 kw-N, ND2; N33 31 29 W86 47 10
P.O. Box 3003, Blue Bell, PA 19422 US
(205) 879-3324, *Fax:* (205) 802-4555
www.101wyde.com
thejunction@wdjconline.com
License: Birmingham, AL held by Kimtron Inc.
Group Owner: Crawford Broadcasting Co.; (acq 1994)
Nat'l Reps: McGavren Guild
Arbitron Metro Market: Birmingham, AL *Format:* News, News/Talk, 86
Steve Armstrong, General Manager
Jennifer Paepcke, General Sales Mgr
Melodye Grubb, News Director
Todd Dixon, Chief Engineer

WDJC-FM
04-22-1968; 93.7 mhz FM; 99 kw; 1007 ft.; N33 26 36 W86 52 50
P.O. Box 3003, Blue Bell, PA 19422 US
(205) 879-3324, *Fax:* (205) 802-4555
www.wdjconline.com
thejunction@wdjconline.com
License: Birmingham, Jefferson County, AL held by Kimtron Inc.
Group Owner: Crawford Broadcasting Co.
Arbitron Metro Market: Birmingham, AL *Format:* Christian *Target Audience:* 25-60; conservative middle income
Steve Armstrong, General Manager
Tom LoPresti, General Sales Mgr

WERC
05-25-1925; 960 khz AM
600 Congress Avenue, Suite 1400, Austin, TX 78701 US
(205) 439-9600, *Fax:* (205) 439-8390
www.wercfm.com
aarontrimmer@clearchannel.com
License: Birmingham, AL held by Capstar TX L.P.
Group Owner: Clear Channel Communications Inc.
Arbitron Metro Market: Birmingham, AL *Format:* News, News/Talk, 86 *Target Audience:* Adults.
Ray Quinn, General Sales Mgr
Aaron Trimmer, Programming Director
Lacey Walker, Promotions Manager
Jim Faherty, News Director
Shelia Howell, Traffic Manager
Kevin Klein, Director of Sales

WENN
01-01-1950; 1320 khz AM; 5 kw-D, ND2; 0.111 kw-N, ND2; N33 33 41 W86 51 37
3773 Howard Hughes Pwy, Suite 300n, Las Vegas, NV 89109 US
(205) 916-1100, *Fax:* (205) 290-1061
www.wzzk.com
David.Walls@coxradio.com
License: Birmingham, AL held by Cox Radio Inc.
Group Owner: Cox Radio Inc.; (acq 3-28-97; grpsl)
Nat'l Reps: Christal
Arbitron Metro Market: Birmingham, AL
Ray Nelson, General Manager
David Walls, General Sales Mgr
Paul Orr, Programming Director
Justin Ragland, Promotions Manager
Paul Bankston, National Sales Manager
Kelsey Dollar, Internet Manager

***WGIB**
01-01-1983; 91.9 mhz FM *Hrs Open:* 24; 3.5 kw; 873 ft.; N33 24 59 W86 36 28
1137 10th Place South, Birmingham, AL 35256 US
(205) 323-1516, *Fax:* (205) 323-2747
www.gleniris.net
nmills@gleniris.net
License: Birmingham, Jefferson County, AL held by Glen Iris Baptist School
Arbitron Metro Market: Birmingham, AL *Format:* Christian
Chris Lamb, Chairman
Dan Ratje, Operations Dir

WSPZ(AM)
10-15-1947; 690 khz AM; 50 kw-D, 500 w-N, DA-N; N33 26 56 W86 55 18
244 Goodwin Crest Dr., Suite 300, Birmingham, AL 35209-3714
(205) 945-4646, *Fax:* (205) 945-3999
www.sportstalk570.com
management@espn980.com
License: Birmingham, Jefferson County, AL
Group Owner: Cumulus Media Inc.; (acq 4-26-2001; grpsl)
Wire Services: SportsTicker
Population Served: 375,900 *Arbitron Metro Market:* Birmingham, AL *Format:* Sports *Special Programming:* Gospel 5 hrs wkly *Target Audience:* 25-54.
Kerry Lambert, Operations Dir
Dale Daniels, General Manager
Lenny Frisaro, General Sales Mgr
Ryan Haney, Programming Director
Jennifer Dickson, Promotions Manager
Lisa Holifield, News Director
Steve Harrison, National SalesManager
Will Berry, Public Affairs Director

***WJSR**
08-11-1977; 91.1 mhz FM *Hrs Open:* 24; 0.23 kw; 194 ft.; N33 39 7 W86 42 20
2601 Carson Road, Birmingham, AL 35215 US
(205) 856-6095, *Fax:* (205) 856-7702
www.angelfire.com
License: Birmingham, Jefferson County, AL held by Jefferson State Community College.
Arbitron Metro Market: Birmingham, AL *Format:* Classic Rock *Hrs. of News Programming:* News progmg 4 hrs wkly *Target Audience:* 24-49; college population
Ray Edwards, General Manager

***WLJR**
01-01-1998; 88.5 mhz FM *Hrs Open:* 24; 0 kw horiz, 0.37 kw vert; 600 ft.; N33 23 51 W86 39 41
2200 Briarwood Way, Birmingham, AL 35243 US
(205) 978-2200, *Fax:* (205) 824-8419
www.wljr.org
info@wljr.org
License: Birmingham, Jefferson County, AL held by Briarwood Presbyterian Church.
Nat'l Network: Moody
Arbitron Metro Market: Birmingham, AL *Format:* Variety/Diverse, Religious *Hrs. of News Programming:* News progmg 10 hrs wkly *Target Audience:* General; upper middle class
James Hulgan, General Manager

WMJJ
06-01-1961; 96.5 mhz FM; 100 kw; 1027 ft.; N33 26 38 W86 52 47
600 Congress Avenue, Suite 1400, Austin, TX 78701 US
(205) 439-9600, *Fax:* (205) 439-8390
www.magic96fm.com
License: Birmingham, Jefferson County, AL held by Capstar TX L.P.
Group Owner: Clear Channel Communications Inc.; (acq 8-30-00; grpsl)
Arbitron Metro Market: Birmingham, AL *Format:* Adult Contemp *Target Audience:* 25-54.
L. Lowry Mays, CEO
Jimmy Vineyard, General Manager
Cyndi Lees, General Sales Mgr
Rich McMillan, Programming Director
Cindee Standridge, Promotions Manager
Cynthia Childress, News Director
Bob Newberry, Chief Engineer
BradleySpears, General Sales Manager

WXJC
04-01-1953; 850 khz AM
866 2nd Ave., 2nd Fl, New York, NY 10017 US
(205) 879-3324, *Fax:* (205) 941-1095
www.850wxjc.com
thejunction@wdjconline.com
License: Birmingham, AL held by Kimtron Inc.
Group Owner: Crawford Broadcasting Co.; (acq 11-12-99)
Nat'l Network: USA
Arbitron Metro Market: Birmingham, AL *Format:* Religious *Target Audience:* Under 12.
Steve Armstrong, General Manager
Jennifer Poepcke, General Sales Mgr
Melodye Grubb, News Director
Todd Dixon, Chief Engineer

WUHT
09-15-1969; 107.7 mhz FM *Hrs Open:* 24; 42 kw; 1345 ft.; N33 29 4 W86 48 25
Attn: David Henderlight, PO Box 11167, Knoxville, TN 37939 US
(205) 945-4646, *Fax:* (205) 942-3175
www.hot1077radio.com
License: Birmingham, Jefferson County, AL held by Citadel Broadcasting Co.
Group Owner: Cumulus Media Inc
Arbitron Metro Market: Birmingham, AL *Format:* Blues *Target Audience:* 18-34.
Dale Daniels, General Manager
Jane Mitchell, General Sales Mgr

***WVSU-FM**
04-06-1967; 91.1 mhz FM *Hrs Open:* 17; 500 w vert; Ant 413 ft; N33 27 47 W86 46 08
Samford Univ., Birmingham, AL 35209
(205) 726-2877, *Fax:* (205) 726-4032
www.samford.edu/wvsu
wvsu@samford.edu
License: Birmingham, Jefferson County, AL held by Samford University.
Population Served: 212,413 *Arbitron Metro Market:* Birmingham, AL *Hrs. of News Programming:* News progmg one hr wkly *Target Audience:* General.

Andy Parrish, General Manager

WJOX-FM
01-01-1947; 94.5 mhz FM; 100 kw; 1014 ft.; N33 27 45 W86 50 59
244 Goodwin Crest Drive, Suite 300, Birmingham, AL 35209 US
(205) 942-1004, *Fax:* (205) 917-1906
www.wjoxfm.com
License: Birmingham, Jefferson County, AL held by Citadel Broadcasting Co.
Group Owner: Cumulus Media Inc
Nat'l Network: ESPN Radio
Arbitron Metro Market: Birmingham, AL *Format:* Sports, Talk
Target Audience: 25-54; general
Austin Davis, Programming Director
Sherry Flick, News Director
Jill Gleeson, Disc Jockey
Kenny Marks, Disc Jockey
Laura Mack, Disc Jockey
Tor Michaels, News Reporter

WZRR
12-01-1975; 99.5 mhz FM; 100 kw; 1014 ft.; N33 27 45 W86 50 59
244 Goodwin Crest Drive, Suite 300, Birmingham, AL 35209 US
(205) 945-4646, *Fax:* (205) 942-3175
www.wzrr.com
sir.laurence@cumulus.com
License: Birmingham, Jefferson County, AL
Group Owner: Cumulus Media Ine
Nat'l Reps: Christal *Wire Services:* Accu-Weather
Arbitron Metro Market: Birmingham, AL *Format:* Classic Rock
John Walker, General Manager
Laurence Salvary, Promotions Manager
Hertisene Riley, National Sales Manager

WZZK-FM
01-01-1948; 104.7 mhz FM *Hrs Open:* 24; 97.8 kw; 1325 ft.; N33 29 4 W86 48 25
3773 Howard Hughes Pwy, Suite 300n, Las Vegas, NV 89109 US
(205) 916-1100, *Fax:* (205) 290-1061
www.wzzk.com
David.Walls@coxradio.com
License: Birmingham, Jefferson County, AL held by Cox Radio Inc.
Group Owner: Cox Radio Inc.; (acq 3-28-97; grpsl)
Arbitron Metro Market: Birmingham, AL *Format:* Country *Hrs. of News Programming:* news progmg 10 hrs wkly *No. News Employees:* 2 *Target Audience:* 25-54.
Ray Nelson, General Manager
David Wells, General Sales Mgr
Paul Orr, Programming Director
Justin Ragland, Promotions Manager
Paul Bankston, National Sales Manager
Kelsey Dollar, Internet Manager

Boaz

WBSA
10-01-1959; 1300 khz AM; 1 kw-D, ND1; 0.037 kw-N, ND1; N34 12 50 W86 9 10
1525 Wills Road, Boaz, AL 35957 US
(256) 593-4264, *Fax:* (256) 593-4265
www.wbsaam.com
1300@wbsaam.com
License: Boaz, AL held by Watkins Broadcasting Inc.
Arbitron Metro Market: Boaz, Al *Format:* Gospel *Target Audience:* General. *Adv. Rates:* 7; 7; 7
Roger Watkins, General Manager
Dale Johnson, Programming Director

Boligee

WQZZ
107.3 mhz FM; kw
US
(205)345-4787, *Fax:* (205)345-4790
License: Boligee, AL
Group Owner: Mildred R Porter
Format: Adult Contemp
Mildred R. Porter, President

Brantley

WEZZ
12-06-1982; 920 khz AM; 5 kw-D, ND1; 0.048 kw-N, ND1; N31 29 40 W87 21 29
1016 C South Alabama Ave, Monroeville, AL 36460 US
(205) 618-2020
License: Brantley, AL held by Brantley Broadcast Associates LLC
Arbitron Metro Market: Brantley, AL
Wendy Smith, General Manager

Brewton

WEBJ
08-01-1947; 1240 khz AM *Hrs Open:* 6 AM-8 PM; 1 kw-U, ND1; N31 6 35 W87 3 36
301 Downing Street, Brewton, AL 36426 US
(251) 867-5717, *Fax:* (251) 867-5718
info@webj.com
License: Brewton, AL held by Candy Cashman Smith, individual.
Arbitron Metro Market: Brewton, AL *Format:* Oldies *Hrs. of News Programming:* news progmg 20 hrs wkly *No. News Employees:* 1 *Target Audience:* 21 plus; 60% female, 40% male
Dennis Dunnaway, General Manager

WKNU
08-19-1974; 106.3 mhz FM *Hrs Open:* 24; 3.8 kw; 417 ft.; N31 6 42 W87 1 17
Mailing Address: P.O. Box 468, Brewton, AL 36427 US
Second Address: 2832 Ridge Rd., Brewton, AL 36426
(251) 867-4824, *Fax:* (251) 867-7003
www.wnku.org
wknubroadcasting@bellsouth.net
License: Brewton, Escambia County, AL held by Ellington Radio Inc.
Format: Country *Special Programming:* Gospel 2 hrs, relg 2 hrs wkly *Hrs. of News Programming:* News progmg 8 hrs wkly
Target Audience: General. *Adv. Rates:* 10; 10; 10; 10
Jack Floyd, President
Carol Ellington, General Manager

***WOWB**
01-01-1998; 90.9 mhz FM; 45 kw; Ant 502 ft; N31 18 13 W87 02 50
Mailing Address: Box 347, Brewton, AL 36502
Second Address: 42676 Hwy. 31, Brewton, AL 36427
(251) 809-1915, *Fax:* (251) 809-1916
gradio@bellsouth.net
License: Brewton, Escambia County, AL held by Gateway Public Radio

Ruth Thompson, General Manager
Debra Johnson, Station Manager

Bridgeport

WGNQ
09-19-1961; 1480 khz AM *Hrs Open:* 24; 1 kw-D, ND1; 0.039 kw-N, ND1; N34 56 34 W85 42 26
P.O. Box 459, Scottsboro, AL 35768 US
(256) 495-2500, *Fax:* (914) 730-9820
www.wgnq.net
manager@wgnq.net
License: Bridgeport, AL held by MG Media Inc.
Nat'l Network: Salem Radio Network *Regional Network:* Alabama Radio Net.
Format: Christian, Talk *Adv. Rates:* 3; 3; 3; N/A
Marvin Glass, President

Brookwood

WRTR
06-01-1966; 105.9 mhz FM *Hrs Open:* 24; 25 kw; 269 ft.; N33 14 17 W87 29 6
Mailing Address: 600 Congress Avenue, Suite 1400, Austin, TX 78701 US
Second Address: 3900 11th Ave. S., Tuscaloosa, AL 35401
(205) 344-4589, *Fax:* (205) 366-9774
www.news1420.com
License: Brookwood, Tuscaloosa County, AL held by Capstar TX L.P.
Group Owner: Clear Channel Communications Inc.
Nat'l Network: USA
Arbitron Metro Market: Tuscaloosa, AL *Format:* Talk *Target Audience:* 25 plus.
Gigi South, General Manager
Bill Seckbach, Programming Director
Tom Canterbury, Promotions Manager

Brundidge

WTBF-FM
10-01-1997; 94.7 mhz FM *Hrs Open:* 24; 14.5 kw; 433 ft.; N31 40 38 W85 56 43
67 Court Square, Troy, AL 36081 US
(334) 566-0300, *Fax:* (334) 566-5689
www.wtbf947.com
wtbf@radio.com
License: Brundidge, Pike County, AL held by Troy Broadcasting Corp.
Nat'l Network: Moody *Regional Network:* Alabama Radio Net.
Wire Services: National Weather Network
Format: Oldies *Hrs. of News Programming:* News progmg 20 hrs wkly *Target Audience:* 28-60. *Adv. Rates:* 25; 10; 25; 5
Doc Kirby, Operations Dir
Jim Roling, General Manager

Butler

***WMLV**
11-20-1978; 93.5 mhz FM; 32 kw; 610 ft.; N32 9 26 W88 29 17
P. O. Box 566, Butler, AL 36904 US
(601) 693-2661, *Fax:* (601) 483-0826
www.klove.com
License: Butler, Choctaw County, AL held by Mississippi Broadcasters L.L.C.
Group Owner: Mississippi Broadcasters L.L.C.; (acq 10-30-2002; $771,500)
Format: Adult Contemp
Scott Stevens, Operations Dir
Clay Holladay, Station Manager

WHSL(AM)
07-11-1959; 1330 khz AM; 5 kw-D; N32 06 02 W88 14 07
909 W. Pushmataha St., Butler, AL 36904-2441
(205) 459-3222, *Fax:* (205) 459-4140
License: Butler, Choctaw County, AL held by Butler Broadcasting Corp.
Population Served: 25,000
Daryl Jackson, General Manager

Carrollton

***WALN**
01-01-1997; 89.3 mhz FM *Hrs Open:* 24; 9.5 kw vert; 699 ft.; N33 13 6 W88 5 46
P.O. Drawer 2440, Tupelo, MS 38803 US
(662) 844-8888, *Fax:* (662) 842-6791
www.afr.net
faq@afr.net
License: Carrollton, Pickens County, AL held by American Family Association.
Group Owner: American Family Radio
Arbitron Metro Market: Carrollton, AL *Format:* Christian, Religious
Tim Waldmon, President
Marvin Sanders, General Manager
John Riley, Programming Director
Fred Jackson, News Director
Joey Moody, Engineering Dir

WZBQ
02-01-1970; 94.1 mhz FM; 98 kw; 1007 ft.; N33 13 7 W88 5 47
600 Congress Avenue, Suite 1400, Austin, TX 78701 US
(205) 344-4589, *Fax:* (205) 752-9269
www.941zbq.com
info@941zbq.com
License: Carrollton, Pickens County, AL held by Capstar TX L.P.
Group Owner: Clear Channel Communications Inc.; (acq 8-30-2000; grpsl)
Arbitron Metro Market: Tuscaloosa, AL *Format:* Contemporary Hits/Top 40 *Target Audience:* 18-49.
Bill Seckbach, Operations Dir
Ray Quinn, General Manager
Lori Moore, General Sales Mgr
Louis Linguini, Programming Director
Laurie Mundy, News Director
Ross Swaner, Chief Engineer

Carrville

WALQ
06-30-1979; 1130 khz AM *Hrs Open:* Sunrise-sunset; 1 kw-D; N32 33 22 W85 52 17
320 Barnett Blvd., Tallassee, AL 36078
(334) 283-6888, *Fax:* (334) 283-6358
wacqradio.com
WACQradio@elmore.rr.com
License: Carrville, Tallapoosa County, AL held by Hughey Communications Inc.
Nat'l Network: ABC *Regional Network:* Alabama Radio Net. *Wire Services:* AP
Population Served: 400,000*Special Programming:* Farm one hr, gospel 5 hrs wkly *Hrs. of News Programming:* news progmg 7 hrs wkly *No. News Employees:* 1 *Target Audience:* 25-54; baby boomers *Adv. Rates:* 10; 10; 10; na
Randall Hughey, General Manager
Debra Hughey, News Director

Centre

WZTQ
11-09-1962; 1560 khz AM *Hrs Open:* 6 AM-sunset; 1 kw-D; N34 07 41 W85 38 27
Box 2, Centre, AL 35960
(256) 927-4027, *Fax:* (205) 295-1238
www.joychristian.com
License: Centre, Cherokee County, AL held by Joy Christian Communications Inc.
Regional Network: Tenn. Radio Net.
Population Served: 245,000*Special Programming:* Farm one hr wkly *Hrs. of News Programming:* news progmg 7 hrs wkly *No. News Employees:* 1 *Target Audience:* 25-55; working middle class, rural
Ed Smith, President
Marie Smith, Operations Dir

WEIS
09-30-1961; 990 khz AM *Hrs Open:* 24
P.O. Box 297, Centre, AL 35960 US
(256) 927-4232, *Fax:* (256) 927-6503
www.weis990am.com
License: Centre, AL held by Baker Enterprises Inc.
Arbitron Metro Market: Centre, AL *Format:* Country, Gospel *Hrs. of News Programming:* news progmg 10 hrs wkly *No. News Employees:* 1 *Target Audience:* General. *Adv. Rates:* 10; 8; 10; 6
Jerry Baker, President

Centreville

WBIB
12-14-1964; 1110 khz AM *Hrs Open:* Sunrise-sunset; 1 kw-D, NDD; N32 58 1 W87 9 1
P.O. Box 584, Alabaster, AL 35007 US
(205) 926-6286, *Fax:* (205) 926-6288
www.wbibradio.com
wbibradio@att.net
License: Centreville, AL held by James DeLoach
Nat'l Reps: Keystone (unwired net)
Arbitron Metro Market: Centreville,AL *Format:* Country, Gospel
Target Audience: Adults. *Adv. Rates:* 10; 7; 10; na
Bo DeLoach, President
Horrace Cruchfield, General Manager
Kim DeLoach, Vice President

Citronelle

*WQUA
06-25-1989; 102.1 mhz FM *Hrs Open:* 24; 15 kw; 427 ft.; N31 5 4 W88 23 51
Mailing Address: 5321 Albert Evans Rd, Wilmer, AL 36587 US
Second Address: 8919 World Ministry Ave., Baton Rouge, LA 70810
(225) 768-3688,(225) 768-8300, *Fax:* (225) 768-3729
www.jsm.org
kawikfish@yahoo.com
License: Citronelle, Mobile County, AL held by Family Worship Center Church Inc.
Group Owner: Family Worship Center Church Inc.; (acq 8-25-2005; $1.25 million)
Arbitron Metro Market: Mobile, AL *Format:* Christian
David Whitelaw, COO
Jimmy Swaggart, President

Coaling

WFFN
06-22-1987; 95.3 mhz FM
142 Skyland Blvd., Tuscaloosa, AL 35504
(205) 750-0929, *Fax:* (205) 349-1715
www.953thebear.com
monk.monk@townsquaremedia.com
License: Coaling, Tuscaloosa County, AL
Group Owner: Townsquare Media; (acq 7-12-2005; grpsl).
Population Served: 1,684 *Arbitron Metro Market:* Coaling, AL
Target Audience: 25-54
Greg Thomas, Operations Dir
Todd Livingston, General Manager
Tammy Boyd, Director of Sales
Meg Summers, Promotions Manager
Monk, Brand Manager

Columbia

WJJN
09-01-1992; 92.1 mhz FM; 2.55 kw; 499 ft.; N31 10 25 W85 12 49
808 N. Oates St., Dothan, AL 36303 US
(334) 671-1753, *Fax:* (334) 677-6923
www.wjjn.com
wtraffic@graceba.net
License: Columbia, Houston County, AL held by Wilson Broadcasting Inc.
Group Owner: Wilson Broadcasting Inc.
Arbitron Metro Market: Dothan, AL *Format:* Urban Contemporary
James Wilson III, General Manager

Columbiana

*WQEM
01-01-2000; 101.5 mhz FM; 1.8 kw; 607 ft.; N33 13 45 W86 42 56
600 Congress Avenue, Suite 1400, Austin, TX 78701 US
(205) 323-1516, *Fax:* (205) 323-2747 (Phone/Fax)
www.gleniris.net
License: Columbiana, Shelby County, AL held by Glen Iris Baptist School
Arbitron Metro Market: Birmingham, AL *Format:* Gospel
Chris Lamb, Chairman

Coosada

WACV
93.1 mhz FM; 3.1 kw; 464 ft.; N32 28 41 W86 24 28 US
(334) 244-0961, *Fax:* (334) 279-9563
www.newstalk931.com
License: Coosada, AL held by Liberty Aquisitions 825 LC
Format: News, News/Talk, 86
Terry Barber, General Manager

Cordova

WXJC-FM
01-01-1997; 92.5 mhz FM *Hrs Open:* 24; 2.2 kw; 548 ft.; N33 38 55 W87 9 19
1406 Cabin Hill Rd, Birmingham, AL 35235 US
(205) 879-3324, *Fax:* (205) 802-4555
thejunction@wdjconline.com
License: Cordova, Walker County, AL held by Kimtron Inc.
Group Owner: Crawford Broadcasting Co.; (acq 7-15-2004; $1.15 million)
Arbitron Metro Market: Birmingham, AL *Format:* Gospel
Steve Armstrong, General Manager
Jennifer Paepcke, General Sales Mgr
Melodye Grubb, News Director
Todd Dixon, Chief Engineer

Cullman

WMCJ
03-25-1950; 1460 khz AM *Hrs Open:* 24; 5 kw-D, DAN; 0.5 kw-N, DAN; N34 10 44 W86 51 58
1707 Warnke Road NW, Cullman, AL 35055 US
(256) 734-3271, *Fax:* (256) 734-3622
License: Cullman, AL held by Walton E. Williams III
Format: Gospel
Walt Williams, General Manager
Susan Hackney, Programming Director

WKUL
09-01-1967; 92.1 mhz FM; 6 kw; 328 ft; N34 11 41 W86 43 52
Box 803, 214 1st Ave. S.E., Cullman, AL 35033
(256) 734-0183, *Fax:* (256) 739-2999
www.wkul.com
License: Cullman, Cullman County, AL held by Jonathan Christian Corp.
Population Served: 1,200,000*Special Programming:* Farm 15 hrs wkly *Hrs. of News Programming:* news progmg 20 hrs wkly *No. News Employees:* 1 *Target Audience:* 25-54. *Adv. Rates:* 28; 22; 28; 18
Ron Mosley, President
Rick Nix, Operations Dir
Grant Smith, News Director

WYDE-FM
08-06-1949; 101.1 mhz FM *Hrs Open:* 24; 100 kw; 1345 ft.; N34 4 56 W86 54 15
1707 Warnke Road NW, Cullman, AL 35055 US
(205) 879-3324, *Fax:* (205) 802-4555
thejunction@wdjconline.com
License: Cullman, Cullman County, AL held by Kimtron Inc.
Group Owner: Crawford Broadcasting Co.; (acq 6-14-2002; $8.5 million)
Arbitron Metro Market: Birmingham, AL *Format:* Adult Contemp
Steve Armstrong, General Manager
Jennifer Paepcke, General Sales Mgr
Melodye Grubb, News Director
Todd Dexon, Chief Engineer

WFMH
10-01-1946; 1340 khz AM *Hrs Open:* 24
1707 Warnke Road, N.W., Cullman, AL 35055 US
(256) 734-3271, *Fax:* (256) 734-3622
wfmh@adelphia.net
License: Cullman, AL held by Walton E. Williams III
Nat'l Reps: Keystone (unwired net)
Arbitron Metro Market: Cullman, AL *Format:* News, News/Talk, 84, Talk *Hrs. of News Programming:* News progmg 18 hrs wkly
Target Audience: 25-54; middle & upper income adults *Adv. Rates:* 6; 6; 6; 4
Walt Williams, General Manager
Susan Hackney, Programming Director

Dadeville

WDLK
08-11-1980; 1450 khz AM; 1 kw-U, ND1; N32 50 56 W85 46 10
Dr. Jim Nichols, Trustee, 212 N. Broadnax St., Dadeville, AL 36853 US
(256) 825-0332, *Fax:* (205) 825-4270
License: Dadeville, AL held by Progressive United Communications Inc.
Arbitron Metro Market: Montgomery, AL *Format:* Gospel
Walter Gilmore, General Manager

Daphne

WASG
11-12-1981; 540 khz AM *Hrs Open:* 24
2070 N Palafox St., Pensacola, FL 32501 US
(850) 434-1230, *Fax:* (850) 469-9698
License: Daphne, AL held by 550 AM Inc.
Arbitron Metro Market: Mobile, AL
Michael Glinter, President
Dara Glinter, Executive Vice President

WAVH
05-15-1993; 106.5 mhz FM *Hrs Open:* 24; 50 kw; 449 ft.; N30 44 44 W88 5 40
4510 North 35th Street, Arlington, VA 22207 US
(207) 622-1340, *Fax:* (207) 623-2874
www.worshipradionetwork.org
denise@lworshipradionetwork.org
License: Daphne, Baldwin County, AL held by Bigler Broadcasting LLC
Nat'l Reps: McGavren Guild
Arbitron Metro Market: Oakland ME *Format:* Christian, Country
Hrs. of News Programming: News progmg one hr wkly
Ray Bouchard, CEO/COO
Ryan Gagne, Operations Dir
Denise Lafountain, General Manager
Roger Jackson, Programming Director

Decatur

WDRM
09-01-1951; 102.1 mhz FM *Hrs Open:* 24; 100 kw; 981 ft.; N34 47 36 W86 37 51
Mailing Address: 600 Congress Ave., Suite 1400, Austin, TX 78701 US
Second Address: 26869 Peoples Rd., Madison, AL 35756
(256) 309-2400, *Fax:* (256) 350-2653
www.wdrm.com
info@wdrm.com
License: Decatur, Morgan County, AL held by Capstar TX L.P.
Group Owner: Clear Channel Communications Inc.
Arbitron Metro Market: Decatur, AL *Format:* Country
George Roberts, Operations Dir
Rick Roberts, Station Manager
Lynn Bieritz, General Sales Mgr
Al Shannon, Operations Manager
Kris Cooper, Promotions Director
Dan Gainey, Regional Sales Manager

WHOS
10-01-1948; 800 khz AM *Hrs Open:* 24; 1 kw-D, ND1; 0.215 kw-N, ND1; N34 35 55 W87 0 24
Mailing Address: 600 Congress Ave., Suite 1400, Austin, TX 78701 US
Second Address: 26869 Peoples Rd., Madison, AL 35756
(256) 353-1750, *Fax:* (256) 350-2653
License: Decatur, AL held by Capstar TX L.P.
Group Owner: Clear Channel Communications Inc.; (acq 7-18-2000; grpsl)
Arbitron Metro Market: Huntsville, AL *Format:* Oldies *No. News Employees:* 3 *Target Audience:* 25-54.
Rick Brown, General Manager
Carmelita Palmer, General Sales Mgr

***WYFD**
05-07-1975; 91.7 mhz FM *Hrs Open:* 24; 9 kw; 787 ft.; N34 47 53 W86 38 24
8030 Arrowridge Blvd., Charlotte, NC 28273 US
(704) 523-5555, *Fax:* (704) 522-1967
www.bbnradio.org
bbn@bbnradio.org
License: Decatur, Morgan County, AL held by Bible Broadcasting Network.
Group Owner: Bible Broadcasting Network; acq 10-19-90; $75,000;
Arbitron Metro Market: Decatur, AL *Format:* Religious
Lowell Davey, President
Hank Crull, General Manager
Dave Phillips, Station Manager

WWTM
05-01-1935; 1400 khz AM; 1 kw-U, ND1; N34 36 44 W86 59 28
P.O. Box 248, Decatur, GA 35602 US
(256) 353-1400, *Fax:* (256) 353-0363
espn1400.info
License: Decatur, AL held by R & B Communications Inc.
Nat'l Network: ESPN Radio
Arbitron Metro Market: Decature, AL *Format:* Sports *Target Audience:* 25-54.
Joe Burns, General Manager

WEKI
1490 khz; 1000 w; N34 35 14 W86 59 13
Mailing Address: 1301 Central Parkway SW, Decatur, AL 35601
Second Address: 2305 Holmes Ave. NW, Huntsville, AL 35816
(256) 533-1450, *Fax:* (256) 551-9865
www.wekiradio.com
License: Decatur, Morgan County, AL
Group Owner: Focus Radio Communications

Demopolis

WXAL
11-09-1947; 1400 khz AM; 0.79 kw-U, ND1; N32 30 8 W87 49 7
1028 Highway 80, Demopolis, AL 36732 US
(334) 289-1400, *Fax:* (334) 289-9811
www.wxal1400.com
valerie@mywin98.com
License: Demopolis, AL held by West Alabama Radio Inc.
Group Owner: West Alabama Radio Inc.; (acq 8-18-98; $456,300 with co-located FM)
Nat'l Network: Westwood One; USA
Arbitron Metro Market: Demopolis, AL *Format:* Black, Gospel, 60, News/Talk, Talk *Target Audience:* 25-54.
Amy Ward, CEO
Amy Ross, General Manager
Sean Park, General Sales Mgr
Larry Carr, Programming Director
Valerie Webb, News Director

WZNJ
01-01-1975; 106.5 mhz FM; 25 kw; 305 ft.; N32 30 8 W87 49 7
1028 Highway 80, Demopolis, AL 36732 US
(334) 289-1106
www.znj1065.com
sales@mywin98.com
License: Demopolis, Marengo County, AL held by West Alabama Radio Inc.
Group Owner: West Alabama Radio Inc.
Nat'l Network: Westwood One; USA
Arbitron Metro Market: Demopolis, AL *Format:* Oldies, Sports *Target Audience:* 18-49.
Morgan Dowdy, CEO
Buddy Baylor, General Manager
Beth Hancock
Sarah James

***WMWI**
88.7 mhz FM; 0.1 kw; 157 ft.; N32 30 43 W87 51 0
US
(205) 929-1609
License: Demopolis, Marengo County, AL held by Miles College.
Arbitron Metro Market: Demopolis, AL
Kenneth Jones, General Manager

Dixons Mills

***WMBV**
08-15-1988; 91.9 mhz FM *Hrs Open:* 24; 62 kw; 614 ft.; N32 7 45 W87 44 16
Mailing Address: 820 N. Lasalee Drive, Chicago, IL 60610 US
Second Address: 10564 Marengo County Rd. 30, Dixons Mills, AL 36736
(334) 992-2425, *Fax:* (205)758-0059
www.moodyradiosouth.fm
wmbv@moody.edu
License: Dixons Mills, Marengo County, AL held by Moody Bible Institute.
Group Owner: The Moody Bible Institute of Chicago; (acq 3-31-88)
Nat'l Network: Moody
Arbitron Metro Market: Dixon Mills, AL *Format:* Religious *Special Programming:* Financial 3 hrs, children 3 hrs, sports one hr wkl *Hrs. of News Programming:* News progmg 10 hrs wkly *Target Audience:* 35-55;general
Rob Moore, General Manager

Dora

WCOC
04-01-1982; 1010 khz AM; 5 kw-D, ND1; 0.041 kw-N, ND1; N33 48 4 W87 6 42
P. O. Box 460, Dora, AL 35062 US
(619) 929-9186
License: Dora, AL held by Azteca Communications of Alabama Inc.
Arbitron Metro Market: Birmingham, AL
Patricia Perez, General Manager

Dothan

WAGF
09-29-1932; 1320 khz AM
808 N. Oates St., Dothan, AL 36303 US
(334) 671-1753, *Fax:* (334) 677-6923
www.wjjn.com
wjjnmusic@gmail.com
License: Dothan, AL held by Wilson Broadcasting Inc.
Group Owner: Wilson Broadcasting Inc.; acq 8-13-92; $60,000;
Arbitron Metro Market: Dothan, AL *Format:* Gospel
James R. Wilson, President
James Wilson III, General Manager
Jamar M. Wilson, Programming Director

WAGF-FM
01-01-1991; 101.3 mhz FM *Hrs Open:* 24; 1.15 kw; 535 ft.; N31 12 4 W85 20 4
808 N. Oates St., Dothan, AL 36303 US
(334) 671-1753, *Fax:* (334) 677-6923
www.wjjn.com
wjjnmusic@gmail.com
License: Dothan, Houston County, AL held by Wilson Broadcasting Inc.
Group Owner: Wilson Broadcasting Inc.
Nat'l Network: Jones Radio Networks *Regional Network:* Alabama Radio Net. *Nat'l Reps:* Rgnl Reps
Arbitron Metro Market: Dothan, AL *Format:* Adult Contemp *Target Audience:* 25-54; female *Adv. Rates:* 20; 18; 20; 12
James R. Wilson, President
Jimmy Doctrie, Operations Dir
James Wilson III, General Manager
J.R. Wilson, General Sales Mgr
Jamar M. Wilson, Programming Director

WESP
09-01-1989; 102.5 mhz FM *Hrs Open:* 24; 16.5 kw; 404 ft.; N31 15 48 W85 18 24
2236 Montgomery Highway, Dothan, AL 36304 US
(334) 671-1025(334) 712-9233, *Fax:* (334) 712-0374
www.rock1025.com
ron@wdjr.com
License: Dothan, Houston County, AL held by Gulf South Communications Inc.
Nat'l Reps: McGavren Guild
Arbitron Metro Market: Dothan, AL *Target Audience:* 25-54; men
Misty Huff, Operations Dir
Ron Eubanks, General Manager
Bill Moody, General Sales Mgr
Jess Bailey, Programming Director
April Granger, News Director

***WGTF**
09-01-1988; 89.5 mhz FM *Hrs Open:* 24; 19 kw; 210 ft.; N31 14 2 W85 26 2
107 Wanda Court, Dothan, AL 36303 US
(334) 794-4770, *Fax:* (334) 794-4770
www.bbnradio.org
wgtf@bbnradio.org
License: Dothan, Houston County, AL held by Dothan Community Educational Radio Inc.
Nat'l Network: Bible Bcstg Net
Arbitron Metro Market: Dothan, AL *Format:* Religious
Raymond Brown, General Manager

WCNF
07-03-1995; 700 khz AM *Hrs Open:* Sunrise-sunset; 1.6 kw-D; N31 26 19 W85 17 22
3385 Reeves St., Dothan, AL 31820
(502) 776-1240
License: Dothan, Houston County, AL held by Jalo Broadcasting Corp.
Arbitron Metro Market: Dothan, AL
Argie Dale Sr., General Manager

WOOF
02-17-1947; 560 khz AM; 5 kw-D, ND2; 0.118 kw-N, ND2; N31 13 5 W85 21 10
Mailing Address: P. O. Box 1427, Dothan, AL 36301 US
Second Address: 2518 Columbia Hwy., Dothan, AL 36303
(334) 792-1149, *Fax:* (334) 677-4612
www.woofradio.com/ballindex.html
woof@ala.net
License: Dothan, AL held by WOOF Inc.
Arbitron Metro Market: Dothan, AL *TV Affiliate:* Sports *Format:* Black, Gospel

WOOF-FM
09-18-1964; 99.7 mhz FM; 100 kw; 981 ft.; N31 15 7 W85 17 12
Mailing Address: P. O. Box 1427, Dothan, AL 36301 US
Second Address: 2518 Columbia Hwy., Dothan, AL 36303
(334) 792-1149, *Fax:* (334) 677-4612
www.997wooffm.com
woof@ala.net
License: Dothan, Houston County, AL held by WOOF Inc.
Nat'l Reps: Christal
Arbitron Metro Market: Dothan, AL *TV Affiliate:* Adult contemp *Special Programming:* news progmg 3 hrs wkly *Hrs. of News Programming:* 2 *No. News Employees:* 25-54; women 18-49 domina
Disc Jockey, Rick Patrick
Disc Jockey

***WRWA**
12-01-1985; 88.7 mhz FM *Hrs Open:* 6 AM-midnight; 50 kw; 469 ft.; N31 12 30 W85 36 51 *Rebroadcasts:* Rebroadcasts WTSU(FM) Troy 100%
University Ave, Troy, AL 36082 US
(334) 670-3268, *Fax:* (334) 670-3934
www.troypublicradio.org/
wtsu@troy.edu
License: Dothan, Houston County, AL held by Troy State University.
Nat'l Network: NPR; PRI
Arbitron Metro Market: Dothan, AL *Format:* News *Special Programming:* Children one hr wkly *Hrs. of News Programming:* News progmg 25 hrs wkly *Target Audience:* General.
Judy Davis, Operations Dir
James Clower, General Manager
Joanne Jacobs, General Sales Mgr
Fred Azbell, Programming Director
John Brunson, Chief Engineer

WTVY-FM
09-20-1968; 95.5 mhz FM *Hrs Open:* 24; 100 kw; 1060 ft.; N31 15 16 W85 15 39
Mailing Address: P.O. Box 2088, Dothan, AL 36302 US
Second Address: 285 N. Foster, 8th Fl., Dothan, AL 36303
(334) 792-0047, *Fax:* (334) 712-9346
www.955wtvy.com
melody@trpdothan.com
License: Dothan, Houston County, AL held by Magic Broadcasting Alabama Licensing LLC.
Group Owner: Magic Broadcasting LLC; (acq 7-27-2001)
Nat'l Reps: Christal
Arbitron Metro Market: Dothan, AL *Format:* Country *Special Programming:* Farm 5 hrs, gospel 4 hrs, religion 3 hrs wkly *Hrs. of News Programming:* News progmg 5 hrs wkly *Target Audience:* 25-54. *Adv. Rates:* 35; 32; 32; 15
Melody Lee, General Manager

***WVOB**
12-08-1988; 91.3 mhz FM *Hrs Open:* 24; 2.5 kw; 328 ft.; N31 10 57 W85 24 21
Mailing Address: P.O. Box 1944, Dothan, AL 36302 US
Second Address: 2573 Hodgesville Rd., Dothan, AL 36301
(334) 671-9862, *Fax:* (334) 793-4344
www.gospel91.com
wvob913fm@bethanybc.edu
License: Dothan, Houston County, AL held by Bethany Divinity College & Seminary Inc.
Nat'l Network: USA
Arbitron Metro Market: Dothan, AL *Format:* Gospel *Hrs. of News Programming:* news progmg 6 hrs wkly *No. News Employees:* 1 *Target Audience:* General; college students & relg community
Dr. H. D. Shuemake, CEO
Keithy Brady, Operations Dir
Dr.H.D.Shuemake, General Manager
Dr. Samuel Shuemake, Station Manager
Sylvia Green, Programming Director

WWNT
04-30-1947; 1450 khz AM; 1 kw-U, ND1; N31 13 10 W85 22 14
1733 Columbia Hwy, Dothan, AL 36303 US
(334) 671-0075, *Fax:* (334) 671-0091
www.wwntradio.com
info@wwntradio.com
License: Dothan, AL held by WWNT LLC
Nat'l Network: USA
Arbitron Metro Market: Dothan, AL *Format:* News, Talk *No. News Employees:* 2 *Target Audience:* 25-54 men; 25-54 males
Larry Williams, General Manager

***WDYF**
01-01-2004; 90.3 mhz FM; 9.2 kw; 561 ft.; N31 19 29 W85 36 6
Mailing Address: Post Office Box 210789, Montgomery, AL 36121 US
Second Address: 381 Mendel Parkway, Montgomery, AL 36117
(334) 271-8900, *Fax:* (334) 260-8962
www.faithradio.org
mail@faithradio.org
License: Dothan, Houston County, AL held by Faith Broadcasting Inc.
Arbitron Metro Market: Montgomery, AL *Format:* Adult Contemp, Religious
Mark Williams, President
Andrew Leuthold, Operations Dir
Russell Dean, General Manager
Gary Hundley, General Sales Mgr
Bob Crittenden, Programming Director
Wiely Boswell, Chief Engineer
Bob Crittenden, Director of SpecialProjects
Billy Irvin, Director of Ministry Relation
Jeremy Smith, Operations Manager
Donna Spears, Office Manger
Ramona Henson, Graphic Design Coordinator
Beth Garland, Bookkeeper

Dozier

***WVPL**
12-01-2011; 90.5 mhz FM; 0.3 kw; 243 ft.; N31 25 38 W86 21 21 US
License: Dozier, Crenshaw County, AL
Group Owner: Townsend Broadcasting Enterprise
Special Programming: Religious

Elba

WELB
11-16-1958; 1350 khz AM *Hrs Open:* 11; 1 kw-D, ND1; 0.044 kw-N, ND1; N31 27 10 W86 4 0
1800 Neil Grantham Drive, Elba, AL 36323 US
(334) 897-2216(334) 897-2217, *Fax:* (334) 897-3694
welbam1350@yahoo.com
License: Elba, AL held by Elba Radio Co.
Arbitron Metro Market: Elba, AL *Format:* Country *Special Programming:* Gospel 12 hrs wkly *Hrs. of News Programming:* News progmg 6 hrs wkly *Target Audience:* General.
Doug Holderfield, General Manager
Mike Holderfield, Programming Director
Eddie Phillips, News Director

WVVL
10-01-1986; 101.1 mhz FM *Hrs Open:* 19; 0.64 kw; 682 ft.; N31 24 41 W85 57 32
1800 Neil Grantham Drive, Elba, AL 36323 US
(334) 347-5621, *Fax:* (334) 347-5631
www.weevil101.com
wvvl@weevil101.com
License: Elba, Coffee County, AL
Arbitron Metro Market: Enterprise, AL *Format:* Country
Doug Holderfielf, General Manager

Enterprise

WDJR
07-01-1968; 96.9 mhz FM; 100 kw; 1037 ft.; N30 55 19 W85 44 41
Box 9663, Dothan, AL 36304 US
(334) 712-9233, *Fax:* (334) 712-0374
www.mix969.net
ron@wdjr.com
License: Enterprise, Coffee County, AL held by Gulf South Communications Inc.
Nat'l Reps: McGavren Guild
Arbitron Metro Market: Dothan, AL *Format:* Country
Misty Huff, Operations Dir
Ron Eubanks, General Manager
Bill Moody, General Sales Mgr
Brett Mason, Programming Director
April Granger, News Director

WKMX
11-27-1974; 106.7 mhz FM *Hrs Open:* 24; 100 kw; 1070 ft.; N31 24 41 W85 57 32
P. O. Box 840, Enterprise, AL 36330 US
(334) 792-0047, *Fax:* (334) 712-9346
www.wkmx.com
info@wkmx.com
License: Enterprise, Coffee County, AL held by Magic Broadcasting Alabama Licensing LLC.
Group Owner: Magic Broadcasting LLC; (acq 9-3-2004; $4.5 million)
Arbitron Metro Market: Dothan, AL *Format:* Contemporary Hits/Top 40 *Hrs. of News Programming:* News progmg 2 hrs wkly *Target Audience:* Females; 18-49
Doc Thompson, Operations Dir
Dan Bradley, General Manager
Richard Reinhardt, General Sales Mgr
John Houston, Promotions Manager
Sue Hughes, General Manager
Chris Green, General Sales Manager
Amie Pollard, National SalesManager
Richard Reomjardt, Operations Manager

Equality

***WBNB**
91.3 mhz FM; kw
US
(334) 430-4296
License: Equality, Coosa County, AL held by Equality Broadcasting Network.
Arbitron Metro Market: Equality, AL
Benny Newton, President

Eufaula

WYDK
03-16-1992; 97.9 mhz FM *Hrs Open:* 24; 6 kw; Ant 328 ft; N31 56 04 W85 12 27
Mailing Address: Box 1419, Eufaula, AL 36027
Second Address: 1347 S. Eufaula Ave., Eufaula, AL 36027
(334) 616-0097, *Fax:* (334) 687-3600
lake98fm@gmail.com
License: Eufaula, Barbour County, AL held by River Valley Media L.L.C.
Nat'l Network: Jones Radio Networks
Target Audience: 24 plus. *Adv. Rates:* 9; 6; 8; 5
Clyde Earnest, General Manager
Pam Sharp, General Sales Mgr
John Crumpton, Programming Director
Terry Harper, Engineering Dir

WKZJ
01-01-1969; 92.7 mhz FM; 39 kw; 551 ft.; N32 7 58 W85 4 13
P O Box 2127, Columus, GA 31902 US
(706) 576-3565, *Fax:* (706) 576-3683
www.theriverrocks.com
riversales@kenology.net
License: Eufaula, Barbour County, AL held by Davis Broadcasting Inc.
Group Owner: Davis Broadcasting Inc.; (acq 7-20-2004; $2.7 million).
Arbitron Metro Market: Columbus, GA *Format:* Adult Contemp *Hrs. of News Programming:* news progmg 6 hrs wkly *No. News Employees:* 2
Gregory Davis, President
Cheryl Davis, Operations Dir
Janet Armstead, General Manager
Angela Verdejo, General Sales Mgr
Carl Conner, Programming Director
Bernie Corcoran, Operations Manager

WNRA
01-01-1948; 1240 khz AM; 1 kw-U; N31 54 30 W85 09 51
Box 1419, Eufaula, AL 30143
(334) 616-0097, *Fax:* (334) 687-3600
lake98fm@gmail.com
License: Eufaula, Barbour County, AL held by River Valley Media LLC
Population Served: 20,000*Special Programming:* Farm 2 hrs, Black 3 hrs wkly *Target Audience:* 25-54; adults *Adv. Rates:* 6.50; 4.50; 5.50; 4.50
John Burns, President

Eutaw

WWPG
08-01-1990; 104.3 mhz FM *Hrs Open:* 24; 2.3 kw; 370 ft; N32 54 16 W87 50 09
Mailing Address: Box 70427, Tuscaloosa, AL 35407
Second Address: 601 Greensboro Ave., Suite 507, Tuscaloosa, AL 35401
(205) 345-4787, *Fax:* (205) 345-4790
jwlawson@bellsouth.net
License: Eutaw, Greene County, AL held by Jim Lawson Communications Inc.
Arbitron Metro Market: Tuscaloosa, AL
Jim Lawson, General Manager

Eva

WRJL-FM
01-01-1996; 99.9 mhz FM *Hrs Open:* 24; 25 kw; 318 ft.; N34 18 43 W86 43 54
Rt. 2, Box 27, Eva, AL 35621 US
(256) 796-8000, *Fax:* (256) 796-8515
License: Eva, Morgan County, AL held by Rojo Inc.
Format: Gospel
Jo French, General Manager
Amy Holland, Programming Director

Evergreen

WEVG
07-01-1957; 1470 khz AM *Hrs Open:* 24; 1 kw-D; N31 26 29 W86 56 08
Mailing Address: Box 705, Evergreen, AL 36561
Second Address: Hwy. 31 S, Evergreen, AL 36401
(251) 578-2780, *Fax:* (251) 578-5399
powerpig@bellsouth.net
License: Evergreen, Conecuh County, AL held by Star Broadcasting Inc.
Group Owner: Star Broadcasting Inc.; (acq 4-13-2004; $2.75 million with co-located FM).
Population Served: 20,000*Hrs. of News Programming:* news progmg 20 hrs wkly *No. News Employees:* 3 *Target Audience:* 34-64.
Luther Upton, General Manager

Fairfield

WJLD(AM)
01-01-1942; 1400 khz AM *Hrs Open:* 24; 1 kw-U; N33 28 36 W86 53 01
Mailing Address: Box 19123, Birmingham, AL 35219-9123
Second Address: 1449 Spaulding Ishkooda Rd., Birmingham, AL 35211-5059
(205) 942-1776, *Fax:* (205) 942-4814
www.wjldfm.com
wjld@juno.com
License: Fairfield, Jefferson County, AL held by Richardson Broadcasting Corp.
Nat'l Network: American Urban; CNN Radio
Population Served: 900,000 *Arbitron Metro Market:* Birmingham, AL *Format:* Blues, Gospel, 86 *Special Programming:* ""Morning Talk"" 6-8AM M-F *Hrs. of News Programming:* TOH 6A-9P *Target Audience:* 35+;majority Black, adult, blue and white collar working class *Adv. Rates:* 35; 15; 10
Gary Richardson, President
Bob Friedman, Operations Dir
Tonja Leath, News Director

Fairhope

WABF
08-12-1961; 1220 khz AM *Hrs Open:* 24
Mailing Address: P.O. Box 679, Orange Beach, AL 36561 US
Second Address: 460 S. Section St., Fairhope, AL 36533
(608) 273-1000, *Fax:* (608) 271-8182
www.q106.com
License: Fairhope, AL held by Gulf Coast Broadcasting Co. Inc.
Nat'l Network: CBS Radio
Arbitron Metro Market: Redding CA *Format:* Country *Target Audience:* 25-54; general *Adv. Rates:* 11;10;11;8
Tom Walker, General Manager
Ted Waldbillig, General Sales Mgr
Brad Austin, Programming Director
John Bauer, Chief Engineer

WXQW
04-22-1965; 660 khz AM *Hrs Open:* 24; 10 kw-D, DAN; 0.85 kw-N, DAN; N30 35 51 W87 52 57 *Rebroadcasts:* Simulcast with WGOK(AM(Mobile 100%
One Independence Plaza, 280 Highway 35, Red Bank, NJ 07701 US
(251) 652-2000, *Fax:* (251) 652-2007
www.gospel900.com
carmen.brown@cumulus.com
License: Fairhope, AL held by Cumulus Licensing Corp.
Group Owner: Cumulus Media Inc.; (acq 10-18-99; grpsl)
Arbitron Metro Market: Mobile, AL *Format:* Gospel *Target Audience:* 18-54; Black adults
James Alexander, Operations Dir
Steve Sandman, General Manager

Angel Taylor, Regional VP/Sales
Felicia Allbritton, Programming Director
Vinny Duncan, Promotions Manager

WZEW
08-28-1966; 92.1 mhz FM *Hrs Open:* 24; 20.5 kw; 363 ft.; N30 31 23 W88 6 32
1827 Jefferson Place, N.W., Washington, DC 20036 US
(251) 433-9236, *Fax:* (251) 438-5462
www.92zew.net
wzewfm@wzewfm.com
License: Fairhope, Baldwin County, AL held by Baldwin Broadcasting Co.
Arbitron Metro Market: Mobile, AL *Format:* Alternative, Blues
Special Programming: Jazz 6 hrs wkly *Hrs. of News Programming:* news progmg 6 hrs wkly *No. News Employees:* 1 *Target Audience:* 25-44.
Ken Johnson, General Manager
Gene Murrell, Programming Director

Fayette

WLDX
09-03-1949; 990 khz AM; 1 kw-D, ND1; 0.042 kw-N, ND1; N33 41 6 W87 49 16
733 Columbus Street East, Fayette, AL 35555 US
(205) 932-3318, *Fax:* (205) 932-3318
www.wldx.com
wldx@wldx.com
License: Fayette, AL held by Dean Broadcasting Inc.
Format: Country *Target Audience:* 25-55; middle-income adults
J. Wiley Dean, President
Jill Dean, Operations Dir
Joe Redker, Programming Director

WTXT
01-29-1977; 98.1 mhz FM *Hrs Open:* 24; 100 kw; 906 ft.; N33 19 17 W87 46 29
600 Congress Avenue, Suite 1400, Austin, TX 78701 US
(205) 344-4589, *Fax:* (205) 366-9774
www.98txt.com
ddhamric@clearchannel.com
License: Fayette, Fayette County, AL held by Clear Channel Communications
Group Owner: Clear Channel Communications Inc.; (acq 8-30-00; grpsl).
Nat'l Network: ABC *Nat'l Reps:* Christal *Wire Services:* Direct Line Weather Wire
Arbitron Metro Market: Tuscaloosa, AL *Format:* Country *No. News Employees:* 1 *Target Audience:* 25-54.
Gigi South, General Manager
Bill Seckbach, Programming Director
Tom Canterberry, Promotions Manager
Kyle.D.Pierce, Digital & Content

Five Points

***WJBE**
88.5 mhz FM; 0 kw horiz, 0.5 kw vert; 200 ft.; N33 57 51 W87 12 34
US
(205) 295-2055
License: Five Points, Chambers County, AL held by Big South Community Broadcasting Inc.
Arbitron Metro Market: Five Points, AL
Brett Elmore, President

Florala

WKWL
11-03-1979; 1230 khz AM *Hrs Open:* 6 AM-6 PM; 1 kw-U, ND1; N31 0 20 W86 19 53
Mailing Address: P.O. Box 158, South 6th St, Florala, AL 36442 US
Second Address: 427 S Sixth St, Florala, AL 36442
(334) 858-6162, *Fax:* (334) 858-6162
wkwl.ezstream.com
wkwl@alaweb.com
License: Florala, AL held by Florala Broadcasting Co. Inc.
Nat'l Network: USA
Format: Christian, Country, 44 *Special Programming:* Farm one hr, relg 12 hrs wkly *Hrs. of News Programming:* news progmg 15 hrs wkly *No. News Employees:* 1 *Target Audience:* 5 plus; general
Robert Williamson, President

Florence

WBCF
01-01-1946; 1240 khz AM *Hrs Open:* 24; 1 kw-U, ND1; N34 47 1 W87 42 15
Mailing Address: 525 E. Tennessee St, Florence, AL 35631 US
Second Address: 525 E. Tennessee St., Florence, AL 35630
(800) 877-5600, *Fax:* (916) 251-1650
www.klove.com
License: Florence, AL held by BCB Inc.
Nat'l Network: Westwood One; Fox News Radio; CBS Radio; ABC; Talk Radio Network
Arbitron Metro Market: Ely NV *Format:* Christian
Mike Novak, President

***WFIX**
03-20-1988; 91.3 mhz FM *Hrs Open:* 12am-12am; 100 kw; 869 ft.; N34 40 24 W87 42 56
2806 West Mall Drive, Florence, AL 35630 US
(256) 760-9191, *Fax:* (256) 764-9154
www.wfix.net
wfix@wfix.net
License: Florence, Lauderdale County, AL held by Tri-State Inspirational Broadcasting Inc.
Nat'l Network: USA
Arbitron Metro Market: Florence, AL *Format:* Adult Contemp, Christian *Special Programming:* Friday & Saturday Night Youth Shows *Hrs. of News Programming:* News progmg 2 hrs wkly *Target Audience:* 25-54; upscalefamily oriented women & men
Mark Allen, General Manager

WQLT-FM
05-29-1967; 107.3 mhz FM *Hrs Open:* 24; 93 kw; 1017 ft.; N34 40 24 W87 42 56
Mailing Address: 624 Sam Phillips Street, Florence, AL 35631 US
Second Address: 624 Sam Phillips Street, Florence, AL 35630
(256) 764-8121, *Fax:* (256) 764-8169
www.wqlt.com
License: Florence, Lauderdale County, AL held by Big River Broadcasting Corp.
Group Owner: Big River Broadcasting Corp.
Arbitron Metro Market: Florence-Muscle Shoals, AL *Format:* Adult Contemp *Target Audience:* 25-54.
Jeff Thomas, Operations Dir
Nick Martin, General Manager
Rocky Reich, General Sales Mgr
Jimmy Oliver, Promotions Manager
Leisa Johnson, News Director
Greg Pace, Chief Engineer
Sharon Brook, General Sales Manager

WSBM
03-29-1946; 1340 khz AM *Hrs Open:* 24; 1 kw-U, ND1; N34 47 50 W87 39 54
Mailing Address: 624 Sam Phillips Street, Florence, AL 35631 US
Second Address: 624 Sam Phillips Street, Florence, AL 35630
(256) 764-8121, *Fax:* (256) 764-8169
www.1340theref.com
License: Florence, AL held by Big River Broadcasting Corp.
Group Owner: Big River Broadcasting Corp.; (Acq 2-21-73)
Nat'l Network: Fox Sports
Arbitron Metro Market: Florence-Muscle *Format:* Sports
Jeff Thomas, Operations Dir
Nick Martin, General Manager
Rocky Reich, General Sales Mgr
Leisa Johnson, News Director
Greg Pace, Engineering Dir
Sharon Brook, General Sales Manager

WXFL
02-01-1992; 96.1 mhz FM *Hrs Open:* 24; 20.5 kw; 781 ft.; N34 54 17 W87 24 2
Mailing Address: 624 Sam Phillips Street, Florence, AL 35631 US
Second Address: 624 Phillips Street, Florence, AL 35630
(256) 764-8121, *Fax:* (256) 764-8169
www.kix96country.com
License: Florence, Lauderdale County, AL held by Big River Broadcasting Corp.
Group Owner: Big River Broadcasting Corp.
Arbitron Metro Market: Florence, AL *Format:* Country *Target Audience:* 18-49; general
Knox Phillips, President
Jerry Phillips, Operations Dir
Nick Martin, General Manager
Rocky Reich, General Sales Mgr
Fletch Brown, Programming Director
Leisa Johnson, News Director
Greg Pace, Engineering Dir
Sharon Brook,General Sales Manager
Jeff Thomas, Operations Manager

Foley

WHEP
05-31-1953; 1310 khz AM *Hrs Open:* 24
Mailing Address: P. O. Box 1747, Foley, AL 36536 US
Second Address: 20109 Hadley Rd., Foley, AL 36535
(251) 943-7131, *Fax:* (251) 943-7031
www.whep1310.com
whepsports@yahoo.com
License: Foley, AL held by Stewart Broadcasting Co. Inc.
Nat'l Network: CNN Radio; Talk Radio Network; Westwood One
Regional Network: Alabama Radio Net.
Arbitron Metro Market: Mobile, AL *Format:* Adult Contemp, News, 62, Sports, Talk *Special Programming:* Farm 2 hrs wkly *No. News Employees:* 2 *Target Audience:* 25 plus. *Adv. Rates:* 8.75; 8.75; 8.75; na
Clark Stewart, President

Fort Deposit

WKXN
07-18-1977; 95.7 mhz FM *Hrs Open:* 24; 4 kw; 226 ft.; N31 50 43 W86 38 56 *Rebroadcasts:* Simulcasts WKXK(FM) Pine Hill 100%
Mailing Address: Manningham Road At I-65, P. O. Box 369, Greenville, AL 36037 US
Second Address: 563 Manningham Rd., Greenville, AL 36037
(334) 382-6555, *Fax:* (334) 382-7770
www.wkxn.com
wkxn@wkxn.com
License: Fort Deposit, Butler County, AL held by Autaugaville Radio Inc.
Format: Blues
Roscoe Miller, General Manager

Fort Mitchell

WBFA
01-01-1988; 98.3 mhz FM; 6 kw; 328 ft.; N32 21 48 W85 3 6
111 East Kilbourn Avenue, Suite 2700, Milwaukee, WI 53202 US
(706) 576-3000, *Fax:* (706) 576-3010
www.thebeatcolumbus.com
derrickgreene@clearchannel.com
License: Fort Mitchell, Russell County, AL held by CC Licenses LLC.
Group Owner: Clear Channel Communications Inc.; (acq 2-21-2002; grpsl)
Arbitron Metro Market: Columbus, GA *Format:* Adult Contemp
Special Programming: Relg 6 hrs wkly
Brian Waters, Operations Dir
James Martin, General Manager

Fort Payne

WFPA
12-01-1949; 1400 khz AM *Hrs Open:* 24; 1 kw-U, ND1; N34 26 21 W85 42 9
5 D'Arbonne Court, Kenner, LA 70065 US
(256) 845-7721, *Fax:* (256) 845-6593
www.1400wfpa.com
wfpa@1400wfpa.com
License: Fort Payne, AL held by J.A.R. Services LLC
Nat'l Network: CBS Radio; Premiere Radio Networks; Talk Radio Network; Jones Radio Networks
Arbitron Metro Market: Huntsville, AL *Format:* News, News/Talk, 86 *Hrs. of News Programming:* news progmg 15 hrs wkly *No. News Employees:* 1 *Target Audience:* 25-59; women/men *Adv. Rates:* 10;10;10;10
Mike Wallace, General Manager
Tammy Wallace, Chief Engineer

WZOB
07-02-1950; 1250 khz AM *Hrs Open:* 24 hrs; 5 kw-D, ND1; 0.122 kw-N, ND1; N34 26 23 W85 45 12
Mailing Address: P. O. Box 967, Dublin, GA 31021 US
Second Address: Hwy. 35 W., Radio Dr., Fort Payne, AL 35968
(256) 845-2810, *Fax:* (256) 845-7521
wzobam@windjammer.net
License: Fort Payne, AL held by Central Broadcasting Co. Inc.
Regional Reps: Dora-Clayton. *Wire Services:* NOAA Weather
Arbitron Metro Market: Fort Payne, AL *Format:* Country *Special Programming:* Farm 2 hrs, gospel 5 hrs, relg 5 hrs wkly *No. News Employees:* 1
Mike Kirby, President
Doris Hobbs, Station Manager

Fort Rucker

WJRL-FM
10-05-1968; 103.9 mhz FM *Hrs Open:* 24; 25 kw; Ant 292 ft; N31 26 25 W85 33 49
285 N. Foster St., Dothan, AL 36302

(334) 792-0047, *Fax:* (334) 712-9346
License: Fort Rucker, Dale County, AL held by Magic Broadcasting Alabama Licensing LLC.
Group Owner: Magic Broadcasting LLC; (acq 8-1-2002; $750,000 with co-located AM)
Nat'l Network: Moody
Arbitron Metro Market: Dothan, AL *Special Programming:* Gospel 8 hrs, jazz 4 hrs, oldies 6 hrs wkly *Hrs. of News Programming:* news progmg 15 hrs wkly *No. News Employees:* 1

Greg Kamishlian, General Manager
Chris Green, General Sales Mgr
John Houston, Programming Director
Steve Youngblood, Chief Engineer

Fruithurst

WCKS
05-09-1994; 102.7 mhz FM; 1.65 kw; 630 ft.; N33 37 24 W85 20 14
2225 Victory Church Road, Bowdon, GA 30174 US
(770) 834-5477, *Fax:* (770) 830-1027
www.gradickcommunications.com
cworthington@newstalk1330.com
License: Fruithurst, Cleburne County, AL held by WCKS LLC.
Arbitron Metro Market: Atlanta, GA *Format:* Adult Contemp
Target Audience: 25-44.

Steve Gradick, President
Colin Worthington, News Director
Michael Vincent, Production Director
Mitch Grey, Sports Director

Fulton

***WJIK**
89.3 mhz FM; 2.1 kw; 545 ft.; N31 53 28 W87 42 45
3000 W Macarthur Blvd, Santa Ana, CA 92704 US
(208) 734-6633, *Fax:* (208) 736-1958
www.csnradio.com
License: Fulton, Monroe County, AL held by CSN International.
Group Owner: CSN International
Arbitron Metro Market: Fulton, AL

Michael Kestler, President
Mike Stockland, General Manager
Don Mills, Programming Director

Gadsden

WAAX
10-18-1947; 570 khz AM; 5 kw-D, DAN; 0.5 kw-N, DAN; N33 58 45 W86 0 9 *Rebroadcasts:* Rebroadcasts WERC(AM) Birmingham 80%
600 Congress Avenue, Suite 1400, Austin, TX 78701 US
(509) 548-1011, *Fax:* (509) 548-3222
koho@kohoradio.com
License: Gadsden, AL held by Capstar TX L.P.
Group Owner: Clear Channel Communications Inc.; (acq 8-30-2000; grpsl).
Arbitron Metro Market: Commerce TX *Format:* Jazz, Smooth Jazz *Adv. Rates:* 50; 40; 25; 10

Harriet Bullitt, President
Gary Mathews, General Manager

WGAD
05-26-1947; 1350 khz AM *Hrs Open:* 24; 5 kw-D, 1 kw-N, DA-N; N34 01 03 W86 05 15
Mailing Address: Box 1350, Gadsden, AL 35901
Second Address: 750 Walnut St., Gadsden, AL 35901
(256) 546-1611, *Fax:* (256) 547-9062
License: Gadsden, Etowah County, AL held by The DR Group LLC
Population Served: 100,000*Adv. Rates:* 13; 13; 13; 10

Dave Hedrick, General Manager

WMGJ
09-11-1985; 1240 khz AM; 1 kw-U, ND1; N34 0 4 W86 1 48
P. O. Box 408, Gadsden, AL 35902 US
(256) 546-4434, *Fax:* (256) 546-9645
www.wmgj.com
floyddddonald@aol.com
License: Gadsden, AL held by Floyd L. Donald Broadcasting Co. Inc.
Nat'l Reps: Roslin
Arbitron Metro Market: GADSDEN, AL *Format:* Urban Contemporary

Floyd Donald, General Manager

***WSGN**
02-11-1975; 91.5 mhz FM *Hrs Open:* 24; 6.3 kw vert; 522 ft.; N34 4 29 W86 1 11 *Rebroadcasts:* Rebroadcasts WBHM(FM) Birmingham 80%
1001 George Wallace Dr., P.O. Box 27, Gadsden, AL 35902 US
(256) 549-8200
www.gadsdenstate.edu
nmullin@gadsdenstate.edu
License: Gadsden, Etowah County, AL held by Gadsden State Community College.
Format: News *Special Programming:* Folk 2 hrs, new age 10 hrs wkly *Hrs. of News Programming:* News progmg 34 hrs wkly
Target Audience: General.

Dr. Renee Culverhouse, President
Neil Mullin, General Manager

***WTBB**
07-20-1999; 89.9 mhz FM *Hrs Open:* 24; 4.8 kw; Ant 515 ft; N34 06 03 W85 59 37 *Rebroadcasts:* Rebroadcasts WTBJ(FM) Oxford 100%
Trinity Christian Academy, 1500 Airport Rd., Oxford, AL 36203
(256) 831-3333, *Fax:* (256) 831-5895
www.trinityoxford.org
truth@trinityoxford.org
License: Gadsden, Etowah County, AL held by Trinity Christian Academy.
Population Served: 500,000*Special Programming:* Sp one hr wkly

Dr. C.O. Grinstead, General Manager

Geneva

WGEA
03-17-1953; 1150 khz AM; 1 kw-D, ND1; 0.035 kw-N, ND1; N31 1 21 W85 52 16
Mailing Address: 409 East Broad Street, Ozark, AL 36360 US
Second Address: 420 Riverside Ave., Geneva, AL 36340
(334) 774-7673, *Fax:* (334) 774-6450
www.wgea.us
yell@wgea.us
License: Geneva, AL held by Shelley Broadcasting Co.
Arbitron Metro Market: Dothan, AL *Format:* Country, Gospel, 60, News/Talk, Talk *Target Audience:* 30 plus.

Jack Mizell, President
Doc Parker, General Manager

WDBT
09-12-1969; 93.7 mhz FM *Hrs Open:* 24; 100 kw; Ant 853 ft; N31 02 42 W85 57 33
285 E. Broad St., Ozark, AL 36360
(334) 774-7673, *Fax:* (334) 774-6450
www.wrjm.com
hjmizell@wrjm.com
License: Geneva, Geneva County, AL held by Stage Door Development, William C. Carn, Trustee
Nat'l Network: ABC; Westwood One *Nat'l Reps:* Rgnl Reps
Population Served: 790,000 *Arbitron Metro Market:* Dothan, AL
Target Audience: 30 plus. *Adv. Rates:* 40; 35; 30; 25

Jack Mizell, President
Susannah Hodges, Station Manager
Boyd Mizell, Engineering Dir

Georgiana

WFXX
01-01-1999; 107.7 mhz FM *Hrs Open:* 24; 42 kw; 535 ft.; N31 27 8 W86 37 7
108 Stanfield St, Greenville, AL 36037 US
(334) 222-2222, *Fax:* (334) 427-8888
www.fox107.com
wfxx@alaweb.com
License: Georgiana, Butler County, AL held by Star Broadcasting Inc.
Format: Adult Contemp

Jeffrey Haynes, President
Kelly Haynes, General Manager

Glencoe

WGMZ
10-11-1993; 93.1 mhz FM *Hrs Open:* 24; 1.65 kw; 620 ft.; N33 57 16 W85 51 40
Mailing Address: 600 Congress Avenue, Suite 1400, Austin, TX 78701 US
Second Address: 304 S. 4th St., Gadsden, AL 35901
(256) 549-0931, *Fax:* (256) 543-8777
www.wgmz.com
gadsdenthoduction@clearchannel.com
License: Glencoe, Etowah County, AL held by Capstar TX L.P.
Group Owner: Clear Channel Communications Inc.; (acq 8-30-00; grpsl).
Format: Oldies *No. News Employees:* 1 *Target Audience:* 35 plus.

Mark Mayes, President
Kathy Boggs, General Manager
Rick Sisk, Programming Director

Goodwater

WKGA
04-04-1990; 97.5 mhz FM *Hrs Open:* 24; 5.1 kw; 354 ft.; N33 1 42 W85 59 23
Mailing Address: P.O. Drawer 1270, Talladega Shopp'g Center, Talladega, AL 35161 US
Second Address: 1051 Tallapoosa St., Alexander City, AL 35011
(256) 234-6977, *Fax:* (256) 234-6976
www.wkgacountry.com
info@wkgacountry.com
License: Goodwater, Coosa County, AL held by Lake Broadcasting Inc.
Format: Country

John Kennedy, President

***WFAZ**
91.1 mhz FM; 700 w; Ant 220 ft; N33 07 01 W86 07 01
908 Opelika Rd., Auburn, AL
(334) 821-0744, *Fax:* (334) 821-4031
jimmy@jimmyscarstereo.com
License: Goodwater, Coosa County, AL held by Jimmy Jarrell Communications Foundation Inc.

Jimmy Jarrell, President

Goshen

WAOQ
06-03-1999; 100.3 mhz FM *Hrs Open:* 24; 6 kw; 328 ft.; N31 42 26 W86 13 12
P.O. Box 83, Clanton, AL 35045 US
(334) 335-2877, *Fax:* (205) 755- 3329
www.waoq.com
office@waoq.com
License: Goshen, Crenshaw County, AL held by Alatron Corp. Inc.
Arbitron Metro Market: Brantley, Al *Format:* Country *Special Programming:* Gospel 14 hrs wkly *Hrs. of News Programming:* News progmg 14 hrs wkly

Robert Williams, President
Christopher Johnson, General Manager
Ken Lyons, Station Manager

Greensboro

WDGM
03-03-2002; 99.1 mhz FM *Hrs Open:* 24; 25 kw; Ant 328 ft; N32 49 46 W87 40 19
142 Skyland Blvd., Tuscaloosa, AL 35476
(205) 339-4953, *Fax:* (205) 349-1715
www.991wdgm.com
todd.livingston@townsquaremedia.com
License: Greensboro, Hale County, AL
Group Owner: Townsquare Media; (acq 7-12-2005; grpsl).
Nat'l Network: ESPN Radio *Nat'l Reps:* Roslin
Population Served: 91,605 *Arbitron Metro Market:* Tuscaloosa, AL *Target Audience:* 25 plus; male & female

Todd Livingston, General Manager
Tammy Boyd, General Sales Mgr
Greg Thomas, Programming Director
Meg Summers, Promotions Manager
Tammy Boyd, Director of Sales

Greenville

WGYV
08-18-1948; 1380 khz AM; 1 kw-D, NDD; N31 50 1 W86 36 7
PO Box 585, Greenville, AL 36037 US
(334) 382-5444, *Fax:* (334) 382-5444
www.wgyv.com
wgyv@alaweb.com
License: Greenville, AL held by Robert John Williamson
Format: News, News/Talk, 64, Talk *Special Programming:* Black 6 hrs wkly *Target Audience:* 25-54; general *Adv. Rates:* 6.95; 6.95; 6.95; na

Robert Williamson, General Manager
Bob Luman, Chief Engineer

WQZX
08-19-1985; 94.3 mhz FM *Hrs Open:* 24; 3.9 kw; 410 ft.; N31 54 40 W86 36 19
205 West Commerce Street, Greenville, AL 36037 US
(334) 382-6633, *Fax:* (334) 382-6634
www.q94.net
q94@q94.net
License: Greenville, Butler County, AL held by Haynes Broadcasting Inc.
Nat'l Network: ABC
Format: Country

Kyle Haynes, President
Mark Ritchie, Programming Director
Chris Johnson, Chief Engineer

Grove Hill

WBMH
05-01-1999; 106.1 mhz FM; 12 kw; 472 ft.; N31 43 30 W87 54 58
Mailing Address: 324 Bradford Street, NW, Gainesville, GA 30501 US
Second Address: 4428 N College Ave, Jackson, AL 36545
(251) 246-4431, *Fax:* (251) 246-1980
www.bamadixie.com
bama1061@yahoo.com
License: Grove Hill, Clarke County, AL held by Capital Assets Inc.
Group Owner: Bennie E. Hewett Stns
Format: Country
Paul McVay, Operations Dir
Benney Hewitt, General Manager

Guntersville

WGSV
04-16-1950; 1270 khz AM; 1 kw-D, NDD; 0.124 kw-N, ND1; N34 18 31 W86 17 44
Mailing Address: P. O. Box 220, Guntersville, AL 35970 US
Second Address: 2301 Thomas Ave., Guntersville, AL
(256) 582-8131, *Fax:* (256) 582-4347
www.wgsv.com
am1270@cwgsv.com
License: Guntersville, AL held by Guntersville Broadcasting Co. Inc.
Nat'l Network: ABC
Format: News, News/Talk, 86
Lavell Jackson, President
Kerry Jackson, Operations Dir

*WJIA
09-01-1995; 88.5 mhz FM; 2.2 kw vert; 427 ft.; N34 25 33 W86 18 25
5025 Spring Creek Drive, Guntersville, AL 35976 US
(256) 505-0885, *Fax:* (256) 505-0886
www.wjia.org
jfm@wjia.org
License: Guntersville, Marshall County, AL held by Lake City Educational Broadcasting Inc.
Format: Christian
Stan Broadus, General Manager
Kevin Guffey, Station Manager

WTWX-FM
08-01-1969; 95.9 mhz FM; 10.5 kw; 515 ft.; N34 20 14 W86 16 46
Mailing Address: P. O. Box 220, Guntersville, AL 35976 US
Second Address: 2301 Thomas Ave., Guntersville, AL
(256) 582-4946, *Fax:* (256) 582-4347
www.wtwx.com
wtwx@wtwx.com
License: Guntersville, Marshall County, AL held by Guntersville Broadcasting Co., Inc.
Nat'l Network: ABC
Arbitron Metro Market: Huntsville, AL *Format:* Country
Lavell Jackson, President
Kerry Jackson, General Manager

Gurley

WHRP
06-08-1995; 94.1 mhz FM *Hrs Open:* 24; 0.71 kw; 945 ft.; N34 40 50 W86 30 55
600 Congress Avenue, Suite 1400, Austin, TX 78701 US
(256) 830-8300, *Fax:* (256) 232-6842
www.whrpfm.com
toni.terrell@cumulus.com
License: Gurley, Madison County, AL held by Cumulus Licensing LLC.
Group Owner: Cumulus Media Inc.; (acq 4-4-2006; $3.3 million with WVNN-FM Trinity)
Nat'l Reps: Katz Radio
Arbitron Metro Market: Huntsville, AL *Format:* Urban Contemporary *Hrs. of News Programming:* 4 hrs per wk
Brian Zaborny, Operations Dir
Bill West, General Manager
Tracy Flesch, General Sales Mgr
Toni Terrell, Programming Director
Aaron Hurd, Promotions Manager
Audrey Raines, News Director
Chuck Miller, Engineering Dir

Hackleburg

WFMH-FM
01-01-1996; 95.5 mhz FM *Hrs Open:* 24; 4.1 kw; 400 ft.; N34 18 38 W87 56 13
1707 Warnke Road, N.W., Cullman, AL 35055 US
(205) 935-3730, *Fax:* (205) 935-3734
www.big955.com
License: Hackleburg, Marion County, AL held by Williams Communications.
Group Owner: Williams Communications Inc.; (acq 8-18-2004; $2.45 million with WFMH(AM) Cullman).
Wire Services: AP
Format: Country *Hrs. of News Programming:* News progmg 15 hrs wkly *Target Audience:* 35-64.
Bryan Walker, Programming Director

Haleyville

WWWH
04-01-1949; 1230 khz AM *Hrs Open:* 24; 1 kw-U; N34 14 00 W87 37 32
Drawer 370, 807 Hwy. 13 N., Haleyville, AL 35565
(205) 486-2277,(205) 486-2278, *Fax:* (205) 486-3905
advertising@wjbbfm.com
License: Haleyville, Winston County, AL held by Haleyville Broadcasting Co. Inc.
Nat'l Reps: Rgnl Reps
Population Served: 87,000*Special Programming:* Farm 3 hrs wkly *Hrs. of News Programming:* news progmg 36 hrs wkly *No. News Employees:* 1 *Target Audience:* 25-55; professionals
John Slatton, President
Terry Slatton, General Manager
Debby Aderholt, General Sales Mgr
Robert Wakefield, Programming Director
Sherron Hayes, News Director
Larry Gardner, Public Affairs Director
Aubrey Haynes, Sales VP

WWWH-FM
07-14-1979; 92.7 mhz FM; 3.9 kw; Ant 240 ft; N34 14 00 W87 37 32
Mailing Address: Drawer 370, Haleyville, AL 35565
Second Address: 807 Hwy. 13 N., Haleyville, AL 35565
(205) 486-2277,(205) 486-2278, *Fax:* (205) 486-3905
wjbb@southnet.net
License: Haleyville, Winston County, AL held by Haleyville Broadcasting Co. Inc.
Population Served: 118,000*Target Audience:* 24-55.
John Slatton, CEO
Terry Slatton, President
Andy Marbutt, Operations Dir
Aubrey Haynes, General Sales Mgr
Keith Page, Programming Director
Sherron Hayes, News Director
Misty Sawyer, Disc Jockey

Hamilton

WERH
08-24-1950; 970 khz AM; 5 kw-D, NDD; N34 7 1 W87 59 29
P.O. Box 1119, Hamilton, AL 35570 US
(205) 921-3195, *Fax:* (205) 921-7187
werh@sonet.net
License: Hamilton, AL held by Kate F. Fite.
Arbitron Metro Market: Hamilton, AL *Format:* Country, Gospel
Special Programming: Farm *Target Audience:* General. *Adv. Rates:* 6; 6; 6; 6
James Fowler, General Manager
Geraldine Miller, General Sales Mgr
Bryan Williams, Programming Director
Bill Moates, Chief Engineer

WERH-FM
04-01-1968; 92.1 mhz FM *Hrs Open:* 24; 3 kw; 121 ft.; N34 7 1 W87 59 29
P.O. Box 1119, Hamilton, AL 35570 US
(205) 921-3481, *Fax:* (205) 921-7187
License: Hamilton, Marion County, AL
Arbitron Metro Market: Hamilton, AL *Format:* Classic Rock *Adv. Rates:* Same as AM
Mark Burleson, News Director
Geraldine Miller, Traffic Manager

Hanceville

WQHC
04-01-1986; 1170 khz AM *Hrs Open:* Sunrise-sunset
401 College Drive Ne, Hanceville, AL 35077 US
(256) 352-1115, *Fax:* (205) 295-1238
www.joychristianradio.com
License: Hanceville, AL held by Queen of Heaven Catholic Radio Inc.
Arbitron Metro Market: Hanceville, AL *Format:* Gospel
Ralph Jolly, General Manager

Hartselle

WTAK-FM
08-01-1992; 106.1 mhz FM *Hrs Open:* 24; 5.4 kw; 725 ft.; N34 27 45 W86 38 36
Mailing Address: 600 Congress Avenue, Suite 1400, Austin, TX 78701 US
Second Address: 26869 Peoples Rd., Madison, AL 35756
(256) 353-1750, *Fax:* (256) 350-2653
www.wtak.com
info@wtak.com
License: Hartselle, Morgan County, AL held by Clear Channel Communications
Group Owner: Clear Channel Communications Inc.; (acq 8-30-00; grpsl)
Arbitron Metro Market: Huntsville, AL *Format:* Classic Rock
Erich West, Operations Dir
Rick Brown, General Manager
Carmelilta Palmer, General Sales Mgr
Stephanie McGee, News Director
Carl Ampieri, Chief Engineer

WYAM
10-01-1956; 890 khz AM *Hrs Open:* 12; 2.5 kw-D, NDD; N34 34 0 W86 54 46
3002 Riley Road, Huntsville, AL 35801 US
(256) 355-4567, *Fax:* (256) 351-1234
wileywg@acninc.net
License: Hartselle, AL held by Decatur Communications Properties LLC
Arbitron Metro Market: Huntsville, AL *Format:* Spanish *Hrs. of News Programming:* news progmg 6 hrs wkly *No. News Employees:* 2 *Target Audience:* 18-60; General
William Wiley, President

Harvest

*WAYH
01-01-2003; 88.1 mhz FM *Hrs Open:* 24; 3.5 kw; 669 ft.; N34 49 8 W86 44 19
P.O. Box 887, Brentwood, TN 37024 US
(256) 837-9293, *Fax:* (256) 772-6731
www.wayh.wayfm.com
supportservices@wayfm.com
License: Harvest, Madison County, AL held by WAY-FM Media Group Inc.
Group Owner: WAY-FM Media Group Inc.
Arbitron Metro Market: Harvest, AL *Format:* Christian *Target Audience:* 18-34; youth & young adults
Lloyd Parker, COO
Bob Augsburg, President
Jack Davis, Operations Dir
Thom Ewing, General Manager
Lisa Shelton, General Sales Mgr
Tina Dimarco, Promotions Manager
Linda Cashin, Administrative Service Manager
Bob Augsburg,Founder

Hazel Green

WBXR
12-11-1970; 1140 khz AM *Hrs Open:* Sunrise-sunset; 7.5 kw-C, DAD; 15 kw-D, DAD; N34 57 11 W86 38 46
2926-D Huntsville Hwy, Fayetteville, TN 37334 US
(931) 433-7017(888) 570-7286, *Fax:* (931) 433-8282
wilkinsradio.com
janet@wilkinsradio.com.
License: Hazel Green, AL held by New England Communications Inc.
Group Owner: Wilkins Communications Network Inc.; (acq 9-16-97; $150,000).
Nat'l Network: Salem Radio Network
Arbitron Metro Market: Fayetteville, TN *Format:* Christian, Talk
Target Audience: 35 plus. *Adv. Rates:* 35; 35, 35, 35
Mitchell Mathis, CEO/COO
Mitchell Mathis, President
Mitchell Mathis, Operations Dir
Carla Payne, Station Manager
Don Roden, Engineering Dir
Kevin Kidd, Engineer
Greg Garrett, Operations Manager

Headland

WECB
09-01-1992; 105.3 mhz FM *Hrs Open:* 24; 11.5 kw; Ant 485 ft; N31 15 48 W85 18 24
3245 Montgomery Hwy., Suite 1, Dothan, AL 36305
(334) 712-9233, *Fax:* (334) 712-0374
www.legends1053.com
ron@wdjr.com

License: Headland, Henry County, AL held by Gulf South Communications Inc.
Group Owner: Woodward Communications Inc
Nat'l Reps: McGavren Guild
Arbitron Metro Market: Dothan, AL *No. News Employees:* 7
Misty Huff, Operations Dir
Ron Eubanks, General Manager
Bill Moody, General Sales Mgr
April Granger, News Director

Heflin

*WPIL
01-01-2003; 91.7 mhz FM; 1.3 kw; 85 ft.; N33 36 55 W85 32 41
321 Freeman Circle, Norcross, GA 30071 US
(256) 463-4226, *Fax:* (256) 463-4232
www.wpilfm.com
wpil@wpilfm.com
License: Heflin, Cleburne County, AL held by Jimmy Jarrell Communications Foundation Inc.
Arbitron Metro Market: Heflin, AL *Format:* Country, Gospel
Jimmy Jarrell, President
Robert Jarrell, General Manager
Dale Hamilton, Programer
Jean Hemby, Accounts Executive Manager

*WKNG-FM
05-01-2005; 89.1 mhz FM; 0.25 kw; 719 ft.; N33 33 18 W85 27 25
102 Parkwood Circle, Carrollton, GA 30117 US
(770) 574-0891, *Fax:* (770) 574-0892
www.rejoice891.com
doug@rejoice891.com
License: Heflin, Cleburne County, AL held by Covenant Communications Inc.
Arbitron Metro Market: Heflin, AL *Format:* Gospel
Steven Gradick, President

Hobson City

WHMA-FM
10-04-1984; 95.5 mhz FM *Hrs Open:* 24; 0.53 kw; 1089 ft.; N33 37 38 W85 53 25
P.O. Box 343, Wedowee, AL 36278 US
(256) 236-1274, *Fax:* (256) 236-9414
www.whmabig95.com
texbig95@cableone.net
License: Hobson City, Calhoun County, AL held by Williams Communications Inc.
Group Owner: Williams Communications Inc.; (acq 8-2-2002; $2.88 million with WZZX(AM) Lineville).
Arbitron Metro Market: Hobson City, AL *Format:* Country *Special Programming:* Black 6 hrs wkly *Target Audience:* 18-54.
Walt Williams Jr., General Manager
Tex Carter, Programming Director

WHOG
04-15-1991; 1120 khz AM *Hrs Open:* Sunrise-sunset; 500 w-D; N33 36 50 W85 51 19
1330 Noble Street, Suite 25, Anniston, AL 36201
(256) 236-6484, *Fax:* (256) 236-6484
www.newsdaytonabeach.com
hog1120@aol.com
License: Hobson City, Calhoun County, AL held by Hobson City Broadcasting Co.
Nat'l Reps: Dora-Clayton
Population Served: 200,000*Target Audience:* General.
Joe Vines, Operations Dir
Leah Jarrell, General Manager
Donna Fillion, General Sales Mgr
Frank Scott, Programming Director
Rex Smith, Chief Engineer

Holly Pond

WRSA-FM
11-23-1965; 96.9 mhz FM *Hrs Open:* 24; 100 kw; 1,010 ft; N34 29 19 W86 37 08
8402 Memorial Pkwy SW, Huntsville, AL 35754
(256) 885-9797, *Fax:* (256) 885-9796
www.lite969.com
License: Holly Pond, Cullman County, AL held by NCA Inc.
Nat'l Reps: Local Focus
Population Served: 500,000 *Arbitron Metro Market:* Huntsville, AL *Hrs. of News Programming:* news progmg one hr wkly *No. News Employees:* 1 *Target Audience:* Women 25-54
Penny Nielson, CEO
Nate Adams, Operations Dir
Tom Panucci, General Sales Mgr
John Malone, Programming Director
Don Roden, Chief Engineer

Homewood

WBPT
06-01-1959; 106.9 mhz FM; 97 kw; 1325 ft.; N33 29 4 W86 48 25
3773 Howard Hughes Pwy, Suite 300n, Las Vegas, NV 89109 US
(205) 916-1100, *Fax:* (205) 290-1061
http://www.birminghamseagle.com/
License: Homewood, Jefferson County, AL held by Cox Radio Inc.
Group Owner: Cox Radio Inc.; (acq 3-28-97; grpsl)
Nat'l Reps: Katz Radio
Arbitron Metro Market: Birmingham, AL *TV Affiliate:* Classic hits
Special Programming: news progmg 15 hrs wkly *Hrs. of News Programming:* 1 *No. News Employees:* 25-54; affluent baby boom
Program Director, Justin Ragland
Promotions Director, Don Daley
Traffic Manager

Huntsville

WAHR
07-28-1959; 99.1 mhz FM; 100 kw; 984 ft.; N34 47 53 W86 38 24 US
(256) 536-1568, *Fax:* (256) 536-4416
www.rocketcitynews.com
lorand@rocketcitybroadcasting.com
License: Huntsville, Madison County, AL held by BCA Radio LLC.
Group Owner: Black Crow Media Group LLC; (acq 11-15-2001; grpsl).
Arbitron Metro Market: Huntsville, AL *Format:* Adult Contemp
Target Audience: 25-55.
Eric Jewell, General Manager
Laura Orand, Director of Sales
Chris Calloway, Programming Director
Don Phelps, News Director
Nick Emmons, Chief Engineer
Brianna Bragdon, Traffic Manager

WBHP
05-23-1937; 1230 khz AM; 1 kw-U, ND1; N34 43 9 W86 35 42
Mailing Address: 600 Congress Ave., Suite 1400, Austin, TX 78701 US
Second Address: 266869 Peoples Rd., Madison, AL 35758
(256) 309-2400, *Fax:* (256) 350-2653
www.wbhpam.com
sales@wdrm.com
License: Huntsville, AL held by Capstar TX L.P.
Group Owner: Clear Channel Communications Inc.; (acq 8-30-00; grpsl).
Arbitron Metro Market: Madison, AL *Format:* Talk *Target Audience:* General.
Rick Brown, General Manager
Stuart Langston, Programming Director
Carmelita Palmer, ADVERTISING

WDJL
10-01-1968; 1000 khz AM *Hrs Open:* Sunrise-sunset
603 Governors Drive, Huntsville, AL 35801 US
(256) 852-1223, *Fax:* (256) 852-1900
www.love1000am.com
info@wjdl.com
License: Huntsville, AL held by James K. Sharp dba 5th Avenue Broadcasting.
Nat'l Network: Westwood One
Arbitron Metro Market: Huntsville, AL *Format:* Gospel *Special Programming:* Gospel comedy 6 hrs wkly *Target Audience:* 35-65; upscale decision makers that enjoy hits of the 40s, 50s & 60s
Dorothy Sandifer, CEO/COO
Walter Peavy, President
Dorothy Sandifer and Antonio Acklin, Programming Director

WHIY
03-20-1958; 1600 khz AM; 5 kw-D, DAN; 0.5 kw-N, DAN; N34 45 32 W86 38 35
P. O. Box 920, Huntsville, AL 35804 US
(256) 837-9387, *Fax:* (256) 837-9404
www.whiyam.com
hundley@103weup.com
License: Huntsville, AL held by Hundley Batts Sr. & Virginia Caples.
Arbitron Metro Market: Huntsville, AL *Format:* Blues *Target Audience:* 25-65.
Hundley Batts Sr., President
Hundley Batts, General Manager
Steve Murry, Programming Director

*WJAB
05-09-1991; 90.9 mhz FM *Hrs Open:* 24; 100 kw; 335 ft.; N34 47 9 W86 34 0
Mailing Address: PO Box 174, Normal, AL 35762 US
Second Address: 3409 Meridian St., Huntsville, AL 35811
(256) 372-5795, *Fax:* (256) 372-5907
www2.aamu.edu/wjab
License: Huntsville, Madison County, AL held by Board of Trustees Alabama A&M University.
Nat'l Network: NPR; PRI *Wire Services:* AP
Arbitron Metro Market: Huntsville, AL *Format:* Blues, Jazz
Special Programming: Black 3 hrs, oldies 8 hrs, reggae 4 hrs, Latin one *No. News Employees:* 1
Michael Burns, Operations Dir
Elizabeth Sloan-Ragland, General Manager
Erica Fox Colman, News Director
Michael Moms, Chief Engineer
Elizabeth Sloan-Ragland, Director of Telecommunication
Rita Hayes, Traffic Manager
Lois Watkins,Production Manager
Jerome Foster, Producer

WLOR
06-01-1948; 1550 khz AM *Hrs Open:* 24
P.O. Box 5936, Huntsville, AL 35814 US
(256) 536-1568, *Fax:* (256) 536-4416
www.jammin1550.am
ed@jammin1550.am
License: Huntsville, AL held by BCA Radio LLC.
Group Owner: Black Crow Media Group LLC; (acq 11-15-2001; grpsl)
Nat'l Network: ABC
Arbitron Metro Market: Huntsville, AL *Format:* Oldies *Hrs. of News Programming:* news progmg one hr wkly *No. News Employees:* 1 *Target Audience:* General. *Adv. Rates:* 25; 20; 10; 10
Eric Jewell, General Manager
Ed Gaines, Programming Director

*WLRH
10-13-1976; 89.3 mhz FM *Hrs Open:* 24; 100 kw; 810 ft.; N34 37 41 W86 30 59
2112 11th Ave., South, Birmingham, AL 35256 US
(256) 895-9574, *Fax:* (256) 830-4577
www.wlrh.org
wlrhnews@highway.net
License: Huntsville, Madison County, AL held by Alabama ETV Commission.
Nat'l Network: PRI; NPR
Arbitron Metro Market: Huntsville, AL *Format:* News *Hrs. of News Programming:* news progmg 40 hrs wkly *No. News Employees:* 1 *Target Audience:* General.
Cheryl Carlson, General Manager
Jennifer Jaudon-Johnston, General Sales Mgr
Oliver Stultner, Programming Director

WRTT-FM
10-06-1960; 95.1 mhz FM *Hrs Open:* 24; 12 kw; 909 ft.; N34 47 53 W86 38 24
2407 9th Avenue Sw, Huntsville, AL 35805 US
(256) 536-1568, *Fax:* (256) 536-4416
www.therocket951.com
info@rocket951.fm
License: Huntsville, Madison County, AL held by BCA Radio LLC.
Group Owner: Black Crow Media Group LLC; (acq 11-15-2001; grpsl).
Arbitron Metro Market: Huntsville, AL *Format:* Rock/AOR *Special Programming:* Relg *No. News Employees:* 1 *Target Audience:* 24-54; male
Eric Jewell, General Manager
Clay Sanders, Programming Director

*WJOU
12-01-1978; 90.1 mhz FM; 25 kw; 230 ft.; N34 45 28 W86 39 44
Oakwood Road, NW, Huntsville, AL 35806 US
(256) 722-9990, *Fax:* (256) 837-7918
www.wocg.org
wjou@oakwood.edu
License: Huntsville, Madison County, AL held by Oakwood College.
Nat'l Network: USA
Arbitron Metro Market: Huntsville, AL *TV Affiliate:* Relg *Special Programming:* News progmg 14 hrs wkly *No. News Employees:* 34-55; families with inte
General Manager, General Manager

WTKI
11-01-1946; 1450 khz AM *Hrs Open:* 24; 1 kw-U, ND1; N34 43 30 W86 36 15
223 East Side Square, Huntsville, AL 35801 US

RADIO - U.S.

(256) 533-1450, *Fax:* (256) 551-9865
www.wtkiradio.com
info@wtkiradio.com
License: Huntsville, AL held by Christian Voice of Central Ohio Inc.
Group Owner: Christian Voice of Central Ohio Inc.; (acq 3-9-2007; $460,000)
Arbitron Metro Market: Huntsville, AL *Format:* Sports
Dan Baughman, General Manager

WEUP
01-01-2001; 1700 khz AM
PO Box 920, Huntsville, AL 35804 US
(256) 837-9387, *Fax:* (256) 837-9404
www.weupam.com
hundley@103weup.com
License: Huntsville, AL held by Hundley Batts Sr. & Virginia Caples.
Arbitron Metro Market: Huntsville, AL *Format:* Gospel
Hundley Batts, General Manager
Steve Murry, Programming Director

Irondale

WQOH
12-05-1960; 1480 khz AM *Hrs Open:* 24
645 Church Street, Suite 400, Norfolk, VA 23510 US
(205) 744-4456
www.queenofheavenradio.com
jack@queenofheavenradio.com
License: Irondale, AL held by Queen of Heaven Catholic Radio Inc.
Nat'l Network: EWTN Radio
Arbitron Metro Market: Birmingham, AL *Format:* Christian
Marc Corsini, President

Jackson

WRJX
06-01-1950; 1230 khz AM *Hrs Open:* 5 AM-midnight; 1 kw-U, ND1; N31 32 38 W87 52 30
Mailing Address: 311 Green St, NESte 211, Gainesville, GA 30501 US
Second Address: 4428 College Ave., Jackson, AL 36545
(251) 246-4431, *Fax:* (251) 246-1980
radiocenter@starband.com
License: Jackson, AL held by Capital Assets Inc.
Group Owner: Bennie E. Hewett Stns
Format: Black, Gospel *No. News Employees:* 1 *Target Audience:* 25-54; business minded, baby-boomers
Shirley Chandler, General Sales Mgr
Paul McVay, Programming Director
Kelly Snell, News Director

WHOD
08-01-1964; 94.5 mhz FM *Hrs Open:* 5 AM-midnight; 30 kw; 640 ft.; N31 28 59 W87 47 27
Mailing Address: 324 Bradford Street NW, Gainesville, GA 30501 US
Second Address: 4428 College Ave., Jackson, AL 36545
(251) 246-4431, *Fax:* (251) 246-1980
License: Jackson, Clarke County, AL
Group Owner: Bennie E. Hewett Stns
Nat'l Network: ABC
Format: Adult Contemp *Hrs. of News Programming:* news progmg 2 hrs wkly *No. News Employees:* 1
Scott Meier, General Manager
Scott Stein, Programming Director

Jacksonville

***WLJS-FM**
09-29-1975; 91.9 mhz FM; 0.61 kw; 1024 ft.; N33 50 12 W85 43 59
700 North Pelham Road, Jacksonville, AL 36265 US
(256) 782-5300, *Fax:* (256) 782-5645
www.919fm.webs.com
programdirectorwljs@gmail.com
License: Jacksonville, Calhoun County, AL held by Board of Trustees-Jacksonville State University.
Nat'l Network: NPR
Format: Variety/Diverse *Special Programming:* Relg 3 hrs wkly *Target Audience:* 18-34; college, young adult
Mike Stedham, General Manager
Thad Burton, Programming Director
Scott Simpson, News Director
Andrew Holderfield, Assistant Program Director
Billy Ramsey, Patrons Director

WCKA
01-01-1986; 810 khz AM *Hrs Open:* 24; 50 kw-D, DA2; 0.5 kw-N, DA2; N33 50 58 W85 45 46
Mailing Address: 3 River Street, White Springs, FL 32096 US
Second Address: 188 Broadcast Blvd., Jacksonville, AL 36265
(256) 237-0810, *Fax:* (256) 782-2489
alabama810@alabama810.com
License: Jacksonville, AL held by Alabama 810 LLC
Nat'l Network: USA *Regional Network:* Alabama Radio Net.
Arbitron Metro Market: Calhoun, AL *Format:* Country *Special Programming:* Gospel 2 hrs wkly *Hrs. of News Programming:* news progmg 15 hrs wkly *No. News Employees:* 2 *Target Audience:* 25 plus; adults*Adv. Rates:* 25; 25; 25; 15
Leslie Gradick, General Manager
Mike Mitchell, News Director

Jasper

WJLX
03-01-1957; 1240 khz AM *Hrs Open:* 24; 1 kw-U, ND1; N33 48 54 W87 16 19
1499 North Airport Road, Jasper, AL 35504 US
(205) 221-2222
License: Jasper, AL held by Wal Win LLC
Arbitron Metro Market: Birmingham, AL *Format:* Gospel
Brett Elmore, General Manager

WDXB
03-28-1962; 102.5 mhz FM; 79 kw; 2,096 ft; N33 28 51 W87 24 03
600 Beacon Pkwy. W., Suite 400, Birmingham, AL 78701
(205) 439-9600, *Fax:* (205) 439-8390
www.1025thebull.com
License: Jasper, Walker County, AL held by Capstar TX L.P.
Group Owner: Clear Channel Communications Inc.; (acq 8-30-00; grpsl).
Population Served: 400,000 *Arbitron Metro Market:* Birmingham, AL
Ray Quinn, General Manager
Cyndi Lees, General Sales Mgr
Tom Hanrahan, Programming Director
Aaron Trimmer, News Director
Bob Newberry, Chief Engineer
Cynthia Childress, Traffic Manager

WIXI
11-02-1946; 1360 khz AM *Hrs Open:* 14
Post Office Box 2499, Robertsdale, AL 36567 US
(205) 384-3461, *Fax:* (205) 384-3462
www.wixi1360.com
wixi@1360wixi.com
License: Jasper, AL held by James T. Lee
Arbitron Metro Market: Jasper, AL *Format:* Christian, Gospel *Special Programming:* Gospel 6 hrs wkly *Hrs. of News Programming:* News progmg 4 hrs wkly *Target Audience:* General. *Adv. Rates:* 6; 6; 6; 3
Joe Cook, General Manager
Joe Cooke, Programming Director

Jemison

WHPH
05-15-1953; 97.7 mhz FM *Hrs Open:* 24; 13 kw; 459 ft.; N32 58 55 W86 51 2
P.O. Box 1820, Clanton, AL 35045 US
(205) 949-4584
www.977thepeach.com
977thepeach@gmail.com
License: Jemison, Chilton County, AL held by Great South Wireless LLC.
Arbitron Metro Market: Jemison, AL *Format:* Oldies
Steven Salter, General Manager

***WPJN**
89.3 mhz FM; 500 w; Ant 187 ft; N33 00 25 W86 44 03
908 Opelika Rd., Auburn, AL
(334) 821-0744, *Fax:* (334) 821-4031
License: Jemison, Chilton County, AL held by Jimmy Jarrell Communications Foundation Inc.
Jimmy Jarrell, President

Langdale

***WEBT**
01-17-1986; 91.5 mhz FM; 0.38 kw; 85 ft.; N32 48 15 W85 10 43
2615 64th Blvd, Valley, AL 36854 US
(334) 756-6923, *Fax:* (334) 756-8430
License: Langdale, Chambers County, AL held by Langdale Educational Broadcasting Foundation.
Format: Gospel *Special Programming:* Southern gospel *Target Audience:* General.
Tim Foster, Station Manager

Level Plains

WIRB
1490 khz AM
US
(334) 894-5047, *Fax:* (334) 894-6684
www.myspace.com
License: Level Plains, AL held by Virgle Leon Strictland, individually.
Arbitron Metro Market: Level Plains, AL *Format:* Gospel
Virgle Strictland, General Manager

Lexington

WJHX
02-20-1981; 620 khz AM; 5 kw-D, ND1; 0.099 kw-N, ND1; N34 58 37 W87 22 10
17967 Brownsferry Road, Athens, AL 35611 US
(256) 353-5959
www.lajefamanda.com
License: Lexington, AL held by BAR Broadcasting Inc.
Pedro Zamora, President
Moises Gomez, General Manager

Linden

WINL
04-01-1991; 98.5 mhz FM *Hrs Open:* 24; 100 kw; 817 ft.; N32 7 34 W87 44 2
110 8th Ave., West, Linden, AL 36748 US
(334) 289-9850, *Fax:* (334) 289-9811
www.bestcountryaround.com
valerie@mywin98.com
License: Linden, Marengo County, AL held by West Alabama Communications Inc.
Group Owner: West Alabama Radio Inc.; (acq 2-12-2001; $1.28 million)
Nat'l Network: ABC *Nat'l Reps:* Dora-Clayton
Format: Country *Special Programming:* Gospel 5 hrs, farm 10 hrs wkly *Target Audience:* 25-54.
Amy Douglas, General Manager

Lineville

WZZX
01-01-1967; 780 khz AM
P.O. Box 343, Wedowee, AL 36278 US
(256) 236-1880, *Fax:* (256) 236-4480
License: Lineville, AL held by Williams Communications Inc.
Group Owner: Williams Communications Inc.; (acq 7-25-2002; $2.88 million).
Arbitron Metro Market: Anniston, AL *Format:* Country
Walt Williams Jr., President
Eva Gibson, General Manager

WZEV
90.5 mhz FM; 500 w; 31 m; N33 18 22 W85 44 42
828 20th St. SW, Lanett, AL
(706) 518-3911
License: Lineville, Clay County, AL held by B. Jordan Communications Corp.

Benjamin Ray Jordan, President

Lisman

WHSL
01-01-1997; 107.7 mhz FM; 6 kw; Ant 328 ft; N32 05 27 W88 13 57
909 W. Pushmataha St., Butler, AL 39604
(205) 459-3222, *Fax:* (205) 459-4140
wprn@tds.net
License: Lisman, Choctaw County, AL held by Butler Broadcasting Corp.
Daryl Jackson, General Manager
Virginia Hummer, News Director

Littleville

WLAY-FM
09-12-1986; 103.5 mhz FM *Hrs Open:* 24; 3.3 kw; 386 ft.; N34 40 27 W87 42 48
111 East Kilbourn Avenue, Suite 2700, Milwaukee, WI 53202 US
(251) 343-4900, *Fax:* (251) 343-4905
www.mix1035.com
License: Littleville, Colbert County, AL held by Urban Radio Licenses LLC.
Group Owner: Urban Radio Licenses LLC; (acq 5-13-2005; grpsl)
Arbitron Metro Market: Florence-Muscle Shoals, AL *Format:* Oldies *No. News Employees:* 1 *Target Audience:* 18-49.
Kevin Wagner, CEO
Todd Mannesses, Operations Dir

Laura Crosby, News Director
Rob Green, Chief Engineer

Luverne

WHLW
01-01-1997; 104.3 mhz FM; 13.5 kw; 1831 ft.; N31 58 28 W86 9 44
600 Congress Avenue, Suite 1400, Austin, TX 78701 US
(334) 274-6464, *Fax:* (334) 274-6465
www1043hallelujahfm.com
License: Luverne, Crenshaw County, AL held by Capstar TX L.P.
Group Owner: Clear Channel Communications Inc.; (acq 8-30-2000; grpsl).
Arbitron Metro Market: Montgomery, AL *Format:* Gospel *Target Audience:* 18-49.
Michael Long, Operations Dir
James Belton, General Manager
Alberta Jackson, General Sales Mgr
Connye Bryant, Programming Director
Nikita Pogue, Promotions Manager

Madison

WUMP
03-29-1983; 730 khz AM *Hrs Open:* 24; 1 kw-D, ND1; 0.129 kw-N, ND1; N34 41 46 W86 44 19
P.O. Box 389, Athens, AL 35611 US
(256) 830-8300, *Fax:* (256) 232-6842
www.730ump.com
jason.marks@cumulus.com
License: Madison, AL held by Cumulus Licensing LLC.
Group Owner: Cumulus Media Inc.; (acq 7-21-2003; grpsl).
Nat'l Network: ESPN Radio *Nat'l Reps:* Katz Radio
Arbitron Metro Market: Athens, AL *Format:* Sports *Special Programming:* Univ. of Alabama Sports *Target Audience:* 18-54; males
Brian Zaborny, Operations Dir
Bill West, General Manager
Tracy Flesch, General Sales Mgr
Zack Bennett, Programming Director
Aaron Hurd, Promotions Manager
Audrey Raines, News Director
Jason Marks, Contact Person

Marion

WJUS
12-08-1951; 1310 khz AM
P.O. Box 930, Marion, AL 36756 US
(334) 683-2043, *Fax:* (334) 872-2329
www.partybluesandoldies.com
License: Marion, AL held by Marion Radio Inc.
Format: Urban Contemporary
Rev. Glenn King, General Manager

WNPT-FM
12-19-1990; 102.9 mhz FM *Hrs Open:* 24; 24 kw; 663 ft.; N32 49 46 W87 25 46
645 Church Street, Suite 400, Norfolk, VA 23510 US
(205) 758-5523, *Fax:* (205) 752-9696
wtbc@dbtech.net
License: Marion, Perry County, AL held by John Sisty Enterprises Inc.
Arbitron Metro Market: Marion, AL *Format:* Country
John Sisty, President
Ronnie Quarles, General Manager
Nancy Wilson, General Sales Mgr
Jay Bronson, Programming Director

Meridianville

WQRV
05-02-1962; 100.3 mhz FM *Hrs Open:* 24; 8.5 kw; 981 ft.; N34 47 36 W86 37 51
509 North Main Street, Tuscumbia, AL 35674 US
(256) 309-2400, *Fax:* (256) 389-1912
www.103theriver.com
License: Meridianville, Colbert County, AL held by CC Licenses LLC.
Group Owner: Clear Channel Communications Inc.; (acq 12-19-2000; grpsl)
Arbitron Metro Market: Meridianville, AL *Format:* Country *Hrs. of News Programming:* news progmg 60 hrs wkly *No. News Employees:* 2 *Target Audience:* 18-34.
Rick Brown, General Manager
Carmelita Palmer, General Sales Mgr
Erich West, Programming Director
Carl Sampieri, Chief Engineer
Stuart Langston, Production
Stephen Hardy, Website Content

Midfield

WBHJ
01-01-1952; 95.7 mhz FM *Hrs Open:* 24; 12 kw; 1004 ft.; N33 27 37 W86 51 7
3773 Howard Hughes Pwy, Suite 300n, Las Vegas, NV 89109 US
(205) 322-2987, *Fax:* (205) 322-2390
www.957jamz.com
maryk@957jamz.com
License: Midfield, Jefferson County, AL held by Cox Radio Inc.
Group Owner: Cox Radio Inc.; (acq 10-6-98; $17 million with WBHK(FM) Warrior)
Nat'l Network: Westwood One *Nat'l Reps:* Christal
Arbitron Metro Market: Birmingham, AL *Format:* Blues *Hrs. of News Programming:* news progmg one hr wkly *No. News Employees:* 1 *Target Audience:* 18-34; upscale baby boomers
Adv. Rates: 250; 150; 200; 125
David DuBose, General Manager
Paul Bankston, Local Sales Manager
Mary Kay Schmitt, Programming Director
Bmoney, Promotions Manager
Hans Heilmann, National Sales Manager
Lil Home, Music Director

Millbrook

WWMG
08-01-1993; 97.1 mhz FM *Hrs Open:* 24; 5.4 kw; 702 ft.; N32 20 6 W86 17 16
600 Congress Avenue, Suite 1400, Austin, TX 78701 US
(334) 274-6464, *Fax:* (334) 274-6467
www.mymagic97.com
License: Millbrook, Elmore County, AL held by Capstar TX L.P.
Group Owner: Clear Channel Communications Inc.; (acq 8-30-2000; grpsl).
Nat'l Network: American Urban; Westwood One
Arbitron Metro Market: Montgomery, AL *Format:* Adult Contemp *Target Audience:* 25-54.
Michael Long, Operations Dir
James Belton, General Manager
Alberta Jackson, General Sales Mgr
Darryl Elliott, Programming Director
Nikita Pogue, Promotions Manager

Mobile

WABB
11-01-1948; 1480 khz AM *Hrs Open:* 24; 5 kw-D, DAN; 4.4 kw-N, DAN; N30 43 11 W88 4 16
Mailing Address: P.O. Box 2148, Moblie, AL 36652 US
Second Address: 1551 Springhill Ave., Mobile, AL 36604
(434) 534-6100, *Fax:* (434) 534-6101
www.espninva.com
wblt@inbox.com
License: Mobile, AL held by WABB-FM Inc.
Nat'l Reps: Christal
Arbitron Metro Market: Eugene-Springfield OR *Format:* Sports
Gary Burns, President
Devin Taylor, Operations Dir

WLVM(FM)
02-05-1973; 97.5 mhz FM *Hrs Open:* 24; 100 kw; Ant 1,551 ft; N30 41 20 W87 49 49
Mailing Address: Box 2148, Mobile, AL 36652-2148
Second Address: 1551 Springhill Ave., Mobile, AL 36604
(251) 432-5572, *Fax:* (251) 438-4044
www.wabb.com
b.dittman@wabb.com
License: Mobile, Mobile County, AL held by WABB-FM Inc.
Group Owner: Cumulus Media Ine
Nat'l Reps: Christal
Population Served: 1,092,100 *Arbitron Metro Market:* Mobile, AL
Bernard Dittman, President
Laura English, General Sales Mgr

WBHY
12-09-1943; 840 khz AM; 10 kw-D, NDD; N30 45 50 W88 6 36
Mailing Address: P.O. Box 1328, Mobile, AL 36633 US
Second Address: 6530 Spanish Fort Blvd., Suite B, Spanish Fort, AL 36527
(251) 473-8488
www.goforth.org
License: Mobile, AL held by Goforth Media Inc.
Group Owner: Goforth Media Inc.; (Acq 4-11-86)
Nat'l Reps: Salem
Arbitron Metro Market: Mobile, AL *Format:* Christian *Target Audience:* 34-64; Christians
Wilbur Goforth, President
Robert Barber, Station Manager
Wilbur Goforth, General Sales Mgr
Kenny Fowler, Music Director

*WBHY-FM
03-20-1992; 88.5 mhz FM *Hrs Open:* 24; 33 kw; 624 ft; N30 40 55 W87 49 41
Mailing Address: Box 1328, Mobile, AL 36633
Second Address: 6530 Spanish Fort Blvd., Suite B, Spanish Fort, AL 36527
(251) 473-8488, *Fax:* na
www.goforth.org
power88.5@goforth.org
License: Mobile, Mobile County, AL held by Goforth Media Inc.
Group Owner: Goforth Media Inc.; acq 6-27-90;
Population Served: 1,000,000 *Arbitron Metro Market:* Mobile, AL *Hrs. of News Programming:* News progmg 7 hrs wkly *Target Audience:* 18-34.
Wayne Taylor, CEO/COO
Clayton Roberts, President
Mark Hard, Operations Dir
Wilbur Goforth, General Manager
Charles Smith, General Sales Mgr
Jean Williams, News Director
Steve Riggs, Chief Engineer

WBLX-FM
04-01-1976; 92.9 mhz FM; 98 kw; 1708 ft.; N30 36 45 W87 38 43
One Independence Plaza, 280 Highway 35, Red Bank, NJ 07701 US
(251)471-9393, *Fax:* (251)652-2007
www.thebigstation93blx.com
chuck.sullivan@cumulus.com
License: Mobile, Mobile County, AL
Group Owner: Cumulus Media Inc.
Nat'l Network: ABC *Nat'l Reps:* Katz Radio
Arbitron Metro Market: Mobile, AL *Format:* Urban Contemporary
Target Audience: 12 plus; primarily Black women, 18-34
James Alexander, Operations Dir
Dean Clinton, General Sales Mgr
Vinny D., Promotions Manager
Chuck Sullivan, Market Manager

WGOK
11-21-1958; 900 khz AM
1 Office Park, Suite 215, Mobile, AL 36609 US
(251) 652-2000, *Fax:* (251) 652-2001
www.gospel900.com
chuck.sullivan@cumulus.com
License: Mobile, AL held by Cumulus Licensing Corp.
Group Owner: Cumulus Media Inc.; (acq 10-18-99; $6 million with WYOK(FM) Atmore)
Nat'l Reps: Roslin
Arbitron Metro Market: Mobile, AL *Format:* Gospel *Target Audience:* 18-54; Black adults
Dickie Roberts, President
Gary Pizzati, General Manager
Kevin Wagner, Station Manager
Dean Clinton, General Sales Mgr
Felicia Allbritton, Programming Director
Vinny Duncan, Promotions Manager
Chcuk Sullivan, Market Manager
YamaScott, Key Account Manager

*WHIL-FM
09-05-1979; 91.3 mhz FM *Hrs Open:* 24; 100 kw; 1066 ft.; N30 41 20 W87 49 49
Mailing Address: P O Box 8509, Mobile, AL 36689 US
Second Address: AL
(251) 380-4685, *Fax:* (251) 460-2189
www.whil.org
whil@whil.org
License: Mobile, Mobile County, AL held by Spring Hill College.
Nat'l Network: PRI; NPR
Arbitron Metro Market: Mobile, AL *Format:* Classical *Hrs. of News Programming:* News progmg 40 hrs wkly *No. News Employees:* 2 *Target Audience:* 35 plus.
Brad Martin, Operations Dir
Mario Mazza, General Manager

WKSJ-FM
04-12-1971; 94.9 mhz FM; 98 kw; 1708 ft.; N30 36 45 W87 38 43
200 Concord Plaza, Suite 600, San Antonio, TX 78216 US
(251) 450-0100, *Fax:* (251) 479-3418
www.95ksj.com
stevepowers@clearchannel.com
License: Mobile, Mobile County, AL held by CC Licenses LLC.
Group Owner: Clear Channel Communications Inc.; (acq 11-21-97; grpsl)
Regional Reps: David Coppock
Arbitron Metro Market: Mobile, AL *Format:* Country *Hrs. of News Programming:* news progmg 25 hrs wkly *No. News Employees:* 2 *Target Audience:* 25-54; mid level to high class country music listeners *Adv. Rates:* 115; 105; 110; 60

David Coppock, Operations Dir
Jeanie Hufford, Station Manager
Bo Clark, General Sales Mgr
Bill Black, Programming Director
Mike Sloan, News Director

WNGL
02-07-1930; 1410 khz AM *Hrs Open:* 24; 5 kw-U, DA-N; N30 40 52 W88 00 02
1263 Battleship Pkwy., Spanish Fort, AL 77520
(251) 626-1090, *Fax:* (251) 626-1099
wlvv@bellsouth.net
License: Mobile, Mobile County, AL held by WLVV Inc.
Group Owner: Martin Broadcasting Inc.; (acq 4-14-99; $263,750)
Nat'l Network: American Urban *Nat'l Reps:* Katz Radio
Arbitron Metro Market: Mobile, AL *Target Audience:* 18-44; Black
Tom Alexander, General Manager

WMOB
01-25-1961; 1360 khz AM *Hrs Open:* 24; 5 kw-D, DA2; 0.212 kw-N, DA2; N30 41 26 W88 1 33
Mailing Address: P. O. Box 63, Mobile, AL 36601 US
Second Address: 200 Addsco Rd. Causeway, Mobile, AL 36601
(251) 432-1360, *Fax:* (251) 432-1396
www.buddytuckerassociation.org
License: Mobile, AL held by Buddy Tucker Association Inc.
Group Owner: Buddy Tucker Association Inc.; (acq 4-84; $395,000;
Arbitron Metro Market: Mobile, AL *Format:* Talk, Religious
Theodore Tucker, President
LeVaughn Tucker, Operations Dir
Buddy Tucker, General Manager
Don Tucker, Operations Manager

WMXC
10-16-1947; 99.9 mhz FM; 94 kw; 1755 ft.; N30 41 20 W87 49 49
200 Concord Plaza, Suite 600, San Antonio, TX 78216 US
(251) 450-0100, *Fax:* (251) 479-3418
www.litemix.com
stevepowers@clearchannel.com
License: Mobile, Mobile County, AL held by CC Licenses LLC
Group Owner: Clear Channel Communications Inc.
Arbitron Metro Market: Mobile, AL *Format:* Adult Contemp *Target Audience:* 25-54.
Dan Mason, Programming Director

WNTM
01-01-1946; 710 khz AM
Mailing Address: 200 Concord Plaza, Suite 600, San Antonio, TX 78216 US
Second Address: 555 Broadcast Dr., Mobile, AL 36606
(251) 450-0100, *Fax:* (251) 479-3418
www.newsradio710.com
stevepowers@clearchannel.com
License: Mobile, AL held by CC Licenses LLC.
Group Owner: Clear Channel Communications Inc.; (acq 11-21-97; grpsl)
Nat'l Network: CBS
Arbitron Metro Market: Mobile, AL *Format:* News, News/Talk, 84, Talk *Target Audience:* 25 plus.
Dave Cappock, President
Ronnie Bloodworth, General Manager
Scott O'Brien, Programming Director
Bill King, News Director

WRKH
12-05-1964; 96.1 mhz FM *Hrs Open:* 24; 73 kw; 1755 ft.; N30 41 20 W87 49 49
200 Concord Plaza, Suite 600, San Antonio, TX 78216 US
(251) 450-0100,(251) 770-9600, *Fax:* (251) 479-3418
www.961therocket.com
stevepowers@clearchannel.com
License: Mobile, Mobile County, AL held by CC Licenses LLC.
Group Owner: Clear Channel Communications Inc.; (acq 11-21-97; grpsl)
Nat'l Reps: D & R Radio
Arbitron Metro Market: Mobile, AL *Format:* Classic Rock *Hrs. of News Programming:* news progmg 2 hrs wkly *No. News Employees:* 2 *Target Audience:* 25-49; front edge baby boomers *Adv. Rates:* 100; 85; 90; 45
David Coppock, Operations Dir
Jeanie Hufford, Station Manager
Steve Powers, Programming Director

Monroeville

WMFC(AM)
04-01-1952; 1360 khz AM; 780 w-D; N31 30 51 W87 17 55
Mailing Address: Box 645, Monroeville, AL 36461
Second Address: 961 Pineville Rd., Monroeville, AL 36460
(251) 575-3281, *Fax:* (251) 575-3280
nmfc@frontiernet.net
License: Monroeville, Monroe County, AL held by Monroe Broadcasting Co. Inc.
Wire Services: NOAA Weather
Population Served: 18,000 *Arbitron Metro Market:* Monroeville, AL *Format:* Oldies *Target Audience:* 25-54.
Carolyn Stewart, Chairman
David Stewart, President
Carol Casey, Programming Director

WMFC
12-01-1965; 99.3 mhz FM *Hrs Open:* 5 AM-midnight; 30 kw; 308 ft.; N31 30 51 W87 17 55
P.O. Box 645, Monroeville, AL 36461 US
(251) 575-3281, *Fax:* (251) 575-3280
License: Monroeville, Monroe County, AL held by Monroe Broadcasting Co. Inc.
Nat'l Network: Jones Radio Networks *Regional Network:* Alabama Radio Net.
Arbitron Metro Market: Monroeville, AL *Format:* Oldies *Target Audience:* General.
Dave Cobb, General Manager
Kevin Peterson, Programming Director
Gerald Wilson, Chief Engineer

Montgomery

WGMP
01-16-1939; 1170 khz AM *Hrs Open:* 24; 10 kw-D, 1 kw-N, DA-2; N32 27 16 W86 17 21
4101 Wal St., Montgomery, AL 36121
(334) 244-0961, *Fax:* (334) 279-9563
www.1049thegump.com
License: Montgomery, Montgomery County, AL held by Bluewater Broadcasting Co. LLC
Nat'l Network: CBS
Population Served: 250,000 *Arbitron Metro Market:* Montgomery, AL *Special Programming:* Farm 5 hrs wkly *No. News Employees:* 1 *Target Audience:* 25 plus.
Terry Barber, General Manager
Rick Peters, Programming Director

WBAM-FM
01-01-1961; 98.9 mhz FM *Hrs Open:* 24; 100 kw; 981 ft.; N31 58 28 W86 11 31
4740 Radio Road, Montgomery, AL 36116 US
(419) 423-3285
www.wtkc897.com
wtkc89.7@sbcglobal.net
License: Montgomery, Montgomery County, AL held by Bluewater Broadcasting Co. LLC
Nat'l Reps: Christal
Arbitron Metro Market: Findlay OH *Format:* Christian, Talk
Juan Salinas, General Manager
Richard Lugo, Programming Director

WLWI
04-30-1930; 1440 khz AM; 5 kw-D, DAN; 1 kw-N, DAN; N32 18 24 W86 16 35
One Office Park Circle, Suite 300, Birmingham, AL 35223 US
(334) 240-9274, *Fax:* (334) 240-9211
www.cumulus.com
whhv@whhvradio.com
License: Montgomery, AL held by Cumulus Licensing Corp.
Group Owner: Cumulus Media Inc.
Nat'l Network: CNN Radio
Arbitron Metro Market: Montgomery, AL *Format:* News, News/Talk, 86 *No. News Employees:* 1 *Target Audience:* 18 plus.
Steve Smith, Programming Director
Bernie Barker, Promotions Manager
Gwen Pierce, News Director

WHHY-FM
01-09-1962; 101.9 mhz FM; 100 kw; 1096 ft.; N32 24 13 W86 11 47
One Office Park Circle, Suite 300, Birmingham, AL 35223 US
(334) 240-9274, *Fax:* (334) 240-9219
www.y102montgomery.com
kevin.waltman@cumulus.com
License: Montgomery, Montgomery County, AL held by Cumulus Licensing Corp.
Group Owner: Cumulus Media Inc.; (acq 3-12-01; grpsl)
Nat'l Reps: McGavren Guild
Arbitron Metro Market: Montgomery, AL *Format:* Contemporary Hits/Top 40, Variety/Diverse *Hrs. of News Programming:* News progmg one hr wkly *Target Audience:* 18-40.
Bill Jones, Operations Dir
Kevin Waltman, General Manager
Joy Melton, General Sales Mgr
Rex Long, Programming Director
Bill Hardin, Promotions Manager
Crystal Palmer Lund, News Director
Herb Connellan, Chief Engineer
JennniferCarter, Business Manager

***WLBF**
04-04-1984; 89.1 mhz FM *Hrs Open:* 24; 100 kw; 538 ft.; N32 24 13 W86 11 50
Mailing Address: P.O. Box 210789, Montgomery, AL 36121 US
Second Address: 381 Mendel Parkway, Montgomery, AL 36117
(334) 271-8900, *Fax:* (334) 260-8962
www.faithradio.org
mail@faithradio.org
License: Montgomery, Montgomery County, AL held by Faith Broadcasting Inc.
Nat'l Network: Moody; USA
Arbitron Metro Market: Montgomery, AL *Format:* Adult Contemp, Religious *Hrs. of News Programming:* News progmg 14 hrs wkly *Target Audience:* General.
Russell Dean, General Manager
Gary Hundley, General Sales Mgr
Donna Spears, News Director

WLWI-FM
07-15-1969; 92.3 mhz FM; 100 kw; 1096 ft.; N32 24 13 W86 11 47
111 East Kilborn Avenue, Suite 2700, Milwaukee, WI 53202 US
(334) 240-9274, *Fax:* (334) 240-9219
www.wlwi.com
bill.dollar@cumulus.com
License: Montgomery, Montgomery County, AL held by Cumulus Licensing Corp.
Group Owner: Cumulus Media Inc.
Nat'l Network: CNN Radio
Arbitron Metro Market: Montgomery, AL *Format:* Country *Special Programming:* Gospel 4 hrs wkly *No. News Employees:* 1 *Target Audience:* 25-54.
Bernie Barker, General Manager
Bill Dollar, Programming Director
Bill Hardin, Promotions Manager
Marcus Hyles, News Director
Herb Connellan, Chief Engineer
Andi Scott, Disc Jockey
Barry McKnight, Sports Commentator
JohnLongshore, Sports Commentator
Gwen Pierce, Traffic Manager

WMGY
06-01-1946; 800 khz AM *Hrs Open:* 6 AM-midnight; 1 kw-D, ND2; 0.143 kw-N, ND2; N32 24 48 W86 17 25
2305 Upper Wetumpka Rd, Montgomery, AL 36107 US
(334) 834-3710, *Fax:* (334) 834-3711
www.wmgyradio.com
admin@wmgyradio.com
License: Montgomery, AL held by WMGY Radio Inc.
Group Owner: GHB Radio Group; (acq 7-75)
Nat'l Network: USA
Arbitron Metro Market: Montgomery, AL *Format:* Gospel *Special Programming:* Black 15 hrs, sports 6 hrs wkly *Hrs. of News Programming:* News progmg 7 hrs wkly *Target Audience:* 35 plus. *Adv. Rates:* 6; 6; 6;5
Dane Harris, General Manager

WMSP
01-01-1953; 740 khz AM
111 East Kilborn Avenue, Suite 2700, Milwaukee, WI 53202 US
(334) 240-9274, *Fax:* (334) 240-9219
www.sportsradio740.com
bob.wooddy@cumulus.com
License: Montgomery, AL held by Cumulus Licensing Corp.
Group Owner: Cumulus Media Inc.; (acq 12-12-98; grpsl)
Nat'l Network: ESPN Radio
Arbitron Metro Market: Montgomery, AL *Format:* Sports *Target Audience:* Adults 18 plus.
Bill Jones, Operations Dir
Bernie Barker, General Manager
Bob Wooddy, Programming Director
Bill Hardin, Promotions Manager
Barry McKnight, News Director
Herb Connellan, Chief Engineer
Bill Hardin, Promotions Director
JohnLongshore, Sports Commentator

WMXS
07-09-1961; 103.3 mhz FM; 100 kw; 1096 ft.; N32 24 13 W86 11 47
111 East Kilborn Avenue, Suite 2700, Milwaukee, WI 53202 US
(334) 240-9274, *Fax:* (334) 240-9219
www.mix103.com
jamie.thompson@cumulus.com
License: Montgomery, Montgomery County, AL held by Cumulus Licensing Corp.

Group Owner: Cumulus Media Partners LLC
Nat'l Network: CNN Radio
Arbitron Metro Market: Montgomery, AL *Format:* Adult Contemp
Target Audience: 25-54.
Bernie Barker, General Manager
Jamie Thompson, Programming Director
Bill Hardin, Promotions Manager
Marcus Hyles, News Director
Herb Connellan, Chief Engineer
Leanne Thompson, Disc Jockey
J.T. Thompson, Disc Jockey
Jay St.John, Disc Jockey

WNZZ
05-08-1953; 950 khz AM; 1 kw-U, DA-N; N32 26 23 W86 15 49
One Commerce St., Suite 300, Montgomery, AL 53202
(334) 240-9274, *Fax:* (334) 240-9219
www.cumulus.com
License: Montgomery, Montgomery County, AL held by Volt Radio LLC
Group Owner: Cumulus Media Inc.; (acq 12-12-98; grpsl)
Population Served: 133,386 *Arbitron Metro Market:* Montgomery, AL *No. News Employees:* 1
Bill Jones, Operations Dir
Bernie Barker, General Manager
Bob Wooddy, Programming Director
Herb Connellan, Chief Engineer
Bill Hardin, Promotions Director

WQKS-FM
12-01-1990; 96.1 mhz FM *Hrs Open:* 24; 0.9 kw; 820 ft.; N32 22 3 W86 15 42
P.O. Box 210723, Montgomery, AL 36121 US
(334) 244-0961, *Fax:* (334) 279-9563
www.alice961.com
License: Montgomery, Montgomery County, AL held by Bluewater Broadcasting Co. LLC
Nat'l Network: ABC
Arbitron Metro Market: Montgomery, AL *Format:* Oldies *Hrs. of News Programming:* News progmg one hr wkly *Target Audience:* 25-54.
Terry Barber, General Manager
Rick Peters, Programming Director
Mary Brazell, News Director
Tom Jones, Chief Engineer

***WVAS**
06-15-1984; 90.7 mhz FM *Hrs Open:* 24 (M-F); 24 (S, Su); 80 kw; 348 ft.; N32 21 58 W86 17 40
P.O. Box 271, Montgomery, AL 36101 US
(334) 229-4708, *Fax:* (334) 269-4995
www.wvasfm.org
License: Montgomery, Montgomery County, AL held by Alabama State University.
Nat'l Network: NPR *Wire Services:* AP
Arbitron Metro Market: Montgomery, AL *Format:* Jazz *Special Programming:* Gospel 5 hrs, Blues 9 hrs, news/talk 7 hrs wkly *Hrs. of News Programming:* news progmg 5 hrs wkly *No. News Employees:* 5 *TargetAudience:* General; African-American community
John Knight, General Manager
Candy Capel, Station Manager
Mel Marshall, Programming Director
Shedd Johnson, News Director
Jay Holcey, Music Director
Temeki Tolbert, Program Assistant
Marcus Hyles, Senior News Correspondent

WXVI
05-01-1947; 1600 khz AM *Hrs Open:* 24; 5 kw-D, DA2; 1 kw-N, DA2; N32 23 40 W86 17 21
207 Montgomery Street, Suite 1025, Montgomery, AL 36104 US
(334) 263-4141, *Fax:* (334) 263-9191
License: Montgomery, AL held by New Life Ministries Inc.
Nat'l Network: American Urban *Nat'l Reps:* Roslin
Arbitron Metro Market: Montgomery, AL *Format:* Christian *Target Audience:* 35 plus; urban *Adv. Rates:* 25; 17; 25; 12
Terry Ellison, CEO
Glenda Perkins, Programming Director

Montgomery-Troy

***WTSU**
03-01-1977; 89.9 mhz FM *Hrs Open:* 24; 100 kw; 755 ft.; N32 3 40 W86 1 19 *Rebroadcasts:* Rebroadcasts WTJB(FM) Columbus 100%
University Ave, Tv Dept, Troy, AL 36082 US
(800) 800-6616, *Fax:* (334) 670-3934
wtsu.troyst.edu
publicradio@troy.edu
License: Montgomery-Troy, Montgomery County, AL held by Troy State University.
Nat'l Network: NPR; PRI
Arbitron Metro Market: Montgomery, AL *Format:* Classical, News *Special Programming:* Children one hr wkly *Hrs. of News Programming:* News progmg 25 hrs wkly *Target Audience:* General.
Judy Davis, Operations Dir
James Clower, General Manager
Fred Azbell, Programming Director
John Brunson, Chief Engineer
Robert Barner, Production Coordinator
Wade Giddens, Broadcast Engineer
Ann Hart, Program Assistant
JoshuaYohn, Digital Media Web Manager

Moody

WURL
10-01-1984; 760 khz AM; 1 kw-D, NDD; N33 35 13 W86 28 18
2999 Radio Park, Moody, AL 35004 US
(205) 699-9875, *Fax:* (205) 640-4379
www.wurlradio.com
wurlradio@aol.com
License: Moody, AL held by Bill Davison Evangelistic Assn.
Nat'l Network: USA
Arbitron Metro Market: Moody, AL *Format:* Gospel *Target Audience:* General.
William Davison Sr., President

Moulton

WEUV
12-11-1963; 1190 khz AM; 2.5 kw-D, NDD; N34 28 55 W87 18 4
P.O. Box 920, Huntsville, AL 35804 US
(256) 974-0681
License: Moulton, AL held by Hundley Batts Sr. and Virginia Caples
Format: Black, Gospel *Target Audience:* General.
Steve Murry, Programming Director

WEUP-FM
09-01-1991; 103.1 mhz FM *Hrs Open:* 20; 11.5 kw; 492 ft.; N34 27 8 W87 6 20
P.O. Box 920, Huntsville, AL 35804 US
(256) 837-9387, *Fax:* (256) 837-9404
103weup.com
info@103weup.com
License: Moulton, Lawrence County, AL held by Hundley Batts Sr. and Virginia Caples
Nat'l Network: USA *Nat'l Reps:* Rgnl Reps *Wire Services:* NOAA Weather
Arbitron Metro Market: Moulton, AL *Format:* Adult Contemp *Special Programming:* Relg one hr wkly *No. News Employees:* 1 *Target Audience:* 21-55.
Huntley Batts, General Manager
Big Ant, Programming Director

Moundville

WKUA
88.5 mhz FM; 5500 w; 272 ft; N33 04 00 W87 42 01
5704 Pineglen Lane, Irondale, AL
License: Moundville, AL
Group Owner: TBTA Ministries

Muscle Shoals

WLAY
01-15-1933; 1450 khz AM
111 East Kilbourn Avenue, Suite 2700, Milwaukee, WI 53202 US
(256) 383-2525, *Fax:* (256) 389-1912
www.wlay1035.com
donnajohnson@clearchannel.com
License: Muscle Shoals, AL held by Urban Radio Licenses LLC.
Group Owner: Urban Radio Licenses LLC; (acq 5-13-2005; grpsl).
Format: Sports *Target Audience:* 18-54.
Brian Rickman, Operations Dir
Cheryl Self, General Sales Mgr

WVNA-FM
10-28-1964; 105.5 mhz FM; 4.4 kw; 387 ft.; N34 40 27 W87 42 48
111 East Kilbourn Avenue, Suite 2700, Milwaukee, WI 53202 US
(256) 383-2525, *Fax:* (256) 389- 1912
www.wlay1035.com
donnajohnson@clearchannel.com
License: Muscle Shoals, Sheffield County, AL
Group Owner: Urban Radio Licenses LLC
Format: Classic Rock
Alan Goodman, President
Bill Shannon, Programming Director
Michelle Hurley, Promotions Manager

***WQPR**
11-01-1987; 88.7 mhz FM *Hrs Open:* 24; 20 kw; 429 ft.; N34 34 41 W87 47 2 *Rebroadcasts:* Rebroadcasts WUAL-FM Tuscaloosa 95%
Box 870370, #17 Bryce La, Tuscaloosa, AL 35487 US
(205) 348-6644, *Fax:* (205) 348-6648
www.apr.org
apr@apr.org
License: Muscle Shoals, Sheffield County, AL held by Board of Trustees University of Alabama.
Nat'l Network: PRI; NPR
Format: Jazz, News *Special Programming:* Bluegrass, blues, folk 5 hrs, new age 19 hrs wkly *Hrs. of News Programming:* news progmg 5 hrs wkly *No. News Employees:* 1
Elizabeth Brock, Station Manager

New Hope

WHWT
01-01-2007; 103.5 mhz FM; 0.29 kw; 1473 ft.; N34 38 11 W86 30 42
, New Hope, AL 0 US
(256) 489-9498, *Fax:* (256) 489-5035
www.hot1035fm.com
License: New Hope, Madison County, AL held by Stroh Communications Corp.
Arbitron Metro Market: New Hope, AL *Format:* Urban Contemporary
Allan Stroh, President
Karen Porter, Director of Sales & Marketing

New Market

WWFF-FM
07-01-1962; 93.3 mhz FM *Hrs Open:* 24; 14.5 kw; 914 ft.; N34 47 37 W86 37 51
405 North Jackson St, Tullahoma, TN 37388 US
(256) 830-8300, *Fax:* (256) 232-6842
www.wolf933.com
License: New Market, Madison County, AL held by Cumulus Licensing LLC.
Group Owner: Cumulus Media Inc.; (acq 7-21-2003; grpsl)
Nat'l Reps: Katz Radio
Arbitron Metro Market: Huntsville, AL *Format:* Country *No. News Employees:* 3 *Target Audience:* Adult; 25-54
Brian Zaborny, Operations Dir
Bill West, General Manager
Tracy Flesch, General Sales Mgr
Buzz Stphens, Programming Director
Aaron Hurd, Promotions Manager
Audrey Raines, News Director
Chuck Miller, Chief Engineer

Northport

WAPI-FM
07-15-1991; 100.5 mhz FM *Hrs Open:* 24; 85 kw; Ant 912 ft; N33 05 42 W87 15 16
244 Goodwin Crest Dr., Suite 300, Helena, AL 35405
(205) 945-4646, *Fax:* (205) 945-3999
www.live1005online.com
License: Northport, Tuscaloosa County, AL
Group Owner: Cumulus Media Inc.; (acq 7-12-2005; grpsl)
Arbitron Metro Market: Tuscaloosa, AL
Dale Daniels, General Manager
Lenny Frisaro, General Sales Mgr
Ryan Haney, Programming Director
Jennifer Dickson, Promotions Manager

WTUG-FM
03-01-1979; 92.9 mhz FM *Hrs Open:* 24; 100 kw; Ant 980 ft; N33 03 15 W87 32 57
142 Skyland Blvd., Tuscaloosa, AL 35405
(205) 345-7200, *Fax:* (205) 349-1715
www.wtug.com
Charles.Anthony@townsquaremedia.com
License: Northport, Tuscaloosa County, AL
Group Owner: Townsquare Media
Population Served: 91,605 *Arbitron Metro Market:* Tuscaloosa, AL *Target Audience:* 25-54.
Greg Thomas, Operations Dir
Todd Livingston, General Manager
Tammy Boyd, General Sales Mgr
Charles Anthony, Programming Director
Meg Summers, Promotions Manager
Jade Nicole, Community Affairs Director

Oneonta

WCRL
07-29-1952; 1570 khz AM; 2.5 kw-D, ND2; 0.064 kw-N, ND2; N33 57 16 W86 28 20

Mailing Address: P.O. Box 490, Oneonta, AL 35121 US
Second Address: 908 2nd Ave. E., Oneonta, AL 35121
(205) 274-9530, *Fax:* (205) 625-5433
www.wcrlradio.com
info@wcrlradio.com
License: Oneonta, AL held by Blount County Broadcasting Service Inc.
Nat'l Network: Jones Radio Networks
Arbitron Metro Market: Oneonta, AL *Format:* Spanish *Adv. Rates:* 8; 7; 8; 6
L.D. Bentley, President
Danny Bentley, General Manager

WZZN
07-12-1968; 97.7 mhz FM; 3.2 kw; Ant 367 ft; N33 56 48 W86 29 06
Mailing Address: Box 490, Oneonta, AL 35121
Second Address: 908 2nd Ave. E., Oneonta, AL 35121
www.wkld.com
License: Oneonta, Blount County, AL
Population Served: 200,000 *Arbitron Metro Market:* Birmingham, AL *Special Programming:* Atlanta Braves baseball *Adv. Rates:* $8; $7; $8; $6
L.D. Bentley, General Sales Mgr
James Bentley, Programming Director
Danny Bentley, Disc Jockey

Opelika

WANI
06-03-1940; 1400 khz AM *Hrs Open:* 24; 1 kw-U; N32 38 13 W85 24 23
Mailing Address: Box 950, Auburn, AL 36831
Second Address: 197 E. University Dr., Auburn, AL 36830
(334) 826-2929, *Fax:* (334) 826-9151
www.wani1400.com
aburcham@aunetwork.com
License: Opelika, Lee County, AL held by Auburn Network Inc.
Nat'l Network: ABC; Fox News Radio; Business Talk Radio; Radio America; Talk Radio Network *Wire Services:* AP
Population Served: 120,000*No. News Employees:* 1
Mike Hubbard, President
Andy Burcham, General Manager
Ann Bergman, General Sales Mgr
Julie Burns, News Director
Kevin Duvall, Engineering Dir
Larry Wilkins, Chief Engineer
Rich Perkins, Traffic Manager

WMXA
07-01-1991; 96.7 mhz FM *Hrs Open:* 24; 3.5 kw; 430 ft.; N32 33 54 W85 22 13
Mailing Address: 139 Executive Circle, Suite 203, Daytona Beach, FL 32114 US
Second Address: 915 Veterans Pkwy., Opelika, AL 36801
(334) 745-4656, *Fax:* (334) 749-1520
www.mix967inline.com
mix97online@gmail.com
License: Opelika, Lee County, AL
Group Owner: Qantum Communications Corp.
Arbitron Metro Market: Opelika, AL *Format:* Adult Contemp *Hrs. of News Programming:* news progmg 2 hrs wkly *No. News Employees:* 1 *Target Audience:* 18-49.
William Spry Jr., President
Terry Harper, Chief Engineer

WTLM
08-12-1968; 1520 khz AM *Hrs Open:* Sunrise-sunset
Mailing Address: 139 Executive Circle, Suite 203, Daytona Beach, FL 32114 US
Second Address: 915 Veterans Pkwy., Opelika, AL 36801
(334) 745-4656, *Fax:* (334) 749-1520
oaadvertising.com
john.bodiford@qantumofauburn.com
License: Opelika, AL held by Qantum of Auburn License Co. LLC.
Group Owner: Qantum Communications Corp.; (acq 7-2-03; grpsl).
Arbitron Metro Market: Opelika, AL *Format:* Adult Contemp *No. News Employees:* 1 *Target Audience:* 35 plus.
Sandy Matthews, General Sales Mgr
Woody Russ, Programming Director
Jim Powell, Promotions Manager
John Bodiford, Market Manager
Ben Taylor, Sales Director

Opp

WAMI
12-12-1952; 860 khz AM; 1 kw-D, 47 w-N; N31 18 54 W86 15 45
Box 40, Opp, AL 36467
(334) 493-3588, *Fax:* (334) 493-4182
wami@oppcatv.com
License: Opp, Covington County, AL held by Opp Broadcasting Co. Inc.
Population Served: 150,000*Special Programming:* 24 hours *No. News Employees:* 3 *Target Audience:* 25-65; agricultural & garment industry workers *Adv. Rates:* 9; 8; 8; 8
Harry Phillips, General Manager
Harry Phillips, General Sales Mgr
Virginia Phillips, Bookkeeper

WAMI-FM
11-09-1973; 102.3 mhz FM; 3.4 kw; 230 ft; N31 18 54 W86 15 45
Mailing Address: Box 40, Opp, AL 36467
Second Address: 1807 N. Main, Opp, AL 36467
(334) 493-3588, *Fax:* (334) 493-4182
wami@oppcatv.com
License: Opp, Covington County, AL held by OPP Broadcasting Co, Inc
Population Served: 175,000*Hrs. of News Programming:* 9 hours *No. News Employees:* 3 *Adv. Rates:* Same as AM
Harry Phillips, General Manager
Harry Phillips, General Sales Mgr
Virginia Phillips, Programming Director

***WJIF**
01-01-1986; 91.9 mhz FM; 0.38 kw; 164 ft.; N31 15 50 W86 13 26
700 Hwy 52, Opp, AL 36467 US
(334) 493-4947, *Fax:* (334) 493-4947
License: Opp, Covington County, AL held by Opp Educational Broadcasting Foundation.
Format: Gospel
Heywood Nyland, General Manager

WOPP
09-19-1980; 1290 khz AM; 2.5 kw-D, DA2; 0.5 kw-N, DA2; N31 17 27 W86 13 51
P. O. Box 560, Opp, AL 36467 US
(334) 493-4545, *Fax:* (334) 493-4546
www.wopp.com
wopp@wopp.com
License: Opp, AL held by E & R Broadcasting Inc.
Nat'l Network: Salem Radio Network *Regional Reps:* Rgnl Reps.
TV Affiliate: Country *Format:* Black, Gospel *Special Programming:* news progmg 16 hrs wkly *Hrs. of News Programming:* 1 *No. News Employees:* 19-58; progsv & highly lo *Adv. Rates:* 10; 9; 10; 9
General Manager, General Manager

Orange Beach

WCSN-FM
07-02-1996; 105.7 mhz FM *Hrs Open:* 24; 5 kw; 246 ft.; N30 17 45 W87 33 42
Mailing Address: Post Office Box 679, Orange Beach, AL 36561 US
Second Address: 2421 E. Second St., Gulf Shores, AL 36542
(251) 967-1057, *Fax:* (251) 967-1050
www.sunny105.com
sunny105@gulftel.com
License: Orange Beach, Baldwin County, AL held by Gulf Coast Broadcasting Co. Inc.
Arbitron Metro Market: Mobile, AL *Format:* Adult Contemp *Target Audience:* 25-54; upscale
R. Lee Hagan, President
Kathryn Hagan, General Manager
Don Brown, General Sales Mgr
Randy Frawley, Promotions Manager

Orrville

WALX
12-12-1973; 100.9 mhz FM; 50 kw; 492 ft.; N32 21 40 W86 52 28
273 Persimmon Tree Rd., Selma, AL 36701 US
(334) 875-9360, *Fax:* (334) 875-1340
License: Orrville, Dallas County, AL held by Scott Communications Inc.
Group Owner: Scott Communications Inc.
Arbitron Metro Market: Orrville, AL *Format:* Adult Contemp *Target Audience:* 18-40.
Mike Lee, Programming Director

Oxford

WVOK
04-01-1956; 1580 khz AM *Hrs Open:* 24; 2.5 kw-D, ND1; 0.0218 kw-N, ND1; N33 35 27 W85 49 54; N33 26 55 W86 3 54
Mailing Address: P. O. Box 3770, Oxford, AL 36203 US
Second Address: 1215 Church St., Oxford, AL 36203
(256) 835-1580, *Fax:* (256) 831-1500
License: Oxford, AL held by Woodard Broadcasting Co.
Nat'l Network: ABC
Format: Oldies *Target Audience:* 25-54. *Adv. Rates:* 20; 12; 12; 8
Steve Stevens, Operations Dir
Chuck Woodard, General Manager
Whit McGhee, Assistant Programming Director

***WTBJ**
05-29-1994; 91.3 mhz FM *Hrs Open:* 24; 0.17 kw; 1578 ft.; N33 29 7 W85 48 33
1500 Airport Road, Oxford, AL 36203 US
(256) 831-3333, *Fax:* (256) 831-5895
www.trinityoxford.org
truth@trinityoxford.org
License: Oxford, Calhoun County, AL held by Trinity Christian Academy.
Format: Religious *Special Programming:* Sp one hr wkly *Target Audience:* General.
Dr. C.O. Grinstead, General Manager

WVOK-FM
02-19-1990; 97.9 mhz FM *Hrs Open:* 24; 510 w; Ant 1,109 ft; N33 37 20 W85 52 19
Mailing Address: PO Box 3770, Oxford, AL 36203
Second Address: 1215 Church St., Oxford, AL 36203
(256) 835-1500, *Fax:* (256) 831-1500
www.979wvok.com
production@979wvok.com
License: Oxford, Calhoun County, AL
Population Served: 40,000
Jimmy E. Woodard, President
Steve Stevens, Operations Dir
Chuck Woodward, General Manager
Jock Burgess, Programming Director

Ozark

***WAQG**
06-01-1998; 91.7 mhz FM; 5 kw; 377 ft.; N31 26 25 W85 33 49
P.O. Drawer 2440, Tupelo, MS 38803 US
(601) 844-8888, *Fax:* (601) 842-6791
www.afr.net
faq@afr.net
License: Ozark, Dale County, AL held by American Family Radio.
Group Owner: American Family Radio
Arbitron Metro Market: Ozark, AL *Format:* Christian, Religious
Marvin Sanders, General Manager
John Riley, Programming Director
Joe Moody, Engineering Dir

WOAB
07-09-1967; 104.9 mhz FM; 6 kw; 269 ft.; N31 27 19 W85 40 58
P. O. Box 911, Ozark, AL 36361 US
(334) 774-5600, *Fax:* (334) 774-1148
License: Ozark, Dale County, AL held by Ozark Broadcasting Corp.
Arbitron Metro Market: Dothan, AL *TV Affiliate:* Hits of the 40s, 50s & 60s

WOZK
05-03-1953; 900 khz AM; 1 kw-D, ND1; 0.07 kw-N, ND1; N31 27 19 W85 40 58
P. O. Box 911, Ozark, AL 36361 US
(334) 774-5600, *Fax:* (334) 774-1148
wozk@alaweb.com
License: Ozark, AL held by Ozark Broadcasting Corp.
Arbitron Metro Market: Dothan, AL *Format:* Adult Contemp *Adv. Rates:* 7; 7; 7; 7
John Stein, General Manager

Pell City

WFHK
01-07-1956; 1430 khz AM *Hrs Open:* 6 AM-6 PM; 5 kw-D, NDD; N33 35 10 W86 19 35
Talladega Shopping Ctr. Brzwy, Suite A, Talladegta, AL 35161 US
(205) 338-1430, *Fax:* (205) 814-1430
License: Pell City, AL held by Stocks Broadcasting Inc.
Regional Network: Alaska Pub.
Arbitron Metro Market: Pell City, AL *Format:* Country *Adv. Rates:* 7.25; 6.25; 6.25; na
John Simpson, General Manager

Pepperell

WZMG
10-01-1979; 910 khz AM *Hrs Open:* 24; 0.65 kw-D, ND1; 0.056 kw-N, ND1; N32 39 26 W85 25 27
139 Executive Circle, Suite 203, Daytona Beach, FL 32114 US
(334) 745-4656, *Fax:* (334) 749-1520
www.intouch910am.com

john.bodiford@qantumofauburn.com, ben.taylor@qantumofauburn.com
License: Pepperell, AL held by Qantum of Auburn License Co. LLC.
Group Owner: Qantum Communications Corp.; (acq 7-2-03; grpsl).
Nat'l Network: ABC
Arbitron Metro Market: Pepperell, AL *Format:* Urban Contemporary *Target Audience:* 25-54; African Americans *Adv. Rates:* 18;15;17;10
Van Riggs, Operations Dir
John Bodiford, General Manager
Richard LeGrand, Programming Director
Donny Blankenship, Production Director
John Bodiford, Market Manager
Ben Taylor, Director of Sales

Phenix City

WGSY
03-04-1971; 100.1 mhz FM *Hrs Open:* 24; 6 kw; 328 ft.; N32 30 42 W85 0 41
Mailing Address: 111 East Kilbourn Ave., Suite 2700, Milwaukee, WI 53202 US
Second Address: 1501 13th Ave., Columbus, GA 31901
(706) 576-3000, *Fax:* (706) 576-3010
www.sunny100columbus.com
info@sunny100columbus.com
License: Phenix City, Russell County, AL held by CC Licenses LLC.
Group Owner: Clear Channel Communications Inc.; (acq 2-21-2002; grpsl).
Nat'l Reps: McGavren Guild
Arbitron Metro Market: Columbus, GA *Format:* Adult Contemp *Target Audience:* 25-54; women
Brian Waters, Operations Dir
Jim Martin, General Manager

Phenix City/Columbus

WHAL
01-01-1951; 1460 khz AM; 4 kw-D, ND1; 0.14 kw-N, ND1; N32 25 58 W84 57 2
Mailing Address: 111 East Kilbourn, Suite 2700, Milwaukee, WI 53202 US
Second Address: Box 687, Columbus, GA 31902
(706) 576-3000, *Fax:* (706) 576-3010
www.whal1460.com
marshawhitney@clearchannel.com
License: Phenix City/Columbus, AL held by CC Licenses LLC.
Group Owner: Clear Channel Communications Inc.; (acq 2-21-2002; grpsl).
Nat'l Reps: McGavren Guild
Arbitron Metro Market: Columbus, GA *Target Audience:* 25 plus.
Jim Martin, General Manager

Piedmont

*WJCK
04-01-1994; 88.3 mhz FM *Hrs Open:* 24; 2.7 kw vert; 968 ft.; N33 50 12 W85 43 59
P.O. Box 1000, Cartersville, GA 30120 US
(256)447-6008, *Fax:* 770-387-2856
www.ibn.org
jo@ibn.org
License: Piedmont, Calhoun County, AL held by Immanuel Broadcasting Network
Format: Religious
Patrick Miller, CFO
Ed Tuten, President
Neil Hopper, General Manager
Jo Kirk, Station Manager
Billy Williams, Programming Director

WPID
06-01-1953; 1280 khz AM *Hrs Open:* 6 AM-10 PM; 1 kw-D, ND1; 0.084 kw-N, ND1; N33 55 50 W85 35 0
P.O. Box 227, Piedmont, AL 36272 US
(256) 447-9096, *Fax:* (256) 447-6669
License: Piedmont, AL held by Piedmont Radio Co.
Format: Adult Contemp, Oldies *Hrs. of News Programming:* News progmg 2 hrs wkly *Target Audience:* 25-55.
Andy Kennedy, Operations Dir
Jimmy Kennedy, General Manager

Pike Road

WTXK
04-01-1968; 1210 khz AM; 10 kw-D, 3 w-N, 5 kw-CH; N31 28 40 W85 41 07
Box 250, Ozark, AL 36302
(334) 445-1612, *Fax:* (334) 445-9266
License: Pike Road, Dale County, AL held by Horizon Broadcasting Co.
Arbitron Metro Market: Dothan, AL *Target Audience:* 25-64.
Wayne North, General Manager

Pine Hill

WKXK
01-01-2000; 96.7 mhz FM; 41 kw; 535 ft.; N32 4 24 W87 35 27
Rebroadcasts: Simulcast of WKXN(FM) Greenville 100%
Mailing Address: Manningham Road At I-65, P. O. Box 369, Greenville, AL 36037 US
Second Address: 563 Manningham Rd., Greenville, AL 36037
(334) 382-6555, *Fax:* (334) 382-7770
www.wkxn.com
wkxn@alaweb.com
License: Pine Hill, Wilcox County, AL held by Autaugaville Radio Inc.
Format: Blues, Gospel
Roscoe Miller, General Manager
Mike Morris, General Sales Mgr
Shelley Merritt, News Director
Bob Luman, Chief Engineer

Pine Level

WVRV
01-01-2008; 97.5 mhz FM; 6 kw; Ant 328 ft; N31 58 32 W85 58 27
1359 Carmichael Way, Montgomery, AL
(334) 239-9750, *Fax:* (334) 356-9776
www.wvrvfmtheriver.com
License: Pine Level, Montgomery County, AL held by Back Door Broadcasting LLC.
Allan Stroh, President
Mike Alan, Operations Dir
Ann Callister, General Manager
Ann Callister, General Sales Mgr
Mike Alan, Programming Director
Terry Harper, Engineering Dir

Prattville

WIQR
03-01-1969; 1410 khz AM; 5 kw-D, DA2; 1 kw-N, DA2; N32 25 23 W86 26 21
319 17th Street North, Birmingham, AL 35203 US
(334) 358-0410
www.wiqr.net
wiqr@hotmail.com
License: Prattville, AL held by Star Power Communications Corp.
Regional Reps: Alabama Net.
Arbitron Metro Market: Montgomery, AL *Format:* Sports *Target Audience:* General.
Greg Meadows, General Manager

WXFX
08-01-1977; 95.1 mhz FM *Hrs Open:* 24; 5.4 kw; 333.8 meters; N32 28 01 W86 24 15
1 Commerce St., Suite 300, Montgomery, AL 35223
(334) 240-9274, *Fax:* (334) 240-9219
www.wxfx.com
License: Prattville, Montgomery County, AL held by Cumulus Licensing Corp.
Group Owner: Cumulus Media Inc.; (acq 3-12-01; grpsl)
Nat'l Network: CNN Radio; Motor Racing Net *Regional Network:* Alabama Radio Net. *Nat'l Reps:* Katz Radio
Population Served: 280,000 *Arbitron Metro Market:* Montgomery, AL *No. News Employees:* 1 *Target Audience:* 25-54; upscale adults, two paycheck households
Bill Jones, Operations Dir
Bernie Barker, General Manager
Donna Headley, General Sales Mgr
Rick Hendricks, Programming Director
Larry Wilkins, Chief Engineer

Priceville

WKZD
08-01-1986; 1310 khz AM *Hrs Open:* Sunrise-sunset
Mailing Address: 1431 Hwy 31 N, Hartselle, AL 35640 US
Second Address: 303 2nd Ave. S.E., Decatur, AL 35601
(256) 773-4114, *Fax:* (256) 773-6915
License: Priceville, AL held by Abercrombie Broadcasting AM Inc.
Arbitron Metro Market: Huntsville, AL *Format:* Oldies *Target Audience:* 25-65.
Percy Yarbrough, General Manager

Prichard

WIJD
06-13-1966; 1270 khz AM *Hrs Open:* 24; 5 kw-D, ND1; 0.103 kw-N, ND1; N30 44 44 W88 5 40
200 Concord Plaza, Suite 600, San Antonio, TX 78216 US
(251) 340-0442
www.wilkinsradio.com
wijd@wilkinsradio.com
License: Prichard, AL held by Mobile Bay Corp.
Group Owner: Wilkins Communications Network Inc.; (acq 7-18-2006; $450,000)
Arbitron Metro Market: Mobile, AL *Format:* Christian, Talk *Target Audience:* 35 plus.
Bob Wilkins, CEO
Mitchell Mathis, President
Mike Pickett, Station Manager
Greg Garrett, Programming Director

WLPR
12-31-1986; 960 khz AM *Hrs Open:* 24
P.O. Box 1328, Mobile, AL 36633 US
(251) 473-8488
www.goforth.org
info@wlpr.com
License: Prichard, AL held by Goforth Media Inc.
Nat'l Network: Salem Radio Network *Nat'l Reps:* Salem
Arbitron Metro Market: Mobile, AL *Format:* Gospel *Hrs. of News Programming:* News progmg 6 hrs wkly *Target Audience:* 35 plus.
Robert Barber, Operations Dir
Wilbur Goforth, General Manager
Charlie Smith, General Sales Mgr
Kenny Fowler, Programming Director
Jean Williams, News Director
Steve Riggs, Chief Engineer

Rainbow City

WJBY
01-01-1926; 930 khz AM *Hrs Open:* 17; 5 kw-D, 500 w-N, DA-2; N33 59 09 W86 02 15
Mailing Address: Box 1350, Gadsden, AL 35906
Second Address: 750 Walnut St, Gadsen, AL 35901
(256) 546-1611, *Fax:* (256) 547-9062
www.wgad.com
dhedrick@wgad.com
License: Rainbow City, Etowah County, AL held by Coosa River Communications Inc.
Nat'l Network: ABC
Population Served: 200,000*Hrs. of News Programming:* News progmg 16 hrs wkly *Target Audience:* 25 plus; general *Adv. Rates:* 15; 12; 15; 12
Dave Hedrick, General Manager

Rainsville

WVSM
05-16-1967; 1500 khz AM *Hrs Open:* Sunrise-sunset; 1 kw-C, NDD; 1 kw-D, NDD; N34 29 56 W85 50 34
P.O. Box 339, Rainsville, AL 35986 US
(256) 638-2137
www.wvsmam.com
wvsm@farmerstel.com
License: Rainsville, AL held by Sand Mountain Advertising Co. Inc.
Arbitron Metro Market: Rainsville, AL *Format:* Gospel *Hrs. of News Programming:* news progmg 9 hrs wkly *No. News Employees:* 3 *Target Audience:* General. *Adv. Rates:* 15; 15
Mark Huber, President
Kayron Guffey, Operations Dir
Annie Ruth Huber, General Sales Mgr
Jesse Finley, Disc Jockey
Ann Spears, Disc Jockey

Red Bay

WRMG
06-29-1968; 1430 khz AM; 1 kw-D, NDD; N34 24 51 W88 8 11
277 County Rd 171, Iuka, MS 38852 US
(256) 356-4458
License: Red Bay, AL held by Jack W. Ivy Sr.
Format: Country, Gospel
Jack Ivy Sr., President

Reform

WBEI
05-07-1991; 101.7 mhz FM *Hrs Open:* 24; 22.5 kw; Ant 725 ft; N33 13 48 W87 50 50
142 Skyland Blvd., Tuscaloosa, AL 35405

RADIO - U.S.

(205) 345-7200, *Fax:* (205) 349-1715
www.b1017online.com
todd.livingston@townsquaremedia.com
License: Reform, Pickens County, AL
Group Owner: Townsquare Media; (acq 7-21-2012; grpsl).
Population Served: 91,605 *Arbitron Metro Market:* Tuscaloosa, AL *Target Audience:* 18-49
Todd Livingston, General Manager
Tammy Boyd, General Sales Mgr
Greg Thomas, Programming Director
Meg Summers, Promotions Manager

Repton

WPPG
10-01-2002; 101.1 mhz FM *Hrs Open:* 24; 3.1 kw; 459 ft.; N31 26 45 W87 16 59
415 North College Street, Greenville, AL 36037 US
(251) 575-7601, *Fax:* (251) 575-7703
fun101@frontiernet.net
License: Repton, Conecuh County, AL held by Wolff Broadcasting Corp.
Arbitron Metro Market: Repton, AL *Format:* Classic Rock
Wendy Smith, General Manager
Robert Williams, Chief Engineer

Roanoke

WELR
04-01-1954; 1360 khz AM; 1 kw-D, ND2; 0.054 kw-N, ND2; N33 9 45 W85 22 30
P.O. Box 709, Roanoke, AL 36274 US
(334) 863-4139, *Fax:* (334) 863-2540
www.eagle1023.com
WELR@Eagle1023.com
License: Roanoke, AL held by Eagle's Nest Inc.
Group Owner: Eagle's Nest Inc.; acq 10-15-88)
Nat'l Network: ESPN Radio
Arbitron Metro Market: Roanoke, AL. *Format:* Sports
Jim Vice, President
Kay Vice, Operations Dir
Coleman Vice, General Sales Mgr
Don Strength, Promotions Manager
Al Haynes, News Director

WELR-FM
02-14-1969; 102.3 mhz FM *Hrs Open:* 24; 8.9 kw; 545 ft.; N33 2 39 W85 20 15
P.O. Box 709, Roanoke, AL 36274 US
(334) 863-4139, *Fax:* (334) 863-2540
www.eagle1023.com
WELR@Eagle1023.com
License: Roanoke, Randolph County, AL held by Eagle's Nest Inc.
Group Owner: Eagle's Nest Inc.; (acq 1988)
Arbitron Metro Market: Roanoke, AL. *Format:* Country *No. News Employees:* 2
Kay Vice, Operations Dir
Jim Vice, General Manager
Coleman Vice, General Sales Mgr
Don Strength, Programming Director
Al Haynes, News Director

Robertsdale

WBZR
03-01-1985; 1000 khz AM *Hrs Open:* 6 am-6 pm; 1 kw-D; N30 32 10 W87 42 55 *Rebroadcasts:* Simulcast with WBZR(FM) Atmore 100%
Box 578, Robertsdale, AL 36561
(251) 947-2346, *Fax:* (251) 947-2347
www.wnsiradio.com
wnsiradio@gulftel.com
License: Robertsdale, Baldwin County, AL held by Great American Radio Network Inc.
Population Served: 40,000 *Arbitron Metro Market:* Mobile, AL *Special Programming:* Religion 6 hrs wkly *Hrs. of News Programming:* news progmg 2 hrs wkly *No. News Employees:* 1 *Target Audience:* 45 plus;upscale
Walter Bowen, General Manager

Rogersville

WYTK
01-01-1994; 93.9 mhz FM *Hrs Open:* 24; 2.25 kw; 531 ft.; N34 51 52 W87 23 43
1725 Rodeo Drive, Tuscumbia, AL 35674 US
(256) 764-9390, *Fax:* (256) 764-7760
www.939thescore.com
thescore@939thescore.com
License: Rogersville, Lauderdale County, AL held by Valley Broadcasting Inc.
Arbitron Metro Market: Florence-Muscle Shoals, AL *Format:* Sports *Hrs. of News Programming:* sports news progmg 28 hrs wkly *Target Audience:* 25-54; male *Adv. Rates:* 22; 18; 20; 16
Greg Thornton, President
Al Mann, Operations Dir
J.D. Byars, General Sales Mgr
Mike Greenberg, News Reporter and Sports Commentator
Mike Golic, News Reporter and Sports Commentator
Tim Brando, Sports Commentator
Harold Bugg,Sports Commentator
Brett Beaird, Sports Commentator
Paul Finebaum, Sports Commentator

Russellville

WGOL
05-29-1949; 920 khz AM *Hrs Open:* 16; 1 kw-D, ND1; 0.04 kw-N, ND1; N34 30 50 W87 42 55
Underwood Road, Russellville, AL 35653 US
(256) 332-0214, *Fax:* (256) 332-7430
www.wgolam.com
License: Russellville, AL held by Pilati Investments Corp.
Regional Network: Alaska Pub.
Format: Country *Special Programming:* Black gospel 4 hrs, relg 10 hrs wkly *Hrs. of News Programming:* News progmg 9 hrs wkly *Target Audience:* 25-60.
John Pilati, General Manager
John Pilati, Station Manager
Thomas Foster, Engineering Dir
Christopher Arthur, Chief Engineer
Buddy Matthues, Sales & Assistant Operator

WKAX
04-03-1974; 1500 khz AM; 1 kw-D, NDD; N34 31 42 W87 42 41
112 Washington Avenue, Russellville, AL 35653 US
(256) 332-6103, *Fax:* (256) 332-7430
www.wkaxam.com
License: Russellville, AL held by Jamar Communications Inc.
Format: Gospel *Special Programming:* Black 4 hrs wkly *Target Audience:* 21-54. *Adv. Rates:* 6; 6; 6; na
Marshall Moore, President

Saraland

WDLT-FM
07-23-2012; 104.1 mhz; 98000 w; 1667 ft; N30 36 45 W87 38 42
One Office Park, Suite 215, Mobile, AL 36609
(334)652-2020, *Fax:* (334)652-2001
www.983wdlt.com
dean.clinton@cumulus.com
License: Saraland, AL held by Cumulus Licensing
Group Owner: Cumulus Licensing
Chuck Sullivan, Vice President/Market Manager
Dean Clinton, General Sales Manager
Yama Scott, Key Account Manager
Catherine Barlow, Music Director

Scottsboro

WKEA-FM
11-03-1965; 98.3 mhz FM *Hrs Open:* 24; 11 kw; 492 ft.; N34 32 0 W85 55 20
P.O. Box 966, Scottsboro, AL 35768 US
(256) 259-2341, *Fax:* (256) 574-2156
www.wkeafm.com
ron@wkeafm.com
License: Scottsboro, Jackson County, AL held by KEA Radio Inc.
Group Owner: KEA Radio Inc.
Format: Country *Special Programming:* Farm one hr, relg 4 hrs wkly *Hrs. of News Programming:* news progmg 2 hrs wkly *No. News Employees:* 1 *Target Audience:* 25-54.
Ronald Livengood, CEO
Gene Sisk, Operations Dir
Campbell Smith, Operations Manager

WWIC
06-13-1950; 1050 khz AM *Hrs Open:* 24; 1 kw-D, ND1; 0.1 kw-N, ND1; N34 40 23 W86 3 11
815 West Willow St., Scottsboro, AL 35768 US
(256) 259-1050, *Fax:* (256) 575-2411
www.wwicradio.com
wwic@scottsboro.org
License: Scottsboro, AL held by Scottsboro Broadcasting Co. Inc.
Nat'l Network: ABC *Regional Network:* Alabama Radio Net.
Arbitron Metro Market: Jackson County, AL *Format:* Country, Sports *Adv. Rates:* 7.62; 6.24; 6.79; 6.24
Greg Bell, President

WZCT
06-11-1952; 1330 khz AM *Hrs Open:* 24; 5 kw-D, ND1; 0.038 kw-N, ND1; N34 42 7 W86 0 15
P. O. Drawer A, Scottsboro, AL 35768 US
(256) 574-1330, *Fax:* (256) 218-3013
License: Scottsboro, AL held by Bonner and Carlile Enterprises.
Nat'l Network: Reach Satellite; USA
Arbitron Metro Market: Scottsboro, AL *Format:* Gospel *Special Programming:* Sports 19 hrs wkly *Hrs. of News Programming:* News progmg 14 hrs wkly *Target Audience:* 25 plus. *Adv. Rates:* 108; 96; 108; 96
Rob Carlile, Station Manager

Selma

*WAPR
05-05-1996; 88.3 mhz FM; 53 kw vert; 1401 ft.; N32 8 30 W86 44 43 *Rebroadcasts:* Rebroadcasts WUAL-FM Tuscaloosa 100%
The Univ. of Alabama, Box 870370, Tuscaloosa, AL 35487 US
(205) 348-6644, *Fax:* (205) 348-6648
www.apr.org
apr@apr.org
License: Selma, Dallas County, AL held by Ua-Asu-Tsu Educational Radio Corp.
Nat'l Network: NPR; PRI
Arbitron Metro Market: Selma, AL. *Format:* Jazz, News
Brian Poellnitz, Operations Dir
Elizabeth Brock, Station Manager
Pat Duggins, News Director

*WAQU
03-01-1998; 91.1 mhz FM; 21.5 kw; 335 ft.; N32 24 17 W87 25 32
P.O. Drawer 2440, Tupelo, MS 38803 US
(662) 844-8888, *Fax:* (662) 842-6791
www.afr.net
faq@afr.net
License: Selma, Dallas County, AL held by American Family Association.
Group Owner: American Family Radio
Arbitron Metro Market: Selma, AL *Format:* Christian, Religious
Don Wildmon, CEO
Tim Wildmon, President
Marvin Sanders, General Manager
John Riley, Programming Director
Fred Jackson, News Director
Shan Easterling, Chief Engineer

WHBB
11-11-1935; 1490 khz AM *Hrs Open:* 24; 1 kw-U, ND1; N32 26 2 W87 0 40
Mailing Address: 505 Lauderdale Street, PO Box 1055, Selma, AL 36706 US
Second Address: 505 Lauderdale St., Selma, AL 36701
(334) 875-3350, *Fax:* (334) 874-6959
www.wdxx.com
info@wdxx.com
License: Selma, AL held by Broadsouth Communications Inc.
Nat'l Reps: Rgnl Reps
Format: News, News/Talk, 86 *Special Programming:* Black 18 hrs, farm 10 hrs wkly *Hrs. of News Programming:* news progmg 13 hrs wkly *No. News Employees:* 1 *Target Audience:* 25-54. *Adv. Rates:* 26; 20; 22;10
Mike Reynolds, General Manager
Evelyn Ogle, General Sales Mgr
George Henry, Programming Director

WJAM
12-19-1946; 1340 khz AM; 1 kw-U, ND1; N32 25 31 W86 59 47
273 Persimmon Tree Rd, Selma, AL 36701 US
(334) 875-9360, *Fax:* (334) 875-1340
License: Selma, AL held by Scott Communications Inc.
Group Owner: Scott Communications Inc.; (acq 12-30-2005; $29,500 for 47.2% of stock with co-located FM)
Arbitron Metro Market: Selma, AL *Format:* Adult Contemp *Target Audience:* 25-49.
Scott Alexander, President
Betty Alexander, Music Director

*WRNF
01-01-2007; 89.5 mhz FM; 6 kw vert; 328 ft.; N32 32 50 W86 55 33
820 North Lasalle Blvd., Chicago, IL 60610 US

wrnf@moody.edu
License: Selma, Dallas County, AL held by The Moody Bible Institute of Chicago.
Arbitron Metro Market: Selma, AL *Format:* Religious
Rob Moore, General Manager

Sheffield

*WAKD
01-01-1996; 89.9 mhz FM; 7.4 kw vert; 236 ft.; N34 50 11 W87 37 20

P.O. Drawer 2440, Tupelo, MS 38803 US
(662) 844-8888, *Fax:* (662) 842-6791
www.afr.net
faq@afr.net
License: Sheffield, Colbert County, AL held by American Family Association.
Group Owner: American Family Radio
Arbitron Metro Market: Shoals, AL *Format:* Christian, Religious
Marvin Sanders, General Manager
John Riley, Programming Director
Joey Moody, Chief Engineer

WBTG
11-06-1963; 1290 khz AM *Hrs Open:* 24; 1 kw-D, ND1; 0.079 kw-N, ND1; N34 46 27 W87 40 14
Mailing Address: P. O. Box 518, Sheffield, AL 35660 US
Second Address: 1605 Gospel Rd., Sheffield, AL 35660
(256) 381-6800, *Fax:* (256) 381-6801
www.wbtgradio.com
announcements@wbtgradio.com
License: Sheffield, AL held by Slatton & Associates.
Nat'l Network: Salem Radio Network *Regional Network:* Ill. Radio Net.
Arbitron Metro Market: Sheffield, Al *Format:* Sports *Target Audience:* 25 up; conservative, mainstream family audience
Paul Slatton, President
Dan Michaels, Programming Director
Kerri Melton, News Director

WBTG-FM
07-02-1969; 106.3 mhz FM *Hrs Open:* 24; 6 kw; 682 ft.; N34 41 34 W87 47 49
Mailing Address: P.O. Box 518, Sheffield, AL 35660 US
Second Address: 1605 Gospel Rd., Sheffield, AL 35660
(256) 381-6800, *Fax:* (256) 381-6801
www.wbtgradio.com
announcements@wbtgradio.com
License: Sheffield, Colbert County, AL
Arbitron Metro Market: Sheffield, Al *Format:* Sports *Hrs. of News Programming:* News progmg 12 hrs wkly
Paul Slatton, General Manager
Dan Michaels, Programming Director
Kerri Melton, News Director

Shorter

WMRK-FM
08-01-1994; 107.9 mhz FM; 25 kw; 328 ft.; N32 21 9 W86 3 6
Mailing Address: 273 Persimmon Tree Rd, Selma, AL 36701 US
Second Address: 273 Persimmon Tree Rd, Selma, AL 36701
(334) 244-0961, *Fax:* (334) 279-9563
www.newstalk1079.com
tbarber@bluewaterbroadcasting.com
License: Shorter, Perry County, AL held by Scott Communications Inc.
Group Owner: Scott Communications Inc.; (acq 10-13-94)
Format: Urban Contemporary
Rick Peters, CEO/COO
Terry Barber, General Manager
Lanier Harris, General Sales Mgr
CJ Hall, Promotions Manager
Greg Rickaby, Chief Engineer
Jay Scott, Production Director

Slocomb

WLDA
01-01-1991; 100.5 mhz FM *Hrs Open:* 24; 16.5 kw; 408 ft.; N31 11 0 W85 24 23
P.O. Box 1129, Daleville, AL 36322 US
(334) 792-0049, *Fax:* (334) 712-9346
License: Slocomb, Dale County, AL held by Magic Broadcasting Alabama Licensing LLC.
Group Owner: Magic Broadcasting LLC; (acq 10-1-2003; $750,000)
Arbitron Metro Market: Dothan, AL *Format:* Adult Contemp *No. News Employees:* 1 *Target Audience:* 25-54; upscale baby boomers, acitive duty & retired military *Adv. Rates:* 15; 12; 12; 9
Doc Thompson, Operations Dir
Dan Bradley, General Manager
Chris Green, General Sales Mgr

Smiths

WAGH
01-01-1998; 101.3 mhz FM; 18 kw; 354 ft.; N32 25 35 W85 8 20
Mailing Address: Suite 2700, 111 E. Kilbourn Avenue, Milwaukee, WI 53202 US
Second Address: 1501 13th Ave., Columbus, GA 31901
(706) 576-3000, *Fax:* (706) 576-3010
www.magic98online.com
License: Smiths, Lee County, AL held by CC Licenses LLC.
Group Owner: Clear Channel Communications Inc.; (acq 2-21-2002; grpsl)
Arbitron Metro Market: Milwaukee,WI *Format:* Adult Contemp
Target Audience: 25-54; working Black adults
Jim Martin, General Manager
Henry Holt, General Sales Mgr
Rasheeda Ali, Programming Director
Frank McLemore, Chief Engineer

Southside

WFXO
10-10-1992; 105.9 mhz FM *Hrs Open:* 24; 1.6 kw; 196 meters; N34 12 51 W85 46 20
801 Nobel St., Fl. 8, Anniston, AL 35203
(256) 236-1880, *Fax:* (256) 236-4480
www.y-106.com
License: Southside, Cherokee County, AL held by Williams Communications Inc.
Group Owner: Williams Communications Inc.; (acq 6-99; $380,000)
Nat'l Network: Motor Racing Net; PRI
Population Served: 440,000*Hrs. of News Programming:* News progmg one hr wkly *Target Audience:* 25-54.
Walt Williams, General Manager
Dan Pullman, General Sales Mgr
Tex Carter, Programming Director
Mike Mote, News Director

St. Florian

WWFA
102.7 mhz FM; 10 kw; 463 ft.; N34 45 28 W87 30 6 US
(256) 349-2041, *Fax:* (256) 349-2088
www.1027kiss.fm
License: St. Florian, Lauderdale County, AL held by George S. Flinn Jr.
Arbitron Metro Market: Saint Florian, AL *Format:* Adult Contemp, Contemporary Hits/Top 40
George Flinn Jr., General Manager

Steele

*WAYU
91.1 mhz FM; 0.15 kw vert; 755 ft.; N33 57 29.6 W86 13 1 US
(888) 239-2936, *Fax:* (719) 278-4339
www.wayu.wayfm.com
supportservices@wayfm.com
License: Steele, St. Clair County, AL held by WAY-FM Media Group Inc.
Group Owner: WAY-FM Media Group Inc.
Arbitron Metro Market: Steele, AL *Format:* Christian
Robert Augsburg, President

Stevenson

WMXN-FM
06-13-1977; 101.7 mhz FM; 2.3 kw; 541 ft.; N34 41 2 W85 48 4
PO Box 966, Scottsboro, AL 35768 US
(256) 259-2341, *Fax:* (256) 574-2156
www.1017thestorm.com
production@wkeafm.com
License: Stevenson, Jackson County, AL held by KEA Radio Inc.
Group Owner: KEA Radio Inc.; (acq 1996).
Wire Services: AP
Arbitron Metro Market: Stevenson, Al *Format:* Contemporary Hits/Top 40
Ron Livengood, President
Danny Lee, Operations Dir
David Kennamer, Chief Engineer
Campbell Smith, Operations Director

Sumiton

WKDG
06-27-1978; 1540 khz AM; 1 kw-D; N33 45 50 W87 03 47
Box 11385, Birmingham, AL 35148
(205) 326-8844
License: Sumiton, Walker County, AL held by Sumiton Broadcasting Co. Inc.
Arbitron Metro Market: Birmingham, AL
Earl F. Hilliard, President

Sylacauga

WFEB
03-01-1945; 1340 khz AM *Hrs Open:* 16; 1 kw-U, ND1; N33 10 16 W86 13 57
P. O. Box 450, Sylacauga, AL 35150 US
(256) 245-3281, *Fax:* (256) 245-3050
License: Sylacauga, AL held by Powers Broadcasting Co LLC
Regional Reps: Keystone (unwired net).
Arbitron Metro Market: Sylacauga, AL *Format:* News, News/Talk, 84, Talk *Special Programming:* Gospel 6 hrs wkly *Hrs. of News Programming:* news progmg 17 hrs wkly *No. News Employees:* 3 *Target Audience:* 25-54.
Bruce Carr, General Manager

WYEA
05-16-1948; 1290 khz AM *Hrs Open:* 6 AM-8 PM
1 Motes Road, PO Box 629, Sylacauga, AL 35150 US
(256) 249-4263, *Fax:* (256) 245-4355
wyea@rocketmail.com
License: Sylacauga, AL held by Spirit Broadcasting Co. Inc.
Nat'l Network: USA *Regional Network:* Alabama Radio Net. *Nat'l Reps:* Salem
Arbitron Metro Market: Sylacauga, AL *Format:* Christian, Country *Hrs. of News Programming:* News progmg 7 hrs wkly *Target Audience:* General. *Adv. Rates:* 6.25; 5.25; 6.25; na
John Vogel, President
Nelda Vogel, Operations Dir

Talladega

WTDR-FM
11-10-1972; 92.7 mhz FM *Hrs Open:* 24; 2.6 kw; Ant 505 ft; N33 29 12 W85 59 15
Box 7785, 1913 Barry St., Suite B, Oxford, AL 35161
(256) 741-6000, *Fax:* (256) 741-6080
www.wtdrthunder.com
jimj@wtdrthunder.com
License: Talladega, Talladega County, AL held by Jacobs Broadcast Group Inc.
Nat'l Network: AP Radio *Wire Services:* AP
Population Served: 300,000*No. News Employees:* 1 *Target Audience:* 25-54; adults *Adv. Rates:* 30; 26; 27; 18
Jim Jacobs, President
Laura Jacobs, Operations Dir
Laura Jacobs, News Director
Bill Moats, Engineering Dir
Grady Sapp, Operations Manager

Tallassee

WQNR
10-29-1992; 99.9 mhz FM; 2.85 kw; 479 ft.; N32 26 32 W85 47 28
320 Barnett Blvd., Tallassee, AL 36078 US
(250) 723-2455, *Fax:* (250) 723-0797
www.933thepeak.com
info@933thepeak.com
License: Tallassee, Elmore County, AL held by Tiger Communications Inc.
Group Owner: Tiger Communications Inc.; (acq 1999)
Arbitron Metro Market: Sedalia MO *Format:* Contemporary Hits/Top 40, Adult Contemp *Target Audience:* 25-54; Adults *Adv. Rates:* 28; 22; 25; 18
Chris Talbot, Operations Dir
Rob Bye, General Manager
Evan Hammond, Programming Director
Pam Doherty, News Director
Cathy Johns, Administration Director

WTLS
06-01-1954; 1300 khz AM
Mailing Address: 1702 Gilmer Ave, Tallassee, AL 36078 US
Second Address: 2045 Hwy 229, Tallassee, AL 36078
(334) 283-8200, *Fax:* (334) 283-8622
www.1300wtls.com
mbutler@1300wtls.com
License: Tallassee, AL held by Michael Butler Broadcasting LLC
Arbitron Metro Market: Tallassee, AL *Format:* Sports, Talk
Special Programming: Farm 6 hrs wkly,gospel 6 hrs wkly *Adv. Rates:* 11; 8; 10; 7
Michael Butler, President
Leigh Anne Butler, General Sales Mgr
Steve Butler, Programming Director
Miles Hathcock, Promotions Manager
Terry Harper, Chief Engineer

Thomaston

WTID
01-01-2001; 103.9 mhz FM; 0.5 kw; 46 ft.; N32 16 49 W87 38 6
2730 Cozumel Drive, #1404, Melbourne, FL 32935 US
(303) 702-9293, *Fax:* (303) 485-1929
www.wayfm.com
License: Thomaston, Marengo County, AL held by Great South Wireless LLC.
Arbitron Metro Market: Trinidad CO *Format:* Christian
Zach Cochran, General Manager

Thomasville

WJDB
07-16-1956; 630 khz AM *Hrs Open:* Sunrise-sunset; 1 kw-D, ND2; 0.049 kw-N, ND2; N31 52 58 W87 44 42
P.O. 219, Thomasville, AL 36784 US
(334) 636-4438, *Fax:* (334) 636-4439
www.wjbdradio.com
wjdb@dixienet1.com
License: Thomasville, AL held by Griffin Broadcasting Corp.
Nat'l Network: CBS *Regional Network:* Ark. Radio Net.
Format: Oldies *Hrs. of News Programming:* news progmg 10 hrs wkly *No. News Employees:* 1 *Target Audience:* General.
Ivy Griffin, General Manager

WJDB-FM
11-02-1972; 95.5 mhz FM *Hrs Open:* 24; 9.6 kw; 525 ft.; N31 44 25 W87 45 43
Mailing Address: P.O. Box 219, Thomasville, AL 36784 US
Second Address: 2211 Hwy. 43 S., Thomasville, AL 36784
(334) 636-4438, *Fax:* (334) 636-4439
www.wjbdradio.com
wjdb@dixienet1.com
License: Thomasville, Clarke County, AL held by Griffin Broadcasting Corp.
Format: Contemporary Hits/Top 40, Country *Hrs. of News Programming:* News progmg 10 hrs wkly *Target Audience:* General.
Mike Kestler, President
Mike Stockland, General Manager
Don Mills, Programming Director

***WDLG**
01-01-2007; 90.1 mhz FM; 0.5 kw; 249 ft.; N31 44 24 W87 45 43
503 Wood St, Fenton, MI 48430 US
(850) 438-7667
www.catholicradio.us
mglin@aol.com
License: Thomasville, Clarke County, AL held by Nationwide Inspirational Broadcasting.
Arbitron Metro Market: Thomasville, AL *Format:* Christian, Religious
Michael Glinter, President

Trinity

WVNN-FM
10-04-1992; 92.5 mhz FM *Hrs Open:* 24; 3.1 kw; 423 ft.; N34 42 36 W87 4 54 *Rebroadcasts:* Simulcasts WVNN-AM 100%
600 Congress Avenue, Suite 1400, Austin, TX 78701 US
(256) 830-8300, *Fax:* (256) 232-6842
www.wvnn.com
programdirector@wvnn.com
License: Trinity, Morgan County, AL held by Cumulus Licensing LLC.
Group Owner: Cumulus Media Inc.; (acq 4-4-2006; $3.3 million with WXQW(FM) Meridianville)
Nat'l Network: ABC *Nat'l Reps:* Katz Radio
Arbitron Metro Market: Huntsville, AL *Format:* News, News/Talk, 86 *Hrs. of News Programming:* 7 hrs news prgmg wkly *No. News Employees:* 3
Bill West, General Manager
Tracy Flesch, General Sales Mgr

Troy

***WAXU**
01-01-2001; 91.1 mhz FM *Hrs Open:* 24; 1.089 kw; 246 ft.; N31 47 22 W85 58 58
P O Drawer 2440, Tupelo, MS 38803 US
(530) 345-0021, *Fax:* (530) 893-2121
License: Troy, Pike County, AL held by American Family Association.
Group Owner: American Family Radio
Format: Sports
Scott Donohue, President
Dino Corbin, General Manager
Mike Wessels, Programming Director

WTBF
02-25-1947; 970 khz AM *Hrs Open:* 24
67 Court Sq., Troy, AL 36081 US
(334) 566-0300, *Fax:* (334) 566-5689
www.wtbf.com
wtbf@radio.com
License: Troy, AL held by Troy Broadcasting Corp.
Format: Talk *Special Programming:* Farm 17 hrs wkly *Hrs. of News Programming:* News progmg 20 hrs wkly *Target Audience:* 35 plus; general *Adv. Rates:* 25; 15; 25; 7:50
Joe Gilchrist, President
Jim Roling, Operations Dir
Dave Kirby, Operations Manager

WZHT
02-28-1973; 105.7 mhz FM; 100 kw; 1831 ft.; N31 58 28 W86 9 44
600 Congress Avenue, Suite 1400, Austin, TX 78701 US
(334) 274-6464, *Fax:* (334) 274-6465
www.myhot105.com
License: Troy, Pike County, AL held by Capstar TX L.P.
Group Owner: Clear Channel Communications Inc.; (acq 8-30-00; grpsl)
Nat'l Network: ABC; Westwood One *Nat'l Reps:* McGavren Guild
Arbitron Metro Market: Montgomery, AL *Format:* Urban Contemporary *Target Audience:* 18-49.
Michael Long, Operations Dir
James Belton, General Manager
Alberta Jackson, General Sales Mgr
Nikita Pogue, Promotions Manager
Connye Bryant, News Director

Trussville

WQEN
10-07-1966; 103.7 mhz FM; 100 kw; 935 ft.; N33 26 38 W86 52 47
600 Congress Avenue, Suite 1400, Austin, TX 78701 US
(205) 439-9600, *Fax:* (205) 439-8390
www.1037theq.com
License: Trussville, Jefferson County, AL held by Capstar TX L.P.
Group Owner: Clear Channel Communications Inc.; (acq 8-30-2000; grpsl)
Arbitron Metro Market: Birmingham, AL *Format:* Contemporary Hits/Top 40
Jimmy Vineyard, General Manager
Keith Allen, Programming Director

Tuscaloosa

WACT
09-01-1958; 1420 khz AM *Hrs Open:* 24; 5 kw-D, ND1; 0.108 kw-N, ND1; N33 10 30 W87 33 18
Mailing Address: 600 Congress Avenue, Suite 1400, Austin, TX 78701 US
Second Address: 2121 9th St., Suite B, Tuscaloosa, AL 35401
License: Tuscaloosa, AL held by Capstar TX L.P.
Group Owner: Clear Channel Communications Inc.; (acq 8-30-2000; grpsl)
Arbitron Metro Market: Vermillion SD
Rosa Cuellar-Khraish, General Manager

WJRD
10-10-1936; 1150 khz AM *Hrs Open:* 24; 20 kw-D, 1 kw-N, DA-N; N33 15 02 W87 36 35
Box 70937, Tuscaloosa, AL 23510
(205) 345-9573, *Fax:* (205) 366-9480
License: Tuscaloosa, Tuscaloosa County, AL held by JRD Inc.
Nat'l Network: ABC
Population Served: 100,000 *Arbitron Metro Market:* Tuscaloosa, AL *Target Audience:* Adults 35 plus.
Jimmy Shaw, President

WTBC
12-23-1946; 1230 khz AM *Hrs Open:* 24
Mailing Address: 3869 Pine Lane, Suite 205-D, Bessemer, AL 35022 US
Second Address: 2110 McFarland Blvd. E., Suite C, Tuscaloosa, AL 35404
(205) 758-5523,(205) 732-9822, *Fax:* (205) 752-9696
www.wtbc1230.com
wtbc@dbtech.net
License: Tuscaloosa, AL held by John Sisty Enterprises Inc.
Nat'l Network: ABC; ESPN Radio *Regional Reps:* Alabama Net.
Arbitron Metro Market: Tuscaloosa, AL *Format:* News, News/Talk, 84, Talk *Special Programming:* Relg 3 hrs wkly *Hrs. of News Programming:* News progmg 3 hrs wkly *Target Audience:* 25-54; upscale, affluent *Adv.Rates:* 28; 30; 28; 10
John Sisty, CEO
Dave McDaniel, Operations Dir
Nancy Wilson, General Sales Mgr
Tesha Price, News Director
Ronnie Quarles, COO

WTSK
02-01-1958; 790 khz AM; 5 kw-D, 36 w-N; N33 11 17 W87 35 23
142 Skyland Blvd., Tuscaloosa, AL 35405
(205) 345-7200, *Fax:* (205) 349-1715
790wtsk.com
Todd.Livingston@townsquaremedia.com
License: Tuscaloosa, Tuscaloosa County, AL
Group Owner: Townsquare Media; (acq 7-31-2012; grpsl).
Population Served: 91,605 *Arbitron Metro Market:* Tuscaloosa, AL *Target Audience:* 35 plus.
Greg Thomas, Operations Dir
Todd Livingston, General Manager
Tammy Boyd, General Sales Mgr
Charles Anthony, Programming Director
Jade Nicole, Promotions Manager
Tammy Boyd, Sales Director

***WUAL-FM**
01-04-1982; 91.5 mhz FM *Hrs Open:* 24; 100 kw; 518 ft.; N33 5 40 W87 24 47
P.O. Box 870370, Tuscaloosa, AL 35487 US
(205) 348-6644, *Fax:* (205) 348-6648
apr.org
aprnews@apr.org
License: Tuscaloosa, Tuscaloosa County, AL held by Board of Trustees of the University of Alabama.
Nat'l Network: PRI; NPR *Regional Reps:* Alabama Net.
Arbitron Metro Market: Tuscaloosa, AL *Format:* Jazz, News, 62, Talk *Special Programming:* Folk 5 hrs, new age 20 hrs wkly *Hrs. of News Programming:* news progmg 5 hrs wkly *No. News Employees:* 3 *TargetAudience:* 35 plus.
Brian Poellnitz, Operations Manager & Fill-In Host
Elizabeth Brock, General Manager
Pat Duggins, News Director
Kathy Henslee, Development Director
David Duff, Music Director
Eva Lynch, Program Assistant
Jackie Howell, MembershipCoordinator

***WVUA-FM**
09-07-1972; 90.7 mhz FM; 0 kw horiz, 0.22 kw vert; 184 ft.; N33 12 34 W87 32 56
P.O. Box 870152, Tuscaloosa, AL 35487 US
(205) 348-6461, *Fax:* (205) 348-0375
www.wvuafm.ua.edu
wvua@sa.ua.edu
License: Tuscaloosa, Tuscaloosa County, AL held by Board of Trustees University of Alabama.
Arbitron Metro Market: Tuscaloosa, AL *Format:* Alternative *Special Programming:* Christian 3 hrs, hardcore 3 hrs, blues 3 hrs, heav *Target Audience:* 18-25; high school & college students
Loy Singleton, General Manager
Cliff Kyle, Station Manager
Chad Haynie, Sports Director
Dusty Fields, Music Director

WMXB
12-10-1951; 1280 khz AM; 5 kw-D, 500 w-N, DA-N; N33 13 07 W87 34 05
601 Greensboro Ave., Suite 507, Tuscaloosa, AL 35407
(205) 345-4787, *Fax:* (205) 345-4790
jwlawson@bellsouth.net
License: Tuscaloosa, Tuscaloosa County, AL held by Lawson of Tuscaloosa Inc.
Nat'l Network: Westwood One
Population Served: 75,000 *Arbitron Metro Market:* Tuscaloosa, AL *Special Programming:* Jazz 2 hrs wkly *Target Audience:* 24-54; mature business audience
Jim Lawson, President
Mildred Porter, Operations Dir

***WMFT**
06-06-2005; 88.9 mhz FM *Hrs Open:* 24; 100 kw vert; 522 ft.; N33 20 19 W87 21 32 *Rebroadcasts:* Rebroadcasts WMBV(FM) Dixon Mills
820 N Lasalle Blvd, Chicago, IL 60610 US
(205) 758-7900, *Fax:* (205) 758-0059
www.wmft.fm
wmft@moody.edu
License: Tuscaloosa, Tuscaloosa County, AL held by The Moody Bible Institute of Chicago
Group Owner: The Moody Bible Institute of Chicago
Nat'l Network: Moody *Wire Services:* AP
Arbitron Metro Market: Tuscaloosa, AL *Format:* Christian *Hrs. of News Programming:* News progmg 6 hrs wkly *Target Audience:* 35-54.
Rob Moore, Station Manager
John Rogers, Programming Director

Tuscumbia

WVNA
04-05-1955; 1590 khz AM *Hrs Open:* 24; 5 kw-D, DAN; 1 kw-N, DAN; N34 45 24 W87 41 10
P.O. Box 477, Tuscumbia, AL 35674 US
(256) 383-2727
www.newstalkwvna.com
License: Tuscumbia, AL held by Urban Radio Licenses LLC.
Group Owner: Urban Radio Licenses LLC; (acq 5-13-2005; grpsl).
Nat'l Network: CBS

Arbitron Metro Market: Tuscumbia, AL *Format:* News, News/Talk, 84, Talk *Special Programming:* News *Hrs. of News Programming:* news progmg 60 hrs wkly *No. News Employees:* 3 *Target Audience:* 25-64.

WZZA
04-17-1960; 1410 khz AM *Hrs Open:* 24; 0.5 kw-D, ND1; 0.051 kw-N, ND1; N34 42 29 W87 41 35
1570 Woodmont Drive, Tuscumbia, AL 35674 US
(256) 381-1862, *Fax:* (256) 381-6006
www.WZZARadio.com
ToriBailey@WZZARadio.com
License: Tuscumbia, AL held by Muscle Shoals Broadcasting
Nat'l Network: American Urban *Wire Services:* Bloomberg Financial
Arbitron Metro Market: Tuscumbia, AL *Format:* Black, Blues, 44, Jazz *Hrs. of News Programming:* news-talk progmg 15 hrs wkly *No. News Employees:* 3 *Target Audience:* Black *Adv. Rates:* 20.00; 15.00; 15.00;12.50
Tori Bailey, CEO
Dorothy Owens, Operations Dir
Leonard Skipworth, Air Personality and Sales Manager
Darryl Luster, Programming Director
Tonyia Carter, News Director / Gospel Music Director
Odessa Bailey, CFO
Peter Smith, GospelProgram Director
LaFredia Thompson, Public Service Director
Theodore Lindsey, Sales Executive
Darryl Luster, Air Personality/Sales Associate/Music Director
Dorothy Owens, Office Manager

Tuskegee

WACQ(AM)
07-01-1952; 580 khz AM; 500 w-D, 139 w-N; N32 22 36 W85 39 28
320 Barnett Blvd, PO Box, Tuskegee, AL 36078
(205) 283-6888, *Fax:* (205) 283-2152
www.wacqradio.com
wacqradio@elmore.rr.com
License: Tuskegee, Macon County, AL held by Tiger Communications Inc.
Group Owner: Tiger Communications Inc.; (acq 4-6-2006; $350,000 with WQSI(FM) Union Springs)
Population Served: 4,852 *Arbitron Metro Market:* Tallassee, AL *Format:* Gospel *Target Audience:* adults 25+.
Bernita Luke, General Manager
Randall Hughey, General Sales Mgr
Sylvester McPherson, Programming Director
Terry Harper, Chief Engineer

WQSI
07-12-1975; 95.9 mhz FM; 4.3 kw; 377 ft; N32 28 17 W85 34 28
2514 S. College St., Suite 104, Auburn, AL 36078
(334) 887-9999, *Fax:* (334) 826-9599
www.thetiger.fm
info@thetiger.fm
License: Tuskegee, Macon County, AL held by Tiger Communications Inc.
Group Owner: Tiger Communications Inc.; (acq 2-26-98; $450,000)
Arbitron Metro Market: Montgomery, AL *Target Audience:* 18-34. *Adv. Rates:* 27; 20; 25; 18
Chris Bailey, General Manager

Union Springs

WTGZ
10-15-1975; 93.9 mhz FM *Hrs Open:* 24; 12.5 kw; Ant 469 ft; N32 19 04 W85 40 16
2514 S. College St., Suite 104, Auburn, AL 23510
(334) 887-9999
wacqradio@elmore.rr.com
License: Union Springs, Bullock County, AL held by Tiger Communications Inc.
Group Owner: Tiger Communications Inc.; (acq 4-6-2006; $350,000 with WBIL(AM) Tuskegee)
Regional Network: Alabama Radio Net.
Population Served: 620,000 *Arbitron Metro Market:* Montgomery, AL *Hrs. of News Programming:* News progmg 15 wkly *Target Audience:* 25-54; 40+ boomers, active, affluent southerners *Adv. Rates:* 18; 18; 18; 12
Marvin Sanders, General Manager

***WBIL**
91.3 mhz FM; 13 kw; 113 meters; N32 07 06 W85 43 10
Box 5725, Twin Falls, ID
(208) 733-3551
www.edgewaterbroadcasing.com
License: Union Springs, Bullock County, AL held by Edgewater Broadcasting Inc
Clark Parrish, President

Valley

WRLD
05-17-1993; 95.3 mhz FM *Hrs Open:* 24; 25 kw; 253 ft.; N32 44 7 W85 8 55
PO Box 639, Valley, AL 36854 US
(706) 327-1217, *Fax:* (706) 596-4600
www.boomer.fm
License: Valley, Chambers County, AL held by PMB Broadcasting LLC.
Group Owner: PMB Broadcasting LLC; (acq 10-1-2008; grpsl)
Arbitron Metro Market: Columbus, GA *Format:* Oldies *Target Audience:* 35 plus.
Chuck Thompson, General Manager

Valley Head

WQRX
02-10-1986; 870 khz AM *Hrs Open:* Sunrise-sunset
220 Jeff Conk Drive, Valley Head, AL 35989 US
(706) 309-9610
www.gnnradio.org
ctbarinowski@comcast.net
License: Valley Head, AL held by Barinowski Investment Company
Group Owner: Good News Network; (acq 10-13-99).
Target Audience: All Sp
Clarence Barinowski, President

Vernon

WJEC
04-01-1991; 106.5 mhz FM *Hrs Open:* 24; 6 kw; 328 ft.; N33 51 15 W88 1 55
P.O. Box 630, Vernon, AL 35592 US
(205) 695-9191, *Fax:* (205) 695-9131
www.wjec1065.com
sales@wjec1065.com
License: Vernon, Lamar County, AL
Format: Gospel *Adv. Rates:* 5; 5; 5; 5
R. William Davis, CEO
Brandon Crawford, President
Brandon Crawford, General Manager
Curt Smith, Station Manager
Glenn Crawford, Vice-President
Eric Otts, Disc Jockey
Randy Wright, Disc Jockey
Greg Fields, Disc Jockey
WayneBarnes, Sales
Teresa Cantrell, Sales

WVSA
07-04-1966; 1380 khz AM; 5 kw-D, ND1; 0.039 kw-N, ND1; N33 47 45 W88 7 3
P.O. Box 630, Vernon, AL 35592 US
(205) 695-9191, *Fax:* (205) 695-9131
www.wvsa1380.com
info@wjec1065.com
License: Vernon, AL held by Lamar County Broadcasting Co. Inc.
Arbitron Metro Market: Vernon, AL *Format:* Sports *Adv. Rates:* 3.50; 3.50; 3.50
Brandon Crawford, President & General Manager
Curtis Smith, Station Manager
Kim Fowlkes, Sales
Glenn Crawford, Vice President
Teresa Cantrell, Sales

Warrior

WBHK
04-22-1992; 98.7 mhz FM; 39 kw; 1339 ft.; N33 29 4 W86 48 25
3773 Howard Hughes Pwy, Suite 300n, Las Vegas, NV 89109 US
(205) 322-2987, *Fax:* (205) 322-2390
www.987kiss.com
david.dubose@coxradio.com
License: Warrior, Jefferson County, AL held by Cox Radio Inc.
Group Owner: Cox Radio Inc.; (acq 10-6-98; $17 million with WBHJ(FM) Tuscaloosa)
Nat'l Reps: Christal *Wire Services:* Metro Weather Service Inc.
Arbitron Metro Market: Birmingham, AL *Format:* Black, Blues *Hrs. of News Programming:* news progmg 5 hrs wkly *No. News Employees:* 2 *Target Audience:* 25-54; general *Adv. Rates:* 400; 250; 250; 125
Kori White, Operations Dir
David DuBose, General Manager
Paul Bankston, General Sales Mgr
Darryl Johnson, Programming Director
Kori White, Promotions Manager
Reginald Green, News Director
Dan Goodman, Chief Engineer
ChrisColeman, Music Director

Waverly

***WELL-FM**
03-01-1990; 88.7 mhz FM *Hrs Open:* 24; 60 kw vert; 423 ft.; N32 44 11 W85 29 54
P.O. Box 284, Dadeville, AL 36853 US
(334) 705-8004, *Fax:* (334) 705-8006
www.praise887.com/
cassiekeyes@hotmail.com
License: Waverly, Tallapoosa County, AL held by Jimmy Jarrell Communications Foundation Inc.
Nat'l Network: USA
Arbitron Metro Market: Waverly, AL. *Format:* Christian *No. News Employees:* 1 *Target Audience:* 24 plus.
Jimmy Jarrell, President
Cassie Keyes, General Manager
Joe May, Programming Director

WGZZ
07-23-1989; 94.3 mhz FM; 4.2 kw; 394 ft.; N32 44 10.5 W85 29 54.2
Mailing Address: Box 909, Alexander City, AL 35011 US
Second Address: 13263 Hwy. 280, Jacksons Gap, AL 36861
(334) 826-2929, *Fax:* (334) 826-9151
www.wingsfm.com
hubbard@aunetwork.com
License: Waverly, Tallapoosa County, AL held by Auburn Network Inc.
Arbitron Metro Market: Waverly, AL *Format:* Country *Special Programming:* Gospel 3 hrs wkly *Target Audience:* 18-55.
Mike Hubbard, President/CEO
Cameron Reynolds, General Manager
Chris Hines, Senior Vice-President
Al Mason, Vice-President/Programming & Production
Tracy Ledbetter, Office Manager
Ashley James, Director of Marketing
Leah Sherriff,Account Executive
Rich Perkins, Traffic Manager/Radio Host

Wetumpka

WRBZ
10-02-1954; 1250 khz AM *Hrs Open:* 24 hours; 5 kw-D, 80 w-N; N32 29 06 W86 12 25 *Rebroadcasts:* 95.7 FM
2821 U.S. Hwy. 231, Wetumpka, AL 36092
(334) 512-1250, *Fax:* (334) 567-7971
www.wapz1250.com
wapz@wapz1250.com
License: Wetumpka, Elmore County, AL held by J&W L.L.C.
Population Served: 450,000 *Arbitron Metro Market:* Montgomery, AL *Special Programming:* HIspanic *Hrs. of News Programming:* 10 *Target Audience:* 12-100. *Adv. Rates:* 22; 22; 22; 18
Johnny Roland, President
Pat Sullivan, Operations Dir
Roz Dorsey, General Manager
Rusty Aldridge, Programming Director

WJWZ
01-01-1998; 97.9 mhz FM; 3.7 kw; 303 ft.; N32 26 50 W86 12 37
4101-A Wall Street, Montgomery, AL 36121 US
(334) 244-0961, *Fax:* (334) 279-9563
www.979-jamz.com
License: Wetumpka, Elmore County, AL held by Bluewater Broadcasting Co. LLC
Arbitron Metro Market: Montgomery, AL *Format:* Urban Contemporary
Terry Barber, General Manager
Marvin Nugent, Programming Director

Winfield

WKXM
08-23-1965; 1300 khz AM; 5 kw-D, ND1; 0.03 kw-N, ND1; N33 55 52 W87 48 36
Mailing Address: PO Box 608, Winfield, AL 35594 US
Second Address: 655 Fairview Rd., Winfield, AL 35594
(205) 487-3261, *Fax:* (205) 487-6991
wkxm@dlis.net
License: Winfield, AL held by Ad-Media Management Corp.
Nat'l Network: Westwood One; ESPN Radio; NBC Radio
Regional Network: Alabama Radio Net.
Format: Sports, Talk *Target Audience:* General. *Adv. Rates:* 9; 7; 9; 7
Maxine Harper, President
Teresa Benton, Operations Dir
Doug Threadgill, News Director
Olen Booth, Engineering Dir

WKXM-FM
01-01-1991; 97.7 mhz FM *Hrs Open:* 24; 3.9 kw; 404 ft.; N34 1 53 W87 48 6
Mailing Address: PO Box 608, Winfield, AL 35594 US
Second Address: 655 Fairview Rd., Winfield, AL 35594
(205) 487-3261, *Fax:* (205) 487-6991
License: Winfield, Marion County, AL
Nat'l Network: ABC
Format: Oldies *Target Audience:* General. *Adv. Rates:* 10; 8; 10; 8
Teresa Benton, News Director

York

WSLY
09-01-1976; 104.9 mhz FM *Hrs Open:* 24; 50 kw; 492 ft.; N32 16 54 W88 15 23
11474 Highway 11 North, York, AL 36925 US
(205) 392-5234, *Fax:* (203) 392-5536
www.espn1049.com
License: York, Sumter County, AL held by Sarah P. Grant.
Nat'l Network: Fox Sports
Format: Sports *Target Audience:* 18-54; male & female
Dan Mecca, General Manager

WYLS
11-01-1970; 670 khz AM *Hrs Open:* 7 AM-4:30 PM; 4.8 kw-D, NDD; N32 31 24 W88 15 28
11474 Us Hwy 11, York, AL 36925 US
(205) 392-5234, *Fax:* (205) 392-5536
ken@1049jackfm.com
License: York, AL held by Grantell Broadcasting Co.
Arbitron Metro Market: York, AL *Format:* Gospel *Target Audience:* 25-54+.
Ken Michaels, Operations Dir

Alaska

Akiachak

*KHKY
01-01-2007; 92.7 mhz FM; 0.05 kw vert; 92 ft.; N60 54 35.6 W161 25 56.6
US
(907) 825-3600, *Fax:* (907) 825-3655
www.yupiit.org
License: Akiachak, Bethel County, AK held by Yupiit School District.
Arbitron Metro Market: Akiachak, AK *Format:* Christian
Trevor Snyder, General Manager

Anchorage

KAFC
04-04-1999; 93.7 mhz FM; 27 kw; 663 ft.; N61 4 2 W149 44 36
Mailing Address: 6401 E. Northern Lights, Suite 201, Anchorage, AK 99504 US
Second Address: 6401 E. Northern Lights Blvd., Anchorage, AK 99504
(907) 222-4826, *Fax:* (907) 337-0003
www.kafc.org
skip@cbimediagroup.com
License: Anchorage, Anchorage County, AK held by Christian Broadcasting Inc.
Arbitron Metro Market: Anchorage, AK *Format:* Christian
Tom Steigleman, General Manager

KUDO
05-10-1975; 1080 khz AM; 10 kw-U, ND1; N61 7 12 W149 53 43
3601 ""C"" Street, Suite 290, Anchorage, AK 99503 US
(907) 522-1018, *Fax:* (907) 522-1027
www.1080theticket.com
klef@klef.com
License: Anchorage, AK held by IBEW Local 1547 Investments LLC
Arbitron Metro Market: Anchorage, AK *Format:* Talk *Target Audience:* 25 plus.
Rich McClear, General Manager

KASH-FM
12-01-1985; 107.5 mhz FM *Hrs Open:* 24; 100 kw; 981 ft.; N61 20 11 W149 30 48
600 Congress Avenue, Suite 1400, Austin, TX 78701 US
(907) 522-1515, *Fax:* (907) 743-5184
www.kashcountry1075.com
garydonovan@clearchannel.com
License: Anchorage, Anchorage County, AK held by Clear Channel Radio Licenses Inc.
Group Owner: Clear Channel Communications Inc.; (acq 8-30-00; grpsl).
Arbitron Metro Market: Anchorage, AK *Format:* Country *Target Audience:* 25-54.
Gary Donovan, President
Gary Donovan, General Manager
Jimmy O'Brien, Programming Director

*KATB
06-01-1985; 89.3 mhz FM *Hrs Open:* 24; 4.9 kw; 663 ft.; N61 4 2 W149 44 36
Mailing Address: 6401 E. Northern Lights, Anchorage, AK 99504 US
Second Address: 6401 E. Northern Lights Blvd., Anchorage, AK 99504
(907) 333-5282, *Fax:* (907) 337-0003
www.katb.org .
tom@katb.org
License: Anchorage, Anchorage County, AK held by Christian Broadcasting Inc.
Nat'l Network: Moody
Arbitron Metro Market: Anchorage, AK *Format:* Religious *Hrs. of News Programming:* News progmg 5 hrs wkly *Target Audience:* 25-49; women
Tom Steigleman, General Manager

KBFX
10-01-1978; 100.5 mhz FM; 25 kw; 174 ft.; N61 11 52 W149 52 31
600 Congress Avenue, Suite 1400, Austin, TX 78701 US
(907) 522-1515, *Fax:* (907) 743-5184
www.1005thefox.com
anchorage@clearchannel.com
License: Anchorage, Anchorage County, AK held by Capstar TX L.P.
Group Owner: Clear Channel Communications Inc.; (acq 8-7-00; grpsl).
Arbitron Metro Market: Anchorage, AK *Format:* Classic Rock
Gray Donavan, President
Mark Murphy, Operations Dir
Andy Lohman, General Manager
Kim Williams, General Sales Mgr
Jeremy Hegna, Programming Director

KBRJ
11-01-1966; 104.1 mhz FM *Hrs Open:* 24; 55 kw; 62 ft.; N61 7 12 W149 53 43
725 Broad St., P.O. Box 936, Augusta, GA 30903 US
(907) 344-9622, *Fax:* (907) 349-7326
kbrj.com
news@kfqd.com
License: Anchorage, Anchorage County, AK held by MCC Radio LLC.
Group Owner: Morris Radio LLC
Arbitron Metro Market: Anchorage, AK *Format:* Country *Target Audience:* 18-49.
Matt Valley, Programming Director

KBYR
01-01-1948; 700 khz AM *Hrs Open:* 24; 10 kw-U, ND1; N61 12 25 W149 55 20
1007 West 32nd Ave., Anchorage, AK 99501 US
(907) 344-4045, *Fax:* (907) 522-6053
www.kbyr.com
dubs@kbyram.com
License: Anchorage, AK held by Cobb Communications Inc.
Nat'l Network: ABC
Arbitron Metro Market: Anchorage, AK *Format:* News, News/Talk, 86 *No. News Employees:* 1 *Target Audience:* 25-54.
Justin McDonald, General Manager
Debbie Rinckey, General Sales Mgr
Kathy Phillips, News Director

KEAG
01-01-1987; 97.3 mhz FM *Hrs Open:* 24; 55 kw; 62 ft.; N61 7 12 W149 53 43
725 Broad St., P.O. Box 936, Augusta, GA 30903 US
(907) 344-9622, *Fax:* (907) 349-7326
www.kool973.com
news@kqfd.com
License: Anchorage, Anchorage County, AK held by Morris Communications Corp.
Group Owner: Morris Radio LLC; (acq 10-15-98; grpsl)
Arbitron Metro Market: Anchorage, AK *Format:* Oldies *Hrs. of News Programming:* news progmg 3 hrs wkly *No. News Employees:* 1 *Target Audience:* 35-49.
Scott Smith, General Manager
Dave Stroh, Programming Director

KENI
07-15-1967; 650 khz AM *Hrs Open:* 24; 50 kw-U, ND1; N61 9 58 W149 49 34
600 Congress Avenue, Suite 1400, Austin, TX 78701 US
(907) 522-1515, *Fax:* (907) 743-5186
www.keni650.com
info@keni.com
License: Anchorage, AK held by Capstar TX L.P.
Group Owner: Clear Channel Communications Inc.; (acq 8-30-2000; grpsl)
Nat'l Reps: Christal
Arbitron Metro Market: Anchorage, AK *Format:* Talk *Hrs. of News Programming:* news progmg 5 hrs wkly *No. News Employees:* 1 *Target Audience:* 25-64.
Andy Lowman, General Manager

KFAT
04-01-1997; 92.9 mhz FM *Hrs Open:* 24; 10 kw; 886 ft.; N61 20 11 W149 30 48
5455 Highland Drive, Bellevue, WA 98006 US
(907) 344-4045
www.kfat929.com
info@kfat929.com
License: Anchorage, Anchorage County, AK
Group Owner: Ohana Media Group LLC; (acq 7-30-99)
Nat'l Network: ABC
Arbitron Metro Market: Anchorage, AK *TV Affiliate:* KYES(TV) affil. *Format:* Christian *Target Audience:* 18-34; adults
Pete Benedetti, CEO
Tom Oakes, Operations Dir
Tom Oakes, General Manager
Derek Moran, Station Manager
McConnell Adams, Programming Director
Trila Bumstead, CFO
Trila Bumstead, Owner

KFQD
01-01-1924; 750 khz AM
725 Broad St., P.O. Box 936, Augusta, GA 30903 US
(907) 344-9622, *Fax:* (907) 349-7326
www.kfqd.com
news@kfqd.com
License: Anchorage, AK held by Morris Communications Corp.
Group Owner: Morris Radio LLC; (acq 12-1-98; grpsl)
Nat'l Reps: Katz Radio
Arbitron Metro Market: Anchorage, AK *TV Affiliate:* KTUU
Format: News, News/Talk, 86 *Special Programming:* Red eye radio 24 hrs wkly *Hrs. of News Programming:* News progmg 140 hrs wkly *Target Audience:* 35plus; higher income, upper demo
Dennis Bookey, General Manager
Scott Smith, General Sales Mgr
Sharon Leighow, News Director
Paul Jewusiak, Chief Engineer

KGOT
09-15-1975; 101.3 mhz FM *Hrs Open:* 24; 26 kw; -66 ft.; N61 9 58 W149 49 34
600 Congress Avenue, Suite 1400, Austin, TX 78701 US
(907) 522-1515, *Fax:* (907) 522-0672
www.kgot.com
anchorage@clearchannel.com
License: Anchorage, Anchorage County, AK held by Capstar TX L.P.
Group Owner: Clear Channel Communications Inc.
Arbitron Metro Market: Anchorage, AK *Format:* Contemporary Hits/Top 40 *Hrs. of News Programming:* News progmg 2 hrs wkly *Target Audience:* 12-44.
Mark Murphy, Operations Dir

KHAR
01-07-1961; 590 khz AM *Hrs Open:* 24; 5 kw-U, ND1; N61 7 12 W149 53 43
725 Broad St., P.O. Box 936, Augusta, GA 30903 US
(907) 344-9622, *Fax:* (907) 349-7326
khar590.com
ron.clement@achoragemediagroup.com
License: Anchorage, AK held by MCC Radio LLC.
Group Owner: Morris Radio LLC; (acq 12-1-98; grpsl)
Nat'l Reps: International Media
Arbitron Metro Market: Anchorage, AK *Format:* Adult Contemp *Special Programming:* Religious 20 hrs wkly *Hrs. of News Programming:* News progmg 3 hrs wkly *Target Audience:* 35 plus; white collar, professional,upper-income demographics
Dennis Bookey, General Manager
Ron Clement, General Sales Mgr
Paul Jewusiak, Chief Engineer

KDBZ
02-01-1973; 102.1 mhz FM; 23 kw; 82 ft.; N61 7 12 W149 53 43
Post Office Box 5210, Yelm, WA 98597 US
(907) 344-4045, *Fax:* (907) 522-6053
www.buzz1021.com
info@buzz1021.com
License: Anchorage, Anchorage County, AK
Group Owner: Ohana Media Group LLC; acq 8-12-99; $1.3 million).

Wire Services: AP
Arbitron Metro Market: Anchorage, AK *Format:* Adult Contemp
Target Audience: 18-44; women
Pete Benedetti, CEO
Tom Oakes, General Manager
Carla Wyrick, General Sales Mgr
Tom Oaks, Programming Director
Trila Bumstead, CFO

KLEF
09-16-1988; 98.1 mhz FM *Hrs Open:* 24; 25 kw; Ant -85 ft; N61 11 17 W149 52 57
165 E. 56th Ave., Ste. 10, Anchorage, AK 99503
(907) 562-4434, *Fax:* (907) 562-4433
www.klef.com
klef@klef.com
License: Anchorage, Anchorage County, AK held by Chinook Concert Broadcasters Inc.
Regional Reps: None
Population Served: 300,000 *Arbitron Metro Market:* Anchorage, AK *Special Programming:* Children two hr wkly *Target Audience:* 25-64; highly educated, affluent adults *Adv. Rates:* Variable
Rick Goodfellow, President
Rick Goodfellow, Operations Dir
Rick Goodfellow, General Manager
Rick Goodfellow, Station Manager
Rick Goodfellow, General Sales Mgr
Rick Goodfellow, Programming Director
Rick Goodfellow, PromotionsManager
Ron Zastrow, Chief Engineer
Evelyn Burdick, Traffic Director

KMXS
09-01-1987; 103.1 mhz FM *Hrs Open:* 24; 100 kw; 105 ft.; N61 11 33 W149 54 1
9200 Lake Otis Parkway, P.O. Box 936, Anchorage, AK 99507 US
(907) 344-9622, *Fax:* (907) 349-7326
www.kmxs.com
news@kftq.com
License: Anchorage, Anchorage County, AK held by Morris Communications Corp.
Group Owner: Morris Radio LLC; (acq 10-15-98; grpsl)
Nat'l Reps: McGavren Guild
Arbitron Metro Market: Anchorage, AK *Format:* Adult Contemp *Hrs. of News Programming:* news progmg 5 hrs wkly *No. News Employees:* 1 *Target Audience:* 25-44; female listeners
Scott Smith, General Manager
Roxy Lennox, Programming Director

***KNBA**
09-01-1996; 90.3 mhz FM *Hrs Open:* 24; 100 kw; 640 ft.; N61 25 22 W149 52 20
810 E. 9th Avenue, Anchorage, AK 99501 US
(907) 793-3500, *Fax:* (907) 793-3536
www.knba.org
feedback@knba.org
License: Anchorage, Anchorage County, AK held by Koahnic Broadcast Corp.
Arbitron Metro Market: Anchorage, AK *Format:* Variety/Diverse *Hrs. of News Programming:* news progmg 8 hrs wkly *No. News Employees:* 3 *Target Audience:* 20-50; well off, public radio listeners *Adv. Rates:* 25; 25; 25; 25.
Jaclyn Sallee, CEO
Loren Dixon, Programming Director
Larry Cleland, Underwriting Director

KNLT
09-15-1960; 105.7 mhz FM *Hrs Open:* 24; 51 kw; Ant 1,069 ft; N61 20 11 W149 30 48
4700 Business Park Blvd., Bldg. E 44A, Anchorage, AK 99501
(907) 522-1018, *Fax:* (907) 522-1027
www.knik.com
License: Anchorage, Anchorage County, AK held by Ubik Corp.
Nat'l Reps: Interep
Population Served: 360,000 *Arbitron Metro Market:* Anchorage, AK *Hrs. of News Programming:* news progmg 9 hrs wkly *No. News Employees:* 1 *Target Audience:* 25-54 plus. *Adv. Rates:* 30; 28; 32; 18
Mike Robbins, General Manager
Dan Thomas, Programming Director

***KRUA**
02-14-1992; 88.1 mhz FM *Hrs Open:* 24; 0.155 kw; 833 ft.; N61 20 11 W149 30 48
P. O. Box 755300, Fairbanks, AK 99775 US
(907) 786-6800, *Fax:* (907) 786-6806
www.krua.uaa.alaska.edu
aykrua1@uaa.alaska.edu
License: Anchorage, Anchorage County, AK held by University of Alaska-Anchorage.
Arbitron Metro Market: Anchorage, AK *Format:* Alternative
Special Programming: Var/div music 20 hrs, sports one hr wklyVar/div music 20 hrs, American Indian 3 hrs, sports one hr wkly *Hrs. of News Programming:* newsprogmg 10 hrs wkly *No. News Employees:* 4 *Target Audience:* General; college community/div
Neil Torquiano, Station Manager

***KSKA**
08-15-1978; 91.1 mhz FM *Hrs Open:* 24; 100 kw; 617 ft.; N61 25 22 W149 52 20
3877 Universtiy Drive, Anchorage, AK 99508 US
(907) 550-8400, *Fax:* (907) 550-8401(907) 550-8403
www.kska.org
info@ksml.com
License: Anchorage, Anchorage County, AK held by Alaska Public Telecommunications Inc.
Nat'l Network: NPR; PRI *Regional Network:* Alaska Pub.
Arbitron Metro Market: Anchorage, AK *Format:* News *Hrs. of News Programming:* news progmg 70 hrs wkly *No. News Employees:* 2 *Target Audience:* 24 plus; professionals
Paul Stankavich, President
Bede Trantina, Station Manager
Bede Trantina, Programming Director
Lori Townsend, News Director

KTZN
05-02-1948; 550 khz AM
600 Congress Avenue, Suite 1400, Austin, TX 78701 US
(907) 522-1515, *Fax:* (907) 743-5184
www.550thezone.com
anchorage@clearchannel.com
License: Anchorage, AK held by Capstar TX L.P.
Group Owner: Clear Channel Communications Inc.; (acq 8-30-00; grpsl).
Nat'l Reps: D & R Radio
Arbitron Metro Market: Anchorage, AK *Format:* Sports *Target Audience:* 25-54.
Gary Donovan, President
Andy Lohman, General Manager
Kim Williams, General Sales Mgr
Mark Murphy, Programming Director

KWHL
09-18-1982; 106.5 mhz FM; 100 kw; 66 ft.; N61 7 14 W149 53 42
925 Lake Otis Parkway, Anchorage, AK 99507 US
(907) 344-9622, *Fax:* (907) 344-0742
www.kwhl.com
studio@kwhl.com
License: Anchorage, Anchorage County, AK held by Morris Communications Corp.
Group Owner: Morris Radio LLC
Arbitron Metro Market: Anchorage, AK *Format:* Rock/AOR *Target Audience:* 18-44; medium income adults, mostly men
Kim Shuck, General Sales Mgr
Brad Stennett, Programming Director
Mathew Grabowy, Promotions Manager

KYMG
01-01-1989; 98.9 mhz FM *Hrs Open:* 24; 100 kw; -151 ft.; N61 9 58 W149 49 34
600 Congress Avenue, Suite 1400, Austin, TX 78701 US
(907) 743-5239, *Fax:* (907) 743-5184
www.magic989fm.com
jobsanchorage@ClearChannel.com'
License: Anchorage, Anchorage County, AK held by Clear Channel Radio Licenses Inc.
Group Owner: Clear Channel Communications Inc.; (acq 8-30-00; grpsl).
Arbitron Metro Market: Anchorage, AK *Format:* Adult Contemp *Special Programming:* Relg one hr wkly *Hrs. of News Programming:* news progmg 4 hrs wkly *No. News Employees:* 1 *Target Audience:* 25-49; mostlywomen
Gary Donovan, President
Mark Murphy, Operations Dir
Andy Lohman, General Manager
Kim Williams, General Sales Mgr
Dave Flavin, Programming Director

***KAKL**
01-01-2004; 88.5 mhz FM *Hrs Open:* 24; 11 kw; -82 ft.; N61 7 14 W149 53 42
1425 North Market Blvd, Suite 9, Sacramento, CA 95834 US
(800) 525-5683, *Fax:* (916) 251-1650
www.klove.com
klove@klove.com
License: Anchorage, Anchorage County, AK held by Educational Media Foundation.
Group Owner: EMF Broadcasting
Nat'l Network: K-Love
Arbitron Metro Market: Anchorage, AK *Format:* Christian *No. News Employees:* 3 *Target Audience:* 25-44; Judeo Chrisitan, female
Darrell Chambliss, Chairman
Mike Novak, President and CEO
Jeff Harris, Operations Dir
Eric Allen, General Sales Mgr
David Pierce, Programming Director
Ed Lenane, News Director
Sam Wallington, Engineering Dir
Tracy Butler,Traffic Manager
Laura Daniels, News Reporter
Tim Luttrell, News Reporter
Kenny Noble Cortes, News Reporter
Darren Vinson, News Reporter
D. Kevin Blair, Secretary and General Counsel

***KAUG**
01-01-2007; 89.9 mhz FM; 0.004 kw horiz; 98 ft.; N61 24 33 W149 25 15
US
(907) 742-4000, *Fax:* (907) 742-3545
License: Anchorage, Anchorage County, AK held by Anchorage School District.
Arbitron Metro Market: Anchorage, AK *Format:* Variety/Diverse
Carol Comeau, General Manager

Barrow

***KBRW**
12-22-1975; 680 khz AM *Hrs Open:* 24; 10 kw-D, ND1; 10 kw-N, ND1; N71 15 24 W156 31 32
P.O. Box 109, Barrow, AK 99723 US
(907) 852-6811, *Fax:* (907) 852-2274
www.kbrw.org
info@kbrw.org
License: Barrow, AK held by Silakkuagvik Communications Inc.
Nat'l Network: PRI; NPR *Regional Network:* Alaska Pub.
Format: Variety/Diverse *Special Programming:* Class 2 hrs, jazz 6 hrs, relg one hr, Filipino 2 h *Hrs. of News Programming:* news progmg 24 hrs wkly *No. News Employees:* 1 *Target Audience:* General.
Jim Vorderstrasse, President
Robert Sommer, Operations Dir
Jason Gilbert, General Sales Mgr
Isaac Tuckfield, Programming Director
Janelle Everett, News Director
Charles Laykatis, Chief Engineer
Doreen Simmonds, News Reporter
Kai Saxton, Operations Manager
Earl Finkler, Reporter

***KBRW-FM**
09-01-1996; 91.9 mhz FM *Hrs Open:* 7 AM-midnight; 0.89 kw; 72 ft.; N71 17 20 W156 45 31
P.O. Box 109, 1695 Okpik St, Barrow, AK 99723 US
(907) 852-6811, *Fax:* (907) 852-2274
License: Barrow, North Slope County, AK held by Silakkuagvik Communications Inc.
Nat'l Network: NPR; PRI *Regional Network:* Alaska Pub.
Format: Adult Contemp, Big Band *Hrs. of News Programming:* news progmg 80 hrs wkly *No. News Employees:* 1 *Target Audience:* General.
Jason Gilbert, General Sales Mgr
Issac Tuckfield, Programming Director
Diana Gish, News Director
Robert Sommer, Chief Engineer

Bethel

KYKD
11-01-1994; 100.1 mhz FM *Hrs Open:* 24; 12 kw; 72 ft; N60 48 20 W161 47 14
P.O. Box 2428, Bethel, AK 99760
(907) 543-5953, *Fax:* (907) 543-5952
www.vfcm.org/kykd
kykd@vfcm.org
License: Bethel, Bethel County, AK held by Voice For Christ Ministries Inc.
Nat'l Network: Salem Radio Network; Moody
Special Programming: Christian Native *Target Audience:* Native and Rural Alaskans *Adv. Rates:* 20;20;20;20
Palmer Bailey, Station Manager

***KYUK**
05-13-1971; 640 khz AM; 10 kw-U, ND1; N60 46 57 W161 53 0
Pouch 468- 640 Radio St., Bethel, AK 99559 US
(907) 543-3131, *Fax:* (907) 543-3130
www.kyuk.org
webmaster@kyuk.org
License: Bethel, AK held by Bethel Broadcasting Inc.
Nat'l Network: PRI; NPR *Regional Network:* Alaska Pub.

RADIO - U.S.

Arbitron Metro Market: Bethel, AK *TV Affiliate:* *KYUK-TV affil
Format: Talk, Variety/Diverse *Special Programming:* Class 4 hrs, country 4 hrs wkly *Target Audience:* General.
Joan Hamilton, Chairman
Shane Iverson, Operations Dir
Mike Martz, General Manager
Angela Denning Barnes, News Director
Joseph Siebert, Chief Engineer

Big Lake

*KAGV
11-01-2004; 1110 khz AM *Hrs Open:* 24/7
US
(907) 832-5426, *Fax:* (907) 892-8825
www.vfcm.org/kagv.htm
alaskaradio@vfcm.org
License: Big Lake, AK held by Voice for Christ Ministries Inc.
Nat'l Network: Salem Radio Network; Moody
Arbitron Metro Market: Big Lake, AK *Format:* Christian, News, 62, Talk *Special Programming:* Native Alaskan 3 hrs wkly *Hrs. of News Programming:* News progmg 20 hrs wkly *Target Audience:* Native and Rural Alaska
Greg Pippin, Chairman
Karl Thieme, Station Manager

Chevak

*KCUK
01-01-1990; 88.1 mhz FM; 6 kw; 79 ft.; N61 31 46 W165 35 20
985 Ksd Way, Chevak, AK 99563 US
(907) 858-7015, *Fax:* (907) 858-7279
www.nv1.org/kcuk.htm
Nauliaran@yahoo.com
License: Chevak, Wade Hampton County, AK held by Kashunamiut School District.
Nat'l Network: NPR *Regional Network:* Alaska Pub.
Arbitron Metro Market: Chevak, AK *Format:* Variety/Diverse
Peter Tuluk, General Manager
Peter Tuluk, Station Manager

College

KTDZ
09-06-1984; 103.9 mhz FM; 2.95 kw; 823 ft.; N64 55 20 W147 42 55
C/O Fisher Wayland: Glm, 2001 Penn Ave,NW,#400, Washington, DC 20006 US
(907) 451-5910, *Fax:* (907) 451-5999
www.mytedfm.com
1039koolfm@nnbradio.com
License: College, Fairbanks County, AK
Group Owner: Last Frontier Mediactive LLC; (acq 10-26-99; grpsl)
Nat'l Reps: Tacher
Arbitron Metro Market: College, AK *Format:* Adult Contemp
Glenn Anderson, Operations Dir
Perry Walley, General Manager

Cordova

KCDV
100.9 mhz FM; 1.2 kw; -417 ft.; N60 32 20 W145 45 35
Haley Bader & Potts, 4350 N. Fairfax Dr, Arlington, VA 22203 US
(907) 424-3796, *Fax:* (907) 424-3737
License: Cordova, Valdez Cordova County, AK
Format: Adult Contemp
Raul Salvador, CFO
Adam Nathanson, President
Mike Anthony, Operations Dir
Dale Hendry, General Manager
Jodi Morgan, General Sales Mgr
Sybil DeAngelo, Promotions Manager

KLAM
05-01-1953; 1450 khz AM; 0.25 kw-U, ND1; N60 32 20 W145 45 35
P.O. Box 60, #1 Forestry Way, Cordova, AK 99574 US
(907) 424-3796, *Fax:* (907) 424-3737
www.cordovaradio.com
License: Cordova, AK held by Bayview Communications Inc.
Nat'l Network: ABC
Arbitron Metro Market: Anchorage, AK *Format:* Classic Rock, Country, 60 *Target Audience:* General.
J.R. Lewis, General Manager

Dillingham

*KDLG
07-22-1975; 670 khz AM *Hrs Open:* 18; 10 kw-U, ND1; N59 2 43 W158 27 7
Box 670, Dillingham, AK 99576 US
(907) 842-5281, *Fax:* (907) 842-5645
www.kdlg.org
kdlgnews@kdlg.org
License: Dillingham, AK held by Dillingham City School District.
Nat'l Network: NPR *Regional Network:* Alaska Pub.
Arbitron Metro Market: Dillingham, AK *Format:* Adult Contemp, Country *Special Programming:* Yupik one hr wkly *Hrs. of News Programming:* news progmg 20 hrs wkly *No. News Employees:* 1
Buchi Lind, President
Rob Carpenter, General Manager
Jason Sear, Programming Director
Mike Mason, News Director

KRUP
08-01-1995; 99.1 mhz FM *Hrs Open:* 24; 6 kw; 128 ft.; N59 2 31 W158 31 19
Mailing Address: P.O. Box 157, 301 Airport Road, Dillingham, AK 99576 US
Second Address: 301 Airport Rd., Dillingham, AK 99576
(907) 842-5364
License: Dillingham, Dillingham County, AK held by McCormick Broadcasting.
Format: Talk
Jackson McCormick, President

*KDLG-FM
89.9 mhz FM; 0.25 kw; 82 ft.; N59 2 37 W158 27 47
US
(907) 842-5281, *Fax:* (907) 842-5645
www.kdlg.org
License: Dillingham, Dillingham County, AK held by Dillingham City School District.
Arbitron Metro Market: Dillingham, AK *Format:* Religious
Rob Carpenter, General Manager

El Jebel

KGHT-FM
100.5 mhz FM; 2 kw; 475 meters; N64 52 47.5 W148 03 09.7
5551 Ridgewood Drive, Suite 501, Naples, FL 34108
(239) 514-1000
License: El Jebel, CO held by BS & T Wireless Inc

Ester

KDJF
07-01-2007; 93.5 mhz FM; 20.5 kw; 1578 ft.; N64 52 45 W148 3 14
US
(907) 452-3697, *Fax:* (907) 456-3428
www.tvtv.com
chris@tvtv.com
License: Ester, Fairbanks North Star County, AK held by Tanana Valley Television Co.
Group Owner: Tanana Valley Television Co.; (acq 1-10-2008; $173,000 for CP)
Arbitron Metro Market: Ester, AK
William St. Pierre, President
Chris Fry, General Manager
Sam Oxman, News Director
Brian Virgin, Department Supervisor

Fairbanks

KAKQ-FM
04-04-1981; 101.1 mhz FM *Hrs Open:* 24; 46.2 kw; 571 ft.; N64 54 55 W147 38 52
600 Congress Avenue, Suite 1400, Austin, TX 78701 US
(907) 450-1000, *Fax:* (907) 450-1092
www.101magic.com
info@101clearchannel.com
License: Fairbanks, Fairbanks North Star County, AK held by Capstar TX L.P.
Group Owner: Clear Channel Communications Inc.; (acq 8-30-00; grpsl).
Nat'l Network: Westwood One *Nat'l Reps:* Christal
Arbitron Metro Market: Fairbanks, AK *Format:* Contemporary Hits/Top 40 *Hrs. of News Programming:* news progmg one hr wkly *No. News Employees:* 2 *Target Audience:* 25-44; working families & adults *Adv. Rates:* 25; 18; 25; 14
Gary Donovan, Operations Dir
Pete Hutton, General Manager
Missey Kohler, Programming Director

KCBF
01-01-1948; 820 khz AM *Hrs Open:* 24; 10 kw-U, ND1; N64 52 44 W147 40 6
630 West Fourth Avenue, Suite 300, Anchorage, AK 99501 US
(907) 451-5910, *Fax:* (907) 451-5999
www.lfmediactive.com
License: Fairbanks, AK
Group Owner: Last Frontier Mediactive LLC; acq 8-12-99; grpsl).
Nat'l Network: CBS; Westwood One
Arbitron Metro Market: Fairbanks, AK *Format:* Sports *Hrs. of News Programming:* news progmg 4 hrs wkly *No. News Employees:* 1 *Target Audience:* 35-54. *Adv. Rates:* 10; 8; 10; 5
Perry Walley, General Manager
Glenn Anderson, Programming Director
Paige Smith, Chief Engineer

KFAR
01-01-1939; 660 khz AM; 10 kw-U, ND1; N64 48 29 W147 29 34
1060 Aspen Street, Fairbanks, AK 99709 US
(907) 451-5910, *Fax:* (907) 451-5999
www.akradio.com
License: Fairbanks, AK
Group Owner: Last Frontier Mediactive LLC; (acq 9-8-81; $675,000;
Arbitron Metro Market: Fairbanks, AK *Format:* News, News/Talk, 86 *Special Programming:* Gospel 2 hrs wkly *Target Audience:* 25 plus.
Glen Anderson, Operations Dir
Perry Walley, General Manager

KFBX
09-18-1972; 970 khz AM *Hrs Open:* 24
600 Congress Avenue, Suite 1400, Austin, TX 78701 US
(907) 450-1000, *Fax:* (907) 457-2128
www.970kfbx.com
kfbx@clearchannel.com
License: Fairbanks, AK held by Capstar TX L.P.
Group Owner: Clear Channel Communications Inc.; (acq 8-30-2000; grpsl)
Nat'l Reps: Christal
Format: News, Talk *Special Programming:* The Wall Street Journal 7 hrs wkly *Hrs. of News Programming:* news progmg 30 hrs wkly *No. News Employees:* 1 *Target Audience:* 35 plus; males
Pete Hutton, General Manager
Charlie O'Toole, Programming Director
Cheys Castle, Promotions Manager
April LaFever, Disc Jockey
Marc Daly, Disc Jockey

KIAK-FM
09-21-1983; 102.5 mhz FM; 92 kw; 571 ft.; N64 54 55 W147 38 52
600 Congress Avenue, Suite 1400, Austin, TX 78701 US
(907) 450-1000, *Fax:* (907) 457-2128
www.kiak.com
kiak@clearchannel.com
License: Fairbanks, Fairbanks North Star County, AK held by Capstar TX L.P.
Group Owner: Clear Channel Communications Inc.
Format: Country *Target Audience:* 18 plus; general *Adv. Rates:* 35; 30; 35; 20
Pete Van Nort, Programming Director
Doug Burnside, News Director
Kathryn Harris, Disc Jockey
J.B. Carnahan, Disc Jockey
Peter Van Nort, Disc Jockey
Monte Brown, Local News Editor

KKED
09-20-1962; 104.7 mhz FM *Hrs Open:* 24; 46 kw; 571 ft.; N64 54 55 W147 38 52
600 Congress Avenue, Suite 1400, Austin, TX 78701 US
(907) 450-1000, *Fax:* (907) 450-1092
www.1047theedge.com
theedge@clearchannel.com
License: Fairbanks, Fairbanks North Star County, AK held by Capstar TX L.P.
Group Owner: Clear Channel Communications Inc.; (acq 8-30-00; grpsl).
Arbitron Metro Market: Anchorage, AK *Format:* Rock/AOR
Kim Williams, General Manager
Mike Crosby, Programming Director

*KSUA
10-10-1985; 91.5 mhz FM *Hrs Open:* 24; 3 kw; -16 ft.; N64 51 32 W147 49 41
202 Butrovich Building, Fairbanks, AK 99775 US
(907) 474-7054, *Fax:* (907) 474-6314
www.uaf.edu/ksua
fyksua@uaf.edu
License: Fairbanks, Fairbanks North Star County, AK held by The University of Alaska Board of Regents.
Arbitron Metro Market: Fairbanks, AK *Format:* Alternative *Special Programming:* Black 8 hrs, Sp 3 hrs, var/div music 19 hrs wkly *Target Audience:* 14-35.
Nick Brewer, General Manager
Sean Bledsoe, Programming Director

***KUAC**
01-01-1962; 89.9 mhz FM *Hrs Open:* 24; 38 kw; 1660 ft.; N64 52 49 W148 3 8
P.O. Box 755620, Fairbanks, AK 99775 US
(907) 474-7491, *Fax:* (907) 474-5064
www.kuac.org
info@kuac.com
License: Fairbanks, Fairbanks North Star County, AK held by University of Alaska.
Nat'l Network: NPR; PRI *Regional Network:* Alaska Pub. *Wire Services:* AP
Arbitron Metro Market: Fairbanks, AK *TV Affiliate:* *KUAC-TV affil. *Format:* News, News/Talk, 86, Variety/Diverse *Special Programming:* Jazz 15 hrs, folk 10 hrs, blues 4 hrs, new age 3 hrs wkly *Hrs. of NewsProgramming:* news progmg 32 hrs wkly *No. News Employees:* 3 *Target Audience:* General.
Greg Petrowich, CEO
Matthew Schroder, Operations & Traffic Coordinator
Keith Martin, General Manager & Dir. of Engineering & Technology
Scott Diseth, Station Manager
Gretchen Gordon, Assistant General Manager & Director ofDevelopmen
Jerry Evans, Director of FM Programming & Production
Chris Wadeson, Chief Engineer
Patty Dyer-Smith, Director of Finance and Administration
Donna Olesen, Corporate Support Manager
Wanda Peros, Corporate Support Manager
LisaScerbak, Communications Manager
Hollie Seiler, Donor Services Coordinator
Sarah Arnold, Donor Relations Manager

KWLF
10-31-1987; 98.1 mhz FM; 28 kw; 764 ft.; N64 55 20 W147 42 55
1060 Aspen Street, Fairbanks, AK 99709 US
(907) 451-5910, *Fax:* (907) 451-5999
www.kwolf981.com
info@akradio.com
License: Fairbanks, Fairbanks North Star County, AK
Group Owner: Last Frontier Mediactive LLC
Arbitron Metro Market: Fairbanks, AK *Format:* Contemporary Hits/Top 40 *Target Audience:* 18 plus; general
Jim Smith, CFO
Paul Armes, President
Glen Anderson, Operations Dir
Perry Walley, General Manager
Paul Sutton, Programming Director
David Carr, Chief Engineer
Bill Hardage, Executive Vice President
Betty Donaldson, VicePresident

KXLR
07-01-1989; 95.9 mhz FM *Hrs Open:* 24; 25 kw; -16 ft.; N64 52 38 W147 48 46
630 West Fourth Avenue, Suite 300, Anchorage, AK 99501 US
(907) 451-5910, *Fax:* (907) 451-5999
xrock959.com/
License: Fairbanks, Fairbanks North Star County, AK
Group Owner: Last Frontier Mediactive LLC
Arbitron Metro Market: Fairbanks, AK *TV Affiliate:* KTVF(TV) affil *Format:* Classic Rock *Target Audience:* 25-49. *Adv. Rates:* 14; 13; 14; 10
Crys Castle, Programming Director

KYSC
01-01-2001; 96.9 mhz FM *Hrs Open:* 24; 5.8 kw; 1608 ft.; N64 52 45 W148 3 14
P.O. Box 671003, Chugiak, AK 99567 US
(907) 452-3697, *Fax:* (907) 456-3428
www.tvtv.com
chris@tvtv.com
License: Fairbanks, Fairbanks North Star County, AK held by Tanana Valley Radio LLC
Group Owner: Tanana Valley Television Co.; (acq 9-28-2005; $700,000)
Nat'l Network: ABC
Arbitron Metro Market: Anchorage, AK *TV Affiliate:* KFXF(TV) affil *Format:* Adult Contemp *Adv. Rates:* 15; 11; 13; 9
Chris Fry, General Manager
Terry Walley, Station Manager
Sam Oxman, News Director
Brian Virgin, Production Department Supervisor

KWDD(FM)
94.3 mhz FM; 28 kw; 233 meters; N64 55 21 W147 42 55
819 First Avenue, Suite A, Fairbanks, AK 99701-4449
(907) 451-5910, *Fax:* (907)451-5999
lfmediaactive.com
License: Fairbanks, North Star Borough County, AK held by Last Frontier Mediactive LLC
Group Owner: Last Frontier Mediactive LLC
Perry Walley, General Manager

Fort Yukon

***KZPA**
09-30-1993; 900 khz AM; 5 kw-U, ND1; N66 33 24 W145 12 4
East Third Avenue, PO Box 50, Fort Yukon, AK 99740 US
(907 662-6356 OR (907) 662-8255, *Fax:* (907) 662-2915
kzparadio@hotmail.com
License: Fort Yukon, AK held by Gwandak Public Broadcasting Inc.
Arbitron Metro Market: Fort Yukon, AK *Format:* Variety/Diverse *Hrs. of News Programming:* News progmg 6 hrs wkly *Target Audience:* All ages.
Arlene Joseph, President
John Alexander, Programming Director

Galena

***KIYU**
07-04-1986; 910 khz AM *Hrs Open:* 24; 5 kw-U, ND1; N64 41 18 W156 43 29
Pob 165, Galena, AK 99741 US
(907) 656-1488, *Fax:* (907) 656-1734
www.kiyu.com
raven@kiyu.com
License: Galena, AK held by Big River Public Broadcasting Corp.
Nat'l Network: NPR *Regional Network:* Alaska Pub.
Format: Variety/Diverse *Special Programming:* Jazz 4 hrs, Alaska native 2 hrs wkly *Hrs. of News Programming:* news progmg 35 hrs wkly *No. News Employees:* 1 *Target Audience:* General.
Susie Sam, President
Tim Bodony, Operations Dir
Shadow Steele, General Manager

***KIYU-FM**
01-01-2008; 97.1 mhz FM; 0.1 kw; 49 ft.; N64 44 34 W156 50 30 US
(907) 656-1488, *Fax:* (907) 656-1734
www.kiyu.com
raven@kiyu.com
License: Galena, Yukon Koyukuk County, AK held by Big River Public Broadcasting Corp.
Arbitron Metro Market: Galena, AK *Format:* Variety/Diverse
Russ Sweetsir, President
Jeremy Scott, Operations/ Program Director
Shadow Steele, General Manager
Rex Charger, Programming Director
Suzette Lapine Rosecrans, Secretary / Treasurer
Jeremy Scott, Acting General Manager

Girdwood

***KEUL**
09-01-1998; 88.9 mhz FM *Hrs Open:* 24; 1.4 kw horiz, 0 kw vert; 636 ft.; N60 57 44 W149 4 38
P O Box 29, Girdwood, AK 99587 US
(907) 754-2489
www.glaciercity.us
radio@glaciercity.us
License: Girdwood, Anchorage County, AK held by Girdwood Community Club Inc.
Arbitron Metro Market: Anchorage, AK *Format:* Variety/Diverse *Target Audience:* Sole service provider.
Lewis Leonard, General Manager

Glennallen

KCAM
04-16-1964; 790 khz AM *Hrs Open:* 24; 5 kw-U; N62 06 52 W145 32 07
Box 249, Glennallen, AK 99833
(907) 822-5226, *Fax:* (907) 822-3761
www.kcam.org
kcam@kcam.org
License: Glennallen, Valdez-Cordova County, AK held by Northern Light Network.
Nat'l Network: Moody; USA
Population Served: 10,000 *Arbitron Metro Market:* Glennallen, AK *Special Programming:* American Indian one hr, class 10 hrs, contemp Chri *Hrs. of News Programming:* News progmg 28 hrs wkly *Target Audience:* General.
Scott Yahr, Station Manager
George Reichman, General Sales Mgr
Michael Eastty, Programming Director
Corey Emery, Engineering Dir
Scott Hill, Chief Engineer

***KXGA**
10-01-1994; 90.5 mhz FM *Hrs Open:* 24; 3.2 kw; 751 ft.; N62 6 31 W146 10 25 *Rebroadcasts:* Rebroadcasts KCHU(AM) Valdez 100%
Mailing Address: P.O. Box 467, Valdez, AK 99686 US
Second Address: c/o KCHU(AM), 128 Pioneer Dr., Valdez, AK 99686
(907) 835-4665, *Fax:* (907) 835-2847
www.kchu.org
kchu@cvinternet.net
License: Glennallen, Valdez-Cordova County, AK held by Terminal Radio Inc.
Arbitron Metro Market: Valdez, AK *Format:* Variety/Diverse
John Anderson, Operations Dir
Danny Sparrell, General Manager
Tony Gorman, News Director
Nancy Meador, Development Coordinator

Haines

***KHNS**
10-04-1980; 102.3 mhz FM *Hrs Open:* 24; 3 kw; -1220 ft.; N59 13 6 W135 25 29
P.O. Box 1109, Haines, AK 99827 US
(907) 766-2020, *Fax:* (907) 766-2022
www.khns.org
gm@khns.org
License: Haines, Haines County, AK held by Lynn Canal Broadcasting.
Nat'l Network: NPR *Regional Network:* Alaska Pub.
Format: Talk *Special Programming:* Country 10 hrs wkly, Variety *Hrs. of News Programming:* news progmg 100 hrs wkly *No. News Employees:* 2 *Target Audience:* General.
Emily Seward, President
Steven Scarrott, Operations Dir
Kay Clements, General Manager
Mary Giovanini, Programming Director
Leslie Ross, Development Director
Amelia Nash, Program Director

Homer

***KBBI**
08-04-1979; 890 khz AM *Hrs Open:* 24; 10 kw-U, ND1; N59 40 14 W151 26 38
3913 Kachemak Way, Homer, AK 99603 US
(907) 235-7721, *Fax:* (907) 235-2357
www.kbbi.org
dorle@kbbi.org
License: Homer, AK held by Kachemak Bay Broadcasting Inc.
Nat'l Network: PRI; NPR; AP Radio *Regional Network:* Alaska Pub. *Wire Services:* AP
Arbitron Metro Market: Homer, AK *Format:* News/Talk *Special Programming:* APM, AAA, jazz, rock *Hrs. of News Programming:* news progmg 84 hrs wkly *No. News Employees:* 15 *Target Audience:* General.
David Anderson, General Manager
Jonathan Coke, General Sales Mgr
Terry Rensel, Programming Director
Aaron Selbig, News Director
Paulette Wellington, Music Director

KGTL
02-11-1981; 620 khz AM *Hrs Open:* 24; 5 kw-U, ND1; N59 41 3 W151 37 51
P.O. Box 109, Homer, AK 99603 US
(907) 235-6000, *Fax:* (907) 235-6683
kwavefm@xyz.net
License: Homer, AK held by Peninsula Communications Inc.
Group Owner: Peninsula Communications Inc.
Nat'l Network: USA
Format: Adult Contemp *Hrs. of News Programming:* News progmg 20 hrs wkly *Target Audience:* 35 plus; professionals
David Becker, President

KWVV-FM
09-22-1979; 103.5 mhz FM *Hrs Open:* 24; 100 kw horiz; 1152 ft.; N59 41 3 W151 37 51
P.O. Box 109, Homer, AK 99603 US
(907) 235-6000, *Fax:* (907) 235-6683
kwavefm@xyz.net
License: Homer, Kenai Peninsula County, AK held by Peninsula Communications Inc.
Group Owner: Peninsula Communications Inc.
Format: Adult Contemp *Hrs. of News Programming:* News progmg 14 hrs wkly *Target Audience:* 18-49. *Adv. Rates:* 240; 240; 240; 192
Marvin Sanders, General Manager

***KMJG**
01-01-2000; 88.9 mhz FM; 0.25 kw; 666 ft.; N59 40 19 W151 30 30
P. O. Box 1121, Kasilof, AK 99610 US
(907) 260-7702, *Fax:* (907) 262-1069
www.kwjg.org
kwjg915@gci.net
License: Homer, Kenai Peninsula County, AK held by Kasilof Public Broadcasting Inc.
Format: Oldies, Variety/Diverse
William Glynn, President

***KHGO**
89.9 mhz FM; 3 kw vert; -187 ft.; N59 42 41 W151 19 58 US
(907) 235-7931
homernewlife.org
License: Homer, Kenai Peninsula County, AK held by New Life Tabernacle Homer AK.
Arbitron Metro Market: Homer, AK
Jon Springer, President

KGTL(AM)
620 khz AM; 5000 watts; non-directional; 59 41 03N 151 37 51W
PO Box 109, Homer, AK 99603 USA
(907) 235-6000, *Fax:* (907) 235-6683
License: Homer, AK
Group Owner: Penninsula Communications Inc

Houston

KZND-FM
04-01-1998; 94.7 mhz FM *Hrs Open:* 24; 15 kw; 869 ft.; N61 20 12 W149 30 45
C/O Amer. Radio Brokers, 1255 Post St., Ste. 1011, San Francisco, CA 94109 US
(907) 522-1018, *Fax:* (907) 522-1027
www.947kznd.com
License: Houston, Matanuska Susitna County, AK held by Tati Broadcasting LLC
Arbitron Metro Market: Anchorage, AK *Target Audience:* 25-44; general
Mike Robbins, General Manager

***KJHA**
07-08-1998; 88.7 mhz FM *Hrs Open:* 24; 1 kw; -131 ft.; N61 37 53 W149 48 46 *Rebroadcasts:* Rebroadcasts KJNP-FM North Pole midnight-7 AM and rebroadcasts KJNP(AM) North Pole 7 AM-midnight
P.O. Box 56359, North Pole, AK 99705 US
(907) 488-2216, *Fax:* (907) 488-5246
www.mosquitonet.com/~kjnp
kjnp@mosquitonet.com
License: Houston, Matanuska Susitna County, AK held by Evangelistic Alaska Missionary Fellowship Inc.
Format: Country, Gospel *Special Programming:* Athabaskan Indian 2 hrs, Eskimo one hr wkly
Yvonne Carriker, President
Richerd T. Olson, Operations Dir

KBBO-FM
01-01-1997; 92.1 mhz FM *Hrs Open:* 24; 10 kw; 886 ft.; N61 20 11 W149 30 48
3700 Woodland Drive, Suite 700, Anchorage, AK 99217 US
(907) 344-4045, *Fax:* (907) 522-6053
www.921bob.fm
info@921bob.fm
License: Houston, Matanuska Susitna County, AK
Group Owner: Ohana Media Group LLC; (acq 8-12-99; $1.1 million).
Wire Services: AP
Arbitron Metro Market: Anchorage, AK *Format:* Adult Contemp
Pete Benedetti, CEO
Bill Sigmar, General Manager
Bill Sigmar, General Sales Mgr
Derek Moran, Programming Director
Trila Bumstead, CFO

KXLW
01-01-2000; 96.3 mhz FM; 10 kw; 886 ft.; N61 20 11 W149 30 48
5455 Highland Drive, Bellevue, WA 98006 US
(907) 344-4045, *Fax:* (907) 522-6053
www.963thewolf.com
bill.sigmar@ohanamediagroup.com
License: Houston, Matanuska Susitna County, AK
Group Owner: Ohana Media Group LLC; (acq 7-30-99)
Wire Services: AP
Arbitron Metro Market: Anchorage, AK *Target Audience:* 20-49; men
Pete Benedetti, CEO
Bill Sigmar, General Manager & Director of Sales
Tom Oakes, Programming Director
Trila Bumstead, CFO

Juneau

***KRNN**
01-01-1999; 102.7 mhz FM; 6 kw; -417 ft.; N58 17 9 W134 25 40
411 Russell Avenue, Santa Rosa, CA 95403 US
(907) 586-1670, *Fax:* (907) 586-3612
www.ktoo.org
License: Juneau, Juneau County, AK held by Capital Community Broadcasting Inc.
Group Owner: Capital Community Broadcasting Inc.; (acq 12-27-2006; $676,400 with KXLL(FM) Juneau)
Arbitron Metro Market: Juneau, AK *Format:* Variety/Diverse
Barbara Sheinberg, Chairman
Bill Legere, President
Bill Legere, General Manager
Cheryl Levitt, Station Manager
John Beiler, General Sales Mgr
Jeff Brown, Programming Director
Rosemarie Alexander, News Director
Jeff Brown,Music Director

***KXLL**
10-01-1999; 100.7 mhz FM; 6 kw; -417 ft.; N58 17 9 W134 25 40
411 Russell Avenue, Santa Rosa, CA 95403 US
(907) 586-1670, *Fax:* (907) 586-5692
www.kxll.org
License: Juneau, Juneau County, AK held by Capital Community Broadcasting Inc.
Group Owner: Capital Community Broadcasting Inc.; (acq 12-27-2006; $676,400 with KRNN(FM) Juneau)
Arbitron Metro Market: Juneau, AK *Format:* Alternative, Triple A
Bill Legere, President
Mike Sakarias, Operations Dir
Cheryl Levitt Snyder, General Manager
Andy Kline, Programming Director
Rosemarie Alexander, News Director
Brian Zittlau, Engineering Dir

KINY
05-28-1935; 800 khz AM *Hrs Open:* 24
1107 West 8th St., No. 2, Juneau, AK 99802 US
(907) 586-1800, *Fax:* (907) 586-3266
www.kinyradio.com
kiny@ptialaska.net
License: Juneau, AK held by Alaska-Juneau Communications Inc.
Format: Adult Contemp *Hrs. of News Programming:* news progmg 4 hrs wkly *No. News Employees:* 2 *Target Audience:* General.
Dennis Egan, President
Kelly Peres, Operations Dir
Tim Armstrong, General Sales Mgr
Christine Personnet, Programming Director
Jim Morgan, Promotions Manager
Charlie Gray, Engineering Dir
Chris Burns, Disc Jockey
Ron Davis, DiscJockey

KJNO
10-19-1952; 630 khz AM *Hrs Open:* 24
3161 Channel Dr., Ste 202, Juneau, AK 99801 US
(907) 586-3630, *Fax:* (907) 463-3685
www.kjno.com
License: Juneau, AK held by Alaska Broadcast Communications Inc.
Group Owner: Alaska Broadcast Communications Inc.; (acq 1972; with co-located FM)
Nat'l Network: CBS Radio *Nat'l Reps:* Tacher *Regional Reps:* Tacher
Format: Talk *Target Audience:* 25-54.
Roy Paschal, President
Richard Burns, Operations Dir
Jeff McCoy, Programming Director

KSUP
12-01-1984; 106.3 mhz FM *Hrs Open:* 24; 10 kw; -1007 ft.; N58 18 5 W134 26 26
1107 West 8th Street, Suite #2, Juneau, AK 99801 US
(907) 586-1063, *Fax:* (907) 586-3266
www.ksupradio.com
ksup@ptialaska.net
License: Juneau, Juneau County, AK held by Alaska-Juneau Communications Inc.
Arbitron Metro Market: Juneau, AK *Format:* Classic Rock, Contemporary Hits/Top 40, 76
Kelly Peres, Programming Director

KTKU
07-09-1984; 105.1 mhz FM *Hrs Open:* 24; 3.8 kw; -1060 ft.; N58 19 47 W134 28 17
3161 Channel Dr. Suite 2, Juneau, AK 99801 US
(907) 586-3630, *Fax:* (907) 463-3685
www.kjno.com
License: Juneau, Juneau County, AK held by Alaska Broadcast Communications Inc.
Group Owner: Alaska Broadcast Communications Inc.
Arbitron Metro Market: Juneau, AK *Format:* Country
Douglas Fisher, Chairman
James Fisher, President
Sheryl Lehman, General Sales Mgr
J.T. Gerlt, Programming Director

***KTOO**
01-27-1974; 104.3 mhz FM *Hrs Open:* 24; 1.4 kw; -1043 ft.; N58 18 4 W134 25 21
360 Egan Drive, Juneau, AK 99801 US
(907) 586-1670, *Fax:* (907) 586-3612(907) 586-2561 (news)
www.ktoo.org
info@ktoo.org
License: Juneau, Juneau County, AK held by Capital Community Broadcasting Inc.
Group Owner: Capital Community Broadcasting Inc.
Nat'l Network: NPR; PRI *Regional Network:* Alaska Pub.
Arbitron Metro Market: Juneau, AK *TV Affiliate:* *KTOO-TV affil.
Format: News, Variety/Diverse *Special Programming:* Children one hrs, folk 8 hrs, Sp 2 hsr, French 2 hrs, jazz 14 hrs, Alaska native one hr wkly *Hrs.of News Programming:* news progmg 48 hrs wkly *No. News Employees:* 14 *Target Audience:* General.
Bill Legere, President
Mike Sakarias, Operations Dir
Bill Legere, General Manager
Cheryl Levitt, Station Manager
Jeff Brown, Programming Director
Rosemarie Alexander, News Director

KXXJ
01-01-2008; 1330 khz AM; 10 kw-D, 3 kw-N; N58 18 05 W134 26 26
Box 1471, Evergreen, CO
(303) 688-5162, (907) 562-5363, *Fax:* (303) 660-4930
www.kxljradio.com
License: Juneau, Juneau County, AK held by Seattle Streaming Radio LLC.
Group Owner: Seattle Streaming Radio LLC; (acq 6-24-2006; $150,000 for CP)
Nat'l Network: ESPN Radio
David Drucker, General Manager

***KAKI**
88.1 mhz FM; 10 kw vert; Ant -1,214 ft; N58 18 05 W134 26 26
Rebroadcasts: KLRD(FM) Yucaipa, California 100%
2351 Sunset Blvd., Suite 170-218, Rocklin, CA
(916) 251-1600, *Fax:* (916) 251-1650
License: Juneau, Juneau County, AK held by Educational Media Foundation
Group Owner: EMF Broadcasting
Mike Novak, President

***KNGW**
88.9 mhz FM; 0.125 kw; -420 ft.; N58 21 57 W134 37 58 US
(818) 779-8444, *Fax:* (818) 779-8411
www.ktlw.net
License: Juneau, Juneau County, AK held by Life On The Way Communications Inc.
Arbitron Metro Market: Juneau, AK *Format:* Christian
Gary Curtis, General Manager

Kaltag

***KALG**
98.1 mhz FM; 0.1 kw; -253 ft.; N64 19 40 W158 43 36 US
(907) 656-1488, *Fax:* (907) 656-1734
www.kiyu.com
raven@kiyu.com
License: Kaltag, Yukon Koyukuk County, AK held by Big River Public Broadcasting Corp.
Arbitron Metro Market: Galena, AK *Format:* Variety/Diverse
Russ Sweetsir, President
Jeremy Scott, Operations, Program Director and Acting General Ma
Suzette Lapine Rosecrans, Secretary / Treasurer

Kasilof

***KWJG**
07-29-1998; 91.5 mhz FM *Hrs Open:* 24; 1 kw; 262 ft.; N60 22 44 W151 11 30

P O Box 1121, Kasilof, AK 99610 US
(907) 260-7702, *Fax:* (907) 262-1069
www.kwjg.org
info@kwjg.com
License: Kasilof, Kenai Peninsula County, AK held by Kasilof Public Broadcasting Inc.
Arbitron Metro Market: Kasilof, AR *Format:* Oldies, Variety/Diverse
William Glynn Jr., President

***KRAW**
01-01-2003; 90.5 mhz FM; 500 w horiz; Ant 197 ft; N60 22 44 W151 11 30
3700 Woodland Dr., Suite 800, Anchorage, AK 99517
(800) 974-6525
aers@oneskyradio.com,kwmd@oneskyradio.com
License: Kasilof, Kenai Peninsula County, AK held by Alaska Educational Radio System Inc.
Larry Snider, Operations Dir
Keith Shipman, General Manager
Bryon Mengle, Promotions Manager
Bill Baker, News Director
Regan Brick, Business Manager

***KABN-FM**
01-01-2003; 88.9 mhz FM; 3.2 kw vert; 335 ft.; N60 31 58 W151 4 52
3700 Woodland Drive, Suite 800, Anchorage, AK 99517 US
(907) 783-2256
www.oneskyradio.com
License: Kasilof, Kenai Peninsula County, AK held by Alaska Educational Radio System Inc.
Arbitron Metro Market: Kasilof, AK
Jeremy Lansman, General Manager

KFSE
11-22-2007; 106.9 mhz FM *Hrs Open:* 24; 8 kw; 203 ft.; N60 25 55 W151 8 26
P.O. Box 769, Kasilof, AK 99610 US
(907) 283-8700, *Fax:* (907) 283-9177
info@radiokenai.com
License: Kasilof, Kenai Peninsula County, AK held by KSRM Inc.
Group Owner: KSRM Inc.; (acq 3-22-2007; $210,000 for CP)
Arbitron Metro Market: Medford-Ashland, OR
John Davis, President
Cherie Curry, General Manager

Kenai

***KDLL**
01-01-1981; 91.9 mhz FM *Hrs Open:* 24; 4.9 kw; 72 ft; N60 34 03 W151 07 25
Box 2111, Kenai, AK 99611
(907) 283-8433, *Fax:* (907) 283-6701
www.kdllradio.org
allen@kdllradio.org
License: Kenai, Kenai Peninsula County, AK held by Pickle Hill Public Broadcasting Inc.
Nat'l Network: NPR; PRI *Regional Network:* Alaska Pub.
Population Served: 30,000*Special Programming:* American Indian 10 hrs wkly *Hrs. of News Programming:* news progmg 60 hrs wkly *No. News Employees:* 1 *Target Audience:* Affluent.
Terry Bookey, President
Dave Anderson, General Manager
Allen Auxier, Station Manager
Terry Rensel, Programming Director
Aaron Selbig, News Director
Bobby Blue, Chief Engineer

KWHQ-FM
11-18-1976; 100.1 mhz FM *Hrs Open:* 24; 25 kw; 190 ft.; N60 30 49 W151 11 19
Route #2 Box 852, Soldotna, AK 99669 US
(907) 283-9430, *Fax:* (907) 283-9177
www.radiokenai.com
info@radiokenai.com
License: Kenai, Kenai Peninsula County, AK held by KSRM Inc.
Group Owner: KSRM Inc.
Wire Services: AP
Arbitron Metro Market: Kenai, AK *Format:* Country *Hrs. of News Programming:* news progmg 12 hrs wkly *No. News Employees:* 2 *Target Audience:* 18-49.
John Davis, CEO/President
J.R. Kitchens, Programming/ Operations
Matt Wilson, General Manager/ Marketing Manager
Andrew Rogers, News Director
Dan Gensel, Sports Director
Mark Gage, Marketing Consultant
Myra Arbelovsky, OfficeManager/ Administrative Assistant/ Bookkeep
Nathan Jonhson, Marketing Consultant

***KOGJ**
88.1 mhz FM; 1.1 kw vert; 87 m; N60 31 58 W151 04 52
Box 2418, Homer, AK
(907)235-7931
License: Kenai, Kenai Peninsula County, AK held by New Life Tabernacle Homer AK
John R. Springer, President

Ketchikan

KFMJ
09-23-1996; 99.9 mhz FM *Hrs Open:* 24; 0.115 kw; 2234 ft.; N55 21 40 W131 47 43
516 Stedman Street, Ketchikan, AK 58202 US
(907) 247-3699, *Fax:* (907) 247-5365
http://www.alaska.fm/kfmj/index.html
kfmj@alaska.fm
License: Ketchikan, Ketchikan County, AK held by TLP Communications Inc.
Nat'l Network: ABC; USA *Wire Services:* AP
Arbitron Metro Market: Ketchikan, AK *Format:* Oldies *Hrs. of News Programming:* News progmg 18.5 hrs wkly *Target Audience:* 30 plus, high disposable income adults *Adv. Rates:* 15; 15; 15; 13.50
Robert Kern, Chairman
Julie Slanaker, General Sales Mgr
Stewart White, Programming Director

KGTW
11-01-1987; 106.7 mhz FM *Hrs Open:* 24; 0.44 kw; 2185 ft.; N55 21 39 W131 47 43
3161 Channel Drive, Suite 202, Juneau, AK 22203 US
(907) 225-2193, *Fax:* (907) 225-0444
gateway1067.com
License: Ketchikan, Ketchikan County, AK
Group Owner: Alaska Broadcast Communications Inc.
Format: Country *Target Audience:* 18 plus.
John Hunt, Programming Director

***KRBD**
05-01-1976; 105.3 mhz FM *Hrs Open:* 24; 3.4 kw; 69 ft.; N55 20 23 W131 37 29
123 Stedman Street, Ketchikan, AK 99901 US
(907) 225-9655, *Fax:* (907) 247-0808
www.krbd.org
License: Ketchikan, Ketchikan County, AK held by Rainbird Community Broadcasting Corp.
Nat'l Network: NPR; PRI *Regional Network:* Alaska Pub. *Wire Services:* AP
Arbitron Metro Market: AK Panhandle *Special Programming:* Class 11 hrs, C&W 14 hrs, folk 10 hrs, jazz 10 hrs *Hrs. of News Programming:* news progmg 2 hrs wkly *No. News Employees:* 2 *Target Audience:* General.
Nathan Grambau, General Manager
Maria Dudzak, Programming Director
Leila Kheiry, News Director
Deb Turnbull, Development Director

KTKN
01-01-1942; 930 khz AM *Hrs Open:* 24; 5 kw-D, ND1; 1 kw-N, ND1; N55 20 22 W131 38 12
3161 Channel Dr. Suite 2, Juneau, AK 99801 US
(907) 225-2193, *Fax:* (907) 225-0444
www.ktkn.com
bmesser@gci.net
License: Ketchikan, AK held by Alaska Broadcast Communications Inc.
Group Owner: Alaska Broadcast Communications Inc.
Regional Reps: Tacher.
Arbitron Metro Market: Ketchikan, AK *Format:* Adult Contemp, News, 62, Talk *Hrs. of News Programming:* news progmg 20 hrs wkly *No. News Employees:* 5 *Target Audience:* 25 plus. *Adv. Rates:* 20; 20; 20; 18
Blake Messer, General Manager
Jamie Beldo, Programming Director

Kodiak

***KMXT**
06-01-1976; 100.1 mhz FM *Hrs Open:* 24; 0.275 kw; 1020 ft.; N57 47 23 W152 25 56
620 Egan Way, Kodiak, AK 99615 US
(907) 486-3181, *Fax:* (907) 486-2733
www.kmxt.org
kmxt@kmxt.org
License: Kodiak, Kodiak Island County, AK held by Kodiak Public Broadcasting Corp.
Nat'l Network: NPR; PRI *Regional Network:* Alaska Pub.
Format: News, Variety/Diverse *Hrs. of News Programming:* news progmg 5 hrs wkly *No. News Employees:* 2 *Target Audience:* General.
Mike Wall, General Manager
Fred Hawley, General Sales Mgr

KRXX
01-01-1987; 101.1 mhz FM; 3.1 kw; 23 ft.; N57 47 3 W152 23 57
Mailing Address: 2435 Chilligan Drive, Anchorage, AK 99517 US
Second Address: 1315 Mill Bay Rd., Kodiak, AK 99615
(907) 486-5159, *Fax:* (907) 486-3044
www.jackfmkodiak.com
kvok@ak.net
License: Kodiak, Kodiak Island County, AK
Arbitron Metro Market: Kodiak, AK *Target Audience:* 18-56.
JR KItchens, Operations Dir
Ellen Simeonoff, General Manager

KVOK
11-07-1974; 560 khz AM *Hrs Open:* 24; 1 kw-U, ND1; N57 46 33 W152 32 7
Mailing Address: 2435 Chilligan Drive, Anchorage, AK 99517 US
Second Address: 1315 Mill Bay Rd., Kodiak, AK 99615
(907) 486-5159, *Fax:* (907) 486-3044
www.kvok.com
kvok@ak.net
License: Kodiak, AK held by Kodiak Island Broadcasting Co. Inc.
Nat'l Network: ABC *Wire Services:* AP
Arbitron Metro Market: Kodiak, AK *Format:* Country, Talk *Target Audience:* 25-56. *Adv. Rates:* 180; 156; 132; 120
Chuck Wright, Operations Dir
Ellen Simeonoff, General Manager
Lesile Ann Heglin, Traffic/ Billing
Denise Simeonoff, Account Executive

***KBKO**
06-29-2012; 88.3 mhz FM; 0.1 kw; -26 ft.; N57 48 40 W152 21 40 US
(800) 949-1050, *Fax:* (425) 867-2340
www.scaredheartradio.org
info@sacredheartradio.org
License: Kodiak, AK held by Sacred Heart Radio, Inc.
Format: Religious *Special Programming:* Religious Forums
Dr Tom Curran, General Manager

Kotzebue

***KOTZ**
03-01-1973; 720 khz AM *Hrs Open:* 0600 - 0000; 10 kw-U, ND1; N66 50 22 W162 34 5
P.O Box 78, 396 Lagoon Street, Kotzebue, AK 99752 US
(907) 442-3434, *Fax:* (907) 442-2292
License: Kotzebue, AK held by Kotzebue Broadcasting Inc.
Nat'l Network: NPR *Regional Network:* Alaska Pub.
Format: Variety/Diverse *Target Audience:* General; 90% rural Eskimo, 10% white-collar caucasian
Suzy Erlich, General Manager
Johnson Greene, Programming Director
Pierre Lonewolf, Chief Engineer

***KHZK**
01-01-2007; 103.9 mhz FM; 0.2 kw; 46 ft.; N66 54 11 W162 34 16 *Rebroadcasts:* Rebroadcasts KSRD(FM) Saint Joseph, MO 100%
US
(858) 277-4991, *Fax:* (858) 277-1365
www.horizonradio.org
License: Kotzebue, Northwest Arctic County, AK held by Horizon Christian Fellowship.
Group Owner: Horizon Christian Fellowship; (acq 2-9-2006; grpsl)
Arbitron Metro Market: Kotzebue, AK *Format:* Christian
Mike MacIntosh, President

***KINU**
06-04-2009; 89.9 mhz FM *Hrs Open:* 24; 0.1 kw; 82 ft.; N66 53 46 W162 35 46
US
(907) 442-3434, *Fax:* (907) 442-2292
www.kotz.org
message@kotz.org
License: Kotzebue, Northwest Arctic County, AK held by Kotzebue Broadcasting Inc.
Nat'l Network: NPR *Regional Network:* Alaska Pub.
Arbitron Metro Market: Kotzebue, AK *Format:* Variety/Diverse
Chester Ballot, Chairman
Rosie Hensley, General Manager
Johnson Greene, Programming Director
Pierre Lonewolf, Chief Engineer

Koyukuk

***KOYU**
98.1 mhz FM; 0.1 kw; -23 ft.; N64 52 58 W157 42 10
US
(907) 656-1488, *Fax:* (907) 656-1734
www.kiyu.com
raven@kiyu.com
License: Koyukuk, Yukon Koyukuk County, AK held by Big River Public Broadcasting Corp.
Arbitron Metro Market: Galena, AK *Format:* Variety/Diverse
Russ Sweetsir, President
Jeremy Scott, Operations, Program Director and Acting General Ma
Shadow Steele, General Manager
Suzette Lapine Rosecrans, Secretary / Treasurer

McCarthy

***KXKM**
10-01-1994; 89.7 mhz FM *Hrs Open:* 24; 102 w; -169 ft; N61 24 58 W143 01 19 *Rebroadcasts:* Rebroadcasts KCHU(AM) Valdez 100%
Mailing Address: c/o KCHU(AM), Box 467, Valdez, AK 99686
Second Address: c/o KCHU(AM), 128 Pioneer Dr., Valdez, AK 99686
(907) 835-4665, *Fax:* (907) 835-2847
www.kchu.org
kchu@cvinternet.net
License: McCarthy, Valdez-Cordova County, AK held by Terminal Radio Inc.
Nat'l Network: NPR; PRI *Regional Network:* Alaska Pub.
Hrs. of News Programming: news progmg 10 hrs wkly *No. News Employees:* 1 *Target Audience:* General.
John Anderson, Operations Dir
Lisa West, General Manager
David Delahunt, Engineering Dir

McGrath

***KMCG**
90.3 mhz FM; kw
US
(907) 524-3182
radiomcgrath@yahoo.com
License: McGrath, Yukon Koyukuk County, AK held by McGrath Community Radio.
Arbitron Metro Market: Carlsbad, CA
Jack Collins, General Manager

***KOGB**
91.3 mhz FM; kw
US
(907) 262-0920
License: McGrath, Yukon Koyukuk County, AK held by Blessed Hope Baptist Mission.
Arbitron Metro Market: McGrath, AK
David McElwain, President

Meadow Lakes

KMVV
03-13-2008; 104.9 mhz FM; 45 kw; 663 ft.; N61 4 2 W149 44 36
US
(907) 522-1018, *Fax:* (907) 522-1027
www.rudolphradio.com
License: Meadow Lakes, Kenai Peninsula County, AK held by World Radio Link Inc.
Group Owner: World Radio Link Inc.
Arbitron Metro Market: Meadow Lakes, AK *Format:* Adult Contemp
Mike Robbins, General Manager
Cary Carrigan, Programming Director

Naknek

KAKN
05-01-1987; 100.9 mhz FM *Hrs Open:* 24; 3 kw; 299 ft.; N58 44 40 W156 58 32
Mailing Address: P.O. Box 214, Naknek, AK 99633 US
Second Address: Mile 2 AK Peninsula Hwy., Naknek, AK 99633
(907) 246-7492, *Fax:* (907) 246-7462
www.kaknradio.org
studio@victoryradionetwork.com
License: Naknek, Bristol Bay County, AK held by Association of Free Lutheran Congregations Mission Corp.
Nat'l Network: USA
Arbitron Metro Market: Naknek, AK *Format:* Adult Contemp, Christian *Hrs. of News Programming:* News progmg 15 hrs wkly *Target Audience:* General; mobile town/village population & coml fishermen *Adv. Rates:* 12.75; 12.75; 12.75; 29
Richard Long, President
Michael Johnson, Operations Dir
Thomas Olsen, General Manager
Anita Karlsson, Station Manager

Nenana

KIAM
06-28-1985; 630 khz AM *Hrs Open:* 24; 10 kw-D, ND1; 3.1 kw-N, ND1; N64 28 43 W149 5 10
P.O. Box 474, Nenana, AK 99760 US
(907) 832-5426, *Fax:* (907) 832-5450
www.vfcm.org
Alaskaradio@vfcm.org
License: Nenana, AK held by Voice for Christ Ministries.
Nat'l Network: Salem Radio Network; Moody
Format: Christian, News, 62, Talk *Special Programming:* American Indian 3 hrs, class one hr wkly, family 3 hrs wkly *Hrs. of News Programming:* News progm 10 hrs wkly *Target Audience:* General.
Brian Blair, Station Manager

Nikiski

KXBA
03-04-2000; 93.3 mhz FM; 50 kw; 243 ft.; N60 30 39 W151 16 12
P O Box 109, Homer, AK 99603 US
(907) 262-6000(907) 283-7423, *Fax:* (907) 283-8461
kpenfm@acsalaska.net
License: Nikiski, Kenai Peninsula County, AK held by Peninsula Communications Inc.
Group Owner: Peninsula Communications Inc.
Format: Oldies *Hrs. of News Programming:* News progmg 8 hrs wkly *Target Audience:* 25-54. *Adv. Rates:* 216; 216; 216; 180
David Becker, President
Tim White, News Director

Nome

KICY
04-17-1960; 850 khz AM *Hrs Open:* 24
Mailing Address: P. O. Box 820, Nome, AK 99762 US
Second Address: 408 West D St., Nome, AK 99762
(907) 443-2213, *Fax:* (907) 443-2344
www.kicy.org
office@kicy.org; dennisw@kicy.org
License: Nome, AK held by Arctic Broadcasting Association
Nat'l Network: ABC; Moody; Salem Radio Network *Regional Reps:* Alaska Broadcast Media
Format: Gospel, Russian *No. News Employees:* 1 *Target Audience:* 25-64. *Adv. Rates:* 13; 10; 10; 7
Ted Haney, President
Dennis Weidler, General Manager
Stephen Palmatier, News & Sports Director

KICY-FM
09-11-1977; 100.3 mhz FM *Hrs Open:* 24; 1 kw; -361 ft.; N64 30 9 W165 24 37
Mailing Address: P.O. Box 820, Nome, AK 99762 US
Second Address: 408 West D St., Nome, AK 99762
(907) 443-2213, *Fax:* (907) 443-2344
www.kicy.org
office@kicy.org; dennisw@kicy.org
License: Nome, AK held by Arctic Broadcasting Association.
Nat'l Network: Salem Radio Network *Regional Reps:* Alaska Broadcast Media *Wire Services:* AP
Format: Christian *No. News Employees:* 1 *Target Audience:* 18-35. *Adv. Rates:* 13; 10; 10; 7
Ted Haney, President
Dennis Weidler, General Manager
Stephen Palmatier, News & Sports Director

***KNOM**
07-14-1971; 780 khz AM *Hrs Open:* 24; 25 kw-D, ND1; 14 kw-N, ND1; N64 29 16 W165 17 58
1316 Peger Road, Fairbanks, AK 99709 US
(907) 443-5221, *Fax:* (907) 443-5757
www.knom.org
info@knom.org
License: Nome, AK held by Catholic Bishop of Northern Alaska.
Wire Services: AP
Format: News, News/Talk, 86, Variety/Diverse, Religious *Special Programming:* Eskimo 6 hrs, CHR 12 hrs, relg 20 hrs, class 5 hrs *Hrs. of News Programming:* news progmg 30 hrs wkly *No. News Employees:* 2 *TargetAudience:* General.
Thomas Busch, CFO
Ric Schmidt, General Manager
Kelly Brabec, Programming Director
Paul Korchin, News Director

***KNOM-FM**
05-17-1993; 96.1 mhz FM *Hrs Open:* 24; 1 kw; -138 ft.; N64 29 56 W165 23 56
1316 Peger Rd., Fairbanks, AK 99709 US
(907) 443-5221, *Fax:* (907) 443-5757
License: Nome, Nome County, AK
Nat'l Network: AP Radio *Wire Services:* AP
Hrs. of News Programming: news progmg 30 hrs wkly *No. News Employees:* 2
Marcos Romero, Station Manager
Mariana Romero, Programming Director
Concepcion Borrayo, News Director

North Nenana

***KIAM-FM**
04-10-2008; 91.9 mhz FM *Hrs Open:* 24; 0.26 kw; -10 ft.; N64 33 50 W149 5 21
US
(907) 832-5426, *Fax:* (907) 832-5450
www.vfcm.org
alaskaradio@vfcm.org
License: North Nenana, Yukon Koyukuk County, AK held by Voice for Christ Ministries Inc.
Nat'l Network: Salem Radio Network; Moody
Arbitron Metro Market: North Nenana, AK *Format:* Christian
Greg Pippin, Chairman
Brian Blair, Station Manager

North Pole

***KJNP**
10-11-1967; 1170 khz AM *Hrs Open:* 19 hrs; 50 kw-D, ND1; 21 kw-N, ND1; N64 45 34 W147 19 26
PO Box 56359, North Pole, AK 99705 US
(907) 488-2216, *Fax:* (907) 488-5246
www.mosquitonet.com
kjnp@mosquitonet.com
License: North Pole, AK held by Evangelistic Alaska Missionary Fellowship.
Format: Religious, Country *Special Programming:* Athabaskan Indian 2 hrs, Eskimo one hr wkly
Yvonne Carriker, President
Richerd Olson, Operations Dir

***KJNP-FM**
10-11-1977; 100.3 mhz FM; 25 kw; 1572 ft.; N64 52 44 W148 3 10
P.O. Box 56359, North Pole, AK 99705 US
(907) 488-2216, *Fax:* (907) 488-5246
License: North Pole, Fairbanks North Star County, AK held by Evangelistic Alaska Missionary Fellowship.
TV Affiliate: *KJNP-TV affil.. *Format:* Religious
Yvonne Carriker, President
Richard Olson, Operations Dir

Nulato

***KNUL**
99.1 mhz FM; 0.1 kw; 16 ft.; N64 43 59 W158 6 25
US
License: Nulato, Yukon Koyukuk County, AK held by Big River Public Broadcasting Corp.
Arbitron Metro Market: Nulato, AK
Shadow Steel, General Manager

Palmer

KMVN
08-07-1957; 95.5 mhz FM *Hrs Open:* 24; kw
US
(818) 525-5000, *Fax:* (818) 525-5002
www.movin939.fm
webmaster@movin939.com
License: Palmer, Los Angeles County, AK held by KMVN License LLC.
Group Owner: Emmis Communications Corp.; (acq 9-26-2000; grpsl)
Arbitron Metro Market: Burbank, CA *Format:* Adult Contemp
Janet Brainin, General Sales Mgr
Jimmy Steal, Programming Director
Dianna Jason, Promotions Manager
Dean Carter, General Sales Manager

***KJLP**
08-01-2005; 88.9 mhz FM; 0.25 kw; -210 ft.; N61 37 18 W149 1 16
Mailing Address: 6401 E Northern Lights B, Anchorage, AK 99504 US
Second Address: 6401 E. Northern Lights, Anchorage, AK 99521

(907) 333-5282, *Fax:* (907) 337-0003
www.katb.org
tom@katb.org
License: Palmer, Matanuska-Susitna County, AK held by Christian Broadcasting Inc.
Arbitron Metro Market: Palmer, AK *Format:* Christian
Tom Steigleman, General Manager

KNLT(FM)
95.5 mhz FM; 100 kw; 114 meters; N61 29 06 W149 45 46
3650 Braddock Street, Suite 2, Fairbanks, AK 99701
(907) 452-3697, *Fax:* (907) 456-3428
License: Palmer, AK held by Tanana Valley Television Company
Group Owner: Tanana Valley Television Co.
William St Pierre, President

Petersburg

***KFSK**
09-01-1977; 100.9 mhz FM *Hrs Open:* 24; 2 kw; -482 ft.; N56 48 57 W132 57 6
Mailing Address: P. O. Box 149, Petersburg, AK 99833 US
Second Address: 404 N Second St, Petersburg, AK
(907) 772-3808, *Fax:* (907) 772-9296
www.kfsk.org
License: Petersburg, Wrangell Petersburg County, AK held by Narrows Broadcasting Corp.
Nat'l Network: PRI; NPR; AP Network News *Regional Network:* Alaska Pub. *Wire Services:* AP
Arbitron Metro Market: Petersburg, AK *Format:* News, News/Talk, 86 *Special Programming:* Jazz 2 hrs wkly *Hrs. of News Programming:* news prgmg 24 hrs wkly *No. News Employees:* 2
Craig Olsen, President
Tom Abbott, General Manager
Suzanne Fuqua, General Sales Mgr
Matt Lichtenstein, News Director
Joe Viechnicki, News Reporter

KRSA
09-24-1982; 580 khz AM *Hrs Open:* 24; 5 kw-U, DA1; N56 40 23 W132 55 0
P.O. Box 650, Petersburg, AK 99833 US
(907) 772-3891, *Fax:* (907) 772-4538
www.krsa.net
krsa@krsa.net
License: Petersburg, AK held by Northern Light Network.
Arbitron Metro Market: Southeast AK *Format:* Religious *Special Programming:* Class 5 hrs, children, oldies 5 hrs wkly *Hrs. of News Programming:* News progmg 20 hrs wkly *Target Audience:* General.
Andrew Mazzella, President
Daryl Carlson, Programming Director
Scott Hill, Chief Engineer
Joe Garness, Music Director

Port Alsworth

***KGCU**
90.3 mhz FM; kw
US
(907) 781-2243
License: Port Alsworth, Lake and Peninsula Boroug County, AK held by Lake Clark Bible Church.
Arbitron Metro Market: Port Alsworth, AK
James Walsh, General Manager

Ruby

***KRBY**
98.1 mhz FM; 0.1 kw; -69 ft.; N64 44 20 W155 28 48
US
(907) 656-1488, *Fax:* (907) 656-1734
www.kiyu.com
License: Ruby, Yukon Koyukuk County, AK held by Big River Public Broadcasting Corp.
Arbitron Metro Market: Ruby, AK
Russ Sweetsir, President
Jeremy Scott, Operations/ Program Director

Sand Point

***KSDP**
03-02-1983; 830 khz AM *Hrs Open:* 24; 1 kw-U; N55 21 06 W160 28 02 *Rebroadcasts:* Rebroadcasts KDLG(AM) Dillingham
Box 328, City Bldg, Sand Point, AK 99661
(907) 383-5737, *Fax:* (907) 383-5737
www.ksdpradio.org
gm@ksdpradio.com
License: Sand Point, Aleutians East Borough County, AK held by Aleutian Peninsula Broadcasting Inc.
Nat'l Network: NPR; PRI
Population Served: 6,000*Special Programming:* Gospel *Target Audience:* General.
Austin Roof, General Manager
Virgil Porter, Programming Director

***KSPM**
90.3 mhz FM; kw
US
(907) 383-4551
www.sandpointchurch.com
radiosandpoint@yahoo.com
License: Sand Point, Aleutians East Borough County, AK held by Sand Point Baptist Church.
Arbitron Metro Market: Sand Point, AK
Craig Furlough, General Manager

Seward

KSEW
11-01-1948; 950 khz AM; 1 kw-U, ND1; N60 5 27 W149 20 20
10914 E. 46th Avenue, Spokane, WA 99206 US
(907) 224-5793, *Fax:* (907) 224-4702
www.sewardradio.com
License: Seward, AK held by Seward Media Partners LLC
Arbitron Metro Market: Seaward, AK *Format:* Country
Wolfgang Kurtz, General Manager
James Spanos, Station Manager

Sitka

***KCAW**
02-19-1982; 104.7 mhz FM *Hrs Open:* 24; 3.6 kw; -610 ft.; N57 3 13 W135 21 7
2b Lincoln Street, Sitka, AK 99835 US
(907) 747-5877, *Fax:* (907) 747-5977
www.kcaw.org
License: Sitka, Sitka County, AK held by Raven Radio Foundation.
Nat'l Network: NPR; PRI *Regional Network:* Alaska Pub.
Arbitron Metro Market: Sitka, AK *Format:* News, Variety/Diverse *Special Programming:* Class 15 hrs, Indian 3 hrs wkly *Target Audience:* General.
Ted Laufenberg, President
Ken Fate, General Manager
Kayla Boettcher, Programming Director
Robert Woolsey, News Director

KIFW
09-01-1949; 1230 khz AM *Hrs Open:* 24; 1 kw-U, ND1; N57 3 27 W135 20 2
3161 Channel Dr. Suite 2, Juneau, AK 99801 US
(907) 747-6626, *Fax:* (907) 747-8455
kifw@ptialaska.net
License: Sitka, AK held by Alaska Broadcast Communications Inc.
Group Owner: Alaska Broadcast Communications Inc.; (acq 12-21-2000; grpsl)
Arbitron Metro Market: Sitka, AK *Format:* Adult Contemp, News, 62, Oldies, Talk *Hrs. of News Programming:* News progmg 60 hrs wkly *Target Audience:* 18-49; all demographics
Steve Rhyner, President
Blake Messer, Station Manager
Bobbie Rusk, General Sales Mgr
Devin Reiter, Programming Director
Clint Daniels, News Director
Chris Kobger, Chief Engineer

KSBZ
10-18-1990; 103.1 mhz FM *Hrs Open:* 24; 3 kw; Ant 144 ft; N57 03 27 W135 20 02
611 Lake St., Sitka, AK 99801
(907) 747-6627, *Fax:* (907) 747-8455
www.ksbz.com
License: Sitka, Sitka County, AK held by Alaska Broadcast Communications Inc.
Group Owner: Alaska Broadcast Communications Inc.
Nat'l Reps: Tacher
Hrs. of News Programming: 2 hours *No. News Employees:* 4
Target Audience: 25-54 *Adv. Rates:* 12 dollars per station/combo 1
Roy Paschal, Chairman
Richard Burns, President
Dan Belair, Operations Dir
Larry Snider, General Manager
Terry Thomas, General Sales Mgr
Mike Leonard, Promotions Manager
Trish Durham, News Director
Dominic Pavonne, EngineeringDir

Soldotna

KKIS-FM
03-02-1994; 96.5 mhz FM *Hrs Open:* 24; 10 kw; 259 ft.; N60 31 26 W151 3 23
44619 Sterling Highway, Soldotna, AK 99669 US
(907) 283-8700, *Fax:* (907) 283-9177
www.radiokenai.com
rken18@radokenai.com
License: Soldotna, Kenai Peninsula County, AK held by KSRM Inc.
Group Owner: KSRM Inc.; (acq 12-7-2001; $350,000 with co-located AM)
Nat'l Network: ABC
Arbitron Metro Market: Anchorage, AK *Format:* Adult Contemp *Hrs. of News Programming:* news progmg 2 hrs wkly *No. News Employees:* 1 *Target Audience:* 18-49.
John Davis, CEO
Steve Holloway, Operations Dir
Joe Nicks, News Director

KPEN-FM
12-01-1984; 101.7 mhz FM *Hrs Open:* 24; 25 kw; 240 ft.; N60 30 40 W151 16 12
P.O. Box 109, Homer, AK 99603 US
(907) 262-6000,(907) 283-7451, *Fax:* (907) 235-6683
kwavefm@xyz.net
License: Soldotna, Kenai Peninsula County, AK held by Peninsula Communications Inc.
Group Owner: Peninsula Communications Inc.
Nat'l Network: USA
Format: Country *Target Audience:* 25-54. *Adv. Rates:* 240; 240; 240; 180
David Becker, President
Tim White, News Director

KSLD
04-06-1985; 1140 khz AM *Hrs Open:* 24; 10 kw-U, ND1; N60 31 26 W151 3 23
44619 Sterling Hwy, Soldotna, AK 99669 US
(907) 283-8700
www.radiokenai.com
info@radiokenai.com
License: Soldotna, AK held by KSRM Inc.
Group Owner: KSRM Inc.
Nat'l Network: Westwood One
Arbitron Metro Market: Kenai, AK *Format:* Classic Rock *Hrs. of News Programming:* News progmg one hr wkly *Target Audience:* 25-59.
Bruce Reese, CEO
John C Davis, President
Monica Leger, Operations Dir
Matt Wilson, General Manager
Lora Woodbury, General Sales Mgr
Kevin Larue, Programming Director
Andrew Rogers, News Director
John Dehnel, Chief Engineer
Robert Johnson, CFO
Paulette Cary, Regional Sales Manager
Greg Wrubell, Sports Commentator

KSRM
09-27-1967; 920 khz AM *Hrs Open:* 24; 5 kw-U, ND1; N60 30 49 W151 11 19
Hc-2 Box 852, Soldotna, AK 99669 US
(907) 283-5959, *Fax:* (907) 283-5811
www.radiokenai.com
info@radiokenai.com
License: Soldotna, AK held by KSRM Inc.
Group Owner: KSRM Inc.; (acq 4-72)
Arbitron Metro Market: Kenai, AK *Format:* News, News/Talk, 86 *Hrs. of News Programming:* news progmg 105 hrs wkly *No. News Employees:* 1 *Target Audience:* 25-54.
John Davis, CEO
Steve Holloway, Operations Dir
Matt Wilson, General Manager
Jake Thompson, Programming Director
Andrew Rogers, News Director
Dayne Clark, Executive Vice President

St. Paul

***KUHB-FM**
07-04-1984; 91.9 mhz FM; 15 kw horiz, 0.23 kw vert; 52 ft.; N57 7 14 W170 16 45
930 Tolstoi St, Box 905, St. Paul Island, AK 99660 US
(907) 546-2254, *Fax:* (907) 546-2367
www.kuhbradio.org
kuhbinfo@gmail.com
License: St. Paul, Pribios Islands County, AK held by Pribilof School District.

Nat'l Network: NPR
Arbitron Metro Market: Saint Paul, AK *Format:* Adult Contemp, Alternative, 22, Contemporary Hits/Top 40, Disco, News
Walt Gregg, General Manager
Walt Gregg, Station Manager
B.J. Kibbe, News Director

Sterling

KKNI
01-01-1998; 105.3 mhz FM; 7 kw; 284 ft.; N60 29 19.33 W150 44 42.83
10914 E. 46th Avenue, Spokane, WA 99206 US
(907) 224-5793, *Fax:* (907) 224-4702
License: Sterling, Kenai Peninsula County, AK held by Seward Media Partners LLC

Wolfgang Kurtz, General Manager
James Spanos, Station Manager

***KWMD**
01-01-2006; 90.1 mhz FM; 1.2 kw horiz; Ant 20 ft; N60 29 16 W150 47 38
3700 Woodland Dr., Anchorage, AK 99517
(800) 974-6525
License: Sterling, Kenai Peninsula County, AK held by Alaska Educational Radio System Inc.
Wolfgang Kurtz, President

Talkeetna

***KTNA**
02-01-1993; 88.9 mhz FM *Hrs Open:* 24; 7.2 kw; 72 ft.; N62 19 5 W150 17 52
P.O. Box 300, Talkeetna, AK 99676 US
(907) 733-1700, *Fax:* (907) 733-1781
www.ktna.org
info@ktna.org
License: Talkeetna, Matanuska Susitna County, AK held by Talkeetna Community Radio Inc.
Nat'l Network: NPR; PRI
Arbitron Metro Market: Talkeentna, AK *Format:* News, News/Talk, 86 *Special Programming:* Blues 5 hrs, light rock 5 hrs wkly *Hrs. of News Programming:* news progmg 15 hrs wkly *No. News Employees:* 1 *TargetAudience:* General; rural Alaskans
Will Peterson, General Manager
Kirsten Merkley, General Sales Mgr
Deborah Brock, Programming Director
Lorien Nettleton, News Director
Kristin Merkley-Business Manager

Tok

***KUDU**
03-03-1998; 91.9 mhz FM; 0.2 kw; -121 ft.; N63 19 53 W143 7 2
402 E Yakima Avenue, Suite 1320, Yakima, WA 98901 US
(800) 775-4673, *Fax:* (907) 883-5245
www.lifetalk.net
office@lifetalk.net
License: Tok, Southeast Fairbanks County, AK held by Lifetalk Broadcasting Association.
Arbitron Metro Market: Tok, AK *Format:* Religious, Talk
John Geli, Program/Operations Manager
Francine Lee, General Manager
Debby Wade, Administration/Station Relations Director
Paul Willis, Engineering Dir
Warren Judd, Director
Connie Vandeman Jeffery, Administration
Nancy Reider,Administrative Receptionist
Seth Wade, Webmaster
Randy Schornstein, Engineer
Marcelo Vallado, Engineer

Unalakleet

KNSA
01-01-1998; 930 khz AM
P.O. Box 178, Unalakleet, AK 99684 US
(907) 624-3100, *Fax:* (907) 624-3130
License: Unalakleet, AK held by Unalakleet Broadcasting Inc.
Format: Variety/Diverse
Henry Ivanoff, Station Manager

Unalaska

***KUCB**
10-01-2008; 89.7 mhz FM; 0.66 kw; -308 ft.; N53 52 35 W166 32 24
US
(907) 581-1888, *Fax:* (907) 581-1634
www.kucb.org
info@kucb.org
License: Unalaska, Aleutian Islands County, AK held by Unalaska Community Broadcasting Inc.
Nat'l Network: NPR *Regional Network:* Alaska Pub.
Arbitron Metro Market: Unalaska, AK *Format:* Public Affairs, News
Pipa Escalante, Operations Dir
Lauren Adams, General Manager
Alexandra Gutierrez, News Director
Daniel Weirich, Producer
Jane Bye, Development Director
Joe Redmon, Music Director

Valdez

***KCHU**
08-03-1986; 770 khz AM *Hrs Open:* 24; 9.7 kw-U, ND1; N61 6 40 W146 15 39
Mailing Address: Box 467, Valdez, AK 99686 US
Second Address: 128 Poineer Dr., Valdez, AK
(907) 835-4665, *Fax:* (907) 835-2847
www.kchu.org
gm@kchu.org
License: Valdez, AK held by Terminal Radio Inc.
Nat'l Network: NPR; PRI *Regional Network:* Alaska Pub.
Arbitron Metro Market: Valdez-Cordova Census Area, AK *Format:* Variety/Diverse *Hrs. of News Programming:* news progmg 40 hrs wkly *No. News Employees:* 1 *Target Audience:* General.
Dan Schally, President
John Anderson, Operations Dir
Danny Sparrell, General Manager
Amy Dunkin, General Sales Mgr
Tony Gorman, News Director
John Anderson, Operations Manager
Nancy Meador, Development Coordinator
Paul Nylund,Vice President
Tori Rego, Secretary
Sue Bergstrom, Treasurer

KVAK
01-01-1983; 1230 khz AM *Hrs Open:* 24; 1 kw-U, ND1; N61 7 16 W146 15 25
Mailing Address: 501 East Bremner, Valdez, AK 99686 US
Second Address: 501 E. Bremner St., Valdez, AK 99686
(907) 835-5825, *Fax:* (907) 835-5158
www.kvakradio.com
kvaksales@gci.net
License: Valdez, AK held by North Wave Communications Inc.
Arbitron Metro Market: Valdez, AK *Format:* Country, Talk *Hrs. of News Programming:* News progmg one hr wkly *Target Audience:* General.
Laurie Prax, President
Laurie Prax, General Manager
Gary Pauly, Sales & Marketing
Brooke Alexander, News Director
Margaret Henry, Traffic & Billing

KVAK-FM
05-28-1999; 93.3 mhz FM; 1.2 kw; -1959 ft.; N61 7 16 W146 15 25
C/O Haley Bader & Potts, 4350 North Fairfax Dr, Arlington, VA 22203 US
(907) 835-5825, *Fax:* (907) 835-5158
www.kvakradio.com
kvaksales@gci.net
License: Valdez, Valdez Cordova County, AK
Arbitron Metro Market: Valdez, AK *Format:* Adult Contemp *Adv. Rates:* 10; 9; 10; 9
Mark Bolland, CEO
Laurie Prax, General Manager
Gary Pauly, Sales & Marketing
Mark Bone, Programming Director
Brooke Alexander, News Director
Margaret Henry, Traffic & Billing

Wasilla

KMBQ-FM
03-15-1985; 99.7 mhz FM *Hrs Open:* 24; 51 kw; -187 ft; N61 38 03 W149 26 25
2200 E. Parks Hwy., Wasilla, AK 99654
(907) 373-0222, *Fax:* (907) 376-1575
www.kmbq.com
john@kmbq
License: Wasilla, Matanuska Susitna County, AK held by KMBQ Corp.
Nat'l Network: CNN Radio
Population Served: 91,000 *Arbitron Metro Market:* Anchorage, AK *Hrs. of News Programming:* news progmg 13 wkly *No. News Employees:* 2 *Target Audience:* 25-54; mid-upper class suburbanites & farm community *Adv.Rates:* 30; 25; 30; 20
John Klapperich, CEO
Terri Bush, General Sales Mgr
Roxi Lennox, Programming Director
Van Craft, Chief Engineer

KAYO
01-23-2009; 100.9 mhz FM; 50 kw; -276 ft.; N61 38 21 W148 59 56
US
(907) 631-0493, *Fax:* (907) 631-0483
www.countrylegends1009.com
License: Wasilla, Matanuska Susitna County, AK held by MCC Radio LLC.
Group Owner: Morris Radio LLC
Arbitron Metro Market: Wasilla, AK *Format:* Country
Scott Smith, General Sales Mgr
Eddie Maxwell, Programming Director
Paul Jewusiak, Chief Engineer
Margie Vanness, Account Executive
Sandy Weihs, Account Executive
Sandy Baker, Account Executive

KWAP
01-01-2008; 1430 khz AM; 1 kw-U; N61 37 09 W149 17 17
2200 E. Parks Hwy., Wasilla, AK
(907) 373-0222, *Fax:* (907) 376-1575
www.kmbq.com
License: Wasilla, Matanuska Susitna County, AK held by Spirit of Alaska Broadcasting Inc.
Arbitron Metro Market: Anchorage, AK
John Klapperich, President

Wrangell

***KSTK**
07-02-1977; 101.7 mhz FM *Hrs Open:* 24; 3 kw; -184 ft.; N56 27 14 W132 22 54
Mailing Address: P.O. Box 1141, Wrangell, AK 99929 US
Second Address: 202 St. Michael's, Wrangell, AK 99929
(907) 874-2345, *Fax:* (907) 874-3293
www.kstk.org
info@kstk.com
License: Wrangell, Wrangell Petersburg County, AK held by Wrangell Radio Group Inc.
Nat'l Network: NPR; PRI *Regional Network:* Alaska Pub.
Arbitron Metro Market: Wrangell, AK *Format:* Variety/Diverse *Special Programming:* Class 4 hrs, country 16 hrs, jazz 8 hrs wkly *Hrs. of News Programming:* news progmg 20 hrs wkly *No. News Employees:* 2 *TargetAudience:* General. *Adv. Rates:* 11.80; 11.80; 11.80; na
Peter Helgeson, General Manager
Cindy Sweat, General Sales Mgr
Dawn Stevens, Programming Director

American Samoa

Fagaitua

WVUV-FM
01-01-2008; 103.1 mhz FM; 1.3 kw; 1591 ft.; S14 19 21 W170 45 47
US
(684) 633-7793, *Fax:* (684) 633-4493
www.wvuv.com
License: Fagaitua, AS held by Horizon Christian Fellowship.
Group Owner: Horizon Christian Fellowship; (acq 2-9-2006; grpsl)
Arbitron Metro Market: Faga'itua, AS
Shannon Cummings, General Manager

Leone

KNWJ
01-01-2001; 104.7 mhz FM *Hrs Open:* 24; 0.28 kw; 1499 ft.; S14 19 21 W170 45 47
Harnack Engineering, Inc, 211 Lowery Road, Boyle, MS 38730 US
(684) 699 8127, *Fax:* (684) 699-8126
www.fm104.org
info@fm104.org
License: Leone, AS held by Showers of Blessings Radio
Format: Christian *Target Audience:* Christian Adults
Dan Dalle, General Manager

Nu'uuli

***KMOA**
89.7 mhz FM; 1.5 kw; 1463 ft.; S14 16 12 W170 41 10

US
(684) 699-2635
www.teenchallengeamericansamoa.org
License: Nu'uuli, AS held by Society of Pure Truth Ministries Inc.
Arbitron Metro Market: Pago Pago, AS
Shannon Cummings, President

Pago Pago

KKHJ-FM
05-01-2000; 93.1 mhz FM *Hrs Open:* 24; 1.1 kw; 1490 ft.; S14 16 12 W170 41 10
Mailing Address: P.O. Box 1787, Cleveland, MS 38732 US
Second Address: 9408 Grand Gate St., Las Vegas, AS 89143
(684) 633-7793, *Fax:* (684) 633-4493
License: Pago Pago, AS held by South Seas Broadcasting.
Group Owner: Contemporary Communications
Format: Adult Contemp *Target Audience:* General. *Adv. Rates:* 7; 6; 6.50; 5.50
Larry Fuss, President
Joey Cummings, General Manager

KSBS-FM
04-14-1988; 92.1 mhz FM *Hrs Open:* 6:00am-Midnight; 15 kw; -92 feet; S14 17 41 W170 39 44
Box 793, Pago Pago, AS 96799
(684) 633-7000, *Fax:* (684) 633-5727
www.ksbsfm.com
prescott.esther@ksbsfm.com
License: Pago Pago, AS held by Samoa Technologies Inc.
Target Audience: Working adults.
Barney Sene, President
Esther Prescott, General Manager

Tafuna

KJAL
01-01-2005; 585 khz AM
US
(417) 862-2781
www.apmedia.org/site
contact@apmedia.org
License: Tafuna, AS held by District Council of the Assemblies of God in AS.
Arbitron Metro Market: Tafuna, AS *Format:* Christian
Viliamu Paaga, General Manager
Bill Snider, Director

Arizona

Apache Junction

KBSZ
01-27-1960; 1260 khz AM *Hrs Open:* 24; 3.5 kw-D, 50 w-N; N33 22 56 W111 32 09
340 W. Wickenburg Way, Suite. B, Wickenburg, AZ 20036
(928) 668-1250, *Fax:* (928) 668-1251
www.kbsz-am.com
amradio1tv@yahoo.com
License: Apache Junction, Maricopa County, AZ held by 1TV.Com Inc.
Group Owner: 1TV.Com Inc.; (acq 3-31-2008; $500,000)
Population Served: 25,000 *Arbitron Metro Market:* Phoenix, AZ *Adv. Rates:* 5; 5; 5; na
Pete Peterson, General Manager

KVVA-FM
07-01-1973; 107.1 mhz FM; 23.5 kw; 335 ft.; N33 26 48 W111 37 32
1436 Auburn Boulevard, Sacramento, CA 95815 US
(602) 266-2005, *Fax:* (602) 279-2921
www.josephoenix.com
License: Apache Junction, Pinal County, AZ held by Entravision Holdings LLC.
Group Owner: Entravision Communications Corp.; (acq 7-28-00; grpsl).
Arbitron Metro Market: Apache Junction, AZ *Format:* Spanish *Target Audience:* 18-49; Hispanic
Tom Duran, General Manager
Chris Moncayo, General Sales Mgr
Edgar Pineda, Programming Director

Arizona City

KKMR
04-13-1985; 106.5 mhz FM *Hrs Open:* 24; 6 kw; 292 ft.; N32 50 4 W111 38 15
7434 E. Stetson Dr., Ste 255, Scottsdale, AZ 85251 US
(602) 308-7900, *Fax:* (602) 308-7979
www.univision.com
License: Arizona City, Pinal County, AZ held by HBC License Corp.
Group Owner: Univision Radio; (acq 9-22-2003; grpsl).
Arbitron Metro Market: Phoenix, AZ *Format:* Spanish *Target Audience:* 25-54. *Adv. Rates:* 50; 50; 50; 50
Mary McEvilly-Hernandez, Operations Dir

Bagdad

KFTT
01-01-2002; 107.7 mhz FM; 1 kw horiz; 1250 ft.; N34 33 25 W113 16 0
P.O. Box 1866, Lake Havasu City, AZ 86405 US
(928) 855-1051, *Fax:* (928) 855-7996
www.maddogwireless.net
info@maddog.net
License: Bagdad, Yava County, AZ held by Smoke and Mirrors LLC.
Group Owner: Smoke and Mirrors LLC; (acq 4-18-2001)
Arbitron Metro Market: Lake Havasu City, AZ *Format:* Adult Contemp
Chris Rolando, General Manager

Benson

KAVV
04-01-1983; 97.7 mhz FM *Hrs Open:* 24; 6 kw; 590 ft; N31 54 24 W110 27 08
Mailing Address: Box 18899, Tucson, AZ 85731
Second Address: 156 W. 5th St., Benson, AZ 85602
(520) 586-9797
www.cavefm.com
cave@gainbroadband.com
License: Benson, Cochise County, AZ held by Stereo 97 Inc.
Population Served: 60,000*Special Programming:* Relg 3 hrs wkly *Target Audience:* 25-49.
Paul Lotsof, General Manager

Bisbee

*KRMB
01-01-1997; 90.1 mhz FM; 0.115 kw; 2208 ft.; N31 28 55 W109 57 31 *Rebroadcasts:* Rebroadcasts KRMC(FM) Douglas 100%
Box 3333, McAllen, TX 78502 US
(520) 364-5392, *Fax:* (520) 364-5392
www.moodyradio.org
License: Bisbee, Cochise County, AZ held by World Radio Network Inc.
Group Owner: World Radio Network Inc.
Format: Christian
Glen Lafitte, General Manager

KWCD
10-12-1979; 92.3 mhz FM *Hrs Open:* 24; 0.09 kw; 2129 ft.; N31 28 52 W109 57 30
P.O. Box 2770, Sierra Vista, AZ 85636 US
(520) 458-4313, *Fax:* (520) 458-4317
www.kwcdcountry.com
KWCD@cherrycreekradio.com
License: Bisbee, Cochise County, AZ held by CCR-Sierra Vista IV LLC.
Group Owner: Cherry Creek Radio LLC; (acq 12-19-2003; grpsl).
Nat'l Network: Westwood One *Nat'l Reps:* Tacher
Arbitron Metro Market: Sierra Vista, AZ *Format:* Country *Hrs. of News Programming:* news progmg one hr wkly *No. News Employees:* 1 *Target Audience:* 25-54; financially secure adults & military personnel
Grady Butler, Operations Dir
Randy Sueskind, General Manager

*KWRB
12-01-1996; 90.9 mhz FM *Hrs Open:* 24; 0.99 kw vert; 2093 ft.; N31 28 58 W109 57 29
P.O. Box 3333, McAllen, TX 78502 US
(520) 452-8022, *Fax:* (520) 452-0927
www.kwrb.org
kwrb@lwpn.org
License: Bisbee, Cochise County, AZ held by World Radio Network Inc.
Arbitron Metro Market: Sierra Vista, AZ *Format:* Christian, Religious *Target Audience:* Women 35+.
Laia Daniels, Operations Dir
Dwight Lind, General Manager

Black Canyon City

KBMB
09-01-1981; 710 khz AM *Hrs Open:* 24; 22 kw-D, 3.9 kw-N, DA-2; N34 04 48 W112 09 15
501 N. 44th St., Suite 425, Phoenix, AZ 20006
(602) 776-1400, *Fax:* (602) 279-2921
info@entravision.com
License: Black Canyon City, Yavapai County, AZ held by Entravision Holdings LLC.
Group Owner: Entravision Communications Corp.; (acq 7-28-00; grpsl).
Arbitron Metro Market: Phoenix, AZ *Target Audience:* 18-54. *Adv. Rates:* 75; 75; 75; 50
Tom Duran, General Manager

Buckeye

KDVA
01-01-1993; 106.9 mhz FM; 6 kw; 305 ft.; N33 27 1 W112 35 58
8401 Colesville Rd, Suite 300, Silver Spring, MD 20910 US
(602) 776-1400, *Fax:* (602) 279-2921
License: Buckeye, Maricopa County, AZ held by Entravision Holdings LLC.
Group Owner: Entravision Communications Corp.; (acq 6-14-2001; $10 million)
Arbitron Metro Market: Phoenix, AZ *Format:* Ethnic *Special Programming:* Black 6 hrs, gospel 7 hrs wkly
Tom Duran, General Manager
Chris Moncayo, General Sales Mgr
Edgar Pineda, Programming Director

Bullhead City

KZZZ
11-15-1981; 1490 khz AM
113 East 7th Street, Tyler, TX 75701 US
(928) 763-5586, *Fax:* (928) 763-3775
www.talkatoz.com
License: Bullhead City, AZ held by Cameron Broadcasting Inc.
Group Owner: Cameron Broadcasting Inc.; acq 7-91; $1.28 million with KNKK(FM) Needles, CA;
Nat'l Network: Fox News Radio
Arbitron Metro Market: Bullhead City, AZ *Format:* Talk *No. News Employees:* 1 *Target Audience:* 35 plus.
William Jaeger, CEO
Craig Powers, Operations Dir
Don Jaeger, General Manager
Mike Fletcher, General Sales Mgr
Dave Cooper, Chief Engineer

KFLG
10-01-1978; 1000 khz AM; 1 kw-D, NDD; N35 10 10 W114 38 2
50 E. Rivercenter Blvd, Suite 180, Covington, KY 41011 US
(928) 763-5586, *Fax:* (520) 763-3775
http://www.kflg947.com
License: Bullhead City, AZ held by Cameron Broadcasting Inc.
Group Owner: Cameron Broadcasting Inc.; acq 11-24-99).
Arbitron Metro Market: Bullhead City, AZ *Format:* Country *Special Programming:* Country Classic Sunday 10-2, American Country Countdown Sunday am *Target Audience:* 18-64
Billy Williams, CEO
Craig Powers, Operations Dir
Don Jaeger, General Manager
Mike Fletcher, General Sales Mgr
Dave Cooper, Chief Engineer

*KVIR
89.9 mhz FM; 9.1 kw vert; 2329 ft.; N35 15 8 W114 44 58
3000 W. Macarthur Blvd., Santa Ana, CA 92704 US
(800) 357-4226, *Fax:* (208) 736-1958
www.csnradio.com
License: Bullhead City, Mohave County, AZ held by CSN International.
Group Owner: CSN International
Arbitron Metro Market: Bullhead City, AZ *Format:* Christian
Mike Kestler, President
Daniel Davidson, Operations Dir
Don Mills, Programming Director
Kelly Carlson, Engineering Dir
Ray Gorney, Assistant Director of Engineering
Austin Morris, Accounting

Camp Verde

KAJM
07-04-1984; 104.3 mhz FM *Hrs Open:* 24; 40 kw; 2648 ft.; N34 13 47 W112 21 3
7434 E. Stetson Drive, Suite 255, Scottsdale, AZ 85251 US
(480) 994-9100, *Fax:* (480) 423-8770
www.mega1043.com
info@mega1043.com
License: Camp Verde, Yavapai County, AZ held by Sierra H. Broadcasting Inc.
Nat'l Network: Westwood One; CNN Radio *Nat'l Reps:* Roslin
Arbitron Metro Market: Scottsdale, AZ *Format:* Blues *Target Audience:* 25-54; general *Adv. Rates:* 100; 80; 100; 60
Steven Szalay, Operations Dir
Michael Mallace, General Manager
Jack Preda, General Sales Mgr
Fred Rico, Programming Director
Matt Kirkpatrick, Promotions Manager

Michael Day, Chief Engineer
Alex Santa Maria, Music Director

Casas Adobes

KZLZ
08-31-1991; 105.3 mhz FM *Hrs Open:* 24; 0.58 kw; 1906 ft.; N32 14 56 W111 6 58
1436 Auburn Bluevard, Sacramento, CA 95815 US
(530) 325-3054, *Fax:* (530) 325-3495
www.lapoderosakzlz.com
sonia@kzlzradio.com
License: Casas Adobes, Pinal County, AZ held by KZLZ LLC.
Group Owner: KZLZ LLC; (acq 12-1-2006; $4.75 million)
Arbitron Metro Market: Casas Adobes, AZ *Target Audience:* General.
Sonya Tabanico, General Manager
Cesar Zalciora, Programming Director

Cave Creek

KFNX
06-27-1997; 1100 khz AM *Hrs Open:* 24; 50 kw-D, DA2; 1 kw-N, DA2; N33 47 52 W111 59 30
1185 N. Main Street, Providence, RI 02904 US
(602) 277-1100, *Fax:* (602) 248-1478
www.1100kfnx.com
info@1100kfnx.com
License: Cave Creek, AZ held by Premier Radio Stations, LLC
Nat'l Network: CNN Radio *Regional Network:* Arizona News Radio *Wire Services:* CNN
Arbitron Metro Market: Phoenix, AZ *Format:* Talk *No. News Employees:* 1 *Target Audience:* 35 plus; Upscale *Adv. Rates:* 75; 75; 75; 50
Francis Battaglia, CEO

Chandler

KMLE
04-18-1980; 107.9 mhz FM *Hrs Open:* 24; 96 kw; 1736 ft.; N33 20 3 W112 3 43
C/O 300 Crescent Court, Suite 600, Dallas, TX 75201 US
(602) 452-1000, *Fax:* (602) 230-2116
www.kmle108.com
License: Chandler, Maricopa County, AZ held by Infinity Radio Inc.
Group Owner: CBS Radio; (acq 8-7-00; grpsl).
Arbitron Metro Market: Phoenix, AZ *Format:* Country *Special Programming:* Camel Views one hr wkly *No. News Employees:* 2 *Target Audience:* 25-54.
Amy Leimbach, General Sales Mgr
Kris Abrams, Programming Director
Mark Waters, Promotions Manager
Doc Holiday, Music Director

Chinle

KFXR-FM
08-01-1995; 107.3 mhz FM *Hrs Open:* 24; 3.6 kw; 1631 ft.; N36 21 7 W109 49 54 *Rebroadcasts:* Rebroadcasts KGLX(FM) Gallup
427 Bedford Road, Pleasantville, NY 10570 US
(505) 863-9391, *Fax:* (505) 863-9393
License: Chinle, Apache County, AZ held by CC Licenses LLC.
Group Owner: Clear Channel Communications Inc.; (acq 8-18-2000).
Arbitron Metro Market: Dallas, TX *Format:* Country
Mary Armijo, General Manager

Chino Valley

KDDL
01-01-1999; 94.3 mhz FM; 4.1 kw; 810 ft.; N34 49 32 W112 34 9
530 Wilshire Blvd., Suite 301, Santa Monica, CA 90401 US
(928) 775-2530, *Fax:* (928) 775-2532
www.kfpbradio.com
License: Chino Valley, Yavapai County, AZ held by Prescott Valley Broadcasting Co. Inc.
Group Owner: Prescott Valley Broadcasting Co. Inc.; (acq 10-15-2007; $1.2 million)
Format: Country
Patti Esell, General Manager

Claypool

KIKO-FM
08-01-1991; 97.3 mhz FM *Hrs Open:* 24; 0.67 kw; 3323 ft.; N33 17 20 W110 49 45
4501 Broadway, Miami, AZ 85539 US
(928) 425-4471, *Fax:* (928) 425-9393
radiokiko@cableone.net
License: Claypool, Gila County, AZ held by 1TV.com Inc.
Group Owner: 1TV.Com Inc.; (acq 4-30-2008; $1.025 million with KIKO(AM) Miami)
Nat'l Network: Jones Radio Networks
Format: Adult Contemp *Hrs. of News Programming:* news progmg 6 hrs wkly *No. News Employees:* 1 *Target Audience:* 21-55; blue collar, housewives, white collar *Adv. Rates:* 12; 12; 12; 12
Shelly Harrison, General Manager
Chelle Hodson, Office Manager

Clifton

KCUZ
07-31-1969; 1490 khz AM *Hrs Open:* 24; 1 kw-U, ND1; N33 2 30 W109 17 40 *Rebroadcasts:* Rebroadcasts KFMM(FM) Thatcher 100%
Mailing Address: C/O Frank H. Newell, P.O. Box 567, Green Valley, AZ 85622 US
Second Address: 301 B Hwy. 70 E., Safford, AZ 85546
(928) 428-0916, *Fax:* (928) 428-7797
www.saffordradio.com
kfmm@eaznet.com
License: Clifton, AZ held by Cochise Broadcasting LLC.
Group Owner: Cochise Broadcasting LLC; (acq 6-30-2007; $330,000 with KFMM(FM) Thatcher)
Format: Classic Rock *Special Programming:* Relg 2 hrs, loc talk 8 hrs wkly *Hrs. of News Programming:* news progmg 7 hrs wkly *No. News Employees:* 1 *Target Audience:* 25-54. *Adv. Rates:* 12; 12; 12; 12.
Rick Schneider, General Manager
Darwin Morris, Programming Director

KWRQ
10-01-1986; 102.3 mhz FM *Hrs Open:* 24; 4.3 kw; 2264 ft.; N32 53 23 W109 19 26
Mailing Address: 1413 Santa Paula Drive, Modesto, CA 95355 US
Second Address: 3335 West 8th St., Thatcher, AZ 85552
(928) 428-1020, *Fax:* (928) 428-6818(928) 428-1311
www.mysouthernaz.com
traffic@mcmurrayradio.com
License: Clifton, Greenlee County, AZ held by McMurray Communications Inc.
Group Owner: McMurray Communications Inc.; acq 11-97; $350,000)
Nat'l Network: Jones Radio Networks
Arbitron Metro Market: Safford, AZ *Format:* Adult Contemp
Target Audience: 20-35; working females
Bud McMurray, President
Reed Richins, Operations Dir
Davis Nathan, General Manager
William Perry, News Director
Davis Nathan, Radio Ad Sales
Lee Patterson, Sports

Colorado City

KXFF
01-01-1993; 107.3 mhz FM *Hrs Open:* 24; 35 kw; 1138 ft.; N37 5 41 W113 11 6
P.O. Box 711, Colorado City, AZ 86021 US
(435) 673-3579, *Fax:* (435) 673-8900
www.107thefoxonline.com
dhiatt@cherrycreekradio.com
License: Colorado City, Mohave County, AZ held by CCR-St. George IV LLC.
Group Owner: Cherry Creek Radio LLC; (acq 5-3-2006; grpsl)
Arbitron Metro Market: St. George, UT *Format:* Oldies
Chris McCarthy, General Sales Mgr
Rick Parrish, Promotions Manager

Coolidge

KCKY
11-19-1964; 1150 khz AM *Hrs Open:* 18; 5 kw-D, DA2; 1 kw-N, DA2; N33 0 27 W111 32 54
13968 N Harmony Road, Coolidge, AZ 85228 US
(602) 426-1150, *Fax:* (602) 276-8119
License: Coolidge, AZ held by Cortaro Broadcasting Corp.
Arbitron Metro Market: Phoenix, AZ *Format:* Christian *No. News Employees:* 1 *Target Audience:* General.
Moses Herrera, President
Moses Herrera Jr., Station Manager

Cordes Lakes

KNRJ
01-01-2000; 101.1 mhz FM *Hrs Open:* 24; 40 kw; 807 meters; N34 13 47 W112 21 03
7434 E. Stetson Dr., Suite 255, Scottsdale, AZ 85377
(480) 994-9100,(800) 254-7510, *Fax:* (480) 423-8770
www.azthebeat.com
info@energyarizonafm.com
License: Cordes Lakes, Gila County, AZ held by Sierra H. Broadcasting Inc.
Nat'l Network: Westwood One; CNN Radio
Arbitron Metro Market: Phoenix, AZ *Adv. Rates:* 100; 80; 100; 60
Steve Szalay, Operations Dir
Michael Mallace, General Manager
Rod Carrillo, Programming Director

Cortaro

KVOI
09-23-1953; 1030 khz AM; 10 kw-D, DA2; 1 kw-N, DA2; N32 20 51 W111 4 19
16418 South 43rd Place, Phoenix, AZ 85044 US
(520) 790-2440, *Fax:* (520) 790-2937
www.kvoi.com
info@kvoi.com
License: Cortaro, AZ held by Good News Broadcasting Inc.
Group Owner: Good News Communications Inc.; (acq 9-53).
Nat'l Reps: Salem
Arbitron Metro Market: Tucson, AZ *Format:* News, Talk *Hrs. of News Programming:* news progmg 10 hrs wkly *No. News Employees:* 1 *Target Audience:* 35 plus.
Doug Martin, President
Ray Alan, Operations Dir
Mary Martin, General Sales Mgr
Larry Massey, Chief Engineer

Cottonwood

KVRD-FM
07-01-1991; 105.7 mhz FM *Hrs Open:* 24; 0.3 kw; 2556 ft.; N34 41 12 W112 7 0
Mailing Address: P.O. Box 187, Cottonwood, AZ 86326 US
Second Address: 3405 E. Hwy. 89 A, Bldg. A, Cottonwood, AZ 86326
(928) 634-2286, *Fax:* (928) 634-2295
www.kvrdfm.com
License: Cottonwood, Yavapai County, AZ
Group Owner: Yavapai Broadcasting Corp.
Arbitron Metro Market: Cottonwood, AZ *Format:* Country *Hrs. of News Programming:* News progmg 2 hrs wkly *Target Audience:* General.
Mark Bachman, Programming Director
Paul David, News Director

KYBC
12-20-1964; 1600 khz AM *Hrs Open:* 24; 1 kw-D, ND1; 0.046 kw-N, ND1; N34 43 15 W111 59 55
Mailing Address: P.O. Box 187, Cottonwood, AZ 86326 US
Second Address: 3405 E. Hwy. 89 A, Bldg. A, Cottonwood, AZ 86326
(928) 634-2286, *Fax:* (928) 634-2295
www.myradioplace.com
kybc@myradioplace.com
License: Cottonwood, AZ held by Yavapai Broadcasting Corp.
Group Owner: Yavapai Broadcasting Corp.; acq 1-96; $750,000 with co-located FM).
Nat'l Network: Westwood One
Arbitron Metro Market: Cottowood, AZ *Format:* Adult Contemp
No. News Employees: 2 *Target Audience:* 18-plus.
W. Grant Hafley, President
David Kessel, General Manager
Mike Puetz, General Sales Mgr
Paul Siabe, Programming Director
Paul David, News Director

KKLD
08-01-1983; 95.9 mhz FM *Hrs Open:* 24; 21 kw; 2621 ft.; N34 41 12 W112 7 2
2690 E. Huntington Drive, Flagstaff, AZ 86004 US
(928) 634-2286, *Fax:* (928) 634-2295
www.kkld.com
License: Cottonwood, Yavapai County, AZ held by Yavapai Broadcasting Corp.
Group Owner: Yavapai Broadcasting Corp.; (acq 10-1-2000; grpsl).
Arbitron Metro Market: Cottonwood, AZ *Format:* Oldies *Hrs. of News Programming:* News progmg 7 hrs wkly *Target Audience:* 18-49.
W. Grant Hafley, President
Rich Malone, Operations Dir
David Kessel, General Manager

Desert Hills

KRRK
09-09-1974; 100.7 mhz FM *Hrs Open:* 24; 0.275 kw; 2697 ft.; N34 33 6 W114 11 37

2068 McCulloch Blvd, Lake Havasu City, AZ 86403 US
(928) 855-1051, *Fax:* (928) 855-7996
www.maddog.net
info@maddog.net
License: Desert Hills, Mohave County, AZ held by Smoke and Mirrors LLC.
Group Owner: Smoke and Mirrors LLC; (acq 11-29-99)
Arbitron Metro Market: Lake Havasu City, AZ *Format:* Light Rock *Hrs. of News Programming:* news progmg 5 hrs wkly *No. News Employees:* 1 *Target Audience:* 18-34.
Kim Turner, Operations Dir
Scott Gosselin, General Manager

Dewey-Humboldt

KMVA
01-15-1988; 97.5 mhz FM *Hrs Open:* 24; 42 kw; 2785 ft.; N34 14 5 W112 22 2
2690 E. Huntington Drive, Flagstaff, AZ 86004 US
(602) 222-9750, *Fax:* (602) 222-2297
www.movin975.com
License: Dewey-Humboldt, Yavapai County, AZ held by Trumper Communications III License LLC
Arbitron Metro Market: Phoenix, AZ *Format:* Oldies
Jeff Trumper, CEO
Jim Ryan, General Sales Mgr
Bob Lewis, Programming Director

Dolan Springs

KOAS
01-07-1976; 105.7 mhz FM *Hrs Open:* 24; kw
50 E. Rivercenter Blvd., Suite 180, Covington, KY 41011 US
(702) 730-0030, *Fax:* (702) 736-8447
www.1057theoasis.com
License: Dolan Springs, Mohave County, AZ held by RBG Las Vegas Licenses LLC.
Group Owner: Riviera Broadcast Group LLC; (acq 10-3-2005; $38 million with KVGS(FM) Laughlin, NV)
Arbitron Metro Market: Las Vegas, NV *Format:* Jazz, Smooth Jazz *Target Audience:* 25-64 *Adv. Rates:* 55; 55; 55; 35
Justin Chase, Operations Dir
Tom Humm, General Manager
Lee Grau, General Sales Mgr
Courtney Smith, Promotions Manager
Ray Fodge, Chief Engineer

*KLKI
91.9 mhz FM; 30 kw vert; Ant 2,893 ft; N35 06 35 W113 52 51
Box 2440, Tupelo, MS 38803
(662) 844-8888, *Fax:* (662) 842-6791
License: Dolan Springs, Mohave County, AZ held by American Family Association.
Group Owner: American Family Radio
Donald Wildmon, Chairman

Doney Park

KZXK
01-01-2009; 98.9 mhz FM; 0.14 kw; 2001 ft.; N35 14 26 W111 35 51
US
(703) 812-0482
License: Doney Park, Coconino County, AZ held by Cochise Broadcasting LLC.
Group Owner: Cochise Broadcasting LLC
Arbitron Metro Market: Doney Park, AZ
Ted Tucker, General Manager

Douglas

KAPR
03-08-1958; 930 khz AM *Hrs Open:* 24; 2.5 kw-D, ND1; 0.071 kw-N, ND1; N31 22 8 W109 31 45 *Rebroadcasts:* KVOI
3434 Washington Avenue, Douglas, AZ 85607 US
(520) 790-2440, *Fax:* (520) 790-2937
www.kvoi.com
info@kvoi.com
License: Douglas, AZ held by Good Music Inc.
Group Owner: Good News Communications Inc.; (acq 6-8-2001; $187,500)
Nat'l Network: Salem Radio Network *Nat'l Reps:* Salem
Arbitron Metro Market: Tuscon, AZ *Format:* News, News/Talk, 86 *Hrs. of News Programming:* News progmg 2 hrs wkly *Target Audience:* General. *Adv. Rates:* 5; 5; 5; 5
Doug Martin, CEO
Ed Alexander, Operations Dir
Mary Martin, General Sales Mgr
Mary Martin, Promotions Manager
Rhonda Curtis, CFO

KDAP
01-01-1946; 1450 khz AM; 1 kw-U, ND1; N31 21 18 W109 33 6
Mailing Address: 1445 West Baseline Road, Phoenix, AZ 85041 US
Second Address: 2031 N. Sulphur Springs St., Douglas, AZ 85607
(520) 364-3486(520) 364-3484, *Fax:* (520) 364-3483
License: Douglas, AZ held by Howard N. Henderson
Target Audience: General; loc Hispanic & Mexican residents
Howard Henderson, General Manager

KCDQ
03-15-1979; 95.3 mhz FM *Hrs Open:* 24; 0.8 kw; 39 ft.; N31 22 8 W109 31 45
3434 Washington Avenue, Douglas, AZ 85607 US
(520) 459-8201, *Fax:* (520) 458-7104
www.kcdq.com
License: Douglas, Cochise County, AZ held by Cochise Broadcasting LLC
Group Owner: Cochise Broadcasting LLC; (acq 6-8-2001; $137,500).
Nat'l Network: Westwood One
Arbitron Metro Market: Sierra Vista, AZ *Format:* Contemporary Hits/Top 40 *Hrs. of News Programming:* News progmg 11 hrs wkly *Target Audience:* 29-49.
Ted Tucker, General Manager
Jeff Davenport, Station Manager

*KRMC
01-01-1996; 91.7 mhz FM; 3 kw; 236 ft.; N31 20 52 W109 28 42
Box 3333, McAllen, TX 78502 US
(520) 287-5206, *Fax:* (520) 364-5392
www.knog.org
License: Douglas, Cochise County, AZ held by World Radio Network Inc.
Arbitron Metro Market: Nogalas, AZ *Format:* Spanish
David Johnson, President
Glen Lafitte, General Manager
James Heck, Engineering Dir

Drake

*KJZA
89.5 mhz FM *Hrs Open:* 24; 0.25 kw; 2526 ft.; N35 12 0 W112 12 18
R.R. Box 308, Perkinsville, AZ 86334 US
(928) 541-1008
www.kjza.org
kjzafm@yahoo.com
License: Drake, Yavapai County, AZ held by St. Paul Bible College.
Nat'l Network: NPR; PRI
Arbitron Metro Market: Kingman, AZ *Format:* Jazz
Nichole Erickson, Director & President
Tom Erickson, General Manager
Tom Erickson, KJZA Sales

Duncan

KJIK
01-01-2003; 100.7 mhz FM *Hrs Open:* 24; 9.73 kw; 2349 ft.; N32 53 21 W109 19 20
1491 Thatcher Blvd., Safford, AZ 85546 US
(928) 428-4100, *Fax:* (928) 348-9581
www.kjik.fm
traffic@kjk.fm
License: Duncan, Greenlee County, AZ held by Country Mountain Airwaves LLC.
Group Owner: Country Mountain Airwaves LLC
Arbitron Metro Market: Duncan, AZ *Format:* Adult Contemp
Dan Curtis, General Manager
Roger Martin, Advertising
Roger Martin, Account Manager

Eagar

KTHQ
01-01-1996; 92.5 mhz FM *Hrs Open:* 24; 62 kw; 1178 ft.; N34 15 6 W109 35 6
1491 Thatcher Blvd, Safford, AZ 85546 US
(928) 532-1010, *Fax:* (928) 532-0101
www.Qcountry92.com
mail@qcountry92.com
License: Eagar, Apache County, AZ held by Country Mountain Airwaves LLC.
Group Owner: Country Mountain Airwaves LLC
Arbitron Metro Market: Show Low, AZ *Format:* Country
Camden Smith, General Manager
Laurie Pogson, News Director

Flagstaff

KAFF
10-15-1963; 930 khz AM *Hrs Open:* 5 AM-midnight; 5 kw-D, 50 w-N; N35 11 26 W111 40 37
Mailing Address: 1117 W. Rt. 66, Flagstaff, AZ 86001
Second Address: 1117 W. Hwy. 66, Flagstaff, AZ 86001
(928) 774-5231, *Fax:* (928) 779-2988
ww.kaff.com
License: Flagstaff, Coconino County, AZ held by Guyann Inc.
Group Owner: Guyann Corp.; (acq 9-7-2005; grpsl).
Wire Services: AP
Population Served: 492,000 *Arbitron Metro Market:* Flagstaff, AZ *No. News Employees:* 2 *Target Audience:* 25-54.
Janie Richardson, General Manager
Chris Halstead, Programming Director
Val Barret, Promotions Manager
George Davis, News Director
Jon Swett, Chief Engineer
Hugh Morris, Music Director

KAFF-FM
10-01-1968; 92.9 mhz FM *Hrs Open:* 24; 98 kw; 1512 ft.; N34 58 7 W111 30 24
P. O. Box 1930, Flagstaff, AZ 86002 US
(928) 774-5231, *Fax:* (928) 779-2988
www.kaff.com
production@kaff.com
License: Flagstaff, Coconino County, AZ held by Guyann Inc.
Group Owner: Guyann Corp.
Nat'l Network: ABC *Wire Services:* AP
Arbitron Metro Market: Flagstaff, AZ *Hrs. of News Programming:* News progmg 4 hrs wkly *No. News Employees:* 2
Don Hurley, Programming Director
Scotty Kvipers, Promotions Manager
Bill Baker, News Reporter
Steve Sandmeyer, News Reporter
Mikelanne Burk, News Reporter
Krista Kay, Disc Jockey
Like Caus, Disc Jockey
Lynn Roberts, DiscJockey

*KJTA
12-19-2001; 89.9 mhz FM *Hrs Open:* 24; 1 kw; 1988 ft.; N35 14 25 W111 35 49
341 S. Washington, Lancaster, WI 53813 US
(928) 774-9514, *Fax:* (928) 774-9515
License: Flagstaff, Coconino County, AZ held by Family Life Broadcasting Inc.
Group Owner: Family Life Communications Inc.; (acq 5-23-2007; grpsl)
Format: Christian
Dawn Bumstead, Programming Director

KVNA-FM
01-01-1999; 100.1 mhz FM *Hrs Open:* 24; 5.2 kw; 1434 ft.; N34 58 5 W111 30 29
P. O. Box 1488, Sedona, AZ 86339 US
(928) 526-2700, *Fax:* (928) 634-2295
www.myradioplace.com
License: Flagstaff, Coconino County, AZ held by Yavapai Broadcasting Corp.
Group Owner: Yavapai Broadcasting Corp.; (acq 5-2-2005; $1.5 million).
Arbitron Metro Market: Flagstaff, AZ *Format:* Adult Contemp
Dave Kessel, General Manager

KMGN
01-01-1975; 93.9 mhz FM *Hrs Open:* 24; 96 kw; 1509 ft.; N34 58 8 W111 30 28
Mailing Address: P.O. Box 1930, Flagstaff, AZ 86002 US
Second Address: 1117 W Rt. 66, Flagstaff, AZ 86001
(928) 774-5231, *Fax:* (928) 779-2988
www.kmgn.com
info@kmgn.com
License: Flagstaff, Coconino County, AZ held by Guyann Corp.
Group Owner: Guyann Corp.; (acq 9-7-2005; grpsl)
Nat'l Network: ABC *Wire Services:* AP
Format: Classic Rock *Hrs. of News Programming:* news progmg 4 hrs wkly *No. News Employees:* 2 *Target Audience:* 25-54; upscale, educated, rgnl audience
Janie Richardson, General Manager
Rob Dowers, Programming Director

*KPUB
10-01-1995; 91.7 mhz FM *Hrs Open:* 24; 0.5 kw; 1837 ft.; N35 14 34 W111 36 40
Post Office Box 5764, Flagstaff, AZ 87011 US
(928) 523-5628, *Fax:* (928) 523-7647
www.knau.org
knau@nau.edu

RADIO - U.S.

License: Flagstaff, Coconino County, AZ held by Northern Arizona University.
Nat'l Network: NPR; PRI
Format: News *Hrs. of News Programming:* News progmg 50 hrs wkly *Target Audience:* 25-54; educated, socially conscious achievers
Dave Riek, Operations Dir
John Stark, General Manager
Liz Gumerman, General Sales Mgr
Jeff Norcross, Programming Director
Don Kraker, News Director
Lisa Skinner, Traffic Manager

***KNAU**
11-24-1970; 88.7 mhz FM *Hrs Open:* 24; 100 kw; 1460 ft.; N34 58 7 W111 30 24
P.O. Box 5764, Flagstaff, AZ 86001 US
(928) 523-5628, *Fax:* (928) 523-7647
www.knau.org
knau@nau.edu
License: Flagstaff, Coconino County, AZ held by Arizona Board of Regents for and on behalf of Northern Arizona University.
Nat'l Network: NPR; PRI
Format: News *Hrs. of News Programming:* news progmg 50 hrs wkly *No. News Employees:* 3 *Target Audience:* 25-54; educated, socially conscious achievers
Dave Riek, Operations Dir
John Stark, General Manager
Liz Gumerman, General Sales Mgr
Jeff Norcross, Programming Director
Dan Kraker, News Director
Jon Swett, Chief Engineer
Annie Cushler, Business Manager

KVNA
08-08-1950; 600 khz AM *Hrs Open:* 24; 1 kw-D, ND1; 0.048 kw-N, ND1; N35 12 2 W111 36 49
2690 E. Huntington Drive, Flagstaff, AZ 86004 US
(928) 526-2700, *Fax:* (928) 774-5852
www.myradioplace.com/am600/am600.htm
am600@radioflagstaff.com
License: Flagstaff, AZ held by Yavapai Broadcasting Corp.
Group Owner: Yavapai Broadcasting Corp.; (acq 9-30-2000; grpsl).
Nat'l Network: Westwood One; AP Network News; Jones Radio Networks *Regional Network:* Arizona News Radio
Arbitron Metro Market: Flagstaff-Prescott, AZ *Format:* News, News/Talk, 84, Talk *Special Programming:* Sp 3 hrs wkly, folk music 4hrs wkly *Hrs. of News Programming:* news progmg 25 hrs wkly *No. News Employees:* 1*Target Audience:* General.
Adv. Rates: 12; 12; 12; 12
W. Hafley, President
Mike Dougal, Operations Dir
David Kessel, General Manager
Mike Dougall, News Director

KZGL
01-01-2007; 103.7 mhz FM; 0.56 kw; 1959 ft.; N35 14 25 W111 35 53
US
(928) 779-1037
www.eagle1037.fm
studio@eagle1037.fm
License: Flagstaff, Coconino County, AZ held by Walker Radio Inc.
Format: Triple A
James Walker, President
Rob Dowers, Operations Dir
Paul Lancaster, General Manager

Florence

KCDX
01-01-1999; 103.1 mhz FM; 2.7 kw; 3058 ft.; N33 17 55 W110 50 28
P.O. Box 36717, Tucson, AZ 85740 US
(520) 459-8201, *Fax:* (520) 458-7104
www.kcdx.com
License: Florence, Pinal County, AZ held by Desert West Air Ranchers Corp.
Format: Classic Rock
Ted Tucker, General Manager

Fountain Hills

***KLVK**
05-01-2000; 89.1 mhz FM *Hrs Open:* 24; 30 kw; 2306 ft.; N33 35 33 W112 34 49
1425 N. Market Blvd., Suite 9, Sacramento, CA 95834 US
(800) 525-5683
www.klove.com
klove@klove.com
License: Fountain Hills, Maricopa County, AZ held by Educational Media Foundation.
Group Owner: EMF Broadcasting; (acq 3-11-03; grpsl).
Nat'l Network: K-Love
Arbitron Metro Market: Omaha, NB *Format:* Christian *No. News Employees:* 3 *Target Audience:* 25-33; Judeo Christian, female
Darrell Chambliss, Chairman
Mike Novak, President
Dan Beck, General Sales Mgr
David Pierce, Programming Director
Ed Lenane, News Director
Sam Wallington, Engineering Dir
Marya Morgan, News Reporter
Richard Hunt, NewsReporter

Gilbert

KEXX(FM)
02-25-1981; 103.9 mhz FM *Hrs Open:* 24; 99.59 kw; Ant 620 ft; N33 14 50 W111 31 49
7434 E. Stetson Dr., Suite 265, Scottsdale, AZ 85251
(480) 423-9255, *Fax:* (480) 423-9382
www.theedge1039.com
nat@theedge1039.com
License: Gilbert, Pinal County, AZ held by RBG Phoenix Licenses LLC
Group Owner: Riviera Broadcast Group LLC; (acq 11-21-2005; $30 million).
Nat'l Reps: Roslin
Population Served: 1,446,948 *Arbitron Metro Market:* Phoenix, AZ *Hrs. of News Programming:* News progmg 2 hrs wkly *Target Audience:* 18-34. *Adv. Rates:* 200; 175; 175; 125
Tim Pohlman, CEO
Nat Galvin, Operations Dir

Glendale

KPXQ
01-01-1946; 1360 khz AM *Hrs Open:* 24
4880 Santa Rosa Road, Suite 300, Camarillo, CA 93012 US
(602) 955-9600, *Fax:* (602) 955-7860
www.kpxq1360.com
info@kpxq1360.com
License: Glendale, AZ held by Common Ground Broadcasting Inc.
Group Owner: Salem Communications Corp.; (acq 6-23-99; $5 million)
Nat'l Network: Salem Radio Network *Nat'l Reps:* Salem
Arbitron Metro Market: Phoenix, AZ *Format:* Talk, Religious *Hrs. of News Programming:* news progmg 6 hrs wkly *No. News Employees:* 1 *Target Audience:* 25-54; adults
Edward Atsinger, CEO
Stuart Epperson, President
Jon Horton, Operations Dir
Diane Zapponi-Paisley, General Manager
Heath Garlutzo, General Sales Mgr
Rachel Van Hofwegen, Promotions Manager
Diane Johnson, News Director
JohnBortowski, Chief Engineer
Joe Davis, Executive Vice President
Laurie Larson, Operations Manager

KTAR-FM
12-19-1979; 92.3 mhz FM; 98 kw; 1788 ft.; N33 19 58 W112 3 48
300 Crescent Court, Suite 600, Austin, TX 75201 US
(602) 274-6200, *Fax:* (602) 266-3858
www.ktar.com
newsradio620@ktar.com
License: Glendale, Maricopa County, AZ held by Bonneville Holding Co.
Group Owner: Bonneville International Corporation; (acq 7-11-2006; $77.5 million).
Arbitron Metro Market: Phoenix, AZ *Format:* News, News/Talk, 86 *Target Audience:* 18-49.
Erik Hellum, Operations Dir
Brett Rogers, General Sales Mgr
Russ Hill, Programming Director

KLNZ
09-01-1997; 103.5 mhz FM *Hrs Open:* 24; 48 kw; 2428 ft.; N33 35 33 W112 34 49
1436 Auburn Boulevard, Sacramento, CA 95815 US
(602) 266-2005, *Fax:* (602) 279-2921
www.entravision.com
info@entravision.com
License: Glendale, Maricopa County, AZ held by Entravision Holdings LLC.
Group Owner: Entravision Communications Corp.; (acq 7-28-00; grpsl).
Arbitron Metro Market: Phoenix, AZ *Format:* Tejano *Target Audience:* General.
Tom Duran, General Manager
Chris Moncayo, General Sales Mgr
Carrie Strait, Programming Director
Ryan Oller, Chief Engineer

Globe

KQMR
09-25-1980; 100.3 mhz FM *Hrs Open:* 24; 90 kw; 2047 ft.; N33 17 23 W110 51 53
11 Skyline Drive, Hawthorne, NY 10532 US
(602) 308-7900, *Fax:* (602) 308-7979
www.univision.com
License: Globe, Gila County, AZ held by Univision Radio License Corp.
Group Owner: Univision Radio; (acq 9-22-2003; grpsl).
Arbitron Metro Market: Phoenix, AZ *Format:* Spanish *Target Audience:* 18-49; upscale, well-educated, affluent adults
Mary McEvilly-Hernandez, Operations Dir
Chris Morris, General Sales Mgr
Dobby White, News Director
Nelson Oseida, Operations Director
Kevin Norgaard, Research Director

KJAA
01-01-1971; 1240 khz AM *Hrs Open:* 24; 1 kw-U, ND1; N33 22 51 W110 45 25 *Rebroadcasts:* KVOI
1240 South Saguaro Drive, Globe, AZ 85501 US
(520) 790-2440, *Fax:* (520) 790-2937
www.kvoi.com
info@kvoi.com
License: Globe, AZ held by 1TV.Com Inc.
Group Owner: 1TV.Com Inc.; (acq 11-7-2008; $300,000)
Format: News, News/Talk, 86 *Hrs. of News Programming:* 3 hrs wkly *No. News Employees:* 3 *Target Audience:* 35 plus. *Adv. Rates:* 5; 5; 5; 5
Doug Martin, General Manager

KRDE
10-13-1995; 94.1 mhz FM *Hrs Open:* 24; 4.7 kw; 1039 Meters HAAT; N33 17 37 W110 50 09
Mailing Address: Box 1660, Globe, AZ 85203
Second Address: 800 N. Main St., Globe, AZ 85501
(928) 402-9222, *Fax:* (928) 425-5063
www.krde.com
krde@cableone.net
License: Globe, Gila County, AZ held by Linda C. Corso.
Nat'l Network: Fox News Radio; Westwood One *Regional Network:* Arizona News Radio *Regional Reps:* Arizona News Network
Population Served: 2,000,000 *Arbitron Metro Market:* Phoenix, AZ *Special Programming:* Country Convoy *Hrs. of News Programming:* news progmg 20 hrs wkly *No. News Employees:* 1 *Target Audience:* 25-54;active, family building, western suburban *Adv. Rates:* 45; 35; 15; 10
Linda Corso, Operations Dir
Linda Corso, General Manager
Mindy Ersey, Station Manager
Mindy Ersey, Programming Director
Mondy Ersey, Promotions Manager
Sean Cram, News/Web Director
Brad Hartman, Sport - Fishing

***KVJC**
01-01-2003; 91.9 mhz FM *Hrs Open:* 24; 0.66 kw; 3396 ft.; N33 17 37 W110 50 9
3000 W. Macarthur Blvd., Santa Ana, CA 92704 US
(800) 357-4226, *Fax:* (208) 736-1958
www.csnradio.com
csn@csnradio.com
License: Globe, Gila County, AZ held by CSN International
Group Owner: CSN International
Arbitron Metro Market: Phoenix, AZ *Format:* Christian
Mike Kestler, President
Daniel Davidson, Operations Dir
Mike Stocklin, General Manager
Don Mills, Network Programming Director / Music Director
Kelly Carlson, Engineering Dir
Jerry Johnson, Engineering Dir
Ray Gorney, AssistantDirector of Engineering
Dustin Pamplona, Engineer
Nolan Mather, Graphics / Website Maintenance
Mike Stocklin, National Underwriting
Austin Morris, Accounting
Lois Mills, FCC Applications / Translator Site Manager

***KLKA**
01-01-2008; 88.5 mhz FM; 1.5 kw vert; 2986 ft.; N33 17 55 W110 50 28 *Rebroadcasts:* Rebroadcasts KVLT(FM) Temple, TX 100%
1601 Belvedere Rd 204 E, West Palm Beach, FL 33406 US

(800) 525-5683, *Fax:* (916) 251-1650
www.klove.com
klove@klove.com
License: Globe, Gila County, AZ held by American Educational Broadcasting Inc.
Nat'l Network: K-Love
Arbitron Metro Market: Globe, AZ *Format:* Christian *No. News Employees:* 13
Darrell Chambliss, Chairman
Mike Novak, President and CEO
James Auel, General Manager
David Pierce, Programming Director
Ed Lenane, News Director
Sam Wallington, Engineering Dir
Dan Antonelli, Chief Business DevelopmentOfficer
Eric Moser, Chief Financial Officer
Brian Burger, Vice President of Human Resources
D. Kevin Blair, Secretary and General Counsel
Tim Luttrell, News Reporter

Golden Valley

KYET
08-17-1992; 1170 khz AM *Hrs Open:* 24; 10 kw-D, ND1; 0.25 kw-N, ND1; N35 15 38 W112 10 55
138 West Bill Williams Avenue, Williams, AZ 86046 US
(928) 753-9100, *Fax:* (928) 753-1978
License: Golden Valley, AZ held by Grand Canyon Gateway Broadcasting L.L.C.
Rhonda Hart, President
Joe Hart, General Manager
Steve Levin, Programming Director
Dave Hawkins, News Director
Matt Krick, Engineering Dir
Deana Campbell, Traffic Manager

Grand Canyon

*KNAG
90.3 mhz FM; 3 kw; 295 ft.; N35 56 44 W112 10 16
Rebroadcasts: KNAU-FM Flagstaff 100%
P . O. Box 5764, Flagstaff, AZ 86011 US
(928) 523-5628, *Fax:* (928) 523-7647
www.knau.org
knau@nau.edu
License: Grand Canyon, Coconino County, AZ held by Arizona Board of Regents/Northern Arizona University.
Arbitron Metro Market: Flagstaff, AZ *Format:* News
Brian Sanders, Operations Director, Announcer
John Stark, General Manager
Liz Gumerman, General Sales Mgr
Cory Sheeley, Underwriting Sales Associate
Estevan Bellino, Traffic Coordinator
Howard Fischer, State Capitol Reporter
Laurel Morales, Fronteras Reporter
Mark Bevis, Content Manager
Shelly Watkins, Underwriting Manager

Green Valley

KFMA
02-20-1983; 92.1 mhz FM *Hrs Open:* 24; 50 kw; 492 ft.; N32 0 11 W110 47 49
6290 Sunset Boulevard, Hollywood, CA 90028 US
(520) 407-4500
www.kfma.com
License: Green Valley, Pima County, AZ held by Arizona Lotus Corp.
Group Owner: Lotus Communications Corp.; (acq 5-10-93; $1.26 million;
Nat'l Reps: Christal
Arbitron Metro Market: Tucson, AZ *Format:* Alternative *Special Programming:* Love night 20 hrs wkly *Target Audience:* 18-34.
Steve Groesbeck, General Manager
Ken Kwilosz, General Sales Mgr
Matt Spry, Programming Director
Jessica Allen, Promotions Manager

KNST-FM
10-21-1990; 97.1 mhz FM *Hrs Open:* 24; 1.75 kw; Ant 613 ft; N31 58 37 W111 06 04
3202 N. Oracle Rd., Tucson, AZ 85713
(520) 618-2100, *Fax:* (520) 610-2200
www.lapreclosa.com
info@lapribsa.tucson.com
License: Green Valley, Pima County, AZ held by Capstar TX L.P.
Group Owner: Clear Channel Communications Inc.
Arbitron Metro Market: Tucson, AZ *Hrs. of News Programming:* news progmg 2 hrs wkly *No. News Employees:* 2 *Target Audience:* 18-35.
Tim Richards, Operations Dir
Debbie Wagner, General Manager
Tom Zlaket, General Sales Mgr
Ruppert Pacheco, Programming Director
Nikki Van Doran, Promotions Manager
Mike Irby, Chief Engineer
Bob Seinman, Director, HispanicOperations

KGVY
09-23-1981; 1080 khz AM *Hrs Open:* 6 AM-sunset; 1 kw-D, NDD; N31 55 34 W110 59 45
Mailing Address: 1 Broadcast Center, Plano, IL 60545 US
Second Address: 1510 W. Camino Antigua, Sahuarita, AZ 85629
(520) 399-1000, *Fax:* (520) 399-9300
www.kgvy1080.com
DeAnnaS@kgvy1080.com
License: Green Valley, AZ held by KGVY LLC
Nat'l Network: ABC
Arbitron Metro Market: Tucson, AZ *Format:* Oldies *Hrs. of News Programming:* news progmg 13 hrs wkly *No. News Employees:* 2 *Target Audience:* 35 plus; mature, well educated, higher income, retired *Adv. Rates:* 31.75; 31.75; 31.75; na
James Walker, General Manager
Joey Lessa, Public Service Director

Holbrook

*KBMH
01-01-2002; 90.3 mhz FM; 0.25 kw; 141 ft.; N34 55 5 W110 8 25
P O Drawer 2440, Tupelo, MS 38803 US
(601) 844-8888, *Fax:* (662) 842-6791
License: Holbrook, Navajo County, AZ held by American Family Association.
Group Owner: American Family Radio
Format: Christian
Marvin Sanders, General Manager
John Riley, Programming Director
Joey Moody, Chief Engineer

KDJI
10-01-1955; 1270 khz AM *Hrs Open:* 9 AM-4 PM
250 N. Broadcast Lane, Holbrook, AZ 86025 US
(928) 368-8100, *Fax:* (928) 368-8108
www.970kvwm.com
production@whitemountainradio.com
License: Holbrook, AZ held by Petracom of Holbrook L.L.C.
Group Owner: White Mountain Radio
Nat'l Network: ABC; Westwood One
Format: News, News/Talk, 86 *Special Programming:* Sports 10 hrs, farm 8 hrs wkly *Target Audience:* 35-65; 46% female, 54% male
Beth Muschel, Programming Director
Kevin McCarthy, Promotions Manager

KZUA
12-06-1993; 92.1 mhz FM; 100 kw; 256 ft.; N34 55 13 W110 7 53
250 North Broadcast Dr., Holbrook, AZ 86025 US
(928) 368-8100, *Fax:* (928) 368-8108
www.921kzua.com/
production@whitemountainradio.com
License: Holbrook, Navajo County, AZ held by Petracom of Holbrook L.L.C.
Group Owner: White Mountain Radio; (acq 2-26-2002; $650,000 with co-located AM)
Nat'l Network: Westwood One; CNN Radio
Arbitron Metro Market: Holbrook, AZ. *Format:* Country *Target Audience:* 18-54; 57% female, 43% male *Adv. Rates:* 15; 12; 12; 10
Steve Johnson, General Manager
Lisa Ames, News Director

Hotevilla

*KUYI
12-20-2000; 88.1 mhz FM *Hrs Open:* 24; 69 kw; 407 ft.; N35 48 29 W110 16 23
P.O. Box 705, Hotevilla, AZ 86030 US
(928) 738-5505, *Fax:* (928) 738-5501
www.kuyi.net
info@kuyi.net
License: Hotevilla, Navajo County, AZ held by Hopi Foundation.
Arbitron Metro Market: Hotevilla, AZ *Format:* News *Hrs. of News Programming:* news progmg 6 hrs wkly *No. News Employees:* 2 *Target Audience:* 30 plus.
Maria Garcia, Operations Dir
Richard Alun Davis, Station Manager
Davis Maho, Operations Manager
Macadio Namoki, Development and Marketing Coordinator

Kachina Village

KBTK(FM)
02-01-1995; 105.1 mhz FM *Hrs Open:* 24; 1 kw; 1,968 ft; N35 14 26 W111 35 48
112 E. Rt. 66, Suite 105, Flagstaff, AZ 86001
(928) 779-1177, *Fax:* (928) 774-5179
www.1051thecanyon.com
ann@northlandradio.com
License: Kachina Village, Coconino County, AZ held by Grenax Broadcasting II LLC.
Group Owner: Grenax Broadcasting LLC; (acq 1-6-2006; grpsl)
Hrs. of News Programming: news progmg 4 hrs wkly *No. News Employees:* 1 *Target Audience:* 28-54; males
Greg Dinetz, President
Bill McAdams, Operations Dir
Jim Shipp, General Manager
Mike Mentor, Programming Director
Jon Sweat, Chief Engineer
Ann Bielinski, Business Manager
Samantha Ward, Public Affairs Director

Kaibito

*KECU
88.5 mhz FM; kw
US
(580) 265-9475
License: Kaibito, Coconino County, AZ held by Union Valley Baptist Church Inc.
Arbitron Metro Market: Eureka, CA
Steve Vandegrift, General Manager

*KCHB
90.1 mhz FM; kw
US
(918) 333-8700, *Fax:* (918) 333-3526
License: Kaibito, Coconino County, AZ held by Pearl Communications Group.
Arbitron Metro Market: Kaibito, AZ
Danny Hester, President

Kingman

KAAA
10-07-1949; 1230 khz AM
50 E. Rivercenter Blvd., Suite 180, Covington, KY 41011 US
(928) 753-2537, *Fax:* (928) 753-1551
www.talkatoz.com
office@cameronbroadcasting.com
License: Kingman, AZ held by Cameron Broadcasting Inc.
Group Owner: Cameron Broadcasting Inc.; (acq 11-24-99; grpsl)
Arbitron Metro Market: Kingman, AZ *Format:* News, News/Talk, 86 *Special Programming:* Sports *Target Audience:* 25 plus.
Don Jaeger, General Manager

KGMN
02-14-1984; 100.1 mhz FM *Hrs Open:* 24; 0.91 kw; 2897 ft.; N35 6 37 W113 52 55
812 East Beale Street, Kingman, AZ 86401 US
(928) 753-9100, *Fax:* (928) 753-1978
www.kgmn.net
rhonda@kgmn.com
License: Kingman, Mohave County, AZ held by New West Broadcasting Systems Inc.
Nat'l Network: AP Radio; Jones Radio Networks
Format: Country *Target Audience:* General
Joe Hart, CEO
Deana Campell, Operations Dir
Rhonda Hart, General Manager
Tim Andrews, Station Manager
Brian Winters, Programming Director
Deana Campell, News Director

*KJZK
90.7 mhz FM; 4.5 kw; 715 ft.; N35 10 37 W113 39 57
US
(928) 541-1008
www.kjza.org
kjzafm@yahoo.com
License: Kingman, Mohave County, AZ held by St. Paul Bible College.
Arbitron Metro Market: Kingman, AZ, Laughlin - Las Vegas, NV
Nichole Erickson, Director & President
Tom Erickson, General Manager

Lake Havasu City

KNTR
09-23-1970; 980 khz AM *Hrs Open:* 24
2068 McCulloch Blvd, Lake Havasu City, AZ 86403 US
(928) 855-9336, *Fax:* (928) 855-9333
www.kntram.com
office@myradiocentral.com
License: Lake Havasu City, AZ held by Steven M. Greeley.
Nat'l Network: PRI

Arbitron Metro Market: Lake Havasu City, AZ *Format:* News, News/Talk, 86 *Hrs. of News Programming:* news progmg 12 hrs wkly *No. News Employees:* 1 *Target Audience:* 35-64.
Steve Greeley, CEO
Traceye Jones, General Manager

KRCY-FM
01-01-1999; 96.7 mhz FM; 0.26 kw; 2707 ft.; N34 33 6 W114 11 37
1620 S. Palo Verde Ave, Lake Havasu City, AZ 86403 US
(928) 855-1051, *Fax:* (928) 855-7996
www.maddog.net
express@maddog.net
License: Lake Havasu City, Mohave County, AZ held by Rick L. Murphy.
Arbitron Metro Market: Lake Havasu City, AZ *Format:* Oldies
Rick Murphy, President

***KNLB**
07-01-1983; 91.1 mhz FM *Hrs Open:* 24; 8 kw; 453 ft.; N34 29 10 W114 13 6
Mailing Address: 510 North Acoma Blvd, Lake Havasu City, AZ 86403 US
Second Address: 510 N. Acoma Blvd., Lake Havasu City, AZ 86403
(928) 855-9110, *Fax:* (928) 453-2588
www.knlb.com
info@knlb.com
License: Lake Havasu City, Mohave County, AZ held by Advance Ministries.
Nat'l Network: USA
Format: Christian, Religious *Hrs. of News Programming:* News progmg 8 hrs wkly *Target Audience:* General.
Richard Tatham, President
Faron Eckelbarger, Station Manager

KZUL-FM
01-01-1986; 104.5 mhz FM *Hrs Open:* 24; 0.23 kw; 2671 ft.; N34 33 6 W114 11 37
2068 McCulloch Blvd, Lake Havasu City, AZ 86403 US
(928) 855-4560, *Fax:* (928) 855-7996
www.hitsandfavorites.com
epress@maddog.net
License: Lake Havasu City, Mohave County, AZ held by Mad Dog Wireless Inc.
Nat'l Network: ABC
Arbitron Metro Market: Lake Havasu City, AZ *Format:* Adult Contemp, Classic Rock *Target Audience:* 25-54.
Rick Murphy, President
Chris Rolando, Operations Dir
Ron Nickle, General Sales Mgr
Faron Ecklebarger, Chief Engineer

***KAIH**
01-01-2008; 89.3 mhz FM; 1.7 kw vert; -219 ft.; N34 27 52 W114 16 2 *Rebroadcasts:* Rebroadcasts KLRD(FM) Yucaipa, CA 100%
1425 N. Market Blvd, Suite 9, Sacramento, CA 95834 US
(888) 937-2471, *Fax:* (916) 251-1650
www.air1.com
info@air1.com
License: Lake Havasu City, Mohave County, AZ held by Educational Media Foundation.
Group Owner: EMF Broadcasting
Nat'l Network: Air 1
Arbitron Metro Market: Lake Havasu City, AZ *Format:* Alternative, Christian
Darrell Chambliss, Chairman
Alan Mason, COO
Mike Novak, President and CEO
Dan Beck, Operations Dir
David Pierce, Programming Director
Ed Lenane, News Director
Sam Wallington, Engineering Dir
Marya Morgan, News Reporter
Richard Hunt, News Reporter
Eric Moser, Chief Financial Officer
Brian Burger, Vice President of Human Resources
D. Kevin Blair, Secretary and General Counsel
Larry Moody, Director

Lake of the Woods

KZXQ
01-01-2005; 104.5 mhz FM; 0.5 kw; -751 ft.; N33 42 35 W108 45 56
P O Box 509, Ruidoso Downs, NM 88346 US
(623) 907-0267
License: Lake of the Woods, Catron County, AZ held by New Star Broadcasting LLC
Format: Talk
Karey Barbee, President
Vance Barbee, General Manager

Leupp

KQLP
101.5 mhz FM; kw
US
(512) 329-5843, *Fax:* (512) 329-5847
www.matineemedia.com
License: Leupp, McKinley County, AZ held by Ace Radio Corp.
Group Owner: Ace Radio Corp.
Arbitron Metro Market: Leupp, AZ
Stephen Hackerman, President

Mammoth

***KLTU**
88.1 mhz FM; 16 kw; 1939 ft.; N32 14 57 W111 6 57
P.O. Box 187, Humble, TX 77347 US
(800) 525-5683, *Fax:* (916) 251-1650
www.klove.com
klove@klove.com
License: Mammoth, Pinal County, AZ held by Good News Radio Broadcasting Inc.
Arbitron Metro Market: Mammoth, AZ *Format:* Christian, Gospel *No. News Employees:* 13
Darrell Chambliss, Chairman
Mike Novak, President and CEO
Doug Martin, General Manager
David Pierce, Programming Director
Ed Lenane, News Director
Sam Wallington, Engineering Dir
Dan Antonelli, Chief Business DevelopmentOfficer
Eric Moser, Chief Financial Officer
Brian Burger, Vice President of Human Resources
D. Kevin Blair, Secretary and General Counsel
Tim Luttrell, News Reporter

Marana

KOHT
10-01-1984; 98.3 mhz FM *Hrs Open:* 24; 6 kw; 184 ft.; N32 27 9 W111 5 11
889 West El Puente Lane, Tucson, AZ 85713 US
(520) 618-2100, *Fax:* (520) 618-2200
www.hot983.com
hot983comments@yahoo.com
License: Marana, Pima County, AZ held by CC Licenses LLC.
Group Owner: Clear Channel Communications Inc.; (acq 6-22-2001; grpsl).
Arbitron Metro Market: Tucson, AZ *Format:* Blues *Hrs. of News Programming:* news progmg 4 hrs wkly *No. News Employees:* 2 *Target Audience:* 18-49; Sp, contemp, white collar adults
Tim Richards, Operations Dir
Debbie Wagner, General Manager
Steve Clement, General Sales Mgr
Fred Rico, Programming Director
Mike Irby, Chief Engineer

KSAZ
01-01-1990; 580 khz AM
6381 E. Grant Road, Tucson, AZ 85715 US
(520) 298-6880, *Fax:* (520) 298-6077
www.radioebenezer580am.com/
amradio1@cox.com
License: Marana, AZ held by Owl Broadcasting & Development Inc.
Nat'l Network: ABC
Arbitron Metro Market: Tucson, AZ *Format:* Country *Special Programming:* International 2 hrs wkly *Target Audience:* 35 plus.
Benny Bee, President
Mark Wagner, General Manager

Maricopa

***KLVA**
04-08-1976; 105.5 mhz FM *Hrs Open:* 24; 50 kw; 492 ft.; N33 0 14 W111 58 53
1425 N. Market Blvd., Suite 9, Sacramento, CA 95834 US
707-528-9236, *Fax:* 707-528-9246
www.klove.com
klove@klove.com
License: Maricopa, Pinal County, AZ held by Educational Media Foundation.
Group Owner: EMF Broadcasting; (acq 7-19-99).
Nat'l Network: K-Love
Format: Christian *Special Programming:* Sports 7 hrs wkly *Target Audience:* 25-44; Judeo-Christian, female
Darell Chambliss, Chairman
Mike Novak, President
Dan Beck, Operations Dir
Eric Allen, General Sales Mgr
David Pierce, Programming Director
Ed Lenane, News Director
Sam Wallington, Engineering Dir
Scott Smith, Music Director
Marya Morgan, Scott Smith
Richard Hunt, News Reporter
Tracy Butler, Traffic Manager

Mayer

KKFR
05-24-1996; 98.3 mhz FM *Hrs Open:* 24; 41 kw; Ant 2,795 ft; N34 14 03 W112 22 01
4745 N. 7th St., Suite 410, Phoenix, AZ 86326
(602) 648-9800, *Fax:* (602) 248-4402
www.power983fm.com
License: Mayer, Yavapai County, AZ held by RBG Phoenix Licenses LLC.
Group Owner: Riviera Broadcast Group LLC; (acq 1-1-2007)
Nat'l Reps: Katz Eastman
Population Served: 75,000 *Arbitron Metro Market:* Phoenix, AZ
Michael Cutchall, CEO
Marc Young, Operations Dir
Jose Rodilles, COO
Todd Burden, General Sales Mgr

Meadview

KVGS
01-01-1991; 107.9 mhz FM *Hrs Open:* 24; 98 kw; Ant 1,984 ft; N35 39 07 W114 18 42
2725 E. Desert Inn Rd, Suite 180, Las Vegas, NV 92374
(702) 784-4000, *Fax:* (702) 784-4040
www.v108fm.com
info@v108fm.com
License: Meadview, Mohave County, AZ held by RBG Las Vegas Licenses LLC
Group Owner: Riviera Broadcast Group LLC; (acq 10-3-2005; $38 million with KOAS(FM) Dolan Springs, AZ)
Nat'l Network: ABC
Arbitron Metro Market: Las Vegas, NV *Target Audience:* 25-54; adults
Dave Presher, General Manager
Joshua Mednick, General Sales Mgr
Tony Rankin, Programming Director
Joey Sparks, Promotions Manager
Theresa Dunbar, News Director
Ray Fodge, Chief Engineer
Craig Knight, Promotions Director

Mesa

KDKB
04-20-1968; 93.3 mhz FM *Hrs Open:* 24; 100 kw; 1667 ft.; N33 20 0.8 W112 3 44.4
1167 West Javelina, Mesa, AZ 85210 US
(480) 897-9300
www.kdkb.com
rock@kdkg.com
License: Mesa, Maricopa County, AZ held by Mesa Radio Inc.
Group Owner: Sandusky Radio; (acq 1977)
Nat'l Reps: Christal
Arbitron Metro Market: Phoenix, AZ *Format:* Rock/AOR
Norman Rau, President
Chuck Artigue, General Manager
Bob Weaver, General Sales Mgr
Buzz Casey, Programming Director
Kathy Perschke, News Director
Clayton Creekmore, Chief Engineer

KFNN
11-01-1962; 1510 khz AM *Hrs Open:* 24; 22 kw-D, DA2; 0.1 kw-N, DA2; N33 41 34 W112 0 9
4800 N. Centrl Avenue, Phoenix, AZ 85012 US
(602) 241-1510, *Fax:* (602) 241-1540
www.kfnn.com
License: Mesa, AZ held by CRC Broadcasting Co. Inc.
Nat'l Network: CNN Radio *Wire Services:* Metro Weather Service Inc.
Arbitron Metro Market: Scottsdale, AZ *Format:* News, News/Talk, 86 *Special Programming:* Real estate 10 hrs wkly *Hrs. of News Programming:* news progmg 84 hrs wkly *No. News Employees:* 3 *Target Audience:* 30 plus; upscale, investment-oriented professionals & entrepreneurs; decision makers *Adv. Rates:* 70; 50; 60; 25
Ronald Cohen, President
Brian DuBose, Operations Dir
Brian Du Bose, Programming Director
Renee Yorks, Operations Manager

KIHP
01-01-1946; 1310 khz AM *Hrs Open:* 24; 5 kw-D, 500 w-N, DA-N; N33 26 23 W111 50 09
4725 N. Scottsdale Rd., Suite 234, Scottsdale, AZ 85251
(480) 423-1310, *Fax:* (480) 423-3867
www.kxam.com
kxam@aol.com
License: Mesa, Maricopa County, AZ held by Embee Broadcasting Inc.
Nat'l Network: Westwood One; ABC
Population Served: 2,500,000 *Arbitron Metro Market:* Phoenix, AZ *Hrs. of News Programming:* News progmg 14 hrs wkly *Target Audience:* 35-64.
Byron Gerson, President
Don Sandler, General Manager

KZZP
01-01-1967; 104.7 mhz FM *Hrs Open:* 24; 100 kw; 1549 ft.; N33 20 4 W112 3 35
50 East Rivercenter Boulevard, Suite 1200, Covington, KY 41011 US
(602) 374-6000, *Fax:* (602) 230-2781
www.1047kissfm.com
License: Mesa, Maricopa County, AZ held by Citicasters Licenses L.P.
Group Owner: Clear Channel Communications Inc.; (acq 6-99; grpsl).
Arbitron Metro Market: Phoenix, AZ *Format:* Contemporary Hits/Top 40 *Hrs. of News Programming:* news progmg 7 hrs wkly *No. News Employees:* 1 *Target Audience:* 18-34; women
Randy Michaels, Chairman
Lowry Mays, CEO
John Hogan, President
Alan Sledge, Operations Dir
Susan Karis-Madigan, General Manager
Cathy Burau, General Sales Mgr

Miami

KIKO
06-13-1958; 97.3 mhz AM *Hrs Open:* 24; 56 w; N33 24 41 W110 50 17
4501 Broadway, Miami, AZ 85539
(928) 425-7500 Business,(928) 425-4471 Contest, *Fax:* (928) 425-9393
www.kikonews.blogspot.com
radiokiko@cableone.net
License: Miami, Gila County, AZ held by 1TV.com Inc.
Group Owner: 1TV.Com Inc.; (acq 4-30-2008; $1.025 million with KIKO-FM Claypool)
Nat'l Network: Westwood One; ABC
Population Served: 35,000*Hrs. of News Programming:* news progmg 8 hrs wkly *No. News Employees:* 1 *Target Audience:* 21-70; industrial/blue collar workers in loc copper mines, highest hourly wage earners *Adv.Rates:* 15; 15; 15; 11
John Low, President
Shelly Harrison, General Manager
Roland Foster, News Director
Chelle Hodson, Office Manager
Randy Escobedo, Sports Commentator

KQSS
03-30-1987; 101.9 mhz FM *Hrs Open:* 24; 6 kw; -79 ft.; N33 24 30 W110 48 14
Mailing Address: P.O. Box 292, Miami, AZ 85539 US
Second Address: 5734 McKinney, Globe, AZ 85501
(928) 425-7186, *Fax:* (928) 425-7982
www.gila1019.com
bill@gila1019.com
License: Miami, Gila County, AZ held by William D. Taylor.
Arbitron Metro Market: Globe, AZ *Format:* Country *Hrs. of News Programming:* news progmg 5 hrs wkly *No. News Employees:* 1 *Target Audience:* 25-54.
Bill Taylor, General Manager

Mohave Valley

KVYL
93.7 mhz FM; 6 kw horiz; -89 ft.; N34 58 6 W114 31 58 US
(928) 855-9336
www.kvylfm.com
Office@MyRadioCentral.com
License: Mohave Valley, Mohave County, AZ held by Smoke and Mirrors LLC.
Group Owner: Smoke and Mirrors LLC
Arbitron Metro Market: Mohave Valley, AZ *Format:* Oldies
Traceye Jones, General Manager
Carol Vasel, Account Executive

Morristown

KRPH
99.5 mhz FM; 50 kw; 492 ft.; N34 8 45.7 W112 41 56.1 US
(713) 528-2517
kdao@kdao.com
License: Morristown, Yavapai County, AZ held by Ace Radio Corp.
Group Owner: Ace Radio Corp.
Arbitron Metro Market: Morristown, AZ
Stephen Hackerman, President

Munds Park

KFSZ
01-01-2009; 106.1 mhz FM; 4.3 kw; 1535 ft.; N34 58 6 W111 30 29 US
(928) 774-5231, *Fax:* (928) 779-2988
www.hits1061.com
info@lkcm.com
License: Munds Park, Coconino County, AZ held by LKCM Radio Group LP.
Group Owner: LKCM Radio Group L.P.
Arbitron Metro Market: Munds Park, AZ *Format:* Contemporary Hits/Top 40
Gerry Schlegel, President
Joel Gough, General Sales Mgr
Chuck Taylor, Programming Director
Molly Prince, Promotions Manager
Jane Wasson, News Director
Michael Margrave, Chief Engineer

Nogales

***KNOG**
12-16-1995; 90.7 mhz FM *Hrs Open:* 24; 100 w horiz, 50 kw vert; 52 meters; N31 21 33 W110 53 54
Mailing Address: Box 1614, Nogales, AZ 78502
Second Address: 150 W. First St., Nogales, AZ 85628
(520) 287-5206, *Fax:* (520) 287-3606
www.knog.org
knog@hcjb.org
License: Nogales, Santa Cruz County, AZ held by World Radio Network Inc.
Nat'l Network: Moody
Population Served: 600,000*Special Programming:* Btfl music 5 hrs wkly *Hrs. of News Programming:* News progmg 5 hrs wkly *Target Audience:* 18-55; Hispanics
Marcos Romero, Station Manager
Mariana Romero, Programming Director
Concepcion Borrayo, News Director

KOFH
04-01-1999; 99.1 mhz FM; 6 kw; 167 ft.; N31 23 19 W110 56 35
934 N. Bejarano Street, Nogales, AZ 85621 US
(520) 287-6885, *Fax:* (520) 287-8290
www.maxima991.fm
noticieroalmaximo@hotmail.com
License: Nogales, Santa Cruz County, AZ held by Felix Corp.
Format: Contemporary Hits/Top 40
Oscar Felix Sr., General Manager
Rene Saylor, Programming Director

Oracle

KTGV
12-01-1984; 106.3 mhz FM *Hrs Open:* 24; 430 w vert, 440 w horiz; 4,172 ft; N32 26 26 W110 47 12
3438 N. Country Club Rd., Tucson, AZ 89102
(520) 795-1490, *Fax:* (520) 327-2260
License: Oracle, Pinal County, AZ held by Journal Broadcast Corp.
Group Owner: Journal Communications Inc.; (acq 4-15-98; $5.8 million)
Nat'l Reps: Christal
Population Served: 600,000 *Arbitron Metro Market:* Tucson, AZ *Hrs. of News Programming:* News progmg 2 hrs wkly *Target Audience:* 25-54; Hispanic and Anglo adults
Julie Brinks, General Manager
Bobby Rich, Programming Director
Larkin Gassman, Promotions Manager

Oro Valley

KSZR
04-28-1992; 97.5 mhz FM *Hrs Open:* 24; 6 kw; 93 meters; N32 19 45 W111 03 40
575 W. Roger Rd., Tuscon, AZ 85705
(520) 887-1000, *Fax:* (520) 887-6397
www.bob975.com
License: Oro Valley, Pima County, AZ
Group Owner: Cumulus Media Inc.; (acq 4-26-01; grpsl).
Population Served: 800,000 *Arbitron Metro Market:* Tucson, AZ *Hrs. of News Programming:* news progmg 60 hrs wkly *No. News Employees:* 2 *Target Audience:* 25-54.
Farid Suleman, CEO
Herb Crowe, Operations Dir
Ken Kowalcek, General Manager
Keith Rosenblatt, General Sales Mgr

KCMT
01-01-2003; 102.1 mhz FM; 100 kw; 266 ft.; N32 17 23 W111 1 6
6290 Sunset Blvd, Suite 1600, Los Angeles, CA 90028 US
(520) 407-4500, *Fax:* (520) 407-4600
www.kcmt.com
steve@kcmt.com
License: Oro Valley, Pima County, AZ held by Arizona Lotus Corp.
Group Owner: Lotus Communications Corp.
Arbitron Metro Market: Tucson, AZ *Format:* Tejano
Steve Groesbeck, General Manager
Tara Hungate, General Sales Mgr
Enrique Mayans, Programming Director
Carlos Gonzales, Promotions Manager
Tara Hungate, Director of Sales
Jorge Leyva, Promotions Coordinator

Page

***KNAD**
01-01-1998; 91.7 mhz FM; 1 kw; 1634 ft.; N36 41 51 W111 37 57
Rebroadcasts: Rebroadcasts KNAU(FM) Flagstaff
P.O. Box 5764, Flagstaff, AZ 86011 US
(928) 523-5628, *Fax:* (928) 523-7647
www.knau.org
knau@nau.edu
License: Page, Coconino County, AZ held by Arizona Board of Regents on behalf of Northern Arizona University.
Format: News
Dave Riek, Operations Dir
John Stark, General Manager
Jeff Norcross, Programming Director
Don Kraker, News Director
Lisa Skinner, Traffic Manager

KPGE
05-15-1971; 1340 khz AM *Hrs Open:* 24; 1 kw-U, ND1; N36 54 23 W111 27 32
P.O. Box 1030, Page, AZ 86040 US
(928) 645-8181, *Fax:* (928) 645-3347
www.kpge.com
License: Page, AZ held by Lake Powell Communications Inc.
Nat'l Network: ABC
Arbitron Metro Market: Page-Lake Powell-Kanab-Fredonia *Format:* Country *Hrs. of News Programming:* news progmg 15 hrs wkly *No. News Employees:* 4 *Target Audience:* 25-54.
Dan Brown, General Manager
Janet Brown, General Sales Mgr
Dave Weaver, Programming Director
Jim Wagoner, News Director
Dan the Man, DJ
Rachel Cates, Webmaster and DJ

KXAZ
09-22-1980; 93.3 mhz FM *Hrs Open:* 24; 12.5 kw; 922 ft.; N37 0 42 W111 40 48
P O Box 1030, Page, AZ 86040 US
(928) 645-8181, *Fax:* (928) 645-3347
kxaz.com
sales@kxaz.com
License: Page, Coconino County, AZ
Arbitron Metro Market: Page, AZ *Format:* Contemporary Hits/Top 40
Dudley Waller, General Manager
Chris Ousley, General Sales Mgr
Victor Covarrubias, Programming Director

Paradise Valley

KHOT-FM
01-01-1996; 105.9 mhz FM *Hrs Open:* 24; 36 kw; 577 ft.; N33 35 16 W111 45 38
3102 Oak Lawn Ave., Suite 215, Dallas, TX 75219 US
(602) 308-7900, *Fax:* (602) 308-7979
www.univision.com
License: Paradise Valley, Maricopa County, AZ held by Univision Radio License Corp.
Group Owner: Univision Radio; (acq 9-22-2003; grpsl).
Arbitron Metro Market: Phoenix, AZ *Target Audience:* 18-49.
Mary McEvilly-Hernandez, Operations Dir
Chris Morris, General Sales Mgr
Dobby White, News Director

Nelson Oreida, Operations Director
Kevin Norgaard, Research Director

Parker

KLPZ
09-07-1974; 1380 khz AM *Hrs Open:* 24; 2.5 kw-D, ND1; 0.058 kw-N, ND1; N34 9 14 W114 17 15
P.O. Box 1247, Williston, ND 58802 US
(928) 669-9274, *Fax:* (928) 669-9300
www.klpz1380.com
info@klpz1380.com
License: Parker, AZ held by Keith Douglas Learn
Nat'l Network: Jones Radio Networks
Arbitron Metro Market: Phoenix, AZ *Format:* Country, News, 62, Talk *Special Programming:* Farm one hr wkly *Hrs. of News Programming:* news progmg 2 hrs wkly *No. News Employees:* 2 *Target Audience:* 25-55.*Adv. Rates:* 14; 14; 14; na
Keith Learn, President

***KWFH**
11-01-1984; 90.3 mhz FM *Hrs Open:* 24; 800 w; 760 meters; N34 08 53 W114 16 44
Box 747, Parker, AZ 85344
(928) 669-5683,(928) 855-9110, *Fax:* (928) 669-5683
www.kwfh.org
License: Parker, La Paz County, AZ held by Desert View Baptist Church.
Nat'l Network: Moody
Population Served: 12,000*Target Audience:* General.
Gary Covert, Station Manager
Faron Eckelbarger, Programming Director

KRIT
01-01-2003; 93.9 mhz FM *Hrs Open:* 24; 7.6 kw; -154 ft.; N34 8 30 W114 17 50
P O Box 62, Keene, CA 93531 US
(602) 269-3121, *Fax:* (602) 269-3020
www.campesina.com
achavez@campesina.com
License: Parker, La Paz County, AZ held by Farmworker Educational Radio Network Inc.
Arbitron Metro Market: Parker, AZ *Format:* Spanish
Bill Barquin, COO
Anthony Chavez, President
Kevin Lein, Station Manager
Barbara Lein, General Sales Mgr
Maria Barquin, Programming Director
Maria Vrrutia, News Director
Dave Whitehead, Chief Engineer
Michael Nowakowski,Executive Vice-President
Monica Nowakowski, Administration Manager
Veronica Gonzalez, Executive Assistant
Gilbert Ochoa, National Sales

KPKR
12-23-2007; 97.3 mhz FM *Hrs Open:* 24; 3.2 kw; 928 ft.; N34 7 29 W114 12 38
Mailing Address: US
Second Address: 1713 S. Kofa Ave., Suite E, Parker, AZ 85344
(928) 669-9999, *Fax:* (928) 669-8957
www.riverratradio.com
License: Parker, La Paz County, AZ held by Prescott Valley Broadcasting Co. Inc.
Group Owner: Prescott Valley Broadcasting Co. Inc.
Nat'l Network: Jones Radio Networks
Arbitron Metro Market: Parker, AZ *Format:* Blues, Classic Rock
Target Audience: 25-54; fun loving recreationists
Sanford Cohen, President
Terry Cohen, Executive Vice President

Payson

KMOG
11-01-1983; 1420 khz AM *Hrs Open:* 24; 2.5 kw-D, DAN; 0.5 kw-N, DAN; N34 16 0 W111 18 54
500 E. Taylor Parkway, Payson, AZ 85541 US
(928) 474-5214, *Fax:* (928) 474-0236
http://and02.info/index.html
kmog@1420kmog.com
License: Payson, AZ held by Farrell Enterprises L.L.C.
Format: Country *Hrs. of News Programming:* news progmg 2 hrs wkly *No. News Employees:* 1 *Target Audience:* 25-54; working adults *Adv. Rates:* 12; 16; 12; 10
Mike Farrell, President
Blaine Kimball, General Manager

KMZQ-FM
01-01-2007; 99.3 mhz FM; 17 kw; 404 ft.; N34 11 4 W111 20 16 US
(702) 736-6161
License: Payson, Gila County, AZ held by Kemp Communications Inc.
Group Owner: Kemp Communications Inc.
Arbitron Metro Market: Payson, AZ
Will Kemp, President

Phoenix

KASA
01-06-1967; 1540 khz AM; 10 kw-D, DA2; 0.019 kw-N, DA2; N33 22 36 W112 5 25
1445 West Baseline Road, Phoenix, AZ 85041 US
(602) 276-4241, *Fax:* (602) 276-8119
License: Phoenix, AZ held by KASA Radio Hogar Inc.
Arbitron Metro Market: Phoenix, AZ *Format:* Religious *Target Audience:* General.
Moses Herrera, President

***KBAQ**
04-26-1993; 89.5 mhz FM *Hrs Open:* 24; 29.7 kw; 1555 ft.; N33 19 58 W112 3 53
1435 S. Dobson Road, Mesa, AZ 85202 US
(480) 833-1122, *Fax:* (480) 774-8475
www.kbaq.org
kbaq.mail@kbaq.org
License: Phoenix, Maricopa County, AZ held by College District.
Nat'l Network: NPR; PRI *Regional Reps:* Public Radio Partners
Wire Services: AP
Arbitron Metro Market: Tempe, AZ *Format:* News
Carl Matthusen, General Manager
Lou Stanley, General Sales Mgr
Scott Williams, Programming Director
Ralph Hogan, Director of Engineering
Sterling Beeaff, Music Director

KESZ
07-01-1982; 99.9 mhz FM *Hrs Open:* 24; 99 kw; 1703 ft.; N33 20 1 W112 3 44
200 Concord Plaza, Siute 600, San Antonio, TX 78216 US
(602) 374-6000, *Fax:* (602) 374-6035
www.kez999.com
License: Phoenix, Maricopa County, AZ held by CC Licenses LLC.
Group Owner: Clear Channel Communications Inc.; (acq 5-14-99; $58 million)
Nat'l Network: AP Radio *Nat'l Reps:* Katz Radio
Arbitron Metro Market: Phoenix, AZ *Format:* Adult Contemp
Target Audience: General.
Joe Puglise, General Manager
Kevin Gossett, Promotions Manager

***KFLR-FM**
12-01-1985; 90.3 mhz FM *Hrs Open:* 24; 100 kw; 1585 ft.; N33 20 2 W112 3 44
7355 North Oracle # 200, Tucson, AZ 85704 US
(602) 978-0903, *Fax:* (602) 548-8089
www.myflc.org
kflr@flc.org
License: Phoenix, Maricopa County, AZ held by Family Life Broadcasting Inc.
Group Owner: Family Life Communications Inc.; (acq 7-30-78)
Nat'l Network: Salem Radio Network
Arbitron Metro Market: Albuquerque, NM *Format:* Christian, Religious
Randy Carlson, President
Fred Morse, Operations Dir
Alan Cook, General Manager
Bruce Thurman, Promotions Manager
Walter Ellis, Engineering Dir

KGME
01-01-1940; 910 khz AM *Hrs Open:* 24; 5 kw-D, DAN; 5 kw-N, DAN; N33 32 0 W112 7 18
300 Crescent Court, Suite 600, Austin, TX 75201 US
(602) 374-6000, *Fax:* (602) 374-6035
www.xtra910.com
License: Phoenix, AZ held by AMFM Radio Licenses L.L.C.
Group Owner: Clear Channel Communications Inc.; (acq 8-30-00; grpsl)
Nat'l Network: CBS; Westwood One
Arbitron Metro Market: Phoenix, AZ *Format:* Sports, Talk *Special Programming:* Fantasy 2 hrs wkly *No. News Employees:* 7
Target Audience: General.
Brad Gould, Station Manager

KFYI
10-01-1921; 550 khz AM *Hrs Open:* 24; 5 kw-D, ND1; 1 kw-N, ND1; N33 23 17 W112 0 22
840 North Central, Phoenix, AZ 85004 US
(602) 374-6000, *Fax:* (602) 374-6032
www.kfyi.com
info@kfyi.com
License: Phoenix, AZ held by AMFM Radio Licenses LLC
Group Owner: Clear Channel Communications Inc.
Nat'l Network: Westwood One *Nat'l Reps:* Christal
Arbitron Metro Market: Phoenix, AZ *Format:* News, News/Talk, 86 *Special Programming:* Relg 2 hrs wkly *Target Audience:* 50 plus.
Brad Gould, Station Manager
Laurie Canfillo, Programming Director

KIDR
02-01-1958; 740 khz AM *Hrs Open:* 24; 1 kw-D, DA2; 0.292 kw-N, DA2; N33 21 55 W112 6 30
8400 N.W. 52nd St., Ste-101, Miami, FL 33166 US
(702) 253-9800, *Fax:* (602) 234-8993
www.kydz.radio.com
cat.thomas@cbsradio.com; juicy.balaro@cbsradio.com; leah.hovig@cbsradio.com
License: Phoenix, AZ held by Force Broadcasting LLC
TV Affiliate: CBS *Format:* Children *Hrs. of News Programming:* news progmg 10 hrs wkly *No. News Employees:* 2 *Target Audience:* Under 18
Arthur Liu, CFO
Arturo Galvez, General Manager
Frank Feder, General Sales Mgr
Cat Thomas, Program Director
Juicy Balaoro, Promotions Director

***KJZZ**
01-01-1951; 91.5 mhz FM *Hrs Open:* 24; 100 kw; 1608 ft.; N33 19 58 W112 3 53
1435 South Dobson Road, Mesa, AZ 85202 US
(480) 834-5627, *Fax:* (480) 774-8475
www.kjzz.org
License: Phoenix, Maricopa County, AZ held by Maricopa County Community College District.
Nat'l Network: NPR; PRI *Regional Reps:* Public radio partners
Wire Services: NOAA Weather; AP
Arbitron Metro Market: Phoenix, AZ *Format:* Jazz, News *Hrs. of News Programming:* news progmg 50 hrs wkly *No. News Employees:* 6 *Target Audience:* 25-54.
Bill Shedd, Operations Dir
Jon Hoban, General Manager
Lou Stanley, General Sales Mgr
Scott Williams, Programming Director
Mark Moran, News Director
Ralph Hogan, Engineering Dir
Louis Stanley, Development Director

KPKX
07-01-1960; 98.7 mhz FM *Hrs Open:* 24; 97 kw; 1788 ft.; N33 19 58 W112 3 48
888 - 7th Avenue, New York, NY 10106 US
(602) 274-6200, *Fax:* (602) 266-3858
www.987thepeak.com
newsradio620@ktar.com
License: Phoenix, Maricopa County, AZ
Group Owner: Bonneville International Corporation
Arbitron Metro Market: Phoenix, AZ *Format:* Adult Contemp *Hrs. of News Programming:* news progmg 2 hrs wkly *No. News Employees:* 1 *Target Audience:* Adults 25-54; lite rock *Adv. Rates:* 400; 300; 350; 150.
Mark Bentz, General Sales Mgr
Jodi Hamilton, Promotions Manager
Gary Smith, Engineering Dir

KMVP
11-23-1949; 860 khz AM *Hrs Open:* 24
888 - 7th Avenue, New York, NY 10106 US
(602) 274-6200, *Fax:* (602) 266-3858
www.ktar.com
newsradio620@ktar.com
License: Phoenix, AZ held by Bonneville Holding Co.
Group Owner: Bonneville International Corporation; (acq 1-14-2005; grpsl)
Nat'l Network: ESPN Radio
Arbitron Metro Market: Phoenix, AZ *Format:* Sports, Talk *Target Audience:* 25-54; sports enthusiast
Bruce Reese, CEO
David Brown, General Sales Mgr
Tisa Vrable, Programming Director
Randy Eccles, Promotions Manager
Gary Smith, Engineering Dir
Mike Fadelli, General Sales Manager
Dawn Paugh

KMXP
10-01-1964; 96.9 mhz FM *Hrs Open:* 24; 98 kw; 1558 ft.; N33 20 3 W112 3 36
50 East Rivercenter Boulevard, Suite 1200, Covington, KY 41011 US
(602) 279-5577, *Fax:* (602) 230-2781
www.mix969.com

License: Phoenix, Maricopa County, AZ held by Citicasters Licenses L.P.
Group Owner: Clear Channel Communications Inc.; (acq 5-4-99; grpsl).
Arbitron Metro Market: Phoenix, AZ *Format:* Adult Contemp *No. News Employees:* 1
Randy Michaels, Chairman
Lowry Mays, CEO
John Hogan, President
Alan Sledge, Operations Dir
Susan Karis-Madigan, General Manager
Shanna McCoy, General Sales Mgr

***KNAI**
10-23-1991; 88.3 mhz FM *Hrs Open:* 4 AM-7:30 PM; 22.5 kw; 997 ft.; N33 35 47 W112 5 29
P. O. Box 62, Keene, CA 93531 US
(602) 269-3121, *Fax:* (602) 269-3020
www.campesina.com
info@campesinainfo.com
License: Phoenix, Maricopa County, AZ held by National Farm Workers Service Center Inc.
Regional Reps: Vision Marketing
Arbitron Metro Market: Phoenix, AZ *Format:* Spanish, Public Affairs *Target Audience:* 24-54; Hispanic market *Adv. Rates:* 110; 100; 90; 0
Paul Chavez, President
Anthony Chavez, Operations Dir
Michael Nowakowski, General Manager
Bill Barquin, General Sales Mgr
Cesar Chavez, Programming Director
Maria Barquin, Public Relations Director

KNIX-FM
09-01-1969; 102.5 mhz FM *Hrs Open:* 24; 98 kw; 1621 ft.; N33 19 58 W112 3 53
200 Cocord Plaza, Suite 600, San Antonio, TX 78216 US
(602) 374-6000, *Fax:* (602) 374-6035
www.knixcountry.com
License: Phoenix, Maricopa County, AZ held by CC Licenses LLC.
Group Owner: Clear Channel Communications Inc.; (acq 6-1-99; $84 million)
Arbitron Metro Market: Phoenix, AZ *Format:* Country *Hrs. of News Programming:* news progmg one hr wkly *No. News Employees:* 3 *Target Audience:* 25-54.
Joe Puglise, General Manager

KOOL-FM
05-01-1956; 94.5 mhz FM *Hrs Open:* 24; 95.6 kw; 1654 ft.; N33 20 2 W112 3 42
4745 North 7th, Suite 210, Phoenix, AZ 85014 US
(602) 956-9696, *Fax:* (602) 285-1450
www.koolradio.com
License: Phoenix, Maricopa County, AZ held by Infinity Radio Inc.
Group Owner: CBS Radio; (acq 8-7-00; grpsl).
Nat'l Reps: Christal
Arbitron Metro Market: Phoenix, AZ *Format:* Oldies *Target Audience:* 25-54.
Charlie Lake, Programming Director

KOY
05-01-1949; 1230 khz AM *Hrs Open:* 24; 1 kw-U, ND1; N33 26 10 W112 6 34
840 N. Central Ave., Phoenix, AZ 85014 US
(602) 374-6000, *Fax:* (602) 374-6035
www.am1230koy.com
info@am1230koy.com
License: Phoenix, AZ held by AMFM Radio Licenses LLC.
Group Owner: Clear Channel Communications Inc.; (acq 8-30-00; grpsl).
Arbitron Metro Market: Phoenix, AZ *Format:* Oldies
Susan Karis-Madigan, General Manager

***KPHF**
12-01-1991; 88.3 mhz FM *Hrs Open:* 7:30 PM-4:30 AM; 22.5 kw; 974 ft.; N33 35 47 W112 5 31
Mailing Address: 4135 Northgate Blvd #1, Sacramento, CA 95834 US
Second Address: 290 Hegenberger Rd., Oakland, CA 94621
(800) 835-4810, *Fax:* (916) 641-8238
www.familyradio.com
info@familyradio.com
License: Phoenix, Maricopa County, AZ held by Family Stations Inc.
Group Owner: Family Stations Inc.; acq 12-91)
Arbitron Metro Market: Phoenix, AZ *Format:* Christian, Religious
Harold Camping, President
David Manzi, Operations Dir

KPHX
06-10-1958; 1480 khz AM; 5 kw-D, DA2; 0.5 kw-N, DA2; N33 24 2 W112 6 28
803 N. Rexford Dr., Beverly Hills, CA 90210 US
(602) 257-1351, *Fax:* (602) 256-0741
www.1480kphx.com
License: Phoenix, AZ held by Continental Broadcasting Corp. of Arizona Inc.
Nat'l Network: Music of Your Life
Arbitron Metro Market: Phoenix, AZ *Format:* Talk
Kent Ennoms, CEO
Jonathan Molina, Operations Dir
Arthur Mobley, General Manager
Cam Maxwell, Station Manager

KKNT
06-01-1947; 960 khz AM *Hrs Open:* 24; 5 kw-D, DAN; 5 kw-N, DAN; N33 41 34 W112 0 9
4880 Santa Rosa Road, Suite 300, Camarillo, CA 93012 US
(602) 955-9600, *Fax:* (602) 955-7860
www.960thepatriot.com
jtimm@kknt960.com
License: Phoenix, AZ held by Common Ground Broadcasting Inc.
Group Owner: Salem Communications Corp.; (acq 1996; $6.5 million).
Nat'l Network: Salem Radio Network
Arbitron Metro Market: Phoenix, AZ *Format:* News, News/Talk, 86 *Special Programming:* Insight bowl *Hrs. of News Programming:* 6 hrs. news progmg wkly *No. News Employees:* 2 *Target Audience:* 25-54; 35-64;upscale adults
Stuart Epperson, Chairman
Edward Atsinger, CEO
Joe Davis, President
Jon Horton, Operations Dir
James Ryan, General Manager
Heath Garlutzo, General Sales Mgr
Chris Llewellyn, Programming Director
Jean Laneri, PromotionsManager
Laurie Larson, Operations Director

KTAR
06-21-1922; 620 khz AM *Hrs Open:* 24; 5 kw-D, DAN; 5 kw-N, DAN; N33 28 44 W112 0 6
888 - 7th Avenue, New York, NY 10106 US
(602) 274-6200, *Fax:* (602) 266-3858
www.ktar.com
newsradio620@ktar.com
License: Phoenix, AZ held by Bonneville Holding Co.
Group Owner: Bonneville International Corporation; (acq 1-14-2005; grpsl)
Nat'l Reps: Interep; D & R Radio *Wire Services:* UPI
Arbitron Metro Market: Phoenix, AZ *Format:* Sports
Jessica Webb, General Sales Mgr
Ryan Hatch, Programming Director
Tyler Bassett, News Director

KXEG
01-01-1956; 1280 khz AM *Hrs Open:* 24; 2.5 kw-D, ND1; 0.049 kw-N, ND1; N33 29 32 W112 8 28
100 West Clarendon, #720, Phoenix, AZ 85013 US
(602) 296-3600, *Fax:* (602) 296-3624
www.kxeg1280.com
jess@kxeg1280.com
License: Phoenix, AZ held by Communicom Co. of Phoenix L.P.
Group Owner: Communicom Broadcasting LLC; (acq 12-14-2005; grpsl).
Nat'l Reps: Salem; Commercial Media Sales
Arbitron Metro Market: Phoenix, AZ *Format:* Christian *Special Programming:* Sp 5 hrs wkly *Target Audience:* 25 plus; educated adults with disposable income
Jess Spurgin, General Manager

KYOT-FM
10-31-1963; 95.5 mhz FM *Hrs Open:* 24; 96 kw; 1572 ft.; N33 20 6 W112 3 39
840 North Central, Phoenix, AZ 85004 US
(602) 374-6000, *Fax:* (602) 374-6035
www.kyot.com
info@am1230koy.com
License: Phoenix, Maricopa County, AZ held by AMFM Radio Licenses LLC
Group Owner: Clear Channel Communications Inc.; (acq 8-30-00; grpsl).
Arbitron Metro Market: Phoenix, AZ *Format:* Jazz *No. News Employees:* 1 *Target Audience:* 25-54.
Susan Karis-Madigan, General Manager
Angie Handa, Programming Director
John Baker, Chief Engineer

KZON
07-05-1964; 101.5 mhz FM *Hrs Open:* 24; 100 kw; 1739 ft.; N33 19 52 W112 3 46
840 North Central, Phoenix, AZ 85004 US
(602) 452-1000, *Fax:* (602) 420-9916(602) 440-6530
www.1015jamz.cbslocal.com/
info@kzon.com
License: Phoenix, Maricopa County, AZ held by Infinity Radio Inc.
Group Owner: CBS Radio; (acq 12-20-99; grpsl)
Arbitron Metro Market: Phoenix, AZ *Format:* Talk *No. News Employees:* 1 *Adv. Rates:* 300; 250; 250; 150
Greg Garber, General Sales Mgr
Chris Patyk, Programming Director
Mark Waters, Promotions Manager

Pinetop

KNKI
106.7 mhz FM; 61.42 kw; 1171 ft.; N34 15 6 W109 35 6
1491 Thatcher Boulevard, Safford, AZ 85546 US
(928) 532-1010
www.italk1067.com
License: Pinetop, Navajo County, AZ held by William S. Konopnicki.
Arbitron Metro Market: Pinetop, AZ *Format:* Talk, News/Talk
William Konopnicki, General Manager
Suzanne Barr, Chief of Staff

Pinetop-Lakeside

***KRCI**
01-01-2009; 89.5 mhz FM; 1 kw; 1125 ft.; N34 12 22 W109 58 34 US
(928) 368-6766
License: Pinetop-Lakeside, Navajo County, AZ held by Truth and Life Ministries.
Arbitron Metro Market: Lakeside, AZ *Format:* Religious
Kevin Hansen, General Manager

Prescott

KAHM
09-09-1981; 102.1 mhz FM *Hrs Open:* 24; 54 kw; 2526 ft.; N34 41 14 W112 7 1
Mailing Address: P.O. Box 2529, Prescott, AZ 86302 US
Second Address: 510 Henry St., Prescott, AZ 86301
(928) 445-7800
Kahm.info
License: Prescott, Yavapai County, AZ held by Southwest FM Broadcasting Co.
Arbitron Metro Market: Prescott, AZ *Format:* Easy Listening *Hrs. of News Programming:* news progmg 7 hrs wkly *No. News Employees:* 3 *Target Audience:* 35-64; mature, affluent *Adv. Rates:* 31; 24; 31; 20
Lou Silverstein, General Manager
Nancy Silverstein, Programming Director
Sue Mapp, News Director
Al Hartsell, Engineering Dir

***KGCB**
12-05-1994; 90.9 mhz FM *Hrs Open:* 24; 58 kw; 2,532 ft; N34 41 15 W112 07 02
3741 Karicio Ln., Prescott, AZ 86301
(928) 776-0909, *Fax:* (928) 776-1736
www.kgcb.org
info@radioshine.org
License: Prescott, Yavapai County, AZ held by Grand Canyon Broadcasters Inc.
Nat'l Network: Salem Radio Network
Target Audience: 25-54; adult, family audience
Sally Barton, Station Manager
Virginia Rayner, General Sales Mgr
Dan Young, Programming Director
Daniel White, Operations Director
Dave Schreiber, Production Director

KNOT
06-22-1957; 1450 khz AM *Hrs Open:* 24; 1 kw-U, ND1; N34 32 42 W112 26 46
Mailing Address: P.O. Box 151, 116 S. Alto (86303), Prescott, AZ 86302 US
Second Address: 2225 E. Hwy. 69, Prescott, AZ 86301
(928) 445-6880, *Fax:* (928) 445-6852
www.magic991.com
pamela.flaherty@kaff.com
License: Prescott, AZ held by Guyann Corp.
Group Owner: Guyann Corp.; (acq 9-7-2005; grpsl).
Format: Country *Special Programming:* Jazz 2 hrs, sports 8 hrs wkly *No. News Employees:* 1 *Target Audience:* 35 plus.
Tamie Phillips, General Manager
C.J. Murri, Programming Director

Leza La Chapelle Dandos, News Director
Mark Hill, Chief Engineer
Leza La Chapple Dandos, Local News Editor

KTMG
11-11-1977; 99.1 mhz FM *Hrs Open:* 24; 6 kw; 200 ft.; N34 34 29 W112 28 45
Mailing Address: P.O. Box 151, 116 S. Alto (86303), Prescott, AZ 86302 US
Second Address: 2225 E. Hwy. 69, Prescott, AZ 86301
(928) 445-6880, *Fax:* (928) 445-6852
pamela.flaherty@kaff.com
License: Prescott, Yavapai County, AZ
Group Owner: Guyann Corp.
Nat'l Network: ABC
Format: Adult Contemp *No. News Employees:* 1 *Target Audience:* 35 plus.
Lee Anderson, General Manager

***KNAQ**
09-01-1997; 89.3 mhz FM; 0.1 kw; 1585 ft.; N34 29 24 W112 31 59 *Rebroadcasts:* Rebroadcasts KNAU-FM Flagstaff 100%
P O Box 5764, Flagstaff, AZ 86011 US
(928) 523-5628, *Fax:* (928) 523-7647
www.knau.org
knau@nau.edu
License: Prescott, Yavapai County, AZ held by Northern Arizona University.
Format: News, Talk
Dave Riek, Operations Dir
John Stark, General Manager
Dan Kraker, News Director
Lisa Skinner, Traffic Manager

KYCA
08-01-1940; 1490 khz AM *Hrs Open:* 5 AM-1 AM; 1 kw-U, ND1; N34 33 3 W112 27 45
Mailing Address: P.O. Box 1631, Prescott, AZ 86302 US
Second Address: 500 Henry St., Prescott, AZ 86301
(928) 445-1700, *Fax:* (928) 445-5365
info@kyca.com
License: Prescott, AZ held by Southwest Broadcasting Co.
Nat'l Network: CBS; Westwood One
Arbitron Metro Market: Flagstaff-Prescott, AZ *Format:* News, News/Talk, 86 *Hrs. of News Programming:* news progmg 20 hrs wkly *No. News Employees:* 4 *Target Audience:* 35-64; mature adults *Adv. Rates:* 20;16; 20; 16
Lou Silverstein, General Manager

***KJZP**
90.1 mhz FM; 0.027 kw; 1594 ft.; N34 29 24 W112 32 3 US
(928) 541-1008
www.kjza.org
kjzafm@yahoo.com
License: Prescott, Yavapai County, AZ held by St. Paul Bible College.
Nat'l Network: NPR
Arbitron Metro Market: Prescott, AZ *Format:* Classical, Jazz, 80
Nichole Erickson, Director & President
Tom Erickson, General Manager

Prescott Valley

KPPV
09-01-1985; 106.7 mhz FM *Hrs Open:* 24; 3.7 kw; 1617 ft.; N34 29 25 W112 32 0
Post Office Box 26523, Prescott Valley, AZ 86312 US
(928) 445-8289, *Fax:* (928) 442-0448
www.kppv.com
contact@kppv.com
License: Prescott Valley, Yavapai County, AZ
Group Owner: Prescott Valley Broadcasting Co. Inc.
Nat'l Network: Jones Radio Networks *Regional Network:* Arizona News Radio
Arbitron Metro Market: Flagstaff-Prescott, AZ *Format:* Adult Contemp *Hrs. of News Programming:* news progmg 6 hrs wkly *No. News Employees:* 2 *Target Audience:* 25-54; middle to upper income professionals withfamilies and disposable income
Sanford Cohen, President
Terry Cohen, Executive Vice President

KQNA
06-28-1986; 1130 khz AM; 1 kw-D, NDD; N34 37 46 W112 18 56
Mailing Address: P.O. Box 26523, Prescott Valley, AZ 86312 US
Second Address: 3755 Karicio Ln., Suite 2-C, Prescott, AZ 86303
(928) 445-8289, *Fax:* (928) 442-0448
www.kqna.com
info@kppv.com
License: Prescott Valley, AZ held by Prescott Valley Broadcasting Co.
Group Owner: Prescott Valley Broadcasting Co. Inc.; (acq 12-27-93; $75,000;
Nat'l Network: Fox News Radio; Salem Radio Network; CNN Radio *Regional Network:* Arizona News Radio
Arbitron Metro Market: Prescott, AZ *Format:* News, News/Talk, 84, Talk *Hrs. of News Programming:* news progmg 84 hrs wkly *No. News Employees:* 3 *Target Audience:* 35-64; middle - upper income, professionals & newconsumers
Sanford Cohen, President
Ken Byers, Operations Dir
Allison Flannery, General Sales Mgr
Bill Monroe, News Director
Mark Hills, Engineering Dir
Terry Cohen, Executive Vice President
Mike Austin, Sports Commentator

Quartzsite

KBUX
11-01-1988; 94.3 mhz FM *Hrs Open:* 6 AM-10 PM; 0.205 kw; -161 ft.; N33 40 58 W114 13 59
P.O. Box 1, Quartzsite, AZ 85346 US
(928) 927-5111
www.kbuxradio.tripod.com
kbuxradio@hotmail.com
License: Quartzsite, La Paz County, AZ held by Maude J. Burdette.
Arbitron Metro Market: Quartzite, AZ *Format:* Country, Oldies, 94 *Target Audience:* General; retired motor home & trailer owners wintering in warmer climate
Maude Burdette, General Manager
Marvin Vosper, Programming Director

Red Mesa

***KRMH**
01-01-1998; 89.7 mhz FM; 4.5 kw; 135 ft.; N36 57 48 W109 22 39
Hcr 6100 Box 40, Teec Nos Pos, AZ 86514 US
(928) 656-4100, *Fax:* (928) 656-4106
www.rmusd.net
License: Red Mesa, Apache County, AZ held by Red Mesa Unified School District No. 27.
Format: Variety/Diverse
Dan Lawrie, General Manager
Chris Kelly, Programming Director
Wayne Smith, Chief Engineer

Safford

KATO
05-05-1961; 1230 khz AM *Hrs Open:* 5 AM-midnight; 1 kw-U; N32 49 30 W109 45 30
Mailing Address: Drawer L, Safford, AZ 85548
Second Address: 3335 W. 8th St., Thatcher, AZ 85552
(928) 428-1230, *Fax:* (928) 428-1311
www.mysouthernaz.com
davis@mcmurrayradio.com
License: Safford, Graham County, AZ held by McMurray Communications Inc.
Group Owner: McMurray Communications Inc.; acq 12-17-92; $10,000 with co-locat
Nat'l Network: ABC
Population Served: 36,000*Hrs. of News Programming:* news progmg 25 hrs wkly *No. News Employees:* 7 *Target Audience:* 25-54; upscale, intelligent *Adv. Rates:* 15; 12; 14; 10
Bud McMurray, President
Reed Richins, Operations Dir
Davis Nathan, General Manager

KXKQ
08-11-1979; 94.1 mhz FM *Hrs Open:* 24; 1 kw; Ant 4,287 ft; N32 39 01 W109 50 53
3335 W. 8th St., Thatcher, AZ 95355
(928) 428-1230, *Fax:* (928) 428-1311
davis@mcmurrayradio.com
License: Safford, Graham County, AZ held by McMurray Communications Inc.
Group Owner: McMurray Communications Inc.
Population Served: 40,000*Hrs. of News Programming:* News progmg one hr wkly *Target Audience:* 25-54.
Lee Patterson, News Director
Reed Richins, Engineering Dir

Sahuarita

KEVT
10-12-1985; 1210 khz AM
P.O. Box 1511, Tuscon, AZ 85702 US
(520) 628-1200, *Fax:* (520) 326-4927
www.radiounica.com
contact@kevtradio.net
License: Sahuarita, AZ held by One Mart Corp.
Arbitron Metro Market: Tucson, AZ *Format:* Tejano
Francisco Zazueta, General Manager

Salome

KVGG
101.9 mhz FM; 5 kw; -164 ft.; N33 47 47.6 W113 33 27.9 US
(702) 385-6000, *Fax:* (702) 385-6001
License: Salome, La Paz County, AZ held by Kemp Communications Inc.
Group Owner: Kemp Communications Inc.
Arbitron Metro Market: Salome, AZ
Will Kemp, President

Scottsdale

KAZG
01-01-1956; 1440 khz AM *Hrs Open:* 8:30 AM - 5:30 PM; 5 kw-D, ND1; 0.052 kw-N, ND1; N33 28 43 W111 56 24
One Nationwide Plaza, 27th Floor, Columbus, OH 43216 US
(480) 941-1007, *Fax:* (602) 260-5759
www.kazg1440.com
kslx@kslx.com
License: Scottsdale, AZ held by Cactus Radio Inc.
Group Owner: Sandusky Radio; (acq 6-5-98; with co-located FM).
Arbitron Metro Market: Phoenix, AZ *Format:* Oldies
Chuck Artigue, General Manager
Bob Weaver, General Sales Mgr
Dave Cooper, Programming Director
Michael Bradford, Promotions Manager
Chuck Artigue, News Director

KSLX-FM
08-01-1969; 100.7 mhz FM; 100 kw; 1841 ft.; N33 19 53 W112 3 47
One Nationwide Plaza, 27th Floor, Columbus, OH 43216 US
(480) 941-1007, *Fax:* (602) 260-1007
www.kslx.com
kslx@kslx.com
License: Scottsdale, Maricopa County, AZ held by Cactus Radio Inc.
Group Owner: Sandusky Radio
Arbitron Metro Market: Phoenix, AZ *Format:* Classic Rock
H. Robert Gourley III, President

Sedona

KAZM
11-01-1974; 780 khz AM *Hrs Open:* 24; 5 kw-D, 250 w-N, DA-N; N34 51 38 W111 49 10
Box 1525, Sedona, AZ 86339
(928) 282-4154, *Fax:* (928) 282-2230
www.kazmradio.com
info@kazmradio.com
License: Sedona, Yavapai County, AZ held by Tabback Broadcasting Co.
Nat'l Network: Westwood One; ESPN Radio; Fox News Radio
Population Served: 280,000*Hrs. of News Programming:* news progmg 16 hrs wkly *No. News Employees:* 2 *Target Audience:* 25 plus; baby boomers, professions, tourists *Adv. Rates:* 20; 20; 20; 14
Tom Tabback, General Manager

KQST
05-01-1984; 102.9 mhz FM *Hrs Open:* 24; 90 kw; 1480 ft.; N34 58 5 W111 30 29
P.O. Box 1488, Sedona, AZ 86339 US
(928) 634-2286, *Fax:* (928) 634-2295
www.myradioplace.com
License: Sedona, Coconino County, AZ held by Yavapai Broadcasting Corp.
Group Owner: Yavapai Broadcasting Corp.; (acq 12-1-2004; $3 million).
Arbitron Metro Market: Flagstaff-Prescott, AZ *Format:* Contemporary Hits/Top 40 *Target Audience:* 24-59.
W. Grant Hafley, President
Dave Kessel, General Manager
Mike Puetz, General Sales Mgr
John Herring, Programming Director

KSED
08-01-1994; 107.5 mhz FM *Hrs Open:* 24; 96 kw; 1463 ft.; N34 58 7 W111 30 24
112 E Route 66, Ste 105, Flagstaff, AZ 86001 US
(928) 779-1177, *Fax:* (928) 774-5179
www.koltcountry.com
ann@northlandradio.com
License: Sedona, Coconino County, AZ held by Grenax Broadcasting II LLC.

Group Owner: Grenax Broadcasting LLC; (acq 1-6-2006; grpsl)
Nat'l Network: NBC
Arbitron Metro Market: Flagstaff, AZ *Format:* Country *No. News Employees:* 1
Greg Dinetz, President
Bill McAdams, Operations Dir
Jim Shipp, General Manager
Mike Mentor, Programming Director
Jon Sweat, Chief Engineer
Ann Bielinski, Business Manager

Seligman

KZKE
01-01-1995; 103.3 mhz FM *Hrs Open:* 24; 7.7 kw; 453 ft.; N35 19 28 W112 45 52
422 West Highwy 66, Seligman, AZ 86337 US
(928) 753-9100, *Fax:* (928) 753-1978
www.kgmn.net/KZKE.htm
joe@kgmn.net
License: Seligman, Yavapai County, AZ held by Route 66 Broadcasting L.L.C.
Arbitron Metro Market: Seligman, AZ *Format:* Oldies
Joe Hart, President
Deana Campbell, Operations Dir
Rhonda Hart, General Manager
JoAnn Oxsen, General Sales Mgr
Tim Andrews, Programming Director
Dave Hawkins, News Director

Sells

*KOHN
01-01-2004; 91.9 mhz FM; 10 kw; 1657 ft.; N32 7 59 W112 9 31 US
(520) 361-5011, *Fax:* (520) 361-3931
www.kohnfm.tonation-nsn.gov/kohn919/Welcome.html
kohn@hotmail.com
License: Sells, Pima County, AZ held by Tohono O'Odham Nation.
Arbitron Metro Market: Sells, AZ *Format:* Native American
Mary Lopez, Operations Dir
Sial Thonolig, General Manager

Show Low

*KNAA
10-01-1997; 90.7 mhz FM; 3 kw; 817 ft.; N34 3 42 W109 54 22
Rebroadcasts: Rebroadcasts KNAU(FM) Flagstaff 100%
P.O. Box 5764, Flagstaff, AZ 86011 US
(928) 523-5628, *Fax:* (928) 523-7647
www.knau.org
knau@nau.edu
License: Show Low, Navajo County, AZ held by Arizona Board of Regents.
Nat'l Network: NPR
Format: News
Dave Riek, Operations Dir
John Stark, General Manager

KRFM
07-01-1983; 96.5 mhz FM; 100 kw; 994 ft.; N34 12 20 W109 56 26
3051 S. White Mountain Rd., Show Low, AZ 85901 US
(928) 368-8100, *Fax:* (928) 368-8108
www.965krfm.com
info@965krfm.com
License: Show Low, Navajo County, AZ
Group Owner: White Mountain Radio
Nat'l Network: Jones Radio Networks
Arbitron Metro Market: White Mountains (AZ) *Format:* Adult Contemp *Target Audience:* 18-34; 65% female & 35% male
Thomas Kigin, President

KSNX(FM)
09-13-1964; 93.5 mhz FM; 25 kw; Ant 150 ft; N34 13 14 W110 01 49
1838 W. Commerce Dr., Suite A, Lakeside, AZ 85929
(928) 368-8100, *Fax:* (928) 368-8108
www.ksnx.com
info@ksnx.com
License: Show Low, Navajo County, AZ
Group Owner: White Mountain Radio
Arbitron Metro Market: Heber, AZ *Format:* Oldies *Target Audience:* 25-54; 50% female & 50% male
Mike Henry, General Manager

KVSL
07-06-1968; 1450 khz AM
3051 S. White Mountain Rd., Show Low, AZ 85901 US
(928) 368-8100, *Fax:* (928) 368-8108
www.whitemountainradio.com
production@whitemountainradio.com
License: Show Low, AZ held by Petracom of Holbrook LLC.
Group Owner: White Mountain Radio; (acq 11-17-2005; grpsl)
Nat'l Network: ABC; Fox News Radio
Arbitron Metro Market: Lakeside, AZ *Format:* Oldies *Special Programming:* Farm 2 hrs wkly *Target Audience:* 45-65; 46% female, 54% male
Steve Johnson, General Manager

KVWM
05-17-1957; 970 khz AM
3051 S White Mountain Rd, Ste D, Show Low, AZ 85901 US
(520) 535-3232, *Fax:* (520) 537-3991
www.970kvwm.com
production@whitemountainradio.com
License: Show Low, AZ held by Petracom of Holbrook LLC.
Group Owner: White Mountain Radio; (acq 11-17-2005; grpsl)
Nat'l Network: ABC; Westwood One
Arbitron Metro Market: Show low, AZ *Format:* News, News/Talk, 86 *Target Audience:* 35-65; 46% female & 54% male
Steve Johnson, General Manager
Lisa Ames, News Director

Sierra Vista

KKYZ
01-01-1995; 101.7 mhz FM *Hrs Open:* 24; 3 kw; 328 ft.; N31 33 59 W110 13 57
P.O. Box 3037, Sierra Vista, AZ 85635 US
(520) 459-8201, *Fax:* (520) 458-7104
www.kkyz.com
info@kkyz.com
License: Sierra Vista, Cochise County, AZ held by Cochise Broadcasting L.L.C.
Group Owner: Cochise Broadcasting LLC; (acq 1-12-2001)
Arbitron Metro Market: Tucson, AZ *Format:* Oldies *Target Audience:* 25-54.
Ted Tucker, General Manager
Jeff Davenport, Station Manager

KNXN
06-20-1980; 1470 khz AM *Hrs Open:* 24
680 Avenida Del Sol, Sierra Vista, AZ 85635 US
(520) 790-2440, *Fax:* (520) 790-2937
www.kgms.com
doug@kvoi.com
License: Sierra Vista, AZ held by Good Music Inc.
Group Owner: Good News Communications Inc.; (acq 4-16-01; $300,000).
Format: Christian, Religious, 86 *Hrs. of News Programming:* news progmg 5 hrs wkly *No. News Employees:* 1
Jeff Davenport, Operations Dir
Doug Martin, General Manager

KTAN
03-01-1957; 1420 khz AM *Hrs Open:* 24
Mailing Address: P.O. Box 2770, Sierra Vista, AZ 85636 US
Second Address: 2300 Busby Dr., Sierra Vista, AZ 85636
(520) 458-4313, *Fax:* (520) 458-4317
ktan@wavmax.com
License: Sierra Vista, AZ held by CCR-Sierra Vista IV LLC.
Group Owner: Cherry Creek Radio LLC; (acq 12-19-2003; grpsl).
Nat'l Network: CBS *Nat'l Reps:* Tacher
Arbitron Metro Market: Sierra Vista, AZ *Format:* News, News/Talk, 84, Talk *Hrs. of News Programming:* news progmg 20 hrs wkly *No. News Employees:* 1 *Target Audience:* 25-54.
Paul Orlando, General Manager
Rudy Sueskind, General Sales Mgr
Debbie Simmons, News Director

KZMK
09-01-1973; 100.9 mhz FM *Hrs Open:* 24; 3 kw; -46 ft.; N31 32 47 W110 16 29
Mailing Address: P.O. Box 2770, Sierra Vista, AZ 85636 US
Second Address: 2300 Busby Dr., Sierra Vista, AZ 85636
(520) 458-4313, *Fax:* (520) 458-4317
www.allhitskzmk.com/
tdriskill@cherrycreekradio.com
License: Sierra Vista, Cochise County, AZ
Group Owner: Cherry Creek Radio LLC
Arbitron Metro Market: Sierra Vista, AZ *Format:* Adult Contemp *Hrs. of News Programming:* news progmg one hr wkly *No. News Employees:* 1 *Target Audience:* 18-49.
Frances Poppe, CFO
Edward Poppe Jr., President
Grady Butler ,III, Operations Dir
Tony Driskill, General Manager
Edward Poppe III, Executive Vice President

South Tucson

KWFM
01-01-1957; 1330 khz AM; 2 kw-D, 5 kw-N, DA-N; N32 18 51 W110 50 17
4433 E. Broadway, Suite 210, Tucson, AZ 85718
(520) 529-5865, *Fax:* (520) 529-9324
www.tucsonsjolt.com
info@kjllam.com
License: South Tucson, Pima County, AZ held by Hudson Communications Inc.
Population Served: 600,000 *Arbitron Metro Market:* Tucson, AZ
Kimberly Lopez, General Manager

KXEW
05-10-1963; 1600 khz AM *Hrs Open:* 24
889 W. El Puente Lane, Tucson, AZ 85713 US
(520) 618-2100, *Fax:* (520) 618-2165
www.tejano1600.com
glynnalan@clearchannel.com
License: South Tucson, AZ held by CC Licenses LLC.
Group Owner: Clear Channel Communications Inc.; (acq 9-25-2003).
Arbitron Metro Market: Tucson, AZ *Format:* Tejano *Target Audience:* 25-54; blue collar Hispanics
Chris Kelly, Operations Dir
Glynn Alan, General Manager
Tom Zlaket, General Sales Mgr
Rupert Pacheco, Programming Director
Nikki Van Doran, Promotions Manager
Mary Palin, News Director
Mike Irby, Chief Engineer
Patti Ruiz,General Sales Manager
Melissa Santa Cruz, Promotions Director
Dan Gibson, Website Support
Nikki Van Doran, Marketing Director
Chris Kelly, Program Director

Springerville

KQAZ
07-15-1984; 101.7 mhz FM; 55 kw; 1243 ft.; N34 15 6 W109 35 6
Mailing Address: P.O. Box 1069, Springerville, AZ 85938 US
Second Address: 691 E. Deuce of Clubs, Show Low, AZ 85901
(928) 532-1010, *Fax:* (928) 532-0101
www.majik101.com
mail@majik101.com
License: Springerville, Apache County, AZ held by Country Mountain Airwaves LLC.
Group Owner: Country Mountain Airwaves LLC; (acq 7-30-99; $175,000 with KRVZ(AM) Springerville)
Nat'l Network: AP Radio
Arbitron Metro Market: Show Low, AZ *Format:* Adult Contemp
Camden Smith, General Manager
Laurie Pogson, News Director
Jack Jacobs, Disc Jockey

KRVZ
06-11-1982; 1400 khz AM *Hrs Open:* 24; 1 kw-U; N34 08 17 W109 16 10
Box 2020, Show Low, AZ 85938
(928) 532-1010, *Fax:* (928) 532-0101
krvz@frontiernet.net
License: Springerville, Apache County, AZ held by Country Mountain Airwaves LLC.
Group Owner: Country Mountain Airwaves LLC; (acq 7-30-99; $175,000 with KQAZ(FM) Springerville)
Nat'l Network: Jones Radio Networks

William Konopnicki, President
Dan Curtis, Operations Dir
Camden Smith, General Manager
Laurie Pogson, News Director

St. Johns

KWKM
01-01-2001; 95.7 mhz FM *Hrs Open:* 24 hours; 100 kw; 1193 ft.; N34 14 58 W109 35 11
3654 West Jarvis Avenue, Skokie, IL 60076 US
(928) 532-2949, *Fax:* (928) 532-3176
www.kwkm.com
program@kwkm.com
License: St. Johns, Apache County, AZ held by KM Radio of St. Johns L.L.C.
Group Owner: KM Communications Inc.; (acq 5-3-99)
Nat'l Network: ABC
Arbitron Metro Market: Show low, AZ *Format:* Adult Contemp *Special Programming:* local high school sports, tradio, local morning show *Hrs. of News Programming:* 1 hour *No. News Employees:* 1 *Target Audience:* 18-35 female
Jean Barton, General Manager

Sun City

KOMR
03-07-1975; 106.3 mhz FM *Hrs Open:* 24; 23 kw; 725 ft.; N33 57 21 W112 28 34
11 Skyline Drive, Hawthorne, NY 10532 US
(602) 308-7900, *Fax:* (602) 308-7979
www.univision.com
License: Sun City, Maricopa County, AZ held by HBC License Corp.
Group Owner: Univision Radio; (acq 9-22-2003; grpsl).
Arbitron Metro Market: Phoenix, AZ *Format:* Spanish *Target Audience:* 25-54.
Mary McEvilly-Hernandez, Operations Dir
Chris Morris, General Sales Mgr
Aide Gonzalez, Promotions Manager
Dobby White, News Director
Nelson Oseida, Operations Director
Kevin Norgaard, Research Director

Sun City West

KVIB
01-01-2005; 95.1 mhz FM *Hrs Open:* 24; 41 kw; Ant 2,785 ft; N34 14 05 W112 22 02
4745 N. 7th Street, #410, Phoenix, AZ 85740
(602) 648-9800, *Fax:* (602) 648-4402
www.951latinovibefm.com
License: Sun City West, Maricopa County, AZ held by Riviera Broadcasting
Nat'l Reps: Katz Eastman
Target Audience: 18-34; Hispanic 2nd & 3rd generation
Michael Cutchall, CEO
Marc Young, Operations Dir
Jose Rodilles, COO
Jacqueline Bosque Diaz, General Sales Mgr
Kristin Minichiello, National Sales Manager

Superior

*KZAI
01-01-2004; 89.9 mhz FM; 45 kw vert; 2031 ft.; N33 43 52 W111 20 39
P.O. Box 637, Bishop, CA 93515 US
(888) 937-2471, *Fax:* (916) 251-1650
www.air1.com
info@air1.com
License: Superior, Pinal County, AZ held by Educational Media Foundation.
Group Owner: EMF Broadcasting; (acq 2-10-2006; $2.5 million).
Nat'l Network: Air 1
Arbitron Metro Market: Superior, AZ *Format:* Alternative, Christian
Darrell Chambliss, Chairman
Alan Mason, COO
Mike Novak, President and CEO
Dan Beck, Operations Dir
David Pierce, Programming Director
Ed Lenane, News Director
Sam Wallington, Engineering Dir
Marya Morgan, News Reporter
Richard Hunt, News Reporter
Eric Moser, Chief Financial Officer
Brian Burger, Vice President of Human Resources
D. Kevin Blair, Secretary and General Counsel
Larry Moody, Director

Tanque Verde

KWCX-FM
07-08-1976; 104.9 mhz FM *Hrs Open:* 24; 730 w; Ant 3,175 ft; N32 13 01 W109 36 26
Box 1250, Willcox, AZ 85546
(520) 384-4626, *Fax:* (520) 384-4627
License: Tanque Verde, Cochise County, AZ held by KZLZ LLC.
Group Owner: KZLZ LLC; (acq 8-8-2007; $900,000 with KHIL(AM) Willcox)
Dan Curtis, General Manager
Mark Lucke, Programming Director

Teec Nos Pos

KNDN-FM
96.5 mhz FM *Hrs Open:* 24 hours; 100 kw; 81 meters; N36 53 03 W109 03 53
1515 West Main Street, Farmington, NM
(505) 325-1996, *Fax:* (505) 327-2019
License: Teec Nos Pos, AZ held by KRJG Inc
Group Owner: Basin Broadcasting Company
Kerwin D Gober, President

Tempe

KDUS
04-16-1960; 1060 khz AM *Hrs Open:* 24; 5 kw-D, DAN; 0.5 kw-N, DAN; N33 21 43 W111 58 3
1167 W. Javelina Avenue, Mesa, AZ 85201 US
(480) 838-0400, *Fax:* (480) 820-8469
www.kdus.com
info@kdus.com
License: Tempe, AZ held by Tempe Radio Inc.
Group Owner: Sandusky Radio; (acq 1994; $20 million with co-located FM)
Arbitron Metro Market: Phoenix, AZ *Format:* Sports *No. News Employees:* 1 *Target Audience:* 18-34 males.
Chuck Artigue, General Manager
Dana Beaudin, General Sales Mgr
Angel Velasquez, Programming Director

KMIK
06-23-1960; 1580 khz AM *Hrs Open:* 24; 50 kw-D, DAN; 50 kw-N, DAN; N33 27 22 W111 50 1
77 West 66th Street, 16th Floor, New York, NY 10023 US
(602) 381-1580, *Fax:* (602) 840-1488
www.radiodisney.com
marni.gerber@abc.com
License: Tempe, AZ held by Radio Disney Group LLC.
Group Owner: ABC Inc.; (acq 9-10-98; $5.85 million)
Nat'l Network: Radio Disney *Nat'l Reps:* McGavren Guild
Arbitron Metro Market: Phoenix, AZ *Format:* Children
Marni Gerber, Station Manager
Carl Jimenez, Promotions Manager

KUPD
04-01-1960; 97.9 mhz FM; 96 kw; 1621 ft.; N33 19 58 W112 3 53
1900 West Carmen, Tempe, AZ 85283 US
(480) 838-0400, *Fax:* (480) 820-8469
www.98kupd.com
mcfeelie@98kupd.com
License: Tempe, Maricopa County, AZ held by Tempe Radio Inc.
Group Owner: Sandusky Radio
Arbitron Metro Market: Phoenix, AZ *Format:* Rock/AOR
J.J. Jeffries, Programming Director

Thatcher

KFMM
12-07-1981; 99.1 mhz FM *Hrs Open:* 24; 50 kw; 2280 ft.; N32 53 22 W109 19 23 *Rebroadcasts:* Rebroadcasts KCUZ (AM) Safford 100%.
Mailing Address: C/O Frank Newell, P.O. Box 567, Green Valley, AZ 85622 US
Second Address: 301 B Hwy. 70 E., Safford, AZ 85546
(928) 428-0916, *Fax:* (928) 428-7797
http://www.991theplanet.com/
License: Thatcher, Graham County, AZ held by Cochise Broadcasting LLC.
Group Owner: Cochise Broadcasting LLC
Arbitron Metro Market: Thatcher, AZ *Special Programming:* Children 2 hrs wkly *Hrs. of News Programming:* news progmg 7 hrs wkly *No. News Employees:* 1 *Adv. Rates:* Same as AM
Darwin Morris, Chief Engineer

Tolleson

KNUV
01-23-1961; 1190 khz AM *Hrs Open:* 24; 5 kw-D, 250 w-N, DA-2; N33 26 42 W112 15 54
Mailing Address: 1582 So. Parker Rd., Suite 204, Denver, CO 92667
Second Address: 8547 E. Arapahoe Rd. #J-451, Greenwood Village, CO 80112
(303) 696-5967, *Fax:* (303) 200-9190
www.onda1190am.com
hebertolv@limarccapital.com
License: Tolleson, Maricopa County, AZ held by Amigo Multimedia Inc.
Population Served: 2,000,000 *Arbitron Metro Market:* Phoenix, AZ
Heberto Limas-Villers, President

KXXT
12-12-1962; 1010 khz AM *Hrs Open:* 24
PO Box 8085, Mitchell, IL 62040 US
(602) 296-3600, *Fax:* (602) 296-3624
www.familyvaluesradio.net
jspurgin@communicom.com
License: Tolleson, AZ held by Communicom Co. of Arizona L.P.
Group Owner: Communicom Broadcasting LLC; (acq 12-14-2005; grpsl).
Arbitron Metro Market: Phoenix, AZ *Format:* Religious *No. News Employees:* 1
Ramon Bonilla, Operations Dir
Bob Christy, General Manager
Willis Girdner, Chief Engineer
Jess Spurgin, National Sales Director
Clayton Creekmore, Studio and Transmitter Engineer
Phillip French, Radio Management Services

Tuba City

*KGHR
11-27-1991; 91.3 mhz FM *Hrs Open:* 24; 100 kw horiz; 1056 ft.; N36 21 27 W111 12 12
P.O. Box 160 Warrior Dr, Tuba City, AZ 86045 US
(928) 283-5555, *Fax:* (928) 283-5557
info@kghr.org
License: Tuba City, Coconino County, AZ held by Tuba City High School Board Inc.
Nat'l Network: NPR
Format: Native American, Triple A *Special Programming:* Pub affrs 5 hrs wkly *Hrs. of News Programming:* News progmg 20 hrs wkly *Target Audience:* General; Native American/Navajo
John Bittner, Station Manager

KTBA
01-01-1980; 760 khz AM
P.O. Box 9090, Window Rock, AZ 86515 US
(505) 371-5587
License: Tuba City, AZ held by Western Indian Ministries Inc.
Arbitron Metro Market: Window Rock, AZ *Format:* Adult Contemp *Target Audience:* English & Navajo
Larry Harper, General Manager

Tucson

KGMS
08-10-1963; 940 khz AM *Hrs Open:* 24
600 Congress Ave., Suite 1400, Austin, TX 78701 US
(520) 790-2440, *Fax:* (520) 790-2937
kgms.com
info@kgms.com
License: Tucson, AZ held by Good Music Inc.
Group Owner: Good News Communications Inc.; (acq 11-27-00; swap with KCEE(FM) Green Valley).
Nat'l Reps: Salem
Arbitron Metro Market: Tucson, AZ *Format:* Christian, Talk *Target Audience:* 25-54. *Adv. Rates:* 25; 25; 25; 25
Doug Martin, CEO
Matt Manis, Operations Dir

KCUB
08-01-1929; 1290 khz AM *Hrs Open:* 24; 1 kw-U; N32 16 37 W110 58 50
575 W. Roger Rd., Tucson, AZ 85705
(520) 887-1000, *Fax:* (520) 887-6397
www.fox1290.com
License: Tucson, Pima County, AZ
Group Owner: Cumulus Media Inc.; (acq 4-26-2001; grpsl)
Population Served: 525,796 *Arbitron Metro Market:* Tucson, AZ *No. News Employees:* 1 *Target Audience:* 25-54.
Herb Crowe, Operations Dir
Ken Kowalcek, General Manager
Keith Rosenblatt, General Sales Mgr

KCEE
01-01-1994; 690 khz AM *Hrs Open:* 24
3222 S. Richey Avenue, Tucson, AZ 85713 US
(520) 889-8904, *Fax:* (520) 889-8573
www.1030kcee.com
info@kceeam.com
License: Tucson, AZ held by Slone Broadcasting LLC
Arbitron Metro Market: Tucson, AZ *Format:* Oldies *Target Audience:* 24-54. *Adv. Rates:* 30; 30; 25; 25
Araceli Espinoza, Operations Dir
Armando Zamora, General Manager
Steve Nunez, General Sales Mgr
Frank Luna, Engineering Dir

KFFN
01-01-1957; 1490 khz AM *Hrs Open:* 24; 1 kw-U, ND1; N32 14 56 W110 55 29
P.O. Box 693, Milwaukee, WI 53201 US
(520) 795-1490, *Fax:* (520) 327-2260
www.espntucson.com
License: Tucson, AZ held by Journal Broadcast Corp.
Group Owner: Journal Communications Inc.
Nat'l Network: ESPN Radio
Arbitron Metro Market: Tucson, AZ *Format:* Sports *Hrs. of News Programming:* News progmg 2 hrs wkly *Target Audience:* 18-49.
Julie Brinks, General Manager
Frank Arrotta, General Sales Mgr
Ryan McCredden, Programming Director

***KFLT**
10-01-1977; 830 khz AM *Hrs Open:* 24; 50 kw-D, DAN; 1 kw-N, DAN; N32 26 39 W111 5 27
Mailing Address: P.O. Box 35300, Tuscan, AZ 85740 US
Second Address: 7355 N. Oracle Rd., Suite 102, Tucson, AZ 85704
(520) 797-3700, *Fax:* (520) 742-3375
www.myflr.org
abiddel@flr.org
License: Tucson, AZ held by Family Life Broadcasting System Inc.
Group Owner: Family Life Communications Inc.; (acq 10-86; $125,000;
Nat'l Network: Moody
Arbitron Metro Market: Tucson, AZ *Format:* Christian, Religious *Hrs. of News Programming:* news progmg 15 hrs wkly *No. News Employees:* 1 *Target Audience:* 25-45; Christian families
Randy Carlson, President
Evan Carlson, Operations Dir
Adam Biddell, General Manager
Dawn Bumsted, Programming Director
Joe Rother, Chief Engineer
Bill Ronning, Music Director

KHYT
08-01-1993; 107.5 mhz FM; 92 kw; 620 meters; N32 24 54 W110 42 56
575 W. Roger, Tucson, AZ 85705
(520) 887-1000, *Fax:* (520) 887-6397
www.khit1075.com
License: Tucson, Pima County, AZ
Group Owner: Cumulus Media Inc.; (acq 4-26-01; grpsl).
Arbitron Metro Market: Tucson, AZ *Target Audience:* 25-54; adults
Farid Suleman, CEO
Herb Crowe, Operations Dir
Ken Kowalcek, General Manager
Keith Rosenblatt, General Sales Mgr
Amber Crowe, Promotions Manager

KIIM-FM
03-01-1954; 99.5 mhz FM *Hrs Open:* 24; 90 kw; 2037 ft.; N32 14 56 W111 6 59
575 W. Roger Road, Tucson, AZ 85705 US
(520) 887-1000, *Fax:* (520) 887-6397
www.kiimfm.com
License: Tucson, Pima County, AZ
Group Owner: Cumulus Media Inc.
Nat'l Network: ABC; Premiere Radio Networks
Arbitron Metro Market: Tucson, AZ *TV Affiliate:* CMT *Format:* Country *Special Programming:* CMT radio live 25 hrs wkly *Target Audience:* Adult: 25-54.
Gary Knehans, Operations Dir
Mike Edwards, General Manager
Keith Rosenblatt, General Sales Mgr
Amber Crowe, Promotions Manager
Warren Goforth, News Director
Dan Boucher, Engineering Dir
Buzz Jackson, Program Director

KLPX
06-01-1967; 96.1 mhz FM; 82 kw; 1952 ft.; N32 14 56 W111 6 59
6290 Sunset Blvd., Suite 1600, Hollywood, CA 90028 US
(520) 407-4500, *Fax:* (520) 407-4600
www.klpx.com
License: Tucson, Pima County, AZ
Group Owner: Lotus Communications Corp.; (Acq 6-79)
Nat'l Reps: D & R Radio
Arbitron Metro Market: Tucson, AZ *Format:* Classic Rock *Target Audience:* 25-54.
Tim McDonald, General Manager
Steve Leslie, Programming Director
Marcy Frankenberg, News Director
John Covington, Local News Editor

KMXZ-FM
04-11-1973; 94.9 mhz FM *Hrs Open:* 24; 97 kw; 1952 ft.; N32 14 56 W111 6 59
P.O. Box 693, Milwaukee, WI 53201 US
(520) 795-1490, *Fax:* (520) 327-2260
www.mixfm.com
mixfm@mixfm.com
License: Tucson, Pima County, AZ held by Journal Broadcast Corp.
Group Owner: Journal Communications Inc.; (acq 1996; grpsl)
Nat'l Network: AP Radio *Wire Services:* AP
Arbitron Metro Market: Tucson, AZ *Format:* Adult Contemp *Hrs. of News Programming:* news progmg 3 hrs wkly *No. News Employees:* 1 *Target Audience:* 25-54.
Darla Thomas, Operations Dir
Julie Brinks, General Manager
Jennifer Nunn, General Sales Mgr
Bobby Rich, Programming Director
Larkin Gassman, Promotions Manager

KNST
10-01-1958; 790 khz AM *Hrs Open:* 24; 5 kw-D, DA1; 0.5 kw-N, DA1; N32 14 54 W111 0 30
600 Congress Ave., Suite 1400, Austin, TX 78701 US
(520) 618-2100, *Fax:* (520) 618-2135
clearchannel.com
info@clearchannel.com
License: Tucson, AZ held by Capstar TX L.P.
Group Owner: Clear Channel Communications Inc.; (acq 8-30-2000; grpsl)
Nat'l Network: Moody *Nat'l Reps:* McGavren Guild
Arbitron Metro Market: Tucson, AZ *Format:* News, News/Talk, 86 *No. News Employees:* 3 *Target Audience:* 25-54.
Tim Richards, Operations Dir
Debbie Wagner, General Manager
Tom Zlaket, General Sales Mgr
Nikki Van Doran, Promotions Manager
Mary Palin, News Director
Mike Irby, Chief Engineer

KRQQ
02-01-1971; 93.7 mhz FM; 93 kw; 2011 ft.; N32 14 56 W111 6 59
600 Congress Ave., Suite 1400, Austin, TX 78701 US
(520) 618-2100, *Fax:* (520) 618-2165
www.krq.com
info@clearchannel.com
License: Tucson, Pima County, AZ
Group Owner: Clear Channel Communications Inc.
Arbitron Metro Market: Tucson, AZ *Format:* Contemporary Hits/Top 40 *No. News Employees:* 1 *Target Audience:* 18-54.
Chris Kelly, Operations Dir
Glynn Alan, General Manager
Rochelle Lang, General Sales Mgr
Chris Kelly, Programming Director
Nikki Van Doran, Promotions Manager
Ryan Brainard, News Director
Scott Wilcox, Chief Engineer
MikeMeilly, Traffic Manager

KTKT
12-01-1949; 990 khz AM; 10 kw-D, DA2; 1 kw-N, DA2; N32 15 19 W111 0 32
C/O Jerome S. Boros, Esq, 1290 Ave of the Americas, New York, NY 10104 US
(520) 407-4500, *Fax:* (520) 407-4600
www.ktktam.com
License: Tucson, AZ held by Arizona Lotus Corp.
Group Owner: Lotus Communications Corp.; (acq 1973).
Nat'l Network: AP Radio *Nat'l Reps:* Lotus Entravision Reps LLC
Arbitron Metro Market: Tucson, AZ *Format:* Sports *Special Programming:* Black one hr, relg 2 hrs wkly *Target Audience:* 25-54.
Steve Groesbeck, General Manager

KTUC
07-10-1926; 1400 khz AM
575 W. Roger Rd., Tucson, AZ 85705 US
(520) 887-1000, *Fax:* (520) 887-6397
www.ktucam.com
Jim.Bednarek@citcomm.com
License: Tucson, AZ
Group Owner: Cumulus Media Inc.; (acq 4-26-01; grpsl).
Nat'l Network: CBS *Nat'l Reps:* Katz Radio
Arbitron Metro Market: Tucson, AZ *Format:* Adult Contemp *Target Audience:* General; college educated, upper income, politically active adults
Ken Kowalcek, General Manager
Keith Rosenblatt, Director of Sales

KTZR
02-27-1947; 1450 khz AM; 1 kw-U; N32 12 04 W110 56 48
3202 N. Oracle Rd., Tucson, AZ 85713
(520) 618-2100, *Fax:* (520) 618-2200
www.cool1450am.com
License: Tucson, Pima County, AZ held by CC Licenses LLC.
Group Owner: Clear Channel Communications Inc.; (acq 6-28-2001; grpsl).
Arbitron Metro Market: Tucson, AZ
Tim Richards, Operations Dir
Debbie Wagner, General Manager
Tom Zlaket, General Sales Mgr
Alan Cook, Programming Director
Nikki Van Doran, Promotions Manager
Mary Palin, News Director
Mike Irby, Chief Engineer
Deeanne Thomas,General Sales Manager
Joan Lee, Promotions Director

***KUAZ**
10-07-1968; 1550 khz AM *Hrs Open:* Sunrise-sunset; 50 kw-D, NDD; N32 22 21 W111 5 52
Mailing Address: Modern Lang Bldg, U of A, Tucson, AZ 85721 US
Second Address: Box 210067, Tucson, AZ
(520) 621-5828, *Fax:* (520) 621-3360
www.kuaz.org
License: Tucson, AZ held by Arizona Board of Regents for the Benefit of The University of Arizona.
Nat'l Network: NPR; PRI *Regional Reps:* Dana Horner *Wire Services:* AP
Arbitron Metro Market: Tucson, AZ *Format:* Jazz, News, 86 *Hrs. of News Programming:* 95+ hours per week *No. News Employees:* 5
Jack Gibson, Director & General Manager
Achilles Calenti, Engineering Dir
Sara Atalla, Underwriting Consultant
Pat Callahan, Director of Membership
Luis Carrin, Content Producer
Michael Chihak, Online Director
ChristopherConover, Producer
Mark Duggan, Producer/Reporter

***KUAT-FM**
05-19-1975; 90.5 mhz FM *Hrs Open:* 24; 12 kw; 3652 ft.; N32 24 55.1 W110 42 51.9
Mailing Address: University of Az, PO Box 210067, Tucson, AZ 85721 US
Second Address: Box 2100067, Tucson, AZ 85721-0067
(520) 621-5828, *Fax:* (520) 621-3360
www.kuatfm.org
License: Tucson, Pima County, AZ held by Arizona Board of Regents for the Benefit of The University of Arizona.
Nat'l Network: PRI *Regional Reps:* Dana Horner *Wire Services:* AP
Arbitron Metro Market: Tucson, AZ *Format:* Classical *Target Audience:* 35 plus.
Jack Gibson, Director & General Manager
Achilles Calenti, Engineering Dir
Sara Atalla, Underwriting Consultant
Pat Callahan, Director of Membership
Luis Carrin, Content Producer
Michael Chihak, Online Director
ChristopherConover, Producer
Mark Duggan, Producer/Reporter

***KUAZ-FM**
04-27-1992; 89.1 mhz FM *Hrs Open:* 24; 1.6 kw; 614 ft.; N32 12 53 W111 0 21
Mailing Address: Unv. of Az, P O Box 210067, Tucson, AZ 85721 US
Second Address: Box 210067, Tucson, AZ
(520) 621-5828, *Fax:* (520) 621-3360
www.kuaz.org
kuaz@arizona.edu, kuaz@kuat.org
License: Tucson, Pima County, AZ held by Arizona Board of Regents for Benefit of the University of Arizona.
Nat'l Network: NPR; PRI *Wire Services:* AP
Arbitron Metro Market: Tucson, AZ *TV Affiliate:* KUAT-TV affil *Format:* Jazz, News, 62, Talk *Hrs. of News Programming:* news progmg 95+ hrs wkly *No. News Employees:* 5 *Target Audience:* General.
Jack Gibson, Director & General Manager
John Kelley, Station Manager
Lyle Kesterson, Programming Director
Achilles Calenti, Engineering Dir
Sara Atalla, Underwriting Consultant
Pat Callahan, Director of Membership
Luis Carrin,Content Producer
Michael Chihak, Online Director
Christopher Conover, Producer
Mark Duggan, Producer/Reporter

KMIY
05-18-1970; 92.9 mhz FM *Hrs Open:* 24; 90 kw; 2,037 ft; N32 14 56 W111 06 59
3202 N. Oracle Rd., Tucson, AZ 78701
(520) 618-2100, *Fax:* (520) 618-2200
www.929themountain.com
License: Tucson, Pima County, AZ held by Capstar TX L.P.
Group Owner: Clear Channel Communications Inc.
Population Served: 452,000 *Arbitron Metro Market:* Tucson, AZ *Hrs. of News Programming:* news progmg 21 hrs wkly *No. News Employees:* 2
Tim Richards, Operations Dir
Debbie Wagner, General Manager
Deanne Thomas, General Sales Mgr
Blake Rogers, Programming Director

RADIO - U.S.

***KXCI**
12-17-1983; 91.3 mhz FM *Hrs Open:* 24; 0.34 kw; 3642 ft.; N32 24 54 W110 42 56
220 South Fourth Avenue, Tucson, AZ 85701 US
(520) 623-1000 EXT. 11(520) 622-5924, *Fax:* (520) 623-0758
www.kxci.org
onfo@kxci.org
License: Tucson, Pima County, AZ held by Foundation for Creative Broadcasting Inc.
Arbitron Metro Market: Tucson, AZ *Format:* Triple A *Special Programming:* American Indian 2 hrs, Black 4 hrs, folk 2 hrs, gospel 2 hrs, jazz 2 hrs, Sp 4 hrs wkly *Hrs. of News Programming:* News progmg 4 hrs wkly*Target Audience:* 18-49.
Amanda Shauger, Operations Dir
Randy Peterson, General Manager/ Development Development/ Acting P
Jill Nunes, General Sales Mgr
Ginger Doran, Programming Director
Doug Groenhoff, Chief Engineer
Duncan Hudson, Music Director
Michelle Boulet-Stephenson, Membership Director

KQTH
05-04-1994; 104.1 mhz FM *Hrs Open:* 24; 3 kw; 328 ft.; N32 17 23 W111 1 6
3438 N Country Club, Tucson, AZ 85716 US
(520) 722-5486, *Fax:* (520) 327-2260
www.1041thetruth.com
License: Tucson, Pima County, AZ held by Journal Broadcast Corp.
Group Owner: Journal Communications Inc.
Arbitron Metro Market: Tucson, AZ *Format:* News *Target Audience:* 25-54; males, persons
Darla Thomas, Operations Dir
Julie Brinks, General Manager
Jennifer Nunn, General Sales Mgr
Ryan McCredden, Programming Director

***KFLT-FM**
01-01-2006; 88.5 mhz FM; 1.5 kw vert; 377 ft.; N32 0 11 W110 47 49
Mailing Address: 7355 N. Oracle, #200, Tucson, AZ 85740 US
Second Address: 7355 N. Oracle Rd., Suite 102, Tucson, AZ 85704
(800) 776-1070, *Fax:* (520) 742-6979
www.myflr.org
abiddel@flr.org
License: Tucson, Pima County, AZ held by Family Life Broadcasting Inc.
Group Owner: Family Life Communications Inc.
Arbitron Metro Market: Tucson, AZ *Format:* Christian, Religious
Dr. Randy L. Carlson, President
Evan Carlson, Operations Dir
Adam Biddell, General Manager
Adam Biddell, Programming Director
Joe Rother, Chief Engineer
Bill Ronning, Music Director
Alonzo Williams, Vice President ofOperations
Rod Robison, Vice President of Development
Doug Goodall, Controller
Evan Carlson, Executive Director of Marketing and Community Tran

***KAIC**
01-01-2006; 88.9 mhz FM; 1.8 kw vert; 26 ft.; N32 36 56 W110 38 38 *Rebroadcasts:* Rebroadcasts KLRD(FM) Yucaipa, CA 100%
1425 N Market Blvd., Suite 9, Sacramento, CA 95834 US
(888) 937-2471, *Fax:* (916) 251-1650
www.air1.com
info@air1.com
License: Tucson, Pima County, AZ held by Educational Media Foundation.
Group Owner: EMF Broadcasting
Nat'l Network: Air 1
Arbitron Metro Market: Tucson, AZ *Format:* Alternative, Christian
Darrell Chambliss, Chairman
Alan Mason, COO
Mike Novak, President and CEO
Dan Beck, Operations Dir
Eric Allen, General Sales Mgr
David Pierce, Programming Director
Ed Lenane, News Director
Sam Wallington, Engineering Dir
Marya Morgan, News Reporter
Richard Hunt, News Reporter
Eric Moser, Chief Financial Officer
Brian Burger, Vice President of Human Resources
D. Kevin Blair, Secretary and General Counsel
Larry Moody, Director

Vail

KRDX
06-01-1978; 98.5 mhz FM *Hrs Open:* 24; 3.9 kw; 410 ft.; N31 55 39 W110 37 57
Post Office Box 36717, Tucson, AZ 85740 US
(520) 459-8201, *Fax:* (520) 458-7104
www.fox985.com
comments@krdx.com
License: Vail, Pima County, AZ held by Desert West Air Ranchers Corp.
Arbitron Metro Market: Tucson, AZ *Format:* Variety/Diverse
Ted Tucker, General Manager

KXZK
01-01-2008; 103.7 mhz FM; 0.79 kw; 476 ft.; N31 55 39 W110 37 57
US
(520) 459-8201, *Fax:* (520) 458-7104
License: Vail, Pima County, AZ held by Cochise Broadcasting LLC.
Group Owner: Cochise Broadcasting LLC
Arbitron Metro Market: Vail, AZ
Ted Tucker, General Manager

Wellton

KCEC-FM
10-01-2000; 104.5 mhz FM *Hrs Open:* 24; 1.75 kw; 1250 ft.; N32 40 22 W114 20 14
PO Box 62, Keene, CA 93531 US
(928) 782-5995, *Fax:* (928) 782-3874
www.campesina.com
info@kcecfm.com
License: Wellton, Yuma County, AZ held by Farmworker Educational Radio Network Inc.
Arbitron Metro Market: Yuma, AZ *Format:* Tejano *Target Audience:* 25-54; Hispanic market
Anthony Chavez, President
Rosella Lopez, General Manager
Barbara Lane, General Sales Mgr
Pepe Escamilla, Programming Director
Isabel Eggert, News Director
Dave Whitehead, Chief Engineer

KUKY
95.9 mhz FM; 1.6 kw; 1263 ft.; N32 40 22 W114 20 11.2
US
(928) 344-3727, *Fax:* (202) 293-7783
www.amigo959fm.com
radio.amigo@yahoo.com
License: Wellton, Yuma County, AZ held by Hispanic Target Media Inc.
Arbitron Metro Market: Wellton, AZ *Format:* Tejano
Meredith Senter, General Manager
Guillermo Meza, Sales Executive and Marketing Consultant
Jose Vasquez, Marketing Director

Whiteriver

***KNNB**
09-11-1982; 88.1 mhz FM *Hrs Open:* 18; 0.63 kw; 600 ft.; N33 45 47 W109 57 39
P. O. Box 700, Whiteriver, AZ 85941 US
(928) 338-5229, *Fax:* (928) 338-1744
License: Whiteriver, Navajo County, AZ held by Apache Radio Broadcasting Corp.
Format: Variety/Diverse *Special Programming:* Apache 8 hrs wkly *Hrs. of News Programming:* news progmg 3 hrs wkly *No. News Employees:* 1 *Target Audience:* 15-60.
Udell Opah, Station Manager
Sylvia Browning, Programming Director

Wickenburg

KHOV-FM
12-02-1983; 105.3 mhz FM *Hrs Open:* 24; 6 kw; 1365 ft.; N34 11 32 W112 45 13
1740 W. Katella Avenue, Suite A, Orange, CA 92667 US
(602) 308-7900, *Fax:* (602) 308-7979
www.univisionradio.com
License: Wickenburg, Maricopa County, AZ held by HBC License Corp.
Group Owner: Univision Radio; (acq 9-22-2003; grpsl).
Nat'l Network: Jones Radio Networks
Arbitron Metro Market: Phoenix, AZ *Target Audience:* 18-49.
Mary McEvilly-Hernandez, Operations Dir
Chris Morris, General Sales Mgr
Dobby White, News Director
Nelson Oseida, Operations Director
Kevin Norgaard

KSWG
01-01-1993; 96.3 mhz FM *Hrs Open:* 24; 6.4 kw; 646 ft.; N33 55 34 W112 47 40
801 West Wickenburg Way, Wickenburg, AZ 85390 US
(928) 684-7804, *Fax:* (928) 684-7805
www.kswgradio.com
kswg@directpc.com
License: Wickenburg, Maricopa County, AZ held by Circle S. Broadcasting Co. Inc.
Arbitron Metro Market: Wickenburg, AZ *Format:* Country *Adv. Rates:* 10; 10; 10; 10
Harold Shumway, President
Mike Shumway, General Manager

Willcox

KHIL
12-02-1959; 1250 khz AM; 5 kw-D, ND1; 0.196 kw-N, ND1; N32 16 0 W109 49 58
Mailing Address: 1491 Thatcher Blvd, Safford, AZ 85546 US
Second Address: 900 West Patte Rd., Willcox, AZ 85643
(520) 384-4626, *Fax:* (520) 384-4627
www.xwave1049.com
markelucke@qwestoffice.net
License: Willcox, AZ held by KZLZ LLC.
Group Owner: KZLZ LLC; (acq 8-8-2007; $900,000 with KWCX-FM Willcox)
Nat'l Network: USA
Format: Country
Mark Lucke, General Manager
Cat Scalzo, Account Manager
Stephanie Childers, Media Arts

Williams

KWMX
01-01-1998; 96.7 mhz FM; 10.5 kw; 1066 ft.; N35 7 52 W112 8 3
2370 West Highway 89a, Suite 11-131, Sedona, AZ 86336 US
(928) 779-1177, *Fax:* (928) 774-5179
www.thewolf.com
ann@northlandradio.com
License: Williams, Coconino County, AZ held by Grenax Broadcasting II LLC.
Group Owner: Grenax Broadcasting LLC; (acq 4-14-2005; grpsl)
Format: Classic Rock
Greg Dinetz, President
Bill McAdams, Operations Dir
Jim Shipp, General Manager
Mike Mentor, Programming Director
Jon Sweat, Chief Engineer
Ann Bielinski, Business Manager

Window Rock

KTNN
02-26-1986; 660 khz AM *Hrs Open:* 12A - 12A; 50 kw-D, DAN; 50 kw-N, DAN; N35 53 42 W109 8 29
P.O.Box 2569, Window Rock, AZ 86515 US
(928) 871-3553, *Fax:* (928) 871-3479
www.ktnnonline.com
webmaster@ktnonline.com
License: Window Rock, AZ held by The Navajo Nation
Wire Services: CNN
Arbitron Metro Market: Window Rock, AZ *Format:* Country *Special Programming:* Native American *Hrs. of News Programming:* 1 *Target Audience:* Navajo Tribe of Native Americans
Troy LIttle, General Manager
L.A. Williams, Programming Director
Marcia Peshlakai, Promotions Manager
Paul Jones, News Director

***KWIM**
09-21-1995; 104.9 mhz FM; 30 kw; 299 ft.; N35 39 19 W109 1 59
Post Office Box 9090, Window Rock, AZ 86515 US
(505) 371-5749, *Fax:* (505) 371-5588
www.westernindian.org
wim@westernindian.org
License: Window Rock, Apache County, AZ held by Western Indian Ministries Inc.
Arbitron Metro Market: Window Rock, AZ *Format:* Adult Contemp, Christian, 74 *Adv. Rates:* 9; 9; 9; 9
Larry Harpor, General Manager

KWRK
10-01-1996; 96.1 mhz FM *Hrs Open:* 24; 94 kw; 584 ft.; N35 33 36 W109 6 30
P. O. Box 2569, Window Rock, AZ 86515 US
(928) 871-3553, *Fax:* (928) 871-3479
License: Window Rock, Apache County, AZ held by The Navajo Nation.
Nat'l Network: Jones Radio Networks *Wire Services:* AP

Arbitron Metro Market: Window Rock, AZ *Format:* Country
Troy Little, General Manager
Stewart Begay, General Sales Mgr
L.A. Williams, Programming Director
Marcia Peshlakai, Promotions Manager
Leander Moffit, Program Coordinator

Winslow

KINO
12-18-1962; 1230 khz AM; 1 kw-U, ND1; N35 2 15 W110 43 0
Drawer K, East End of Easy Street, Winslow, AZ 86047 US
(928) 289-3364, *Fax:* (928) 289-3366
kinoradio@cableone.net
License: Winslow, AZ held by Sunflower Communications.
Nat'l Network: CBS; ESPN Radio *Regional Network:* Arizona News Radio
Format: Country *Special Programming:* Sp 4 hrs wkly *Target Audience:* General. *Adv. Rates:* 7.75; na; na; na
Loy Engelhardt, General Manager

***KAWN**
91.3 mhz FM; 0.3 kw; 118 ft.; N35 1 36 W110 41 50 US
(662) 844-5036, *Fax:* (662) 842-7798
www.afr.net
contact@afa.net
License: Winslow, Navajo County, AZ held by American Family Association.
Group Owner: American Family Radio
Arbitron Metro Market: Winslow, AZ *Format:* Christian
Donald E. Wildmon, Founder
Buster Wilson, General Manager
Jennifer Hagman, Programming Director

Yuma

***KAWC**
07-11-1970; 1320 khz AM *Hrs Open:* 6 AM-6 PM
Mailing Address: PO Box 929, Yuma, AZ 85364 US
Second Address: 2020 S. Ave., # 8E, Yuma, AZ 85366
(928) 317-7690, *Fax:* (928) 317-7740
kawcradio.org
License: Yuma, AZ held by Arizona Western College.
Nat'l Network: NPR; PRI
Arbitron Metro Market: Yuma, AZ *Format:* News, News/Talk, 86 *Special Programming:* Sp 15 hrs wkly *No. News Employees:* 1 *Target Audience:* General.
Dave Riek, General Manager

***KAWC-FM**
03-27-1992; 88.9 mhz FM *Hrs Open:* 6 AM-9 PM; 2.4 kw; 108 ft.; N32 41 23 W114 30 1
9500 S. Avenue 8e, Yuma, AZ 85365 US
(928) 317-7690, *Fax:* (928) 317-7740
kawcradio.org
License: Yuma, Yuma County, AZ held by Arizona Western College
Arbitron Metro Market: Yuma, AZ *Format:* Jazz, News *No. News Employees:* 1
Dwyan Calvert, Chairman
Dave Riek, General Manager
Al Ross, Station Manager
Lou Gum, News Director

KBLU
03-01-1940; 560 khz AM *Hrs Open:* 24; 1 kw-D, DAN; 1 kw-N, DAN; N32 43 25 W114 38 39
600 Congress Avenue, Suite 1400, Austin, TX 78701 US
(928) 344-4980, *Fax:* (928) 344-4983
www.kbluam.com
License: Yuma, AZ held by EDB Yuma License LLC
Group Owner: Frontier Radio Management Inc.
Nat'l Network: ABC; Fox News Radio; Fox Sports; Premiere Radio Networks *Regional Network:* Southwest Agri-Radio
Arbitron Metro Market: Yuma, AZ *Format:* News, News/Talk, 86 *Target Audience:* Adults 25-54.
Jeff Harris, General Manager
Russ Egan, Programming Director
Chris Reichman, News Director
Starr Favreau, Office Manager

***KCFY**
03-01-1992; 88.1 mhz FM *Hrs Open:* 24; 3 kw; 240 ft.; N32 38 31 W114 33 34
Mailing Address: P.O. Box 1669, Yuma, AZ 85366 US
Second Address: 1921 S. Rail Ave., Yuma, AZ 85365
(928) 341-9730, *Fax:* (928) 341-9099
www.kcfyfm.com
kcfy@kcfyfm.com
License: Yuma, Yuma County, AZ held by Relevant Media Inc.
Format: Christian *Hrs. of News Programming:* News progmg 4 hrs wkly *Target Audience:* 25-45; young to middle aged families
Greg Myers, General Manager
Lynette Toepfer, General Sales Mgr
Brandon Sweet, Programming Director
Mike Bondora, Promotions Manager
Mikie Francher, News Director

KCYK
12-11-1950; 1400 khz AM *Hrs Open:* 24; 1 kw; N32 39 06 W114 39 00
949 S. Avenue B, Yuma, AZ 85364
(928) 782-4321, *Fax:* (928) 343-1710
www.kjokyuma.com
oldiesradio@kjokyuma.com
License: Yuma, Yuma County, AZ held by MonsterMedia L.L.C.
Nat'l Network: Jones Radio Networks *Nat'l Reps:* McGavren Guild
Population Served: 160,000*Hrs. of News Programming:* News progmg 6 hrs wkly *Target Audience:* 35 plus. *Adv. Rates:* 24; 24; 24; 15
Keith Lewis, CEO
Jennifer Blackwell, News Director

KLJZ
08-20-1972; 93.1 mhz FM *Hrs Open:* 24; 100 kw; 82 ft.; N32 39 6 W114 39 4
Aztec Plaza, 949 S. Avenue B, Yuma, AZ 85364 US
(928) 782-4321, *Fax:* (928) 343-1710
www.z93yuma.com
todaysbestmusic@z93yuma.com
License: Yuma, Yuma County, AZ held by MonsterMedia L.L.C.
Nat'l Network: Jones Radio Networks *Nat'l Reps:* McGavren Guild
Arbitron Metro Market: Phoenix, AZ *Format:* Adult Contemp *Hrs. of News Programming:* News progmg 2 hrs wkly *Target Audience:* 18-49. *Adv. Rates:* 42; 42; 42; 30
Richard Jenkins, President
Mike Novak, Operations Dir
Keith Whipple, General Sales Mgr
David Pierce, Programming Director
Ed Lenane, News Director
Sam Wallington, Engineering Dir
Karen Johnson, News Reporter
Marya Morgan,Richard Hunt
News Reporter, Jennifer Lohman
Regional Manager

KTTI
11-06-1970; 95.1 mhz FM *Hrs Open:* 24; 50 kw; 246 ft.; N32 38 31 W114 33 34
600 Congress Avenue, Suite 1400, Austin, TX 78701 US
(928) 344-4980, *Fax:* (928) 344-4983
www.kttifm.com
kathiwebber@edbroadcasters.com
License: Yuma, Yuma County, AZ held by EDB Yuma License LLC
Group Owner: Frontier Radio Management Inc.; (acq 11-30-2007; grpsl)
Nat'l Network: Jones Radio Networks *Regional Network:* Southwest Agri-Radio
Arbitron Metro Market: Yuma, AZ *Format:* Country *No. News Employees:* 3 *Target Audience:* 25-54; Adults
Jeff Edwards, Operations Dir
Jeff Harris, General Manager
Starr Favreau, Business Manager

KQSR
09-05-1986; 100.9 mhz FM *Hrs Open:* 24; 3 kw; 262 ft.; N32 38 31 W114 33 34
600 Congress Avenue, Suite 1400, Austin, TX 78701 US
(928) 344-4980, *Fax:* (928) 344-4983
www.kqsrfm.com
License: Yuma, Yuma County, AZ held by EDB Yuma License LLC.
Group Owner: Frontier Radio Management Inc.; (acq 11-30-2007; grpsl)
Arbitron Metro Market: Yuma, AZ *Format:* Adult Contemp *Target Audience:* 25-54.
Jeff Harris, General Manager
Jay Wachs, General Sales Mgr
Jeff Edwards, Programming Director

***KYRM**
04-01-2000; 91.9 mhz FM *Hrs Open:* 24; 6.3 kw; 1335 ft.; N33 3 18 W114 49 37
Mailing Address: Box 3765, McAllen, TX 78502 US
Second Address: 2690 3rd Ave., Yuma, AZ 85364
(928) 341-0919, *Fax:* (928) 314-4141
www.manantialyuma.org
kyrm@lwrn.org
License: Yuma, Yuma County, AZ held by World Radio Network.
Group Owner: World Radio Network Inc.
Arbitron Metro Market: Yuma, AZ. *Format:* Christian, Religious *Special Programming:* Children 6 hrs *Hrs. of News Programming:* News progmg 6 hrs wkly *Target Audience:* Hispanic population
Douglas Swanson, Station Manager
Rachel Swanson, Programming Director

Arkansas

Arkadelphia

KDEL-FM
06-12-1977; 100.9 mhz FM *Hrs Open:* 24; 3 kw; 95 ft.; N34 6 39 W93 3 1
Mailing Address: P.O. Box 40, Arkadelphia, AR 71923 US
Second Address: 601 S. 7th St., Arkadelphia, AR 71923
(870) 246-9272, *Fax:* (870) 246-5878
www.arkadelphiaradio.com
License: Arkadelphia, Clark County, AR held by Noalmark Broadcasting Corp.
Group Owner: Noalmark Broadcasting Corp.
Arbitron Metro Market: Arkadelphia, AR *Format:* Classic Rock
Pete Osteen, General Manager
Debbie Thompson, Station Manager
Dina Angel, Office Manager
Kevin Hrabal, Production Manager

***KSWH-FM**
09-25-1969; 91.1 mhz FM *Hrs Open:* 6 AM-midnight; 0.015 kw horiz; 49 ft.; N34 7 32 W93 3 48
Radio Station Kswh(Fm), P.O. Box 7872, Arkadelphia, AR 71923 US
(870) 230-5185, *Fax:* (870) 230-5144
www.kswh.org
kswh@hsu.edu
License: Arkadelphia, Clark County, AR held by Henderson State University.
Arbitron Metro Market: Arkadelphia, AR *Special Programming:* Alternative 15 hrs, contemp Christian 2 hrs, rap 15 hrs wkly *Hrs. of News Programming:* news progmg 2 hrs wkly *No. News Employees:* 2 *Target Audience:* 18-36; activity-orienated youthful females
Jaris Johnson, Operations Dir
Michael Taggart, General Manager
Annie Benoit, General Sales Mgr
Cody Graves, News Director

KVRC
09-25-1947; 1240 khz AM *Hrs Open:* 24; 1 kw-U, ND1; N34 6 39 W93 3 1
Mailing Address: P. O. Box 40, Arkadelphia, AR 71923 US
Second Address: 601 S. 7th St., Arkadelphia, AR 71923
(870) 246-9272, *Fax:* (870) 246-5878
www.arkadelphiaradio.com
License: Arkadelphia, AR held by Noalmark Broadcasting Corp.
Group Owner: Noalmark Broadcasting Corp.; (acq 6-29-2007; grpsl)
Arbitron Metro Market: Arkadelphia, AR *Format:* News, News/Talk, 86
Pete Osteen, General Manager
Debbie Thompson, Station Manager
Randy Seale, Programming Director
Ronna Pennington, News Director
Gina Angel, Office and Traffic Manager
Kevin Hrabal, DJ/ Production Manager

***KHED**
91.9 mhz FM; kw
1100 Henderson Street, Arkadelpjia, AR 71999 US
(870) 230-5091
khedfm@kswhgmail.com
License: Arkadelphia, Clark County, AR held by Henderson State University.
Charles Dunn, President

Ash Flat

KFCM
05-18-1981; 98.3 mhz FM *Hrs Open:* 24; 25 kw; 318 ft.; N36 21 58 W91 28 35
PO Box 909, Cherokee Village, AR 72525 US
(870) 856-4408, *Fax:* (870) 895-4088
hometownradio@centurytel.net
License: Ash Flat, Sharp County, AR held by KFCM Inc.
Arbitron Metro Market: Cherokee Village, AR *Format:* Oldies *Hrs. of News Programming:* news progmg 25 hrs wkly *No. News Employees:* 3 *Target Audience:* 25-54. *Adv. Rates:* 18; 14; 16; 12
James Bragg, President

Ashdown

KMJI
05-25-1985; 93.3 mhz FM *Hrs Open:* 24; 7.4 kw; 597 ft.; N33 30 24 W94 12 25
P O Box 311, Dequeen, AR 71832 US
(870) 772-3771, *Fax:* (870) 772-0364
www.mix933fm.com
wesspicher@gapbroadcasting.com
License: Ashdown, Little River County, AR held by GAP Broadcasting Texarkana License LLC.
Group Owner: GAP Broadcasting LLC; (acq 8-3-2007; grpsl)
Arbitron Metro Market: Texarkana, AR *Format:* Adult Contemp *Special Programming:* Relg 4 hrs wkly *Hrs. of News Programming:* news progmg 7 hrs wkly *No. News Employees:* 1 *Target Audience:* General.
Ron Bird, General Manager
Wes Spicher, Programming Director

KPGG
05-19-1972; 103.9 mhz FM *Hrs Open:* 24; 5.1 kw; 354 ft.; N33 36 6 W94 4 38
1578 Boston Road, New Boston, TX 75570 US
(903) 793-1109, *Fax:* (903) 794-4717
License: Ashdown, Little River County, AR held by American Media Investments Inc.
Group Owner: American Media Investments Inc.; (acq 2-17-2009; grpsl)
Nat'l Reps: Katz Radio
Arbitron Metro Market: Ashtown, AK *Format:* Country *No. News Employees:* 1 *Adv. Rates:* 35; 30; 30; 15
Mike Basso, General Manager

Atkins

KVLD
10-01-1999; 99.3 mhz FM *Hrs Open:* 24; 4.1 kw; 394 ft.; N35 14 41 W92 52 51
P O Box 541, Morrilton, AR 72110 US
(479) 968-6816, *Fax:* (479) 968-6016
www.oldies993.com
rich@rivervalleyradio.com
License: Atkins, Pope County, AR held by MMA License LLC.
Group Owner: MAX Media L.L.C.; (acq 6-6-2003; grpsl)
Nat'l Reps: Christal *Wire Services:* AP
Format: Oldies
Aaron Thomas, Operations Dir
Rich Moellers, General Manager
Rhonda Dilbeck, General Sales Mgr
Johnny Story, Programming Director
Jim Alexander, Chief Engineer

Augusta

***KJSM-FM**
08-27-1979; 97.7 mhz FM; 100 kw; 620 ft.; N35 10 36 W91 23 49
Mailing Address: 1206 No. Main, Beebe, AR 72012 US
Second Address: 8919 World Ministry Ave., Baton Rouge, LA 70810
(225) 768-3688
www.jsm.org
kawikfish@yahoo.com
License: Augusta, Woodruff County, AR held by Family Worship Center Church Inc.
Group Owner: Family Worship Center Church Inc.; acq 3-4-2003; $2.75 million)
Arbitron Metro Market: Augusta, AR *Format:* Christian
David Whitelaw, COO
Jimmy Swaggart, President
John Santiago, Programming Director

Barling

KFPW-FM
09-01-1987; 94.5 mhz FM *Hrs Open:* 24; 18.5 kw; Ant 269 ft; N35 15 54 W94 21 52
Box 908, Fort Smith, AR 72736
(479) 288-1047, *Fax:* (479) 785-2638
www.fort_94.htm
License: Barling, Sebastian County, AR held by Pharis Broadcasting Inc.
Group Owner: Pharis Broadcasting Inc.; (acq 3-14-2002;. $350,000 with KFPW
Nat'l Reps: Local Focus
Arbitron Metro Market: Fort Smith, AR *Target Audience:* 25-54; general *Adv. Rates:* 20; 20; 20; 20
William Pharis, President
Jessica Aaron, Operations Dir
Karen Pharis, General Manager
Dennis Snow, Programming Director
Jim Barnes, Chief Engineer

Batesville

KAAB
08-01-1980; 1130 khz AM; 1 kw-D, DA2; 0.02 kw-N, DA2; N35 44 40 W91 38 21
Mailing Address: Post Office Box 2077, Batesville, AR 72503 US
Second Address: Box 2077, Batesville, AR 72503
(870) 793-4196, *Fax:* (870) 793-5222
arweekly@cei.net,arkansas1-3@hotmail.com
License: Batesville, AR held by WRD Entertainment Inc.
Group Owner: WRD Entertainment Inc.
Regional Network: Ark. Radio Net.
Arbitron Metro Market: Batesville, AR *Format:* Tejano *Special Programming:* Farm 5 hrs wkly *Target Audience:* 18-44.
John Grace, President
Gary Bridgman, General Manager

KBTA
06-30-1950; 1340 khz AM *Hrs Open:* 24; 1 kw-U, ND1; N35 44 39 W91 38 21
P.O. Box 2077, Batesville, AR 72503 US
(870) 793-4196, *Fax:* (870) 793-5222
maxfm.com
info@maxfm.com
License: Batesville, AR held by W.R.D. Entertainment Inc.
Group Owner: WRD Entertainment Inc.; acq 12-15-95).
Wire Services: AP
Format: Sports *Hrs. of News Programming:* news progmg 22 hrs wkly *No. News Employees:* 2 *Target Audience:* 18 plus.
Rob Grace, President
Gary Bridgman, General Manager
Ben Johnson, Programming Director
Dale Johnson, Chief Engineer

KBTA-FM
01-01-1999; 99.5 mhz FM; 3.4 kw; 427 ft.; N35 52 7 W91 35 14
P.O. Box 2077, Batesville, AR 72503 US
(870) 793-4196, *Fax:* (870) 793-5222
www.995hitsnow.com
garyb@swbell.net
License: Batesville, Independence County, AR held by W.R.D. Entertainment Inc.
Group Owner: WRD Entertainment Inc.
Arbitron Metro Market: Batesville, AR *Format:* Adult Contemp
Rob Grace, President
Gary Bridgman, General Manager
Matt Johnson, General Sales Mgr
Rob Stanley, Programming Director
Bill Beck, News Director
Dale Johnson, Chief Engineer

KZLE
03-03-1982; 93.1 mhz FM; 99 kw; 984 ft.; N35 53 29 W91 43 31
720 Ramsey Street, P.O. Box 2037, Batesville, AR 72503 US
(870) 793-4196, *Fax:* (870) 793-5222
maxfm.com
rob@maxfm.com
License: Batesville, Independence County, AR held by W.R.D. Entertainment Inc.
Group Owner: WRD Entertainment Inc.
Wire Services: AP
Arbitron Metro Market: Batesville, AR *Target Audience:* 24 plus.
Rob Grace, Programming Director
Dale Johnson, Engineering Dir

Beebe

***KOAR**
06-22-1991; 101.5 mhz FM *Hrs Open:* 24; 6 kw; 328 ft.; N35 11 26 W91 54 45
1206 N. Main, Beebe, AR 72012 US
(916) 251-1600, *Fax:* (916) 251-1650
www.air1.com
info@air1.com
License: Beebe, White County, AR held by Educational Media Foundation.
Group Owner: EMF Broadcasting; (acq 6-9-2005; $525,000).
Nat'l Network: Air 1
Arbitron Metro Market: Searcy, AZ *Format:* Christian
Darrell Chambliss, Chairman
Mike Novak, CEO
Mike Novak, President
Alan Mason, Operations Dir
Eric Moser, CFO

Bella Vista

KBVA
11-01-1991; 106.5 mhz FM *Hrs Open:* 24; 37 kw; 567 ft; N36 18 21 W94 27 29
1512 Hwy. 72 S.E., Gravette, AR 72736
(479) 787-6411, *Fax:* (479) 787-6116
www.variety1065.com
gayla@variety1065.com
License: Bella Vista, Benton County, AR held by Gayla Joy McKenzie.
Arbitron Metro Market: Gravette, AR
Gayla Joy McKenzie, President

Bellefonte

KNWA
01-01-1986; 1600 khz AM; 5 kw-D, ND1; 0.05 kw-N, ND1; N36 14 49 W93 5 6
Mailing Address: P.O. Box 2639, Gulfport, MS 39505 US
Second Address: 600 S. Pine, Harrison, AR 72601
(870) 741-1402, *Fax:* (870) 741-9702
kcwd@all.net
License: Bellefonte, AR held by Harrison Radio Stations Inc.
Format: Gospel
Tom Arnold, General Manager
Phillip Cary, Programming Director

Benton

KEWI
06-26-1953; 690 khz AM *Hrs Open:* 5 AM-10 PM; 0.25 kw-D, ND1; 0.073 kw-N, ND1; N34 31 57 W92 34 16
102 W. South Street, Benton, AR 72015 US
(501) 778-6677, *Fax:* (501) 778-7717
www.kewi690.com
kewi690@yahoo.com
License: Benton, AR held by Landers Broadcasting Co. Inc.
Nat'l Network: USA *Regional Network:* Ark. Radio Net.
Arbitron Metro Market: Benton, AR *Format:* Country, News, 64, Sports, Talk *Special Programming:* Farm 4 hrs, gospel 10 hrs, relg 5 hrs wkly *Hrs. of News Programming:* news progmg 10 hrs wkly *No. News Employees:* 1 *Target Audience:* 25-65; all income levels *Adv. Rates:* 13; 10; 12; 7
Jim Landers, CEO
Doris Landers, President

KHLR
01-01-1971; 106.7 mhz FM *Hrs Open:* 24; kw
200 Concord Plaza, Suite 600, San Antonio, TX 78216 US
(501) 217-5000, *Fax:* (501) 228-9547
www.cool 95.com
cool95@cei.net
License: Benton, Pulaski County, AR held by CC Licenses LLC.
Group Owner: Clear Channel Communications Inc.; (acq 9-12-97; grpsl).
Nat'l Reps: D & R Radio
Arbitron Metro Market: Little Rock, AR *Format:* Adult Contemp *Hrs. of News Programming:* news progmg 5 hrs wkly *No. News Employees:* 1 *Target Audience:* 25-54; baby boomers
Jeff Peterson, Operations Dir
Kim Pyle, General Manager
Keli Williams, General Sales Mgr
Torrez Harris, Programming Director

Bentonville

KKEG
10-16-1964; 98.3 mhz FM *Hrs Open:* 24; 100 kw; 617 ft.; N36 7 38 W93 59 23
111 East Kilbourn Avenue, Suite 2700, Milwaukee, WI 53202 US
(479) 521-5566, *Fax:* (479) 521-0751
www.921thekeg.com
License: Bentonville, Washington County, AR held by Cumulus Licensing Corp.
Group Owner: Cumulus Media Inc.; (acq 2-1-99; grpsl)
Nat'l Reps: Roslin
Arbitron Metro Market: Fatetteville, AR *Format:* Classic Rock, Rock/AOR *No. News Employees:* 1 *Target Audience:* 18-49.
Joe Conway, General Manager
Becky Dole, General Sales Mgr
Chris Baker, Programming Director
Jay Phillips, News Director
Gregg Judd, Chief Engineer

KSEC
95.7 mhz FM *Hrs Open:* 24; 6 kw; 328 ft.; N36 17 54 W94 10 21
Highway 72 East, Route 5, Gravette, AR 72736 US
(479) 756-8686, *Fax:* (479) 756-8687
www.ezspanishmedia.com
info@ezspanishmedia.com
License: Bentonville, Benton County, AR held by Lazeta 957 Co.
Arbitron Metro Market: Fayetteville, AR *Format:* Tejano
Edwards Vega, General Manager

***KAPG**
01-01-2006; 88.1 mhz FM; 0.75 kw; 230 ft.; N36 23 37 W94 10 53

P O Drawer 2440, Tupelo, MS 38803 US
(662) 844-8888, *Fax:* (662) 842-6791
www.afr.net
faq@afr.net
License: Bentonville, Benton County, AR held by American Family Association.
Group Owner: American Family Radio
Arbitron Metro Market: Fayetteville, AR *Format:* Christian
Marvin Sanders, General Manager
John Riley, Programming Director
Fred Jackson, News Director
Joey Moody, Chief Engineer

Bentonville-Bella

KREB
02-05-1979; 1190 khz AM *Hrs Open:* Sunrise-sunset
10826 Hw 412, Alpena, AR 72611 US
(479) 582-3776, *Fax:* (479) 571-0995
www.newrock1049x.com
License: Bentonville-Bella, AR held by Butler Broadcasting Co. LLC
Nat'l Network: USA
Arbitron Metro Market: Fayetteville (Northwest Arkansas), AR *Format:* Sports, Talk *Target Audience:* 35 plus.
Steve Butler, General Manager
Dave Jackson, Programming Director

Berryville

KTHS
02-01-1958; 1480 khz AM *Hrs Open:* 24; 5 kw-D, ND1; 0.064 kw-N, ND1; N36 21 42 W93 33 40 *Rebroadcasts:* KUOA FM
Mailing Address: P.O. Bx 191, Berryville, AR 72616 US
Second Address: One Radio Dr., Berryville, AR 72616
(870) 423-2147, *Fax:* (870) 423-2146
www.kthsradio.com
studio@kthsradio.com
License: Berryville, AR held by Carroll County Broadcasting Inc.
Arbitron Metro Market: Springfield, MO *Format:* Sports, Talk *Special Programming:* Farm 15 hrs wkly *No. News Employees:* 1 *Target Audience:* General. *Adv. Rates:* $10 6a - 7p
Jay Bunyard, President
Tim Poynter, General Manager
William Autry, General Sales Mgr
Linda Boyer, Programming Director
Zeb Huffmaster, Chief Engineer
Sherri Linz, Traffic Manager

KTHS-FM
12-19-1974; 107.1 mhz FM *Hrs Open:* 24; 3.6 kw; 627 ft.; N36 20 45 W93 29 17
P.O. Bx 191, Berryville, AR 72616 US
(870) 423-2147, *Fax:* (870) 423-2146
www.kthsradio.com
frontdesk@kthsradio.com
License: Berryville, Carroll County, AR held by Carroll County Broadcasting
Nat'l Network: ABC
Arbitron Metro Market: Springfield, MO *Format:* Country *Special Programming:* Tradio 8:30a - 10a *Hrs. of News Programming:* news progmg 21.5 hrs wkly *No. News Employees:* 1 *Target Audience:* General.*Adv. Rates:* :30 $10, :60 $13.50 net
Jay Bunyard, President
Tim Poynter, General Manager
Linda Boyer, Programming Director
Sherri Linz, News Director
Eddie Keever, Sports

Blytheville

*KBCM
01-01-2000; 88.3 mhz FM *Hrs Open:* 24; 1.2 kw; 190 ft.; N35 54 45 W89 53 28
Po Drawer 2440, Tupelo, MS 38803 US
(662) 844-8888, *Fax:* (662) 842-6797
www.afr.net
info@afa.net
License: Blytheville, Mississippi County, AR held by American Family Association.
Group Owner: American Family Radio
Arbitron Metro Market: Tupelo, MS *Format:* Christian
Marvin Sanders, General Manager
John Riley, Programming Director

KHLS
01-01-1948; 96.3 mhz FM; 100 kw; 433 ft.; N35 53 56 W89 52 48
Mailing Address: P. O. Box 989, Blytheville, AR 72315 US
Second Address: 125 S. Second St., Blytheville, AR 72315
(870) 762-2093, *Fax:* (870) 763-8459
www.thundercountry963.com
jwhite@sudburybroadcastinggroup.com
License: Blytheville, Mississippi County, AR
Group Owner: Sudbury Services Inc.
Arbitron Metro Market: Memphis, TN *Format:* Country
Keith Micheals, Operations Dir
Jean Anderson, General Manager
Christina Moore, General Sales Mgr
Torrez Harris, Programming Director
Tom Hill, Chief Engineer
Debbie Polk, Traffic Department

KLCN
01-01-1922; 910 khz AM; 5 kw-D, ND2; 0.085 kw-N, ND2; N35 55 27 W89 52 18
Mailing Address: P. O. Box 989, Blytheville, AR 72316 US
Second Address: 125 S. Second St., Blytheville, AR 72315
(870) 762-2093, *Fax:* (870) 763-8459
License: Blytheville, AR held by Sudbury Services Inc.
Group Owner: Sudbury Services Inc.
Arbitron Metro Market: Memphis, TN *Format:* News, News/Talk, 86
Dave Clark, General Manager
Tom Hill, Chief Engineer

Booneville

KQBK
11-01-1981; 104.7 mhz FM *Hrs Open:* 24; 50 kw; 492 ft.; N35 11 1 W94 7 44
523 Garrison Ave., Suite 201, Ft. Smith, AR 72901 US
(479) 288-1047, *Fax:* (479) 785-2638
www.fox94.com
License: Booneville, Logan County, AR held by Pharis Broadcasting Inc.
Group Owner: Pharis Broadcasting Inc.; acq 11-20-97; $800,000)
Regional Network: Ark. Radio Net. *Nat'l Reps:* Commercial Media Sales *Regional Reps:* BRI
Arbitron Metro Market: Fort Smith, AR *Format:* Oldies *Hrs. of News Programming:* news progmg 10 hrs wkly *No. News Employees:* 1 *Target Audience:* 18-54. *Adv. Rates:* 20; 20; 20; 20
Bill Pharis, President
Ernie Witt, Operations Dir
Karen Pharis, General Manager

*KBHN
01-01-2005; 89.7 mhz FM; 59 kw; 302 ft.; N35 8 25 W94 3 43
Box 6210, Fort Smith, AR 72906 US
(479) 646-6700, *Fax:* (479) 646-1373
www.kzkzfm.com
kzkzfm@kzkzfm.com
License: Booneville, Logan County, AR held by Vision Ministries Inc.
Arbitron Metro Market: Booneville, AR *Format:* Christian
Marilyn Lynch, President
Jay Lynch, Owner/General Manager
Jay Lynch, Station Manager
Al Ross, Programming Director
Ashley Baker, Account Executives/Sales
Tiffany Snow, Account Executives/Sales

Brinkley

KBRI
10-25-1959; 1570 khz AM *Hrs Open:* 6 AM-10 PM; 0.25 kw-D, ND2; 0.023 kw-N, ND2; N34 52 2 W91 12 4
P.O. Box 789, Highway 64 West, Wynne, AR 72396 US
(870) 734-1570, *Fax:* (870) 734-1571
License: Brinkley, AR held by East Arkansas Broadcasters Inc.
Group Owner: East Arkansas Broadcasters Inc.
Regional Network: Ark. Radio Net.
Format: Gospel *No. News Employees:* 1 *Target Audience:* General.
Bobby Caldwell, Station Manager
David Sills, General Sales Mgr
Lane Goodwin, Chief Engineer

Bryant

KKSP
04-01-1989; 93.3 mhz FM *Hrs Open:* 24; 5.6 kw; 699 ft.; N34 47 31 W92 28 38
1402 Highway 270, Malvern, AR 72104 US
(501) 219-1919, *Fax:* (501) 225-4610
www.spirit933.com
donburns@crainmedia.com
License: Bryant, Saline County, AR held by Crain Media Group LLC.
Group Owner: Crain Media Group LLC; (acq 2-1-2008; grpsl)
Arbitron Metro Market: Little Rock, AR *Format:* Christian
Don Burns, Programming Director

Cabot

KPZK-FM
05-01-1993; 102.5 mhz FM *Hrs Open:* 24; 3 kw; 328 ft.; N34 55 22 W92 0 32
City Center West, 7201 W. Lake Mead Blvd, Las Vegas, NV 89128 US
(501) 401-0200, *Fax:* (501) 401-0366
www.praisepage.com
License: Cabot, Lonoke County, AR held by The Last Bastion Station Trust LLC, as Trustee
Nat'l Network: ABC *Nat'l Reps:* McGavren Guild
Arbitron Metro Market: Little Rock, AZ *Format:* Gospel *No. News Employees:* 4 *Target Audience:* 25-49.
Jim Beard, Promotions Manager

KZTD
11-16-1980; 1350 khz AM; 2.5 kw-D, ND1; 0.073 kw-N, ND1; N34 59 59 W92 1 41
#1 Shackleford Drive, Suite 400, Little Rock, AR 72211 US
(501) 378-0104, *Fax:* (501) 305-2977
kztd1350@hotmail.com
License: Cabot, AR held by New World LLC
Arbitron Metro Market: Cabot, AR *Target Audience:* 18-49.
Arik Lev, President
Robert Tindle, Operations Dir
Phil Hall, General Manager
Christy Flynn, General Sales Mgr

Cale

*KEJA
91.7 mhz FM; 3 kw; 446 ft.; N33 28 34 W93 16 23 US
(864) 297-0216, *Fax:* (864) 297-0344
networkofglory.com
info@networkofglory.org
License: Cale, Nevada County, AR held by Network of Glory Inc.
Arbitron Metro Market: Cale, AR *Format:* Christian, Gospel
Lola Richey, President

Calico Rock

KJMT
03-01-2007; 97.1 mhz FM *Hrs Open:* 24; 5.2 kw; 715 ft.; N36 5 31 W92 15 46
US
(870) 425-4971, *Fax:* (870) 424-9717
www.mountaintalk97.com
License: Calico Rock, Izard County, AR held by Malvern Entertainment Corp.
Nat'l Network: Fox News Radio; Premiere Radio Networks; Talk Radio Network; Radio America
Arbitron Metro Market: Calico Rock, AR *Format:* News, News/Talk, 86 *Hrs. of News Programming:* news progmg 29 hrs/week *No. News Employees:* 1
Scott Gray, CEO, General Manager
Kim Szecksi, News Director
Mike Wiseman, Engineering Dir
Dale Hoffman, Host, Producer
Roy Roane, Sales Representative

Camden

KAMD-FM
12-01-1968; 97.1 mhz FM *Hrs Open:* 24; 50 kw; Ant 456 ft; N33 30 14 W92 48 38
612 Fairview Rd, Camden, AR 71701
(870) 836-9567, *Fax:* (870) 836-9500
www.k97online.com
radioworks@cablelynx.com
License: Camden, Ouachita County, AR held by Radio Works Inc.
Group Owner: Radio Works Inc.; (acq 12-13-2004; grpsl).
Population Served: 50,000 *Arbitron Metro Market:* Camden, AR
Greg Arnold, Operations Dir
Donna Stewart, Station Manager
Helen Aregood, News Director
Steve Halatyn, Chief Engineer

*KCAC
06-11-1990; 89.5 mhz FM *Hrs Open:* 8 AM-midnight; 10 kw horiz, 9.9 kw vert; 324 ft.; N33 39 16 W92 40 34
327 Stewart Street S.W., Camden, AR 71701 US
(501) 836-5289, *Fax:* (501) 836-4917
License: Camden, Ouachita County, AR held by Southern Arkansas University Tech
Nat'l Network: ABC
Arbitron Metro Market: Camden. AR *Format:* Alternative *Target Audience:* 18-35.
Quintin Green, Operations Dir
Rachelle Moore, General Manager

KMGC
11-18-1994; 104.5 mhz FM *Hrs Open:* 24; 3 kw; 328 ft; N33 30 14 W92 48 38
133 Washington St., Camden, AR 71701
(870) 836-0104, *Fax:* (870) 836-9500
www.yesradioworks.com
cmbdenradioworks@hotmail.com
License: Camden, Ouachita County, AR held by Radio Works Inc.
Group Owner: Radio Works Inc.; (acq 12-13-2004; grpsl).
Helen Aregood, General Manager
Dan Murphy, General Sales Mgr

KNHD
08-08-1963; 1450 khz AM *Hrs Open:* 24; 1 kw-U, ND1; N33 33 49 W92 50 37
Mailing Address: 3109 Carlisle, Suite 212, Dallas, TX 75204 US
Second Address: 8917 World Ministry Ave., Baton Rouge, LA 70810
(225) 768-3688, *Fax:* (225) 768-3729
www.jsm.org
kawikfish@yahoo.com
License: Camden, AR held by Family Worship Center Church Inc.
Group Owner: Family Worship Center Church Inc.; (acq 3-7-2002; grpsl).
Format: Gospel *No. News Employees:* 1 *Target Audience:* 35 plus.
David Whitelaw, COO
Jimmy Swaggart, President
John Santiago, Programming Director

Cash

KJBX
02-01-1991; 106.3 mhz FM *Hrs Open:* 24; 25 kw; 312 ft.; N35 44 49 W90 37 50
314 Union Street, Jonesboro, AR 72401 US
(870) 933-8800, *Fax:* (870) 933-0403
www.themix1067.com
trey@triplefm.com
License: Cash, Poinsett County, AR held by Saga Communications of Arkansas LLC.
Group Owner: Saga Communications Inc.; (acq 11-8-02; grpsl).
Arbitron Metro Market: Jonesboro, AR *Format:* Adult Contemp *Hrs. of News Programming:* News progmg 2 hrs wkly *Target Audience:* 25-54; women *Adv. Rates:* 34; 43; 34; 59
Trey Stafford, President
Bill Pressly, Station Manager
Kevin Neathery, General Sales Mgr
James Dean, News Director
Al Simpson, Chief Engineer

Cave City

***KVMN**
01-01-1981; 89.9 mhz FM; 3.3 kw; 351 ft.; N35 57 7 W91 32 58
P.O. Box 190, Cave City, AR 72521 US
(870) 283-5331, *Fax:* (870) 283-3255
bsisk@cavecity.ncsc.k12.ar.us
License: Cave City, Sharp County, AR held by Cave City Schools.
Nat'l Network: USA
Arbitron Metro Market: Cave City, AR *Format:* Variety/Diverse, Religious *Target Audience:* General.
Becky Sisk, General Manager

Centerton

KLTK
03-02-1977; 1140 khz AM
1912 South Walton Blvd, Suite A, Bentonville, AR 72712 US
(479) 899-6952, *Fax:* (479) 899-6953
www.lamasmexicana1140.com
sales@lamasmexicana1140.com
License: Centerton, AR held by La Mas Mexicana LLC
Genaro Salas, General Manager

Cherry Valley

***KXRL**
01-01-2007; 90.1 mhz FM; 9 kw; 377 ft.; N35 22 31 W90 43 22
Rebroadcasts: Rebroadcasts WXHL-FM Christiana, DE 100%
3076 Glenfinnan Road, Memphis, TN 38128 US
(800) 220-8078, *Fax:* (302) 738-3090
www.thereachfm.com
info@thereachfm.com
License: Cherry Valley, Cross County, AR held by Priority Radio Inc.
Group Owner: Priority Radio Inc.; (acq 10-14-2005; $200,000 for CP)
Arbitron Metro Market: Cherry Valley, AR *Format:* Christian
Steve Hare, President

Clarksville

KLYR
03-18-1957; 1360 khz AM *Hrs Open:* 16; 0.5 kw-D, ND2; 0.098 kw-N, ND2; N35 28 21 W93 29 28
P.O.188, Clarksville, AR 72830 US
(479) 754-3092
www.klyr.net
License: Clarksville, AR held by Randall P. Forrester.
Arbitron Metro Market: Fatetteville, AR *Format:* Country *Special Programming:* Relg 8 hrs wkly *Hrs. of News Programming:* News progmg 12 hrs wkly *Target Audience:* General.
Randy Forrester, General Manager

KLYR-FM
01-01-1974; 92.7 mhz FM *Hrs Open:* 16; 3 kw; 292 ft.; N35 29 38 W93 32 21
P.O. 188, Clarksville, AR 72830 US
(479) 754-3092
License: Clarksville, Johnson County, AR
Arbitron Metro Market: Fatetteville, AR *Format:* Country
Randy Forrester, General Manager

KXIO
04-01-1991; 106.9 mhz FM; 5.9 kw; 112 ft.; N35 33 7 W93 24 33
205 Amy Lyn Place, Russellville, AR 72801 US
(479) 705-1069, *Fax:* (479) 754-5518
www.kxio-radio.net
office@kxioradio.com
License: Clarksville, Johnson County, AR held by Jody Copeland
Format: Country
Gary Barnett, General Manager
Kelley Ray, Programming Director

Clinton

KGFL
10-01-1977; 1110 khz AM; 5 kw-D; N35 33 30 W92 27 32
Mailing Address: Box 1349, Clinton, AR 72031
Second Address: Corner of Main & Griggs, Clinton, AR 72031
(501) 745-4474, *Fax:* (501) 745-4084
sid@khpq.com
License: Clinton, Van Buren County, AR held by King-Sulivan Radio
Population Served: 20,000*Target Audience:* 35 plus.
Sid King, General Manager
Ali Sugg, General Sales Mgr
Sid King, Programming Director
Dixie Carter, News Director
David Britton

KHPQ
12-23-1982; 92.1 mhz FM; 10 kw; 512 ft.; N35 38 37 W92 27 33
Mailing Address: Post Office Box 33, Clinton, AR 72031 US
Second Address: Corner of Main & Griggs, Clinton, AR 72031
(501) 745-4474, *Fax:* (501) 745-4084
www.infozark.net
sid@khpq.com
License: Clinton, Van Buren County, AR held by King-Sulivan Radio.
Nat'l Network: Jones Radio Networks
Format: Country *Target Audience:* 25 plus.
Dave Britton, Chief Engineer

Colt

KTRQ
10-01-1969; 102.3 mhz FM; 40 kw; 548 ft.; N35 3 16 W90 44 36
Mailing Address: P.O. Box 789, Highway 64 West, Wynne, AR 72396 US
Second Address: Hwy. 70 W., Brinkley, AR 72021
(870) 734-1570, *Fax:* (870) 734-1571
www.ktrq.com
License: Colt, St. Francis County, AR held by East Arkansas Broadcasters Inc.
Group Owner: East Arkansas Broadcasters Inc.
Arbitron Metro Market: Brinkley, AR *Format:* Oldies
Vickie Hooker, General Manager

Conway

***KHDX**
05-01-1973; 93.1 mhz FM; 0.008 kw; 59 ft.; N35 6 1 W92 26 29
Washington & Indpendence, Conway, AR 72032 US
(501) 450-1339, *Fax:* (501) 450-1200
www.hendrix.edu
khdx@hendrix.edu
License: Conway, Faulkner County, AR held by Hendrix College.
Regional Network: Ark. Radio Net.
Format: Variety/Diverse
Julie Marvin, General Manager

KMJX
06-01-1967; 105.1 mhz FM *Hrs Open:* 24; 79 kw; 1053 ft.; N34 47 53 W92 29 33
200 Concord Plaza, Suite 600, San Antonio, TX 78216 US
(501) 217-5000, *Fax:* (501) 228-9547
www.classiccountry1067.com
License: Conway, Faulkner County, AR held by CC Licenses LLC.
Group Owner: Clear Channel Communications Inc.; (acq 5-5-96; grpsl)
Nat'l Reps: Clear Channel
Arbitron Metro Market: Little Rock, AR *Format:* Country *Hrs. of News Programming:* news progmg 3 hrs wkly *No. News Employees:* 1 *Target Audience:* 18-34.
Llowrey Mays, Chairman
Randall Mays, CFO
Mark Mays, President
Bruce Demps, Operations Dir
Joe Rook, General Sales Mgr
Jeff Peterson, Operations Manager

KXXA(AM)
05-26-1961; 1330 khz AM; 500 watts; N35 06 00 W92 26 41
Box 1266, 1117 Oak Street, Suite 300, Conway, AR 72033-1266
(501) 327-6611, *Fax:* (501) 327-7920
License: Conway, Faulkner County, AR held by Creative Media Inc.
Arbitron Metro Market: Little Rock, AR *Format:* Sports *Special Programming:* Farm 6 hrs wkly
Michael Harrison, President
Elaine Harrison, Promotions Manager

***KUCA**
10-10-1966; 91.3 mhz FM *Hrs Open:* 24; 5 kw; 154 ft; N35 02 55 W92 27 49
Mailing Address: Box U-5144, Univ of Central Arkansas, Conway, AR 72032
Second Address: 201 Donaghey Ave., Conway, AR
(501) 450-3326, *Fax:* (501) 450-5874
Montyr@uca.edu
License: Conway, Faulkner County, AR held by University of Central Arkansas.
Population Served: 80,000*Hrs. of News Programming:* News progmg 10 hrs wkly *Target Audience:* 18-54; educated adults
Monty Rowell, General Manager
Dale Johnson, Engineering Dir
Steve Owens, Assistant General Manager

Corning

KBKG
09-15-1983; 93.5 mhz FM; 3 kw; 138 ft.; N36 24 0 W90 35 5
P.O. Box 398, Corning, AR 72422 US
(870) 857-6646, *Fax:* (870) 857-6795
License: Corning, Clay County, AR held by Shields-Adkins Broadcasting Inc.
Nat'l Network: ABC
Arbitron Metro Market: Corning, AR *Format:* Adult Contemp, Oldies
Jim Adkins, CEO

KCCB
02-19-1959; 1260 khz AM; 1 kw-D, ND2; 0.031 kw-N, ND2; N36 24 0 W90 35 5
P.O. Box 398, Corning, AR 72422 US
(870) 857-6646, *Fax:* (870) 857-6795
License: Corning, AR held by Shields-Adkins Broadcasting Inc.
Nat'l Reps: Keystone (unwired net)
Arbitron Metro Market: Corning, AR *Format:* Classic Rock *Target Audience:* General.
Jim Adkins, President
Tina Privett, General Manager
Neil Raines, Programming Director
Palmer Johnson, Chief Engineer

Cotton Plant

KERL
01-01-2008; 99.3 mhz FM; 6 kw; Ant 328 ft; N34 58 07 W90 59 48
Box 711, Wynne, AR
(870) 238-8141, *Fax:* (870) 238-5997
bradfordcaldwell@yahoo.com
License: Cotton Plant, Woodruff County, AR held by Caldwell Media LLC.
Bradfoed Caldwell, CEO/COO
Bradford Caldwell, General Manager

Crossett

KAGH
01-01-1951; 800 khz AM *Hrs Open:* 24; 0.24 kw-D, NDD; N33 8 5 W91 56 49
P.O. Box 697, 117 Ashley 252, Crossett, AR 71635 US
(870) 364-2181, *Fax:* (501) 364-2183
kagh@alltell.net
License: Crossett, AR held by Ashley County Broadcasters Inc.
Nat'l Network: Westwood One *Regional Network:* Ark. Radio Net.
Arbitron Metro Market: Crossett, AR *Format:* Country
Kevin Medlin, President
Russ Miller, Programming Director
Bryan Bailey, News Director

KAGH-FM
03-16-1967; 104.9 mhz FM; 6 kw; 328 ft.; N33 8 5 W91 56 49
P.O. Box 697, 117 Ashley 252, Crossett, AR 71635 US
(870) 364-2181, *Fax:* (501) 364-2183
www.crossettradio.com/todayscountry1049
kagh@alltell.net
License: Crossett, Ashley County, AR held by Ashley County Broadcasters Inc.
Arbitron Metro Market: Crossett, AR *Format:* Country
Jan Stott, General Manager
Nathan Peacock, General Sales Mgr
Jennifer Allen, Programming Director
Stacy Colvin, News Director
Ed Loftus, Chief Engineer
Kathy Vaughan, General Sales Manager

Danville

KYEL
105.5 mhz FM *Hrs Open:* 5am - 11pm; 4.4 kw; 381 ft.; N35 6 11 W93 13 58
3004 Kay Lane, Springdale, AR 72762 US
(479) 890-7207, *Fax:* (479) 967-5278
karv-kyel@yahoo
License: Danville, Yell County, AR held by Danville FM Inc.
Arbitron Metro Market: Russellville, AZ *Format:* Country *Special Programming:* Cardinal Baseball
Diane Womack, General Manager
Chris Womack, Station Manager

Dardanelle

KCAB
03-24-1964; 980 khz AM
Mailing Address: 797 Winrock Drive, Morrilton, AR 72110 US
Second Address: 2705 E. Pkwy., Russellville, AR 72802
(479) 968-6816, *Fax:* (479) 968-2946
www.rivertalk980.com
aaron@rivervalleyradio.com
License: Dardanelle, AR held by MMA License LLC.
Group Owner: MAX Media L.L.C.; (acq 6-6-2003; grpsl)
Nat'l Network: Premiere Radio Networks *Regional Network:* Ark. Radio Net. *Nat'l Reps:* Christal *Wire Services:* AP
Arbitron Metro Market: Russellville, AR *Format:* News, News/Talk, 86 *Target Audience:* 25-54; adults
Aaron Thomas, Operations Dir
Rich Moellers, General Manager
Rhonda Dilbeck, General Sales Mgr
Johnny Story, Programming Director
Jim Alexander, Chief Engineer

KCJC
01-26-1966; 102.3 mhz FM; 1.45 kw; 1322 ft.; N35 13 41 W93 15 20
797 Winrock Drive, Morrilton, AR 72110 US
(757) 437-9800, *Fax:* (479) 968-2946
www.rivervalleyradio.com
rich@rivervalleyradio.com
License: Dardanelle, Yell County, AR held by MMA License LLC.
Group Owner: MAX Media L.L.C.
Nat'l Network: ABC *Regional Network:* Ark. Radio Net. *Nat'l Reps:* Christal *Wire Services:* AP
Arbitron Metro Market: Dardanelle, AR *Format:* Country
Aaron Thomas, Operations Dir
Rich Moellers, General Manager
Rhonda Dilbeck, General Sales Mgr
Johnny Story, Programming Director
Jim Alexander, Chief Engineer
Rhonda Dilbeck, Director of Sales
Aaron Thomas, Operations Manager

KWXT
10-01-1987; 1490 khz AM; 1 kw-U, ND1; N35 13 8 W93 7 38
701 East Main Street, Russellville, AR 72801 US
(479) 754-3399, *Fax:* (479) 968-1337
www.kwxt1490am.com
kwxt1490am@ahoo.com

License: Dardanelle, AR held by George V. Domerese/Sherwood Broadcasting Co.
Arbitron Metro Market: Clarksville, AR *Format:* Christian, Country, 44
Tim Domerese, General Manager
Jim Alexander, Chief Engineer

De Queen

*KBPU
01-01-2002; 88.7 mhz FM; 0.25 kw; 122 ft.; N34 2 38 W94 17 41
P. O. Box 1452, Washington, DC 20013 US
(208) 733-3551, *Fax:* (208) 734-0674
www.edgewaterbroadcasting.com
License: De Queen, Sevier County, AR held by Edgewater Broadcasting Inc.
Format: Christian
Clark Parrish, President

KDQN
08-01-1956; 1390 khz AM; 0.5 kw-D, ND1; N34 1 57 W94 19 43
Mailing Address: P.O. Box 311, Dequeen, AR 71832 US
Second Address: 921 W Collin Raye Dr., De Queen, AR 71832
(870) 642-2446, *Fax:* (870) 642-2442
wwww.kdqn.net
numberonecountry@yahoo.com
License: De Queen, AR held by Jay W. Bunyard & Anne W. Bunyard.
Regional Network: Ark. Radio Net.
Arbitron Metro Market: De Queen, AR
Jay Bunyard, President
Jon Bunyard, General Manager
Victor Rojas, General Sales Mgr

KDQN-FM
10-06-1978; 92.1 mhz FM; 50 kw; 492 ft.; N34 13 35 W94 17 35
Mailing Address: P.O. Box 311, Dequeen, AR 71832 US
Second Address: 921 West Collin Raye Dr, DeQueen, AR 71832
(870) 642-2446, *Fax:* (870) 642-2442
www.kdqn.net
numberonecountry@yahoo.com
License: De Queen, Sevier County, AR held by Jay W. Bunyard & Anne W. Bunyard.
Arbitron Metro Market: De Queen, AR *Format:* Country
Jon Bunyard, General Manager

De Witt

KDEW-FM
09-01-1970; 97.3 mhz FM *Hrs Open:* 24; 50 kw; 272 ft.; N34 25 52 W91 26 8
P.O. Box 907, Stuttgart, AR 72160 US
(870) 673-1595, *Fax:* (870)673-8445
www.country973.com
kdew973@yahoo.com
License: De Witt, Arkansas County, AR held by Arkansas County Broadcasters Inc.
Group Owner: Arkansas County Broadcasters Inc.; acq 3-5-97; $150,000).
Format: Country *No. News Employees:* 1 *Adv. Rates:* 16; 12; 12; 10
Scott Siler, General Manager
Keith Hill, Programming Director
Jonathan Reaves, News Director
Jim Alexander, Engineering Dir
Sandi Levy, Traffic Manager

Dermott

KXSA-FM
08-24-1924; 103.1 mhz FM *Hrs Open:* 24; 5.5 kw; 328 ft.; N33 31 56 W91 34 28
539 W. Gaines, Monticello, AR 71655 US
(870) 367-8528, *Fax:* (870) 367-9564
pinesradio@global.net
License: Dermott, Chicot County, AR held by Pines Broadcasting Inc.
Group Owner: Pines Broadcasting Inc.; (acq 3-14-2007; grpsl)
Arbitron Metro Market: Monticello, AR *Format:* Country
Jimmy Sledge, President

Des Arc

KBDO
01-01-1999; 91.7 mhz FM; 56 kw vert; 682 ft.; N35 0 8 W91 44 41
Po Drawer 2440, Tupelo, MS 38803 US
(662) 844-8888, *Fax:* (662) 842-6791
www.afa.net
License: Des Arc, Prairie County, AR held by American Family Association.
Group Owner: American Family Radio

Arbitron Metro Market: Tupelo, MS *Format:* Religious
Marvin Sanders, General Manager
Gary Vaile, Station Manager
John Riley, Programming Director
Joey Moody, Chief Engineer

KFLI
01-01-2003; 104.7 mhz FM; 25 kw; 328 ft.; N35 0 23 W91 40 20
188 South Bellevue, Suite 222, Memphis, TN 38104 US
(800) 833-9211, *Fax:* (304) 455-1170
www.oldiesradioonline.com
webmaster@greatestmojo.com
License: Des Arc, Prairie County, AR held by George S. Flinn Jr.
Arbitron Metro Market: Little Rock, AR *Format:* Oldies
Ken Madden, General Manager

Dumas

KXFE
09-01-1980; 106.9 mhz FM; 25 kw; Ant 269 ft; N33 58 11 W91 32 58
Box 789, Wynne, AR 71601
(870) 238-8141, *Fax:* (870) 238-5997
License: Dumas, Desha County, AR held by Arkansas County Broadcasters Inc.
Group Owner: East Arkansas Broadcasters; (acq 8-31-2004; $130,000)
Population Served: 12,500
Bobby Caldwell, CEO
Scott Siler, General Manager

Earle

KCJF
01-01-2004; 103.9 mhz FM; 12.5 kw; 469 ft.; N35 27 1 W90 42 11
1515 Jefferson Davis Hyw, Arlington, VA 22202 US
(870) 236-0424, *Fax:* (870) 336-3810
www.1039thegame.com
License: Earle, Crittenden County, AR held by Catherine Joanna Flinn.
Arbitron Metro Market: Jonesboro, AR *Format:* Sports, Talk
Bobby Caldwell, CEO

East Camden

KCXY
09-28-1987; 95.3 mhz FM *Hrs Open:* 24; 100 kw; Ant 456 ft; N33 30 14 W92 48 38
Mailing Address: Box 957, 612 Fairvew Road, Camden, AR 71701
Second Address: 133 Washington St. S.W., Camden, AR 71701
(870) 836-9567, *Fax:* (870) 836-9500
www.camdenfm.net
radioworks@cablelynx.com
License: East Camden, Ouachita County, AR held by Radio Works Inc.
Group Owner: Radio Works Inc.; (acq 12-13-2004; grpsl).
Regional Network: Ark. Radio Net.
Population Served: 12,072 *Arbitron Metro Market:* Camden, AR *Hrs. of News Programming:* news progmg 15 hrs wkly *No. News Employees:* 1 *Target Audience:* 25-54.
Greg Arnold, Operations Dir
Donna Stewart, General Manager

El Dorado

KAGL
09-29-1993; 93.3 mhz FM *Hrs Open:* 24; 18 kw; 354 ft.; N33 16 16 W92 39 17
202 West 19th Street, El Dorado, AR 71730 US
(870) 863-6126, *Fax:* (870) 863-4555
www.eagle933.com
info@totalradio.com
License: El Dorado, Union County, AR held by Noalmark Broadcasting Corp.
Group Owner: Noalmark Broadcasting Corp.; acq 1-8-93; $10,000;
Nat'l Reps: Target Broadcast Sales
Arbitron Metro Market: El Dorado, AR *Format:* Classic Rock *Hrs. of News Programming:* news progmg 15 hrs wkly *No. News Employees:* 1 *Target Audience:* 25-54; general
William Nolan, President
Sandy Sanford, General Manager
Edwin Alderson, Executive Vice President

*KBSA
12-01-1987; 90.9 mhz FM *Hrs Open:* 24; 3 kw; 587 ft.; N33 16 19 W92 42 12 *Rebroadcasts:* Rebroadcasts KDAQ(FM) Shreveport, LA 100%
8515 Youree Drive, Shreveport, LA 71115 US

(800) 552-8502, *Fax:* (318) 797-5265
www.redriverradio.org
listenermail@redriverradio.org
License: El Dorado, Union County, AR held by Board of Supervisors of Louisiana State University & A&M College.
Nat'l Network: NPR; PRI
Format: Classical, Jazz, 60 *Target Audience:* 25+.
Rick Shelton, Operations Dir
Kermit Poling, General Manager

KMRX
05-12-1984; 96.1 mhz FM *Hrs Open:* 24; 100 kw; 446 ft.; N33 16 16 W92 39 17
202 West 19th Street, El Dorado, AR 71730 US
(870) 863-6126, *Fax:* (870) 863-4555
www.totalradio.com
info@totalradio.com
License: El Dorado, Union County, AR held by Noalmark Broadcasting Corp.
Group Owner: Noalmark Broadcasting Corp.; acq 7-31-97).
Arbitron Metro Market: El Dorado, AR *Format:* Adult Contemp *Hrs. of News Programming:* news progmg 2 hrs wkly *No. News Employees:* 1 *Target Audience:* 18-34. *Adv. Rates:* 21; 11; 11; 11
Chase Roberts, Operations Dir
Sandy Sanford, General Manager

KDMS
05-08-1950; 1290 khz AM
1904 W. Hillsboro, El Dorado, AR 71730 US
(870) 863-5121, *Fax:* (870) 863-6221
www.klbq99.com
klbq@suddenlink.com
License: El Dorado, AR held by El Dorado Broadcasting Co.
Arbitron Metro Market: El Dorado, AR *Format:* Adult Contemp
Rosh Partridge, President
Dan Murphy, Operations Dir
Don Travis, General Sales Mgr
Norm Mason, Chief Engineer

KELD
10-17-1935; 1400 khz AM *Hrs Open:* 24; 1 kw-U, ND1; N33 14 14 W92 39 54
202 West 19th Street, El Dorado, AR 71730 US
(870) 863-6126(870) 862-1400, *Fax:* (870) 863-4555
www.totalradio.com
info@totalradio.com
License: El Dorado, Union County, AR held by Noalmark Broadcasting Corp.
Group Owner: Noalmark Broadcasting Corp.; (acq 7-73)
Nat'l Network: Fox Sports *Nat'l Reps:* Target Broadcast Sales
Arbitron Metro Market: El Dorado, AR *Format:* Sports *Target Audience:* General.
William Nolan Jr., President
Patrick Thomas, Operations Dir
Sandy Sanford, General Manager
Steven Gray, Chief Engineer
Edwin Alderson, Executive Vice President

KMLK
01-01-2000; 101.5 mhz FM; 6 kw; 328 ft.; N33 9 32 W92 37 47
4401 Fairgate Drive, Midland, TX 79707 US
(870) 875-1015, *Fax:* (870) 863-4555
www.randbandoldschool.com
License: El Dorado, Union County, AR held by Noalmark Broadcasting Corp.
Group Owner: Noalmark Broadcasting Corp.; acq 6-14-01).
Format: Adult Contemp *Special Programming:* Gospel 5 hrs wkly
Patrick Thomas, Operations Dir
Sandy Sanford, General Manager
Harry Dyer, General Sales Mgr
Cyndal Thompson, News Director
Steven Gay, Chief Engineer

KIXB
12-09-1963; 103.3 mhz FM *Hrs Open:* 24; 100 kw; 571 ft.; N33 13 20 W92 55 28
202 West 19th Street, El Dorado, AR 71730 US
(870) 864-0103, *Fax:* (870) 863-4555
www.totalradio.com
kix103@noalmark.com
License: El Dorado, Union County, AR held by Noalmark Broadcasting Corp.
Group Owner: Noalmark Broadcasting Corp.
Format: Country *Hrs. of News Programming:* News progmg 15 hrs wkly *Target Audience:* 18-54.
Tom Hoyt, Operations Dir
Kim Jennings, General Sales Mgr
Joe Pagano, Programming Director

KLBQ
12-23-1963; 98.7 mhz FM; 14 kw; 299 ft.; N33 12 30 W92 41 16
1904 W. Hillsboro, El Dorado, AR 71730 US
(870) 863-5121, *Fax:* (870) 863-6221
klbq@suddenlink.com
License: El Dorado, Union County, AR held by El Dorado Broadcasting Co.
Arbitron Metro Market: Monroe, LA *Format:* Adult Contemp, Contemporary Hits/Top 40
Dan Murphy, Programming Director

*KAKV
01-01-2003; 88.9 mhz FM *Hrs Open:* 24; 26 kw; 377 ft.; N33 12 30 W92 42 30
188 S Bellevue, Suite 222, Memphis, TN 38104 US
(800) 525-5683, *Fax:* (916) 251-1650
www.klove.com
klove@klove.com
License: El Dorado, Union County, AR held by Educational Media Foundation.
Group Owner: EMF Broadcasting; (acq 1-23-2008; $320,000 with WLRK(FM) Greenville, MS)
Nat'l Network: K-Love
Arbitron Metro Market: El Dorado, AR *Format:* Christian
Darrell Chambliss, Chairman
Mike Novak, President and CEO
Glenn Goodwin, Operations Dir
David Pierce, Programming Director
Ed Lenane, News Director
Sam Wallington, Engineering Dir
Laura Daniels, News Reporter
Tim Luttrell, NewsReporter
Kenny Noble Cortes, News Reporter
Darren Vinson, News Reporter
Brian Burger, Vice President of Human Resources
D. Kevin Blair, Secretary and General Counsel

England

KVDW
08-31-1979; 1530 khz AM *Hrs Open:* 24
#1 Shackleford Drive, Suite 400, Little Rock, AR 72211 US
(501) 864-7120, *Fax:* (501) 842-9308
www.vern1530am.com
victory1530@yahoo.com
License: England, AR held by Wells Broadcasting Inc.
Arbitron Metro Market: Little Rock, AR *Format:* Gospel, Religious, 86 *Special Programming:* Farm 5 hrs, talk 10 hrs wkly *Target Audience:* 18-54; professionals, farmers, college educated
Vernon Wells, General Manager

KHTE-FM
09-26-1988; 96.5 mhz FM *Hrs Open:* 24; 10.5 kw; 495 ft.; N34 29 10 W92 9 27
#1 Shackleford Drive, Suite 400, Little Rock, AR 72211 US
(501) 219-1919, *Fax:* (501) 225-6140
www.khits965.com
donburns@crainmedia.com
License: England, Lonoke County, AR held by Crain Media Group LLC.
Group Owner: Crain Media Group LLC; (acq 2-1-2008; grpsl)
Arbitron Metro Market: Little Rock, AR *Format:* Contemporary Hits/Top 40
Neal Gladner, General Manager
Vince Fruge, General Sales Mgr
Ed Johnson, Programming Director
Chris Duncan, Chief Engineer

Eudora

KAVH
01-01-2001; 101.5 mhz FM *Hrs Open:* 24; 6 kw; 328 ft.; N33 11 58 W91 15 39
1991 West Greenwood Road, Glendale, WI 53209 US
(414) 764-4953
info@kavh.com
License: Eudora, Chicot County, AR held by Joel J. Kinlow.
Arbitron Metro Market: Eudora, AR *Format:* Variety/Diverse
Bruce Herz, Operations Dir
Joel Kinlow, General Manager

Eureka Springs

KESA
05-13-1985; 100.9 mhz FM *Hrs Open:* 6 AM-10 PM; 2 kw; 509 ft.; N36 22 48 W93 44 52
1411 Locust Street, St. Louis, MO 63103 US
(479) 253-9001, *Fax:* 4(79) 253-9002
License: Eureka Springs, Carroll County, AR held by Northeast Oklahoma Broadcast Network Inc.
Group Owner: Northeast Oklahoma Broadcast Network Inc.; (acq 5-7-2008; $302,000)
Regional Network: Ark. Radio Net.
Arbitron Metro Market: Grove, AR *Format:* Adult Contemp *Special Programming:* Class 10 hrs, hits of the 50s & 60s 2 hrs wkly *Hrs. of News Programming:* news progmg 20 hrs wkly *No. News Employees:* 1 *TargetAudience:* 35 plus; upper income & retired
Larry Hestand, President

Fairfield Bay

KFFB
12-31-1981; 106.1 mhz FM *Hrs Open:* 24; 15.5 kw; 879 ft.; N35 44 0 W92 15 37
130 Liberty Lane, Batesville, AR 72501 US
(501) 884-6812, *Fax:* (501) 723-4861
www.kffb.com
kffb@kffb.com
License: Fairfield Bay, Van Buren County, AR held by Freedom Broadcasting Inc.
Group Owner: 2510 Licenses LLC
Nat'l Network: ABC *Regional Network:* Ark. Radio Net.
Arbitron Metro Market: Fairfield Bay, AR *Format:* Adult Contemp *Hrs. of News Programming:* news progmg 8 hrs wkly *No. News Employees:* 2 *Target Audience:* 35 plus; middle & upper income
Bob Connell, President
Chad Whiteaker, Operations Dir
Bob Connell, General Manager
Chick Watkins, Music Director
Vic Schedler, Weather Director

Farmington

KFAY
12-15-1946; 1030 khz AM *Hrs Open:* 24; 10 kw-D, DA2; 1 kw-N, DA2; N36 6 34 W94 10 59
111 East Kilbourn Avenue, Suite 2700, Milwaukee, WI 53202 US
(479) 521-5566, *Fax:* (479) 521-0751
www.newstalk1030.com
info@kfayam.com
License: Farmington, AR held by Cumulus Licensing Corp.
Group Owner: Cumulus Media Inc.; (acq 2-1-99; grpsl)
Arbitron Metro Market: Fayetteville (Northwest Arkansas), AR *Format:* News, News/Talk, 86 *Hrs. of News Programming:* news progmg 20 hrs wkly *No. News Employees:* 6 *Target Audience:* 25-64; general
Joe Conway, General Manager
Dan Hentschel, Programming Director
Anita Cowan, Promotions Manager
Dale Daniels, Market Manager

Fayetteville

*KAYH
06-26-2000; 89.3 mhz FM *Hrs Open:* 24; 6 kw; 381 ft.; N36 10 48 W94 5 10
Box 6210, Forth Smith, AR 72906 US
(479) 750-7893, *Fax:* (479) 927-1250
License: Fayetteville, Washington County, AR held by Community Broadcasting Inc.
Group Owner: Bott Radio Network; (acq 1-14-2008; $450,000)
Arbitron Metro Market: Fayetteville (Northwest Arkansas), AR *Format:* Christian, Talk
Mike Disney, General Sales Mgr

*KBNV
01-01-2000; 90.1 mhz FM *Hrs Open:* 24; 7.1 kw horiz, 16 kw vert; 466 ft.; N36 7 38 W93 59 23
P O Drawer 2440, Tupelo, MS 38803 US
(662) 844-8888, *Fax:* (662) 844-9090
info@afa.net
License: Fayetteville, Washington County, AR held by American Family Association.
Group Owner: American Family Radio
Arbitron Metro Market: Fayetteville (Northwest AR), AR *Format:* Christian
John Riley, Programming Director

KEZA
09-06-1983; 107.9 mhz FM; 99 kw; 1260 ft.; N35 51 12 W94 1 33
600 Congress Ave., Suite 1400, Austin, TX 78701 US
(479) 582-1079, *Fax:* (479) 587-8255
www.magic1079.com
License: Fayetteville, Washington County, AR held by Capstar TX L.P.
Group Owner: Clear Channel Communications Inc.; (acq 8-30-00; grpsl).
Arbitron Metro Market: Fayetteville (Northwest Arkansas), AR *Format:* Adult Contemp *Special Programming:* Jazz, oldies *Target Audience:* 25-54.
Tony Beringer, General Manager
Jim Harvill, Programming Director
Jess Smith, News Director
Zeb Huffmaster, Chief Engineer

KQSM-FM
11-07-1983; 92.1 mhz FM *Hrs Open:* 24; 7.6 kw; 531 ft.; N36 7 38 W93 59 23
111 East Kilbourn Avenue, Suite 2700, Milwaukee, WI 53202 US
(479) 521-5566, *Fax:* (479) 521-0751
www.921theticket.com
License: Fayetteville, Benton County, AR held by Cumulus Licensing Corp.
Group Owner: Cumulus Media Inc.; (acq 2-1-99; grpsl).
Arbitron Metro Market: Fayetteville (Northwest Arkansas), AR *Format:* Country *Special Programming:* Class 2 hrs wkly *Target Audience:* 25-54.
Joe Conway, General Manager
Josh Bertaccini, Programming Director
Dale Daniels, Market Manager

KKIX
10-01-1966; 103.9 mhz FM *Hrs Open:* 24; 100 kw; 482 ft.; N36 1 17 W94 13 4
600 Congress Ave., Suite 1400, Austin, TX 78701 US
(479) 521-0104, *Fax:* (479) 444-8600
www.kix104.com
info@kkixfm.com
License: Fayetteville, Washington County, AR held by Capstar TX L.P.
Group Owner: Clear Channel Communications Inc.; (acq 8-30-00; grpsl).
Arbitron Metro Market: Fatetteville, AR *Format:* Country *Hrs. of News Programming:* news progmg 2 hrs wkly *No. News Employees:* 1 *Target Audience:* 25-54.
Tony Beringer, General Manager
Jay Steele, Programming Director
Zeb Huffmaster, Chief Engineer

KOFC
06-10-1957; 1250 khz AM *Hrs Open:* 16
1658 Carolyn, Fayetteville, AR 72701 US
(479) 750-7893, *Fax:* (479) 927-1250
License: Fayetteville, AR held by Community Broadcasting Inc.
Group Owner: Bott Radio Network; (acq 1-15-2008)
Arbitron Metro Market: Fayetteville (Northwest Arkansas), AR *Format:* Christian, Talk *Target Audience:* 35 plus; traditional Christian families
Michael Disney, Operations Dir

***KUAF**
01-15-1973; 91.3 mhz FM *Hrs Open:* 24; 100 kw; 1089 ft.; N35 51 12 W94 1 32
406 Administration Bldg., Fayetteville, AR 72701 US
(479) 575-2556, *Fax:* (479) 575-8440
www.kuaf.com
kuaf.info@uark.edu
License: Fayetteville, Washington County, AR held by Board of Trustees University of Arkansas.
Nat'l Network: NPR
Arbitron Metro Market: Fayetteville, AR *Format:* Jazz, News *Special Programming:* Folk 5 hrs, Black 5 hrs wkly *Hrs. of News Programming:* news progmg 45 hrs wkly *No. News Employees:* 3 *Target Audience:* 25-65.
Pete Hartman, Operations Dir
Rick Stockdell, Station Manager
Rhonda Dillard, General Sales Mgr
P.J. Robowski, Programming Director
Kyle Kellams, News Director
Doyle Garner, Chief Engineer
Molly Rawn, Major Giving/Membership
Rhonda Dillard, Underwriting Director
Christina Thomas, Development Coordinator/OAL Producer
Katy Henriksen, Classical Music/OAL & Arts Producer
Jacqueline Froelich, Ozarks at Large Producer/NPR Correspondent
Antoinette Grajeda, Ozarks AtLarge Producer

***KXUA**
04-04-2000; 88.3 mhz FM *Hrs Open:* 24; 0 kw horiz, 0.47 kw vert; 262 ft.; N36 3 56 W94 10 30
406 Administration Bldg., Fayetteville, AR 72701 US
(479) 575-4273, *Fax:* (479) 575-2019
www.kxua.com
info@kxua.com
License: Fayetteville, Washington County, AR held by Board of Trustees of University of Arkansas.
Arbitron Metro Market: Fayetteville, AR *Format:* Variety/Diverse *Target Audience:* 12-24; high school and colege students
Richard Adams, General Manager
David Zeek Martin, Station Manager
Tyler Eck, Programming Director
Terry Johnson, Promotions Manager
TG Keas, Music Director
Harrison Grimwood, Production Manager

Fordyce

KBJT
08-01-1959; 1590 khz AM *Hrs Open:* 24
303 Spring Street, Fordyce, AR 72742 US
(870) 352-7137, *Fax:* (870) 352-7139
kbjtkq.com
kbjt@windstream.net
License: Fordyce, AR held by KBJT Inc.
Arbitron Metro Market: Fordyce, AR *Format:* News, News/Talk, 86 *Special Programming:* Gospel 11 hrs wkly *Target Audience:* General. *Adv. Rates:* 8; 8; 8; 8
Gary Coates, President
Gary Coates, General Manager
Carna Coates, Programming Director
Saxon Coates, News Director

KQEW
02-23-1982; 102.3 mhz FM; 25 kw; 328 ft.; N33 48 10 W92 26 10
303 Spring Street, Fordyce, AR 71742 US
(870) 352-7137, *Fax:* (870) 352-7139
www.kbjtkq.com
License: Fordyce, Dallas County, AR held by Dallas Properties Inc.
Format: News, Talk *Target Audience:* General. *Adv. Rates:* 12; 12; 12; 12

Forrest City

***KARH**
01-01-2000; 88.1 mhz FM; 4.2 kw; 508 ft.; N35 12 11 W90 33 57
P.O. Drawer 2440, Tupelo, MS 38803 US
(662) 844-8888, *Fax:* (662) 842-6791
www.afr.net
License: Forrest City, St. Francis County, AR held by American Family Association.
Group Owner: American Family Radio
Arbitron Metro Market: Tupelo, MO *Format:* Religious
Marvin Sanders, General Manager
John Riley, Programming Director
Joey Moody, Chief Engineer

KXJK
04-29-1949; 950 khz AM *Hrs Open:* 24; 5 kw-D, ND1; 0.087 kw-N, ND1; N34 58 53 W90 51 27
P. O. Box 707, Forrest City, AR 72336 US
(870) 633-1252, *Fax:* (870) 633-1259
www.kxjk.com
radio@arkansas.net
License: Forrest City, AR held by Forrest City Broadcasting Co. Inc.
Regional Network: Ark. Radio Net. *Regional Reps:* Midsouth
Format: Classic Rock, News, 62, Talk *Special Programming:* Farm 16 hrs wkly *Hrs. of News Programming:* news progmg 24 hrs wkly *No. News Employees:* 2 *Target Audience:* General.
William Fogg, General Manager

Fort Smith

***KAOW**
01-01-1999; 88.9 mhz FM *Hrs Open:* 24; 1.387 kw; 482 ft.; N35 26 50 W94 21 54
P.O. Drawer 2440, Tupelo, MS 38803 US
(479) 883-8131
www.889radio.com
info@thelightsoutherngospelradio.com
License: Fort Smith, Sebastian County, AR held by American Family Association.
Group Owner: American Family Radio
Arbitron Metro Market: Fort Smith, AR *Format:* Religious
Marvin Sanders, General Manager
Bruce Park, Station Manager
John Riley, Programming Director
Joey Moody, Chief Engineer

KLSZ-FM
07-27-1978; 100.7 mhz FM *Hrs Open:* 24; 50 kw; 459 ft.; N35 13 32 W94 20 29
323 North Greenwood, Fort Smith, AR 72901 US
(479) 452-0681, *Fax:* (479) 452-0873
www.rock1007.com
info@rock1007.com
License: Fort Smith, Sebastian County, AR held by Cumulus Licensing Corp.
Group Owner: Cumulus Media Inc.; (acq 5-1-99; $1 million)
Arbitron Metro Market: Fort Smith, AR *Format:* Oldies *Hrs. of News Programming:* News progmg 7 hrs wkly *Target Audience:* 25-64.
Smitty O'Loughlin, General Manager
Matt Miller, Programming Director

KENA
07-01-1950; 1450 khz AM *Hrs Open:* 24; 1 kw-U, ND1; N34 34 23 W94 14 55
Mailing Address: P.O. Box 1450, Mena, AR 71953 US
Second Address: 1600 S. Reine St., Mena, AR 71953
(501) 394-1450, *Fax:* (501) 394-1459
License: Fort Smith, AR held by Ouachita Broadcasting Inc.
Group Owner: Ouachita Broadcasting Inc.; (acq 1-14-99; $750,000 with co-located FM)
Format: Gospel *Hrs. of News Programming:* news progmg 10 hrs wkly *No. News Employees:* 1 *Target Audience:* 18 plus; industrial & agricultural workers, retirees, tourists & professionals
Dwight Douglas, General Manager
Matt Stone, News Director
Sue Canner, Promotions Director

KFPW
07-27-1930; 1230 khz AM *Hrs Open:* 24
Mailing Address: 323 North Greenwood, Fort Smith, AR 72901 US
Second Address: 323 N. Greenwood, Fort Smith, AR 72902
(479) 288-1047, *Fax:* (479) 785-2638

http://www.sportshog1031.com/
billpharis40@yahoo.com
License: Fort Smith, AR held by Pharis Broadcasting Inc.
Group Owner: Pharis Broadcasting Inc.; (acq 3-14-2002; $850,000 with KFPW-FM Barling).
Nat'l Network: ABC *Regional Network:* Ark. Radio Net. *Nat'l Reps:* Commercial Media Sales
Arbitron Metro Market: Fort Smith, AR *Format:* News, Talk *Special Programming:* Sports 15 hrs wkly *Hrs. of News Programming:* News progmg 13 hrs wkly *Target Audience:* 35 plus; affluent *Adv. Rates:* 12; 12;12; 12
Bill Pharis, President
Karen Pharis, Operations Dir
Dennis McCaslin, Traffic Manager

KFSA
02-13-1947; 950 khz AM; 1 kw-D, DA2; 0.5 kw-N, DA2; N35 25 58 W94 28 13
Four Glen Haven Dr., Fort Smith, AK 72901 US
(501) 646-6700, *Fax:* (501) 646-1373
License: Fort Smith, AR held by Fred H. Baker Sr.
Arbitron Metro Market: Fort Smith, AR *Format:* Religious *Target Audience:* General.
Fred Baker Sr., President
Jerry Lynch, General Manager
David Burdue, Programming Director

KISR
08-13-1971; 93.7 mhz FM *Hrs Open:* 24; 100 kw; 1250 ft.; N35 31 22 W94 23 32
Mailing Address: 4 Glen Haven Drive, Fort Smith, AR 72901 US
Second Address: 601 N. Greenwood, Fort Smith, AR 72901
(501) 785-2526, *Fax:* (479) 782-9127
www.kisr.net
info@kisr.net
License: Fort Smith, Sebastian County, AR held by Stereo 93 Inc.
Arbitron Metro Market: Fort Smith, AR *Format:* Contemporary Hits/Top 40 *No. News Employees:* 1 *Target Audience:* 18-39.
Fred Baker Jr., General Manager
Gary Keifer, Station Manager
Carol Patterson, General Sales Mgr
Dale Davenport, Engineering Dir
Rick Hayes, Music Director

KMAG
12-31-1964; 99.1 mhz FM *Hrs Open:* 24; 94 kw; 1969 ft.; N35 4 26 W94 40 48
600 Congress Ave., Suite 1400, Austin, TX 78701 US
(479) 782-8888, *Fax:* (479) 785-5946
www.kmag991.com
info@kmag991.com
License: Fort Smith, Sebastian County, AR held by Capstar TX L.P.
Group Owner: Clear Channel Communications Inc.; (acq 8-30-00; grpsl).
Arbitron Metro Market: Fort Smith, AR *Format:* Country *No. News Employees:* 2 *Target Audience:* 25-54; females
Ralph Cherry, Operations Dir
Paul Swint, General Manager
Phil Robken, General Sales Mgr
Gary Elmore, News Director
Allan Riley, Chief Engineer

KTCS
03-01-1956; 1410 khz AM; 1 kw-D, ND2; 0.13 kw-N, ND2; N35 16 40 W94 22 35

Mailing Address: PO Box 180188, Fort Smith, AR 72918 US
Second Address: 5304 Hwy. 45 E, Fort Smith, AR 72916
(479) 646-6151, Fax: (479) 646-3509
www.ktcs.com
info@ktcs.com
License: Fort Smith, AR held by Big Chief Broadcasting Co.
Arbitron Metro Market: Fort Smith, AR Format: Gospel
Lee Young, Station Manager
Lee Young, General Sales Mgr
Troy Eckelhoff, Programming Director
Melissa Eckelhoff, Promotions Manager
Sandy Hunter, News Director

KTCS-FM
08-15-1964; 99.9 mhz FM; 100 kw; 1919 ft.; N35 4 20 W94 40 50
Mailing Address: P. O. Box 6321, Fort Smith, AR 72906 US
Second Address: 5304 Hwy. 45 E., Fort Smith, AR 72916
(479) 646-6151, Fax: (479) 646-3509
www.ktcs.com
info@ktcs.com
License: Fort Smith, Sebastian County, AR held by Big Chief Broadcasting Co.
Arbitron Metro Market: Fort Smith, AR Format: Country
Melissa Harper, Operations Dir
Lee Young, General Manager
Lee Young, Station Manager
Lee Young, General Sales Mgr
Troy Eckelhoff, Programming Director
Melissa Eckelhoff, Promotions Manager
Mary Livingston, News Director
ScottReeves, Chief Engineer
Sandy Hunter, Traffic Manager

KWHN
11-22-1947; 1320 khz AM Hrs Open: 24; 5 kw-D, DAN; 5 kw-N, DAN; N35 24 36 W94 21 30
600 Congress Ave., Suite 1400, Austin, TX 78701 US
(479) 782-8888, Fax: (479) 785—5946
www.kwhn.com
License: Fort Smith, AR held by Capstar TX L.P.
Group Owner: Clear Channel Communications Inc.
Arbitron Metro Market: Fort Smith, AR Format: News, News/Talk, 86 Hrs. of News Programming: news progmg 40 hrs wkly No. News Employees: 6 Target Audience: 25-54.
Paul Swint, General Manager
Phil Robken, General Sales Mgr
Maverick, Programming Director
Mike Burgess, Director of Sales

***KEAF**
01-01-2009; 90.7 mhz FM; 26 kw vert; 2087 ft.; N35 9 56 W93 40 36 Rebroadcasts: Rebroadcasts WBFR(FM) Birmingham, AL 100%
4135 Northgate Blvd, Suite 1, Sacramento, CA 95834 US
(800) 543-1495, Fax: (510) 568-6190
www.familyradio.com
info@familyradio.com
License: Fort Smith, Sebastian County, AR held by Family Stations Inc.
Group Owner: Family Stations Inc.
Arbitron Metro Market: Fort Smith, AR Format: Christian
Harold Camping, General Manager

Fouke

***KPOS**
01-01-2001; 104.3 mhz FM Hrs Open: 24; 5 kw; 361 ft.; N33 21 5 W93 50 41
707 Green Cook Rd, Sunbury, OH 43074 US
(916) 251-1600, Fax: (916) 251-1650
www.air1.com
info@air1.com
License: Fouke, Miller County, AR held by Educational Media Foundation.
Group Owner: EMF Broadcasting; (acq 1-15-2004; $500,000)
Nat'l Network: Air 1
Format: Alternative, Christian No. News Employees: 3 Target Audience: 25-44; Judeo Christian, female
Darrell Chambliss, Chairman
Mike Novak, CEO
Mike Novak, President
Alan Mason, Operations Dir
Eric Allen, General Sales Mgr
David Pierce, Programming Director
Ed Lenane, News Director
Sam Wallington, Engineering Dir
MaryaMorgan, News Reporter
Richard Hunt

Ft. Smith

KYHN
01-01-2001; 1650 khz AM
600 Congress Ave., Suite 1400, Austin, TX 78701 US
(479) 782-8888, Fax: (479) 782-0366
www.kwhn.com
info@kwhn.com
License: Ft. Smith, AR held by Capstar TX L.P.
Group Owner: Clear Channel Communications Inc.
Arbitron Metro Market: Fort Smith, AR Format: News, News/Talk, 86
Paul Swint, General Manager
Tony Montgomery, General Sales Mgr

Glenwood

KWXI
05-12-1980; 670 khz AM Hrs Open: 6 AM-midnight; 5 kw-D, NDD; N34 19 32 W93 33 27
Mailing Address: P.O. Box 831, Arkadelphia, AR 71923 US
Second Address: 180 Hwy. 70 E., Suite 11, Glenwood, AR 71943
(870) 356-2151(870) 356-2181, Fax: (870) 356-4684
www.kwxi.net
info@kwxi.net
License: Glenwood, AR held by US Stations LLC.
Group Owner: US Stations LLC; (acq 2-9-2005; $530,000 with co-located FM).
Regional Reps: Rgnl Reps
Arbitron Metro Market: Glenwood, AR Format: Gospel Hrs. of News Programming: News progmg 8 hrs wkly Target Audience: 34-54; affluent professionals Adv. Rates: 10.59; 10.59; 10.59; 10.59
Lenny Brothers, Operations Dir
Bob DelGiorno, GM, News Director, Sports Director and Sales Mgr
Doug Dumont, Programming Director
Jamie Allan, News Director
Tony Evans, Chief Engineer
Ted Kelly, VP Programming, Webmaster
JanaBradford, Attorney
Meghan DelGiorno, Owner, Human Resources, Chief Financial Officer

Gosnell

KAMJ
02-01-1999; 93.9 mhz FM Hrs Open: 24; 1 kw; 489 ft.; N35 53 56 W89 52 48
P.O. Box 989, Blytheville, AR 72315 US
(870) 762-2093, Fax: (870) 763-8459
License: Gosnell, Mississippi County, AR held by Phoenix Broadcasting Group Inc.
Group Owner: Sudbury Services Inc.
Arbitron Metro Market: Gosnell, AR Format: Urban Contemporary
Dave Clark, General Manager

Gould

KOTN(FM)
04-15-1999; 102.5 mhz FM Hrs Open: 24; 6 kw; Ant 177 ft; N33 58 11 W91 32 58
Mailing Address: Box 910, Stuttgart, AR 92160
Second Address: 1818 S. Buerkle, Stuttgart, AR 92160
(870) 673-1595, Fax: (870) 673-8445
kdew973@yahoo.com
License: Gould, Lincoln County, AR held by Arkansas County Broadcasters Inc.
Group Owner: Arkansas County Broadcasters Inc.; acq 12-30-2003; $90,000)
Arbitron Metro Market: Gould, AR Format: Country
Scott Siler, Station Manager
Sandi Levey, News Director

KOTN
03-12-1934; 102.5 mhz FM Hrs Open: 24; 6 kw; 177 ft.; N33 58 11 W91 32 58
City Center West, 7201 W. Lake Mead Blvd, Las Vegas, NV 89128 US
(870) 534-8911,(501) 534-8978, Fax: (870) 534-8984
License: Gould, Jefferson County, AR held by M.R.S. Ventures Inc.
Group Owner: M.R.S. Ventures Inc.; (acq 4-29-2003; $350,000).
Nat'l Network: Westwood One
Format: Adult Contemp, News, 62, Sports, Talk Hrs. of News Programming: news progmg 7 hrs wkly No. News Employees: 1 Target Audience: 25-54.
Andy Hodges, General Manager

Gravette

KURM-FM
10-01-1989; 100.3 mhz FM; 1.75 kw; 610 ft.; N36 25 54 W94 30 46
1912 South Walton Blvd, Sutie A, Bentonville, AR 72712 US
(479) 633-0790, Fax: (479) 631-9711
www.kurm.net
kurm@kurm.net
License: Gravette, Benton County, AR held by KERM Inc.
Group Owner: KERM Inc.; (acq 4-4-2002; $350,000 with KLTK(AM) Centerton)
Arbitron Metro Market: Rogers, AK Format: News, News/Talk, 86
Kermit Womack, General Manager

Green Forest

***KGSF**
01-01-2008; 88.7 mhz FM; 5 kw vert; 595 ft.; N36 21 38 W93 44 54 Rebroadcasts: Rebroadcasts KAWZ(FM) Twin Falls, ID 100%
3000 W Macarthur Blvd., Santa Ana, MO 92704 US
(208) 734-6633, Fax: (208) 736-1958
www.csnradio.com
License: Green Forest, Carroll County, AR held by Calvary Chapel of Twin Falls Inc.
Group Owner: CSN International
Arbitron Metro Market: Green Forest, AR Format: Christian
Mike Kestler, President

Greenbrier

KCNY
10-15-1984; 107.1 mhz FM; 12.5 kw; 466 ft.; N35 17 47 W92 19 11
914 James Street, Searcy, AR 72143 US
(501) 832-0925, Fax: (501) 279-2900
www.y107fm.com
jrrunyon@crainmedia.com
License: Greenbrier, White County, AR held by Crain Media Group LLC
Group Owner: Crain Media Group LLC
Format: Adult Contemp
Florence Rogers, President
Phil Burger, Operations Dir
Melanie Canon, General Sales Mgr
JR Runyon, Programming Director
Lynn Dyer, Promotions Manager
Warren Brown, Chief Engineer
Jay Bartos, Public Affairs Director

Greenwood

KZKZ-FM
12-01-1981; 106.3 mhz FM Hrs Open: 24; 15 kw; 397 ft.; N35 13 44 W94 15 45
6420 South Zero, Fort Smith, AR 72903 US
(479) 646-6700, Fax: (479) 646-1373
www.kzkzfm.com
kzkzfm@kzkzfm.com
License: Greenwood, Pike County, AR held by Family Communications Inc.
Arbitron Metro Market: Greenwood, AR Format: Christian
Jerry Lynch, General Manager
Jay Lynch, Station Manager
Dave Burdul, Programming Director

Gurdon

KYXK
12-01-1984; 106.9 mhz FM Hrs Open: 24; 17.5 kw; 302 ft.; N33 56 42 W93 10 43
Mailing Address: P.O. Box 831, Arkadelphia, AR 71923 US
Second Address: 601 S. 7th St., Arkadelphia, AR 71923
(870) 246-9272, Fax: (870) 246-5878
www.clarkcountybroadcasting.com
License: Gurdon, Clark County, AR held by Noalmark Broadcasting Corp.
Group Owner: Noalmark Broadcasting Corp.; (acq 6-29-2007; grpsl)
Arbitron Metro Market: Gurdon, AR Format: Country Target Audience: 25-54; adults
William Nolan Jr., President
Stephanie Collie, General Sales Mgr
Randy Seale, Programming Director
Ronna Pennington, News Director

Hamburg

KHMB
01-01-1996; 99.5 mhz FM Hrs Open: 24; 3.2 kw; 312 ft.; N33 17 19 W91 52 45

1707 Louisa Street, Rayville, LA 71269 US
(870) 364-4700, *Fax:* (870) 364-4770
www.QLiteradio.com
qlite@arkansas.net
License: Hamburg, Ash County, AR held by R&M Broadcasting
Format: Adult Contemp *Target Audience:* 25-54
Dennis Maxwell, General Manager
Jane Jordan, General Sales Mgr

Hampton

KELD-FM
11-26-1984; 107.1 mhz FM *Hrs Open:* 24; 17.5 kw; 302 ft.; N33 32 23 W92 34 59
P O Box 831, Arkadelphia, AR 71923 US
(870) 863-6126, *Fax:* (870) 863-4555
www.keldfm.com
info@totalradio.com
License: Hampton, Calhoun County, AR held by Noalmark Broadcasting Corp.
Group Owner: Noalmark Broadcasting Corp.; acq 2-21-03; $250,000).
Nat'l Network: ABC; Fox News Radio
Arbitron Metro Market: Monroe, LA *Format:* News, News/Talk, 86
Sandy Sanford, General Manager

*KBPW
01-01-2001; 88.1 mhz FM; 60 kw vert; 338 ft.; N33 32 11 W92 28 7
P O Box 1452, Washington, DC 20013 US
(662) 844-8888, *Fax:* (662) 842-6791
License: Hampton, Calhoun County, AR held by American Family Association Inc.
Group Owner: American Family Radio; (acq 4-19-01).
Arbitron Metro Market: Tupelo, MS *Format:* Christian
Marvin Sanders, General Manager
John Riley, Programming Director
Joey Moody, Chief Engineer

Hardy

KOOU
10-04-1993; 104.7 mhz FM *Hrs Open:* 24; 5.4 kw; 305 ft.; N36 16 29 W91 30 18
P.O. Box 480, Hardy, AR 72542 US
(870) 856-3240, *Fax:* (870) 856-4408
hometownradio@centurytec.net
License: Hardy, Sharp County, AR held by KOOU Inc.
Regional Network: Ark. Radio Net.
Format: Adult Contemp *Hrs. of News Programming:* news progmg 10 hrs wkly *No. News Employees:* 2 *Target Audience:* 25-60; female/professional *Adv. Rates:* 12; 10; 11; 7
James Bragg, General Manager

Harrisburg

KWHF
05-15-1999; 95.9 mhz FM *Hrs Open:* 24; 34 kw; 489 ft.; N35 47 42 W90 47 35
Mailing Address: P.O. Box 540, Jonesboro, AR 72403 US
Second Address: 407 W. Parker Rd., Jonesboro, AR 72404
(870) 932-8400, *Fax:* (870) 932-3814
License: Harrisburg, Poinsett County, AR held by CC Licenses LLC.
Group Owner: Clear Channel Communications Inc.; (acq 6-13-2002; $2.05 million with KNEA(AM) Jonesboro).
Arbitron Metro Market: Jonesboro, AR *Format:* Country *Hrs. of News Programming:* news progmg 3 hrs wkly *No. News Employees:* 2 *Target Audience:* 28-65; affluent baby boomers who have spendable income *Adv.Rates:* 16; 14; 16; 10
Scott Silar, General Manager
Dennis Rogers, News Director

Harrison

*KBPB
01-01-2001; 91.9 mhz FM *Hrs Open:* 24; 5.5 kw; 341 ft.; N36 22 12 W93 13 23
1411 Locust Street, St. Louis, MO 63103 US
(800) 228-5284, *Fax:* (573) 896-4376
License: Harrison, Boone County, AR held by New Life Evangelistic Center Inc.
Format: Christian, Gospel
Larry Rice, General Manager

KCWD
01-01-1982; 96.1 mhz FM *Hrs Open:* 24; 8 kw; 1191 ft.; N36 6 41 W93 2 0
Mailing Address: P.O. Box 2639, Gulfport, MS 39505 US
Second Address: 600 S. Pine, Harrison, AR 72601
(870) 741-1402, *Fax:* (870) 741-9702
www.kcwdradio.com/index.php
kcwd@all.net
License: Harrison, Boone County, AR held by Harrison Radio Station Inc.
Arbitron Metro Market: Harrison, AR *Format:* Classic Rock
Roger Lowery, General Manager
Linda Peter, General Sales Mgr
Barbara Dean, Office Manager

KHOZ
09-28-1946; 900 khz AM *Hrs Open:* 24; 1 kw-D, ND1; 0.062 kw-N, ND1; N36 14 35 W93 6 43
Pob 430 One Radio Aven., Harrison, AR 72601 US
(870) 741-2302, *Fax:* (870) 741-3299
www.khoz.com
scottieearls@krzk.com
License: Harrison, AR held by KHOZ LLC.
Group Owner: Earls Broadcasting Co.; (acq 6-16-2005; $3.7 million with co-located FM)
Nat'l Network: CBS *Wire Services:* AP
Format: Country *Special Programming:* Sports 20 hrs wkly *Hrs. of News Programming:* news progmg 15 hrs wkly *No. News Employees:* 3 *Target Audience:* General. *Adv. Rates:* 8.50; 8.50; 8.50; 8.50
Charles Earls, CEO
Rob McBee, Operations Dir
Scottie Earls, General Manager
Marilyn Wallus, Station Manager
Tammy Stevens, Office Manager
Lesli Bruce, Administrative Assistant

KHOZ-FM
03-25-1963; 102.9 mhz FM *Hrs Open:* 24; 100 kw; 981 ft.; N36 26 11 W93 14 43
P.O. Box 430, One Radio Avenue, Harrison, AR 72601 US
(870) 741-2301, *Fax:* (870) 741-3299
www.khoz.com
scottieearls@krzk.com
License: Harrison, Boone County, AR held by KHOZ LLC.
Group Owner: Earls Broadcasting Co.
Nat'l Network: CBS Radio *Wire Services:* AP
Format: Country *Hrs. of News Programming:* news progmg 15 hrs wkly *No. News Employees:* 2 *Target Audience:* 25-54. *Adv. Rates:* 37; 37; 37; 37
Rob McBee, Operations Dir
Scottie Earls, General Manager
Marilyn Wallus, Station Manager
Brent Klein, Programming Director
Patty Eddings, News Director
Tammy Stevens, Office Manager
Lesli Bruce, Administrative Assistant
JerryBowman, Disc Jockey
Jamie Cooleg, News Reporter
Tom Parker, Reporter

Hatfield

KILX
01-01-2001; 104.1 mhz FM *Hrs Open:* 24; 28.5 kw; 469 ft.; N34 32 42 W94 18 21
P.O. Box 311, Dequeen, AR 71832 US
(479) 394-1450
License: Hatfield, Polk County, AR held by Ouachita Broadcasting Inc.
Group Owner: Ouachita Broadcasting Inc.; (acq 3-8-99).
Arbitron Metro Market: Hatfield, AR *Format:* Adult Contemp
Dwight Douglas, General Manager

Heber Springs

KAWW
07-15-1967; 1370 khz AM *Hrs Open:* 6 AM-sunset (2 hrs past); 1 kw-D, NDD; N35 29 10 W92 2 5
#1 Shackleford Dr., Suite 400, Little Rock, AR 72211 US
(501) 268-7123, *Fax:* (501) 279-2900
jrrunyon@crainmedia.com
License: Heber Springs, AR held by Crain Media Group LLC
Group Owner: Crain Media Group LLC; acq 8-7-02; grpsl).
Regional Network: Ark. Radio Net.
Arbitron Metro Market: Heber Springs, AR *Format:* News, News/Talk, 86 *Hrs. of News Programming:* news progmg one hr wkly *No. News Employees:* 1 *Target Audience:* 25-65. *Adv. Rates:* 8; 8; 8; 8
Larry Crain, CEO
J.R. Runyon, General Manager

KEAZ
09-01-1972; 100.7 mhz FM *Hrs Open:* 24; 50 kw; 328 ft.; N35 27 26 W92 2 11
#1 Shackleford Dr., Suite 400, Little Rock, AR 72211 US
(501) 268-7123, *Fax:* (501) 279-2900
jrrunyon@crainmedia.com
License: Heber Springs, Cleburne County, AR held by Crain Media Group LLC.
Group Owner: Crain Media Group LLC; (acq 8-7-2002; grpsl)
Arbitron Metro Market: Heber Springs, AR *Format:* Adult Contemp *Target Audience:* 25-54.
Larry Crain, CEO
J.R. Runyon, General Manager

*KBMJ
01-01-2002; 89.5 mhz FM *Hrs Open:* 24; 70 kw vert; 735 ft.; N35 44 0 W92 15 37
P.O. Drawer 2440, Tupelo, MS 38803 US
(662) 844-8888
info@kbmjfm.com
License: Heber Springs, Cleburne County, AR held by American Family Association.
Group Owner: American Family Radio
Format: Christian
Marvin Sanders, General Manager

Helena

KFFA
11-19-1941; 1360 khz AM *Hrs Open:* 24; 1 kw-D, ND1; 0.09 kw-N, ND1; N34 31 39 W90 37 48
P.O. Box 430, Helena, AR 72342 US
(870) 338-8361(870) 338-8331, *Fax:* (870) 338-8332
www.kffa.com
kffa@arkansas.net
License: Helena, AR held by Delta Broadcasting Inc.
Arbitron Metro Market: Helana, AR *Format:* Country *Special Programming:* Farm 16 hrs, blues 8 hrs, Black 10 hrs, sports 15 hrs, gospel 4 hrs wkly *Hrs. of News Programming:* News progmg 25 hrs wkly *Target Audience:* 18-54.
Jim Howe, President
Rose Seaton, Operations Dir
Louis Smith, Programming Director
Nancy Howie, News Director
Jerry Campbell, Engineering Dir

KFFA-FM
01-01-1972; 103.1 mhz FM *Hrs Open:* 24; 13 kw; 318 ft.; N34 31 39 W90 37 46
Mailing Address: P.O. Box 430, Helena, AR 72342 US
Second Address: 1360 Radio Dr., Helena, AR 72342
(870) 338-8361(870) 338-8331, *Fax:* (870) 338-8332
www.kffa.com
kffa@arkansas.net
License: Helena, Phillips County, AR held by Delta Broadcasting Inc.
Arbitron Metro Market: Helana, AR *Format:* Adult Contemp, Sports *Hrs. of News Programming:* News progmg 4 hrs wkly
Jim Howe, CEO
Rose Seaton, Programming Director
Kacye Patton, News Director
Louis Smith, Music Critic

KJIW-FM
01-05-1989; 94.5 mhz FM *Hrs Open:* 24; 14 kw; 413 ft.; N34 31 28 W90 35 47
204 Moore Street, Helena, AR 72342 US
(870) 338-2700
kjiwfm@ipa.net
License: Helena, Phillips County, AR held by Elijah Mondy Jr.
Format: Gospel
Elijah Mondy Jr., General Manager
April Mondy, Programming Director
Zipporah Mondy, Music Director

Hope

KHPA
04-21-1977; 104.9 mhz FM; 6 kw; 328 ft.; N33 43 12 W93 29 11
Mailing Address: P. O. Box 989, Blytheville, AR 72316 US
Second Address: 1600 S. Elm, Hope, AR 71801
(870) 777-8868, *Fax:* (870) 777-8888
www.supercountry105.com
SonyaOdom@supercountry105.com
License: Hope, Hempstead County, AR held by Newport Broadcasting Co.
Group Owner: Sudbury Services Inc.
Format: Country *Target Audience:* General.
Kelley Ray, Operations Dir
Sonya Odom, General Manager
Kathy Davis, General Sales Mgr
Amanda Smith, News Director
Kevin McKinnon, Chief Engineer

KXAR
12-12-1947; 1490 khz AM; 0.7 kw-U, ND1; N33 41 20 W93 35 55

Mailing Address: Box 320 Hwy 29 At I-30, Hope, AR 71801 US
Second Address: 1600 S. Elm, Hope, AR 71801
(870) 777-8868, *Fax:* (870) 777-8888
khpafm@supercountry105.com
License: Hope, AR held by Newport Broadcast Co.
Group Owner: Sudbury Services Inc.; (Acq 8-26-99; $51,000)
Regional Network: Ark. Radio Net.
Arbitron Metro Market: Hope, AR *Format:* Talk *Target Audience:* General; double income, stable, adult households
Byron Gerson, President
Don Sandler, General Manager

KBYB
12-31-1984; 101.7 mhz FM *Hrs Open:* 24; 50 kw; 492 ft.; N33 40 46 W93 49 42
Highway 29 At I-30, Hope, AR 72801 US
(903) 793-4671, *Fax:* (903) 792-4261
www.1017bobfm.com
License: Hope, Hempstead County, AR held by Arklatex LLC.
Group Owner: Arklatex LLC; (acq 1-3-2007; grpsl)
Nat'l Reps: Interep
Arbitron Metro Market: Texarkana, TX *Format:* Adult Contemp *Target Audience:* 25-54.
Scott Gray, CFO

Horseshoe Bend

KKIK
01-01-2004; 106.5 mhz FM; 12 kw; 476 ft.; N36 15 22 W91 55 23
720 Ramsey Street, Batesville, AR 72503 US
(870) 793-4196, *Fax:* (870) 793-5222
License: Horseshoe Bend, Izard County, AR held by WRD Entertainment Inc.
Group Owner: WRD Entertainment Inc.
Arbitron Metro Market: Horseshoe Bend, AR *Format:* Oldies
Gary Bridgman, General Manager

Hot Springs

***KALR**
05-01-1989; 91.5 mhz FM *Hrs Open:* 24; 4.5 kw; 486 ft.; N34 37 31 W93 0 37
P.O. Box 8500, Hot Springs, AR 71910 US
(888) 937-2471
www.air1.com
info@air1.com
License: Hot Springs, Garland County, AR held by Educational Media Foundation.
Group Owner: EMF Broadcasting; (acq 6-28-2007; $275,000)
Nat'l Network: Air 1
Arbitron Metro Market: Omaha, NB *Format:* Alternative, Christian
Darrell Chambliss, Chairman
Mike Novak, CEO
Mike Novak, President

KZHS
03-10-1953; 590 khz AM; 5 kw-D, ND2; 0.067 kw-N, ND2; N34 29 55 W92 58 45
P.O. Box 6021, Hot Springs, AR 71901 US
(501) 525-4600, *Fax:* (501) 525-4344
License: Hot Springs, AR held by Noalmark Broadcasting Corp.
Group Owner: Noalmark Broadcasting Corp.; (acq 12-13-2004; $140,000)
Nat'l Network: Fox Sports
Arbitron Metro Market: Hot Springs, AR *Format:* News, News/Talk, 84, Talk
Eddie Tarpley, General Manager

KLAZ
10-01-1971; 105.9 mhz FM; 95 kw; 994 ft.; N34 22 20 W93 2 51
202 West 19th Street, El Dorado, AR 71730 US
(510) 525-1301, *Fax:* (501) 525-4344
License: Hot Springs, Garland County, AR held by Noalmark Broadcasting Corp.
Group Owner: Noalmark Broadcasting Corp.
Arbitron Metro Market: Little Rock, AR *Format:* Adult Contemp *Target Audience:* 18-49.
Raul Alarcon Jr., CEO
Peter Remington, General Manager
Jason Wilberding, General Sales Mgr
Juan Hidalog, Programming Director
Patty Castor, Promotions Manager

KYDL(FM)
06-18-1965; 96.7 mhz FM *Hrs Open:* 24; 940 w; Ant 807 ft; N34 24 13 W93 07 14
125 Corporate Terr., Hot Springs, AR 71913-7248
(501) 525-9700, *Fax:* (501) 525-9739
www.star96fm.com
hot967@ussations.com
License: Hot Springs, Garland County, AR held by US Stations LLC.
Group Owner: US Stations LLC; (acq 2-1-2005; grpsl).
Population Served: 65,631*Format:* Adult Contemp *Target Audience:* 18 plus.
Craig Dale, Operations Dir
Gary Terrell, General Manager
Neal Gladner, General Sales Mgr
Melissa Waters, News Director

KQUS-FM
02-07-1969; 97.5 mhz FM *Hrs Open:* 24; 100 kw; 860 ft; N34 24 11 W93 07 13
125 Corporate Terr., Hot Springs, AR 72702
(501) 525-9700, *Fax:* (501) 525-9739
www.us97country.com
info@usstations.com
License: Hot Springs, Garland County, AR
Group Owner: US Stations LLC; 10/1/2004
Nat'l Network: CBS *Nat'l Reps:* Local Focus *Wire Services:* AP
Population Served: 128,000 *Arbitron Metro Market:* Hot Springs, AR *No. News Employees:* 1 *Target Audience:* 18-54.
Gary Terrell, General Manager
Paul Swint, General Sales Mgr
Craig Dale, Programming Director
Craig Dale, News Director
Gary Terrell, Chief Engineer
Tom Duke, Music Director

***KLRO**
03-20-1984; 90.1 mhz FM *Hrs Open:* 24; 38 kw; 971 ft.; N34 30 18 W93 4 42
600 Garland Avenue, Hot Springs, AR 71913 US
(916) 251-1600, *Fax:* (916) 251-1650
www.klove.com
License: Hot Springs, Garland County, AR held by Educational Media Foundation.
Group Owner: EMF Broadcasting; (acq 9-24-2004; $1.2 million).
Nat'l Network: K-Love
Arbitron Metro Market: Rocklin, CA *Format:* Christian
Darrell Chambliss, Chairman
Mike Novak, CEO/COO
Mike Novak, President
Glenn Goodwin, Operations Dir
Eric Allen, General Sales Mgr
David Pierce, Programming Director
Ed Lenane, News Director
Sam Wallington, Engineering Dir
Marya Morgan, News Reporter
Richard Hunt, News Reporter

KBHS
10-06-1966; 1420 khz AM; 5 kw-D, ND1; 0.087 kw-N, ND1; N34 27 19 W93 3 26
Mailing Address: 202 West 19th Street, El Dorado, AR 71730 US
Second Address: 208 Buena Vista Rd., Hot Springs, AR 71902
(501) 525-1301, *Fax:* (501) 525-4344
www.klaz.com
klaz@klaz.com
License: Hot Springs, AR held by Noalmark Broadcasting Corp.
Group Owner: Noalmark Broadcasting Corp.
Nat'l Reps: Target Broadcast Sales
Format: Adult Contemp *Target Audience:* 35 plus; upscale, high-income residents & business people
Eddie Tarpley, General Manager

KZNG
01-01-1953; 1340 khz AM *Hrs Open:* 24; 1 kw-U, ND1; N34 29 43 W93 1 27
P.O. Box 459, Cave Springs, AR 72718 US
(501) 525-9700, *Fax:* (501) 525-9739
www.myhotsprings.com
dck_antoine@yahoo.com
License: Hot Springs, AR held by US Stations LLC.
Group Owner: US Stations LLC; (acq 2-1-2005; grpsl).
Nat'l Network: ABC; Premiere Radio Networks; Westwood One
Regional Network: Ark. Radio Net. *Wire Services:* AP
Arbitron Metro Market: Hot Springs, AR *Format:* News, News/Talk, 86 *Hrs. of News Programming:* news progmg 10 hrs wkly *No. News Employees:* 1 *Target Audience:* 18 plus.
Gary Terrell, General Manager
Paul Swint, Director Of Sales
Craig Dale, Programming Director
Melissa Walters, News Director

Hot Springs Village

KVRE
02-01-1994; 92.9 mhz FM *Hrs Open:* 24; 25 kw; 328 ft.; N34 38 34 W93 4 8
P. O. Box 8439, Hot Springs Village, AR 71909 US
(501) 922-5678(501) 922-5880(501) 922-9444, *Fax:* (501) 922-6626
kvre@kvre.com
License: Hot Springs Village, Garland County, AR held by Caddo Broadcasting Co.
Nat'l Network: Music of Your Life
Arbitron Metro Market: Hot Springs, AR *Format:* Adult Contemp *Target Audience:* 35 plus; general
Alice Bates, Operations Dir
Polly Nichols, General Manager
Cyrie Wright, General Sales Mgr
Tom Nichols, Programming Director
John Chapman, News Director
Scotty Mack, Production Manager

Hoxie

***KJLV**
01-20-1988; 105.3 mhz FM *Hrs Open:* 24; 25 kw; 328 ft.; N36 3 36 W91 2 44
Post Office Box 540, Jonesboro, AR 72403 US
(707) 528-9236, *Fax:* (707) 528-9246,(916) 251-1650
www.klove.com
License: Hoxie, Lawrence County, AR held by Educational Media Foundation.
Group Owner: EMF Broadcasting; (acq 11-1-01; $1.3 million with KJBR(FM) Marked Tree).
Arbitron Metro Market: Jonesboro, AR *Format:* Christian *Adv. Rates:* 10; 7; 10; na
Jon Taylor, CFO
Mike Novak, President
David Wolf, Operations Dir
Eric Allen, Programming Director
David Pierce, Promotions Manager
Ed Lenane, News Director
Sam Wallington, Engineering Dir
Richard Hunt, News Reporter
MaryaMorgan, News Reporter

Humnoke

KVLO
01-01-1996; 101.7 mhz FM; 6 kw; 328 ft.; N34 32 58 W91 45 26
City Center West, 7201 W. Lake Mead Blvd, Las Vegas, NV 89128 US
(501) 401-0200, *Fax:* (501) 401-0366
License: Humnoke, Lonoke County, AR held by The Last Bastion Station Trust LLC, as Trustee
Arbitron Metro Market: Little Rock, AR *Format:* Adult Contemp
Jim Beard, Operations Dir

Huntsville

KAKS
01-01-1955; 99.5 mhz FM; 14 kw; 443 ft.; N36 7 37 W93 51 57
70 North East St., Suite 100, Fayetteville, AR 72701 US
(479) 443-9960, *Fax:* (479) 444-9670
License: Huntsville, Madison County, AR held by Davidson Media Station KREB-FM Licensee LLC.
Group Owner: Davidson Media Group LLC; (acq 2-10-2005; $3.9 million with KCZZ(AM) Mission, KS).
Nat'l Network: ABC
Arbitron Metro Market: Fayetteville (Northwest Arkansas), AR *Format:* Sports *Target Audience:* 25-54; general
Steve Butler, General Manager

Jacksonville

KDJE
09-29-1969; 100.3 mhz FM *Hrs Open:* 24; 83 kw; 1053 ft.; N34 47 53 W92 29 33
200 Concord Plaza, Suite 600, San Antonio, TX 78216 US
(501) 217-5000, *Fax:* (501) 374-0808
www.edgelittlerock.com
jeffcage@clearchannel.com
License: Jacksonville, Pulaski County, AR held by CC Licenses LLC.
Group Owner: Clear Channel Communications Inc.; (acq 5-15-96; grpsl).
Nat'l Reps: Clear Channel
Arbitron Metro Market: Little Rock, AR *Format:* Rock/AOR *Hrs. of News Programming:* news progmg 3 hrs wkly *No. News Employees:* 1 *Target Audience:* 18-49.
Jeff Peterson, Operations Dir
Keli Williams, General Sales Mgr

Jonesboro

***KAOG**
01-01-1999; 90.5 mhz FM; 40 kw; 397 ft.; N35 48 36 W90 48 45
P O Drawer 2440, Tupelo, MS 38803 US
(662) 844-8888, *Fax:* (662) 842-6191
www.afr.net
License: Jonesboro, Craighead County, AR held by American Family Association.

Group Owner: American Family Radio
Arbitron Metro Market: Tupelo, MO *Format:* Religious
Marvin Sanders, General Manager
John Riley, Programming Director
Joey Moody, Chief Engineer

***KASU**
05-17-1957; 91.9 mhz FM *Hrs Open:* 24; 100 kw; 689 ft.; N35 53 27 W90 40 26
P.O. Box 2160, State University, AR 72467 US
(870) 972-2200, *Fax:* (870) 972-2997
www.kasu.org
kasu@astate.edu
License: Jonesboro, Craighead County, AR held by Arkansas State University.
Nat'l Network: PRI; NPR *Wire Services:* AP
Arbitron Metro Market: State University, AZ *Format:* Classical, Jazz, 60 *Special Programming:* New age, blues, folk 4 hrs, big band 2 hrs wkly *Hrs. of News Programming:* news progmg 45 hrs wkly *No. News Employees:* 1 *Target Audience:* General.
June Taylor, Operations Dir
Micheal Doyle, Station Manager
Marty Scarbrough, Programming Director
Greg Chance, News Director
Eddy Arnold, Chief Engineer
Osa Amienyi, Director of Broadcasting
Mark Smith, Morning Edition Host
Greg Chance, News Director
Marty Scarbrough, Programming Director

KBTM
03-15-1930; 1230 khz AM *Hrs Open:* 24
Mailing Address: P.O. Drawer 1737, Jonesboro, AK 72403 US
Second Address: 407 W. Parker Rd., Jonesboro, AR 72404
(870) 935-5598, *Fax:* (870) 932-3814
License: Jonesboro, AR held by Capstar TX L.P.
Group Owner: Clear Channel Communications Inc.
Regional Network: Ark. Radio Net.
Arbitron Metro Market: Jonesboro, AR *Format:* News, News/Talk, 86 *Hrs. of News Programming:* news progmg 14 hrs wkly *No. News Employees:* 2 *Target Audience:* 45 plus; upscale adults
Barbara Nelson, General Sales Mgr
Kevin Box, Promotions Manager
Janice Reid, News Director

KEGI
11-21-1986; 100.5 mhz FM *Hrs Open:* 24; 38 kw; Ant 558 ft; N35 56 59 W90 39 58
314 Union Ave., Jonesboro, AR 72401
(870) 933-8800, *Fax:* (870) 933-0403
eagle1005.com
trey@triplefm.com
License: Jonesboro, Craighead County, AR held by Saga Communications of Arkansas LLC.
Group Owner: Saga Communications Inc.; (acq 11-8-2002; grpsl)
Arbitron Metro Market: Jonesboro, AR *Hrs. of News Programming:* news progmg one hr wkly *No. News Employees:* 1 *Target Audience:* 18-49. *Adv. Rates:* 31; 36; 31; 11
Trey Stafford, President
Kevin Neathery, General Sales Mgr
Bill Pressly, Group Program Director
Al Simpson, Chief Engineer
Rick Christian, Programming Director

KFIN
03-04-1974; 107.9 mhz FM *Hrs Open:* 24; 98 kw; 600 ft.; N35 47 56 W90 44 31
Mailing Address: P.O. Drawer 1737, Jonesboro, AR 72403 US
Second Address: 407 W. Parker Rd., Jonesboro, AR 72404
(870) 932-1079, *Fax:* (870) 932-0892
www.kfin.com
info@kfin.com
License: Jonesboro, Craighead County, AR held by Capstar TX L.P.
Group Owner: Clear Channel Communications Inc.; (acq 1-18-01; grpsl).
Arbitron Metro Market: Jonesboro, AR *Format:* Country *Special Programming:* Farm 13 hrs wkly *Hrs. of News Programming:* news progmg 9 hrs wkly *No. News Employees:* 1 *Target Audience:* 25-54; broaddemographics
Brandon Baxter, Operations Dir
Larry James, General Manager
Barbara Nelson, Station Manager
Dennis Rogers, News Director

KNEA
09-20-1950; 970 khz AM *Hrs Open:* 24
Post Office Box 540, Jonesboro, AR 72403 US
(870) 932-8400, *Fax:* (870) 932-3814
www.knea970.com
License: Jonesboro, AR held by CC Licenses LLC.
Group Owner: Clear Channel Communications Inc.; (acq 6-13-2002; $2.05 million with KWHF(FM) Harrisburg).
Regional Network: Ark. Radio Net.
Arbitron Metro Market: Jonesboro, AR *Format:* Gospel *Special Programming:* Farm 6 hrs wkly *No. News Employees:* 5 *Target Audience:* General.
Scott Silar, General Manager
Ray Sharp, Programming Director
Dennis Rogers, News Director

***KJSB**
88.3 mhz FM; 1.9 kw vert; 299 ft.; N35 48 36 W90 48 45 US
(662) 844-5036, *Fax:* (662) 842-7798
www.afr.net
contact@afa.net
License: Jonesboro, Craighead County, AR held by Solid Rock Broadcasting Inc.
Arbitron Metro Market: Jonesboro, AR *Format:* Christian
Donald E. Wildmon, Founder
Barbara Coggin, President
Buster Wilson, General Manager
Jennifer Hagman, Programming Director

Judsonia

KVHU
01-01-2006; 95.3 mhz FM *Hrs Open:* 24; 14 kw; Ant 440 ft; N35 13 41 W91 29 19
Box 10765, Searcy, AR
(501) 279-4886, *Fax:* (501) 279-4065
www.kvhu.harding.edu
kvhu@harding.edu
License: Judsonia, White County, AR held by George S. Flinn Jr.
Target Audience: 35+.
Dutch Hoggatt, General Manager

Kensett

KHAN(FM)
01-01-2007; 105.7 mhz FM; 15 kw; Ant 426 ft; N35 17 20 W91 46 17
401 S. Spring St., Searcy, AR 72143
(501) 268-9700
License: Kensett, White County, AR held by Malvern Entertainment Corp.
Population Served: 1,284 *Arbitron Metro Market:* Deadwood, SD *Format:* Adult Contemp
Scott Gray, President
Amber Carson, General Manager

Lake City

KDXY
10-04-1971; 104.9 mhz FM *Hrs Open:* 24; 25 kw; 480 ft; N35 49 29 W90 33 54
314 Union Ave., Jonesboro, AR 72401
(870) 933-8800, *Fax:* (870) 933-0403
www.thefox1049.com
trey@triplefm.com
License: Lake City, Craighead County, AR held by Saga Communications of Arkansas LLC.
Group Owner: Saga Communications Inc.; (acq 11-8-02; grpsl).
Population Served: 120,000*Hrs. of News Programming:* news progmg 6 hrs wkly *No. News Employees:* 1 *Target Audience:* 25-49. *Adv. Rates:* 82; 76; 54; 10
Trey Stafford, President
Kevin Neathery, General Sales Mgr
Christy Matthews, Programming Director
Al Simpson, Chief Engineer

Lake Village

***KUUZ**
07-30-1977; 95.9 mhz FM *Hrs Open:* 24; 20 kw; 302 ft.; N33 20 7 W91 7 33
Mailing Address: P. O. Box 1794, Greenville, MS 38702 US
Second Address: 8919 World Ministry Ave., Baton Rouge, LA 70810
(225) 768-3288, *Fax:* (225) 768-3729
www.jsm.org
onair@jsm.org
License: Lake Village, Chicot County, AR held by Family Worship Center Church Inc.
Group Owner: Family Worship Center Church Inc.; acq 6-12-02; $500,000).
Arbitron Metro Market: Lake Village, AR *Format:* Religious
David Whitelaw, COO
Van Michael, President
John Santiago, Programming Director

Lakeview

KKTZ
05-01-1999; 93.5 mhz FM; 7.1 kw; 623 ft.; N36 29 13 W92 29 39
P.O. Box 2639, Gulfport, MS 39502 US
(870) 492-6022, *Fax:* (870) 492-2137
www.kktz.net
stewartbrunner@twinlakesradio.com
License: Lakeview, Baxter County, AR held by John M. Dowdy.
Arbitron Metro Market: Mountain Home, AR *Format:* Adult Contemp *Target Audience:* 24-25.
Morgan Dowdy, CEO
Stewart Brunner, Operations Dir
Stewart Brunner, General Manager
Roger Lowery, Station Manager

Little Rock

KAAY
12-20-1924; 1090 khz AM; 50 kw-D, DAN; 50 kw-N, DAN; N34 36 0 W92 13 30
City Center West, 7201 W. Lake Mead Blvd, Las Vegas, NV 89128 US
(501) 401-0200, *Fax:* (501) 401-0387
www.1090kaay.com
info@1090kaay.com
License: Little Rock, AR
Group Owner: Cumulus Media Inc.; (acq 9-30-98; $5 million).
Nat'l Network: USA
Arbitron Metro Market: Little Rock, AR *Format:* Gospel, Religious *Special Programming:* Sp 2 hrs wkly *Adv. Rates:* 14; 14; 14; 14
Joe Booker, Operations Dir
John Scuderi, General Sales Mgr
Jim Beard, Promotions Manager

***KABF**
09-30-1984; 88.3 mhz FM *Hrs Open:* 24; 91 kw; 778 ft.; N34 47 31 W92 28 38
2101 S Main Street, Suite 200, Little Rock, AR 72206 US
(501) 372-6119, *Fax:* (501) 376-3952
www.kabf.us
radiokabf@yahoo.com
License: Little Rock, Pulaski County, AR held by Arkansas Broadcasting Foundation.
Arbitron Metro Market: Little Rock, AR *Format:* Black, Gospel, 52, Variety/Diverse *Special Programming:* Sp 10 hrs, folk 10 hrs, American Indian 3 hrs, blu *Hrs. of News Programming:* news progmg 12 hrs wkly *No. NewsEmployees:* 1 *Target Audience:* General; low-moderate income & politically disenfranchised
Pat House, General Manager
John Cain, Programming Director

KARN
01-01-1928; 920 khz AM *Hrs Open:* 24; 5 kw-D, DAN; 5 kw-N, DAN; N34 46 20 W92 14 45
City Center West, 7201 W. Lake Mead Blvd, Las Vegas, NV 89128 US
(501) 401-0200, *Fax:* (501) 401-0387
www.karnnewsradio.com
karn@karnnewsradio.com
License: Little Rock, AR
Group Owner: Cumulus Media Inc.; (acq 8-27-97; grpsl).
Nat'l Network: CBS *Regional Network:* Ark. Radio Net. *Wire Services:* ESSA Weather Service
Arbitron Metro Market: Little Rock, AZ *Format:* News, News/Talk, 86 *Hrs. of News Programming:* news progmg 28 hrs wkly *No. News Employees:* 10 *Target Audience:* 35-64.
Jim Beard, Promotions Manager

KTUV
10-01-1956; 1440 khz AM *Hrs Open:* 24; 5 kw-D, DAN; 0.24 kw-N, DAN; N34 42 46 W92 16 48
723 West 14th Street, Little Rock, AK 72202 US
(501) 375-1440, *Fax:* (877) 426-1447
kita1440@earthlink.net
License: Little Rock, AR held by Birach Broadcasting Corp.
Group Owner: Birach Broadcasting Corp.; (acq 1-31-2008; $1.5 million with KJMU(AM) Sand Springs, OK)
Arbitron Metro Market: Little Rock, AR *Adv. Rates:* 35; 25; 35; 15
John Rice, General Manager
Sam Scott, Programming Director
Wilma Scott, Traffic Manager

KJBN
01-01-1946; 1050 khz AM; 1 kw-D, ND1; 0.019 kw-N, ND1; N34 45 58 W92 17 38
1800 Maple Street, North Little Rock, AR 72114 US
(501) 791-1000, *Fax:* (501) 791-7121
License: Little Rock, AR held by Joshua Ministries and Community Development Corp.

Arbitron Metro Market: Little Rock, AR *Format:* Gospel *Target Audience:* Career-oriented people.
James Smith, General Manager
Chris Bryant, Station Manager

KKPT
10-26-1960; 94.1 mhz FM *Hrs Open:* 24; 100 kw; 1601 ft.; N34 47 56 W92 29 44
P.O. Box 795365, Dallas, TX 75379 US
(501) 664-9410, *Fax:* (501) 664-5871
www.kkpt.com,signalmedia.com
License: Little Rock, Pulaski County, AR held by Signal Media of Arkansas.
Nat'l Reps: D & R Radio *Wire Services:* AP
Arbitron Metro Market: Little Rock, AR *Format:* Contemporary Hits/Top 40, Adult Contemp *Hrs. of News Programming:* news progmg one hr wkly *No. News Employees:* 1 *Target Audience:* 25-54; adults *Adv. Rates:* 90; 80; 85; 25
Philip Jonsson, President
Mike Kennedy, Programming Director
Chuck Gatlin, Promotions Manager

KPZK
01-01-1929; 1250 khz AM *Hrs Open:* 24; 2 kw-D, DA2; 1.2 kw-N, DA2; N34 42 5 W92 13 2
City Center West, 7201 W. Lake Mead Blvd, Las Vegas, NV 89128 US
(501) 401-0200, *Fax:* (501) 401-0366
License: Little Rock, AR
Group Owner: Cumulus Media Inc.; (acq 9-19-97; grpsl)
Nat'l Reps: D & R Radio
Arbitron Metro Market: Little Rock, AR *Format:* Gospel *No. News Employees:* 1 *Target Audience:* 50 plus.
Jim Beard, Promotions Manager

***KLRE-FM**
02-01-1973; 90.5 mhz FM *Hrs Open:* 24; 40 kw; 246 ft.; N34 40 33.7 W92 19 7.5
2801 S University Avenue, Little Rock, AR 72204 US
(501) 569-8485, *Fax:* (501) 569-8488
www.ualr.edu,kuar.org
License: Little Rock, Pulaski County, AR held by University of Arkansas.
Nat'l Network: PRI; NPR
Arbitron Metro Market: Little Rock, AR *Format:* Talk *Target Audience:* 35-54.
Ben Fry, General Manager
Mary Waldo, General Sales Mgr
Ron Dreeding, Programming Director

KSSN
01-01-1966; 95.7 mhz FM *Hrs Open:* 24; 92 kw; 1663 ft.; N34 47 57 W92 29 29
200 Concord Plaza, Suite 600, San Antonio, TX 78216 US
(501) 217-5000, *Fax:* (501) 228-9547
www.kssn.com
kssn@cei.net
License: Little Rock, Pulaski County, AR held by CC Licenses LLC.
Group Owner: Clear Channel Communications Inc.; (acq 9-12-97; grpsl)
Nat'l Reps: Clear Channel
Arbitron Metro Market: Little Rock, AR *Format:* Country *Hrs. of News Programming:* news progmg 2 hrs wkly *No. News Employees:* 1 *Target Audience:* 25-54.
Chad Heritage, Operations Dir
Kevin Waltman, General Sales Mgr

KABZ
01-01-1967; 103.7 mhz FM *Hrs Open:* 24; 100 kw; 1499 ft.; N34 47 56 W92 29 44
2400 Cottondale Lane, Little Rock, AR 72202 US
(501) 661-1037, *Fax:* (501) 664-5871
www.1037thebuzz.com,signalmedia.com
License: Little Rock, Pulaski County, AR held by Signal Media of Arkansas Inc.
Nat'l Network: ESPN Radio; Westwood One
Arbitron Metro Market: Little Rock, AR *Format:* Talk *Hrs. of News Programming:* news progmg 10 hrs wkly *No. News Employees:* 1 *Target Audience:* 18-49.
Philip Jonsson, President
Steve Jonsson, General Manager
Justin Acri, Programming Director
Lindy Blackstone, Promotions Manager

***KUAR**
09-16-1986; 89.1 mhz FM *Hrs Open:* 24; 63 kw; 1122 ft.; N34 47 49 W92 29 20
2801 S University Avenue, Little Rock, AR 72204 US
(501) 569-8485, *Fax:* (501) 569-8488
www.kuar.org
ben@kuar.org
License: Little Rock, Pulaski County, AR held by Board of Trustees of the University of Arkansas.
Nat'l Network: NPR; PRI
Arbitron Metro Market: Little Rock, AR *Format:* Jazz, News, 62, Talk *Special Programming:* Folk 3 hrs wkly *Hrs. of News Programming:* news progmg 86 hrs wkly *No. News Employees:* 1 *Target Audience:* 35-54.
William Wagner, Operations Dir
Ben Fry, General Manager
Mary Waldo, General Sales Mgr
Mary Waldo, Development Director
Laurie Pierce, Development Assistant
Karen Tricot Steward, Web Communications Manager
Benita Norwood, OfficeAdminstrator

KURB
07-07-1972; 98.5 mhz FM *Hrs Open:* 24; 99 kw; 1286 ft.; N34 47 56 W92 29 44
City Center West, 7201 W. Lake Mead Blvd, Las Vegas, NV 89128 US
(501) 401-0200, *Fax:* (501) 401-0349
www.b98.com
info@b98.com
License: Little Rock, Pulaski County, AR
Group Owner: Cumulus Media Inc.
Arbitron Metro Market: Little Rock, AR *Format:* Adult Contemp
Jim Beard, Promotions Manager

KDIS-FM
08-14-1992; 99.5 mhz FM; 3 kw; 312 ft.; N34 45 58 W92 17 38
13910 Cooper Orbit Cove, Little Rock, AR 72210 US
(501) 663-3300, *Fax:* (501) 663-3723
www.radiodisney.com
info@kdis.com
License: Little Rock, Pulaski County, AR held by Radio Disney Group LLC.
Group Owner: ABC Inc.; (acq 5-30-03; $2.56 million).
Arbitron Metro Market: Little Rock, AR *Format:* Children
John Campbell, Station Manager
Lauren Eddins, Promotions Manager

Lonoke

KOLL
06-01-1982; 106.3 mhz FM; 50 kw; 492 ft.; N34 36 6 W91 51 40
1 Shackleford Drive, Suite 400, Little Rock, AR 72211 US
(501) 219-1919, *Fax:* (501) 225-4610
www.refreshingmix.com
sonnyvictory@crainmedia.com; neilgladner@crainmedia.com
License: Lonoke, Lonoke County, AR held by Crain Media Group LLC.
Group Owner: Crain Media Group LLC; (acq 2-1-2008; grpsl)
Arbitron Metro Market: Little Rock, AR *Format:* Adult Contemp
Neal Gladner, General Manager
Don Burns, Programming Director

Lowell

KMXF
06-30-1992; 101.9 mhz FM *Hrs Open:* 24; 23 kw; 709 ft.; N36 26 28 W93 58 22
600 Congress Ave., Suite 1400, Austin, TX 78701 US
(479) 442-0102, *Fax:* (479) 587-8255
www.hotmix1019.com
License: Lowell, Benton County, AR held by Capstar TX L.P.
Group Owner: Clear Channel Communications Inc.; (acq 8-30-00; grpsl).
Wire Services: AP
Arbitron Metro Market: Fatetteville, AR *Format:* Contemporary Hits/Top 40 *Hrs. of News Programming:* news progmg one hr wkly *No. News Employees:* 1 *Target Audience:* 18-34; women *Adv. Rates:* 45; 40; 40; 35
Dave Ashcraft, Operations Dir
Tony Beringer, General Manager
Jay Steele, Programming Director

Magnolia

KVMA
04-01-1948; 630 khz AM *Hrs Open:* 24; 1 kw-D, NDD; 0.03 kw-N, ND1; N33 17 59 W93 13 57
Mailing Address: PO Box 430, Magnolia, AR 71753 US
Second Address: 131 S. Jackson, Magnolia, AR 71753
(880) 822-5862, *Fax:* (870) 234-5865
www.magnoliaradio.com
kvmakvmz@magnoliaradio.com
License: Magnolia, AR held by Noalmark Broadcasting Corp.
Group Owner: Noalmark Broadcasting Corp.; (acq 8-1-2005; $165,000)
Nat'l Network: ABC *Regional Network:* Ark. Radio Net.
Arbitron Metro Market: Magnolia, AR *Format:* Talk, Country *Special Programming:* Farm 2 hrs wkly *Hrs. of News Programming:* 20 hrs news progmg wkly *Target Audience:* General. *Adv. Rates:* 11; 8; 9; 5
William Nolan Jr., President
Ed Alderson, Operations Dir
Ken Sibley, General Manager
Dan Gregory, Accounts Executive/Sports Director
Amanda Smith, Account Executive
Megan Black, Office Manager/ Accounting

Malvern

KBOK
08-01-1951; 1310 khz AM *Hrs Open:* Sunrise-sunset; 1 kw-D, NDD; N34 22 25 W92 49 52
1402 Hwy 270 West, Malvern, AR 72104 US
(501) 332-6981, *Fax:* (501) 332-6984
License: Malvern, AR held by Noalmark Broadcasting Corp.
Group Owner: Noalmark Broadcasting Corp.; acq 4-1-03; $62,500).
Regional Network: Ark. Radio Net.
Arbitron Metro Market: Little Rock, AR *Format:* Country, News *Special Programming:* Talk 6 hrs, gospel 8 hrs wkly *Hrs. of News Programming:* News progmg 20 hrs wkly *Target Audience:* General.
Malia Brown, General Manager

KIXV(FM)
04-01-1991; 101.5 mhz FM *Hrs Open:* 24; 6 kw; Ant 322 ft; N34 28 24 W92 55 51
208 Buena Vista Rd., Hot Springs, AR 71913
(501) 525-4600, *Fax:* (501) 525-4344
www.klez.com
pob@klaz.com
License: Malvern, Hot Spring County, AR held by Noalmark Broadcasting Corp.
Group Owner: Noalmark Broadcasting Corp.; (acq 1-21-2003; $437,500).
Population Served: 120,000*Format:* Easy Listening *Hrs. of News Programming:* News progmg 3 hrs wkly *Target Audience:* 35-60.
William Nolan Jr., President
Brad Hutcheson, General Manager
Kevin Krebbs, General Sales Mgr
Larry K, Programming Director
Doc Bryce, Chief Engineer

Mammoth Spring

KAMS
01-01-1956; 95.1 mhz FM *Hrs Open:* 24; 100 kw; 650 ft.; N36 32 49 W91 25 47
Mailing Address: P. O. Box 193, Mammoth Spring, AR 72554 US
Second Address: N. Hwy. 63, Thayer, MO 65791
(417) 264-7211, *Fax:* (417) 264-7212
www.kkountry.com
peggy@kkountry.com
License: Mammoth Spring, Fulton County, AR held by E-Communications LLC
Nat'l Network: ABC Daytime Direction *Nat'l Reps:* Rgnl Reps
Regional Reps: Regional Reps
Arbitron Metro Market: Thayer, MT *Format:* Country *Hrs. of News Programming:* news progmg 11 hrs wkly *No. News Employees:* 1 *Target Audience:* General. *Adv. Rates:* :60-$30.50 :30-$20.50
Robert Eckman, President

Marianna

KAKJ
01-01-1994; 105.3 mhz FM *Hrs Open:* 24; 6 kw; 328 ft.; N34 47 14 W90 46 3 *Rebroadcasts:* Rebroadcasts KCLT(FM) West Helena 90%
P.O. Box 2870, West Helena, AR 72390 US
(870) 572-9506, *Fax:* (870) 572-1845
www.force2radio.com
force2@sbcglobal.net
License: Marianna, Lee County, AR held by Raymond & L.T. Simes II.
Nat'l Network: ABC
Arbitron Metro Market: Helena-West Helena, AR *Format:* Black *No. News Employees:* 1 *Target Audience:* All ages.
Raymond Simes, President
L.T. Simes, Operations Dir
Raymond Simes, General Manager
Elaine Simes, Station Manager
Earnest Simes, Programming Director
Elaine Sims, Promotions Manager
Larry Evans, Operations Manager
Peter Turner,Promotions Director

Marion

KXHT
02-01-1986; 107.1 mhz FM; 2.75 kw; 479 ft.; N35 9 23 W90 5 46
188 South Bellevue, Suite 222, Memphis, TN 38104 US
(901) 375-9324, *Fax:* (901) 375-9331
www.flinn.com
info@kxht.com
License: Marion, Crittenden County, AR held by Flinn Broadcasting Corp.
Arbitron Metro Market: Memphis, TN *Format:* Urban Contemporary
Lloyd Hetzer, General Manager
Duane Hargrove, Station Manager

Marked Tree

***KJBR**
01-01-1993; 93.7 mhz FM *Hrs Open:* 24; 6 kw; 279 ft.; N35 34 34 W90 29 51
P.O. Box 540, Jonesboro, AR 72403 US
(916) 251-1600, *Fax:* (916) 251-1650
www.air1.com
info@air1.com
License: Marked Tree, Poinsett County, AR held by Educational Media Foundation.
Group Owner: EMF Broadcasting; (acq 11-1-01; $1.3 million with KJLV(FM) Hoxie).
Nat'l Network: Air 1
Format: Alternative, Christian
Mike Novak, President
Eric Allen, General Sales Mgr
David Pierce, Programming Director
Ed Lenane, News Director
Sam Wallington, Engineering Dir
Marya Morgan, News Reporter
Richard Hunt, News Reporter

Marshall

KBCN-FM
04-25-1983; 104.3 mhz FM *Hrs Open:* 24; 100 kw; 820 ft; N35 52 17 W92 39 10
100 Blue Bird St., Harrison, AR 23225
(870) 743-1157, *Fax:* (870) 743-1168
ESPNArkansas.net
License: Marshall, Searcy County, AR held by Pearson Broadcasting of Marshall Inc.
Group Owner: Pearson Broadcasting; (acq 4-30-93; $450,000; *Special Programming:* ESPN/Arkansas Razorbacks *Adv. Rates:* Call for rates
Tommy Craft, Market Manager
Jamie Holt, General Manager
Kevin Reeman, Operations Manager

KCGS
05-24-1975; 960 khz AM *Hrs Open:* 24
Mailing Address: P.O. Box 178, Marshall, AR 72650 US
Second Address: 208 Battle St., Marshall, AR 72650
(870) 448-5567, *Fax:* (870) 448-5384
www.kcgs.com
kcgs@alltel.net
License: Marshall, AR held by Southland Broadcasting Corp.
Nat'l Network: USA
Format: Gospel *Special Programming:* Bible answers live 7 hrs wkly *Hrs. of News Programming:* news progmg 10 hrs wkly *No. News Employees:* 2 *Target Audience:* General. *Adv. Rates:* 84; 84; 84; na
Ronald Woolsey, President
Karl Leukert, General Manager

***KCAV**
04-27-2009; 90.3 mhz FM *Hrs Open:* 24/7; 0.057 kw; 676 ft.; N35 52 16 W92 39 10 *Rebroadcasts:* KCMH US
(870) 425-2525, *Fax:* (870) 424-2626
www.kcmhradio.com
kyle@anonymous.com
License: Marshall, Searcy County, AR held by Christian Broadcasting Group of Mountain Home Inc.
Nat'l Network: Moody; USA
Arbitron Metro Market: Marshall, AR *Format:* Religious
Jim Holsted, President
Kyle Sexton, Station Manager
Michael Coolidge, Vice President
Lila Doyel, Secretary
Sondra McNelley, Receptionist

Marvell

***KLMK**
01-01-1999; 90.7 mhz FM *Hrs Open:* 24; 50 kw; 486 ft.; N34 37 20 W90 58 44 *Rebroadcasts:* Rebroadcasts KLVR(FM) Middletown, CA 100%
113 Quapaw Trail, Helena, AR 72342 US
(916) 251-1600, *Fax:* (916) 251-1650
www.klove.com
License: Marvell, Phillips County, AR held by Educational Media Foundation.
Group Owner: EMF Broadcasting; (acq 8-28-2007; $300,000)
Nat'l Network: K-Love
Arbitron Metro Market: Marvell, AR *Format:* Christian
Mike Novak, President

Maumelle

KHKN
01-01-1979; 94.9 mhz FM *Hrs Open:* 24; 96 kw; 1844 ft.; N34 26 31 W92 13 3
200 Concord Plaza, Suite 600, San Antonio, TX 78216 US
(501) 217-5000, *Fax:* (501) 228-9547(501) 227-5776
www.949tommfm.com
License: Maumelle, Saline County, AR held by CC Licenses LLC.
Group Owner: Clear Channel Communications Inc.; (acq 9-12-97; grpsl)
Arbitron Metro Market: Little Rock, AR *Format:* Classic Rock
Target Audience: 18-49.
Kim Pyle, General Manager
Kevin Waltman, General Sales Mgr
Sonny Victory, Programming Director
Tom Rusk, Chief Engineer

KWLR
01-01-1998; 96.9 mhz FM; 4.6 kw; 377 ft.; N34 53 33 W92 24 50
188 South Bellevue, Suite 222, Memphis, TN 38104 US
(501) 812 9700, *Fax:* (501) 812 9690
www.klove.com
kwlrword97@aol.com
License: Maumelle, Pulaski County, AR held by Flinn Broadcasting Corp.
Arbitron Metro Market: Memphis, TN *Format:* Religious
Mike Novak, President
Eric Allen, Programming Director
David Pierce, Promotions Manager
Ed Lenane, News Director
Tracy Butler, Traffic Manager

McGehee

KVSA
06-29-1953; 1220 khz AM *Hrs Open:* 6 AM-6:30 PM; 1 kw-D, ND1; 0.04 kw-N, ND1; N33 33 39 W91 23 6
P.O. Box 110, McGehee, AR 71654 US
(870) 222-4200(870) 538-5200, *Fax:* (870) 538-3389
kvsa1220@yahoo.com
License: McGehee, AR held by Southeast Arkansas Broadcasters Inc.
Regional Network: Ark. Radio Net. *Nat'l Reps:* Keystone (unwired net)
Arbitron Metro Market: McGehee, AR *Format:* Variety/Diverse
Special Programming: Farm 5 hrs wkly *Hrs. of News Programming:* 10 hrs wkly *No. News Employees:* 2 *Adv. Rates:* 5.25; 5.25; 5.25; 5.25
Joyce Kinney, President
Dale Jones, Programming Director

Melbourne

***KLRM**
01-01-2008; 90.7 mhz FM; 7 kw vert; 617 ft.; N36 5 31 W92 15 46 *Rebroadcasts:* Rebroadcasts KLVR(FM) Middletown, CA 100%
88 Casey Jones Blvd., Jackson, TN 38305 US
(800) 877-5600, *Fax:* (916) 251-1650
www.klove.com
License: Melbourne, Izard County, AR held by Educational Media Foundation.
Group Owner: EMF Broadcasting; (acq 3-23-2007; grpsl)
Nat'l Network: K-Love
Arbitron Metro Market: Melbourne, AR *Format:* Christian
Mike Novak, President

Mena

KQOR
01-01-2001; 105.3 mhz FM; 12.5 kw; 469 ft.; N34 32 42 W94 18 21
P.O. Box 311, Dequeen, AR 71832 US
www.classichitsradioonline.com
License: Mena, Polk County, AR held by Ouachita Broadcasting Inc.
Group Owner: Ouachita Broadcasting Inc.; (acq 3-8-99).
Arbitron Metro Market: Dallas, TX *Format:* Oldies
Dwight Douglas, General Manager

KENA-FM
01-01-1969; 102.1 mhz FM *Hrs Open:* 24; 12.5 kw; 469 ft.; N34 32 42 W94 18 21
Mailing Address: P.O. Box 311, Dequeen, AR 71832 US
Second Address: 1600 S. Reine St., Mena, AR 71953
(501) 394-1450, *Fax:* (501) 394-1459
License: Mena, Polk County, AR held by Ouachita Broadcasting Inc.
Group Owner: Ouachita Broadcasting Inc.
Nat'l Network: ABC
Format: Country *Hrs. of News Programming:* news progmg 6 hrs wkly *No. News Employees:* 1
Dwight Douglas, Station Manager
Bevona Williams, News Director
Curt Teasdale, Disc Jockey
Mark Hobson, Disc Jockey
Matt Stone, Local News Editor

KTTG
12-01-1994; 96.3 mhz FM *Hrs Open:* 24; 47 kw; 1316 ft.; N34 41 24 W93 56 35
2937 Highway 71 North, Mean, AR 71593 US
(479) 394-6198, *Fax:* (479) 784-7290
www.espnradio.com
info@kttg.com
License: Mena, Polk County, AR held by Pearson Broadcasting of Mena Inc.
Group Owner: Pearson Broadcasting; (acq 1995; $175,000)
Nat'l Network: ESPN Radio *Nat'l Reps:* ABC Radio Sales
Arbitron Metro Market: Mena, AR *Format:* Sports, Talk *No. News Employees:* 1 *Target Audience:* 18-49. *Adv. Rates:* 14; 12; 14; 8
Max Pearson, CEO
Tommy Craft, General Manager
Jason Wade, Programming Director
Bruce Hale, CFO

Monticello

KGPQ
05-01-1997; 99.9 mhz FM; 25 kw; 328 ft.; N33 43 49 W91 48 56
P.O. Box 308, Monticello, AR 71655 US
(870) 367-8525, *Fax:* (870) 367-9564
pinesradio@sbcglobal.net
License: Monticello, Drew County, AR held by Pines Broadcasting Inc.
Group Owner: Pines Broadcasting Inc.; (acq 3-14-2007; grpsl)
Format: Adult Contemp
Jimmy Sledge, President

KHBM
04-01-1955; 1430 khz AM *Hrs Open:* 24; 1 kw-D, ND2; 0.03 kw-N, ND2; N33 36 18 W91 47 14
539 W. Gaines, Monticello, AR 71655 US
(870) 367-6854, *Fax:* (870) 367-9564
pinesradio@sbcglobal.com
License: Monticello, AR held by Pines Broadcasting Inc.
Group Owner: Pines Broadcasting Inc.; (acq 3-14-2007; grpsl)
Regional Network: Ark. Radio Net.
Format: Contemporary Hits/Top 40 *Hrs. of News Programming:* news progmg 10 hrs wkly *No. News Employees:* 1 *Target Audience:* General.
Jimmy Sledge, President
Bonnie Ellis, General Manager

KHBM-FM
09-01-1967; 93.7 mhz FM *Hrs Open:* 24; 23 kw; 417 ft.; N33 46 35 W91 43 2
539 W. Gaines, Monticello, AR 71655 US
(870) 367-6854, *Fax:* (870) 367-9564
pinesradio@sbcglobal.net
License: Monticello, Drew County, AR held by Pines Broadcasting Inc.
Group Owner: Pines Broadcasting Inc.; (acq 3-14-2007; grpsl)
Regional Network: Ark. Radio Net.
Format: Contemporary Hits/Top 40, Adult Contemp *Hrs. of News Programming:* news progmg 8 hrs wkly *No. News Employees:* 1
Jimmy Sledge, President

Morrilton

KVOM
12-25-1952; 800 khz AM; 0.25 kw-D, ND1; 0.04 kw-N, ND1; N35 9 32 W92 46 13
PO Box 541, Morrilton, AR 72110 US

(501) 354-2484, *Fax:* (501) 354-5629
www.kvom.com
newsroom@kvom.cm
License: Morrilton, AR held by MMA License LLC.
Group Owner: MAX Media L.L.C.; (acq 6-6-2003; grpsl)
Nat'l Network: ESPN Radio *Regional Network:* Ark. Radio Net.
Nat'l Reps: Christal *Wire Services:* AP
Arbitron Metro Market: Morriton, AR *Format:* Sports *Hrs. of News Programming:* news progmg 20 hrs wkly *No. News Employees:* 2 *Target Audience:* General. *Adv. Rates:* 14; 13; 14; 10
Rich Moellers, General Manager
Ashton Tyler, Program Director/ Host
Eric Tyler, News and Sports Director

KVOM-FM
01-01-1981; 101.7 mhz FM *Hrs Open:* 24; 6 kw; 226 ft.; N35 9 32 W92 46 13
PO Box 541, Morrilton, AR 72110 US
(501) 354-2484, *Fax:* (501) 354-5629
www.kvom.com
newsroom@kvom.cm
License: Morrilton, Conway County, AR
Group Owner: MAX Media L.L.C.
Nat'l Reps: Christal
Arbitron Metro Market: Morriton, AR *Format:* Country *Hrs. of News Programming:* news progmg 5 hrs wkly *No. News Employees:* 2 *Target Audience:* General.
Ken Eubanks, Operations Dir
Rich Moellers, General Manager
Ashton Tyler, Program Director/ Host
Eric Tyler, News and Sports Director

Mountain Home

***KCMH**
06-28-1988; 91.5 mhz FM *Hrs Open:* 24; 26 kw vert; 472 ft.; N36 16 17 W92 25 20
P.O. Box 93, Mountain Home, AR 72653 US
(870) 425-2525, *Fax:* (870) 424-2626
www.kcmhradio.com
lorra@kcmhradio.com
License: Mountain Home, Baxter County, AR held by Christian Broadcasting Group of Mountain Home Inc.
Nat'l Network: Moody; USA
Arbitron Metro Market: Mountain Home, AR *Format:* Religious *Hrs. of News Programming:* News progmg 9 hrs wkly *Target Audience:* General.
Jim Holsted, President
Michael Coolidge, Operations Dir
Kyle Sexton, Station Manager
Sondra McNelley, Receptionist
Michael Coolidge, Vice President
Lila Doyel, Secretary

KOMT
10-25-1985; 107.5 mhz FM *Hrs Open:* 24; 100 kw; 1017 ft.; N36 29 13 W92 29 39
P.O. Box 2639, Gulfport, MS 39505 US
(870) 492-6022, *Fax:* (870) 492-2137
www.twinlakesradio.com
radio@mountainhome.com
License: Mountain Home, Baxter County, AR held by MAC Partners.
Nat'l Network: ABC
Arbitron Metro Market: Fayetteville, AR *Format:* Adult Contemp *Target Audience:* 25-54; females
Morgan Dowdy, CEO
Stewart Brunner, General Manager
Roger Lowery, Station Manager
Bob Van Haaren, Programming Director
Kristen Speer, Marketing Specialist
Kim Garrett, Office Manager

KPFM
06-06-1984; 105.5 mhz FM *Hrs Open:* 24; 19 kw; 797 ft.; N36 29 13 W92 29 39
P.O. Box 2639, Gulfport, MS 39505 US
(870) 492-6022, *Fax:* (870) 492-2137
www.twinlakesradio.com
radio@mountainhome.com
License: Mountain Home, Baxter County, AR held by Mountain Home Radio Station Inc.
Nat'l Network: ABC
Format: Country *Hrs. of News Programming:* news progmg 15 hrs wkly *No. News Employees:* 1 *Target Audience:* 24-54.
Morgan Dowdy, CEO
Stewart Brunner, Operations Dir
Roger Lowery, Station Manager

KTLO
05-30-1953; 1240 khz AM *Hrs Open:* 24
Mailing Address: 620 Highway 5 North, P.O. Box C, Mountain Home, AR 72653 US
Second Address: 620 Hwy. 5 N., Mountain Home, AR 72654
(870) 425-3101, *Fax:* (870) 424-4314
www.ktlo.com
bob@ktlo.com
License: Mountain Home, AR held by KTLO L.L.C.
Group Owner: KTLO LLC; (acq 5-1-91)
Arbitron Metro Market: Mountain Home, AR *Format:* Country *Hrs. of News Programming:* news progmg 11 hrs wkly *No. News Employees:* 3 *Target Audience:* 18-55; general
Bob Knight, General Manager
Danny Ward, Station Manager
Patty Sindlinger-Traffic Director

KTLO-FM
01-11-1971; 97.9 mhz FM; 30 kw; 636 ft.; N36 20 55 W92 23 59
Mailing Address: Post Office Box C, Mountain Home, AR 72653 US
Second Address: 620 Hwy. 5 N., Mountain Home, AR 72654
(870) 425-3101, *Fax:* (870) 424-4314
www.ktlo.com
bob@ktlo.com
License: Mountain Home, Baxter County, AR
Group Owner: KTLO LLC
Regional Network: Ark. Radio Net.
Arbitron Metro Market: Mountain Home, AR *Format:* Adult Contemp *Target Audience:* 40 plus.
Ronald Curtis, Operations Dir
Chuck Miller, General Manager
Danny Ward, Station Manager
Karen Anklam, General Sales Mgr
Fred Kasten, Programming Director
Patty Sindlinger-Traffic Director

Mountain Pine

KLXQ
01-01-1996; 101.9 mhz FM; 3.1 kw; 407 ft.; N34 26 56 W93 15 59
125 Corporate Terrace, Hot Springs, AR 71913 US
(501) 525-9700, *Fax:* (501) 525-9739
www.myhotsprings.com
info@usstations.com
License: Mountain Pine, Garland County, AR held by US Stations LLC.
Group Owner: US Stations LLC; (acq 2-1-2005; grpsl)
Arbitron Metro Market: Mountain Pine, AR *Format:* Classic Rock *Target Audience:* 25-54.
Gary Terrell, General Manager
Paul Swint, Director Of Sales
Craig Dale, Programming Director
Melissa Walters, News Director

Mountain View

KWOZ
12-01-1981; 103.3 mhz FM; 100 kw; 988 ft.; N35 47 6 W91 57 44
Ridgeview Drive, N. County Road 269, Mountain View, AR 72560 US
(870) 793-4196, *Fax:* (870) 793-5222
www.arkansas103.com
arkansas103@hotmail.com
License: Mountain View, Stone County, AR held by WRD Entertainment Inc.
Group Owner: WRD Entertainment Inc.
Nat'l Network: ABC *Wire Services:* AP
Arbitron Metro Market: Batesville, AR *Format:* Country *Hrs. of News Programming:* news progmg 3 hrs wkly *No. News Employees:* 2 *Target Audience:* 18-54.
Matt Johnson, General Sales Mgr
Rob Stanley, Programming Director
Bill Beck, News Director

Murfreesboro

KMTB
05-18-1983; 99.5 mhz FM *Hrs Open:* 24; 25 kw; 262 ft.; N34 0 41 W93 52 3
1513 South Fourth St., Nashville, AR 71852 US
(870) 845-3601, *Fax:* (870) 845-3680
operations@southwestarkansasradio.com
License: Murfreesboro, Pike County, AR held by ARKLATEX Radio Inc.
Group Owner: ARKLATEX Radio Inc.; acq 8-28-2001; grpsl).
Format: Country
Scott Dunson, Operations Dir
Brent Pinkerton, General Manager

Nashville

KBHC
05-01-1959; 1260 khz AM; 0.5 kw-D, NDD; N33 55 45 W93 51 1
1513 South Fourth Street, Nashville, AR 71852 US
(870) 845-3601, *Fax:* (870) 845-3680
operations@southwestarkansasradio.com
License: Nashville, AR held by ARKLATEX Radio Inc.
Group Owner: ARKLATEX Radio Inc.; (acq 8-23-2001; grpsl).
Regional Network: Ark. Radio Net. *Nat'l Reps:* Keystone (unwired net)
Arbitron Metro Market: Nashville, AR *Format:* Tejano
Scott Dunson, Operations Dir
Brent Pinkerton, General Manager

KNAS
02-14-1977; 105.5 mhz FM; 6 kw; 203 ft.; N34 0 41 W93 52 3
1513 South Fourth Street, Nashville, AR 71852 US
(870) 845-3601, *Fax:* (870) 845-9012
License: Nashville, Howard County, AR held by ARKLATEX Radio Inc.
Group Owner: ARKLATEX Radio Inc.
Format: Adult Contemp
Richard Jenkins, President
Mike Novak, Operations Dir
Keith Whipple, General Sales Mgr
David Pierce, Programming Director
Ed Lenane, News Director
Sam Wallington, Engineering Dir
Marya Morgan, News Reporter
Richard Hunt, MaryaMorgan
Karen Johnson, News Reporter
Felipe Aguilar, Regional Manager

***KSSW**
01-01-2003; 96.9 mhz FM; 6 kw; 328 ft.; N34 0 41 W93 52 3
P O Box 989, Blytheville, AR 72316 US
(225)768-3224
www.jsm.org
onair@jsm.org
License: Nashville, Howard County, AR held by Family Worship Center Church Inc.
Group Owner: Family Worship Center Church Inc.; (acq 9-15-2005; $400,000)
Arbitron Metro Market: Texarkana, TX *Format:* Religious
Van Michael, President
John Santiago, General Manager

***KNLL**
01-01-2008; 90.5 mhz FM; 100 kw vert; 481 ft.; N33 30 17 W93 34 47 *Rebroadcasts:* Rebroadcasts WAFR(FM) Tupelo, MS 100%
P O Drawer 2440, Tupelo, MS 38803 US
(662) 844-5036, *Fax:* (662) 842-6791
www.afr.net
contact@afa.net
License: Nashville, Howard County, AR held by American Family Association.
Group Owner: American Family Radio
Nat'l Network: American Family Radio
Arbitron Metro Market: Nashville, AR *Format:* Christian
Donald E. Wildmon, Founder
Buster Wilson, General Manager
Jennifer Hagman, Programming Director

Newark

***KLLN**
01-01-1985; 90.9 mhz FM; 4 kw; 456 ft.; N35 43 25 W91 26 40
1502 N. Hill Street, Newark, AR 72562 US
(870) 799-8969, *Fax:* (870) 799-8647
www.klln.fm
kllnfm@yahoo.com
License: Newark, Independence County, AR held by Newark Public School.
Arbitron Metro Market: Jonesboro, AR *Format:* Gospel
Fred Ahlborn, General Manager

Newport

KNBY
10-12-1949; 1280 khz AM *Hrs Open:* 24; 1 kw-D, ND2; 0.088 kw-N, ND2; N35 36 38 W91 15 2
Mailing Address: P. O. Box 989, Blytheville, AR 72316 US
Second Address: 2025 McCarty Dr., Newport, AR 72112
(870) 523-5891, *Fax:* (870) 523-2967
daleturner@suddenlinkmail.com
License: Newport, AR held by Newport Broadcasting Co.
Group Owner: Sudbury Services Inc.
Format: News, News/Talk, 86 *Adv. Rates:* 9; 8; 9; 6

Harold Sudbury, President
Dale Turner, General Manager
Doug Holt, Programming Director

KOKR
09-01-1966; 96.7 mhz FM; 40 kw; 548 ft.; N35 29 16 W91 26 13
Mailing Address: P. O. Box 989, Blytheville, AR 72316 US
Second Address: 401 S. Spring Street, Searcy, AR 72143
(870) 523-5891, *Fax:* (870) 523_2967
rhondap@searcyradiogroup.com
License: Newport, Jackson County, AR
Group Owner: Sudbury Services Inc.
Format: Country *Adv. Rates:* 10; 9; 10; 8
Art Laboe, General Manager
Anna Avila, General Sales Mgr
Paul Mendoza, Programming Director

North Crossett

KWLT
05-01-1995; 102.7 mhz FM *Hrs Open:* 24; 25 kw; 328 ft.; N33 8 5 W91 56 49
P.O. Box 697, Crossett, AR 71635 US
(870) 364-2181, *Fax:* (870) 364-2183
www.crossettradio.com
kagh@alltel.net
License: North Crossett, Ashley County, AR held by South Ark Broadcasting Inc.
Nat'l Network: ABC
Arbitron Metro Market: Crosset, AR *Format:* Classic Rock *Hrs. of News Programming:* News progmg 2 hrs wkly *Target Audience:* General. *Adv. Rates:* 14; 14; 14; 14
Kevin Medlin, President
Barry Medlin, General Sales Mgr
Russell Miller, Programming Director
Brian Bailey, News Director
Sylvia Walker, General Sales Manager

North Little Rock

KDXE
05-09-1957; 1380 khz AM *Hrs Open:* 24; 5 kw-D, DA2; 2.5 kw-N, DA2; N34 52 49 W92 14 1
10301 N. Rodney Parham Road, Suite C6, Little Rock, AR 72227 US
(501) 819-0625, *Fax:* (501) 835-4992
www.laquebuena1380.com
kdxe1380@sbcglobal.net
License: North Little Rock, AR held by Simmons Austin, LS LLC.
Group Owner: Simmons Media Group; (acq 3-8-2006; $350,000)
Nat'l Network: ESPN Radio
Arbitron Metro Market: Little Rock, AR *Format:* Spanish *Special Programming:* 3 hrs wkly *Hrs. of News Programming:* 2 hrs *No. News Employees:* 1 *Target Audience:* 25-54; men *Adv. Rates:* 12; 10; 12;10
Albert Phipps, President
Lee Malcolm, Operations Dir
Arlen Horn, General Manager
Eric Kailin, General Sales Mgr
Mark Hill, Engineering Dir
David Graves, Engineer

Ola

KARV-FM
01-01-1998; 101.3 mhz FM; 0.74 kw; 909 ft.; N34 59 34 W93 11 35
201 West Second, Russellville, AR 72801 US
(479) 968-1184, *Fax:* (479) 967-5278
karv-kyel@yahoo.com
License: Ola, Yell County, AR held by KERM Inc.
Group Owner: KERM Inc.
Arbitron Metro Market: Ola, AR *Format:* News, News/Talk, 86 *Hrs. of News Programming:* news progmg 20 hrs wkly *No. News Employees:* 2 *Adv. Rates:* 120; 108; 108; 108
Kermit Womack, President
Chris Womack, General Manager

Osceola

KQMJ(FM)
09-01-1996; 107.3 mhz FM; 1.6 kw; Ant 335 ft; N35 45 59 W89 55 43
Box 989, Blytheville, AR 72316
(870) 762-2093, *Fax:* (870) 763-8459
License: Osceola, Mississippi County, AR held by Phoenix Broadcasting Group Inc.
Group Owner: Sudbury Services Inc.
Arbitron Metro Market: Memphis, TN *Format:* Contemporary Hits/Top 40, Adult Contemp
Noel Showers, Programming Director

Ozark

KDYN
02-05-1969; 1540 khz AM *Hrs Open:* Sunrise-sunset; 0.5 kw-D, ND2; 0.001 kw-N, ND2; N35 29 16 W93 48 43
P. O. Box 1086, Ozark, AR 72949 US
(479) 667-4567, *Fax:* (479) 667-5214
www.kdyn.com
kdyn@centurytel.net
License: Ozark, AR held by Ozark Communications Inc.
Regional Network: Ark. Radio Net.
Arbitron Metro Market: Ozark, AR *Format:* Country *Hrs. of News Programming:* news progmg 20 hrs wkly *No. News Employees:* 1 *Target Audience:* General. *Adv. Rates:* 10; 10; 10; 7
Marc Dietz, President

KDYN-FM
10-02-1980; 96.7 mhz FM *Hrs Open:* 24; 10 kw; 486 ft.; N35 29 9.11 W93 53 29.49
Mailing Address: Highway 64, East Ozark, AR 72949 US
Second Address: 9331 Puddin Ridge Rd., Ozark, AR 72949
(479) 667-4567, *Fax:* (479) 667-5214
www.kdyn.com
kdyn@centurytel.net
License: Ozark, Franklin County, AR held by Ozark Communications Inc.
Arbitron Metro Market: Ozark, AR
Trey Stafford, President
Kevin Neathery, General Sales Mgr
Christy Matthews, Programming Director
James Dean, News Director
Al Simpson, Chief Engineer

Pangburn

KSMD
11-02-2003; 99.1 mhz FM *Hrs Open:* 24; 25 kw; 328 ft.; N35 23 43 W91 44 17
P.O. Box 1488, Searcy, AR 72145 US
(501) 268-7123, *Fax:* (501) 279-2900
www.newstalk991.com
production@heartarkansas.com
License: Pangburn, White County, AR held by Crain Media Group LLC
Group Owner: Crain Media Group LLC; acq 10-15-02; $180,000 for CP).
Arbitron Metro Market: Pangburn, AR *Format:* News, News/Talk, 86
J.R. Runyon, Operations Dir
Dave Clark, Chief Engineer

Paragould

KDRS
01-01-1947; 1490 khz AM *Hrs Open:* 24; 1 kw-U; N36 02 56 W90 27 44
400 Tower Dr., Paragould, AR 72401
(870) 236-7627, *Fax:* (870) 239-4583
www.kdrs.com
dina@kdrs.com
License: Paragould, Greene County, AR held by MOR Media Inc.
Regional Network: Ark. Radio Net.
Population Served: 50,000*Hrs. of News Programming:* News progmg 7 hrs wkly *Adv. Rates:* 12; 12; 12; 12
Dina Mason, President
Brian Osborn, Operations Dir

KDRS-FM
03-05-1983; 107.1 mhz FM *Hrs Open:* 24; 3 kw; 410 ft; N36 01 48 W90 35 49
400 Tower Dr., Paragould, AR 72401
(870) 236-7627, *Fax:* (870) 239-4583
www.kdrs.com
dina@kdrs.com
License: Paragould, Greene County, AR held by MOR Media Inc.
Target Audience: 18-44. *Adv. Rates:* Same as AM
Dina Mason, General Manager
Dina Mason, General Sales Mgr
Brian Osborn, Programming Director
Leisa Rae, Public Service Director
Leisa Rae, Traffic Manager

Paris

KERX
05-01-1981; 95.3 mhz FM; 50 kw; 459 ft.; N35 17 13 W94 2 51
P. O. Box 6610, Branson, MO 65615 US
(479) 484-7285, *Fax:* (479) 784-7390
www.953maxfm.com/index2/
tommy@pearsonbroadcasting.com
License: Paris, Logan County, AR held by Pearson Broadcasting of Paris Inc.
Group Owner: Pearson Broadcasting; (acq 10-18-93; $42,000;
Wire Services: AP
Arbitron Metro Market: Paris, AR *Format:* Rock/AOR *Special Programming:* Blues 3 hrs wkly *Target Audience:* 18-44; men & women *Adv. Rates:* 16; 14; 16; 10
Bruce Hale, CFO
Tommy Craft, General Manager
Jeff Clunn, General Sales Mgr
Ray Miller, Programming Director

Pearcy

KLBL
11-18-1991; 104.5 mhz FM *Hrs Open:* 24; 3 kw; 407 ft.; N34 26 56 W93 15 59
P.O. Box 831, Arkadelphia, AR 71923 US
(501) 525-9700, *Fax:* (501) 525-9739
www.myhotsprings.com
pobriant@usstations.com
License: Pearcy, Garland County, AR held by US Stations LLC.
Group Owner: US Stations LLC
Nat'l Network: CBS Radio *Regional Reps:* Rgnl Reps
Arbitron Metro Market: Hot Springs, AR *Format:* Country *Hrs. of News Programming:* News progmg 7 hrs wkly *Target Audience:* 25-50; general *Adv. Rates:* 11.77; 11.77; 11.77; 11.77
Gary Terrel, General Manager
Neil Gladner, General Sales Mgr

Piggott

KBOA-FM
10-15-1983; 105.5 mhz FM *Hrs Open:* 24; 6 kw; 299 ft.; N36 19 50 W90 7 24
342 River Oaks Road, Memphis, TN 38120 US
(573) 888-4616, *Fax:* (573) 888-4890
www.semoradio.com
perry@semoradio.com
License: Piggott, Clay County, AR held by Pollack Broadcasting Co.
Group Owner: Pollack Broadcasting Co.; acq 9-25-98; $450,000 with KBOA(AM) Kennett, MO)
Format: Adult Contemp *Special Programming:* Farm 5 hrs wkly *Hrs. of News Programming:* news progmg 5 hrs wkly *No. News Employees:* 1 *Target Audience:* 18-55; young adults, young professionals, farmers
William Pollack, President
Perry Jones, General Manager
Monte Lyons, Programming Director
Charles Isbell, News Director
Palmer Johnson, Chief Engineer

Pine Bluff

***KCAT**
04-01-1963; 1340 khz AM; 1 kw-U, ND1; N34 12 47 W92 1 53
P.O. Box 8808, Pine Bluff, AR 71601 US
(870) 534-5001, *Fax:* (870) 534-7985
www.kcatam.com
april@lordradio.com
License: Pine Bluff, AR held by Monday Burke Smith Broadcasting Network
Arbitron Metro Market: Pine Bluff, AR *Format:* Gospel *Target Audience:* 18-55. *Adv. Rates:* 20; 20; 20; 20
Elijah Mondy, General Manager
Darren Smith, General Sales Mgr
April Mondy, Programming Director
Belinda Mondy, News Director

KIPR
01-01-1963; 92.3 mhz FM; 100 kw; Ant 938 ft; N34 22 12 W92 10 07
700 Wellington Hills Rd., Little Rock, AR 89128
(501) 401-0200, *Fax:* (501) 401-0366
www.power923.com
License: Pine Bluff, Jefferson County, AR
Group Owner: Cumulus Media Inc.; (acq 7-29-97; grpsl)
Population Served: 200,000 *Arbitron Metro Market:* Little Rock, AR *Target Audience:* 18-44.
Jim Beard, Promotions Manager

KPBQ-FM
12-23-1991; 101.3 mhz FM *Hrs Open:* 24; 25 kw; Ant 328 ft; N34 15 13 W92 03 58
920 Commerce Rd., Pine Bluff, AR 71601
(870) 534-8911, *Fax:* (870) 534-8984
delta4radio@netscape.net
License: Pine Bluff, Jefferson County, AR held by M.R.S. Ventures Inc.
Group Owner: M.R.S. Ventures Inc.; (acq 4-29-2003; grpsl).
Nat'l Network: ABC
Population Served: 150,000*Format:* Country *Special Programming:* Farm 2 hrs wkly *Target Audience:* 12-60.

Andy Hodges, General Manager

***KUAP**
01-01-1995; 89.7 mhz FM; 50 kw; 268 ft.; N34 14 33 W92 1 2
P.O. Box 4145, Little Rock, AR 71601 US
(870) 575-8000, *Fax:* (870) 575-4666
www.uapb.edu
webadmin@uapb.edu
License: Pine Bluff, Jefferson County, AR held by Board of Trustees of Univ. of Arkansas.
Arbitron Metro Market: Pine Bluff, AR *Format:* Jazz, Smooth Jazz
Finley Hill, Station Manager

Pocahontas

KPOC
11-15-1950; 1420 khz AM *Hrs Open:* 24
Mailing Address: P. O. Box 508, Pocahontas, AR 72455 US
Second Address: One Radio Dr., Pocahontas, AR 72455
(870) 892-5234, *Fax:* (870) 892-5235
info@kpoc.com
License: Pocahontas, AR held by Combined Media Group Inc.
Group Owner: Combined Media Group Inc.; (acq 12-20-2001; $410,000 with co-located FM).
Regional Network: Ark. Radio Net.
Format: Adult Contemp *Special Programming:* Farm 10 hrs wkly *No. News Employees:* 1 *Target Audience:* 25-54; general
Timothy Scott, President
Jamie Ward, General Sales Mgr
Larry Caldwell, Chief Engineer

KPOC-FM
04-25-1969; 104.1 mhz FM *Hrs Open:* 24; 6 kw; 144 ft.; N36 16 38 W90 57 16
P. O. Box 508, Pocahontas, AR 72455 US
(870) 892-5234, *Fax:* (870) 892-5235
info@kpoc.com
License: Pocahontas, Randolph County, AR
Format: Adult Contemp
Eddie Johnson, CFO
Pamela Tsutsui, General Manager

Prarie Grove

KMCK-FM
01-01-1947; 105.7 mhz FM; 100 kw; 476 ft; N36 11 07 W94 17 49
4209 N Frontage Road, Fayetteville, AR 53202
(479) 521-5566, *Fax:* (479) 521-0751
www.power1057.com
License: Prarie Grove, Benton County, AR held by Cumulus Licensing Corp.
Group Owner: Cumulus Media Inc.; (acq 12-10-98; grpsl)
Nat'l Reps: Christal
Population Served: 300,000 *Arbitron Metro Market:* Fayetteville (Northwest Arkansas), AR *Target Audience:* 18-49; contemp adults
Joe Conway, General Manager
J.J. Ryan, Programming Director

Prescott

KTPA
12-01-1959; 1370 khz AM; 1 kw-D, NDD; N33 47 36 W93 23 42
Mailing Address: P.O. Box 424, Hope, AR 71801 US
Second Address: 1600 So. Elm St., Hope, AZ 71802
(870) 777-8868(870) 777-8869, *Fax:* (870) 777-8888
khpafm@supercountry105.com
License: Prescott, AR held by Newport Broadcasting Co.
Group Owner: Sudbury Services Inc.; (acq 5-14-66)
Regional Network: Ark. Radio Net.
Arbitron Metro Market: Hope, AR *Format:* Gospel
Robert Hill, General Manager
Sonya Odom, General Sales Mgr

Rogers

KAMO-FM
01-01-1971; 94.3 mhz FM *Hrs Open:* 24; 25 kw; 692 ft.; N36 26 30 W93 58 26
111 East Kilbourn Avenue, Suite 2700, Milwaukee, WI 53202 US
(479) 521-5566, *Fax:* (479) 521-0751
www.us94.com
dale.daniels@cumulus.com
License: Rogers, Benton County, AR held by Cumulus Licensing Corp.
Group Owner: Cumulus Media Inc.; (acq 12-10-98; grpsl)
Arbitron Metro Market: Fayetteville, AZ *Format:* Oldies
Joe Conway, General Manager
Dan Hinschell, Programming Director

KFFK
09-16-1954; 1390 khz AM *Hrs Open:* 24
70 North East Street, Suite 100, Fayetteville, AR 72701 US
(479) 582-3776, *Fax:* (479) 571-0995
License: Rogers, AR held by Butler Broadcasting Co. LLC
Nat'l Network: Fox Sports
Arbitron Metro Market: Fayetteville (Northwest Arkansas), AR *Format:* News, News/Talk, 82, Talk *Target Audience:* 25-54.
Steve Butler, President
Steve Bulter, General Manager
Dave Jackson, Programming Director

KURM
11-09-1979; 790 khz AM *Hrs Open:* 5 AM-11 PM; 5 kw-D, DAN; 0.5 kw-N, DAN; N36 18 10 W94 6 47
212 North 2nd Street, Rogers, AR 72756 US
(479) 633-0790, *Fax:* (479) 631-9711
www.kurm.net
kurm@kurm.net
License: Rogers, AR held by KERM Inc.
Group Owner: KERM Inc.
Nat'l Network: CBS *Regional Network:* Okla. News Net.
Arbitron Metro Market: Rogers, AR *Format:* Variety/Diverse *Special Programming:* Farm 10 hrs wkly *Hrs. of News Programming:* news progmg 15 hrs wkly *No. News Employees:* 2 *Target Audience:* 35
Kermit Womack, President
Diane Womack, General Sales Mgr

Russellville

KARV
02-25-1947; 610 khz AM *Hrs Open:* 24; 1 kw-D, DA2; 0.5 kw-N, DA2; N35 17 56 W93 9 9
201 West Second, Russellville, AR 72801 US
(479) 968-1184, *Fax:* (479) 967-5278
karv-kyet@yahoo.com
License: Russellville, AR held by KERM Inc.
Group Owner: KERM Inc.; acq 10-22-92; $250,000;
Nat'l Network: CBS *Regional Network:* Ark. Radio Net.
Arbitron Metro Market: Ola, AR *Format:* Sports, Talk *Special Programming:* Farm 5 hrs wkly *Hrs. of News Programming:* news progmg 38 hrs wkly *No. News Employees:* 4 *Target Audience:* 35 plus; affluentadults
Chris Womack, General Manager

***KMTC**
06-01-1987; 91.1 mhz FM *Hrs Open:* 24; 360 w; 62 ft; N35 18 11 W93 08 42
Mailing Address: Box 570, Russellville, AR 72811
Second Address: 305 Lake Front Dr., Russellville, AR 72802
(479) 967-7400, *Fax:* (479) 967-7894
License: Russellville, Pope County, AR held by Russellville Educational Broadcasting Foundation.
Nat'l Network: USA
Population Served: 30,000*Hrs. of News Programming:* News progmg one hr wkly *Target Audience:* 18-55; Christian
Tom Underhill, CEO
Debbie Bewley, General Manager
Melissa Krueger, Station Manager
Jim Alexander, Chief Engineer

KWKK
09-29-1985; 100.9 mhz FM *Hrs Open:* 24; 6 kw; 328 ft.; N35 17 37 W93 10 39
797 Winrock Drive, Morrilton, AR 72110 US
(479) 968-6816, *Fax:* (479) 968-2946
www.mykwkk.com
aaron@rivervalleyradio.com
License: Russellville, Pope County, AR held by MMA License LLC.
Group Owner: MAX Media L.L.C.; (acq 6-6-2003; grpsl)
Nat'l Network: ABC *Nat'l Reps:* Christal *Wire Services:* AP
Arbitron Metro Market: Russellville, AR *Format:* Adult Contemp *Special Programming:* Arkansas Tech University Sports *Hrs. of News Programming:* news progmg 5 hrs wkly *No. News Employees:* 1 *Target Audience:* 18-49; young adults
Aaron Thomas, Operations Dir
Rich Moellers, General Manager
Rhonda Dilbeck, General Sales Mgr
Johnny Story, Programming Director
Jim Alexander, Chief Engineer

***KXRJ**
04-03-1989; 91.9 mhz FM *Hrs Open:* 24; 0.1 kw horiz; -92 ft.; N35 17 47 W93 8 18
Hwy 7 North, Russellville, AR 72801 US
(479) 964-0806(479) 964-3282, *Fax:* (479) 498-6024
www.broadcast.atu.edu
info@kxrj.edu
License: Russellville, Pope County, AR held by Arkansas Tech University.
Format: Jazz, Variety/Diverse *Special Programming:* Educ, jazz 15 hrs wkly *Hrs. of News Programming:* News progmg 10 hrs wkly *Target Audience:* General.
George Cotton, Chief Engineer

Salem

KHOM
09-01-1977; 100.9 mhz FM; 50 kw; 492 ft.; N36 35 38 W91 40 3
Post Office Box 458, Salem, AR 72576 US
(417) 255-0427, *Fax:* (417) 255-2907
www.threeriversdailynews.com
khom@centurytel.net
License: Salem, Fulton County, AR held by Three Rivers Communications, LLC
Nat'l Network: ABC
Arbitron Metro Market: West Plains, MO *Format:* Country *No. News Employees:* 1 *Target Audience:* 35-54; adults
Paul Coates, CEO
Connie Pfeifer, Station Manager

Searcy

KWCK
08-25-1951; 1300 khz AM; 5 kw-D, NDD; N35 15 27 W91 43 49
100 East Arch, Searcy, AR 72143 US
(501) 268-7123, *Fax:* (501) 279-2900
www.kwck999.com
larrynokes@crainmedia.com
License: Searcy, AR held by Crain Media Group LLC.
Group Owner: Crain Media Group LLC; (acq 10-21-2002; grpsl).
Arbitron Metro Market: Searcy, AR *Format:* Talk *Special Programming:* Farm 10 hrs wkly *Target Audience:* 25-64.
Grant Carey, Operations Dir
Larry Nokes, General Manager
Mike Horne, General Sales Mgr
Heath Shelby, Program Director/ Music Director
Bill Bumpass, News Director
Shannon Scott, Sales
Tonya Abraham, Sales

KWCK-FM
10-01-1973; 99.9 mhz FM *Hrs Open:* 24; 50 kw; 492 ft.; N35 26 50 W91 56 52
Post Office Box 1300, Searcy, AR 72143 US
(501) 268-7123, *Fax:* (501) 279-2900
www.kwck999.com
larrynokes@crainmedia.com
License: Searcy, White County, AR
Group Owner: Crain Media Group LLC
Arbitron Metro Market: Searcy, AR *Format:* Country *Hrs. of News Programming:* news progmg 3 hrs wkly *No. News Employees:* 1 *Target Audience:* 18-49.
Grant Carey, Operations Dir
Larry Nokes, General Manager
Mike Horne, General Sales Mgr
Heath Shelby, Program Director/ Music Director
Bill Bumpass, News Director
Shannon Scott, Sales
Tonya Abraham, Sales

Sheridan

***KANX**
01-01-1999; 91.1 mhz FM; 40 kw; 522 ft.; N34 17 26 W92 29 36
P.O. Drawer 2440, Tupelo, MS 38803 US
(601) 844-8888, *Fax:* (601) 842-6191
www.afr.net
License: Sheridan, Grant County, AR held by American Family Association.
Group Owner: American Family Radio
Arbitron Metro Market: Tupelo, MO *Format:* Religious
Marvin Sanders, General Manager
John Riley, Programming Director

KARN-FM
11-01-1984; 102.9 mhz FM *Hrs Open:* 24; 50 kw; 492 ft.; N34 32 6 W92 24 33
City Center West, 7201 W. Lake Mead Blvd, Las Vegas, NV 89128 US
(501) 401-0200, *Fax:* (501) 401-0387
www.sportsanimal920.com
info@920karn.com
License: Sheridan, Grant County, AR held by The Last Bastion Station Trust LLC, as Trustee
Arbitron Metro Market: Little Rock, AR *Format:* News, Talk *Hrs. of News Programming:* news progmg 2 hrs wkly *No. News Employees:* 1 *Target Audience:* 35-64.

John Scuderi, General Sales Mgr
Dave Elswick, Programming Director
Jim Beard, Promotions Manager

Sherwood

KMTL
10-31-1983; 760 khz AM; 10 kw-D, NDD; N34 49 34 W92 12 19
P.O. Box 6460, North Little Rock, AR 72124 US
(501) 835-1554
kmtl76am@bcglobal
License: Sherwood, AR held by George V. Domerese.
Arbitron Metro Market: Little Rock, AR *Format:* Religious
George Domerese, General Manager
Tom Rusk, Chief Engineer

KOKY
01-01-1994; 102.1 mhz FM; 4.1 kw; 387 ft; N34 44 38 W92 16 32
700 Wellington Hills Rd., Little Rock, AR 89128
(501) 401-0200, *Fax:* (501) 401-0366
www.koky.com
License: Sherwood, Pulaski County, AR
Group Owner: Cumulus Media Inc.; (acq 10-23-97; grpsl).
Population Served: 525,000 *Arbitron Metro Market:* Little Rock, AR
Jim Beard, Promotions Manager

Siloam Springs

*KLRC
10-01-1981; 101.1 mhz FM; 3.1 kw; 453 ft.; N36 11 28 W94 33 58
2000 West Univ. Street, Siloam Springs, AR 72761 US
(479) 524-7101, *Fax:* (479) 524-7451
www.klrc.com
klrc@klrc.edu
License: Siloam Springs, Benton County, AR held by John Brown University.
Nat'l Network: USA *Wire Services:* UPI
Arbitron Metro Market: Fatetteville, AR *Format:* Christian, Religious *Hrs. of News Programming:* News progmg 2 hrs wkly *Target Audience:* 25-49.
Charles Pollard, President
Sean Sawatzky, General Manager
Mark Michaels, Programming Director

KUOA
04-12-1923; 1290 khz AM *Hrs Open:* 24
Box 3145 John Brown Univ, Siloam Springs, AR 72761 US
(479) 303-2034, *Fax:* (479) 303-2037
www.hogsportsradio.com
dan@hogsportsradio.com
License: Siloam Springs, AR held by Hog Radio Inc.
Arbitron Metro Market: Siloam Springs, AR *Format:* Sports
Jay Bunyard, President
Dan Storrs, General Manager
Lori Storrs, Local Sales Manager
Joe Morris, Production Director / Show Producer
Viktoria Baker, Traffic Director
Jennifer Adams, Account Executive

Springdale

KXNA
09-19-1968; 104.9 mhz FM; 2.75 kw; 486 ft.; N36 10 48 W94 5 7
70 North East Street, Suite 100, Fayetteville, AR 72701 US
(479) 582-3776, *Fax:* (479) 571-0995
License: Springdale, Washington County, AR held by Bulter Broadcasting LLC.
Nat'l Reps: Christal
Arbitron Metro Market: Fayetteville (Northwest AR), AR *Format:* Alternative
Steve Butler, General Manager

KYNG
07-15-1966; 1590 khz AM
111 East Kilbourn Avenue, Suite 2700, Milwaukee, WI 53202 US
(479) 521-5566, *Fax:* (479) 521-0751
License: Springdale, AR held by Cumulus Licensing Corp.
Group Owner: Cumulus Media Inc.; (acq 12-10-98; grpsl)
Arbitron Metro Market: Springdale, AR *Target Audience:* 18-54.
Joe Conway, General Manager
Mariposa Salas, Programming Director

Stamps

KZHE
10-01-1980; 100.5 mhz FM *Hrs Open:* 24; 50 kw; 492 ft.; N33 28 34 W93 16 23
909 East Main, Magnolia, AR 71753 US
(870) 234-7790, *Fax:* (870) 234-7791
www.kzhe.com
kzhe@kzhe.com
License: Stamps, Lafayette County, AR held by A-1 Communications Inc.
Arbitron Metro Market: Stamps, AR *Format:* Country *Special Programming:* Gospel 8 hrs wkly *Target Audience:* 25-54.
Troy Alphin, President
Sharon Alphin, Operations Dir
Dave Sehon, General Manager

Stuttgart

KWAK
05-15-1948; 1240 khz AM *Hrs Open:* 24
P.O. Box 789, Highway 64, Wynne, AR 72396 US
(870) 673-1595, *Fax:* (870) 673-8445
kdew973@yahoo.com
License: Stuttgart, AR held by Arkansas County Broadcasters Inc.
Group Owner: Arkansas County Broadcasters Inc.
Arbitron Metro Market: Stuttgart, AR *Format:* News *Special Programming:* Farm 6 hrs wkly *No. News Employees:* 1 *Target Audience:* General.
Bobby Caldwell, President
Scott Siler, Station Manager
Johnathan Reaves, News Director
Sandi Levey, Music Director
Sandy Levey, Traffic Manager

KWAK-FM
12-15-1987; 105.5 mhz FM *Hrs Open:* 24; 2.7 kw; 344 ft.; N34 25 52 W91 26 8
P.O. Box 789, Highway 64 West, Wynne, AR 72396 US
(870) 673-1595, *Fax:* (870) 673-8445
kdew973@yahoo.com
License: Stuttgart, Arkansas County, AR
Group Owner: Arkansas County Broadcasters Inc.
Nat'l Network: ABC
Arbitron Metro Market: Stuttgart, AR *Format:* Oldies *Hrs. of News Programming:* one.
Scott Siler, General Manager
Johnathan Reeves, News Director
Sandi Levey, Traffic Director

Texarkana

KOSY
11-15-1951; 790 khz AM *Hrs Open:* 24; 1 kw-D, DAN; 0.5 kw-N, DAN; N33 22 30 W94 1 0
600 Congress Avenue, Suite 1400, Austin, TX 78701 US
(870) 772-3771, *Fax:* (870) 772-0364
www.kkyr.com
wesspicher@gapbroadcasting.com
License: Texarkana, AR held by GAP Broadcasting Texarkana License LLC.
Group Owner: GAP Broadcasting LLC; (acq 8-3-2007; grpsl)
Arbitron Metro Market: Texarkana, TX *Format:* Country *No. News Employees:* 1 *Target Audience:* General.
Ron Bird, General Manager
Wes Spicher, Programming Director

KFYX(FM)
06-11-1968; 107.1 mhz FM *Hrs Open:* 24; 2.9 kw; Ant 479 ft; N33 25 45 W94 07 11
615 Olive St., Texarkana, TX 75501
(903) 793-4671, *Fax:* (903) 792-4261
License: Texarkana, Miller County, AR held by ArkLaTex LLC.
Group Owner: Arklatex LLC; (acq 1-3-2007; grpsl)
Population Served: 36,501 *Arbitron Metro Market:* Texarkana TX *Format:* Contemporary Hits/Top 40 *Target Audience:* 18-34.
Harold Sudbury, CEO
Scott Gray, CFO/Vice President

KYGL
01-01-1995; 106.3 mhz FM; 50 kw; 492 ft.; N33 18 30 W93 56 54
600 Congress Avenue, Suite 1400, Austin, TX 78701 US
(870) 772-3771, *Fax:* (870) 770-0364
www.kygl.com
License: Texarkana, Miller County, AR
Group Owner: GAP Broadcasting LLC
Arbitron Metro Market: Texarkana, AR *Format:* Classic Rock
Wes Spicher, Chief Engineer

*KKLT
01-01-2004; 89.3 mhz FM; 0.001 kw horiz, 23 kw vert; 505 ft.; N33 23 36 W93 51 34 *Rebroadcasts:* Rebroadcasts KLVR(FM) Santa Rosa, CA 100%
188 South Bellevue, Suite 222, Memphis, TN 38104 US
(800) 525-5683, *Fax:* (916) 251-1650
www.klove.com
klove@klove.com
License: Texarkana, Miller County, AR held by Educational Media Foundation.
Group Owner: EMF Broadcasting; (acq 1-11-2005; $125,000 for CP).
Nat'l Network: K-Love
Arbitron Metro Market: Texarkana, AR *Format:* Christian *No. News Employees:* 13
Darrell Chambliss, Chairman
Mike Novak, President and CEO
Eric Allen, General Sales Mgr
David Pierce, Chief Creative Officer and Programming Director
Ed Lenane, News Director
Sam Wallington, Engineering Dir
Richard Hunt, NewsReporter
Marya Morgan, News Reporter
Glenn Goodwin, Regional Manager
Alan Mason, Chief Operating Officer
Dan Antonelli, Chief Business Development Officer
Eric Moser, Chief Financial Officer

KTOY
01-01-1993; 104.7 mhz FM *Hrs Open:* 24; 3.1 kw; 453 ft.; N33 25 45 W94 7 11
2409 College Drive, Texarkana, TX 75501 US
(903) 793-4671, *Fax:* (903) 792-4261
www.ktoy1047.com
scott@texarkanaradio.com
License: Texarkana, Miller County, AR held by Jo-Al Broadcasting Inc.
Group Owner: Arklatex LLC; (acq 1-3-2007; grpsl)
Nat'l Network: ABC *Nat'l Reps:* Interep
Arbitron Metro Market: Texarkana, AR *Format:* Adult Contemp *Target Audience:* 25-54; blacks
John McCoy, Operations Dir
Scott Gray, General Sales Mgr
Soulman Billy Bland, Programming Director
Dee Dee Woods, Asst Program Director

Turrell

*KXIQ(AM)
04-01-1987; 1180 khz AM *Hrs Open:* 24 hours; 5 kw-D, 26 w-N, 3.5 kw-CH; N35 08 31 W90 08 06
5500 Poplar Ave., Suite 1, Memphis, TN 38119-3716
(901) 683-3993, *Fax:* (901) 685-3995
License: Turrell, Crittenden County, AR held by Pollack Broadcasting Co.
Group Owner: Pollack Broadcasting Co.; (acq 10-20-2000; grpsl)
Population Served: 1,500,000 *Arbitron Metro Market:* Memphis, TN *No. News Employees:* 3 *Target Audience:* 18-49 male
William H. Pollack, President

Van Buren

KOAI
09-06-1979; 1060 khz AM
P.O. Box 5084, Fort Smith, AR 72913 US
(479) 452-0681, *Fax:* (479) 452-0873
License: Van Buren, AR held by Cumulus Licensing Corp.
Group Owner: Cumulus Media Inc.
Arbitron Metro Market: Fort Smith, AR
Smitty O'Loughlin, General Manager

KHGG
11-24-1958; 1580 khz AM *Hrs Open:* 24
P.O. Box 573, 523 Garrison Ave., #201, Fort Smith, AR 72902 US
(479) 288-1047, *Fax:* (479) 785-2638
www.fortsmithradiogroup.com
koolproduction@sbcglobal.net
License: Van Buren, AR held by Pharis Broadcasting Inc.
Group Owner: Pharis Broadcasting Inc.; acq 9-20-93; $110,000;
Nat'l Network: Fox Sports *Regional Network:* Ark. Radio Net.
Nat'l Reps: Commercial Media Sales
Arbitron Metro Market: Fort Smith, AR *Format:* Sports, Talk
Target Audience: General. *Adv. Rates:* 15; 15; 15; 15
William Pharis, CEO
Ernie Witt, Programming Director
Karen Pharis, Executive Vice President

KBBQ-FM
05-22-1983; 102.7 mhz FM; 17 kw; 574 ft.; N35 26 51 W94 21 54
111 East Kilbourn Avenue, Suite 2700, Milwaukee, WI 53202 US
(479) 452-0681, *Fax:* (479) 452-0873
www.1027thevibe.com
info@1027thevibe.com
License: Van Buren, Crawford County, AR held by Cumulus Licensing Corp.
Group Owner: Cumulus Media Inc.; (acq 8-99; $1.15 million)
Arbitron Metro Market: Fort Smith, AR *Format:* Contemporary Hits/Top 40

Smitty O'Loughlin, General Manager
Dale Daniels, General Sales Mgr
JJ Ryan, Programming Director
Dina Godfrey, Promotions Manager
Michael Young, Business Manager
Anita Cowan, Events Manager

***KLFS**
01-01-2004; 90.3 mhz FM *Hrs Open:* 24; 2.4 kw vert; 256 ft.; N35 23 37 W94 33 7
1425 N Market Blvd., Suite 9, Sacramento, CA 95834 US
(800) 525-5683, *Fax:* (916) 251-1650
www.klove.com
klove@klove.com
License: Van Buren, Crawford County, AR held by Educational Media Foundation.
Group Owner: EMF Broadcasting
Nat'l Network: K-Love
Arbitron Metro Market: Van Buren, AR *Format:* Christian *No. News Employees:* 3 *Target Audience:* 25-44; Judeo Chrisitan, female
Darrell Chambliss, Chairman
Mike Novak, President and CEO
Glenn Goodwin, Operations Dir
David Pierce, Programming Director
Ed Lenane, News Director
Sam Wallington, Engineering Dir
Marya Morgan, News Reporter
Richard Hunt, NewsReporter
Laura Daniels, News Reporter
Tim Luttrell, News Reporter
Kenny Noble Cortes, News Reporter
Darren Vinson, News Reporter

Vilonia

KASR
04-01-1984; 92.7 mhz FM; 25 kw; 328 ft.; N35 3 26 W92 4 16
1117 Oak Street, Suite 300, Conway, AR 72032 US
(501) 327-6611, *Fax:* (501) 327-6614
www.kasr.com
kasr@sbcglobal.net
License: Vilonia, Faulkner County, AR
Arbitron Metro Market: Conway, AR *Format:* Sports
Mike Harrison, President
Josh Harrison, Operations Dir
Mike Harrison, General Manager
Michel Mace, Station Manager

Viola

KCMC-FM
05-01-2007; 94.3 mhz FM *Hrs Open:* 24/7; 8.1 kw; Ant 571 ft; N36 19 30 W91 58 41
223 Russell St., Mountain Home, AR
(870) 425-4971, *Fax:* (870) 424-9717
License: Viola, Fulton County, AR held by MJFM LLC.
Population Served: 219,194*Target Audience:* 25-54.
Mike Wiseman, COO
Scott Gray, General Manager

Waldo

KVMZ
01-01-2002; 99.1 mhz FM; 4.1 kw; 400 ft.; N33 17 59 W93 14 0
188 South Bellevue, Suite 222, Memphis, TN 38104 US
(870) 234-9901, *Fax:* (870) 234-5865
www.magnoliaradio.com
kvmakvmz@magnoliaradio.com
License: Waldo, Columbia County, AR held by Noalmark Broadcasting Corp.
Group Owner: Noalmark Broadcasting Corp.; (acq 8-1-2005; $430,000)
Regional Network: Ark. Radio Net.
Arbitron Metro Market: Magnolia, AR *Format:* Country *Adv. Rates:* 10.59; 10.59; 10.59; 10.59
Ken Sibley, General Manager
Dan Gregory, Account Executive/Sports Director
Amanda Smith, Account Executive
Megan Black, Office Manager

Waldron

KHGG-FM
05-18-1982; 103.1 mhz FM; 6.1 kw; 1352 ft.; N34 58 44 W93 56 42 *Rebroadcasts:* Rebroadcasts KHGG(AM) 100%
2708 Rannoch Circle, Fort Smith, AR 72903 US
(479) 288-1047, *Fax:* (479) 288-0942
www.fortsmithradiogroup.com/sportshog103.htm
License: Waldron, Scott County, AR held by Pharis Broadcasting Inc.
Group Owner: Pharis Broadcasting Inc.; (acq 6-1-2003; $360,000).
Nat'l Network: Fox Sports *Nat'l Reps:* Commercial Media Sales
Regional Reps: BRI
Format: Sports, Talk *Hrs. of News Programming:* news progmg 10 hrs wkly *No. News Employees:* 1 *Target Audience:* 25-54.
Adv. Rates: 12; 12; 12; 12
William Pharis, President
Ernie Witt, Operations Dir
Karen Pharis, General Manager

Walnut Ridge

KIYS
01-01-1947; 101.7 mhz FM *Hrs Open:* 24; 10.5 kw; 1073 ft.; N35 57 14 W90 41 41
Mailing Address: PO Box 30, Walnut Ridge, AR 72476 US
Second Address: 407 W. Parker Rd, Jonesboro, AR 72404
(870) 935-5598, *Fax:* (870) 932-3814
www.1019kiysfm.com
License: Walnut Ridge, Craighead County, AR held by Capstar TX L.P.
Group Owner: Clear Channel Communications Inc.; (acq 1-18-01; grpsl).
Arbitron Metro Market: Jonesboro, AR *Format:* Contemporary Hits/Top 40 *Target Audience:* 18-49; middle to upper middle income
Larry James, General Manager
Katy Wiliamson, General Sales Mgr
Kevin Box, Programming Director
Duce Foreman, Promotions Manager
Janice Reed, News Director
Troy Owens, Chief Engineer

KRLW
06-29-1951; 1320 khz AM *Hrs Open:* 12; 1 kw-D, ND2; 0.152 kw-N, ND2; N36 3 58 W90 56 24
PO Box 30, Walnut Ridge, AR 72476 US
(870) 886-6666, *Fax:* (870) 886-5719
krlw@nex.net
License: Walnut Ridge, AR held by Combined Media Group Inc.
Group Owner: Combined Media Group Inc.; acq 7-25-01; with co-located FM).
Nat'l Network: CBS *Regional Network:* Ark. Radio Net.
Arbitron Metro Market: Jonesboro, AR *Format:* Oldies
Tim Scott, President

KIYS-FM
03-27-1977; 106.3 mhz FM *Hrs Open:* 24; 3 kw; 328 ft; N36 03 58 W90 56 24
1 Radio Dr., Pocohantas, AR 72455
(870) 934-5000, *Fax:* (870) 932-3814
www.kissjonesboro.com
info@krlw.com
License: Walnut Ridge, Lawrence County, AR
Nat'l Network: CBS *Regional Network:* Ark. Radio Net.
Population Served: 20,000 *Arbitron Metro Market:* Jonesboro, AR *Format:* Contemporary Hits/Top 40
Mike Novak, President
Chuck Crossno, General Sales Mgr

Warren

KWRF
08-01-1953; 860 khz AM *Hrs Open:* 24; 0.25 kw-D, ND1; 0.055 kw-N, ND1; N33 37 59 W92 3 51
1255 North Myrtle St, Warren, AR 71671 US
(870) 226-2653(870) 226-2654, *Fax:* (870) 226-3039
pines.broadcasting@sbcglobal.net
License: Warren, AR held by Pines Broadcasting Inc.
Regional Network: Ark. Radio Net.
Arbitron Metro Market: Warren, AR *Format:* Classic Rock *Special Programming:* Gospel 8 hrs wkly *Hrs. of News Programming:* news progmg 10 hrs wkly *No. News Employees:* 1 *Target Audience:* General.
Jimmy Sledge, President
Gwen Sledge, Operations Dir
Richard Garrison, Disc Jockey

KWRF-FM
06-21-1976; 105.5 mhz FM *Hrs Open:* 24; 3 kw; 243 ft.; N33 38 8 W92 3 56
1255 N. Myrtle Street, Warren, AR 71671 US
(870) 226-2653, *Fax:* (870) 226-3039
License: Warren, Bradley County, AR
Arbitron Metro Market: Warren, AR
Gwen Sledge, President
Judy Moore, Programming Director
Richard Garrison, Disc Jockey
Allen Weise, Disc Jockey

West Helena

KCLT
12-17-1984; 104.9 mhz FM *Hrs Open:* 24; 3 kw; 299 ft.; N34 30 56 W90 40 13
Mailing Address: P.O. Box 2870, West Helena, AR 72390 US
Second Address: 700 Dr. Martin Luther King Dr., Suite 1, West Helena, AR 72390
(870) 572-9506, *Fax:* (870) 572-1845
www.force2radio.com
force2@sbcglobal.net
License: West Helena, Phillips County, AR held by West Helena Broadcasters Inc.
Arbitron Metro Market: West Helena, AR *Format:* Urban Contemporary *Special Programming:* Gospel 15 hrs wkly *Hrs. of News Programming:* news progmg one hr wkly *No. News Employees:* 1 *Target Audience:* 25-54;general, mainly African-Americans
Raymond Simes, President
Larry Evans, Operations Dir
Elaine Sims, Station Manager

West Memphis

KQPN
12-01-1961; 730 khz AM *Hrs Open:* 24
342 River Oaks Blvd., Memphis, TN 38120 US
(901) 522-1919, *Fax:* (901) 522-1920
www.730espn.com
Harry.Long@730espn.com
License: West Memphis, AR held by Simmons Austin, LS LLC.
Group Owner: Simmons Media Group; (acq 6-14-2006; $2 million)
Nat'l Network: ESPN Radio
Arbitron Metro Market: Memphis, TN *Format:* Sports *Target Audience:* 25-54; family types *Adv. Rates:* 25; 25; 25; 20
Kosta Panidis, General Manager
Dean Allen, Programming Director
Kent Abendroth, Chief Engineer

White Hall

KTRN
11-01-1997; 104.5 mhz FM *Hrs Open:* 24; 3 kw; 289 ft.; N34 13 13 W92 4 37
6257 Brisa Del Mar, El Paso, TX 79925 US
(870) 536-5876 (on air)(870) 536 3282 (office), *Fax:* (870) 536-3475
License: White Hall, Jefferson County, AR held by Bayou Broadcasting Inc.
Arbitron Metro Market: Pine Bluff, AR *Format:* Classic Rock *Target Audience:* Women; 20 & up
Vickie Hooker, General Manager

Wilson

KOSE
10-11-1949; 860 khz AM; 1 kw-D, ND1; 0.021 kw-N, ND1; N35 41 3 W89 58 57
125 S. Second St, Blytheville, AR 72315 US
(870) 762-2093, *Fax:* (870) 763-8459
License: Wilson, AR held by Newport Broadcasting Co.
Group Owner: Sudbury Services Inc.; (acq 1996)
Regional Network: Ark. Radio Net. *Nat'l Reps:* Roslin
Arbitron Metro Market: Memphis, TN *Format:* Gospel *Special Programming:* Black 6 hrs, farm 5 hrs wkly *Target Audience:* 24-55; middle-class, blue/white collar workers
Tom Hill, Chief Engineer

Wrightsville

KLAL
03-01-1992; 107.7 mhz FM; 100 kw; Ant 741 ft; N34 36 34 W92 14 14
700 Wellington Hills Rd., Little Rock, AR 89128
(501) 401-0200, *Fax:* (501) 401-0349
www.alice1077.com
info@alice1077.com
License: Wrightsville, Pulaski County, AR
Group Owner: Cumulus Media Inc.; (acq 9-4-97).
Arbitron Metro Market: Little Rock, AR
Jim Beard, Promotions Manager

Wynne

KWYN
09-28-1956; 1400 khz AM *Hrs Open:* 24; 1 kw-U, ND1; N35 15 21 W90 47 49
P.O. Box 789, Highway 64 West, Wynne, AR 72396 US
(870) 238-8141, *Fax:* (870) 238-5997
www.kwyn.com
eabwynne@cablelynx.com

License: Wynne, AR held by East Arkansas Broadcasters Inc.
Group Owner: East Arkansas Broadcasters Inc.
Nat'l Network: CBS; Westwood One *Regional Network:* Ark. Radio Net.
Arbitron Metro Market: Wynne, AR *Format:* Talk *Special Programming:* Farm 6 hrs wkly *Target Audience:* General.
Bobby Caldwell, CEO
David Sills, General Sales Mgr
Lindell Staggs, News Director
Lane Goodwin, Engineering Dir
Jim Alexander, Engineer
Jennifer Lynch, Traffic Manager
Renae Smith, Sales Representtive

KWYN-FM
05-15-1969; 92.5 mhz FM *Hrs Open:* 24; 35 kw; 335 ft.; N35 11 59 W90 43 23
P.O. Box 789, Wynne, AR 72396 US
(870) 238-8141, *Fax:* (870) 238-5997
www.kwyn.com
eabwynne@cablelynx.com
License: Wynne, Cross County, AR held by East Arkansas Broadcasters Inc.
Group Owner: East Arkansas Broadcasters Inc.
Regional Network: Ark. Radio Net.
Arbitron Metro Market: Wynne, AR *Format:* Country
Bobby Caldwell, CEO
David Sills, General Sales Mgr
Lindell Staggs, News Director
Jim Alexander, Engineering Dir
Lane Goodwin, Engineer
Lindell Staggs, News/Programming Director
Jennifer Lynch, Traffic Manager
Ranae Smith, SalesRepresentative

Yellville

KCTT-FM
01-01-1986; 101.7 mhz FM; 6 kw; 285 ft.; N36 17 18 W92 30 37
P.O. Box 100, Yellville, AR 72687 US
(870) 449-4001(870) 425-3101, *Fax:* (870) 424-4314
www.ktlo.com
bob@ktlo.com
License: Yellville, Marion County, AR held by KTLO L.L.C.
Group Owner: KTLO LLC; (acq 5-29-98; $215,000)
Nat'l Network: ABC
Arbitron Metro Market: Mountain Home, AR *Format:* Oldies
Special Programming: Folk 10 hrs wkly
Bob Knight, CEO
Brad Haworth, Operations Dir
Bob Knight, General Manager
Danny Ward, Station Manager
Jim Bodenhamer, News Director

California

Adelanto

KLSN
92.7 mhz FM; 0.28 kw; 1473 ft.; N34 36 44 W117 17 27
3101 North Federal Highway, Suite 601, Ft. Lauderdale, FL 33306 US
(949) 454-2475, *Fax:* (949) 454-1710
www.playlist927.com
License: Adelanto, Gallatin County, CA held by Gallatin Valley Community Radio.
Arbitron Metro Market: Adelanto, CA *Format:* Adult Contemp
Susan Cole, Chairman
Rick Shaw, Programming Director
Matthew Rodriguez, General Manager
Pat Duffy, Station Manager
Justin Schuvie, Promotions Manager
Chris Hicks, Chief Engineer
Betsy Zook, Business Manager
Jake Hagen, TrafficDirector/Asst Program Director
Doug Eldred, Public Service Director
Linda Perry, Senior Account Executive

Alameda

KREV
08-01-1959; 92.7 mhz FM; 3.6 kw; 420 ft.; N37 47 54 W122 24 59
50 East Rivercenter Blvd., #1200, Covington, KY 41011 US
(415) 356-1600, *Fax:* (415) 356-1601
www.927rev.com
autumn@927rev.com
License: Alameda, Alameda County, CA held by Golden State Broadcasting LLC
Arbitron Metro Market: San Francisco, CA *Format:* Contemporary Hits/Top 40
Ed Stolz, CEO
Autumn Larrick, Station Manager

Alturas

KALT-FM
07-01-2002; 106.5 mhz FM; 0.5 kw; 272 ft.; N41 29 57 W120 37 30
Post Office Box 509, Ruidoso Downs, NM 88346 US
(530) 233-4842, *Fax:* (530) 233-4173
kalt@hdo.net
License: Alturas, Modoc County, CA held by Woodrow Michael Warren.
Group Owner: Woodrow Michael Warren Stns
Arbitron Metro Market: Alturas, CA *Format:* Classic Rock
Mike Warren, General Manager

KCNO
12-04-1990; 94.5 mhz FM *Hrs Open:* 14; 100 kw horiz; -194 ft.; N41 33 50 W120 24 55
P.O. Box 570, Alturas, CA 96101 US
(530) 233-3570, *Fax:* (530) 233-5470
englishradio@edimediainc.com
License: Alturas, Modoc County, CA held by EDI Media Inc.
Arbitron Metro Market: Alturas, CA *Format:* Country *Hrs. of News Programming:* News progmg 17 hrs wkly *Target Audience:* General.
Bill Hansen, General Manager
Dodie McGoregh, News Director

KCFJ
06-04-1951; 570 khz AM *Hrs Open:* 6 AM-10 PM; 5 kw-D, 200 w-N; N41 30 07 W120 30 01
Box 580, Alturas, CA 96101
(530) 233-3570, *Fax:* (530) 233-5470
License: Alturas, Modoc County, CA held by EDI Media Inc.
Nat'l Network: USA
Population Served: 100,000*Special Programming:* Farm one hr wkly *Hrs. of News Programming:* news progmg 3 hrs wkly *No. News Employees:* 1 *Target Audience:* General.
Bill Hansen, General Manager
Dodie McGough, News Director

Anderson

KEWB
03-20-1983; 94.7 mhz FM; 4.2 kw; 1565 ft.; N40 39 6 W122 31 32
1588 Charles Drive, Redding, CA 96003 US
(530) 244-9700, *Fax:* (530) 244-9707
www.power94booty.com
rhealy@resultsradiomail.com
License: Anderson, Shasta County, CA held by Results Radio of Redding Licensee LLC.
Group Owner: Fritz Communications Inc.; (acq 6-28-2000; grpsl).
Arbitron Metro Market: Redding, CA *Format:* Contemporary Hits/Top 40 *Target Audience:* 18-49.
Beth Tappan, General Manager
Laurie Curto, General Sales Mgr
Rico Garcia, Programming Director

Angwin

***KDFC**
09-01-1947; 89.9 mhz FM *Hrs Open:* 24; 0.8 kw; 3035 ft.; N38 40 9 W122 37 53
PO Box 89, Angwin, CA 94508 US
(415) 764-1021, *Fax:* (415) 777-2291
www.kdfc.com
info@kdfc.com
License: Angwin, San Francisco County, CA held by Entercom San Francisco License LLC.
Group Owner: Entercom Communications Corp.; (acq 3-14-2008; grpsl)
Arbitron Metro Market: San Francisco *Format:* Talk *Target Audience:* 25-54; educated, upscale
Bill Lueth, President
Dwight Walker, General Manager
Paul Duckett, General Sales Mgr
Rick Malone, Programming Director
Jude Heller, Promotions Manager
Rik Malone, Music Director

***KNDL(FM)**
05-20-1961; 89.9 mhz FM *Hrs Open:* 24; 794 w; Ant 3,010 ft; N38 40 09 W122 37 53
95 La Jota Dr., Angwin, CA 94508
(707) 965-4155, *Fax:* (707) 965-4161
www.thecandle.com
kndl@thecandle.com
License: Angwin, Napa County, CA held by Howell Mountain Broadcasting Co. Inc.
Format: Christian *Target Audience:* 35-49; general
Jim Aldred, General Manager

Apple Valley

KIXW
06-05-1954; 960 khz AM *Hrs Open:* 8:30 AM-5:30 PM; 5 kw-D, ND2; 0.02 kw-N, ND2; N34 31 0 W117 13 35
12370 Hesperia Road, Suite 17, Victorville, CA 92932 US
(760) 241-1313, *Fax:* (760) 241-0205
www.talk960.com
kimjennings@edbroadcasters.com
License: Apple Valley, CA held by EDB VV License LLC.
Group Owner: Frontier Radio Management Inc.; (acq 11-30-2007; grpsl)
Nat'l Reps: Christal
Format: Talk *Target Audience:* 35+.
Tom Hoyt, Operations Dir
Kim Jennings, General Sales Mgr
Joe Pagano, Programming Director

KWRN
01-26-1991; 1550 khz AM *Hrs Open:* 24; 5 kw-D, DAN; 0.5 kw-N, DA2; N34 32 12 W117 9 22 *Rebroadcasts:* Rebroadcasts KWRM(AM) Corona 100%
Mailing Address: 210 Radio Road, Corona, CA 91719 US
Second Address: 15165 7th St., Ste D, Victorville, CA 92392
(760) 955-8722, *Fax:* (760) 955-5751
www.lapoderosa1550am.com
kwrn@majormarket.com
License: Apple Valley, CA held by Major Market Stations Inc.
Nat'l Network: ABC
Arbitron Metro Market: Victorville, CA *Format:* Contemporary Hits/Top 40 *Target Audience:* 34-54; adults with a stable job and disposable income *Adv. Rates:* 20; 20; 20; 20
Marilynn Kramar, President
Iris Gutierrez, Promotions Manager
kathy DeCastro, News Director
Dick Vosper, Chief Engineer

KZXY-FM
05-17-1968; 102.3 mhz FM; 6 kw; 328 ft.; N34 24 40 W117 11 9
Mr. Chuck Mc Kay, 12370 Hesperia Rd, Covington, KY 92392 US
(760) 241-1313, *Fax:* (760) 241-0205
www.y102fm.com
kimjennings@edbroadcasters.com
License: Apple Valley, San Bernardino County, CA held by EDB VV License LLC.
Group Owner: Frontier Radio Management Inc.
Nat'l Reps: Christal
Arbitron Metro Market: Apple Valley, CA *Format:* Adult Contemp *Target Audience:* 25-54; women *Adv. Rates:* 25-75
Tom Hoyt, Operations Dir
Kim Jennings, General Sales Mgr
Colleen Quinn, Programming Director

Arcadia

KSSE
12-03-1960; 107.1 mhz FM *Hrs Open:* 24; 6 kw; -43 ft.; N34 10 51 W118 1 38
11 Skyline Drive, Hawthorne, NY 10532 US
(323) 900-6100, *Fax:* (323) 900-6200
www.viva1071.com
info@viva1071.com
License: Arcadia, Los Angeles County, CA held by Entravision Holdings LLC.
Group Owner: Entravision Communications Corp.; (acq 4-1-03; grpsl).
Wire Services: SportsTicker
Arbitron Metro Market: Los Angeles, CA *Target Audience:* 24-39; general
Karl Meyer, General Manager
Nestor Rocha, Programming Director
Elias Autran, Programming Director

Arcata

KATA
11-15-1957; 1340 khz AM; 1 kw-U, ND1; N40 51 12 W124 5 0
Pmb 333, 1 Blackfield Dr, Tiburon, CA 94920 US
(707) 442-2000, *Fax:* (707) 443-6848
www.kata1340.com
ddaniels@bicoastalmedia.com
License: Arcata, CA held by Bicoastal Media LLC.
Group Owner: Bicoastal Media L.L.C.; acq 7-28-99; grpsl)
Nat'l Network: ABC
Arbitron Metro Market: Eureka, CA *Format:* Sports *Target Audience:* 25-54; upscale adults
Mike Wilson, President
Laurie Tate, General Manager

Victoria Bennington, General Sales Mgr
Tom Sebourn, Programming Director

***KHSU**
10-01-1960; 90.5 mhz FM *Hrs Open:* 24; 8.5 kw; 1506 ft.; N40 43 37 W123 58 22
Radio Station Khsu-Fm, Arcata, CA 95521 US
(707) 826-4807, *Fax:* (707) 826-6082
www.khsu.org
khsu@humboldt.edu
License: Arcata, Humboldt County, CA held by Humboldt State University.
Nat'l Network: NPR; PRI
Format: News *Special Programming:* World 14 hrs, jazz 10 hrs wkly *Hrs. of News Programming:* News progmg 28 hrs wkly
Kate Whiteside, Operations Dir
Ed Subkis, General Manager
David Reed, General Sales Mgr
Kevin Sanders, Chief Engineer
Mark Shikuma, Music Director
Lorna Bryant, Administrative Assistant

KXGO
01-01-1970; 93.1 mhz FM; 50 kw; Ant 1,666 ft; N40 43 38 W123 58 22
1400 Main Street, Suite 104, Ferndale, CA 95501
(707) 786-5104, *Fax:* (707) 786-5100
www.theclassicrockstation.com
brnda@khum.com
License: Arcata, Humboldt County, CA held by Lost Coast Communications
Group Owner: Lost Coast Communications; (acq 11-1-97).
Nat'l Reps: Christal
Population Served: 210,000*Target Audience:* 25-54; upscale adults
Patrick Cleary, President
Brenda Boyd, Operations Dir
Patrick Cleary, General Sales Mgr
Charlie Fuentes, Programming Director

Arnold

KBYN
09-01-1995; 95.9 mhz FM *Hrs Open:* 24; 0.86 kw; 863 ft.; N38 22 40 W120 11 33
4043 Geer Rd, P.O. Box 1039, Hughson, CA 95326 US
(209) 883-8760, *Fax:* (209) 883-8769
www.lafavorita.net
ngomez@lafavorita.net
License: Arnold, Calaveras County, CA held by KBYN Inc.
Nat'l Network: CBS
Arbitron Metro Market: Hughson, CA *Format:* Country *Hrs. of News Programming:* news progmg 3 hrs wkly *No. News Employees:* 1 *Target Audience:* 25-54; general
Nelson Gomez, General Manager

KCFA
10-02-1995; 106.1 mhz FM *Hrs Open:* 24; 3.8 kw; 843 ft.; N38 22 40 W120 11 33
3003 Snelling Avenue North, St. Paul, MN 55113 US
(209) 883-8760, *Fax:* (209) 883-8769
www.lafavorita.net
ngomez@lafavorita.net
License: Arnold, Calaveras County, CA held by KCFA Inc.
Format: Ethnic *Hrs. of News Programming:* news progmg 5 hrs wkly *No. News Employees:* 1 *Target Audience:* 30-50; Families
Nelson Gomez, General Manager
Marisol Valenzuela, Programming Director
Chuck Hughes, Chief Engineer

Arroyo Grande

KXTK
06-29-1962; 1280 khz AM *Hrs Open:* 24
10209 Southeast Division Street, Portland, OR 97266 US
(805) 547-1280, *Fax:* (805) 543-1508
espnradio1280.com
sports@espnradio1280.com
License: Arroyo Grande, CA held by Pacific Coast Media LLC
Nat'l Network: ESPN Radio; Westwood One
Arbitron Metro Market: San Luis Obispo, CA *Format:* Sports
Target Audience: 25 plus.
Mike Chellsen, General Manager
Tom Barket, News Director
Bill Bordeaux, Engineering Dir

KLFF
09-01-2002; 890 khz AM
1159 Fair Oaks Ave., Arroyo Grande, CA 93420 US
(805) 541-4343, *Fax:* (805) 541-9101
www.890online.com
info@klfie.org
License: Arroyo Grande, CA held by Jerry J. Collins.
Arbitron Metro Market: San Luis Obispo, CA *Format:* Religious
Jerry Collins, President
Joel Riley, General Manager
Noonie Fugler, Promotions Manager

Arvin

KMYX-FM
06-30-1999; 92.5 mhz FM *Hrs Open:* 24; 0.62 kw; 1024 ft.; N35 11 41.1 W118 42 16
P.O. Box 62, Keene, CA 93531 US
(661) 837-0745, *Fax:* (661) 837-1612
www.campesina.net
achavez@campesina.com
License: Arvin, Kern County, CA held by Farmworker Educ. Radio Network Inc.
Arbitron Metro Market: Bakersfield, CA *Format:* Tejano *Target Audience:* 25-54; Hispanic market
Anthony Chavez, President
Cesar Chavez, General Manager
Cesar Chavez, Programming Director
Maria Urrutia, News Director
Dave Whitehead, Chief Engineer

Atascadero

KIQO
05-19-1979; 104.5 mhz FM *Hrs Open:* 24; 4.7 kw; 1444 ft.; N35 21 40 W120 39 21
1400 Easton Drive, Suite 129, Bakersfield, CA 93309 US
(805) 781-2750, *Fax:* (805) 781-2758
www.kiqo104.5.com
info@kiqo104.5.com
License: Atascadero, San Luis Obispo County, CA held by AGM California.
Group Owner: American General Media; (acq 2-10-99; $1.5 million).
Nat'l Network: ABC
Arbitron Metro Market: San Luis Obispo, CA *Format:* Oldies
Target Audience: 25-55.
Kathy Signorelli, General Manager
Mark Tobin, General Sales Mgr
Seth Blackburn, Programming Director
Pat Mallon, News Director
Bill Bordeaux, Chief Engineer

Atherton

***KCEA**
06-02-1979; 89.1 mhz FM *Hrs Open:* 24; 0.1 kw; 128 ft.; N37 29 32 W122 16 28
555 Middlefield Road, Atherton, CA 94027 US
(650) 306-8823,(650) 306-8822, *Fax:* (650) 306-8834
www.kcea.org
info@kcea.org
License: Atherton, San Mateo County, CA held by Sequoia Union High School District.
Format: Big Band, Oldies *Target Audience:* General.
Trish Millet, Operations Dir
Michael Isaacs, General Manager
John Mylod, News Director

Atwater

KBRE
10-01-1995; 92.5 mhz FM *Hrs Open:* 24; 6 kw; 328 ft.; N37 16 41 W120 37 35
1175 Fairview Drive, Suite N, Carson City, NV 89701 US
(209) 723-2191, *Fax:* (209) 383-2950
www.925thebear.com
info@925thebear.com
License: Atwater, Merced County, CA held by Mapleton License of Merced LLC.
Group Owner: Mapleton Communications LLC; (acq 6-1-2002; grpsl)
Format: Rock/AOR *Hrs. of News Programming:* news progmg 3 hrs wkly *No. News Employees:* 1 *Target Audience:* Men 25-49
Andrew Adams, General Manager
Damian Galaarza, General Sales Mgr
Jason LaChance, Programming Director

Auberry

KKBZ
07-12-1992; 105.1 mhz FM *Hrs Open:* 24; 0.6 kw; 1870 ft.; N37 4 25 W119 25 52
6290 Sunset Boulevard, Los Angeles, CA 90028 US
(559) 497-1100, *Fax:* (559) 497-1125
mginsburg@lotusfresno.com
License: Auberry, Fresno County, CA held by Lotus Communications Corp.
Group Owner: Lotus Communications Corp.
Nat'l Reps: Lotus Entravision Reps LLC
Arbitron Metro Market: Fresno, CA *Format:* Classic Rock *Adv. Rates:* 40; 40; 40; 25
Howard Kalmenson, President
Mike Ginsburg, General Manager

Auburn

KAHI
11-13-1957; 950 khz AM *Hrs Open:* 24; 5 kw-D, DA2; 5 kw-N, DA2; N38 51 28 W121 1 39
605 West Lake Blvd., Suite 5, Tahoe City, CA 96145 US
(530) 885-5636, *Fax:* (530) 885-0166
www.kahi.com
info@KAHI.com
License: Auburn, CA held by IHR Educational Broadcasting.
Group Owner: IHR Educational Broadcasting; (acq 4-28-99; $475,000 with KSMH(AM) West Sacramento)
Nat'l Network: Radio America
Arbitron Metro Market: Auburm, CA *Format:* Variety/Diverse
Special Programming: community *Hrs. of News Programming:* 6-9am, 12-1pm, 4-7pm *Target Audience:* 25-54; Community focused *Adv. Rates:* 25; 25; 25;18
Dave Rosenthal, Operations Dir
Jerry Henry, General Manager

KHYL
12-21-1961; 101.1 mhz FM *Hrs Open:* 24; 36 kw; 577 ft.; N38 51 28 W121 1 39
1440 Ethan Way, Suite 200, Sacramento, CA 95825 US
(916) 929-5325, *Fax:* (916) 925-0118
www.v101fm.com
info@khylfm.com
License: Auburn, Placer County, CA held by AMFM Broadcasting Licenses LLC.
Group Owner: Clear Channel Communications Inc.; (acq 8-30-2000; grpsl).
Arbitron Metro Market: Sacramento, CA *Format:* Adult Contemp, Oldies *Special Programming:* Soul 5 hrs wkly *Hrs. of News Programming:* News progmg one hr wkly *Target Audience:* 25-54.
Jeff Holden, General Manager
Rob Worden, General Sales Mgr
Jeff McMurray, Programming Director
Amy Bingham, Promotions Manager

Avalon

KBRT
06-01-1952; 740 khz AM; 10 kw-D, DA2; 0.113 kw-N, DA2; N33 21 36 W118 22 18
PO Box 3003, Blue Bell, PA 19422 US
(714) 754-4450, *Fax:* (714) 754-0735
www.kbrt740.com
kbrtinfo@crawfordbroadcasting.com
License: Avalon, CA held by Kierton Inc.
Group Owner: Crawford Broadcasting Co.; (acq 5-21-80)
Arbitron Metro Market: Los Angeles *Format:* Talk, Religious
Target Audience: Christian adult.
Todd Stickler, Operations Dir
Sarah Davis, General Sales Mgr

***KISL**
01-01-2000; 88.7 mhz FM; 0.2 kw; 20 ft.; N33 20 32 W118 19 11
P.O. Box 1980, Avalon, CA 90704 US
(310) 510-7469, *Fax:* (310) 510-1025
www.kisl.org
arts@cipas.org
License: Avalon, Los Angeles County, CA held by Catalina Island Performing Arts Foundation
Format: Variety/Diverse
Aaron Pitts, Station Manager

Avenal

***KAAX**
106.9 mhz FM; kw
12550 Brookhurst Street, Suite A, Garden Grove, CA 92840 US
License: Avenal, Kings County, CA held by Avenal Educational Services Inc.
Arbitron Metro Market: Garden Grove, CA
Abel DeLuna, President
Denny Jackson, Programming Director

Baker

KIXF
03-01-1994; 101.5 mhz FM *Hrs Open:* 24; 4.3 kw; 1322 ft.; N35 26 10 W115 55 25 *Rebroadcasts:* Rebroadcasts KIXW-FM Lenwood 100%
12381 Wilshire Blvd, Suite 105, Los Angeles, CA 25606 US

(760) 256-0326, *Fax:* (760) 256-9507
www.thehighwaystations.com
time@highwayradio.com
License: Baker, San Bernardino County, CA held by KHWY Inc.
Group Owner: KHWY Inc.; (acq 2-18-98; $1,741,444 with KIXW-FM Lenwood).
Nat'l Network: Westwood One; CNN Radio
Format: Country *Special Programming:* Hourly traf report to service interstate travelers *No. News Employees:* 1 *Target Audience:* 25-54; interstate travelers to Las Vegas & Laughlin, NV
Howard Anderson, CEO
Timothy Anderson, Operations Dir
Judy Robinson, General Sales Mgr
Lance Todd, Programming Director
John Gregg, Promotions Manager
Keith Hayes, News Director
Thomas McNeill, Engineering Dir
Kirk Anderson,Executive Vice President

KHRQ
01-01-2002; 94.9 mhz FM; 1.45 kw; 1325 ft.; N35 26 10 W115 55 25
12381 Wilshire Boulevard, Suite 105, Los Angeles, CA 90025 US
(760) 256-0326, *Fax:* (760) 256-9507
www.highwayrock.com
highwayradio@highwayradio.com
License: Baker, San Bernardino County, CA held by The Drive LLC.
Group Owner: KHWY Inc.; (acq 5-31-2003).
Nat'l Network: Jones Radio Networks
Arbitron Metro Market: Baker, CA *Format:* Classic Rock
Howard Anderson, CEO
Timothy Anderson, Operations Dir
Judy Robinson, General Sales Mgr
Lance Todd, Programming Director
John Gregg, Promotions Manager
Thomas McNeill, Engineering Dir
Kirk Anderson, Executive Vice President

Bakersfield

KHTY
10-01-1946; 970 khz AM *Hrs Open:* 24; 1 kw-D, DA2; 5 kw-N, DA2; N35 27 0 W118 56 48
16501 N.W. 16th Court, Miami, FL 33169 US
(661) 322-9929, *Fax:* (661) 322-7239
www.foxsports970am.com
A Jimbell@clearchannel.com
License: Bakersfield, CA held by AMFM Radio Licenses LLC.
Group Owner: Clear Channel Communications Inc.; (acq 12-22-2000; $1.4 million)
Nat'l Network: Fox Sports
Arbitron Metro Market: Bakersfield, CA *Format:* Sports
Jim Bell, Operations Dir
Ron Fisher, General Sales Mgr
Steve King, Programming Director
Steve Mull, Chief Engineer

KLHC
02-01-1958; 1350 khz AM *Hrs Open:* 24; 1 kw-D, ND1; 0.033 kw-N, ND1; N35 21 0 W118 58 58
1400 Easton Road, Bakersfield, CA 93309 US
(661) 847-1450, *Fax:* (661) 847-1350
www.klhcradio.com
klhc@klhcradio.com
License: Bakersfield, CA held by Force Broadcasting LLC.
Group Owner: Gore-Overgaard Broadcasting Inc.; (acq 1-6-2006; $925,000)
Arbitron Metro Market: Bakersfield, CA *Format:* Religious
Maria Ochoa, General Manager

KCWR
03-21-1990; 107.1 mhz FM *Hrs Open:* 24; 6 kw; 157 ft.; N35 22 11 W119 0 18
3223 Sillect Ave, Bakersfield, CA 93308 US
(661) 326-1011, *Fax:* (661) 328-7503(661) 328-7537(news)
License: Bakersfield, Kern County, CA held by Owens One Co. Inc.
Group Owner: Buck Owens Productions Inc.; (acq 5-24-2006; grpsl).
Arbitron Metro Market: Bakersfield, CA *Format:* Country
Mel Owens Jr., CEO
Julie Randolph, General Sales Manager

KERI
01-03-1932; 1410 khz AM *Hrs Open:* 24; 1 kw-U, ND1; N35 21 7 W118 57 29
Mailing Address: P.O. Box 2700, Bakersfield, CA 93303 US
Second Address: 1400 Easton Dr., Suite 144, Bakersfield, CA 93309
(661) 328-1410, *Fax:* (661) 328-0873
www.keri.com
License: Bakersfield, CA held by AGM California.
Group Owner: American General Media; (acq 5-1-75)
Nat'l Reps: Christal Wire Services: AP
Arbitron Metro Market: Bakersfield, CA *Format:* Christian *Target Audience:* 25-54.
Toni Snyder, General Manager
Toni Snyder, General Sales Mgr
D.C. Carter, Programming Director

***KFRB**
08-01-1996; 91.3 mhz FM *Hrs Open:* 24; 2.8 kw vert; 1368 ft.; N35 26 17 W118 44 22
Mailing Address: 4135 Northgate Blvd, Suite 1, Sacramento, CA 95834 US
Second Address: 290 Hegenberger Rd., Oakland, CA 94621
(805) 363-5576, *Fax:* (209) 389-0215
www.familyradio.com
familyradio@familyradio.org; info@familyradio.org; international@familyradio.org
License: Bakersfield, Kern County, CA held by Family Stations Inc.
Group Owner: Family Stations Inc.
Arbitron Metro Market: Bakersfield, CA *Format:* Christian, Religious *Special Programming:* Children's 10 hrs wkly
Harold Camping, President
David Manzi, Operations Dir

KGEO
01-01-1946; 1230 khz AM; 1 kw-U, ND1; N35 20 53 W119 0 33
PO Box 2700, Bakersfield, CA 93303 US
(661) 631-1410, *Fax:* (661) 328-0873
www.kernradio.com
tsynder@americangeneralmedia.com
License: Bakersfield, CA held by AGM California.
Group Owner: American General Media; (acq 12-9-92; $1.75 million with co-located FM;
Nat'l Network: Westwood One; ESPN Radio; CBS *Nat'l Reps:* McGavren Guild
Arbitron Metro Market: Bakersfield, CA *Format:* News, News/Talk, 86 *Special Programming:* Finance 13 hrs wkly *Hrs. of News Programming:* news progmg 130 hrs wkly
Toni Synder, General Manager
Steve Nicklaus, Programming Director
Jeff Lemucchi, News Director

KGFM
10-01-1964; 101.5 mhz FM; 6.7 kw; 1299 ft.; N35 26 17 W118 44 22
P.O. Box 2700, Bakersfield, CA 93303 US
(661) 631-1410, *Fax:* (661) 328-0873
www.kgfm.com
tsnyder@americangeneralmedia.com
License: Bakersfield, Kern County, CA held by AGM California.
Group Owner: American General Media
Arbitron Metro Market: Bakersfield, CA *Format:* Classic Rock *Target Audience:* 25-54
Toni Synder, General Manager
Chris Edwards, Programming Director

KBFP
01-01-1959; 800 khz AM *Hrs Open:* 6 AM-12 AM; 1 kw-D, DA2; 0.44 kw-N, DA2; N35 20 44 W118 59 33
966 East Essex Drive, Fresno, CA 93720 US
(661) 322-9929, *Fax:* (661) 322-9239
http://www.lapreciosa1053.com
stacydodson@clearchannel.com
License: Bakersfield, CA held by CC Licenses LLC.
Group Owner: Clear Channel Communications Inc.; (acq 10-11-2000; grpsl)
Arbitron Metro Market: Bakersfield, CA *Format:* Spanish *Target Audience:* 25-54, Spanish Adults
Jim Bell, Operations Dir
Tony Manes, Programming Director
Steve Mull, Chief Engineer
Stacy Dodson, Human Resources

KISV
01-01-1948; 94.1 mhz FM *Hrs Open:* 24; 4.5 kw; 1332 ft.; N35 26 17 W118 44 22
Mailing Address: P.O. Box 2700, Bakersfield, CA 93303 US
Second Address: 1400 Easton Dr., Suite 144, Bakersfield, CA 93309
(661) 328-1410, *Fax:* (661) 328-0873
www.hot941.com
jreed@americangeneralmedia.com
License: Bakersfield, Kern County, CA held by AGM California.
Group Owner: American General Media
Arbitron Metro Market: Bakersfield, CA *Format:* Contemporary Hits/Top 40 *Special Programming:* Farm one hr, relg one hr wkly
Roger Fessler, General Manager

KPSL-FM
12-15-1985; 96.5 mhz FM *Hrs Open:* 24; 50 kw; 499 ft.; N35 29 8 W118 53 19
966 East Essex Drive, Fresno, CA 93720 US
(661) 327-9711, *Fax:* (661) 327-0797
info@thespanishradio.com
License: Bakersfield, Kern County, CA held by Illinois Lotus Corp.
Group Owner: Lotus Communications Corp.; (acq 8-24-99; grpsl).
Arbitron Metro Market: Bakersfield, CA *Format:* Spanish
Greg Holcomb, General Manager
Isidro Roman, Programming Director

KKBB
11-01-1991; 99.3 mhz FM *Hrs Open:* 24; 10 kw; 390 ft.; N35 27 33 W119 1 13
Mailing Address: 166 West Putnam Ave, Greenwich, CT 06830 US
Second Address: 3651 Pegasus Dr., Suite 107, Bakersfield, CA 93380
(661) 393-1900, *Fax:* (661) 393-1915
www.groove993.com
jlove@kkbb.com
License: Bakersfield, Kern County, CA held by Buckley Communications Inc.
Group Owner: Buckley Broadcasting Corp.; (acq 10-3-94; $1 million;
Nat'l Reps: D & R Radio
Arbitron Metro Market: Bakersfield, CA *Format:* Oldies *Target Audience:* 25-54; adults
Steve Darnell, General Manager
Otis Warren, General Sales Mgr
Louie Cruz, Programming Director
Kathy King, News Director
Bob Turner, Chief Engineer

KVMX
08-24-1963; 92.1 mhz FM; 4.2 kw; 397 ft.; N35 29 11 W118 53 21
5200 Standard St, Bakersfield, CA 93308 US
(661) 322-9929, *Fax:* (661) 322-9239
www.965maxfm.com
License: Bakersfield, Kern County, CA held by Texas Lotus Corp.
Group Owner: Lotus Communications Corp.; (acq 7-29-2008; with KWID(FM) Las Vegas, NV in exchange for KZEP-FM San Antonio, TX)
Nat'l Reps: McGavren Guild
Arbitron Metro Market: Bakersfield, CA *Format:* Classic Rock
Greg Holcomb, General Manager
Sandy Ozuna, General Sales Mgr
Kenn McCloud, Programming Director

KNZR
01-01-1933; 1560 khz AM *Hrs Open:* 24; 25 kw-D, DAN; 10 kw-N, DAN; N35 18 30 W119 2 46
Mailing Address: 166 West Putnam Ave, Greenwich, CT 06830 US
Second Address: 3651 Pegasus Dr., Suite 107, Bakersfield, CA 93380
(661) 393-1900, *Fax:* (661) 393-1915
www.knzr.com
info@knzr.com
License: Bakersfield, CA held by Buckley Broadcasting of California LLC.
Group Owner: Buckley Broadcasting Corp.; (acq 1-25-90; $1 million;
Nat'l Network: CBS *Nat'l Reps:* D & R Radio
Arbitron Metro Market: Bakersfield, CA *Format:* News, News/Talk, 86 *Special Programming:* L.A. Dodgers *Hrs. of News Programming:* news progmg 40 hrs wkly *No. News Employees:* 4 *Target Audience:* 25-54.
Steve Darnell, General Manager

***KPRX**
02-28-1987; 89.1 mhz FM; 11 kw; 499 ft.; N35 29 10 W118 53 20
Rebroadcasts: Rebroadcasts KVPR(FM) Fresno 100%
3437 W. Shaw #101, Fresno, CA 93711 US
(559) 275-0764, *Fax:* (559) 275-2202
www.kvpr.org
kvpr@kvpr.org
License: Bakersfield, Kern County, CA held by White Ash Broadcasting Inc.
Nat'l Network: NPR
Arbitron Metro Market: San Joaquin Valley, CA *Format:* News
Mariam Stepanian, President
Mariam Stepanian, General Manager
Jim Meyers, Station Manager
Joe Moore, Programming Director
Steve Mull, Chief Engineer

***KTQX**
04-14-1989; 90.1 mhz FM *Hrs Open:* 24; 0.57 kw; 3622 ft.; N35 27 11 W118 35 25
5005 E. Belmont Avenue, Fresno, CA 93727 US
(559) 455-5777, *Fax:* (559) 455-5778
www.radiobilingue.org
mail@radiobilingue.org
License: Bakersfield, Kern County, CA held by Radio Bilingue Inc.
Arbitron Metro Market: Bakersfield, CA *Format:* Ethnic *Hrs. of News Programming:* news progmg 11 hrs wkly *No. News Employees:* 5 *Target Audience:* 16-60; Latino
Hugo Morales, CEO
Maria Erana, General Manager
Phil Traynor, General Sales Mgr
Samuel Orozco, News Director
Bill Bach, Chief Engineer

KUZZ
10-01-1946; 550 khz AM; 5 kw-U, DA-N; N35 20 25 W118 56 14
3223 Sillect Ave., Bakersfield, CA 93308
(661) 326-1011, *Fax:* (661) 328-7503
www.kuzz.com
License: Bakersfield, Kern County, CA held by Buck Owens Productions Co., Inc.
Group Owner: Buck Owens Productions Inc.; (acq 5-24-2006; grpsl).
Population Served: 100,000 *Arbitron Metro Market:* Bakersfield, CA *Target Audience:* 25-54.
Mel Owens Jr., CEO
Harvey Campbell, General Sales Mgr
Tom Jordan, Programming Director
Jerry Hufford, Promotions Manager
Suzanne Grant, News Director
Terry Gaiser, Chief Engineer
Toni Marie Faria, Music Director
HarveyCampbell, National Sales Manager

KUZZ-FM
01-01-1968; 107.9 mhz FM; kw
3223 Sillect Ave, Bakersfield, CA 93308 US
(661) 326-1011, *Fax:* (661)328-7503
www.kuzz.com
hcampbell@buckowens.com
License: Bakersfield, Kern County, CA
Group Owner: Buck Owens Productions Inc.
Arbitron Metro Market: Bakersfield, CA *Format:* Country
Harvey Campbell, General Sales Mgr
Tom Jordan, Programming Director
Jerry Hufford, Promotions Manager
Suzanne Grant, News Director
Chris Conner, Disc Jockey
K.C. Adams, Disc Jockey
Casey McBride, Disc Jockey
Peter Samore, NewsReporter
Gerri Barrett, Manager
Dianna Prather, Manager

KWAC
01-01-1954; 1490 khz AM *Hrs Open:* 24
5200 Standard Street, Bakersfield, CA 93308 US
(661) 327-9711, *Fax:* (661) 327-0797
kwac.com
info@thespanishradio.com
License: Bakersfield, CA held by Illinois Lotus Corp.
Group Owner: Lotus Communications Corp.; (acq 8-24-99; grpsl).
Nat'l Network: ESPN Radio *Nat'l Reps:* Lotus Entravision Reps LLC
Arbitron Metro Market: Bakersfield, CA *Format:* Tejano *Hrs. of News Programming:* News progmg 5 hrs wkly *Target Audience:* General. *Adv. Rates:* 25; 25; 25; 15
Howard Kalmenson, President
Anna Gallegos, Operations Dir
Mike Allen, General Manager
Juan Martinez, Programming Director
Lloyd Moss, Chief Engineer
Jesus Valdez, Disc Jockey
Manolo Martinez, Disc Jockey

KAFY
01-01-2000; 1100 khz AM *Hrs Open:* 24
2960 Coral Way, Miami, FL 33145 US
(209) 883-8760, *Fax:* (209) 883-8769
www.lafavorita.net
ngomez@lafavorita.net
License: Bakersfield, CA held by KAFY Inc.
Arbitron Metro Market: Bakersfield, CA *Format:* Talk
Nelson Gomez, General Manager

Banning

KMET
01-01-1948; 1490 khz AM *Hrs Open:* 24; 1 kw-U; N33 55 49 W116 55 20
700 E. Redlands Blvd., Suite U, PMB 323, Redlands, CA 92026
(951) 849-4644,(909) 319-1177, *Fax:* NA
kmet1490talkradio@yahoo.com
License: Banning, Riverside County, CA held by Sunset Broadcasting Inc.
Nat'l Network: Talk Radio Network
Population Served: 375,000 *Arbitron Metro Market:* Riverside-San Bernardino, CA *Hrs. of News Programming:* News progmg 3 hrs wkly *Target Audience:* General; 25-54, 35-65
Mitch McClellan, General Manager
Sean Nickerson, Production Manager

Barstow

KDUC
06-04-1986; 94.3 mhz FM; 4.6 kw; 784 ft.; N34 58 15 W117 2 22
320 West College Avenue, Pleasant Gap, PA 16823 US
(760) 256-2121, *Fax:* (760) 256-5090
doscostascommunications@yahoo.com
License: Barstow, San Bernardino County, CA held by Dos Costas Communications Corp.
Group Owner: Dos Costas Communications Corp.; acq 6-18-03; grpsl).
Format: Contemporary Hits/Top 40 *Target Audience:* 12-44.
Adv. Rates: Same as AM
Roland Ulloa, General Manager
Manny Lopez, General Sales Mgr
Mike Garcia, Programming Director

KIQQ
09-29-1960; 1310 khz AM *Hrs Open:* 24*Rebroadcasts:* Simulcast with KAEH(FM) Beaumont 100%
16435 Wimbleton Drive, Victorville, CA 92392 US
(760) 255-2636, *Fax:* (760) 255-3236
moonbroadcasting.com,lamaquinamusical.net
jramirez@lamaquinaamusical.net
License: Barstow, CA held by MBR Licensee LLC.
Group Owner: Moon Broadcasting; (acq 8-7-2000).
Nat'l Network: Westwood One
Format: Tejano *Target Audience:* 45 plus.
Alicia Avila, General Manager

KSZL
06-25-1986; 1230 khz AM *Hrs Open:* 24; 1 kw-U, ND1; N34 54 44 W117 1 39
320 West College Avenue, Pleasant Gap, PA 16823 US
(760) 256-2121(760) 256-5382, *Fax:* (760) 256-5090
am1230kszl@yahoo.com
License: Barstow, CA held by Dos Costas Communications Corp.
Nat'l Network: Westwood One *Nat'l Reps:* Western Regional Broadcast Sales
Arbitron Metro Market: Barstow, CA *Format:* News, Talk *Hrs. of News Programming:* news progmg 12 hrs wkly *No. News Employees:* 2 *Target Audience:* 25 plus; Adults 35 years + *Adv. Rates:* 15; 15; 15; 10
Michael Garcia, Operations Dir
Roland Ulloa, General Manager
Manny Lopez, General Sales Mgr
Steve Hastings, News Director

KXXZ
01-01-1989; 95.9 mhz FM *Hrs Open:* 24; 8.9 kw; 486 ft.; N34 51 22 W117 3 0
320 West College Ave., Pleasant Gap, PA 16823 US
(760) 256-2121, *Fax:* (760) 256-5090
doscostas@yahoo.com
License: Barstow, San Bernardino County, CA held by Dos Costas Communications Corp.
Group Owner: Dos Costas Communications Corp.; acq 6-18-03; grpsl).
Arbitron Metro Market: Barstow *Format:* Tejano
Roland Ulloa, General Manager
Manny Lopez, General Sales Mgr
Mike Garcia, Programming Director
Steve Hastings, News Director

***KWTH**
01-01-2006; 91.3 mhz FM; 1.55 kw; 2296 ft.; N34 38 39 W116 37 38 *Rebroadcasts:* Rebroadcasts KWTW(FM) Bishop 100%
P O Box 637, Bishop, CA 93515 US
(866) 466-5989, *Fax:* (714) 979-8916
www.kwtw.org
recep@kwtw.org
License: Barstow, San Bernardino County, CA held by Living Proof Inc.
Arbitron Metro Market: Barstow, CA *Format:* Christian, Religious
Daniel McClenaghan, President

***KODV**
01-01-2005; 89.1 mhz FM; 5.8 kw; 768 ft.; N34 58 15.09 W117 2 21.51
Mailing Address: US
Second Address: 18280 Atlantic St., Hesperia, CA 92345
(760) 947-4300, *Fax:* (760) 245-6268
www.ondasdevida.com
comentarios@ondadevida.com
License: Barstow, San Bernardino County, CA held by Ondas de Vida Network Inc.
Arbitron Metro Market: Barstow, CA
Hector Manzo, CEO

Bayside

***KNHM**
04-15-1992; 91.5 mhz FM *Hrs Open:* 24; 0.48 kw; 1722 ft.; N40 43 38 W123 58 22
2803 Greenwood Hgts Road, Kneeland, CA 95549 US
(541) 552-6301, *Fax:* (541) 552-8565
www.ijpr.org
info@ijpr.org
License: Bayside, Humboldt County, CA held by JPR Foundation Inc.
Arbitron Metro Market: Bayside CA
Ronald Kramer, General Manager
Paul Westhelle, General Sales Mgr

Beaumont

KAEH
01-01-1996; 100.9 mhz FM *Hrs Open:* 24; 1.5 kw; 479 ft.; N33 54 29 W116 59 45
PO Box 2235, Beaumont, CA 92223 US
(909) 381-0969, *Fax:* (909) 381-0943
www.lamaquinamusical.net
License: Beaumont, Riverside County, CA held by MBR Licensee LLC.
Group Owner: Moon Broadcasting; (acq 2-13-2002; $1.7 million).
Arbitron Metro Market: Beaumont, CA
Abel DeLuna, President
Alicia Avila, General Manager
Juan Ramirez, Programming Director
Manuel Garcia, News Director
Rick Hunt, Chief Engineer

Bella Vista

***KKRN**
88.5 mhz FM; 0.6 kw; 2001 ft.; N40 54 23 W121 49 39 US
(530) 337-6736, *Fax:* (530) 337-6567
www.kkrn.org
info@kkrn.org
License: Bella Vista, Shasta County, CA held by Acorn Community Enterprises.
Arbitron Metro Market: Bella Vista, CA
Staci Wadley, General Manager

Berkeley

***KALX**
10-01-1967; 90.7 mhz FM *Hrs Open:* 24; 0.5 kw; 781 ft.; N37 52 40 W122 14 44
300 Lakeside Dr. 8th Flr, Oakland, CA 94612 US
(510) 642-1111
kalx.berkeley.edu
mail@kalx.berkeley.edu
License: Berkeley, Alameda County, CA held by The Regents of the University of California.
Arbitron Metro Market: San Francisco, CA *Format:* Variety/Diverse *Hrs. of News Programming:* News progmg 4 hrs wkly
Erin Ruiz-Prunchak, Operations Dir
Sandra Wasson, General Manager
Lindsay Melnyk, Programming Director
Tristan Parker, News Director
Joe Tysl, Chief Engineer
Brittney Stanley, Music Director
Jackie Sloves, News Director

KBLX-FM
04-29-1949; 102.9 mhz FM *Hrs Open:* 24; 6.6 kw; 1289 ft.; N37 41 20 W122 26 7
55 Hawthorne St #900, San Francisco, CA 94105 US
((415) 284-1029, *Fax:* (415) 764-4959
www.kblx.com
info@kblx.com
License: Berkeley, Alameda County, CA

Group Owner: Inner City Broadcasting
Wire Services: Bay City News Service
Arbitron Metro Market: San Francisco *Format:* Adult Contemp
Hrs. of News Programming: Feature only *No. News Employees:* 1 *Target Audience:* 25-54; adults
Harvey Stone, President
Renee Guillory, Operations Dir
Barry Rose, General Sales Mgr
Kevin Brown, Programming Director
Michelle Heller, Promotions Manager
Paul Marks, Chief Engineer
Rhonda Amoe, National Sales Director
AaronJones, Local Sales Manager
Kimmie Taylor, Music Director
Susie Lee, Public Service Director

KPFA
04-01-1949; 94.1 mhz FM *Hrs Open:* 24; 59 kw horiz; 1329 ft.; N37 51 55 W122 13 12
1929 Mlk Jr Way, Berkeley, CA 94704 US
(510) 848-6767, *Fax:* (510) 848-3812
www.kpfa.org
info@kpfa.org
License: Berkeley, Alameda County, CA held by Pacifica Foundation.
Group Owner: Pacifica Foundation Inc.
Wire Services: Reuters; Pacifica Network News
Arbitron Metro Market: San Francisco *Format:* Variety/Diverse
Special Programming: C&W 18 hrs, Black 18 hrs, jazz 15 hrs, folk 10 hrs, women 10 hrs, world 18 hrs wkly *Hrs. of News Programming:* news progmg 11 hrs wkly*No. News Employees:* 4 *Target Audience:* 25-50.
Lem Lem Rijio, General Manager
Luis Medina, Programming Director
Mark Mericle, News Director
Michael Yoshida, Chief Engineer
Aileen Alfandary, News Director

***KPFB**
02-01-1954; 89.3 mhz FM; 0.46 kw horiz; -98 ft.; N37 52 20 W122 16 18 *Rebroadcasts:* Simulcasts with *KPFA(FM) Berkeley except for pub affrs & special events progmg
1929 Martin L King Jr Wy, Berkley, CA 94704 US
License: Berkeley, Alameda County, CA held by Pacifica Foundation Inc.
Group Owner: Pacifica Foundation Inc.
Arbitron Metro Market: San Francisco
Lem Lem Rigio, General Manager
Luis Medina, Programming Director
Mark Mericle, News Director
Michael Yoshida, Chief Engineer

KVTO
05-22-1922; 1400 khz AM *Hrs Open:* 24; 1 kw-U, ND1; N37 50 58 W122 17 44
55 Hawthorne Street, San Francisco, CA 94105 US
(415) 284-1029, *Fax:* (415) 764-4959
www.chineseradio.com
info@kblx.com
License: Berkeley, CA held by Urban Radio III L.L.C.
Group Owner: Inner City Broadcasting; (acq 1979)
Nat'l Reps: D & R Radio
Arbitron Metro Market: San Francisco, CA *Format:* Japanese, Korean, 18 *Target Audience:* 25-54.
Harvey Stone, President
Barry Rose, General Sales Mgr
Jaime Arbona, Programming Director
Paul Marks, Chief Engineer
Rhonda Amoe, National Sales Manager

Big Bear City

KBHR
12-17-1995; 93.3 mhz FM *Hrs Open:* 24; 1.5 kw; 663 ft; N34 16 41 W116 47 31
Box 2979, ., Big Bear City, CA 92314
(909) 584-5247, *Fax:* (909) 584-5347
www.kbhr933.com,www.bigbearnews.com
info@kbhr933.com
License: Big Bear City, San Bernardino County, CA held by Parallel Broadcasting Inc.
Nat'l Network: NBC News Radio
Population Served: 25,000 *Arbitron Metro Market:* Riverside-San B *Special Programming:* NBC News Radio 8 hrs, ski report, fish report *Hrs. of News Programming:* news progmg 11 hrs wkly *No. News Employees:* 1*Target Audience:* 25-54; upscale second home owners, resort visitors *Adv. Rates:* 30; 27; 30; 25
Rick Herrick, President
Cathy Herrick, Operations Dir
Jay Tunnell, General Sales Mgr
Mike Evans, Programming Director

Big Bear Lake

KXSB
05-01-1975; 101.7 mhz FM *Hrs Open:* 24; 0.3 kw; 1414 ft.; N34 12 47 W116 51 59 *Rebroadcasts:* Rebroadcasts KXLM(FM) Oxnard 80%
200 South a Street, Suite 400, Oxnard, CA 93030 US
(909) 384-9750, *Fax:* (909) 884-5844(909) 890-3849
www.radiolazer.com
edith@radiolazer.com
License: Big Bear Lake, San Bernardino County, CA held by Lazer Broadcasting Corp.
Group Owner: Lazer Broadcasting Corp.; acq 1995; $750,000)
Nat'l Reps: Lotus Entravision Reps LLC
Arbitron Metro Market: Riverside-San Bernardino, CA *Format:* Contemporary Hits/Top 40, Spanish *Hrs. of News Programming:* news progmg 2 hrs wkly *No. News Employees:* 1 *Target Audience:* 25-54; adults, seriousminded *Adv. Rates:* 75; 65; 65; 50
Alfredo Plascencia, CEO
Vicki Bails, Operations Dir
Salvador Prieto, Programming Director
Gerardo Palafox, Promotions Manager
Ralph Jones, Chief Engineer

Big Pine

KRHV
01-01-1999; 93.3 mhz FM; 0.89 kw; 2904 ft.; N37 24 48 W118 11 8
Mailing Address: P.O. Box 1284, Mammoth Lakes, CA 93546 US
Second Address: 94 Laurel Mountain Rd., Mammouth Lakes, CA 93546
(760) 934-8888, *Fax:* (760) 934-2429
www.kmmtradio.com
kmmtradioworks@yahoo.com
License: Big Pine, Inyo County, CA held by David & Mary Digerness.
Format: Variety/Diverse, Classic Rock
Maryann Digerness, President
Shellie Woods, General Manager
Paul Payne, Station Manager
Paul Payne, General Sales Mgr
Spencer Myers, Programming Director
Ron Nelson, Engineering Dir

Big River

KFLG-FM
12-06-1974; 94.7 mhz FM *Hrs Open:* 24; 19.5 kw; 2736 ft.; N34 33 6 W114 11 37
50 E. Rivercenter Blvd., Suite 180, Covington, KY 41011 US
(928) 763-5586, *Fax:* (928) 763-3775
www.kflg947.com
License: Big River, San Bernardino County, CA held by Cameron Broadcasting Inc.
Group Owner: Cameron Broadcasting Inc.
Arbitron Metro Market: Big River, CA *Format:* Country *No. News Employees:* 1 *Target Audience:* 25-54
William Jaeger, CEO
Don Jaeger, Operations Dir
Mike Fletcher, General Sales Mgr
Dave Cooper, Chief Engineer
Craig Powers, Operations Manager

Big Sur

KMZT-FM
95.9 mhz FM; 1 kw horiz; -111 meters; N36 13 24 W121 45 27
1500 Cotner Avenue, Los Angeles, CA
(310) 478-5540, *Fax:* (310) 445-1439
www.mountwilsoninc.com
License: Big Sur, Monterey County, CA held by Mount Wilson FM Broadcasters
Saul Levine, President

Bishop

KBOV
04-01-1953; 1230 khz AM; 1 kw-U, ND1; N37 20 44 W118 23 43
P. O. Box 757, Bishop, CA 93515 US
(760) 873-6324, *Fax:* (760) 872-2639
www.kibskbov.com
kibskbov@qnet.com
License: Bishop, CA held by Great Country Broadcasting Inc.
Nat'l Reps: Western Regional Broadcast Sales
Format: Oldies *Hrs. of News Programming:* news progmg 8 hrs wkly *No. News Employees:* 1 *Target Audience:* General. *Adv. Rates:* 8; 8; 8; 8
Lauren Brandt, General Manager

KIBS
11-01-1974; 100.7 mhz FM *Hrs Open:* 24; 1 kw; 2959 ft.; N37 25 0 W118 11 0
PO Box 757, Bishop, CA 93515 US
(760) 873-6324, *Fax:* (760) 872-2639
www.kibskbov.com
kibskbov@kibskbov.com
License: Bishop, Inyo County, CA held by Great Country Broadcasting Inc.
Format: Country *Special Programming:* Sports 20 hrs wkly *Hrs. of News Programming:* news progmg 8 hrs wkly *No. News Employees:* 1 *Adv. Rates:* 12; 12; 13; 12
Steve Miller, Operations Dir
Steve Miller, General Manager
Arnie Palu, News Director
Gary Young, Music & Program Director
Ron Knox, Sports Engineer
Mike Cheuvront, Disc Jockey
John Young, Disc Jockey

***KWTW**
01-01-2002; 88.5 mhz FM *Hrs Open:* 24; 0.9 kw; 2917 ft.; N37 24 48 W118 11 8
Mailing Address: P.O. Box 637, Bishop, CA 93515 US
Second Address: 125 S. Main St., Bishop, CA 93514
(760) 872-4225(866) 466-5989, *Fax:* (760) 872-4155
www.kwtw.org
recep@kwtw.org
License: Bishop, Inyo County, CA held by Living Proof Inc.
Arbitron Metro Market: Bishop, CA *Format:* Christian, Religious
Target Audience: General; all who want to hear the gospel
Daniel McClenaghan, President

Blythe

KJMB-FM
04-01-1975; 100.3 mhz FM *Hrs Open:* 24; 36 kw horiz; 56 ft.; N33 37 16 W114 35 28
681 North 4th Street, Blythe, CA 92507 US
(760) 922-7143, *Fax:* (760) 922-2844
info@kjmbfm.com
License: Blythe, Riverside County, CA held by Blythe Radio Inc.
Nat'l Network: USA
Format: Adult Contemp *Special Programming:* Farm 5 hrs wkly *Hrs. of News Programming:* news progmg 10 hrs wkly *No. News Employees:* 1 *Target Audience:* 18-40; adults *Adv. Rates:* 16; 16; 16; 16
Jim Mayson, President
James Morris, General Manager

Borrego Springs

***KKJD**
91.3 mhz FM; 6 kw; -347 m; N33 14 39 W116 22 30
Box 2429, Borrego SpringsCA
(760)767-7447
www.kkjdradio.com
License: Borrego Springs, San Diego County, CA held by Borrego Springs Christian Center
Steve Mellor, President

Brawley

KROP
11-01-1946; 1300 khz AM *Hrs Open:* 24
2550 Fifth Ave., Suite 723, San Diego, CA 42102 US
(760) 344-1300, *Fax:* (760) 344-1763
q96radio@yahoo.com
License: Brawley, CA held by CCR-Brawley IV LLC.
Group Owner: Cherry Creek Radio LLC; acq 6-99; $2 million with co-located FM).
Arbitron Metro Market: Palm Springs, CA *Format:* Country *Target Audience:* 25-54; male
Tony Driskill, General Manager
Lisa Aguirre, General Sales Mgr

KSEH
04-04-1988; 94.5 mhz FM *Hrs Open:* 24; 50 kw; 302 ft.; N32 54 40 W115 31 40
11900 Olympic Boulevard, Los Angeles, CA 90064 US
(760) 482-7777, *Fax:* (760) 482-0099
www.jose945.com
License: Brawley, Imperial County, CA held by Entravision Holdings LLC.
Group Owner: Entravision Communications Corp.
Nat'l Network: ABC
Arbitron Metro Market: El Centro, CA *Format:* Ethnic *Target Audience:* 25-54.
Eric Chavez, General Manager

Buena Park

*KBPK
07-06-1970; 90.1 mhz FM; 0.019 kw; 10 ft.; N33 51 35 W118 0 53
6885 Orangethorpe Avenue, Buena Park, CA 90620 US
(714) 732-5459
kbpk-fm.com
License: Buena Park, Orange County, CA held by Buena Park School District.
Wire Services: AP
Arbitron Metro Market: Los Angeles *Format:* Adult Contemp
Target Audience: 25-54.
Edward Ford, Operations Dir
Peg Berger, Programming Director
Tracy Thackrah, Music Director

Burbank

KIEV
01-01-1986; 1500 khz AM
801 K Streeet 27th Fl, Sacramento, CA 95814 US
(916) 813-1065
License: Burbank, CA held by Royce International Broadcasting Co.
Nat'l Reps: McGavren Guild
Arbitron Metro Market: Los Angeles
Edward Stolz II, President

Burney

*KIBC
11-15-1985; 90.5 mhz FM *Hrs Open:* 24; 3 kw; 1457 ft.; N40 52 29 W121 46 13
P. O. Box 1717, Burney, CA 96013 US
(530) 335-5422, *Fax:* (530) 335-5422
www.kibcfm.org
bud@norcalis.net
License: Burney, Shasta County, CA held by Burney Educational Broadcasting Foundation.
Format: Gospel *Target Audience:* General.
Wayne Hennessey, General Manager
Alvin Hennessey, Programming Director

*KNCA
07-01-1992; 89.7 mhz FM *Hrs Open:* 5 AM-2 AM; 29 kw; 2064 ft.; N40 54 21 W121 49 38
P.O. Box 3175, Eugene, OR 97403 US
(541) 552-6301
www.ijpr.org
info@ijpr.org
License: Burney, Shasta County, CA held by The State of Oregon, acting by and through the State Board of Higher Education.
Nat'l Network: NPR; PRI
Arbitron Metro Market: Redding, CA *Format:* Jazz, News, 90
Special Programming: Blues 6 hrs, folk 3 hrs, pub affrs 7 hrs wkly *Hrs. of News Programming:* news progmg 45 hrs wkly *No. News Employees:* 1 *TargetAudience:* General.
Ronald Kramer, CEO
Bryon Lambert, Operations Dir
Paul Westhelle, General Sales Mgr
Mitchell Christian, CFO

KRRX
05-01-1985; 106.1 mhz FM *Hrs Open:* 24; 100 kw; 1969 ft.; N40 54 21 W121 49 38
Mr. Mel Dolezal/Gm, 4352 Caterpillar Road, Redding, CA 95928 US
(530) 226-9500, *Fax:* (530) 221-4940
www.106x.com
Clark@reddingradio.com; Duane@reddingradio.com
License: Burney, Shasta County, CA held by Mapleton License of Redding LLC.
Group Owner: Mapleton Communications LLC; (acq 11-30-2006; grpsl)
Arbitron Metro Market: Northern CA *Format:* Rock/AOR *No. News Employees:* 2 *Target Audience:* 25-54; upscale
Vince Shadrick, General Manager
Clark Schopflin, Programming Director

Calexico

*KQVO
03-01-1984; 97.7 mhz FM *Hrs Open:* 24; 6 kw; 305 ft.; N32 40 48 W115 25 36 *Rebroadcasts:* Rebroadcasts KPBS-FM San Diego 100%
2925 East Exposition Ave., Denver, CO 80209 US
(619) 594-6983, *Fax:* (619) 594-3812
www.kpbs.org
letters@kpbs.org
License: Calexico, Imperial County, CA held by State of California, San Diego State University
Nat'l Network: NPR; PRI
Arbitron Metro Market: San Diego, CA
Kathryn Nelson, Operations Dir
Tom Karlo, General Manager
Deanna Mackey, Station Manager
John Decker, Programming Director
Suzanne Marmion, News Director

*KUBO
01-01-1989; 88.7 mhz FM *Hrs Open:* 24; 3 kw; 272 ft.; N32 47 57 W115 30 12
5005 E. Belmont, Fresno, CA 93727 US
(559) 264-9191, *Fax:* (559) 455-5778
www.radiobilingue.org
ricardo@radiobilingue.org
License: Calexico, Imperial County, CA held by Radio Bilingue Inc.
Arbitron Metro Market: Calexico, CA *Format:* Ethnic *Hrs. of News Programming:* news progmg 3 hrs wkly *No. News Employees:* 5
Target Audience: 16-60; Latino
Hugo Morales, CEO
Maria Erana, Operations Dir
Maria Esana, Programming Director

California City

KMVE
05-22-1999; 106.9 mhz FM *Hrs Open:* 24; 2.35 kw; 522 ft.; N35 12 44 W117 45 11
8401 California City, Blvd., #9, California City, CA 93505 US
(760) 373-1069, *Fax:* (760) 373-8808
License: California City, Kern County, CA held by Point Broadcasting Co.
Group Owner: Point Broadcasting Company; (acq 12-29-2003; $500,000)
Nat'l Network: ABC
Format: Tejano *Special Programming:* Gospel 3 hrs wkly *No. News Employees:* 1 *Target Audience:* General. *Adv. Rates:* 16; 16; 16; 14
Brent Foster, General Manager
Josh Branch, Station Manager

Calipatria

KSSB
02-08-1997; 100.9 mhz FM *Hrs Open:* 24; 3 kw horiz; 66 ft.; N33 7 12 W115 30 47
620 S. Park Ave., Calipatria, CA 92233 US
(909) 825-5020, *Fax:* (909) 884-5844
License: Calipatria, Imperial County, CA held by Lazer Licenses LLC.
Group Owner: Lazer Broadcasting Corp.; (acq 9-22-2006; $925,000)
Arbitron Metro Market: Calipatria, CA *Special Programming:* Religious 6 hrs wkly *Hrs. of News Programming:* news progmg 6 hrs wkly *No. News Employees:* 1 *Target Audience:* 25 plus; female/male *Adv. Rates:* 12:50; 12:50; 12:50; 12:50
Alfredo Plascencia, CEO
Vickie Balesz, General Manager

Calistoga

*KBBF
05-30-1973; 89.1 mhz FM; 0.42 kw; 2767 ft.; N38 39 23 W122 36 54
P. O. Box 7189, Santa Rosa, CA 95401 US
(707) 545-8833, *Fax:* (707) 545-6244
www.kbbf-fm.org
kbbfradio@aol.com
License: Calistoga, Napa County, CA held by Bilingual Broadcasting Foundation Inc.
Arbitron Metro Market: Santa Rosa, CA *Format:* Spanish
Roy Brown, Operations Dir
Jesus Lozano, General Manager
Roy Brown, Promotions Manager

Camarillo

*KMRO
01-19-1987; 90.3 mhz FM *Hrs Open:* 24; 10.5 kw; 920 ft.; N34 24 40 W119 10 28
2310 Ponderosa Drive, Camarillo, CA 93010 US
(805) 482-4797, *Fax:* (805) 388-5202
www.nuevavida.com
info@nuevavida.com
License: Camarillo, Ventura County, CA held by The Association for Community Education Inc.
Arbitron Metro Market: Oxnard, CA *Format:* Religious *Target Audience:* General; Hispanics
Phil Guthrie, President
Mary Guthrie, General Manager

KOCP
08-15-1972; 95.9 mhz FM *Hrs Open:* 24; 1.2 kw; 1457 ft.; N34 20 55 W119 20 13
100 Wilshire Blvd, Suite 1000, Santa Monica, CA 90401 US
(805) 289-1400, *Fax:* (805) 644-7906
www.theoctopus959.com
perryinthemorning@yahoo.com
License: Camarillo, Ventura County, CA held by Gold Coast Broadcasting LLC
Group Owner: Gold Coast Broadcasting LLC; acq 1995; $1.2 million with KMXO(AM) Santa Paula).
Nat'l Reps: Katz Radio
Arbitron Metro Market: Oxnard-Ventura, CA *Format:* Classic Rock *Target Audience:* 25-54.
Chip Ehrhardt, General Manager
Perry Van Houten, Programming Director

Camino

*KYCJ
01-01-2005; 88.3 mhz FM *Hrs Open:* 24; 0.055 kw vert; 446 ft.; N38 44 18 W120 42 8 *Rebroadcasts:* Rebroadcasts KYCC(FM) Stockton 100%
US
(209) 477-3690, *Fax:* (209) 477-2762
www.kycc.org
kycc@kycc.org
License: Camino, El Dorado County, CA held by Your Christian Companion Network Inc.
Arbitron Metro Market: Kerville, TX *Format:* Gospel, Religious
Target Audience: 35-55.
Shirley Garner, General Manager

Canyon Country

KHTS
06-01-1989; 1220 khz AM *Hrs Open:* 24; 1 kw-D, 500 w-N, DA-2; N34 27 55 W118 24 08
27225 Camp Plenty Rd., Suite 8, Santa Clarita, CA 41011
(661) 298-1220, *Fax:* (661) 298-2020
www.hometownstation.com
License: Canyon Country, Los Angeles County, CA held by Jeri Lyn Broadcasting Inc.
Arbitron Metro Market: Los Angeles
Carl Goldman, General Manager
Jen Serati, Station Manager
Kyle Jellings, Programming Director
Carol Rock, News Director
Bruce Smith, Chief Engineer

Carlsbad

KUSS(FM)
08-22-1965; 95.7 mhz FM *Hrs Open:* 24; 29 kw; 639 ft; N32 50 24 W117 14 52
9660 Granite Ridge Rd., San Diego, CA 92123
(858) 292-2000, *Fax:* (858) 278-7957
www.us957.com
info@kussfm.com
License: Carlsbad, San Diego County, CA held by Citicasters Licenses L.P.
Group Owner: Clear Channel Communications Inc.; (acq 5-4-99; grpsl).
Nat'l Network: ABC
Population Served: 600,000 *Arbitron Metro Market:* San Diego, CA *Format:* Oldies *Target Audience:* 25-54; general
Bob Bolinger, General Manager
Mike O'Brian, Programming Director
Geoff Alan, Promotions Manager

Carmel

KKHK
12-04-1993; 95.5 mhz FM *Hrs Open:* 24; 1.7 kw; 630 ft.; N36 33 9 W121 47 17
2511 Garden Rd, Se C-150, Carmel, CA 93940 US
(831) 658-5200, *Fax:* (831) 658-5299
www.hankcountry.com
License: Carmel, Monterey County, CA held by Mapleton License of Monterey LLC.
Group Owner: Mapleton Communications LLC; (acq 6-7-2005; $3.75 million)
Nat'l Reps: McGavren Guild
Arbitron Metro Market: Monterey-Salinas-Santa Cruz, CA
Format: Country
Adam Nathanson, President
Mike Anthony, General Manager
Jodi Morgan, General Sales Mgr
Kenny Allen, Programming Director

Sybil DeAngelo, Promotions Manager
Tom Hughes, Chief Engineer

KCDU
04-29-1971; 101.7 mhz FM *Hrs Open:* 24; 2.35 kw; 528 ft.; N36 33 9 W121 47 17
4150 Pinnacle, El Paso, TX 79902 US
(831) 658-5200, *Fax:* (831) 658-5299
www.1017thebeach.com
thebeach1017@yahoo.com
License: Carmel, Monterey County, CA held by Mapleton License of Monterey LLC.
Group Owner: Mapleton Communications LLC; (acq 1-17-2002; grpsl)
Nat'l Reps: McGavren Guild
Arbitron Metro Market: Monterey-Salinas-Santa Cruz, CA
Format: Adult Contemp *Target Audience:* Women 25-54; upscale, educated, above average income
Raul Salvador, CFO
Adam Nathanson, President
Kenny Allen, Operations Dir
Mike Anthony, General Manager
Jodi Morgan, General Sales Mgr
Sybil DeAngelo, Promotions Manager

KRML
12-25-1957; 1410 khz AM *Hrs Open:* 24; 0.5 kw-D, ND1; 0.016 kw-N, ND1; N36 32 11 W121 54 13 *Rebroadcasts:* live streaming from www.krmlradio.com
Mailing Address: P.O. Drawer 22440, Carmel, CA 93922 US
Second Address: San Carlos near 5th, Carmel, CA 93921
(831) 624-6431, *Fax:* (831) 625-2417
www.krml.com
info@thejazzandbluescompany.com
License: Carmel, CA held by Wisdom Broadcasting Co. Inc.
Regional Reps: McGavern Guild
Arbitron Metro Market: Monterey Bay *Format:* Jazz *Special Programming:* Gospel 6 hrs wkly *Hrs. of News Programming:* 10.5 hrs wkly *Target Audience:* 35+. *Adv. Rates:* 50; 40; 50; 25
David Kimball, General Manager

Carmel Valley

KRXA
07-10-1989; 540 khz AM *Hrs Open:* 18
2360 N.E. Coachman Road, Clearwater, FL 33765 US
(831) 394-5792
www.krxa540.com
hal@krxa540.com
License: Carmel Valley, CA held by KRFA-AM, LLC
Arbitron Metro Market: Monterey-Salinas-Santa Cruz, CA
Format: Talk *Special Programming:* Religious 5 hrs wkly, Health 2 hrs wkly *Hrs. of News Programming:* News progmg 60 hrs wkly
Hal Ginsberg, General Manager
Larry Wrathall, General Sales Mgr
Fia Karim, Programming Director
Annabel Lund, News Director

Carmichael

KFIA
01-11-1979; 710 khz AM; 25 kw-D, 1 kw-N, DA-2; N38 49 58 W121 19 03
1425 River Park Dr., Suite 520, Sacramento, CA 93012
(916) 924-0710, *Fax:* (916) 924-1587
www.kfia.com
info@kfia.com
License: Carmichael, Sacramento County, CA held by New Inspiration Broadcasting Co. Inc.
Group Owner: Salem Communications Corp.; (acq 2-15-95; *Population Served:* 7,000,000 *Arbitron Metro Market:* Sacramento, CA *Target Audience:* 35 plus; general
Edward Atsinger III, President
Steve Gasser, Operations Dir
Dale Hendry, General Manager
Max Miller, Programming Director

Carnelian Bay

KODS
01-01-1970; 103.7 mhz FM; 5.9 kw; 2986 ft.; N39 18 38 W119 53 1
1900 Avenue of the Stars, Suite 1880, Los Angeles, CA 90067 US
(775) 829-1964, *Fax:* (775) 825-3183
www.river1037.com
License: Carnelian Bay, Placer County, CA held by Americom, a Nevada L.P.
Nat'l Reps: CBS Radio
Arbitron Metro Market: Reno, NV *Format:* Oldies

Tom Quinn, President
Daniel Cook, General Manager
Heather Forcier, General Sales Mgr
Beej ., Programming Director
Sandy Vance, News Director
Steve Weber, Chief Engineer

Carpinteria

KIST-FM
01-01-1998; 107.7 mhz FM *Hrs Open:* 24; 930 w; Ant 1,627 ft; N34 30 10 W119 50 56
414 East Cota Street, Santa Barbara, CA 41011
(805) 879-8300, *Fax:* (805) 879-8430
License: Carpinteria, Santa Barbara County, CA held by Rincon License Subsidiary LLC.
Group Owner: Rincon Broadcasting LLC; (acq 7-11-2007; grpsl)
Nat'l Reps: Katz Radio
Arbitron Metro Market: Santa Barbara, CA
Keith Royer, Operations Dir
Tom Baker, General Manager
Vince Holian, General Sales Mgr
Peter Bie, News Director
Andrea Shaparenko, Traffic Manager

Cartago

KWTY
11-01-1989; 94.5 mhz FM *Hrs Open:* 24; 2 kw horiz; -1788 ft.; N36 19 16 W118 1 22
P.O. Box 773, Big Pine, CA 93513 US
(760) 764-1111, *Fax:* (760) 764-1111
gm@kwty.com
License: Cartago, Inyo County, CA held by Mark A. Miller
Wire Services: UPI
Format: Classic Rock *Hrs. of News Programming:* News progmg 7 hrs wkly *Target Audience:* General; 15-55 years (M-F), recreation/resort commuters *Adv. Rates:* 5; 5; 5; 3
Mark Miller, General Manager
Dan Owen, General Sales Mgr

Cathedral City

KDES-FM
02-10-1963; 98.5 mhz FM; 43 kw; 528 ft.; N33 51 56 W116 26 4
68700 Dinah Shore Drive, Palm Springs, CA 92263 US
(760) 325-2582, *Fax:* (760) 322-3562
www.kdes.com
kdes@aol.com
License: Cathedral City, Riverside County, CA
Group Owner: RR Broadcasting
Arbitron Metro Market: Palm Springs, CA *Format:* Oldies
Gregg Aratin, General Sales Mgr
Brian Garris, Promotions Manager
Gene Nichols, News Director

KWXY(FM)
01-19-1969; 98.5 mhz FM *Hrs Open:* 24; 50 kw; 499 ft; N33 51 55 W116 26 10
KWXY Broadcast Centre, Box 5470, Palm Springs, CA 92263
(760) 328-1104, *Fax:* (760) 328-7814
www.kwxy.com
License: Cathedral City, Riverside County, CA held by Glen Barnett Inc.
Wire Services: AP
Population Served: 45,573 *Arbitron Metro Market:* Palm Springs, CA *Format:* Adult Contemp *Special Programming:* Canadian news 2 hrs wkly *Hrs. of News Programming:* news progmg 16 hrs wkly *No. News Employees:* 1 *Target Audience:* 35 plus; affluent adults *Adv. Rates:* 37; 37; 37; 30
Glen Barnett, President
Bob Wetherall, Operations Dir
Jim Keye, General Sales Mgr
Estelle Layton, Executive Vice President

Cayucos

KPYG
10-01-1984; 94.9 mhz FM *Hrs Open:* 24; 25 kw; 328 ft.; N35 31 26 W121 3 40
840 Shefield Street, Cambria, CA 93428 US
(805) 786-2570, *Fax:* (805) 547-9860
www.mapletoncommunications.com
License: Cayucos, San Luis Obispo County, CA held by Mapleton License of San Luis Obispo LLC
Group Owner: Mapleton Communications LLC; (acq 7-19-2002; grpsl)
Arbitron Metro Market: San Luis Obispo, CA *Format:* Triple A *Target Audience:* 25-54.
Adam Nathanson, President
Bill Heirendt, Programming Director

David Atwood, News Director
Tom Hughes, Chief Engineer

Cazadero

KTRY(FM)
106.3 mhz FM; 1620 watts; 194 meters; 38 29 20N 123 01 53W
3392 Mendocino Avenue, PO Box 100, Santa Rosa, CA 95402 USA
(707) 528-4434
www.ktry.com
License: Cazadero, Sonoma County, CA
Group Owner: Redwood Empire Stereocasters

Cedarville

KHAL
01-01-2008; 95.5 mhz FM; kw
US
(541) 298-4141
License: Cedarville, Gilliam County, CA held by Haystack Broadcasting Inc.
Arbitron Metro Market: Omaha-Council Bluffs, NE-IA
Danny Manciu, President

***KDUP**
01-01-2008; 88.1 mhz FM; 0.27 kw; -105 ft.; N41 38 13 W120 5 28
US
(775) 279-6677
openskyradio.org
klap@klap.fm
License: Cedarville, Modoc County, CA held by OpenSkyRadio Corp.
Arbitron Metro Market: Cedarville, CA *Format:* Variety/Diverse
Jeffrey Cotton, General Manager

Ceres

***KBES**
09-01-1979; 89.5 mhz FM; 0.15 kw; 131 ft.; N37 35 21 W120 57 23
P.O. Box 4116, Modesto, CA 95352 US
(209) 538-4130, *Fax:* (209) 538-2795
www.betnahrain.org
info@kbesfm.com
License: Ceres, Stanislaus County, CA held by Bet Nahrain Inc.
Arbitron Metro Market: Modesto, CA *Format:* Ethnic
Dr. Sargon Dadisho, General Manager
Janet Shamon, Programming Director
Seimon Mamio, Chief Engineer

KVIN
09-15-1963; 920 khz AM; 0.5 kw-D, DA2; 2.5 kw-N, DA2; N37 35 49 W121 4 15; N37 37 55 W120 45 6
1436 Auburn Boulevard, Llc, Sacramento, CA 95815 US
(209) 544-1055, *Fax:* (209) 544-1055
www.krvr.com
theriver@krvr.com
License: Ceres, CA held by Threshold Communications
Nat'l Reps: Interep
Arbitron Metro Market: Modesto, CA *Format:* Adult Contemp *Target Audience:* 35-64.
Doug Wulff, Operations Dir
Jim Bryan, General Manager
Brian Henry, Chief Engineer
Sally Waterman, Office Manager

Chester

***KWLU**
04-06-1989; 98.9 mhz FM *Hrs Open:* 24; 1 kw; 2474 ft.; N40 14 0 W121 1 11
395 Main St., Quincy, CA 95971 US
(916) 251-1600, *Fax:* (916) 251-1650
www.klove.com
License: Chester, Plumas County, CA held by Educational Media Foundation.
Group Owner: EMF Broadcasting; (acq 6-30-2005; $900,000 with KPCO(AM) Quincy)
Nat'l Network: K-Love
Format: Christian
Mike Novak, President
Ed Lenane, News Director
Sam Wallington, Engineering Dir
Marya Morgan, News Reporter
Richard Hunt, News Reporter

Chico

***KCHO**
04-22-1969; 91.7 mhz FM *Hrs Open:* 24; 7.7 kw; 1220 ft.; N39 57 30 W121 42 48
First & Normal Sts., Chico, CA 95929 US
(530) 898-5896, *Fax:* (530) 898-4348
www.kcho.org
info@kcho.org
License: Chico, Butte County, CA held by California State University, Chico Research Foundation.
Nat'l Network: PRI; NPR
Arbitron Metro Market: Chico, CA *Format:* Jazz, News *Hrs. of News Programming:* news progmg 37 hrs wkly *No. News Employees:* 1 *Target Audience:* General.
Beth Heberle, Operations Dir
Brian Terhorst, General Manager
Lorraine Dechter, News Director
Jim Moore, Engineering Dir
Mike Birdsill, Chief Engineer

KFMF
02-01-1974; 93.9 mhz FM *Hrs Open:* 24; 2 kw; 1129 ft.; N39 56 46 W121 43 17
1459 Humbolt Road, Suite D, Chico, CA 95928 US
(530) 899-3600, *Fax:* (530) 343-0243
License: Chico, Butte County, CA held by Mapleton License of Chico LLC.
Group Owner: Mapleton Communications LLC; (acq 11-30-2006; grpsl)
Nat'l Reps: Christal
Arbitron Metro Market: Chico, CA *Format:* Rock/AOR *Hrs. of News Programming:* news progmg one hr wkly *No. News Employees:* 1 *Target Audience:* 18-44.
Coyote McGee, Operations Dir
Kenny Allen, Programming Director
Chad Gammage, Promotions Manager
Linda Patterson, Business Manager

***KHAP**
01-01-1999; 89.1 mhz FM; 12 kw; 285 ft.; N39 43 37 W121 40 45
Mailing Address: 4135 Northgate Blvd #1, Sacramento, CA 95834 US
Second Address: 290 Hegenberger Rd., Oakland, CA 94621
(916) 641-8191, *Fax:* (916) 641-8238
www.familyradio.com
info@familyradio.com
License: Chico, Butte County, CA held by Family Stations Inc.
Group Owner: Family Stations Inc.
Arbitron Metro Market: Chico, CA *Format:* Christian, Religious *Special Programming:* Family 25 hrs wkly *Target Audience:* Christian Adults
Harold Camping, President
Matt Pearce, Operations Dir

KBQB
06-01-1993; 92.7 mhz FM; 1.5 kw; 643 ft.; N39 48 25 W121 37 35
Post Office Box 7568, Chico, CA 95927 US
(530) 342-2200, *Fax:* (530) 342-2260
www.927bobfm.com
bob@927bobfm.com
License: Chico, Butte County, CA held by Results Radio Licensee L.L.C.
Group Owner: Fritz Communications Inc.; (acq 6-11-99; grpsl)
Arbitron Metro Market: Chico, CA *Format:* Adult Contemp
Jon Graham, General Manager
Chad Perry, Programming Director
Candy Mason, News Director
J.D. Davis, Chief Engineer

KMXI
11-16-1972; 95.1 mhz FM; 8.7 kw; 1171 ft.; N39 56 46 W121 43 17
4700 Sw Macadam Avenue, Portland, OR 97201 US
(530) 345-0021, *Fax:* (530) 893-2121
www.kmxi.com
License: Chico, Butte County, CA held by Deer Creek Broadcasting LLC
Group Owner: Deer Creek Broadcasting LLC
Arbitron Metro Market: Chico, CA *Format:* Adult Contemp
Dino Corbin, General Manager
Bill Meyer, General Sales Mgr
Larry Scott, Programming Director
Heather Welch, News Director
Jaime Perry, Local Sales Manager

KPAY
04-17-1935; 1290 khz AM
4700 S.W. Macadam Ave., Portland, OR 97201 US
(530) 345-0021, *Fax:* (530) 893-2121
www.kpay.com
License: Chico, CA held by Deer Creek Broadcasting LLC.
Group Owner: Deer Creek Broadcasting LLC; (acq 9-8-2004; grpsl).
Nat'l Reps: Katz Radio
Arbitron Metro Market: Chico, CA *Format:* News, News/Talk, 86 *Target Audience:* 25 plus.
Dino Corbin, General Manager
Larry Scott, Programming Director
Lisa Fitzgerald, Promotions Manager
Matt Ray, News Director

***KZFR**
07-06-1990; 90.1 mhz FM *Hrs Open:* 24; 6.3 kw; 587 ft.; N39 48 25 W121 37 35
Mailing Address: P.O. Box 3173, Chico, CA 95927 US
Second Address: 341 Broadway, Suite 411, Chico, CA 95928
(530) 895-0706/895-0788, *Fax:* (530) 895-0775
www.kzfr.org
info@kzfr.org
License: Chico, Butte County, CA held by Golden Valley Community Broadcasters.
Arbitron Metro Market: Chico, CA *Format:* News, News/Talk, 86, Variety/Diverse *Special Programming:* American Indian 2 hrs, Sp 6 hrs wkly *Hrs. of News Programming:* News progmg 8 hrs wkly
Jill Paydon, General Manager
Shelly Mariposa, General Sales Mgr
Stacey Wear, Office Manager

China Lake

KSSI
01-01-1995; 102.7 mhz FM *Hrs Open:* 24; 3 kw; -23 ft.; N35 39 6 W117 40 58
701 C. Inyokern Road, Ridgecrest, CA 93555 US
(760) 446-5774, *Fax:* (760) 446-5774
www.kssifm.com
john@kssifm.com
License: China Lake, Kern County, CA held by Sound Enterprises.
Arbitron Metro Market: Ridgecrest, CA *Format:* Rock/AOR *Target Audience:* 25-54; general
John Perrige, General Manager
Christine Williams, Programming Director
Lisa Garcia, News Director

***KFRJ**
06-01-2005; 91.1 mhz FM *Hrs Open:* 24; 5.5 kw; 1266 ft.; N35 28 38 W117 41 59
Mailing Address: 4135 Northgate Blve, Suite 1, Sacramenta, CA 95834 US
Second Address: 290 Hegenberger Rd., Oakland, CA 94621
(800) 543-1495, *Fax:* (916) 641-8238
www.familyradio.com
info@familyradio.com
License: China Lake, Kern County, CA held by Family Stations Inc.
Group Owner: Family Stations Inc.
Arbitron Metro Market: China Lake, CA *Format:* Christian, Religious
Harold Camping, President

Chowchilla

KNTO
08-01-1992; 93.3 mhz FM *Hrs Open:* 24; 2.95 kw; 335 ft.; N37 13 2 W120 11 56
1425 N Market Boulevard, Sacramento, CA 95834 US
(209) 883-8760, *Fax:* (209) 883-8769
www.lafavorita.net
ngomez@lafavorita.net
License: Chowchilla, Madera County, CA held by KSKD Inc.
Arbitron Metro Market: Hughson, CA *Format:* Spanish *Target Audience:* 18-35; teens, young adults
Nelson Gomez, General Manager

Chualar

***KHDC**
06-28-1981; 90.9 mhz FM; 3 kw; 194 ft.; N36 34 54 W121 26 34
5005 E. Belmont, Fresno, CA 93727 US
(831) 757-8039, *Fax:* (831) 757-9854
www.radiobilingue.org
info@khdcfm.com
License: Chualar, Monterey County, CA held by Radio Bilingue Inc.
Format: Ethnic, Talk
Hugo Morales, CEO
Delia Saldivar, Station Manager
Maria de Jesus, Programming Director

Citrus Heights

***KLVB**
11-01-1985; 99.5 mhz FM *Hrs Open:* 24; 5.1 kw; 358 ft.; N38 38 32 W121 5 25 *Rebroadcasts:* Rebroadcasts KLVC(FM) Magalia 100%
1425 North Market Blvd., Suite 9, Sacramento, CA 95834 US
(916) 251-1600, *Fax:* (916) 251-1650
www.klove.com
klove@klove.com
License: Citrus Heights, Tehama County, CA held by Educational Media Foundation.
Group Owner: EMF Broadcasting; (acq 1-11-2001; $750,000).
Nat'l Network: K-Love *Nat'l Reps:* D & R Radio
Arbitron Metro Market: Redding, CA *Format:* Christian *No. News Employees:* 3 *Target Audience:* 25-44; Judeo Christian, female
Darrell Chambliss, Chairman
Mike Novak, CEO/COO
Mike Novak, President
David Pierce, Programming Director
Ed Lenane, News Director
Sam Wallington, Engineering Dir
Richard Hunt, News Reporter
Marya Morgan, News Reporter
TracyButler, Traffic Manager

Claremont

***KSPC**
02-01-1956; 88.7 mhz FM; 0.4 kw; 69 ft.; N34 8 33 W117 43 17
340 N. College Avenue, Claremont, CA 91711 US
(909) 621-8157
www.kspc.org
director@kspc.org
License: Claremont, Los Angeles County, CA held by Pomona College.
Arbitron Metro Market: Los Angeles *Format:* Alternative, Jazz, 94 *Special Programming:* Pol 3 hrs, reggae 4 hrs, blues 4 hrs, pub affrs 3 hrs, hip hop/rap 6 hrs wkly *Target Audience:* General.
Clio Beauvoir, General Manager
Erica Tyron, General Sales Mgr
Cameron Quevedo, Programming Director
Rachel Smith, Music Director

Cloverdale

KSRT
01-01-2002; 107.1 mhz FM *Hrs Open:* 24; 3.5 kw; 430 ft.; N38 48 34 W123 2 56
759 South State St #133, Ukiah, CA 95482 US
(707) 284-3069, *Fax:* (707) 284-3174
www.radiolazer.com
License: Cloverdale, Sonoma County, CA held by Lazer Licenses LLC.
Group Owner: Lazer Broadcasting Corp.; (acq 6-29-2006; $6.85 million with KJOR(FM) Windsor).
Format: Tejano
Ken Kuhl, General Manager
Salvador Prieto, Programming Director

Clovis

KFPT
05-02-1977; 790 khz AM *Hrs Open:* 24
600 New Hampshire Avenue, N.W., Suite 1200, Washington, DC 20037 US
(559) 447-3570, *Fax:* (559) 447-3579
www.1430espn.com
comments@1430espn.com
License: Clovis, CA held by Peak Broadcasting of Fresno Licenses LLC.
Group Owner: Peak Broadcasting LLC; (acq 3-30-2007; grpsl)
Nat'l Network: ESPN Radio
Arbitron Metro Market: Fresno, CA *Format:* Sports
Paul Swearengin, General Manager

KOND
09-30-1974; 92.1 mhz FM; 39 kw; 558 ft.; N37 7 40 W119 40 39
1436 Auburn Boulevard, Sacramento, CA 95815 US
(559) 456-4000, *Fax:* (559) 251-9555
www.univision.com
License: Clovis, Fresno County, CA held by Univision Radio License Corp.
Group Owner: Univision Radio; (acq 2-18-2004; $8 million).
Arbitron Metro Market: Fresno, CA
Angela Navarrete, General Manager

Coachella

KNWZ
01-01-1954; 970 khz AM; 5 kw-D, DA2; 1 kw-N, DA2; N33 41 12 W116 9 34

736 Broad St., P.O. Box 936, Augusta, GA 30903 US
(760) 322-7890, *Fax:* (760) 322-5493
www.943knews.com
jay.white@morris.com?subject=Knewsradio.com
License: Coachella, CA held by Morris Communications Corp.
Group Owner: Morris Radio LLC; (acq 1998; $7 million with co-located FM)
Arbitron Metro Market: Palm Springs, CA *Format:* Talk *Target Audience:* 18-49.
Angela Powers, Operations Dir
Jay White, General Manager
Scott Smith, General Sales Mgr
Virginia Nelson, Programming Director
John McMullen, Program Director
Jamie Kanai, Marketing Director
Jose Rodriguez, PromotionsCoordinator
Cristine Constantinescu, Director of Digital Media

KCLB-FM
09-01-1960; 93.7 mhz FM; 26.5 kw; 646 ft.; N33 48 6 W116 13 28
736 Broad St., P.O. Box 936, Augusta, GA 30903 US
(760) 322-7890, *Fax:* (760) 322-5493
www.937kclb.com
jay.white@morris.com?subject=Knewsradio.com
License: Coachella, Riverside County, CA
Arbitron Metro Market: Palm Springs, CA *Format:* Rock/AOR *Target Audience:* 18-49
Angela Powers, Operations Dir
Jay White, General Manager
Scott Smith, General Sales Mgr
Jennifer Shevlin, Program Director / Operations Manager
Jose Rodriguez, Program Director / Operations Manager
Kevin Conklin, Assistant ProgramDirector / Music Director
Jamie Kanai, Marketing Director
Cristine Constantinescu, Director of Digital Media
Cristine Constantinescu, Director of Digital Media

***KPSH**
90.9 mhz FM; 0.23 kw; 623 ft.; N33 52 3 W116 25 58
Mailing Address: 1905 Columbia Blvd, St Helens, OR 97051 US
Second Address: 8919 World Ministry Ave., Baton Rouge, LA 70826
(225) 768-3288, *Fax:* (225) 768-3729
www.jsm.org
onair@jsm.org
License: Coachella, Riverside County, CA held by Family Worship Center Church Inc.
Group Owner: Family Worship Center Church Inc.; acq 2-18-2004; $750,000 for CP).
Arbitron Metro Market: Coachella, CA *Format:* Christian, Religious
David Whitelow, COO
Van Michael, President
John Santiago, Programming Director

Coalinga

***KDKL**
01-01-1999; 88.3 mhz FM; 1.4 kw vert; 2352 ft.; N36 22 11 W120 38 37
1601 Belvedere Rd, Suite 204e, West Palm Beach, FL 33406 US
(916) 251-1600, *Fax:* (916) 251-1650
www.klove.com
License: Coalinga, Fresno County, CA held by Educational Media Foundation
Group Owner: EMF Broadcasting; (acq 10-20-00; $80,000 for CP).
Nat'l Network: K-Love
Format: Christian
Mike Novak, President
David Pierce, Programming Director
Ed Lenane, News Director
Sam Wallington, Engineering Dir
Richard Hunt, News Reporter
Tracy Butler, Traffic Manager

KNGS
100.1 mhz FM; kw
12550 Brookhurst Street, Garden Grove, CA 92640 US
License: Coalinga, Fresno County, CA held by William L. Zawila.
Arbitron Metro Market: Fresno, CA
William Zawila, General Manager

***KFRP**
11-01-2005; 90.7 mhz FM; 2.5 kw vert; 1253 ft.; N35 55 39 W120 22 46
Mailing Address: 4135 Northgate Blvd, Suite 1, Sacramento, CA 95834 US
Second Address: 290 Hegenberger Rd., Oakland, CA 94621
(800) 543-1495, *Fax:* (916) 641-8238
www.familyradio.com
info@familyradio.com
License: Coalinga, Fresno County, CA held by Family Stations Inc.
Group Owner: Family Stations Inc.
Arbitron Metro Market: Coalinga, CA *Format:* Christian, Religious
Harold Camping, President

KQNO
97.3 mhz FM; 6.5 kw; 180 ft.; N36 7 46 W120 26 52 US
(512) 329-5843
www.matineemedia.com
License: Coalinga, Fresno County, CA held by Ace Radio Corp.
Group Owner: Ace Radio Corp.
Arbitron Metro Market: Coalinga, CA
Stephen Hackerman, President

Coarsegold

KRPW(FM)
94.5 mhz FM; 6 kw; Ant 103 ft; N37 15 56 W119 41 11
980 N. Michigan Ave., Suite 1880, Chicago, IL 60611
(312) 204-9900
License: Coarsegold, Madera County, CA held by College Creek Media LLC.
Group Owner: College Creek Media LLC
Population Served: 1,840 *Arbitron Metro Market:* Coarsegold, CA
Neal Robinson, President

Columbia

KCVR-FM
08-01-1995; 98.9 mhz FM; 6 kw; 328 ft.; N38 2 15 W120 22 5
1436 Auburn Boulevard, Sacramento, CA 95815 US
(209) 474-0154, *Fax:* (209) 474-0316
www.entravision.com
info@entravision.com
License: Columbia, Tuolumne County, CA held by Entravision Holdings LLC.
Group Owner: Entravision Communications Corp.; (acq 7-28-2000; grpsl).
Arbitron Metro Market: Stockton, CA *Format:* Spanish
Walter F. Ulloa, Chairman
Jeffery A Liberman, Operations Dir
Lisa Vela, General Manager

Colusa

KKCY
05-01-1990; 103.1 mhz FM *Hrs Open:* 24; 0.135 kw; 1965 ft.; N39 12 21 W121 49 11
P.O. Box 7568, Chico, CA 95927 US
(530) 673-2200, *Fax:* (530) 673-3010
www.kkcy.com
ccarothers@results.com
License: Colusa, Colusa County, CA held by Results Radio of Chico Licensee LLC.
Group Owner: Fritz Communications Inc.; (acq 6-11-99; grpsl)
Nat'l Reps: Katz Radio
Arbitron Metro Market: Chico, CA *Format:* Country *Special Programming:* Sp one hr wkly *Hrs. of News Programming:* news progmg 7 hrs wkly *No. News Employees:* 1 *Target Audience:* 18-64.
Jack Fritz, President
Chris Carothers, Operations Dir
Gordon Rowntree, General Manager
Gordon Rowntree, General Sales Mgr
Chris Carothers, Programming Director
Matthew Reisz, WebMaster

KQPT
09-01-1986; 107.5 mhz FM; 28 kw; 633 ft.; N39 17 17 W122 20 2
1459 Humbolt Road, Suite D, Chico, CA 95928 US
(530) 899-3600, *Fax:* (530) 343-0243
www.107thepoint.com
License: Colusa, Colusa County, CA held by Mapleton License of Chico LLC.
Group Owner: Mapleton Communications LLC; (acq 11-30-2006; grpsl)
Nat'l Reps: Christal
Arbitron Metro Market: Chico, CA *Format:* Contemporary Hits/Top 40 *Target Audience:* 24-48.
Coyote McGee, Operations Dir
Kenny Allen, Programming Director
Chad Gammage, Promotions Manager
Linda Patterson, Business Manager

Compton

KJLH
04-01-1965; 102.3 mhz FM *Hrs Open:* 24; 5.6 kw; 338 ft.; N33 59 52 W118 21 32
161 North La Brea Ave, Inglewood, CA 90301 US
(310) 330-2200, *Fax:* (310) 330-5555,(310) 330-2244
www.kjlhradio.com
sales@kjlhradio.com
License: Compton, Los Angeles County, CA held by TAXI Productions Inc.
Nat'l Network: American Urban; ABC *Nat'l Reps:* McGavren Guild
Arbitron Metro Market: Los Angeles *Format:* Blues *Special Programming:* Relg 7 hrs, gospel 6 hrs, talk 8.5 hrs, Christian 6 hrs wkly *Hrs. of News Programming:* news progmg 8.5 hrs wkly *No. News Employees:* 2*Target Audience:* 25-49; African-American audience
Stevland Morris, CEO
Lawrence Williams, Operations Dir
Karen Slade, General Manager
Aundrae Russell, Programming Director
Jacquie Stephens, News Director
Barry Clark, Chief Engineer
Carrie Haynes, Traffic Manager

Concord

***KVHS**
05-16-1969; 90.5 mhz FM *Hrs Open:* 25.?Â ?; 0.41 kw; 449 ft.; N38 1 49 W122 0 3
1101 Alberta Way, Concord, CA 94521 US
(925) 682-5847, *Fax:* (925) 609-5847
www.kvhs.com
License: Concord, Contra Costa County, CA held by Clayton Valley High School.
Wire Services: Bay City News Service
Arbitron Metro Market: Concord, CA *Format:* Rock/AOR *Special Programming:* Flashback Show(Classic Rock); Punk & SKA Show; Metal Show(Hard Rock), Klub KVHS (Dance Mix) *Target Audience:* 18-34.(P-1) 18-49(P-2) 12+.*Adv. Rates:* 10.00 per CTBR
Melissa McConnell Wilson, General Manager

Copperopolis

KRVR
01-01-1995; 105.5 mhz FM *Hrs Open:* 24; 1 kw; 781 ft; N37 56 55 W120 42 16
961 N. Emerald Ave., Suite A, Modesto, CA 95351
(209) 544-1055, *Fax:* (209) 544-8105
krvr.com
TheRiver@krvr.com
License: Copperopolis, Calaveras County, CA held by Threshold Communications.
Nat'l Reps: Interep
Population Served: 750,000 *Arbitron Metro Market:* Modesto, CA *Target Audience:* 35-64.
Doug Wulff, Operations Dir
Jim Bryan, General Manager
Cheryl Miller, General Sales Mgr
James Arata, Programming Director
Sally Waterman, News Director
R.J. Rose, Production Director

Corcoran

KBLO
01-01-1999; 102.3 mhz FM *Hrs Open:* 24; 19.5 kw; 381 ft.; N36 11 4 W119 24 1
2171 Ralph Avenue, Stockton, CA 95206 US
(559) 740-4172, *Fax:* (559) 740-4177
www.radiolobo987.com
License: Corcoran, Kings County, CA held by Mapleton License of Visalia LLC
Group Owner: Mapleton Communications LLC; (acq 2-27-2009; $8 million)
Arbitron Metro Market: Corcoran, CA
Andrew Adams, General Manager
Dora Deltora, General Sales Mgr
Jaun Davbla, Promotions Manager
Rick McMillion, Chief Engineer

Corning

KTHU
04-08-1988; 100.7 mhz FM *Hrs Open:* 24; 50 kw; 272 ft.; N39 53 17 W122 37 38
P.O. Box 7568, Chico, CA 95927 US
(530) 342-2200, *Fax:* (530) 342-2260
www.chicothunderheads.com

License: Corning, Tehama County, CA held by Results Radio Licensee L.L.C.
Group Owner: Fritz Communications Inc.; (acq 6-11-99; grpsl)
Arbitron Metro Market: Chico, CA *Format:* Classic Rock *Special Programming:* Sp one hr wkly *No. News Employees:* 1 *Target Audience:* 25-54.
Jack Fritz, President
Jon Graham, General Manager
Ron Woodward, Programming Director
Candy Mason, News Director
J. D. Davis, Engineering Dir

Corona

KWRM
01-01-1948; 1370 khz AM *Hrs Open:* 24; 5 kw-D, DA2; 2.5 kw-N, DA2; N33 52 52 W117 32 33
Mailing Address: 210 Radio Road, Corona, CA 91719 US
Second Address: 210 Radio Rd., Corona, CA 92879
(951) 737-1370, *Fax:* (951) 735-9572
kwrm1370am.com
kwrm@majormarket.com
License: Corona, CA held by Major Market Stations Inc.
Arbitron Metro Market: Corona, CA *Format:* Sports, Variety/Diverse *Hrs. of News Programming:* news progmg 20 hrs wkly *No. News Employees:* 2 *Target Audience:* 18-49; young Hispanic adults
Marilynn Kramar, President
Damian Vasquez, Operations Dir

Crescent City

KCRE-FM
03-21-1980; 94.3 mhz FM; 25 kw; Ant -305 ft; N41 45 35 W124 09 49
Mailing Address: Box 1089, Crescent City, CA 95531
Second Address: 1345 Northcrest Dr., Crescent City, CA 95531
(707) 464-9561, *Fax:* (707) 464-4303
www.kcrefm.com
kcre@charter.net
License: Crescent City, Del Norte County, CA held by Bicoastal Media Licenses II, LLC
Nat'l Network: ABC
Population Served: 35,000
Mike Wilson, CEO/COO
Mike Wilson, President
Ernie Garza, Operations Dir
Rene Shanle-Hutzell, General Manager
John Pritchett, News Director
Kevin Sanders, Chief Engineer

KFVR
07-01-1950; 1310 khz AM *Hrs Open:* 24
PO Box 1089, Crescent City, CA 95531 US
(435) 623-4010, *Fax:* (435) 623-1451
www.lanueva1090.com
License: Crescent City, CA held by Del Rosario Talpa Inc.
Arbitron Metro Market: Beulah, CO *Format:* Religious, Spanish
Mario Meza, General Manager

*KHSR
07-01-1999; 91.9 mhz FM *Hrs Open:* 24; 4.5 kw; -194 ft.; N41 45 35 W124 11 28 *Rebroadcasts:* Rebroadcasts KHSU-FM Arcata 100%
Khsu Humboldt State Univ, Arcata, CA 95521 US
(707) 826-4807, *Fax:* (707) 826-6082
www.khsu.org
khsu@humboldt.edu
License: Crescent City, Del Norte County, CA held by Humboldt State University.
Nat'l Network: NPR; PRI
Format: News *Special Programming:* World 14 hrs, jazz 10 hrs wkly
Katie Whiteside, Operations Dir
Ed Subkis, General Manager
David Reed, General Sales Mgr
Kevin Sanders, Chief Engineer
Mark Shikuma, Music Director
Lorna Bryant, Administrative Assistant

KPOD
12-05-1959; 1240 khz AM *Hrs Open:* 24; 778 w-U; N41 45 35 W124 11 28
Mailing Address: Box 1089, Crescent City, CA 95531
Second Address: 1345 Northcrest Dr., Crescent City, CA 95531
(707) 464-3183, *Fax:* (707) 464-4303
www.kpod.com
kcre@charter.net
License: Crescent City, Del Norte County, CA held by Bicoastal Media Licenses II, LLC
Group Owner: Bicoastal Media L.L.C.; (acq 3-31-00; $850,000 with co-loca
Nat'l Network: ABC
Population Served: 60,000*Adv. Rates:* 12; 11; 11; 11
Mike Wilson, President
Rene Shanle-Hutzell, General Manager
Kevin Sanders, Chief Engineer

KPOD-FM
01-01-1989; 97.9 mhz FM *Hrs Open:* 24; 6 kw; Ant -128 ft; N41 45 35 W124 11 28
Mailing Address: Box 1089, Crescent City, CA 95531
Second Address: 1345 Northcrest Dr., Crescent City, CA 95531
(707) 464-1000, *Fax:* (707) 464-4303
www.kpodfm.com
kcre@charter.net
License: Crescent City, Del Norte County, CA held by Bicoastal Media Licenses II, LLC
Group Owner: Bicoastal Media L.L.C.
Chuck Clifford, Operations Dir

*KHEC
91.1 mhz FM; 0.125 kw; 177 ft.; N41 48 11 W124 4 9 US
(713) 944-8181
License: Crescent City, Del Norte County, CA held by Centro Cristiano Cosecha Final.
Arbitron Metro Market: Crescent City, CA
Francisco Diaz, President

Cupertino

*KKUP
05-15-1972; 91.5 mhz FM *Hrs Open:* 24; 0.2 kw; 2582 ft.; N37 6 40 W121 50 36
P. O. Box 820, Cupertino, CA 95015 US
(408) 260-2999
www.kkup.org
webmeister@kkup.org
License: Cupertino, Santa Clara County, CA held by Assurance Sciences Foundation Inc.
Arbitron Metro Market: San Jose, CA *Format:* Alternative, Blues
Special Programming: Brazilian 2 hrs, African 6 hrs, Indian 3 hrs, Sp 3 *Target Audience:* General.
Jim Thomas, Chairman
Jim Thomas, General Manager
Tim Adelman, Programming Director
Dave Barnett, Chief Engineer
Peter Schwartz, Music Director
David Stafford, Studio Engineer

Cutten

KHUM
01-01-1996; 104.7 mhz FM *Hrs Open:* 24; 50 kw; 2651 ft.; N40 7 15 W123 41 27
Mailing Address: PO Box 25, Ferndale, CA 95536 US
Second Address: 1400 Main St., Suite 104, Ferndale, CA 95536
(707) 786-5104, *Fax:* (707) 786-5100
www.khum.com
studio@khum.com
License: Cutten, Humboldt County, CA held by Lost Coast Communications Inc.
Group Owner: Lost Coast Communications Inc.; (acq 11-5-2001)
Nat'l Reps: McGavren Guild
Format: Triple A *Special Programming:* Jazz 20 hrs wkly *Target Audience:* 25-54; general *Adv. Rates:* 19; 19; 19; 9.
Cliff Berkowitz, Operations Dir
Patrick Cleary, General Manager
Jennefer White, General Sales Mgr
Mike Dronkers, Programming Director
Gregg Foster, Promotions Manager
Kevin Sanders, Chief Engineer
Kara Hochner, PromotionsDirector

Davis

*KDVS
01-01-1968; 90.3 mhz FM *Hrs Open:* 24; 9.2 kw; 105 ft.; N38 32 29 W121 45 3
1111 Franklin Street, 7th Floor, Oakland, CA 94607 US
(530) 752-0728, *Fax:* (530) 752-8548
www.kdvs.org
gm@kdvs.org
License: Davis, Yolo County, CA held by Regents of the University of California.
Arbitron Metro Market: Sacramento, CA *Format:* Talk, Variety/Diverse *Hrs. of News Programming:* News progmg 13 hrs wkly *Target Audience:* General; loc community
Renner Burkle, General Manager
Mike Mastrangelo, General Sales Mgr
Michael Taber, Programming Director
Elizabeth Stitt, News Director
Rich Luscher, Chief Engineer
Sean Carson, Music Director
Natalie Roman, Music Director
GregCotta, Sports Director

KXSE
02-01-1979; 104.3 mhz FM *Hrs Open:* 24; 3.4 kw; 436 ft.; N38 39 26 W121 43 12
1436 Auburn Boulevard, Sacramento, CA 95815 US
(916) 646-4000, *Fax:* (916) 646-1958
www.jose1043.com
jdanzer@entravision.com; promociones@jose1043.com
License: Davis, Sacramento County, CA held by Entravision Holdings LLC.
Group Owner: Entravision Communications Corp.; (acq 7-28-2000; grpsl).
Nat'l Network: ABC; Westwood One; CBS
Arbitron Metro Market: Sacramento, CA *Format:* Adult Contemp
Target Audience: 25-54.
Allyson Maiman, General Manager
Jim Danzer, General Sales Mgr
Salvador Lopez, Promotions Manager
Website is in Spanish

Delano

KCHJ
12-01-1951; 1010 khz AM *Hrs Open:* 24; 5 kw-D, DA2; 1 kw-N, DA2; N35 48 40 W119 19 18
5200 Standard Street, Bakersfield, CA 93308 US
(661) 327-9711, *Fax:* (661) 327-0797
info@thespanishradio.com
License: Delano, CA held by Illinois Lotus Corp.
Group Owner: Lotus Communications Corp.; (acq 8-24-99; grpsl)
Wire Services: UPI
Arbitron Metro Market: Bakersfield, CA *Format:* Oldies, Spanish
Special Programming: Sp 24 hrs, 7days a wk *No. News Employees:* 2 *Target Audience:* 18 plus; Sp speaking adults
Howard Kalmenson, President
Greg Holcomb, General Manager
Vicente Arias, Programming Director
Lloyd Moss, Chief Engineer

KBFP-FM
10-02-1986; 105.3 mhz FM; 35 kw; 581 ft.; N35 30 53 W119 3 41
C/O Jodi M. Krame, 966 East Essex Drive, Fresno, CA 93720 US
(661) 322-9929, *Fax:* (661) 283-2963
www.lapreciosa1053.com
License: Delano, Kern County, CA held by CC Licenses LLC.
Group Owner: Clear Channel Communications Inc.; (acq 4-94)
Nat'l Reps: McGavren Guild
Arbitron Metro Market: Bakersfield, CA *Format:* Adult Contemp
Target Audience: 18-44.
Jim Bell, Operations Dir
Bell, General Manager
Steve King, Station Manager
Ron Fisher, General Sales Mgr
Kenn McCloud, Programming Director
Billy Smith, Promotions Manager
Steve Mull, Chief Engineer
Public Affairs, LindseyPonce

KDFO
11-01-1968; 98.5 mhz FM *Hrs Open:* 24; 8 kw; 581 ft.; N35 30 53 W119 3 41
C/O Arter & Hadden, 1801 K St, NW, Ste. 400k, Washington, DC 20006 US
(661) 322-9929, *Fax:* (661) 283-2963
www.985thefox.com
jimbell@clearchannel.com
License: Delano, Kern County, CA held by CC Licenses LLC.
Group Owner: Clear Channel Communications Inc.; (acq 10-16-2000; grpsl)
Arbitron Metro Market: Bakersfield, CA *Format:* Classic Rock
Target Audience: 18-44.
Jim Bell, Operations Dir
Steve King, Station Manager
Ron Fisher, General Sales Mgr
Kenn McCloud, Programming Director
Billy Smith, Promotions Manager
Steve Mull, Chief Engineer

Dinuba

KRDU
12-26-1946; 1130 khz AM *Hrs Open:* 24; 5 kw-D, DA2; 6.2 kw-N, DA2; N36 29 3 W119 15 57
Mailing Address: 600 Congress Ave., Suite 1400, Austin, TX 78701 US
Second Address: 83 East Shaw, Fresno, CA 93727
(559) 591-1130, *Fax:* (559) 591-4822
www.krdu1130.com

License: Dinuba, CA held by Capstar TX L.P.
Group Owner: Clear Channel Communications Inc.; (acq 8-30-00; grpsl).
Arbitron Metro Market: Fresno-Visalia, CA *Format:* Christian, Talk *Hrs. of News Programming:* news progmg 7 hrs wkly *No. News Employees:* 1 *Target Audience:* 18-65.
Jim Tuck, General Manager
Doug Diedrich, Programming Director
Mike Hauber, Chief Engineer
Steve Carloon, Local News Editor

KSOF
06-05-1975; 98.9 mhz FM *Hrs Open:* 24; 19 kw; 820 ft.; N36 38 15 W118 56 35
600 Congress Ave., Suite 1400, Austin, TX 78701 US
(559) 243-4300, *Fax:* (559) 243-4301
www.softrock989.com
info@softrock989.com
License: Dinuba, Tulare County, CA held by Capstar TX L.P.
Group Owner: Clear Channel Communications Inc.
Arbitron Metro Market: Fresno, CA *Format:* Classic Rock *Hrs. of News Programming:* News progmg 2 hrs wkly *Target Audience:* 25-54; women
Paul Wilson, Operations Dir
Jeff Negrete, General Manager
Tim Rapp, General Sales Mgr
Mike Brady, Programming Director
Dave Case, Chief Engineer

Dunnigan

KSAC-FM
09-01-1983; 105.5 mhz FM *Hrs Open:* 24; 2.55 kw; 1010 ft.; N38 47 17 W122 6 52
296 H Street, Third Floor, Chula Vista, CA 91910 US
(916) 924-0710, *Fax:* (916) 924-1587
www.ksfm1025.com
License: Dunnigan, Yolo County, CA held by Caron Broadcasting Inc.
Group Owner: Salem Communications Corp.; (acq 1-11-2002; $8 million)
Format: Religious
Dale Hendry, General Manager
Max Miller, Programming Director
Veldon Leverich, Engineering Dir

Dunsmuir

KZRO
12-08-1992; 100.1 mhz FM *Hrs Open:* 24; 12.5 kw; 233 ft.; N41 17 30 W122 14 21
Mailing Address: 111 E. Alma Street, Mt. Shasta, CA 96067 US
Second Address: 113 E. Alma St., Mt. Shasta, CA 96067
(530) 926-1332, *Fax:* (530) 926-0737
www.z100fm.net/
zmail@zchannelradio.com
License: Dunsmuir, Siskiyou County, CA held by Dennis Michael Crepps dba Big Tree Communications
Nat'l Network: Westwood One
Arbitron Metro Market: Dunsmuir, CA *Format:* Classic Rock, Oldies *Special Programming:* Children 2 hrs wkly *No. News Employees:* 1 *Target Audience:* 18-55; general
Dennis Michaels, General Manager
Rob Hanson, Chief Engineer

Earlimart

***KNAC**
93.5 mhz FM; kw
12550 Brookhurst St. #A, Garden Grove, CA 92640 US

www.knac.com
License: Earlimart, Tulare County, CA held by Earlimart Educational Foundation Inc.

William Zawila, General Manager

East Los Angeles

KLAX-FM
04-22-1949; 97.9 mhz FM; 33 kw; 604 ft.; N34 9 49 W118 11 44
3191 Coral Way, Suite 805, Miami, FL 33145 US
(310) 203-0900, *Fax:* (310) 843-4961
www.979laraza.com
info@979laraza.com
License: East Los Angeles, Los Angeles County, CA held by KLAX Licensing Inc.
Group Owner: Spanish Broadcasting System Inc.; (acq 2-87)
Arbitron Metro Market: Los Angeles, CA *Format:* Spanish *Target Audience:* 18-34.
Raul Alarcon Jr., CEO
Peter Remington, General Manager
Jason Wilberding, General Sales Mgr
Juan Hidalog, Programming Director
Patty Castor, Promotions Manager

East Porterville

KMQA
12-01-1989; 100.5 mhz FM; 2 kw; 2009 ft.; N35 45 36 W118 45 32
18319 Hart St., #19, Reseda, CA 91335 US
(559) 687-3170, *Fax:* (559) 687-3175
www.lamaquinamusical.net
traffic@lunacommunications.net
License: East Porterville, Tulare County, CA held by MBP Licensee LLC.
Group Owner: Moon Broadcasting; (acq 12-29-98).
Nat'l Network: CNN Radio
Arbitron Metro Market: Visalia, CA *Format:* Tejano *Target Audience:* 25-40.
George Rayo, Operations Dir
Rey Ponce, Promotions Manager

Edwards

KGBB
03-01-1990; 103.9 mhz FM *Hrs Open:* 24; 6 kw; 328 ft.; N34 58 45 W118 10 2
731 North Balsam Street, Ridgecrest, CA 94555 US
(760) 371-1700, *Fax:* (760) 371-1824
www.bobfm1039.com
radio@iwvisp.com
License: Edwards, Kern County, CA held by Adelman Broadcasting Inc.
Group Owner: Adelman Broadcasting Inc.
Arbitron Metro Market: Ridgecrest, CA *Format:* Adult Contemp *Target Audience:* 18-54.
Robert Adelman, President

El Cajon

***KECR**
01-01-1955; 910 khz AM *Hrs Open:* 24
4135 Northgate Blvd, Suite 1, Sacramento, CA 95834 US
(619) 390-3481, *Fax:* (619) 443-7693
www.familyradio.com
kecr@nethere.com
License: El Cajon, CA held by Family Stations Inc.
Group Owner: Family Stations Inc.; acq 6-9-63)
Arbitron Metro Market: Lakeside, CA *Format:* Religious *Target Audience:* All ages; families
Bill Babcock, Operations Dir
Jeff Zimmer, Chief Engineer
David Manzi, Regional Manager

KHTS-FM
01-01-1961; 93.3 mhz FM *Hrs Open:* 24; 50 kw; 482 ft.; N32 43 48 W117 5 2
50 East Rivercenter Blvd, Suite 1200, Covington, KY 41011 US
(858) 292-2000, *Fax:* (858) 522-5707
www.channel933.com
bgann@jrn.com; dthompson@rendabroadcasting.com
License: El Cajon, San Diego County, CA held by Citicasters Licenses L.P.
Group Owner: Clear Channel Communications Inc.; (acq 5-4-99; grpsl).
Arbitron Metro Market: San Diego, CA *Format:* Contemporary Hits/Top 40 *Target Audience:* 18-34.
Bob Bolinger, General Manager
Terry King, General Sales Mgr
Jimmy Steele, Programming Director
Jean Arrollado, Promotions Manager
Mary Ayala, News Director
John Rigg, Chief Engineer
Geoff Alan, Promotions Director

El Centro

KWST
06-21-1958; 1430 khz AM *Hrs Open:* 24; 1 kw-D, ND1; 0.036 kw-N, ND1; N32 48 27 W115 32 18
11900 Olympic Blvd., Los Angeles, CA 90064 US
(760) 482-7777
www.jose945.com
License: El Centro, CA held by Entravision Holding L.L.C.
Group Owner: Entravision Communications Corp.; (acq 1998; $4.8 million)
Arbitron Metro Market: El Centro, CA *Format:* Country *Target Audience:* 25-49.
Albert Valdez, Operations Dir
Eric Chavez, General Manager

KXO
01-01-1927; 1230 khz AM *Hrs Open:* 24
420 Main Street, El Centro, CA 92243 US
(760) 352-1230
www.kxoradio.com
kxoamfm@kxoradio.com
License: El Centro, CA held by KXO Inc.
Nat'l Network: CBS *Nat'l Reps:* McGavren Guild
Arbitron Metro Market: El Centro, CA *Format:* Oldies *Special Programming:* Farm 7 hrs wkly *Hrs. of News Programming:* news progmg 10 hrs wkly *No. News Employees:* 1 *Target Audience:* 18-49. *Adv. Rates:* 24; 23; 24; 23
Gene Brister, President
Caroll Buckley, Operations Dir
Doug Melanson, Chief Engineer

KXO-FM
08-02-1976; 107.5 mhz FM *Hrs Open:* 24; 50 kw; 285 ft.; N32 48 24 W115 32 44
420 Main Street, El Centro, CA 92243 US
(760) 352-1230, *Fax:* (760) 352-0858
www.kxoradio.com
kxoamfm@kxoradio.com
License: El Centro, Imperial County, CA held by kxo.inc
Nat'l Reps: McGavren Guild
Arbitron Metro Market: El Centro, CA *Format:* Adult Contemp *Hrs. of News Programming:* News progmg 3 hrs wkly *No. News Employees:* 1 *Target Audience:* 25-49. *Adv. Rates:* 26; 24; 26; 24
Gene Brister, General Manager

El Cerrito

***KECG**
09-01-1978; 88.1 mhz FM *Hrs Open:* 24; 0.017 kw; -95 ft.; N37 54 20 W122 17 34
Mailing Address: 540 Ashbury Avenue, El Cerrito, CA 94530 US
Second Address: 540 Ashbury Ave., El Cerrito, CA 94530
(510) 869-9910
www.morepublicradiointernational.org; www.jazzbeatradio.tv
prentisswoods@yahoo.com
License: El Cerrito, Contra Costa County, CA held by West Contra Costa Unified School District.
Arbitron Metro Market: San Francisco *Format:* Jazz, Variety/Diverse *Special Programming:* Gospel 5 hrs, Sp 3 hrs, Filipino 2 hrs wkly *Hrs. of News Programming:* News progmg 5 hrs wkly *Target Audience:* General.
Prentiss Woods, Station Manager
Corey Mason, Programming Director

El Rio

KMLA
10-01-1996; 103.7 mhz FM; 1 kw; 804 ft.; N34 18 10 W119 13 41
555 South ""A"" Street, Suite 175, Oxnard, CA 93030 US
(805) 385-5656, *Fax:* (805) 385-5690
www.lam1037.com
willy@lam1037.com
License: El Rio, Ventura County, CA held by Gold Coast Radio L.L.C.
Arbitron Metro Market: Oxnard, CA
Guillermo Gonzalez, General Manager
Sonia Lopez, Station Manager
Gerardo Ceja, Programming Director
Rosa Rodriguez, Promotions Manager
Charles Hastings, Chief Engineer

Ellwood

KSPE-FM
02-06-1989; 94.5 mhz FM *Hrs Open:* 24; 81 kw; Ant 2,949 ft; N34 31 32 W119 57 28
414 E. Cota St., Santa Barbara, CA 93101
(805) 879-8300, *Fax:* (805) 879-8430
License: Ellwood, Santa Barbara County, CA held by Rincon License Subsidiary LLC.
Group Owner: Point Broadcasting Company; (acq 7-11-2007; grpsl)
Population Served: 89,054 *Arbitron Metro Market:* Santa Barbara, CA *Format:* Oldies
Roxy Cruz, Programming Director
Stacy Wood, Music Director

Encinitas

KPRI
01-20-1962; 102.1 mhz FM *Hrs Open:* 24; 30 kw; 632 ft.; N32 50 24 W117 14 52
5015 Shoreman Place, Suite 102, San Diego, CA 92122 US
(858) 678-0102, *Fax:* (858) 320-7024
www.kprifm.com
info@kprifm.com

License: Encinitas, San Diego County, CA held by Compass Radio of San Diego Inc.
Nat'l Reps: Katz Radio
Arbitron Metro Market: San Diego, CA *Format:* Triple A *Hrs. of News Programming:* news progmg 2 hrs wkly *No. News Employees:* 1 *Target Audience:* 18-34; upscale, well educated, young adult contemp mus fans
Jonathan Schwartz, CFO
Bob Hughes, General Manager
Robert Burch, Station Manager
Patrick Osburn, General Sales Mgr
Keith Miller, Promotions Manager

Escondido

KSOQ-FM
07-01-1966; 92.1 mhz FM *Hrs Open:* 24; 0.58 kw; 1024 ft.; N33 6 39 W117 9 13 *Rebroadcasts:* Rebroadcasts KSON-FM San Diego 100%
Mailing Address: 550 Laguna Drive, Carlsbad, CA 92008 US
Second Address: 1615 Murray Canyon Rd., Suite 710, San Diego, CA 92108-4321
(619) 291-9797, *Fax:* (619) 543-1353
www.kson.com
ksonstudio@kson.com
License: Escondido, San Diego County, CA held by Jefferson-Pilot Communications Co. of California.
Group Owner: Lincoln Financial Media; (acq 4-1-2004; $18 million).
Arbitron Metro Market: Escondido, CA *Format:* Country *Special Programming:* Bluegrass Special 2 hrs wkly *Target Audience:* 25-54
Rick Jackson, General Manager
Steve Sklenar, General Sales Mgr
Kevin Callahan, Programming Director
Bill Eisenhamer, Chief Engineer

KFSD
06-01-1958; 1450 khz AM *Hrs Open:* 24
550 Laguna Drive, Carlsbad, CA 92008 US
(760) 729-1000, *Fax:* (760) 476-9604
www.am1510kspa.com
reception@astorbroadcastgroup.com
License: Escondido, CA held by North County Broadcasting Corp.
Group Owner: Astor Broadcast Group; (acq 9-15-87; $3 million with co-located FM;
Arbitron Metro Market: Escondido, CA *Format:* Adult Contemp *Hrs. of News Programming:* News progmg 2 hrs wkly *Target Audience:* 35-64.
Arthur Astor, CEO
Rick Roome, General Manager

Esparto

KLMG
01-01-1996; 97.9 mhz FM; 6 kw; 328 ft.; N38 45 33 W121 52 33
296 H Street, Suite 300, Chula Vista, CA 91910 US
(916) 368-6300, *Fax:* (916) 473-0146
www.latino979.com
acadenas@adelantemediagroup.com
License: Esparto, Yolo County, CA
Group Owner: Adelante Media Group LLC; (acq 12-15-2004; $21.7 million with KBBU(FM) Modesto)
Arbitron Metro Market: Esparto, CA *Format:* Spanish, Christian
John Bustos, General Manager
Juan Gonzalez, Programming Director
Javier Gonzalez, Promotions Manager
Cynthia Sanchez, News Director
Mark Sedaka, Chief Engineer

Essex

KHWY
05-01-1991; 98.9 mhz FM *Hrs Open:* 24; 9 kw; 1142 ft.; N34 52 50 W115 4 6 *Rebroadcasts:* Rebroadcasts KRXV(FM) Yermo 100%
12381 Wilshire Blvd. Suite 105, Los Angeles, CA 90025 US
(760) 256-0326, *Fax:* (760) 256-9507
www.thehighwaystations.com
highwayradio@highwayradio.com
License: Essex, San Bernardino County, CA held by KHWY Inc.
Group Owner: KHWY Inc.
Nat'l Network: AP Radio
Format: Adult Contemp *Hrs. of News Programming:* news progmg 28 hrs wkly *No. News Employees:* 1 *Target Audience:* 35 plus; travelers on I-40 & I-15 & Mojave Desert residents
Howard Anderson, CEO
Timothy Anderson, Operations Dir
Judy Robinson, General Sales Mgr
Lance Todd, Programming Director
John Gregg, Promotions Manager

Keith Hayes, News Director
Thomas McNeill, Engineering Dir
Kirk Anderson,Executive Vice President

Eureka

KEKA-FM
11-01-1983; 101.5 mhz FM; 89 kw; 2051 ft.; N40 25 12 W124 5 0
1101 Marsh Road, Eureka, CA 95501 US
(707) 442-5744
www.keka101.com/info/contact-us/
License: Eureka, Humboldt County, CA held by Eureka Broadcasting.
Group Owner: Eureka Broadcasting Co.; (acq 12-13-90; $430,189;
Nat'l Network: ABC *Nat'l Reps:* Katz Radio
Arbitron Metro Market: Eureka, CA *Format:* Country *Target Audience:* 25-54.
Brian Papstein, General Manager

KFMI
01-01-1973; 96.3 mhz FM; 30 kw; 1581 ft.; N40 43 36 W123 58 18
775 East Blithedale Avenue, #143, Mill Valley, CA 94941 US
(707) 442-2000, *Fax:* (707) 443-6848
www.power963.com
power963@hotmail.com
License: Eureka, Humboldt County, CA held by Bicoastal Media LLC.
Group Owner: Bicoastal Media L.L.C.; acq 7-28-99; grpsl)
Nat'l Network: Jones Radio Networks
Arbitron Metro Market: Eureka, CA *Format:* Adult Contemp *Special Programming:* Loveline 10 hrs wkly *Target Audience:* 18-36; upscale adults
Ken Dennis, CEO
Mike Wilson, President
Laurie Tate, General Manager
Victoria Bennington, General Sales Mgr
Tom Sebourn, Programming Director

KGOE
05-12-1933; 1480 khz AM *Hrs Open:* 24; 5 kw-D, ND2; 1 kw-N, ND2; N40 44 28 W124 12 5
775 East Blithedale Avenue, #143, Mill Valley, CA 94941 US
(707) 442-2000, *Fax:* (707) 443-6848
www.kgoe.com
ltate@bicoastalmedia.com
License: Eureka, CA held by Bicoastal Media LLC.
Group Owner: Bicoastal Media L.L.C.; acq 7-28-99; grpsl)
Nat'l Network: Jones Radio Networks
Format: News, News/Talk, 86 *Hrs. of News Programming:* news progmg 100 hrs wkly *No. News Employees:* 1 *Target Audience:* 25-54.
Laurie Tate, General Manager
Victoria Bennington, General Sales Mgr
Tom Sebourn, Programming Director
Rollin Treehearn, Promotions Manager
Kevin Sanders, Chief Engineer

KWSW(AM)
01-01-1946; 980 khz AM *Hrs Open:* 24; 5 kw-D, 500 w-N, DA-N; N40 48 02 W124 07 39
1101 Marsh Rd., Eureka, CA 95501
(707) 442-5744
License: Eureka, Humboldt County, CA held by Eureka Broadcasting Co.
Group Owner: Eureka Broadcasting Co.; (acq 3-1-58).
Nat'l Network: CBS; Wall Street
Population Served: 28,936*Format:* News, News/Talk, 86 *No. News Employees:* 2 *Target Audience:* 35 plus; upscale, educated
Brian Papstein, President
Mark Householter, Chief Engineer

KKHB
01-01-1994; 105.5 mhz FM; 28 kw; 1588 ft.; N40 43 50 W123 57 7 *Rebroadcasts:* Rebroadcasts KGO(AM) San Francisco
775 East Blithedale Avenue, #143, Mill Valley, CA 94941 US
(707) 442-2000, *Fax:* (707) 443-6848
www.cool1055.com
ltate@bicoastalmedia.com
License: Eureka, Humboldt County, CA held by Bicoastal Media L.L.C.
Group Owner: Bicoastal Media L.L.C.; acq 11-9-98; grpsl)
Arbitron Metro Market: Redding, CA *Format:* Oldies
Laurie Tate, General Manager
Victoria Bennington, General Sales Mgr
Tom Sebourn, Programming Director

*KMUE
08-09-1996; 88.1 mhz FM; 10 kw; 1621 ft.; N40 43 39 W123 58 17 *Rebroadcasts:* Rebroadcasts KMUD(FM) Garberville 100%
Mailing Address: P.O. Box 135, Redway, CA 95560 US
Second Address: 1144 Redway Dr., Redway, CA 95560
(707) 923-2513, *Fax:* (707) 923-2501
www.kmud.org
kmud@kmud.org
License: Eureka, Humboldt County, CA held by Redwood Community Radio Inc.
Format: Talk, Variety/Diverse
David Lippe, Operations Dir
Brenda Starr, General Manager
Marianne Knorzer, Programming Director

KRED-FM
12-17-1979; 92.3 mhz FM; 25 kw; 1539 ft.; N40 43 37 W123 58 25
775 East Blithedale Avenue, #143, Mill Valley, CA 94941 US
(707) 442-2000, *Fax:* (707) 443-6848
www.kred923.com
mail@kred923.com
License: Eureka, Humboldt County, CA held by Bicoastal Media LLC.
Group Owner: Bicoastal Media L.L.C.
Arbitron Metro Market: Eureka, CA *Format:* Country *Hrs. of News Programming:* news progmg 7 hrs wkly *No. News Employees:* 1
Rollin Treehearn, Programming Director

KWSW
12-20-1979; 980 khz AM
1101 Marsh Road, Eureka, CA 95501 US
(707) 442-5744
License: Eureka, CA held by Eureka Broadcasting Co. Inc.
Group Owner: Eureka Broadcasting Co.; (acq 11-30-92; $105,000;
Arbitron Metro Market: Eureka, CA *Format:* Talk *Target Audience:* 35 plus; baby boomers with discretionary income
Brian Papstein, President
Mark Householter, Chief Engineer

KEJY
01-01-2007; 790 khz AM; 5 kw-D, ND1; 0.11 kw-N, ND1; Ant 1,692 ft; N40 48 9 W124 8 20
1101 Marsh Road, Eureka, CA 95501 US
(707) 442-5744
www.kins1063.com
License: Eureka, CA held by Eureka Broadcasting Co. Inc.
Group Owner: Eureka Broadcasting Co.
Arbitron Metro Market: Eureka, CA *Format:* Adult Contemp
Brian Papstein, President

KIHH
07-26-2008; 1400 khz AM
US
(916) 535-0500, *Fax:* (916) 535-0504
www.ihradio.org
info@ihradio.org
License: Eureka, CA held by IHR Educational Broadcasting.
Group Owner: IHR Educational Broadcasting
Nat'l Network: EWTN Radio
Arbitron Metro Market: Eureka, CA *Format:* Christian
Douglas Sherman, President
Lori Brown, General Manager

Fair Oaks

KSSJ(FM)
11-25-1970; 94.7 mhz FM; 86.6 kw; 2,072 ft; N39 15 30 W119 42 36
5345 Madison Ave., Sacramento, CA 95841-3141
(916) 334-7777, *Fax:* (916) 339-4559
www.kssj.com
info@kssj.com
License: Fair Oaks, Sacramento County, CA held by Entercom Sacramento License L.L.C.
Group Owner: Entercom Communications Corp.; (acq 11-4-97; $15.9 million)
Population Served: 472,178 *Arbitron Metro Market:* Sacramento, CA *Format:* Jazz, Smooth Jazz
John Geary, General Manager
Lee Hansen, Station Manager
Fred Hormel, General Sales Mgr
Lizann Hunt, Promotions Manager

Fairfield

*KASK
91.5 mhz FM; 0.075 kw horiz; 650 ft.; N38 19 9 W121 59 31
160 Lighthouse Way, Vacaville, CA 95688 US
(707) 449-9300, *Fax:* (707) 447-0680
kaskradio..com
info@kaskfm.com
License: Fairfield, Solano County, CA held by Maranatha Broadcasting.

Arbitron Metro Market: Fairfield, CA *Format:* Religious
Bob Michaels, Operations Dir
Michel Mace, Station Manager

Fairmead

***KLVY**
01-01-1998; 91.1 mhz FM *Hrs Open:* 24; 39 kw; 558 ft.; N37 7 40 W119 40 39 *Rebroadcasts:* Rebroadcasts KLVN(FM) Livingston 100%
1425 N.Market Blvd,Ste.9, Sacramento, CA 95834 US
(707) 528-9236, *Fax:* (707) 528-9246
www.klove.com
klove@klove.com
License: Fairmead, Madera County, CA held by Educational Media Foundation Inc.
Group Owner: EMF Broadcasting
Nat'l Network: K-Love
Format: Christian *No. News Employees:* 3 *Target Audience:* 25-44; Judeo-Christian, female
Darell Chambliss, Chairman
Mike Novak, President
David Pierce, Programming Director
Ed Lenane, News Director
Sam Wallington, Engineering Dir
Marya Morgan, News Reporter
Richard Hunt, Marya Morgan

Fall River Mills

***KKLC**
11-26-1977; 107.9 mhz FM *Hrs Open:* 24; 13 kw; 2103 ft.; N40 54 23 W121 49 43 *Rebroadcasts:* Rebroadcasts KLVR(FM) Santa Rosa 100%
P. O. Box 448, Mount Shasta, CA 96067 US
(916) 251-1600, *Fax:* (916) 251-1650
www.klove.com
klove@klove.com
License: Fall River Mills, Siskiyou County, CA held by Educational Media Foundation
Group Owner: EMF Broadcasting; (acq 12-27-2002; $400,000).
Nat'l Network: K-Love
Format: Christian *No. News Employees:* 3 *Target Audience:* 25-44; Judeo Christian, female
Mike Novak, President
David Pierce, Programming Director
Ed Lenane, News Director
Sam Wallington, Engineering Dir
Richard Hunt, News Director
Marya Morgan

Fallbrook

KSSD
11-22-1977; 107.1 mhz FM *Hrs Open:* 24; 3 kw; 299 ft.; N33 23 1 W117 11 20
11 Skyline Drive, Hawthorne, NY 10532 US
(323) 900-6100, *Fax:* (323) 900-6127
www.superestrella.com
License: Fallbrook, San Diego County, CA held by Entravision Holdings LLC.
Group Owner: Entravision Communications Corp.; (acq 4-1-03; grpsl).
Nat'l Reps: Lotus Entravision Reps LLC
Arbitron Metro Market: Los Angeles, CA *Format:* Spanish, Christian *Target Audience:* 18-34. *Adv. Rates:* 100; 100; 150; 50
Jeff Liberman, Operations Dir
Karl Meyer, General Manager
Elias Autran, Programming Director
Pam McCaffrey, News Director
Eugene McAffe, Engineering Dir

Felton

KXZM
01-01-1999; 93.7 mhz FM; 0.41 kw; 2264 ft.; N37 9 35 W121 54 32
Leventhal Senter Lerman, 2000 K St, NW, Ste 600, Washington, DC 20006 US
(805) 240-2070, *Fax:* (805) 240-5960
License: Felton, Santa Cruz County, CA held by Lazer Broadcasting Corp.
Group Owner: Lazer Broadcasting Corp.; (acq 7-25-2005; $2.88 million with KXSM(FM) Hollister).
Alfredo Plascencia, President
Daniel Osuna, General Manager

Firebaugh

***KYAF**
01-01-2006; 94.7 mhz FM; kw
C/O William Zawila, Esq., 12550 Brookhurst St. #A, Garden Grove, CA 92840 US
(559) 659-0100
kyafm.com
info@kayfm.com
License: Firebaugh, Fresno County, CA held by Central Valley Educational Services Inc.
Arbitron Metro Market: Firebaugh, CA *Format:* Oldies
Verne White, President

***KYCI**
01-01-2008; 90.5 mhz FM; 0.395 kw horiz; 1089 ft.; N36 43 32 W120 45 49 *Rebroadcasts:* Rebroadcasts KYCC(FM) Stockton 100%
9019 West Lane, Stockton, CA 95210 US
(209) 477-3690, *Fax:* (209) 477-2762
www.kycc.org
kycc@kycc.org
License: Firebaugh, Fresno County, CA held by Your Christian Companion Network Inc.
Arbitron Metro Market: Firebaugh, CA *Format:* Gospel, Religious
Shirley Garner, President
Shirley Garner, General Manager
Scott Mearns, Programming Director
John Ramos, Promotions Manager
Vanessa Kudenov, Office Manager
Gary Harding, Production Manager

Ford City

KZPE
102.1 mhz FM; kw
12550 Brookhurst St. #A, Garden Grove, CA 92840 US
(714) 636-5040, *Fax:* (714) 636-5042
License: Ford City, Kern County, CA held by Estate of H.L. Charles, Robert Willing, executor
Arbitron Metro Market: Ford City, CA
William Zawila, Operations Dir

Forestville

KSXY
01-01-1996; 100.9 mhz FM; 2.5 kw; 513 ft.; N38 44 8 W122 50 55
3565 Standish Ave., Santa Rosa, CA 95407 US
(707) 588-0707, *Fax:* (707) 588-0777
www.allthehits.fm
License: Forestville, SONOMA County, CA held by Sinclair Telecable Inc.
Group Owner: Sinclair Communications Inc.; (acq 8-3-2001; $3.5 million)
Format: Adult Contemp *Target Audience:* 18-45 *Adv. Rates:* 35; 30; 35; 20
Bob Sinclair, President
Debbie Morton, General Manager

Fort Bragg

KDAC
06-01-1948; 1230 khz AM *Hrs Open:* 24; 1 kw-U, ND1; N39 26 35 W123 46 48 *Rebroadcasts:* Rebroadcasts KUKI(AM)Ukiah 100%
PO Box 77766, Stockton, CA 95267 US
(707) 466-5868, *Fax:* (707) 466-5852
ukiah@bicoastalspots.com
License: Fort Bragg, CA held by Bicoastal Media Licenses, LLC
Group Owner: Bicoastal Media L.L.C.; (acq 9-15-2003; grpsl).
Format: Spanish *Hrs. of News Programming:* news progmg 24 hrs wkly *No. News Employees:* 1 *Target Audience:* 35 plus.
Alan Mathews, General Manager
Kevin Mostyn, Chief Engineer

KOZT
12-05-1981; 95.3 mhz FM *Hrs Open:* 24; 35 kw; 515 ft.; N39 24 24 W123 44 4
110 South Franklin Stree, Fort Bragg, CA 95437 US
(707) 964-7277, *Fax:* (707) 964-9536
www.kozt.com
thecoast@kozt.com
License: Fort Bragg, Mendocino County, CA held by California Radio Partners Inc.
Format: Triple A *Hrs. of News Programming:* news progmg one hr wkly *No. News Employees:* 1 *Target Audience:* 25-49; affluent, educated consumers
Vicky Watts, Chairman
Tom Yates, CEO

***KJCU**
01-01-2004; 89.9 mhz FM; 0.13 kw; 348 ft.; N39 26 35 W123 43 58
3000 W Macarthur Blvd, Santa Ana, CA 92704 US
(866) 466-5989, *Fax:* (714) 979-8916
www.kwtw.org/kjcu.html
recep@kwtw.org
License: Fort Bragg, Mendocino County, CA held by Calvary Chapel of Costa Mesa Inc.
Group Owner: CSN International
Nat'l Network: CSN
Arbitron Metro Market: Fort Bragg, CA *Format:* Christian, Religious, 86
Richard McIntosh, General Manager
Jan Beaty, Programming Director

Fortuna

KNCR
10-31-1966; 1090 khz AM *Hrs Open:* Sunrise-sunset; 10 kw-D; N40 33 30 W124 07 24
Box 109, Eureka, CA 95501
(707) 725-9363, *Fax:* (707) 726-9446
www.lanueva1090.com
mario@lanueva1090.com
License: Fortuna, Humboldt County, CA held by Del Rosario Talpa Inc.
Hrs. of News Programming: News progmg 2 hrs wkly *Target Audience:* 25-54.
Mario Meza, General Manager
Sylvia Meza, General Sales Mgr

KWPT
05-15-1992; 100.3 mhz FM *Hrs Open:* 24; 12 kw; 1894 ft.; N40 25 30.6 W124 6 18.9
1713 Main Street, Fortuna, CA 95540 US
(707) 786-5104, *Fax:* (707) 786-5100
www.kwpt.com
studio@kwpt.com
License: Fortuna, Humboldt County, CA held by KWPT Inc.
Group Owner: Lost Coast Communications Inc.; (acq 5-12-2005; $650,000)
Arbitron Metro Market: Eureka, CA *Format:* Contemporary Hits/Top 40, Adult Contemp *Target Audience:* 30-54; affluent, college educated
Patrick Cleary, General Manager
Jennefer White, General Sales Mgr
Cliff Berkowitz, Programming Director
Gregg Foster, Promotions Manager
Kara Hochner, Promotions Director

Fountain Valley

KJLL(FM)
01-01-1993; 92.7 mhz FM *Hrs Open:* 24; 690 w; Ant 961 ft; N33 36 20 W117 48 35 *Rebroadcasts:* Rebroadcasts KHJL(FM) Thousand Oaks 100%
99 Long Ct., Suite 200, Thousand Oaks, CA 91360
(805) 497-8511, *Fax:* (805) 497-8514
www.927jillfm.com
reception@927jillfm.com
License: Fountain Valley, Orange County, CA held by Amaturo Group of L.A. Ltd.
Group Owner: Amaturo Groups; (acq 1996; $5.5 million)
Nat'l Network: ABC
Population Served: 4,000,000*Format:* Adult Contemp *Target Audience:* 25-54.
Joseph Amaturo, CEO
Robert Christy, General Manager
Aaron Fonesca, Programming Director

Fowler

KALZ
11-07-1980; 96.7 mhz FM *Hrs Open:* 24; 25 kw; 328 ft.; N36 41 42 W119 43 56
600 Congress Ave., Suite 1400, Austin, TX 78701 US
(559) 230-4300, *Fax:* (559) 243-4301
www.alice967.com
info@alice967.com
License: Fowler, Fresno County, CA held by Clear Channel Radio Licenses Inc.
Group Owner: Clear Channel Communications Inc.; (acq 8-30-2000; grpsl)
Arbitron Metro Market: Fresno, CA *Format:* Adult Contemp *Target Audience:* 25-54; women
Paul Wilson, Operations Dir
Jeff Negrete, General Manager
Tony Rainaldi, General Sales Mgr
Paul Wilson, Programming Director
David Abenojar, Promotions Manager
Dave Case, Chief Engineer

KQEQ
07-01-1962; 1210 khz AM
2171 Ralph Avenue, Stockton, CA 95206 US

(559) 233-8803, *Fax:* (559) 233-8871
www.thehmongradio.com
rakradio@comcast.net
License: Fowler, CA held by RAK Communications Inc.
Arbitron Metro Market: Fresno, CA *Hrs. of News Programming:* news progmg 10 hrs wkly *No. News Employees:* 1 *Target Audience:* 13-Senior; Hmong and Lao *Adv. Rates:* 12.10; 12.10; 12.10; 12.10
Dr. Daniel Moua, CEO
Pahoua Moua, General Manager

Frazier Park

KJPG
01-01-1994; 1050 khz AM
P.O. Box 9775, Bakersfield, CA 93389 US
(916) 535-0500, *Fax:* (916) 535-0504
www.ihradio.org
info@ihradio.org
License: Frazier Park, CA held by IHR Educational Broadcasting.
Group Owner: IHR Educational Broadcasting; (acq 11-15-2003; $700,000).
Arbitron Metro Market: Bakersfield, CA *Format:* Religious, Christian
Douglas Sherman, President

Freedom

KPIG-FM
12-01-1987; 107.5 mhz FM *Hrs Open:* 24; 5.4 kw; 338 ft.; N36 50 6 W121 42 22
Mailing Address: 4150 Pinnacle, El Paso, TX 79902 US
Second Address: 1110 Main St., Suite 16, Watsonville, CA 95076-3700
(831) 722-9000, *Fax:* (831) 722-7548
www.kpig.com
frank@kpig.com
License: Freedom, Santa Cruz County, CA held by Mapleton License of Monterey LLC.
Group Owner: Mapleton Communications LLC; (acq 11-16-2001; grpsl)
Nat'l Reps: McGavren Guild
Arbitron Metro Market: Monterey-Salinas-Santa Cruz, CA *Format:* Blues, Country *Target Audience:* 25-54.
Frank Caprista, Operations Dir
Mike Anthony, General Manager
Jodi Morgan, General Sales Mgr
Sybil DeAngelo, Promotions Manager
Tom Hughes, Chief Engineer
Bill Goldsmith, Webmaster

Fremont

*KOHL
09-23-1974; 89.3 mhz FM *Hrs Open:* 24; 0.145 kw horiz, 0.115 kw vert; 407 ft.; N37 32 14 W121 54 14
43600 Mission Blvd., Fremont, CA 94539 US
(510) 659-6221, *Fax:* (510) 659-6001
www.kohlradio.com
kohl@kohlradio.com
License: Fremont, Alameda County, CA held by Fremont-Newark Community College Dist.
Format: Contemporary Hits/Top 40 *Hrs. of News Programming:* News progmg one hr wkly *Target Audience:* 18-34.
Robert Dochterman, General Manager
Tom Gomez, Programming Director

Fresno

KHGE
01-06-1962; 102.7 mhz FM *Hrs Open:* 24; 50 kw; 499 ft.; N36 49 7 W119 30 33
600 Congress Ave., Suite 1400, Austin, TX 78701 US
(559) 230-4300, *Fax:* (559) 243-4301
www.bigcountry1027.com
info@bigcountry1027.com
License: Fresno, Fresno County, CA held by Capstar TX L.P.
Group Owner: Clear Channel Communications Inc.; (acq 8-30-2000; grpsl)
Nat'l Reps: Clear Channel
Arbitron Metro Market: Fresno, CA *Format:* Country *Hrs. of News Programming:* news progmg 20 hrs wkly *No. News Employees:* 1 *Target Audience:* 25-54; women
Jeff Negrete, Operations Dir
Tony Rainaldi, General Sales Mgr
Paul Wilson, Programming Director
David Abenojar, Promotions Manager
Rita Walls, Regional Sales Manager

KGED
01-01-2003; 1680 khz AM
2171 Ralph Ave., Stockton, CA 95206 US
(559) 233-8803, *Fax:* (559) 233-8871
rakradio@comcast.net
License: Fresno, CA held by RAK Communications Inc.
Arbitron Metro Market: Fresno, CA *Format:* Christian, Religious
Albert Perez, General Manager
Paul Kramer, Chief Engineer

KBIF
11-17-1947; 900 khz AM *Hrs Open:* 24; 1 kw-D, DAN; 0.5 kw-N, DAN; N36 41 30 W119 40 46
1000 Olde Doubloon Drive, Vero Beach, FL 32963 US
(559) 222-0900, *Fax:* (559) 222-1573
www.warpradio.com
kbifkirv@aol.com
License: Fresno, CA held by Gore-Overgaard Broadcasting Inc.
Group Owner: Gore-Overgaard Broadcasting Inc.
Nat'l Network: USA
Arbitron Metro Market: Fresno, CA *Format:* Japanese, Korean, 18 *Special Programming:* Sp 6 hrs, Punjabi 16 hrs wkly *Hrs. of News Programming:* news progmg 10 hrs wkly *No. News Employees:* 4 *Target Audience:* 25 plus; Asian adults
Dana Kennon, Operations Dir
Tony Donato, Operations Director

KCBL
06-26-1953; 1340 khz AM; 1 kw-U, ND1; N36 45 51 W119 47 8
600 Congress Ave., Suite 1400, Austin, TX 78701 US
(559) 230-4300, *Fax:* (559) 243-4301
www.foxsportsradio1340.com
info@foxsportsradio1340.com
License: Fresno, CA held by Capstar TX L.P.
Group Owner: Clear Channel Communications Inc.; (acq 8-30-00; grpsl)
Nat'l Network: CNN Radio; Fox Sports *Nat'l Reps:* Clear Channel
Arbitron Metro Market: Fresno, CA *Format:* Sports *Target Audience:* 18-49.
Jeff Negrete, Operations Dir
Tony Rainaldi, General Sales Mgr
Greg Hoffman, Programming Director
Paul Wilson, Operations Manager

*KEYQ
10-14-1957; 980 khz AM *Hrs Open:* 24; 0.5 kw-D, ND1; 0.048 kw-N, ND1; N36 44 28 W119 51 12 *Rebroadcasts:* Rebroadcasts KMRO(FM) Camarillo 100%
2310 Ponderosa Drive, #28, Camarillo, CA 93010 US
(805) 482-4797, *Fax:* (805) 388-5202
www.nuevavida.com
info@nuevavida.com
License: Fresno, CA held by The Association for Community Education Inc.
Arbitron Metro Market: Camarillo, CA *Format:* Religious *Target Audience:* General; Sp-speaking
Phil Guthrie, President
Mary Guthrie, General Manager

*KFCF
06-09-1975; 88.1 mhz FM *Hrs Open:* 24; 2.4 kw; 1900 ft.; N37 4 23 W119 25 51 *Rebroadcasts:* Rebroadcasts KPFA(FM) Berkeley 85%
Mailing Address: PO Box 4364, Fresno, CA 93744 US
Second Address: 1449 N. Wishon Ave., Fresno, CA 93728 US
(559) 233-2221, *Fax:* (559) 233-5776
www.kfcf.org
kfcf@kfcf.org
License: Fresno, Fresno County, CA held by Fresno Free College Foundation.
Arbitron Metro Market: Fresno, CA *Format:* Variety/Diverse *Special Programming:* Southeast Asian languages one hr, American Indian 2 hrs, Sp 5 hrs wkly *Hrs. of News Programming:* News progmg 12 hrs wkly *No. NewsEmployees:* 2 *Target Audience:* General; intelligent, discerning, questioning
Rebecca Caraveo, Operations Dir
Rychard Withers, General Manager
Frank Delgado, Promotions Manager
Rick Flores, Music Director

KFIG
01-01-1938; 1430 khz AM; 5 kw-U, DA-1; N36 50 49 W119 40 46
351 W. Cromwell, Suite 108, Fresno, CA 93711
(559) 447-3570, *Fax:* (559) 447-3579
License: Fresno, Fresno County, CA held by Fat Dawgs 7 Broadcasting LLC
Nat'l Network: ESPN Radio
Population Served: 500,000 *Arbitron Metro Market:* Fresno, CA *Target Audience:* 25 plus.
Joe Pacheco, President
Paul Swearengin, General Manager
Mehhi Honarvar, General Sales Mgr
Nick Washington, Programming Director
Paul Kleinkramer, Chief Engineer

*KFNO
02-12-1992; 90.3 mhz FM; 2.2 kw; 1949 ft.; N37 4 25 W119 25 52
4135 Northgate Blvd #1, Sacramento, CA 95834 US
1-(800) 543-1495, *Fax:* (916) 641-8238
http://www.familyradio.com
familyradio@familyradio.org; info@familyradio.org; international@familyradio.org
License: Fresno, Fresno County, CA held by Family Stations Inc.
Group Owner: Family Stations Inc.
Arbitron Metro Market: Fresno, CA *Format:* Religious *Special Programming:* Children's 10 hrs wkly
Harold Camping, President
Peggy Renschler, General Manager

KWRU
01-01-1937; 940 khz AM; 50 kw-U, DA-2; N36 50 49 W119 39 46
4910 E. Clinton Ave., Suite 107, Fresno, CA 93720
(559) 251-6128, *Fax:* (559) 452-0948
www.radiovidaabundante.com
info@kwruam.com
License: Fresno, Fresno County, CA held by Multicultural Radio Broadcasting Licensee LLC.
Group Owner: Multicultural Radio Broadcasting Inc.; (acq 2-4-2004; grpsl).
Population Served: 180,500 *Arbitron Metro Market:* Fresno, CA *Target Audience:* 25-54.
Arthur Liu, President
Alberto Felix, General Manager

*KFSR
10-30-1982; 90.7 mhz FM *Hrs Open:* 24; 2.55 kw; 66 ft.; N36 48 42 W119 44 43
5201 N. Maple Ave., Fresno, CA 93740 US
(559) 278-2598, *Fax:* (559) 278-6985
www.kfsr.org
kfsrfresno@hotmail.com
License: Fresno, Fresno County, CA held by California State University Fresno.
Arbitron Metro Market: Fresno, CA *Format:* Jazz *Special Programming:* Evening eclectic 24 hrs wkly, *Hrs. of News Programming:* News progmg 2 hrs wkly *Target Audience:* General.
Don Priest, General Manager
Mike Stephens, Station Manager
Kyle Wheeler, Programming Director

KGST
01-01-1949; 1600 khz AM; 5 kw-D, DAN; 5 kw-N, DAN; N36 42 36 W119 50 6
6290 Sunset Blvd, Ste 1600, Hollywood, CA 90028 US
(559) 497-1100, *Fax:* (559) 497-1125
www.espn1600am.com
mginsburg@lotusfresno.com
License: Fresno, CA held by Lotus Communications Inc.
Group Owner: Lotus Communications Corp.; (acq 8-1-85; $1.76 million;
Nat'l Reps: Lotus Entravision Reps LLC
Arbitron Metro Market: Fresno, CA *TV Affiliate:* ESPN *Format:* Sports *Hrs. of News Programming:* news progmg 2 hrs wkly *No. News Employees:* 1 *Target Audience:* 18 plus; Hispanic adults *Adv. Rates:* 30; 25; 25; 15
Howard Kalmenson, President
Daniel Crotty, General Manager

KIRV
10-01-1962; 1510 khz AM; 10 kw-D, DAD; N36 42 42 W119 49 59
1000 Olde Doubloon Drive, Vero Beach, FL 32963 US
(559) 222-0900, *Fax:* (559) 222-1573
www.kirv.com
License: Fresno, CA held by Gore-Overgaard Broadcasting Inc.
Group Owner: Gore-Overgaard Broadcasting Inc.; (acq 4-24-99)
Arbitron Metro Market: Fresno, CA *Format:* Christian, Talk *Target Audience:* 25-54.
Dana Kennon, Operations Dir
Tony Donato, Operations Director

KJFX
05-15-1970; 95.7 mhz FM *Hrs Open:* 24; 17.5 kw; 850 ft.; N36 56 55 W119 29 9
966 East Essex Drive, Fresno, CA 93720 US
(559) 255-1041, *Fax:* (559) 230-0177
www.957thefox.com
License: Fresno, Fresno County, CA held by Wilks License Co.-Fresno LLC.
Group Owner: Wilks Broadcast Group LLC; (acq 6-1-2005; grpsl)
Nat'l Reps: McGavren Guild
Arbitron Metro Market: Fresno, CA *Format:* Classic Rock

Kevin O'Rorke, General Manager
Rob Hasson, General Sales Mgr
Andrea Carter, Programming Director

KJWL

04-29-1994; 99.3 mhz FM *Hrs Open:* 24; 14.5 kw; 344 ft.; N36 44 7 W119 47 9
670 P Street, Fresno, CA 93721 US
(559) 497-5118, *Fax:* (559) 497-9760
www.kjwl.com
License: Fresno, Fresno County, CA held by John E. Ostlund
Nat'l Network: CNN Radio
Arbitron Metro Market: Fresno, CA *Format:* Classic Rock *Target Audience:* 35 plus; upscale
John Ostlund, President
Bruce Campbell, Operations Dir
Mary Lou Gunn, General Manager
Dave Hull, General Sales Mgr
E. Curtis Johnson, Programming Director
Chris Gentile, Promotions Manager
Juanita Stevenson, News Director
LizRay, General Sales Manager
Jim Roberts, Production Manager
Joe Garcia, Traffic Manager
Kaarin Rosso, Business Administrator

KMGV

03-15-1948; 97.9 mhz FM; 2.1 kw; 2005 ft.; N37 4 29 W119 25 52
600 New Hampshire Avenue, N.W., Suite 1200, Washington, DC 20037 US
(559) 490-9800, *Fax:* (559) 490-4199
www.mega979.com
info@mega979.com
License: Fresno, Fresno County, CA held by Peak Broadcasting of Fresno Licenses LLC.
Group Owner: Peak Broadcasting LLC; (acq 3-30-2007; grpsl)
Wire Services: UPI
Arbitron Metro Market: Fresno, CA *Format:* Oldies *Target Audience:* 25-54. *Adv. Rates:* 100; 90; 90; 50
Patty Hixson, General Manager

KMJ

06-01-1925; 580 khz AM *Hrs Open:* 24
600 New Hampshire Avenue, N.W., Suite 1200, Washington, DC 20037 US
(559) 490-5800, *Fax:* (559) 490-5977
www.kmjnow.com
info@kmjam.com
License: Fresno, CA held by Peak Broadcasting of Fresno Licenses LLC.
Group Owner: Peak Broadcasting LLC; (acq 3-30-2007; grpsl)
Nat'l Network: ABC
Arbitron Metro Market: Fresno, CA *Format:* News, News/Talk, 86 *Hrs. of News Programming:* news progmg 44 hrs wkly *No. News Employees:* 13 *Target Audience:* 25-64.
Patty Hixson, General Manager
Joe Mauk, Chief Engineer

KLBN

03-15-1948; 101.9 mhz FM *Hrs Open:* 24; 2.25 kw; 1959 ft.; N37 4 22 W119 25 53
600 New Hampshire Avenue, N.W., Suite 1200, Washington, DC 20037 US
(559) 497-1100, *Fax:* (559) 497-1125
www.1019labuena.com
License: Fresno, Fresno County, CA held by Lotus Fresno Corp.
Group Owner: Lotus Communications Corp.; (acq 11-1-2007; $8.4 million)
Nat'l Reps: Lotus Entravision Reps LLC
Arbitron Metro Market: Fresno, CA *Format:* Tejano *Hrs. of News Programming:* news progmg one hr wkly *No. News Employees:* 1 *Target Audience:* 25-54; adults
Howard Kalmenson, President
Tony Bonnici, Operations Dir
Kevin O'Rourke, General Manager
Vince Cantu, News Director
Rich Smith, News Director

KMJ-FM

12-08-1979; 105.9 mhz FM *Hrs Open:* 24; 2.4 kw; 1959 ft.; N37 4 23 W119 25 51
600 New Hampshire Avenue, N.W., Suite 1200, Washington, DC 20037 US
(559) 490-5800, *Fax:* (559) 490-5878
www.kmj580.com
info@kmjfm.com
License: Fresno, Fresno County, CA held by Peak Broadcasting of Fresno Licenses LLC.
Group Owner: Peak Broadcasting LLC; (acq 3-30-2007; grpsl)
Arbitron Metro Market: Fresno, CA *Format:* Talk
Patty Hixson, General Manager
Lori Garcia, General Sales Mgr
Skip Essick, Programming Director
Chris Miller, Promotions Manager

*KSJV

07-04-1980; 91.5 mhz FM *Hrs Open:* 24; 16 kw; 869 ft.; N36 38 15 W118 56 35
5005 E. Belmont, Fresno, CA 93727 US
(559) 455-5777, *Fax:* (559) 455-5778
www.radiobilingue.org
mail@radiobilingue.org
License: Fresno, Fresno County, CA held by Radio Bilingue Inc.
Arbitron Metro Market: Fresno, CA *Format:* Ethnic *Hrs. of News Programming:* news progmg 11 hrs wkly *No. News Employees:* 5 *Target Audience:* 16-60; Latino
Hugo Morales, CEO
Maria Erana, General Manager
Phil Traynor, General Sales Mgr
Samuel Orozco, News Director
Bill Bach, Chief Engineer

KSKS

01-01-1946; 93.7 mhz FM; 68 kw; 1903 ft.; N37 4 39 W119 26 1
600 New Hampshire Ave., N.W., Suite 1200, Washington, DC 20037 US
(559) 490-9300, *Fax:* (559) 490-5944
www.ksks.com
info@ksks.com
License: Fresno, Fresno County, CA
Group Owner: Peak Broadcasting LLC
Arbitron Metro Market: Fresno, CA *Format:* Country
Patty Hixson, General Manager
Lori Garcia, General Sales Mgr
Mac Daniels, Programming Director

*KVPR

10-15-1978; 89.3 mhz FM *Hrs Open:* 24; 2.45 kw; 1890 ft.; N37 4 25 W119 25 52
3437 W. Shaw #101, Fresno, CA 93711 US
(559) 275-0764, *Fax:* (559) 275-2202
www.kvpr.org
kvpr@kvpr.org
License: Fresno, Fresno County, CA held by White Ash Broadcasting Inc.
Nat'l Network: NPR
Arbitron Metro Market: Fresno, CA *Format:* News *Hrs. of News Programming:* News progmg 52 hrs wkly
Ed Palacious, Chairman
Mariam Stepanian, President
Don Weaver, Production/ operations
Jim Meyers, Station Manager
David Parker, Secretary
Jim moore, Direct of Programme Content
Kristiana Richerdson, Assistant to President/General Manager
Shirin Sohraci, Business Manager
Shrin Sohrabi, Business Manager

KWYE

01-01-1963; 101.1 mhz FM *Hrs Open:* 24; 10 kw; 1076 ft.; N36 55 48 W119 38 27
600 New Hampshire Ave., N.W., Suite 1200, Washington, DC 20037 US
(559) 490-1011
www.y101hits.com
info@y101hits.com
License: Fresno, Fresno County, CA held by Peak Broadcasting of Fresno Licenses LLC.
Group Owner: Peak Broadcasting LLC; (acq 3-30-2007; grpsl)
Nat'l Reps: Katz Radio
Arbitron Metro Market: Fresno, CA *Format:* Contemporary Hits/Top 40 *Target Audience:* 18-49; emphasis on women
Todd Lawley, CEO
Patty Hixson, General Manager
Gina Massenzi, General Sales Mgr
Tim Lyons, CFO
Lori Garcia, National Sales Manager
Chris Miller, Marketing Director
Miggy Santos, Assistant Program Director

KXEX

09-01-1962; 1550 khz AM; 5 kw-D, DA2; 2.5 kw-N, DA2; N36 46 14 W119 55 20
2171 Ralph Avenue, Stockton, CA 95206 US
(559) 233-8803, *Fax:* (559) 233-8871
rakradio@comcast.net
License: Fresno, CA held by RAK Communications Inc.
Arbitron Metro Market: Fresno, CA *Format:* Religious
Ray Carrasco, General Manager
Paul Kramer, Chief Engineer

KYNO

10-01-1947; 1300 khz AM *Hrs Open:* 24; 5 kw-D, 1 kw-N, DA-N; N36 46 14 W119 45 00
1415 Fulton Street, Fresno, CA 93277
(559) 497-5118, *Fax:* (559) 452-0948
www.940espnfresno.com
info@940espnfresno.com
License: Fresno, Fresno County, CA held by John Ostlund and Katrina Ostlund
Population Served: 165,972 *Arbitron Metro Market:* Fresno, CA
Ray Carrasco, General Manager

Ft. Bragg

KSAY

11-01-1988; 98.5 mhz FM *Hrs Open:* 24; 3.5 kw; 453 ft.; N39 28 3 W123 45 34
P.O. Box 2269, Fort Bragg, CA 95437 US
(707) 964-5729, *Fax:* (707) 964-5729
ksayfm@yahoo.com
License: Ft. Bragg, Mendocino County, CA held by Axell Broadcasting.
Arbitron Metro Market: Fort Bragg, CA *Format:* Adult Contemp *Hrs. of News Programming:* news progmg 9 hrs wkly *No. News Employees:* 1 *Target Audience:* 18-49; primarily women
Wade Axell, General Manager

Garberville

*KLVG

01-01-1999; 103.7 mhz FM *Hrs Open:* 24; 11 kw; 2349 ft.; N40 20 5 W124 6 32
1425 North Market Blvd, Suite 9, Sacramento, CA 95834 US
(727) 528-9236, *Fax:* (727) 528-9246
www.klove.com
klove@klove.com
License: Garberville, Humboldt County, CA held by Educational Media Foundation.
Group Owner: EMF Broadcasting
Nat'l Network: K-Love
Format: Christian *No. News Employees:* 3 *Target Audience:* 25-44; female (Judeo-Christian)
Darell Chambliss, Chairman
Mike Novak, President
Eric Allen, General Sales Mgr
David Pierce, Programming Director
Ed Lenane, News Director
Sam Wallington, Engineering Dir
Scott Smith, Music Director
Marya Morgan, ScottSmith
Richard Hunt, News Reporter
Tracy Butler, Traffic Manager

*KMUD

05-28-1987; 91.1 mhz FM *Hrs Open:* 24; 0 kw horiz, 5.5 kw vert; 2602 ft.; N40 7 13 W123 41 31
Mailing Address: PO Box 135, 1144 Redway Drive, Redway, CA 95560 US
Second Address: 1144 Redway Dr., Redway, CA 95560
(707) 923-2513, *Fax:* (707) 923-2501
www.kmud.org
kmud@kmud.org
License: Garberville, Humboldt County, CA held by Redwood Community Radio Inc.
Format: Talk, Variety/Diverse *Special Programming:* Black 3 hrs, ethnic one hr, jazz 6 hrs, Sp 2 hrs, *Hrs. of News Programming:* news progmg 6 hrs wkly *No. News Employees:* 1 *Target Audience:* General.
David Lippe, Operations Dir
Brenda Starr, General Manager
Marianne Knorzer, Programming Director
Terri Klemetson, News Director
Simon Frech, Chief Engineer
Cynthia Elkins, News Coordinator

*KXBC

01-01-2009; 89.1 mhz FM; 1.3 kw vert; 2510 ft.; N40 7 14 W123 41 31 *Rebroadcasts:* Rebroadcasts KEAR-FM Sacramento 100%
Mailing Address: 4135 Northgate Blvd, Suite 1, Sacramento, CA 95834 US
Second Address: 290 Hegenberger Rd., Oakland, CA 94621
(800) 543-1495, *Fax:* (916) 641-8238
www.familyradio.com
info@familyradio.com
License: Garberville, Humboldt County, CA held by Family Stations Inc.
Group Owner: Family Stations Inc.
Nat'l Network: Family Radio
Arbitron Metro Market: Garberville, CA *Format:* Christian, Religious

Harold Camping, General Manager

Garden Grove

KEBN
06-21-1961; 94.3 mhz FM *Hrs Open:* 24; 6 kw; 240 ft.; N33 46 51 W117 53 33
1045 South East Street, Anaheim, CA 92805 US
(817) 522-3143, *Fax:* (818) 729-5683
www.kebnradio.com
advertising@aquisuena.com
License: Garden Grove, Orange County, CA held by LBI Radio License Corp.
Group Owner: Liberman Broadcasting Inc.; (acq 5-15-03; $35 million).
Arbitron Metro Market: Los Angeles
Andrew Mars, General Manager
Daisy Ortiz, General Sales Mgr
Edward Leon, Programming Director
Gustave Aviles, News Director
Shannon Murdock, Chief Engineer

George

KATJ-FM
06-29-1989; 100.7 mhz FM; 0.26 kw; 1549 ft.; N34 36 38 W117 17 18
15650 Seneca Road, Building A, Victorville, CA 92392 US
(760) 241-1313, *Fax:* (760) 241-0205
www.katcountry1007.com
kimjennings@edbroadcasters.com
License: George, San Bernardino County, CA held by EDB VV License LLC.
Group Owner: Frontier Radio Management Inc.; (acq 11-30-2007; grpsl)
Nat'l Network: CNN Radio *Nat'l Reps:* Christal
Arbitron Metro Market: Victorville,CA *Format:* Country *Target Audience:* 25-54; adults *Adv. Rates:* 25-60
Tom Hoyt, Operations Dir
Tim Anderson, General Manager
Kim Jennings, General Sales Mgr
Gregg Thomas, Programming Director

Gerber

KTOR
01-01-2003; 99.7 mhz FM *Hrs Open:* 24; 0.09 kw; 2484 ft.; N40 14 21 W121 1 52
P O Box 1074, Chico, CA 95927 US
(530) 256-2400, *Fax:* (530) 256-3780
ktor@frontiernet.net
License: Gerber, Lassen County, CA held by Sierra Radio Inc.
Nat'l Network: ABC
Arbitron Metro Market: Chico, CA *Format:* Classic Rock
Greg Heller, General Manager
Cari Catron, General Sales Mgr

Geyserville

KXTS
12-01-1993; 98.7 mhz FM; 2.65 kw; 503 ft.; N38 44 8 W122 50 55
2121 Diamond Mountain Ro, Calistoga, CA 94515 US
(707) 588-0707, *Fax:* (707) 588-0777
www.exitos98.7.fm
License: Geyserville, Sonoma County, CA held by Commonwealth Broadcasting LLC.
Group Owner: Sinclair Communications Inc.; (acq 8-3-2001; $5.5 million)
Arbitron Metro Market: San Francisco *Format:* Tejano
Debbie Morton, General Manager
Alex Ballesteros, Programming Director

Gilroy

KAZA
09-01-1957; 1290 khz AM *Hrs Open:* 6 AM-midnight; 5 kw-D, DA2; 0.088 kw-N, DA2; N37 9 48 W121 38 28
355 Twn & Cntry Villiage, San Jose, CA 95128 US
(408) 776-3090, *Fax:* (408) 881-1292
sakes@kazaradio.com
License: Gilroy, CA held by Radio Fiesta Corp.
Arbitron Metro Market: San Jose, CA *Format:* Oldies
Sonia Rodriquez, President
Juan Sidhu, Operations Dir

KBAY
01-01-1970; 94.5 mhz FM *Hrs Open:* 24; 44 kw; 518 ft.; N37 12 32 W121 46 27
600 New Hampshire Ave,NW, Suite 1200, Washington, DC 20037 US
(408) 287-5775, *Fax:* (408) 293-3341
www.kbay.com
djang@nextmediagroup.net
License: Gilroy, Santa Clara County, CA held by NM Licensing LLC.
Group Owner: NextMedia Group Inc.; (acq 12-6-2005; $80 million with KEZR(FM) San Jose).
Nat'l Reps: D & R Radio
Arbitron Metro Market: San Jose, CA *Format:* Adult Contemp *Hrs. of News Programming:* news progmg 4 hrs wkly *No. News Employees:* 1 *Target Audience:* 35-54. *Adv. Rates:* 300; 300; 300; 100
John Leathers, General Manager
Judy Dixon, General Sales Mgr
Dana Jang, Programming Director
Lissa Kreisler, News Director
Michael Stockwell, Chief Engineer

Glendale

KRLA
01-01-1928; 870 khz AM *Hrs Open:* 24
4880 Santa Rosa Road, Suite 300, Camarillo, CA 93012 US
(818) 956-5552, *Fax:* (818) 551-1110
www.krla870.com
License: Glendale, CA held by New Inspiration Broadcasting Co. Inc.
Group Owner: Salem Communications Corp.; (acq 6-23-98; $33.4 million).
Nat'l Network: Salem Radio Network *Nat'l Reps:* Christal
Regional Reps: SRR *Wire Services:* Metro Weather Service Inc.
Arbitron Metro Market: Los Angeles *Format:* News, News/Talk, 86 *Special Programming:* Special Programming 20 hrs wkly, health 2 hrs wkly *Hrs. of News Programming:* News progmg 100 hrs wkly *Target Audience:* 35plus.
Jim Tinker, Operations Dir
Mark Pennington, General Sales Mgr
Craig Edwards, Programming Director
Kristi Charley, News Director
Bill Sheets, Chief Engineer

KSCA
03-01-1951; 101.9 mhz FM *Hrs Open:* 24; 4.8 kw; 2831 ft.; N34 13 26 W118 3 45
3102 Oak Lawn Avenue, Suite 215, Dallas, TX 75219 US
(818) 500-4500, *Fax:* (818) 500-4580
www.univision.com
License: Glendale, Los Angeles County, CA held by HBC License Corp.
Group Owner: Univision Radio; (acq 9-22-2003; grpsl).
Arbitron Metro Market: Los Angeles *Format:* Spanish *Target Audience:* 25-54.
Michelle Hohman, Operations Dir
Victor Camino, General Sales Mgr
Veronica Nava, Programming Director
Tom Koza, Chief Engineer
Haz Montana, Operations Director
Georgia Carrera, Public Affairs Director

Goleta

KMGQ(FM)
01-30-1982; 106.3 mhz FM *Hrs Open:* 24; 250 w; 827 ft; N34 27 55 W119 40 38
403 E. Montecito St., Suite A, Santa Barbara, CA 93101-1759
(805) 966-1755, *Fax:* (805) 650-6172
www.kmgq1063.com
License: Goleta, Santa Barbara County, CA held by Cumulus Licensing Corp.
Group Owner: Cumulus Media Inc.; (acq 3-12-2001; grpsl).
Nat'l Reps: McGavren Guild
Population Served: 350,000 *Arbitron Metro Market:* Santa Barbara, CA *Format:* Adult Contemp, Jazz *Target Audience:* 35-64; upscale, educated, professional, affluent *Adv. Rates:* 30; 30; 30; 10
Nery Reyes, General Manager
Bruce Pollock, General Sales Mgr
Matt Stone, Programming Director
Tammy Myers, Promotions Manager
John Straker, Chief Engineer

Gonzales

KKMC
09-22-1984; 880 khz AM *Hrs Open:* 24
30 E. San Joaquin St., #105, Salinas, CA 93901 US
(831) 424-5562, *Fax:* (831) 424-6437
www.kkmc.com
info@kkmc.com
License: Gonzales, CA held by Monterey County Broadcasters Inc.
Nat'l Network: USA *Nat'l Reps:* Salem
Arbitron Metro Market: Monterey, CA *Format:* Christian, Talk, 74 *Special Programming:* Sp 3 hrs wkly *Hrs. of News Programming:* News progmg 7 hrs wkly *Target Audience:* 25 plus; family oriented *Adv. Rates:* Call for4 rates and Packages
Carl Auel, President
John Dick, General Manager
Lorraine Dick, General Sales Mgr

KHIP
10-25-1990; 104.3 mhz FM *Hrs Open:* 24; 2.6 kw; 509 ft.; N36 40 6 W121 31 9
2000 K Street NW, Suite 600, Washington, DC 20006 US
(831) 658-5200, *Fax:* (831) 658-5299
www.thehippo.com
info@thehippo.com
License: Gonzales, Monterey County, CA held by Mapleton License of Monterey LLC.
Group Owner: Mapleton Communications LLC; (acq 11-16-2001; grpsl)
Nat'l Reps: McGavren Guild
Arbitron Metro Market: Monterey, CA *Format:* Classic Rock
Target Audience: 18-49; upscale, active young professionals
Mike Anthony, General Manager
Jodi Morgan, General Sales Mgr
Kenny Allen, Programming Director
Sybil DeAngelo, Promotions Manager

Grass Valley

KNCO
10-01-1978; 830 khz AM *Hrs Open:* 24
1255 East Main St., A, Grass Valley, CA 95945 US
(530) 272-3424, *Fax:* (530) 272-2872
www.knco.com
info@knco.com
License: Grass Valley, CA held by Nevada County Broadcasters Inc.
Group Owner: Nevada County Broadcasters Inc.
Nat'l Network: CNN Radio; ABC; CBS Radio *Wire Services:* AP
Arbitron Metro Market: Sacramento, CA *Format:* News, News/Talk, 86 *Special Programming:* Christian 4 hrs wkly *Hrs. of News Programming:* news progmg 30 hrs wkly *No. News Employees:* 4 *Target Audience:* 35plus; adults of western Nevada County
Edward Sylvester, Chairman
Bob Breck, CEO
Scott Robertson, President
Tom Fitzsimmons, Operations Dir
Barbara Juneau, News Director
Tim Parish, Chief Engineer

KNCO-FM
09-07-1982; 94.1 mhz FM *Hrs Open:* 24; 0.66 kw; 981 ft.; N39 14 44 W120 57 52
Mailing Address: 1255 E. Main Street, Grass Valley, CA 95945 US
Second Address: 1479 Sanborn Rd., Yuba City, CA 95993
(530) 272-3424, *Fax:* (530) 272-2872
www.mystarradio.com
info@mystarradio.com
License: Grass Valley, Nevada County, CA
Group Owner: Nevada County Broadcasters Inc.
Nat'l Network: Westwood One
Format: Adult Contemp *Hrs. of News Programming:* news progmg 2 hrs wkly *No. News Employees:* 1 *Target Audience:* 25-54; residents of western Nevada County
Tom Fitzsimmons, Programming Director
Hollie Grimaldi-Flores, Promotions Manager

KBAA
05-03-2004; 103.3 mhz FM *Hrs Open:* 24; 0.53 kw; 1102 ft.; N39 14 45 W120 57 56
4880 Santa Rosa Rd, Camarillo, CA 93012 US
(916) 368-6300, *Fax:* (916) 473-0146
www.latino979.com
acadenas@adelantemediagroup.com
License: Grass Valley, Nevada County, CA
Group Owner: Adelante Media Group LLC; (acq 5-12-2006; $500,000)
Arbitron Metro Market: Grass Valley, CA *Format:* Tejano
John Bustos, General Manager

Greenacres

***KAXL**
05-04-1994; 88.3 mhz FM *Hrs Open:* 24; 21 kw; 328 ft.; N35 24 55 W119 14 1
110 South Montclair, Suite 205, Bakersfield, CA 93309 US
(661) 832-2800, *Fax:* (661) 832-3164
www.kaxl.com
kaxl@kaxl.com

License: Greenacres, Kern County, CA held by Skyride Unlimted Inc.
Arbitron Metro Market: Bakersfield, CA *Format:* Religious *Hrs. of News Programming:* News progmg 4 hrs wkly *Target Audience:* 35 plus; women *Adv. Rates:* 25; 25; 25; 20
Dan Schaffer, Operations Dir
Terri Blankenship, Station Manager
Sheryl Giesbrecht, Promotions Manager
Matt Pelischek, Production Director

KRAB
10-01-1991; 106.1 mhz FM *Hrs Open:* 24; 25 kw; 328 ft.; N35 21 33 W118 43 45
966 East Essex Drive, Fresno, CA 93720 US
(661) 322-9929, *Fax:* (661) 716-1616
www.krab.com
A jimbell@clearchannel.com
License: Greenacres, Kern County, CA held by CC Licenses LLC.
Group Owner: Clear Channel Communications Inc.
Nat'l Reps: McGavren Guild
Arbitron Metro Market: Bakersfield, CA *Format:* Rock/AOR
Target Audience: 18-49; predominantly male
Jim Bell, Operations Dir
Ron Fisher, General Sales Mgr
Danny Spanks, Programming Director
Steve Mull, Chief Engineer

Greenfield

KLOK-FM
08-07-1989; 99.5 mhz FM; 30 kw; 640 ft.; N36 27 51 W121 17 52
2905 South King Road, San Jose, CA 95122 US
(831) 373-6767, *Fax:* (831) 373-6700
www.tricolor995.com
tvalenca@entravision.com
License: Greenfield, Monterey County, CA held by Entravision Holdings LLC.
Group Owner: Entravision Communications Corp.; (acq 3-14-00; grpsl).
Nat'l Reps: Lotus Entravision Reps LLC
Arbitron Metro Market: Monterey, CA
Aaron Scoby, General Manager
Tony Valencia, Programming Director
Fidel Soto, News Director
Abraham Trejo, Chief Engineer

KSEA
01-01-1998; 107.9 mhz FM *Hrs Open:* 24; 0.87 kw; 1637 ft.; N36 23 0 W121 25 40
P O Box 62, Keene, CA 93531 US
(831) 754-1469, *Fax:* (831) 754-1563
www.campesina.com
paco@campesina.com
License: Greenfield, Monterey County, CA held by Farmworker Educational Radio Network Inc.
Arbitron Metro Market: Monterey-Salinas-Santa Cruz, CA
Format: Spanish *Target Audience:* 18-54; Hispanic market
Bill Barquin, COO
Francisco Jacobo, General Manager
Maria Barquin, Programming Director

Greenville

***KPJP**
09-15-2004; 89.3 mhz FM; 4.5 kw vert; 2349 ft.; N40 13 59 W121 1 8
P. O. Box 180, Tahoma, CA 96142 US
(916) 535-0500, *Fax:* (916) 535-0504
www.ihradio.org
info@ihradio.org
License: Greenville, Plumas County, CA held by IHR Educational Broadcasting
Group Owner: IHR Educational Broadcasting
Arbitron Metro Market: Greenville, CA *Format:* Religious
Douglas Sherman, President
Lori Erown, General Manager

Gridley

KHHZ
07-06-1979; 97.7 mhz FM *Hrs Open:* 24; 1.5 kw; 1276 ft.; N39 30 18 W121 18 35
1436 Auburn Bloulevard, Sacramento, CA 95815 US
(530) 345-0021, *Fax:* (530) 893-2121
www.khhz.com
License: Gridley, Butte County, CA held by Deer Creek Broadcasting LLC.
Group Owner: Deer Creek Broadcasting LLC; (acq 9-8-2004; grpsl)
Nat'l Reps: Katz Radio
Arbitron Metro Market: Gridley, CA *Format:* Spanish *Target Audience:* 18-49.
Dino Corbin, General Manager
Bill Meyer, General Sales Mgr
Juan Villagrana, Programming Director
Matt Ray, News Director
Mark Miller, Chief Engineer
Heather Welch, Traffic Manager

Groveland

***KXSR**
05-08-1992; 91.7 mhz FM *Hrs Open:* 24; 4 kw; 1591 ft.; N38 3 46 W120 14 45 *Rebroadcasts:* Rebroadcasts KXPR(FM) Sacramento 100%
3416 American River Dr., Suite B, Sacramento, CA 95864 US
(916) 278-8900 (877) 480-5900, *Fax:* (916) 278-8989
www.capradio.org
info@capradio.org
License: Groveland, Tuolumne County, CA held by California State University Sacramento.
Nat'l Network: NPR; PRI
Arbitron Metro Market: Sacramento, CA *Format:* Talk *Target Audience:* General; NPR listeners, eg. professionals, educators & administrators
John Brenneise, Operations Dir
Carl Watanabe, Station Manager
Joe Barr, Director of News and Information
Jeff Browne, Engineering Dir
Jason Buddell, Traffic Director
Mark Jones, Production Manager
Arla Gibson, Director ofDevelopment
Constance Crawford, Director of Marketing & Public Relations

Grover Beach

KURQ
07-04-1984; 107.3 mhz FM *Hrs Open:* 24; 3.5 kw; 1650 ft.; N35 21 37 W120 39 18
966 East Essex Drive, Fresno, CA 93720 US
(805) 545-0101, *Fax:* (805) 541-5303
www.newrock1073.com
info@107therock.com
License: Grover Beach, San Luis Obispo County, CA held by EDB SLO License LLC.
Group Owner: Frontier Radio Management Inc.; (acq 11-30-2007; grpsl)
Arbitron Metro Market: San Luis Obispo *Format:* Rock/AOR *Hrs. of News Programming:* news progmg 8 hrs wkly *No. News Employees:* 1 *Target Audience:* 18-44; emphasis on 25-34 year olds *Adv. Rates:* 18; 18;18; 10
Ron Roy, VP
Rich Hawkins, General Manager
Pattie Wagner, General Sales Mgr
Tristan, Programming Director
Rebecca Crites, Promotions Manager

Guadalupe

KRTO
01-01-1992; 97.1 mhz FM *Hrs Open:* 24; 0.36 kw; 1325 ft.; N34 53 52 W120 35 23
104 West Chapel Avenue, Santa Maria, CA 93454 US
(805) 928-4334, *Fax:* (805) 349-2765
www.mega971.com
mega971@gmail.com
License: Guadalupe, Santa Barbara County, CA held by Emerald Wave Media.
Group Owner: Emerald Wave Media; (acq 5-1-97; $475,000 with KTAP(AM) Santa Maria)
Arbitron Metro Market: Santa Maria-Lom *Format:* Contemporary Hits/Top 40
August Ruiz, General Manager

Gualala

KTDE
08-01-1993; 100.5 mhz FM *Hrs Open:* 24; 6 kw; 669 ft.; N38 49 33 W123 34 12
Mailing Address: P.O. Box 3463, Carefree, AZ 85377 US
Second Address: 38958 Cypress Way, Gualala, CA 95445
(707) 884-1000, *Fax:* (707) 884-1229
www.ktde.com
thetide@mcn.org
License: Gualala, Mendocino County, CA held by Four Rivers Broadcasting Inc.
Group Owner: Four Rivers Broadcasting Inc.; (acq 7-21-2005; grpsl)
Nat'l Network: CBS
Arbitron Metro Market: Gualala, CA *Format:* Adult Contemp, Variety/Diverse *Special Programming:* Gospel one hr wkly *Target Audience:* 30-55.
John Power, CEO
Diana Schmidt, Operations Dir
Paula Power, General Manager

***KGUA**
88.3 mhz FM; 2.8 kw; 787 ft.; N38 49 30 W123 34 19 US
(707) 884-4883, *Fax:* (707) 884-4883
www.kgua.org
License: Gualala, Mendocino County, CA held by Native Media Resource Center.
Arbitron Metro Market: Gualala, CA
Peggy Berryhill, President

Hamilton City

KCKS
09-01-1978; 101.7 mhz FM *Hrs Open:* 24; 0.53 kw; 1099 ft.; N39 56 46 W121 43 17
Mailing Address: US
Second Address: Rt. 1 W. 11th St., Concordia, KS 66901
(530) 345-0021, *Fax:* (530) 894-4837
www.1340foxsports.com
jperry@dcbchico.com
License: Hamilton City, Cloud County, CA held by KNCK, Inc.
Wire Services: National Weather Network
Arbitron Metro Market: Chico, CA *Format:* Sports, Talk
Joe Jindra, President
Jaime Perry, General Sales Mgr

Hanford

KGEN-FM
01-01-1997; 94.5 mhz FM *Hrs Open:* 24; 3.3 kw; 446 ft.; N36 12 16 W119 33 53
323 East San Joaquin St., Tulare, CA 93274 US
(559) 686-1370, *Fax:* (559) 685-1394
kgen@sbcglobal.net
License: Hanford, Kings County, CA held by Azteca Broadcasting Corp.
Group Owner: Azteca Broadcasting Corp.
Arbitron Metro Market: Visalia-Tulare, CA *Format:* Tejano *Target Audience:* 18 plus.
Margreta Hernandez, General Manager
Isabel Duran, General Sales Mgr
Ernesto Gaytan, Programming Director

KIGS
02-01-1948; 620 khz AM *Hrs Open:* 24
6165 East Lacey Blvd., Hanford, CA 93230 US
(559) 582-0361, *Fax:* (559) 582-3981
info@kigs.com
License: Hanford, CA held by Perreira Broadcasting
Arbitron Metro Market: Hanford, CA *Format:* Portugese *Hrs. of News Programming:* News progmg 35 hrs wkly *Target Audience:* 18-49, Portuguese
Tony Vieira, General Manager

KRDA
09-01-1976; 107.5 mhz FM *Hrs Open:* 24; 24.6 kw; 705 ft.; N36 38 12 W118 56 34
500 S. Chinowth Road, Visalia, CA 93277 US
(559) 456-4000, *Fax:* (559) 251-9555
License: Hanford, Tulare County, CA held by Univision Radio License Corp.
Group Owner: Univision Radio; (acq 1-3-2006; $10 million).
Nat'l Reps: Lotus Entravision Reps LLC
Arbitron Metro Market: Fresno, CA *Format:* Adult Contemp
Target Audience: 35-54; high quality FM oriented news/talk listeners *Adv. Rates:* 42; 38; 41; 20
Angela Navarrete, General Manager

Hayward

***KCRH**
04-10-1981; 89.9 mhz FM; 0.018 kw; -135 ft.; N37 38 23 W122 6 16
Po 25555 Hesperian Blvd, Hayward, CA 94545 US
(510) 723-6954
www.kcrhradio.com
kcrhradio@gmail.com
License: Hayward, Alameda County, CA held by South County Community College District.
Arbitron Metro Market: Hayward, CA *Format:* Variety/Diverse, Adult Contemp *Special Programming:* Instructional one hr, pub affrs 5 hrs wkly *Hrs. of News Programming:* News progmg 5 hrs wkly *Target Audience:* 17-35; general
Chad Mark Glen, Operations Dir
Chad Mark Glen, General Manager
Reid Alexander, Programming Director
Jesse Clark, Promotions Manager
Josh Hewitt, News Director

RADIO - U.S.

Healdsburg

KFGY
12-21-1979; 92.9 mhz FM; 2.3 kw; 1949 ft.; N38 45 45 W122 50 24
1410 Neotomas Avenue, Suite 200, Santa Rosa, CA 95405 US
(707) 543-0100, *Fax:* (707) 571-1097
www.froggy929.com
License: Healdsburg, Sonoma County, CA held by Maverick Media of Santa Rosa License LLC
Group Owner: Maverick Media LLC
Arbitron Metro Market: San Francisco *Format:* Country *Special Programming:* Jazz 5 hrs wkly *Target Audience:* 18-44.
Kent Bjugstad, General Manager
Micheal Mitchell, General Sales Mgr
Jim Murphy, Programming Director
Dano, Promotions Manager
Stacy Hoblitzell, Music Director

KRSH
02-01-1996; 95.9 mhz FM; 2.65 kw; 502 ft.; N38 44 8 W122 50 55
126 Mill Street, Healdsburg, CA 95448 US
(707) 588-0707, *Fax:* (707) 588-0777
www.krsh.com
studio@krsh.com
License: Healdsburg, Sonoma County, CA held by Deas Communications Inc.
Group Owner: Sinclair Communications Inc.; (acq 8-3-2001; $2.1 million).
Arbitron Metro Market: Santa Rosa, CA *Format:* Triple A *Target Audience:* 25-49.
Debbie Morton, General Manager
Dan Ethan, Chief Engineer

KNOB
01-01-2002; 96.7 mhz FM; 2.4 kw; 525 ft.; N38 44 8 W122 50 55
P O Box 968, Healdsburg, CA 95448 US
(707) 588-0707, *Fax:* (707) 588-0777
www.967bobfm.com
Bobfm@winecountryradio.net
License: Healdsburg, Sonoma County, CA held by JYH Broadcasting.
Arbitron Metro Market: Santa Rosa, CA *Format:* Adult Contemp
Judy Hughes, General Manager
Nate Campbell, Programming Director
Dan Ethan, Chief Engineer

Heber

KGBA
04-06-1946; 1490 khz AM *Hrs Open:* 24
2925 East Exposition Ave., Denver, CO 80209 US
(760) 357-5055, *Fax:* (760) 357-4168
www.kgba.com
License: Heber, CA held by The Voice of International Christian Evangelism Inc.
Arbitron Metro Market: Heber, CA *Format:* Christian *Target Audience:* 18-49; Hispanic
Douglas Hanson, General Manager
Paul Raine, General Sales Mgr
Noe Diaz, Programming Director

Hemet

KSDT
04-10-1959; 1320 khz AM *Hrs Open:* 24; 0.5 kw-D, DAD; 0.3 kw-N, DA2; N33 44 59 W116 59 53
200 S. a Street, Suite 400, Oxnard, CA 93030 US
(909) 925-1320, *Fax:* (909) 658-4843
www.radioimpacto.org
License: Hemet, CA held by Rudex Broadcasting Ltd.
Arbitron Metro Market: Riverside-San Bernardino, CA *Format:* Christian
John Cooper, President

KXRS
11-09-1963; 105.7 mhz FM *Hrs Open:* 24; 0.17 kw; 1024 ft.; N33 41 17 W116 55 32
200 S. a Street, Suite 400, Oxnard, CA 93030 US
(909) 384-9750, *Fax:* (909) 884-5844
www.radiolazer.com
vb@radiolazer.com
License: Hemet, Riverside County, CA held by Lazer Broadcasting Corp.
Group Owner: Lazer Broadcasting Corp.; acq 2-94).
Arbitron Metro Market: Riverside-San Bernardino, CA
Vicki Bails, General Manager
Salvador Prieto, Programming Director
Armando Gutierrez, Promotions Manager

Hesperia

KRAK
02-01-1990; 910 khz AM *Hrs Open:* 24
320 West College Avenue, Pleasant Gap, PA 16823 US
(760) 244-2000, *Fax:* (760) 244-1198
www.910espn.com
kimberly.maetinez@cbsradio.com
License: Hesperia, CA held by CBS Radio Stations Inc.
Group Owner: CBS Radio; (acq 7-19-2000; $3,537,500 with KVFG(FM) Victorville).
Nat'l Network: ABC
Arbitron Metro Market: Hesperia, CA *Format:* Oldies *Target Audience:* 40 plus.
Tom Hoyt, General Manager
Bill Pettus, Station Manager

Hollister

KXSM
01-01-1979; 93.1 mhz FM; 0.48 kw; 2110 ft.; N36 54 13 W121 13 45
79 Chestnut Ridge Road, Saddle River, NJ 07458 US
(805) 240-2070, *Fax:* (805) 240-5960
License: Hollister, San Benito County, CA held by Lazer Broadcasting Corp.
Group Owner: Lazer Broadcasting Corp.; (acq 7-25-2005; $2.88 million with KXZM(FM) Felton).
Arbitron Metro Market: Monterey-Salinas-Santa Cruz, CA
Alfredo Plascencia, President
Daniel Osuna, General Manager

KMPG
01-01-1966; 1520 khz AM *Hrs Open:* 14
P.O. Box 369, Hollister, CA 95024 US
(831) 722-4477, *Fax:* (831) 637-4031
kmpgradio@netzero.net
License: Hollister, CA held by Promo Radio Corp.
Format: Spanish, Tejano *Target Audience:* 18-49.
Adala Martinez, General Manager
Rafael Meza, Station Manager

***KHRI**
12-17-2000; 90.7 mhz FM *Hrs Open:* 24; 0.17 kw; -364 ft.; N36 52 2 W121 23 58 *Rebroadcasts:* Rebroadcasts KLRD(FM) Yucaipa 100%
1601 Belvedere Rd., 204, West Palm Beach, FL 33406 US
(888) 937-2471, *Fax:* (916) 251-1650
www.air1.com
info@air1.com
License: Hollister, San Benito County, CA held by Educational Media Foundation.
Group Owner: EMF Broadcasting; (acq 11-7-00; $30,000 for CP).
Nat'l Network: Air 1
Arbitron Metro Market: Omaha, NE *Format:* Alternative, Christian *No. News Employees:* 3 *Target Audience:* 18-35; Judeo-Christian, female
Darrell Chambliss, Chairman
Mike Novak, President & CEO
Eric Allen, General Sales Mgr
David Pierce, Programming Director
Ed Lenane, News Director
Sam Wallington, Engineering Dir
Paul Goldsmith, Music Director
Marya Morgan, NewsReporter
Richard Hunt, News Reporter
Larry Moody, Director
Tracy Butler, Traffic Manager
Mitch Barnhart, Director

Holtville

KGBA-FM
08-08-1983; 100.1 mhz FM *Hrs Open:* 24; 6 kw; 328 ft.; N32 48 10 W115 29 54
605 State Street, El Centro, CA 92243 US
(406)243-6758, *Fax:* (760) 352-1883
www.kgba.org
kgba@kgba.org
License: Holtville, Imperial County, CA held by The Voice of International Christian Evangelism Inc.
Arbitron Metro Market: Missoula, MT *Format:* Easy Listening *Special Programming:* Politics 5 hrs wkly *Hrs. of News Programming:* News progmg 3 hrs wkly *Target Audience:* College Students
Chris Justice, General Manager
Mike Leonard, General Sales Mgr
Jon Van Dyke, Programming Director
Dean Imhof, Chief Engineer

Hoopa

***KIDE**
12-01-1980; 91.3 mhz FM *Hrs Open:* 24; 0.195 kw; -1558 ft.; N41 3 51 W123 41 5
P.O.Box 1220, Hoopa, CA 95546 US
(530) 625-4245, *Fax:* (530) 625-4046
www.hoopa-nsn.gov
kide@koopa-nsn.gov
License: Hoopa, Humboldt County, CA held by Hoopa Valley Tribe.
Format: Easy Listening *Special Programming:* Native American 55 hrs wkly, youth 2 hrs wkly, Alternative 10 hrs wkly
Joseph Orozco, Station Manager
Floriene McCovey, Traffic Controller/Announcer
Jay Renzulli, Music Director/Announcer
Marian Mattz, Front Office/Traffic Assistant

Hopland

***KORB**
01-01-2009; 88.7 mhz FM; 0.1 kw vert; -1086 ft.; N38 58 15 W123 6 50
1425 North Market Blvd., Suite 9, Sacramento, CA 95834 US
(707) 526-2765
www.broken.fm
korb@broken.fm
License: Hopland, Mendocino County, CA held by One Ministries Inc.
Arbitron Metro Market: Hopland, CA *Format:* Christian
Keith Leitch, President
Rynie Leitch, General Manager

Hornbrook

KRVC
01-01-2007; 98.9 mhz FM; 1.25 kw; 2484 ft.; N42 5 0 W122 42 0 US
(541) 772-0322, *Fax:* (541) 772-4233
www.hot989fm.com
License: Hornbrook, Siskiyou County, CA held by Opus Broadcasting Systems Inc.
Group Owner: Opus Broadcasting Systems Inc.
Nat'l Reps: Tacher
Arbitron Metro Market: Hornbrook, CA *Format:* Contemporary Hits/Top 40
Dean Flock, General Manager
Brian Fraser, General Sales Mgr

Hydesville

KSLG-FM
04-13-2001; 94.1 mhz FM; 4.5 kw; 1731 ft.; N40 30 3.1 W124 17 8.1
Mailing Address: 1400 Main Street, #104, P.O. Box 25, Ferndale, CA 95536 US
Second Address: 1400 Main St., Suite 104, Ferndale, CA 95536
(707) 786-5104, *Fax:* (707) 786-5104
www.kslg.com
941@kslg.com
License: Hydesville, Humboldt County, CA held by Lost Coast Communications Inc.
Group Owner: Lost Coast Communications Inc.; (acq 11-5-2001)
Nat'l Reps: McGavren Guild
Arbitron Metro Market: Ferndale, CA *Format:* Rock/AOR *Target Audience:* 18-49. *Adv. Rates:* 19; 19; 19; 9
Cliff Berkowitz, Operations Dir
Patrick Cleary, General Manager
Jennefer White, General Sales Mgr
Mike Dronkers, Programming Director
Gregg Foster, Promotions Manager
Kevin Sanders, Chief Engineer
Kara Hochner, PromotionsDirector

Idyllwild

KATY-FM
12-01-1989; 101.3 mhz FM *Hrs Open:* 24; 1.55 kw; 656 ft.; N33 43 31 W116 44 58
2519 Dundee Way, Vista, CA 92083 US
(951) 506-1222, *Fax:* (951) 506-1213
www.katyfm.com
katytraffic@linkline.com
License: Idyllwild, Riverside County, CA held by All Pro Broadcasting Inc.
Arbitron Metro Market: Riverside-San B *Format:* Adult Contemp *Hrs. of News Programming:* news progmg 2 hrs wkly *No. News Employees:* 1 *Target Audience:* 25-49; affluent, upwardly mobile *Adv. Rates:* 65; 65;65; 30
Willie Davis, CEO
Duane Davis, President
Bill McNulty, General Manager

Kevin Watson, Station Manager
Tom Lazar, Programming Director

Imperial

KMXX
09-17-1980; 99.3 mhz FM *Hrs Open:* 24; 6 kw; 302 ft.; N32 54 40 W115 31 40
11900 Olympic Boulevard, Los Angeles, CA 90064 US
(760) 352-2277, *Fax:* (760) 482-0099
www.entravision.com
License: Imperial, Imperial County, CA held by Entravision Holdings LLC.
Group Owner: Entravision Communications Corp.; (acq 7-31-00; grpsl)
Target Audience: 18-49.
Eric Chavez, General Manager

Independence

KSRW
04-12-1996; 92.5 mhz FM *Hrs Open:* 24; 0.87 kw; 2949 ft.; N36 58 38 W118 7 13
P.O. Box 275, Independence, CA 93526 US
(760) 873-5329, *Fax:* (760) 873-5328
sierrawave.net
ksrw@sierrawave.net
License: Independence, Inyo County, CA held by Ms. Benett Kessler
Nat'l Network: CNN Radio
Arbitron Metro Market: Bishop, CA *TV Affiliate:* KSRW TV33
Format: Adult Contemp *Hrs. of News Programming:* news progmg 10 hrs wkly *No. News Employees:* 3 *Target Audience:* 30-65; professionals & retireeswith average to above average buying power
Benett Kessler, CEO/COO
Benett Kessler, News Director

Indian Wells

KAJR
08-25-2007; 95.9 mhz FM; 1.75 kw; 620 ft.; N33 48 4 W116 13 28
Mailing Address: US
Second Address: 441 S. Calle Encilia, Palm Springs, CA 92262
(760) 568-4550, *Fax:* (760) 541-7900
www.959theoasis.com
License: Indian Wells, Riverside County, CA held by A & J Media LLC.
Arbitron Metro Market: Indian Wells, CA *Format:* Adult Contemp
Target Audience: Mostly Adults 45+, about 45% Women, 55% Men.
Arthur Rivkin, General Manager
Ken White, General Sales Mgr
Scott Herman, Digital Manager

Indio

***KCRI**
01-01-1995; 89.3 mhz FM; 3.2 kw; 571 ft.; N33 48 5.7 W116 13 26.9 *Rebroadcasts:* Rebroadcasts KCRW(FM) Santa Monica 100%
1900 Pico Blvd., Santa Monica, CA 90405 US
(310) 450-5183(888) 600-kcrw, *Fax:* (310) 450-7172
www.kcrw.com
mail@kcrw.org
License: Indio, Riverside County, CA held by Santa Monica Community College.
Nat'l Network: NPR *Wire Services:* AP
Arbitron Metro Market: Indio, CA *Format:* News
Mike Newport, Operations Dir
Ruth Seymour, General Manager
Jennifer Ferro, Station Manager
David Kleinbart, General Sales Mgr

KESQ
01-01-1946; 1400 khz AM *Hrs Open:* 24; 1 kw-U, ND1; N33 43 37 W116 15 10
42-650 Melanie Place, Palm Desert, CA 92211 US
(760) 773-0342, *Fax:* (760) 568-3984
License: Indio, CA held by Gulf-California Broadcast Co.
Group Owner: News-Press & Gazette Co.
Arbitron Metro Market: Palm Springs, CA *Format:* Tejano *Hrs. of News Programming:* news progmg 7 hrs wkly *No. News Employees:* 1 *Target Audience:* General. *Adv. Rates:* 30; 25; 22; 12
Martin Serna, General Manager

KJJZ
03-01-1993; 102.3 mhz FM *Hrs Open:* 24; 2.6 kw; 331 ft.; N33 52 14 W116 13 39
P.O. Box 1825, Palm Springs, CA 92263 US
(760) 320-4550, *Fax:* (760) 320-3037
www.102kjjz.com
License: Indio, Riverside County, CA held by R.M. Broadcasting L.L.C.
Nat'l Network: Westwood One *Nat'l Reps:* McGavren Guild
Arbitron Metro Market: Palm Springs, CA *Format:* Jazz, Smooth Jazz *Hrs. of News Programming:* news progmg 3 hrs wkly *No. News Employees:* 1 *Target Audience:* 25-49; Palm Springs baby boomers *Adv. Rates:* 50; 30; 30; 25
Todd Marker, Operations Dir
Hughes Hilles, General Sales Mgr
Jim Fitzgerald, Programming Director
Cary James, Promotions Manager
Jeff Michaels, News Director
Ben Manierre, Chief Engineer

KKUU
04-13-1984; 92.7 mhz FM *Hrs Open:* 24; 4.2 kw; 394 ft.; N33 52 15 W116 13 37
725 Broad St., P.O. Box 936, Augusta, GA 30903 US
(760) 322-7890, *Fax:* (760) 322-5493
info@desertfun.com
License: Indio, Riverside County, CA held by MCC Radio LLC.
Group Owner: Morris Radio LLC; (acq 1998; $4.5 million).
Nat'l Reps: Christal
Arbitron Metro Market: Palm Springs, CA *Format:* Urban Contemporary *Target Audience:* 25-54.
Angela Powers, Operations Dir
Norman Feuer, General Manager
Cos Cappellino, General Sales Mgr
Virginia Nelson, Programming Director
Anthony ""Ant Dog"" Quiroz, Program Director

Inglewood

KRCD
01-01-1959; 103.9 mhz FM *Hrs Open:* 24; 4.1 kw; 387 ft.; N34 0 26 W118 21 54
610 S. Ardmore Ave., Los Angeles, CA 90005 US
(818) 500-4500, *Fax:* (818) 500-4560
www.univision.com
License: Inglewood, Los Angeles County, CA held by Univision Radio License Corp.
Group Owner: Univision Radio; (acq 9-22-2003; grpsl).
Arbitron Metro Market: Los Angeles *Format:* Adult Contemp
Target Audience: 25-44; women, 60% African-American, 30% Hispanic
Haz Montana, Operations Dir
Michelle Hohman, General Manager
Jason Strongin, General Sales Mgr
Amalia Gonzalez, Programming Director
Olga Jaramillo, Promotions Manager
Tom Koza, Chief Engineer

KTYM
02-14-1958; 1460 khz AM *Hrs Open:* 24; 5 kw-D, DA2; 0.5 kw-N, DA2; N34 0 24 W118 21 52
6803 West Boulevard, Inglewood, CA 90302 US
(310) 672-3700, *Fax:* (310) 673-2259
www.ktym.com
gray@ktym.com
License: Inglewood, CA held by Trans America Broadcasting Corp.
Arbitron Metro Market: Inglewood, CA *TV Affiliate:* KAIL(TV) affil
Format: Black, Variety/Diverse *Special Programming:* Japanese one hr, Pol 2 hrs, Russian 2 hrs wkly *Hrs. of News Programming:* news progmg 2 hrswkly *No. News Employees:* 2 *Target Audience:* 18-54.
Gerardo Borrego, President & General Manager
Gary Rehers, General Sales Mgr
Paul Wiren, Chief Engineer
Gary Rehers, Sales Director
Bobby Howe, Public Affairs
Jean Yamashita, Bookkeeper

Inyokern

***KZLU**
01-01-2008; 88.5 mhz FM; 1 kw; 1299 ft.; N35 28 39 W117 41 58
Rebroadcasts: Rebroadcasts KLVR(FM) Middletown 100%
P.O. Box 637, Bishop, CA 93515 US
(800) 877-5600, *Fax:* (916) 251-1650
www.klove.com
License: Inyokern, Kern County, CA held by Educational Media Foundation.
Group Owner: EMF Broadcasting; (acq 9-14-2005)
Nat'l Network: K-Love
Arbitron Metro Market: Inyokern, CA *Format:* Christian
Mike Novak, President
David Pierce, Programming Director
Ed Lenane, News Director
Sam Wallington, Engineering Dir
Marya Morgan, News Reporter
Richard Hunt, News Reporter

Irvine

***KUCI**
10-01-1969; 88.9 mhz FM *Hrs Open:* 24; 200 w; -10 ft; N33 38 41 W117 50 36
Box 4362, Irvine, CA 94612
(949) 824-6868
www.kuci.org
kuci@kuci.org
License: Irvine, Orange County, CA held by Regents of the University of California.
Population Served: 215,529 *Arbitron Metro Market:* Irvine, CA
Barbara DeMarco-Barrett, Operations Dir
Kevin Stockdale, General Manager
Heather McCoy, Programming Director
Lily Colovic, Promotions Manager
Adam O'Neal, News Director
Mike Boyle, Engineering Dir
Elaine Hawkes, ChiefEngineer
Matt Buga, Music Director
Angela Taslakian, Music Co-Director
Michelle Ma, Music Co-Director
Lauren Quijano, Public Affairs Director
Athena Matsudo, Marketing Director
Lily Colovic, Operations Manager

Isla Vista

KSBL
06-01-1981; 101.7 mhz FM *Hrs Open:* 24; 6.9 kw; 389 meters; N34 27 55 W119 40 37
414 E. Cota St., Santa Barbara, CA 41011
(805) 879-8300, *Fax:* (805) 879-8430
www.ksbl.com
License: Isla Vista, Santa Barbara County, CA held by Rincon License Subsidiary LLC.
Group Owner: Rincon Broadcasting LLC; (acq 7-11-2007; grpsl)
Population Served: 89,045 *Arbitron Metro Market:* Santa Barbara, CA *Hrs. of News Programming:* news progmg 2 hrs wkly *No. News Employees:* 1 *Target Audience:* 25-54; women
Keith Royer, Operations Dir
Keith Royer, General Manager
Jack Clarke, General Sales Mgr
Lin Aubuchon, Promotions Manager
Peter Bie, News Director
Andrea Shaparenko, Traffic Manager

Jackson

KTTA(FM)
08-16-1973; 94.3 mhz FM; 4.3 kw; Ant 790 ft; N38 24 10 W120 39 15
500 Media Place, Sacramento, CA 95815
(916) 368-6300, *Fax:* (916) 441-6480
www.lakebuena.com
License: Jackson, Amador County, CA held by Bustos Media of California License LLC.
Group Owner: Bustos Media LLC; (acq 5-12-2006; swap for KKFS(FM) Lincoln)
Population Served: 60,000
John Bustos, General Manager
Juan Gonzalez, Programming Director
Bobby Reynoso, Promotions Manager
Cynthia Sanchez, News Director
Mark Sedaka, Chief Engineer

KGRB(FM)
94.3 mhz FM; 4300 watts; 241 meters; non directional
PO Box 609, Jackson, CA 95642 USA
(916) 368-6300
www.radiogrande.com
License: Jackson, Amador County, CA
Group Owner: Adelante Media Of California License LLC

Johannesburg

KGIL
10-01-1947; 98.5 mhz FM *Hrs Open:* 24; kw
US
(310) 478-5540, *Fax:* (310) 445-1439
www.kmozart.com
kbiscaya@mountwilsoninc.com
License: Johannesburg, Los Angeles County, CA held by Mount Wilson FM Broadcasters Inc.
Nat'l Network: AP Radio *Nat'l Reps:* D & R Radio
Arbitron Metro Market: Los Angeles *Format:* Classical *Special Programming:* Theater 2 hrs wkly

Saul Levine, President
Mike Johnson, Operations Dir
Kane Biscaya, General Sales Mgr

KRAJ
10-01-1998; 100.9 mhz FM *Hrs Open:* 24; 1.5 kw; 1309 ft.; N35 28 38 W117 41 59
632 Glen Court, Ridgecrest, CA 93555 US
(661) 718-1552, *Fax:* (661) 718-1553
www.adelmanbroadcasting.com; www.theheat1009.com
radio@iwvisp.com
License: Johannesburg, Kern County, CA held by Adelman Broadcasting Inc.
Group Owner: Adelman Broadcasting Inc.; (acq 12-28-99; $45,000).
Nat'l Network: Jones Radio Networks
Arbitron Metro Market: Antelope Valley *Format:* Christian *Target Audience:* 18-54.
Robert Adelman, President

Joshua Tree

KXCM
04-01-1965; 96.3 mhz FM *Hrs Open:* 24; 6 kw; 243 ft.; N34 9 15 W116 11 50
P.O. Box 908, Twentynine Palms, CA 92277 US
(760) 362-4264
www.kxcmradio.com
coppermountainbroadcasting@yahoo.com
License: Joshua Tree, San Bernardino County, CA held by Copper Mountain Broadcasting Co.
Nat'l Network: Westwood One; Jones Radio Networks *Nat'l Reps:* Interep
Arbitron Metro Market: Palm Springs, CA *Format:* Country
Gary Demaroney, President
Carol Vaughn, Operations Dir
Gary Demaroney, General Manager
Scott Sear, Promotions Manager

Julian

***KLVJ**
10-23-1991; 100.1 mhz FM *Hrs Open:* 24; 0.11 kw; 2228 ft.; N33 9 33 W116 36 53
1425 North Market Blvd, Ste 9, Sacramento, CA 95834 US
(727) 528-9236, *Fax:* (727) 528-9246
www.klove.com
klove@klove.com
License: Julian, San Diego County, CA held by Educational Media Foundation.
Group Owner: EMF Broadcasting; (acq 1-30-97; $34,168).
Nat'l Network: K-Love
Arbitron Metro Market: San Diego, CA *Format:* Christian *No. News Employees:* 3 *Target Audience:* 25-44; Judeo-Christian, female
Darell Chambliss, Chairman
Mike Novak, President
Fernando Chaidez, General Sales Mgr
David Pierce, Programming Director
Ed Lenane, News Director
Sam Wallington, Engineering Dir
Marya Morgan, News Reporter
Richard Hunt, MaryaMorgan

June Lake

***KWTM**
01-01-2002; 90.9 mhz FM *Hrs Open:* 24; 0.91 kw; 344 ft.; N38 5 14 W119 10 31 *Rebroadcasts:* Rebroadcasts KWTW(FM) Bishop 100%
Mailing Address: 3000 W. Macarthur Blvd, Santa Ana, CA 92704 US
Second Address: 125 S. Main St., Bishop, CA 93514
(760) 872-4225, *Fax:* (760) 872-4155
www.kwtw.org
recep@kwtw.org
License: June Lake, Mono County, CA held by Living Proof Inc.
Format: Christian *Special Programming:* Talk 15 hrs wkly *Target Audience:* Christian Families
Daniel McClenaghan, President
Brian Law, Operations Dir
Robert Branch, Chief Engineer

Kerman

KBHH
03-01-2001; 95.3 mhz FM; 6 kw; 328 ft.; N36 39 40 W120 9 59
Mailing Address: P O Box 62, Keene, CA 93531 US
Second Address: 2502 Merced St., Fresno, CA 93721
(661) 837-0745, *Fax:* (661) 837-1612
www.campesina.net
Achavez@campesina.com
License: Kerman, Fresno County, CA held by Farmworker Educational Radio Network Inc.
Arbitron Metro Market: Bakersfield, CA *Format:* Spanish, Tejano *Target Audience:* 25-54; Hispanic market
Cesar Chavez, General Manager
Cesar Chavez, Programming Director
Maria Urrutia, News Director
Dave Whitehead, Chief Engineer

KOKO-FM
04-16-1990; 94.3 mhz FM *Hrs Open:* 24; 6 kw; 328 ft.; N36 44 29 W120 5 8
7120 Sunset Blvd., Hollywood, CA 90046 US
(559) 292-9494, *Fax:* (559) 294-7041
www.kok94.com
info@kokofm.com
License: Kerman, Fresno County, CA held by Big Broadcasting Inc.
Arbitron Metro Market: Fresno, CA *Format:* Oldies *Hrs. of News Programming:* news progmg 14 hrs wkly *No. News Employees:* 4 *Target Audience:* 18-54; Hispanic men & women
Art Laboe, General Manager
Anna Avila, General Sales Mgr
Paul Mendoza, Programming Director

Kernville

KCNQ
11-01-1985; 102.5 mhz FM *Hrs Open:* 24; 0.13 kw; 1230 ft.; N35 37 21 W118 26 16
Mailing Address: 55 Valley View, Kernville, CA 93238 US
Second Address: 14 Sierra Dr., Kernville, CA 93238
(760) 379-4500, *Fax:* (760) 376-3119
todaysbestcountryonline.com
License: Kernville, Kern County, CA held by Robert J. Bohn & Katherine M. Bohn.
Nat'l Network: ABC
Arbitron Metro Market: Bakersfield, CA *Format:* Country *Special Programming:* Relg one hr wkly *Hrs. of News Programming:* news progmg 18 hrs wkly *No. News Employees:* 1 *Target Audience:* General. *Adv.Rates:* 28; 28; 28; 24
Anthony Bohn, CEO
Robert Bohn, President
Gary Huff, General Sales Mgr
Bob Jamison, Programming Director
Scott Costa, News Director
Jullian King, Traffic Manager
Chris Potter, Webmaster

Kettleman City

***KWDS**
01-01-2006; 89.9 mhz FM; 50 kw vert; 251 ft.; N35 59 42 W119 58 6
P.O. Box 637, Bishop, CA 93515 US
(858) 277-4991, *Fax:* (858) 277-1365
www.horizonradio.org
kwoods@horizonsd.org
License: Kettleman City, Kings County, CA held by Horizon Christian Fellowship
Group Owner: Horizon Christian Fellowship; (acq 5-21-2004; $150,000 for CP).
Arbitron Metro Market: Excelsior Springs, MO *Format:* Christian
Mike MacIntosh, President

King City

***KDRH**
01-01-2001; 91.3 mhz FM; 0.3 kw vert; 75 ft.; N36 16 22 W121 5 2
1601 Belvedere Road, 204, West Palm Beach, FL 33406 US

www.air1.com
info@air1.com
License: King City, Monterey County, CA held by Educational Media Foundation.
Group Owner: EMF Broadcasting; (acq 11-7-00; $30,000 for CP).
Nat'l Network: Air 1
Arbitron Metro Market: Omaha, NB *Format:* Alternative, Christian *Hrs. of News Programming:* News progmg one hr wkly *Target Audience:* 18-25; teen, young adult
Mike Novak, President
David Pierce, Programming Director
Ed Lenane, News Director
Sam Wallington, Engineering Dir
Marya Morgan, News Reporter
Richard Hunt, News Reporter
Tracy Butler, Traffic Manager

KRKC
09-21-1958; 1490 khz AM *Hrs Open:* 24; 1 kw-U, ND1; N36 13 34 W121 7 26
Mailing Address: P.O. Box B, King City, CA 93930 US
Second Address: 1134 San Antonio Dr., King City, CA 93930
(831) 385-5421, *Fax:* (831) 385-0635
www.krkc.com
bill@krkc.com
License: King City, CA held by Radio Del Rey.
Nat'l Network: CBS *Nat'l Reps:* Farmakis; Katz Radio
Arbitron Metro Market: South Monterey County *Format:* Country *Special Programming:* Farm 10 hrs, sports 9 hrs wkly *No. News Employees:* 1 *Target Audience:* 25-54.
Bill Gittler, President
Bill Gittler, General Manager

KRKC-FM
01-30-1989; 102.1 mhz FM *Hrs Open:* 24; 2.6 kw; 1821 ft.; N35 57 6 W121 0 3
P.O. Box B, King City, CA 93930 US
(831) 385-5421, *Fax:* (831) 385-0635
www.krkc.com
bill@krkc.com
License: King City, Monterey County, CA held by King City Communications Corp.
Nat'l Network: AP Radio
Arbitron Metro Market: Monterey-Salina *Format:* Adult Contemp *Hrs. of News Programming:* news progmg 1 hr wkly *No. News Employees:* 1 *Target Audience:* 18-49; men and women
Bill Gittler, President
Jim Barker, Operations Dir
Bill Gittler, General Manager
David Magnum, News Director
Ron Warren, Chief Engineer

KEXA
01-01-1981; 93.9 mhz FM *Hrs Open:* 24; 5.4 kw; 702 ft.; N36 22 48 W121 12 57
Mailing Address: 548 East Alisal Ste A, Salinas, CA 93905 US
Second Address: 548 E. Alisal St., Salinas, CA 93905
(831) 757-1910, *Fax:* (831) 757-8015
wolfhouseradio@yahoo.es
License: King City, Monterey County, CA held by Wolfhouse Radio Group Inc.
Group Owner: Wolfhouse Radio Group Inc.; (acq 8-31-2001; grpsl)
Arbitron Metro Market: King City, CA *Format:* Tejano *Target Audience:* General.
Ramon Castro, General Manager

Kings Beach

KSRN
01-01-1990; 107.7 mhz FM; 0.23 kw; 2867 ft.; N39 18 48 W119 52 59
805 Virginia Street, Reno, NV 89502 US
(775) 324-4819, *Fax:* (775) 324-4832
vickyo@radiolazer.com
License: Kings Beach, Placer County, CA held by Lazer Broadcasting Corp.
Group Owner: Lazer Broadcasting Corp.; (acq 12-12-2003; $2.5 million)
Nat'l Network: ABC *Nat'l Reps:* Katz Radio
Arbitron Metro Market: Sacramento, CA *Format:* Tejano *Special Programming:* Gospel one hr wkly *Hrs. of News Programming:* News progmg 5 hrs wkly *Target Audience:* 35-54; affluent, business professionals *Adv.Rates:* 12; 10; 10; 10
Eduardo Rios, Operations Dir
Vicky Orozco, General Manager
Salvador Prieto, Programming Director

Kingsburg

***KVPW**
01-01-1992; 106.3 mhz FM *Hrs Open:* 24; 16 kw; 420 ft.; N36 26 50 W119 37 10
1425 N Market Boulevard, Suite 9, Sacramento, CA 95834 US
707-528-9236, *Fax:* 707-528-9246
www.air1.com
License: Kingsburg, Fresno County, CA held by Pro-Active Communications-Fresno LLC
Arbitron Metro Market: Fresno, CA *Format:* Christian
Darell Chambliss, Chairman
Gerald Clifton, CEO
Mike Novak, President
Brenda Brown, General Manager

La Mirada

KFSH-FM
04-16-1961; 95.9 mhz FM; 6 kw; 328 ft.; N33 49 53 W117 48 33
50 E. Rivercenter Blvd., Suite 1200, Covington, KY 41011 US
(714) 796-4458, *Fax:* (818) 551-1110
www.thefish959.com
License: La Mirada, Orange County, CA

Group Owner: Salem Communications Corp.
Arbitron Metro Market: Glendale, CA *Format:* Christian *Target Audience:* 18-49.
John Davis, President
Cherie Curry, General Manager

La Quinta

KUNA-FM
08-01-1987; 96.7 mhz FM *Hrs Open:* 24; 0.97 kw; 581 ft.; N33 48 8 W116 13 30
42-650 Melanie Place, Palm Desert, CA 92211 US
(760) 568-6830, *Fax:* (760) 568-3984
www.kesq.com
License: La Quinta, Riverside County, CA held by Gulf California Broadcasting Co.
Group Owner: News-Press & Gazette Co.
Nat'l Reps: Univision Radio National Sales
Arbitron Metro Market: La Quinta, CA *Hrs. of News Programming:* news progmg 25 hrs wkly *No. News Employees:* 1 *Target Audience:* 25-54. *Adv. Rates:* 65; 60; 55; 40
Adolpho Iniguez, Operations Dir
Mike Stutz, General Manager and Corporate Director of News
Alex Silver, General Sales Mgr
Sonia Montano, Programming Director
Bob Smith, News Director
Barry Gorfine, Director of Sales
SusanTruesdale, Business Manager
Catherine Furguson, HR Coordinator
Kent Kay, Creative Services Director
Linda Gaston, Community Affairs Director
Tim Kiley, Assistant News Director

La Selva Beach

KOMY
01-01-1937; 1340 khz AM *Hrs Open:* 5 AM-midnight (M-S); 1 kw-D, ND2; 0.85 kw-N, ND2; N36 57 43 W121 58 51
2300 Portola Drive, Santa Cruz, CA 95062 US
(831) 475-1080, *Fax:* (831) 475-2967
www.1340komy.com
rosie@ksco.com
License: La Selva Beach, CA held by Zwerling Broadcasting System Ltd.
Format: Oldies, Sports *Target Audience:* 25-64; people with an investment at risk in the community *Adv. Rates:* 20; 20; 20; 15
Michael Zwerling, CEO
Ron Stevens, President
Michael Olson, General Manager
Rosemary Chalmers, Station Manager

Lake Arrowhead

KCXX
06-01-1978; 103.9 mhz FM *Hrs Open:* 24; 400 w; Ant 1,797 ft; N34 14 03 W117 08 25
242 E. Airport Dr., Suite 106, San Bernardino, CA 90301
(909) 890-5904, *Fax:* (909) 890-9035
www.x1039.com
License: Lake Arrowhead, San Bernardino County, CA held by All-Pro Broadcasting Inc.
Nat'l Reps: Christal
Population Served: 1,300,000 *Arbitron Metro Market:* Riverside-San B *Target Audience:* 18-49. *Adv. Rates:* 120; 120; 120; 50
Willie Davis, CEO
Bill McNulty, General Manager
Coleen Bambrick, General Sales Mgr
John DeSantis, Programming Director
Monica Alonso, Promotions Manager

Lake Isabella

KQAB(AM)
07-15-1977; 1140 khz AM *Hrs Open:* Sunrise-sunset; 1 kw-D; N35 38 20 W118 28 22
14 Sierra Dr., PO Box 2008, Kernville, CA 93238
(760) 379-5636, *Fax:* (760) 376-3119
License: Lake Isabella, Kern County, CA held by Robert J. and Katherine M. Bohn.
Nat'l Network: ABC
Population Served: 29,000 *Arbitron Metro Market:* Bakersfield, CA *Format:* News, Talk *Hrs. of News Programming:* news progmg 14 hrs wkly *No. News Employees:* 1 *Target Audience:* 40 plus; mature *Adv.Rates:* 11; 11; 11; 8.80
Robert Bohn, President
Anthony Bohn, General Manager
Gary Huff, General Sales Mgr
Bob Jamison, Programming Director
Scott Costa, News Director
Jillian King, Traffic Manager

KVLI(FM)
10-29-1992; 104.5 mhz FM *Hrs Open:* 24; 200 w; 1,260 ft; N35 37 21 W118 26 16
Box 2008, 14 Sierra Dr., Kernville, CA 93238
(760) 376-4500, *Fax:* (760) 376-3119
www.classichitsradioonline.com
License: Lake Isabella, Kern County, CA held by Robert J. Bohn & Katerine M. Bohn
Nat'l Network: ABC
Population Served: 29,000 *Arbitron Metro Market:* Kernville, CA *Format:* Oldies *Hrs. of News Programming:* news progmg 12 hrs wkly *No. News Employees:* 1 *Target Audience:* 25-54. *Adv. Rates:* 28; 28;28; 24
Anthony Bohn, Station Manager
Gary Huff, General Sales Mgr
Scott Cosa, News Director
Bob Jamison, Engineering Dir
Jillian King, Traffic Manager

KRVQ-FM
05-01-2005; 104.5 mhz FM; 0.2 kw; 1260 ft.; N35 37 21 W118 26 16
55 Valley View, Kernville, CA 93238 US
(307) 732-0384
www.923theriver.com
bstphnsn@gmail.com
License: Lake Isabella, Teton County, CA held by Jackson Radio Group Inc.
Group Owner: Northeast Broadcasting Company Inc.; (acq 3-31-2006; $900,000 with KVRG(FM) Victor)
Arbitron Metro Market: Lake Isabella, CA *Format:* Classic Rock
Steven Silberberg, President
Bruce Pollock, General Manager
Shay Richardson, Sales Manager
Bob Stephenson, Operations Mgr/Program Director
Mason Tibbs, Marketing Consultant/On Air

Lakeport

KNTI
10-21-1984; 99.5 mhz FM *Hrs Open:* 24; 2.4 kw; 1919 ft.; N39 7 50 W123 4 32
140 N. Main Street, Lakeport, CA 95453 US
(707) 263-6113, *Fax:* (707) 263-0939
www.knti.com
mwilson@9tbicoastalmedia.com
License: Lakeport, Lake County, CA held by Bicoastal Media L.L.C.
Group Owner: Bicoastal Media L.L.C.; acq 7-28-99; grpsl)
Nat'l Network: CNN Radio
Format: Contemporary Hits/Top 40, Adult Contemp *Special Programming:* Sp 3 hrs, new adult contemp 3 hrs wkly *Hrs. of News Programming:* news progmg 8 hrs wkly *No. News Employees:* 1 *Target Audience:* 25-54;family oriented, upscale, professional adults
Ken Dennis, CEO
Mike Wilson, President
Eric Patrick, Operations Dir
Tony Calumet, General Manager
Alan Mathews, General Sales Mgr
Paul Reading, News Director
Kevin Mostyn, Chief Engineer

KXBX
06-17-1966; 1270 khz AM *Hrs Open:* 24; 0.5 kw-D, ND1; 0.097 kw-N, ND1; N39 0 50 W122 53 39
775 East Blithedale Avenue, #143, Mill Valley, CA 94941 US
(707) 263-6113, *Fax:* (707) 263-0939
www.kxkx.com
mwilson@ncradio.com
License: Lakeport, CA held by Bicoastal Media LLC.
Group Owner: Bicoastal Media L.L.C.; acq 7-28-99; grpsl)
Nat'l Network: Westwood One
Arbitron Metro Market: Lakeport, CA *Format:* Adult Contemp, Oldies *Special Programming:* Sp 3 hrs, loc talk & info 5 hrs wkly *Hrs. of News Programming:* news progmg 4 hrs wkly *No. News Employees:* 1 *TargetAudience:* 40 plus; retirees *Adv. Rates:* 16; 14; 16; 12
Mike Wilson, President
Alan Matthews, General Sales Mgr
Bill Moen, Programming Director
Kevin Mostyn, Engineering Dir
Juan Huerta, Min Affairs Director

KXBX-FM
08-31-1984; 98.3 mhz FM; 4.8 kw; 367 ft.; N39 2 56 W122 46 3
775 East Blithedale Avenue, #143, Mill Valley, CA 94941 US
(707) 263-6113, *Fax:* (707) 263-0939
www.kxbxfm.com
License: Lakeport, Lake County, CA
Arbitron Metro Market: Lakeport, CA *Format:* Adult Contemp
Jerry Del Core, General Manager

*KPFZ-FM
01-01-2008; 88.1 mhz FM; 0.1 kw vert; 2185 ft.; N38 59 23 W122 46 5
P O Box 1494, Lucerne, CA 95458 US
(707) 263-3640, *Fax:* (707) 263-3890
www.kpfz.org
kpfz@mchsi.com
License: Lakeport, Lake County, CA held by Lake County Community Radio Inc.
Arbitron Metro Market: Lakeport, CA *Format:* Talk
Andy Weiss, Operations Dir
Andy Weiss, Station Manager
Tim Hoff, Programming Director
Bill Rett, Chief Engineer
Tee Watts, Music Director
Sandra Wade, Public/Cultural Affairs Director

Lancaster

KAVL
09-08-1950; 610 khz AM *Hrs Open:* 24; 4.9 kw-D, DA2; 4 kw-N, DA2; N34 42 22 W118 10 36
50 E. Rivercenter Blvd., #1200, Covington, KY 41011 US
(661) 942-1121, *Fax:* (661) 723-5512
www.foxsports610.com
info@foxsports610.com
License: Lancaster, CA held by Aloha Station Trust LLC, as Trustee
Nat'l Network: USA
Arbitron Metro Market: Los Angeles *Format:* Sports *No. News Employees:* 2 *Target Audience:* 25-44; predominantly male, commuters, sports fans
Mark Mitchell, Operations Dir
Jim Bell, General Manager
Shaun Palmer, General Sales Mgr

KGMX
10-28-1970; 106.3 mhz FM *Hrs Open:* 24; 3 kw; 135 ft.; N34 44 41 W118 7 30
100 Wilshire Blvd., Suite 1000, Santa Monica, CA 90401 US
(661) 947-3107, *Fax:* (661) 272-5688
www.kmix1063.com
psa@highdesertbroadcasting.com
License: Lancaster, Los Angeles County, CA held by High Desert Broadcasting LLC.
Group Owner: High Desert Broadcasting LLC
Arbitron Metro Market: Los Angeles *Format:* Adult Contemp *Hrs. of News Programming:* News 25 hrs wkly *Target Audience:* 24-54.
Nelson Rasse, General Manager

KOSS
08-01-1956; 1380 khz AM *Hrs Open:* 24
100 Wilshire Blvd., Suite 1000, Santa Monica, CA 90401 US
(661) 947-3107, *Fax:* (661) 272-5688
www.newstalk1380.com
License: Lancaster, CA held by High Desert Broadcasting LLC.
Group Owner: High Desert Broadcasting LLC; (acq 1-21-97; with co-located FM)
Arbitron Metro Market: Los Angeles *Format:* News, News/Talk, 86 *Special Programming:* Local 21 hrs wkly, finance 2 hrs wkly, good day Doug Stephan 4 hrs wkly *Target Audience:* 18-49; homeowners, married couples withdiscretionary income
Gary Wilson, Operations Dir
Nelson Rasse, General Manager
Jeff McElfresh, Promotions Manager
Bob Montague, News Director
Ella Rice, Traffic Manager

*KTLW
07-03-1997; 88.9 mhz FM *Hrs Open:* 24; 5.8 kw; Ant 272 ft; N34 51 03 W118 09 22
14820 Sherman Way, Life On The Way Communications, Van Nuys, CA 91405
(818) 779-8444
www.ktlw.net
ktlwinfo@ktlw.net
License: Lancaster, Los Angeles County, CA held by Life On The Way Communications Inc.
Nat'l Network: AP Network News
Population Served: 4,500,000*Hrs. of News Programming:* News progmg 6 hrs wkly *Target Audience:* 25-54; 50% male, 50% female
Gary Curtis, Operations Dir
Rita Medall, Operations Manager

RADIO - U.S.

Laytonville

*KHKL
01-01-2002; 91.9 mhz FM *Hrs Open:* 24; 0.1 kw; 2372 ft.; N39 41 38 W123 34 43
US
(800) 525-5683, *Fax:* (916) 251-1650
www.klove.com
klove@klove.com
License: Laytonville, Mendocino County, CA held by Educational Media Foundation.
Group Owner: EMF Broadcasting
Nat'l Network: K-Love
Arbitron Metro Market: Laytonville, CA *Format:* Christian *No. News Employees:* 3 *Target Audience:* 25-44; Judeo Christian, female
Darrell Chambliss, Chairman
Mike Novak, President and CEO
Eric Allen, General Sales Mgr
David Pierce, Programming Director
Ed Lenane, News Director
Sam Wallington, Engineering Dir
Scott Smith, Music Director
Marya Morgan, NewsReporter
Richard Hunt, News Reporter
Tracy Butler, Traffic Manager
Laura Daniels, News Reporter
Tim Luttrell, News Reporter

*KVUH
01-01-2005; 88.5 mhz FM; 1 kw vert; 2431 ft.; N39 41 38 W123 34 43 *Rebroadcasts:* Rebroadcasts KSJV(FM) Fresno 100%
4135 Northgate Blvd., Suite 1, Sacramento, CA 95834 US
(559) 264-9191, *Fax:* (559) 455-5778
www.radiobilingue.org
ricardo@radiobilingue.org
License: Laytonville, Mendocino County, CA held by Radio Bilingue Inc.
Arbitron Metro Market: Fresno, CA *Format:* Ethnic
Hugo Morales, CEO
Maria Erana, General Manager
Phil Traynor, General Sales Mgr
Samuel Orozco, News Director
Bill Bach, Chief Engineer

*KLAI
01-01-2006; 90.3 mhz FM; 0.5 kw vert; 2431 ft.; N39 41 38 W123 34 43
Mailing Address: P O Box 135, Redway, CA 95560 US
Second Address: 1144 Redway Drive, Redway, CA 95560
(707) 923-2513, *Fax:* (707) 923-2501
www.kmud.org
kmud@kmud.org
License: Laytonville, Mendocino County, CA held by Redwood Community Radio Inc.
Arbitron Metro Market: Laytonville, CA *Format:* Variety/Diverse
Michael Jacinto, Operations Dir
Brenda Starr, General Manager
Jeanette Todd, Interim Station Manager
Marianne Knorzer, Programming Director
Cynthia Elkins, News Coordinator
Simon Frech, Engineering Dir
Cynthia Click, MusicDirector and Volunteer Coordinator
Beth Comes-Westkamper, Traffic Cordinator
Terri Klemetson, News Coordinator
Dave Smith, Production Assistant
BR Graham, Underwriting Representative

Le Grand

*KEFR
01-11-1985; 89.9 mhz FM; 1.8 kw; 2142 ft.; N37 32 1 W120 1 50
Mailing Address: 4135 Northgate Blvd #1, Sacramento, CA 95834 US
Second Address: 290 Hegenberger Rd., Oakland, CA 94621
(916) 641-8191 (510) 568-6200, *Fax:* (916) 641-8238 (510) 633-7983
www.familyradio.com
kefr@k66.com
License: Le Grand, Merced County, CA held by Family Stations Inc.
Group Owner: Family Stations Inc.
Arbitron Metro Market: Oakland, CA *Format:* Christian, Religious *Target Audience:* General.
Harold Camping, President
Matt Pearce, Operations Dir
Larry Milliken, Station Manager
Craig Hulsebos, Programming Director

Lemoore

KJOP
12-23-1963; 1240 khz AM
15279 Hanford Armona Road, Lemoore, CA 93245 US
(916) 535-0500, *Fax:* (916) 535-0504
www.ihradio.org
info@ihradio.org
License: Lemoore, CA held by IHR Educational Broadcasting.
Group Owner: IHR Educational Broadcasting; (acq 12-22-2000; $125,000)
Arbitron Metro Market: Visalia, CA *Format:* Religious, Christian
Doug Sherman, President

Lenwood

KBTW
04-01-2001; 104.5 mhz FM *Hrs Open:* 24; 1.1 kw; 768 ft.; N34 58 15 W117 2 22 *Rebroadcasts:* Rebroadcasts KXLM (FM) Oxnard 80%
Mailing Address: 1145 Mansiones Lane, Chula Vista, CA 91910 US
Second Address: 125 E. Fredericks St., Barstow, CA 92311
(909) 384-9750, *Fax:* (909) 884-5844
www.radiolazer.com
info@radiolazer.com
License: Lenwood, San Bernardino County, CA held by Lazer Broadcasting Corp.
Group Owner: Lazer Broadcasting Corp.; (acq 10-27-99; 450,000).
Nat'l Reps: Lotus Entravision Reps LLC
Arbitron Metro Market: San Bernardino, CA *Format:* Tejano *Hrs. of News Programming:* News progmg 2 hrs wkly *Target Audience:* 25-54; adult
Vicki Bails, General Sales Mgr
Salvador Prieto, Programming Director
Armando Gutierrez, Promotions Manager
Ralph Jones, Chief Engineer

KIXW-FM
11-01-1994; 107.3 mhz FM; 1 kw; 781 ft.; N34 58 15 W117 2 22
12381 Wilshire Blvd, Suite 105, Los Angeles, CA 90025 US
(760) 256-0326, *Fax:* (760) 256-9507
www.thehighwaystations.com
tim@highwayradio.com
License: Lenwood, San Bernardino County, CA held by KHWY Inc.
Group Owner: KHWY Inc.; (acq 2-18-98; $1,741,444 with KIXF(FM) Baker).
Nat'l Network: CNN Radio; Westwood One
Format: Country
Howard Anderson, CEO
Timothy Anderson, Operations Dir
Judy Robinson, General Sales Mgr
Lance Todd, Programming Director
John Gregg, Promotions Manager
Keith Hayes, News Director
Thomas McNeill, Engineering Dir
Kirk Anderson,Executive Vice President

KHDR
12-20-2002; 96.9 mhz FM *Hrs Open:* 24; 1 kw; 801 ft.; N34 58 15 W117 2 23 *Rebroadcasts:* Rebroadcasts KHRQ(FM) Baker 100%
12381 Wilshire Blvd, Suite 105, Los Angeles, CA 90025 US
(760) 256-0326, *Fax:* (760) 256-9507
www.thehighwaystations.com
highwayradio@highwayradio.com
License: Lenwood, San Bernardino County, CA held by The Drive LLC.
Group Owner: KHWY Inc.; (acq 2-25-2003).
Nat'l Network: AP Radio
Arbitron Metro Market: Lenwood, CA *Format:* Classic Rock, Rock/AOR *No. News Employees:* 1 *Target Audience:* General; travelers on I-15 and I-40
Howard Anderson, CEO
Timothy Anderson, Operations Dir
Judy Robinson, General Sales Mgr
Lance Todd, Programming Director
Kirk Anderson, Executive Vice President

Lincoln

KKFS
11-08-1974; 103.9 mhz FM *Hrs Open:* 24; 6 kw; 328 ft.; N38 52 33 W121 7 30
P.O. Box 232, Yuba City, CA 95992 US
(916) 924-0710, *Fax:* (916) 924-1587
www.1039thefish.com
info@1039thefish.com
License: Lincoln, Placer County, CA held by Golden Gate Broadcasting Co. Inc.
Group Owner: Salem Communications Corp.; (acq 5-12-2006; swap for KTTA(FM) Jackson)
Arbitron Metro Market: Sacramento, CA *Format:* Christian
Dale Hendry, General Manager
Max Miller, Programming Director
Veldon Leverich, Engineering Dir

Lindsay

KZPO
01-01-1999; 103.3 mhz FM; 0.28 kw; 2625 ft.; N36 17 14 W118 50 17
12550 Brookhurst St., #A, Garden Grove, CA 92840 US

members.aol.com/kingradio
kim.novak@cattenlaw.com
License: Lindsay, Tulare County, CA held by Estate of Linda Ware, Cynthia Ramage, executor
Arbitron Metro Market: Lindsay, CA *Format:* Oldies
Susan Crawford, General Manager

Livermore

KKIQ
05-01-1969; 101.7 mhz FM *Hrs Open:* 24; 4.5 kw; 381 ft.; N37 35 42 W121 39 42
142 West Santa Clara St., San Jose, CA 95113 US
(925) 455-4500, *Fax:* (925) 416-1211
www.kkiq.com
License: Livermore, Alameda County, CA held by KKIQ Inc.
Group Owner: Coast Radio Company Inc.; (acq 6-19-98; $9 million)
Nat'l Network: AP Radio
Arbitron Metro Market: San Francisco, CA *Format:* Adult Contemp *Hrs. of News Programming:* news progmg 28 hrs wkly *No. News Employees:* 1 *Target Audience:* 25-54; high income & highly educated adults *Adv.Rates:* 120; 110; 120; 60
John Levitt, General Manager
Jim Hampton, Programming Director
Ted Asregadoo, Promotions Manager
John Higdon, Chief Engineer

*KLVS
09-01-1997; 107.3 mhz FM *Hrs Open:* 24; 8.1 kw horiz; 1611 ft.; N37 49 17 W121 46 49 *Rebroadcasts:* Rebroadcasts KLVR(FM) Middletown, CA 100%
2171 Ralph Avenue, Stockton, CA 95206 US
(707) 528-9236, *Fax:* (707) 528-9246
www.klove.com
klove@klove.com
License: Livermore, Sacramento County, CA held by Educational Media Foundation.
Group Owner: EMF Broadcasting; (acq 9-12-96; $65,000).
Nat'l Network: K-Love
Arbitron Metro Market: Sacramento, CA *Format:* Christian *No. News Employees:* 3 *Target Audience:* 25-44; Judeo-Christian, female
Darell Chambliss, Chairman
Mike Novak, President
David Pierce, Programming Director
Ed Lenane, News Director
Sam Wallington, Engineering Dir
Marya Morgan, News Reporter
Richard Hunt, Marya Morgan

Livingston

*KLVN
01-01-1998; 88.3 mhz FM *Hrs Open:* 24; 7.5 kw; 344 ft.; N37 36 31 W120 39 2 *Rebroadcasts:* Rebroadcasts KLVY(FM) Fairmead 100%
1425 N. Market Boulevard, Suite 9, Sacramento, CA 95834 US
(707) 528-9236, *Fax:* (707) 528-9246
www.klove.com
klove@klove.com
License: Livingston, Merced County, CA held by Educational Media Foundation.
Group Owner: EMF Broadcasting
Nat'l Network: K-Love
Arbitron Metro Market: Merced, CA *Format:* Christian *No. News Employees:* 3 *Target Audience:* 25-44; female (Judeo-Christian)
Darell Chambliss, Chairman
Mike Novak, President
David Pierce, Programming Director
Ed Lenane, News Director
Sam Wallington, Engineering Dir
Marya Morgan, News Reporter
Richard Hunt, Marya Morgan

KSKD
11-01-1984; 95.9 mhz FM; 3 kw; 305 ft.; N37 18 57 W120 43 20
2859 Greer Rd., Ste C, Turlock, CA 95382 US

(209) 883-8760, *Fax:* (209) 883-8769
www.lafavorita.net
ngomez@lafavorita.net
License: Livingston, Merced County, CA held by All American Broadcasting Co.
Nat'l Reps: Lotus Entravision Reps LLC
Arbitron Metro Market: Modesto, CA *Format:* Adult Contemp
Nelson Gomez, President

***KCJH**
01-01-1997; 89.1 mhz FM *Hrs Open:* 24; 13.5 kw vert; 305 ft.; N37 18 57 W120 43 20 *Rebroadcasts:* Rebroadcasts KYCC(FM) Stockton 100%
9019 West Lane, Stockton, CA 95210 US
(209) 477-3690, *Fax:* (209) 477-2762
www.kycc.org
kycc@kycc.org
License: Livingston, Merced County, CA held by Your Christian Companion Network Inc.
Arbitron Metro Market: Stockton, CA *Format:* Adult Contemp, Gospel, 74 *Target Audience:* 35-55.
Kenneth Haney, President
Shirley Garner, General Manager
Scott Mearns, Programming Director
John Ramos, Promotions Manager
Shirley Garner, Executive Vice President
Marina Tahod, Music Director
Vanessa Kudenov, Office Manager
Sharla Ogden, Accounting
Gary Harding, Production Manager

Lodi

KCVR
01-01-1946; 1570 khz AM; 5 kw-D, DA2; 0.5 kw-N, DA2; N38 5 10 W121 12 57
1436 Auburn Boulevard, Sacramento, CA 95815 US
(209) 474-0154, *Fax:* (209) 474-0316
www.entravision.com
info@entravision.com
License: Lodi, CA held by Entravision Holdings LLC.
Group Owner: Entravision Communications Corp.; (acq 7-28-2000; grpsl).
Arbitron Metro Market: Stockton, CA *Format:* Spanish
Walter F. Ulloa, Chairman
Walter F. Ulloa, CEO/COO
Lisa Vela, General Manager
Esperanza Lopez, News Director
Christopher T. Young, Treasurer
Jules G. Buenabenta, Director
Mario M. Carrera, Chief Revenue Officer

KWIN
12-24-1959; 97.7 mhz FM *Hrs Open:* 24; 6 kw; 328 ft.; N38 4 17 W121 15 25
Mailing Address: 6820 Pacific Ave., S#2, Stockton, CA 95207 US
Second Address: 1581 Cummins Dr., Suite 135, Modesto, CA 95358
(209) 476-1230, *Fax:* (209) 957-1833
www.kwin.com
info@kwin.com
License: Lodi, San Joaquin County, CA
Group Owner: Cumulus Media Inc.; (acq 5-9-03; grpsl).
Arbitron Metro Market: Stockton, CA *Format:* Contemporary Hits/Top 40
Joanne Matteri, Operations Dir
Roy Williams, General Manager
Jean Western, General Sales Mgr
Raymond Baca, Chief Engineer

***KCAI**
89.7 mhz FM; 6.8 kw vert; Ant 396 ft; N38 23 01 W121 17 15
2351 Sunset Blvd., Suite 170-218, Rocklin, CA 95834
(916) 251-1600, *Fax:* (916) 251-1650
www.klove.com
License: Lodi, San Joaquin County, CA held by Educational Media Foundation.
Group Owner: EMF Broadcasting
Nat'l Network: K-Love
Arbitron Metro Market: Sacramento, CA
Mike Novak, President

Loma Linda

KCAA
11-01-1964; 1050 khz AM *Hrs Open:* 24
Mailing Address: 19939 Gatling Court, Katy, TX 77449 US
Second Address: 19939 Gatling Ct., Katy, TX 77449
(909) 885-8497, *Fax:* (909) 381-8935
www.KCAAradio.com
info@kcaaradio.com
License: Loma Linda, CA held by Broadcast Management Services Inc.
Nat'l Network: NBC Radio
Arbitron Metro Market: San Bernardino, CA *Format:* News, Talk
Special Programming: Polka, swing era, sports *Hrs. of News Programming:* news progmg 15 hrs wkly *No. News Employees:* 3 *Target Audience:* General. *Adv. Rates:* various
Fred Lundgren, CEO
Jim Hill, Operations Dir
Dennis Baxter, General Manager
Dick Vosper, Chief Engineer
Bill Bruns, Operations Manager
Paul Lane, Production Director

Lompoc

KSMY
01-01-1997; 106.7 mhz FM; 3.5 kw; 879 ft.; N34 44 31 W120 26 46
2100 West Northwest Highway, Suite 1150, Grapevine, TX 76051 US
(805) 925-2582, *Fax:* (805) 928-1544
www.elcompa1067.com
ronroy@edbroadcaster.com
License: Lompoc, Santa Barbara County, CA held by EDB SLO License LLC.
Group Owner: Frontier Radio Management Inc.; (acq 11-30-2007; grpsl)
Arbitron Metro Market: Santa Maria, CA *Format:* Spanish, Tejano
Ron Roy, General Manager
Kathy Mansell, General Sales Mgr
Armando Lopez, Programming Director
Danny Fogle, Chief Engineer

KIDI-FM
01-01-1999; 105.1 mhz FM *Hrs Open:* 24; 3.4 kw; 902 ft.; N34 44 31 W120 26 46
15275 Old Cazadero, Guerneville, CA 95446 US
(805) 928-4334, *Fax:* (805) 349-2765
www.labuena.fm
License: Lompoc, Santa Barbara County, CA held by Emerald Wave Media.
Group Owner: Emerald Wave Media; (acq 7-7-2006; $1.5 million)
Arbitron Metro Market: Santa Maria, CA *Format:* Spanish *Hrs. of News Programming:* news progmg 5 hrs wkly *No. News Employees:* 1 *Target Audience:* 18-45; second generation bilingual Mexican Americans
August Ruiz, General Manager
Sofia Lariz, Regional Sales Manager

KBOX
12-24-1968; 104.1 mhz FM *Hrs Open:* 24; 3.3 kw; 899 ft.; N34 44 30 W120 26 45
P.O. Box 518, Santa Maria, CA 93456 US
(805) 922-1041, *Fax:* (805) 928-3069
License: Lompoc, Santa Barbara County, CA held by AGM-Santa Maria LP.
Group Owner: American General Media; (acq 2-1-2000)
Arbitron Metro Market: Santa Maria-Lompoc, CA *Format:* Adult Contemp *No. News Employees:* 1 *Target Audience:* 25-54.
Rich Watson, President
Emily Stich, General Sales Mgr
luis Diaz, Programming Director
John Bartel, Chief Engineer

KRQK
12-18-1979; 100.3 mhz FM *Hrs Open:* 24; 3.7 kw; 863 ft.; N34 44 30 W120 26 45
296 H Street, Suite 300, Chula Vista, CA 91910 US
(805) 922-1041, *Fax:* (805) 928-3069
License: Lompoc, Santa Barbara County, CA held by AGM-Santa Maria LP.
Group Owner: American General Media; (acq 10-29-99; $1.3 million).
Arbitron Metro Market: Santa Maria-Lom *Format:* Tejano *Target Audience:* 18-49.
Rich Watson, General Manager
Emily Stich, General Sales Mgr
Salvador Ponce, Programming Director

KSMA
05-25-1963; 1410 khz AM *Hrs Open:* 24*Rebroadcasts:* Rebroadcasts KUHL(AM) Santa Maria 100%
P.O. Box 1964, Santa Maria, CA 93456 US
(805) 922-7727, *Fax:* (805) 349-0265
www.rangeradio.com
Shawn@knightbroadcasting.com
License: Lompoc, CA held by Knight Broadcasting Inc.
Group Owner: Knight Broadcasting Inc.; (acq 7-31-2006; $1.2 million with KUHL(AM) Santa Maria)
Nat'l Network: ABC
Arbitron Metro Market: Santa Maria-Lompoc, CA *Format:* News, News/Talk, 86 *Target Audience:* 25-54.
Jeff Williams, General Manager
Shawn Knight, General Manager

***KRQZ**
09-03-2000; 91.5 mhz FM *Hrs Open:* 24; 4 kw; 781 ft.; N34 50 8 W120 24 6 *Rebroadcasts:* Rebroadcasts WUFM(FM) Columbus, OH 60%.
500 East North Avenue, Lompoc, CA 93436 US
(614) 839-7100, *Fax:* (805) 736-2642
www.radiou.com
krqz@trinaz.com
License: Lompoc, Santa Barbara County, CA held by Trinity Church of the Nazarene.
Arbitron Metro Market: Westerville, OH *Format:* Christian *Target Audience:* 12-24 years.
Mark Hostand, Station Manager
Chris Hill, Chief Engineer

***KLWG**
01-01-2006; 88.1 mhz FM *Hrs Open:* 24; 2.5 kw; 1873 ft.; N34 54 36 W120 11 10
P O Box 1241, Lompoc, CA 93436 US
(805) 735-1511
www.calvarychapellompoc.com/radio_ministry.htm
License: Lompoc, Santa Barbara County, CA held by Calvary Chapel of Lompoc.
Arbitron Metro Market: Lompoc, CA *Format:* Religious
Mark Galvan, General Manager
Landon Galvan, Programming Director

Long Beach

KBUE
08-01-1961; 105.5 mhz FM *Hrs Open:* 24; 3 kw; 466 ft.; N33 51 29 W118 13 24
5724 Hollywood Boulevard, Los Angeles, CA 90028 US
(818) 729-5300, *Fax:* (818) 729-5678
www.aquisuena.com
info@lbimedia.com
License: Long Beach, Los Angeles County, CA held by LBI Radio License Corp.
Group Owner: Liberman Broadcasting Inc.; (acq 1995; $13 million)
Arbitron Metro Market: Los Angeles, CA *Format:* Spanish *Target Audience:* 18-49; Spanish speaking adults
Andy Mars, General Manager
Daisy Ortiz, General Sales Mgr
Pepe Garza, Programming Director
Chris Buchanan, Chief Engineer
Xavier Ortiz, National Sales Manager
Luis Hernandez, Regional Sales Manager

***KFRN**
09-19-1977; 1280 khz AM *Hrs Open:* 24
4135 Northgate Blvd, Suite1, Sacramento, CA 95834 US
(562) 427-7773, *Fax:* (562) 427-7723
www.familyradio.com
kfrn@familyradio.com
License: Long Beach, CA held by Family Stations Inc.
Group Owner: Family Stations Inc.; acq 9-19-77)
Nat'l Network: Family Radio *Regional Reps:* David Manzi
Arbitron Metro Market: Los Angeles, CA *Format:* Christian, News *Hrs. of News Programming:* News progmg 70 hrs wkly *Target Audience:* Family spectrum.
Harold Camping, President
Ward Cayot, Operations Dir
Suong Tran, Public Affairs Director

***KKJZ**
01-03-1950; 88.1 mhz FM *Hrs Open:* 24; 30 kw; 449 ft.; N33 47 58 W118 9 43
1250 Bellflower Blvd., Long Beach, CA 90840 US
(562) 985-2999, *Fax:* (562) 985-2982
www.jazzandblues.org
info@kkjz.org
License: Long Beach, Los Angeles County, CA held by California State University, Long Beach Foundation
Nat'l Network: NPR
Arbitron Metro Market: Los Angeles, CA *Format:* Jazz *Special Programming:* Blues 15 hrs wkly *Hrs. of News Programming:* news progmg 5 hrs wkly *No. News Employees:* 1 *Target Audience:* 25-64; educated,opinion leaders, jazz & mus lovers
Mike Johnson, Operations Dir
Stephanie Levine-Fried, General Manager
Michael Levine, Programming Director
Denise Maynard, Promotions Manager

KLTX
01-01-1926; 1390 khz AM *Hrs Open:* 24; 5 kw-D, DA2; 3.6 kw-N, DA2; N33 53 30 W118 11 3

4880 Santa Rosa Rd, #300, Camarillo, CA 93012 US
(805) 482-4797, *Fax:* (805) 388-5202
www.nuevavida.com
info@kltxam.com
License: Long Beach, CA held by Hi-Favor Broadcasting LLC
Group Owner: Hi-Favor Broadcasting LLC; acq 8-4-00; $30 million).
Arbitron Metro Market: Los Angeles, CA *Format:* Religious
Target Audience: 35 plus; mature audience
Mary Guthrie, Operations Dir

Los Altos

KFFG

10-17-1960; 97.7 mhz FM; kw*Rebroadcasts:* Rebroadcasts KFOG(FM) San Francisco 100%
140 East Market Street, York, PA 17401 US
(415) 817-5364, *Fax:* (415) 995-7007
www.kfog.com
kfog@kfog.com
License: Los Altos, Santa Clara County, CA held by KFFG Lico Inc.
Group Owner: Cumulus Media Partners LLC; (acq 1995; $8.25 million)
Arbitron Metro Market: San Francisco *Format:* Classic Rock
Target Audience: 18-49.
Lee Hammer, General Manager
Peter Schwartz, General Sales Mgr
Sheri Nelson, Promotions Manager
Omari Patterson, General Sales Manager
Kelly Ransford, Music Director

*KFJC

12-04-1959; 89.7 mhz FM *Hrs Open:* 24; 0.11 kw; 1844 ft.; N37 19 14 W122 8 29
12345 - El Monte Road, Los Altos Hill, CA 94022 US
(650) 949-7260, *Fax:* (650) 948-1085
www.kfjc.org
info@kfjc.org
License: Los Altos, Santa Clara County, CA held by Foothill Community College Board of Trustees.
Arbitron Metro Market: Los Altos Hills, CA *Format:* Variety/Diverse *Special Programming:* Country 8 hrs, bluegrass 8 hrs, jazz 7 hrs, progsv *Hrs. of News Programming:* News progmg 9 hrs wkly *Target Audience:* 8-80; psychedelic speed freaks, radicals & other social outcasts
Eric Johnson, General Manager
Doc Penzel, Station Manager
Liz Clark, Promotions Manager
Mark Laubach, Chief Engineer
Dale Self
Brian Gilligan, Music Director

Los Angeles

KABC

11-15-1929; 790 khz AM; 5 kw-D, DAN; 5 kw-N, DAN; N34 1 41 W118 22 22
77 West 66th St, 16th Floor, New York, NY 10023 US
(310) 840-4900, *Fax:* (310) 558-5635
www.kabc.com
License: Los Angeles, CA
Group Owner: Cumulus Media Inc.; (acq 6-12-2007; grpsl)
Nat'l Network: ABC
Arbitron Metro Market: Los Angeles, CA *Format:* Talk *Target Audience:* 35 plus; upscale, affluent, college educated
John Davidson, President
Nelkane Benton, Operations Dir
Joe Schwartz, General Sales Mgr
Erik Braverman, Programming Director
Shelley Wagner, Promotions Manager
Norm Avery, Chief Engineer
Pete Dominguez, National Sales Manager

KBIG-FM

02-15-1959; 104.3 mhz FM; 65 kw; 3045 ft.; N34 13 36 W118 3 59
300 Cresent Court, Siute 600, Dallas, TX 75201 US
(818) 559-2252, *Fax:* (818) 637-2267
www.1043myfm.com
License: Los Angeles, Los Angeles County, CA
Group Owner: Clear Channel Communications Inc.
Arbitron Metro Market: Burbank, CA *Format:* Adult Contemp
Target Audience: 25-54.
Bruce Reese, CEO
Tracy Barrios, News Director

KCBS-FM

01-01-1948; 93.1 mhz FM *Hrs Open:* 24; 27.5 kw; 3524 ft.; N34 13 55 W118 4 18
600 New Hampshire Avenue, NW, Suite 1200, Washington, DC 20037 US
(323) 569-1070, *Fax:* (323) 463-9270
www.931jackfm.cbslocal.com
License: Los Angeles, Los Angeles County, CA
Nat'l Network: Westwood One *Nat'l Reps:* Interep
Arbitron Metro Market: Los Angeles, CA *TV Affiliate:* KCBS-TV affil *Format:* Rock/AOR *Hrs. of News Programming:* news progmg 3 hrs wkly *No. News Employees:* 1 *Target Audience:* 25-49.
Mel Karmazin, CEO
Dan Mason, President
Brad West, General Sales Mgr
Jaime Korzenieski, Promotions Manager
Fario Suledian, CFO

KSWD

06-01-1957; 100.3 mhz FM *Hrs Open:* 24; 5.4 kw; 2917 ft.; N34 13 35 W118 3 58
Mailing Address: 33o N. Blvd., Suite 800, Glendale, CA 91203 US
Second Address: 5900 Wilshire Blvd., 19th Floor, Los Angeles, CA 90036
(323) 634-1800, *Fax:* (323) 634-1888
www.thesoundla.com
heysound@thesoundla.com
License: Los Angeles, Los Angeles County, CA held by Bonneville Holding Co.
Group Owner: Bonneville International Corporation; (acq 5-30-2008; $137.5 million)
Arbitron Metro Market: Los Angeles, CA *Format:* Triple A *Target Audience:* 25-54.
Peter Burton, General Manager
Ron Turner, General Sales Mgr
Dave Beasing, Programming Director
Leonard McGee, Promotions Manager

KMPC

09-22-1952; 1540 khz AM
26 West 56th St, New York, NY 90064 US
(310) 452-7100, *Fax:* (310) 452-7880
www.radiokorea.com
rnadel@sportingnews.com
License: Los Angeles, CA held by P&Y Broadcasting Inc.
Arbitron Metro Market: Los Angeles *Format:* Korean
Chris Canning, President

KSPN

02-18-1927; 710 khz AM *Hrs Open:* 24
77 West 66th St, 16th Floor, New York, NY 10023 US
(310) 840-2800, *Fax:* (310) 840-2848
www.espnradio710.com
info@kspnam.com
License: Los Angeles, CA held by KABC-AM Radio Inc.
Group Owner: ABC Inc.; (acq 2-27-95; $17.5 million).
Nat'l Network: ABC
Arbitron Metro Market: Los Angeles *Format:* Sports *No. News Employees:* 2 *Target Audience:* General; famlies and moms
John Davison, President

KFI

04-16-1922; 640 khz AM
610 S. Admore Ave., Los Angeles, CA 90005 US
(818) 559-2252
www.kfi640.com
License: Los Angeles, CA held by Capstar TX L.P.
Group Owner: Clear Channel Communications Inc.; (acq 8-7-2000; grpsl)
Nat'l Reps: Christal
Arbitron Metro Market: Los Angeles *Format:* Talk *Target Audience:* 25-54.
Greg Ashlock, General Manager

KXOL-FM

01-01-1949; 96.3 mhz FM *Hrs Open:* 24; 6.6 kw; 1306 ft.; N34 11 48 W118 15 30
1910 W. Sunset Blvd, Suite 200, Los Angeles, CA 90026 US
(213) 483-5374, *Fax:* (213) 484-8304
www.elsol963.com
info@elsol963.com
License: Los Angeles, Los Angeles County, CA held by KXOL Licensing Inc.
Group Owner: Spanish Broadcasting System Inc.; (acq 10-30-2003; $250 million).
Arbitron Metro Market: Los Angeles *Target Audience:* 18-54.
Raul Alcarcon Jr., CEO
Raul Alarcon Jr., President
Peter Remington, General Manager
Jason Wilberding, General Sales Mgr
Juan Hidalgo, Programming Director
Patty Castor, Promotions Manager

KFWB

03-25-1925; 980 khz AM *Hrs Open:* 24; 5 kw-U, ND1; N34 4 11 W118 11 35
600 New Hampshire Avenue, NW, Suite 1200, Washington, DC 20037 US
(323) 525-0980, *Fax:* (323) 930-8729
www.kfwb.com
License: Los Angeles, CA held by Infinity Broadcasting East Inc.
Group Owner: CBS Radio; (acq 11-13-98; grpsl).
Nat'l Network: CNN Radio *Nat'l Reps:* CBS Radio *Wire Services:* AP; Bloomberg News
Arbitron Metro Market: Los Angeles,CA *Format:* News *Special Programming:* Real Estate 3 hrs wkly, Finance 2 hrs wkly *Hrs. of News Programming:* news progmg 160 hrs wkly
Pat Duffy, Operations Dir
Sean O'Neil, General Sales Mgr
Andy Ludlum, Programming Director
Joe Edward, Promotions Manager
Paul Gomez, News Director
Paul Sakrison, Chief Engineer

KIIS-FM

01-01-1948; 102.7 mhz FM; 8 kw; 2959 ft.; N34 13 36 W118 3 57
50 East Rivercenter Blvd, Ste 1200, Covington, KY 41011 US
(818) 559-2252, *Fax:* (818) 295-6466
www.kiisfm.com
License: Los Angeles, Los Angeles County, CA
Group Owner: Clear Channel Communications Inc.
Arbitron Metro Market: Los Angeles *Format:* Contemporary Hits/Top 40 *Special Programming:* Ryan Seacrest, Dr. Drew
Target Audience: 18-34.
Roy Laughlin, General Manager

KHHT

12-29-1948; 92.3 mhz FM *Hrs Open:* 24; 42 kw; 2910 ft.; N34 13 36 W118 3 57
5900 Wilshire Blvd., Suite 1900, Los Angeles, CA 90036 US
(818) 559-2252, *Fax:* (818) 566-4517
info@hot92jams.com
info@hot92jamz.com
License: Los Angeles, Los Angeles County, CA held by AMFM Broadcasting Licenses LLC.
Group Owner: Clear Channel Communications Inc.; (acq 8-30-2000; grpsl).
Arbitron Metro Market: Los Angeles, CA *Format:* Urban Contemporary *Target Audience:* 18-49; females
Val Maki, General Manager
Mike Marino, Programming Director

KKGO

02-18-1959; 105.1 mhz FM *Hrs Open:* 24; 18 kw; 2887 ft.; N34 13 45 W118 4 4
1500 Cotner Ave., Los Angeles, CA 90024 US
(310) 478-5540, *Fax:* (310) 445-1439
gocountry.am
info@gocountry105.com
License: Los Angeles, Los Angeles County, CA held by Mt. Wilson FM Broadcasters Inc.
Nat'l Network: AP Radio
Arbitron Metro Market: Los Angeles, CA *Format:* Country
Saul Levine, President
Linda Vali, General Sales Mgr
Dave Wagner, Programming Director
Michael Levine, Promotions Manager
Susan Foreman, Promotions Director

KHJ

04-13-1922; 930 khz AM *Hrs Open:* 24
5724 Hollywood Blvd., Los Angeles, CA 90028 US
(818) 729-5300, *Fax:* (818) 729-5678
info@lbimedia.com
License: Los Angeles, CA held by LBI Radio License Corp.
Group Owner: Liberman Broadcasting Inc.; (acq 3-27-90)
Arbitron Metro Market: Los Angeles, CA *No. News Employees:* 1
Target Audience: 18-49.
Jose Liberman, President
Andy Mars, General Manager
Disy Ortiz, General Sales Mgr
Eddie Leon, Programming Director
Lenard Liberman, Executive Vice President

KKLA-FM

01-01-1985; 99.5 mhz FM *Hrs Open:* 24; 10 kw; 2959 ft.; N34 13 26 W118 3 44
Mailing Address: 4880 Santa Rosa Rd, #300, Camarillo, CA 93012 US
Second Address: 701 N. Brand Blvd., Suite 550, Glendale, CA 91203
(818) 956-5552, *Fax:* (818) 551-1110
www.kkla.com
info@kkla.com

License: Los Angeles, Los Angeles County, CA held by New Inspiration Broadcasting Inc.
Group Owner: Salem Communications Corp.
Nat'l Network: Salem Radio Network *Nat'l Reps:* Salem *Wire Services:* Metro Weather Service Inc.
Arbitron Metro Market: Los Angeles, CA *Format:* Christian *Target Audience:* 25-55.
Jim Tinker, Operations Dir
Terry Fahy, General Manager
Bill Price, General Sales Mgr
Chuck Tyler, Programming Director
Larry Marino, Operations Director

KLAC
01-01-1924; 570 khz AM *Hrs Open:* 24; 5 kw-D, DAN; 5 kw-N, DAN; N34 4 11 W118 11 36
433 E. Las Colina Blvd, #1130, Irving, TX 75039 US
(818) 559-2252
www.xtrasportsradio.com
info@klacam.com
License: Los Angeles, CA held by AMFM Broadcasting Licenses LLC.
Group Owner: Clear Channel Communications Inc.; (acq 8-30-2000; grpsl).
Arbitron Metro Market: Los Angeles, CA *Format:* Sports *Target Audience:* 35-54.
Mark Austin Thomas, Operations Dir
Ed Krampf, General Manager
Jeff Thomas, General Sales Mgr
Robin Bertoluci, Programming Director
V. Freeman, Promotions Manager
Chris Little, News Director
John Paoli, Engineering Dir
BillLewis, Marketing Director

KLOS
12-30-1947; 95.5 mhz FM; 61 kw; 3130 ft.; N34 13 37 W118 3 58
77 West 66th St., 16th Floor, New York, NY 10023 US
(310) 840-4800, *Fax:* (310) 558-7685
www.955klos.com
john.h.davison@citcomm.com
License: Los Angeles, Los Angeles County, CA
Group Owner: Cumulus Media Inc.
Arbitron Metro Market: Los Angeles, CA *Format:* Classic Rock
John Davison, General Manager
Leonard Madrid, General Sales Mgr
Rita Wilde, Programming Director
Norm Avery, Engineering Dir
C.W. West, Advertising Director
Jim Villanueva

KLVE
05-02-1959; 107.5 mhz FM *Hrs Open:* 24; 29.5 kw; 2999 ft.; N34 13 44 W118 4 2
3102 Oak Lawn Avenue, Suite 215, Dallas, TX 75219 US
(818) 500-4500, *Fax:* (818) 500-4480
www.iloveklove.univision.com
License: Los Angeles, Los Angeles County, CA
Group Owner: Univision Radio
Wire Services: Reuters
Arbitron Metro Market: Los Angeles, CA *Format:* Adult Contemp *Target Audience:* 18-49.
Make Montana, COO
Georgia Carrera, Operations Dir
Jason Strongin, General Sales Mgr
Maria Nava, Programming Director
Olga Jaramillo, Marketing Director

KNX
09-10-1920; 1070 khz AM *Hrs Open:* 24; 50 kw-U, ND1; N33 51 35 W118 20 56
600 New Hampshire Avenue, NW, Suite 1200, Washington, DC 20037 US
(323) 569-1070, *Fax:* (323) 930-8798
www.knx1070.com
License: Los Angeles, CA held by CBS Radio East Inc.
Group Owner: CBS Radio; (acq 9-36).
Nat'l Network: CBS *Nat'l Reps:* CBS Radio *Wire Services:* Reuters
Arbitron Metro Market: Los Angeles *Format:* News *No. News Employees:* 40 *Target Audience:* General.
Pat Duffy, Operations Dir
Rosemary Hernadez, General Sales Mgr
David Hall, Programming Director
Howard Freshman, Promotions Manager
Julie Chin, News Director
Paul Sakrison, Chief Engineer
Amanda Arrington, National SalesManager
Dick Helton, Political Ed
Vivian Porter, Public Affairs Director
Terri Boysaw, Traffic Manager

KOST
10-09-1957; 103.5 mhz FM; 12.5 kw; 3114 ft.; N34 13 32 W118 3 52
610 S. Ardmore Avenue, Los Angeles, CA 90005 US
(818) 559-2252, *Fax:* (818) 637-2267
www.kost1035.com
License: Los Angeles, Los Angeles County, CA held by AMFM Broadcasting Licenses LLC.
Group Owner: Clear Channel Communications Inc.
Arbitron Metro Market: Los Angeles *Format:* Adult Contemp
Craig Rossi, Station Manager
Stella Schwartz, Programming Director

*KPFK
07-26-1959; 90.7 mhz FM *Hrs Open:* 24; 110 kw; 2831 ft.; N34 13 45 W118 4 3
3729 Cahuenga Blvd West, North Hollywood, CA 91604 US
(818) 985-2711, *Fax:* (818) 763-7526
www.kpfk.org
gm@kpfk.org
License: Los Angeles, Los Angeles County, CA held by Pacifica Foundation.
Group Owner: Pacifica Foundation Inc.
Wire Services: AP; Catholic News Service; Reuters
Arbitron Metro Market: Los Angeles *Format:* News, News/Talk, 86, Variety/Diverse *Special Programming:* Children one hr, jazz 5 hrs, gospel 2 hrs, Sp 15 hrs wkly *Hrs. of News Programming:* news progmg 11 hrs wkly *No.News Employees:* 4 *Target Audience:* 25-55.
Zuberi Fields, Operations Dir
Eva Georgia, Station Manager
Sue Welsh, General Sales Mgr
Armando Gudino, Programming Director
Molly Paige, News Director
Fernando Velasquez, News Director

KPWR
12-20-1956; 105.9 mhz FM *Hrs Open:* 24; 25 kw; 3035 ft.; N34 13 38 W118 4 0
3500 West Olive Avenue, Suite 300, Burbank, CA 91505 US
(818) 953-4200, *Fax:* (818) 848-0961
www.power106.com
power106info@power106.com
License: Los Angeles, Los Angeles County, CA held by Emmis Radio License LLC.
Group Owner: Emmis Communications Corp.; (acq 1-84; grpsl;
Nat'l Reps: D & R Radio
Arbitron Metro Market: Greater Los Angeles *Format:* Contemporary Hits/Top 40 *Target Audience:* 18-34; males
Val Maki, Operations Dir
Janet Brainin, General Sales Mgr
Jimmy Steal, Programming Director
Dianna Jason, Promotions Manager
Dennis Martin, Chief Engineer

KRTH
01-01-1941; 101.1 mhz FM; 51 kw; 3133 ft.; N34 13 38 W118 4 0
600 New Hampshire Ave., N.W., Suite 1200, Washington, DC 20037 US
(323) 936-5784, *Fax:* (323) 464-6101
www.kearth101.com
License: Los Angeles, Los Angeles County, CA held by Infinity Broadcasting East Inc.
Group Owner: CBS Radio; (acq 2-2-94; $116 million;
Nat'l Network: AP Network News *Nat'l Reps:* CBS Radio
Arbitron Metro Market: Los Angeles, CA *TV Affiliate:* KCBS-TV affil *Format:* Oldies *Target Audience:* 25-64.
Maureen Lesourd, Operations Dir
Steve Carver, General Manager
Amber Perry, General Sales Mgr
Jahni Kaye, Programming Director
Karen Tobin, Promotions Manager
Lynn Duke, Chief Engineer

KTNQ
01-01-1925; 1020 khz AM *Hrs Open:* 24; 50 kw-D, DA2; 50 kw-N, DA2; N34 2 0 W117 59 0
3102 Oak Lawn Avenue, Suite 215, Dallas, TX 75219 US
(818) 500-4500, *Fax:* (818) 500-4307
www.ktnq.com
License: Los Angeles, CA held by KTNQ-AM License Corp.
Group Owner: Univision Radio; (acq 9-22-2003; grpsl).
Wire Services: Reuters
Arbitron Metro Market: Los Angeles *Format:* News, News/Talk, 86 *Target Audience:* 25-54.
Haz Montana, Operations Dir
Michelle Hohman, General Manager
Eric Osuna, General Sales Mgr
Santiago Nieto, Programming Director
Offad Vallejo, Promotions Manager

KTWV
03-07-1961; 94.7 mhz FM *Hrs Open:* 24; 52 kw; 2831 ft.; N34 13 29 W118 3 47
600 New Hampshire Avenue, NW, Suite 1200, Washington, DC 20037 US
(323) 937-9283, *Fax:* (323) 634-0947
www.947wave.com
wave@947thewave.com?subject=E-Mail%20For%20Promotions%20Department
License: Los Angeles, Los Angeles County, CA held by Infinity Broadcasting East Inc.
Group Owner: CBS Radio; (acq 11-13-98; grpsl).
Arbitron Metro Market: Los Angeles, CA *Format:* Jazz, Smooth Jazz *Target Audience:* 25-54.
Bob Moore, Operations Dir
Steve Carver, General Manager
John Bassanelli, General Sales Mgr
Jhani Kaye, Programming Director
Patty Pastor, Promotions Manager
Lynn Duke, Chief Engineer
Paul Ciliano, Assistant Program Director/MusicDirector
Ron Turner, Local Sales Manager
Adam Bookbinder, Web Content Manager

*KUSC
10-24-1946; 91.5 mhz FM *Hrs Open:* 24; 39 kw; 2923 ft.; N34 12 48 W118 3 41
Mailing Address: P. O. Box 77913, Los Angeles, CA 90007 US
Second Address: 515 S. Figueroa St., Suite 2050, Los Angeles, CA 90071
(213) 225-7400, *Fax:* (213) 225-7410
www.kusc.org
kusc@kusc.org
License: Los Angeles, Los Angeles County, CA held by University of Southern California.
Nat'l Network: PRI; NPR
Arbitron Metro Market: Los Angeles, CA *Format:* Talk *Target Audience:* 35 plus.
Brenda Barnes, President
Steve Coghill, Operations Dir
Eric DeWeese, General Manager
Janet McIntyre, General Sales Mgr
Bill Lueth, Programming Director
Ron Thompson, Engineering Dir
Amy Iwata, Office Manager
Rina Romero, Sr.Business Manager
Gail Eichenthal, Executive Director of Arts Programming
Brian Lauritzen, Producer
James Paisley, Music Director
Bill Kappelman, Director of Compliance

KWKW
04-14-1931; 1330 khz AM *Hrs Open:* 24
6290 Sunset Blvd, Ste 1600, Hollywood, CA 90028 US
(323) 851-5959, *Fax:* (323) 461-7347
www.radiodeportes.com
kwkw1330@aol.com
License: Los Angeles, CA held by Lotus Communications Corp.
Group Owner: Lotus Communications Corp.; (acq 1962)
Nat'l Reps: Lotus Entravision Reps LLC
Arbitron Metro Market: Los Angeles, CA *Format:* Sports *No. News Employees:* 30 *Target Audience:* 18-34 and 25 -54 males
Adv. Rates: upon request
Jim Kalmenson, President
Mike Addison, General Sales Mgr
Juan Rodriguez, Programming Director

*KXLU
02-01-1957; 88.9 mhz FM *Hrs Open:* 24; 2.9 kw horiz; 10 ft.; N33 58 16 W118 24 56
7900 Loyola Blvd, Los Angeles, CA 90045 US
(310) 338-2866(310) 338-5958, *Fax:* (310) 338-5959
www.kxlu.com
kxlu889fm@hotmail.com
License: Los Angeles, Los Angeles County, CA held by Loyola Marymount University Board of Trustees.
Arbitron Metro Market: Los Angeles, CA *Special Programming:* Black 10 hrs, Children one hr, folk one hr wkly *Hrs. of News Programming:* News progmg 2 hrs wkly *Target Audience:* 16-30.
Bennett Kongon, General Manager
Marcel Borbon, Programming Director
Mukta Mohan, Promotions Manager
Maki Tamura, Chief Engineer
Domenico DeCaro, Music Director
Robert Cifuentes, Production Director
Yolanda McClamb, Fine ArtsDirector
Lydia Ammossow, KXLU Advicer

KTLK
01-01-1927; 1150 khz AM

50 E. Rivercenter Blvd, Suite 1200, Covington, KY 41011 US
(818) 559-2252
License: Los Angeles, CA held by Citicasters Licenses L.P.
Group Owner: Clear Channel Communications Inc.; (acq 5-4-99; grpsl).
Arbitron Metro Market: Burbank, CA *Format:* Alternative, Talk
Greg Ashlock, General Manager
Don Martin, Station Manager

KYPA
01-01-1926; 1230 khz AM *Hrs Open:* 24; 1 kw-U, ND1; N34 2 15 W118 16 35
449 Broadway, New York, NY 10013 US
(213) 487-1300, *Fax:* (213) 251-2017
www.radiokorea.com
info@radiokorea.com
License: Los Angeles, CA held by Multicultural Radio Broadcasting Licensee LLC.
Group Owner: Multicultural Radio Broadcasting Inc.; (acq 2-20-98; grpsl).
Nat'l Network: ABC
Arbitron Metro Market: Los Angeles, CA *Format:* Korean
David Sweeney, General Manager

KYSR
06-30-1954; 98.7 mhz FM *Hrs Open:* 24; 75 kw; 1181 ft.; N34 7 8 W118 23 30
433 E. Las Colinas Blvd, #1130, Irving, TX 75039 US
(818) 559-2252, *Fax:* (818) 566-4517
www.987fm.com/
starprogramming@clearchannel.com
License: Los Angeles, Los Angeles County, CA held by AMFM Broadcasting Licenses LLC.
Group Owner: Clear Channel Communications Inc.; (acq 8-30-2000; grpsl).
Arbitron Metro Market: Los Angeles, CA *Format:* Adult Contemp *Special Programming:* Pub affrs 2 hrs wkly *Target Audience:* 25-54.
Greg Ashlock, General Manager

Los Banos

KLBS
05-01-1961; 1330 khz AM *Hrs Open:* 24 hrs. a day; 0.42 kw-D, DAN; 5 kw-N, DAN; N37 5 51 W120 49 51
401 Pacheco Blvd., Los Banos, CA 93635 US
(209) 826-0578, *Fax:* (209) 826-1906
www.klbs.com
pr@klbs.com
License: Los Banos, CA held by Ethnic Radio Los Banos Inc.
Arbitron Metro Market: Merced, CA *Format:* Portugese *Special Programming:* Relg 8 hrs wkly
Jose Encarnacao, General Manager

KQLB
11-01-1992; 106.9 mhz FM *Hrs Open:* 24; 6 kw; 328 ft.; N36 55 35 W120 50 42
401-A Pacheco Boulevard, Los Banos, CA 93635 US
(209) 827-0123, *Fax:* (209) 826-1906
www.kqlb.com
pr@kqlb.com
License: Los Banos, Merced County, CA held by VLB Broadcasting Inc.
Arbitron Metro Market: Merced, CA *Format:* Spanish
Batista Vieira, Chairman
Cidalia Sequeira, Operations Dir
J.J. Encarnacao, General Manager
Jose Berumen, Programming Director

Los Gatos

KRTY
07-09-1966; 95.3 mhz FM *Hrs Open:* 24; 0.87 kw; 860 ft.; N37 12 17 W121 56 56
PO Box 995, 750 Story Rd, San Jose, CA 95108 US
(408) 293-8030, *Fax:* (408) 293-6124(408) 995-0823(studio)
www.krty.com
License: Los Gatos, Santa Clara County, CA held by KRTY Ltd.
Group Owner: Empire Broadcasting Corp.; (acq 2-93; $3.31 million;
Arbitron Metro Market: San Jose, CA *Format:* Country *No. News Employees:* 1 *Target Audience:* 25-54.
Bob Kieve, President
Nate Deaton, General Manager
Stuart Hinkle, General Sales Mgr
Julie Stevens, Programming Director
George Sampson, News Director
Mike Danberger, Chief Engineer
Tina Ferguson, General Sales Manager
JamiePauhl, Promotions Director

Los Molinos

KCEZ
01-01-1999; 102.1 mhz FM; 25 kw; 220 ft.; N39 53 17 W122 37 38
Post Office Box 2371, Chico, CA 95927 US
(530) 342-2200, *Fax:* (530) 342-2260
www.chicooldies.com
License: Los Molinos, Tehama County, CA held by Results Radio Licensee L.L.C.
Group Owner: Fritz Communications Inc.; (acq 6-11-99; grpsl)
Arbitron Metro Market: Chico, CA *Format:* Oldies
Jon Graham, General Manager
Steve Michaels, Programming Director
Candy Mason, News Director
J.D. Davis, Chief Engineer

Los Osos-Baywood Par

KSTT-FM
01-01-1987; 101.3 mhz FM *Hrs Open:* 24; 3.6 kw; 1647 ft.; N35 21 37 W120 39 18
966 East Essex Drive, Fresno, CA 93720 US
(805) 545-0101, *Fax:* (805) 541-5303
www.kstt.com
info@kstt.com
License: Los Osos-Baywood Par, San Luis Obispo County, CA held by EDB SLO License LLC.
Group Owner: Frontier Radio Management Inc.; (acq 11-30-2007; grpsl)
Arbitron Metro Market: San Luis Obispo, CA *Format:* Adult Contemp *Hrs. of News Programming:* news progmg 5 hrs wkly *No. News Employees:* 1 *Target Audience:* 25-54.
Andrew Winford, Operations Dir
Rich Hawkins, General Manager
Josh Riley, General Sales Mgr
Andrew Cannon, Programming Director
Rebecca Crites, Promotions Manager

Lost Hills

KEBT
12-10-1995; 96.9 mhz FM; 15.5 kw; 413 ft.; N35 19 40 W119 42 58
1416 Hollister Lane, Los Osos, CA 93402 US
(661) 328-1410, *Fax:* (661) 328-0873
License: Lost Hills, Kern County, CA held by AGM California.
Group Owner: American General Media; (acq 6-5-2006; $2.05 million)
Arbitron Metro Market: Bakersfield, CA *Special Programming:* Piolin Por La Manana *Target Audience:* 25-54.
Roger Fessler, General Manager
Toni Snyder, General Sales Mgr
Ricky Perez, Programming Director

KQMX
105.7 mhz FM; 24.4 kw; 331 ft.; N35 30 54 W119 57 30 US
(512) 329-5843, *Fax:* (512) 329-5847
www.matineemedia.com
License: Lost Hills, Kern County, CA held by Ace Radio Corp.
Group Owner: Ace Radio Corp.
Arbitron Metro Market: Lost Hills, CA
Stephen Hackerman, President

Lucerne Valley

KIXA
11-01-1992; 106.5 mhz FM *Hrs Open:* 24; 0.56 kw; 1066 ft.; N34 23 9 W117 3 24
50 E. Rivercenter Blvd, #180, Covington, KY 41011 US
(760) 241-1313, *Fax:* (760) 241-0205
www.thefox1065.com
kimjennings@edbroadcasters.com
License: Lucerne Valley, San Bernardino County, CA held by EDB VV License LLC.
Group Owner: Frontier Radio Management Inc.; (acq 11-30-2007; grpsl)
Nat'l Reps: Christal
Format: Classic Rock *Hrs. of News Programming:* News progmg 18 hrs wkly *Target Audience:* 16-45. *Adv. Rates:* 25-60
Tom Hoyt, Operations Dir
Kim Jennings, General Sales Mgr
Joe Pagano, Programming Director

Ludlow

KDUQ
07-07-1995; 102.5 mhz FM *Hrs Open:* 24; 6 kw; -164 ft.; N34 43 21 W116 10 4 *Rebroadcasts:* Rebroadcasts KDUC(FM) Barstow 100%
320 West College Avenue, Pleasant Gap, PA 16823 US
(760) 256-2121, *Fax:* (760) 256-5090
doscostas@yahoo.com
License: Ludlow, San Bernardino County, CA held by Dos Costas Communications Corp.
Group Owner: Dos Costas Communications Corp.; (acq 6-18-03; grpsl).
Nat'l Network: ABC; CBS *Nat'l Reps:* Western Regional Broadcast Sales
Format: Contemporary Hits/Top 40 *Special Programming:* Relg one hr wkly *Hrs. of News Programming:* news progmg 7 hrs wkly *No. News Employees:* 1 *Target Audience:* 25-54; adults
Roland Ulloa, Station Manager
Manny Lopez, General Sales Mgr
Mike Garcia, Programming Director
Brad Sobel, Chief Engineer

KHWZ
01-01-1992; 100.1 mhz FM *Hrs Open:* 24; 25 kw; 249 ft.; N34 42 34 W116 9 2 *Rebroadcasts:* Rebroadcasts KHDR 100%
12381 Wilshire Blvd. Suite 105, Los Angeles, CA 90025 US
(760) 256-0326, *Fax:* (760) 256-9507
www.thehighwaystations.com
highwayradio@highwayradio.com
License: Ludlow, San Bernardino County, CA held by KHWY Inc.
Group Owner: KHWY Inc.
Nat'l Network: Jones Radio Networks
Format: Rock/AOR *Special Programming:* Real time traffic and weather reports *Target Audience:* 35 plus; travelers on I-15 & I-40
Gary Shorman, President
Timothy Anderson, Operations Dir
Judy Robinson, General Sales Mgr
Kirk Anderson, Executive Vice President
Howard Anderson, President

Madera

KHOT
12-31-1956; 1250 khz AM *Hrs Open:* 24
1436 Auburn Boulevard, Sacramento, CA 95815 US
(916) 535-0500, *Fax:* (916) 535-0504
www.ihradio.org
info@ihradio.org
License: Madera, CA held by Redwood Family Services Inc.
Arbitron Metro Market: Fresno, CA *Format:* Religious *Special Programming:* Talk 70 hrs wkly *Hrs. of News Programming:* news progmg 30 hrs wkly *No. News Employees:* 1 *Target Audience:* 25-54.
Doug Sherman, President

KHIT-FM
10-01-1992; 107.1 mhz FM; 9.9 kw; 515 ft.; N37 7 40 W119 40 38
211 East 6th Street, Madera, CA 93638 US
(559) 497-1100, *Fax:* (559) 497-1125
mginsburg@lotusfresno.com
License: Madera, Madera County, CA held by Lotus Communications Corp.
Group Owner: Lotus Communications Corp.; (acq 3-10-99)
Nat'l Reps: Lotus Entravision Reps LLC
Arbitron Metro Market: Fresno, CA *Format:* Spanish *Target Audience:* 18-49. *Adv. Rates:* 35; 35; 35; 30
Dan Crotty, General Manager
Mike Ginsburg, General Sales Mgr
Jose Berumen, Programming Director
Paul Klein Kramer, Chief Engineer

Magalia

*KLVC
01-01-1993; 88.3 mhz FM *Hrs Open:* 24; 5.7 kw; 1378 ft.; N39 57 45 W121 42 40 *Rebroadcasts:* Rebroadcasts KLVB-FM Red Bluff 100%
1425 N. Market Blvd. #9, Sacramento, CA 95834 US
(707) 528-9236, *Fax:* (707) 528-9246
www.klove.com
klove@klove.com
License: Magalia, Butte County, CA held by Educational Media Foundation Inc.
Group Owner: EMF Broadcasting
Nat'l Network: K-Love
Format: Christian *No. News Employees:* 3 *Target Audience:* 33—40; Judeo-Christian, female
Darell Chambliss, Chairman
Mike Novak, President
Marya Morgan, News Director
Sam Wallington, Engineering Dir
Richard Hunt, News Reporter

Mammoth Lakes

KMMT
04-03-1973; 106.5 mhz FM *Hrs Open:* 24; 0.36 kw; 2372 ft.; N37 37 42 W119 1 47
P. O. Box 1284, Mammoth Lakes, CA 93546 US
(760) 934-8888, *Fax:* (760) 934-2429
kmmtradioworks@yahoo.com
License: Mammoth Lakes, Mono County, CA held by Mammoth Mountain F.M. Associates Inc.
Format: Adult Contemp *Special Programming:* Jazz 2 hrs, classic rock 4 hrs wkly *Hrs. of News Programming:* news progmg 2 hrs wkly *No. News Employees:* 1 *Target Audience:* 18-54; active, athletic, affluent adults*Adv. Rates:* 15; 12; 15; 10
David Digerness, President
Shellie Woods, General Manager

Manteca

KCBC
04-05-1987; 770 khz AM *Hrs Open:* 24
P. O. Box 3003, Blue Bell, PA 19422 US
(209) 847-7700, *Fax:* (209) 847-1769
www.770kcbc.com
kcbcradio@surfside.net
License: Manteca, CA held by Kiertron Inc.
Group Owner: Crawford Broadcasting Co.; (acq 12-30-92; $1 million;
Arbitron Metro Market: Modesto, CA *Format:* Religious *Hrs. of News Programming:* news progmg 25 hrs wkly *No. News Employees:* 1 *Target Audience:* 25-49.
Don Crawford Sr., President
John Yazel, Operations Dir
Laura Scotti, General Manager
Sarah Davis, Programming Director
Steve Minshall, Chief Engineer

Maricopa

KXTT
94.9 mhz FM; 6 kw; 312 ft.; N35 5 39 W119 27 40
US
(805) 240-2070
License: Maricopa, Kern County, CA held by Lazer Licenses LLC.
Group Owner: Lazer Broadcasting Corp.; (acq 6-11-2007; $3.85 million with KEAL(FM) Taft)
Arbitron Metro Market: Altus, OK
Neal Robinson, President

Marina

KTOM-FM
04-06-1982; 92.7 mhz FM *Hrs Open:* 24; 6.9 kw; 620 ft.; N36 33 9 W121 47 17
220 Concord Plaza, Suite 600, San Antonio, TX 78216 US
(831) 755-8181, *Fax:* (831) 755-8193
www.ktom.com
License: Marina, Monterey County, CA held by CC Licenses LLC.
Group Owner: Clear Channel Communications Inc.; (acq 9-22-97; grpsl).
Nat'l Reps: D & R Radio
Arbitron Metro Market: Monterey-Salina *Format:* Country *Hrs. of News Programming:* news progmg 5 hrs wkly *No. News Employees:* 1 *Target Audience:* 25-54; men
Sam Diggedy, Operations Dir
Rhonda McCormack, General Manager
Monica Tovar, General Sales Mgr
Sam Diggedy, Programming Director
Angel Jarquin, Promotions Manager
Jim Pearson, Production and Music Director

Mariposa

KDJK
01-01-1994; 103.9 mhz FM *Hrs Open:* 24; 0.071 kw; 2047 ft.; N37 32 0 W120 1 29 *Rebroadcasts:* Simulcasts KHKK(FM) Modesto 95%
City Center West, 7201 W. Lake Mead Blvd, Las Vegas, NV 89128 US
(209) 766-5000, *Fax:* (209) 522-2061
www.104thehawk.com
info@104thehawk.com
License: Mariposa, Mariposa County, CA
Group Owner: Cumulus Media Inc.; (acq 7-30-93; $6 million;
Nat'l Reps: Christal
Arbitron Metro Market: Merced, CA *Format:* Classic Rock *Target Audience:* 18-54.
Roy Williams, General Manager
Jean Western, General Sales Mgr
Richard Perry, Programming Director
Raymond Baca, Chief Engineer

KUBB
07-04-1977; 96.3 mhz FM *Hrs Open:* 24; 1.9 kw; 2096 ft.; N37 32 1 W120 1 46
166 West Putnam Ave., Greenwich, CT 06830 US
(209) 383-7900, *Fax:* (209) 723-8461
www.kubb.com
emonroe@kubb.com
License: Mariposa, Mariposa County, CA held by Buckley Broadcasting of Monterey.
Group Owner: Buckley Broadcasting Corp.; (acq 7-1-85; $640,000;
Nat'l Network: Westwood One *Nat'l Reps:* D & R Radio
Arbitron Metro Market: Mariposa, CA *Format:* Country *Special Programming:* Farm 2 hrs wkly *Hrs. of News Programming:* news progmg 2 hrs wkly *No. News Employees:* 1 *Target Audience:* 25-54. *Adv. Rates:* 36; 32; 36; 22
Mike McAdam, Operations Dir
Ed Monroe, General Sales Mgr
Rene Roberts, Operations Manager

Marysville

KMYC
01-01-1940; 1410 khz AM *Hrs Open:* 6 AM-midnight; 5 kw-D, DA2; 1 kw-N, DA2; N39 8 18 W121 33 15
2905 South King Road, San Jose, CA 95122 US
(530) 742-5555, *Fax:* (530) 741-3758
www.kmyc.com
kmyc@xyix.com
License: Marysville, CA held by Thomas Huth.
Group Owner: Huth Broadcasting; .
Format: Talk *Special Programming:* Indian/Punjabi 2 hrs wkly *No. News Employees:* 1 *Target Audience:* 18 plus; general
Thomas Huth, CEO
Jerry Snaper, Engineering Dir

KRCX-FM
10-12-1994; 99.9 mhz FM *Hrs Open:* 24; 1.75 kw; 2182 ft.; N39 12 20 W121 49 10
2905 South King Road, San Jose, CA 95122 US
(916) 646-4000, *Fax:* (916) 646-1958
www.tricolor999.com
slopez@entravision.com
License: Marysville, Yuba County, CA held by Entravision Holdings LLC.
Group Owner: Entravision Communications Corp.; (acq 3-14-2000; grpsl).
Arbitron Metro Market: Sacramento, CA *Format:* Tejano *No. News Employees:* 2 *Target Audience:* 18-49.
Allyson Maiman, General Manager
Salvador Lopez, Promotions Manager

McCloud

***KLDD**
01-01-2008; 91.9 mhz FM; 0.035 kw; 2375 ft.; N41 20 43 W122 11 42
P.O. Box 3175, Eugene, OR 97403 US
(541) 552-6301, *Fax:* (541) 552-8565
www.ijpr.org
jprinfo@sou.edu
License: McCloud, Siskiyou County, CA held by The State of Oregon Acting By and Through the Oregon State Board of Higher Education for Southern Oregon University.
Nat'l Network: NPR
Arbitron Metro Market: McCloud, CA *Format:* Classical, News
Ron Kramer, General Manager
Valerie Ing-Miller, Programming Director
Darin Ransom, Engineering Dir
Betsy Byers, Administrative Assistant
Mitchell Christian, Director of Finance & Administration
Jill Hernandez, AccountantTechnician
Paul Westhelle, Executive Director

McFarland

KIWI
07-11-1989; 102.9 mhz FM *Hrs Open:* 24; 25 kw; 322 ft.; N35 19 16 W119 42 26
Suite 102, 3701 Pegasus Dr., Bakersville, CA 93308 US
(661) 327-9711, *Fax:* (661) 327-0797
www.kiwifm.co.nz
napo@radiolobo.com
License: McFarland, Kern County, CA
Group Owner: Lotus Communications Corp.; (Acq 12-18-00; $2.5 million including a $10,000 three-year noncompete agreement).
Nat'l Reps: Lotus Entravision Reps LLC
Arbitron Metro Market: Bakersfield, CA *Format:* Tejano *Target Audience:* General.
Bryan King, General Manager

KBQF
104.3 mhz FM; 6 kw; 327 ft.; N35 31 35 W119 18 43
US
(805) 486-4400
License: McFarland, Kern County, CA held by JAB Broadcasting LLC.
Arbitron Metro Market: McFarland, CA *Format:* Spanish
Javier Orosco, General Manager

McKinleyville

***KNDZ**
01-01-2009; 89.3 mhz FM; 750 w vert; Ant 1,005 ft; N40 49 32 W124 00 05 *Rebroadcasts:* Rebroadcasts KVIP-FM Redding 100%
1139 Hartnell Ave., Redding, CA 94508
(530) 222-4455, *Fax:* (530) 222-4484
www.kvip.org
info@kvip.org
License: McKinleyville, Humboldt County, CA held by Pacific Cascade Communications Corp.
Group Owner: Pacific Cascade Communications Corp.; (acq 2-9-2009; $62,500 for CP)
David Morrow, Operations Dir
Steve Hafen, General Manager
Paul Brown, Chief Engineer

KMDR
95.1 mhz FM; 2.3 kw; 1070 ft.; N40 49 32 W124 0 5
US
(707) 445-3699, *Fax:* (707) 445-3906
www.951mixfm.com
License: McKinleyville, Humboldt County, CA held by William W. McCutchen III.
Group Owner: William W. McCutchen III Stns
Arbitron Metro Market: McKinleyville, CA *Format:* Adult Contemp
Randy Flavers, General Manager
Teresa Wold, Business Manager
Barbara Kennon, Account Manager

Mecca

KRCK-FM
01-01-2001; 97.7 mhz FM; 2 kw; 571 ft.; N33 48 4 W116 13 28
1425 River Park Drive, Sacramento, CA 95815 US
(760) 341-0123, *Fax:* (760) 341-7455
www.krck.com
joshua@krck.com
License: Mecca, Riverside County, CA held by Playa Del Sol Broadcasters.
Arbitron Metro Market: Palm Springs, CA *Format:* Contemporary Hits/Top 40 *Target Audience:* w18-49, A18-49
Edward Stolz, General Manager
Edward Morowski, Station Manager
Robert Scorpio, Programming Director
Debby McKay, National Sales Executive

Mendocino

***KAKX**
01-15-1997; 89.3 mhz FM *Hrs Open:* 24; 0.25 kw vert; 233 ft.; N39 18 46 W123 46 57
Post Office Box 1154, Mendocino, CA 95460 US
(707) 937-1200
audio@mcn.org
License: Mendocino, Mendocino County, CA held by Mendocino Unified School District.
Arbitron Metro Market: Mendocino, CA *Format:* Rock/AOR, Variety/Diverse
Peter Davidson, President
Marshall Brown, General Manager

KMFB(FM)
11-01-1966; 92.7 mhz FM *Hrs Open:* 24; 3 kw; 165 ft; N39 20 33 W123 46 51
101-E Boatyard Dr., Fort Bragg, CA 95437
(707) 964-5307, *Fax:* (707) 964-3299
www.kmfb(FM).com
generalmail@kmfb(FM).com
License: Mendocino, Mendocino County, CA held by Four Rivers Broadcasting Inc.
Group Owner: Four Rivers Broadcasting Inc.; (acq 7-21-2005; grpsl).
Wire Services: Agence France-Presse (AFP)
Population Served: 75,000*Format:* Sports *No. News Employees:* 4 *Target Audience:* 35-54. *Adv. Rates:* 16; 14; 14; 12
Bob Woelfel, General Manager
Ed Kowas, News Director
Liz Helenchild, Music Director

***KPMO**
11-16-1966; 1300 khz AM *Hrs Open:* 24 hrs
1906 Coralino Drive, Henderson, NV 89014 US
(541) 552-6301, *Fax:* (541) 552-8565
www.ijpr.org
jprinfo@sou.edu
License: Mendocino, CA held by JPR Foundation Inc.
Nat'l Network: NPR; PRI *Wire Services:* AP
Format: News, News/Talk, 86 *No. News Employees:* 1 *Target Audience:* General.
Ronald Kramer, CEO
Bryon Lambert, Operations Dir
Ronald Kramer, General Manager
Darin Ransom, Engineering Dir

Mendota

KMEN
01-01-2007; 100.5 mhz FM; 6 kw; 144 ft.; N36 38 50 W120 21 2
40 Bellan Blvd, No 10101, San Rafael, CA 94912 US
(213) 745-6224, *Fax:* (213) 745-7577
mmartinez@lunacommunication.net
License: Mendota, Fresno County, CA held by MBP Licensee LLC.
Group Owner: Moon Broadcasting; (acq 3-30-2001; $350,000).
Arbitron Metro Market: Tulare, CA
Abel de Luna, President
Angelica Figueroa, General Sales Mgr
Yesenia de Luna, Programming Director

Merced

KABX-FM
12-18-1975; 97.5 mhz FM *Hrs Open:* 24; 8.8 kw; 1161 ft.; N37 26 44 W120 8 37
1360 W. 18th St., Merced, CA 95340 US
(209) 723-2191, *Fax:* (209) 383-2950
www.975kabx.com
License: Merced, Merced County, CA
Group Owner: Mapleton Communications LLC
Arbitron Metro Market: Merced, CA *Format:* Oldies
Andrew Adams, General Manager
Damian Galaarza, General Sales Mgr
Dave Luna, Programming Director

***KAMB**
11-06-1967; 101.5 mhz FM *Hrs Open:* 24; 1.85 kw; 2093 ft.; N37 32 1 W120 1 46
90 East 16th Street, Merced, CA 95340 US
(209) 723-1015, *Fax:* (209) 723-1945
www.celebrationradio.com
kamb@celebrationradio.com
License: Merced, Merced County, CA held by Central Valley Broadcasting Co. Inc.
Nat'l Network: AP Radio; Moody
Arbitron Metro Market: Merced, CA *Format:* Christian *Hrs. of News Programming:* news progmg 5 hrs wkly *No. News Employees:* 1 *Target Audience:* 29-54; Christian adults in central California
Tim Land, CEO
Mike Boster, President
Dave Benton, Operations Dir
Tim Land, General Manager
Jinous Vartan, Promotions Manager

KTIQ
11-01-1999; 1660 khz AM *Hrs Open:* 24
Mailing Address: 1175 Fairview Drive, Suite N, Carson City, NV 89701 US
Second Address: 1020 Main St., Merced, CA 95340
(209) 577-2860
www.amistad1660.com
radioamistad1660@hotmail.com
License: Merced, CA held by Mapleton License of Merced LLC.
Group Owner: Mapleton Communications LLC; (acq 6-1-2002; grpsl)
Arbitron Metro Market: Modesto, CA *Format:* Christian, Talk
Target Audience: 25-54.
Pastor Juan Montes, General Manager
Rick McMillion, Chief Engineer

KBKY
01-01-2002; 94.1 mhz FM; 6 kw; 328 ft.; N37 27 59 W120 14 9
1436 Auburn Blvd., Sacramento, CA 95815 US
(209) 385-9994, *Fax:* (209) 385-9982
y94@comcast.net
License: Merced, Merced County, CA held by KM Radio of Merced L.L.C.
Arbitron Metro Market: Merced, CA *Format:* Adult Contemp
Target Audience: Women Ages 24-54 Two Income Families
Adv. Rates: 20; 15; 20; 12.
Cynthia Masterson, General Manager
Roman Scanlon, General Sales Mgr
Matthew Stone, Programming Director

KGAM
01-01-1969; 106.3 mhz FM *Hrs Open:* 24; 4 kw; 404 ft.; N37 25 35 W120 26 25
PO Box 717, Merced, CA 95341 US
(760) 325-2582, *Fax:* (760) 322-3562
www.kgam.com
info@kgam.com
License: Merced, Riverside County, CA held by R & R Radio Corp.
Group Owner: RR Broadcasting; (acq 4-8-2002; with co-located FM)
Nat'l Reps: Christal
Arbitron Metro Market: Palm Springs, CA *Format:* News, News/Talk, 86 *Hrs. of News Programming:* news progmg 5 hrs wkly *No. News Employees:* 2 *Target Audience:* 25 plus; upscale, informed, involved adults
Rozene Supple, President
Mike Keane, General Manager
Mel Hill, General Sales Mgr
Steve Kelly, Programming Director
Geoff Allan, Promotions Manager
Gene Nichols, News Director
Barry O'Connor, Chief Engineer

KGAM(FM)
05-14-1992; 106.3 mhz FM *Hrs Open:* 24; 4 kw; Ant 403 ft; N37 25 35 W120 26 25
1020 W. Main St., Merced, CA 95340-4521
(209) 723-2191, *Fax:* (209) 383-2950
www.hank1063.com
License: Merced, Merced County, CA held by Mapleton License of Merced LLC.
Group Owner: Mapleton Communications LLC; (acq 6-1-2002; grpsl)
Arbitron Metro Market: Merced, CA *Format:* Country *Target Audience:* 25-54; upscale professionals
Andrew Adams, General Manager
Damian Galaarza, General Sales Mgr
Brian Montgomery, Programming Director
Rick McMillion, Chief Engineer
Appears to no longer be broadcasting.

KYOS
10-01-1936; 1480 khz AM *Hrs Open:* 24
1360 W. 18th St., Merced, CA 95340 US
(209) 723-2191, *Fax:* (209) 205-1013
www.1480kyos.com
kyos@radiomerced.com
License: Merced, CA held by Mapleton License of Merced LLC.
Group Owner: Mapleton Communications LLC; acq 6-5-2002; grpsl)
Nat'l Network: CBS *Nat'l Reps:* Christal
Arbitron Metro Market: Merced, CA *Format:* News, News/Talk, 86 *Special Programming:* Farm 5 hrs, gospel one hr wkly *Hrs. of News Programming:* news progmg 20 hrs wkly *No. News Employees:* 2 *Target Audience:* 25-54.
Adam Nathanson, President
Andrew Adams, General Manager
Damian Galaarza, General Sales Mgr

Middletown

***KLVR**
10-15-1982; 91.9 mhz FM *Hrs Open:* 24; 0.83 kw; 2989 ft.; N38 40 9 W122 37 53
1425 N. Market St, #9, Sacramento, CA 95834 US
(707) 528-9236, *Fax:* (707) 528-9236
www.klove.com
klove@klove.com
License: Middletown, Lake County, CA held by Educational Media Foundation.
Group Owner: EMF Broadcasting; (acq 1986).
Nat'l Network: K-Love
Arbitron Metro Market: San Francisco, CA *Format:* Christian *No. News Employees:* 3 *Target Audience:* 25-44; Judeo-Christian females
Darell Chambliss, Chairman
Mike Novak, President
David Pierce, Programming Director
Ed Lenane, News Director
Sam Wallington, Engineering Dir
Tracy Butler, Traffic Manager

Millers Ranch

KRBO(FM)
01-01-2012; 89.3 mhz FM; 100 w; -65.5 meters; N36 12 06 W121 27 48.9
975 West First Street, Azusa, CA 91702
(626) 969-7945
License: Millers Ranch, CA held by Christian Faith Center of the Valley
Samuel Martinez, President

Mission Viejo

***KSBR**
05-07-1979; 88.5 mhz FM; 620 w; 600 ft; N33 30 10 W117 36 06
28000 Marguerite Pkwy., Mission Viejo, CA 92675
(949) 582-5727, *Fax:* (949) 347-9693
www.ksbr.net
License: Mission Viejo, Orange County, CA held by South Orange County Community College District.
Nat'l Network: AP Network News *Wire Services:* AP
Population Served: 500,000*Special Programming:* Latin 3 hrs, blues 3 hrs, reggae 3 hrs, electronic 4 hrs, ragtime 2 hrs, folk 2 hrs wkly *No. News Employees:* 1 *Target Audience:* 25-54.
Terry Wedel, Operations Dir
Dawn Kamber, News Director
Mark Schiffelbein, Engineering Dir

Modesto

***KADV**
11-01-1988; 90.5 mhz FM *Hrs Open:* 24; 1.5 kw; 141 ft.; N37 36 26 W120 57 26
2031 Academy Place, Ceres, CA 95307 US
(559) 627-5276
www.mypromisefm.com
License: Modesto, Stanislaus County, CA held by Modesto Adventist Academy.
Nat'l Network: Moody; Salem Radio Network
Arbitron Metro Market: Visalia, CA *Format:* Religious *Special Programming:* Sp one hr wkly *Hrs. of News Programming:* News progmg 14 hrs wkly *Target Audience:* 30 plus.
Steve White, General Manager
Jerry Moore, Chief Engineer

KESP
01-01-1951; 970 khz AM *Hrs Open:* 24
City Center West, 7201 W. Lake Mead Blvd, Las Vegas, NV 89128 US
(209) 577-6970, *Fax:* (209) 593-7970
www.espnradio970.com
info@espnradio970.com
License: Modesto, CA
Group Owner: Cumulus Media Inc.; (acq 5-18-92; $12.5 million grpsl, including co-located FM;
Nat'l Network: ESPN Radio; Cumulus Media Inc. *Nat'l Reps:* McGavren Guild
Arbitron Metro Market: Modesto, CA *Format:* Sports *Target Audience:* 35 plus.
Roy Williams, General Manager
Jean Western, General Sales Mgr
Richard Perry, Programming Director

KATM
01-01-1948; 103.3 mhz FM; 50 kw; 499 ft.; N37 34 30 W121 21 13
City Center West, 7201 W. Lake Mead Blvd., Las Vegas, NV 89128 US
(209) 956-5103, *Fax:* (209) 571-1033
www.katm.com
info@katmfm.com
License: Modesto, Stanislaus County, CA
Group Owner: Cumulus Media Inc.
Arbitron Metro Market: Stockton, CA *Format:* Country *Target Audience:* 25-64; mass appeal
Randy ""Bubba"" Black, Programming Director

KBBU
01-01-1999; 93.9 mhz FM *Hrs Open:* 24; 4 kw; 404 ft.; N37 39 0 W121 1 24 *Rebroadcasts:* Simulcast with KTTA(FM) Esparto 100%
P.O. Box 1022, Manteca, CA 95336 US
(916) 368-6300, *Fax:* (916) 441-6480
www.lakebuena.com
abalderas@bustosmedia.com
License: Modesto, Stanislaus County, CA
Group Owner: Adelante Media Group LLC; (acq 12-15-2004; $21.7 million with KLMG(FM) Esparto)
Arbitron Metro Market: Modesto, CA
John Bustos, General Manager
Juan Gonzalez, Programming Director
Javier Gonzalez, Promotions Manager
Adela Garcia, News Director
Mark Sedaka, Chief Engineer
Cynthia Sanchez, Traffic Manager

KFIV
01-01-1950; 1360 khz AM
600 Congress Avenue, Suite 1400, Auston, TX 78701 US
(209) 551-1306, *Fax:* (209) 551-1359
www.kfiv1360.com
License: Modesto, CA held by Capstar TX L.P.
Group Owner: Clear Channel Communications Inc.; (acq 8-30-2000; grpsl)
Nat'l Network: ABC
Arbitron Metro Market: Modesto, CA *Format:* News, News/Talk, 86 *Special Programming:* Afternoons live, 20 hrs wkly *Hrs. of News Programming:* news progmg 148 hrs wkly *Target Audience:* 25-54.
Rich Hawkins, General Manager
Rick Myers, General Sales Mgr
Matthew Hobley, Programming Director
Kacie Marshall, Promotions Manager

KHKK
01-01-1949; 104.1 mhz FM *Hrs Open:* 24; 50 kw; 499 ft.; N37 39 10 W121 28 38
City Center West, 7201 W. Lake Mead Blvd, Las Vegas, NV 89128 US
(209) 766-5000, *Fax:* (209) 522-0540
www.104thehawk.com
thehawk@104thehawk.com
License: Modesto, Stanislaus County, CA
Group Owner: Cumulus Media Inc.; (acq 10-1-93).
Nat'l Reps: McGavren Guild
Arbitron Metro Market: Modesto, CA *Format:* Classic Rock *Hrs. of News Programming:* news progmg 5 hrs wkly *No. News Employees:* 1 *Target Audience:* 25-49; baby boomers who grew up with rock and roll
Roy Williams, General Manager
Richard Perry, Programming Director
Raymond Baca, Chief Engineer

KJSN
07-04-1977; 102.3 mhz FM; 6 kw; 289 ft.; N37 40 50 W120 55 26
600 Congress Avenue, Suite 1400, Auston, TX 78701 US
(209) 551-1306, *Fax:* (209) 551-1359
www.sunny102fm.com
License: Modesto, Stanislaus County, CA held by Capstar TX L.P.
Group Owner: Clear Channel Communications Inc.
Arbitron Metro Market: Modesto, CA *Format:* Adult Contemp *Target Audience:* 25-49.
Matthew Hobley, Operations Dir
Gary Michaels, Programming Director
Steve Minshall, Chief Engineer

***KMPO**
01-01-1984; 88.7 mhz FM *Hrs Open:* 24; 2.05 kw; 2041 ft.; N37 32 0 W120 1 29
5005 E. Belmont, Fresno, CA 93727 US
(559) 455-5777, *Fax:* (559) 455-5778
www.radiobilingue.org
mail@radiobilingue.org
License: Modesto, Stanislaus County, CA held by Radio Bilingue Inc.
Arbitron Metro Market: Modesto, CA *Format:* Ethnic *Special Programming:* Black 3 hrs, folk 4 hrs, Filipino one hr wkly *Hrs. of News Programming:* news progmg 11 hrs wkly *No. News Employees:* 5 *Target Audience:* 16 plus; Latinos
Hugo Morales, CEO
Maria Erana, General Manager
Phil Traynor, General Sales Mgr
Samuel Orozco, News Director
Bill Bach, Chief Engineer

KMPH
07-10-2006; 840 khz AM
US
(209) 527-8400, *Fax:* (209) 526-0820
www.kmph840.com
jpappas@kmph840.com
License: Modesto, CA held by Pappas Radio of Modesto LLC.
Group Owner: Pappas Telecasting Companies; (acq 11-5-2003)
Nat'l Network: Salem Radio Network; Premiere Radio Networks; Talk Radio Network *Nat'l Reps:* McGavren Guild
Arbitron Metro Market: Modesto, CA *Format:* News, News/Talk, 86 *Hrs. of News Programming:* M-F 6am - 9am and Top of Each Hour *No. News Employees:* 1 *Target Audience:* Adults: 35-64
Harry J. Pappas, CEO
Jim Pappas, Operations Dir
Jim P. Pappas, General Manager
Kevin Barrett, Programming Director

Mojave

KTPI
05-01-1958; 1340 khz AM *Hrs Open:* 24; 1 kw-U, ND1; N35 2 23 W118 8 57
190 Sierra Court, B-2, Palmdale, CA 93550 US
(661) 942-1121, *Fax:* (661) 723-5512
License: Mojave, CA held by CC Licenses LLC.
Group Owner: Clear Channel Communications Inc.; (acq 11-21-2003; grpsl).
Nat'l Reps: Christal
Arbitron Metro Market: Lancaster, CA *Target Audience:* 35 plus; Adult Christian community
Mark Mitchell, Operations Dir
Larry Thornhill, General Manager
Shaun Palmer, General Sales Mgr

KTPI-FM
05-01-1966; 97.7 mhz FM *Hrs Open:* 24; 3 kw; 299 ft.; N34 58 45 W118 10 2
50 E. Rivercenter Blvd., #1200, Covington, KY 41011 US
(661) 942-1121, *Fax:* (661) 723-5512
www.ktpi.com
info@ktpi.com
License: Mojave, Kern County, CA held by Aloha Station Trust LLC, as Trustee
Arbitron Metro Market: Mojave, CA *Format:* Country *No. News Employees:* 1 *Target Audience:* 25-54. *Adv. Rates:* 30; 22; 30; 24
Jim Bell, General Manager
Ron Vacchina, General Sales Mgr
John Ivey, Programming Director

***KCRY**
06-01-2000; 88.1 mhz FM; 10.5 kw; -95 ft.; N35 7 20 W118 12 25
Rebroadcasts: Rebroadcasts KCRW(FM) Santa Monica 100%
1900 Pico Blvd, Santa Monica, CA 90405 US
(310) 450-5183, *Fax:* (310) 450-7172
www.kcrw.com
mail@kcrw.org
License: Mojave, Kern County, CA held by Santa Monica Community College District.
Nat'l Network: NPR *Wire Services:* AP
Arbitron Metro Market: Santa Monica, CA *Format:* News
Michael Fleming, Chairman
Jennifer Ferro, President
Stu Bloomberg, Vice Chair
Tom Donner, Secretary/Treasurer

KCEL
01-01-2009; 96.1 mhz FM; 0.63 kw; 823 ft.; N35 5 38 W118 16 0 US
(661) 947-3107, *Fax:* (661) 256-8254
laquebuena961.com
psa@highdesertbroadcasting.com
License: Mojave, Kern County, CA held by Coloma Mojave LLC.
Arbitron Metro Market: Mojave, CA
Scott Donohue, CEO
Bijan Omidi, General Manager

Monte Rio

KVRV
11-20-1977; 97.7 mhz FM *Hrs Open:* 24; 2.05 kw; 1122 ft.; N38 32 25 W122 57 40
Mailing Address: 1410 Neotomas Avenue, Suite 200, Santa Rosa, CA 95405 US
Second Address: 1410 Neotomas Ave., Suite 200, Santa Rosa, CA 95405
(707) 543-0100, *Fax:* (707) 571-1097
www.977theriver.com
License: Monte Rio, Sonoma County, CA held by Maverick Media of Santa Rosa License LLC.
Group Owner: Maverick Media LLC; (acq 12-16-02; grpsl).
Arbitron Metro Market: San Francisco, CA *Format:* Classic Rock *Target Audience:* 25-54.
Jeff Clark, General Manager

Montecito

KJEE
03-01-1994; 92.9 mhz FM; 0.82 kw; 886 ft.; N34 27 57 W119 40 37
P. O. Box 22105, Santa Barbara, CA 93121 US
(805) 963-4676, *Fax:* (805) 963-8166
www.kjee.com
sales@kjee.com
License: Montecito, Santa Barbara County, CA held by Montecito FM Inc.
Arbitron Metro Market: Santa Barbara, CA *Format:* Rock/AOR *Target Audience:* 18-34; general
Eddie Gutierrez, General Manager
Steve Meade, General Sales Mgr
Ryan Zoldas, Promotions Manager
John Palmmentari, News Director
Dean Burt, Chief Engineer

Monterey

KIDD
10-12-1995; 630 khz AM *Hrs Open:* 12a-12a; 1 kw-D, DA2; 1 kw-N, DA2; N36 41 28 W121 48 0
166 West Putnam Avenue, Greenwich, CT 06830 US
(831) 649-0969, *Fax:* (831) 649-3335
www.espn630.com
sstade@kwav.com
License: Monterey, CA held by Buckley Communications Inc.
Group Owner: Buckley Broadcasting Corp.; (acq 1995; $200,000)
Nat'l Reps: Eastman Radio *Wire Services:* AP
Arbitron Metro Market: Monterey-Salina *TV Affiliate:* ESPN
Format: Sports, Talk
Sean Stade, General Manager
Jim Souza, General Sales Mgr
Kevin Kahl, Programming Director

KWAV
10-14-1961; 96.9 mhz FM; 18 kw; 2451 ft.; N36 32 5 W121 37 14
166 West Putnam Avenue, Greenwich, CT 06830 US
(831) 649-0969, *Fax:* (831) 649-3335
www.kwav.com
sstade@kwav.com
License: Monterey, Monterey County, CA held by Buckley Broadcasting Corp. of Monterey
Group Owner: Buckley Broadcasting Corp.; (acq 5-1-80; $700,000;
Nat'l Reps: Eastman Radio *Wire Services:* AP
Arbitron Metro Market: Monterey-Salinas-Santa Cruz, CA
Format: Adult Contemp *Target Audience:* 18-54; primarily women
Melanie Swain, Operations Dir
Kathy Baker, General Manager
Sean Stade, General Sales Mgr
Bernie Moody, Programming Director
Ron Warren, Chief Engineer
Karen Hamilton, News Director

Monterey Bay

KNRY
10-01-1935; 1240 khz AM *Hrs Open:* 24
2360 N.E. Coachman Road, Clearwater, FL 34625 US
(831) 372-1074, *Fax:* (831) 372-3585
www.knry.com
Natalie@knry.com
License: Monterey Bay, CA held by People's Radio Inc.
Nat'l Network: CBS
Arbitron Metro Market: Monterey, CA *Format:* News, News/Talk, 86 *Target Audience:* 35 plus.
Jim Vossen, Operations Dir

Moraga

***KSMC**
09-22-1977; 89.5 mhz FM *Hrs Open:* 24; 0.8 kw horiz; 79 ft.; N37 50 25 W122 6 36
1928 St. Mary's Road, Moraga, CA 94575 US
(925) 631-4252(925) 631-4772, *Fax:* (925) 376-5766
www.ksmc895.com
ksmc@stmarys-ca.edu
License: Moraga, Contra Costa County, CA held by Associated Students of St. Mary's College of California.
Wire Services: Dow Jones News Service
Arbitron Metro Market: Moraga, CA *Format:* Contemporary Hits/Top 40, News, 30 *Special Programming:* Relg 2 hrs, class 4 hrs, Sp 3 hrs, jazz 5 hrs wkly *Target Audience:* 15-30; young, urban & willing to experiment
Noel Cilker, General Manager
Will McCoster, Programming Director
Jessica Fajardo, Promotions Manager
Ed Tywoniak, Chief Engineer
Nick McAlpine, Music Director

Moreno Valley

KHPY
01-16-2003; 1670 khz AM
PO Box 87, Colton, CA 92324 US
(909) 247-5479, *Fax:* (909) 247-2790
License: Moreno Valley, CA held by Delbert L. Van Voorhis.
Format: Religious
Bill DeGeorge, General Manager

Morgan Hill

KSQQ
12-01-1990; 96.1 mhz FM; 4.7 kw; 161 ft.; N37 11 1 W121 48 9
1629-C Alum Rock Avenue, San Jose, CA 95116 US
(408) 258-9699, *Fax:* (408) 258-9770
www.ksqq.com
pr@ksqq.com
License: Morgan Hill, Santa Clara County, CA held by Coyote Communications Inc.
Arbitron Metro Market: San Jose, CA *Format:* Ethnic
Batista Vieira, President
Peter Mieuli, Operations Dir
Alvaro Aguiar, General Sales Mgr
Elza Bettencourt-office manager

Morro Bay

*KESC
05-01-1991; 99.7 mhz FM *Hrs Open:* 24; 0.285 kw; 1490 ft.; N35 21 40 W120 39 21 *Rebroadcasts:* Rebroadcasts KUSC(FM) Los Angeles 100%
P.O. Box 987, San Luis Obispo, CA 93406 US
(213) 225-7400, *Fax:* (213) 225-7410
www.kusc.org
kusc@kusc.org
License: Morro Bay, San Luis Obispo County, CA held by University of Southern California
Nat'l Reps: Michigan Spot Sales
Arbitron Metro Market: Los Angeles, CA *Format:* Classical
Brenda Barnes, President
Steve Coghill, Operations Dir
Eric DeWeese, General Manager
Ron Thompson, Engineering Dir
Amy Lwata, Office Manager
Rina Romero, Business Manager
Bill Lueth, Program Director
James Paisley, MusicDirector
Mark Hatwan, Production Manager
Craig Saunders, IT Director

Mount Bullion

KCIV
04-24-1989; 99.9 mhz FM *Hrs Open:* 24; 1.9 kw; 2094 ft.; N37 32 0 W120 1 29
10550 Barkley, Ste 108, Overland Park, KS 66212 US
(913) 642-7770, *Fax:* (913) 642-1319
bottradionetwork.com
comments@bottradionetwork.com
License: Mount Bullion, Stanislaus County, CA held by Bott Communications Inc.
Group Owner: Bott Radio Network
Arbitron Metro Market: Merced, CA *Format:* Christian *Target Audience:* 25-54; Christian family audience *Adv. Rates:* 29; 25; 26; 12
Richard (Dick) Bott, Sr., Founder & Chairman
Tom Holdeman, CFO
Richard (Rich) Bott, II, President/CEO
Eben Fowler, Operations Dir
Kathleen Reynolds, Station Manager
Tim Lumpkin, Corporate Controller
Pat Rulon, Director, NationalSales
Ken Monroe, Corporate Production
Larry Ross, Assistant Production
Helaine Parish, Production
John Dale, Director of Marketing

Mount Shasta

KMJC
06-12-1947; 620 khz AM *Hrs Open:* 24
P. O. Box 448, Mt. Shasta, CA 96067 US
(541) 552-6301, *Fax:* (541) 552-8565
www.ijpr.org
info@ijpr.org
License: Mount Shasta, CA held by JPR Foundation Inc.
Nat'l Network: NPR; PRI *Wire Services:* AP
Format: News, News/Talk, 86 *No. News Employees:* 1 *Target Audience:* General.
Bryon Lambert, Operations Dir
Ronald Kramer, General Manager
Paul Westhelle, General Sales Mgr

*KNSQ
01-01-1994; 88.1 mhz FM *Hrs Open:* 5 AM-2 AM; 5 kw; 889 ft.; N41 13 22 W122 17 51
P.O. Box 3175, Eugene, OR 97403 US
(541) 552-6301, *Fax:* (541) 552-8565
www.ijpr.org
info@ijpr.org
License: Mount Shasta, Siskiyou County, CA held by The State of Oregon, acting by and through the State Board of Higher Education, for the benefit of Southern Oregon University.
Nat'l Network: NPR; PRI
Format: Jazz, News, 90 *Special Programming:* Blues 6 hrs, folk 3 hrs, pub affrs 7 hrs wkly *Hrs. of News Programming:* news progmg 45 hrs wkly *No. News Employees:* 1 *Target Audience:* General.
Ronald Kramer, CEO
Bryon Lambert, Operations Dir
Paul Westhelle, General Sales Mgr
Mitchell Christian, CFO

Mountain Pass

KHYZ
04-01-1980; 99.7 mhz FM *Hrs Open:* 24; 8.4 kw; 1808 ft.; N35 29 27 W115 33 27
12381 Wilshire Blvd. Suite 105, Los Angeles, CA 90025 US
(760) 256-0326, *Fax:* (760) 256-9507
www.thehighwaystations.com
highwayradio@highwayradio.com
License: Mountain Pass, San Bernardino County, CA held by KHWY Inc.
Group Owner: KHWY Inc.
Nat'l Network: AP Radio
Format: Adult Contemp *Hrs. of News Programming:* news progmg 16 hrs wkly *No. News Employees:* 1 *Target Audience:* 35 plus; travelers & loc communities
Howard Anderson, CEO
Timothy Anderson, Operations Dir
Judy Robinson, General Sales Mgr
Lance Todd, Programming Director
John Gregg, Promotions Manager
Keith Hayes, News Director
Thomas McNeill, Engineering Dir
Kirk Anderson,Executive Vice President

Mountain View

*KSFH
01-01-1974; 87.9 mhz FM *Hrs Open:* 1 PM-9 PM (M-F); 0.01 kw; -246 ft.; N37 22 8 W122 5 2
1885 Miramonte Avenue, Mountain View, CA 94040 US
(650) 210-2435, *Fax:* (650) 968-1706
www.ksfh.com
License: Mountain View, Santa Clara County, CA held by St. Francis High School of Mountain View California Inc.
Arbitron Metro Market: Mountain, CA *Format:* Rock/AOR *Hrs. of News Programming:* News progmg 5 hrs wkly *Target Audience:* General; young adult, high school, college
Bob Lautenslager, General Manager

Napa

KVON
12-17-1947; 1440 khz AM *Hrs Open:* 24; 5 kw-D, DA2; 1 kw-N, DA2; N38 15 45 W122 16 56
1124 Foster Road, Napa, CA 94558 US
(707) 258-1111, *Fax:* (707) 226-7544
www.kvon.com
License: Napa, CA held by Wine Country Broadcasting Co.
Nat'l Reps: Christal
Arbitron Metro Market: Napa, CA *Format:* News, News/Talk, 86 *Special Programming:* Sp 2 hrs *Hrs. of News Programming:* news progmg 30 hrs wkly *No. News Employees:* 3 *Target Audience:* 35 plus. *Adv.Rates:* 60; 50; 60; 20
Jeff Schechtman, General Manager
Erica Pickett, Promotions Manager
Ben Webster, Chief Engineer
Dan Darnielle, Advertising & Sales Director

Needles

KLUK
05-01-1984; 97.9 mhz FM; 29.5 kw; 1552 ft.; N35 2 6 W114 22 9
1531 Jill Way, Suite 5, Bullhead City, AZ 86426 US
(928) 763-5586, *Fax:* (928) 763-3775
www.lucky98fm.com
License: Needles, San Bernardino County, CA held by Cameron Broadcasting Inc.
Group Owner: Cameron Broadcasting Inc.; acq 1-18-02; grpsl).
Format: Classic Rock *No. News Employees:* 1 *Target Audience:* 25-54
William Jaeger, CEO
Craig Powers, Operations Dir
Don Jaeger, General Manager
Mike Fletcher, General Sales Mgr
Dave Cooper, Chief Engineer

KTOX
10-01-1952; 1340 khz AM *Hrs Open:* 24; 1 kw-U, ND1; N34 51 10 W114 37 19
Mailing Address: 2281 Mc Culloch Blvd., Suite 18, Lake Havasu City, AZ 86403 US
Second Address: P.O. Box 8766, Ft. Mahaur, AZ 86427
(760) 326-4500, *Fax:* (760) 326-6849
www.ktox1340am.com
ktox1340@citlink.net
License: Needles, CA held by Creative Broadcasting Services Inc.
Nat'l Network: Jones Radio Networks; Premiere Radio Networks
Arbitron Metro Market: Needles, CA *Format:* News, News/Talk, 86 *Special Programming:* Rt 66 program, 22 hrs of personalities and live local programming wkly *Hrs. of News Programming:* news progmg 24 hrs wkly *No.News Employees:* 1 *Target Audience:* 18 plus. *Adv. Rates:* 11;10; 11; 9
Robert Hayes, CEO
David Hayes, President
Paul Fix, Operations Dir
Kelly Hayes, General Sales Mgr

KNKK
107.1 mhz FM *Hrs Open:* 24; 15.5 kw; 1909 ft.; N35 1 58 W114 21 57
225 N. Mill Street, Aspen, CO 81611 US
(928) 763-5586, *Fax:* (928) 763-3775
www.theknack107.com
info@theknack107.com
License: Needles, San Bernardino County, CA held by Cameron Broadcasting Inc.
Group Owner: Cameron Broadcasting Inc.; acq 3-13-01).
Arbitron Metro Market: Bullhead City, AZ *Format:* Contemporary Hits/Top 40 *Target Audience:* 18-49
William Jaeger, CEO
Craig Powers, Operations Dir
Don Jaeger, General Manager
Mike Fletcher, General Sales Mgr
Dave Cooper, Chief Engineer

*KJLC-FM
08-07-2012; 90.7 mhz FM; 1 kw; -259 ft.; N34 54 13 W114 38 38 US
(909)882-5330
License: Needles, San Bernadino County, CA held by Centro Cristiano Vida Abundante
Ramiro Lopez, President

Nevada City

*KVMR
07-17-1978; 89.5 mhz FM *Hrs Open:* 24; 1.75 kw; 1132 ft.; N39 14 47 W120 57 48
401 Spring Street, Nevada City, CA 95959 US
(530) 265-9073, *Fax:* (530) 265-9077
www.kvmr.org
office@KVMR.org
License: Nevada City, Nevada County, CA held by Nevada City Community Broadcast Group.
Arbitron Metro Market: Nevada City, CA *Format:* Variety/Diverse *Special Programming:* Country 7 hrs, Black 4 hrs, folk 13 hrs, blues 7 hrs, foreign/ethnic 20 hrs wkly *Hrs. of News Programming:* news progmg 1 hr dailymon-fri *No. News Employees:* 2 *Target Audience:* Full spectrum community radio *Adv. Rates:* Upon Request
Erica Randall, Operations Dir
David Levin, General Manager
Brianna Caldwell, General Sales Mgr
Steve Baker, Programming Director
Felton Pruitt, News Director
Paul Patterson, Chief Engineer
Alice MacAllister, Music Director
Felton Pruitt, News Producer
John Button, Webmaster
Adrianna Kelly, Membership Coordinator
Briana Ezzell, Development Director
Julie Chiarelli, Business Manager

Newberry Springs

KIQQ-FM
01-01-2001; 103.7 mhz FM *Hrs Open:* 24; 6 kw; 282 ft.; N34 53 7 W116 53 45 *Rebroadcasts:* Simulcast with KAEH(FM) Beaumont 100%
P.O. Box 191747, Atlanta, GA 31119 US
(760) 255-2636, *Fax:* (760) 255-3236
www.moonbroadcasting.com
jramirez@lamaquinamusical.net
License: Newberry Springs, San Bernardino County, CA held by MBR Licensee LLC.
Group Owner: Moon Broadcasting; (acq 11-5-99).

Arbitron Metro Market: Barstow, CA
Alicia Avila, General Manager

Newport Beach

KDLE

01-31-1964; 103.1 mhz FM *Hrs Open:* 24; 0.3 kw; 965 ft.; N33 36 19 W117 48 38 *Rebroadcasts:* Simulcast with KDLD(FM) Santa Monica 100%
50 East Rivercenter Blvd, #1200, Covington, KY 41011 US
(323) 900-6100, *Fax:* (323) 900-6200
www.indie1031.com
feedback@indie1031.com
License: Newport Beach, Orange County, CA held by Entravision Holdings LLC.
Group Owner: Entravision Communications Corp.; (acq 2000; grpsl)
Arbitron Metro Market: Los Angeles, CA
Karl Meyer, General Manager
Penelope Wakeman, Station Manager

North Fork

KLLE

01-01-1996; 107.9 mhz FM; 1.75 kw; 1227 ft.; N37 17 42 W119 33 51
1360 W. 18th Street, Merced, CA 95341 US
(559) 456-4000, *Fax:* (559) 251-9555
www.univision.com
License: North Fork, Madera County, CA held by Univision Radio License Corp.
Group Owner: Univision Radio; (acq 9-22-2003; grpsl).
Arbitron Metro Market: Fresno, CA *Format:* Spanish
Angela Navarrete, General Manager

North Highlands

*KQEI-FM

02-21-1992; 89.3 mhz FM *Hrs Open:* 24; 3.3 kw; 354 ft.; N38 42 38 W121 28 54 *Rebroadcasts:* Rebroadcasts KQED-FM San Francisco 98%
4135 Northgate Blvd, Suite 1, Sacramento, CA 95834 US
(415) 864-2000, *Fax:* (415) 553-2241
www.kqed.org
fm@kqed.org
License: North Highlands, Sacramento County, CA held by KQED Inc.
Arbitron Metro Market: San Francisco, CA *Format:* News
Jo Anne Wallace, General Manager
Traci Eckels, General Sales Mgr
Raul Ramirez, News Director
Sinclair Crockett, Director
Georgi Kelly, Senior Director
Jeff Rutledge, Project Manager

Northridge

*KCSN

11-01-1963; 88.5 mhz FM *Hrs Open:* 24; 0.37 kw; 1644 ft.; N34 19 10 W118 33 15
18111 Nordhoff Street, Northridge, CA 91330 US
(818) 677-3090, *Fax:* (818) 677-3069
www.kcsn.org
info@kcsn.org
License: Northridge, Los Angeles County, CA held by California State University Northridge.
Nat'l Network: PRI; NPR
Arbitron Metro Market: Northridge, CA *Format:* Variety/Diverse *Special Programming:* German 3 hrs, Jewish 3 hrs, bluegrass 5 hrs wkly *Hrs. of News Programming:* news progmg 12 hrs wkly *No. News Employees:* 1 *Target Audience:* 35 plus; middle/upper middle-class, well educated
Sky Daniels, General Manager
Laura Kelly, General Sales Mgr
Sky Daniels, Programming Director
Keith Goldstein, News Director
Conor S. Watson, Chief Engineer

Oakdale

KHOP

03-11-1985; 95.1 mhz FM *Hrs Open:* 24; 29.5 kw; 633 ft.; N37 47 34 W120 31 8
City Center West, 7201 W. Lake Mead Blvd, Las Vegas, NV 89128 US
(209) 766-5000, *Fax:* (209) 522-2061
www.khop.com
khop@khop.com
License: Oakdale, Stanislaus County, CA
Group Owner: Cumulus Media Inc.; (acq 1996; $5 million).
Arbitron Metro Market: Modesto, CA *Format:* Contemporary Hits/Top 40 *Special Programming:* Perez Hilton 20 hrs wkly *Hrs. of News Programming:* news progmg 3 hrs wkly *No. News Employees:* 1 *Target Audience:* 18-49.
Roy Williams, General Manager
Jean Western, General Sales Mgr
Joe Roberts, Program Director

Oakhurst

KAAT

11-01-1982; 103.1 mhz FM *Hrs Open:* 24; 25 kw; -194 ft.; N37 27 10 W119 37 54
40356 Oak Park Way, Oakhurst, CA 93644 US
(559) 683-1031, *Fax:* (559) 683-5488
www.kaat.com
mtkaat@sierratel.com
License: Oakhurst, Madera County, CA held by California Sierra Corp.
Group Owner: Moon Broadcasting; (acq 3-3-2005; $4.75 million with co-located AM).
Arbitron Metro Market: Fresno, CA *Format:* Spanish *Special Programming:* Relg 2 hrs wkly *Target Audience:* 25-54; general
Abel DeLuna, President
Denny Jackson, Programming Director

KTNS

11-20-1982; 1060 khz AM *Hrs Open:* 24
40356 Oak Pk Wy Box 2020, Oakhurst, CA 93644 US
(559) 683-1060(559) 683-1060, *Fax:* (559) 683-5488
www.ktnsradio.com
tammy@kaat.com
License: Oakhurst, CA held by California Sierra Corp.
Group Owner: Moon Broadcasting
Nat'l Network: CNN Radio; Westwood One
Arbitron Metro Market: Oakhurst, CA *Format:* Adult Contemp *No. News Employees:* 3 *Target Audience:* 25-49.
Becky Deaver, General Sales Mgr
Jesse Taylor, Programming Director

Oakland

KNEW(AM)

01-01-1925; 960 khz AM *Hrs Open:* 24; 5 kw-U, DA-1; N37 49 40 W122 18 53
340 Townsend St., San Francisco, CA 94107
(415) 975-5555, *Fax:* (415) 538-5953
www.960knew.com
John@Green960.com
License: Oakland, Alameda County, CA held by AMFM Broadcasting Licenses LLC.
Group Owner: Clear Channel Communications Inc.; (acq 8-30-2000; grpsl)
Nat'l Reps: Christal
Population Served: 715,674 *Arbitron Metro Market:* San Francisco, CA *Format:* Talk
Don Parker, Operations Dir
Dave Pugh, General Manager
Alan Eisenson, Programming Director
Ramona Gutierrez, Promotions Manager

KKSF

11-03-1947; 910 khz AM *Hrs Open:* 24; 1,470 ft
750 Battery Road, Suite 200, San Francisco, CA 94111 US
(415) 356-5500, *Fax:* (415) 975-5573
www.1037theband.com
License: Oakland, CA held by AMFM Broadcasting Licenses LLC.
Group Owner: Clear Channel Communications Inc.; (acq 8-30-2000; grpsl).
Arbitron Metro Market: San Francisco, CA *Format:* Classic Rock *Hrs. of News Programming:* news progmg 5 hrs wkly *No. News Employees:* 1 *Target Audience:* 25-49.
Don Parker, Operations Dir
Dave Pugh, General Manager
Dave Logan, Programming Director
Ramona Gutierrez, Promotions Manager

KMKY

07-01-1922; 1310 khz AM *Hrs Open:* 24; 5 kw-U, DA1; N37 49 27 W122 19 10
77 West 66th Street, 16th Floor, New York, NY 10023 US
(650) 637-8800
www.radiodisney.com
License: Oakland, CA held by KGO-AM Radio Inc.
Group Owner: ABC Inc.; (acq 12-18-97; $6.25 million)
Nat'l Network: Radio Disney *Nat'l Reps:* Interep
Arbitron Metro Market: San Francisco, CA *Format:* Children *Target Audience:* 2-14; kids, tweens & moms 25-54 *Adv. Rates:* 200; 150; 250; 100
Lynn Dooley, Station Manager
Shalon Rogers, Promotions Manager

KNEW

07-02-1921; 960 khz AM *Hrs Open:* 24; 5 kw-U, DA1; N37 49 40 W122 18 53
750 Battery St., Suite 200, San Francisco, CA 94111 US
(415) 356-5500, *Fax:* (415) 975-5573
www.talk910.com
kenjones@clearchannel.com
License: Oakland, CA held by AMFM Broadcasting Licenses LLC.
Group Owner: Clear Channel Communications Inc.; (acq 8-30-2000; grpsl).
Arbitron Metro Market: San Francisco, CA *Format:* News, News/Talk, 86 *Hrs. of News Programming:* news progmg 65 hrs wkly *No. News Employees:* 8 *Target Audience:* 25-54.
Don Parker, Operations Dir
Dave Pugh, General Manager
John Scott, Programming Director
Ramona Gutierrez, Promotions Manager

Oceano

KLMM

09-01-1997; 94.1 mhz FM *Hrs Open:* 24; 0.34 kw; 1371 ft.; N34 53 52 W120 35 21
1200 W. Venice Blvd., Los Angeles, CA 90006 US
(805) 928-9796, *Fax:* (805) 928-4896
www.radiolazer.com
joseg@radiolazer.com
License: Oceano, San Luis Obispo County, CA held by Lazer Broadcasting Corp.
Group Owner: Lazer Broadcasting Corp.; (acq 8-7-2000; $1.115 million with KLUN(FM) Paso Robles)
Arbitron Metro Market: San Luis Obispo, CA *Format:* Adult Contemp *Hrs. of News Programming:* News progmg 6 hrs wkly *Target Audience:* 25-54; general
Jose Guzman, General Manager
Salvador Prieto, Programming Director

Oceanside

*KKSM

07-04-1956; 1320 khz AM *Hrs Open:* 24; 0.5 kw-U, DA1; N33 12 8 W117 20 17
1140 West Mission Road, San Marcos, CA 92069 US
(760) 744-1150
www.kksm.palomar.edu
License: Oceanside, CA held by Palomar Community College District.
Arbitron Metro Market: San Diego, CA *Format:* Variety/Diverse *Hrs. of News Programming:* news progmg 10 hrs wkly *No. News Employees:* 1 *Target Audience:* 18-25; college age, mid-upper income, diverse ethnic*Adv. Rates:* 15; 10; 10; 8
Zeb Navarro, General Manager
Matt O'Brien, Programming Director
Christa Lynch, Promotions Manager
Josh Diaz, News Director
Joan Rubin, Music Director
David Quera, Music Director
Joan Rubin, Music Director
Lindsay Lutz, NewsDirector
Ken Chapman

Oildale

KWVE(AM)

07-04-1988; 660 khz AM *Hrs Open:* 24; 10 kw-D, 1 kw-N, DA-2; N34 57 04 W120 22 38
1416 Hollister Ln., Los Osos, CA 93402
(805) 928-7707, *Fax:* (805) 922-8582
www.kgdp660.com
kgdp660@yahoo.com
License: Oildale, Santa Barbara County, CA held by Radio Representatives Inc.
Nat'l Network: USA
Population Served: 650,000 *Arbitron Metro Market:* Santa Maria, CA *Format:* Christian, Talk *Target Audience:* 35-65. *Adv. Rates:* 22; 20; 19; 18
Crystal Stahl, Operations Dir
Steve Cox, General Manager
Bill Greenelsh, Promotions Manager
Gretchen England, News Director

KLLY

01-01-1985; 95.3 mhz FM *Hrs Open:* 24; 12.5 kw; 463 ft.; N35 27 33 W119 1 13
Mailing Address: 166 West Putnam Avenue, Greenwich, CT 06830 US
Second Address: 3651 Pegasus, Suite 107, Bakersfield, CA 93308

(661) 393-1900, *Fax:* (661) 393-1915
www.klly.com
info@klly.com
License: Oildale, Kern County, CA held by Buckley Broadcasting of California LLC.
Group Owner: Buckley Broadcasting Corp.; (acq 12-86; $1.3 million;
Nat'l Reps: D & R Radio
Arbitron Metro Market: Bakersfield, CA *Format:* Adult Contemp
Target Audience: 25-44; adults
Steve Darnell, General Manager
Otis Warren, General Sales Mgr
E.J. Tyler, Programming Director

Ojai

KFYV

01-04-1972; 105.5 mhz FM *Hrs Open:* 24; 0.31 kw; 1437 ft.; N34 20 55 W119 20 13
100 Wilshire Blvd., Suite 1000, Santa Monica, CA 90401 US
(805) 289-1400, *Fax:* (805) 644-7906
www.live1055.fm
info@live1055.fm
License: Ojai, Ventura County, CA held by Gold Coast Broadcasting LLC
Group Owner: Gold Coast Broadcasting LLC; (acq 5-15-97; $2 million with KUNX(AM) Ventura)
Nat'l Network: AP Radio *Nat'l Reps:* Katz Radio
Arbitron Metro Market: Oxnard, CA *Format:* Adult Contemp *Hrs. of News Programming:* news progmg 3 hrs wkly *No. News Employees:* 1 *Target Audience:* 25-49; fun, upscale, classy adults
Chip Ehrhardt, General Manager
Jack Clarke, General Sales Mgr
Mark Elliot, Programming Director

*KLFH

01-01-2003; 89.5 mhz FM; 0.097 kw; 1322 ft.; N34 24 45 W119 11 16
35225 Avenue A, #204, Yucaipa, CA 92399 US
(805) 541-4343, *Fax:* (805) 541-9101
www.klife.org
info@klife.org
License: Ojai, Ventura County, CA held by Logos Broadcasting Corp.
Arbitron Metro Market: Ojai, CA *Format:* Contemporary Hits/Top 40
Jim Fugler, General Manager
Noonie Fugler, Promotions Manager

Ontario

KSPA

01-26-1947; 1510 khz AM *Hrs Open:* 24; 10 kw-D, DA2; 1 kw-N, DA2; N34 5 41 W117 36 46
1045 South East, Anaheim, CA 97805 US
(909) 483-1500, *Fax:* (909) 483-1515
www.thesparadio.com
kspa1510@aol.com
License: Ontario, CA held by Ontario Broadcasting L.L.C.
Group Owner: Astor Broadcast Group; (acq 11-4-99)
Arbitron Metro Market: Riverside, CA *Format:* Adult Contemp, Contemporary Hits/Top 40 *No. News Employees:* 1 *Target Audience:* 35+ *Adv. Rates:* 50; 50; 50; 30
Art Astor, President
Joe Lyons, Operations Dir
Peri Corso, General Manager
Susan Burke, Executive Vice President

KDEY(FM)

01-26-1947; 93.5 mhz FM *Hrs Open:* 24; 5 kw; Ant -131 ft; N34 10 32 W117 34 26
5055 Wilshire Blvd. #720, Los Angeles, CA 90036
(323) 337-1600, *Fax:* (323) 337-1633
www.935kday.com
sales@935kday.com
License: Ontario, San Bernardino County, CA held by KDAI Licensing LLC.
Group Owner: Magic Broadcasting LLC; (acq 1-31-2006; $120 million with KDAY(FM) Redondo Beach)
Population Served: 2,000,000 *Arbitron Metro Market:* Riverside-San Bernardino *Format:* Urban Contemporary
Kimberly Fletcher, General Manager

Orange

KLAA

01-13-1992; 830 khz AM *Hrs Open:* 24
8910 University Center Lane, #130, San Diego, CA 92122 US
(818) 528-2050, *Fax:* (818) 784-8824
www.830am.com
License: Orange, CA held by LAA 1 LLC
Nat'l Network: NBC Radio
Arbitron Metro Market: Los Angeles *Format:* News, Sports, 86 *Special Programming:* Sports *Hrs. of News Programming:* News progmg 28 hrs wkly *Target Audience:* 25-54; Male & female, high income, professionals*Adv. Rates:* 350; 350; 350; 75
Alan Fuller, General Manager

Orange Cove

KMAK

10-27-1990; 100.3 mhz FM *Hrs Open:* 24; 0.072 kw; 2073 ft.; N36 44 45 W119 16 58
Mailing Address: 611 Willow Street, Visalia, CA 93291 US
Second Address: 640 Park Blvd., Orange Cove, CA 93646
(559) 626-7922, *Fax:* (559) 896-1631
kmakfm@sbcglobal.net
License: Orange Cove, Fresno County, CA held by Mr. Richard B. Smith.
Nat'l Network: CNN Radio
Arbitron Metro Market: Fresno, CA *No. News Employees:* 1
Target Audience: 18-94. *Adv. Rates:* 25; 25; 20; 15
Ms. Sue Jones, General Manager
Mr. Nelson Gomez, Promotions Manager
Mr. Richard Smith, Chief Engineer

Orcutt

KPAT

01-01-1993; 95.7 mhz FM; 3.3 kw; 899 ft.; N34 44 30 W120 26 45
1416 Hollister Lane, Los Osos, CA 93402 US
(805) 922-1041, *Fax:* (805) 928-3069
www.957thebeatfm.com
info@957thebeatfm.com
License: Orcutt, Santa Barbara County, CA held by AGM-Santa Maria LP.
Group Owner: American General Media; (acq 12-1-99; $900,000).
Nat'l Network: USA
Arbitron Metro Market: Santa Maria-Lompoc, CA *Format:* Blues
Rich Watson, General Manager
Emily Stich, General Sales Mgr
Luis Diaz, Programming Director
Jeff Lyons, Promotions Manager

Orland

KRQR

01-01-1994; 106.7 mhz FM *Hrs Open:* 24; 50 kw; 308 ft.; N39 53 16 W122 37 38
P. O. Box 7568, Chico, CA 95927 US
(530) 342-2200, *Fax:* (530) 342-2260
www.zrockfm.com
info@zrockfm.com
License: Orland, Glenn County, CA held by Results Radio Licensee L.L.C.
Group Owner: Fritz Communications Inc.; (acq 6-11-99; grpsl)
Arbitron Metro Market: Chico, CA *Format:* Rock/AOR
Jack Fritz, President
Jon Graham, General Manager
Neil Randall, Programming Director
Candy Mason, News Director
J.D. Davis, Chief Engineer

Oroville

KEWE

08-04-1962; 1340 khz AM *Hrs Open:* 24*Rebroadcasts:* Rebroadcasts KRER(FM) Hamilton City
1436 Auburn Boulevard, Sacramento, CA 95815 US
(530) 345-0021, *Fax:* (530) 893-2121
License: Oroville, CA held by Deer Creek Broadcasting LLC
Group Owner: Deer Creek Broadcasting LLC
Arbitron Metro Market: Chico, CA *Format:* Sports
Rosa Ramos, Programming Director

Oxnard

KCAQ

09-27-1958; 104.7 mhz FM; 4.5 kw; 1522 ft.; N34 19 49 W119 1 24
100 Wilshire Blvd., Suite 1000, Santa Monica, CA 90401 US
(805) 289-1400, *Fax:* (805) 644-7906
www.q1047.com
info@q1047.com
License: Oxnard, Ventura County, CA held by Gold Coast Broadcasting LLC
Group Owner: Gold Coast Broadcasting LLC; acq 1996; $3.65 million with KVTA(AM) Port Hueneme).
Nat'l Reps: Katz Radio
Arbitron Metro Market: Ventura, CA *Format:* Contemporary Hits/Top 40 *Target Audience:* 18-44.
Chip Ehrhardt, General Manager
Steve Hess, General Sales Mgr
Brian Davis, Programming Director

*KCRU

01-01-1993; 89.1 mhz FM; 0.85 kw; 853 ft.; N34 6 47 W119 3 34
Rebroadcasts: Rebroadcasts KCRW(FM) Santa Monica 98%
1900 Pico Blvd, Santa Monica, CA 90405 US
(310) 450-5183(888) 660-kcrw, *Fax:* (310) 450-7172
www.kcrw.com
mail@kcrw.org
License: Oxnard, Ventura County, CA held by Santa Monica Community College District.
Arbitron Metro Market: Oxnard, CA *Format:* News
Mike Newport, Operations Dir
Ruth Seymour, General Manager
Jennifer Ferro, Station Manager
David Kleinbart, General Sales Mgr
Ariana Morgenstern, Programming Director
Steve Herbert, Chief Engineer

KDAR

10-28-1974; 98.3 mhz FM *Hrs Open:* 24; 1.5 kw; 1289 ft.; N34 20 55 W119 19 57
Mailing Address: 500 Esplanade Drive, Oxnard, CA 93030 US
Second Address: 500 Esplanade Dr., Suite 1500, Oxnard, CA 93036
(805) 485-8881, *Fax:* (805) 656-5330
www.kdar.com
radiomail@kdar.com
License: Oxnard, Ventura County, CA held by New Inspiration Broadcasting Co. Inc.
Group Owner: Salem Communications Corp.
Arbitron Metro Market: Oxnard-Ventura, CA *Format:* Christian, Talk *Hrs. of News Programming:* News progmg 2 hrs wkly
Target Audience: 25-54; upscale adults with large families
Ed Atsinger, President
Richard Trejo, General Manager
Terri Dawson, General Sales Mgr
Jeff Hunter, Programming Director

KOXR

06-11-1955; 910 khz AM *Hrs Open:* 24; 5 kw-D, DA2; 1 kw-N, DA2; N34 16 58 W119 7 36
200 South ""A"" Street, 4th Floor, Oxnard, CA 93030 US
(805) 240-2070, *Fax:* (805) 240-5960
License: Oxnard, CA held by Lazer Broadcasting Corp.
Group Owner: Lazer Broadcasting Corp.; acq 1-11-99)
Nat'l Reps: Lotus Entravision Reps LLC
Arbitron Metro Market: Oxnard-Ventura, CA *Target Audience:* 25-54.
Alfredo Plascencia, CEO
Salvador Prieto, Operations Dir

KXLM

01-01-1991; 102.9 mhz FM *Hrs Open:* 24; 5.5 kw; 112 ft.; N34 14 12 W119 12 11
Mailing Address: 200 S. a Street, Ste 400, Oxnard, CA 93030 US
Second Address: Box 6940, Oxnard, CA 93030
(805) 240-2070, *Fax:* (805) 240-5960
radiolazer.com
info@radiolazer.com
License: Oxnard, Ventura County, CA held by Kext Broadcasters Inc.
Arbitron Metro Market: Oxnard, CA *Format:* Adult Contemp *Hrs. of News Programming:* news progmg 2 hrs wkly *No. News Employees:* 1 *Target Audience:* 25-59. *Adv. Rates:* 65; 65; 65; 50
Alfredo Plascencia, President
Terry Janisch, General Sales Mgr

Pacific Grove

*KAZU

10-01-1977; 90.3 mhz FM *Hrs Open:* 24; 3.4 kw; 551 ft.; N36 33 9 W121 47 17
P.O. Box 210, Pacific Grove, CA 93950 US
(831) 582-5298, *Fax:* (831) 582-5299
www.kazu.org
programming@kazu.org
License: Pacific Grove, Monterey County, CA held by Foundation of California State University Monterey Bay
Nat'l Network: NPR
Arbitron Metro Market: Seaside, CA *Format:* News *Special Programming:* Country 6 hrs, women's mus 6 hrs, gospel 4 hrs, fo *Hrs. of News Programming:* News progmg 8 hrs wkly *Target Audience:* 25-65; general
Mik Benedek, General Manager
Krista Almanzan, News Director

KOCN
04-10-1977; 105.1 mhz FM *Hrs Open:* 24; 1.8 kw; 600 ft.; N36 33 9 W121 47 17
220 Concord Plaza, Suite 600, San Antonio, TX 78216 US
(831) 755-8181, *Fax:* (831) 755-8193
www.kocean105.com
License: Pacific Grove, Monterey County, CA held by CC Licenses LLC.
Group Owner: Clear Channel Communications Inc.; (acq 9-22-97; grpsl)
Nat'l Network: Westwood One *Nat'l Reps:* Clear Channel
Arbitron Metro Market: Monterey-Salinas-Santa Cruz, CA *Format:* Oldies *No. News Employees:* 1 *Target Audience:* 25-54; at work, double income households
Rhonda McCormack, General Manager
Sam Diggedy, Programming Director
Angel Jarquin, Promotions Manager

Pala

***KOPA(FM)**
91.3 mhz FM; 100 w; Ant -1,066 ft; N33 22 00 W117 04 05
35008 Pala Temecula Road, Pala, CA 92059
(760) 891-3500
www.palatribe.com
hr@palatribe.com
License: Pala, San Diego County, CA held by Pala Band of Mission Indians.
Population Served: 1,326,179 *Arbitron Metro Market:* San Diego, California *Format:* Variety/Diverse
Robert Smith, Chairman
Leroy Miranda, Vice Chairman
Theressa Villa, Secretary
Theresa J. Nieto, Treasurer
Dion Perez, Council Member
Sheila Lopez, Council Member

Palm Desert

KEZN
11-28-1977; 103.1 mhz FM *Hrs Open:* 24; 1.9 kw; 591 ft.; N33 51 58 W116 25 56
Mailing Address: 600 New Hampshire N.W., Suite 1200, Washington, DC 20037 US
Second Address: Box 291, Palm Desert, CA 92260
(760) 340-9383, *Fax:* (760) 340-5756
www.ez103.com
info@ez103.com
License: Palm Desert, Riverside County, CA held by Infinity Radio Holdings Inc.
Group Owner: CBS Radio; (acq 11-13-98; grpsl).
Nat'l Network: Westwood One
Arbitron Metro Market: Palm Springs, CA *Format:* Adult Contemp *No. News Employees:* 1 *Target Audience:* 25-64.
Tom Hoyt, General Manager
Doug Kratky, General Sales Mgr
Rick Shaw, Programming Director
Frank Torok, Promotions Manager

***KHCS**
01-01-1993; 91.7 mhz FM *Hrs Open:* 24; 0.96 kw; 574 ft.; N33 51 57 W116 25 56
5855 Naples Plaza, Long Beach, CA 90803 US
(760) 864-9620, *Fax:* (760) 864-9633
www.khcs.us
email@khcb.org
License: Palm Desert, Riverside County, CA held by Prairie Avenue Gospel Center.
Format: Christian, Religious *Target Audience:* 20-85.
Dan Pike, President
R.F. Watts, Chief Engineer

Palm Springs

KNWQ
02-12-1946; 1140 khz AM; 10 kw-D, DA2; 2.5 kw-N, DA2; N33 51 39 W116 28 20
725 Broad St., P.O. Box 936, Augusta, GA 30903 US
(760) 322-7890, *Fax:* (760) 322-5493
www.943knews.com
jay.white@morris.com?subject=Knewsradio.com
License: Palm Springs, CA held by Morris Communications Corp.
Group Owner: Morris Radio LLC; (acq 12-24-97; $4.5 million)
Nat'l Network: CBS *Nat'l Reps:* McGavren Guild
Arbitron Metro Market: Palm Springs, CA *Format:* News, News/Talk, 86 *Target Audience:* 35-65.
Angela Powers, Operations Dir
Jay White, General Manager
Scott Smith, General Sales Mgr
Virginia Nelson, Programming Director
Jose Rodriguez, Promotions Manager
John McMullen, Program Director
Jamie Kanai, Marketing Director
Cristine Constantinescu, Director of Digital Media
Michael Knight, News Department
Charlie Dyer, News Department

KPLM
01-24-1983; 106.1 mhz FM *Hrs Open:* 24; 50 kw; 397 ft.; N33 52 14 W116 13 39
P.O. Box 1825, Palm Springs, CA 92263 US
(760) 568-4550, *Fax:* (760) 341-7600
thebig106.com
kplm@markerbroadcasting.com
License: Palm Springs, Riverside County, CA held by RM Broadcasting L.L.C.
Nat'l Reps: Katz Radio
Arbitron Metro Market: Palm Springs, CA *Format:* Country *Hrs. of News Programming:* news progmg 9 hrs wkly *No. News Employees:* 1 *Target Audience:* 25-54.
Todd Marker, General Manager
Hughes Hilles, General Sales Mgr
Al Gordon, Programming Director
Kory James, Promotions Manager
Jeff Michaels, News Director
Nick Summers, Production Manager

***KPSC**
04-01-1978; 88.5 mhz FM *Hrs Open:* 24; 1.25 kw; 587 ft.; N33 51 56 W116 26 4 *Rebroadcasts:* Rebroadcasts KUSC 100%
Mailing Address: P. O. Box 77913, Los Angeles, CA 90007 US
Second Address: 515 S. Figueroa St., Suite 2050, Los Angeles, CA 90071
(213) 225-7400, *Fax:* (213) 225-7410
www.kusc.org
memberservices@kusc.org
License: Palm Springs, Riverside County, CA held by University of Southern California.
Nat'l Network: PRI; NPR
Arbitron Metro Market: Palm Springs, CA *Format:* News/Talk, Classical *Target Audience:* 35 plus; general
Brenda Barnes, President
Steve Coghill, Operations Dir
Eric DeWeese, General Manager
Amy Iwata, Station Manager
Janet McIntyre, General Sales Mgr
Gail Eichenthal, Programming Director
Stephanie Ross, Promotions Manager
RonThompson, Engineering Dir

KPSI
10-29-1956; 920 khz AM; 5 kw-D, DA2; 1 kw-N, DA2; N33 51 29 W116 29 39
2100 E Tahquitz-Canyon W, Palm Springs, CA 92262 US
(760) 325-2582, *Fax:* (760) 322-3562
www.newstalk920.com
info@newstalk920.com
License: Palm Springs, CA held by R & R Radio Corp.
Group Owner: RR Broadcasting
Nat'l Reps: Christal
Arbitron Metro Market: Palm Springs, CA *Format:* News, Talk
Special Programming: American Indian 2 hrs wkly *Hrs. of News Programming:* news progmg 16 hrs wkly *No. News Employees:* 4 *Target Audience:* 25-54.
Mike Keane, General Manager
Gregg Aratin, General Sales Mgr
Steve Kelly, Programming Director
Brian Garris, Promotions Manager
Gregg Nichols, News Director

KPSI-FM
06-01-1980; 100.5 mhz FM *Hrs Open:* 24; 25 kw; Ant 121 ft; N33 56 44 W116 24 34
2100 E. Tahquitz Canyon Way, Palm Springs, CA 92262
(760) 325-2582, *Fax:* (760) 320-4632
www.mix1005.fm
License: Palm Springs, Riverside County, CA held by R & R Radio Corp.
Group Owner: RR Broadcasting
Population Served: 358,000 *Arbitron Metro Market:* Palm Springs, C
Scott Chrisman, CEO/COO
Ric Supple, President
Jack Brody, Operations Dir
Jack Brody, General Manager
Jack Brody, Station Manager
Gregg Aratin, General Sales Mgr
Bradley Ryan, Programming Director
Brian Garris, PromotionsManager
Gene Nichols, News Director
Barry O'Connor, Engineering Dir
Barry O'Connor, Chief Engineer

KPTR
10-04-1964; 1450 khz AM *Hrs Open:* 24
2100 E Tahquitz, Canyon Way, Palm Springs, CA 92262 US
(760) 325-2582, *Fax:* (760) 322-3562
www.kptr1450.com
gregg@rrbroadcasting.com
License: Palm Springs, CA held by R & R Radio Corp.
Group Owner: RR Broadcasting; (acq 7-27-2006; $2.3 million).
Arbitron Metro Market: Palm Springs, CA *Format:* Alternative, Talk *No. News Employees:* 1
0, Chairman
Mike Keane, General Manager
Gregg Aratin, Gen. Sales Mgr.
Steve Kelly, Program Director
Lisa Childs, Program Director
Scott Cristman, Financial Officer
Mell Hill, Local Sales Mgr.
Ken Vincent, News Anchor/Reporter
Jazmin Anderson, Accounting
Jack Broady, Production Director
Kacy Broady, Traffic Director

Palmdale

KUTY
08-01-1957; 1470 khz AM *Hrs Open:* 24; 5 kw-D, DA2; 5 kw-N, DA2; N34 39 55 W118 0 40
100 Wilshire Boulevard, Suite 1000, Santa Monica, CA 90401 US
(661) 947-3107, *Fax:* (661) 272-5688
www.lameramera1470.com
info@lameramera1470.com
License: Palmdale, CA held by High Desert Broadcasting LLC.
Group Owner: High Desert Broadcasting LLC; (acq 3-5-97)
Arbitron Metro Market: Palmdale, CA
Nelson Rasse, General Manager

Palo Alto

KDOW
01-01-1947; 1220 khz AM *Hrs Open:* 24; 5 kw-D, ND1; 0.145 kw-N, ND1; N37 29 4 W122 8 4
114 Sansome St, Sutie 1410, San Francisco, CA 94104 US
(510) 713-1100, *Fax:* (510) 505-1448
www.kdow.biz
comments@kdow.biz
License: Palo Alto, CA held by SCA-Palo Alto LLC.
Group Owner: Salem Communications Corp.; (acq 6-28-2001; $9 million)
Nat'l Network: Salem Radio Network *Nat'l Reps:* Salem
Arbitron Metro Market: Fremont, CA *Format:* Talk, News *Hrs. of News Programming:* news progmg 70 hrs wkly *No. News Employees:* 5 *Target Audience:* 25-54; general
Greg Edwards, Operations Dir
Mike Shields, General Manager
Mike Ginsburg, General Sales Mgr
Craig Roberts, Programming Director
Amy Nyquist, Promotions Manager
Craig Roberts, Chief Engineer

Palo Cedro

KWCA
101.1 mhz FM; 4.9 kw; 1476 ft.; N40 39 15 W122 31 12
188 South Bellevue, Suite 222, Memphis, TN 38104 US
(530) 727-8181, *Fax:* (530) 243-6642
www.mixredding.com
radio@mia101.com
License: Palo Cedro, Trinity County, CA held by George S. Flinn Jr.
Arbitron Metro Market: Palo Cedro, CA
George S. Flinn Jr., President
Jose Pacheco, General Manager

Paradise

KHSL-FM
10-15-1983; 103.5 mhz FM *Hrs Open:* 24; 1.5 kw; 1312 ft.; N39 57 29 W121 42 49
4700 S.W. Macadam Ave., Portland, OR 97201 US
(530) 345-0021, *Fax:* (530) 893-2121
www.khsl.com
jperry@dcbchico.com; dcorbin@dcbchico.com
License: Paradise, Butte County, CA held by Deer Creek Broadcasting LLC.
Group Owner: Deer Creek Broadcasting LLC; (acq 9-8-2004; grpsl).
Nat'l Reps: Katz Radio
Arbitron Metro Market: Chico, CA *Format:* Country *Hrs. of News Programming:* news progmg 6 hrs wkly *No. News Employees:* 1 *Target Audience:* 25-54; active

Dino Corbin, General Manager
Bill Meyer, General Sales Mgr
Lisa Fitzgerald, Promotions Manager

KKXX
09-01-1960; 930 khz AM
1601 Belvedere Road, West Palm Beach, FL 33406 US
(530) 894-7325, *Fax:* (530) 894-5372
www.kkxx.net
info@kkxx.net
License: Paradise, CA held by Butte Broadcasting Co.
Arbitron Metro Market: Chico, CA *Format:* News, News/Talk, 86, Religious
Carl Auel, President
Andrew Palmquist, General Manager

KZAP
06-15-2007; 96.7 mhz FM *Hrs Open:* 24; 1.5 kw; 1289 ft.; N39 57 45 W121 42 40 *Rebroadcasts:* Simulcast with KPIG-FM Freedom 100%
407 West 9th Street, Chico, CA 95928 US
(530) 899-3600, *Fax:* (530) 343-0243
www.kpig.com
License: Paradise, Butte County, CA held by Mapleton License of Chico LLC.
Group Owner: Mapleton Communications LLC; (acq 11-30-2006; grpsl)
Nat'l Reps: Christal
Arbitron Metro Market: Paradise, CA *Format:* Triple A *Target Audience:* 25-49.
Coyote McGee, Operations Dir
Frank Caprista, Programming Director
Chad Gammage, Promotions Manager
Linda Patterson, Business Manager

Pasadena

KAZN
09-12-1942; 1300 khz AM *Hrs Open:* 24
449 Broadway, New York, NY 10013 US
(626) 568-1300, *Fax:* (626) 568-3666
www.am1300.com
License: Pasadena, CA held by Multicultural Radio Broadcasting Licensee LLC.
Group Owner: Multicultural Radio Broadcasting Inc.; (acq 5-11-98; $12 million).
Arbitron Metro Market: Pasadena, CA *Format:* Chinese *Hrs. of News Programming:* News progmg 90 hrs wkly *Target Audience:* Chinese. *Adv. Rates:* 235; 205; 225; 195
Arthur Liu, President
Hsiang Lee, Programming Director

***KPCC**
09-01-1957; 89.3 mhz FM *Hrs Open:* 24; 680 w; 2,922 ft; N34 13 35 W118 03 58
1570 E. Colorado Blvd., Pasadena, CA 91106
(626) 585-7000, *Fax:* (626) 585-7916
www.kpcc.org
mail@kpcc.org
License: Pasadena, Los Angeles County, CA held by Pasadena Area Community College District Board of Trustees.
Nat'l Network: NPR; PRI; CBC Radio One
Population Served: 342,000 *Arbitron Metro Market:* Los Angeles *Hrs. of News Programming:* News progmg 6 hrs wkly *Target Audience:* 25-55.
Bill Davis, CEO
Doug Johnson, Operations Dir
Julie Allen, General Sales Mgr
Craig Curtis, Programming Director
Paul Glickman, News Director

KDIS
02-07-1942; 1110 khz AM; 50 kw-D, DA2; 20 kw-N, DA2; N34 6 50 W117 59 51
600 New Hampshrie Ave., N.W., Suite 1200, Washington, DC 20037 US
(818) 569-5035
www.radiodisney.com/kdisam1110
License: Pasadena, CA held by KABC-AM Radio Inc.
Group Owner: ABC Inc.; (acq 12-19-00; $65 million).
Nat'l Network: Radio Disney
Arbitron Metro Market: Los Angeles *Format:* Children
John Davison, President
Natalie Eig, General Manager

KROQ-FM
01-01-1974; 106.7 mhz FM *Hrs Open:* 24; 5.5 kw; 1388 ft.; N34 11 49 W118 15 30
600 New Hampshire Ave., N.W., Suite 1200, Washington, DC 20037 US
(323) 930-1067, *Fax:* (323) 931-1067
www.kroq.com
Tips@kroq.com
License: Pasadena, Los Angeles County, CA held by Infinity Broadcasting of Los Angeles Inc.
Group Owner: CBS Radio; (acq 11-13-98; grpsl).
Arbitron Metro Market: Greater Los Angeles *Format:* Rock/AOR *Target Audience:* 18-34.
Jeff Federman, General Manager
Bill Denton, General Sales Mgr
Kevin Weatherly, Programming Director

Paso Robles

KLUN
08-01-1995; 103.1 mhz FM *Hrs Open:* 24; 1.1 kw; 761 ft.; N35 38 45 W120 44 16
1200 W. Venice Blvd., Los Angeles, CA 90006 US
(805) 928-9796, *Fax:* (805) 928-4896
www.radiolazer.com
joseg@radiolazer.com
License: Paso Robles, San Luis Obispo County, CA held by Lazer Broadcasting Corp.
Group Owner: Lazer Broadcasting Corp.; acq 8-7-00; $1.115 million with KLMM(FM) Morro Bay)
Arbitron Metro Market: Santa Maria, CA *Target Audience:* 18-49; general
Alfredo Placencia, President
Jose Guzman, General Manager
Salvador Prieto, Programming Director
Bill Bordoux, Chief Engineer

KKAL
11-20-1972; 92.5 mhz FM *Hrs Open:* 24; 4.8 kw; 1486 ft.; N35 21 40 W120 39 21
P.O. Box 2700, Bakersfield, CA 93303 US
(805) 781-2750, *Fax:* (805) 781-2758
www.kkalonline.com
License: Paso Robles, San Luis Obispo County, CA held by AGM California.
Group Owner: American General Media; (acq 1997; $675,000)
Arbitron Metro Market: San Luis Obispo, CA *Format:* Adult Contemp *Hrs. of News Programming:* news progmg 12 hrs wkly *No. News Employees:* 1 *Target Audience:* 18 plus.
Kathy Signorelli, General Manager
Mark Tobin, General Sales Mgr
Pepper Daniels, Programming Director

KPRL
10-01-1946; 1230 khz AM; 1 kw-U, ND1; N35 39 15 W120 40 52
P.O. Box 5365, Santa Barbara, CA 93150 US
(805) 238-1230, *Fax:* (805) 238-5332
www.kprl.com
reception@kprl.com
License: Paso Robles, CA held by North County Communications LLC
Nat'l Reps: Western Regional Broadcast Sales
Arbitron Metro Market: San Luis Obispo *Format:* News, News/Talk, 84, Talk *Hrs. of News Programming:* news progmg one hr wkly *No. News Employees:* 1 *Target Audience:* 25 plus. *Adv. Rates:* 19; 17; 15; 12
Kevin Will, CEO

Patterson

KOSO
06-06-1966; 92.9 mhz FM *Hrs Open:* 24; 6 kw; 328 ft.; N37 36 24.2 W121 2 37.2
600 Congress Ave., Suite 1400, Austin, TX 78701 US
(209) 551-1306, *Fax:* (209) 551-1359
www.b929.com
License: Patterson, Stanislaus County, CA held by Capstar TX L.P.
Group Owner: Clear Channel Communications Inc.; (acq 8-30-00; grpsl).
Arbitron Metro Market: Modesto, CA *Format:* Alternative *Hrs. of News Programming:* news progmg 5 hrs wkly *No. News Employees:* 1 *Target Audience:* 25-54.
Rich Hawkins, General Manager
Rick Myers, General Sales Mgr
Angie Good, Programming Director

KTSE-FM
01-01-1996; 97.1 mhz FM *Hrs Open:* 24; 1.35 kw; 495 ft.; N37 29 34 W121 13 29
162o N. Carpenter Road, Suite C-17, Modesto, CA 95351 US
(408) 540-5600, *Fax:* (408) 540-5587
www.jose971.com
info@entravision.com
License: Patterson, Stanislaus County, CA held by Entravision Holdings LLC.
Group Owner: Entravision Communications Corp.; (acq 7-28-00; grpsl).
Arbitron Metro Market: Patterson, CA
Lisa Vela, General Manager
Esperanza Lopez, News Director
Paul Shinn, Chief Engineer

Pebble Beach

***KSPB**
09-22-1978; 91.9 mhz FM; 1 kw; 486 ft.; N36 35 11 W121 55 21
P.O. Box 657, Pebble Beach, CA 93953 US
(831) 626-5300(831) 625-5078, *Fax:* (831) 625-5208
www.kspb.org
webmaster@kspb.org
License: Pebble Beach, Monterey County, CA held by Robert Louis Stevenson School.
Arbitron Metro Market: Pebble Beach, CA *Format:* Alternative
Special Programming: Black 18 hrs, oldies 4 hrs, reggae 2 hrs, hard rock 2 hrs wkly
Matthew Arruda, Station Manager

Pescadero

***KPDO**
01-01-2006; 89.3 mhz FM; 0.1 kw; -118 ft.; N37 15 11.5 W122 24 37.2
Mailing Address: P O Box 25, Loma Mar, CA 94021 US
Second Address: 20748 Powder Horn Rd., Hidden Valley Lake, CA 95467
(831) 459-2811, *Fax:* (831) 459-4734
www.kpdo.org
License: Pescadero, San Mateo County, CA held by Pescadero Public Radio Service Inc.
Arbitron Metro Market: Pescadero, CA
Michael Bryant, General Manager

Petaluma

KTOB
01-10-1950; 1490 khz AM *Hrs Open:* 24; 1 kw-U; N35 39 15 W120 40 52
c/o Radio Station KRRS(AM), 1410 Neotomas Ave., Suite 104, Santa Rosa, CA 94953
(707) 545-1460, *Fax:* (707) 545-0112
www.moonradios.com
krrs@sonic.net
License: Petaluma, Sonoma County, CA held by California Broadcasting Corp LLC
Group Owner: Moon Broadcasting; (acq 12-13-2001; $1.28 million).
Nat'l Reps: Interep
Population Served: 812,826 *Arbitron Metro Market:* San Francisco *Target Audience:* 25-54; contemporary Hispanic families *Adv. Rates:* 45; 35; 45; 35
Abel DeLuna, CEO
Miriam Gomez, General Manager
Arelia DeLuna, CFO

Philo

***KZYX**
10-01-1989; 90.7 mhz FM; 3.4 kw; 1686 ft.; N39 1 22 W123 31 17
PO Box 1, 9300 Hwy 128, Philo, CA 95466 US
(707) 895-2324, *Fax:* (707) 895-2451
www.kzyx.org
uw@kzyx.org.
License: Philo, Mendocino County, CA held by Mendocino County Public Broadcasting.
Nat'l Network: NPR
Arbitron Metro Market: Philo, CA *Format:* News, Talk, 94 *Special Programming:* Black 8 hrs, class 14 hrs, folk 8 hrs, gospel 2 hrs, jazz 11 hrs, blues 3 hrs *Target Audience:* General.
Rich Culbertson, Operations Dir
John Coate, General Manager
David Steffen, General Sales Mgr
Mary Aigner, Programming Director
Paul Hanson, News Director

Piedmont

KSFN(AM)
05-01-1947; 1510 khz AM *Hrs Open:* 24; 8 kw-D, 230 w-N, DA-2; N37 49 02 W122 17 10 *Rebroadcasts:* Simulcast with KPIG-FM Freedom 100%
Mailing Address: 28 Second St., Suite 501, San Francisco, CA 94105
Second Address: 1110 Main St., Suite 16, Watsonville, CA 95076

(415) 744-1510, *Fax:* (415) 495-1510
www.kpig.com
emonroe@kpig.com
License: Piedmont, Alameda County, CA held by Mapleton License of San Francisco LLC.
Group Owner: Mapleton Communications LLC; (acq 7-27-2005; $5.1 million)
Nat'l Reps: McGavren Guild
Population Served: 245,000 *Arbitron Metro Market:* San Francisco, CA *Format:* Triple A

Frank Caprista, Operations Dir
Ed Monroe, General Manager
Mike Martindale, Chief Engineer

Pismo Beach

KXTZ
12-07-1974; 95.3 mhz FM *Hrs Open:* 24; 4.2 kw; 390 ft.; N35 9 24 W120 38 11
1303 Grande Avenue, Suite 229, Arroyo Grande, CA 93420 US
(805) 786-2570, *Fax:* (805) 547-9860
www.953thebeach.com
License: Pismo Beach, San Luis Obispo County, CA held by Mapleton License of San Luis Obispo LLC.
Group Owner: Mapleton Communications LLC; (acq 7-19-2002; grpsl)
Arbitron Metro Market: San Luis Obispo, CA *Format:* Contemporary Hits/Top 40, Adult Contemp *Special Programming:* Talk one hr wkly *Hrs. of News Programming:* news progmg one hr wkly *No. News Employees:* 1*Target Audience:* 18-49.

Adam Nathanson, President
Aaron Criswell, General Manager
Drew Ross, Programming Director
David Atwood, News Director
Tom Hughes, Chief Engineer

Pittsburg

KATD
09-01-1949; 990 khz AM *Hrs Open:* 24*Rebroadcasts:* Rebroadcasts KIQI(AM) San Francisco 100%
1251 Monument Blvd, #260, Concord, CA 94520 US
(415) 978-5378, *Fax:* (415) 978-5380
www.kiqi1010am.com
License: Pittsburg, CA held by Way Broadcasting Licensee LLC.
Group Owner: Multicultural Radio Broadcasting Inc.; (acq 2-4-2004; grpsl).
Arbitron Metro Market: San Francisco, CA *Format:* Spanish *Hrs. of News Programming:* News progmg 50 hrs wkly *Target Audience:* 25-54; middle upper income

Arthur Liu, President
Omar Gallegos, Operations Dir
Judy Re, General Manager
Andrea Yamazaki, General Sales Mgr

Placerville

KCCL
12-09-1982; 92.1 mhz FM *Hrs Open:* 24; 6 kw; Ant 328 ft; 38Â° 38' 10"" N, 120Â° 38' 14"" W
298 Commerce Cir., Sacramento, CA 95815
(916) 576-7333, *Fax:* (916) 929-5330
www.921khits.com
rico@921khits.com
License: Placerville, El Dorado County, CA held by Results Radio of Sacramento LLC.
Group Owner: Fritz Communications Inc.; (acq 6-18-2008)
Nat'l Reps: McGavren Guild
Arbitron Metro Market: Sacramento, CA *Target Audience:* Adults 35-64 *Adv. Rates:* 30; 40; 40; 20

Jack Fritz, CEO
Jack Fritz, General Manager
Kelly Andrews, General Sales Mgr
Rico Garcia, Programming Director
Rico Garcia, Promotions Manager
Ron Castro, Engineering Dir

Planada

KHTN
01-01-1966; 104.7 mhz FM *Hrs Open:* 24; 1.95 kw; 2080 ft.; N37 32 1 W120 1 46
166 West Putnam Ave., Greenwich, CT 06830 US
(209) 383-7900, *Fax:* (209) 723-8461
www.hot1047fm.com
hot1047email@aol.com
License: Planada, Merced County, CA held by Buckley Communications Inc.
Group Owner: Buckley Broadcasting Corp.; (acq 9-21-95; $500,000).
Nat'l Reps: D & R Radio
Arbitron Metro Market: Merced, CA *Format:* Contemporary Hits/Top 40 *Target Audience:* 21-34; women *Adv. Rates:* 36; 32; 36; 22

Mike McAdam, Operations Dir
John Sterling, General Sales Mgr
Rene Roberts, Operations Manager

Point Arena

KYOE
01-01-2003; 102.3 mhz FM; 1.2 kw; 1417 ft.; N38 53 44 W123 32 34
P. O. Box 1152, Fort Bragg, CA 95437 US
(707) 882-2323, *Fax:* (707) 882-3258
License: Point Arena, Mendocino County, CA held by Del Mar Trust.
Arbitron Metro Market: Point Arena, CA *Format:* Country

Karen Hay, General Manager

Point Reyes Station

***KWMR**
05-02-1999; 90.5 mhz FM *Hrs Open:* 7 AM-12 AM; 0.235 kw; 1076 ft.; N38 4 48 W122 51 57
Mailing Address: P.O. Box 1262, Point Reyes Station, CA 94956 US
Second Address: 11431 State Rte. One #8, Point Reyes Station, CA 94956
(415) 663-8068, *Fax:* (415) 663-0746
www.kwmr.org
kwmr@kwmr.org
License: Point Reyes Station, Marin County, CA held by West Marin Community Radio Inc.
Arbitron Metro Market: Point Reyes Station, CA *Format:* Talk

Kay Clements, General Manager
Amanda Eichstaedt, Executive Director/ Station Manager
Janet Galea, General Sales Mgr
Lyons Filmer, Programming Director
Alex Horvath, News Director
Richard Dillman, Chief Operator/ TransmitterWrangler
Marc Matheson, Office Administration/ Membership/ Volunteer Coord
Mia Jhonson, Underwriting
Ian Mcmurray, IT Desk
Janet Robbins, Classical Music Director

Pollock Pines

KHLX
08-19-1976; 93.1 mhz FM; 20.5 kw; 364 ft.; N38 38 10.5 W120 38 14
3015 Johnstonville Road, Susanville, CA 96130 US
(916) 929-5325, *Fax:* (916) 925-0118
www.classic931.com
License: Pollock Pines, El Dorado County, CA held by CC Licenses LLC.
Group Owner: Clear Channel Communications Inc.; (acq 3-6-2008; $2.75 million)
Format: Oldies

Jeff Holden, General Manager

Pomona

KAHZ
05-12-1947; 1600 khz AM *Hrs Open:* 24; 5 kw-D, DAN; 5 kw-N, DAN; N34 1 48 W117 43 35
449 Broadway, New York, NY 10013 US
(626) 844-8882, *Fax:* (626) 844-2928
www.mrbi.net
infor@kahzam.com
License: Pomona, CA held by Multicultural Radio Broadcasting Licensee LLC.
Group Owner: Multicultural Radio Broadcasting Inc.; (acq 11-17-98; $7.55 million).
Arbitron Metro Market: Los Angeles, CA *Format:* Chinese, News, 62, Talk *Target Audience:* 30 plus; money oriented

Arthur Liu, President

KWKU
12-23-1960; 1220 khz AM *Hrs Open:* 20; 0.25 kw-D, DA2; 0.25 kw-N, DA2; N34 1 11 W117 43 3 *Rebroadcasts:* Rebroadcasts KWKW(AM) Los Angeles 60%
449 Broadway, New York, NY 10013 US
(909) 865-3323, *Fax:* (909) 865-0342
www.kwkuradio.com
jrodriguez@kwkuradio.com
License: Pomona, CA held by Lotus Communications Corp.
Group Owner: Lotus Communications Corp.; acq 2-00; $750,000).
Arbitron Metro Market: Pomona, CA *Format:* News, News/Talk, 84, Talk *Special Programming:* Relg 15 hrs wkly *Hrs. of News Programming:* news progmg 7 hrs wkly *No. News Employees:* 1 *Target Audience:* 24-64.

Juan Rodriguez, General Manager
Mike Addison, General Sales Mgr
Maria Diaz, News Director

Port Hueneme

KVTA
07-01-1958; 1520 khz AM; 10 kw-D, DA2; 1 kw-N, DA2; N34 10 2 W119 8 2
100 Wilshire Blvd., Suite 1000, Santa Monica, CA 90401 US
(805) 289-1400, *Fax:* (805) 644-7906
www.kvta.com
License: Port Hueneme, CA held by Gold Coast Broadcasting LLC
Group Owner: Gold Coast Broadcasting LLC; (acq 1996; $3.65 million with KCAQ(FM) Oxnard)
Arbitron Metro Market: Oxnard-Ventura, CA *Format:* News, News/Talk, 86 *Target Audience:* 25-54.

Chip Ehrhardt, General Manager
Steve Hess, General Sales Mgr
Tom Spence, Programming Director
Jack Claeke, National Sales Manager

Porterville

KIOO
08-01-1972; 99.7 mhz FM *Hrs Open:* 24; 24 kw; 689 ft.; N36 6 26 W119 1 45
166 W Putnam Ave, Greenwich, CT 06830 US
(559) 627-9710, *Fax:* (559) 627-1590
www.997classicrock.com
License: Porterville, Tulare County, CA held by Buckley Broadcasting Corp.
Group Owner: Buckley Broadcasting Corp.; acq 3-1-94; $360,000;
Nat'l Reps: Eastman Radio
Arbitron Metro Market: Visalia-Tulare-Hanford, CA *Format:* Classic Rock *Target Audience:* 25-44.

Rick Buckley, President
Ray McCarty, Operations Dir
Tommy Del Rio, Operations Manager

KTIP
01-01-1947; 1450 khz AM *Hrs Open:* 24; 1 kw-U, ND1; N36 5 44 W119 3 10
1660 North Newcomb St, Porterville, CA 93257 US
(559) 784-1450, *Fax:* (559) 784-2482
www.ktip.com
live@ktip.com
License: Porterville, CA held by Mayberry Broadcasting Co. Inc.
Nat'l Network: ABC; Westwood One *Regional Reps:* Rgnl Reps.
Arbitron Metro Market: Visalia-Tulare-Hanford, CA *Format:* News, News/Talk, 86 *Special Programming:* Health show one hr, loc travel one hr wkly, national health 3hrs.,Trader's Market *Hrs. of News Programming:* newsprogmg 23 hrs wkly *No. News Employees:* 2 *Target Audience:* 25 plus. *Adv. Rates:* 25; 23; 20; 10

Larry Stoneburner, President
Kent Hopper, Operations Dir
Larry & Mimi Stoneburner, General Manager
Michael Partipilo, General Sales Mgr
Mimi Stoneburner, Promotions Manager
P.K. Whitmire, News Director
Ron Neil, ChiefEngineer
Janice Dawson, Traffic Manager

Prunedale

***KLVM**
02-28-1986; 89.7 mhz FM *Hrs Open:* 24; 0.45 kw; 2346 ft.; N36 45 22 W121 30 6 *Rebroadcasts:* Rebroadcasts KLVR(FM) Santa Rosa 100%
Mailing Address: 8145 Prunedale North Rd., Prunedale, CA 93907 US
Second Address: 8145 Prunedale N. Rd., Salinas, CA 93907
(707) 528-9236, *Fax:* (707) 528-9246
www.klove.com
klove@klove.com
License: Prunedale, Monterey County, CA held by Prunedale Educational Association
Nat'l Network: K-Love
Format: Christian *Target Audience:* 25-35; Judeo-Christian female

Darell Chambliss, Chairman
Mike Novak, President
David Pierce, Programming Director
Scott Smith, Music Director

RADIO - U.S.

Quincy

KNLF

06-10-1996; 95.9 mhz FM *Hrs Open:* 24; 500 w; -499 ft; N39 58 03 W120 53 34
Box 117, 440 Lawrence St., Quincy, CA 95971
(530) 283-4144, *Fax:* (530) 283-5135
www.knlfradio.com
rtrumbo@excite.com
License: Quincy, Plumas County, CA held by New Life Broadcasting.
Nat'l Network: American Family Radio
Population Served: 20,000*Hrs. of News Programming:* News progmg 10 hrs wkly *Target Audience:* 18-54. *Adv. Rates:* 8; 8; 8; 8
Ron Trumbo, President
Kip Sobel, Chief Engineer

KRAC

08-16-1963; 1370 khz AM *Hrs Open:* 24; 5 kw-D, DA2; 0.5 kw-N, DA2; N39 56 54 W120 53 54
395 Main St., Quincy, CA 95971 US
(530) 742-5555, *Fax:* (530) 741-3758
License: Quincy, CA held by Tom F. Huth
Group Owner: Huth Broadcasting; (acq 2-2-2006; $100,000)
Format: Talk
Cal Hunter, President
Tom Huth, General Manager

KVXX

01-01-1934; 100.3 mhz FM; 0.2 kw; -719 ft.; N39 56 25 W120 55 39
P.O. Box 77766, Stockton, CA 95267 US
(503) 223-1441, *Fax:* (503) 223-6909
www.espndeportesradio.com
License: Quincy, Marion County, CA held by Entercom Portland License LLC.
Group Owner: Entercom Communications Corp.; (acq 10-22-98; $605,000)
Nat'l Network: ESPN Deportes *Regional Reps:* Allied Radio Partners.
Arbitron Metro Market: Portland, OR *Format:* Sports
David Field, President
Jack Hutchison, Executive Vice President

*KQNC

01-01-2005; 88.1 mhz FM; 0.5 kw; -1135 ft.; N39 56 14 W120 56 51 *Rebroadcasts:* Simulcast with KXJZ(FM) Sacramento 100% US
(916) 278-8900, *Fax:* (916) 278-8989
www.csus.edu/npr
npr@csus.edu
License: Quincy, Plumas County, CA held by California State University, Sacramento.
Nat'l Network: NPR
Arbitron Metro Market: Quincy, CA *Format:* Jazz, News
Kevin O'Brien, Chairman
Rick Eytcheson, President & General Manager
John Brenneise, Director of Operations/Producer of JazzStream
Carl Watanabe, Station Manager
Joe Barr, Director of News and Information
Jeff Browne, EngineeringDir
John L. Lewis, Treasurer
Ben Adler, Capitol Bureau Chief
Paul Conley, Senior Producer, News
Constance Crawford, Director of Marketing & Public Relations
Arla Gibson, Director of Development
Al Gibes, Director of Digital Content

*KQNY

91.9 mhz FM; 2.7 kw; -1122 ft.; N39 56 15 W120 56 49 US
(530) 283-5494
License: Quincy, Plumas County, CA held by Plumas Community Radio
Arbitron Metro Market: Quincy, CA *Format:* Blues, Rock/AOR
Mark Houston, President

Rancho Cordova

KSTE

04-19-1990; 650 khz AM *Hrs Open:* 24
1440 Ethan Way, Ste 200, Scaramento, CA 95825 US
(916) 929-5325, *Fax:* (916) 929-0118
www.talk650kste.com
info@kste.com
License: Rancho Cordova, CA held by AMFM Broadcasting Licenses LLC.
Group Owner: Clear Channel Communications Inc.; (acq 8-30-2000; grpsl).
Nat'l Network: ABC; Westwood One
Arbitron Metro Market: Sacramento, CA *Format:* Talk *Hrs. of News Programming:* news progmg 15 hrs wkly *No. News Employees:* 4 *Target Audience:* 25-54.
Alan Eisenson, Operations Dir
Jeff Holden, General Manager

Rancho Mirage

KMRJ

07-17-1998; 99.5 mhz FM *Hrs Open:* 24; 3 kw; 328 ft.; N33 52 15 W116 13 37
25601 Paseo De La Paz, San Juan Capistrano, CA 92675 US
(760) 778-6995, *Fax:* (760) 778-1249
www.995theheat.com
info@995theheat.com
License: Rancho Mirage, Riverside County, CA held by Mitchell Media Inc.
Nat'l Network: Westwood One *Nat'l Reps:* Katz Radio
Arbitron Metro Market: Palm Springs, CA *Format:* Classic Rock *Hrs. of News Programming:* News progmg 2 hrs wkly *Target Audience:* 35-64; mid age families, working adults *Adv. Rates:* 45; 30; 35; 20
Daniel Mitchell III, Chairman
Maurine Mitchell, CFO
Thomas Carr Mitchell, Station Manager
Adam Carolla, Programming Director
Veronica Ochoa, Promotions Manager
Carolina O'Connel, News Director
Mark Moceri, Engineering Dir
LordTim Hudson, Disc Jockey
Jeff Larsen

*DKCPC

1200 khz AM; Ant 446 ft
875 Comstock Avenue, Los Angeles, CA 90024 US
(713) 520-5200
www.khcb.org
email@khcb.org
License: Rancho Mirage, CA held by Houston Christian Broadcasters Inc.
Group Owner: Houston Christian Broadcasters Inc.
Arbitron Metro Market: Houston, TX *Format:* Christian *Hrs. of News Programming:* News progmg 6 hrs wkly
Bruce Munsterman, President
Bruce Munsterman, General Manager
Bonnie BeMent, News Director

Randsburg

*KGBM

12-01-2001; 89.7 mhz FM *Hrs Open:* 24; 6.8 kw; 1302 ft.; N35 28 39 W117 41 58
2009 South Sweet Gum Ave, Broken Arrow, OK 74012 US
(888) 937-2471, *Fax:* (916) 251-1650
www.air1.com
info@air1.com
License: Randsburg, Kern County, CA held by Educational Media Foundation.
Group Owner: EMF Broadcasting; (acq 4-19-02).
Nat'l Network: Air 1
Arbitron Metro Market: Bakersfield, CA *Format:* Alternative, Christian *No. News Employees:* 3 *Target Audience:* 18-35; Judeo-Christian female
Darrell Chambliss, Chairman
Alan Mason, COO
Mike Novak, President and CEO
David Pierce, Programming Director
David R. Ferry, Promotions Manager
Ed Lenane, News Director
Sam Wallington, Engineering Dir
Marya Morgan, NewsReporter
Richard Hunt, News Reporter
Larry Moody, Director
Mitch Barnhart, Director
Walter Golembeski, Director

Red Bluff

KALF

01-01-1978; 95.7 mhz FM *Hrs Open:* 24; 7 kw; 1266 ft.; N39 55 2 W122 40 10
1459 Humbolt Road, Suite D, Chico, CA 95928 US
(530) 899-3600, *Fax:* (530) 343-0243
www.957thewolfonline.com
smichaels@radiochicocomm.com
License: Red Bluff, Tehama County, CA held by Mapleton License of Chico LLC.
Group Owner: Mapleton Communications LLC; (acq 11-30-2006; grpsl)
Nat'l Reps: Christal
Arbitron Metro Market: Chico, CA *Format:* Country *Hrs. of News Programming:* news progmg 10 hrs wkly *No. News Employees:* 1 *Target Audience:* 25-54.
Scott Michaels, Operations Dir
Mert Ahlstrom, General Sales Mgr
Chad Gammage, Promotions Manager
Linda Patterson, Business Manager

KBLF

01-01-1946; 1490 khz AM; 1 kw-U, ND1; N40 11 28 W122 12 54
113 East Alma, Mount Shasta, CA 95207 US
(530) 527-1490, *Fax:* (530) 527-3525
www.kblfam.com
kblfam@yahoo.com
License: Red Bluff, CA held by Tom Huth.
Group Owner: Huth Broadcasting; (acq 8-11-98; $5,000).
Nat'l Network: Westwood One; PRI
Arbitron Metro Market: Red Bluff, CA *Format:* Oldies *Special Programming:* Farm 5 hrs, Sp 4 hrs wkly *Target Audience:* 35-64. *Adv. Rates:* 12; 8; 10; 5
Cal Hunter, General Manager

*KKRO

11-15-2002; 102.7 mhz FM *Hrs Open:* 24; 5.5 kw; 1414 ft.; N40 20 41 W121 56 48 *Rebroadcasts:* Rebroadcasts KLRD(FM) Yucaipa 100%
1588 Charles Drive, Redding, CA 96003 US
(888) 937-2471, *Fax:* (916) 251-1650
www.air1.com
info@air1.com
License: Red Bluff, Shasta County, CA held by Educational Media Foundation Inc.
Group Owner: EMF Broadcasting
Nat'l Network: Air 1
Arbitron Metro Market: Redding, CA *Format:* Alternative, Christian *No. News Employees:* 3 *Target Audience:* 27-33; Judeo-Christian female
Darrell Chambliss, Chairman
Alan Mason, COO
Mike Novak, President and CEO
David Pierce, Programming Director
Ed Lenane, News Director
Sam Wallington, Engineering Dir
Marya Morgan, News Reporter
Richard Hunt, News Reporter
Larry Moody, Director
Mitch Barnhart, Director
David R. Ferry, Director
Walter Golembeski, Director

*KTHM

90.7 mhz FM; 0.1 kw vert; -135 ft.; N40 10 27 W122 13 55
P O Box 855, Los Molinos, CA 96055 US
(530) 347-0138
info@kthmradio.org
License: Red Bluff, Tehama County, CA held by Tehama County Community Broadcasters.
Arbitron Metro Market: Red Bluff, CA *Format:* Variety/Diverse
Erik Mathisen, Station Manager

Redding

KNRO

01-01-2001; 1670 khz AM
PO Box 3463, Carefree, AZ 85377 US
(530) 226-9500, *Fax:* (530) 221-4940
www.reddingradio.com
don@reddingradio.com
License: Redding, CA held by Mapleton License of Redding LLC.
Group Owner: Mapleton Communications LLC; (acq 11-30-2006; grpsl)
Nat'l Network: Fox Sports
Arbitron Metro Market: Redding, CA *Format:* Sports
Vince Shadrick, General Manager

*KFPR

11-17-1994; 88.9 mhz FM; 0.75 kw; 3579 ft.; N40 36 10 W122 38 58 *Rebroadcasts:* Rebroadcasts KCHO(FM) Chico 100%
First and Normal, Chico, CA 95929 US
(530) 241-5246, *Fax:* (530) 241-5246
www.kcho.org
bterhorst@csuchico.edu
License: Redding, Shasta County, CA held by California State University, Chico Research Foundation.
Nat'l Network: NPR; PRI
Arbitron Metro Market: Redding, CA *Format:* Jazz, News *Special Programming:* Sp 4 hrs wkly, BBC 40 hrs wkly *Hrs. of News Programming:* news progmg 55 hrs wkly *Target Audience:* General.
Brian Terhorst, General Manager
Mike Birdsill, Chief Engineer

KLXR
08-01-1956; 1230 khz AM *Hrs Open:* 24; 1 kw-U, ND1; N40 33 14 W122 22 53
P.O. Box 3463, Carefree, AZ 85377 US
(530) 244-5082, *Fax:* (530) 244-5698
KLXR1230@yahoo.com
License: Redding, CA held by Michael R. Quinn
Nat'l Network: Jones Radio Networks *Wire Services:* AP
Arbitron Metro Market: Redding, CA *Format:* Adult Contemp
Target Audience: 35 plus.
Mike Quinn, Programming Director
MIke Quinn, Promotions Manager

KNCQ
10-29-1985; 97.3 mhz FM; 28 kw; 3570 ft.; N40 36 10 W122 38 58
1588 Charles Drive, Redding, CA 96003 US
(530) 244-9700, *Fax:* (530) 244-9707
www.q97country.com
rhealy@resultsradiomail.com
License: Redding, Shasta County, CA held by Results Radio of Redding Licensee LLC.
Group Owner: Fritz Communications Inc.
Nat'l Reps: D & R Radio
Arbitron Metro Market: Redding, CA *Format:* Country *Target Audience:* 25-54.
Beth Tappan, General Manager
Laurie Curto, General Sales Mgr
Rick Healy, Programming Director
Patrick Johnson, News Director

KQMS
09-14-1954; 1400 khz AM; 1 kw-U, ND1; N40 33 31 W122 19 48
3360 Alta Mesa Drive, Redding, CA 96002 US
(530) 226-9500, *Fax:* (530) 221-6653
www.kqms.com
jim@kqms.com
License: Redding, CA held by Mapleton License of Redding LLC.
Group Owner: Mapleton Communications LLC; (acq 11-30-2006; grpsl)
Nat'l Reps: McGavren Guild
Arbitron Metro Market: Northern CA *Format:* News, News/Talk, 86
Adam Nathanson, President
Don Burton, Operations Dir
Vince Shadrick, General Manager
Randie Meyer, General Sales Mgr
Erin Gilmer, Programming Director
Steve Gibson, News Director

KSHA
09-01-1981; 104.3 mhz FM; 100 kw; 1558 ft.; N40 39 14 W122 31 12
3360 Alta Mesa Drive, Redding, CA 96002 US
(530) 226-9500, *Fax:* (530) 221-4940
www.kshasta.com
don@reddingradio.com
License: Redding, Shasta County, CA
Group Owner: Mapleton Communications LLC
Arbitron Metro Market: Redding, CA *Format:* Adult Contemp
Duane Davis, Operations Dir
Vince Shadrick, General Manager
Don Burton, Programming Director
Jill Fontana, Business Manager

***KSTN-FM**
01-01-1962; 91.5 mhz FM; 0.42 kw vert; 1234 ft.; N40 54 27 W122 26 37
1425 N Market Blvd, Suite 9, Sacramento, CA 95834 US
(209) 948-5786
www.nuevavida.com
License: Redding, San Joaquin County, CA held by San Joaquin Broadcasting Co.
Arbitron Metro Market: Stockton, CA *Special Programming:* Sp, Por 4 hrs wkly *Target Audience:* General.
Knox LaRue, President
Jose Rodriguez, Programming Director
Paul Shinn, Chief Engineer

***KVIP**
01-04-1970; 540 khz AM *Hrs Open:* 24; 2.5 kw-D, 17 w-N; N40 37 25 W122 16 49
1139 Hartnell Ave., Redding, CA 96049
(530) 222-4455
www.kvip.org
info@kvip.org
License: Redding, Shasta County, CA held by Pacific Cascade Communications Corp.
Group Owner: Pacific Cascade Communications Corp.; (acq 12-69)
Nat'l Network: Moody; Salem Radio Network
Population Served: 200,000 *Arbitron Metro Market:* Redding, CA
Hrs. of News Programming: news progmg 14 hrs wkly *No. News Employees:* 2 *Target Audience:* General.
David Morrow, Operations Dir
Steve Hafen, General Manager
Ted Hering, Programming Director
Larry Cardoza, Engineering Dir
Paul Brown, Chief Engineer

***KVIP-FM**
10-19-1975; 98.1 mhz FM *Hrs Open:* 24; 30 kw; Ant 1,710 ft; N40 36 10 W122 38 58
1139 Hartnell Ave., Redding, CA 96099
(530) 222-4455
www.kvip.org
info@kvip.org
License: Redding, Shasta County, CA held by Pacific Cascade Communications Corp.
Group Owner: Pacific Cascade Communications Corp.
Nat'l Network: Moody; Salem Radio Network *Wire Services:* AP
Population Served: 250,000 *Arbitron Metro Market:* Redding, CA
No. News Employees: 2
David Morrow, President
Steve Hafen, General Manager
Ted Hering, Programming Director
Paul Brown, Chief Engineer

Redlands

KCAL(AM)
04-01-1959; 1410 khz AM *Hrs Open:* 24; 5 kw-D, 4 kw-N, DA-N; N34 04 08 W117 12 06
1950 S. Sunwest Lane, Suite 302, San Bernardino, CA 92408
(909) 304-9750, *Fax:* (909) 884-5844
www.radiolazer.com
jmdiaz@radiolazer.com
License: Redlands, San Bernardino County, CA held by Lazer Broadcasting Corp.
Group Owner: Lazer Broadcasting Corp.; acq 8-7-01; $2.35 million).
Population Served: 680,000 *Arbitron Metro Market:* Riverside-San Bernardino, CA *No. News Employees:* 2 *Target Audience:* 18-49, 25-64; Mexican origin, Latin American *Adv. Rates:* 40; 40; 40; na.
Alfredo Plascencia, CEO
Vicki Bails, Operations Dir
Arturo Costa, Programming Director
Armando Gutierrez, Promotions Manager

KCAL-FM
01-01-1965; 96.7 mhz FM; 1.75 kw; 377 ft.; N34 11 51 W117 17 10
437 S. Highway 101, Suite 201, Solana Beach, CA 92075 US
(909) 793-3554, *Fax:* (909) 793-7225
www.kcalfm.com
info@kcalfm.com
License: Redlands, San Bernardino County, CA held by Anaheim Broadcasting Corp.
Group Owner: Anaheim Broadcasting Corp.
Nat'l Reps: D & R Radio
Arbitron Metro Market: Redlands, CA *Format:* Rock/AOR *Target Audience:* 16-30.
Jeff Parke, Operations Dir
Beverly Trout, General Sales Mgr
Steve Hoffman, Operations Manager

***KUOR-FM**
10-01-1966; 89.1 mhz FM; 0.035 kw; 2782 ft.; N34 11 47 W117 2 56 *Rebroadcasts:* Rebroadcasts KPCC(FM) Pasadena 100%
1200 East Colton Avenue, Redlands, CA 92374 US

www.scpr.org
License: Redlands, San Bernardino County, CA held by University of Redlands.
Nat'l Network: NPR
Arbitron Metro Market: Pasadena, CA *Format:* Talk
Bill Davis, CEO
John Brenneise, Operations Dir
Mark Crowley, Vice President
Cheryl Dring, Programming Director
Joe Barr, News Director
Lance Harper, Chief Engineer
Russ Stanton, Vice President of Content
Melanie Sill, ExecutiveEditor
Bianca Ramirez, Associate Producer

Redondo Beach

KDAY
08-04-1961; 93.5 mhz FM *Hrs Open:* 24; 4.2 kw; 384 ft.; N34 0 19 W118 21 44
222 North Sepulveda Blvd, Suite 1324, El Segundo, CA 90245 US
(760) 873-5329, *Fax:* (760) 873-5328
www.935kday.com
info@kday.com
License: Redondo Beach, Los Angeles County, CA held by KDAY Licensing LLC.
Group Owner: Magic Broadcasting LLC; (acq 1-31-2006; $120 million with KDAI(FM) Ontario)
Arbitron Metro Market: Los Angeles *Format:* Urban Contemporary
Kimberly Fletcher, General Manager
Lisa Alta Moreno, General Sales Mgr
Anthony Acampora, Programming Director
Larry Slover, Chief Engineer

Ridgecrest

KLOA
12-11-1956; 1240 khz AM
731 North Balsam, Ridgecrest, CA 93555 US
(760) 375-8888, *Fax:* (760) 371-1824
www.kloaam.com
radio@iwvisp.com
License: Ridgecrest, CA held by Adelman Broadcasting Inc.
Group Owner: Adelman Broadcasting Inc.
Arbitron Metro Market: Bakersfield, CA *Format:* Oldies
Robert Adelman, President
Eric Kauffman, Programming Director
James Rowles, Chief Engineer

KLOA(FM)
01-01-1979; 104.9 mhz FM; 1.5 kw; Ant 1,289 ft; N35 28 38 W117 41 59
731 N. Balsam St., Ridgecrest, CA 93555
(760) 375-8888, *Fax:* (760) 371-1824
www.kloafm.com
info@kloafm.com
License: Ridgecrest, Kern County, CA held by Adelman Broadcasting Inc.
Group Owner: Adelman Broadcasting Inc.
Population Served: 70,000 *Arbitron Metro Market:* Bakersfield, CA *Format:* Country
Tom Duran, General Manager
Chris Moncayo, General Sales Mgr
Carrie Strait, Programming Director
Ryan Oller, Chief Engineer

KWDJ
04-07-1974; 1360 khz AM *Hrs Open:* 24; 1 kw-D, ND1; 0.031 kw-N, ND1; N35 36 58 W117 38 35
121 W. Ridgecrest Blvd, Ridgecrest, CA 93555 US
(760) 384-4937, *Fax:* (760) 384-4978
foxtalk1360.com
eric@kziq.com
License: Ridgecrest, CA held by James & Donna Knudsen.
Nat'l Network: Fox News Radio; Jones Radio Networks; Premiere Radio Networks *Regional Reps:* Kim Kauffman
Arbitron Metro Market: Ridgecrest, CA *Format:* News, Sports
Hrs. of News Programming: news progmg 168 hrs wkly *No. News Employees:* 1 *Target Audience:* 25-54; educated adults with high disposable income
James Knudsen, President
Eric Kauffman, General Manager
Kim Kauffman, General Sales Mgr

KZIQ-FM
01-01-1978; 92.7 mhz FM *Hrs Open:* 24; 3 kw; -131 ft.; N35 36 58 W117 38 35
121 West Ridgecrest Blvd, Ridgecrest, CA 93555 US
(760) 384-4937, *Fax:* (760) 384-4978
www.kziq.com
eric@kziq.com
License: Ridgecrest, Kern County, CA held by James & Donna Knudsen.
Arbitron Metro Market: Ridgecrest, CA *Format:* Country *Hrs. of News Programming:* News progmg 2 hrs wkly
Eric Kauffman, General Manager

***KWTD**
05-01-2005; 91.9 mhz FM; 7 kw; 1281 ft.; N35 28 38 W117 41 58
Rebroadcasts: Rebroadcasts KWTW(FM) Bishop 100%
P O Box 637, Bishop, CA 93515 US
(866) 466-5989, *Fax:* (760) 872-4155
www.kwtw.org
recep@kwtw.org
License: Ridgecrest, Kern County, CA held by Living Proof Inc.
Arbitron Metro Market: Ridgecrest, CA *Format:* Christian
Daniel McClenaghan, President

***KRSF**
89.3 mhz FM; 4 kw horiz; 1480 ft.; N35 53 52.6 W117 17 18.3

Mailing Address: US
Second Address: 1209 W. Robert Ave., Ridgecrest, CA 93555-5936
(760) 375-2355
www.radio74.net
ejwitzel@mchsi.com
License: Ridgecrest, Kern County, CA held by Radio 74 Internationale.
Arbitron Metro Market: Ridgecrest, CA
Everet Witzel, President

Rio Dell

*KNHT

01-01-1999; 107.3 mhz FM *Hrs Open:* 5AM-2AM; 3.3 kw; 1703 ft.; N40 30 3 W124 17 10
67 Lakeview Terrace, Sandy Hook, CT 06482 US
(541) 552-6301, *Fax:* (541) 552-8565
www.ijpr.org
jprinfo@sou.edu
License: Rio Dell, Humboldt County, CA held by The State of Oregon, acting by and through the State Board of Higher Education, for the benefit of Southern Oregon University.
Nat'l Network: NPR; PRI *Wire Services:* AP
Format: Classical, News *Hrs. of News Programming:* news progmg 35 hrs wkly *No. News Employees:* 1
Ronald Kramer, CEO
Bryon Lambert, Operations Dir
Paul Westhelle, General Sales Mgr
Darin Ransom, Engineering Dir
Mitchell Christian, CFO

Rio Vista

*KRVH

11-07-1972; 91.5 mhz FM; 0.05 kw; 102 ft.; N38 9 17 W121 41 48
410 S. 4th Street, Rio Vista, CA 94571 US
(707) 374-6336, *Fax:* (707) 374-6810
www.radiorio.us
info@radiorio.us
License: Rio Vista, Solano County, CA held by River Delta Unified School District.
Arbitron Metro Market: Rio Vista, CA *Format:* Classic Rock *Target Audience:* 13-19; young adult
Kevin MacGregor, General Manager

Riverbank

KMRQ

01-15-1979; 96.7 mhz FM *Hrs Open:* 24; 6 kw; 299 ft.; N37 40 49.8 W120 55 25.5
600 Congress Avenue, Suite 1400, Auston, TX 78701 US
(209) 551-1306, *Fax:* (209) 551-1359
www.rock967.com
License: Riverbank, San Joaquin County, CA held by Capstar TX L.P.
Group Owner: Clear Channel Communications Inc.; (acq 8-30-2000; grpsl)
Arbitron Metro Market: Modesto, CA *Format:* Rock/AOR *No. News Employees:* 1 *Target Audience:* 25-54.
Matthew Hobley, Programming Director

Riverdale

KZLA

01-01-2003; 98.3 mhz FM; 0.1 kw; 43 ft.; N36 12 5 W120 5 53
Gammon & Grange Pc, 8280 Greensboro Dr, McLean, VA 22102 US
(559) 935-4191, *Fax:* (559) 935-4191
License: Riverdale, Fresno County, CA held by Huron Broadcasting LLC.
Arbitron Metro Market: Riverdale, CA *Format:* Oldies
Rebecca Sexton, General Manager

Riverside

KGGI

01-23-1965; 99.1 mhz FM *Hrs Open:* 24; 2.55 kw; 1844 ft.; N34 14 4 W117 8 24
2001 Iowa Ave, Suite 200, Riverside, CA 92507 US
(951) 684-1991, *Fax:* (951) 274-4911
www.991kggifm.com
jesseduran991@hotmail.com
License: Riverside, Riverside County, CA held by AMFM Broadcasting Licenses LLC.
Group Owner: Clear Channel Communications Inc.; (acq 8-30-2000; grpsl).
Nat'l Reps: McGavren Guild
Arbitron Metro Market: Riverside-San Bernardino, CA *Format:* Contemporary Hits/Top 40 *Special Programming:* Discussion 7 hrs wkly *Target Audience:* 18-49.
Bob Ridzak, General Manager
Scott Welsh, General Sales Mgr
Jesse Duran, Programming Director
Justin Garcia, Promotions Manager
Rich Mena, Engineering Dir
Jesse Garcia, Promotions Director

KPRO

06-22-1957; 1570 khz AM *Hrs Open:* 24; 5 kw-D, DA2; 0.194 kw-N, DA2; N33 55 54 W117 23 47
7351 Lincoln Avenue, Riverside, CA 92504 US
(951) 688-1570, *Fax:* (951) 688-7009
www.bristar.com
kproval@aol.com
License: Riverside, CA held by Impact Radio Inc.
Arbitron Metro Market: Riverside-San Bernardino, CA *Format:* Christian, Religious *Target Audience:* 18+ *Adv. Rates:* 20; 20; 20; 20
Ronnie Olenick, President
Valorie Stitely, General Manager

*KSGN

01-01-1970; 89.7 mhz FM *Hrs Open:* 24; 2.75 kw; 322 ft.; N34 11 50.9 W117 17 9.2
11498 Pierce Street, Riverside, CA 92505 US
(909) 583-2150, *Fax:* (909) 583-2170
www.ksgn.com
info@ksgn.com
License: Riverside, Riverside County, CA held by Good News Radio.
Arbitron Metro Market: Redlands, CA *Format:* Christian, Religious *Hrs. of News Programming:* News progmg 12 hrs wkly *Target Audience:* General; Christians & church goers
Dennis Johnson, Chairman
Dawn Hibbard, General Manager
Bryan O'Neal, Programming Director
Brandi Lanai, News Director
Bruce Potterton, Chief Engineer
Heather Clough, Traffic Manager

KLYY

03-17-1959; 97.5 mhz FM *Hrs Open:* 24; 72 kw; 1827 ft.; N34 14 4 W117 8 24
2905 South King Road, San Jose, CA 95122 US
(323) 900-6100, *Fax:* (323) 900-6127
www.oye975.com
License: Riverside, Riverside County, CA held by Entravision Holdings LLC.
Group Owner: Entravision Communications Corp.; (acq 4-20-00; grpsl).
Nat'l Reps: Lotus Entravision Reps LLC
Arbitron Metro Market: Los Angeles *Format:* Spanish *Target Audience:* 18-49.
Jeff Liberman, Operations Dir
Karl Meyer, General Manager
Nestor Rocha, Programming Director
Pam McCaffrey, News Director
Eugene McAfel, Engineering Dir
Elias Autran, Programming Director

*KUCR

10-01-1966; 88.3 mhz FM; 0.15 kw; 1621 ft.; N33 57 58 W117 17 14
300 Lakeside Dr. 8th Flr, Oakland, CA 94612 US
(951) 827-3737, *Fax:* (951) 827-3240
www.kucr.org
kucrinfo@kucr.org
License: Riverside, Riverside County, CA held by The Regents of the University of California.
Arbitron Metro Market: Riverside, CA *Format:* Alternative, Variety/Diverse *Special Programming:* Black 18 hrs, class 14 hrs, jazz 6 hrs wkly
Jeff Armantrout, Operations Dir
Louis Vandenberg, General Manager
Walter Douglas, Promotions Manager
Bill Elledge, Chief Engineer

Rock Creek

*KRBP

09-07-2012; 90.7 mhz FM; 1 kw; -2569 ft.; N39 54 20 W121 20 41
Mailing Address: US
Second Address: , (626) 969-7945,
License: Rock Creek, Plumas County, CA held by Christian Faith Center of the Valley
Format: Religious
Samuel Martinez, President

Rocklin

*KEBR

07-27-1988; 1210 khz AM *Hrs Open:* 24
Mailing Address: 4135 Northgate Blvd #1, Sacramento, CA 95834 US
Second Address: 290 Hegenberger Rd., Oakland, CA 94621
(916) 641-8191, *Fax:* (916) 641-8238
www.familyradio.com
info@familyradio.com
License: Rocklin, CA held by Family Stations Inc.
Group Owner: Family Stations Inc.; 1988
Arbitron Metro Market: Sacramento, CA *Format:* Religious *Target Audience:* General.
Harold Camping, President
Peggy Renschler, Station Manager

Rohnert Park

KMHX

03-04-1986; 104.9 mhz FM *Hrs Open:* 24; 6.6 kw; 548 ft.; N38 23 31 W122 40 40
6640 Redwood Drive, Suite 202, Rohnert Park, CA 94928 US
(707) 543-0100, *Fax:* (707) 543-1097
www.mix1049fm.com
License: Rohnert Park, Sonoma County, CA held by Maverick Media of Santa Rosa Licensee LLC.
Group Owner: Maverick Media LLC; (acq 6-5-2006; $7.7 million)
Arbitron Metro Market: Santa Rosa, CA *Format:* Adult Contemp *Target Audience:* 25-54.
Neysa Hinton, General Manager
Kent Bjugstad, General Sales Mgr
Danny White, Programming Director
Monika Weber, Promotions Manager

Rosamond

KLKX(FM)

09-01-1993; 93.5 mhz FM *Hrs Open:* 24; 3 kw; Ant 207 ft; N34 51 03 W118 09 22
570 East Ave., Q-9, Palmdale, CA 93550
(661) 947-3107, *Fax:* (661) 272-5688
www.935thequake.com
info@thequake.com
License: Rosamond, Kern County, CA held by High Desert Broadcasting LLC
Group Owner: High Desert Broadcasting LLC; acq 3-7-2002; grpsl).
Nat'l Network: Westwood One
Population Served: 300,000 *Arbitron Metro Market:* Bakersfield, CA *Format:* Classic Rock, News *Target Audience:* 25-54.
Gary Wilson, Operations Dir
Nelson Rosse, General Manager
Greg Wood, General Sales Mgr
Jeff McElfresh, Promotions Manager
Amir Raheem, News Director

KVVS

03-01-1985; 105.5 mhz FM *Hrs Open:* 24; 6 kw; 308 ft.; N34 51 3 W118 9 22 *Rebroadcasts:* Simulcast with KIIS-FM Los Angeles 100%
50 E. Rivercenter Blvd., Suite 180, Covington, KY 41011 US
(818) 559-2252, *Fax:* (818) 729-2502
www.kiisfm.com
License: Rosamond, Kern County, CA held by CC Licenses LLC.
Group Owner: Clear Channel Communications Inc.; (acq 11-21-2003; grpsl)
Arbitron Metro Market: Los Angeles *Format:* Contemporary Hits/Top 40
Greg Ashlock, General Manager

Roseville

KLIB

04-01-1968; 1110 khz AM *Hrs Open:* 24; 5 kw-D, DA2; 0.5 kw-N, DA2; N38 44 22 W121 12 50
127 Mamanasco Road, Ridgefield, CT 06877 US
(916) 456-3288, *Fax:* (916) 456-3324
klib_1110@yahoo.com
License: Roseville, CA held by Way Broadcasting Licensee LLC
Arbitron Metro Market: Sacramento, CA *Format:* Ethnic *Target Audience:* 18 plus; Hispanic
Rosario Delatorre, General Manager
Yuri Reyes, Programming Director

KFSG

01-01-2001; 1690 khz AM
127 Mamanasco Road, Ridgefield, CT 06877 US
(916) 456-3288, *Fax:* (916) 456-3324
klib_1110@yahoo.com
License: Roseville, CA held by Way Broadcasting Licensee LLC
Arbitron Metro Market: Sacramento, CA *Format:* Ethnic

Rosario Delatorre, General Manager
Yuri Reyes, Programming Director

KQJK
06-01-1970; 93.7 mhz FM *Hrs Open:* 24; 25 kw; 328 ft.; N38 44 22 W121 12 50
600 New Hampshire Ave, NW, Suite 1200, Washington, DC 20037 US
(916) 929-9370, *Fax:* (916) 925-0118
www.937jackfm.com
License: Roseville, Placer County, CA held by AMFM Texas Licenses L.P.
Group Owner: Clear Channel Communications Inc.; (acq 4-1-2009; grpsl)
Arbitron Metro Market: Sacramento, CA *Format:* Adult Contemp *Hrs. of News Programming:* news progmg 2 hrs wkly *No. News Employees:* 1 *Target Audience:* 25-54.
Jeff Holden, General Manager

Sacramento

KBMB(FM)
10-01-1996; 103.5 mhz FM *Hrs Open:* 24; 6 kw; 312 ft; N38 33 59 W121 28 47
1436 Auburn Blvd., Sacramento, CA 95815
(916) 646-4000, *Fax:* (916) 927-7376
www.hot1035radio.com
info@kbmb.com
License: Sacramento, Sacramento County, CA held by Entravision Holdings LLC.
Group Owner: Entravision Communications Corp.; (acq 9-30-2004; $16.1 million).
Arbitron Metro Market: Sacramento, CA *Format:* Urban Contemporary *Target Audience:* 18-49.
Allyson Maiman, General Manager
Jim Danzer, General Sales Mgr
Patti Moreno, Programming Director
Alex Guerra, Promotions Manager
Paul Waegele, Chief Engineer

KDND
08-01-1945; 107.9 mhz FM *Hrs Open:* 24; 50 kw; 404 ft.; N38 42 38 W121 28 54
401 City Avenue, Suite 409, Bala Cynwyd, PA 19004 US
(916) 334-7777, *Fax:* (916) 334-1092
www.endonline.com
License: Sacramento, Sacramento County, CA held by Entercom Sacramento License L.L.C.
Group Owner: Entercom Communications Corp.; (acq 6-3-97; $27.5 million).
Nat'l Reps: D & R Radio
Arbitron Metro Market: Sacramento, CA *Format:* Contemporary Hits/Top 40 *No. News Employees:* 1 *Target Audience:* 25-44.
John Geary, Operations Dir
Dan Mason, Station Manager
Butch Mitchell, General Sales Mgr
Dayne Damme, Promotions Manager
Kat Maudru, News Director
Kristin Wong, General Sales Manager

***KEAR-FM**
05-01-1997; 88.1 mhz FM *Hrs Open:* 24; 8.4 kw vert; 994 ft.; N38 14 50 W121 30 3
Mailing Address: 4135 Northgate Blvd., Suite 1, Sacramento, CA 95834 US
Second Address: 290 Hegenberger Rd., Oakland, CA 94621
(916) 641-8191, *Fax:* (916) 641-8238
www.familyradio.com
info@familyradio.com
License: Sacramento, Sacramento County, CA held by Family Stations Inc.
Group Owner: Family Stations Inc.; Built 1997
Arbitron Metro Market: Sacramento, CA *Format:* Religious
Harold Camping, President
Peggy Renschler, General Manager

KFBK
01-01-1922; 1530 khz AM *Hrs Open:* 24; 50 kw-D, DA2; 50 kw-N, DA2; N38 50 54 W121 28 58
1440 Ethan Way, Suite 200, Sacramento, CA 95825 US
(916) 929-5325, *Fax:* (916) 925-0118
www.kfbk.com
info@kfbk.com
License: Sacramento, CA held by AMFM Broadcasting Licenses LLC.
Group Owner: Clear Channel Communications Inc.; (acq 8-30-2000; grpsl)
Wire Services: PR Newswire
Arbitron Metro Market: Sacramento, CA *Format:* News, News/Talk, 86 *Hrs. of News Programming:* news progmg 45 hrs wkly *No. News Employees:* 8
Jeff Holden, Operations Dir
Rob Worden, General Sales Mgr
Amy Bingham, Promotions Manager
Judy Farah, News Director
Gregg Garcia, Chief Engineer
Alan Eisenson, Operations Director

KFBK-FM
01-01-1946; 92.5 mhz FM *Hrs Open:* 24; 50 kw; Ant 499 ft; N38 42 26 W121 28 33
2525 South Danville, Abilene, TX 79605
(325) 793-9700, *Fax:* (325) 692-1576
www.kcby.com
jim.christoferson@culumus.com
License: Sacramento, Sacramento County, CA held by AMFM Broadcasting Licenses LLC.
Group Owner: Clear Channel Communications Inc.
Arbitron Metro Market: Sacramento, CA *Format:* Country *Special Programming:* West Texas Saturday Nights *Hrs. of News Programming:* News progmg one hr wkly *Target Audience:* 18-35
Jim Christoferson, General Sales Mgr
Kelly Jay, Programming Director
Amy Bingham, Promotions Manager
Chris Andrews, Engineering Dir

KHTK
11-01-1926; 1140 khz AM *Hrs Open:* 24
600 New Hampshire Avenue, N.W., Suite 1200, Washington, DC 20037 US
(916) 338-9200, *Fax:* (916) 338-9208
www.khtkam.com
dongeronimo@khtk.com
License: Sacramento, CA held by CBS Radio Holdings Inc.
Group Owner: CBS Radio; (acq 11-13-98; grpsl)
Nat'l Network: Fox Sports; Westwood One
Arbitron Metro Market: Sacramento, CA *TV Affiliate:* CBS *Format:* Sports *Hrs. of News Programming:* News progmg 10 hrs wkly *Target Audience:* 25-44.
Steve Cottingim, General Manager
Brandon Bettar, General Sales Mgr
Mark Evans, Programming Director
Don Geronimo, Program Director
Joe Pittman, Assistant Program Director

KJAY
05-23-1963; 1430 khz AM *Hrs Open:* 6 AM-8 PM; 0.5 kw-D, DAD; 0.02 kw-N, DA2; N38 30 17 W121 33 39
P.O. Box 1384, Carmichael, CA 95609 US
(916) 371-5101,(916) 371-5104, *Fax:* (916) 371-1459
kjay1430am@yahoo.com
License: Sacramento, CA held by KJAY L.L.C.
Arbitron Metro Market: Sacramento, CA *Format:* Religious *Target Audience:* 25-64.
Trudi Powell, President
Jerry Sieber, General Manager
Tiffany Powell, Co-President

KNCI
02-21-1960; 105.1 mhz FM; 50 kw; 499 ft.; N38 38 31 W121 5 25
600 New Hampshire Ave, Suite 1200, Washington, DC 20037 US
(916) 338-9200, *Fax:* (916) 338-9208
www.kncifm.com
info@kncifm.com
License: Sacramento, Sacramento County, CA held by CBS Radio Holdings Inc.
Group Owner: CBS Radio
Arbitron Metro Market: Sacramento, CA *Format:* Country
Mark Evans, Operations Dir
Steve Cottingim, General Manager
Dell Goetz, General Sales Mgr
Walt Shaw, News Director
Bruce Hirsch, Chief Engineer

KIID
08-01-1945; 1470 khz AM
600 New Hampshire Ave., N.W., Suite 1200, Washington, DC 20037 US
(972) 448-3352, *Fax:* (916) 780-1493
www.radiodisney.com
License: Sacramento, CA held by Radio Disney Group LLC.
Group Owner: ABC Inc.; (acq 12-19-00; $3.31 million).
Nat'l Network: Radio Disney
Arbitron Metro Market: Sacramento, CA *Format:* Children
Drew Korzeniewski, VP Radio Disney
Judy Remy, Station Manager

KRXQ
11-01-1959; 98.5 mhz FM *Hrs Open:* 24; 50 kw; 495 ft.; N38 38 53 W121 5 51
401 City Avenue, Suite 409, Bala Cynwyd, PA 19004 US
(916) 334-7777, *Fax:* (916) 339-4274
www.krxq.net
License: Sacramento, Sacramento County, CA held by Entercom Sacramento License L.L.C.
Group Owner: Entercom Communications Corp.; (acq 7-28-98; grpsl)
Nat'l Reps: McGavren Guild
Arbitron Metro Market: Sacramento, CA *Format:* Rock/AOR *Special Programming:* Blues one hr wkly *No. News Employees:* 1 *Target Audience:* 25-40; males
John Geary, Operations Dir
Jim Fox, Programming Director
John Boyle, Promotions Manager

KSEG
01-01-1959; 96.9 mhz FM; 50 kw; 499 ft.; N38 38 53 W121 28 38
401 City Avenue, Ste 409, Bala Cynwyd, PA 19004 US
(916) 334-7777, *Fax:* (916) 339-4559
www.eagle969.com
License: Sacramento, Sacramento County, CA held by Entercom Sacramento License L.L.C.
Group Owner: Entercom Communications Corp.; (acq 1-7-97; $45 million with KRAK(FM) Roseville).
Nat'l Reps: D & R Radio
Arbitron Metro Market: Sacramento, CA *Format:* Classic Rock *Target Audience:* 18-49.
John Geary, Operations Dir
Rich Ripley, General Sales Mgr
Curtiss Johnson, Programming Director
Lizann Hunt, Promotions Manager

KTKZ
01-01-1952; 1380 khz AM; 5 kw-U, DA-2; N38 33 19 W121 10 51
1425 River Park Dr., Suite 520, Sacramento, CA 93012
(916) 924-0710, *Fax:* (916) 924-1587
www.ktkz.com
info@ktkz.com
License: Sacramento, Sacramento County, CA held by New Inspiration Broadcasting Co. Inc.
Group Owner: Salem Communications Corp.; (acq 3-11-97; $1.5 million).
Population Served: 1,110,000 *Arbitron Metro Market:* Sacramento, CA *Target Audience:* 35 plus; general
Steve Gasser, Operations Dir
Dale Hendry, General Manager
Max Miller, Programming Director

KBZC
04-01-1957; 106.5 mhz FM *Hrs Open:* 24; 50 kw; 410 ft.; N38 38 30 W121 5 25
801 K St, 27th Floor, Sacramento, CA 95814 US
(916) 334-7777, *Fax:* (916) 339-4559
www.90sbuzz.com
License: Sacramento, Sacramento County, CA held by Entercom Sacramento License LLC.
Group Owner: Entercom Communications Corp.; (acq 5-19-2003; $25 million).
Arbitron Metro Market: Sacramento, CA *Format:* Adult Contemp *Target Audience:* 18-49; new rock, mass appeal
John Geary, Operations Dir
Dan Mason, Station Manager
Butch Mitchell, General Sales Mgr
Lizann Hunt, Promotions Manager

***KXPR**
07-01-1991; 88.9 mhz FM *Hrs Open:* 24; 50 kw; 492 ft.; N38 16 25 W121 30 11
3416 American River Dr., Suite B, Sacramento, CA 95864 US
(916) 278-8900, *Fax:* (916) 278-8989
www.capradio.org
npr@csus.edu
License: Sacramento, Sacramento County, CA held by California State University, Sacramento.
Nat'l Network: NPR; PRI
Arbitron Metro Market: Sacramento, CA *Format:* Classical *Target Audience:* General; NPR Listeners, eg. professionals, educators, administrators
John Brenneise, Operations Dir
Tom Livingston, General Manager
Carl Watanabe, Station Manager
Joe Barr, News Director
Jeff Brown, Engineering Dir
Cheryl Dring, Music Director

***KXJZ**
10-01-1964; 90.9 mhz FM *Hrs Open:* 24; 50 kw; 482 ft.; N38 42 38 W121 28 54
3416 American River Dr, Suite B, Sacramento, CA 95864 US
(916) 278-8900, *Fax:* (916) 278-8989
www.capradio.org
npr@csus.edu

License: Sacramento, Sacramento County, CA held by California State University, Sacramento.
Nat'l Network: NPR; PRI; AP Radio
Arbitron Metro Market: Sacramento, CA *Format:* Jazz, News
Special Programming: World mus 2 hrs, blues 7 hrs wkly. *Hrs. of News Programming:* news progmg 90 hrs wkly *No. News Employees:* 5 *Target Audience:* General; NPR listeners,ex. professionals, educators & administrators
John Brenneise, Operations Dir
Carl Watanabe, Station Manager
Joe Barr, News Director
Jeff Browne, Engineering Dir

*KYDS
01-24-1979; 91.5 mhz FM *Hrs Open:* 7 AM-3:30 PM; 0.41 kw; 108 ft.; N38 36 33 W121 21 38
3738 Walnut Avenue, Carmichael, CA 95609 US
(916) 971-7430, *Fax:* (916) 971-7429
www.sanjuan.edu
kyds915station@live.com
License: Sacramento, Sacramento County, CA held by San Juan Unified School District.
Arbitron Metro Market: Sacramento, CA *Format:* Variety/Diverse
Ed Santillanes, General Manager

KYMX
01-01-1947; 96.1 mhz FM; 50 kw; 476 ft.; N38 38 9 W121 33 11
600 New Hampshire Ave., N.W., Suite 1200, Washington, DC 20037 US
(916) 923-6800, *Fax:* (916) 922-2830
www.kymx.cbslocal.com
butch.mitchell@cbsradio.com
License: Sacramento, Sacramento County, CA held by Infinity Radio Inc.
Group Owner: CBS Radio; (acq 11-13-98; grpsl).
Arbitron Metro Market: Sacramento, CA *Format:* Adult Contemp
Hrs. of News Programming: news progmg 3 hrs wkly *No. News Employees:* 1 *Target Audience:* 25-54; Women ages 25-54
Jacque Tortorolli, CFO
Joel Hollander, President
Lisa Decker, Operations Dir
Butch Mitchell, General Sales Mgr
Bryan Jackson, Programming Director
Ashly Vicini, Promotions Manager
Jacqui Freeman, News Director

KZZO
10-01-1958; 100.5 mhz FM; 115 kw; 328 ft.; N38 38 30 W121 5 25
600 New Hampshire Ave., N.W., Suite 1200, Washington, DC 20037 US
(916) 923-6800, *Fax:* (916) 922-2830
now100fm.cbslocal.com/
christian.salisbury@cbsradio.com
License: Sacramento, Sacramento County, CA held by Infinity Radio Inc.
Group Owner: CBS Radio; (acq 11-13-98; grpsl).
Nat'l Reps: Christal
Arbitron Metro Market: Sacramento, CA *Format:* Adult Contemp
Hrs. of News Programming: news progmg 3 hrs wkly *No. News Employees:* 1 *Target Audience:* 25-44.
Steve Cottingim, General Manager
Christian Salisbury, General Sales Mgr
Chad Rufer, Programming Director
Chad Skinner, Promotions Manager
Karen Silben, Promotions Director

Salinas

KDBV
07-17-1963; 980 khz AM *Hrs Open:* 24
1436 Auburn Boulevard, Sacramento, CA 95815 US
(805) 406-9157
www.radioabundante.com
info@kdbvam.com
License: Salinas, CA held by Centro Cristiano Vida Abundante Inc.
Wire Services: Accu-Weather
Arbitron Metro Market: Monterey-Salinas-Santa Cruz, CA
Format: Christian *Target Audience:* 18-49; Hispanics
Ronald Stevens, General Manager

KDON-FM
12-01-1959; 102.5 mhz FM; 15 kw; 2372 ft.; N36 45 23 W121 30 5
220 Concord Plaza, Suite 600, San Antonio, TX 78216 US
(831) 755-8181, *Fax:* (831) 755-8193
www.kdon.com
License: Salinas, Monterey County, CA held by CC Licenses LLC.
Group Owner: Clear Channel Communications Inc.; (acq 9-22-97; grpsl)
Nat'l Reps: Christal
Arbitron Metro Market: Monterey-Salinas-Santa Cruz, CA
Format: Urban Contemporary *No. News Employees:* 1 *Target Audience:* 18-54.
Rhonda McCormack, General Manager
Sam Diggedy, Programming Director
Angel Jarquin, Promotions Manager
Irma Gonzalez, News Director
Ray Franklin, Chief Engineer

KYZZ
03-10-1997; 97.9 mhz FM *Hrs Open:* 24; 2.9 kw; 479 ft.; N36 40 20 W121 31 28
1437 Auburn Boulevard, Sacramento, CA 95815 US
(831) 649-0969, *Fax:* (831) 649-3335
www.espnfm979.com
frontdesk@kwav.com
License: Salinas, Monterey County, CA held by Buckley Broadcasting Corp. of Salinas.
Group Owner: Buckley Broadcasting Corp.; (acq 12-21-2005; $3 million) .
Arbitron Metro Market: Monterey, CA *Format:* Contemporary Hits/Top 40 *Target Audience:* 18-34; women
Kathy Baker, General Manager
Sean Stade, General Sales Mgr
Amy Challis, Programming Director
Ron Wharton, Chief Engineer

KRAY-FM
12-05-1977; 103.5 mhz FM *Hrs Open:* 24; 2.5 kw; 512 ft.; N36 40 20 W121 31 28
Mailing Address: 1436 Auburn Boulevard, Sacramento, CA 95815 US
Second Address: 548 E. Alisal St., Salinas, CA 93905
(831) 757-1910, *Fax:* (831) 757-8015
wolfhouseradio@yahoo.es
License: Salinas, Monterey County, CA held by Wolfhouse Radio Group Inc.
Group Owner: Wolfhouse Radio Group Inc.; (acq 7-13-2001; grpsl).
Arbitron Metro Market: Santa Cruz, CA *Format:* Tejano
Ramon Castro, General Manager

KTGE
07-04-1963; 1570 khz AM *Hrs Open:* 24; 5 kw-D, DA2; 0.5 kw-N, DA2; N36 39 38 W121 32 29
Mailing Address: 548 East Alisal Suite A, Salinas, CA 93905 US
Second Address: 548 E. Alisal St., Salinas, CA 93905
(831) 757-5911, *Fax:* (831) 757-8015
wolfhouseradio@yahoo.es
License: Salinas, CA held by Wolfhouse Radio Group Inc.
Group Owner: Wolfhouse Radio Group Inc.; (acq 7-13-2001; grpsl).
Arbitron Metro Market: Salinas, CA *Format:* Tejano *Target Audience:* Adults 24-54.
Ramon Castro, General Manager
Vicente Romero, Programming Director
Ron Warren, Chief Engineer

KPRC-FM
09-16-1964; 100.7 mhz FM; 1.4 kw; 2385 ft.; N36 32 5 W121 37 14
220 Concord Plaza, Suite 600, San Antonio, TX 78216 US
(831) 755-8181, *Fax:* (831) 755-8193
www.salinas.lapreciosa.com
License: Salinas, Monterey County, CA held by CC Licenses LLC.
Group Owner: Clear Channel Communications Inc.; (acq 9-22-97; grpsl)
Arbitron Metro Market: Monterey-Salinas-Santa Cruz, CA
Rhonda mcCormack, General Manager
Alex Luca, Programming Director
Maggie Fernandez, Promotions Manager

KION
01-01-1947; 1460 khz AM *Hrs Open:* 24; 10 kw-D, DA1; 10 kw-N, DA1; N36 43 59 W121 35 32
220 Concord Plaza, Suite 600, San Antonio, TX 78216 US
(831) 755-8181, *Fax:* (831) 755-8193
www.1460kion.com
markcarbonaro@clearchannel.com
License: Salinas, CA held by CC Licenses LLC.
Group Owner: Clear Channel Communications Inc.
Arbitron Metro Market: Salinas, CA *Format:* News, News/Talk, 86
Rhonda McCormack, Market Manager, National Sales Manager, Director o
Mark Carbonero, Programming Director
Monica Tovar, Sales Manager

San Andreas

*KARQ
01-01-2005; 89.3 mhz FM *Hrs Open:* 24; 0.45 kw vert; 1926 ft.; N38 7 10 W120 43 27 *Rebroadcasts:* Rebroadcasts KLRD(FM) Yucaipa 100%
1425 N Market Blvd., Suite 9, Sacramento, CA 95834 US
(888) 937-2471, *Fax:* (916) 251-1650
www.air1.com
info@air1.com
License: San Andreas, Tuolumne County, CA held by Educational Media Foundation.
Group Owner: EMF Broadcasting
Nat'l Network: Air 1
Arbitron Metro Market: Ashdown, AR *Format:* Alternative, Christian *No. News Employees:* 3 *Target Audience:* 25-44; Judeo Christian, female
Darrell Chambliss, Chairman
Alan Mason, COO
Mike Novak, President and CEO
Ed Lenane, News Director
Sam Wallington, Engineering Dir
Tracy Butler, Traffic Manager
Larry Moody, Director
Mitch Barnhart, Director
David R. Ferry,Director
Walter Golembeski, Director
David Pierce, Chief Creative Officer

San Ardo

*KNBX
01-21-2001; 91.7 mhz FM; 2.7 kw; 1781 ft.; N35 57 6 W121 0 3
Rebroadcasts: Rebroadcasts KCBX(FM) San Luis Obispo 100%
P.O. 423, Santa Cruz, CA 95061 US
(805) 549-8855
www.kcbx.org
kcbx@kcbx.org
License: San Ardo, Monterey County, CA held by KCBX, Inc.
Nat'l Network: NPR; PRI
Arbitron Metro Market: San Ardo, CA *Format:* Variety/Diverse
Hrs. of News Programming: News progmg 44 hrs wkly
Frank Lanzone, General Manager
Paul Severtson, General Sales Mgr
Neal Losey, Programming Director
Ken Schreiner, Chief Engineer
Guy Rathbun, Programming Director

San Bernardino

KTDD
10-15-1947; 1350 khz AM *Hrs Open:* 24; 5 kw-D, DA2; 0.6 kw-N, DA2; N34 5 37 W117 17 57
50 East Rivercenter Blvd, #1200, Covington, KY 41011 US
(951) 684-1991, *Fax:* (951) 274-4911
www.am1350thetoad.com/main.html
teresahutchinson@clearchannel.com
License: San Bernardino, CA held by Citicasters Licenses L.P.
Group Owner: Clear Channel Communications Inc.; (acq 5-4-99; grpsl).
Nat'l Reps: McGavren Guild
Arbitron Metro Market: Riverside-San Bernardino, CA *Format:* Country *Hrs. of News Programming:* News progmg 15 hrs wkly
Target Audience: 25-64.
Bob Ridzak, General Manager
Bill Georgi, Programming Director

KFRG
08-01-1974; 95.1 mhz FM *Hrs Open:* 24; 50 kw; 489 ft.; N34 11 51 W117 17 10
600 New Hampshire Avenue, N.W., Suite 1200, Washington, DC 20037 US
(909) 825-9525, *Fax:* (909) 825-0441
www.kfrog.com
License: San Bernardino, San Bernardino County, CA held by Infinity Radio Inc.
Group Owner: CBS Radio; (acq 11-13-98; grpsl).
Nat'l Reps: McGavren Guild
Arbitron Metro Market: Colton, CA *Format:* Country *Hrs. of News Programming:* news progmg 3 hrs wkly *No. News Employees:* 1 *Target Audience:* 25-54; dual income families
Kimberly Martinez, General Sales Mgr
Lee Douglas, Operations Manager

KKDD
01-01-1947; 1290 khz AM *Hrs Open:* 24; 5 kw-D, DA2; 5 kw-N, DA2; N34 7 27 W117 14 14
2001 Iowa Avenue, Suite 200, Riverside, CA 92507 US
(951) 684-1991, *Fax:* (951) 274-4911
www.radiodisney.com
info@radiodisney.com

License: San Bernardino, CA held by AMFM Broadcasting Licenses LLC.
Group Owner: Clear Channel Communications Inc.; (acq 8-30-2000; grpsl).
Arbitron Metro Market: Riverside-San B *Format:* Children *Hrs. of News Programming:* news progmg 10 hrs wkly *No. News Employees:* 1
Bob Ridzak, General Manager
Scott Welsh, Programming Director

KEZY
08-01-1947; 1240 khz AM *Hrs Open:* 24; 1 kw-U, ND1; N34 4 55 W117 18 17
4880 Santa Rosa Rd, #300, Camarillo, CA 93012 US
(626) 356-4230, *Fax:* (626) 795-9185
info@enuevavida.com
License: San Bernardino, CA held by Hi-Favor Broadcasting LLC
Group Owner: Hi-Favor Broadcasting LLC; acq 8-27-01; $4 million).
Nat'l Network: USA
Arbitron Metro Market: Riverside-San B *Format:* Religious *Hrs. of News Programming:* News progmg 2 hrs wkly *Target Audience:* 30 plus.
Roland Hinz, President
Sergio Martinez, General Sales Mgr
Mary Guthrie, Programming Director

KOLA
06-15-1959; 99.9 mhz FM *Hrs Open:* 24; 29.5 kw; 1663 ft.; N33 57 59 W117 17 16
437 S. Highway 101, Suite 201, Solana Beach, CA 92075 US
(909) 793-3554, *Fax:* (909) 798-6627
www.imakolanut.com
info@imakolanut.com
License: San Bernardino, San Bernardino County, CA held by Anaheim Broadcasting Corp.
Group Owner: Anaheim Broadcasting Corp.; acq 1995; $5 million)
Arbitron Metro Market: Riverside-San Bernardino, CA *Format:* Oldies *Hrs. of News Programming:* News progmg one hr wkly *Target Audience:* 25-54.
Jeff Parke, General Manager
Gary Springfield, Programming Director

KTIE
01-01-1929; 590 khz AM *Hrs Open:* 24
2905 South King Road, San Jose, CA 95122 US
(909) 885-6555 Ext. 101, *Fax:* (909) 383-8889
www.590ktie.com
License: San Bernardino, CA held by Caron Broadcasting Inc.
Group Owner: Salem Communications Corp.; (acq 8-29-2001; $7 million).
Arbitron Metro Market: San Bernardino, CA *Format:* News, News/Talk, 86 *Target Audience:* 35-54; male /female upscale, educated, home owners, business decision makers
Jim Tinker, Operations Dir
Terry Fahy, General Manager
Brad Anderson, General Sales Mgr
Chuck Tyler, Programming Director
Pamela Tyus, Promotions Manager
Craig Edwards, Programming Director

*KVCR
12-01-1953; 91.9 mhz FM *Hrs Open:* 24; 3.8 kw; 1621 ft.; N33 57 57 W117 17 5
701 S. Mt. Vernon Ave., San Bernardino, CA 92410 US
(909) 384-4444, *Fax:* (909) 885-2116
www.kvcr.org
info@kvcr.org; memberservices@kvcr.org
License: San Bernardino, San Bernardino County, CA held by San Bernardino Community College Dist.
Nat'l Network: NPR
Arbitron Metro Market: Riverside-San Bernardino, CA *TV Affiliate:* KVCR-TV affil *Format:* News, Talk *Hrs. of News Programming:* news progmg 50 hrs wkly *No. News Employees:* 3 *Target Audience:* General.
Steve Ward, Operations Director
Larry Ciecalone, General Manager
Duncan Lively, Station Manager
Ben Holland, Programming Director
Lillian Vasquez, Promotions Manager
Ken Vincent, News Director
Rick Dulock, Programme Manager
Devid Fleming, Producer
Jim Walker, R-F Engineer
Yendis Battle, Senior Accountant
Gina Guerrero, Secretary
Jessica James, Program Operations

San Clemente

KWVE-FM
11-16-1971; 107.9 mhz FM *Hrs Open:* 24; 0.53 kw; 3793 ft.; N33 42 40 W117 31 55
3800 South Fairview, Santa Ana, CA 92704 US
(714) 918-6207, *Fax:* (714) 918-6256
www.kwve.com
kwve@kwve.com
License: San Clemente, Orange County, CA held by Calvary Chapel of Costa Mesa Inc.
Arbitron Metro Market: Santa Ana, CA *Format:* Christian, Talk, 74 *Special Programming:* Children 3 hrs wkly *Hrs. of News Programming:* news progmg 3-5 hrs wkly *No. News Employees:* 2 *Target Audience:* General. *Adv. Rates:* 120; 90; 90; 45
Charles Smith, President
Jeffrey Dorman, General Manager

San Diego

KBZT
03-06-1960; 94.9 mhz FM; 26.5 kw; 686 ft.; N32 50 17 W117 14 57
P.O. Box 21008, Greensboro, NC 27420 US
(619) 297-9595, *Fax:* (619) 543-1353
www.fm49sd.com
License: San Diego, San Diego County, CA held by Lincoln Financial Media Co. of California.
Group Owner: Lincoln Financial Media; (acq 9-13-96; $25 million for stock)
Arbitron Metro Market: San Diego, CA *Format:* Alternative *Target Audience:* 18-49.
Darrel Goodin, Station Manager
John Marks, Programming Director
Chris Turner, Promotions Manager
Eric Schecter, Chief Engineer
Copeland Isaac, Promotions Manager

KCBQ
01-01-1946; 1170 khz AM *Hrs Open:* 24
11521 Innfields Drive, Odessa, FL 33556 US
(858) 535-1210, *Fax:* (858) 535-1212
www.kcbq.com
info@kcbq.com
License: San Diego, CA held by New Inspiration Broadcasting Co. Inc.
Group Owner: Salem Communications Corp.; (acq 8-23-2000; $5 million).
Nat'l Network: AP Radio; ABC
Arbitron Metro Market: San Diego, CA *Format:* News, News/Talk, 86 *Hrs. of News Programming:* News progmg 5 hrs wkly *Target Audience:* 35-64; baby boomers that grew up in the 50s & early 60s
Heather Lloyd, Operations Dir
Dave Armstrong, General Manager
Dawn Hockaday, Promotions Manager
Craig Caston, Chief Engineer

KFMB
05-19-1941; 760 khz AM *Hrs Open:* 24; 5 kw-D, DAN; 50 kw-N, DAN; N32 50 33 W117 1 30
Mailing Address: 7677 Engineer Road, San Diego, CA 92111 US
Second Address: 7677 Engineer Rd., San Diego, CA 92186
(619) 495-7548, *Fax:* (619) 279-7676
www.760kfmb.com
info@kdmbam.com
License: San Diego, CA held by Midwest Television Inc.
Nat'l Network: CBS *Nat'l Reps:* McGavren Guild
Arbitron Metro Market: San Diego, CA *Format:* News, News/Talk, 86 *Special Programming:* Financial 8 hrs wkly *Hrs. of News Programming:* News 125 hrs wkly *No. News Employees:* 10 *Target Audience:* 25-54.
August Meyer Jr., CEO
Ed Trimble, President
Tracy Johnson, General Manager
John Marquiss, General Sales Mgr
Dave Sniff, Programming Director
Fred D'Ambrosi, News Director
Mike Sommerville, Chief Engineer
Dayna Monroe, PublicAffairs Director
Melanie Kartalija, Research Director

KFMB-FM
09-21-1959; 100.7 mhz FM; 30 kw; 620 ft.; N32 50 17 W117 14 57
Mailing Address: 7677 Engineer Road, San Diego, CA 92111 US
Second Address: 7677 Engineer Rd., San Diego, CA 92186
(619) 495-7548, *Fax:* (619) 279-7676
www.sandiegojack.com/
info@kfmbfm.com
License: San Diego, San Diego County, CA held by Midwest Television Inc.
Arbitron Metro Market: San Diego, CA *TV Affiliate:* KFMB-TV affil. *Format:* Adult Contemp *Target Audience:* 18-35
Gina Landau, General Sales Mgr
Scott Sands, Programming Director
Kim Leeds, Promotions Manager
Jen Sewell, Music Director
Lynn Yuen, Research Director

KGB-FM
01-01-1956; 101.5 mhz FM *Hrs Open:* 24; 50 kw; 499 ft.; N32 43 48 W117 5 3
50 E Rivercenter Blvd, Suite 1200, Covington, KY 41011 US
(858) 292-2000, *Fax:* (858) 715-3372
www.101kgb.com
License: San Diego, San Diego County, CA
Group Owner: Clear Channel Communications Inc.
Arbitron Metro Market: San Diego, CA *Format:* Classic Rock *Target Audience:* 25-54.
Dave Saunders, General Sales Mgr
Jim Richards, Programming Director
Jay Isbell, Promotions Manager

KIFM
02-04-1960; 98.1 mhz FM *Hrs Open:* 24; 26.5 kw; 686 ft.; N32 50 17 W117 14 57
1615 Murray Canyon Road, Suite 710, San Diego, CA 92108 US
(619) 297-3698, *Fax:* (619) 543-1353
www.981smoothfm.com
mikev@kifm.net; john.dangelo@lincolnfinancialmedia.com
License: San Diego, San Diego County, CA held by Lincoln Financial Media Co. of California.
Group Owner: Lincoln Financial Media; (acq 8-1-96; $28.75 million)
Nat'l Reps: CBS Radio
Arbitron Metro Market: San Diego, CA *Format:* Jazz, Smooth Jazz *Special Programming:* Living Better San Diego 5 hrs wkly *Hrs. of News Programming:* News progmg 2 hrs wkly *Target Audience:* 25-54; upscale adults
Rick Jackson, General Manager
Mike Vasquez, Programming Director
John D'Angelo, Promotions Manager
Bill Eisenhamer, Chief Engineer
Mike Vasquez, Program Director

KIOZ
01-01-1954; 105.3 mhz FM *Hrs Open:* 24; 26 kw; 689 ft.; N32 50 20 W117 14 56
50 East Rivercenter Blvd, Suite 1200, Covington, KY 41011 US
(858) 292-2000, *Fax:* (858) 715-3180
www.rock1053.com
info@kiozfm.com
License: San Diego, San Diego County, CA held by Citicasters Licenses L.P.
Group Owner: Clear Channel Communications Inc.; (acq 5-4-99; grpsl).
Arbitron Metro Market: San Diego, CA *Hrs. of News Programming:* news progmg one hr wkly *No. News Employees:* 1 *Target Audience:* 18-49; upscale, well educated, young adult rock fans
Bob Bolinger, General Manager
Shauna Moran, Programming Director
Jay Isbell, Promotions Manager

KMYI
01-01-1949; 94.1 mhz FM *Hrs Open:* 24; 77 kw; 689 ft.; N32 50 20 W117 14 56
3102 Oak Lawn Ave., Suite 215, Dallas, TX 75219 US
(858) 292-2000, *Fax:* (858) 715-3336
www.star941fm.com
License: San Diego, San Diego County, CA held by Citicasters Licenses L.P.
Group Owner: Clear Channel Communications Inc.; (acq 5-4-99; grpsl).
Arbitron Metro Market: San Diego, CA *Format:* Adult Contemp *Target Audience:* 35-54; general, women
Debbie Wagner, President
Jim Richards, Operations Dir
Bob Bolinger, General Manager
Terry King, General Sales Mgr
Jimmy Steele, Programming Director
Kristin Ferguson, Promotions Manager
Melissa Forrest, Market Manager

KLNV
06-26-1960; 106.5 mhz FM; 50 kw; 440 ft.; N32 43 19 W117 4 7
100 Crescent Court, Suite 1777, Dallas, TX 75201 US
(619) 235-0600, *Fax:* (619) 744-4300
www.lanueva1065.com
License: San Diego, San Diego County, CA held by HBC San Diego License Corp.

Group Owner: Univision Radio; (acq 9-22-2003; grpsl).
Wire Services: UPI
Arbitron Metro Market: San Diego, CA *Format:* Tejano *Target Audience:* 18-49; young adult, contemp mus fans, upscale, well-educated *Adv. Rates:* 250; 250; 250; 125
Peter Moore, General Manager
Michael Donavan, General Sales Mgr
Jose Gadea, Programming Director
Nate Mendez, Promotions Manager
Angel Ramos, Chief Engineer

KLQV
05-20-1963; 102.9 mhz FM *Hrs Open:* 24; 30 kw; 632 ft.; N32 50 24 W117 14 52
100 Crescent Court, Suite 1777, Dallas, TX 75201 US
(619) 235-0600, *Fax:* (619) 744-4300
www.univison.com
License: San Diego, San Diego County, CA held by HBC San Diego License Corp.
Group Owner: Univision Radio; (acq 9-22-2003; grpsl).
Arbitron Metro Market: San Diego, CA *Target Audience:* 25-44.
Adv. Rates: 350; 350; 350; 200
Peter Moore, General Manager

KOGO
01-01-1926; 600 khz AM *Hrs Open:* 24
201 East Fifth Street, Suite 1300, Cincinnati, OH 45202 US
(858) 292-2000, *Fax:* (858) 715-3364
www.kogo.com
kogo@clearchannel.com
License: San Diego, CA held by Citicasters Licenses L.P.
Group Owner: Clear Channel Communications Inc.; (acq 1999; grpsl).
Nat'l Network: Fox News Radio *Wire Services:* AP
Arbitron Metro Market: San Diego, CA *Format:* News, News/Talk, 86 *Hrs. of News Programming:* news progmg 22 hrs wkly *No. News Employees:* 10 *Target Audience:* 25-54; issue oriented talk radio listeners
Debra Wagner, General Manager
Cliff Albert, Programming Director
Sherry Toennies, Promotions Manager
John Rigg, Chief Engineer

*KPBS-FM
09-12-1960; 89.5 mhz FM *Hrs Open:* 24; 2.7 kw; 1804 ft.; N32 41 53 W116 56 3
5200 Campanile Drive, Mc 5400, San Diego, CA 92182 US
(619) 594-1515, (619) 594-8100, *Fax:* (619) 594-3812
www.kpbs.org
letters@kpbs.org
License: San Diego, San Diego County, CA held by San Diego State University.
Nat'l Network: PRI; NPR *Wire Services:* AP
Arbitron Metro Market: San Diego, CA *Format:* News, News/Talk, 86 *Hrs. of News Programming:* news progmg 11 hrs wkly *No. News Employees:* 15 *Target Audience:* 35 plus.
Tom Karlo, General Manager
John Decker, Programming Director

KEGY(FM)
01-01-1965; 103.7 mhz FM *Hrs Open:* 24; 26.5 kw; Ant 689 ft; N32 50 20 W117 14 56
8033 Linda Vista Rd., San Diego, CA 92111-5108
(858) 561-7600, *Fax:* (858) 571-0326
www.energy1037.com
pa@energy1037.com
License: San Diego, San Diego County, CA held by CBS Stations Inc.
Group Owner: CBS Radio; (acq 8-7-2000; grpsl)
Nat'l Reps: Christal
Population Served: 300,000 *Arbitron Metro Market:* San Diego, CA *Format:* Adult Contemp
Charlie Quinn, Operations Dir
Bob Bolinger, General Manager
Charese Fruge, Programming Director

KLSD
07-14-1922; 1360 khz AM; 5 kw-D, ND1; 1 kw-N, ND1; N32 43 49 W117 5 1
201 East Fifth Street, Suite 1300, Cincinnati, OH 45202 US
(858) 292-2000, *Fax:* (858) 715-3372
www.extrasports1360.com
cliffalbert@clearchannel.com
License: San Diego, CA held by Citicasters Licenses L.P.
Group Owner: Clear Channel Communications Inc.; (acq 1999; grpsl)
Nat'l Reps: CBS Radio
Arbitron Metro Market: San Diego, CA *Format:* Sports
Cliff Albert, Station Manager
Scotty Morache, General Sales Mgr
Sherry Toennies, Promotions Manager

Mary Ayala, News Director
Bill Thompson, Chief Engineer

KSDO
10-01-1947; 1130 khz AM *Hrs Open:* 24; 10 kw-D, DA2; 10 kw-N, DA2; N32 51 4 W116 57 51
50 E. Rivercenter Blvd, Suite 1200, Covington, KY 41011 US
(626) 356-4230, *Fax:* (626) 795-9185
www.ksdo.com
info@enuevavida.com
License: San Diego, CA held by Hi-Favor Broadcasting LLC
Group Owner: Hi-Favor Broadcasting LLC; acq 4-1-03; $10 million). .
Nat'l Network: ABC
Arbitron Metro Market: San Diego, CA *Format:* Religious *No. News Employees:* 10 *Target Audience:* 25-54.
Sean McCoy, General Manager
Sergio Martinez, General Sales Mgr
Mary Guthrie, Programming Director
Carlos Ortega, News Director
Rudy Agus, Chief Engineer

*KSDS
12-01-1951; 88.3 mhz FM *Hrs Open:* 24; 22 kw vert; Ant 246 ft; N32 48 19 W117 10 09
1313 Park Blvd., San Diego, CA 92108
(619) 388-3037, *Fax:* (619) 388-3928
www.jazzs88.org
markd@jazz88.org
License: San Diego, San Diego County, CA held by San Diego Community College District.
Nat'l Network: NPR
Population Served: 696,679 *Arbitron Metro Market:* San Diego, CA *Hrs. of News Programming:* news progmg 7 hrs wkly *No. News Employees:* 1 *Target Audience:* 25-65 plus; affluent, professional adults
Joseph Kocherhans, Operations Dir
Mark DeBoskey, Station Manager
Ann Bauer, General Sales Mgr
Claudia Russell, Programming Director
Natasha Collins, Promotions Manager
Bob Broms, News Director
Larry Quick, Chief Engineer
Jennifer Weddel, Development Director
April Pendergraft, Membership Director
Joe Kocherhans, Music Director
Chad Fox, Assistant Music Director

KNSN
01-01-1946; 1240 khz AM; non directional
1615 Murray Canyon Road, Suite 710, San Diego, CA 92108 US
(619) 291-9797
www.esneradio.com
License: San Diego, CA held by Multicultural Radio Broadcasting Licensee, LLC
Group Owner: Multicultural Radio Broadcasting Inc.; (acq 4-3-2006; grpsl)
Arbitron Metro Market: San Diego, CA *Format:* Chinese
Darrel Goodin, General Manager
Eric Schecter, Chief Engineer

KSON
01-15-1964; 97.3 mhz FM; 50 kw; 440 ft.; N32 43 13 W117 4 14
1615 Murray Canyon Road, Suite 710, San Diego, CA 92108 US
(619) 291-9797, *Fax:* (619) 543-1353
www.kson.com
License: San Diego, San Diego County, CA held by Lincoln Financial Media Co. of California.
Group Owner: Lincoln Financial Media; (acq 2-7-85)
Arbitron Metro Market: San Diego, CA *Format:* Country
Darrel Goodin, General Manager
John Marks, Programming Director
Chris Turner, Promotions Manager
Eric Schecter, Chief Engineer
Copeland Isaac, Promotions Manager

KURS
11-01-1992; 1040 khz AM *Hrs Open:* 24
296 H Street, Suite 300, Chuka Vista, CA 91910 US
(619) 426-5645, *Fax:* (619) 425-1000
www.espnradio620am.com
jc@psnradio.com
License: San Diego, CA held by Quetzal Bilingual Communications Inc.
Wire Services: UPI
Arbitron Metro Market: San Diego, CA *Format:* Oldies
Jaime Bonilla, President
Jose Carbajal, General Manager

KYXY
01-01-1960; 96.5 mhz FM *Hrs Open:* 24; 26.5 kw; 689 ft.; N32 50 20 W117 14 56
600 Congress Ave., Suite 1400, Austin, TX 78701 US
(858) 571-7600, *Fax:* (858) 571-0326
www.kyxy.cbslocal.com/
webmaster@kyxy.com
License: San Diego, San Diego County, CA held by CBS Stations Inc.
Group Owner: CBS Radio; (acq 8-7-00; grpsl).
Nat'l Reps: Christal
Arbitron Metro Market: San Diego, CA *Format:* Classic Rock
Target Audience: 25-54; adults, women
Charlie Quinn, Operations Dir
Bob Bolinger, General Manager

San Fernando

KBUA
11-14-1958; 94.3 mhz FM *Hrs Open:* 24; 6 kw; 85 ft.; N34 17 3 W118 28 17 *Rebroadcasts:* Rebroadcasts KBUE(FM) Long Beach 100%
5724 Hollywood Blvd., Los Angeles, CA 90028 US
(818) 729-5300, *Fax:* (818) 729-5678
www.aquisuena.com
License: San Fernando, Los Angeles County, CA held by LBI Radio License Corp.
Group Owner: Liberman Broadcasting Inc.; (acq 1997; $10.8 million)
Arbitron Metro Market: Los Angeles, CA *Format:* Tejano
Lenard Liberman, President
Pepe Garza, Station Manager
Chris Buchanan, Chief Engineer

San Francisco

*KALW
03-20-1941; 91.7 mhz FM *Hrs Open:* 24; 1.9 kw; 919 ft.; N37 45 17 W122 26 44
500 Mansell Street, San Francisco, CA 94134 US
(415) 841-4121, *Fax:* (415) 841-4125
www.kalw.org
kalw@kalw.org
License: San Francisco, San Francisco County, CA held by San Francisco Unified School District.
Nat'l Network: PRI; NPR
Arbitron Metro Market: San Francisco, CA *Format:* Oldies, Variety/Diverse *Special Programming:* Diversified *Hrs. of News Programming:* News progmg 68 hrs wkly *Target Audience:* General; news & info-orientedlisteners
William Helgeson, Operations Dir
Matt Martin, General Manager
Dianne Keogh, General Sales Mgr

KCBS
04-01-1909; 740 khz AM; 50 kw-D, DA2; 50 kw-N, DA2; N38 8 23 W122 31 45
600 New Hampshire Avenue, NW, Suite 1200, Washington, DC 20037 US
(415) 765-4000, *Fax:* (415) 765-4080
www.kcbs.com
kcbscomments@kcbs.com
License: San Francisco, CA held by CBS Radio East Inc.
Group Owner: CBS Radio; (acq 1996)
Nat'l Network: CBS *Wire Services:* Reuters; Bay City News Service; U.S. Weather Service
Arbitron Metro Market: San Francisco, CA *Format:* News *Target Audience:* 25-54.
Doug Harvill, General Manager
David Bramnick, Station Manager
Ed Cavagnaro, News Director

KFRC-FM
01-01-1958; 106.9 mhz FM *Hrs Open:* 24; 80 kw; 1001 ft.; N37 51 4 W122 29 50 *Rebroadcasts:* Simulcast with KCBS(AM) San Francisco 100%
4135 Northgate Blvd #1, Sacramento, CA 95834 US
(415) 765-4000, *Fax:* (415) 765-4080
www.kcbs.com
License: San Francisco, San Francisco County, CA held by CBS Radio Stations Inc.
Group Owner: CBS Radio; (acq 12-7-2005; $95 million)
Nat'l Network: CBS Radio *Nat'l Reps:* CBS Radio
Arbitron Metro Market: San Francisco *Format:* News *No. News Employees:* 2
Doug Harvill, General Manager

KEST
01-01-1926; 1450 khz AM *Hrs Open:* 24; 1 kw-U, ND1; N37 45 37 W122 22 56
499 Hamilton Avenue, Suite 140, Palo Alto, CA 94301 US
(415) 978-5378, *Fax:* (415) 865-0738
www.kestradio.com
info@kestradio.com

License: San Francisco, CA held by Multicultural Radio Broadcasting Licensee LLC.
Group Owner: Multicultural Radio Broadcasting Inc.; (acq 3-31-98; grpsl).
Arbitron Metro Market: San Francisco *Format:* Talk *Special Programming:* Chinese, Japanese, Indian, gospel, new age *Hrs. of News Programming:* news progmg 6 hrs wkly *No. News Employees:* 1 *Target Audience:* 25 plus.
Arthur Liu, President
Omar Gallegos, Operations Dir
Judy Re, General Manager

KFAX
01-01-1925; 1100 khz AM *Hrs Open:* 24
4880 Santa Rosa Rd, #300, Camarillo, CA 93012 US
(510) 713-1100, *Fax:* (510) 505-1448
www.kfax.com
info@kfax.com
License: San Francisco, CA held by Golden Gate Broadcasting Co. Inc.
Group Owner: Salem Communications Corp.; (acq 9-1-84)
Nat'l Network: Salem Radio Network *Nat'l Reps:* Salem
Arbitron Metro Market: San Francisco *Format:* Talk, Religious *Special Programming:* Contemp Christian music 5 hrs weekly, children one hr wkly *Hrs. of News Programming:* News progmg 4 hrs wkly *Target Audience:* 25-54; females, families, college educated
Greg Edwards, Operations Dir
Mike Shields, General Manager
Mike Ginsburg, General Sales Mgr
Wanda Cornelius, Promotions Manager
Craig Roberts, Chief Engineer

KFOG
03-01-1963; 104.5 mhz FM *Hrs Open:* 24; 7.1 kw; 1506 ft.; N37 45 19 W122 27 6
140 East Market Street, York, PA 17401 US
(415) 817-5364, *Fax:* (415) 995-7090
www.kfog.com
kfog@kfog.com
License: San Francisco, San Francisco County, CA held by KFFG Lico Inc.
Group Owner: Cumulus Media Partners LLC
Arbitron Metro Market: San Francisco, CA *Format:* Classic Rock *Special Programming:* Acoustic 10 hrs wkly, international 2 hrs wkly *Hrs. of News Programming:* news progmg 4 hrs wkly *No. News Employees:* 1*Target Audience:* 25-54
Lee Hammer, General Manager
Omari Patterson, General Sales Mgr
Sheri Nelson, Promotions Manager
Michele Mercer, News Director

KEAR
09-24-1924; 610 khz AM
Mailing Address: 600 New Hampshire Ave NW, Suite 1200, Washington, DC 20037 US
Second Address: 290 Hegenberger Rd., Oakland, CA 94621-1436
(805) 363-5576, *Fax:* (209) 389-0215
www.familyradio.com
info@familyradio.com
License: San Francisco, CA held by Family Stations Inc.
Group Owner: Family Stations Inc.; (acq 4-28-2005; $35 million).
Nat'l Network: Family Radio
Arbitron Metro Market: Banning, CA *Format:* Christian, Religious *Target Audience:* General.
Harold Camping, President
Matt Pearce, Operations Dir

KMVQ-FM
01-01-1949; 99.7 mhz FM; 40 kw; 1299 ft.; N37 41 15 W122 26 4
600 New Hampshire Ave NW, Suite 1200, Washington, DC 20037 US
(415) 391-9970, *Fax:* (415) 951-2329
http://997now.cbslocal.com/
cat.ong@movin997.com
License: San Francisco, San Francisco County, CA held by CBS Radio KFRC-FM Inc.
Group Owner: CBS Radio; (acq 1-96; grpsl)
Arbitron Metro Market: San Francisco *Format:* Adult Contemp
Doug Harvill, General Manager
Larry Blumhagen, General Sales Mgr
Mike Preston, Programming Director
Cat Ong, Promotions Manager
Phil Lerza, Chief Engineer
Stephanie Saporita, Local Sales Manager

KGO
01-08-1924; 810 khz AM; 50 kw-U, DA1; N37 31 35 W122 6 2
900 Front Street, 16th Floor, San Francisco, CA 94111 US
(415) 261-0810, *Fax:* (415) 995-7099
www.kgoam810.com
producers@kgoradio.com
License: San Francisco, CA
Group Owner: Cumulus Media Inc.; (acq 6-12-2007; grpsl)
Arbitron Metro Market: San Francisco, CA *Format:* News, News/Talk, 86 *Hrs. of News Programming:* news progmg 80 hrs wkly *Target Audience:* 25-54; general
Michael Luckoff, President
Rob Rossi, General Sales Mgr
Jack Swanson, Programming Director
Ken Berry, News Director
Joe Talbot, Chief Engineer
Cathy Whitman, Producer

KIOI
10-27-1957; 101.3 mhz FM *Hrs Open:* 24; 125 kw; 1161 ft.; N37 41 24 W122 26 13
300 Crescent Court, Suite 600, Dallas, TX 75201 US
(415) 356-5500, *Fax:* (415) 975-5573
www.star1013fm.com
License: San Francisco, San Francisco County, CA held by AMFM Broadcasting Licenses LLC.
Group Owner: Clear Channel Communications Inc.; (acq 8-30-2000; grpsl).
Nat'l Reps: Christal
Arbitron Metro Market: San Francisco *Format:* Adult Contemp *Hrs. of News Programming:* news progmg one hr wkly *No. News Employees:* 1 *Target Audience:* 25-54.
Don Parker, Operations Dir
Dave Pugh, General Sales Mgr
Andrew Jeffries, Programming Director
Alicia Kimbrell, Promotions Manager
David Williams, Chief Engineer

KIQI
01-01-1957; 1010 khz AM *Hrs Open:* 24; 10 kw-D, DA2; 0.5 kw-N, DA2; N37 49 33 W122 18 39
8400 N.W. 52nd St., Suite 101, Miami, FL 33166 US
(415) 978-5378, *Fax:* (415) 978-5380
www.kiqi1010am.com
License: San Francisco, CA held by Multicultural Radio Broadcasting Licensee LLC.
Group Owner: Multicultural Radio Broadcasting Inc.; (acq 2-4-2004; grpsl).
Arbitron Metro Market: San Francisco *Format:* Urban Contemporary *No. News Employees:* 3 *Target Audience:* 24-54.
Arthur Liu, President
Omar Gallegos, Operations Dir
Judy Re, General Manager

KISQ
07-17-1958; 98.1 mhz FM *Hrs Open:* 8 AM-5:30 PM; 75 kw; 1016 ft.; N37 51 4 W122 29 50
750 Battery St., Suite 200, San Francisco, CA 94111 US
(415) 356-5500, *Fax:* (877) 547-7329
www.981kissfm.com
info@kisqfm.com
License: San Francisco, San Francisco County, CA held by AMFM Broadcasting Licenses LLC.
Group Owner: Clear Channel Communications Inc.; (acq 8-30-2000; grpsl).
Nat'l Reps: McGavren Guild
Arbitron Metro Market: San Francisco *Format:* Oldies *Special Programming:* Gospel 3 hrs wkly *Target Audience:* 25-54; women
Don Parker, Operations Dir
Dave Pugh, General Manager
Stacy Cunningham, Programming Director
David Williams, Chief Engineer

KITS
06-01-1964; 105.3 mhz FM; 15 kw; 1201 ft.; N37 41 20 W122 26 7
600 New Hampshire Avenue, NW, Suite 1200, Washington, DC 20037 US
(415) 512-1053,(415) 402-6700, *Fax:* (415) 777-0608
www.live105.com
info@kitsfm.com
License: San Francisco, San Francisco County, CA held by Infinity Broadcasting East Inc.
Group Owner: CBS Radio; (acq 5-7-97).
Arbitron Metro Market: San Francisco *Format:* Alternative
Doug Harvill, General Manager
Karl Isotalo, General Sales Mgr
Michael Martin, Programming Director

KLLC
02-01-1948; 97.3 mhz FM *Hrs Open:* 24; 82 kw; 1014 ft.; N37 51 3 W122 29 51
600 New Hampshire Avenue, NW, Suite 1200, Washington, DC 20037 US
(415) 765-4097, *Fax:* (415) 765-4084
www.radioalice.com
studio@radioalice.com
License: San Francisco, San Francisco County, CA held by Infinity Broadcasting East Inc.
Group Owner: CBS Radio
Nat'l Reps: CBS Radio
Arbitron Metro Market: San Francisco, CA *Format:* Adult Contemp *Target Audience:* 18-54.
Doug Harvill, General Manager

KMEL
11-30-1960; 106.1 mhz FM *Hrs Open:* 24; 69 kw; 1289 ft.; N37 41 24 W122 26 13
433 E. Las Colinas Blvd, #1130, Irving, TX 75039 US
(415) 356-5500, *Fax:* (415) 975-5573
www.106kmel.com
License: San Francisco, San Francisco County, CA held by AMFM Broadcasting Licenses LLC.
Group Owner: Clear Channel Communications Inc.; (acq 8-30-2000; grpsl).
Nat'l Reps: Christal
Arbitron Metro Market: San Francisco, CA *Format:* Contemporary Hits/Top 40
Don Parker, Operations Dir
Dave Pugh, General Manager
John Plesses, General Sales Mgr
Stacy Cunningham, Programming Director
Tony Ng, Promotions Manager

KNBR
01-01-1922; 680 khz AM *Hrs Open:* 24; 50 kw-U, ND1; N37 32 50 W122 14 0
140 East Market St., York, PA 17401 US
(415) 995-6800, *Fax:* (415) 995-6867
www.knbr.com
sports@knbr.com
License: San Francisco, CA held by KNBR Lico Inc.
Group Owner: Cumulus Media Partners LLC; (acq 5-24-89; $17.5 million;
Nat'l Network: ABC; Westwood One
Arbitron Metro Market: San Francisco, CA *Format:* Sports, Talk *Target Audience:* 18 plus; predominently men
Lee Hammer, Operations Dir
Peter Schwartz, General Sales Mgr
Lyell Perry, Promotions Manager
Judi Ratto, General Sales Manager
Sheri Nelson, Judi Ratto
Daniel Erman, Sales Manager

KSFB
01-01-1926; 1260 khz AM
P.O. Box 1160, Salt Lake City, UT 84110 US
(916) 535-0500, *Fax:* (916) 535-0504
www.ihradio.org
info@ihradio.org
License: San Francisco, CA held by IHR Educational Broadcasting.
Group Owner: IHR Educational Broadcasting; (acq 7-16-2007; $14 million)
Nat'l Network: EWTN Radio
Arbitron Metro Market: San Francisco *Format:* Christian
Douglas Sherman, President
Lori Brown, General Manager

KOIT
01-01-1959; 96.5 mhz FM; 24 kw; 1575 ft.; N37 45 19 W122 27 6
P.O. Box 1160, Salt Lake City, UT 84110 US
(415) 777-0965, *Fax:* (415) 896-0965
www.koit.com
koit@koit.com
License: San Francisco, San Francisco County, CA held by Entercom San Francisco License LLC.
Group Owner: Entercom Communications Corp.; (acq 3-14-2008; grpsl)
Arbitron Metro Market: San Francisco *Format:* Adult Contemp *Target Audience:* 25-54; upscale adults who earn an average of $30,000
Dwight Walker, General Manager
Scotty Bastable, General Sales Mgr
Bill Conway, Programming Director
Jude Heller, Promotions Manager
Julie Deppish, Assistant Music Director
Payton Raymond, National Sales Manager
Dave Milner, SalesDirector

*KPOO
04-01-1971; 89.5 mhz FM; 0.27 kw horiz; 541 ft.; N37 47 33 W122 24 52
Mailing Address: P.O. Box 11008, San Francisco, CA 94101 US
Second Address: 1329 Divisadero St., San Francisco, CA 94142

RADIO - U.S.

(415) 346-5373, *Fax:* (415) 346-5173
www.kpoo.com
info@kpoo.com
License: San Francisco, San Francisco County, CA held by Poor Peoples' Radio Inc.
Arbitron Metro Market: San Francisco Bay Area *Format:* Variety/Diverse
Terry Collins, President
Marilyn Fowler, Operations Dir
Jerome Parsons, General Manager
Harrison Chastang, News Director
Dave Billicci, Chief Engineer

***KQED-FM**
06-01-1969; 88.5 mhz FM *Hrs Open:* 24; 110 kw; 1270 ft.; N37 41 23 W122 26 13
2601 Mariposa Street, San Francisco, CA 94110 US
(415) 553-2129, *Fax:* (415) 553-2241
www.kqed.org
fm@kqed.org
License: San Francisco, San Francisco County, CA held by KQED Inc.
Nat'l Network: NPR; PRI *Wire Services:* Bay City News Service
Arbitron Metro Market: San Francisco-Oakland-San Jose-Sacramento *TV Affiliate:* KQED(TV) affil. *Hrs. of News Programming:* news progmg 160 hrs wkly *No. News Employees:* 9 *Target Audience:* General.
Monty Carlos, Operations Dir
Jo Anne Wallace, General Manager
Traci Eckels, General Sales Mgr
Raul Ramirez, News Director

KSFO
08-01-1925; 560 khz AM; 5 kw-D, DAN; 5 kw-N, DAN; N37 44 44 W122 22 40
77 West 66th St, 16th Floor, New York, NY 10023 US
(415) 398-5600, *Fax:* (415) 391-2795
www.ksfo.com
License: San Francisco, CA
Group Owner: Cumulus Media Inc.; (acq 6-12-2007; grpsl)
Arbitron Metro Market: San Francisco *Format:* News, Talk *Target Audience:* 25-54.
Michael Luckoff, President
Melissa Galliani, General Sales Mgr
Jack Swanson, Programming Director
Joe Talbot, Chief Engineer

KSOL
12-10-1959; 98.9 mhz FM *Hrs Open:* 24; 6.1 kw; 1342 ft.; N37 45 19 W122 27 6
3102 Oak Lawn Ave., Suite 215, Dallas, TX 75219 US
(415) 733-5765, *Fax:* (415) 733-5766
www.univision.com
License: San Francisco, San Francisco County, CA held by TMS License California Inc.
Group Owner: Univision Radio; (acq 9-22-2003; grpsl).
Arbitron Metro Market: San Francisco *Format:* Spanish *No. News Employees:* 1 *Target Audience:* 18-54.
Tony Perlongo, General Manager
Mary Lou Gunn, General Sales Mgr
Jose Gonzalez, Programming Director
Luz Rodriguez, Promotions Manager

KTRB
06-18-1933; 860 khz AM
1192 Norwegian Avenue, Modesto, CA 95350 US
(415) 362-8686, *Fax:* (415) 391-6860
www.ktrb860.com
jpappas@ktrb860.com
License: San Francisco, CA held by Pappas Radio of California, a California L.P.
Group Owner: Pappas Telecasting Companies; (acq 3-30-2000)
Nat'l Network: Fox Sports; Sporting News Radio Network *Nat'l Reps:* McGavren Guild
Arbitron Metro Market: San Francisco *Format:* Sports *Special Programming:* Oakland A's, Stanford Football and Men's Basketball *Target Audience:* Men: 25-54.
Harry Pappas, CEO
Jim Pappas, Operations Dir
Kevin Barrett, Programming Director
Georgette Rodarakis, Promotions Manager
John Burger, Chief Engineer

KZDG(AM)
01-01-1947; 1550 khz AM *Hrs Open:* 24; 10 kw-U, DA-2; N37 31 49 W122 16 29
865 Battery St., 3rd Fl., San Francisco, CA 94111-1513
(415) 391-9970, *Fax:* (415) 397-7655
www.kfrc.com
License: San Francisco, San Francisco County, CA held by CBS Radio East Inc.
Group Owner: CBS Radio; (acq 12-14-2000; grpsl)
Population Served: 715,674 *Arbitron Metro Market:* San Francisco *Format:* Oldies *Special Programming:* Jazz *Target Audience:* 12 plus; affluent, home-owning, highly educated, business professionals
Stephen Paige, Station Manager
Greg Nemitz, General Sales Mgr

KRZZ
02-01-1959; 93.3 mhz FM *Hrs Open:* 24; 6 kw; 1362 ft.; N37 41 13 W122 26 3
600 New Hampshire Ave NW, Suite 1200, Washington, DC 20037 US
(415) 543-9330, *Fax:* (415) 543-3753
www.yosoyraza.com
License: San Francisco, San Francisco County, CA held by KRZZ Licensing LLC.
Group Owner: Spanish Broadcasting System Inc.; (acq 12-7-2004).
Arbitron Metro Market: San Francisco *Target Audience:* 18-49; Hispanics
Joe Cunningham, General Manager
Lisa Kruglov, General Sales Mgr

KYLD
03-12-1958; 94.9 mhz FM; 30 kw; 1211 ft.; N37 41 22 W122 26 10
340 Townsend St., #4-949, San Francisco, CA 94107 US
(415) 541-5555, *Fax:* (415) 541-3087
www.wild949.com
License: San Francisco, San Francisco County, CA held by AMFM Broadcasting Licenses LLC.
Group Owner: Clear Channel Communications Inc.; (acq 8-30-2000; grpsl).
Arbitron Metro Market: San Francisco, CA *Format:* Urban Contemporary, Christian *Target Audience:* 25-54.
Don Parker, Operations Dir
Dave Pugh, General Manager
Anne Hudson, General Sales Mgr
Cat Collins, Programming Director
Tony Ng, Promotions Manager
Jay Plus, Assistant Promotions Director

KGMZ(FM)
01-01-1959; 95.7 mhz FM *Hrs Open:* 24; 6.9 kw; Ant 1,500 ft; N37 41 23 W122 26 12
201 Third St., Suite 1200, San Francisco, CA 94103-3143
(415) 957-0957, *Fax:* (415) 356-8394
www.957thegame.com/
thegame@957thegame.com
License: San Francisco, San Francisco County, CA held by Entercom San Francisco License LLC.
Group Owner: Entercom Communications Corp.; (acq 3-14-2008; grpsl)
Population Served: 812,846 *Arbitron Metro Market:* San Francisco,CA *Format:* Country *Target Audience:* 25-54.
Dwight Walker, General Manager
Mike Fadelli, General Sales Mgr
Jason Barrett, Programming Director
Josh Pearlman, Promotions Manager

San Gabriel

KMRB
01-01-1942; 1430 khz AM *Hrs Open:* 24
747 E. Green Street, 4th Floor, Pasadena, CA 91101 US
(626) 844-8882, *Fax:* (626) 792-8890
info@kmrbam.com
License: San Gabriel, CA held by Polyethnic Broadcasting Licensee LLC
Arbitron Metro Market: Los Angeles, CA *Format:* Japanese, Korean, 18 *Special Programming:* Thai 2 hrs, Ethiopian 2 hrs wkly *Target Audience:* General.
Arthur Liu, President
Kevin Chu, Station Manager
Katherine Lieu, General Sales Mgr
Alan Mok, Programming Director
Hon Vu, Chief Engineer
David Sweeney, Executive Vice President

San Jacinto

KRQB
09-23-1990; 96.1 mhz FM *Hrs Open:* 24; 1.4 kw; 686 ft.; N34 2 13 W116 58 7
475 W. Stetson, Ste. U, Hemet, CA 92543 US
(909) 663-1961, *Fax:* (909) 663-1996
aquisuena.estrellatv.com
advertising@quebuena961.com
License: San Jacinto, Riverside County, CA held by LBI Radio License LLC.
Group Owner: Liberman Broadcasting Inc.; (acq 9-6-2007; $25 million)
Arbitron Metro Market: Riverside-San Bernardino, CA *Adv. Rates:* 47; 47; 47; na
Jose Liberman, President
Cristian Garcia, Operations Dir
Winter Horton, General Manager
Carlos Santos, General Sales Mgr
Pepe Garza, Programming Director

San Joaquin

KJZN
01-01-1999; 105.5 mhz FM *Hrs Open:* 24; 25 kw; 328 ft.; N36 36 28 W119 59 49
966 East Essex Drive, Fresno, CA 93720 US
(559) 230-0104, *Fax:* (559) 230-0177
www.fresnostruth.com
License: San Joaquin, Fresno County, CA held by Wilks License Co.-Fresno LLC.
Group Owner: Wilks Broadcast Group LLC; (acq 6-1-2005; grpsl)
Nat'l Reps: McGavren Guild
Arbitron Metro Market: Fresno, CA *Format:* Talk *Target Audience:* Adults 25-54. *Adv. Rates:* 40; 40; 40; 10
Kevin O'Rorke, General Manager
Stephen Brown, Programming Director

San Jose

KBRG
03-04-1963; 100.3 mhz FM *Hrs Open:* 24; 14.5 kw; 2579 ft.; N37 6 40 W121 50 34
2905 South King Road, San Jose, CA 95122 US
(415) 733-5765, *Fax:* (415) 733-5766
www.univision.com
License: San Jose, Santa Clara County, CA held by Univision Radio License Corp.
Group Owner: Univision Radio; (acq 1-1-2006; $90 million with KLOK(AM) San Jose).
Arbitron Metro Market: San Francisco
Tony Perlongo, General Manager
Mary Lou Gunn, General Sales Mgr
Ramon Lopez, Programming Director
Luz Maria Rodriguez, Promotions Manager

KEZR
07-03-1967; 106.5 mhz FM; 42 kw; 535 ft.; N37 12 32 W121 46 27
600 New Hampshire Avenue, N.W., Suite 1200, Washington, DC 20037 US
(408) 287-5775, *Fax:* (408) 293-3341
www.mymix1065.com
License: San Jose, Santa Clara County, CA held by NM Licensing LLC.
Group Owner: NextMedia Group Inc.; (acq 12-6-2005; $80 million with KBAY(FM) Gilroy)
Nat'l Reps: Christal
Arbitron Metro Market: San Jose, CA *Format:* Adult Contemp *Hrs. of News Programming:* news progmg 4 hrs wkly *No. News Employees:* 1 *Target Audience:* 25-44. *Adv. Rates:* 300; 300; 300; 100
John Leathers, General Manager
Judy Dixon, General Sales Mgr
Dana Jang, Programming Director
Marla Davies, News Director

***KMTG**
05-17-1977; 89.3 mhz FM; 0.3 kw; -312 ft.; N37 12 6 W121 51 42
Mailing Address: 6677 Camden Avenue, San Jose, CA 95120 US
Second Address: 855 Linden Ave., San Jose, CA 95126
(408) 535-6310, *Fax:* (408) 535-2357
www.pioneerhigh.org
steve_dini@sjusd.org
License: San Jose, Santa Clara County, CA held by San Jose Unified School District.
Arbitron Metro Market: San Francisco, CA *Format:* Variety/Diverse
Steve Dini, General Manager

KLIV
01-01-1946; 1590 khz AM *Hrs Open:* 24; 5 kw-D, DAN; 5 kw-N, DAN; N37 19 45 W121 51 23
P.O. Box 995, San Jose, CA 95108 US
(408) 293-8030, *Fax:* (408) 293-6124
www.kliv.com
License: San Jose, CA held by Empire Broadcasting Corp.
Group Owner: Empire Broadcasting Corp.; acq 7-1-67)
Nat'l Network: CNN Radio *Nat'l Reps:* Christal *Wire Services:* AP; Bay City News Service
Arbitron Metro Market: San Jose, CA *Format:* News *Special Programming:* San Jose soccer earthquakes *No. News Employees:* 8 *Target Audience:* General. *Adv. Rates:* 75; 65; 65; 20

Robert Kieve, President
Tina Ferguson, General Sales Mgr
George Sampson, Programming Director
George Sampson, News Director
Shawn Murphy, Sports Director

KLOK
10-19-1946; 1170 khz AM *Hrs Open:* 24
Mailing Address: 2905 South King Road, San Jose, CA 95122 US
Second Address: 2905 South King Rd., San Jose, CA 95122
(408) 440-0851, *Fax:* (408) 440-0853
www.klok1170am.com
klok1170am@aol.com
License: San Jose, CA held by Principle Bay Area Holding Co., LLC
Group Owner: Univision Radio
Arbitron Metro Market: San Francisco, CA *Format:* Ethnic *Target Audience:* 18-49.
Brad Behnke, General Manager

KSJO
12-01-1946; 92.3 mhz FM; 32 kw; 446 ft.; N37 12 32 W121 46 27
50 East Rivercenter Blvd., Suite 1200, Covington, KY 41011 US
(408) 453-5400, *Fax:* (408) 452-1330
www.channel923.com
License: San Jose, Santa Clara County, CA held by Aloha Station Trust LLC, as Trustee
Nat'l Reps: McGavren Guild
Arbitron Metro Market: San Jose, CA *Format:* Alternative *Target Audience:* 18-49; active adults
Dave Pugh, General Manager
Jaysson Reno, General Sales Mgr
Michael Solari, Programming Director

***KSJS**
02-22-1963; 90.5 mhz FM *Hrs Open:* 24; 1.5 kw; 472 ft.; N37 12 33 W121 46 30
1 Washington Square, Theatre Arts Dept, San Jose, CA 95192 US
(408) 924-5757(408) 924-4545, *Fax:* (408) 924-4558
www.ksjs.org
ksjs@ksjs.org
License: San Jose, Santa Clara County, CA held by San Jose State University.
Arbitron Metro Market: San Jose, CA *Format:* Variety/Diverse *Target Audience:* 18-34; students & community members
Nick Martinez, General Manager
Mike Adams, General Sales Mgr
Vincente Heredia, Programming Director

KSJX
06-24-1948; 1500 khz AM *Hrs Open:* 24; 10 kw-D, DA2; 5 kw-N, DA2; N37 21 28 W121 52 17
449 Broadway, New York, NY 10013 US
(408) 280-1515, *Fax:* (408) 280-1585
www.mrbi.net
ksjx1500@sbcglobal.net
License: San Jose, CA held by Multicultural Radio Broadcasting Licensee LLC.
Group Owner: Multicultural Radio Broadcasting Inc.; (acq 2-20-98; grpsl).
Arbitron Metro Market: San Jose, CA *Format:* Vietnamese
Special Programming: Mandarin Chinese 10 hrs, Vietnamese
No. News Employees: 2 *Target Audience:* 25-54; managerial, professional, homeowners *Adv.Rates:* 80; 80; 80; 65
Arthur Liu, President
Victor Nguyen, Operations Dir
Andrea Yamazaki, General Manager

KUFX
07-01-1959; 98.5 mhz FM *Hrs Open:* 24; 10 kw; 879 ft.; N37 12 17 W121 56 56
50 East Rivercenter Boulevard, Suite 1200, Covington, KY 41011 US
(408) 200-9850, *Fax:* (408) 452-1330
www.kfox.com
ggoin@kfox.com?subject=KFOX%20Programming
License: San Jose, Santa Clara County, CA held by Aloha Station Trust LLC, as Trustee
Nat'l Reps: CBS Radio
Arbitron Metro Market: San Jose, CA *Format:* Classic Rock
Target Audience: 18-49; general
Dave Pugh, General Manager
Rob Rossi, Sales Manager
Garner Goin, Programming Director
Sharon Kenney, Promotions Manager
Andy Drake, Web Director

KZSF
06-21-1947; 1370 khz AM *Hrs Open:* 24; 5 kw-U, DA1; N37 21 28 W121 52 17
1436 Auburn Boulevard, Sacramento, CA 95815 US
(408) 546-7201, *Fax:* (408) 247-4353
www.1370am.com
info@1370am.com
License: San Jose, CA held by Carlos A. Duharte
Regional Reps: Interep
Arbitron Metro Market: San Jose, CA *Format:* Tejano *Target Audience:* 18-49. *Adv. Rates:* 150; 75; 75; 60
Carlos Duharte, CEO
Reyna Santillan, Promotions Manager

San Luis Obispo

***KCBX**
07-25-1975; 90.1 mhz FM *Hrs Open:* 24; 5.3 kw; 1421 ft.; N35 21 37 W120 39 17 *Rebroadcasts:* Rebroadcasts KSBX(FM) Santa Barbara 100%
4100 Vachell Lane, San Luis Obispo, CA 93401 US
(805) 549-8855, *Fax:* (805) 781-3025
www.kcbx.org
901kcbx@kcbx.org
License: San Luis Obispo, San Luis Obispo County, CA held by KCBX Inc.
Nat'l Network: NPR
Arbitron Metro Market: San Luis Obispo, CA *Format:* Jazz, News
Special Programming: Folk 15 hrs wkly *Hrs. of News Programming:* News progmg 32 hrs wkly *Target Audience:* General.
Frank Lanzone, President
Hank Hadley, Operations Dir
Paul Severtson, General Sales Mgr
Guy Rathbun, Programming Director
Katherine Johnson, Business Manager

***KCPR**
01-01-1968; 91.3 mhz FM *Hrs Open:* 24; 0.31 kw; 1417 ft.; N35 21 38 W120 39 21
Graphic Arts Bldg 201, San Luis Obispo, CA 93407 US
(805) 756-5998
www.kcpr.org
kcpr.internet@gmail.com
License: San Luis Obispo, San Luis Obispo County, CA held by California Polytechnic State University.
Arbitron Metro Market: San Luis Obispo, CA *Format:* Variety/Diverse *Special Programming:* Sp 3 hrs, metal 3 hrs, blues 3 hrs *Hrs. of News Programming:* News progmg 4 hrs wkly
Target Audience: General; Cal Polystudents, San Luis Obispo community
Alyssa Duhe, General Manager
Megan Keith, Programming Director
Brian Powell, Promotions Manager
Brian Hildebrand, General Manager
Eric Buckthal, Music Director
Maddie Mori, Music Director
Biba Pickles, Music Director
TylerDeitz, Business Director
Laurie Fraser, Business Director

KYNS
12-13-1949; 1340 khz AM *Hrs Open:* 24
PO Box 170, Arroyo Grande, CA 93421 US
(805) 786-2570, *Fax:* (805) 547-9860
www.mapletoncommunications.com.com
License: San Luis Obispo, CA held by Mapleton License of San Luis Obispo LLC.
Group Owner: Mapleton Communications LLC; (acq 3-19-2003; $370,000)
Arbitron Metro Market: San Luis Obispo, CA *Format:* Alternative, News, 62, Talk
Adam Nathanson, President
Nancy Leichter, General Manager

KJDJ
02-08-1988; 1030 khz AM; 2.5 kw-D, ND1; 0.7 kw-N, ND1; N35 17 58 W120 40 24
296 H Street, Suite 300, Chula Vista, CA 91910 US
(805) 928-1030
www.radiovidaabundante.com
oracion@radiovidaabundante.com
License: San Luis Obispo, CA held by Padre Serra Communications Inc.
Arbitron Metro Market: San Luis Obispo, CA *Format:* Religious
Manuel Salvador, General Manager
Manny Aram, Programming Director

KKJG
01-01-1984; 98.1 mhz FM; 4.5 kw; 1519 ft.; N35 21 40 W120 39 21
PO Box 2700, Bakersfield, CA 93303 US
(805) 781-2750, *Fax:* (805) 781-2758
www.jugcountry.com
License: San Luis Obispo, San Luis Obispo County, CA held by AGM San Luis Obispo L.P.
Group Owner: American General Media; (acq 7-1-97; $1.5 million).
Arbitron Metro Market: San Luis Obispo, CA *Format:* Country
Target Audience: 25-54.
Kathy Signorelli, General Manager
Pepper Daniels, Programming Director

KKJL
02-06-1960; 1400 khz AM *Hrs Open:* 24; 1 kw-U, ND1; N35 15 51 W120 39 56
Mailing Address: P.O. Box 1400, San Luis Obispo, CA 93406 US
Second Address: 51 Zaca Ln., Suite 90, San Luis Obispo, CA 93401
(805) 543-9400, *Fax:* (805) 543-0787
www.kkjl1400.com
info@kkjl1400.com
License: San Luis Obispo, CA held by San Luis Obispo Broadcasting Inc.
Nat'l Network: CNN Radio
Arbitron Metro Market: San Luis Obispo, CA *Format:* Sports, Adult Contemp *Special Programming:* SF Giants, SF 49ers, LA Lakers *Target Audience:* 35 plus; adults males & females *Adv. Rates:* 22; 22; 22; 16
Guy Hackman, President
Kyle Ronemus, Operations Dir
Mary Brown, Operations Manager

***KLFF-FM**
09-26-1995; 89.3 mhz FM *Hrs Open:* 24; 4.4 kw; 1529 ft.; N35 21 37 W120 39 17
P.O. Box 1561, San Luis Obispo, CA 93406 US
(805) 541-4343, *Fax:* (805) 541-9101
www.klife.org
info@klife.org
License: San Luis Obispo, San Luis Obispo County, CA held by Logos Broadcasting Corp.
Nat'l Network: Salem Radio Network
Arbitron Metro Market: San Luis Obispo, CA *Format:* Christian
Target Audience: 18-34; Christians *Adv. Rates:* 15; 15; 15; 15
Dr. Daniel Woods, CFO
Dan Lemburg, President
Jon Fugler, General Manager
Noonie Fugler, Promotions Manager

***KLVH**
03-25-1999; 88.5 mhz FM *Hrs Open:* 24; 2.8 kw; 1493 ft.; N35 21 37 W120 39 20
1425 N. Market Blvd., Suite 9, Sacramento, CA 95839 US
(707) 528-9236, *Fax:* (707) 528-9246
www.klove.com
klove@klove.com
License: San Luis Obispo, San Luis Obispo County, CA held by Educational Media Foundation.
Group Owner: EMF Broadcasting; (acq 5-12-99).
Nat'l Network: K-Love
Arbitron Metro Market: San Luis Obispo, CA *Format:* Christian
No. News Employees: 3 *Target Audience:* 25-44; Judeo Christian, female
Darell Chambliss, Chairman
Mike Novak, President
Fernando Chaidez, General Sales Mgr
David Pierce, Programming Director
Ed Lenane, News Director
Sam Wallington, Engineering Dir
Marya Morgan, News Reporter
Richard Hunt, MaryaMorgan

KSLY-FM
12-01-1959; 96.1 mhz FM; 3.6 kw; 1647 ft.; N35 21 37 W120 39 18
966 East Essex Drive, Fresno, CA 93720 US
(805) 545-0101, *Fax:* (805) 541-5303
www.ksly.com
info@ksly.com
License: San Luis Obispo, San Luis Obispo County, CA held by EDB SLO License LLC.
Group Owner: Frontier Radio Management Inc.; (acq 11-30-2007; grpsl)
Arbitron Metro Market: San Luis Obispo, CA *Format:* Country
Dave Daniels, Operations Dir
Rich Hawkins, General Manager
Kathy Mansell, General Sales Mgr
Jay Turner, Programming Director
Teresa Lara, Promotions Manager
Ben Grenaway, News Director

KVEC
05-01-1937; 920 khz AM *Hrs Open:* 24; 1 kw-D, ND2; 0.5 kw-N, ND2; N35 17 58 W120 40 24
1329 Chorro St., San Luis Obispo, CA 93401 US

(805) 545-0101, *Fax:* (805) 541-5303
www.920kvec.com
info@920kvec.com
License: San Luis Obispo, CA held by EDB SLO License LLC.
Group Owner: Frontier Radio Management Inc.; (acq 11-30-2007; grpsl)
Nat'l Network: ABC; Fox News Radio
Arbitron Metro Market: San Luis Obispo, CA *Format:* News, News/Talk, 86 *Special Programming:* Dodgers baseball, NFL/NCAA football, finance, senior focus, health, real estate *Hrs. of News Programming:* news progmg 45hrs wkly *No. News Employees:* 4 *Target Audience:* 35 plus; affluent decision & newsmakers, sports fans, business owners & retirees *Adv. Rates:* 19; 17; 19; 17
Rich Hawkins, General Manager
Andrew Cannon, Programming Director
King Harris, News Director
Greg Russo, Webmaster
Ron Roy, Regional Vice President

KZOZ
01-01-1962; 93.3 mhz FM; 23 kw; 1549 ft.; N35 21 40 W120 39 21
4115 Broad St. Suite B-4, San Luis Obispo, CA 93401 US
(805) 781-2750, *Fax:* (805) 781-2758
www.kzoz.com
sales@americangeneralmedia.com
License: San Luis Obispo, San Luis Obispo County, CA held by AGM California.
Group Owner: American General Media; (acq 6-89; grpsl).
Arbitron Metro Market: San Luis Obispo, CA *Format:* Classic Rock, Rock/AOR
Bill Heirendt, Operations Dir
Kathy Signorelli, General Manager
David Atwood, Programming Director

San Marcos-Poway

KPRZ
01-01-1986; 1210 khz AM *Hrs Open:* 24
4880 Santa Rosa Rd, #300, Camarillo, CA 93012 US
(858) 535-1210, *Fax:* (858) 535-1212
www.kprz.com
slopez@kprz.com
License: San Marcos-Poway, CA held by New Inspiration Broadcasting Co. Inc.
Group Owner: Salem Communications Corp.; (acq 1986)
Nat'l Network: Salem Radio Network
Arbitron Metro Market: San Diego, CA *Format:* Christian, Talk, 74 *Special Programming:* Sp 22 hrs wkly *Hrs. of News Programming:* News progmg 15 hrs wkly *Target Audience:* 25-54; conservative, pro-family
Edward Astinger III, CEO
Heather Lloyd, Operations Dir
Dave Armstrong, General Manager
Dawn Hockaday, Promotions Manager
Craig Caston, Chief Engineer
David Evans, CFO

San Martin

KZSJ
11-01-1995; 1120 khz AM *Hrs Open:* 24; 5 kw-D, ND1; 0.15 kw-N, ND1; N36 57 49 W121 29 22
1436 Auburn Blvd., Sacramento, CA 95815 US
(408) 223-3130, *Fax:* (408) 223-3131
www.quehuongmedia.com
qhradio@aol.com
License: San Martin, CA held by Bustos Media Holdings, LLC
Group Owner: Bustos Media LLC; (acq 2-26-99).
Arbitron Metro Market: San Martin, CA *Format:* Vietnamese *Target Audience:* Vietnamese *Adv. Rates:* 50; 45; 50; 30
Amador Bustos, Chairman
Carlos A. Duharte, Operations Dir
Khoi Nguyen, General Manager

San Mateo

*KCSM
10-01-1964; 91.1 mhz FM; 11 kw; 372 ft.; N37 32 8.1 W122 20 0
3401 Csm Drive, San Mateo, CA 94402 US
(650) 574-6586, *Fax:* (650) 524-6975
www.kcsm.org
info@kcsm.org
License: San Mateo, San Mateo County, CA held by San Mateo County Community College District.
Nat'l Network: PRI; NPR
Arbitron Metro Market: San Mateo, CA *TV Affiliate:* *KCSM-TV affil. *Format:* Jazz *Special Programming:* Blues 3 hrs wkly *Target Audience:* 40 plus; males
Alisa Clancy, Operations Dir
Marilyn Lawrence, General Manager
Melanie Berzon, Programming Director
Michele Muller, Engineering Dir

KSAN
09-01-1963; 107.7 mhz FM; 8.9 kw; 1161 ft.; N37 41 20 W122 26 7
140 East Market Street, York, PA 17401 US
(415) 981-5726, *Fax:* (415) 995-7061
www.1077thebone.com
License: San Mateo, San Mateo County, CA held by Susquehanna Radio Corp.
Group Owner: Cumulus Media Partners LLC; acq 5-29-97; $44 million)
Nat'l Reps: McGavren Guild
Arbitron Metro Market: San Francisco, CA *Format:* Classic Rock *Target Audience:* 25-54.
Lee Hammer, General Manager
Michael Seghieri, General Sales Mgr
Sheri Nelson, Promotions Manager
James Ly, News Director
Chuck Bullett, Chief Engineer
Peter Schwartz, Sales Director

KTCT
01-01-1948; 1050 khz AM *Hrs Open:* 24; 10 kw-N, DA2; N37 39 2 W122 9 2
140 East Market Street, York, PA 17401 US
(415) 995-6867, *Fax:* (415) 995-6867
www.knbr.com
License: San Mateo, CA
Group Owner: Cumulus Media Partners LLC; (Acq 7-21-97; $15 million)
Nat'l Network: Westwood One
Arbitron Metro Market: San Francisco, CA *Format:* Sports *Target Audience:* 25-54.
Lee Hammer, Operations Dir
David Drutz, General Sales Mgr
Lee Hammer, Programming Director

San Rafael

KVVZ
06-01-1961; 100.7 mhz FM; 6 kw; 328 ft.; N37 58 49 W122 31 39
Rebroadcasts: Simulcasts KVVF-FM Santa Clara 100%
1500 Cotner Avenue, P. O. Box 250028, Los Angeles, CA 90025 US
(415) 733-5765, *Fax:* (415) 733-5766
www.univision.com
License: San Rafael, Marin County, CA held by Univision Radio License Corp.
Group Owner: Univision Radio; (acq 3-1-2005; exchange for KOSL(FM) Jackson).
Arbitron Metro Market: San Francisco, CA *Format:* Spanish
Tony Perlongo, General Manager

*KSRH
05-01-1980; 88.1 mhz FM *Hrs Open:* 9 AM-3 PM; 0.007 kw; 66 ft.; N37 58 16 W122 30 47
185 Mission Street, San Rafael, CA 94901 US
(415) 485-2309 ext. 5213
info@ksrh.com
License: San Rafael, Marin County, CA held by San Rafael High School District.
Format: Black, Variety/Diverse *Special Programming:* Fr one hr wkly *Hrs. of News Programming:* News progmg 5 hrs wkly *Target Audience:* 12-29.
Agnes Thomas, General Manager

Santa Ana

KALI-FM
02-06-1980; 106.3 mhz FM; 6 kw; 302 ft.; N33 45 21 W117 51 18
449 Broadway, New York, NY 10013 US
(877) 595-3424, *Fax:* (626) 844-0156
www.kalifm.com
info@kalifm.com
License: Santa Ana, Orange County, CA held by KALI-FM Licensee LLC.
Arbitron Metro Market: Los Angeles, CA *Format:* Japanese, Korean, 18 *Target Audience:* 18-44.
Arthur Liu, President
David Sweeney, General Manager
Alan Mok, Programming Director

KVNR
11-26-1926; 1480 khz AM; 5 kw-D, DA2; 5 kw-N, DA2; N33 45 6 W117 54 38
5724 Hollywood Blvd., Los Angeles, CA 90028 US
(714) 554-5000, *Fax:* (714) 554-9362
www.littlesoiganradio.com
radio@littlesoigonradio.com
License: Santa Ana, CA held by LBI Radio License Corp.
Group Owner: Liberman Broadcasting Inc.; (Acq 1-88; $6.25 million with co-located FM;
Arbitron Metro Market: Los Angeles *Format:* Vietnamese *Target Audience:* 18-49.
Ninh Vu, President
Kathleen Bui, General Manager
Joe Dinh, Chief Engineer

KWIZ
01-01-1947; 96.7 mhz FM *Hrs Open:* 24; 6 kw; 203 ft.; N33 48 8 W117 47 43
5724 Hollywood Blvd., Los Angeles, CA 90028 US
(714) 554-5000, *Fax:* (714) 554-9362
www.larockola967.com
License: Santa Ana, Orange County, CA held by LBI Radio License Corp.
Group Owner: Liberman Broadcasting Inc.; (acq 1997; $11.2 million).
Arbitron Metro Market: Los Angeles, CA *Target Audience:* 18 plus; Asian
Winnie Coombs, Station Manager
Edwardo Leon, Programming Director
Francisco Morales, Promotions Manager
Patty Diaz, News Director
Shannon Murdock, Chief Engineer
Jesus Mar, Music Director

Santa Barbara

*KCSB-FM
11-01-1964; 91.9 mhz FM *Hrs Open:* 24; 0.62 kw; 2884 ft.; N34 31 31 W119 57 29
300 Lakeside Dr. 8th Flr, Oakland, CA 94612 US
(805) 893-3757, *Fax:* (805) 893-7832
www.kcsb.org
info@kcsb.org
License: Santa Barbara, Santa Barbara County, CA held by Regents of the University of California.
Arbitron Metro Market: Santa Barbara, CA *Format:* Variety/Diverse *Special Programming:* Sp 12 hrs, Japanese pop one hr, East Indian 2 hrs, reggae 6 hrs, American Indian 3 hrs wkly *Hrs. of News Programming:* news progmg9 hrs wkly *No. News Employees:* 2 *Target Audience:* Community radio/college radio
Michael Kenney, General Manager
Elizabeth Robinson, Station Manager
Navid Ebrahimzadeh, Programming Director
Nick Werth, Promotions Manager

KDB
02-14-1960; 93.7 mhz FM *Hrs Open:* 24; 12.5 kw; 870 ft; N34 27 58 W119 40 37
Box 91660, Santa Barbara, CA 93101
(805) 966-4131, *Fax:* (805) 966-4788
www.kdb.com
kdb@kdb.com
License: Santa Barbara, Santa Barbara County, CA held by Pacific Broadcasting Co.
Population Served: 600,000 *Arbitron Metro Market:* Santa Barbara, CA *Hrs. of News Programming:* News progmg one hr wkly *Target Audience:* Adults; affluent, influential & educated *Adv. Rates:* 30; 30; 30; 24
Richard Bickle, Operations Dir
Tim Owens, General Manager
Roby Scott, Station Manager
Roby Scott, General Sales Mgr
Steve Murphy, Programming Director
Roby Scott, Promotions Manager

KZER
10-31-1937; 1250 khz AM *Hrs Open:* 24; 2.5 kw-D, DA2; 1 kw-N, DA2; N34 25 6 W119 49 5
3839 4th St., North, Suite 420, St. Petersburg, FL 33703 US
(805) 240-2070, *Fax:* (805) 240-5960
www.radiolazer.com
terryj@radiolazer.com
License: Santa Barbara, CA held by Lazer Broadcasting Corp.
Group Owner: Lazer Broadcasting Corp.; acq 12-18-2003; $1.5 million).
Arbitron Metro Market: Oxnard, CA *Hrs. of News Programming:* news progmg 140 hrs wkly *No. News Employees:* 5 *Target Audience:* 25 plus; upscale, educated listeners
Terry Janisch, Station Manager
Salvador Prieto, Programming Director

*KQSC
07-01-1985; 88.7 mhz FM *Hrs Open:* 24; 12 kw; 866 ft.; N34 27 55 W119 40 37 *Rebroadcasts:* Rebroadcasts KUSC 100%
P.O. Box 77913, Los Angeles, CA 90007 US
(213) 225-7400, *Fax:* (213) 225-7410
www.kusc.org
kusc@kusc.org

License: Santa Barbara, Santa Barbara County, CA held by University of Southern California.
Nat'l Network: PRI; NPR
Arbitron Metro Market: Los Angeles, CA *Format:* Talk *Hrs. of News Programming:* News progmg 3 hrs wkly *Target Audience:* 35 plus.
Brenda Barnes, President
Eric DeWeese, General Manager
Bill Lueth, Programming Director

KRUZ
09-01-1957; 97.5 mhz FM *Hrs Open:* 24; 17.5 kw; 890 meters; N34 31 31 W119 57 29
403 E Montecito Street, Suite A, Santa Barbara, CA 93103
(805) 966-1755, *Fax:* (805) 650-6172
www.kruz.com
License: Santa Barbara, Santa Barbara County, CA held by Cumulus Licensing LLC
Group Owner: Cumulus Media Inc.; (acq 3-12-2001; grpsl).
Nat'l Reps: McGavren Guild *Wire Services:* AP
Population Served: 650,000 *Arbitron Metro Market:* Santa Barbara, CA *Target Audience:* 35-64; young, educated, upscale adults *Adv. Rates:* 50; 50; 50; 20
Nery Reyes, General Manager
Bruce Pollock, General Sales Mgr
Matt Stone, Programming Director
Tammy Myers, Promotions Manager
John Straker, Chief Engineer

KVYB
08-08-1961; 103.3 mhz FM *Hrs Open:* 24; 105 kw; 2969 ft.; N34 31 29 W119 57 32
C/O Fletcher Head, 1300 N 17th St, 11th Fl, Arlington, VA 22209 US
(805) 642-8595, *Fax:* (805) 656-5838
www.1033thevibe.com
info@1033thevibe.com
License: Santa Barbara, Santa Barbara County, CA held by Cumulus Licensing Corp.
Group Owner: Cumulus Media Inc.; (acq 4-2000).
Nat'l Reps: McGavren Guild
Arbitron Metro Market: Ventura, CA *Format:* Adult Contemp
Target Audience: 18-54; general *Adv. Rates:* 75; 75;75; 20
Jonathon Pinch, COO
Lewis Dickey Jr., President
Gail Furillo, General Sales Mgr
Daniel Herejon, Programming Director
Barbara Haser, News Director
J.D. Strahler, Chief Engineer
Martin Gausvik, CFO
John Dickey, Executive VicePresident

KTMS
08-11-1962; 990 khz AM *Hrs Open:* 24; 5 kw-D, DA2; 0.5 kw-N, DA2; N34 28 15 W119 40 33
50 East Rivercenter Blvd. Suite 1200, Covington, KY 41011 US
(805) 879-8300
www.990am.com
info@990am.com
License: Santa Barbara, CA held by Rincon Broadcasting LS LLC.
Group Owner: Rincon Broadcasting LLC; (acq 7-11-2007; grpsl)
Nat'l Network: ABC; CNN Radio
Arbitron Metro Market: Santa Barbara, CA *Format:* Talk *Hrs. of News Programming:* news progmg 4 hrs wkly *No. News Employees:* 2 *Target Audience:* 25 plus; upscale adults
Keith Royer, Operations Dir
Tom Baker, General Manager
Lin Aubuchon, Promotions Manager

KTYD
08-11-1972; 99.9 mhz FM *Hrs Open:* 24; 34 kw; 1280 ft.; N34 28 15 W119 40 33
50 East Rivercenter Blvd, Suite 1200, Covington, KY 41011 US
(805) 879-8300, *Fax:* (805)879-8430
www.ktyd.com
keith.royer@rinconbroadcasting.com
License: Santa Barbara, Santa Barbara County, CA held by Rincon License Subsidiary LLC.
Group Owner: Rincon Broadcasting LLC; (acq 7-11-2007; grpsl)
Nat'l Reps: Katz Radio
Arbitron Metro Market: Santa Barbara, CA *Format:* Rock/AOR
Special Programming: Pub affrs one hr wkly *Hrs. of News Programming:* news progmg 3 hrs wkly *No. News Employees:* 1
Target Audience: 18-49;upscale adults
Keith Royer, Operations Dir
Keith Royer, Executive VP/General Manager
Vince Hollian, General Sales Mgr
Lin Aubuchon, Promotions Manager
Peter Bie, News Director
Ran Bullard, Chief Engineer

Andrea Shaparenko, Traffic Manager
Jack Clarke, National Sales Manager
Steve Hess, Local Sales Manager

KCLU
01-01-1946; 1340 khz AM *Rebroadcasts:* Simulcast with KCLU-FM Thousand Oaks 100%
50 East Rivercenter Boulevard, Suite 1200, Covington, KY 41011 US
(805) 493-3900, *Fax:* (805) 493-3982
www.kclu.org
molson@callutheran.edu
License: Santa Barbara, CA held by California Lutheran University
Nat'l Network: NPR
Arbitron Metro Market: Thousand Oaks, CA *Format:* News, News/Talk, 86
Jim Rondeau, Director of Operations and Programming
Mary Olson, General Manager
Lance Orozco, News Director
Mia Karnatz, Director of Member Services

KZSB
03-01-1961; 1290 khz AM *Hrs Open:* 24; 0.5 kw-D, ND1; 0.122 kw-N, ND1; N34 25 7 W119 41 10
1875 Century Pk E.#2250, Los Angeles, CA 90067 US
(805) 564-2000, *Fax:* (805) 966-6258
www.newspress.com
dkatich@newspress.com
License: Santa Barbara, CA held by Santa Barbara Broadcasting Inc.
Nat'l Network: Westwood One
Arbitron Metro Market: Santa Barbara, CA *Format:* News, News/Talk, 86 *Target Audience:* 35-64.
Dennis Weibling, President
Richard Dugan, Operations Dir
Les Carroll, General Manager
Don Katich, News Director
Patrice Cardenas, Public Affairs Director

***KSBX**
04-01-2003; 89.5 mhz FM *Hrs Open:* 24; 0.05 kw; 899 ft.; N34 27 57 W119 40 37 *Rebroadcasts:* Rebroadcassts KCBX(FM) San Luis Obispo 99%
4100 Vachell Lane, San Luis Obispo, CA 93401 US
(805) 549-8855
www.kcbx.org
901kcbx@kcbx.org
License: Santa Barbara, Santa Barbara County, CA held by KCBX Inc.
Nat'l Network: NPR *Regional Reps:* Margaret Merisante
Arbitron Metro Market: Santa Barbara, CA *Format:* Jazz *Hrs. of News Programming:* News progmg 30 hrs wkly
Hank Hadley, Operations Dir
Frank Lanzone, General Manager
Paul Severtson, General Sales Mgr
Marisa Waddell, Director of Programming & New Media
Katherine Johnson, Business Manager
Hank Hadley, Operations Manager
KatherineJohnson, Assistant General Manager
Neal Losey, Music Director
Rodger Mastako, Senior Account Executive
Greg Perry, KCBXnet Manager

Santa Clara

KVVF
09-25-1964; 105.7 mhz FM *Hrs Open:* 24; 50 kw; 499 ft.; N37 21 32 W121 45 22
P. O. Box 995, San Jose, CA 95108 US
(415) 989-5765, *Fax:* (415) 733-5766
www.latinomixsf.univision.com
jrojo@univisionradio.com
License: Santa Clara, Santa Clara County, CA held by Univision Radio License Corp.
Group Owner: Univision Radio; (acq 9-22-2003; grpsl).
Arbitron Metro Market: San Francisco, CA *Format:* Spanish
Tony Perlongo, General Manager
Jose Rojo, General Sales Mgr
Jose Luis Gonzalez, Programming Director

***KSCU**
07-01-1978; 103.3 mhz FM *Hrs Open:* 24; 0.03 kw; -7 ft.; N37 20 50 W121 56 21
500 El Camino Real, Santa Clara, CA 95053 US
(408) 554-4413, *Fax:* (408) 554-5738
www.kscu.org
music@kscu.org
License: Santa Clara, Santa Clara County, CA held by President and Board of Trustees of Santa Clara University.
Arbitron Metro Market: San Francisco *Format:* Alternative *Special Programming:* Hip-hop 15 hrs, Blues 3 hrs, loud rock 6 hrs, world one hr wkly *Hrs. of News Programming:* News progmg one hr wkly *Target Audience:* 14-34; Young adult who like modern music
Sam Duarte, General Manager
Tyler Kogura, Programming Director
Gordon Young, News Director
Bill Orr, Engineering Dir

KVVN
12-18-1964; 1430 khz AM *Hrs Open:* 24
55 Hawthorne Street, San Francisco, CA 94015 US
(408) 998-0612, *Fax:* (408) 998-0583
kvvn@inlanguageradio.com
License: Santa Clara, CA held by Urban Radio III L.L.C.
Group Owner: Inner City Broadcasting; (acq 3-24-97; $2.2 million).
Regional Reps: In-Language Radio, SF
Arbitron Metro Market: Santa Clara, CA *Format:* Vietnamese *Hrs. of News Programming:* news progmg 14 hrs wkly *No. News Employees:* 1 *Target Audience:* 23-34; Hispanic
Phung Dang, Operations Dir
Harvey Stone, General Manager
Andrew Luu, Station Manager
Paul Marks, Chief Engineer

RADIO • U.S.

Santa Cruz

***KFER**
01-01-1992; 89.9 mhz FM *Hrs Open:* 24; 0.2 kw; 26 ft.; N37 0 45 W121 58 25
PO Box 13, Santa Cruz, CA 95063 US
(831) 475-6651, *Fax:* (831) 464-8427
www.radioliberty.com
License: Santa Cruz, Santa Cruz County, CA held by Santa Cruz Educational Broadcasting Foundation.
Nat'l Network: Moody *Regional Reps:* Moody
Arbitron Metro Market: Monterey-Salinas-Santa Cruz, CA *Format:* Variety/Diverse *Hrs. of News Programming:* News progmg 15 hrs wkly *Target Audience:* General.
Mildred Holmes, President
Dr. Stan Monteith, General Manager

***KSRI**
02-28-2001; 90.7 mhz FM *Hrs Open:* 24; 0.32 kw; 364 ft.; N37 0 10 W122 3 5 *Rebroadcasts:* Rebroadcasts KHRI(FM) Hollister 100%
500 Redwood Heights Road, Santa Cruz, CA 95003 US
(916) 251-1600, *Fax:* (916) 251-1650
www.air1.com
info@air1.com
License: Santa Cruz, Santa Cruz County, CA held by Educational Media Foundation.
Group Owner: EMF Broadcasting; (acq 8-17-00; $295,000).
Nat'l Network: Air 1
Format: Alternative, Christian *No. News Employees:* 3 *Target Audience:* 18-35; Judeo-Christian, female
Mike Novak, President
David Pierce, Programming Director
Ed Lenane, News Director
Sam Wallington, Engineering Dir
Marya Morgan, News Reporter
Richard Hunt, Marya Morgan
Tracy Butler, Traffic Manager

KSCO
09-21-1947; 1080 khz AM *Hrs Open:* 24; 10 kw-D, DAN; 5 kw-N, DAN; N36 57 43 W121 58 51
2300 Portola Dr., Santa Cruz, CA 95062 US
(831) 475-1080, *Fax:* (831) 475-2967
www.ksco.com
License: Santa Cruz, CA held by Zwerling Broadcasting System Ltd.
Arbitron Metro Market: Monterey-Salinas-Santa Cruz, CA *Format:* News, News/Talk, 86 *Hrs. of News Programming:* news progmg 35 hrs wkly *No. News Employees:* 8 *Target Audience:* 25 plus; well educatedprofessionals, managers *Adv. Rates:* 50; 50; 50; 35
Michael Zwerling, CEO
Michael Olson, General Manager
Michael Olson, General Sales Mgr
Rosemary Chalmers, Programming Director

***KUSP**
04-14-1972; 88.9 mhz FM; 1.25 kw; 2497 ft.; N36 32 5 W121 37 14
P. O. Box 423, Santa Cruz, CA 95061 US
(831) 476-2800, *Fax:* (831) 476-2802
www.kusp.org
kusp@kusp.org
License: Santa Cruz, Santa Cruz County, CA held by Pataphysical Broadcasting Foundation Inc.
Nat'l Network: NPR

Arbitron Metro Market: Santa Cruz, CA *Format:* Variety/Diverse *Hrs. of News Programming:* News progmg 44 hrs wkly
Duncan Lively, Operations Dir
Terry Green, General Manager
Johnny Simmons, Programming Director
J.D. Hillard, Director of News, Talk and Information Programs
J. D. Hillard, Producer
Steve Laufer, Director of New Media &kusp.org
Jen Switzer, Director of Individual Giving
Meera Collier-Mitchell, Underwriting Account Executive
Sally Heine, Bookkeeping and Member Services
Geo Warner, Volunteer Coordinator for Music Programming

KSQL
09-02-1961; 99.1 mhz FM *Hrs Open:* 24; 1.1 kw; 2612 ft.; N37 6 39 W121 50 37 *Rebroadcasts:* Simulcasts KSOL-FM San Francisco 100%
3102 Oak Lawn Ave., Suite 215, Dallas, TX 75219 US
(415) 733-5765, *Fax:* (415) 733-5766
www.univision.com
License: Santa Cruz, Santa Cruz County, CA held by TMS License California Inc.
Group Owner: Univision Radio; (acq 9-22-2003; grpsl).
Arbitron Metro Market: Santa Cruz, CA *Format:* Spanish *Hrs. of News Programming:* news progmg 4 hrs wkly *No. News Employees:* 1 *Target Audience:* 25-54.
Tony Perlongo, General Manager

***KZSC**
08-01-1974; 88.1 mhz FM *Hrs Open:* 24; 20 kw; 436 ft.; N37 0 10 W122 3 4
1111 Franklin Street, Oakland, CA 94607 US
(831) 459-5173, *Fax:* (831) 459-4734
www.kzsc.org
stationmanager@kzsc.org
License: Santa Cruz, Santa Cruz County, CA held by Regents of University of California.
Arbitron Metro Market: Santa Cruz, CA *Format:* Variety/Diverse *Hrs. of News Programming:* News progmg 40 hrs wkly *Target Audience:* 18-plus; college students up till late 30's *Adv. Rates:* 5; 15; 15; 15
Michael Bryant, General Manager
Valerie Ross, Station Manager
Lois Rosson, Programming Director

Santa Margarita

KWWV
07-21-1986; 106.1 mhz FM *Hrs Open:* 24; 1.1 kw; 1447 ft.; N35 21 40 W120 39 21
300 E Lombard Street, Suite 620, Baltimore, MD 21202 US
(805) 786-2570, *Fax:* (805) 547-9860
www.wild1061.com
License: Santa Margarita, San Luis Obispo County, CA held by Mapleton License of San Luis Obispo LLC.
Group Owner: Mapleton Communications LLC; (acq 1-1-2007)
Arbitron Metro Market: San Luis Obispo, CA *Format:* Contemporary Hits/Top 40 *Hrs. of News Programming:* news progmg 6 hrs wkly *No. News Employees:* 2 *Target Audience:* 18-34; upscale homeowners
Bill Heirendt, General Manager

Santa Maria

KSBQ
09-01-1961; 1480 khz AM *Hrs Open:* 24; 1 kw-D, ND1; 0.061 kw-N, ND1; N34 57 2 W120 29 22
296 H Street, Suite 300, Chula Vista, CA 91910 US
(805) 240-2070(805) 928-9796, *Fax:* (805) 240-5960(805) 928-3367
www.radiolazer.com/estrella/index.html
License: Santa Maria, CA held by Lazer Broadcasting Corp.
Group Owner: Lazer Broadcasting Corp.; acq 12-29-99; $225,000)
Nat'l Reps: Lotus Entravision Reps LLC
Arbitron Metro Market: Santa Maria-Lompoc, CA *Format:* Christian *Target Audience:* 18-49; adults *Adv. Rates:* 10; na; na; 5
Alfredo Plascencia, CEO
Salvador Prieto, Operations Dir
Jose Guzman, General Sales Mgr

KSMX
01-01-1946; 1240 khz AM; 1 kw-U, ND1; N34 57 2 W120 29 27
2215 Skyway Drive, Santa Maria, CA 93455 US
(805) 925-2582, *Fax:* (805) 361-1366
www.1240ksmx.com
License: Santa Maria, CA held by EDB SLO License LLC.
Group Owner: Frontier Radio Management Inc.; (acq 11-30-2007; grpsl)
Nat'l Network: Premiere Radio Networks; Westwood One; Talk Radio Network
Arbitron Metro Market: Santa Maria-Lompoc, CA *Format:* News, News/Talk, 86
Dave Daniels, Operations Dir
Ron Roy, General Manager
Kathy Mansell, General Sales Mgr
Jennifer Grant, Programming Director

KSNI-FM
01-01-1960; 102.5 mhz FM; 13.5 kw; 860 ft.; N34 50 8 W120 24 6
US
(805) 925-2582, *Fax:* (805) 928-1544
www.sunnycountry.com
License: Santa Maria, Santa Barbara County, CA held by EDB SLO License LLC.
Group Owner: Frontier Radio Management Inc.
Arbitron Metro Market: Santa Maria-Lompoc, CA *Format:* Country
Kathey Mansell, General Sales Mgr
Jay Turner, Programming Director
Mitch Kelly, News Director
Tree Lee, Engineering Dir

KTAP
06-10-1962; 1600 khz AM *Hrs Open:* 6 AM-midnight; 0.47 kw-D, ND2; 0.026 kw-N, ND2; N34 58 48 W120 27 12
104 West Chapel Ave., Santa Maria, CA 93454 US
(805) 928-4334, *Fax:* (805) 349-2765
License: Santa Maria, CA held by Emerald Wave Media.
Group Owner: Emerald Wave Media; (acq 3-6-97; $475,000 with KRTO(FM) Guadalupe)
Arbitron Metro Market: Santa Maria-Lompoc, CA *Format:* Spanish *Hrs. of News Programming:* news progmg 4 hrs wkly *No. News Employees:* 1 *Target Audience:* General; first generation Mexicans
August Ruiz, General Manager

KUHL
04-01-1946; 1440 khz AM; 5 kw-D, DAN; 1 kw-N, DAN; N34 59 2 W120 27 10
211 East Fesler, Santa Maria, CA 93456 US
(805) 922-7727, *Fax:* (805) 349-0265
www.am1440.com
Shawn@knightbroadcasting.com
License: Santa Maria, CA held by Knight Broadcasting Inc.
Group Owner: Knight Broadcasting Inc.; (acq 7-31-2006; $1.2 million with KSMA(AM) Lompoc).
Arbitron Metro Market: Santa Maria, CA *Format:* News, News/Talk, 86 *Target Audience:* 35-64; upscale news & sports listeners
Jeff Williams, Operations Dir
Shawn Knight, General Manager

KXFM
01-01-1959; 99.1 mhz FM; 2.3 kw; 1906 ft.; N34 54 37 W120 11 8
966 East Essex Drive, Fresno, CA 93720 US
(805) 925-2582, *Fax:* (805) 928-1544
www.991thefox.com
davedaniels@edbroadcasters.com
License: Santa Maria, Santa Barbara County, CA held by EDB SLO License LLC.
Group Owner: Frontier Radio Management Inc.; (acq 11-30-2007; grpsl)
Arbitron Metro Market: Santa Maria-Lompoc, CA *Format:* Classic Rock *Target Audience:* 18-49; contemp, active adults
Jennifer Grant, Operations Dir
Rich Hawkins, General Manager
Pattie Wagner, General Sales Mgr
Milos Nemicik, Chief Engineer

***KHFR**
06-21-2005; 89.7 mhz FM *Hrs Open:* 24; 2.45 kw vert; 1867 ft.; N34 54 37 W120 11 8
Mailing Address: 4135 Northgate Blvd, Suite 1, Sacramento, CA 95834 US
Second Address: 290 Hegenberger Rd., Oakland, CA 94621
(800) 543-1495, *Fax:* (916) 641-8238
www.familyradio.com
info@familyradio.com
License: Santa Maria, Santa Barbara County, CA held by Family Stations Inc.
Group Owner: Family Stations Inc.
Arbitron Metro Market: Santa Maria, CA *Format:* Christian, Religious
Harol Camping, President
David Manzi, Operations Dir
Peggy Renschler, Assistant Secretary

***KGDP-FM**
01-01-2003; 90.5 mhz FM; 17.5 kw; 827 ft.; N34 44 30 W120 26 45
1416 Hollister Lane, Los Osos, CA 93402 US
(800) 776-1070, *Fax:* (805) 922-8582
www.myflr.org
feedback@flc.org?subject=The%20Intentional%20Living%20Program%20website%20contact
License: Santa Maria, Santa Barbara County, CA held by People of Action.
Arbitron Metro Market: Santa Maria, CA *Format:* Christian, Talk
Warren J. Bolthouse, Chairman
Dr. Randy L. Carlson, President
Steve Cox, General Manager
Adam Biddell, Programming Director
Alonzo Williams, Vice President of Operations
Rod Robison, Vice President of Development
Doug Goodall,Controller
Evan Carlson, Executive Director of Marketing and Community Tran

Santa Monica

KDLD
01-01-1963; 103.1 mhz FM *Hrs Open:* 24; 3.7 kw; 269 ft.; N34 0 53 W118 22 50 *Rebroadcasts:* Simulcast with KDLE(FM) Newport Beach 100%
50 East Rivercenter Blvd, Suite 1200, Covington, KY 41011 US
(323) 900-6100, *Fax:* (323) 900-6127
www.elgato1031.com
License: Santa Monica, Los Angeles County, CA held by Entravision Holdings LLC.
Group Owner: Entravision Communications Corp.; (acq 2000)
Arbitron Metro Market: Los Angeles *Target Audience:* 25-54; upscale adults in Los Angeles' westside *Adv. Rates:* 150; 100; 125; 100
Karl Meyer, General Manager

KBLA
01-01-1947; 1580 khz AM; 50 kw-D, DA2; 50 kw-N, DA2; N34 5 8 W118 15 24
8400 N.W. 52nd Street, Suite 101, Miami, FL 33166 US
(626) 844-8882, *Fax:* (626) 844-0156
www.mrbi.net
info@mrbi.net
License: Santa Monica, CA held by Multicultural Radio Broadcasting Licensee LLC.
Group Owner: Multicultural Radio Broadcasting Inc.; (acq 2-4-2004; grpsl).
Arbitron Metro Market: Los Angeles, CA *Format:* Christian, Spanish *No. News Employees:* 1
David Sweeney, General Manager
Jose Calles, Station Manager

***KCRW**
01-01-1946; 89.9 mhz FM *Hrs Open:* 24; 6.9 kw; 1109 ft.; N34 7 8 W118 23 30
1900 Pico Blvd., Santa Monica, CA 90405 US
(310) 450-5183, *Fax:* (310) 450-7172
www.kcrw.org
mail@kcrw.org
License: Santa Monica, Los Angeles County, CA held by Santa Monica College District.
Nat'l Network: NPR; PRI *Wire Services:* AP
Arbitron Metro Market: Santa Monica, CA *Format:* News *Hrs. of News Programming:* news progmg 14 hrs wkly *No. News Employees:* 3 *Target Audience:* General; 18-55 year old consumers
Mike Newport, Operations Dir
Ruth Seymour, General Manager
David Kleinbart, General Sales Mgr
Nic Harcourt, Programming Director
Steve Herbert, Chief Engineer
Jennifer Ferro, Assistant General Manager

Santa Paula

KLJR-FM
10-04-1976; 96.7 mhz FM *Hrs Open:* 24; 0.28 kw; 1499 ft.; N34 19 33 W119 2 18
200 South ""A"" St., 4th Floor, Oxnard, CA 93030 US
(805) 240-2070, *Fax:* (805) 240-5960
License: Santa Paula, Ventura County, CA held by Lazer Broadcasting Corp.
Group Owner: Lazer Broadcasting Corp.; (acq 3-31-98; $925,000;
Nat'l Reps: Lotus Entravision Reps LLC
Arbitron Metro Market: Oxnard-Ventura, CA *Format:* Adult Contemp *Target Audience:* 25-54; general
Alfredo Plascencia, CEO
Terry Janisch, General Sales Mgr
Salvador Prieto, Programming Director

KKZZ
01-01-1948; 1400 khz AM; 1 kw-U, ND1; N34 19 48 W119 5 31

100 Wilshire Blvd, Suite 1000, Santa Monica, CA 90401 US
(805) 289-1400, *Fax:* (805) 644-7906
info@1590kkzz.com
License: Santa Paula, CA held by Gold Coast Broadcasting LLC
Group Owner: Gold Coast Broadcasting LLC; (acq 8-18-99; grpsl)
Arbitron Metro Market: Oxnard, CA *Format:* News, News/Talk, 86
Target Audience: 25-54.
Chip Ehrhardt, General Manager
Mark Elliott, Programming Director

Santa Rosa

KRRS
04-01-1962; 1460 khz AM *Hrs Open:* 24; 1 kw-D, 33 w-N, DA-2; N38 22 13 W122 43 39
1410 Neotomas Ave. #104, Santa Rosa, CA 90006
(707) 545-1460, *Fax:* (707) 545-0112
krrs@sonic.net
License: Santa Rosa, Sonoma County, CA held by Claifornia Broadcasting Corp LLC
Group Owner: Moon Broadcasting; (acq 1993; $400,000;
Nat'l Reps: Interep
Population Served: 500,000 *Arbitron Metro Market:* Santa Rosa
Target Audience: 25-54; contemporary Hispanic families *Adv. Rates:* 45; 35; 45; 35
Abel DeLuna, CEO
Miriam Gomez, General Manager
Arelia DeLuna, CFO

KSRO
05-01-1937; 1350 khz AM; 5 kw-D, DAN; 5 kw-N, DAN; N38 26 22 W122 44 51
Mailing Address: 1410 Neotomas Avenue, Suite 200, Santa Rosa, CA 95405 US
Second Address: 1410 Neotomas Ave., Suite 200, Santa Rosa, CA 95405
(707) 543-0100, *Fax:* (707) 571-1097
www.ksro.com
License: Santa Rosa, CA held by Maverick Media of Santa Rosa License LLC.
Group Owner: Maverick Media LLC; (acq 12-16-02; grpsl).
Arbitron Metro Market: Santa Rosa, CA *Format:* News, News/Talk, 86 *Target Audience:* 35-64.
Gary Rozynek, President
Kent Bjugstad, General Manager
Kent Bjusgastad, General Sales Mgr
Kent Bjugstad, Programming Director
Michelle Marques, Promotions Manager
Renee Bakos, News Director
Mick Rush, Chief Engineer

KZST
04-18-1971; 100.1 mhz FM *Hrs Open:* 24; 6 kw; 246 ft.; N38 25 7 W122 40 33
Mailing Address: P.O Box 100, Santa Rosa, CA 95402 US
Second Address: 3392 Mendocino Ave., Santa Rosa, CA 95403
(707) 528-4434, *Fax:* (707) 527-8216
www.kzst.com
toms@kzst.com
License: Santa Rosa, Sonoma County, CA held by Redwood Empire Stereocasters.
Group Owner: Redwood Empire Stereocasters
Nat'l Reps: McGavren Guild *Wire Services:* AP; Bay City News Service
Arbitron Metro Market: Santa Rosa, CA *Format:* Adult Contemp
No. News Employees: 2 *Target Audience:* 25-54.
Tom Skinner, General Manager

Santa Ynez

KRAZ
01-01-2001; 105.9 mhz FM *Hrs Open:* 24; 0.065 kw; 2933 ft.; N34 31 32 W119 57 29
4350 N Fairfax Dr, Suite 900, Arlington, VA 22203 US
(805) 688-8386, *Fax:* (805) 688-2271
www.krazfm.com
kathy@knightbroadcasting.com
License: Santa Ynez, Santa Barbara County, CA held by Knight Broadcasting Inc.
Group Owner: Knight Broadcasting Inc.; (acq 5-21-2001; $325,000 for CP).
Nat'l Network: ABC
Arbitron Metro Market: Santa Barbara, CA *Format:* Country
Shawn Knight, General Manager

Seaside

KBOQ
10-01-1996; 103.9 mhz FM *Hrs Open:* 24; 1.4 kw; Ant 604 ft; N36 30 17 W121 54 21
60 Garden Court, Suite 300, Monterey, CA 93940
(831) 658-5200, *Fax:* (831) 658-5299
www.kbach.com
kallen@radiomontereybay.com
License: Seaside, Monterey County, CA held by Mapleton License of Monterey LLC.
Group Owner: Mapleton Communications LLC; (acq 1-24-2002; $1.85 million)
Nat'l Reps: McGavren Guild
Population Served: 500,000 *Arbitron Metro Market:* Monterey-Salinas-Santa Cruz, CA
Jim Shea Jr, CEO/COO
Kenny Allen, Operations Dir
Jodi Morgan, General Manager
Jodi Morgan, General Sales Mgr
Kenny Allen, Programming Director
Alyson Hess, Promotions Manager
Tom Hughes, Chief Engineer

KSES-FM
11-22-1972; 107.1 mhz FM; 1.85 kw; 587 ft.; N36 33 9 W121 47 17
2905 South King Road, San Jose, CA 95122 US
(831) 333-9735, *Fax:* (831) 333-9750
www.1071se.com
ascoby@entravision.com
License: Seaside, Monterey County, CA held by Entravision Holdings LLC.
Group Owner: Entravision Communications Corp.; (acq 3-14-00; grpsl).
Arbitron Metro Market: Monterey-Salinas-Santa Cruz, CA
Format: Spanish *Target Audience:* 18-49.
Aaron Scoby, CEO
Tony Valencia, Promotions Manager
Fidel M. Soto, News Director
Abraham Trejo, Chief Engineer
Chip Thomas, National Sales Manager
Karla Maciel, Internet Sales Manager
Joanne Dempsey, Office Manager
Zaida Rosado,Traffic Manager
Silka Saavendra, Production Manager
Ernesto Altamirano, Director of Research

Sebastopol

KJZY
11-05-1995; 93.7 mhz FM *Hrs Open:* 24; 6 kw; 217 ft.; N38 25 7 W122 40 33
P.O. Box 100, Santa Rosa, CA 95402 US
(707) 528-9393, *Fax:* (707) 527-8216
www.kjzy.com
info@kjzy.com
License: Sebastopol, Sonoma County, CA held by Redwood Empire Sterocasters.
Group Owner: Redwood Empire Stereocasters
Nat'l Reps: McGavren Guild *Wire Services:* AP
Format: Jazz
Gordon Zlot, President
Tom Skinner, General Manager
Patrick Stelzner, General Sales Mgr
Brent Farrs, Programming Director
Steve Zabrskie, News Director
Eric Peter, Chief Engineer
Darlene Evart, Traffc Director

Selma

*KQKL
08-06-2003; 88.5 mhz FM *Hrs Open:* 24; 50 kw; 492 ft.; N36 26 50 W119 37 10
1425 N Market Blvd, Suite 9, Sacramento, CA 95834 US
(800) 525-5683, *Fax:* (916) 251-1650
www.klove.com
klove@klove.com
License: Selma, Fresno County, CA held by Educational Media Foundation.
Group Owner: EMF Broadcasting
Nat'l Network: K-Love
Arbitron Metro Market: Selma, CA *Format:* Christian *No. News Employees:* 3 *Target Audience:* 25-44; Judeo Christian, female
Darrell Chambliss, Chairman
Mike Novak, President and CEO
David Pierce, Programming Director
Ed Lenane, News Director
Sam Wallington, Engineering Dir
Marya Morgan, News Reporter
Richard Hunt, News Reporter
Laura Daniels, NewsReporter
Tim Luttrell, News Reporter
Kenny Noble Cortes, News Reporter
Darren Vinson, News Reporter

Shafter

KKXX-FM
01-01-1994; 93.1 mhz FM *Hrs Open:* 24; 4 kw; 404 ft.; N35 28 21 W119 1 40
1400 Easton Road, Bakersfield, CA 93309 US
(661) 328-1410, *Fax:* (661) 328-0873
www.hits931fm.com
rachel@hothits931.com
License: Shafter, Kern County, CA held by AGM California.
Group Owner: American General Media; (acq 7-25-97; $1.5 million with KBID(AM) Bakersfield).
Arbitron Metro Market: Bakersfield, CA *Format:* Adult Contemp
Hrs. of News Programming: news progmg 2 hrs wkly *No. News Employees:* 4 *Target Audience:* 18-49; men
Roger Fessler, General Manager
Toni Snyder, General Sales Mgr
Chris Edwards, Programming Director

*KGZO
06-06-1996; 90.9 mhz FM *Hrs Open:* 24; 1.9 kw; 2070 ft.; N35 16 51 W119 44 52 *Rebroadcasts:* Rebroadcasts KMRO(FM) Camarillo 100%
2310 Ponderosa Drive, Suite 28, Camarillo, CA 93010 US
(805) 482-4797, *Fax:* (805) 388-5202
www.nuevavida.com
info@nuevavida.com
License: Shafter, Kern County, CA held by The Association for Community Education Inc.
Arbitron Metro Market: Bakersfield, CA *Format:* Religious *Target Audience:* General.
Phil Guthrie, President
Mary Guthrie, General Manager

KSMJ
03-03-1978; 97.7 mhz FM *Hrs Open:* 24; 4.1 kw; 397 ft.; N35 27 33 W119 1 13
Suite 102, 3701 Pegasus Dr., Bakersfield, CA 93308 US
(661) 393-1900, *Fax:* (661) 393-1915
www.knzr.com
License: Shafter, Kern County, CA held by Buckley Broadcasting of California LLC.
Group Owner: Buckley Broadcasting Corp.; (acq 2-1-2001; $2 million).
Arbitron Metro Market: Bakersfield, CA *Format:* News, News/Talk, 86 *Target Audience:* 18-49.
E.J. Tyler, Operations Dir
Steve Darnell, General Manager
Otis Warren, General Sales Mgr
Steve Darnell, Programming Director
Kathy King, News Director

*KAIB
01-01-2006; 89.5 mhz FM; 50 kw; 358 ft.; N35 36 53 W119 28 16
Rebroadcasts: Rebroadcasts KLRD(FM) Yucaipa 100%
US
(888) 937-2471, *Fax:* (916) 251-1650
www.air1.com
info@air1.com
License: Shafter, Kern County, CA held by Educational Media Foundation.
Group Owner: EMF Broadcasting; (acq 1-14-2005).
Nat'l Network: Air 1
Arbitron Metro Market: Shafter, CA *Format:* Alternative, Christian
Darrell Chambliss, Chairman
Alan Mason, COO
Mike Novak, President and CEO
David Pierce, Programming Director
Ed Lenane, News Director
Sam Wallington, Engineering Dir
Tracy Butler, Traffic Manager
Eric Moser, Chief FinancialOfficer
Brian Burger, Vice President of Human Resources
D. Kevin Blair, Secretary and General Counsel
Larry Moody, Director
Mitch Barnhart, Director

Shasta

KCNR
08-13-1967; 1460 khz AM
4531 Shannon Place, Redding, CA 96001 US
(530) 244-5082, *Fax:* (530) 244-5698
License: Shasta, CA held by M C Allen Productions
Arbitron Metro Market: Redding, CA *Format:* Sports, Talk *Target Audience:* 24-55.
Mike Quinn, General Manager

Shasta Lake City

KESR
01-01-1998; 107.1 mhz FM *Hrs Open:* 24; 1.4 kw; 1362 ft.; N40 39 6 W122 31 32
1588 Charles Drive, Redding, CA 96003 US
(530) 244-9700, *Fax:* (530) 244-9707
rhealy@resultsradiomail.com
License: Shasta Lake City, Shasta County, CA held by Results Radio of Redding Licensee LLC.
Group Owner: Fritz Communications Inc.; (acq 5-28-2000; grpsl).
Arbitron Metro Market: Redding, CA *Format:* Adult Contemp
Jack Fritz, President
Rick Healy, Operations Dir
Beth Tappan, General Manager
Laurie Curto, General Sales Mgr
Rob Reid, Programming Director
Bryant Smith, Chief Engineer

KNNN(FM)
10-26-1989; 99.3 mhz FM; 1.6 kw; Ant 1,525 ft; N40 39 15 W122 31 12
3360 Alta Mesa Dr., Redding, CA 96002
(530) 226-9500, *Fax:* (530) 221-4940
www.reddingradio.com
License: Shasta Lake City, Shasta County, CA held by Mapleton License of Redding LLC.
Group Owner: Mapleton Communications LLC; (acq 11-30-2006; grpsl)
Arbitron Metro Market: Redding, CA *Format:* Country *Special Programming:* Jazz 3 hrs wkly *Target Audience:* 25-54.
Vince Shadrick, General Manager
Ryan James, Programming Director

KJPR
01-01-2005; 1330 khz AM *Hrs Open:* 24 hrs
US
(541) 552-6301, *Fax:* (541) 552-8565
www.ijpr.org
jprinfo@sou.edu
License: Shasta Lake City, CA held by JPR Foundation Inc.
Arbitron Metro Market: Redding, CA *Format:* News
Bryon Lambert, Operations Dir
Ronald Kramer, General Manager
Paul Westhelle, General Sales Mgr
Darin Ransom, Engineering Dir
Betsy Byers, Administrative Assistant
Mitchell Christian, Director of Finance & Administration
JillHernandez, Accountant Technician
Valerie Ing-Miller, Northern CA Program Coordinator
Abby Kraft, Development Associate / Editor Jefferson Monthly
John Matthews, Classical Music Director

Shingle Springs

KNTY
05-01-1989; 101.9 mhz FM *Hrs Open:* 24; 47 kw; 505 ft.; N38 51 12 W120 56 23
2905 South King Road, San Jose, CA 95122 US
(916) 646-4000, *Fax:* (916) 646-6020
www.1019thewolf.com
License: Shingle Springs, El Dorado County, CA held by Entravision Holdings LLC.
Group Owner: Entravision Communications Corp.; (acq 3-14-2000; grpsl).
Arbitron Metro Market: Sacramento, CA *Format:* Country *Target Audience:* 25-54.
Allyson Maiman, General Manager
Bob McNeill, Programming Director
Alex Guerra, Promotions Manager

Shingletown

KKXS
01-01-2001; 96.1 mhz FM; 1.9 kw; 1175 ft.; N40 29 18 W121 53 58
555 East Lindo Avenue, Chico, CA 95927 US
(530) 244-9700, *Fax:* (530) 244-9707
www.xs961.com
License: Shingletown, Shasta County, CA held by Results Radio of Redding Licensee LLC.
Group Owner: Fritz Communications Inc.; (acq 3-29-99; $125,000 for 50%).
Arbitron Metro Market: Redding, CA *Format:* Jazz, Smooth Jazz
Rick Healy, Operations Dir
Beth Tappan, General Manager
Laurie Curto, General Sales Mgr
Bryant Smith, Chief Engineer

KRDG
08-01-1995; 105.3 mhz FM *Hrs Open:* 24; 28 kw; 1243 ft.; N40 29 19 W121 54 23
Mr. Mel Dolezal, Gm, 4352 Catepillar Road, Redding, CA 95928 US
(530) 226-9500, *Fax:* (530) 221-4940
www.oldies1053.com
License: Shingletown, Shasta County, CA held by Mapleton License of Redding LLC.
Group Owner: Mapleton Communications LLC; (acq 11-30-2006; grpsl)
Arbitron Metro Market: Northern CA *Format:* Oldies *Target Audience:* 25-54; active adults with families
Vince Shadrick, General Manager
Randie Meyer, General Sales Mgr
Steve Mena, Programming Director

Simi Valley

KIRN
09-21-1984; 670 khz AM *Hrs Open:* 24; 5 kw-D, DA1; 3 kw-N, DA1; N34 19 10 W118 42 56
6290 Sunset Boulevard, Suite #1600, Los Angeles, CA 90028 US
(323) 851-5476, *Fax:* (323) 512-7452
www.670amkirn.com
jimk@670amkirn.com
License: Simi Valley, CA held by Lotus Oxnard Corp.
Group Owner: Lotus Communications Corp.; (acq 12-11-96; $4.2 million)
Arbitron Metro Market: Simi Valley, CA *Format:* Adult Contemp, Farsi, 60, News/Talk, Sports, Talk *Hrs. of News Programming:* news progmg 14 hrs wkly *No. News Employees:* 3 *Target Audience:* Persian, Iranian,Farsi Speaking Middle Eastern *Adv. Rates:* $225 for 60""; $180 for 30""
Howard Kalmenson, President
John Paley, Operations Dir
Jim Kalmenson, General Manager
Poopak Mozaffari, Director of Administration & Sales
Afshin Gorgin, Programming Director
Poopak Mozaffari, Promotions Manager
Jason Houts,Chief Engineer

Soledad

*KFRS
04-04-2002; 89.9 mhz FM; 0.25 kw vert; 305 ft.; N36 16 25 W121 16 12
Mailing Address: 4135 Northgate Blvd., Suite 1, Sacramento, CA 95834 US
Second Address: 290 Hegenberger Rd., Oakland, CA 94621
(916) 641-8191, *Fax:* (916) 641-8238
www.familyradio.com
info@familyradio.com
License: Soledad, Monterey County, CA held by Family Stations Inc.
Group Owner: Family Stations Inc.
Arbitron Metro Market: Soledad, CA *Format:* Christian, Religious *Target Audience:* Christian Adults
Matt Pearce, Operations Dir

KMJV
10-01-1991; 106.3 mhz FM *Hrs Open:* 24; 4.7 kw; 371 ft.; N36 16 27 W121 16 15
600 New Hampshire Ave., N.W., Suite 1200, Washington, DC 20037 US
(831) 766-1200, *Fax:* (831) 757-8015
wolfhouseradio@yahoo.es
License: Soledad, Monterey County, CA held by Wolfhouse Radio Group Inc.
Group Owner: Wolfhouse Radio Group Inc.; (acq 7-13-2001; grpsl).
Arbitron Metro Market: Monterey, CA *Format:* Tejano *Target Audience:* 18-44.
Roman Castro, General Manager

KMBX
01-01-1992; 700 khz AM; 2.5 kw-D, ND1; 0.7 kw-N, ND1; N36 27 51 W121 17 52
2905 South King Road, San Jose, CA 95122 US
(831) 333-9735, *Fax:* (831) 333-9750
www.jose1071.com
ascoby@entravision.com
License: Soledad, CA held by Entravision Holdings LLC.
Group Owner: Entravision Communications Corp.; (acq 3-14-00; grpsl).
Arbitron Metro Market: Monterey-Salinas-Santa Cruz, CA *Format:* Spanish *Target Audience:* 18-49.
Aaron Scoby, CEO
Jeff Liberman, Operations Dir
Tony Valencia, Promotions Manager
Fidel M. Soto, News Director
Abraham Trejo, Chief Engineer
Chip Thomas, National Sales Manager
Karla Maciel, Internet Sales Manager
JoanneDempsey, Office Manager
Zaida Rosado, Traffic Manager
Silka Saavendra, Production Manager
Ernesto Altamirano, Director of Research

Solvang

KSYV
09-22-1982; 96.7 mhz FM *Hrs Open:* 24; 0.42 kw; 1217 ft.; N34 41 28 W120 15 58
1693 Mission Drive, Solvang, CA 93463 US
(805) 688-5798, *Fax:* (805) 688-2271
www.mix96.com
kathy@knightbroadcasting.com
License: Solvang, Santa Barbara County, CA held by Knight Broadcasting Inc.
Group Owner: Knight Broadcasting Inc.; (acq 2-8-2002).
Nat'l Network: AP Network News
Arbitron Metro Market: Santa Maria-Lompoc, CA *Format:* Adult Contemp *Hrs. of News Programming:* News progmg 126 hrs wkly *Target Audience:* 24-54; female 60%, male 40%
Jeff Williams, Operations Dir
Shawn Knight, General Manager

Sonoma

*KSVY
01-01-2005; 91.3 mhz FM; 0 kw horiz, 2.5 kw vert; -305 ft.; N38 16 47 W122 26 47
470 Third Street West, Sonoma, CA 95476 US
(707) 933-0808, *Fax:* (707) 933-1573
www.ksvy.org
mail@sonomasunfm.com
License: Sonoma, Sonoma County, CA held by Commonbond Foundation.
Arbitron Metro Market: Sonoma, CA *Format:* Talk
Bill Hammett, President
Bob Taylor, General Manager

Sonora

KVML
01-01-1949; 1450 khz AM *Hrs Open:* 24; 1 kw-U; N38 00 30 W120 21 45
342 S. Washington, Sonora, CA 89701
(209) 533-1450, *Fax:* (209) 533-9520
www.kvml.com
License: Sonora, Tuolumne County, CA held by Clarke Broadcasting Corp.
Group Owner: Clarke Broadcasting Corp.; acq 12-86; with co-located FM;
Nat'l Network: ABC; Fox News Radio
Population Served: 200,000*Special Programming:* Relg 3 hrs *Hrs. of News Programming:* news progmg 50 hrs wkly *No. News Employees:* 3 *Target Audience:* 25 plus; general
H. Randolph Holder Jr., President
Larry England, General Manager
Larry England, General Sales Mgr
Mark Truppner, Programming Director
B.J. Hansen, News Director
John Petter, Chief Engineer
D.J. Riendeau, Traffic Manager

KZSQ-FM
10-03-1973; 92.7 mhz FM *Hrs Open:* 24; 380 w; Ant 1,289 ft; N38 00 30 W120 21 45
342 S. Washington, Sonora, CA 89701
(209) 533-1450, *Fax:* (209) 533-9520
License: Sonora, Tuolumne County, CA held by Clarke Broadcasting Corp.
Group Owner: Clarke Broadcasting Corp.; (acq 1986)
Nat'l Network: Fox News Radio
Population Served: 500,000*Hrs. of News Programming:* news progmg 4 hrs wkly *No. News Employees:* 3 *Target Audience:* 25-54.
Randolph Holder, CEO
Larry England, General Manager
Justin Flores, Programming Director
Maryann Curmi, Promotions Manager
B J Hansen, News Director
John Petter, Engineering Dir

Soquel

KYAA
01-01-2001; 1200 khz AM
5420 T Street, Sacramento, CA 95819 US
(831) 372-1074; (866) 895-2829, *Fax:* (831) 372-3585
www.knry.com
License: Soquel, CA held by People's Radio Inc.

Arbitron Metro Market: Monterey-Salinas-Santa Cruz, CA
Format: Ethnic
Jasvir Sandhu, Programming Director

South Lake Tahoe

KRLT
06-23-1976; 93.9 mhz FM *Hrs Open:* 24; 3 kw; -105 ft.; N38 57 38 W119 56 32
Mailing Address: 2435 E. Venice Drive, Suite 120, South Lake Tahoe, CA 96150 US
Second Address: 276 Kingsbury Grade, Suite 203, Stateline, NV 89449
(775) 580-7130
www.krltfm.com
steve@krltfm.com
License: South Lake Tahoe, El Dorado County, CA held by CCR-Lake Tahoe IV LLC.
Group Owner: Cherry Creek Radio LLC; (acq 12-19-2003; grpsl).
Arbitron Metro Market: Lake Tahoe, CA/NE *Format:* Contemporary Hits/Top 40 *Hrs. of News Programming:* News progmg 10 hrs wkly *Target Audience:* 25-54.
Tony Driskill, General Manager
George Alm, General Sales Mgr
Steve Harness, Programming Director

KTHO
03-17-1963; 590 khz AM *Hrs Open:* 24; 2.5 kw-D, DAN; 0.5 kw-N, DAN; N38 55 0 W119 57 46
Mailing Address: P.O Box 1590, South Lake Tahoe, CA 96156 US
Second Address: 2520 Lake Tahoe Blvd., Ste 5, South Lake Tahoe, CA 96150
(530) 543-0590, *Fax:* (530) 543-1101
www.kthoradio.com
ed@590ktho.com
License: South Lake Tahoe, CA held by Live Wire Media Partners LLC
Nat'l Network: ABC
Arbitron Metro Market: Reno, NV *Format:* Oldies *Special Programming:* Jazz Trax Sundays 8pm *Hrs. of News Programming:* news progmg 40 hrs wkly *No. News Employees:* 1 *Target Audience:* 35-55; locals &visitors, working population and retired
Darrell Wampler, President
Ed Crook, Station Manager

KWYL
01-01-1995; 102.9 mhz FM *Hrs Open:* 24; 39 kw; 2927 ft.; N39 18 38 W119 53 1
1960 Idaho Street, Carson City, NV 89701 US
(775) 789-6700, *Fax:* (775) 789-6767
www.wild1029.com
r.boogie@cumulus.com
License: South Lake Tahoe, El Dorado County, CA
Group Owner: Cumulus Media Inc.; (acq 5-9-03; grpsl).
Arbitron Metro Market: South Lake Tahoe, CA *Format:* Adult Contemp, Oldies *Target Audience:* 25-54.
Andrew Perini, General Manager
Kathy Williams, General Sales Mgr
R. Boogie, Programming Director
Jay Schell, Promotions Manager
Martin Stabbert, Chief Engineer

KOWL
11-01-1956; 1490 khz AM; 1 kw-U, ND1; N38 56 34 W119 57 25
Mailing Address: 2435 E. Venice Drive, Suite 120, South Lake Tahoe, CA 96150 US
Second Address: 276 Kingsbury Grade, Suite 203, Stateline, NV 89449
(775) 580-7130
www.krltfm.com
steve@krltfm.com
License: South Lake Tahoe, CA held by CCR-Lake Tahoe IV LLC.
Group Owner: Cherry Creek Radio LLC; (acq 12-19-2003; grpsl).
Arbitron Metro Market: South Lake Tahoe, CA *Format:* News, News/Talk, 86
Tony Driskill, General Manager
Steve Harness, Programming Director

South Oroville

KYIX
02-01-1994; 104.9 mhz FM; 0.26 kw; 1549 ft.; N39 39 4 W121 27 43
1601 Belvedere Rd, West Palm Beach, FL 33406 US
(530) 894-7325, *Fax:* (530) 894-5372
www.air1.com
info@kkxx.net/ info@air1.com
License: South Oroville, Butte County, CA held by Butte Broadcasting Co.
Arbitron Metro Market: Chico, CA *Format:* Alternative, Christian
Andrew Palmquist, General Manager

St. Helena

KVYN
11-01-1976; 99.3 mhz FM; 6 kw; 259 ft.; N38 25 34 W122 19 33
1124 Foster Road, Napa, CA 94558 US
(707) 252-1440(707) 258-1111, *Fax:* (707) 226-7544
www.kvyn.com
License: St. Helena, Napa County, CA held by Wine Country Broadcasting Co.
Nat'l Network: ABC *Nat'l Reps:* Christal
Arbitron Metro Market: Saint Helena, CA *Format:* Adult Contemp
Special Programming: Folk 2 hrs wkly. *Target Audience:* 25-45.
Adv. Rates: 60; 60; 55; 35
Roger Walther, President
Jeff Schechtman, General Manager
Erica Pickett, Promotions Manager
Megan Goldsby, News Director
Ben Webster, Chief Engineer

Stanford

*KZSU
10-10-1964; 90.1 mhz FM *Hrs Open:* 24; 500 w; -10 ft; N37 24 42 W122 10 41
Box 20510, Stanford, CA 94309
(650) 725-5865, *Fax:* (650) 725-5865
www.kzsu.stanford.edu
gm@kzsu.stanford.edu
License: Stanford, Santa Clara County, CA held by Trustees of Leland Stanford Jr. University.
Population Served: 13,000 *Arbitron Metro Market:* San Francisco *Hrs. of News Programming:* news progmg 15 hrs wkly *No. News Employees:* 40 *Target Audience:* 13-plus; independent-thinking individuals who valueunique programming
John Pearson, Chairman
Francis Dickerson, Operations Dir
Sophia Vo, General Manager
Abra Jeffers, General Sales Mgr
Mark Mollineaux, Programming Director
Molly Vorweck, News Director
Mark Lawrence, Chief Engineer
George Lu,Assistant General Manager
Sam Fisher, Sports Director
Diego Aguilar-Canabal, Music Director
Lilly Oh, Financial Director
Andy Stuhl, Training Director

Stockton

*KYCC
02-24-1975; 90.1 mhz FM; 41 kw; 351 ft.; N37 57 30 W121 16 55
9019 West Lane, Stockton, CA 95210 US
(209) 477-3690, *Fax:* (209) 477-2762
www.kycc.org
kycc@kycc.org
License: Stockton, San Joaquin County, CA held by Your Christian Companion Network Inc.
Arbitron Metro Market: Stockton, CA *Format:* Adult Contemp, Gospel, 74 *Special Programming:* Black 6 hrs, health one hr wkly *Target Audience:* 35-55.
Shirley Garner, President
Shirley Garner, General Manager
Scott Mearns, Programming Director
John Ramos, Promotions Manager
Vanessa Kudenov, Office Manager
Sharla Ogden, Accounting
Sandy Guerrero, Donor Relations
Gary Harding,Production Manager

KWSX
01-01-1947; 1280 khz AM *Hrs Open:* 24; 1 kw-D, DAN; 1 kw-N, DAN; N37 58 58 W121 13 46; N37 58 55 W121 13 44
600 Congress Avenue, Suite 1400, Auston, TX 78701 US
(209) 551-1306, *Fax:* (209) 551-1359
License: Stockton, CA held by Capstar TX L.P.
Group Owner: Clear Channel Communications Inc.; (acq 8-30-2000; grpsl)
Arbitron Metro Market: Stockton, CA *Format:* Talk *Target Audience:* 25-64.
Rich Hawkins, General Manager
Matthew Hobley, Programming Director

KJOY
06-15-1968; 99.3 mhz FM *Hrs Open:* 24; 4 kw; 322 ft.; N37 59 30 W121 17 17
Mailing Address: 6820 Pacific Ave., Suite 2, Stockton, CA 95207 US
Second Address: 1581 Cummins Dr., Suite 135, Modesto, CA 95358
(209) 476-1230, *Fax:* (209) 956-0907
www.993kjoy.com
info@993kjoy.com
License: Stockton, San Joaquin County, CA
Group Owner: Cumulus Media Inc.; (acq 5-9-03; grpsl).
Arbitron Metro Market: Stockton, CA *Format:* Adult Contemp
Target Audience: 25-54.
Ort Lofthus, President
Roy Williams, General Manager
Jonathan Carlos, General Sales Mgr
Dirk Kooyman, Programming Director
Jeff Bayani, Promotions Manager

KQOD
01-24-1980; 100.1 mhz FM; 6 kw; 328 ft.; N37 59 47.8 W121 12 15.9
1120 N. San Joaquin St., Stockton, CA 95202 US
(209) 551-1306, *Fax:* (209) 551-53193791
www.mega100online.com
License: Stockton, San Joaquin County, CA held by Capstar TX L.P.
Group Owner: Clear Channel Communications Inc.; (acq 11-18-99).
Arbitron Metro Market: Stockton/Modesto *Format:* Oldies *Target Audience:* 25-54.
Matthew Hobley, Operations Dir
Rich Hawkins, General Manager
Rick Myers, General Sales Mgr
Tony Bear, Programming Director
Kacie Marshall, Promotions Manager
Mayra Hernandez, News Director

KSTN
11-01-1949; 1420 khz AM *Hrs Open:* 24; 5 kw-D, DA2; 1 kw-N, DA2; N37 55 32 W121 14 44
2171 Ralph Avenue, Stockton, CA 95206 US
(209) 948-5786
www.valleyradio.org/kstn/
License: Stockton, CA held by San Joaquin Broadcasting Co.
Arbitron Metro Market: Stockton, CA *Format:* Oldies *Special Programming:* Farm 3 hrs, relg 5 hrs wkly *Hrs. of News Programming:* news progmg 20 hrs wkly *No. News Employees:* 1 *Target Audience:* 18-40.
Knox LaRue, President
John Hampton, Music Director

*KUOP
09-22-1947; 91.3 mhz FM *Hrs Open:* 24; 7 kw; 1220 ft.; N37 28 48 W121 21 2
3601 Pacific Avenue, Stockton, CA 95211 US
(916) 278-8900, *Fax:* (916) 278-8989
www.capradio.org
npr@csus.edu
License: Stockton, San Joaquin County, CA held by University of the Pacific.
Nat'l Network: NPR; PRI
Arbitron Metro Market: Stockton, CA *Format:* News *Hrs. of News Programming:* news progmg 90 hrs wkly *No. News Employees:* 1 *Target Audience:* General; NPR listeners, eg. professionals, educators, administrators
Kevin O'Brien, Chairman
John Brenneise, Operations Dir
Cheryl Dring, Programming Director
Joe Barr, News Director
Jeff Browne, Chief Engineer
John L. Lewis, Treasurer
Ben Adler, Capitol Bureau Chief
Nick Brunner, Blue Dog JamHost, Producer & Operations Assistant
Paul Conley, Senior Producer, News
Elaine Corn, Food & Lifestyle Reporter
Constance Crawford, Director of Marketing & Public Relations

*KWG
11-22-1921; 1230 khz AM
1120 N. San Joaquin Street, Stockton, CA 95202 US
(209) 462-8307
www.ihradio.org
info@ihradio.org
License: Stockton, CA held by IHR Educational Broadcasting
Group Owner: IHR Educational Broadcasting; acq 10-18-99; $441,227).
Wire Services: Dow Jones News Service
Arbitron Metro Market: Loomis, CA *Format:* Religious, Christian
Target Audience: 25-54.
Joseph Nesta, Station Manager
Dale Harry, Chief Engineer

RADIO - U.S.

Sun City

KXFG
03-01-1997; 92.9 mhz FM; 6 kw; 328 ft.; N33 35 34.3 W117 8 50.8 *Rebroadcasts:* Rebroadcasts KFRG(FM) San Bernardino 100%
600 New Hampshire Avenue, N.W., Suite 1200, Washington, DC 20037 US
(909) 825-9525, *Fax:* (909) 825-0441
www.kfrog.com
webmaster@kfrog.net
License: Sun City, Riverside County, CA held by Infinity Radio Inc.
Group Owner: CBS Radio; (acq 11-13-98; grpsl).
Arbitron Metro Market: Colton, CA *Format:* Country
Lee Douglas, Operations Dir
Kimberly Martinz, General Manager
Mixhael Valen, General Sales Mgr
Harvey Wells, SVP Market Manager
Steve Hay, Digital Sales Manager
Leslie Bischoff, Marketing Director
Michael Valenzuela, Director ofSales
Scott Ward, Music Director
Jorge Lopz, Web Directoe

Sunnyvale

KXSC(FM)
01-01-1961; 104.9 mhz FM; 6 kw; Ant -154 ft; N37 19 23 W121 45 15
1420 Koll Cir., Suite A, San Jose, CA 95112
(408) 453-5400, *Fax:* (408) 452-1330
www.iheart.com
License: Sunnyvale, Santa Clara County, CA held by CC Licenses LLC.
Group Owner: Clear Channel Communications Inc.; (acq 2-2-2004; grpsl)
Population Served: 967,487 *Arbitron Metro Market:* San Jose, CA *Format:* Tejano *Target Audience:* 18-49.
Dave Pugh, General Manager
Paul Dela Rosa, General Sales Mgr
Jose Reyes, Programming Director
Carmen Torres, Promotions Manager
David Williams, Chief Engineer

Susanville

KJDX
05-25-1983; 93.3 mhz FM *Hrs Open:* 24; 100 kw; 1155 ft.; N40 27 13 W120 34 14
3015 Johnstonville Road, Susanville, CA 96130 US
(530) 257-2121, *Fax:* (530) 257-6955
www.theradionetwork.com
radiorod11@aol.com
License: Susanville, Lassen County, CA held by Sierra Broadcasting Corp.
Format: Country *Special Programming:* Class 5 hrs wkly
Rodney Chambers, General Manager

KSUE
04-22-1948; 1240 khz AM
3015 Johnstonville Rd, Susanville, CA 96130 US
(530) 257-2121, *Fax:* (530) 257-6955
www.theradionetwork.com
radiorod11@aol.com
License: Susanville, CA held by Sierra Broadcasting Corp.
Arbitron Metro Market: Susanville, CA *Format:* News, News/Talk, 86 *Special Programming:* Relg 3 hrs wkly *Target Audience:* 35-54.
Rod Chambers, President
Ruth Dike, Operations Dir
Mike Smith, News Director
Mike Martindale, Chief Engineer
Kristin Volberg, Public Affairs Director

KLZN
01-01-2006; 1490 khz AM; Ant -528 ft
US
(530) 257-6100, *Fax:* (530) 257-6107
dennis@jackfm963.com
License: Susanville, CA held by Gary Katz.
Arbitron Metro Market: Yakima, WA *Format:* Adult Contemp
Gary Katz, President
Dennis Carlson, General Manager

***KJLC(FM)**
90.9 mhz FM; 12 kw; Ant 2,266 ft; N40 26 48 W120 21 27
478-200 Hwy. 139, Susanville, CA 96130
(530) 310-3303
License: Susanville, Lassen County, CA held by Lassen Community College.
Population Served: 4,917 *Arbitron Metro Market:* Needles, CA
Kam Vento, General Manager

Sutter

***KXJS**
01-01-2004; 88.7 mhz FM; 0.55 kw; 1978 ft.; N39 12 20 W121 49 10
3416 American River Dr, Suite B, Sacramento, CA 95864 US
(916) 278-8900, *Fax:* (916) 278-8989
www.csus.edu/npr
npr@csus.edu
License: Sutter, Sutter County, CA held by California State University, Sacramento.
Arbitron Metro Market: Sutter, CA *Format:* Jazz, News
Kevin O'Brien, Chairman
Larry Gilbert, VP & Chief Information Officer
Rick Eytcheson, President & General Manager
John Brenneise, Operations Dir
Carl Watanabe, Station Manager
Joe Barr, Director of News and Information
JeffBrowne, Engineering Dir

Taft

KBDS
06-01-1986; 103.9 mhz FM *Hrs Open:* 24; 6 kw; 328 ft.; N35 7 4 W119 27 33
PO Box 62, Keene, CA 93531 US
(661) 837-0745, *Fax:* (661) 837-1612
achavez@campesina.com
License: Taft, Kern County, CA held by Radio Campesina Bakersfield Inc.
Arbitron Metro Market: Bakersfield, CA
Anthony Chavez, General Manager

KEAL
106.5 mhz FM; 6 kw; 285 ft.; N35 5 39 W119 27 40
US
(805) 240-2070
License: Taft, Kern County, CA held by Lazer Licenses LLC.
Group Owner: Lazer Broadcasting Corp.; (acq 6-11-2007; $3.85 million with KXTT(FM) Maricopa)
Arbitron Metro Market: Duluth-Superior, MN-WI
Neal Robinson, President

Tahoe City

***KKTO**
10-03-1997; 90.5 mhz FM *Hrs Open:* 24; 38 kw vert; 2940 ft.; N39 18 38 W119 53 1
Suite B, 3416 American River Dr., Sacramento, CA 95864 US
(916) 278-8900, *Fax:* (916) 278-8989
www.capradio.org
npr@csus.edu
License: Tahoe City, Placer County, CA held by California State University, Sacramento.
Nat'l Network: NPR; PRI
Arbitron Metro Market: Reno, NV *Format:* News *Hrs. of News Programming:* news progmg 90 hrs wkly *No. News Employees:* 4 *Target Audience:* General; NPR listeners, eg. professionals, educators, administrators
Vincent Johnson, Operations Dir
Rick Eytcheson, General Manager
Carl Watanabe, Station Manager
Arla Gibson, General Sales Mgr
Joe Barr, News Director
Brian Witt, Engineering Dir
Linda Onstad, Advertising Director
Cheryl Dring,Music Director

KLCA
04-05-1985; 96.5 mhz FM *Hrs Open:* 24; 6.1 kw; 2963 ft.; N39 18 38 W119 53 1
1900 Avenue of the Stars, Suite 1880, Los Angeles, CA 90067 US
(775) 829-1964, *Fax:* (775) 825-3183
www.alice965.com
License: Tahoe City, Placer County, CA held by Americom Broadcasting.
Group Owner: Americom; (acq 1996; $1.225 million)
Arbitron Metro Market: Reno, NV *Format:* Contemporary Hits/Top 40 *Special Programming:* Metal shop 2 hrs wkly *Hrs. of News Programming:* News progmg 3 hrs wkly *Target Audience:* 18-34.
Tom Quinn, President
Daniel Cook, General Manager
Carrie Carano, General Sales Mgr
Beej ., Programming Director
Tina ., News Director
Steve Weber, Chief Engineer

Tehachapi

KKZQ
01-01-2001; 100.1 mhz FM; 0.34 kw; 620 ft.; N35 4 30 W118 22 7
715 Broadway, Suite 320, Santa Monica, CA 90401 US
(661) 947-3107, *Fax:* (661) 272-5688
www.edge100.com
info@edge100.com
License: Tehachapi, Kern County, CA held by High Desert Broadcasting LLC
Group Owner: High Desert Broadcasting LLC
Arbitron Metro Market: Bakersfield, CA *Format:* Alternative
Target Audience: 18-49.
Gary Wilson, Operations Dir
Nelson Rasse, General Manager
Greg Wood, General Sales Mgr
Jeff McElfresh, Promotions Manager
Amir Raheem, News Director

KSRY
01-08-1982; 103.1 mhz FM *Hrs Open:* 24; 1.9 kw; 577 ft.; N35 4 30 W118 22 8
190 Sierra Court, B-2, Palmdale, CA 93550 US
(818) 559-2252, *Fax:* (818) 729-2502
www.987fm.com/main.html
License: Tehachapi, Kern County, CA held by CC Licenses LLC.
Group Owner: Clear Channel Communications Inc.; (acq 11-21-2003; grpsl)
Nat'l Reps: Christal
Arbitron Metro Market: Los Angeles *Format:* Alternative *Hrs. of News Programming:* news progmg 2 hrs wkly *No. News Employees:* 1
Greg Ashlock, General Manager

***KBLV**
01-01-2006; 88.7 mhz FM; 0.39 kw; 3694 ft.; N35 27 11 W118 35 25 *Rebroadcasts:* Rebroadcasts KLVR(FM) Middletown 100%
US
(800) 877-5600, *Fax:* (916) 251-1650
www.klove.com
License: Tehachapi, Kern County, CA held by Educational Media Foundation.
Group Owner: EMF Broadcasting
Nat'l Network: K-Love
Arbitron Metro Market: Tehachapi, CA *Format:* Christian
Mike Novak, President
David Pierce, Programming Director
Ed Lenane, News Director
Sam Wallington, Engineering Dir
Marya Morgan, News Reporter
Richard Hunt, News Reporter

Temecula

KMYT
01-01-2000; 94.5 mhz FM *Hrs Open:* 24; 0.54 kw; 771 ft.; N33 28 51 W117 10 58 *Rebroadcasts:* Rebroadcasts KOGO(AM) San Diego
41220 Calle Contento, Temecula, CA 92390 US
(951) 296-9050, *Fax:* (951) 296-9077
www.kmyt945.com
michaeldellinger@clearchannel.com
License: Temecula, Riverside County, CA held by CC Licenses LLC.
Group Owner: Clear Channel Communications Inc.; (acq 6-11-2001; $4.5 million including five-year noncompete agreement).
Arbitron Metro Market: Temecula, CA *Format:* Jazz, Smooth Jazz
Bill Georgi, Operations Dir
Bob Ridzak, General Manager
Kevin Lein, Station Manager
Robyn Bedessem, General Sales Mgr
Allen Keppler, Programming Director
Mike Dellinger, Promotions Manager
Rich Mena, Chief Engineer
MikeDellinger, Promotions
Bob Ridzak, Market Manager

KTMQ
01-01-2001; 103.3 mhz FM; 1.25 kw; 715 ft.; N33 28 51 W117 10 58
29771 Bonanaza Place, Canyon Lake, CA 92587 US
(951) 684-1991, *Fax:* (951) 296-9077
www.q1033.com
teresahutchinson@clearchannel.com
License: Temecula, Riverside County, CA held by CC Licenses LLC.
Group Owner: Clear Channel Communications Inc.; (acq 7-31-2001; $6.225 million).

Arbitron Metro Market: Temecula, CA *Format:* Classic Rock
Bob Ridzak, General Manager
Mike Dellinger, Promotions Manager

Templeton

KXDZ
01-01-2004; 100.5 mhz FM; 1.35 kw; 361 ft.; N35 30 19 W120 37 18
P.O. Box 938, Capitola, CA 95010 US
(805) 786-2570, *Fax:* (805) 547-9860
www.953thebeach.com
aaron@radiocentralcoast.com
License: Templeton, San Luis Obispo County, CA held by Mapleton License of San Luis Obispo LLC.
Group Owner: Mapleton Communications LLC; (acq 7-19-2002;. grpsl)
Arbitron Metro Market: San Luis Obispo, CA *Format:* Contemporary Hits/Top 40, Adult Contemp
Adam Nathanson, President
Aaron Criswell, General Manager
Drew Ross, Programming Director
David Atwood, News Director
Tom Hughes, Chief Engineer

Thermal

KKCM
03-12-1993; 92.1 mhz FM *Hrs Open:* 24; 1.3 kw; 215 m; N33 39 18.00 W115 59 13.00
Box 1437, Joshua Tree, CA 92277
(760) 362-4264
www.kxcmradio.com
coppermountainbroadcasting@yahoo.com
License: Thermal, Riverside County, CA held by Copper Mountain Broadcasting Co.
Nat'l Network: Dial Global; Premiere *Nat'l Reps:* Interep
Population Served: 350,000 *Arbitron Metro Market:* Palm Springs *Target Audience:* 25-54.
Gary DeMaroney, President
Gary DeMaroney, General Manager
Carol Vaughn, Business Manager
Scott Sear, News Director

Thousand Oaks

*KCLU-FM
10-20-1994; 88.3 mhz FM *Hrs Open:* 24; 3.2 kw; 518 ft.; N34 13 5 W118 56 42
60 West Olsen Road, Thousand Oaks, CA 91360 US
(805) 493-3900, *Fax:* (805) 493-3982
www.kclu.org
kclu@callutheran.edu
License: Thousand Oaks, Ventura County, CA held by California Lutheran University.
Nat'l Network: NPR; PRI *Wire Services:* AP
Arbitron Metro Market: Ventura County-Santa Barbara, CA *Format:* News *Special Programming:* Jazz & blues 5 hrs wkly *Hrs. of News Programming:* news progmg 125 hrs wkly *No. News Employees:* 2 *Target Audience:* General.
Jim Rondeau, Director of Operations and Programming
Mary Olson, General Manager
Lance Orozco, News Director
Mia Karnatz-Shifflett, Director of Member Services
Rick Pack, Sponsorships

*KDSC
12-04-1979; 91.1 mhz FM *Hrs Open:* 24; 4.8 kw; 1280 ft.; N34 24 47 W119 11 10 *Rebroadcasts:* Rebroadcasts KUSC(FM) Los Angeles 100%
Mailing Address: P. O. Box 77913, Los Angeles, CA 90007 US
Second Address: 515 S. Figueroa St., Suite 2050, Los Angeles, CA 90071
(213) 225-7400, *Fax:* (213) 225-7410
www.kusc.org
kusc@kusc.org
License: Thousand Oaks, Ventura County, CA held by University of Southern California
Nat'l Network: PRI; NPR
Arbitron Metro Market: Thousand Oaks, CA *Format:* Talk *Target Audience:* 35 plus.
Brenda Barnes, President
Steve Coghill, Operations Dir
Eric DeWeese, General Manager
Janet McIntyre, General Sales Mgr
Bill Lueth, Programming Director
Ron Thompson, Engineering Dir
Amy Iwata, Office Manager
Rina Romero, Sr.Business Manager
Gail Eichenthal, Executive Director of Arts Programming
Brian Lauritzen, Producer
Kelsey McConnell, Production Manager
Mark Hatwan, Production Director

KHJL(FM)
04-01-1963; 92.7 mhz FM *Hrs Open:* 24; 3.1 kw; Ant 462 ft; N34 12 21 W118 49 04
99 Long Court, Suite 200, Thousand Oaks, CA 91360
(805) 497-8511, *Fax:* (805) 497-8514
www.927jillfm.com
reception@927jillfm.com
License: Thousand Oaks, Ventura County, CA held by Amaturo Group of L.A. Ltd.
Group Owner: Amaturo Groups; (acq 1996; $2 million)
Population Served: 700,000*Format:* Adult Contemp *No. News Employees:* 1 *Target Audience:* 25-54; employed professional adults, especially women *Adv. Rates:* 60; 65; 60; 50
Joseph Amaturo, CEO
Robert Christy, General Manager

KLSI
05-01-2006; 92.7 mhz FM *Hrs Open:* 24; 3.1 kw; 463 ft.; N34 12 21 W118 49 4 *Rebroadcasts:* Rebroadcasts WAZQ(FM) Layton, FL 100%.
3101 North Federal, Highway, Suite 601, Ft. Lauderdale, FL 33306 US
(877) 927-4927, *Fax:* (949) 454-1710
www.playlist927.com
matt@playlist927.com?subject=Email%20from%20Website
License: Thousand Oaks, San Mateo County, CA held by Educational Public Radio Inc.
Arbitron Metro Market: Malibu Vista, CA *Format:* Adult Contemp *Target Audience:* 18-54; adults
Bill Lacy, President
Matthew Rodriguez, General Manager
Pat Duffy, Station Manager
Rick Shaw, Operations Manager/Program Director
Justin Schuvie, Operations Manager/Program Director
Chris Hicks, Chief Engineer
Betsy Zook,Business Manager
Jake Hagen, Traffic Director/Asst Program Director
Doug Eldred, Public Service Director
Linda Perry, Senior Account Executive
Jan Bussman, Account Executive
Charles Hoyes, Account Executive

Thousand Palms

KLOB
04-21-1994; 94.7 mhz FM; 1.65 kw; 640 ft.; N33 51 56 W116 25 58
11900 Olympic Blvd, Suite 590, Los Angeles, CA 90064 US
(760) 341-5837, *Fax:* (760) 341-0951
www.entravision.com
klobtraffic@entravision.com
License: Thousand Palms, Riverside County, CA held by Entravision Holdings LLC.
Group Owner: Entravision Communications Corp.; (acq 2-27-97).
Arbitron Metro Market: Palm Springs, CA *Format:* Spanish
Philip Wilkinson, President
Victor Tocco, General Manager
Edgar Pineda, Programming Director
Sandra Cano, Promotions Manager
Martha Saldana, News Director
Sergio De la Torre, Chief Engineer

KXPS
11-14-1992; 1010 khz AM *Hrs Open:* 24; 3.6 kw-D, DA2; 0.4 kw-N, DA2; N33 50 35 W116 25 39
725 Broad St., P.O. Box 936, Augusta, GA 30903 US
(760) 322-7890, *Fax:* (760) 322-5493
www.1010kxps.com
info@desertfun.com
License: Thousand Palms, CA held by Morris Communications Corp.
Group Owner: Morris Radio LLC; (acq 12-24-97; $2.25 million with KDGL(FM) Yucca Valley).
Arbitron Metro Market: Palm Springs, CA *Format:* Sports, Talk *Special Programming:* Relg 17 hrs wkly
Angela Powers, Operations Dir
Norman Feuer, General Manager
Cos Cappellino, General Sales Mgr
Virginia Nelson, Programming Director
John McMullen, Program Director

KFUT
12-07-1963; 1270 khz AM *Hrs Open:* 24; 5 kw-D, DA2; 0.75 kw-N, DA2; N33 51 4 W116 23 36
725 Broad St., P.O. Box 936, Augusta, GA 30903 US
(760) 322-7890, *Fax:* (760) 322-5493
1207kfut.com
info@desertfun.com
License: Thousand Palms, CA held by MCC Radio LLC.
Group Owner: Morris Radio LLC; (acq 12-24-97; $2.25 million with KDGL(FM) Yucca Valley)
Arbitron Metro Market: Palm Springs, CA *Format:* Talk *Hrs. of News Programming:* news progmg 20 hrs wkly *No. News Employees:* 3 *Target Audience:* 25 plus.
Angela Powers, Operations Dir
Norman Feuer, General Manager
Cos Cappellino, General Sales Mgr
Virginia Nelson, Programming Director
Jennifer Shevlin, Program Director

Tipton

KCRZ
01-01-1997; 104.9 mhz FM *Hrs Open:* 24; 2.3 kw; 528 ft.; N36 10 7 W119 15 4
9440 Santa Monica Blvd, Beverly Hills, CA 90210 US
(559) 553-1500, *Fax:* (559) 627-1496
www.z1049.com
License: Tipton, Tulare County, CA held by Lemoore Wireless Co. Inc.
Nat'l Network: ABC
Arbitron Metro Market: Visalia-Tulare-Hanford, CA *Format:* Adult Contemp *Target Audience:* 25-54. *Adv. Rates:* 30; 25; 20; na
Genia Taylor, General Manager
Randy Hendrix, Programming Director

Torrance

KFOX
01-01-1998; 1650 khz AM
1500 Cotner Avenue, Los Angeles, CA 90025 US
(323) 935-0606, *Fax:* (323) 935-8885
www.radioseoul1650.com
info@kfoxam.com
License: Torrance, CA held by Chagal Communications Inc.
Format: Adult Contemp, Korean
Grant Chang, General Manager

Tracy

KMIX
12-14-1966; 100.9 mhz FM; 6 kw; 328 ft.; N37 37 32 W121 23 58
1436 Auburn Boulevard, Sacramento, CA 95815 US
(209) 474-0154, *Fax:* (209) 474-0316
www.entravision.com
info@entravision.com
License: Tracy, San Joaquin County, CA held by Entravision Holdings LLC.
Group Owner: Entravision Communications Corp.; (acq 7-28-00; grpsl).
Arbitron Metro Market: Stockton, CA
Lisa Vela, General Manager

*KAIS(FM)
01-01-2004; 90.7 mhz FM *Hrs Open:* 24; 210 w; Ant 1,745 ft; N37 33 37 W121 36 19
PO Box 2098, Omaha, NE 68103-2098
(800) 525-5683, *Fax:* (916) 251-1650
www.klove.com
klove@klove.com
License: Tracy, San Joaquin County, CA held by Educational Media Foundation.
Group Owner: EMF Broadcasting
Nat'l Network: K-Love
Population Served: 967,487 *Arbitron Metro Market:* San Jose, CA *Format:* Christian *No. News Employees:* 3 *Target Audience:* 25-44; Judeo Christian, female
Darrell Chambliss, Chairman
Mike Novak, President and CEO
David Pierce, Programming Director
Ed Lenane, News Director
Sam Wallington, Engineering Dir
Marya Morgan, News Reporter
Richard Hunt, News Reporter
Laura Daniels, NewsReporter
Tim Luttrell, News Reporter
Kenny Noble Cortes, News Reporter
Darren Vinson, News Reporter

Truckee

KTKE
01-01-2003; 101.5 mhz FM *Hrs Open:* 24; 0.14 kw; 1988 ft.; N39 14 29 W120 8 20
Gammon & Grange Pc, 8280 Greensboro Drive, McLean, VA 22102 US
(530) 587-9999, *Fax:* (530) 587-9119
www.truckeetahoeradio.com
info@truckeetahoeradio.com
License: Truckee, Nevada County, CA held by Todd Robinson, Inc

Arbitron Metro Market: Truckee, CA *Format:* Triple A
Jon Robinson, President
Lindsay Romack, General Manager
Keith Thomas, Sales Manager
Lindsay Romack, Program Manager
Sue Waters, Music Director

Tulare

KBOS-FM
01-01-1965; 94.9 mhz FM *Hrs Open:* 24; 16.5 kw; 850 ft.; N36 38 15 W118 56 35
600 Congress Ave., Suite 1400, Austin, TX 78701 US
(559) 230-4300, *Fax:* (559) 243-4301
www.b95forlife.com
info@b95forlife.com
License: Tulare, Tulare County, CA held by Capstar TX L.P.
Group Owner: Clear Channel Communications Inc.; (acq 8-30-00; grpsl).
Arbitron Metro Market: Fresno, CA *Format:* Christian *Target Audience:* 12-34.
Jeff Negrete, Operations Dir
Tony Rainaldi, General Sales Mgr
Greg Hoffman, Programming Director
Dave Case, Chief Engineer
Paul Wilson, Operations Manager

KGEN
01-01-1957; 1370 khz AM *Hrs Open:* 24
Mailing Address: 323 East San Joaquin St., Tulare, CA 93274 US
Second Address: 323 E. San Joaquin Ave., Tulare, CA 93274
(559) 686-1370, *Fax:* (559) 685-1394
License: Tulare, CA held by Azteca Broadcasting Corp.
Group Owner: Azteca Broadcasting Corp.
Arbitron Metro Market: Visalia-Tulare, CA *Format:* Spanish *Target Audience:* General.
Margaretia Hernandez, General Manager

KJUG
08-01-1946; 1270 khz AM *Hrs Open:* 24; 5 kw-D, DAN; 1 kw-N, DAN; N36 10 6 W119 15 12
717 N. Mooney Blvd, Tulare, CA 93274 US
(559) 553-1500, *Fax:* (559) 627-1496
www.kjugam.com
License: Tulare, CA held by Westcoast Broadcasting Inc.
Nat'l Network: ABC *Nat'l Reps:* Interep
Arbitron Metro Market: Visalia, CA *Format:* Country *Special Programming:* Farm 5 hrs wkly *Hrs. of News Programming:* news progmg 7 hrs wkly *No. News Employees:* 1 *Target Audience:* 25-64.
Bill Lynch, General Manager
Wayne Foster, General Sales Mgr
Dave Daniels, Promotions Manager
Darrin Cantrell, News Director
Jamie Moore, Traffic Manager

KJUG-FM
05-06-1965; 106.7 mhz FM *Hrs Open:* 24; 1.2 kw; 2552 ft.; N36 17 8 W118 50 17
717 North Mooney Blvd, Tulare, CA 93274 US
(559) 553-1500, *Fax:* (559) 627-1496
www.kjug.com
studio@kjug.com
License: Tulare, Tulare County, CA held by Westcoast Broadcasting Inc.
Arbitron Metro Market: Visalia, CA *Format:* Country *Target Audience:* 18-54.
Randy Carlson, President
Bill Lynch, General Manager
Dawn Bumstead, Programming Director

Tulelake

KFLS-FM
07-23-1993; 96.5 mhz FM *Hrs Open:* 24; 20 kw; 2156 ft.; N42 5 50 W121 37 59
Mailing Address: 1338 Oregon Avenue, Klamath Falls, OR 97601 US
Second Address: 1338 Oregon Ave., Klamath Falls, OR 97601
(541) 882-4656, *Fax:* (541) 884-2845
www.klamathradio.com
traffic@klamathradio.com
License: Tulelake, Siskiyou County, CA held by Wynne Enterprises LLC
Group Owner: Wynne Enterprises LLC
Regional Reps: Tacher.
Arbitron Metro Market: Klamath Falls, OR *Format:* Country *Target Audience:* 18-49.
Robert Wynne, CEO
Leslie Hougan, General Sales Mgr
Randy Adams, Programming Director

Lyle Ahrens, News Director
Russ Jump, Chief Engineer
Carol Fritch, Traffic Manager

Turlock

*KBDG
01-01-1977; 90.9 mhz FM *Hrs Open:* 24; 0.73 kw; 39 ft.; N37 31 1 W120 52 10
Mailing Address: P O Box 192, Turlock, CA 95381 US
Second Address: 1600 E. Canal Dr., Turlock, CA 95380
(209) 668-7176, *Fax:* (209) 668-2322
www.aaccot.org
License: Turlock, Stanislaus County, CA held by Assyrian American Civic Club.
Arbitron Metro Market: Turlock, CA *Format:* Talk
Zaya Sargis, Station Manager

*KCSS
08-13-1975; 91.9 mhz FM *Hrs Open:* 20; 0.4 kw vert; 105 ft.; N37 31 35 W120 51 25
801 W. Monte Vista Ave., Turlock, CA 95382 US
(209) 667-3378 (office)(209) 667-3900 (stn), *Fax:* (209) 667-3901
www.kcss.net
info@kcss.net
License: Turlock, Stanislaus County, CA held by California State University, Stanislaus.
Arbitron Metro Market: Turlock, CA *Format:* Variety/Diverse
Special Programming: Class 9 hrs, jazz 4 hrs, Americana 10 hrs, wkly *Target Audience:* 18-54.
Greg Jacquay, General Manager
Garrett Neely, Station Manager
Clay Hobbs, Promotions Manager

KLOC
10-01-1949; 1390 khz AM; 5 kw-D, DA2; 5 kw-N, DA2; N37 31 48 W120 41 37
961 North Emerald Avenue, Suite A, Modesto, CA 95351 US
(209) 883-8760, *Fax:* (209) 883-8769
www.lafavorita.net
ngomez@lafavorita.net
License: Turlock, CA held by La Favorita Broadcasting Inc.
Arbitron Metro Market: Hughson, CA
Nelson Gomez, General Manager

KWNN
03-03-1978; 98.3 mhz FM *Hrs Open:* 24; 2 kw; 390 ft.; N37 34 46 W120 50 48 *Rebroadcasts:* Simulcasts KWIN(FM) Lodi 95%
Mailing Address: 6820 Pacific Ave #2, Stockton, CA 95207 US
Second Address: 1581 Cummins Dr., Suite 135, Modesto, CA 95358
(209) 476-1230, *Fax:* (209) 957-1833
www.kwin.com
info@kwin.com
License: Turlock, Stanislaus County, CA
Group Owner: Cumulus Media Inc.; (acq 12-12-03).
Nat'l Reps: Christal
Arbitron Metro Market: Stockton, CA *Format:* Contemporary Hits/Top 40
Roy Williams, General Manager
Jean Western, General Sales Mgr

Twain Harte

KKBN
10-19-1985; 93.5 mhz FM *Hrs Open:* 24; 0.4 kw; 1262 ft.; N38 0 30 W120 21 44
P.O. Box 708, Twain Harte, CA 95383 US
(209) 533-1450, *Fax:* (209) 533-9520
www.kkbn.com
lenglandcbc@mlode.com
License: Twain Harte, Tuolumne County, CA held by Clarke Broadcasting Corp.
Group Owner: Clarke Broadcasting Corp.; (acq 3-1-2000; $2.2 million)
Nat'l Network: Fox News Radio *Wire Services:* AP
Arbitron Metro Market: Modesto, CA *Format:* Country *Hrs. of News Programming:* news progmg 4 hrs wkly *No. News Employees:* 3 *Target Audience:* 25-54; general
H. Randolph Holder Jr., President
Larry England, General Manager
Larry England, General Sales Mgr
Joe Marshall, Programming Director
Maryann Curmi, Promotions Manager

Twentynine Palms

KCDZ
07-15-1989; 107.7 mhz FM *Hrs Open:* 24; 6.7 kw; 305 ft.; N34 9 15 W116 11 50
6448 Hallee Road, #5, Joshua Tree, CA 92252 US
(760) 366-8471, *Fax:* (760) 366-2976
www.kcdzfm.com
z1077fm@gnail.com
License: Twentynine Palms, San Bernardino County, CA held by Morongo Basin Broadcasting Corp.
Nat'l Network: ABC *Wire Services:* AP
Format: Adult Contemp *Hrs. of News Programming:* news progmg 10 hrs wkly *No. News Employees:* 6 *Target Audience:* 25-54 *Adv. Rates:* 18; 17; 18; 15
Cynthia Daigneault, President
Eddie Hernandez, Chief Engineer
Gary Daigneault, Executive Vice President

KRSX-FM
12-01-1996; 105.3 mhz FM *Hrs Open:* 24; 6 kw
PO Box 1437, Joshua Tree, CA 41011
(760) 362-4264
License: Twentynine Palms, San Bernardino County, CA held by S & H Broadcasting
Nat'l Network: Fox News; Fox Sports *Nat'l Reps:* Christal
Population Served: 64,000*No. News Employees:* 1 *Target Audience:* 25-54
Greg Smith, President

Ukiah

*KPRA
05-01-1987; 89.5 mhz FM *Hrs Open:* 24; 1.6 kw; 1135 ft.; N39 7 1 W123 13 54
Mailing Address: 4135 Northgate Blvd #1, Sacramento, CA 95834 US
Second Address: 290 Hegenberger Rd., Oakland, CA 94621
(916) 641-8191, *Fax:* (916) 641-8238
www.familyradio.com
info@familyradio.com
License: Ukiah, Mendocino County, CA held by Family Stations Inc.
Group Owner: Family Stations Inc.; acq 2-3-86)
Format: Christian, Religious
Matt Pearce, Operations Dir

KQPM
02-01-1989; 105.9 mhz FM *Hrs Open:* 24; 1.9 kw; 2018 ft.; N39 7 50 W123 4 32
775 East Blithedale Avenue, #143, Mill Valley, CA 94941 US
(707) 263-6113, *Fax:* (707) 263-0939
www.kqpm.com
License: Ukiah, Mendocino County, CA held by Bicoastal Media L.L.C.
Group Owner: Bicoastal Media L.L.C.; acq 7-28-99; grpsl)
Format: Country *Adv. Rates:* 20; 18; 20; 16
Ken Dennis, CEO
Mike Wilson, President
Eric Patrick, Operations Dir
Alan Mathews, General Sales Mgr
Kevin Mostyn, Chief Engineer

KUKI
10-01-1950; 1400 khz AM *Hrs Open:* 24
P.O. Box 77766, Stockton, CA 95267 US
(707) 466-5868, *Fax:* (707) 466-5852
www.kukifm.com
ukiah@bicoastalspots.com
License: Ukiah, CA held by Bicoastal Media Licenses, LLC
Group Owner: Bicoastal Media L.L.C.; (acq 7-28-2006; grpsl)
Arbitron Metro Market: Ukiah, CA *Format:* Spanish *Hrs. of News Programming:* news progmg 25 hrs wkly *No. News Employees:* 2 *Target Audience:* 25 plus; upwardly mobile adults
Alan Mathews, General Manager
Kevin Mostyn, Chief Engineer

KUKI-FM
10-16-1974; 103.3 mhz FM; 2.9 kw; 1778 ft.; N39 19 35 W123 16 11
P.O. Box 77766, Stockton, CA 95267 US
(707) 466-5868, *Fax:* (707) 466-5852
www.kukifm.com
ukiah@bicoastalspots.com
License: Ukiah, Mendocino County, CA held by Bicoastal Media Licenses, LLC
Group Owner: Bicoastal Media L.L.C.
Nat'l Network: ABC
Arbitron Metro Market: Ukiah, CA *Format:* Country *Hrs. of News Programming:* news progmg 7 hrs wkly *No. News Employees:* 1 *Target Audience:* 25-54.
Alan Mathews, General Manager
Kevin Mostyn, Chief Engineer

KWNE
01-01-1968; 94.5 mhz FM *Hrs Open:* 24; 2.2 kw; 1965 ft.; N39 7 50 W123 4 32

Mailing Address: P.O. Box 1056, Ukiah, CA 95482 US
Second Address: 1100 Hastings Rd., Suite B, Ukiah, CA 95482
(707) 462-1451(707) 462-0945, *Fax:* (707) 462-4670
www.kwine.com
kwine@kwine.com
License: Ukiah, Mendocino County, CA held by Broadcasting Corp of Mendocino County.
Arbitron Metro Market: Ukiah, CA *Format:* Adult Contemp *Special Programming:* Sp 4 hrs, farm one hr wkly *Hrs. of News Programming:* news progmg 12 hrs wkly *No. News Employees:* 1 *Target Audience:* 18-54;young adult *Adv. Rates:* 30; 28; 30; 24
Guilford Dye, President
Gudrun Dye, Operations Dir
Mike Spencer, Station Manager

***KULV**
09-22-2003; 97.1 mhz FM *Hrs Open:* 24; 0.13 kw; 1978 ft.; N39 7 50 W123 4 32
1425 North Market Blvd, Suite 9, Sacramento, CA 95834 US
(800) 525-5683, *Fax:* (916) 251-1650
www.klove.com
klove@klove.com
License: Ukiah, Mendocino County, CA held by Educational Media Foundation.
Group Owner: EMF Broadcasting
Nat'l Network: K-Love
Arbitron Metro Market: Ukiah, CA *Format:* Christian *No. News Employees:* 3 *Target Audience:* 25-44; Judeo Christian, female
Darrell Chambliss, Chairman
Mike Novak, President and CEO
Eric Allen, General Sales Mgr
David Pierce, Programming Director
Ed Lenane, News Director
Sam Wallington, Engineering Dir
Richard Hunt, News Reporter
Marya Morgan, NewsReporter
Laura Daniels, News Reporter
Tim Luttrell, News Reporter
Kenny Noble Cortes, News Reporter
Darren Vinson, News Reporter

Vacaville

KUIC
11-01-1968; 95.3 mhz FM *Hrs Open:* 24; 0.49 kw; 2024 ft.; N38 23 44 W122 5 56
Suite 525, 7901 Stoneridge Drive, Pleasanton, CA 94588 US
(707) 446-0200, *Fax:* (707) 446-0122
www.kuic.com
gm@KUIC.com
License: Vacaville, Solano County, CA held by KUIC Inc.
Group Owner: Coast Radio Company Inc.; (acq 10-6-98)
Arbitron Metro Market: Vacaville, CA *Format:* Adult Contemp *Hrs. of News Programming:* news progmg one hr wkly *No. News Employees:* 3 *Target Audience:* General; middle class, professionals *Adv. Rates:* 120;110; 120; 90
Jim Levitt, CEO
John Levitt, President

Vallejo

KDIA
03-19-1996; 1640 khz AM *Hrs Open:* 24
600 East Main Street, Vacaville, CA 95688 US
(510) 222-4242, *Fax:* (510) 262-9054
www.kdia.com
andy.santamaria@kdia.com
License: Vallejo, CA held by Baybridge Communications L.L.C.
Arbitron Metro Market: San Francisco *Format:* Religious *Special Programming:* Relg 5 hrs, Black 2 hrs, gospel 7 hrs wkly *Hrs. of News Programming:* News progmg 5 hrs wkly *Target Audience:* 25-54.
Clifford Brown, Operations Dir
Andy Santamaria, General Manager

KDYA
08-01-1947; 1190 khz AM *Hrs Open:* 24; 1 kw-D, NDD; N38 7 2 W122 15 20
600 East Main Street, Vacaville, CA 95688 US
(510) 222-4242, *Fax:* (510) 262-9054
www.gospel1190.net
andysantamaria@gospel1190.net
License: Vallejo, CA held by Baybridge Communications L.L.C.
Arbitron Metro Market: San Francisco *Format:* Gospel *Special Programming:* Relg 5 hrs, Black 2 hrs, gospel 7 hrs wkly *Hrs. of News Programming:* News progmg 5 hrs wkly *Target Audience:* 25-54.
Andy Santamaria, President
Clifford Brown, Programming Director

Ventura

KBBY-FM
12-27-1962; 95.1 mhz FM; 12.5 kw; 876 ft.; N34 6 47 W119 3 34
P.O. Box 699, Ventura, CA 93002 US
(805) 642-8595, *Fax:* (805) 656-5838
www.b951.com
info@cumulus.com
License: Ventura, Ventura County, CA held by Cumulus Licensing Corp.
Group Owner: Cumulus Media Inc.; (acq 9-22-00; grpsl)
Nat'l Network: Westwood One
Arbitron Metro Market: Ventura, CA *Format:* Adult Contemp *Target Audience:* 18-54.
Tom Watson, Operations Dir
Gail Furillo, General Manager
Todd Violet, Programming Director

KHAY
01-01-1962; 100.7 mhz FM; 39 kw; 1211 ft.; N34 20 55 W119 19 57
P.O. Box 699, Ventura, CA 93002 US
(805) 642-8595, *Fax:* (805) 656-5838
www.khay.com
info@cumulus.com
License: Ventura, Ventura County, CA
Group Owner: Cumulus Media Inc.
Arbitron Metro Market: Oxnard-Ventura, CA *Format:* Country *Target Audience:* 18-54.
Tom Watson, Programming Director
Chris Cox, Program Director
Dave Bradley, Production Director

KUNX
10-15-1994; 1590 khz AM; 5 kw-D, DA2; 5 kw-N, DA2; N34 14 13 W119 12 9
715 Broadway, Ste 320, Santa Monica, CA 90401 US
(805) 289-1400, *Fax:* (805) 644-7906
info@kunx.com
License: Ventura, CA held by Gold Coast Broadcasting LLC.
Group Owner: Gold Coast Broadcasting LLC; (acq 2-10-97; $2 million with KFYV(FM) Ojai)
Arbitron Metro Market: Ventura, CA *Format:* News, News/Talk, 86 *Target Audience:* 35 plus.
Chip Ehrhardt, General Manager
Mark Elliott, Programming Director

KVEN
03-01-1948; 1450 khz AM; 1 kw-U, ND1; N34 15 39 W119 14 28
One Office Park Circle, Suite 300, Birmingham, AL 35223 US
(805) 642-8595, *Fax:* (805) 656-5838
www.kven.com
info@cumulus.com
License: Ventura, CA held by Cumulus Licensing Corp.
Group Owner: Cumulus Media Inc.; (acq 9-22-00; grpsl)
Arbitron Metro Market: Oxnard, CA *Format:* Oldies *Target Audience:* 25 plus; affluent, educated, professional with above average income
Gail Furillo, General Manager
Ernie Bingham, General Sales Mgr
Bo Jaxson, Programming Director
Jennifer Caldwell, Promotions Manager
Cyndy Abarre, News Director
J.D. Strahler, Chief Engineer
Sommer Frisk, Director of Sales
NeryReyes, Human Resources Manager

KSSC
11-01-1989; 107.1 mhz FM *Hrs Open:* 24; 0.37 kw; 1296 ft.; N34 20 55 W119 19 57
11 Skyline Drive, Hawthorne, NY 10532 US
(323) 90-6100, *Fax:* (323) 900-6119
www.superestrella.com
comments@superestrella.com
License: Ventura, Ventura County, CA held by Entravision Holdings LLC.
Group Owner: Entravision Communications Corp.; (acq 4-1-03; grpsl).
Arbitron Metro Market: Oxnard-Ventura, CA *Format:* Spanish
Karl Meyer, General Manager
Juan Navarro, Interactive Sales Manager
Elias Autran, Promotions Manager
John Regalado, Multimedia Programming Chief

Victorville

KVFG
08-18-1980; 103.1 mhz FM *Hrs Open:* 24; 0.25 kw; 1558 ft.; N34 36 44 W117 17 29
320 West College Avenue, Pleasant Gap, PA 16823 US
(909) 825-9525, *Fax:* (909) 825-2948
www.kfrog103.com
Kimberly.Martinez@cbsradio.com
License: Victorville, San Bernardino County, CA held by CBS Radio Station Inc.
Group Owner: CBS Radio; (acq 7-19-00; $3,537,500 with KRAK(AM) Hesperia).
Nat'l Network: ABC
TV Affiliate: ESPN *Format:* News, News/Talk, 84, Talk *Target Audience:* 25-54.
Tom Hoyt, General Manager
Bill Pettus, Station Manager

***KHMS**
01-03-1993; 88.5 mhz FM *Hrs Open:* 24; 0.2 kw; 1512 ft.; N34 36 40 W117 17 20 *Rebroadcasts:* Rebroadcasts KSOS(FM) Las Vegas 100%
2201 South 6th Street, Las Vegas, NV 89104 US
(702) 731-5452, *Fax:* (702) 731-1992
www.sosradio.net
brad@sosradio.net
License: Victorville, San Bernardino County, CA held by Faith Communications Corp.
Group Owner: Faith Communications Corp.; (acq 4-5-91;
Format: Adult Contemp, Christian *Special Programming:* Family 2 hrs wkly *Target Audience:* 25-44; young families
Jack French, CEO
Brad Staley, General Manager
Scott Herrold, Programming Director
Chris Staley, Promotions Manager
Rick Hall, Music Director

***KXRD**
10-18-1994; 89.5 mhz FM *Hrs Open:* 24; 1.25 kw; 1411 ft.; N34 36 44 W117 17 27 *Rebroadcasts:* Rebroadcasts KLRD(FM) Yucaipa 100%
1425 North Market Blvd, Suite 9, Sacramento, CA 95834 US
(888) 937-2471, *Fax:* (916) 251-1650 (700) 528-9246
www.air1.com
info@air1.com
License: Victorville, San Bernardino County, CA held by Educational Media Foundation.
Group Owner: EMF Broadcasting; (acq 1-22-99).
Nat'l Network: Air 1
Arbitron Metro Market: Omaha, NE *Format:* Alternative, Christian *Hrs. of News Programming:* News progmg 7 hrs wkly *Target Audience:* 18-34.
Mike Novak, President
Fernando Chaidez, Operations Dir
David Pierce, Programming Director
Ed Lenane, News Director
Sam Wallington, Engineering Dir
Marya Morgan, News Reporter
Richard Hunt, News Reporter

Visalia

***KARM**
01-01-1990; 89.7 mhz FM; 1 kw; 810 ft.; N36 38 10 W118 56 32
1300 South Woodland Dr., Visalia, CA 93291 US
(559) 627-5276, *Fax:* (559) 627-5288
www.mypromisefm.com
info@promisefm.com
License: Visalia, Tulare County, CA held by Harvest Broadcasting Co.
Nat'l Network: ABC
Arbitron Metro Market: Visalia, CA *Format:* Christian, Religious
Dr. Richard Dunn, Chairman
Loren Olson, General Manager

***KDUV**
01-01-1992; 88.9 mhz FM; 1 kw; 2648 ft.; N36 17 14 W118 50 17
130 N. Kelsey, Ste H-123, Visalia, CA 93291 US
(559) 651-4111, *Fax:* (559) 651-4115
www.kduvfm.com
info@kduvfm.com
License: Visalia, Tulare County, CA held by Community Educational Broadcasting Inc.
Arbitron Metro Market: Visalia-Tulare-Hanford, CA *Format:* Christian
Bob Croft, President
Bob Croft, General Manager
Jeremy Morris, Programming Director
Jeremy Morris, News Director

KFSO-FM
09-01-1951; 92.9 mhz FM; 17.5 kw; 853 ft.; N36 38 10 W118 56 34
600 Congress Ave., Suite 1400, Austin, TX 78701 US
(559) 230-4300, *Fax:* (559) 243-4301
www.lapreciosa929.com
info@lapreciosa929.com

License: Visalia, Tulare County, CA held by Capstar TX L.P.
Group Owner: Clear Channel Communications Inc.; (acq 2-4-2009)
Arbitron Metro Market: Visalia, CA *Format:* Tejano *Special Programming:* Religious 3 hrs wkly
Jeff Negrete, General Manager
Tony Rainaldi, General Sales Mgr
Greg Hoffman, Programming Director

KRZR
12-24-1976; 1400 khz AM *Hrs Open:* 24; 1 kw-U, ND1; 499 ft; N36 21 14 W119 17 2
600 Congress Ave., Suite 1400, Austin, TX 78701 US
(559) 230-4300, *Fax:* (559) 243-4301
www.krzr.com
info@krzr.com
License: Visalia, CA held by Capstar TX L.P.
Group Owner: Clear Channel Communications Inc.; (acq 8-30-00; grpsl).
Arbitron Metro Market: Fresno, CA *Format:* Rock/AOR *Hrs. of News Programming:* News progmg one hr wkly *Target Audience:* 18-34; male *Adv. Rates:* 80; 80; 80; 50
Jeff Megrete, General Manager
Tony Rainaldi, General Sales Mgr
Paul Wilson, Programming Director
Dave Case, Chief Engineer

KSEQ
10-01-1984; 97.1 mhz FM; 17 kw; 778 ft.; N36 38 8 W118 56 32
166 West Putnam St., Greenwich, CT 06830 US
(559) 627-9710, *Fax:* (559) 627-1590
www.q97.com
License: Visalia, Tulare County, CA held by Buckley Broadcasting of Monterey.
Group Owner: Buckley Broadcasting Corp.; (acq 12-87)
Nat'l Reps: Eastman Radio
Arbitron Metro Market: Visalia-Tulare-Hanford, CA *Format:* Contemporary Hits/Top 40 *Target Audience:* 18-49.
Rick Buckley, President
Ray McCarty, Operations Dir
John Sterling, General Manager
Tommy Del Rio, Operations Manager

KSLK
11-22-1994; 96.1 mhz FM *Hrs Open:* 24; 4.8 kw; Ant 360 ft; N36 21 59 W119 10 46
7179 N. Van Ness Blvd., Fresno, CA 93711
(559) 259-5455, *Fax:* (559) 439-5714
bobeurich@aol.com
License: Visalia, Tulare County, CA held by New Visalia Broadcasting Inc.
Nat'l Network: ESPN Deportes Radio Network
Population Served: 1,500,000 *Arbitron Metro Market:* Visalia-Tulare *No. News Employees:* 2
Robert Eurich, President

KEZL(AM)
01-01-1948; 1400 khz AM; 1 kw-U; N36 21 14 W119 17 02
Rebroadcasts: Rebroadcasts KCBL(AM) Fresno 100%
83 E. Shaw Ave, Suite 150, Fresno, CA 93710-7616
(559) 230-4300, *Fax:* (559) 243-4301
www.foxsportsradio1340.com
greghoffman@clearchannel.com
License: Visalia, Tulare County, CA held by Capstar TX L.P.
Group Owner: Clear Channel Communications Inc.; (acq 8-30-2000; grpsl)
Nat'l Reps: McGavren Guild
Population Served: 501,362 *Arbitron Metro Market:* Fresno, CA *Format:* Sports *Target Audience:* 25-64; general
Tony Rainaldi, General Sales Mgr
Greg Hoffman, Programming Director

Vista

KCEO
11-03-1967; 1000 khz AM *Hrs Open:* 24
550 Laguna Drive, Carlsbad, CA 92008 US
(760) 729-1000, *Fax:* (760) 476-9604
www.kceoradio.com
reception@astorbroadcastgroup.com
License: Vista, CA held by North County Broadcasting Corp.
Group Owner: Astor Broadcast Group; (acq 4-30-97; $2.6 million).
Nat'l Network: Westwood One
Arbitron Metro Market: San Diego, CA *Format:* Talk *Hrs. of News Programming:* News progmg 20 hrs wkly *Target Audience:* 35 plus.
Arthur Astor, President
Rick Roome, Operations Dir
Susan Burke, Executive Vice President

Walnut

***KSAK**
01-10-1974; 90.1 mhz FM *Hrs Open:* 24; 0.004 kw; 417 ft.; N34 2 46 W117 51 37
1100 N. Grand Avenue, Walnut, CA 91789 US
(909) 594-5611 EXT. 4678
www.ksak.com
ksak@mtsac.edu
License: Walnut, Los Angeles County, CA held by Mount San Antonio Community College District.
Wire Services: UPI
Arbitron Metro Market: Walnut, CA *Format:* Christian *Target Audience:* 18-25; students
Cason Smith, General Manager

Walnut Creek

KKDV
12-10-1959; 92.1 mhz FM; 3 kw; 79 ft.; N37 54 2 W122 5 7
200 Concord Plaza, Suite 600, San Antonio, TX 78216 US
(925) 944-6300, *Fax:* (925) 416-1211
www.kkdv.com
License: Walnut Creek, Contra Costa County, CA held by Contra Costa County Radio Inc.
Group Owner: Coast Radio Company Inc.; (acq 7-29-2005; $7 million)
Regional Reps: Lotus.
Arbitron Metro Market: San Francisco *Format:* Adult Contemp *Special Programming:* Hometown Mornings 24 hrs wkly *Target Audience:* Adults; 25-54 *Adv. Rates:* 65; 65; 65;65
John Levitt, General Manager
Jim Hampton, Programming Director

Wasco

***KFHL**
01-01-2005; 91.7 mhz FM; 6 kw; 240 ft.; N35 24 55 W119 14 1
P O Box 7346, Las Vegas, NV 89125 US
(661) 872-0030
www.kfhlradio.com
kfhlradio@yahoo.com
License: Wasco, Kern County, CA held by Mary V. Harris Foundation.
Arbitron Metro Market: Wasco, CA *Format:* Christian, Talk
Robin Wade, Programming Director

Wasco-Greenacres

KERN
05-17-1950; 1180 khz AM *Hrs Open:* 24; 50 kw-D, DA2; 10 kw-N, DA2; N35 34 17 W119 19 26
Mailing Address: 110 S. Montclair St.#205, Bakersfield, CA 93309 US
Second Address: 1400 Easton Dr., Suite 144, Bakersfield, CA 93309
(661) 328-1410, *Fax:* (661) 283-7992
www.kernradio.com
news@kernradio.com
License: Wasco-Greenacres, CA held by AGM California.
Group Owner: American General Media; (acq 9-27-2004; $1.83 million)
Nat'l Reps: Salem
Arbitron Metro Market: Bakersfield, CA *Format:* News, News/Talk, 86
Toni Snyder, General Manager
Toni Snyder, General Sales Mgr
Chris Squires, Programming Director

Weaverville

KHRD
01-01-2000; 103.1 mhz FM *Hrs Open:* 24; 0.6 kw; 3593 ft.; N40 36 10 W122 38 58
P. O. Box 7568, Chico, CA 95927 US
(530) 244-9700, *Fax:* (530) 342-2260
www.red1031.com
rhealy@resultsradiomail.com
License: Weaverville, Trinity County, CA held by Results Radio of Redding Licensee LLC.
Group Owner: Fritz Communications Inc.; (acq 6-11-99; grpsl).
Arbitron Metro Market: Redding, CA *Format:* Classic Rock
Beth Tappan, General Manager
Laurie Curto, General Sales Mgr
Rob Reid, Programming Director
Bryant Smith, Chief Engineer

Weed

KCWH
11-01-1983; 102.3 mhz FM *Hrs Open:* 24; 15.5 kw; 1942 ft.; N41 21 30 W122 12 21
113 East Alma, Mt. Shasta, CA 96067 US
(530) 926-5946, *Fax:* (530) 926-0830
kcwhfm@yahoo.com
License: Weed, Siskiyou County, CA held by TRC Enterprises, LLC
Format: Contemporary Hits/Top 40, Adult Contemp *Special Programming:* Nostalgia 2 hrs wkly *Hrs. of News Programming:* news progmg 6 hrs wkly *No. News Employees:* 1 *Target Audience:* 25-54. *Adv. Rates:* 13;12; 10; na
Rick Martin, General Manager
Al Blackmore, General Sales Mgr

West Covina

KALI
09-25-1963; 900 khz AM *Hrs Open:* 24; 0.5 kw-D, DA2; 0.079 kw-N, DA2; N34 1 54 W117 56 6
449 Broadway, New York, NY 10013 US
(562) 401-4030, *Fax:* (562) 401-4032
www.radiozion.net
contactenos@zionmultimedia.com
License: West Covina, CA held by Multicultural Radio Broadcasting Licensee LLC.
Group Owner: Multicultural Radio Broadcasting Inc.; (acq 10-5-98; $9 million).
Arbitron Metro Market: Downet, CA *Format:* Christian
Arthur Liu, President
David Sweeney, Operations Dir
Alan Mok, Programming Director

KRCV
11-18-1957; 98.3 mhz FM *Hrs Open:* 24; 6 kw; 299 ft.; N34 4 18 W117 48 46
610 South Ardmore Avenue, Los Angeles, CA 90005 US
(818) 500-4500, *Fax:* (818) 500-4560
www.univision.com
License: West Covina, Los Angeles County, CA held by HBC License Corp.
Group Owner: Univision Radio; (acq 9-22-2003; grpsl).
Arbitron Metro Market: Los Angeles, CA *Format:* Oldies *Hrs. of News Programming:* News progmg 3 hrs wkly *Target Audience:* 18-49; Sp speaking Hispanics, primarily of Mexican origin
Jason Strongin, General Sales Mgr
Amalia Gonzalez, Programming Director
Tom Koza, Chief Engineer

West Sacramento

KCTC
04-01-1945; 1320 khz AM *Hrs Open:* 24
401 City Avenue, Suite 409, Bala Cynwyd, PA 19004 US
(916) 334-7777, *Fax:* (916) 339-4280
www.espn1320.net
License: West Sacramento, CA held by Entercom Sacramento License LLC.
Group Owner: Entercom Communications Corp.; (acq 10-17-97)
Nat'l Network: ESPN Radio
Arbitron Metro Market: Sacramento, CA *Format:* Sports
John Geary, Operations Dir
Rich Ripley, General Sales Mgr
Brian Lopez, Programming Director
Lizann Hunt, Promotions Manager

KSMH
02-01-1999; 1620 khz AM *Hrs Open:* 24
605 West Lake Blvd., Suite 5, Tahoe City, CA 96145 US
(916) 535-0500, *Fax:* (916) 535-0504
www.ihradio.org
info@ihradio.org
License: West Sacramento, CA held by IHR Educational Broadcasting.
Group Owner: IHR Educational Broadcasting; (acq 4-28-99; $475,000 with KAHI(AM) Auburn).
Arbitron Metro Market: Loomis, CA *Format:* Religious
David Hornbek, Station Manager

Westwood

***KJCQ**
01-01-2006; 88.5 mhz FM; 0.8 kw vert; 2352 ft.; N40 14 0 W121 1 11 *Rebroadcasts:* Rebroadcasts KJCU(FM) Fort Bragg 100% US
(866) 466-5989, *Fax:* (573) 449-7770
www.kwtw.org
recep@kwtw.org
License: Westwood, Lassen County, CA held by Calvary Chapel of Costa Mesa Inc.
Group Owner: CSN International
Arbitron Metro Market: Westwood, CA *Format:* Religious
Charles Smith, President

Williams

***KARA**
10-28-2003; 99.1 mhz FM *Hrs Open:* 24; 0.9 kw; 108 ft.; N39 8 7 W122 7 58
1425 N Market Blvd, Suite 9, Sacramento, CA 95834 US
(888) 937-2471, *Fax:* (916) 251-1650
www.air1.com
info@air1.com
License: Williams, Colusa County, CA held by Educational Media Foundation.
Group Owner: EMF Broadcasting
Nat'l Network: Air 1
Arbitron Metro Market: Sacramento, CA *Format:* Alternative, Christian *No. News Employees:* 3 *Target Audience:* 18-35; Judeo-Christian, female
Darrell Chambliss, Chairman
Alan Mason, COO
Mike Novak, President and CEO
Ed Lenane, News Director
Sam Wallington, Engineering Dir
Tracy Butler, Traffic Manager
Larry Moody, Director
Mitch Barnhart, Director
David R. Ferry,Director
Walter Golembeski, Director
David Pierce, Chief Creative Officer

Willits

KLLK
08-05-1985; 1250 khz AM *Hrs Open:* 5 AM-midnight; 5 kw-D, DA2; 2.5 kw-N, DA2; N39 23 58 W123 19 20 *Rebroadcasts:* Rebroadcasts KUKI(AM) Ukiah 100%
1799-2 Silverado Trail, Napa, CA 94558 US
(707) 263-6113, *Fax:* (707) 466-5852
ukiah@bicoastalspots.com
License: Willits, CA held by Bicoastal Media Licenses, LLC
Group Owner: Bicoastal Media L.L.C.; (acq 7-28-2006; grpsl)
Arbitron Metro Market: San Francisco, CA *Format:* Spanish *Hrs. of News Programming:* News progmg 8 hrs wkly *Target Audience:* 18-49; adults who like a progsv mix of modern rock mus
Alan Mathews, General Manager
Kevin Mostyn, Chief Engineer

KMKX
02-19-2000; 93.5 mhz FM *Hrs Open:* 24; 0.89 kw; 2874 ft.; N39 30 59 W123 5 21
12 West Valley Street, 1799-2 Silverado Trail, Napa, CA 94558 US
(707) 462-1483, *Fax:* (707) 462-4670
www.maxrock.com
License: Willits, Mendocino County, CA held by Radio Millennium L L C
Nat'l Network: Westwood One
Arbitron Metro Market: Redding, CA *Format:* Rock/AOR *Hrs. of News Programming:* news progmg 1 hr wkly *No. News Employees:* 1 *Target Audience:* 18-60; adults *Adv. Rates:* 24; 22; 24; 18
Guilford Dye, President
Gudrun Dye, Operations Dir
Guil Dye, General Manager
Mike Spencer, Station Manager

***KZYZ**
01-01-1995; 91.5 mhz FM *Hrs Open:* 18; 1.7 kw; 1788 ft.; N39 19 35 W123 16 10 *Rebroadcasts:* Rebroadcasts KZYX(FM) Philo 100%
P.O. Box 1, Philo, CA 95466 US
(707) 895-2324, *Fax:* (707) 895-2451
www.kzyx.org
uw@kzyx.org.
License: Willits, Mendocino County, CA held by Mendocino County Public Broadcasting.
Arbitron Metro Market: Willits, CA *Format:* News, Talk, 94
Rich Culbertson, Operations Dir
John Coate, General Manager
David Steffen, General Sales Mgr
Mary Aigner, Programming Director

Willows

KIQS
12-29-1961; 1560 khz AM; 0.25 kw-D, NDD; N39 31 44 W122 10 9
P. O. Box 7, Willows, CA 95988 US
(209) 277-8433, *Fax:* (209) 430-2733
avianhelpprogramcoordinator@yahoo.com
License: Willows, CA held by Radio Pan de Vida LLC
Format: Christian
Martin Godinez, General Manager

Windsor

KJOR
06-20-1997; 104.1 mhz FM *Hrs Open:* 24; 0.9 kw; 305 ft.; N38 32 28 W122 54 5
Mailing Address: 6640 Redwood Drive, Suite 202, Rohnert Park, CA 94928 US
Second Address: P.O. Box 6940, Oxnard, CA 93031
(805) 240-2070, *Fax:* (805) 240-5960
www.radiolazer.com
alfredop@radiolazer.com
License: Windsor, Sonoma County, CA held by Lazer Licenses LLC.
Group Owner: Lazer Broadcasting Corp.; (acq 6-29-2006; $6.85 million with KSRT(FM) Cloverdale).
Nat'l Reps: Christal
Format: Oldies *Target Audience:* 25-54.
Alfredo Plascencia, CEO

***KRCB-FM**
09-01-1993; 91.1 mhz FM *Hrs Open:* 24; 0.12 kw; 732 ft.; N38 44 25 W122 50 46
5850 Labath Avenue, Rohnert Park, CA 94928 US
(707) 584-2000, *Fax:* (707) 585-1363
www.krcb.org
listener@krcb.org
License: Windsor, Sonoma County, CA held by Rural California Broadcasting Corp.
Nat'l Network: NPR; PRI *Wire Services:* DAC
Arbitron Metro Market: Santa Rosa, CA *TV Affiliate:* *KRCB-TV affil. *Format:* News, News/Talk, 86 *Special Programming:* Folk 6 hrs, jazz 6 hrs wkly *Hrs. of News Programming:* news progmg 15 hrs wkly *No. NewsEmployees:* 1 *Target Audience:* General.
Nancy Dobbs, CEO
Nancy Dobbs, President
Robin Pressman, Programming Director
Larry Stratton, COO

***DKEZD**
1580 khz AM; Ant 43 ft
502 a Avenida Sevilla, Laguna Hills, CA 92653 US
(970) 669-9200
License: Windsor, CA held by Cedar Cove Broadcasting Inc.
Group Owner: Cedar Cove Broadcasting Inc.
Arbitron Metro Market: Estes Park, CO
Victor Michael Jr., President

Winton

KLOQ-FM
01-01-1994; 98.7 mhz FM *Hrs Open:* 24; 6 kw; 299 ft.; N37 16 41 W120 37 35
1176 Fairview Drive, Suite N, Carson City, NV 89701 US
(209) 723-2191, *Fax:* (209) 383-2950
www.radiolobo987.com
License: Winton, Merced County, CA held by Mapleton License of Merced LLC.
Group Owner: Mapleton Communications LLC; acq 6-1-2002; grpsl)
Arbitron Metro Market: Merced, CA *Format:* Tejano *Target Audience:* 25-49; Hispanic
Andrew Adams, General Manager
Damian Galaarza, General Sales Mgr

Woodlake

KFRR
09-01-1994; 104.1 mhz FM *Hrs Open:* 24; 17 kw; 853 ft.; N36 38 12 W118 56 34
966 East Essex Drive, Fresno, CA 93720 US
(559) 230-0104, *Fax:* (559) 230-0177
License: Woodlake, Tulare County, CA held by Wilks License Co.-Fresno LLC.
Group Owner: Wilks Broadcast Group LLC; (acq 6-1-2005; grpsl)
Nat'l Reps: McGavren Guild
Arbitron Metro Market: Fresno, CA *Format:* Alternative *Target Audience:* 18-34; young affluent adults
Kevin O'Rorke, General Manager
Jason Squires, Programming Director

Woodland

KMJE
10-01-1996; 101.5 mhz FM; 0.14 kw; 1975 ft.; N39 12 21 W121 49 11
Post Office Box 7568, Chico, CA 95927 US
(530) 673-2200, *Fax:* (530) 673-3010
www.gosunny.com
ccarothers@results.com
License: Woodland, Butte County, CA held by Results Radio Licensee L.L.C.
Group Owner: Fritz Communications Inc.; (acq 6-11-99; grpsl)
Arbitron Metro Market: Chico, CA *Format:* Adult Contemp *Hrs. of News Programming:* news progmg 7 hrs wkly *No. News Employees:* 1
Jack Fritz, President
Chris Carothers, Operations Dir
Gordon Rowntree, General Sales Mgr

KSFM
02-04-1961; 102.5 mhz FM; 50 kw; 499 ft.; N38 35 20 W121 43 30
600 New Hampshire Ave., N.W., Suite 1200, Washington, DC 20037 US
(916) 923-6800, *Fax:* (916) 922-2830
www.ksfm.com
info@ksfm.com
License: Woodland, Yolo County, CA held by Infinity Radio of Sacramento Inc.
Group Owner: CBS Radio; (acq 11-13-98; grpsl).
Nat'l Network: Westwood One
Arbitron Metro Market: Sacramento, CA *Format:* Blues *Target Audience:* 12-44.
Steve Cottingim, General Manager
Christian Salisbury, General Sales Mgr
Byron Kennedy, Programming Director
Kim Piazza, Promotions Manager
Mike DaSilva, Chief Engineer

Yermo

KRXV
04-01-1980; 98.1 mhz FM *Hrs Open:* 24; 1.55 kw; 2280 ft.; N34 59 43 W116 50 15
12381 Wilshire Blvd. Suite 105, Los Angeles, CA 90025 US
(760) 256-0326, *Fax:* (760) 256-9507
www.thehighwaystations.com
tim@highwayradio.com
License: Yermo, San Bernardino County, CA held by KHWY Inc.
Group Owner: KHWY Inc.
Nat'l Network: AP Radio
Arbitron Metro Market: Barstow, CA *Format:* Adult Contemp *Target Audience:* 25-54; travelers on I-15 & I-40 & loc communities
Howard Anderson, CEO
Timothy Anderson, Operations Dir
Judy Robinson, General Sales Mgr
Lance Todd, Programming Director
Thomas McNeill, Chief Engineer
Kirk Anderson, Executive Vice President

Yreka

***KSYC**
07-27-1947; 1490 khz AM *Hrs Open:* 24 hrs
P.O. Box 3463, Carefree, AZ 85377 US
(541) 552-6301, *Fax:* (541) 552-8565
www.ijpr.org
info@ijpr.org
License: Yreka, CA held by JPR Foundation Inc.
Nat'l Network: NPR; PRI
Arbitron Metro Market: Ashland, OR *Hrs. of News Programming:* news progmg 35 hrs wkly *No. News Employees:* 1
Ronald Kramer, CEO
Bryon Lambert, Operations Dir
Paul Westhelle, General Sales Mgr
Eric Teel, Programming Director
Ransom,Darin, News Director
Darin Ransom, Engineering Dir
Mitchell Christian, CFO
Eric Alan, Music Director

KSYC-FM
06-01-1983; 103.9 mhz FM; 10 kw; 2359 ft.; N41 36 36 W122 37 26
Mailing Address: P.O. Box 3463, Carefree, AZ 85377 US
Second Address: 316 Lawrence Ln., Yreka, CA 96097
(530) 842-4158, *Fax:* (530) 842-7635
www.ksyc1039.com
ksyc@4fast.net
License: Yreka, Siskiyou County, CA held by Jamison-Wolf Enterprises, Inc.
Arbitron Metro Market: Yreka, CA *Format:* Country *Adv. Rates:* 21; 21; 21; 18
Lee Jamison, General Manager
Kevin Sponsler, Programming Director

***KNYR**
01-01-1995; 91.3 mhz FM *Hrs Open:* 5AM-2am; 0.4 kw; 2365 ft.; N41 36 36 W122 37 26
P.O. Box 3175, Eugene, OR 97403 US
(541) 552-6301, *Fax:* (541) 552-8565
www.ijpr.org
jprinfo@sou.edu

License: Yreka, Siskiyou County, CA held by The State of Oregon, Acting By and Through the State Board of Higher Education for the Benefit of Southern Oregon University.
Nat'l Network: NPR; PRI
Arbitron Metro Market: Yreka, CA *Format:* News *Hrs. of News Programming:* news progmg 35 hrs wkly *No. News Employees:* 1
Ronald Kramer, CEO
Bryon Lambert, Operations Dir
Paul Westhelle, General Sales Mgr
Eric Teel, Programming Director
Darin Ransom, Engineering Dir
Kurt Katzmar, Disc Jockey
Valerie Ing-Miller, Disc Jockey
Eric Alan, MusicDirector
Betsy Byers, Administrative Assistant
Mitchell Christian, Director of Finance & Administration
Jill Hernandez, Accountant Technician

Yuba City

KOBO
06-01-1953; 1450 khz AM
449 Broadway, New York, NY 10013 US
(530) 742-5555, *Fax:* (530) 741-3758
License: Yuba City, CA held by Tom F. Huth.
Group Owner: Huth Broadcasting; (acq 12-17-2003; $200,000).
Format: Ethnic *Special Programming:* East Indian 3 hrs wkly
Thomas Huth, CEO

KUBA
01-01-1948; 1600 khz AM *Hrs Open:* 24
P.O. Box 309, Yuba City, CA 95992 US
(530) 673-1600, *Fax:* (530) 673-3010
www.kubaradio.com
info@lbimedia.com
License: Yuba City, CA held by Nevada County Broadcasters Inc.
Group Owner: Nevada County Broadcasters Inc.; (acq 8-9-2004; $500,000).
Nat'l Network: CBS Radio *Regional Network:* Calif. Agri-Radio
Wire Services: AP
Arbitron Metro Market: Yuba City, CA *Format:* News, News/Talk, 86 *Special Programming:* Farm 4 hrs, gospel 2 hrs, relg 2 hrs wkly *Hrs. of News Programming:* news progmg 15 hrs wkly *No. News Employees:* 2*Target Audience:* 35-64; community oriented *Adv. Rates:* 29; 24; 24; 13
Dave Bear, Operations Dir
Robert Harlan, General Manager
Chris Gilbert, News Director
John Black, Promotions Director
Lucy Spears, Public Affairs Director

Yucaipa

***KLRD**
07-15-1986; 90.1 mhz FM *Hrs Open:* 24; 0.55 kw; 3642 ft.; N34 3 18 W116 53 35
1425 North Market Blvd, Suite 9, Sacramento, CA 95834 US
(707) 528-9236, *Fax:* (916) 251-1650
www.air1.com
info@air1.com; aramirez@emfbroadcasting.com
License: Yucaipa, San Bernardino County, CA held by Educational Media Foundation.
Group Owner: EMF Broadcasting; (acq 1-22-99).
Nat'l Network: Air 1
Format: Alternative, Christian *Hrs. of News Programming:* News progmg 7 hrs wkly *Target Audience:* 18-34; Christians
Mike Novak, President
Fernando Chaidez, Operations Dir
Eric Allen, General Sales Mgr
David Pierce, Programming Director
Ed Lenane, News Director
Sam Wallington, Engineering Dir
Paul Goldsmith, Music Director

Yucca Valley

KNWH
04-03-1961; 1250 khz AM *Rebroadcasts:* Rebroadcasts KNWQ(AM) Palm Springs 100%
P.O. Box 908, 68474 29 Palms Hwy, Twentynine Palms, CA 92277 US
(760) 322-7890, *Fax:* (760) 322-5493
www.943knews.com
info@desertfun.com
License: Yucca Valley, CA held by MCC Radio LLC.
Group Owner: Morris Radio LLC; (acq 1-12-2005; $100,000)
Format: News, News/Talk, 86 *Hrs. of News Programming:* 4.5 hrs. news progmg wkly *No. News Employees:* 4 *Target Audience:* 25-54.
Angela Powers, Operations Dir
Jay White, General Manager
Scott Smith, General Sales Mgr
Virginia Nelson, Programming Director
Jose Rodriguez, Promotions Manager
John McMullen, News Director
John McMullen, Program Director

***KRTM**
01-01-1989; 88.1 mhz FM *Hrs Open:* 24; 0.14 kw; 1437 ft.; N34 4 55 W116 20 32
3000 W. Macarthur Blvd., Santa Ana, CA 92704 US
(951) 296-9694
www.krtmradio.com
steve@krtmradio.com
License: Yucca Valley, Riverside County, CA held by Penfold Communications Inc.
Arbitron Metro Market: Temecula, CA *Format:* Christian *Target Audience:* 25-54.
Chuck Smith, President
Jeff Smith, Operations Dir
Steve Bessette, General Manager

KDGL
08-01-1988; 106.9 mhz FM *Hrs Open:* 24; 4 kw horiz; 1371 ft.; N34 4 55 W116 20 32
725 Broad St., P.O. Box 936, Augusta, GA 30903 US
(760) 322-9890, *Fax:* (760) 322-5493
www.theeagle1069.com/
jennifer.shevlin@desertradiogroup.com
License: Yucca Valley, San Bernardino County, CA held by MCC Radio LLC.
Group Owner: Morris Radio LLC; (acq 1998; $2.25 million with KXPS(AM) Thousand Palms)
Nat'l Network: USA
Arbitron Metro Market: Yucca Valley, CA *Format:* Contemporary Hits/Top 40, Adult Contemp *Target Audience:* 25-54
Angela Powers, Operations Dir
Jay White, General Manager
Scott Smith, General Sales Mgr
Jennifer Shevlin, Programming Director
Jamie Kanai, Promotions Manager
Jennifer Shevlin, Program Director

Colorado

Alamosa

KALQ-FM
06-26-1969; 93.5 mhz FM; 2.8 kw; 131 ft.; N37 28 20 W105 51 13
Mailing Address: Box 179, Alamosa, CO 81101 US
Second Address: 292 Santa Fe, Alamosa, CO 81101
(719) 589-6644, *Fax:* (719) 589-0993
www.kalq935.com
info@kgiwkalq.com
License: Alamosa, Alamosa County, CO held by Community Broadcasting Corp.
Nat'l Network: ABC
Arbitron Metro Market: Alamosa, CO *Format:* Country
Dale Burns, President
Marilyn Burns, Operations Dir
Neil Hammer, General Manager
Evan Slack, General Sales Mgr
Mark Beatty, News Director
Will Williams, Chief Engineer
Helen Lozoya, Public Affairs Director

***KASF**
01-01-1967; 90.9 mhz FM *Hrs Open:* 24; 1.1 kw; 89 ft.; N37 28 20 W105 52 39
110 Richardson Ave., Alamosa, CO 81101 US
(719) 587-7871, *Fax:* (719) 587-7522
www.adams.edu
License: Alamosa, Alamosa County, CO held by Adams State College.
Arbitron Metro Market: Alamosa, CO *Format:* Contemporary Hits/Top 40 *Special Programming:* Gospel 4 hrs, talk 6 hrs, blues/jazz 6 hrs, reggae *Hrs. of News Programming:* News progmg one hr wkly *Target Audience:* Community; college and local
Beth Dussault, General Manager

KGIW
02-27-1929; 1450 khz AM *Hrs Open:* 6 AM-11 PM; 1 kw-U, ND1; N37 28 20 W105 51 13
Box 179, Alamosa, CO 81101 US
(719) 589-6644, *Fax:* (719) 589-0993
www.kgiwk450.com
info@kgiwkalq.com
License: Alamosa, CO held by Community Broadcasting Corp.
Nat'l Network: ABC
Format: Adult Contemp *Special Programming:* Sp 6 hrs, farm 6 hrs wkly *Hrs. of News Programming:* news progmg 25 hrs wkly *No. News Employees:* 1 *Target Audience:* 18-60.
Dale Burns, President
Neil Hammer, General Manager
Helen Lozoya, General Sales Mgr
Mark Beatty, News Director
Will Williams, Chief Engineer
Marilyn Burns, Executive Vice President
Evan Slack, Promotions Manager

***KHUI**
03-01-1993; 89.1 mhz FM *Hrs Open:* 24; 0.2 kw; 131 ft.; N37 30 33 W105 51 9
US
(808) 533-0065, *Fax:* (808) 524-2104
www.khuiradio.com
License: Alamosa, Honolulu County, CO held by Salem Media of Hawaii Inc.
Group Owner: Salem Communications Corp.; (acq 8-13-2004; $3.7 million with KHNR-FM Honolulu).
Nat'l Reps: McGavren Guild
Arbitron Metro Market: Honolulu, HI *Format:* Ethnic
Steve Miller, General Manager
Rudi Camello, General Sales Mgr

***KRZA**
10-26-1985; 88.7 mhz FM *Hrs Open:* 5 AM-midnight; 9.8 kw; 2077 ft.; N36 51 32 W106 0 28
528 Ninth Street, Alamasa, CO 81101 US
(719) 589-8844, *Fax:* (719) 587-0032
www.krza.org
manager@krza.org
License: Alamosa, Alamosa County, CO held by Equal Representation of Media Advocacy Corp.
Nat'l Network: NPR
Arbitron Metro Market: Alamosa, CO *Format:* Jazz, News *Special Programming:* Sp 14 hrs, Latin American 3 hrs, news 4 hrs wkly *Hrs. of News Programming:* news progmg 18 hrs wkly *No. News Employees:* 1 *TargetAudience:* General; adult progsv community oriented rural area
David Guerrero, President
Holly Felmlee, General Manager

Arvada

KDDZ
06-01-1998; 1690 khz AM
77 West 66th Street, 16th Floor, New York, NY 10023 US
(303) 783-0880, *Fax:* (303) 761-1774
www.radiodisney.com
License: Arvada, CO held by Radio Disney Group LLC.
Group Owner: ABC Inc.; (acq 7-16-98; $3.5 million with KADZ Arvada).
Nat'l Network: Radio Disney
Arbitron Metro Market: Lakewood, CO *Format:* Children
Tracy Wells, General Manager

Aspen

***KAJX**
07-07-1987; 91.5 mhz FM *Hrs Open:* 24; 0.38 kw horiz, 0.37 kw vert; -988 ft.; N39 11 48 W106 48 14
110 E Hallam St #134, Aspen, CO 81611 US
(970) 920-9000, *Fax:* (970) 544-8002
www.kajx.org
info@kajx.org
License: Aspen, Pitkin County, CO held by Roaring Fork Public Radio Inc.
Nat'l Network: NPR; PRI *Wire Services:* AP
Arbitron Metro Market: Aspen, CO *Format:* Jazz, News *Special Programming:* Bluegrass 2 hrs wkly *Hrs. of News Programming:* news progmg 50 hrs wkly *No. News Employees:* 3 *Target Audience:* General; Aspenresidents & tourists
Brent Gardner-Smith, General Manager
Steve Cole, Programming Director
Kirk Siegler, News Director

KSPN-FM
02-14-1970; 103.1 mhz FM *Hrs Open:* 24; 3 kw; -85 ft.; N39 13 33 W106 50 0
C/O Jerome S. Boros, 1290 Avenue of Americas, New York, NY 10104 US
(970) 925-5776, *Fax:* (970) 925-1142
www.kspnradio.com
studio@kspnradio.com
License: Aspen, Pitkin County, CO held by NRC Broadcasting Mountain Group LLC.
Group Owner: NRC Broadcasting Inc.; (acq 5-1-2007; grpsl)
Nat'l Reps: Christal

Arbitron Metro Market: Aspen, CO *Format:* Triple A *Hrs. of News Programming:* news progmg 6 hrs wkly *No. News Employees:* 2 *Target Audience:* 25-49; affluent, well educated people who live in resort areas
David Bach, Operations Dir
Colleen Barill, General Manager

KPVW
01-01-2000; 107.1 mhz FM *Hrs Open:* 24; 20.5 kw; 361 ft.; N39 18 56 W106 57 32
5770 Ruffin Rd., San Diego, CA 92123 US
(970) 927-7600, *Fax:* (970) 927-8001
jeloy@entravision.com
License: Aspen, Pitkin County, CO held by Entravision Holdings LLC.
Group Owner: Entravision Communications Corp.; (acq 12-13-01; $57,500).
Arbitron Metro Market: Grand Junction, CO *Format:* Tejano
Target Audience: Latino; 18-34
Walter Ulloa, CEO
Jeffery Liberman, President
Mario Carrera, General Manager
John DeLorenzo, CFO
Philip Wilkinson, COO

Aurora

KEZW
01-01-1954; 1430 khz AM *Hrs Open:* 24
10200 E. Girard Ave, Suite B131, Denver, CO 80321 US
(303) 967-2700, *Fax:* (303) 967-2747
www.kezw.com
info@kezw.com
License: Aurora, CO held by Entercom Denver License LLC.
Group Owner: Entercom Communications Corp.; (acq 7-24-02; with KOSI(FM) Denver).
Nat'l Reps: Katz Radio
Arbitron Metro Market: Denver-Boulder, CO *Format:* Adult Contemp, Big Band, 64 *Hrs. of News Programming:* News progmg 4 hrs wkly *Target Audience:* 35 plus; general
Joby Koren, General Sales Mgr
Rick Crandall, Programming Director
Tina Lorraine, Promotions Manager
Stephanie Walrath, News Director
Jeff Garrett, Chief Engineer

KMXA
09-12-1972; 1090 khz AM
2905 South King Road, San Jose, CA 95122 US
(303) 721-9210, *Fax:* (303) 832-3410
License: Aurora, CO held by Entravision Holdings LLC.
Group Owner: Entravision Communications Corp.; (acq 3-14-2000; grpsl).
Arbitron Metro Market: Denver, CO *Format:* Spanish *Target Audience:* 18-54; Hispanics
Mario Carrera, General Manager

Avon

KZYR
12-24-1984; 97.7 mhz FM *Hrs Open:* 24; 15 kw; 440 ft.; N39 38 5 W106 26 47
1400 Easton Road, Bakersfield, CA 93303 US
(970) 949-0140, *Fax:* (970) 949-1464
www.kzyr.com
tony@kzyr.com
License: Avon, Eagle County, CO held by Cool Radio LLC
Arbitron Metro Market: Avon, CO. *Format:* Triple A *Target Audience:* 18-54.
Thomas Dobrez, President
Tony Mauro, General Manager

Basalt

KNFO
07-01-1995; 106.1 mhz FM *Hrs Open:* 24; 1.6 kw; 364 ft.; N39 18 55 W106 57 36
C/O Jerome S. Boros, 1290 Avenue of Americas, New York, NY 10104 US
(970) 544-9100, *Fax:* (970) 544-9101
License: Basalt, Eagle County, CO held by NRC Broadcasting Mountain Group LLC.
Group Owner: NRC Broadcasting Inc.; (acq 5-1-2007; grpsl)
Nat'l Network: CBS
Format: News, Sports, 86 *Hrs. of News Programming:* news progmg 13 hrs wkly *No. News Employees:* 2 *Target Audience:* 35-64.
Tim Brown, CEO
David Bach, Operations Dir
Colleen Barill, General Manager
Dave Rogers, CFO

Bayfield

KLJH
07-01-2003; 107.1 mhz FM; 100 kw horiz; 1883 ft.; N37 21 46 W107 47 40
1105 West Apache, Farmington, NM 87401 US
(505) 327-7202, *Fax:* (505) 327-2163
www.kpcl.org
kpcl@kpcl.org
License: Bayfield, La Plata County, CO held by Voice Ministries of Farmington Inc.
Nat'l Reps: Salem
Arbitron Metro Market: Farmington, NM *Format:* Christian
Fareed Ayoub, General Manager

KAYF
01-01-2008; 92.5 mhz FM; 0.1 kw horiz; -272 ft.; N37 13 51 W107 35 11
US
(312) 204-9900
License: Bayfield, La Plata County, CO held by College Creek Media LLC.
Group Owner: College Creek Media LLC
Arbitron Metro Market: Bayfield, CO
Neal Robinson, President

Bennett

KONN-FM
01-01-1978; 107.1 mhz FM *Hrs Open:* 24; 100 kw; Ant 1,932 ft; N39 55 22 W103 58 18
3033 S. Parker Rd., Suite 700, Aurora, CO 80014
(303) 872-1500, *Fax:* (303) 872-1501
www.hot1071denver.com
License: Bennett, Adams County, CO held by Max Radio of Denver LLC
Group Owner: MAX Media L.L.C.; (acq 10-24-2005; $14 million)
Population Served: 332,354 *Arbitron Metro Market:* Aurora, CO
Format: Contemporary Hits/Top 40
Louise Espinosa, CFO
Jeff Norman, General Manager
Zac Davis, Programming Director
Lee Damschroder, Chief Engineer

Bethany

***KKWD(FM)**
104.9 mhz FM; 25 kw; Ant 341 ft; N37 58 43 W103 34 48
3290 Peachtree Lane NW, Altanta, GA 67864-0991
(404) 949-0700
www.kjil.com
kjil@kjil.com
License: Bethany, OK held by Radio License Holding CBC LLC
Population Served: 74,523 *Arbitron Metro Market:* Dodge City - Garden City - Liberal, KS *Format:* Christian, Religious
Robert Hughes, CEO
Glenn Hascall, Station Manager
Bill Lurwick, Program Director and Music Director
Delvin Kinser, News Director

Beulah

KFVR-FM
01-01-2001; 94.7 mhz FM *Hrs Open:* 24; 18 kw; 387 ft.; N37 52 40 W104 57 19
1470 Ben Sawyer Blvd, Suite 16, Mount Pleasant, SC 29464 US
(719) 254-6300, *Fax:* (719) 254-6303
License: Beulah, Otero County, CO held by Greeley Broadcasting Corp.
Group Owner: Greeley Broadcasting Corp.; (acq 11-30-2006; $125,000)
Format: Tejano
Ricardo Salazar, General Manager

Billings

KEWF(FM)
98.5 mhz FM; 100,000 watts; 113 meters; 45 45 51N 108 27 18W
4915 South Vine Street, Cherry Hills Village, CO 80113 USA
(425) 466-4628
www.985thewolf.com
License: Billings, Yellowstone County, MT
Group Owner: Benedetti Media Group

Black Forest

KLIM
05-08-1984; 1120 khz AM *Hrs Open:* 6 AM-sunset; 0.25 kw-D, NDD; N39 16 27 W103 42 49
Box 87, 165 E. Ave., Limon, CO 80828 US
(719) 775-8199
License: Black Forest, CO held by Kona Coast Radio II LLC
Group Owner: Kona Coast Radio LLC; (acq 3-7-96; $8,000).
Arbitron Metro Market: Colorado Sping, CO *Format:* Oldies
Alan Olson, General Manager

Boulder

KBCO
10-01-1955; 97.3 mhz FM; 94 kw horiz, 80 kw vert; 1539 ft.; N39 54 48 W105 17 32
Mailing Address: 50 East Rivercenter Blvd, Suite 1200, Covington, KY 41011 US
Second Address: 2500 Pearl St., Suite 315, Boulder, CO 80302
(303) 713-8000, *Fax:* (303) 930-6890
www.kbco.com
kbco@kbco.com
License: Boulder, Boulder County, CO held by Citicasters Licenses L.P.
Group Owner: Clear Channel Communications Inc.
Arbitron Metro Market: Denver, CO *Format:* Triple A
Lee Larsen, General Manager
Brigid Walje, General Sales Mgr
Scott Arbough, Programming Director

***KGNU-FM**
05-22-1978; 88.5 mhz FM *Hrs Open:* 24; 4 kw; 213 ft.; N39 59 33 W105 9 16
P.O. Box 885, Boulder, CO 80306 US
(303) 449-4885
www.kgnu.org
marty@kgnu.org
License: Boulder, Boulder County, CO held by Boulder Community Broadcast Association Inc.
Nat'l Network: PRI; NPR *Regional Network:* Colo. Pub.
Arbitron Metro Market: Denver-Boulder, CO *Format:* Variety/Diverse *Special Programming:* Black 7 hrs, folk 20 hrs, Sp 3 hrs, jazz 15 hrs, c *Hrs. of News Programming:* news progmg 30 hrs wkly *No. News Employees:* 2 *Target Audience:* General.
Evan Perkins, Operations Dir
Sam Fuqua, Station Manager
Faye Lamb, General Sales Mgr
John Schaefer, Programming Director
Maeve Conran, News Director
Joel Edelstein, News Director

KVCU
11-14-1973; 1190 khz AM *Hrs Open:* 24
1305 University Avenue, Boulder, CO 80306 US
(303) 492-5031, *Fax:* (303) 492-1369
www.radio1190.org
dj@radio1190.org
License: Boulder, CO held by The University of Colorado Foundation.
Arbitron Metro Market: Denver-Boulder, CO *Format:* Variety/Diverse *Special Programming:* Jazz 3 hrs wkly *Hrs. of News Programming:* news progmg 3 hrs wkly *No. News Employees:* 3 *Target Audience:* 25-44.
Mike Goldenberg, General Manager
Alex Sequin, Promotions Manager
Joe Oria, News Director
Henry Moffly, Production Director
Sam Goldner, Music Director
Michael Odbert, Student Operations Manager
Amy Moore-Shipley, Program Director& In-Studio/Interview Contact
Gracie Tomczak, Volunteer Coordinator
Allen Miller, Membership Coordinator

KCFC
02-15-1947; 1490 khz AM
701 Montgomery St., Fourth Floor, San Francisco, CA 94111 US
(303) 871-9191, *Fax:* (303) 733-3319
www.cpr.org
License: Boulder, CO held by Public Broadcasting of Colorado Inc.
Nat'l Network: NPR
Arbitron Metro Market: Centennail, CO *Format:* News *Target Audience:* General. *Adv. Rates:* 20; 20; 20; na
Max Wycisk, President
Sue Coughlin, General Sales Mgr

Breckenridge

KSMT
09-12-1975; 102.1 mhz FM *Hrs Open:* 24; 6 kw; -210 ft.; N39 29 44 W106 1 44
Mailing Address: 1400 Easton Road, Bakersfield, CA 93303 US
Second Address: 130 Ski Hill Rd., Suite 240, Breckenridge, CO 80424

RADIO - U.S.

(970) 453-2234, *Fax:* (970) 453-5425
www.ksmtradio.com
ksmtstudio@nrcbroadcasting.com
License: Breckenridge, Summit County, CO held by NRC Broadcasting Mountain Group LLC.
Group Owner: NRC Broadcasting Inc.; (acq 5-1-2007; grpsl)
Arbitron Metro Market: Breckenridge, CO *Format:* Triple A
Special Programming: Funk, hip hop, local & reggae *Hrs. of News Programming:* news progmg 12 hrs wkly *No. News Employees:* 1 *Target Audience:* 18-44; upscale adults, heavy ski & outdoor industry consumers *Adv. Rates:* 35; 30; 35; 27
Lisa Korry-Cheek, General Manager

***KMPB**
06-01-2008; 88.7 mhz FM *Hrs Open:* 24; 0.3 kw; -249 ft.; N39 29 44 W106 1 44
Mailing Address: US
Second Address: Ship 136 Lake Dillon Drive, Dillon, CO 80435
(970) 468-0905, *Fax:* (970) 468-0286
www.mountainpublicradio.org
comments@mountainpublicradio.org
License: Breckenridge, Summit County, CO held by Cedar Cove Broadcasting Inc.
Group Owner: Cedar Cove Broadcasting Inc.; (acq 8-10-2007; $280,000)
Nat'l Network: AP Network News *Wire Services:* AP
Arbitron Metro Market: Breckenridge, CO *Format:* Variety/Diverse *Hrs. of News Programming:* news progmg 3 hrs wkly *No. News Employees:* 2 *Target Audience:* 35+
M.R. Murray, President
Victor Michael Jr., Operations Dir

Breen

KLLV
09-19-1984; 550 khz AM *Hrs Open:* 24; 1.8 kw-D, NDD; N37 11 2 W108 4 54
Mailing Address: 14780 Hwy 140, Breen, CO 81326 US
Second Address: 14780 Hwy. 140, Breen, CO 81326
(970) 247-8955
License: Breen, CO held by Daystar Radio Ltd.
Arbitron Metro Market: Breen, CO *Format:* Christian, Gospel, 74 *Hrs. of News Programming:* New progmg 2 hrs wkly *Target Audience:* General.
Sharon Harper, General Manager
Debbie Baker, Programming Director
Jim Alexander, Chief Engineer

Brighton

KLVZ
04-26-1956; 810 khz AM
P.O. Box 3003, Blue Bell, PA 19422 US
(303) 433-5500, *Fax:* (303) 433-1555
www.810klvz.com
klvz@crawfordbroadcasting.com
License: Brighton, CO held by KLZ Radio Inc.
Group Owner: Crawford Broadcasting Co.; (acq 12-10-93; $700,000;
Arbitron Metro Market: Denver, CO *Format:* Christian *Target Audience:* 18-49.
Donald Crawford, President
Mike Triem, General Manager
Teresa Johnston, Station Manager

Broomfield

KWOF
06-01-1967; 92.5 mhz FM *Hrs Open:* 24; 57 kw horiz, 56 kw vert; 1237 ft.; N40 5 47 W104 54 4
433 E. Las Colina Blvd, #1130, Irving, TX 75039 US
(303) 832-5665, *Fax:* (303) 832-7000
www.925thewolf.com
info@925thewolf.com
License: Broomfield, Boulder County, CO held by Wilks License Co.-Denver LLC.
Group Owner: Wilks Broadcast Group LLC; (acq 3-5-2009; grpsl)
Arbitron Metro Market: Denver-Boulder, CO *Format:* Country *Hrs. of News Programming:* news progmg 2 hrs wkly *No. News Employees:* 1 *Target Audience:* 35-64; educated, upscale, active professionals, ethnic
Barry Remington, General Manager
Brenda Egger, General Sales Mgr
Randy ""Shotgun"" Shannon, Programming Director
Barry Walters, Chief Engineer

Brush

KPRB
11-02-1998; 106.3 mhz FM *Hrs Open:* 24; 7 kw; 249 ft.; N40 13 2 W103 41 46.1
Mailing Address: 231 Main Street, Fort Morgan, CO 80701 US
Second Address: 220 State St., Suite 106, Fort Morgan, CO 80701
(970) 867-7271, *Fax:* (970) 867-2676
www.b106.com
b106@b106.com
License: Brush, Morgan County, CO
Group Owner: Northeast Colorado Broadcasting LLC
Nat'l Network: ABC *Wire Services:* AP
Format: Adult Contemp *Hrs. of News Programming:* news progmg one hr wkly *No. News Employees:* 1 *Target Audience:* 18-45; females
Alec Creighton, Programming Director

KSIR
08-01-1977; 1010 khz AM *Hrs Open:* 24; 25 kw-D, DA1; 0.28 kw-N, DA1; N40 18 50 W103 35 30
Mailing Address: 231 Main St, Ft Morgan, CO 80701 US
Second Address: 220 State St., Suite 106, Fort Morgan, CO 80701
(970) 867-7271, *Fax:* (970) 867-2676
www.ksir.com
ksir@necolorado.com
License: Brush, CO held by Northeast Colorado Broadcasting LLC
Group Owner: Northeast Colorado Broadcasting LLC; acq 7-1-2003; grpsl).
Nat'l Network: ABC *Wire Services:* AP
Arbitron Metro Market: Fort Morgan, CO *Format:* Agriculture, Sports, 86 *Hrs. of News Programming:* news progmg 5 hrs wkly *No. News Employees:* 2 *Target Audience:* 25-65; farmers, ranchers, sports fans
Alec Creighton, General Manager
Theresa Leake, General Sales Mgr
Lorrie Boyer, Programming Director

***KLZV**
91.3 mhz FM; 6 kw; 423 ft.; N40 8 56 W103 17 4
16075 W Belleview Ave, Morrison, CO 80465 US
(800) 525-5683, *Fax:* (916) 251-1650
www.klove.com
klove@klove.com
License: Brush, Logan County, CO held by Educational Media Foundation.
Group Owner: EMF Broadcasting; (acq 10-2-2003; grpsl).
Nat'l Network: K-Love
Arbitron Metro Market: Brush, CO *Format:* Christian *No. News Employees:* 13 *Target Audience:* 25-44; Judeo Christian, female
Darrell Chambliss, Chairman
Mike Novak, President and CEO
Jennifer Lohman, Operations Dir
Eric Allen, General Sales Mgr
David Pierce, Chief Creative Officer and Programming Director
Ed Lenane, News Director
Sam Wallington,Engineering Dir
Scott Smith, Music Director
Richard Hunt, News Reporter
Marya Morgan, News Reporter
Tracy Butler, Traffic Manager
Alan Mason, Chief Operating Officer
Dan Antonelli, Chief Business Development Officer

***KBWA**
01-01-2006; 89.1 mhz FM; 6 kw vert; 145 ft.; N40 13 2.1 W103 41 46.2 *Rebroadcasts:* Rebroadcasts KXWA(FM) Loveland 100%
188 South Bellevue, Suite 222, Memphis, TN 38104 US
(877) 702-9293, *Fax:* (303) 702-9293
www.wayfm.com
supportservices@wayfm.com
License: Brush, Morgan County, CO held by WAY-FM Media Group Inc.
Group Owner: WAY-FM Media Group Inc.; (acq 2-23-2005; $25,000 for CP).
Arbitron Metro Market: Brush, CO *Format:* Christian
Robert Augsburg, President

Buena Vista

KBVC
01-01-1997; 104.1 mhz FM; 0.6 kw; 1188 ft.; N38 44 45 W106 11 55
P.O. Box 4030, Buena Vista, CO 81211 US
(719) 539-2575, *Fax:* (719) 539-4851
www.kbvcfm.com
kvrh@kvrh.com
License: Buena Vista, Chaffee County, CO held by Three Eagles Communications of Colorado LLC
Arbitron Metro Market: Salida, CO *Format:* Country
Dean Johnson, Operations Dir
Ron Gates, General Manager
Cassandra Peterson, Programming Director
Chad Franzen, News Director

KSKE
08-22-1986; 1450 khz AM *Hrs Open:* 24*Rebroadcasts:* Simulcasts KVLE(AM) Vail
54 Monument Circle, Indianapolis, IN 46204 US
(303) 776-2323, *Fax:* (303) 776-1377
www.kvleradio.com
cduncan@bcdworldwide.com
License: Buena Vista, CO held by Pilgrim Communications Inc.
Group Owner: Pilgrim Communications Inc.; (acq 12-11-97)
Nat'l Network: NBC Radio *Nat'l Reps:* Interep
Arbitron Metro Market: Buena Vista, CO *Format:* Talk *Hrs. of News Programming:* news progmg 12 hrs wkly *No. News Employees:* 3 *Target Audience:* Adults 25-54. *Adv. Rates:* 40; 40; 40; 30
Chuck Duncan, CEO
Roger Cridelbaugh, Operations Dir
Nancy Smith, Business Manager
Gene Hood, Owner

Burlington

KNAB
07-11-1967; 1140 khz AM; 1 kw-D, NDD; N39 17 41 W102 15 37
17534 County Road 49, Burlington, CO 80807 US
(719) 346-8600, *Fax:* (719) 346-8656
www.knabradio.com
knab@centurytel.net
License: Burlington, CO held by KNAB Inc.
Format: Adult Contemp *Target Audience:* 18 plus.
Bette Bailly, CEO
Bette Bailly, General Manager
Paul O'Reilly, Programming Director
Beverly Schott, News Director
Chris Baylock, Disc Jockey

KNAB-FM
03-07-1980; 104.1 mhz FM *Hrs Open:* 24; 51 kw; 361 ft.; N39 17 41 W102 15 37
P.O. Box 516, 17534 Colorado Road, Burlington, CO 80807 US
(719) 346-8600, *Fax:* (719) 346-8656
www.knabradio.com
knab@centurytel.net
License: Burlington, Kit Carson County, CO held by KNAB Inc.
Format: Country *Adv. Rates:* 35; 30; 20; 12.50
Bette Bailly, General Manager

Burns

KIDN-FM
02-15-1985; 95.9 mhz FM; 6 kw; 650 ft.; N40 31 16 W107 17 46
1400 Easton Road, Bakersfield, CA 93303 US
(970) 879-5368, *Fax:* (970) 879-5843
www.alwaysmountaintime.com/kidn
ecampbell@nrcbroadcasting.com
License: Burns, Routt County, CO held by NRC Broadcasting Mountain Group LLC.
Group Owner: NRC Broadcasting Inc.; (acq 5-1-2007; grpsl)
Format: Contemporary Hits/Top 40 *Target Audience:* 21-54.
Steve Wodlinger, General Manager

Calhan

KKCS(FM)
104.7 mhz FM; 400 w horiz; Ant 476 ft; N38 59 57 W104 18 47
4843 South Ulster Street, Suite 700, Denver, CO 60611
(303) 446-5926
License: Calhan, El Paso County, CO held by Superior Broadcasting of Denver LLC.
Population Served: 2,707,120 *Arbitron Metro Market:* Chicago, IL
Christopher Devine, President

Canon City

KRLN
08-15-1947; 1400 khz AM *Hrs Open:* 24; 1 kw-U, ND1; N38 27 35 W105 13 26
4343 ""O"" Street, Lincoln, NE 68510 US
(719) 275-7488, *Fax:* (719) 275-5132
starads@krln.cc
License: Canon City, CO held by Royal Gorge Broadcasting LLC.
Nat'l Network: CBS
Arbitron Metro Market: Fremont County *Format:* News, News/Talk, 86 *Hrs. of News Programming:* news progmg 25 hrs wkly *No. News Employees:* 1 *Target Audience:* 25-54; two income families & older discretionaryincome *Adv. Rates:* 16; 12; 16; 12

Joan Wood, General Manager
Rosemary Lamberson, General Sales Mgr
Melissa Nunn, News Director

KSTY
06-01-1975; 104.5 mhz FM; 8.6 kw; 46 ft.; N38 18 54 W105 12 40
P. O. Box 30181, Lincoln, NE 68503 US
(719) 275-7488, *Fax:* (719) 275-5132
License: Canon City, Fremont County, CO held by Royal Gorge Broadcasting LLC.
Arbitron Metro Market: Canon City, CO *Format:* Country *Target Audience:* 25-60. *Adv. Rates:* 30; 29; 30; 27
Missi Nunn, Operations Dir
Joan Wood, General Manager
Rosemary Lamberson, General Sales Mgr
Dennis Bloomquist, Programming Director
Harry Russell, Engineering Dir
Ed Norden, Chief Engineer
Tanner Brandt, Music Director

***KTLC**
05-01-2001; 89.1 mhz FM *Hrs Open:* 24; 1.15 kw; 1476 ft.; N38 45 21 W105 13 2 *Rebroadcasts:* Rebroadcasts KTLF(FM) Colorado Springs 100%
1665 Briargate Blvd, Colorado Springs, CO 80920 US
(719) 593-0600, *Fax:* (719) 593-2399
www.ktlf.org
lightpraise@ktlf.org
License: Canon City, Fremont County, CO held by Make a Difference Foundation Inc.
Arbitron Metro Market: Colorado Springs, CO *Format:* Christian *Target Audience:* 45-60; Christian
James Felix, Operations Dir
Tom Sullivan, General Manager
Sharick Wade, Programming Director
Robert Mumm, Chief Engineer

Carbondale

***KVOV**
04-15-1983; 90.5 mhz FM; 0.45 kw; 2543 ft.; N39 25 8 W107 22 10 *Rebroadcasts:* Rebroadcasts KVOD(FM) Denver 100%
P.O. Box 1388, Carbondale, CO 81623 US
(303) 871-9191, *Fax:* (303) 733-3319
www.cpr.org
License: Carbondale, Garfield County, CO held by Public Broadcasting of Colorado Inc.
Regional Network: Colo. Pub.
Arbitron Metro Market: Centennial, CO *Format:* Classical
Max Wycisk, President
Mike Flanagan, Programming Director
Kelley Griffin, News Director

***KCJX**
09-06-2004; 88.9 mhz FM; 4 kw horiz, 3.5 kw vert; 2543 ft.; N39 25 8 W107 22 10
530 E. Main Street, Aspen, CO 81611 US
(970) 920-9000, *Fax:* (970) 544-8002
www.kajx.org
psa@aspenpublicradio.org
License: Carbondale, Garfield County, CO held by Roaring Fork Public Radio Inc.
Wire Services: AP
Arbitron Metro Market: West Glenwood Spring, CO *Format:* Jazz, News *No. News Employees:* 3
Tom Egan, Operations Dir
Brent Gardner-Smith, General Manager
Roger Adams, News Director
Andrew Todd, Executive Director
Collins Kelly, Membership Director
Debbie Welden, Director of Development & Corporate Support
Christy Gair,Underwriting Sales Director

KUUR
01-01-2007; 96.7 mhz FM; 90 w; Ant 2,507 ft; N39 25 08 W107 22 10
Mailing Address: Box 11657, Aspen, CO
Second Address: 132 W. Main St., Aspen, CO 81611
(970) 920-9600, *Fax:* (970) 544-5239
www.aspenglenwood.com
sales@aspenglenwood.com
License: Carbondale, Garfield County, CO held by Colorado Radio Marketing LLC.
Marcos Rodriguez, General Manager

Castle Rock

KJMN
02-26-1978; 92.1 mhz FM *Hrs Open:* 24; 42 kw; 535 ft.; N39 23 7 W105 2 52
C/O Excl Communs, Inc., 2905 S. King Road, San Jose, CA 95122 US
(303) 721-9210, *Fax:* (303) 832-3410
License: Castle Rock, Douglas County, CO held by Entravision Holdings LLC.
Group Owner: Entravision Communications Corp.; (acq 3-14-00; grpsl).
Arbitron Metro Market: Denver-Boulder, CO *Target Audience:* 25-54.
Mario Carrera, General Manager

Centennial

KXWA
03-11-2004; 101.9 mhz FM *Hrs Open:* 24; 9.5 kw; 535 ft.; N39 23 7 W105 2 52
5145 Centennial Blvd, Ste 200, Colorado Springs, CO 80949 US
(303) 702-9293, *Fax:* (303) 485-1929
www.wayfm.com
supportservices@wayfm.com
License: Centennial, Larimer County, CO held by WAY-FM Media Group Inc.
Group Owner: WAY-FM Media Group Inc.; (acq 11-19-2002).
Arbitron Metro Market: Centennial, CO *Format:* Christian *Target Audience:* 18-34.
Lloyd Parker, COO
Bob Augsburg, President/Founder
Zach Cochran, General Manager
Jeff Connell, Programming Director

Center

KPAU
103.5 mhz FM; 0.46 kw horiz; 26 ft.; N37 47 20 W106 6 43 US
(312) 204-9900
License: Center, Saguache County, CO held by College Creek Media LLC.
Group Owner: College Creek Media LLC
Arbitron Metro Market: Center, CO
Neal Robinson, President

Central City

***KDAB**
88.9 mhz FM; 0.005 kw vert; 1604 ft.; N39 52 1 W105 32 37 US
(970) 669-9200
License: Central City, Gilpin County, CO held by Cedar Cove Broadcasting Inc.
Group Owner: Cedar Cove Broadcasting Inc.
Arbitron Metro Market: Central City, CO
Victor Michael Jr., President

Clifton

KMZK
09-08-1946; 106.9 mhz FM *Hrs Open:* 24; 100 kw; 1444 ft.; N39 34 52 W108 57 36 US
(406) 245-3121, *Fax:* (406) 245-0822
www.kmzk.com
www.genmgr@kmzk.com
License: Clifton, Yellowstone County, CO held by Elenbaas Media Inc.
Nat'l Network: Salem Radio Network *Wire Services:* AP
Arbitron Metro Market: Billings, MT *Format:* Christian *Target Audience:* 18-44; young & energetic high school & college students & young adults
Herm Elenbaas, President
Holly Howard, Operations Dir
John Black, Programming Director
Deb Padilla, News Director

Colona

KAVP
09-30-2000; 1450 khz AM *Hrs Open:* 24*Rebroadcasts:* Rebroadcasts KWGL(FM) Ouray 100%
C/O Brill & Meisel, 488 Madison Ave, 5th Flr, New York, NY 10022 US
(970) 241-6460, *Fax:* (970) 241-6452
License: Colona, CO held by WS Communications LLC.
Group Owner: Western Slope Communications LLC
Format: Country
John Reid, General Manager

Colorado City

KJQY
103.3 mhz FM; 100 kw; 541 ft.; N37 46 52 W104 32 3 US
(719)-542-1033, *Fax:* (877) 842-6336
power1033.com
License: Colorado City, Huerfano County, CO held by Steven R. Bartholomew.
Arbitron Metro Market: Colorado City, CO *Format:* Black
Steven Bartholomew, General Manager
Mike Knar, Station Manager

Colorado Springs

***KEPC**
02-15-1957; 89.7 mhz FM *Hrs Open:* 24; 10 kw; -256 ft.; N38 45 41 W104 47 4
5675 S. Academy Blvd., Colorado Springs, CO 80906 US
(719) 502-3131 (719) 502-3128
www.ppcc.edu/news/kepc-897-fm
kepc@ppcc.edu
License: Colorado Springs, El Paso County, CO held by Pikes Peak Community College.
Arbitron Metro Market: Colorado Springs, CO *Format:* Variety/Diverse *Target Audience:* General.
Sharon Hogg, General Manager

KILO
01-21-1966; 94.3 mhz FM; 59.2 kw; 2198 ft.; N38 44 44 W104 51 42
Mailing Address: P.O. Box 2080, 1805 E. Cheyenne Rd, Colorado Springs, CO 80901 US
Second Address: 1805 E. Cheyenne Rd., Colorado Springs, CO 80905
(719) 634-4896, *Fax:* (719) 634-5837
www.kilo943.com
License: Colorado Springs, El Paso County, CO held by Colorado Springs Radio Broadcasters Inc.
Group Owner: Bahakel Communications; acq 8-14-84)
Arbitron Metro Market: Colorado Spring *Format:* Triple A
Lou Mellini, General Manager
Lana Janc, General Sales Mgr
Ross Ford, Programming Director

KZNT
12-15-1956; 1460 khz AM *Hrs Open:* 24
5145 Centennial Blvd., Ste 200, Colorado Springs, CO 80949 US
(719) 531-5438, *Fax:* (719) 531-5588
www.newstalk1460.com
info@kznt.com
License: Colorado Springs, CO held by Bison Media Inc.
Group Owner: Salem Communications Corp.; (acq 10-6-03; $1.5 million).
Arbitron Metro Market: Colorado Spring, CO *Format:* News, News/Talk, 86
Carrie Lakey, General Manager
Carrie Lakey, Station Manager

KKFM
01-01-1958; 98.1 mhz FM *Hrs Open:* 24; 71 kw; 2290 ft.; N38 44 36 W104 51 44
City Center West, 7201 W. Lake Mead Blvd, Las Vegas, NV 89128 US
(719) 593-2700, *Fax:* (719) 593-2727
www.kkfm.com
info@kkfm.com
License: Colorado Springs, El Paso County, CO
Group Owner: Cumulus Media Inc.; (acq 1-86; $2.5 million;
Nat'l Reps: McGavren Guild
Arbitron Metro Market: Colorado Spring, CO *Format:* Classic Rock *Hrs. of News Programming:* News progmg one hr wkly
Target Audience: 25-54.
Farid Suleman, CEO
Bobby Irwin, Operations Dir
Judy Ellis, COO

***KRCC**
10-02-1951; 91.5 mhz FM *Hrs Open:* 24; 2.1 kw; 2254 ft.; N38 44 43 W104 51 42
912 North Weber, Colorado Springs, CO 80903 US
(719) 473-4801, *Fax:* (719) 473-7863
www.krcc.org
info@krcc.org
License: Colorado Springs, El Paso County, CO held by The Colorado College.
Nat'l Network: NPR; PRI
Arbitron Metro Market: CO Springs, CO *Format:* News/Talk
Special Programming: Celtic 5 hrs, reggae 6 hrs, jazz 15 hrs, blues 5 h *Hrs. of News Programming:* News progmg 42 hrs wkly
Target Audience: 25-54;general
Mike Procell, Operations Dir
Delaney Utterback, General Manager
Jeff Bieri, Promotions Manager

KRDO
03-01-1947; 1240 khz AM *Hrs Open:* 24

P.O. Box 1457, Colorado Springs, CO 80901 US
(719) 632-1515, *Fax:* (719) 475-0815
www.krdo.com
m.lewis@krdo.com
License: Colorado Springs, CO held by Pikes Peak Radio LLC.
Group Owner: News-Press & Gazette Co.; (acq 6-26-2006; grpsl).
Nat'l Reps: D & R Radio
Arbitron Metro Market: CO Spring *TV Affiliate:* KRDO-TV affil.
Format: News, News/Talk, 86
David Bradley Jr., President
Tim Larson, General Manager
Phill Emmert, General Sales Mgr
Mike Lewis, Programming Director
J.R. Reed, Chief Engineer

KATC-FM
10-01-1969; 95.1 mhz FM *Hrs Open:* 24; 58 kw; 2280 ft.; N38 44 43 W104 51 39
P.O. Box 1457, Colorado Springs, CO 80901 US
(719) 593-2700, *Fax:* (719) 593-2727
www.catcountry951.com
info@catcountry951.com
License: Colorado Springs, El Paso County, CO
Group Owner: Cumulus Media Inc.; (acq 8-25-2006; $8.5 million).
Arbitron Metro Market: CO Spring, Pueblo CO *Format:* Country
Bobby Irwin, Operations Dir
Mike Knar, General Manager
Kent Hildebrand, General Sales Mgr
Chris Brooks, Programming Director
Stomie Yeasel, Promotions Manager

KKPK
02-01-1960; 92.9 mhz FM; 60 kw; 2198 ft.; N38 44 44 W104 51 42
City Center West 2701 W. Lake Mead Blvd, Suite 400, Las Vegas, NV 89128 US
(719) 593-2700, *Fax:* (719) 593-2727
www.929peakfm.com
info@929peakfm.com
License: Colorado Springs, El Paso County, CO
Group Owner: Cumulus Media Inc.
Wire Services: UPI
Arbitron Metro Market: Colorado Springs, CO *Format:* Adult Contemp *Target Audience:* 25-54.
Dan Hardee, Programming Director

*KTLF
02-27-1989; 90.5 mhz FM *Hrs Open:* 24; 0 kw horiz, 20 kw vert; 2208 ft.; N38 44 43 W104 51 39
1665 Briargate Blvd., Colorado Springs, CO 80920 US
(719) 593-0600, *Fax:* (719) 593-2399
www.ktlf.org
lightpraise@ktlf.org
License: Colorado Springs, El Paso County, CO held by Educational Communications of Colorado Springs Inc.
Arbitron Metro Market: Colorado Springs, CO *Format:* Christian *Target Audience:* 45-60; Christian
Dr. Ron Johnson, Chairman
Sharick Wade, Operations Dir
Lynn Carmichael, Programming Director

KCSF
09-22-1922; 1300 khz AM *Hrs Open:* 24; 5 kw-D, ND1; 1 kw-N, ND1; N38 48 46 W104 48 51
City Center West 2701 W. Lake Mead Blvd, Suite 400, Las Vegas, NV 89128 US
(719) 593-2700
www.kcs1300am.com
License: Colorado Springs, CO
Group Owner: Cumulus Media Inc.; (acq 1999; grpsl)
Nat'l Reps: McGavren Guild
Arbitron Metro Market: Colorado Springs, CO *Format:* Country
Farid Suleman, CEO
Bobby Irwin, Operations Dir
Kent Hildebrand, General Manager
Bobby Irwin, Programming Director
Gina Kavali, Interactive Director

KREL
05-11-1951; 1580 khz AM *Hrs Open:* 6 AM-sunset
54 Monument Circle, Indianapolis, IN 46204 US
(940) 663-5711
www.krel1580.com
info@krel.com
License: Colorado Springs, CO held by First Broadcasters Investment Partners LLC.
Group Owner: First Broadcasting Operating Inc.; (acq 6-13-2005; grpsl)
Arbitron Metro Market: Dallas, TX *Format:* Country *Target Audience:* General.
Dean Goodman, President
Richard Womack, General Manager
Kimberly Long, Station Manager
Scott Kubala, Programming Director
Kevin Brooks, Chief Engineer

KVOR
09-22-1922; 740 khz AM; 3.3 kw-D, DA2; 1.5 kw-N, DA2; N39 5 2 W104 42 41
City Center West 2701 W. Lake Mead Blvd, Suite 400, Las Vegas, NV 89128 US
(719) 593-2700, *Fax:* (719) 593-2727
www.kvor.com
bobby.irwin@cumulus.com
License: Colorado Springs, CO
Group Owner: Cumulus Media Inc.; (acq 1999; grpsl).
Nat'l Network: CBS; Wall Street
Arbitron Metro Market: Colorado Springs, CO *Format:* News, News/Talk, 84, Talk *Target Audience:* General.
Bobby Irwin, Operations Dir
Kent Hildebrand, General Sales Mgr
Dan Mandis, Programming Director
Jim Arthur, Promotions Manager
Charlie Stone, News Director
Gina Kavali, Community Officer & Interactive Director

Commerce City

KLTT
01-01-1996; 670 khz AM
P.O. Box 3003, Blue Bell, PA 19422 US
(303) 433-5500, *Fax:* (303) 433-1555
www.670kltt.com
kltt@crawfordbroadcasting.com
License: Commerce City, CO held by KLZ Radio Inc.
Group Owner: Crawford Broadcasting Co.; (acq 1995; $750,000)
Arbitron Metro Market: Denver-Boulder, *Format:* Religious *Target Audience:* 30 plus; general
Mike Triem, General Manager

Cortez

KISZ-FM
09-28-1978; 97.9 mhz FM *Hrs Open:* 20; 100 kw; 1309 ft.; N37 21 48 W108 9 0
Mailing Address: 427 Bedford Road, Pleasantville, CO 10570 US
Second Address: 2402 Hawkins, Cortez, CO 81321
(505) 325-3541, *Fax:* (505) 327-5796
www.kisscountry979fm.com
License: Cortez, Montezuma County, CO held by Winton Road Broadcasting Co. LLC
Group Owner: Winton Road Broadcasting Co. LLC; (acq 5-3-01; grpsl).
Format: Country *Hrs. of News Programming:* news progmg 4 hrs wkly *No. News Employees:* 1 *Target Audience:* 18-49; young sophisticated adults *Adv. Rates:* 350; 300; 350; 200
Dan Buchta, General Manager
Randy KLock, General Sales Mgr

KRTZ
12-01-1981; 98.7 mhz FM *Hrs Open:* 24; 27 kw; 2900 ft.; N37 13 10 W108 48 26
1400 Easton Road, Bakersfield, CA 93303 US
(970) 565-6565, *Fax:* (970) 565-8567
krtzradio.com
radio@krtzradio.com
License: Cortez, Montezuma County, CO
Arbitron Metro Market: Cortez, CO *Format:* Adult Contemp
Special Programming: American Indian one hr, gospel one hr wkly *Hrs. of News Programming:* news progmg 3 hrs wkly *No. News Employees:* 1 *TargetAudience:* 20-55. *Adv. Rates:* 228; 228; 228; 192
Kelly Turner, Programming Director
Desiree Burnham, Promotions Manager
Jim Burt, Engineering Dir

*KSJD
07-01-1990; 91.5 mhz FM *Hrs Open:* 24; 1.2 kw; 312 ft.; N37 28 57 W108 30 34
P.O. Box 970, Cortez, CO 81321 US
(970) 564-9727 (970) 564-0808
www.ksjd.org
info@ksjd.org
License: Cortez, Montezuma County, CO held by Community Radio Project, Inc.
Arbitron Metro Market: Mancos, CO *Format:* Variety/Diverse
Special Programming: Relg one hr wkly *No. News Employees:* 1 *Target Audience:* 16-30; college level
Kristine Nunn, President
Jeff Pope, General Manager
Melissa Betrone, General Sales Mgr
Karen Mooneyhan, Programming Director

KVFC
02-27-1955; 740 khz AM *Hrs Open:* 24; 1 kw-D, DAN; 0.25 kw-N, DAN; N37 20 58 W108 32 29
1400 Easton Road, Bakersfield, CA 93303 US
(505) 325-3541, *Fax:* (505) 327-5796
www.kvfcradio.com
feedback@kvfcradio.com
License: Cortez, CO held by Winton Road Broadcasting Co. LLC
Group Owner: Winton Road Broadcasting Co. LLC; (acq 12-18-01; with co-located FM).
Nat'l Network: ABC; CNN Radio; Westwood One
Arbitron Metro Market: Farmington, NM *Format:* News, News/Talk, 86 *Hrs. of News Programming:* news progmg 15 hrs wkly *No. News Employees:* 2 *Target Audience:* 18-54; young adults
Anthony Brandon, CEO
Kelly Turner, Operations Dir
Bill Kruger, General Manager
Keri-Lyn Riley, General Sales Mgr
Jim Burt, Chief Engineer
L. Rogers Brandon, COO

*KZET
09-03-2011; 90.5 mhz FM; 2 kw; 2865 ft.; N37 13 13 W108 48 24 US
(970) 749-9117
License: Cortez, Montezuma County, CO held by Community Radio Project.
Arbitron Metro Market: Cortez, CO *Format:* Variety/Diverse
Jeffery Pope, General Manager

Craig

KRAI
01-01-1948; 550 khz AM *Hrs Open:* 19; 5 kw-D, DAN; 0.5 kw-N, DAN; N40 32 45 W107 31 52
Mailing Address: 1111 W. Victory Way, Craig, CO 81626 US
Second Address: 1111 W. Victory Way., Craig, CO 81626
(970) 824-6574, *Fax:* (970) 826-4581
www.krai.com
krai@krai.com
License: Craig, CO held by Wild West Radio Inc.
Nat'l Network: Westwood Edge; CNN Radio *Wire Services:* AP
Format: Country, News, 84 *Special Programming:* Farm one hr wkly *Hrs. of News Programming:* news progmg 12 hrs wkly *No. News Employees:* 3 *Target Audience:* 25-54.
Frank Hanel, General Manager
Tammie Hanel, Station Manager

KRAI-FM
04-01-1976; 93.7 mhz FM *Hrs Open:* 24; 100 kw; 980 ft; N40 34 35 W107 36 29
Mailing Address: 1111 West Victory Way, Craig, CO 81625
Second Address: 1111 W. Victory Way., Craig, CO 81626
(970) 824-6574, *Fax:* (970) 826-4581
www.krai.com
krai@krai.com
License: Craig, Moffat County, CO
Wire Services: AP
Population Served: 45,000*Hrs. of News Programming:* news progmg 4 hrs wkly *No. News Employees:* 3 *Target Audience:* 18-49.
Frank Hanel, General Manager
Tammie Hanel, Station Manager
Marci Marumoto, Account Executive

*KPYR
01-01-2005; 88.3 mhz FM; 0.25 kw; 889 ft.; N40 33 50 W107 36 40 *Rebroadcasts:* Rebroadcasts KCFR(AM) Denver 100%
2249 S. Josephine St., Denver, CO 80210 US
(303) 871-9191, *Fax:* (303) 733-3319
www.cpr.org
License: Craig, Moffat County, CO held by Public Broadcasting of Colorado Inc.
Arbitron Metro Market: Craig, CO *Format:* News
Max Wycisk, President

Crested Butte

*KBUT
12-20-1986; 90.3 mhz FM *Hrs Open:* 24; 0.225 kw; -636 ft.; N38 54 11 W106 58 23
Mailing Address: Box 308, Crested Butte, CO 81224 US
Second Address: 508 Maroon Ave., Crested Butte, CO 81224
(970) 349-5225, *Fax:* (970) 349-6440
www.kbut.org
kbut@kbut.org
License: Crested Butte, Gunnison County, CO held by Crested Butte Mountain Educational Radio Inc.
Nat'l Network: NPR; PRI

Arbitron Metro Market: Crested Butte, CO *Format:* Variety/Diverse *Hrs. of News Programming:* news progmg 72 hrs wkly *No. News Employees:* 1 *Target Audience:* General. *Adv. Rates:* 80; 80; 80; 70
Ryan Stringfellow, General Manager
Chad Reich, Programming Director

Del Norte

KSLV-FM
96.5 mhz FM; 930 w; Ant 1,589 ft; N37 43 47 W106 35 18
Box 631, Monte Vista, CO
(719) 852-3581, *Fax:* (719) 852-3583
www.kslvradio.com
kslv@amigo.net
License: Del Norte, Rio Grande County, CO held by San Luis Valley Broadcasting Inc.
Group Owner: San Luis Valley Broadcasting Inc.; 7-Jun
Nat'l Network: Dial Global Networks *Wire Services:* AP
Special Programming: Local sports *Hrs. of News Programming:* 2 hours weekly *No. News Employees:* 1 *Target Audience:* 25 to 55 Adults
H. Robert Gourley III, President
Steven Howard, Operations Dir
Gerald Vigil, General Manager
Linda Pacheco, News Director

Delta

KDTA
01-14-1955; 1400 khz AM *Hrs Open:* 24; 1 kw-U; N38 45 38 W108 05 28 *Rebroadcasts:* Simulcast of KJOL(AM) Grand Junction 100%
1354 E. Sherwood Dr., Grand Junction, CO 81416
(970) 254-5565, *Fax:* (970) 254-5550
www.kjol.org
info@kjol.org
License: Delta, Delta County, CO held by United Ministries.
Group Owner: United Ministries; (acq 11-16-2004; $88,000).
Population Served: 30,000 *Arbitron Metro Market:* Grand Junction, CO
Ken Andrews, General Manager
Ken Andrews, Station Manager

KKNN
12-01-1985; 95.1 mhz FM *Hrs Open:* 24; 100 kw; 969 ft; N38 52 40 W108 13 30
315 Kennedy Ave., Grand Junction, CO 81506
(970) 242-7788, *Fax:* (970) 243-0567
www.95rockfm.com
95rock@cumulus.com
License: Delta, Delta County, CO held by Townsquare Media Grand Junction
Group Owner: Cumulus Media Inc.; (acq 1-00).
Nat'l Reps: Katz Radio
Population Served: 225,000 *Arbitron Metro Market:* Grand Junction, CO *Hrs. of News Programming:* news progmg 6 hrs wkly *No. News Employees:* 1 *Target Audience:* 18-49; men
Lewis Dickey, CEO
John Dickey, President
Ed Chandler, Operations Dir
Kevin Wodlinger, General Manager

*KPRU
01-01-2001; 103.3 mhz FM; 12 kw; 988 ft.; N38 52 40 W108 13 32
2249 S Josephine St, Denver, CO 80210 US
(303) 871-9191, *Fax:* (303) 733-3319
www.cpr.org
License: Delta, Delta County, CO held by Public Broadcasting of Colorado Inc.
Format: Country
Max Wycisk, President
Sue Coughlin, General Sales Mgr
Sean Nethery, Programming Director
David Gomez, News Director
Bob Hensler, Chief Engineer

Denver

KALC
06-21-1965; 105.9 mhz FM; 96 kw; 1719 ft.; N39 43 58 W105 14 8
1200 17th Street, Suiye 2300, Denver, CO 80202 US
(303) 967-2700, *Fax:* (303) 967-2747
www.alice1059.com
info@alice1059.com
License: Denver, Denver County, CO held by Entercom Denver License LLC.
Group Owner: Entercom Communications Corp.; (acq 5-1-2002; $88 million).
Nat'l Reps: Christal
Arbitron Metro Market: Denver, CO *Format:* Adult Contemp
Target Audience: 18-34; women
Jeff Silver, General Sales Mgr
Mike Peterson, Programming Director
Tina Lorraine, Promotions Manager
Stephanie Walrath, News Director
Jeff Garrett, Chief Engineer

KBJD
01-01-2001; 1650 khz AM *Hrs Open:* 24
4880 Santa Rosa Rd, Camarillo, CA 93012 US
(303) 283-0118
www.1650radioluz.com
production@salemdenver.com
License: Denver, CO held by Salem Media of Colorado Inc.
Group Owner: Salem Communications Corp.
Arbitron Metro Market: Aurora, CO *Format:* Religious, Spanish, 86 *Hrs. of News Programming:* news progmg 15 hrs wkly *No. News Employees:* 3
Brian Taylor, General Manager

KLDC
06-05-1954; 1220 khz AM; 0.66 kw-D, ND1; 0.011 kw-N, ND1; N39 41 0 W105 0 24
2727 Bryant St., Ste.100, Denver, CO 80211 US
(303) 433-5500, *Fax:* (303) 433-1555
www.1220kldc.com
License: Denver, CO held by KLZ Radio Inc.
Group Owner: Crawford Broadcasting Co.; (acq 8-11-99; $1.5 million)
Arbitron Metro Market: Denver-Boulder, CO *Format:* Gospel
Special Programming: Black 2 hrs wkly *Target Audience:* 24-55; general
Mike Triem, General Manager

KBPI
06-19-1962; 106.7 mhz FM *Hrs Open:* 24; 100 kw; 1339 ft.; N39 43 58 W105 14 8
50 East Rivercenter Blvd, Suite 1200, Covington, KY 41011 US
(303) 713-8000, *Fax:* (303) 713-8744
www.kbpi.com
info@kbpi.com
License: Denver, Denver County, CO held by Citicasters Licenses Inc. (NEW).
Group Owner: Clear Channel Communications Inc.; (acq 5-4-99; grpsl).
Nat'l Network: ABC
Arbitron Metro Market: Denver-Boulder, CO *Format:* Rock/AOR
Target Audience: 25-34; men
Lee Larsen, General Manager
Jack Lambiotte, General Sales Mgr
Willie Hung, Programming Director

*KCFR-FM
11-01-1970; 90.1 mhz FM *Hrs Open:* 24; 44 kw; 909 ft.; N39 43 49 W105 14 59
2249 South Josephine St., Denver, CO 80210 US
(303) 871-9191, *Fax:* (303) 733-3319
www.cpr.org
info@cpr.org
License: Denver, Denver County, CO held by Public Broadcasting of Colorado Inc.
Nat'l Network: NPR
Arbitron Metro Market: Denver-Boulder, CO *Format:* News, News/Talk, 86 *Hrs. of News Programming:* news progmg 50 hrs wkly *No. News Employees:* 8 *Target Audience:* General.
Max Wycisk, President
Sue Coughlin, General Sales Mgr
Sean Nethery, Programming Director
Robert Hensler, Engineering Dir
Jenny Gentry, Executive Vice President

KPTT
03-31-1968; 95.7 mhz FM; 100 kw; 1135 ft.; N39 43 59 W105 14 10
50 East Rivercenter Blvd, Suite 1200, Covington, KY 41011 US
(303) 713-8000, *Fax:* (303) 713-8738
www.957theparty.com
License: Denver, Denver County, CO held by Citicasters Licenses L.P.
Group Owner: Clear Channel Communications Inc.
Arbitron Metro Market: Denver-Boulder, CO *Format:* Adult Contemp *Target Audience:* General.
Joe Bevilacqua, Programming Director

KHOW
01-01-1925; 630 khz AM *Hrs Open:* 24; 5 kw-D, DA2; 5 kw-N, DA2; N39 54 36 W104 54 50
50 East Rivercenter Blvd, Suite 1200, Covington, KY 41011 US
(303) 713-8000, *Fax:* (303) 713-8738
www.khow.com
RosemaryBennett@clearchannel.com;
JessicaFarias@clearchannel.com;
InternetSalesDenver@ClearChannel.c
License: Denver, CO held by Citicasters Licenses L.P.
Group Owner: Clear Channel Communications Inc.; (acq 5-4-99; grpsl)
Arbitron Metro Market: Denver-Boulder, CO *Format:* Talk *Target Audience:* 25-54.
Lee Larsen, General Manager
Rosemary Bennett, General Sales Mgr
Kristine Olinger, Programming Director
Jan Chadwell, Chief Engineer
Jessica Farias, Local Sales Manager

KIMN
08-01-1959; 100.3 mhz FM *Hrs Open:* 24; 97 kw; 1132 ft.; N39 40 18 W105 13 12
1200 17th Street, Suite 2300, Denver, CO 80202 US
(303) 832-5665, *Fax:* (303) 832-7000
www.mix100.com
info@mix100.com
License: Denver, Denver County, CO held by Wilks License Co.-Denver LLC.
Group Owner: Wilks Broadcast Group LLC; (acq 3-5-2009; grpsl)
Nat'l Reps: Christal
Arbitron Metro Market: Denver-Boulder, *Format:* Adult Contemp
Special Programming: Pub affrs 2 hrs wkly *Target Audience:* 35-44; women
Barry Remington, General Manager
Geronimo, Programming Director

*KGNU
01-01-1954; 1390 khz AM *Hrs Open:* 24*Rebroadcasts:* Simulcast of KGNU-FM, Boulder 95%
828 Santa Fe Drive, Denver, CO 80204 US
(303) 449-4885
www.kgnu.org
sam@kgnu.org
License: Denver, CO held by Boulder Community Broadcast Association Inc.
Arbitron Metro Market: Denver-Boulder, CO *Format:* Easy Listening
Sam Fuqua, General Manager

KQMT
10-02-1959; 99.5 mhz FM *Hrs Open:* 24; 74 kw; 1624 ft.; N39 43 45 W105 14 6
10200 E. Girard Avenue, Suite B131, Denver, CO 80231 US
(303) 967-2700, *Fax:* (303) 967-2747
www.995themountain.com
info@995themountain.com
License: Denver, Denver County, CO held by Entercom Denver License LLC.
Group Owner: Entercom Communications Corp.; (acq 3-21-03).
Arbitron Metro Market: Denver, CO *Format:* Classic Rock *Hrs. of News Programming:* News progmg 4 hrs wkly *Target Audience:* 25-54; upscale, educated
Amy Griesheimer, General Manager
Greg Carpenter, General Sales Mgr
Dylan Sprague, Programming Director

*KVOQ(AM)
03-04-1956; 1340 khz AM *Hrs Open:* 24; 1 kw-U; N39 39 34 W105 00 44
7409 S. Alton Ct., Centennial, CO 80112
(303) 871-9191, *Fax:* (303) 733-3319
www.cpr.org
License: Denver, Denver County, CO held by Public Broadcasting of Colorado Inc.
Population Served: 1,250,000 *Arbitron Metro Market:* Denver, CO *Format:* News
Max Wycisk, President
Sue Coughlin, General Sales Mgr

KLZ
03-10-1922; 560 khz AM *Hrs Open:* 24
P. O. Box 3003, Blue Bell, PA 19422 US
(303) 433-5500, *Fax:* (303) 433-1555
www.560thesource.com
License: Denver, CO held by KLZ Radio Inc.
Group Owner: Crawford Broadcasting Co.; (acq 6-30-92; $1.5 million).
Arbitron Metro Market: Denver, CO *Format:* Christian, Talk
Target Audience: 25-54; men
Mike Triem, General Manager

KNUS
01-01-1941; 710 khz AM *Hrs Open:* 24; 5 kw-U, DA1; N39 57 19 W104 51 1
4880 Santa Rosa Road, Suite 300, Camarillo, CA 93012 US
(303) 750-5687, *Fax:* (303) 696-8063
www.710knus.com
production@salemdenver.com

License: Denver, CO held by Salem Media of Colorado Inc.
Group Owner: Salem Communications Corp.; (acq 1996; $1.2 million)
Arbitron Metro Market: Denver-Boulder, CO *Format:* News, News/Talk, 86 *Hrs. of News Programming:* news progmg 15 hrs wkly *No. News Employees:* 3 *Target Audience:* 35-54; Adults
Brian Taylor, General Manager

KOA
12-15-1924; 850 khz AM *Hrs Open:* 24; 50 kw-U, ND1; N39 30 22 W104 45 57
50 East Rivercenter Blvd, Suite 1200, Covington, KY 41011 US
(303) 713-8000, *Fax:* (303) 713-8735
www.850koa.com
info@850koa.com
License: Denver, CO held by Citicasters Licenses Inc. (NEW).
Group Owner: Clear Channel Communications Inc.; (acq 5-4-99; grpsl).
Nat'l Network: CBS *Wire Services:* CBS
Arbitron Metro Market: Denver-Boulder, CO *Format:* News, News/Talk, 84, Talk *Target Audience:* 25-54.
Lee Larsen, General Manager
Kristine Olinger, Programming Director
Jan Chadwell, Chief Engineer

KOSI
03-03-1968; 101.1 mhz FM *Hrs Open:* 24; 74 kw; 1624 ft.; N39 43 45 W105 14 6
10200 E. Girard Avenue, Suite B-131, Denver, CO 80231 US
(303) 967-2700, *Fax:* (303) 967-2747
www.kosi101.com
info@kosi101.com
License: Denver, Denver County, CO held by Entercom Denver License LLC.
Group Owner: Entercom Communications Corp.; (acq 7-24-02; with KEZW(AM) Aurora).
Arbitron Metro Market: Denver-Boulder, CO *Format:* Adult Contemp *Hrs. of News Programming:* news progmg 5 hrs wkly *No. News Employees:* 1 *Target Audience:* 25-54; women/families
Glynn Alan, General Sales Mgr
Dave Symonds, Programming Director

*KPOF
03-09-1928; 910 khz AM *Hrs Open:* 24; 5 kw-D, ND1; 1 kw-N, ND1; N39 50 47 W105 1 59
1302 Sherman St, Denver, CO 80203 US
(303) 428-0910, *Fax:* (303) 429-0910
www.am91.org
info@am91.org
License: Denver, CO held by Pillar of Fire Corp.
Group Owner: Pillar of Fire Inc.; acq 1928)
Nat'l Network: Moody
Arbitron Metro Market: Denver-Boulder, CO *Format:* Christian, Religious *Target Audience:* 18-plus; mature adult and families
Robert Dallenbach, President
Jerry Bauer, Operations Dir
Jack Pelon, General Manager

KRFX
06-01-1961; 103.5 mhz FM; 100 kw; 1135 ft.; N39 43 59 W105 14 10
50 East Rivercenter Blvd, Suite 1200, Covington, KY 41011 US
(303) 713-8000, *Fax:* (303) 713-8744
www.thefox.com
License: Denver, Denver County, CO
Group Owner: Clear Channel Communications Inc.
Arbitron Metro Market: Denver, CO *Format:* Classic Rock *Target Audience:* 25-54.
Lee Larsen, General Manager
Jack Lambiotte, General Sales Mgr
Joe Bevilacqua, Programming Director

KRKS
08-01-1953; 990 khz AM *Hrs Open:* 24
4880 Santa Rosa Rd #300, Carmarillo, CA 93012 US
(303) 750-5687, *Fax:* (303) 696-8063
www.krks.com
krks@krks.com
License: Denver, CO held by Salem Media of Colorado Inc.
Group Owner: Salem Communications Corp.; (acq 10-93; $400,000)
Arbitron Metro Market: Denver-Boulder, CO *Format:* Christian *Target Audience:* 25 plus.
Brian Taylor, VP
Jules Dygert, General Sales Mgr
Cliff Mikkelson, Engineering Dir

*KUVO
08-29-1985; 89.3 mhz FM *Hrs Open:* 24; 22.5 kw; 912 ft.; N39 43 49 W105 14 59
Mailing Address: P.O. Box 11111, Denver, CO 80211 US
Second Address: 2900 Welton St., Suite 200, Denver, CO 80205
(303) 480-9272, *Fax:* (303) 291-0757
www.kuvo.org
alfredo@kuvo.org
License: Denver, Denver County, CO held by Denver Educational Broadcasting.
Nat'l Network: NPR; PRI
Arbitron Metro Market: Denver, CO *Format:* Jazz *Special Programming:* Sp 15 hrs wkly *Target Audience:* 25-49.
Carlos Lando, COO/Program Director
Alfredo Cruz, CEO/President
Joey Kloss, Engineer/ISDN
Mike Pappas, Chief Engineer
Laura Jorstad, Business Manager
Tina Cartagena, Director of Development & Marketing
Victor Cooper, ProductionManager
Arturo Gmez, Music Director
Martha Griego, Underwriting Account Executive
Denise Meny, Web Content Coordinator

KBNO
05-15-1948; 1280 khz AM *Hrs Open:* 24; 5 kw-D, DA2; 5 kw-N, DA2; N39 36 5 W104 58 48
1560 Broadway, Suite 1100, Denver, CO 80202 US
(303) 733-5266, *Fax:* (303) 733-5242
www.radioquebueno.com
kbno@kbno.net
License: Denver, CO held by Latino Communications LLC
Group Owner: Latino Communications LLC; acq 11-21-00; $3.3 million).
Arbitron Metro Market: Denver-Boulder, CO *Hrs. of News Programming:* news progmg 21 hrs wkly *No. News Employees:* 27 *Target Audience:* 25-54; male
Zee Ferrufino, CEO
Michael Ferrufino, Operations Dir

KXKL-FM
12-01-1956; 105.1 mhz FM *Hrs Open:* 24; 100 kw; 1168 ft.; N39 36 0 W105 12 35
433 E. Las Colina Blvd, #1130, Irving, TX 75039 US
(303) 228-2000, *Fax:* (303) 832-7000
www.kool105.com
info@kool105.com
License: Denver, Denver County, CO held by Wilks License Co.-Denver LLC.
Group Owner: Wilks Broadcast Group LLC; (acq 3-5-2009; grpsl)
Arbitron Metro Market: Denver, CO *Format:* Oldies
Barry Remington, General Manager
Brenda Egger, General Sales Mgr
Cha Cha, Programming Director
Barry Walters, Chief Engineer

KYGO-FM
12-01-1953; 98.5 mhz FM *Hrs Open:* 24; 96.6 kw; 1821 ft.; N39 40 35 W105 29 9
1095 South Monaco Pky, Denver, CO 80224 US
(303) 321—0950, *Fax:* (303) 333-2987
www.kygo.com
License: Denver, Denver County, CO
Group Owner: Lincoln Financial Media
Arbitron Metro Market: Greenwood Village, CO *Format:* Country *Target Audience:* 25-54.
Joel Burke, Programming Director
Garret Doll, Promotions Manager
Garret Doll, Music Director
Randy Weidner, National Sales
Rita Gillespie-Stein, Webmaser
John ""JT"" Thomas, Program Director

Dolores

*KTCF
01-01-2004; 89.5 mhz FM; 0.5 kw; 174 ft.; N37 28 7 W108 32 48
Rebroadcasts: Rebroadcasts KTLF(FM) Colorado Springs 100%
1665 Briargate Blvd, Colorado Springs, CO 80920 US
(719) 593-0600, *Fax:* (719) 593-2399
www.ktlf.org
awagnon@ktlf.org
License: Dolores, Montezuma County, CO held by Educational Communications of Colorado Springs Inc.
Arbitron Metro Market: Crosby, MN *Format:* Christian *Target Audience:* 45-60; Christian
James Felix, Operations Dir
Tom Sullivan, General Manager
Lynn Carmichael, Programming Director
Marge Wallace, Office Manager
Alleen Wagnon, Office Assistant
Sharick Wade, KTPL Program Director

KKDC
01-06-2004; 93.3 mhz FM; 50 kw; 338 ft.; N37 27 59 W108 31 28
Mailing Address: 185 Suttle Street, Suite 203, Durango, CO 81301 US
Second Address: 310 Railroad, Dolores, CO
(970) 259-4444, *Fax:* (970) 247-1005
www.radiodolores.com
raycrow23@yahoo.com
License: Dolores, Montezuma County, CO held by Four Corners Broadcasting L.L.C.
Group Owner: Four Corners Broadcasting L.L.C.
Arbitron Metro Market: Dolores, CO *Format:* Classic Rock *No. News Employees:* 1 *Target Audience:* 35-54.
Allen Brill, CEO
Ward Holmes, Operations Dir
Ray McDonnell, Station Manager
Ed Lacy, Programming Director
Kristin Dills, Business Manager

Durango

KDGO
04-18-1958; 1240 khz AM *Hrs Open:* 24; 1 kw-U, ND1; N37 18 18 W107 51 25
427 Bedford Rd, Pleasantville, NY 10570 US
(970) 247-1240, *Fax:* (970) 247-1771
www.kdgoam.com
kdgo@kdgoam.com
License: Durango, CO held by Winton Road Broadcasting Co. LLC.
Group Owner: Winton Road Broadcasting Co. LLC; (acq 6-1-2001; grpsl)
Nat'l Network: ABC
Arbitron Metro Market: Durango, CO *Format:* News, News/Talk, 86 *No. News Employees:* 1 *Target Audience:* 35-55.
Dan Buchta, General Manager
Ryan Nutter, Programming Director

*KDUR
01-01-1975; 91.9 mhz FM; 6 kw vert; -512 ft.; N37 16 41 W107 52 21
Fort Lewis College, 1000 Rim Drive, Durango, CO 81301 US
(970) 247-7262, *Fax:* (970) 247-7487
www.kdur.org
KDUR@fortlewis.edu
License: Durango, La Plata County, CO held by Board of Trustees for Fort Lewis College.
Nat'l Network: PRI
Arbitron Metro Market: Durango, CO *Format:* Variety/Diverse
Special Programming: Bluegrass 6 hrs, blues 6 hrs, class 6 hrs, jazz 9 hrs, Native American folk 3 hrs wkly
Bryant Liggett, Station Manager
Ellen Stein, General Sales Mgr
Jon Lynch, Programming Director
Rachel Perrault, Development Director
Jennifer Cossey, Office Manager

KIQX
10-15-1982; 101.3 mhz FM *Hrs Open:* 24; 29.5 kw; 1995 ft.; N37 21 46 W107 47 37
Mailing Address: 488 Madison Avenue, Fifth Floor, New York, NY 10022 US
Second Address: 190 Turner Drive, Suite G, Durango, CO 81303
(970) 259-4444, *Fax:* (970) 247-1005
www.radiodurango.com
fcb@frontier.net
License: Durango, La Plata County, CO held by Four Corners Broadcasting L.L.C.
Group Owner: Four Corners Broadcasting L.L.C.
Nat'l Network: CBS
Arbitron Metro Market: Albuquerque, NM *Format:* Adult Contemp
Special Programming: Jazz 7 hrs wkly *Hrs. of News Programming:* news progmg 5 hrs wkly *No. News Employees:* 2 *Target Audience:* 25-54;mainstream business professionals & families *Adv. Rates:* 15; 13; 15; 10
Allen Brill, Chairman
Ward Holmes, Operations Dir
Kristin Dills, Business Manager

KIUP
12-10-1935; 930 khz AM *Hrs Open:* 24; 5 kw-D, ND1; 0.1 kw-N, ND1; N37 18 18 W107 51 25
Mailing Address: 185 Suttle Street, Suite 203, Durango, CO 81302 US
Second Address: 190 Turner Drive, Suite G, Durango, CO 81303
(970) 259-4444, *Fax:* (970) 247-1005
www.radiodurango.com
fcb@frontier.net
License: Durango, CO held by Four Corners Broadcasting LLC.
Group Owner: Four Corners Broadcasting L.L.C.; (acq 4-1-96; with co-located FM)
Nat'l Network: ESPN Radio *Wire Services:* AP

Format: Sports *Special Programming:* Rockies-AV's-Flc sports *Hrs. of News Programming:* news progmg 5 hrs wkly *No. News Employees:* 2 *Target Audience:* 12 plus. *Adv. Rates:* 15; 18; 15; 10
Allen Brill, CEO
Ward Holmes, Operations Dir

KPTE
07-01-1995; 99.7 mhz FM; 9.2 kw; 1129 ft.; N37 20 21 W107 49 25
427 Bedford Rd, Pleasantville, NY 10570 US
(970) 247-1240, *Fax:* (970) 247-1771
99xdurango.com
kpte@997thepoint.com
License: Durango, La Plata County, CO held by Winton Road Broadcasting Co. LLC.
Group Owner: Winton Road Broadcasting Co. LLC
Arbitron Metro Market: Four Corners *Format:* Adult Contemp, Contemporary Hits/Top 40 *Target Audience:* 18-44.
Dr. David Bryant, President
Russell Guthrie, General Manager

KRSJ
12-04-1972; 100.5 mhz FM *Hrs Open:* 24; 29.7 kw; 1995 ft.; N37 21 46 W107 47 37
Mailing Address: Fifth Floor, 488 Madison Ave., New York, NY 10022 US
Second Address: 190 Turner Drive, Suite G, Durango, CO 81303
(970) 259-4444, *Fax:* (970) 247-1005
www.radiodurango.com
fcb@frontier.net
License: Durango, La Plata County, CO held by Four Corners Broadcasting LLC.
Group Owner: Four Corners Broadcasting L.L.C.
Nat'l Network: Fox News Radio *Wire Services:* AP
Arbitron Metro Market: Durango,CO *Format:* Country *Hrs. of News Programming:* news progmg 6 hrs wkly *No. News Employees:* 2 *Target Audience:* 25 plus. *Adv. Rates:* 15; 12; 15; 10
Allen Brill, CEO
Ward Holmes, Operations Dir
Kim Emanual, General Sales Mgr
Ed Lacy, Programming Director
Clark Hoffer, Chief Engineer
Kritin Dills, Business Manager

***KTDU**
05-02-2005; 88.5 mhz FM; 0 kw horiz, 4 kw vert; 371 ft.; N37 15 43 W107 54 24 *Rebroadcasts:* Rebroadcasts KTLF(FM) Colorado Springs 100%
1665 Briargate Blvd, Colorado Springs, CO 80920 US
(719) 593-0600, *Fax:* (719) 593-2399
www.ktlf.org
awagnon@ktlf.org
License: Durango, La Plata County, CO held by Educational Communications of Colorado Springs Inc.
Arbitron Metro Market: Durango, CO *Format:* Christian *Target Audience:* 45-60; Christian
James Felix, Operations Dir
Tom Sullivan, General Manager
Lynn Carmichael, Programming Director
Marge Wallace, Office Manager
Alleen Wagnon, Office Assistant
Sharick Wade, KTPL Program Director

***KDNG**
89.3 mhz FM; 0.2 kw; 322 ft.; N37 15 44 W107 53 58
P.O. Box 737, Ignacio, CO 81137 US
(970) 563-0255, *Fax:* (970) 563-0399
www.ksut.org
info@ksut.org
License: Durango, La Plata County, CO held by KUTE Inc.
Group Owner: KUTE Inc.
Arbitron Metro Market: Durango, CO
Eddie Box Jr., President

Eagle

KSKE-FM
01-01-1997; 101.7 mhz FM *Hrs Open:* 24; 12 kw; 2188 ft.; N39 44 18 W106 47 58
Mailing Address: 225 N. Mill Street, Aspen, CO 81611 US
Second Address: 182 Avon Rd., Avon, CO 81620
(970) 949-0140, *Fax:* (970) 949-1464
www.kskeradio.com
info@kskeradio.com
License: Eagle, Eagle County, CO held by Superior Broadcasting of Denver LLC
Arbitron Metro Market: Avon, CO *Format:* Country
Meredith Fox, Operations Dir
Steve Wodlinger, General Manager
Holli Snyder, General Sales Mgr
David Bach, News Director
Ken Laughlin, Chief Engineer

Eckley

KECK
95.3 mhz FM; 100 kw; 339 ft.; N40 0 33 W102 45 35
US
(719) 336-4227
License: Eckley, Yuma County, CO held by Arnold Broadcasting Inc.
Group Owner: Arnold Broadcasting Inc.; (acq 7-31-2008; grpsl)
Arbitron Metro Market: Eckley, CO
William Arnold, General Manager

El Jebel

KGHT
03-01-1982; 100.5 mhz FM *Hrs Open:* 24; 6 kw; 295 ft.; N39 18 56 W106 57 32
US
(501) 985-0880, *Fax:* (501) 985-0260
License: El Jebel, Grant County, CO held by Metropolitan Radio Group Inc.
Group Owner: Metropolitan Radio Group Inc.; acq 1-97)
Nat'l Network: Salem Radio Network
Arbitron Metro Market: Little Rock, AR *Format:* Gospel *Target Audience:* WF 35-64. *Adv. Rates:* 28; 28; 28; na
Larry Skinner, General Manager
Lloyd Denney, General Sales Mgr
Paula Johnson, Programming Director
Ed Roupe, Sales

KGHT(FM)
01-01-2006; 100.5 mhz FM; 6 kw; Ant 295 ft; N39 18 56 W106 57 32
5551 Ridgewood Dr., Suite 501, Naples, FL 34108
(239) 263-7700, *Fax:* (239) 263-0998
License: El Jebel, Eagle County, CO held by BS&T Wireless Inc.
Population Served: 373,698 *Arbitron Metro Market:* Arlington, TX
David Budd, General Manager

Englewood

KNRV
01-01-1951; 1150 khz AM *Hrs Open:* 24; 10 kw-D, 1 kw-N, DA-2; N39 36 18 W104 50 25
1582 So. Parker Rd., Suite 204, Denver, CO 80203
(303) 696-5966, *Fax:* (303) 200-9190
www.onda1150am.com
hebertolv@limarccapital.com
License: Englewood, Arapahoe County, CO held by Amigo Multimedia Inc.
Population Served: 400,000 *Arbitron Metro Market:* Denver-Boulder,
Heberto Limas-Villers, President

Estes Park

KDEB(AM)
08-19-1967; 1470 khz AM *Hrs Open:* 24; 1 kw-D, 53 w-N; N40 20 15 W105 31 36
Mailing Address: Box 2810, Estes Park, CO 80517
Second Address: 184 E. Elkhorn Ave., Estes Park, CO 80517
(970) 586-9555, *Fax:* (970) 586-9561
keplradio@yahoo.com
License: Estes Park, Larimer County, CO held by WP Broadcasting of Colorado LLC.
Group Owner: Westburg Media Capital LP; (acq 6-30-2007)
Population Served: 5,976 *Arbitron Metro Market:* Estes Park, CO *Format:* Talk *Target Audience:* General. *Adv. Rates:* 17; 16; 17; 10
Vince Lupo, General Manager

KRKY-FM
04-06-1998; 102.1 mhz FM *Hrs Open:* 24; 6 kw horiz, 0 kw vert; 82 ft.; N40 21 38 W105 31 12
6807 Foxglove Drive, Cheyenne, WY 82009 US
(970) 453-2234, *Fax:* (970) 453-5425
www.alwaysmountaintime.com
jen@NRC365.com
License: Estes Park, Larimer County, CO held by NRC Broadcasting Inc.
Group Owner: United States CP LLC; (acq 8-31-2006; exchange for KSKE-FM Vail)
Nat'l Network: ABC
Arbitron Metro Market: Fort Collins, CO *Format:* Spanish *Target Audience:* Urban adults 19-34; Black, Hispanic, White *Adv. Rates:* 120;120;120;80
Jen Radueg, General Manager
Tonya Everist, General Sales Mgr

***KHIH**
88.7 mhz FM; 0.1 kw vert; -161 ft.; N40 21 44 W105 31 4
US
(970) 669-9200
License: Estes Park, Lincoln County, CO held by Kona Coast Radio LLC.
Group Owner: Kona Coast Radio LLC
Arbitron Metro Market: Estes Park, CO
Victor Michael Jr., General Manager

Evergreen

KXPK
06-08-1994; 96.5 mhz FM *Hrs Open:* 24; 100 kw; 1739 ft.; N39 40 35 W105 29 9
12655 N. Central Expressway, Suite 405, Dallas, TX 75243 US
(303) 832-0050, *Fax:* (303) 832-3410
www.965tricolor.com
License: Evergreen, Jefferson County, CO held by Entravision Holdings LLC.
Group Owner: Entravision Communications Corp.; (acq 5-1-02; $47.5 million).
Arbitron Metro Market: Denver-Boulder, CO *No. News Employees:* 1
Mario Carrera, General Manager

Fleming

KMAP
95.9 mhz FM; kw
US
(970) 669-9200
www.klove.com
License: Fleming, Lincoln County, CO held by Kona Coast Radio LLC.
Group Owner: Kona Coast Radio LLC
Arbitron Metro Market: Fleming, CO *Format:* Christian
Victor Michael Jr., General Manager

Fort Collins

KIIX
03-01-1947; 1410 khz AM *Hrs Open:* 24; 1 kw-D, DAN; 1 kw-N, DAN; N40 35 34 W105 6 18
201 East Fifth Street, Suite 1300, Cincinnati, OH 45202 US
(970) 461-2560, *Fax:* (970) 461-0118
www.1410kiix.com
info@1410kiix.com
License: Fort Collins, CO held by Citicasters Licenses Inc. (NEW).
Group Owner: Clear Channel Communications Inc.; (acq 5-4-99; grpsl)
Arbitron Metro Market: Fort Collins, CO *Format:* Sports *Hrs. of News Programming:* news progmg 35 hrs wkly *No. News Employees:* 2 *Target Audience:* 18-54; educated, affluent, professional
Stu Haskell, Operations Dir
Kathy Arias, General Sales Mgr
Chris Kelly, Programming Director
Mike Sanchez, Promotions Manager
Dave Agnew, Chief Engineer

***KCSU-FM**
09-20-1964; 90.5 mhz FM *Hrs Open:* 24; 10 kw; -354 ft.; N40 36 0 W105 9 21
110 16th Street, Denver, CO 80202 US
(970) 491-7611, *Fax:* (970) 491-1690
www.kcsufm.com
program@colostate.edu
License: Fort Collins, Larimer County, CO held by Colorado State Board of Agriculture.
Arbitron Metro Market: Fort Collins, CO *Format:* Alternative *Special Programming:* Hip-hop 3 hrs, jazz 3 hrs, Black 3 hrs wkly *Hrs. of News Programming:* News progmg 3 hrs wkly *Target Audience:* 18-34; general
Nick Sbesta, Station Manager
Mario Caballero, General Sales Mgr

KPAW
07-27-1975; 107.9 mhz FM *Hrs Open:* 24; 100 kw; 722 ft.; N40 53 42 W105 11 38
50 East Rivercenter Blvd, Suite 1200, Covington, KY 41011 US
(970) 461-2560, *Fax:* (970) 461-0118
www.1079thebear.com
info@1079thebear.com
License: Fort Collins, Larimer County, CO held by Citicasters Licenses Inc. (NEW).
Group Owner: Clear Channel Communications Inc.
Arbitron Metro Market: Fort Collins-Greeley, CO *Format:* Classic Rock *Target Audience:* 25-54; men

Stu Haskell, General Manager
Doc Jarnagin, Programming Director
Mike Sanchez, Promotions Manager

***KGCO**
01-01-2005; 88.3 mhz FM *Hrs Open:* 24; 0.15 kw vert; 1194 ft.; N40 37 3 W105 19 40
P.O. Box 887, Brentwood, TN 37034 US
(800) 260-5676
www.nuevavida.com
info@nuevavida.com
License: Fort Collins, Larimer County, CO held by Educational Media Foundation.
Group Owner: EMF Broadcasting; (acq 10-2-2003; grpsl)
Arbitron Metro Market: Fort Collins, CO *Format:* Christian *No. News Employees:* 3 *Target Audience:* 25-44; Judeo Christian female
Mike Novak, President

***KRFC**
88.9 mhz FM *Hrs Open:* 24; 0.01 kw horiz, 3 kw vert; 217 ft.; N40 34 53 W104 54 20
1840 Wallenberg Dr, Fort Collins, CO 80526 US
(970) 221-5075, *Fax:* (970) 221-5075
www.krfcfm.org
dj@krfcfm.org
License: Fort Collins, Larimer County, CO held by Public Radio for the Front Range.
Arbitron Metro Market: Fort Collins, CO *Format:* Variety/Diverse
Chris Kennison, Station Manager
Kristen Rasmussen, General Sales Mgr
Dennis Bigelow, Programming Director
Brian Hughes, Executive Director
Danielle Hastings, Development Director
Andrea Bradstreet, Volunteer Coordinator
AndrewSchneider, Web & Social Media

Fort Morgan

KFTM
05-22-1949; 1400 khz AM; 1 kw-U, ND1; N40 15 31 W103 51 7
Mailing Address: 803 West Main, Sterling, CO 80751 US
Second Address: 16041 Hwy. 34, Fort Morgan, CO 80701
(970) 867-5674, *Fax:* (970) 542-1023
www.kftm.net
kftm@medialogic.com
License: Fort Morgan, CO held by Media Logic LLC
Group Owner: Media Logic LLC; acq 9-29-03; $415,000).
Nat'l Network: AP Radio; Jones Radio Networks *Wire Services:* AP
Arbitron Metro Market: Fort Morgan, CO *Format:* Adult Contemp, News, 62, Talk *Special Programming:* Farm news 6 hrs, talk 5 hrs, sports 10 hrs, local 3 hrs wkly *Hrs. of News Programming:* news progmg 16 hrs wkly *No.News Employees:* 1 *Target Audience:* General; the people of (Morgan county) Colorado
Wayne Johnson, President
Wayne Johnson, General Manager
Dana Marini, General Sales Mgr
John Waters, Programming Director
Micheal Schaus, News Director

Fountain

KIBT
09-25-1992; 96.1 mhz FM *Hrs Open:* 24; 0.46 kw; 2169 ft.; N38 44 44 W104 51 42
4880 Santa Rosa Road, Suite 300, Camarillo, CA 93012 US
(719) 540-9200, *Fax:* (719) 579-0882
www.beatcolorado.com
info@beatcolorado.com
License: Fountain, El Paso County, CO held by AMFM Radio Licenses LLC.
Group Owner: Clear Channel Communications Inc.; (acq 7-1-2000; grpsl).
Nat'l Reps: Clear Channel
Arbitron Metro Market: CO Springs, CO Pueblo, CO *Format:* Contemporary Hits/Top 40 *Special Programming:* Blues 3 hrs wkly *Hrs. of News Programming:* News progmg 8-5 Monday - Friday *No. News Employees:* 1*Target Audience:* 25-44; men
Adv. Rates: 40; 35; 35; 15
Bill Fuerst, General Manager
Bill Fuerst, General Sales Mgr
Adam Burnes, Programming Director
Alex Ryden, Promotions Manager
Daren McMullin, Chief Engineer

KJME
890 khz AM; 5 kw-D, 580w-N, DA-2; 274 meters; N38 31 07 W104 36 03
965 South Irving Street, Denver, CO
(303) 937-1900
www.890kjme.com
License: Fountain, CO held by Timothy C Cutforth
Tim Cutforth, General Manager

Fowler

KPCR
99.3 mhz FM; 0.1 kw horiz; -98 ft.; N38 7 49 W104 1 22 US
(314) 909-8569, *Fax:* (314) 835-9739
www.joyfmonline.org
License: Fowler, Kit Carson County, CO held by Youngers Colorado Broadcasting LLC.
Arbitron Metro Market: Fowler, CO
Sandi Brown, General Manager
Nick Spiniolas, Promotions Manager
Kelly Corday, News Director
Kim Underwood, Social Media Director
Jill Willis, Events Manager
Brenda Pacini, Office/Accounting Manager

Fraser

***KPOY(FM)**
90.3 mhz FM; 150 w vert; Ant -1,007 ft; N39 56 49 W105 48 57
87 Jasper Lake Rd., Loveland, CO 80537
(970) 669-9200, *Fax:* (970) 669-0800
License: Fraser, Grand County, CO held by Cedar Cove Broadcasting Inc.
Group Owner: Cedar Cove Broadcasting Inc.
Population Served: 1,199 *Arbitron Metro Market:* Fraser, CO
Victor Michael Jr., President

Frisco

KYSL
05-27-1988; 93.9 mhz FM *Hrs Open:* 24; 560 w; 1,050 ft; N39 33 22 W106 06 53
P.O. Box 27, Frisco, CO 80443
(970) 513-9393, *Fax:* (970) 262-3677
www.krystal93.com
feedback@krystal93.com
License: Frisco, Summit County, CO held by Krystal Broadcasting Inc.
Nat'l Network: AP Radio *Nat'l Reps:* Interep
Hrs. of News Programming: news progmg 8 hrs wkly *No. News Employees:* 1 *Target Audience:* 25-49; upscale adults *Adv. Rates:* 27; 25; 27; 14
Ann Penny, President
John O'Connor, General Manager

Fruita

KEKB
05-24-1984; 99.9 mhz FM *Hrs Open:* 24; 79 kw; 1,380 ft; N39 03 56 W108 44 52
315 Kennedy Ave., Grand Junction, CO 53202
(970) 242-7788, *Fax:* (970) 243-0567
www.kekbfm.com
kekb@cumulus.com
License: Fruita, Mesa County, CO held by Townsquare Media Grand Junction
Group Owner: Cumulus Media Inc.; (acq 7-9-98; grpsl).
Population Served: 100,000 *Arbitron Metro Market:* Grand Junction, CO *Hrs. of News Programming:* news progmg 6 hrs wkly *No. News Employees:* 2 *Target Audience:* 25-54.
Lewis Dickey, CEO
John Dickey, President
Dave Noll, Operations Dir
Kevin Wodlinger, General Manager
Mack Dodge, Programming Director
Marty Gausvik, CFO
Ed Chandler, Operations Manager

KGJX
07-30-2012; 101.5 mhz FM; 3.15 kw; 418 m; N39 04 00 W108 44 45
3180 N. Mountain View Drive, San Diego, CA
(970)986-4900
License: Fruita, Mesa County, CO held by KBDX LLC

Glenwood Springs

***KLXV**
08-01-1995; 91.9 mhz FM *Hrs Open:* 24; 0.75 kw horiz, 0.185 kw vert; 2661 ft.; N39 25 30 W107 22 46
16075 W. Belleview Ave., Morrison, CO 80465 US
(916) 251-1600, *Fax:* (916) 251-1650
www.klove.com
klove@klove.com
License: Glenwood Springs, Garfield County, CO held by Educational Media Foundation.
Group Owner: EMF Broadcasting; (acq 12-28-00; grpsl).
Nat'l Network: K-Love
Arbitron Metro Market: Rocklin, CA *Format:* Christian *No. News Employees:* 3 *Target Audience:* 25-44; Judeo Christian, female
Darrell Chambliss, Chairman
Mike Novak, CEO/COO
Mike Novak, President
Jennifer Lohman, Operations Dir
David Pierce, Programming Director
Ed Lenane, News Director
Sam Wallington, Engineering Dir
Marya Morgan, News Reporter
Richard Hunt, News Reporter
Tracy Butler, Traffic Manager

KGLN
05-14-1950; 980 khz AM *Hrs Open:* 24
P.O. Box 1028, Glenwood Springs, CO 81602 US
(970) 254-2150, *Fax:* (970) 245-1100
www.kgln.com
jimt@gjradio.com
License: Glenwood Springs, CO held by MBC Grand Broadcasting Inc.
Group Owner: MBC Grand Broadcasting Inc.; (acq 1-16-2008; $250,000)
Nat'l Network: Fox News Radio
Format: Talk *Special Programming:* Finance 20 hrs wkly, religious 4 hrs wkly *Hrs. of News Programming:* news 140 hrs wkly *No. News Employees:* 1
David Hinson, President
Jim Ter Louw, General Manager

KKCH
09-01-1997; 92.7 mhz FM; 55.2 kw; 2503 ft.; N39 25 7 W107 22 6
1400 Easton Road, Bakersfield, CA 93303 US
(970) 949-0140, *Fax:* (970) 949-1464
mfox@rcbroadcasting.com
License: Glenwood Springs, Garfield County, CO held by NRC Broadcasting Mountain Group LLC.
Group Owner: NRC Broadcasting Inc.; (acq 5-1-2007; grpsl)
Steve Wodlinger, General Manager

KMTS
06-06-1977; 99.1 mhz FM; 10 kw; -226 ft.; N39 31 57 W107 20 30
P.O. Box 1028, Glenwood Springs, CO 81602 US
(970) 945-9124, *Fax:* (970) 945-5409
www.kmts.com
kmts@kmts.com
License: Glenwood Springs, Garfield County, CO held by Colorado West Broadcasting Inc.
Format: Country *Target Audience:* 25-50.
Gabe Chenoweth, President
Kimberly Henrie, General Sales Mgr
Ron Milhorn, News Director

KRVG
10-01-2000; 95.5 mhz FM *Hrs Open:* 24; 1 kw; 2416 ft.; N39 25 5 W107 22 1
488 Madison Ave, New York, NY 10022 US
(970) 241-6460, *Fax:* (970) 241-6452
www.wscradio.net
frank@wscradio.net
License: Glenwood Springs, Garfield County, CO held by Western Slope Communications LLC.
Group Owner: Western Slope Communications LLC
Arbitron Metro Market: Grand Junction, CO *Format:* Classic Rock *Hrs. of News Programming:* news progmg 20 hrs wkly *No. News Employees:* 1
John Reid, General Manager
Frank Ladd, Station Manager

***KDNK**
01-01-2004; 88.1 mhz FM *Hrs Open:* 6 AM-1 AM (M-F); 7 AM-1 AM (S, Su); 1.2 kw horiz, 1.07 kw vert; 2543 ft.; N39 25 8 W107 22 10
2249 S Josephine Street, Denver, CO 80210 US
(970) 963-0139, *Fax:* (970) 963-0810
www.kdnk.org
kdnk@kdnk.org
License: Glenwood Springs, Garfield County, CO held by Carbondale Community Access Radio Inc.
Nat'l Network: NPR
Arbitron Metro Market: Grand Junction, CO *Format:* News *Hrs. of News Programming:* News progmg 21 hrs wkly
Nancy Emerson, President
Steve Skinner, Station Manager
Amy Kimberly, General Sales Mgr
Luke Nestler, Programming Director
Wick Moses, Advertising Director
Laura McCormick, Vice President

Nancy Smith, Treasurer
Susan Darrow,Secretary

Granby

KRKY
07-03-1986; 930 khz AM *Hrs Open:* 24; 4.5 kw-D, ND1; 0.121 kw-N, ND1; N40 2 26 W105 56 11
P.O.Drawer J, Dillon, CO 80435 US
(970) 453-2234, *Fax:* (970) 453-5425
www.alwaysmountaintime.com
jen@NRC365.com
License: Granby, CO held by New Field Broadcasting LLC
Format: Country *Special Programming:* Agriculture one hr, Sp one hr wkly *Hrs. of News Programming:* news progmg 5 hrs wkly *No. News Employees:* 2 *Target Audience:* 24-49; adults *Adv. Rates:* 15; 12; 10; 8
Jen Radueg, General Manager
Tonya Everist, General Sales Mgr
Brandon Spence, Programming Director

Grand Junction

*KAFM
01-01-1999; 88.1 mhz FM *Hrs Open:* 24; 0.3 kw; 1301 ft.; N39 4 0 W108 44 41
3684 G 4/10 Road, Palisade, CO 81526 US
(970) 241-8801
www.kafmradio.org
kafm@kafmradio.org
License: Grand Junction, Mesa County, CO held by Grand Valley Public Radio Co. Inc.
Arbitron Metro Market: Grand Junction, CO *Format:* Talk *Hrs. of News Programming:* News progmg 20 hrs wkly *Target Audience:* 25-80.
Barry Barak, President
Tracy Baker, Operations Dir
Ryan Stringfellow, General Manager
Jon Rizzo, Programming Director
Marc Foster, Music Director

KBKL
01-01-1993; 107.9 mhz FM *Hrs Open:* 24; 100 kw; 1,305 ft; N39 04 00 W108 44 41
315 Kennedy Ave., Grand Junction, CO 53202
(970) 242-7788, *Fax:* (970) 243-0567
www.kool1079.com
kool1079@cumulus.com
License: Grand Junction, Mesa County, CO held by Townsquare Media Grand Junction License LLC
Group Owner: Cumulus Media Inc.; (acq 3-10-98; grpsl)
Arbitron Metro Market: Grand Junction, CO *Target Audience:* 25-54.
Lewis Dickey, CEO
John Dickey, President
Ed Chandler, Operations Dir
Kevin Wodlinger, General Manager
Marty Gausvik, CFO
Jonathan Pinch, COO

*KCIC
03-04-1979; 88.5 mhz FM *Hrs Open:* 24; 0.44 kw; -351 ft.; N39 4 41 W108 28 36
3102 E Road, Grand Junction, CO 81504 US
(970) 434-4113
info@kcicfm.com
License: Grand Junction, Mesa County, CO held by Pear Park Baptist Schools.
Arbitron Metro Market: Grand Junction, CO *Format:* Religious *Special Programming:* Class 14 hrs wkly *Hrs. of News Programming:* 2 hrs wkly
Randy David, President
Glenn Gardner, General Manager

KEXO
01-01-1942; 1230 khz AM *Hrs Open:* 24; 1 kw-U, ND1; N39 5 41 W108 34 41
715 Horizon Drive, Suite 430, Grand Junction, CO 81506 US
(970) 242-7788, *Fax:* (970) 243-0567
www.kexo1230.com
kexo1230@cumulus.com
License: Grand Junction, CO held by Cumulus Licensing Corp.
Group Owner: Cumulus Media Inc.; (acq 1-2000)
Arbitron Metro Market: Grand Junction, CO *Format:* Talk *No. News Employees:* 1 *Target Audience:* General.
Lewis Dickey, CEO
Ed Chandler, Operations Dir
Kevin Wodlinger, General Manager
Kim Gordon, Programming Director
Marty Gausvik, CFO

*KLFV
04-24-1982; 90.3 mhz FM *Hrs Open:* 24; 3 kw; 1309 ft.; N39 3 57 W108 44 48
16075 W. Belleview Ave., Morrison, CO 80465 US
(916) 251-1600, *Fax:* (916) 251-1650
www.klove.com
klove@klove.com
License: Grand Junction, Mesa County, CO held by Educational Media Foundation.
Group Owner: EMF Broadcasting; (acq 12-28-00; grpsl).
Nat'l Network: K-Love
Arbitron Metro Market: Grand Junction, CO *Format:* Christian *Special Programming:* Sp 2 hrs wkly *No. News Employees:* 3 *Target Audience:* 25-44; Judeo Christian, female
Darrell Chambliss, Chairman
Mke Novak, CEO
Mike Novak, President
Jennifer Lohman, Operations Dir
Eric Moser, General Sales Mgr
David Pierce, Programming Director
Ed Lenane, News Director
Sam Wallington, Engineering Dir
AlanMason, Chief Operating Officer
D. Kevin Blair, Secretary and General Counsel
Amy Baumann, News Anchor
Jennifer James, News Anchor
Jennifer James, News Anchor
Mitch Barnhart, Director

KKVT(FM)
05-01-1960; 92.3 mhz FM *Hrs Open:* 24; 100 kw; 1,378 ft; N39 04 00 W108 44 41
1360 E. Sherwood Dr., Grand Junction, CO 81501
(970) 254-2100, *Fax:* (970) 245-7551
www.gjradio.com
License: Grand Junction, Mesa County, CO held by MBC Grand Broadcasting Inc
Group Owner: MBC Grand Broadcasting Inc.
Wire Services: AP
Population Served: 240,000 *Arbitron Metro Market:* Grand Junction, CO *Hrs. of News Programming:* News progmg 8 hrs wkly *Target Audience:* Adults; 25-54
David Hinson, President

*KMSA
02-18-1975; 91.3 mhz FM *Hrs Open:* 24; 3 kw; 1274 ft.; N39 3 58 W108 44 50
1175 Texas, Grand Junction, CO 81501 US
(970) 248-1442, *Fax:* (970) 248-1834
www.mesastate.edu
rtucci@mesastate.edu
License: Grand Junction, Mesa County, CO held by Mesa State College.
Arbitron Metro Market: Grand Junction, CO *Format:* Alternative, Reggae, 92 *Special Programming:* Black 6 hrs, folk 2 hrs, jazz 12 hrs wkly *Hrs. of News Programming:* news progmg 10 hrs wkly *No. News Employees:* 2*Target Audience:* 18-60; college students and gen pub

KMXY
01-01-1996; 104.3 mhz FM; 100 kw; 1,296 ft
315 Kennedy Ave., Grand Junction, CO 53202
(970) 242-7788, *Fax:* (970) 243-0567
www.mix1043fm.com
mix1043@cumulus.com
License: Grand Junction, Mesa County, CO held by Townsquare Media Grand Junction
Group Owner: Cumulus Media Inc.; (acq 7-9-98; grpsl).
Arbitron Metro Market: Grand Junction, CO
Lewis Dickey, CEO
John Dickey, President
Dave Noll, Operations Dir
Kevin Wodlinger, General Manager
Marty Gausvik, CFO

KNZZ
05-01-1926; 1100 khz AM *Hrs Open:* 24; 36 kw-C, DAN; 50 kw-D, DAN; DAN; 10 kw-N; N38 57 6 W108 25 10
1360 E. Sherwood Drive, Grand Junction, CO 81501 US
(970) 254-2100, *Fax:* (970) 245-7551
www.gjradio.com
License: Grand Junction, CO held by MBC Grand Broadcasting Inc.
Group Owner: MBC Grand Broadcasting Inc.; (acq 8-30-89).
Nat'l Network: Fox News Radio *Wire Services:* AP
Arbitron Metro Market: Grand Junction, CO *Format:* News, News/Talk, 86 *Hrs. of News Programming:* news progmg 44 hrs wkly *No. News Employees:* 3 *Target Audience:* 25-64.
David Hinson, President
Jim TerLouw, General Manager
Dave Beck, General Sales Mgr

Libby Jackson, News Director
Robert Bowe, Engineering Dir

*KPRN
04-01-1985; 89.5 mhz FM *Hrs Open:* 24; 19.83 kw; 1319 ft.; N39 3 58 W108 44 43
2249 S Josephine Street, Denver, CO 80210 US
(303) 871-9191, *Fax:* (303) 733-3319
www.cpr.org
info@cpr.org
License: Grand Junction, Mesa County, CO held by Public Broadcasting of Colorado Inc.
Nat'l Network: NPR *Regional Network:* Colo. Pub.
Arbitron Metro Market: Grand Junction, CO *Format:* News *Hrs. of News Programming:* news progmg 28 hrs wkly *No. News Employees:* 1 *Target Audience:* 25 plus.
Max Wycisk, President
Sue Coughlin, General Sales Mgr
Sean Nethery, Programming Director
Robert Hensler, Engineering Dir
Jenny Gentry, Executive Vice President

KTMM
01-01-1959; 1340 khz AM *Hrs Open:* 24
715 Horizon Drive, Suite 430, Grand Junction, CO 81506 US
(970) 242-1340, *Fax:* (970) 245-7551
www.theteam1340.com
jimd@gjradio.com
License: Grand Junction, CO held by MBC Grand Broadcasting Inc.
Group Owner: MBC Grand Broadcasting Inc.
Nat'l Network: ESPN Radio
Arbitron Metro Market: Grand Junction, CO *Format:* Sports *Hrs. of News Programming:* news progmg 10 hrs wkly *No. News Employees:* 1 *Target Audience:* 25-54; men
Jim Davis, Programming Director

KMGJ
11-01-1973; 93.1 mhz FM *Hrs Open:* 24; 100 kw; 1434 ft.; N39 3 59 W108 44 41
715 Horizon Drive, Suite 430, Grand Junction, CO 81506 US
(970) 241-9393, *Fax:* (970) 245-7551
www.931magic.com
931magic@gmail.com
License: Grand Junction, Mesa County, CO held by MBC Grand Broadcasting, Inc.
Group Owner: MBC Grand Broadcasting Inc.; acq 5-94; with co-located AM).
Arbitron Metro Market: Grand Junction, CO *Format:* Contemporary Hits/Top 40 *Hrs. of News Programming:* news progmg 6 hrs wkly *No. News Employees:* 1 *Target Audience:* 18-49; women
Robert St. John, Operations Dir
Jim Terlouw, General Manager
Dave Beck, General Sales Mgr
Chris Britt, Programming Director

KJOL
06-19-1957; 620 khz AM *Hrs Open:* 24; 5 kw-D, ND2; 0.079 kw-N, ND2; N39 7 35 W108 38 13
660 Rood Avenue, Grand Junction, CO 81501 US
(970) 254-5565, *Fax:* (970) 254-5550
www.kjol.org
info@kjol.org
License: Grand Junction, CO held by United Ministries.
Group Owner: United Ministries; (acq 5-1-2003).
Arbitron Metro Market: Grand Junction, *Format:* Christian
Ken Andrews, General Manager
Ken Andrews, Station Manager
Rhonda Repshire, Promotions Manager
Kurt Neuswanger, Music Director

KMOZ-FM
03-27-1999; 100.7 mhz FM *Hrs Open:* 24; 30 kw; 1558 ft.; N39 3 59.36 W108 44 40.94
300 East Rock Road, Allentown, PA 18103 US
(970) 254-2100, *Fax:* (970) 245-7551
www.gjradio.com
License: Grand Junction, Mesa County, CO held by MBC Grand Broadcasting Inc.
Group Owner: MBC Grand Broadcasting Inc.
Arbitron Metro Market: Grand Junction, CO *Format:* Country *Hrs. of News Programming:* news progmg 2 hrs wkly *No. News Employees:* 2 *Target Audience:* 25-54.
Dave Beck, General Manager

Greeley

KFKA
05-21-1921; 1310 khz AM *Hrs Open:* 24; 5 kw-D, DAN; 1 kw-N, DAN; N40 21 56 W104 43 56
P.O. Box K, Greely, CO 80632 US

(970) 356-1310, *Fax:* (970) 356-1314
www.1310kfka.com
info@1310kfka.com
License: Greeley, CO held by Music Ventures LLC dba Broadcast Media LLC
Nat'l Network: CBS Radio
Arbitron Metro Market: Greely, CO *Format:* News, News/Talk, 86
Special Programming: Farm 15 hrs, Ger one hr, relg 4 hrs wkly
Hrs. of News Programming: news progmg 25 hrs wkly *No. News Employees:* 2 *TargetAudience:* 25-54; community-minded, active people
Damon Sasso, Operations Dir
Justin Sasso, General Manager
Brady Hull, General Sales Mgr
Troy Coverdale, News Director
Joe Cross, Chief Engineer

KSME
12-25-1975; 96.1 mhz FM *Hrs Open:* 24; 100 kw; 735 ft.; N40 40 50 W104 56 32
50 East Rivercenter Blvd., #1200, Covington, KY 41011 US
(970) 461-2560, *Fax:* (970) 461-0118
www.kissfmcolorado.com
stuhaskell@clearchannelradio.com
License: Greeley, Weld County, CO held by Citicasters Licenses Inc. (NEW).
Group Owner: Clear Channel Communications Inc.; (acq 5-4-99; grpsl).
Nat'l Network: ABC
Arbitron Metro Market: Fort Collins-Gr, IA *Format:* Contemporary Hits/Top 40 *No. News Employees:* 2 *Target Audience:* 10-44.
Stu Haskell, Operations Dir
Kathy Arias, General Sales Mgr
Ryan Kramer, Programming Director
Mike Sanchez, Promotions Manager

KGRE
08-24-1948; 1450 khz AM *Hrs Open:* 24; 1 kw-U, ND1; N40 26 15 W104 43 25
2132 N. Valley Street, Burbank, CA 91505 US
(970) 356-1450, *Fax:* (970) 356-8522
www.tigrecolorado.com
kgre@msn.com
License: Greeley, CO held by Greeley Broadcasting Corp.
Group Owner: Greeley Broadcasting Corp.; (acq 3-24-98)
Arbitron Metro Market: Fort Collins, CO *Special Programming:* Bienvenidos a America one hr wkly *Target Audience:* 25-54; Hispanic *Adv. Rates:* 25; 25; 25; 20
Ricardo Salazar, President

*KUNC
01-01-1967; 91.5 mhz FM *Hrs Open:* 24; 36 kw; 1260 ft.; N40 37 3 W105 19 39
University of N Colorado, Greeley, CO 80639 US
(970) 378-2579, *Fax:* (970) 378-2580
www.kunc.org
comment@kunc.org
License: Greeley, Weld County, CO held by Community Radio for Northern Colorado
Nat'l Network: NPR; PRI *Wire Services:* AP
Arbitron Metro Market: Greeley, CO *Format:* News, Variety/Diverse *Hrs. of News Programming:* news progmg 65 hrs wkly *No. News Employees:* 5 *Target Audience:* General.
Jamie Wood, CFO
Neil Best, President & CEO
Ryan Thompson, Operations Dir
Neil Best, General Manager
Michelle Kornrich, General Sales Mgr
Kirk Mowens, Programming Director
Brian Larson, News Director
Ken Broeffle, ChiefEngineer
Robert Leja, Director of Corporate Support and Marketing
Netanya Hearne, Membership Associate
Kirk Mowers, Content Director
Nancy D'Albergaria, Development Director
Jim Hill, Digital Media Manager
Benjamin McPhail, MusicDirector

Greenwood Village

KDSP(FM)
07-19-1995; 102.3 mhz FM *Hrs Open:* 24; 6 kw; Ant 210 ft; N39 39 55 W104 51 38 *Rebroadcasts:* Simulcast with KJAC(FM) Timnath 100%
1201 18th St., Suite 250, Denver, CO 80202
(303) 296-7025, *Fax:* (303) 296-7030
www.kcuvradio.com
info@kcuvradio.com
License: Greenwood Village, Arapahoe County, CO held by NRC Broadcasting Inc.
Group Owner: NRC Broadcasting Inc.; (acq 11-9-2005; $16 million)
Arbitron Metro Market: Denver, CO *Format:* Adult Contemp
Timothy Brown, General Manager

Gunnison

KEJJ
01-01-1980; 98.3 mhz FM *Hrs Open:* 24-7; 3 kw; 299 ft.; N38 31 22 W106 54 28 *Rebroadcasts:* at crested butte/lake city
P.O. Box 970, Montrose, CO 81401 US
(970) 641-4000, *Fax:* (970) 641-3300
kpkeharv@hotmail.com
License: Gunnison, Gunnison County, CO held by John Harvey Rees
Nat'l Network: Fox News Radio
Format: Oldies *No. News Employees:* 2 *Target Audience:* 25-54. *Adv. Rates:* 15; 12.50; 15; 6.50
John Rees, CEO
Matt Rees, Operations Dir

KPKE
08-23-1960; 1490 khz AM *Hrs Open:* 24; 1 kw-U, ND1; N38 33 57 W106 55 32
Box 1288, Gunnison, CO 81230 US
(970) 641-4000, *Fax:* (970) 641-3300
http://www.visitgunnison.com/businesspage.cfm?businessid=833
kpke@gunnison.com
License: Gunnison, CO held by John Harvey Rees.
Nat'l Network: Fox News Radio
Format: Country *Special Programming:* Den Broncos *Hrs. of News Programming:* news progmg 2 hrs wkly *No. News Employees:* 1 *Target Audience:* 25-54. *Adv. Rates:* 9.50; 4; 5; 2
John Rees, CEO
Matt Rees, Operations Dir

KVLE-FM
04-18-1980; 102.3 mhz FM *Hrs Open:* 24; 3 kw; -459 ft.; N38 33 53 W106 55 38
54 Monument Circle, Indianapolis, IN 46204 US
(303) 776-2323, *Fax:* (303) 776-1377
www.kvleradio.com
feedback@radioonetwork.com
License: Gunnison, Gunnison County, CO held by Pilgrim Communications Inc.
Group Owner: Pilgrim Communications Inc.; (acq 4-30-98; $300,000)
Nat'l Network: ABC *Wire Services:* CBS
Arbitron Metro Market: Longmont,CO *Format:* Classic Rock *Hrs. of News Programming:* News progmg 12 hrs wkly *Target Audience:* 25-54; males: 35-54.
Chuck Duncan, CEO
Roger Cridelbaugh, Operations Dir
Tyler Kincaid, General Manager
Gary Montgomery, General Sales Mgr
Nancy Smith, Business Manager
Gene Hood, Owner

*KWSB-FM
01-26-1968; 91.1 mhz FM *Hrs Open:* 18; 0.135 kw; 299 ft.; N38 31 22 W106 54 28
Kwsb Taylor Hall Rm. 111, Gunnison, CO 81231 US
(970) 943-3222, *Fax:* (970) 943-7069
www.kwsb.org
kwsb@western.edu
License: Gunnison, Gunnison County, CO held by Western State College of Colorado.
Nat'l Network: AP Radio
Arbitron Metro Market: Gunnison, CO *Format:* Variety/Diverse
Special Programming: Jazz 3 hrs, reggae 6 hrs, blues 3 hrs, 60s hits 3 hrs, Sp one hr wkly *Hrs. of News Programming:* News progmg 2 hrs wkly *TargetAudience:* 18-25.
Tory Maurer, General Manager
Brendan Kholer, Station Manager
Scott Stewart, Programming Director
Stephanie Bollini, Promotions Manager
Rusty Spydell, Production Director
Kelsey Hollenbaugh, Music Director
Trevor Bartez, StationTrainer

Gypsum

*KLRY
01-01-2003; 91.3 mhz FM *Hrs Open:* 24; 0.11 kw; 2818 ft.; N39 46 30 W106 50 45 *Rebroadcasts:* Rebroadcasts KLVR(FM) Santa Rosa, CA 100%
16075 W Belleview Ave., Morrison, CO 80465 US
(800) 525-5683, *Fax:* (916) 251-1650
www.klove.com
klove@klove.com
License: Gypsum, Eagle County, CO held by Educational Media Foundation.
Group Owner: EMF Broadcasting; (acq 10-2-2003; grpsl).
Nat'l Network: K-Love
Arbitron Metro Market: Gypsum, CO *Format:* Christian *No. News Employees:* 13 *Target Audience:* 25-44; Judeo Christian female
Darrell Chambliss, Chairman
Mike Novak, President and CEO
Jennifer Lohman, General Sales Mgr
David Pierce, Programming Director
Ed Lenane, News Director
Sam Wallington, Engineering Dir
Scott Smith, Music Director
Richard Hunt,News Reporter
Marya Morgan, News Reporter
Tracy Butler, Traffic Manager
Dan Antonelli, Chief Business Development Officer

KQSE
03-01-2005; 102.5 mhz FM; 1.35 kw; 2165 ft.; N39 44 18 W106 47 58
165 E Avenue, P O Box 87, Limon, CO 80828 US
(970) 949-0140, *Fax:* (970) 949-1464
www.alwaysmountaintime.com/kqse
holli@NRC365.com
License: Gypsum, Eagle County, CO held by Wildcat Communications L.L.C.
Arbitron Metro Market: Gypsum, CO
Holli Snyder, General Sales Mgr
Tonya Everist, Director of Sales

Hayden

KQZR
01-01-2000; 107.3 mhz FM; 29 kw; 650 ft.; N40 31 16 W107 17 46
300 East Lombard, Suite #620, Baltimore, MD 21202 US
(970) 879-5368, *Fax:* (970) 879-5843
www.alwaysmountaintime.com/zrock
ecampbell@nrcbroadcasting.com
License: Hayden, Routt County, CO held by NRC Broadcasting Mountain Group LLC.
Group Owner: NRC Broadcasting Inc.; (acq 5-1-2007; grpsl)
Arbitron Metro Market: Hayden, CO *Format:* Classic Rock
Steve Wodlinger, General Manager
Eli Campbell, General Sales Mgr
John Johnston, Programming Director

*KHCO
01-01-2005; 90.1 mhz FM; 1.8 kw vert; 1713 ft.; N40 27 4 W106 45 6 *Rebroadcasts:* Rebroadcasts KLRD(FM) Yucaipa, CA 100%
188 South Bellevue, Suite 222, Memphis, TN 38104 US
(888) 937-2471, *Fax:* (916) 251-1650
www.air1.com
info@air1.com
License: Hayden, Routt County, CO held by Educational Media Foundation.
Group Owner: EMF Broadcasting; (acq 6-8-2005; $25,000 for CP).
Nat'l Network: Air 1
Arbitron Metro Market: Hayden, CO *Format:* Alternative, Christian
Darrell Chambliss, Chairman
Alan Mason, COO
Mike Novak, President and CEO
Jennifer Lohman, Operations Dir
David Pierce, Programming Director
Ed Lenane, News Director
Sam Wallington, Engineering Dir
Marya Morgan, NewsReporter
Richard Hunt, News Reporter
Dan Antonelli, Chief Business Development Officer
Eric Moser, Chief Financial Officer
Brian Burger, Vice President of Human Resources
D. Kevin Blair, Secretary and General Counsel

Holyoke

KSTH
01-01-2002; 92.3 mhz FM; 1 kw; 210 ft.; N40 34 49 W102 19 11
P.O. Box 71, McCook, NE 69001 US
(308) 345-5400, *Fax:* (308) 345-4720
www.plansreporter.k2radio.net/ksth
License: Holyoke, Phillips County, CO held by Armada Media - McCook Inc.
Group Owner: Armada Media Corp.; (acq 1-17-2007; grpsl)
Format: Adult Contemp
Andrew Stossmeister, Operations Dir
Bryan Loker, General Manager

Idalia

KWDI
94.1 mhz FM; 0.1 kw; 190 ft.; N39 42 10 W102 17 32 US
(858) 277-4991, *Fax:* (858) 277-1365
License: Idalia, Yuma County, CO held by Horizon Christian Fellowship.
Group Owner: Horizon Christian Fellowship; (acq 2-9-2006; grpsl).
Arbitron Metro Market: Idalia, CO
Mike MacIntosh, President

Ignacio

*KSUT
06-09-1976; 91.3 mhz FM *Hrs Open:* 24; 2 kw; 1631 ft.; N37 11 3 W107 29 6
Mailing Address: P.O. Box 737, Ignacio, CO 81137 US
Second Address: 123 Capote Dr., Ignacio, CO 81137
(970) 563-0255, *Fax:* (970) 563-0399
www.ksut.org
info@ksut.org
License: Ignacio, La Plata County, CO held by KUTE Inc.
Group Owner: KUTE Inc.
Nat'l Network: NPR; PRI
Arbitron Metro Market: Ignacio, CO *Format:* Native American
Special Programming: American Indian 7 hrs, class 8 hrs, jazz 15 hrs wkly *Hrs. of News Programming:* News progmg 30 hrs wkly *Target Audience:* 24 plus;public radio audience
Ken Brott, Operations Dir
Stasia Lanier, Station Manager
Jim Belcher, Programming Director
Beth Warren, Promotions Manager

*KUTE
06-01-1998; 90.1 mhz FM; 3 kw vert; 1965 ft.; N37 21 51 W107 46 56
P O Box 737, Ignacio, CO 81137 US
(970) 563-0255, *Fax:* (970) 563-0399
www.ksut.org
bruce@ksut.org
License: Ignacio, La Plata County, CO held by KUTE Inc.
Group Owner: KUTE Inc.
Nat'l Network: NPR; PRI
Arbitron Metro Market: Ignacio, CO *Format:* Triple A
Stasia Lanier, Station Manager
Beth Warren, Promotions Manager

Johnstown

KHNC
01-01-1993; 1360 khz AM
26886 W.C.R. 17, Johnstown, CO 80534 US
(970) 587-5175, *Fax:* (970) 587-5450
www.americanewsnet.com
comments@americanewsnet.com; don@americanewsnet.com; danette@americanewsnet.com; mike@americanewsnet
License: Johnstown, CO held by Donald A. and Sharon A. Wiedeman.
Format: News, News/Talk, 86 *Hrs. of News Programming:* news progmg 100 hrs wkly *No. News Employees:* 5
Donald Wiedeman, President
Michael Golden, Operations Dir

Julesburg

KJBL
01-01-2002; 96.5 mhz FM; 0.265 kw; -106 ft.; N40 59 18 W102 15 44
P.O. Box 71, McCook, NE 69001 US
(308) 345-5400, *Fax:* (308) 345-4720
www.plainsreporter.k2radio.net
bryan@highplainsradio.net?subject=Email%20for%20further%20details%20here
License: Julesburg, Sedgwick County, CO held by Armada Media - McCook Inc.
Group Owner: Armada Media Corp.; (acq 1-17-2007; grpsl)
Arbitron Metro Market: Julesburg, CO *Format:* Country
Andrew Stossmeister, Operations Dir
Bryan Loker, General Manager

Kremmling

KIFT(FM)
11-01-1987; 106.3 mhz FM *Hrs Open:* 24; 2.5 kw; 1,050 ft; N40 00 18 W106 26 57
130 Ski Hill Rd. #240, Breckenridge, CO 80424
(970) 453-2234, *Fax:* (970) 453-5425
www.alwaysmountaintime.com
jen@NRC365.com
License: Kremmling, Grand County, CO held by New Field Broadcasting LLC
Population Served: 25,000*Format:* Contemporary Hits/Top 40
Hrs. of News Programming: news progmg 5 hrs wkly *No. News Employees:* 2 *Target Audience:* 24-49. *Adv. Rates:* 20; 15; 17; 12
Jen Radueg, General Manager
Tonya Everist, General Sales Mgr
Brandon Spence, Programming Director

La Jara

KZBR
97.1 mhz FM; 25 kw; 180 ft.; N37 22 5 W106 6 44 US
(719) 206-3013, *Fax:* (719) 480-6008
www.kzbr971.com
admin@kzbr971.com
License: La Jara, Conejos County, CO held by Lendsi Radio LLC.
Arbitron Metro Market: Alamosa, CO *Format:* Variety/Diverse
Lina Jones, General Manager

La Junta

KTHN
08-28-1974; 92.1 mhz FM; 3 kw; 299 ft.; N37 59 15 W103 34 2
P. O. Box 485, La Junta, CO 81050 US
(719) 384-5456, *Fax:* (719) 384-5450
www.cherrycreekradio.com
kblj@secom.net
License: La Junta, Otero County, CO held by CCR-La Junta IV LLC
Group Owner: Cherry Creek Radio LLC
Arbitron Metro Market: La Junta, CO *Format:* Country
Joe Swartz, CEO
Pat Gittings, General Manager
Adrian Hart, General Sales Mgr
Pat McGee, Programming Director

KBLJ
07-23-1937; 1400 khz AM; 1 kw-U, ND1; N37 59 14 W103 34 1
P. O. Box 485, La Junta, CO 81050 US
(719) 384-5456, *Fax:* (719) 384-5450
www.cherrycreekradio.com
pgittings@cherrycreekradio.com
License: La Junta, CO held by CCR-La Junta IV LLC.
Group Owner: Cherry Creek Radio LLC; (acq 12-19-2003; grpsl).
Nat'l Network: ABC
Arbitron Metro Market: La Junta, CO *Format:* Contemporary Hits/Top 40, Adult Contemp *Target Audience:* 30 plus; general
Adv. Rates: 21; 15; 15; 10
Pat Gittings, General Manager
Adrian Hart, General Sales Mgr
Pat McGee, Programming Director

*KECC
08-01-2002; 89.1 mhz FM *Hrs Open:* 24; 0.74 kw; 299 ft.; N37 58 43 W103 34 48 *Rebroadcasts:* Rebroadcasts KRCC(FM) Colorado Springs 100%
14 East Cache La Poudre, Colorado Springs, CO 80903 US
(719) 473-4801, *Fax:* (719) 473-7863
www.krcc.org
info@krcc.org
License: La Junta, Otero County, CO held by The Colorado College.
Nat'l Network: NPR; PRI
Arbitron Metro Market: Colorado Springs, CO *Format:* News, Variety/Diverse
Mike Procell, Operations Dir
Delaney Utterback, General Manager
Jeff Bieri, Promotions Manager
Joel Belik, Chief Engineer
Barbara Wilson, Human Resources

Lafayette

KRKS-FM
03-15-1971; 94.7 mhz FM *Hrs Open:* 24; 100 kw; 984 ft.; N40 4 19 W105 21 14
4880 Santa Rosa Road, Suite 300, Camarillo, CA 93012 US
(303) 750-5687, *Fax:* (303) 696-8063
www.krks.com
krks@krks.com
License: Lafayette, Boulder County, CO held by Salem Media of Colorado Inc.
Group Owner: Salem Communications Corp.; (acq 12-15-93; $5 million;
Arbitron Metro Market: Denver-Boulder, CO *Format:* Christian, Talk
Edward Atsinger, President
Joe Davis, Operations Dir
Brian Taylor, VP
Jules Dygert, General Sales Mgr
Cliff Mikkelson, Engineering Dir
Rob Adair, Regional Vice President

Lakewood

KEPN
01-08-1955; 1600 khz AM; 5 kw-D, DAN; 5 kw-N, DAN; N39 39 20 W105 4 28
1095 South Monaco Pakway, Denver, CO 80224 US
(303) 321-0950, *Fax:* (303) 321-3383
www.1600thezone.com
comments @1600thezone.com
License: Lakewood, CO held by Lincoln Financial Media Co. of Colorado.
Group Owner: Lincoln Financial Media; (acq 4-3-2006; grpsl)
Nat'l Network: ESPN Radio *Nat'l Reps:* CBS Radio
Arbitron Metro Market: Denver-Lakewood-Boulder, CO *Format:* Sports
Clarke Brown, President
Robert Call, Operations Dir
Steve Price, General Sales Mgr
Tim Spence, Programming Director
J.J. Pelini, Promotions Manager
Simone Seiklay, News Director
Brad Hart, Engineering Dir
Randy Weidner,National Sales Manager
Simone Seikaly, Public Affairs Director

KQKS
07-09-1966; 107.5 mhz FM; 91 kw; 1198 ft.; N39 41 45 W105 9 54
1095 S. Monaco Parkway, Denver, CO 80224 US
(303) 321-0950, *Fax:* (303) 321-3383
www.ks1075.com
License: Lakewood, Jefferson County, CO held by Lincoln Financial Media Co. of Colorado.
Group Owner: Lincoln Financial Media
Arbitron Metro Market: Denver-Boulder, CO *Format:* Contemporary Hits/Top 40 *Target Audience:* 12-34.
Wendy Davis, General Sales Mgr
John E. Kage, Programming Director
JJ Pellini, Promotions Manager

*KVOD
01-01-2005; 88.1 mhz FM; 1.2 kw vert; Ant 1,053 ft; N39 40 18 W105 13 05
Bridges Broadcast Center, 7409 S. Alton Ct., Centennial, CO 80226
(303) 871-9191, *Fax:* (303) 733-3319
www.cpr.org
info@cpr.org
License: Lakewood, Jefferson County, CO held by PRC Denver-I LLC
Regional Network: Colo. Pub.
Population Served: 2,548,279 *Arbitron Metro Market:* Denver-Boulder, CO *Special Programming:* 24 Hour Classsical
No. News Employees: 20 *Target Audience:* 18 Plus
Max Wycisk, President
Max Wycisk, General Manager
Jackie Purmort, General Sales Mgr
Doug Clifton, Programming Director
Jim East, Membership Director
Kelley Griffin, VP News
Bob Hensler, Engineering Dir

Lamar

KLMR
12-01-1948; 920 khz AM *Hrs Open:* 24; 5 kw-D, DAN; 0.5 kw-N, DAN; N38 6 53 W102 37 16
Mailing Address: 1200 Rosewood Dr., Loveland, CO 80537 US
Second Address: 7350 US Hwy. 50, Lamar, CO 81052
(719) 336-2206, *Fax:* (719) 336-7973
klmraudio@yahoo.com
License: Lamar, CO held by CCR-Lamar IV LLC.
Group Owner: Cherry Creek Radio LLC; (acq 12-19-2003; grpsl).
Nat'l Network: ABC
Arbitron Metro Market: Pueblo *Format:* Country *Hrs. of News Programming:* News progmg 12 hrs wkly *Target Audience:* 25-54.
Pat Gittings, General Manager
Ty Harmon, Programming Director
Erik Stone, News Director

KLMR-FM
11-01-1978; 93.5 mhz FM *Hrs Open:* 24; 100 kw; 479 ft.; N38 2 10 W102 35 58
1200 Rosewood Dr., Loveland, CO 80537 US
(719) 336-2206, *Fax:* (719) 336-7973
klmraudio@yahoo.com

License: Lamar, Prowers County, CO
Group Owner: Cherry Creek Radio LLC
Arbitron Metro Market: Lamar, CO *Format:* Classic Rock *Target Audience:* 25-54.
Pat Gittings, General Manager

KVAY
08-05-1991; 105.7 mhz FM *Hrs Open:* 24; 100 kw; 479 ft.; N38 6 44 W102 57 39
P.O. Box 1176, 224 South Main, Lamar, CO 81052 US
(719) 336-8734, *Fax:* (719) 336-5977
www.kvay.com
deb@kvay.com
License: Lamar, Prowers County, CO held by Beacon Broadcasting LLC
Nat'l Network: AP Radio
Arbitron Metro Market: Lamar, CO *Format:* Country *Special Programming:* Gospel 4 hrs, classic rock 4 hrs wkly *No. News Employees:* 1 *Target Audience:* 25-55. *Adv. Rates:* 15; 12; 12; 6
Cory Alan Forgue, Chief of Operations Engineer
Debbie Ellis, General Manager
Rich Lingle, Sales
Travis Williams, Assistant Program Director and Music Director
Cory Alan Forgue, News Contact
Frankie Carrillo, Office Manager/TrafficDirectors
Kayla Bronson, Sales
Anthony LaTour, Sports Team
Matthew Sizemore, Sports Team
Cory Alan Forgue, Sports Team

Las Animas

***KRKV**
08-01-2008; 107.3 mhz FM; 80 kw; 354 ft.; N37 56 23 W103 26 8
Mailing Address: US
Second Address: 709 Coleman Ave., Athens, AL 35611
(256) 497-4502, *Fax:* NA
varietyrock@hotmail.com
License: Las Animas, Bent County, CO held by Alleycat Communications.
Arbitron Metro Market: Tulsa, OK *Format:* Variety/Diverse, Rock/AOR *Target Audience:* 18-54.
Richard Dabney, General Manager

Leadville

***KTOL**
01-01-2006; 90.9 mhz FM; 0.45 kw; -679 ft.; N39 14 5 W106 17 59 *Rebroadcasts:* Rebroadcasts KTLF(FM) Colorado Springs 100%
1665 Briargate Blvd, Colorado Springs, CO 80920 US
(719) 593-0600, *Fax:* (719) 593-2399
www.ktlf.org
lightpraise@ktlf.org
License: Leadville, Lake County, CO held by Educational Communications of Colorado Springs Inc.
Arbitron Metro Market: Leadville, CO *Format:* Christian *Target Audience:* 45-60; Christian
James Felix, Operations Dir
Tom Sullivan, General Manager
Sharick Wade, Programming Director
Robert Mumm, Chief Engineer
Skip Rice, Sonrise Host
Marge Wallace, Office Manager
Alleen Wagnon, Office Assistant

Limon

KWFA(FM)
01-01-2003; 103.1 mhz FM; 100 kw; Ant 443 ft; N39 28 12 W103 38 14
1211 Chuck Dawley Blvd., Suite 202, Mount Pleasant, SC 29464
(843) 849-0076
License: Limon, Lincoln County, CO held by Coloradio Inc.
Edward Seeger, General Manager

***KYCO**
89.1 mhz FM; 1.8 kw; 328 ft.; N39 22 13 W103 42 50
US
(517) 999-3737
www.foundationradio.org
License: Limon, CO held by Saidnewsfoundation.
Arbitron Metro Market: Limon, CO
David Schaberg, General Manager

Littleton

KCKK
08-22-1957; 1510 khz AM
2559 Welton Street, Denver, CO 80205 US
(303) 650-1795, *Fax:* (303) 524-3410
www.milehighsports.com
License: Littleton, CO held by People's Wireless Inc.
Group Owner: NRC Broadcasting Inc.; (acq 4-26-2002; $2.7 million)
Arbitron Metro Market: Denver-Boulder, CO *Format:* Sports
James Merilatt, General Manager

Loma

KDVC
01-01-2008; 102.5 mhz FM; 3.8 kw horiz; 1047 ft.; N37 56 29 W108 54 27
US
(312) 204-9900
License: Loma, Delores County, CO held by College Creek Media LLC.
Group Owner: College Creek Media LLC
Arbitron Metro Market: Loma, CO
Neal Robinson, President

Longmont

***KGUD**
09-01-1975; 90.7 mhz FM *Hrs Open:* 24; 100 w; Ant 270 ft; N40 14 24 W105 03 19
Mailing Address: Box 1534, Longmont, CO 80501
Second Address: Studio: 457 Fourth Ave., Longmont, CO 80501
(303) 485-9811
kgud907@gmail.com
License: Longmont, Boulder County, CO held by Longmont Community Radio
Population Served: 180,000 *Arbitron Metro Market:* Denver-Boulder, *No. News Employees:* 2 *Target Audience:* 45 plus; retirees
George Baskos, General Manager
James Boynton Sr., Station Manager
N/A, Promotions Manager
N/A, News Director
N/A, Engineering Dir
N/A, Chief Engineer

KKFN
09-01-1964; 104.3 mhz FM *Hrs Open:* 24; 91 kw; 676 ft.; N39 41 45 W105 9 54
1095 S Monaco Parkway, Denver, CO 80224 US
(303) 321-0950, *Fax:* (303) 321-3383
www.fm1043thefan.com
License: Longmont, Boulder County, CO held by Lincoln Financial Media Co. of Colorado.
Group Owner: Lincoln Financial Media; (acq 4-3-2006; grpsl)
Nat'l Network: Fox Sports
Arbitron Metro Market: Denver-Boulder, CO *Format:* Sports
Target Audience: 18-34; hip
Bob Call, Operations Dir
Steve Price, General Manager
Steven Price, General Sales Mgr
Nate Lundy, Programming Director
Andrew Joynt, Promotions Manager
Brad Hart, Chief Engineer

KRCN
12-01-1949; 1060 khz AM *Hrs Open:* 15; 18 (summer)
54 Monument Circle, Ste 250, Indianapolis, IN 46204 US
(303) 776-2323, *Fax:* (303) 776-1377
License: Longmont, CO held by Pilgrim Communications Inc.
Group Owner: Pilgrim Communications Inc.; (acq 5-27-98; $575,000)
Nat'l Network: ABC *Nat'l Reps:* McGavren Guild
Arbitron Metro Market: Denver-Boulder, *Format:* Talk *Hrs. of News Programming:* news progmg 12 hrs wkly *No. News Employees:* 3 *Target Audience:* 25-64; news & sports listeners
Adv. Rates: 150; 150; 150;120
Chuck Duncan, CEO
Roger Cridelbaugh, Operations Dir
Nancy Smith, Business Manager
Gene Hood, Nancy Smith

Loveland

KPIO
01-21-1955; 1570 khz AM *Hrs Open:* 24
1200 Rosewood Dr., Loveland, CO 80537 US
(816) 630-1090
www.thecatholicradionetwork.com
info@thecatholicradionetwork.com
License: Loveland, CO held by Catholic Radio Network Inc.
Group Owner: Catholic Radio Network Inc.; (acq 1-28-2009; $740,000)
Nat'l Network: EWTN Radio
Format: Christian *Target Audience:* Christian Women
James O'Laughlin, General Manager

KTRR
02-05-1966; 102.5 mhz FM; 17 kw; 768 ft.; N40 38 31 W104 49 3
P.O. Box 3353, Evansville, IN 47732 US
(970) 674-2700, *Fax:* (970) 686-7491
www.tri1025.com
chall@regentcomm.com
License: Loveland, Larimer County, CO
Group Owner: Townsquare Media; (acq 2-25-03).
Arbitron Metro Market: Windsor, CO *Format:* Adult Contemp
Target Audience: 25-54.
Mark Callaghan, Operations Dir
Pete Hanson, General Manager
Zandi Wilcox, General Sales Mgr
George King, Programming Director

***KXGR**
89.7 mhz FM; 0.1 kw horiz, 80 kw vert; 1220 ft.; N40 37 3 W105 19 40
16075 W Belleview Ave, Morrison, CO 80465 US
(303)628-7200
License: Loveland, CO held by Calvary Chapel Aurora
Format: Christian
Ed Taylor, President

Manitou Springs

KBIQ
05-01-1952; 102.7 mhz FM *Hrs Open:* 24; 57 kw; 2280 ft.; N38 44 43 W104 51 39
4880 Santa Rosa Road, Suite 300, Camarillo, CA 93012 US
(719) 531-5438, *Fax:* (719) 531-5588
www.kbiqradio.com
clakey@kbiqradio.com
License: Manitou Springs, El Paso County, CO held by Bison Media Inc.
Group Owner: Salem Communications Corp.; (acq 10-8-96; $2.825 million)
Arbitron Metro Market: CO Springs, CO *Format:* Adult Contemp, Christian *No. News Employees:* 1 *Target Audience:* 18-54.
Bret Stevens, Operations Dir
Carrie Lakey, General Manager
Jon Cobb, General Sales Mgr
Julie Smith, Promotions Manager

***KCME**
09-01-1979; 88.7 mhz FM *Hrs Open:* 24; 8.9 kw; 9,570 ft; N38 44 40 W104 51 41
1921 N. Weber St., Colorado Springs, CO 80907
(719) 578-5263, *Fax:* (719) 578-1033
www.kcme.org
kcme@kcme.org
License: Manitou Springs, El Paso County, CO held by Cheyenne Mt. Public Broadcast House Inc.
Population Served: 1,200,000 *Arbitron Metro Market:* Colorado Springs, CO *Target Audience:* 45 plus; upper-middle class, mostly college graduates *Adv. Rates:* 21; 21; 21; 21
Joseph Bennet McCoy, President
Jeanna Wearing, General Manager
Jeanna Wearing, General Sales Mgr
Jana Lee, Programming Director
Cynthis Bullock, Development Director
John Hassebrock, Chief Engineer
Brenda Bratton, Chief FinancialOfficer
Keith Kauspedas, Traffic Director

KXRE
11-01-1956; 1490 khz AM *Hrs Open:* 24
PO Box 1471, Evergreen, CO 80439 US
(303) 733-5266, *Fax:* (303) 733-5242
www.radioquebueno.net
kbno@kbno.net
License: Manitou Springs, CO held by Latino Communications LLC
Group Owner: Latino Communications LLC; acq 1-23-03; $350,000 with KAVA(AM) Pueblo).
Arbitron Metro Market: Denver, CO *Hrs. of News Programming:* 21 hrs wkly *No. News Employees:* 5 *Target Audience:* 25-54.
Adv. Rates: 35; 35; 35; 35
Zee Ferrufino, General Manager

Meeker

KAYW
09-30-2000; 98.1 mhz FM *Hrs Open:* 24; 100 kw; 1145 ft.; N40 11 45 W107 56 0 *Rebroadcasts:* Rebroadcasts KZKS(FM) Rifle 100%
C/O Brill & Meisel, 488 Madison Ave, 5th Floor, New York, NY 10022 US
(970) 241-6460, *Fax:* (970) 241-6452
License: Meeker, Rio Blanco County, CO held by Western Slope Communications LLC.

Group Owner: Western Slope Communications LLC
Arbitron Metro Market: Meeker, CO *Format:* Adult Contemp *Hrs. of News Programming:* News progmg 20 hrs wkly
John Reid, General Manager

Merino

KRFD(FM)
01-01-2008; 94.5 mhz FM; 6.5 kw; Ant 226 ft; N40 28 33 W103 13 28
87 Jasper Lake Rd., Loveland, CO 80537
(970) 669-9200
License: Merino, Logan County, CO held by Northeast Colorado Broadcasting
Population Served: 37,395 *Arbitron Metro Market:* Roy, UT
Victor Michael Jr., General Manager

Monte Vista

KSLV
02-01-1954; 1240 khz AM *Hrs Open:* 24; 1 kw-U, ND1; N37 36 10 W106 8 58
P.O. Box 631, Monte Vista, CO 81144 US
(719) 852-3581, *Fax:* (719) 852-3583
www.kslvradio.com
kslv@amigo.net
License: Monte Vista, CO held by San Luis Valley Broadcasting Inc.
Group Owner: San Luis Valley Broadcasting Inc.; (acq 4-1-79)
Nat'l Network: Jones Radio Networks *Wire Services:* AP
Arbitron Metro Market: Monte Vista, CO *Format:* Country *Special Programming:* Sp 10 hrs, farm one hr, gospel 4 hrs wkly *Hrs. of News Programming:* news progmg 1 hour weekly *No. News Employees:* 1 *TargetAudience:* 25-54.
Gerald Vigil, General Manager
Jerry Medina, Programming Director
Linda Pacheco, News Director

KYDN
01-01-1986; 95.3 mhz FM *Hrs Open:* 24; 6 kw; 89 ft.; N37 36 10 W106 8 58
P. O. Box 631, Monte Vista, CO 81144 US
(719) 852-3581, *Fax:* (719) 852-3583
www.kslvradio.com
kslv@amigo.net
License: Monte Vista, Rio Grande County, CO held by San Luis Valley Broadcasting Inc.
Group Owner: San Luis Valley Broadcasting Inc.
Nat'l Network: Jones Radio Networks *Wire Services:* AP
Arbitron Metro Market: Monte Vista, CO *Format:* Country *Hrs. of News Programming:* News progmg 6 hrs wkly
Gerald Vigil, General Manager
Jerry Medina, Programming Director
Linda Pacheco, News Director

Montrose

KKXK
12-01-1976; 94.1 mhz FM *Hrs Open:* 24; 90 kw; 1883 ft.; N38 20 16 W107 38 23
Mailing Address: P.O. Box 970, Montrose, CO 81401 US
Second Address: 106 Rose Ln., Montrose, CO 81401
(970) 249-4546, *Fax:* (970) 249-2229
www.coloradoradio.com
porlando@cherrycreekradio.com
License: Montrose, Montrose County, CO held by Cherry Creek Radio IV, LLC
Group Owner: Cherry Creek Radio LLC
Nat'l Network: ABC
Arbitron Metro Market: Grand Junction, CO *Format:* Country *Hrs. of News Programming:* news progmg 4 hrs wkly *No. News Employees:* 2 *Target Audience:* 25-54. Adults *Adv. Rates:* 28; 28; 28; 17
Joe Schwartz, President
Bee Haddock, Operations Dir
Jay D. Austin, General Manager
Scott Staley, Programming Director
Jim Kerschner, Sports Director
Heather Glassman, Traffic Manager

*KPRH
10-01-1998; 88.3 mhz FM; 3.5 kw; 1677 ft.; N38 23 14 W107 40 28 *Rebroadcasts:* Rebroadcasts KCFR(FM) Denver 100%
2249 S Josephine St, Denver, CO 80210 US
(303) 871-9191, *Fax:* (303) 733-3319
www.cpr.org
License: Montrose, Montrose County, CO held by Public Broadcasting of Colorado Inc.
Nat'l Network: NPR
Format: News *Target Audience:* General.
Max Wycisk, President
Sue Coughlin, General Sales Mgr
Sean Nethery, Programming Director
David Gomez, News Director
Robert Hensler, Engineering Dir

KSTR-FM
04-10-1980; 96.1 mhz FM; 91 kw; 1099 ft.; N38 52 40 W108 13 33
660 Road Avenue, Grand Junction, CO 81501 US
(970) 254-2100, *Fax:* (970) 245-7551
www.gjradio.com
License: Montrose, Montrose County, CO held by MBC Grand Broadcasting Inc.
Group Owner: MBC Grand Broadcasting Inc.; (acq 5-25-2005; $600,000).
Arbitron Metro Market: Grand Junction, CO
David Hinson, President
Dave Beck, General Manager
Dave Beck, General Sales Mgr

KUBC
09-25-1947; 580 khz AM *Hrs Open:* 24; 5 kw-D, 1 kw-N, DA-N; N38 25 32 W107 52 57
Mailing Address: Box 970, Montrose, CO 81401
Second Address: 106 Rose Ln., Montrose, CO 81401
(970) 249-4546, *Fax:* (970) 249-2229
www.coloradoradio.com
porlando@cherrycreekradio.com
License: Montrose, Montrose County, CO held by CCR-Montrose IV LLC.
Group Owner: Cherry Creek Radio LLC; (acq 8-19-2004; grpsl).
Nat'l Network: ABC *Nat'l Reps:* TACHER
Population Served: 150,000 *Arbitron Metro Market:* Grand Junction, *Special Programming:* Sports 5 hrs, relg 3 hrs wkly *Hrs. of News Programming:* News progmg 4 hrs wkly *Target Audience:* 35+ *Adv. Rates:* 14; 14; 14; 10
Joseph Schwartz, President
Bee Haddock, Operations Dir
Paul Orlando, General Manager
Scott Staley, Programming Director
James MacDonald, News Director
Jim Frank, Chief Engineer
James MacDonald, News Director
Heather Glassman,Traffic Manager

*KVMT
01-01-1999; 89.1 mhz FM *Hrs Open:* 24; 8 kw; 1581 ft.; N38 18 52 W108 12 2 *Rebroadcasts:* Rebroadcasts KVNF (FM) Paonia 100%
P.O. Box 1350, Paonia, CO 81428 US
(970) 527-4866, *Fax:* (970) 527-4865
www.kvnf.org
sally@kvnf.org; events@kvnf.org
License: Montrose, Montrose County, CO held by North Fork Valley Public Radio Inc.
Arbitron Metro Market: Paonia, CO *Format:* News *Hrs. of News Programming:* News progmg 35 hrs wkly
Jeff Reynolds, Operations Dir
Ali Lightfoot, Programming Director
Ariana Brocious, News Director
Candy Pennetta, Music Director
Gretchen Astonpuckett, Development Director

*KTMH
01-01-2005; 89.9 mhz FM; 0 kw horiz, 4 kw vert; 1634 ft.; N38 23 15 W107 40 31 *Rebroadcasts:* Rebroadcasts KTLF(FM) Colorado Springs 100%
1665 Briargate Blvd, Colorado Springs, CO 80920 US
(719) 593-0600, *Fax:* (719) 593-2399
www.ktlf.org
awagnon@ktlf.org
License: Montrose, Ouray County, CO held by Educational Communications of Colorado Springs Inc.
Arbitron Metro Market: Montrose, CO *Format:* Christian *Target Audience:* 45-60; Christian
James Felix, Operations Dir
Tom Sullivan, General Manager
Lynn Carmichael, Programming Director
Marge Wallace, Office Manager
Alleen Wagnon, Office Assistant
Sharick Wade, KTPL Program Director

*KJOL-FM
91.9 mhz FM; 0.475 kw; -276 ft.; N38 28 8 W107 53 5 US
(970) 254-5565, *Fax:* (970) 254-5550
www.kjol.org
info@kjol.org
License: Montrose, Montrose County, CO held by United Ministries.
Arbitron Metro Market: Montrose, CO
Ken Andrews, General Manager
Ken Andrews, Station Manager
Rhonda Repshire, Promotions Manager
Kurt Neuswanger, Music Director
Dave Andrews, Public Affairs Director

Monument

KCBR
07-20-1986; 1040 khz AM *Hrs Open:* Sunrise-sunset
P.O. Box 3003, Blue Bell, PA 19422 US
(719) 570-1530, *Fax:* (719) 570-1007
License: Monument, CO held by DJR Broadcasting, LLC
Group Owner: United States CP LLC; (acq 1999; $750,000 with KCMN(AM) Colorado Springs)
Arbitron Metro Market: Colorado Springs, CO *Format:* Christian, Talk *Target Audience:* 25-54; 70% male, upper-middle income or higher
Don Crawford Jr., CEO
Don Crawford Sr, President
Tron Simpson, Operations Dir

Morrison

*KLDV
03-27-1971; 91.1 mhz FM *Hrs Open:* 24; 100 kw; 1168 ft.; N39 36 0 W105 12 35 *Rebroadcasts:* Rebroadcasts KLVR(FM) Middletown, CA 100%
16075 W. Belleview Ave., Morrison, CO 80465 US
(916) 251-1600, *Fax:* (916) 251-1650
www.klove.com
klove@klove.com
License: Morrison, Jefferson County, CO held by Educational Media Foundation.
Group Owner: EMF Broadcasting; (acq 12-28-2000; grpsl)
Nat'l Network: K-Love
Arbitron Metro Market: Morrison, CO *Format:* Christian *No. News Employees:* 3 *Target Audience:* 25-44; Judeo Christian, female
Mike Novak, President
Jennifer Lohman, Operations Dir

Mountain Village

KRKQ
95.5 mhz FM; 0.25 kw; 1470 ft.; N37 59 29 W107 58 21 US
(888) 948-1640
www.mountainchill.com
License: Mountain Village, San Miguel County, CO held by Lorenz E. Proietti.
Arbitron Metro Market: Mountain Village, CO *Format:* Easy Listening
Lorenz Proietti, General Manager

New Castle

KTUN
04-16-1984; 94.5 mhz FM *Hrs Open:* 24; 25 kw; -397 ft.; N39 33 56 W107 32 1 US
(970) 949-0140, *Fax:* (970) 949-1464
www.alwaysmountaintime.com
info@kskeradio.com
License: New Castle, Eagle County, CO held by NRC Broadcasting Mountain Group LLC.
Group Owner: NRC Broadcasting Inc.; (acq 5-1-2007; grpsl)
Arbitron Metro Market: New Castle, CO *Format:* Classic Rock *Hrs. of News Programming:* news progmg 4 hrs wkly *No. News Employees:* 2 *Target Audience:* 25-63; affluent locals & tourists *Adv. Rates:* 40; 38;40; 25
Meredith Fox, Operations Dir
Steve Wodlinger, General Manager

Norwood

KRYD
01-01-1998; 104.9 mhz FM *Hrs Open:* 24; 23.62 kw; 1678 ft.; N38 18 59 W108 11 55
Mailing Address: C/O Kkco-Tv, 2325 Interstate Avenue, Grand Junction, CO 81505 US
Second Address: 475 Water St., Monrose, CO 81401
(970) 263-4100, *Fax:* (970) 263-9600
www.krydfm.com
billv@taousa.tv
License: Norwood, San Miguel County, CO held by Rocky III Investments Inc.
Arbitron Metro Market: Grand Junction, CO *Format:* Country *Hrs. of News Programming:* news progmg one hr wkly *No. News Employees:* 3 *Target Audience:* 18 plus. *Adv. Rates:* 45; 40; 45; 35
Bill Varecha, CEO
Jon Donofrio, Operations Dir
Paul Varecha, General Sales Mgr
Debbie Varecha, CFO

Nunn

KIMX

01-01-2002; 96.9 mhz FM; 4.8 kw; 1027 ft.; N41 17 15 W105 26 38
2232 Dell Range Blvd., Cheyenne, WY 82009 US
(307) 745-5208, *Fax:* (307) 745-8570
mix967@fiberpipe.net
License: Nunn, Albany County, CO held by Appaloosa Broadcasting Co. Inc.
Group Owner: Northeast Broadcasting Company Inc.; (acq 11-12-2003; $775,000).
Format: Adult Contemp
Jim O'Reilly, General Manager

Oak Creek

KFMU-FM

09-22-1975; 104.1 mhz FM *Hrs Open:* 24; 1.4 kw; 1073 ft.; N40 14 10 W106 52 30
Mailing Address: C/O Jerome S. Boros, 1290 Avenue of Americas, New York, NY 10104 US
Second Address: 2955 Village Dr., Steamboat Springs, CO 80487
(970) 879-5368, *Fax:* (970) 879-5843
http://alwaysmountaintime.com/kfmu/
ecampbell@nrcbroadcasting.com
License: Oak Creek, Routt County, CO held by NRC Broadcasting Mountain Group LLC.
Group Owner: NRC Broadcasting Inc.; (acq 5-1-2007; grpsl)
Arbitron Metro Market: Oak Creek, CO *Format:* Triple A *Special Programming:* Jazz 4 hrs, modern mus 4 hrs wkly *Hrs. of News Programming:* news progmg 10 hrs wkly *No. News Employees:* 2 *Target Audience:* 21-54. *Adv. Rates:* 18; 16; 16; 12
Steve Wodlinger, General Manager

Olathe

*KUSZ

01-01-2000; 106.5 mhz FM; kw
US
(307) 745-5208, *Fax:* (307) 745-8570
mix967@fiberpipe.net
License: Olathe, Albany County, CO held by Laramie Mountain Broadcasting LLC.
Format: Oldies
Jim O'Reilly, General Manager

Olney Springs

KRYE

01-01-2008; 104.9 mhz FM; 100 kw; 79 meters; N37 56 40 W104 59 56
2099 U.S. Hwy 50 W., #130A, Pueblo, CO
(970) 356-1452, *Fax:* (719) 562-0947
www.tigrecolorado.com
krye104.9@hotmail.com
License: Olney Springs, Pueblo County, CO held by United States CP LLC.
Group Owner: United States CP LLC
Population Served: 348 *Arbitron Metro Market:* Olney Springs, CO
Ricardo Salazar, General Manager

Ouray

KWGL

06-16-1986; 105.7 mhz FM *Hrs Open:* 24; 60 kw horiz; 1752 ft.; N38 23 16 W107 40 28
P.O. Box 60040, Grand Junction, CO 81506 US
(970) 241-6460, *Fax:* (970) 241-6452
www.range105.net
frank@wscradio.net
License: Ouray, Ouray County, CO held by WS Communications L.L.C.
Nat'l Network: Jones Radio Networks
Arbitron Metro Market: Grand Junction, CO *Format:* Country *Hrs. of News Programming:* news progmg 15 hrs wkly *No. News Employees:* 1
Tom Little, General Manager
Michael Johnson, Programming Director
Katie Robblie, Business Manager
Bryan Fleming, Account Executive

Pagosa Springs

KWUF

08-27-1975; 1400 khz AM *Hrs Open:* 24; 1 kw-U, ND1; N37 15 24 W107 1 6
Mailing Address: C/O J. Randolph Torbert, Esq., 320 East Costilla, Colorado Springs, CO 80903 US
Second Address: 702 S. 10th St., Pagosa Springs, CO 81147
(970) 264-5983, *Fax:* (970) 264-5129
www.kwuf.com
admin@kwuf.com
License: Pagosa Springs, CO held by Wolf Creek Broadcasting L.L.C.
Nat'l Network: Westwood One
Arbitron Metro Market: Pagosa Springs, CO *Format:* Country, News, 62, Sports, Talk *Hrs. of News Programming:* News progmg 10 hrs wkly *No. News Employees:* 1 *Target Audience:* General. *Adv. Rates:* Same asFM
Will Spears, CEO
Christie Spears, General Sales Mgr
Chris Olivarez, Programming Director
Jodie Blankenship, News Director

KWUF-FM

05-01-1986; 106.3 mhz FM *Hrs Open:* 24; 0.255 kw; 1280 ft.; N37 11 32 W107 5 55
Mailing Address: C/O J. Randolph Torbert, Esq., 320 East Costilla, Colorado Springs, CO 80903 US
Second Address: 702 S. 10th St., Pagosa Springs, CO 81147
(970) 264-5983, *Fax:* (970) 264-5129
www.kwuf.com
admin@kwuf.com
License: Pagosa Springs, Archuleta County, CO held by Wolf Creek Broadcasting L.L.C.
Nat'l Network: Westwood One
Arbitron Metro Market: Pagosa Springs, CO *Format:* Adult Contemp *Special Programming:* Blues 10 hrs, jazz 10 hrs wkly *Hrs. of News Programming:* News progmg 10 hrs wkly *No. News Employees:* 1 *Target Audience:* 18 plus. *Adv. Rates:* 9; 9; 9; na
Will Spears, CEO
Christie Spears, General Sales Mgr
Jodie Blankenship, Programming Director
Chris Olivarez, Music/Sports/News

*KTPS

01-01-2003; 89.7 mhz FM; 0.2 kw; 1273 ft.; N37 11 35 W107 5 58 *Rebroadcasts:* Rebroadcasts KTLF(FM) Colorado Springs 100%
1665 Briargate Blvd., Colorado Springs, CO 80920 US
(719) 593-0600, *Fax:* (719) 593-2399
www.ktlf.org
awagnon@ktlf.org
License: Pagosa Springs, Archuleta County, CO held by Educational Communications of Colorado Springs Inc.
Arbitron Metro Market: Tacoma, WA *Format:* Christian *Target Audience:* 45-60; Christian
James Felix, Operations Dir
Tom Sullivan, General Manager
Lynn Carmichael, Programming Director
Marge Wallace, Office Manager
Alleen Wagnon, Office Assistant
Sharick Wade, KTPL Program Director

*KPGS

01-01-2008; 88.1 mhz FM; 1 kw vert; 1365 ft.; N37 11 48 W107 7 1 *Rebroadcasts:* Rebroadcasts KUTE(FM) Ignacio 100%
US
(970) 563-0255, *Fax:* (970) 563-0399
www.ksut.org
info@ksut.org
License: Pagosa Springs, Archuleta County, CO held by KUTE Inc.
Group Owner: KUTE Inc.
Nat'l Network: NPR
Arbitron Metro Market: Grand Junction, CO *Format:* Triple A
Eddie Box Jr., President
Beth Warren, General Manager

Palisade

*KAAI

01-01-2007; 98.5 mhz FM; 0.26 kw; 2989 ft.; N39 3 14 W108 15 13
US
(888) 937-2471, *Fax:* (916) 251-1650
www.air1.com
info@air1.com
License: Palisade, Mesa County, CO held by Covenant Educational Media Inc.
Arbitron Metro Market: Palisade, CO *Format:* Alternative, Christian
Darrell Chambliss, Chairman
Alan Mason, CEO/COO
Mike Novak, CEO
Doug Price, General Manager
David Pierce, Chief Creative Officer
Dan Antonelli, Chief Business Development Officer
Eric Moser, Chief Financial Officer
BrianBurger, Vice President of Human Resources

Paonia

*KVNF

10-05-1979; 90.9 mhz FM *Hrs Open:* 18; 2.6 kw; -72 ft.; N38 52 28 W107 39 40
Mailing Address: P. O. Box 1350, Paonia, CO 81428 US
Second Address: 233 Grand Ave., Paonia, CO 81428
(970) 527-4866, *Fax:* (970) 527-4865
www.kvnf.org
sally@kvnf.org; events@kvnf.org
License: Paonia, Delta County, CO held by North Fork Valley Public Radio Inc.
Nat'l Network: NPR
Arbitron Metro Market: Paonia, CO *Format:* News *Special Programming:* Class 15 hrs, jazz 17 hrs, blues 3 hrs, C&W 5 hrs, new age 6 hrs, Sp 2 hrs, gospel 3 hrs wkly
Jeff Reynolds, Operations Dir
Sally Kane, General Manager
Ali Lightfoot, Programming Director
Ariana Brocious, News Director
Candy Pennetta, Music Director
Getchen Astor, Development Director

Parker

KRWZ

07-04-1922; 950 khz AM *Hrs Open:* 24; 5 kw-U, DA1; N39 52 30 W104 56 0
1095 S. Monaco Pky, Denver, CO 80224 US
(303) 321-0950, *Fax:* (303) 321-3383
www.cruisinoldies950.com
License: Parker, CO held by Lincoln Financial Media Co. of Colorado.
Group Owner: Lincoln Financial Media; (acq 4-3-2006; grpsl)
Nat'l Reps: CBS Radio
Arbitron Metro Market: Denver-Boulder, *Format:* Oldies
Robert Call, Operations Dir
Steve Price, General Sales Mgr
Joel Burke, Programming Director
Nikki Swarn, Promotions Manager
Simone Seikaly, News Director
Brad Hart, Engineering Dir
Randy Weidner, National Sales Manager

Phippsburg

KEZZ

94.1 mhz FM; 1.75 kw; 1247 ft.; N40 22 3 W106 41 28
US
(970) 302-8444
License: Phippsburg, Jackson County, CO held by Youngers Colorado Broadcasting LLC.
Arbitron Metro Market: Phippsburg, CO
Kevin Youngers, General Manager

Pierce

KJMP

01-01-2004; 870 khz AM
US
(307) 638-8921
License: Pierce, CO held by White Park Broadcasting Inc
Group Owner: Northeast Broadcasting Company Inc.; (acq 2-1-2006; $350,000)
Arbitron Metro Market: Fort Collins, CO *Format:* Sports
Steven Silverburg., General Manager

Placerville

*KTEI

90.7 mhz FM; 0.25 kw horiz; 1474 ft.; N37 59 30 W107 58 21
Rebroadcasts: KTLF (FM) Colorado Springs 100%
1665 Briargate Blvd., Colorado Springs, CO 80920 US
(719) 593-0600, *Fax:* (719) 593-2399
www.ktlf.org
awagnon@ktlf.org
License: Placerville, San Miguel County, CO held by Educational Communications of Colorado Springs Inc.
Arbitron Metro Market: Placerville, CO *Format:* Christian *Target Audience:* 45-60; Christian
James Felix, Operations Dir
Tom Sullivan, General Manager
Lynn Carmichael, Programming Director
Marge Wallace, Office Manager
Alleen Wagnon, Office Assistant
Sharick Wade, KTPL Program Director

Poncha Springs

KWUZ

01-01-2008; 97.5 mhz FM; 0.029 kw; 2927 ft.; N38 27 11 W106 1 2

US
(719) 539-2575, *Fax:* (719) 539-4851
www.hippieradio975.com
kvrh@kvrh.com
License: Poncha Springs, Chaffee County, CO held by Three Eagles Communications of Colorado LLC
Arbitron Metro Market: Poncha Springs, CO *Format:* Contemporary Hits/Top 40, Adult Contemp
Rolland Johnson, CEO
Dean Johnson, Operations Dir
Ron Gates, General Sales Manager

Pueblo

KAVA
06-01-1963; 1480 khz AM; 1 kw-D, DA2; 0.107 kw-N, DA2; N38 18 56 W104 37 3
PO Box 1471, Evergreen, CO 80439 US
(303) 733-5266, *Fax:* (303) 733-5242
www.radioquebueno.com
kbno@kbno.net
License: Pueblo, CO held by Latino Communications LLC
Group Owner: Latino Communications LLC; acq 1-23-03; $350,000 with KXRE(AM) Manitou Springs).
Arbitron Metro Market: Pueblo, CO *Hrs. of News Programming:* 21 hrs wkly *No. News Employees:* 6 *Target Audience:* 25-54. *Adv. Rates:* 25; 25; 25; 25
Zee Ferrufino, General Manager

KCCY-FM
08-23-1975; 96.9 mhz FM; 58 kw; 2280 ft.; N38 44 43 W104 51 41
4700 Southwest Macadam, Portland, OR 97201 US
(719) 540-9200, *Fax:* (719) 579-0882
www.y969.com
License: Pueblo, Pueblo County, CO held by Clear Channel Radio Licenses, Inc.
Group Owner: Clear Channel Communications Inc.; (acq 11-22-00; with KDZA-FM Pueblo).
Nat'l Reps: Christal
Arbitron Metro Market: CO Springs, CO *Format:* Country *Target Audience:* 25-54; general
Paul Kelley, Operations Dir
Bill Fuerst, General Manager
Adam Burnes, Programming Director
Angela Cortez, Promotions Manager
Paul Richards, News Director
Daren McMullin, Chief Engineer

***KCFP**
06-01-1986; 91.9 mhz FM *Hrs Open:* 24; 0.6 kw horiz; 633 ft.; N38 22 23 W104 33 42 *Rebroadcasts:* Rebroadcasts KCFR(FM) Denver 100%
2249 South Josephine St, Denver, CO 80210 US
(303) 871-9191, *Fax:* (303) 733-3319
www.cpr.org
License: Pueblo, Pueblo County, CO held by Public Broadcasting of Colorado Inc.
Nat'l Network: NPR
Arbitron Metro Market: Pueblo, CO *Format:* News *Hrs. of News Programming:* news progmg 50 hrs wkly *No. News Employees:* 8 *Target Audience:* General.
Max Wycisk, President
Sue Coughlin, General Sales Mgr

KCSJ
01-01-1947; 590 khz AM *Hrs Open:* 24
Post Office Box 2080, Colorado Springs, CO 80901 US
(719) 545-2080, *Fax:* (719) 543-9898
www.590kcsj.com
webmaster@590kcsj.com
License: Pueblo, CO held by CC Licenses LLC.
Group Owner: Clear Channel Communications Inc.; (acq 6-14-2001; with KDZA(AM) Pueblo)
Nat'l Network: ABC *Nat'l Reps:* Christal
Arbitron Metro Market: Pueblo, CO *Format:* News, News/Talk, 84, Talk *Hrs. of News Programming:* news progmg 41 hrs wkly *No. News Employees:* 2 *Target Audience:* 35-64; upscale *Adv. Rates:* 20; 18; 18; 14
Paul Kelley, Operations Dir
Bill Fuerst, General Manager
Paul Richards, Programming Director
Angela Cortez, Promotions Manager

KDZA-FM
03-03-1987; 107.9 mhz FM; 32 kw; 2211 ft.; N38 44 41 W104 51 46
4700 S.W. Macadam Avenue, Portland, OR 47201 US
(719) 540-9200, *Fax:* (719) 579-0882
www.1079kdza.com
License: Pueblo, Pueblo County, CO held by Capstar TX L.P.
Group Owner: Clear Channel Communications Inc.; (acq 11-22-2000; with KCCY(FM) Pueblo)
Arbitron Metro Market: Pueblo, CO
Bob Richards, General Manager
Alex Ryden, Promotions Manager

KFEL
08-01-1956; 970 khz AM
P.O. Box 8055, Pueblo, CO 81008 US
(719) 543-7506 (970) 669-8000, *Fax:* (719) 543—0432 (970) 669-8000
www.thecatholicradionetwork.com
kfel970am@gmail.com
License: Pueblo, CO held by Catholic Radio Network Inc.
Group Owner: Catholic Radio Network Inc.; (acq 11-3-2006; $475,000)
Arbitron Metro Market: Pueblo, CO *Format:* Religious *Target Audience:* 25 plus.
John Koenig, Station Manager

KGFT
03-31-1988; 100.7 mhz FM *Hrs Open:* 24; 77 kw; 2218 ft.; N38 44 43 W104 51 39
4880 Santa Rosa Road, Suite 300, Camarillo, CA 93012 US
(719) 531-5438, *Fax:* (719) 531-5588
www.kgftradio.com
questions@kgft.com
License: Pueblo, Pueblo County, CO held by Salem Communications Corp.
Group Owner: Salem Communications Corp.; (acq 1996; $3 million).
Nat'l Network: AP Radio
Arbitron Metro Market: Colorado Springs, CO *Format:* Christian, News, 62, Talk, Religious *Special Programming:* Gospel 3 hrs, old time radio 11 hrs wkly *Hrs. of News Programming:* news progmg 4 hrs wkly *No. NewsEmployees:* 1 *Target Audience:* 25 plus; Christian
Carrie Lakey, General Manager
Kim Bratton, Station Manager
Jon Cobb, General Sales Mgr
Bret Stevens, Programming Director
Julie Smith, Promotions Manager
Steve Altmaier, News Director

KCCY(AM)
02-01-1928; 1350 khz AM *Hrs Open:* 24; 5 kw-D, 1 kw-N, DA-N; N38 18 29 W104 38 24
2864 S. Circle Drive, Suite 300, Colorado Springs, CO 80906
(719) 540-9200, *Fax:* (719) 543-9898
www.z1079rocks.com
License: Pueblo, Pueblo County, CO held by CC Licenses LLC.
Group Owner: Clear Channel Communications Inc.; (acq 6-14-2001; with KCSJ(AM) Pueblo)
Population Served: 130,000*Format:* Classic Rock *Hrs. of News Programming:* news progmg one hr wkly *No. News Employees:* 1 *Target Audience:* 35 plus.
Paul Kelley, Operations Dir
Bill Feurst, General Manager
Paul Kelley, Programming Director
Angela Cortez, Promotions Manager
Daren McMullin, Chief Engineer

KKMG
01-01-1967; 98.9 mhz FM *Hrs Open:* 24; 57 kw; 2280 ft.; N38 44 43 W104 51 41
City Center West, 7201 W. Lake Mead Blvd, Las Vegas, NV 89128 US
(719) 593-2700, *Fax:* (719) 593-2727
www.989magicfm.com
info@989magicfm.com
License: Pueblo, Pueblo County, CO
Group Owner: Cumulus Media Inc.; (acq 3-21-94; $912,500;
Nat'l Reps: McGavren Guild
Arbitron Metro Market: Colorado Spring, CO *Format:* Contemporary Hits/Top 40 *Target Audience:* 18-44.
Bobby Irwin, Operations Dir
John Fox, Programming Director

KKPC
12-29-1947; 1230 khz AM *Hrs Open:* 24
900 West Orman, Pueblo, CO 81004 US
(303) 871-9191, *Fax:* (303) 733-3319
www.cpr.org
info@cpr.org
License: Pueblo, CO held by Public Broadcasting of Colorado Inc.
Arbitron Metro Market: Pueblo, CO *Format:* News
Max Wycisk, President
Sean Nethery, Programming Director
Jenny Gentry, Executive Vice President

KNKN(FM)
11-01-1979; 106.9 mhz FM; 27.5 kw; Ant 666 ft; N38 06 22 W104 29 18
30 N. Electronic Dr., Pueblo West, CO 81007
(719) 547-0411, *Fax:* (719) 547-9301
knfoffice@qwestoffice.net
License: Pueblo, Pueblo County, CO held by United States CP LLC.
Group Owner: United States CP LLC; (acq 3-10-2008; $1.75 million with KRMX(AM) Pueblo)
Population Served: 159,361 *Arbitron Metro Market:* Pueblo, CO *Format:* Spanish *Target Audience:* 18-54.
Lupe Brown, General Manager

***KTSC-FM**
10-01-1970; 89.5 mhz FM; 8 kw; 180 ft.; N38 18 38 W104 34 40
2200 Bonforte Blvd., Pueblo, CO 81001 US
(719) 549-2821 (719) 549-2822, *Fax:* (719) 549-2120
www.rev89radio.com
info@ktsc.com
License: Pueblo, Pueblo County, CO held by University of Southern Colorado.
Arbitron Metro Market: Pueblo, CO *Format:* Blues
Mike Atencio, Station Manager

KVUU
01-01-1976; 99.9 mhz FM *Hrs Open:* 24; 57 kw; 2198 ft.; N38 44 44 W104 51 42
600 Congress Avenue, Suite 1400, Austin, TX 78701 US
(719) 540-9200, *Fax:* (719) 579-0882
www.my999radio.com
info@my999radio.com
License: Pueblo, Pueblo County, CO held by Capstar TX L.P.
Group Owner: Clear Channel Communications Inc.; (acq 8-30-00; grpsl).
Nat'l Reps: Clear Channel
Arbitron Metro Market: Pueblo, CO *Format:* Adult Contemp *Hrs. of News Programming:* news progmg 3 hrs wkly *No. News Employees:* 1 *Target Audience:* 25-54; upscale young adults
Adv. Rates: 80; 75; 75; 50
Bob Richards, General Manager
Bill Fuerst, General Sales Mgr
Chris Pickett, Programming Director
Daren McMullin, Chief Engineer

***KTPL**
01-01-2005; 88.3 mhz FM; 65 kw; 226 ft.; N37 56 40 W104 59 56
16075 W. Belleview Ave., Morrison, CO 80465 US
(719) 593-0600, *Fax:* (719) 593-2399
www.ktpl.org
ktpl@ktpl.org
License: Pueblo, Pueblo County, CO held by Educational Communications of Colorado Springs Inc.
Arbitron Metro Market: Pueblo, CO *Format:* Christian, Religious *Target Audience:* 18-35; Christian
James Felix, Operations Dir
Tom Sullivan, General Manager
Sharick Wade, Programming Director
Robert Mumm, Chief Engineer
Marge Wallace, Office Manager
Alleen Wagnon, Office Assistant

***KFRY**
01-01-2006; 89.9 mhz FM; 0.87 kw; 2123 ft.; N38 2 29 W105 11 5 *Rebroadcasts:* Rebroadcasts KUFR(FM) Salt Lake City, UT 100%
4135 Northgate Blvd, Suite 1, Sacramento, CA 95834 US
(800) 543-1495, *Fax:* (916) 641-8238
www.familyradio.com
info@familyradio.com
License: Pueblo, Pueblo County, CO held by Family Stations Inc.
Group Owner: Family Stations Inc.
Arbitron Metro Market: Pueblo, CO *Format:* Christian, Religious
Harold Camping, President

KIQN-FM
106.9 mhz FM; 27,500 watts; 203 meters; 38 06 22N 104 29 18W
800 Compton, Suite 33, Cincinnati, OH 45231 USA
(336) 307-3828
www.1069kissfm.com
License: Pueblo, Pueblo County, CO
Group Owner: United States CP LLC

Pueblo West

KRXP
01-01-1993; 103.9 mhz FM *Hrs Open:* 24; 1.75 kw; 2156 ft.; N38 44 44 W104 51 42
Mailing Address: Post Office Box 236, Pueblo, CO 81002 US
Second Address: 1805 E. Cheyenne Rd., Colorado Springs, CO 80905

(719) 634-4896, *Fax:* (719) 634-5837
www.1039rxp.com
License: Pueblo West, Pueblo County, CO held by Colorado Springs Radio Broadcasters Inc.
Group Owner: Bahakel Communications; (acq 2-22-99; grpsl)
Arbitron Metro Market: Pueblo, CO *Hrs. of News Programming:* news progmg one hr wkly *No. News Employees:* 1 *Target Audience:* 25-49; general
Lou Mellini, General Manager
Lana Janc, General Sales Mgr
Jason Janc, Programming Director

Red Feather Lakes

*KMKZ(FM)
88.7 mhz FM; 26 w; Ant 853 ft; N40 52 04 W105 38 33
5944 Kenosha St., Cheyenne, WY 82001
(307) 460-4224
License: Red Feather Lakes, Larimer County, CO held by Red Feather Lakes Co
Population Served: 230,482 *Arbitron Metro Market:* Glendale, Az
Tara Parker, President

Redlands

KRZX
03-31-2010; 106.1 mhz FM; 0.87 kw; 1257 ft.; N39 4 1 W108 44 39
US
(520) 797-4434
in@krzxfm.com
License: Redlands, San Juan County, CO held by Cochise Media Licenses LLC
Group Owner: SkyWest Media L.L.C.
Arbitron Metro Market: Redlands, CO
Ted Tucker, General Manager

Rico

*KICO
89.5 mhz FM; 125 kw horiz; -1319 ft.; N37 41 32 W108 1 55
US
(970) 564-9727, *Fax:* (970) 516-1927
www.ksjd.org
License: Rico, Dolores County, CO held by Community Radio Project.
Arbitron Metro Market: Rico, CO
Kristine Nunn, President
Deborah Gangloff, Vice President
Katrina Roberts, Secretary
Jeffrey Pope, Executive Director
Lindsay Isbell, Music Director
Tom Yoder, Programming & Media Director
Melissa Betrone, DevelopmentCoordinator

Ridgway

KSNN-FM
01-01-2002; 103.7 mhz FM *Hrs Open:* 24; 4.1 kw; Ant 1,574 ft; N38 23 15 W107 40 31
Mailing Address: Box 970, Montrose, CO 81402
Second Address: 106 Rose Lane, Montrose, CO 81401
(970) 249-4546, *Fax:* (970) 249-2229
www.coloradoradio.com
License: Ridgway, Ouray County, CO held by CCR-Montrose IV, LLC.
Group Owner: Cherry Creek Radio LLC; (acq 8-19-2004; grpsl).
Nat'l Reps: Tacher
No. News Employees: 1.5 *Target Audience:* 18-44 Adults *Adv. Rates:* 15; 15; 15; 15
Joseph Schwartz, President
Bee Haddock, Operations Dir
Paul Orlando, General Manager
Scott Staley, Programming Director
James MacDonald, News Director
Jim Frank, Chief Engineer

Rifle

KRGS
06-09-1967; 690 khz AM *Hrs Open:* 24; 0.9 kw-D, ND1; 0.012 kw-N, ND1; N39 32 56 W107 46 11
P.O. Box 60040, Grand Junction, CO 81506 US
(970) 241-6460, *Fax:* (970) 241-6452
License: Rifle, CO held by Western Slope Communications L.L.C.
Group Owner: Western Slope Communications LLC
Format: Sports *Target Audience:* 18-54; males
John Reid, General Manager

KZKS
01-01-1994; 105.3 mhz FM *Hrs Open:* 24; 60 kw; 2,437 ft; N39 25 57 W108 07 46
751 Horizon Ct., Suite 225, Grand Junction, CO 81506
(970) 241-6460, *Fax:* (970) 241-6452
License: Rifle, Garfield County, CO
Group Owner: Western Slope Communications LLC
Population Served: 320,000*Hrs. of News Programming:* news progmg 20 hrs wkly *No. News Employees:* 1
Katie Robley, Operations Dir
Tom Little, General Manager
Tom Little, Station Manager
Michael Johnson, Programming Director
Ryan Baker, Chief Engineer

Rocky Ford

KPHT
01-01-2002; 95.5 mhz FM; 100 kw; 735 ft.; N37 54 8 W104 16 0
1470 Ben Sawyer Blvd, Suite 16, Mout Pleasant, SC 29464 US
(719) 545-2080, *Fax:* (719) 543-9898
www.kpht955.com
License: Rocky Ford, Otero County, CO held by Capstar TX L.P.
Group Owner: Clear Channel Communications Inc.; (acq 2-12-2001; $1 million).
Format: Oldies
Scott Jones, General Manager
Charnell Mayer, Programming Director

Rye

*KRWA
08-24-2007; 90.9 mhz FM; 10 kw; 114 ft.; N37 56 40 W104 59 56
P.O. Box 704, Rye, CO 81069 US
(877) 702-9293, *Fax:* (719) 278-4339
www.kxwy.wayfm.com
supportservices@wayfm.com
License: Rye, Pueblo County, CO held by WAY-FM Media Group Inc.
Group Owner: WAY-FM Media Group Inc.; (acq 6-17-2005; $200,000 for CP)
Arbitron Metro Market: Rye, CO *Format:* Christian
Robert Augsburg, President

Salida

KVRH
12-10-1948; 1340 khz AM *Hrs Open:* 24; 1 kw-U, ND1; N38 31 55 W106 0 54
7600 County Road 120, Salida, CO 81201 US
(719) 539-2575, *Fax:* (719) 539-4851
www.kvrh.com
kvrh@kvrh.com
License: Salida, CO held by Headwaters Media L.L.C.
Arbitron Metro Market: Salida,CO *Format:* Oldies *Hrs. of News Programming:* news progmg 10 hrs wkly *No. News Employees:* 1 *Target Audience:* 25-54; general
Dean Jhonson, Operations Dir
Ron Gates, General Manager and General Sales Manager

KVRH-FM
01-01-1971; 92.3 mhz FM *Hrs Open:* 24; 0.22 kw; 2938 ft.; N38 27 11 W106 1 2
7600 County Road 120, Salida, CO 81201 US
(719) 539-2575, *Fax:* (719) 539-4851
www.kvrh.com
kvrh@kvrh.com
License: Salida, Chaffee County, CO held by Three Eagles Communications of Colorado LLC
Arbitron Metro Market: Salida,CO *Format:* Adult Contemp *Hrs. of News Programming:* news progmg 10 hrs wkly *No. News Employees:* 1
Dean Jhonson, Operations Dir
Ron Gates, General Manager and General Sales Manager

KSBV
01-01-2002; 93.7 mhz FM *Hrs Open:* 24; 1 kw; 2723 ft.; N38 26 47 W106 0 37
403 Route South, Cape May Court House, NJ 08210 US
(719) 539-9377, *Fax:* (719) 539-7904
www.ksbv.net
ksbvradio@bresnan.net
License: Salida, Chaffee County, CO held by Arkansas Valley Broadcasting L.L.C.
Arbitron Metro Market: Salida, CO *Format:* Classic Rock, Sports *Target Audience:* 25-65.
Marc Scott, President
Melissa Scott, News Director

*KTPF
01-01-2007; 91.3 mhz FM; 0.39 kw; 2953 ft.; N38 26 48 W106 0 36 *Rebroadcasts:* Rebroadcasts KTLF(FM) Colorado Springs 100%
1665 Briargate Blvd., Colorado Springs, CO 80920 US
(719) 593-0600, *Fax:* (719) 593-2399
www.ktlf.org
lightpraise@ktlf.org
License: Salida, Chaffee County, CO held by Educational Communications of Colorado Springs Inc.
Arbitron Metro Market: Salida, CO *Format:* Christian *Target Audience:* 45-60; Christian
James Felix, Operations Dir
Tom Sullivan, General Manager
Sharick Wade, Programming Director
Robert Mumm, Chief Engineer
Skip Rice, Sonrise Host
Marge Wallace, Office Manager
Alleen Wagnon, Office Assistant

*KMPZ
88.1 mhz FM; 0.2 kw; 2713 ft.; N38 26 48 W106 0 36
US
(719) 578-5263
www.kcme.org
genmanager@kcme.org
License: Salida, Chaffee County, CO held by Cheyenne Mountain Public Broadcast House Inc.
Arbitron Metro Market: Salida, CO *Format:* Classical
John Haralson, President
Jeanna Wearing, General Manager
Cynthia Bullock, Interim Development Director
Brenda Bratton, Finance/Office Manager

*KADE
89.7 mhz FM; 0.18 kw vert; 1096 ft.; N38 44 45 W106 11 52
US
(970) 669-9200
License: Salida, Chaffee County, CO held by Cedar Cove Broadcasting Inc.
Group Owner: Cedar Cove Broadcasting Inc.
Arbitron Metro Market: Loveland, CO *Format:* Country
Victor Michael Jr., President

Security

KRDO-FM
04-08-1973; 105.5 mhz FM *Hrs Open:* 24; 1.6 kw horiz, 1.47 kw vert; 2238 ft.; N38 44 40 W104 51 41 *Rebroadcasts:* Simulcasts KRDO(AM) Colorado Springs 100%
1201 Connecticut Ave.450, Washington, DC 20036 US
(719) 632-1515 (719) 473-1240, *Fax:* (719) 475-0815
www.krdo.com
m.lewis@krdo.com
License: Security, El Paso County, CO held by Optima Communications Inc.
Arbitron Metro Market: Colorado Springs, CO *Format:* News, News/Talk, 86
James Bond Jr., CFO
J.B. McCoy III, President
Edward Klimek, Operations Dir
Tim Larson, General Manager
Mike Lewis, Programming Director
Baaron Pittenger, News Director

Severance

KYEN
03-13-2008; 103.9 mhz FM; 16.5 kw; 1220 ft.; N40 37 3 W105 19 40
US
(312) 204-9900
rocktherockies.com
Guru@rocktherockies.com
License: Severance, Weld County, CO held by College Creek Media LLC.
Group Owner: College Creek Media LLC
Arbitron Metro Market: Severance, CO *Format:* Classic Rock
Neal Robinson, President

Snowmass Village

KSNO-FM
04-01-1985; 103.9 mhz FM *Hrs Open:* 24; 6 kw; 325 ft.; N39 14 51 W106 55 13
1400 Easton Road, Bakersfield, CA 93303 US
(970) 925-4111, *Fax:* (970) 925-7190
www.ksno.us
don@thesoundfm.com
License: Snowmass Village, Pitkin County, CO held by Cool Radio LLC.
Nat'l Reps: Katz Radio *Wire Services:* AP

Arbitron Metro Market: Aspen, CO *Format:* Triple A *Hrs. of News Programming:* news progmg 2 hrs wkly *No. News Employees:* 1 *Target Audience:* 25-54.
Don Chaney, General Manager

South Fork

***KTML**
01-01-2009; 91.5 mhz FM; 0 kw horiz, 0.28 kw vert; 1614 ft.; N37 43 47 W106 35 18 *Rebroadcasts:* Rebroadcasts KTLF(FM) Colorado Springs 100%
US
(719) 593-0600, *Fax:* (719) 593-2399
www.ktlf.org
lightpraise@ktlf.org
License: South Fork, Rio Grande County, CO held by Educational Communications of Colorado Springs Inc.
Arbitron Metro Market: South Fork, CO *Format:* Christian
Tom Sullivan, General Manager
Sharick Wade, Programming Director
Robert Mumm, Chief Engineer
James Felix, Operations Manager & Sonrise Co-Host
Marge Wallace, Office Manager
Alleen Wagnon, Office Assistant

Springfield

***KLXD**
91.7 mhz FM; 0.25 kw; 151 ft.; N37 24 1 W102 37 8
US
(405) 380-3516
www.klxfm.com
info@bpba.us
License: Springfield, Baca County, CO held by Better Public Broadcasting Association.
Arbitron Metro Market: Springfield, CO
Dennis Burton, General Manager

Starkville

***KCCS**
01-01-2008; 91.7 mhz FM; 0.37 kw; 994 ft.; N36 59 33 W104 28 24 *Rebroadcasts:* Rebroadcasts KRCC(FM) Colorado Springs 100%
14 East Cache La Poudre, Colorado Springs, CO 80903 US
(719) 473-4801, *Fax:* (719) 473-7863
www.krcc.org
info@krcc.org
License: Starkville, Las Animas County, CO held by The Colorado College.
Nat'l Network: NPR; PRI
Arbitron Metro Market: Starkville, CO
Delaney Utterback, General Manager

Steamboat Springs

KBCR
08-01-1976; 1230 khz AM *Hrs Open:* 24; 1 kw-U, ND1; N40 29 19 W106 50 57
Mailing Address: 815 Reed St, Lakewood, CO 80477 US
Second Address: 2110 Mt. Werner Rd., Steamboat Springs, CO 80487
(970) 879-2270, *Fax:* (970) 879-1404
kbcr.com
brian@kbcr.com
License: Steamboat Springs, CO held by Cool Radio LLC.
Nat'l Network: ESPN Radio
Arbitron Metro Market: Steamboat Springs, CO *Format:* Sports *No. News Employees:* 1 *Target Audience:* 24-55.
Brian Harvey, General Manager
Dave Lancaster, News Director

KBCR-FM
07-25-1974; 96.9 mhz FM; 10 kw; Ant 666 ft; N40 27 43 W106 50 57
Box 774050, Steamboat Springs, CO 80215
(970) 879-2270, *Fax:* (970) 879-1404
kbcr.com
tony@kbcr.com
License: Steamboat Springs, Routt County, CO held by Cool Radio LLC
Nat'l Network: ABC
Population Served: 25,000
Tom Dobrel, CEO
Tony Mauro, Operations Dir
Craig Roehn, General Manager

***KLBV**
01-01-2005; 89.3 mhz FM *Hrs Open:* 24; 2.6 kw vert; 1732 ft.; N40 27 4 W106 45 6
16075 West Belleview Ave, Morrison, CO 80465 US
(800) 525-5683, *Fax:* (916) 251-1650
www.klove.com
klove@klove.com
License: Steamboat Springs, Routt County, CO held by Educational Media Foundation.
Group Owner: EMF Broadcasting; (acq 10-2-03; grpsl).
Nat'l Network: K-Love
Arbitron Metro Market: Steamboat Springs, CO *Format:* Christian *No. News Employees:* 13 *Target Audience:* 25-44; Judeo Christian, female
Darrell Chambliss, Chairman
Mike Novak, President and CEO
Jennifer Lohman, Operations Dir
David Pierce, Chief Creative Officer and Programming Director
Ed Lenane, News Director
Sam Wallington, Engineering Dir
Marya Morgan, NewsReporter
Richard Hunt, News Reporter
Alan Mason, Chief Operating Officer
Dan Antonelli, Chief Business Development Officer
Eric Moser, Chief Financial Officer
Brian Burger, Vice President of Human Resources

***KRNC**
01-23-2006; 88.5 mhz FM; 0.24 kw; 600 ft.; N40 27 43 W106 50 57 *Rebroadcasts:* Rebroadcasts KUNC(FM) Greeley 100%
US
(970) 378-2579, *Fax:* (970) 378-2580
www.kunc.org
comment@kunc.org
License: Steamboat Springs, Routt County, CO held by Community Radio of Northern Colorado
Nat'l Network: NPR; PRI *Wire Services:* AP
Arbitron Metro Market: Steamboat Springs, CO *Format:* News, Variety/Diverse
Jamie Wood, CFO
Neil Best, President and CEO
Ryan Thompson, Operations Dir
Michelle Komanich, General Sales Mgr
Kirk Mowers, Programming Director
Brian Larson, News Director
Ken Broeffle, Chief Engineer
Benjamin McPhail, MusicDirector
Dave Dennis, Corporate Support Associate
Robert Leja, Director of Corporate Support and Marketing
Jim Hill, Digital Media Manager
Kirk Mowers, Content Director
Marc Applegate, Announcer/Producer

***KTSG**
01-01-2006; 91.7 mhz FM; 2.5 kw horiz, 0 kw vert; N40 27 43 W106 50 58 *Rebroadcasts:* Rebroadcasts KTLF(FM) Colorado Springs 100%
1665 Briargate Blvd., Colordo Springs, CO 80920 US
(719) 593-0600, *Fax:* (719) 593-2399
www.ktlf.org
lightpraise@ktlf.org
License: Steamboat Springs, Routt County, CO held by Educational Communications of Colorado Springs Inc.
Arbitron Metro Market: Steamboat Springs, CO *Format:* Christian *Target Audience:* 45-60; Christian
James Felix, Operations Dir
Tom Sullivan, General Manager
Sharick Wade, Programming Director
Robert Mumm, Chief Engineer
Skip Rice, Sonrise Host
Marge Wallace, Office Manager
Alleen Wagnon, Office Assistant

Sterling

KNNG
02-08-1974; 104.7 mhz FM *Hrs Open:* 24; 100 kw; 650 ft.; N40 34 57 W103 1 56
P.O. Box 830, Sterling, CO 80751 US
(970) 522-1607, *Fax:* (970) 522-1322
knng@kci.net
License: Sterling, Logan County, CO held by Arnold Broadcasting Inc.
Group Owner: Arnold Broadcasting Inc.; (acq 7-31-2008; grpsl)
Nat'l Network: Jones Radio Networks; ABC
Format: Country *Hrs. of News Programming:* news progmg 10 hrs wkly *No. News Employees:* 1 *Target Audience:* General; country listeners
William Arnold, CEO

KPMX
08-19-1983; 105.7 mhz FM *Hrs Open:* 24; 12 kw; 479 ft.; N40 31 57 W103 7 22
101 So. Division Ave, Sterling, CO 80751 US
(970) 522-4800, *Fax:* (970) 522-3997
www.kpmx.com
andy@kpmx.com
License: Sterling, Logan County, CO held by Northeast Colorado Broadcasting LLC
Group Owner: Northeast Colorado Broadcasting LLC; acq 7-1-2003; grpsl).
Format: Adult Contemp *Target Audience:* 18-54. *Adv. Rates:* 12
Alec Creighton, General Manager

KSTC
01-03-1925; 1230 khz AM *Hrs Open:* 24
P.O. Box 830, Sterling, CO 80751 US
(970) 522-1607, *Fax:* (970) 522-1322
knng@kci.net
License: Sterling, CO held by Arnold Broadcasting Inc.
Group Owner: Arnold Broadcasting Inc.; (acq 7-31-2008; grpsl)
Nat'l Network: ABC; Jones Radio Networks
Arbitron Metro Market: Sterling, CO *Format:* Oldies *Special Programming:* Farm 15 hrs wkly *Hrs. of News Programming:* news progmg 12 hrs wkly *No. News Employees:* 1 *Target Audience:* General.
William Arnold, CEO
Betty Carlson, General Manager
Mike Walker, Programming Director
Montica Loft, Assistant Manager

***KDRE**
01-01-2005; 90.7 mhz FM; 1.6 kw vert; 506 ft.; N40 36 56 W103 2 2 *Rebroadcasts:* Rebroadcasts KLRD(FM) Yucaipa, CA 100%
188 South Bellevue, Suite 222, Memphis, TN 38104 US
(888) 937-2471, *Fax:* (916) 251-1650
www.air1.com
info@air1.com
License: Sterling, Logan County, CO held by Educational Media Foundation.
Group Owner: EMF Broadcasting; (acq 9-22-2005; $17,000 for CP)
Nat'l Network: Air 1
Arbitron Metro Market: Sterling, CO *Format:* Alternative, Christian
Darrell Chambliss, Chairman
Alan Mason, COO
Mike Novak, President and CEO
Jennifer Lohman, Operations Dir
David Pierce, Programming Director
Ed Lenane, News Director
Sam Wallington, Engineering Dir
Marya Morgan, NewsReporter
Richard Hunt, News Reporter
Tracy Butler, Traffic Manager
Dan Antonelli, Chief Business Development Officer
Eric Moser, Chief Financial Officer
Brian Burger, Vice President of Human Resources

***KTAD**
01-01-2005; 89.9 mhz FM; 5 kw vert; 407 ft.; N40 31 57 W103 7 22 *Rebroadcasts:* Rebroadcasts KTPL(FM) Pueblo 100%
1665 Briargate Blvd., Colorado Springs, CO 80920 US
(719) 593-0600, *Fax:* (719) 593-2399
www.ktlf.org
Tom@ktlf.org
License: Sterling, Logan County, CO held by Educational Communications of Colorado Springs Inc.
Arbitron Metro Market: Sterling, CO *Format:* Christian, Religious *Target Audience:* 18-35; Christian
James Felix, Operations Dir
Tom Sullivan, General Manager
Sharick Wade, Programming Director
Robert Mumm, Chief Engineer
Marge Wallace, Office Manager
Alleen Wagnon, Office Assistant

KSRX
01-01-2008; 97.5 mhz FM; 17 kw; Ant 561 ft; N40 27 15.1 W103 09 6.1
P.O. Box 430, Fort Morgan, CO
(970) 867-5674, *Fax:* (970) 542-1023
License: Sterling, Logan County, CO held by Media Logic LLC.
Group Owner: Media Logic LLC
Target Audience: 18-45; female, male
Wayne Johnson, President
Marc Romero, Station Manager

Strasburg

***KSJL**
97.7 mhz FM; 25 kw horiz; 52 ft.; N39 42 19 W104 12 17
P.O. Box 7346, Las Vegas, NV 89125 US
(210) 736-9700, *Fax:* (210) 735-8811
License: Strasburg, Adams County, CO held by Mary V. Harris Foundation.
Arbitron Metro Market: Strasburg, CO *Format:* Oldies

Linda De Romanett, President

Telluride

*KOTO
10-01-1975; 91.7 mhz FM; 8.4 kw; -223 ft.; N37 55 59 W107 49 59
P.O. Box 1069, Telluride, CO 81435 US
(970) 728-4334, *Fax:* (970) 728-4326
www.koto.org
koto@telluridecolorado.net
License: Telluride, San Miguel County, CO held by San Miguel Educational Fund.
Nat'l Network: NPR; PRI
Format: Variety/Diverse *Special Programming:* Class 9 hrs, country 12 hrs, jazz 9 hrs, blues 7 hrs, drama 3 hrs wkly *Hrs. of News Programming:* news progmg 2 hrs wkly *No. News Employees:* 2 *Target Audience:* General; community
Bob Biener, President
Janice Zink, Operations Dir
Ben Kerr, Station Manager
Steve Kennedy, General Sales Mgr
Stephen Barrett, News Director
Suzanne Cheavens, Music Director

Thornton

KKZN
05-30-1987; 760 khz AM
50 East Rivercenter Blvd, Suite 1200, Covington, KY 41011 US
(303) 713-8000, *Fax:* (303) 713-8738
www.am760.net
License: Thornton, CO held by Citicasters Licenses Inc. (NEW).
Group Owner: Clear Channel Communications Inc.; (acq 5-4-99; grpsl).
Arbitron Metro Market: Denver-Boulder, CO *Format:* Alternative, Talk
Lee Larsen, General Manager
Kristine Olinger, Programming Director
Jan Chadwell, Chief Engineer

Timnath

KJAC
04-10-1989; 105.5 mhz FM *Hrs Open:* 24; 50 kw; 1302 ft.; N40 37 3 W105 19 39
1806 Capitol Avenue, Cheyenne, WY 82001 US
(303) 296-7025, *Fax:* (303) 296-7030
www.1055jackfm.com
info@1055jackfm.com
License: Timnath, Larimer County, CO held by NRC Broadcasting Inc.
Group Owner: NRC Broadcasting Inc.; (acq 4-13-2004; $15 million)
Nat'l Network: Westwood One *Nat'l Reps:* Target Broadcast Sales
Arbitron Metro Market: Fort Collins-Greeley, CO *Hrs. of News Programming:* News progmg 10 hrs wkly *Target Audience:* 18-54; general
Timothy Brown, General Manager
Roger Tighe, Chief Engineer

Trinidad

KCRT
05-21-1946; 1240 khz AM *Hrs Open:* 24; 0.25 kw-U, ND1; N37 8 45 W104 30 42
100 Fisher Drive, Trinidad, CO 81082 US
(719) 846-3355, *Fax:* (719) 846-4711
www.kcrtradio.com
kcrt@comcast.net
License: Trinidad, CO held by Phillips Broadcasting Inc.
Group Owner: Phillips Broadcasting Inc.; (acq 3-30-92; $235,000 with co-located FM;
Nat'l Network: ABC; Jones Radio Networks
Arbitron Metro Market: Trinidad, CO *Format:* Country *Special Programming:* Farm one hr, relg 5 hrs wkly *Hrs. of News Programming:* news progmg 15 hrs wkly *No. News Employees:* 1 *Target Audience:* General.*Adv. Rates:* 8; 7; 6; 6
Anita Phillips, President
Lory Phillips, General Manager
David Phillips, Station Manager
Rick Neurauter, Advertising Director

KCRT-FM
08-01-1981; 92.5 mhz FM *Hrs Open:* 24; 38.5 kw; 1020 ft.; N36 59 33 W104 28 24
100 Fisher Drive, Trinidad, CO 81082 US
(719) 846-3355, *Fax:* (719) 846-4711
www.kcrtradio.com
krct@comcast.net
License: Trinidad, Las Animas County, CO held by Phillips Broadcasting Inc.
Group Owner: Phillips Broadcasting Inc.
Arbitron Metro Market: Trinidad, CO *Format:* Classic Rock *Target Audience:* 25-54. *Adv. Rates:* 12; 10; 8; 8
Anita Phillips, President
Lory Phillips, General Manager
David Phillips, Station Manager

*KJWA
89.7 mhz FM; 0.9 kw; 791 ft.; N37 14 14 W104 30 52
Rebroadcasts: Rebroadcasts KXWA(FM) Loveland 100%
P.O. Box 704, Rye, CO 81069 US
(303) 702-9293, *Fax:* (303) 485-1929
www.wayfm.com
License: Trinidad, Pueblo County, CO held by WAY-FM Media Group Inc.
Group Owner: WAY-FM Media Group Inc.; (acq 6-19-2007)
Arbitron Metro Market: Trinidad, CO *Format:* Christian
Zach Cochran, General Manager

*KTDL
01-01-2007; 90.7 mhz FM; 0.45 kw; 971 ft.; N36 59 33 W104 28 24 *Rebroadcasts:* Rebroadcasts KTLF(FM) Colorado Springs 100%
1665 Briargate Blvd, Colorado Springs, CO 80920 US
(719) 593-0600, *Fax:* (719) 593-2399
www.ktlf.org
lightpraise@ktlf.org
License: Trinidad, Las Animas County, CO held by Educational Communications of Colorado Springs Inc.
Arbitron Metro Market: Trinidad, CO *Format:* Christian *Target Audience:* 45-60; Christian
James Felix, Operations Dir
Tom Sullivan, General Manager
Sharick Wade, Programming Director
Robert Mumm, Chief Engineer
Skip Rice, Sonrise Host
Marge Wallace, Office Manager
Alleen Wagnon, Office Assistant

Vail

*KPRE
09-01-1994; 89.9 mhz FM *Hrs Open:* 24; 1.5 kw; 295 ft.; N39 38 5 W106 26 47 *Rebroadcasts:* Rebroadcasts KCFR(FM) Denver 100%
2249 S. Josephine Street, Denver, CO 80210 US
(303) 871-9191, *Fax:* (303) 733-3319
www.cpr.org
info@cpr.org
License: Vail, Eagle County, CO held by Public Broadcasting of Colorado Inc.
Nat'l Network: NPR
Format: News *Hrs. of News Programming:* news progmg 50 hrs wkly *No. News Employees:* 8 *Target Audience:* General.
Warren Olsen, Chairman
Max Wycisk, President
Sue Coughlin, General Sales Mgr
Bob Hensler, Engineering Dir

KVLE
07-25-1983; 610 khz AM; 5 kw-D, ND1; 0.217 kw-N, ND1; N39 34 47 W106 24 54 *Rebroadcasts:* Simulcasts KSKE(AM) Buena Vista
1768 Coral Way North, Vero Beach, FL 32963 US
(303) 776-2323, *Fax:* (303) 776-1377
www.kvleradio.com
cduncan@bcdworldwide.com
License: Vail, CO held by Pilgrim Communications Inc.
Group Owner: Pilgrim Communications Inc.; (acq 3-2-2000; $150,000)
Nat'l Network: ABC
Arbitron Metro Market: Longmont, CO *Format:* Talk *Hrs. of News Programming:* news progmg 12 hrs wkly *No. News Employees:* 3 *Target Audience:* 25-65. *Adv. Rates:* 40; 40; 40; 30
Chuck Duncan, CEO
Roger Cridelbaugh, Operations Dir
Nancy Smith, Business Manager
Gene Hood, Owner

*KVJZ
88.5 mhz FM; 5 kw; -791 ft.; N39 36 56 W106 26 57
P O Box 11111, Denver, CO 80211 US
(303) 480-9272, *Fax:* (303) 291-0757
www.kuvo.org
info@kuvo.org
License: Vail, Eagle County, CO held by Denver Educational Broadcasting Inc.
Arbitron Metro Market: Vail, CO
Carlos Lando, COO
Gene Craven, President

Walsenburg

KSPK-FM
03-01-1985; 102.3 mhz FM *Hrs Open:* 24; 100 kw; 430 ft.; N37 37 39 W104 49 17
516 Main Street, Walsenburg, CO 81089 US
(719) 738-3636, *Fax:* (719) 738-2010
www.kspk.com
info@kspk.com
License: Walsenburg, Huerfano County, CO held by Mainstreet Broadcasting Co. Inc.
Nat'l Network: ABC *Wire Services:* ABC
Arbitron Metro Market: Walsenburg, CO *TV Affiliate:* KSPK-TV
Format: Country, Sports *Special Programming:* Relg 2 hrs wkly *Hrs. of News Programming:* news progmg 3 hrs wkly *No. News Employees:* 2 *TargetAudience:* 24-59; upwardly mobile, two-income families *Adv. Rates:* 20; 16; 18; 14
David Raye, Operations Dir
Paul Richards, General Manager
Paul Bossert, Chief Engineer
Michelle Lessar, Traffic Manager

*KTAW
01-01-2008; 89.3 mhz FM; 0 kw horiz, 0.5 kw vert; 377 ft.; N37 37 39 W104 49 17 *Rebroadcasts:* Rebroadcasts KTLF(FM) Colorado Springs 100%
1665 Briargate Blvd, Colorado Sorings, CO 80920 US
(719) 593-0600, *Fax:* (719) 593-2399
www.ktlf.org
litepraise@ktlf.org
License: Walsenburg, Huerfano County, CO held by Educational Communications of Colorado Springs Inc.
Arbitron Metro Market: Walsenburg, CO *Format:* Christian *Target Audience:* 45-60; Christian
James Felix, Operations Dir
Tom Sullivan, General Manager
Sharick Wade, Programming Director
Robert Mumm, Chief Engineer
Skip Rice, Sonrise Host
Marge Wallace, Office Manager
Alleen Wagnon, Office Assistant

KFEZ(FM)
01-01-2009; 101.3 mhz FM; 95.5 kw; Ant 1,000 ft; N37 47 20 W104 29 12
516 Main St., Walsenburg, CO 81089
(773) 592-9800
License: Walsenburg, Huerfano County, CO held by Edward Magnus.
Population Served: 2,980 *Arbitron Metro Market:* Walsenburg, CO
Edward Magnus, General Manager

Weldona

KFWA(FM)
103.1 mhz FM; 25,000 watts; 135 meters; 39 28 12N 103 38 14W
1707 Ben Sawyer Blvd, Suite 16, Mount Pleasant, SC 29464 USA
kxwa.wayfm.com
License: Weldona, Morgan County, CO
Group Owner: Way-FM Media Inc

Wellington

KCOL
01-12-1959; 600 khz AM; 5 kw-D, DA2; 0.5 kw-N, DA2; N40 39 0 W105 2 51
50 E. Rivercenter Blvd., Suite 1200, Covington, KY 41011 US
(970) 461-2560, *Fax:* (970) 461-0118
www.600kcol.com
stuhaskell@clearchannel.com; kathyarias@clearchannel.com
License: Wellington, CO held by Jacor Broadcasting of Colorado Inc.
Group Owner: Clear Channel Communications Inc.; (acq 5-8-98; $6.1 million with co-located FM)
Nat'l Reps: McGavren Guild
TV Affiliate: Fox *Format:* News, News/Talk, 86 *Special Programming:* Farm 2 hrs, relg one hr, sports talk 7 hrs wkly *Hrs. of News Programming:* News progmg 120 hrs wkly *Target Audience:* 35 plus.
Stu Haskell, General Manager
Kathy Arias, General Sales Mgr
Scott James, Programming Director
Mike Sanchez, Promotions Manager
Dave Agnew, Chief Engineer
Sue Sutton, Producer

KMAX-FM
01-01-2003; 94.3 mhz FM *Hrs Open:* 24; 8.7 kw; 551 ft.; N40 55 41 W105 8 36

C/O Brill Media Co Lp, P O Box 3353, Evansville, IN 47732 US
(970) 674-2700, *Fax:* (970) 686-7491
www.943maxfm.com
george.king@townsquaremedia.com
License: Wellington, Larimer County, CO
Group Owner: Townsquare Media; (acq 2-25-2003)
Arbitron Metro Market: Wellington, CO *Format:* Classic Rock
Mark Callaghan, Operations Dir
Pete Hanson, General Manager
Miles Schallert, General Sales Mgr
Susan Moore, News Director
Kerry Richards, Chief Engineer
George Kings, Brand Manager
Zandi Wilcox, Director of Sales

Westcliffe

KXCL
01-01-2008; 101.7 mhz FM; 125 w; 655 meters; N38 08 09 W105 27 07
1200 W. Cornwallis, Greensboro, NC
(336) 286-2087
License: Westcliffe, Custer County, CO held by United States CP LLC.
Group Owner: United States CP LLC
Population Served: 58 *Arbitron Metro Market:* Rock Creek Park, CO
W. Philip Robinson, General Manager

***KLZR**
91.9 mhz FM; kw
US
(785)843-1320, *Fax:* (785)841-1320
www.1059kissfm.com
License: Westcliffe, Custer County, CO
Group Owner: Cedar Cove Broadcasting Inc.
Jay Wachs, General Manager
Ammber Lee, Programming Director
Rebecca Supernaw, Advertising

Wheat Ridge

KTCL
09-01-1965; 93.3 mhz FM; 71 kw; 1135 ft.; N39 43 59 W105 14 10
50 E. Rivercenter Blvd, Suite 1200, Covington, KY 41011 US
(303) 713-8000, *Fax:* (303) 713-8744
www.area93.com
info@ktcl.com
License: Wheat Ridge, Jefferson County, CO held by Jacor Broadcasting of Colorado Inc.
Group Owner: Clear Channel Communications Inc.; (acq 5-8-98; $6.1 million with co-located AM)
Arbitron Metro Market: Denver-Boulder, CO *Format:* Alternative *Special Programming:* Comedy one hr, loc bands one hr, reggae 2 hrs wkly *Target Audience:* 18 plus.
Lee Larsen, General Manager
Jack Lambiotte, General Sales Mgr
Nerf, Programming Director

Widefield

KKLI
03-23-1987; 106.3 mhz FM *Hrs Open:* 24; 1.6 kw; 2224 ft.; N38 44 41 W104 51 46
600 Congress Avenue, Suite 1400, Austin, TX 78701 US
(719) 540-9200, *Fax:* (719) 579-0882
www.klite1063.com
License: Widefield, El Paso County, CO held by Capstar TX L.P.
Group Owner: Clear Channel Communications Inc.; (acq 8-30-00; grpsl).
Nat'l Reps: Clear Channel
Arbitron Metro Market: Colorado Spring, CO *Format:* Adult Contemp *Hrs. of News Programming:* news progmg 4 hrs wkly *No. News Employees:* 1 *Target Audience:* 25-54; family-oriented, educated *Adv. Rates:* 100; 90; 90; 60
Bob Richards, General Manager
Chrissy Adsit, General Sales Mgr
David Black, Programming Director
Paul Richards, News Director
Daren McMullin, Chief Engineer

Windsor

KUAD-FM
05-31-1975; 99.1 mhz FM; 100 kw; 837 ft.; N40 38 31 W104 49 3
P.O.Box 3353, Evansville, IN 47732 US
(970) 674-2700, *Fax:* (970) 686-7491
www.k99.com
chall@regentcomm.com
License: Windsor, Weld County, CO
Group Owner: Townsquare Media; (acq 2-25-03).
Arbitron Metro Market: Windsor, CO *Format:* Country *Target Audience:* 25-54; upscale country listeners, 60% women *Adv. Rates:* 35; 35; 35; 25
Mark Callaghan, Operations Dir
Pete Hanson, General Manager
Zandi Wilcox, Director of Sales
Shelley Heier, Promotions Manager
Meg Sprague, News Director
George King, Brand Manager

KJJD
04-12-1969; 1170 khz AM *Hrs Open:* Sunrise-sunset; 1 kw-D, NDD; N40 27 46 W104 54 47
Mailing Address: P.O. Box 698, Windsor, CO 80550 US
Second Address: PO Box 698, Windsor, CO 80550
(970) 686-1170, *Fax:* (970) 686-5751
www.laley1170.com
secretaria1170@yahoo.com
License: Windsor, CO held by Rodriguez-Gallegos Broadcasting Corporation.
Format: Spanish *Special Programming:* Pub affrs *Hrs. of News Programming:* News progmg 5 hrs wkly *Target Audience:* 18-54; general
Jesse Rodriguez, General Manager
Danny Casas, Station Manager

Woodland Park

***KILE-FM**
89.5 mhz FM; 100 w vert; Ant -407 ft; N38 59 37 W105 02 21
4703 Orkney Dr., Missouri City, TX
(281) 923-7100, *Fax:* 713-559-8517
radioguy@airmail.net
License: Woodland Park, Teller County, CO held by Grace Public Radio.
Population Served: 10,200 *Arbitron Metro Market:* Colorado Springs, CO *Target Audience:* Adults, 25-54
Fred Morton, Member
KT Morton, Member

Wray

KATR-FM
09-01-1983; 98.3 mhz FM *Hrs Open:* 24; 100 kw; 554 ft.; N40 25 13 W102 58 10
P.O. Box 2224, Greeley, CO 80632 US
(970) 521-2732, *Fax:* (970) 521-2733
www.katcountry983.com
medialogic@kci.net
License: Wray, Washington County, CO held by Media Logic LLC
Group Owner: Media Logic LLC; acq 10-28-2002; $700,000).
Arbitron Metro Market: Sterling, CO *Format:* Country *Hrs. of News Programming:* news progmg 15 hrs wkly *No. News Employees:* 3 *Target Audience:* 16-70; males & females
Wayne Johnson, General Manager
Marc Romero, Station Manager
Dana Marini, General Sales Mgr
Michael Schaus, News Director

KRDZ
01-11-1978; 1440 khz AM *Hrs Open:* 4:50 AM-midnight; 5 kw-D, ND1; 0.212 kw-N, ND1; N40 4 56 W102 11 25
P.O. Box 466, Wray, CO 80758 US
(970) 332-4171, *Fax:* (970) 332-4172
www.krdz.com
krdz@medialogicradio.com
License: Wray, CO held by Media Logic LLC
Group Owner: Media Logic LLC; acq 10-31-2002).
Nat'l Network: Jones Radio Networks *Regional Network:* Brownfield
Format: Contemporary Hits/Top 40 *Special Programming:* Focus on family 2 hrs, farm 10 hrs wkly *Hrs. of News Programming:* News progmg 10 hrs wkly *Target Audience:* Farmers & ranchers.
Wayne Johnson/Owner, General Manager
Keith Lippoldt, Station Manager
Dana Marini, General Sales Mgr
Robert Lovell, Sports Director

***KGCD**
01-01-2006; 90.3 mhz FM *Hrs Open:* 24; 0.43 kw vert; 253 ft.; N40 3 13 W102 13 32
US
(785) 694-2877, *Fax:* (785) 694-2875
www.wordpress.kgcr.org
kgcr@kgcr.org
License: Wray, Burleigh County, CO held by Educational Media Foundation.
Group Owner: EMF Broadcasting
Nat'l Network: K-Love
Arbitron Metro Market: Wray, CO *Format:* Country, Gospel *No. News Employees:* 3 *Target Audience:* 25-44; Judeo Christian, female
Mike Novak, President

Yuma

KNEC
01-01-1999; 100.9 mhz FM; 23 kw; 348 ft.; N40 0 33 W102 45 35
P O Box 830, 803 W Main St, Sterling, CO 80751 US
(970) 848-2302, *Fax:* (970) 848-2240
knec@plains.net
License: Yuma, Yuma County, CO held by Arnold Broadcasting Inc.
Group Owner: Arnold Broadcasting Inc.; (acq 7-31-2008; grpsl)
Format: Adult Contemp
Ashley Lynch, General Manager

Connecticut

Ansonia

WADS
05-08-1956; 690 khz AM; 3.2 kw-D, DAD; N41 20 46 W73 6 51
P.O. Box 384, New Haven, CT 06513 US
(662) 844-8888, *Fax:* (662) 842-6791
www.afr.net
License: Ansonia, CT held by Radio Amor Inc.
Format: Christian, Religious
Marvin Sanders, General Manager

Berlin

***WERB**
01-12-1979; 94.5 mhz FM *Hrs Open:* 24; 27.5 w; 95 ft; N41 37 18 W72 45 13
Berlin High School Media Center, 139 Patterson Way, Berlin, CT 06037
(860) 828-0606,(860) 828-6577, *Fax:* (860) 829-0526
www.berlinwall.org
werb@berlinschools.org
License: Berlin, Hartford County, CT held by Berlin Board of Education.
Target Audience: Teenage listeners from Berlin High School
Chris Wolfe, General Manager

Bloomfield

WSDK
02-01-1964; 1550 khz AM *Hrs Open:* 24; 5 kw-D, DA2; 2.4 kw-N, DA2; N41 51 47 W72 44 1
866 2nd Ave., 2nd Fl, New York, NY 10017 US
(860) 643-3912, *Fax:* (860) 643-3910
www.radiodisney.com
paul.o.robertson.@disney.com
License: Bloomfield, CT held by Radio Disney Group LLC.
Group Owner: ABC Inc.; (acq 11-21-00; grpsl).
Nat'l Network: ABC
Arbitron Metro Market: Bloomfield, CT *Format:* Children *Hrs. of News Programming:* news progmg 11 hrs wkly *No. News Employees:* 1 *Target Audience:* 18-80; general *Adv. Rates:* 32; 30; 32; 22
Paul Robertson, General Manager

Bridgeport

WCUM
09-01-1941; 1450 khz AM *Hrs Open:* 24; 1 kw-U, ND1; N41 13 10 W73 12 8
Mailing Address: 1862-1902 St Str Exten, Bridgeport, CT 06605 US
Second Address: P.O. Box 3975, Bridgeport, CT 6605
(203) 335-1450
www.radiocumbre.am
radiocumbre1450@aol.com
License: Bridgeport, CT held by Radio Cumbre Broadcasting Inc.
Arbitron Metro Market: Bridgeport, CT *Hrs. of News Programming:* news progmg 14 hrs wkly *No. News Employees:* 2 *Target Audience:* 25 plus.
Pablo De Jesus Colon Hijo, CEO
Migdalia Ramos Colon, Operations Dir
Allison Sheahan, General Manager

WDJZ
04-30-1977; 1530 khz AM; 5 kw-D, DAD; N41 10 9 W73 13 14
175 Church Street, 3rd Floor, Naugatuck, CT 06770 US
(203) 368-4392, *Fax:* (203) 367-4551
www.wdjzradio.com
wdjzradio@sbcglobal.net
License: Bridgeport, CT held by People's Broadcast Network LLC
Arbitron Metro Market: Bridgeport, CT *Format:* Ethnic, Gospel
Target Audience: 35 plus.

Milford Edwards Sr., General Manager

WEZN-FM
10-24-1960; 99.9 mhz FM; 27.5 kw; 669 ft.; N41 16 44 W73 11 8
3773 Howard Hughes Prwy, Suite 300n, Las Vegas, NV 89109 US
(203) 783-8200, *Fax:* (203) 783-8383
www.star999.com
kristin.okesson@coxinc.com
License: Bridgeport, Fairfield County, CT held by Cox Radio Inc.
Group Owner: Cox Radio Inc.; (acq 3-28-97; grpsl)
Arbitron Metro Market: Bridgeport, CT *Format:* Adult Contemp
Target Audience: 25-54. *Adv. Rates:* 275; 275; 275; 100
Kim Guthrie, President
Andy Alcosser, General Sales Mgr
Samantha Stevens, Programming Director
Stephen Donnarummo, Promotions Manager
Carol Roberts, News Director
Dom Bordonaro, Chief Engineer
Helaine Greenbaum, National SalesManager
Jennifer Chaves, Local Sales Manager
Kristin Okesson, VP/Market Manager

WICC
01-01-1926; 600 khz AM *Hrs Open:* 24; 1 kw-D, 500 w-N, DA-2; N41 09 36 W73 09 53
2 Lafayette Sq., Bridgeport, CT 06840
(203) 366-6000, *Fax:* (203) 384-0600,
www.wicc600.com
License: Bridgeport, Fairfield County, CT held by Cumulus Licensing Corp.
Group Owner: Cumulus Media Inc.; (acq 3-14-02; grpsl).
Nat'l Reps: Christal
Population Served: 450,000 *Arbitron Metro Market:* Bridgeport, CT *Special Programming:* It 5 hrs wkly *Hrs. of News Programming:* news progmg 25 hrs wkly *No. News Employees:* 3 *Target Audience:* 35-64.
Ann McManus, Market Manager
Marrie Klebat, Sales Manager
Danny Lyons, Programming Director
Alissa Balouskus, Promotions Manager
Mike Bellamy, News Director
Curt Hansen, Operations Manager

***WPKN**
10-10-1963; 89.5 mhz FM *Hrs Open:* 24; 10 kw; 554 ft.; N41 16 44 W73 11 8
244 University Ave., Bridgeport, CT 06601 US
(203) 331-9756
www.wpkn.org
wpkn@wpkn.org
License: Bridgeport, Fairfield County, CT held by WPKN Inc.
Arbitron Metro Market: Bridgeport, CT *Format:* Variety/Diverse *Special Programming:* Class 2 hrs, Sp 4 hrs, Black 4 hrs, Fr 2 hrs, jazz 16 hrs wkly
Henry Minot, General Manager

Bristol

WPRX
11-22-1993; 1120 khz AM *Hrs Open:* 24; 1 kw-D, DAN; 0.5 kw-N, DAN; N41 39 29 W72 56 51
81 West Main Street, Suite G, New Britain, CT 06050 US
(860) 348-0667, *Fax:* (860) 348-0711
www.wprx1120.net
wprx1120@comcast.net
License: Bristol, CT held by Nievezquez Production Inc.
Arbitron Metro Market: Hartford-New Britain-Middletown, CT *Format:* News, News/Talk, 86 *Special Programming:* Pol 2 hrs wkly *Hrs. of News Programming:* news progmg 12 hrs wkly *No. News Employees:* 2 *TargetAudience:* 23-54; Hispanic adults *Adv. Rates:* 65; 60; 52; 30
Oscar Nieves, General Manager

Brookfield

WINE
05-09-1966; 940 khz AM; 0.68 kw-D, ND1; 0.004 kw-N, ND1; N41 29 35 W73 25 45
600 14th Street, N.W., Suite 800, Washington, DC 20005 US
(203) 775-1212, *Fax:* (203) 775-6452
www.wineradio.com
info@cumulus.com
License: Brookfield, CT held by Cumulus Licensing Corp.
Group Owner: Cumulus Media Inc.; (acq 1-23-2002; grpsl)
Nat'l Network: ESPN Radio
Arbitron Metro Market: Danbury, CT *Format:* Sports *Target Audience:* 25-54.
Tim Sheehan, Operations Dir
Brett Beshore, General Manager
Matt Carey, Programming Director

Lisa Harris, News Director
Peter Partenio, Chief Engineer

WRKI
12-24-1976; 95.1 mhz FM; 29.5 kw; 636 ft.; N41 29 36 W73 25 45
600 14th St., N.W., Suite800, Washington, DC 20005 US
(203) 775-1212, *Fax:* (203) 775-6452
www.i95rock.com
info@i95rock.com
License: Brookfield, Fairfield County, CT held by Cumulus Licensing Corp.
Group Owner: Cumulus Media Inc.
Arbitron Metro Market: Danbury, CT *Format:* Classic Rock
Tom Principi, General Sales Mgr
Taryn Polites, Promotions Manager

Danbury

WDAQ
12-01-1953; 98.3 mhz FM *Hrs Open:* 24; 1.3 kw; 460 ft; N41 22 27 W73 26 47
98 Mill Plain Road, Danbury, CT 06810
(203) 744-4800, *Fax:* (203) 778-4655
www.98q.com
License: Danbury, Fairfield County, CT held by Berkshire Broadcasting Corp.
Group Owner: Berkshire Broadcasting Corp.
Nat'l Reps: D & R Radio
Population Served: 250,000 *Arbitron Metro Market:* Danbury, CT
Ian Goldstein, CEO/COO
Ian Goldstein, General Manager
Mike Delpha, General Sales Mgr
Rich Minor, Programming Director

***WFAR**
07-19-1981; 93.3 mhz FM; 0.015 kw; 203 ft.; N41 23 44 W73 25 24
78 Liberty Street, Danbury, CT 06810 US
(203) 748-0001, *Fax:* (203) 748-1101
www.radiofamilia.com
david@radiofamilia.com
License: Danbury, Fairfield County, CT held by Danbury Community Radio Inc.
Arbitron Metro Market: Danbury, CT *Format:* Religious *Special Programming:* Sp 2 hrs wkly *No. News Employees:* 1 *Target Audience:* Portuguese, Sp & It
David Abrantes, President
Helena Abrantes, Operations Dir
Joe Mingachos, News Director
David Abrantes, Director
Elio Ferreira, Director
Teresa Azevedo, Director
Octavio Rebelo, Director
Manuel Ramos, Director
Americo Ventura,Director

WLAD
10-01-1947; 800 khz AM *Hrs Open:* 24; 1 kw-D, 287 w-N; N41 22 27 W73 26 47
98 Mill Plain Road, Danbury, CT 06810
(203) 744-4800, *Fax:* (203)778-4655
www.wlad.com
radio80wlad@aol.com
License: Danbury, Fairfield County, CT held by Berkshire Broadcasting Corp.
Group Owner: Berkshire Broadcasting Corp.
Nat'l Network: NBC; Dial Global *Nat'l Reps:* Katz
Population Served: 250,000 *Arbitron Metro Market:* Danbury, CT
Irv Goldstein, CEO/COO
Irv Goldstein, General Manager
Mike Delpha, General Sales Mgr
Bart Buiterma, Programming Director

***WXCI**
02-10-1973; 91.7 mhz FM *Hrs Open:* 6 AM-2 AM; 3 kw; 220 ft.; N41 23 42 W73 29 14
White Hall, 181 White Street, Danbury, CT 06810 US
(203) 837-9924
www.wxci.org
wxci@yahoo.com,wxcigm@yahoo.com
License: Danbury, Fairfield County, CT held by Western Connecticut State University Board of Trustees.
Arbitron Metro Market: Danbury, CT *Format:* Alternative *Special Programming:* Club mus 3 hrs, jazz 3 hrs, reggae 2 hrs, new age *Hrs. of News Programming:* News progmg 3 hrs wkly *Target Audience:* 14-25.
Justin Mazzarese, General Manager
John Selwyn, Programming Director
Chris Merkle, Promotions Manager
Travis Cuddy, Chief Engineer
Tom Carpenter, Music Director

East Lyme

WNLC
04-01-1994; 98.7 mhz FM *Hrs Open:* 24; 5.5 kw; 269 ft.; N41 23 6 W72 4 13
Mailing Address: P.O. Box 4368, Lancaster, PA 17604 US
Second Address: 89 Broad St., New London, CT 6320
(860) 442-5328, *Fax:* (860) 442-6532
www.wnlc.com
arussell@hallradio.com
License: East Lyme, New London County, CT held by Hall Communication Inc.
Group Owner: Hall Communications Inc.; acq 6-16-97; $2 million)
Nat'l Reps: Eastman Radio
Arbitron Metro Market: New London, CT *Format:* Contemporary Hits/Top 40 *Target Audience:* Adults 25-49
Bonnie Rowbotham, Chairman
Arthur Rowbotham, President
Bill Baldwin, Operations Dir
Andy Russell, General Manager

Enfield

WMAS-FM
12-01-1947; 94.7 mhz FM; 50 kw; 55 meters; N42 6 33 W72 36 40
101 West Street, Springfield, MA 01104 US
(413) 737-1414, *Fax:* (413) 737-1488
www.947wmas.com
info@947wmas.com
License: Enfield, Hampden County, CT
Group Owner: Cumulus Media Inc.
Arbitron Metro Market: Springfield, MA *Format:* Adult Contemp
Paul Cannon, Programming Director

Fairfield

***WSHU-FM**
02-01-1964; 91.1 mhz FM *Hrs Open:* 24; 20 kw; 624 ft.; N41 16 45 W73 11 9
5151 Park Avenue, Fairfield, CT 06432 US
(203) 365-6604, *Fax:* (203) 371-7991
www.wshu.org
lombardi@wshu.org
License: Fairfield, Fairfield County, CT held by Sacred Heart University Inc.
Nat'l Network: NPR; PRI *Wire Services:* AP
Format: News *Special Programming:* Folk 5 hrs, new age 6 hrs wkly *Hrs. of News Programming:* news progmg 43 hrs wkly *No. News Employees:* 4 *Target Audience:* General; all ages
Barbara Bashar, Operations Dir
George Lombardi, General Manager
Gillian Anderson, General Sales Mgr
Tom Kuser, Programming Director
Naomi Starobin, News Director
Paul Litwinovich, Chief Engineer

***WVOF**
09-01-1970; 88.5 mhz FM *Hrs Open:* 5 AM-2 AM; 0.1 kw; 33 ft.; N41 9 32 W73 15 35
North Benson Road, Barone Campus Center Box, Fairfield, CT 06430 US
(203) 254-4144, *Fax:* (203) 254-4224
www.wvof.org
License: Fairfield, Fairfield County, CT held by Fairfield University.
Arbitron Metro Market: Fairfield, CT *Format:* Variety/Diverse *Hrs. of News Programming:* news progmg 4 hrs wkly *No. News Employees:* 5 *Target Audience:* 18-35.
Matt Dinnan, General Manager
Angelika Zbikowski, Station Manager
Robert Miller, Programming Director
Sarah Markham, Promotions Manager
Catherine Wolk, Music Director
Brian Alexander, Business Director
William Hollingsworth,Sports Director

Greenwich

WGCH
09-14-1964; 1490 khz AM *Hrs Open:* 24; 1 kw-U, ND1; N41 1 37 W73 37 59
1490 Dayton Ave., Greenwich, CT 06830 US
(203) 869-1490, *Fax:* (203) 869-3636
www.wgch.com
bob.small@wgch.com
License: Greenwich, CT held by BTR Greenwich Inc.
Group Owner: BusinessTalkRadio.Net Inc.; (acq 6-18-2003; $1.1 million)
Nat'l Network: Fox News Radio
Arbitron Metro Market: New York *Format:* News, Talk *Special Programming:* High school sports 6 hrs, educ 2 hrs, Pol one hr,

Hrs. of News Programming: news progmg 35 hrs wkly *No. News Employees:* 2 *TargetAudience:* 35 plus; very upscale, active, athletic, community-minded *Adv. Rates:* 50; 50; 50; 50
Michael Metter, CEO
Michael Metter, President
Bob Small, Operations Dir
Elizabeth Kopyscinski, General Sales Mgr
Tony Savino, News Director
Jeff Weber, Executive Vice President
Rob Adams, Sports Commentator
Bob Small, TrafficManager

Groton

WQGN-FM
01-01-1971; 105.5 mhz FM; 3 kw; 276 ft.; N41 23 5 W72 4 13
1750 Rockville Pike, Suite 20, Rockville, MD 20852 US
(860) 443-1980, *Fax:* (860) 444-7970
www.q105.fm
info@q105.fm.com
License: Groton, New London County, CT
Arbitron Metro Market: New London, CT *Format:* Contemporary Hits/Top 40 *Target Audience:* 18-49. *Adv. Rates:* 100; 90; 100; 50
Shawn Murphy, Programming Director

WXLM
07-26-1958; 980 khz AM; 1 kw-D; N41 23 05 W72 04 13
7 Governor Winthrop Blvd., New London, CT 20852
(860) 443-1980, *Fax:* (860) 444-7970
www.caliente980am.com
info@caliente980.com
License: Groton, New London County, CT
Group Owner: Cumulus Media Inc.; (acq 4-26-2001; grpsl).
Nat'l Network: ABC
Population Served: 43,000 *Arbitron Metro Market:* New London, CT *Target Audience:* 25-49; middle income professionals
Wayne Leland, Operations Dir
Bonnie Gomes, General Manager
Kevin Palana, Programming Director
Frank Doremus, Chief Engineer

Guilford

***WGRS**
12-27-1993; 91.5 mhz FM *Hrs Open:* 24; 3.1 kw; 82 ft.; N41 17 19 W72 39 32 *Rebroadcasts:* Rebroadcasts WMNR(FM) Monroe 100%
375 Monroe Turnpike, Monroe, CT 06468 US
(203) 268-9667
www.wmnr.org
info@wmnr.org
License: Guilford, New Haven County, CT held by Monroe Board of Education.
Nat'l Network: PRI
Arbitron Metro Market: New Haven, CT *Format:* Talk *Special Programming:* Big band 8 hrs, folk 2 hrs, new age one hr, Broadw
Jane Stadler, Operations Dir
Kurt Anderson, General Manager
Carol Babina, General Sales Mgr

Hamden

WKCI-FM
02-10-1969; 101.3 mhz FM; 12 kw; 915 ft.; N41 26 1 W72 56 45
3305 W. Spring Mt. Road, #60, Las Vegas, NV 89102 US
(203) 281-9600, *Fax:* (203) 407-4652
www.kc101.com
comments@kc101.com
License: Hamden, New Haven County, CT
Group Owner: Clear Channel Communications Inc.; (Acq 7-24-92).
Arbitron Metro Market: New Haven, CT *Format:* Contemporary Hits/Top 40
Chaz Kelly, Programming Director

***WQAQ**
02-01-1973; 98.1 mhz FM *Hrs Open:* Noon-2 AM (S-Su); 8 AM-2 AM (M-F); 0.018 kw; -79 ft.; N41 25 10.6 W72 54 22.6
275 Mount Carmel Avenue, Hamden, CT 06518 US
(203) 582-5278, *Fax:* (203) 582-8098
www.angelfire.com/ct2/wqaqradio/
License: Hamden, New Haven County, CT
Arbitron Metro Market: New Haven, CT *Format:* Alternative, News, 62, Rock/AOR, Talk *Hrs. of News Programming:* News progmg 10 hrs wkly *Target Audience:* 18-30.
Bill Shoulders, Operations Dir
Chris Cooper, General Manager
Sally Densa, General Sales Mgr
Glenn Giangrande, Programming Director
Carlos Lanesee, Promotions Manager
Alison Keller, News Director
Jessie Elgarten, ProgrammingDirector

WQUN
07-17-1960; 1220 khz AM *Hrs Open:* 24
275 Mt. Carmel Avenue, Hamden, CT 06518 US
(203) 582-8984, *Fax:* (203) 582-5372
www.wqun.com
ray.andrewsen@quinnipiac.edu
License: Hamden, CT held by Quinnipiac University
Nat'l Network: CBS; Jones Radio Networks
Arbitron Metro Market: New Haven, CT *Format:* News *Special Programming:* Irish 2 hrs, Broadway 2hrs, big bands 4 hrs wkly *No. News Employees:* 2 *Target Audience:* General; community, business & cultural leaders
Ray Andrewsen, General Manager
Greg Little, News Director
Bob Radil, Chief Engineer

Hartford

WCCC-FM
06-07-1960; 106.9 mhz FM *Hrs Open:* 24; 23 kw; 725 ft.; N41 47 48 W72 47 52
32 Fairfield Street, Boston, MA 02116 US
(860) 525-1069, *Fax:* (860) 246-9084
www.wccc.com
License: Hartford, Hartford County, CT
Nat'l Reps: Eastman Radio
Arbitron Metro Market: Hartford, CT *Format:* Rock/AOR *Target Audience:* 18-49; adult men
Howard (Woody) Tanger, CEO/COO
Howard ""Woody"" Tanger, President
Jon Skonieczny, Promotions Manager

WDRC
12-10-1922; 1360 khz AM *Hrs Open:* 24
166 West Putnam Avenue, Greenwich, CT 06830 US
(860) 243-1115, *Fax:* (860) 286-8257
talkofconnecticut.com
wdrc@talkofconnecticut.com
License: Hartford, CT held by Buckley Broadcasting of Connecticut LLC.
Group Owner: Buckley Broadcasting Corp.; (acq 8-1-59).
Nat'l Network: Westwood One; AP Radio *Regional Network:* CRN *Nat'l Reps:* Katz Radio *Wire Services:* AP
Arbitron Metro Market: Hartford, CT *Format:* News, News/Talk, 86 *No. News Employees:* 1 *Target Audience:* 40+.
Richard Buckley, President
Eric Fahnoe, Operations Dir
Michael Markowitz, General Sales Mgr
Grahame Winters, Programming Director
Laura Kittell, Operations Manager

WDRC-FM
01-01-1939; 102.9 mhz FM *Hrs Open:* 24; 19.5 kw; Ant 810 ft; N41 33 44 W72 50 40
869 Blue Hills Ave., Bloomfield, CT 06830
(860) 243-1115, *Fax:* (860) 286-8257
drcfm.com
info@drcfm.com
License: Hartford, Hartford County, CT
Group Owner: Buckley Broadcasting Corp.
Wire Services: AP; Metro Weather Service Inc.
Population Served: 1,030,500 *Arbitron Metro Market:* Hartford-New Britain-Middletown, CT *No. News Employees:* 1 *Target Audience:* 25-64.
Joe Bilotta, President
Eric Fahnoe, General Manager
Grahame Winters, Programming Director
Kelly Colonghi, Promotions Manager
Richard Price, News Director
Scott Brown, Chief Engineer

WHCN
01-01-1939; 105.9 mhz FM *Hrs Open:* 24; 16 kw; 866 ft.; N41 33 47 W72 50 42
600 Congress Ave., Suite 1400, Austin, TX 78701 US
(860) 723-6000, *Fax:* (860) 723-7090
www.theriver1059.com
License: Hartford, Hartford County, CT held by Capstar TX L.P.
Group Owner: Clear Channel Communications Inc.; (acq 8-30-00; grpsl).
Nat'l Reps: Christal
Arbitron Metro Market: Hartford-New Britain-Middletown, CT *Format:* Rock/AOR
Tom McConnell, General Manager
Steve Honeycomb, General Sales Mgr
Todd Thomas, Programming Director
Rick Walsh, Chief Engineer

***WJMJ**
10-18-1976; 88.9 mhz FM *Hrs Open:* 5 am-Midnight; 6.2 kw; 607 ft.; N41 45 9 W72 59 40
Archdioces of Hartford, 785 Asylum Avenue, Hartford, CT 06105 US
(860) 242-8800, *Fax:* (860) 242-4886
www.wjmj.org
info@wjmj.org
License: Hartford, Hartford County, CT held by St. Thomas Seminary-Archdiocese of Hartford.
Nat'l Network: ABC *Wire Services:* AP
Arbitron Metro Market: Hartford-New Britain-Middletown, CT *Format:* Religious *Special Programming:* Educ, foreign one hr wkly *Hrs. of News Programming:* news progmg 10 hrs wkly *No. News Employees:* 1 *TargetAudience:* 40-65; working, middle-class, family group
Archbishop Henry Mansell, President
John Ellinger, General Manager
John Masternak, Programming Director
Ivor Hugh, Music Director

WPOP
07-01-1935; 1410 khz AM *Hrs Open:* 24; 5 kw-D, DA2; 5 kw-N, DA2; N41 41 35 W72 45 30
600 Congress Ave., Suite 1400, Austin, TX 78701 US
(860) 723-6000, *Fax:* (860) 723-7090
www.espnradio1410.com
License: Hartford, CT held by Capstar TX L.P.
Group Owner: Clear Channel Communications Inc.
Nat'l Network: ESPN Radio
Arbitron Metro Market: Hartford-New Britain-Middletown, CT *Format:* Sports *Hrs. of News Programming:* news progmg 25 hrs wkly *No. News Employees:* 8 *Target Audience:* 35 plus.
Jimmie James, Operations Dir
Sima Birach, General Manager

***WQTQ**
11-01-1961; 89.9 mhz FM *Hrs Open:* 24; 0.115 kw; 85 ft.; N41 47 47 W72 41 42
153 Market Street, 8th Floor, Hartford, CT 06103 US
(860) 695-1899,(860) 695-1900, *Fax:* (860) 722-6605
www.wqtq.com/wqtq
wqtqfm@yahoo.com
License: Hartford, Hartford County, CT held by Hartford Board of Education.
Arbitron Metro Market: Hartford-New Britain-Middletown, CT *Format:* Gospel, Jazz, 72, Smooth Jazz *Special Programming:* Gospel 12 hrs, clean hip hop rap 19 hrs, reggae/calypso 6 hrs, jazz 12 hrs, Rhythm and blues 18 hrs wkly*Target Audience:* 15-45; literate, professional, quality mus listeners
Thomas Smith, COO
Connie Coles, President
Tom Smith, Operations Dir
Shirley Minnifield, CFO

***WRTC-FM**
02-01-1958; 89.3 mhz FM *Hrs Open:* 24; 0.3 kw; 95 ft.; N41 45 6 W72 41 29
300 Summit Street, Hartford, CT 06106 US
(860) 297-2450, *Fax:* (860) 987-6214
www.wrtcfm.com
License: Hartford, Hartford County, CT held by Trustees of Trinity College.
Arbitron Metro Market: Hartford-New Br *Format:* Variety/Diverse *Special Programming:* Class 4 hrs, gospel 6 hrs, West Indian 6 hrs, Pol *Target Audience:* 15 plus.
Devon MacGillivary, General Manager
Matthew Mainuli, Station Manager
Benton Bair, Programming Director
Jonathan Costello, Promotions Manager

WTIC
02-10-1925; 1080 khz AM *Hrs Open:* 24
600 New Hampshire Ave., N.W., Suite 1200, Washington, DC 20037 US
(860) 677-6700, *Fax:* (860) 284-9842
www.wtic.com
info@wtic.com
License: Hartford, CT held by Infinity Radio Inc.
Group Owner: CBS Radio; (acq 11-13-98; grpsl).
Nat'l Network: CBS
Arbitron Metro Market: Hartford, CT *Format:* News, News/Talk, 86 *Hrs. of News Programming:* News progmg 30 hrs wkly *Target Audience:* 35-59; intelligent, mature adults
Suzanne McDonald, Operations Dir
Stephanie McNamara, General Sales Mgr
Tristano Korlou, Promotions Manager
Dana Whalen, News Director
Jeff Hugabone, Chief Engineer
Geri DeRosa, National Sales Manager
Steve Salhany, OperationsManager

WTIC-FM
02-05-1940; 96.5 mhz FM *Hrs Open:* 24; 20 kw; 784 ft.; N41 46 27 W72 48 20
600 New Hampshire Avenue, N.W., Suite 1200, Washington, DC 20037 US
(860) 677-6700, *Fax:* (860) 678-3952
965tic.cbslocal.com
ryan.jones@cbsradio.com
License: Hartford, Hartford County, CT
Arbitron Metro Market: Hartford, CT *Format:* Adult Contemp *Hrs. of News Programming:* News progmg 8 hrs wkly *Target Audience:* 18-34; intelligent, spirited, youthful adults
Henry Hinton, General Manager
Stephanie Perl, General Sales Mgr
Ryan Jones, Programming Director
Tristano Korlou, Marketing Director
Mike McKenzie, Internship Coordinator

WZMX
01-01-1939; 93.7 mhz FM *Hrs Open:* 24; 17 kw; 850 ft.; N41 33 44 W72 50 42
600 New Hampshire Ave., N.W., Suite 1200, Washington, DC 20037 US
(860) 677-6700, *Fax:* (860) 674-8427
www.hot937.com
DJ.Buck@cbsradio.com
License: Hartford, Hartford County, CT held by Infinity Radio Inc.
Group Owner: CBS Radio; (acq 6-8-98; grpsl).
Arbitron Metro Market: Hartford, CT *Format:* Urban Contemporary *Target Audience:* 18-34; adults in Hartford & New Haven
Suzanne McDonald, Operations Dir
Stephanie Perl, Sales Manager
DJ Buck, Programming Director
Jason Ricketts, Promotions Manager
Steve Salhany, Operations Manager
Mike McKenzie, Internship Coordinator

Hartford-Meriden

WKSS
06-01-1947; 95.7 mhz FM; 16.5 kw; 879 ft.; N41 33 41 W72 50 39
600 Congress Ave., Suite 1400, Austin, TX 78701 US
(860) 723-6000, *Fax:* (860) 493-7090
www.kiss957.com
License: Hartford-Meriden, Hartford County, CT held by Capstar TX L.P.
Group Owner: Clear Channel Communications Inc.; (acq 8-30-00; grpsl).
Regional Network: Conn. Radio Net. *Nat'l Reps:* Christal
Arbitron Metro Market: Hartford-New Britain-Middletown, CT *Format:* Contemporary Hits/Top 40 *Target Audience:* 18-34.
Tom McConnell, General Manager
Stan Priest, Programming Director

Ledyard

WWRX
11-30-1995; 107.7 mhz FM *Hrs Open:* 24; 1.4 kw; 492 ft.; N41 27 35 W71 55 40
1110 Central Avenue, Pawtucket, RI 02861 US
(860) 464-1065, *Fax:* (860) 464-8143
www.jammin1077.com
License: Ledyard, New London County, CT held by Fuller Broadcasting International LLC
Arbitron Metro Market: New London, CT *Format:* Contemporary Hits/Top 40 *Hrs. of News Programming:* News progmg one hr wkly *Target Audience:* 25-54; mobile, upscale
John Fuller, President
Scott Bradshaw, Operations Dir

Litchfield

WZBG
07-08-1992; 97.3 mhz FM *Hrs Open:* 24; 3 kw; 328 ft.; N41 48 8 W73 9 50
P.O. Box 1497, Litchfield, CT 06759 US
(860) 567-3697, *Fax:* (860) 567-3292
www.wzbg.com
info@wzbg.com
License: Litchfield, Litchfield County, CT held by Local Girls & Boys Broadcasting Corp.
Nat'l Network: CBS
Arbitron Metro Market: Litchfield, CT *Format:* Adult Contemp, News *Special Programming:* Jazz 2 hrs wkly *No. News Employees:* 3 *Target Audience:* 25-54.
Jennifer Parsons, General Manager

Manchester

WNEZ
05-18-1958; 1230 khz AM *Hrs Open:* 24
8121 Georgia Ave., 10th Floor, Silver Spring, MD 20910 US
(860) 524-0001, *Fax:* (860) 548-1922
mtanderson2942@sbcglobal.net
License: Manchester, CT held by Freedom Communications of Connecticut Inc.
Group Owner: Freedom Communications of Connecticut Inc.; (acq 6-1-2004; $3 million with WLAT(AM) New Britain)
Arbitron Metro Market: Hartford-New Britain-Middletown, CT *Format:* News, News/Talk, 86
Lowell Register, CEO
Debbie Hart, General Manager

Meriden

WMMW
01-01-1946; 1470 khz AM *Hrs Open:* 24; 2.5 kw-D, DA2; 2.5 kw-N, DA2; N41 33 14 W72 48 7 *Rebroadcasts:* Rebroadcast WDRC (AM) Hartford 100%
166 West Putnam Ave, Greenwich, CT 06830 US
(860) 243-1115, *Fax:* (860) 286-8257
www.talkofconnecticut.com
License: Meriden, CT held by Buckley Broadcasting of Connecticut LLC.
Group Owner: Buckley Broadcasting Corp.; (acq 10-21-98; $630,000).
Nat'l Network: Westwood One; AP Radio; ABC *Regional Network:* CRN *Nat'l Reps:* McGavren Guild *Wire Services:* ABC
Arbitron Metro Market: New Haven, CT *Format:* News, Talk
Target Audience: 40 plus; middle income, grassroots America
Richard Buckley, President
Wayne Mulligan, Operations Dir
Michael Markowitz, General Sales Mgr
Dave Nagel, Programming Director
Grahame Winters, Promotions Manager
Dan Lovallo, News Director
Scott Baron, Chief Engineer
LauraKittell, Operations Manager
Joe Orlando, Traffic Manager

***WNPR**
06-11-1978; 90.5 mhz FM *Hrs Open:* 24; 18.5 kw horiz, 13.5 kw vert; Ant 1,148 ft; N41 33 42 W72 50 41
1049 Asylum Ave., Hartford, CT 06126
(860) 278-5310, *Fax:* (860) 275-7403
www.wnpr.org
info@wnpr.org
License: Meriden, New Haven County, CT held by Connecticut Public Television & Radio.
Nat'l Network: NPR; PRI
Population Served: 2,000,000*Hrs. of News Programming:* news progmg 26 hrs wkly *No. News Employees:* 5
Jerry Franklin, CEO
Kim Grehn, Operations Dir
Nancy Bauer, Promotions Manager
John Dankosky, News Director
Joseph Zareski, Chief Engineer

Middletown

***WESU**
09-01-1939; 88.1 mhz FM *Hrs Open:* 24; 6 kw; 36 ft.; N41 33 12 W72 39 29
Box 2300,Wesleyan Stat., Middletown, CT 06457 US
(860) 685-7703/685-7700/685-7707, *Fax:* (860) 704-0608
www.wesufm.org
president@wesufm.org
License: Middletown, Middlesex County, CT held by Wesleyan University
Nat'l Network: NPR *Wire Services:* UPI
Arbitron Metro Market: Middletown, CT *Format:* Variety/Diverse
Special Programming: NPR, Paacifica and Local Public affairs by day, Free form music at nighit and weekends Blues 10 hrs, gospel 6 hrs, reggae 10 hrs, metal 5hrs wkly *Hrs. of News Programming:* 12hrs /day *Target Audience:* discerning listeners
Adv. Rates: sliding scale underwriting opp
Sam Long, President
Ben Michael, General Manager
Josh Sharp, Programming Director
Mickey Capper, Tech Director
Adrien DeFontaine, Vice President
Bryan Skowera, Personnel Director
Dan DeBonis, Production Director
AveryTrufelman, Public Affairs Director
Ben Fitzelle, Public Relations Director
Jesse Brent, Music Director

***WIHS**
10-11-1969; 104.9 mhz FM *Hrs Open:* 24; 3 kw; 300 ft; N41 30 18 W72 39 32
1933 S. Main St., Hartford, CT 06457
(860) 346-1049, *Fax:* (860) 347-1049
www.wihsradio.org
wihs@snet.net
License: Middletown, Middlesex County, CT held by Connecticut Radio Fellowship Inc.
Nat'l Network: Moody
Population Served: 2,000,000*Special Programming:* Children 9 hrs wkly *Hrs. of News Programming:* News progmg 18 hrs wkly *No. News Employees:* 2 *Target Audience:* General. *Adv. Rates:* none
William Bacon, President
Paul Kretschmer, Operations Dir
G.J. Gerard, General Manager
Ron Gangwer, Programming Manager
Paul Kretschmer, News Director
G.J. Gerard, Chief Engineer

WMRD
12-12-1948; 1150 khz AM *Hrs Open:* 24; 2.5 kw-D, ND1; 0.046 kw-N, ND1; N41 33 26 W72 37 13
167 North Seir Hill Rd, Norwalk, CT 06850 US
(860) 347-9673, *Fax:* (860) 347-7704
www.wliswmrd.net
radio@wliswmrd.net
License: Middletown, CT held by Crossroads Communications L.L.C.
Nat'l Network: Westwood One; CBS Radio; Jones Radio Networks *Regional Network:* Conn. Radio Net.
Arbitron Metro Market: Hartford, CT *Format:* Talk *Special Programming:* Pol 2 hrs, It 2 hrs, Celtic one hr, Caribbean one *Hrs. of News Programming:* news progmg 8 hrs wkly *No. News Employees:* 1 *TargetAudience:* 25-54; adults *Adv. Rates:* 58; 47; 43; 38
Don DeCesare, President

Milford

WFIF
09-04-1965; 1500 khz AM *Hrs Open:* Sunrise-sunset; 5 kw-D, DAD; N41 11 33 W73 6 5
90 Kay Avenue, Milford, CT 06460 US
(203) 878-5915
www.wfif.net
info@wfif.net
License: Milford, CT held by K.W. Dolmar Broadcasting Co. Inc.
Group Owner: Blount Communications Group; (acq 4-82; $425,000;
Nat'l Network: Salem Radio Network
Arbitron Metro Market: Milford, CT *Format:* Religious *Special Programming:* Black 6 hrs wkly *Target Audience:* General.
William Blount, President
Jon Vaught, Station Manager
William Barnett, Chief Engineer
Dave Young, Executive Vice President

Monroe

***WMNR**
01-31-1974; 88.1 mhz FM *Hrs Open:* 24; 5 kw; 404 ft.; N41 19 8 W73 15 13
375 Monroe Turnpike, Monroe, CT 06468 US
(203) 268-9667
www.wmnr.org
info@wmnr.org
License: Monroe, Fairfield County, CT held by Monroe Board of Education.
Nat'l Network: PRI
Arbitron Metro Market: Bridgeport, CT *Format:* Talk *Special Programming:* Big band 8 hrs, folk 2 hrs, new age one hr, Broadw
Jane Stadler, Operations Dir
Kurt Anderson, General Manager
Carol Babina, General Sales Mgr

Naugatuck

WFNW
02-26-1961; 1380 khz AM; 5 kw-D, DA2; 0.5 kw-N, DA2; N41 30 35 W73 3 20
175 Church Street, 3rd Floor, Naugatuck, CT 06770 US
(203) 755-4960, *Fax:* (203) 755-4957
License: Naugatuck, CT held by Candido Dias Carrelo.
Placido Acevedo, President
Candido Carrelo, General Manager

New Britain

*WFCS
10-17-1972; 107.7 mhz FM *Hrs Open:* 24; 0.036 kw; 108 ft.; N41 41 36 W72 45 49
1615 Stanley Street, New Britain, CT 06050 US
(860) 832-1883, *Fax:* (860) 832-3757
www.ccsu.collegiatelink.net
License: New Britain, Hartford County, CT held by Trustees of Central Connecticut State University.
Arbitron Metro Market: New Britain, CT *Special Programming:* Blues 12 hrs, Sp 2 hrs wkly *Hrs. of News Programming:* news progmg 10 hrs wkly *No. News Employees:* 4 *Target Audience:* 14-50.
Adam Morgan, General Manager
Mike McDonald, General Sales Mgr
Matt Rockwell, Programming Director
John Ramsey, Chief Engineer

WLAT
05-20-1949; 910 khz AM *Hrs Open:* 24
8121 Georgia Ave 10th Fl, Silver Spring, MD 20910 US
(860) 524-0001, *Fax:* (860) 548-1922
mtanderson2942@sbcglobal.net
License: New Britain, CT held by Freedom Communications of Connecticut Inc.
Group Owner: Freedom Communications of Connecticut Inc.; (acq 6-1-2004; $3 million with WNEZ(AM) Manchester)
Arbitron Metro Market: Hartford, CT *Format:* Spanish
James Sigler, General Manager

WRCH
07-01-1968; 100.5 mhz FM *Hrs Open:* 24; 7.5 kw; 1250 ft.; N41 42 13 W72 49 57
600 New Hampshire Ave., N.W., Suite 1200, Washington, DC 20037 US
(860) 677-6700, *Fax:* (860) 677-5483
www.wrch.com
wrch@cbs.com
License: New Britain, Hartford County, CT held by Infinity Radio Inc.
Group Owner: CBS Radio; (acq 6-8-98; grpsl).
Arbitron Metro Market: Hartford-New Britain-Middletown, CT *Format:* Adult Contemp *Target Audience:* 25-54; women, adults
Suzanne McDonald, Operations Dir
Steve Salhany, Operations Manager

WRYM
08-01-1946; 840 khz AM *Hrs Open:* 24; 1 kw-D, DAN; 0.125 kw-N, DAN; N41 41 10 W72 43 47
1056 Willard Ave., Newington, CT 06111 US
(860) 666-5646, *Fax:* (860) 666-5647
www.wrymradio.com
radio@wyrm840.com
License: New Britain, CT held by Eight Forty Broadcasting Corp.
Nat'l Network: CNN Radio *Nat'l Reps:* McGavren Guild
Arbitron Metro Market: Hartford-New Br *Special Programming:* Pol 5 hrs wkly, Italian 2 hrs wkly *Hrs. of News Programming:* news progmg 8 hrs wkly *No. News Employees:* 4 *Target Audience:* General; Hispanic
Dina Cassarino, Operations Dir
Walter Martinez, General Manager
Danny Delgado, News Director
Silvina Martinez, Traffic Manager

New Canaan

*WSLX
01-01-1975; 91.9 mhz FM; 0.019 kw horiz; 174 ft.; N41 11 32 W73 29 46
377 North Wilton Road, New Canaan, CT 06840 US
(203) 966-5612, *Fax:* (203) 966-3409
www.wslx.org
info@stlukesct.org
License: New Canaan, Fairfield County, CT held by St. Luke's Foundation Inc.
Format: Variety/Diverse

New Haven

WAVZ
09-01-1947; 1300 khz AM *Hrs Open:* 24; 1 kw-D, DAN; 1 kw-N, DAN; N41 17 16 W72 56 48
3305 W Spring Mount. Rd, Suite 60, Las Vegas, NV 89102 US
(800) 877-5600, *Fax:* (916) 251-1650
www.klove.com
License: New Haven, CT held by CC Licenses LLC.
Group Owner: Clear Channel Communications Inc.; (acq 12-18-92; $10 with WKCI-FM Hamden;
Nat'l Network: ESPN Radio *Nat'l Reps:* Clear Channel
Arbitron Metro Market: Bozeman MT *Format:* Christian
Darrell Chambliss, Chairman
Mike Novak, CEO, President
Mike Lee, Operations Dir
Dr. David R. Ferry, Chief Engineer
Mitch Barnhart, Director
Larry Moody, Director

WELI
10-01-1935; 960 khz AM; 5 kw-D, DAN; 5 kw-N, DAN; N41 22 14 W72 56 15
3305 W. Mountain Rd, Suite 60, Las Vegas, NV 89102 US
(203) 281-9600, *Fax:* (203) 407-4652
www.960weli.com
comments@weli.com
License: New Haven, CT held by CC Licenses LLC.
Group Owner: Clear Channel Communications Inc.; (acq 8-5-85).
Regional Network: Conn. Radio Net. *Nat'l Reps:* Katz Radio
Arbitron Metro Market: New Haven, CT *Format:* News, News/Talk, 86 *Target Audience:* 18 plus.
L. Lowry Mays, President
Tom McConnel, General Manager
Jerry Kristafer, Programming Director

WPLR
01-01-1944; 99.1 mhz FM; 15 kw; 906 ft.; N41 25 22 W72 57 6
600 Congress Ave., Suite 1400, Austin, TX 78701 US
(203) 783-8200, *Fax:* (203) 783-8373
www.wplr.com
License: New Haven, New Haven County, CT held by CXR Holdings Inc.
Group Owner: Cox Radio Inc.; (acq 8-2000; grpsl)
Arbitron Metro Market: New Haven, CT *Format:* Rock/AOR
Stu Gorlick, General Sales Mgr
Ed Sabatino, Programming Director
Samuel Tilery, Promotions Manager

WYBC
01-01-1944; 1340 khz AM
P.O. Box 209050, New Haven, CT 06520 US
(203) 365-0425, *Fax:* (203) 776-2446
www.wshu.org
info@wybc.com
License: New Haven, CT held by Yale Broadcasting Co. Inc.
Regional Network: Conn. Radio Net.
Arbitron Metro Market: New Haven, CT *Format:* Easy Listening
Special Programming: Sp one hr wkly
George Lombardi, General Manager
Tom Kuser, Programming Director
Naomi Starobin, News Director
Paul Litwinovich, Chief Engineer
Gillian Anderson, Development Director
Kat Ariano, Production Assistant
Barbara Bashar, BusinessManager
Teri McCready, Host
Kate Remington, Music Director

WYBC-FM
03-09-1959; 94.3 mhz FM *Hrs Open:* 24; 3 kw horiz, 2.6 kw vert; 472 ft.; N41 20 59 W72 58 23
165 Elm Street, P.O. Box 209050, New Haven, CT 06520 US
(203) 783-8200, *Fax:* (203) 783-8383
www.943wybc.com
License: New Haven, New Haven County, CT held by Yale Broadcasting Co.
Nat'l Network: ABC
Arbitron Metro Market: Milford, CT *Format:* Urban Contemporary
Special Programming: Gospel 8 hrs, jazz 8 hrs, folk 3 hrs wkly
Hrs. of News Programming: News progmg 10 hrs wkly *Target Audience:* Urban & collegeage listeners.

New London

*WCNI
01-01-1974; 90.9 mhz FM *Hrs Open:* 1 PM-5 PM (M-F); 2 kw vert; 187 ft.; N41 22 53 W72 6 28
Box 4972, New London, CT 06320 US
(860) 439-2853 (860) 439-2850, *Fax:* (860) 439-2805
www.wcniradio.org
wnci@conncoll.edu
License: New London, New London County, CT held by Connecticut College Broadcasting Association Inc.
Arbitron Metro Market: New London, CT *Format:* Variety/Diverse
Special Programming: Black 3 hrs, class 6 hrs, folk 9 hrs, gospel 3 hrs, jazz 9 hrs, Pol 3 hrs, Sp 3 hrs, women's 3 hrs wkly *Target Audience:* General;all musical audiences except pop
Bridgett Ellis, General Manager
John Tyler, Chief Engineer

WKNL
01-01-1970; 100.9 mhz FM *Hrs Open:* 24; 6 kw; 325 ft.; N41 26 27 W72 8 29
Mailing Address: P.O. Box 4368, Lancaster, PA 17604 US
Second Address: 89 Broad St., New London, CT 6320
(860) 442-5328, *Fax:* (860) 442-6532
www.kool101fm.com
arussell@hallradio.com
License: New London, New London County, CT held by Hall Communications Inc.
Group Owner: Hall Communications Inc.; acq 1-19-95; $3.5 million with co-located AM;
Nat'l Reps: Eastman Radio
Arbitron Metro Market: New London, CT *Format:* Oldies *Hrs. of News Programming:* News progmg 2 hrs wkly *Target Audience:* 25-54.
Bonnie Rowbotham, Chairman
Arthur Rowbotham, President
Bill Baldwin, Operations Dir
Andy Russell, VP/General Manager
Bob Houde, Local Sales Manager
Jim Reed, Programming Director

Norfolk

*WSGG
05-17-2001; 89.3 mhz FM *Hrs Open:* 24; 0.14 kw vert; 92 ft.; N42 0 38 W73 12 8
P. O. Box 4594, Hartfordd, CT 06147 US
(860) 243-5630
www.revivalfm.com
License: Norfolk, Litchfield County, CT held by Revival Christian Ministries Inc.
Arbitron Metro Market: Hartford, CT *Format:* Christian
Samuel Girona, General Manager

North Granby

*WWQA
11-21-2011; 89.9 mhz FM; kw
US
(877) 700-8047
www.thelifefm.com
License: North Granby, CT held by The Power Foundation

Norwalk

WFOX
01-01-1966; 95.9 mhz FM; 3 kw; 299 ft.; N41 6 54 W73 26 6
600 Congress Ave., Suite 1400, Austin, TX 78701 US
(203) 783-8200, *Fax:* (203) 783-8383
www.959thefox.com/
steve.soyland@coxinc.com
License: Norwalk, Fairfield County, CT held by Cox Radio Inc.
Group Owner: Cox Radio Inc.
Arbitron Metro Market: Norwalk, CT *Format:* Classic Rock
Christopher Gabrelcik, President
Michael Barone, Station Manager
Steve Soyland, Promotions Manager

WNLK
01-01-1948; 1350 khz AM *Hrs Open:* 24*Rebroadcasts:* Rebroadcasts WSTC(AM) Stamford 100%
600 Congress Ave., Suite 1400, Austin, TX 78701 US
(203) 365-6604, *Fax:* (203) 371-7991
www.wshu.org
License: Norwalk, CT held by Cox Radio Inc.
Group Owner: Cox Radio Inc.; (acq 8-25-2000; grpsl).
Regional Network: Conn. Radio Net.
Arbitron Metro Market: Norwalk, CT *Format:* News, News/Talk, 86 *Hrs. of News Programming:* news progmg 20 hrs wkly *No. News Employees:* 4 *Target Audience:* 25-54.
George Lombardi, General Manager
Tom Kuser, Programming Director
Naomi Starobin, News Director
Paul Litwinovich, Chief Engineer

Norwich

WCTY
05-01-1968; 97.7 mhz FM *Hrs Open:* 24; 1.9 kw; 410 ft.; N41 28 28 W72 6 14
Mailing Address: P.O. Box 4368, Lancaster, PA 17604 US
Second Address: 40 Cuprak Rd., Norwich, CT 6360
(860) 887-3511, *Fax:* (860) 886-7649
www.wcty.com
dave@wcty.com
License: Norwich, New London County, CT held by WICH Inc.
Group Owner: Hall Communications Inc.
Nat'l Reps: Eastman Radio *Wire Services:* AP
Arbitron Metro Market: New London, CT *Format:* Country *Target Audience:* 25-54.
Andy Russell, Operations Dir
Andy Rusell, General Manager
Dave Elder, Programming Director

RADIO - U.S.

WICH
09-01-1946; 1310 khz AM *Hrs Open:* 24; 5 kw-U, DA-2; N41 33 10 W72 04 34
Box 551, 40 Cuprak Rd., Norwich, CT 17604
(860) 887-3511, *Fax:* (860) 886-7649
www.wich.com
License: Norwich, New London County, CT held by WICH Inc.
Group Owner: Hall Communications Inc.; (acq 7-1-65)
Nat'l Network: ABC *Regional Network:* Conn. Radio Net. *Nat'l Reps:* Eastman Radio *Wire Services:* AP
Population Served: 220,000 *Arbitron Metro Market:* New London, CT *Special Programming:* Pol 2 hrs wkly *Hrs. of News Programming:* 5 *No. News Employees:* 2 *Target Audience:* 35 plus.
Bonnie Rowbotham, Chairman
Arthur Rowbotham, President
Bill Baldwin, Operations Dir
Andy Russell, General Manager
Bob Reed, Station Manager
Bob Houde, Local Sales Manager
Stu Bryer, Programming Director
Susan Harley, PromotionsManager
Roger Arnold, Chief Engineer

***WPKT**
10-17-1981; 89.1 mhz FM *Hrs Open:* 24; 5.1 kw; Ant 590 ft; N41 31 11 W72 10 04 *Rebroadcasts:* Rebroadcasts WPKT(FM) Meriden 100%
1049 Asylum Ave., Hartford, CT 06106
(860) 278-5310, *Fax:* (860) 244-9624
www.wnpr.org
wherewelive@wnpr.org
License: Norwich, New London County, CT held by Connecticut Public Television & Radio.
Nat'l Network: NPR; PRI; AP Radio
Arbitron Metro Market: New London, CT *Hrs. of News Programming:* news progmg 38 hrs wkly *No. News Employees:* 13 *Target Audience:* General.
Jerry Franklin, CEO
Kim Grehn, Operations Dir
Nancy Bauer, Promotions Manager
John Dankosky, News Director
Joe Zareski, Chief Engineer
Gene Amatruda, Operations Manager

Old Saybrook

WLIS
09-27-1956; 1420 khz AM *Hrs Open:* 24 hrs; 5 kw-D, DAN; 0.5 kw-N, DAN; N41 19 38 W72 23 21 *Rebroadcasts:* Rebroadcasts WMRD(AM) Middletown 90%
167 N. Seir Hill Road, Norwalk, CT 06850 US
(860) 347-9673, *Fax:* (860) 347-7704
www.wliswmrd.net
radio@wliswmrd.net
License: Old Saybrook, CT held by Crossroads Communications of Old Saybrook L.L.C.
Nat'l Network: CNN Radio; Westwood One; Talk Radio Network
Regional Network: Conn. Radio Net.
Format: Talk *Special Programming:* Jazz 4 hrs wkly *Hrs. of News Programming:* news progmg 8 hrs wkly *No. News Employees:* 1 *Target Audience:* 25-64; Adults
Don DeCesare, President

Pawcatuck

WBMW
12-24-1992; 106.5 mhz FM *Hrs Open:* 24; 3.1 kw; 459 ft.; N41 27 43 W72 1 27
756 Colonel Ledyard Hwy, Ledyard, CT 06339 US
(860) 464-1066, *Fax:* (860) 464-8143
www.wbmw.com
production@wbmw.com
License: Pawcatuck, New London County, CT held by Redwolf Broadcasting Corp.
Nat'l Network: USA
Arbitron Metro Market: New London, CT *Format:* Adult Contemp *No. News Employees:* 1 *Target Audience:* Adults 25-54 & women 25-54
John Fuller, President
Scott Bradshaw, Operations Dir
John Fuller, General Manager

Pomfret

***WBVC**
01-01-2001; 91.1 mhz FM; 0.1 kw vert; 289 ft.; N41 53 27 W71 57 24
P O Box 128, Pomfret, CT 06258 US
(860) 963-5911, *Fax:* (860) 963-2086
www.web.pomfretschool.org/wbvc/
wbvc@pomfretschool.org
License: Pomfret, Windham County, CT held by Pomfret School.
Format: Variety/Diverse
Tim Peck, General Manager
Ben Tules, Co-Manager
Seth Fargnoli, Student Manager

Putnam

WINY
05-03-1953; 1350 khz AM *Hrs Open:* 24; 5 kw-D, ND1; 0.079 kw-N, ND1; N41 54 10 W71 53 43
P.O. Box 231, Putnam, CT 06260 US
(860) 928-1350, *Fax:* (860) 928-7878
www.winyradio.com
info@winyradio.com
License: Putnam, CT held by Osbrey Broadcasting Co.
Nat'l Network: AP Radio; Jones Radio Networks *Wire Services:* AP
Format: Adult Contemp *Special Programming:* Talk 11 hrs wkly *Hrs. of News Programming:* news progmg 18 hrs wkly *No. News Employees:* 3 *Target Audience:* 25-54 plus; adults *Adv. Rates:* 31; 27; 31; 25
Gary Osbrey, President
Karen Osbrey, Operations Dir
Karen Osbrey, General Sales Mgr
Shaina Smith, News Director
John Wilbur, Sports Director
Kerri LeClerc, Traffic Manager
Adam Heath, Disc Jockey
Bill Alley, Disc Jockey
JasonBleau, Disc Jockey
Alyssa Moody, News Reporter

Ridgefield

WAXB
03-15-1985; 850 khz AM *Hrs Open:* 6 AM-10 PM; 2.5 kw; N41 17 27 W73 29 16
198 Main St., Danbury, CT 06810
(203) 744-4800, *Fax:* (203) 778-4655
trueoldies850@hotmail.com
License: Ridgefield, Fairfield County, CT held by Berkshire Broadcasting Corp.
Group Owner: Berkshire Broadcasting Corp.; (acq 3-31-97; $550,000)
Nat'l Network: ABC *Nat'l Reps:* D & R Radio
Population Served: 500,000 *Arbitron Metro Market:* Danbury, CT
Irv Goldstein, President

Salisbury

WKZE-FM
09-01-1992; 98.1 mhz FM *Hrs Open:* 24; 1.8 kw; 604 ft.; N41 55 8 W73 34 22
67 Main Street, Sharon, CT 06069 US
(845) 758-9810, *Fax:* (845) 758-9819
www.wkze.com
info@wkze.com
License: Salisbury, Litchfield County, CT held by Willpower Radio L.L.C.
Nat'l Network: AP Radio
Arbitron Metro Market: Poughkeepsie, NY *Format:* Triple A *Hrs. of News Programming:* news progmg 2 hrs wkly *No. News Employees:* 1 *Target Audience:* 25-54. *Adv. Rates:* 35; 35; 35; na
Dave Doud, General Manager
Pete Nugent, General Sales Mgr
Paul Higgins, Sales

Sharon

WHDD
12-23-1986; 1020 khz AM *Hrs Open:* 6 AM-6 PM; 1.8 kw-C, NDD; 2.5 kw-D, NDD; N41 58 35 W73 31 27
67 Main Street, Sharon, CT 06069 US
(860) 364-4640, *Fax:* (860) 364-7035
www.am1020whdd.com
jg@robinhoodradio.com
License: Sharon, CT held by Willpower Radio L.L.C.
Arbitron Metro Market: Poughkeepsie, NY *Format:* Talk
Marshall Miles, General Manager

WQQQ
10-07-1993; 103.3 mhz FM *Hrs Open:* 24; 1.5 kw; 610 ft.; N41 55 8 W73 34 22
19 Boas Lane, Wilton, CT 06897 US
(860) 435-3333, *Fax:* (860) 435-3334
www.wqqq.com
WQQQfm@yahoo.com
License: Sharon, Litchfield County, CT held by The Ridgefield Broadcasting Corp.
Wire Services: AP
Format: Adult Contemp *Special Programming:* Oldies, Jazz, MOR *Hrs. of News Programming:* news progmg 14 hrs wkly *No. News Employees:* 1 *Target Audience:* Upscale adults; 25-54
Dennis Jackson, President
Joe Loverro, General Manager

***WHDD-FM**
05-05-2008; 91.9 mhz FM *Hrs Open:* 24; 0.65 kw; -62 ft.; N41 53 32 W73 27 16 US
(860) 364-4640, *Fax:* (860) 364-7035
www.robinhoodradio.com
jg@robinhoodradio.com
License: Sharon, Litchfield County, CT held by Tri-State Public Communications Inc.
Nat'l Network: NPR; PRI
Arbitron Metro Market: Sharon, CT *Format:* Public Affairs, News
Marshall Miles, President

Shelton

***WRXC**
01-01-1977; 90.1 mhz FM *Hrs Open:* 24; 0.045 kw; 482 ft.; N41 21 43 W73 6 48 *Rebroadcasts:* Rebroadcasts WMNR(FM) Monroe 100%
375 Monroe Turnpike, Monroe, CT 06468 US
(203) 268-9667
www.wmnr.org
info@wmnr.org
License: Shelton, Fairfield County, CT held by Monroe Board of Education.
Nat'l Network: PRI
Format: Talk *Special Programming:* Big band 8 hrs, folk 2 hrs, new age one hr, Broadw
Jane Stadler, Operations Dir
Kurt Anderson, General Manager
Carol Babina, General Sales Mgr

Somers

***WDJW**
10-06-1986; 89.7 mhz FM; 0.009 kw horiz; -59 ft.; N41 57 43 W72 27 51 *Rebroadcasts:* Rebroadcasts WWUH(FM) West Hartford
Ninth District Road, Somers, CT 06071 US
(860) 749-2501(860) 749-0719, *Fax:* (860) 749-9264
License: Somers, Tolland County, CT held by Somers Board of Education.
Arbitron Metro Market: Somers, CT *Format:* Alternative, Jazz
Peter Stone, President

South Kent

***WGSK**
12-25-1987; 90.1 mhz FM *Hrs Open:* 24; 0.077 kw; 128 ft.; N41 40 54 W73 29 13 *Rebroadcasts:* Rebroadcasts WMNR(FM) Monroe 100%
375 Monroe Turnpike, Monroe, CT 06468 US
(203) 268-9667
www.wmnr.org
info@wmnr.org
License: South Kent, Litchfield County, CT held by Monroe Board of Education.
Nat'l Network: PRI
Format: Talk *Special Programming:* Big band 8 hrs, folk 2 hrs, new age one hr, Broadw
Jane Stadler, Operations Dir
Kurt Anderson, General Manager
Carol Babina, General Sales Mgr

Southington

WXCT
09-02-1969; 990 khz AM *Hrs Open:* 24; 2.5 kw-D, DA2; 0.08 kw-N, DA2; N41 34 59 W72 53 1
5 Division Street, East Greenwich, RI 02818 US
(860) 621-1754, *Fax:* (860) 426-1172
www.canticonuevoradio.com
License: Southington, CT held by Davidson Media Station WXCT LLC.
Group Owner: Davidson Media Group LLC; (acq 4-30-2004; $1.4 million)
Arbitron Metro Market: Hartford, CT *Format:* Christian
Eric Salgado, President
Alejandro Torres, Station Manager

Stamford

***WEDW-FM**
02-17-1992; 88.5 mhz FM; 2 kw horiz, 1.8 kw vert; 302 ft.; N41 2 49 W73 31 36 *Rebroadcasts:* Rebroadcasts WPKT (FM) Meriden100%
240 New Britain Avenue, Hartford, CT 06126 US
(860) 275-7550, *Fax:* (860) 244-9624
www.cpbn.org/
info@wnpr.org
License: Stamford, Fairfield County, CT held by Connecticut Public Broadcasting Inc.
Arbitron Metro Market: Stamford, CT *Format:* News, News/Talk, 86
Kim Grehn, Station Manager
Nancy Bauer, Promotions Manager
John Dankosky, News Director
Joe Zareski, Chief Engineer

WSTC
09-18-1941; 1400 khz AM *Hrs Open:* 24
600 Congress Ave., Suite 1400, Austin, TX 78701 US
(203) 845-3030, *Fax:* (203) 229-1765
wstcwnlk.com
info@wstc.com
License: Stamford, CT held by Cox Radio Inc.
Group Owner: Cox Radio Inc.
Nat'l Network: CNN Radio; Westwood One *Regional Network:* Conn. Radio Net. *Nat'l Reps:* Katz Radio
Arbitron Metro Market: New York *Format:* News, News/Talk, 86 *Hrs. of News Programming:* news progmg 16 hrs wkly *No. News Employees:* 4 *Target Audience:* 25-54.
Robin Faller, Operations Dir
Eric McDonald, Programming Director
Dawn Wachner, Promotions Manager

Stonington

WMOS
11-01-1981; 102.3 mhz FM *Hrs Open:* 24; 3 kw; Ant 328 ft; N41 24 23 W71 50 15
7 Governor Winthrop Blvd., New London, CT 06355
(860) 443-1980, *Fax:* (860) 444-7970
www.1023thewolf.com
info@thewolf.mohegansun.com
License: Stonington, New London County, CT
Group Owner: Cumulus Media Inc.; (acq 4-26-2001; grpsl)
Nat'l Reps: D & R Radio
Population Served: 927 *Arbitron Metro Market:* Stonington, CT *No. News Employees:* 1 *Target Audience:* 25-45.
Judy Ellis, CFO
Fahrid Soleman, President
Bonnie Gomes, General Manager
Matt Chase, General Sales Mgr
Kevin O'Connor, Programming Director
Jackie Steele, Promotions Manager
Frank Doremus, Chief Engineer
Dave Holmes, TrafficManager
Mark Stachowski, Director of Sales

Storrs

***WHUS**
01-01-1956; 91.7 mhz FM *Hrs Open:* 24; 1.2 kw horiz, 4.4 kw vert; 492 ft.; N41 48 50 W72 15 36
Student U. Bldg Bx U-8r, Storrs, CT 06269 US
(860) 486-4007, *Fax:* (860) 486-2955
www.whus.org
info@whus.org
License: Storrs, Tolland County, CT held by Board of Trustees University of Connecticut.
Nat'l Network: AP Radio; NPR *Wire Services:* AP
Arbitron Metro Market: Hartford-New Britain-Middletown, CT *Format:* Variety/Diverse *Special Programming:* Sp 3 hrs wkly *Hrs. of News Programming:* 18 hrs wkly *No. News Employees:* 2 *Adv. Rates:* 25; 25; 25;25
Ben Shaiken, Operations Dir
John Murphy, General Manager

Torrington

***WAPJ**
01-01-1997; 89.9 mhz FM; 0.04 kw; 276 ft.; N41 48 9 W73 9 54.3 *Rebroadcasts:* WWUH(FM) West Hartford
855 University Drive, Torrington, CT 06790 US
(860) 489-9033, *Fax:* (860) 482-7614
www.wapjfm.com
info@wapj.org
License: Torrington, Litchfield County, CT held by The I.B. and Zena H. Temkin Foundation Inc.
Arbitron Metro Market: Torrington, CT *Format:* Variety/Diverse *Hrs. of News Programming:* News progmg 10 hrs wkly *Target Audience:* General; any and all
Dick Williams, General Manager

WSNG
610 khz AM *Hrs Open:* 24; 1 kw-D, DA2; 0.5 kw-N, DA2; N41 45 28 W73 3 6 *Rebroadcasts:* Rebroadcast WDRC (AM) Hartford 100%
166 West Putnam Ave., Greenwich, CT 06790 US
(860) 243-1115, *Fax:* (860) 286-8257
www.talkofconnecticut.com
License: Torrington, CT held by Buckley Broadcasting of Connecticut LLC.
Group Owner: Buckley Broadcasting Corp.
Nat'l Network: Westwood One; AP Radio *Regional Network:* CRN *Nat'l Reps:* Katz Radio *Wire Services:* AP
Arbitron Metro Market: Hartford-New Britain-Middletown, CT *Format:* News, Talk *Target Audience:* 40 plus; middle income, grassroots America
Richard Buckley, President
Laura Kittell, Operations Dir
Eric Fahnoe, General Manager
Grahame Winters, Programming Director
Dan Lovallo, News Director
Scott Baron, Chief Engineer
Joe Orlando, Traffic Manager

Vernon

***WCTF**
11-21-1982; 1170 khz AM
4135 Northgate Blvd, Suite 1, Sacramento, CA 95834 US
(800) 543-1495, *Fax:* (916) 641-8238 (510) 633-7983
www.familyradio.com
familyradio@familyradio.org
License: Vernon, CT held by Family Stations Inc.
Group Owner: Family Stations Inc.; acq 1-86; $136,000;
Arbitron Metro Market: Hartford, CT *Format:* Religious
Harold Camping, President

Wallingford

***WWEB**
11-10-1976; 89.9 mhz FM; 0.015 kw horiz; -16 ft.; N41 27 34 W72 48 48 *Rebroadcasts:* Rebroadcasts WWUH (FM) West Hartford 80%
333 Christian Street, Wallingford, CT 06492 US
(203) 697-2506, *Fax:* (203) 697-2186
www.wwebfm.org
StationManager@WWEBfm.org
License: Wallingford, New Haven County, CT held by Choate Rosemary Hall Foundation.
Arbitron Metro Market: Wallingford, CT *Format:* Variety/Diverse *Special Programming:* Class 2 hrs, C&W 2 hrs wkly *Target Audience:* High school students.
Chris Bielizna, General Manager

Waterbury

WATR
06-15-1934; 1320 khz AM *Hrs Open:* 24; 5 kw-D, DA2; 1 kw-N, DA2; N41 32 12 W73 1 52
79 Baldwin Ave, Waterbury, CT 06702 US
(203) 755-1121, *Fax:* (203) 574-3025
www.watr.com
talkback@watr.com
License: Waterbury, CT held by WATR Inc.
Nat'l Network: AP Radio
Arbitron Metro Market: Waterbury, CT *Format:* News, News/Talk, 64, Talk *Special Programming:* Pol 2 hrs, It 3 hrs wkly *Hrs. of News Programming:* news progmg 15 hrs wkly *No. News Employees:* 2 *Target Audience:* 35-64.
Dave Deville, Operations Dir
Tom Chute, General Manager
Trish Torello, General Sales Mgr

WMRQ-FM)
12-25-1967; 104.1 mhz FM *Hrs Open:* 24; 50 kw; Ant 859 ft; N41 33 41 W72 50 39
131 New London Turnpike, Suite 101, Glastonbury, CT 6033
(860) 723-6000, *Fax:* (860) 657-1042
www.radio1041.fm
sales@radio1041.fm
License: Waterbury, New Haven County, CT held by Aloha Station Trust LLC
Nat'l Network: ABC *Nat'l Reps:* Christal
Population Served: 900,000 *Arbitron Metro Market:* Hartford, CT *Format:* Adult Contemp *Target Audience:* 18-49.
Tom McConnell, General Manager
Michael Maguire, Programming Director

WWCO
01-01-1946; 1240 khz AM *Hrs Open:* 24; 1 kw-U, ND1; N41 33 59 W73 3 23 *Rebroadcasts:* Rebroadcasts WDRC(AM) Bloomfield 90%
166 West Putnam Avenue, Greenwich, CT 06708 US
(860) 243-1115, *Fax:* (860) 274-9734
www.talkofconnecticut.com
wwco@talkofconnecticut.com
License: Waterbury, CT held by Buckley Broadcasting of Connecticut LLC.
Group Owner: Buckley Broadcasting Corp.; (acq 4-97; $500,000).
Arbitron Metro Market: Waterbury, CT *Format:* News, News/Talk, 86 *No. News Employees:* 2 *Target Audience:* 35 plus.
Richard Buckley, President
Laura Kittell, Operations Dir
Wayne Mulligan, General Manager

WWYZ
08-01-1961; 92.5 mhz FM *Hrs Open:* 24; 17 kw; 879 ft.; N41 33 47 W72 50 42
600 Congress Ave., Suite 1400, Austin, TX 78701 US
(860) 723-6000, *Fax:* (860) 493-7090
www.country925.com
License: Waterbury, New Haven County, CT held by Capstar TX L.P.
Group Owner: Clear Channel Communications Inc.; (acq 8-30-00; grpsl).
Nat'l Network: Westwood One *Nat'l Reps:* Christal
Arbitron Metro Market: Waterbury, CT *Format:* Country *Hrs. of News Programming:* news progmg 5 hrs wkly *No. News Employees:* 1 *Target Audience:* 25-54.
Todd Thomas, Operations Dir
Tom McConnell, General Manager
Pete Salant, Programming Director

West Hartford

WCCC
01-01-1947; 1290 khz AM *Hrs Open:* 24
32 Fairfield Street, Boston, MA 02116 US
(860) 525-1069, *Fax:* (860) 246-9084
www.beethoven.com
info@wccc.com
License: West Hartford, CT held by Marlin Broadcasting of Hartford LLC
Nat'l Reps: Eastman Radio
Arbitron Metro Market: Hartford, CT *Format:* Talk *Target Audience:* 18-54.
Woody Tanger, CEO
Boyd Arnold, Operations Dir
Jay Schultz, General Sales Mgr
Nicole Godburn, Promotions Manager
John Ramsey, Chief Engineer
Michelle Bassoss, National Sales Manager
Michael Picozzi, Operations Manager

***WWUH**
07-15-1968; 91.3 mhz FM *Hrs Open:* 24; 0.44 kw; 784 ft.; N41 46 27 W72 48 20
200 Bloomfield Avenue, West Hartford, CT 06117 US
(860) 768-4701, *Fax:* (860) 768-5701
www.wwuh.org
wwuh@hartford.edu
License: West Hartford, Hartford County, CT held by University of Hartford.
Wire Services: Pacifica Network News
Arbitron Metro Market: Hartford, CT *Format:* Variety/Diverse *Special Programming:* It 3 hrs, Por 3 hrs, Pol 3 hrs, It 3 hrs, foreign/ *Hrs. of News Programming:* News progmg 8 hrs wkly *Target Audience:* General.
John Ramsey, President
Stephanie Lloukis, Operations Dir
Susan Mullis, General Sales Mgr
Joe Rush, Programming Director
Jim Christensen, Assistant Programming Director
Andy Taylor, Music Director
Mike DeRosa, Public AffairsDirector

West Haven

***WNHU**
01-01-1973; 88.7 mhz FM *Hrs Open:* 6 AM-2 AM; 1.7 kw; 161 ft.; N41 17 29 W72 57 40
300 Orange Avenue, West Haven, CT 06516 US
(203) 479-8800
www.wnhu.net
wnhu887@gmail.com
License: West Haven, New Haven County, CT held by University of New Haven Inc.

Arbitron Metro Market: New Haven, CT *Format:* Variety/Diverse *Special Programming:* Jazz 12 hrs, folk 6 hrs, Irish 5 hrs, metal 9 hrs, *Hrs. of News Programming:* News progmg 12 hrs wkly *Target Audience:* General.
Bryan Lane, General Manager

Westport

WEBE
09-01-1962; 107.9 mhz FM *Hrs Open:* 24; 50 kw; 384 ft.; N41 10 14 W73 11 5
350 Park Avenue, 16th Floor, New York, NY 10022 US
(203) 333-9108, *Fax:* (203) 333-9108
www.webe108.com
danny@webe108.com
License: Westport, Fairfield County, CT held by Cumulus Licensing Corp.
Group Owner: Cumulus Media Inc.; (acq 3-14-02; grpsl).
Nat'l Reps: Christal
Arbitron Metro Market: Westport, CT *Format:* Adult Contemp *Special Programming:* Talk one hr wkly *Hrs. of News Programming:* news progmg 3 hrs wkly *No. News Employees:* 1 *Target Audience:* 25-54; upscalefemales *Adv. Rates:* 330; 330; 330; 100
Curtis Hansen, Operations Dir
Ann McManus, General Manager
Valerie Thompson, News Director

*WSHU
04-15-1959; 1260 khz AM *Hrs Open:* 6 AM-7 PM; 1 kw-D, DA2; 0.009 kw-N, DA2; N41 7 44 W73 23 20 *Rebroadcasts:* Rebroadcasts WSHU(FM) Fairfield 30%
5151 Park Avenue, Fairfield, CT 06432 US
(203) 365-0425, *Fax:* (203) 371-7991
www.wshu.org
lombardi@wshu.org
License: Westport, CT held by Sacred Heart University Inc.
Nat'l Network: NPR; PRI *Wire Services:* AP
Arbitron Metro Market: New York, NY *Format:* News, News/Talk, 86 *Hrs. of News Programming:* news progmg 45 hrs wkly *No. News Employees:* 2 *Target Audience:* General.
George Lombardi, General Manager
Gillian Anderson, General Sales Mgr
Tom Kuser, Programming Director
Naomi Starobin, News Director
Paul Litwinovich, Chief Engineer

*WWPT
01-01-1975; 90.3 mhz FM; 0.33 kw; 128 ft.; N41 10 19 W73 19 43
Mailing Address: 110 Myrtle Avenue, Westport, CT 06880 US
Second Address: 110 Myrtle Ave., Westport, CT 6880
(203) 341-1381, *Fax:* (203) 226-6875
www.shs.westport.k12.ct.us
License: Westport, Fairfield County, CT held by Board of Education, Town of Westport.
Arbitron Metro Market: Westport, CT *Format:* Variety/Diverse *Special Programming:* Slovak 3 hrs wkly *Target Audience:* 14-24; youth
Mike Zito, Operations Dir
Will Kanter, Station Manager
Brendan Burris, Promotions Manager
Hannah Foley, News Director
Jim Honeycutt, Faculty Advisor
Alex Zuckerman, Music Director
Ryan Jacobs, Sports Director

Willimantic

*WECS
02-06-1982; 90.1 mhz FM; 0.43 kw; 381 ft.; N41 41 0 W72 13 1
83 Windham St., Willimantic, CT 06226 US
(860) 465-5354, *Fax:* (860) 465-5073
www.easternct.edu/wecs/
wecs@easternct.edu
License: Willimantic, Windham County, CT held by Eastern Connecticut State University.
Arbitron Metro Market: Willimantic, CT *Format:* Rock/AOR *Special Programming:* Jazz 16 hrs, relg 3 hrs, Sp 9 hrs wkly
John Zatowski, General Manager

WILI
10-05-1957; 1400 khz AM *Hrs Open:* 24; 1 kw-U, ND1; N41 42 54 W72 11 23
720 Main Street, Willimantic, CT 06226 US
(860) 456-1111, *Fax:* (860) 456-9501
www.wili.com
donna@wili.com
License: Willimantic, CT held by Nutmeg Broadcasting Co.
Group Owner: Hall Communications Inc.; (acq 8-30-2005; $1.8 million with co-located FM)
Nat'l Network: ABC *Regional Network:* Conn. Radio Net. *Nat'l Reps:* Eastman Radio *Wire Services:* AP
Format: Adult Contemp, News *Special Programming:* Ukrainian one hr, Sp one hr, relg 2 hrs, *Hrs. of News Programming:* news progmg 10 hrs wkly *No. News Employees:* 3 *Target Audience:* 25 plus; general *Adv.Rates:* 21; 18; 21; 15
Colin Rice, Operations Dir
Andy Russell, General Manager
Donna Evan, General Sales Mgr

WILI-FM
06-16-1975; 98.3 mhz FM *Hrs Open:* 24; 1.05 kw; 525 ft.; N41 41 0 W72 12 59
720 Main Street, Williamantic, CT 06226 US
(860) 456-1111, *Fax:* (860) 456-9501
www.wili.com
donna@wili.com
License: Willimantic, Windham County, CT held by Nutmeg Broadcasting Co.
Group Owner: Hall Communications Inc.; 8/30/2005
Nat'l Reps: Eastman Radio *Wire Services:* AP
Arbitron Metro Market: New London, CT *Format:* Contemporary Hits/Top 40 *Hrs. of News Programming:* news progmg 6 hrs wkly *No. News Employees:* 1 *Target Audience:* 22-44; college students, young married couples,young families *Adv. Rates:* 38;34;38;32
Colin Rice, President
Andy Russell, General Manager
Donna Evan, General Sales Mgr

Windsor

WKND
05-04-1961; 1480 khz AM; 0.5 kw-D, DA2; 0.014 kw-N, DA2; N41 51 10 W72 40 43
544-J Windsor Ave, Windsor, CT 06095 US
(860) 524-0001, *Fax:* (860) 524-0336
www.wknd.fm
mtanderson2942@sbcglobal.net
License: Windsor, CT held by Freedom Communications of Connecticut Inc.
Group Owner: Freedom Communications of Connecticut Inc.; (acq 11-29-2004)
Nat'l Network: ABC
Arbitron Metro Market: Hartford-New Britain-Middletown, CT *Format:* Blues, Talk *Special Programming:* Gospel 5 hrs, jazz 3 hrs wkly
Richard Weaver-Bey, President
Marion Anderson, General Sales Mgr

Windsor Locks

WUCS
07-01-1990; 97.9 mhz FM; 3.4 kw; 528 ft; N42 05 05 W72 42 14
1331 Main St., Springfield, MA 78701
(413) 781-1011, *Fax:* (413) 734-4434
www.kix979.com
License: Windsor Locks, Hartford County, CT held by Capstar TX L.P.
Group Owner: Clear Channel Communications Inc.; (acq 8-30-00; grpsl).
Arbitron Metro Market: Springfield, MA *Target Audience:* 25-54. *Adv. Rates:* 110; 100; 105; 55
Pat McKay, Operations Dir
Sean Davey, General Manager

Delaware

Bethany Beach

WJKI
01-01-1996; 103.5 mhz FM; 1.45 kw; 479 ft.; N38 34 21 W75 6 58 *Rebroadcasts:* Simulcast w/ WGBG (FM) Seaford 100%
224 Maugers Will Road, Pottstown, PA 19464 US
(302) 856-2567, *Fax:* (302) 856-7633
www.bigclassicrock.com
wgbg@bigclassicrock.com
License: Bethany Beach, Sussex County, DE held by Great Scott Broadcasting.
Group Owner: Great Scott Broadcasting
Format: Classic Rock
Sue Timmons, General Manager
Sean McHugh, Programming Director
Tracy Baker, News Director

WKZP
01-01-1974; 95.9 mhz FM; 10.5 kw; Ant 469 ft; N38 25 20 W75 08 23
Gateway Crossing, 351 Tilghman Rd., Salisbury, MD 53202
(410) 742-1923, *Fax:* (410) 742-2329
www.96rocksyou.com
License: Bethany Beach, Sussex County, DE held by Capstar TX L.P.
Group Owner: Clear Channel Communications Inc.; (acq 8-7-2000; grpsl).
Nat'l Reps: Clear Channel
Arbitron Metro Market: Salisbury-Ocean City, MD *Target Audience:* 18-34.
Brian Cleary, Operations Dir
Frank Hamilton, General Manager
Dixie Penner, Promotions Manager
Marie Merrill, News Director

Christiana

*WXHL-FM
08-01-1994; 89.1 mhz FM *Hrs Open:* 24; 0.001 kw horiz, 1.2 kw vert; 66 ft.; N39 40 38 W75 39 47
P.O. Box 372, Wilmington, DE 19899 US
(302) 731-0690, *Fax:* (302) 738-3090
www.thereachfm.com
listenercare@myreachradio.com
License: Christiana, New Castle County, DE held by Priority Radio Inc.
Group Owner: Priority Radio Inc.; (acq 12-10-99)
Arbitron Metro Market: Christiana, DE *Format:* Christian, Religious
Dan Edwards, Operations Dir
Steve Hare, General Manager
Larry Humm, General Sales Mgr
Dave Kirby, Programming Director

Dover

WDOV
01-01-1948; 1410 khz AM *Hrs Open:* 24; 5 kw-D, DA2; 5 kw-N, DA2; N39 12 3 W75 33 55
600 Congress Avenue, Suite 1400, Austin, TX 78701 US
(302) 395-9800, *Fax:* (302) 674-5978
www.wdov.com
ericfendt@clearchannel.com
License: Dover, DE held by Capstar TX L.P.
Group Owner: Clear Channel Communications Inc.; (acq 8-30-2000; grpsl)
Nat'l Network: Westwood One *Nat'l Reps:* Clear Channel
Arbitron Metro Market: Dover, DE *Format:* News, News/Talk, 84, Talk *Hrs. of News Programming:* news progmg 162 hrs wkly *No. News Employees:* 2 *Target Audience:* 25-54.
Bob Walton, Operations Dir
Heidi Piazza, General Sales Mgr
Andy Harris, Programming Director
Paige Lamers, Promotions Manager
Phil Feliciangeli, News Director

WDSD
01-01-1956; 94.7 mhz FM; 50 kw; 377 ft.; N39 12 3 W75 33 55
600 Congress Avenue, Suite 1400, Austin, TX 78701 US
(302) 395-9800, *Fax:* (302) 395-9808
www.wdsd.com
wdsd@clearchannel.com
License: Dover, Kent County, DE held by Capstar TX L.P.
Group Owner: Clear Channel Communications Inc.
Nat'l Network: Motor Racing Net *Nat'l Reps:* Clear Channel
Arbitron Metro Market: Wilmington, DE *Format:* Country *Hrs. of News Programming:* news progmg 2 hrs wkly *No. News Employees:* 1 *Target Audience:* 18-49.
Paige Lamers, General Manager
Heidi Piazza, General Sales Mgr
Andy Harris, Programming Director
Eric Fendt, Promotions Manager
Rob Reb, Chief Engineer

*WRTX
04-05-1995; 91.7 mhz FM *Hrs Open:* 24; 0 kw horiz, 0.58 kw vert; 315 ft.; N39 12 3 W75 33 55 *Rebroadcasts:* Rebroadcasts WRTI(FM) Philadelphia, PA 100%
Anneberg Hall (011-00), Philadelphia, PA 19122 US
(215) 204-8405, *Fax:* (215) 204-7027
www.wrti.org
comments@wrti.org
License: Dover, Kent County, DE held by Temple University of the Commonwealth System of Higher Education.
Nat'l Network: NPR; AP Radio
Format: Jazz *No. News Employees:* 1 *Target Audience:* 30-65.
Tobias Poole, Operations Dir
David Conant, General Manager
William Johnson, Station Manager
Brick Torpey, General Sales Mgr
Jack Moore, Programming Director
Jeffrey DePolo, Engineering Dir
Dave Conant, Executive Director

WRJE
09-28-2005; 1600 khz AM *Hrs Open:* 24; 5 kw-D, DA2; 1 kw-N, DA2; N39 10 11 W75 33 13
400 Walker Road, P.O. Box 553, Dover, DE 19901 US
License: Dover, DE held by K-5 Communications LLC

Fenwick Island

***WLBW**
04-01-1994; 92.1 mhz FM; 3 kw; 469 ft.; N38 25 20 W75 8 23
111 East Kilbourn Avenue, Suite 2700, Milwaukee, WI 53202 US
(410) 742-1923, *Fax:* (410) 742-2329
www.isurfthewave.com
wave@intercom.net
License: Fenwick Island, Sussex County, DE held by Aloha Station Trust LLC
Arbitron Metro Market: Salisbury-Ocean City, MD *Format:* Oldies *Target Audience:* 25-54. *Adv. Rates:* 50; 40; 50; 25
Frank Hamilton, General Manager
Marie Merrill, News Director

Georgetown

WJWL
06-23-1951; 900 khz AM *Hrs Open:* 24; 10.5 kw-D, DA2; 1.08 kw-N, DA2; N38 42 29 W75 24 28
224 Maugers Mill Road, Pottstown, PA 19464 US
(302) 422-2600, *Fax:* (302) 424-1630
www.digital900.com
digital900@aol.com
License: Georgetown, DE held by Great Scott Broadcasting Ltd.
Group Owner: Great Scott Broadcasting
Nat'l Network: CNN Radio *Nat'l Reps:* ABC Radio Sales
Arbitron Metro Market: Salisbury-Ocean City, MD *Format:* Spanish *Special Programming:* Relg 6 hrs wkly *Hrs. of News Programming:* news progmg 10 hrs wkly *No. News Employees:* 11 *Target Audience:* 25-54;mature adults
Faye Scott, President
Danny Perez, General Manager
Lisette Perez, Programming Director

WZBH
07-04-1969; 93.5 mhz FM *Hrs Open:* 24; 11 kw; 486 ft.; N38 31 24 W75 17 55
224 Maugers Mill Road, Pottstown, PA 19464 US
(302) 856-2567, *Fax:* (302) 856-7633
License: Georgetown, Sussex County, DE
Group Owner: Great Scott Broadcasting
Arbitron Metro Market: Salisbury-Ocean *Format:* Contemporary Hits/Top 40 *Target Audience:* Adults; baby boomers
C. Marcus, General Sales Mgr
Shawn Murphy, Programming Director
Terry Dalton, Chief Engineer
H. Lasren, Disc Jockey
B. Graxston, Disc Jockey
Donna Cavender, Women's Int Ed

Harrington

***WKNZ**
88.7 mhz FM; 0 kw horiz, 25 kw vert; 322 ft.; N38 53 30 W75 34 48
R. D. #1 Box 169-M, Milton, DE 19968 US
(302) 684-3149, *Fax:* (302) 684-2905
www.887thebridge.com
License: Harrington, Kent County, DE held by Eagle's Nest Fellowship Church.
Arbitron Metro Market: Harrington, DE
William Sammons Sr., President

Laurel

WKDB
11-19-1991; 95.3 mhz FM *Hrs Open:* 24; 6 kw; 328 ft.; N38 30 12 W75 39 39
224 Maugers Mill Rd., Pottstown, PA 19464 US
(302) 856-2567, *Fax:* (302) 856-7633
www.musicontheb.com
myhitsongs@gmail.com
License: Laurel, Sussex County, DE held by Great Scott Broadcasting
Group Owner: Great Scott Broadcasting; acq 2-13-98; $1.5 million).
Arbitron Metro Market: Salisbury-Ocean City, MD *Format:* Adult Contemp *Hrs. of News Programming:* News progmg 6 hrs wkly *Target Audience:* 25-49.
Sue Timmons, General Manager
Tracy Baker, News Director

Lewes

WXDE
06-01-1991; 105.9 mhz FM *Hrs Open:* 24; 6 kw; Ant 341 ft; N38 38 36 W75 13 00 *Rebroadcasts:* Rebroadcasts WKTT(FM) Salisbury, MD 100%
Box 909, Salisbury, MD 19803
(410) 219-3500,(410) 548-1543, *Fax:* (410) 548-1543
www.catcountryradio.com
catcountry@radiocenter.com
License: Lewes, Sussex County, DE held by Delmarva Broadcasting Co.
Group Owner: Delmarva Broadcasting Co.; (acq 6-26-97; grpsl)
Nat'l Network: Motor Racing Net *Nat'l Reps:* Katz Radio *Wire Services:* AP
Population Served: 225,000 *Arbitron Metro Market:* Salisbury-Ocean City, MD *Special Programming:* NASCAR *Hrs. of News Programming:* news progmg 3 hrs wkly *No. News Employees:* 1 *Target Audience:* 25-54.
Joe Edwards, Operations Dir
Joe Beail, General Manager
E. J. Fox, Programming Director
Brian K. Hall, Promotions Manager
Jeff Twilley, Chief Engineer

***WPBD**
06-20-2012; 91.5 mhz FM; kw
US
License: Lewes, DE held by Allied Communications Network Two

Middletown

***WXHM**
91.9 mhz FM; 0.28 kw vert; 319 ft.; N39 26 37 W75 43 24
US
(302) 731-0690, *Fax:* (302) 738-3090
www.thereachfm.com
License: Middletown, New Castle County, DE held by Priority Radio Inc.
Group Owner: Priority Radio Inc.
Arbitron Metro Market: Middletown, DE
Steve Hare, General Manager

Milford

WAFL
05-19-1973; 97.7 mhz FM; 3 kw; 328 ft.; N38 55 39 W75 29 20
Mailing Address: 2727 Shipley Rd., P.O. Box 7492, Wilmington, DE 19803 US
Second Address: 1666 Blairs Pond Rd., Milford, DE 19963
(302) 422-7575, *Fax:* (302) 422-3069
www.eagle977.com
mcobo@dbcmedia.com
License: Milford, Sussex County, DE held by Delmarva Broadcasting Co.
Group Owner: Delmarva Broadcasting Co.; (acq 6-26-97; grpsl).
Nat'l Network: Westwood One
Arbitron Metro Market: Salisbury-Ocean City, MD *Format:* Adult Contemp *Special Programming:* Southern gospel 2 hrs wkly *Target Audience:* 18-49; active, affluent adults in central & southern Delaware
Steve Monz, Operations Dir
Melody Booker, General Manager
Jody Trinsey, General Sales Mgr
Gary John, Programming Director
Jeff Twilly, Chief Engineer

WNCL
11-05-1990; 101.3 mhz FM *Hrs Open:* 24; 3 kw; 328 ft.; N38 51 21 W75 29 2
Mailing Address: Wxpz County Road 626, Lincoln, DE 19960 US
Second Address: 1666 Blairs Pond Rd., Milford, DE 19963-5263
(302) 422-7575, *Fax:* (302) 422-3069
www.cool1013.com
cool@cool1013.com
License: Milford, Sussex County, DE held by Delmarva Broadcasting Co.
Group Owner: Delmarva Broadcasting Co.; acq 1-17-2003; $1.6 million).
Arbitron Metro Market: Salisbury-Ocean, MD *Format:* Oldies *Hrs. of News Programming:* News progmg 7 hrs wkly *Target Audience:* 35-54; adults
Melody Booker, General Manager
Jody Trinsey, General Sales Mgr
Steve Monz, Programming Director
Jeff Twilly, Chief Engineer

WYUS
01-01-1953; 930 khz AM *Hrs Open:* 6 AM-midnight; 0.5 kw-D, DA2; 0.081 kw-N, DA2; N38 55 39 W75 29 20
Mailing Address: 2727 Shipley Rd., P.O. Box 7492, Wilmington, DE 19803 US
Second Address: 1666 Blairs Pond Rd., Milford, DE 19963
(302) 422-2428
www.laexitosa.com
rafael@wyusam.com
License: Milford, DE held by Delmarva Broadcasting Co.
Group Owner: Delmarva Broadcasting Co.
Arbitron Metro Market: Salisbury-Ocean *Special Programming:* Relg 10 hrs, Haitian 3 hrs wkly *Target Audience:* 18 plus; Hispanic
Rafael Dosman, Programming Director

Newark

***WVUD**
10-04-1976; 91.3 mhz FM; 0.79 kw horiz, 6.8 kw vert; 135 ft.; N39 41 26 W75 45 23
Perkins Student Center, Newark, DE 19716 US
(302) 831-2701, *Fax:* (302) 831-1399
www.wvud.org
ud.wvud@gmail.com
License: Newark, New Castle County, DE held by University of Delaware.
Nat'l Network: AP Radio
Arbitron Metro Market: Newark, DE *Format:* Variety/Diverse *Special Programming:* Class 10 hrs, black 10 hrs, jazz 15 hrs, folk 15 h *Target Audience:* General.
Trish Saccomanno, General Manager
Steve Kramarck, Station Manager
Kelsi Skeens, Programming Director
Jake Kairis, Promotions Manager
David Mackenzie, Chief Engineer
Matt Wolfson, Business Manager
Mike Tsarouhas, ProductionDirector
Anna Kamensky, Music Director
Jake Glickman, Music Director

Ocean View

WZEB
01-12-1986; 101.7 mhz FM; 3.3 kw; 446 ft.; N38 31 24 W75 17 55 *Rebroadcasts:* Simulcast of WKDB (FM) Laurel 100%
224 Maugers Mill Road, Pottstown, PA 19464 US
(302) 856-2567, *Fax:* (302) 856-7633
www.musicontheb.com
License: Ocean View, Sussex County, DE held by Great Scott Broadcasting.
Group Owner: Great Scott Broadcasting; acq 5-29-98; $1.5 million)
Arbitron Metro Market: Salisbury-Ocean City, MD *Format:* Adult Contemp
Sue Timmons, General Manager
Tracy Baker, News Director

Pike Creek

***WMHS**
04-01-2000; 88.1 mhz FM *Hrs Open:* 24; 0.088 kw vert; 121 ft.; N39 45 27 W75 40 2
Mailing Address: 1400 Washington Street, P O Box 869, Wilmington, DE 19899 US
Second Address: 301 McKennans Church Rd., Wilmington, DE 19808
(302) 636-5652
www.wmhs881.info
wmhs881@gmail.com
License: Pike Creek, New Castle County, DE held by Red Clay Consolidated School District.
Wire Services: AP
Arbitron Metro Market: Pike Creek, DE *Format:* Oldies *Hrs. of News Programming:* news progmg 20 hrs wkly *No. News Employees:* 11 *Target Audience:* 25-54; adults-baby boomers
Eric Stancell, Operations Dir
Sherry Gross, Principal

Rehoboth Beach

WGMD
09-21-1975; 92.7 mhz FM *Hrs Open:* 24; 2.6 kw; 433 ft.; N38 42 14.4 W75 12 0.6
1000 Connecticut Ave., NW, Ste-201, Washington, DC 20036 US
(302) 945-2050, *Fax:* (302) 945-3781
www.wgmd.com
wgmd@wgmd.com
License: Rehoboth Beach, Sussex County, DE held by Resort Broadcasting Co. L.L.C.
Nat'l Reps: ABC Radio Sales
Arbitron Metro Market: Salisbury-Ocean City, MD *Format:* News, News/Talk, 86 *Special Programming:* Farm 2 hrs, jazz 2 hrs, relg 2 hrs wkly *Hrs. of News Programming:* news progmg 16 hrs wkly

No. News Employees: 3*Target Audience:* 35 plus. *Adv. Rates:* 50; 40; 50; 30
Jared Morris, Operations Dir
Dan Gaffney, General Manager
Marie Moulinier, General Sales Mgr

Seaford

WGBG
02-01-1972; 98.5 mhz FM *Hrs Open:* 24; 6 kw; 322 ft.; N38 36 47 W75 35 12
759 Garfield Parkway, Bethany Beach, DE 19930 US
(302) 856-2567, *Fax:* (302) 856-7633
www.bigclassicrock.com
wgbg@bigclassicrock.com
License: Seaford, Sussex County, DE held by Great Scott Broadcasting
Group Owner: Great Scott Broadcasting; (acq 4-27-98; $1.2 million with co-located AM)
Nat'l Network: CBS
Arbitron Metro Market: Salisbury-Ocean City, MD *Format:* Classic Rock *Special Programming:* Farm one hr wkly *Hrs. of News Programming:* News progmg 4 hrs wkly *Target Audience:* 18-49; secondary 25-54, tertiary 35plus
Sue Timmons, General Manager
Sean McHugh, Programming Director
Tracy Baker, News Director
Terry Dalton, Chief Engineer

WJWK
01-01-1955; 1280 khz AM *Hrs Open:* 6 AM-midnight; 0.84 kw-D, ND1; 0.211 kw-N, ND1; N38 36 47 W75 35 12 *Rebroadcasts:* Simulcast with WKHI(FM) Fruitland 100%
759 Garfield Parkway, Bethany Beach, DE 19930 US
(302) 856-2567, *Fax:* (302) 856-7633
License: Seaford, DE held by Great Scott Broadcasting
Group Owner: Great Scott Broadcasting
Arbitron Metro Market: Salisbury-Ocean City, MD *Format:* News/Talk *Hrs. of News Programming:* News progmg 4 hrs wkly *Target Audience:* Black adults.
Adam Davis, Programming Director
Tracy Baker, News Director

Selbyville

WOCM
03-01-1993; 98.1 mhz FM *Hrs Open:* 24; 3 kw; 469 ft.; N38 25 20 W75 8 23
P.O. Box 169, 57 W. Church Street, Selbyville, DE 19975 US
(410) 723-3683, *Fax:* (410) 723-3698
www.irieradio.com
License: Selbyville, Sussex County, DE held by Irie Radio Inc.
Arbitron Metro Market: Salisbury-Ocean *Format:* Triple A *Target Audience:* 25-54; seasonal, beach residents & loc urban/farm
Adv. Rates: 20;20;20;20
Leighton Moore, President
David Rothner, General Manager

Smyrna

WRDX
11-10-1993; 92.9 mhz FM *Hrs Open:* 24; 1.7 kw; 377 ft.; N39 12 3 W75 33 55
600 Congress Avenue, Suite 1400, Austin, TX 78701 US
(302) 395-9800, *Fax:* (302) 395-9808
929tomfm.com
ericfendt@clearchannel.com
License: Smyrna, Kent County, DE held by Capstar TX L.P.
Group Owner: Clear Channel Communications Inc.; (acq 8-30-2000; grpsl)
Nat'l Network: Westwood One *Nat'l Reps:* Clear Channel
Arbitron Metro Market: Smyrna, DE *Format:* Contemporary Hits/Top 40, Adult Contemp *Target Audience:* 25-54.
Bob Walton, Operations Dir
Marco Acevedo, General Sales Mgr
Paige Lamers, Promotions Manager

Wilmington

WTMC
01-01-1947; 1380 khz AM
115 South Justison St., Wilmington, DE 19801 US
(410) 964-5700, *Fax:* (410) 964-6478
www.deldot.net
info@wtmc.net
License: Wilmington, DE held by State of Delaware Department of Transportation.
Arbitron Metro Market: Wilmington, DE *Format:* Talk
Jonathan Weishaupt, President
William Brooks, General Manager

WDEL
01-01-1922; 1150 khz AM *Hrs Open:* 24
2727 Shipley Road, Wilmington, DE 19803 US
(302) 478-2700, *Fax:* (302) 478-0100
www.wdel.com
rgilbert@dbcmedia.com
License: Wilmington, DE held by Delmarva Broadcasting Co. Inc.
Group Owner: Delmarva Broadcasting Co.
Nat'l Network: Westwood One *Nat'l Reps:* Katz Radio
Arbitron Metro Market: Wilmington, DE *Format:* News, News/Talk, 86 *Special Programming:* Sp 2 hrs wkly *Hrs. of News Programming:* news progmg 70 hrs wkly *No. News Employees:* 10 *Target Audience:* 35-64.
Julian Booker, CEO
Michael Reath, General Manager
Ruth Gilbert, General Sales Mgr

WILM
10-01-1923; 1450 khz AM *Hrs Open:* 24; 1 kw-U, ND1; N39 43 46 W75 33 7
1215 French Street, Wilmington, DE 19801 US
(302) 395-9800, *Fax:* (302) 395-9808
www.wilm.com
mail@wilm.com
License: Wilmington, DE held by Citicasters Licenses L.P.
Group Owner: Clear Channel Communications Inc.; (acq 10-29-2004; $3,986,000)
Nat'l Network: Wall Street; Fox News Radio *Nat'l Reps:* Clear Channel *Wire Services:* AP
Arbitron Metro Market: Wilmington, DE *Format:* News, News/Talk, 86 *Special Programming:* Community Spotlight, Delaware Radio Magazine *Hrs. of News Programming:* news progmg 168 hrs wkly *No. News Employees:* 6*Target Audience:* Adults 25-54. *Adv. Rates:* na
Paige Lamers, General Manager
Martha Burns, General Sales Mgr
Mark Fowser, Programming Director
Eric Fendt, Promotions Manager

WWTX
04-21-1947; 1290 khz AM *Hrs Open:* 24; 2.5 kw-D, ND1; 0.032 kw-N, ND1; N39 44 3 W75 31 44
600 Congress Avenue, Suite 1400, Austin, TX 78701 US
(302) 395-9800, *Fax:* (302) 395-9808
www.1290theticket.com
wwtx@clearchannel.com
License: Wilmington, DE held by Capstar TX L.P.
Group Owner: Clear Channel Communications Inc.
Nat'l Reps: Clear Channel
Arbitron Metro Market: Wilmington, DE *Format:* Sports, Talk *Target Audience:* Males: 18-45. *Adv. Rates:* na
Paige Lamers, General Manager
Martha Burns, General Sales Mgr

WJBR-FM
01-01-1957; 99.5 mhz FM *Hrs Open:* 24; 50 kw; 499 ft.; N39 50 2 W75 31 27
3001 Philadelphia Pike, Claymont, DE 19703 US
(302) 765-1160, *Fax:* (302) 765-1192
www.wjbr.com
info@wjbr.com
License: Wilmington, New Castle County, DE held by NM Licensing LLC.
Group Owner: NextMedia Group Inc.; (acq 3-7-00; $32.4 million).
Nat'l Reps: Christal
Arbitron Metro Market: Wilmington, DE *Format:* Adult Contemp
No. News Employees: 1 *Target Audience:* 25-54.
Bruce Beasley, President
Jane Bartsch, Operations Dir
Michael Waite, Vice President, Operations

***WMPH**
10-01-1969; 91.7 mhz FM *Hrs Open:* 24; 0.1 kw vert; 144 ft.; N39 46 23 W75 30 25
5201 Washington St Ext, Wilmington, DE 19809 US
(302) 762-3671
www.brandywineschools.org/wmph
91.7wmph@gmail.com
License: Wilmington, New Castle County, DE held by Brandywine School District, Brd of Educ
Arbitron Metro Market: Wilmington, DE *Format:* Variety/Diverse *Hrs. of News Programming:* news progmg 2 hrs wkly *No. News Employees:* 1 *Target Audience:* 13-27; high school & college students
Pat Bush, General Manager
Paul Wishengrad, Station Manager

WSTW
01-01-1950; 93.7 mhz FM *Hrs Open:* 24; 47.1 kw; 502 ft.; N39 48 57 W75 31 47
2727 Shipley Road, P.O. Box 7492, Wilmington, DE 19803 US
(302) 478-2700, *Fax:* (302) 478-0100
info@wstwfm.com
License: Wilmington, New Castle County, DE
Group Owner: Delmarva Broadcasting Co.
Arbitron Metro Market: Wilmington, DE *Format:* Adult Contemp
Special Programming: Relg one hr, pub affrs one hr wkly *Hrs. of News Programming:* News progmg 10 hrs wkly *Target Audience:* 25-54.
Brian Sands, General Manager

District of Columbia

Washington

***WAMU**
10-23-1961; 88.5 mhz FM *Hrs Open:* 24; 50 kw; 499 ft.; N38 56 10 W77 5 33
4400 Mass., Avenue N.W., Washington, DC 20016 US
(202) 885-1200, *Fax:* (202) 885-1269
www.wamu.org
feedback@wamu.org
License: Washington, DC held by American University.
Nat'l Network: NPR; PRI
Arbitron Metro Market: Washington, DC *Format:* News, News/Talk, 86 *Special Programming:* Vintage radio 4 hrs, country 4 hrs, jazz 3 hrs wkly *Hrs. of News Programming:* news progmg 120 hrs wkly *No. News Employees:* 6 *Target Audience:* 25-54.
Caryn Mathes, General Manager
Mark McDonald, Programming Director
Jim Asendio, News Director

WASH
01-01-1948; 97.1 mhz FM; 17.5 kw; 794 ft.; N38 57 1 W77 4 47
1801 Rockville Pike, 6th Floor, Rockville, MD 20852 US
(301) 984-9710, *Fax:* (301) 255-4314
www.washfm.com
info@wash.com
License: Washington, DC held by AMFM Radio Licenses LLC.
Group Owner: Clear Channel Communications Inc.; (acq 8-30-00; grpsl).
Arbitron Metro Market: Washington, DC *Format:* Adult Contemp
Dave Pugh, President
Bill Hess, Operations Dir
Loretta Lage, General Sales Mgr

WBIG-FM
06-03-1994; 100.3 mhz FM *Hrs Open:* 24; 50 kw; 489 ft.; N38 53 13 W77 12 3
11300 Rockville Pike, Suite 905, Rockville, MD 20852 US
(240) 747-2700, *Fax:* (301) 770-0236
www.thebigdc.com
billcahill@clearchannel.com
License: Washington, DC held by AMFM Radio Licenses LLC.
Group Owner: Clear Channel Communications Inc.; (acq 8-30-2000; grpsl)
Arbitron Metro Market: Rockville, MD *Format:* Oldies *Hrs. of News Programming:* news progmg one hr wkly *No. News Employees:* 2 *Target Audience:* 35-54; professional, college, upscale
Dave Pugh, General Manager
Jeff Boden, General Sales Mgr
Bill Cahill, Programming Director
Dave Hennessy, Promotions Manager

***WCSP-FM**
05-08-1982; 90.1 mhz FM *Hrs Open:* 24; 36 kw; 568 ft.; N38 57 44 W77 1 36
400 North Capitol St, NW, Suite 650, Washington, DC 20001 US
(202) 737-3220, *Fax:* (202) 737-5554
www.c-span.org
radio@c-span.org
License: Washington, DC held by National Cable Satellite Corp.
Arbitron Metro Market: Washington, DC *Format:* Public Affairs
Target Audience: General.
Brian Lamb, CEO
Kate Mills, General Manager

***WETA**
04-19-1970; 90.9 mhz FM *Hrs Open:* 24; 75 kw; 610 ft.; N38 53 30 W77 7 55
PO Box 2626, Washington, DC 20013 US
(703) 998-2600
www.weta.org/fm
radio@weta.com
License: Washington, DC held by Greater Washington Educational Telecommunications Association Inc.
Nat'l Network: NPR; PRI
Arbitron Metro Market: Washington, DC *TV Affiliate:* *WETA-TV affil *Format:* Talk *Target Audience:* General; educated adults

Timothy C. Coughlin, Chairman
Sharon Percy Rockefeller, President and Chief Executive Officer
Dan Devany, General Manager
Joseph B. Bruns, Executive Vice President and Chief Operating Offic
Dalton Delan, Executive Vice President andChief Programming Off
Polly Povejsil Heath, Senior Vice President and Chief Financial Officer

WWRC
01-01-1941; 1260 khz AM *Hrs Open:* 24
300 Crescent Court, Suite 600, Dallas, TX 75201 US
(301)231-7798, *Fax:* (301)881-8030
redzebea@broadcasting.com
License: Washington, DC held by Red Zebra Broadcasting Licensee LLC.
Group Owner: Red Zebra Holdings LLC; (acq 7-29-2008; grpsl)
Nat'l Network: Westwood One *Nat'l Reps:* Clear Channel
Arbitron Metro Market: Washington, DC *Format:* Talk *Target Audience:* 25-54; adults
Bill Hess, Operations Dir
Heather Steffan, General Sales Mgr
Dave Pugh, Promotions Manager
Jerry Phillips, News Director
Shaun Sandoval, Chief Engineer
Kathy Lennhoff, Promotions Director

WTOP-FM
09-01-1948; 103.5 mhz FM *Hrs Open:* 24; 44 kw; 518 ft.; N38 56 10 W77 5 33
P.O. Box 1160, Salt Lake City, UT 84110 US
(202) 895-5000, *Fax:* (202) 895-5016
www.wtop.com
info@wtop.com
License: Washington, DC held by Bonneville Holding Co.
Group Owner: Bonneville International Corporation; (acq 1-30-98; grpsl)
Nat'l Network: CBS Radio *Nat'l Reps:* Katz Radio *Wire Services:* Reuters
Arbitron Metro Market: Washington, DC *Format:* News *Target Audience:* General.
Bruce Reese, President
Joel Oxley, General Manager
Matt Mills, General Sales Mgr

***WHUR-FM**
12-10-1971; 96.3 mhz FM *Hrs Open:* 24; 16.5 kw; 801 ft.; N38 57 1 W77 4 47
2400 Sixth Street N.W., Washington, DC 20059 US
(202) 806-3500, *Fax:* (202) 806-3522
www.whur.com
dickinson@whur.com
License: Washington, DC held by Howard University Board of Trustees.
Nat'l Network: CNN Radio; ABC *Nat'l Reps:* D & R Radio *Wire Services:* UPI
Arbitron Metro Market: Washington, DC *Format:* Adult Contemp *Special Programming:* Gospel 14 hrs, Caribbean 6 hrs wkly *Hrs. of News Programming:* news progmg 7 hrs wkly *No. News Employees:* 3 *Target Audience:* 25-54.
Dr. H. Patrick Swygert, President
Millard Watkins III, General Manager
Jeanette Tyce, General Sales Mgr
David Dickinson, Programming Director

WIHT
01-01-1960; 99.5 mhz FM *Hrs Open:* 24; 22 kw; 751 ft.; N38 57 49 W77 6 18
300 Crescent Court, Suite 600, Dallas, TX 75201 US
(301) 255-4300, *Fax:* (301) 770-3541
www.hot995.com
info@hot995.com
License: Washington, DC held by AMFM Radio Licenses L.L.C.
Group Owner: Clear Channel Communications Inc.; (acq 9-00).
Arbitron Metro Market: Washington, DC *Format:* Contemporary Hits/Top 40
Bill Hess, Operations Dir
Dave Pugh, General Manager
Melissa Kelly, General Sales Mgr
Sarah Fraser, Programming Director
Jessica Ritch, Promotions Manager

WKYS
08-01-1947; 93.9 mhz FM *Hrs Open:* 24; 24.5 kw; 705 ft.; N38 56 24 W77 4 54
5900 Princess Grdn Pkwy, 7th Floor, Lanham, MD 20706 US
(301) 306-1111, *Fax:* (301) 306-9510
www.939wkys.com
info@939wkys.com
License: Washington, DC held by Radio One Licenses LLC
Group Owner: Radio One Inc.; (acq 6-95; $34 million;
Nat'l Reps: McGavren Guild
Arbitron Metro Market: Washington, DC *Format:* Blues *Hrs. of News Programming:* news progmg 4 hrs wkly *No. News Employees:* 3 *Target Audience:* 25-54; upscale Black adults
Michele Williams, General Manager
Jack Murray, General Sales Mgr
Steve Hegwood, Programming Director
Sheila Stewart, News Director
Scott Tanner, Chief Engineer
Russ Parr, Disc Jockey
Paul Stewart, Music Director
Ezio Torres,National Sales Manager
Cynthia Bullock, Traffic Manager

WMAL
10-12-1925; 630 khz AM *Hrs Open:* 24
4400 Jenifer Street, N.W, Washington, DC 20015 US
(202) 686-3100, *Fax:* (202) 686-3061
www.wmal.com
info@wmal.com
License: Washington, DC
Group Owner: Cumulus Media Inc.; (acq 6-12-2007; grpsl)
Nat'l Reps: ABC Radio Sales
Arbitron Metro Market: Washington, DC *Format:* News, News/Talk, 86 *Target Audience:* General
Chris Berry, President
Paul Duckworth, Operations Dir
Ernie Fears Jr., General Sales Mgr
John Matthews, News Director
David Sproul, Engineering Dir
Bryan Nehman, News Reporter
Chuck Eisenhauer, Traffic Manager

WMZQ-FM
09-01-1968; 98.7 mhz FM *Hrs Open:* 24; 50 kw; 489 ft.; N38 53 13 W77 12 3
300 Crescent Court, Suite 600, Dallas, TX 75201 US
(240) 747-2700, *Fax:* (301) 984-4895
www.wmzq.com
megstevens@clearchannel.com
License: Washington, DC held by Clear Channel Radio Licenses, Inc.
Group Owner: Clear Channel Communications Inc.; (acq 8-30-00; grpsl)
Nat'l Reps: Christal
Arbitron Metro Market: Washington, DC *Format:* Country *No. News Employees:* 1 *Target Audience:* 25-54.
Bill Hess, Operations Dir
Dave Pugh, General Manager
Bill McIntyre, General Sales Mgr
Meg Stevens, Programming Director
Kim Sauer, Promotions Manager
Oswald Pinott, Chief Engineer

WOL
01-01-1924; 1450 khz AM
5900 Princess Garden Pky, Lanham, MD 20706 US
301-306-1111, *Fax:* 301-306-9540
http://woldcnews.com
mwilliams@radio-one.com
License: Washington, DC held by Radio One Licenses LLC
Group Owner: Radio One Inc.; (Acq 6-95)
Arbitron Metro Market: Washington, DC *TV Affiliate:* Talk

***WPFW**
02-28-1977; 89.3 mhz FM *Hrs Open:* 24; 50 kw; 410 ft.; N38 56 9 W77 5 33
1929 Mlk, Jr Way, Berkeley, CA 94704 US
(202) 588-0999, *Fax:* (202) 588-0561
www.wpfw.org
bmwpfw@aol.com
License: Washington, DC held by Pacifica Foundation Inc.
Group Owner: Pacifica Foundation Inc.
Arbitron Metro Market: Washington, DC *Format:* Jazz, News, 62, Talk *Special Programming:* Oldies 3 hrs, women 3 hrs, health one hr wkly *Hrs. of News Programming:* News progmg 9 hrs wkly *Target Audience:* 25-55.
Ron Pinchback, General Manager
Tiffany Jordan, General Sales Mgr

WRQX
05-15-1948; 107.3 mhz FM; 19.5 kw; 807 ft.; N38 57 1 W77 4 47
4400 Jenifer Street, N.W, Washington, DC 20015 US
(202) 686-3100, *Fax:* (202) 686-3091
www.mix1073fm.com
License: Washington, DC
Group Owner: Cumulus Media Inc.
Nat'l Network: ABC *Nat'l Reps:* Christal
Arbitron Metro Market: Washington, DC *Format:* Adult Contemp *Target Audience:* 25-54.
Jeff Boden, President
Tom Grooms, Operations Dir
Carol Parker, Programming Director
Stella Pressley, News Director
David Sproul, Engineering Dir

WTEM
08-01-1923; 980 khz AM *Hrs Open:* 24; 50 kw-D, DA2; 5 kw-N, DA2; N38 57 43 W76 58 24
11300 Rockville Pike, Suite 707, Rockville, MD 20852 US
(301) 220-0980, *Fax:* (301) 255-4314
www.espn980.com
management@espn980.com
License: Washington, DC held by Red Zebra Broadcasting Licensee LLC.
Group Owner: Red Zebra Holdings LLC; (acq 7-29-2008; grpsl)
Nat'l Network: ESPN Radio *Wire Services:* The Sports Network
Arbitron Metro Market: Washington, DC *Format:* Sports, Talk *Target Audience:* 25-54; men
Bruce Gilbert, President
Hartley Adkins, General Manager

WFED
09-25-1926; 1500 khz AM *Hrs Open:* 24
P.O. Box 1160, Salt Lake City, UT 84110 US
(202) 895-5000, *Fax:* (202) 895-5144
www.federalnewsradio.com
info@federalnewsradio.com
License: Washington, DC held by Bonneville Holding Co.
Group Owner: Bonneville International Corporation; (acq 4-27-98; grpsl)
Arbitron Metro Market: Washington, DC *Format:* News *No. News Employees:* 4 *Target Audience:* General.
Bruce Reese, President
Julia Ziegler, Operations Dir
Joel Oxley, General Manager
Lisa Wolfe, Programming Director
Ralph Renzi, Director of Federal Sales
Jeffrey Wolinsky, Sports Sales and Team Relations

WUST
01-01-1949; 1120 khz AM; 3 kw-C, NDD; 20 kw-D, NDD; N38 54 15 W77 9 54
2131crimmins Lane, Falls Church, VA 22043 US
(703) 532-0400
www.wust1120.com
contactwithwust@wust1120.com
License: Washington, DC held by New World Radio Inc.
Arbitron Metro Market: Falls Church, VA *Format:* Ethnic *Special Programming:* Fr 15 hrs, Sp 15 hrs, Ger 7 hrs, Ethiopian 6 hrs,
Brian Edwards, Operations Dir
Alan Pendleton, General Manager

WWDC
01-01-1947; 101.1 mhz FM *Hrs Open:* 24; 22.5 kw; 761 ft.; N38 59 59 W77 3 27
300 Crescent Court, Suite 600, Dallas, TX 75201 US
(301) 587-7100, *Fax:* (301) 587-0225
www.dc101.com
License: Washington, DC held by AMFM Radio Licenses L.L.C.
Group Owner: Clear Channel Communications Inc.; (acq 8-30-00; grpsl).
Arbitron Metro Market: Washington, DC
Dave Pugh, General Manager
Beth Cohen, General Sales Mgr
James Howard, Programming Director
Dave Hennessy, Promotions Manager
Oswald Pinott, Chief Engineer
Greg Roche, Music Director
Paul Krakovsky, Online Sales

WYCB
01-01-1978; 1340 khz AM
5900 Princess Garden, Parkway, 8th Floor, Lanham, MD 20706 US
(301) 306-1111, *Fax:* (301) 306-9540
www.myspiritdc.com
info@1340wycb.com
License: Washington, DC held by Radio One Licenses LLC.
Group Owner: Radio One Inc.; (acq 11-8-01; grpsl).
Nat'l Network: American Urban
Arbitron Metro Market: Washington, DC *Format:* Gospel
Cathy Hughes, Chairman
Alfred Liggins, CEO
Alfred Liggins, President
Chris Wegman, General Manager
Karen Jackson, General Sales Mgr
Sheila Stewart, News Director
Scott Tanner, Chief Engineer
Scott Royster, CFO

Florida

Alachua

WNDT
01-01-1996; 92.5 mhz FM *Hrs Open:* 24; 3.2 kw; 443 ft.; N29 44 22 W82 23 9 *Rebroadcasts:* Rebroadcasts WNDD(FM) Silver Springs 100%
3602 NE20th Place, Ocala, FL 32670 US
(352) 373-6644, *Fax:* (352) 375-1700
www.windfm.com
rkassi@windwogksales.com
License: Alachua, Alachua County, FL held by Ocala Broadcasting Corp. L.L.C.
Group Owner: Wooster Republican Printing Co.; (acq 10-22-97; $675,000 for stock)
Nat'l Reps: Katz Radio
Arbitron Metro Market: Gainesville, FL *Format:* Light Rock *Target Audience:* Adults; 25-54 *Adv. Rates:* 55; 70; 60; 25
Jim Robertson, Operations Dir
Robert Kassi, General Sales Mgr
Kevin Davis, Programming Director
Cheree Carr, News Director

Altamonte Springs

WORL
01-01-1986; 660 khz AM
1601 Belvedere Rd., 204 E, West Palm Beach, FL 33406 US
(407) 682-9494, *Fax:* (407) 682-7005
www.worl660.com
License: Altamonte Springs, FL held by Salem Media of Illinois LLC.
Group Owner: Salem Communications Corp.; (acq 2-3-2006; swap in exchange for KNIT(AM) Dallas, TX)
Nat'l Reps: Salem
Arbitron Metro Market: Orlando, FL *TV Affiliate:* Talk *No. News Employees:* 35-64; adult, male
CEO, CEO/COO
General Manager, General Manager
General Sales Manager, General Sales Mgr
Promotions Director, Promotions Manager

Apalachicola

WOYS
07-01-1988; 100.5 mhz FM *Hrs Open:* 24; 12 kw; Ant 476 ft; N29 43 57 W84 53 24
Point Mall 35 Island Dr. #16, Eastpoint, FL 32328
(850) 670-8450, *Fax:* (850) 670-8492
www.oysterradio.com
manager@oysterradio.com
License: Apalachicola, Franklin County, FL held by Oyster Radio Inc.
No. News Employees: 1 *Target Audience:* General.
Bonnie Gomes, Chairman
Bonnie Gomes, CEO/COO
Bonnie Gomes, President
Michael Allen, Operations Dir
Michael Allen, General Manager
Michael Allen, Station Manager
Bonnie Gomes, General Sales Mgr

WFCT
11-01-1997; 105.5 mhz FM *Hrs Open:* 24; 50 kw; 315 ft.; N29 45 2 W84 52 18
4500 Illinois, Midland, TX 79703 US
(850) 227-9048, *Fax:* (850) 227-1101
wfct@gtcom.net
License: Apalachicola, Franklin County, FL held by Williams Communications Inc.
Group Owner: Williams Communications Inc.; acq 3-27-02; $650,000).
Arbitron Metro Market: Apalachicola, FL *Format:* Adult Contemp
John Nichols, General Manager
Ken Carey, News Director

Arcadia

WFLN
09-03-1955; 1480 khz AM *Hrs Open:* 24; 1 kw-D, ND1; 0.131 kw-N, ND1; N27 13 43 W81 51 28
300 Kilispie Drive, Punta Gorda, FL 33950 US
(863) 993-1480, *Fax:* (863) 499-1489
www.wflnradio.com
wflnradio@aol.com
License: Arcadia, FL held by Integrity Radio of Florida LLC.
Nat'l Network: CBS Radio; CNN Radio *Regional Network:* Florida's Radio Networks
Arbitron Metro Market: Arcadia, FL *Format:* News, News/Talk, 86 *Target Audience:* 25-65; upscale adults
George S Kalman, President/General Manager
Rosemarie Carlucci, General Sales Mgr
Jack Welch, Programming Director
Phill Scott, Engineer
Kayo Keen, On Air Personality/Sales
Yerica Toscano, Office Manager

Atlantic Beach

WFYV-FM
03-10-1980; 104.5 mhz FM *Hrs Open:* 24; 99 kw; 1014 ft.; N30 16 34 W81 33 53
600 Congress Avenue, Suite 1400, Austin, TX 78701 US
(904) 245-8500, *Fax:* (904) 245-8501
www.rock105i.com
todd.shannon@coxinc.com
License: Atlantic Beach, Duval County, FL held by Cox Radio Inc.
Group Owner: Cox Radio Inc.; (acq 2000; grpsl)
Nat'l Network: Fox News Radio *Nat'l Reps:* Katz Radio
Arbitron Metro Market: Jacksonville, FL *Format:* Classic Rock *Target Audience:* 18-49; male oriented
Bill Hendrich, General Manager
Jenny Sutton, General Sales Mgr
Andy Meyer, Programming Director
Beth Gettys, Promotions Manager
Jodi Rainey, National Sales Manager
Beth Gettys, Promotions and Marketing Director

WZNZ
08-01-1942; 1600 khz AM
Post Office Box 51585, Jacksonville Beach, FL 32240 US
(904) 241-3311, *Fax:* (904) 241-1402
www.qopradio.com
queenofpeaceradio @ yahoo .com
License: Atlantic Beach, FL held by Queen of Peace Radio Inc.
Nat'l Network: EWTN Radio
Arbitron Metro Market: Jacksonville, FL *Format:* Christian *Special Programming:* 2 days - The 2012 Fall Sharethon *Target Audience:* 25-54.
Tom Moran, General Manager

Auburndale

WTWB
10-10-1956; 1570 khz AM *Hrs Open:* 24; 5 kw-D, ND1; 0.013 kw-N, ND1; N28 4 32 W81 49 19
205 S. Hoover St., #400, Tampa, FL 33609 US
(863) 967-1570, *Fax:* (206) 350-6874
www.laraza1570.com
laraza1570@gmail.com
License: Auburndale, FL held by La Raza Media Group LLC
Arbitron Metro Market: Auburndale, FL *Format:* Christian, News, 62, Talk *Hrs. of News Programming:* news progmg 13 hrs wkly
No. News Employees: 1 *Target Audience:* 30 plus; middle income, 2-income family *Adv.Rates:* 15; 20; 20; 15
Lynne Breidenbach, General Manager
Justin Sargent, Programming Director

Avon Park

WFHT
10-01-1970; 1390 khz AM *Hrs Open:* 6 AM-10 PM
1020 North Church Avenue, Mulberry, FL 33860 US
(970) 356-1452, *Fax:* (719) 562-0947
www.tigrecolorado.com
krye104.9@hotmail.com
License: Avon Park, FL held by Odyssey Broadcasting Co. Inc.
Nat'l Network: Jones Radio Networks
Arbitron Metro Market: Olney Springs, CO
Ricardo Salazar, General Manager

WWOJ
08-01-1982; 99.1 mhz FM *Hrs Open:* 24; 10 kw; 515 ft.; N27 30 39 W81 31 54
Peter L. Coughlin, 3750 Usn Hwy., Ste. 1, Sebring, FL 33870 US
(863) 382-9999, *Fax:* (863) 382-1982
www.cohanradiogroup.com
cohanradiogroup@htn.net
License: Avon Park, Highlands County, FL held by Cohan Radio Group Inc.
Group Owner: Cohan Radio Group Inc.; acq 11-1-98; $910,000 with WWTK(AM) Lake Placid)
Nat'l Network: ABC *Regional Network:* Florida's Radio Networks
Nat'l Reps: Interep *Wire Services:* AP
Arbitron Metro Market: Sebring, FL *Format:* Country *Special Programming:* Bluegrass 2 hrs wkly *Hrs. of News Programming:* news progmg 7 hrs wkly *No. News Employees:* 1 *Target Audience:* 18 plus.
Peter Coughlin, President & General Manager
Rob Ellis, Programming Director

Baker

*WTJT
05-01-1987; 90.1 mhz FM *Hrs Open:* 24; 50 kw; 417 ft.; N30 49 19 W86 42 37
Rt 2, Box 204, Baker, FL 32531 US
(850) 537-2009, *Fax:* (850) 537-4663
www.wtjt901fm.com
wtjtradio@yahoo.com
License: Baker, Okaloosa County, FL held by Okaloosa Public Radio Inc.
Nat'l Network: USA
Arbitron Metro Market: Fort Walton Beach, FL *Format:* Christian, Gospel, 86 *Target Audience:* 45 plus.
Earl Thompson, President
Jessica Walker, Station Manager
Ruth Thompson, Programming Director
Randy Henry, Chief Engineer

Baldwin

WJGM(FM)
07-30-1992; 105.7 mhz FM; 25 kw; Ant 328 ft; N30 22 28 W82 01 42
9090 Hogan Rd., Suite B, Jacksonville, FL 32216
(904) 425-3482
www.whjx.biz
License: Baldwin, Duval County, FL held by Tama Radio Licenses of Jacksonville, FL, Inc.
Group Owner: Tama Broadcasting Inc.; (acq 12-2-2001; $1.5 million)
Population Served: 827,908 *Arbitron Metro Market:* Jacksonville, FL *Format:* Talk
Andy Johnson, General Manager

Bartow

WQXM
09-28-1953; 1460 khz AM *Hrs Open:* 24 hrs.; 1 kw-D, ND1; 0.155 kw-N, ND1; N27 54 34 W81 51 29
P.O. Box 820, Bartow, FL 33831 US
(360) 330-0777, *Fax:* (360) 736-0150
www.kmnt.com
License: Bartow, FL held by Florida Broadcasting Media LLC
Arbitron Metro Market: Chehalis WA *Format:* Country *Special Programming:* NFL Football *Hrs. of News Programming:* 60 minutes weekly *No. News Employees:* 1 *Adv. Rates:* 32
John DiMeo Jr., General Manager

WWBF
09-16-1969; 1130 khz AM *Hrs Open:* 24; 2.5 kw-D, DAN; 0.5 kw-N, DAN; N27 54 31 W81 49 33
1130 Radio Road, Bartow, FL 33830 US
(863) 533-0744, *Fax:* (863) 533-8546
www.wwbf.com
tom@wwbf.com
License: Bartow, FL held by Thornburg Communications Inc.
Nat'l Network: CNN Radio *Regional Network:* Florida's Radio Networks
Arbitron Metro Market: Bartow, FL *Format:* Oldies *Special Programming:* Sports *Hrs. of News Programming:* news progmg 10 hrs wkly *No. News Employees:* 1 *Target Audience:* 35-54; affluent adults
Thomas Thornburg, President
Jeffrey Thornburg, Operations Dir
Susan Thornburg, Station Manager

Belle Glade

WBGF
05-31-1965; 93.5 mhz FM; 15.5 kw; 419 ft.; N26 41 0 W80 43 39
Mailing Address: P.O. Box 1505, Belle Glade, FL 33430 US
Second Address: 2001 State Rd. 715, Belle Glade, FL 33430
(561) 996-2063, *Fax:* (561) 996-1852
www.lobo935.com/
jjorgeavina@aol.com
License: Belle Glade, Palm Beach County, FL held by BGI Broadcasting LP.
Nat'l Network: ABC *Regional Network:* Florida's Radio Networks
Regional Reps: Interep
Arbitron Metro Market: Belle Glade, FL *Format:* Sports *Special Programming:* Farm 5 hrs wkly *Target Audience:* 25-54.
Mike Diagostine, Programming Director

WSWN
10-07-1947; 900 khz AM; 1 kw-D, ND1; 0.022 kw-N, ND1; N26 42 43 W80 40 59
Mailing Address: PO Box 1505, Belle Glade, FL 33430 US
Second Address: 2001 State Rd. 715, Belle Glade, FL 33430
(561) 996-2063, *Fax:* (561) 996-1852
wswnwbgfa@bellsouth.net
License: Belle Glade, FL held by BGI Inc.

Nat'l Network: ABC; Jones Radio Networks *Regional Network:* Florida's Radio Networks; Southeast AgNet *Nat'l Reps:* Interep *Arbitron Metro Market:* West Palm Beach-Boca Raton, FL *Format:* Gospel, Religious *Special Programming:* Sports *Target Audience:* 25-54.
David Lampel, General Manager
Harvey Poole Jr., Programming Director
Rick Rieke, Chief Engineer

Belleview

*WYFZ
04-01-2001; 91.3 mhz FM *Hrs Open:* 24; 0.9 kw; 318 ft.; N29 10 38 W82 8 42
6883 NE79th Terrace, Wildwood, FL 34785 US
(704) 523-5555, *Fax:* (704) 522-1967
bbnradio.org
License: Belleview, Marion County, FL held by Bible Broadcasting Network Inc.
Group Owner: Bible Broadcasting Network; (acq 12-1-2005; $250,000)
Arbitron Metro Market: Belleview, FL *Format:* Religious
Lowell Davey, President

Beverly Beach

WBHQ
01-01-1978; 92.7 mhz FM *Hrs Open:* 24; 5.5 kw; 341 ft.; N29 32 7 W81 15 50
50 East Rivercenter Blvd, Suite 1200, Covington, KY 41011 US
(386) 437-1992, *Fax:* (386) 437-8728
www.beach927.com
david@wnzf.com
License: Beverly Beach, Flagler County, FL held by Flagler County Broadcasting LLC
Format: Variety/Diverse
David Ayres, General Manager
Mary Hendley, General Sales Mgr
Marc Gilliland, Programming Director
Ron Charles, News Director
Dave Shy, Underwriting Manager
Mary Gergely, Office Manager
Dr. Dave West, Sports Director

Big Pine Key

WWUS
09-22-1980; 104.1 mhz FM *Hrs Open:* 24; 100 kw horiz, 90.25 kw vert; 453 ft.; N24 39 39.8 W81 25 10.4
1400 Woodbridge Ave, Detroit, MI 48207 US
(305) 872-9100, *Fax:* (305) 872-1603
www.us1radio.com
us1radio@aol.com
License: Big Pine Key, Monroe County, FL held by Vox Communications Group LLC.
Group Owner: Vox Communications; (acq 8-31-2005; grpsl).
Nat'l Network: AP Radio
Arbitron Metro Market: Big Pine Key, FL *Format:* Contemporary Hits/Top 40, Adult Contemp *Special Programming:* Island mus 4 hrs wkly *Hrs. of News Programming:* news progmg 2 hrs wkly *No. News Employees:* 1 *Target Audience:* 30-50. *Adv. Rates:* 25; 25; 25; 25
Kevin LeRoux, General Manager
Race Ashlyn, Station Manager
Mark Humenik, Director of Sales
Erica Bowman, Programming Director
Bill Becker, News Director
Randy Perry, Chief Engineer
Tanya Rossi, Traffic Manager

Bithlo

WNTF
07-31-1974; 1580 khz AM
Network, Inc., P.O. Box 100, Ruskin, FL 33570 US
(407) 291-1395, *Fax:* (407) 293-2870
www.wntf1580.com
License: Bithlo, FL held by Rama Communications Inc.
Group Owner: Rama Communications Inc.; (acq 10-29-2002; $600,000 with WGAF(AM) Alachua)
Arbitron Metro Market: Orlando, FL
Sabita Persaud, President
Steve January, General Manager
Steve De Lay, Chief Engineer

Blountstown

WPHK
12-18-1968; 102.7 mhz FM; 13 kw; 318 ft.; N30 27 15 W85 2 32
269 Kelly Avenue, Blountstown, FL 32424 US
License: Blountstown, Calhoun County, FL held by Blountstown Communications
Format: Country *Special Programming:* Black 12 hrs wkly
Harry Hagen, General Manager

WYBT
09-08-1962; 1000 khz AM
269 Kelly Avenue, Blountstown, FL 32424 US
(850) 674-5101, *Fax:* (850) 674-2965
License: Blountstown, FL held by Blountstown Communications
Arbitron Metro Market: Blountstown, FL *Format:* Oldies *Special Programming:* Gospel & relg 15 hrs wkly
Shelley Shell

Boca Raton

WKIS
10-01-1965; 99.9 mhz FM *Hrs Open:* 24; 100 kw; 984 ft.; N25 59 34 W80 10 27
9881 Sheridan Street, Hollywood, FL 33021 US
(305) 654-1700, *Fax:* (305) 654-1715
www.wkis.com
info@wkis.com
License: Boca Raton, Palm Beach County, FL
Group Owner: Beasley Broadcast Group Inc.
Nat'l Network: Westwood One
Arbitron Metro Market: Miami-Fort Lauderdale-Hollywood, FL *Format:* Country *Hrs. of News Programming:* news progmg 2 hrs wkly *No. News Employees:* 1 *Target Audience:* 25-54.
George Corso, CEO
Joe Bell, Operations Dir
Carole Bowen, General Sales Mgr
Bob Barnett, Programming Director

WSBR
04-01-1965; 740 khz AM; 2.5 kw-D, DA2; 0.94 kw-N, DA2; N26 20 6 W80 15 55
6699 N. Federal Highway, Boca Raton, FL 33487 US
(561) 997-0074, *Fax:* (561) 997-0476
www.wsbradio.com
info@wsbr.com
License: Boca Raton, FL held by WWNN License LLC.
Group Owner: Beasley Broadcast Group Inc.; (acq 3-14-2000; grpsl).
Arbitron Metro Market: West Palm Beach *Format:* Talk
Karen Ruggerie, Operations Dir
Bob Morency, General Manager
Duff Lindsey, Programming Director
Greg Cooper, Operations Manager

Bonifay

WYYX
04-23-1983; 97.7 mhz FM *Hrs Open:* 24; 100 kw; 830 ft.; N30 30 41 W85 29 24
3018 Thompson Lane, Murfreesboro, TN 37129 US
(850) 233-6606, *Fax:* (850) 233-1541
www.wyyx.com
info@wyyx.com
License: Bonifay, Holmes County, FL held by Magic Broadcasting Florida Licensing LLC.
Group Owner: Magic Broadcasting LLC; (acq 9-30-2002; grpsl)
Arbitron Metro Market: Panama City, FL *Format:* Rock/AOR *No. News Employees:* 1 *Target Audience:* 18-49.
Jim Storey, COO
J.P. Ferrell, General Sales Mgr
Karla Melvin, News Director

Bonita Springs

WRXK-FM
09-01-1974; 96.1 mhz FM; 100 kw; 1119 ft.; N26 25 22 W81 37 49
20125 S. Tamiami Trail, Estero, FL 33928 US
(239) 495-2100, *Fax:* (239) 992-8165
www.96krock.com
info@96krock.com
License: Bonita Springs, Lee County, FL held by Beasley Broadcasting of Western Florida Inc.
Group Owner: Beasley Broadcast Group Inc.; (acq 8-12-86).
Nat'l Network: ABC *Nat'l Reps:* Katz Radio
Arbitron Metro Market: Fort Myers-Napl *Format:* Classic Rock *Target Audience:* 18-49.
George Beasley, President
Shane Reilly, Operations Dir
Brad Beasley, General Manager
Robert Hallman, General Sales Mgr
Jeff Hickcox, Promotions Manager

Boynton Beach

WLVJ
01-23-1973; 1040 khz AM *Hrs Open:* 24
3071 Continental Drive, West Palm Beach, FL 33407 US
(954) 315-1515, *Fax:* (954) 315-1555
www.wlvj.com
info@wlvj.com
License: Boynton Beach, FL held by Communicom Co. of Florida L.P.
Group Owner: Communicom Broadcasting LLC; (acq 12-14-2005; grpsl).
Arbitron Metro Market: West Palm Beach-Boca Raton, FL
Format: Religious
Rick Hindes, CFO
Steve Lapa, General Manager

*WRMB
04-15-1979; 89.3 mhz FM *Hrs Open:* 24; 100 kw; 469 ft.; N26 31 4 W80 10 14
820 North, Lasalle Boulevard, Chicago, IL 60610 US
(561) 737-9762, *Fax:* (561) 737-9899
www.wrmb.org
wrmb@moody.edu
License: Boynton Beach, Palm Beach County, FL held by Moody Bible Institute of Chicago.
Group Owner: The Moody Bible Institute of Chicago
Nat'l Network: Moody Wire Services: AP
Format: Religious *No. News Employees:* 1 *Target Audience:* General.
Dr. Paul Nyquist, President
Jennifer Epperson, Station Manager

Bradenton

*WJIS
01-01-1989; 88.1 mhz FM; 100 kw; 397 ft.; N27 7 54 W82 23 39
Post Office Box 7217, Lakeland, FL 33807 US
(941) 753-0401, *Fax:* (941) 753-2963
www.thejoyfm.com
thejoyfm@thejoyfm.com
License: Bradenton, Manatee County, FL held by WJIS FM Radio.
Arbitron Metro Market: Sarasota-Bradenton, FL *Format:* Adult Contemp, Christian
Jeff McFarlane, General Manager
Steve Swanson, Programming Director
Carmen Brown, Promotions Manager
Steve Rieker, Chief Engineer

WWPR
01-01-1946; 1490 khz AM *Hrs Open:* 24
670 Ridge Pike, Lafayette Hill, PA 19444 US
(941) 761-8843, *Fax:* (941) 761-8683
www.1490wwpr.com
manager@1490wwpr.com
License: Bradenton, FL held by Greenrose Broadcasting Services Inc.
Nat'l Network: Talk Radio Network
Arbitron Metro Market: Tampa, FL *Format:* Talk *Special Programming:* Community talk15 hrs, relg 6 hrs, gospel 6 hrs, sp *Hrs. of News Programming:* news progmg 15 hrs wkly *No. News Employees:* 1 *TargetAudience:* 35-64; general *Adv. Rates:* 40; 30; 40; 20
Valerie Silver, General Manager

Brandon

WLCC
02-01-1988; 760 khz AM
8121 Georgia Ave., 10th, Silver Spring, MD 20910 US
(813) 871-1819, *Fax:* (813) 871-1155
www.laleytampa.com
License: Brandon, FL held by Minority Media and Telecommunications Council Inc.
Arbitron Metro Market: Tampa-St. Petersburg-Clearwater, FL *Target Audience:* 25-54.
Angela Cotto, CFO
Rafael Grullon, President

Brooksville

WWJB
10-11-1958; 1450 khz AM *Hrs Open:* 24
Mailing Address: P.O. Box 1507, Brooksville, FL 34605 US
Second Address: 55 W. Fort Dade Ave., Brooksville, FL 34605-1507
(352) 796-7469, *Fax:* (352) 796-5074
www.wwjb.com
info@wwjb.com
License: Brooksville, FL held by Hernando Broadcasting Co.
Nat'l Network: Westwood One; ABC *Regional Network:* Florida's Radio Networks *Nat'l Reps:* Dora-Clayton
Arbitron Metro Market: Tampa, FL *Format:* News, News/Talk, 84, Talk *No. News Employees:* 1 *Target Audience:* 25 plus.
Steve Manuel, President
Bill Willamson, General Sales Mgr

Peggy Hope, Promotions Manager
Bob Haa, News Director

Bunnell

WNZF

01-01-2008; 1550 khz AM *Hrs Open:* 24
US
(386) 437-1992
wnzf.com
newsradio@wnzf.com
License: Bunnell, FL held by Flagler County Broadcasting LLC
Nat'l Network: Fox Sports
Format: News, News/Talk, 86
David Ayers, General Manager
Ron Charles, News Director

Bushnell

WKFL

01-01-1987; 1170 khz AM *Hrs Open:* 6 AM-9 PM varies by season; 1 kw-D, NDD; N28 42 31 W82 7 36
P.O. Box 1000, Bushnell, FL 33513 US
(352) 568-3204, *Fax:* (407) 322-0431
www.talknsports.net
License: Bushnell, FL held by TalknSports Inc.
Nat'l Network: Salem Radio Network
Format: News, News/Talk, 84, Talk *Hrs. of News Programming:* news progmg 8 hrs wkly *No. News Employees:* 1 *Target Audience:* 18-54; those who enjoy family progmg *Adv. Rates:* 14; 13; 14; 13
Bruce Cox, President
Jan Hall, General Manager

Callahan

WEWC

01-01-1999; 1160 khz AM; 5 kw-D, DAD; 0.25 kw-N, DAD; N30 22 28 W81 44 28
9373 West Sample Road, Coral Springs, FL 33065 US
(904) 549-2218, *Fax:* (904) 359-0070
www.1160latinohits.com
License: Callahan, FL held by Norsan Consulting and Management Inc.
Group Owner: Norsan Consulting and Management Inc.; (acq 9-25-2007; $650,000)
Arbitron Metro Market: Callahan, FL
George Lopez, General Manager

WJBT

06-01-1983; 93.3 mhz FM *Hrs Open:* 24; kw
200 Concord Plaza, Suite 600, San Antonio, TX 78216 US
(904) 636-0507, *Fax:* (904) 997-7713
www.wjbt.com
rhondagroff@clearchannel.com
License: Callahan, Nassau County, FL held by Clear Channel Radio Licenses Inc.
Group Owner: Clear Channel Communications Inc.; (acq 11-21-97; grpsl)
Arbitron Metro Market: Jacksonville, FL *Format:* Urban Contemporary *Target Audience:* 12-54; the young & young-at-heart
Gail Austin, Operations Dir
Norm Feuer, General Manager
Chad Chumley, Programming Director

Callaway

WAKT-FM

02-01-1990; 103.5 mhz FM *Hrs Open:* 24; 100 kw; 423 ft.; N30 10 51 W85 29 45
Two Bala Plaza, Suite 801, Bala-Cynwyd, PA 19004 US
(850) 234-8858, *Fax:* (850) 234-6592
www.1035hankfm.com
MelissaMiller@PanamaCityRadio.com
License: Callaway, Bay County, FL held by Double O Radio Corp.
Group Owner: Double O Radio L.L.C.; acq 3-10-2004; grpsl).
Nat'l Reps: Christal
Arbitron Metro Market: Panama City, FL *Format:* Country *Adv. Rates:* 50; 40; 40; 25
Harry Finch, General Manager
Melissa Miller, Programming Director

WKNK(FM)

103.5 mhz FM; 100,000 watts; 129 meters; 30 10 51N 85 29 45W
Two Bala Plaza, Suite 801, Bala Cynwyd, PA 19004 USA
(270) 432-0847, *Fax:* (270) 432-7601
License: Callaway, Bay County, FL
Group Owner: Powell Briadcasting Company LLC

Cantonment

WNVY

12-01-1955; 1070 khz AM
2070 N Palafox, Pensacola, FL 32501 US
(850) 435-1115
http://www.wilkinsradio.com/
License: Cantonment, FL held by Pensacola Radio Corp.
Group Owner: Wilkins Communications Network Inc.; (acq 11-30-2006; $430,000)
Arbitron Metro Market: Pensacola, FL *TV Affiliate:* Relg
CEO, Mitchell Mathis
Operations Director, Operations Dir
Station Manager, Station Manager

Cape Coral

WXKB

01-01-1975; 103.9 mhz FM; 100 kw; 1119 ft.; N26 25 22 W81 37 49
20125 Tamiami Trail, Estero, FL 33928 US
(239) 495-2100, *Fax:* (239) 992-8165
www.b1039.com
info@bbgi.com
License: Cape Coral, Lee County, FL held by Beasley Broadcasting.
Group Owner: Beasley Broadcast Group Inc.; (acq 11-18-94; $3.7 million;
Arbitron Metro Market: Fort Myers, FL *Format:* Contemporary Hits/Top 40 *Target Audience:* General.
George Beasley, President
Shane Reilly, Operations Dir
Brad Beasley, General Manager
Robert Halls, Sales Director
Matt Johnson, Programming Director
Jeff Hickcox, Promotions Manager
AJ Lurie, National Sales Manager
DianaBeasley, Webmaster
Dawn Krause, Business Manager

Carrabelle

WOCY

01-01-1999; 106.5 mhz FM; 100 kw; 482 ft.; N29 43 57 W84 53 24
Unit 16, 35 Island Drive, Eastpoint, FL 32328 US
(850) 670-8450, *Fax:* (850) 670-8492
http://www.hitz106fm.com/
manager@oysterradio.com
License: Carrabelle, Franklin County, FL held by Oyster Radio Inc.
Regional Network: Florida's Radio Networks
TV Affiliate: Top 40
Program Director, Jason Harrop
Promotions Director, Promotions Manager

Cedar Creek

*WKSG

01-01-1999; 89.5 mhz FM; 22 kw; 375 ft.; N29 11 16 W81 52 55
1403 Indian River Ave., Titusville, FL 32780 US
(352) 369-8950, *Fax:* (352) 369-1109
www.daystarradio.com
daystar@ocalapro.com
License: Cedar Creek, Marion County, FL held by Daystar Public Radio Inc.
Format: Adult Contemp, Christian
Gary Linkus, General Manager

Cedar Key

WRGO

09-01-1996; 102.7 mhz FM *Hrs Open:* 24; 12.5 kw; 459 ft.; N29 11 45 W82 59 46
3131 Bermuda Dunes Dr, Lecanto, FL 34461 US
(352) 795-1027, *Fax:* (352) 795-0002
License: Cedar Key, Levy County, FL held by WRGO Radio LLC.
Nat'l Network: Jones Radio Networks
Format: Oldies *Target Audience:* 25-64. *Adv. Rates:* 24; 20; 24; 18
Lou Cerra, General Manager

Century

WPFL

07-01-1989; 105.1 mhz FM; 8.6 kw; 558 ft.; N31 7 9 W87 16 5
Mailing Address: P.O. Box 1203, Century, FL 32535 US
Second Address: 2059 Old Fannie Rd., Flomaton, AL 36441
(251) 296-1051, *Fax:* (251) 296-1055
www.oldiesradioonline.com
wpflradio@bellsouth.net
License: Century, Escambia County, FL held by Tri-County Broadcasting Inc.
Arbitron Metro Market: Pensacola, FL *Format:* Oldies
Ronnie Hammond, General Manager
Howard Macht, Chief Engineer

Charlotte Harbor

WIKX

09-01-1970; 92.9 mhz FM *Hrs Open:* 24; 100 kw; 807 ft.; N26 53 47 W82 14 27
50 East Rivercenter Boulevard, #1200, Covington, KY 41011 US
(941) 206-1188, *Fax:* (941) 206-9296
www.wikx.com
kixcountry@hotmail.com
License: Charlotte Harbor, Charlotte County, FL
Format: Country *Hrs. of News Programming:* News progmg 10 hrs wkly *Target Audience:* 25-54.
Richard Jenkins, President

Chattahoochee

WTCL

11-01-1963; 1580 khz AM; 10 kw-D, NDD; N30 40 14 W84 50 8
5004 - 27th Ave, Rockford, IL 61125 US
(850) 663-3857, *Fax:* (850) 663-8543
info@wtcl.com
License: Chattahoochee, FL held by Metz Inc.
Nat'l Network: USA *Regional Network:* Florida's Radio Networks
Arbitron Metro Market: Chattahoochee, FL *Format:* Gospel
Target Audience: General.
Don Metz, President
David Garcia, General Manager

Chiefland

WLQH

06-06-1968; 940 khz AM *Hrs Open:* Sunrise-sunset
P.O. Box 99, Chiefland, FL 32626 US
(352) 498-0304, *Fax:* (352) 493-9909
www.suncoastradio.com
john@suncoastradio.com
License: Chiefland, FL held by Ocala Broadcasting Corp.
Format: Contemporary Hits/Top 40 *Special Programming:* Relg 9 hrs wkly
Bob Moody, Station Manager

WNDN

01-01-1991; 107.9 mhz FM *Hrs Open:* 6 AM-midnight; 6 kw; 328 ft.; N29 30 54.9 W82 53 5
P.O. Box 99, Chiefland, FL 32626 US
(352) 493-4940, *Fax:* (352) 493-9909
www.windfm.com
hunter@windfm.com
License: Chiefland, Levy County, FL held by Ocala Broadcasting Corp.
Nat'l Network: Jones Radio Networks
Format: Rock/AOR
Robert McLimans, Operations Dir
Bob Kassi, General Sales Mgr
Rick Small, Operations Director
Emily Carey, Business Manager
Cheree Carr, Traffic

Chipley

WBGC

04-10-1956; 1240 khz AM; 1 kw-U, ND1; N30 46 19 W85 33 31
1513 South Blvd, Chipley, FL 32428 US
(850) 638-0234, *Fax:* (850) 638-4333
License: Chipley, FL held by Jacquelyn Collier Pembroke
Regional Network: Florida's Radio Networks *Nat'l Reps:* Keystone (unwired net)
Arbitron Metro Market: Chipley,FL *Format:* Variety/Diverse
Todd Burnett, General Manager

Clearwater

WBTP

08-19-1963; 95.7 mhz FM *Hrs Open:* 24; 100 kw; 607 ft.; N27 52 0 W82 37 27
200 Concord Plaza, Suite 600, San Antonio, TX 78216 US
(813) 832-1000, *Fax:* (813) 832-1090
www.957thebeat.com
License: Clearwater, Pinellas County, FL held by Clear Channel Broadcasting Licenses Inc.
Group Owner: Clear Channel Communications Inc.; (acq 10-94).
Nat'l Reps: Katz Radio *Wire Services:* AP
Arbitron Metro Market: Tampa-St. Petersburg-Clearwater, FL
Format: Adult Contemp *Target Audience:* 18-49; upwardly mobile adults

Russell Link, CFO
Dan DiLoreto, Operations Dir
Ron Shepard, Programming Director
Misty Pittman, News Director
John McMartin, Engineering Dir
Doug Hammond, Operations Manager

WTAN
06-01-1948; 1340 khz AM *Hrs Open:* 24
2360 N.E. Coachman Road, Clearwater, FL 33765 US
(727) 441-3311, *Fax:* (727) 441-1300
www.tantalk1340.com
lola@tantalk.net
License: Clearwater, FL held by Wagenvoord Advertising Group Inc.
Group Owner: Wagenvoord Advertising Group Inc.; acq 12-29-99; $100,000).
Arbitron Metro Market: Tampa-St. Petersburg-Clearwater, FL *Format:* News, Talk *Special Programming:* Big band 40 hrs wkly *Hrs. of News Programming:* news progmg 12 hrs wkly *No. News Employees:* 2 *TargetAudience:* 35-64.
Dave Wagenvoord, CEO
Lola Wagenvoord, General Manager

WXTB
12-01-1967; 97.9 mhz FM *Hrs Open:* 24; 100 kw; 1503 ft.; N28 10 56 W82 46 6
50 East Rivercenter Blvd, Suite 1200, Covington, KY 41011 US
(813) 832-1000, *Fax:* (813) 831-9898
www.98rock.com
doubledown@clearchannel.com
License: Clearwater, Pinellas County, FL held by Citicasters Licenses L.P.
Group Owner: Clear Channel Communications Inc.; (acq 5-6-99; grpsl).
Nat'l Network: Premiere Radio Networks *Nat'l Reps:* Katz Radio
Wire Services: AP
Arbitron Metro Market: Tampa-St. Peter, FL *Special Programming:* Pub affrs 4 hrs wkly *Hrs. of News Programming:* news progmg 2 hrs wkly *No. News Employees:* 1 *Target Audience:* 18-49; men
Russell Link, CFO
Daniel DiLoreto, Operations Dir
Jason Fulmino, General Sales Mgr
James Howard, Programming Director
Kim Cusmano, Promotions Manager
Anqunette Wilson, News Director
John McMartin, Engineering Dir
Norm,Prodution Director
Ethan Youker, Public Services Director
Rachel Pitts, Internship Director

Clermont

***WMYZ**
07-18-1997; 88.7 mhz FM *Hrs Open:* 24; 1.2 kw; 350 ft.; N28 38 56 W81 44 9 *Rebroadcasts:* Rebroadcasts WPOZ(FM) Union Park 100%
P. O. Box 980, Quebradillas, PR 0678 US
(407) 869-8000, *Fax:* (407) 869-0380
www.zradio.org
zcrew@zradio.org
License: Clermont, Lake County, FL held by Central Florida Educational Foundation Inc.
Format: Christian
James Hoge, President

WWFL
01-01-1962; 1340 khz AM *Hrs Open:* 24; 1 kw-U, ND1; N28 34 59 W81 42 19
5601 Windover Drive, Orland0, FL 32819 US
(407) 351-3350, *Fax:* (407) 370-3524
www.cflradio.net
License: Clermont, FL held by Central Florida Investments Inc.
Arbitron Metro Market: Clermont, FL *Format:* Adult Contemp
David Siegal, President

Clewiston

WAFC
02-16-1988; 590 khz AM *Hrs Open:* 24; 0.93 kw-D, ND1; 0.47 kw-N, ND1; N26 43 46 W80 54 49
530 East Alverdez Ave., Clewiston, FL 33440 US
(863) 983-5900, *Fax:* (863) 983-6109
www.wafcfm.com
RADIOFIESTA1061@WAFCFM.COM
License: Clewiston, FL held by Glades Media Company LLP
Nat'l Reps: Interep
Arbitron Metro Market: West Palm Beach-Boca Raton, FL *Hrs. of News Programming:* News progmg 10 hrs wkly *Target Audience:* General. *Adv. Rates:* 20; 20; 20; 18
Robert Castellanos, CEO
KC Kelly, General Manager
Larry Parrish, General Sales Mgr
Jesus Castro, Programming Director
Debbie Pattison, News Director
Jim Johnson, CFO

***WJCB**
88.5 mhz FM; 3 kw; 292 ft.; N26 43 46 W80 54 49
1150 West King Street, Cocoa, FL 32922 US
(321) 632-1000, *Fax:* (321) 636-0000
www.wjfp.com/site/page.php?pid=home
info@wjfp.com
License: Clewiston, Hendry County, FL held by Black Media Works Inc.
Group Owner: Black Media Works Inc.
Arbitron Metro Market: West Palm Beach, FL *Format:* Gospel
Ray Kassis, General Manager

***WPSF**
01-01-2008; 91.5 mhz FM; 0.7 kw vert; 387 ft.; N26 41 27 W80 47 18
1601 Belvedere Rd, 204 E, W Palm Beach, FL 33406 US
(786) 429-3606, *Fax:* (305) 251-2293
www.callfm.com
rob@callfm.com
License: Clewiston, Hendry County, FL held by American Educational Broadcasting Inc.
Arbitron Metro Market: Clewiston, FL *Format:* Christian
Tim Pappas, Chairman
Rob Robbins, Ph.D., President
Rob Robbins, General Manager
Rob Robbins, Ph.D., Programming Director

Cocoa

***WMIE-FM**
12-01-1984; 91.5 mhz FM *Hrs Open:* 24; 20 kw horiz, 19 kw vert; 98 ft.; N28 21 21 W80 44 47
1150 West King Street, Cocoa, FL 32922 US
(321) 632-1000, *Fax:* (321) 636-0000
www.wjfp.com
info@wjfp.com
License: Cocoa, Brevard County, FL held by National Christian Network.
Arbitron Metro Market: Melbourne, FL *Format:* Urban Contemporary *Target Audience:* 18-49.
Raymond Kassis, President
Paul Esposito, General Manager
Jim Conn, Programming Director
Jan Ferguson, Chief Engineer

WMMV
10-04-1957; 1350 khz AM; 1 kw-D, DAN; 1 kw-N, DAN; N28 21 58 W80 45 8
600 Congress Ave., Suite 1400, Austin, TX 78701 US
(321) 733-1000, *Fax:* (321) 733-0904
www.wmmvdm.com
billmick@clearchannel.com
License: Cocoa, FL held by Capstar TX L.P.
Group Owner: Clear Channel Communications Inc.; (acq 8-30-00; grpsl).
Nat'l Network: ABC; Westwood One *Regional Network:* Florida's Radio Networks
Arbitron Metro Market: Melbourne, FL *Format:* News, News/Talk, 86 *Target Audience:* General
Ken Holiday, Operations Dir
Barbara Latham, General Manager
Bill Mick, Programming Director

WWBC
07-01-1965; 1510 khz AM *Hrs Open:* Sunrise-sunset
1150 West King Street, Cocoa, FL 32922 US
(321) 632-1000, *Fax:* (321) 636-0000
www.wmiefm.com
josh@ncnradio.com
License: Cocoa, FL held by Astro Enterprises.
Arbitron Metro Market: Cocoa, FL *Format:* Gospel, Talk, 74
Target Audience: 25 plus.
Ray Kassis, President
Paul Esposito, General Manager

Cocoa Beach

WJRR
07-19-1962; 101.1 mhz FM; 95 kw; 1598 ft.; N28 34 51 W81 4 32
200 Concord Plaza, Suite 600, San Antonio, TX 78216 US
(407) 916-7800, *Fax:* (407) 916-7407
www.realrock1011.com
info@realrock1011.com
License: Cocoa Beach, Brevard County, FL held by Clear Channel Broadcasting Licenses Inc.
Group Owner: Clear Channel Communications Inc.; (acq 1-27-2009; with KYRK(FM) Houma, LA)
Arbitron Metro Market: Orlando, FL *Format:* Rock/AOR *Target Audience:* 18-34; men *Adv. Rates:* 200.;180.,225.,50.
Linda Byrd, General Manager
Aaron Miller, General Sales Mgr
Chris Kampmeier, Programming Director
Rick Everett, Promotions Manager
Pat Lynch, Programming Director
Josh Egolf, Promotions Manager

WTKS-FM
05-08-1962; 104.1 mhz FM *Hrs Open:* 24; 94 kw; 1598 ft.; N28 34 51 W81 4 32
200 Concord Plaza, Suite 600, San Antonio, TX 78216 US
(407) 916-7800, *Fax:* (407) 916-7511
www.wtks.com
ProgramDirector@wtks.com
License: Cocoa Beach, Brevard County, FL held by Clear Channel Broadcasting Licenses Inc.
Group Owner: Clear Channel Communications Inc.; (acq 11-21-97; grpsl).
Nat'l Network: Premiere Radio Networks *Nat'l Reps:* Clear Channel
Arbitron Metro Market: Orlando, FL *Format:* Talk *Target Audience:* Adults; 25-54 *Adv. Rates:* 300; 250; 450; 100
Linda Byrd, General Manager
Pam Volkman, General Sales Mgr
Katherine Brown, Programming Director
Rick Everett, Promotions Manager
Ed Kennedy, General Sales Manager
Rick Everett, Marketing
Frank Celebre, National Sales Manager
Chris Kampmeier, Programming Director
Erika Plak, Promotions Manager
Dan Stone, APD

WMEL
06-22-1959; 1300 khz AM *Hrs Open:* 24; 5 kw-D, DA2; 1 kw-N, DA2; N28 20 38 W80 46 6
8263 Conroy Windmere Rd, Orlando, FL 32801 US
(321) 631-1300, *Fax:* (321) 631-9113
www.1300wmel.com
wmelradiojohn@gmail.com
License: Cocoa Beach, FL held by Rama Communications Inc.
Group Owner: Rama Communications Inc.; (acq 10-13-93; $950,000 with WLAA(AM) Winter Garden;
Nat'l Network: ABC; Talk Radio Network
Arbitron Metro Market: Cocoa Beach, FL *Format:* News, News/Talk, 84, Talk *Hrs. of News Programming:* news progmg 144 hrs wky *No. News Employees:* 2 *Target Audience:* 35-64; decision making men & women
John Harper, President

Columbia City

WJTK
01-01-2006; 96.5 mhz FM; 5 kw; 359 ft.; N30 9 20 W82 38 14 US
(386) 758-9696, *Fax:* (386) 269-4361
www.northfloridanow.com
cest@965wjtkfm.com
License: Columbia City, Columbia County, FL held by ABC Media Inc.
Arbitron Metro Market: Columbia City, FL *Format:* News, News/Talk, 86
Cesta Newman, President

Coral Cove

WSRZ-FM
03-25-1995; 107.9 mhz FM *Hrs Open:* 24; 47 kw; 509 ft.; N27 9 3 W82 27 51
50 East Rivercenter Blvd, Suite 1200, Covington, KY 41011 US
(941) 552-4800, *Fax:* (941) 552-4900
www.oldies108.com
info@oldies108.com
License: Coral Cove, Sarasota County, FL held by Citicasters Licenses L.P.
Group Owner: Clear Channel Communications Inc.; (acq 5-4-99; grpsl).
Arbitron Metro Market: Sarasota-Bradenton, FL *Format:* Oldies
Target Audience: 25-54.
Buddy Lee, General Manager

Coral Gables

WHIM
05-04-1964; 1080 khz AM *Hrs Open:* 24
2828 W. Flagler St, Miami, FL 33135 US

(407) 682-9494, *Fax:* (407) 682-7005
www.1520whim.com
whim@salemorlando.com
License: Coral Gables, FL held by Pennsylvania Media Associates Inc.
Group Owner: Salem Communications Corp.; (acq 1-23-2006; $600,000)
Nat'l Network: Salem Radio Network *Nat'l Reps:* Salem
Arbitron Metro Market: Orlando, FL *Format:* Christian, Talk
Target Audience: 35-64.
Edward Atsinger III, President
Dale Forbis, Operations Dir
David Koon, General Manager
John Stolz, General Sales Mgr

WHQT
11-15-1958; 105.1 mhz FM; 98 kw; 1007 ft.; N25 58 2 W80 12 34
2741 N. 29th Ave., Hollywood, FL 33020 US
(305) 444-4404, *Fax:* (954) 847-3240
www.hot105fm.com
pmt@coxradio.com
License: Coral Gables, Dade County, FL held by Cox Radio Inc.
Group Owner: Cox Radio Inc.; (acq 12-28-92;
Nat'l Reps: Christal
Arbitron Metro Market: Miami-Fort Lauderdale-Hollywood, FL *Format:* Adult Contemp *Target Audience:* 18-49.
Jerry Rushin, General Manager
Mumball, General Sales Mgr
Phil Michaels-Trueba, Programming Director
Janine Dupont, Promotions Manager
Missy Bailey, Promotions Manager
Susan Isreal, National Sales Manager
Dian Massa Rattner,Customer Service Director
Jose Pagan, Web Producer
Derick Pitts, Director of Marketing Services

WRHC
01-01-1963; 1550 khz AM *Hrs Open:* 24; 10 kw-D, 500 k-N, DA-2; N25 51 27 W80 28 52
330 S.W. 27th Ave., Suite 207, Miami, FL 33135
(305) 541-3300, *Fax:* (305) 541-7470
www.wrhc.com
anavidal@lapoderosa.com
License: Coral Gables, Dade County, FL held by WRHC Broadcasting Corp.
Nat'l Reps: Lotus Entravision Reps LLC
Population Served: 1,800,000 *Arbitron Metro Market:* Miami-Fort Lauderdale-Hollywood, FL *Hrs. of News Programming:* news progmg 4 hrs wkly *No. News Employees:* 4 *Target Audience:* Central & South Americans
Jorge Rodriguez, President
Ana Vidal Rodriguez, Vice President
Miguel Melanio, Programming Director
Eduardo Aleman, News Director
Eduardo Rodriguez, Chief Engineer

WHIM(AM)
02-18-1949; 1080 khz AM *Hrs Open:* 24; 50 kw-D, 20 kw-N, DA-2; N25 44 53 W80 32 47
2828 W. Flagler St., Miami, FL 33135
(305) 644-0800, *Fax:* (305) 677-7585
www.1080theanswer.com
info@1080theanswer.com
License: Coral Gables, Dade County, FL held by Caron Broadcasting Inc.
Group Owner: Salem Communications Corp.; (acq 4-11-2008; $12.25 million)
Population Served: 408,750 *Arbitron Metro Market:* Miami, FL *Format:* Christian, Religious
Tony Calatayud, General Manager
Jorge Guevara, General Sales Mgr
Mike Hernandez, Promotions Manager
Steve James, Chief Engineer
John Davitt, Traffic Director
Dania Hernandez, Media Specialist

***WVUM**
05-01-1968; 90.5 mhz FM *Hrs Open:* 24; 0.1 kw horiz, 1.3 kw vert; 174 ft.; N25 43 2 W80 16 48
P.O. Box 248127, Coral Gables, FL 33124 US
(305) 284-3131, *Fax:* (305) 284-3132
www.wvum.org
info@wvum.org
License: Coral Gables, Dade County, FL held by WVUM Inc.
Arbitron Metro Market: Coral Gables, FL *Format:* Alternative, Variety/Diverse *Special Programming:* Sports 5 hrs, Black 7 hrs, relg 6 hrs, Sp 2 hrs, o *Hrs. of News Programming:* news progmg 3 hrs wkly *No. NewsEmployees:* 1 *Target Audience:* 13-plus.
Paul Driscoll, Operations Dir
Savanna Stiff, General Manager
Jackson Alexander Parodi, Programming Director

Ashley Gonzalez, Promotions Manager
Ben Hampton, News and Public Affairs Director
Alex Faron, Engineering Dir
ZoeBrown, Digital Music Director
Christopher Lloyd, Office Manager
Giovanna Stallings-Blanche, Music Director
Demetris Antoniou, Training Director

Coral Springs

WFNX
1120 khz AM; 9.5 kw-d; n26 16 54 w80 17 39
94 St Rose Street, Boston, MA
(617) 522-4889
License: Coral Springs, FL held by Langer Bradcasting Group LLC
Group Owner: Langer Broadcasting Group LLC
Alexander Langer, General Manager

Crawfordville

WAKU
01-01-1996; 94.1 mhz FM *Hrs Open:* 24; 3 kw; 459 ft.; N30 4 34 W84 18 5
Mailing Address: P.O. Box 4106, Tallahassee, FL 32315 US
Second Address: 3225 Harstfield Rd., Tallahassee, FL 32303
(850) 926-8000, *Fax:* (850) 562-2730
www.wave94.com
dougapple@wave94.com
License: Crawfordville, Wakulla County, FL held by Altrua Investments International Corp.
Nat'l Network: Salem Radio Network
Arbitron Metro Market: Tallahassee, FL *Format:* Christian *Hrs. of News Programming:* News progmg 10 hrs wkly *Target Audience:* 35-54; Adults *Adv. Rates:* 20; 18; 18; 15
Mike Floyd, CEO
Doug Apple, General Manager

Crestview

WAAZ-FM
07-15-1965; 104.7 mhz FM *Hrs Open:* 5 AM - MIDNIGHT; 100 kw; 486 ft.; N30 46 1 W86 35 7 *Rebroadcasts:* Simulcast with WJSB(AM) Crestview 100%
Mailing Address: P. O. Box 267, Crestview, FL 32536 US
Second Address: 506 W. First Ave., Crestview, FL 32536
(519) 357-1310, *Fax:* (519) 357-1897
www.945thebull.ca
License: Crestview, Okaloosa County, FL held by Crestview Broadcasting Co.
Nat'l Network: CBS Radio
Format: Rock/AOR
John Weese, General Manager

WJSB
1050 khz AM *Hrs Open:* daytime sunrise to sunset; Ant 485 ft*Rebroadcasts:* Simulcast with WAAZ - FM Crestview 100%
Mailing Address: P.O. Box 267, Crestview, FL 32536 US
Second Address: 506 W. FIRST AVE., Crestview, FL 32536
(850) 682-3040, *Fax:* (850) 682-5232
waazwjsb@embarqmail.com
License: Crestview, FL held by Crestview Broadcasting Co.
Nat'l Network: CBS Radio
Arbitron Metro Market: Fort Walton Beach, FL *Format:* Country
Special Programming: ATLANTA BRAVES BASEBALL *No. News Employees:* 1
James T. Whitaker, General Manager
Cal Zethmayer, General Sales Mgr
Claude T. Strickland, Programming Director
Joe Dunn, Announcer
Buddy Shuman, Announcer
Sallie Stapleton, Office Manager
Tim English, Sports Director

Cross City

WZCC
11-01-1985; 1240 khz AM *Hrs Open:* 24; 1 kw-U, ND1; N29 36 35 W83 8 3
P.O. Box 2220, Cross City, FL 32628 US
(352) 498-0304, *Fax:* (352) 795-0002
www.suncoastradio.com
john@suncoastradio.com
License: Cross City, FL held by WRGO Radio LLC
Arbitron Metro Market: Gainesville-Ocala, FL *Format:* Country
Lou Cerra, General Manager

WKZY
11-16-1987; 106.9 mhz FM; 100 kw; 469 ft.; N29 36 29 W82 51 1
P.O. Box 2220, Cross City, FL 32628 US

(352) 313-3150, *Fax:* (352) 313-3166
www.1069kzy.com
kevin.mangan@marcradio.com
License: Cross City, Dixie County, FL held by 6 Johnson Road Licenses Inc.
Group Owner: Pamal Broadcasting Ltd.; (acq 1-5-2007; grpsl)
Arbitron Metro Market: Gainesville-Ocala, FL *Format:* Adult Contemp
Shawn Portmann, General Manager
Jeanie Edwards, General Sales Mgr
Kevin McKay, Programming Director
Alan Ritchie, National Sales Manager

***WWLC**
01-01-2006; 88.5 mhz FM *Hrs Open:* 24; 1,000 w; Ant 193 ft; N29 39 09 W83 10 08
Spirit Radio of North Florida Inc., 500 N.E. 16th Ave., Gainesville, FL
(352) 372-2191, *Fax:* (352) 376-0575
www.sprintradio.org
License: Cross City, Dixie County, FL held by Spirit Radio of North Florida Inc.
Fr. Roland Julien, General Manager

WURB
97.7 mhz FM; 25 kw; 79 meters; N29 44 17 W82 51 26
25 East 86th Street, Apt 13B, New York, NY
(917) 535-0419
License: Cross City, Dixie County, FL held by Alex Media Inc
Group Owner: Alex Media Inc.
Alexander Berger, President

Crystal River

***WAQV**
01-01-1999; 90.9 mhz FM *Hrs Open:* 24; 3.7 kw; 331 ft.; N29 1 54 W82 27 8 *Rebroadcasts:* Rebroadcasts WHIJ(FM) Ocala 100%
4741 S.W. 20th Street, Ocala, FL 34474 US
(800)456-8910, *Fax:* (352) 351-8917
www.thejoyfm.com
thejoyfm@thejoy.com
License: Crystal River, Citrus County, FL held by Radio Training Network Inc.
Arbitron Metro Market: Crystal River, FL *Format:* Adult Contemp, Christian
Jeff MacFarlane, General Manager

WKTK
02-13-1976; 98.5 mhz FM *Hrs Open:* 24; 100 kw; 981 ft.; N29 15 34 W82 34 5
401 City Ave., Suite 409, Bala Cynwyd, PA 19004 US
(352) 377-0985, *Fax:* (352) 377-1884
www.ktk985.com
dickoneil@entercom.com
License: Crystal River, Citrus County, FL held by Entercom Gainesville License LLC.
Group Owner: Entercom Communications Corp.; (acq 11-13-86; $3.6 million;
Arbitron Metro Market: Gainesville-Ocala, FL *Format:* Adult Contemp *Hrs. of News Programming:* news progmg 6 hrs wkly *No. News Employees:* 1 *Target Audience:* 25-54.
Joseph Field, Chairman
David Field, CEO
Dick O'Neil, Operations Dir
Chris Malone, Programming Director

***WHGN**
11-01-1992; 91.9 mhz FM *Hrs Open:* 24; 41 kw horiz, 39.3 kw vert; 541 ft.; N28 50 29 W82 30 21
Mailing Address: 7311 Grover Cleveland, Blvd, Homosassa, FL 34446 US
Second Address: P.O. Box 8889, St. Petersburg, FL 33738
(727) 391-9994, *Fax:* (727) 397-6425
www.moodyradioflorida.fm
wkes@moody.com
License: Crystal River, Citrus County, FL held by The Moody Bible Institute of Chicago
Group Owner: The Moody Bible Institute of Chicago; acq 4-11-03; $500,000).
Arbitron Metro Market: Crystal River, FL *Format:* Christian
Andrew Leuthold, Operations Dir
David Boyer, General Manager
Pierre Chestang, Station Manager
Ron Maxwell, Programming Director
John Stortz, Chief Engineer
Ruth Dinwiddie, Office Assistant
Alicia Gandre, Office Assistant

Cypress Gardens

WHNR
11-29-1958; 1360 khz AM *Hrs Open:* 6 AM-midnight; 5 kw-D, DA2; 2.5 kw-N, DA2; N28 1 16 W81 42 2
1505 Dundee Road, Winter Haven, FL 33884 US
(863) 299-1141, *Fax:* (863) 293-6397
www.whnr1360am.com
info@whnr1360am.com
License: Cypress Gardens, FL held by GB Enterprises Communication Corp.
Regional Network: Florida's Radio Networks
Arbitron Metro Market: Lakeland-Winter Haven, FL *Format:* Urban Contemporary *Special Programming:* Relg 10 hrs wkly *Hrs. of News Programming:* news progmg 20 hrs wkly *No. News Employees:* 1 *Target Audience:* 55 plus.
P.J. Allen, Station Manager

Cypress Quarters

***WREH**
01-01-2004; 90.5 mhz FM; 100 kw horiz, 91.7 kw vert; 249 ft.; N27 20 51 W80 57 4
P. O. Box 637, Bishop, CA 93515 US
(954) 315-4315, *Fax:* (954) 315-4231
www.reachfm.org
License: Cypress Quarters, Okeechobee County, FL held by Reach Communications Inc.
Format: Christian
Carl Mims, General Manager
John Boone, Programming Director

Dade City

WDCF
12-01-1954; 1350 khz AM; 1 kw-D, DAN; 0.5 kw-N, DAN; N28 20 4 W82 11 23
38141 Fifth Avenue, Zephyrhills, FL 33540 US
(727) 441-3311, *Fax:* (727) 441-1300
www.wdcf.tantalknetwork.com
lola@tantalk1340.com
License: Dade City, FL held by Wagenvoord Advertising Group Inc.
Group Owner: Wagenvoord Advertising Group Inc.; acq 2-13-02).
Nat'l Network: ABC *Regional Network:* Florida's Radio Networks
Arbitron Metro Market: Pasco County, Fl *Format:* Religious
Target Audience: 25 plus; basic country demographics
Dave Wagenvoord, President
Lola Wagenvoord, Operations Dir

WTMP-FM
09-03-1993; 96.1 mhz FM *Hrs Open:* 24; 2.8 kw; 482 ft.; N28 28 22 W82 17 45
8121 Georgia Ave 10th Fl, Silver Spring, MD 20910 US
(813) 259-9867, *Fax:* (813) 254-9867
www.wtmp.com
info@tamabroadcasting.com
License: Dade City, Pasco County, FL held by Tama Radio Licenses of Tampa, FL, Inc.
Group Owner: Tama Broadcasting Inc.; (acq 12-21-2001; $4.1 million).
Arbitron Metro Market: Tampa, FL *Format:* Spanish *Target Audience:* 35 plus; general
Glenn Cherry, CEO
Chris McMurray, General Manager
Lynn Tolliver, Programming Director

Davie

WAVS
08-21-1970; 1170 khz AM *Hrs Open:* 24; 5 kw-D, DAN; 0.25 kw-N, DAN; N26 4 39 W80 13 3
6360 Southwest 41st Pl., Davie, FL 33314 US
(601) 883-0848
www.vicksburgv105.com
mark@vicksburgv105.com
License: Davie, FL held by Alliance Broadcasting Inc.
Arbitron Metro Market: Redwood MS *Format:* Oldies
Darrell Chambliss, Chairman
Mark Jones, CEO/COO
Dailon Huskey, Operations Dir
Lina Jones, General Manager
Stephen Donnovan, Engineering Dir

Daytona Beach

WCFB
03-01-1947; 94.5 mhz FM *Hrs Open:* 24; 97.5 kw horiz, 100 kw vert; 1480 ft.; N28 58 47 W81 27 20
1400 Lake Hearn Drive, N.E., Atlanta, GA 30319 US
(321) 281-2000, *Fax:* (407) 290-6631
www.star94fm.com
Tammie.McGrath@coxinc.com
License: Daytona Beach, Volusia County, FL held by Cox Radio Inc.
Group Owner: Cox Radio Inc.; (acq 3-28-97; grpsl)
Arbitron Metro Market: Orlando, FL *Format:* Adult Contemp
Steve Holbrook, Operations Dir
Brian Elam, General Manager
Tammie McGrath, General Sales Mgr
Michael Saunders, Programming Director
Keith Memoly, Promotions Manager

WJHM
11-01-1967; 101.9 mhz FM; 90 kw; 1585 ft.; N28 55 10 W81 19 8
433 E. Las Colina Blvd, #1130, Irving, TX 75039 US
(407) 919-1000, *Fax:* (407) 919-1190
www.102jamzorlando.com
License: Daytona Beach, Volusia County, FL held by Infinity Radio Inc.
Group Owner: CBS Radio; (acq 8-7-00; grpsl).
Nat'l Network: AP Radio
Arbitron Metro Market: Orlando, FL *Format:* Christian *Target Audience:* 18-34.
Earnest James, Operations Dir
James Black, General Sales Mgr
Stevie DeMann, Programming Director
Dawn Campbell, Promotions Director

WMFJ
04-16-1935; 1450 khz AM *Hrs Open:* 24; 1 kw-U, ND1; N29 13 30 W81 1 30
4295 Ridgewood Ave., Port Orange, FL 32127 US
(386) 756-9094, *Fax:* (386) 760-7107
www.cornerstoneministry.org
wjlu@wjlu.org
License: Daytona Beach, FL held by Cornerstone Broadcasting Corp.
Nat'l Network: Moody; USA
Arbitron Metro Market: Daytona Beach, FL *Format:* Religious
Target Audience: General.
Bill Powell, President
William Powell, General Manager
Chris Johnson, Programming Director

WNDB
04-01-1948; 1150 khz AM *Hrs Open:* 24; 1 kw-D, DAN; 1 kw-N, DAN; N29 14 6 W81 4 19
126 West International Speedway Blvd., Daytona Beach, FL 32214 US
(386) 257-1150, *Fax:* (386) 271-0137
www.wndb1150.com
newsdaytonabeach@gmail.com
License: Daytona Beach, FL held by Black Crow LLC.
Group Owner: Black Crow Media Group LLC; (acq 9-21-2001; grpsl).
Nat'l Network: CBS; Motor Racing Net *Wire Services:* UPI
Arbitron Metro Market: Daytona Beach, FL *Format:* News, News/Talk, 84, Talk *Special Programming:* Relg 5 hrs, NASCAR auto racing wkly *No. News Employees:* 2 *Target Audience:* 25-64; general
J. Michael Linn, President
Frank Scott, Operations Dir
Stacey Knerler, General Manager
Mike Moltane, General Sales Mgr
Dave Laing, Programming Director

WROD
01-01-1947; 1340 khz AM *Hrs Open:* 24; 1 kw-U, ND1; N29 11 19 W81 0 28
Mailing Address: 1000 Olde Doubloon Drive, Vero Beach, FL 32963 US
Second Address: 2400 S. Ridgewood Ave., Suite 51, South Daytona, FL 32119
(386) 253-0000, *Fax:* (386) 255-3178
www.wrod.net
production@wrodam.com
License: Daytona Beach, FL held by Volusia Broadcasting Co., LLC
Group Owner: Wilderness Communications LLC; 2008
Nat'l Network: NBC
Arbitron Metro Market: Daytona Beach, FL *Format:* Adult Contemp, Contemporary Hits/Top 40 *Hrs. of News Programming:* news progmg 15 hrs wkly *No. News Employees:* 1 *Target Audience:* 50 plus; adult standards*Adv. Rates:* 30; 30; 30; 30
Joseph Hopkins, President
Lori Bailey, Station Manager

De Funiak Springs

WDSP
03-01-1956; 1280 khz AM *Hrs Open:* 24; 5 kw-D, NDD; 0.046 kw-N, ND1; N30 42 41 W86 6 25
633 S. Second St., P.O. Box 90, Defuniak Springs, FL 32435 US
(850) 951-1280, *Fax:* (850) 951-1282
info@wdsp1280.com
License: De Funiak Springs, FL held by The Sportzmax Inc.
Nat'l Network: ABC
Format: Country *Special Programming:* High School Sports
Target Audience: 25-54. *Adv. Rates:* 10; 7; 10; na
Stephen Riggs III, President
Max Howell, Operations Dir
Arty Goodman, General Manager
Carolyn Mora, General Sales Mgr
Joshua Smith, Sales

WZEP
10-17-1955; 1460 khz AM *Hrs Open:* 24; 10 kw-D, 186 w-N; Single tower unipole; N30 43 45 W86 07 04
Mailing Address: 449 N. 12th St., De Funiak Springs, FL 32435
Second Address: Box 627, De Funiak Springs, FL 32435-0627
(850) 892-3158, *Fax:* (850) 892-9675
www.wzep1460.com
wzep@wzep1460.com
License: De Funiak Springs, Walton County, FL held by Walton County Broadcasting Inc.
Nat'l Network: CBS *Regional Network:* Florida News Network
Population Served: 75,000 *Arbitron Metro Market:* Panama City, FL *Special Programming:* Gospel 13 hrs wkly *Hrs. of News Programming:* news progmg 60 hrs wkly *No. News Employees:* 1 *Target Audience:* General; residents & visitors to Walton & Holmes counties
Arthur Dees, President
Wes Richardson, Operations Dir
Arthur Dees, General Manager
Marty Dees, Station Manager
Rebecca King, General Sales Mgr
Stephanie King, Programming Director
Marty Dees, Promotions Manager
Kevin Chilcutt,News Director
Kevin Chilcutt, Engineering Dir
Terry Reeves, Chief Engineer
Wes Richardson, Traffic Manager

Defuniak Springs

***WAKJ**
01-01-1996; 91.3 mhz FM *Hrs Open:* 24; 1.2 kw; 226 ft.; N30 41 5 W86 8 28
Mailing Address: Post Office Box 1305, Defuniak Springs, FL 32433 US
Second Address: 295 Hwy. 90 W., De Funiak Springs, FL 32435
(850) 892-2107, *Fax:* (866) 309-6532
www.eridan.websrvcs.com
WAKJradio@gmail.com
License: Defuniak Springs, Walton County, FL held by First Baptist Church Inc.
Arbitron Metro Market: De Funiak Springs, FL *Format:* Christian
Zane Welch, General Manager
Jesse Knapp, Station Manager
John Gradick, Promotions Manager

Deland

WOCL
07-10-1967; 105.9 mhz FM; 96 kw; 1588 ft.; N28 55 10 W81 19 8
2101 West State Rd. 434, Siute 305, Longwood, FL 32779 US
(407) 919-1000, *Fax:* (407) 919-1190
www.sunny1059.com
License: Deland, Volusia County, FL held by CBS Radio Stations Inc.
Group Owner: CBS Radio; (acq 8-7-2000; grpsl)
Nat'l Reps: Christal
Arbitron Metro Market: Orlando, FL *TV Affiliate:* Classic hits
Special Programming: news progmg 20 hrs wkly *Hrs. of News Programming:* 1 *No. News Employees:* 25-54.
Program Director, Angela Schlesman
Promotions Director, Promotions Manager

WTJV
09-10-1948; 1490 khz AM
P.O. Box 1777, 220 East Hubbard Avenue, Deland, FL 32721 US
(386) 255-9300, *Fax:* (386) 239-0966
www.radiovidaorlando.com
License: Deland, FL held by J&V Communications Inc.
Group Owner: J&V Communications Inc.; (acq 12-7-2005; $370,000)
Regional Network: Florida's Radio Networks

Arbitron Metro Market: Daytona Beach, FL *Format:* News, News/Talk, 84, Talk *Target Audience:* 35 plus.
Frank Scott, Operations Dir
Stacey Knerler, General Manager

WYND
12-07-1956; 1310 khz AM *Hrs Open:* 24
316 E. Taylor Road, Deland, FL 32724 US
(386) 734-1310, *Fax:* (386) 734-8885
License: Deland, FL held by Buddy Tucker Association Inc.
Group Owner: Buddy Tucker Association Inc.; (acq 12-30-86; $255,000;
Nat'l Network: USA
Arbitron Metro Market: De Land, FL *Format:* Christian, News, 62, Talk *Hrs. of News Programming:* news progmg 45 hrs wkly *No. News Employees:* 1 *Target Audience:* 25-55. *Adv. Rates:* 20; 15; 20; 10
Buddy Tucker, General Manager
Art Taylor, Chief Engineer

Delray Beach

WDJA
02-01-1952; 1420 khz AM *Hrs Open:* 24; 5 kw-D, DA2; 0.5 kw-N, DA2; N26 27 22 W80 5 58
%Fletcher,Heald & Hildre, 1300 N 17th St- 11th Flr, Arlington, VA 22209 US
(561) 278-1420, *Fax:* (561) 278-7515
www.universo1420.com
info@universo1420.com
License: Delray Beach, FL held by Professional Broadcasting LLC
Arbitron Metro Market: West Palm Beach-Boca Raton, FL *Format:* Reggae
Stan Rain, Operations Dir
Roy Bresky, General Manager

Deltona

WNUE-FM
09-01-1968; 98.1 mhz FM *Hrs Open:* 24; kw
200 Concord Plaza, Suite 600, San Antonio, TX 78216 US
(407) 331-1777, *Fax:* (407) 830-6223
www.mega981.com
jstein@megastations.net
License: Deltona, Brevard County, FL held by Entravision Holdings LLC.
Group Owner: Entravision Communications Corp.; (acq 3-24-2008; $24 million)
Nat'l Reps: SBS/Interep
Arbitron Metro Market: Daytona Beach, FL *Format:* Spanish *Hrs. of News Programming:* news progmg 2 hrs wkly *No. News Employees:* 1 *Target Audience:* 25-54; Hispanic adults 25-54
Walter Ulloa, CEO
Rafael Grullon, President
Jeff Stein, General Sales Mgr

Destin

WNWF
01-01-2000; 1120 khz AM *Hrs Open:* 6 AM-6 PM; 1 kw-D, NDD; N30 30 34 W86 28 34
Mailing Address: Box 5780, Gainesville, FL 32602 US
Second Address: 415 Mountain Dr., Suite 7, Destin, FL 32541
(850) 654-1718, *Fax:* (850) 650-1619
www.destin1120am.com/
wnwf@destin1120am.com
License: Destin, FL held by Flagship Communications Inc.
Arbitron Metro Market: Pensacola, FL *Format:* News, News/Talk, 86 *No. News Employees:* 1 *Target Audience:* 35-64. *Adv. Rates:* 12; 12; 12; 12
Dale Riddick, General Manager

WECQ(FM)
09-24-1981; 92.1 mhz FM; 25 kw; 279 ft; N30 31 06 W86 28 01
743 Harbor Blvd., Suite 6, Destin, FL 32541
(850) 654-1031, *Fax:* (850) 654-6510
www.fly921.com
License: Destin, Okaloosa County, FL held by Qantum of Ft. Walton Beach License Company LLC.
Group Owner: Qantum Communications Corp.
Nat'l Reps: Katz Radio
Arbitron Metro Market: Fort Walton Beach, FL *Format:* Christian *Target Audience:* 18-49; general *Adv. Rates:* 60; 60; 60; 30
Frank Osborne, President
Georgia Edmiston, General Manager
Allyson Buckner, General Sales Mgr

Dogwood Lakes Estate

***WJED**
01-15-1992; 91.1 mhz FM; 0.7 kw; 180 ft.; N30 51 34 W85 47 45
Mailing Address: P.O. Box 1944, Dothan, AL 36301 US
Second Address: 2573 Hodgesville Rd, Dothan, AL 36302
(334) 793-3189, *Fax:* (334) 793-4344
www.bethanybc.edu
wjed911fm@bethanybc.edu
License: Dogwood Lakes Estate, Holmes County, FL held by Bethany Bible College & Bethany Theological Seminary Inc.
Nat'l Network: USA
Format: Gospel, Religious *Target Audience:* General; college students & relg community
Dr. H.D. Shuemake, CEO
Sylvia Green, Operations Dir
Dr. Samuel Shuemake, Station Manager

Dunedin

WGUL
11-21-1959; 860 khz AM *Hrs Open:* 24; 5 kw-D, 1.5 kw-N, DA-2; N27 59 55 W82 42 01
5211 W. Laurel St., Tampa, FL 34684
(813) 639-1903, *Fax:* (813) 639-1272
www.860wgul.com
barb@salemtampa.com
License: Dunedin, Pinellas County, FL held by Caron Broadcasting Inc.
Group Owner: Salem Communications Corp.; (acq 8-12-2005; $9.5 million with W
Nat'l Network: Salem Radio Network *Nat'l Reps:* Salem
Population Served: 4,000,000 *Arbitron Metro Market:* Tampa-St. Peter
Joe Weaver, Operations Dir
Barbara Yoder, General Manager

Dunnellon

WTRS
03-11-1969; 102.3 mhz FM *Hrs Open:* 24; 50 kw; 489 ft.; N29 11 15 W82 23 40
1429 N. Federal Highway, Ft Lauderdale, FL 33304 US
(352) 867-1023, *Fax:* (888) 450-1049
www.wtrs.fm
shane@wtrs.fm
License: Dunnellon, Marion County, FL held by Asterisk Communications Inc.
Arbitron Metro Market: Ocala, FL *Format:* Country
Shane Finch, Operations & Program Director
Dean Johnson, General Manager
Sam Gerace, General Sales Mgr
Shirley Sapp, Traffic Manager
Dave Tyler, Music Director

Eatonville

WRLZ
01-01-1957; 1270 khz AM *Hrs Open:* 24
Mailing Address: 4151 West Oakridge Road, Orlando, FL 32839 US
Second Address: 6106 B Hoffner Ave., Orlando, FL 32822
(407) 345-0700, *Fax:* (407) 345-1492
www.radioluz1270.com
info@radioluz1270.com
License: Eatonville, FL held by Radio Luz Inc.
Arbitron Metro Market: Orlando, FL *Format:* Spanish *Target Audience:* General; Family *Adv. Rates:* 35; 35; 35; 30.
Saturnino Gonzalez, President
John Maldonado, General Manager

Ebro

WBPC
07-15-2005; 95.1 mhz FM *Hrs Open:* 24; 25 kw; Ant 285 ft; N30 34 06 W85 48 28
Box 27272, Panama City Beach, FL
(850) 235-2195, *Fax:* (850) 235-2795
www.beach951.com
License: Ebro, Washington County, FL held by Beach Radio Inc.
Group Owner: Randy Sheffield-Wayne Bishop; Startup
Nat'l Network: ABC News
Arbitron Metro Market: Panama City, FL *Target Audience:* 35-64; adults *Adv. Rates:* 40; 25; 30; 15
Randy Sheffield, President
David Nolan, Operations Dir
Randy Sheffield, General Manager
Wayne Bishop, General Sales Mgr

Edgewater

***WKTO**
11-01-1997; 88.9 mhz FM *Hrs Open:* 24; 25 kw; 395 ft.; N29 1 30 W81 8 52
P O Box 677, Mims, FL 32754 US
(386) 427-1095, *Fax:* (386) 427-8970
www.wkto.net
info@wkto.net
License: Edgewater, Volusia County, FL held by Mims Community Radio Inc.
Format: Religious *Special Programming:* Jazz 4 hrs, Pol 1.5 hrs, Ger 1.5 hrs, Sp 2 hr wkly *Target Audience:* 18-50.
Carol Henry, CEO

Egypt Lake

WMGG
01-01-1955; 1470 khz AM
Haley, Bader & Potts, 4350 N Fairfax Dr, Suite 9, Arlington, VA 22203 US
(813) 281-1040, *Fax:* (813) 281-1948
www.newstalkflorida.com
contactus@radiogenesis.com
License: Egypt Lake, FL held by Genesis Communications of Tampa Bay Inc.
Group Owner: Genesis Communications Inc.; (acq 3-5-2001; $2 million)
Regional Network: Florida's Radio Networks *Nat'l Reps:* Interep; McGavren Guild *Wire Services:* AP
Arbitron Metro Market: Tampa, FL *Format:* Oldies *Special Programming:* Relg 2 hrs wkly *Target Audience:* 40 plus. *Adv. Rates:* 75; 55; 80; 40
Adam Lindemann, Chairman
Bruce Maduri, CEO
Steven Baltimore, General Manager
Dro Silva, Programming Director
Cindy Scheffer, News Director
Jerry Smith, Chief Engineer
Kimo Gray, Information Technology Director

WTMP
01-01-1954; 1150 khz AM *Hrs Open:* 24
5207 Washington Blvd, Tampa, FL 33619 US
(813) 259-9867, *Fax:* (813) 254-9867
www.wtmp.com
info@tamabroadcasting.com
License: Egypt Lake, FL held by Tama Radio Licenses of Tampa, FL, Inc.
Group Owner: Tama Broadcasting Inc.; (acq 12-18-2001).
Nat'l Network: American Urban
Arbitron Metro Market: Tampa, FL *Format:* Adult Contemp *Target Audience:* 18-49; urban contemporary music listeners & adults *Adv. Rates:* 80; 75; 80; 65
Dr. Glenn Cherry, CEO
Louis Muhammad, Operations Dir
Glenn Cherry, General Manager
Lynn Tolliver, Programming Director

Emeralda

***WGTT**
91.5 mhz FM; 1.1 kw; 135 ft.; N28 57 8 W81 47 29
P. O. Box 4291, Enterprise, FL 32725 US
License: Emeralda, Lake County, FL held by Sunbelt Educational Broadcasting Inc.
Raul Ortiz, President

Englewood

WENG
11-15-1964; 1530 khz AM *Hrs Open:* 24
Mailing Address: P.O. Box 2908, Englewood, FL 34295 US
Second Address: 1355 S. River Rd., Englewood, FL 34223
(941) 474-3231, *Fax:* (941) 475-2205
www.wengradio.com/
Info@wengradio.com
License: Englewood, FL held by Viper Communications Inc.
Group Owner: Viper Communications Broadcast Group; (acq 10-21-02).
Nat'l Network: ABC *Regional Network:* Florida's Radio Networks
Arbitron Metro Market: Englewood, FL *Format:* News, News/Talk, 86 *Special Programming:* Religious 2 hrs wkly *Hrs. of News Programming:* news progmg 50 hrs wkly *No. News Employees:* 1 *Target Audience:* 18plus; securely established, financially independent
Kenneth Kuenzie, President
Scott Holcomb, Operations Dir
Kenneth Birdsong, General Manager
Dennis Klautzer, Executive Vice President

***WSEB**
05-01-1989; 91.3 mhz FM *Hrs Open:* 24; 62 kw horiz, 60 kw vert; 282 ft.; N26 51 48 W82 17 54
517 Paul Morris Drive, Suite 4-2, Englewood, FL 34223 US
(941) 475-9732, *Fax:* (941) 473-7308
www.wsebfm.com
comments@wsebfm.com

License: Englewood, Sarasota County, FL held by Suncoast Educational Broadcasting Corp.
Arbitron Metro Market: Sarasota-Braden *Format:* Religious *Target Audience:* 35 plus; Christian families

WTZB
04-05-1999; 105.9 mhz FM; 25 kw; 295 ft.; N27 6 19 W82 23 59
50 East Rivercenter Blvd, Suite 1200, Covington, KY 41011 US
(941) 552-4800, *Fax:* (941) 552-4900
www.1059thebuzz.com
info@1059thebuzz.com
License: Englewood, Sarasota County, FL held by Citicasters Licenses L.P.
Group Owner: Clear Channel Communications Inc.; (acq 5-4-99; grpsl).
Arbitron Metro Market: Sarasota-Braden *Format:* Alternative
Ron White, Operations Dir
Buddy Lee, General Manager

Estero

WFSX-FM
12-16-1978; 92.5 mhz FM *Hrs Open:* 24; 25 kw; Ant 620 ft; N26 19 00 W81 47 13
2824 Palm Beach Blvd., Ft. Myers, FL 33916
(239) 337-2346, *Fax:* (239) 332-0767
randy.marsh@us985.com
License: Estero, Lee County, FL held by Meridian Broadcasting Inc.
Group Owner: Meridian Broadcasting Inc.; (acq 9-14-2000; $7 million)
Nat'l Reps: McGavren Guild *Wire Services:* AP
Population Served: 63,512 *Arbitron Metro Market:* Fort Myers, FL *Format:* Oldies *Target Audience:* 25-44.
Joseph Schwartzel, President
Jim Schwartzel, General Sales Mgr
Lance Hale, Programming Director
Keith Stuhlman, Engineering Dir
Randy Marsh, Programming Director

Eustis

WKIQ
06-01-1955; 1240 khz AM; 0.79 kw-U, ND1; N28 50 19 W81 41 46
P.O. Box 878, Marion, IL 62959 US
(407) 291-1395, *Fax:* (407) 293-2870
License: Eustis, FL held by Rama Communications Inc.
Group Owner: Rama Communications Inc.; (acq 10-15-2004; $180,000 with WQBQ(AM) Leesburg).
Format: Urban Contemporary
Sabeta Persaud, President
Steve January, General Manager

***WIGW**
90.3 mhz FM; 9.4 kw; 233 ft.; N28 58 18 W81 45 15 US
(714) 545-7868, *Fax:* (208) 736-1958
www.csnradio.com
License: Eustis, Lake County, FL held by CSN International.
Group Owner: CSN International
Arbitron Metro Market: Whitehouse, OH
Mike Kestler, President
Don Mills, Network Programming Director / Music Director
Kelly Carlson, Engineering Dir
Ray Gorney, Assistant Director of Engineering
Jerry Johnson, Engineer / Outage Coordinator
Dustin Pamplona,Engineer
O.J. Edwards, Engineer
Jeremy Estabrooks, Engineer
Mickel Pruden, Engineer

Everglades City

***WBGY**
08-01-2004; 88.1 mhz FM; 0 kw horiz, 0.11 kw vert; 59 ft.; N25 51 56 W81 23 9
1601 Belvedere Rd, 204 E, West Palm Beach, FL 33406 US
(239) 404-9849
wbby@earthlink.net
License: Everglades City, Collier County, FL held by Everglades City Broadcasting Co. Inc.
Arbitron Metro Market: West Palm Beach, FL *Format:* Country
Robert Ladd, President

Fernandina Beach

WVOJ
01-01-1955; 1570 khz AM *Hrs Open:* 24
1218 S. Park Street, Kalamazoo, MI 49001 US
(904) 739-3660, *Fax:* (904) 739-9409
License: Fernandina Beach, FL held by Norsan Consulting and Management Inc.
Group Owner: Norsan Consulting and Management Inc.; (acq 9-14-2005; $2.1 million with WNNR(AM) Jacksonville).
Arbitron Metro Market: Jacksonville, FL *Format:* Spanish, Christian
Norberto Sanchez, President
Bernie Daigle, General Manager

WJSJ
01-01-2000; 105.3 mhz FM; 3.9 kw; 410 ft.; N30 30 4 W81 35 14
Rebroadcasts: Simulcast with WJXL(AM) Jacksonville Beach 100%
1801 K St NW, Suite 400k, Washington, DC 20006 US
(904) 641-1011, *Fax:* (904) 641-1022
www.1010xl.com
SteveG@1010XL.com
License: Fernandina Beach, Nassau County, FL held by Tama Radio Licenses of Jacksonville, FL, Inc.
Group Owner: Tama Broadcasting Inc.; (acq 2-28-2003; $8.5 million with WSJF(FM) Saint Augustine Beach)
Nat'l Network: ESPN Radio
Arbitron Metro Market: Jacksonville, FL *Format:* Sports
Steve Griffin, General Manager
Ken Brady, General Sales Mgr
Jason Dixon, Programming Director
Tom Champion, Promotions Manager
Michelle Thomas, Business Manager
Chadd Scott, Assistant Program Director
Terri Hill, AdministrativeAssistant
Steve Bute, Producer
Donna Murphy, Producer
Jessica Blaylock, Producer/Jaguars Reporter

Five Points

WCJX
01-01-1996; 106.5 mhz FM *Hrs Open:* 24; 3.8 kw; 341 ft.; N30 15 14 W82 40 56
Mailing Address: P.O. Box 39, Lake City, FL 32056 US
Second Address: 5348 NW US Highway 41, Lake City, FL 32055
(386) 755-9259, *Fax:* (386) 755-1557
www.wcjx.com
audio@wcjx106.5.com
License: Five Points, Columbia County, FL held by RTG Radio LLC.
Group Owner: Black Crow Media Group LLC; (acq 11-9-2001; grpsl).
Nat'l Network: ABC; Premiere Radio Networks
Arbitron Metro Market: Lake City, Florida *Format:* Classic Rock
Dean Blackwell, General Manager
Steve Johnson, Station Manager

Flagler Beach

***WJLH**
08-23-1996; 90.3 mhz FM; 15 kw; 177 ft.; N29 22 26 W81 10 49
Rebroadcasts: Rebroadcasts WJLU(FM) New Smyrna Beach 100%
4295 Ridgewood Avenue, Port Orange, FL 32127 US
(386) 756-9094, *Fax:* (386) 760-7107
www.cornerstoneministry.org
thecornerstone@cornerstoneministry.org
License: Flagler Beach, Flagler County, FL held by Cornerstone Broadcasting Corp.
Format: Christian
Sandra Leisner, Operations Dir
William Powell, General Manager

Florida City

***WMFL**
10-01-1998; 88.5 mhz FM *Hrs Open:* 24; 7.7 kw; 171 ft.; N25 19 31 W80 24 16
Mailing Address: 1601 Belvedere Road, West Palm Beach, FL 33406 US
Second Address: 290 Hegenberger Rd., OaklandCA 94621
(916) 641-8191, *Fax:* (916) 641-8238
www.familyradio.com
info@familyradio.com
License: Florida City, Dade County, FL held by Family Stations Inc.
Group Owner: Family Stations Inc.; acq 11-15-00; $75,000).
Nat'l Network: Family Radio
Arbitron Metro Market: Sacramento, CA *Format:* Christian, Religious
Harold Camping, President
Stanley Jackson, Operations Dir
Rob Robbins, Operations Manager

Fort Lauderdale

***WYBP**
01-01-1974; 90.3 mhz FM *Hrs Open:* 24; 3 kw; 280 ft; N26 11 48 W80 06 45
11530 Carmel Commons Blvd., Charlotte, NC 33308
(704) 523-5555
www.bbnradio.org
License: Fort Lauderdale, Broward County, FL held by Bible Broadcasting Network Inc.
Population Served: 1,700,000 *Arbitron Metro Market:* Miami-Fort Lauderdale-Hollywood, FL *Target Audience:* 30 plus; general
Lowell L. Davey, President

WBGG-FM
07-01-1960; 105.9 mhz FM; 100 kw; 1030 ft.; N25 59 34 W80 10 27
3305 W Spring Mountain, Road, Ste 60, Las Vegas, NV 89102 US
(954) 862-2000, *Fax:* (954) 862-4013
www.big1059.com
JoeBonadonna@clearchannel.com
License: Fort Lauderdale, Broward County, FL held by Clear Channel Radio Licenses Inc.
Group Owner: Clear Channel Communications Inc.; (acq 2-24-94; $14 million;
Arbitron Metro Market: Miramar, FL *Format:* Classic Rock
Todd Winick, Sales Manager
Joe Bonadonna, Programming Director
Ken Charles, PSD Director
Arthur Rodriguez, Promotions road crew
Russell Wein, Digital & Integrated Media Sales Director

WFLL
09-16-1946; 1400 khz AM *Hrs Open:* 24; 1 kw-U, ND1; N26 9 13 W80 10 11
200 Concord Plaza, Suite 600, San Antonio, TX 78216 US
(954) 315-1515, *Fax:* (954) 315-1555
info@1400espn.com
License: Fort Lauderdale, FL held by James Crystal Licenses L.L.C.
Group Owner: James Crystal Inc.; (acq 6-17-98; grpsl)
Nat'l Network: ESPN Radio
Arbitron Metro Market: Miami-Fort Lauderdale-Hollywood, FL *Format:* Sports *Target Audience:* 25 plus.
Steve Lapa, General Manager

WHYI-FM
07-31-1960; 100.7 mhz FM; 98 kw; 1007 ft.; N25 58 2 W80 12 34
200 Concord Plaza, Suite 600, San Antonio, TX 78216 US
(954) 862-2000, *Fax:* (954) 862-4012
www.y100.7miami.com
info@y100.7miami.com
License: Fort Lauderdale, Broward County, FL held by Clear Channel Radio Licenses Inc.
Group Owner: Clear Channel Communications Inc.; (acq 11-94; grpsl)
Nat'l Reps: McGavren Guild
Arbitron Metro Market: Miami-Fort Lauderdale-Hollywood, FL *Format:* Contemporary Hits/Top 40
David D'Dugenio, General Sales Mgr

WSHE-FM
10-17-1959; 103.5 mhz FM; 100 kw; 1,007 ft; N25 57 59 W80 12 33
7601 Riviera Blvd., Miramar, FL 33023
(954) 862-2000, *Fax:* (954) 862-4012
www.thebeatmiami.com
info@thebeatmiami.com
License: Fort Lauderdale, Broward County, FL held by Clear Channel Broadcasting Licenses Inc.
Group Owner: Clear Channel Communications Inc.; (acq 11-21-97; grpsl).
Population Served: 3,000,000 *Arbitron Metro Market:* Miami-Fort Lauderdale-Hollywood, FL *Format:* Blues
Kevin Hemmings, General Sales Mgr

WRMA
08-15-1962; 106.7 mhz FM *Hrs Open:* 24; 100 kw; 984 ft.; N25 59 34 W80 10 27
3191 Coral Way, Suite 805, Miami, FL 33145 US
(305) 444-9292, *Fax:* (305) 461-4466
www.romance106fm.com
License: Fort Lauderdale, Broward County, FL held by WRMA Licensing Inc.
Group Owner: Spanish Broadcasting System Inc.; (acq 7-11-97; $110 million with WXDJ(FM) North Miami Beach)
Nat'l Reps: D & R Radio
Arbitron Metro Market: Miami-Fort Lauderdale-Hollywood, FL *Format:* Ethnic *No. News Employees:* 1 *Target Audience:* 18-54; Hispanic adults

Raoul Alarcon, President
Jackie Nosti-Cambo, General Manager
Albert Rodriguez, General Sales Mgr
Tony Campos, Programming Director
John Caride, Promotions Manager
Tomas Regalado, News Director
Ralph Chambers, Chief Engineer
Yoli Machado, Traffic Manager

WSRF
01-01-1955; 1580 khz AM *Hrs Open:* 24; 10 kw-D, 5 kw-N, DA-2; N26 04 54 W80 13 34
1510 N.E. 162 St., Miami, FL 33314
(305) 940-1580, *Fax:* (305) 947-8050
info@wsrf.com
License: Fort Lauderdale, Broward County, FL held by Niche Radio Inc.
Population Served: 2,000,000 *Arbitron Metro Market:* Miami-Fort Lauderdale *No. News Employees:* 8 *Target Audience:* Haitian-Creole
Jean Cherubin, CEO/COO
Emmanuel Cherubin, President
Rose P Coriolan, Operations Dir
Jean Cherubin, General Manager
Rose P Coriolan, General Sales Mgr
Ed Lozama, Programming Director
Rose P Coriolan, Promotions Manager
EdLozama, News Director
Ralph Chambers, Engineering Dir
Ralph Chambers, Chief Engineer

Fort Meade

WWRZ
03-07-1977; 98.3 mhz FM *Hrs Open:* 24; 27 kw; 666 ft.; N27 51 10 W81 52 2
Mailing Address: One Cuprak Road, Norwich, CT 06360 US
Second Address: 404 West Lime Street, Lakeland, FL 33815-4651
(863) 682-8184, *Fax:* (863) 683-2409
www.max983fm.com
mjames@halllakeland.com
License: Fort Meade, Polk County, FL held by Hall Communications Inc.
Group Owner: Hall Communications Inc.; acq 10-1-96; $1,750,000).
Nat'l Reps: Eastman Radio *Wire Services:* AP
Arbitron Metro Market: Lakeland, FL *Format:* Adult Contemp *Hrs. of News Programming:* news progmg 2 hrs wkly *No. News Employees:* 3 *Target Audience:* 25-54; women
Bonnie Rowbotham, Chairman
Art Rowbotham, Operations Dir
Nancy Cattarius, General Manager
Mike James, Programming Director
Jessica Brown, Promotions Manager
Andrea Oliver, News & Public Affairs Director
Mike James, OperationsManager

Fort Myers

WCRM
08-22-1964; 1350 khz AM *Hrs Open:* 19; 2 kw-D, ND1; 0.15 kw-N, ND1; N26 37 31 W81 50 29
3448 Canal Street, Fort Meyers, FL 33916 US
(239) 334-1350 / (941) 332-1350, *Fax:* (305)969-8755
www.aleluya.com/1350_am.htm
radio1350office@aol.com
License: Fort Myers, FL held by Manna Christian Missions Inc.
Nat'l Network: USA
Arbitron Metro Market: Fort Myers, FL *Format:* Christian *Hrs. of News Programming:* news progmg 5 hrs wkly *No. News Employees:* 1 *Target Audience:* General.
Salvador Santana, General Manager

***WGCU-FM**
09-12-1983; 90.1 mhz FM *Hrs Open:* 24; 100 kw; 813 ft; N26 48 54 W81 45 44
10501 FGCU Blvd., Fort Myers, FL 33965
(239) 590-2500, *Fax:* (239) 590-2520
www.wgcu.org
License: Fort Myers, Lee County, FL held by Board of Trustees, Florida Gulf Coast University
Nat'l Network: NPR; PRI; BBC; APM *Regional Network:* Fla. Pub. Radio; Fla. News Exchange
Population Served: 830,000 *Arbitron Metro Market:* Fort Myers-Napl *TV Affiliate:* WGCU *No. News Employees:* 4 *Target Audience:* 24 plus.
Luc Martin, Operations Dir
Rick Johnson, General Manager
Amy Tardif, Station Manager
Terry Brennen, General Sales Mgr
Amy Tardif, Programming Director
Amy Tardif, News Director
Rick Carroll, Engineering Dir
Rick Carroll, ChiefEngineer

WINK-FM
10-10-1964; 96.9 mhz FM *Hrs Open:* 24; 98 kw; 1499 ft.; N26 48 1 W81 45 48
2824 Palm Beach Blvd., Fort Myers, FL 33916 US
(239) 334-1111, *Fax:* (239) 334-0744
www.winkfm.com
wayne.simons@fmbcmail.com
License: Fort Myers, Lee County, FL held by Fort Myers Broadcasting Co.
Group Owner: Fort Myers Broadcasting Co.
Nat'l Reps: McGavren Guild
Arbitron Metro Market: Fort Myers-Naples-Marco Island, FL *TV Affiliate:* WINK-TV affil. *Format:* Adult Contemp *Target Audience:* 25-54; females
Wayne Simons, General Manager
Brad Foster, General Sales Mgr
Michael Hayes, Programming Director
Chad Rufer, Promotions Manager

***WJYO**
01-01-1988; 91.5 mhz FM *Hrs Open:* 24; 3 kw; 285 ft.; N26 30 18 W81 51 14 *Rebroadcasts:* Rebroadcasts WBIY(FM) LaBelle 100%
Falls Road, Toccoa Falls, GA 30598 US
(239) 274-9150, *Fax:* (239) 274-0191
airwavesforJesus.com
wjyo@aol.com
License: Fort Myers, Lee County, FL held by Airwaves for Jesus Inc.
Arbitron Metro Market: Fort Myers-Naples-Marco Island, FL *Format:* Christian *Special Programming:* Children 5 hrs wkly *Hrs. of News Programming:* News progmg 10 hrs wkly *Target Audience:* 44 plus; traditionalminded persons
Art Ramos, CEO
Jasmin Ramos, Operations Dir

WMYR
11-11-1952; 1410 khz AM *Hrs Open:* 24; 5 kw-D, DAN; 5 kw-N, DAN; N26 37 23 W81 51 18
P.O. Box 216, Fort Myers, FL 33902 US
(239) 732-9369, *Fax:* (239) 732-7267
www.avenuefla.com
wmyr@mail.com
License: Fort Myers, FL held by J&B WMYR LLC
Nat'l Network: USA *Regional Network:* Florida's Radio Networks
Arbitron Metro Market: Fort Myers, FL *Format:* News, Oldies *No. News Employees:* 1 *Adv. Rates:* 35; 35; 35; 35
Bob Ladd, Operations Dir

WOLZ
01-01-1970; 95.3 mhz FM; 79 kw; 476 ft.; N26 30 18 W81 51 14
200 Concord Plaza, Suite 600, San Antonio, TX 78216 US
(239) 225-4300, *Fax:* (239) 225-4329
www.wolz.com
info@wolz.com
License: Fort Myers, Lee County, FL held by Clear Channel Radio Licenses Inc.
Group Owner: Clear Channel Communications Inc.; (acq 2-18-97; grpsl)
Nat'l Reps: Clear Channel
Arbitron Metro Market: Fort Myers-Napl *TV Affiliate:* Oldies *Special Programming:* news progmg 2 hrs wkly *Hrs. of News Programming:* 1 *No. News Employees:* 35-54; upbeat, fun oldies

WWGR
12-02-1969; 101.9 mhz FM *Hrs Open:* 24; 100 kw; 1119 ft.; N26 25 22 W81 37 49
Broadcast Plaza, Crane Ave., Pittsburgh, PA 15220 US
(239) 495-8383, *Fax:* (239) 495-0883
www.gatorcountry1019.com
wwgr@rendabroadcasting.com
License: Fort Myers, Lee County, FL held by Renda Broadcast Corp.
Group Owner: Renda Broadcasting Corp.; (acq 7-13-94; $4 million;
Arbitron Metro Market: Fort Myers, FL *Format:* Country
Roger Harris, General Manager
Camellia Pflum, General Sales Mgr
Randy Savage, Programming Director
Buzzy Ford, Promotions Manager

***WMYE**
01-01-2008; 91.9 mhz FM; 1.2 kw; 328 ft.; N26 47 7.5 W81 47 46.6
US
(786) 429-3606, *Fax:* (305) 251-2293
www.callfm.com
rob@callfm.com
License: Fort Myers, Lee County, FL held by Call Communications Group Inc.
Arbitron Metro Market: Fort Myers, FL *Format:* Christian *Target Audience:* 13-25.
Tim Pappas, Chairman
Rob Robbins, Ph.D., Programming Director and General Manager

Fort Myers Beach

WJBX
01-01-1983; 99.3 mhz FM; 45 kw; 466 ft.; N26 29 16 W81 55 46
3033 Riviera Drive, Suite 200, Naples, FL 34103 US
(239) 495-2100, *Fax:* (239) 992-8165
www.99xwjbx.com
info@99xwjbx.com
License: Fort Myers Beach, Lee County, FL held by Dillon License L.P.
Group Owner: Beasley Broadcast Group Inc.; (acq 10-16-97; $6 million).
Arbitron Metro Market: Fort Myers-Naples-Marco Island, FL *Format:* Alternative *Target Audience:* 18-49; adults
Brad Beasley, General Manager
Robert Hallman, General Sales Mgr
Chris Delozier, Programming Director
Jeff Hickcox, Promotions Manager
Dawn Krause, New Business Manager
AJ Lurie, National Sales Manager
Diana Beasley, Webmaster

Fort Myers Villas

WJPT
07-31-1991; 106.3 mhz FM; 50 kw; Ant 472 ft; N26 29 16 W81 55 49
20125 S. Tamiami Tr., Estero, FL 34103
(239) 495-2100, *Fax:* (239) 992-8165
www.sunny1063.com
randy@morningshow.net
License: Fort Myers Villas, Lee County, FL held by WJST License L.P.
Group Owner: Beasley Broadcast Group Inc.; (acq 12-11-97; $5 million)
Arbitron Metro Market: Fort Myers-Naples-Marco Island, FL *Target Audience:* 45 plus.
Brad Beasley, General Manager
Randy Sherwyn, Programming Director
Jeff Hickcox, Promotions Manager
Richard Gallow, Engineering Dir
Richard Gallow, Chief Engineer

Fort Pierce

WIRA
05-18-1946; 1400 khz AM *Hrs Open:* 24; 1 kw-U, ND1; N27 26 7 W80 21 41
200 Concord Plaza, Suite 600, San Antonio, TX 78216 US
(772) 460-9356, *Fax:* (772) 460-2700
License: Fort Pierce, FL held by Team One Media LLC
Nat'l Network: ABC
Arbitron Metro Market: Fort Pierce-Stuart-Vero Beach, FL *Format:* Gospel *Special Programming:* Relg one hr, pub affrs one hr wkly *Target Audience:* 45 plus; male & female
Al Richards, General Manager

***WJFP**
01-15-1995; 91.1 mhz FM *Hrs Open:* 6 AM-midnight; 6 kw; 157 ft.; N27 27 7 W80 21 34
1150 W. King Street, Cocoa, FL 32922 US
(772) 467-2400, *Fax:* (772) 467-9400
www.wjfp.com
info@wjfp.com
License: Fort Pierce, St. Lucie County, FL held by Black Media Works Inc.
Group Owner: Black Media Works Inc.; acq 1-21-98).
Arbitron Metro Market: Fort Pierce-Stuart-Vero Beach, FL *Format:* Religious *Special Programming:* Sp 2 hrs, Haitian 8 hrs wkly *Target Audience:* 12-49.
Kimberly Kassis, President

WJNX
12-24-1952; 1330 khz AM *Hrs Open:* 24; 5 kw-D, DA2; 1 kw-N, DA2; N27 27 20 W80 22 2
200 Concord Plaza, Suite 600, San Antonio, TX 78216 US
(772) 340-1590, *Fax:* (772) 340-3245
www.lagigante1330.com
wpsl@wpsl.com
License: Fort Pierce, FL held by Port St. Lucie Broadcasters Inc.
Nat'l Network: ESPN Deportes

Arbitron Metro Market: Fort Pierce-Stuart-Vero Beach, FL *Format:* News, News/Talk, 86 *No. News Employees:* 1 *Target Audience:* 25-54. *Adv. Rates:* 50; 30; 50; 40
Carol Wyatt, CEO
Greg Wyatt, General Manager

*WQCS
04-01-1982; 88.9 mhz FM; 100 kw; 436 ft.; N27 25 17 W80 21 23
3209 Virginia Aveue, Fort Pierce, FL 33454 US
(772) 462-4744, *Fax:* (772) 462-4743
www.wqcs.org
info@wqcs.org
License: Fort Pierce, St. Lucie County, FL held by Indian River State College.
Nat'l Network: NPR; PRI; AP Radio
Arbitron Metro Market: Fort Pierce-Stuart-Vero Beach, FL *Format:* News
Michelle Rhinesmith, Operations Dir
Madison Hodges, General Manager

Fort Walton Beach

WEDM(AM)
01-01-1956; 1400 khz AM; 1 kw-U; N30 24 38 W86 37 23
21 Miracle Strip Pkwy. S.E., Fort Walton Beach, FL 32548
(850) 244-1400, *Fax:* (850) 243-1471
License: Fort Walton Beach, Okaloosa County, FL held by Star Broadcasting Inc.
Group Owner: Star Broadcasting Inc.; (acq 7-11-2005)
Population Served: 19,793 *Arbitron Metro Market:* Fort Walton Beach, FL *Format:* Oldies *Special Programming:* Church program one hr wkly *Target Audience:* 50 plus.
Ron Hale Sr., General Manager
David Kuntz, General Sales Mgr
Frank Hale, Programming Director

WFTW
11-20-1953; 1260 khz AM *Hrs Open:* 24; 2.5 kw-D, ND1; 0.131 kw-N, ND1; N30 24 49 W86 37 40
P.O. Box 2347, Fort Walton Beach, FL 32549 US
(850) 243-7676, *Fax:* (850) 664-0203
www.wftw.com
ken@wftw.com
License: Fort Walton Beach, FL held by Cumulus Licensing Corp.
Group Owner: Cumulus Media Inc.; (acq 1-10-03; grpsl).
Regional Network: Florida's Radio Networks
Arbitron Metro Market: Fort Walton Beach, FL *Format:* News, News/Talk, 86 *Special Programming:* Rush Limbaugh affiliate
Lou Dickey, President
Ron Raybourne, General Manager
Georgia Edmiston, General Sales Mgr
Steve Williams, Programming Director
Lisa Captain, Promotions Manager
Gerald Lee, News Director
Bruce Campbell, Chief Engineer

WKSM
05-28-1965; 99.5 mhz FM; 50 kw; 438 ft.; N30 24 50 W86 37 40
P.O. Box 1699, Meridian, FL 39302 US
(850) 243-7676, *Fax:* (850) 243-6806
www.wksm.com
info@wksm.com
License: Fort Walton Beach, Okaloosa County, FL
Arbitron Metro Market: Fort Walton Beach, FL
Lee Leonard, General Sales Mgr
Nicci Garmon, Programming Director
Steve O'Day, Promotions Manager
Aimee Shaffer, News Director
Anthony Proffitt, Music Director
Steve Williams, Special Events Coordinator
Gerald Lee, TrafficManager

*WPSM
07-01-1985; 91.1 mhz FM *Hrs Open:* 24; 11 kw horiz, 10.78 kw vert; 344 ft.; N30 24 38 W86 37 22
Mailing Address: P.O. Box 1474, Ft. Walton Beach, FL 32549 US
Second Address: 233 N. Hill Ave., Fort Walton Beach, FL 32548
(850) 244-7667, *Fax:* (850) 244-3254
www.wpsm.com
contact@wpsm.com
License: Fort Walton Beach, Okaloosa County, FL held by Fort Walton Beach Educ. Broadcasting Corp.
Nat'l Network: USA
Arbitron Metro Market: Fort Walton Beach, FL *Format:* Christian *Hrs. of News Programming:* news progmg 14 hrs wkly *No. News Employees:* 1 *Target Audience:* 25-55; young to middle-age adult Christians
Terry Thorne, General Manager

WZNS
01-01-1997; 96.5 mhz FM *Hrs Open:* 24; 100 kw; 438 ft.; N30 24 50 W86 37 40
P.O. Box 1699, Meridian, MS 39302 US
(850) 664-0965, *Fax:* (850) 243-6806
www.z96.com
hayden@z96.com, gilligan@z96.com
License: Fort Walton Beach, Okaloosa County, FL held by Cumulus Licensing Corp.
Group Owner: Cumulus Media Inc.; (acq 1-10-03; grpsl).
Arbitron Metro Market: Fort Walton Beach, FL *Format:* Contemporary Hits/Top 40
Hayden Green, Programming Director

Fruit Cove

WSOS-FM
07-17-1982; 94.1 mhz FM *Hrs Open:* 24; 5.5 kw; 505 ft.; N30 4 8 W81 38 50
2715 Stratton Blvd, St. Augustine, FL 32095 US
(904) 824-0833,(904) 722-9606, *Fax:* (904) 721-9322
www.wsosfm.com
tbryan@rendabroadcasting.com
License: Fruit Cove, St. Johns County, FL held by Renda Broadcasting Corp. of Nevada.
Group Owner: Renda Broadcasting Corp.; (acq 4-27-2005; $7.75 million).
Nat'l Reps: McGavren Guild
Arbitron Metro Market: Jacksonville, FL *Format:* Adult Contemp *Target Audience:* 25-54; upscale audience
Tony Renda, CEO
Tim Bryan, General Manager
Don Runk, General Sales Mgr
Briggs Bickley, Programming Director
Stacey Steiner, Promotions Manager
Brenda McArthur, News Director
Bob Dillehay, Chief Engineer
Jim Byard, PublicService Director

Gainesville

WAJD
05-31-1961; 1390 khz AM; 5 kw-D, ND1; 0.051 kw-N, ND1; N29 39 56 W82 17 26
7120 Sw 24th Avenue, Gainesville, FL 32607 US
(352) 331-2200, *Fax:* (352) 331-0401
www.kiss1053.com
info@kiss1053.com
License: Gainesville, FL held by Gillen Broadcasting Corp.
Arbitron Metro Market: Gainesville, FL *Format:* Children *Target Audience:* 12-49.
Douglas Gillen, President
Doug Gillen, General Sales Manager

WGGG
02-01-1948; 1230 khz AM; 1 kw-U, ND1; N29 40 56 W82 24 48
Mailing Address: P.O. Box 3930, Ocala, FL 34478 US
Second Address: 101 S.E. 2nd Pl., Grainesville, FL 32601
(352) 378-7378, *Fax:* (352) 629-1614
www.cflradio.net
License: Gainesville, FL held by Florida Sportstalk Inc.
Arbitron Metro Market: Gainesville-Ocala, FL *Format:* Sports
Doug Gillen, General Manager

*WJLF
08-26-1990; 91.7 mhz FM *Hrs Open:* 24; 2 kw; 400 ft.; N29 38 34 W82 25 13 *Rebroadcasts:* Rebroadcasts WJIS(FM) Brandenton
2925 N.W. 39th Avenue, Gainesville, FL 32605 US
(352) 373-9553, *Fax:* (352) 373-9888
thejoyfm.com
thejoyfm@thejoyfm.com
License: Gainesville, Alachua County, FL held by Radio Training Network Inc.
Arbitron Metro Market: Gainesville-Ocala, FL *Format:* Christian *Special Programming:* Youth 5 hrs, jazz 2 hrs, children 1 hr wkly *Hrs. of News Programming:* news progmg 2 hrs wkly *No. News Employees:* 1 *TargetAudience:* 18-49; young adults & young families
James Campbell, President
Andy Haynes, Station Manager

WDVH
10-01-1954; 980 khz AM *Hrs Open:* 6 AM-10 PM; 5 kw-D, ND1; 0.166 kw-N, ND1; N29 37 26 W82 17 19
9421 Holiday Drive, Indianapolis, IN 46260 US
(352) 313-3150, *Fax:* (352) 313-3199
www.flafnr.com
jbrand@sunshinebroadcasting.com
License: Gainesville, FL held by 6 Johnson Road Licenses Inc.
Group Owner: Pamal Broadcasting Ltd.; (acq 1-5-2007; grpsl)
Nat'l Reps: Roslin
Arbitron Metro Market: Gainesville, FL *Format:* News, News/Talk, 86 *Target Audience:* 35 plus.
Shawn Portmann, General Manager

WRUF
01-01-1928; 850 khz AM *Hrs Open:* 24; 5 kw-D, DAN; 5 kw-N, DAN; N29 38 34 W82 25 13
Mailing Address: P. O. Box 14444, Gainesville, FL 32604 US
Second Address: Univ. Of Florida, 3200 Wiemer Hall, Gainesville, FL 32611
(352) 392-0771, *Fax:* (352) 392-0519
www.am850.com
info@am850.com
License: Gainesville, FL held by University of Florida, Board of Trustees
Nat'l Network: CBS; Westwood One *Regional Network:* Florida's Radio Networks *Wire Services:* CBS
Arbitron Metro Market: Gainesville-Oca *TV Affiliate:* WUFT-TV, WLUF-TV affils. *Format:* News, News/Talk, 84, Talk *Special Programming:* Black 4 hrs wkly *Hrs. of News Programming:* news progmg 54 hrs wkly *No.News Employees:* 3 *Target Audience:* 35-54; middle-to-upper income, decision makers
Robert Lawrence, Operations Dir
Larry Dankner, General Sales Mgr
Tom Ksynski, News Director
Don Rice, Chief Engineer
Steve Russell, Sports Commentator

WRUF-FM
01-01-1948; 103.7 mhz FM *Hrs Open:* 24; 100 kw; 768 ft.; N29 42 34 W82 23 40
Mailing Address: 3200 Wimer Hall, P.O. Box 14444, Gainesville, FL 32604 US
Second Address: Univ. of Florida, 3200 Wiemer Hall, Gainesville, FL 32611
(352) 392-0771, *Fax:* (352) 392-0519
www.rock104.com
info@rock104.com
License: Gainesville, Alachua County, FL held by University of Florida, Board of Trustees
Arbitron Metro Market: Gainesville-Oca *Format:* Contemporary Hits/Top 40 *Special Programming:* Alternative 6 hrs wkly *Hrs. of News Programming:* news progmg 5 hrs wkly *No. News Employees:* 3 *Target Audience:* 25-34; urban rockers
Harry Guscott, Operations Dir
Larry Dankner, General Manager
Tom Kymski, News Director
Don Rice, Chief Engineer
Monica Richs, Disc Jockey
Matt Lehtola, Disc Jockey
Cathy Ferguson, Traffic Manager

*WUFT-FM
09-27-1981; 89.1 mhz FM *Hrs Open:* 24; 100 kw; 771 ft.; N29 42 34 W82 23 40
2208 Weimer Hall, Gainesville, FL 32611 US
(352) 392-5551, *Fax:* (352) 392-5731
www.wuft.org
info@wuft.org
License: Gainesville, Alachua County, FL held by Board of Trustees, University of Florida.
Nat'l Network: NPR; PRI *Regional Network:* Fla. Pub.
Arbitron Metro Market: Gainesville, FL *TV Affiliate:* *WUFT-TV affl. *Format:* Jazz *Special Programming:* Black 4 hrs, folk one hr, wkly *Hrs. of News Programming:* news progmg 15 hrs wkly *No. News Employees:* 3 *Target Audience:* 35-65; general, educated (some college or degree)
Steve Seipp, Operations Dir
Larry Dankner, General Manager
Henri Pensis, Station Manager
Bill Beckett, Programming Director
Kevin Allen, News Director
Manis Samons, Chief Engineer
Richard Drake, Music Director

WTMN
01-01-1990; 1430 khz AM
249 W. University Ave., Suite B, Gainesville, FL 32601 US
(352) 313-3150, *Fax:* (352) 338-0566
rejoice@musicalsoulfood.com
License: Gainesville, FL held by 6 Johnson Road Licenses Inc.
Group Owner: Pamal Broadcasting Ltd.; (acq 1-5-2007; grpsl)
Arbitron Metro Market: Gainesville, FL *Format:* Gospel
Benjamin Hill, General Manager

*WYFB
08-04-1985; 90.5 mhz FM *Hrs Open:* 24; 97 kw; 679 ft.; N29 52 8 W82 12 4
8030 Arrowridge Blvd., Charlotte, NC 28273 US

(704) 523-5555, *Fax:* (704) 522-1967
www.bbnradio.org
bbn@bbnradio.org
License: Gainesville, Alachua County, FL held by Bible Broadcasting Network Inc.
Group Owner: Bible Broadcasting Network
Nat'l Network: Bible Bcstg Net; USA
Arbitron Metro Market: Gainesville, FL *Format:* Religious *Hrs. of News Programming:* News progmg 12 hrs wkly *Target Audience:* General.
Lowell Davey, President
David Nichols, General Manager

WXJZ
05-01-1982; 100.9 mhz FM *Hrs Open:* 24; 6 kw; 299 ft.; N29 38 3 W82 18 50
1429 N. Federal Hwy, Ft. Lauderdale, FL 33304 US
(352) 375-1317, *Fax:* (352) 375-6961
www.wxjz.fm
feedback@wxjz.fm
License: Gainesville, Alachua County, FL held by Asterisk Communications Inc.
Group Owner: Asterisk Inc.; (acq 10-4-93; $1.4 million;
Nat'l Network: Jones Radio Networks *Nat'l Reps:* McGavren Guild
Arbitron Metro Market: Gainesville, FL *Format:* Jazz, Smooth Jazz *Target Audience:* 25-54; upscale, affluent, sophisticated
Adv. Rates: 30; 35; 30; 20
John Starr, General Manager
Bill Elliott, Programming Director

WYKS
05-04-1970; 105.3 mhz FM; 3 kw; 466 ft.; N29 37 53 W82 25 8
7120 Sw 24th Avenue, Gainesville, FL 32607 US
(352)331- 2200, *Fax:* (352) 331-0401
www.kiss1053.com
info@kiss1053.com
License: Gainesville, Alachua County, FL
Arbitron Metro Market: Gainesville, FL *Format:* Contemporary Hits/Top 40
Stephen Puffer, President
Teresa Puffer, Operations Dir
Don Smith, Chief Engineer

Gifford

WSYR-FM
06-01-1994; 94.7 mhz FM; 25 kw; 295 ft; N27 33 21 W80 22 08
290 Hegenberger Rd, Oakland, CA 94621
1-800-543-1495, *Fax:* (801) 359-8112
www.familyradio.com
info@familyradio.com
License: Gifford, Indian River County, FL held by Aloha Station Trust LLC
Population Served: 33,704 *Arbitron Metro Market:* Butte MT
Format: Christian, Religious
Harold Camping, General Manager

Golden Gate

WNPL
09-01-2008; 1460 khz AM
US
(239) 334-1111, *Fax:* (239) 332-0767
www.foxsportsradio1200.com
License: Golden Gate, FL held by Fort Myers Broadcasting Co.
Group Owner: Fort Myers Broadcasting Co.; (acq 6-18-2007; $975,000 for CP)
Nat'l Network: Fox Sports *Nat'l Reps:* McGavren Guild
Arbitron Metro Market: Denison, IA *Format:* Sports
Wayne Simons, Operations Dir
Brad Foster, General Sales Mgr

Goulds

WRTO-FM
02-01-1976; 98.3 mhz FM *Hrs Open:* 24; 100 kw; 1407 ft.; N25 32 24 W80 28 7
3102 Oak Lawn Avenue, Suite 215, Dallas, TX 75219 US
(305) 447-1140, *Fax:* (305) 529-6631
www.univision.com
License: Goulds, Dade County, FL held by License Corp. #2.
Group Owner: Univision Radio; (acq 9-22-2003; grpsl).
Arbitron Metro Market: Miami-Fort Laud
Claudia Puig, General Manager
Monica Rabassa, Promotions Manager

Graceville

WTOT-FM
01-01-1996; 101.7 mhz FM *Hrs Open:* 24; 6 kw; 328 ft.; N30 57 21 W85 29 53
9102 North Meridian St, Suite 500, Indianapolis, IN 46260 US
(850) 482-3046, *Fax:* (850) 482-3049
License: Graceville, Jackson County, FL held by GFR Inc.
Nat'l Network: ABC
Arbitron Metro Market: Graceville, FL *Format:* Adult Contemp
Target Audience: 25+; female *Adv. Rates:* 10; 8; 9; 6
Ed Cearley, General Manager

Greenville

*WYJC
01-01-2005; 90.3 mhz FM; 0.325 kw vert; 184 ft.; N30 23 56 W83 39 24 *Rebroadcasts:* Rebroadcasts WUJC(FM) Saint Marks 100%
US
(800) 357-4226, *Fax:* (208) 736-1958
www.csnradio.com
csn@csnradio.com
License: Greenville, Madison County, FL held by CSN International
Group Owner: CSN International
Arbitron Metro Market: Greenville, FL *Format:* Christian
Mike Kestler, President
Daniel Davidson, Operations Dir
Don Mills, Network Programming Director / Music Director
Kelly Carlson, Engineering Dir
Jerry Johnson, Engineering Dir
Ray Gorney, Assistant Director of Engineering
DustinPamplona, Engineer
Nolan Mather, Graphics / Website Maintenance
Mike Stocklin, National Underwriting
Austin Morris, Accounting
Lois Mills, FCC Applications / Translator Site Manager

Gretna

WGWD
10-02-1989; 93.3 mhz FM *Hrs Open:* 24; 8.7 kw; 499 ft.; N30 29 48 W84 27 33
Mailing Address: P.O.Box 919, 8 West Washington Street, Quincy, FL 32351 US
Second Address: 8 W. Washington, Quincy, FL 32351
(850) 627-7086, *Fax:* (850) 627-3422
License: Gretna, Gadsden County, FL held by De Col Inc.
Nat'l Network: USA
Format: Country *Special Programming:* Black 20 hrs wkly *Hrs. of News Programming:* News progmg 21 hrs wkly *Target Audience:* 25-54.
Pat Bitner, Operations Dir
Monte Bitner, General Manager
Jan Rogers, News Director
Jeff Fallaway, Chief Engineer

Gulf Breeze

WNRP
02-01-1998; 1620 khz AM
P.O. Box 10, 805 N. Main St., Atmore, AL 36502 US
(850) 494-2800, *Fax:* (850) 494-0778
www.newsradio1620.com
License: Gulf Breeze, FL held by ADX Communications of Escambia
Arbitron Metro Market: Pensacola, FL *Format:* News, News/Talk, 86 *Target Audience:* 35-64; 60% male, 40% female
Mary Hoxeng, General Manager
Bob Nieman, Station Manager
Jeff Wayne, General Sales Mgr
Tracey Castillo, Promotions Manager
Tim McEvoy, Engineering Dir

WRNE
11-01-1957; 980 khz AM *Hrs Open:* 24
312 E. Nine Mile Road, Pensacola, FL 32514 US
(850) 478-6000, *Fax:* (850) 484-8080
www.wrne980.com
hill@wrne980.com
License: Gulf Breeze, FL held by Media One Communications Inc.
Nat'l Reps: Dora-Clayton
Arbitron Metro Market: Pensacola, FL *Format:* Gospel *Special Programming:* Gospel, talk *Hrs. of News Programming:* news progmg 5 hrs wkly *No. News Employees:* 1 *Target Audience:* 25-54; minorities
Robert Hill, President

WRRX
106.1 mhz FM; 3.9 kw; 407 ft.; N30 26 36 W87 14 4
300 East Rock Rd., (Wfmz-Tv), Allentown, PA 18103 US
(404) 949-0700, *Fax:* (404) 949-0740
www.cumulus.com
webmaster@cumulus.com
License: Gulf Breeze, Santa Rosa County, FL held by Cumulus Licensing Corp.
Arbitron Metro Market: Atlanta, GA *Format:* Urban Contemporary
Lewis W. Dickey, Jr., Chairman, President & CEO
Debbie Dingwall, Operations Dir
Liz Hanlon, General Manager
Jonathan G. Pinch, Executive Vice President & Co-Chief Operating Offi
John W. Dickey, Executive Vice President & Co-ChiefOperating Offi
Richard S. Denning, Senior Vice President, Secretary & General Counsel
Joseph P. Hannan, Senior Vice President, Treasurer & Chief Financial
Linda A. Hill, Vice President, Corporate Controller & Chief Accou

Gulfport

WFUS
10-01-1963; 103.5 mhz FM; 66 kw; 1549 ft.; N27 49 9.7 W82 15 38.7
50 East Rivercenter Blvd, Suite 1200, Covington, KY 41011 US
(813) 832-1000, *Fax:* (813) 832-1090
www.us1035.com
License: Gulfport, Pinellas County, FL held by Citicasters Licenses L.P.
Group Owner: Clear Channel Communications Inc.; (acq 6-99; grpsl)
Wire Services: AP
Arbitron Metro Market: Tampa, FL *Format:* Country *Target Audience:* 25-54; men
Russell Linker, CFO
Dan DiLoreto, Operations Dir
Lisa Rice, General Sales Mgr
Travis Daily, Programming Director
Rebecca Kaplan, Promotions Manager
Sandra Ambrosino, News Director
John McMartin, Chief Engineer
Ryan Nelson,Music Director
Josh Jenson, Creative Services Director
Rachel Pitts, Internship Director
Ethan Youker, Public Services Director

Haines City

*WLVF-FM
04-11-1986; 90.3 mhz FM *Hrs Open:* 24; 0.75 kw; 315 ft.; N28 6 49 W81 37 23
110 W. Scenic Highway, Haines City, FL 33844 US
(863) 422-5175, *Fax:* (863) 422-0110
www.gospel903.com
info@gospel903.com
License: Haines City, Polk County, FL held by Landmark Baptist Church
Nat'l Network: USA
Arbitron Metro Market: Haines City, FL *Format:* Gospel
Lewis Cruz, Operations Dir
Steven Carter, General Manager
Lewis Cruz, Station Manager
Bobby Ogden, General Sales Mgr
Jeff Crews, Chief Engineer

Hammocks

*WMKL
10-01-1998; 91.9 mhz FM *Hrs Open:* 24; 25 kw vert; 318 ft.; N25 45 41.63 W80 49 10.77
1601 Belvedere Rd., 204e, West Palm Beach, FL 33406 US
(786) 429-3606, *Fax:* (305) 251-2293
www.callfm.com
callfm@callfm.com
License: Hammocks, Monroe County, FL held by Call Communications Group Inc.
Arbitron Metro Market: Hammocks, FL *Format:* Christian *Target Audience:* 13-25.
Robert Robbins, President
Kelly Downing, Programming Director
Jim Sorensen, Chief Engineer

Havana

WHTF
01-01-1986; 104.9 mhz FM *Hrs Open:* 24; 47 kw; 505 ft.; N30 35 11 W84 14 11
25 Reliance Drive, Bristol, RI 02809 US

(850) 386-8004, *Fax:* (850) 442-1897
www.hot1049.com
License: Havana, Gadsden County, FL held by Opus Broadcasting Tallahassee LLC.
Group Owner: Opus Media Holdings LLC; (acq 9-2-2005; grpsl)
Nat'l Reps: McGavren Guild
Arbitron Metro Market: Tallahassee, FL *Format:* Contemporary Hits/Top 40 *Target Audience:* 18-49.
Doug Purtee, Operations Dir
Hank Kestenbaum, General Manager

Hernando

WRZN
06-01-1989; 720 khz AM; 10 kw-D, DAN; 0.25 kw-N, DAN; N28 55 21 W82 22 21
Mailing Address: 3974 Patch Drive, Tallahassee, FL 32308 US
Second Address: 3938 N. Roscoe Rd., Hernando, FL 34442
(352) 726-7221, *Fax:* (352) 726-3172
License: Hernando, FL held by 6 Johnson Road Licenses Inc.
Group Owner: Pamal Broadcasting Ltd.; (acq 1-5-2007; grpsl)
Format: Adult Contemp *Special Programming:* Loc news 4 hrs wkly *Target Audience:* 45 plus.
Ben Hill, General Manager
Reggie Thomas, General Sales Mgr
Jim Brand, Programming Director

Hialeah

WACC
12-01-1987; 830 khz AM *Hrs Open:* 24; 1 kw-D, DA2; 1 kw-N, DA2; N25 46 22 W80 25 16
3785 N.W. 82nd Ave., Suite 312, Miami, FL 33166 US
(956) 487-8015
License: Hialeah, FL held by Radio Peace Catholic Broadcasting Inc.
Arbitron Metro Market: Reno NV *Adv. Rates:* 100; 100; 100; 50
Eloy Vera, General Manager

WCMQ-FM
12-22-1969; 92.3 mhz FM; 31 kw; 617 ft.; N25 46 24 W80 11 18
3191 Coral Way, Suite 805, Miami, FL 33145 US
(305) 444-9292, *Fax:* (305) 883-7701
www.z92miami.com
saludos@clasica92fm.com
License: Hialeah, Dade County, FL held by WCMQ Licensing Inc.
Group Owner: Spanish Broadcasting System Inc.; (acq 12-22-86; grpsl;
Arbitron Metro Market: Miami-Fort Lauderdale-Hollywood, FL
Format: Adult Contemp
Tony Campos, Operations Dir
Jackie Nosti-Combo, General Manager
Albert Rodriguez, General Sales Mgr
John Caride, Promotions Manager

High Springs

***WUBA**
01-01-1923; 88.1 mhz FM *Hrs Open:* 24; kw
US
(610) 617-8500, *Fax:* (610) 617-8501
www.rumba1045.com
License: High Springs, Philadelphia County, FL held by AMFM Radio Licenses LLC.
Group Owner: Clear Channel Communications Inc.; (acq 8-30-2000; grpsl)
Arbitron Metro Market: Philadelphia, PA
Joseph Tamburro, General Manager

WYGC
01-31-1984; 104.9 mhz FM *Hrs Open:* 24; 3.2 kw; 449 ft.; N29 49 16 W82 34 25
2848 East Oakland Park Boulevard, Fort Lauderdale, FL 33306 US
(352) 375-1317, *Fax:* (352) 375-6961
www.105thegame.com
sales@thestar.fm
License: High Springs, Alachua County, FL held by Asterisk Communications Inc.
Group Owner: Asterisk Inc.; (acq 2-99; $825,000).
Nat'l Network: CNN Radio; Westwood One
Arbitron Metro Market: Gainesville, FL *Format:* Country *Hrs. of News Programming:* News progmg 4 hrs wkly *Target Audience:* 25-54. *Adv. Rates:* 60; 60; 60; 20
Dean Johnson, General Manager
Joey Cuffari, Contact Person

Hobe Sound

WOLL
01-01-2002; 105.5 mhz FM; 50 kw; 456 ft.; N26 45 42 W80 4 42
200 Concord Plaza, Suite 600, San Antonio, TX 78216 US
(561) 616-6600, *Fax:* (561) 616-6677
www.1055online.com
info@1055online.com
License: Hobe Sound, Martin County, FL held by Aloha Station Trust LLC, as Trustee
Arbitron Metro Market: West Palm Beach *TV Affiliate:* Classic Hits *No. News Employees:* 25-54.
Promotions, Promotions Manager

Holiday

WSUN-FM
01-01-1979; 97.1 mhz FM *Hrs Open:* 24; 11.5 kw; 735 ft.; N28 10 56 W82 46 6
11521 Innfields Drive, Odessa, FL 33556 US
(727) 579-2000, *Fax:* (727) 579-2662,(727) 579-2271
www.97xonline.com
97xcomments@97xonline.com
License: Holiday, Pasco County, FL held by Cox Radio Inc.
Group Owner: Cox Radio Inc.; (acq 11-20-98)
Arbitron Metro Market: Tampa-St. Petersburg-Clearwater, FL
Format: Alternative *Target Audience:* 35 plus. *Adv. Rates:* 60; 50; 60; 40
Bob Neil, CEO
Keith Lawless, Operations Dir
Dan Connelly, Promotions Manager
Tom Paleveda, Operations Manager

Holly Hill

***WAPN**
10-01-1985; 91.5 mhz FM *Hrs Open:* 24; 1.8 kw; 285 ft.; N29 15 6 W81 2 53
Mailing Address: 1508 State Avenue, Holly Hill, FL 32117 US
Second Address: 1508 State Ave., Daytona Beach, FL 32125
(386) 677-4272(386) 672-3333, *Fax:* (386) 677-7095
www.wapn.net
wapn@wapn.net
License: Holly Hill, Volusia County, FL held by Public Radio Capital Florida
Arbitron Metro Market: Holly Hill, FL *Format:* Religious *Special Programming:* Sp 4 hrs wkly *Target Audience:* General.
Shellye Lund-Vallance, General Manager
Earlyne Lund, Owner

WVYB
01-01-1997; 103.3 mhz FM *Hrs Open:* 24; 6 kw; 295 ft.; N29 14 11 W81 4 22
126 West International Speedway Blvd., Daytona Beach, FL 32214 US
(386) 255-9300, *Fax:* (386) 238-6071
www.newsdaytonabeach.com
fargo@blackcrow.fm
License: Holly Hill, Volusia County, FL held by Black Crow LLC.
Group Owner: Black Crow Media Group LLC; (acq 9-21-2001; grpsl).
Arbitron Metro Market: Daytona Beach, FL *Format:* Adult Contemp *Hrs. of News Programming:* News progmg 2 hrs wkly *Target Audience:* 18-49.
Stacey Knerler, General Manager
Donna Filon, Director of Sales
Fargo, Programming Director
DJ Tremble, Music Director

Hollywood

WLQY
04-01-1953; 1320 khz AM
1436 Auburn Boulevard, Sacramento, CA 95815 US
(305) 891-1729, *Fax:* (305) 891-1583
www.entravision.com
wlqy@bellsouth.net
License: Hollywood, FL held by Entravision Holdings LLC.
Group Owner: Entravision Communications Corp.; (acq 7-28-00; grpsl).
Arbitron Metro Market: Miami-Fort Lauderdale-Hollywood, FL
Format: Ethnic *Target Audience:* 35 plus; female
Jeff Liberman, President
Rick Santos, General Manager

Holmes Beach

WHFS-FM
98.7 mhz; 50000 w; 489 ft; N27 50 32 W82 48 52
600 New Hampshire Avenue, Suite 200, Washington, DC 20037
(301)306-0091, *Fax:* (301)731-0431
www.b1063fm.com
License: Holmes Beach, Manatee County, FL
Group Owner: CBS Radio Stations
Patrice Wright, Programming
Kailey Mills, Promotions Manager

Homestead

WOIR
11-04-1957; 1430 khz AM
206 Washington Ave, Homestead, FL 33030 US
(305) 270-1430
http://www.zoe1430.com/
lenriquez@vida1430am.com
License: Homestead, FL held by Amanecer Christian Network Inc.
Arbitron Metro Market: Miami-Fort Laud *TV Affiliate:* Sp

***WRGP**
01-01-1999; 88.1 mhz FM *Hrs Open:* 24; 0.165 kw; 423 ft.; N25 32 24 W80 28 7
University Park Campus, 11200 S.W. 8th Street, Miami, FL 33199 US
(305) 348-3071, *Fax:* (305) 348-6665
wrgp.org
wrgp@fiu.edu
License: Homestead, Dade County, FL held by Florida International University.
Arbitron Metro Market: Miami-Fort Lauderdale-Hollywood, FL
Format: Variety/Diverse *Special Programming:* Hip hop 12 hrs, news 3 hrs, raggae 3 hrs wkly *Hrs. of News Programming:* News progmg 4 hrs wkly *TargetAudience:* General; young adults, mainly university students
Brennan Forsyth, General Manager
Jennifer Mojena, Programming Director

Homosassa Springs

WXCV
03-01-1983; 95.3 mhz FM *Hrs Open:* 24; 6 kw; 328 ft.; N28 50 3 W82 39 34
P.O. Box 1408, Crystal River, FL 34423 US
(352) 628-4444, *Fax:* (352) 628-4450
www.citrus953.com
staff@citrus.com
License: Homosassa Springs, Citrus County, FL held by Westwind Broadcasting Inc.
Arbitron Metro Market: Homosassa Springs, FL *Format:* Classic Rock *Special Programming:* Jazz 7 hrs, oldies 6 hrs wkly *Hrs. of News Programming:* news progmg 7 hrs wkly *No. News Employees:* 1 *Target Audience:* 25-54.
Laura Grady, General Manager
Ryan Downs, Programming Director
Jody Boles, Traffic Director
Annette Kimball, Senior Account Executive
Brittany Jones, Account Executive
Mary Castro, Account Executive

Immokalee

WAFZ
10-14-1964; 1490 khz AM *Hrs Open:* 24
2105 W. Immokalee Dr., Immokalee, FL 33934 US
(239) 657-9210, *Fax:* (239) 658-6109
www.wafz.com
iza@gladesmedia.com
License: Immokalee, FL held by Glades Media Company LLP.
Nat'l Network: CNN Radio *Nat'l Reps:* Univision Radio National Sales
Arbitron Metro Market: Fort Myers-Naples-Marco Island, FL
Target Audience: Sp
Ricardo Chairez, Operations Dir
KC Kelly, General Manager
Jesus Castro, Programming Director
Robbie Castellanos, Partner

WAFZ-FM
01-01-1995; 92.1 mhz FM *Hrs Open:* 24; 5.6 kw; 328 ft.; N26 26 54 W81 16 17
3061 Terrace Ave., Naples, FL 34104 US
(239) 657-9210, *Fax:* (239) 658-6109
www.radiofiesta.com
robbie@gladesmedia.com
License: Immokalee, Collier County, FL held by Glades Media Co. LLC
Nat'l Network: CNN Radio *Nat'l Reps:* Univision Radio National Sales
Arbitron Metro Market: Fort Myers-Naples-Marco Island, FL
Format: Tejano *Target Audience:* 18 plus; general *Adv. Rates:* 20; 15; 20; 15
Robbie Castellanos, President
Ricardlo Chairez, Operations Dir
Alfredo Hernandez, General Manager

Indian Lakes Estates

*WLOQ
01-01-1966; 88.7 mhz FM *Hrs Open:* 24; kw
US
(407) 647-5557, *Fax:* (407) 647-4495
www.wloq.com
frontdesk@wloq.com
License: Indian Lakes Estates, Orange County, FL held by Gross Communications Corp.
Nat'l Reps: Interep
Arbitron Metro Market: Orlando, FL *Format:* Jazz *Target Audience:* 25-54; white collar/professionals
John Gross, CFO
Herbert Gross, President
Rick Weinkauf, Operations Dir
Ken Marks, General Sales Mgr

Indian River Shores

WOSN
01-01-1996; 97.1 mhz FM; 23 kw; 348 ft.; N27 44 6 W80 27 27
3825 Forrestgate Drive, Suite 100, Winston-Salem, NC 27103
US
(772) 567-0937, *Fax:* (772) 562-4747
www.wosnfm.com
License: Indian River Shores, Indian River County, FL held by Vero Beach Broadcasters LLC
Group Owner: Vero Beach Broadcasters LLC; acq 2-15-01; $4.1 million).
Arbitron Metro Market: Fort Pierce-Stuart-Vero Beach, FL *Format:* Adult Contemp
Jim Davis, General Manager
Hamp Elliott, Programming Director
John Rotolante, Promotions Manager

Indian Rocks Beach

WXYB
05-11-1963; 1520 khz AM *Hrs Open:* Sunrise-sunset; 0.6 kw-D, NDD; N27 50 45 W82 46 21
27873 U.S. 19 North, Clearwater, FL 34621 US
(727) 725-5555, *Fax:* (813) 814-7500
www.wpso.com
wpso@wpso.com
License: Indian Rocks Beach, FL held by ASA Broadcasting Inc.
Arbitron Metro Market: Indian Rocks Beach, FL *Format:* Ethnic, Greek, 60, News/Talk, Talk *Special Programming:* Indian 3 hrs, It 2 hrs, Pol 2 hrs, East Indian one *Hrs. of News Programming:* News progmg 7 hrs wkly*Target Audience:* General; international, ethnic
Sam Agelatos, President
Angelo Agelatos, Station Manager

Indiantown

WIRK
08-01-1965; 103.1 mhz FM; 90 kw; 974 ft.; N27 1 31 W80 10 43
701 Northpoint Pkwy, Suite 500, West Palm Beach, FL 33407
US
(561) 686-9505, *Fax:* (561) 686-0157
www.wirk.com
info@wirk.com
License: Indiantown, Palm Beach County, FL held by CBS Radio Inc.
Group Owner: CBS Radio; (acq 11-13-98; grpsl).
Arbitron Metro Market: West Palm Beach-Boca Raton, FL *Format:* Country
Lee Strasser, Operations Dir
Tony Bonvini, General Sales Mgr

WIRK(FM)
07-04-1965; 103.1 mhz FM *Hrs Open:* 24; 90 kw; 974 ft; N27 01 32 W80 10 43
701 Northpoint Pkwy., Suite 400, West Palm Beach, FL 33407
(561) 616-4600, *Fax:* (561) 684-6311
www.buzz103.com
mcmeatal169@buzz103.com
License: Indiantown, Martin County, FL held by Infinity Radio Inc.
Group Owner: CBS Radio; (acq 12-14-00; grpsl).
Arbitron Metro Market: West Palm Beach-Boca Raton, FL *Format:* Alternative *Hrs. of News Programming:* news progmg 12 hrs wkly *No. News Employees:* 1 *Target Audience:* 18-34; men
John O'Connell, Operations Dir
Lee Strasser, General Manager
Fran Marcone, General Sales Mgr
Lynette Shady, Promotions Manager
Lane Racette, News Director
Chuck Herlihey, Chief Engineer
Jason Davis, Disc Jockey
Nik Rivers,Music Director
Susan Oland, National Sales Manager

Inglis

WYKE(FM)
10-01-1994; 104.3 mhz FM *Hrs Open:* 24; 4.4 kw; Ant 380 ft; N29 01 18 W82 41 20
11928 N. William St., Dunnellon, FL 34432
(352) 522-0172, *Fax:* (352) 564-8750
www.wow104.com
wifl@xtalwind.net
License: Inglis, Levy County, FL held by Nature Coast Broadcasting Inc.
Regional Network: Florida's Radio Networks
Population Served: 350,000 *Arbitron Metro Market:* Gainesville-Ocala, FL *Format:* Adult Contemp *Hrs. of News Programming:* News progmg one hr wkly *Target Audience:* 25-54. *Adv. Rates:* 20; 10; 15; 10
Lisa Cuppelli, CEO
Sab Cupelli, President
Marc Tyll, Operations Dir
Jeremy Howard, General Sales Mgr
Jon Kay, Operations Manager

WXRA
01-01-2008; 99.3 mhz FM; 3.7 kw; 420 ft.; N29 9 19 W82 27 1
US
(901) 375-9324, *Fax:* (901) 375-5889
www.flinn.com
mail@flinn.com
License: Inglis, Levy County, FL held by George S. Flinn Jr.
Arbitron Metro Market: Inglis, FL *Format:* Christian
George Flinn Jr., President

Inverness

*WJUF
10-01-1995; 90.1 mhz FM *Hrs Open:* 24; 21 kw; 397 ft.; N28 46 39 W82 28 5 *Rebroadcasts:* Rebroadcasts WUFT-FM Gainesville 100%
2208 Weimer Hall, University of Florida, Gainesville, FL 32611
US
(352) 392-5200, *Fax:* (352) 392-5741
www.wuft.org
info@wuft.org
License: Inverness, Citrus County, FL held by Board of Trustees, University of Florida.
Nat'l Network: NPR; PRI *Regional Network:* Fla. Pub.
TV Affiliate: *WUFT-TV affil. *Format:* Classical, Jazz, 60 *Hrs. of News Programming:* news progmg 15 hrs wkly *No. News Employees:* 3 *Target Audience:* General.
Larry Dankner, General Manager
Henri Pensis, Station Manager

Islamorada

WWWK
10-15-1984; 105.5 mhz FM; 50 kw; 430 ft.; N25 5 29 W80 26 37
200 Concord Plaza, Suite 600, San Antonio, TX 78216 US
(270) 389-1550, *Fax:* (270) 389-1553
www.wmskamfm.com
wmsk@bellsouth.net
License: Islamorada, Monroe County, FL held by LSM Radio Partners LLC
Arbitron Metro Market: Morganfield KY *Format:* Country, Religious *Hrs. of News Programming:* News progmg 20 hrs wkly *Target Audience:* General; adults 25-64
Edward Henson, President
Bob Hite, Operations Dir
John Robinson, General Manager
Don Sheridan, General Sales Mgr
Rhonda Gibson, Traffic Manager

*WAZQ
89.3 mhz FM; kw
US
(561) 912-9002
License: Islamorada, Monroe County, FL held by Educational Public Radio Inc.
Arbitron Metro Market: Islamorada, FL *Format:* Adult Contemp *No. News Employees:* 12 *Target Audience:* 18-54; adults
Bill Lacy, President

Jacksonville

WAPE-FM
04-01-1949; 95.1 mhz FM; 100 kw; 984 ft.; N30 19 22 W81 38 34
600 Congress Avenue, Suite 1400, Austin, TX 78701 US
(904) 245-8500, *Fax:* (904) 245-8501
www.wape.com
kane@wape.com
License: Jacksonville, Duval County, FL held by Cox Radio Inc.
Group Owner: Cox Radio Inc.; (acq 8-00; grpsl).
Nat'l Network: Fox News Radio *Nat'l Reps:* Christal *Wire Services:* AP
Arbitron Metro Market: Jacksonville, FL *Format:* Contemporary Hits/Top 40
David Isreal, General Manager
Matt Urban, General Sales Mgr
Kane, Programming Director
Beth Gettys, Promotions Manager
Mark Frank, National Sales Manager

WBOB(AM)
12-09-1933; 600 khz AM *Hrs Open:* 24; 5 kw-D, 5.4 kw-N, DA-N; N30 18 00 W81 45 34
10245 Centurion Pkwy., Suite 109, Jacksonville, FL 32256
(904) 646-1100(904) 783-3711, *Fax:* (904) 646-1117
www.radiodisney.com
License: Jacksonville, Duval County, FL held by Radio Disney Group LLC.
Group Owner: ABC Inc.; (acq 8-1-02; $2.5 million).
Nat'l Network: Radio Disney
Population Served: 827,908 *Arbitron Metro Market:* Jacksonville, FL *Format:* Children
Jay Schneider, Station Manager

WCGL
01-01-1948; 1360 khz AM *Hrs Open:* 24; 5 kw-D, ND2; 0.089 kw-N, ND2; N30 16 33 W81 38 12
6050-6 Moncrief Road, Jacksonville, FL 32209 US
(904) 766-9955, *Fax:* (904) 765-9214
www.wcgl1360.com
wcgl@aol.com
License: Jacksonville, FL held by JBD Communications Inc.
Arbitron Metro Market: Jacksonville, FL *Format:* Religious *Target Audience:* 25 plus.
Deborah Maiden, President
Kelvin Postell, Operations Dir

WEJZ
01-01-1949; 96.1 mhz FM; 100 kw; 984 ft.; N30 19 22 W81 38 34
Broadcast Plaza, Crane Ave., Pittsburgh, PA 15220 US
(904) 727-9696, *Fax:* (904) 721-9322
www.wejz.com
breese@rendabroadcasting.com
License: Jacksonville, Duval County, FL held by Renda Broadcasting Corp.
Group Owner: Renda Broadcasting Corp.; acq 6-90; grpsl;
Nat'l Reps: McGavren Guild *Wire Services:* Metro Weather Service Inc.
Arbitron Metro Market: Jacksonville, FL *Format:* Adult Contemp *Target Audience:* 25-54; office, home & in-the-car audience
Tony Renda Sr., CEO
Bill Scull, General Manager
Bill Reese, General Sales Mgr
Chuck Beck, Programming Director
Woody Carlson, Promotions Manager
Jim Byard, News Director
Bob Dillehay, Chief Engineer
Jim Byard, Public ServiceDirector

WJAX
01-01-1958; 1220 khz AM *Hrs Open:* 24; 1 kw-D, ND2; 0.036 kw-N, ND2; N30 19 30 W81 34 15
5353 Arlington Expreway, Jacksonville, FL 32211 US
(904) 680-1220
www.wktz.jones.edu
kjones@jones.edu
License: Jacksonville, FL held by Jones College
Nat'l Network: CNN Radio
Arbitron Metro Market: Jacksonville, FL *Format:* Adult Contemp *Target Audience:* 40 plus.
Jamey Styer, Operations Dir
John Wharff III, General Manager
Andy Rex, Programming Director
Ralph Matheny, Chief Engineer

*WJCT-FM
04-17-1972; 89.9 mhz FM; 98 kw; 823 ft.; N30 16 51 W81 34 12
100 Festival Park Avenue, Jacksonville, FL 32206 US
(904) 353-7770, *Fax:* (904) 358-6352
www.wjct.org
wjct@wjct.org
License: Jacksonville, Duval County, FL held by WJCT Inc.
Nat'l Network: NPR; PRI *Regional Network:* Fla. Pub.
Arbitron Metro Market: Jacksonville, FL *TV Affiliate:* *WJCT-TV affil. *Format:* News, News/Talk, 86
Michael Boylan, CEO
Tom Patton, News Director

*WJFR
09-15-1987; 88.7 mhz FM; 8 kw; 351 ft.; N30 19 43 W81 41 42

4135 Northgate Blvd, Suite1, Sacramento, CA 95834 US
(904) 389-9088
www.familyradio.com
License: Jacksonville, Duval County, FL held by Family Stations Inc.
Arbitron Metro Market: Jacksonville, FL *Format:* Religious *Target Audience:* Conservative Christians.
Harold Camping, President
Harold Camping, General Manager
Marcy Morrison-Pearce, Programming Director
Phyllis Johnston, Music Director

WBOB
01-01-1945; 600 khz AM
600 Congress Ave., Suite 1400, Austin, TX 78701 US
(904) 470-4615, *Fax:* (904) 296-1683
www.wbobradio.com
robin719@comes.net
License: Jacksonville, FL held by Chesapeake-Portsmouth Broadcasting Corp.
Group Owner: Chesapeake-Portsmouth Broadcasting Corp.; (acq 12-5-2006; $1.8 million with WZNZ(AM) Jacksonville)
Arbitron Metro Market: Jacksonville, FL *Format:* News, News/Talk, 86 *Target Audience:* 25-54.
Calvin Grabau, Operations Dir
Henry Hoot, General Manager

WJGL
07-01-1969; 96.9 mhz FM *Hrs Open:* 24; 98 kw; 1014 ft.; N30 16 34 W81 33 53
600 Congress Ave., Suite 1400, Austin, TX 78701 US
(904) 245-8500, *Fax:* (904) 245-8501
www.969TheEagle.com
todd.shannon@coxinc.com
License: Jacksonville, Duval County, FL held by Cox Radio Inc.
Group Owner: Cox Radio Inc.
Nat'l Network: Fox News Radio *Nat'l Reps:* Christal
Arbitron Metro Market: Jacksonville, FL *Format:* Contemporary Hits/Top 40, Adult Contemp *No. News Employees:* 1 *Target Audience:* Adults 25-54
Bill Hendrich, General Manager
Jenny Sutton, General Sales Mgr
Todd Shannon, Programming Director
Laura Hermanson, Promotions Manager
A.J. Vanghan, Local Sales Manager
Jodi Rainey, National Sales Manager

***WKTZ-FM**
02-08-1973; 90.9 mhz FM *Hrs Open:* 24; 50 kw; 463 ft.; N30 16 36 W81 33 47
5353 Arlington Expressway, Jacksonville, FL 32211 US
(904) 731-1184
wktz.jones.edu
License: Jacksonville, Duval County, FL held by Jones College
Nat'l Network: AP Network News
Arbitron Metro Market: Jacksonville, FL *Format:* Easy Listening *Target Audience:* 40+.
Kenneth Jones, General Manager
Dick Jones, Chief Engineer
Tom Buetow, Music Director

WXXJ
11-01-1965; 102.9 mhz FM *Hrs Open:* 24; 98 kw; 1014 ft.; N30 16 34 W81 33 53
600 Congress Ave., Suite 1400, Austin, TX 78701 US
(904) 245-8500, *Fax:* (904) 245-8501
www.x1029.com
aaron.schachter@coxinc.com
License: Jacksonville, Duval County, FL held by Cox Radio Inc.
Group Owner: Cox Radio Inc.; (acq 2-23-2000; grpsl)
Nat'l Network: Fox News Radio *Nat'l Reps:* Christal
Arbitron Metro Market: Jacksonville, FL *Format:* Rock/AOR *Target Audience:* Men 18-34
David Isreal, General Manager
Matt Urban, General Sales Mgr
Aaron Schachter, Programming Director
Liz Goshert, Promotions Manager
Mark Frank, National Sales Manager

***WCRJ**
03-16-1984; 88.1 mhz FM *Hrs Open:* 24; 8 kw; 495 ft.; N30 16 34 W81 33 53
2361 Cortez Rd., Jacksonville, FL 32246 US
(904) 641-9626, *Fax:* (904) 645-9626
www.klove.com
calvin@fm88.org
License: Jacksonville, Duval County, FL held by The River Educational Media Inc.
Arbitron Metro Market: Jacksonville, FL *Format:* Christian *Target Audience:* 25-55; women
Roger Henderson, Operations Dir
Calvin Grabau, General Manager

WFXJ
11-01-1925; 930 khz AM; 5 kw-D, DAN; 5 kw-N, DAN; N30 17 9 W81 44 52
200 Concord Plaza, Suite 600, San Antonio, TX 78216 US
(904) 636-0507, *Fax:* (904) 997-7713
www.930thefox.com
victoriagowan@clearchannel.com
License: Jacksonville, FL held by Clear Channel Radio Licenses Inc.
Group Owner: Clear Channel Communications Inc.
Arbitron Metro Market: Jacksonville, F *TV Affiliate:* Sports *No. News Employees:* 25-49; men
Executive Producer

WYMM
11-18-1976; 1530 khz AM; 50 kw-D, DAD; N30 21 50 W81 44 54
3801 Skillern Blvd, Flower Mound, TX 75028 US
(904) 786-2820, *Fax:* (904) 786-2661
am1530jax@yahoo.com
License: Jacksonville, FL held by Word Broadcasting Network Inc.
Group Owner: Word Broadcasting Network Inc.; (acq 7-29-2003; $1.25 million with WYRM(AM) Norfolk, VA).
Arbitron Metro Market: Jacksonville, F *TV Affiliate:* Sp *Adv. Rates:* varies

WQIK-FM
09-01-1964; 99.1 mhz FM *Hrs Open:* 24; 100 kw; 991 ft.; N30 16 51 W81 34 13
50 East Rivercenter Blvd, Suite 1200, Covington, KY 41011 US
(904) 642-3030, *Fax:* (904) 997-7707
www.wqik.com
tanderson@ccjax.com
License: Jacksonville, Duval County, FL held by Citicasters Licenses L.P.
Group Owner: Clear Channel Communications Inc.; (acq 5-4-99; grpsl).
Nat'l Network: ABC
Arbitron Metro Market: Jacksonville, FL *Format:* Country *Hrs. of News Programming:* news progmg 4 hrs wkly *No. News Employees:* 1 *Target Audience:* 18-54.
John Hogan, Operations Dir
Norm Feuer, General Manager
Tony Anderson, Promotions Manager
Gail Austin, Operations Director

WQOP
01-30-1958; 1460 khz AM
Mailing Address: 11521 Innfields Drive, Odessa, FL 33556 US
Second Address: 391 S. 14th Ave., Jacksonville Beach, FL 32250
(904) 241-3311, *Fax:* (904) 241-1402
www.qopradio.com
radioqop@aol.com
License: Jacksonville, FL held by Queen of Peace Radio, Inc.
Nat'l Network: USA
Arbitron Metro Market: Jacksonville, FL *Format:* Talk, Religious
C. Williams, President
Tom Moran, General Manager

WROS
07-01-1955; 1050 khz AM *Hrs Open:* 6 AM-sunset; 5 kw-D, DA2; 0.013 kw-N, DA2; N30 21 14 W81 44 21
5590 Rio Grande, Jacksonville, FL 32205 US
(904) 353-1050, *Fax:* (904) 353-7076
www.wros.net
wros@wros.net
License: Jacksonville, FL held by The Rose of Jacksonville
Nat'l Network: USA *Regional Reps:* NRB
Arbitron Metro Market: Jacksonville, FL *Format:* Christian *Hrs. of News Programming:* news progmg 7 hrs wkly *No. News Employees:* 1 *Target Audience:* 25-65; Christians & secular
Adv. Rates: 45; 45; 45; 45
Elwyn Hall, CEO
Robyne Hall, Station Manager
Yisrael Freedman, Programming Director
Jerry Smith, Chief Engineer

WNNR
01-01-1969; 970 khz AM; 1 kw-D, DA2; 0.164 kw-N, DA2; N30 23 8 W81 40 4
2427 University Blvd. N., Jacksonville, FL 32211 US
(904) 739-3660, *Fax:* (904) 739-9409
www.larazalaraza.com
License: Jacksonville, FL held by Norsan Consulting and Management Inc.
Group Owner: Norsan Consulting and Management Inc.; (acq 9-15-2005; $2.1 million with WVOJ(AM) Fernandina Beach)
Arbitron Metro Market: Jacksonville, FL *Format:* Sports *Target Audience:* General.
Norberto Sanchez, President
Bernie Daigle, General Manager
Marci Koziolek, News Director

WZAZ
07-04-1950; 1400 khz AM *Hrs Open:* 24; 1 kw-U, ND1; N30 19 43 W81 41 42
8889 Pelican Bay Blvd., Suite 5100, Naples, FL 34108 US
(904) 470-4615, *Fax:* (904) 296-1683
www.1400wzaz.com
ronin719@comes.net
License: Jacksonville, FL held by Caron Broadcasting Inc.
Group Owner: Salem Communications Corp.; (acq 5-30-03; grpsl).
Nat'l Reps: Roslin
Arbitron Metro Market: Jacksonville, F *Format:* Gospel *Hrs. of News Programming:* news progmg 5 hrs wkly *No. News Employees:* 2 *Target Audience:* 25-54; adult Black listeners
Henry Hoot, General Manager
Calvin Grabau, Programming Director

Jacksonville Beach

WJXL
01-01-1946; 1010 khz AM *Hrs Open:* 24
P.O. Box 16907, Jacksonville, FL 32245 US
(904) 641-1011, *Fax:* (904) 641-1022
www.1010xl.com
JasonD@1010XL.com
License: Jacksonville Beach, FL held by Seven Bridges Radio LLC
Nat'l Network: ESPN Radio; Motor Racing Net *Wire Services:* AP
Arbitron Metro Market: Jacksonville, FL *Format:* Sports *Special Programming:* NASCAR (MRN, PRN) Jacksonville University *Target Audience:* M 25-54. *Adv. Rates:* 30; 30; 30; 30
Steven Griffin, President
Jack O'Brien, General Sales Mgr
Jason Dixon, Programming Director

WFJO
11-01-1989; 92.5 mhz FM; 1.7 kw; 627 ft.; N30 16 34 W81 33 51
P.O. Box 1448, Kingsland, GA 31548 US
(904) 425-3482
www.radiofreejax.com
License: Jacksonville Beach, Charlton County, FL held by Tama Radio Licenses of Jacksonville, FL Inc.
Group Owner: Tama Broadcasting Inc.; (acq 6-4-2003)
TV Affiliate: Talk *No. News Employees:* General.

Jensen Beach

WMBX
12-10-1980; 102.3 mhz FM *Hrs Open:* 24; 100 kw; 974 ft.; N27 1 31 W80 10 43
701 North Point Parkway, West Palm Beach, FL 33407 US
(561) 686-9505, *Fax:* (561) 684-6311
mcmeatal69@buzz103.com
License: Jensen Beach, Martin County, FL held by Infinity Radio Operations Inc.
Group Owner: CBS Radio; (acq 12-14-00; grpsl).
Arbitron Metro Market: West Palm Beach, FL *Format:* Contemporary Hits/Top 40 *Hrs. of News Programming:* news progmg 17 hrs wkly *No. News Employees:* 1 *Target Audience:* 25-54; women
Patricia Larschan, Operations Dir
Mark Krieger, General Sales Mgr
Danelle Sarvas, Promotions Manager
Pam Crosby, News Director
Jeff Clarke, Music Director
John O'Connell, Operations Manager

Juno Beach

WLDI
10-30-1969; 95.5 mhz FM; 100 kw; 925 ft.; N27 7 19 W80 23 20
200 Concord Plaza, Suite 600, San Antonio, TX 78216 US
(561) 616-6600, *Fax:* (561) 616-6677
www.wild955.com
info@wild955.com
License: Juno Beach, St. Lucie County, FL held by Clear Channel Radio Licenses Inc.
Group Owner: Clear Channel Communications Inc.; (acq 6-17-98; grpsl).
Arbitron Metro Market: West Palm Beach-Boca Raton, FL *Format:* Contemporary Hits/Top 40 *Target Audience:* 18-49; active, contemp
Dave Denver, Operations Dir
John Hunt, General Manager

Jupiter

WJBW
01-01-1997; 1000 khz AM *Hrs Open:* 24
2255 Glades Road, Suite 237w, Boca Raton, FL 33431 US
(772) 567-0937, *Fax:* (772) 562-4747
www.wjbwam.com
License: Jupiter, FL held by AM of Palm Beach Inc.
Arbitron Metro Market: West Palm Beach-Boca Raton, FL
Format: News, News/Talk, 86
Laurie Silvers, President
Jim Davis, General Manager
Karen Franke, Director of Sales
Brittany Hinger, Promotions Manager
Brittany Hinger, Webmaster

WUUB
106.3 mhz FM; 19000 w; 374 ft; N26 47 59 W80 04 33
2255 Glades Road, Suite 237W, Boca Raton, FL 33431
www.b1063fm.com
License: Jupiter, Palm Beach County, FL
Group Owner: CBS Radio Stations Inc.

Kendall

WURN
08-01-1999; 1020 khz AM
1662 Willowmont Ave., San Jose, CA 95124 US
(305) 446-5444, *Fax:* (305) 493-1111
www.radiomega.net
License: Kendall, FL held by New World Broadcasting Inc.
Format: Ethnic *Target Audience:* 25-55; adult
Alex Saintsuin, General Manager

Key Colony Beach

WKYZ
04-15-1999; 101.7 mhz FM *Hrs Open:* 24; 100 kw horiz, 90.25 kw vert; 453 ft.; N24 39 39.8 W81 25 10.4
10144 Seagrape Way, Palm Beach Gardens, FL 33480 US
(305) 289-1013, *Fax:* (305) 743-9441
www.pirateradiokeywest.com
info@pirateradiokeywest.com
License: Key Colony Beach, Monroe County, FL held by Keys Media Co. Inc.
Format: Classic Rock *Target Audience:* 25-54.
Joe Nascone, General Manager

Key Largo

***WLFE-FM**
01-01-2004; 90.9 mhz FM; 33 kw; Ant 308 ft; N25 14 07 W80 19 35
The New 88.3 19620 Pines Blvd, # 114, Pembroke Pines, FL 33029
(305) 406-2883, *Fax:* (305) 551-2737
www.lanuevafm.net
info@lanuevafm.net
License: Key Largo, Monroe County, FL held by Genesis License Subsidiary LLC.
Population Served: 408,750 *Arbitron Metro Market:* Miami, FL
Format: Christian
Kenny Reyes, General Manager

Key West

WAIL
12-01-1978; 99.5 mhz FM *Hrs Open:* 24; 100 kw; 240 ft.; N24 39 32 W81 32 18
200 Concord Plaza, Suite 600, San Antonio, TX 78216 US
(305) 296-7511, *Fax:* (305) 296-0358
www.sun103.com
randallperry@clearchannel.com
License: Key West, Monroe County, FL held by Clear Channel Radio Licenses Inc.
Group Owner: Clear Channel Communications Inc.; (acq 6-5-98; $2.6 million with WEOW(FM) Key West)
Regional Network: Florida's Radio Networks
Arbitron Metro Market: Key West, FL *Format:* Classic Rock
Target Audience: 25-54; men
Greg Capogna, Operations Dir
Sherry Russo, Station Manager
Randall Perry, Chief Engineer
Ken MacKenzie, Operations Director

WCNK
01-01-1986; 98.7 mhz FM *Hrs Open:* 24; 100 kw horiz, 81 kw vert; 453 ft.; N24 39 39.8 W81 25 10.4
1400 Woodbridge Ave., Detroit, MI 48207 US
(305) 872-9100, *Fax:* (305) 872-1603
www.conchcountry.com
mark@us1radio.com
License: Key West, Monroe County, FL held by Vox Communications Group LLC.
Group Owner: Vox Communications; (acq 8-31-2005; grpsl).
Arbitron Metro Market: Key West, Fl *Format:* Country *Special Programming:* Armed Forces news one hr wkly *Hrs. of News Programming:* News progmg one hr wkly *Target Audience:* 24-55; military, baby boomers &largest income holders
Kevin LeRoux, General Manager
Erika Bowman, Programming Director

WEOW
02-01-1967; 92.7 mhz FM *Hrs Open:* 24; 100 kw; 551 ft.; N24 40 36 W81 30 39
200 Concord Plaza, Suite 600, San Antonio, TX 78216 US
(305) 296-7511, *Fax:* (305) 296-0358
www.weow927.com
randallperry@clearchannel.com
License: Key West, Monroe County, FL held by Clear Channel Radio Licenses Inc.
Group Owner: Clear Channel Communications Inc.; (acq 6-5-98; $2.6 million with WAIL(FM) Key West)
Regional Network: Florida's Radio Networks
Arbitron Metro Market: Key West, FL *Format:* Contemporary Hits/Top 40
Mark Mays, President
Sherry Russo, General Manager
Randall Perry, Chief Engineer
Bill Bravo, Assistant Music Director

WIIS
06-01-1978; 107.1 mhz FM *Hrs Open:* 24; 2.5 kw; 203 ft.; N24 33 18 W81 48 7
517 Eaton Street, Key West, FL 33040 US
(305) 292-1133, *Fax:* (305) 292-6936
www.radiokeywest.com
johnrussin@hotmail.com
License: Key West, Monroe County, FL held by The Keyed Up Communications Co.
Format: Alternative *Special Programming:* Reggae 4 hrs, Metropolitan opera 4 hrs wkly *Hrs. of News Programming:* news progmg 5 hrs wkly *No. News Employees:* 1 *Target Audience:* 18-44; young, educated, activespenders for goods & svcs *Adv. Rates:* 28; 24; 28; 17
John Russin, CEO
Linda Russin, COO

***WJIR**
12-01-1986; 90.9 mhz FM *Hrs Open:* 24; 0.39 kw; 121 ft.; N24 33 7 W81 47 53
1209 United Street, Key West, FL 33040 US
(305) 296-4306, *Fax:* (305) 294-9547
www.wjir.org
pastorernie@bellsouth
License: Key West, Monroe County, FL held by Key West Educational Broadcasting.
Format: Christian, Religious *Hrs. of News Programming:* News progmg 12 hrs wkly *Target Audience:* General.
Ernie DeLoach, Station Manager

WKIZ
02-02-1959; 1500 khz AM *Hrs Open:* 24
P.O. Box 1471, Evergreen, CO 80439 US
(305) 296-1630, *Fax:* (305) 768-0282
www.konknet.com
wkizradio@aol.com
License: Key West, FL held by Seattle Streaming Radio L.L.C.
Group Owner: Seattle Streaming Radio LLC
Nat'l Network: CBS
Format: Religious, Spanish
Jim Spreitzer, General Sales Mgr

WKEY-FM
11-17-1985; 93.5 mhz FM *Hrs Open:* 24; 32 kw; 138 ft.; N24 34 17 W81 44 25
200 Concord Plaza, Suite 600, San Antonio, TX 78216 US
(305) 296-7511, *Fax:* (305) 296-0358
www.key93.com
kenmackenzie@clearchannel.com
License: Key West, Monroe County, FL held by Aloha Station Trust LLC, as Trustee
Regional Network: Florida's Radio Networks *Nat'l Reps:* Clear Channel
Format: Adult Contemp *Special Programming:* Classical 4 hrs, Sp 3 hrs wkly *Hrs. of News Programming:* news progmg 8 hrs wkly *No. News Employees:* 1 *Target Audience:* 25-54; affluent, upscale, culturallysupportive
Greg Capogna, General Manager
Sherry Russo, Station Manager
John Stuempfig, Promotions Manager

WKWF
10-01-1945; 1600 khz AM *Hrs Open:* 24
500 Fleming Road, Key West, FL 33010 US
(305) 296-7511, *Fax:* (305) 296-0358
www.keysradio.com,www.sportsradio1600.com
Toddswofford@clearchannel.com
License: Key West, FL held by Spottswood Partners II Ltd.
Format: Sports
Greg Capogna, Operations Dir
Sherry Russo, Station Manager
Todd Swofford, Programming Director

WMFM
01-01-1995; 107.9 mhz FM; 100 kw; 548 ft.; N24 40 35 W81 30 41 *Rebroadcasts:* Rebroadcasts WXDJ (FM) North Miami Beach 100%
26 West 56th Street, New York, NY 10019 US
(305) 447-9292, *Fax:* (305) 461-4466
www.lamusica.com
License: Key West, Monroe County, FL held by South Broadcasting System Inc.
Arbitron Metro Market: Coral Gables, FL
Jackie Nosti-Combo, General Manager
Albert Rodriguez, General Sales Mgr
Andrew Polsky, Advertising Contact

***WYBX(FM)**
06-01-2005; 88.3 mhz FM *Hrs Open:* 24; 2kw; 31m; N24 34 20 W81 44 25 *Rebroadcasts:* Rebroadcasts WAFG(FM) Fort Lauderdale 100%
5555 N. Federal Hwy., Fort Lauderdale, FL 33308
(954) 776-7705, *Fax:* (954) 771-2633
www.wafg.org
wafg@wafg.org
License: Key West, Monroe County, FL held by Bible Broadcasting Network Inc
Nat'l Network: Salem Radio Network
Population Served: 168,528 *Arbitron Metro Market:* Fort Lauderdale, FL *Format:* Christian, News, 62, Talk, Religious
Target Audience: 25+
Dolores King-St. George, General Manager

***WKWR**
01-01-2005; 90.1 mhz FM; 0.25 kw; 69 ft.; N24 34 5 W81 44 53
188 South Bellevue, Suite 222, Memphis, TN 38104 US
(800) 525-5683, *Fax:* (916) 251-1650
www.klove.com
klove@klove.com
License: Key West, Monroe County, FL held by Broadcasting for the Challenged Inc.
Nat'l Network: K-Love
Arbitron Metro Market: Key West, FL *Format:* Christian *No. News Employees:* 13
Darrell Chambliss, Chairman
Mike Novak, President and CEO
George Flinn Jr., General Manager
David Pierce, Chief Creative Officer and Programming Director
Ed Lenane, News Director
Sam Wallington, Engineering Dir
Alan Mason, ChiefOperating Officer
Dan Antonelli, Chief Business Development Officer
Eric Moser, Chief Financial Officer
Brian Burger, Vice President of Human Resources
D. Kevin Blair, Secretary and General Counsel
Tim Luttrell, News Reporter

Kissimmee

WHOO
04-01-1965; 1080 khz AM *Hrs Open:* 18
1084 Country Blvd., Kissimmee, FL 34741 US
(407) 380-9255, *Fax:* (407) 382-7565
www.sportstalkflorida.com
mytake@espnflorida.com
License: Kissimmee, FL held by Genesis Communications I Inc.
Group Owner: Genesis Communications Inc.; (acq 10-19-99)
Nat'l Network: ESPN Radio *Regional Network:* Florida's Radio Networks *Nat'l Reps:* Interep
Arbitron Metro Market: Orlando, FL *Format:* Sports, Talk *Target Audience:* 25-54; men *Adv. Rates:* 75; 50; 100; 35
Bruce Maduri, President
Colin Cantwell, Operations Dir
Sabrina Lavender, General Sales Mgr
Jerry O'Neill, Programming Director
Simon Luke, Operations Manager

WOTS
10-23-1978; 1220 khz AM *Hrs Open:* 24; 1 kw-D; N28 19 27 W81 23 44
222 Hazard St., Orlando, FL 32804
(407) 841-8282, *Fax:* (407) 841-8250
License: Kissimmee, Osceola County, FL held by J&V Communications Inc.

Group Owner: J&V Communications Inc.; acq 1-12-99)
Arbitron Metro Market: Orlando, FL *Special Programming:* Imus in the Morning *No. News Employees:* 1 *Target Audience:* Tourists
John Torrado, CEO & President
Jocelyn Torrado, Operations Dir
Lucas Soto, CO & GM
Jocelyn Torrado, Vice President & CFO
Jocelyn Torrado, Programming Director
Lou Mueller, Chief Engineer
Virgen Torrado, CEO
Janice Torrado, PSADirector

*WLAZ

01-01-2000; 89.1 mhz FM *Hrs Open:* 24; 5.2 kw vert; 522 ft.; N28 10 27 W81 17 1
Box 980, Quebradillas, PR 0678 US
(407) 518-7150, *Fax:* (407) 518-0062
www.laestaciondelafamilia.com
License: Kissimmee, Osceola County, FL held by Caguas Educational TV Inc.
Arbitron Metro Market: Kissimmee, FL *Format:* Christian *Hrs. of News Programming:* news progmg 10 hrs wkly *No. News Employees:* 2
William Gutierrez, General Manager

La Belle

*WBIY

01-01-1999; 88.3 mhz FM *Hrs Open:* 24; 9 kw; 230 ft.; N26 43 22 W81 30 4
Falls Road, Toccoa Falls, GA 30598 US
1(888)400-9904, *Fax:* (863) 675-7584
www.oscaragueroministry.com
apostol@oscaraguero.com
License: La Belle, Hendry County, FL held by Oscar Aguero Ministry Inc.
Arbitron Metro Market: LaBelle, Fl *Format:* Christian
Oscar Aguero, President
Roger Martinez, Station Manager

La Crosse

WBXY

10-01-1993; 99.5 mhz FM *Hrs Open:* 24; 2.2 kw; 472 ft.; N29 44 22 W82 23 9
2848 East Oakland Park Blvd., Fort Lauderdale, FL 33306 US
(352) 375-1317, *Fax:* (352) 375-6961
www.thestar.fm
sales@thestar.fm
License: La Crosse, Alachua County, FL held by Asterisk Communications Inc.
Nat'l Network: Westwood One; Talk Radio Network; ABC; Fox Sports *Nat'l Reps:* McGavren Guild
Arbitron Metro Market: Gainesville-Ocala, FL *Format:* News, Sports, 86 *Target Audience:* 25-54; primarily baby boomers-upscale *Adv. Rates:* 35; 30; 30; 20
John Starr, General Manager
Steve Cox, Programming Director

Lake City

WJOE

05-13-1956; 1450 khz AM *Hrs Open:* Sunrise-sunset
Mailing Address: US
Second Address: 660 E. Main St., Orange, MA 1364
(978) 630-8700, *Fax:* (978) 630-3011
www.wjoeam.com/
wjoe@wjoeam.com
License: Lake City, FL held by County Broadcasting Co. LLC.
Group Owner: Northeast Broadcasting Company Inc.; (acq 10-6-2003; $650,000 with WXRG(FM) Athol)
Arbitron Metro Market: Worcester, MA *Format:* Oldies *Target Audience:* 45 plus.
Glenn Cardinal, General Manager
Spencer Marshall, Programming Director
Chris Thompson, General Manager
Billy Curtis, Programming Director

WDSR

05-06-1946; 1340 khz AM *Hrs Open:* 24; 1 kw-U, ND1; N30 9 20 W82 38 14
1914 Maple Leaf Drive, Windermere, FL 34786 US
(386) 961-9494, *Fax:* (386) 755-9369
www.northfloridanow.com/
John@Mix943.com
License: Lake City, FL held by Newman Media Inc.
Nat'l Network: CBS *Regional Network:* Florida's Radio Networks
Regional Reps: Florida's Radio Net.
Arbitron Metro Market: Lake City, FL *Format:* Oldies *Special Programming:* Black 1 hr wkly *Target Audience:* 40-65. *Adv. Rates:* 20; 20; 20; 15
John Newman, President
Barry Cole, Programming Director

WGRO

11-14-1958; 960 khz AM *Hrs Open:* 6 AM-midnight (M-S); 7 AM-11 PM (Su; 0.5 kw-D, DAN; 1 kw-N, DAN; N30 11 47 W82 40 48
Rt 13, Box 318, Lake City, FL 32055 US
(386) 755-4102, *Fax:* (386) 752-9861
bandk@ISgroup.net
License: Lake City, FL held by Power Country Inc.
Regional Network: Florida's Radio Networks
Format: Country, Gospel
Louis Bolton II, President
Bob Hendrickson, General Manager

WNFB

05-28-1969; 94.3 mhz FM *Hrs Open:* 24; 50 kw; 492 ft.; N30 7 44 W82 52 49
1914 Maple Leaf Drive, Windermere, FL 34786 US
(386) 961-9494, *Fax:* (386) 754-6915
www.northfloridanow.com
License: Lake City, Columbia County, FL held by Newman Media Inc.
Arbitron Metro Market: Lake City, FL *Format:* Adult Contemp *Target Audience:* 25-54. *Adv. Rates:* 38; 35; 38; 25
John Newman, President
Barry Cole, Programming Director
Jack Wiley, Music Director

*WOLR

09-11-1986; 91.3 mhz FM; 0 kw horiz, 18 kw vert; 285 ft.; N30 2 56 W82 48 44
P O Box 1448, Live Oak, FL 32064 US
904-935-3300, *Fax:* (386) 935-2684
www.christianhitradio.net
License: Lake City, Columbia County, FL held by WOLR 91.3 FM Inc.
TV Affiliate: Relg

Lake Placid

WWTK

01-01-1989; 730 khz AM *Hrs Open:* 24; 0.5 kw-D, DA2; 0.34 kw-N, DA2; N27 24 25 W81 25 56
Peter L. Coughlin, 3750 Usn Hwy. 27, Ste. 1, Sebring, FL 33870 US
(863) 382-9999, *Fax:* (863) 382-1982
www.cohanradiogroup.com
cohanradiogroup@htn.net
License: Lake Placid, FL held by Cohan Radio Group Inc.
Group Owner: Cohan Radio Group Inc.; (acq 11-1-98; $910,000 with WWOJ(FM) Avon Park).
Nat'l Network: USA; CBS Radio; ABC; Premiere Radio Networks; Talk Radio Network *Regional Network:* Florida's Radio Networks
Nat'l Reps: Interep *Wire Services:* AP
Arbitron Metro Market: Sebring, FL *Format:* Talk *Hrs. of News Programming:* news progmg 120 hrs wkly *No. News Employees:* 1 *Target Audience:* 35 plus.
Peter Coughlin, President
Barry Foster, News Director
Phil Scott, Chief Engineer
Libby Coughlin, Regional Sales Manager
Kim McPherson, Traffic Manager

Lake Wales

WIPC

07-01-1951; 1280 khz AM *Hrs Open:* 24; 1 kw-D, DAN; 0.5 kw-N, DAN; N27 55 34 W81 36 4; N27 55 30 W81 36 16
2000 Universal Studios, Fl Suite 604, Orlando, FL 32819 US
(863) 679-7178, *Fax:* (863) 679-9395
wipc1280@yahoo.com
License: Lake Wales, FL held by Super W Media Group Inc.
Arbitron Metro Market: Lakeland-Winter Haven, FL *Hrs. of News Programming:* news progmg 10 hrs wkly *No. News Employees:* 1 *Target Audience:* 18+ Hispanics. *Adv. Rates:* 29; 22; 29; 20
Robert Cubero, President
Carl Czuchaj, Operations Dir
Raul Centeno, Programming Director
Guadalupe Gonzales, News Director
Linda Perez, Music Director
Guadalupe Gonzalez, Operations Manager

Lake Worth

WWRF

05-01-1959; 1380 khz AM *Hrs Open:* 24; 1 kw-D, ND1; 0.103 kw-N, ND1; N26 37 22 W80 4 20
1939 7th Avenue North, Lake Worth, FL 33461 US
(561) 721-9950, *Fax:* (561) 721-9973
www.la1380.com/
info@gladesmedia.com
License: Lake Worth, FL held by Radio Fiesta Inc.
Arbitron Metro Market: West Palm Beach, FL *Format:* Tejano
Special Programming: Sp relg 4 hrs wkly *No. News Employees:* 1 *Target Audience:* 25-54; Hispanic
Robbie Castellanos, President
Gigi Mitre, Operations Dir
Liza Flores, General Manager
Paul Danitz, General Sales Mgr
Jesus Ybaez, Programming Director
Paola Cartay, Office Manager

Lakeland

*WKES

05-20-1975; 91.1 mhz FM *Hrs Open:* 24; 100 kw; 420 ft.; N28 4 46 W82 2 27
820 N. Lasalle Boulevard, Chicago, IL 60610 US
(727) 391-9994, *Fax:* (727) 397-6425
www.wkes.fm
wkes@moody.edu
License: Lakeland, Polk County, FL held by The Moody Bible Institute of Chicago.
Group Owner: The Moody Bible Institute of Chicago; acq 10-10-96; $5 million)
Arbitron Metro Market: Lakeland-Winter Haven, FL *Format:* Religious
Michael Easley, President
Michael Gleichman, Operations Dir
Pierre Chestang, Station Manager
John Stortz, Chief Engineer

WLKF

01-01-1936; 1430 khz AM *Hrs Open:* 24; 5 kw-D, ND1; 1 kw-N, ND1; N28 2 27 W81 56 8
Mailing Address: P.O. Box 4368, Lancaster, PA 17604 US
Second Address: 404 W. Lime St., Lakeland, FL 33815-4651
(863) 682-8184, *Fax:* (863) 683-2409
www.wlkf.com
talk1430@wlkf.com
License: Lakeland, FL held by Hall Communications Ltd.
Group Owner: Hall Communications Inc.; (acq 10-1-96; $550,000)
Nat'l Network: ABC *Regional Network:* Florida's Radio Networks
Nat'l Reps: Eastman Radio *Wire Services:* AP
Arbitron Metro Market: Lakeland-Winter Haven, FL *Format:* News, News/Talk, 86 *Hrs. of News Programming:* News progmg 15 hrs wkly *No. News Employees:* 3 *Target Audience:* 35 plus; middle to upper income adults
Bonnie Rowbotham, Chairman
Arthur Rowbotham, President
Nancy Cattarius, Station Manager
Bill Baldwin, Executive Vice President

WLLD

01-27-1992; 94.1 mhz FM *Hrs Open:* 24; 100 kw; 1493 ft.; N27 40 23 W82 6 35
200 Concord Plaza, Suite 600, San Antonio, TX 78216 US
(727) 579-1925, *Fax:* (727) 579-8888
www.wild987.com
beata@infinitybroadcasting.com
License: Lakeland, Manatee County, FL held by Infinity Radio Inc.
Group Owner: CBS Radio; (acq 11-13-98; grpsl).
Nat'l Network: CNN Radio
Arbitron Metro Market: Sarasota-Bradenton, FL *Format:* Urban Contemporary *Target Audience:* 25 plus; professional, educated, upscale audience
Ross Block, Operations Dir
Charlie Ochs, General Manager
Marvin Kapman, General Sales Mgr
Orlando Davis, Programming Director

WONN

09-15-1949; 1230 khz AM; 1 kw-U, ND1; N28 2 23 W81 57 39
Mailing Address: P.O. Box 4368, Lancaster, PA 17604 US
Second Address: 404 W. Lime St., Lakeland, FL 33815-4651
(863) 682-8184, *Fax:* (863) 683-2409
www.wonn.com
wonn@wonn.com
License: Lakeland, FL held by Hall Communications Inc.
Group Owner: Hall Communications Inc.; acq 10-1-81; $2 million with co-located FM;
Nat'l Network: CNN Radio *Nat'l Reps:* Eastman Radio
Arbitron Metro Market: Lakeland-Winter *TV Affiliate:* MOR
Format: Religious *Special Programming:* News progmg 20 hrs wkly *Hrs. of News Programming:* 3 *No. News Employees:* 35 plus. *Target Audience:* Bonnie Rowbotham

RADIO - U.S.

WLLD(FM)
09-11-1967; 94.1 mhz FM *Hrs Open:* 24; 100 kw; Ant 1,492 ft; N27 40 23 W82 06 35
9721 Executive Center Dr. N., Suite 200, St. Petersburg, FL 33702-2439
(727) 568-0941, *Fax:* (727) 568-9758
www.wsjt.com
smoothjazz@wsjt.com
License: Lakeland, Polk County, FL held by Infinity Radio Inc.
Group Owner: CBS Radio; (acq 1999; grpsl).
Nat'l Reps: CBS Radio
Population Served: 4,000,000 *Arbitron Metro Market:* Tampa-St. Peter *Format:* Jazz *No. News Employees:* 1 *Target Audience:* 25-54; middle to upper income adults, skews towards females
Adv. Rates: 12; 12;12; 200
Ross Block, Operations Dir
Charlie Ochs, General Manager
Rose Bobier, Promotions Manager

WWAB
09-01-1957; 1330 khz AM; 1 kw-D, ND2; 0.118 kw-N, ND2; N28 2 40 W81 58 28
Mailing Address: P.O. Box 65, Lakeland, FL 33802 US
Second Address: 1203 Chase St., Lakeland, FL 33802
(863) 682-2998, *Fax:* (863) 683-9922
wwab@verizon.net
License: Lakeland, FL held by WWAB Inc.
Arbitron Metro Market: Lakeland, FL *Format:* Blues, Talk *Special Programming:* Gospel 12 hrs wkly *Target Audience:* 18-49.
Frank Clark, Operations Dir
Jerry Hughes, General Manager
Hugh Hughes, General Sales Mgr

***WYFO**
03-01-1988; 91.9 mhz FM; 25 kw horiz, 23 kw vert; 328 ft.; N27 56 35 W81 54 45
8030 Arrowridge Blvd, Charlotte, NC 28273 US
(704) 523-5555, *Fax:* (704) 522-1967
www.bbnradio.org
bbn@bbnradio.org
License: Lakeland, Polk County, FL held by Bible Broadcasting Network Inc.
Group Owner: Bible Broadcasting Network; acq 9-21-89; $200,000;
Arbitron Metro Market: Lakeland, FL *Format:* Christian
Doug Roby, Station Manager

Lantana

WPBR
01-01-1941; 1340 khz AM *Hrs Open:* 25.?Â ?; 0.81 kw-U, ND1; N26 37 12 W80 4 51
130 North Dixie Highway, Lake North, FL 33460 US
(561) 641-8882, *Fax:* (561) 641-8629
www.talk1340wpbram.com
adminandsales@1340wpbr.com
License: Lantana, FL held by Omni-Lingual Broadcasting Corp.
Nat'l Network: USA
Arbitron Metro Market: West Palm Beach-Boca Raton, FL
Format: News, News/Talk, 86 *Special Programming:* Financial 9 hrs, medical 8 hrs, Jewish 3 hrs, Creole 30 hrs wkly *Target Audience:* 35-64.
Emil Antonoff, President
Markes Pierre Louis, General Manager

Largo

WWBA
05-29-1972; 820 khz AM *Hrs Open:* 24; 50 kw-D, DA2; 1 kw-N, DA2; N27 54 30 W82 46 51
8121 Georgia Avenue, 10th Floor, Silver Spring, MD 20910 US
(813) 281-1040, *Fax:* (813) 281-1948
www.newstalk820.com
contactus@radiogenesis.com
License: Largo, FL held by Genesis Communications of Tampa Bay Inc.
Group Owner: Genesis Communications Inc.; (acq 1-13-2009; $3 million)
Nat'l Network: ABC
Arbitron Metro Market: Largo, FL *Format:* News, News/Talk, 86 *No. News Employees:* 3 *Target Audience:* 25-54.
Luis Diaz-Albertini, General Manager
Roger Schulman, News Director

Leesburg

WQBQ
09-12-1962; 1410 khz AM; 5 kw-D, ND1; 0.09 kw-N, ND1; N28 47 13 W81 53 26
888 East Keene Road, Apopka, FL 32703 US
(407) 222-6628, *Fax:* (407) 656-3487
License: Leesburg, FL held by Rama Communications Inc.
Group Owner: Rama Communications Inc.; (acq 10-15-2004; $180,000 with WKIQ(AM) Eustis).
Format: Spanish
Sabeta Persaud, President
Jose Lopez, General Manager

Leesburg-Eustis

WLBE
08-01-1949; 790 khz AM *Hrs Open:* 24; 5 kw-D, DAN; 1 kw-N, DAN; N28 49 42 W81 47 10
32900 Radio Road, Leesburg, FL 34788 US
(352) 787-7900, *Fax:* (352) 787-1402
www.my790am.com
info@am790wlbe.com
License: Leesburg-Eustis, FL held by WLBE 790 Inc.
Nat'l Network: CBS *Regional Network:* Florida's Radio Networks
Nat'l Reps: Dora-Clayton
Format: Talk *Special Programming:* Black 3 hrs, farm 3 hrs, gospel 4 hrs, Pol 2 hrs w *Hrs. of News Programming:* News progmg 25 hrs wkly *Target Audience:* 45 plus.
MJ McNair, General Manager

Lehigh Acres

WCKT
01-01-1976; 107.1 mhz FM *Hrs Open:* 24; 23.5 kw; 722 ft.; N26 19 0 W81 47 13
200 Concord Plz., Ste 600, San Antonio, TX 78216 US
(239) 225-4300(800) 827-1071, *Fax:* (239) 275-4669
www.catcountry1071.com
License: Lehigh Acres, Lee County, FL held by Clear Channel Broadcasting Licenses Inc.
Group Owner: Clear Channel Communications Inc.; (acq 1996; grpsl)
Nat'l Reps: Clear Channel
Arbitron Metro Market: Fort Myers, FL *Format:* Country *Hrs. of News Programming:* news progmg 20 hrs wkly *No. News Employees:* 1 *Target Audience:* 25-54.
Lowry Mays, Chairman
Randall Mays, CFO
Mark Mays, President
Jay Meyers, Operations Dir
Jim Keating, General Manager
Robin Craig, General Sales Mgr
Dave Logan, Programming Director
Church Morgan, News Director
Dick Parrish,Chief Engineer
Steve Amari, Operations Director

WWCL
04-29-1970; 1440 khz AM; 5 kw-D, DA2; 1 kw-N, DA2; N26 36 5 W81 33 30
P.O. Box 61239, Fort Myers, FL 33906 US
(239) 337-1440, *Fax:* (239) 369-3386
energi1440@aol.com
License: Lehigh Acres, FL held by Latino Media Corp.
Arbitron Metro Market: Fort Myers, FL *Format:* Christian
Angel Ramos, General Manager

Leisure City

WRAZ-FM
01-20-1990; 106.3 mhz FM; 50 kw; 308 ft.; N25 14 7 W80 19 35
3191 Coral Way, Suite 805, Miami, FL 33145 US
(305) 445-1063, *Fax:* (305) 446-9339
www.cima1063.com
info@cima1063.com
License: Leisure City, Miami-Dade County, FL held by South Broadcasting System Inc.
Arbitron Metro Market: Leisure City, FL
Raoul Alarcon, President
Yanin Mesa, Assistant to Vice President/General Manager
John Fina, General Sales Mgr
John Caride, Promotions Manager
Ralph Chambers, Chief Engineer
Berry Jasin, National Sales Manager
Barbara Guerra,Local Sales Manager
Vice President of Sales, Felix Lopez

Live Oak

WQHL
06-16-1949; 1250 khz AM *Hrs Open:* 24; 1 kw-D, ND2; 0.083 kw-N, ND2; N30 17 14 W82 57 56
P. O. Box 130, Live Oak, FL 32060 US
(386) 362-1250,(386) 364-3502, *Fax:* (386) 364-3504
www.wqhl981.com
audio@wqhl981.com
License: Live Oak, FL held by RTG Radio LLC.
Group Owner: Black Crow Media Group LLC; (acq 11-9-2001; grpsl).
Nat'l Network: ABC *Regional Network:* Florida's Radio Networks
Format: Contemporary Hits/Top 40, Adult Contemp *Special Programming:* Gospel 7 hrs, relg 6 hrs wkly *Hrs. of News Programming:* News progmg 12 hrs wkly *Target Audience:* General.
Dean Blackwell, General Manager

WQHL-FM
10-01-1973; 98.1 mhz FM *Hrs Open:* 24; 50 kw; 444 ft.; N30 17 14 W82 57 56
P.O. Box 130, Live Oak, FL 32064 US
(386) 362-1250,(386) 364-3502, *Fax:* (386) 364-3504
wqhl981.com
audio@wqhl981.com
License: Live Oak, Suwannee County, FL
Group Owner: Black Crow Media Group LLC
Nat'l Network: ABC *Regional Network:* Southeast AgNet
Format: Country *Special Programming:* Nascar Racing, High School Football *Target Audience:* General.
Dean Blackwell, General Manager
Rob Harder, Programming Director
Jim Smith, Chief Engineer

WILA
100.1 mhz FM; 6 kw; 328 feet; N30 13 43 W82 58 05
15722 96th Street, Live Oak, FL
(386) 364-6005
License: Live Oak, Suwannee County, FL held by Learning Avenue Inc
Sergio Martins, President

Lynn Haven

WBYW(FM)
104.3 mhz FM; 6 kw; Ant 249 ft; N30 10 47 W85 38 11
1670 N.W. Federal Hwy., Stuart, FL 34994
(772) 692-9454, *Fax:* (772) 692-0258
License: Lynn Haven, Bay County, FL held by Horizon Broadcasting Co. Inc.
Population Served: 18,607 *Arbitron Metro Market:* Lynn Haven, FL
George Metcalf, President

Macclenny

WJXR
09-01-1978; 92.1 mhz FM *Hrs Open:* 24; 25 kw; 328 ft; N30 17 54 W82 00 55
Box One, Jacksonville, FL 32063
(904) 259-2292, *Fax:* (904) 259-4488
www.wjxr.com
License: Macclenny, Baker County, FL held by WJXR Inc.
Nat'l Network: ABC *Regional Network:* Florida's Radio Networks
Arbitron Metro Market: Jacksonville, F *Hrs. of News Programming:* news progmg 7 hrs wkly *No. News Employees:* 1 *Target Audience:* 25-54; middle class & upscale families *Adv. Rates:* 30; 30; 30; 25
Gregory Perich, CEO
Sarah Perich, Operations Dir
Doug Rudowich, Station Manager
Avery Perich, Programming Director
Jerry Smith, Chief Engineer

Madison

WMAF
12-06-1956; 1230 khz AM; 1 kw-U, ND1; N30 28 23 W83 26 9
Mailing Address: P. O. Box 776, Perry, FL 32347 US
Second Address: 2 Captain Brown Rd., Madison, FL 32341
(850) 973-3233, *Fax:* (850) 973-3097
www.wmafcountry.com
countrywmaf@embarkmail.com
License: Madison, FL held by Geneva Walker.
Regional Network: Florida's Radio Networks
Arbitron Metro Market: Madison, FL *Format:* Country *Special Programming:* Oldies, gospel
Betty Evertt, General Manager

WXHT
11-01-2000; 102.7 mhz FM; 19 kw; 377 ft.; N30 38 23 W83 26 52
P. O. Box 177, Pinetta, FL 32350 US
(229) 244-8642, *Fax:* (229) 242-7620
www.valdostatoday.com
cwhittle@blackcrow.fm
License: Madison, Madison County, FL held by RTG Radio L.L.C.
Group Owner: Black Crow Media Group LLC; (acq 6-4-2004; $3.4 million with WSTI-FM Quitman, GA).
Arbitron Metro Market: Valdosta, GA *Format:* Contemporary Hits/Top 40 *Target Audience:* Adults 18-49.
Robert Ganzak, President
Jay Mathews, Programming Director

Kim Pelkowski, Director of Sales
Lee Mayhew Smothers, Account Executive
Jennifer Johnson, Account Executive
Lynn Loftus, Account Executive
Blake Brown, AccountExecutive
Mike Gebora, Account Executive

***WAPB**
01-01-2005; 91.7 mhz FM; 0.2 kw; 224 ft.; N30 27 13 W83 24 17
Mailing Address: 1508 State Street, Holly Hill, FL 32117 US
Second Address: 1508 State Ave., Dayton Beach, FL 32125
(386) 677-4272, *Fax:* (386) 677-7095
www.wapb.net
wapn@wapn.net
License: Madison, Madison County, FL held by Public Radio Inc.
Arbitron Metro Market: Madison, FL *Format:* Religious
Shellye Lund-Vallance, President
Earlyne Lund, Owner

Maitland

WPYO
09-01-1968; 95.3 mhz FM *Hrs Open:* 24; 12 kw; 472 ft.; N28 34 27 W81 27 46
1400 Lake Hearn Drive, N.E., Atlanta, GA 30319 US
(407) 422-9696, *Fax:* (407) 422-5883
www.power953.com
info@power953.com
License: Maitland, Orange County, FL held by Cox Radio Inc.
Group Owner: Cox Radio Inc.; (acq 1999; $14.5 million)
Arbitron Metro Market: Orlando, FL *Format:* Urban Contemporary *Target Audience:* General.
Brian Elam, General Manager

Marathon

WFFG
04-07-1962; 1300 khz AM *Hrs Open:* 24; 2.5 kw-U, DA1; N24 41 28 W81 6 30
One Boot Key, P.O. Box 500940, Marathon, FL 33050 US
(305) 743-5563(305) 743-5564, *Fax:* (305) 743-9441
keysradiogroup@aol.com
License: Marathon, FL held by The Great Marathon Radio Co.
Nat'l Network: Westwood One
Arbitron Metro Market: Marathon, FL *Format:* News, News/Talk, 84, Talk *Hrs. of News Programming:* News progmg 10 hrs wkly *Target Audience:* 25-54; general
Joe Mascone, General Manager
Jane Martin, News Director
Vince Cacone, Engineering Dir

WGMX
12-01-1976; 94.3 mhz FM *Hrs Open:* 24; 50 kw; 276 ft.; N24 41 30 W81 6 31
P. O. Box 500940, Marathon, FL 33050 US
(305) 743-5563, *Fax:* (305) 743-9441
www.wgmxfm.com
keysradiogroup@aol.com
License: Marathon, Monroe County, FL
Nat'l Network: Westwood One
Format: Adult Contemp *Adv. Rates:* Same as AM
John Bartus, Operations Dir
Dannielle Alderman, Programming Director
John Perry, News Director

WAVK
01-01-2002; 97.7 mhz FM *Hrs Open:* 24; 50 kw horiz, 49 kw vert; 213 ft.; N24 46 2 W80 56 42
331 Lookout Point, Hot Springs, AR 71913 US
(305) 827-9100, *Fax:* (305) 872-1603
mail@wave-fm.com
License: Marathon, Monroe County, FL held by Vox Communications Group LLC.
Group Owner: Vox Communications; (acq 8-31-2005; grpsl)
Format: Adult Contemp
Kevin LeRoux, General Manager

***WKWM**
01-01-2008; 91.5 mhz FM *Hrs Open:* 24; 12 kw; 462 ft.; N24 39 40 W81 25 10 *Rebroadcasts:* Rebroadcasts WLRN-FM Miami 100%
US
(305) 995-1717, *Fax:* (305) 995-2299
www.wlrn.org
info@wlrn.org
License: Marathon, Monroe County, FL held by The School Board of Miami-Dade County, FL.
Nat'l Network: NPR; PRI *Regional Network:* Fla. Pub. *Wire Services:* AP
Arbitron Metro Market: Bakersfield, CA *Format:* News, News/Talk, 86 *Special Programming:* Haitian 3 hrs wkly *Hrs. of News Programming:* news progmg 111 hrs wkly *No. News*

Employees: 7 *Target Audience:* General; well educated, moderate to high income bracket
John LaBonia, General Manager
Ted Eldredge, Station Manager
Peter J. Moerz, Programming Director
Irina Lellemand, News Director

Marco

WGUF
01-01-1990; 98.9 mhz FM *Hrs Open:* 24; 6 kw; 328 ft.; N26 1 50 W81 38 33
1459 Crane Ave, Pittsburgh, PA 15220 US
(239) 495-8383, *Fax:* (239) 495-0883
www.thegulf989.com
wguf@rendabroadcasting.com
License: Marco, Collier County, FL held by Renda Broadcasting Corp. of Nevada.
Group Owner: Renda Broadcasting Corp.; (acq 4-17-97; $2 million).
Arbitron Metro Market: Fort Myers-Naples-Marco Island, FL *Format:* News, News/Talk, 86 *Hrs. of News Programming:* News progmg 7 hrs wkly *Target Audience:* 35 plus; affluent southwest FL residents *Adv. Rates:* 38;38; 38; 25
Tony Renda Jr., General Manager
Randy Savage, Programming Director

***WMKO**
02-08-1999; 91.7 mhz FM *Hrs Open:* 24; 6.9 kw; 369 ft.; N26 3 10 W81 42 11 *Rebroadcasts:* Rebroadcasts WGCU-FM Fort Myers100%
10501 Fgcu Blvd S., Ft Myers, FL 33965 US
(239) 590-2500, *Fax:* (239) 590-2520
www.wgcu.org
wgcufm@fgcu.edu
License: Marco, Collier County, FL held by Board of Trustees, Florida Gulf Coast University
Nat'l Network: NPR
Arbitron Metro Market: Fort Myers, FL
Rick Johnson, General Manager

Marco Island

***WCNZ**
05-01-1999; 1660 khz AM *Hrs Open:* 24
462 Merrimack Street, Methuen, MA 01844 US
(239) 732-9369, *Fax:* (239) 732-7267
www.avenuefla.com
bladd@mail.com
License: Marco Island, FL held by J & B WCNZ LLC
Nat'l Network: USA *Regional Network:* Florida's Radio Networks
Arbitron Metro Market: Fort Myers, FL *Format:* Jazz *Hrs. of News Programming:* news progmg 10 hrs wkly *No. News Employees:* 1
Robert Ladd, Station Manager

WVOI
01-01-1975; 1480 khz AM; 1 kw-D, DA2; 1 kw-N, DA2; N25 59 30 W81 37 30
462 Merrimack Street, Methuen, MA 01844 US
(239) 732-9369, *Fax:* (239) 732-7267
http://www.avenue1410and1660.com/
bladd@mail.com
License: Marco Island, FL held by J&J WCNZ LLC
Nat'l Network: USA *Regional Network:* Florida's Radio Networks
Arbitron Metro Market: Fort Myers-Napl *TV Affiliate:* AAA *Special Programming:* news progmg 5.5 hrs wkly *Hrs. of News Programming:* 1 *No. News Employees:* 45 plus; upscale & profes *Adv. Rates:* 10; 10; 10;10

Marianna

WTYS-FM
08-04-1995; 94.1 mhz FM *Hrs Open:* 24; 4.4 kw; 384 ft.; N30 45 47 W85 13 52
Mailing Address: 2483 Jefferson, Marianna, FL 32448 US
Second Address: 2725 Jefferson St., Marianna, FL 32448
(850) 482-2131, *Fax:* (850) 526-3687
www.wtys.cc
wtysradio@embarqmail.com
License: Marianna, Jackson County, FL held by James L. Adams Jr.
Nat'l Network: CBS *Regional Network:* Florida's Radio Networks
Arbitron Metro Market: Marianna, Fl *Format:* Gospel *Hrs. of News Programming:* news progmg 5 hrs wkly *No. News Employees:* 1 *Target Audience:* 25-64; adults in Jackson county, FL & surrounding area
Jerry Jackson, Operations Dir
James Adams, General Manager
Tom O'Brien, News Director

WJAQ
09-01-1964; 100.9 mhz FM *Hrs Open:* 24; 5.9 kw horiz; 331 ft.; N30 47 1 W85 15 18
P.O. Box 569, Marianna, FL 32447 US
(850) 482-3046, *Fax:* (850) 482-3049
wjaq@phon1.com
License: Marianna, Jackson County, FL
Nat'l Network: ABC *Wire Services:* UPI
Format: Country *Hrs. of News Programming:* news progmg 3 hrs wkly *No. News Employees:* 1 *Target Audience:* General. *Adv. Rates:* 25; 20; 22; 12
Bill Jones, Operations Dir
Gregory Kamishlian, Promotions Manager

***WAYP**
05-01-1985; 88.3 mhz FM *Hrs Open:* 24; 0.75 kw horiz, 70 kw vert; 344 ft.; N30 26 18.1 W85 25 27
P. O. Box 450, Marianna, FL 32446 US
(850) 422-1929, *Fax:* (850) 297-1888
wayp.wayfm.com
License: Marianna, Jackson County, FL held by WAY-FM Media Group Inc.
Group Owner: WAY-FM Media Group Inc.; (acq 11-13-2007; $210,000)
Arbitron Metro Market: Panama City, FL *Format:* Christian
Steve Young, General Manager

WTOT
09-24-1958; 980 khz AM *Hrs Open:* 24; 1 kw-D, ND1; 0.34 kw-N, ND1; N30 47 1 W85 15 18
Mailing Address: 9102 N. Meridian Street, Ste 500, Indianapolis, IN 46260 US
Second Address: 4376 Lafayette St., Suite A, Marianna, FL 32446-3300
(850) 482-3046, *Fax:* (850) 482-3049
wjaq@phon1.com
License: Marianna, FL held by MFR Inc.
Nat'l Network: ABC
Arbitron Metro Market: Marianna, FL *Format:* Christian *Target Audience:* 25 plus. *Adv. Rates:* 10; 8; 9; 6
John Biddinger, CEO
Ed Cearley, President
Don Moore, General Sales Mgr
Curtis Blount, Chief Engineer

WTYS
04-03-1947; 1340 khz AM *Hrs Open:* 24
Mailing Address: P.O. Box 777, Marianna, FL 32447 US
Second Address: 2725 Jefferson St., Marianna, FL 32448
(850) 482-2131, *Fax:* (850) 526-3687
www.wtys.cc
wtysradio@embarqmail.com
License: Marianna, FL held by James L. Adams Jr.
Regional Network: Florida's Radio Networks
Arbitron Metro Market: Dotham, AL *Format:* Country *Special Programming:* Farm one hr, gospel 11 hrs wkly *Hrs. of News Programming:* news progmg 7 hrs wkly *No. News Employees:* 1 *Target Audience:* 25-64;adults in Jackson County & the surrounding area
Jerry Jackson, Operations Dir
James Adams, General Manager

***WHMF**
91.1 mhz FM; kw
US
(850) 763-6489
License: Marianna, Jackson County, FL held by Health and Happiness Radio Inc.
Arbitron Metro Market: Panama City, FL
Leonard Moore, President

Mary Esther

WYZB
05-01-1986; 105.5 mhz FM; 25 kw; 305 ft.; N30 24 42 W86 37 14
P.O. Box 2347, Fort Walton Beach, FL 32549 US
(850) 244-1055
www.wyzb.com
sales@wyzb.com
License: Mary Esther, Okaloosa County, FL held by Cumulus Licensing Corp.
Group Owner: Cumulus Media Inc.; (acq 1-10-2003; grpsl)
Arbitron Metro Market: Fort Walton Bea *Format:* Country *Target Audience:* 25-54.
Georgia Edmiston, General Manager

Mayo

***WGSG**
01-01-1991; 89.5 mhz FM; 2.5 kw horiz, 20 kw vert; 249 ft.; N30 2 30 W83 7 45
P.O. Box 644, Mayo, FL 32066 US

(386) 294-2525, *Fax:* (386) 294-2525
License: Mayo, Lafayette County, FL held by True Concepts of Levy County Inc.
Format: Religious
Terri Simmons, General Manager

Melbourne

WAOA-FM
11-09-1972; 107.1 mhz FM; 100 kw; 486 ft.; N28 8 11 W80 42 12
316 Banyan Blvd, W Palm Beach, FL 33401 US
(321) 984-1000, *Fax:* (321) 724-1565
www.wa1a.com
Jennifer.Armstrong@Cumulus.com
License: Melbourne, Brevard County, FL held by Cumulus Licensing Corp.
Group Owner: Cumulus Media Inc.
Arbitron Metro Market: Melbourne, FL *Format:* Contemporary Hits/Top 40 *Target Audience:* 25-54.
Terry Forcht, CEO
Pete DeSimone, General Manager
Jennifer Armstrong, Promotions Manager
Jon Roberts, Chief Engineer

WFKS(FM)
12-25-1965; 95.1 mhz FM *Hrs Open:* 24; 1.2 kw; Ant 210 ft; N28 04 41 W80 35 57
1388 S. Babcock St., Melbourne, FL 32901
(321) 821-7100, *Fax:* (321) 725-6821
www.mykiss951.com
kevincampbell@clearchannel.com
License: Melbourne, Brevard County, FL held by Capstar TX LP
Group Owner: Clear Channel Communications Inc.
Population Served: 76,095 *Arbitron Metro Market:* Melbourne, FL *Format:* Contemporary Hits/Top 40 *Hrs. of News Programming:* News progmg one hr wkly
Ken Holiday, Operations Dir
Jeff McKeel, General Sales Mgr
Kevin Campbell, Programming Director
Deano Chaple, Promotions Manager
Doug Remington, Engineering Dir
Laurie Reid, Business Manager
Adam Schanz, Webmaster

WCIF
01-01-1980; 106.3 mhz FM; 13.5 kw; 446 ft.; N28 8 15 W80 42 11
Mailing Address: 702 East New Haven Ave, Melbourne, FL 32901 US
Second Address: 3301 Dairy Rd., Melbourne, FL 32904
(321) 725-9243
www.wcif.com
info@wcif.com
License: Melbourne, Brevard County, FL held by First Baptist Church Inc.
Arbitron Metro Market: Melbourne-Palm bay, FL *Format:* Religious
Martha Root, Operations Dir
Lee Martinez, General Manager

*WFIT
04-01-1975; 89.5 mhz FM *Hrs Open:* 24; 900 w horiz, 4.6 kw vert; 112 ft; N28 03 51 W80 37 25
150 W. University Blvd., Melbourne, FL 32901
(321) 674-8950, *Fax:* (321) 674-8139
www.wfit.org
wfit@fit.edu
License: Melbourne, Brevard County, FL held by Florida Institute of Technology.
Population Served: 76,095 *Arbitron Metro Market:* Melbourne, FL *Hrs. of News Programming:* News progmg 40 hrs wkly *Target Audience:* 25-54; pub radio listeners
Terri Wright, General Manager
Todd Kennedy, Programming Director
Barbara Bingnear, Director of Gifts and Outreach
George Wilson, Sr. Underwriting Executive
Rose Mantle, Public Service Announcement Director, Membership S

WFKS
08-01-1965; 95.1 mhz FM *Hrs Open:* 24; 4.3 kw; 387 ft.; N28 8 12 W80 42 13
600 Congress Ave., Suite 1400, Austin, TX 78701 US
(904) 636-0507, *Fax:* (904) 997-7713
www.979kissfm.com
info@979kissfm.com
License: Melbourne, Duval County, FL held by Clear Channel Broadcasting Licenses Inc.
Group Owner: Clear Channel Communications Inc.; (acq 11-21-97; grpsl)
Arbitron Metro Market: Jacksonville, FL *Format:* Contemporary Hits/Top 40 *Hrs. of News Programming:* news progmg one hr wkly *No. News Employees:* 1 *Target Audience:* 35-54; general
Gail Austin, Operations Dir
Norm Feuer, Station Manager

WDMC
01-04-1956; 920 khz AM *Hrs Open:* 24; 5 kw-D, DA2; 1 kw-N, DA2; N28 8 11 W80 41 20
1800 Turtle Mound Road, Melbourne, FL 32934 US
(321) 757-7717, *Fax:* (321) 757-7705
info@divinemercyradio.com
License: Melbourne, FL held by Divine Mercy Communications Inc.
Arbitron Metro Market: Melbourne, FL *Format:* Christian
Robert Groppe, President

WMMB
01-01-1947; 1240 khz AM *Hrs Open:* 24; 1 kw-U, ND1; N28 4 40 W80 35 55
600 Congress Ave., Suite 1400, Austin, TX 78701 US
(321) 733-7100, *Fax:* (321) 733-0904
www.wmmbam.com
billmick@clearchannel.com
License: Melbourne, FL held by Capstar TX L.P.
Group Owner: Clear Channel Communications Inc.; (acq 8-30-00; grpsl)
Nat'l Network: Westwood One *Regional Network:* Florida's Radio Networks
Arbitron Metro Market: Melbourne, FL *Format:* News, News/Talk, 86 *Hrs. of News Programming:* news progmg 4 hrs wkly *No. News Employees:* 3 *Target Audience:* 35 plus.
Ken Holiday, Operations Dir
Bill Mick, General Manager
Larry Brewer, Programming Director

WLZR(AM)
03-08-1968; 1560 khz AM *Hrs Open:* 6 AM-7 PM; 5 kw-D; N28 07 40 W80 42 29
1800 W. Hibiscus Blvd., Suite 138, Melbourne, FL 32901
(321) 984-1000, *Fax:* (321) 724-1565
www.espn1560.com
License: Melbourne, Brevard County, FL held by Cumulus Licensing Corp.
Group Owner: Cumulus Media Inc.; (acq 5-23-2001; with co-located FM)
Nat'l Network: ESPN Radio
Population Served: 76,095 *Arbitron Metro Market:* Melbourne, FL *Format:* Sports *Target Audience:* 35-64.
Sue Garrett, General Manager

Mexico Beach

WEBZ
11-28-1990; 99.3 mhz FM *Hrs Open:* 24; 50 kw; 492 ft.; N30 0 21 W85 20 36
200 Concord Plaza, Suite 600, San Antonio, TX 78216 US
(850) 769-1408, *Fax:* (850) 769-0659
www.993thebeat.com
info@panamacity@clearchannel.com
License: Mexico Beach, Bay County, FL held by Clear Channel Broadcasting Licenses Inc.
Group Owner: Clear Channel Communications Inc.; (acq 11-21-97; grpsl)
Format: Oldies *Target Audience:* 30 plus; professional adults
Todd Berry, Operations Dir
Jackie Rinker, General Manager
Darrell Johnson, General Sales Mgr
Derby Strength, Promotions Manager

Miami

WAMR-FM
06-07-1974; 107.5 mhz FM; 93 kw; 1007 ft.; N25 58 2 W80 12 34
3102 Oak Lawn Ave., Suite 215, Dallas, TX 75219 US
(305) 447-1140, *Fax:* (305) 643-1075
www.univision.com
info@wamr.com
License: Miami, Dade County, FL held by WQBA-FM License Corp.
Group Owner: Univision Radio; (acq 9-22-2003; grpsl).
Arbitron Metro Market: Miami, FL *Format:* Adult Contemp
Claudia Puig, General Manager

WAQI
01-01-1939; 710 khz AM; 50 kw-D, DA2; 50 kw-N, DA2; N25 58 7 W80 22 44
3102 Oak Lawn Avenue, Suite 215, Dallas, TX 75219 US
(305) 447-1140, *Fax:* (305) 442-7676
www.radiomambi710.univision.com
gfernandez@univisionradio.com
License: Miami, FL held by Licensee Corporation #1.
Group Owner: Univision Radio; (acq 9-22-2003; grpsl).
Arbitron Metro Market: Miami, FL *Format:* News, News/Talk, 86
Claudia Puig, Operations Dir
Yvette Sanguilty, General Sales Mgr
Armando Perez-Roura, Programming Director
Monica Rabassa, Promotions Manager
Max Fitero, Chief Engineer

*WDNA
06-10-1980; 88.9 mhz FM *Hrs Open:* 24; 7.4 kw horiz, 6.3 kw vert; 1145 ft.; N25 32 24 W80 28 7
P.O. Box 558636, Miami, FL 33255 US
(305) 662-8889, *Fax:* (305) 662-1975
www.wdna.org
feedback@wdna.org
License: Miami, Dade County, FL held by Bascomb Memorial Broadcasting Foundation Inc.
Arbitron Metro Market: Miami-Dade, FL *Format:* Jazz *Special Programming:* World music 10 hrs wkly *Hrs. of News Programming:* News progmg 10 hrs wkly *Target Audience:* General; minorities *Adv. Rates:* 30;25; 30; 20
Maggie Pelleya, General Manager

WEDR
05-18-1963; 99.1 mhz FM; 100 kw; 919 ft.; N25 58 3 W80 12 34
3790 N.W. 167 Th St, Miami, FL 33054 US
(305) 623-7711 / (305) 444-4404, *Fax:* (305) 624-2736
www.wedr.com
info@wedr.com
License: Miami, Dade County, FL held by Cox Radio Inc.
Group Owner: Cox Radio Inc.; (acq 8-00; grpsl).
Arbitron Metro Market: Miami, FL *Format:* Urban Contemporary
Jerry Rushin, General Manager
Jo Castro, General Sales Mgr
Derrick Baker, Programming Director
Lindsey "Maestro" Powell, Promotions Manager

WMYM
08-15-1997; 990 khz AM *Hrs Open:* 24; 5 kw-D, DA2; 5 kw-N, DA2; N25 50 34 W80 25 12
11300 N.W. 87th Court, Suite 151, Hialeah Gardens, FL 33018 US
(305) 823-0990, *Fax:* (305) 823-9322
www.radio.disney.go.com
kimberly.r.munoz@disney.com
License: Miami, FL held by Radio Disney Group LLC.
Group Owner: ABC Inc.; (acq 7-30-99; $7.4 million).
Arbitron Metro Market: Miami, FL *Format:* Contemporary Hits/Top 40 *Target Audience:* Kids and families
Jeff Schwartz, Operations Dir
Gilbert Salguero, General Manager
John Craveno, General Sales Mgr
John Hurni, Chief Engineer

WFLC
07-20-1951; 97.3 mhz FM; 98 kw; 1007 ft.; N25 58 2 W80 12 34
2741 N. 29th Ave., Hollywood, FL 33020 US
(305) 444-4404, *Fax:* (954) 847-3223
www.coastfm.com
ryan.sherwin@coxinc.com
License: Miami, Dade County, FL held by Cox Radio Inc.
Group Owner: Cox Radio Inc.
Nat'l Reps: Christal
Arbitron Metro Market: Miami-Fort Lauderdale-Hollywood, FL *Format:* Blues *Target Audience:* 25-54.
Mike G. Disney, General Manager
Tony Yip, General Sales Mgr
Gary Williams, Programming Director
Ryan Sherwin, Promotions Manager
Jerry Rushin, Vice President and Market Manager
Jeanne Griswold, National Sales Manager
Dian MassaRattner, Customer Service Director
Derick Pitts, Director of Marketing Services
Jose Pagan, Web Producer

WINZ
01-01-1946; 940 khz AM *Hrs Open:* 24; 50 kw-D, DAN; 10 kw-N, DAN; N25 57 36 W80 16 13
200 Concord Plaza, Suite 600, San Antonio, TX 78216 US
(954) 862-2000, *Fax:* (954) 862-4012
www.am940southflorida.com
info@am940southflorida.com
License: Miami, FL held by Clear Channel Broadcasting Licenses Inc.
Group Owner: Clear Channel Communications Inc.; (acq 11-21-97; grpsl).
Nat'l Network: ABC *Regional Network:* Florida's Radio Networks
Nat'l Reps: Clear Channel
Arbitron Metro Market: Miami-Fort Lauderdale-Hollywood, FL *Format:* Talk *No. News Employees:* 20 *Target Audience:* 35-64; upscale, professional, managerial adults
Ken Brady, General Sales Mgr

WIOD
01-19-1926; 610 khz AM; 5 kw-D, DA2; 5 kw-N, DA2; N25 50 58 W80 9 18
200 Concord Plaza, Suite 600, San Antonio, TX 78216 US
(954) 862-2000, *Fax:* (954) 862-4012
www.newsradio610.com
newsradio610@ccmiami.com
License: Miami, FL held by Clear Channel Radio Licenses Inc.
Group Owner: Clear Channel Communications Inc.; (acq 11-21-97; grpsl)
Wire Services: UPI
Arbitron Metro Market: Miami-Fort Lauderdale-Hollywood, FL
Format: News, News/Talk, 86 *Target Audience:* 25-64.
Michael Crusham, Operations Dir
Gary Reyes, General Sales Mgr
Ken Charles, Programming Director
Jessie Trujillo, Promotions Manager
Russell Wein, Digital and Integrated Media Sales Director

***WLRN-FM**
02-01-1948; 91.3 mhz FM *Hrs Open:* 24; 47 kw; 935 ft.; N25 58 46 W80 11 46
172 Northeast 15 Th Str., Miami, FL 33132 US
(305) 995-1717, *Fax:* (305) 995-2299
www.wlrn.org
info@wlrn.org
License: Miami, Dade County, FL held by School Board of Miami Dade County Florida.
Nat'l Network: NPR; PRI *Regional Network:* Fla. Pub. *Wire Services:* AP
Arbitron Metro Market: Miami-Fort Lauderdale-Hollywood, FL *TV Affiliate:* *WLRN-TV affil. *Format:* News, News/Talk, 86 *Special Programming:* Haitian 3 hrs wkly *Hrs. of News Programming:* news progmg 111 hrs wkly*No. News Employees:* 7 *Target Audience:* General; well educated, moderate to high income bracket
Karen Echols, CFO
Antonio Zayas, Operations Dir
John Labonia, General Manager
Ted Eldredge, Station Manager
Peter J. Maerz, Programming Director
Irina Lallemond, News Director
Jack Yaghdjian, Chief Engineer

WLYF
01-01-1948; 101.5 mhz FM *Hrs Open:* 24; 100 kw; 814 ft.; N25 58 0 W80 12 42.8
20450 NW Second Aveune, Miami, FL 33169 US
(305) 521-5100, *Fax:* (305) 652-0098
www.litemiami.com
litefm@litemiami.com
License: Miami, Miami-Dade County, FL held by Lincoln Financial Media Co. of Florida.
Group Owner: Lincoln Financial Media; (acq 4-3-2006; grpsl).
Nat'l Reps: Interep *Wire Services:* AP
Arbitron Metro Market: Miami, FL *Format:* Adult Contemp *Hrs. of News Programming:* News progmg 2 hrs wkly *Target Audience:* 25-54; women
Jon Boscia, CEO
Don Benson, President
Dennis Collins, Operations Dir
Rosemary Zimmerman, General Sales Mgr
Nicole Gates, Promotions Manager
Gary Blau, Engineering Dir
Rob Sidney, Operations Director
Danielle Webb, RegionalSales Manager

***WKCP**
08-24-1970; 89.7 mhz FM *Hrs Open:* 24; 100 kw; 1014 ft.; N25 32 24 W80 28 7
2065 Half Day Road, Deerfield, IL 60015 US
(954)522-8755
classicalsouthflorida.publicradio.org
License: Miami, Miami-Dade County, FL held by American Public Media Group
Arbitron Metro Market: Miami, FL *Format:* Talk
Douglas Evans, General Manager

WOCN
12-22-1956; 1450 khz AM
350 N.E. 71 Street, Miami, FL 33138 US
(305) 759-7280, *Fax:* (305) 759-2276
Daniel@1450espndeportes.com
License: Miami, FL held by IM FL Licenses LLC.
Group Owner: Independence Media Holdings LLC; (acq 7-12-2006; $6 million)
Nat'l Network: ESPN Deportes *Wire Services:* AP
Arbitron Metro Market: Miami-Fort Laud *TV Affiliate:* Sp No. *News Employees:* General. *Adv. Rates:* 50; 50; 50; 40

WPOW
06-15-1985; 96.5 mhz FM; 98 kw; 1007 ft.; N25 58 2 W80 12 34
20295 N.W. 2nd Ave, #300, Miami, FL 33169 US
(305) 653-6796, *Fax:* (305) 770-1456
www.power96.com
License: Miami, Dade County, FL held by Beasley FM Acquisition Corp.
Group Owner: Beasley Broadcast Group Inc.; (acq 8-94).
Arbitron Metro Market: Miami-Fort Lauderdale-Hollywood, FL
Format: Contemporary Hits/Top 40
George Beasley, President
Ira Wolf, Operations Dir
Matthew Bell, General Manager
John Jaras, General Sales Mgr

WQAM
05-01-1921; 560 khz AM *Hrs Open:* 24; 5 kw-D, ND1; 1 kw-N, ND1; N25 44 36 W80 9 14
3033 Riviera Drive, Naples, FL 33940 US
(305) 654-1700, *Fax:* (305) 654-1717
www.wqam.com
info@wqam.com
License: Miami, FL held by Beasley-Reed Broadcasting.
Group Owner: Beasley Broadcast Group Inc.
Nat'l Network: Sporting News Radio Network *Nat'l Reps:* Eastman Radio
Arbitron Metro Market: Miami-Fort Lauderdale-Hollywood, FL
Format: Sports *Target Audience:* 25-54; males
Joe Bell, General Manager
Chris Jones, General Sales Mgr
Josh Darrow, Programming Director
George Corso, Chief Engineer
Ray Perry, Director of Network
Lisa Blum, National Sales Manager
Lee ""Flee"" Feldman, PromotionsDirector/

WQBA
01-01-1947; 1140 khz AM; 50 kw-D, DA2; 10 kw-N, DA2; N25 46 3 W80 29 10
3102 Oak Lawn Ave., Suite 215, Dallas, TX 75219 US
(305) 447-1140, *Fax:* (305) 441-2454
www.wqba.com
License: Miami, FL held by WQBA-AM License Corp.
Group Owner: Univision Radio; (acq 9-22-2003; grpsl).
Arbitron Metro Market: Miami-Fort Lauderdale-Hollywood, FL
Format: News, News/Talk, 86
Claudia Puig, Operations Dir

WSUA
06-20-1969; 1260 khz AM *Hrs Open:* 24
2100 Coral Way, Miami, FL 33145 US
(305) 285-1260, *Fax:* (305) 858-5907
www.caracolusa.com
info@wsua.com
License: Miami, FL held by WSUA Broadcasting Corp.
Arbitron Metro Market: Miami-Fort Lauderdale-Hollywood, FL
Format: News, News/Talk, 86 *Hrs. of News Programming:* news progmg 31 hrs wkly *No. News Employees:* 7 *Target Audience:* 18-54; Latin American audience
Tomas Martinez, General Manager

WFEZ(FM)
11-01-1960; 93.1 mhz FM *Hrs Open:* 24; 100 kw; Ant 1,007 ft; N25 58 03 W80 12 34
2741 N. 29th Ave., Hollywood, FL 33020
(305) 444-4404, *Fax:* (954) 847-3223
93rock.com
rry.rushin@coxinc.com
License: Miami, Dade County, FL held by Cox Radio Inc.
Group Owner: Cox Radio Inc.; (acq 5-18-2000; grpsl)
Nat'l Reps: Christal
Population Served: 143,357 *Arbitron Metro Market:* Hollywood, FL *Format:* Rock/AOR *Target Audience:* 18-49; upscale, educ adults with hip active lifestyles *Adv. Rates:* 210; 215; 265; 150
Jerry Rushin, Vice President & Market Manager
Michael Disney, General Manager
Jeanne Griswold, General Sales Mgr
Gary Williams, Programming Director
Ryan Sherwin, Promotions Manager
Dian Massa Rattner, Customer Service Director,Sales
Derick Pitts, Director of Marketing Services
Jose Pagan, Web Producer

WWFE
07-01-1989; 670 khz AM *Hrs Open:* 24; 50 kw-D, 2.5 kw-N, DA-2; N25 51 27 W80 28 52
330 S.W. 27th Ave., Suite 207, Miami, FL 33135
(305) 541-3300, *Fax:* (305) 541-7470
www.lapoderosa.com
anavidal@lapoderosa.com
License: Miami, Dade County, FL held by Fenix Broadcasting Corp.
Nat'l Reps: Lotus Entravision Reps LLC
Population Served: 1,800,000 *Arbitron Metro Market:* Miami-Fort Lauderdale-Hollywood, FL *Hrs. of News Programming:* news progmg 27 hrs wkly *No. News Employees:* 4 *Target Audience:* 25-54.
Jorge Rodriguez, President
Ana Vidal Rodriguez, Vice President
Miguel Melanio, Programming Director
Eduardo Aleman, News Director
Eduardo Rodriguez, Chief Engineer

Miami Beach

WMIA-FM
07-01-1968; 93.9 mhz FM; 98 kw; 1007 ft.; N25 58 2 W80 12 34
200 Concord Plaza, Suite 600, San Antonio, TX 78216 US
(954) 862-2000, *Fax:* (954) 862-4013
www.939mia.com
RayHernandez@clearchannel.com
License: Miami Beach, Dade County, FL held by Clear Channel Radio Licenses Inc.
Group Owner: Clear Channel Communications Inc.; (acq 11-21-97; grpsl)
Arbitron Metro Market: Miami Beach, FL *Format:* Adult Contemp *Target Audience:* 25-54.
Jamie Kaufman, General Manager
Matthew Bell, General Sales Mgr
Ray Hernandez, Programming Director
Jessie Trujillo, Promotions Manager

WMBM
01-01-1949; 1490 khz AM *Hrs Open:* 24; 1 kw-U; N25 46 10 W80 08 11
13242 NW 7 Ave., North Miami, FL 33139
(305) 769-1100, *Fax:* (305) 769-9975
www.wmbm.com
wmbm@wmbm.com
License: Miami Beach, Dade County, FL held by New Birth Broadcasting Corp.
Nat'l Network: American Urban; Westwood One
Population Served: 50,000 *Arbitron Metro Market:* Miami, FL *Hrs. of News Programming:* news progmg 3 hrs wkly *No. News Employees:* 1 *Target Audience:* 25 plus; mature Black, self-motivated, Christian,professionals *Adv. Rates:* 140; 95; 140; 65
Victor Curry, President
Caroline Kelly, Operations Dir
Gregory Cooper, Programming Director

WMGE
01-01-1961; 94.9 mhz FM; 98 kw; 1007 ft.; N25 58 2 W80 12 34
200 Concord Plaza, Suite 600, San Antonio, TX 78216 US
(954) 862-2000, *Fax:* (305) 862-4012
www.mega949.com
RayHernandez@clearchannel.com
License: Miami Beach, Dade County, FL held by Clear Channel Broadcasting Licenses Inc.
Group Owner: Clear Channel Communications Inc.; (acq 11-21-97; grpsl).
Nat'l Network: Westwood One
Arbitron Metro Market: Miramar. FL *Format:* Ethnic *Target Audience:* 18-34.
Victor Olaniel, Sales Manager
Ray Hernandez, Station Program Director
Sergio Duarte, Station Program Director
Russell Wein, Digital & Integrated Media Sales Director

Miami Springs

WNMA
05-18-1958; 1210 khz AM *Hrs Open:* 24
8400 N.W. 52nd St., Suite 101, Miami, FL 33166 US
(305) 759 7280, *Fax:* (305) 759-2276
www.espndeportesmiami.com
eduardor@mrbi.net
License: Miami Springs, FL held by Multicultural Radio Broadcasting Licensee LLC.
Group Owner: Multicultural Radio Broadcasting Inc.; (acq 2-4-2004; grpsl).
Arbitron Metro Market: Miami, FL *Format:* Sports, Talk
Eduardo Rueda, General Manager

Micanopy

WSKY-FM
09-07-1985; 97.3 mhz FM *Hrs Open:* 24; 50 kw; 492 ft.; N29 32 9 W82 19 18
401 City Ave., Suite 409, Bala Cynwyd, PA 19004 US
(352) 377-0985, *Fax:* (352) 337-2968
www.thesky973.com

License: Micanopy, Alachua County, FL held by Entercom Gainesville License L.L.C.
Group Owner: Entercom Communications Corp.; (acq 3-18-98; $2.8 million).
Nat'l Reps: Christal
Arbitron Metro Market: Gainesville-Oca *Format:* News, News/Talk, 86 *Target Audience:* 18-54. *Adv. Rates:* 26; 22; 24; 19
Dick O'Neill, General Manager
Eric Jewell, General Sales Mgr
Nick Allen, Programming Director
John Boyer, News Director

Middleburg

WGNE-FM
12-13-1973; 99.9 mhz FM; 48 kw; 984 ft.; N30 19 22 W81 38 34
Broadcast Plaza, Crane Ave., Pittsburgh, PA 15220 US
(904) 727-9696, *Fax:* (904) 721-9322
www.cflradio.net
info@gatercountry.com
License: Middleburg, Putnam County, FL held by Renda Broadcasting Corp.
Group Owner: Renda Broadcasting Corp.; (acq 1996; $6.5 million with WMUV(FM) Brunswick, GA)
Arbitron Metro Market: Daytona Beach, FL *Format:* Country
Target Audience: 18-49. *Adv. Rates:* 95; 65; 85; 55
Toney Renda, President
Gary Spurgeon, General Manager
Randy Hill, Programming Director

Midway

WFLA-FM
01-01-1996; 100.7 mhz FM; 11.5 kw; 489 ft.; N30 29 32 W84 17 13
200 Concord Plaza, Suite 600, San Antonio, TX 78216 US
(850) 422-3107, *Fax:* (850) 383-0747
www.1270wfla.com
mattmillar@clearchannel.com
License: Midway, Gadsden County, FL held by Clear Channel Broadcasting Licenses Inc.
Group Owner: Clear Channel Communications Inc.; (acq 11-21-97; grpsl).
Arbitron Metro Market: Tallahassee, FL *Format:* Talk
Jeff Horn, Operations Dir
Lisa Rice, General Manager
Jason Sauer, Promotions Manager

Milton

WEBY
01-01-1978; 1330 khz AM *Hrs Open:* 24
7179 Printers Alley, Milton, FL 32583 US
(850) 983-2242, *Fax:* (850) 983-3231
www.1330weby.com
weby@1330weby.com
License: Milton, FL held by Spinnaker License Corp.
Nat'l Network: Jones Radio Networks
Arbitron Metro Market: Milton, FL *Format:* News, Talk *Special Programming:* Christian 7 hrs wkly / Florida State football *Hrs. of News Programming:* News progmg 15 hrs wkly *No. News Employees:* 1 *TargetAudience:* 35 plus; affuent, educated adults *Adv. Rates:* 25; 25; 25; 25
Mike Bates, President
Anthony Daughtery, Operations Dir
Dave Daughtry, News Director

*WEGS
10-15-1985; 91.7 mhz FM; 20 kw; 367 ft.; N30 37 20 W87 5 12
Mailing Address: 505 Josephine St, Titusville, FL 32796 US
Second Address: 505 Josephine St., Titusville, FL 32796
(904) 474-1223, *Fax:* (850) 447-9650
www.olivebaptist.org
wegs917@aol.com
License: Milton, Santa Rosa County, FL held by Florida Public Radio Inc.
Arbitron Metro Market: Milton, FL *Format:* Christian, Talk
Dave Talley, General Manager

WXBM-FM
04-28-1964; 102.7 mhz FM; 100 kw; 1601 ft.; N30 36 40 W87 36 26
600 Congress Ave., Suite 1400, Austin, TX 78701 US
(850) 994-5357, *Fax:* (850) 994-7191
www.wxbm.com
feedback@wxbm.com
License: Milton, Santa Rosa County, FL held by 6 Johnson Road Licenses Inc.
Group Owner: Pamal Broadcasting Ltd.; (acq 10-19-2001; grpsl).
Arbitron Metro Market: Milton, FL *Format:* Country
Dave Cobb, General Manager

Mims

WPGS
05-05-1986; 840 khz AM *Hrs Open:* Sunrise-sunset
805 North Dixie Ave, Titusville, FL 32796 US
(321) 383-1000
www.talkstar840.com
wpgs840@aol.com
License: Mims, FL held by WPGS Inc.
Nat'l Network: USA
Arbitron Metro Market: Melbourne-Titusville-Cocoa, FL *Format:* Talk
Ed Shiflett, President
Jay Rowan, Chief Engineer

Miramar Beach

WSBZ
10-18-1994; 106.3 mhz FM; 6 kw; 328 ft.; N30 23 7 W86 18 3
690 Little Canal Drive, Santa Rosa Beach, FL 32459 US
(850) 267-3279, *Fax:* (850) 231-1775
www.seabreeze.fm
office@wsbz.com
License: Miramar Beach, Walton County, FL held by Carter Broadcasting Inc.
Arbitron Metro Market: Fort Walton Bea *Format:* Adult Contemp
Renee Carter, CFO
Mark Carter, General Manager

Monticello

*WFRF-FM
12-01-1996; 105.7 mhz FM *Hrs Open:* 24; 16 kw; 410 ft.; N30 23 8 W83 50 5
2906 Clardy Road, Dothan, AL 36303 US
(850) 201-1070, *Fax:* (850) 201-1071
www.faithradio.us
mailbox@faithradio.us
License: Monticello, Jefferson County, FL held by Faith Radio Network Inc.
Nat'l Network: CBS
Arbitron Metro Market: Tallahassee, FL *Format:* Religious *Target Audience:* 12+. *Adv. Rates:* 15; 25; 20; 13
Scott Beigle, President
Steve Huffman, Operations Dir
Brenda Beigle, Vice President
Suzanne Farrar, Administrative Assistant
Anna Moore, Administrative Assistant

*WKVH
03-01-2003; 91.9 mhz FM *Hrs Open:* 24; 1.5 kw; 1322 ft.; N30 40 13 W83 56 26
1425 N. Market Blvd, Suite 9, Sacramento, CA 95834 US
(800) 525-5683, *Fax:* (916) 251-1650
www.klove.com
klove@klove.com
License: Monticello, Jefferson County, FL held by Educational Media Foundation.
Group Owner: EMF Broadcasting
Nat'l Network: K-Love
Arbitron Metro Market: Tallahassee, FL *Format:* Christian *No. News Employees:* 3 *Target Audience:* 25-44; Judeo Christian, female
Darrell Chambliss, Chairman
Mike Novak, President and CEO
Chip Bailey, Operations Dir
Eric Allen, General Sales Mgr
David Pierce, Programming Director
Ed Lenane, News Director
Sam Wallington, Engineering Dir
Marya Morgan, NewsReporter
Richard Hunt, News Reporter
Laura Daniels, News Reporter
Tim Luttrell, News Reporter
Kenny Noble Cortes, News Reporter
Darren Vinson, News Reporter

Mount Dora

WMGF
01-01-1966; 107.7 mhz FM *Hrs Open:* 24; 98 kw; 1588 ft.; N28 55 10.1 W81 19 7.4
200 Concord Plaza, Suite 600, San Antonio, TX 78216 US
(407) 916-7800, *Fax:* (407) 916-0329
www.magic107.com
info@magic107.com
License: Mount Dora, Lake County, FL held by Clear Channel Radio Licenses Inc.
Group Owner: Clear Channel Communications Inc.; (acq 11-21-97; grpsl)
Regional Reps: Paul Rogers
Arbitron Metro Market: Orlando, FL *Format:* Adult Contemp
Special Programming: Contemp Christian mus 20 hrs wkly *Hrs. of News Programming:* news progmg 2 hrs wkly *No. News Employees:* 1 *Target Audience:* 25-54; working women *Adv. Rates:* 350.;350.;350.;170.
Linda Byrd, General Manager
Shannon Fraser, General Sales Mgr
Ken Payne, Programming Director
Laura Kam, Promotions Manager
Shawn Williams, News Director
Chris Kampmeier, Programming Director

Murdock

WBCG
10-22-2001; 98.9 mhz FM *Hrs Open:* 24; 5.5 kw; 341 ft.; N27 0 9 W82 10 54
9148 Bonita Beach Road, Suite 205, Bonita Springs, FL 34135 US
(941) 639-1112, *Fax:* (941) 206-9296
www.989thebeach.com
wbcgbeachradio@cs.com
License: Murdock, Charlotte County, FL held by Concord Media Group Inc.
Regional Network: Florida's Radio Networks
Format: Adult Contemp *Hrs. of News Programming:* News progmg 2 hrs wkly *Target Audience:* Adults 25+; core 35-54 female *Adv. Rates:* 20; 10; 10; 10
Mark Jorgenson, General Manager
Michael Keating, Programming Director

Naples

WARO
05-08-1962; 94.5 mhz FM *Hrs Open:* 24; 99 kw; 1014 ft.; N26 20 26 W81 42 48
2824 Palm Beach Blvd., Fort Myers, FL 33916 US
(239) 337-2346, *Fax:* (239) 479-5581
www.classicrock945.com
License: Naples, Collier County, FL held by Meridian Broadcasting Inc.
Group Owner: Meridian Broadcasting Inc.
Arbitron Metro Market: Fort Myers, FL *Format:* Classic Rock
Special Programming: Relg 2 hrs wkly *Target Audience:* 25-54; men
Mike Allen, Programming Director

*WAYJ
10-01-1987; 89.5 mhz FM *Hrs Open:* 24; 100 kw; 309 ft.; N26 7 12 W81 40 58
Mailing Address: 2132 Shadowlawn Drive, Naples, FL 33962 US
Second Address: 1860 Boy Scout Dr., Suite 202, Fort Myers, FL 33906
(800) 877-5600, *Fax:* (916) 251-1650
www.air1.com
info@air1.com
License: Naples, Lee County, FL held by WAY-FM Media Group Inc.
Group Owner: WAY-FM Media Group Inc.
Nat'l Network: USA
Arbitron Metro Market: Laramie WY *Format:* Alternative, Christian
Darrell Chambliss, Chairman
Mike Novak, President
Alan Mason, Operations Dir
David Pierce, Programming Director
Ed Lenane, News Director
Sam Wallington, Engineering Dir
Marya Morgan, News Reporter
Richard Hunt, News Reporter

WNOG
10-14-1954; 1270 khz AM *Hrs Open:* 24*Rebroadcasts:* Rebroadcasts WINK(AM) Fort Myers 100%
2824 Palm Beach Blvd., Fort Myers, FL 33916 US
(239) 337-2346, *Fax:* (239) 479-5583
www.925foxnews.com
License: Naples, FL held by Meridian Broadcasting Inc.
Group Owner: Meridian Broadcasting Inc.; (acq 12-1-96; grpsl)
Nat'l Network: CBS *Nat'l Reps:* McGavren Guild
Arbitron Metro Market: Fort Myers, FL *Format:* News, News/Talk, 86 *Target Audience:* 35 plus.
Joseph Schwantzel, President
Paul Thomas, General Manager
Wayne Simons, General Sales Mgr
Jim Watkins, Programming Director
Keith Stulhmann, Engineering Dir

WSGL
05-10-1980; 104.7 mhz FM *Hrs Open:* 24; 20 kw; 433 ft.; N26 7 35 W81 43 17
1459 Crane Avenue, Pittsburgh, PA 15220 US

(239) 495-8383, *Fax:* (239) 495-0883
www.wsgl1047.com
webguy@1047mixfm.com
License: Naples, Collier County, FL held by Renda Broadcasting Corp. of Nevada.
Group Owner: Renda Broadcasting Corp.; (acq 11-10-98; $3.65 million).
Arbitron Metro Market: Fort Myers-Napl *Format:* Adult Contemp *Special Programming:* Classic rock 70s & 80s music 5 hrs wkly *Hrs. of News Programming:* News progmg one hr wkly *Target Audience:* 25-54; women
Buzzy Ford, Promotions Manager

***WSOR**
01-01-1989; 90.9 mhz FM *Hrs Open:* 24; 36 kw; 902 ft.; N26 20 29 W81 42 38
820 N. Lasalle Blvd., Chcago, IL 60610 US
(727) 391-9994, *Fax:* (727) 397-6425
www.wkes.fm
wkes@moody.edu
License: Naples, Collier County, FL held by Moody Bible Institute.
Nat'l Network: Salem Radio Network *Wire Services:* AP
Arbitron Metro Market: Fort Myers-Naples-Marco Island, FL *Format:* Christian, Talk *No. News Employees:* 1 *Target Audience:* 40 plus.
Mike Gleichman, Operations Dir
Pierre Chestang, General Manager
John Stortz, Chief Engineer

***WAYJ(FM)**
08-01-1988; 89.5 mhz FM *Hrs Open:* 24; 100 kw; Ant 309 ft; N26 07 12 W81 40 58
3805 The Lords Way, Naples, FL 34114
(239) 775-8950, *Fax:* (239) 774-5889
www.praisefm.com
praisefm895@msn.com
License: Naples, Collier County, FL held by Shadowlawn Association Inc.
Arbitron Metro Market: Fort Myers-Naples-Marco Island, FL *Format:* Christian *Target Audience:* 18-40.
Arnie Coones, General Manager

Naples Park

WAVV
05-30-1987; 101.1 mhz FM *Hrs Open:* 24; 100 kw; Ant 980 ft; N26 10 58 W81 34 30
11800 Tamiami Tr. E., Naples, FL 33962
(239) 793-1011, *Fax:* (239) 793-7000
wavv101.com
w.tiburski@wavv101.com
License: Naples Park, Collier County, FL held by Alpine Broadcasting Corp.
Nat'l Network: AP Radio *Nat'l Reps:* Christal
Arbitron Metro Market: Fort Myers-Napl *Special Programming:* Jazz 3 hrs wkly *Hrs. of News Programming:* News progmg 8 hrs wkly *Target Audience:* 35 plus; an economically qualified audience that is somewhat moreaffluent *Adv. Rates:* 80; 80; 80; 50
Donna Alpert, CFO
Norman Alpert, President
Kenny Lamb, Operations Dir
Walt Tiburski, General Manager

WBTT
10-22-1987; 105.5 mhz FM; 23.5 kw; 722 ft.; N26 19 0 W81 47 13
200 Concord Plaza, Suite 600, San Antonio, TX 78216 US
(914) 225-4300,(866) 843-2328, *Fax:* (239) 225-4329
www.1055thebeat.com
License: Naples Park, Collier County, FL held by Clear Channel Radio Licenses Inc.
Group Owner: Clear Channel Communications Inc.; (acq 1996; grpsl)
Arbitron Metro Market: Fort Myers-Naples-Marco Island, FL *Format:* Christian *Target Audience:* 18-34.
Jim Keating, General Manager

Navarre

WKFP(FM)
01-01-1999; 95.7 mhz FM; 25 kw; Ant 282 ft; N30 27 02 W86 51 59
2070 N. Palafax St., Pensacola, FL 32501
(850) 434-1230, *Fax:* (850) 469-9698
www.praise95.net,www.pensacolachristianradio.com
praise957@hotmail.com
License: Navarre, Santa Rosa County, FL held by 550 AM Inc.
Arbitron Metro Market: Pensacola, FL *Format:* Christian
Michael Glinter, President
Dara Glinter, Executive Vice President

New Port Richey

WDUV
09-19-1969; 105.5 mhz FM *Hrs Open:* 24; 33 kw; 1503 ft.; N28 10 56 W82 46 6
3773 Howard Hughes Pwy, Suite 300n, Las Vegas, NV 89109 US
(727) 579-2000, *Fax:* (727) 579-2662(727) 579-2271
www.wduv.com
info@coxradio.com
License: New Port Richey, Pasco County, FL held by Cox Radio Inc.
Group Owner: Cox Radio Inc.; (acq 5-99)
Arbitron Metro Market: New Port Richey, FL *Format:* Adult Contemp *Special Programming:* It one hr wkly *Target Audience:* 25-54.
Howard Tuuri, Operations Dir
Paul DeFazio, General Sales Mgr
John Larson, Programming Director
Julia Freeman, Promotions Manager
Tom Paleveda, Operations Manager

***WCIE**
04-10-1985; 91.5 mhz FM *Hrs Open:* 24; 16.5 kw; 305 ft.; N28 16 58 W82 42 43
5015 South Florida Ave, Suite 104, Lakeland, FL 33813 US
(727) 848-9150, *Fax:* (727) 848-1233
www.thejoyfm.com
jeff@thejoyfm.com
License: New Port Richey, Pasco County, FL held by Radio Training Network Inc.
Arbitron Metro Market: Tampa-St. Petersburg-Clearwater, FL *Format:* Adult Contemp, Christian
James Campbell, President
Jeff MacFarlane, General Manager
Carmen Brown, Promotions Manager
Steve Rieker, Chief Engineer

WPSO
10-31-1963; 1500 khz AM *Hrs Open:* Sunrise-sunset
27873 U.S. 19 North, Clearwater, FL 34621 US
(727) 725-3500,(727) 725-5555, *Fax:* (813) 814-7500
www.wpso.com
wzra48@yahoo.com
License: New Port Richey, FL held by AKMA Broadcast Network Inc.
Arbitron Metro Market: Tampa-St. Petersburg-Clearwater, FL *Format:* Greek, News, 62, Talk *Special Programming:* Pol two hrs, quiz/trivia program, relg 8 hrs, East Indian one hr, It 3 hrs wkly, Ethnic *Hrs. of NewsProgramming:* news progmg 35 hrs wkly *No. News Employees:* 1 *Target Audience:* General; international, ethnic
Sam Agelatos, President
Angelo Agelatos, Operations Dir

New Smyrna Beach

***WJLU**
09-07-1989; 89.7 mhz FM *Hrs Open:* 24; 10 kw; 328 ft.; N29 0 32 W80 58 27
4295 Ridgewood Avenue, Port Orange, FL 32127 US
(386) 756-9094, *Fax:* (386) 760-7107
www.cornerstoneministry.org
thecornerstone@cornerstoneministry.org
License: New Smyrna Beach, Volusia County, FL held by Cornerstone Broadcasting Corp.
Nat'l Network: USA; Moody
Arbitron Metro Market: Daytona Beach, FL *Format:* Religious *Hrs. of News Programming:* News progmg 18 hrs wkly *Target Audience:* General; families
Sandra Leisner, Operations Dir
William Powell, General Manager

WSBB
01-01-1950; 1230 khz AM *Hrs Open:* 24; 1 kw-U; N29 01 57 W80 55 03
229 Canal St., New Smyrna Beach, FL 32170
(386) 428-9091, *Fax:* (386) 428-1924
barbdiegel@wsbbradio.com
License: New Smyrna Beach, Volusia County, FL held by Diegel Communications LLC
Nat'l Network: CNN Radio *Regional Network:* Florida's Radio Networks
Population Served: 240,000 *Arbitron Metro Market:* Daytona Beach, FL *Special Programming:* Sundays: Boston Pops show, Jazz Journey show, Back To Live show, When Radio Was, Florida Roundtable, Best of Broadway *Hrs. of NewsProgramming:* News progmg 120 hrs wkly *No. News Employees:* 1 *Target Audience:* 45 plus. *Adv. Rates:* available on request
Skip Diegel, President
Skip Diegel, President/Owner/General Manager

Newberry

WHHZ
02-01-1999; 100.5 mhz FM; 44 kw; 469 ft.; N29 36 29 W82 51 1
2912 NW 62nd Terrace, Gainesville, FL 32606 US
(352) 313-3130 / 3135, *Fax:* (352) 313-3166
www.1005thebuzz.com
themorningbuzz2004@yahoo.com
License: Newberry, Alachua County, FL held by 6 Johnson Road Licenses Inc.
Group Owner: Pamal Broadcasting Ltd.; (acq 1-5-2007; grpsl)
Arbitron Metro Market: Gainesville-Ocala, FL *Format:* Rock/AOR
Benjamin Hill, General Manager

Niceville

WTKE-FM
07-01-1950; 100.3 mhz FM; 3 kw; 469 ft.; N30 24 38 W86 37 22
P O Box 1699, Meridian, MS 39302 US
(850) 244-1400, *Fax:* (850) 243-1471
www.sportstalktheticket.com
info@sportstalktheticket.com
License: Niceville, Okaloosa County, FL held by Star Broadcasting Inc.
Group Owner: Star Broadcasting Inc.; (acq 2-14-2003)
Nat'l Reps: Roslin
Arbitron Metro Market: Fort Walton Beach, FL *Format:* Sports, Talk *Target Audience:* 25-54.
Ron Hale,Sr., General Manager
David Kuntz, General Sales Mgr
Frank Hale, Programming Director

Nocatee

WZSP
08-27-1998; 105.3 mhz FM *Hrs Open:* 24; 4.1 kw; 400 ft.; N27 11 1 W81 56 57
300 Klispie Drive, Punta Gorda, FL 33950 US
(863) 494-4111, *Fax:* (863) 494-4443
www.lazeta.fm
info@lazeta.fm
License: Nocatee, De Soto County, FL held by Heartland Broadcasting Corp.
Regional Network: Florida's Radio Networks *Nat'l Reps:* Lotus Entravision Reps LLC *Regional Reps:* Lotus-Entravision
Arbitron Metro Market: Zolfo Springs, FL *Target Audience:* General; Sp speaking audience, Charlotte, Desto, Hardee, Sarasota, Polk & Highlands counties *Adv. Rates:* 35; 30; 30; 24
Harold (Hal) Kneller Jr., President
Casey Williams, Sales & Station Manager
Sherry Good, Office Manager

North Fort Myers

WWCN
12-17-1983; 770 khz AM
20125 S. Tamiami Trail, Estero, FL 33928 US
(239) 495-2100, *Fax:* (239) 992-8165
www.770espn.com
info@am770.com
License: North Fort Myers, FL held by Beasley Radio Co.
Group Owner: Beasley Broadcast Group Inc.; (acq 12-16-87).
Arbitron Metro Market: Fort Myers, FL *Format:* Sports, Talk
George Beasley, President
John Rozz, Operations Dir
Bradley Beasley, General Manager
AJ Lurie, General Sales Mgr
Eric Willard, Programming Director
Jeff Hickcox, Promotions Manager
Dawn Krause, Business Manager

North Miami

WKAT
11-01-1937; 1360 khz AM; 5 kw-D, ND1; 1 kw-N, ND1; N25 44 36 W80 9 14
13499 Biscayne Blvd., #1, North Miami, FL 33181 US
(305) 503-1340, *Fax:* (305) 677-7585
www.1360wkat.com
info@qwkat.com
License: North Miami, FL held by Caron Broadcasting Inc.
Group Owner: Salem Communications Corp.; (acq 1-31-2005; $10 million)
Arbitron Metro Market: Miami-Fort Lauderdale-Hollywood, FL *Format:* Classical, News, 62, Talk
Stephen James, Operations Dir
Tony Calatayud, General Manager

North Miami Beach

WXDJ
01-01-1986; 95.7 mhz FM *Hrs Open:* 24; 40 kw; 548 ft.; N25 46 24 W80 11 18
3191 Coral Way, Suite 805, Miami, FL 33145 US
(305) 444-9292, *Fax:* (305) 461-4466
www.lamusica.com
License: North Miami Beach, Dade County, FL held by WXDJ Licensing Inc.
Group Owner: Spanish Broadcasting System Inc.; (acq 7-11-97; $110 million with WRMA(FM) Fort Lauderdale)
Arbitron Metro Market: North Miami Beach, FL *Hrs. of News Programming:* News progmg 4 hrs wkly *Target Audience:* 18-54; Hispanic Adults
Jackie Nosti-Combo, General Manager
John Caride, Promotions Manager

North Palm Beach

WSVU
01-01-2006; 960 khz AM
US
(561) 627-9966
www.seaviewam960.com
Chet@SeaviewRadio.com
License: North Palm Beach, FL held by North Palm Beach Broadcasting Inc.
Nat'l Network: CBS Radio
Arbitron Metro Market: North Palm Beach, FL *Format:* Classic Rock
Mike Balsamo, Operations Dir
Chet Tart, General Manager
Patty Palmer, Promotions Manager
Maryann Mckee, Traffic/Office Manager
Caroline Tart, Creative/Web Director
Harry Kaufman, Sales
Barry Horowitz, Sales

Ocala

*WHIJ
03-30-1990; 88.1 mhz FM *Hrs Open:* 24; 1.25 kw vert; 394 ft.; N29 14 17 W82 7 17
814 N.E. 2nd Street, Ocala, FL 32670 US
(352) 351-8810, *Fax:* (352) 351-8917
www.thejoyfm.com
thejoyfm@thejoyfm.com
License: Ocala, Marion County, FL held by Radio Training Network Inc.
Arbitron Metro Market: Gainesville-Ocala, FL *Format:* Adult Contemp, Christian *Target Audience:* 20-50.
Jeff MacFarlane, General Manager

WMFQ
07-11-1977; 92.9 mhz FM *Hrs Open:* 24; 50 kw; 476 ft.; N29 4 45 W82 5 31
1429 N. Federal Highway, Ft. Lauderdale, FL 33304 US
(352) 732-9877, *Fax:* (352) 622-6675
www.radio92q.com
License: Ocala, Marion County, FL held by Asterisk Communications Inc.
Group Owner: Asterisk Inc.; (acq 1995; $2.1 million)
Nat'l Reps: McGavren Guild
Arbitron Metro Market: Ocala, FL *Format:* Adult Contemp *Hrs. of News Programming:* news progmg 5 hrs wkly *No. News Employees:* 1 *Target Audience:* 35 plus; upscale, female
Shane Finch, Operations Dir
Dean Johnson, General Manager
Same Gerace, General Sales Mgr
Bill Barr, Programming Director

WMOP
12-18-1953; 900 khz AM *Hrs Open:* 24; 2.7 kw-D, ND1; 0.023 kw-N, ND1; N29 14 16 W82 7 16
P.O. Box 3930, Ocala, FL 34478 US
(352) 732-2010, *Fax:* (352) 629-1614
http://www.espngo1.com
thesportsfix@espngo1.com
License: Ocala, FL held by Florida Sportstalk Inc.
Nat'l Network: ABC *Nat'l Reps:* Dora-Clayton
Arbitron Metro Market: Gainesville, FL *Format:* Sports, Talk *Hrs. of News Programming:* news progmg 3 hrs wkly *No. News Employees:* 1 *Target Audience:* 35 plus.
Don DePew, Operations Dir
Tom Catalano, General Manager
Carey David, General Sales Mgr
Chris Doering, Programming Director
Bill Boyer, Chief Engineer

WOCA
05-01-1957; 1370 khz AM
Mailing Address: P.O. Box 1056, Ocala, FL 34478 US
Second Address: 1515 E. Silver Springs Blvd., Suite 134, Ocala, FL 34470
(352) 732-8000, *Fax:* 352-240-3858
www.woca.com
woca@woca.com
License: Ocala, FL held by Westshore Broadcasting Inc.
Nat'l Network: ABC *Regional Network:* Florida's Radio Networks
Arbitron Metro Market: Gainesville-Oca *TV Affiliate:* News/talk *Format:* Black *Special Programming:* news progmg 16 hrs wkly *Hrs. of News Programming:* 2 *No. News Employees:* 35 plus.

WOGK
11-07-1960; 93.7 mhz FM; 100 kw; 1348 ft.; N29 16 5 W82 4 51
3502 N.E. 20th Place, Ocala, FL 32670 US
(352) 622-5600, *Fax:* (352) 622-7822
http://www.937kcountry.com/
ncfmrbob@earthlink.net
License: Ocala, Marion County, FL held by Ocala Broadcasting L.L.C.
Group Owner: Wooster Republican Printing Co.; (acq 9-27-86)
Nat'l Reps: Katz Radio
Arbitron Metro Market: Gainesville-Oca *TV Affiliate:* Country *Special Programming:* news progmg 3 hrs wkly *Hrs. of News Programming:* 1 *No. News Employees:* 25-54; general *Adv. Rates:* 70; 75; 70; 25

Ocoee

WUNA
10-25-1962; 1480 khz AM; 1 kw-D, ND1; 0.071 kw-N, ND1; N28 33 28 W81 32 28
127 Mamanasco Road, Ridgefield, CT 06877 US
(407) 656-9823, *Fax:* (407) 656-2092
www.lajefa1480.com
License: Ocoee, FL held by Way Broadcasting Licensee LLC
Regional Network: Florida's Radio Networks
Arbitron Metro Market: Ocoee, FL *Format:* Spanish
Juan Nieves, General Manager
Sheila Rodriguez, General Sales Mgr
Lou Muller, Chief Engineer

Okeechobee

WAFC-FM
07-02-1979; 106.1 mhz FM *Hrs Open:* 24; 12.5 kw; 279 ft.; N27 13 16.8 W80 52 5.8
US
(863) 902-0995, *Fax:* (863) 983-6109
www.trueoldieswafc.com
License: Okeechobee, Hendry County, FL held by Glades Media Co. LLP.
Arbitron Metro Market: West Palm Beach-Boca Raton, FL *Target Audience:* 18-49.
KC Kelly, General Manager
Jesus Castro, Programming Director

WOKC
02-06-1962; 1570 khz AM
PO Box 1247, Okeechobee, FL 34973 US
(863) 467-1570, *Fax:* (863) 763-3171
www.gladesmedia.com
wokc@gladesmedia.com
License: Okeechobee, FL held by Glades Media Co. LLC
Regional Network: Florida's Radio Networks; Southeast AgNet
TV Affiliate: Country *Special Programming:* news progmg 10 hrs wkly *Hrs. of News Programming:* 1 *No. News Employees:* General. *Adv. Rates:* 12; 12; 12; 12
CEO, CEO/COO

Orange Park

*WAYR
05-28-1960; 550 khz AM *Hrs Open:* 24; 5 kw-D, DA2; 0.065 kw-N, DA2; N30 4 21 W81 47 24
2500 Russell Rd, Green Cove Springs, FL 32043 US
(800) 877-5600, *Fax:* (916) 251-1650
www.air1.com
info@air1.com
License: Orange Park, FL held by Good Tidings Trust Inc.
Arbitron Metro Market: McQueeney TX *Format:* Alternative, Christian
Mike Novak, President
David Pierce, Programming Director
Ed Lenane, News Director
Sam Wallington, Engineering Dir
Marya Morgan, News Reporter
Richard Hunt, News Reporter

Orlando

WDBO
05-24-1924; 580 khz AM
1400 Lake Hearn Drive, N.E., Atlanta, GA 30319 US
(407) 295-5858(321) 281-2000, *Fax:* (407) 297-0156
www.wdbo.com
news@wdbo.com
License: Orlando, FL held by Cox Radio Inc.
Group Owner: Cox Radio Inc.; (acq 3-28-97; grpsl)
Arbitron Metro Market: Orlando, FL *Format:* News, News/Talk, 86
Steve Holbrook, Operations Dir
Bill Hendrich, General Manager
Jimmy Farrell, General Sales Mgr
Drew Anderssen, Programming & Promotions Director
Rich Mastroberte, Programming & Promotions Director
Marsha Taylor, News Director
Steve Fluker, Chief Engineer
Steve Avellone, National Sales Manager

WDYZ
12-05-1947; 990 khz AM
1400 Lake Hearn Dr, Ne, Atlanta, GA 30319 US
(407) 566-2033, *Fax:* (407) 566-2034
www.radiodisney.com
michele.bastone@disney.com
License: Orlando, FL held by Radio Disney Group LLC.
Group Owner: ABC Inc.; (acq 1-23-01; $5 million cash).
Nat'l Network: Radio Disney *Nat'l Reps:* Interep
Arbitron Metro Market: Orlando, FL *Format:* Children *Target Audience:* 4-16;25-49; children; mothers
Paul Proly, Station Manager
Robin Jones, Programming Director
Pren Rashbury, Promotions Manager

WHTQ(FM)
01-01-1952; 96.5 mhz FM *Hrs Open:* 24; 100 kw; 1,600 ft; N28 34 51 W81 04 32
4192 John Young Pkwy, Orlando, FL 32804
(407) 422-9696, *Fax:* (407) 422-5883
www.whtq.com
info@whtq.com
License: Orlando, Orange County, FL held by Cox Radio Inc.
Group Owner: Cox Radio Inc.; (acq 1997)
Nat'l Reps: Christal
Population Served: 99,006 *Arbitron Metro Market:* Orlando, FL *Format:* Classic Rock *Hrs. of News Programming:* news progmg 2 hrs wkly *No. News Employees:* 1 *Target Audience:* 25-54; adult male
Debbie Morel, Operations Dir

*WMFE-FM
07-14-1980; 90.7 mhz FM *Hrs Open:* 24; 100 kw; 732 ft.; N28 36 8 W81 5 37
11510 East Colonial Driv, Orlando, FL 32817 US
(407) 273-2300, *Fax:* (407) 273-8462
www.wmfe.org
info@wmfe.org
License: Orlando, Orange County, FL held by Community Communications Inc.
Nat'l Network: PRI; NPR
Arbitron Metro Market: Orlando, FL *Format:* News *Special Programming:* New instrumental 4 hrs wkly *Hrs. of News Programming:* news progmg 48 hrs wkly *No. News Employees:* 4 *Target Audience:* 35 plus;well-educated, executive, professional, upper-income
Jos A. Fajardo, CEO
Sherry Alexander, General Sales Mgr

WMMO
08-19-1990; 98.9 mhz FM *Hrs Open:* 24; 44 kw; 522 ft.; N28 34 27 W81 27 46
1400 Lake Hearn Drive, Atlanta, GA 30319 US
(321) 281-2000, *Fax:* (407) 536-2556
www.wmmo.com
info@wmmo.com
License: Orlando, Orange County, FL held by Cox Radio Inc.
Group Owner: Cox Radio Inc.
Nat'l Reps: Christal
Arbitron Metro Market: Orlando, FL *Format:* Adult Contemp *Hrs. of News Programming:* News progmg one hr wkly *Target Audience:* 25-49.
Debbie Morel, Operations Dir
Chris Ganoudis, General Sales Mgr
Michael Saunders, Programming Director

WOMX-FM
08-15-1967; 105.1 mhz FM; 94 kw; 1598 ft.; N28 34 51 W81 4 32
1801 Lee Road Suite 270, Winter Park, FL 32790 US
(407) 919-1000, *Fax:* (407) 919-1190
www.mix1051.com
License: Orlando, Orange County, FL held by Infinity Radio Inc.

Group Owner: CBS Radio; (acq 12-14-00; grpsl).
Arbitron Metro Market: Orlando, FL *TV Affiliate:* Hot adult contemp *Hrs. of News Programming:* 1

WRMQ
10-21-1985; 1140 khz AM
1033 East Semoran Blvd, #253, Casselberry, FL 32707 US
(407) 830-0800, *Fax:* (407) 260-6100
mannyarroyo@qbcflorida.com
License: Orlando, FL held by Florida Broadcasters.
Arbitron Metro Market: Orlando, FL *Format:* Gospel *Target Audience:* 25-54.
George Arroyo, President

WRUM
07-01-1971; 100.3 mhz FM *Hrs Open:* 24; 95 kw; 1588 ft.; N28 34 51 W81 4 32
200 Concord Plaza, Suite 600, San Antonio, TX 78216 US
(407) 916-1003, *Fax:* (407) 916-0329
www.rumba1003.com
raymondtorres@rumba100.com
License: Orlando, Orange County, FL held by Clear Channel Broadcasting Licenses Inc.
Group Owner: Clear Channel Communications Inc.; (acq 1997; grpsl).
Arbitron Metro Market: Orlando, FL *Format:* Tejano *Target Audience:* 18-49. *Adv. Rates:* 225; 200; 225; 125
Fernando Bauermeister, General Sales Mgr
Raymond Torres, Programming Director
Suheiley Gonzalez, Promotions Manager

WTLN
04-01-1940; 950 khz AM *Hrs Open:* 24
901 Douglas Ave, Ste 100, Altamonte Springs, FL 32714 US
(407) 618-1761, *Fax:* (407) 682-7005
www.wtln.com
office@salemorlando.com
License: Orlando, FL held by Pennsylvania Media Associates Inc.
Group Owner: Salem Communications Corp.; (acq 12-7-2005; $9.4 million)
Nat'l Reps: Salem
Arbitron Metro Market: Orlando, FL *Format:* Christian, Talk *Target Audience:* 35-64.
Edward Atsinger III, President
Dale Forbis, Operations Dir
David Koon, General Manager
John Stolz, General Sales Mgr
Allan Dempsey, Programming Director
Joe Ferraro, Promotions Manager
Pete Paquette, Operations Manager
JeffSenas, Producer/Production Assistant
Jim Turner, Weekend Board Operator/Producer
John Stolz, Director of Ministry Development
Christy Siron, Executive Assistant
Debrah Hayden, Traffic Manager

***WUCF-FM**
01-30-1978; 89.9 mhz FM *Hrs Open:* 24; 0.36 kw horiz, 5.6 kw vert; 486 ft.; N28 35 27 W81 12 17
Mailing Address: P.O. Box 162199, Orlando, FL 32816 US
Second Address: 4000 Central Florida Blvd., Bldg. 75, Rm. 130, Orlando, FL 32816
(407) 823-0899, *Fax:* (407) 823-6364
wucf.org
wucfhost@mail.ucf.edu
License: Orlando, Orange County, FL held by University of Central Florida.
Nat'l Network: NPR; PRI
Arbitron Metro Market: Orlando, FL *Format:* Jazz *Special Programming:* blues 4 hrs; seasonal opera *Hrs. of News Programming:* news progmg 16 hrs wkly *No. News Employees:* 10 *Adv. Rates:* $25/25-sec spot
John Hitt, President
Kayonne Riley, General Manager
Bruce Doerle, Engineering Dir
Patricia Stucky, Ofice Manager
Jan Whitehouse, Marketing Specialist
John Segers, Library Coordinator

WWKA
04-24-1952; 92.3 mhz FM *Hrs Open:* 24; 99 kw; 1490 ft.; N28 34 7 W81 3 16
1400 Lake Hearn Drive, N.E., Atlanta, GA 30319 US
(407) 298-9292, *Fax:* (407) 299-4947
www.wwka.com
info@wwka.com
License: Orlando, Orange County, FL
Arbitron Metro Market: Orlando, FL *Format:* Country
Tammie McGrath, General Sales Mgr
Len Shackelford, Programming Director
Amy Lynch, Promotions Manager

Steve Fluker, Engineering Dir
Shadow Stevens, Music Director
Anna Hards, Promotions Coordinator
Dennis Hopkins, ProductionDirector

WYGM
01-01-1947; 740 khz AM *Hrs Open:* 25.?Â ?; 50 kw-D, DA2; 50 kw-N, DA2; N28 28 53 W81 39 43
200 Concord Plaza, Suite 600, San Antonio, TX 78216 US
(407) 916-7800, *Fax:* (407) 916-0329
www.740thegame.com
rickeverett@clearchannel.com
License: Orlando, FL held by Clear Channel Radio Licenses Inc.
Group Owner: Clear Channel Communications Inc.; (acq 11-21-97; grpsl)
Wire Services: AP
Arbitron Metro Market: Orlando, FL *Format:* Sports *Adv. Rates:* 65.; 65.; 65.; 35.
Linda Byrd, Operations Dir
Mark McCauley, General Sales Mgr
Rick Everett, Programming Director
Josh Egolf, Promotions Manager
Scott Harris, Program Coordinator

Orlovista

WRSO(AM)
01-01-2006; 810 khz AM *Hrs Open:* 24 hrs; 10 kw-D, 400 w-N, DA-2; N28 34 18 W81 26 02
999 Douglas Ave., Attamonte, FL 32714
(407) 774-8810, *Fax:* (407) 774-8895
License: Orlovista, Orange County, FL held by Star Over Orlando Inc.
Population Served: 243,195 *Arbitron Metro Market:* Orlando, FL *Format:* Religious
Carl Tutera, President

Ormond Beach

WELE
08-01-1957; 1380 khz AM; 5 kw-D, DA2; 2.5 kw-N, DA2; N29 16 9 W81 4 54
432 South Nova Road, Ormond Beach, FL 32174 US
(386) 523-1870, *Fax:* (386) 677-4123
www.goliathradio.com/
doug@wele1380.com
License: Ormond Beach, FL held by Wings Communications Inc.
Nat'l Network: CNN Radio; Westwood One
Arbitron Metro Market: Ormond Beach, FL *Format:* News, News/Talk, 86 *Target Audience:* General; mature, adults interested in sports & local current events *Adv. Rates:* 45; 45; 45; na
F. Douglas Wilhite, President
Kristin Cobb, Operations Dir
Mike Matsin, General Sales Mgr
Mike Johnson, Programming Director
Mike Johnson, News Director
Doug Wilhite, Engineering Dir
Greg Lake, Production Director

Ormond-By-The-Sea

WHOG-FM
01-01-1995; 95.7 mhz FM; 25 kw; 328 ft.; N29 14 11 W81 4 22
126 West International Speedway Blvd., Daytona Beach, FL 32214 US
(386) 255-9300, *Fax:* (386) 238-6071
www.newsdaytonabeach.com
License: Ormond-By-The-Sea, Volusia County, FL held by Black Crow LLC.
Group Owner: Black Crow Media Group LLC; (acq 9-21-2001; grpsl).
Arbitron Metro Market: Daytona Beach, FL *Format:* Classic Rock, Rock/AOR
Stacey Knerler, General Manager
Donna Fillion, General Sales Mgr

Oviedo

WONQ
11-21-1992; 1030 khz AM
1033 Sermoran Blvd.#253, Summit Plaza, Casselberry, FL 32707 US
(407) 830-0800, *Fax:* (407) 260-6100
www.1030lagrande.com/
info@lagrande1030am.com
License: Oviedo, FL held by Florida Broadcasters.
Arbitron Metro Market: Orlando, FL *TV Affiliate:* Sp *No. News Employees:* 25-54.

Palatka

***WHIF**
03-29-1996; 91.3 mhz FM; 1.7 kw; 318 ft.; N29 39 7 W81 35 32
3111 St. Johns Avenue, Palatka, FL 32177 US
(386) 325-3334, *Fax:* (386) 325-0934
www.whif.org
whif@gbso.net
License: Palatka, Putnam County, FL held by Putnam Radio Ministries Inc.
Format: Adult Contemp, Christian *Special Programming:* Relg educ 10 hrs wkly *Target Audience:* 25-54; family-oriented, middle-class
Robin Toole, General Manager

WIYD
02-14-1947; 1260 khz AM *Hrs Open:* 24
P.O. Box 918, Palatka, FL 32078 US
(386) 325-4556, *Fax:* (386) 328-5161
www.wiydradio.com
wiyd@atlantic.net
License: Palatka, FL held by Hall Broadcasting Co.
Nat'l Network: ABC *Regional Network:* Florida's Radio Networks
Format: Country *Special Programming:* Relg 5 hrs wkly *Hrs. of News Programming:* news progmg 6 hrs wkly *No. News Employees:* 1 *Target Audience:* 18-49; rich & powerful *Adv. Rates:* 15; 15; 15; 10
Wayne Bullock, President
Mary Connor, Station Manager

WPLK
01-01-1957; 800 khz AM *Hrs Open:* 24; 1 kw-D, ND1; 0.334 kw-N, ND1; N29 39 7 W81 35 32
Mailing Address: P. O. Box 335, Palatka, FL 32178 US
Second Address: 1428 St. John's Ave., Palatka, FL 32177
(386) 325-5800, *Fax:* (386) 328-8725
wplk.com
wplk@wplk.com
License: Palatka, FL held by Radio Palatka Inc.
Nat'l Network: ABC
Format: Oldies *Hrs. of News Programming:* news progmg 2 hrs wkly *No. News Employees:* 1 *Target Audience:* General.
Wayne Bullock, President

Palm Bay

***WEJF**
01-01-1993; 90.3 mhz FM; 0.1 kw horiz, 10 kw vert; 404 ft.; N28 2 49 W80 40 34
505 Josephine Street, Titusville, FL 32796 US
(321) 722-9998, *Fax:* (321) 724-0845
www.ggrn.info/
wejf@bellsouth.net
License: Palm Bay, Brevard County, FL held by Florida Public Radio Inc.
Arbitron Metro Market: Palm Bay, FL *Format:* Adult Contemp, Christian
Eric Sabo, Operations Dir

***WHYZ(FM)**
07-01-1997; 88.5 mhz FM *Hrs Open:* 24; 600 w vert; Ant 108 ft; N28 02 54 W80 40 34
1065 Rainer Dr., Altamonte Springs, FL 32714-3847
(407) 869-8000, *Fax:* (407) 869-0380
www.zradio.org
License: Palm Bay, Brevard County, FL held by Central Florida Educational Foundation Inc.
Population Served: 41,727 *Arbitron Metro Market:* Altamonte Springs, FL *Format:* Christian *Target Audience:* Christian.
Jim Hoge, Founder, President andCEO
James Hoge, President
Dean O'Neal, Vice President, General Manager, Program Director
Carol Baker Ellingson, Promotions Manager
Mark Chambers, Chief Engineer
Judy Wise, HR/ Office Manager
TateLuck, Assistant Program Director
Tim Wolf, Music Director
Jen Rose, Production
Jessica Bonano, Promotions Assistant
Randy Woods, Technical Director

Palm Beach

WRMF
01-01-1957; 97.9 mhz FM *Hrs Open:* 24; 100 kw; 1348 ft.; N26 34 37 W80 14 32
2406 South Congress Aven, West Palm Beach, FL 33406 US
(561) 868-1100, *Fax:* (561) 868-1111
www.wrmf.com
License: Palm Beach, West Palm Beach County, FL held by Cobalt LLC

RADIO - U.S.

Nat'l Reps: McGavren Guild
Arbitron Metro Market: West Palm Beach-Boca Raton, FL
Format: Adult Contemp *Target Audience:* 25-54; general
Mike Catchall, CEO
Elizabeth Hamma, Operations Dir
Mark Krieger, General Sales Mgr
Bob Neumann, Programming Director
Erika Ewald, Promotions Manager
Doris Dupee, CFO

Palm City

*WCNO
04-01-1990; 89.9 mhz FM; 100 kw; 614 ft.; N27 7 20 W80 23 21
1150 West King Street, Cocoa, FL 32922 US
(772) 221-1100, *Fax:* (772) 221-8716
www.wcno.com
wcno@wcno.com
License: Palm City, Martin County, FL held by National Christian Network Inc.
Arbitron Metro Market: West Palm Beach,FL *Format:* Adult Contemp, Christian
Ray Kassis, President
Tom Craton, General Manager

Palm Coast

*WHYZ
91.1 mhz FM; 9.2 kw horiz, 9.16 kw vert; 175 ft.; N29 26 8 W81 9 21
P. O. Box 607883, Orlando, FL 32860 US
(407) 869-8000, *Fax:* (407) 869-0380
www.zradio.org
License: Palm Coast, Flagler County, FL held by Central Florida Educational Foundation Inc.
Arbitron Metro Market: Palm Coast, FL *Format:* Christian
James Hoge, President

Palmetto

WBRD
10-01-1957; 1420 khz AM; 2.5 kw-D, DA2; 1 kw-N, DA2; N27 32 42 W82 34 28
2101 Hammock Pl., Sarasota, FL 34235 US
(248) 557-3500, *Fax:* (248) 557-2950
www.birach.com/wbrd.htm
sima@BIRACH.Com
License: Palmetto, FL held by Metropolitan Radio Group Inc.
Group Owner: Metropolitan Radio Group Inc.; acq 6-96)
Arbitron Metro Market: Southfield, MI *Format:* Gospel *Target Audience:* 35 plus. *Adv. Rates:* 20; 25; 15; na
Sima Birach, Operations Dir
Bill Bailey, General Manager

Panama City

WDIZ
04-01-1940; 590 khz AM; 1.7 kw-D, DAN; 2.5 kw-N, DAN; N30 10 20 W85 36 49
Mailing Address: 200 Concord Plaza, Suite 600, San Antonio, TX 78216 US
Second Address: 1834 Lisenby Ave., Panama City, FL 32405
(850) 769-1408, *Fax:* (850) 769-0659
www.espn590.com
info@panamacity@clearchannel.com
License: Panama City, FL held by Clear Channel Broadcasting Licenses Inc.
Group Owner: Clear Channel Communications Inc.; (acq 11-21-97; grpsl)
Arbitron Metro Market: Panama City, FL *Format:* Oldies
Todd Berry, Operations Dir
Jackie Rinker, General Manager
Darrell Johnson, General Sales Mgr
Derby Strength, Promotions Manager

*WFSW
01-01-1995; 89.1 mhz FM; 100 kw; 404 ft.; N30 22 2 W85 55 29
1600 Red Barber Plaza, Tallahassee, FL 32310 US
(850) 487-3086, *Fax:* (850) 487-3293
www.wfsu.org
License: Panama City, Bay County, FL held by Florida State University.
Nat'l Network: NPR
Arbitron Metro Market: Panama City, FL *Format:* News, Talk
Pat Keating, General Manager
Caroline Austin, Station Manager
Aron Myers, Promotions Manager
Tom Flanigan, News Director
Andy Hanus, Engineering Dir

WFSY
10-01-1971; 98.5 mhz FM; 100 kw; 1089 ft.; N30 30 41 W85 29 24
Mailing Address: 200 Concord Plaza, Suite 600, San Antonio, TX 78216 US
Second Address: 1834 Lisenby Ave., Panama City, FL 32405
(850) 769-1408, *Fax:* (850) 769-0659
www.beachfm.com
info@panamacity@clearchannel.com
License: Panama City, Bay County, FL held by Clear Channel Broadcasting Licenses Inc.
Group Owner: Clear Channel Communications Inc.
Arbitron Metro Market: Panama City, FL *Format:* Adult Contemp *Target Audience:* 25-54.
Jackie Rinker, General Manager
Caroline Austin, Station Manager
Darrell Johnson, General Sales Mgr
Derby Strength, Promotions Manager
Todd Berry, Operations Manager
James MacDaniel, Production Director
Mike Baker, Webmaster

WILN
04-11-1985; 105.9 mhz FM *Hrs Open:* 24; 50 kw; 384 ft.; N30 10 44 W85 46 55
8317 Front Beach Rd, Suite 21, Panama City, FL 32407 US
(850) 230-5855, *Fax:* (850) 230-6988
www.island106.com
License: Panama City, Bay County, FL held by Magic Broadcasting Florida Licensing LLC.
Group Owner: Magic Broadcasting LLC; (acq 1-31-2003; grpsl)
Arbitron Metro Market: Panama City, FL *Format:* Contemporary Hits/Top 40 *Hrs. of News Programming:* news progmg 2 hrs wkly *No. News Employees:* 1 *Target Audience:* 18-49.
Jeff Storey, COO
Mike Preble, Operations Dir

*WJTF
10-15-1998; 89.9 mhz FM; 100 kw; 105 ft.; N30 10 5 W85 40 30
341 S. Washington, Lancaster, WI 53813 US
(850) 874-9900, *Fax:* (850) 874-9930
www.myfln.org
wjtf@bellsouth.net
License: Panama City, Bay County, FL held by Family Life Broadcasting Inc
Group Owner: Family Life Communications Inc.; (acq 5-23-2007; grpsl)
Nat'l Network: Moody
Arbitron Metro Market: Panama City, FL *Format:* Religious *Target Audience:* 35-90; general
Kelly Dickson, Operations Dir
Tom Bush, General Manager
Mickey Jacobs, Programming Director

*WKGC-FM
10-01-1982; 90.7 mhz FM; 100 kw; 356 ft.; N30 17 45 W85 39 42
5230 West Highway 98, Panama City, FL 32401 US
(850) 873-3500, *Fax:* (850) 913-3299
www.wkgc.org
fsundram@gulfcoast.edu
License: Panama City, Bay County, FL held by Gulf Coast Community College.
Nat'l Network: NPR; PRI *Regional Network:* Fla. Pub.
Arbitron Metro Market: Panama City, FL *Format:* News *Special Programming:* Black 6 hrs wkly *Target Audience:* General.
Robert Spadden, President
Reed Kinney, Operations Dir
Frank Sundram, General Manager

WPFM-FM
09-01-1963; 107.9 mhz FM *Hrs Open:* 24; 98.5 kw; 781 ft.; N30 25 59 W85 24 51
Two Bala Plaza, Suite 801, Bala-Cynwyd, PA 19004 US
(850) 234-8858, *Fax:* (850) 234-6592
www.hot1079pc.com
neilknight@panamacityradio.com
License: Panama City, Bay County, FL
Group Owner: Powell Broadcasting Co. L.L.C.; acq 3-10-2004; grpsl).
Nat'l Reps: Christal
Arbitron Metro Market: Panama City, FL *Format:* Contemporary Hits/Top 40 *Target Audience:* 18-49; active lifestyle, young adult audience *Adv. Rates:* 50; 40; 40; 25
Neil Knight, Operations Dir
Harry Finch, General Manager
Neil Knight, Programming Director
Ira Rosenblatt, Market Manager

WLTG
12-11-1949; 1430 khz AM; 5 kw-D, DA2; 5 kw-N, DA2; N30 9 55 W85 35 19
Mailing Address: P.O. Box 15635, Panama City, FL 32406 US
Second Address: 3100 E. 15th St., Springfield, FL 32405
(850) 784-9873, *Fax:* (850) 784-6908
www.1430newstalk.com
wltg@bellsouth.net
License: Panama City, FL held by Williams Communications Inc.
Group Owner: Williams Communications Inc.; acq 8-12-03; $500,000).
Nat'l Network: Premiere Radio Networks; Salem Radio Network
Nat'l Reps: Commercial Media Sales
Arbitron Metro Market: Panama City, FL *Format:* News, News/Talk, 84, Talk *Special Programming:* Black gospel 7 hrs wkly *Target Audience:* General.
John Gay, General Manager

WPAP-FM
03-30-1967; 92.5 mhz FM *Hrs Open:* 24; 100 kw; 922 ft.; N30 30 41 W85 29 24
200 Concord Plaza, Suite 600, San Antonio, TX 78216 US
(850) 769-1408, *Fax:* (850) 769-0659
www.wpapfm.com
info@panamacity@clearchannel.com
License: Panama City, Bay County, FL held by Clear Channel Radio Licenses Inc.
Group Owner: Clear Channel Communications Inc.; (acq 11-21-97; grpsl)
Nat'l Reps: McGavren Guild
Arbitron Metro Market: Panama City, FL *Format:* Country *Target Audience:* 25-54.
Pete Norton, General Manager

*WFFL
01-01-2007; 91.7 mhz FM; 0.31 kw horiz, 0.304 kw vert; 207 ft.; N30 10 48 W85 38 10 *Rebroadcasts:* Rebroadcasts WJFM(FM) Baton Rouge, LA 100%
Mailing Address: 8030 Arrowridge Blvd, Charlotte, VA 28273 US
Second Address: 8919 World Ministry Ave., Baton Rouge, FL 70810
(225) 768-3224
www.jsm.org
License: Panama City, Bay County, FL held by Family Worship Center Church Inc.
Group Owner: Family Worship Center Church Inc.; (acq 10-12-2006; grpsl)
Arbitron Metro Market: Tucson, AZ *Format:* Christian
David Whitelaw, COO

Panama City Beach

WASJ
01-01-1993; 105.1 mhz FM *Hrs Open:* 24; 50 kw; 335 ft.; N30 10 44 W85 46 55
Two Bala Plaza, Suite 801, Bala-Cynwyd, PA 19004 US
(850) 234-8858, *Fax:* (850) 234-6592
www.bobatthebeach.com
ira.rosenblatt@panamacityradio.com
License: Panama City Beach, Bay County, FL
Group Owner: Powell Broadcasting Co. L.L.C.; acq 3-10-2004; grpsl)
Nat'l Network: ESPN Radio *Nat'l Reps:* Christal
Arbitron Metro Market: Panama City, FL *Format:* Sports *Adv. Rates:* 50; 40; 40; 25
Harry Finch, General Manager
Melissa Miller, Programming Director

WPCF
09-23-1958; 1290 khz AM; 0.27 kw-D, ND2; 0.055 kw-N, ND2; N30 10 44 W85 46 55
7106 Laird Street, Suite 102, Panama City, FL 32408 US
(850) 230-5855, *Fax:* (850) 230-6988
www.troprock1290.com
syoungblood@magicfl.com
License: Panama City Beach, FL held by Magic Broadcasting Florida Licensing LLC.
Group Owner: Magic Broadcasting LLC; (acq 9-30-2002; grpsl)
Arbitron Metro Market: Panama City, FL *Format:* Country
Jeff Storey, CEO
Mike Preble, Operations Dir
Kim Styles, General Manager
Joe Valentine, Station Manager
Steven, Programming Director

WVVE
06-01-1988; 100.1 mhz FM *Hrs Open:* 24; 12 kw; 404 ft.; N30 10 44 W85 46 55
P.O. Box 16626, Panama City, FL 32406 US
(850) 230-5855, *Fax:* (850) 230-6988
License: Panama City Beach, Bay County, FL held by Magic Broadcasting Florida Licensing LLC.
Group Owner: Magic Broadcasting LLC; (acq 9-30-2002; grpsl)
Arbitron Metro Market: Panama City, FL *Format:* Adult Contemp *Adv. Rates:* 20; 20; 20; na

Jeff Storey, CEO
Mike Prebke, Operations Dir

Parker

WFLF-FM
08-01-1977; 94.5 mhz FM *Hrs Open:* 24; 100 kw; 994 ft.; N29 49 9 W85 15 34
200 Concord Plaza, Suite 600, San Antonio, TX 78216 US
(850) 769-1408, *Fax:* (850) 769-0659
www.945thefox.com
info@panamacity@clearchannel.com
License: Parker, Bay County, FL held by Clear Channel Broadcasting Licenses Inc.
Group Owner: Clear Channel Communications Inc.; (acq 11-21-97; grpsl)
Nat'l Network: Fox News Radio
Arbitron Metro Market: Panama City, FL *Format:* News, News/Talk, 86 *Special Programming:* Relg 5 hrs wkly
Pete Norden, General Manager

Pennsuco

*WGNK
01-01-1999; 88.3 mhz FM *Hrs Open:* 24; 6 kw; 282 ft.; N25 52 24 W80 28 59
7205 S.W. 125 Avenue, Miami, FL 33183 US
(305) 406-2883, *Fax:* (305) 406-3030
www.lanueva883fm.com
LANUEVA@FM.COM
License: Pennsuco, Dade County, FL held by Genesis License Subsidiary LLC
Format: Christian *Special Programming:* Children 6 hrs *Hrs. of News Programming:* news progmg 3 hrs wkly *No. News Employees:* 1 *Target Audience:* 18-35; Hispanic Christians
Edwin Ortiz, President
Mauricio Quintana, General Manager

Pensacola

WYCT
11-28-2003; 98.7 mhz FM; 100 kw; 981 ft.; N30 37 30 W87 26 39
130 Aylesbury Dr., San Antonio, TX 78209 US
(850) 430-1987, *Fax:* (850) 494-0778
www.catcountry987.com
comments@CatCountry987.com
License: Pensacola, Escambia County, FL held by ADX Communications of Pensacola.
Arbitron Metro Market: Pensacola, FL *Format:* Country
David Hoxeng, CEO
Kevin King, Operations Dir
Mary Hoxeng, General Manager
Mary Hoxeng, General Sales Mgr
Paul Stadden, Promotions Manager
Tim McEvoy, Engineering Dir

WBSR
09-01-1946; 1450 khz AM *Hrs Open:* 24; 1 kw-D, ND1; 1 kw-N, ND1; N30 25 44 W87 14 27
Mailing Address: P. O. Box 8057, Pensacola, FL 32505 US
Second Address: 1601 N. Pace Blvd., Pensacola, FL 32505
(850) 438-4982, *Fax:* (850) 433-7932
www.espnpensacola.com
doug@espnpensacola.com
License: Pensacola, FL held by Easy Media Inc.
Arbitron Metro Market: Pensacola, FL *Format:* Adult Contemp *Target Audience:* 35-54.
Frederic Brewer, President
Gene Pfalzer, Station Manager

WCOA
02-03-1926; 1370 khz AM *Hrs Open:* 24; 5 kw-D, DAN; 5 kw-N, DAN; N30 26 57 W87 15 46
6565 North W. Street, Pensacola, FL 32505 US
(850) 478-6011, *Fax:* (850) 478-3971
www.wcoapensacola.com
alan.caudle@cumulus.com
License: Pensacola, FL held by Cumulus Licensing Corp.
Group Owner: Cumulus Media Inc.; (acq 10-25-99; with co-located FM)
Nat'l Network: ABC *Nat'l Reps:* Katz Radio
Arbitron Metro Market: Vicinity-Pensacola, FL *Format:* News, News/Talk, 86 *Special Programming:* Relg 3 hrs wkly *Target Audience:* 25-54.
Brian Weil, General Manager
Alan Caudle, Programming Director
Jim Roberts, News Director
Yancy McNair, Chief Engineer

WMEZ
11-11-1960; 94.1 mhz FM; 77 kw; 1601 ft.; N30 36 40 W87 36 26
600 Congress Ave., Suite 1400, Austin, TX 78701 US
(850) 994-5357, *Fax:* (850) 994-7191
www.softrock941.com
info@softrock941.com
License: Pensacola, Escambia County, FL held by 6 Johnson Road Licenses Inc.
Group Owner: Pamal Broadcasting Ltd.; (acq 10-19-2001; grpsl).
Nat'l Network: Westwood One
Arbitron Metro Market: Pensacola, FL *Format:* Adult Contemp *Target Audience:* 25-54. females
Dave Cobb, General Manager
Kevin Peterson, Programming Director
Gerald Wilson, Chief Engineer

*WPCS
06-22-1971; 89.5 mhz FM *Hrs Open:* 24; 95 kw; Ant 1,358 ft; N30 35 16 W87 33 13
Box 18000, Pensacola, FL 32503
(850) 479-6570, *Fax:* (850) 969-1638
www.rejoice.org
rbn@rejoice.org
License: Pensacola, Escambia County, FL held by Pensacola Christian College Inc.
Population Served: 1,025,018 *Arbitron Metro Market:* Pensacola, FL
Troy Shoemaker, President
Caleb Keener, Station Manager
Tonita Ohman, Programming Director
Ryan See, Chief Engineer

WPNN
10-01-1956; 790 khz AM; 1 kw-D; N30 27 18 W87 14 22
3801 N. Pace Blvd., Pensacola, FL 32505
(850) 433-1141, *Fax:* (850) 433-1142
www.cnnpensacola.com
License: Pensacola, Escambia County, FL held by Miracle Radio Inc.
Population Served: 62,507 *Arbitron Metro Market:* Pensacola, FL
Gerald Schroeder, President
Gerald Schroeder, Operations Dir
Scott Schroeder, General Manager
Scott Schroeder, Station Manager

WTKX-FM
01-01-1971; 101.5 mhz FM *Hrs Open:* 24; 100 kw; 1601 ft.; N30 36 40 W87 36 26.4
200 Concord Plaza, Suite 600, San Antonio, TX 78216 US
(850) 473-0400, *Fax:* (850) 473-0907
www.tk101.com
radio@tk101.com
License: Pensacola, Escambia County, FL held by Clear Channel Broadcasting Licenses Inc.
Group Owner: Clear Channel Communications Inc.; (acq 11-21-97; grpsl).
Arbitron Metro Market: Pensacola, FL *Format:* Rock/AOR *Target Audience:* 18-49; general
Lowry Mays, CEO
Mark Mays, President
Randall Mays, CFO

*WUWF
01-01-1981; 88.1 mhz FM *Hrs Open:* 24; 100 kw; 614 ft.; N30 24 13 W86 59 34
11000 University Parkway, Pensacola, FL 32514 US
(850) 474-2787
www.wuwf.org
wuwf@wuwf.org
License: Pensacola, Escambia County, FL held by Board of Trustees, University of West Florida
Nat'l Network: PRI; NPR *Regional Network:* Fla. Pub.
Arbitron Metro Market: Pensacola, GA *Format:* Alternative, News *Hrs. of News Programming:* news progmg 34 hrs wkly *No. News Employees:* 2 *Target Audience:* General.
Joe Vincenza, Station Manager
Lynne Marshall, Promotions Manager
Sandra Averhart, News Director
Dale Riegle, Technical Director
Pat Crawford, Executive Director
John Macdonell, IT Services Director
Theresa Clark, BusinessManager
Dave Dunwoody, Assistant News Director

WVTJ
11-01-1959; 610 khz AM *Hrs Open:* 24; 500 w-D, 157 w-N; N30 27 18 W87 14 22
2070 N. Palafox St., Pensacola, FL 32505
(850) 432-3658
www.wilkinsradio.com
wvtj@wilkinsradio.com
License: Pensacola, Escambia County, FL held by Pensacola Radio Corp.
Group Owner: Wilkins Communications Network Inc.; (acq 4-23-2007; $545,000)
Population Served: 480,000 *Arbitron Metro Market:* Pensacola, FL *Target Audience:* 18-64.
Robert Wilkins, President
Jessica Jordan, General Manager

WCOA-FM
09-01-1965; 100.7 mhz FM; 100 kw; 1,555 ft; N30 37 35 W87 38 50
6565 N. W St., Pensacola, FL 32505
(850) 478-6011, *Fax:* (850) 478-3971
www.wcoapensacola.com
alan.caudle@cumulus.com
License: Pensacola, Escambia County, FL
Population Served: 52,197 *Arbitron Metro Market:* Pensacola, FL *Format:* News, News/Talk, 86 *Target Audience:* 25-44.
Alan Caudle, Programming Director
Yancy McNair, Chief Engineer
Brian Newkirk, Assistant Program Director
Monte Saunders, Business Manager
Monica Ard, Traffic

WDWR
01-01-1947; 1230 khz AM *Hrs Open:* 24
2070 North Palafox St., Pensacola, FL 32501 US
(850) 438-7667, *Fax:* (850) 437-3733
www.divinewordradio.com
info@divinewordradio.com
License: Pensacola, FL held by Divine Word Communications
Nat'l Network: EWTN Radio
Arbitron Metro Market: Pensacola, FL *Format:* Christian
Gene Church, President

Perry

WNFK
12-01-1989; 92.1 mhz FM; 6 kw; 328 ft.; N30 5 17 W83 29 46
P.O. Box 779, Perry, FL 32347 US
(850) 584-9210, *Fax:* (850) 223-3492
www.powercountry102.com
powercountry921@wildblue.net
License: Perry, Taylor County, FL held by Taylor County Broadcasting Inc.
Arbitron Metro Market: Perry, FL *Format:* Country
Bob Hendrickson, General Manager
Keith Conway, Programming Director

WPRY
01-01-1953; 1400 khz AM *Hrs Open:* 24; 1 kw-U, ND1; N30 6 27 W83 34 0
P.O. Box 779, Perry, FL 32347 US
(850) 223-1400, *Fax:* (850) 223-3501
www.wpry.com
License: Perry, FL held by HF Broadcasting Perry LC
Format: Contemporary Hits/Top 40, Adult Contemp *Special Programming:* Black 2 hrs wkly *Hrs. of News Programming:* 15 hrs news progmg wkly *Target Audience:* 18 plus.
Gary Williams, General Manager

WFDZ
93.5 mhz FM; 6 kw; 252 ft.; N30 8 0 W83 35 45
US
(573) 701-4708
License: Perry, Taylor County, FL held by Dockins Telecommunications Inc.
Arbitron Metro Market: Perry, FL
Fred Dockins, General Manager

Pine Castle Sky Lake

WAMT
01-28-1977; 1190 khz AM *Hrs Open:* 24
1160 South Semoran Blvd, Suite A, Orlando, FL 32807 US
(813) 281-1040, *Fax:* (407) 382-7565
www.newstalkflorida.com
contactus@radiogenesis.com
License: Pine Castle Sky Lake, FL held by Genesis Communications I Inc.
Group Owner: Genesis Communications Inc.; (acq 3-20-2000; $2.1 million)
Nat'l Network: ABC; Westwood One *Regional Network:* Florida's Radio Networks *Nat'l Reps:* Interep *Wire Services:* AP; Metro Weather Service Inc.
Arbitron Metro Market: Orlando, FL *Format:* News, News/Talk, 86 *Target Audience:* 25-65; general *Adv. Rates:* 50; 40; 50; 30
Bruce Maduri, President
Colin Cantwell, Operations Dir
Sabrina Lavender, General Sales Mgr

RADIO - U.S.

Pine Hills

WFLF
09-09-1955; 540 khz AM *Hrs Open:* 24
200 Concord Plaza, Suite 600, San Antonio, TX 78216 US
(407) 916-7800, *Fax:* (407) 661-1940
www.540wfla.com
kaystelling@clearchannel.com
License: Pine Hills, FL held by Clear Channel Radio Licenses Inc.
Group Owner: Clear Channel Communications Inc.; (acq 11-21-97; grpsl)
Nat'l Network: Fox News Radio *Regional Network:* Florida's Radio Networks *Wire Services:* AP
Arbitron Metro Market: Orlando, FL *Format:* News, News/Talk, 86 *Special Programming:* Florida Gaton football & basketball, Florida Marlins, Miami Dolphins *Hrs. of News Programming:* news progmg 168 hrs wkly *No. NewsEmployees:* 5 *Target Audience:* 35-64. *Adv. Rates:* 125; 150; 135; 25
Linda Byrd, General Manager
Kay Stelling, General Sales Mgr
Chris Kampmeier, Programming Director
Rick Everett, Promotions Manager
Tom Benson, Programming Director

Pine Island Center

WINK
03-01-1940; 1200 khz AM *Rebroadcasts:* Rebroadcasts WNOG(AM) Naples 100%
2824 Palm Beach Blvd., Fort Myers, FL 33916 US
(239) 337-2346, *Fax:* (239) 334-0744
www.winkfm.com
wayne.simons@fmbcmail.com
License: Pine Island Center, FL held by Meridian Broadcasting Inc.
Group Owner: Meridian Broadcasting Inc.
Nat'l Network: Jones Radio Networks *Nat'l Reps:* McGavren Guild
Arbitron Metro Market: Fort Myers-Naples-Marco Island, FL *Format:* News, News/Talk, 86 *Target Audience:* 35 plus.
Joe Schwartzel, President
Wayne Simons, General Manager
Brad Foster, General Sales Mgr
Michael Hayes, Programming Director

Pinellas Park

WHBO
11-01-1948; 1040 khz AM
2970 Peachtree Rd. N.W., Suite 970, Atlanta, GA 30305 US
(813) 281-1040, *Fax:* (813) 281-1948
www.sportstalkflorida.com
License: Pinellas Park, FL held by Genesis Communications of Tampa Bay Inc.
Group Owner: Genesis Communications Inc.; (acq 12-17-97; $1.5 million)
Nat'l Network: ESPN Radio *Regional Network:* Florida's Radio Networks *Nat'l Reps:* Interep; McGavren Guild *Wire Services:* AP
Arbitron Metro Market: Tampa, FL *Format:* Sports *Target Audience:* 25-54. *Adv. Rates:* 85; 50; 80; 45
Bruce Maduri, CEO
Steven Baltimore, General Manager
Dro Silve, Programming Director
Kimo Gray, Information Technology Director

Pinellas Park,

WTBN
11-12-1966; 570 khz AM *Hrs Open:* 24
200 Concord Plaza, Suite 600, San Antonio, TX 78216 US
(813) 639-1903, *Fax:* (813) 639-1272
www.bayword.com
info@bayword.com
License: Pinellas Park, FL held by Common Ground Broadcasting Inc.
Group Owner: Salem Communications Corp.; (acq 8-7-2001; $6.75 million).
Nat'l Network: Salem Radio Network *Nat'l Reps:* Salem
Arbitron Metro Market: Tampa-St. Petersburg-Clearwater, FL *Format:* Christian, Talk *Special Programming:* College (USF) sports football & basketball *Hrs. of News Programming:* news progmg 30 hrs wkly *No. NewsEmployees:* 2 *Target Audience:* 25-64.
Mike Serio, Operations Dir
Chris Gould, General Manager
Rey Noriega, News Director
Dee Addison, Account Executive
Rinita Anderson, Account Executive
Horance Andrews, On-Air Studio Engineer
Barbara Backman, Account Executive
Tammy Bancroft, Administrative Assistant
Merry Brocket, Executive Sales Director

Plant City

WTWD
07-01-1949; 910 khz AM *Hrs Open:* 24; 5 kw-U, DA1; N27 59 26 W82 12 31 *Rebroadcasts:* Rebroadcasts WTBN Pinnellas Park 100%
877 Executive Center Drive, #300, St. Petersburg, FL 33702 US
(813) 639-1903, *Fax:* (813) 639-1272
www.baywood.com
info@baywood.com
License: Plant City, FL held by South Texas Broadcasting Inc.
Group Owner: Salem Communications Corp.; (acq 7-27-00; grpsl).
Nat'l Network: Salem Radio Network *Nat'l Reps:* Salem
Arbitron Metro Market: Tampa-St. Petersburg-Clearwater, FL *Format:* Christian, Talk *Target Audience:* 25-54.
Mike Serio, Operations Dir
Christopher Gould, Sr, General Manager

Plantation Key

WCTH
07-01-1969; 100.3 mhz FM *Hrs Open:* 24; 100 kw; 463 ft.; N24 57 34 W80 34 30
200 Concord Plaza, Suite 600, San Antonio, TX 78216 US
(305) 852-9085, *Fax:* (305) 852-2304
www.thundercountry.com,keysradio.com
randallperry@clearchannel.com
License: Plantation Key, Monroe County, FL held by Clear Channel Radio Licenses Inc.
Group Owner: Clear Channel Communications Inc.; (acq 2-99; $1.8 million)
Nat'l Network: Westwood One; Motor Racing Net *Regional Network:* Florida's Radio Networks *Nat'l Reps:* Clear Channel
Arbitron Metro Market: Tavernier,FL *Format:* Country *Special Programming:* NASCAR 3 hrs wkly *Hrs. of News Programming:* news progmg 4 hrs wkly *No. News Employees:* 1 *Target Audience:* 25-54; residents &tourists *Adv. Rates:* 35; 30; 35; 20
John Hogan, CEO
Greg Capgna, Operations Dir
Mark Mills, General Manager
Scott Hamilton, Programming Director

WFKZ
01-02-1984; 103.1 mhz FM *Hrs Open:* 24; 50 kw; 449 ft.; N24 57 33 W80 34 30
200 Concord Plaza, Suite 600, San Antonio, TX 78216 US
(305) 852-9085, *Fax:* (305) 852-5586
www.sun103.com
randallperry@clearchannel.com
License: Plantation Key, Monroe County, FL held by Clear Channel Radio Licenses Inc.
Group Owner: Clear Channel Communications Inc.; (acq 11-21-97; grpsl)
Format: Rock/AOR *Hrs. of News Programming:* news progmg 8 hrs wkly *No. News Employees:* 2 *Target Audience:* 25-54; adults *Adv. Rates:* 28; 24; 28; 10
Greg Capgna, Operations Dir
Mark Mills, General Manager
Randall Perry, Chief Engineer
Doug Hitchcock, Assistant Music Director
Bill Bravo, Assistant Music Director

Pompano Beach

WHSR
01-01-1959; 980 khz AM
6699 N. Federal Highway, Ste 200, Boca Raton, FL 33487 US
(561) 997-0074, *Fax:* (561) 997-0476
www.whsrradio.com
info@wshrradio.com
License: Pompano Beach, FL held by WWNN License L.L.C.
Group Owner: Beasley Broadcast Group Inc.; (acq 3-17-2000; grpsl).
Arbitron Metro Market: Miami-Fort Lauderdale-Hollywood, FL *Format:* Ethnic, Talk *Target Audience:* 25-54; baby boomers weaned on electronic media as an info source
Bob Morency, Operations Dir
Greg Cooper, Operations Manager

WMXJ
01-01-1960; 102.7 mhz FM; 98 kw; 1007 ft.; N25 58 2 W80 12 34
20450 NW 2nd Avenue, Miami, FL 33169 US
(305) 521-5100, *Fax:* (305) 652-1888
www.majic1027.com
webmasterWMXJ@wmxj.com
License: Pompano Beach, Broward County, FL held by Lincoln Financial Media Co. of Florida.
Group Owner: Lincoln Financial Media; (acq 4-3-2006; grpsl).
Nat'l Reps: CBS Radio *Wire Services:* AP
Arbitron Metro Market: Miami, FL *Format:* Contemporary Hits/Top 40 *Target Audience:* 35-64.
Dennis Collins, Operations Dir
Daryl Leoce, General Sales Mgr
Robert Hamilton, Programming Director
Connie Estopinan, Promotions Manager
Gary Blau, Engineering Dir

WWNN
01-01-1959; 1470 khz AM *Hrs Open:* 24; 50 kw-D, DA2; 2.5 kw-N, DA2; N26 10 46 W80 13 15
6699 N. Federal Highway, Boca Raton, FL 33487 US
(561) 997-0074, *Fax:* (561) 997-0476
www.wwnnradio.com
info@wwnn.com
License: Pompano Beach, FL held by WWNN License LLC.
Group Owner: Beasley Broadcast Group Inc.; (acq 3-14-2000; grpsl).
Arbitron Metro Market: Pompano Beach, FL *Format:* Public Affairs
Bob Morency, Operations Dir
Bob Morency, General Manager
Duff Lindsey, Programming Director
Karen Ruggerie, Business Manager
Jodi Mibaum, Traffic Manager

Ponte Vedra Beach

WOKV-FM
01-01-1996; 106.5 mhz FM *Hrs Open:* 24; 6 kw; 328 ft.; N30 16 35 W81 33 58
11521 Innfields Drive, Odessa, FL 33556 US
(904) 245-8500, *Fax:* (904) 245-8501
www.wokv.com
news@wokv.com
License: Ponte Vedra Beach, St. Johns County, FL held by Cox Radio Inc.
Group Owner: Cox Radio Inc.; (acq 9-18-2006; $7.65 million)
Arbitron Metro Market: Jacksonville, FL *Format:* Christian *Target Audience:* 25-44.
Calvin Grabau, General Manager
Bob DeBlois, General Sales Mgr
Mike Dorwart, Programming Director
Laura Hermanson, Promotions Manager
Rich Jones, News Director
Jodi Rainey, National Sales Manager

Port Charlotte

WZJZ
10-01-1976; 100.1 mhz FM *Hrs Open:* 24; 84 kw; 1060 ft.; N26 47 7 W81 47 47
200 Concord Plaza, Suite 600, San Antonio, TX 78216 US
(239) 225-4300
www.smoothjazz1071.com
License: Port Charlotte, Charlotte County, FL held by Clear Channel Broadcasting Licenses Inc.
Group Owner: Clear Channel Communications Inc.; (acq 2-18-97; grpsl)
Arbitron Metro Market: Fort Myers-Naples-Marco Island, FL *Format:* Jazz, Smooth Jazz *Target Audience:* 25-54.
Jim Keating, General Manager

***WVIJ**
07-26-1987; 91.7 mhz FM; 1.9 kw; 207 ft.; N26 58 49 W82 4 3
3279 Sherwood Road, Port Charlotte, FL 33980 US
(941) 624-5000, *Fax:* (775) 243-0586
www.wvij.com
wvij@wvij.com
License: Port Charlotte, Charlotte County, FL held by Port Charlotte Educational Broadcasting Foundation Inc.
Arbitron Metro Market: Port Charlotte, FL *Format:* Religious *Target Audience:* 35 plus.
Daniel Kolenda Jr., General Manager

Port Orange

WKRO-FM
01-01-1993; 93.1 mhz FM *Hrs Open:* 24; 15 kw; 427 ft.; N28 53 40 W80 53 8
126 West Inernational, Speedway Blvd, Daytona Beach, FL 32114 US
(386) 255-9300, *Fax:* (386) 238-6071
License: Port Orange, Volusia County, FL held by Black Crow LLC.
Group Owner: Black Crow Media Group LLC; (acq 9-21-2001; grpsl).
Arbitron Metro Market: Daytona Beach, FL *Format:* Country
Stacey Knerler, General Manager

Port St. Lucie

WHLG
11-16-1998; 101.3 mhz FM *Hrs Open:* 24; 6 kw; 299 ft.; N27 12 53 W80 15 24
1000 NW Alice Avenue, Stuart, FL 34994 US
(772) 692-9454, *Fax:* (772) 692-0258
www.coast1013.com
info@coast1013.com
License: Port St. Lucie, St. Lucie County, FL held by Horton Broadcasting Co. Inc.
Nat'l Network: Jones Radio Networks *Nat'l Reps:* Interep *Format:* Adult Contemp *No. News Employees:* 10 *Target Audience:* 25-54; female/male 60/40%, 35 years old *Adv. Rates:* 365; 40; 30; 20
George Metcalf, CEO
Lorna Potter, General Manager

WPSL
10-26-1985; 1590 khz AM *Hrs Open:* 24; 5 kw-D, ND1; 0.063 kw-N, ND1; N27 18 28 W80 18 26
8245 Business Park Drive, Port St Lucie, FL 34952 US
(772) 340-1590, *Fax:* (772) 340-3245
www.wpsl.com
wpsl@wpsl.com
License: Port St. Lucie, FL held by Port St. Lucie Broadcasters Inc.
Nat'l Network: CBS; ESPN Radio *Regional Network:* Florida's Radio Networks
Arbitron Metro Market: Fort Pierce-Stuart-Vero Beach, FL *Format:* News, News/Talk, 84, Talk *Special Programming:* Relg 6 hrs wkly *Hrs. of News Programming:* news progmg 4 hrs wkly *No. News Employees:* 1 *TargetAudience:* 45 plus; established families *Adv. Rates:* 50 for:60—40 for :30
Carol Wyatt, CEO
Greg Wyatt, Operations Dir

Punta Gorda

WCCF
09-15-1961; 1580 khz AM; 1.25 kw-D, ND1; 0.11 kw-N, ND1; N26 53 37 W82 3 3
50 East Rivercenter Boulevard, #1200, Covington, KY 41011 US
(941) 206-1188, *Fax:* (941) 206-9296
www.wccfam.com
info@wccfam.com
License: Punta Gorda, FL held by Citicasters Licenses L.P.
Group Owner: Clear Channel Communications Inc.; (acq 2-1-99; grpsl).
Format: News, News/Talk, 86 *Target Audience:* 45 plus. *Adv. Rates:* 35; 35; 35; 25
Chris Monk, Operations Dir
Mike Moody, General Manager

Punta Rassa

WTLQ-FM
05-03-1999; 97.7 mhz FM *Hrs Open:* 24; 14.5 kw; 430 ft.; N26 29 16 W81 55 46
9148 Bonita Beach Road, Suite 205, Bonita Springs, FL 34135 US
(239) 334-1111 / (239) 338-4325, *Fax:* (239) 334-0744
www.latino977.com
License: Punta Rassa, Lee County, FL held by Fort Myers Broadcasting Co.
Group Owner: Fort Myers Broadcasting Co.; acq 9-13-00; $7 million).
Nat'l Reps: McGavren Guild
Arbitron Metro Market: Fort Myers, FL *Target Audience:* 18-49; adults
Wayne Simons, General Manager
Brad Foster, General Sales Mgr
Hector Velazquez, Programming Director
Keith Stuhlmann, Engineering Dir

Quincy

WXSR
12-01-1966; 101.5 mhz FM; 37 kw; 489 ft.; N30 29 32 W84 17 13
200 Concord Plaza, Suite 600, San Antonio, TX 78216 US
(850) 422-3107, *Fax:* (850) 383-0747
www.x1015.com
License: Quincy, Gadsden County, FL held by Clear Channel Radio Licenses Inc.
Group Owner: Clear Channel Communications Inc.; (acq 11-21-97; grpsl)
Arbitron Metro Market: Tallahassee, FL *Format:* Alternative *Target Audience:* 18-34. *Adv. Rates:* 50; 60; 60; 30
Jeff Horn, Operations Dir
Lisa Rice, General Manager
AJ Malone, Programming Director
Jason Taylor, Webmaster

***WFRU**
06-25-2008; 90.1 mhz FM; 32 kw vert; 328 ft.; N30 42 22 W84 37 39
954 Hwy C4-A, Baker, FL 32531 US
(850) 201-1070, *Fax:* (850) 201-1071
www.faithradio.us
License: Quincy, Gadsden County, FL held by Okaloosa Public Radio Inc.
Arbitron Metro Market: Quincy, FL *Format:* Religious
Scott Beigle, General Manager
Steve Huffman, Operations Dir
Brenda Beigle, Vice President
Suzanne Farrar, Administrative Assistant
Anna Moore, Administrative Assistant

Riviera Beach

WHTY
02-26-1965; 1600 khz AM *Hrs Open:* 24; 456 ft
866 2nd Avenue, 2nd Floor, New York, NY 10017 US
(765) 288-4403, *Fax:* (765) 378-2091
www.maxrocks.net
maxstudio@maxrocks.com
License: Riviera Beach, FL held by Indiana Sabrecom Inc.
Group Owner: Backyard Broadcasting LLC; (acq 12-1-02; grpsl).
Nat'l Network: Westwood One *Nat'l Reps:* Rgnl Reps *Wire Services:* UPI
Format: Classic Rock *Hrs. of News Programming:* news progmg one hr wkly *No. News Employees:* 1 *Target Audience:* 25-54.
Steve Lindell, General Manager
Bret Beshore, Promotions Manager

WHTY(AM)
08-17-1959; 1600 khz AM *Hrs Open:* 24; 5 kw-D, 4.7 kw-N, DA-2; N26 44 55 W80 08 02
824 US Hwy. 1, North Palm Beach, FL 33408
(561) 694-7636
www.radiodisney.com
License: Riviera Beach, Palm Beach County, FL held by Radio Disney Group LLC.
Group Owner: ABC Inc.; (acq 8-22-00; grpsl).
Nat'l Reps: Roslin
Arbitron Metro Market: West Palm Beach-Boca Raton, FL *Format:* Children *Special Programming:* Sp *Hrs. of News Programming:* news progmg 30 hrs wkly *No. News Employees:* 2 *Target Audience:* Local Blacks &Hispanics
Neil Orlikoff, General Manager

WZZR
01-01-1971; 94.3 mhz FM; 50 kw; 456 ft.; N26 45 42 W80 4 42
200 Concord Plaza, Suite 600, San Antonio, TX 78216 US
(561) 616-6600, *Fax:* (561) 616-6677
www.wzzr.com
AndrewBednar@clearchannel.com
License: Riviera Beach, West Palm Beach County, FL held by Clear Channel Broadcasting Licenses Inc.
Group Owner: Clear Channel Communications Inc.; (acq 11-21-97; grpsl).
Arbitron Metro Market: West Palm Beach, FL *Format:* Talk *Target Audience:* 25-54. *Adv. Rates:* 90; 75; 90; 60
Mike Michaels, Operations Dir
Mark Bass, General Manager
Mike Scott, Director of Sales
Andrew Bednar, Promotions Manager
Chad Tyson, Webmaster
Erika Ewald, Digital Sales Manager

Rock Harbor

WKLG
11-01-1984; 102.1 mhz FM *Hrs Open:* 24; 100 kw; 430 ft.; N25 5 29 W80 26 37
Mailing Address: 513 Southard Street, Key West, FL 33040 US
Second Address: 1452 N. Krome Ave., Suite 103 E., Florida City, FL 33034
(305) 451-2202, *Fax:* (305) 453-2265
www.wklginc.com/radio
cs@wklginc.com
License: Rock Harbor, Monroe County, FL held by WKLG Inc.
Format: Adult Contemp *Target Audience:* 25-54; majority are female 18 plus
Douglas LaRue, President

Rockledge

WHKR
11-25-1989; 102.7 mhz FM *Hrs Open:* 24; 50 kw; 433 ft.; N28 20 59 W80 46 29
600 Congress Ave., Suite 1400, Austin, TX 78701 US
(321) 984-1000, *Fax:* (321) 724-1565
www.thehitkicker.com
Pete.DeSimone@cumulus.com
License: Rockledge, Brevard County, FL held by Cumulus Licensing Corp.
Group Owner: Cumulus Media Inc.; (acq 8-7-2000; grpsl).
Arbitron Metro Market: Melbourne-Titusville-Cocoa, FL *Format:* Country *Special Programming:* Pub service one hr wkly *Hrs. of News Programming:* news progmg 6 hrs wkly *No. News Employees:* 2 *Target Audience:* 25-54.
Pete DeSimone, General Manager
Jim Callahan, Programming Director
Jennifer Armstrong, Promotions Manager
Jon Roberts, Chief Engineer
Christina Volonnino, Traffic Director

Royal Palm Beach

WMEN
04-01-1987; 640 khz AM *Hrs Open:* 24; 7.5 kw-D, DA2; 0.46 kw-N, DA2; N26 45 18 W80 22 0
1601 Belvedere Rd., 204e, West Palm Beach, FL 33406 US
(954) 315-1515, *Fax:* (954) 315-1555
www.wftlsports.com
info@wlvj.com
License: Royal Palm Beach, FL held by JCE Licenses L.L.C.
Group Owner: James Crystal Inc.; (acq 11-18-99; $3,945,500 for stock)
Nat'l Network: Fox Sports
Arbitron Metro Market: Royal Palm Beach, FL *Format:* Sports
James Hilliard, CEO
Steve Lapa, General Manager

WPSP
02-01-1991; 1190 khz AM *Hrs Open:* 18
1033 East Semoran Blvd., #253, Casselberry, FL 32707 US
(561) 681-9777, *Fax:* (561) 687-3398
diaz1190am@aol.com
License: Royal Palm Beach, FL held by George M. Arroyo.
Arbitron Metro Market: West Palm Beach-Boca Raton, FL *Format:* Spanish *Hrs. of News Programming:* news progmg 20 hrs wkly *No. News Employees:* 2 *Target Audience:* 25-54. *Adv. Rates:* 30; 25; 30; 20
George Arroyo, President
Lissette Diaz, General Manager

Safety Harbor

WYUU
10-01-1983; 92.5 mhz FM; 50 kw; 489 ft.; N27 50 32 W82 48 52
600 New Hampshire Avenue, NW, Suite 1200, Washington, DC 20037 US
(727) 579-1925, *Fax:* (813) 287-1833
lanueva925.com
info@lanueva925.com
License: Safety Harbor, Pinellas County, FL held by CBS Radio Stations Inc.
Group Owner: CBS Radio; (acq 10-15-98; $75 million with WLLD(FM) Holmes Beach).
Arbitron Metro Market: Tampa-St. Peter *Format:* Spanish *Target Audience:* 18-49.
John Fennessy, General Sales Mgr

Saint Augustine

WAOC
12-01-1953; 1420 khz AM *Hrs Open:* 24; 2.18 kw-D, 250 w-N; N29 51 00 W81 19 50
Mailing Address: Box 3847, Saint Augustine, FL 93720
Second Address: 567 Lewis Point Rd. Ext., Saint Augustine, FL 32086
(904) 797-4444, *Fax:* (904) 797-3446
www.1420sports.com
kris@1420sports.com
License: Saint Augustine, St. Johns County, FL held by Phillips Broadcasting LLC
Nat'l Network: ESPN Radio *Nat'l Reps:* Rgnl Reps *Regional Reps:* Rgnl Reps
Population Served: 150,000 *Arbitron Metro Market:* Jacksonville, FL *Special Programming:* University of Florida sports, NFL Jaguar affiliate, NASCAR *Hrs. of News Programming:* news progmg 8 hrs wkly *No. NewsEmployees:* 1 *Target Audience:* 26 plus; affluent adults *Adv. Rates:* 24; 18; 24; 12
Kristine Phillips, President
Matt Kraycinovich, Operations Dir

Saint Augustine Beach

WYRE-FM
09-01-1995; 105.5 mhz FM *Hrs Open:* 24; 16 kw; Ant 410 ft; N29 51 00 W81 19 50
9550 Regency Sq. Blvd., Suite 200, Jacksonville, FL 32225
(904) 680-1050, *Fax:* (904) 680-1051
www.tamabroadcasting.com
jaxproduction@tamabroadcasting.com

License: Saint Augustine Beach, St. Johns County, FL held by Tama Radio Licenses of Jacksonville, FL, Inc.
Group Owner: Tama Broadcasting Inc.; (acq 2-28-2003; $8.5 million with WJSJ(FM) Fernandina Beach)
Population Served: 175,000 *Arbitron Metro Market:* Jacksonville, FL *Format:* Oldies *Target Audience:* 20-45; general
Joel Widdows, Operations Dir
Linda Fructuoso, General Manager
Gerry Smith, Chief Engineer

San Carlos Park

WDEO-FM
01-01-1995; 98.5 mhz FM *Hrs Open:* 24; 18.5 kw; 371 ft.; N26 30 18 W81 51 14
7290 College Parkway, Suite 100, Fort Myers, FL 33907 US
(734) 930-5200, *Fax:* (734) 930-3179
www.avemariaradio.net
License: San Carlos Park, Lee County, FL held by Ave Maria University Inc.
Arbitron Metro Market: San Carlos Park, FL *Format:* News, News/Talk, 86, Christian *Target Audience:* 21 plus; adult Christian
Michael Jones, General Manager

Sanford

WSDO
05-20-1947; 1400 khz AM *Hrs Open:* 24; 1 kw-U, ND1; N28 48 4 W81 15 6
222 Hazard St, Orlando, FL 32804 US
(407) 841-8282, *Fax:* (407) 841-8250
www.wprd.com
wprd1440@hotmail.com
License: Sanford, FL held by J & V Communications Co.
Group Owner: J&V Communications Inc.; (acq 6-5-92; $300,000;
Nat'l Network: Westwood One *Regional Network:* Florida's Radio Networks
Arbitron Metro Market: Orlando, FL *Format:* News, News/Talk, 86
Special Programming: Relg 3 hrs wkly *Target Audience:* 21 plus.
John Torrado, CEO
Jocelyn Torrado, Operations Dir
Hector Reyes, General Manager
Virgen Torrado, CEO

Sanibel

WTLT
12-01-1971; 93.7 mhz FM *Hrs Open:* 24; 43 kw; 476 ft.; N26 30 18 W81 51 14
9838 Red Reef Court, Fort Myers, FL 33919 US
(239) 334-1111, *Fax:* (239) 479-5535
www.lite973.com
kristen@lite937.com
License: Sanibel, Collier County, FL held by Meridian Broadcasting Inc.
Group Owner: Meridian Broadcasting Inc.; acq 12-1-96; grpsl)
Nat'l Reps: McGavren Guild *Wire Services:* AP
Arbitron Metro Market: Fort Myers, FL *Format:* Adult Contemp
Hrs. of News Programming: news progmg 2 hrs wkly *No. News Employees:* 3 *Target Audience:* 25-54; women
Joseph Schwartzel, CEO
Jim Schwartzel, General Sales Mgr
Lance Ballance, Programming Director
Matt Mangas, Promotions Manager
Keith Stuhlmann, Engineering Dir

Santa Rosa Beach

WWAV
04-03-1985; 102.1 mhz FM *Hrs Open:* 24; 50 kw; 374 ft.; N30 23 10 W86 17 48
Two Bala Plaza, Suite 801, Bala-Cynwyd, PA 19004 US
(850) 654-1000, *Fax:* (850) 654-5102
www.1021thewave.com
rraybourne@apexbroadcasting.com
License: Santa Rosa Beach, FL held by Qantum of Fort Walton Beach License Co. LLC.
Group Owner: Qantum Communications Corp.; (acq 7-2-2003; grpsl).
Nat'l Reps: Katz Radio
Arbitron Metro Market: Santa Rosa Beach, FL *Format:* Adult Contemp *Hrs. of News Programming:* News progmg one hr wkly
Target Audience: 25-54; general *Adv. Rates:* 50; 50; 50; 25
Frank Osborne, President
Dan Collins, Program Director/Operations Director
Ron Raybourne, General Manager
Judy Hoepfl, General Sales Mgr

Sarasota

WCTQ
06-30-1965; 106.5 mhz FM *Hrs Open:* 24; 13 kw; 584 ft.; N27 32 42 W82 34 27
50 East Rivercenter Blvd, Suite 1200, Covington, KY 41011 US
(941) 552-4800, *Fax:* (941) 55-4900
www.1065ctq.com
eddierupp@clearchannel.com
License: Sarasota, Sarasota County, FL
Group Owner: Clear Channel Communications Inc.
Arbitron Metro Market: Sarasota-Bradenton, FL *Format:* Country
Hrs. of News Programming: News progmg one hr wkly *Target Audience:* 25-54.
Mark Wilson, Operations Dir
Matt Howell, Engineering Dir
Heidi Decker, Disc Jockey
Sammi Austin, Disc Jockey
Maverick Johnson, Disc Jockey
Tracy Black, Public Affairs Director

WHPT
01-01-1973; 102.5 mhz FM *Hrs Open:* 24; 100 kw; 1650 ft.; N27 24 30 W82 15 0
3773 Howard Hughes Pwy, Suite 300n, Las Vegas, NV 89109 US
(727) 579-2000, *Fax:* (727) 579-2662
theboneonline.com
info@coxradio.com
License: Sarasota, Sarasota County, FL held by Cox Radio Inc.
Group Owner: Cox Radio Inc.; (acq 5-99; grpsl)
Nat'l Reps: Clear Channel
Arbitron Metro Market: Sarasota-Bradenton, FL *Format:* Light Rock *Target Audience:* 25-54.
Keith Lawless, Operations Dir

WLSS
05-23-1949; 930 khz AM *Hrs Open:* 24
2500 10th Street, Sarasota, FL 34237 US
(813) 639-1903, *Fax:* (813) 639-1272
www.wlssradio.com
wlss@wlssradio.com
License: Sarasota, FL held by Caron Broadcasting Inc.
Group Owner: Salem Communications Corp.; (acq 8-12-2005; $9.5 million with WGUL(AM) Dunedin).
Nat'l Network: Salem Radio Network *Nat'l Reps:* Salem
Arbitron Metro Market: Sarasota-Bradenton, FL *Format:* News, News/Talk, 86
Mike Serio, Operations Dir
Chris Gould, General Manager
Casey Bell, Promotions Manager

*WKZM
10-21-1974; 104.3 mhz FM *Hrs Open:* 24; 6 kw; 266 ft.; N27 16 30 W82 28 54 *Rebroadcasts:* Rebroadcasts WKES(FM) Lakeland 100%
P.O. Box 7627, Sarasota, FL 34278 US
(727) 391-9994, *Fax:* (727) 397-6425
www.wkes.org
wkes@moody.edu
License: Sarasota, Sarasota County, FL held by The Moody Bible Institute of Chicago.
Group Owner: The Moody Bible Institute of Chicago; acq 10-15-99)
Arbitron Metro Market: Sarasota-Bradenton, FL *Format:* Religious *Hrs. of News Programming:* News progmg 14 hrs wkly
Target Audience: General.
Pierre Chestang, General Manager

WSRQ
01-01-1961; 1220 khz AM; 1 kw-D, DAD; 0.159 kw-N, DA2; N27 19 27 W82 29 47
3135 S.E. 27th Street, Gainesville, FL 32641 US
(941) 952-1220, *Fax:* (941) 365-2900
www.newstalk1220.com
1220@newstalk1220.com
License: Sarasota, FL held by SRQ Radio LLC
Regional Network: Florida's Radio Networks
Arbitron Metro Market: Sarasota-Bradenton, FL *Format:* News, News/Talk, 84, Talk *Target Audience:* 25-64; men
James Grady, General Manager

*WSMR
01-01-1993; 89.1 mhz FM *Hrs Open:* 24; 54 kw; 443 ft.; N27 9 3 W82 27 51
3003 North Snelling Ave., St. Paul, MN 55113 US
(941) 906-9767, *Fax:* (941) 362-0377
www.wsmr.org
License: Sarasota, Sarasota County, FL held by Northwestern College.
Group Owner: Northwestern College & Radio; (acq 10-4-96; $400,000).
Arbitron Metro Market: Sarasota-Bradenton, FL *Format:* Christian
Hrs. of News Programming: News progmg 6 hrs wkly *Target Audience:* 30-55; with kids still at home
Dr. Alan Cureton, CEO
Harv Hendrickson, General Manager
Douglas Poll, Station Manager

WSDV
12-07-1939; 1450 khz AM *Hrs Open:* 24; 1 kw-U, ND1; N27 20 11 W82 34 25
50 East Rivercenter Blvd, Suite 1200, Covington, KY 41011 US
(941) 552-4800, *Fax:* (941) 552-4900
www.doveradio.com
nancylee@doveradio.com
License: Sarasota, FL held by Citicasters Licenses L.P.
Group Owner: Clear Channel Communications Inc.; (acq 5-4-99; grpsl).
Arbitron Metro Market: Sarasota-Bradenton, FL *Format:* Adult Contemp *Hrs. of News Programming:* news progmg 40 hrs wkly
No. News Employees: 3 *Target Audience:* 25-54; general
Sherri Carlson, Operations Dir

WTMY
12-02-1961; 1280 khz AM *Hrs Open:* 24
3801 Skillern Blvd., Flower Mound, TX 75028 US
(941) 955-9387, *Fax:* (941) 955-9062
www.wtmy.com
Traffic.wtmy@gmail.com
License: Sarasota, FL held by Metropolitan Radio Group Inc.
Group Owner: Metropolitan Radio Group Inc.; acq 8-96)
Arbitron Metro Market: Sarasota, FL *Format:* Talk *Special Programming:* Pol one hr, gospel 6 hrs, full service 2 hrs wkly
Target Audience: 40 plus; wealth & health oriented *Adv. Rates:* 15; 15; 15; na
Mark Acker, President
Alex Smith, Operations Dir
Phil Russell, General Manager
Gino Norman, Programming Director
Ryan Williams, Producer & Show Host
Sean Osborne, Sports Director

Satellite Beach

WSBH
98.5 mhz FM; 6 kw; 328 ft.; N28 8 11 W80 42 12 US
(321) 752-9850, *Fax:* (321) 752-8717
www.beach985.com
License: Satellite Beach, Brevard County, FL held by Horton Broadcasting Co. Inc.
Arbitron Metro Market: Satellite Beach, FL
George Metcalf, President

Sebastian

WSJZ-FM
01-01-2001; 95.9 mhz FM; 25 kw; 289 ft.; N27 49 5 W80 37 18
72 Dunbar Road, Palm Beach Gardens, FL 33418 US
(321) 984-1000, *Fax:* (321) 724-1565
www.espn959.com/
jennifer.armstrong@cumulus.com
License: Sebastian, Indian River County, FL held by Cumulus Licensing LLC.
Group Owner: Cumulus Media Inc.; (acq 11-8-2004; $5 million).
Arbitron Metro Market: Melbourne-Titusville-Cocoa, FL *Format:* Sports
Dan Carelli, General Manager
Jon Roberts, Programming Director

Sebring

WITS
11-24-1959; 1340 khz AM *Hrs Open:* 24
16 Woodshire Court, Ballston Lake, NY 12019 US
(863) 382-9999, *Fax:* (863) 382-1982
www.cohanradiogroup.com
cohanradiogroup@htn.net
License: Sebring, FL held by Cohan Radio Group Inc.
Group Owner: Cohan Radio Group Inc.; (acq 11-1-98; $735,000 with co-located FM plus WJCM(AM) Sebring)
Nat'l Network: ABC *Nat'l Reps:* Interep *Wire Services:* AP
Arbitron Metro Market: Sebring, FL *Format:* Adult Contemp *Hrs. of News Programming:* news progmg 5 hrs wkly *No. News Employees:* 1 *Target Audience:* 40 plus; mature adults
Peter Coughlin, President
Libby Coughlin, General Sales Mgr
Kim McPherson, News Director

WJCM
05-22-1950; 1050 khz AM *Hrs Open:* 24; 1 kw-D, ND1; 0.011 kw-N, ND1; N27 30 30 W81 25 20
16 Woodshire Court, Ballston Lake, NY 12019 US

(863) 382-9999, *Fax:* (863) 382-1982
www.cohanradiogroup.com
cohanradiogroup@htn.net
License: Sebring, FL held by Cohan Radio Group Inc.
Group Owner: Cohan Radio Group Inc.; (acq 11-1-98; $150,000).
Regional Network: Florida's Radio Networks *Nat'l Reps:* Interep
Regional Reps: Interep *Wire Services:* AP
Arbitron Metro Market: Sebring, FL *Format:* Oldies *Hrs. of News Programming:* news progmg 8 hrs wkly *No. News Employees:* 1 *Target Audience:* 45+.
Stacy Clark, Operations Dir
Peter Coughlin, General Manager
Alan Gray, Programming Director
Barry Foster, News Director
Phil Scott, Chief Engineer
Libby Coughlin, Regional Sales Manager

WWLL
07-01-1967; 105.7 mhz FM *Hrs Open:* 24; 19 kw; Ant 351 ft; N27 21 29 W81 28 22
3750 U.S. 27 N., Suite 1, Sebring, FL 12019
(863) 382-9999, *Fax:* (863) 382-1982
www.cohanradiogroup.com
License: Sebring, Highlands County, FL held by Cohan Radio Group Inc.
Group Owner: Cohan Radio Group Inc.; (acq 11-1-98)
Nat'l Network: NBC Radio *Nat'l Reps:* Interep *Wire Services:* AP
Population Served: 90,000 *Arbitron Metro Market:* Sebring, FL *Hrs. of News Programming:* news progmg 2 hrs wkly *No. News Employees:* 1 *Target Audience:* 25-54; adults
Peter Coughlin, President
Libby Coughlin, General Sales Mgr
Les Jacoby, Programming Director

***WJFH**
01-01-2007; 91.5 mhz FM; 16 kw horiz, 15.7 kw vert; 454 ft.; N27 22 52 W81 29 28
P.O. Box 7217, 5015 South Florida Ave., Lakeland, FL 33813 US
(800)456-8910, *Fax:* (863) 646-5326
www.thejoyfm.com
License: Sebring, Highlands County, FL held by Radio Training Network Inc.
Arbitron Metro Market: Sebring, FL *Format:* Christian
James Campbell, President

Seffner

WHFS(AM)
11-07-1960; 1010 khz AM *Hrs Open:* 24; 50 kw-D, 5 kw-N, DA-2; N27 59 25 W82 15 06
9721 Executive Center Dr. N., Suite 200, Saint Petersburg, FL 33702
(727) 579-1925, *Fax:* (727) 563-8204
www.1010sportsonline.com
License: Seffner, Hillsborough County, FL held by CBS Radio Inc. of Tampa.
Group Owner: CBS Radio; (acq 11-21-87).
Nat'l Network: Sporting News Radio Network; Westwood One
Nat'l Reps: CBS Radio
Arbitron Metro Market: Tampa-St. Petersburg-Clearwater, FL
Format: Sports
Don Howe, Operations Dir
Mike Culotta, Operations Manager

Shalimar

WNCV
10-25-1982; 93.3 mhz FM *Hrs Open:* 24; 50 kw; 469 ft.; N30 24 38 W86 37 22
P.O. Box 679, Orange Beach, AL 36561 US
(850) 243-7676, *Fax:* (850) 243-6806
www.wncv.com
coastoffice@wncv.com
License: Shalimar, Okaloosa County, FL held by Cumulus Licensing LLC.
Group Owner: Cumulus Media Inc.; (acq 8-2-2006; swap for WRKN(FM) Niceville)
Arbitron Metro Market: Fort Walton Beach, FL *Format:* Adult Contemp
Mike DeMarco, General Manager
Skip Davis, Programming Director

Silver Springs

WNDD
02-01-1991; 95.5 mhz FM *Hrs Open:* 24; 6 kw; 328 ft.; N29 16 55 W82 2 50
3602 NE20th Place, Ocala, FL 32670 US
(352) 622-9500, *Fax:* (352) 622-1900
www.windfm.com
rkassi@windwogksales.com
License: Silver Springs, Marion County, FL held by Ocala Broadcasting Corp. L.L.C.
Group Owner: Wooster Republican Printing Co.; (acq 9-1-97).
Nat'l Reps: Katz Radio
Arbitron Metro Market: Gainesville, FL *Format:* Light Rock *Target Audience:* 25-54; adults *Adv. Rates:* 70; 80; 70; 30
Jim Robertson, General Manager
Bob Kassi, General Sales Mgr
Hunter, Programming Director

Solana

WCVU
01-01-1994; 104.9 mhz FM; 6 kw; 318 ft.; N26 53 37.5 W82 3 2.7
50 East Rivercenter Boulevard, #1200, Covington, KY 41011 US
(941) 206-1188, *Fax:* (941) 206-9296
www.wcvu.com
toddmatthews@clearchannel.com.
License: Solana, Charlotte County, FL held by Citicasters Licenses L.P.
Group Owner: Clear Channel Communications Inc.; (acq 2-1-99; grpsl).
Nat'l Network: CNN Radio
Arbitron Metro Market: Fort Myers, FL *Format:* Adult Contemp
Adv. Rates: 35; 30; 35; 25
Michael Moody, General Manager
David Ayres, General Sales Mgr
Todd Matthews, Programming Director

WKII
11-19-1986; 1070 khz AM *Hrs Open:* 24
3305 W. Spring Mountain, Rd., #60, Las Vegas, NV 89102 US
(941) 206-1188, *Fax:* (941) 206-9296
www.kixclassics.com
License: Solana, FL held by Clear Channel Broadcasting Licenses Inc.
Group Owner: Clear Channel Communications Inc.
Regional Network: Florida's Radio Networks
Format: Adult Contemp *Hrs. of News Programming:* news progmg 2 hrs wkly *No. News Employees:* 1 *Target Audience:* 35 plus.
Mike Moody, Station Manager
David Ayres, General Sales Mgr
Ron Bigley, News Director
Paul Wolf, Chief Engineer

South Daytona

WPUL
06-13-1957; 1590 khz AM *Hrs Open:* 6 am-12 pm; 1 kw-D, ND1; 0.032 kw-N, ND1; N29 9 16 W81 1 20
Box 4010, South Daytona, FL 32121 US
(386) 239-7080 (Studio),(386) 226-2398, *Fax:* (386) 254-7510
ccherry2@aol.com
License: South Daytona, FL held by PSI Communications Inc.
Nat'l Network: American Urban
Arbitron Metro Market: Daytona Beach, FL *Format:* Gospel, Talk
Target Audience: General. *Adv. Rates:* 50; 40; 50; 35
Charles Cherry, CEO
Charles Cherry II, General Manager
Phinesse Demps, Programming Director

South Miami

WAXY
09-15-1947; 790 khz AM *Hrs Open:* 24; 25 kw-U, DA-2; N25 46 25 W80 38 13
20450 N.W. 2nd Ave., Miami, FL 33169
(305) 521-5100 / (887) 790-1015, *Fax:* (305) 521-1416
www.waxy.com
License: South Miami, Dade County, FL held by Lincoln Financial Media Co. of Florida.
Group Owner: Lincoln Financial Media; (acq 4-3-2006; grpsl).
Nat'l Reps: CBS Radio
Population Served: 2,800,000 *Arbitron Metro Market:* Miami-Fort Lauderdale-Hollywood, FL *Target Audience:* 35 plus.
Gary Aybar, Operations Dir
Dennis Collins, General Manager

Southport

***WKGC**
06-25-1965; 1480 khz AM *Hrs Open:* 6 AM-9 PM
5230 W. Highway 98, Panama City, FL 32401 US
(850) 873-3500, *Fax:* (850) 913-3299
www.wkgc.org
fsundram@gnfcoast.edu
License: Southport, FL held by Gulf Coast Community College.
Nat'l Network: NPR
Arbitron Metro Market: Panama City, FL *Format:* Easy Listening
Special Programming: Folk 2 hrs, educ 8 hrs wkly *Hrs. of News Programming:* News progmg 25 hrs wkly *Target Audience:* General; college students &older high school students
Robert McSpadden, President
Reed Kinney, Operations Dir
Frank Sundram, General Manager

Sparr

***WTYG**
91.5 mhz FM; 0.1 kw; 95 ft.; N29 20 21 W82 6 10 US
(913) 669-8101
www.wtygfm.com/careers.htm
wtygfm@yahoo.com
License: Sparr, Marion County, FL held by Arts for the Community Inc.
Arbitron Metro Market: Mount Dora, FL *Format:* Talk
De Miller, President

Spring Hill

WJQB
10-01-1992; 106.3 mhz FM *Hrs Open:* 24 hours; 25 kw; 315 ft.; N28 31 41 W82 32 45
35048 U.S. Highway 19 N, Palm Harbor, FL 34684 US
(727) 697-1063, *Fax:* (727) 817-1063
www.trueoldies1063.com
wjqbsteve@wjqb.com
License: Spring Hill, Hernando County, FL held by WGUL-FM Inc.
Nat'l Network: ABC Music Radio
Arbitron Metro Market: Tampa-St. Petersburg-Clearwater, FL
Format: Oldies *Target Audience:* adults 35-64 adults 35+ *Adv. Rates:* 55; 45; 55; 15
Betty Marcocci, Chairman
Steve Schurdell, General Manager

Springfield

WRBA
06-01-1986; 95.9 mhz FM *Hrs Open:* 24; 50 kw; 282 ft.; N30 12 12 W85 36 57
Two Bala Plaza, Suite 801, Bala-Cynwyd, PA 19004 US
(850) 234-8858, *Fax:* (850) 234-6592
www.arrow959.com
billyoung@panamacityradio.com
License: Springfield, Bay County, FL
Group Owner: Powell Broadcasting Co. L.L.C.; acq 3-10-2004; grpsl).
Arbitron Metro Market: Panama City, FL *Format:* Classic Rock
Target Audience: 30-54; general *Adv. Rates:* 50; 40; 40; 25
Harry Finch, General Manager

WYOO
03-02-1993; 101.1 mhz FM *Hrs Open:* 24; 12 kw; 404 ft.; N30 10 44 W85 46 55
P.O. Box 16626, Panama City, FL 32406 US
(850) 230-5855, *Fax:* (850) 230-6988
www.talkradio101.com
License: Springfield, Bay County, FL held by Magic Broadcasting Florida Licensing LLC.
Group Owner: Magic Broadcasting LLC; (acq 9-30-2002; grpsl)
Regional Network: Florida's Radio Networks *Nat'l Reps:* Christal
Arbitron Metro Market: Panama City, FL *Format:* Talk *Hrs. of News Programming:* news progmg 28 hrs wkly *No. News Employees:* 1 *Target Audience:* 25-54; educated, upscale
Jeff Storey, COO
Mike Preble, Operations Dir

St. Augustine

***WAYL**
05-22-1994; 91.9 mhz FM *Hrs Open:* 24; 5 kw; 207 ft.; N29 51 0 W81 19 50
Mailing Address: 2701 Hodges Blvd., Jacksonville, FL 32225 US
Second Address: 1485 US Rt. 1 S., Saint Augustine, FL 32086
(906) 774-5731, *Fax:* (906) 774-4542
www.1067themountain.com
peterson.trisha@gmail.com
License: St. Augustine, St. Johns County, FL held by New Covenant Educational Ministries Inc.
Nat'l Network: Salem Radio Network
Arbitron Metro Market: Iron Mountain MI *Format:* Oldies
Trisha Peterson, General Manager

***WFCF**
11-01-1993; 88.5 mhz FM *Hrs Open:* 7 AM-midnight; 10 kw horiz, 9.8 kw vert; 201 ft.; N29 51 17 W81 20 9
P. O. Box 1027, St. Augustine, FL 32085 US
(904) 829-6481, *Fax:* (904) 826-3471
www.flagler.edu
wfcf@flagler.edu

License: St. Augustine, St. Johns County, FL held by Flagler College.
Arbitron Metro Market: St. Augustine, FL *Format:* Variety/Diverse *Special Programming:* Sp 4 hrs, new age 4 hrs, folk 3 hrs, reggae 4 hrs, world 4 hrs, blues 4 hrs wkly *Hrs. of News Programming:* News progmg one hrwkly *Target Audience:* General.
Donna DeLorenzo Webb, General Manager
Daniel McCook, Station Manager
Chris Smith, Programming Director

WFOY
07-07-1936; 1240 khz AM *Hrs Open:* 24
Mailing Address: One Radio Road, St. Augustine, FL 32085 US
Second Address: 567 Lewis Point Rd. Ext., Saint Augustine, FL 32086
(904) 797-1955, *Fax:* (904) 797-3446
www.1240news.com
kris@1240news.com
License: St. Augustine, FL held by Phillips Broadcasting LLC
Nat'l Network: Fox News Radio; Westwood One; Talk Radio Network *Regional Network:* Florida's Radio Networks *Nat'l Reps:* Rgnl Reps *Regional Reps:* Rgnl Reps
Arbitron Metro Market: Jacksonville, FL *Format:* News, News/Talk, 84, Talk *Special Programming:* Rush Limbaugh affiliate *Hrs. of News Programming:* news progmg 8 hrs wkly *No. News Employees:* 1 *TargetAudience:* 26 plus; affluent adults
Adv. Rates: 29; 18; 29; 12
Kristine Phillips, President
Jenny Hayes, General Manager

St. Augustine Beach

WSOS
10-15-1986; 1170 khz AM *Hrs Open:* 6 AM-9 PM
2820 Lewis Speedway, St. Augustine, FL 32084 US
(904) 739-3660, *Fax:* (904) 739-9409
www.classicrock941.com
License: St. Augustine Beach, FL held by Norsan Consulting and Management Inc.
Group Owner: Norsan Consulting and Management Inc.; (acq 1-13-2006; $300,000)
Arbitron Metro Market: Jacksonville, FL
Jorge Lopez, General Manager

St. Catherine

***WKFA**
01-01-2005; 89.3 mhz FM; 0 kw horiz, 3.9 kw vert; 322 ft.; N28 32 22 W82 4 48
P O Box 1089, Silver Springs, FL 34489 US
(321) 267-3000, *Fax:* (321) 264-9370
www.noncomradio.com
wpio@gate.net
License: St. Catherine, Sumter County, FL held by Florida Public Radio Inc.
Arbitron Metro Market: Saint Catherine, FL *Format:* Public Affairs, Religious
Randy Henry, President

St. Cloud

WIWA
01-01-2005; 1160 khz AM
US
(407) 770-2500, *Fax:* (407) 770-2503
www.viva1160.com
info@viva1160.com
License: St. Cloud, FL held by Centro de la Familia Cristiana Inc.
Arbitron Metro Market: Saint Cloud, FL *Format:* News, News/Talk, 82, Talk
Roberto Candelario, President

St. Marks

***WUJC**
01-01-2005; 91.1 mhz FM; 7 kw vert; 312 ft.; N30 8 32 W83 54 58
US
(800) 357-4226, *Fax:* (208) 736-1958
www.csnradio.com
csn@csnradio.com
License: St. Marks, Wakulla County, FL held by CSN International
Group Owner: CSN International
Arbitron Metro Market: Saint Marks, FL *Format:* Religious
Mike Kestler, President
Daniel Davidson, Operations Dir
Don Mills, Network Programming Director / Music Director
Kelly Carlson, Engineering Dir
Jerry Johnson, Engineering Dir
Ray Gorney, Assistant Director of Engineering
DustinPamplona, Engineer
Nolan Mather, Graphics / Website Maintenance
Mike Stocklin, National Underwriting
Austin Morris, Accounting
Lois Mills, FCC Applications / Translator Site Manager

St. Petersburg

WXGL
01-01-1958; 107.3 mhz FM *Hrs Open:* 24; 100 kw; 597 ft.; N28 2 22 W82 39 12
877 Executive Center Dr, Saint Petersburg, FL 33702 US
(727) 579-2000, *Fax:* (727) 579-2662
www.1073theeagle.com
1073comments@coxtampa.com
License: St. Petersburg, Pinellas County, FL held by Cox Radio Inc.
Group Owner: Cox Radio Inc.; (acq 7-1-88).
Nat'l Reps: Commercial Media Sales
Arbitron Metro Market: Tampa-St. Petersburg-Clearwater, FL
Format: Contemporary Hits/Top 40, Adult Contemp
Keith Lawless, Operations Dir
Mary Rogers, General Sales Mgr
John Larson, Programming Director
Tom Paleveda, Operations Manager

WPOI
07-01-1961; 101.5 mhz FM *Hrs Open:* 24; 97.1 kw; 1542 ft.; N27 49 10 W82 15 39
3773 Howard Hughes Pwy, Suite 300n, Las Vegas, NV 89109 US
(727) 579-2000, *Fax:* (727) 579-2662
info@doxradio.com
License: St. Petersburg, Pinellas County, FL held by Cox Radio Inc.
Group Owner: Cox Radio Inc.; (acq 1999; grpsl)
Nat'l Reps: Clear Channel
Arbitron Metro Market: Tampa-St. Petersburg-Clearwater, FL
Format: Oldies *Target Audience:* 25-54.
Howard Tuuri, Operations Dir
Bernadette Osdal, General Sales Mgr
Gerry Brauer, Promotions Manager
Tom Paleveda, Operations Manager

***WFTI-FM**
06-01-1988; 91.7 mhz FM *Hrs Open:* 24; 3 kw; 282 ft.; N27 46 15 W82 38 19
4135 Northgate Blvd., Suite 1, Sacramento, CA 95834 US
(727) 823-1140, *Fax:* (727) 823-5753
www.familyradio.com
WFTIFM@hotmail.com
License: St. Petersburg, Pinellas County, FL held by Family Stations Inc.
Group Owner: Family Stations Inc.; acq 11-19-88)
Nat'l Network: Family Radio
Arbitron Metro Market: Tampa-St. Petersburg-Clearwater, FLsburg-Clearwate *Format:* Religious *Hrs. of News Programming:* News progmg 9 hrs wkly *Target Audience:* General.
Bob Barnes, Station Manager

WQYK-FM
05-01-1958; 99.5 mhz FM *Hrs Open:* 24; 99 kw; 571 ft.; N27 55 53.8 W82 24 4.6
600 New Hampshire Ave., Suite 1200, Washington, DC 20037 US
(727) 579-1925
www.wqyk.com
License: St. Petersburg, Pinellas County, FL held by CBS Radio Inc. of Florida.
Group Owner: CBS Radio; (acq 12-1-86;
Nat'l Network: CBS *Nat'l Reps:* Interep
Arbitron Metro Market: Tampa-St. Petersburg-Clearwater, FL *TV Affiliate:* WTOG(TV) affil *Format:* Country *Hrs. of News Programming:* news progmg 6 hrs wkly *No. News Employees:* 1 *Target Audience:* 25-54.
Charlie Ochs, Operations Dir
Mike Culotta, General Manager
Luis Albertini, Vice President

WGES
05-05-1950; 680 khz AM; 0.69 kw-D, ND1; 0.125 kw-N, ND1; N27 51 24 W82 37 26
2700 W Martin Luther, King Blvd, Tampa, FL 34607 US
(813) 319-5757,(813) 637-8000, *Fax:* (813) 319-0029,(813) 637-8001
www.genesis680.com
info@genesis680.com
License: St. Petersburg, FL held by ZGS Broadcasting of Tampa Inc.
Regional Reps: Katz Hispanic Media
Arbitron Metro Market: Tampa-St. Petersburg-Clearwater, FL
Format: Spanish *Target Audience:* General; adults 18-49
Patricia Omana, General Manager

WDAE
11-01-1927; 620 khz AM *Hrs Open:* 24
11521 Innfields Drive, Odessa, FL 33556 US
(813) 832-1000, *Fax:* (813) 832-1090
www.620wdae.com
License: St. Petersburg, FL held by Clear Channel Broadcasting Licenses Inc.
Nat'l Network: Fox Sports *Nat'l Reps:* Katz Radio *Wire Services:* AP
Arbitron Metro Market: Tampa-St. Peter *Format:* Sports
Russell Link, CFO
Dan Diloreto, Operations Dir
Mark Warlaumont, General Sales Mgr
Steve Versnick, Programming Director
Greg Wolf, Promotions Manager
Gwen Shuler, News Director
John McMartin, Chief Engineer

WWMI
01-01-1939; 1380 khz AM *Hrs Open:* 24
16th Floor, 77 West 66th Street, New York, NY 10023 US
(727) 577-4500, *Fax:* (727) 579-1340
www.radiodisney.com
License: St. Petersburg, FL held by Radio Disney Group LLC.
Group Owner: ABC Inc.; (acq 1999; grpsl).
Nat'l Reps: Clear Channel *Wire Services:* NOAA Weather
Arbitron Metro Market: Tampa-St. Peter, FL *Format:* Contemporary Hits/Top 40 *No. News Employees:* 2 *Target Audience:* 25-54.
Ted Wolfe, Station Manager
Drew Rashbaum, Promotions Manager

St. Petersburg Beach

WRXB
01-01-1957; 1590 khz AM; 5 kw-D, DA2; 1 kw-N, DA2; N27 44 3 W82 41 8
3801 Skillern Blvd., Flower Mound, TX 75028 US
(727) 865-1591, *Fax:* (727) 866-1728
www.wrxb.com
wrxb@juno.com
License: St. Petersburg Beach, FL held by Metropolitan Radio Group of Florida Inc.
Group Owner: Metropolitan Radio Group Inc.
Arbitron Metro Market: Tampa-St. Peter *Format:* Adult Contemp *Special Programming:* Jazz 15 hrs wkly *Target Audience:* 23-54; urban contemp
Ed Edwards, General Manager

Starke

***WTLG**
01-01-1982; 88.3 mhz FM *Hrs Open:* 24; 7 kw; 285 ft.; N29 54 34 W82 6 2
163 W. Jefferson At, At Clark St., Starke, FL 32091 US
(662) 844-5036, *Fax:* (662) 842-6791
www.afr.net
License: Starke, Bradford County, FL held by American Family Association.
Group Owner: American Family Radio; (acq 3-31-2008; $225,000)
Nat'l Network: American Family Radio
Arbitron Metro Market: Tupelo, MS *Format:* Christian
Donald Wildmon, Chairman

Stuart

WSTU
12-09-1954; 1450 khz AM *Hrs Open:* 24; 1 kw-U, ND1; N27 12 53 W80 15 24
2435 S.E. Dixie Hgwy, Stuart, FL 34996 US
(772) 220-9788, *Fax:* (772) 340-3245
www.wstu1450.com
wpsl@wpsl.com
License: Stuart, FL held by Treasure Coast Broadcasters Inc.
Nat'l Network: ESPN Radio; ABC *Regional Network:* Florida's Radio Networks
Arbitron Metro Market: Fort Pierce-Stuart-Vero Beach, FL
Format: News, News/Talk, 84, Talk *No. News Employees:* 2 *Target Audience:* 35 plus. *Adv. Rates:* 50 for :60— 40 for :30
Carol Wyatt, President

***WWFR**
01-01-1988; 91.7 mhz FM *Hrs Open:* 24; 2.65 kw; 499 ft.; N27 7 14 W80 23 59
Mailing Address: 4135 Northgate Blvd, Suite1, Sacramento, CA 95834 US
Second Address: 10400 NW 240th st, Okeechobee, FL 34973

(800) 543-1495
www.familyradio.com
info@familyradio.org
License: Stuart, Martin County, FL held by Family Stations Inc.
Group Owner: Family Stations Inc.
Nat'l Network: Family Radio
Arbitron Metro Market: Stuart, FL *Format:* Christian *Special Programming:* Pub affrs 2 hrs wkly *Hrs. of News Programming:* News progmg 11 hrs wkly *Target Audience:* General.
Ed Dearborn, Operations Dir

WAVW
12-24-1964; 92.7 mhz FM; 50 kw; 482 ft.; N27 16 29 W80 17 11
600 Congress Ave., Suite 1400, Austin, TX 78701 US
(772) 335-9300, *Fax:* (772) 335-3291
www.wavw.com
mikescott@clearchannel.com
License: Stuart, Martin County, FL held by Capstar TX L.P.
Group Owner: Clear Channel Communications Inc.; (acq 8-30-00; grpsl).
Arbitron Metro Market: Port St. Lucie, FL *Format:* Country
John Hunt, General Manager
Heath West, Programming Director
Mike Kerley, Chief Engineer
Mike Scott, Director of Sales
Erika Ewald, Digital Sales Manager
Chad Tyson, Webmaster

Summerland Key

WPIK
12-01-1991; 102.5 mhz FM *Hrs Open:* 24; 50 kw; 413 ft.; N24 40 36 W81 30 39
Mailing Address: P.O. Box 420249, Summerland Key, FL 33042 US
Second Address: 22500 Pieces of Eight Rd., Cudjoe Key, FL 33042
(305) 745-9988, *Fax:* (305) 745-4165
www.myradioritmo.com
info@myradioritmo.com
License: Summerland Key, Monroe County, FL held by Summerland Media LLC
Format: Ethnic
Lilliam Sierra, General Manager
Pepin Navarro, Programming Director

Sunrise

***WKPX**
02-14-1983; 88.5 mhz FM *Hrs Open:* 12; 3 kw; 98 ft.; N26 10 38 W80 15 23
8000 N.W. 44th Street, Sunrise, FL 33351 US
(754) 321-1000, *Fax:* (754) 321-1180
www.becon.tv
info@becon.tv
License: Sunrise, Broward County, FL held by School Board of Broward County.
Format: Alternative *Special Programming:* Black 3 hrs, blues 3 hrs wkly *Target Audience:* 15-35; people interested in alternative progmg
Pat Swank, Station Manager
Jim Sorensen, Chief Engineer

Sweetwater

WZAB
01-01-2008; 880 khz AM
85 East Harris Street, La Grange, IL 60525 US
(305) 503-1340, *Fax:* (305) 677-7585
www.880thebiz.com
License: Sweetwater, FL held by Florida City Radio.
Arbitron Metro Market: Sweetwater, FL *Format:* News/Talk, News
Tony Calatayud, General Manager

Tallahassee

WWOF(FM)
06-17-1976; 103.1 mhz FM *Hrs Open:* 24; 50 kw; 295 ft; N30 29 43 W84 13 51
Opus Broadcasting, 3000 Olson Rd., Tallahassee, FL 32308
(850) 386-8004, *Fax:* (850) 422-1897
www.1031thewolf.com
hkestenbaum@opusbroadcasting.com
License: Tallahassee, Leon County, FL held by Opus Broadcasting Tallahassee LLC.
Group Owner: Opus Media Holdings LLC; (acq 9-2-2005; grpsl)
Nat'l Reps: McGavren Guild
Population Served: 182,965 *Arbitron Metro Market:* Tallahassee, FL *Format:* Country *Target Audience:* 25-54.
Doug Purtee, Operations Dir
Hank Kestenbaum, General Manager

***WANM**
11-01-1976; 90.5 mhz FM *Hrs Open:* 24; 1.6 kw vert; 167 ft.; N30 25 49 W84 17 27
P. O. Box 6202, Tallahassee, FL 32314 US
(850) 599-3000, *Fax:* (850) 561-2829
www.famu.edu/famcast
info@wanm.com
License: Tallahassee, Leon County, FL held by The Board of Trustees of Florida A&M University.
Nat'l Network: AP Radio *Wire Services:* AP
Arbitron Metro Market: Tallahassee, FL *Format:* News, Sports *Special Programming:* Reggae 3 hrs wkly, Gospel 18 hrs wkly, Jazz 15 hrs wkly. *Hrs. of News Programming:* News progmg 5 hrs wkly *Target Audience:* General; urban African-American in area
Greg Bishop, Operations Dir
Keith Miles, General Manager

WBZE
07-15-1962; 98.9 mhz FM *Hrs Open:* 24; 99.2 kw; 604 ft.; N30 29 32 W84 17 2
111 East Kilbourn Ave., Suite 2700, Milwaukee, WI 53202 US
(850) 201-3000, *Fax:* (850) 561-8903
www.mystar98.com
john.dawson@cumulus.com
License: Tallahassee, Leon County, FL held by Cumulus Licensing Corp.
Group Owner: Cumulus Media Inc.
Nat'l Reps: Katz Radio
Arbitron Metro Market: Tallahassee, FL *Format:* Adult Contemp *Target Audience:* 25-54. *Adv. Rates:* 90; 75; 75; 50
John Dawson, Programming Director
Carl Anthony, Promotions Manager

WCVC
11-05-1953; 1330 khz AM *Hrs Open:* 6:30 AM-7 PM; 5 kw-D, NDD; N30 29 3 W84 17 13
117 1/2 Henderson Road, Tallahassee, FL 32312 US
(850) 386-1330
www.lordoflorida.com
alanmccal@hotmail.com
License: Tallahassee, FL held by WCVC Inc.
Arbitron Metro Market: Tallahassee, FL
Wendell Borrink, President
Erwin O'Conner, General Manager

***WFRF**
08-01-1974; 1070 khz AM *Hrs Open:* Sunrise-senset
Mailing Address: P.O. Box 7617, Tallahassee, FL 32314 US
Second Address: 4015 N. Monroe St., Tallahassee, FL 32303
(850) 201-1070, *Fax:* (850) 201-1071
www.faithradio.us
mailbox@faithradio.us
License: Tallahassee, FL held by Faith Radio Network Inc.
Arbitron Metro Market: Tallahassee, FL *Format:* Christian *Target Audience:* 12 plus.
Scott Beigle, General Manager

***WFSQ**
05-01-1954; 91.5 mhz FM *Hrs Open:* 24; 86 kw; 735 ft.; N30 21 31 W84 36 38
The Public Broadcast Cen, 1600 Red Barber Plaza, Tallahasse, FL 32310 US
(850) 487-3170, *Fax:* (850) 487-3093
www.wfsu.org
mail@wfsu.org
License: Tallahassee, Leon County, FL held by The Board of Regents of Florida acting for and on behalf of Florida State University.
Nat'l Network: NPR; PRI
Arbitron Metro Market: Tallahassee, FL *TV Affiliate:* WFSU TV *Format:* Talk *Hrs. of News Programming:* News progmg one hr wkly *Target Audience:* 35 plus; highly educated
Patrick Keating, General Manager
Caroline Austin, Station Manager
Cary Martin, Engineering Dir

***WFSU-FM**
10-14-1990; 88.9 mhz FM *Hrs Open:* 24; 90 kw; 1243 ft.; N30 40 13 W83 56 26
The Public B/Cast Center, 1600 Red Barber Plaza, Tallahassee, FL 32310 US
(850) 487-3086, *Fax:* (850) 487-2611
www.wfsu.org
License: Tallahassee, Leon County, FL held by The Board of Regents of Florida acting for and on behalf of Florida State University.
Nat'l Network: NPR; PRI *Regional Network:* Fla. Pub.
Arbitron Metro Market: Tallahassee, FL *Format:* News, News/Talk, 86 *Special Programming:* Jazz 8 hrs wkly *No. News Employees:* 9 *Target Audience:* 35-54; highly educated
Pat Keating, General Manager
Caroline Austin, Station Manager
Aron Meyers, Promotions Manager
Cary Martin, Engineering Dir

WGLF
12-01-1967; 104.1 mhz FM *Hrs Open:* 24; 100 kw; 1411 ft.; N30 27 4 W84 0 42
P.O. Box 14369, Tallahassee, FL 32317 US
(850) 201-3000, *Fax:* (850) 561-8903
www.gulf104.com
john.baker@cumulus.com
License: Tallahassee, Leon County, FL held by Cumulus Licensing Corp.
Group Owner: Cumulus Media Inc.; (acq 6-22-99; $4 million)
Nat'l Reps: Katz Radio
Arbitron Metro Market: Tallahassee, FL *Format:* Classic Rock, Rock/AOR *Target Audience:* 25-54. *Adv. Rates:* 75; 65; 60; 50
Barry Kaye, General Manager
John Baker, Programming Director
Carl Anthony, Promotions Manager
Carl Anthony, Marketing Director

WHBT
08-06-1959; 1410 khz AM *Hrs Open:* 24; 5 kw-D, ND1; 0.018 kw-N, ND1; N30 29 3 W84 17 13
111 East Kilbourn Ave., Suite 2700, Milwaukee, WI 53202 US
(850) 201-3000, *Fax:* (850) 561-8903
www.heaven1410.com
License: Tallahassee, FL held by Cumulus Licensing Corp.
Group Owner: Cumulus Media Inc.; (acq 10-28-97; grpsl)
Nat'l Reps: Katz Radio
Arbitron Metro Market: Tallahassee, FL *Format:* Gospel *Target Audience:* 18-54. *Adv. Rates:* 15; 15; 15; 15
Barry Kaye, General Manager
Peter Walkowiak, Chief Engineer

WHBX
06-28-1982; 96.1 mhz FM *Hrs Open:* 24; 37 kw; 479 ft.; N30 16 8 W84 16 32
111 East Kilbourn Ave., Suite 2700, Milwaukee, WI 53202 US
(850) 201-3000, *Fax:* (850) 561-8903
961jamz.com
License: Tallahassee, Leon County, FL held by Cumulus Licensing Corp.
Group Owner: Cumulus Media Inc.; (acq 10-28-97; grpsl)
Nat'l Reps: Katz Radio
Arbitron Metro Market: Tallahassee, FL *Format:* Urban Contemporary *Target Audience:* 25-54. *Adv. Rates:* 95; 90; 90; 50
Barry Kaye, General Manager
Joe Bullard, Programming Director

WNLS
10-15-1946; 1270 khz AM *Hrs Open:* 24
200 Concord Plaza, Suite 600, San Antonio, TX 78216 US
(850) 422-3107, *Fax:* (850) 383-0747
www.1270theteam.com
mattmillar@clearchannel.com
License: Tallahassee, FL held by Clear Channel Radio Licenses Inc.
Group Owner: Clear Channel Communications Inc.
Arbitron Metro Market: Tallahassee, FL *Format:* Sports *Hrs. of News Programming:* news progmg 25 hrs wkly *No. News Employees:* 1
Matt Millar, Programming Director
Jason Sauer, Promotions Manager
Sandra Lee, News Director

WTAL
01-01-1935; 1450 khz AM *Hrs Open:* 24
1820 E. Park Ave, Tallahassee, FL 32301 US
(850) 671-1450,(850) 877-0105, *Fax:* (850) 877-5110
www.wtal1450.com
wtaal@nettally.com
License: Tallahassee, FL held by Live Communications Inc.
Nat'l Network: CBS *Nat'l Reps:* Roslin
Arbitron Metro Market: Tallahassee, FL *Format:* Christian, News, 62, Talk *Hrs. of News Programming:* news progmg 21 hrs wkly *No. News Employees:* 4 *Target Audience:* 25-54; educated, intelligent, affluent,involved, conservative *Adv. Rates:* 15; 25; 20; 15
Dr. R.B. Holmes Jr., CEO
Richard Henderson, General Manager

WTNT-FM
07-24-1967; 94.9 mhz FM; 98 kw; 840 ft.; N30 34 42 W84 15 48
200 Concord Plaza, Suite 600, San Antonio, TX 78216 US
(850) 422-3107, *Fax:* (850) 383-0747
www.wtntfm.com
jeff@949tnt.com

License: Tallahassee, Leon County, FL held by Clear Channel Radio Licenses Inc.
Group Owner: Clear Channel Communications Inc.; (acq 11-21-97; grpsl)
Nat'l Reps: Christal
Arbitron Metro Market: Tallahassee, FL *Format:* Country *Hrs. of News Programming:* News progmg one hr wkly *Target Audience:* 25-54.
Lisa Rice, General Manager
Jeff Horn, Programming Director
Jason Taylor, Promotions Manager
Sandra Lee, News Director
Randy Moore, Engineering Dir

***WVFS**
09-01-1987; 89.7 mhz FM *Hrs Open:* 24; 7 kw vert; 180 ft.; N30 26 22 W84 17 29
420 Diffenbaugh Hall, Tallahassee, FL 32306 US
(850) 644-9692, *Fax:* (850) 644-8753
www.wvfs.fsu.edu
wvfs@wvfs.fsu.edu
License: Tallahassee, Leon County, FL held by Florida State University.
Arbitron Metro Market: Tallahassee, FL *Format:* Alternative *Special Programming:* Black 8 hrs, folk 3 hrs, Sp 2 hrs wkly *Hrs. of News Programming:* News progmg 2 hrs wkly *Target Audience:* General.
Misha Laurents, Ph.D., General Manager
Misha.H.Laurents, Programming Director

WQTL
05-01-1992; 106.1 mhz FM *Hrs Open:* 24; 2.25 kw; 543 ft.; N30 29 39 W84 14 0
111 East Kilbourn Ave., Suite 2700, Milwaukee, WI 53202 US
(850) 386-8004, *Fax:* (850) 422-1897
www.1061thepath.com
hkestenbaum@opusbroadcasting.com
License: Tallahassee, Leon County, FL held by Opus Broadcasting Tallahassee LLC.
Group Owner: Opus Media Holdings LLC; (acq 9-2-2005;. grpsl)
Arbitron Metro Market: Tallahassee, FL *Format:* Rock/AOR *Target Audience:* 18-49.
Hank Kestenbaum, Operations Dir
Doug Purtee, Operations Manager

Tampa

WMTX
11-01-1947; 100.7 mhz FM *Hrs Open:* 24; 96 kw; 1549 ft.; N27 49 9.7 W82 15 38.7
50 E. Rivercenter Blvd., 12th Floor, Covington, KY 41011 US
(813) 832-1000, *Fax:* (813) 832-1090
www.tampabaysmix.com
License: Tampa, Hillsborough County, FL held by Citicasters Licenses L.P.
Group Owner: Clear Channel Communications Inc.
Nat'l Network: Premiere Radio Networks *Nat'l Reps:* Katz Radio *Wire Services:* AP
Arbitron Metro Market: Tampa, FL *Format:* Adult Contemp
Russell Link, CFO
Dan DiLoreto, Operations Dir
Chris Soechtig, General Sales Mgr
Randi West, Programming Director
Rebecca Kaplan, Promotions Manager
Sandra Ambrosino, News Director
John McMartin, Chief Engineer
Doug Hamand,Operations Manager
Josh Jensen, Creative Services Director

WAMA
01-01-1961; 1550 khz AM *Hrs Open:* 24; 10 kw-D, ND1; 0.133 kw-N, ND1; N27 55 16 W82 23 41
2000 North 14th Street, Suite 400, Arlington, VA 22201 US
(813) 319-1550, *Fax:* (813) 289-1554
www.holaciudad.com/tampa/home.html
trafficlainvasora@gmail.com
License: Tampa, FL held by WAMA Inc.
Nat'l Reps: Univision Radio National Sales *Wire Services:* UPI
Arbitron Metro Market: Tampa, FL *Format:* Tejano *No. News Employees:* 1 *Target Audience:* 25-54; Hispanic Adults *Adv. Rates:* 70; 60; 65; 45
Ron Gordon, Chairman
Norberto Vallejo, President

***WBVM**
05-27-1986; 90.5 mhz FM *Hrs Open:* 24; 77 kw horiz, 74.7 kw vert; 965 ft.; N27 50 50.4 W82 15 50.1
Mailing Address: P.O. Box 18081, Tampa, FL 33679 US
Second Address: 3816 Morrison Ave., Tampa, FL 33629
(813) 289-8040, *Fax:* (813) 282-3580
www.spiritfm905.com
contact@spiritfm905.com
License: Tampa, Hillsborough County, FL held by The Bishop of the Diocese of St. Petersburg.
Arbitron Metro Market: Tampa, FL *Format:* Christian *Special Programming:* Black 4 hrs, children 4 hrs, Sp 4 hrs wkly *Target Audience:* 35 plus; families
John Morris, Operations Dir
Abby, Promotions Manager
Chris Sampson, Operations Manager

WHNZ
05-15-1922; 1250 khz AM
4002 Gandy Blvd., Tampa, FL 33611 US
(813) 832-1000, *Fax:* (813) 832-1090
www.whnz.com
License: Tampa, FL held by Citicasters Licenses L.P.
Group Owner: Clear Channel Communications Inc.; (acq 5-4-99; grpsl)
Nat'l Reps: Katz Radio
Arbitron Metro Market: Tampa, FL *Format:* News, News/Talk, 86 *Target Audience:* 25-54.
Russell Link, CFO
Dan DiLorette, Operations Dir
Chris Soechtig, General Sales Mgr
Steve Versnick, Programming Director
Greg Wolf, Promotions Manager
Misty Pittman, News Director
John McMartin, Chief Engineer
Mike Baker,Webmaster

WFLA
01-01-1924; 970 khz AM; 25 kw-D, DA2; 11 kw-N, DA2; N28 1 14 W82 36 34
200 Concord Plaza, Suite 600, San Antonio, TX 78216 US
(813) 832-1000, *Fax:* (813) 832-1090
www.970wfla.com
License: Tampa, FL held by Citicasters Licenses L.P.
Group Owner: Clear Channel Communications Inc.; (acq 5-4-99; grpsl).
Nat'l Network: Fox News Radio *Nat'l Reps:* Katz Radio *Wire Services:* AP
Arbitron Metro Market: Tampa-St. Petersburg-Clearwater, FLsburg-Clearwate *Format:* News, News/Talk, 86 *Special Programming:* home imporvement, gardening 4 hrs wkly *Hrs. of News Programming:* news progrmg 28 hrs wkly*No. News Employees:* 5 *Target Audience:* 25-54.
Russell Link, CFO
Dan Diloreto, Operations Dir
Dan Deloreto, General Manager
Mark Warlaumont, General Sales Mgr
Steve Vernick, Programming Director
Greg Wolf, Promotions Manager
Steve Hall, News Director
John McMartin, ChiefEngineer
Kristy Knight, Production Director
Phil Azoon, Creative Services Director
Ethan Youker, Public Service Director
Ryan Lang, Webmaster
Rachhel Pitts, Internship Director

WFLZ-FM
01-01-1948; 93.3 mhz FM; 97 kw; 1549 ft.; N27 49 9.7 W82 15 38.7
50 East Rivercenter Blvd, Suite 1200, Covington, KY 41011 US
(813) 839-9393, *Fax:* (813) 831-4475
www.933flz.com
License: Tampa, Hillsborough County, FL
Nat'l Reps: Katz Radio *Wire Services:* AP
Arbitron Metro Market: Tampa-St. Petersburg-Clearwater, FL *Format:* Contemporary Hits/Top 40 *Target Audience:* 18-34.
Russell Link, CFO
Doug Hamand, Operations Dir
Dan Diloreto, General Manager
Chris Soechtig, General Sales Mgr
Tommy Chuck, Programming Director
Misty Pittman, News Director
John McMartin, Chief Engineer

***WMNF**
09-14-1979; 88.5 mhz FM *Hrs Open:* 24; 70 kw; 1550 feet; N27 49 04 W82 14 31
1210 E. Martin Luther King Jr. Blvd., Tampa, FL 33603
(813) 238-8001
www.wmnf.org
wmnf@wmnf.org
License: Tampa, Hillsborough County, FL held by The Nathan B. Stubblefield Foundation.
Nat'l Network: NPR
Population Served: 2,800,000 *Arbitron Metro Market:* Tampa-St. Peter *Hrs. of News Programming:* news progmg 24 hrs wkly *No. News Employees:* 3 *Target Audience:* General.
Sheila Cowley, Operations Dir
Dr. Sydney White, Station Manager
Randy Wynne, Programming Director
Bill Brown, Chief Engineer

WRBQ-FM
01-01-1954; 104.7 mhz FM; 99 kw; 571 ft.; N27 55 53.8 W82 24 4.6
200 Concord Plaza, Suite 600, San Antonio, TX 78216 US
(813) 287-1047, *Fax:* (813) 637-7908
www.tampabaysq105.com
License: Tampa, Hillsborough County, FL held by Infinity Radio Inc.
Group Owner: CBS Radio; (acq 5-99).
Arbitron Metro Market: Tampa-St. Petersburg-Clearwater, FL *Format:* Oldies *Target Audience:* 18-49.
Charlie Ochs, General Manager
Mason Dixon, Programming Director

WTIS
01-01-1946; 1110 khz AM; 10 kw-D, DAD; N27 52 26 W82 37 53
311 112th Ave., N.E., St Petersburg, FL 33716 US
(727) 576-1110, *Fax:* (727) 578-1110
wtis1110.com
operations@wtis1110.comm
License: Tampa, FL held by WTIS-AM Inc.
Arbitron Metro Market: St. Petersburg, FL *Format:* Ethnic, Religious *Special Programming:* Sp one hr wkly *Target Audience:* 25-54.
Ron Roseman, President
Tom Connolly, Operations/Program Director
Mike Smith, General Manager
Pete O'Shea, Promotions Manager
Ed Roseman, Executive Vice President
Joe Sparra, Sales Executive
Jodi Long, Sales Executive
DeborahRay Roseman, Executive

***WUSF**
09-01-1963; 89.7 mhz FM *Hrs Open:* 24; 71 kw; 942 ft.; N27 50 53 W82 15 48
4202 East Fowler Ave, Tampa, FL 33620 US
(813) 974-8700, *Fax:* (813) 974-5016
www.wusf.org
info@wusf.org
License: Tampa, Hillsborough County, FL held by Board of Trustees, University of South Florida.
Nat'l Network: NPR; PRI *Regional Network:* Fla. Pub. *Wire Services:* AP
Arbitron Metro Market: Tampa, FL *TV Affiliate:* *WUSF-TV affil *Format:* Jazz, News *Hrs. of News Programming:* news progmg 38 hrs wkly *No. News Employees:* 8 *Target Audience:* General.
Jo Ann Urofsky, General Manager
Tom Dollenmayer, Station Manager
Scot Kaufman, General Sales Mgr
Scott Finn, News Director
Gregory Forget, Director of Engineering & Operations
Cathy Coccia, Development Director
Patrick Morris,Special Projects Manager
Patricia J. Hickok, Member Services Director

WWRM
01-01-1958; 94.9 mhz FM *Hrs Open:* 24; 97.3 kw; 1542 ft.; N27 49 10 W82 15 39
877 Executive Ctr W., Suite 300, St. Petersburg, FL 33702 US
(727) 579-2000, *Fax:* (727) 579-2271
www.949online.com
info@coxradio.com
License: Tampa, Hillsborough County, FL held by Cox Radio Inc.
Group Owner: Cox Radio Inc.; (acq 7-1-88).
Nat'l Reps: Christal
Arbitron Metro Market: Tampa, FL *Format:* Adult Contemp *Target Audience:* 25-54.
Tom Paleveda, Operations Dir
Howard Tuuri, General Manager
Mary Rogers, General Sales Mgr
John Larson, Programming Director
Julia Freeman, Promotions Manager
Jodi Rainey, National Sales Manager
Keith Lawless, Vice President andMarket Manager

Tarpon Springs

***WYFE**
06-14-1988; 88.9 mhz FM; 60 kw; 449 ft.; N28 22 39 W82 40 25
8030 Arrowridge Blvd., Charlotte, NC 28273 US
(704) 523-5555, *Fax:* (704) 522-1967
www.bbnradio.org
bbn@bbnradio.org
License: Tarpon Springs, Pinellas County, FL held by Bible Broadcasting Network Inc.
Group Owner: Bible Broadcasting Network; acq 8-11-89)

Arbitron Metro Market: Tarpon Springs, FL *Format:* Religious *Target Audience:* General; Christians
Lowell Davey, President
Jack Long, General Manager

Tavares

WXXL

02-12-1969; 106.7 mhz FM *Hrs Open:* 24; 100 kw; 823 ft.; N28 33 31 W81 35 38
337 S. Northlake Blvd., Suite 1024, Altamonte Springs, FL 32701 US
(407) 916-7800, *Fax:* (407) 916-7510
www.wxxl.com
info@wxxl.com
License: Tavares, Lake County, FL held by AMFM Radio Licenses L.L.C.
Group Owner: Clear Channel Communications Inc.; (acq 8-30-00; grpsl)
Arbitron Metro Market: Orlando, FL *Format:* Contemporary Hits/Top 40 *Special Programming:* Alternative 6 hrs wkly *No. News Employees:* 1 *Target Audience:* 18-49; general *Adv. Rates:* 350.;200.;260.;125.
Linda Byrd, Operations Dir
Shannon Fraser, General Sales Mgr
Jordan, Programming Director
Glory Adona-Langston, Promotions Manager
Donna Carmichael, News Director
Jana, Assistant Program/Music Director

Tavernier

WKEZ-FM

01-01-1999; 96.9 mhz FM; 25 kw; 223 ft.; N25 1 35 W80 30 30
200 Concord Plaza, Suite 600, San Antonio, TX 78216 US
(305) 852-9085, *Fax:* (305) 852-5586
www.easy969.com
License: Tavernier, Monroe County, FL held by Aloha Station Trust LLC, as Trustee
Format: Easy Listening
Scott Hamilton, Operations Dir
Mark Mills, Station Manager
Greg Capgna, Promotions Manager

Temple Terrace

WQBN

01-01-1956; 1300 khz AM *Hrs Open:* 6 AM-midnight
Mailing Address: PO Box 151300, Tampa, FL 33684 US
Second Address: 5203 N. Armenia Ave., Tampa, FL 33603
(813) 871-1333, *Fax:* (813) 876-1333
www.superq1300am.com
superq1300@hotmail.com
License: Temple Terrace, FL held by Radio Tropical Inc.
Arbitron Metro Market: Tampa-St. Petersburg-Clearwater, FL *Format:* Tejano, Variety/Diverse *Hrs. of News Programming:* news progmg 20 hrs wkly *No. News Employees:* 3 *Target Audience:* 25 plus; Hispanics
Efrain Archilla, President
Marc Vila, Operations Dir

Tequesta

WEFL

08-01-2002; 760 khz AM *Hrs Open:* 24
P.O. Box 1635, Tacoma, WA 98401 US
(519) 832-9800, *Fax:* (519) 371-4242
www.98thebeach.ca
License: Tequesta, FL held by Good Karma Broadcasting L.L.C.
Group Owner: Good Karma Broadcasting L.L.C.; (acq 1-3-2006; $2.8 million)
Nat'l Network: ESPN Radio; Westwood One
Arbitron Metro Market: Bryan-College Station TX *Format:* Adult Contemp *Target Audience:* 18-54.
Ross Kentner, General Manager
Rob Brignell, General Sales Mgr
Don Vail, Programming Director
John Divinski, News Director

Tice

WJGO

03-01-2000; 102.9 mhz FM; 96 kw; 466 ft.; N26 29 16 W81 55 46
1766 Marlyn Rd., Fort Myers, FL 33901 US
(239) 495-8383, *Fax:* (239) 495-0883
www.1029bobfm.com
webguy@1029bobfm.com
License: Tice, Lee County, FL held by Renda Broadcasting Corp. of Nevada.
Group Owner: Renda Broadcasting Corp.; (acq 10-5-2000; $7 million)
Arbitron Metro Market: Fort Myers, FL *Format:* Adult Contemp
Roger Harris, General Manager
Randy Savage, Programming Director
Buzzy Ford, Promotions Manager

Titusville

WIXC

11-20-1957; 1060 khz AM *Hrs Open:* 24
3909 Champion Road, Titusville, FL 32796 US
(813) 281-1040, *Fax:* (321) 264-4246
www.newstalkflorida.com
contactus@radiogenesis.com
License: Titusville, FL held by Genesis Communications I Inc.
Group Owner: Genesis Communications Inc.; (acq 4-19-2000; $650,000)
Arbitron Metro Market: Titusville, FL *Format:* News, News/Talk, 86 *Target Audience:* 35 plus.
Bruce Maouri, CEO
Kevin Fennessy, General Manager
Steve Potter, General Sales Mgr
Greg Sherlock, News Director
Jerry Smith, Chief Engineer

*WPIO

10-19-1975; 89.3 mhz FM; 7.1 kw; 335 ft.; N28 34 49 W80 51 0
505 Josephine Street, Titusville, FL 32796 US
(321) 267-3000, *Fax:* (321) 264-9370
www.noncomradio.net
License: Titusville, Brevard County, FL held by Florida Public Radio Inc.
Format: Religious
Randy Henry, President

Trenton

WLVW(FM)

02-01-1988; 101.7 mhz FM *Hrs Open:* 24; 3 kw; 328 ft; N29 36 40 W82 51 14
100 NW 76th Dr., Suite 2, Gainesville, FL 32607
(352) 313-3150, *Fax:* (352) 313-3166
www.pulse1017fm.com
kevin.mangan@marcradio.com
License: Trenton, Gilchrist County, FL held by 6 Johnson Road Licenses Inc.
Group Owner: Pamal Broadcasting Ltd.; (acq 1-5-2007; grpsl)
Population Served: 181,843 *Arbitron Metro Market:* Gainesville-Ocala, FL *Format:* Country *Special Programming:* Farm 2 hrs wkly *Hrs. of News Programming:* News progmg 7 hrs wkly *Target Audience:* 25 plus;working class & professionals
Shawn Portmann, Sales Manager
Kevin Mangan, Programming Director

Union Park

*WPOZ

08-09-1995; 88.3 mhz FM *Hrs Open:* 24; 13 kw; 1333 ft.; N28 36 7 W81 5 37
P O Box 60883, Orlando, FL 32871 US
(407) 869-8000, *Fax:* (407) 869-0380
www.zradio.org
zcrew@zradio.org
License: Union Park, Orange County, FL held by Central Florida Educational Foundation Inc.
Arbitron Metro Market: Orlando, FL *Format:* Christian *Target Audience:* 25-44.
James Hoge, President

Venice

WDDV

02-01-1960; 1320 khz AM
50 East Rivercenter Blvd, Suite 1200, Covington, KY 41011 US
(941) 552-4800, *Fax:* (941) 552-4900
www.doveradio.com
webmaster@doveradio.com
License: Venice, FL held by Citicasters Licenses L.P.
Group Owner: Clear Channel Communications Inc.; (acq 5-4-99; grpsl).
Arbitron Metro Market: Venice, FL *Format:* Adult Contemp *Target Audience:* 25-54; active, upscale, affluent
JJ Paone, Promotions Manager

WLTQ-FM

03-01-1974; 92.1 mhz FM *Hrs Open:* 24; 11.5 kw; 476 ft.; N27 9 3 W82 27 51
50 East Rivercenter Blvd, Suite 1200, Covington, KY 41011 US
(941)552-4800, *Fax:* (941) 552-4900
www.921thecoast.com
eddierupp@clearchannel.com
License: Venice, Sarasota County, FL
Group Owner: Clear Channel Communications Inc.
Arbitron Metro Market: Sarasota, FL *Format:* Oldies, Classic Rock *Target Audience:* 25-54; female
Randy Wanek, General Sales Mgr
Jeff Lynn, Programming Director
Joanne Jelinek, News Director
Bryan Kelly, Director of Sales

Vero Beach

WZTA

05-01-1954; 1370 khz AM; 1 kw-D, ND1; 0.074 kw-N, ND1; N27 36 1 W80 23 33
600 Congress Ave., Suite 1400, Austin, TX 78701 US
(325) 673-3045, *Fax:* (325) 672-7938
www.kgnz.com
studio@kgnz.com
License: Vero Beach, FL held by Capstar TX L.P.
Group Owner: Clear Channel Communications Inc.; (acq 8-30-2000; grpsl).
Arbitron Metro Market: San Angelo TX *Format:* Christian
Gary Hill, General Manager

WCZR

05-29-1986; 101.7 mhz FM; 4.2 kw; 394 ft.; N27 44 7 W80 27 27
600 Congress Ave., Suite 1400, Austin, TX 78701 US
(450) 243-6285, *Fax:* (450) 243-1041
www.sunnymead.org/cidi
deweydurrell@axion.ca
License: Vero Beach, Indian River County, FL held by Aloha Station Trust LLC
Arbitron Metro Market: Redding CA *Format:* Talk *Hrs. of News Programming:* news progmg 21 hrs wkly *No. News Employees:* 3 *Target Audience:* 18-60.
Lana Littlechief, General Manager

WGYL

11-01-1970; 93.7 mhz FM; 50 kw; 479 ft.; N27 36 4 W80 23 33
2201 Old Court Road, Baltimore, MD 21208 US
(772) 567-0937, *Fax:* (772) 562-4747
www.wgylfm.com
jimd@wgylfm.com
License: Vero Beach, Indian River County, FL
Group Owner: Vero Beach Broadcasters LLC
Arbitron Metro Market: Fort Pierce-Stuart-Vero Beach, FL *Format:* Adult Contemp, Jazz, 80 *Target Audience:* 35-64; upscale adult
Jim Davis, Operations Dir
Jim Davis, General Manager
Karen Franke, Station Manager
Karen Franke, General Sales Mgr
Hamp Elliott, Programming Director
Jason Carr, Promotions Manager
Ballard Fore, Engineering Dir

WJKD

01-01-1995; 99.7 mhz FM; 50 kw; 440 ft.; N27 44 7 W80 27 27
Fletcher Heald &Hildreth, 1300 N 17th St, 11th Fl, Arlington, VA 22209 US
(772) 567-0937, *Fax:* (772) 562-4747
www.997jackfm.com
jack@997jackfm.com
License: Vero Beach, Indian River County, FL held by Vero Beach FM Radio Partnership.
Group Owner: Vero Beach Broadcasters LLC; (acq 2-11-2002).
Arbitron Metro Market: Fort Pierce-Stuart-Vero Beach, FL
Format: Adult Contemp
Jim Davis, General Manager

WQOL

09-01-1979; 103.7 mhz FM; 50 kw; 476 ft.; N27 44 7 W80 27 27
600 Congress Ave., Suite 1400, Austin, TX 78701 US
(772) 335-9300, *Fax:* (772) 335-3291
www.wqolfm.com
License: Vero Beach, Indian River County, FL held by Capstar TX L.P.
Group Owner: Clear Channel Communications Inc.; (acq 8-30-00; grpsl).
Nat'l Network: Westwood One
Arbitron Metro Market: Fort Pierce-Stu *Format:* Oldies *Target Audience:* 35-64; baby boomers
Mike Michaels, Operations Dir
Heath West, Programming Director
Mike Kerley, Engineering Dir

*WSCF-FM

02-01-1990; 91.9 mhz FM *Hrs Open:* 24; 15.5 kw; 305 ft.; N27 38 10 W80 27 59
6767 20th Street, Vero Beach, FL 32966 US
(772) 569-0919, *Fax:* (772) 562-4892
www.wscf.com
License: Vero Beach, Indian River County, FL held by Central Educational Broadcasting Inc.

Nat'l Network: USA
Arbitron Metro Market: Fort Pierce-Stu *Format:* Religious
Jon Hamilton, General Manager
Brad Bacon, General Sales Mgr
Paul Tipton, Programming Director
Bruce Douglas, News Director

WTTB
06-07-1954; 1490 khz AM; 1 kw-U, ND1; N27 37 12 W80 25 1
2201 Old Court Road, Baltimore, MD 21208 US
(772) 569-8367, *Fax:* (772) 562-4747
www.wttbam.com
License: Vero Beach, FL held by Vero Beach Broadcasters LLC
Group Owner: Vero Beach Broadcasters LLC; acq 6-19-00; $5.15 million with co-located FM).
Nat'l Network: ABC *Regional Network:* Florida's Radio Networks
Arbitron Metro Market: Vero Beach, FL *Format:* Talk *Target Audience:* General.
Jim Davis, General Manager
Karen Franke, Station Manager
Jason Carr, Promotions Manager
Ballard Fore, Engineering Dir

Watertown

WQLC
10-06-1990; 102.1 mhz FM; 9 kw; 531 ft.; N30 13 58 W82 48 18
3821 Cove Drive, Birmingham, AL 35213 US
(386) 755-4102, *Fax:* (386) 752-9861
www.powercountry102.com
bandk@ISgroup.net
License: Watertown, Columbia County, FL held by Power Country Inc.
Format: Country *Special Programming:* Gospel 4 hrs wkly
Target Audience: 18-54.
Louis Bolton II, President
Bob Hendrickson, General Manager

Wauchula

WAUC
01-07-1958; 1310 khz AM *Hrs Open:* 6 AM-midnight; 5 kw-D, DA2; 0.5 kw-N, DA2; N27 31 48 W81 49 8
Mailing Address: 1310 South Florida Avenue, Wauchula, FL 33873 US
Second Address: 1310 S. Florida Ave., Wauchula, FL 33873
(863) 773-9282(863) 773-5008(813) 773-5088, *Fax:* (863) 773-2032
wauc.radiostation@earthlink.net
License: Wauchula, FL held by Dora A. Cruz.
Regional Network: Florida's Radio Networks
Arbitron Metro Market: Grand Junction, CO *Format:* Tejano
Target Audience: 35-54.
Robert Ayala, General Manager

Wellington

WKGR
05-01-1961; 98.7 mhz FM; 100 kw; 981 ft.; N27 1 31 W80 10 43
200 Concord Plaza, Suite 600, San Antonio, TX 78216 US
(561) 616-6600, *Fax:* (561) 616-6677
www.gater.com
info@gator.com
License: Wellington, St. Lucie County, FL held by Clear Channel Radio Licenses Inc.
Group Owner: Clear Channel Communications Inc.; (acq 9-16-97; grpsl)
Arbitron Metro Market: West Palm Beach-Boca Raton, FL
Format: Classic Rock *Target Audience:* 25-54.
Dave Denver, Operations Dir
John Hunt, General Manager
Roger Koch, General Sales Mgr

West Palm Beach

***WAYF**
11-11-1993; 88.1 mhz FM *Hrs Open:* 24; 0.05 kw horiz, 50 kw vert; 1053 ft.; N26 35 20 W80 12 44
P.O. Box 061275, Fort Meyers, FL 33906 US
(307) 745-5208, *Fax:* (307) 745-8570
mix967@fiberpipe.net
License: West Palm Beach, Palm Beach County, FL held by WAY-FM Media Group Inc.
Group Owner: WAY-FM Media Group Inc.
Arbitron Metro Market: Medicine Bow WY *Format:* Classic Rock
Steven Silberberg, President
Jim O'Reilly, General Manager

WJNO
07-15-1947; 1290 khz AM
200 Concord Plaza, Suite 600, San Antonio, TX 78216 US
(561) 616-6600, *Fax:* (561) 616-6677
www.wjno.com
mikescott@clearchannel.com
License: West Palm Beach, FL held by Clear Channel Radio Licenses Inc.
Group Owner: Clear Channel Communications Inc.; (acq 9-16-97; grpsl)
Nat'l Reps: Clear Channel
Arbitron Metro Market: West Palm Beach, FL *Format:* News, News/Talk, 84, Talk *Target Audience:* Adults; 25-64
Dave Denver, Operations Dir
John Hunt, General Manager
Mike Scott, Director of Sales
Brian Mudd, Programming Director
Jim Leifer, Chief Engineer
Erika Ewald, Digital Sales Manager
Chad Tyson, Webmaster

WFTL
01-01-1948; 850 khz AM *Hrs Open:* 24; 50 kw-D, 24 kw-N, DA-2; N26 32 30 W80 44 30
2100 Park Central Blvd, Suite 100, Fort Lauderdale, FL 22203
(954) 315-1515, *Fax:* (954) 315-1555
www.850wftl.com
info@850wftl.com
License: West Palm Beach, Palm Beach County, FL held by JCE Licenses L.L.C.
Group Owner: James Crystal Inc.; (acq 5-15-98; $1.5 million).
Nat'l Network: ABC; NBC *Nat'l Reps:* Steve Lapa *Regional Reps:* Andrew Herbert; Scott Courant; Linda Stein
Arbitron Metro Market: West Palm Beach-Boca Raton, FL *Target Audience:* 35 plus.
Rick Hindes, CFO
James Hilliard, President
Brennan Forsythe, Operations Dir
Steve Lapa, General Manager
Tim Reever, General Sales Mgr
Tony Hernandez, Promotions Manager
Dave McBride, News Director
Matt Greeney, EngineeringDir
Rick Rieke, Chief Engineer

WEAT
08-30-1969; 107.9 mhz FM; 100 kw; 427 ft.; N26 45 47 W80 12 19
600 New Hampshire Avenue, N.W., Suite 1200, Washington, DC 20037 US
(561) 616-4777, *Fax:* (561) 686-0157(561) 686-4043
www.sunny1043.com
jeff.greenwald@palmbeach-broadcasting.com
License: West Palm Beach, Palm Beach County, FL held by CBS Radio Inc.
Group Owner: CBS Radio; (acq 11-13-98; grpsl).
Nat'l Reps: Katz Radio
Arbitron Metro Market: West Palm Beach, FL *Format:* Adult Contemp *Target Audience:* 25-54.
Lee Strasser, Operations Dir

WBZT
07-31-1936; 1230 khz AM *Hrs Open:* 24; 1 kw-U, ND1; 0.8 kw-U, ND1; N26 45 33 W80 8 40; N26 15 18 W80 8 49
4401 S. Ocean Blvd., Suite 7, Highland Beach, FL 33487 US
(561) 616-6600, *Fax:* (561) 616-6677
www.wbzt.com
info@wbzt.com
License: West Palm Beach, FL held by Capstar TX L.P.
Group Owner: Clear Channel Communications Inc.; (acq 9-27-00; grpsl).
Arbitron Metro Market: West Palm Beach-Boca Raton, FL
Format: Talk
John Hunt, General Manager

WRLX
12-13-1975; 92.1 mhz FM; 7.2 kw; 499 ft.; N26 47 58 W80 4 33
4401 S. Ocean Blvd., Suite 7, Highland Beach, FL 33487 US
(561) 616-6600, *Fax:* (561) 616-6677
www.mia921.com
info@mia921.com
License: West Palm Beach, Palm Beach County, FL held by Clear Channel Broadcasting Licenses
Group Owner: Clear Channel Communications Inc.; (acq 9-27-2000; grpsl)
Nat'l Reps: Clear Channel
Arbitron Metro Market: West Palm Beach-Boca Raton, FL
Dave Denver, Operations Dir
John Hunt, General Manager

***WPBI(FM)**
11-24-1969; 90.7 mhz FM *Hrs Open:* 24; 38 kw; Ant 1,115 ft; N26 35 20 W80 12 44
Mailing Address: Box 6607, West Palm Beach, FL 33405
Second Address: 3401 S. Congress Ave., Boynton Beach, FL 33426
(561) 737-8000, *Fax:* (561) 369-3067
www.wxel.org
info@wxel.org
License: West Palm Beach, Palm Beach County, FL held by Barry Telecommunications Inc.
Nat'l Network: NPR *Regional Network:* Fla. Pub. *Wire Services:* AP
Population Served: 101,043 *Arbitron Metro Market:* West Palm Beach, FL *Format:* News *No. News Employees:* 7 *Target Audience:* 35 plus; career oriented (news & info)
Sr. Linda Bevilacqua, Chairman
Jerry Carr, CEO
Joanna Marie, Operations Dir
Bernard Henneberg, CFO

WAXY-FM
104.3 mhz FM; 100 kw; 1273 ft.; N26 34 37 W80 14 32
600 New Hampshire Ave., N.W., Suite 1200, Washington, DC 20037 US
(305)521-5100, *Fax:* (305)521-1416
www.theticketmiami.com
tod.castleberry@lincolnfinancialmedia.com
License: West Palm Beach, Palm Beach County, FL
Group Owner: CBS Radio Stations Inc.

Tod Castleberry, Programming Director
Rick Malette, Market Controller
Von Freeman, Director of Marketing

White City

WFLM
12-01-1993; 104.7 mhz FM *Hrs Open:* 24; 17.5 kw; 390 ft.; N27 26 8 W80 22 40
6803 South Federal Hwy., Port St. Lucie, FL 34952 US
(772) 460-9356, *Fax:* (772) 460-2700
www.wflm.cc
info@wflm.cc, requests@wflm.cc
License: White City, St. Lucie County, FL held by Midway Broadcasting Co.
Arbitron Metro Market: Fort Pierce-Stuart-Vero Beach, FLart-Vero Beach, F *Format:* Blues *Special Programming:* Gospel 20 hrs, jazz 4 hrs, reggae 4 hrs wkly *Target Audience:* 18-54.
Alice Lee, President

Wildwood

WVLG
09-01-1987; 640 khz AM *Hrs Open:* 6 AM-midnight; 930 w-D, 860 w-N; N28 54 16 W81 57 36
1161 Main St., The Villages, FL 34785
(352) 753-1119, *Fax:* (352) 259-4819
thevillagesdailysun.com/wvlg/WVLG.html
License: Wildwood, Sumter County, FL held by Senior Broadcasting Corp.
Regional Network: Southeast AgNet
Arbitron Metro Market: Gainesville-Ocala, FL *Target Audience:* 18 plus; general
Frank Messing, Operations Dir
Rob Newton, General Manager
Ed Newlands, Station Manager
Laurie Shaw, General Sales Mgr
Ed Newlands, Programming Director
Rob Newton, Promotions Manager

Williston

WTMG
07-01-1983; 101.3 mhz FM *Hrs Open:* 24; 3.5 kw; 433 ft.; N29 25 4 W82 32 58
249 University Avenue, Suite B, Gainesville, FL 32601 US
(352) 313-3150, *Fax:* (352) 313-3166
www.magic1013.com
rallen@marcradio.com
License: Williston, Levy County, FL held by 6 Johnson Road Licenses Inc.
Group Owner: Pamal Broadcasting Ltd.; (acq 1-5-2007; grpsl)
Arbitron Metro Market: Gainesville, FL *Format:* Adult Contemp
Hrs. of News Programming: news progmg 2 hrs wkly *No. News Employees:* 1
Shawn Portmann, President
Benjamin Hill, General Manager
Russ Allen, Programming,Music & Promotion Director
Max Sitero, Chief Engineer
Keith Feeney, Business/ Finance
DJ Terrah, Mix Show Director

Wilton Manors

WEXY
06-01-1963; 1520 khz AM
412 W Oakland Park Blvd., Ft. Lauderdale, FL 33311 US
(954) 561-1520, *Fax:* (954) 561-9830
License: Wilton Manors, FL held by Multicultural Radio Broadcasting Licensee LLC.
Group Owner: Multicultural Radio Broadcasting Inc.; (acq 4-4-03; $2.75 million).
Nat'l Network: American Urban
Arbitron Metro Market: Wilton Manors, FL *Format:* Gospel
Arthur Liu, CEO
Jim Glogowski, Operations Dir
Eduardo Ruedo, General Manager
Doug DeVos, Operations Manager

Winter Garden

WLAA
01-01-1958; 1600 khz AM
8263 Conroy Windmere Rd, Orlando, FL 32801 US
(407) 296-4747, *Fax:* (407) 293-2870
License: Winter Garden, FL held by Rama Communications Inc.
Group Owner: Rama Communications Inc.; (acq 10-13-93; $950,000 with WMEL(AM) Cocoa Beach;
Arbitron Metro Market: Orlando, FL *TV Affiliate:* Sp

WOKB
02-22-2000; 1680 khz AM
PO Box 680889, Orlando, FL 32868 US
(407) 291-1395, *Fax:* (407) 293-2870
www.wokbradio.com
info@wokbradio.com
License: Winter Garden, FL held by Rama Communications Inc.
Group Owner: Rama Communications Inc.
Arbitron Metro Market: Orlando, FL *Format:* Gospel, Talk *Target Audience:* 25-64; adults
Joel Marquez, President
Shanti Persaud, General Manager

Winter Haven

WPCV
01-01-1962; 97.5 mhz FM *Hrs Open:* 24; 100 kw; 1017 ft.; N28 7 35 W81 33 3
Mailing Address: P.O. Bo.X 4368, Lancaster, PA 17604 US
Second Address: 404 W. Lime St., Lakeland, FL 33815-4651
(863) 682-8184, *Fax:* (863) 683-2409
www.wpcv.com
wpcv@wpcv.com
License: Winter Haven, Polk County, FL held by Hall Communications Inc.
Group Owner: Hall Communications Inc.
Nat'l Reps: Eastman Radio *Wire Services:* AP
Arbitron Metro Market: Lakeland-Winter Haven, FL *Format:* Country *Hrs. of News Programming:* news progmg 4 hrs wkly *No. News Employees:* 3 *Target Audience:* 25-54.
Bonnie Rowbotham, Chairman
Art Rowbotham, President
Nancy Cattarius, Station Manager
Jeff Crews, Chief Engineer

WSIR
02-14-1947; 1490 khz AM *Hrs Open:* 24; 1 kw-U; N28 00 50 W81 45 02
665 Southwest Lake Howard Dr., Winter Haven, FL 33860
(863) 295-9411, *Fax:* (863) 401-9365
www.familyradio1490.com
joe.fisher@familyradio1490.com
License: Winter Haven, Polk County, FL held by Anscombe Broadcasting Group Ltd.
Nat'l Network: AURN; Sheridan Gospel Network *Regional Network:* Florida's Radio Networks
Population Served: 683,000 *Arbitron Metro Market:* Lakeland-Winter *Special Programming:* Relg 8090 *Hrs. of News Programming:* News progmg 5 hrs wkly *Target Audience:* 25-54 *Adv. Rates:* 40-60s / 35-30s
Steve Reszka, CEO
Tony Charles, Operations Dir
Joe Fisher, General Manager
Joe Fisher, General Sales Mgr
Joe Fisher, Programming Director
Pat Hughes, Promotions Manager
Steve Zagony, Engineering Dir
Steve Zagony, ChiefEngineer

Winter Park

WPRD
09-01-1954; 1440 khz AM *Hrs Open:* 24; 5 kw-D, DAN; 1 kw-N, DAN; N28 35 18 W81 22 53
222 Hazard St, Orlando, FL 32804 US
(407) 841-8282, *Fax:* (407) 841-8250
wprd1440@hotmail.com
License: Winter Park, FL held by J & V Communications Inc.
Group Owner: J&V Communications Inc.; acq 11-94; $300,000)
Arbitron Metro Market: Orlando, FL *Format:* News, News/Talk, 86 *Target Audience:* 25-64; upscale
John Torrado, CEO
Jocelyn Torrado, Operations Dir
Hector Reyes, General Manager
Virgen Torrado, CEO

***WPRK**
12-10-1952; 91.5 mhz FM *Hrs Open:* 24; 1.3 kw; 105 ft.; N28 35 28 W81 20 55.7
1000 Holt Ave - 2745, Winter Park, FL 32789 US
(407) 646-2915,(407) 646-2241
www.rollins.edu/wprk
License: Winter Park, Orange County, FL held by Rollins College.
Arbitron Metro Market: Orlando, FL *Format:* Urban Contemporary
Special Programming: Jazz 3 hrs wkly *Hrs. of News Programming:* News progmg 2 hrs wkly *Target Audience:* General; non-traditional class and/or rocklisteners
Whitney Coulter, Operations Dir
Dan Seeger, General Manager

Woodville

WTSM(FM)
09-01-2003; 97.9 mhz FM *Hrs Open:* 8:30 AM-5:30 PM; 6 kw; Ant 328 ft; N30 16 30 W84 07 39
435 St. Francis St., Tallahassee, FL 32301
(850) 561-8400, *Fax:* (850) 224-1553
www.wjztfm.com
epetrone@wjztfm.com,ccooper@wjztfm.com
License: Woodville, Leon County, FL held by 97.9 WJZTFM Inc.
Population Served: 182,965 *Arbitron Metro Market:* Tallahassee, FL *Format:* Jazz, Smooth Jazz *Target Audience:* 25-55. *Adv. Rates:* 20; 15; 10; 8
Ernest Petrone, General Manager
Chris Cooper, Station Manager

Yankeetown

WXOF
01-01-1998; 96.3 mhz FM; 3.5 kw; 433 ft.; N29 1 18 W82 41 20
35048 U.S. Highway 19, North, Palm Harbor, FL 34684 US
(352) 628-4444, *Fax:* (352) 628-4450
www.citrus95.com
staff@citrus95radio.com
License: Yankeetown, Levy County, FL held by WGUL-FM Inc.
Arbitron Metro Market: Yankeetown, FL *Format:* Classic Rock
Laura Grady, General Manager
Ryan Downs, Programming Director
Annette Kimball, Senior Account Executive
Mary Castro, Account Executive
Jim Hathaway, Account Executive

Zephyrhills

WZHR
05-09-1962; 1400 khz AM *Hrs Open:* 24; 1 kw-U, ND1; N28 16 54 W82 12 30
38141 Fifth Avenue, Zephyrhills, FL 33540 US
(727) 441-3311, *Fax:* (727) 441-1300
www.tantalk1340.com
lola@tantalk1340.com
License: Zephyrhills, FL held by Wagenvoord Advertising Group Inc.
Group Owner: Wagenvoord Advertising Group Inc.; acq 2-13-02).
Nat'l Network: CNN Radio; CBS Radio
Arbitron Metro Market: Tampa-St. Peter *Format:* Gospel, Talk *Special Programming:* CHR 10 hrs wkly *Target Audience:* 35-64; men & women *Adv. Rates:* 65; 65; 65; 65;
Dave Wagenvoord, CEO
Lola Wagenvoord, Operations Dir

Zolfo Springs

WZZS
11-01-1992; 106.9 mhz FM *Hrs Open:* 24; 5 kw; 358 ft.; N27 21 59 W81 47 52
300 Klispie Drive, Punta Gorda, FL 33950 US
(863) 494-4111, *Fax:* (863) 494-4443
www.bull.fm
Info@Bull.fm
License: Zolfo Springs, Hardee County, FL held by Heartland Broadcasting Corp.
Regional Network: Florida's Radio Networks
Arbitron Metro Market: Zolfo Springs, FL *Format:* Country *Special Programming:* Gospel 2 hrs, farm one hr daily *Hrs. of News Programming:* news progmg one hr wkly *No. News Employees:* 1 *Target Audience:* General; DeSoto, Hardee and Highlands counties
Harold Kneller Jr., President
Janet Kneller, Operations Dir
Casey Williams, Sales & Station Manager
Casey Williams, Sales & Station Manager
Michael Williams, Sales Representative
Billy Brown, Mornings/Program Director
SherryGood, Office Manager

Georgia

Adel

WDDQ
10-01-1979; 92.1 mhz FM *Hrs Open:* 24; 2.6 kw; 506 ft.; N31 8 15 W83 23 41
1203 West 4th Street, Ste 11, Adel, GA 31620 US
(229) 259-9301, *Fax:* (229) 559-1332
www.talk921.com
lauren@talk921.com
License: Adel, Cook County, GA held by Adventure Radio Group LLC
Arbitron Metro Market: Valdosta, GA *Format:* Talk *Target Audience:* 18-50.
Ron Hester, General Manager
Scott James, Owner/Manager

Albany

WALG
01-01-1940; 1590 khz AM *Hrs Open:* 24; 5 kw-D, DA2; 1 kw-N, DA2; N31 37 19 W84 9 9
330 E. Kilbourn Ave., Suite 250, Milwaukee, WI 53202 US
(912) 436-7233, *Fax:* (912) 888-6018
www.1590walg.com
matt.patrick@cumulus.com
License: Albany, GA held by Cumulus Licensing Corp.
Group Owner: Cumulus Media Inc.; (acq 11-3-98; grpsl).
Nat'l Network: ABC *Regional Network:* Southern Farm *Nat'l Reps:* Katz Radio
Arbitron Metro Market: Albany, GA *Format:* News, News/Talk, 86 *Target Audience:* General.
George Francis, President
Bill Jones, Programming Director
Joey Falgout, Chief Engineer
Jenna McKay, Public Affairs Director

WSRA
07-10-1962; 1250 khz AM; 1 kw-D, ND1; 0.053 kw-N, ND1; N31 37 0 W84 9 32
P. O. Box 90, Thomasville, GA 31799 US
(229) 432-1250, *Fax:* (229) 432-1927
www.wsraradio.com
info@wsra.com
License: Albany, GA held by Livingston Fulton
Arbitron Metro Market: Albany, GA *Format:* Sports *Target Audience:* 25-54.
Livingston Fulton, President

***WWVO**
07-12-1990; 90.7 mhz FM *Hrs Open:* 16; 5.5 kw; 305 ft.; N31 38 42 W84 21 15
2724 Ledo Road, Albany, GA 31707 US
(229) 698-3473, *Fax:* (229) 874-5015
www.wwvothevoice.com
wwvothevoice@gmail.com
License: Albany, Dougherty County, GA held by Lamad Ministries Inc.
Arbitron Metro Market: Albany, GA *Format:* Religious *Hrs. of News Programming:* News progmg 4 hrs wkly *Target Audience:* 35 plus.
C. William Eidenire, President
Eric Eidenire, General Manager

WGPC
01-01-1933; 1450 khz AM *Hrs Open:* 24; 1 kw-U, ND1; N31 34 55 W84 11 58
111 East Kilbourn Ave., Suite 2700, Milwaukee, WI 53202 US
(229) 888-5000, *Fax:* (229) 888-5960
License: Albany, GA held by Cumulus Licensing Corp.
Group Owner: Cumulus Media Inc.; (acq 11-3-98; $2.25 million with co-locatd FM).
Nat'l Network: CBS; Fox Sports *Regional Network:* Ga. News Net.
Arbitron Metro Market: Albany, GA *Format:* Sports, Easy Listening *Hrs. of News Programming:* News progmg 20 hrs wkly *Target Audience:* 25 plus; middle to upper income

George Francis, President
Bill Jones, Programming Director
Joey Falgout, Chief Engineer

WJIZ-FM
01-01-1965; 96.3 mhz FM; 100 kw; 466 ft.; N31 39 16 W84 10 36
2700 N. Slappy Blvd., Albany, GA 31702 US
(229) 439-9704, *Fax:* (229) 439-1509
www.wjiz.com
License: Albany, Dougherty County, GA
Group Owner: Clear Channel Communications Inc.
Nat'l Network: American Urban
Arbitron Metro Market: Albany, GA *Format:* Urban Contemporary
Target Audience: 18-54. *Adv. Rates:* 60; 40; 60; 40
John Richards, General Manager
Adrian Guyton, Programming Director

WJYZ
11-01-1952; 960 khz AM *Hrs Open:* 24; 5 kw-D, DA2; 0.39 kw-N, DA2; N31 37 5 W84 10 31
225 Green Street, Suite 906, Fayetteville, NC 28301 US
(229) 439-9704, *Fax:* (229) 439-1509
www.wjyz.com
frankc@wjyz.com
License: Albany, GA held by CC Licenses LLC.
Group Owner: Clear Channel Communications Inc.; (acq 7-12-2000; grpsl).
Nat'l Network: American Urban *Nat'l Reps:* D & R Radio
Arbitron Metro Market: Albany, GA *Format:* Gospel *Hrs. of News Programming:* News progmg 3.5 hrs wkly *Target Audience:* 25-54. *Adv. Rates:* 12; 15; 12; 10
John Richards, General Manager
Frank Crapp, Programming Director

WKAK
02-22-1963; 104.5 mhz FM *Hrs Open:* 24; 98 kw; 981 ft.; N31 32 57 W84 0 19
111 East Kilbourn Ave., Suite 2700, Milwaukee, WI 53202 US
(229) 888-5000, *Fax:* (229) 888-5960
www.kcountry104.com
License: Albany, Dougherty County, GA
Arbitron Metro Market: Albany, GA *Format:* Country *Hrs. of News Programming:* News progmg 25 hrs wkly
Claire Peeples, General Sales Mgr
Genna McKay, Programming Director
Mason Dixon, Disc Jockey
Candy O'Reilley, Disc Jockey

WQVE
12-17-1972; 101.7 mhz FM; 6 kw; 299 ft.; N31 37 15 W84 9 11
330 E. Kilbourn Ave., Suite 250, Milwaukee, WI 53202 US
(229) 888-5000, *Fax:* (912) 888-5960
www.wqvealbany.com
matt.patrick@cumulus.com
License: Albany, Dougherty County, GA
Group Owner: Cumulus Media Inc.
Arbitron Metro Market: Albany, GA *Format:* Contemporary Hits/Top 40
Ken O'Brien, Operations Dir
Mark McGee, Programming Director
Jenna McKay, News Director
Al Crumpton, Disc Jockey
Staci Cates, Disc Jockey
Mason Dixon, Disc Jockey
Kurt Baker, Disc Jockey
Dotti Davis, Disc Jockey

***WUNV**
01-01-1990; 91.7 mhz FM *Hrs Open:* 24; 3 kw; 328 ft.; N31 40 20 W84 3 27 *Rebroadcasts:* Rebroadcasts WJSP-FM Warm Springs 100%
260 - 14th Street, N.W., Atlanta, GA 30318 US
(404) 685-2690, *Fax:* (404) 685-2684
www.gpb.org
ask@gpb.org
License: Albany, Dougherty County, GA held by Georgia Public Telecommunications Commission.
Nat'l Network: PRI; NPR *Wire Services:* AP
Arbitron Metro Market: Atlanta, GA *TV Affiliate:* GBP-TV *Format:* News *Hrs. of News Programming:* news progmg 40 hrs wkly *No. News Employees:* 10 *Target Audience:* Adults: 35 plus.
Nancy Hall, CEO
Teya Ryan, President
Tom Barclay, Operations Dir
Bob Houghton, General Manager
Rob Maynard, Programming Director
Nancy Zintak, Promotions Manager
Susanna Capelouto, News Director
Bonnie Bean, CFO

Alma

WAWO
10-01-1957; 1400 khz AM *Hrs Open:* 24; 1 kw-U; N31 31 50 W82 27 45
Drawer F, 208 Douglas St., Alma, GA 31510
(912) 632-1000, *Fax:* (912) 632-9696
License: Alma, Bacon County, GA held by Blueberry Broadcasting Co. Inc.
Nat'l Network: CNN Radio *Regional Network:* Ga. News Net.
Population Served: 35,000*Special Programming:* Farm 2 hrs wkly *Hrs. of News Programming:* news progmg 6 hrs wkly *No. News Employees:* 1 *Target Audience:* General.
Debra Deen, General Manager

WAJQ-FM
05-14-1987; 104.3 mhz FM; 4.5 kw; 371 ft.; N31 36 26 W82 32 46
208 Douglas Street, PO Box F, Alma, GA 31510 US
(912) 632-1000, *Fax:* (912) 632-9696
License: Alma, Bacon County, GA
Arbitron Metro Market: Brunswick GA *Format:* Country *Target Audience:* General.
Bob Sass, Promotions Manager

Alpharetta

WLTA
08-25-1986; 1400 khz AM; 1 kw-U, ND1; N34 3 49 W84 16 34
Rebroadcasts: Rebroadcasts WNIV(AM) Atlanta 80%
2970 Peachtree Rd., N.W., Suite 970, Atlanta, GA 30305 US
(404) 995-7300, *Fax:* (404) 816-0748
www.faithtalk970.com
adam.asher@salematlanta.com
License: Alpharetta, GA held by South Texas Broadcasting Inc.
Group Owner: Salem Communications Corp.; (acq 11-17-99; $8 million with WNIV(AM) Atlanta)
Arbitron Metro Market: Atlanta, GA *Format:* News, Talk, 74
Target Audience: 25-49; upper middle to upper income
Jeff Carter, Operations Dir
Mike Moran, General Manager
Adam Asher, Station Manager
Mitch Ambler, General Sales Mgr
John Stirzaker, Programming Director

Ambrose

WDMG-FM
12-01-1983; 97.9 mhz FM *Hrs Open:* 24; 3.5 kw; 316 ft.; N31 31 51 W82 54 34
603 West 2nd Street, PO Box 7, Tifton, GA 31754 US
(912) 389-0995, *Fax:* (912) 383-8552
www.979thebigdog.com
traffic@charter.net
License: Ambrose, Coffee County, GA held by Broadcast South LLC.
Group Owner: Broadcast South LLC; (acq 11-15-2006; grpsl)
Format: Classic Rock
John Higgs, General Manager

Americus

***WBJY**
01-01-2002; 89.3 mhz FM; 65 kw vert; 614 ft.; N31 38 22 W83 44 58
P O Drawer 2440, Tupelo, MS 38803 US
(662) 844-8888, *Fax:* (662) 842-6791
www.afa.net/Radio/
License: Americus, Sumter County, GA held by American Family Association.
Group Owner: American Family Radio
Arbitron Metro Market: Americus, GA *Format:* Christian
Marvin Sanders, General Manager

WDEC-FM
09-12-1964; 94.7 mhz FM; 25 kw; 328 ft.; N31 53 52 W84 18 53
Mailing Address: P O Box 727, 215 Ga Highway 30 West, Americus, GA 31709 US
Second Address: 1028 Adderton St., Americus, GA 31719
(229) 924-1390, *Fax:* (229) 928-2337
www.americusradio.com
wiskwdec@mchsi.com
License: Americus, Sumter County, GA held by Sumter Broadcasting Co.
Group Owner: Sumter Broadcasting Co. Inc.; (acq 1994; with co-located AM)
Nat'l Reps: Rgnl Reps
Arbitron Metro Market: Albany, GA *Format:* Adult Contemp
Special Programming: Black 5 hrs, farm one hr wkly *Hrs. of News Programming:* news progmg 2 hrs wkly *No. News Employees:* 2
Steve Lashley, President
Steve Lashley, General Manager
Thurston Clary, Programming Director
Donnie McCrary, News Director

WISK-FM
09-01-1973; 98.7 mhz FM *Hrs Open:* 24; 25 kw; 302 ft.; N32 4 51 W84 15 20
Mailing Address: P.O. Box 727, Americus, GA 31709 US
Second Address: 1028 Adderton St., Americus, GA 31709
(229) 924-1390, *Fax:* (229) 928-2337
www.americusradio.com
wisk.wdec@mehsi.com
License: Americus, Sumter County, GA held by Sumter Broadcasting Co. Inc.
Group Owner: Sumter Broadcasting Co. Inc.
Nat'l Reps: Rgnl Reps
Format: Country
Dana Withers, General Manager

***WFRP**
01-01-2005; 88.7 mhz FM; 4.2 kw; 230 ft.; N32 5 34 W84 16 56
Rebroadcasts: Rebroadcasts WBFR(FM) Birmingham, AL 100%
Mailing Address: 4135 Nothgate, Suite 1, Sacramento, CA 95834 US
Second Address: 290 Hegenberger Rd., Oakland, CA 94621
(800) 543-1495, *Fax:* (916) 641-8238
www.familyradio.com
info@familyradio.com
License: Americus, Sumter County, GA held by Family Stations Inc.
Group Owner: Family Stations Inc.
Arbitron Metro Market: Americus, GA *Format:* Christian, Religious
Harold Camping, President
Stanley Jackson, Operations Dir

Aragon

WTSH-FM
08-01-1989; 107.1 mhz FM; 45 kw; Ant 518 ft; N34 15 03 W84 59 05
20 John Davenport Dr.; Rome, GA 30160
(706) 291-9496, *Fax:* (706) 235-7107
www.south107.com
License: Aragon, Polk County, GA held by Woman's World Broadcasting Inc.
Population Served: 496,000*Target Audience:* 25-54. *Adv. Rates:* 32; 29; 32; 28
Randy Quick, General Manager

Arcade

WNGC
11-01-1947; 106.1 mhz FM *Hrs Open:* 24; 100 kw; 1,132 ft; N34 43 46 W83 29 29
850 Bobbin Mill Rd., Athens, GA 30622
(706) 549-1340,(706) 549-6222, *Fax:* (706) 546-0441
www.1061wngc.com
wngc@negia.net
License: Arcade, Stephens County, GA held by Cox Radio Inc.
Group Owner: Cox Radio Inc.; (acq 8-1-2008; grpsl)
Population Served: 850,000*Hrs. of News Programming:* news progmg 10 hrs wkly *No. News Employees:* 1 *Target Audience:* 25-54; adults with disposable income
Robert Neil, President
Scott Smith, Operations Dir
Kevin Steele, Programming Director

Ashburn

WFFM
12-01-1989; 105.7 mhz FM; 6 kw; 328 ft.; N31 41 17 W83 38 38
P.O. Box 306, Adel, GA 31620 US
(229) 382-1340, *Fax:* (229) 386-8658
www.hookfmoline.com
contact@hookfmonline.com
License: Ashburn, Turner County, GA held by Three Trees Communications Inc.
Group Owner: Three Trees Communications Inc.; (acq 10-31-2007; $150,000)
Arbitron Metro Market: Ashburn, GA *Format:* Christian
James Howard, President

Athens

WFSH-FM
01-01-1964; 104.7 mhz FM *Hrs Open:* 24; 24 kw; 1657 ft.; N33 52 2 W83 49 44
2970 Peachtree Road, NW, Suite 700, Atlanta, GA 30305 US
(404) 995-7300, *Fax:* (404) 816-0748
www.thefishatlanta.com

License: Athens, Clarke County, GA held by South Texas Broadcasting Inc.
Group Owner: Salem Communications Corp.; (acq 7-27-2000; grpsl).
Arbitron Metro Market: Atlanta, GA *Format:* Christian *Special Programming:* Gospel 2 hrs wkly
Mike Moran, General Manager
Kevin Isaacs, Sales Director
Mike Blakemore, Programming Director
Chad Davis:, Promotions Manager
C. J. Jackson, Chief Engineer
Mike Stoudt, Music Director

WGAU
05-01-1938; 1340 khz AM *Hrs Open:* 24; 1 kw-U; N33 56 28 W83 24 13
850 Bobbin Mill Rd., Athens, GA 30622
(706) 549-1340, *Fax:* (706) 353-1220
www.1340wgau.com
matt.caesar@coxinc.com
License: Athens, Clarke County, GA held by Cox Radio Inc.
Group Owner: Cox Radio Inc.; (acq 8-1-2008; grpsl)
Nat'l Network: ABC
Population Served: 175,000*No. News Employees:* 3 *Target Audience:* 25 plus; educated, middle to upper-income, news & info oriented
Robert Neil, President
Scott Smith, General Manager
Matt Caesar, Programming Director
Tim Bryant, News Director

*WMSL
10-01-1987; 88.9 mhz FM *Hrs Open:* 24; 20 kw; 299 ft.; N33 54 25 W83 29 35
585 Prince Avenue, Athens, GA 30601 US
(770) 725-8890, *Fax:* (678) 753-0088
www.wmsl.fm
gm@wmsl.fm
License: Athens, Clarke County, GA held by Prince Avenue Baptist Christian School.
Nat'l Network: USA
Arbitron Metro Market: Athens, GA *Format:* Christian *Hrs. of News Programming:* news progmg 11 hrs wkly *No. News Employees:* 1 *Target Audience:* 25-54; women
George McKay, Operations Dir
Jim Hutto, General Manager
Nathan Collins, Programming Director
Dianne Hutto, Promotions Manager
Mitch Kimbrell, News Director
James Hutto, Music Director

WRFC
05-01-1948; 960 khz AM *Hrs Open:* 24; 5 kw-D, DAN; 2.5 kw-N, DAN; N33 59 58 W83 26 0
1010 Tower Place, Bogart, GA 30622 US
(706) 549-6222, *Fax:* (706) 353-1967
www.960theref.com
License: Athens, GA held by Cox Radio Inc.
Group Owner: Cox Radio Inc.; (acq 8-1-2008; grpsl)
Nat'l Network: ESPN Radio
Format: Sports, Talk *Special Programming:* Black 15 hrs wkly *Hrs. of News Programming:* news progmg 10 hrs wkly *No. News Employees:* 3 *Target Audience:* 25-54; community-minded adults
Robert Neil, President
Scott Smith, Operations Dir
David Johnston, Programming Director

*WUGA
08-28-1987; 91.7 mhz FM *Hrs Open:* 24; 6 kw; 325 ft.; N33 55 13 W83 14 46
Mailing Address: 260 - 14th Street, N.W., Atlanta, GA 30318 US
Second Address: Georgia Public Radio (HQ), 260 14th St. N.W., Atlanta, GA 30318
(706) 542-9842, *Fax:* (706) 542-6718
www.wuga.org
wuga@uga.edu
License: Athens, Clarke County, GA held by Georgia Public Telecommunications Commission.
Nat'l Network: PRI; NPR *Regional Network:* Georgia Public Radio *Wire Services:* AP
Arbitron Metro Market: Athens, GA *Format:* News *Special Programming:* Folk 4 hrs, jazz 4 hrs wkly *Hrs. of News Programming:* news progmg 5 hrs wkly *No. News Employees:* 3 *Target Audience:* Adults: 35 plus.
Nancy Hall, CEO
Michael Cardin, Operations Dir
Bob Houghton, General Manager
Jimmy Sanders, Station Manager
Rob Maynard, Programming Director
Jeff Dantre, News Director
Walt Howard, Chief Engineer
Abbie Thaxton, TrafficManager
Robb Holmes, Music Director
Michael Cardin, Production and Operations Manager

*WUOG
10-16-1972; 90.5 mhz FM *Hrs Open:* 24; 26 kw; 180 ft.; N33 56 59 W83 22 58
P.O. Box 2065, Athens, GA 30612 US
(706) 542-7100, *Fax:* (706) 542-0070
www.wuog.org
info@wuog.org
License: Athens, Clarke County, GA held by University of Georgia.
Regional Network: Ga. News Net.
Arbitron Metro Market: Athens, GA *Format:* Alternative *Hrs. of News Programming:* news progmg 4 hrs wkly *No. News Employees:* 3 *Target Audience:* 18-25; students & faculty of Univ
Akeeme Martin, Operations Dir
Sarah Lawrence, General Manager
Eli Gaultney, Programming Director
Ella Grace Downs, Promotions Manager
Jason Flynn, News Director
David Sanders, Sports Director
Ryan Rudder, Music Director
Caroline Marchildon, Public Affairs Director

WXAG
06-10-1957; 1470 khz AM
3166 Robinwood Trail, Decatur, GA 30034 US
(706) 552-1470, *Fax:* (706) 425-0847
www.1470wxag.com
License: Athens, GA held by Mecca Communications Inc.
Arbitron Metro Market: Athens, GA *Format:* Gospel, Religious
Michael Thurmond, General Manager

Atlanta

*WABE
09-13-1948; 90.1 mhz FM *Hrs Open:* 24; 100 kw; 1096 ft.; N33 45 33 W84 20 5
740 Bismark Road, N. E., Atlanta, GA 30324 US
(760) 954-6655, *Fax:* (760) 872-4155
License: Atlanta, Fulton County, GA held by Board of Education of the City of Atlanta.
Nat'l Network: NPR; PRI *Wire Services:* AP
Arbitron Metro Market: Tucson AZ
Daniel McClenaghan, President

WAEC
01-01-1947; 860 khz AM; 2.5 kw-C, DAN; 5 kw-D, DAN; DAN; 0.5 kw-; N33 43 45 W84 19 19
9600 Koger Blvd, Suite 202, St. Petersburg, FL 33702 US
(662) 844-8888, *Fax:* (662 842-6791
www.afr.net
License: Atlanta, GA held by WAEC License L.P.
Group Owner: Beasley Broadcast Group Inc.; (acq 10-29-99)
Arbitron Metro Market: Visalia-Tulare-Hanford CA *Format:* Christian, Religious *Adv. Rates:* 40; 35; 35; 20
Marvin Sanders, General Manager

WGKA
03-17-1922; 920 khz AM
Suite 200, Bldg. 15, 1820 Powers Ferry Rd., Atlanta, GA 30339 US
(404) 995-7300, *Fax:* (404) 816-0748
www.talk920.com
adam.asher@salematlanta.com
License: Atlanta, GA held by Pennsylvania Media Associates Inc.
Group Owner: Salem Communications Corp.; (acq 6-28-2004; $16.4 million).
Arbitron Metro Market: Atlanta, GA *Format:* News, News/Talk, 86 *Target Audience:* General.
Jeff Carter, Operations Dir
Mike Moran, General Manager
David Koon, General Sales Mgr

WIFN
11-20-1965; 1340 khz AM *Hrs Open:* 24; 1 kw-U; N33 44 56 W84 24 26
3535 Piedmont Rd., Bldg. 14, Suite 1200, Atlanta, GA 30305
(404) 688-0068, *Fax:* (404) 995-4045
www.talkradio1340.com
scottmcfarlane@680thefan.com
License: Atlanta, Fulton County, GA held by Dickey Broadcasting Co.
Group Owner: Dickey Broadcasting Co.; (acq 8-31-2000; grpsl)
Nat'l Network: Fox Sports *Nat'l Reps:* McGavren Guild *Wire Services:* AP
Population Served: 496,973 *Arbitron Metro Market:* Atlanta, GA *Adv. Rates:* 100; 100; 100; 50
Scott McFarlane, Operations Dir
David Dickey, General Manager
Rob Hasson, General Sales Mgr

WAOK
03-15-1954; 1380 khz AM
600 New Hampshire Ave, N.W., Suite 1200, Washington, DC 20037 US
(404) 898-8900, *Fax:* (404) 898-8915
www.atlanta.cbslocal.com/station/waok-am/
Shelice.Smith@cbsradio.com
License: Atlanta, GA held by Infinity Broadcasting East Inc.
Group Owner: CBS Radio; (acq 1996; grpsl).
Nat'l Network: CBS
Arbitron Metro Market: Atlanta, GA *Format:* News, News/Talk, 86 *Hrs. of News Programming:* news progmg 50 hrs wkly *No. News Employees:* 5 *Target Audience:* 25-54.
Mel Karmazin, CEO
Tasha Brown, Operations Dir
Ben Segarra, General Sales Mgr
Reggie Rouse, Programming Director
Rick Caffey, Promotions Manager
Sid Daniel, Chief Engineer
Tasha Love, Programming Director
Monique McCoy,Promotions Manager
Brenda Yelling, Research Director

*WCLK
04-10-1974; 91.9 mhz FM; 6 kw; 308 ft.; N33 44 56 W84 24 26
111 James P Brawley Dr, S.W., Atlanta, GA 30314 US
(404) 880-8284(404) 880-8278, *Fax:* (404) 880-8869
www.wclk.com
wclkfm@cau.edu
License: Atlanta, Fulton County, GA held by Clark Atlanta University.
Nat'l Network: NPR; PRI
Arbitron Metro Market: Atlanta, GA *Format:* Jazz *Special Programming:* Gospel 17 hrs, reggae 3 hrs, blues 3 hrs, info/talk 12 hrs wkly *No. News Employees:* 16 *Target Audience:* 25-49; upscale, college educated,primarily African American
Glen Simmonds, Operations Dir
Wendy Williams, General Manager
Tammy Nobles, Station Manager
Aaron Cohen, Programming Director
Shelley Trotter, Promotions Manager
Traci Ross, News Director
Gary Owens, Chief Engineer
Rose Holmes,Edit Manager
Renee Williams, Music Director

WDWD
07-01-1938; 590 khz AM
77 West 66th Street, 16th Fl, New York, NY 10023 US
(770) 541-0590, *Fax:* (770) 952-7461
www.radiodisney.com/atlanta
License: Atlanta, GA held by Radio Disney Atlanta LLC.
Group Owner: ABC Inc.; (acq 5-17-85; $6.85 million;
Nat'l Network: ABC *Nat'l Reps:* Interep
Arbitron Metro Market: Atlanta, GA *Format:* Children *Target Audience:* Children 6-14 Adults 25-54. *Adv. Rates:* 125; 125; 125; 125
Melissa Munro, Operations Dir
Shawn Serra, Station Manager

WAFS
09-01-1955; 1190 khz AM *Hrs Open:* Sunrise-sunset
2999 Piedmont Rd, N.E., Atlanta, GA 30327 US
(404) 995-7300, *Fax:* (404) 816-0748
www.biz1190.com
License: Atlanta, GA held by South Texas Broadcasting Inc.
Group Owner: Salem Communications Corp.; (acq 4-4-2000; $8 million).
Arbitron Metro Market: Atlanta, GA *Format:* Gospel *Target Audience:* 35-64.
Jeff Carter, Operations Dir
Mike Marmon, General Manager

WGST
04-07-1988; 640 khz AM *Hrs Open:* 24; 50 kw-D, DA2; 1 kw-N, DA2; N33 45 43 W84 27 29 *Rebroadcasts:* Rebroadcasts WHEL(FM) Helen 100%
50 East Rivercenter Blvd, Suite 1200, Covington, KY 41011 US
(404) 367-0640, *Fax:* (404) 367-1100
www.wgst.com
License: Atlanta, GA held by Citicasters Licenses L.P.
Group Owner: Clear Channel Communications Inc.
Wire Services: AP
Arbitron Metro Market: Atlanta, GA *Format:* News, News/Talk, 86 *Target Audience:* 25-54.
Tim Dukes, Operations Dir
Pat McDonnell, General Manager

Jared Blass, General Sales Mgr
Tom Parker, Programming Director
Jim Oktavec, Promotions Manager
Paul Mann, News Director
Mike Lawing, Chief Engineer
Pam Rahal, PromotionsDirector

WGUN
07-01-1947; 1010 khz AM *Hrs Open:* 24
2901 Mt. Industrial Blvd, Tucker, GA 30084 US
(770) 491-1010, *Fax:* (770) 491-3019
wgunstudio@bellsouth.net
License: Atlanta, GA held by Dee Rivers Group.
Arbitron Metro Market: Atlanta, GA *Format:* Talk, Religious *Hrs. of News Programming:* News progmg one hr wkly *Target Audience:* 25-54; working class
Georgia Salva, CEO
Erwin Hill, Operations Dir
Darrell Vick, General Manager

WWPW(FM)
12-02-1960; 96.1 mhz FM *Hrs Open:* 24; 99 kw; Ant 984 ft; N33 48 27 W84 20 26
1819 Peachtree St., Suite 700, Atlanta, GA 30309
(404) 325-0960, *Fax:* (404) 367-1155
www.project961.com
info@project961.com
License: Atlanta, Fulton County, GA held by Citicasters Licenses L.P.
Group Owner: Clear Channel Communications Inc.; (acq 5-4-99; grpsl)
Population Served: 3,500,000 *Arbitron Metro Market:* Atlanta, GA *Format:* Rock/AOR *Hrs. of News Programming:* News progmg 7 hrs wkly *Target Audience:* 25-49; primarily male
Mike Wheeler, Operations Dir
Jerry Del Core, General Manager
Jeff McMurray, Programming Director
Susan De Bonis, Promotions Manager

WNIV
01-01-1948; 970 khz AM *Hrs Open:* 24; 5 kw-D, ND2; 0.039 kw-N, ND2; N33 48 35 W84 21 14
2970 Peachtree Road, 8th Floor, Atlanta, GA 30305 US
(404) 995-7300, *Fax:* (404) 816-0748
www.faithtalk970.com
adam.asher@salematlanta.com
License: Atlanta, GA held by South Texas Broadcasting Inc.
Group Owner: Salem Communications Corp.; (acq 11-17-99; $8 million with WLTA(AM) Alpharetta)
Arbitron Metro Market: Atlanta, GA *Format:* Christian, Talk *Hrs. of News Programming:* news progmg 7 hrs wkly *No. News Employees:* 1 *Target Audience:* 25-49; educated adults, upper middle to upper income
Stuart Epperson, Chairman
Edward Atsinger III, President
Jeff Carter, Operations Dir
Mike Moran, General Manager
Adam Asher, Station Manager
Mitch Ambler, General Sales Mgr
John Stirzaker, Programming Director
Joel Foster,Promotions Manager
Cynthia Weaver, News Director
C. J. Jackson, Chief Engineer

WWWQ
11-01-1963; 99.7 mhz FM; 96.6 kw; 1115 ft.; N33 48 26 W84 20 22
140 East Market Street, York, PA 17401 US
(404) 497-4700, *Fax:* (404) 497-4735
www.q100atlanta.com
License: Atlanta, Fulton County, GA held by Susquehanna Radio Corp.
Group Owner: Cumulus Media Partners LLC; (acq 2-28-74)
Nat'l Reps: Cumulus Radio Sales
Arbitron Metro Market: Atlanta, GA *Format:* Contemporary Hits/Top 40
Joyce Harms, Operations Dir
Gary Lewis, General Manager
Rob Roberts, Programming Director

WUBL
02-18-1962; 94.9 mhz FM *Hrs Open:* 24; 99 kw; 978 ft.; N33 48 27 W84 20 27
50 East Rivercenter Blvd, Suite 1200, Covington, KY 41011 US
(404) 367-0949, *Fax:* (404) 367-9490
www.bullatlanta.com
info@bullatlanta.com
License: Atlanta, Fulton County, GA
Group Owner: Clear Channel Communications Inc.
Nat'l Network: ABC
Arbitron Metro Market: Atlanta, GA *Format:* Country

Cheryl Ervin, General Sales Mgr
Louis Kaplan, Programming Director
Scott Baker, Promotions Manager
Steve Goss, Music Director

WQXI
10-01-1947; 790 khz AM
3350 Peachtree Road, N.E, Atlanta, GA 30326 US
(404) 237-0079, *Fax:* (404) 231-5923
www.790thezone.com
feedback@790thezone.com
License: Atlanta, GA held by Jefferson Pilot Communications Co.
Group Owner: Lincoln Financial Media; (acq 3-1-74).
Arbitron Metro Market: Atlanta, GA *Format:* Sports, Talk *Target Audience:* 18-54; men
Andrew Saltzman, President
Neal Maziar, Operations Dir
Neal Maziiar, General Manager
Chris Young, General Sales Mgr
Leslie Smith, Promotions Manager
Jim Heilman, National Sales Manager
Eric Tepe, Operations Manager
StephenShapiro, Operations Manager
Leslie Hoar, Promotions Manager

***WRAS**
01-18-1971; 88.5 mhz FM *Hrs Open:* 24; 100 kw; 436 ft.; N33 41 4 W84 17 23
University Plaza, Atlanta, GA 30303 US
(404) 413-1630, *Fax:* (404) 463-9535
www.wras.org
License: Atlanta, Fulton County, GA held by Georgia State University.
Arbitron Metro Market: Atlanta, GA *Format:* Talk *Special Programming:* Classical 3 hrs, world 3 hrs, reggae 4 hrs, new age 3 hrs, rap/hip-hop 6 hrs wkly *Hrs. of News Programming:* News progmg 6 hrs wkly *TargetAudience:* 18-34; college students
Dr. Kurt Keppler, CEO
Brady Rainey, General Manager
Andy Hawley, Programming Director
Michael Valania, Promotions Manager
Tom Taylor, Chief Engineer
Todd Wiese, Music Director

***WREK**
04-01-1968; 91.1 mhz FM *Hrs Open:* 24; 100 kw; 335 ft.; N33 46 41 W84 24 22
165 Eighth Street, Atlanta, GA 30332 US
(404) 894-2468, *Fax:* (404) 894-6872
www.wrek.org
wrek@gatech.edu
License: Atlanta, Fulton County, GA held by Radio Communications Board, Georgia Institute of Technology.
Regional Network: Ga. News Net.
Arbitron Metro Market: Atlanta, GA *Format:* Ethnic, Variety/Diverse *Special Programming:* Experimental 18 hrs, jazz 15 hrs, class 15 hrs wkly *Target Audience:* General.
Jeremy Varner, Operations Dir
Aakash Jariwala, General Manager
Steve Fenton, Programming Director

***WRFG**
07-15-1973; 89.3 mhz FM *Hrs Open:* 24; 65 kw; 486 ft.; N33 48 26 W84 20 22
1083 Austin Avenue Ne, Atlanta, GA 30307 US
(404) 523-3471, *Fax:* (404) 523-8990
www.wrfg.org
info@wrfg.org
License: Atlanta, Fulton County, GA held by Radio Free Georgia Broadcasting Foundation Inc.
Arbitron Metro Market: Atlanta, GA *Format:* Easy Listening *Special Programming:* , Indian 3 hrs, Sp 5 hrs wkly *Hrs. of News Programming:* News progmg 3 hrs wkly *Target Audience:* 18-45; socially consciousAfrican-Americans
Wanique Shabazz, Operations Dir
Joan Baptist, Station Manager

WSB
03-15-1922; 750 khz AM *Hrs Open:* 24; 50 kw-U, ND1; N33 50 38 W84 15 12
3773 Howard Hughes Pwy, Suite 300n, Las Vegas, NV 89109 US
(404) 897-7500, *Fax:* (404) 897-7363
www.wsbradio.com
License: Atlanta, GA held by Cox Radio Inc.
Group Owner: Cox Radio Inc.
Nat'l Reps: Christal
Arbitron Metro Market: Atlanta, GA *Format:* News, News/Talk, 86 *Hrs. of News Programming:* news progmg 168 hrs wkly *No. News Employees:* 9 *Target Audience:* 25-54.

Walt Phillips, General Sales Mgr
Pete Spriggs, Programming Director
Michael Dobson, Promotions Manager
Charles Kinney, Chief Engineer
Tony Kidd, VP, Market Manager

WSB-FM
11-10-1944; 98.5 mhz FM; 100 kw; 1027 ft.; N33 45 33 W84 20 5
3773 Howard Hughes Pwy, Suite 300n, Las Vegas, NV 89109 US
(404) 897-7500, *Fax:* (404) 897-7363
www.b985.com
License: Atlanta, Fulton County, GA
Group Owner: Cox Radio Inc.
Arbitron Metro Market: Atlanta, GA *TV Affiliate:* WSB-TV affil *Format:* Adult Contemp *Hrs. of News Programming:* news progmg 3.5 hrs wkly *No. News Employees:* 1 *Target Audience:* 25-54.
Francisco Luciano, General Sales Mgr
Chris Eagan, Programming Director
Dave Clapper, Promotions Manager
Dan Kearney, VP, Market Manager

WVEE
07-01-1948; 103.3 mhz FM; 100 kw; 1017 ft.; N33 45 33 W84 20 5
600 New Hampshire Ave., Suite 1200, Washington, DC 20037 US
(404) 898-8900, *Fax:* (404) 898-8915
www.v-103.com
Ben.Segarra@cbsradio.com
License: Atlanta, Fulton County, GA
Nat'l Network: Westwood One
Arbitron Metro Market: Atlanta, GA *Format:* Urban Contemporary *No. News Employees:* 2 *Target Audience:* 18-49.
Katrina Noles, Operations Dir
Susan Palmer, General Sales Mgr
Reggie Rouse, Programming Director
Ben Segarra, Advertising Contact
Ashley Roberson, Digital Sales Manager

WYZE
06-01-1957; 1480 khz AM
1776 Briarcliff Rd, Atlanta, GA 30306 US
(404) 622-7802, *Fax:* (404) 622-6767
www.wyze1480.com
am1480wyze@aol.com
License: Atlanta, GA held by GHB Broadcasting Inc.
Group Owner: GHB Radio Group
Regional Network: Ga. News Net.
Arbitron Metro Market: Atlanta, GA *Format:* Black, Gospel
George Buck Jr., President
Jacob Bogan, Station Manager

WZGC
09-01-1965; 92.9 mhz FM *Hrs Open:* 24; 64 kw; 1115 ft.; N33 48 26 W84 20 21.8
600 New Hampshire Avenue, Suite 1200, Washington, DC 20037 US
(404) 898-8900, *Fax:* (404) 843-3541
www.929dave.fm
info@929dave.fm
License: Atlanta, Fulton County, GA held by CBS Radio Inc. of Atlanta.
Group Owner: CBS Radio; (acq 11-13-98; grpsl).
Nat'l Network: Westwood One *Nat'l Reps:* Katz Radio
Arbitron Metro Market: Atlanta, GA *Format:* Triple A *Hrs. of News Programming:* news progmg 2 hrs wkly *No. News Employees:* 1 *Target Audience:* 25-54; upscale baby boomers
Rick Caffey, Operations Dir
John Riemenschneider, General Sales Mgr
Scott Jameson, Programming Director
Robert Lafore, Chief Engineer
Mara Davis, Disc Jockey
Sully, Disc Jockey
Susan Palmer, National Sales Manager

Augusta

***WACG-FM**
06-02-1970; 90.7 mhz FM *Hrs Open:* 24; 3.7 kw horiz; 1381 ft.; N33 24 18 W81 50 15 *Rebroadcasts:* Rebroadcasts WJSP-FM Warm Springs 75%
Mailing Address: 260 - 14th Street, N.W., Atlanta, GA 30318 US
Second Address: 2500 Walton Way, Augusta, GA 30904
(956) 487-8015
License: Augusta, Richmond County, GA held by Georgia Public Telecommunications Commission.
Nat'l Network: PRI; NPR *Wire Services:* AP
Arbitron Metro Market: De Queen AR
Eloy Vera, General Manager

WRDW
01-01-2001; 1630 khz AM
1537 Flagler Rd, Augusta, GA 30909 US
(808) 935-2924, *Fax:* (808) 244-8247
License: Augusta, GA held by WCHZ License LLC.
Group Owner: Beasley Broadcast Group Inc.; (acq 2-23-2000).
Arbitron Metro Market: Kurtistown HI *Format:* Adult Contemp
John Detz, President

WYNF
01-12-1947; 1340 khz AM *Hrs Open:* 24; 1 kw-U; N33 27 46 W82 00 29
2743 Perimeter Pkwy., Bldg. 100, Augusta, GA 53202
(706) 396-6000, *Fax:* (706) 396-6010
License: Augusta, Richmond County, GA held by Clear Channel Broadcasting Licenses Inc.
Group Owner: Clear Channel Communications Inc.
Population Served: 425,000 *Arbitron Metro Market:* Augusta, GA *Target Audience:* Children.
Art Sutton, President
Terry Carter, Operations Dir
Marty Lee, Chief Engineer
Opal Coleman, Office Manager
Ron Shuller, Operations Manager
Carl Pundt, Vice President

WBBQ-FM
03-01-1955; 104.3 mhz FM *Hrs Open:* 24; 78 kw; 1430 ft.; N33 25 16.6 W81 50 18.6
111 East Kilbourn Ave., Suite 2700, Milwaukee, WI 53202 US
(662) 844-8888, *Fax:* (662) 842-6791
www.afr.net
License: Augusta, Richmond County, GA held by Clear Channel Broadcasting Licenses Inc.
Group Owner: Clear Channel Communications Inc.; (acq 12-19-2000; grpsl).
Arbitron Metro Market: El Dorado AR *Format:* Christian
Marvin Sanders, General Manager

WZNY
11-11-1967; 102.3 mhz FM *Hrs Open:* 24; 1.5 kw; Ant 666 ft; N33 26 15 W82 05 27
2743 Perimeter Pkwy., Bldg. 100, Suite 200, Augusta, GA 53202

www.bullcountry.com
License: Augusta, Richmond County, GA held by Aloha Station Trust LLC
Arbitron Metro Market: Augusta, GA *Hrs. of News Programming:* news progmg 3 hrs wkly *No. News Employees:* 1 *Target Audience:* 18-34.
Tim Lawandus, General Sales Mgr
Bill West, Programming Director
Robb Tomas, Promotions Manager

WFAM
03-10-1952; 1050 khz AM *Hrs Open:* 24; 5 kw-D, ND2; 0.082 kw-N, ND2; N33 27 21 W81 56 20
P.O. Box 444, Spartanburg, SC 29304 US
(864) 585-1885, *Fax:* (864) 597-0687
www.wilkinsradio.com
barry@wilkinsradio.com
License: Augusta, GA held by J.J. & B. Broadcasting Inc.
Group Owner: Wilkins Communications Network Inc.; (acq 11-22-96; $330,000).
Nat'l Network: Salem Radio Network *Nat'l Reps:* Salem
Arbitron Metro Market: Augusta, GA *Format:* Religious *Hrs. of News Programming:* News progmg 2 hrs wkly *Target Audience:* 35 plus. *Adv. Rates:* 30; 30; 30; 30
Bob Wilkins, CEO
Mitchell Mathis, President/Chief Operating Officer
Mitchell Mathis, Operations Dir
Paul Lindsey, Station Manager
LuAnn Wilkins, Executive Vice President
Greg Garrett, Operations Manager
Barry Bright, SeniorDirector, Client Development
Paige Carrick, Network Media Coordinator
Joel Perkins, Director, Client Development
Amy Cleveland, Network Media Coordinator

WFXA-FM
07-11-1968; 103.1 mhz FM *Hrs Open:* 24; 6 kw; 302 ft.; N33 30 0 W81 56 3
Mailing Address: P.O. Box 1584, Augusta, GA 30903 US
Second Address: 104 Bennett Ln., North Augusta, SC 29841
(803) 279-2330, *Fax:* (803) 279-8149
www.103jamzthefox.com
info@perrybroadcasting.net
License: Augusta, Richmond County, GA held by Perry Broadcasting of Augusta Inc.
Group Owner: Perry Publishing & Broadcasting Co.; (acq 12-12-2007; grpsl)
Arbitron Metro Market: Augusta, GA *Format:* Black *Target Audience:* 25-34; females *Adv. Rates:* 85; 80; 85; 75
Ron Thomas, Operations Dir
Velvet Perry, General Sales Mgr
Lakeshia Collins, News Director
Walter Brumbeloe, Chief Engineer
Jamie Langley, Traffic Manager
TJ Peterson, Technology Director

WGAC
01-01-1940; 580 khz AM *Rebroadcasts:* Simulcast with WGAC-FM Warrenton
PO Box 211045, Augusta, GA 30917 US
(706) 396-7000, *Fax:* (706) 396-7092
www.wgac.com
wgac@wgac.com
License: Augusta, GA held by WGAC License LLC.
Group Owner: Beasley Broadcast Group Inc.; (acq 5-19-92; assumption of debt;
Nat'l Network: CBS *Nat'l Reps:* D & R Radio
Arbitron Metro Market: Augusta, GA *Format:* News, News/Talk, 84, Talk *Special Programming:* Farm 4 hrs, military 3 hrs wkly, Rush Limbaugh Affil. *No. News Employees:* 5 *Target Audience:* 35-65.
George Beasley, Chairman
Kent Dunn, Operations Dir
Terry Kellems, General Sales Mgr
Mary Liz Nolan, News Director
Charlie McCoy, Chief Engineer
Keith Beckum, Farm Director
Harley Drew, Operations Director
Diane Underwood,Traffic Manager

WEZO
11-01-1993; 1230 khz AM *Hrs Open:* 24; 1 kw-U; N33 27 14 W82 01 47
1286 Broad St., Augusta, GA 30906
(706) 922-3834, *Fax:* (706) 922-3831
www.newsradio1230.com
will@newsradio1230.com
License: Augusta, Richmond County, GA held by Will Nunley Broadcasting LLC
Nat'l Network: CNN Radio; Premiere Radio Networks; Westwood One *Regional Network:* Ga. News Net.
Population Served: 350,000 *Arbitron Metro Market:* Augusta, GA *Hrs. of News Programming:* 24 hrs wkly *No. News Employees:* 3 *Target Audience:* 25- women; 25+ men. *Adv. Rates:* 7; 7; 7; 7
Will Nunley, General Manager
Teri Exrleben, General Sales Mgr

***WLPE**
11-17-1984; 91.7 mhz FM *Hrs Open:* 24; 1.15 kw; 589 ft.; N33 34 21 W81 55 23
3213 Huxley Dr, Augusta, GA 30909 US
(706) 309-9610, *Fax:* (706) 309-9669
www.gnnradio.org
ctbarinowski@comcast.net
License: Augusta, Richmond County, GA held by Augusta Radio Fellowship Institute Inc.
Arbitron Metro Market: Augusta, GA *Format:* Christian *Hrs. of News Programming:* News progmg 12 hrs wkly *Target Audience:* General.
Clarence Barinowski, General Manager

WCHZ
07-01-1930; 1480 khz AM; 5 kw-U, DA-N; N33 31 00 W82 00 36
Rebroadcasts: Simulcast WGUS-FM
4051 Jimmie Dyess Pkwy., Augusta, GA 30909
(706) 396-7000, *Fax:* (706) 396-7100
info@wgus.com
License: Augusta, Richmond County, GA held by WCHZ License LLC.
Group Owner: Beasley Broadcast Group Inc.; (acq 5-3-2000; $800,000 with WGAC-FM Warrenton)
Population Served: 66,800 *Arbitron Metro Market:* Augusta, GA *Target Audience:* 18-49; well educated
Richard Chambers, General Manager
Chris O'Kelley, Programming Director
Kent Dunn, General Manager

WTHB
05-01-1960; 1550 khz AM; 5 kw-D, ND2; 0.011 kw-N, ND2; N33 30 0 W81 56 3
Mailing Address: P.O. Box 1584, Augusta, GA 30903 US
Second Address: 104 Bennett Ln., North Augusta, GA 29841
(803) 279-2330, *Fax:* (803) 279-8149
praise969.com
info@perrybroadcasting.net
License: Augusta, GA held by Perry Broadcasting of Augusta Inc.
Group Owner: Perry Publishing & Broadcasting Co.
Nat'l Network: American Urban
Arbitron Metro Market: Augusta, GA *Format:* Gospel *Adv. Rates:* 40; 35; 40; 35
Mary Kingcannon, Programming Director
Walter Brumbeloe, Chief Engineer
Velvet Perry, VP Director of Sales
Tj Peterson, IT Director

WEKL
03-10-1952; 105.7 mhz FM *Hrs Open:* 24; 100 kw; 1217 ft.; N33 25 17 W81 50 19
808 Greene Street, Suite 210, Augusta, GA 30901 US
(706) 396-6000, *Fax:* (706) 396-6010
eagle102.com
travisdylan@clearchannel.com
License: Augusta, Richmond County, GA held by Clear Channel Broadcasting Licenses Inc.
Group Owner: Clear Channel Communications Inc.; (acq 12-19-2000; grpsl)
Arbitron Metro Market: Augusta, GA *Format:* Classic Rock *Target Audience:* 18-44.
Mark Bass, General Manager
Brett Pomykala, General Sales Mgr
Cliff Bennett, Program Director/Digital Content Director
Amanda Washington, Program Director/Digital Content Director
Andrew Harman, Promotions Coordinator
Travis Dylan,Operations Manager

Austell

WAOS
04-16-1968; 1600 khz AM *Hrs Open:* 24 hrs
5815 Westside Road, Austell, GA 30001 US
(770) 944-0900, *Fax:* (770) 944-9794
www.lamejorestacion.com
sammy@lamejorestacion.com
License: Austell, GA held by La Favorita Inc.
Group Owner: La Favorita Inc.; acq 1-24-90).
Arbitron Metro Market: Atlanta, GA *Target Audience:* 18 plus; Hispanics in metro Atlanta & northeast GA
Samuel Zamarron, President
Gracie Zamarron, Station Manager

Avondale Estates

WMLB
11-01-2003; 1690 khz AM *Hrs Open:* 24
1200 West 4th Street, Adel, GA 31620 US
(307) 733-4030
www.jhcr.org
info@jhcr.org
License: Avondale Estates, GA held by JW Broadcasting Inc.
Format: Variety/Diverse
Jim Tallichet, General Manager

Bainbridge

WMGR
08-17-1947; 930 khz AM *Hrs Open:* 18; 5 kw-D, DAN; 0.5 kw-N, DAN; N30 54 25 W84 33 2
809 S. Westover Blvd., Albany, GA 31707 US
(229) 246-1650, *Fax:* (229) 246-1403
www.wmgr.net
wmgr@wmgr.net
License: Bainbridge, GA held by Decatur Broadcasting Inc.
Regional Network: Ga. News Net.
Arbitron Metro Market: Bainbridge, GA *Format:* Oldies *Hrs. of News Programming:* News progmg 10 hrs wkly *Target Audience:* 30 plus.
Coley Voyles, President

WGEX
12-20-1967; 97.3 mhz FM *Hrs Open:* 24; 100 kw; 1,200 ft; N31 09 12 W84 32 42
809 S. Westover Blvd., Albany, GA 28301
(229) 439-9704, *Fax:* (229) 439-1509
www.magic973radio.com
License: Bainbridge, Decatur County, GA held by CC Licenses LLC.
Group Owner: Clear Channel Communications Inc.; (acq 7-11-2000; grpsl).
Nat'l Reps: Christal
Population Served: 900,000 *Arbitron Metro Market:* Albany, GA *Hrs. of News Programming:* News progmg 2 hrs wkly *Target Audience:* 18-49. *Adv. Rates:* 45; 40; 45; 35
John Richards, General Manager
Jasmine Phoenix, Programming Director

WBGE
05-01-2001; 101.9 mhz FM; 6 kw; 328 ft.; N31 0 33 W84 25 16
4143 East River Road, Camilla, GA 31730 US

(229) 246-7776, *Fax:* (229) 246-9995
www.live1019.com
kevin @live1019.com
License: Bainbridge, Decatur County, GA held by Flint Media Inc.
Group Owner: Flint Media Inc.; (acq 7-15-2005; $485,000)
Format: Adult Contemp
Kevin Dowdy, General Manager

Barnesville

WBAF
07-23-1966; 1090 khz AM; 1 kw-D, NDD; N33 3 13 W84 8 7
645 Forsyth Street, Barnesville, GA 30204 US
(309) 834-1100, *Fax:* (309) 834-4390
www.magic1007.fm
License: Barnesville, GA held by Barnesville Broadcasting Inc.
Regional Network: Ga. News Net.
Format: Adult Contemp *Target Audience:* 25-54; adult
Jack Swart, General Manager
Grant Thompson, General Sales Mgr
Chad Fasig, Programming Director
Mark Hill, Chief Engineer

Baxley

WBYZ
07-01-1983; 94.5 mhz FM *Hrs Open:* 24; 100 kw; Ant 1,014 ft; N31 47 10 W82 27 03
Mailing Address: Box 390, Baxley, GA 31513
Second Address: 4005 Golden Isles W., Baxley, GA 31515
(912) 367-3000, *Fax:* (912) 367-9779
www.wbyz.com
peggy@wbyz94.com
License: Baxley, Appling County, GA
Nat'l Network: ABC *Regional Network:* Ga. News Net.
Target Audience: 20-55; those with buying power
Al Graham, President
Peggy Miles, Operations Dir
Peggy Miles, General Manager
Peggy Miles, Station Manager
Peggy Miles, General Sales Mgr
Al Graham, Programming Director
Peggy Miles, Promotions Manager
Cole Younger, NewsDirector
Dick Boekloo, Chief Engineer
Alan DuPriest, Music Director

WUFE
12-01-1954; 1260 khz AM *Hrs Open:* 6 AM-sunset; 5 kw-D; N31 48 00 W82 24 40
Mailing Address: Box 390, Baxley, GA 31513
Second Address: Hwy. 341 W., Baxley, GA 31515
(912) 367-3000, *Fax:* (912) 367-9779
License: Baxley, Appling County, GA held by South Georgia Broadcasters Inc.
Regional Network: Ga. News Net.
Population Served: 75,000*Hrs. of News Programming:* News progmg 6 hrs wkly *Target Audience:* General.
Al Graham, President
Peggy Miles, General Manager
Peggy Miles, Station Manager
Peggy Miles, General Sales Mgr
Dick Boeklod, Chief Engineer

Blackshear

WFNS
03-10-1961; 1350 khz AM; 2.5 kw-D, ND1; 0.117 kw-N, ND1; N31 18 44 W82 14 0
245 Main Street, Blackshear, GA 31516 US
(912) 285-5002, *Fax:* (912) 285-3877
wgaradio@yahoo.com
License: Blackshear, GA held by MarMac Communications LLC.
Group Owner: MarMac Communications LLC; (acq 7-19-2001; $60,000)
Nat'l Network: CNN Radio *Regional Network:* Ga. News Net.
Format: Sports *Special Programming:* Atlanta Braves, Hawks, Falcons, Ga Tech *Target Audience:* General; families *Adv. Rates:* 6; 5; 6; 5
Gary Marmitt, President
Sharon McKeand, Operations Dir
Charlie Kanons, General Sales Mgr
Kevin Thomas, News Director

WKUB
12-01-1979; 105.1 mhz FM *Hrs Open:* 24; 50 kw; 348 ft.; N31 10 54 W82 22 51
Mailing Address: P.O. Box 112, Blackshear, GA 31516 US
Second Address: Box 1472, Waycross, GA 31502
(912) 449-3391, *Fax:* (912) 449-6284
www.waycrossradio.com
wkub@almatel.net
License: Blackshear, Pierce County, GA held by Mattox Broadcasting Inc.
Nat'l Network: ABC *Regional Network:* Ga. News Net. *Nat'l Reps:* Dora-Clayton
Format: Country *Hrs. of News Programming:* News progmg 4 hrs wkly *Target Audience:* 25 plus.
G. Troy Mattox, President
Jim MIller, General Sales Mgr

Blakely

WBBK-FM
11-01-1984; 93.1 mhz FM; 45 kw; 328 ft.; N31 17 55 W85 3 18
P.O. Box 87, Donalsonville, GA 31745 US
(910) 253-6593
www.kjbbfm.com
info@kjbbfm.com
License: Blakely, Early County, GA held by Magic Broadcasting Alabama Licensing LLC.
Group Owner: Magic Broadcasting LLC; (acq 5-13-2004; grpsl)
Arbitron Metro Market: Modesto CA *Format:* Christian
Danny Hawkins, President

Blue Ridge

WPPL
01-01-1971; 103.9 mhz FM *Hrs Open:* 24; 5.5 kw; 341 ft.; N34 52 3 W84 20 2
Mailing Address: 3350 Comberland Cirlcl, Suite 1700 Riverwood, Atlanta, GA 30339 US
Second Address: 333 W. Highland St., Blue Ridge, GA 35013
(706) 632-9775, *Fax:* (706) 632-5922
www.mountaincountryradio.com
mcwolf@etcmail.com
License: Blue Ridge, Fannin County, GA held by Fannin County Broadcasting Co. Inc.
Nat'l Network: AP Radio *Regional Network:* Ga. News Net.
Arbitron Metro Market: Chattanooga, TN *Format:* Country *No. News Employees:* 9 *Target Audience:* 25-54; adults *Adv. Rates:* 14; 14; 14; 12
Tim White, President
Jim Quinton, Operations Dir
Vicky Pulliam, General Manager

Bolingbroke

WWWD
01-01-2005; 102.1 mhz FM; 4.5 kw; 377 ft.; N32 54 30 W83 46 37
188 South Bellevue, Suite 222, Memphis, TN 38104 US
(901) 375-9324, *Fax:* (901) 375-0041
www.flinn.com
mail@flinn.com
License: Bolingbroke, Monroe County, GA held by George S. Flinn Jr.
Arbitron Metro Market: Memphis, TN
George Flinn Jr., General Manager

Boston

WTUF
07-18-1988; 106.3 mhz FM *Hrs Open:* 24; 6 kw; 328 ft.; N30 47 40 W83 46 54
Mailing Address: P. O. Box 129, Thomasville, GA 31799 US
Second Address: 117 Remington Ave., Thomasville, GA 31792
(229) 225-1063, *Fax:* (229) 226-1361
www.wtufradio.com
lenrob@rose.net
License: Boston, Thomas County, GA held by Boston Radio Co.
Nat'l Network: AP Network News *Regional Network:* Agrinet; Ga. News Net. *Nat'l Reps:* Rgnl Reps
Arbitron Metro Market: Boston, GA *Format:* Country *Special Programming:* Bluegrass 5 hrs, gospel 7 hrs wkly *Target Audience:* 18-65; adults
Len Robinson, President

Bostwick

WMOQ
01-01-1994; 92.3 mhz FM; 3 kw; 328 ft.; N33 44 49 W83 33 23
Mailing Address: 1081 N. Cherokee Road, Social Circle, GA 30275 US
Second Address: 1610 Launius Rd., Good Hope, GA
(770) 267-0923, *Fax:* (770) 342-8135
www.wmoqfm.com
julio@wmoqfm.com
License: Bostwick, Morgan County, GA held by Bostwick Broadcasting Group Inc.
Arbitron Metro Market: Bostwick, GA *Format:* Country
B.R. Anderson, Sr, President
Julio, Operations Dir
David Malcolm, General Manager
Melanie Ann, News Director

Bowdon

WBZY
12-09-1996; 105.3 mhz FM; 61 kw; 1204 ft.; N33 24 41 W84 49 48
107 Marie Lane, Tallapoosa, GA 30176 US
(404)741-1053, *Fax:* (404) 367-1111
1053elpatron.com
License: Bowdon, Carroll County, GA held by CC Licenses LLC.
Group Owner: Clear Channel Communications Inc.; (acq 11-24-2000; at least $7 million)
Arbitron Metro Market: Atlanta, GA
Jerry DelCore, General Manager
Liz Leos, Programming Director
Gabriel Diaz, Assistant Director

Bremen

WGMI
10-01-1957; 1440 khz AM *Hrs Open:* 24; 2.5 kw-D, NDD; 0.062 kw-N, ND1; N33 42 56 W85 9 34
613 Tallapoosa Street, Bremen, GA 30110 US
(770) 537-0840, *Fax:* (770) 406-2324
www.wgmiradio.com
wgmi1440@yahoo.com
License: Bremen, GA held by Garner Ministries Inc.
Format: Christian, Gospel, 74 *Special Programming:* High School Sports *Hrs. of News Programming:* news progmg 3 hrs wkly *No. News Employees:* 1 *Target Audience:* 25-54; majority married women with children*Adv. Rates:* Contact us for rates
Horace Garner, CEO
Peggy Garner, Operations Dir

Broxton

WULS
11-01-1993; 103.7 mhz FM; 6 kw; 328 ft.; N31 35 12 W82 52 25
P.O. Box 2450, Douglas, GA 31533 US
(912) 384-9857, *Fax:* (912) 384-0016
www.wuls1037.com
wuls@windstream.net
License: Broxton, Coffee County, GA held by WULS Inc.
Arbitron Metro Market: Broxton, GA *Format:* Christian, Gospel
Wyndel Burnsed, Owner
Leona.M.Burnsed, Owner

Brunswick

*WAYR-FM
01-01-1996; 90.7 mhz FM; 14 kw; 328 ft.; N31 11 39 W81 29 30
2500 Russell Road, Green Cove Springs, FL 32043 US
(406) 721-6800, *Fax:* (406) 329-1850
www.trail1033.com
rharsell@simmonsmedia.com
License: Brunswick, Glynn County, GA held by Good Tidings Trust Inc.
Arbitron Metro Market: Florence MT *Format:* Triple A *No. News Employees:* 1 *Target Audience:* 25-54; adults
Rod Harsell, General Manager
Robert Chase, Programming Director

WGIG
03-05-1949; 1440 khz AM; 5 kw-D, DAN; 1 kw-N, DAN; N31 10 7 W81 32 14
Two Bala Plaza, Suite 801, Bala-Cynwyd, PA 19004 US
(912) 267-1025, *Fax:* (912) 264-5462
www.1440wgig.net
ryfun@adelphia.net
License: Brunswick, GA held by Qantum of Brunswick License Co. LLC.
Group Owner: Qantum Communications Corp.; (acq 7-2-03; grpsl).
Nat'l Network: CBS *Regional Network:* Ga. News Net.
Arbitron Metro Market: Brunswick, GA *Format:* News, News/Talk, 86
Scott Ryfun, Operations Dir
Jonathan Havens, General Manager
Gerri Landrum, Director of Sales
Larry Landrum, Director of Sales

WMOG
06-01-1940; 1490 khz AM *Hrs Open:* 24; 0.6 kw-U, ND1; N31 9 42 W81 28 28
Two Bala Plaza, Suite 801, Bala-Cynwyd, PA 19004 US
(912) 267-1025, *Fax:* (912) 264-5462
www.1490wmog.net
scottrysun@gmail.com
License: Brunswick, GA held by Qantum of Brunswick License Co. LLC.

Group Owner: Qantum Communications Corp.; (acq 7-2-2003; grpsl).
Nat'l Reps: McGavren Guild
Arbitron Metro Market: Brunswick, GA *Format:* Sports *Special Programming:* Black 8 hrs, class one hr wkly *Hrs. of News Programming:* news progmg 20 hrs wkly *No. News Employees:* 1 *Target Audience:* 35 plus.
Larry Landrum, General Manager
Scott Ryfun, Programming Director

WRJY
06-30-1994; 104.1 mhz FM *Hrs Open:* 24; 4.2 kw; 390 ft.; N31 11 39 W81 29 30
108 Benedict Road, Brunswick, GA 31525 US
(912) 261-1000, *Fax:* (912) 265-8391
www.thewave1041.com
License: Brunswick, Glynn County, GA held by Golden Isles Broadcasting LLC
Nat'l Reps: Rgnl Reps
Arbitron Metro Market: Brunswick, GA *Format:* Country *Hrs. of News Programming:* News progmg 168 hrs wkly *Target Audience:* 25-54; urban female *Adv. Rates:* 15; 15; 15; 10
Ed Strang Steel, Operations Dir
Joe Willie Sousa, General Manager
Cathy Trimble, General Sales Mgr
Mark Douglas, Programming Director
Dick Boekeloo, Chief Engineer
Mike Cornell, Production Manager

WSFN
09-01-1966; 790 khz AM; 0.5 kw-D, DA2; 0.115 kw-N, DA2; N31 8 40 W81 34 56
7515 Blythe Island Hwy, Brunswick, GA 31523 US
(912) 264-6251, *Fax:* (912) 264-9991
thefanradio@aol.com
License: Brunswick, GA held by MarMac Communications L.L.C.
Group Owner: MarMac Communications LLC; (acq 4-98; $350,000)
Nat'l Network: ABC *Regional Network:* Ga. News Net.
Arbitron Metro Market: Brunswick, GA *Format:* Sports
Gary Marmitt, President

WSOL-FM
09-01-1966; 101.5 mhz FM *Hrs Open:* 24; 100 kw; 1463 ft.; N30 49 16 W81 44 14
50 East Rivercenter Blvd, Suite 1200, Covington, KY 41011 US
(904) 996-0400 / (904) 642-3030, *Fax:* (904) 997-7713
www.v1015.com
karmenbrooks@clearchannel.com
License: Brunswick, Glynn County, GA held by Citicasters Licenses L.P.
Group Owner: Clear Channel Communications Inc.; (acq 5-4-99; grpsl).
Arbitron Metro Market: Jacksonville, FL *Format:* Urban Contemporary
Norm Fever, General Manager

***WWIO-FM**
02-28-1993; 88.9 mhz FM *Hrs Open:* 24; 11.5 kw; 151 ft.; N31 11 20 W81 29 5 *Rebroadcasts:* Rebroadcasts WSVH(FM) Savannah 100%
260 - 14th Street, N.W., Atlanta, GA 30318 US
(404) 685-2690, *Fax:* (404) 685-2684
www.gpb.org
ask@gpb.org
License: Brunswick, Glynn County, GA held by Georgia Public Telecommunications Commission.
Nat'l Network: NPR; PRI *Wire Services:* AP
Arbitron Metro Market: Brunswick, GA *Format:* Classical, News *Hrs. of News Programming:* news progmg 51 hrs wkly *No. News Employees:* 10 *Target Audience:* Adults: 35 plus.
Michael H. McDougald, Chairman
Nancy Hall, CEO
Teya Ryan, President
Russell Wells, Operations Dir
Bob Houghton, General Manager
Eric Nauert, Station Manager
Rob Maynard, Programming Director
Susanna Capelouto, News Director
Bonnie Bean, CFO
Tom Barclay, Operations Manager
Janice Paul, Vice Chair

WMUV
11-08-1965; 100.7 mhz FM *Hrs Open:* 24; 62 kw; 1473 ft.; N30 49 16 W81 44 14
Broadcast Plaza, Crane Ave., Pittsburgh, PA 15220 US
(904) 727-9696, *Fax:* (904) 721-9322
www.countrylegends1007.com
info@kool1007.com
License: Brunswick, Glynn County, GA held by Renda Broadcasting Corp.
Group Owner: Renda Broadcasting Corp.; (acq 1996; $6.5 million with WGNE-FM Palatka, FL)
Nat'l Reps: McGavren Guild
Arbitron Metro Market: Jacksonville, FL *Format:* Country *Adv. Rates:* 50; 45; 60; 35
Tony Renda Sr., CEO
Bill Reese, General Manager
Charlie Jennings, General Sales Mgr
Chuck Beck, Programming Director
Stacey Steiner, Promotions Manager
Judy Riley, News Director
Bob Dillehay, Chief Engineer
Jim Byard, PublicService Director
Buffy Daum, Interactive Sales Manager
Leslie Rimer, Web Content Manager/ Web Designer

Buckhead

***WPMA**
12-01-2002; 102.7 mhz FM *Hrs Open:* 24; 7.5 kw; 594 ft.; N33 30 10 W83 15 37
3213 Huxley Drive, Augusta, GA 30909 US
(706) 309-9610
www.gnnradio.org
ctbarinowski@comcast.net
License: Buckhead, Morgan County, GA held by Barinowski Investment Co. L.P.
Group Owner: Good News Network
Format: Christian
Clarence Barinowski, General Manager

Buena Vista

WEAM-FM
06-21-2001; 100.7 mhz FM *Hrs Open:* 24; 2.6 kw; 502 ft.; N32 20 33 W84 39 18
P.O. Box 180, Hawkinsville, GA 31036 US
(706) 576-3565, *Fax:* (706) 576-3683
www.weamfm.com
foxie1049@aol.com
License: Buena Vista, Marion County, GA held by Davis Broadcasting Inc. of Columbus.
Group Owner: Davis Broadcasting Inc.; (acq 7-30-2003).
Arbitron Metro Market: Columbus, GA *Format:* Gospel
Gregory Davis, Owner
Carl Conner, Operations Dir
Angela Verdejo, General Sales Mgr
Pam Dixon, Programming Director
Nicole Buffong, Promotions Manager
Anitra Strickland, Traffic Manager

Buford

WLKQ-FM
01-01-1970; 102.3 mhz FM *Hrs Open:* 24; 4.2 kw; 390 ft.; N34 7 16 W83 58 35
6259 Woodlake Drive, Buford, GA 30518 US
(770) 623-8772, *Fax:* (770) 623-4722
www.laraza1023.com
info@laraza1023.com
License: Buford, Gwinnett County, GA held by Davis Broadcasting of Atlanta L.L.C.
Group Owner: Davis Broadcasting Inc.; (acq 9-30-2003; $5.25 million)
Regional Network: Ga. News Net.
Arbitron Metro Market: Atlanta, GA *Hrs. of News Programming:* news progmg 6 hrs wkly *No. News Employees:* 2 *Target Audience:* 35-54; upper-middle class professionals
Gregory Davis, President
Brian Barber, General Manager

WXEM
12-12-1957; 1460 khz AM; 5 kw-D, ND1; 0.193 kw-N, ND1; N34 7 15 W83 58 35
5815 Westside Road, PO Box 746, Austell, GA 30001 US
(770) 944-0900, *Fax:* (770) 944-9794
www.lamejorestacion.com
ammy@lamejorestacion.com
License: Buford, GA held by La Favorita Inc.
Group Owner: La Favorita Inc.; acq 6-12-91;
Arbitron Metro Market: Buford, GA *Target Audience:* Hispanic.
Samuel Zamarron, CEO
Gracie Zamarron, Station Manager
Sammy, Programming Director
Gracie, Advertising

Byron

***WPWB**
01-01-1988; 90.5 mhz FM *Hrs Open:* 24; 16.5 kw; 453 ft.; N32 40 55 W83 22 10
3213 Huxley Drive, Augusta, GA 30909 US
(706) 309-9610, *Fax:* (706) 309-9669
www.gnnradio.org
ctbarinowski@comcast.net
License: Byron, Peach County, GA held by Augusta Radio Fellowship Institute Inc.
Group Owner: Good News Network
Format: Christian *Hrs. of News Programming:* News progmg 12 hrs wkly *Target Audience:* General.
Clarence Barinowski, General Manager

Cairo

WGRA
10-01-1949; 790 khz AM; 1 kw-D, ND2; 0.11 kw-N, ND2; N30 54 8 W84 14 3
Mailing Address: PO Box 120, Cairo, GA 31728 US
Second Address: 1809 U.S. 84 W., Cairo, GA 39828
(229) 377-4392, *Fax:* (229) 377-4564
www.wgra.net
jeff@wgra.net
License: Cairo, GA held by Lovett Broadcasting Enterprises Inc.
Regional Network: Ga. News Net. *Nat'l Reps:* Rgnl Reps
Format: News, News/Talk, 86 *Special Programming:* Black 6 hrs wkly *Target Audience:* 30 plus; mainly women
Jeffrey Lovett, President

WWLD
06-01-1983; 102.3 mhz FM; 27 kw; 604 ft.; N30 29 32 W84 17 2
PO Box 120, Cairo, GA 31728 US
(850) 201-3000, *Fax:* (850) 205-3711
blazin1023.com
License: Cairo, Grady County, GA held by Cumulus Licensing LLC.
Group Owner: Cumulus Media Inc.; (acq 10-10-01; $1.5 million including noncompete agreement).
Nat'l Reps: Katz Radio
Arbitron Metro Market: Tallahassee, FL *Format:* Urban Contemporary *Target Audience:* 18-34. *Adv. Rates:* 45; 40; 45; 50
Barry Kaye, General Manager
Jay Blaze, Programming Director

Calhoun

WEBS
11-01-1966; 1030 khz AM
Mailing Address: Post Office Box 1299, Calhoun, GA 30701 US
Second Address: 427 S. Wall St., Calhoun, GA 30703
(706) 629-1110, *Fax:* (706) 629-7092
www.webscalhoun.com/
webs@webscalhoun.com
License: Calhoun, GA held by Radio WEBS Inc.
Nat'l Network: Jones Radio Networks
Arbitron Metro Market: Calhoun GA *Format:* Oldies *Special Programming:* Black 2 hrs wkly *Target Audience:* 18-52. *Adv. Rates:* 18; 20; 20; 15
Ken Payne, President

WJTH
06-16-1977; 900 khz AM *Hrs Open:* 24; 1 kw-D, 266 w-N; 256 feet; N34 27 40 W84 53 44
Mailing Address: Box 1119, 329 RICHARDSON RD SE, Calhoun, GA 30701
Second Address: 329 Richardson Rd. S.E., Calhoun, GA 30701
(706) 629-6397, *Fax:* (706) 629-8463
www.wjth.com
am900@wjth.com
License: Calhoun, Gordon County, GA held by Cherokee Broadcasting Co.
Nat'l Network: ABC; Dial Global *Regional Network:* Ga. News Net.; Southeast Agnet *Nat'l Reps:* Rgnl Reps
Population Served: 50,000 *Arbitron Metro Market:* Atlanta, GA *Special Programming:* Farm one hr, gospel 2 hrs, relg 16 hrs wkly *Hrs. of News Programming:* news progmg 20 hrs wkly *No. News Employees:* 1 *TargetAudience:* 18-64; general *Adv. Rates:* 15; 14; 15; 14
Sam Thomas, General Manager
Keith Thomas, Station Manager
Gloria Cooley, General Sales Mgr
Sam Thomas, Programming Director
Phil Baker, Chief Engineer

Camilla

WZBN
04-01-1977; 105.5 mhz FM *Hrs Open:* 24; 6 kw; 276 ft.; N31 18 51 W84 12 18
970 Martin Luther King Jr., Dr, Sw, Suite 202, Atlanta, GA 30314 US
(229) 888-5000, *Fax:* (912) 888-5960
matt.patrick@cumulus.com

License: Camilla, Mitchell County, GA held by Extreme Media Group LLC
Regional Network: Ga. News Net. *Nat'l Reps:* Katz Radio
Arbitron Metro Market: Albany, GA *Format:* Urban Contemporary
Special Programming: Blues 5 hrs, gospel 16 hrs wkly *Hrs. of News Programming:* news progmg 3 hrs wkly *No. News Employees:* 1 *Target Audience:* 25-54; female
Paul Bucurel, General Manager

Canton

WCHK
04-11-1957; 1290 khz AM
P. O. Box 1290, Canton, GA 30114 US
(770) 623-8772, *Fax:* (770) 623-4722
www.laraza1023.com/inicio1/index.php/es/
License: Canton, GA held by Davis Broadcasting of Atlanta L.L.C.
Group Owner: Davis Broadcasting Inc.; (acq 1-17-2007; $3.8 million with WNSY(FM) Talking Rock)
Arbitron Metro Market: Suwanee,GA
Brian Barber, General Manager

WWVA-FM
08-01-1964; 105.7 mhz FM *Hrs Open:* 24; 20 kw; 781 ft.; N34 3 58 W84 27 15
P. O. Box 1290, Canton, GA 30114 US
(404) 607-1336, *Fax:* (404) 367-1105
www.vivaatlanta.com
License: Canton, Cherokee County, GA held by CC Licenses LLC.
Group Owner: Clear Channel Communications Inc.; (acq 3-29-2004; $31 million).
Arbitron Metro Market: Atlanta, GA *Format:* Spanish
Ricardo Villalona, General Manager

Carrollton

WLBB
11-19-1975; 1330 khz AM *Hrs Open:* 24
100 Wexford Place, Athens, GA 30606 US
(678) 601-1330, *Fax:* (678) 601-8256
www.gradickcommunications.com
cworthington@newstalk1330.com
License: Carrollton, GA held by WYAI Inc.
Nat'l Network: CBS
Arbitron Metro Market: Carrollton, GA, *Format:* News, News/Talk, 86 *No. News Employees:* 2
Steve Gradick, President
Colin Worthington, News Director
Michael Vincent, Production Director
Mitch Grey, Sports Director

WBTR-FM
01-01-1964; 92.1 mhz FM *Hrs Open:* 24; 0.58 kw; 636 ft.; N33 33 54 W85 1 2
305 Courtyard Square, Carrollton, GA 30117 US
(770) 832-9685, *Fax:* (770) 830-1027
www.gradickcommunications.com
cworthington@newstalk1330.com
License: Carrollton, Carroll County, GA held by WYAI Inc.
Regional Network: Ga. News Net.
Arbitron Metro Market: Carrollton, GA, *Format:* Country *Special Programming:* Black 5 hrs wkly *Hrs. of News Programming:* news progmg 3 hrs wkly *No. News Employees:* 1 *Target Audience:* 25-49.
Steven Gradick, President
Colin Worthington, News Director
Michael Vincent, Production Director
Mitch Grey, Sports Director

***WUWG**
02-19-1973; 90.7 mhz FM *Hrs Open:* 24; 0.43 kw; 495 ft.; N33 33 50 W85 1 4 *Rebroadcasts:* WJSP, Warm Springs/Columbus, GA, 75%
Learning Resources Cntr, Carrollton, GA 30118 US
(404) 685-2690, *Fax:* (404) 685-2684
www.gpb.org
ask@gpb.org
License: Carrollton, Carroll County, GA held by Georgia Public Telecommunications Commission
Nat'l Network: NPR; PRI *Wire Services:* AP
Arbitron Metro Market: Carrollton, GA *Format:* Classical, News *Special Programming:* Folk 2 hrs, bluegrass 2 hrs, new age 3 hrs *Hrs. of News Programming:* news progmg 25-30 hrs wkly *No. News Employees:* 10*Target Audience:* General; students & area residents
Nancy Hall, CEO
Tom Barclay, Operations Dir
Bob Houghton, General Manager
Rob Maynard, Programming Director
Nancy Zintak, Promotions Manager
Susanna Capelouto, News Director
Bonnie Bean, CFO
Steve Carey, Vice President ofProduction

Cartersville

WBHF
07-17-1946; 1450 khz AM *Hrs Open:* 24
406 Old Mill Road, Cartersville, GA 30120 US
(770) 386-1450, *Fax:* (770) 382-5390
www.wbhfradio.org/
news@wbhfradio.org
License: Cartersville, GA held by Anverse Inc.
Nat'l Network: ABC; AP Radio *Wire Services:* AP
Arbitron Metro Market: Atlanta, GA *Format:* News, Oldies, 84 *Hrs. of News Programming:* news progmg 10 hrs wkly *No. News Employees:* 3
Ernestine Jones, Operations Dir
Matt Santini, General Manager

***WCCV**
01-24-1983; 91.7 mhz FM *Hrs Open:* 6am-8pm; 7.3 kw; 935 ft.; N34 9 34 W85 2 13
779 South Erwin Street, Cartersville, GA 30120 US
(770) 387-0917, *Fax:* (770) 387-2856
www.ibn.org
License: Cartersville, Bartow County, GA held by Immanuel Broadcasting.
Arbitron Metro Market: Cartersville, GA *Format:* Religious
Patrick Miller, CFO
Ed Tuten, President
Neil Hopper, General Manager
Howard Tuten, Station Manager
Billy Williams, Programming Director

WYXC
09-21-1961; 1270 khz AM *Hrs Open:* 24
1410 Highway 411, N.E., Cartersville, GA 30120 US
(770) 382-1306
www.newstalk1270.com
info@newstalk1270.com
License: Cartersville, GA held by Clarion Communications Inc.
Arbitron Metro Market: Atlanta, GA *Format:* News, Sports, 86 *Hrs. of News Programming:* news progmg 15 hrs. wkly *No. News Employees:* 1 *Target Audience:* 25-55.
Charles Shiflett, President
Jim Adams, Station Manager
Connie Dixon, General Sales Mgr
Charles Brachel, Programming Director
Allen Schmelz, Chief Engineer
Manny Garrett, Chief of Engineering

Chatsworth

***WNGH-FM**
11-13-1976; 98.9 mhz FM *Hrs Open:* 24; 0.42 kw; 1729 ft.; N34 45 6 W84 42 54
613 Silver Circle, Dalton, GA 30721 US
(404) 685-2415
www.gpb.org
License: Chatsworth, Murray County, GA held by The Foundation for Public Broadcasting in Georgia Inc.
Nat'l Network: NPR; PRI *Wire Services:* AP
TV Affiliate: WNGH-TV affil *Format:* Classical, News *Special Programming:* Jazz 16 hrs wkly *Hrs. of News Programming:* news progmg 41 hrs wkly *No. News Employees:* 10 *Target Audience:* 35 plus; adults
Nancy Hall, CEO
Tom Barclay, Operations Dir
Bob Houghton, General Manager
Rob Maynard, Programming Director
Susanna Capelouto, News Director
Bonnie Bean, CFO
John Sepulvado, N.W. GA Bureau Chief

Chauncey

WQIL
10-20-1995; 101.3 mhz FM *Hrs Open:* 24; 50 kw; 492 ft.; N32 22 59 W83 7 8
P. O. Box 98, Milan, GA 31060 US
(478) 272-4422, *Fax:* (478) 275-4657
www.1013wqil.com
webmaster@1013wqil.com
License: Chauncey, Dodge County, GA held by GSW Inc.
Regional Reps: Regional Reps
Arbitron Metro Market: Macon, GA *Format:* Gospel *Hrs. of News Programming:* News progmg one hr wkly *Target Audience:* 30 plus; Christians
G.S. Walker, Operations Dir
Rick Humphrey, General Manager
J. Morgan Dowdy, Partner

Clarkesville

WCHM
12-01-1989; 1490 khz AM *Hrs Open:* 24
Mailing Address: W Waters St, Clarkesville, GA 30523 US
Second Address: 1331 Washington St., Clarkesville, GA 30523
(706) 839-1490, *Fax:* (706) 754-8621
www.wchmradio.com/
northgeorgiaradio@hemc.net
License: Clarkesville, GA held by Brian Rothell.
Nat'l Network: USA
Arbitron Metro Market: Clarkesville, GA *Format:* Christian *Hrs. of News Programming:* news progmg 5 hrs wkly *No. News Employees:* 1 *Target Audience:* 25-62.
Brian Rothell, General Manager

WDUN-FM
01-01-1990; 102.9 mhz FM *Hrs Open:* 24; 16 kw; 413 ft; N34 29 05 W83 38 24
Mailing Address: PO Box 10, Gainesville, GA 30503
Second Address: 1102 Thompson Bridge Rd. N.E., Gainesville, GA 30501
(770) 532-9921, *Fax:* (770) 532-0459
MAJIC1029.com and AccessNorthGa.com
jay.jacobs@jacobsmedia.net
License: Clarkesville, Habersham County, GA held by JWJ Properties Inc.
Group Owner: Jacobs Media Corp.; (acq 3-19-92).
Nat'l Network: Westwood One *Wire Services:* AP
Population Served: 500,000*Target Audience:* 25-54; females with a median age of 41
John W. Jacobs Jr., Chairman
John W. Jacobs III, CEO
Joel Williams, General Manager
Bill Maine, Programming Director

Claxton

WCLA
07-20-1958; 1470 khz AM *Hrs Open:* 24; 1 kw-D, ND1; 0.26 kw-N, ND1; N32 10 12 W81 53 56
316 N. River St, Claxton, GA 30714 US
(912) 739-9252, *Fax:* (912) 739-0050
www.wclaradio.net
radioevans@bellsouth.net
License: Claxton, GA held by W. Danny Swain
Nat'l Network: ABC *Regional Network:* Ga. News Net.
Arbitron Metro Market: Claxton, GA *Format:* Oldies *Special Programming:* Farm 1.5 hrs, Hispanic 6 hrs, relg 4 hrs wkly *No. News Employees:* 1 *Target Audience:* 35-64; adults *Adv. Rates:* 10; 10; 10; 7
W. Swain, President
Herman Moody, Operations Dir
W. Smith, General Manager
Martin Foglia, Chief Engineer

WMCD
09-15-1972; 107.3 mhz FM *Hrs Open:* 24; 25 kw; 328 ft.; N32 10 1 W81 54 7
Mailing Address: 607 Cricklewood Circle, Heathrow, FL 32746 US
Second Address: 561 E. Olliff St., Statesboro, GA 30458
(912) 764-6000, *Fax:* (912) 764-8827
spots@georgiaeagleradio.com
License: Claxton, Evans County, GA held by Georgia Eagle Broadcasting Inc..
Group Owner: Georgia Eagle Broadcasting Inc.; (acq 5-21-2007; grpsl)
Nat'l Network: Westwood One *Regional Reps:* Rgnl Reps
Arbitron Metro Market: Heathrow, FL *Format:* Adult Contemp *Hrs. of News Programming:* news progmg 7 hrs wkly *No. News Employees:* 1 *Target Audience:* 25-50; general *Adv. Rates:* 12; 12; 12; 12
Jeff Anderson, General Manager
Buddy Horne, Programming Director
Cornell Burgess, News Director

Clayton

WGHC(AM)
05-08-2009; 1400 khz AM *Hrs Open:* 24/7; 1KW-U; N34 51 41 W83 24 25
Box 1149, 18 Radio Lane, Clayton, GA 30525
(706) 782-1041, *Fax:* (706) 782-4252
www.sky104.com
sky104wrbn@gmail.com
License: Clayton, Rabun County, GA held by Tugart Properties, LLC
Group Owner: Georgia-Carolina Radiocasting Companies
Nat'l Network: CBS Radio *Regional Network:* Ga. News Net.
Population Served: 13,351*Format:* Adult Contemp, Talk *Special Programming:* Local News *Hrs. of News Programming:* news

progmg 5 hrs wkly *No. News Employees:* 1 *Target Audience:* 35 plus; upper income
Art Sutton, President
Tug Carter, Operations Dir
Adam Wright, VP and General Manager
Robin Dake, Programming Director
Marty Lee, Chief Engineer
Kathern S. Granberg, Sales Representative
John Durham, Disc Jockey
Jewell WilbanksSpeed, Office Manager

WRBN
06-11-1990; 104.1 mhz FM *Hrs Open:* 24; 0.37 kw; 1296 ft.; N34 54 24 W83 24 56
Mailing Address: 164 Tanner Bluff, Athens, GA 30606 US
Second Address: 18 Radio Lane, Clayton, GA 30525
(706) 782-4251,(706) 782-1041, *Fax:* (706) 782-4252
sky104@rabun.net
License: Clayton, Rabun County, GA held by Sutton Radiocasting Corp.
Group Owner: Georgia-Carolina Radiocasting Companies
Nat'l Network: ABC
Format: Adult Contemp, News *Special Programming:* NASCAR/Local Sports *Hrs. of News Programming:* news progmg 2 hrs wkly *No. News Employees:* 1 *Target Audience:* 25 plus
Douglas M. Sutton, Jr, President
John Durham, Operations Dir
Robin Dake, Programming Director
Marty Lee, Chief Engineer
M. Terry Carter, Vice President
Vicki Childs, Vice President

WGHC
05-08-2009; 1400 khz AM *Hrs Open:* 24/7
US
(706) 782 4251, *Fax:* (706) 782 4252
www.rabunradio.com
License: Clayton, GA held by Tugart Properties LLC.
Group Owner: Georgia-Carolina Radiocasting Companies
Nat'l Network: CBS Radio *Regional Network:* Ga. News Net.
Arbitron Metro Market: Clayton, GA *Format:* News *Special Programming:* Local News *Hrs. of News Programming:* 15 hours weekly *No. News Employees:* 2
Douglas M Sutton Jr., President
John Durham, Operations Dir
Scott Kimbler, Programming Director
Marty Lee, Chief Engineer
M. Terry Carter, Vice President
Vickie Childs, Vice President

Clermont

WNGA
12-06-1993; 105.1 mhz FM *Hrs Open:* 24; 1.7 kw; 614 ft.; N34 44 55 W83 43 43
Mailing Address: 50 East Rivercenter Blvd., Suite 1200, Covington, KY 41011 US
Second Address: 705 Brucken Strasse, Suite 201, Helen, GA 30545
(706) 878-1051, *Fax:* (706) 878-1433
www.georgia1051.com
jkyzer@gacaradio.com
License: Clermont, White County, GA held by Tugart Properties, LLC
Group Owner: Georgia-Carolina Radiocasting Companies; (acq 6-01-2009; $705,000).
Nat'l Network: AP Radio
Format: Country *Special Programming:* Local News/Classic Country(Nights) *Hrs. of News Programming:* 5 *No. News Employees:* 1 *Target Audience:* 25 plus
Art Sutton, President
Misty Reid Richardson, Station Manager
Scott Kimbler, Programming Director
Marty Lee, Chief Engineer
Tug Carter, Vice President
Jason Kyzer, Vice President

Cleveland

WAZX-FM
01-01-1989; 101.9 mhz FM; 0.35 kw; 1344 ft.; N34 30 32 W83 48 27
5113 Powers Ferry Road, Atlanta, GA 30327 US
(406) 657-2941, *Fax:* (406) 657-2977
www.yellowstonepublicradio.org
License: Cleveland, White County, GA held by WAZX-FM Inc.
Format: Classical, Jazz, 60
Lois Bent, General Manager

WRWH
09-27-1958; 1350 khz AM *Hrs Open:* 6 AM-sunset; 1 kw-D, ND2; 0.093 kw-N, ND2; N34 35 11 W83 46 1
Mailing Address: Box 181, Cleveland, GA 30528 US
Second Address: 681 Hood St., Cleveland, GA 30528
(706) 865-3181, *Fax:* (706) 865-0421
wrwh.com
wrwh@windstream.net
License: Cleveland, GA held by White County Media LLC
Regional Network: Ga. News Net.
Format: Religious *Target Audience:* 35 plus.
Dean Dyer, President
Dean Dyer, General Manager

Cochran

***WMUM-FM**
02-04-1985; 89.7 mhz FM *Hrs Open:* 24; 43 kw horiz, 100 kw vert; 998 ft.; N32 28 11 W83 15 17 *Rebroadcasts:* Rebroadcasts WJSP-FM Warm Springs 80%
260 - 14th Street, N.W., Atlanta, GA 30318 US
(478) 301-5760, *Fax:* (404) 685-2684
www.gpb.org
ask@gpb.org
License: Cochran, Bleckley County, GA held by Georgia Public Telecommunications Commission.
Nat'l Network: NPR; PRI *Wire Services:* AP
Arbitron Metro Market: Macon, GA *TV Affiliate:* WMUM-TV affil
Format: Classical, News *Special Programming:* Jazz 18 hrs wkly *Hrs. of News Programming:* news progmg 40 hrs wkly *No. News Employees:* 10*Target Audience:* Adults 35+
Nancy Hall, CEO
Tom Barclay, Operations Dir
Bob Houghton, General Manager
Rob Maynard, Programming Director
Nancy Zintak, Promotions Manager
Susanna Capelonto, News Director
Bonnie Bean, CFO

WDXQ
07-04-1965; 1440 khz AM *Hrs Open:* 24; 1 kw-D; N32 24 43 W83 21 42
157 Jac Arts Rd., Cochran, GA 31014
(478) 934-6337, *Fax:* (478) 934-0929
taylor@ham.net
License: Cochran, Bleckley County, GA held by Georgia Eagle Broadcasting Co.
Group Owner: Georgia Eagle Broadcasting Inc.; (acq 5-21-2007; grpsl)
Population Served: 30,000*Special Programming:* Black 6 hrs, farm 3 hrs, gospel 6 hrs wkly *Target Audience:* 18-54; adults
Tommy Palmer, General Manager
James Gay, Chief Engineer

WRWR-FM
07-04-1968; 96.7 mhz FM; 3 kw; 319 ft; N32 24 43 W83 21 42
Box 766, 157 Jac Arts Rd., Cochran, GA 31014
(478) 934-6337, *Fax:* (478) 934-0929
License: Cochran, Bleckley County, GA
Group Owner: Georgia Eagle Broadcasting Inc.
Nat'l Network: ABC *Nat'l Reps:* Clear Channel *Wire Services:* UPI
Population Served: 10,291*Target Audience:* Adults 18-54.
Carl Strandell, General Sales Mgr

College Park

WNNX
01-12-2001; 100.5 mhz FM *Hrs Open:* 24; 12.5 kw; 978 ft.; N33 45 34 W84 23 19
140 East Market Street, York, PA 17401 US
(404) 497-4700, *Fax:* (404) 497-4735
www.atlantasrockstation.com
rob.hamilton@cumulus.com
License: College Park, Fulton County, GA held by Susquehanna Radio Corp.
Group Owner: Cumulus Media Partners LLC; (acq 1-27-97; with co-located AM)
Nat'l Reps: Cumulus Radio Sales
Arbitron Metro Market: Atlanta, GA *Format:* Rock/AOR
Joyce Harms, Operations Dir
Gary Lewis, General Manager
Rob Roberts, Programming Director

Colquitt

***WCOQ**
01-01-2008; 90.5 mhz FM; 4.5 kw vert; 154 ft.; N31 10 24 W84 43 33
10142 East County Rd 22, Columbia, AL 36319 US
(334) 798-6664
wcoqfm@yahoo.com
License: Colquitt, Miller County, GA held by D & K Communications Inc.
Arbitron Metro Market: Colquitt, GA *Format:* Oldies
Robert Rogers, President

Columbus

WCGQ
07-15-1966; 107.3 mhz FM *Hrs Open:* 24; 100 kw; 1010 ft.; N32 28 0 W85 3 20
P. O. Box 1537, Columbus, GA 31994 US
(706) 327-1217, *Fax:* (706) 596-4600
www.q1073.com
info@q1073.com
License: Columbus, Muscogee County, GA held by PMB Broadcasting LLC.
Group Owner: PMB Broadcasting LLC; (acq 10-1-2008; grpsl)
Arbitron Metro Market: Columbus, GA *Format:* Contemporary Hits/Top 40 *Target Audience:* 18-49. *Adv. Rates:* 41; 41; 41; 41
Al Haynes, Programming Director
Chuck Thompson, Promotions Manager

WDAK
08-01-1940; 540 khz AM
Mailing Address: C/O Haley, Bader & Potts, 4350 N. Fairfax Dr, #900, Arlington, VA 22203 US
Second Address: 1501 13th Ave., Columbus, GA 31901
(706) 576-3000, *Fax:* (706) 576-3010
www.newsradio540.com
scottmiller@clearchannel.com
License: Columbus, GA held by CC Licenses LLC.
Group Owner: Clear Channel Communications Inc.; (acq 5-9-2003; $2.73 million with WSTH-FM Alexander City, AL).
Nat'l Network: USA; Westwood One
Arbitron Metro Market: Columbus, GA *Format:* News *Target Audience:* 18-49; men
Brian Waters, Operations Dir
Jennifer Newman, General Manager
Chuck Thompson, General Sales Mgr
Scott Miller, Programming Director

WIOL
12-01-1954; 1580 khz AM *Hrs Open:* 20; 2.3 kw-D, 1 kw-N, DA-N; N32 27 55 W85 01 22
Box 1998, Columbus, GA 36107
(706) 576-3565, *Fax:* (706) 576-3683
INFO@DBICOLUMBUS.COM
License: Columbus, Muscogee County, GA held by Davis Broadcasting Inc. of Columbus.
Group Owner: Davis Broadcasting Inc.; (acq 4-20-01; $400,000).
Nat'l Network: USA
Population Served: 250,000 *Arbitron Metro Market:* Columbus, GA *Hrs. of News Programming:* News progmg 15 hrs wkly
Target Audience: General.
Gregory Davis, CFO

***WFRC**
06-14-1985; 90.5 mhz FM; 25 kw; 240 ft.; N32 25 58 W84 57 2
4135 Northgate Blvd, Suite 1, Sacramento, CA 95834 US
(334) 291-0399, *Fax:* (510) 633-7983
www.familyradio.com
familyradio@familyradio.com
License: Columbus, Muscogee County, GA held by Family Stations Inc.
Group Owner: Family Stations Inc.
Arbitron Metro Market: Columbus, GA *Format:* Religious *Special Programming:* Call-in 8 hrs wkly
Harold Camping, President
Sandra Salewski, Operations Dir

WFXE
09-22-1969; 104.9 mhz FM; 2.3 kw; 538 ft.; N32 27 59 W85 3 22
P.O. Box 1998, Columbus, GA 31994 US
(706) 576-3565, *Fax:* (706) 576-3683
info@dbicolumbus.com
License: Columbus, Muscogee County, GA held by Davis Broadcasting Inc.
Arbitron Metro Market: Columbus, GA *Format:* Urban Contemporary
Gregory Davis, CEO
Bernie Corcoran, CFO

WSHE
01-01-1947; 1270 khz AM *Hrs Open:* 19; 5 kw-D, ND1; 0.188 kw-N, ND1; N32 26 16 W85 1 10
Mailing Address: 111 East Kilbourn Ave., Suite 2700, Milwaukee, WI 53202 US
Second Address: 1501 13th Ave., Columbus, GA 31901
(706) 576-3000, *Fax:* (706) 576-3010
www.am1270radio.com
scottmiller@clearchannel.com
License: Columbus, GA held by CC Licenses LLC.

Group Owner: Clear Channel Communications Inc.; (acq 2-21-2002; grpsl).
Nat'l Reps: McGavren Guild
Arbitron Metro Market: Columbus, GA *Format:* Gospel *Hrs. of News Programming:* News progmg 20 hrs wkly *Target Audience:* 35-60.
Brian Waters, Operations Dir
Jim Martin, General Manager
Jennifer Newman, General Sales Mgr
Jim Foster, Programming Director

WOKS
03-02-1959; 1340 khz AM; 1 kw-U, ND1; N32 27 7 W84 58 25
Mailing Address: P.O. Box 1998, Columbus, GA 31902 US
Second Address: 2203 Wynnton Rd., Columbus, GA 31906
(706) 576-3565, *Fax:* (706) 576-3683
info@dbicolumbus.com
License: Columbus, GA held by Davis Broadcasting Inc.
Group Owner: Davis Broadcasting Inc.; acq 7-24-92).
Nat'l Network: American Urban *Nat'l Reps:* Katz Radio
Arbitron Metro Market: Columbus, GA *TV Affiliate:* Urban contemp *No. News Employees:* 35-64.

WRCG
05-10-1928; 1420 khz AM *Hrs Open:* 24
PO Box 1537, Columbus, GA 31994 US
(706) 327-1217, *Fax:* (706) 596-4600
www.wrcg.com
info@wrcg.com
License: Columbus, GA held by PMB Broadcasting LLC.
Group Owner: PMB Broadcasting LLC; (acq 10-1-2008; grpsl)
Nat'l Network: CBS *Regional Network:* Ga. News Net. *Nat'l Reps:* Christal
Arbitron Metro Market: Columbus, GA *Format:* News, News/Talk, 84, Talk *Special Programming:* Farm 3 hrs wkly *Hrs. of News Programming:* news progmg 24 hrs wkly *No. News Employees:* 1 *Target Audience:* 35plus; adults with discretionary income *Adv. Rates:* 21; 21; 21; 21
Bob Quick, Operations Dir
Chuck Thompson, General Manager

***WTJB**
12-15-1984; 91.7 mhz FM *Hrs Open:* 6 AM-midnight; 5 kw horiz, 3.33 kw vert; 299 ft.; N32 25 20 W85 1 50 *Rebroadcasts:* Rebroadcasts WTSU(FM) Troy 100%
University Avenue, Department of Radio & Tv, Troy, AL 36082 US
(334) 670-3268, *Fax:* (334) 670-3934
www.troy.edu
wtsu@troy.edu
License: Columbus, Muscogee County, GA held by Troy State University.
Nat'l Network: NPR; PRI
Arbitron Metro Market: Phoenix City, AL *Format:* News *Special Programming:* Children one hr wkly *Hrs. of News Programming:* News progmg 25 hrs wkly *Target Audience:* General.
Judy Davis, Operations Dir
James Clower, General Manager
Fred Azbell, Programming Director
John Brunson, Chief Engineer
Donna Schubert, Associate Vice Chancellor for Marketing and Commun
Wade Giddens, Broadcast Engineer
DavidGriffin, Radio Engineer
Robert Barner, Production Coordinator

WVRK
11-16-1946; 102.9 mhz FM; 98 kw; 1568 ft.; N32 19 25.5 W84 46 46
Mailing Address: 111 East Kilbourn Avenue, Suite 2700, Milwaukee, WI 53202 US
Second Address: Box 687, Columbus, GA 31902
(706) 576-3000, *Fax:* (706) 576-3010
www.rock103online.com
chuckthompson@clearchannel.com
License: Columbus, Muscogee County, GA
Group Owner: Clear Channel Communications Inc.
Arbitron Metro Market: Columbus, GA *Format:* Classic Rock, Rock/AOR
Jerri Northington, General Sales Mgr
Brian Waters, Programming Director
Terri Avery, Contact Person

***WYFK**
07-01-1987; 89.5 mhz FM; 50 kw; 440 ft.; N32 40 3 W84 57 19
8030 Arrowridge Blvd, Charlotte, NC 28273 US
(704) 523-5555, *Fax:* (704) 522-1967
www.bbnradio.org
bbn@bnnradio.org
License: Columbus, Muscogee County, GA held by Bible Broadcasting Network Inc.
Group Owner: Bible Broadcasting Network
Arbitron Metro Market: Columbus, GA *Format:* Religious *Target Audience:* General.
Lowell Davey, President

Commerce

WJJC
06-27-1957; 1270 khz AM *Hrs Open:* 24; 5 kw-D, ND1; 0.173 kw-N, ND1; N34 12 57 W83 26 9
Mailing Address: Company, Inc., PO Box 379, Commerce, GA 30529 US
Second Address: 1801 N. Elm St., Commerce, GA 30529
(706) 335-1270, *Fax:* (706) 335-1905
www.wjjc.net
wjjc@windstream.net
License: Commerce, GA held by Side Communications Inc.
Regional Network: Ga. News Net. *Nat'l Reps:* Rgnl Reps
Arbitron Metro Market: Atlanta, GA *Format:* Talk *Special Programming:* Glenn Beck, Jim Rome, Dr. Laura *Target Audience:* 25-55.
Rob Jordan, General Manager
Craig Fischer, Assistant General Manager

Conyers

WPBS
11-01-1979; 1040 khz AM *Hrs Open:* 12
1151 Flat Shoals Road, Conyers, GA 30208 US
(404) 932-5006
License: Conyers, GA held by PacificStar Media Corp.
Arbitron Metro Market: Atlanta, GA *Format:* Christian, Spanish
Charles Kim, General Manager

Coosa

WSRM
01-01-2005; 93.5 mhz FM; 1.2 kw; 741 ft.; N34 14 2 W85 13 50
Rebroadcasts: Simulcast with WRGA(AM) Rome 100%
32 Saddle Mountain Rd, Rome, GA 30161 US
(706) 291-9496, *Fax:* (706) 235-7107
www.wrgarome.com
info@wrgarome.com
License: Coosa, Floyd County, GA held by Coosa Broadcasting Corp.
Group Owner: Southern Broadcasting Companies Inc.; (acq 5-31-2005; $1.1 million)
Arbitron Metro Market: Coosa, GA *Format:* News, News/Talk, 86
Paul Stone, President
Randy Quick, General Manager

Cordele

***WAEF**
01-01-2001; 90.3 mhz FM; 11 kw vert; 505 ft.; N31 38 22 W83 44 58
P.O. Drawer 2440, Tupelo, MS 38803 US
(312) 461-8540 or (219) 309-9327, *Fax:* (312) 588-0168
www.waur.relevantradio.com
aciabattari@relevantradio.com
License: Cordele, Crisp County, GA held by American Family Association.
Group Owner: American Family Radio
Arbitron Metro Market: Hutchinson MN *Format:* Talk, Christian *Special Programming:* Farm 15 hrs wkly *Target Audience:* 25-54.
Armand Ciabattari, General Manager

Cornelia

WCON
03-28-1953; 1450 khz AM *Hrs Open:* 24; 1 kw-U, ND1; N34 30 57 W83 32 20
Mailing Address: P. O. Box 100, Cornelia, GA 30531 US
Second Address: 540 N. Main St., Cornelia, GA 30531
(706) 778-2241, *Fax:* (706) 778-0576
www.wconfm.com
wcon@windstream.net
License: Cornelia, GA held by Habersham Broadcasting Co.
Nat'l Network: ABC *Regional Network:* Ga. News Net.
Arbitron Metro Market: Cornelia,GA *Format:* Country, Gospel *No. News Employees:* 1 *Target Audience:* Adults. *Adv. Rates:* 7; 6; 7; 5
Bobbie C. Foster, GM
John Foster, Operations Dir
Michael Harvey, News Director
Jimmy Dillard, Chief Engineer

WCON-FM
03-27-1965; 99.3 mhz FM *Hrs Open:* 24; 19 kw; 807 ft.; N34 31 24 W83 40 46
Mailing Address: P.O. Box 100, Cornelia, GA 30531 US
Second Address: 540 N. Main St., Cornelia, GA 30531
(706) 778-2241, *Fax:* (706) 778-0576
www.wconfm.com
wcon@windstream.net
License: Cornelia, Habersham County, GA held by Habersham Broadcasting Co.
Arbitron Metro Market: Cornelia,GA *Format:* Country *No. News Employees:* 1 *Target Audience:* 18 plus. *Adv. Rates:* 13; 11; 13; na.
Bobbie C. Foster, GM
Tom Thon, General Manager

Covington

WGFS
10-09-1946; 1430 khz AM *Hrs Open:* 6 AM-7 PM
Mailing Address: P. O. Box 869, Covington, GA 30209 US
Second Address: 1151 Hendricks St., Covington, GA 30014
(770) 786-1430, *Fax:* (770) 784-9892
License: Covington, GA held by Multicultural Radio Broadcasting Licensee LLC.
Group Owner: Multicultural Radio Broadcasting Inc.; (acq 11-21-03; $700,000).
Nat'l Network: CBS *Regional Network:* Ga. News Net. *Wire Services:* CBS
Arbitron Metro Market: Atlanta, GA *Format:* Oldies *Hrs. of News Programming:* news progmg 20 hrs wkly *No. News Employees:* 1 *Target Audience:* General.
Arthur Liu, President
Mike Shumate, Station Manager

Crawford

WGMG
04-01-1990; 102.1 mhz FM; 10 kw; 328 ft.; N33 55 18 W83 14 14
3360 Capital Circle Ne, Tallahassee, FL 32308 US
(706) 549-6222, *Fax:* (706) 546-0411
www.magic1021fm.com
scott.smith@coxinc.com
License: Crawford, Oglethorpe County, GA held by Cox Radio Inc.
Group Owner: Cox Radio Inc.; (acq 8-1-2008; grpsl)
Format: Adult Contemp *Target Audience:* 18-49; general
Robert Neil, President
Scott Smith, Operations Dir
Scott Smith, General Manager
Eric Lauer, General Sales Mgr
Tod Tucker, Programming Director
David Ratz, Promotions Manager
Tim Bryant, News Director

Cumming

***WWEV-FM**
12-04-1981; 91.5 mhz FM *Hrs Open:* 24; 8.9 kw; 961 ft.; N34 14 13 W84 9 36
Mailing Address: P.O. Box 248, Cumming, GA 30130 US
Second Address: 1705 Sawnee Dr., Cumming, GA 30040
(770) 781-9150, *Fax:* (770) 781-5003
www.wwev.org
info@wwev.org
License: Cumming, Forsyth County, GA held by Curriculum Development Foundation Inc.
Arbitron Metro Market: Cumming, GA *Format:* Religious *Target Audience:* 18-49; the family unit
Ray Haynes, General Manager
Ray Haynes, Promotions Manager
Marty Passmore, Chief Engineer
Denise Bell, Office Manager
Judy McDearis, Office Manager
Rhonda Haynes, Sales Rep
Suzan Cook, Sales Rep
Holly Bader, Sales Rep

Cusseta

WLTC
103.7 mhz FM; 6 kw; Ant 328 ft; N32 18 39 W84 45 45
1820 Wynnton Rd Suite B, Columbus, GA 31906
(706) 324-5850, *Fax:* (706) 256-2984
1037thetruth.com
License: Cusseta, Chattahoochee County, GA held by Signature Broadcasting Ltd.
Arbitron Metro Market: Columbus, GA
Shirley Thrasher, General Manager

Dahlonega

WDGR
03-01-1982; 1210 khz AM; 2.5 kw-C, NDD; 10 kw-D, NDD; N34 31 45 W84 0 23

9110 Four Mile Creek Rd, Dahlonega, GA 30506 US
(706) 864-4477, *Fax:* (404) 446-5981
License: Dahlonega, GA held by USK Broadcasting Inc.
Hye Kim, General Manager

WZTR
12-16-1996; 104.3 mhz FM *Hrs Open:* 24; 3.7 kw; 417 ft.; N34 29 56 W84 8 32
1376 Ben Higgins Road, Dahlonega, GA 30533 US
(706) 867-9542, *Fax:* (706) 864-4364
www.thunder1043fm.com
License: Dahlonega, Lumpkin County, GA held by Grady W. Turner
Nat'l Network: ABC *Regional Network:* Ga. News Net.
Format: Classic Rock, Country *Hrs. of News Programming:* news progmg 4 hrs wkly *No. News Employees:* 1 *Target Audience:* 25-54; general *Adv. Rates:* 30; 22; 30; 15
Bo Wilson, Station Manager

***WNGU**
01-01-1998; 89.5 mhz FM *Hrs Open:* 24; 0.75 kw; 459 ft.; N34 31 29 W83 59 50 *Rebroadcasts:* Rebroadcast WJSP, Warm Springs, Colombus, 100%
260 - 14th Street, N.W., Altanta, GA 30318 US
(404) 685-2690, *Fax:* (404) 685-2684
www.gpb.org
ask@gpb.org
License: Dahlonega, Lumpkin County, GA held by Georgia Public Telecommunications Commission.
Nat'l Network: NPR; PRI *Wire Services:* AP
Arbitron Metro Market: Atlanta, GA *Format:* Classical, News
Special Programming: Jazz *Hrs. of News Programming:* news progmg 40 hrs wkly *No. News Employees:* 10
Nancy Hall, CEO
Tom Barclay, Operations Dir
Bob Houghton, General Manager
Rob Maynard, Programming Director
Nancy Zintak, Promotions Manager
Susanna Capelonto, News Director
Bonnie Bean, CFO

Dallas

WDPC
09-21-1979; 1500 khz AM
8451 S. Cherokee Blvd, Suite B, Dougladcille, CA 30134 US
(770) 920-1520, *Fax:* (770) 920-4600
www.wordchristianbroadcasting.com
License: Dallas, GA held by Word Christian Broadcasting Inc.
Arbitron Metro Market: Dallas, GA *Format:* Gospel, Religious
Target Audience: General.
Ken Johns, President

Dalton

WBLJ
04-08-1940; 1230 khz AM *Hrs Open:* 24; 1 kw-U, ND1; N34 45 23 W84 57 2
P.O. Box 809, Dalton, GA 30720 US
(706) 278-5511, *Fax:* (706) 226-8766
wblj1230.com
pscoggins@ngaradio.com
License: Dalton, GA held by North Georgia Radio Group L.P.
Group Owner: North Georgia Radio Group L.P.; (acq 3-20-2006; grpsl)
Nat'l Network: CBS Radio *Regional Network:* Ga. News Net.
Arbitron Metro Market: Dalton, GA *Format:* News, News/Talk, 86
Special Programming: Relg mus *Hrs. of News Programming:* news progmg 28 hrs wkly *No. News Employees:* 2 *Target Audience:* 18-54. *Adv.Rates:* 20; 30; 25; 10
Mark Cooper, General Manager
Larry Gibson, Programming Director

WDAL
10-01-1954; 1430 khz AM *Hrs Open:* 24
Mailing Address: 1899 Cleveland Hwy, Dalton, GA 30720 US
Second Address: 613 Silver Cir., Dalton, GA 30721
(706) 278-5511(706) 278-3300, *Fax:* (706) 278-7966
License: Dalton, GA held by North Georgia Radio Group L.P.
Group Owner: North Georgia Radio Group L.P.; (acq 3-20-2006; grpsl)
Nat'l Network: CBS *Nat'l Reps:* Rgnl Reps
Arbitron Metro Market: Chattanooga, TN *Format:* Tejano *Hrs. of News Programming:* news progmg 30 hrs wkly *No. News Employees:* 3 *Target Audience:* 25-45.
Rich Phillips, General Manager

WYYU
08-01-1995; 104.5 mhz FM *Hrs Open:* 24; 6 kw; 328 ft.; N34 49 42 W84 53 41
Mailing Address: 104 South Pentz Street, Dalton, GA 30721 US
Second Address: 613 Silver Cir, Dalton, GA 30721
(706) 278-5511, *Fax:* (706) 278-7966
License: Dalton, Whitfield County, GA
Group Owner: North Georgia Radio Group L.P.
Arbitron Metro Market: Dalton, GA *Format:* Adult Contemp *No. News Employees:* 3
Lamar Studstill, Chairman
Cole Studstill, CFO
Lee Studstill, President

WTTI
06-17-1965; 1530 khz AM; 10 kw-C, DAD; 10 kw-D, DAD; N34 47 9 W85 2 40
Mailing Address: P.O. Box 216, Dalton, GA 30720 US
Second Address: 111 W. Crawford St., Dalton, GA 30720
(706) 673-2222, *Fax:* (706) 673-7141
www.wttiradio.com
License: Dalton, GA held by Troy L. Hall.
Arbitron Metro Market: Dalton, GA *Format:* Christian *Target Audience:* 25-54; family, relg
Troy Hall, CEO
C.W. Queen, Station Manager

Darien

WHFX
05-13-1993; 107.7 mhz FM *Hrs Open:* 24; 50 kw; 482 ft.; N31 10 9 W81 32 14
Two Bala Plaza, Suite 801, Bala-Cynwyd, PA 19004 US
(912) 267-1025, *Fax:* (912) 264-5462
1077thefox.net
scottrysun@gmail.com
License: Darien, McIntosh County, GA held by Qantum of Brunswick License Co. LLC.
Group Owner: Qantum Communications Corp.; (acq 7-2-2003; grpsl).
Nat'l Reps: McGavren Guild
Arbitron Metro Market: Brunswick, GA *Hrs. of News Programming:* news progmg 4 hrs wkly *No. News Employees:* 1 *Target Audience:* 25 plus; general *Adv. Rates:* 25; 18; 20; 12
Joe Sousa, Operations Dir
Jonathan Havens, General Manager
Jim Hendrick, General Sales Mgr
Mark Douglas, Programming Director
Mike Hamens, News Director
Dick Boekeloo, Chief Engineer
Kat Blackstone, Disc Jockey
Robin Rowe,Special Events Coordinator

Dawson

WMRZ
06-01-2005; 98.1 mhz FM; 25 kw; 262 ft.; N31 37 29 W84 19 20
P.O. Box 180, Hawkinsville, GA 31036 US
(229) 439-9704, *Fax:* (229) 439-1509
www.kissalbany.com
jackietoye@clearchannel.com
License: Dawson, Terrell County, GA held by CC Licenses LLC.
Group Owner: Clear Channel Communications Inc.; (acq 11-16-2005; $875,000)
Arbitron Metro Market: Dawson, GA *Format:* Blues, Oldies
John Richards, General Manager
Paul Edwards, Programming Director

Decatur

WATB
07-19-1958; 1420 khz AM; 1 kw-D, DA2; 0.051 kw-N, DA2; N33 47 13 W84 14 53
127 Mamanasco Road, Ridgefield, CT 06877 US
(404) 508-1420, *Fax:* (404) 508-8930
www.watb1420.com/
benv@mrbi.net
License: Decatur, GA held by Way Broadcasting Licensee LLC
Arbitron Metro Market: Atlanta, GA *Format:* Ethnic *Target Audience:* General; ethnic groups from around the world
Benjamin Vannoy Jr., General Manager

WPBC
08-11-1964; 1310 khz AM *Hrs Open:* 24
3300 Buckeye Road, Suite 800, Atlanta, GA 30341 US
(678) 200-8540
License: Decatur, GA held by Hanmi Broadcasting Inc.
Arbitron Metro Market: Atlanta, GA
Chang Kim, General Manager

Demorest

***WPPR**
01-01-1997; 88.3 mhz FM *Hrs Open:* 24; 7.3 kw; 636 ft.; N34 31 24 W83 40 46 *Rebroadcasts:* Rebroadcasts WJSP-FM Warm Springs 85%
260 - 14th Street, N.W., Atlanta, GA 30318 US
(404) 685-2690, *Fax:* (404) 685-2684
www.gpb.org
ask@spb.org
License: Demorest, Habersham County, GA held by Georgia Public Telecommunications Commission.
Nat'l Network: NPR; PRI *Wire Services:* AP
Format: News *Special Programming:* Jazz *Hrs. of News Programming:* news progmg 40 hrs wkly *No. News Employees:* 10 *Target Audience:* Adults 35+
Nancy Hall, CEO
Tom Barclay, Operations Dir
Bob Houghton, General Manager
Rob Maynard, Programming Director
Nancy Zintak, Promotions Manager
Susanna Capelouto, News Director
Bonnie Bean, CFO

Dock Junction

WXMK
05-01-1991; 105.9 mhz FM *Hrs Open:* 24; 15 kw; 420 ft.; N31 11 39 W81 29 30
522 Old Mission Rd, Brunswick, GA 31520 US
(912) 261-1000, *Fax:* (912) 265-8391
www.magic1059.com
info@magic1059.com
License: Dock Junction, Glynn County, GA held by Golden Isles Broadcasting L.L C.
Arbitron Metro Market: Brunswick, GA *Format:* Adult Contemp, Contemporary Hits/Top 40 *Target Audience:* 25-54; women *Adv. Rates:* 25; 25; 25; 20
Mark Douglas, Operations Dir
Joe Willie Sousa, General Manager
Cathy Trimble, General Sales Mgr
Dick Boekeloo, Chief Engineer
Everett Armstrong, Business Manager
Laura Wisham, Senior Account Executive
Joey Miller, AccountExecutive
Mike Cornell, Production Director

Donalsonville

WGMK
09-01-1980; 106.3 mhz FM; 5.9 kw; 331 ft.; N31 4 26 W84 52 47
Mailing Address: P. O. Box 236, Donalsonville, GA 31745 US
Second Address: 91 North Way, Donalsonville, GA 31743
(229) 524-5123, *Fax:* (229) 524-2265
License: Donalsonville, Seminole County, GA
Group Owner: Flint Media Inc.
Format: Adult Contemp
Robert Neil, President
Scott Smith, Operations Dir
Kevin Steele, Programming Director

WSEM
02-12-1963; 1500 khz AM; 1 kw-D, NDD; N31 4 26 W84 52 47
Mailing Address: P. O. Box 87, Donalsonville, GA 31745 US
Second Address: 91 North Way, Donalsonville, GA 31743
(229) 524-5123, *Fax:* (229) 524-2265
wgmk@alltel.net
License: Donalsonville, GA held by Flint Media Inc.
Group Owner: Flint Media Inc.; (acq 6-22-2006; grpsl).
Regional Network: Ga. News Net.
Format: News, Talk *Target Audience:* 25-49. *Adv. Rates:* 20; 20; 20; na
Kevin Dowdy, President
Gilbert Kelley Jr., General Manager
Grace Kelley, General Sales Mgr

***WWGF**
08-01-1998; 107.5 mhz FM *Hrs Open:* 24; 6 kw; 315 ft.; N30 58 45 W84 57 27
3213 Huxley Drive, Augusta, GA 30909 US
(706) 309-9610
www.gnnradio.org
ctbarinowski@comcast.net
License: Donalsonville, Seminole County, GA held by Barinowski Investment Co.
Group Owner: Good News Network; (acq 1-21-99)
Arbitron Metro Market: Grovetown, GA *Format:* Christian *Target Audience:* All.
Clarence Barinowski, General Manager

Doraville

WSSB(FM)
05-01-1948; 95.5 mhz FM *Hrs Open:* 24; 40 kw; Ant 1,417 ft; N34 07 32 W83 51 32
1601 W. Peachtree St. N.E., Atlanta, GA 30309
(404) 897-7500, *Fax:* (404) 897-6211
www.955thebeat.com
License: Doraville, De Kalb County, GA held by Cox Radio Inc.

Group Owner: Cox Radio Inc.; (acq 7-19-99; $78 million)
Population Served: 2,500,000 *Arbitron Metro Market:* Atlanta, GA *Target Audience:* 25-54; blue collar to executive, modern country mus lovers
Dan Kearney, Promotions Manager
Tony Kidd, VP, Market Manager

Douglas

WDMG
03-01-1947; 860 khz AM; 5 kw-D, DAN; 5 kw-N, DAN; N31 30 23 W82 49 10
620 East Ward Street, Douglas, GA 31533 US
(912) 389-0995, *Fax:* (912) 383-8552
www.laescandalosa.webs.com
traffic@charter.net
License: Douglas, GA held by Broadcast South LLC.
Group Owner: Broadcast South LLC; (acq 11-15-2006; grpsl)
Nat'l Network: USA
Arbitron Metro Market: Albany, GA *Format:* Sports *Special Programming:* Farm 4 hrs, relg 6 hrs wkly *Hrs. of News Programming:* news progmg 20 hrs wkly *No. News Employees:* 1 *Target Audience:* 25-54. *Adv.Rates:* 10; 9; 9; 6.
John Higgs, Station Manager

WOKA
12-10-1962; 1310 khz AM; 3.9 kw-D, ND1; 0.039 kw-N, ND1; N31 31 24 W82 52 22
1310 W. Walker St., Douglas, GA 31533 US
(912) 384-1310, *Fax:* (912) 383-6328
License: Douglas, GA held by Coffee County Broadcasters Inc.
TV Affiliate: Sp *No. News Employees:* General. *Adv. Rates:* 12; 10; 12; 4.
CEO, Dwayne Gillis

WOKA-FM
07-01-1971; 106.7 mhz FM; 100 kw; 981 ft.; N31 40 21 W82 51 28
PO Box 471, Douglas, GA 31533 US
(912) 384-8153, *Fax:* (912) 383-6328
www.dixiecountry.com
production@atc.cc
License: Douglas, Coffee County, GA held by Coffee County Broadcasters Inc.
TV Affiliate: Country *Format:* Gospel *No. News Employees:* Adults 25-54. *Adv. Rates:* 25; 18; 20; 10
Disc Jockey

Douglasville

WXJO
09-01-1969; 1120 khz AM
6070 Rock Springs Road, Lithonia, GA 30038 US
(706) 276-2016, *Fax:* (706) 635-1018
wxjo1120.blogspot.com
License: Douglasville, GA held by Exponent Broadcasting Inc.
Arbitron Metro Market: Atlanta, GA *Format:* Oldies
Randy Gravley, President

WDCY
05-05-1993; 1520 khz AM *Hrs Open:* Sunrise-sunset
8451 Cherokee Blvd., Suite B, Douglasville, GA 30134 US
(770) 920-1520, *Fax:* (770) 920-4600
www.wordchristianbroadcasting.com
info@wordchristianbroadcasting.com
License: Douglasville, GA held by Word Christian Broadcasting Inc.
Arbitron Metro Market: Atlanta, GA *Format:* Religious *Hrs. of News Programming:* News progmg 10 hrs wkly *Target Audience:* General.
Ken Johns, President

Dry Branch

WPLA(AM)
04-15-1998; 1670 khz AM *Hrs Open:* 24; 10 kw-D, 1 kw-N; N32 48 16 W83 36 16
7080 Industrial Hwy., Macon, GA 31216
(478) 781-1063, *Fax:* (478) 781-6711
huston@965thebuzz.net
License: Dry Branch, Twiggs County, GA held by AMFM Radio Licenses LLC.
Group Owner: Clear Channel Communications Inc.; (acq. 2-15-2001; grpsl)
Nat'l Reps: Clear Channel
Population Served: 250,000 *Arbitron Metro Market:* Macon, GA *Target Audience:* General; adults
Bill Clark, General Manager

WPLA
05-09-1977; 1670 khz AM *Hrs Open:* 24; Ant 705 ft
750 West Sandtown Road, S.W., Marietta, GA 30054 US
(904) 636-0507, *Fax:* (904) 997-7713
License: Dry Branch, GA held by Clear Channel Radio Licenses Inc.
Group Owner: Clear Channel Communications Inc.; (acq 11-21-97; grpsl)
Regional Network: Florida's Radio Networks *Nat'l Reps:* Clear Channel
Arbitron Metro Market: Jacksonville, FL *TV Affiliate:* WAWS(TV) affil *Format:* Country *Special Programming:* Relg 2 hrs wkly *No. News Employees:* 1 *Target Audience:* 25-49.
Gail Austin, Operations Dir
Norm Feuer, General Manager

Dublin

*WAWH
01-01-2000; 88.3 mhz FM; 0.4 kw; 82 ft.; N32 32 27 W82 57 27
Po Drawer 2440, Tupelo, MS 38803 US
(307) 638-8921, *Fax:* (307) 638-8922
License: Dublin, Laurens County, GA held by American Family Association.
Group Owner: American Family Radio
Arbitron Metro Market: Bar Nunn WY *Format:* Rock/AOR
Steven Silberberg, President
Roger Ingram, General Manager

WKKZ
04-04-1967; 92.7 mhz FM *Hrs Open:* 24; 50 kw; 417 ft.; N32 31 21 W82 54 0
Mailing Address: Post Office Box 967, Dublin, GA 31040 US
Second Address: 1006 Martin Luther King Blvd., Dublin, GA 31021
(478) 272-9270, *Fax:* (478) 275-3592
www.wkkz927.com
License: Dublin, Laurens County, GA held by Kirby Broadcasting Co.
Nat'l Network: ABC *Nat'l Reps:* Dora-Clayton
Arbitron Metro Market: Macon, GA *Format:* Contemporary Hits/Top 40
Ray Beck, General Manager

WMLT
01-12-1945; 1330 khz AM *Hrs Open:* 24; 5 kw-D, DAN; 0.5 kw-N, DAN; N32 33 50 W82 52 0
Mailing Address: PO Box 2639, Gulfport, MS 39505 US
Second Address: 807 Bellevue Ave., Dublin, GA 31021
(478) 272-4422, *Fax:* (478) 275-4657
www.1330wmlt.com
richhumphrey@wqzy.com
License: Dublin, GA held by State Broadcasting Corporation.
Regional Network: Ga. News Net. *Nat'l Reps:* Rgnl Reps
Regional Reps: Regional Reps
Arbitron Metro Market: Dublin, GA *Format:* Gospel *No. News Employees:* 2 *Target Audience:* 25-54.
J. Morgan Dowdy, President
Rick Humphrey, General Manager

WQZY
01-01-1978; 95.9 mhz FM *Hrs Open:* 24; 100 kw; 1024 ft.; N32 40 42 W82 33 26
P.O Box 2639, Gulfport, MS 39505 US
(478) 272-4422, *Fax:* (478) 275-4657
www.wqzy.com
webmaster@wqzy.com
License: Dublin, Laurens County, GA held by State Broadcasting Corporation
Regional Network: Ga. News Net. *Regional Reps:* Regional Reps
Format: Country *Target Audience:* 18-54. *Adv. Rates:* 28; 28; 26; 10
J. Morgan Dowdy, President
Rick Humphrey, General Manager
Robert Whitt, Programming Director

WXLI
03-16-1958; 1230 khz AM; 0.7 kw-U, ND1; N32 31 21 W82 54 0
Mailing Address: P.O. Box 967, Dublin, GA 31040 US
Second Address: 1006 Martin Luther King Blvd., Dublin, GA 31021
(478) 272-4282, *Fax:* (478) 275-3592
License: Dublin, GA held by Laurens County Broadcasting Co.
Nat'l Network: CBS *Nat'l Reps:* Dora-Clayton
Arbitron Metro Market: Dublin, GA *Format:* Country, Gospel
Ray Beck, General Manager

East Dublin

WEDB
12-18-1966; 98.1 mhz FM; 9.6 kw; 525 ft.; N32 32 55 W82 38 49
P.O. Box 1590 2 Radio Loop, Swainsboro, GA 30401 US
(478) 237-1590, *Fax:* (478) 237-3559
www.magic98wedb.com/
License: East Dublin, Laurens County, GA held by RadioJones LLC.
Group Owner: RadioJones LLC
Arbitron Metro Market: East Dublin, GA *Format:* Contemporary Hits/Top 40 *Hrs. of News Programming:* news progmg 10 hrs wkly *No. News Employees:* 1 *Target Audience:* 18-50. *Adv. Rates:* 16; 14; 14; 8
Dennis Jones, President
John Wagner, Operations Dir
Jolly Martin, General Sales Mgr
Bobby Duncan, Programming Director

East Point

WCFO
10-09-1994; 1160 khz AM *Hrs Open:* 24
1935 Sixth Street, Chamblee, GA 30341 US
(404) 681-9307, *Fax:* (404) 870-8859
www.newstalk1160.com
listeners@jwbroadcasting.com
License: East Point, GA held by JW Broadcasting Inc.
Arbitron Metro Market: Atlanta, GA *Format:* News, News/Talk, 86
Jeff Davis, Operations Dir

WTJH
12-01-1949; 1260 khz AM; 5 kw-D, ND2; 0.039 kw-N, ND2; N33 41 47 W84 28 29
645 Church St., Ste. 400, Norfolk, VA 23510 US
(404) 344-2233, *Fax:* (404) 346-0647
License: East Point, GA held by Christian Broadcasting of East Point Inc.
Group Owner: Willis Broadcasting Corp.
Arbitron Metro Market: Atlanta, GA *Format:* Gospel, Religious
Christine Willis-Wiggs, General Manager

Eastman

WUFF
09-01-1961; 710 khz AM
Mailing Address: 731 College Street, Eastman, GA 31023 US
Second Address: 855 College St., Eastman, GA
(478) 374-3437, *Fax:* (478) 374-3585
License: Eastman, GA held by Dodge Broadcasting Inc.
Arbitron Metro Market: Eastman,GA *Format:* Country *Special Programming:* Black 5 hrs wkly

WUFF-FM
01-01-1976; 97.5 mhz FM; 4.62 kw; 371 ft.; N32 13 18 W83 13 4
Mailing Address: 731 College Street, Eastman, GA 31023 US
Second Address: 855 College St., Eastman, GA 31023
(478) 374-3437, *Fax:* (478) 374-3585
wolfcountry975.com
Greg@wolfcountry975.com
License: Eastman, Dodge County, GA
Arbitron Metro Market: Eastman, GA *Format:* Gospel, News
Greg Grantham, General Manager/Program Director
Scott Morrison, Station Manager
Wanda Lancaster, General Sales Mgr
Quint Bush, News Director
Mike Cowan, Traffic/Billing

Eatonton

WKVQ
12-15-1966; 1540 khz AM *Rebroadcasts:* Simulcast with WKRR(FM) Milledgeville
P.O. Box 3965, Eatonton, GA 31024 US
(706) 485-8792, *Fax:* (706) 485-3555
starstation@bellsouth.net
License: Eatonton, GA held by Craig Baker.
Format: Adult Contemp *Target Audience:* General.
Craig Baker, President

WMGZ
02-08-1988; 97.7 mhz FM *Hrs Open:* 24; 8.5 kw; 554 ft.; N33 20 41 W83 13 41
Mailing Address: P. O. Box 832, Milledgeville, GA 31061 US
Second Address: 156 Lake Laurel Rd., Milledgeville, GA 31061
(478) 453-9406, *Fax:* (478) 453-3298
www.z97.fm/
z97mail@yahoo.com
License: Eatonton, Putnam County, GA held by Southern Stone Broadcasting Inc.
Group Owner: Southern Broadcasting Companies Inc.; (acq 7-6-2005; $1.1 million with WKGQ(AM) Milledgeville)
Nat'l Network: ABC
Arbitron Metro Market: Eatonton, GA *Format:* Adult Contemp *Hrs. of News Programming:* news progmg 4 hrs wkly *No. News Employees:* 1 *Target Audience:* 18-49. *Adv. Rates:* 12; 10; 12; 8

Tony Taylor, Operations Dir
Tom Ptak, General Manager
Walter Reynolds, Promotions Manager

Elberton

WSGC-FM
05-15-1998; 105.3 mhz FM *Hrs Open:* 24; 6 kw; Ant 328 ft; N33 59 22 W82 46 23
Mailing Address: Box 340, Elberton, GA 30606
Second Address: 562 Jones St., Elberton, GA 30635
(706) 213-1051, *Fax:* (706) 283-8710
www.wsgcradio.com
pundt@gacaradio.com
License: Elberton, Elbert County, GA held by Georgia-Carolina Radiocasting Co. LLC.
Group Owner: Georgia-Carolina Radiocasting Companies; (acq 7-25-2002; grpsl)
Nat'l Network: ABC
Population Served: 27,724*Hrs. of News Programming:* news progmg 5 hrs wkly *No. News Employees:* 1 *Target Audience:* 25-54; general
Douglas M. Sutton, Jr., President
David Thompson, Operations Dir
Carl T Pundt, General Manager
Jennifer Long, General Sales Mgr
David Thompson, Programming Director
David Stephens, News Director
Marty Lee, Chief Engineer
CarlPundt, Vice President
Terry Carter, Vice President

WSGC
01-01-1947; 1400 khz AM *Hrs Open:* 24*Rebroadcasts:* FM translator W243CI
P.O. Box 638, Elberton, GA 30458 US
(706) 213-1051, *Fax:* (706) 283-8710
www.wsgcradio.com
wsgc@elbertonradio.com
License: Elberton, GA held by Georgia-Carolina Radiocasting Co. LLC.
Group Owner: Georgia-Carolina Radiocasting Companies; (acq 7-25-2002; grpsl)
Nat'l Network: CBS Radio *Regional Network:* Ga. News Net.
Arbitron Metro Market: Elberton, GA *Format:* News, Oldies, 84
Hrs. of News Programming: news progmg 12 hrs wkly *No. News Employees:* 1 *Target Audience:* 35+.
Art Sutton, President
Ron Shuler, Operations Dir
Carl Pundt, Vice-President/General Manager
Lori Vickery, Programming Director
David Stephens, News Director
Marty Lee, Chief Engineer
Susie Larson, Office Manager
Jennifer Long,Advertising Sales Representative

Ellaville

WLEL
01-01-2009; 94.3 mhz FM; 4.8 kw; 328 ft.; N32 15 10 W84 13 50 US
(229) 937-9967, *Fax:* (229) 591-5743
www.wlelclassichits.com
License: Ellaville, Schley County, GA held by Gary S. Hess
Arbitron Metro Market: Ellaville, GA *Format:* Contemporary Hits/Top 40, Adult Contemp
Roy Janes, General Manager
Cary Moore, Account Executive

Ellijay

WPGY
05-10-1978; 1580 khz AM
P.O. Box 545, Ellijay, GA 30540 US
(706) 276-2016, *Fax:* (706) 635-1018
wlja@ellijay.com
License: Ellijay, GA held by Exponent Broadcasting Inc.
Format: Country *Target Audience:* 18-75. *Adv. Rates:* 15; 12; 15; 12
Randy Gravley, Operations Dir
Byron Dobbs, General Manager

WLJA-FM
11-01-1985; 101.1 mhz FM *Hrs Open:* 6 AM-10 PM; 19 kw; 276 ft.; N34 42 59 W84 30 50
P.O. Box 545, Ellijay, GA 30540 US
(678) 454-9350, *Fax:* (678) 454-3950
www.wljaradio.com
License: Ellijay, Gilmer County, GA held by Tri-State Communications Inc.
Format: Country, Gospel *Target Audience:* 18-75. *Adv. Rates:* $15; 12; 15; 12

Millard Oakley, President
Craig Cantrell, Operations Dir
Joel Upton, General Manager
Carolyn Peterman, Station Manager
Mark Young, General Sales Mgr
Shirley Burnette, News Director
Austin Stinnett, Chief Engineer
Roger Ealey,News & Sports Director

Evans

WAEG
11-01-1991; 92.3 mhz FM; 6 kw; 328 ft.; N33 35 24.5 W82 13 52.5
Mailing Address: P.O. Box 1100, Columbus, GA 31994 US
Second Address: 104 Bennett Ln., North Augusta, SC 29841
(269) 471-3400, *Fax:* (269) 471-3804
www.waus.org
waus@andrews.edu
License: Evans, Columbia County, GA held by Perry Broadcasting of Augusta Inc.
Group Owner: Perry Publishing & Broadcasting Co.; (acq 12-12-2007; grpsl)
Nat'l Reps: Christal
Arbitron Metro Market: Tyler-Longview TX *Format:* Talk *Special Programming:* Relg 10 hrs wkly *Hrs. of News Programming:* News progmg 3 hrs wkly *Target Audience:* 35 plus; listeners with interest in classicalmusic *Adv. Rates:* 35; 30; 30; 25
Niels-Erik Andreasen, Chairman
Sharon Dudgeon, General Manager
Bill Brent, Programming Director

Fayetteville

WUMJ
03-08-1966; 97.5 mhz FM; 7.9 kw; 574 ft.; N33 29 29 W84 35 0
5900 Princess Garden Parkway, 8th Floor, Lanham, MD 20706 US
(404) 765-9750, *Fax:* (404) 688-7686
www.majicatl.com
License: Fayetteville, Fayette County, GA held by ROA Licenses LLC.
Group Owner: Radio One Inc.; (acq 11-8-2001; grpsl)
Arbitron Metro Market: Atlanta, GA *Format:* Blues
Tim Davies, General Manager
Derek Harper, Programming Director
Corey Punzi, Promotions Manager

Fitzgerald

WBHB
10-08-1946; 1240 khz AM; 1 kw-U, ND1; N31 42 23 W83 15 40
Box 100, Fitzgerald, GA 31750 US
(229) 423-2077, *Fax:* (229) 423-8313
jank@rtgmedia.net
License: Fitzgerald, GA held by Broadcast South LLC.
Group Owner: Broadcast South LLC; (acq 11-15-2006; grpsl)
Nat'l Network: Westwood One
Format: Black, Gospel *Target Audience:* General.
John Higgs, General Manager

WRDO
01-01-1991; 96.9 mhz FM *Hrs Open:* 24; 6 kw; 328 ft.; N31 44 33 W83 14 39
603 West 2nd Street, Pobox 7, Tifton, GA 31754 US
(912) 389-0995, *Fax:* (912) 383-8552
traffic@charter.net
License: Fitzgerald, Ben Hill County, GA held by Broadcast South LLC.
Group Owner: Broadcast South LLC; (acq 11-15-2006; grpsl)
Nat'l Network: USA
Format: Adult Contemp *Special Programming:* Gospel 6 hrs wkly *No. News Employees:* 1 *Target Audience:* 25-55; baby boomers
John Higgs, General Manager

Folkston

***WATY**
01-01-2000; 91.3 mhz FM *Hrs Open:* 24; 0.6 kw; 322 ft.; N30 52 29 W82 1 10
Box 1448, Kingsland, GA 31548 US
(912)496-4484, *Fax:* (912)496-4086
www.gpb.org
ask@gpb.org
License: Folkston, Charlton County, GA held by The Foundation for Public Broadcasting in Georgia Inc.
Nat'l Network: NPR *Regional Network:* Georgia Public Radio
Arbitron Metro Market: Jacksonville, FL
Teya Ryan, President
Bonnie Bean, Programming Director

***WECC-FM**
03-17-2002; 89.3 mhz FM; 30 kw; 489 ft.; N30 55 54 W81 42 30
P O Box 1190, St. Marys, GA 31558 US
(912) 882-8930, *Fax:* (912) 882-9322
www.thelighthousefm.org
mail@thelighthousefm.org
License: Folkston, Charlton County, GA held by Lighthouse Christian Broadcasting Corp.
Nat'l Network: Salem Radio Network
Arbitron Metro Market: Folkston, GA *Format:* Christian
Paul Hafer, General Manager

Forsyth

WQMJ
11-22-1973; 100.1 mhz FM; 3 kw; 299 ft.; N32 58 27 W83 52 2
6070 Rock Springs Road, Lithonia, GA 30038 US
(478) 745-3301, *Fax:* (478) 742-2293
productionrci@aol.com
License: Forsyth, Monroe County, GA held by Roberts Communications Inc.
Arbitron Metro Market: Macon, GA *Format:* Urban Contemporary
Mike Roberts, General Manager

***WBIB-FM**
89.1 mhz FM; 0.1 kw; 174 ft.; N33 3 1 W83 57 10 US
(478) 932-0036
www.wbibfm.com
wbibfm@yahoo.com
License: Forsyth, Monroe County, GA held by Believers in Broadcasting Inc.
Arbitron Metro Market: Forsyth, GA *Format:* Christian
Travis Nunn, President
Jennifer Nunn, General Manager
Travis Nunn, Programming Director

Fort Benning South

WKCN
11-06-1992; 99.3 mhz FM *Hrs Open:* 24; 29 kw; 548 ft.; N32 27 59 W85 3 22
1353 13th Avenue, Columbus, GA 31901 US
(706) 596-9000, *Fax:* (706) 596-4600
www.kissin993.com
info@kissin993.com
License: Fort Benning South, Stewart County, GA held by PMB Broadcasting LLC.
Group Owner: PMB Broadcasting LLC; (acq 10-1-2008; grpsl)
Nat'l Reps: Christal
Arbitron Metro Market: Columbus, GA *Format:* Country *Target Audience:* 25-54; general
Chuck Thompson, General Manager

Fort Gaines

***WJWV**
02-28-1993; 90.9 mhz FM *Hrs Open:* 24; 20.5 kw horiz, 81 kw vert; 254 ft.; N31 36 16 W85 2 2 *Rebroadcasts:* Rebroadcasts WJSP-FM Warm Springs 100%
260 - 14th Street, N.W., Atlanta, GA 30318 US
(404) 685-2690, *Fax:* (404) 685-2684
www.gpb.org
ask@gpb.org
License: Fort Gaines, Clay County, GA held by Georgia Public Telecommunications Commission.
Arbitron Metro Market: Dothan, AL *Format:* News *Special Programming:* Jazz 16 hrs wkly *No. News Employees:* 10
Nancy Hall, CEO
Tom Barclay, Operations Dir
Bob Houghton, General Manager
Rob Maynard, Programming Director
Nancy Zintak, Promotions Manager
Susanna Capelouto, News Director
Bonnie Bean, CFO

Fort Valley

WIBB-FM
03-03-1993; 97.9 mhz FM *Hrs Open:* 24; 10.5 kw; 499 ft.; N32 34 12 W83 45 26
750 West Sandtown Road, S.W., Marietta, GA 30064 US
(478) 781-1063, *Fax:* (478) 781-6711
www.wibb.com
info@wibb.com
License: Fort Valley, Peach County, GA held by AMFM Radio Licenses LLC.
Group Owner: Clear Channel Communications Inc.; (acq 2-15-2001; grpsl).
Arbitron Metro Market: Macon, GA *Format:* Blues *Hrs. of News Programming:* news progmg 14 hrs wkly *No. News Employees:* 1 *Target Audience:* 18-44.

Bill Clark, General Manager

***WJTG**
03-01-1989; 91.3 mhz FM *Hrs Open:* 24; 100 kw; 459 ft.; N32 41 27 W83 51 45
341 S Washington, Lancaster, WI 53813 US
(478) 956-0085, *Fax:* (478) 956-0913
www.wjtg.org
wjtg913@aol.com
License: Fort Valley, Peach County, GA held by Family Life Broadcasting Inc.
Group Owner: Family Life Communications Inc.; (acq 5-23-2007; grpsl)
Nat'l Network: USA
Arbitron Metro Market: Macon, GA *Format:* Gospel *Target Audience:* General.
Tracy O. Wells, Operations Dir

WQBZ
04-06-1981; 106.3 mhz FM *Hrs Open:* 24; 48 kw; 492 ft.; N32 45 31 W83 44 49
598 West Sandtown Rd, Sw, Marietta, GA 30064 US
(478) 781-1063, *Fax:* (478) 781-6711
www.q106.fm
info@q106.fm
License: Fort Valley, Peach County, GA held by AMFM Radio Licenses LLC.
Group Owner: Clear Channel Communications Inc.; (acq 2-15-2001; grpsl).
Arbitron Metro Market: Macon, GA *Format:* Classic Rock *Target Audience:* 18-49.
Bill Clark, General Manager

WXKO
06-01-1951; 1150 khz AM *Hrs Open:* 24; 1 kw-D, ND1; 0.062 kw-N, ND1; N32 34 34 W83 54 17
6070 Rock Springs Road, Lithonia, GA 30038 US
(912) 825-5547, *Fax:* (912) 827-1273
clmurray11@aol.com
License: Fort Valley, GA held by WVKX-FM Radio LLC
Regional Network: Ga. News Net.
Arbitron Metro Market: Macon, GA *Format:* Country *Hrs. of News Programming:* news progmg 10 hrs wkly *No. News Employees:* 1 *Target Audience:* 25 plus; Black
Christopher Murray, President

Gainesville

***WBCX**
01-01-1977; 89.1 mhz FM *Hrs Open:* 24; 0.84 kw; 545 ft.; N34 19 1 W83 49 45
One Centinnial Circle, Gainesville, GA 30501 US
(307) 638-8921, *Fax:* (307) 638-8922
License: Gainesville, Hall County, GA held by Brenau University.
Nat'l Network: PRI; Jones Radio Networks
Arbitron Metro Market: Auburn WA *Format:* Rock/AOR *Adv. Rates:* 22; 15; 22; 15
Steven Silberberg, President
Roger Ingram, General Manager

WDUN
04-02-1949; 550 khz AM *Hrs Open:* 24; 10 kw-D, DAN; 2.5 kw-N, DAN; N34 20 8 W83 47 32
Mailing Address: P. O. Box 10, Gainesville, GA 30503 US
Second Address: 1102 Thompson Bridge Rd. N.E., Gainesville, GA 30501
(770) 532-9921, *Fax:* (770) 532-0459
WDUN.com or AccessNorthGA.com
jay.jacobs@jacobsmedia.net
License: Gainesville, GA held by JWJ Properties Inc.
Group Owner: Jacobs Media Corp.; (acq 9-83;
Nat'l Network: Fox News Radio *Regional Network:* Ga. News Net. *Wire Services:* AP
Arbitron Metro Market: Atlanta, GA *Format:* News, News/Talk, 86 *Hrs. of News Programming:* Hourly *No. News Employees:* 10 *Target Audience:* 25-65. *Adv. Rates:* Varies
John W. Jacobs Jr., Chairman
Jay Jacobs, CEO
Bill Maine, Operations Dir
Joel Williams, General Manager
Jean Pethel, General Sales Mgr
Bill Maine, Programming Director

WSRV
11-01-1965; 97.1 mhz FM; 98 kw; 1585 ft.; N34 7 32 W83 51 32
2000 Riveredge Parkway, Suite 797, Atlanta, GA 30328 US
(404) 897-7500, *Fax:* (404) 876-5126
www.971theriver.com
lee.cagle@coxinc.com
License: Gainesville, Hall County, GA held by Cox Radio Inc.
Group Owner: Cox Radio Inc.; (acq 8-16-2000; grpsl)
Arbitron Metro Market: Atlanta, GA *Format:* Contemporary Hits/Top 40, Adult Contemp *Hrs. of News Programming:* News progmg 3 hrs wkly *Target Audience:* 35-54; baby boomers
Francisco Luciano, General Sales Mgr
Lee Cagle, Programming Director
Dave Clapper, Promotions Manager
Tony Kidd, VP, Market Manager
Karyn Cerulli, General Sales Manager
Hans Heilmann, National Sales Manager
Andrew Rudd, Directorof Client Services

WGGA
10-10-1941; 1240 khz AM *Hrs Open:* 24
Mailing Address: P.O. Box 10, Gainesville, GA 30503 US
Second Address: 1102 Thompson Bridge Rd. N.E., Gainesville, GA 30501
(770) 532-9921, *Fax:* (770) 532-0459
www.1240Theticket.com,www.AccessNorthGA.com
jay.jacobs@jacobsmedia.net
License: Gainesville, GA held by JWJ Properties Inc.
Group Owner: Jacobs Media Corp.; (acq 4-20-93; $360,000;
Nat'l Network: NBC *Regional Network:* Ga. News Net.
Arbitron Metro Market: Atlanta, GA *Format:* Sports, Talk *Hrs. of News Programming:* Hourly *No. News Employees:* 1 *Target Audience:* 18-49 men *Adv. Rates:* Varies
John W. Jacobs Jr., Chairman
John W. Jacobs III, CEO
Joel Williams, General Manager

WLBA
01-26-1957; 1130 khz AM *Hrs Open:* Sunrise-sunset; 1 kw-C, NDD; 10 kw-D, NDD; N34 16 45 W83 46 33
PO Box 746, Austell, GA 30001 US
(770) 944-0900, *Fax:* (770) 944-9794
www.radiolafavorita.com
ariel@radiolafavorita.com
License: Gainesville, GA held by La Favorita Inc.
Group Owner: La Favorita Inc.; acq 2-18-97; $275,000)

Samuel Zamarron, President
Ariel Zamarron, Station Manager

WYAY
04-03-1949; 106.7 mhz FM; 77 kw; 1657 ft.; N33 52 2 W83 49 44
210 Interstate N. 6th Fl, Atlanta, GA 30339 US
(404) 521-1007, *Fax:* (404) 499-1067
www.allnews1067.com
License: Gainesville, Hall County, GA
Group Owner: Cumulus Media Inc.; (acq 6-12-2007; grpsl)
Nat'l Network: ABC *Nat'l Reps:* ABC Radio Sales
Arbitron Metro Market: Atlanta, GA *Format:* Country *Target Audience:* 25-54.
Victor Sansone, President
Mark Richards, Operations Dir
Lisa C. McMahon, General Sales Mgr
Marshall Adams, Programming Director
Christy Ullman, Promotions Manager
Glenda Dodd, News Director
Matt Scarano, General Sales Manager
Nancy Barre, National Sales Manager
Mary Gordon, Regional Sales Manager

Gibson

***WTHP**
01-01-2006; 94.3 mhz FM; 6.3 kw; 571 ft.; N33 17 5 W82 35 45
966 Athol Avenue, Aiken, SC 29803 US
(800) -926-4669
www.gnnradio.org
ctbarinowski@comcast.net
License: Gibson, Glascock County, GA held by Barinowski Investment Co. L.P.
Group Owner: Good News Network; (acq 2-15-2006)
Arbitron Metro Market: Grovetown, GA *Format:* Christian
Clarence Barinowski, General Manager

Glennville

WOAH
11-18-1977; 106.3 mhz FM *Hrs Open:* 24; 6 kw; Ant 394 ft; N32 00 27 W81 54 51
25 Bristlecone Dr., Savannah, GA 30427
(912) 408-1063, *Fax:* (912) 876-6920
www.hotkiss1063.com
jimlewis@coastalnow.net
License: Glennville, Tattnall County, GA held by Broadcast Executives Corp.
James Lewis, General Manager

Gordon

WFXM
03-30-1976; 107.1 mhz FM *Hrs Open:* 24; 3 kw; 466 ft.; N32 50 55 W83 28 29
6070 Rock Springs Road, Lithonia, GA 30038 US
(478) 745-3301(478) 745-1077, *Fax:* (478) 742-2293
www.powermacon.com
productionrci@aol.com
License: Gordon, Wilkinson County, GA held by WFXM-FM Radio LLC
Arbitron Metro Market: Macon, GA *Format:* Urban Contemporary
Special Programming: Jazz 3 hrs wkly *Target Audience:* Middle & upper class Georgians
Mike Roberts, General Manager

Gray

WPCH
01-01-1994; 96.5 mhz FM *Hrs Open:* 24; 8 kw; 571 ft.; N32 58 31 W83 47 59
750 West Sandtown Road, S.W., Marietta, GA 30064 US
(478) 781-1063, *Fax:* (478) 781-6711
www.peach965.com
License: Gray, Jones County, GA held by AMFM Radio Licenses LLC.
Group Owner: Clear Channel Communications Inc.; (acq 2-1-2001; grpsl).
Arbitron Metro Market: Macon, GA *Format:* Contemporary Hits/Top 40, Adult Contemp *Target Audience:* 18-54; adults
John Lund, Operations Dir
Bill Clark, General Manager

Grayson

WPLO
01-07-1959; 610 khz AM *Hrs Open:* 24; 1.5 kw-D, ND1; 0.225 kw-N, ND1; N33 57 11 W83 58 15
3055 Sugarloaf Club Dr, Duluth, GA 30097 US
(770) 237-9897, *Fax:* (770) 246-0054
www.radiomex610atlanta.com
laleysales@covat.net
License: Grayson, GA held by Teresa Prieto
Arbitron Metro Market: Atlanta, GA *Format:* Spanish, Christian
Franca Vera, General Manager

Greensboro

WDDK
07-12-1980; 103.9 mhz FM *Hrs Open:* 24; 5.3 kw; 328 ft.; N33 28 29 W83 14 46
1271-B East Broad Street, Greensboro, GA 30642 US
(706) 453-4140, *Fax:* (706) 453-7179
www.dock1039.com/wddk/
chip@dock1039.com
License: Greensboro, Greene County, GA held by Wyche Services Corp.
Nat'l Network: ABC *Regional Network:* Ga. News Net.
Arbitron Metro Market: Greensboro, GA *Format:* Oldies, Talk *Hrs. of News Programming:* news progmg 4 hrs wkly *No. News Employees:* 1 *Target Audience:* 24-60. *Adv. Rates:* 12; 12; 12; 12
K.B. Travis, Operations Dir
Chip Lyness, General Manager
K.B. Travis, Operations Director

Griffin

WHIE
12-15-1952; 1320 khz AM; 5 kw-D, ND1; 0.083 kw-N, ND1; N33 14 30 W84 18 17
3707 Randall Mill Road, NW, Atlanta, GA 30327 US
(770) 227-9451, *Fax:* (770) 229-2291
License: Griffin, GA held by Chappell Communications L.L.C.
Arbitron Metro Market: Atlanta, GA *Format:* Country, News, 62, Sports, Talk
Robert Chappell Jr., President

WKEU
01-01-1933; 1450 khz AM; 1 kw-U, ND1; N33 14 24 W84 14 55
Mailing Address: P.O. Box 997, Griffin, GA 30224 US
Second Address: 1000 Memorial Dr., Griffin, GA 30224
(770) 227-5507, *Fax:* (770) 229-2291
www.wkeuradio.com
wkeu@aol.com
License: Griffin, GA held by WLT & Associates L.P.
Regional Network: Ga. News Net. *Nat'l Reps:* Rgnl Reps
Arbitron Metro Market: Atlanta, GA *Format:* News, Oldies *Target Audience:* 25 plus.
William Taylor, President

***WMVV**
04-16-1995; 90.7 mhz FM *Hrs Open:* 24; 18 kw; 472 ft.; N33 22 12 W84 8 0
Mailing Address: 1984 Old Peachtree Rd, Lawrenceville, GA 30043 US
Second Address: 100 S. Hill St., Suite 100, Griffin, GA 30223
(770) 229-2020
www.newlife.fm
contactus@newlife.fm
License: Griffin, Spalding County, GA held by Life Radio Ministries Inc.
Nat'l Network: American Family Radio *Wire Services:* AP
Arbitron Metro Market: Atlanta, GA *Format:* Christian, Religious
Joseph Emert, President
James Stewart, Operations Dir

Hahira

WTHV
01-01-1990; 810 khz AM *Hrs Open:* 15; 2.5 kw-D; N30 52 33.7N 83 16 22.5W
4198 Rebecca Circle, Valdosta, GA 31602
(229) 245-9848, *Fax:* (229) 262-0809
wthv810am@yahoo.com
License: Hahira, Lowndes County, GA held by Eternal Life Ministries Inc.
Nat'l Network: Salem Radio Network
Population Served: 90,000 *Arbitron Metro Market:* Valdosta, GA
Special Programming: Spanish 5 hrs wkly *Target Audience:* 24-55. *Adv. Rates:* 84; 84; 84; na
Cody Fender, President
Phyllis Fender, Operations Dir
Cory Fender, General Manager
Cory Fender, Station Manager
Cory Fender, General Sales Mgr
Cory Fender, Programming Director
Cory Fender, Promotions Manager
Cory Fender, ChiefEngineer

Hampton

WHTA
10-19-1973; 107.9 mhz FM; kw
544 Mulberry St, Suite 700, Macon, GA 31201 US
(404) 765-9750, *Fax:* (404) 688-7686
www.hot1079atl.com
License: Hampton, Henry County, GA held by Radio One Licenses LLC.
Group Owner: Radio One Inc.; (acq 8-20-01; $60 million).
Arbitron Metro Market: Atlanta, GA *Format:* Urban Contemporary
Wayne Brown, General Manager

Hapeville

WWWE
01-07-1947; 1100 khz AM *Hrs Open:* Sunrise-sunset; 3.8 kw-C, NDD; 5 kw-D, NDD; N33 43 43 W84 19 20
9600 Koger Boulrvard, Suite 202, St. Petersburg, FL 33702 US
(404) 352-9993, *Fax:* (404) 355-0291
License: Hapeville, GA held by WAEC License L.P.
Group Owner: Beasley Broadcast Group Inc.; (acq 10-29-99; $10 million with WAEC(AM) Atlanta)
Arbitron Metro Market: Atlanta, GA *Format:* Sports, Talk *Special Programming:* Relg 12 hrs, news/talk 14 hrs, Ethiopian 2 hrs wk *Hrs. of News Programming:* news progmg 8 hrs wkly *No. News Employees:* 1 *TargetAudience:* 35 plus; mature audience
George Beasley, Chairman
Caroline Beasley, CFO
Bruce Beasley, President
Chris Edmonds, General Manager
Brian Beasley, Executive Vice President

Harlem

WGAC-FM
11-23-1992; 95.1 mhz FM; 5.7 kw; 440 ft; N33 31 34 W82 15 55
4051 Jimmie Dyess Pkwy., Augusta, GA 33940
(706) 396-7000, *Fax:* (706) 396-7100
www.95rock.com
info@wchz.com
License: Harlem, Columbia County, GA held by WCHZ License LLC
Group Owner: Beasley Broadcast Group Inc.; (acq 1-13-97; $1.2 million).
Arbitron Metro Market: Augusta, GA *Target Audience:* 18-34; well-educated adults, upper demographics
Kent Dunn, General Manager
Greg Mclaughlin, General Sales Mgr

Hartwell

WKLY
09-05-1947; 980 khz AM *Hrs Open:* 18; 1 kw-D, ND1; 0.149 kw-N, ND1; N34 21 28 W82 58 35
Mailing Address: PO Box 636, Hartwell, GA 30643 US
Second Address: 2235 Bowersville Hwy., Hartwell, GA 30643
(706) 376-2233, *Fax:* (706) 376-3100
www.wklyradio.com
wklyradio@hartcom.net
License: Hartwell, GA held by WKLY Broadcasting Co.
Nat'l Network: ABC Music Radio *Regional Network:* Ga. News Net.
Format: Country, Gospel *Hrs. of News Programming:* news progmg 18 hrs wkly *No. News Employees:* 2 *Target Audience:* 30 plus; middle class, working adults *Adv. Rates:* 15; 15; 15; 10
Bruce Hicks, CFO
Bryan Hicks, General Manager

Hawkinsville

WCEH
12-11-1952; 610 khz AM *Hrs Open:* 24; 0.5 kw-D, ND1; 0.126 kw-N, ND1; N32 16 50 W83 26 37
500 Commerce Street, P.O. Box 180, Hawkinsville, GA 31036 US
(478) 892-9061, *Fax:* (478) 892-9063
www.houstoncountyradio.com/WCEH.html
information@houstoncountyradio.com
License: Hawkinsville, GA held by Georgia Eagle Broadcasting Inc.
Group Owner: Georgia Eagle Broadcasting Inc.; (acq 1-12-2007; grpsl)
Arbitron Metro Market: Warner Robins, GA *Format:* News, Sports *Hrs. of News Programming:* 7 *Target Audience:* men 24-65 *Adv. Rates:* 8; 6; 8; 6
Cecil Staton, President
Jay Braswell, General Manager

WQXZ
09-26-1968; 103.9 mhz FM; 10.5 kw; 495 ft.; N32 10 3 W83 37 51
P. O. Box 489, Hawkinsville, GA 31036 US
(478) 892-9061, *Fax:* (478) 892-8663
qwixie983@georgiaeagleradio.com
License: Hawkinsville, Pulaski County, GA held by Georgia Eagle Broadcasting Inc.
Group Owner: Georgia Eagle Broadcasting Inc.; 2007
Nat'l Network: CNN Radio *Regional Network:* Ga. News Net.
Arbitron Metro Market: Macon, GA *Format:* Oldies *Hrs. of News Programming:* 7 *No. News Employees:* 1 *Target Audience:* male and female, 25-65 *Adv. Rates:* 14; 12; 14; 12
Cecil Station, President
Jay Braswell, General Manager

Hazlehurst

WHJD
09-06-1962; 920 khz AM *Hrs Open:* 24; 500 w-D, 39 w-N; N31 51 02 W82 33 19
546 Baxley Hwy., Hazlehurst, GA 31539
(912) 375-4511, *Fax:* (912) 375-4512
www.wvohradio.com
wvoh@wvohradio.com
License: Hazlehurst, Jeff Davis County, GA held by Broadcast South, LLC
Group Owner: Broadcast South LLC
Nat'l Network: Fox News Radio *Regional Network:* Ga. News Net.
Population Served: 10,000*TV Affiliate:* WVOH-LP affil *Special Programming:* Farm 2 hrs wkly *No. News Employees:* 1 *Adv. Rates:* 11.00/60sec—9.00/30 sec 24/7
Tony Deloach, Station Manager

Helen

***WTFH**
02-01-2001; 89.9 mhz FM *Hrs Open:* 24; 0.015 kw; 561 ft.; N34 44 55 W83 43 43
Mailing Address: Falls Road, Toccoa Falls, GA 30598 US
Second Address: 292 Old Clarksville Hwy., Toccoa Falls, GA 30577
(800) 251-8326, *Fax:* (706) 282-6090
www.toccoafallsradio.org
radio@tfc.edu
License: Helen, White County, GA held by Toccoa Falls College.
Arbitron Metro Market: Helen, GA *Format:* Christian
Marty Lee, Operations Dir
David Cornelius, General Manager
Bryan Race, Station Manager
Bryan Race, Programming Director
Mike Shelley, Assistant Manager
Mike Shelley, Music Director

Hephzibah

WAKB
01-01-1975; 100.9 mhz FM *Hrs Open:* 24; 16 kw; 302 ft.; N33 22 40 W82 4 37
Mailing Address: P.O. Box 1100, Columbus, GA 31994 US
Second Address: 104 Bennett Ln., North Augusta, SC 29841
(662) 844-8888(662) 844-8893, *Fax:* (662) 842-6791
www.afr.net
comments@afr.net
License: Hephzibah, Burke County, GA held by Perry Broadcasting of Augusta Inc.
Group Owner: Perry Publishing & Broadcasting Co.; (acq 12-12-2007; grpsl)
Arbitron Metro Market: Devil's Lake ND *Format:* Religious
Marvin Sanders, General Manager

Hiawassee

WJUL
1230 khz AM; 1 kw-U; N34 56 34 W83 46 27
Mailing Address: 101 S. Main St., Ste 6, Hiawassee, GA
Second Address: 38 Kenmare Hall, N.E., Atlanta, GA 30324
(706 896-1230,(404) 266-2257
info@wngm1230.com
License: Hiawassee, Towns County, GA held by BMG Broadcasting Inc.
Rick Morris, General Manager
John Allen, Programming Director
Jackie Grizzle, Chief Engineer

Hinesville

WGML
12-09-1958; 990 khz AM *Hrs Open:* Sunrise-sunset; 0.25 kw-D, ND1; 0.076 kw-N, ND1; N31 51 1 W81 36 4
Mailing Address: P.O. Box 93, Hinesville, GA 31310 US
Second Address: 308 Rolland St., Hinesville, GA 31313
(912) 368-3399, *Fax:* (912) 368-4191
wgml@coastalnow.net
License: Hinesville, GA held by Powerhouse of Deliverance Church Inc.
Format: Gospel, Religious *Special Programming:* Sp one hr wkly *Hrs. of News Programming:* News progmg 10 hrs wkly *Target Audience:* General. *Adv. Rates:* 7.50; 7; 7.50
Bishop Raymond Napper, CEO
Elder Mary Napper, President
Emanuel White, General Manager

WTHG
01-01-1994; 104.7 mhz FM *Hrs Open:* 24; 12 kw; 469 ft.; N31 51 18 W81 44 28
Mailing Address: 120 Liberty St./#Cd-104, Hinesville, GA 31313 US
Second Address: 120 D Liberty St., Hinesville, GA 31313
(912) 368-9258, *Fax:* (912) 368-5526
rjp106@aol.com
License: Hinesville, Liberty County, GA held by Tama Radio Licenses of Savannah, GA Inc.
Group Owner: Tama Broadcasting Inc.; (acq 4-8-2004).
Arbitron Metro Market: Savannah, GA *Format:* Classic Rock
Yvonne Clark, General Manager

WSGA
08-02-1982; 92.3 mhz FM *Hrs Open:* 24; 50 kw; 482 ft.; N31 41 37 W81 23 27
Mailing Address: P.O. Box 1280, Hinesville, GA 31313 US
Second Address: 120 D Liberty St., Hinesville, GA 31313
(912) 368-9258, *Fax:* (912) 368-5526
www.freedom923.com
office@923classiccountry.com
License: Hinesville, Liberty County, GA held by Tama Radio Licenses of Savannah, GA, Inc.
Group Owner: Tama Broadcasting Inc.; (acq 4-8-2004; $2.79 million).
Nat'l Reps: Rgnl Reps
Format: Adult Contemp *Hrs. of News Programming:* News progmg 2 hrs wkly *Target Audience:* 25-54; Savannah, Hinesville, Brunswick, 15 county area
Yvonne Clark, General Manager

Hogansville

WVCC
08-12-1985; 720 khz AM *Hrs Open:* Sunrise-sunset; 7.97 kw-D, NDD; N33 3 54 W84 57 23
50 E. Rivercenter Blvd., Suite 1299, Covington, KY 41011 US

(770) 683-7234, *Fax:* (770) 683-9846
www.720thevoice.com
johnlund@clearchannel.com
License: Hogansville, GA held by Citicasters Licenses L.P.
Group Owner: Clear Channel Communications Inc.
Nat'l Network: Fox News Radio; Premiere Radio Networks; Salem Radio Network *Regional Network:* Ga. News Net.
Arbitron Metro Market: Newnan, GA *Format:* News, News/Talk, 86
Bill Clark, Promotions Manager

WMGP
09-03-1992; 98.1 mhz FM *Hrs Open:* 24; 25 kw; 328 ft.; N33 3 54 W84 57 23
50 E. Rivercenter Blvd., Suite 200, Covington, KY 41011 US
(770) 683-7234, *Fax:* (770) 683-9846
www.magic981.com
JaniceHorne@clearchannel.com
License: Hogansville, Troup County, GA held by Citicasters Licenses L.P.
Group Owner: Clear Channel Communications Inc.; (acq 1999; grpsl).
Arbitron Metro Market: Hogansville, GA *Format:* Contemporary Hits/Top 40, Adult Contemp *Target Audience:* 17-64; non-country listeners
Bill Clark, Promotions Manager

Homerville

WBTY
12-01-1980; 98.7 mhz FM; 6 kw; 299 ft.; N31 2 4 W82 51 50
Mailing Address: PO Bix 577, Homerville, GA 31634 US
Second Address: Intersection of Hwy's 168 & 37, Homerville, GA 31634
(781) 891-2808, *Fax:* (912) 487-3414
www.radiobentley.com
RadioBentley@gmail.com
License: Homerville, Clinch County, GA held by Southern Broadcasting & Investments.
Arbitron Metro Market: Waltham, MA *Format:* Contemporary Hits/Top 40, Adult Contemp *Target Audience:* General.
Nicholas Smits, President
Jim Strickland, Operations Dir
Michael Primes, General Manager
Vincent Menechino, Station Manager
Brian Irvine, Programming Director
Robbie LaBrie, Sports Director

Irwinton

WVKX
09-01-1995; 103.7 mhz FM; 6 kw; 328 ft.; N32 52 48 W83 11 7
P.O. Box 569, 104 High Hill Street, Irwinton, GA 31042 US
(478) 946-3445, *Fax:* (478) 946-2406
blackmaconweb.com
biggeorgeradio@cox.net
License: Irwinton, Wilkinson County, GA held by Wilkinson Broadcasting Inc.
Arbitron Metro Market: Irwinton, GA *Format:* Blues, Gospel
Stan Carter, General Manager

Jackson

WJGA-FM
04-24-1967; 92.1 mhz FM *Hrs Open:* 24; 2.15 kw; 374 ft.; N33 16 37 W83 57 59
P.O. Box 878, Jackson, GA 30233 US
(770) 775-3151, *Fax:* (770) 775-3153
License: Jackson, Butts County, GA held by Earnhart Broadcasting Co. Inc.
Nat'l Reps: Keystone (unwired net) *Regional Reps:* Rgnl Reps.
Wire Services: AP
Format: Adult Contemp, Black *Special Programming:* Gospel 15 hrs wkly *Hrs. of News Programming:* news progmg 20 hrs wkly *No. News Employees:* 1 *Target Audience:* General. *Adv. Rates:* 15; 15; 15; 15
Don Earnhart, President

Jacksonville

WSIZ-FM
102.3 mhz FM; 5.5 kw; 335 ft.; N31 46 42 W83 5 7
US
(208) 733-3551
www.wayx.net
License: Jacksonville, Telfair County, GA held by World Radio Link Inc.
Group Owner: World Radio Link Inc.
Arbitron Metro Market: Jacksonville, GA *Format:* Classic Rock, News, 86
Earl Williamson, President

Jasper

***WIVL**
01-01-1999; 88.3 mhz FM *Hrs Open:* 24; 0.2 kw; 3 ft.; N34 28 1 W84 25 49
321 Freeman Circle, Norcross, GA 30071 US
(770) 596-0739, *Fax:* (706) 425-1840
communitypublicradio@prodigy.net
License: Jasper, Pickens County, GA held by Community Public Radio Inc.
Arbitron Metro Market: Jasper, GA *Format:* Adult Contemp
Target Audience: 35-55; upper middle class, educated, Christian
Penny Jackson, President

WYYZ
05-25-1973; 1490 khz AM; 1 kw-U, ND1; N34 28 32 W84 26 13
P.O. Box 280, Jasper, GA 30143 US
(706) 692-4100, *Fax:* (706) 692-4012
License: Jasper, GA held by Enlightment LLC
Nat'l Network: CBS
Arbitron Metro Market: Atlanta, GA *Format:* Classic Rock
Mark Hellinger, General Manager

Jeffersonville

WPEZ
09-27-1993; 93.7 mhz FM *Hrs Open:* 24; 100 kw; 679 ft.; N32 45 12 W83 33 46
173 First Street, Macon, GA 31202 US
(478) 746-6286, *Fax:* (478) 745-4383
www.z937.com
info@z937.com
License: Jeffersonville, Twiggs County, GA held by Cumulus Licensing Corp.
Group Owner: Cumulus Media Inc.; (acq 12-20-02; grpsl).
Arbitron Metro Market: Macon, GA *Format:* Classic Rock *Hrs. of News Programming:* News progmg one hr wkly *Target Audience:* 25-54. *Adv. Rates:* 120; 110; 110; 30
John Sheftic, General Manager

Jesup

***WTLD**
01-01-2004; 90.5 mhz FM *Hrs Open:* 24; 6 kw; 171 ft.; N31 35 49 W81 56 14
207 Greenview Street, Jesup, GA 31545 US
(912) 695-7169, *Fax:* (912) 588-1822
www.wtldradio.com
WTLDFM@AOL.COM
License: Jesup, Wayne County, GA held by Resurrection House Ministries Inc.
Arbitron Metro Market: JESUP, GA *Format:* Gospel *Hrs. of News Programming:* News progmg 12 hrs wkly *Target Audience:* 18 plus.
Dr. Leonard Small, CEO
Evangelist Marie Butler, General Manager

WIFO-FM
07-01-1968; 105.5 mhz FM *Hrs Open:* 24; 25 kw; 308 ft.; N31 36 6 W81 56 0
P. O. Box 647, Jesup, GA 31545 US
(912) 427-3711, *Fax:* (912) 530-7717
www.bigdogcountry.com
bigdogstaff@bellsouth.net
License: Jesup, Wayne County, GA held by Jesup Broadcasting Corp.
Nat'l Network: ABC Information & Entertainment *Regional Network:* Ga. News Net. *Nat'l Reps:* Rgnl Reps
Format: Country *No. News Employees:* 1 *Target Audience:* General.
Charles Hubbard, CEO
Matt Hubbard, General Manager

WLOP
07-12-1949; 1370 khz AM; 5 kw-D, ND1; 0.035 kw-N, ND1; N31 36 6 W81 56 0
Mailing Address: P. O. Box 647, Jesup, GA 31545 US
Second Address: 2420 Waycross Hwy, Jesup, GA 31545
(912) 427-3711, *Fax:* (912) 530-7717
bigdogstaff@bellsouth.net
License: Jesup, GA held by Jesup Broadcasting Corp.
Regional Network: Ga. News Net. *Nat'l Reps:* Rgnl Reps
Format: Sports *Target Audience:* General.
Charles Hubbard Jr., President
Matt Hubbard, General Manager

***WLPT**
01-01-1988; 88.3 mhz FM *Hrs Open:* 24; 20 kw; 801 ft.; N31 40 27 W81 53 12
3213 Huxley Drive, Augusta, GA 30909 US
(706) 309-9610
www.gnnradio.org
ctbarinowski@comcast.net
License: Jesup, Wayne County, GA held by Augusta Radio Fellowship Institute Inc.
Format: Christian *Hrs. of News Programming:* News progmg 12 hrs wkly *Target Audience:* General.
Clarence Barinowski, General Manager

Kingsland

WKBX
02-23-1987; 106.3 mhz FM *Hrs Open:* 24; 6 kw; 328 ft.; N30 48 4 W81 40 43
P.O. Box 2525, 111 N. Grove Boulevard, Kingsland, GA 31548 US
(912) 729-6106, *Fax:* (912) 729-4106
www.k-bay106.com
wkbx@k-bay106.com
License: Kingsland, Camden County, GA held by Radio Kings Bay Inc.
Nat'l Network: ABC
Format: Country *Hrs. of News Programming:* news progmg one hr wkly *No. News Employees:* 1 *Target Audience:* 18-54; contemp country audience *Adv. Rates:* 20; 15.29; 20; 15.29
James Steele, President
John Fluery, Programming Director
Susan Pope, News Director
Wendy Steele, Executive Vice President
Jason Bishop, News Director

La Fayette

WQCH
11-01-1954; 1590 khz AM *Hrs Open:* 12; 5 kw-D; N34 42 57 W85 16 06
Box 746, La Fayette, GA 30728
(706) 638-3276, *Fax:* (706) 638-3896
www.wqch.net
WQCHRadio@aol.com
License: La Fayette, Walker County, GA held by Radix Broadcasting Inc.
Nat'l Network: AP Network News *Regional Network:* Ga. News Net. *Nat'l Reps:* Rgnl Reps
Arbitron Metro Market: Chattanooga, TN *Special Programming:* Farm 2 hrs wkly *Hrs. of News Programming:* news progmg 10 hrs wkly *No. News Employees:* 1 *Target Audience:* 25 plus. *Adv. Rates:* 11.50; 11.50;11.50; 11.50
C Rich Gwyn, General Manager

La Grange

WLAG
05-01-1941; 1240 khz AM *Hrs Open:* 24; 1 kw-U, ND1; N33 2 24 W85 1 27
Mailing Address: P.O. Box 1429, Lagrange, GA 30241 US
Second Address: 304 Broome St., La Grange, GA 30240
(706) 845-1023, *Fax:* (706) 845-8642
www.eagle1023.com
wlag@eagle1023.com
License: La Grange, GA held by Eagle's Nest Inc.
Group Owner: Eagle's Nest Inc.; acq 4-3-92; $10;
Format: Sports *Hrs. of News Programming:* news progmg 4 hrs wkly *No. News Employees:* 1 *Target Audience:* 25-54; general
Jim Vice, General Manager

***WOAK**
06-11-1984; 90.9 mhz FM; 3.4 kw; 299 ft.; N32 57 57 W84 59 8
1921 Hamilton Rd., Lagrange, GA 30240 US
(706) 884-2950, *Fax:* (706) 884-2930
woak.com
woak@woak.org
License: La Grange, Troup County, GA held by Oakside Christian School.
Nat'l Network: USA
TV Affiliate: Relg

WTRP
01-09-1953; 620 khz AM
806 New Franklin Rd., Lagrange, GA 30240 US
(706) 407-7230
wtrp620.com
620wtrp@gmail.com
License: La Grange, GA held by Tiger Communications Inc.
Group Owner: Tiger Communications Inc.; (acq 10-19-2006; $279,000 with WRLA(AM) West Point)
Arbitron Metro Market: Lagrange, GA *Format:* News, Sports
Walter Douglas, Air Staff
Barbara Douglas, Air Staff

***WBRQ**
91.9 mhz FM; 1 kw; 43 ft.; N33 0 48 W85 2 58

321 Freeman Circle, Norcross, GA 30071 US
(787) 529-8917
License: La Grange, Troup County, GA held by Family Educational Association Inc.
Arbitron Metro Market: La Grange, GA
Juan Carlos Matos, President

Lakeland

WVGA
01-01-1994; 105.9 mhz FM; 10 kw; 328 ft.; N31 3 21 W83 13 54
1707-A Al Brooks Drive, Valdosta, GA 31601 US
(229) 244-8642, *Fax:* (229) 242-7620
www.newstalk1059wvga.com
info@newstalk1059wvga.com
License: Lakeland, Lanier County, GA held by RTG Radio LLC.
Group Owner: Black Crow Media Group LLC; (acq 11-9-2001; grpsl).
Arbitron Metro Market: Valdosta, GA *Format:* News, News/Talk, 86
Robert Ganzak, President

Lavonia

WLHR-FM
05-15-2008; 92.1 mhz FM; 5.6 kw; Ant 338 ft; N34 22 51 W83 07 28
Mailing Address: P O Box 228, Lavonia, GA 30635
Second Address: 12715 Augusta Road, Lavonia, GA 30553
(706) 356-0921, *Fax:* (706) 356-5921
www.921wlhr.com
dbrown@gacaradio.com
License: Lavonia, Franklin County, GA held by Lake Hartwell Radio Inc.
Group Owner: Georgia-Carolina Radiocasting Companies; (acq 12-31-2008; $158,185 assumption of debt)
Nat'l Network: AP Network News
Population Served: 85,118*Special Programming:* Local News *Hrs. of News Programming:* local news progmg 11 hrs wkly *No. News Employees:* 1 *Target Audience:* 25 plus. *Adv. Rates:* Please Contact
Art Sutton, President
Daniel Brown, Operations Dir
Daniel Brown, General Manager
Daniel Brown, Programming Director
MJ Kneiser, News Director
Marty Lee, Chief Engineer
Brian Rothell, Music Director
Terry Carter, VicePresident

Lawrenceville

WISK
08-28-1962; 990 khz AM *Hrs Open:* Sunrise-sunset
P. O. Box 727, Americus, GA 31709 US
(229) 924-1390, *Fax:* (229) 928-2337
www.americusradio.com
License: Lawrenceville, GA held by Sumter Broadcasting Co. Inc.
Group Owner: Sumter Broadcasting Co. Inc.
Regional Network: Ga. News Net.
Format: Oldies *No. News Employees:* 1 *Target Audience:* 19-65.
Steve Lashley, General Manager
Donnie McCreary, News Director

Leesburg

WJAD
10-01-1989; 103.5 mhz FM; 12.5 kw; 463 ft.; N31 40 18 W84 3 32
330 E. Kilbourn Ave., Suite 250, Milwaukee, WI 53202 US
(229) 888-5000, *Fax:* (229) 888-5960
www.wjad.com
License: Leesburg, Lee County, GA held by Cumulus Licensing Corp.
Group Owner: Cumulus Media Inc.; (acq 7-7-98)
Nat'l Reps: Katz Radio
Arbitron Metro Market: Albany, GA *Target Audience:* 25-40; Generation X, tail end of baby boomers
Bill Jones, Operations Dir
Gregory Kamishlian, Promotions Manager

Lithia Springs

WJTP
04-15-1959; 890 khz AM *Hrs Open:* Sunrise-sunset
P.O. Box 10, Walhalla, SC 29691 US
(239) 485-2100, *Fax:* (239) 992-8165
www.sunny1063.com
randy@sunny1063.com
License: Lithia Springs, GA held by New Life Broadcasting Inc.
Nat'l Network: ABC
Format: Oldies, Talk *Hrs. of News Programming:* news progmg 6 hrs wkly *No. News Employees:* 1 *Target Audience:* 25-54; emphasis on women
Juan Carlos Matos, President
Gary Butts, Operations Dir
Brad Beasley, General Manager
Randy Sherwyn, Programming Director
Jeff Hickcox, Promotions Manager
Dick Mangrum, News Director
Tim Stephens, Chief Engineer
Robert Hallman,Director of Sales
Dawn Krause, New Business Manager
AJ Lurie, National Sales Manager
Diana Beasley, Webmaster

Louisville

WPEH
09-10-1960; 1420 khz AM *Hrs Open:* 6 AM-midnight; 1 kw-D, ND1; 0.159 kw-N, ND1; N33 0 48 W82 23 33
PO Box 425, Louisville, GA 30434 US
(912) 625-7248, *Fax:* (912) 625-7249
www.wpeh.com
License: Louisville, GA held by Peach Broadcasting Co. Inc.
Regional Network: Ga. News Net.
Format: Country, Oldies *Hrs. of News Programming:* News progmg 11 hrs wkly *Target Audience:* General.
Ottis Stephens, President
Wendell Stephens, Programming Director

WPEH-FM
05-06-1971; 92.1 mhz FM; 6 kw; 299 ft.; N33 0 48 W82 23 33
PO Box 425, Louisville, GA 30434 US
(912) 625-7248, *Fax:* (912) 625-7249
wpeh@classicsouth.net
License: Louisville, Jefferson County, GA held by Peach Broadcasting Co. Inc.
Target Audience: 25 plus.
Otis Stephens, General Manager

Lumber City

*WMOC
04-01-1997; 88.7 mhz FM; 50 kw; 210 ft.; N31 55 48 W82 41 6
Mailing Address: P.O. Box 176, Lumber City, GA 31549 US
Second Address: 412 Renwick St., Lumber City, GA 31549
(912) 363-2203, *Fax:* (912) 363-2106
http://www.mocradio.com
wmoc887@yahoo.com
License: Lumber City, Telfair County, GA held by Full Gospel Church of God Written in Heaven.
Arbitron Metro Market: Lumber City, GA *Format:* Gospel *Target Audience:* General , urban
Eddie Conaway, General Manager

Lumpkin

*WBOJ
01-01-2008; 88.5 mhz FM; 23 kw; Ant 538 ft; N31 59 19 W84 55 59
Box 9382, Columbus, GA 31908
(706) 413-0342
www.wtmq.com
License: Lumpkin, Stewart County, GA held by Spanish Cultural Education Inc.
Victor Molina, President

*WXIV
90.1 mhz FM; kw
US
(205) 951-3700
License: Lumpkin, Stewart County, GA held by TBTA Ministries.
Arbitron Metro Market: Lumpkin, GA
Kenneth Layton, President

Lyons

WBBT
03-12-1959; 1340 khz AM *Hrs Open:* 24; 1 kw-U; N32 12 50 W82 19 51
P.O. Box 629, 473 N. Victory Dr., Lyons, GA 30436
(912) 526-8122,(912) 526-6333, *Fax:* (912) 526-9155
rockinrobin_y101@yahoo.com
License: Lyons, Toombs County, GA held by T.C.B. Broadcasting Inc.
Nat'l Network: ABC
Population Served: 85,000*Hrs. of News Programming:* news progmg 20 hrs wkly *No. News Employees:* 2 *Target Audience:* General. *Adv. Rates:* 5; 5; 5; 5
Ray Bilbrey, CEO
Robin Watson, Programming Director

WLYU
01-01-1989; 100.9 mhz FM *Hrs Open:* 24; 6 kw; 328 ft.; N32 6 48 W82 23 52
P.O. Box 111, Lyons, GA 30436 US
(912) 526-8122, *Fax:* (912) 526-9155
www.toombsnow.com/y-101radio.html
barney@toombsnow.com
License: Lyons, Toombs County, GA
Nat'l Network: Fox News Radio
Arbitron Metro Market: Lyons, GA *Format:* Country *Hrs. of News Programming:* news progmg 8 hrs wkly *No. News Employees:* 3 *Target Audience:* General. *Adv. Rates:* 8; 8; 8; 7
Ray Bilbrey, President
Robin Watson, News Director

Mableton

WPZE
01-01-2001; 102.5 mhz FM; 3 kw; 469 ft.; N33 41 20 W84 30 38
150 Eason Way, Mableton, GA 30126 US
(850) 235-2195, *Fax:* (850) 235-2795
www.beach951.com
License: Mableton, Cobb County, GA held by ROA Licenses LLC.
Group Owner: Radio One Inc.; (acq 7-8-2004; $31.5 million)
Arbitron Metro Market: Ebro FL *Format:* Oldies *Target Audience:* 35-64; adults
Charles Shapiro, CEO

Macon

WDEN-FM
02-17-1947; 99.1 mhz FM *Hrs Open:* 24; 100 kw; 581 ft.; N32 45 51 W83 33 32
P.O. Box 900, Macon, GA 31202 US
(800) 877-5600, *Fax:* (916) 251-1650
www.klove.com
License: Macon, Bibb County, GA held by Cumulus Licensing Corp.
Group Owner: Cumulus Media Inc.
Nat'l Reps: Christal
Arbitron Metro Market: Whitehall MT *Format:* Christian *Adv. Rates:* 45; 45; 45; 15
Mike Novak, President
Mike Lee, Operations Dir

*WBKG
01-01-2002; 88.9 mhz FM; 5.5 kw; 502 ft.; N32 45 51 W83 33 32
P.O. Drawer 2440, Tupelo, MS 38803 US
(662) 844-8888, *Fax:* (662) 842-6791
www.afa.net/Radio/
License: Macon, Bibb County, GA held by American Family Association.
Group Owner: American Family Radio
Arbitron Metro Market: Macon, GA *Format:* Adult Contemp
Marvin Sanders, General Manager
John Riley, Programming Director

WBML
10-15-1940; 900 khz AM; 2 kw-D, ND1; 0.145 kw-N, ND1; N32 50 58 W83 36 8; N32 50 58 W83 36 6
Mailing Address: 2301 West Main Street, Richmond, IN 47374 US
Second Address: 735 Reese St., Macon, GA 31217
(478) 743-5453, *Fax:* (912) 743-5453
info@wbml.com,info@wbml.com
License: Macon, GA held by WBML Inc.
Group Owner: Rodgers Broadcasting Corp.
Arbitron Metro Market: Richmond, IN *Format:* Religious *Target Audience:* 35 plus.
David Rogers, President

WDDO
11-25-1957; 1240 khz AM *Hrs Open:* 24; 1 kw-U, ND1; N32 50 18 W83 39 2
173 First Street, Macon, GA 31202 US
(478) 746-6286, *Fax:* (478) 745-4383
www.wddoam.com/info/contact.php
willie.collins@cumulus.com
License: Macon, GA held by Cumulus Licensing Corp.
Group Owner: Cumulus Media Inc.; (acq 12-20-02; grpsl).
Nat'l Network: American Urban *Nat'l Reps:* Christal
Arbitron Metro Market: Macon, GA *Format:* Black, Gospel
John Sheftic, General Manager

WAYS
08-01-1967; 1500 khz AM; 1 kw-D, NDD; N32 48 47 W83 37 36
P. O. Box 46, Macon, GA 31297 US
(478) 746-6286, *Fax:* (478) 742-8061
www.waysam.com
info@ways.com
License: Macon, GA held by Cumulus Licensing Corp.

Group Owner: Cumulus Media Inc.; (acq 12-20-2002; grpsl).
Nat'l Network: Westwood One *Nat'l Reps:* Christal
Arbitron Metro Market: Macon, GA *Format:* Oldies *Target Audience:* 25-54.
Steve Hazen, President
John Sheftic, General Manager

WROK-FM
06-10-1968; 105.5 mhz FM *Hrs Open:* 24; 6.1 kw; Ant 659 ft; N32 53 48 W83 32 05
544 Mulberry St., Suite 500, Macon, GA 31297
(478) 746-6286
info@wifn.com
License: Macon, Bibb County, GA held by Volt Radio LLC
Group Owner: Cumulus Media Inc.
Nat'l Network: ESPN Radio
Population Served: 300,000 *Arbitron Metro Market:* Macon, GA
Jim Jones, General Sales Mgr
David Nolin, Programming Director

WIBB
11-01-1948; 1280 khz AM *Hrs Open:* 24; 5 kw-D, ND1; 0.099 kw-N, ND1; N32 48 16 W83 36 16
750 West Sandtown Road, S.W., Marietta, GA 30064 US
(478) 781-1063, *Fax:* (478) 781-6711
www.peach965.com
ccw@clearchannel.com
License: Macon, GA held by AMFM Radio Licenses LLC.
Group Owner: Clear Channel Communications Inc.; (acq 2-15-2001; grpsl)
Nat'l Reps: Clear Channel
Arbitron Metro Market: Macon, GA *Format:* Black, Talk *Target Audience:* General.
Bill Clark, General Manager

WMAC
10-30-1922; 940 khz AM *Hrs Open:* 24; 50 kw-D, DAN; 10 kw-N, DAN; N32 53 6 W83 43 50
P.O. Box 900, Macon, GA 31202 US
(478) 746-6286, *Fax:* (478) 742-8061
www.wmac-am.com
info@middlegeorgia.com
License: Macon, GA held by Cumulus Licensing Corp.
Group Owner: Cumulus Media Inc.; (acq 12-20-02; grpsl).
Nat'l Network: ABC; Westwood One *Nat'l Reps:* McGavren Guild
Arbitron Metro Market: Macon, GA *Format:* News, News/Talk, 86
Special Programming: Relg 4 hrs wkly *Hrs. of News Programming:* news progmg 40 hrs wkly *No. News Employees:* 2 *Target Audience:* 40 plus;upscale, college educated, household income $50K plus *Adv. Rates:* 40; 40; 40; 10
Bill Hazen, General Manager

WNEX
04-01-1945; 1400 khz AM
5962 Zebulon Road, Suite 306, Macon, GA 31210 US
(478) 745-5858, *Fax:* (478) 745-0500
phil@upga.tv
License: Macon, GA held by Radio Peach Inc.
Nat'l Network: Radio Disney
Arbitron Metro Market: Macon, GA *Format:* Gospel
Lowell Register, CEO
Debbie Hart, General Manager

WLZN
08-01-1992; 92.3 mhz FM *Hrs Open:* 24; 3 kw; 328 ft.; N32 46 26 W83 38 15
173 First Street, Macon, GA 31202 US
(478) 746-6286, *Fax:* (478) 742-8061
info@middlegeorgia.com
License: Macon, Bibb County, GA held by Cumulus Licensing Corp.
Group Owner: Cumulus Media Inc.; (acq 12-20-2002; grpsl).
Arbitron Metro Market: Macon, GA *Format:* Urban Contemporary *Hrs. of News Programming:* News progmg one hr wkly *Adv. Rates:* 55; 60; 60; 20
Bill Hazen, General Manager
Doug Rice, General Sales Mgr
Brian Rayes, Programming Director
Joe Meredith, Chief Engineer

Madison

WYTH
06-01-1955; 1250 khz AM *Hrs Open:* 6 AM-sunset; 1 kw-D, ND2; 0.079 kw-N, ND2; N33 34 45 W83 28 40
Mailing Address: P. O. Box 635, Madison, GA 30650 US
Second Address: 869 Church St., Eaton, GA 31024
(706) 485-8792, *Fax:* (706) 485-3555
starstation@bellsouth.net
License: Madison, GA held by Craig Baker and Debra Baker
Regional Network: Ga. News Net.
Arbitron Metro Market: Madison, GA *Format:* Adult Contemp *Hrs. of News Programming:* news progmg 15 hrs wkly *No. News Employees:* 1 *Target Audience:* General.
Craig Baker, President

Manchester

WFDR
06-01-1957; 1370 khz AM *Hrs Open:* 6 AM-6 PM
PO Box 510, Manchester, GA 31816 US
(770) 487-4500, *Fax:* (706) 866-3494
www.georgia.thejoyfm.com
License: Manchester, GA held by Ploener Radio Group LLC
Arbitron Metro Market: Manchester, GA *Format:* Gospel
Paul Ploener, President
Rick Davison, General Manager
Johanna Antes, Director of Support
Ken Hammock, Underwriting Specialist
Roxanne Davison, Office Manager

WVFJ-FM
01-01-1967; 93.3 mhz FM *Hrs Open:* 24; 27 kw; 1611 ft.; N33 5 10 W84 46 10
P.O. Box 7217, 5015 South Florida Ave, Lakeland, FL 33813 US
(770) 487-4500, *Fax:* (770) 486-6400
www.j933.com
License: Manchester, Meriwether County, GA held by Provident Broadcasting Co.
Nat'l Reps: Rgnl Reps
Arbitron Metro Market: Atlanta, GA *Format:* Christian *No. News Employees:* 1 *Target Audience:* 25-45; women
Rick Davison, General Manager
John Zeiler, General Sales Mgr
Don Schaeffer, Programming Director
Steve Williams, Promotions Manager
Susan Ricards, News Director
Brian Chin, Chief Engineer
Dian Pena, Traffic Manager
RoxanneDavison, Office Manager

Marietta

WFOM
10-13-1946; 1230 khz AM *Hrs Open:* 24; 1 kw-D, ND2; 1 kw-N, ND2; N33 55 38 W84 30 8
2970 Peachtree Road, NW, Suite 700, Atlanta, GA 30305 US
(404) 688-0068, *Fax:* (404) 995-4045
www.1230thefan2.com
License: Marietta, GA held by Dickey Broadcasting Co.
Group Owner: Dickey Broadcasting Co.; (acq 8-31-2000; grpsl)
Nat'l Network: ESPN Radio *Nat'l Reps:* McGavren Guild *Wire Services:* AP
Arbitron Metro Market: Atlanta, GA *Format:* Sports *Special Programming:* Notre Dame football (fall) *Target Audience:* 25-64. *Adv. Rates:* 100; 100; 100; 50
David Dickey, President
Jim Mahanay, Operations Dir
David Dickey, General Manager
Colan Wheat, General Sales Mgr
Scott McFarlane, Programming Director
Laura Cowart, Controller
Rob Jenners, Creative Production Director
LindaPorter, Director of Traffic and Business Affairs
Josh Kluchka, Creative Production Assistant
Katie Kochman, Sales Coordinator

WFTD
11-14-1955; 1080 khz AM *Hrs Open:* Sunrise-sunset
3939 Gentlly Road, New Orleans, LA 70126 US
(770) 825-0095, *Fax:* (770) 246-0054
License: Marietta, GA held by Prieto Enterprises Inc.
Group Owner: Prieto Broadcasting Inc.; (acq 12-20-2001)
Arbitron Metro Market: Atlanta, GA *Target Audience:* 21-45.
Filiberto Prieto, President

WKHX-FM
11-01-1960; 101.5 mhz FM *Hrs Open:* 24; 100 kw; 1079 ft.; N33 48 26 W84 20 22
77 West 66th Street, 16th Floor, New York, NY 10023 US
(404) 497-4701, *Fax:* (404) 499-1015
www.kicks1015.com
info@kicks1015.com
License: Marietta, Cobb County, GA
Group Owner: Cumulus Media Inc.; (acq 6-12-2007; grpsl)
Nat'l Reps: ABC Radio Sales
Arbitron Metro Market: Atlanta, GA *Format:* Country *No. News Employees:* 1 *Target Audience:* 25-54.
Victor Sansone, President
Mark Richards, Operations Dir
Rick Mack, General Sales Mgr
Mike Macho, Programming Director
Christy Ullman, Promotions Manager
Glenda Sanders, News Director
Matt Scarano, General Sales Manager
NancyBarre, National Sales Manager
Mary Gordon, Regional Sales Manager

Martinez

WDRR
05-31-1984; 93.9 mhz FM *Hrs Open:* 24; 13 kw; 456 ft.; N33 26 17 W82 5 19
124 North Blair Rd, Evans, GA 30809 US
(706) 396-7000, *Fax:* (706) 396-7092
License: Martinez, Columbia County, GA held by WGOR License LLC.
Group Owner: Beasley Broadcast Group Inc.; (acq 11-10-92; $810,000;
Arbitron Metro Market: Augusta, GA *Format:* Contemporary Hits/Top 40, Adult Contemp *Target Audience:* 25 plus.
Kent Dunn, General Manager
Kent Murphy, General Sales Mgr
Chris O'Kelley, Programming Director

WPRW-FM
01-01-1994; 107.7 mhz FM; 24.5 kw; 577 ft.; N33 36 47 W82 17 51
111 East Kilbourn Ave, Suite 2700, Milwaukee, WI 53202 US
(706) 396-6000, *Fax:* (706) 396-6010
www.power107.net
travisdylan@clearchannel.com
License: Martinez, Columbia County, GA held by Capstar TX L.P.
Group Owner: Clear Channel Communications Inc.; (acq 6-30-97; grpsl)
Arbitron Metro Market: Augusta, GA *Format:* Urban Contemporary *Target Audience:* General.
Travis Dylan, Operations Dir
Mark Bass, General Manager
Brett Pomykala, General Sales Mgr
Minnesota Fattz, Programming Director
Cher Best, Promotions Manager
Cliff Bennett, Digital Content Director

Maysville

WXKT
12-01-1988; 103.7 mhz FM *Hrs Open:* 24; 25 kw; Ant 328 ft; N34 14 13 W83 16 03
1010 Tower Pl., Bogart, GA 30622
(706) 549-6222, *Fax:* (706) 353-1967
www.bulldog1037.com
License: Maysville, Franklin County, GA held by Cox Radio Inc.
Group Owner: Cox Radio Inc.; (acq 8-1-2008; grpsl)
Population Served: 190,000
Robert Neil, President
Scott Smith, Operations Dir
Kevin Steele, Programming Director

McDonough

WKKP
04-02-1979; 1410 khz AM *Hrs Open:* 24; 2.5 kw-D, ND1; 0.058 kw-N, ND1; N33 25 47 W84 7 52 *Rebroadcasts:* Solid Gospel Network
Mailing Address: P.O. Box 878, Jackson, GA 30233 US
Second Address: 940 Brownlee Rd., Jackson, GA 30233
(770) 504-8410, *Fax:* (770) 775-3153
donaldwearnhart@bellsouth.net
License: McDonough, GA held by Henry County Radio Co. Inc.
Nat'l Network: Jones Radio Networks *Nat'l Reps:* Rgnl Reps
Arbitron Metro Market: Atlanta, GA *Format:* Country *Hrs. of News Programming:* News progmg 20 hrs wkly *Target Audience:* General. *Adv. Rates:* 8; 8; 8; 8
Susanne Earnhart, President
Tom Lynde, Operations Dir
Don Earnhardt, General Manager

McRae

WYIS
07-27-1957; 1410 khz AM; 1 kw-D, NDD; N32 3 25 W82 51 56
Highway 341 South, McRae, GA 31055 US
(229) 868-5611, *Fax:* (229) 868-7552
License: McRae, GA held by Cinecom Broadcasting Systems Inc.
Nat'l Reps: Rgnl Reps
Arbitron Metro Market: McRae, GA *Format:* Oldies *Special Programming:* Black 4 hrs wkly *Target Audience:* 25-50; mature, wage earners
Jimmy Hussey, General Manager

Meigs

WQLI
09-08-2000; 92.3 mhz FM; 6 kw; 328 ft.; N31 5 12 W84 12 10
Rt 3 Box 514, Pelham, GA 31779 US
(229) 294-1909
License: Meigs, Mitchell County, GA held by Mitchell County Television.
Arbitron Metro Market: Pelham, GA *Format:* Adult Contemp
Greg Jessen, Operations Dir
Buck Hein, General Sales Mgr
Brian Stenzel, Promotions Manager
Mark Heller, Chief Engineer
Jimmy Clark, Operations Manager

Metter

WBMZ
08-01-1971; 104.9 mhz FM *Hrs Open:* 24; 3 kw; 299 ft.; N32 23 56 W82 2 36
Mailing Address: P. O. Box 238, Metter, GA 30439 US
Second Address: 1075 East Lillian Street, Metter, GA 30439
(912) 685-2136, *Fax:* (912) 685-2137
www.wbmzfm.com
License: Metter, Candler County, GA held by Radio Metter Inc.
Regional Network: Ga. News Net.
Format: Contemporary Hits/Top 40, Adult Contemp *Target Audience:* General. *Adv. Rates:* 8; 8; 8; 6
Jimmy Page, CEO

WHCG
12-22-1961; 1360 khz AM; 1 kw-D, ND2; 0.059 kw-N, ND2; N32 23 56 W82 2 36
Mailing Address: P.O.Box 238, Metter, GA 30439 US
Second Address: 1075 E. Lillian St., Metter, GA 30439
(912) 685-2136, *Fax:* (912) 685-2137
License: Metter, GA held by Radio Metter Inc.
Format: Gospel *Target Audience:* General.
Jimmy Page, President

Midway

WGCO
01-01-1974; 98.3 mhz FM *Hrs Open:* 24; 100 kw; 981 ft.; N31 36 45 W81 21 37
100 Bluefield Avenue, Suite 3, Bluefield, WV 24701 US
(912) 351-9830, *Fax:* (912) 352-4821
www.big983.com
jtaylor@adventureradio.fm
License: Midway, Liberty County, GA held by Monterey Licenses LLC.
Group Owner: Triad Broadcasting Co. L.L.C.; (acq 9-1-2000; grpsl)
Nat'l Reps: Christal
Arbitron Metro Market: Savannah, GA *Format:* Oldies *Hrs. of News Programming:* news progmg 2 hrs wkly *No. News Employees:* 3 *Target Audience:* 25-54; yuppies *Adv. Rates:* 50; 50; 50; 50
Robert Leonard, General Manager

Milan

WMCG
01-01-1982; 104.9 mhz FM *Hrs Open:* 24; 36 kw; 564 ft.; N32 7 16 W83 16 5
P.O. Box 2639, Gulfport, GA 39505 US
(478) 272-4422, *Fax:* (478) 275-4657
www.1049wmcg.com
webmaster@1049wmcg.com
License: Milan, Telfair County, GA held by Tel-Dodge Broadcasting Inc.
Regional Reps: Dora-Clayton
Arbitron Metro Market: Macon, GA *Format:* Country *Special Programming:* Farm one hr wkly *Hrs. of News Programming:* News progmg 1 hr wkly *Target Audience:* 35+.
J. Morgan Dowdy, Operations Dir
Rick Humphrey, General Manager

Milledgeville

***WGUR**
08-01-1975; 95.3 mhz FM; 85 w; Ant 3 ft; N33 04 44 W83 13 55
Box 3124, Georgia College & State University, Milledgeville, GA 31061
(478) 445-8256
License: Milledgeville, Baldwin County, GA held by Georgia College & State University
Population Served: 4,500*Target Audience:* 18-24; college students
Sonya Barnes, General Manager

WKZR
06-30-1966; 102.3 mhz FM; 3.3 kw; 299 ft.; N33 4 58 W83 15 1
Box 519, Milledgeville, GA 31061 US
(478) 452-0586, *Fax:* (478) 452-5886
www.country102fm.com
License: Milledgeville, Baldwin County, GA held by WMVG Inc.
Format: Country
Carl Hirsch, Chairman
Steven Dinetz, CEO
Skip Weller, President
Barry Brown, General Manager
Art Greene, General Sales Mgr
Mark McKinney, Programming Director
Liza Van Horne, Promotions Manager
Trimeshia Jeffery, NewsDirector
Paul Matthews, Chief Engineer
Jeff Dinetz, COO

WLRR
07-24-1990; 100.7 mhz FM; 3 kw; 328 ft.; N33 6 50 W83 13 8
Rebroadcasts: Rebroadcasts WKVQ(AM) Eatonton 100%
P. O. Box 793, Milledgeville, GA 31061 US
(706) 485-8792, *Fax:* (706) 485-3555
License: Milledgeville, Baldwin County, GA held by Preston W. Small.
Format: Adult Contemp *Target Audience:* 18-35.
Craig Baker, President

WMVG
03-29-1946; 1450 khz AM *Hrs Open:* 24; 1 kw-U, ND1; N33 4 58 W83 15 1
P. O. Box 519, Milledgeville, GA 31061 US
(478) 452-0586, *Fax:* (478) 452-5886
www.country102fm.com
License: Milledgeville, GA held by WMVG Inc.
Nat'l Reps: Rgnl Reps
Arbitron Metro Market: Milledgeville, GA *Format:* News, Sports *Special Programming:* Black 4 hrs wkly *Hrs. of News Programming:* news progmg 25 hrs wkly *No. News Employees:* 1 *Target Audience:* 18-49.
Randy Beasley, President

***WRGC-FM**
88.3 mhz FM; 4.8 kw; Ant 384 ft; N33 04 05 W83 16 30
Campus Box 97, Milledgeville, GA 31061-3375
(478) 445-6804, *Fax:* (478) 445-2364
License: Milledgeville, Baldwin County, GA held by Georgia College & State University.
Population Served: 17,499 *Arbitron Metro Market:* Milledgeville, GA
Dorothy Leland, President
Angela Criscoe, General Manager

Millen

WHKN
12-04-1989; 94.9 mhz FM *Hrs Open:* 24; 14.5 kw; 400 ft.; N32 43 57 W81 51 43
P.O. Box 180, Hawkinsville, GA 32069 US
(912) 764-5496, *Fax:* (912) 764-8827
radiocenter@frontiernet.net
License: Millen, Jenkins County, GA held by Georgia Eagle Broadcasting Inc.
Group Owner: Georgia Eagle Broadcasting Inc.; acq 1-12-2007; grpsl)
Nat'l Network: ABC
Format: Country *Special Programming:* Farm 10 hrs, relg 2 hrs wkly *Hrs. of News Programming:* news progmg 8 hrs wkly *No. News Employees:* 1 *Target Audience:* 25-54; adults
Jeff Anderson, General Manager
Buddy Horne, Programming Director

Monroe

WKUN
02-04-1971; 1490 khz AM *Hrs Open:* 6 AM-6 PM
Mailing Address: 1081 Cherokee Road, Social Circle, GA 30279 US
Second Address: 1610 Launius Rd., Good Hope, GA 30641
(770) 267-0923, *Fax:* (706) 342-8135
www.wmoqfm.com
info@wmoqfm.com
License: Monroe, GA held by B.R. Anderson Sr. dba Radio Station WKUN
Regional Network: Ga. News Net.
Arbitron Metro Market: Atlanta, GA *Format:* Gospel *Hrs. of News Programming:* News progmg 3 hrs wkly *Target Audience:* 25-65. *Adv. Rates:* 8; 8; 8; na
B. R. Anderson Sr., President
Melanie Jackson, General Manager

Montezuma

WMNZ
11-29-1961; 1050 khz AM; 0.25 kw-D, ND1; 0.041 kw-N, ND1; N32 17 53 W84 2 2
Mailing Address: P. O. Box 610, Montezuma, GA 31063 US
Second Address: 115 1/2 Cherry St., Montezuma, GA 31063
(478) 472-8386, *Fax:* (478) 472-8296
License: Montezuma, GA held by Macon County Broadcasting Co.
Arbitron Metro Market: Montezuma, GA *Format:* Country, Gospel, 64
Danny Blizzard, President

WMGB
08-10-2001; 95.1 mhz FM *Hrs Open:* 24; 46 kw; 390 ft.; N32 33 20 W83 44 14
P. O. Box 180, Hawkinsville, GA 31036 US
(478) 646-9510, *Fax:* (478) 745-4383
www.allthehitsb951.com
info@allthehitsB951.com
License: Montezuma, Macon County, GA held by Cumulus Licensing Corp.
Group Owner: Cumulus Media Inc.; (acq 12-20-02; grpsl).
Nat'l Network: Westwood One
Arbitron Metro Market: Macon, GA *Format:* Contemporary Hits/Top 40
John Sheftic, General Manager

Morgan

WMRG
93.5 mhz; 25 kw; 328 ft; N31 44 05 W84 30 06
25 East 86th Street, Apt 13B, New York, NY
(917)535-0419
License: Morgan, GA held by Alex Media Inc.
Group Owner: Alex Media Inc.
Alexander Berger, President

Morrow

WIGO
11-01-1956; 1570 khz AM; 5 kw-D, ND1; 0.05 kw-N, ND1; N33 36 5 W84 18 40
2424 Old Rex Morrow Road, Morrow, GA 30260 US
(404) 361-1570, *Fax:* (404) 366-9772
www.wigoam.com
pploener@wigo.com
License: Morrow, GA held by MCL/MCM Georgia LLC.
Group Owner: Sheridan Broadcasting Corp.; (acq 12-29-2006; $1.75 million)
Arbitron Metro Market: Atlanta, GA *Format:* Black, Gospel *Target Audience:* 24-55. *Adv. Rates:* 12;30 12;20 12;25
Larry Young, Operations Dir
Paul Ploener, General Manager

Moultrie

WMTM
11-10-1953; 1300 khz AM *Hrs Open:* 6 AM-sunset; 5 kw-D, ND2; 0.06 kw-N, ND2; N31 10 12 W83 44 50
Mailing Address: P.O. Box 788, Moultrie, GA 31776 US
Second Address: 100 WMTM Rd., Moultrie, GA 31768
(229) 985-1300, *Fax:* (229) 890-0905
www.cruisin94.com
jay@cruisin9.4.com
License: Moultrie, GA held by Colquitt Broadcasting Co. L.L.C.
Nat'l Reps: Rgnl Reps
Arbitron Metro Market: Moultrie, GA *Format:* Gospel, News *Special Programming:* Farm 16 hrs wkly *No. News Employees:* 1 *Target Audience:* General.
Jim Turner, President

WMTM-FM
11-17-1964; 93.9 mhz FM *Hrs Open:* 6 AM-midnight; 100 kw; 554 ft.; N31 12 54 W83 47 13
P.O. Box 788, Moultrie, GA 31776 US
(229) 985-1300, *Fax:* (229) 890-0905
www.cruisin94.com
License: Moultrie, Colquitt County, GA held by Colquitt Broadcasting Co. LLC
Arbitron Metro Market: Albany, GA *Format:* Contemporary Hits/Top 40
Jim Turner, Operations Dir

WHLJ(AM)
01-01-2002; 1400 khz AM *Hrs Open:* 24; 1 kw-U; N31 09 56 W83 46 01
Mailing Address: 1643 South Blvd., Moultrie, GA 31768
Second Address: Box 1305, Valdosta, GA 31603
(229) 890-2900, *Fax:* (229) 890-1497
whbsam1400.com

RADIO - U.S.

License: Moultrie, Colquitt County, GA held by Lataurus Productions Two LLC
Population Served: 77,683 *Arbitron Metro Market:* Albany, GA
Ronnie Barnes, General Manager

***WBGP**
01-02-2012; 91.3 mhz
PO Box 181000, Tallahassee, FL
(877)801-1070, *Fax:* (850)201-1071
www.faithradio.us
scott@faithradio.us
License: Moultrie, GA
Group Owner: Faith Radio
Scott Beigle, President
Steve Huffman, Operations Dir
Brenda Beigle, Vice President

Mount Vernon

WYUM
08-03-1998; 101.7 mhz FM; 3.6 kw; 427 ft.; N32 13 12 W82 26 7
1501 Mount Vernon Road, Vidalia, GA 30474 US
(912) 537-9202, *Fax:* (912) 537-4477
www.vidaliacommunications.com
zfowler@vidaliacommunications.com,wyum@vidialiacommunications.com
License: Mount Vernon, Montgomery County, GA held by Vidalia Communications Corp.
Group Owner: Vidalia Communications Corp.
Regional Network: Ga. News Net. *Regional Reps:* Rgnl Reps.
Arbitron Metro Market: Mount Vernon, GA *Format:* Country
Target Audience: 25-49.
John Ladson III, President
Collins Knightor, Operations Dir
Zack Fowler, General Manager

Mountain City

WALH
05-01-1986; 1340 khz AM *Hrs Open:* 24/7
Box F, Hwy 441 North, Mountain City, GA 30562 US
(706) 746-2256, *Fax:* (706) 746-2259
www.walhradio.com
walh@windstream.net
License: Mountain City, GA held by Tugart Properties, LLC
Group Owner: Georgia-Carolina Radiocasting Companies; 5-8-2009; $75,000
Nat'l Network: AP Radio *Regional Network:* Ga. News Net.
Arbitron Metro Market: Mountain City, GA *Format:* Country, Gospel *Special Programming:* Local News *No. News Employees:* 1 *Target Audience:* 35 plus; low to middle income
Art Sutton, President
John Durham, Operations Dir
Robin Dake, Programming Director
Marty Lee, Chief Engineer
Tug Carter, Vice President
David Skinner, Vice President

Murrayville

WGTJ
11-01-1986; 1330 khz AM *Hrs Open:* 6 AM-sunset; 1 kw-D, NDD; N34 22 16 W83 56 47
Mailing Address: Post Office Box 907038, Gainesville, GA 30503 US
Second Address: 1716 Cleveland Hwy., Gainesville, GA 30501
(770) 297-7485, *Fax:* (770) 297-8030
www.glory1330.com
mail@glory1330.com
License: Murrayville, GA held by Vision Communications Inc.
Format: Christian *No. News Employees:* 1 *Target Audience:* General.
Mike Wofford, President

Nashville

***WVKV**
11-26-1986; 95.3 mhz FM *Hrs Open:* 24; 29 kw; 522 ft.; N31 10 18 W83 21 57
104 E 7th Street, Tifton, GA 31794 US
(916) 251-1600, *Fax:* (916) 251-1650
www.klove.com
License: Nashville, Berrien County, GA held by Educational Media Foundation.
Group Owner: EMF Broadcasting; (acq 5-10-2007; $1.3 million)
Nat'l Network: K-Love
Arbitron Metro Market: Valdosta, GA *Format:* Christian
Mike Novak, President

***WGCN**
01-01-2005; 90.5 mhz FM; 0.001 kw horiz, 50 kw vert; 292 ft.; N31 9 26 W83 22 28
US
(916) 251-1600, *Fax:* (916) 251-1650
www.nuevavida.com
info@nuevavida.com
License: Nashville, Berrien County, GA held by Educational Media Foundation.
Group Owner: EMF Broadcasting; (acq 1-7-2004)
Arbitron Metro Market: Nashville, GA *Format:* Country, Gospel
Mike Novak, President

Newnan

WCOH
12-01-1947; 1400 khz AM; 1 kw-U, ND1; N33 21 53 W84 48 42
50 E. Rivercenter Blvd., Suite 1200, Covington, KY 41011 US
(770) 683-7234, *Fax:* (770) 683-9846
www.foxsports1400.com
johnlund@clearchannel.com
License: Newnan, GA held by Citicasters Licenses L.P.
Group Owner: Clear Channel Communications Inc.; (acq 5-4-99; grpsl)
Nat'l Network: Fox Sports *Regional Network:* Ga. News Net.
Arbitron Metro Market: Atlanta, GA *Format:* Sports *Target Audience:* 25-54.
Bill Clark, Promotions Manager

WNEA
04-18-1962; 1300 khz AM; 1 kw-D, ND1; 0.05 kw-N, ND1; N33 22 31 W84 47 8
8 Madison Street, Newnan, GA 30264 US
(770) 920-1520, *Fax:* (770) 253-4711
www.wordchristianbroadcasting.com
License: Newnan, GA held by Word Christian Broadcasting Inc.
Regional Network: Ga. News Net.
Arbitron Metro Market: Atlanta, GA *Format:* Religious *Special Programming:* Black, relg, gospel 15 hrs wkly *Target Audience:* 18-64.
Ken Johns, CEO

Nicholls

WVOH-FM
12-09-1975; 93.5 mhz FM; 25 kw; 315 ft; N31 51 15 W82 34 00
546 Baxley Hwy., Hazlehurst, GA 31539
(912) 375-4511, *Fax:* (912) 375-4512
License: Nicholls, Coffee County, GA
Group Owner: Broadcast South LLC
Nat'l Network: Jones Radio Networks *Regional Network:* Ga. News Net.
Tony DeLoach, Station Manager

North Atlanta

WCNN
12-04-1967; 680 khz AM *Hrs Open:* 24; 50 kw-D, DA2; 10 kw-N, DA2; N33 57 42 W84 15 48
2970 Peachtree Rd, Atlanta, GA 30305 US
(404) 688-0068, *Fax:* (404) 995-4045
www.680thefan.com
cwheat@680thefan.com
License: North Atlanta, GA held by Dickey Broadcasting Co.
Group Owner: Dickey Broadcasting Co.; acq 8-31-00; grpsl).
Regional Network: Nebraska Public Radio
Arbitron Metro Market: Atlanta, GA *Format:* News, Sports
David Dickey, GM
Robert Hasson, General Sales Mgr
Scott McFarlane, Programming Director

Ochlocknee

WSBX
06-04-1984; 1020 khz AM *Hrs Open:* Sunrise-sunset; 10 kw-D, NDD; N30 54 0 W83 59 55
Mailing Address: PO Box 90, Thomasville, GA 31799 US
Second Address: 540 Daisy Ln., Thomasville, GA 31792
(912) 228-5683, *Fax:* (912) 436-0544
www.wsbxradio.com
wjep@rose.net
License: Ochlocknee, GA held by Doreen A. Blood
Format: Talk *Special Programming:* Black 2 hrs, southern gospel 3 hrs wkly
Jimmy Bennett, General Manager

Ocilla

***WLPF**
12-01-1993; 98.5 mhz FM *Hrs Open:* 24; 2.3 kw; 522 ft.; N31 28 11 W83 14 11
3213 Huxley Drive, Augusta, GA 30909 US
(706) 309-9610, *Fax:* (706) 309-9669
www.gnnradio.org
ctbarinowski@comcast.net
License: Ocilla, Irwin County, GA held by Barinowski Investment Co.
Group Owner: Good News Network; (acq 11-17-92; for CP;
Format: Christian *Hrs. of News Programming:* News progmg 12 hrs wkly *Target Audience:* General.
Clarence Barinowski, General Manager

Omega

WTIF-FM
04-01-1993; 107.5 mhz FM *Hrs Open:* 24; 6 kw; 328 ft.; N31 30 34 W83 31 13
P.O. Box 968, Tifton, GA 31793 US
(229) 382-1075, *Fax:* (229) 386-8658
www.-wtif1075.-com
mornings@wtif1075.com
License: Omega, Tift County, GA held by Three Trees Communications Inc.
Group Owner: Three Trees Communications Inc.; (acq 6-28-2004; grpsl).
Regional Network: Ga. News Net.
Arbitron Metro Market: Tifton,GA *Format:* Christian *Hrs. of News Programming:* news progmg 5 hrs wkly *No. News Employees:* 6 *Target Audience:* 18 plus.
Matt Baldrich, General Manager

Palmetto

WALR-FM
09-01-1947; 104.1 mhz FM; 100 kw; 1217 ft.; N33 24 43 W84 50 3
3773 Howard Hughes Pwy, Suite 300n, Las Vegas, NV 89109 US
(404) 897-7500, *Fax:* (404) 897-6495
www.kiss1041fm.com
License: Palmetto, Troup County, GA held by Cox Radio Inc.
Group Owner: Cox Radio Inc.; (acq 8-2000; $280 million)
Nat'l Reps: McGavren Guild
Arbitron Metro Market: Atlanta, GA *Format:* Adult Contemp
Target Audience: 25-54.
Tony Kidd, General Manager

Patterson

***WNEE**
88.1 mhz FM; 6 kw; 161 ft.; N34 0 43 W83 17 38
US
(770) 596-0739
License: Patterson, Pierce County, GA held by Community Public Radio Inc.
Arbitron Metro Market: Patterson, GA
Penny Jackson, President

Peachtree City

WWLG
01-01-1948; 96.7 mhz FM; 2.15 kw; 551 ft.; N33 29 22 W84 34 7
50 E. Rivercenter Blvd., Suite 200, Covington, KY 41011 US
(404) 875-8080, *Fax:* (404) 367-9490
www.wildatlanta.com
info@976thelegend.com
License: Peachtree City, Fayette County, GA held by Citicasters Licenses L.P.
Group Owner: Clear Channel Communications Inc.; (acq 5-4-99; grpsl)
Arbitron Metro Market: Atlanta, GA *Format:* Christian
Chuck Deskins, General Manager
JB Wilde, Programming Director
Liz Leos, Promotions Manager
Mike Lawing, Chief Engineer

***WMVW**
91.7 mhz FM; 13 kw; 246 ft.; N33 14 39 W84 25 49
P O Box 100, Lovejoy, GA 30250 US
(770) 229-2020
www.newlife.fm
License: Peachtree City, Fayette County, GA held by Life Radio Ministries Inc.
Arbitron Metro Market: Peachtree City, GA *Format:* Christian
Joseph Emert, President
Jim Stewart, Operations Dir
Doug Doran, Vice President
Pete Chagnon, Production Director
Jenny Emert, Business Manager
Glenna Stewart, Administrative Assistant

Pearson

WPNG
08-01-1999; 101.9 mhz FM *Hrs Open:* 24; 13 kw; 459 ft.; N31 19 36 W82 51 54

Mailing Address: 3654 West Jarvis Avenue, Skokie, IL 60076 US
Second Address: 2232 Old Douglas Hwy., Pearson, GA 31642
(912) 422-6122, *Fax:* (912) 422-7840
www.hitsandfavorites.com
freedom1019@planttel.net
License: Pearson, Atkinson County, GA held by KM Radio of Pearson L.L.C.
Group Owner: KM Communications Inc.; (acq 5-3-99)
Format: Adult Contemp *Target Audience:* 25-49; women ages 25-49 *Adv. Rates:* 17; 14; 16; 13
Myoung Hwa Bae, President
Kevin Bae, General Manager

Pembroke

WBAW-FM
08-31-1966; 99.3 mhz FM; 25 kw; 328 ft.; N33 13 25 W81 21 35
120 Liberty St., Ste. C&D, Hinesville, GA 31313 US
(605) 352-1933, *Fax:* (605) 352-1934
www.bigjimrocks.com
mlyon@kokk.com
License: Pembroke, Bryan County, GA held by Bullie Broadcasting Corp.
Format: Classic Rock
Linda Marcus, General Manager
Mike Lyon, General Sales Mgr

Perry

WPGA
01-01-1955; 980 khz AM *Hrs Open:* 24
P. O. Box 980, Perry, GA 31069 US
(478) 745-5858, *Fax:* (478) 745-5800
www.58abc.com
info@58abc.com
License: Perry, GA held by Register Communications Inc.
Arbitron Metro Market: Macon, GA *Format:* Children *No. News Employees:* 1 *Target Audience:* Children up to 12.
Loel Register, President
Debbie Hart, General Manager
Janice Register, Programming Director

WPGA-FM
05-03-1966; 100.9 mhz FM; 3.3 kw; 446 ft.; N32 33 20 W83 44 14
P.O. Box 5858, Macon, GA 31208 US
(478) 745-5500, *Fax:* (478) 745-5800
www.58abc.com
info@58abc.com
License: Perry, Houston County, GA held by Register Communications Inc.
Arbitron Metro Market: Macon, GA *TV Affiliate:* WPGA-TV affil
Format: Adult Contemp *No. News Employees:* 1
Kristy Turner, General Sales Mgr
Janice Register, Programming Director

Pinehurst

WSSY
02-22-1969; 98.3 mhz FM *Hrs Open:* 24; 3.1 kw; 459 ft.; N32 10 3 W83 37 51
500 Commerce Street, P O Box 180, Hawkinsville, GA 31036 US
(478) 892-9061, *Fax:* (478) 892-9063
braswell@broadcast.net
License: Pinehurst, Dooly County, GA held by Georgia Eagle Broadcasting Inc.
Group Owner: Georgia Eagle Broadcasting Inc.; (acq 1-12-2007; grpsl)
Nat'l Network: CNN Radio; Jones Radio Networks *Regional Network:* Ga. News Net.
Arbitron Metro Market: Macon, GA *Format:* Adult Contemp *Hrs. of News Programming:* news progmg 15 hrs wkly *No. News Employees:* 1 *Target Audience:* 35-64 *Adv. Rates:* 18; 12; 15; 10
Dr. Joe S. Robinson, Chairman
Cecil P. Staton, Jr., CEO

Plainville

WRBF
104.9 mhz FM; 0.95 kw; 606 ft.; N34 20 35 W85 2 20
US
(817) 846-9535
www.1049therebel.com
License: Plainville, Gordon County, GA held by Howard C. Toole.
Arbitron Metro Market: Plainville, GA *Format:* Classic Rock
Howard Toole, CEO/COO
Kevin Daniels, Operations Dir
Randy Quick, General Manager
Howard Toole, General Sales Mgr
Dustin Sledge, Programming Director
Cheryl Scott, Business Manager & Human Resource Director
Samantha Bell, BrandsManager
Rick Bradley, Production & Imaging Director
Nelle Reagan, Public Service Director

Port Wentworth

*WLFS
01-01-2001; 91.9 mhz FM; 23.5 kw horiz, 23 kw vert; 338 ft.; N32 9 28 W80 59 31
P.O. Box 7217, 5015 South Florida Ave, Lakeland, FL 33813 US
(707) 526-2765
www.broken.fm
korb@broken.fm
License: Port Wentworth, Chatham County, GA held by Radio Training Network Inc.
Arbitron Metro Market: Hopland CA *Format:* Christian
Keith Leitch, President
Rynie Leitch, General Manager

Portal

WXRS-FM
08-02-1982; 100.5 mhz FM *Hrs Open:* 24; 3 kw; 299 ft.; N32 34 52 W82 23 14
P. O. Box 1590, Swainsboro, GA 30401 US
(478) 237-1590, *Fax:* (478) 237-3559
www.radiojones.com
License: Portal, Emanuel County, GA
Group Owner: RadioJones LLC
Arbitron Metro Market: Portal, GA *Format:* Country *Hrs. of News Programming:* news progmg 10 hrs wkly *No. News Employees:* 1 *Target Audience:* 25 plus. *Adv. Rates:* 16; 14; 14; 8
John Wagner, Operations Dir
Dennis Jones, General Manager
Jolly Martin, General Sales Mgr
Marty Foglia, Engineering Dir

Quitman

WSFB
11-19-1955; 1490 khz AM; 1 kw-U, ND1; N30 46 51 W83 34 30
Rte 2 Bx 533, Tallahassee, FL 32311 US
(912) 263-4373
License: Quitman, GA held by Scott Matheson
Format: Contemporary Hits/Top 40, Adult Contemp *Target Audience:* 30+.
Scott Matheson, General Manager

WSTI-FM
09-12-1986; 105.3 mhz FM; 25 kw; 318 ft.; N30 38 23 W83 26 52
P O Box 5286, Valdosta, GA 31603 US
(229) 244-8642, *Fax:* (229) 242-7620
License: Quitman, Brooks County, GA held by RTG Radio L.L.C.
Group Owner: Black Crow Media Group LLC; (acq 6-4-2004; $3.4 million with WXHT(FM) Madison, FL).
Arbitron Metro Market: Valdosta, GA *Format:* Urban Contemporary *Special Programming:* Farm 5 hrs wkly *Target Audience:* 25-54; white collar
Scott James, General Manager

Reidsville

WRBX
07-01-1993; 104.1 mhz FM *Hrs Open:* 24; 4.9 kw; 361 ft.; N32 5 14 W82 7 48
P. O. Box 69, Reidsville, GA 30453 US
(912) 557-4140
License: Reidsville, Tattnall County, GA
Nat'l Network: USA
Format: Gospel *Target Audience:* 8 plus; religious
William Keith Register, General Manager

WTNL
06-25-1976; 1390 khz AM *Hrs Open:* 6 AM-sunset; 0.5 kw-D, NDD; N32 5 14 W82 7 47
P.O. Box 69, 125 Friar Tuck Circle, Reidsville, GA 30453 US
(912) 557-3777, *Fax:* (912) 557-6956
License: Reidsville, GA held by WRBX/WTNL L.L.C.
Nat'l Network: USA
Arbitron Metro Market: Reidsville, GA *Format:* Gospel *Target Audience:* General.
Gary Frank, CEO
Jerry Richmond, News Director
Lisa Frank, COO

Richmond Hill

WRHQ
05-13-1991; 105.3 mhz FM *Hrs Open:* 24; 11 kw; 485 ft; N32 02 52 W81 07 26
1102 E. 52nd St., Savannah, GA 31324
(912) 234-1053, *Fax:* (912) 354-6600
www.wrhq.com
qualityrock@wrhq.com
License: Richmond Hill, Bryan County, GA held by Thoroughbred Communications Inc.
Nat'l Network: AP Radio *Nat'l Reps:* Christal
Arbitron Metro Market: Savannah, GA *Hrs. of News Programming:* News progmg 2 hrs wkly *Target Audience:* 25-54; 35-64; affluent
Jerry Rogers, President
Lyndy Brannan, Operations Dir
Mike Roberts, Programming Director
Phyllis Bright, News Director
Marty Foglia, Chief Engineer
Ray Williams, Regional Sales Manager

Rincon

WSSJ
05-01-1967; 100.1 mhz FM *Hrs Open:* 24; 50 kw; 492 ft.; N32 16 49 W81 11 40
Mailing Address: 561 East Oliff Street, Statesboro, GA 30458 US
Second Address: 120 D. Liberty, Hinesville, GA 31313
(912) 691-1934, *Fax:* (912) 691-1936
www.myjoy100.com
rjp106@aol.com
License: Rincon, Effingham County, GA held by Tama Radio Licenses of Savannah, GA Inc.
Group Owner: Tama Broadcasting Inc.; (acq 4-28-2004)
Arbitron Metro Market: Savannah, GA *Format:* Gospel *No. News Employees:* 1 *Target Audience:* 18-45. *Adv. Rates:* 14; 12; 14; na
Yvonne Clark, General Manager

Ringgold

WOCE
03-01-1989; 101.9 mhz FM; 1.3 kw; 702 ft.; N34 58 11 W85 5 10
P.O. 814, Ringgold, GA 30736 US
(423) 485-8987, *Fax:* (423) 553-9490
http://www.quebuena1019.com/
License: Ringgold, Catoosa County, GA held by North Georgia Radio Group L.P.
Group Owner: North Georgia Radio Group L.P.; (acq 7-28-2006; $2.15 milion)
Arbitron Metro Market: Chattanooga, TN *Format:* Religious
Paul Fink, General Manager

Rochelle

WWKM
93.1 mhz FM; kw
US
(478)757-0983, *Fax:* (478)757-1305
License: Rochelle, Wilcox County, GA held by Georgia Eagle Media Inc.

Cecil P. Staton, President

Rockmart

WZOT
08-28-1959; 1220 khz AM; 0.5 kw-D, ND2; 0.103 kw-N, ND2; N34 0 14 W85 3 22
20 John Daveport Drive, Rome, GA 30161 US
(770) 684-7848, *Fax:* (770) 684-7848
www.hometown1220.com
samanthab@hometown1220.com
License: Rockmart, GA held by Triple J's Broadcasting LLC
Regional Network: Ga. News Net.
Arbitron Metro Market: Rockmart, GA *Format:* Gospel *Target Audience:* 18-45.
Paul Stone, President
Kevin Daniels, Operations Dir
Randy Quick, General Manager
Dustin Sledge, Programming Director
Luke Brannon, Director of Engineering & IT
Cheryl Scott, Business Manager
Howard Tole, Sales Manager
SamanthaBell, Brands Manager
Rick Bradley, Production / Imaging Director
Nelle Reagan, Public Service Director

Rocky Ford

WZBX
09-06-1991; 106.5 mhz FM; 25 kw; 311 ft.; N32 43 57 W81 51 43
910 West Ogeechee Street, Sylvania, GA 30467 US
(912) 564-7461, *Fax:* (912) 564-7462
info@wzbx.com
License: Rocky Ford, Screven County, GA
Group Owner: Georgia Eagle Broadcasting Inc.

Arbitron Metro Market: Rocky Ford, GA *Format:* Classic Rock
Nate Hirsch, Station Manager
Scott Kidd, General Sales Mgr

Rome

*WGPB
05-22-1965; 97.7 mhz FM *Hrs Open:* 24; 4.2 kw; 791 ft.; N34 14 5 W85 13 48
Mailing Address: 710 Turner McCall Blvd., Rome, GA 30165 US
Second Address: Heritage Hall, 415 E. Third Ave., Rome, GA 30162
(706) 204-2276
www.gpb.org
ask@gpb.org
License: Rome, Floyd County, GA held by Georgia Public Telecommunications Commission
Nat'l Network: NPR; PRI *Wire Services:* AP
Format: Classical, News *Special Programming:* Jazz 16 hrs wkly. *Hrs. of News Programming:* news progmg 40 hrs wkly *No. News Employees:* 10 *Target Audience:* Adults: 35 plus.
Nancy Hall, CEO
Tom Barclay, Operations Dir
Bob Houghton, General Manager
Rob Maynard, Programming Director
Nancy Zintak, Promotions Manager
Susanna Capelouto, News Director
John Sepulvado, Bureau Chief
Bonnie Bean, CFO

WLAQ
01-01-1947; 1410 khz AM
2 Mt. Alto Road, Rome, GA 30165 US
(706) 232-7767, *Fax:* (706) 295-9225
www.wlaq1410.com
wlaq@comcast.net
License: Rome, GA held by Cripple Creek Broadcasting Co.
Nat'l Network: CBS
Format: News, News/Talk, 84, Talk
Randy Davis, President

WQTU
05-02-1966; 102.3 mhz FM *Hrs Open:* 24; 1.1 kw; 745 ft.; N34 14 2 W85 13 50
P.O. Box 1187, Rome, GA 30162 US
(706) 295-1023, *Fax:* (706) 235-7107
q102rome.com
q102rome@q102rome.com
License: Rome, Floyd County, GA held by McDougald Broadcasting Corp.
Group Owner: Southern Broadcasting Companies Inc.
Wire Services: National Weather Network
Format: Adult Contemp *Hrs. of News Programming:* news progmg 6 hrs wkly *No. News Employees:* 1 *Target Audience:* 25-54; upscale *Adv. Rates:* 22; 18; 20; 12
Randy Quick, General Manager

WRGA
11-01-1929; 1470 khz AM *Hrs Open:* 24; 5 kw-D, DAN; 5 kw-N, DAN; N34 18 5 W85 9 19
P. O. Box 1187, Rome, GA 30161 US
(706) 291-9496, *Fax:* (706) 235-7107
www.wrgarome.com
south107@aol.com
License: Rome, GA held by McDougald Broadcasting Corp.
Group Owner: Southern Broadcasting Companies Inc.; (acq 1-28-2002; $1.6 million with co-located FM).
Nat'l Network: ABC; CNN Radio *Regional Network:* Ga. News Net. *Wire Services:* National Weather Network
Format: News, News/Talk, 86 *Hrs. of News Programming:* news progmg 168 hrs wkly *No. News Employees:* 2 *Target Audience:* General; upscale, involved, upwardly mobile
Paul Stone, President
Gregory Kamishlian, General Manager

WROM
12-26-1946; 710 khz AM *Hrs Open:* Sunrise-sunset
725 Calloway Dr., Rockmart, GA 30153 US
(706) 234-7171, *Fax:* (706) 234-8043
www.wromradio.com
wromradio@comcast.net
License: Rome, GA held by LGV Broadcasting Inc.
Nat'l Network: USA
Format: Gospel *Special Programming:* Christian teaching, contemp Christian mus *Hrs. of News Programming:* news progmg 14 hrs wkly *No. News Employees:* 1 *Target Audience:* 35 plus; middle class families, women,homeowners
Mark Lumpkin, General Manager

WGJK
08-01-1962; 1360 khz AM *Hrs Open:* 6 AM-12 PM; 0.5 kw-D, ND1; 0.047 kw-N, ND1; N34 16 15 W85 11 0
20 John Davenport Drive, Rome, GA 30161 US
(706) 291-9496, *Fax:* (706) 235-7107
www.magic1360.com
sales@q102rome.com
License: Rome, GA held by Woman's World Broadcasting Inc.
Arbitron Metro Market: Rome, GA *Format:* Urban Contemporary
Howard Toole, CEO
Randy Quick, General Manager
Kevin Daniels, Operation Manager & Programming Director
Luke Brannon, Engineering Director & IT
Dana Clark, Traffic Manager
Samantha Bell, Brands Manager
Nelle Reagan, Public ServiceDirector
Rick Bradley, Production & Imaging Director
Cheryl Scott, Business Manager & Human Resources Director

Rossville

WDYN
11-11-1958; 980 khz AM *Hrs Open:* Sunrise-sunset; 500 w-D; N34 58 03 W85 18 00
7413 Old Lee Hwy., Chattanooga, TN 53202
(423) 892-3333, *Fax:* (423) 899-7224
License: Rossville, Walker County, GA held by 3 Daughters Media Inc.
Group Owner: 3 Daughters Media Inc.; (acq 6-22-2007; grpsl)
Nat'l Reps: Clear Channel
Arbitron Metro Market: Chattanooga, TN *Hrs. of News Programming:* news progmg 4 hrs wkly *No. News Employees:* 1 *Target Audience:* 35-64; adults
Sammy George, General Manager

WRXR-FM
06-08-1966; 105.5 mhz FM *Hrs Open:* 24; 1.8 kw; 604 ft.; N34 57 23 W85 17 32
330 East Kilbourn Avenue, Suite 250, Milwaukee, WI 53202 US
(423) 892-3333, *Fax:* (423) 899-7224
www.rock105.com
jcruze@clearchannel.com
License: Rossville, Walker County, GA held by Capstar TX L.P.
Group Owner: Clear Channel Communications Inc.; (acq 8-7-2000; grpsl)
Nat'l Reps: Clear Channel
Arbitron Metro Market: Chattanooga, TN *Format:* Rock/AOR *Hrs. of News Programming:* News progmg one hr wkly *Adv. Rates:* 75; 45; 65; 20
Sammy George, General Manager

Roswell

WAMJ
01-01-1997; 107.5 mhz FM; 18 kw horiz, 33 kw vert; 607 ft.; N33 55 1 W84 12 6
5900 Princess Garden Prk, 8th Floor, Lanham, MD 20706 US
(404) 765-9750, *Fax:* (404) 688-7686
www.majicatl.com
License: Roswell, Fulton County, GA held by ROA Licenses LLC.
Group Owner: Radio One Inc.; (acq 11-8-2001; grpsl)
Arbitron Metro Market: Atlanta, GA *Format:* Blues
Tim Davies, General Manager
Derek Harper, Programming Director
Corey Punzi, Promotions Manager

Royston

WXFO
01-01-1971; 810 khz AM *Hrs Open:* Sunrise-sunset; 0.23 kw-D, NDD; N34 16 50 W83 7 9
1010 Tower Place, Bogart, GA 30622 US
(706) 246-0059, *Fax:* (706) 245-0890
www.newstalk810.com
studio@familycountry.com
License: Royston, GA held by Oconee River Broadcasting LLC
Nat'l Network: Fox News Radio *Regional Network:* Ga. News Net.
Arbitron Metro Market: Royston, GA *Format:* Talk *Hrs. of News Programming:* news progmg 7 hrs wkly *No. News Employees:* 3 *Target Audience:* General. *Adv. Rates:* 7.50; 5.75; 7.50; 5.75
KJ Allen, General Manager

Sandersville

WSNT
05-11-1956; 1490 khz AM; 1 kw-U; N32 58 23 W82 48 34
Mailing Address: Box 150, Sandersville, GA 30401
Second Address: 312 Morningside Dr., Sandersville, GA 31082
(478) 552-5182, *Fax:* (478) 553-0800
sales@waco100fm.com
License: Sandersville, Washington County, GA held by Radio Station WSNT Inc.
Nat'l Network: Salem Gospel *Regional Network:* Ga. News Net.
Nat'l Reps: Rgnl Reps *Regional Reps:* SE AgNet
Capers Brazzell, General Manager
Nancy Craig, General Sales Mgr
Jerry Knight, Programming Director
Taylor Everett, Promotions Manager

WSNT-FM
01-01-1975; 99.9 mhz FM *Hrs Open:* 24; 6 kw; Ant 184 ft; N32 58 23 W82 48 34
Mailing Address: Box 150, Sandersville, GA 31082
Second Address: 312 Morningside Dr., Sandersville, GA 31082
(478) 552-5182, *Fax:* (478) 553-0800
www.waco100fm.com
sales@waco100fm.com
License: Sandersville, Washington County, GA held by Radio Station WSNT, Inc.
Nat'l Network: ABC Music Radio *Regional Network:* Ga. News Net. *Nat'l Reps:* Rgnl Reps *Regional Reps:* SE AgNet
Hrs. of News Programming: 2 *No. News Employees:* 1
Mary Foster, Operations Dir
Capers Brazzell, General Manager
Nancy Craig, General Sales Mgr
Jerry Knight, Programming Director
Taylor Everett, Promotions Manager
Buddy Wommack, Chief Engineer

Sasser

WEGC
01-01-1995; 107.7 mhz FM; 11.5 kw; 312 ft.; N31 38 42 W84 21 15
330 E. Kilbourn Ave., Suite 250, Milwaukee, WI 53202 US
(229) 888-5000(229) 878-1077, *Fax:* (229) 888-5960
www.mix107albany.com
april.bailey@cumulus.com
License: Sasser, Terrell County, GA held by Cumulus Licensing Corp.
Group Owner: Cumulus Media Inc.; (acq 7-7-98)
Nat'l Reps: Katz Radio
Arbitron Metro Market: Sasser, GA. *Format:* Adult Contemp
Gregory Kamishlian, General Manager
Katy Edwards, Promotions Manager

Savannah

WAEV
02-04-1969; 97.3 mhz FM; 100 kw; 1299 ft.; N32 2 45 W81 20 27
600 Congress Ave., Suite 1400, Austin, TX 78701 US
(912) 964-7794, *Fax:* (912) 964-9414
www.973kissfm.com
info@973kissfm.com
License: Savannah, Chatham County, GA
Group Owner: Clear Channel Communications Inc.
Nat'l Network: Westwood One
Arbitron Metro Market: Savannah, GA *Format:* Contemporary Hits/Top 40 *Target Audience:* 25-54; affluent
Steve Richards, Operations Dir
Sheryl Collison, Programming Director
Craig Scott, Promotions Manager
Marty Foglia, Chief Engineer
Mark Robertson, PSA Director

WBMQ
12-29-1939; 630 khz AM
330 East Kilbourn Avenue, Suite 250, Milwaukee, WI 53202 US
(912) 961-9000, *Fax:* (912) 961-7070
www.wbmq.com
Gil.Jones@cumulus.com
License: Savannah, GA held by Cumulus Licensing Corp.
Group Owner: Cumulus Media Inc.; (acq 3-26-98; grpsl)
Nat'l Network: CBS
Arbitron Metro Market: Savannah, GA *Format:* News, News/Talk, 86 *Target Audience:* 35 plus.
Dale Powers, General Manager
Gill Jones, Promotions Manager

WTKS
10-15-1929; 1290 khz AM; 5 kw-D, DAN; 5 kw-N, DAN; N32 5 26 W81 8 55
600 Congress Ave., Suite 1400, Austin, TX 78701 US
(912) 927-1290, *Fax:* (912) 964-9414
www.newsradio1290wtks.com
community@newsradio1290.com
License: Savannah, GA held by Capstar TX L.P.
Group Owner: Clear Channel Communications Inc.; (acq 8-30-00; grpsl).
Arbitron Metro Market: Savannah, GA *Format:* News, Talk *Target Audience:* 25-64.
Steve Richards, Operations Dir
Wesley Peper, General Sales Mgr
Sheryl Collison, Programming Director
Craig Scott, Promotions Manager
Marty Foglia, Chief Engineer

Bill Edwards, News Director
Mark Robertson, PSA Director

***WHCJ**
08-18-1975; 90.3 mhz FM *Hrs Open:* 16; 6 kw; 223 ft.; N32 1 28 W81 3 23
P. O. Box 20484, Savannah, GA 31404 US
(912) 356-2399, *Fax:* (912) 356-2041
www.savstate.edu/whcj
WHCJ@savstate.edu
License: Savannah, Chatham County, GA held by Savannah State University.
Arbitron Metro Market: Savannah, GA *Format:* Variety/Diverse
Target Audience: 17-65; interested in jazz, reggae, blues & gospel
Theron Ike Carter, General Manager

WIXV
04-24-1972; 95.5 mhz FM; 98 kw; 988 ft.; N32 3 29 W81 20 19
330 East Kilbourn Avenue, Suite 250, Milwaukee, WI 53202 US
(912) 961-9000, *Fax:* (912) 961-7070
www.rockofsavannah.com
info@diane.hubelcumulus.com
License: Savannah, Chatham County, GA
Group Owner: Cumulus Media Inc.
Arbitron Metro Market: Savannah, GA *Format:* Classic Rock
Target Audience: 18-49.
Greg Park, Station Manager
Steve Entrekin, Programming Director
Paul Galvin, Promotions Manager

WJCL-FM
06-18-1972; 96.5 mhz FM *Hrs Open:* 24; 100 kw; 1161 ft.; N32 3 29 W81 20 19
330 East Kilbourn Ave., N.W., Suite 250, Milwaukee, WI 53202 US
(912) 961-9000, *Fax:* (912) 961-7070
www.kix96.com
boomer.lee@cumulus.com
License: Savannah, Chatham County, GA held by Cumulus Licensing Corp.
Group Owner: Cumulus Media Inc.; (acq 3-12-98; $7.25 million)
Arbitron Metro Market: Savannah, GA *Format:* Country *No. News Employees:* 1 *Target Audience:* 25-54.
Lewis Dickey Jr., CEO
Sam Nelson, Operations Dir
Dale Powers, General Manager
Tom Hennessey, General Sales Mgr
Martin Gausvik, CFO

WJLG
10-06-1950; 900 khz AM; 4.35 kw-D, ND1; 0.152 kw-N, ND1; N32 4 29 W81 4 17
330 East Kilbourn Ave., Suite 250, Milwaukee, WI 53202 US
(912) 961-9000, *Fax:* (912) 961-7070
www.cumulus.com
info@diane.hubelcumulus.com
License: Savannah, GA held by Cumulus Licensing Corp.
Group Owner: Cumulus Media Inc.; (acq 7-29-98; $5.25 million with co-located FM)
Nat'l Network: Fox Sports
Arbitron Metro Market: Savannah, GA *Format:* Sports
Dale Power, General Manager

***WLXP**
01-01-2002; 88.1 mhz FM *Hrs Open:* 24; 5.5 kw; 341 ft.; N32 3 48 W81 2 56
P.O. Box 246, Savannah, GA 31402 US
(888) 937-2471, *Fax:* (916) 251-1650
www.air1.com
info@air1.com
License: Savannah, Chatham County, GA held by Christian Multimedia Network Inc.
Nat'l Network: Air 1
Arbitron Metro Market: Savannah, GA *Format:* Christian *No. News Employees:* 3 *Target Audience:* 18-35; Judeo-Christian, female *Adv. Rates:* 12; 9; 12; 7.50
Mike Novak, CEO/COO
Mike Novak, President
Chip Bailey, Operations Dir

WQBT
11-29-1946; 94.1 mhz FM; 100 kw; 1299 ft.; N32 2 45 W81 20 27
600 Congress Ave., Suite 1400, Austin, TX 78701 US
(912) 964-7794, *Fax:* (912) 964-9414
www.941thebeat.com
info@941thebeat.com
License: Savannah, Chatham County, GA
Arbitron Metro Market: Savannah, GA *Format:* Urban Contemporary
Steve Richards, Operations Dir
Chase, Programming Director
Craig Scott, Promotions Manager
Marty Foglia, Chief Engineer
Sheryl Collison, Sales Director

WSEG
05-01-1956; 1400 khz AM *Hrs Open:* 24; 0.65 kw-D, ND1; 0.65 kw-N, ND1; N32 4 29 W81 4 17
2970 Peachtree Road, NW, Suite 970, Eighth Floor, Atlanta, GA 30305 US
(912) 264-6251
License: Savannah, GA held by MarMac Communications LLC.
Group Owner: MarMac Communications LLC; (acq 6-26-2007; $300,000)
Arbitron Metro Market: Savannah, GA *Format:* Contemporary Hits/Top 40, Adult Contemp
Gary Marmitt, General Manager

WSOK
10-01-1946; 1230 khz AM; 1 kw-U, ND1; N32 4 20 W81 4 35
600 Congress Ave., Suite 1400, Austin, TX 78701 US
(912) 964-7794, *Fax:* (912) 964-9414
License: Savannah, GA held by Capstar TX L.P.
Group Owner: Clear Channel Communications Inc.; (acq 8-30-00; grpsl).
Nat'l Network: American Urban
Arbitron Metro Market: Savannah, GA *Format:* Gospel
Steve Richards, Operations Dir
Sheryl Collison, Programming Director
Craig Scott, Promotions Manager
Marty Foglia, Chief Engineer
E. Larry McDuffie, Disc Jockey
Gary Young, Program Director

***WSVH**
04-20-1981; 91.1 mhz FM *Hrs Open:* 24; 96 kw vert; 1414 ft.; N32 8 48 W81 37 5 *Rebroadcasts:* WJSP, Warm Springs, GA, 50-60%
Mailing Address: 260 - 14th Street, N.W., Atlanta, GA 30318 US
Second Address: 12 Ocean Science Cir., Savannah, GA 30602
(404) 685-2690 HQ, *Fax:* (404) 685-2684 HQ
www.gpb.org
ask@gpb.org
License: Savannah, Chatham County, GA held by Georgia Public Telecommunications Commission.
Nat'l Network: PRI; NPR *Wire Services:* AP
Arbitron Metro Market: Savannah, GA *Format:* Jazz, News *Hrs. of News Programming:* news progmg 51 hrs wkly *No. News Employees:* 10 *Target Audience:* Adults: 35 plus.
Nancy Hall, CEO
Tom Barclay, Operations Dir
Bob Houghton, General Manager
Eric Nauert, Station Manager
Rob Maynard, Programming Director
Susanna Capelouto, News Director
Bonnie Bean, CFO
Orlando Montoya, News Reporter
RussellWells, Wsvh Operations manager

***WYFS**
11-01-1986; 89.5 mhz FM *Hrs Open:* 24; 100 kw horiz, 91 kw vert; 600 ft.; N32 4 4 W81 21 17
Mailing Address: 8030 Arrowridge Blvd., Charlotte, NC 28273 US
Second Address: Bible Broadcasting Network, Charlotte, GA 28241-7300
(704) 523-5555, *Fax:* (704) 522-1967
www.bbnradio.org
bbn@bbnradio.org
License: Savannah, Chatham County, GA held by Bible Broadcasting Network Inc.
Group Owner: Bible Broadcasting Network
Arbitron Metro Market: Savannah, GA *Format:* Christian, Religious *Target Audience:* General; christian progmg for the entire family
Lowell Davey, President
Rob Ferguson, General Manager

Smithboro

***WAKP**
89.1 mhz FM; 2.9 kw vert; 220 ft.; N33 19 0 W83 31 40 US
(864) 297-0216
info@networkofglory.org
License: Smithboro, Jasper County, GA held by Network of Glory Inc.
Arbitron Metro Market: Smithboro, GA
Lola Richey, General Manager

Smithville

WZIQ
01-01-1996; 106.5 mhz FM *Hrs Open:* 24; 2.45 kw; 515 ft; N31 47 59 W84 14 54
2278 Wortham Ln., Grovetown, GA 30909
(706) 309-9610
www.gnnradio.org
ctbarinowski@comcast.net
License: Smithville, Lee County, GA held by Barinowski Investment Co.
Group Owner: Good News Network; (acq 1-21-98)
Population Served: 110,000 *Arbitron Metro Market:* Albany, GA
Clarence Barinowski, General Manager

Smyrna

WAZX
03-01-1962; 1550 khz AM *Hrs Open:* 24
2460 Atlanta Road, Smyrna, GA 30080 US
(559) 935-4191, *Fax:* (559) 935-4191
License: Smyrna, GA held by GA-MEX Broadcasting Inc.
Arbitron Metro Market: Riverdale CA *Format:* Oldies
Rebecca Sexton, General Manager

WSTR
05-01-1966; 94.1 mhz FM; 100 kw; 1018 ft.; N33 45 33 W84 20 5
3350 Peachtree Road, Ne, Atlanta, GA 30326 US
(404) 261-2970, *Fax:* (404) 365-9026
www.star94.com
star94frontdesk@star94.com
License: Smyrna, Cobb County, GA held by Jefferson Pilot Communications Co.
Group Owner: Lincoln Financial Media; acq 3-1-74)
Arbitron Metro Market: Atlanta, GA *Format:* Contemporary Hits/Top 40 *Target Audience:* 18-49; general
Don Benson, President
Mark Kanov, General Manager
Dan Bowen, Programming Director

Soperton

***WKTM**
11-23-1982; 106.1 mhz FM *Hrs Open:* 24; 6 kw; 299 ft.; N32 25 31 W82 33 26
3213 Huxley Drive, Augusta, GA 30909 US
(706) 309-9610
www.gnnradio.org
ctbarinowski@comcast.net
License: Soperton, Treutlen County, GA held by Barinowski Investment Co.
Clarence Barinowski, General Manager

Sparta

***WJDS**
88.7 mhz FM; 0 kw horiz, 2 kw vert; 135 ft.; N33 18 48 W83 0 5
3213 Huxley Drive, Augusta, GA 30909 US
(800) 926-4669
www.gnnradio.org
brian@gnnradio.org
License: Sparta, Hancock County, GA held by Augusta Radio Fellowship Institute Inc.
Arbitron Metro Market: Appling, GA
Clarence Barinowski, General Manager

Springfield

WEAS-FM
08-01-1967; 93.1 mhz FM; 96.64 kw; 981 ft.; N32 2 45 W81 20 27
330 East Kilbourn Ave., Suite 250, Milwaukee, WI 53202 US
(912) 961-9000, *Fax:* (912) 961-7070
www.e93fm.com/
lg@cumulus.com
License: Springfield, Effingham County, GA held by Cumulus Licensing Corp.
Group Owner: Cumulus Media Inc.
Arbitron Metro Market: Springfield, GA *Format:* Urban Contemporary
Barbara Haynes, General Manager
Lil G, Programming Director
Gil Jones, Promotions Manager
Duffy Egan, Chief Engineer

St. Marys

WWIO
10-15-1985; 1190 khz AM *Hrs Open:* Daytime
2101 Hwy 40 E., St. Marys, GA 31558 US

RADIO - U.S.

(912) 344-3565, *Fax:* (912) 344-3411
www.wsvh.org
publicradio@wsvh.org
License: St. Marys, GA held by Lighthouse Christian Broadcasting Corp.
Nat'l Network: USA; NPR *Regional Network:* Georgia Public Radio *Nat'l Reps:* Rgnl Reps *Wire Services:* AP
Arbitron Metro Market: Savannah, GA *Format:* Classical, News *Hrs. of News Programming:* news progmg 40 hrs wkly *No. News Employees:* 6 *Target Audience:* General; 35 yrs +
Russell Wells, Operations Dir
Eric Nauert, Station Manager
St. John Flynn, Programming Director
Mark Sehlig, Chief Engineer

St. Simons Island

WBGA
01-01-1990; 92.7 mhz FM *Hrs Open:* 24; 6 kw; 328 ft.; N31 9 42 W81 28 28
Two Bala Plaza, Suite 801, Bala-Cynwyd, PA 19004 US
(912) 265-9300, *Fax:* (912) 264-5462
scottrysun@gmail.com
License: St. Simons Island, Glynn County, GA held by Quantum of Brunswick License Co. LLC
Group Owner: Qantum Communications Corp.
Nat'l Network: ABC
Arbitron Metro Market: Brunswick, GA *Format:* Urban Contemporary *Target Audience:* 24-45.
Jonthan Havens, General Manager

Statenville

WHLJ-FM
01-01-1999; 97.5 mhz FM; 6 kw; Ant 328 ft; N30 46 47 W82 52 43
LaTaurus Productions Inc., Box 1305, Valdosta, GA 31601
(229) 242-9997, *Fax:* (229) 249-9765
WHLJ@BELLSOUTH.NET
License: Statenville, Echols County, GA held by LaTaurus Productions Inc.
Arbitron Metro Market: Valdosta, GA
Warren Lee, General Manager

Statesboro

WPMX
01-01-1995; 102.9 mhz FM *Hrs Open:* 24; 25 kw; 328 ft.; N32 26 43 W81 58 7
P.O. Box 180, Hawkinsville, GA 31036 US
(912) 764-6000, *Fax:* (912) 764-8827
radiocenter@frontiernet.net
License: Statesboro, Bulloch County, GA held by Georgia Eagle Broadcasting Inc.
Group Owner: Georgia Eagle Broadcasting Inc.; acq 1-12-2007; grpsl)
Nat'l Network: ABC *Regional Network:* Ga. News Net.
Format: Adult Contemp *Target Audience:* General.
Jeff Anderson, General Manager
Buddy Horne, Programming Director

WPTB
04-04-1976; 850 khz AM *Hrs Open:* 24
1201 Third Avenue, Suite 3600, Seattle, WA 98101 US
(912) 764-6621, *Fax:* (912) 764-6622
www.radiostatesboro.com
espn850@frontiernet.net
License: Statesboro, GA held by Georgia Eagle Broadcasting Inc.
Group Owner: Georgia Eagle Broadcasting Inc.; (acq 5-21-2007; grpsl)
Nat'l Network: ESPN Radio *Nat'l Reps:* Dora-Clayton *Regional Reps:* Regional Reps
Format: Sports *Special Programming:* Gospel 6 hrs wkly *Hrs. of News Programming:* news progmg 7 hrs wkly *No. News Employees:* 1 *Target Audience:* General.
Sandi Kirkland, Operations Dir
Nate Hirsch, General Manager
Bill Kent, Programming Director

***WVGS**
01-01-1975; 91.9 mhz FM *Hrs Open:* 24; 1 kw; 161 ft.; N32 25 32 W81 46 58
Lb 8128, Statesboro, GA 30460 US
(912) 681-0877, *Fax:* (912) 486-7113
class.georgiasouthern.edu
wvgs@georgiasouthern.edu
License: Statesboro, Bulloch County, GA held by Georgia Southern University
Arbitron Metro Market: Statesboro, GA *Format:* Alternative *Target Audience:* 18-25; college kids
Melonie Stone, General Manager

WWNS
12-01-1946; 1240 khz AM *Hrs Open:* 24; 0.71 kw-U, ND1; N32 27 19 W81 46 28
Mailing Address: 561 East Olliff St Bx958, Statesboro, GA 30458 US
Second Address: 561 E. Olliff St., Statesboro, GA 30458
(912) 764-5446, *Fax:* (912) 764-8827
spots@georgiaeagleradio.com
License: Statesboro, GA held by Georgia Eagle Broadcasting Inc.
Group Owner: Georgia Eagle Broadcasting Inc.; (acq 5-21-2007; grpsl)
Nat'l Network: USA *Regional Reps:* Rgnl Reps
Arbitron Metro Market: Statesboro, GA *Format:* News, News/Talk, 84, Talk *Hrs. of News Programming:* news progmg 20 hrs wkly *No. News Employees:* 1 *Target Audience:* 25-death.
Cornell Burgess, Operations Dir
Jeff Anderson, General Manager
Buddy Horne, Programming Director

***WSLT**
88.5 mhz FM; 6 kw; 197 ft.; N32 38 9 W81 41 36 US
(912) 826-3833
License: Statesboro, Bulloch County, GA held by Salt and Light Communications Inc.
Arbitron Metro Market: Statesboro, GA
Linda Hand, CEO

Summerville

WGTA
08-27-1950; 950 khz AM *Hrs Open:* 6 AM-7 PM; 5 kw-D, ND2; 0.11 kw-N, ND2; N34 27 53 W85 21 12
2 Mount Alto Road, Rome, GA 30165 US
(770) 436-6171, *Fax:* (770) 436-0100
License: Summerville, GA held by Azteca Communications Inc.
Javier Macias, President
Patty Perez, General Manager

Swainsboro

WJAT
01-01-1950; 800 khz AM *Hrs Open:* 24
P.O. Box 1590 2 Radio Loop, Swainsboro, GA 30401 US
(478) 237-1590, *Fax:* (478) 237-3559
License: Swainsboro, GA held by RadioJones LLC.
Group Owner: RadioJones LLC; (acq 4-2-2004; grpsl)
Format: News, Sports, 86 *Special Programming:* Farm 5 hrs wkly; high school sports *Hrs. of News Programming:* news progmg 10 hrs wkly *No. News Employees:* 1 *Target Audience:* 25-64. *Adv. Rates:* 10; 8; 8;5
Dennis Jones, President
Jolly Martin, General Sales Mgr
John Wagner, Programming Director
Marty Foglia, Engineering Dir

WXRS
03-10-1978; 1590 khz AM *Hrs Open:* 24; 2.5 kw-D, ND1; 0.023 kw-N, ND1; N32 33 25 W82 20 29
2 Radio Loop, PO Box 1590, Swainsboro, GA 30401 US
(478) 237-1590, *Fax:* (478) 237-3559
www.radiojones.com
License: Swainsboro, GA held by RadioJones LLC.
Group Owner: RadioJones LLC; (acq 4-2-2004; grpsl).
Arbitron Metro Market: Portal, GA *Format:* Oldies *Hrs. of News Programming:* news progmg 10 per day *No. News Employees:* 1 *Target Audience:* 25-64. *Adv. Rates:* 8; 6; 6; 3
Dennis Jones, President
John Wagner, Operations Dir
Jolly Martin, General Sales Mgr
Marty Foglia, Engineering Dir

Sylvania

WSYL
12-01-1955; 1490 khz AM *Hrs Open:* 24; 1 kw-U, ND1; N32 43 51 W81 37 4
910 W. Ogeechee Street, Sylvania, GA 30467 US
(912) 564-7461, *Fax:* (912) 564-7462
info@wsyl.com
License: Sylvania, GA held by Georgia Eagle Broadcasting Inc.
Group Owner: Georgia Eagle Broadcasting Inc.; (acq 5-21-2007; grpsl)
Regional Network: Ga. News Net. *Nat'l Reps:* Rgnl Reps
Special Programming: Farm 5 hrs wkly
Nathan Hirsch, General Manager
Mary Lou Clontz, Programming Director
David Hartley, News Director

Sylvester

***WHKV**
01-27-1993; 106.1 mhz FM; 6 kw; 328 ft.; N31 30 15 W83 55 46
1121 East Franklin St., Sylvester, GA 31791 US
(800) 525-5683
www.klove.com
klove@klove.com
License: Sylvester, Worth County, GA held by Educational Media Foundation.
Group Owner: EMF Broadcasting; (acq 4-30-2007; $615,000 with WFFM(FM) Ashburn)
Nat'l Network: K-Love
Arbitron Metro Market: Albany, GA *Format:* Religious
Darrell Chambliss, Chairman
Alan Mason, COO
Mike Novak, President

WNUQ
08-01-1999; 102.1 mhz FM; 6 kw; 259 ft.; N31 31 40 W83 50 22
P.O. Box 364, Sylvester, GA 31791 US
(229) 888-5000, *Fax:* (229) 888-5960
www.q102albany.com
info18@cumulus.com
License: Sylvester, Worth County, GA held by Cumulus Licensing Corp.
Group Owner: Cumulus Media Inc.; (acq 3-12-2001; $550,000).
Nat'l Reps: Katz Radio
Arbitron Metro Market: Sylvester, GA *Format:* Blues
Gregory Kamishlian, General Manager
Roshon Vance, Programming Director
Katy Edwards, Promotions Manager
April Bailey, Business Manager
Kelly Carpenter, Asst. Business Mgr. & Traffic
Angel Taylor, Vice President of Sales
MicheleHicks, Account Executive
Tiffany Cox, Account Executive
Susan Vancel, Account Executive

Talking Rock

WNSY
01-01-1999; 100.1 mhz FM; 7 kw; 617 ft.; N34 37 50 W84 29 29
Rebroadcasts: Rebroadcasts WLKQ-FM Buford 100%
1353 13th Avenue, Columbus, GA 31901 US
(770) 623-8772, *Fax:* (770) 623-4722
www.laraza1023.com
License: Talking Rock, Pickens County, GA held by Davis Broadcasting of Atlanta L.L.C.
Group Owner: Davis Broadcasting Inc.; (acq 1-17-2007; $3.8 million with WCHK(AM) Canton)
Arbitron Metro Market: Pickens, GA
Brian Barber, General Manager

Tallapoosa

WKNG
09-01-1977; 1060 khz AM
Mailing Address: P.O. Box 606, Tallapoosa, GA 30176 US
Second Address: Hwy. 78, Golf Course Rd., Tallapoosa, GA 30176
(770) 574-1060, *Fax:* (770) 574-1062
www.wkng.com
info@wkng.com
License: Tallapoosa, GA held by WKNG LLC.
Nat'l Network: ABC *Regional Network:* Ga. News Net.
Format: Country *Target Audience:* 25-54.
Steven Gradick, President

***WEYY**
88.7 mhz FM; 0.25 kw; 98 ft.; N33 44 42.6 W85 17 16.2 US
(706) 965-2355
License: Tallapoosa, Haralson County, GA held by Old Time Gospel Ministries.
Arbitron Metro Market: Tallapoosa, GA
Robert Jarrell, President

WWGA
98.9 mhz; 1850 w; 597 ft; N33 39 03 W85 17 41
1 Golf Course Road, Tallapoosa, GA
(770)574-1060, *Fax:* (770)574-1062
www.gradickcommunications.com
License: Tallapoosa, GA held by Wkng LLC
Kim Fitzgerald Buhl, Traffic/Promotions
Colin Worthington, News Director
Michael Vincent, Production Director
Mitch Grey, Production Director

Tallulah Falls

***WNGM(FM)**
91.7 mhz FM; 130 w; Ant 1,030 ft; N34 43 46 W83 29 42
179 Cross Creek Dr., Toccoa, GA 30577
(706) 491-4457
License: Tallulah Falls, Habersham and Rabun County, GA held by Toccoa Foundation Inc.
Population Served: 2,986 *Arbitron Metro Market:* Pendleton, SC
Douglas Sutton, President

***WNGM(FM)**
90.3 mhz FM; 2.25 kw; Ant 325 ft; N33 49 50.4 W82 45 19.2
179 Cross Creek Drive, Toccoa, GA 30577
(706) 491-4457
License: Tallulah Falls, Wilkes County, GA held by Toccoa Foundation Inc.
Population Served: 168 *Arbitron Metro Market:* Tallulah Falls, GA
Douglas Sutton Jr., Operations Dir

WNGM
91.7 mhz; 60 w; 1264 ft; N34 50 42 W83 30 02
License: Tallulah Falls, GA held by Toccoa Foundation
Group Owner: Toccoa Foundation

Tennille

WJFL
10-14-1993; 101.9 mhz FM; 6 kw; 328 ft.; N32 54 49 W82 53 6
P.O. Box 1097, Sandersville, GA 31082 US
(478) 553-1019, *Fax:* (478) 553-1123
www.wjfl.com
wjfl@wjfl.com
License: Tennille, Washington County, GA held by Middle Georgia Broadcasting, Inc.
Format: Contemporary Hits/Top 40, Oldies
Michael Cowan, General Manager
Andrea Turner, Programming Director
Reba Barlow, Production Assistant
Tina Walker, Production Assistant

The Rock

***WKEU-FM**
01-01-2000; 88.9 mhz FM; 5 kw; 764 ft.; N32 59 11 W84 21 56
Mailing Address: 1000 Memorial Drive, Griffin, GA 30223 US
Second Address: 1000 Memorial Dr., Griffin, GA 30224
(770) 227-5507, *Fax:* (770) 229-2291
www.wkeuradio.com
wkeu@aol.com
License: The Rock, Upson County, GA held by Georgia Public Radio Inc.
Format: Classic Rock
William Taylor, Jr., President

Thomaston

WTGA
11-01-1962; 1590 khz AM; 0.5 kw-D, ND1; 0.025 kw-N, ND1; N32 53 45 W84 18 10
Mailing Address: 208 South Center St, Thomaston, GA 30286 US
Second Address: Box 550, Thomaston, GA
(706) 647-7121, *Fax:* (706) 647-7122
License: Thomaston, GA held by Radio Georgia Inc.
Arbitron Metro Market: Thomaston, GA *Format:* Adult Contemp
Special Programming: Black 4 hrs wkly
David Piper, President
Bill Bailey, General Sales Mgr
Robert Lyons, Chief Engineer

WTGA-FM
11-15-1982; 101.1 mhz FM; 6 kw; 308 ft; N32 51 49 W84 25 10
Mailing Address: 208 S. Center St., Thomaston, GA 30286
Second Address: Box 550, Thomaston, GA 30286
(706) 647-7121, *Fax:* (706) 647-7122
www.wtga.com
License: Thomaston, Upson County, GA
Population Served: 15,000
Dave Piper, President
Dave Piper, General Manager
Carl Pruett, General Sales Mgr
Charlie Steele, Programming Director
Bill Gentry, Promotions Manager
Mickey Thresher, News Director
Al Rhymeburg, Chief Engineer

Thomasville

WGMI(FM)
01-01-1971; 107.1 mhz FM; 100 kw; 981 ft; N30 43 55 W84 08 45
325 John Knox Rd., Building G, Tallahassee, FL 32303
(850) 422-3107, *Fax:* (850) 383-0747,
www.magic1071.com
jeffhorn@clearchannel.com
License: Thomasville, Thomas County, GA held by CC Licenses LLC.
Group Owner: Clear Channel Communications Inc.; (acq 11-21-97; grpsl)
Population Served: 400,000 *Arbitron Metro Market:* Tallahassee, FL *TV Affiliate:* Adult Contemp *Special Programming:* news progmg 5 hrs wkly *Hrs. of News Programming:* 1 *No. News Employees:* 25-54.
Program Director, Programming Director

WPAX
12-27-1922; 1240 khz AM *Hrs Open:* 24; 1 kw-U, ND1; N30 50 10 W83 59 19
Mailing Address: 117 Remington Ave, Thomasville, GA 31799 US
Second Address: 117 Remington Ave., Thomasville, GA 31799
(229) 226-1240, *Fax:* (229) 226-1361
www.wpaxradio.com
lenrob@rose.net
License: Thomasville, GA held by LenRob Inc.
Nat'l Network: CBS *Regional Network:* Ga. News Net. *Nat'l Reps:* Rgnl Reps
Format: Contemporary Hits/Top 40 *Hrs. of News Programming:* news progmg 20 hrs wkly *No. News Employees:* 1 *Target Audience:* 25 plus; mature with disposable income
Len Robinson, President

WSTT
01-01-1947; 730 khz AM *Hrs Open:* 5:30 AM-9 PM; 5 kw-D, NDD; 0.027 kw-N, ND1; N30 42 47 W84 8 20
7606 Harold Avenue, Gary, IN 46403 US
(229) 377-2337, *Fax:* (229) 377-0023
sgulfbroadcasting@att.net
License: Thomasville, GA held by Marion R. Williams.
Group Owner: Marion R. Williams Stns; (acq 7-26-99; $300,000)
Nat'l Network: CBS
Arbitron Metro Market: Tallahassee, FL *Format:* Gospel *Target Audience:* 25-54; general
Marion Williams, General Manager

***WAYT**
01-01-2003; 88.1 mhz FM; 35 kw; 1286 ft.; N30 40 6 W83 58 10
P.O. Box 14884, Tallahassee, FL 32317 US
(850) 422-9293, *Fax:* (850) 297-1888
wayt.wayfm.com
supportservices@wayfm.com
License: Thomasville, Thomas County, GA held by WAY-FM Media Group Inc.
Group Owner: WAY-FM Media Group Inc.; acq 10-24-02).
Arbitron Metro Market: Tallahassee, FL *Format:* Christian
Bob Augsburg, President/Founder
Steve Young, Station Manager

***WFSL**
03-01-2005; 90.7 mhz FM; 0.25 kw; 154 ft.; N30 50 12 W83 58 57
Florida St University, 1600 Red Baber Plaza, Talleahassee, FL 32310 US
(850) 487-3170, *Fax:* (850) 487-3093
www.wfsu.org
fpm@wfsu.org
License: Thomasville, Thomas County, GA held by Florida State University Board of Trustees.
Arbitron Metro Market: Tallahassee, FL *Format:* Talk
Patrick Keating, General Manager
Caroline Austin, Station Manager
Krysta Brown, News Director
Doug Crall, Engineering Dir
Leo Barfield, Chief Engineer
Denison Graham, Finance Director
Sherri Leggett, Accounting Supervisor
Amanda DiLullo, Accounting Associate
Jacqueline Roark, Financial Specialist
Zhonta Stapleton, Accounting Associate
Melissa Roy, Administrative Specialist/HR

WGMY
107.1 mhz FM; 100 kw; 823 ft.; N30 35 12 W84 14 11
200 Concord Plaza, Suite 600, San Antonio, TX 78216 US
(850) 422-3107
www.1071hitmusicnow.com
License: Thomasville, Orange County, GA held by River Broadcasting Inc.
Arbitron Metro Market: Thomasville, GA *Format:* Adult Contemp
John Katonah, President
Scott Dwyer, Programming Director
Jason Taylor, Promotions Manager

Thomson

WTHO-FM
02-22-1971; 101.7 mhz FM; 5.1 kw; 354 ft.; N33 28 20 W82 31 2
P.O. Box 900, 788 Cedar Rock Road NW, Thomson, GA 30824 US
(706) 595-5122, *Fax:* (706) 595-3021
wtho.com
traffic@wtho.com
License: Thomson, McDuffie County, GA held by Camellia City Communications Inc.
Regional Network: Ga. News Net. *Nat'l Reps:* Rgnl Reps
Arbitron Metro Market: Augusta, GA *Format:* Country *Special Programming:* Farm 3 hrs, gospel one hr, relg 6 hrs wkly *Hrs. of News Programming:* News progmg 2 hrs wkly *No. News Employees:* 1 *Target Audience:* 25-54.
Mike Wall, General Manager
Mike Wall, General Sales Mgr
Steve Ferguson, Programming Director
Donna Branch, News Director
Mary Thomaston, Traffic Manager
Mike Wall, Station Owner

WTWA
01-10-1948; 1240 khz AM *Hrs Open:* 19; 1 kw-U, ND1; N33 28 20 W82 31 2
P.O. Box 900, Thomson, GA 30824 US
(706) 595-5122, *Fax:* (706) 595-3021
www.wtho.com
traffic@wtho.com
License: Thomson, GA held by Camellia City Communications Inc.
Arbitron Metro Market: Augusta, GA *Format:* Adult Contemp *No. News Employees:* 1 *Target Audience:* 35 plus.
Tom Thon, Operations Dir
Mike Wall, Station Manager
Steve Ferguson, Programming Director
Donna Branch, News Director

***WQAI**
89.5 mhz FM; 0.05 kw horiz, 49 kw vert; 476 ft.; N33 44 32 W82 31 17 *Rebroadcasts:* Rebroadcasts KLRD(FM) Yucaipa, CA 100%
P O Box 2440, Tupelo, MS 38803 US
(916) 251-1600, *Fax:* (916) 251-1650
www.air1.com
info@air1.com
License: Thomson, McDuffie County, GA held by Educational Media Foundation.
Group Owner: EMF Broadcasting; (acq 3-23-2007; grpsl)
Nat'l Network: Air 1
Arbitron Metro Market: Denison, IA *Format:* Alternative, Christian
Mike Novak, President

Tifton

***WABR**
12-01-1973; 91.1 mhz FM; 30 kw; 249 ft.; N31 29 30 W83 31 49
Rebroadcasts: Rebroadcasts WJSP-FM Warm Springs 100%
260 - 14th Street, N.W., Atlanta, GA 30318 US
(308) 632-5667, *Fax:* (308) 635-1905
License: Tifton, Tift County, GA held by Georgia Public Telecommunications Commission.
Nat'l Network: NPR *Regional Network:* Georgia Public Radio
Wire Services: AP
Arbitron Metro Market: Centennial CO *Format:* Country
Julie Marshall, General Manager

WKZZ
01-01-2000; 92.5 mhz FM; 20.5 kw; 361 ft.; N31 31 40 W83 20 1
Box 100, Fitzgerald, GA 31750 US
(912) 389-0995, *Fax:* (912) 383-8552
traffic@charter.net
License: Tifton, Tift County, GA held by Broadcast South LLC.
Group Owner: Broadcast South LLC; (acq 11-15-2006; grpsl)
Format: Adult Contemp
John Higgs, General Manager

WOBB
01-01-1975; 100.3 mhz FM; 100 kw; 997 ft.; N31 25 51 W83 45 10
225 Green St, #906, Fayetteville, NC 28301 US
(229) 439-9704, *Fax:* (229) 439-1509
www.b100wobb.com
kurtbaker@clearchannel.com
License: Tifton, Tift County, GA held by CC Licenses LLC.

Group Owner: Clear Channel Communications Inc.; (acq 7-12-2000; grpsl).
Nat'l Reps: Christal
Arbitron Metro Market: Albany, GA *TV Affiliate:* Country *Special Programming:* News progmg 2 hrs wkly *No. News Employees:* 25-49. *Adv. Rates:* 45; 40; 45; 35
Program Director, Programming Director

***WPLH**
01-01-1988; 103.1 mhz FM; 0.029 kw horiz; 177 ft.; N31 28 51 W83 31 38
Mailing Address: P.O. Box 20 Abac Station, Tifton, GA 31794 US
Second Address: 2802 Moore Hwy, Tifton, GA 31793
(229) 391-4977,(229) 391-4957, *Fax:* (229) 386-7158
wplh@abac.edu
License: Tifton, Tift County, GA held by Abraham Baldwin Agriculture College.
Regional Network: Georgia Public Radio
Format: Alternative
Eric Cash, General Manager

WTIF
01-01-1957; 1340 khz AM *Hrs Open:* 24; 1 kw-U, ND1; N31 28 16 W83 29 12
P.O. Box 968, Tiftion, GA 31793 US
(229) 382-1340, *Fax:* (229) 386-8658
License: Tifton, GA held by Plant Broadcasting
Group Owner: Plant Broadcasting; (acq 8-1-2011)
Nat'l Network: FOX *Regional Network:* Ga. News Net.
Arbitron Metro Market: Tifton,GA *Format:* Country, Talk *Special Programming:* Farm 5 hrs wkly *Hrs. of News Programming:* news progmg 15 hrs wkly *No. News Employees:* 1 *Target Audience:* 18 plus.
James Howard, President
Ron Yontz, General Manager
Andy Reeves, Station Manager

Toccoa

WNEG
04-21-1956; 630 khz AM *Hrs Open:* 24
121 West Doyle St PO Box, Toccoa, GA 30577 US
(706) 886-2191, *Fax:* (706) 282-0189
www.wnegradio.com
wneg@windstream.net
License: Toccoa, GA held by Georgia-Carolina Radiocasting Co. LLC.
Group Owner: Georgia-Carolina Radiocasting Companies; (acq 7-25-2002; grpsl)
Nat'l Network: CBS Radio *Regional Network:* Ga. News Net.
Arbitron Metro Market: Toccoa, GA *Format:* Adult Contemp, News, 64 *Hrs. of News Programming:* news progmg 18 hrs wkly *No. News Employees:* 1 *Target Audience:* General; adult working class
Douglas M. Sutton Jr., President
Connie Gaines, Operations Dir
Phil Hobbs, General Manager
Ken Brady, General Sales Mgr
Charlie Bauder, News Director
Marty Lee, Chief Engineer
Connie Gaines, Operations Manager
Terry Carter,Vice President

Toccoa Falls

***WRAF**
09-04-1980; 90.9 mhz FM *Hrs Open:* 24; 100 kw; 564 ft.; N34 35 57 W83 21 55
Mailing Address: Toccoa Falls College, Toccoa, GA 30598 US
Second Address: 292 Old Clarksville Hwy., Toccoa, GA 30577
(800) 251-8326,(706) 282-6030, *Fax:* (706) 282-6090
www.myfavoritestation.net
radio@tfc.edu
License: Toccoa Falls, Stephens County, GA held by Toccoa Falls College.
Nat'l Network: USA
Format: Adult Contemp, Religious *Target Audience:* General; families
David Cornelius, General Manager

***WTXR**
09-01-1996; 89.7 mhz FM *Hrs Open:* 24; 0.4 kw; 138 ft.; N34 35 57 W83 21 55
Mailing Address: Falls Road, Toccoa Falls, GA 30598 US
Second Address: 292 Old Clarkesville Hwy., Toccoa, GA 30577
(706) 282-6030, *Fax:* (706) 282-6090
www.wtxr.com
radio@tfc.edu
License: Toccoa Falls, Stephens County, GA held by Toccoa Falls College.
Arbitron Metro Market: Toccoa Falls, GA *Format:* Christian *Target Audience:* 18-35; college students, young adults
David Cornelius, General Manager
Craig Salmon, Station Manager
Jennifer Doll, Programming Director
Kyle Atkins, Administrative Assistant
Allyn Griffith, Social Media Director

Toomsboro

***WZZG**
01-01-2009; 91.9 mhz FM; 2.3 kw; 479 ft.; N33 4 37.78 W83 8 48.25
US
(800) 926-4669, *Fax:* (706) 309-9669
www.gnnradio.org
License: Toomsboro, Wilkinson County, GA held by Augusta Radio Fellowship Institute Inc.
Arbitron Metro Market: Toomsboro, GA
C.T. Barinowski, President

Trenton

WBDX
01-01-1989; 102.7 mhz FM *Hrs Open:* 24; 0.32 kw; 1375 ft.; N34 51 48 W85 23 35
2288 Gumbarrel Road, Ste. 111, Chattanooga, TN 37421 US
(254) 772-1900
www.kbderadio.net
License: Trenton, Dade County, GA held by Partners for Christian Media Inc.
Arbitron Metro Market: Eagle Pass TX *Format:* Christian
Marvin Sanders, General Manager

WKWN
04-04-1982; 1420 khz AM *Hrs Open:* 24; 2.5 kw-D, ND2; 0.112 kw-N, ND2; N34 51 43 W85 29 59
Mailing Address: 11980 South Maine, Trenton, GA 30752 US
Second Address: 12544 N. Main St., Trenton, GA 30752
(706) 657-7594, *Fax:* (706) 657-6767
www.discoverdade.com
License: Trenton, GA held by Dade County Broadcasting Inc.
Regional Network: Ga. News Net.
Arbitron Metro Market: Chattanooga, TN *Format:* News, News/Talk, 86 *Target Audience:* 25-54; locals
Evan Stone, CEO

Trion

WATG
01-01-1997; 95.7 mhz FM *Hrs Open:* 24; 1.3 kw; 699 ft.; N34 28 10 W85 17 48
Mailing Address: 2 Mount Alto Road, Rome, GA 30165 US
Second Address: 10143 Commerce St., Summerville, GA 30747
(706) 857-2000, *Fax:* (706) 857-3652
www.theridge957.com/
oldies957@aol.com
License: Trion, Chattooga County, GA held by TTA Broadcasting Inc.
Nat'l Network: ABC *Nat'l Reps:* Rgnl Reps
Arbitron Metro Market: Summerville,MA *Format:* Oldies *Hrs. of News Programming:* News progmg one hr wkly *Target Audience:* 25-54; general
Jim Bojo, CFO
Randy Davis, President

WZQZ
04-01-1985; 1180 khz AM *Hrs Open:* 6am-10pm; 5 kw-D, NDD; N34 28 22 W85 19 31
Mailing Address: 3213 Huxley Dr., Augusta, GA 30909 US
Second Address: 4689 US Hwy. 27, Summerville, GA 30747
(706) 857-5555, *Fax:* (706) 857-2006
wzqz@alltel.net
License: Trion, GA held by HS Productions Inc.
Nat'l Network: USA; CNN Radio *Regional Network:* Ga. News Net.
Format: Talk *Target Audience:* All ages; Northwest Georgia
Lebron Jimmy Charles Holbrook Jr., President
Terry Adams, General Manager

Tybee Island

WZAT
10-19-1971; 102.1 mhz FM *Hrs Open:* 24; 98 kw; 1328 ft.; N32 3 29 W81 20 19
330 East Kilbourn Avenue, Suite 250, Milwaukee, WI 53202 US
(912) 961-9000, *Fax:* (912) 961-7070
www.z102.net
brian.rickman@z102.net
License: Tybee Island, Chatham County, GA held by Cumulus Licensing Corp.
Group Owner: Cumulus Media Inc.; (acq 7-29-98; $3.5 million)
Arbitron Metro Market: Savannah, GA *Format:* Contemporary Hits/Top 40, Variety/Diverse
Lewis Dickey Jr., CEO
Sam Nelson, Operations Dir
Dale Powers, General Manager
Robert Combs, Engineering Dir
Martin Gausvik, CFO

Unadilla

WNNG-FM
06-01-1995; 99.9 mhz FM *Hrs Open:* 24; 6 kw; 328 ft.; N32 18 29 W83 46 30
PO Box 2127, Warner Robins, GA 31099 US
(478) 923-3416
www.espn999.com
news@wrwr.com
License: Unadilla, Dooly County, GA held by Georgia Eagle Broadcasting Inc
Group Owner: Georgia Eagle Broadcasting Inc.; (acq 10-8-2007; $350,000)
Arbitron Metro Market: Unadilla, GA *Format:* Adult Contemp
Cecil Staton, President
Karrie Sudbrack, General Manager
Tom Edwards, General Sales Mgr
Bobby Dayer, Programming Director
Rodney Edmondson, Programming

Valdosta

WAAC
01-01-1968; 92.9 mhz FM; 100 kw; 502 ft.; N30 48 13 W83 21 20
Mailing Address: Highway 84 West, Valdosta, GA 31601 US
Second Address: 2973 Hwy. 84 W., Valdosta, GA 31601
(229) 242-4513, *Fax:* (229) 247-7676
www.waacradio.com
mail@waacradio.com
License: Valdosta, Lowndes County, GA
Group Owner: Dee Rivers Radio Group
Nat'l Network: ABC
Arbitron Metro Market: Valdosta, GA *Format:* Country *Target Audience:* 25-54. *Adv. Rates:* 53; 45; 53; 37
Robert Whitt, Operations Dir

***WAFT**
11-25-1971; 101.1 mhz FM *Hrs Open:* 24; 100 kw; 558 ft; N30 51 50 W83 23 39
215 Waft Hill Ln., Valdosta, GA 31603
(229) 244-5180, *Fax:* (229) 242-8808
www.waft.org
mail@waft.org
License: Valdosta, Lowndes County, GA held by Christian Radio Fellowship Inc.
Population Served: 56,019 *Arbitron Metro Market:* Valdosta, GA *Hrs. of News Programming:* News progmg 3 hrs wkly *Target Audience:* 40+ empty nesters
Bill Tidwell, GM

WRFV
11-03-1951; 910 khz AM; 5 kw-D, DAN; 5 kw-N, DAN; N30 52 21 W83 20 36
C/O Douglas Perreault, PO Box 7140, Sun City, FL 33586 US
(407) 291-1395
License: Valdosta, GA held by Rama Communications Inc.
Group Owner: Rama Communications Inc.; (acq 2-28-2002; $255,000)
Arbitron Metro Market: Valdosta, GA
Sabeta Persaud, President

WGOV
01-01-1939; 950 khz AM *Hrs Open:* 24; 3.5 kw-D, ND2; 0.063 kw-N, ND2; N30 48 13 W83 21 20
Mailing Address: Highway 84 West, Valdosta, GA 31601 US
Second Address: 2973 Hwy. 84 W., Valdosta, GA 31601
(229) 244-9590, *Fax:* (229) 247-7676
www.wgovradio.com
wgovradio@bellsouth.net
License: Valdosta, GA held by WGOV Inc.
Group Owner: Dee Rivers Radio Group
Nat'l Reps: Rgnl Reps
Arbitron Metro Market: Valdosta, GA *Format:* Blues, Religious *Special Programming:* Gospel 14 hrs, oldies 10 hrs wkly *Hrs. of News Programming:* news progmg 3 hrs wkly *No. News Employees:* 1 *Target Audience:* 18-45; Black *Adv. Rates:* 28; 24; 28; 17
Lamar Freeman, Operations Dir
Loretta Grecco, General Sales Mgr
Jammie Brooks, Music Director

WQPW
09-01-1977; 95.7 mhz FM *Hrs Open:* 24; 32 kw; 607 ft.; N30 42 7 W83 6 54

P.O. Box 1327, Valdosta, GA 31603 US
(229) 244-8642, *Fax:* (229) 242-7620
www.957themix.com
info@957themix.com
License: Valdosta, Lowndes County, GA held by RTG Radio LLC.
Group Owner: Black Crow Media Group LLC; (acq 11-9-2001; grpsl).
Arbitron Metro Market: Valdosta, GA *Format:* Adult Contemp *No. News Employees:* 14 *Target Audience:* 18-44.
Scott James, General Manager

WVLD
09-03-1959; 1450 khz AM *Hrs Open:* 24
P.O. Box 1327, Valdosta, GA 31603 US
(229) 244-8642, *Fax:* (229) 242-7620
License: Valdosta, GA held by RTG Media.
Group Owner: Black Crow Media Group LLC; (acq 11-9-2001; grpsl).
Nat'l Network: CBS
Arbitron Metro Market: Valdosta, GA *Format:* Sports, Talk
Special Programming: Gospel 2 hrs wkly *Hrs. of News Programming:* News progmg 10 hrs wkly *Target Audience:* 35 plus.
Robert Ganzack, President

***WVVS-FM**
07-26-1971; 90.9 mhz FM; 5.3 kw horiz; 69 ft.; N30 50 50 W83 17 26
Vsu Box 142, Valdosta, GA 31698 US
(229) 259-2015
www.valdosta.edu/wvvs/
License: Valdosta, Lowndes County, GA held by Valdosta State University.
Arbitron Metro Market: Valdosta, GA *Format:* Alternative *Target Audience:* 18-25; students of VSU, population at large
Michael Taylor, General Manager
Daniel Oakes, Station Manager
Brian Auten, Promotions Manager

***WWET**
12-01-1989; 91.7 mhz FM *Hrs Open:* 24; 0 kw horiz, 0.43 kw vert; 85 ft.; N30 49 35 W83 16 40 *Rebroadcasts:* Rebroadcasts WJSP-FM Warm Springs 100%
260 - 14th Street, N.W., Atlanta, GA 30318 US
(404) 685-2690, *Fax:* (404) 685-2684
www.gpb.org
ask@gpb.org
License: Valdosta, Lowndes County, GA held by Georgia Public Telecommunications Commission.
Nat'l Network: NPR; PRI *Wire Services:* AP
Arbitron Metro Market: Valdosta, GA *Format:* News *Special Programming:* Jazz 16 hrs *Hrs. of News Programming:* news progmg 40 hrs wkly *No. News Employees:* 10 *Target Audience:* Adults: 35 plus.
Nancy Hall, CEO
Tom Barclay, Operations Dir
Bob Houghton, General Manager
Rob Maynard, Programming Director
Nancy Zintak, Promotions Manager
Susanna Capelouto, News Director
Bonnie Bean, CFO
Steve Carey, Vice President ofProduction

WWRQ-FM
02-01-1992; 107.9 mhz FM; 50 kw; 269 ft.; N31 3 21 W83 13 54
1707 a Al Brooks Dr., Valdosta, GA 31601 US
(229) 244-8642, *Fax:* (229) 247-7620
www.valdostatoday.com/Rock108.html
cjohnson@blackcrowfm.com
License: Valdosta, Lowndes County, GA held by RTG Radio LLC.
Group Owner: Black Crow Media Group LLC; (acq 11-9-2001; grpsl).
Arbitron Metro Market: Valdosta, GA *Format:* Classic Rock, Rock/AOR *Target Audience:* 25-49; upscale suburban couples
Kim Pelkowski, General Manager
Lee Mayhew Smothers, Account Executive
Jennifer Johnson, Account Executive
Lynn Loftus, Account Executive

WGOV-FM
06-01-1985; 96.7 mhz FM *Hrs Open:* 24; 50 kw; Ant 328 ft; N30 48 13 W83 21 20
Mailing Address: Box 1207, Valdosta, GA 31601
Second Address: 2973 Hwy. 84 W., Valdosta, GA 31601
(229) 242-4513, *Fax:* (229) 247-7676
www.wgovradio.com
info@govradio.com
License: Valdosta, Lowndes County, GA held by W.G.O.V. Inc.
Group Owner: Dee Rivers Radio Group; (acq 4-19-2006; $2 million).

Arbitron Metro Market: Valdosta, GA *Target Audience:* 18-49.
Joseph Jones, Operations Dir
Lamar Freeman, General Manager
Loretta Grecco, General Sales Mgr

***WVDA**
01-01-2006; 88.5 mhz FM; 18.5 kw vert; 217 ft.; N30 47 50 W83 1 1 *Rebroadcasts:* Rebroadcasts KLRD(FM) Yucaipa, CA 100% US
(888) 937-2471, *Fax:* (916) 251-1650
www.air1.com
info@air1.com
License: Valdosta, Lowndes County, GA held by Educational Media Foundation.
Group Owner: EMF Broadcasting; (acq 5-10-2007; $350,000)
Nat'l Network: Air 1
Arbitron Metro Market: Valdosta, GA *Format:* Alternative, Christian
Darrell Chambliss, Chairman
Alan Mason, COO
Mike Novak, President and CEO
Ed Lenane, News Director
Sam Wallington, Engineering Dir
Dan Antonelli, Chief Business Development Officer
Eric Moser, Chief Financial Officer
BrianBurger, Vice President of Human Resources
D. Kevin Blair, Secretary and General Counsel
Larry Moody, Director
Mitch Barnhart, Director

WJEM
08-01-1955; 1150 khz AM; 5 kw-D, DA2; 0.101 kw-N, DA2; N30 50 49 W83 14 14
PO Box 5883, Valdosta, GA 31635 US
(229) 241-9797
www.thejock1150.com
License: Valdosta, GA held by WJEM Inc.
Arbitron Metro Market: Valdosta, GA *Format:* Sports, Talk
John Staub, President
Joanna Staub, Operations Dir
Louis Scally, Programming Director
Tom Bradley, News Director
Jackie Hall, Traffic Manager

Vidalia

***WGPH**
01-01-1988; 91.5 mhz FM *Hrs Open:* 24; 31 kw; 604 ft.; N32 13 58 W82 28 51
3213 Huxley Drive, Augusta, GA 30909 US
(706) 309-9610
www.gnnradio.org
ctbarinowski@comcast.net
License: Vidalia, Toombs County, GA held by Augusta Radio Fellowship Institute Inc.
Group Owner: Good News Network
Format: Christian *Hrs. of News Programming:* News progmg 12 hrs wkly *Target Audience:* General.
Clarence Barinowski, General Manager

WTCQ
03-05-1969; 97.7 mhz FM; 4.3 kw; 387 ft.; N32 13 12 W82 26 7
Mailing Address: Po.Box 900, Vidalia, GA 30474 US
Second Address: 1501 Mt. Vernon Rd., Vidalia, GA 30474
(912) 537-9202, *Fax:* (912) 537-4477
www.southeastgeorgiatoday.com
License: Vidalia, Toombs County, GA
Nat'l Reps: Rgnl Reps
Arbitron Metro Market: Vidalia, GA *Format:* Adult Contemp
Target Audience: 18-34.
Zack Fowler, Station Manager
John Koon, General Sales Mgr
Joyce Foskey, Account Executive and Office Manager
Helen Harris, IT Manager and Web Design

WVOP
12-02-1946; 970 khz AM *Hrs Open:* 24
Mailing Address: P.O. Box 900 Hwy 280 W., Vidalia, GA 30474 US
Second Address: 1501 Mt. Vernon Rd., Vidalia, GA 30474
(912) 537-9202, *Fax:* (912) 537-4477
www.southeastgeorgiatoday.com
License: Vidalia, GA held by Vidalia Communications Corp.
Group Owner: Vidalia Communications Corp.
Regional Network: Ga. News Net. *Nat'l Reps:* Rgnl Reps
Arbitron Metro Market: Vidalia, GA *Format:* News, Oldies, 84
Special Programming: Pub affrs 2 hrs, relg 8 hrs wkly *Hrs. of News Programming:* news progmg 18 hrs wkly *No. News Employees:* 1 *Target Audience:* 25-54.
John Ladson, President
Jim Perry, Operations Dir
Zack Fowler, Station Manager
Marvin McIntyre, General Sales Mgr
Zack Fowler, Programming Director
Joyce Foskey, News Director
Dick Boekeloo, Chief Engineer
John Koon, SalesManager
Jeff Raiford, Account Executive
Helen Harris, Traffic, IT Manager
Warren Sowell, Financial Editor for Vidalia Communications

Vienna

WKTF
11-17-1979; 1550 khz AM *Hrs Open:* 24
404 N. 6th Street, Vienna, GA 31092 US
(229) 268-1550
License: Vienna, GA held by LEN Radio Broadcasting of Vienna, Georgia LLC.
Arbitron Metro Market: Vienna, GA *Format:* Christian, Contemporary Hits/Top 40
Thomas McCoy, General Manager

***WHHR**
92.1 mhz FM; 5.1 kw; 348 ft.; N32 9 16 W83 47 55 US
(208) 733-3551, *Fax:* (208) 734-0674
www.edgewaterbroadcasting.com
License: Vienna, Dooly County, GA held by Radio Assist Ministry Inc.
Arbitron Metro Market: Vienna, GA
Clark Parrish, President
Jim Long, General Manager
Robert L. Jackson, Programming Director
Steve Atkin, Executive Director
Clark Parrish, Technical Director
Ben Mccarron, Chief Operating Engineer
Diana Atkin, Vice President
Earl Williamson, Secretary / Treasurer

Wadley

***WZAE**
93.3 mhz FM; 4 kw; 144 ft.; N32 50 55 W82 24 10 US
(863) 644-3464, *Fax:* (863) 646-5326
License: Wadley, Jefferson County, GA held by Radio Training Network Inc.
Arbitron Metro Market: Wadley, GA
James Campbell, President

Warm Springs

***WJSP-FM**
02-03-1985; 88.1 mhz FM *Hrs Open:* 24; 42 kw; 1368 ft.; N32 51 8 W84 42 4
260 - 14th Street, N.W., Atlanta, GA 30318 US
(404) 685-2690, *Fax:* (404) 685-2684
www.gpb.org
ask@gpb.org
License: Warm Springs, Meriwether County, GA held by Georgia Public Telecommunications Commission.
Nat'l Network: NPR; PRI *Wire Services:* AP
Arbitron Metro Market: Columbus, GA *Format:* News, Talk
Special Programming: Jazz 18 hrs wkly *Hrs. of News Programming:* news progmg 40 hrs wkly *No. News Employees:* 10 *Target Audience:* 35-54; NPR-demo
Nancy Hall, CEO
Tom Barclay, Operations Dir
Bob Houghton, General Manager
Rob Maynard, Programming Director
Nancy Zintak, Promotions Manager
Susanna Capelouto, News Director
Bonnie Bean, CFO

Warner Robins

WRWR
10-13-1954; 1350 khz AM *Hrs Open:* 24; 15 kw-D, 500 w-N, DA-N; N32 37 00 W83 39 00
1350 Radio Loop, Warner Robins, GA 31099
(478) 923-3416, *Fax:* (478) 923-3236
www.wnngthepatriot.com
License: Warner Robins, Houston County, GA held by Georgia Eagle Broadcasting Inc.
Group Owner: Georgia Eagle Broadcasting Inc.; (acq 1-3-2007; $650,000)
Nat'l Network: Fox News Radio; Westwood One; Talk Radio Network; Salem Radio Network *Regional Network:* Ga. News Net.
Population Served: 200,000 *Arbitron Metro Market:* Macon, GA *Hrs. of News Programming:* 12 *No. News Employees:* 2 *Target Audience:* 35-74; middle to upper class, working class, miltary, retired, business owners*Adv. Rates:* 18; 12; 18; 12

Cecil Staton, President
Jeff Scott, Programming Director

***WZCH**
09-01-1994; 102.5 mhz FM *Hrs Open:* 24; 4 kw; 328 ft.; N32 34 20 W83 40 13
750 West Sandtown Road, S.W., Marietta, GA 30064 US
(478) 781-1063, *Fax:* (478) 781-6711
www.peach965.com
ccw@clearchannel.com
License: Warner Robins, Houston County, GA held by Aloha Station Trust LLC, as Trustee
Arbitron Metro Market: Macon, GA *Format:* Contemporary Hits/Top 40, Adult Contemp *Target Audience:* 25-64.
John Lund, Operations Dir
Bill Clark, General Manager

WRBV
08-01-1969; 101.7 mhz FM *Hrs Open:* 24; 4.9 kw; 354 ft.; N32 38 19 W83 38 33
750 West Sandtown Road, S.W., Marietta, GA 30064 US
(478) 781-1063, *Fax:* (478) 781-6711
www.1017.com
info@1017.com
License: Warner Robins, Houston County, GA held by AMFM Radio Licenses LLC.
Group Owner: Clear Channel Communications Inc.; (acq 2-1-2001; grpsl).
Nat'l Network: ABC
Arbitron Metro Market: Macon, GA *Format:* Blues *Hrs. of News Programming:* News progmg one hr wkly *Target Audience:* 21-54.
Bill Clark, General Manager

Warrenton

WCHZ-FM
01-01-1998; 93.1 mhz FM; 4.1 kw; Ant 400 ft; N33 29 59 W82 37 09 *Rebroadcasts:* Simulcast with WGAC(AM) Augusta
4051 Jimmie Dyess Pkwy., Augusta, GA 30909
(706) 396-7000, *Fax:* (706) 396-7092
www.wgac.com
wgac@wgac.com
License: Warrenton, Warren County, GA held by WCHZ License LLC.
Group Owner: Beasley Broadcast Group Inc.; (acq 5-3-2000; $800,000 with WGUS(AM) Augusta).
Arbitron Metro Market: Augusta, GA *No. News Employees:* 5
Kent Dunn, General Manager
Kent Murphy, General Sales Mgr
Harley Drew, Programming Director

Washington

WLOV
09-01-1955; 1370 khz AM
Mailing Address: 330 Kilbourn Ave., Suite 250, Milwaukee, WI 53202 US
Second Address: 312 Old First National Bank Bldg., Elberton, GA 30635
(706) 678-0100, *Fax:* (706) 678-3394
www.wlovradio.com
License: Washington, GA held by Southern Stone Broadcasting Inc.
Group Owner: Southern Broadcasting Companies Inc.
Regional Network: Ga. News Net.
Format: Classic Rock
Leisa McCurley, News Director

Watkinsville

WPUP
06-01-1970; 100.1 mhz FM *Hrs Open:* 24; 4.3 kw; 289 ft.; N33 56 28 W83 23 55
330 Kilbourn Ave., Suite 250, Milwaukee, WI 53202 US
(706) 549-6222, *Fax:* (706) 546-0441
www.powerathens.com
tod.tucker@coxinc.com
License: Watkinsville, Oconee County, GA held by Cox Radio Inc.
Group Owner: Cox Radio Inc.; (acq 8-1-2008; grpsl)
Arbitron Metro Market: Watkinsville, GA *Format:* Classic Rock
Scott Smith, VP/General Manager
Eric Lauer, General Sales Mgr
Tod Tucker, Programming Director
David Ratz, Promotions Manager
Evan Delaney, Music Director
Mel Stovall, PSA Director

Waverly Hall

WIOL-FM
07-04-1994; 95.7 mhz FM *Hrs Open:* 24; 6 kw; Ant 876 ft; N32 50 48 W84 41 27
Box 1998, Columbus, GA 31902
(706) 576-3565, *Fax:* (706) 576-3683
info@dbicolumbus.com
License: Waverly Hall, Meriwether County, GA held by Davis Broadcasting of Columbus Inc.
Group Owner: Davis Broadcasting Inc.; (acq 11-4-97; $450,000).
Nat'l Network: CBS
Population Served: 250,000 *Arbitron Metro Market:* Columbus, GA *Hrs. of News Programming:* news progmg 6 hrs wkly *No. News Employees:* 2 *Target Audience:* 18-49; females 18-35 specifically
Gregory Davis, CEO

Waycross

***WASW**
06-01-1998; 91.9 mhz FM; 18 kw; 289 ft.; N31 16 13 W82 39 19
P.O Drawer 2440, Tupelo, MS 38803 US
(662) 844-8888, *Fax:* (662) 842-6791
www.afr.net
faq@afr.net
License: Waycross, Ware County, GA held by American Family Radio.
Group Owner: American Family Radio
Arbitron Metro Market: Waycross, GA *Format:* Christian, Religious
Marvin Sanders, General Manager
Lauren Brigman, Station Manager
Rick Robertson, Programming Director
Alex Gulledge, Promotions Manager

WYNR
10-10-1971; 102.5 mhz FM *Hrs Open:* 24; 97 kw; 994 ft.; N31 9 22 W81 58 19
Two Bala Plaza, Suite 801, Bala-Cynwyd, PA 19004 US
(912) 267-1025, *Fax:* (912) 264-5462
www.1025wynr.net
joeportagee@hotmail.com
License: Waycross, Ware County, GA held by Qantum of Brunswick License Co. LLC.
Group Owner: Qantum Communications Corp.; (acq 7-2-03; grpsl).
Nat'l Reps: McGavren Guild
Arbitron Metro Market: Brunswick, GA *Format:* Country *Hrs. of News Programming:* news progmg one hr wkly *No. News Employees:* 1 *Target Audience:* 25-54.
Mike Mangen, CFO
Frank Osborne, President
Scott Ryfun, Operations Dir
Jonathan Havens, General Manager
Joe Sousa, Station Manager
Gerri Landrum, Director of Sales
Christy Alan, Programming Director
Jonathan Brewster, ExecutiveVice President
Larry Landrum, Director of Sales

WQGA
06-03-1972; 103.3 mhz FM; 100 kw; 1,100 ft; N31 15 42 W82 19 26
3833 US Hwy. 82, Brunswick, GA 19004
(912) 267-1025, *Fax:* (912) 264-5462
www.sunny103.net
ryfun@adelphia.net
License: Waycross, Ware County, GA held by Qantum of Brunswick License Co. LLC.
Group Owner: Qantum Communications Corp.; (acq 7-2-03; grpsl).
Nat'l Reps: McGavren Guild
Population Served: 250,000 *Arbitron Metro Market:* Brunswick, GA *Special Programming:* Jazz 5 hrs wkly *Target Audience:* 25-54. *Adv. Rates:* 24; 20; 22; 12
Scott Ryfun, Operations Dir
Jonathan Havens, General Manager

WWUF
01-25-1986; 97.7 mhz FM *Hrs Open:* 24; 6 kw; 325 ft.; N31 11 5 W82 15 24
Mailing Address: 1350 Paces Forest Dr. NW, Atlanta, GA 30327 US
Second Address: 2132 Hwy. 84, Blackshear, GA 31516
(912) 449-3391, *Fax:* (912) 449-6284
www.waycrossradio.com/977/
wkub@almatel.net
License: Waycross, Ware County, GA held by Mattox Broadcasting Inc.
Nat'l Network: ABC *Regional Network:* Ga. News Net. *Nat'l Reps:* Dora-Clayton
Arbitron Metro Market: Waycross, GA *Format:* Contemporary Hits/Top 40, Adult Contemp *Target Audience:* 25-54; general
Troy Mattox, President
Ray Williamson, Operations Dir
Jim Miller, General Sales Mgr

***WXVS**
12-01-1985; 90.1 mhz FM *Hrs Open:* 24; 79 kw horiz, 77.6 kw vert; 919 ft.; N31 13 17 W82 34 24 *Rebroadcasts:* WJSP, Warm Springs/Columbus, GA, 100%
260 - 14th Street, N.W., Atlanta, GA 30318 US
(404) 685-2690, *Fax:* (404) 685-2684
www.gpb.org
ask@gpb.org
License: Waycross, Ware County, GA held by Georgia Public Telecommunications Commission.
Nat'l Network: NPR; PRI *Wire Services:* AP
Arbitron Metro Market: Waycross, GA *Format:* Classical, News *Special Programming:* Jazz 16 hrs *Hrs. of News Programming:* news progmg 40 hrs wkly *No. News Employees:* 10
Nancy Hall, CEO
Teya Ryan, President
Tom Barclay, Operations Dir
Bob Houghton, General Manager
Rob Maynard, Programming Director
Nancy Zintak, Promotions Manager
Susanna Capelouto, News Director
Bonnie Bean, CFO

WWGA(AM)
01-01-2004; 1230 khz AM *Hrs Open:* 24; 1 kw-U; N31 12 45 W82 22 20
1766 Memorial Dr., Suite 1, Waycross, GA 31501
(912) 285-5002, *Fax:* (912) 264-1991
www.gradickcommunications.com
License: Waycross, Ware County, GA held by MarMac Communications L.L.C.
Group Owner: MarMac Communications LLC
Format: News, News/Talk, 86
Gary Marmitt, General Manager
Dick Eoekeloo, Chief Engineer

Waynesboro

***WYFA**
08-01-1991; 107.1 mhz FM *Hrs Open:* 24; 25 kw; 295 ft.; N33 10 42 W81 59 24
Mailing Address: 8030 Arrowridge Blvd, Charlotte, NC 28273 US
Second Address: Bible Broadcasting Network, 11530 Carmel Commons Blvd., Charlotte, GA 28226
(704) 523-5555, *Fax:* (704) 522-1967
www.bbnradio.org
License: Waynesboro, Burke County, GA held by Bible Broadcasting Network Inc.
Group Owner: Bible Broadcasting Network; acq 8-26-92; $225,000;
Arbitron Metro Market: Waynesboro, GA *Format:* Religious
Scott Curtis, Operations Dir

West Point

WCJM-FM
07-18-1966; 100.9 mhz FM; 5.8 kw; 328 ft.; N32 51 7 W85 8 14
139 Executive Circle, Suite 203, Daytona Beach, FL 32114 US
(706) 645-2991, *Fax:* (706) 645-3364
www.wcjmthebull.com
wjcm@qantumofauburn.com
License: West Point, Troup County, GA held by Qantum of Auburn License Co. LLC.
Group Owner: Qantum Communications Corp.; (acq 7-2-03; grpsl).
Regional Network: Ga. News Net.
Arbitron Metro Market: West Point, GA *Format:* Country
Steve Wheeler, General Manager
Anthony Lovelady, Programming Director

WRLA
05-01-1944; 1490 khz AM *Hrs Open:* 24; 1 kw-U, ND1; N32 52 26 W85 11 32
602 N. Cherry Drive, Lanett, AL 36863 US
(706) 645-1490, *Fax:* (706) 645-1497
wrla@wrla1490.com
License: West Point, GA held by Tiger Communications Inc.
Group Owner: Tiger Communications Inc.; (acq 10-19-2006; $279,000 with WTRP(AM) La Grange)
Regional Network: Ga. News Net.
Arbitron Metro Market: West Point, GA *Format:* Oldies *Hrs. of News Programming:* news progmg 9 hrs wkly *No. News Employees:* 1 *Target Audience:* 18-55.
Vince Smith, General Manager

WPLV
08-01-1958; 1310 khz AM *Hrs Open:* 24
7050 Greenbower Lane, College Park, GA 30349 US
(706) 645-1310, *Fax:* (706) 645-3364
wcjm@quantumofauburn.com
License: West Point, GA held by Qantum of Auburn License Co. LLC.
Group Owner: Qantum Communications Corp.; (acq 7-2-03; grpsl).
Format: Talk
Steve Wheeler, General Manager
Terry Harper, Chief Engineer

Willacoochee

WKAA
04-07-1978; 99.5 mhz FM *Hrs Open:* 24; 73 kw; 754 ft.; N31 10 18 W83 21 57
620 East Ward Street, Douglas, GA 31533 US
(229) 244-8642, *Fax:* (229) 242-7620
www.valdostatoday.com
kpelkowski@blackcrow.fm
License: Willacoochee, Atkinson County, GA held by RTG Radio LLC.
Group Owner: Black Crow Media Group LLC; (acq 11-9-2001; grpsl).
Arbitron Metro Market: Valdosta, GA *Format:* Country *Hrs. of News Programming:* news progmg 10 hrs wkly *No. News Employees:* 1 *Target Audience:* 25-54.
Robert Ganzak, President
Kim Pelkowski, Director of Sales

Winder

WIMO
11-04-1952; 1300 khz AM
P.O. Box 1540, Winder, GA 30680 US
(770) 867-1300, *Fax:* (770) 868-1962
www.wimo1300am.com
quincos@aol.com
License: Winder, GA held by Mark Myers
Nat'l Network: Salem Radio Network; Radio America; Fox News Radio *Regional Network:* Ga. News Net.
Arbitron Metro Market: Atlanta, GA *Format:* Gospel, Talk *Target Audience:* General.
Jon Graham, Operations Dir
John Boyd, General Manager
Kurt Andrews, Programming Director

***WYFW**
12-01-1987; 89.5 mhz FM *Hrs Open:* 24; 6 kw; 200 ft.; N33 59 29 W83 45 46
8030 Arrowridge Blvd, Charlotte, NC 28273 US
(704) 523-5555, *Fax:* (704) 522-1967
www.bbnradio.org
bbn@bbnradio.org
License: Winder, Barrow County, GA held by Bible Broadcasting Network Inc.
Group Owner: Bible Broadcasting Network; acq 6-24-93; $104,000;
Arbitron Metro Market: Winder, GA *Format:* Adult Contemp, Religious *Hrs. of News Programming:* News progmg 7 hrs wkly *Target Audience:* 35-44.
Lowell Davey, President
Paul Montgomery, General Manager

Woodbine

WCGA
06-15-1987; 1100 khz AM
Route 9, Box 280e, St. Simons Island, GA 31522 US
(912) 634-1100
wescox@adelphia.net
License: Woodbine, GA held by Cox Broadcast Group Inc.
Arbitron Metro Market: St. Simons Island,GA *Format:* News, News/Talk, 86 *Hrs. of News Programming:* news progmg 2 hrs wkly *No. News Employees:* 2 *Target Audience:* Adults; 35-64
Adv. Rates: 25; 22; 23; 15.
Wesley Cox, General Manager

Woodbury

WFDR-FM
01-01-2007; 94.5 mhz FM; 2.75 kw; 492 ft.; N32 50 40 W84 37 25
US
(770) 487-4500, *Fax:* (706) 846-3494
www.georgia.thejoyfm.com
License: Woodbury, Meriwether County, GA held by Ploener Radio Group LLC.
Arbitron Metro Market: Manchester, GA *Format:* Christian
Rick Davison, General Manager
Roxanne Davison, Office Manager

Wrens

WTHB-FM
06-10-1979; 96.9 mhz FM; 6.2 kw; 397 ft.; N33 15 32.2 W82 19 10.1
Mailing Address: P O Box 1584, Augusta, GA 30903 US
Second Address: Box 1584, Augusta, GA 30903
(803) 279-2330, *Fax:* (803) 279-8149
www.praise969.com
vperry@perrybroadcasting.net
License: Wrens, Jefferson County, GA held by Perry Broadcasting of Augusta Inc.
Group Owner: Perry Publishing & Broadcasting Co.; (acq 12-12-2007; grpsl)
Arbitron Metro Market: Augusta, GA *Format:* Gospel *Target Audience:* Teen-49.
Dennis Jackson, General Manager
Velvet Perry, VP Director of Sales
Walter Brumbeloe, Chief Engineer

Wrightsville

WDBN
05-27-1986; 107.9 mhz FM *Hrs Open:* 24; 25 kw; 328 ft.; N32 37 5 W82 46 5
P.O. Box 2639, Gulfport, MS 39505 US
(478) 272-4422, *Fax:* (478) 275-4657
www.1079thebuzz.com
kris.bjorkman@statebroadcasting.com
License: Wrightsville, Johnson County, GA held by State Broadcasting Corp.
Regional Reps: Regional Reps
Arbitron Metro Market: Macon, GA *Target Audience:* 12 plus.
J. Morgan Dowdy, President
Kris Bjorkman, General Manager

Young Harris

WACF
01-01-2007; 95.1 mhz FM; 0.2 kw; 1585 ft.; N34 56 26 W83 55 8 US
(706) 379-9770, *Fax:* (706) 379-4104
License: Young Harris, Towns County, GA held by Wolf Creek Broadcasting Inc.
Group Owner: Wolf Creek Broadcasting Inc.
Arbitron Metro Market: Young Harris, GA
A.D. Frazier, President
Rebecca St. John, General Manager

Zebulon

WEKS
02-01-1994; 92.5 mhz FM *Hrs Open:* 24; 12 kw; 476 ft.; N33 8 20 W84 31 31
4 Plum Lane, Newnan, GA 30263 US
(770) 412-8700, *Fax:* (770) 412-8080
www.925fmthebear.com
bear925@bellsouth.net
License: Zebulon, Pike County, GA held by Spalding Broadcasting Inc.
Arbitron Metro Market: Griffin, GA *Format:* Country *No. News Employees:* 1 *Target Audience:* 25-54.
Stephen Tarkenton, CEO
Les Reed, General Manager

Guam

Agana

***KPRG**
01-27-1994; 89.3 mhz FM *Hrs Open:* 24; 9.2 kw; 531 ft.; N13 29 17 E144 49 53
303 University Drive, Uog Station, Mangilao, GU 96923 US
(671) 734-8930, *Fax:* (671) 734-2958
www.kprgfm.org
kprg@kprg.org,kprg@guam.net
License: Agana, GU held by Guam Educational Radio Foundation.
Nat'l Network: NPR
Arbitron Metro Market: Guam *Format:* Jazz, Talk
Denise Mendiola, General Manager
Olympia Terral, General Sales Mgr
Lydia Taleu, Programming Director

KSTO
09-01-1973; 95.5 mhz FM *Hrs Open:* 24; 25 kw; 583 ft.; N13 29 16.8 E144 49 53
P.O. Box 20249, Guam Main Facility, GU 96921 US
(671) 477-7108(671) 477-5786, *Fax:* (671) 477-6411
ksto@ite.net
License: Agana, GU held by Inter-Island Communications Inc.
Group Owner: Inter-Island Communications Inc.; acq 11-77).
Arbitron Metro Market: Hagatna, GU *Format:* Adult Contemp
Special Programming: Country 12 hrs, gospel 6 hrs wkly *Hrs. of News Programming:* news progmg 14 hrs wkly *No. News Employees:* 1 *Target Audience:* 25-54.
Frances Poppe, CFO
Edward Poppe Jr., President
Joe Tighe, Operations Dir
Rosalin Koss, Programming Director
Edward Poppe III, Executive Vice President

KTWG
08-01-1975; 801 khz AM *Hrs Open:* 24; 10 kw-U, ND1; N13 27 7 E144 42 32 *Rebroadcasts:* Simulcasts KCNM(AM) Saipan, Northern Mariana Islands
PO Box 8700, Cary, NC 27512 US
(671) 477-5894, *Fax:* (671) 477-6411
www.ktwg.com
am800guam@gmail.com
License: Agana, GU held by Edward H. Poppe Jr. and Frances W. Poppe.
Group Owner: Inter-Island Communications Inc.; (acq 2-20-2002).
Arbitron Metro Market: Hagta, GU *Format:* Religious *Hrs. of News Programming:* news progmg 5 hrs wkly *No. News Employees:* 1 *Target Audience:* 25-49; Christian
K. Leilani Dahilig, Station Manager
Richard Dahilig

KUAM
03-14-1954; 630 khz AM
600 Harmon Loop Road, #102, Dededo, GU 96912 US
(671) 637-5826, *Fax:* (671) 637-9865
www.kuam.com
License: Agana, GU held by Pacific Telestations Inc.
Nat'l Network: CBS
Arbitron Metro Market: Hagta, GU *Format:* Adult Contemp
Joey Calvo, General Manager

KISH
01-01-2003; 102.9 mhz FM *Hrs Open:* 24; 25 kw; 583 ft.; N13 29 16.8 E144 49 53
P O Box 20249, Guam Main Facility, Agana, Guam, GU 96921 US
(671) 477-9448, *Fax:* (671) 477-6411
License: Agana, GU held by Inter-Island Communications Inc.
Group Owner: Inter-Island Communications Inc.
Arbitron Metro Market: Hagta, GU *Format:* Ethnic *Hrs. of News Programming:* news progmg 15 hrs wkly *No. News Employees:* 1 *Target Audience:* General; indiginous residents of Marianas Islands
Frances Poppe, CFO
Edward Poppe Jr., President
Joe Tighe, Operations Dir
Rosalin Koss, Programming Director
Edward Poppe III, Executive Vice President

KVOG
1530 khz AM
US
(808) 521-4711, *Fax:* (808) 538-3269
License: Agana, GU held by Guam Power II Inc.
Arbitron Metro Market: Phoenix, AZ
Wagdy Guirguis, President

Agat

***KSDA-FM**
11-22-1990; 91.9 mhz FM *Hrs Open:* 24; 3.8 kw; 1001 ft.; N13 25 53 E144 42 36
12501 Old Columbia Pike, Silver Spring, MD 20904 US
(671) 472-5732, *Fax:* (671) 477-4678
mail@joy92.net
License: Agat, GU held by Good News Broadcasting Corp.
Arbitron Metro Market: Agana Heights, GU *Format:* Christian, Religious *Hrs. of News Programming:* News progmg 7 hrs wkly *Target Audience:* 25-54.
Robert Gibbons, Chairman
Brook Powers, President
Matthew Dodd, General Manager

Barrigada

***KHMG**
03-26-1996; 88.1 mhz FM *Hrs Open:* 24; 8 kw; 472 ft; N13 29 17 W144 49 53
Box 23189, 170C Machaute St., Barrigada, GU 96921

(671) 477-6341, *Fax:* (671) 477-7136
www.hbcguam.net
khmg@hbcguam.net
License: Barrigada, GU held by Harvest Christian Academy.
Population Served: 140,000*Special Programming:* Children 2 hrs wkly *Hrs. of News Programming:* News progmg 5 hrs wkly
Target Audience: General; Christian, church and school families
John Collier, Station Manager

Dededo

KGUM-FM
02-28-1999; 105.1 mhz FM; 12 kw; 502 ft.; N13 29 17 E144 49 30
P.O. Box Gm, Agana, GU 96932 US
(671) 477-5700, *Fax:* (671) 477-3982
www.105therock.com
License: Dededo, GU held by Sorensen Pacific Broadcasting Inc.
Group Owner: Sorensen Pacific Broadcasting Inc.; acq 6-23-03; grpsl).
Rex Sorensen, CEO
Jon Anderson, President
Albert Juan, Station Manager

Hagatna

KGUM
02-01-1975; 567 khz AM *Hrs Open:* 24; 10 kw-U, ND1; N13 23 21 E144 45 34
P.O. Box Gm, Agana, GU 96932 US
(671) 477-5700, *Fax:* (671) 477-3982
www.radiopacific.com
License: Hagatna, GU held by Sorensen Pacific Broadcasting Inc.
Group Owner: Sorensen Pacific Broadcasting Inc.; (acq 6-23-2003; grpsl)
Nat'l Network: CBS; Westwood One
Format: News, News/Talk, 86 *Special Programming:* Educ one hr, computer 3 hrs, police one hr, health *Hrs. of News Programming:* news progmg 20 hrs wkly *No. News Employees:* 5 *Target Audience:* 35 plus; adultswith high income & education
Adv. Rates: 79; 45; 69; 45
Ray Gibson, Operations Dir
Rex Sorensen, General Manager

KOKU
04-28-1984; 100.3 mhz FM *Hrs Open:* 24; 50 kw horiz, 49.7 kw vert; 541 ft.; N13 29 17 E144 49 35
530 West O'Brien Drive, Agana, GU 96910 US
, *Fax:* (671) 477-5658
www.hitradio100.com
marketing@hitradio.com
License: Hagatna, GU held by Moy Communications Inc.
Format: Contemporary Hits/Top 40 *Target Audience:* 18-34; females *Adv. Rates:* 96; 72; 83; 64
Kurt Moylan, President
Vince R. Limuaco, General Sales Mgr
Rick Nauta, Programming Director

KUAM-FM
09-01-1966; 93.9 mhz FM; 2 kw; 950 ft; N13 25 53 E144 42 36
600 Harmon Loop Rd., Suite 102, Dededo, GU 96912
(671) 637-0094, *Fax:* (671) 637-9865
www.kuam.com/i94
License: Hagatna, GU
Joey Calvo, General Manager
Eli Monge, General Sales Mgr
Chris Barnett, Programming Director

KZGZ
12-01-1986; 97.5 mhz FM *Hrs Open:* 24; 40 kw; 538 ft.; N13 29 17 E144 49 30
P. O. Box Gm, Agana, GU 96910 US
(671) 477-5700, *Fax:* (671) 477-3982
www.power98.com/
License: Hagatna, GU held by Sorensen Pacific Broadcasting Inc.
Group Owner: Sorensen Pacific Broadcasting Inc.
Arbitron Metro Market: Agana, GU *Format:* Urban Contemporary
Hrs. of News Programming: News progmg 15 hrs wkly *Target Audience:* 18-34; young affluent adults *Adv. Rates:* 79; 59; 69; 45
Kazie Perkins, Operations Dir
Gene Colliflower, News Director

Tamuning

KNUT
01-01-1999; 101.1 mhz FM; 8 kw; 193 meters; N13 29 15 E144 49 42
1868 Halsey Dr., Piti, GU 96921
(670) 234-7239, *Fax:* (671) 477-6411
www.kcnmkzmi.com
kcnm@ite.net
License: Tamuning, GU held by Inter-Island Communications Inc.
Group Owner: Inter-Island Communications Inc.
Population Served: 65,000*Hrs. of News Programming:* news progmg 16 hrs wkly *No. News Employees:* 1
Frances Poppe, CFO
Edward Poppe Jr., President
Edward Poppe, General Manager
Harry Blalock, Station Manager
Lewis Tenorio, Programming Director

Tumon

KIJI
01-01-2006; 104.3 mhz FM; 12.5 kw; 292 ft.; N13 30 7 E144 47 21
US
(671) 478-0104, *Fax:* (671) 647-7840
www.kijifm104.com
License: Tumon, GU held by Guam Broadcast Services Inc.
Arbitron Metro Market: Tumon, GU *Format:* Oldies
Yasunori Kawauchi, President
Kevin Yamazaki, Operations Dir

Hawaii

Aiea

KKOL-FM
09-01-1992; 107.9 mhz FM *Hrs Open:* 24; 100 kw horiz, 80 kw vert; 1965 ft.; N21 23 51 W158 6 1
970 North Kalaheo Ave., Suite C-107, Kailua, HI 96734 US
(808) 533-0065, *Fax:* (808) 524-2104
www.1079koolgold.com
edkanoi@hawaii-radio.net
License: Aiea, Honolulu County, HI held by Salem Media of Hawaii Inc.
Group Owner: Salem Communications Corp.; (acq 1-3-2005 in exchange for KRTR(AM) Honolulu and KKNE(AM) Waipahu).
Arbitron Metro Market: Honolulu, HI *Format:* Oldies *No. News Employees:* 1 *Target Audience:* 35-54; adults
Steve Miller, General Manager
Rudi Camello, General Sales Mgr
Jenny Clipse, News Director
Bill Davis, Chief Engineer
Ed Kanoi, Program Director

Bellaire

KGOW(AM)
1560 khz AM; 10 kw-U, DA-2; N19 47 02 W155 05 25
4703 Orkney Dr., Missouri City, TX 77459
(281) 923-7100
radioguy@neosoft.com
License: Bellaire, TX held by GOW Communications LLC
Fred Morton, General Manager

Captain Cook

KMWB
01-01-2007; 93.1 mhz FM; 10 kw; 3235 ft.; N19 43 14.9 W155 55 16
US
(808) 935-5461, *Fax:* (808) 935-7761
www.b97hawaii.com
sales@kwxx.com
License: Captain Cook, Hawaii County, HI held by Captain Cook Broadcasting Inc.
Arbitron Metro Market: Captain Cook, HI *Format:* Contemporary Hits/Top 40, Adult Contemp
Joel Sellers, President

Eleele

KUAI
06-30-1965; 720 khz AM *Hrs Open:* 5 AM-midnight; 5 kw-U, ND1; N21 53 37 W159 33 27
P. O. Box 720, Eleele, HI 96705 US
(808) 245-9527, *Fax:* (808) 245-3563
kuai@hawaiian.net
License: Eleele, HI held by Visionary Related Entertainment L.L.C.
Group Owner: Visionary Related Entertainment L.L.C.; acq 2-10-2004; grpsl).
Arbitron Metro Market: Eleele, HI *Format:* Adult Contemp, Country *Special Programming:* Hawaiian 5 hrs, jazz 4 hrs wkly
Hrs. of News Programming: News progmg 21 hrs wkly *Target Audience:* 25-65; loc long-timeresidents, blue & white collar
John Detz, President

Haiku

KUAU
01-01-1995; 1570 khz AM *Hrs Open:* 24
707 Puunene Avenue, Kahului Maui, HI 96732 US
888) 404-7729, *Fax:* (808) 871-9708
www.kingscathedral.com
info@kingscathedral.com
License: Haiku, HI held by First Assembly of God-Kahului, Maui Inc.
Arbitron Metro Market: Haiku, HI
Ron Moody, General Manager
Dr James Marocco

KRYL(FM)
106.5 mhz FM; 72 kw; Ant 2,283 ft; N20 39 36 W156 21 50
Hochman Hawaii Five, 8215 Birch St., New Orleans, LA 70118
(504) 458-5976
License: Haiku, Maui County, HI held by Hochman Hawaii Five Inc
Population Served: 8,118 *Arbitron Metro Market:* Haiku, HI
Joel Sellers, President

Haliimaile

KPMW
01-01-1994; 105.5 mhz FM; 9 kw; 541 ft.; N20 44 40 W156 18 39
230 Hana Highway, Kahului, HI 96732 US
(808) 871-6251, *Fax:* (808) 871-5670
wild105@maui.net
License: Haliimaile, Maui County, HI held by Rey-Cel Broadcasting Inc.
Arbitron Metro Market: Maui, HI *Format:* Contemporary Hits/Top 40
Cecille Piros, General Manager
Cecille Pirose, General Sales Mgr
Bryan Pirose, Programming Director
Ray Piros, News Director

Hanalei

*KKCR
08-02-1997; 90.9 mhz FM *Hrs Open:* 24; 0.9 kw; -308 ft.; N22 13 2 W159 28 53
P.O. Box 825, Hanalei, HI 96714 US
(808) 826-7774, *Fax:* (808) 826-7977
www.kkcr.org
kkcr@kkcr.org
License: Hanalei, Kauai County, HI held by Kekahu Foundation Inc.
Arbitron Metro Market: Honolulu, HI *Format:* Ethnic *Hrs. of News Programming:* News progmg 5 hrs wkly *Target Audience:* General; Kauai County residents
Harvey Cohen, President
Gwen Squyres, General Manager
Dean Rogers, Station Manager
Jessica Dofflemyer, General Sales Mgr
Donna Giarman, Engineering Dir
Erik Coopersmith, Development Director

Hilo

KHBC
10-01-1986; 92.7 mhz FM; 7.5 kw; -256 ft.; N19 50 19 W155 6 43
2447 Makiki Heights Dr, Honolulu, HI 96822 US
(808) 959-5700, *Fax:* (808) 959-5800
License: Hilo, Hawaii County, HI held by Hilo Broadcasting L.L.C.
Arbitron Metro Market: Hilo, HI *Format:* Ethnic
Buddy Gordon, General Manager
Robert Turner, Chief Engineer

*KANO
01-01-2001; 91.1 mhz FM *Hrs Open:* 24; 30 kw; N19 35 31.4 W155 7 36
738 Kaheka Street, Honolulu, HI 96814 US
(808) 955-8821, *Fax:* (808) 946-3963
www.hawaiipublicradio.org
License: Hilo, Hawaii County, HI held by Hawaii Public Radio.
Nat'l Network: NPR; PRI
Arbitron Metro Market: Honolulu, HI *Format:* Talk *Hrs. of News Programming:* news progmg 35 hrs wkly *No. News Employees:* 3
Valerie Yee, Operations Dir
Michael Titterton, General Manager
Kayla Rosenfeld, News Director
Gene Schiller, Music Director
Charles Husson, Operations Director

*KCIF
07-01-1998; 90.3 mhz FM; 5 kw vert; -132 ft.; N19 38 14 W155 3 19
180 Kinoole St., Suite 310, Hilo, HI 96720 US

(808) 935-7434, *Fax:* (808) 961-6022
www.kcifhawaii.org
keepchristinfocus@KCIFradio.com
License: Hilo, Hawaii County, HI held by Hilo Christian Broadcasting.
Arbitron Metro Market: Hilo, HI *Format:* Christian, Religious
Pastor David Shotwell, Chairman

KHLO
04-01-1950; 850 khz AM *Hrs Open:* 24; 5 kw-U, ND1; N19 41 48 W155 3 5
1090 Vermont Avenue, N.W., Suite 800, Washington, DC 20005 US
(808) 961-0651, *Fax:* (808) 934-8088
www.espnhawaii.com
jatebare@pacificradiogroup.com
License: Hilo, HI held by Pacific Radio Group Inc.
Group Owner: Pacific Radio Group Inc.; acq 9-17-03; grpsl).
TV Affiliate: ESPN *Format:* Sports *Hrs. of News Programming:* news progmg 7 hrs wkly *No. News Employees:* 2 *Target Audience:* 25-54.
Ilene Jones, General Manager
Tom Newhouse, Programming Director
Josh Pacheco, Program Director

KAPA
12-01-1988; 100.3 mhz FM *Hrs Open:* 24; 35 kw; -256 ft.; N19 50 19 W155 6 43
688 Kinoole Street, Hilo, HI 96720 US
(808) 962-6633, *Fax:* (808) 934-8088
www.kaparadio.com
studio@kaparadio.com
License: Hilo, Hawaii County, HI held by Pacific Radio Group Inc.
Group Owner: Pacific Radio Group Inc.; (acq 8-11-2005; grpsl).
Format: Ethnic *Target Audience:* 18-49.
Jeanine Atebara, General Manager
Jason Iglesias, Programming Director
Russ Roberts, News Director
Aaron Savage, Chief Engineer
Cobey Patolo, Traffic Manager

KHNU
09-10-1947; 620 khz AM *Hrs Open:* 24; 5 kw-U, ND1; 10 kw-U, DA1; ND1; 5 kw-U; N19 51 2 W155 5 7; N19 44 12 W156 1 56; N19 018 W155 4037
2447 Makiki Heights Dr., Honolulu, HI 96822 US
(808) 329-8090, *Fax:* (808) 443-0888
www.lava105.com
info@lava105.com
License: Hilo, HI held by Mahalo Broadcasting L.L.C.
Group Owner: Mahalo Broadcasting L.L.C.; (acq 8-31-2007; grpsl)
Nat'l Network: ABC
Format: News, Talk *No. News Employees:* 9 *Target Audience:* 35 plus. *Adv. Rates:* 5; 5; 5; 5
Chip Begay, Operations Dir

KKBG
08-05-1980; 97.9 mhz FM *Hrs Open:* 24; 51 kw; -65 ft.; N19 50 19 W155 6 43
1090 Vermont Avenue, N.W., Suite 800, Washington, DC 20005 US
(808) 961-0651, *Fax:* (808) 934-8088
www.kbigfm.com
studio@kbigfm.com
License: Hilo, Hawaii County, HI held by Pacific Radio Group Inc.
Group Owner: Pacific Radio Group Inc.; (acq 9-17-2003; grpsl).
Arbitron Metro Market: Honolulu, HI *Format:* Adult Contemp *Hrs. of News Programming:* news progmg 10 hrs wkly *No. News Employees:* 1
Chuck Bergson, CEO
Llene Alford, General Manager
Darin Gumbs, Programming Director

KNWB
08-03-1985; 97.1 mhz FM *Hrs Open:* 5 AM-10:30 PM; 38 kw; -823 ft.; N19 47 2 W155 5 25
1145 Kilauea Avenue, Hilo, HI 96720 US
(808) 935-5461, *Fax:* (808) 935-7761
www.B97Hawaii.com
sales@kwxx.com
License: Hilo, Hawaii County, HI held by New West Broadcasting Corp.
Group Owner: New West Broadcasting Corp.; acq 1995; $270,000).
Format: Contemporary Hits/Top 40, Adult Contemp *Hrs. of News Programming:* news progmg 8 hrs wkly *No. News Employees:* 1 *Target Audience:* 25-45.
Chris Leonard, President
Gavin Tanouye, Station Manager

KPUA
01-01-1936; 670 khz AM *Hrs Open:* 24
1145 Kilauea Avenue, Hilo, HI 96720 US
(808) 935-5461, *Fax:* (808) 935-7761
www.kpua.net
info@kpua.net
License: Hilo, HI held by New West Broadcasting Corp.
Group Owner: New West Broadcasting Corp.; acq 5-18-92; $370,000 with co-located FM;
Nat'l Network: CBS; Westwood One
Format: News, Sports, 86 *Special Programming:* Japanese 6 hrs wkly *Hrs. of News Programming:* news progmg 22 hrs wkly *No. News Employees:* 3 *Target Audience:* 25 plus; upscale adults with interest in news
Christopher Leonard, General Manager
Ken Hupp, Programming Director
Triska LaRochell, Regional Sales Manager
John Orozco, Regional Sales Manager

KPVS
01-01-1995; 95.9 mhz FM *Hrs Open:* 24; 39 kw; -256 ft.; N19 50 19 W155 6 43 *Rebroadcasts:* Rebroadcasts KLUA(FM) Kailua-Kona 100%
2447 Makiki Heights Dr, Honlulu, HI 96822 US
(808) 961-0651, *Fax:* (808) 934-8088
www.nativefm.com
studio@nativefm.com
License: Hilo, Hawaii County, HI held by Pacific Radio Group Inc.
Group Owner: Pacific Radio Group Inc.; (acq 8-11-2005; grpsl).
Arbitron Metro Market: Hilo, HI *Format:* Reggae *Target Audience:* 25-54; women
Ilene Alford, General Manager
Darin Gumbs, Programming Director
Russ Roberts, News Director
Aaron Savage, Chief Engineer
Cobey Patolo, Traffic Manager

KWXX-FM
12-16-1984; 94.7 mhz FM *Hrs Open:* 24; 51 kw; -758 ft.; N19 47 2 W155 5 25
1145 Kilauea Avenue, Hilo, HI 96720 US
(808) 935-5461, *Fax:* (808) 935-7761
www.kwxx.com
sales@kwxx.com
License: Hilo, Hawaii County, HI
Nat'l Network: Westwood One
Arbitron Metro Market: Hilo, HI *Format:* Adult Contemp *Special Programming:* Contemp Hawaiian 20 hrs, reggae 20 hrs wkly *Hrs. of News Programming:* news progmg 3 hrs wkly *No. News Employees:* 1 *TargetAudience:* 25 plus; upscale adults
Gavin Tawouye, Programming Director
Keoni Johnson, Disc Jockey
G. Kruz, Disc Jockey

***DKEAU**
01-01-2008; 88.1 mhz FM; kw
738 Kaheka Street, Honolulu, HI 96814 US
(406) 761-8816, *Fax:* (406) 454-3484
License: Hilo, Teton County, HI held by College Creek Media LLC.
Group Owner: College Creek Media LLC
Arbitron Metro Market: Great Falls, MT
Neal Robinson, President
Darnell Washington, General Manager

KIPA
01-01-2008; 1060 khz AM; Ant 3,113 ft
P.O. Box 4727, Hilo, HI 96720 US
(217) 607-0017, *Fax:* (808) 959-5800
www.konafm.com
scott@kona.sm
License: Hilo, HI held by Parrott Broadcasting L.P.
Arbitron Metro Market: Hilo, HI *Format:* Classic Rock
Buddy Gordon, General Manager

KHNU(AM)
09-10-1947; 620 khz AM *Hrs Open:* 24; 5 kw-U; N19 51 03 W155 05 09
74-5605 Luhia St., B-7, Kailua-Kona, HI 96740
(808) 329-8090, *Fax:* (808) 443-0888
www.lava105.com
info@lava105.com
License: Hilo, Hawaii County, HI held by Mahalo Broadcasting L.L.C.
Group Owner: Mahalo Broadcasting L.L.C.; (acq 8-31-2007; grpsl)
Nat'l Network: ABC
Population Served: 135,000*No. News Employees:* 9 *Target Audience:* 35 plus. *Adv. Rates:* 5; 5; 5; 5
Chip Begay, Operations Dir

Holualoa

KHWI
09-20-1992; 92.1 mhz FM *Hrs Open:* 24; 4.5 kw; 3114 ft.; N19 43 15 W155 55 16
US
(208) 837-4104
License: Holualoa, Hawaii County, HI held by Parrott Broadcasting L.P.
Arbitron Metro Market: Sun Valley, ID *Format:* Adult Contemp
Scott Parker, General Manager

Honokaa

KLZY
102.9 mhz FM; 1.5 kw; 2283 ft.; N20 39 36 W156 21 50
US
License: Honokaa, Hawaii County, HI held by Chaparral Broadcasting Inc.
Group Owner: Chaparral Communications
Arbitron Metro Market: Paia, HI *Format:* Triple A
Jerrold Lundquist, President

Honolulu

KHCM
08-31-1956; 880 khz AM *Hrs Open:* 24
3555 Harding Avenue, Honolulu, HI 96816 US
(626) 912-3388, *Fax:* (626) 912-5604
www.am980.net
radio88@am880.net
License: Honolulu, HI held by Salem Media of Hawaii Inc.
Group Owner: Salem Communications Corp.; (Acq 11-10-99; with co-located FM)
Arbitron Metro Market: Honolulu, HI *Format:* Chinese
Bruce Munsterman, General Manager
Dolly Martin, Programming Director
Bonnie BeMent, Assistant General Manager

KAIM-FM
11-01-1953; 95.5 mhz FM *Hrs Open:* 24; 100 kw; 1854 ft.; N21 23 45 W158 5 58
3555 Harding Avenue, Honolulu, HI 96816 US
(808) 533-0065, *Fax:* (808) 524-2104
www.thefishhawaii.com
jwaters@salemhawaii.com
License: Honolulu, Honolulu County, HI held by Salem Media of Hawaii Inc.
Group Owner: Salem Communications Corp.; (acq 11-10-99; with co-located AM)
Nat'l Network: Salem Radio Network
Arbitron Metro Market: Honolulu, HI *Format:* Christian *Target Audience:* 25-49; female
Steve Miller, General Manager
Jack Waters, Programming Director

KKEA
11-01-1966; 1420 khz AM; 5 kw-U, ND1; N21 19 26 W157 52 47
12381 Wilshire Blvd., Suite 105, PO Box 25606, Los Angeles, CA 90025 US
(808) 275-1047, *Fax:* (808) 548-0608
www.espn1420am.com
License: Honolulu, HI held by Blow Up LLC
Nat'l Network: CNN Radio; ESPN Radio *Nat'l Reps:* Katz Radio
Arbitron Metro Market: Honolulu, HI *Format:* Sports, Talk *Target Audience:* 25-54; Male *Adv. Rates:* 372; 372; 372; 372.
Randall Ikeda, General Manager
Chris Hart, Programming Director

KCCN-FM
05-21-1990; 100.3 mhz FM; 100 kw horiz, 81 kw vert; 1965 ft.; N21 23 51 W158 6 1
12381 Wilshire Blvd., Suite 105, PO Box 25606, Los Angeles, CA 90025 US
(808) 275-1000, *Fax:* (808) 536-2528
www.kccnfm100.com
info@kccnfm100.com
License: Honolulu, Honolulu County, HI held by Cox Radio Inc.
Group Owner: Cox Radio Inc.; (acq 3-15-2000; grpsl)
Arbitron Metro Market: Honolulu, HI *Format:* Ethnic
Patti Milburn, President
Wayne Maria, Operations Dir
Michol Klabo, General Manager
Stuart Chang, General Sales Mgr
Shannon Scott, Promotions Manager

KHRA
03-01-1992; 1460 khz AM; 5 kw-U, ND1; N21 19 26 W157 52 32
970 North Kalaheo Avenue, No. C-107, Kailua, HI 96734 US
(808) 593-1460, *Fax:* (808) 591-1986
License: Honolulu, HI held by KMC Broadcasting L.L.C.
Arbitron Metro Market: Honolulu, HI *Format:* Korean

RADIO - U.S.

Tony Young Ho Kim, President
Chung Sangkit, General Manager

KGU

05-11-1922; 760 khz AM *Hrs Open:* 24; 10 kw-U, ND1; N21 17 41 W157 51 49
222 N. Sepulveda Blvd, Suite 1324, El Segundo, CA 90245 US
(808) 533-0065, *Fax:* (808) 524-2104
www.kguradio.com
info@kguradio.com
License: Honolulu, HI held by Salem Media of Hawaii Inc.
Group Owner: Salem Communications Corp.; (acq 2-16-00)
Nat'l Network: Salem Radio Network *Nat'l Reps:* Salem
Arbitron Metro Market: Honolulu, HI *Format:* Christian, Talk *Hrs. of News Programming:* News progmg 5 hrs wkly *Target Audience:* 35-54; general
Jack Waters, Operations Dir
T.J. Malievsky, General Manager
David Serrone, Programming Director
Jack Waters, Program Director

KRTR

01-01-1946; 650 khz AM *Hrs Open:* 24; 10 kw-U, ND1; N21 26 43 W158 3 49
222 N Sepulveda Blvd, Suite 1324, El Segundo, CA 90245 US
(808) 533-0065, *Fax:* (808) 524-2104
www.khnr.com
License: Honolulu, HI held by Cox Radio Inc.
Group Owner: Cox Radio Inc.; (acq 1-3-2005 with KKNE(AM) Waipahu in exchange for KKOL-FM Aiea)
Nat'l Network: CNN Radio; CBS Radio *Nat'l Reps:* Salem *Wire Services:* AP
Arbitron Metro Market: Honolulu, HI *Format:* News, Talk *Hrs. of News Programming:* News progmg 55 hrs wkly *Target Audience:* 25-54.
Jack Walters, Operations Dir
T.J. Malievsky, General Manager
Wayne Marla, Programming Director

*KHPR

11-13-1981; 88.1 mhz FM *Hrs Open:* 24; 39 kw; 1686 ft.; N21 20 12 W157 49 3
738 Kaheka Street, Honolulu, HI 96814 US
(808) 955-8821, *Fax:* (808) 946-3863
www.hawaiipublicradio.org
mail@hawaiipublicradio.org
License: Honolulu, Honolulu County, HI held by Hawaii Public Radio.
Nat'l Network: NPR; PRI
Arbitron Metro Market: Honolulu, HI *Format:* News *Hrs. of News Programming:* news progmg 35 hrs wkly *No. News Employees:* 1 *Target Audience:* General.
Charles Husson, Operations Dir
Michael Titterton, General Manager
Kayla Rosenfeld, News Director
Gene schiller, Music Director
Judy Neale, Director of Promotion
Bill Dorman, News Director

KHVH

04-01-1951; 830 khz AM *Hrs Open:* 24; 10 kw-U, ND1; N21 19 26 W157 52 32
600 Congress Ave., Suite 1400, Austin, TX 78701 US
(808) 550-9200, *Fax:* (808) 550-9288
www.khvhradio.com
info@khvh830am.com
License: Honolulu, HI held by Capstar TX L.P.
Group Owner: Clear Channel Communications Inc.; (acq 8-30-2000; grpsl)
Nat'l Reps: Clear Channel *Wire Services:* AP
Arbitron Metro Market: Honolulu, HI *Format:* News, News/Talk, 86 *Hrs. of News Programming:* news progmg 21 hrs wkly *No. News Employees:* 5 *Target Audience:* 25-54.
John Hogan, CEO
Charlie Ramilly, Operations Dir
Chuck Cotton, General Manager
Rob Welsh, General Sales Mgr
Steven Norstrom, Programming Director
Jamie Hartnett, Promotions Manager
Dave Curtis, News Director
Jerry Varoujean,Chief Engineer
Patti Milburn, General Sales Manager

KIKI(AM)

03-18-1957; 990 khz AM *Hrs Open:* 24; 5 kw-U; N21 17 59 W157 51 33
650 Iwilei Rd., Suite 400, Honolulu, HI 96817
(808) 550-9200, *Fax:* (808) 550-9288
www.kikiradio.com
stevennorstrom@clearchannel.com; kevinjones@clearchannel.com; robertwelsh@clearchannel.com; greggmue
License: Honolulu, Honolulu County, HI held by Capstar TX L.P.
Group Owner: Clear Channel Communications Inc.
Nat'l Network: ABC *Nat'l Reps:* Clear Channel
Population Served: 900,000 *Arbitron Metro Market:* Honolulu, HI *Format:* News, News/Talk, 86 *Hrs. of News Programming:* News progmg 20 hrs wkly *Target Audience:* 25-54.
Roger Galle, President
Robert Welsh, General Sales Mgr
Steven Norstrom, Programming Director
Kevin Jones, Promotions Manager

KINE-FM

11-01-1988; 105.1 mhz FM; 100 kw horiz, 81 kw vert; 1965 ft.; N21 23 51 W158 6 1
12381 Wilshire Blvd., Suite 105, PO Box 25606, Los Angeles, CA 90025 US
(808) 275-1000, *Fax:* (808) 536-2528
www.hawaiian105.com
info@hawaiian105.com
License: Honolulu, Honolulu County, HI held by Cox Radio Inc.
Group Owner: Cox Radio Inc.; (acq 3-15-2000; grpsl)
Arbitron Metro Market: Honolulu, HI *Format:* Contemporary Hits/Top 40, Ethnic *Target Audience:* 25-44.
Michael Kelly, Operations Dir
John Aeto, General Sales Mgr
David Daniels, Programming Director
Scott MacKenzie, Promotions Manager
Jane Pascual, News Director
Wade Faildo, Promotions Manager
Ann Boots, Regional Sales Manager

*KIPO

01-01-1989; 89.3 mhz FM *Hrs Open:* 24; 38.5 kw; 1686 ft.; N21 20 12 W157 49 3
738 Kaheka Street, Honolulu, HI 96814 US
(808) 955-8821, *Fax:* (808) 946-3863
www.hawaiipublicradio.org
License: Honolulu, Honolulu County, HI held by Hawaii Public Radio.
Nat'l Network: PRI; NPR
Arbitron Metro Market: Honolulu, HI *Format:* Jazz, News *Hrs. of News Programming:* news progmg 50 hrs wkly *No. News Employees:* 3 *Target Audience:* General.
Valerie Yee, Operations Dir
Michael Titterton, General Manager
Kayla Rosenfeld, News Director
Gene Schiller, Music Director
Charles Husson, Operations Director

KREA

04-24-1973; 1540 khz AM *Hrs Open:* 24; 5 kw-U, ND1; N21 19 27 W157 52 47
1921 Sacramento Street, San Francisco, CA 94109 US
(808) 955-1234, *Fax:* (808) 946-9637
License: Honolulu, HI held by JMK Communications Inc.
Arbitron Metro Market: Honolulu, HI *Format:* Korean
Young Lee, General Manager

KDNN

07-04-1988; 98.5 mhz FM *Hrs Open:* 24; 51 kw; 59 ft.; N21 18 49 W157 51 43
600 Congress Ave., Suite 1400, Austin, TX 78701 US
(808) 550-9200, *Fax:* (808) 550-9510
www.island985.com
info@island985.com
License: Honolulu, Honolulu County, HI held by Capstar TX L.P.
Group Owner: Clear Channel Communications Inc.; (acq 8-30-00; grpsl).
Nat'l Reps: Clear Channel
Arbitron Metro Market: Honolulu, HI *Format:* Ethnic *Target Audience:* 25-54; upscale, white collar, college educated
John Hogan, CEO
Charlie Rahilly, Operations Dir
Chuck Cotton, General Manager

KLHT

01-01-1946; 1040 khz AM *Hrs Open:* 24; 10 kw-U; N21 20 10 W157 53 33
98-1016 Komo Mai Dr., Aiea, HI 96817
(808) 524-1040, *Fax:* (808) 487-1040
www.klight.org
klht@hawaii.rr.com
License: Honolulu, Honolulu County, HI held by Calvary Chapel of Honolulu Inc.
Arbitron Metro Market: Honolulu, HI *Target Audience:* General.
Jake O'Neil, General Manager
Clif Burchfield, General Sales Mgr
Josh Villoria, Programming Director

KPOI-FM

08-03-2000; 105.9 mhz FM *Hrs Open:* 24; 100 kw horiz, 92 kw vert; 1965 ft.; N21 23 51 W158 6 1
45-602 Haamaile St, Kaneohe, HI 96744 US
(808) 947-1500, *Fax:* (808) 947-1506
www.lavarock1059.com
kumu@kumu.com
License: Honolulu, Honolulu County, HI held by Visionary Related Entertainment LLC.
Group Owner: Visionary Related Entertainment L.L.C.; (acq 3-17-2004; grpsl).
Arbitron Metro Market: Honolulu, HI *Format:* Classic Rock *Hrs. of News Programming:* news progmg 23 hrs wkly *No. News Employees:* 1 *Target Audience:* 24-54; families, including single-parent families *Adv.Rates:* 36; 36; 36; 15
John Detz, General Manager
Greg Everett, General Sales Mgr
Dale Parsons, Programming Director
Gary Forsberg, News Director

KNDI

07-11-1960; 1270 khz AM *Hrs Open:* 24; 5 kw-U, ND1; N21 19 26 W157 52 47
Dba. Kndi Radio, 1734 S. King Street, Honolulu, HI 96826 US
(808) 946-2844, *Fax:* (808) 947-3531
www.kndi.com
kndiradio@hawaii.rr.com
License: Honolulu, HI held by Leona Jona dba KNDI Radio.
Arbitron Metro Market: Honolulu, HI *Format:* Ethnic, Filipino *Target Audience:* Limited english proficiency. *Adv. Rates:* 45; 40; 35; 30
Leona Jona, President
Harvey Weinstein, Operations Dir
Ellen Kaiuwailani, Secretary/Office Mgr

KORL

12-01-1959; 1180 khz AM *Hrs Open:* 24
210 North 1000 East, St. George, UT 84770 US
(808) 875-8868, *Fax:* (808) 875-8870
www.korlam.com
License: Honolulu, HI held by Hochman-McCann Hawaii Inc.
Arbitron Metro Market: Honolulu, HI *Format:* Ethnic *Target Audience:* 25 plus.
George Hochman, CEO

KHCM-FM

03-06-1962; 97.5 mhz FM *Hrs Open:* 24; 80 kw; Ant 46 ft; N21 17 37 W157 50 32
1160 N. King St., 2nd Fl., Honolulu, HI 79902
(808) 533-0065, *Fax:* (808) 524-2104
www.hawaiiscountrymusic.com
mtshawaii@yahoo.com
License: Honolulu, Honolulu County, HI held by Salem Media of Hawaii Inc.
Group Owner: Salem Communications Corp.; (acq 8-13-2004; $3.7 million with K
Population Served: 622,900 *Arbitron Metro Market:* Honolulu, HI
Leilani Williams, General Manager
Ed Kanol, Programming Director

KHNR

05-14-1947; 690 khz AM *Hrs Open:* 24; 10 kw-U; N21 17 41 W157 51 49
1160 N. King St., 2nd Fl., Honolulu, HI 79902
(808) 533-0065, *Fax:* (808) 524-2104
www.khnr.com
info@khnr.com
License: Honolulu, Honolulu County, HI held by Salem Media of Hawaii Inc.
Group Owner: Salem Communications; (acq 10-1-2006; exchange for KORL(AM) Honolulu)
Fox News Radio; Salem Radio Network
Population Served: 1,000,000 *Arbitron Metro Market:* Honolulu, HI
Stuart Epperson, Chairman
Edward G Atsinger, CEO/COO
Dave Santrella, President
Linnae Young, Operations Dir
Leilani Williams, General Manager
Jack Waters, Station Manager
Dita Holifield, General Sales Mgr
Jack Waters,Programming Director
Dave Kateley, Promotions Manager
Ernie Nearman, Chief Engineer

KQMQ-FM

10-01-1967; 93.1 mhz FM; 100 kw; 1854 ft.; N21 23 45 W158 5 58
4150 Pinnacle, El Paso, TX 79902 US
(808) 947-1500, *Fax:* (808) 947-1506
www.931dapaina.com
lauriemizuno@ohanabroadcast.com
License: Honolulu, Honolulu County, HI held by Visionary Related Entertainment L.L.C.

Group Owner: Visionary Related Entertainment L.L.C.; acq 7-1-2004; grpsl).
Arbitron Metro Market: Honolulu, HI *Format:* Reggae
John Detz, General Manager
Laurie Mizuno, General Sales Mgr
Sean Lynch, Programming Director
Ryan Sean, Music Director

KSSK
01-01-1929; 590 khz AM *Hrs Open:* 24; 7.5 kw-U, ND1; N21 19 26 W157 52 32
600 Congress Ave., Suite 1400, Austin, TX 78701 US
(808) 550-9200, *Fax:* (808) 550-9507
www.ksskradio.com
info@ksskradio.com
License: Honolulu, HI held by Capstar TX L.P.
Group Owner: Clear Channel Communications Inc.; (acq 3-12-99; grpsl)
Nat'l Reps: Clear Channel *Wire Services:* AP
Arbitron Metro Market: Honolulu, HI *Format:* Adult Contemp *Hrs. of News Programming:* news progmg 15 hrs wkly *No. News Employees:* 5 *Target Audience:* 25-54.
Chuck Cotton, General Manager
Rob Welsh, General Sales Mgr
Jamie Hyatt, Programming Director
kevin Jones, Promotions Manager

***KTUH**
01-01-1969; 90.3 mhz FM *Hrs Open:* 24; 3 kw; -82 ft.; N21 18 14 W157 49 22
2444 Dole Street, Bachman Hall 209, Honolulu, HI 96822 US
(808) 956-7431, *Fax:* (808) 956-5271
www.ktuh.org
gm@ktuh.org
License: Honolulu, Honolulu County, HI held by University of Hawaii.
Arbitron Metro Market: Honolulu, HI *Format:* Variety/Diverse *Target Audience:* 18-59; no target, all kinds of people listen
Monty Anderson, General Manager
Travis Tokuyama, Programming Director
Loriel Macalma, Promotions Manager
Katie McClellen, News Director
Dale Machado, Chief Engineer

KUMU(AM)
03-01-1963; 1500 khz AM *Hrs Open:* 24; 10 kw-U; N21 17 08 W157 48 08
1000 Bishop Street, Suite 200, Honolulu, HI 96813
(808) 947-1500, *Fax:* (808) 947-1506
www.kumu.com
lauriemizuno@ohanabroadcast.com
License: Honolulu, Honolulu County, HI held by Visionary Related Entertainment LLC
Group Owner: Visionary Related Entertainment L.L.C.
Nat'l Network: Westwood One
Population Served: 374,658 *Arbitron Metro Market:* Honolulu, HI *Format:* Talk *Target Audience:* 35-64.
Dave Capps, President
Randy McKone, Operations Dir
Laurie Mizuno, Director of Sales
Butch Thurman, News Director
J.J. Ford, Operations Manager

KUMU-FM
09-01-1967; 94.7 mhz FM; 100 kw; 79 ft.; N21 17 9 W157 50 19
765 Amana Street, Suite 206, Honolulu, HI 96814 US
(808) 947-1500, *Fax:* (808) 947-1506
www.kumu.com
lauriemizuno@ohanabroadcast.com
License: Honolulu, Honolulu County, HI held by Visionary Related Entertainment LLC
Group Owner: Visionary Related Entertainment L.L.C.; (acq 3-17-2004; grpsl)
Arbitron Metro Market: Honolulu, HI *Format:* Adult Contemp *Target Audience:* 25-54.
Jeff Coelho, General Manager
Laurie Mizuno, Director of Sales
Ed Kanoi, Programming Director
Sumee Mikkelson, Promotions Manager
Lilly Yamachika, News Director
Ernie Nearman, Chief Engineer

KWAI
01-21-1972; 1080 khz AM *Hrs Open:* 24; 5 kw-U, ND1; N21 17 41 W157 51 49
100 North Beretania St, Suite 401, Honolulu, HI 96817 US
(808) 523-3868, *Fax:* (808) 531-6532
www.kwai1080am.com
radio@hawaii.com
License: Honolulu, HI held by Radio Hawaii Inc.
Nat'l Network: USA
Arbitron Metro Market: Honolulu, HI *Format:* News, News/Talk, 86 *Special Programming:* Filipino 7 hrs, Hawaiian 3hrs wkly, Samoan 14 hrs wkly *Hrs. of News Programming:* News progmg 72 hrs wkly *Target Audience:* 25-64; general
Sam Wagenvoord, Operations Dir
Barry Wagenvoord, General Manager
Renee Rosehill, Operations Director
Ritchie Koseki, Account Executive
Jose Maldonado, Account Executive
Francis Andaya, Moderator/ Board Operator

KZOO
10-18-1963; 1210 khz AM; 1 kw-U, ND1; N21 17 41 W157 51 49
250 Ward Avenue, Honolulu, HI 96814 US
(808) 593-2880, *Fax:* (808) 596-0083
www.kzoohawaii.com
radio@am1210kzoo.com
License: Honolulu, HI held by Polynesian Broadcasting Inc.
Arbitron Metro Market: Honolulu, HI *Format:* Japanese
David Furuya, President

KPHI
01-01-2008; 1130 khz AM
188 South Bellevue, Ste 222, Memphis, TN 38104 US
(808) 538-1180, *Fax:* (808) 538-9548
www.hhawaiimedia.com
gh5512@aol.com
License: Honolulu, HI held by Hochman-McCann Hawaii Inc.
Arbitron Metro Market: Honolulu, HI *Format:* Ethnic *Target Audience:* 25 plus. *Adv. Rates:* 30; 25; 25; 20
George Hochman, President

Kahaluu

KLEO
01-01-1992; 106.1 mhz FM; 7.3 kw; 2995 ft.; N19 43 16 W155 55 15
1090 Vermont Avenue, N.W., Suite 800, Washington, DC 20005 US
(808) 961-0651, *Fax:* (808) 934-8088
jatebare@pacificradiogroup.com
License: Kahaluu, Hawaii West County, HI held by Pacific Radio Group Inc.
Group Owner: Pacific Radio Group Inc.; acq 9-17-03; grpsl).
Arbitron Metro Market: Honolulu, HI *Format:* Adult Contemp
Jeanine Atebara, General Manager
J.E. Orozco, General Sales Mgr
Russ Roberts, News Director
Aaron Savage, Chief Engineer
Cobey Patolo, Traffic Manager

Kahului

KNUI
09-14-1962; 900 khz AM *Hrs Open:* 24; 5 kw-U, ND1; N20 47 30 W156 28 21
505 Front Street, Suite 215, Lahaina, HI 96761 US
(808) 877-5566, *Fax:* (808) 877-2888
www.foxnews900.com
onair@knuiam900.com
License: Kahului, HI held by Pacific Radio Group Inc.
Group Owner: Pacific Radio Group Inc.; (acq 12-10-99; grpsl)
Nat'l Network: Fox News Radio
Format: News, News/Talk, 86 *Adv. Rates:* 18; 18; 18; 11
Eddie Johnson, CFO
Chuck Bergson, President
Jeff Hunter, Operations Dir
Pamela Tsutsui, General Manager
Debbie Probst, General Sales Mgr
Fred Guzman, Programming Director
Sherri Grimes, Promotions Manager
Dorene Moniz, NewsDirector
Earl Tolley, Chief Engineer

KJKS
06-22-1984; 99.9 mhz FM; 69 kw; 2283 ft.; N20 39 36 W156 21 50
505 Front Street, Suite 215, Lahaina, HI 96761 US
(808) 877-5566, *Fax:* (808) 877-2888
License: Kahului, Maui County, HI
Group Owner: Pacific Radio Group Inc.
Nat'l Network: Westwood One
Format: Adult Contemp *No. News Employees:* 1 *Target Audience:* 25-49. *Adv. Rates:* 24; 24; 24; 15
Jeff Hunter, Programming Director
Sherri Grimes, Promotions Manager
Dorene Moniz, News Director
Kopaa Tita, Disc Jockey

KLHI-FM
10-01-1994; 92.5 mhz FM *Hrs Open:* 24; 1.7 kw; 2211 ft.; N20 39 36 W156 21 50
US
(808) 877-5566, *Fax:* (808)-877-2888
native925.com
studio@native925.com
License: Kahului, Maui County, HI held by Pacific Radio Group Inc.
Group Owner: Pacific Radio Group Inc.; (acq 6-29-2007; swap for KORL-FM Waianae)
Arbitron Metro Market: Kahului, HI *Format:* Contemporary Hits/Top 40 *No. News Employees:* 1 *Target Audience:* Adults 18-49 *Adv. Rates:* 33, 28, 30, 20
Chuck Bergson, CEO/COO
Chuck Bergson, President
Pamela Tsutsui, General Manager
Kawika Veeka, Music Director
Sherri Grimes, Music Director

Kailua

KRTR-FM
10-09-1978; 96.3 mhz FM *Hrs Open:* 24; 74 kw; 2116 ft.; N21 19 49 W157 45 24
970 N. Kalaheo Ave., Suite C-107, Kailua, HI 96734 US
(808) 275-1000, *Fax:* (808) 536-2528
www.krater96.com
License: Kailua, Honolulu County, HI held by Cox Radio Inc.
Group Owner: Cox Radio Inc.; (acq 11-10-99; grpsl)
Arbitron Metro Market: Honolulu, HI *Format:* Adult Contemp *Target Audience:* 25-54.
Bob Neil, CEO
Wayne Maria, Operations Dir
Patti Milburn, General Manager
Wayne Maria, Station Manager
Michol Klabo, General Sales Mgr
Shannon Scott, Promotions Manager
Neil Johnston, CFO
Marc Morgan, COO
Richard Ferguson,Executive Vice President
Mimi Beams, General Sales Manager
Corinne Webb, National Sales Manager

Kailua Kona

KLUA
01-01-1991; 93.9 mhz FM *Hrs Open:* 24; 7.3 kw; 3022 ft.; N19 43 16 W155 55 15 *Rebroadcasts:* Rebroadcasts KPVS(FM) Hilo 100%
688 Kinoole Street, Hilo, HI 96720 US
(808) 935-6858, *Fax:* (808) 969-7949
jatebara@pacificradiogroup.com
License: Kailua Kona, Hawaii County, HI held by Pacific Radio Group Inc.
Group Owner: Pacific Radio Group Inc.; (acq 8-11-2005; grpsl).
Arbitron Metro Market: Kailuna Koa *Format:* Adult Contemp *Target Audience:* 25-54; women
Chuck Bergson, CEO
Ilene Alford, General Manager
Darin Gumbs, Programming Director
Russ Roberts, News Director
Aaron Savage, Chief Engineer
Cobey Patolo, Traffic Manager

Kalaheo

KTOH
06-01-2002; 99.9 mhz FM; 51 kw; 892 ft.; N21 56 10 W159 26 43
P.O. Box 1588, Clayton, GA 30525 US
(808) 246-4444, *Fax:* (808) 246-4405
www.hhawaiimedia.com
info@roostercountry.com
License: Kalaheo, Kauai County, HI held by Hochman Hawaii-One Inc.
Wire Services: AP
Arbitron Metro Market: Lihue, HI *Format:* Contemporary Hits/Top 40, Adult Contemp *Target Audience:* 25-54; adults *Adv. Rates:* 25; 20; 20; 15
Dianna Hochman, General Manager
Mark James, Programming Director
George Hochman, Promotions Manager

Kaneohe

KPHW
10-17-1997; 104.3 mhz FM *Hrs Open:* 24; 74 kw; 2116 ft.; N21 19 49 W157 45 24
970 North Kalaheo Avenue, Suite C-107, Kailua, HI 96734 US
(808) 275-1000, *Fax:* (808) 536-2528
www.power1043.com
patti@power1043.com
License: Kaneohe, Honolulu County, HI held by Cox Radio Inc.
Group Owner: Cox Radio Inc.; (acq 11-10-99; grpsl)

Arbitron Metro Market: Honolulu, HI *Format:* Contemporary Hits/Top 40 *Target Audience:* 18-34.
Bob Neil, CEO
Wayne Maria, Operations Dir
Patti Milburn, VP and General Manager
Mark Haworth, General Sales Mgr
KC Bejerana, Programming Director
Scott McKenzie, Promotions Manager
Neil Johnston, CFO
Marc Morgan, COO
CorinneWebb, National Sales Manager
Aron Dote, Promotions Manager
Rhoda Kihikhi, Human Resources
Alan Yamamoto, National Sales Manager

Kapaa

KITH
01-01-1999; 98.9 mhz FM; 51 kw; 919 ft.; N21 56 10 W159 26 43
P.O. Box 80657, Baton Rouge, LA 70898 US
(808) 246-4444, *Fax:* (808) 246-4405
www.hhawaiimedia.com
License: Kapaa, Kauai County, HI held by Hochman Hawaii-Two Inc.
Wire Services: AP
Arbitron Metro Market: Lihue, HI *Format:* Ethnic *Hrs. of News Programming:* News progmg 10 hrs wkly *Target Audience:* 18-44; adults *Adv. Rates:* 25; 20; 20; 12
Dianna Hochman, General Manager

Kaunakakai

KMKK-FM
03-19-2007; 102.3 mhz FM; 1.9 kw; 1181 ft.; N21 7 55 W157 11 31
US
(808) 947-1500, *Fax:* (808) 244-8247
License: Kaunakakai, Maui County, HI held by Visionary Related Entertainment LLC.
Group Owner: Visionary Related Entertainment L.L.C.
Arbitron Metro Market: Kaunakakai, HI *Format:* Adult Contemp
Jim McKeon, Operations Dir
John Detz, General Manager

Kawaihae

KWYI
11-01-1993; 106.9 mhz FM *Hrs Open:* 6 AM-10 PM; 5.5 kw; 341 ft.; N19 53 9 W155 39 28
P.O.Box 58, Ookala, HI 96774 US
(808) 885-9866, *Fax:* (808) 885-6480
www.kwyi.com
info@kwyi.com
License: Kawaihae, Hawaii County, HI held by Colin H. Naito.
Format: Adult Contemp *Target Audience:* 25-54.
Colin Naito, General Manager

Keaau

KBGX
04-16-2004; 105.3 mhz FM *Hrs Open:* 24; 25.5 kw horiz, 0 kw vert; 92 ft.; N19 43 18 W155 27 23
133 North Superior St, De Pere, WI 54115 US
(808) 329-8090, *Fax:* (808) 443-0888
www.lava105.com
info@lava105.com
License: Keaau, Hawaii County, HI held by Mahalo Broadcasting L.L.C.
Group Owner: Mahalo Broadcasting L.L.C.; (acq 8-31-2007; grpsl)
Nat'l Network: ABC
Arbitron Metro Market: Kea'au, HI *Format:* Oldies *Target Audience:* Adults; 25-54 *Adv. Rates:* 30; 30; 30; 30
Chip Begay, Operations Dir

Kealakekua

KAOY
11-11-1982; 101.5 mhz FM; 6.5 kw; 2982 ft.; N19 43 15 W155 55 16
688 Kinoole St., Hilo, HI 96720 US
(808) 935-5461, *Fax:* (808) 935-7761
www.kwxx.com
sales@kwxx.com
License: Kealakekua, Hawaii County, HI held by New West Broadcasting Corp.
Group Owner: New West Broadcasting Corp.; acq 4-16-2004; $500,000).
Arbitron Metro Market: Hilo, HI *Format:* Adult Contemp *Target Audience:* 18-49.
Christopher Leonard, General Manager
Trisha LaRochelle, General Sales Mgr
Gavin Panouye, Programming Director
Ken Hupp, News Director
Yisa Var, Traffic Manager

KKON
10-01-1963; 790 khz AM *Hrs Open:* 24; 5 kw-U, ND1; N19 31 10 W155 55 8 *Rebroadcasts:* Rebroadcasts Khlo(AM) Hilo 100%
688 Kinoole Street, Hilo, HI 96720 US
(808) 961-0651, *Fax:* (808) 934-8088
www.pacificradiogroup.com
info@kkonam.com
License: Kealakekua, HI held by Pacific Radio Group Inc.
Group Owner: Pacific Radio Group Inc.; (acq 8-11-2005; grpsl).
Arbitron Metro Market: Honolulu, HI *Format:* Sports *Special Programming:* Hawaiian mus *Target Audience:* 35 plus; general
Richard Bergson, CEO
Pamela Tsutsui, General Manager
Sherri Grimes, Promotions Manager
Seth Welcker, Chief Engineer

Kekaha

KSHK
08-10-1999; 103.3 mhz FM; 51 kw; 919 ft.; N21 56 11 W159 26 43
P.O. Box 15261, Santa Rosa, CA 95402 US
(808) 245-9527
www.kongradio.com
knog@hawaiian.net
License: Kekaha, Kauai County, HI held by Visionary Related Entertainment L.L.C.
Group Owner: Visionary Related Entertainment L.L.C.; acq 2-10-2004; grpsl).
Arbitron Metro Market: Lihue, HI *Format:* Contemporary Hits/Top 40
John Detz, President
Jim McKeon, Operations Dir
Denise Roberts, Promotions Manager
Ron Middag, Chief Engineer

Kihei

KAOI
10-11-1979; 1110 khz AM
Mailing Address: P.O. Box 15261, Santa Rosa, CA 95402 US
Second Address: Box 1437, Wailuku, HI 96793
(808) 244-9145, *Fax:* (808) 244-8247
www.vremaui.com
kaoi@kaoi.net
License: Kihei, HI held by Visionary Related Entertainment L.L.C.
Group Owner: Visionary Related Entertainment L.L.C.
Nat'l Network: CBS; Westwood One
Arbitron Metro Market: Wailuku, Hi *Format:* News, Sports, 86 *Target Audience:* 25-54.
J. Detz, News Director
Alex Kowalski, Chief Engineer

KKHI
01-28-1967; 100.7 mhz FM; kw
US
(303) 889-1019, *Fax:* (303) 962-5289
www.kkhi1019.com
License: Kihei, Arapahoe County, HI held by Bustos Media of Colorado License Corp.
Group Owner: Bustos Media LLC; (acq 9-29-2006; $17.5 million)
Arbitron Metro Market: Denver, CO *Format:* Jazz, Smooth Jazz
Ricky Tatum, General Manager

KHEI-FM
01-01-2009; 107.5 mhz FM *Hrs Open:* 24; 0.75 kw horiz; 3133 ft.; N20 46 31 W156 14 49
Mailing Address: US
Second Address: 1900 Main St., Suite 6, Wailuku, HI 96793
(808) 244-9145, *Fax:* (808) 244-8247
www.island1075.com
kaoi@kaoi.net
License: Kihei, Maui County, HI held by Visionary Related Entertainment LLC.
Group Owner: Visionary Related Entertainment L.L.C.
Arbitron Metro Market: Kihei, HI *Format:* Ethnic
Alex Kowalaski, CEO
John Detz, General Manager
jim McKeon, Station Manager

Kilauea

*KAQA
07-03-1997; 91.9 mhz FM; 6 kw horiz; 1690 ft.; N21 58 41 W159 29 55
P.O. Box 825, Hanalei, HI 96714 US
(808) 826-7774, *Fax:* (808) 826-7977
www.kkcr.org
kkcr@kkcr.org
License: Kilauea, Kauai County, HI held by Kekahu Foundation Inc.
Arbitron Metro Market: Hanalei, HI *Format:* Ethnic *Target Audience:* General; Kauai County residents
Harvey Cohen, President
Larry Lasota, General Manager
Dean Rogers, Station Manager
Douvn Jewell, General Sales Mgr
Ken Jannelli, Programming Director
Donna Lewis, News Director
Dean Rogers, Chief Engineer

Kurtistown

KTBH-FM
01-01-2008; 102.1 mhz FM; 50 kw horiz; N19 41 48 W155 3 5
US
(808) 935-2924, *Fax:* (808) 244-8247
License: Kurtistown, Hawaii County, HI held by Visionary Related Entertainment LLC.
Group Owner: Visionary Related Entertainment L.L.C.
Arbitron Metro Market: Kurtistown, HI *Format:* Adult Contemp
John Detz, President

Lahaina

KPOA
10-24-1984; 93.5 mhz FM *Hrs Open:* 24; 69 kw; 2283 ft.; N20 39 36 W156 21 50
505 Front Street, Suite 215, Lahaina, HI 96761 US
(808) 877-5566, *Fax:* (808) 877-2888
www.kpoa.com
studio@kpoa.com
License: Lahaina, Maui County, HI held by Pacific Radio Group Inc.
Group Owner: Pacific Radio Group Inc.; acq 12-10-99; grpsl)
Format: Adult Contemp *Hrs. of News Programming:* top of the hour *No. News Employees:* 1 *Target Audience:* Adults; 25-54 *Adv. Rates:* 50; 40; 45; 30.
Eddie Johnson, CFO
Pamela Tsutsui, General Manager
Alakai Paleka, Programming Director

Lanai City

KONI
11-01-1993; 104.7 mhz FM *Hrs Open:* 24; 69 kw; 2283 ft.; N20 39 36 W156 21 50
300 Ohukai Rd ,Ste C-318, Kihei, HI 96753 US
(808) 875-8866, *Fax:* (808) 875-8870
www.hhawaiimedia.net
koni@hawaii.rr.com
License: Lanai City, Maui County, HI held by Hochman Hawaii Publishing Inc.
Wire Services: AP
Format: Oldies *Hrs. of News Programming:* News progmg one hr wkly *Target Audience:* 25-54; Maui county residents *Adv. Rates:* 25; 20; 20; 12
George Hochman, COO
Jim Carroll, General Manager
Adrienne Owens, General Sales Mgr
Joe Hawkins, Programming Director
Byron McCann, Chief Engineer

Lihue

KJMQ
01-01-2001; 98.1 mhz FM; 51 kw; 13 ft.; N21 59 41 W159 24 36
3460 Torrance Blvd, Suite 303, Torrance, CA 90503 US
(808) 246-4444, *Fax:* (808) 246-4405
www.jamz981.com
License: Lihue, Kauai County, HI held by Hochman Hawaii Four Inc.
Arbitron Metro Market: Lihue, HI *Format:* Contemporary Hits/Top 40
George Hochman, President
Dianna Hochman, General Manager

KFMN
03-07-1988; 96.9 mhz FM *Hrs Open:* 24; 100 kw; 400 ft; N21 59 54 W159 25 35
Box 1566, 1860 Leleiona St., Lihue, HI 96766
(808) 246-1197, *Fax:* (808) 246-9697
john.wada@fm97radio.com
License: Lihue, Kauai County, HI held by FM 97 Associates.
Population Served: 75,000*Hrs. of News Programming:* news progmg 4 hrs wkly *No. News Employees:* 1 *Target Audience:* 25-54; island residents & visitors

John Wada, General Manager
Valarie Rynda, General Sales Mgr
Jason Fujinaka, Programming Director
Jason Fujinaka, News Director
Russell Wada, Chief Engineer

KQNG
01-01-1939; 570 khz AM; 1 kw-U, ND1; N21 59 33 W159 24 24
P.O. Box 15261, Santa Rosa, CA 95402 US
(808) 245-9527, *Fax:* (808) 245-3563
www.kongradio.com
kong@kongradio.com
License: Lihue, HI held by Visionary Related Entertainment L.L.C.
Group Owner: Visionary Related Entertainment L.L.C.; (acq 2-10-2004; grpsl)
Arbitron Metro Market: Kauai *Format:* News, News/Talk, 86 *Target Audience:* 25-54.
John Detz, CEO
Ron Middac, Chief Engineer

KQNG-FM
10-17-1983; 93.5 mhz FM; 51 kw; 226 ft.; N21 59 33 W159 24 24
P.O. Box 15261, Santa Rosa, CA 95402 US
(808) 245-9527, *Fax:* (808) 245-3563
www.kongradio.com
kong@kongradio.com
License: Lihue, Kauai County, HI
Arbitron Metro Market: Kauai *Format:* Contemporary Hits/Top 40 *Target Audience:* 18-49.
John Detz, President
Ron Wiley, Operations Dir

***KHJC**
88.9 mhz FM; 21 kw; 364 ft.; N21 59 54 W159 25 35
Mailing Address: 1911 1/2 19th Street, Santa Monica, CA 90404 US
Second Address: CSN International, 3000 W. MacArthur Blvd., Santa Ana, CA 92704
(800) 357-4226, *Fax:* (208) 736-1958
www.csnradio.com
License: Lihue, Kauai County, HI held by CSN International
Group Owner: CSN International
Arbitron Metro Market: Twin Falls, OD *Format:* Religious
Mike Kestler, President
Daniel Davidson, Operations Dir
Ken Sutherland, Programming Director
Mike Allen, News Director
Kelly Carlson, Engineering Dir
Don Mills, Network Programming Director / Music Director
Ray Gorney, AssistantDirector of Engineering
Austin Morris, Accounting
Lois Mills, FCC Applications / Translator Site Manager
Mike Stocklin, National Underwriting
Sherri Wallace, Local Origination

Makawao

KDLX
12-31-1980; 94.3 mhz FM *Hrs Open:* 24; 0.76 kw horiz; 3061 ft.; N20 46 31 W156 14 49
P.O. Box 15261, Santa Rosa, CA 95402 US
(808) 244-9145, *Fax:* (808) 244-8247
License: Makawao, Maui County, HI held by Visionary Related Entertainment L.L.C.
Group Owner: Visionary Related Entertainment L.L.C.; acq 2-10-2004; grpsl).
Format: Country
John Detz, President
Jack Gist, Programming Director
Gary Forsberg, News Director
Alex Kowalski, Chief Engineer

Nanakuli

KNAN
106.7 mhz FM; 25 kw; -23 ft.; N21 18 46 W158 5 51 US
(702) 385-6000, *Fax:* (702) 385-6001
License: Nanakuli, Honolulu County, HI held by Big D Consulting Inc.
Arbitron Metro Market: Nanakuli, HI
Donald Hildre, President

Paauilo

KNUQ
01-01-1995; 103.7 mhz FM *Hrs Open:* 24; 100 kw horiz; 1509 ft.; N20 38 13 W156 23 21
5501 Excelsior Blvd, Minneapolis, MN 55416 US
(808) 244-9145, *Fax:* (808) 244-8247
www.q103maui.com
License: Paauilo, Hawaii County, HI held by Visionary Related Entertainment LLC
Group Owner: Visionary Related Entertainment L.L.C.; acq 2-10-2004; grpsl).
Format: Ethnic *No. News Employees:* 1 *Target Audience:* 18-49; young active adults
John Detz, CEO
Jim McKeon, Operations Dir
Shaggy Jenkins, Programming Director
Gary Forsberg, News Director
Alex Kowalski, Chief Engineer

Pahala

***KAHU**
91.7 mhz FM; 1.8 kw; -128 ft.; N19 6 2 W155 34 9 US
(808) 959-2726
www.kahufm.com
License: Pahala, Hawaii County, HI held by Haola Inc.
Arbitron Metro Market: Pahala, HI *Format:* Ethnic
Wendell Kaehuaea, Operations Dir

Pearl City

KUPA
05-02-1990; 1370 khz AM *Hrs Open:* 24
738 Kaheka St., Honolulu, HI 96814 US
(801) 273-9200
License: Pearl City, HI held by Broadcasting Corp. of America.
Nat'l Network: Fox Sports
Arbitron Metro Market: Pearl City, HI *Format:* Sports
Nathan Drage, President

KUCD
02-14-1995; 101.9 mhz FM *Hrs Open:* 24; 100 kw horiz, 81 kw vert; 1965 ft.; N21 23 51 W158 6 1
600 Congress Ave., Suite 1400, Austin, TX 78701 US
(808) 550-9200, *Fax:* (808) 550-9288
www.star1019fm.com
jamiehyatt@clearchannel.com
License: Pearl City, Honolulu County, HI held by Capstar TX L.P.
Group Owner: Clear Channel Communications Inc.; (acq 8-30-00; grpsl).
Nat'l Reps: Clear Channel
Arbitron Metro Market: Honolulu, HI *Format:* Alternative *Target Audience:* 25-54; boomers & yuppies
Chuck Cotton, Operations Dir
Laurie Mizuno, General Sales Mgr
Jamie Hyatt, Programming Director
Kevin Jones, Promotions Manager
Damian Balinowski, News Director
Dale Costales, Chief Engineer
Iwalani Costales, Traffic Manager
Jovi Santiago, Sales Manager

Poipu

KSRF
08-14-1999; 95.9 mhz FM; 51 kw; 919 ft.; N21 56 11 W159 26 43
P.O. Box 15261, Santa Rosa, CA 95402 US
(808) 245-9527
www.kongradio.com
kong@hawaiian.net
License: Poipu, Kauai County, HI held by Visionary Related Entertainment L.L.C.
Group Owner: Visionary Related Entertainment L.L.C.; acq 2-10-2004; grpsl).
Arbitron Metro Market: Lihue, HI *Format:* Ethnic
John Detz, President
Shelly Cobb, Programming Director
Denise Roberts, News Director
Ron Middag, Chief Engineer

Pukalani

KJMD
06-15-1984; 98.3 mhz FM *Hrs Open:* 24; 9.4 kw; 2306 ft.; N20 39 36 W156 21 50
5501 Excelsior Blvd, Minneapolis, MN 55416 US
(808) 877-5566, *Fax:* (808) 871-0666
www.dajam983.com
License: Pukalani, Maui County, HI held by Pacific Radio Group Inc.
Group Owner: Pacific Radio Group Inc.; acq 12-10-99; grpsl).
Format: Contemporary Hits/Top 40 *No. News Employees:* 1 *Target Audience:* 18-34; young active adults *Adv. Rates:* 33; 28; 30; 20
Chuck Bergson, CEO
Pamela Tsutsui, General Manager
Trance, Programming Director

Volcano

KKOA
01-01-1996; 107.7 mhz FM *Hrs Open:* 24; 25.5 kw horiz; 92 ft.; N19 43 18 W155 27 23
1090 Vermont Avenue, N.W., Suite 800, Washington, DC 20005 US
(808) 329-8090, *Fax:* (808) 443-0888
www.KOACountry.com
info@KOACountry.com
License: Volcano, Hawaii County, HI held by Mahalo Broadcasting L.L.C.
Group Owner: Mahalo Broadcasting L.L.C.; (acq 9-1-2007; grpsl)
Nat'l Network: ABC
Arbitron Metro Market: Honolulu, HI *Format:* Country *Target Audience:* Adults 18-64. *Adv. Rates:* 30; 30; 30; 30
Chip Begay, Operations Dir

Wahiawa

***KHAI**
01-01-2007; 103.5 mhz FM; 2.2 kw horiz, 1.9 kw vert; 1959 ft.; N21 23 51 W158 6 1 *Rebroadcasts:* Rebroadcasts KLRD(FM) Yucaipa, CA 100%
US
(800) 877-5600, *Fax:* (916) 251-1650
www.air1.com
info@air1.com
License: Wahiawa, Oahu County, HI held by Educational Media Foundation.
Group Owner: EMF Broadcasting; (acq 12-19-2005; $2 million for CP)
Nat'l Network: Air 1
Arbitron Metro Market: McAllen-Brownsville-Harlingen, TX
Format: Alternative, Christian
Mike Novak, President

Wailea-Makena

KRKH
06-04-2008; 97.3 mhz FM; 1.446 kw; 2283 ft.; N20 39 36 W156 21 50
US
(808) 875-8866, *Fax:* (808) 875-8870
www.hhawaiimedia.com
License: Wailea-Makena, Maui County, HI held by Hochman Hawaii Publishing Inc.
Arbitron Metro Market: Wailea, HI *Format:* Classic Rock
George Hochman, President
Jim Carroll, General Manager

Wailuku

KAOI-FM
06-01-1974; 95.1 mhz FM *Hrs Open:* 24; 3.5 kw horiz; 3061 ft.; N20 46 31 W156 14 49
P.O. Box 15261, Santa Rosa, CA 95402 US
(808) 244-9145
License: Wailuku, Maui County, HI held by Visionary Related Entertainment L.L.C.
Group Owner: Visionary Related Entertainment L.L.C.; (acq 2-10-2004; grpsl).
Arbitron Metro Market: Wailuku, Hi *Format:* Adult Contemp *Hrs. of News Programming:* news progmg 5 hrs wkly *No. News Employees:* 1 *Target Audience:* General.
Jim McKeon, Operations Dir
John Detz, General Manager
Dale Parsons, Programming Director
Gary Forsberg, News Director
Alex Kowalski, Chief Engineer

***KKUA**
04-15-1988; 90.7 mhz FM *Hrs Open:* 24; 56 kw; 2556 ft.; N20 39 36 W156 21 50 *Rebroadcasts:* Rebroadcasts KHPR(FM) Honolulu 100%
738 Kaheka Street, Honolulu, HI 96814 US
(808) 955-8821, *Fax:* (808) 942-5477
www.hawaiipublicradio.org
mail@hawaiipublicradio.org
License: Wailuku, Maui County, HI held by Hawaii Public Radio Inc.
Nat'l Network: PRI; NPR
Arbitron Metro Market: Honolulu, HI *Format:* News *Special Programming:* Hawaiian one hr, Pacific Island 2 hrs wkly *Hrs. of News Programming:* news progmg 35 hrs wkly *No. News Employees:* 3 *Target Audience:* General.
Charles Husson, Operations Dir
Michael Titterton, General Manager
Judy Neale, Programming Director
Bill Dorman, News Director
Gene Schiller, Music Director

KMVI
03-17-1947; 550 khz AM *Hrs Open:* 24; 5 kw-U, ND1; N20 53 29 W156 29 23
5501 Excelsior Boulevard, Minneapolis, MN 55416 US
(808) 877-5566, *Fax:* (808) 871-0666
www.espn550.com
License: Wailuku, HI held by Pacific Radio Group Inc.
Group Owner: Pacific Radio Group Inc.; acq 12-10-99; grpsl)
Nat'l Network: ESPN Radio; ABC
Format: Sports *No. News Employees:* 1 *Target Audience:* 18 plus; men, residents/tourists, educated professionals *Adv. Rates:* 18; 18; 18; 11.
Chuck Bergson, President
Pamela Tsutsui, General Manager

***KMNO**
91.7 mhz FM; 140 w; 161.1 m; N20 42 19 W156 21 54
Box 1145, Wailuku, HI
(808)244-2032, *Fax:* (808)243-9626
www.manaoradio.com
License: Wailuku, Maui County, HI
Scott Sherley, President

Waimea

KAGB
01-01-2000; 99.1 mhz FM; 7.3 kw; 2991 ft.; N19 43 16 W155 55 15
C/O Julie O'Connor, General Delivery, Kamuela, HI 96743 US
(808) 329-6633, *Fax:* (808) 934-8088
www.kaparadio.com
studi@kaparadio.com
License: Waimea, Kauai County, HI held by Pacific Radio Group Inc.
Group Owner: Pacific Radio Group Inc.; (acq 8-11-2005; grpsl).
Arbitron Metro Market: Kailua-Kona, HI *Format:* Ethnic
Jeanina Atebara, General Manager
J.E. Orozco, Station Manager
Russ Roberts, News Director
Aaron Savage, Chief Engineer
Cobey Patolo, Traffic Manager

Waipahu

KKNE
09-20-1950; 940 khz AM *Hrs Open:* 24; 10 kw-U, ND1; N21 26 43 W158 3 49
711 Kapiolani Blvd., Suite 750, Honolulu, HI 96813 US
(808) 275-1000, *Fax:* (808) 536-2528
www.am940hawaii.com
info@kkneam.com
License: Waipahu, HI held by Cox Radio Inc.
Group Owner: Cox Radio Inc.; (acq 1-3-2005 with KRTR(AM) Honolulu in exchange for KKOL-FM Aiea)
Regional Network: Waitt Farm Net.
Arbitron Metro Market: Honolulu, HI *Format:* Country *Target Audience:* 25-44.
Patti Milburn, General Manager
Michol Klabo, General Sales Mgr
Kimo Akane, Programming Director
Wade Faildo, Promotions Manager
Rhoda Kihikihi, Human Resources Manager

KDDB
11-23-1988; 102.7 mhz FM; 61 kw horiz, 60 kw vert; 1893 ft.; N21 23 49 W158 5 58
4150 Pinnacle, El Paso, TX 79902 US
(808) 947-1500, *Fax:* (808) 947-1506
License: Waipahu, Honolulu County, HI held by Visionary Related Entertainment L.L.C.
Group Owner: Visionary Related Entertainment L.L.C.; acq 7-1-2004; grpsl).
Nat'l Reps: McGavren Guild
Arbitron Metro Market: Honolulu, HI *Format:* Contemporary Hits/Top 40 *Target Audience:* 18-34; young adults who enjoy many different types of music
John Detz, General Manager

KSSK-FM
12-30-1976; 92.3 mhz FM *Hrs Open:* 24; 100 kw; 1949 ft.; N21 23 49 W158 5 58
600 Congress Ave., Suite 1400, Austin, TX 78701 US
(808) 550-9200, *Fax:* (808) 550-9510
ksskradio.com
info@ksskradio.com
License: Waipahu, Honolulu County, HI held by Clear Channel Broadcasting Licenses Inc.
Group Owner: Clear Channel Communications Inc.; (acq 9-1-00; grpsl)
Nat'l Reps: Clear Channel *Wire Services:* AP; Metro Weather Service Inc.
Arbitron Metro Market: Honolulu, HI *Format:* Adult Contemp *Hrs. of News Programming:* news progmg 6 hrs wkly *No. News Employees:* 3 *Target Audience:* 25-54.
Chuck Cotton, General Manager
Rob Welsh, General Sales Mgr
Jamie Hyatt, Programming Director
kevin Jones, Promotions Manager
Damian Balinowski, News Director
Dale Machado, Chief Engineer
Patti Milburn, General Sales Manager
Larry Price, Traffic Manager

Idaho

Aberdeen

KQPI
01-01-2008; 99.5 mhz FM; 2.2 kw; 1959 ft.; N42 48 31 W112 29 10
US
(312) 204-9900
License: Aberdeen, Bingham County, ID held by College Creek Media LLC.
Group Owner: College Creek Media LLC
Arbitron Metro Market: Aberdeen, ID *Format:* Country
Neal Robinson, President

American Falls

KORR
01-01-1995; 104.1 mhz FM *Hrs Open:* 24; 56 kw; 1109 ft.; N42 51 46 W112 31 3
Mailing Address: P O Box 97, Pocatello, ID 83204 US
Second Address: 436 N. Main St., Pocatello, ID 83204
(208) 234-1290, *Fax:* (208) 234-9451
spots@kzbq.com
License: American Falls, Power County, ID held by Idaho Wireless Corp.
Group Owner: Idaho Wireless Corp.; acq 1996).
Format: Adult Contemp
Paul Anderson, General Manager
Harry Neuhardt, General Sales Mgr

Ammon

KSPZ
11-09-1957; 980 khz AM; 5 kw-D, DA2; 1 kw-N, DA2; N43 31 23 W112 0 36
854 Lindsay Boulevard, Idaho Falls, ID 83401 US
(208) 522-1101, *Fax:* (208) 522-6110
www.lasupercaliente.com
contactus@lasupercalienta.com
License: Ammon, ID held by Sandhill Media Group LLC.
Group Owner: Sand Hill Media Corp.; (acq 2-27-2004; $2.65 million with co-located FM)
Nat'l Reps: McGavren Guild
Arbitron Metro Market: Ammon, ID
James Garshow, President
Ken Walker, General Sales Mgr
Domingo Munoz, Programming Director

Blackfoot

KCVI
09-22-1994; 101.5 mhz FM *Hrs Open:* 24; 95 kw; 1512 ft.; N43 30 3 W112 39 43
810 West 200 North, Logan, UT 84321 US
(208) 785-1400, *Fax:* (208) 785-0184
www.kbear.fm
scott@kbear.fm
License: Blackfoot, Bingham County, ID held by Riverbend Communications LLC.
Group Owner: Riverbend Communications LLC; (acq 4-17-2006; grpsl).
Nat'l Reps: McGavren Guild
Arbitron Metro Market: Blackfoot, ID *Format:* Rock/AOR *Hrs. of News Programming:* news progmg 3 hrs wkly *No. News Employees:* 1 *Target Audience:* 25-44; male
Jim Burgoyne, President
Delyn Hendricks, General Manager
Matt Burgoyne, General Sales Mgr
Scott Taylor, Programming Director
Tisa Cudmore, News Director

KBLI
11-01-1951; 690 khz AM
980 North Michigan Ave, Ste-1880, Chicago, IL 60611 US
(208) 785-1400, *Fax:* (208) 785-0184
www.eastidahonews.com
License: Blackfoot, ID held by Riverbend Communications LLC.
Group Owner: Riverbend Communications LLC; (acq 4-17-2006; grpsl).
Arbitron Metro Market: Blackfoot, ID *Format:* Talk
Mike Nelson, Operations Dir
Delyn Hendricks, General Manager
Tim Lewis, News Director

KLCE
10-15-1975; 97.3 mhz FM; 95 kw; 1512 ft.; N43 30 3 W112 39 43
810 West 200 North, Logan, UT 84321 US
(208) 785-1400, *Fax:* (208) 785-0184
www.klce.com
info@klce.com
License: Blackfoot, Bingham County, ID held by Riverbend Communications LLC
Group Owner: Riverbend Communications LLC
Nat'l Reps: McGavren Guild
Arbitron Metro Market: Boise, ID *Format:* Adult Contemp *Target Audience:* 18-49.
Chris Cross, General Manager
Mary Stapek, General Sales Mgr
Sea Stachura, News Director

Boise

KBOI
05-01-1947; 670 khz AM *Hrs Open:* 24
Mailing Address: City Center West, 7201 W. Lake Mead Blvd, Las Vegas, NV 89128 US
Second Address: 1419 W. Bannock, Boise, ID 83702
(208) 336-3670, *Fax:* (208) 336-3734
www.670kboi.com
andrew.paul@citcomm.com
License: Boise, ID
Group Owner: Cumulus Media Inc.; (acq 12-10-97; grpsl).
Nat'l Reps: Katz Radio *Regional Reps:* Allied Radio Partners
Arbitron Metro Market: Boise, ID *Format:* News, News/Talk, 86 *No. News Employees:* 3 *Target Audience:* 25-54; white collar, upper income
Kevin Godwin, General Manager
Mike Owens, General Sales Mgr
Andrew Paul, Programming Director
Linda Rupe, Promotions Manager
Ken Weaver, News Director

***KBSU-FM**
12-04-1955; 730 khz AM; 15 kw-D, 500 w-N, DA-2; N43 34 13 W116 20 45
213 SMITC, 1910 University Dr., Boise, ID 83725
(208) 426-3663, *Fax:* (208) 344-6631
radio.boisestate.edu/AM730.html
License: Boise, Ada County, ID held by Idaho State Board of Education (Boise State University)
Population Served: 250,000 *Arbitron Metro Market:* Boise, ID *Format:* Jazz, News, 62, Talk *Special Programming:* Folk
Brad Campbell, Operations Dir
John Hess, General Manager
Hy Kloc, General Sales Mgr
Ele Ellis, Programming Director
Sadie Babits, News Director
Tom Taylor, Chief Engineer
Betsy Micone, Business Director
Erik Jones, OperationsManager

***KBSU-FM**
01-16-1977; 90.3 mhz FM *Hrs Open:* 24; 17.5 kw; 2713 ft.; N43 45 21 W116 5 54
1910 University Drive, Boise, ID 83725 US
(208) 426-3663, *Fax:* (208) 344-6631
radio.boisestate.edu
License: Boise, Ada County, ID held by Boise State Board of Education.
Nat'l Network: PRI; NPR
Arbitron Metro Market: Boise, ID *Format:* Talk *Hrs. of News Programming:* News progmg 15 hrs wkly *Target Audience:* General.
Erik Jones, Operations Dir
John Hess, General Manager
Ele Ellis, Programming Director
Sadie Babits, News Director

***KBSX**
01-01-1994; 91.5 mhz FM; 3.7 kw; 2713 ft.; N43 45 21 W116 5 54
1910 University Drive, Boise, ID 83725 US
(208) 426-3663, *Fax:* (208) 344-6631
www.radio.boisestate.edu
License: Boise, Ada County, ID held by Idaho State Board of Education.
Nat'l Network: NPR *Wire Services:* AP
Arbitron Metro Market: Boise, ID *Format:* News *No. News Employees:* 4

Erik Jones, Operations Dir
John Hess, General Manager
Tom Taylor, Chief Engineer

KGEM

01-01-1945; 1140 khz AM *Hrs Open:* 24
P.O. Box 693, Milwaukee, WI 53201 US
(208) 344-4744, *Fax:* (208) 947-6765
www.saltandlightradio.com
License: Boise, ID held by Journal Broadcast Corp.
Group Owner: Journal Communications Inc.; (acq 5-13-98; grpsl)
Nat'l Reps: Katz Radio
Arbitron Metro Market: Boise, ID *Format:* Christian, Religious, 86
Special Programming: Scripture 7 hrs wkly *Target Audience:* 25-54.
Bob Rosenthal, Operations Dir
Cathy Prazenica, General Manager
Brook Bender, General Sales Mgr
Rick Kemp, Programming Director
Kristine Simoni, Promotions Manager
Dan McColly, Operations Manager
Paula Jensen, Traffic Manager

KFXD

11-09-1928; 630 khz AM; 5 kw-D, DA2; 5 kw-N, DA2; N43 30 56 W116 19 43
50 East Rivercenter Blvd., Suite 1200, Covington, KY 41011 US
(208) 344-6363, *Fax:* (208) 344-1134
www.kfxd.com
dave.burnett@peakbroadcasting.com;
kevin.godwin@peakbroadcasting.com;
dave.tester@peakbroadcasting.c
License: Boise, ID held by Peak Broadcasting of Boise Licenses LLC.
Group Owner: Peak Broadcasting LLC; (acq 6-28-2007; grpsl)
Arbitron Metro Market: Boise, ID *Format:* Talk *Special Programming:* Religious 2.5 hrs wkly, finance 6 hrs wkly, gardening 1 hr wkly, gun 3 hr wkly, health 1 hr wkly *Hrs. of News Programming:* news progmg 120 hrs wkly
Dave Burnett, Operations Dir
Kevin Godwin, General Manager
Dave Tester, General Sales Mgr
Dave Burnett, Programming Director

KIZN

08-01-1968; 92.3 mhz FM *Hrs Open:* 24; 48 kw; 2717 ft.; N43 45 21 W116 5 54
City Center West, 7201 W. Lake Mead Blvd, Las Vegas, NV 89128 US
(208) 336-3670, *Fax:* (208) 336-3736
www.kizn.com
rich.summers@citicomm.com
License: Boise, Ada County, ID
Group Owner: Cumulus Media Inc.; (acq 12-24-97; grpsl).
Arbitron Metro Market: Boise, ID *Format:* Country *No. News Employees:* 1 *Target Audience:* 25-54.
Rich Summers, Operations Dir
Adella Stauffer, General Sales Mgr
Don Morin, Promotions Manager
Brenda Mee, News Director
Bill Frahm, Chief Engineer
Patti Hull, Traffic Manager

KJOT

01-01-1979; 105.1 mhz FM *Hrs Open:* 24; 53 kw; 2589 ft.; N43 45 18 W116 5 52
P.O. Box 693, Milwaukee, WI 53201 US
(208) 344-3511, *Fax:* (208) 947-6765
www.varietyrocks.com
License: Boise, Ada County, ID held by Journal Broadcast Corp.
Group Owner: Journal Communications Inc.
Nat'l Reps: Katz Radio
Arbitron Metro Market: Boise, ID *Format:* Classic Rock *Target Audience:* 25-49.
Bob Rosenthal, Operations Dir
Marie McGlynn, General Manager
Brook Bender, General Sales Mgr
Rick Kemp, Programming Director
Kristine Simoni, Promotions Manager
Dan McColly, Operations Manager
Paula Jensen, Traffic Manager
DanMcColly

KMHR(AM)

04-08-1961; 950 khz AM; 5 kw-D, 35 w-N; N43 37 14 W116 17 57
Box 1600, Nampa, ID 83653
(208) 463-1900
info@knjyam.com
License: Boise, Ada County, ID held by First Western Inc.
Arbitron Metro Market: Boise, ID *Format:* Religious *Special Programming:* Farm 5 hrs wkly

Steve Sumner, General Manager

KAWO

11-02-1979; 104.3 mhz FM *Hrs Open:* Monday - Friday 8-5pm; 52 kw; 2579 ft.; N43 45 18 W116 5 52
50 East Rivercenter Blvd., Suite 1200, Covington, KY 41011 US
(208) 344-6363, *Fax:* (208) 342-0444
www.wow1043.com
License: Boise, Ada County, ID held by Peak Broadcasting of Boise Licenses LLC.
Group Owner: Peak Broadcasting LLC
Arbitron Metro Market: Boise, ID *Format:* Country *Target Audience:* General.
Kevin Godwin, General Manager
Dan Matthews, Programming Director
Mike Owens, Promotions Manager

KQFC

11-01-1960; 97.9 mhz FM *Hrs Open:* 24; 48 kw; 2717 ft.; N43 45 21 W116 5 54
City Center West, 7201 W. Lake Mead Blvd, Las Vegas, NV 89128 US
(208) 336-3670, *Fax:* (208) 336-3734
www.98kqfc.com
License: Boise, Ada County, ID
Group Owner: Cumulus Media Inc.
Arbitron Metro Market: Boise metropolitan area *Format:* Country *Target Audience:* 25-54; country lifestyle
Jim Garshow, General Manager
Tom Newman, General Sales Mgr
Rich Summers, Programming Director
Emily Marcum, Promotions Manager

KSPD

04-29-1959; 790 khz AM *Hrs Open:* 24; 1 kw-D, ND2; 0.061 kw-N, ND2; N43 33 57 W116 20 13
1477 South Five Mile Rd., Boise, ID 83709 US
(208) 377-3790, *Fax:* (208) 377-3792
www.myfamilyradio.com
info@myfamilyradio.com
License: Boise, ID held by KSPD Inc.
Group Owner: KSPD Inc.; acq 3-24-83;
Nat'l Network: Salem Radio Network
Arbitron Metro Market: Boise, ID *Format:* Christian, Talk *Target Audience:* 18-54. *Adv. Rates:* 20; 20; 20; 15
Lee Schafer, President
David Schafer, Assistant Manager
Beth Schafer, Executive Vice President

Bonners Ferry

KBFI

09-01-1977; 1450 khz AM; 1 kw-U, ND1; N48 41 20 W116 20 4
327 Marion Avenue, Sandpoint, ID 83864 US
(208) 263-2179, *Fax:* (208) 265-5440
prod@953kpnd.com
License: Bonners Ferry, ID held by Blue Sky Broadcasting.
Arbitron Metro Market: Bonners Ferry, ID *Format:* News, News/Talk, 84, Talk *No. News Employees:* 1 *Target Audience:* General.
Dylan Benefield, General Manager
Jim Tomchek, Programming Director

*KIBX

01-01-2000; 92.1 mhz FM; 0.074 kw; 2749 ft.; N48 36 37 W116 15 24
Mailing Address: 2319 North Monroe Street, Spokane, WA 99205 US
Second Address: , Bonners Ferry, ID
(509) 328-5729, *Fax:* (509) 328-5764
kpbx.org
kpbx@kpbx.org
License: Bonners Ferry, Boundary County, ID held by Spokane Public Radio Inc.
Nat'l Network: NPR; PRI
Arbitron Metro Market: Spokane, WA *Format:* Classical, Jazz, 60 *Target Audience:* General, educated
Tom Parker, Chairman
Cary Boyce, President & General Manager
Kevin Brown, Front Porch Bluegrass Producer
Paige Browning, News Correspondent, Announcer
Mary Cravens, Membership Coordinator
Frank Delaney, Raw Bytes Producer &Host
Brian Flick, Operations Manager, Jazz Host
Mary Harvill, Front Desk Receptionist

Buhl

*KTFY

08-01-2005; 88.1 mhz FM *Hrs Open:* 24; 60 kw vert; 653 ft.; N42 43 48 W114 25 6
16115 South Montana Ave, Caldwell, ID 83605 US
(208) 735-0881, *Fax:* (208) 459-3144
www.881ktfy.org
family@thebridgeinteractive.org
License: Buhl, Twin Falls County, ID held by Southern Idaho Corp. of Seventh-Day Adventists dba Gem State Academy.
Arbitron Metro Market: Buhl, ID *Format:* Christian *Target Audience:* 25-54; women
Donald Klinger, Chairman
Stephen McPherson, President
Michael Agee, General Manager
Jerry Woods, Programming Director

Burley

KBAR

08-31-1946; 1230 khz AM; 1 kw-U, ND1; N42 32 5 W113 48 54
313 7th Avenue East, Jerome, ID 83338 US
(208) 678-2244, *Fax:* (208) 678-2246
kimlee@cableone.net
License: Burley, ID held by KART Broadcasting Co. Inc. and Eagle Rock Broadcasting Inc. as tenants-in-common.
Group Owner: Tri-Market Radio Broadcasters Inc. & Eagle Rock Broadcasting Inc.; (acq 1-30-98; with co-located FM).
Format: Oldies, Talk
Kim Lee, General Manager
Chris Kinzel, General Sales Mgr
Ben Reed, Programming Director

*KBSY

10-01-1998; 88.5 mhz FM; 0.44 kw vert; 2083 ft.; N42 21 42 W113 27 17 *Rebroadcasts:* Rebroadcasts KBSX(FM) Boise 100%
1910 University Drive, Boise, ID 83725 US
(208) 426-3663, *Fax:* (208) 344-6631
radio.boisestate.edu
License: Burley, Cassia County, ID held by Idaho State Board of Education.
Nat'l Network: NPR
Format: News, News/Talk, 86
Erik Jones, Operations Dir
John Hess, General Manager
Ele Ellis, Programming Director
Tom Taylor, Engineering Dir

KZDX

02-15-1975; 99.9 mhz FM; 27 kw; 2450 ft.; N42 20 6 W113 36 15
313 7th Avenue East, Jerome, ID 83338 US
(208) 312-7284, *Fax:* (208) 678-2246
www.hot100now.com/
kzdxblastoff@yahoo.com
License: Burley, Cassia County, ID held by KART Broadcasting Co. Inc.
Group Owner: Tri-Market Radio Broadcasters Inc. & Eagle Rock Broadcasting Inc.
Arbitron Metro Market: Burley, ID *Format:* Rock/AOR
Ted Riley, General Manager
Broc Johnson, Programming Director

Caldwell

KSAS-FM

09-28-1982; 103.3 mhz FM *Hrs Open:* 24; 54 kw; 2579 ft.; N43 45 18 W116 5 52
50 East Rivercenter Blvd., Suite 1200, Covington, KY 41011 US
(208) 344-6363, *Fax:* (208) 385-9064
www.1033kissfm.com
kekeluv@gmail.com
License: Caldwell, Canyon County, ID held by Peak Broadcasting of Boise Licenses LLC.
Group Owner: Peak Broadcasting LLC; (acq 6-28-2007; grpsl)
Arbitron Metro Market: Boise, ID *Format:* Contemporary Hits/Top 40 *Special Programming:* Class 2 hrs, jazz 4 hrs wkly *Hrs. of News Programming:* news progmg one hr wkly *No. News Employees:* 1 *Target Audience:* 25-54; upscale, white collar
Kevin Godwin, General Manager
Mike Sutton, General Sales Mgr
Steve Kicklighter, Programming Director
Crystal Struthers, Promotions Manager
Dave Burnett, News Director
Susan Green, Traffic Manager

KBGN

10-05-1960; 1060 khz AM; 10 kw-D, NDD; N43 43 13 W116 31 58
3303 E. Chicago, Caldwell, ID 83605 US
(208) 459-3635
www.kbgnradio.com
kbgn@kbgnradio.com
License: Caldwell, ID held by Nelson M. Wilson & Karen E. Wilson.
Nat'l Network: USA

Arbitron Metro Market: Caldwell, ID *Format:* Christian, Religious, 86 *Special Programming:* Sp 5 hrs wkly *Target Audience:* General.
Marnie Fillmore, Operations Dir
Nelson Wilson, General Manager

KBXL

02-22-1961; 94.1 mhz FM *Hrs Open:* 24; 39 kw; 2635 ft.; N43 45 18 W116 5 52
1477 South Five Mile Rd, Boise, ID 83709 US
(208) 377-3790, *Fax:* (208) 377-3792
www.myfamilyradio.com
info@myfamilyradio.com
License: Caldwell, Canyon County, ID held by KSPD Inc.
Group Owner: KSPD Inc.; acq 4-26-89;
Nat'l Network: AP Network News *Nat'l Reps:* Salem *Regional Reps:* Tacher
Arbitron Metro Market: Boise, ID *Format:* Christian, Talk, 74 *Target Audience:* 25-54. *Adv. Rates:* 35; 25; 35; 15.
Lee Schafer, President
David Schafer, Operations Dir
Beth Schafer, General Manager
Leigh Ann Schafer, Programming Director

KCID

01-01-1947; 1490 khz AM *Hrs Open:* 24; 1 kw-U, ND1; N43 39 51 W116 38 10
P.O. Box 693, Milwaukee, WI 53201 US
(208) 344-3511, *Fax:* (208) 947-6765
License: Caldwell, ID held by Journal Broadcast Corp.
Group Owner: Journal Communications Inc.; (acq 5-13-98; grpsl)
Nat'l Reps: Katz Radio
Arbitron Metro Market: Boise, ID *Format:* Oldies *Target Audience:* 35 plus.
Bob Rosenthal, Operations Dir
Cathy Prazenica, General Manager
Brook Bender, General Sales Mgr
Rick Kemp, Programming Director
Kristine Simoni, Promotions Manager
Dan McColly, Operations Manager
Paula Jensen, Traffic Manager

KTHI

12-01-1983; 107.1 mhz FM *Hrs Open:* 24; 52 kw; 2579 ft.; N43 45 18 W116 5 52
P.O. Box 693, Milwaukee, WI 53201 US
(208) 344-3511, *Fax:* (208) 947-6765
www.khits.fm
License: Caldwell, Canyon County, ID held by Journal Broadcast Corp.
Group Owner: Journal Communications Inc.
Nat'l Reps: Katz Radio
Arbitron Metro Market: Boise, ID *Format:* Oldies *Target Audience:* General. *Adv. Rates:* 35; 30; 30; 20
Bob Rosenthal, Operations Dir
Cathy Prazenica, General Manager
Brook Bender, General Sales Mgr
Rick Kemp, Programming Director
Kristine Simoni, Promotions Manager
Dan McColly, Operations Manager
KJ Mac, Program Director
PaulaJensen, Traffic Manager

*KTSY

10-14-1990; 89.5 mhz FM *Hrs Open:* 24; 8.3 kw; 2595 ft.; N43 45 18 W116 5 52
16115 S. Montana Avenue, Caldwell, ID 83605 US
(208) 459-5879, *Fax:* (208) 459-3144
www.ktsy.org
family@ktsy.org
License: Caldwell, Canyon County, ID held by Gem State Adventist Academy.
Arbitron Metro Market: Boise, ID *Format:* Christian *Hrs. of News Programming:* News progmg 4 hrs wkly *Target Audience:* 25-45.
Donald Klinger, Chairman
Stephen McPherson, President
Michael Agee, General Manager
Jerry Woods, Programming Director

Chubbuck

KLLP

11-10-1984; 98.5 mhz FM *Hrs Open:* 24; kw*Rebroadcasts:* Rebroadcasts KAWZ(FM) Twin Falls 65%
50 East Rivercenter Blvd., #1200, Covington, KY 41011 US
(208) 233-1133, *Fax:* (208) 232-1240
www.985klite.com,www.star985.com
kellymartinez@gapbroadcasting.com
License: Chubbuck, Bannock County, ID
Group Owner: Rich Broadcasting LLC; (acq 2-13-2008; grpsl)
Arbitron Metro Market: Boise, ID *Format:* Adult Contemp *Special Programming:* Sp 4 hrs wkly *Target Audience:* General. *Adv. Rates:* 6; 4; 6; 4
Jeff Evans, Operations Dir
Ryan Doremus, General Sales Mgr
Kelly Martinez, Programming Director
Cami Chopski, News Director
Rhett Downing, Chief Engineer
Neica Kinney, Sales Manager

KRTK

01-01-1981; 1490 khz AM *Hrs Open:* 24; 1 kw-U, ND1; N42 55 38 W112 30 3
P.O. Box Zee, Pocatello, ID 83206 US
(208) 237-9500, *Fax:* (208) 237-4600
krtk@ltlink.com
License: Chubbuck, ID held by Broken Chains Inc.
Nat'l Network: ABC
Arbitron Metro Market: Pocatello, ID *Format:* Christian *Target Audience:* 35-55. *Adv. Rates:* 12; 10; 12; 5
Stacy Dare, Station Manager

Coeur D'Alene

KICR

10-12-2001; 102.3 mhz FM *Hrs Open:* 24; 0.172 kw; 1844 ft.; N47 39 35 W116 57 12 *Rebroadcasts:* Rebroadcasts KIBR-FM Sandpoint 100%
23547 Schoen Born, West Hills, CA 91304 US
(208) 663-2179, *Fax:* (208) 265-5440
www.themorningstampede.com
dylanb@a53kpwd.com
License: Coeur D'Alene, Kootenai County, ID held by Great Northern Broadcasting Inc.
Arbitron Metro Market: Spokane, ID *Format:* Country
Dylan Benefield, General Manager
Jimmy Silver, Programming Director
Mike Brown, News Director

KVNI

11-01-1946; 1080 khz AM *Hrs Open:* 24
Mailing Address: 500 West Boone Avenue, Spokane, WA 99201 US
Second Address: 500 W. Boone Ave., Spokane, WA 99201
(208) 664-9271, *Fax:* (208) 667-0945
www.kvni.com
License: Coeur D'Alene, ID held by QueenB Radio Inc.
Nat'l Reps: Katz Radio
Arbitron Metro Market: Spokane, WA *Format:* News, Oldies
Special Programming: Relg 3 hrs wkly *No. News Employees:* 2 *Target Audience:* 25 plus.
Roger Nelson, General Manager
Kris Siebers, Programming Director
Tim Anderson, Chief Engineer

Cottonwood

*KNWO

01-01-1994; 90.1 mhz FM *Hrs Open:* 24; 0.25 kw; 2008 ft.; N46 4 9 W116 27 54 *Rebroadcasts:* Rebroadcasts KRFA-FM Moscow, ID
Edu. Telecommns. & Tech., PO Box 642530, Pullman, WA 99164 US
(509) 335-6500, *Fax:* (509) 335-3772
www.nwpr.org
nwpr@wsu.edu
License: Cottonwood, Idaho County, ID held by Washington State University.
Format: News *Hrs. of News Programming:* news progmg 37 hrs wkly *No. News Employees:* 1 *Target Audience:* 25 plus.
Karen Olstad, COO
Scott Weatherly, Operations Dir
Dennis Haarsager, General Manager
Roger Johnson, Station Manager
Sarah McDaniel, General Sales Mgr
Mary Hawkins, Programming Director
Rachael McDonald, News Director
RalphHogan, Engineering Dir
Robin Rilette, Music Director

Culdesac

KZID

01-01-2003; 98.5 mhz FM; 6.3 kw; 420 ft.; N46 27 47 W116 54 25
Gammon & Grange Pc, 8280 Greensboro Dr 7th F, McLean, VA 22102 US
(336) 286-2087
License: Culdesac, Clearwater County, ID held by Torro Broadcasting.
Arbitron Metro Market: Culdesac, ID *Format:* Rock/AOR
Eliot Keller, President
Julie Hein, General Sales Mgr
Greg Runyon, Programming Director
Jamie Burgin, Promotions Manager
Scott Schulte, News Director
Robert Norton Jr., Executive Vice President
Kellie Lala, General SalesManager
Ric Swann, Music Director

Donnelly

KMCL(AM)

10-15-1965; 1240 khz AM; 1 kw-U; N44 46 52 W116 02 51
Mailing Address: Box 813, McCall, ID 83638
Second Address: 204 N. 3rd St., McCall, ID 83638
License: Donnelly, Valley County, ID held by Brundage Mountain Air Inc.
Population Served: 25,000
David Eaton, General Manager

Driggs

KCHQ

02-12-2004; 102.1 mhz FM *Hrs Open:* 24; 4 kw; Ant 1899 ft; N43 42 42 W111 20 56
Mailing Address: 1406 Commerce Way, Idaho Falls, ID 83445
Second Address: P.O. Box 54, Driggs, ID 83422
(208) 524-5900, *Fax:* (208) 522-9696
www.rivercountryfm.com
delyn@richbroadcasting.com
License: Driggs, Teton County, ID held by Rich Broadcasting of Idaho LS
Group Owner: Rich Broadcasting LLC; 06/02/2011
Nat'l Reps: Eastman
Population Served: 95,000*Hrs. of News Programming:* news progmg 8 hrs wkly *No. News Employees:* 1 *Target Audience:* 25-54; adults *Adv. Rates:* 20; 15; 18; 12.
Richard Mecham, President
DeLyn Hendricks, General Manager
Sandie Fulks, General Sales Mgr
Denis Miller, Programming Director

Eagle

KXLT-FM

09-01-1994; 107.9 mhz FM; 45 kw; 2684 ft.; N43 45 18 W116 5 52
50 East Rivercenter Boulevard, Suite 1200, Covington, KY 41011 US
(208) 344-6363, *Fax:* (208) 327-8800
www.lite108.com
lisa.adams@peakbroadcasting.com
License: Eagle, Ada County, ID held by Peak Broadcasting of Boise Licenses LLC.
Group Owner: Peak Broadcasting LLC; (acq 6-28-2007; grpsl)
Nat'l Reps: McGavren Guild
Arbitron Metro Market: Boise, ID *Format:* Adult Contemp *Target Audience:* 25-54.
Kevin Godwin, General Manager
Tobin Jeffries, Programming Director
Dave Burnett, News Director
Susan Green, Traffic Manager

Emmett

KDBI

03-12-1973; 101.9 mhz FM; 57 kw; 2533 ft.; N43 45 18 W116 5 52
3982 Glendale, Boise, ID 83703 US
(208) 463-2900
www.bustosmedia.com
jtovar@bustomedia.com
License: Emmett, Gem County, ID held by First Western Inc.
Group Owner: Adelante Media Group LLC; (acq 11-1-2003; $1.05 million).
Ed Distel, General Manager

Fairfield

KXML

99.9 mhz FM; 0.2 kw; -1312 ft.; N45 10 2 W113 52 14 US
(520) 797-4434
License: Fairfield, Lemhi County, ID held by SkyWest Media L.L.C.
Group Owner: SkyWest Media L.L.C.
Arbitron Metro Market: Fairfield, ID
Ted Tucker, General Manager

Garden City

KCIX
01-01-1985; 105.9 mhz FM; 49 kw; 2700 ft.; N43 45 18 W116 5 52
50 East Rivercenter Boulevard, Suite 1200, Covington, KY 41011 US
(208) 344-6363, *Fax:* (208) 385-9064
www.mix106radio.com
mikeandkate@mix106radio.com
License: Garden City, Ada County, ID held by Peak Broadcasting of Boise Licenses LLC.
Group Owner: Peak Broadcasting LLC; (acq 6-28-2007; grpsl)
Nat'l Reps: McGavren Guild
Arbitron Metro Market: Boise, ID *Format:* Adult Contemp *Target Audience:* 25-54.
Terry Tario, General Manager
Brent Carey, Programming Director
Dave Burnett, News Director
Susan Green, Traffic Manager
Matt Steele

Gooding

KPDA-FM
12-02-1996; 100.7 mhz FM *Hrs Open:* 24; 73 kw; 2192 ft.; N43 14 43 W115 26 12
616 Blue Lakes Blvd, North, #1270, Twin Falls, ID 83301 US
(208) 465-9966, *Fax:* (208) 465-2922
License: Gooding, Gooding County, ID held by FM Idaho Co. LLC.
Group Owner: FM Idaho Co. LLC dba Impact Radio Group; (acq 12-31-2006; grpsl)
Arbitron Metro Market: Boise, ID *Format:* Tejano *No. News Employees:* 35
Elliott Klein, President
Mikey Fuentes, Operations Dir
Darrell Calton, General Manager
Mark Broz, General Sales Mgr
Sarah McBride, Traffic Manager

KRXR
01-01-1992; 1480 khz AM
910 5th St., Rupert, ID 83350 US
, *Fax:* (208) 934-8630
(208) 934-8688
krxr@cableone.net
License: Gooding, ID held by Maria Elena Juarez.
Efrain Ortega, General Manager

Grangeville

KORT(AM/FM)
10-08-1954; 1230 khz AM; 1 kw-U; N45 55 52 W116 07 50
Box 510, Grangeville, ID 83530
(208) 983-1230, *Fax:* (208) 983-2744
License: Grangeville, Idaho County, ID held by 4-K Radio Inc.
Group Owner: 4-K Radio Inc.; (acq 6-1-71)
Population Served: 12,500*Special Programming:* Farm 2 hrs wkly *Hrs. of News Programming:* news progmg 8 hrs wkly *No. News Employees:* 1 *Target Audience:* General. *Adv. Rates:* 15; 15; 15; 15
Mike Ripley, President
Melinda Hall, General Manager
David Forsman, Chief Engineer
Ben Rivers, Disc Jockey
William, Disc Jockey
Tammy Lyson, Disc Jockey

KORT-FM
12-01-1979; 92.7 mhz FM; 360 w; 2,352 ft; N45 51 48 W116 07 24
Box 510, Grangeville, ID 83501
(208) 983-1230, *Fax:* (208) 983-2744
License: Grangeville, Idaho County, ID
Group Owner: 4-K Radio Inc.
Nat'l Network: ABC
Population Served: 8,500
Mike Ripley, President
Mike Ripley, General Manager
Melinda Hall, Station Manager
Melinda Hall, General Sales Mgr
Melinda Hall, Programming Director
Jason Ford, News Director
David Forsman, Chief Engineer

*KKRH
90.9 mhz FM; 1.9 kw; 2324 ft.; N45 51 42 W116 7 25
US
(208) 983-5433
www.calvarychapelgrangeville.com
License: Grangeville, Idaho County, ID held by Calvary Chapel of Grangeville Inc.
Arbitron Metro Market: Grangeville, ID *Format:* Christian
Dean Huibregtse, President

Hailey

KYUN
01-01-2006; 106.7 mhz FM; 97 kw; 1578 ft.; N43 16 45 W114 9 14
US
(208) 735-8300, *Fax:* (208) 733-4196
www.canyoncountryonline.com
License: Hailey, Blaine County, ID held by Locally Owned Radio LLC.
Group Owner: Locally Owned Radio LLC
Arbitron Metro Market: Hailey, ID *Format:* Country
Larry Johnson, President
Jerre Fender, Operations Dir
Deb Uvieu, General Sales Mgr
Denis Jeffs, News Director

Hayden

KHTQ
11-01-1991; 94.5 mhz FM *Hrs Open:* 24; 83 kw; 2182 ft.; N47 39 34 W116 57 48
Mailing Address: 500 West Boone Avenue, Spokane, WA 99201 US
Second Address: 500 W. Boone Ave., Spokane, WA 99201
(509) 324-4200, *Fax:* (208) 667-0945
www.rock945.com
garya@kxly.com
License: Hayden, Kootenai County, ID
Arbitron Metro Market: Spokane, WA *Format:* Rock/AOR *Target Audience:* 18-35
Roger Nelson, General Manager
Tery Garras, General Sales Mgr
Barry Hawbaker, Programming Director
Jolene Longwill, News Director
Gary Allen, Disc Jockey
Barry Bennet, Disc Jockey
Geoff Scott, Disc Jockey
Kris Siebers, MusicDirector

Hazelton

KTPZ
01-01-2007; 92.7 mhz FM; 4.9 kw; 741 ft.; N42 43 54 W114 25 4
US
(208) 735-8300, *Fax:* (208) 733-4196
www.ktpz.com
lorproduction@gmail.com
License: Hazelton, Jerome County, ID held by Locally Owned Radio LLC.
Group Owner: Locally Owned Radio LLC; (acq 9-8-2006; $2,911,000 with KIRQ(FM) Twin Falls)
Arbitron Metro Market: Hazelton, ID *Format:* Christian
Larry Johnson, President
Jerre Fender, Operations Dir
Deb Uvieu, General Sales Mgr
Denis Jeffs, News Director

Homedale

KQTA
12-01-2004; 106.3 mhz FM; 100 kw; 1028 ft.; N43 37 15 W117 12 35
C/O Leopoldo Ramos, 30721 Driftwood Drive, Laguna Beach, CA 92677 US
(916) 368-6300, *Fax:* (916) 283-9614
www.lakebuena.com
info@bustosmedia.com
License: Homedale, Owyhee County, ID
Group Owner: Adelante Media Group LLC; (acq 10-28-2005; $2.25 million)
Ed Distel, General Manager
Jose Tovar, General Sales Mgr

Idaho Falls

KSNA
08-18-1975; 100.7 mhz FM *Hrs Open:* 24; 100 kw; 633 ft.; N43 21 6 W112 0 29
854 Lindsay Boulevard, Idaho Falls, ID 83402 US
(208) 522-1101, *Fax:* (208) 522-6110
www.sunny943.com
License: Idaho Falls, Madison County, ID held by Sand Hill Media Corp.
Group Owner: Sand Hill Media Corp.; acq 9-7-2001; $1.2 million with KQEO(FM) Idaho Falls plus 36-month employment agreement).
Nat'l Network: Jones Radio Networks; USA *Nat'l Reps:* Tacher
Arbitron Metro Market: Idaho Falls, IN *Format:* Contemporary Hits/Top 40
Mike Steele, Operations Dir
Keith Walker, General Manager
Chris Sheetz, General Sales Mgr
John Balginy, News Director

KFTZ
05-24-1986; 103.3 mhz FM *Hrs Open:* 24; 100 kw; 659 ft.; N43 21 6 W112 0 22
Mailing Address: 980 North Michigan Ave., Suite 1880, Chicago, IL 60611 US
Second Address: 1190 Lincoln Rd., Idaho Falls, ID 83401
(208) 785-1400, *Fax:* (208) 785-0184
www.z103.fm
info@z103.fm
License: Idaho Falls, Bonneville County, ID held by Riverbend Communications LLC.
Group Owner: Riverbend Communications LLC; (acq 4-17-2006; grpsl).
Regional Reps: Christal Radio
Arbitron Metro Market: ID Falls, ID *Format:* Contemporary Hits/Top 40 *Target Audience:* 18-34.
Jim Burgoyne, President
Delyn Hendricks, General Manager
Matt Burgoyne, General Sales Mgr
Jeremy Dresen, Programming Director
Tisa Cudmore, News Director

KBLY
09-10-1960; 1260 khz AM; 5 kw-D, ND1; 0.064 kw-N, ND1; N43 31 15 W111 59 33
810 West 200 North, Logan, UT 84321 US
(208) 785-1400, *Fax:* (208) 785-0184
www.eastidahonews.com
tim@eiradio.com; mike@klce.com
License: Idaho Falls, ID held by Riverbend Communications LLC.
Group Owner: Riverbend Communications LLC; (acq 4-17-2006; grpsl).
Format: Talk *Special Programming:* Nutrition 1 hr wkly *Hrs. of News Programming:* news 120 hrs wkly *Target Audience:* 35 plus; upscale, mature adults
Jim Burgoyne, President
Mike Nelson, Operations Dir
Delyn Hendricks, General Manager
Matt Burgoyne, General Sales Mgr
Neal Larson, Programming Director
Tim Lewis, News Director

KID
01-01-1928; 590 khz AM; 5 kw-D, DAN; 1 kw-N, DAN; N43 33 35 W111 55 15
50 East Rivercenter Blvd., Suite 1200, Covington, KY 41011 US
(208) 524-5900, *Fax:* (208) 522-9696
www,590kid.com
neal@590kid.com; DeLyn@radiopandemic.com; Sandie@radiopandemic.com
License: Idaho Falls, ID
Group Owner: Rich Broadcasting LLC; (acq 2-13-2008; grpsl)
Nat'l Network: CBS *Nat'l Reps:* Target Broadcast Sales
Format: News, News/Talk, 86 *Special Programming:* Wall Street Journal 20 hrs wkly, sports 1 hr wkly *Hrs. of News Programming:* News progmg 100 hrs wkly *Target Audience:* 25-54; upscale decision-making professionals
Neica Kinney, General Manager
Sandie Fulks, General Sales Mgr
Bill Hatch, News Director
Neal Larson, Program/News Director
DeLyn Hendricks, Market Manager

KID-FM
05-01-1965; 96.1 mhz FM; 100 kw; 1503 ft.; N43 29 51 W112 39 50
50 East Rivercenter Blvd., Suite 1200, Covington, KY 41011 US
(208) 524-5900, *Fax:* (208) 522-9696
www,590kid.com
neal@590kid.com; DeLyn@radiopandemic.com; Sandie@radiopandemic.com
License: Idaho Falls, Bonneville County, ID
Group Owner: Rich Broadcasting LLC; (acq 2-13-2008; grpsl)
Format: Country *Special Programming:* Wall Street Journal 20 hrs wkly, sports 1 hr wkly
Joseph Orozco, General Manager
Sandie Fulks, General Sales Mgr
Neal Larson, Program/News Director
DeLyn Hendricks, Market Manager

KTHK
10-01-1993; 105.5 mhz FM *Hrs Open:* 24; 100 kw; 659 ft.; N43 21 6 W112 0 22
980 North Michigan Ave., Suite 1880, Chicago, IL 60611 US

(208) 523-3722, *Fax:* (208) 525-2575
www.1055thehawk.com
License: Idaho Falls, Booneville County, ID held by Riverbend Communications LLC.
Group Owner: Riverbend Communications LLC; (acq 4-17-2006; grpsl).
Format: Country
Delyn Hendricks, General Manager
Sandie Fulks, General Sales Mgr

KQEO
04-01-2003; 107.1 mhz FM; 100 kw; 633 ft.; N43 21 6 W112 0 29
Mailing Address: P O Box 17, St Anthony, ID 83445 US
Second Address: 854 Lindsay Blvd., Idaho Falls, ID 83402
(208) 522-1101, *Fax:* (208) 522-6110
www.arrow107.com
contactus@arrow107.com
License: Idaho Falls, Bonneville County, ID held by Sand Hill Media Corp.
Group Owner: Sand Hill Media Corp.; acq 9-7-2001; $1.2 million with KSNA(FM) Rexburg plus 36-month employment agreement).
Arbitron Metro Market: Idaho Falls, ID *Format:* Contemporary Hits/Top 40, Adult Contemp
Jim Garshow, General Manager

***KAIO**
01-01-2006; 90.5 mhz FM; 0.5 kw vert; 528 ft.; N43 32 37 W111 53 7 *Rebroadcasts:* Rebroadcasts KLRD(FM) Yucaipa, CA 100%
1425 North Market Blvd, Suite 9, Sacramento, CA 95834 US
(800) 877-5600, *Fax:* (916) 251-1650
www.air1.com
info@air1.com
License: Idaho Falls, Bonneville County, ID held by Educational Media Foundation.
Group Owner: EMF Broadcasting
Nat'l Network: Air 1
Format: Alternative, Christian
Mike Novak, President
Mike Lee, Operations Dir
David Pierce, Programming Director
Ed Lenane, News Director
Sam Wallington, Engineering Dir
Marya Morgan, News Reporter
Richard Hunt, News Reporter

Island Park

KWYS(FM)
11-01-1998; 102.9 mhz FM *Hrs Open:* 24; 46 kw; 2,732 ft; N44 33 41 W111 26 32
Box 2158, Ketchum, ID 83340
(208) 726-5324, *Fax:* (208) 726-5459
License: Island Park, Fremont County, ID held by Resurgence Development LLC
Population Served: 100,000*Format:* Classic Rock *Hrs. of News Programming:* news progmg 10 hrs wkly *No. News Employees:* 2 *Target Audience:* 18-45; Adults
Scott Anderson, General Manager

Jerome

KART
08-01-1956; 1400 khz AM; 1 kw-U, ND1; N42 43 51 W114 32 17
144 Seminole Circle, Jerome, ID 83338 US
(208) 324-8181, *Fax:* (208) 324-7124
License: Jerome, ID held by KART Broadcasting Co.
Nat'l Network: CBS
Arbitron Metro Market: Jerome, ID *Format:* Country *Target Audience:* 25 plus.
Lamont Summers, Programming Director
Tammy Davis, News Director

KZNO (FM)
08-01-1970; 102.9 mhz FM; 100 kw; 760 ft; N42 43 54 W114 25 04
3219 Laurelwood Dr, Twin Falls, ID 83301
(208) 324-8181, *Fax:* (208) 324-7124
KimLee@leeradio.net
License: Jerome, Jerome County, ID held by KART Broadcasting Co.
Group Owner: Lee Family Broadcasting Inc.; Acq 5-1-2012
Nat'l Reps: McGavren Guild
Target Audience: Men 12-64
Broc Johnson, Operations Dir
Kim Lee, General Manager
Kim Lee, Station Manager
Kim Lee, General Sales Mgr
Broc Johnson, Programming Director
Jerry Thaxon, Chief Engineer
Tammy Davis, Traffic Manager

KDIL
940 khz AM
US
(208) 324-9268
License: Jerome, ID held by Scott Powell.
Arbitron Metro Market: Jerome, ID
Amy Meredith, President
Scott Powell, General Manager

Ketchum

KIKX
12-02-1996; 104.7 mhz FM; 97 kw; 1578 ft.; N43 16 45 W114 9 14
2660 Peachtree Road, N.W, #17f, Atlanta, GA 30305 US
(208) 733-5459, *Fax:* (208) 733-4196
kikx.com
lorproduction@gmail.com
License: Ketchum, Blaine County, ID held by Locally Owned Radio LLC.
Group Owner: Locally Owned Radio LLC; (acq 10-31-2003; grpsl)
Format: News
Larry Johnson, President
Jerre Fender, Operations Dir
Deb Uvieu, General Sales Mgr
Denis Jeffs, News Director

Kootenai

KTPO
01-01-2007; 106.7 mhz FM; 1.3 kw; 1158 ft.; N48 13 45 W116 30 30
US
(208) 263-2179, *Fax:* (208) 265-5440
www.1067thepoint.com
carolynp@953kpnd.com
License: Kootenai, Bonner County, ID held by Hellroaring Communications L.L.C.
Arbitron Metro Market: Kootenai, ID *Format:* Classic Rock
Dylan Benefield, General Manager
Mike Brown, News Director
John Goes, Chief Engineer

Kuna

***KARJ**
01-01-2005; 88.3 mhz FM *Hrs Open:* 24; 23 kw vert; 2161 ft.; N43 0 26 W116 42 23 *Rebroadcasts:* Rebroadcasts KLRD(FM) Yucaipa, CA 100%
1425 North Market Blvd., Suite 9, Sacramento, CA 95834 US
(888) 937-2471, *Fax:* (916) 251-1650
www.air1.com
info@air1.com
License: Kuna, Ada County, ID held by Educational Media Foundation.
Group Owner: EMF Broadcasting
Nat'l Network: Air 1
Arbitron Metro Market: Kuna, ID *Format:* Alternative, Christian *No. News Employees:* 3 *Target Audience:* 18-35; Judeo-Christian, female
Darrell Chambliss, Chairman
Alan Mason, COO
Mike Novak, President and CEO
Mike Lee, Operations Dir
Eric Allen, General Sales Mgr
David Pierce, Programming Director
Ed Lenane, News Director
Sam Wallington, Engineering Dir
Tracy Butler, Traffic Manager
Dan Antonelli, Chief Business Development Officer
Eric Moser, Chief Financial Officer
Brian Burger, Vice President of Human Resources
D. Kevin Blair, Secretary and General Counsel
Walter Golembeski, Director

Lapwai

KZBG
01-01-2005; 97.7 mhz FM; 0.57 kw; 1060 ft.; N46 27 22 W117 2 56
721 South Hillcrest Dr, Colfax, WA 99111 US
(509) 751-0976, *Fax:* (509) 751-0975
bigcountryradio@clearwire.net
License: Lapwai, Nez Perce County, ID held by Xana Duke Radio Partners LLC
Arbitron Metro Market: Lapwai, ID *Format:* Country
Thomas D. Hodgins, General Manager

Lewiston

KATW
10-02-1986; 101.5 mhz FM *Hrs Open:* 24; 100 kw; 846 ft.; N46 27 38 W117 1 0
403 C Street, Lewiston, ID 83501 US
(208) 743-6564, *Fax:* (208) 798-0110
www.catfm.com
markbolland@pacempire.com
License: Lewiston, Nez Perce County, ID held by Bolland Enterprises LLC.
Group Owner: Pacific Empire Radio Corp.; (acq 9-12-2008; grpsl)
Format: Adult Contemp *Target Audience:* 18-49.
Mark Bolland, General Manager
Evan Yeoman, Programming Director
Leslie Gatherer, News Director

***KLCZ**
10-01-1967; 88.9 mhz FM; 0.23 kw; -840 ft.; N46 24 45 W117 1 31
3317 12th St., Lewiston, ID 83501 US
(208) 792-2418, *Fax:* (208) 792-2568
www.klcz.com
klcz@lcmal.lcsc.edu
License: Lewiston, Nez Perce County, ID held by Lewis-Clark State College
Format: Variety/Diverse
Tate Smith, General Manager
Sandra Kelly, Station Manager
Jason Snyder, Music Manager

KMOK
03-01-1983; 106.9 mhz FM *Hrs Open:* 24; 99 kw; 1230 ft.; N46 27 33 W117 2 18
805 Stewart Ave., Lewiston, ID 83501 US
(208) 743-1551, *Fax:* (208) 743-4440
sales@idavend.com
License: Lewiston, Nez Perce County, ID held by Ida-Vend Co. Inc.
Group Owner: IdaVend Broadcasting Inc.
Nat'l Network: AP Radio
Format: Country *Hrs. of News Programming:* news progmg 3 hrs wkly *No. News Employees:* 1 *Target Audience:* 25-49; female
Adv. Rates: 20; 20; 20; 20
Robert Prasil, President
Darin Siebert, Operations Dir
Ben Bonnfield, General Sales Mgr
Jim Nelly, Programming Director
John Thomas, News Director
Steve Franco, Chief Engineer
Zoanne Byers, Traffic Manager

KOZE
10-06-1955; 950 khz AM *Hrs Open:* 24; 5 kw-D, DA2; 1 kw-N, DA2; N46 23 32 W117 2 3
P. O. Box 936, Lewiston, ID 83501 US
(208) 743-2502, *Fax:* (208) 743-1995
License: Lewiston, ID held by 4-K Radio Inc.
Group Owner: 4-K Radio Inc.; acq 6-1-71)
Regional Reps: Tacher Company.
Format: Talk *Special Programming:* Farm 2 hrs wkly *No. News Employees:* 2 *Target Audience:* 25-54. *Adv. Rates:* 15; 15; 15; 13
Michael Ripley, President
Chris Ripley, Station Manager
Lisa Jensen, General Sales Mgr
Jason Ford, News Director
David Forsman, Chief Engineer

KOZE-FM
01-17-1961; 96.5 mhz FM *Hrs Open:* 24; 25 kw; 741 ft.; N46 27 48 W117 0 1
P.O. Box 936, Lewiston, ID 83501 US
(208) 743-2502, *Fax:* (208) 743-1995
License: Lewiston, Nez Perce County, ID
Group Owner: 4-K Radio Inc.
Format: Rock/AOR *Target Audience:* 18-49.
Lee McVey, Programming Director

KVTY
07-20-1998; 105.1 mhz FM *Hrs Open:* 24; 0.5 kw; 1099 ft.; N46 27 33 W117 2 18
805 Stewart Avenue, Lewiston, ID 83501 US
(208) 743-1551, *Fax:* (208) 743-4440
sales@idavend.com
License: Lewiston, Nez Perce County, ID held by IdaVend Co. Inc.
Group Owner: IdaVend Broadcasting Inc.
Nat'l Network: AP Radio
Arbitron Metro Market: Lewiston, ID *Format:* Contemporary Hits/Top 40 *Hrs. of News Programming:* news progmg 1 hr wkly

No. News Employees: 1 *Target Audience:* 18-44. *Adv. Rates:* 20; 20; 20; 20
Robert Prasil, President
Darin Siebert, Operations Dir
Melva Prasil, Station Manager
Ben Bonfield, General Sales Mgr
Jeff Tuchscherer, Programming Director
John Thomas, News Director
Steve Franco, Chief Engineer
Zoanne Byers,Traffic Manager

Lewiston-Clarkston

KRLC
03-01-1935; 1350 khz AM *Hrs Open:* 24; 5 kw-D, DAN; 1 kw-N, DAN; N46 23 39 W116 59 40
805 Stewart Ave., Lewiston, ID 83501 US
(208) 743-1551, *Fax:* (208) 743-4440
sales@idavend.com
License: Lewiston-Clarkston, ID held by Ida-Vend Inc.
Group Owner: IdaVend Broadcasting Inc.; (acq 11-1-81).
Arbitron Metro Market: Lewiston *Format:* Country *Special Programming:* Farm 5 hrs, radio auction one hr wkly *Hrs. of News Programming:* news progmg 10 hrs wkly *No. News Employees:* 1 *Target Audience:* 25plus; adults *Adv. Rates:* 20; 20; 20; 20.
Robert Prasil, President
Melva Prasil, Station Manager
Ben Bonfield, General Sales Mgr
John Thomas, News Director
Steve Franco, Engineering Dir
ZoAnne Byers, Traffic Manager

Marsing

*KAWS
01-01-2007; 89.1 mhz FM; 8.75 kw vert; 2192 ft.; N43 0 25 W116 42 13 *Rebroadcasts:* Rebroadcasts KAWZ(FM) Twin Falls 100%
P.O. Box 271, Twin Falls, ID 83303 US
(800) 357-4226, *Fax:* (208) 736-1958
www.csnradio.com
csn@csnradio.com
License: Marsing, Owyhee County, ID held by Calvary Chapel of Twin Falls Inc.
Arbitron Metro Market: Marsing, ID *Format:* Christian
Mike Kestler, President
Daniel Davidson, Operations Dir
Mike Stocklin, General Manager
Don Mills, Network Programming Director / Music Director
Kelly Carlson, Engineering Dir
Jerry Johnson, Engineering Dir
Ray Gorney, AssistantDirector of Engineering
Dustin Pamplona, Engineer
Nolan Mather, Graphics / Website Maintenance
Mike Stocklin, National Underwriting
Austin Morris, Accounting
Lois Mills, FCC Applications / Translator Site Manager

McCall

*KBSK
01-01-2002; 89.9 mhz FM; 0.22 kw; 1919 ft.; N45 0 38 W116 7 53
1910 University Drive, Boise, ID 83725 US
(208) 426-3663, *Fax:* (208) 344-6631
radio.boisestate.edu
License: McCall, Valley County, ID held by Idaho State Board of Education.
Format: Jazz
Erik Jones, Operations Dir
John Hess, General Manager
Hy Kloc, General Sales Mgr
Ele Ellis, Programming Director
Sadie Babits, News Director
Tom Taylor, Engineering Dir
Betsy Micone, Business Director
Brad Campell, OperationsManager

*KBSM
01-20-1991; 91.7 mhz FM *Hrs Open:* 24; 0.22 kw; 1913 ft.; N45 0 38 W116 7 53
1910 University Drive, Boise, ID 83725 US
(208) 426-3663, *Fax:* (208) 344-6631
radio.boisestate.edu
License: McCall, Valley County, ID held by Idaho State Board of Education.
Nat'l Network: PRI; NPR
Format: News *Special Programming:* Jazz *Hrs. of News Programming:* News progmg 15 hrs wkly *Target Audience:* General.
Erik Jones, Operations Dir
John Hess, General Manager
Hy Kloc, General Sales Mgr
Ele Ellis, Programming Director
Sadie Babits, News Director
Tom Taylor, Engineering Dir
Betsy Micone, Business Director
Brad Campbell, OperationsManager

KDZY
01-01-2001; 98.3 mhz FM *Hrs Open:* 24; 0.5 kw horiz, 0 kw vert; N45 0 18 W116 8 1
2121 Diamond Mountain Road, Calistoga, CA 94515 US
(208) 377-3790(208) 634-3781, *Fax:* (208) 377-3792
www.kdzy98.com
daveh@myfamilyradio.com
License: McCall, Valley County, ID held by KSPD Inc.
Group Owner: KSPD Inc.; acq 4-15-02; $75,000).
Nat'l Network: AP Network News
Arbitron Metro Market: McCall, ID *Format:* Country *Target Audience:* 25 plus. *Adv. Rates:* 13; 13; 13; 13
Lee Schafer, President

*KBSQ
90.7 mhz FM; 0.22 kw; 1919 ft.; N45 0 38 W116 7 53
1910 University Drive, Boise, ID 83725 US
(208) 426-3663, *Fax:* (208) 344-6631
radio.boisestate.edu
boisestatepublicradio@boisestate.edu
License: McCall, Valley County, ID held by Idaho State Board of Education.
Arbitron Metro Market: Boise, ID *Format:* News, Variety/Diverse
Erik Jones, Operations Dir
John Hess, General Manager
Hy Kloc, General Sales Mgr
Ele Ellis, Programming Director
Sadie Babits, News Director
Tom Taylor, Engineering Dir
Betsy Micone, Business Director
Brad Campbell, OperationsManager
Adrienne Zachary, Marketing & Special Events Coordinator
Arthur Balinger, Producer/ Program Host
Carol Wilke, Membership Assistant
Craig Morgan, Web & Graphic Designer

Middleton

*KOAY(FM)
88.7 mhz FM; 5 kw; Ant 2,594 ft; N43 45 18 W116 05 52
16115 S. Montana Ave., Caldwell, ID 83605
(209) 459-5879, *Fax:* (208) 459-3144
fun@ktfy.org
License: Middleton, Canyon County, ID held by Southern Idaho Corp.
Population Served: 5,607 *Arbitron Metro Market:* Middleton, ID
Michael Agee, General Manager

Montpelier

KVSI
07-20-1965; 1450 khz AM
24681 U.S. 89 Box 349, Montpelier, ID 83254 US
(208) 847-1450, *Fax:* (208) 847-1451
kvsi.com
kvsi@dcdi.net
License: Montpelier, ID held by Tri-States Broadcasting LLC
Arbitron Metro Market: Montpelier, ID *Format:* Country *Special Programming:* Farm 4 hrs, relg 2 hrs wkly
Keith Martindale, Owner and General Manager
Ada Hillier, Programming Director
Ada Jane Hillier, Program and Traffic Director

Moscow

*KRFA-FM
09-01-1963; 91.7 mhz FM *Hrs Open:* 24; 28 kw vert; 925 ft.; N46 40 54 W116 58 13
PO Box 642530, Pullman, WA 99164 US
(509) 335-6500, *Fax:* (509) 335-6557
www.nwpr.org
nwpr@wsu.edu
License: Moscow, Latah County, ID held by Washington State University.
Nat'l Network: NPR; PRI
Format: News, News/Talk, 86 *Special Programming:* Folk, jazz *Hrs. of News Programming:* news progmg 37 hrs wkly *No. News Employees:* 1 *Target Audience:* General.
Gillian Coldsnow, Operations Dir
Kerry Swanson, Station Manager
Dave Deeney, General Sales Mgr
Robin Rilette, Programming Director
John Paxson, News Director
Sarah McDaniel, Membership Director

KRPL
05-20-1947; 1400 khz AM *Hrs Open:* 24; 1 kw-U; N46 44 47 W117 01 06
1114 N. Almon, PO Box 8849, Moscow, ID 83843
(208) 882-2551, *Fax:* (208) 883-3571
License: Moscow, Latah County, ID held by KRPL Inc.
Population Served: 60,000 *Arbitron Metro Market:* Pullman-Moscow area *Special Programming:* Farm 4 hrs, relg 2 hrs wkly *Hrs. of News Programming:* news progmg 12 hrs wkly *No. News Employees:* 4 *TargetAudience:* 25-54.
Gary Cummins, General Manager

*KUOI-FM
11-01-1945; 89.3 mhz FM *Hrs Open:* 24; 0.4 kw vert; -115 ft.; N46 43 43 W117 0 22
S.U.B / 3rd Floor, Moscow, ID 83844 US
(208) 885-2218, *Fax:* (208) 885-2222
www.kuoi.org
nae@kuoi.org
License: Moscow, Latah County, ID held by University of Idaho.
Arbitron Metro Market: Moscow, ID *Format:* Variety/Diverse *Special Programming:* Black 3 hrs, folk 3 hrs, jazz 4 hrs wkly *Hrs. of News Programming:* news progmg 2 hrs wkly *No. News Employees:* 3 *TargetAudience:* General; alternative mus listeners
Nae Hakala, Station Manager
Tim Goldy, Programming Director
Joseph Engle, News Director
Jeff Kimberling, Chief Engineer
Lindsay Stribling, Music Director
Nick McGarvey, Production Director and Chief Announcer
Shawn O'Neal,Advisor/Chief Operator

KZFN
02-24-1973; 106.1 mhz FM *Hrs Open:* 24; 62 kw; 922 ft.; N46 40 51 W116 58 26
P. O. Box 8849, Moscow, ID 83843 US
(208) 883-2551, *Fax:* (208) 883-3571
www.zfun106.com
License: Moscow, Latah County, ID
Arbitron Metro Market: Moscow, ID *Format:* Contemporary Hits/Top 40 *Hrs. of News Programming:* news progmg 5 hrs wkly *No. News Employees:* 4 *Target Audience:* 25-54.
Gary Cummings, Programming Director

Mountain Home

KMHI
03-20-1962; 1240 khz AM *Hrs Open:* 24; 1 kw-U, ND1; N43 9 3 W115 42 26
2660 Peachtree Road, N.W, #17f, Atlanta, GA 30305 US
(208) 465-9966, *Fax:* (208) 465-2922
www.impactradiogroup.com
barbara@impactradiogroup.com
License: Mountain Home, ID held by FM Idaho Co. LLC.
Group Owner: FM Idaho Co. LLC dba Impact Radio Group; (acq 12-31-2006; grpsl)
Nat'l Network: Westwood One
Format: Country *Special Programming:* Sp 7 hrs wkly *Hrs. of News Programming:* news progmg 15 hrs wkly *No. News Employees:* 1 *Target Audience:* General.
Elliott Klein, President
Sarah McBride, Operations Dir
Darrell Calton, General Manager
Mark Broz, General Sales Mgr
Mikey Fuentes, Programming Director

Mt Home

KQLZ(FM)
99.1 mhz FM *Hrs Open:* 24 hours; 80 kw; Avt 668 m; N 43 14 43 115 26 12W
5660 Franklin rd. Suite 200, Nampa, ID 83687
208-4659966, *Fax:* 208-465-2922
www.991trueoldies.com
License: Mt Home, Gooding County, ID held by Fm Idaho Inc
Group Owner: Impact Radio LLC
Population Served: 82,755 *Arbitron Metro Market:* Nampa, ID
Format: Oldies
DarrellCalton, General Manager
Mikey Fuentes, Programming Director

Nampa

KIDO
05-17-1920; 580 khz AM *Hrs Open:* 24; 5 kw-D, DAN; 5 kw-N, DAN; N43 33 35 W116 24 2
50 East Rivercenter Boulevard, Suite 1200, Covington, KY 41011 US
(208) 344-6363, *Fax:* (208) 344-1134
www.kidoam.com
dave.burnett@peakbroadcasting.com

License: Nampa, ID held by Peak Broadcasting of Boise Licenses LLC.
Group Owner: Peak Broadcasting LLC; (acq 6-28-2007; grpsl)
Arbitron Metro Market: Boise, ID *Format:* News, Talk *Special Programming:* Religious 1 hr wkly, Gun talk 3 hrs wkly *Target Audience:* 25-54.
Kevin Godwin, General Manager
Dave Burnett, Programming Director

KRVB
01-10-1975; 94.9 mhz FM; 49 kw; 2694 ft.; N43 45 18 W116 5 52
455 Amity Road, Meridian, ID 83642 US
(208) 344-3511, *Fax:* (208) 947-6765
www.riverinteractive.com
License: Nampa, Canyon County, ID held by Journal Broadcast Corp.
Group Owner: Journal Communications Inc.; (acq 4-11-00).
Nat'l Reps: Katz Radio
Arbitron Metro Market: Boise, ID *Format:* Classic Rock *Special Programming:* Talk 20 hrs wkly *Target Audience:* 18-64.
Bob Rosenthal, Operations Dir
Cathy Prazenica, General Manager
Brook Bender, General Sales Mgr
Rich Kemp, Programming Director
Kristine Simoni, Promotions Manager
Tim Johnstone, Music Director
Dan McColly, Operations Manager
Paula Jensen, Traffic Manager

KKGL
02-01-1977; 96.9 mhz FM *Hrs Open:* 24; 48 kw; 2717 ft.; N43 45 21 W116 5 54
City Center West, 7201 W. Lake Mead Blvd, Las Vegas, NV 89128 US
(208) 336-3670, *Fax:* (208) 336-3734
www.96-9meeagle.com
License: Nampa, Canyon County, ID
Group Owner: Cumulus Media Inc.; (acq 12-10-97; grpsl).
Nat'l Reps: Katz Radio
Arbitron Metro Market: Boise, ID *Format:* Classic Rock *Target Audience:* 25-44; upscale baby boomers who listen to primarily 70s based rock *Adv. Rates:* 35; 35; 30; 15
Rich Summers, Operations Dir
Kevin Godwin, General Manager
Rich Bryan, Programming Director
Bill Frahn, Chief Engineer

KTIK
11-01-1962; 1350 khz AM *Hrs Open:* 24
5257 Fairview Ave., Boise, ID 83706 US
(208) 336-3670, *Fax:* (208) 336-3736
www.ktik.com
License: Nampa, ID
Group Owner: Cumulus Media Inc.; (acq 4-1-03; $750,000).
Nat'l Network: ESPN Radio; Westwood One
Arbitron Metro Market: Boise, ID *Format:* Sports, Talk *Hrs. of News Programming:* News progmg one hr wkly *Target Audience:* 25-54; sports oriented men *Adv. Rates:* 25; 20; 25; 15
Tom Newman, General Sales Mgr
Andrew Paul, Programming Director
Don Morin, Promotions Manager

Notus

KWEI
12-01-1947; 1450 khz AM *Hrs Open:* Sunrise-sunset
6885 Highland Valley Rd., Boise, ID 83712 US
(208) 367-1859, *Fax:* (208) 383-9170
www.kweiradio.net
kwei@cableone.net
License: Notus, ID held by Treasure Valley Broadcasting Co.
Arbitron Metro Market: Boise, ID *Format:* News, News/Talk, 86 *No. News Employees:* 1 *Target Audience:* 35-65; mass appeal
Hal Widsten, President
Cindy Aguirre, Operations Dir
Sennett Rockers, News Director
Richard Schuh, Chief Engineer
Sandra Valdez, Business/Traffic Manager
Darren Dunn, Operations Manager

Orofino

KLER
10-15-1958; 1300 khz AM; 5 kw-D, DAN; 1 kw-N, DAN; N46 28 41 W116 14 34
P.O. Box 32, Orofino, ID 83544 US
(208) 476-5702, *Fax:* (208) 476-5703
kler@wildblue.net
License: Orofino, ID held by Central Idaho Broadcasting.
Nat'l Network: ABC; Jones Radio Networks
Arbitron Metro Market: Spokane, WA *Format:* Country *Hrs. of News Programming:* news progmg 8 hrs wkly *No. News Employees:* 2 *Target Audience:* General; family or logging industry-federal employee workers *Adv.Rates:* 15; 15; 15; 15
Ben Dickson, Operations Dir
Jeff Jones, General Manager
Jason Ford, News Director
Jim Sheldon, Chief Engineer

KLER-FM
09-20-1979; 95.1 mhz FM *Hrs Open:* 24; 2.3 kw; 676 ft.; N46 28 9 W116 16 40
P. O. Box 32, Orofino, ID 83544 US
(208) 476-5702, *Fax:* (208) 476-5703
kler@wildblue.net
License: Orofino, Clearwater County, ID
Nat'l Network: Jones Radio Networks
Arbitron Metro Market: Spokane, WA *Format:* Adult Contemp *Hrs. of News Programming:* news progmg 8 hrs wkly *No. News Employees:* 2
Ben Dickson, Operations Dir
Jeff Jones, General Manager
Jason Ford, News Director
Jim Sheldon, Chief Engineer

Parma

KWYD
10-22-1990; 101.1 mhz FM *Hrs Open:* 24; 96 kw; 1001 ft.; N43 24 9 W116 54 9
P.O. Box 813, McCall, ID 83638 US
(208) 465-9966, *Fax:* (208) 465-2922
www.wild101fm.com
License: Parma, Canyon County, ID held by FM Idaho Co. LLC.
Group Owner: FM Idaho Co. LLC dba Impact Radio Group; (acq 9-14-2007; $950,000)
Nat'l Network: ABC
Arbitron Metro Market: Boise, ID *Format:* Contemporary Hits/Top 40 *No. News Employees:* 35 *Target Audience:* 18-34; women
Wendell M Stark, Operations Dir
Elliott Klein, General Manager

Payette

KWEI(AM)
12-20-1957; 1450 khz AM *Hrs Open:* 24; 1 kw-U; N44 03 47 W116 54 27
1406 N. Main St., Suite 107, Meridian, ID 83642-1798
(208) 267-5234, *Fax:* (208) 888-9647
www.kiov.com
sports@kiov.com
License: Payette, Payette County, ID held by Media Enterprises LLC.
Regional Reps: Tacher.
Population Served: 125,000*Format:* Sports *Target Audience:* 18-54; 65% male *Adv. Rates:* 45; 25; 40; 10
Marshall Sage, Operations Dir
David Combes, General Manager

KQXR
12-01-1978; 100.3 mhz FM *Hrs Open:* 24; 98 kw; 708 ft; N43 49 31 W116 30 29
5257 W. Fairview Ave., Suite 260, Boise, ID 53201
(208) 344-3511, *Fax:* (208) 947-6765
www.xrock.com
License: Payette, Payette County, ID held by Journal Broadcast Corp.
Group Owner: Journal Communications Inc.; (acq 5-13-98; grpsl)
Nat'l Reps: Katz Radio
Population Served: 293,600 *Arbitron Metro Market:* Boise, ID *Target Audience:* 18-49.
Bob Rosenthal, Operations Dir
Cathy Prazenica, General Manager
Brook Bender, General Sales Mgr
Rick Kemp, Programming Director
Kristine Simoni, Promotions Manager
Jeremi Smith, Music Director
Dan McColly, Operations Manager
Jeremy Nicolato, Program Director
Paula Jensen, Traffic Manager

Plummer

***KWIS**
88.3 mhz FM; 0 kw horiz, 2.4 kw vert; 945 ft.; N47 19 37 W116 42 55
US
(208) 686-5059, *Fax:* (208) 686-1182
www.cdatribe.com
hkeen@cdatribe-nsn.gov
License: Plummer, Benewah County, ID held by Coeur d'Alene Tribe.
Arbitron Metro Market: Plummer, ID
Chief Allan, Chairman
Helo Hancock, Legislative Director
Heather Keen, Public Relations
Ernie Stensgar, Vice Chairman
John Abraham, Secretary

Pocatello

***KISU-FM**
04-15-1998; 91.1 mhz FM *Hrs Open:* 24; 4.5 kw vert; 1043 ft.; N42 51 46 W112 31 3
Box 8310, Pocatello, ID 83209 US
(208) 282-3691, *Fax:* (208) 282-4600
www.kisu.org
milljerr@isu.edu
License: Pocatello, Bannock County, ID held by Idaho State University.
Nat'l Network: NPR; PRI
Format: Jazz, News, 86, Triple A *Hrs. of News Programming:* 60+ *Adv. Rates:* 20; 18; 20; 12.
Jerry Miller, General Manager

KMGI
04-01-1978; 102.5 mhz FM *Hrs Open:* 24; 100 kw; 1024 ft.; N42 51 57 W112 30 46
403 C Street, Lewiston, ID 83501 US
(208) 233-2121, *Fax:* (208) 234-7682
www.classicrock102.fm
License: Pocatello, Bannock County, ID
Group Owner: Pacific Empire Radio Corp.
Nat'l Network: Westwood One
Format: Classic Rock *Adv. Rates:* 276; 276; 276; 180
C.J. Morrison, Programming Director

KOUU
12-20-1956; 1290 khz AM *Hrs Open:* 24
P.O. Box 97, Pocatello, ID 83204 US
(208) 234-1290, *Fax:* (208) 234-9451
License: Pocatello, ID held by Idaho Wireless Corp.
Group Owner: Idaho Wireless Corp.; (acq 3-86; with co-located FM;
Nat'l Network: ABC
Format: Country *Target Audience:* 35-64; adults
Paul Anderson, General Manager
Harry Newhardt, General Sales Mgr

KPKY
08-18-1975; 94.9 mhz FM; 100 kw; 1004 ft.; N42 52 26 W112 30 48
50 East Rivercenter Blvd., Suite 1200, Covington, KY 41011 US
(208) 233-1133, *Fax:* (208) 232-1240
www.kpky.com
kellymartinez@gapbroadcasting.com
License: Pocatello, Bannock County, ID
Group Owner: Rich Broadcasting LLC; (acq 2-13-2008; grpsl)
Arbitron Metro Market: Pocatello, ID *Format:* Classic Rock
Samuel Weller, President
J.D. Kelly, Operations Dir
Mike Hudson, General Sales Mgr
Marie Mccallister, Programming Director

KSEI
09-23-1926; 930 khz AM *Hrs Open:* 24; 5 kw-D, DAN; 5 kw-N, DAN; N42 57 44 W112 29 50
Mailing Address: 403 C Street, Pocatello, ID 83501 US
Second Address: 544 N. Arthur St., Pocatello, ID 83204
(208) 233-2121, *Fax:* (208) 234-7682
neilmab@pacempire.com
License: Pocatello, ID held by Pacific Empire Radio Corp.
Group Owner: Pacific Empire Radio Corp.; acq 8-28-97; $1.2 million with co-located FM).
Nat'l Reps: Katz Radio
Arbitron Metro Market: Pocatello, ID *Format:* News *Target Audience:* General. *Adv. Rates:* 120; 144; 110; 110
Mark Bolland, President
Neil Mayberry, General Manager
Jim Christopher, News Director
Bill Trowe, Chief Engineer

KWIK
09-01-1946; 1240 khz AM *Hrs Open:* 24
50 East Rivercenter Blvd., Suite 1200, Covington, KY 41011 US
(208) 524-5900, *Fax:* (208) 522-9696
www.590kid.com
kellymartinez@gapbroadcasting.com
License: Pocatello, ID
Group Owner: Rich Broadcasting LLC; (acq 2-13-2008; grpsl)
Regional Reps: Art Moore.
Arbitron Metro Market: Idhao Falls, ID *Format:* News, News/Talk, 84, Talk *Special Programming:* Farm 3 hrs, gospel 2 hrs, relg one hr, American Indian one hr wkly *Hrs. of News Programming:*

news progmg 15 hrs wkly*No. News Employees:* 3 *Target Audience:* 45 plus.
Tim Murphy, General Manager
Jodie Bates, General Sales Mgr
Neal Larson, Program/ News Director
Rhett Downing, Chief Engineer
Delyn Hendricks, Markert Manager
Sandie Fulks, Sales Manager

KZBQ
12-27-1969; 93.7 mhz FM *Hrs Open:* 24; 98 kw; 984 ft.; N42 51 57 W112 30 46
P. O. Box 97, Pocatello, ID 83204 US
(208) 234-1290, *Fax:* (208) 234-9451
www.kzbq.com/
Sales@EastIdahoRadio.com
License: Pocatello, Bannock County, ID
Group Owner: Idaho Wireless Corp.
Nat'l Network: ABC
Arbitron Metro Market: Pocatello, ID *Format:* Country *Target Audience:* 25-54; adults
Paul Anderson, Station Manager

KPTO
12-01-2005; 1440 khz AM *Hrs Open:* 24; 2.5 kw-D, 350 w-N, DA-2; N42 56 30 W112 27 17
Mailing Address: 2975 Valmont Road, St. George, UT
Second Address: 210 North 1000 East, St. George, UT 84770-3155
(208) 234-7000, *Fax:* (208) 232-1440,
legacy1@infowest.com
License: Pocatello, Bannock County, ID held by AM Radio 1440 Inc.
Group Owner: Legacy Media Corporation; (acq 12-6-2004).
Nat'l Network: CNN Radio; Westwood One
Hrs. of News Programming: On-The-Hour *Target Audience:* 25-64.
Lee Weinstein, ESQ, Operations Dir

***KZJB**
01-01-2006; 90.3 mhz FM; 0.91 kw vert; 1031 ft.; N42 51 46 W112 31 3
3000 W Macarthur Blvd., Santa Ana, CA 92704 US
(208) 524-4747, *Fax:* (208) 524-0697
www.revelationradio.fm
radioinfo@calvaryif.org
License: Pocatello, Bannock County, ID held by CSN International
Group Owner: CSN International
Arbitron Metro Market: Pocatello, ID *Format:* Christian, Religious
James Knudsen, Station Manager

KEGE
07-23-2007; 92.1 mhz FM; 12 kw; 988 ft.; N42 52 26 W112 30 48
9148 Bonita Beach Road, Suite 205, Bonita Springs, FL 34135 US
(208) 522-5900, *Fax:* (208) 522-9696
www.590kid.com
neal@590kid.com
License: Pocatello, Bannock County, ID
Group Owner: Rich Broadcasting LLC; (acq 9-3-2008; $1.09 million)
Arbitron Metro Market: Pocatello, ID *Format:* News, Talk
Neica Kinney, General Manager
Sandie Fulks, Sales Manager
Neal Larson, Program / News Director
DeLyn Hendricks, Market Manager

Post Falls

KCDA
06-29-1979; 103.1 mhz FM *Hrs Open:* 24; 18.5 kw; 1742 ft.; N47 34 52 W117 17 47
1400 Easton Road, Suite 129, Bakersfield, CA 93309 US
(509) 242-2400, *Fax:* (509) 448-4043
www.1031kcda.com
michaellacrrosse@clearchannel.com
License: Post Falls, Kootenai County, ID held by Capstar TX L.P.
Group Owner: Clear Channel Communications Inc.; (acq 10-18-00; $4.7 million)
Nat'l Reps: Roslin
Arbitron Metro Market: Spokane, WA *Format:* Alternative *Hrs. of News Programming:* news progmg one hr wkly *No. News Employees:* 2 *Target Audience:* 25-54; active & affluent
Michael La Crosse, Operations Dir
Kosta Panidis, General Manager
Jerry Jensen, General Sales Mgr
Matt Auclair, Promotions Manager

Preston

KACH
09-04-1948; 1340 khz AM *Hrs Open:* 24; 1 kw-U; N42 07 45 W111 51 00
1133 E. Glendale Rd., Preston, ID 83263
(208) 852-1340, *Fax:* (208) 852-1342
kach@plmw.com
License: Preston, Franklin County, ID held by Alan J. White, Nelada G. White.
Nat'l Network: ABC *Nat'l Reps:* Interep *Wire Services:* AP
Population Served: 10,500*Special Programming:* Farm *Hrs. of News Programming:* News progmg 12 hrs wkly *Target Audience:* 18-54; general *Adv. Rates:* 13.50; 10.50; 8.50; 6
Alan White, General Manager

KKEX
12-09-1993; 96.7 mhz FM *Hrs Open:* 24; 100 kw; 217 ft.; N41 52 18 W111 48 31
Mailing Address: P.O. Box 3369, Logan, UT 84323 US
Second Address: 810 W. 200 N., Logan, UT 84321
(435) 752-1390, *Fax:* (435) 752-1392
License: Preston, Franklin County, ID held by Sun Valley Radio Inc.
Group Owner: Sun Valley Radio Inc.; acq 1994).
Format: Country
M. Kent Frandsen, President
Jay Eubanks, General Manager
Lynn Simmons, Programming Director
Dan Baker, Chief Engineer

Rathdrum

***KYMS**
06-01-2006; 89.9 mhz FM *Hrs Open:* 24; 11 kw vert; 1952 ft.; N48 5 38 W116 33 12
3000 W Mscarthur Blvd, Santa Ana, CA 92704 US
(800) 357-4226, *Fax:* (208) 736-1958
www.csnradio.com
csn@csnradio.com
License: Rathdrum, Kootenai County, ID held by Calvary Radio Network Inc.
Group Owner: CSN International
Arbitron Metro Market: Rathdrum, ID *Format:* Religious
Mike Kestler, President
Daniel Davidson, Operations Dir
Charles Sagona, General Manager
Don Mills, Network Programming Director / Music Director
Kelly Carlson, Engineering Dir
Jerry Johnson, Engineering Dir
Ray Gorney, AssistantDirector of Engineering
Dustin Pamplona, Engineer
Nolan Mather, Graphics / Website Maintenance
Mike Stocklin, National Underwriting
Austin Morris, Accounting
Lois Mills, FCC Applications / Translator Site Manager

Rexburg

KGTM
01-17-1986; 98.1 mhz FM *Hrs Open:* 24/7; 100 kw; 636 ft.; N43 32 34 W111 53 7
P.O. Box 3451, 228 E. 1st Street, Idaho Fall, ID 83401 US
(208) 235-7625, *Fax:* (208) 233-1133
www.star98radio.com
kelly@star98radio.com
License: Rexburg, Madison County, ID
Group Owner: Rich Broadcasting LLC; acq 7-25-2000; $495,000 with KRXK(FM) Rexburg).
Format: Contemporary Hits/Top 40, Adult Contemp *Target Audience:* 35 plus. *Adv. Rates:* 15; 15; 15; 6
Phil Jimenez, General Manager
Sandie Fulks, Programming Director
Kelly Martinez, Program Director
DeLyn Hendricks, Market Manager

***KBYI**
11-13-1972; 94.3 mhz FM *Hrs Open:* 24; 99 kw; 692 ft.; N43 45 44 W111 57 30
Spori Building, Room 243, Rexburg, ID 83460 US
(208) 496-2411, *Fax:* (208) 496-2912
www.byuidahoradio.org
newsdesk@byui.edu
License: Rexburg, Madison County, ID held by Brigham Young University-Idaho.
Nat'l Network: NPR; PRI
Arbitron Metro Market: Southeastern ID *Format:* Talk *Hrs. of News Programming:* news progmg 33 hrs wkly *No. News Employees:* 1 *Target Audience:* General.
Jim Clark, General Manager
Michelle Snyder, Promotions Manager
Mark Bailey, News Director

KRXK
01-01-1951; 1230 khz AM; 1 kw-U, ND1; N43 50 50 W111 47 3
Rebroadcasts: Simulcast with KSEI (AM) Pocotello
341 West 1500 North, Rexburg, ID 83440 US
(208) 356-3651, *Fax:* (208) 356-8885
philjimenez@pacempire.com
License: Rexburg, ID
Group Owner: Rich Broadcasting LLC; (acq 7-25-2000; $495,000 with KGTM(FM) Rexburg).
Nat'l Reps: Target Broadcast Sales
Format: Sports *Target Audience:* 25-54; male *Adv. Rates:* 12; 10; 12; 6
Phil Jimenez, General Manager
Sean Green, Programming Director

KUPI-FM
08-16-1975; 99.1 mhz FM; 100 kw; 577 ft.; N43 32 33 W111 53 4
2464 Radio Rd, St. Anthony, ID 83445 US
(208) 522-1101, *Fax:* (208) 522-6110
www.99kupi.com
contactus@99kupi.com
License: Rexburg, Bonneville County, ID
Group Owner: Sand Hill Media Corp.
Arbitron Metro Market: Rexburg, ID *Format:* Country
Tom Marhefka, CEO
Bob Eckman, General Manager
Jonathon Bergman, General Sales Mgr
Gary Lee, Programming Director
Mike Robertson, News Director
Jim White, Chief Engineer

***KBYR-FM**
01-01-1993; 91.5 mhz FM *Hrs Open:* 24; 1 kw; 46 ft.; N43 49 2 W111 46 42
Spori Building, Room 294, Rexburg, ID 83460 US
(208) 496-1411, *Fax:* (208) 496-2912
www.byui.edu/kbyr
newsdesk@byui.edu
License: Rexburg, Madison County, ID held by Ricks College Corp.
Arbitron Metro Market: Rexburg, ID *Format:* Adult Contemp
Target Audience: General.
Jim Clark, General Manager

Rigby

***KLRI**
01-01-2005; 89.5 mhz FM *Hrs Open:* 24; 78 kw vert; 1527 ft.; N43 30 4 W112 39 44 *Rebroadcasts:* Rebroadcasts KLVR(FM) Santa Rosa, CA 100%
1425 North Market Blvd., Suite 9, Sacramento, CA 95834 US
(800) 525-5683, *Fax:* (916) 251-1650
www.klove.com
klove@klove.com
License: Rigby, Jefferson County, ID held by Educational Media Foundation.
Group Owner: EMF Broadcasting
Nat'l Network: K-Love
Arbitron Metro Market: Rigby, ID *Format:* Christian *No. News Employees:* 3 *Target Audience:* 25-44; Judeo Christian, female
Darrell Chambliss, Chairman
Mike Novak, President and CEO
Mike Lee, Operations Dir
David Pierce, Programming Director
Ed Lenane, News Director
Sam Wallington, Engineering Dir
Marya Morgan, News Reporter
Richard Hunt, NewsReporter
Laura Daniels, News Reporter
Tim Luttrell, News Reporter
Kenny Noble Cortes, News Reporter
Darren Vinson, News Reporter

Ririe

***KSQS**
01-01-2006; 91.7 mhz FM; 0.25 kw; 532 ft.; N43 32 37 W111 53 7
2201 S 6th St, Las Vegas, NV 89104 US
(702) 731-5452, *Fax:* (702) 731-1992
www.sosradio.net
info@sosradio.net
License: Ririe, Jefferson County, ID held by Faith Communications Corp.
Group Owner: Faith Communications Corp.
Arbitron Metro Market: Ririe, ID *Format:* Adult Contemp, Christian
Brad Staley, General Manager
Bob Alzugarat, Station Manager
Scott Herrold, Programming Director
Rick Hall, Assistant Program Director/Music Director

Tim Hunt, Director of Network Engineering
Chris Staley, VP of Programming andAdministration

Rupert

KFTA

10-12-1955; 970 khz AM *Hrs Open:* 24; 2.5 kw-D, DAN; 0.9 kw-N, DAN; N42 36 7 W113 43 21; N42 36 10 W113 43 21
144 Seminole Circle, Jerome, ID 83338 US
(208) 436-4757, *Fax:* (208) 436-3050
www.lafantastica970.com
lafantastica970@yahoo.com
License: Rupert, ID held by Tri-Market Radio Broadcasters Inc.
Group Owner: Tri-Market Radio Broadcasters Inc. & Eagle Rock Broadcasting Inc.; (acq 9-24-93; $700,000 with co-located FM;
Arbitron Metro Market: Rupert, ID *No. News Employees:* 1
Kim Lee, General Manager
Ben Reed, Programming Director
Jerry Thaxton, Chief Engineer

KKMV

12-05-1978; 106.1 mhz FM; 25 kw; 2497 ft.; N42 20 6 W113 36 15
144 Seminole Circle, Jerome, ID 83338 US
(208) 436-4757, *Fax:* (208) 436-3050
License: Rupert, Minidoka County, ID held by Tri-Market Radio Broadcasters Inc.
Group Owner: Tri-Market Radio Broadcasters Inc. & Eagle Rock Broadcasting Inc.
Arbitron Metro Market: Boise, ID *Format:* Country *No. News Employees:* 1 *Target Audience:* Adults: 25-54.
Kim Lee, President

Salmon

KSRA

03-01-1959; 960 khz AM; 1 kw-D, ND1; 0.056 kw-N, ND1; N45 11 2 W113 52 12
Box 950, Salmon, ID 83467 US
(208) 756-2218, *Fax:* (208) 756-2098
www.ksrafm.com
ksraradio@ksrafm.com
License: Salmon, ID held by Salmon River Communications Inc.
Nat'l Network: ABC
Arbitron Metro Market: Salmon, ID *Format:* Adult Contemp, Country *Special Programming:* Farm 4 hrs, class one hr wkly *Hrs. of News Programming:* 4
Jim Hone, President
Rick Sessions, General Manager
Leo Marshall, General Sales Mgr
Todd Skeen, Programming Director
Rockwell Smith, Chief Engineer
Shirley Sullivan, Office Manager

KSRA-FM

09-01-1979; 92.7 mhz FM *Hrs Open:* 6 AM-10 PM; 1.5 kw; -879 ft.; N45 11 2 W113 52 12
315 Highway 93 N., Salmon, ID 83467 US
(208) 756-2218, *Fax:* (208) 756-2098
www.ksrafm.com
ksraradio@ksrafm.com
License: Salmon, Lemhi County, ID
Nat'l Network: ABC
Arbitron Metro Market: Salmon, ID
Jim Hone, CEO
Rick Sessions, General Manager
Leo Marshall, General Sales Mgr
Todd Skeen, Programming Director
Todd Skeen, Promotions Manager
Shirley Sullivan, Office Manager

Sandpoint

KIBR

01-01-1994; 102.5 mhz FM *Hrs Open:* 24; 6 kw; -344 ft.; N48 18 16 W116 32 32 *Rebroadcasts:* Rebroadcasts KICR(FM) Coeur d'Alene 100%
327 Marion Ave, Sandpoint, ID 83864 US
(208) 263-2179, *Fax:* (208) 265-5440
carolynp@953kpnd.com
License: Sandpoint, Bonner County, ID held by Benefield Broadcasting Inc.
Nat'l Network: ABC
Arbitron Metro Market: Sandpoint, ID *Format:* Country *No. News Employees:* 1 *Target Audience:* 25-54.
Dylan Benefield, General Manager
Jimmy Silver, Programming Director
Mike Brown, News Director

KPND

05-19-1980; 95.3 mhz FM *Hrs Open:* 24; 56 kw; 2503 ft.; N48 4 44 W116 57 11
327 Marion Avenue, Sandpoint, ID 83864 US
(208) 263-2179, *Fax:* (208) 265-5440
www.953kpnd.com
carolynp@953kpnd.com
License: Sandpoint, Bonner County, ID
Arbitron Metro Market: Spokane, WA *Format:* Triple A
Jim Tomchek, News Director

KSPT

03-23-1949; 1400 khz AM *Hrs Open:* 24; 1 kw-U, ND1; N48 18 16 W116 32 32 *Rebroadcasts:* Rebroadcasts KBFI(AM) Bonners Ferry 100%
327 Marion Avenue, Sandpoint, ID 83864 US
(208) 263-2179, *Fax:* (208) 265-5440
www.kspt.org.pl
carolynp@953kpnd.com
License: Sandpoint, ID held by Blue Sky Broadcasting Inc.
Nat'l Network: ABC; USA *Nat'l Reps:* Tacher
Arbitron Metro Market: Sandpoint, ID *Format:* News, News/Talk, 84, Talk *Special Programming:* Relg 2 hrs wkly *Target Audience:* 25 plus.
Dylan Benefield, General Manager
Mike Davis, News Director
Conrad Agtee, Chief Engineer
Jim Tomchek, Traffic Manager

Shelley

KQEZ(FM)

10-01-1999; 106.3 mhz FM *Hrs Open:* 24/7; 100 kw; 636 ft; N43 06 45 W112 29 34
1406 Commerce Way., Idaho Falls, ID 83401
(208) 524-5900, *Fax:* (208) 529-6927
www.ezrockradio.com
scott@richbroadcasting.com
License: Shelley, Bingham County, ID
Group Owner: Rich Broadcasting LLC; acq 10-6-98; $788,500 with KATW(FM) Lewiston).
Population Served: 80,000 *Arbitron Metro Market:* ID Falls, ID *Format:* Classic Rock *Target Audience:* 25-54; adults *Adv. Rates:* 20; 20; 20; 12
Phil Jimenez, General Manager
Sandie Fulks, General Sales Mgr
JJ Jeffrey, Programming Director

Soda Springs

KBRV

09-22-1957; 790 khz AM
81 S. Main, Soda Springs, ID 83276 US
(208) 547-2400, *Fax:* (208) 547-4593
License: Soda Springs, ID held by Caribou Broadcasting Inc.
Format: Country
Tom Mathis, General Manager

KITT

10-17-1983; 100.1 mhz FM *Hrs Open:* 24; 3 kw horiz; -276 ft.; N42 38 30 W111 36 40
Mailing Address: 81 S. Main, Box 777, Soda Springs, ID 83276 US
Second Address: Box 1450, 210 North 1000 East, St. George, UT 84771
(208) 547-2500, *Fax:* (208) 547-4593
www.kittfm.com
kitt100@kitt100.com
License: Soda Springs, Caribou County, ID held by Tri-State Media Corp.
Group Owner: Legacy Media Corporation; (acq 7-8-2004; $234,000)
Arbitron Metro Market: Soda Springs, ID *Format:* Country *Special Programming:* CNN radio 10 hrs wkly *No. News Employees:* 2 *Target Audience:* 18-35
E. Morgan Skinner, Jr, President
Lavon Randall, Operations Dir
Jeffrey Bate, General Sales Mgr

St. Anthony

KIGO

07-10-1966; 1420 khz AM *Hrs Open:* 24*Rebroadcasts:* 96.7 FM
PO Box 17, St. Anthony, ID 83445 US
(208) 280-1962
License: St. Anthony, ID held by Albino Ortega & Maria Juarez
Arbitron Metro Market: Saint Anthony, ID *Target Audience:* 17-44; adults
Albino Ortega, General Manager

St. Maries

KOFE

03-01-1970; 1240 khz AM *Hrs Open:* 24; 1 kw-D, ND1; 0.5 kw-N, ND1; N47 19 14 W116 32 50
12260 Nacogdoches Road, Suite 102, San Antonio, TX 78217 US
(208) 245-1240, *Fax:* (208) 245-6525
KOFE@sm-email.com
License: St. Maries, ID held by Campbell River Holding Co. L.L.C.
Nat'l Network: Fox News Radio
Format: Contemporary Hits/Top 40, Adult Contemp *Hrs. of News Programming:* news progmg 9 hrs wkly *No. News Employees:* 2 *Target Audience:* 25-55.
Theresa Plank, General Manager
Phil Plank, Engineering Dir

*KXJO

92.1 mhz FM; 0.2 kw; 22 ft.; N47 20 8.4 W116 34 18.2 US
(509) 328-5729, *Fax:* (509) 328-5764
www.kpbx.org
kpbx@kpbx.org
License: St. Maries, Benewah County, ID held by College Creek Media LLC.
Group Owner: College Creek Media LLC
Arbitron Metro Market: Saint Maries, ID
Neal Robinson, President

Sun Valley

KECH-FM

11-21-1988; 95.3 mhz FM *Hrs Open:* 24; 0.1 kw; 2169 ft.; N43 39 42 W114 24 7
P.O. Box 2158, Ketchum, ID 83340 US
(208) 788-7118, *Fax:* (208) 788-7119
www.kech95.com
License: Sun Valley, Blaine County, ID held by Chaparral Broadcasting Inc.
Group Owner: Chaparral Communications; acq 7-30-2004; grpsl).
Arbitron Metro Market: Hailey, ID *Format:* Classic Rock *Special Programming:* Alternative 5 hrs, blues 8 hrs, jazz 6 hrs wkly *Hrs. of News Programming:* news progmg 6 hrs wkly *No. News Employees:* 1 *TargetAudience:* 25-54; upscale adults *Adv. Rates:* 18; 15; 18; 6
Scott Anderson, General Manager
Cathy Nikolaisons, General Sales Mgr
Lenny Joseph, Programming Director
Dayle Ohlau, News Director

KSKI-FM

08-03-1977; 103.7 mhz FM *Hrs Open:* 24; 52 kw; 1909 ft.; N43 38 36 W114 23 49
P.O. Box 2158, Ketchum, ID 83340 US
(208) 726-5324, *Fax:* (208) 726-5459
www.ketsvidaho.net,www.kskilive.com
License: Sun Valley, Blaine County, ID held by Chaparral Broadcasting Inc.
Group Owner: Chaparral Communications; (acq 7-30-2004; grpsl).
Arbitron Metro Market: Hailey, ID *Format:* Alternative *Hrs. of News Programming:* news progmg 2 hrs wkly *No. News Employees:* 1 *Target Audience:* 18-49; affluent, upscale consumers *Adv. Rates:* 18; 12; 18;6
Scott Anderson, General Manager
Cathy Nikolaisons, General Sales Mgr
Bob Thompson, Programming Director
Sue Bailey, News Director

*KWRV

07-29-1993; 91.9 mhz FM; 0.1 kw; 2154 ft.; N43 39 41 W114 24 8
45 East 7th Street, Saint Paul, MN 55101 US
(218) 751-8864, *Fax:* (218) 751-8640
www.mpr.org
kbooth@mpr.org
License: Sun Valley, Blaine County, ID held by Minnesota Public Radio.
Nat'l Network: PRI *Regional Network:* Minn. Pub. Radio
Arbitron Metro Market: Bemidji, MN *Format:* Talk
William Kling, President

KYZK

107.5 mhz FM *Hrs Open:* 24; 0.1 kw; 2169 ft.; N43 39 42 W114 24 7
4350 N. Fairfax Dr.#900, Arlington, VA 22203 US
(208) 726-5324, *Fax:* (208) 726-5459
License: Sun Valley, Blaine County, ID held by Chaparral Broadcasting Inc.
Group Owner: Chaparral Communications; (acq 7-30-2004; grpsl).
Nat'l Network: ABC *Regional Reps:* Allied Radio
Arbitron Metro Market: Sun Valley, OD *Format:* Jazz
Scott Anderson, General Manager
Cathy Nikolaisons, General Sales Mgr

Bob Thompson, Programming Director
Sue Bailey, News Director
Don Mussell, Engineering Dir

***KBSS**
08-01-2004; 91.1 mhz FM; 0.7 kw; 1870 ft.; N43 38 36 W114 23 49
1910 University Drive, Boise, ID 83725 US
(208) 426-3663, *Fax:* (208) 344-6631
radio.boisestate.edu
boisestatepublicradio@boisestate.edu
License: Sun Valley, Blaine County, ID held by Idaho State Board of Education.
Nat'l Network: NPR
Arbitron Metro Market: Boise, ID *Format:* News
Erik Jones, Operations Dir
John Hess, General Manager
Hy Kloc, General Sales Mgr
Ele Ellis, Programming Director
Sadie Babits, News Director
Tom Taylor, Engineering Dir
Betsy Micone, Business Director
Brad Campbell, OperationsManager
Aaron Kunz, EarthFix Environmental Reporter
Adam Cotterell, News Reporter
Adrienne Zachary, Marketing & Special Events Coordinator
Arthur Balinger, Producer/ Program Host

Troy

KQZB
01-01-2008; 100.5 mhz FM; 0.9 kw; 1598 ft.; N46 48 42 W116 54 59
US
(208) 743-4560, *Fax:* (208) 798-0110
License: Troy, Latah County, ID held by Pacific Empire Radio Corp.
Group Owner: Pacific Empire Radio Corp.
Arbitron Metro Market: Salt Lake City-Ogden-Provo, UT *Format:* Jazz, Smooth Jazz
Mark Bolland, President

Twin Falls

***KAWZ**
04-13-1988; 89.9 mhz FM *Hrs Open:* 24; 100 kw vert; 991 ft.; N42 43 47 W114 24 52
Mailing Address: 241 Main Ave., West, Twin Falls, ID 83303 US
Second Address: 4002 N. 3300 E., Twin Falls, ID 83301
(208) 734-6633, *Fax:* (208) 736-1958
www.csnradio.com
csn@csnradio.com
License: Twin Falls, Twin Falls County, ID held by Calvary Chapel of Twin Falls Inc.
Arbitron Metro Market: Twin Falls, ID *Format:* Christian *Hrs. of News Programming:* News progmg 2 hrs wkly *Target Audience:* General; 18-80
Mike Kestler, President
Don Mills, Operations Dir
Mike Stocklin, General Manager

***KBSW**
05-15-1989; 91.7 mhz FM *Hrs Open:* 24; 4.5 kw; 492 ft.; N42 43 48 W114 25 6
1910 University Drive, Boise, ID 83725 US
(208) 426-3663, *Fax:* (208) 344-6631
radio.boisestate.edu
License: Twin Falls, Twin Falls County, ID held by Idaho State Board of Education.
Nat'l Network: PRI; NPR
Format: Talk *Hrs. of News Programming:* news progmg 15 hrs wkly *No. News Employees:* 2 *Target Audience:* General.
Erik Jones, Operations Dir
John Hess, General Manager
Hy Kloc, General Sales Mgr
Ele Ellis, Programming Director
Sadie Babits, News Director
Tom Taylor, Engineering Dir
Betsy Micone, Business Director
Brad Campbell, OperationsManager

***KCIR**
12-12-1982; 90.7 mhz FM *Hrs Open:* 24; 44.1 kw; 2513 ft.; N42 20 7 W113 36 17 *Rebroadcasts:* Rebroadcasts KILA(FM) Las Vegas 97%
2201 S. Sixth St., Las Vegas, NV 89104 US
(208) 734-5777, *Fax:* (702) 731-1992
www.sosradio.net
scott@sosradio.net
License: Twin Falls, Twin Falls County, ID held by Faith Communications Corp.
Group Owner: Faith Communications Corp.; (acq 9-29-82)
Nat'l Network: USA
Arbitron Metro Market: Twin Falls, ID *Format:* Christian *Special Programming:* Children 2 hrs wkly *Hrs. of News Programming:* News progmg 5 hrs wkly *Target Audience:* 25-49; adults with families
Brad Staley, President and General Manager
Duane Luchsinger, Station Manager
Scott Herrold, Programming Director
Tim Hunt, Network Director of Engineering
Gary Thompson, Creative Services Director
Mike Mead, Donor Relations
Marney Domeraski, Donor Relations
Dawn Vincent, Listener Services
Rick Hall, Music Director
Chris Staley, Vice-President of Programming & Administration

***KEFX**
01-01-1996; 88.9 mhz FM; 100 kw vert; 991 ft.; N42 43 47 W114 24 52
241 Main Avenue West, Twin Falls, ID 83303 US
(208) 734-2049, *Fax:* (208) 736-1958
www.effectiveradio.com
effectradio@effectradio.com
License: Twin Falls, Twin Falls County, ID held by Calvary Chapel of Twin Falls Inc.
Group Owner: CSN International
Arbitron Metro Market: Twin Falls, ID *Format:* Christian, Religious
Mike Kestler, President
Matt McNeilly, Station Manager
Drew Hartney, Programming Director
Ray Gorney, Chief Engineer

***KEZJ**
01-01-1946; 1450 khz AM; 1 kw-U, ND1; N42 32 36 W114 28 14
Rebroadcasts: Rebroadcasts KBSU(AM) Boise
315 Falls Avenue, P.O. Box 1238, Twin Falls, ID 83303 US
(208) 733-7512, *Fax:* (208) 736-2188
www.957kezj.com
License: Twin Falls, ID held by College of Southern Idaho.
Arbitron Metro Market: Twin Falls, ID *Format:* Jazz, News, 62, Talk
Janice Degner, General Manager
Amanda Miller, General Sales Mgr
Brad Weiser, Programming Director

KEZJ-FM
03-15-1977; 95.7 mhz FM; 100 kw; 650 ft.; N42 43 42 W114 24 48
Mailing Address: 50 East Rivercenter Blv, Covington, KY 41011 US
Second Address: 415 Park Ave., Twin Falls, ID 83301
(208) 733-7512, *Fax:* (208) 733-7525
www.957kezj.com
bradweiser@clearchannel.com
License: Twin Falls, Twin Falls County, ID held by GAP Broadcasting Twin Falls License LLC.
Group Owner: GAPWEST Broadcasting; (acq 2-13-2008; grpsl)
Nat'l Network: ABC *Nat'l Reps:* Clear Channel *Wire Services:* ABC; AP
Arbitron Metro Market: Twin Falls, ID *Format:* Country *Target Audience:* 25-54.
Janice Degner, Operations Dir
Janice Degner, General Manager
Amanda Miller, General Sales Mgr
Brad Weiser, Programming Director
James Tidmarsh, News Director
Kelly Klaas, Chief Engineer
Brad Weiser, Operations Director

KLIX
12-12-1946; 1310 khz AM *Hrs Open:* 24; 5 kw-D, DAN; 2.5 kw-N, DAN; N42 33 6 W114 22 3
50 East Rivercenter, Blvd., Suite 1200, Covington, KY 41011 US
(208) 733-1310, *Fax:* (208) 733-7525
www.newsradio1310.com
License: Twin Falls, ID held by GAP Broadcasting Twin Falls License LLC.
Group Owner: GAPWEST Broadcasting; (acq 2-13-2008; grpsl)
Nat'l Network: ABC
Arbitron Metro Market: Boise, ID *Format:* News, News/Talk, 86 *Special Programming:* Farm 2 hrs wkly *Hrs. of News Programming:* news progmg 12 hrs wkly *No. News Employees:* 1 *Target Audience:* 35-54. *Adv.Rates:* 16; 22; 16; 10.
Brad Weiser, Operations Dir
Janice Degner, General Manager
Chris Muldaney, General Sales Mgr
Suzanne Jusst, News Director
Kelly Klaas, Chief Engineer

KLIX-FM
06-15-1974; 96.5 mhz FM; 100 kw; 131 ft.; N42 33 5 W114 30 59
50 East Rivercenter Blvd, Covington, KY 41011 US
(208) 733-1310, *Fax:* (208) 733-7525
www.coololdies965.com
License: Twin Falls, Twin Falls County, ID held by GAP Broadcasting Twin Falls License LLC.
Group Owner: GAPWEST Broadcasting; (acq 2-13-2008; grpsl)
Arbitron Metro Market: Boise, ID *Format:* Oldies *Target Audience:* 18-49.
Brad Hollstrom, Operations Dir
Janice Degner, General Sales Mgr
Kelly Klaas, Farm Director

KSNQ
09-01-2004; 98.3 mhz FM; 100 kw; 650 ft.; N42 43 42 W114 24 48
9148 Bonita Beach Road, Suite 205, Bonita Springs, FL 34135 US
(208) 733-7512, *Fax:* (208) 733-7525
www.983thesnake.com
kendra@983thesnake.com
License: Twin Falls, Twin Falls County, ID held by Intermart Broadcasting Twin Falls Inc.
Arbitron Metro Market: Twin Falls, ID *Format:* Classic Rock
Patricia Woods, Operations Dir
Janice Degner, General Manager
Kendra Wolfe, Brand Manager

KIRQ
01-01-2007; 102.1 mhz FM; 5.2 kw; 722 ft.; N42 43 54 W114 25 4
US
(208) 735-8300, *Fax:* (208) 733-4196
www.irock1021.com
License: Twin Falls, Twin Falls County, ID held by Locally Owned Radio LLC.
Group Owner: Locally Owned Radio LLC; (acq 9-8-2006; $2,911,000 with KTPZ(FM) Hazelton)
Arbitron Metro Market: Twin Falls, ID
Rocky Metts, President
Jerre Fender, Operations Dir
Deb Uvieu, General Sales Mgr
Tiffany Seeley, Programming Director
Denis Jeffs, News Director
Charlie Knapp, Vice President

Ucon

KZKY(FM)
104.5 mhz FM; 28 kw; Ant 656 ft; N44 10 35 W111 25 51
980 N. Michigan Ave., Suite 1880, Chicago, IL 60611
(312) 204-9900
License: Ucon, Fremont County, ID held by Rich Broadcasting Idaho LS, LLC
Group Owner: Rich Broadcasting LLC
Population Served: 1,117 *Arbitron Metro Market:* Ashton, ID
Bruce Buzil, General Manager

Victor

KVRG
05-01-2005; 103.7 mhz FM; 0.821 kw; 1086 ft.; N43 29 27 W110 57 16
7901 Stoneridge Drive, Cheyenne, WY 82009 US
(307) 732-0384
www.1037therange.com
info@1037therange.com
License: Victor, Teton County, ID held by Jackson Radio Group Inc.
Group Owner: Northeast Broadcasting Company Inc.; (acq 3-31-2006; $900,000 with KRVQ(FM) Victor)
Arbitron Metro Market: Victor, ID *Format:* Country
Steven Silberberg, President
Bruce Pollock, General Manager

Wallace

***KTWD**
12-01-2000; 97.5 mhz FM *Hrs Open:* 24; 1.6 kw; 2215 ft.; N47 33 49 W115 50 1
5546-3 Century Avenue, Middleton, WI 53562 US
(509) 244-5577, *Fax:* (509) 244-2232
ktwd@csnradio.com
License: Wallace, Shoshone County, ID held by CSN International
Group Owner: CSN International; (acq 2-24-2000; $50,000 for CP)
Format: Christian
Barney Dasovich, General Manager

KWAL
05-01-1938; 620 khz AM *Hrs Open:* 24; 1 kw-D, DAN; 1 kw-N, DAN; N47 30 29 W116 0 17
P. O. Box ""U"", Osburn, ID 83849 US

RADIO - U.S.

(208) 752-1141(208) 752-1142, *Fax:* (208) 753-5111
kwalradio@usamedia.tv
License: Wallace, ID held by Silver Valley Broadcasters Inc.
Nat'l Network: Jones Radio Networks
Arbitron Metro Market: Wallace, ID *Format:* Country
Paul Robinson, President
Paul Robinson, General Manager
George White, General Sales Mgr
John Davis, Programming Director

Weiser

KTRP
1260 khz AM
2001 Penn Ave. NW, Fisher, Wayland Et Al, Washington, DC 20006 US
(208) 367-1859
www.ktrpradio.com
sales@tvbradio.com
License: Weiser, ID held by JNE Investments Inc.
Arbitron Metro Market: Weiser, ID *Format:* Talk

Wendell

KTFI
10-01-1928; 1340 khz AM
Mailing Address: US
Second Address: 21361 Hwy 30, Twin Falls, ID 83301
(208) 735-8300, *Fax:* (208) 733-4196
www.ktfi.com
License: Wendell, ID held by Locally Owned Radio LLC.
Group Owner: Locally Owned Radio LLC; (acq 10-31-2003; grpsl)
Format: Oldies *Special Programming:* Farm 3 hrs, relg 5 hrs, sports 3 hrs wkly *Target Audience:* 35 plus.
Larry Johnson, President
Jerre Fender, Operations Dir
Deb Uvieu, General Sales Mgr
Denis Jeffs, News Director

Weston

KLZX
01-01-2001; 95.9 mhz FM; 25 kw; 217 ft.; N41 52 18 W111 48 31
2001 Pennsylvania Ave NW, Suite 400, Washington, DC 22206 US
(435) 752-5141, *Fax:* (435) 752-1392
www.klzxfm.com
will@cvradio.com
License: Weston, Franklin County, ID held by Sun Valley Radio Inc.
Group Owner: Sun Valley Radio Inc.
Arbitron Metro Market: Logan, UT *Format:* Classic Rock
Lynn Simmons, General Manager
James Murdock, Sales Manager
Will Wheelwright, Programming Director

Illinois

Albion

*WBJW
12-01-1997; 91.7 mhz FM; 1.7 kw; 499 ft.; N38 19 14 W88 2 37
Rebroadcasts: Rebroadcasts WBGW(FM) Fort Branch,
P O Box 4164, Evansville, IN 47724 US
(800)264-5550, *Fax:* (812) 768-5552
www.thyword.org
mail@thyword.org
License: Albion, Edwards County, IL held by Music Ministries Inc.
Arbitron Metro Market: Evansville,IN *Format:* Religious
Floyd Turner, General Manager

Aledo

WRMJ
06-12-1979; 102.3 mhz FM *Hrs Open:* 24; 3 kw; 299 ft.; N41 12 29 W90 48 10
P.O. Box 187, Aledo, IL 61231 US
(309) 582-5666, *Fax:* (309) 582-5667
wrmj.com
contactus@wrmj.com
License: Aledo, Mercer County, IL held by Western Illinois Broadcasting Co.
Regional Network: Brownfield
Arbitron Metro Market: Quad Cities, IA-IL (Davenport-Rock Island-Moline) *Format:* Country, News *Special Programming:* Relg 3 hrs wkly *Hrs. of News Programming:* news progmg 20 hrs wkly *No. News Employees:* 1*Target Audience:* 25-54. *Adv. Rates:* 11; 7; 7; 7
John Hoscheidt, General Manager
Judy Bedford, General Sales Mgr
Terry Tracy, Programming Director
Jim Taylor, News Director

Alton

WBGZ
01-01-1948; 1570 khz AM *Hrs Open:* 24; 1 kw-D, ND1; 0.074 kw-N, ND1; N38 55 44 W90 13 3
P.O. Box 615, Alton, IL 62002 US
(618) 465-1570, *Fax:* (618) 465-3546
www.wbgzradio.com
wbgz@wbgzradio.com
License: Alton, IL held by Metroplex Communications Inc.
Nat'l Network: USA
Arbitron Metro Market: St. Louis, MO *Format:* News, News/Talk, 86 *Special Programming:* Gospel 4 hrs, relg 3 hrs wkly *Hrs. of News Programming:* news progmg 20 hrs wkly *No. News Employees:* 2 *Target Audience:* General.
Sam Stemm, General Manager
Nancy Bivens, Director of Sales
Mark Ellebracht, News Director
Mark Hilgert, Office Manager
Brent Burklund, Sports Director

Anna

WIBH
01-10-1957; 1440 khz AM *Hrs Open:* 24; 0.5 kw-D, ND1; 0.109 kw-N, ND1; N37 26 45 W89 15 0
330 South Main, Anna, IL 62906 US
(618) 833-9424, *Fax:* (618) 833-9091
www.wibhradio.com
wibh@ajinternet.net
License: Anna, IL held by WIBH Inc.
Wire Services: UPI
Format: Country *Hrs. of News Programming:* news progmg 3 hrs wkly *No. News Employees:* 1 *Target Audience:* 25-69. *Adv. Rates:* 12; 12; 12; 11
Ronald Ellis, President
Maury Bass, Operations Dir
Maurice Bass, Programming Director

WKIB
01-13-1958; 96.5 mhz FM *Hrs Open:* 24; 22 kw; 748 ft.; N37 21 44 W89 31 19
6120 Waldo Church Rd., Metropolis, IL 62960 US
(573) 339-7000, *Fax:* (573) 651-4100
www.mix965.net
License: Anna, Union County, IL held by W. Russell Withers Jr.
Group Owner: Withers Broadcasting Co.; (acq 10-22-2001; $2 million)
Nat'l Reps: Katz Radio
Format: Contemporary Hits/Top 40 *Hrs. of News Programming:* news progmg 10 hrs wkly *No. News Employees:* 1 *Target Audience:* 18-45.
Rick Lambert, General Manager
Steve Thomas, Programming Director

Arcola

WUIL
12-19-1974; 107.9 mhz FM *Hrs Open:* 24; 3.6 kw horiz, 3 kw vert; 427 ft.; N39 52 43 W88 11 51
206 South Willow, P.O. Box 988, Effingham, IL 62401 US
(217) 258-6060, *Fax:* (217) 258-6077
www.urock1079.com
License: Arcola, Moultrie County, IL held by Champaign Partners LLC
Arbitron Metro Market: Champaign, IL *Format:* Christian *Hrs. of News Programming:* news progmg 10 hrs wkly *No. News Employees:* 1 *Target Audience:* 25-54.
Shirley Browning, General Manager

Arlington Heights

WCPT-FM
03-10-1960; 92.7 mhz FM *Hrs Open:* 24; 1.8 kw; 381 ft.; N42 8 14 W87 58 57
11 Skyline Drive, Hawthorne, NY 10532 US
(773) 767-1000, *Fax:* (773) 767-1100
www.chicagoprogressivetalk.com
info@wcpt820.com
License: Arlington Heights, Cook County, IL held by WKIE Inc.
Group Owner: Newsweb Corp.; (acq 11-15-2004; grpsl)
Nat'l Network: CNN Radio
Arbitron Metro Market: Chicago, IL *Format:* Alternative, Talk
Harvey Wells, General Manager
Bill Cavanaugh, General Sales Mgr
Roan Davis, News Director
Mike McCarthy, Chief Engineer

*WCLR
11-01-2003; 88.3 mhz FM *Hrs Open:* 24; 0.001 kw horiz, 1 kw vert; 59 ft.; N42 6 45 W87 58 58
502 West Euclid Avenue, Arlington Hiehgts, IL 60004 US
(888) 937-2471, *Fax:* (916) 251-1650
www.air1.com
info@air1.com
License: Arlington Heights, Cook County, IL held by Educational Media Foundation.
Group Owner: EMF Broadcasting; (acq 8-13-03).
Nat'l Network: Air 1
Arbitron Metro Market: Omaha, NE *Format:* Alternative, Christian *No. News Employees:* 3 *Target Audience:* 18-35; Judeo Christian, female
Darrell Chambliss, Chairman
Mike Novak, President & CEO
Ed Lenane, News Director
Sam Wallington, Engineering Dir
Marya Morgan, News Reporter
Richard Hunt, News Reporter
David R. Ferry, Director
Walter Golembeski, Director
David Pierce, Chief Creative Officer
Alan Mason, Chief Operating Officer

Atlanta

WLCN
04-13-2001; 96.3 mhz FM *Hrs Open:* 24; 6 kw; 266 ft.; N40 14 39 W89 15 51
3654 West Jarvis Avenue, Skokie, IL 60076 US
(217) 648-5510, *Fax:* (217) 648-2499
License: Atlanta, Logan County, IL held by KM Radio of Atlanta L.L.C.
Group Owner: KM Communications Inc.; (acq 5-3-99).
Nat'l Network: ABC *Wire Services:* AP; Metro Weather Service Inc.
Arbitron Metro Market: Atlanta, IL *Format:* Country *Target Audience:* 25-54. *Adv. Rates:* 180; 180; 180; 180
Jim Ash, General Manager
Tamera Turner, General Sales Mgr
Jeff Benjamin, News Director

Aurora

WBIG
12-13-1938; 1280 khz AM *Hrs Open:* 24; 1 kw-D, DA2; 0.5 kw-N, DA2; N41 46 10 W88 14 44
C/O K. Richard Jakle, 14 Douglas Ave., Elgin, IL 60120 US
(630) 851-5200, *Fax:* (630) 851-5286
www.wbig1280.com
stevemarten@wbig1280.com
License: Aurora, IL held by Big Broadcasting Co.
Group Owner: McNaughton-Jakle Stations; (acq 1-94; $550,000).
Nat'l Network: Fox Sports
Arbitron Metro Market: Aurora, IL *Format:* News, News/Talk, 84, Talk *Special Programming:* Relg 6 hrs wkly *Hrs. of News Programming:* news progmg 10 hrs wkly *No. News Employees:* 1 *Target Audience:* 25-54;professional, upscale, suburbanites with children
Rick Jakle, President
Jack Davis, Operations Dir
Jim Sauers, General Sales Mgr
Ryan Gatenby, Programming Director
Brien Prenevost, Chief Engineer
Steve Marten, Executive Vice President
Sue Griffin, Radio Shopping ShowCoordinater

WERV-FM
02-12-1961; 95.9 mhz FM; 2.85 kw; 338 ft.; N41 46 9 W88 16 2
1884 Plains Avenue, Aurora, IL 60307 US
(630) 898-1580, *Fax:* (630) 898-2463
www.959theriver.fm
License: Aurora, Du Page County, IL held by NM Licensing LLC.
Group Owner: NextMedia Group Inc.; (acq 11-26-2001; grpsl).
Nat'l Reps: McGavren Guild
Arbitron Metro Market: Chicago, IL *Format:* Contemporary Hits/Top 40, Adult Contemp *Hrs. of News Programming:* news progmg 5 hrs wkly *No. News Employees:* 1 *Target Audience:* 25-54; suburban Chicago adults*Adv. Rates:* 50; 45; 50; 30
Brian Foster, General Manager

WLEY-FM
01-01-1965; 107.9 mhz FM *Hrs Open:* 24; 21 kw; 761 ft.; N41 56 1 W88 4 23
3191 Coral Way, Suite 805, Miami, FL 33145 US
(312) 920-9500, *Fax:* (312) 920-9516
www.laley1079.com
info@laley1079.com
License: Aurora, Du Page County, IL held by WLEY Licensing Inc.

Group Owner: Spanish Broadcasting System Inc.; (acq 12-26-96; $33 million)
Arbitron Metro Market: Chicago, IL *No. News Employees:* 1
Target Audience: 25-54.
Jeff Schrinsky, General Manager
Marylu Ramos, Programming Director
Leticia Aguilera, Promotions Manager
Sam Palerno, Chief Engineer
Mario Paez, General Manager
Joe McKay, General Sales Manager

Ava

WXAN
01-11-1982; 103.9 mhz FM *Hrs Open:* 24; 2.9 kw; 469 ft.; N37 51 19 W89 28 6
9077 Ava Road, Ava, IL 62907 US
(618) 426-3308, *Fax:* (618) 426-3310
www.mysoutherngospel.net
billmac@egyptian.net
License: Ava, Jackson County, IL held by Southern Gospetality LLC.
Nat'l Network: Salem Radio Network
Arbitron Metro Market: Ava, IL *Format:* Gospel, Religious *Hrs. of News Programming:* News progmg 10 hrs wkly *Target Audience:* 30-55; Christians & family-oriented listeners *Adv. Rates:* 12; 12; 12; 12.
Harold Lawder, President
Will Stephens, General Manager
Bill McCarty, Lead Account Representative
Tish Brooks, Radio Jockey

Bartonville

WWCT
02-01-1997; 99.9 mhz FM *Hrs Open:* 24; 1.5 kw; 584 ft.; N40 36 23 W89 32 20
P.O. Box 150846, Nashville, TN 37215 US
(309) 686-0101, *Fax:* (309) 686-0111
www.thebuzzpeoria.com
Studio@TheBuzzPeoria.com
License: Bartonville, Peoria County, IL held by IM IL Licenses LLC.
Group Owner: Independence Media Holdings LLC; (acq 9-19-2006; grpsl)
Arbitron Metro Market: Peoria, IL *Adv. Rates:* 30; 25; 30; 10
David Manning, General Manager
Jason Stuckwisch, General Sales Mgr
Gabe Reynolds, Programming Director

Beardstown

WRMS
11-01-1959; 790 khz AM
108 East Main Street, Beardstown, IL 62618 US
(314) 752-7000
covenantnetwork@juno.com
License: Beardstown, IL held by Covenant Network.
Group Owner: Covenant Network; (acq 7-28-2004)
Format: Christian, Religious
Tony Holman, President
Jim Schaper, Programming Director

WRMS-FM
01-01-1976; 94.3 mhz FM; 6 kw; 299 ft.; N40 4 45 W90 25 58
108 East Main Street, Beardstown, IL 62618 US
(217) 323-1790, *Fax:* (217) 323-1705
wrmsfm@casscomm.com
License: Beardstown, Cass County, IL held by Conner Family Broadcasting Inc.
Format: Country
John Conner, General Manager
Glen Hopkins, Chief Engineer

Belleville

WSDZ
07-13-1947; 1260 khz AM *Hrs Open:* 24
77 West 66th St., 16th Flr : Sam Antar, New York, NY 10023 US
(314) 428-4023, *Fax:* (314) 428-9119
www.radiodisney.com/stlouis
ted.m.zimmerman@disney.com
License: Belleville, IL held by Radio Disney Group LLC.
Group Owner: ABC Inc.
Nat'l Network: ABC
Arbitron Metro Market: St. Louis, MO *Format:* Contemporary Hits/Top 40, Adult Contemp *Special Programming:* Caring is Cool 30 min wkly *Target Audience:* 25-54 plus; 6-14; affluent, well-educated, business &professional Kids
Ted Zimmerman, Station Manager
Jason Miller, General Sales Mgr

Nicole Polley, Promotions Manager
Jacqui Grable, Account Executive

Belvidere

WXRX
02-27-1971; 104.9 mhz FM; 4 kw; 400 ft.; N42 19 21 W88 57 14 US
(815) 874-7861, *Fax:* (815) 874-2202
www.wxrx.com
License: Belvidere, Boone County, IL held by Maverick Media of Rockford License LLC.
Group Owner: Maverick Media LLC; (acq 4-27-2005; grpsl)
Arbitron Metro Market: Rockford, IL *Format:* Rock/AOR *Target Audience:* 18-49.
Gary Rozynek, President
Jay Chapman, General Manager
Jim Stone, Programming Director

Benton

WQRL
10-01-1973; 106.3 mhz FM *Hrs Open:* 24; 12.5 kw; 459 ft.; N37 55 51 W88 40 52
Mailing Address: P.O. 818, Benton, IL 62812 US
Second Address: 303 N. Main St., Benton, IL 62812
(618) 435-8100, *Fax:* (618) 435-8102
wwqrlfm@shawneelink.net
License: Benton, Franklin County, IL held by Dana Communications Corp.
Arbitron Metro Market: Marion-Carbondale (Southern Illinois)
Format: Oldies *Special Programming:* Farm 3 hrs wkly *Hrs. of News Programming:* news progmg 15 hrs wkly *No. News Employees:* 2 *Target Audience:* 25-49; adults & young adults preferring new country
Dana Withers, CEO
Gloria Holland, Station Manager
Jeff Oestreich, Chief Engineer
Bleu Withers, Executive Vice President

Berwyn

WVON
10-07-2003; 1690 khz AM
111 East Kibourn Avenue, Suite 2700, Milwaukee, WI 53202 US
(773) 247-6200, *Fax:* (773) 247-5336
www.wvon.com
info@wvon.com
License: Berwyn, IL held by CC Licenses LLC.
Group Owner: Clear Channel Communications Inc.; (acq 1-18-2001)
Nat'l Network: ABC
Arbitron Metro Market: Chicago, IL *Format:* Talk *Target Audience:* 25-54; urban talk listeners
Melody Spann-Cooper, General Manager

Bethalto

WFUN-FM
04-01-1991; 95.5 mhz FM *Hrs Open:* 24; 24.5 kw; 335 ft.; N38 48 38 W90 17 38
5900 Princess Garden Parkway, 8th Floor, Lanham, MD 20706 US
(314) 989-9550, *Fax:* (314) 989-9551
License: Bethalto, Madison County, IL held by Radio One Licenses LLC.
Group Owner: Radio One Inc.; (acq 11-8-01; grpsl).
Arbitron Metro Market: St. Louis, MO *Format:* Black, Blues *Hrs. of News Programming:* News progmg 2 hrs wkly *Target Audience:* General; families
Alfred Liggins, President
Michael Douglass, General Manager
Laura Steele, General Sales Mgr
Melissa Wakefields, News Director
Gary Bennett, Chief Engineer

Bloomington

WBNQ
01-01-1947; 101.5 mhz FM; 50 kw; 466 ft.; N40 27 1 W89 0 42
P. O. Box 8, Bloomington, IL 61701 US
(309) 829-1221, *Fax:* (309) 827-8071
www.wbnq.com
brian@wbnq.com
License: Bloomington, McLean County, IL
Group Owner: Townsquare Media
Arbitron Metro Market: Bloomington, IL *Format:* Contemporary Hits/Top 40 *Special Programming:* Farm one hr wkly
Dan Westhoff, Station Manager
Julie Penn, Sales Director
Brian Davis, Programming Director
Russell Rush, Music Director

*WESN
01-01-1972; 88.1 mhz FM; 0.12 kw; 98 ft.; N40 29 28 W88 59 37
P. O. Box 2900, Bloomington, IL 61701 US
(309) 556-2638, *Fax:* (309) 556-2949
www.wesn.org
wesn@iwu.edu
License: Bloomington, McLean County, IL held by Illinois Wesleyan University.
Nat'l Network: PRI
Arbitron Metro Market: Bloomington, IL *Format:* Variety/Diverse
Special Programming: Black 18 hrs, class 6 hrs, jazz 6 hrs wkly
Patrick Nevels, Station Manager
Darek Jakubowski, Programming Director
Michael Kocourek, Promotions Manager
Al Maiocco, Technical Director
Patrick Cavanaugh, Music Director
Matt Siegert, Sports Director
Matt Siegert, SportsDirector
Sen "Jules" Wang, Assistant music director
Mike Kistner, Local show director
Rick Lindquist, Advisor

WJBC
01-01-1925; 1230 khz AM; 1 kw-U, ND1; N40 27 1 W89 0 42
P.O. Box 8, Bloomington, IL 61701 US
(309) 829-1221, *Fax:* (309) 827-8071
www.wjbc.com
RCMcBride@wjbc.com
License: Bloomington, IL
Group Owner: Townsquare Media; (acq 5-12-2004; grpsl)
Nat'l Reps: McGavren Guild
Arbitron Metro Market: Bloomington, IL *Format:* Variety/Diverse
Special Programming: Farm 13 hrs wkly
R.C. McBride, Operations Dir
Red Pitcher, General Manager
Julie Penn, General Sales Mgr
R.D. McBride, Programming Director
Colleen Reynolds, News Director
Ron Schott, Chief Engineer

*WJWR
90.3 mhz FM; 18 kw; 327 ft.; N40 40 59.3 W88 45 43
Rr4, Box 184, Bloomington, IL 61704 US
(309) 963-4932
License: Bloomington, McLean County, IL held by Bloomington Normal Broadcasting Corp.
Arbitron Metro Market: Bloomington, IL
Jacqueline Dearing, President

Bluford

*WVYN
90.9 mhz FM; 11 kw; 210 ft.; N38 13 10 W88 37 47 US
(618) 895-3030
www.wvyn.org
License: Bluford, Jefferson County, IL held by Real Life Radio Foundation Inc.
Arbitron Metro Market: Bluford, IL
Randall Lee Olson, President

Breese

WDLJ
01-01-2003; 97.5 mhz FM; 2.5 kw; 512 ft.; N38 36 33 W89 23 35
1320 Eithteenth St, N.W., Suite 400, Washington, DC 20036 US
(618) 594-2620, *Fax:* (618) 594-2659
www.wdlj.com
support@gtshighland.com
License: Breese, Clinton County, IL held by KM Radio of Breese L.L.C.
Arbitron Metro Market: Carlyle, IL *Format:* Classic Rock
Kevin Bae, General Manager
Tim, Salespersons
Michelle, Salespersons
Moose, Salespersons

Brookport

WTHQ
10-01-1987; 750 khz AM; 0.5 kw-D, NDD; N37 8 31 W88 38 58
6120 Waldo Church Road, Metropolis, IL 62960 US
, *Fax:* (618) 564-3202
License: Brookport, IL held by Daniel S. Stratemeyer
Format: Talk
Samuel Stratemeyer, General Manager

Bushnell

WLMD
08-01-1992; 104.7 mhz FM *Hrs Open:* 24; 3.3 kw; 377 ft.; N40 32 45 W90 29 15

RADIO - U.S.

P.O. Box 250, Macomb, IL 61455 US
(309) 833-5561, *Fax:* (309) 833-3460
www.radiomacomb.com
wlmd@macomb.com
License: Bushnell, McDonough County, IL held by WPW Broadcasting Inc.
Group Owner: Prairie Radio Communications; (acq 12-27-99; grpsl)
Nat'l Network: ABC; Jones Radio Networks *Regional Network:* Brownfield; Ill. Radio Net.
Format: Country *Special Programming:* Farm 3 hrs wkly *Hrs. of News Programming:* news progmg 2 hrs wkly *No. News Employees:* 1 *Target Audience:* 25-54; general *Adv. Rates:* 10; 10; 10; na
Vanessa Wetterling, Station Manager
Mike Weaver, Programming Director

Cairo

*WBEL
01-01-2002; 88.5 mhz FM; 64 kw vert; 558 ft.; N36 59 32 W88 59 19
P O Drawer 2440, Tupelo, MS 38803 US
(509) 341-4230
License: Cairo, Alexander County, IL held by American Family Association.
Group Owner: American Family Radio
Arbitron Metro Market: Barling AR *Format:* Triple A
Don Ashford, General Manager

WKRO
01-08-1942; 1490 khz AM *Hrs Open:* 24; 1 kw-U, ND1; N37 2 36 W89 11 2
Rural Route #1 Box 124, Thebes, IL 62990 US
(618) 734-1490, *Fax:* (618) 734-0884
djman75@hotmail.com
License: Cairo, IL held by Alexander Broadcasting Corp.
Nat'l Network: ABC
Format: Adult Contemp *Special Programming:* Gospel 12 hrs, farm 12 hrs wkly *Hrs. of News Programming:* news progmg 12 hrs wkly *No. News Employees:* 1 *Target Audience:* 25-54; general *Adv. Rates:* 8.50;8.50; 8.50; 8.50
Danny McDonald, General Manager
Marti Nicholson, General Sales Mgr

Cambridge

WYEC
05-20-1966; 93.9 mhz FM *Hrs Open:* 24; 4.2 kw; 394 ft.; N41 22 56 W90 10 47
111 W. Main Cr/PO Bx 169, Taylorville, IL 62568 US
(309) 853-4471, *Fax:* (309) 853-4474
www.randyradio.com
regionalradio@verizon.net
License: Cambridge, Henry County, IL held by Virden Broadcasting Corp.
Group Owner: Miller Media Group
Nat'l Network: CNN Radio
Arbitron Metro Market: Quad Cities, IA *Format:* Adult Contemp
Target Audience: 35-64.
Randal Miller, President
Will Stevenson, News Director
Bob McKee, Local News

Canton

WBYS
10-05-1947; 1560 khz AM *Hrs Open:* 6 AM-sunset
1000 East Linn Street, P.O. Box 600, Canton, IL 61520 US
(309) 647-1560, *Fax:* (309) 647-1563
www.1560wbys.com
wbysradio@yahoo.com
License: Canton, IL held by WPW Broadcasting Inc.
Group Owner: Prairie Radio Communications; (acq 1999; $210,000 for stock with co-located FM)
Nat'l Network: ABC
Arbitron Metro Market: Canton, IL *Format:* News, News/Talk, 84, Talk *Special Programming:* Farm 10 hrs wkly *Hrs. of News Programming:* news progmg 25 hrs wkly *No. News Employees:* 1 *Target Audience:* 30plus; community-oriented with above average income *Adv. Rates:* 13; 9; 11; 5
Don Davis, CEO
BJ Stone, General Manager

WCDD
10-07-1968; 107.9 mhz FM *Hrs Open:* 24; 25 kw; 269 ft.; N40 32 40.5 W90 1 15.5
1000 East Linn, Canton, IL 61520 US
(309) 647-1560, *Fax:* (309) 647-1563
www.cd1079.com
bj.stone@prairiecommunications.net
License: Canton, Fulton County, IL
Group Owner: Prairie Radio Communications
Nat'l Network: ABC
Arbitron Metro Market: Canton, IL *Format:* Contemporary Hits/Top 40, Adult Contemp *Special Programming:* High School Sports *Hrs. of News Programming:* news progmg 10 hrs wkly *No. News Employees:* 1 *TargetAudience:* 35-54; males *Adv. Rates:* 15; 11; 13; 9
Don Davis, CEO
BJ Stone, General Manager
Wayne Miller, Chief Engineer

Carbondale

WCIL
11-14-1946; 1020 khz AM *Hrs Open:* Sunrise-sunset; 1 kw-D, NDD; N37 43 31 W89 15 25 *Rebroadcasts:* Rebroadcasts WJPF(AM) Herrin 100%
P.O. Box 1749, Cape Girardeau, MO 63702 US
(618) 985-4843, *Fax:* (618) 985-6529
www.wjpf.com
tomm@riverradio.net
License: Carbondale, IL held by MRR License LLC.
Group Owner: MAX Media L.L.C.; (acq 3-29-2004; grpsl).
Nat'l Reps: Christal
Arbitron Metro Market: Marion-Carbondale, IL *Format:* News, News/Talk, 84, Talk *Special Programming:* Farm one hr wkly *Hrs. of News Programming:* news progmg 10 hrs wkly *No. News Employees:* 2 *Target Audience:* 35 plus.
Tom Miller, Operations Dir
Steve Schimmel, General Manager
Kim Debose, Sales Manager
Tom Miller, Programming Director
Ryan Patrick, Promotions Manager
Felicia Dick, News Director
Jon Brookmyer, Chief Engineer
Richard Cason,News Reporter
Dee James, News Reporter
Steve Falat, Market Manager

WCIL-FM
07-01-1968; 101.5 mhz FM *Hrs Open:* 24; 28.5 kw; 653 ft.; N37 42 4 W89 22 18
P. O. Box 1610, Cape Girardeau, MO 63702 US
(618) 985-4843, *Fax:* (618) 985-6529
www.cilfm.com
Stevef@riverradio.net
License: Carbondale, Jackson County, IL
Nat'l Reps: Christal
Arbitron Metro Market: Marion-Carbondale, IL *Format:* Contemporary Hits/Top 40 *Target Audience:* 18-34; adult females
Tom Miller, Operations Dir
Steve Falat, General Manager
Kim Debose, Sales Manager
Jon Quest, Programming Director
Ryan Patrick, Promotions Manager
Felicia Dick, News Director
Jon Brookmyer, Chief Engineer
Dave McKenzie, EventsCoordinator
Steve Falat, Market Manager

*WDBX
02-01-1996; 91.1 mhz FM *Hrs Open:* 7 AM-4 AM; 3 kw; 131 ft.; N37 43 43 W89 12 57
100 East Jackson Street, Carbondale, IL 62901 US
(618) 457-3691(618) 529-5900
www.wdbx.org
wdbx911@yahoo.com
License: Carbondale, Jackson County, IL held by Heterodyne Broadcasting Co.
Arbitron Metro Market: Marion-Carbondale, IL *Format:* Variety/Diverse *Hrs. of News Programming:* News progmg 2.5 hrs wkly *Adv. Rates:* 5; 5; 5; 5
John Hochheimer, Chairman
Francis Murphy, President
Brian Powell, Station Manager

*WSIU
09-15-1958; 91.9 mhz FM *Hrs Open:* 24; 50 kw; 299 ft.; N37 42 29 W89 14 5 *Rebroadcasts:* Rebroadcasts WUSI(FM) Olney 100%, WVSI(FM) Mt. Venon 100%
Radio Station Wsiu, Carbondale, IL 62901 US
(618) 453-4343, *Fax:* (618) 453-6186
wsiu.org
jeff.williams@wsiu.org
License: Carbondale, Jackson County, IL held by Board of Trustees Southern Illinois University.
Nat'l Network: NPR; PRI *Regional Network:* Ill. Radio Net. *Wire Services:* AP
Arbitron Metro Market: Marion-Carbonda *TV Affiliate:* *WSIU-TV affil *Special Programming:* New age 4 hrs, big band 4 hrs, folk 3 hrs wkly *Hrs. of News Programming:* news progmg 36 hrs wkly *No. News Employees:* 3*Target Audience:* 35-64; highly educated, upper income, socially conscious
Greg Petrowich, CEO
Jeff Williams, General Manager
Renee Dillard, General Sales Mgr
Mike Zelten, Programming Director
Terry Harvey, Chief Engineer
Delores Kerstein, CFO

Carlinville

*WIBI
09-30-1975; 91.1 mhz FM *Hrs Open:* 24; 50 kw; 476 ft.; N39 20 58 W89 48 16
P.O. Box 140, Carlinville, IL 62626 US
(217) 854-4800, *Fax:* (217) 854-4810
www.wibi.org
wibi@wibi.org
License: Carlinville, Macoupin County, IL held by Illinois Bible Institute Inc.
Group Owner: Illinois Bible Institute Inc.
Format: Adult Contemp, Christian *Target Audience:* 25-49.
Barry Copeland, General Manager
Jeremiah Beck, Station Manager
Rob Regal, Programming Director
Jessica Barton, Promotions Manager
Sally Braundmeier, News Director
Joe Buchanan, Music Director
Liz Eilers, Underwriting Director

*WOLG
12-08-1990; 95.9 mhz FM; 6 kw; 325 ft.; N39 14 25 W89 54 27
9 Cougar Road, Glen Carbon, IL 62034 US
(314) 752-7000
http://www.covenantnet.net/
covenantnetwork@juno.com
License: Carlinville, Macoupin County, IL held by Covenant Network.
Group Owner: Covenant Network; (acq 8-10-98; $300,000)
TV Affiliate: Relg

*WTSG
08-11-1997; 90.1 mhz FM *Hrs Open:* 24; 5 kw; 295 ft.; N39 20 58 W89 48 16
Box 140, Carlinville, IL 62626 US
(217) 854-4651, *Fax:* (217) 854-4610
www.wtsg.org
wibi@wibi.org
License: Carlinville, Macoupin County, IL held by Illinois Bible Institute Inc.
Group Owner: Illinois Bible Institute Inc.
Arbitron Metro Market: Carlinville, IL *Format:* Gospel, Religious
Target Audience: 25-44. *Adv. Rates:* 5; 5; 5; 5
Barry Copeland, General Manager
Jeremiah Beck, Station Manager
Rob Regal, Programming Director
Jessica Barton, Promotions Manager
Sally Braundmeier, News Director
Joe Buchanan, Music Director
Liz Eilers, Underwriting Director

Carmi

WROY
12-13-1948; 1460 khz AM *Hrs Open:* 24; 1 kw-D, ND1; 0.085 kw-N, ND1; N38 4 54 W88 12 4
101 North Church Street, Carmi, IL 62821 US
(618) 382-4161, *Fax:* (618) 382-4162
www.wrul.com
wroy1460@verizon.net
License: Carmi, IL held by W. Russell Withers Jr.
Group Owner: Withers Broadcasting Co.
Format: Oldies *Special Programming:* Farm 6 hrs wkly *Hrs. of News Programming:* news progmg 25 hrs wkly *No. News Employees:* 2 *Target Audience:* 35 plus; general *Adv. Rates:* 16; 15; 16; 12
George Hinds, General Manager
Bill Perry Sr., Station Manager

WRUL
01-01-1951; 97.3 mhz FM *Hrs Open:* 24; 50 kw; 489 ft.; N38 4 54 W88 12 4
101 North Church Street, Carmi, IL 62821 US
(618) 382-4161, *Fax:* (618) 382-4162
www.wrul.com
wrul973@verizon.net
License: Carmi, White County, IL held by W. Russell Withers Jr.
Group Owner: Withers Broadcasting Co.; (acq 5-1-2006; $1.1 million with co-located AM)
Nat'l Network: ABC

Format: Country *Hrs. of News Programming:* news progmg 8 hrs wkly *No. News Employees:* 1 *Target Audience:* 25-55. *Adv. Rates:* 19; 17; 19; 13
Russell Withers, President
J.C. Tinsley, General Sales Mgr
Irma O'Dell, Programming Director
Bob Miller, News Director

***WYER**
90.5 mhz FM; 2.5 kw vert; 94 ft.; N38 4 28.6 W88 12 31.9 US
(765) 821-2180
License: Carmi, White County, IL held by Connersville Apostolic Lighthouse Inc.
Arbitron Metro Market: Carmi, IL
Blaine Lucas, Chairman
Sean Sebastian, President
Lee Ferraro, General Manager
Tony Pirollo, General Sales Mgr
Rosemary Welsch, Programming Director
Joe Resch, Disc Jockey

Carpentersville

***WWTG**
88.1 mhz FM; 2 kw vert; Ant 108 ft; N42 06 21 W88 22 38
238 Oak Avenue, Carpentersville, IL 98901
(847) 975-6000, *Fax:* (615) 216-7266
www.lifetalk.net
terryyounce@comcast.net
License: Carpentersville, Kane County, IL held by LifeTalk Radio Inc.
Nat'l Network: Life Talk Radio Network
Arbitron Metro Market: Chicago
Gabriel Bardan, Chairman
Terry Younce, Station Manager
John Geli, Programming Director

Carrier Mills

WBVN
01-08-1990; 104.5 mhz FM *Hrs Open:* 24; 6 kw; 328 ft.; N37 46 25 W88 44 20
Route 7, Box 385b, Marion, IL 62959 US
(618) 252-2999, *Fax:* (618) 997-3194
www.wbvn.org
wbvn@wbvn.org
License: Carrier Mills, Saline County, IL held by Kenneth W. and Jane A. Anderson
Arbitron Metro Market: Marion,IL *Format:* Christian *No. News Employees:* 3 *Target Audience:* 18-45; general
Ken Anderson, President

Carterville

WUEZ
04-02-1992; 95.1 mhz FM *Hrs Open:* 24; 17.6 kw; 390 ft.; N37 43 31 W89 15 25
P.O. Box 1749, Cape Girardeau, MO 63702 US
(618) 985-4843, *Fax:* (618) 985-6529
www.magic951.com
mail@magic951.com
License: Carterville, Williamson County, IL held by MRR License LLC.
Group Owner: MAX Media L.L.C.; (acq 6-2-2004; grpsl)
Nat'l Reps: Christal
Arbitron Metro Market: Carterville, IL *Format:* Adult Contemp *Hrs. of News Programming:* news progmg 18 hrs wkly *No. News Employees:* 2 *Target Audience:* 25-49; 60% women, 40% men, good spendable income; mgrs,supvrs, professionals
Tom Miller, Operations Dir
Mike Smith, General Manager
Kim DeBose, General Sales Mgr
Jake, Programming Director
Ryan Patrick, Promotions Manager
Felicia Dick, News Director
Jon Brookmyer, Chief Engineer
Steve Falat, MarketManager

Carthage

WCAZ
01-01-1922; 990 khz AM; 1 kw-D, ND1; 0.009 kw-N, ND1; N40 24 30 W91 10 15
Mailing Address: 84 South Madison Street, Carthage, IL 62321 US
Second Address: 86 S. Madison, Carthage, IL 62321
(217) 357-3128, *Fax:* (217) 357-2014
www.wcazam990.com
wcazam@adamas.net
License: Carthage, IL held by Ralla Broadcasting Co. Inc.
Arbitron Metro Market: Carthage, IL *Format:* Talk
Rob Dunham, General Manager
Keith Yex, General Sales Mgr
Chuck Porter, Programming Director

WQKQ
11-01-1978; 92.1 mhz FM *Hrs Open:* 24; 25 kw; 328 ft.; N40 35 37 W91 6 48
2220 Avenue L, Ft. Madison, IA 52627 US
(319) 752-5402, *Fax:* (319) 752-4715
www.KQ92rocks.com
kq92rocks@kq92rocks.com
License: Carthage, Hancock County, IL held by Pritchard Broadcasting Corp.
Group Owner: Pritchard Broadcasting Corp.; (acq 12-1-99)
Nat'l Reps: Katz Radio
Arbitron Metro Market: Burlington, IA *Hrs. of News Programming:* news progmg 2 hrs wkly *No. News Employees:* 2 *Target Audience:* 25-54. *Adv. Rates:* 22; 22; 22; 11
John Pritchard, President
Joe Bates, Operations Dir
John Pritchard, General Manager
Chet Young, General Sales Mgr
Mike Savage, Programming Director

WCEZ
01-01-2001; 93.9 mhz FM *Hrs Open:* 24; 6 kw; 328 ft.; N40 24 54 W91 15 11
Mailing Address: P O Box 818, Benton, IL 62812 US
Second Address: 303 N. Main, Carthage, IL 62812
(319) 524-5410, *Fax:* (319) 524-7275
www.keokukradio.com/our-stations/wcez
gary@keokukradio.comm
License: Carthage, Hancock County, IL held by Dana R. Withers.
Group Owner: Withers Broadcasting Co.; Gary M. Folluo, (319) 524-5410
Arbitron Metro Market: Keokuk, IA *Format:* Adult Contemp *Hrs. of News Programming:* news progmg 8 hrs wkly *No. News Employees:* 1 *Target Audience:* 18-45; 60% female, 40% male *Adv. Rates:* 13; 12; 11; 10
Dana Withers, President
Gary Folluo, General Manager
Judy Hall, Sales Manager
Preston Hampton, Program Director/Operations Manager
Matt Frisbee, News Director
Preston Hampton, News Director
Bill Reed, Sports Director
TaraWhitnah, Office Manager

Casey

WCBH
09-19-1988; 104.3 mhz FM *Hrs Open:* 24; 11 kw; 495 ft.; N39 16 24 W87 55 39
937 S.E. 2nd Street, Galva, IL 61434 US
(217) 932-4900, *Fax:* (217) 937-4487
www.1043theparty.com
wcrc@wcrc975.com
License: Casey, Clark County, IL held by Two Petaz Inc.
Group Owner: The Cromwell Group Inc.; (acq 1-9-02; grpsl).
Arbitron Metro Market: Terre Haute, IN *Format:* Christian
Bud Walters, CEO
Marvin Phillips, General Manager
Marvin Phillips, General Sales Mgr
David Wilson, Chief Engineer

WKZI
12-14-1963; 800 khz AM *Hrs Open:* 24; 250 w-U; N39 18 14 W87 58 15
18889 N. 23rd 50th St., Dennison, IL 62420
(217) 826-9673
wordpower.us
wkzi@rr1.net
License: Casey, Clark County, IL held by Word Power Inc.
Nat'l Network: Moody
Population Served: 358,500 *Arbitron Metro Market:* Terre Haute, IN *Hrs. of News Programming:* News progmg 17 hrs wkly *Target Audience:* General; 12 plus *Adv. Rates:* 30; 30; 30; 30
Paul Dean Ford, President
Eleanor Jean Ford, Programming Director
Dan Watson, Engineering Dir

***WLHW**
01-01-2006; 91.5 mhz FM *Hrs Open:* 24; 6 kw; 197 ft.; N39 18 14 W87 58 15
6 East Colorado Alley, P.O. Box 8, Casey, IL 62420 US
(217) 826-9673
www.wordpower.us
wkzi@rrl.net
License: Casey, Clark County, IL
Arbitron Metro Market: Casey, IL *Format:* Christian, Religious
Paul Ford, News Director
Eleanor Ford, Disc Jockey

Centralia

WILY
08-15-1946; 1210 khz AM *Hrs Open:* Sunrise-sunset
Mailing Address: 3501 Broadway, P.O. Box 1508, Mount Vernon, IL 62864 US
Second Address: 302 S. Poplar, Centralia, IL 62801
(618) 533-5700, *Fax:* (618) 533-5737
www.web.ics.purdue.edu
wrxx@mvn.net
License: Centralia, IL held by Withers Broadcasting Co. of West Virginia.
Group Owner: Withers Broadcasting Co.; (acq 11-4-97; $527,500 with co-located FM)
Regional Network: Brownfield *Wire Services:* AP
Format: Oldies *Special Programming:* Business news *Hrs. of News Programming:* news progmg 60 hrs wkly *No. News Employees:* 2 *Target Audience:* 25-54. *Adv. Rates:* 8.50; na; na; na
Russ Withers, President
Brenda Robinson, Operations Dir
Jared Kuhn, General Manager
Barrett Beach, Station Manager
Timmy Willmore, Chief Engineer
Nick Skok, Mobile Manager
Stephanie Domagalski, Public Relations Director
NhigelHinkson, Music Director

WRXX
12-24-1964; 95.3 mhz FM *Hrs Open:* 24; 5.5 kw; 328 ft.; N38 33 46 W88 59 58
Mailing Address: 3501 Broadway, P.O. Box 1508, Mount Vernon, IL 62864 US
Second Address: 302 S. Poplar, Centralia, IL 62801
(618) 533-5700, *Fax:* (618) 533-5737
www.mywithersradio.com
centralia@mywithersradio.com
License: Centralia, Marion County, IL held by Withers Broadcasting Co. of West Virginia.
Group Owner: Withers Broadcasting Co.
Nat'l Network: ABC
Format: Rock/AOR *Hrs. of News Programming:* news progmg 2 hrs wkly *No. News Employees:* 2 *Target Audience:* 18-49.
Barry Drake, President
Curt Peterson, Operations Dir
Brad Stevens, Programming Director

Champaign

***WBGL**
10-31-1982; 91.7 mhz FM *Hrs Open:* 24; 20 kw; Ant 459 ft; N40 09 12 W88 06 56
4101 Fieldstone Road, Champaign, IL 61821
(217) 359-8232, *Fax:* (217) 359-7374
www.wbgl.org
wbgl@wbgl.org
License: Champaign, Champaign County, IL held by Illinois Bible Institute Inc.
Group Owner: Illinois Bible Institute Inc.
Nat'l Network: USA
Arbitron Metro Market: Champaign, IL *No. News Employees:* 1 *Target Audience:* 25-44.
Jeff Scott, Station Manager
Ryan Springer, Programming Director
Jennifer Briski, Promotions Manager
Joe Rother, Engineering Dir
Joe Buchanan, Music Director
Zoe Fuller, Underwriting Director

WDWS
01-24-1937; 1400 khz AM *Hrs Open:* 24; 1 kw-U, ND1; N40 5 4 W88 14 53
P.O. Box 3939, Champaign, IL 61826 US
(217) 351-5300, *Fax:* (217) 351-5385
www.wdws.com
talk@wdws.com
License: Champaign, IL held by D.W.S. Inc.
Nat'l Network: ABC *Regional Network:* Ill. Radio Net. *Nat'l Reps:* Christal *Wire Services:* AP
Arbitron Metro Market: Champaign, IL *Format:* News, News/Talk, 84, Talk *Special Programming:* Farm 10 hrs, relg 4 hrs wkly *Hrs. of News Programming:* news progmg 26 hrs wkly *No. News Employees:* 6 *TargetAudience:* 35-64; adults
Mike Haile, Operations Dir
Mike Halle, General Manager
Dave Burns, General Sales Mgr
Carol Vorel, News Director
Jim Lewis, Operations Manager

***WEFT**
09-21-1981; 90.1 mhz FM *Hrs Open:* 6 AM-2 AM; 10 kw horiz, 8.5 kw vert; 325 ft.; N40 10 51 W88 19 4
113 North Market, Champaign, IL 61820 US
(217) 359-9338
www.weft.org/
weft@weftfm.org
License: Champaign, Champaign County, IL held by Prairie Air Inc.
Nat'l Network: NPR; PRI
Arbitron Metro Market: Champaign, IL *Format:* Variety/Diverse *Special Programming:* Black 8 hrs, blues 10 hrs, folk 10 hrs, pub affrs 5 hrs, Sp 3 hrs wkly *Hrs. of News Programming:* News progmg 10 hrs wkly *TargetAudience:* General.
Mick Woolf, General Manager
George Uricoechea, Programming Director
Darren Martin, Chief Engineer

WHMS-FM
01-01-1948; 97.5 mhz FM *Hrs Open:* 24; 50 kw; 358 ft.; N40 5 4 W88 14 53
Mailing Address: P.O. Box 3939, Champaign, IL 61826 US
Second Address: 2301 S. Neil, Champaign, IL 61820
(217) 351-5300, *Fax:* (217) 351-5385
www.whms.com
literock@whms.com
License: Champaign, Champaign County, IL
Wire Services: AP
Arbitron Metro Market: Champaign, IL *Format:* Adult Contemp *Hrs. of News Programming:* news progmg 10 hrs wkly *No. News Employees:* 4 *Target Audience:* 25-54; adults
Mike Haile, General Manager
Ryan Aurthur, Programming Director

WIXY
06-01-1992; 100.3 mhz FM; 13 kw; 453 ft.; N40 0 45 W88 8 29
2603 W. Bradley Avenue, Champaign, IL 61821 US
(217) 355-4141, *Fax:* (217) 352-1256
www.wixy.com
info@wixy.com
License: Champaign, Champaign County, IL held by Saga Communications of Illinois LLC.
Group Owner: Saga Communications Inc.; (acq 11-4-92; $250,000;
Nat'l Reps: Katz Radio
Arbitron Metro Market: Champaign, IL *Format:* Country *Hrs. of News Programming:* News progmg 5 hrs wkly *Target Audience:* 25 plus.
Ed Christian, CEO
Steve Goldstein, President
Alan Beck, General Manager

WLRW
01-01-1963; 94.5 mhz FM *Hrs Open:* 24; 50 kw; 453 ft.; N40 7 35 W88 17 25
2603 W. Bradley Avenue, Champaign, IL 61821 US
(217) 352-4141, *Fax:* (217) 352-1256
www.mix945.com
info@mix945.com
License: Champaign, Champaign County, IL held by Saga Communications of Illinois LLC.
Group Owner: Saga Communications Inc.; (acq 10-86; grpsl;
Arbitron Metro Market: Champaign, IL *Format:* Adult Contemp *Target Audience:* 18-49.
Alan Beck, General Manager
Jonathan Drake, Programming Director

WPCD
01-01-1978; 88.7 mhz FM; 10.5 kw; 338 ft.; N40 13 27 W88 17 56
2400 West Bradley Avenue, Champaign, IL 61820 US
(217) 351-2450, *Fax:* (217) 351-2581
www.parkland.edu/wpcd/
wpcdradio@parkland.edu
License: Champaign, Champaign County, IL held by Parkland College Community College District No. 505.
Nat'l Network: AP Radio
Arbitron Metro Market: Champaign, IL *Format:* Alternative, Urban Contemporary *Special Programming:* News 8 hrs, spanish 4 hrs wkly *Hrs. of News Programming:* News progmg 8 hrs wkly *Target Audience:* General.
Dan Hughes, General Manager

Charleston

WRJM(AM)
12-10-1954; 1270 khz AM *Hrs Open:* 25.?Â ?; 1 kw-D, 500 w-N, DA-3; N39 30 18 W88 12 54
2560 W. State St., Charleston, IL 61920
(217) 345-2148, *Fax:* (217) 348-7036
www.weic1270.org/
info@weic.com
License: Charleston, Coles County, IL held by Eastern Illinois Christian Broadcasting Inc.
Population Served: 21,852 *Arbitron Metro Market:* Charleston, IL *Format:* Gospel *Special Programming:* Farm 8 hrs wkly *Adv. Rates:* 8; 8; 8; n/a
Brad Lee, General Manager
Steve Hamm, Chief Engineer

***WEIU**
07-01-1985; 88.9 mhz FM *Hrs Open:* 24; 4 kw; 167 ft.; N39 28 43 W88 10 21
Weiu Fm & Tv, Charleston, IL 61920 US
(217) 581-5956, *Fax:* (217) 581-6650
www.weiu.net
weiu@weiu.net
License: Charleston, Coles County, IL held by Eastern Illinois University.
Arbitron Metro Market: Charleston, IL *TV Affiliate:* *WEIU-TV affil *Format:* Variety/Diverse *Special Programming:* Folks 4 hrs, jazz 4 hrs wkly *Hrs. of News Programming:* news progmg 3 hrs wkly *No. NewsEmployees:* 1 *Target Audience:* 12 plus; 25-55 women *Adv. Rates:* 10; 8; 9; 6
Denis Roche, General Manager
Jeff Owens, Station Manager
Linda Kingery, Programming Director
Kelly Runyon, News Director
John Wiley, Underwriting Director

WWGO
10-01-1965; 92.1 mhz FM *Hrs Open:* 24; 6 kw; 328 ft.; N39 31 40 W88 21 23
P.O. Box 150846, Nashville, TN 37215 US
(217) 844-4487, *Fax:* (217) 235-6624
www.myradiolink.com
bub@radiomattoon.com
License: Charleston, Coles County, IL held by The Cromwell Group Inc. of Illinois.
Group Owner: The Cromwell Group Inc.; (acq 1993)
Nat'l Network: ABC
Arbitron Metro Market: Charleston, IL *Format:* Classic Rock *Hrs. of News Programming:* news progmg 20 hrs wkly *No. News Employees:* 1 *Target Audience:* 25-54; upscale, educated adults
Bud Walters, President
Carol Floyd, General Manager
Bub McCullough, Programming Director
Kathie St. Clair, News Director
Josh Jamison, Chief Engineer

***WZGL**
01-01-2008; 88.1 mhz FM; 2.1 kw; 229 ft.; N39 28 38 W88 8 25
Rebroadcasts: Rebroadcasts WBGL(FM) Champaign 100%
P O Box 140, Carlinville, IL 62626 US
(217) 359-8232, *Fax:* (217) 359-7374
www.wbgl.org
License: Charleston, Coles County, IL held by Illinois Bible Institute Inc.
Group Owner: Illinois Bible Institute Inc.
Arbitron Metro Market: Charleston, IL *Format:* Christian
Meridith Foster, Operations Dir
Jeff Scott, Station Manager
Ryan Springer, Programming Director
Jennifer Briski, Promotions Manager
Zoe Fuller, Office Manager/Underwriting Director
Jerilynn Jones, Volunteer Coordinator/Assistant toStation Manager
Sheryl Maxwell, Promotions Assistant
Jason Rackow, Production Director
Steve Thompson, Internet Media Director
Weez Stockton, Assistant Promotions Director

Chatham

WYMG
03-01-1948; 100.5 mhz FM *Hrs Open:* 24; 50 kw; 489 ft.; N39 39 43 W89 55 22
1030 Durkin Drive, Springfield, IL 62704 US
(217) 753-5400, *Fax:* (217) 753-7902
www.wymg.com
wymg@wymg.com
License: Chatham, Sangamon County, IL held by Saga Communications of Illinois LLC.
Group Owner: Saga Communications Inc.; (acq 10-1-86).
Arbitron Metro Market: Chatham, IL *Format:* Classic Rock *Target Audience:* 25-54.
Mike Topoll, General Manager
Jane Cochran, Programming Director

Chester

KSGM
07-05-1947; 980 khz AM *Hrs Open:* 24; 1 kw-D, DAN; 0.47 kw-N, DAN; N37 47 16 W89 54 21 *Rebroadcasts:* Rebroadcasts KBDZ(FM) Perryville, MO
P.O. Box 428, Ste. Genevieve, MO 63670 US
(573) 883-2980 618-826-2980573-547-6780, *Fax:* (573) 883-2866
www.suntimesnews.com
suntimesnews@brick.net
License: Chester, IL held by Donze Communications Inc.
Arbitron Metro Market: Ste. Gene, MO *Format:* Country, News, 62, Talk *Special Programming:* Farm 2 hrs, relg 6 hrs wkly *Hrs. of News Programming:* news progmg 14 hrs wkly *No. News Employees:* 2 *TargetAudience:* General; adults *Adv. Rates:* 16; 14; 16; 14
Don Pritchard, News Director

Chicago

WBBM
11-14-1923; 780 khz AM *Hrs Open:* 24 hours*Rebroadcasts:* WCFS-FM HD2
600 New Hampshire Avenue, NW, Suite 1200, Washington, DC 20037 US
(970) 563-0255, *Fax:* (970) 563-0399
www.ksut.org
info@ksut.org
License: Chicago, IL held by CBS Radio East Inc.
Group Owner: CBS Radio; (acq 1931)
Nat'l Network: CBS; CNN Radio; AP Network News *Regional Network:* Ill. Radio Net. *Wire Services:* AP; CBS; SportsTicker
Arbitron Metro Market: Hobbs NM *Format:* Triple A *Adv. Rates:* call sales dept
Eddie Box Jr., President
Beth Warren, General Manager

WBBM-FM
12-07-1941; 96.3 mhz FM; 3.3 kw; 1555 ft.; N41 52 44 W87 38 8
600 New Hampshire Avenue, NW, Suite 1200, Washington, DC 20037 US
(701) 252-1400, *Fax:* (701) 252-1402
bigdog@daktel.com
License: Chicago, Cook County, IL held by CBS Radio East Inc.
Group Owner: CBS Radio
Nat'l Network: CBS *Nat'l Reps:* CBS Radio
Arbitron Metro Market: Lubbock TX *Target Audience:* 18-54.
Dave Reed, General Manager
Lynn Lambrecht, General Sales Mgr

***WBEZ**
01-01-1942; 91.5 mhz FM *Hrs Open:* 24; 5.7 kw; 1395 ft.; N41 53 56 W87 37 23
848 East Grand Avenue, Chicago, IL 60611 US
(312) 948-4600, *Fax:* (312) 832-3100
www.chicagopublicradio.org
questions@wbez.org
License: Chicago, Cook County, IL held by The WBEZ Alliance Inc.
Nat'l Network: NPR; PRI
Arbitron Metro Market: Chicago,IL *Format:* Jazz, News *Hrs. of News Programming:* news progmg 45 hrs wkly *No. News Employees:* 5 *Target Audience:* General; people who want to know about the world around them
Merrill Smith, Chairman
Donna Moore, CFO
Torey Malatia, President
Sally Eisele, Programming Director
Steve Edwards, Acting Program Manager

***WCRX**
07-29-1975; 88.1 mhz FM *Hrs Open:* 24; 0.1 kw horiz, 0.09 kw vert; 128 ft.; N41 52 22 W87 38 52
600 South Michigan Ave., Chicago, IL 60605 US
(312) 663-3512, *Fax:* (312) 663-5204
www.colum.edu
WCRXDJ@colum.edu.
License: Chicago, Cook County, IL held by Columbia College.
Nat'l Network: AP Radio *Wire Services:* AP
Arbitron Metro Market: Chicago,IL *Format:* News, Sports *Hrs. of News Programming:* news progmg 20 hrs wkly *No. News Employees:* 2 *Target Audience:* 18-24; Men
Cheryl Langston, General Manager
Tony Kwiecinski, Station Manager
Dave Dennis, Chief Engineer

WFMT
12-13-1951; 98.7 mhz FM *Hrs Open:* 24; 6 kw; 1542 ft.; N41 52 44 W87 38 8
5400 N. St. Louis Ave., Chicago, IL 60625 US

(773) 279-2000, *Fax:* (773) 279-2199
www.networkchicago.com
finearts@wfmt.com
License: Chicago, Cook County, IL held by Window to the World Communications Inc.
Arbitron Metro Market: Chicago, IL *TV Affiliate:* WTTW(TV) affil *Format:* Talk *Special Programming:* Folk 4 hrs, jazz 5 hrs wkly *Hrs. of News Programming:* News progmg 7 hrs wkly *Target Audience:* 25-54;upscale, professional, college educated, upper income adults
Dan Schmidt, CEO
Steve Robinson, Operations Dir
Paul Ansell, General Sales Mgr
Peter Whorf, Programming Director
Gordon Carter, Chief Engineer
Don Mueller, Operations Manager

WGRB
01-01-1924; 1390 khz AM; 5 kw-D, DA2; 5 kw-N, DA2; N41 44 13 W87 42 0
332 S. Michigan Ave., Suite 600, Chicago, IL 60604 US
(312) 540-2000, *Fax:* (312) 938-4477
www.wgci.com
License: Chicago, IL held by AMFM Broadcasting Licenses LLC.
Group Owner: Clear Channel Communications Inc.; (acq 8-30-2000; grpsl).
Nat'l Reps: Christal
Arbitron Metro Market: Chicago, IL *Format:* Gospel
Marv Dyson, President
Sandra Robinson, Programming Director

WGCI-FM
12-11-1958; 107.5 mhz FM; 3.7 kw; 1549 ft.; N41 52 44 W87 38 8
300 Crescent Court, Suite 600, Dallas, TX 75201 US
(312) 540-2000, *Fax:* (312) 938-4477
www.wgci.com
License: Chicago, Cook County, IL
Group Owner: Clear Channel Communications Inc.
Arbitron Metro Market: Chicago, IL *Format:* Urban Contemporary
Elroy Smith, Programming Director

WGN(AM)
06-01-1924; 720 khz AM; 50 kw-U; N42 00 42 W88 02 07
435 N. Michigan Ave., Chicago, IL 60611
(312) 222-4700, *Fax:* (312) 222-5165
www.wgnradio.com
info@wgnradio.com
License: Chicago, Cook County, IL held by WGN Continental Broadcasting Company
Group Owner: Tribune Broadcasting Co.; (acq 12-20-2007; grpsl)
Nat'l Network: ABC *Nat'l Reps:* Christal *Wire Services:* AP
Arbitron Metro Market: Chicago, IL *TV Affiliate:* WGN-TV affil *Format:* News, News/Talk, 84, Talk *Special Programming:* Play-by-play: Chicago Cubs (MLB), Chicago Blackhaw *No. News Employees:* 15 *TargetAudience:* 35-64.
Charlene Connaughton, CFO
Tom Langmyer, General Manager
Wendi Power, General Sales Mgr
Kevin Metheny, Programming Director
Jackie Paulus, Promotions Manager
Charlie Meyerson, News Director
Jim Carollo, Engineering Dir
ChenessaRoberson, HR Director

***WHPK-FM**
03-15-1968; 88.5 mhz FM *Hrs Open:* 24; 0.1 kw; 121 ft.; N41 47 40 W87 35 55
5706 S. University Ave, Chicago, IL 60637 US
(773) 702-8289, *Fax:* (773) 702-7718
whpk.uchicago.edu
whpk@uchicago.edu
License: Chicago, Cook County, IL held by The University of Chicago.
Arbitron Metro Market: Chicago, IL *Format:* Jazz, Variety/Diverse *Special Programming:* Class 10 hrs, African one hr, Haitian 3 hrs, Isra *Hrs. of News Programming:* News progmg 5 hrs wkly
Simon Wiener, Station Manager
Alec Mitrovich, Programming Director
Rachel Lazar, Promotions Manager
Theo Shure, Publicity Director
Mario Smith, Sponsorship Director
Rachel Schastock, Treasurer
Keegan Hankes, Music Director
RyanLavery, Training Director
Lillian Seonick, Traffic Director

WIND
01-01-1927; 560 khz AM; 5 kw-D, DA2; 5 kw-N, DA2; N41 33 54 W87 25 11
3102 Oak Lawn Ave., Suite 215, Dallas, TX 75219 US
(847) 437-5200, *Fax:* (847) 956-5040
www.560wind.com
www.560wind.com
License: Chicago, IL held by Salem Media of Illinois LLC.
Group Owner: Salem Communications Corp.; (acq 1-7-2005; with KNIT(AM) Dallas and KKHT-FM Winnie, both TX, in exchange for WPPN(FM) Des Plaines, IL).
Arbitron Metro Market: Chicago, IL *Format:* News, News/Talk, 86
Eric Thomas, Operations Dir
David Santrella, General Manager

WJMK
01-02-1961; 104.3 mhz FM; 4.1 kw; 1575 ft.; N41 52 44 W87 38 8
600 New Hampshire Ave., Suite 1200, Washington, DC 20037 US
(312) 729-3870, *Fax:* (312) 729-3887
www.wjmk.com
wjmk@wjmk.com
License: Chicago, Cook County, IL held by Infinity Broadcasting Corp. of Illinois.
Group Owner: CBS Radio
Nat'l Network: Westwood One
Arbitron Metro Market: Chicago, IL *Format:* Oldies *Target Audience:* 25-54.
Dave Robbins, Operations Dir
Terry Hardin, General Sales Mgr
Charlie Lake, Programming Director
Lisa Piovosi, Promotions Manager
John Galenta, Chief Engineer

***WKKC**
01-01-1975; 89.3 mhz FM; 280 w horiz, 250 w vert; Ant 111 ft; N41 46 48 W87 38 38
Kennedy-King College, 6800 S. Wentworth Ave., Chicago, IL 60621
(773) 602-5540, *Fax:* (773) 602-5532
www.ccc.edu
License: Chicago, Cook County, IL held by District 508 City College of Chicago.
Population Served: 250,000 *Arbitron Metro Market:* Chicago *Target Audience:* 15-50.
Kevin Brown, General Manager

WLIT-FM
04-07-1958; 93.9 mhz FM *Hrs Open:* 24; 4 kw; 1581 ft.; N41 52 44 W87 38 8
1001 Pennsylvania Ave NW, Suite 1300, Washington, DC 20004 US
(312) 540-2000, *Fax:* (312) 938-0111
www.wlit.com
info@wlit.com
License: Chicago, Cook County, IL held by AMFM Broadcasting Licenses LLC.
Group Owner: Clear Channel Communications Inc.; (acq 8-30-2000; grpsl).
Nat'l Network: Premiere Radio Networks *Nat'l Reps:* Clear Channel *Wire Services:* AP
Arbitron Metro Market: Chicago, IL *Format:* Adult Contemp *Hrs. of News Programming:* news progmg one hr wkly *No. News Employees:* 1 *Target Audience:* 25-54; affluent adults
Earl Jones, Operations Dir
Ken Denton, General Sales Mgr
Darren Davis, Programming Director
Bob Fukuda, Chief Engineer
Eric Richeke, Music Director
Rick Zurick, Music Director
Ella Hammitte, Traffic Manager

WLS
04-12-1924; 890 khz AM; 50 kw-U, ND1; N41 33 21 W87 50 54
190 North State Street, Chicago, IL 60601 US
(312) 984-0890, *Fax:* (312) 984-5305
www.wlsam.com
info@wlsam.com
License: Chicago, IL
Group Owner: Cumulus Media Inc.; (acq 6-12-2007; grpsl)
Arbitron Metro Market: Chicago, IL *Format:* News, News/Talk, 86 *Target Audience:* 35-64; listeners involved in Chicago news & community affairs
Zemira Jones, President
Carol O'Keefe, Operations Dir
Bill Gamble, Programming Director

WLUP-FM
01-01-1942; 97.9 mhz FM *Hrs Open:* 24; 4 kw; 1394 ft.; N41 53 56 W87 37 23
P.O. Box 1160, Salt Lake City, UT 84110 US
(312) 245-1200, *Fax:* (312) 527-9587
www.wlup.com
info@wlup.com
License: Chicago, Cook County, IL
Group Owner: Merlin Media LLC; (acq 12-15-2004; swap for KMVP(AM) and KTAR(AM)-KKLT(FM) Phoenix, AZ).
Nat'l Reps: D & R Radio
Arbitron Metro Market: Chicago, IL *Target Audience:* 18-49.
Marv Nyren, General Manager

***WLUW**
09-19-1978; 88.7 mhz FM *Hrs Open:* 24; 0.1 kw; 230 ft.; N42 0 4 W87 39 36
820 North Michigan Ave, Chicago, IL 60611 US
(773) 508-8080, *Fax:* (773) 508-8082
www.wluw.org
wluwradio@wluw.org
License: Chicago, Cook County, IL held by Loyola University, Chicago.
Wire Services: Pacifica Network News
Arbitron Metro Market: Chicago, IL *Format:* Variety/Diverse *Target Audience:* College students.
Danielle Basci, General Manager
Maxx McGathey, Programming Director
Katie Reese, Promotions Manager
Matt Malooly, News Director

WRTO
12-01-1988; 1200 khz AM *Hrs Open:* 24
3102 Oak Lawn Ave., Suite 215, Dallas, TX 75219 US
(312) 981-1800, *Fax:* (312) 981-1806
www.univision.com
License: Chicago, IL held by WLXX-AM License Corp.
Group Owner: Univision Radio; (acq 9-22-2003; grpsl).
Nat'l Reps: McGavren Guild
Arbitron Metro Market: Chicago, IL *Format:* News, News/Talk, 86 *Hrs. of News Programming:* news progmg 10 hrs wkly *No. News Employees:* 4 *Target Audience:* Urban Spanish.
Cesar Canales, Operations Dir
Jerry Ryan, General Manager
Alicia Chavarria, Promotions Manager
Joshua Sigstad, Engineering Dir

WSCR
04-01-1922; 670 khz AM *Hrs Open:* 24; 50 kw-U, ND1; N41 56 1 W88 4 23
600 New Hampshire Avenue, NW, Suite 1200, Washington, DC 20037 US
(312) 245-6000, *Fax:* (312) 245-6099
www.670thescore.com
info@wscr670am.com
License: Chicago, IL held by Infinity Broadcasting East Inc.
Group Owner: CBS Radio; (acq 11-13-98; grpsl).
Nat'l Network: Westwood One *Regional Network:* Ill. Radio Net.
Arbitron Metro Market: Chicago,IL *TV Affiliate:* WBBM-TV *Format:* Sports *Target Audience:* 25-54.
Rod Zimmerman, Operations Dir
Paul Agase, General Sales Mgr
Matt Fishman, Programming Director
Cher Ames, Promotions Manager
George Offman, News Director
Mary Compton, National Sales Manager
Drew Hayes, Operations Director
Jesse Rogers, Public Affairs Director

***WMBI**
07-28-1926; 1110 khz AM *Hrs Open:* Sunrise-sunset; 4.2 kw-D, NDD; N41 55 41 W88 0 25
820 N. Lasalle Boulevard, Chicago, IL 60610 US
(312) 329-4300, *Fax:* (312) 329-4468
www.moodyradiochicago.fm
mbn@moody.edu
License: Chicago, IL held by The Moody Bible Institute of Chicago
Group Owner: The Moody Bible Institute of Chicago
Nat'l Network: Moody *Wire Services:* AP
Arbitron Metro Market: Chicago, IL *Format:* Christian *Special Programming:* Sp 12 hrs wkly *Target Audience:* 35-54; Hispanic Christians, children, English-speaking
John Hayden, Operations Dir
Collin Lambert, Programming Director
Bruce Everhart, Promotions Manager

***WMBI-FM**
07-25-1960; 90.1 mhz FM *Hrs Open:* 24; 100 kw; 440 ft; N41 55 35 W88 00 22
820 N. LaSalle Blvd., Chicago, IL 60610
(312) 329-4300, *Fax:* (312) 329-4468
www.wmbi.org
wmbi@moody.edu
License: Chicago, Cook County, IL held by The Moody Bible Institute of Chicago
Group Owner: The Moody Bible Institute of Chicago
Nat'l Network: Moody *Wire Services:* AP
Population Served: 7,400,000 *Arbitron Metro Market:* Chicago *No. News Employees:* 2 *Target Audience:* 35-54; Christian

Jerry Jenkins, Chairman
Steve Mogck, CEO/COO
Paul Nyquist, President
Vacant, Operations Dir
Doug Hastings, General Manager
Roy Patterson, Station Manager
Calvin Robinson, General Sales Mgr
Dan Craig, Programming Director
George Economos, Promotions Manager
Dave Mitchell, News Director
Mark Williames, Engineering Dir
Rod Simon, Chief Engineer
Collin Lambert, Vice President

WMVP
06-25-1926; 1000 khz AM *Hrs Open:* 24
77 West 66th, 16th Floor, New York, NY 10023 US
(312) 980-1000, *Fax:* (312) 980-1020
www.espnradio.com
jeff.s.schwartz@abc.com
License: Chicago, IL held by Sports Radio Chicago LLC.
Group Owner: ABC Inc.; (acq 4-1-99; $21 million).
Nat'l Network: ESPN Radio *Nat'l Reps:* ABC Radio Sales
Arbitron Metro Market: Chicago, IL *Format:* Comedy, Sports, 86
Target Audience: 25-54.
Jeff Schwartz, Operations Dir
James Pastor, General Manager
John Craveno, General Sales Mgr
Justin Craig, Programming Director
John Hurni, Chief Engineer
Jon Paul Rexing, Regional Sales Manager

WDRV
07-09-1955; 97.1 mhz FM *Hrs Open:* 24; 8.3 kw; 1191 ft.; N41 53 6 W87 37 18
1140 West Erie Street, Chicago, IL 60622 US
(312) 274-9710, *Fax:* (312) 274-1304
www.wdrv.com
License: Chicago, Cook County, IL held by Bonneville Holding Co.
Group Owner: Bonneville International Corporation; (acq 1-25-01; $165 million with WWDV(FM) Zion).
Nat'l Reps: Katz Radio
Arbitron Metro Market: Chicago, IL *Format:* Light Rock
Jerry Schnacke, Operations Dir
Chris Winston, General Sales Mgr
Patty Martin, Programming Director
Eileen Elliot, General Sales Manager
Greg Solk, Vice President, Operations

WILV
01-01-1947; 100.3 mhz FM; 5.7 kw; 1394 ft.; N41 53 56 W87 37 23
Suite1510, 875 N. Michigan Ave., Chicago, IL 60611 US
(312) 297-5100, *Fax:* (312) 297-5143
www.wilv.com
davidj@lovefm.fm
License: Chicago, Cook County, IL held by Bonneville Holding Co.
Group Owner: Bonneville International Corporation; (acq 6-13-97; $75 million).
Arbitron Metro Market: Chicago, IL *Format:* Adult Contemp *Target Audience:* 25-49; women
Barry James, Operations Dir
Sue Werley, General Sales Mgr
Mandy Irwin, Promotions Manager
Keith Warner, Chief Engineer

WNTD
05-01-1922; 950 khz AM; 1 kw-D, DAN; 5 kw-N, DAN; N41 51 39 W87 41 12; N41 38 12 W87 33 10
8400 NW 52nd Street, Suite 101, Miami, FL 33166 US
(312) 467-9755, *Fax:* (312) 467-9603
www.relevantradio.com
WNTD@relevantradio.com
License: Chicago, IL held by Sovereign City Radio Services LLC
Group Owner: Relevant Radio; (acq 10-18-2007; $15 million)
Arbitron Metro Market: Chicago, IL *Format:* Religious *Target Audience:* 25-54.
Scott Wert, General Manager

WNUA
03-09-1959; 95.5 mhz FM; 8.3 kw; 1175 ft.; N41 53 56 W87 37 23
433 E. Las Colinas Blvd, #1130, Irving, TX 75039 US
(312) 540-2000, *Fax:* (312) 938-0712
www.955elpatron.com
License: Chicago, Cook County, IL held by AMFM Broadcasting Licenses LLC.
Group Owner: Clear Channel Communications Inc.; (acq 8-30-2000; grpsl).
Wire Services: UPI
Arbitron Metro Market: Chicago, IL *Format:* Adult Contemp, Jazz, 80 *Target Audience:* 25-54.
Patrick Kelly, General Manager

***WIIT**
06-01-1974; 88.9 mhz FM *Hrs Open:* 24; 0.017 kw horiz; 89 ft.; N41 50 4 W87 37 43
3300 S. Federal St, Chicago, IL 60616 US
(312) 567-3087,(312) 567-3088, *Fax:* (312) 567-7042
wiit@iit.edu
License: Chicago, Cook County, IL held by Illinois Institute of Technology.
Arbitron Metro Market: Chicago *Format:* Variety/Diverse *Special Programming:* Jazz 9 hrs, Ger 3 hrs, relg 2 hrs, Sp 5 hrs wkly *Hrs. of News Programming:* News progmg 5 hrs wkly *Target Audience:* 15-35; college &young urban community
Patrick Schneider, Station Manager

***WRTE**
12-01-1969; 90.5 mhz FM *Hrs Open:* 24; 0.073 kw; 85 ft.; N41 50 26 W87 43 5
Mailing Address: 1401 West 18th Street, Chicago, IL 60608 US
Second Address: c/o Mexican Fine Arts Ctr. Museum, 1852 W. 19th St., Chicago, IL 60608-2706
(312) 455-9455, *Fax:* (312) 455-9755
www.radioarte.org
valdivia@radioarte.org
License: Chicago, Cook County, IL held by Mexican Fine Arts Center Museum.
Arbitron Metro Market: Chicago *Format:* Alternative *Target Audience:* 15-35.
Jorge Valdivia, General Manager
Carlos Mendez, Programming Director
Shaaron Resendiz, Marketing/Underwriting Director
Adriana Diaz, Director of Youth Media Development & Research

WSBC
01-01-1925; 1240 khz AM *Hrs Open:* 24; 1 kw-U, ND1; N41 58 53 W87 46 20
1645 West Fullerton Avenue, Chicago, IL 60614 US
(773) 792-1121, *Fax:* (773) 792-2904
www.accessradiochicago.com
wsbc@wsbcradio.com
License: Chicago, IL held by WSBC Inc.
Group Owner: Newsweb Corp.; (acq 2-23-98)
Arbitron Metro Market: Chicago *Format:* Variety/Diverse *Target Audience:* General.
Harvey Wells, Operations Dir
Mark Pinski, General Manager
Kevin Horan, Programming Director
Mike McCarthy, Chief Engineer
Jorge Murillo, Operations Manager

WYLL
10-13-1924; 1160 khz AM *Hrs Open:* 24; 50 kw-D, DA2; N42 2 30 W87 51 57
600 New Hampshire Ave, N.W., Suite 1200, Washington, DC 20037 US
(847) 956-5030, *Fax:* (847) 956-5040
www.wyll.com
License: Chicago, IL held by Salem Media Group LLC.
Group Owner: Salem Communications Corp.; (acq 12-20-2000; $29 million)
Arbitron Metro Market: Chicago *Format:* Religious *Target Audience:* 25-54; Upscale income adults
Eric Thomas, Operations Dir
Jeff Reisman, General Manager
James Herring, Station Manager
Marcus Brown, Programming Director
Frank McCoy, Chief Engineer

***WSSD**
09-15-1987; 88.1 mhz FM; 0.01 kw; 102 ft.; N41 43 44 W87 33 3
11026 South Wentworth, ', Chicago, IL 60628 US
(773) 928-8800, *Fax:* (773) 928-9009
info@wssd.com
License: Chicago, Cook County, IL held by Lakeside Communications Inc.
Arbitron Metro Market: Chicago *Format:* Blues, Gospel, 86
Special Programming: Gospel, jazz, talk *Target Audience:* 25 plus; Black
Huey Williams, President
Steven McKinney, Station Manager
Willie McPhatter, Programming Director

WKSC-FM
11-01-1957; 103.5 mhz FM *Hrs Open:* 24; 4.3 kw; 1549 ft.; N41 52 44 W87 38 8
875 N. Michigan Ave., Suite 3530, Chicago, IL 60611 US
(312) 540-2000, *Fax:* (312) 938-0712
www.kisschicago.com
chicagolandcommunity@clearchannel.com
License: Chicago, Cook County, IL held by AMFM Broadcasting Licenses LLC.
Group Owner: Clear Channel Communications Inc.; (acq 8-30-2000; grpsl).
Arbitron Metro Market: Chicago, IL *Format:* Contemporary Hits/Top 40 *Hrs. of News Programming:* news progmg 15 hrs wkly *No. News Employees:* 1 *Target Audience:* 18-34; upscale
Dave Scharf, General Sales Mgr
Lynn Clymer, News Director
Bob Fukuda, Chief Engineer
Earl Jones, Regional Vice President
Matt Scarano, Sales Director

WUSN
01-01-1940; 99.5 mhz FM; 5.7 kw; 1394 ft.; N41 53 56 W87 37 23
600 New Hampshire Ave., Suite 1200, Washington, DC 20037 US
(312) 649-0099, *Fax:* (312) 856-9586
www.us99.com
lisa@us99.com
License: Chicago, Cook County, IL held by Infinity Broadcasting Corp. of Chicago.
Group Owner: CBS Radio; (acq 1996; grpsl).
Arbitron Metro Market: Chicago, IL *Format:* Country *Target Audience:* 25-54.
Dave Robbins, Station Manager
Lindsay Cerajewski, General Sales Mgr

WLS-FM
04-01-1949; 94.7 mhz FM; 4.4 kw; 1535 ft.; N41 52 44 W87 38 8
77 W. 66th St., 16th Fl., Wxcd Station, New York, NY 10023 US
(312) 984-9923, *Fax:* (312) 984-5357
www.947wls.com
scott@947wls.com
License: Chicago, Cook County, IL
Group Owner: Cumulus Media Inc.; (acq 6-12-2007; grpsl)
Arbitron Metro Market: Chicago, IL *Format:* Oldies
Jim Pastor, President
Jan Jeffries, Operations Dir
Jeff Smaluk, General Sales Mgr
Lorraine Lynn, Promotions Manager
Donna Baker, VP/Market Manager
Scott Dirks, Production Director

WXRT
01-01-1959; 93.1 mhz FM; 6.7 kw; 1309 ft.; N41 53 56 W87 37 23
600 New Hampshire Avenue, NW, Suite 1200, Washington, DC 20037 US
(312) 649-0099, *Fax:* (312) 240-7973
www.93xrt.com
License: Chicago, Cook County, IL held by CBS Radio East Inc.
Group Owner: CBS Radio; (acq 11-13-98; grpsl)
Nat'l Reps: CBS Radio
Arbitron Metro Market: Chicago, IL *Format:* Alternative, Rock/AOR *No. News Employees:* 1 *Target Audience:* 25-54; upscale adults
Michael Damsky, Operations Dir
Norm Winer, Programming Director
Brad Auerbach, Promotions Manager
Mark Nielson, Chief Engineer
John Farneda, Operations Manager
Adrienne Szarmack, Regional Sales Manager

***WZRD**
07-08-1974; 88.3 mhz FM *Hrs Open:* 11 AM-midnight; 0.1 kw; 72 ft.; N41 58 56 W87 43 7
5500 N. St. Louis Avenue, Chicago, IL 60625 US
(773) 442-4578, *Fax:* (773) 442-4900
www.wzrdchicago.com
wzrdinexile@hotmail.com
License: Chicago, Cook County, IL held by Northeastern Illinois University.
Arbitron Metro Market: Chicago, IL *Format:* Variety/Diverse *Hrs. of News Programming:* news progmg 12 hrs wkly *No. News Employees:* 29 *Target Audience:* General.
Dennis Sagel, Station Manager

Chicago Heights

WCFJ
08-15-1963; 1470 khz AM *Hrs Open:* 24; 1 kw-D, DA2; 1 kw-N, DA2; N41 25 29 W87 38 27
1000 Lincoln Hwy., Ford Heights, IL 60411 US
(773) 792-1121, *Fax:* (773) 792-2904
mp@wsbcradio.com
License: Chicago Heights, IL held by WCFJ Inc.
Group Owner: Newsweb Corp.; (acq 2-23-98)

Arbitron Metro Market: Chicago, Il *Format:* Variety/Diverse *Target Audience:* General
Harvey Wells, Operations Dir
Mark Pinski, General Manager
Mike McCarthy, Chief Engineer
Jorge Murillo, Operations Manager

Chillicothe

WPMJ
05-16-1977; 94.3 mhz FM *Hrs Open:* 24; 6 kw; 299 ft.; N40 49 48 W89 29 54
5555 Gulf of Mexico Dr., Suite 201, Longboat Key, FL 34228 US
(309) 685-5975, *Fax:* (309) 685-9095
www.wpmjradio.com
info@wpmjradio.com
License: Chillicothe, Peoria County, IL held by Kelly Communications Inc.
Arbitron Metro Market: Peoria, IL
Bob Kelly, CEO

Christopher

WXLT
12-25-1990; 103.5 mhz FM *Hrs Open:* 24; 6 kw; 328 ft.; N37 55 55 W88 57 31
P.O. Box 1749, Cape Girardeau, MO 63702 US
(618) 985-4843, *Fax:* (618) 985-6529
www.wxlt.com
mail@wxlt.com
License: Christopher, Franklin County, IL held by MRR License LLC.
Group Owner: MAX Media L.L.C.; (acq 6-2-2004; grpsl)
Nat'l Network: ESPN Radio *Nat'l Reps:* Christal
Arbitron Metro Market: Christopher, IL *Format:* Sports
Tom Miller, Operations Dir
Steve Falat, General Manager
Kim DeBose, General Sales Mgr
Ryan Patrick, Promotions Manager
Felicia Dick, News Director
Jon Brookmyer, Chief Engineer
Dave McKenzie, Events Coordinator

Cicero

WCEV
10-01-1979; 1450 khz AM *Hrs Open:* 1-10PM(M-F);1-8:30PM(S);5AM-10PM(S); 1 kw; 305 ft.; N41 49 57 W87 42 40
5356 W. Belmont Ave., Chicago, IL 60641
(773) 282-6700, *Fax:* (773) 282-0123
www.wcev1450.com
wcev@wcev1450.com
License: Cicero, Cook County, IL held by Migala Communications Corp.
Wire Services: AP
Arbitron Metro Market: Chicago *Special Programming:* Ethnic Languages *Hrs. of News Programming:* News progmg 7 hrs wkly *Target Audience:* Adult ethnic Americans. *Adv. Rates:* 65; 65; 65; 65
Estelle Migala, President
Barbara Holtzinger, Business Manager
George Migala, General Manager
Lucyna Migala, Programming Director
Dave Dybas, Chief Engineer

WRLL
01-01-1979; 1450 khz AM *Hrs Open:* Midnight-1 PM; 1 kw-U, ND1; N41 49 57 W87 42 20
3350 So. Kedzie Ave., Chicago, IL 60623 US
(773) 247-6200, *Fax:* (773) 247-5336
www.wrll1450.com
tom@wpmh1010.com
License: Cicero, IL held by Midway Broadcasting Corp.
Arbitron Metro Market: Chicago, IL
Melody Spann Cooper, Chairman
Pervis Spann, CEO/COO
Pervis Spann, President
Todd Ronczkowski, Operations Dir
Gustavo Rios, Station Manager
Juanita Maze, General Sales Mgr
Coz Carson, Programming Director
Denise King, NewsDirector
Bridget Goins, Executive Assistant

Clinton

WHOW
08-01-1947; 1520 khz AM *Hrs Open:* Sunrise-sunset; 1 kw-C, NDD; 5 kw-D, NDD; N40 5 43 W88 57 51
Rr2, Box 117m, Clinton, IL 61727 US
(217) 935-9590, *Fax:* (217) 935-9909
www.dewittdailynews.com
License: Clinton, IL held by Kaskaskia Broadcasting Inc.
Group Owner: Miller Media Group; (acq 1-4-2008; $400,000 with co-located FM)
Nat'l Network: CNN Radio *Nat'l Reps:* Commercial Media Sales
Format: Agriculture, News, 62, Talk *Hrs. of News Programming:* news progmg 20 hrs wkly *No. News Employees:* 1 *Target Audience:* 35+. *Adv. Rates:* 12; 15; 7; na
Randal Miller, General Manager
Jared White, Programming Director

WEZC
12-15-1975; 95.9 mhz FM *Hrs Open:* 24; 6 kw; 308 ft.; N40 5 43 W88 57 51
R.R.2, Box 117m, Clinton, IL 61727 US
(217) 935-9590, *Fax:* (217) 935-9909
www.dewittdailynews.com
License: Clinton, DeWitt County, IL held by Kaskaskia Broadcasting Inc.
Group Owner: Miller Media Group; (acq 1-4-2008; $400,000 with co-located AM)
Nat'l Network: CNN Radio *Nat'l Reps:* Commercial Media Sales
Format: Adult Contemp *Hrs. of News Programming:* 4 hrs news programing wkly *No. News Employees:* 1 *Target Audience:* 35+.
Randal Miller, General Manager
Jared White, Programming Director

Coal City

WRXQ
02-08-1991; 100.7 mhz FM *Hrs Open:* 24; 2.45 kw; 482 ft.; N41 17 39 W88 10 15
8800 Route 14, Crystal Lake, IL 60012 US
(815) 556-0100, *Fax:* (815) 577-9231
www.wrxq.com
mzander@nextmediachicago.com
License: Coal City, Grundy County, IL held by NM Licensing LLC.
Group Owner: NextMedia Group Inc.; (acq 11-26-01; grpsl).
Nat'l Reps: Christal
Arbitron Metro Market: Crest Hill IL *Format:* Classic Rock *Hrs. of News Programming:* News progmg 5 hrs wkly *Target Audience:* 35-50; adults
Ryan Snow, Operations Dir
Patrick Pendergast, General Manager
Doug Boyd, General Sales Mgr
Mark Zander, Programming Director

Colchester

WMQZ
01-01-1999; 104.1 mhz FM; 6 kw; 328 ft.; N40 32 1 W90 51 45
31 East Side Square, McComb, IL 61455 US
(309) 833-2121, *Fax:* (309) 836-3291
wjeq@macomb.com
License: Colchester, McDonough County, IL held by Colchester Radio Inc.
Arbitron Metro Market: Colchester, IL *Format:* Oldies
Bruce Foster, President
Nancy Foster, General Manager
Karen Kearne, General Sales Mgr
Mike Grillette, News Director
Shana Drake, Traffic Manager

WGNX
01-01-2007; 96.7 mhz FM; 1.8 kw; 328 ft.; N40 23 54 W90 43 55 US
(888) 357-5639, *Fax:* (217) 357-3001
www.wgnx.org
GoodNews@adams.net
License: Colchester, McDonough County, IL held by Patricia Van Zandt.
Arbitron Metro Market: Colchester, IL
Patricia Van Zandt, General Manager

Colfax

WRPW
01-01-1997; 92.9 mhz FM; 6 kw; 328 ft.; N40 29 28 W88 43 14
5555 Gulf of Mexico Drive, Suite 201, Longboat Key, FL 34228 US
(309) 888-4496, *Fax:* (309) 452-9677
www.power929fm.com
License: Colfax, McLean County, IL held by Pilot Media LLC.
Group Owner: Great Plains Media Inc.; (acq 6-19-2007; grpsl)
Format: Contemporary Hits/Top 40
Kevin Trueblood, Operations Dir
Patti Donsbach, General Manager
Don Black, Programming Director
Amber Goodwin, Promotions Manager

Collinsville

KPNT
03-01-1967; 105.7 mhz FM *Hrs Open:* 24; 100 kw; 1375 ft.; N38 13 10 W90 35 44
10706 Beaver Dam Road, Cockeysville, MD 21030 US
(314) 231-1057, *Fax:* (314) 621-3000
www.1057thepoint.com
stl.ms@emies.com
License: Collinsville, Ste. Genevieve County, IL held by Emmis Radio License LLC.
Group Owner: Emmis Communications Corp.
Nat'l Network: ABC
Arbitron Metro Market: St. Louis, MO *Format:* Rock/AOR *Target Audience:* 18-34.
John Beck, General Manager
Becky Duncan, General Sales Mgr
Tommy Mathern, Programming Director
Sam Caputa, Chief Engineer

Columbia

KMJM-FM
02-15-1964; 104.9 mhz FM *Hrs Open:* 24; 7.8 kw; 574 ft.; N38 34 24 W90 19 30
50 East Rivercenter Blvd., Suite 1200, Covington, KY 41011 US
(314) 333-8000
www.kmjm.com
License: Columbia, Monroe County, IL held by Citicasters Licenses L.P.
Group Owner: Clear Channel Communications Inc.; (acq 5-4-99; grpsl).
Arbitron Metro Market: St. Louis, MO *Format:* Adult Contemp *Target Audience:* 25-54; adults *Adv. Rates:* 50; 30; 42; 15
Tommy Austin, Operations Dir
Dennis Lamme, General Manager
Beth Davis, General Sales Mgr
John Helmkamp, Promotions Manager
Kevin Joyce, General Sales Manager

Crest Hill

WCCQ
01-28-1976; 98.3 mhz FM *Hrs Open:* 24; 3 kw; 469 ft.; N41 26 9 W88 11 4
1520 North Rock Run Drive, Joliet, IL 60435 US
(815) 556-0100, *Fax:* (815) 577-9231
www.wccq.com
info@wccq.com
License: Crest Hill, Will County, IL held by Three Eagles of Joliet Inc.
Group Owner: Three Eagles Communications; (acq 1-13-97; grpsl)
Nat'l Network: ABC *Nat'l Reps:* Christal *Wire Services:* UPI
Arbitron Metro Market: Crest Hill IL *Format:* Country *Target Audience:* 25-54; general
Ryan Snow, Operations Dir
Patrick Pendergast, General Manager
Doug Boyd, General Sales Mgr
Roy Gregory, Programming Director
Roy Gregory, Program Director

Crete

***WBMF**
01-01-2002; 88.1 mhz FM; 0.09 kw; 374 ft.; N41 25 17 W87 38 39
P O Drawer 2440, Tupelo, MS 38801 US
(662) 844-8888, *Fax:* (662) 842-6791
www.afa.net/Radio/
License: Crete, Will County, IL held by American Family Association.
Group Owner: American Family Radio
Arbitron Metro Market: Crete, IL *Format:* Christian *Hrs. of News Programming:* News progmg 2 hrs wkly
Charlotte Michael, General Manager

WYCA
09-05-1965; 102.3 mhz FM; 1.05 kw; 499 ft.; N41 19 32 W87 37 15
P O Box 3003, Blue Bell, PA 19422 US
(773) 734-4455, *Fax:* (219) 933-0323
www.wyca1023.com
wybainfo@crawfordbroadcasting.com
License: Crete, Will County, IL held by Dontron Inc.
Group Owner: Crawford Broadcasting Co.; (acq 8-26-97; $1.8 million).
Arbitron Metro Market: Crete, IL *Format:* Christian, Talk *Target Audience:* 35 plus; adult, African-Americans
Donald Crawford, CEO
Taft Harris, General Manager

Crystal Lake

WAIT
10-01-1965; 850 khz AM *Hrs Open:* Sunrise-sunset; 2.5 kw-D, DAD; N42 15 30 W88 21 48
8800 Route 14, Crystal Lake, IL 60012 US
(773) 792-1121, *Fax:* (773) 792-2904
www.thepromise850.com
License: Crystal Lake, IL held by Chicago Newsweb Corp.
Group Owner: Newsweb Corp.; (acq 9-16-2003; $8.25 million)
Arbitron Metro Market: Chicago, IL *Format:* Christian, Spanish
Jorge Murillo, Operations Dir
Mark Pinski, General Manager
Sally Gaigalas, General Sales Mgr
Mike McCarthy, Chief Engineer

Danville

WDAN
10-01-1938; 1490 khz AM; 1 kw-U, ND1; N40 8 58 W87 37 35
3001 Springmill Ste-B, Springfield, IL 62708 US
(217) 442-1700, *Fax:* (217) 431-1489
www.vermilioncountyfirst.com
BillPickett@neuhoffmedia.com
License: Danville, IL held by Neuhoff Family L.P.
Group Owner: Neuhoff Family L.P.; acq 11-5-03; grpsl).
Nat'l Reps: McGavren Guild
Arbitron Metro Market: Danville, Il *Format:* News, News/Talk, 84, Talk *Special Programming:* Farm 20 hrs wkly *Hrs. of News Programming:* news progmg 20 hrs wkly *No. News Employees:* 1 *Target Audience:* 25-54.
Roger Neuhoff, President
Michael Hulvey, Operations Dir
Michelle Campbell, General Sales Mgr
Bill Pickett, News Director
Geoffery Neuhoff, Executive Vice President
Tom Barnes, Operations Manager

WDNL
05-01-1967; 102.1 mhz FM *Hrs Open:* 24; 50 kw; 367 ft.; N40 8 58 W87 37 35
3001 Springmill, Ste-B, Springfield, IL 62708 US
(217) 442-1700, *Fax:* (217) 431-1489
www.wdnlfm.com
infowdnl@cooketech.net
License: Danville, Vermilion County, IL
Group Owner: Neuhoff Family L.P.
Arbitron Metro Market: Danville, Il *Format:* Adult Contemp *Hrs. of News Programming:* News progmg 2 hrs wkly *Target Audience:* 18-49.
Michael Hulvey, Operations Dir
Tom Barnes, Programming Director
Carole Wade, Music Director

WYXY(FM)
03-02-1970; 99.1 mhz FM; 50 kw; Ant 500 ft; N40 08 52 W87 46 20
2603 W. Bradley Ave., Champaign, IL 61821
(217) 352-4141, *Fax:* (217) 352-1256
www.wxrt.cbslocal.com
License: Danville, Vermilion County, IL held by Saga Communications of Illinois LLC.
Group Owner: Saga Communications Inc.; (acq 6-30-2004; $3.25 million).
Nat'l Reps: D & R Radio
Population Served: 469,000 *Arbitron Metro Market:* Champaign, IL *Format:* Classic Rock
Alan Beck, General Manager
Bill Cain, Programming Director

WRHK
11-01-1992; 94.9 mhz FM *Hrs Open:* 24; 6 kw; 328 ft.; N40 10 40 W87 28 55
1904 Oak Creek Road, Springfield, IL 62704 US
(217) 442-1700, *Fax:* (217) 431-1489
www.949krock.com
info@949rock.com
License: Danville, Vermilion County, IL held by Neuhoff Family L.P.
Group Owner: Neuhoff Family L.P.; acq 11-5-03; grpsl).
Nat'l Reps: McGavren Guild
Format: Classic Rock *Hrs. of News Programming:* News progmg 5 hrs wkly *Target Audience:* 18-49.
Roger Neuhoff, Chairman
Pat Odea, CFO
Geoffery Neuhoff, President
Michael Hulvey, General Manager
Michelle Campbell, General Sales Mgr
Tom Barnes, Programming Director
Don Russell, Chief Engineer

Decatur

WDZ
03-17-1921; 1050 khz AM; 1 kw-D, ND1; 0.25 kw-N, ND1; N39 48 54 W89 0 8
1705 West Northwest Highway, Suite 275, Grapevine, TX 76051 US
(217) 423-9744, *Fax:* (217) 423-9764
www.espndecatur.com/
info@magic1050am.com
License: Decatur, IL held by Neuhoff Family L.P.
Group Owner: Neuhoff Family L.P.; (acq 2-23-2009; grpsl)
Nat'l Network: Fox Sports
Arbitron Metro Market: Decatur, IL *Format:* Sports
Mark Hanson, General Manager
Tricia LeVeck, Programming Director

WDZQ
11-01-1976; 95.1 mhz FM; 50 kw; 492 ft.; N39 37 40 W89 4 51
1705 West Northwest Highway, Suite 275, Grapevine, TX 76051 US
(217) 423-9744, *Fax:* (217) 423-9764
www.95q.com
License: Decatur, Macon County, IL held by Neuhoff Family L.P.
Group Owner: Neuhoff Family L.P.; (acq 2-23-2009; grpsl)
Arbitron Metro Market: Decatur, IL *Format:* Country
Mark Hanson, General Manager
Wendy Tohill, General Sales Mgr
Brad Wells, Programming Director
Tammy Moore, Promotions Manager

*WJMU
03-10-1971; 89.5 mhz FM *Hrs Open:* 7 AM-1 AM; 1.65 kw; 85 ft.; N39 50 30 W88 58 29
1184 West Main Street, Decatur, IL 62522 US
(217) 424-6377, *Fax:* (217) 424-3993
www.millikin.edu
wjmu@mail.millikin.edu
License: Decatur, Macon County, IL held by Millikin University.
Arbitron Metro Market: Decatur, IL *Format:* Alternative *Hrs. of News Programming:* News progmg 8 hrs wkly *Target Audience:* 20 plus; students, surrounding community
Dove Zemke, President
Matt Tucker, General Manager
Keith Chandler, Programming Director
Dan Bleyle, Promotions Manager

WSOY
01-01-1925; 1340 khz AM *Hrs Open:* 24
1705 West Northwest Hwy, Ste 275, Grapevine, TX 76051 US
(217) 877-5371, *Fax:* (217) 877-8777
www.wsoy.com
License: Decatur, IL held by Neuhoff Family L.P.
Group Owner: Neuhoff Family L.P.; (acq 2-23-2009; grpsl)
Arbitron Metro Market: Decatur, IL *Format:* News, News/Talk, 84, Talk *Hrs. of News Programming:* news progmg 13 hrs wkly *No. News Employees:* 3 *Target Audience:* 25 plus.
Mark Hanson, General Manager
Ryan Forden, Programming Director

WSOY-FM
11-01-1946; 102.9 mhz FM *Hrs Open:* 24; 54 kw; 443 ft.; N39 52 41 W88 56 32
1100 E. Pershing Road, Decatur, IL 62526 US
(217) 877-5371, *Fax:* (217) 877-8777
www.wsoy.com
info@wsoyfm.com
License: Decatur, Macon County, IL held by Neuhoff Family L.P.
Group Owner: Neuhoff Family L.P.; (acq 2-23-2009; grpsl)
Nat'l Network: CBS *Regional Network:* Ill. Radio Net.
Arbitron Metro Market: Decatur, IL *Format:* Contemporary Hits/Top 40 *Hrs. of News Programming:* news progmg 3 hrs wkly *No. News Employees:* 3 *Target Audience:* 25-54.
Mark Hanson, General Manager
Roy Jaynes, Programming Director

WYDS
01-01-1993; 93.1 mhz FM *Hrs Open:* 24; 6 kw; 328 ft; N39 48 35 W88 59 31
410 N. Water St., Suite B, Decatur, IL 37215
(217) 428-4487, *Fax:* (217) 428-4501
www.partydecatur.com
cbullock@cromwellradio.com
License: Decatur, Macon County, IL held by WEJT Inc.
Group Owner: The Cromwell Group Inc.; (acq 4-9-93; $750,000;
Nat'l Reps: Eastman Radio
Population Served: 200,000 *Arbitron Metro Market:* Decatur, IL *Hrs. of News Programming:* 24/7 *No. News Employees:* 1 *Target Audience:* 18-49; females average age of 26 *Adv. Rates:* 30; 28; 30; 20
Tara Nickerson, Operations Dir
Chris Bullock, General Manager
Larry Timmons, Chief Engineer

Deerfield

WEEF
08-15-1963; 1430 khz AM; 1 kw-D, DA2; 0.029 kw-N, DA2; N42 10 53 W87 57 5
210 Skokie Valley Road, Highland Park, IL 60035 US
(708) 831-5440, *Fax:* (847) 498-5743
www.plcradio.com/1430_weef
info@plcradio.com
License: Deerfield, IL held by Polnet Communications Ltd.
Group Owner: Polnet Communications Ltd.; (acq 5-20-2003; $1 million)
Arbitron Metro Market: Deerfield, IL *Format:* Ethnic *Target Audience:* General; ethnic
Sara Vargas, General Manager

Dekalb

WCPY
12-17-1961; 92.5 mhz FM *Hrs Open:* 24; 20 kw; 489 ft.; N41 52 33 W88 45 16
11 Skyline Drive, Hawthorne, NY 10532 US
(773) 792-0400, *Fax:* (773) 767-1100
www.chicagoprogressivetalk.com
web@newswebradio.net
License: Dekalb, De Kalb County, IL held by WDEK Inc.
Group Owner: Newsweb Corp.; (acq 11-15-2004; grpsl)
Nat'l Network: CNN Radio
Arbitron Metro Market: Chicago, IL *Format:* Alternative, Talk
Harvey Wells, General Manager
Bill Cavanaugh, General Sales Mgr
Mike McCarthy, Chief Engineer

WDKB
08-13-1990; 94.9 mhz FM *Hrs Open:* 24; 3 kw; 328 ft.; N41 56 57 W88 53 44
2201 N. First St., #95, Dekalb, IL 60115 US
(815) 758-0950, (815) 758-4926, *Fax:* (815) 758-6226
www.b95fm.com
ontheair@b95fm.com
License: Dekalb, De Kalb County, IL held by De Kalb County Radio Ltd.
Wire Services: AP
Arbitron Metro Market: DeKalb, Il *Format:* Adult Contemp *Special Programming:* Relg one hr wkly *Hrs. of News Programming:* news progmg 3hrs wkly *No. News Employees:* 1 *Target Audience:* 25-54; adults withmoderate to upper incomes *Adv. Rates:* 29; 29; 29; 20
Tana Knetsch, President
Dave Bavido, General Sales Mgr
Ken Misch, Programming Director

WLBK
12-07-1947; 1360 khz AM *Hrs Open:* 24 hours; 1 kw-D, ND1; 0.024 kw-N, ND1; N41 56 18 W88 45 3
Mailing Address: 11 Skyline Drive, Hawthorne, NY 10532 US
Second Address: 2410 Sycamore Rd. Suite C, De Kalb, IL 60115
(815) 758-8686, *Fax:* (815) 756-9723
www.wlbkradio.com
sales@1360wlbk.com
License: Dekalb, IL held by WPW Broadcasting Inc.
Group Owner: Prairie Radio Communications; (acq 4-12-2000).
Format: News, News/Talk, 86 *Special Programming:* Farm 12 hrs wkly *Hrs. of News Programming:* news progmg 21 hrs wkly *No. News Employees:* 1 *Target Audience:* General. *Adv. Rates:* $35 6-10a.m., 3-7p.m.,$25 6a.
Larry Timpe, General Manager
Terry Ryan, Programming Director
Scott Zak, News Director

*WNIJ
10-01-1954; 89.5 mhz FM *Hrs Open:* 24; 50 kw; 420 ft.; N42 0 55 W89 0 7
801 North Frist Street, Dekalb, IL 60115 US
(815) 753-9000, *Fax:* (815) 753-9938
www.northernpublicradio.org
npr@niu.edu
License: Dekalb, De Kalb County, IL held by Northern Illinois University.
Nat'l Network: PRI; NPR
Arbitron Metro Market: Rockford, IL *Format:* Jazz, News *Special Programming:* Folk 4 hrs wkly *Hrs. of News Programming:* news progmg one hr wkly *No. News Employees:* 2 *Target Audience:* General.
Staci Hoste, General Manager
Jan Kilgard, General Sales Mgr
Bill Drake, Programming Director

Guy Stephens, News Director
Jeff Glass, Chief Engineer

Des Plaines

WPPN
12-03-1971; 106.7 mhz FM *Hrs Open:* 24; 50 kw; 423 ft.; N42 8 14 W87 58 57
Suite 300, 4880 Santa Rosa Road, Camarillo, CA 93012 US
(312) 981-1800, *Fax:* (312) 981-1806
www.univision.com/content/channel.jhtml?chid=9627&schid=9828
License: Des Plaines, Cook County, IL held by Univision Radio License Corp.
Group Owner: Univision Radio; (acq 12-21-2004; asset exchange agreement).
Arbitron Metro Market: Des Plaines, IL *Format:* Oldies, Spanish
Cesar Canales, Operations Dir
Jerry Ryan, General Manager
Victor Cerdo, Programming Director
Joshua Sigstad, Engineering Dir

Dixon

WIXN
07-01-1961; 1460 khz AM *Hrs Open:* 19; 1 kw-D, DA2; 0.023 kw-N, DA2; N41 49 38 W89 29 11
980 North Michigan Avenue, Suite 1880, Chicago, IL 60611 US
(815) 288-3341, *Fax:* (815) 284-1017
www.wixn.com
info@wixn.com
License: Dixon, IL held by NRG License Sub. LLC.
Group Owner: NRG Media LLC; (acq 10-31-2005; grpsl)
Format: News, Oldies *Special Programming:* Farm 11 hrs wkly *Hrs. of News Programming:* news progmg 14 hrs wkly *No. News Employees:* 2 *Target Audience:* 25-54.
Al Knickrehm, General Manager

WRCV
09-01-1965; 101.7 mhz FM *Hrs Open:* 24; 6 kw; 328 ft.; N41 49 29 W89 29 51
980 North Michigan Avenue, Suite 1880, Chicago, IL 60611 US
(815) 288-3341, *Fax:* (815) 284-1017
www.wixn.com
info@wixn.com
License: Dixon, Lee County, IL held by NRG License Sub. LLC.
Group Owner: NRG Media LLC
Format: Country *Hrs. of News Programming:* news progmg 10 hrs wkly *No. News Employees:* 2
Steve Marco, Programming Director

Dorsey

*WARW
01-01-2006; 89.5 mhz FM; 1.5 kw; 318 ft.; N39 0 44 W89 57 13
Rebroadcasts: Rebroadcasts KLRD(FM) Yucaipa, CA 100%.
US
(888) 937-2471, *Fax:* (916) 251-1650
www.air1.com
info@air1.com
License: Dorsey, Madison County, IL held by Educational Media Foundation.
Group Owner: EMF Broadcasting; (acq 9-22-2005; $30,000 for CP)
Nat'l Network: Air 1
Arbitron Metro Market: Dorsey, IL *Format:* Alternative, Christian
Darrell Chambliss, Chairman
Alan Mason, COO
Mike Novak, President and CEO
Ed Lenane, News Director
Sam Wallington, Engineering Dir
Dan Antonelli, Chief Business Development Officer
Eric Moser, Chief Financial Officer
BrianBurger, Vice President of Human Resources
D. Kevin Blair, Secretary and General Counsel
Larry Moody, Director
Mitch Barnhart, Director

Downers Grove

*WDGC-FM
02-28-1969; 88.3 mhz FM *Hrs Open:* 8 AM-10 PM (M-S); 0.25 kw horiz; 131 ft.; N41 48 16 W88 0 44
6301 Springside Avenue, Downers Grove, IL 60516 US
(630) 795-8490(630) 795-8400, *Fax:* (630) 795-8499
www.wdgc.csd99.org/
wdgcfm@hotmail.com
License: Downers Grove, Du Page County, IL held by High School District No. 99 Dupage County.
Arbitron Metro Market: Chicago, IL *Format:* Variety/Diverse
Special Programming: Community affrs 6 hrs wkly *Hrs. of News Programming:* News progmg 5 hrs wkly *Target Audience:* General; all age groups
John Waite, General Manager

Dundee

WWYW
06-08-1967; 103.9 mhz FM *Hrs Open:* 24; 2.55 kw; 322 ft.; N42 6 21 W88 22 37
1436 Auburn Boulevard, Sacramento, CA 95815 US
(815) 459-7000, *Fax:* (815) 459-7027
www.y1039.com
License: Dundee, Kane County, IL held by NM Licensing LLC.
Group Owner: NextMedia Group Inc.; (acq 5-19-2004; $5 million).
Arbitron Metro Market: Chicago *Format:* Oldies
Doug Boyd, General Sales Mgr
Stew Cohen, News Director
Floyd Evans, VP, Regional Manager

Duquoin

WDQN
01-01-1951; 1580 khz AM *Hrs Open:* 5:30 AM-11 PM; 0.17 kw-D, ND1; 0.0066 kw-N, ND1; N38 1 56 W89 14 30
Mailing Address: P.O. Box 190, Duquoin, IL 62832 US
Second Address: 2337 US Rt. 51, Du Quoin, IL 62832
(618) 542-3894, *Fax:* (618) 542-4514
wdqnradio@oneclig.net
License: Duquoin, IL held by Du Quoin Broadcasting Co.
Nat'l Network: ABC; Motor Racing Net *Regional Network:* Brownfield *Wire Services:* AP
Arbitron Metro Market: Du Quoin, IL *Format:* Adult Contemp, Country *Special Programming:* Farm 3 hrs, relg 5 hrs wkly *Target Audience:* 25-64; male & female *Adv. Rates:* 18; 18; 18
Marrianne Showalter, Operations Dir
Greg Showalter, General Manager
Michelle Klein, General Sales Mgr
Gordon Showalter, Programming Director
Ruth Showalter, Traffic & Accounts Rec

WDQN-FM
09-01-1969; 95.9 mhz FM *Hrs Open:* 6 AM-11 PM; 6 kw; 328 ft.; N38 1 56 W89 14 30
Mailing Address: P.O. Box 190, Duquoin, IL 62832 US
Second Address: 3391 Charley Good Rd., West Frankfort, IL 62896
(618) 627-4651, *Fax:* (618) 627-2726
www.3abn.org
info@wdqn.com
License: Duquoin, Perry County, IL held by Three Angels Broadcasting Network Inc.
Arbitron Metro Market: Du Quoin, IL *Format:* Christian
Danny Shelton, President
Mollie Steenson, General Manager
Jim Morris, General Sales Mgr
Sandra Juarez, Programming Director
Moses Primo, Chief Engineer

Dwight

WJEZ
06-09-1997; 98.9 mhz FM; 1.3 kw; 489 ft.; N41 2 6 W88 26 10
315 North Mill Street, Pontiac, IL 61764 US
(815) 844-6101, *Fax:* (815) 844-7235
www.wjez.com
kent.casson@townsquaremedia.com
License: Dwight, Livingston County, IL
Group Owner: Townsquare Media; (acq 5-12-2004; grpsl).
Format: Adult Contemp *Target Audience:* 18-49; general
Red Pitcher, General Manager
Julie Penn, General Sales Mgr
Kent Kasson, Programming Director
Shelley Grove, Promotions Manager
Lane Lindstrom, Chief Engineer

Earlville

WMKB
02-03-2003; 102.9 mhz FM *Hrs Open:* 24; 2.15 kw; 558 ft.; N41 37 16 W89 5 20
3654 W Jarvis Ave, Skokie, IL 60076 US
(815) 538-7500, *Fax:* (866) 816-0064
www.wmkbradio.com
info@wmkbradio.com
License: Earlville, La Salle County, IL held by KM Radio of Earlville L.L.C.
Group Owner: KM Communications Inc.
Nat'l Network: ABC
Arbitron Metro Market: Brandon *Format:* Light Rock *Special Programming:* Blues 5 hrs wkly *Hrs. of News Programming:* News progmg 2 hrs wkly *Target Audience:* 25-54.
Anne Schenck, General Manager

East Moline

KUUL
02-23-1976; 101.3 mhz FM; 50 kw; 499 ft.; N41 37 10 W90 17 41
3535 East Kimberly Road, Davenport, IA 52807 US
(563) 344-7000, *Fax:* (563) 359-8524
www.kuul.com
jeffashcraft@clearchannel.com
License: East Moline, Rock Island County, IL held by Citicasters Licenses L.P.
Group Owner: Clear Channel Communications Inc.; (acq 11-15-00; grpsl).
Nat'l Reps: Katz Radio
Arbitron Metro Market: East Moline, IL *Format:* Classic Rock
Special Programming: Pub affrs 6 hrs, farm one hr wkly *Target Audience:* 25-54; contemp, upscale adults
Jeff Ashcraft, General Sales Mgr
Larry Rosmilso, Promotions Manager
Kevin Allensworth, Chief Engineer
Mike Hamann, General Sales Manager

*WDLM
04-03-1960; 960 khz AM; 1 kw-D, DA2; 0.102 kw-N, DA2; N41 24 57 W90 23 54
820 N. Lasalle St., East Moline, IL 60610 US
(309) 234-5111, *Fax:* (309) 234-5114
www.moodyradioqc.fm
wdlm@moody.edu
License: East Moline, IL held by Moody Bible Institute of Chicago.
Group Owner: The Moody Bible Institute of Chicago
Arbitron Metro Market: Moline-Rock Island-Bettendorf- East Moline, IL-IA *Format:* Religious
Lane Morgan, General Manager
Angie Walters, Promotions Manager
Deborah Gustafson, News Director
John Johnson, Chief Engineer

*WDLM-FM
01-20-1980; 89.3 mhz FM; 100 kw; 499 ft.; N41 32 52 W90 28 30
820 N. Lasalle Blvd, Chicago, IL 60610 US
(309) 234-5111, *Fax:* (309) 234-5114
www.moodyradioqc.fm
wdlm@moody.edu
License: East Moline, Rock Island County, IL
Arbitron Metro Market: Moline-Rock Island-Bettendorf- East Moline, IL-IA
Dave Jolly, Station Manager
Ken Brooks, Programming Director
Angie Walters, Promotions Manager
Deborah Gustafson, News Director
John Johnson, Chief Engineer

East St. Louis

*WCBW-FM
01-01-2001; 89.7 mhz FM; 0.25 kw; 187 ft.; N38 37 53 W90 12 9
1411 Locust Street, St. Louis, MO 63103 US
(314) 421-3020, *Fax:* (314) 421-1702
www.newlifeevangelisticcenter.org
larryr@hereshelpnet.org
License: East St. Louis, St. Clair County, IL held by New Life Evangelistic Center Inc.
Arbitron Metro Market: Saint Louis, MO *Format:* Religious
Larry Rice, General Manager

WFFX(AM)
08-01-1934; 1490 khz AM; 1 kw-U, DA-2; N38 37 16 W90 09 36
6555 Highway 98 West, Suite 8, Hattiesburg, MS 39402
(601) 544-1037, *Fax:* (601) 296-9800
www.1037wffx.com
contact@1037wffx.com
License: East St. Louis, St. Clair County, IL held by Simmons Austin, LS LLC.
Group Owner: Simmons Media Group; (acq 3-31-2005; $1.15 million)
Nat'l Network: American Urban *Nat'l Reps:* Katz Radio
Population Served: 46,626 *Arbitron Metro Market:* Hattiesburg, MS *Format:* Blues, Gospel *Target Audience:* 23-55.
Dave Greene, General Manager
Kahilla Hakimzadeh, General Sales Mgr
Mike Comfort, Market Manager
James Harris, Account Executive
Michael Watkins, Account Executive
Jennifer Forbes, Account Executive
Todd Ellzey, AccountExecutive

WXOS
06-06-1965; 101.1 mhz FM; 100 kw; 986 ft.; N38 28 56 W90 23 53

10706 Beaver Dam Road, Cockeysville, MD 21030 US
(314) 983-6000, *Fax:* (314) 994-9447
www.101espn.com
webmaster@101sports.com
License: East St. Louis, St. Clair County, IL held by Bonneville Holding Co.
Group Owner: Bonneville International Corporation; (acq 9-26-2000; grpsl)
Nat'l Network: ESPN Radio *Nat'l Reps:* McGavren Guild
Arbitron Metro Market: St. Louis, MO *Format:* Sports, Talk *Target Audience:* 25-49.
Bruce Reese, CEO
John Kijowski, Operations Dir
Dave Slazinik, General Sales Mgr
Kent Sterling, Programming Director
Kelly Rebal, Promotions Manager
Trish Gazzal, News Director
Marshall Rice, Chief Engineer
Bob Johnson, CFO
Amanda Koeppe, HR Director
Kim Grant, Digital Media Director

Edwardsville

*WRYT
11-20-1987; 1080 khz AM
664-A Coeur De Royale, Creve Coeur, MO 63141 US
(314) 752-7000
www.covenantnet.net
covenantnetwork@juno.com
License: Edwardsville, IL held by Covenant Network.
Group Owner: Covenant Network; (acq 10-2-97)
Arbitron Metro Market: St. Louis, MO *Format:* Religious *Target Audience:* General.
John Holman, President
Tony Holman, General Manager

*WSIE
09-04-1970; 88.7 mhz FM *Hrs Open:* 24; 50 kw horiz, 41 kw vert; 499 ft.; N38 47 6 W89 59 10
Siue Box 1773, Edwardsville, IL 62026 US
(618) 650-2228, *Fax:* (618) 650-2233
www.wsieradio.com
License: Edwardsville, Madison County, IL held by Board of Trustees, Southern Illinois University.
Nat'l Network: NPR; PRI *Regional Network:* Ill. Radio Net.
Arbitron Metro Market: St. Louis, MO *Format:* Jazz *Special Programming:* New age 10 hrs wkly *Hrs. of News Programming:* news progmg 20 hrs wkly *No. News Employees:* 1 *Target Audience:* 25-49; adults seekinga sophisticated alternative
Gregory Conroy, General Manager
Jason Valentine, Programming Director
Justin Wingerter, News Director
John Masters, Chief Engineer

Effingham

WCRA
06-08-1947; 1090 khz AM; 1 kw-D, NDD; N39 6 26 W88 33 44
937 S.E. 2nd Street, Galva, IL 61434 US
(217) 342-4141, *Fax:* (217) 342-4143
www.wcra1090.com
mphillips@cromwellradio.com
License: Effingham, IL held by Two Petaz Inc.
Group Owner: The Cromwell Group Inc.; (acq 1-9-02; grpsl).
Nat'l Network: CBS
Arbitron Metro Market: Effingham, Illinois *Format:* News, News/Talk, 86 *Target Audience:* 25-54.
Marv Phillips, General Manager

WCRC
06-14-1963; 95.7 mhz FM *Hrs Open:* 24; 50 kw; 479 ft.; N39 6 26 W88 33 44
937 S.E. 2nd Street, Galva, IL 61434 US
(217) 342-4141, *Fax:* (217) 342- 4143
www.wcrc957.com
wcrc@wcrc957.com
License: Effingham, Effingham County, IL held by Two Petaz Inc.
Group Owner: The Cromwell Group Inc.
Arbitron Metro Market: Effingham, Illinois *Format:* Country
Nancy Dieterich, General Manager
Mark Edwards, Programming Director
Tim Neill, Promotions Manager

WXEF
10-04-1982; 97.9 mhz FM *Hrs Open:* 24; 6 kw; 312 ft.; N39 7 25 W88 38 28
P.O. Box 988, Effingham, IL 62401 US
(217) 347-5518, *Fax:* (217) 347-5519
www.thexradio.com
info@thexradio.com
License: Effingham, Effingham County, IL held by Premier Broadcasting Inc.
Nat'l Network: Fox News Radio
Arbitron Metro Market: Effingham, IL *Format:* Adult Contemp *Special Programming:* High school sports *Hrs. of News Programming:* news progmg 15 hrs wkly *No. News Employees:* 2 *Target Audience:* General.
Dave Ring, President
Tonya Siner, VP Operations, Sales Manager
Greg Sapp, Station Manager, News & Sports Directo
Kenna Endebrock, Promotions Manager
Angela James, Certified Radio & Digital Marketing Consultant
Teresa Klinger,Traffic, Office Manager
Mike Walker, Account Representative

*WEFI
01-01-2006; 89.5 mhz FM; 0.4 kw; 164 ft.; N39 8 30 W88 33 36
Rebroadcasts: Rebroadcasts WAFR(FM) Tupelo, MS 100%
P.O. Drawer 2440, Tupelo, MS 38803 US
(662) 844-8888, *Fax:* (662) 842-6791
www.afr.net
License: Effingham, Effingham County, IL held by American Family Association.
Group Owner: American Family Radio
Arbitron Metro Market: Tyler-Longview, TX *Format:* Christian
Marvin Sanders, General Manager

*WGMR
91.3 mhz FM; 0.62 kw; 295 ft.; N39 7 2 W88 32 5 US
(314)752-7000
www.covenantnet.net
webmaster@covenantnet.net
License: Effingham, Effingham County, IL held by Brindisi Consortium.
Nat'l Network: EWTN Radio
Arbitron Metro Market: St. Louis, IL *Format:* Christian
William Bence, President

Eldorado

WEBQ-FM
04-01-1972; 102.3 mhz FM *Hrs Open:* 24; 3 kw; 299 ft.; N37 49 14 W88 27 11
701 South Commercial St, Harrisburg, IL 62946 US
(618) 253-7282, *Fax:* (618) 252-2366
www.webqradio.com
webq@yourclearwave.com
License: Eldorado, Saline County, IL held by W. Russell Withers Jr.
Group Owner: Withers Broadcasting Co.; (acq 7-28-2004; $450,000 with WEBQ(AM) Harrisburg).
Nat'l Network: ABC *Regional Network:* Ill. Radio Net.
Arbitron Metro Market: Harrisburg, IL *Format:* Adult Contemp *Hrs. of News Programming:* news progmg 6 hrs wkly *No. News Employees:* 1 *Target Audience:* 25-45; young middle class adults *Adv. Rates:* 9.79;9.79; 7.79; 4.64
Cathy Horton, General Manager
Cathy Horton, Station Manager
Sonny Dotson, General Sales Mgr
Wyatt Drake, News Director
Bob Romonosky, Chief Engineer
Shelly Reeder, Traffic Manager

Elgin

*WEPS
01-01-1950; 88.9 mhz FM *Hrs Open:* 6; 0.74 kw; 43 ft.; N42 2 11 W88 16 34
355 E. Chicago Street, Elgin, IL 60120 US
(800) 747-7444, *Fax:* (847) 888-0272
www.wpr.org
Listener@wpr.org
License: Elgin, Kane County, IL held by Board of Education, Union School District 46.
Arbitron Metro Market: Elgin, IL *Format:* Variety/Diverse *Special Programming:* Class 5 hrs, jazz 6 hrs, community affrs 3 hrs, educ 13 hrs wkly *Target Audience:* Parents of students.
Steve Johnston, Director of Engineering & Operations
Jackie Olson Kold, Station Manager
Michael Leland, News Director
Mike Crane, Director of Radio
Michael Arnold, Associate Director
Sarah Jacobs, Audience Services Manager
Jeffrey Potter, Marketing Director
Rebecca Dopart, Membership and Corporate Support
Mary Kay Dadisman, Director of Development

WRMN
01-01-1949; 1410 khz AM
14 Douglas Avenue, Elgin, IL 60120 US
(847) 741-7700, *Fax:* (847) 888-4227
www.radioshoppingshow.com,www.wrmn1410.com
mail@wrmn1410.com
License: Elgin, IL held by Elgin Broadcasting Co.
Group Owner: McNaughton-Jakle Stations; (acq 1952)
Arbitron Metro Market: Chicago *Format:* News, News/Talk, 86 *Special Programming:* Sp 10 hrs wkly *Hrs. of News Programming:* news progmg 5 hrs wkly *No. News Employees:* 1 *Target Audience:* General.
Richard Jakle, CEO
Jack Davis, Station Manager
Chuck France, General Sales Mgr

Ellsworth

*WSPI
89.5 mhz FM; 0.29 kw; 312 ft.; N40 24 16.9 W88 35 33.8 US
(309) 807-0100, *Fax:* (570) 644-2232
www.catholicspiritradio.com
License: Ellsworth, McLean County, IL held by 2820 Communications Inc.
Arbitron Metro Market: Ellsworth, IL *Format:* Christian
Morgan Grammer, General Manager

Elmhurst

WJJG
10-10-1974; 1530 khz AM; 760 w-D, DA; N41 52 03 W87 55 07
5629 St. Charles Rd., Suite 208, Berkeley, IL 60163
(708) 493-1530, *Fax:* (708) 493-1537
www.1530wjjg.com
License: Elmhurst, Du Page County, IL held by Joseph J. Gentile Inc.
Population Served: 5,000,000 *Arbitron Metro Market:* Chicago, IL *Target Audience:* 45 plus; affluent adults
Joseph Gentile, President
Mike Baker, Operations Dir

*WRSE
12-07-1962; 88.7 mhz FM *Hrs Open:* 24; 0.32 kw; 95 ft.; N41 53 46 W87 56 45
190 Propect Avenue, Elmhurst, IL 60126 US
(630) 617-3729, *Fax:* (630) 617-3313
www.wrse.com
License: Elmhurst, Du Page County, IL held by Board of Trustees Elmhurst College.
Wire Services: AP
Arbitron Metro Market: Chicago *Format:* Alternative, Oldies *Special Programming:* Metal 3 hrs, hip hop 6 hrs wkly *Hrs. of News Programming:* News progmg one hr wkly *Target Audience:* 17-40; college & general
Jon Morgan, General Manager

Elmwood

WFYR
08-02-1993; 97.3 mhz FM *Hrs Open:* 24; 23.5 kw; 338 ft.; N40 46 22 W89 44 50
P O Box 150846, Nashville, TN 37215 US
(309) 673-0973, *Fax:* (309) 676-2600
www.973rivercountry.com
jgreeley@regentcomm.com
License: Elmwood, Peoria County, IL
Group Owner: Townsquare Media; (acq 7-6-01; grpsl).
Nat'l Reps: Katz Radio
Arbitron Metro Market: Peoria, IL *Format:* Country *Hrs. of News Programming:* News progmg one hr wkly *Target Audience:* 25-54; adults, family oriented & skewing female *Adv. Rates:* 30; 30; 30; 10
Ric Morgan, Operations Dir
J.R. Greeley, General Manager
Brad Creek, General Sales Mgr

Elmwood Park

WCFS-FM
01-01-1947; 105.9 mhz FM *Hrs Open:* 24; 4.1 kw; 1581 ft.; N41 52 44 W87 38 8
600 New Hampshire Ave., Suite 1200, Washington, DC 20037 US
1(800)784-6397, *Fax:* (312) 565-3181
www.chicago.cbslocal.com
License: Elmwood Park, Cook County, IL held by CBS Radio Holdings Corp. of Orlando.
Group Owner: CBS Radio; (acq 1996)
Nat'l Network: Westwood One
Arbitron Metro Market: Chicago,IL *Format:* Adult Contemp *Hrs. of News Programming:* news progmg one hr wkly *No. News Employees:* 1 *Target Audience:* 25-54.
Rob Zimmerman, General Manager
Mike Kennelly, General Sales Mgr

Eureka

WPIA
01-01-1989; 98.5 mhz FM *Hrs Open:* 24; 6 kw; 328 ft.; N40 42 57 W89 27 50 *Rebroadcasts:* Simulcast with WWCT(FM) Farmington 100%
Post Office Box 150846, Nashville, TN 37215 US
(309) 686-0101, *Fax:* (309) 686-0111
www.kisspeoria.com/
mrea@ampillinois.com
License: Eureka, Woodford County, IL held by IM IL Licenses LLC.
Group Owner: Independence Media Holdings LLC; (acq 9-19-2006; grpsl).
Arbitron Metro Market: Eureka, IL *Format:* Contemporary Hits/Top 40
Michael Rea, General Manager
Don Black, Programming Director

Evanston

WKTA
01-01-1953; 1330 khz AM *Hrs Open:* 24; 5 kw-D, DAD; 0.017 kw-N, DAD; N42 8 23 W87 53 9
4320 Dundee Road, Northbrook, IL 60062 US
(847) 498-3350, *Fax:* (847) 498-5743
www.pclradio.com
wkta@inc-us.com
License: Evanston, IL held by Polnet Communications Ltd.
Group Owner: Polnet Communications Ltd.; (acq 5-5-86; $1.66 million;
Arbitron Metro Market: Chicago, IL *Format:* Korean, Rock/AOR, 78 *Special Programming:* Ger 5 hrs wkly *Hrs. of News Programming:* News progmg 5 hrs wkly *Target Audience:* 18-54; Russian, Korean and German speakingaudience
Walter Kotaba, President
Scott Davidson, Operations Dir
Sara Vargas, General Manager

*WNUR-FM
05-08-1950; 89.3 mhz FM *Hrs Open:* 24; 7.2 kw; 98 ft.; N42 3 12 W87 40 33
1905 Sheridan Road, Evanston, IL 60201 US
(847) 491-7101, *Fax:* (847) 467-2058
www.wnur.org
gm@wnur.org
License: Evanston, Cook County, IL held by Northwestern University.
Arbitron Metro Market: Chicago, IL *Format:* Jazz *Special Programming:* Folk 3 hrs, world mus 10 hrs, reggae 4 hrs wkly *Hrs. of News Programming:* News progmg 3 hrs wkly *Target Audience:* 18-34; general
Henry Bienen, President
Monica Yi, Operations Dir
Matt Ludwig, General Manager
Ethan Simonoff, Programming Director
Ashley Ayarza, Promotions Manager

WOJO
01-01-1946; 105.1 mhz FM; 5.7 kw; 1394 ft.; N41 53 56 W87 37 23
3102 Oak Lawn Ave., Suite 215, Dallas, TX 75219 US
312-654-5324, *Fax:* 312-649-9283
http://www.univison.com/content/channel.jhtml?chid=9627&schid=9638
License: Evanston, Cook County, IL held by Tichenor License Corp.
Group Owner: Univision Radio; (acq 9-22-2003; grpsl).
Nat'l Reps: Katz Radio
Arbitron Metro Market: Chicago *TV Affiliate:* Sp *Hrs. of News Programming:* 1 *No. News Employees:* 18-35; regional/Mexican
Programming Director

WCGO
01-01-1947; 1590 khz AM
2100 Lee Street, Evanston, IL 60202 US
(847) 475-1590, *Fax:* (847) 475-1590
www.1590wcgo.com
License: Evanston, IL held by Kovas Communications Inc.
Arbitron Metro Market: Chicago *TV Affiliate:* Sp *Format:* Greek *Special Programming:* News progmg 8 hrs wkly *No. News Employees:* General.

Fairbury

WIBL(FM)
08-08-2000; 107.7 mhz FM *Hrs Open:* 24; 22.5 kw; Ant 351 ft; N40 37 45 W88 46 52
108 Boeykens Pl., Normal, IL 61761
(309) 888-4496, *Fax:* (309) 452-9677
www.star1077.net
star1077@aaabloomington.com
License: Fairbury, Livingston County, IL held by Pilot Media LLC.
Group Owner: Great Plains Media Inc.; (acq 6-19-2007; grpsl)
Nat'l Network: AP Radio *Wire Services:* AP
Population Served: 77,071 *Arbitron Metro Market:* Bloomington, IL *Format:* Adult Contemp *Hrs. of News Programming:* News progmg 2 hrs wkly *Target Audience:* 25+; women
Kevin Trueblood, Operations Dir
Patti Donsbach, General Manager

Fairfield

WFIW
08-21-1953; 1390 khz AM *Hrs Open:* 24; 0.71 kw-D, ND1; 0.058 kw-N, ND1; N38 22 46 W88 19 33
P. O. Box 310, Fairfield, IL 62837 US
(618) 842-2159, *Fax:* (618) 847-5907
www.wfiwradio.com
wfiwwokz@fairfieldwireless.net
License: Fairfield, IL held by Wayne County Broadcasting Co.
Group Owner: Wayne County Broadcasting Co.
Nat'l Network: ABC
Format: News, News/Talk, 86 *Special Programming:* Farm 16 hrs wkly *Hrs. of News Programming:* news progmg 22 hrs wkly *No. News Employees:* 1 *Target Audience:* 45 plus; small town rural, business, farm, olderadults *Adv. Rates:* 23; 23; 23; 16
Thomas Land, Chairman
David Land, President & General Manager
Vicky Strange, Station Manager
Jenny Crippen, Promotions Manager
Len Wells, News Director
Tom Lavine, Music Director and Disc Jockey
Deron Caudle, News Reporter and AMOperator
Derek Dunn, Disc Jockey
Dodie Dickey, Sales Representative
Kathy Bircket, Sales Representative
Diana Lamp, Sales Representative

WFIW-FM
01-01-1965; 104.9 mhz FM *Hrs Open:* 24; 4.9 kw; 364 ft; N38 22 46 W88 19 33
Box 310, Hwy. 15 E., Fairfield, IL 62837
(618) 842-2159, *Fax:* (618) 847-5907
www.wfiwradio.com
License: Fairfield, Wayne County, IL
Group Owner: Wayne County Broadcasting Co.
Population Served: 150,000*Special Programming:* Farm 12 hrs wkly *Hrs. of News Programming:* news progmg 16 hrs wkly *No. News Employees:* 1 *Target Audience:* 25-49; small town rural, young, middle age, business,farm *Adv. Rates:* Same as AM
Mark Lange, President
Len Wells, News Director
Kirk Wallace, Chief Engineer

WOKZ
09-01-1996; 105.9 mhz FM *Hrs Open:* 24; 6 kw; 328 ft; N38 22 46 W88 19 33
Box 310, Hwy. 15 E., Fairfield, IL 62837
(618) 842-2159, *Fax:* (618) 847-5907
www.wfiwradio.com
wfiwwokz@fairfieldwireless.net
License: Fairfield, Wayne County, IL held by Wayne County Broadcasting Co., Inc.
Group Owner: Wayne County Broadcasting Co.
Nat'l Network: Fox News Radio
Population Served: 150,000*Hrs. of News Programming:* news progmg 20 hrs wkly *No. News Employees:* 1 *Target Audience:* 25-54; small town rural, business, farm *Adv. Rates:* 23; 23; 23; 16
Thomas Land, Chairman
David Land, President

Farmer City

WWHP
10-01-1983; 98.3 mhz FM *Hrs Open:* 24; 5.2 kw; 351 ft.; N40 24 17 W88 35 34
401 North Main St, Farmer City, IL 61842 US
(309) 928-9876, *Fax:* (309) 928-3708
www.wwhp.com
wwhp@farmwagon.com
License: Farmer City, De Witt County, IL held by WMS1 Inc.
Arbitron Metro Market: Champaign, IL *Format:* Triple A *Special Programming:* Gospel 3 hrs, comedy 1 hr *Target Audience:* 18-65; reach city, suburbs & rural listeners in east central Illinois *Adv. Rates:* 25; 25;25; 25
Larry Williams, Station Manager

Farmington

WZPN
01-01-1997; 96.5 mhz FM; 4.3 kw; 377 ft.; N40 40 10 W89 53 31
4530 N. Miller Ave., Peoria Heights, IL 61614 US
(309) 282-7625, *Fax:* (309) 686-0111
License: Farmington, Fulton County, IL held by IM IL Licenses LLC.
Group Owner: Independence Media Holdings LLC; (acq 3-30-2007; $600,000)
Nat'l Network: ESPN Radio
Format: Sports, Talk
Michael Rea, General Manager

Fisher

*WGNN
04-07-1996; 102.5 mhz FM *Hrs Open:* 24; 6 kw; 328 ft.; N40 20 21 W88 24 18
Mailing Address: P.O. Box 12345, Champaign, IL 61826 US
Second Address: 2421 N. 1450 E. Rd., White Heath, IL 61884
(217) 897-6333
www.greatnewsradio.org
staff@greatnewsradio.org
License: Fisher, Champaign County, IL held by Good News Radio Inc.
Nat'l Network: Moody; USA; Salem Radio Network
Format: News, News/Talk, 86, Religious *Target Audience:* 35 plus; general
David Herriott, Chairman
Mark Burns, President
Carrie Burns, Operations Dir

Flora

WNOI
05-21-1971; 103.9 mhz FM *Hrs Open:* 24; 3.3 kw; 299 ft.; N38 40 42 W88 29 14
P.O. Box 368, Flora, IL 62839 US
(618) 662-8331, *Fax:* (618) 662-2407
www.wnoi.com
info@wnoi.com
License: Flora, Clay County, IL held by H&R Communications Inc.
Nat'l Network: Jones Radio Networks
Arbitron Metro Market: Flora, IL *Format:* Adult Contemp *Hrs. of News Programming:* news progmg 12 hrs wkly *No. News Employees:* 1 *Target Audience:* General.
Steven Lovellette, President
Patrick Garret, Operations Dir
Randy Poole, General Manager
Brenda Miller, General Sales Mgr
Patrick Garrett, Programming Director
Kirk Wallace, Chief Engineer

Flossmoor

*WHFH
01-01-1965; 88.5 mhz FM *Hrs Open:* 14; 1.5 kw horiz; 92 ft.; N41 32 43 W87 41 30
999 South Kedzie, Flossmoor, IL 60422 US
(708) 798-9434, *Fax:* (708) 799-3142
www.whfh.org
whfh@hfhighschool.org
License: Flossmoor, Cook County, IL held by Community High School District No. 233.
Special Programming: News/talk one hr, sports talk one hr, live sports *Hrs. of News Programming:* News progmg 4 hrs wkly *Target Audience:* Teens-Adult.
Robert Comstock, General Manager
John Henry, Station Manager

Freeport

WFPS
11-01-1970; 92.1 mhz FM *Hrs Open:* 24; 3.6 kw; 423 ft.; N42 19 41 W89 43 30
Mailing Address: 2830 Sandy Hollow Road, Rockford, IL 61109 US
Second Address: 834 N. Tower Rd., Freeport, IL 61032
(815) 235-7191, *Fax:* (815) 235-4318
www.wekz.com
License: Freeport, Stephenson County, IL held by Scott A. Thompson dba Big Radio
Format: Country *Hrs. of News Programming:* news progmg 15 hrs wkly *No. News Employees:* 4 *Target Audience:* 25-49.
Kent McConnell, Operations Dir
Wyatt Herrmann, Programming Director
Brad Hart, News Director
Todd Hausser, Chief Engineer
Becky Koester, Traffic Manager

WFRL
10-28-1947; 1570 khz AM *Hrs Open:* 24; 5 kw-D, 500 w-N, DA-2; N42 18 45 W89 35 38
Mailing Address: P.O. Box 807, Freeport, IL 61109
Second Address: 834 N. Tower Rd., Freeport, IL 61032

(815) 235-7191, *Fax:* (815) 235-4318
License: Freeport, Stephenson County, IL held by Scott A. Thompson dba Big Radio
Nat'l Network: ABC
Population Served: 50,000*Hrs. of News Programming:* news progmg 24 hrs wkly *No. News Employees:* 4 *Target Audience:* 25-34 *Adv. Rates:* 12; 10; 12; 8
Kent McConnell, Operations Dir
Wyatt Herrmann, Programming Director
Brad Hart, News Director
Todd Hausser, Chief Engineer
Becky Koester, Traffic Manager

*WNIE

01-01-1999; 89.1 mhz FM *Hrs Open:* 24; 6 kw; 361 ft.; N42 18 45 W89 35 38 *Rebroadcasts:* Rebroadcasts WNIJ(FM) De Kalb & WNIU(FM) Rockford 50%
801 North First Street, Dekalb, IL 60115 US
(815) 753-9000, *Fax:* (815) 753-9938
www.northernpublicradio.org
npr@niu.edu
License: Freeport, Stephenson County, IL held by Northern Illinois University.
Nat'l Network: PRI; NPR
Arbitron Metro Market: Freeport, IL *Format:* News *No. News Employees:* 2 *Target Audience:* General.
Staci Hoste, General Manager
Jan Kilgard, General Sales Mgr
Bill Drake, Programming Director
Guy Stephens, News Director
Jeff Glass, Chief Engineer

WXXQ

04-11-1965; 98.5 mhz FM *Hrs Open:* 24; 11 kw; 492 ft.; N42 16 48 W89 19 59
C/O Putbrese Hunsaker, P. O. Box 217, Sterling, VA 20167 US
(815) 399-2233, *Fax:* (815) 484-2432
www.q985online.com
License: Freeport, Stephenson County, IL held by Cumulus Licensing Corp.
Group Owner: Cumulus Media Inc.; (acq 3-15-00; grpsl).
Arbitron Metro Market: Freeport, IL *Format:* Country *No. News Employees:* 1 *Target Audience:* 25-54.
Greg Sher, General Manager
Steve Summers, Programming Director
Dawn Plock, Promotions Manager

Galatia

WISH-FM

01-01-2001; 98.9 mhz FM; 4.1 kw; 400 ft.; N37 55 52 W88 40 50
P.O. Box 1508, Mount Vernon, IL 62864 US
(618) 643-2311, *Fax:* (618) 643-3299
License: Galatia, Saline County, IL held by W. Russell Withers Jr.
Group Owner: Withers Broadcasting Co.
Arbitron Metro Market: Mc Leansboro, IL *Format:* Adult Contemp, Contemporary Hits/Top 40
Dana Withers, General Manager

Galena

WDBQ-FM

02-01-1989; 107.5 mhz FM *Hrs Open:* 24; 6 kw; 328 ft.; N42 24 2 W90 23 55
111 East Kilbourn Avenue, Suite 2700, Milwaukee, WI 53202 US
(563) 690-2938, *Fax:* (563) 583-4535
www.myq1075.com
ken.peiffer@cumulus.com
License: Galena, Jo Daviess County, IL held by Cumulus Licensing Corp.
Group Owner: Cumulus Media Inc.; (acq 12-17-98; grpsl)
Arbitron Metro Market: Dubuque, IA *Format:* Contemporary Hits/Top 40, Adult Contemp *No. News Employees:* 1 *Target Audience:* 25-54.
Scott Lindahl, Promotions Manager

Galesburg

WAAG

12-15-1966; 94.9 mhz FM *Hrs Open:* 24; 50 kw; 492 ft.; N40 56 34 W90 20 39
Mailing Address: 154 East Simmons Street, Galesburg, IL 61401 US
Second Address: 154 E. Simmons, Galesburg, IL 61401
(309) 342-5131(309) 342-0840, *Fax:* (309) 342-0619
www.fm95online.com
fm95@fm95online.com
License: Galesburg, Knox County, IL
Group Owner: Galesburg Broadcasting Co.
Wire Services: AP
Arbitron Metro Market: Galesburg, IL *Format:* Country *Hrs. of News Programming:* news progmg 2 hrs wkly *No. News Employees:* 4 *Target Audience:* 25-54.
Jim Lee, General Sales Mgr
Brian Prescott, Programming Director
Mike Perry, News Director

WAIK

01-01-1957; 1590 khz AM *Hrs Open:* 24; 5 kw-D, DA2; 0.055 kw-N, DA2; N40 57 43 W90 18 30
1245 W. North Street, Galesburg, IL 61401 US
(309) 342-3161, *Fax:* (309) 734-3276
www.1590waik.com
Vanessa.Wetterling@prairiecommunications.net
License: Galesburg, IL held by WPW Broadcasting Inc.
Group Owner: Prairie Radio Communications; acq 7-9-98; $439,500)
Nat'l Network: ABC
Arbitron Metro Market: Galesburg, IL *Format:* Adult Contemp, Big Band, 64 *Special Programming:* Talk 10 hrs, loc sports 10 hrs, relg 6 hrs wkly *Hrs. of News Programming:* news progmg 24 hrs wkly *No. News Employees:* 3 *Target Audience:* 25 plus.
Don Davis, CEO
Heidi Aycock, Operations Dir
Vanessa Wetterling, General Manager
Kyle Lester, General Sales Mgr
Greg Ford, Programming Director
Kris Kinney, News Director
Wayne R. Miller, Chief Engineer
Mike Weaver, OperationsManager

WGIL

06-12-1938; 1400 khz AM *Hrs Open:* 24
Mailing Address: 154 East Simmons St., Galesburg, IL 61401 US
Second Address: 154 E. Simmons, Galesburg, IL 61401
(309) 342-5131, *Fax:* (309) 342-0840
www.wgil.com
wgil@wgil.com
License: Galesburg, IL held by Galesburg Broadcasting Co.
Group Owner: Galesburg Broadcasting Co.
Nat'l Network: Westwood One *Regional Network:* Ill. Radio Net.
Nat'l Reps: Interep *Wire Services:* AP
Format: News, News/Talk, 84, Talk *Special Programming:* Farm 10 hrs, relg 4 hrs, sports 15 hrs wkly *Hrs. of News Programming:* news progmg 20 hrs wkly *No. News Employees:* 4 *Target Audience:* 25-54.
John Pritchard, President
Brian Prescott, Operations Dir
Roger Lundeen, General Manager
Chris Postin, General Sales Mgr
Jim Lee, Programming Director
Will Stevenson, News Director
Angie Benson, Marketing Consultant
MichelleBizarri, Marketing Consultant
Vicki Diefendorf, Office Manager
Rick Heath, Engineer
Kyle Schassburger, News Director

WLSR

01-17-1979; 92.7 mhz FM *Hrs Open:* 24; 4.2 kw; 390 ft.; N40 56 34 W90 20 39
154 E. Simmons Street, Galesburg, IL 61401 US
(309) 342-5131, *Fax:* (309) 342-0840
www.thelaseronline.com
thelaser@thelaseronline.com
License: Galesburg, Knox County, IL held by Galesburg Broadcasting Co.
Group Owner: Galesburg Broadcasting Co.; (acq 7-3-97).
Wire Services: AP
Arbitron Metro Market: Galesburg, IL *Format:* Rock/AOR *Special Programming:* 24 Religious; 2 hrs. wkly. *Hrs. of News Programming:* news progmg one hr wkly *No. News Employees:* 4 *Target Audience:* 18-34.
John Pritchard, President
Roger Lundeen, General Manager
Chris Postin, General Sales Mgr
Chris Lagrow, Programming Director
Brian Prescott, Promotions Manager

*WVKC

04-12-1961; 90.7 mhz FM; 1 kw horiz; 102 ft.; N40 56 46 W90 22 11
2 E. South Street, Galesburg, IL 61401 US
(309) 341-7000, *Fax:* (309) 341-7090
www.knox.edu/wvkc.xml
hengelma@knox.edu
License: Galesburg, Knox County, IL held by Knox College.
Arbitron Metro Market: Galesburg, IL *Format:* Variety/Diverse
Special Programming: Black 6 hrs, jazz 15 hrs, class 18 hrs wkly
Roger Moore, President
Mark Iellski, General Manager

Galva

WJRE

10-15-1995; 102.5 mhz FM *Hrs Open:* 24; 6 kw; 293 ft.; N41 13 36 W89 56 5
Mailing Address: 937 Se 2nd Street, P.O. Box 222, Galva, IL 61434 US
Second Address: 133 E. Division St., Kewanee, IL 61443
(309) 853-4471, *Fax:* (309) 853-4474
www.1025wjre.com
regionalradio@verizon.net
License: Galva, Henry County, IL held by Virden Broadcasting Corp.
Group Owner: Miller Media Group; (acq 3-31-2003; $475,000 with WGEN(AM) Geneseo)
Nat'l Reps: Commercial Media Sales
Format: Country *Special Programming:* Southern gospel one hr wkly *No. News Employees:* 1
Randal Miller, President
Kris Wexell, Programming Director

Geneseo

*WAXR

01-01-2001; 88.1 mhz FM; 3 kw vert; 322 ft.; N41 28 47 W90 16 8
P O Drawer 2440, Tupelo, MS 38803 US
(319) 273-6325, *Fax:* (319) 273-2682
www.khke.org
kuni@uni.edu
License: Geneseo, Henry County, IL held by American Family Association.
Group Owner: American Family Radio
Format: Classical
Wayne Jarvis, General Manager
Al Schares, Programming Director
Scott Verdos, Promotions Manager
Greg Shanley, News Director
Steve Schoon, Chief Engineer

Geneva

WSPY

11-11-1961; 1480 khz AM *Hrs Open:* 24; 1 kw-D, DA2; 0.5 kw-N, DA2; N41 54 25 W88 17 43
1215 East Fern Avenue, Saint Charles, IL 60174 US
(630) 552-1000, *Fax:* (630) 552-9300
wspy@nelsonmultimedia.net
License: Geneva, IL held by Nelson Multi Media Inc.
Arbitron Metro Market: Chicago, IL *Format:* Adult Contemp *Hrs. of News Programming:* news progmg 2 hrs wkly *No. News Employees:* 1 *Target Audience:* 35-65; baby boomers *Adv. Rates:* 25; 20; 20; 10
Larry Nelson, President
Chris Schwemlein, Operations Dir
Vori Dhabolt, General Sales Mgr
Jenny Beckman, News Director
Lane Lindstrom, Chief Engineer
Beth Perrie, General Sales Manager

Genoa

WYRB

01-01-2001; 106.3 mhz FM; 3.8 kw; 413 ft.; N42 4 28 W88 49 24
Rebroadcasts: Rebroadcasts WSRB(FM) Lansing 100%
980 North Michigan Avenue, Suite 1880, Chicago, IL 60611 US
(773) 734-4455, *Fax:* (219) 933-0323
www.soul1063radio.com
wycainfo@crawfordbroadcsting.com
License: Genoa, De Kalb County, IL held by Dontron Inc.
Group Owner: Crawford Broadcasting Co.; (acq 9-28-01; $1.5 million).
Format: Black, Blues *Target Audience:* 25-54; adult urban
Donald Crawford, CEO
Taft Harris, General Manager

Gibson City

WGCY

11-28-1983; 106.3 mhz FM *Hrs Open:* 6 AM-midnight; 6 kw; 322 ft.; N40 33 57 W88 20 48
607 South Sangamon, Gibson City, IL 60936 US
(217) 784-8661, *Fax:* (217) 784-8677
www.wgcyradio.com
wgcyproduction@hotmail.com
License: Gibson City, Ford County, IL held by F & G Broadcasting Inc.
Nat'l Network: USA
Format: Easy Listening *No. News Employees:* 1 *Target Audience:* 35 plus.
Gary McCollough, CEO/COO
Gary McCullough, General Manager

Frank McCullough, Sports Director
Tom Benefiel, Sports Commentator
Joni Cox, Sales Accounting
Rod Habermeyer, Sales Associate
Jim Cotter, News Reporter

Gilman

WFAV
01-01-2007; 103.7 mhz FM; 3.6 kw; 433 ft.; N40 53 53.3 W87 59 57.8
US
(815) 933-9287, *Fax:* (815) 933-8696
www.wfav1037.com
License: Gilman, Iroquois County, IL held by Milner Broadcasting Co.
Group Owner: Milner Broadcasting
Arbitron Metro Market: Gilman, IL *Format:* Contemporary Hits/Top 40
Jim Brandt, Operations Dir
Tim Milner, General Manager
Chris Swain, General Sales Mgr
Mickey Milner, Programming Director
Kathy Gagliano, Vice President, Sales
Gordy McCollum, Public Service Director
Chris Nickles, ProductionDirector

Glasford

WHPI
01-01-2000; 101.1 mhz FM *Hrs Open:* 24; 3.3 kw; 449 ft.; N40 39 0 W89 46 46
P.O. Box 150846, Nashville, TN 37215 US
(256) 497-4502, *Fax:* NA
varietyrock@hotmail.com
License: Glasford, Peoria County, IL held by IM IL Licenses LLC.
Group Owner: Independence Media Holdings LLC; (acq 9-19-2006; grpsl)
Arbitron Metro Market: Tulsa OK *Format:* Variety/Diverse, Rock/AOR *Target Audience:* 18-54.
Richard Dabney, General Manager

Glen Ellyn

***WDCB**
07-05-1977; 90.9 mhz FM *Hrs Open:* 24; 5 kw; 300 ft; N41 50 36 W88 05 00
College of DuPage, 425 Fawell Blvd., Glen Ellyn, IL 60137
(630) 942-4200,(630) 942-3708, *Fax:* (630) 942-2788
www.wdcb.org
wdcbmktg@cdnet.cod.edu
License: Glen Ellyn, Du Page County, IL held by College of DuPage.
Special Programming: College classes 12 hrs, folk 12 hrs, gospel 2 hrs, var music 7 hrs wkly *Hrs. of News Programming:* news progmg 13 hrs wkly *No. News Employees:* 3 *Target Audience:* General.
Scott Wager, Station Manager
Ken Scott, General Sales Mgr
Mary Pat LaRue, Programming Director
Ken Scott, Promotions Manager
Brian O'Keefe, News Director
Paul Abella, Music Director

Glendale Heights

***WJKL**
09-01-1960; 94.3 mhz FM *Hrs Open:* 24; 3.5 kw; 440 ft.; N41 51 30 W87 57 16 *Rebroadcasts:* Rebroadcasts KLVR(FM) Santa Rosa, CA 100%
14 Douglas Avenue, Elgin, IL 60120 US
(916) 251-1600, *Fax:* (916) 251-1650
www.klove.com
License: Glendale Heights, Du Page County, IL held by Educational Media Foundation.
Group Owner: EMF Broadcasting; (acq 4-10-2007; $17 million)
Nat'l Network: K-Love
Arbitron Metro Market: Chicago, IL *Format:* Christian
Mike Novak, President

Glenview

***WGBK**
01-13-1979; 88.5 mhz FM *Hrs Open:* 6:30 AM-8:00 AM; 3 PM-10 PM (M-F); 0.185 kw; 105 ft.; N42 6 39 W87 49 56
1835 Landwehr Rd, Glenview, IL 60025 US
(847) 486-4487, *Fax:* (847) 486-4439
www.wcbk.com
contest@wcbk.com
License: Glenview, Cook County, IL held by Glenbrook High School District 225.
Arbitron Metro Market: Chicago, IL *Format:* Alternative, Sports *Special Programming:* Sports talk 5 hrs, live sports 4 hrs *Hrs. of News Programming:* News progmg 1 hr wkly *Target Audience:* General; teens &adults
Dr. Daniel Oswald, General Manager

Godfrey

***WLCA**
01-01-1974; 89.9 mhz FM *Hrs Open:* 18; 1.5 kw; 394 ft.; N38 56 57 W90 11 47
5800 Godfrey Road, Godfrey, IL 62035 US
(618) 466-8936, *Fax:* (618) 466-7458
www.wlcafm.com
mlemons@lc.edu
License: Godfrey, Madison County, IL held by Lewis and Clark Community College.
Nat'l Network: USA
Format: Rock/AOR *Adv. Rates:* 120; 120; 120; na
Mike Lemons, General Manager
Michael Lemons, Station Manager
Matthew Dorman, Programming Director
Dylan Brown, Promotions Manager
Dave Caires, Engineering Dir
Matt Maher, Music Director
Jon Mintert, Production Manager
JohnNeumann, Sports Director

Golconda

WKYX-FM
11-22-1990; 94.3 mhz FM *Hrs Open:* 24; 3.1 kw; 449 ft.; N37 14 4 W88 29 48 *Rebroadcasts:* Simulcast with WKYX(AM) Paducah, KY 100%
P.O. Box 900, Bowling Green, KY 42102 US
(270) 554-8255, *Fax:* (270) 554-5468
www.wkyx.com
info@wkyx.com
License: Golconda, Pope County, IL held by Bristol Broadcasting Co. Inc.
Group Owner: Bristol Broadcasting Co. Inc.; (acq 2-20-2004; grpsl)
Arbitron Metro Market: Golconda, IL *Format:* News, News/Talk, 86 *Special Programming:* Relg one hr wkly *Target Audience:* 25-54.
Pete Ninninger, President
Gary Morse, General Manager

Granite City

WGNU
12-01-1961; 920 khz AM *Hrs Open:* 24; 0.45 kw-D, DA2; 0.5 kw-N, DA2; N38 45 33 W90 3 0
275 Union Blvd., St. Louis, MO 63108 US
(314) 454-0400, *Fax:* (314)448-4999
www.wgnu920am.com
info@wgnu920am.com
License: Granite City, IL held by 920 AM LLC
Arbitron Metro Market: St. Louis, MO *Format:* Christian
Jay Madas, Operations Dir
Dirk Hallemeier, General Manager

WARH
11-24-1965; 106.5 mhz FM; kw
3500 West Olive Avenue, Suite 300, Burbank, CA 91505 US
(314) 983-6000, *Fax:* (314) 994-9447
www.wssm.com
info@wssm.com
License: Granite City, Madison County, IL held by Bonneville Holding Co.
Group Owner: Bonneville International Corporation; (acq 9-26-2000; grpsl)
Arbitron Metro Market: St. Louis, MO *Format:* Jazz, Smooth Jazz
Bruce Reese, CEO
John Kijowski, Operations Dir
Mike Jennewein, General Sales Mgr
Marshall Rice, Chief Engineer
Bob Johnson, CFO
Ben Granger, National Sales Manager
Amanda Koeppe, Public Affairs Director

Greenville

WGEL
12-20-1984; 101.7 mhz FM *Hrs Open:* 24; 6 kw; 295 ft.; N38 48 11 W89 20 56
Box 177 309 W. Main Ave., Greenville, IL 62246 US
(618) 664-3300, *Fax:* (618) 664-3318
www.wgel.com
john@wgel.com
License: Greenville, Bond County, IL held by Bond Broadcasting.
Nat'l Network: USA
Format: Country *Special Programming:* Farm 19 hrs wkly *No. News Employees:* 2 *Target Audience:* 25-64.
John Kennedy, President
Joe Doll, General Sales Mgr
Brad Rogers, Programming Director
Tom Kennedy, News Director

Harrisburg

WEBQ
09-01-1923; 1240 khz AM; 1 kw-U, ND1; N37 43 3 W88 32 37
701 South Commercial, Harrisburg, IL 62946 US
(618) 253-7282, *Fax:* (618) 252-2366
www.webqradio.com
webq@yourclearwave.com
License: Harrisburg, IL held by W. Russell Withers Jr.
Group Owner: Withers Broadcasting Co.; (acq 7-28-2004; $450,000 with WEBQ-FM Eldorado).
Nat'l Network: ABC *Regional Network:* Brownfield
Arbitron Metro Market: Harrisburg, IL *Format:* Country *Special Programming:* Farm 6 hrs wkly *Hrs. of News Programming:* news progmg 6 hrs wkly *No. News Employees:* 1 *Target Audience:* Older area residents.*Adv. Rates:* 9.79; 9.79; 9.79; 4.64
Cathy Horton, General Manager
Sonny Dotson, General Sales Mgr
Shelly Reeder, News Director
Bob Romonosky, Chief Engineer

WOOZ-FM
09-01-1947; 99.9 mhz FM; 32 kw; 620 ft.; N37 36 45 W88 52 3
P.O. Box 1749, Cape Girardeau, MO 63702 US
(618) 985-4843, *Fax:* (618) 985-6529
www.z100fm.com
mail@z100fm.com
License: Harrisburg, Saline County, IL held by MRR License LLC.
Group Owner: MAX Media L.L.C.; (acq 3-29-2004; grpsl).
Nat'l Reps: Christal
Arbitron Metro Market: Marion-Carbonda *TV Affiliate:* Country *No. News Employees:* 18-49.
Events Coordinator

Harvey

WBGX
01-01-1955; 1570 khz AM *Hrs Open:* 24
15700 Campbell, Harvey, IL 60426 US
(800) 877-5600, *Fax:* (916) 251-1650
www.klove.com
License: Harvey, IL held by Great Lakes Radio-Chicago LLC
Arbitron Metro Market: Torrington WY *Format:* Christian *Adv. Rates:* 45; 25; 45; 25
Mike Novak, President

Havana

WDUK
02-27-1970; 99.3 mhz FM; 3 kw horiz; 299 ft.; N40 18 43 W90 3 19
901 N. Promenade, Havana, IL 62644 US
(309) 543-3331
info@wduk.com
License: Havana, Mason County, IL held by Illinois Valley Radio.
Regional Network: Brownfield *Regional Reps:* Brownfield.
Arbitron Metro Market: Havana, IL *Format:* Variety/Diverse, Country *Special Programming:* Farm 8 hrs wkly *Target Audience:* General. *Adv. Rates:* 3.70; 3.70; 3.70; 3.70
Edwin Stimpson, President

Henry

WRVY-FM
07-30-1990; 100.5 mhz FM *Hrs Open:* 24; 3 kw; 328 ft.; N41 4 32 W89 21 10
P. O. Box 140, Carlinville, IL 62262 US
(815) 875-8014, *Fax:* (815) 872-0308
www.wrvy.com
License: Henry, Marshall County, IL held by WZOE Inc.
Group Owner: WZOE Inc.; (acq 5-8-98)
Nat'l Network: CBS; CNN Radio *Regional Network:* Ill. Radio Net.
Format: Country *Special Programming:* Farm 4 hrs wkly *Hrs. of News Programming:* news progmg 3 hrs wkly *No. News Employees:* 3 *Target Audience:* 25-45.
Mary Harmon, Operations Dir
Steve Samet, General Manager
Gregg Stephens, Broadcast Engineer

Herrin

WJPF
08-28-1940; 1340 khz AM *Hrs Open:* 24; 0.77 kw-U, ND1; N37 50 4 W89 1 40
P.O. Box 1749, Cape Girardeau, MO 63702 US
(618) 985-4843, *Fax:* (618) 985-6529
www.wjpf.com
mail@wjpf.com
License: Herrin, IL held by MRR License LLC.
Group Owner: MAX Media L.L.C.; (acq 6-2-2004; grpsl)
Nat'l Network: Westwood One *Regional Network:* Ill. Radio Net.
Nat'l Reps: Christal
Arbitron Metro Market: Marion-Carbondale (Southern Illinois)
Format: News, News/Talk, 84, Talk *Hrs. of News Programming:* news progmg 10 hrs wkly *No. News Employees:* 3 *Target Audience:* 35 plus; mature,middle-income wage earners
Tom Miller, Operations Dir
Steve Falat, General Manager
Kim DeBose, General Sales Mgr
Ryan Patrick, Promotions Manager
Felicia Dick, News Director
Jon Brookmyer, Chief Engineer
Dave McKenzie, Events Coordinator
Richard Cason,News Reporter
Dee James, News Reporter

WTAO-FM
08-01-1972; 92.7 mhz FM *Hrs Open:* 24; 25 kw; 328 ft.; N37 46 28 W89 5 50
330 East Kilbourn Ave., Suite 250, Milwaukee, WI 53202 US
(618) 997-8123, *Fax:* (618) 993-2319
www.105tao.com
License: Herrin, Jackson County, IL held by Withers Broadcasting of Southern Illinois LLC.
Group Owner: Withers Broadcasting Co.; (acq 3-17-2008; grpsl)
Arbitron Metro Market: Marion-Carbondale (Southern Illinois)
Format: Rock/AOR *Target Audience:* M18-49.
Paxton Guy, Operations Dir
Jerry Crouse, General Manager
Mett Mellen, Programming Director
Tim Deterding, Chief Engineer

Heyworth

WBBE
06-06-2005; 97.9 mhz FM; 5.4 kw; Ant 344 ft; N40 27 08 W88 57 48
520 N. Center St., Bloomington, IL
(309) 834-1100, *Fax:* (309) 834-4390
www.bob979.com
License: Heyworth, McLean County, IL held by Connoisseur Media LLC.
Group Owner: Connoisseur Media LLC
Nat'l Reps: Christal
Target Audience: 18-54; Adults
Floyd Evans, General Manager
Michael Mendelssohn, General Sales Mgr
Adam Chandler, Programming Director
Mark Hill, Chief Engineer

Highland

WIJR
12-02-1963; 880 khz AM *Hrs Open:* 24; 1.7 kw-D, DA1; 0.16 kw-N, DA1; N38 45 23 W89 39 18
Mailing Address: 1411 Locust St., St. Louis, MO 63103 US
Second Address: 13063 Winu Dr., Highland, IL 62249
(314) 351-7390
www.laley880.com
hhnjim@hereshelpnet.org
License: Highland, IL held by Birach Broadcasting Corp.
Group Owner: Birach Broadcasting Corp.; (acq 8-15-2006; $1 million).
Regional Network: Brownfield
Arbitron Metro Market: St. Louis, MO *Format:* Christian *Special Programming:* Farm 3 hrs, Ger one hr wkly *Hrs. of News Programming:* news progmg 18 hrs wkly *No. News Employees:* 1 *Target Audience:* General;mature adults *Adv. Rates:* 30; 30; 30; 20
Sima Birach, President
Bernard Turner, Operations Dir
Larry Rice, General Manager

Highland Park

WVIV-FM
08-15-1963; 103.1 mhz FM *Hrs Open:* 24; 6 kw; 328 ft.; N42 8 14 W87 58 57
11 Skyline Drive, Hawthorne, NY 10532 US
(312) 981-1800, *Fax:* (312) 981-1806
www.univision.com/content/channel.jhtml?chid=9627&schid=9808
License: Highland Park, Lake County, IL held by HBC License Corp.
Group Owner: Univision Radio; (acq 9-22-2003; grpsl).
Arbitron Metro Market: Chicago, IL *Format:* Spanish *Target Audience:* 25-54.
Cesar Canales, Operations Dir
Doug Levy, General Manager
Hector Fabregas, General Sales Mgr
Victor Cerda, Programming Director
Alicia Chavarria, Promotions Manager
Joshua Sigstad, Engineering Dir
Lucy Diaz, National SalesManager

Hillsboro

WXAJ
09-01-2000; 99.7 mhz FM *Hrs Open:* 24; 50 kw; 492 ft.; N39 21 12 W89 31 53
#2 Magnolia Drive, Centralia, IL 62801 US
(217) 528-3033, *Fax:* (217) 528-5348
www.997kissfm.com
kevinodea@neuhoffmedia.com
License: Hillsboro, Montgomery County, IL held by Neuhoff Family L.P.
Group Owner: Neuhoff Family L.P.; (acq 8-1-2007; grpsl)
Nat'l Reps: Christal
Arbitron Metro Market: Springfield, IL *Format:* Contemporary Hits/Top 40 *Target Audience:* Adults; 18-49
Kevin O'Dea, General Manager
Kathy Byerly, Local Sales Manager
Frank Konwinski, Chief Engineer
Danielle Outlaw, Director of Sales
Morgan Jenkins, Receptionist
Jessica Ross, Traffic Manager
Dave Comstock, Production

Hinsdale

***WHSD**
12-06-1970; 88.5 mhz FM *Hrs Open:* 3 PM-10 PM; 0.125 kw horiz, 0.08 kw vert; 131 ft.; N41 47 18 W87 56 2
55th and Grant Streets, Hinsdale, IL 60521 US
(630) 570-8463, *Fax:* (630) 887-1362
License: Hinsdale, Du Page County, IL held by Hinsdale Twsp. High School District 86.
Format: Variety/Diverse *Target Audience:* General.
Jerry Edwards, President
Darrel Kelly, Programming Director

Hoopeston

WHPO
05-29-1979; 100.9 mhz FM *Hrs Open:* 24; 3 kw; 299 ft.; N40 28 36 W87 41 36
627 North Market, P.O.Box 55, Hoopeston, IL 60942 US
(217) 283-7744, *Fax:* (217) 283-6090
www.whporadio.com
whporadio@whporadio.com
License: Hoopeston, Vermilion County, IL held by Market Street Broadcasting LLC
Format: Country *Special Programming:* Southern gospel 7 hrs, big band 2 hrs wkly *Hrs. of News Programming:* news progmg 6 hrs wkly *No. News Employees:* 1 *Target Audience:* 25 plus; rural middle class
Blanche Voss, General Manager
Becky Voss, Programming Director

Jacksonville

WJIL
11-01-1961; 1550 khz AM *Hrs Open:* 24; 1 kw-D, DA2; 0.01 kw-N, DA2; N39 43 20 W90 11 43
P.O. Box 1065, Jacksonville, IL 62651 US
(217) 245-5119, *Fax:* (217) 245-1596
www.wjvofm.com
dianawjvo@mchsi.com
License: Jacksonville, IL held by Morgan County Broadcasting Co. Inc.
Nat'l Network: Westwood One *Nat'l Reps:* Roslin
Format: News, News/Talk, 86 *Special Programming:* Farm 8 hrs wkly *Hrs. of News Programming:* news progmg 9 hrs wkly *No. News Employees:* 1 *Target Audience:* 35-64.
Ed Steele, Operations Dir
Sarah Hautala, General Manager
Diana McCutcheon, General Sales Mgr
Matt Lakis, Programming Director
Jeremy Ray, News Director
Glen Hopkiins, Chief Engineer
Julie Cambridge, Music Director
LouEstabrook, Office Manager

WLDS
12-09-1941; 1180 khz AM *Hrs Open:* Sunrise-sunset; 1 kw-D, NDD; N39 44 6 W90 11 50
P.O. Box 1180, Jacksonville, IL 62651 US
(217) 245-7171, *Fax:* (217) 245-6711
www.wlds.com
wlds@wlds.com
License: Jacksonville, IL held by Jacksonville Area Radio Broadcasters Inc.
Nat'l Network: CBS *Regional Network:* Ill. Radio Net. *Nat'l Reps:* Katz Radio *Wire Services:* AP
Format: Adult Contemp, News, 62, Talk *Special Programming:* Farm 20 hrs wkly *Hrs. of News Programming:* news progmg 23 hrs wkly *No. News Employees:* 3 *Target Audience:* 35 plus; business & professional people,farmers & housewives
Sue Shireman, Operations Dir
Gary Scott, General Manager
Mark Whalen, General Sales Mgr
Bob Thomas, Programming Director
Kevin Baxter, News Director
John Coe, Engineering Dir
Marty Megginson, Continuity Director
Gary Ballard,Music Director

Jerseyville

WJBM
10-11-1959; 1480 khz AM; 0.5 kw-D, DA2; 0.032 kw-N, DA2; N39 6 46 W90 18 43
#1 Professional Plaza, P.O. Box 150, Pittsfield, IL 62363 US
(618) 498-8265, *Fax:* (618) 498-9830
www.wjbmradio.com
wjbm@wjbmradio.com
License: Jerseyville, IL held by DJ Two Rivers Radio Inc.
Regional Network: Brownfield
Arbitron Metro Market: St. Louis, MO *Format:* Oldies *Special Programming:* Farm 18 hrs, sports 13 hrs, relg 3 hrs wkly *Target Audience:* 25 plus; general market through retirement
J. Boyd Ingram, General Manager

Johnston City

WDDD-FM
11-22-1970; 107.3 mhz FM *Hrs Open:* 24; 50 kw; 492 ft.; N37 45 15 W88 56 5
330 East Kilbourn Ave., Suite 250, Milwaukee, WI 53202 US
(618) 997-8123, *Fax:* (618) 993-2319
www.mywithersradio.com/w3d/
License: Johnston City, Williamson County, IL held by Withers Broadcasting of Southern Illinois LLC.
Group Owner: Withers Broadcasting Co.; (acq 3-17-2008; grpsl)
Arbitron Metro Market: Marion, IL *Format:* Country *Hrs. of News Programming:* news progmg 5 hrs wkly *No. News Employees:* 2 *Target Audience:* P25-54.
Paxton Guy, Operations Dir
Janet Jensen, General Manager
Tim Deterding, Chief Engineer

Joliet

***WCSF**
09-05-1988; 88.7 mhz FM *Hrs Open:* 7 AM-2 AM (M-F); 0.1 kw; 128 ft.; N41 31 58 W88 5 54
500 North Wilcox Street, Joliet, IL 60435 US
(815) 740-3425(815) 740-3214, *Fax:* (815) 740-3697
www.stfrancis.edu
webmaster@st.francis.edu
License: Joliet, Will County, IL held by University of St. Francis.
Arbitron Metro Market: Chicago,IL *Format:* Rock/AOR *Special Programming:* Black 2 hrs, jazz 2 hrs, talk 4 hrs, requests 4 hrs, classic rock 4 hrs wkly *Target Audience:* 18-45; males
Don Burke, President
Rick Lawrence, General Manager
Jen Marentic, Station Manager

***WJCH**
04-25-1986; 91.9 mhz FM *Hrs Open:* 24; 50 kw; 495 ft.; N41 24 55 W88 16 19
4135 Northgate Blvd.Ste1, Sacramento, CA 95834 US
(815) 725-1331
www.familyradio.com
familyradio@familyradio.org
License: Joliet, Will County, IL held by Family Stations Inc.
Group Owner: Family Stations Inc.
Arbitron Metro Market: Chicago, IL *Format:* Religious *Special Programming:* Class 2 hrs wkly
Harold Camping, President
Virginia Beehn, Operations Dir

WJOL
01-01-1924; 1340 khz AM *Hrs Open:* 24; 1 kw-U, ND1; N41 32 6 W88 3 15
8800 Route 14, Crystal Lake, IL 60012 US
(815) 556-0100, *Fax:* (815) 577-9231
www.wjol.com
License: Joliet, IL held by NM Licensing LLC.
Group Owner: NextMedia Group Inc.; (acq 11-26-2001; grpsl)
Nat'l Reps: Christal *Regional Reps:* Ill. Radio Net.
Arbitron Metro Market: Chicago, IL *Format:* Talk *Special Programming:* Farm 3 hrs, gospel one hr, Pol one hr wkly *Hrs. of News Programming:* news progmg 40 hrs wkly *No. News Employees:* 2 *Target Audience:* 35 plus.
Ryan Snow, Operations Dir
Todd Elbrink, General Manager
Roger Piper, General Sales Mgr
Scott Slocum, Programming Director
Dan Waddick, Promotions Director

WSSR
02-06-1960; 96.7 mhz FM *Hrs Open:* 24; 3.1 kw; 466 ft.; N41 36 1 W87 58 44
8800 Route 14, Crystal Lake, IL 60012 US
(815) 556-0100, *Fax:* (815) 577-9231
www.star967.net
info@star967.net
License: Joliet, Will County, IL held by NM Licensing LLC.
Group Owner: NextMedia Group Inc.
Nat'l Reps: Christal
Arbitron Metro Market: Chicago, IL *Format:* Adult Contemp *No. News Employees:* 1 *Target Audience:* 25-54; Adults
Ryan Snow, Operations Dir
Todd Elbrink, General Manager
Roger Piper, General Sales Mgr
Dan Waddick, Programming Director

WWHN
04-10-1964; 1510 khz AM; 0.6 kw-C, NDD; 1 kw-D, NDD; N41 30 50 W88 3 10
506 S. Dante Avenue, Glenwood, IL 60425 US
(773) 239-2300, *Fax:* (773) 239-9921
wwhn@aol.com
License: Joliet, IL held by Hawkins Broadcasting Co.
Arbitron Metro Market: Chicago, IL *Format:* Gospel *Special Programming:* Sp one hr wkly *Target Audience:* 18-54; affluent adults
Raymond Hawkins, President
Toni Hawkins, General Manager

Kankakee

***WAWF**
01-01-2000; 88.3 mhz FM; 1.25 kw; 285 ft.; N41 4 39 W87 45 22
P.O. Drawer 2440, Tupelo, MS 38803 US
(509) 527-1000, *Fax:* (509) 529-5534
www.kix106online.com
License: Kankakee, Kankakee County, IL held by American Family Radio.
Group Owner: American Family Radio
Arbitron Metro Market: Hewitt TX
Tom Hodgins, President

WKAN
06-01-1947; 1320 khz AM *Hrs Open:* 24; 1 kw-D, DAN; 0.5 kw-N, DAN; N41 8 8 W87 49 10
2 Dearborn Square, Kankakee, IL 60901 US
(815) 935-9555, *Fax:* (815) 935-9593
www.wkan.com
wkan@starradio.com
License: Kankakee, IL held by STARadio Corp.
Group Owner: STARadio Corp.; (acq 2-7-94; $1.31 million with co-located FM;
Wire Services: UPI
Format: Talk *Special Programming:* Farm 10 hrs wkly *Hrs. of News Programming:* news progmg 20 hrs wkly *No. News Employees:* 1 *Target Audience:* 25-54. *Adv. Rates:* 36; 36; 36; 20
Robert Kersmarki, President
Brendan Michaels, Operations Dir
Larry Regnier, General Sales Mgr

WKIF
09-21-1986; 92.7 mhz FM *Hrs Open:* 24; 3 kw; 328 ft.; N41 7 22 W87 53 35
11 Skyline Drive, Hawthorne, NY 10532 US
(773) 767-1000, *Fax:* (773) 767-1100
info@weplayanything.com
License: Kankakee, Kankakee County, IL held by WKIF Inc.
Group Owner: Newsweb Corp.; (acq 11-15-2004; grpsl).
Nat'l Network: CNN Radio
Format: News
Harvey Wells, General Manager
Gary Wright, Programming Director

***WONU**
01-01-1966; 89.7 mhz FM; 35 kw; 413 ft.; N41 9 24 W87 52 16
240 E. Marsile, Bourbonnais, IL 60914 US
(815) 939-5330, *Fax:* (815) 939-5087
www.shine.fm
shine@olivet.edu
License: Kankakee, Kankakee County, IL held by Olivet Nazarene University.
TV Affiliate: Relg *No. News Employees:* 25-49; female, predominan
Director of Broadcast Operations, Justin Knight
General Manager, General Manager
Program Director, Programming Director

***WKCC**
06-01-1992; 91.1 mhz FM *Hrs Open:* 24; 2.6 kw; 254 ft.; N41 9 38.9 W87 52 29.8
1711 Rt. 50 North, Ste 1, Bourbonnais, IL 60914 US
(815) 802-8230, *Fax:* (815) 935-5169
www.kcc.edu
wkcc@kcc.edu
License: Kankakee, Kankakee County, IL held by Kankakee Community College.
Arbitron Metro Market: Kankakee, IL *Format:* Public Affairs *Hrs. of News Programming:* News progmg 3 hrs wkly *No. News Employees:* 1 *Target Audience:* General; travelers in northern IL
Mike Savage, General Manager

WVLI
10-22-1992; 95.1 mhz FM *Hrs Open:* 24; 2.3 kw; 367 ft.; N41 4 39 W87 45 22
Mailing Address: 292 N Convent, Bourbonnais, IL 60914 US
Second Address: 292 N. Convent, Bourbonnais, IL 60914
(815) 933-9287, *Fax:* (815) 933-8696
www.rivervalleyradio.net
License: Kankakee, Kankakee County, IL held by Milner Broadcasting Co.
Group Owner: Milner Broadcasting; (acq 3-17-95; $400,000).
Nat'l Network: AP Network News *Wire Services:* AP
Arbitron Metro Market: Bourbonnais, IL *Format:* Contemporary Hits/Top 40 *Hrs. of News Programming:* news progmg 20 hrs wkly *No. News Employees:* 1 *Target Audience:* 25 plus. *Adv. Rates:* 45; 45; 45; 35
Kathy Gagliano, VP/Sales
Jim Brandt, Operations Dir
Tim Milner, General Manager
Chris Swain, Local Sales Manager
Mickey Milner, Programming Director
Gordy McCollum, Public Service Director
Mike Ruble, Farm Director
Carla,Traffic Manager
Chris Nickles, Production Director

***WEGN**
88.7 mhz FM; 5 kw; 213 ft.; N41 12 26.5 W87 58 21.6 US
(877) 700-8047, *Fax:* (217) 528-2400
www.thelifefm.com
License: Kankakee, Kankakee County, IL held by Cornerstone Community Radio Inc.
Arbitron Metro Market: Kankakee, IL
Richard Van Zandt, President

Kewanee

WKEI
09-11-1952; 1450 khz AM *Hrs Open:* 24
Mailing Address: 111 West Main Cross, P.O. Box 169, Taylorville, IL 62568 US
Second Address: 133 E. Division St., Kewanee, IL 61443
(309) 853-4471, *Fax:* (309) 853-4474
www.randyradio.com
regionalradio@verizon.net
License: Kewanee, IL held by Virden Broadcasting Corp.
Group Owner: Miller Media Group; (acq 11-8-94; $400,000 with co-located FM;
Nat'l Network: CBS Radio *Nat'l Reps:* Commercial Media Sales
Arbitron Metro Market: Quad Cities, IA *Format:* News, News/Talk, 86 *Special Programming:* Farm 20 hrs, relg 6 hrs wkly *No. News Employees:* 1
Randal Miller, President
Kris Wexell, Programming Director
Will Stevenson, News Director
Wayne Miller, Chief Engineer
Jennie Holtschult, Traffic Manager

Knoxville

WKAY
12-13-2001; 105.3 mhz FM *Hrs Open:* 24; 3.7 kw; 423 ft.; N40 56 34 W90 20 39
154 East Simmons St., Galesburg, IL 61401 US
(662) 844-8888, *Fax:* (662) 842-6791
www.afr.net
License: Knoxville, Knox County, IL held by Galesburg Broadcasting Co.
Group Owner: Galesburg Broadcasting Co.; (acq 4-1-99)
Wire Services: AP
Arbitron Metro Market: Eagle Pass TX *Format:* Christian
Marvin Sanders, General Manager

La Grange

***WLTL**
01-05-1968; 88.1 mhz FM *Hrs Open:* 24; 0.18 kw; 138 ft.; N41 48 45 W87 52 51
100 South Brainard Ave., La Grange, IL 60525 US
(708) 482-9585, *Fax:* (708) 482-7051
www.wltl.net
cthomas@wltl.net
License: La Grange, Cook County, IL held by Lyons Township High School.
Arbitron Metro Market: Chicago, IL *Format:* Variety/Diverse, Rock/AOR *Special Programming:* Sports 5 hrs, news & views 10 hrs wkly *Hrs. of News Programming:* News progmg 10 hrs wkly *Target Audience:* 14-35; youngadults
Chris Thomas, General Manager
Jacob Alderman, Programming Director
Evan Boyd, Chief Engineer

WRDZ
10-01-1950; 1300 khz AM; 4.5 kw-D, DA2; 4 kw-N, DA2; N41 40 29 W87 45 45
77 West 66th Street, 16th Floor, New York, NY 10023 US
(312) 683-1300, *Fax:* (312) 577-5994
License: La Grange, IL held by Radio Disney Chicago LLC.
Group Owner: ABC Inc.; (acq 5-12-99; with WPJX(AM) Zion).
Nat'l Network: ABC *Wire Services:* City News Bureau
Arbitron Metro Market: Chicago *Format:* Children *Target Audience:* Children, mom's & dad's
Karyn Esken, Station Manager

La Salle

WAJK
12-04-1964; 99.3 mhz FM; 11 kw; 489 ft.; N41 24 47 W89 16 34
P.O. Box 215, Lasalle, IL 61301 US
(815) 223-3100, *Fax:* (815) 223-3095
wajk.com
generalmanager@993wajk.com
License: La Salle, La Salle County, IL held by La Salle County Broadcasting Corp.
Group Owner: La Salle County Broadcasting Corp.
Arbitron Metro Market: LaSalle-Peru, IL *Format:* Adult Contemp *Target Audience:* 25-49.
Peter Miller, President
Joyce McCullough, General Manager
Mark Lippert, General Sales Mgr
John Spencer, Programming Director
Jennifer Nagle, News Director
Steve Vogler, Engineering Dir
Joyce McCullough, General Manager

***WNIW**
11-01-1998; 91.3 mhz FM *Hrs Open:* 24; 36 kw vert; 331 ft.; N41 24 47 W89 16 34 *Rebroadcasts:* Rebroadcasts WNIJ(FM) De Kalb & WNIU(FM) Rockford 50%
801 North First Street, Dekalb, IL 60115 US
(815) 753-9000, *Fax:* (815) 753-9938
www.northernpublicradio.org
npr@niu.edu
License: La Salle, La Salle County, IL held by Northern Illinois University.
Nat'l Network: PRI; NPR
Arbitron Metro Market: Freeport, IL *Format:* Classical, News *No. News Employees:* 2 *Target Audience:* General.
Staci Hoste, General Manager
Jan Kilgard, General Sales Mgr
Bill Drake, Programming Director
Guy Stephens, News Director

Lake Forest

***WMXM**
09-10-1973; 88.9 mhz FM *Hrs Open:* 18; 0.295 kw; 95 ft.; N42 14 59 W87 49 44
555 N. Sheridan Rd., Lake Forest, IL 60045 US

RADIO - U.S.

(847) 735-5220, *Fax:* (847) 735-6291
www.wmxm.org
wmxmgm@lakeforest.edu
License: Lake Forest, Lake County, IL held by Lake Forest College.
Arbitron Metro Market: Chicago, IL *Format:* Classic Rock, Variety/Diverse *Special Programming:* Black 6 hrs, class 3 hrs, gospel 3 hrs, jazz 6 hrs *Hrs. of News Programming:* news progmg 5 hrs wkly *No. NewsEmployees:* 2 *Target Audience:* 18-25; students
April Arellano, General Manager
Cleo Hehn, Programming Director

Lansing

WSRB
08-28-1961; 106.3 mhz FM *Hrs Open:* 24; 4.1 kw; 397 ft.; N41 34 44 W87 32 47
P.O. Box 3003, Blue Bell, PA 19422 US
(773) 928-9230, *Fax:* (219) 933-4455
www.soul1063radio.com
wycainfo@crawfordbroadcasting.com
License: Lansing, Cook County, IL held by Dontron Inc.
Group Owner: Crawford Broadcasting Co.; (acq 4-10-97; $14.8 million).
Nat'l Network: ABC
Arbitron Metro Market: Chicago *Format:* Black, Blues *Target Audience:* 25-54; urban, adult, African-American

Lasalle

WLPO
11-16-1947; 1220 khz AM *Hrs Open:* 24; 1 kw-D, DA2; 0.5 kw-N, DA2; N41 18 14 W89 5 44
P. O. Box 215, Lasalle, IL 61301 US
(815) 223-3100, *Fax:* (815) 223-3095
wlpo.net
License: Lasalle, IL held by La Salle County Broadcasting Corp.
Group Owner: La Salle County Broadcasting Corp.; (acq 8-1-49)
Format: News, News/Talk, 84, Talk *Hrs. of News Programming:* news progmg 35 hrs wkly *No. News Employees:* 3 *Target Audience:* 30 plus.
Peter Miler, President
Joyce McCullough, Operations Dir
Mark Lippert, General Sales Mgr
John Spencer, Programming Director
Jennifer Nagle, News Director
Steve Vogler, Engineering Dir
Becky Roberts, Office Manager

Lawrenceville

WAKO
06-09-1959; 910 khz AM *Hrs Open:* 5 AM-midnight; 0.5 kw-D, DA2; 0.05 kw-N, DA2; N38 43 23 W87 39 13
P.O. Box 210, Lawrenceville, IL 62439 US
(618) 943-3354, *Fax:* (618) 943-4173
www.wakoradio.com
wakoradio@yahoo.com
License: Lawrenceville, IL held by Lawrenceville Broadcasting Co. Inc.
Nat'l Network: Westwood One *Wire Services:* AP
Arbitron Metro Market: Lawrenceville, IL *Format:* Adult Contemp, Country *Hrs. of News Programming:* news progmg 12 hrs wkly *No. News Employees:* 1 *Target Audience:* 20-65+.
Stuart Kent Lankford, President

WAKO-FM
03-01-1965; 103.1 mhz FM *Hrs Open:* 19; 6 kw; 328 ft.; N38 43 23 W87 39 13
P. O. Box 210, Lawrenceville, IL 62439 US
(618) 943-3354, *Fax:* (618) 943-4173
www.wakoradio.com
wakoradio@yahoo.com
License: Lawrenceville, Lawrence County, IL
Wire Services: CNN; AP
Arbitron Metro Market: Lawrenceville, IL *Adv. Rates:* 15; 30; 20; 60
Stuart Kent Lankford, General Manager
Steve Anderson, News Director

Le Roy

WBWN
10-15-1979; 104.1 mhz FM *Hrs Open:* 24; 47 kw; 328 ft.; N40 25 26 W88 52 27
P.O. Box 8, Bloomington, IL 61702 US
(309) 829-1221, *Fax:* (309) 662-8598
www.wbwn.com
dan@wbwn.com
License: Le Roy, McLean County, IL
Group Owner: Townsquare Media; (acq 5-12-2004; grpsl).
Nat'l Reps: McGavren Guild
Arbitron Metro Market: Bloomington, IL *Format:* Country *Target Audience:* 25-45. *Adv. Rates:* 70; 50; 50; 15
Red Pitcher, Station Manager
Dan Westhoff, Programming Director
Julie Penn, Sales Director

Lemont

WVIX
04-17-1960; 93.5 mhz FM *Hrs Open:* 24; 6 kw; 328 ft.; N41 36 39 W88 0 33 *Rebroadcasts:* Simulcast with WVIV-FM Highland Park
8800 Route 14, Crystal Lake, IL 60012 US
(312) 981-1800, *Fax:* (312) 981-1806
maximamusica.univision.com
License: Lemont, Will County, IL held by HBC License Corp.
Group Owner: Univision Radio; (acq 9-22-2003; grpsl).
Arbitron Metro Market: Chicago, IL *Format:* Spanish *Hrs. of News Programming:* one *No. News Employees:* 1
Cesar Canales, Operations Dir
Jerry Ryan, General Manager
Armando Reyes, Programming Director
Joshua Sigstad, Engineering Dir

Lena

WQLF
08-02-2002; 102.1 mhz FM *Hrs Open:* 24; 5.2 kw; 351 ft.; N42 20 31 W89 48 21
Mailing Address: 530 Quail Drive, Lena, IL 61048 US
Second Address: 834 N. Tower Rd., Freeport, IL 61032
(815) 235-7191, *Fax:* (815) 235-4318
www.bigradio.fm
License: Lena, Stephenson County, IL held by Scott A. Thompson dba Big Radio
Arbitron Metro Market: Freeport, IL *Format:* Contemporary Hits/Top 40, Adult Contemp *Special Programming:* Off the Record with Joe Benson 1 hr; Wolfman Jack Hits of the 70s & 80s 5 hrs; American Top 40 from the 80s *Hrs.of News Programming:* news progmg 3 hrs wkly *No. News Employees:* 4 *Target Audience:* 20-49. *Adv. Rates:* 12; 12; 12; 12
Kent McConnell, Operations Dir
Wyatt Herrmann, Programming Director
Becky Koester, News Director
Todd Hauser, Chief Engineer

Lexington

WZIM(FM)
01-01-2004; 99.5 mhz FM *Hrs Open:* 24; 6 kw; Ant 328 ft; N40 34 30 W88 50 15
108 Boeykens Place, Normal, IL 61761
(309) 888-4496, *Fax:* (309) 452-9677
www.eagleclassicrock.com
cody@gpmbloomington.com?subject=Inquiry%20From%2099.5%20The%20Ticket
License: Lexington, McLean County, IL held by Pilot Media LLC.
Group Owner: Great Plains Media Inc.; (acq 6-19-2007; grpsl)
Wire Services: NBC
Population Served: 52,772 *Arbitron Metro Market:* Normal, IL *Hrs. of News Programming:* News progmg 2 hrs wkly *Target Audience:* 25-54.
Cody Welling, General Sales Manager
Robert Rees, Programming Director

Lincoln

WLLM
04-01-1951; 1370 khz AM *Hrs Open:* 24; 1 kw-D, ND1; 0.035 kw-N, ND1; N40 8 24 W89 23 10
3501 Sangamon Avenue, Springfield, IL 62707 US
(217) 735-9735, *Fax:* (217) 735-9736
www.wllmradio.com
License: Lincoln, IL held by Cornerstone Community Radio Inc.
Nat'l Network: USA
Format: Christian, Easy Listening
Beverly Tibbs, Operations Dir
Richard Van Zandt, General Manager
William Dolan, Station Manager
Pamela Pollard, Executive Assistant

*WLNX
01-28-1974; 88.9 mhz FM *Hrs Open:* 24; 0.225 kw; 69 ft.; N40 9 23 W89 21 40
300 Keokuk Street, Lincoln, IL 62656 US
(217) 732-3155, *Fax:* (217) 732-3715
www.wlnxradio.com
info@wlnxradio.com
License: Lincoln, Logan County, IL held by Lincoln University.
Target Audience: 18-34; adults
John Malone, General Manager

Lincolnshire

*WAES
01-01-2002; 88.1 mhz FM; 0.15 kw; 49 ft.; N42 11 59 W87 56 49
Two Stevenson Drive, Lincolnshire, IL 60069 US
(847) 634-4000 ext. 1710, *Fax:* (847) 634-0983
License: Lincolnshire, Lake County, IL held by Adlai E. Stevenson High School District No. 125.
Format: Variety/Diverse
Greg Sherwin, General Manager

Litchfield

WSMI
11-02-1950; 1540 khz AM; 1 kw-D, NDD; N39 10 21 W89 34 14
Mailing Address: P. O. Box 10, Litchfield, IL 62056 US
Second Address: 6308 IL Rt. 16, Hillsboro, IL 62049
(217) 324-5921, *Fax:* (217) 532-2431
wsmiradio.com
wsmi@wsmiradio.com
License: Litchfield, IL held by Talley Broadcasting Corp.
Group Owner: Talley Radio Stations
Nat'l Network: CNN Radio *Nat'l Reps:* Christal *Wire Services:* AP
Format: Country, News, 62, Talk *Special Programming:* Farm 18 hrs wkly *Hrs. of News Programming:* news progmg 15 hrs wkly *No. News Employees:* 3 *Target Audience:* General.
Hayward Talley, President
Brian Talley, Operations Dir
Michael Niehaus, General Sales Mgr
Kevin Talley, Promotions Manager

WSMI-FM
03-05-1960; 106.1 mhz FM *Hrs Open:* 4:30 AM-midnight; 50 kw; 500 ft; N39 15 21 W89 36 48
Mailing Address: Box 10, WSMI Bldg, Litchfield, IL 62056
Second Address: 6308 IL Rt. 16, Hillsboro, IL 62049
(217) 324-5921, *Fax:* (217) 532-2431
License: Litchfield, Montgomery County, IL
Group Owner: Talley Radio Stations
Nat'l Network: NBC *Nat'l Reps:* Katz Radio; Christal *Wire Services:* AP
Population Served: 600,000*Special Programming:* Farm *No. News Employees:* 3
Haywrd Talley, President
Brian Talley, Operations Dir
Mike Niehaus, General Sales Mgr
Terry Todt, Programming Director
Rick Davis, News Director
Tobin Ott, Local News Editor

Lockport

*WLRA
11-01-1972; 88.1 mhz FM *Hrs Open:* 24; 0.14 kw; 131 ft.; N41 36 10 W88 4 49
500 Independence Blvd, M/C 528, Romeoville, IL 60446 US
(815) 838-0500, *Fax:* (815) 838-9149
www.lewisu.edu/wlra
wlraradio@lewisu.edu
License: Lockport, Will County, IL held by Lewis University.
Nat'l Network: AP Network News *Wire Services:* AP
Arbitron Metro Market: Chicago, IL *Format:* Variety/Diverse *Special Programming:* Black 15 hrs, class 6 hrs, jazz 15 hrs, sports 15 *Hrs. of News Programming:* News progmg 6 hrs wkly *Target Audience:* 13-30;college bound or post-college
John Carey, General Manager

Loves Park

*WGSL
03-28-1988; 91.1 mhz FM; 7 kw; 528 ft.; N42 19 20 W89 0 41
Mailing Address: 5375 Pebble Creek Trail, Rockford, IL 61111 US
Second Address: 5375 Pebble Creek Tr., Loves Park, IL 61111
(815) 654-1200, *Fax:* (815) 282-7779
www.radio91.com
home@radio91.com
License: Loves Park, Winnebago County, IL held by Quest for Life Inc.
Nat'l Network: USA
Arbitron Metro Market: Rockford, IL *Format:* Religious *Target Audience:* 35-50; older families
Ron Tietsort, Operations Dir
Ralph Trendadue, General Manager

WLUV
09-29-1962; 1520 khz AM; 0.5 kw-D, ND2; 0.0125 kw-N, ND2; N42 19 48 W89 4 58
Mailing Address: 2272 Elmwood Rd, Loves Park, IL 61032 US
Second Address: 2272 Elmwood Rd., Rockford, IL 61103
(815) 877-9588, *Fax:* (815) 877-9649
License: Loves Park, IL held by Loves Park Broadcasting Co.

Arbitron Metro Market: Rockford, IL *Format:* Country, Sports *Special Programming:* Farm 6 hrs, polka 6 hrs wkly *Target Audience:* 25-60; blue collar workers
Joe Salvi, General Manager

WKGL-FM
03-25-1964; 96.7 mhz FM; 2.2 kw; 551 ft.; N42 21 48 W89 8 6
2272 Elmwood Rd., Rockford, IL 61103 US
(815) 399-2233, *Fax:* (815) 484-2432
www.967theeagle.net
Becky.Riojas@cumulus.com
License: Loves Park, Winnebago County, IL held by Cumulus Licensing Corp.
Group Owner: Cumulus Media Inc.; (acq 3-12-2001).
Arbitron Metro Market: Rockford, IL *Format:* Classic Rock
Becky Riojas, General Manager
Linda Sweeney, General Sales Mgr
John Brizolla, Programming Director
Allisia Bri-Asperson, Promotions Manager
Paul Hannigan, News Director
John Huntley, Chief Engineer
Jan Thorp, Traffic Manager

Lynnville

WEAI
11-15-1989; 107.1 mhz FM *Hrs Open:* 5 AM-midnight; 6 kw; 328 ft.; N39 37 16 W90 15 28
Mailing Address: P.O. Box 1180, Jacksonville, IL 62651 US
Second Address: 2161 Old State Rd., Jacksonville, IL 62651
(217) 245-7171, *Fax:* (217) 245-6711
www.wlds.com/
weai@weai.com
License: Lynnville, Morgan County, IL held by Jacksonville Area Radio Broadcasters Inc.
Nat'l Network: NBC Radio *Regional Network:* Ill. Radio Net. *Nat'l Reps:* Katz Radio *Wire Services:* AP
Arbitron Metro Market: Jacksonville, IL *Format:* Oldies *Hrs. of News Programming:* news progmg 6 hrs wkly *No. News Employees:* 3 *Target Audience:* 20-40; active young adults
Gary Scott, General Manager
Mark Whalen, General Sales Mgr
Perry Brown, Programming Director
Kevin Baxter, News Director
John Coe, Chief Engineer
Troy Armstrong, Music Director
Marty Megginson, Traffic Manager

Macomb

***WIUM**
05-23-1956; 91.3 mhz FM *Hrs Open:* 24; 50 kw; 486 ft.; N40 25 40 W90 40 58
1 University Circle, Macomb, IL 61455 US
(309) 298-2424, *Fax:* (309) 298-2133
www.tristatesradio.com
publicradio@wiu.edu
License: Macomb, McDonough County, IL held by Western Illinois University.
Nat'l Network: NPR; PRI
Format: News *Special Programming:* Folk/blues 7 hrs, jazz 5 hrs wkly *Hrs. of News Programming:* news progmg 58 hrs wkly *No. News Employees:* 2 *Target Audience:* General.
Ken Thermon, Operations Dir
Dorothy Vallillo, General Manager
Sharon Faust, General Sales Mgr
Rich Egger, News Director
Mark Garrett, Chief Engineer

***WIUS**
02-01-1982; 88.3 mhz FM; 0.12 kw horiz; 82 ft.; N40 27 47 W90 41 0
1 University Circle, Macomb, IL 61455 US
(309) 298-3217, *Fax:* (309) 298-2133
www.wiu.edu/the dog/
License: Macomb, McDonough County, IL held by Western Illinois University.
Format: Alternative, Urban Contemporary *Special Programming:* Jazz 2 hrs, Sp 3 hrs, blues 4 hrs wkly *Target Audience:* 18-30.
Patrick Stout, Station Manager

WJEQ
02-01-1983; 102.7 mhz FM *Hrs Open:* 24; 10 kw; 512 ft.; N40 25 3 W90 36 51
31 East Side Square, Macomb, IL 61455 US
(309) 833-2121, *Fax:* (309) 836-3291
www.wjeq.com
wjeq@macomb.com
License: Macomb, McDonough County, IL held by Central Illinois Broadcasting.
Format: Classic Rock *Special Programming:* Farm one hr wkly *Hrs. of News Programming:* news progmg 10 hrs wkly *No. News Employees:* 1 *Target Audience:* 18-49.
Bruce Foster, President
Nancy Foster, General Manager
Karen Kearne, General Sales Mgr
Mike Grillette, Programming Director
Mick Wilkens, News Director
Shana Drake, Traffic Manager

WKAI
06-06-1966; 100.1 mhz FM *Hrs Open:* 24; 25 kw; 282 ft.; N40 32 1 W90 51 45
P.O. Box 250, Macomb, IL 61455 US
(309) 833-5561, *Fax:* (309) 833-3460
www.radiomacomb.com
wkai@macomb.com
License: Macomb, McDonough County, IL held by WPW Broadcasting Inc.
Group Owner: Prairie Radio Communications
Format: Adult Contemp *Hrs. of News Programming:* news progmg 5 hrs wkly *No. News Employees:* 1 *Target Audience:* 35 plus. *Adv. Rates:* 10; 10; 10; na
Julie Kahn, General Manager

WLRB
07-04-1947; 1510 khz AM *Hrs Open:* Sunrise-sunset; 0.25 kw-C, NDD; 1 kw-D, NDD; N40 29 50 W90 40 30
P.O. Box 250, Macomb, IL 61455 US
(309) 833-5561, *Fax:* (309) 833-3460
www.radiomacomb.com
wlrb@macomb.com
License: Macomb, IL held by WPW Broadcasting Inc.
Group Owner: Prairie Radio Communications; (acq 12-27-99; grpsl)
Nat'l Network: Westwood One; Jones Radio Networks *Regional Network:* Brownfield
Format: Contemporary Hits/Top 40 *Special Programming:* Farm 1.25 hrs wkly *Hrs. of News Programming:* news progmg 6 hrs wkly *No. News Employees:* 1 *Target Audience:* 45 plus. *Adv. Rates:* 10; 10; 10; na
Don Davis, President
Mike Weaver, Operations Dir
Vanessa Wetterling, General Manager
Mike Weave, Programming Director

WNLF
01-01-2003; 95.9 mhz FM; 6 kw; 328 ft.; N40 25 3 W90 36 51
C/O Wjeq Radio, 31 E Side Square, Macomb, IL 91455 US
(309) 833-2121, *Fax:* (309) 836-3291
www.wnlffm.com
radio@prestigeradio.com
License: Macomb, McDonough County, IL held by Nancy L. Foster.
Arbitron Metro Market: Macomb, IL *Format:* Rock/AOR
Bruce Foster, President
Nancy Foster, General Manager
Karen Kearne, General Sales Mgr
Mike Grillette, Programming Director
Mick Wilkens, News Director
Shana Drake, Traffic Manager

Macon

WZUS
05-05-1977; 100.9 mhz FM *Hrs Open:* 24; 6 kw; Ant 328 ft; N39 47 11 W88 59 29
410 N. Water St., Suite B, Decatur, IL 62568
(217) 428-4487, *Fax:* (217) 428-4501
www.decaturradio.com
cbullock@cromwellradio.com
License: Macon, Macon County, IL held by The Cromwell Group Inc. of Illinois.
Group Owner: The Cromwell Group Inc.; (acq 4-16-02; $900,000).
Nat'l Network: Cumulus Radio Network; Premiere Radio Network; Talk Radio Network *Regional Network:* Cromwell Ag Radio Network *Nat'l Reps:* Eastman Radio
Population Served: 200,000 *Arbitron Metro Market:* Decatur, IL *Special Programming:* Farm 8 hrs wkly *Target Audience:* General.
Tara Nickerson, Operations Dir
Chris Bullock, General Manager
Larry Timmons, Chief Engineer

Mahomet

WGKC
12-15-1990; 105.9 mhz FM *Hrs Open:* 24; 2.5 kw; 512 ft.; N40 13 27 W88 17 56
400 North Broadway, Urbana, IL 61801 US
(217) 367-1195, *Fax:* (217) 367-3291
www.wgkc.net
ken.cunningham@sjbroadcasting.com
License: Mahomet, Champaign County, IL held by RadioStar Inc.
Group Owner: RadioStar Inc.; (acq 5-23-2006; grpsl).
Nat'l Reps: McGavren Guild
Arbitron Metro Market: Champaign, IL *Format:* Classic Rock *No. News Employees:* 1 *Target Audience:* 25-54; adult men
Jim Glassman, President
Roxanne Charles, General Manager
Steve Miller, General Sales Mgr
Ken Cunningham, Programming Director
Josh Laskowski, Promotions Manager
Jon Hall, Chief Engineer
Donna Keleher, Office Manager

Marion

***WAWJ**
01-01-2001; 90.1 mhz FM; 3 kw vert; 344 ft.; N37 51 23 W89 8 22
P O Drawer 2440, Tupelo, MS 38803 US
(662) 844-8888, *Fax:* (662) 842-6791
www.afa.net
License: Marion, Williamson County, IL held by American Family Association.
Group Owner: American Family Radio
Arbitron Metro Market: Great Falls MT *Format:* Christian
Marvin Sanders, General Manager

WGGH
09-24-1949; 1150 khz AM *Hrs Open:* 24 hrs; 5 kw-D, DA2; 0.044 kw-N, DA2; N37 43 47 W88 53 44
P.O. Box 340, Marion, IL 62959 US
(618) 993-8102, *Fax:* (618) 997-2305
www.wggh.net
wggh@shawneelink.net,wggh@wggh.net
License: Marion, IL held by Vine Broadcasting Inc.
Nat'l Network: Salem Radio Network *Regional Network:* Ill. Radio Net.
Arbitron Metro Market: Marion-Carbondale (Southern Illinois)
Format: Country, News, 62, Talk *Hrs. of News Programming:* News progmg Hourly *Target Audience:* 18 plus; general
Elaine Gomez, General Manager
Mat Canon, Programming Director
Brenda Bender, News Director
Johnny Gomez, Chief Engineer

Maroa

WDKR
05-01-1996; 107.3 mhz FM *Hrs Open:* 24; 3 kw; 456 ft.; N39 57 56 W89 3 27
602 Woodland Court, Mt. Zion, IL 62549 US
(217) 864-4141, *Fax:* (217) 864-4727
wxfmwdkr@comcast.net
License: Maroa, Macon County, IL held by WDKR Inc.
Arbitron Metro Market: Decatur, IL *Format:* Oldies *Target Audience:* 25-54; general *Adv. Rates:* 23.55; 23.55; 23.55; 23.55
Mary Ellen Burns, General Manager

Marseilles

WLWF(FM)
03-01-1992; 96.5 mhz FM *Hrs Open:* 24; 3 kw; 328 ft; N41 18 40 W88 49 07
1 Broadcast Ln., Oglesby, IL 61348
(815) 233-3100, *Fax:* (815) 223-3095
www.wkot.com
john@wajk.com
License: Marseilles, La Salle County, IL held by La Salle County Broadcasting Corp.
Group Owner: La Salle County Broadcasting Corp.; acq 6-99; $550,000
Nat'l Network: Jones Radio Networks
Format: Contemporary Hits/Top 40, Adult Contemp *Hrs. of News Programming:* news progmg 8 hrs wkly *No. News Employees:* 1 *Target Audience:* 35-54.
Peter Miller, President
Joyce McCullough, Operations Dir
John Spencer, Programming Director
Jennifer Nagle, News Director

Marshall

WMMC
10-02-1989; 105.9 mhz FM *Hrs Open:* 24; 2.3 kw; 528 ft.; N39 21 9 W87 49 19
Mailing Address: 1477 Radcliff Ln., Aurora, IL 60504 US
Second Address: 627 1/2 Archer Ave., Marshall, IL 62441

(217) 826-8017, *Fax:* (217) 826-8519
www.wmmcradio.com/
WMMC106@aol.com
License: Marshall, Clark County, IL held by JDL Broadcasting Inc.
Nat'l Network: ABC
Arbitron Metro Market: Terre Haute, IN *Format:* Oldies *Hrs. of News Programming:* News progmg 8 hrs wkly *Target Audience:* 25-54; career-oriented men and women
J. Spangler, President
Lori Spangler, Operations Dir

Mattoon

WLBH
11-26-1946; 1170 khz AM *Hrs Open:* 6 AM-7 PM; 5 kw-D, DAD; N39 31 5 W88 22 15
PO Box 1848, North Route 45, Mattoon, IL 61938 US
(217) 234-6464, *Fax:* (217) 234-6019
License: Mattoon, IL held by Mattoon Broadcasting Co.
Group Owner: J.R. Livesay Group
Format: Adult Contemp, News, 62, Talk *Special Programming:* Relg 5 hrs wkly *Hrs. of News Programming:* news progmg 20 hrs wkly *No. News Employees:* 3 *Target Audience:* 25 plus.
J.R. Livesay, Chairman
J.R. Livesay II, CEO
Adam Kennedy, News Director
S.L. Herrington, CFO
Chase Arnold, Political Ed

WLBH-FM
08-01-1949; 96.9 mhz FM *Hrs Open:* 24; 50 kw; 499 ft.; N39 31 2 W88 22 13
P. O. Box 1848, Mattoon, IL 61938 US
(217) 234-6464, *Fax:* (217) 234-6019
License: Mattoon, Coles County, IL held by Mattoon Broadcasting Co.
Group Owner: J.R. Livesay Group
Format: Adult Contemp *Hrs. of News Programming:* news progmg 18 hrs wkly *No. News Employees:* 3 *Target Audience:* 25 plus.
S.L. Herrington, CFO
J.R. Livesay II, General Manager
Adam Kennedy, News Director
J.R. Livesay, Chairman/CEO
Chase Arnold, Political Ed

*WLKL
01-20-1975; 89.9 mhz FM *Hrs Open:* 24; 1.3 kw; 203 ft.; N39 25 7 W88 22 55
Lake Land College, 5001 Lake Land Blvd, Mattoon, IL 61938 US
(217) 234-5373, *Fax:* (217) 234-5506
www.899themax.com
gpowers@lakeland.cc.il.us
License: Mattoon, Coles County, IL held by Community College District 517 Lake Land College.
Format: Rock/AOR *Hrs. of News Programming:* news progmg 6 hrs wkly *No. News Employees:* 1 *Target Audience:* 18-34; general *Adv. Rates:* 5; 4; 4; 5
Greg Powers, General Manager

McLeansboro

WMCL
01-26-1968; 1060 khz AM *Hrs Open:* 24; 2.5 kw-D, DAD; 0.002 kw-N, DAD; N38 6 16 W88 33 48
303 North Main, P.O. Box 818, Benton, IL 62812 US
(618) 435-4392, *Fax:* (618) 643-3299
www.wqrlradio.com
wishfm989@gmail.com
License: McLeansboro, IL held by Dana Communications Corp.
Nat'l Network: CNN Radio
Arbitron Metro Market: McLeansboro, IL *Format:* Country *Target Audience:* 25-65; agricultural community
Dana Withers, President
Gloria Holland, Operations Dir

Mendota

WGLC-FM
09-01-1965; 100.1 mhz FM; 6 kw; 328 ft.; N41 32 16 W89 6 25
Mailing Address: P O Box 88, Mendota, IL 61342 US
Second Address: 3905 Progress Blvd., Peru, IL 61354
(815) 224-2100, *Fax:* (815) 225-2066
www.wglc.net
wglc@theradiogroup.net
License: Mendota, La Salle County, IL held by Mendota Broadcasting Inc.
Group Owner: Studstill Broadcasting; (acq 4-8-88)
Nat'l Network: ABC *Nat'l Reps:* Rgnl Reps *Wire Services:* AP
Arbitron Metro Market: La Salle-Peru, IL *Format:* Country *Target Audience:* 35 plus.
Lee Studstill, CEO
Owen Studstill, President
Cole Studstill, Operations Dir
Stuart Hall, Operations Director
Chris Turnow, Operations Manager

Metropolis

WMOK
02-04-1951; 920 khz AM *Hrs Open:* 24
3501 Broadway, P.O. Box 1508, Mount Vernon, IL 62864 US
(618) 524-4400, *Fax:* (618) 524-3133
http://www.920wmok.com
wmok920@frontier.com
License: Metropolis, IL held by Withers Broadcasting Co. of Paducah LLC.
Group Owner: Withers Broadcasting Co.; (acq 9-11-97; grpsl).
Arbitron Metro Market: Metropolis, IL *Format:* Country *Special Programming:* Relg 5 hrs wkly *No. News Employees:* 1 *Target Audience:* General.
Rick Lambert, General Manager
Melanie Shepherd, General Sales Mgr
Evan Spencer, Programming Director
Evan Spencer, News Director
Smokey King, Chief Engineer

WREZ
12-12-1988; 105.5 mhz FM *Hrs Open:* 24; 6 kw; 328 ft.; N37 10 25 W88 42 29
3501 Broadway, P.O. Box 1508, Mount Vernon, IL 62864 US
(270) 538-5251, *Fax:* (270) 415-0599
License: Metropolis, Massac County, IL held by Withers Broadcasting Co. of Paducah LLC
Group Owner: Withers Broadcasting Co.
Format: Adult Contemp
Steve Thompson, Programming Director

WRIK-FM
07-11-1984; 98.3 mhz FM; 100 kw; 699 ft.; N36 45 9 W88 29 58
6120 Waldo Church Rd, Metropolis, IL 62960 US
, *Fax:* (618) 564-3202
K98@hitsandfavs.com
License: Metropolis, Massac County, IL held by Sun Media Inc.
Format: Adult Contemp
Samuel Stratemeyer, President
Willie Kerns, Operations Dir

Milford

*WJCZ
01-01-2005; 91.3 mhz FM; 25 kw; 89 ft.; N40 35 7 W87 57 47 US
(800) 357-4226, *Fax:* (208) 736-1958
www.csnradio.com
csn@csnradio.com
License: Milford, Iroquois County, IL held by CSN International
Group Owner: CSN International
Arbitron Metro Market: Milford, IL *Format:* Christian
Mike Kestler, President
Daniel Davidson, Operations Dir
Mike Stockland, General Manager
Don Mills, Network Programming Director / Music Director
Kelly Carlson, Engineering Dir
Jerry Johnson, Engineering Dir
Ray Gorney, AssistantDirector of Engineering
Dustin Pamplona, Engineer
Nolan Mather, Graphics / Website Maintenance
Mike Stocklin, National Underwriting
Austin Morris, Accounting
Lois Mills, FCC Applications / Translator Site Manager

Moline

WFXN
01-01-1946; 1230 khz AM *Hrs Open:* 24; 1 kw-U, ND1; N41 28 54 W90 31 49
3535 East Kimberly Road, Davenport, IA 52807 US
(563) 344-7000, *Fax:* (563) 359-8524
www.wfxn.net
ronevans@clearchannel.com
License: Moline, IL held by Citicasters Licenses L.P.
Group Owner: Clear Channel Communications Inc.; (acq 11-15-00; grpsl).
Arbitron Metro Market: Quad Cities, IA *Format:* Country *Special Programming:* Sports 8 hrs, pub affrs 4 hrs, farm one hr wkly *Hrs. of News Programming:* news progmg 6 hrs wkly *No. News Employees:* 1 *TargetAudience:* 25-54; upscale/contemp
Jeff Ashcraft, General Sales Mgr
Ron Evans, Programming Director
John Laton, Promotions Manager
Kevin Allensworth, Chief Engineer
Gordon Ehler, General Sales Manager

WXLP
11-22-1970; 96.9 mhz FM; 50 kw; 499 ft.; N41 20 16 W90 22 46
1229 Brady Street, Davenport, IA 52803 US
(563) 326-2541, *Fax:* (563) 326-1819
www.97x.com
License: Moline, Rock Island County, IL held by Cumulus Licensing Corp.
Group Owner: Cumulus Media Inc.; (acq 3-15-2000; grpsl)
Nat'l Network: Westwood One
Arbitron Metro Market: Quad Cities, IA *Format:* Classic Rock *Target Audience:* 25-54.
Darren Pitra, Operations Dir
Jack Swart, General Manager
Julie Derrer, General Sales Mgr
Dave Levora, Programming Director
Tracey Hall, News Director
Andy Andresen, Chief Engineer
Cheryl Riley-Hayles, Market Manager

Monee

*WOTW
11-01-1995; 88.9 mhz FM; 0.1 kw vert; 177 ft.; N41 24 47.9 W87 46 2.8
820 N. Lasalle Blvd., Chicago, IL 60610 US
(312) 329-4300, *Fax:* (312) 329-4339
www.ktlw.org
ktlwinfo@ktlw.net
License: Monee, Will County, IL held by Life on the Way Communications Inc.
Format: Christian, Religious *Target Audience:* General.
Gary Curtis, Operations Dir
Doug Hastings, Station Manager
Pamela McCain, Operations Manager

Monmouth

WMOI
12-06-1967; 97.7 mhz FM *Hrs Open:* 24; 3.4 kw; 440 ft.; N40 53 25 W90 36 31
PO Box 885, Monmouth, IL 61462 US
(309) 734-9452, *Fax:* (309) 734-3276
www.977wmoi.com
License: Monmouth, Warren County, IL
Group Owner: Prairie Radio Communications
Regional Network: Tribune Radio Networks
Arbitron Metro Market: Monouth, IL *Format:* Adult Contemp *Hrs. of News Programming:* news progmg 40 hrs wkly *No. News Employees:* 3 *Target Audience:* General. *Adv. Rates:* 20; 20; 20; 14.50
D. Richard Teubner, President
Gail Teubner, Operations Dir

WRAM
05-01-1957; 1330 khz AM *Hrs Open:* 6 AM-6 PM; 1 kw-D, DA2; 0.05 kw-N, DA2; N40 56 59 W90 34 19
PO Box 885, Monmouth, IL 61462 US
(309) 734-9452, *Fax:* (309) 734-3276
www.977wmoi.com
License: Monmouth, IL held by WPW Broadcasting Inc.
Group Owner: Prairie Radio Communications; (acq 12-24-97; $1.7 million with co-located FM)
Nat'l Network: ABC *Regional Network:* Tribune Radio Networks
Format: Country *Special Programming:* Farm 18 hrs, relg 3 hrs wkly *Hrs. of News Programming:* news progmg 20 hrs wkly *No. News Employees:* 3 *Target Audience:* General; adult, mature
Don Davis, President
David Klockenga, General Manager

Monticello

WCZQ
01-18-1972; 105.5 mhz FM *Hrs Open:* 24; 6 kw; 328 ft.; N40 2 54 W88 34 25
1705 West Northwest Highway, Suite 275, Grapevine, TX 76051 US
(217) 762-2588, *Fax:* (217) 423-9764
www.wczq.piatt.com
wczq@piatt.com
License: Monticello, Piatt County, IL held by Neuhoff Family L.P.
Group Owner: Neuhoff Family L.P.; (acq 2-23-2009; grpsl)
Nat'l Network: ABC
Arbitron Metro Market: Champaign, IL *Format:* Urban Contemporary *Special Programming:* Farm 11 hrs wkly *Hrs. of News Programming:* News progmg 5 hrs wkly *Target Audience:* 25-65; upscale suburban & prosperousfarm *Adv. Rates:* 17; 17; 17; 17
Mark Hanson, General Manager
Wendy Tohill, General Sales Mgr
Jamie Pendleton, Programming Director

Cindy Hansen, News Director
Frank Konwinski, Chief Engineer

Morris

*WCFL
01-01-1962; 104.7 mhz FM *Hrs Open:* 24; 50 kw; 496 ft; N41 21 17 W88 29 55 *Rebroadcasts:* Rebroadcasts WBGL(FM) Champaign 100%
409 North Liberty Street, Suite 403, Morris, IL 62626
(815) 942-4400, *Fax:* (815) 942-4401
www.wbgl.org
wbgl@wbgl.org
License: Morris, Grundy County, IL held by Illinois District Council of Assembly.
Nat'l Network: USA
Population Served: 1,500,000 *Arbitron Metro Market:* Chicago
Target Audience: 24-39.
Jeff Scott, General Manager

WCSJ
01-15-1964; 1550 khz AM *Hrs Open:* 24; 0.25 kw-D, ND1; 0.006 kw-N, ND1; N41 20 29 W88 25 31
1 Broadcast Center, Plano, IL 60545 US
(815) 941-1000, *Fax:* (815) 941-9300
www.wcsjfm.com
news@NelsonMultimedia.net
License: Morris, IL held by Grundy County Broadcasters Inc.
Arbitron Metro Market: Chicago,IL *Format:* Adult Contemp, News, 62, Talk *Target Audience:* 35 plus. *Adv. Rates:* 42; 31; 36; 25
Larry Nelson, President
Jack Daly, General Manager
Susan Pellegrini, General Sales Mgr

WCSJ-FM
01-01-1993; 103.1 mhz FM *Hrs Open:* 24; 6 kw; 328 ft.; N41 17 35 W88 20 4
11 Skyline Drive, Hawthorne, NY 10532 US
(815) 941-1000, *Fax:* (815) 941-9300
License: Morris, Grundy County, IL held by Grundy County Broadcasters Inc.
Nat'l Network: ABC
Arbitron Metro Market: Chicago *Format:* Adult Contemp, News, 62, Talk *Special Programming:* Farm 10 hrs wkly. *Hrs. of News Programming:* news progmg 20 hrs wkly *No. News Employees:* 1 *Target Audience:* 25plus; community oriented *Adv. Rates:* 42; 31; 36; 25
Larry Nelson, President
Kevin Schramm, Operations Dir
Jack Daly, General Manager

*WBEQ
11-01-2003; 90.7 mhz FM; 1.45 kw; 468 ft.; N41 17 9 W88 25 49
Rebroadcasts: Rebroadcasts WBEZ(FM) Chicago 100%
848 East Grand Ave., Chicago, IL 60611 US
(312) 948-4600, *Fax:* (312) 832 3100
www.wbez.org
questions@webq.org
License: Morris, Grundy County, IL held by The WBEZ Alliance Inc.
Nat'l Network: NPR
Arbitron Metro Market: Morris, IL *Format:* Jazz, News, 62, Talk
Merrill Smith, Chairman
Donna Moore, CFO
Torey Malatia, President and Chief Executive Officer
Greg Salustro, General Sales Mgr
Aurora Aguilar, Project Editor, Front & Center
Daniel O. Ash, Vice President, StrategicCommunications
Sally Eisele, Managing Editor, Public Affairs
Heidi Goldfein, Production Director
Matthew Green, Director of Digital Product Management
Vanessa Harris, Marketing Director

Morrison

WZZT
04-10-1991; 95.1 mhz FM; 6 kw; 328 ft.; N41 50 16 W89 55 29
3501 Broadway, P.O. Box 1508, Mount Vernon, IL 62864 US
(815) 625-3400, *Fax:* (815) 625-6940
wsdr1240@theramp.net
License: Morrison, Whiteside County, IL held by Withers Broadcasting Co. of Rock River LLC.
Group Owner: Withers Broadcasting Co.; (acq 1-21-98; grpsl).
Nat'l Network: ABC *Regional Network:* Ill. Radio Net. *Nat'l Reps:* Christal
Arbitron Metro Market: Sterling, IL *Format:* Classic Rock, Sports
Target Audience: 25-54; adults/men
Brian Zschiesche, General Manager
Kathy Wagner, Programming Director
Mary Carlson, News Director
Sherry Smith, Traffic Manager

Morton

WDQX
11-28-1976; 102.3 mhz FM *Hrs Open:* 24; 6 kw; Ant 300 ft; N40 38 27 W89 24 33
331 Fulton St., Suite 1200, Peoria, IL 34228
(309) 637-3700, *Fax:* (309) 272-1476
www.1023maxfm.com
License: Morton, Tazewell County, IL held by Monterey Licenses LLC.
Group Owner: Triad Broadcasting Co. L.L.C.; (acq 4-21-2006; $5.2 million with WXCL(FM) Pekin)
Nat'l Network: Westwood One; CBS *Regional Network:* Ill. Radio Net.
Population Served: 350,000 *Arbitron Metro Market:* Peoria, IL
Special Programming: Relg one hr wkly *Hrs. of News Programming:* news progmg 10 hrs wkly *No. News Employees:* 1 *Target Audience:* 25 plus;active, affluent males
Joe Swanson, General Manager
Brad Ziegler, Station Manager
A J Wyman, Programming Director
Scott Legath, Engineering Dir
Shawn Newell, Music Director

Mount Carmel

WYNG
11-28-1960; 94.9 mhz FM *Hrs Open:* 24; 50 kw; 420 ft.; N38 23 57 W87 47 18
P.O. Box 242, 1309 Old Orchard Road, Vincennes, IN 47591 US
(618) 263-3500, *Fax:* (618) 263-3520
www.wyng949.com
wyng@wyng949.com
License: Mount Carmel, Wabash County, IL held by W. Russell Withers Jr.
Group Owner: Withers Broadcasting Co.; (acq 12-22-2006; $1.5 million)
Arbitron Metro Market: Mount Carmel, IL *Format:* Adult Contemp
Scott Allen, General Manager
Terry Beckerman, General Sales Mgr
Josh Howard, Programming Director
Josh Baxter, News Director
Rodger Beard, Account Executive
Sally Voight, Account Executive
Denise Hodges, Traffic

*WVJC
07-23-1973; 89.1 mhz FM *Hrs Open:* 24; 50 kw; 331 ft.; N38 26 29 W87 45 26
2200 College Drive, Mt. Carmel, IL 62863 US
(618) 262-8641, *Fax:* (618) 262-8989
www.bashradio.com
peachk@iecc.edu
License: Mount Carmel, Wabash County, IL held by Illinois Eastern Community Colleges.
Arbitron Metro Market: Evansville, IN *Format:* Alternative *Target Audience:* 12-24; general *Adv. Rates:* N/A
Ryan Jenkins, Operations Dir
Kyle Peach, Programming Director

Mount Sterling

WPWQ
09-01-1995; 106.7 mhz FM; 25 kw; 328 ft.; N39 56 33 W90 57 44
P.O Box 196, 142 E. Washington Street, Rushville, IL 62681 US
(217) 224-4653, *Fax:* (217) 885-3233
www.oldies1067.com
wpwq106@adams.net
License: Mount Sterling, Brown County, IL held by WPW Broadcasting Inc.
Group Owner: Prairie Radio Communications; (acq 12-6-99; $550,000 with WKXQ(FM) Rushville)
Format: Oldies
Don Davis, President
Phil Alexander, General Manager
Brian Myles, Programming Director

Mount Vernon

WIBV
01-01-2001; 102.1 mhz FM *Hrs Open:* 24; 10.5 kw; 509 ft.; N38 24 7 W89 8 9
6120 Waldo Church Road, Metropolis, IL 62960 US
(618) 249-6025, *Fax:* (618) 564-3202
www.wibv102.com
jack@wibv102.com
License: Mount Vernon, Jefferson County, IL held by Benjamin Stratemeyer
Arbitron Metro Market: Mount Vernon-Centralia, IL *Format:* Country *Target Audience:* 18-54.
Samuel Stratemeyer, General Manager

*WAPO
01-01-1997; 90.5 mhz FM; 1.1 kw; 203 ft.; N38 18 39 W88 56 11
Po Drawer 2440, Tupelo, MS 38803 US
(662) 844-8888, *Fax:* (662) 842-6791
www.afr.net
faq@afr.net
License: Mount Vernon, Jefferson County, IL held by American Family Association.
Group Owner: American Family Radio
Arbitron Metro Market: Mount Vernon, IL *Format:* Christian, Religious
Marvin Sanders, General Manager
John Riley, Programming Director

*WBMV
09-30-1997; 89.7 mhz FM *Hrs Open:* 24; 10.5 kw vert; 492 ft.; N38 22 15 W88 55 20 *Rebroadcasts:* Rebroadcasts WIBI(FM) Carlinville 100%
P.O. Box 140, Carlinville, IL 62626 US
(217) 854-4800, *Fax:* (217) 854-4810
www.wibi.org/
wibi@wibi.org
License: Mount Vernon, Jefferson County, IL held by Illinois Bible Institute Inc.
Group Owner: Illinois Bible Institute Inc.
Arbitron Metro Market: Carlinville, IL *Format:* Adult Contemp, Christian *Target Audience:* 29-45. *Adv. Rates:* 7; 7; 7; 7
Barry Copeland, General Manager
Tom Greene, Station Manager
Rob Regal, Programming Director
Jessica Barton, Promotions Manager
Sally Braundmeier, News Director
Joe Buchanan, Music Director
Liz Eilers, Underwriting Director
Angie Carpenter, Office Manager
Brian Miller, Donor Relations Director

WMIX
01-01-1947; 940 khz AM *Hrs Open:* 24; 5 kw-D, DA2; 1.5 kw-N, DA2; N38 22 14 W88 55 24; N38 21 15 W89 0 29
Mailing Address: 3501 Broadway, Mount Vernon, IL 62864 US
Second Address: 3501 Broadway, Mount Vernon, IL 62864
(618) 242-3500, *Fax:* (618) 242-2490
www.mywithersradio.com
wmix@mvn.net
License: Mount Vernon, IL held by Withers Broadcasting Co. of Illinois LLC.
Group Owner: Withers Broadcasting Co.; (acq 5-30-73).
Nat'l Network: Westwood One *Wire Services:* AP
Arbitron Metro Market: Moutn Vernon, IL *Format:* Adult Contemp
Special Programming: Farm 18 hrs wkly *Hrs. of News Programming:* news progmg 15 hrs wkly *No. News Employees:* 2 *Target Audience:* 25 plus.
W. Russell Withers Jr., President
Dana Withers, General Manager
Scott Smalls, General Sales Mgr
Nicholas Lemay, News Director

WMIX-FM
01-01-1946; 94.1 mhz FM *Hrs Open:* 24; 50 kw horiz; 551 ft.; N38 22 15 W88 55 20
P. O. Box 1238, Mount Vernon, IL 62864 US
(618) 242-3500, *Fax:* (618) 242-2490
www.mywithersradio.com
wmix@mvn.net
License: Mount Vernon, Jefferson County, IL held by Withers Broadcasting Co. of Illinois LLC
Group Owner: Withers Broadcasting Co.
Arbitron Metro Market: Moutn Vernon, IL *Format:* Country
Russell Withers, CEO
D.T. Brown, Programming Director
Craig Warner, News Director

Mount Zion

WXFM-FM
10-01-1984; 99.3 mhz FM *Hrs Open:* 24; 1.15 kw; 495 ft; N39 48 35 W88 59 31
120 Wildwood Dr., Mount Zion, IL 62549
(217) 864-4141, *Fax:* (217) 864-4727
License: Mount Zion, Macon County, IL held by Technicom Inc.
Nat'l Network: CNN Radio *Regional Network:* Brownfield
Population Served: 300,000*Hrs. of News Programming:* News progmg 5 hrs wkly *Target Audience:* Free spending, affluent adults. *Adv. Rates:* 29; 29; 29; 29
Mary Ellen Burns, President

RADIO - U.S.

Mt. Vernon

***WVSI**
01-01-2003; 88.9 mhz FM *Hrs Open:* 24; 1.9 kw horiz, 4 kw vert; 338 ft.; N38 21 13 W88 56 32 *Rebroadcasts:* Rebroadcasts WSIU(FM) Carbondale
US
(618) 453-4343, *Fax:* (618) 453-6186
wsiu.org
jeff.williams@wsiu.org
License: Mt. Vernon, Jefferson County, IL held by The Board of Trustees of Southern Illinois University.
Nat'l Network: NPR; PRI *Regional Network:* Ill. Radio Net. *Wire Services:* AP
Arbitron Metro Market: Carbondale, IL *Format:* News *Hrs. of News Programming:* news progmg 36 hrs wkly *No. News Employees:* 3
Greg Petrowich, CEO
Mike Zelten, Operations Dir
Jeff Williams, Station Manager
Renee Dillard, General Sales Mgr

Murphysboro

WINI
09-15-1954; 1420 khz AM *Hrs Open:* 24; 0.42 kw-D, DAN; 0.5 kw-N, DAN; N37 45 30 W89 14 2
1677 Business Highway 13, Murphysboro, IL 62966 US
(618) 684-2128, *Fax:* (618) 687-4318
www.winiradio.com
wini@intrnet.net
License: Murphysboro, IL held by Radio Station WINI.
Arbitron Metro Market: Marion-Carbondale (Southern Illinois)
Format: News, News/Talk, 86 *Special Programming:* Relg 6 hrs wkly *Hrs. of News Programming:* News progmg 22 hrs wkly
Target Audience: 25-59.
Nancy Engel, Operations Dir
Dale Adkins, General Manager

WVZA
03-01-1994; 105.1 mhz FM *Hrs Open:* 24; 25 kw; 308 ft.; N37 45 15 W89 19 14
330 East Kilbourn Ave., Suite 250, Milwaukee, WI 53202 US
(618) 997-8123, *Fax:* (618) 993-2319
www.mywithersradio.comvza
License: Murphysboro, Williamson County, IL held by Withers Broadcasting of Southern Illinois LLC.
Group Owner: Withers Broadcasting Co.; (acq 3-17-2008; grpsl)
Arbitron Metro Market: Marion-Carbondale, IL *Format:* Adult Contemp *Target Audience:* W18-49, 25-54.
Paxton Guy, Operations Dir
Janet Jensen, General Manager
Gina Heern, General Sales Mgr
April Bennett, News Director
Tim Deterding, Chief Engineer

Naperville

***WONC**
07-01-1968; 89.1 mhz FM; 1.5 kw; 164 ft.; N41 46 34 W88 11 41
30 N. Brainard St., Naperville, IL 60566 US
(630) 637-8989, *Fax:* (630) 637-5900
www.wonc.org
jvmadormo@noctrl.edu
License: Naperville, Du Page County, IL held by North Central College.
Wire Services: AP
Arbitron Metro Market: Chicago *TV Affiliate:* rock and roll *Format:* Alternative, Religious *Special Programming:* 5 *No. News Employees:* 18-44.
General Manager, General Manager

Nashville

WNSV
07-10-1994; 104.7 mhz FM *Hrs Open:* 24; 3.4 kw; 440 ft.; N38 26 2 W89 18 55
P. O. Box 818, Benton, IL 62812 US
(618) 327-4444, *Fax:* (618) 327-3716
www.v1047.com
angie@v1047.com
License: Nashville, Washington County, IL held by Dana K. Withers.
Arbitron Metro Market: Nashville, IL *Format:* Adult Contemp
Target Audience: 30 plus.
Gloria Holland, Operations Dir
Dana Withers, General Manager

Neoga

WHQQ
09-01-1996; 98.9 mhz FM *Hrs Open:* 24; 3.2 kw; 453 ft.; N39 14 59 W88 22 48
Mailing Address: P.O. Box 150846, Nashville, TN 37215 US
Second Address: 405 S. Banker St., #201, Effingham, IL 62401
(615) 361-7560, *Fax:* (615) 366-4313
www.effinghamradio.com
mphillips@cromwellradio.co
License: Neoga, Cumberland County, IL held by WSHY Inc.
Group Owner: The Cromwell Group Inc.
Nat'l Network: Jones Radio Networks
Format: Oldies *Special Programming:* Farm 7 hrs wkly *Hrs. of News Programming:* News progmg 14 hrs wkly *Target Audience:* 25-54; adults *Adv. Rates:* 15; 12; 15; 10
Bayard Walters, Chairman
Tommy Crocker, CFO
Woody Bushue, Operations Dir
Marv Phillips, General Manager
Kathie St. Claire, Business Manager

Neoga B

WMCI
08-24-1989; 101.3 mhz FM *Hrs Open:* 24; 14.5 kw; 433 ft.; N39 31 39 W88 21 23
209 Lakeland Blvd., Mattoon, IL 37215
(217) 235-5624,(217) 348-9292, *Fax:* (217) 235-6624
www.radiomattoon.com
info@radiomattoon.com
License: Neoga B, Cumberland County, IL held by The Cromwell Group Inc. of Illinois.
Group Owner: The Cromwell Group Inc.
Regional Reps: Katz
Population Served: 100,000*Special Programming:* Farm 5 hrs wkly *Hrs. of News Programming:* news progmg 10 hrs wkly *No. News Employees:* 1 *Target Audience:* 25-54. *Adv. Rates:* 25; 18; 20; 15
Bud Walters, President
Carol Floyd, Station Manager
Bob McCullough, Programming Director

Newton

WIKK
05-04-1992; 103.5 mhz FM *Hrs Open:* 24; 25 kw; 328 ft.; N39 6 20 W88 10 21
P.O. Box 304, Newton, IL 62448 US
(618) 783-8000, *Fax:* (618) 783-4040
www.929thelegend.com
wikk1035@psbnewton.com
License: Newton, Jasper County, IL held by V.L.N. Broadcasting Inc.
Group Owner: Key Broadcasting Inc.; (acq 6-25-2002; $600,000)
Nat'l Network: CNN Radio
Format: Classic Rock *Hrs. of News Programming:* news progmg 8 hrs wkly *No. News Employees:* 1 *Target Audience:* 25-49.
Mike Shipman, Operations Dir
Mark Weiler, News Director

Normal

***WGLT**
02-04-1966; 89.1 mhz FM *Hrs Open:* 24; 25 kw; 377 ft.; N40 28 46 W89 3 12
310 Media Center, Normal, IL 61761 US
(309) 438-2255, *Fax:* (309) 438-7870
www.wglt.org
wglt@IllinoisState.edu
License: Normal, McLean County, IL held by Illinois State University.
Nat'l Network: NPR; PRI; AP Radio *Regional Network:* Ill. Radio Net. *Wire Services:* AP
Format: Blues, Jazz *Special Programming:* Folk 4 hrs, musical theater 2 hrs wkly *Hrs. of News Programming:* news progmg 40 hrs wkly *No. News Employees:* 3 *Target Audience:* 35-54.
Bruce Bergethon, General Manager
Aaron Wissmiller, General Sales Mgr
Mike McCurdy, Programming Director
Linda Healy, Promotions Manager
Willis Kern, News Director
Mark Hill, Chief Engineer
Jon Norton, Music Director
TravisMeadors, Broadcast Technologist
Jeff Paxton, Corporate Support Coordinator
Paat Peterson, Individual Giving Director
Chalrie Schlenker, Assistant News Director
Aaron Wissmiller, Development Director

WIHN
12-21-1973; 96.7 mhz FM *Hrs Open:* 24; 3.9 kw; 410 ft.; N40 28 34 W89 2 2
555 Gulf of Mexico Dr, Suite 201, Longboat Key, FL 34228 US
(309) 834-1100, *Fax:* (309) 834-4390
www.967irock.com
License: Normal, McLean County, IL held by Connoisseur Media of Bloomington LLC.
Group Owner: Connoisseur Media LLC; (acq 11-2-2006; $4 million)
Nat'l Network: ABC *Nat'l Reps:* Christal
Arbitron Metro Market: Bloomington, IL *Hrs. of News Programming:* news progmg 9 hrs wkly *No. News Employees:* 1
Target Audience: 18-44.
Jack Swart, General Manager
Grant Thompson, General Sales Mgr
Adam Chandler, Programming Director
Mark Hill, Chief Engineer

Northbrook

WZRK
05-15-1964; 1550 khz AM; 1 kw-D, DA2; 0.001 kw-N, DA2; N42 35 39 W88 23 24
Mailing Address: PO Box 700, Hwy 50 East, Lake Geneva, WI 53147 US
Second Address: 2300 Riverside Dr., Green Bay, WI 54301
(920) 271-1000, *Fax:* (920) 271-1010
www.sovcity.com
License: Northbrook, IL held by Sovereign City Radio Services LLC
Arbitron Metro Market: North Platte, NE
Scott Krusinski, Operations Dir

Oak Lawn

WNWI
12-31-1965; 1080 khz AM
21700 Northwestern, Tower 14, Suite 1190, Southfield, MI 48075 US
(708) 201-9600, *Fax:* (248) 557-2950
infomacja@wietrzneradio.com
License: Oak Lawn, IL held by Birach Broadcasting Corp.
Group Owner: Birach Broadcasting Corp.; (acq 6-30-95; $375,000).
Arbitron Metro Market: Chicago *TV Affiliate:* Foreign language, Pol

Oak Park

WPNA
10-07-1950; 1490 khz AM *Hrs Open:* 24; 1 kw-U, ND1; N41 52 52 W87 47 38
6100 N. Cicero Avenue, Chicago, IL 60646 US
(708) 848-8980, *Fax:* (708) 848-9220
www.wpna1490am.com
email@wpna1490am.com
License: Oak Park, IL held by Alliance Communications Inc.
Wire Services: AP
Arbitron Metro Market: Chicago *Format:* Ethnic, Polish *Special Programming:* Polka 15 hrs, gospel 2 hrs, blues 4 hrs, relg 4 hrs, Irish 3 hrs, Ukranian 2 hrs wkly *Target Audience:* General.
Frank Spula, President
Alan Kearns, Operations Dir
Emily Leszczynski, General Manager
Jerry Obrecki, General Sales Mgr

WVAZ
10-17-1950; 102.7 mhz FM *Hrs Open:* 24; 6 kw; 1171 ft.; N41 53 56 W87 37 23
800 Wouth Wells, Suite 250, Chicago, IL 60607 US
(312) 540-2000, *Fax:* (312) 938-4404
www.wvaz.com
info@wvaz.com
License: Oak Park, Cook County, IL held by AMFM Broadcasting Licenses LLC.
Group Owner: Clear Channel Communications Inc.; (acq 8-30-2000; grpsl).
Arbitron Metro Market: Chicago, IL *Format:* Adult Contemp, Black
Special Programming: Gospel 4 hrs, pub affrs 2 hrs wkly *Hrs. of News Programming:* news progmg one hr wkly *No. News Employees:* 2 *TargetAudience:* 25-54; Black adults
Elroy Smith, Operations Dir
Anita Genes, General Sales Mgr
Armando Rivera, Programming Director
Angela Ingram, Promotions Manager
Wanda Wells, News Director
Tim Wright, Chief Engineer
Troi Tyler, Disc Jockey
Herb Kent, DiscJockey
Jodie Craigen, Traffic Manager

Oglesby

WALS
02-01-1993; 102.1 mhz FM *Hrs Open:* 24; 2.25 kw; 545 ft.; N41 16 30 W88 57 56
P. O. Box 88, Mendota, IL 67342 US
(877) 855-2480, *Fax:* (815) 224-2066
www.walls102.com
walls102@theradiogroup.net
License: Oglesby, La Salle County, IL held by Laco Radio Inc.
Group Owner: Studstill Broadcasting
Arbitron Metro Market: La Salle-Peru, IL *Format:* Country *Hrs. of News Programming:* news progmg 2 hrs wkly *No. News Employees:* 2 *Target Audience:* 25-55.
Lamar Studstill, Chairman
Cole Studstill, CFO
Doris Studstill, General Manager
Kim Miller, Promotions Manager
David Kuharski, News Director

Olney

*WPTH
07-01-1992; 88.1 mhz FM; 2.9 kw; 200 ft.; N38 41 50 W88 2 13
817 Orchard Drive, Olney, IL 62450 US
(618) 863-2765, *Fax:* (618) 395-7064
License: Olney, Richland County, IL held by Olney Voice of Christian Faith Inc.
Format: Christian, Talk
Dr. Thomas Benson, President
Ron James, Operations Dir

WSEI
01-01-1953; 92.9 mhz FM; 50 kw; 289 ft.; N38 42 0 W88 4 49
Mailing Address: P. O. Box 1450, Corbin, KY 40702 US
Second Address: 4667 E. Radio Tower Ln., Olney, IL 62450
(618) 393-2156, *Fax:* (618) 392-4536
www.freedom929.com
929thelegend@forchtbroadcasting.com
License: Olney, Richland County, IL held by V.L.N. Broadcasting Inc.
Group Owner: Key Broadcasting Inc.; (acq 7-21-87; $1.12 million with co-located AM;
Format: Country
Dr. Kenneth Lindow, President
Joy Clark, General Manager
Roger Johnson, Programming Director
Mark Weiler, News Director

*WUSI
11-01-1992; 90.3 mhz FM *Hrs Open:* 24; 25 kw; 472 ft.; N38 50 18 W88 7 46 *Rebroadcasts:* Rebroadcasts WSIU(FM) Carbondale 100%
1048 Commun. Bldg. Siuc, Carbondale, IL 62901 US
(618) 453-4343, *Fax:* (618) 453-6186
www.wsiu.org
wsiuradio@wsiu.org
License: Olney, Richland County, IL held by Southern Illinois University.
Nat'l Network: NPR; PRI *Regional Network:* Ill. Radio Net. *Wire Services:* AP
Arbitron Metro Market: Carbondale, IL *TV Affiliate:* WUSI-TV affil
Format: News *Hrs. of News Programming:* news progmg 36 hrs wkly *No. News Employees:* 3 *Target Audience:* 35-64; highly educated, upperincome, socially conscious
Greg Petrowich, CEO
Mike Zelten, Operations Dir
Jeff Williams, Station Manager

WVLN
11-11-1947; 740 khz AM
Mailing Address: P.O. Box 1450, Corbin, KY 40702 US
Second Address: 4667 E. Radio Tower Ln., Olney, IL 62450
(618) 393-2156, *Fax:* (618) 392-4536
wvlnam.com
License: Olney, IL held by V.L.N. Broadcasting Inc.
Group Owner: Key Broadcasting Inc.; (acq 7-21-87; $1.12 million with co-located FM;
Nat'l Network: ESPN Radio
Arbitron Metro Market: Olney, IL *Format:* Sports
Terry Forcht, President

Oreana

*WDCR
03-04-1958; 88.9 mhz FM *Hrs Open:* 24; 1.1 kw; 163 ft.; N39 55 49.9 W88 51 41
Mailing Address: US
Second Address: 3rd Fl., Robinson Hall, Dartmouth College, Hanover, NH 3826
(603) 646-3313(603) 646-3826, *Fax:* (603) 643-7655
www.webdcr.com
NEWSTIP@WebDCR.COM
License: Oreana, Grafton County, IL held by Trustees of Dartmouth College.
Arbitron Metro Market: Hanover, NH *Format:* Rock/AOR *Hrs. of News Programming:* news progmg 4 hrs wkly *No. News Employees:* 2 *Target Audience:* General.
Heath Cole, Operations Dir
Ryan Zehner, General Manager
Julie Kaye, General Sales Mgr
Gregg Fox, Programming Director
Catherine Treyz, News Director

Oregon

WSEY
12-27-1999; 95.7 mhz FM; 3.2 kw; 358 ft.; N42 4 19 W89 25 8
P.O. Box 630, Marshfield, WI 54449 US
(815) 288-3341, *Fax:* (815) 284-1017
www.koolfm957.com
wixnstaff@wixn.com
License: Oregon, Ogle County, IL held by NRG License Sub. LLC.
Group Owner: NRG Media LLC; (acq 10-31-2005; grpsl)
Format: Oldies
Allan Knickrehm, General Manager
Steve Marco, Programming Director
Danette Dallgas-Frey, News Director
Mark Baker, Chief Engineer

Ottawa

WCMY
03-05-1952; 1430 khz AM *Hrs Open:* 24; 0.5 kw-D, ND2; 0.038 kw-N, ND2; N41 20 53 W88 48 15
980 North Michigan Avenue, Suite 1880, Chicago, IL 60611 US
(815) 434-6050, *Fax:* (815) 434-5311
www.ottawaradio.net
info@wcmy1430.com
License: Ottawa, IL held by NRG License Sub. LLC.
Group Owner: NRG Media LLC; (acq 10-31-2005; grpsl)
Nat'l Network: CBS Radio; Westwood One *Regional Network:* Brownfield *Nat'l Reps:* Interep *Wire Services:* AP
Arbitron Metro Market: LaSalle, Ottawa, IL *Format:* Adult Contemp, News, 62, Talk *Special Programming:* Farm 9 hrs wkly *Hrs. of News Programming:* news progmg 35 hrs wkly *No. News Employees:* 2 *TargetAudience:* 25 plus.
Jay Le Seuve, Operations Dir
Bill Jankowski, General Manager
Jill Williams, Promotions Manager
Rick Koshko, News Director
Kris Michaels, Creative Director

WRKX
09-01-1964; 95.3 mhz FM; 4.3 kw; 200 ft.; N41 23 0 W88 51 16
980 North Michigan Avenue, Suite 1880, Chicago, IL 60611 US
(815) 434-6050, *Fax:* (815) 434-5311
License: Ottawa, La Salle County, IL
Group Owner: NRG Media LLC
Wire Services: AP
Format: Adult Contemp
Jay LeSeure, Operations Dir
Bill Jankowski, General Manager
Kris Michaels, Promotions Manager
Rick Koshko, News Director
Jill Williams, Business Manager

*WWGN
09-24-1994; 88.9 mhz FM *Hrs Open:* 24; 1.4 kw horiz, 4.1 kw vert; 487 ft.; N41 18 5 W88 57 11
P.O. Drawer 2440, Tupelo, MS 38803 US
(662) 844-8888
www.afr.net
wwgn@afo.net
License: Ottawa, La Salle County, IL held by American Family Association
Group Owner: American Family Radio; (acq 1-4-99; $250,000)
Arbitron Metro Market: Tupelo, MS *Format:* Religious *Hrs. of News Programming:* news progmg 14 hrs wkly *No. News Employees:* 2 *Target Audience:* General.
Tim Wildmon, President
Marvin Sanders, General Manager

Palatine

*WHCM
01-01-2003; 88.3 mhz FM; 0.1 kw; 56 ft.; N42 4 54 W88 4 23
1200 W. Algonquin Rd, Palatine, IL 60067 US
(847) 925-6000
www.harpercollege.edu
servicedesk@harpercollege.edu
License: Palatine, Cook County, IL held by William Rainey Harper College.
Arbitron Metro Market: Palatine, IL *Format:* Variety/Diverse
Diane Hill, Chairman
Dave Dluger, General Manager
Rita Canning, Vice-Chair
Walt Mundt, Secretary
Clara Moravec, Student Trustee

Pana

WMKR
07-12-1996; 94.3 mhz FM *Hrs Open:* 24; 5.6 kw; 341 ft.; N39 27 8 W89 17 10
111 W. Main Cross, PO Box 169, Taylorville, IL 62568 US
(217) 824-3395, *Fax:* (217) 824-3301
www.randyradio.com
License: Pana, Christian County, IL held by Miller Communications Inc.
Group Owner: Miller Media Group
Nat'l Network: CNN Radio *Nat'l Reps:* Commercial Media Sales
Arbitron Metro Market: Taylorville, IL *Format:* Country *Target Audience:* 25-54.
Randal Miller, President
Kami Payne, General Manager
Brandon Fellows, Programming Director
Steve Butera, News Director

Paris

WIBQ
01-01-1952; 98.5 mhz FM; 50 kw; 499 ft.; N39 36 20 W87 43 32
Mailing Address: Post Office Box 1450, Corbin, KY 40702 US
Second Address: 824 S. 3rd St., Paris, IL 61944
(956) 487-8015
License: Paris, Edgar County, IL held by Midwest Communications Inc.
Group Owner: Midwest Communications Inc.
Arbitron Metro Market: Bismarck ND
Eloy Vera, General Manager

WPRS
01-01-1951; 1440 khz AM *Hrs Open:* 24
Mailing Address: P.O. Box 1450, Corbin, KY 40702 US
Second Address: 12861 Illinos Hwy. 133, Paris, IL 61944
(217) 465-6336, *Fax:* (217) 466-1408
wacf@comwares.net
License: Paris, IL held by Midwest Communications Inc.
Group Owner: Midwest Communications Inc.; (acq 12-15-2005; $2.55 million with
Arbitron Metro Market: Terre Haute, IN *Format:* News, Sports, 86 *No. News Employees:* 1 *Target Audience:* General.
Duke Wright, President
Steve Hall, Operations Dir
Karl Wertzler, General Manager
Doug Boyd, General Sales Mgr
B.J. Fessant, News Director

Park Forest

WCPQ
01-05-1962; 99.9 mhz FM *Hrs Open:* 24; 50 kw; 492 ft.; N41 18 4 W87 49 35
1436 Auburn Boulevard, Sacramento, CA 95815 US
(773) 792-0400, *Fax:* (773) 767-1100
www.chicagoprogressivetalk.com
info@wcpt820.com
License: Park Forest, Cook County, IL held by WCLR Inc.
Group Owner: Newsweb Corp.; (acq 3-16-2004; $24 million with WNDZ(AM) Portage, IN)
Nat'l Network: CNN Radio
Arbitron Metro Market: Chicago *Format:* Talk
Matt Comings, Operations Dir
Harvey Wells, General Manager
Mark Earnest, General Sales Mgr

Park Ridge

*WMTH
05-22-1960; 90.5 mhz FM; 0.008 kw; 102 ft.; N42 2 14 W87 51 30
1131 South Dee Road, Park Ridge, IL 60068 US
(847) 692-8495, *Fax:* (847) 692-8499
www.wmthalumni.org
dave@wmthalumni.com
License: Park Ridge, Cook County, IL held by Board of Education, Maine Twp. #207.
Arbitron Metro Market: Chicago, IL *Format:* Variety/Diverse
Jim Wunderlich, General Manager

Paxton

***WRTK**
11-01-1963; 90.5 mhz FM; kw
Mailing Address: US
Second Address: 124 N. Park Ave., Warren, OH 44482
(219) 228-2995, *Fax:* (330) 394-7701
www.thekeyfm.com
info@thekeyfm.com
License: Paxton, Trumbull County, IL held by Beacon Broadcasting Inc.
Group Owner: Beacon Broadcasting Inc.; (acq 9-14-2005; $400,000)
Arbitron Metro Market: Youngstown, IN *Format:* Christian, Gospel *Special Programming:* It one hr, Pol one hr wkly
Harold Glunt, President
Dan Wolfe, General Manager
Jody McManus, Programming Director
Mike Azinger, Promotions Manager

WPXN
10-01-1984; 104.9 mhz FM *Hrs Open:* 24; 3 kw; 299 ft.; N40 27 11 W88 6 11
361 N Railroad Avenue, Paxton, IL 60957 US
(217) 379-4333,(217) 892-9796, *Fax:* (217) 379-4334
wpxnradio.com
wpxn@wpxnradio.com
License: Paxton, Ford County, IL held by Paxton Broadcasting Corp.
Nat'l Network: CNN Radio *Regional Network:* Brownfield *Wire Services:* AP
Format: Oldies *Special Programming:* Farm 10 hrs wkly *Hrs. of News Programming:* news progmg 8 hrs wkly *No. News Employees:* 2 *Target Audience:* 25-54.
Dan Daugherity, President
Joel Cluver, Station Manager

Pekin

***WBNH**
12-01-1988; 88.5 mhz FM; 48,000 kw; 495 ft; N40 38 34 W89 32 38
1915 Mayflower Drive, Pekin, IL 61555
(309) 636-8850, *Fax:* (877) 631-8850
www.wbnh.org
wbnh@wbnh.org
License: Pekin, Tazewell County, IL held by Central Illinois Radio Fellowship Inc.
Nat'l Network: Moody
Arbitron Metro Market: Peoria, IL *Target Audience:* General.
Don Rice, President
Keith Lang, Operations Dir
Jim Huber, Station Manager
Wayne Miller, Chief Engineer

***WCIC**
11-02-1983; 91.5 mhz FM *Hrs Open:* 24; 47 kw; 505 ft.; N40 33 28 W89 34 4
3263 Court Street, Pekin, IL 61554 US
(309) 692-9242, *Fax:* (309) 692-9241
www.wcicfm.org
wcic@wcicfm.com
License: Pekin, Tazewell County, IL held by Illinois Bible Institute.
Group Owner: Illinois Bible Institute Inc.
Arbitron Metro Market: Peoria, IL *Format:* Adult Contemp, Christian, 74 *Hrs. of News Programming:* News progmg 2 hrs wkly *Target Audience:* 25-49.
Dave Brooks, General Manager
Dave Brooks, Station Manager
Jessie Browning, Promotions Manager
Joe Buchanan, Music Director
Katie Post, Office Manager
Trevor Moore, Audio/New Media Producer

WGLO
11-18-1971; 95.5 mhz FM; 7 kw; 620 ft.; N40 36 23 W89 32 20
P. O. Box 150846, Nashville, TN 37215 US
(309) 676-5000, *Fax:* (309) 676-2600
www.955glo.com
matt.bahan@townsquaremedia.com
License: Pekin, Tazewell County, IL
Group Owner: Townsquare Media
Nat'l Reps: D & R Radio
Arbitron Metro Market: Peoria, IL *Format:* Classic Rock *Target Audience:* 18-49.
Matt Bahan, Programming Director
Brad Creek, Director of Sales

WVEL
04-21-1948; 1140 khz AM
P. O. Box 150846, Nashville, TN 37215 US
(309) 676-5000, *Fax:* (309) 676-2600
www.wvel.com
jgreeley@regentcomm.com
License: Pekin, IL
Group Owner: Townsquare Media; (acq 7-6-01; grpsl).
Arbitron Metro Market: Peoria, IL *Format:* Gospel *Target Audience:* General.
J.R. Greeley, General Manager
Brad Creek, Director of Sales
Robert Caruth, Programming Director

WXCL
01-01-1973; 104.9 mhz FM *Hrs Open:* 24; 6 kw; 328 ft.; N40 38 34 W89 32 38
5555 Gulf Mexico Dr., Suite 201, Longboat Key, FL 34228 US
(309) 637-3700, *Fax:* (309) 272-1476
www.1049thewolf.com
info@1049.com
License: Pekin, Tazewell County, IL held by Monterey Licenses LLC.
Group Owner: Triad Broadcasting Co. L.L.C.; (acq 4-21-2006; $5.2 million with WDQX(FM) Morton)
Arbitron Metro Market: Peoria, IL *Format:* Country *No. News Employees:* 2 *Target Audience:* 25-54; affluent adults
Mike Wild, General Manager
Kevin Cassulo, General Sales Mgr
Chris Michaels, Programming Director
Dirk Clemens, Promotions Manager
Cindy Austin, Asst. Program Director
Ryan Madden, Production Director
Cody West, Webmaster

Peoria

WZPW
11-01-1992; 92.3 mhz FM; 19.2 kw; 374 ft.; N40 47 10 W89 47 1
516 W. Main St., Peoria, IL 61606 US
(309) 676-5000
www.powerpeoria.com
amanda.king@cumulus.com
License: Peoria, Peoria County, IL held by B&G Broadcasting Inc.
Group Owner: Townsquare Media; (acq 9-19-2006; $11.75 million with WIXO(FM) Peoria).
Arbitron Metro Market: Peoria, IL *Format:* Contemporary Hits/Top 40
J.R. Greeley, General Manager
Brad Creek, Director of Sales
Amanda King, Programming Director

***WCBU**
01-01-1970; 89.9 mhz FM; 26.5 kw; 647 ft.; N40 37 44 W89 34 12
1501 W. Bradley Ave., Peoria, IL 61625 US
(309) 677-3690, *Fax:* (309) 677-3462
www.wcbu.bradley.edu/
wcbu@bradley.edu
License: Peoria, Peoria County, IL held by Bradley University.
Nat'l Network: NPR *Wire Services:* AP
Arbitron Metro Market: Peoria, IL *Format:* Classical, News
Daryl Scott, Operations Dir
Thomas Hunt, General Manager
Cindy Dermody, General Sales Mgr
Nathan Irwin, Programming Director
Betty Beard, Promotions Manager
Jonathan Ahl, News Director
William Porter, Engineering Dir

WIRL
01-01-1947; 1290 khz AM; 5 kw-D, DA2; 5 kw-N, DA2; N40 37 24 W89 35 27
P.O. Box 3335, Peoria, IL 61612 US
(309) 637-3700, *Fax:* (309) 673-9562
www.1290wirl.com
courtneylynne@1290wirl.com
License: Peoria, IL held by Monterey Licenses LLC.
Group Owner: Triad Broadcasting Co. L.L.C.; (acq 3-25-2003; grpsl)
Nat'l Reps: Christal
Arbitron Metro Market: Peoria, IL *Format:* Country *Target Audience:* 25-54; men
David Benjamin III, President
Randy Rundle, Operations Dir
Mike Wild, General Manager
Kevin Cassulo, General Sales Mgr
John Malone, Programming Director
Ed Hammond, News Director
Wayne Miller, Chief Engineer
Brian Rowell,General Sales Manager
Brenda Rundle, Traffic Manager
Mike Wild, Market Manager
Brian Rowell, Director of Sports Sales
Ryan Madden, Production Manager
DeAnna Thomas, Director of Ag Programming

WMBD
01-01-1927; 1470 khz AM *Hrs Open:* 24; 5 kw-D, DA2; 5 kw-N, DA2; N40 34 22 W89 32 0
3131 North University, Peoria, IL 61604 US
(309) 637-3700, *Fax:* (309) 673-9562
www.1470wmbd.com
License: Peoria, IL held by Monterey Licenses LLC.
Group Owner: Triad Broadcasting Co. L.L.C.; (acq 3-25-2003; grpsl).
Nat'l Network: Premiere Radio Networks; Westwood One *Nat'l Reps:* Christal *Wire Services:* U.S. Weather Service
Arbitron Metro Market: Peoria, IL *Format:* News, News/Talk, 86 *Special Programming:* Farm 15 hrs wkly *Hrs. of News Programming:* news progmg 40 hrs wkly *No. News Employees:* 5 *Target Audience:* 35-64;upscale, well educated, professional, conservative
David Benjamin III, President
Mike Wild, General Manager

WOAM
02-08-1960; 1350 khz AM; 1 kw-D, DA2; 1 kw-N, DA2; N40 35 41 W89 35 40
5555 Gulf of Mexico Dr, Suite 201, Longboat Key, FL 34228 US
(309) 685-0977, *Fax:* (309) 685-7150
License: Peoria, IL held by Kelly Communications Inc.
Arbitron Metro Market: Peoria, IL *TV Affiliate:* Hits of the 40s, 50s & 60s

WPBG
01-01-1947; 93.3 mhz FM *Hrs Open:* 24; 40 kw; 551 ft.; N40 38 7 W89 32 19
3131 North University, Peoria, IL 61604 US
, *Fax:* (309) 686-8659
www.933thedrive.com
License: Peoria, Peoria County, IL held by Monterey Licenses LLC
Group Owner: Triad Broadcasting Co. L.L.C.
Arbitron Metro Market: Peoria, IL *Format:* Contemporary Hits/Top 40, Adult Contemp *Target Audience:* 25-54; baby boomers
Brent Millar, General Manager
Lisa Powell, General Sales Mgr
Randy Bliss, Programming Director
Valerie Dickens, News Director
Larry Allen, Chief Engineer
Greg Carpenter, General Sales Manager

WPEO
01-01-1946; 1020 khz AM; 1 kw-D; N40 41 53 W89 31 31
Mailing Address: 1708 Highview Rd., East Peoria, IL 61611
Second Address: Box 1, Peoria, IL 61650
(309) 698-9736, *Fax:* (309) 698-9740
www.wpeo.com
wpeo@wpeo.com
License: Peoria, Peoria County, IL held by Pinebrook Foundation Inc.
Population Served: 500,000 *Arbitron Metro Market:* Peoria, IL *Target Audience:* 35 plus. *Adv. Rates:* 18; 18; 18; 18
John Wieland, President
Robert Ulrich, General Manager
Jeff Wineberry, General Sales Mgr
Nelson Hostetler, Programming Director
Jessica Wieland, News Director

WSWT
01-01-1964; 106.9 mhz FM *Hrs Open:* 24; 50 kw; 479 ft.; N40 43 22 W89 30 40
P.O. Box 3335, Peoria, IL 61612 US
(309) 637-3700, *Fax:* (309) 686-8659
www.literock107.com
License: Peoria, Peoria County, IL held by Monterey Licenses LLC.
Group Owner: Triad Broadcasting Co. L.L.C.
Nat'l Reps: Christal *Wire Services:* AP
Arbitron Metro Market: Peoria, IL *Format:* Adult Contemp *Hrs. of News Programming:* News progmg 2.5 hrs wkly *Target Audience:* 25-54. *Adv. Rates:* 85; 85; 85; 25
Randy Rundle, Operations Dir
Dirk Clemens, Promotions Manager
Wayne Miller, Chief Engineer

WIXO
05-14-1972; 105.7 mhz FM; 39 kw; 555 ft.; N40 43 25 W89 29 4
4701 N. War Memorial Dr., Peoria, IL 61614 US
(309) 676-5000, *Fax:* (309) 686-0111
www.1057thexrocks.com
matt.bahan@cumulus.com
License: Peoria, Peoria County, IL

Group Owner: Townsquare Media; (acq 9-19-2006; $11.75 million with WZPW(FM) Peoria).
Nat'l Reps: Christal
Arbitron Metro Market: Peoria, IL *Format:* Rock/AOR
Michael Rea, General Manager
Becky Riojas, General Sales Mgr
Matt Bahan, Programming Director
Marta Poznaska, Promotions Manager
Brett Ring, Chief Engineer
Brad Creek, Director of Sales

***WAZU**
90.7 mhz FM; 0.5 kw; 266 ft.; N40 46 46 W89 39 18
138 Park Plaza Court, Canton, IL 61520 US
(309) 253-1951
www.wazufm.org
License: Peoria, Peoria County, IL held by Sirius Syncope Inc.
Arbitron Metro Market: Peoria, IL *Format:* Talk
Jeremy Styninger, President

Peru

WBZG
03-15-1970; 100.9 mhz FM *Hrs Open:* 24; 3 kw; 328 ft.; N41 18 9 W89 14 11
3905 Progress Blvd., Peru, IL 61354 US
(815) 224-2100, *Fax:* (815) 224-2066
wbzg.net
wbzg@theradiogroup.net
License: Peru, La Salle County, IL held by Mendota Broadcasting Inc.
Group Owner: Studstill Broadcasting; (acq 7-17-97; $700,000 with WIVQ(FM) Spring Valley).
Nat'l Reps: Rgnl Reps *Wire Services:* AP
Arbitron Metro Market: La Salle-Peru, IL *Format:* Classic Rock
No. News Employees: 2 *Target Audience:* Men 18-54.
Lamar Studstill, Chairman
Owen Studstill, CEO
Cole Charles Studstill, CFO
Cole Studstill, Operations Manager

Petersburg

WLCE
03-01-1987; 97.7 mhz FM *Hrs Open:* 24; 6 kw; 328 ft.; N39 54 35 W89 43 1
906 Gabbert Road, Springfield, IL 62707 US
(217) 629-7077, *Fax:* (217) 629-7952
www.alice.fm
alice@alice.fm
License: Petersburg, Menard County, IL held by Long-Nine Inc.
Group Owner: The Mid-West Family Broadcast Group; (acq 7-27-2001; $3 million)
Wire Services: AP
Arbitron Metro Market: Petersburg, IL *Format:* Triple A *Special Programming:* Relg 5 hrs wkly *Target Audience:* 18-34; female
Mark Birtch, General Manager
Dave Duetsch, General Sales Mgr
Josie O'Donnell, Programming Director
Jim Leach, News Director
Greg Stephens, Chief Engineer
Quinn Fagg, Traffic Manager

***WLWJ**
10-07-2001; 88.1 mhz FM; 6 kw; 328 ft.; N40 0 5 W89 41 49
600 West Mason Street, Springfield, IL 62702 US
(800) 932-9585, *Fax:* (217) 528-2400
www.wluj.org
comments@wluj.org
License: Petersburg, Menard County, IL held by Cornerstone Community Radio Inc.
Nat'l Network: USA
Arbitron Metro Market: Springfield, IL *Format:* Christian, Religious, 86
Howard Fouks, Operations Dir
Richard Van Zandt, General Manager
David King, Station Manager
Richard Beaman, General Sales Mgr
Howard Fouks, Chief Engineer
Lonnie Lein, Production Manager
Richard Beaman, Senior Director ofUnderwriting
John McBride, Director of Special Ministries
Sherri McBride, Relational Phoning
Wayne Langhein, Finance
Claudia King, Office Assistant

Pittsfield

WBBA-FM
08-01-1966; 97.5 mhz FM *Hrs Open:* 24; 10 kw; 305 ft.; N39 34 53 W90 47 52
#1 Professional Plaza, P.O. Box 150, Pittsfield, IL 62363 US
(304) 399-9603, *Fax:* (304) 399-9608
www.magic979.com
License: Pittsfield, Pike County, IL held by DJ Two Rivers Radio Inc.
Arbitron Metro Market: Oakland CA *Format:* Adult Contemp
Newman Adkins, General Manager

***WIPA**
01-04-1993; 89.3 mhz FM *Hrs Open:* 24; 50 kw; 492 ft.; N39 43 25 W90 41 9 *Rebroadcasts:* Rebroadcasts WUIS(FM) Springfield 100%
South Shepherd Road, Springfield, IL 62794 US
(217) 206-6516, *Fax:* (217) 206-6527
www.wuis.org
wuis@uis.org
License: Pittsfield, Pike County, IL held by University of Illinois at Springfield.
Nat'l Network: NPR; PRI
Format: Jazz, News *Hrs. of News Programming:* news progmg 45 hrs wkly *No. News Employees:* 4 *Target Audience:* 25-54.
Sinta Seiber, Operations Dir
Bill Wheelhouse, General Manager
Lisa Clemmons-Stott, General Sales Mgr
Rick Bradley, News Director
Greg Manfroi, Chief Engineer

Plano

WSPY-FM
01-19-1974; 107.1 mhz FM *Hrs Open:* 24; 1.5 kw; 466 ft.; N41 39 55 W88 34 34
1 Broadcast Center, Plano, IL 60545 US
(630) 552-1000, *Fax:* (630) 552-9300
wspy@nelsonmultimedia.net
License: Plano, Kendall County, IL held by Nelson Enterprises Inc.
Nat'l Network: ABC
Arbitron Metro Market: Chicago *Format:* Variety/Diverse *Special Programming:* Farm 18 hrs wkly *Hrs. of News Programming:* News progmg 12 hrs wkly *Target Audience:* 25-54.
Liz Clark, CFO
Larry Nelson, President
Chris Schwemlein, Operations Dir
Vori Dhabolt, General Sales Mgr
Jeni Beckman, News Director
Lane Lindstrom, Chief Engineer
Beth Pierre, General Sales Manager

Polo

WLLT
12-12-1989; 107.7 mhz FM *Hrs Open:* 24; 3 kw; 476 ft.; N41 53 51.9 W89 36 19.6
260 State Route 2, Dixon, IL 61021 US
(815) 284-1077
wllt@comcast.net
License: Polo, Ogle County, IL held by Sauk Valley Broadcasting Co.
Format: Adult Contemp
Bob Burns, President

Pontiac

WJBC-FM
10-06-1985; 93.7 mhz FM; 12 kw; 472 ft.; N40 45 27 W88 37 40
315 N. Mill Street, Pontiac, IL 61764 US
(904) 781-4321
www.wjgmfm.com
info@wjbcfm.com
License: Pontiac, Nassau County, IL held by West Jacksonville Baptist Church Inc.
Arbitron Metro Market: Jacksonville, FL *Format:* Gospel *Target Audience:* General.
Rodney Kelley, President

***WPJC**
01-01-2003; 88.3 mhz FM; 0.5 kw; 207 ft.; N40 56 42 W88 38 46
6910 NW 2nd Terrace, Boca Raton, FL 33487 US
(219) 548-8956, *Fax:* (219) 548-5808
www.wpjcfm.ning.com
info@healthylivingseminars.org
License: Pontiac, Livingston County, IL held by CSN International
Group Owner: CSN International; acq 12-31-2001; $25,000 for CP).
Arbitron Metro Market: Warrenville, IL *Format:* Christian, Talk
Jim Motshagen, General Manager

Princeton

WZOE
10-25-1961; 1490 khz AM *Hrs Open:* 24; 1 kw-U, ND1; N41 21 8 W89 28 5
Mailing Address: P. O. Box 69, Princeton, IL 61356 US
Second Address: S. Main St., Princeton, IL 61356
(815) 875-8014
www.wzoeradio.com
info@wzoeradio.com
License: Princeton, IL held by WZOE Inc.
Group Owner: WZOE Inc.; acq 11-1-73)
Nat'l Network: CBS *Wire Services:* Metro Weather Service Inc.
Arbitron Metro Market: Princeton, IL *Format:* News, News/Talk, 84, Talk *Special Programming:* Farm 15 hrs wkly *Hrs. of News Programming:* news progmg 84 hrs wkly *No. News Employees:* 3
Steve Samet, President
Paul Bomleny, Operations Dir
Steve Samet, General Manager
Mike Samet, General Sales Mgr
Tommy Rose, Programming Director
Scott Mighle, News Director
Greg Stephens, Chief Engineer
Nedda Simon, PublicAffairs Director
Mary Harmon, Traffic Manager
Brad Kloepping, C.P.A., Accountant / Bookkeeping
Marion Rinehart, Office Manager
Gregg Stephens, Broadcast Engineer
Chris Compton, CRMC, Senior Sales Rep

WZOE-FM
07-01-1980; 98.1 mhz FM *Hrs Open:* 24; 6 kw; 299 ft.; N41 21 49 W89 23 36
P.O. Box 69, Princeton, IL 61356 US
(815) 875-8014
www.wzoeradio.com
info@wzoeradio.com
License: Princeton, Bureau County, IL held by WZOE Inc.
Group Owner: WZOE Inc.
Nat'l Network: CNN Radio *Wire Services:* Metro Weather Service Inc.
Arbitron Metro Market: Princeton, IL *Format:* Contemporary Hits/Top 40, Adult Contemp *Hrs. of News Programming:* news progmg 8 hrs wkly *No. News Employees:* 3
Steve Samet, General Manager
Mike Samet, General Sales Mgr
Nedda Simon, Programming Director
Mary Harmon, News Director
Brad Kloepping, C.P.A., Accountant / Bookkeeping
Marion Rinehart, Office Manager
Gregg Stephens, BroadcastEngineer
Chris Compton, CRMC, Senior Sales Rep

Quincy

WLIQ
12-13-1966; 1530 khz AM *Hrs Open:* Sunrise-sunset
15894 Highway 54 Pobox 1, Bowling Greeen, MO 63334 US
(573) 221-3450, *Fax:* (573) 221-5331
hsmith@qraido.com
License: Quincy, IL held by Bick Broadcasting Co.
Group Owner: Bick Broadcasting Co.; (acq 10-14-2003).
Format: Adult Contemp
Ed Foxall, General Manager
Jeff Dorsey, Programming Director
John Hanvelt, News Director
Gary Glaenzer, Chief Engineer

***WGCA-FM**
09-20-1987; 88.5 mhz FM; 40 kw; 449 ft.; N39 58 18 W91 19 42
Post Office Box 467, Quincy, IL 62306 US
(217) 224-9422, *Fax:* (217) 228-0504
www.wgca.org
themix@wgca.org
License: Quincy, Adams County, IL held by Great Commission Broadcasting Corp.
Nat'l Network: USA
Format: Christian *Target Audience:* 25-45.
Jim Tyler, Operations Dir
Bruce Rice, General Manager
Laura Cook, General Sales Mgr
Jim Taylor, Programming Director
Jim Wilson, Chief Engineer
Bruce Rice, Executive Director
Maxine Rice, Associate Director

WGEM
01-01-1948; 1440 khz AM; 5 kw-D, DA2; 1 kw-N, DA2; N39 58 48 W91 19 24
Mailing Address: P.O. Box 80, 513 Hampshire, Quincy, IL 62306 US
Second Address: 513 Hampshire, Quincy, IL 62301
(217) 228-6600, *Fax:* (217) 228-6670
www.wgem.com
aelkins@wgem.com

License: Quincy, IL held by Quincy Broadcasting Co.
Group Owner: Quincy Newspapers Inc.
Nat'l Network: ESPN Radio *Nat'l Reps:* Christal
Format: News, News/Talk, 84, Talk *Hrs. of News Programming:* news progmg 25 hrs wkly *Target Audience:* 25-54; general
Ralph Oakley, President
Carlos Fernandez, General Manager

WGEM-FM
01-01-1947; 105.1 mhz FM *Hrs Open:* 24; 26.5 kw; 686 ft.; N39 57 4 W91 19 53
Mailing Address: 513 Hampshire, PO Box 80, Quincy, IL 62301 US
Second Address: 513 Hampshire, Quincy, IL 62301
(217) 228-6600, *Fax:* (217) 228-6670
www.wgem.com
aelkins@wgem.com
License: Quincy, Adams County, IL
Group Owner: Quincy Newspapers Inc.
Regional Network: Miss. News Net. *Nat'l Reps:* Christal *Wire Services:* AP
Format: News, News/Talk, 86 *Hrs. of News Programming:* News progmg 110 hrs wkly *Target Audience:* 25-54.
Ralph Oakley, President
Carlos Fernandez, General Manager

WQCY
05-08-1989; 103.9 mhz FM; 1.8 kw; 436 ft.; N39 56 30 W91 35 3
2 Dearborn Square, Kankakee, IL 60901 US
(217) 224-4102, *Fax:* (217) 224-4133
www.1039thefox.com
wqcy@staradio.com
License: Quincy, Adams County, IL held by STARadio Corp.
Group Owner: STARadio Corp.; acq 8-13-98; grpsl)
Nat'l Network: CBS
Arbitron Metro Market: Quincy, IL *Format:* Light Rock *Target Audience:* 18-44; general
Michael Moyers, General Manager
Brenda Park, General Sales Mgr
Steve Boll, Programming Director
Mary Griffith, News Director
Phillip Reilly, Chief Engineer
Jerry Shoup, Traffic Manager

WCOY
01-01-1948; 99.5 mhz FM *Hrs Open:* 24; 100 kw; 489 ft.; N39 56 30 W91 35 3
510 Maine Street, Quincy, IL 62306 US
(217) 224-4102, *Fax:* (217) 224-4133
License: Quincy, Adams County, IL
Group Owner: STARadio Corp.
Nat'l Network: CBS
Format: Country
Mike Moyers, Programming Director

***WQUB**
04-01-1974; 90.3 mhz FM *Hrs Open:* 24; 28 kw; 417 ft.; N39 57 22 W91 23 22
1800 College Avenue, Quincy, IL 62301 US
(217) 228-5410, *Fax:* (217) 228-5616
www.wqub.org
info@wqub.org
License: Quincy, Adams County, IL held by Quincy University Corp.
Nat'l Network: NPR; AP Radio
Format: Jazz, News *Special Programming:* Folk 2 hrs, blues 2 hrs, alternative rock 12 hrs, hip hop 2 hrs, oldies 2 hrs wkly *Hrs. of News Programming:* news progmg 31 hrs wkly *No. News Employees:* 2 *Target Audience:* 25-64; male & female
Jim Lenz, Operations Dir
Patrick Mays, General Sales Mgr
Jim Cate, Chief Engineer

WTAD
07-25-1925; 930 khz AM *Hrs Open:* 24; 5 kw-D, DAN; 1 kw-N, DAN; N39 53 31 W91 25 25
2 Dearborn Square, Kankakee, IL 60901 US
(217) 224-4102, *Fax:* (217) 224-4133
www.wtad.com
info@wtad.com
License: Quincy, IL held by STARadio Corp.
Group Owner: STARadio Corp.; (acq 8-13-98; grpsl)
Nat'l Network: CBS *Nat'l Reps:* McGavren Guild
Format: News, News/Talk, 86 *Hrs. of News Programming:* news progmg 22 hrs wkly *No. News Employees:* 1 *Target Audience:* 35 plus; general
Brenda Parks, General Manager
Michael Moyers, General Manager

Ramsey

***WJLY**
01-01-1999; 88.3 mhz FM *Hrs Open:* 24; 25 kw; 502 ft.; N39 8 6 W89 6 2
Mailing Address: P.O. Box 456, Ramsey, IL 62080 US
Second Address: R.R. 2 Box 51A, Ramsey, IL
(618) 423-2082, *Fax:* (618) 423-2394
www.wjly.org
wjly@frontiernet.net
License: Ramsey, Fayette County, IL held by Countryside Broadcasting.
Nat'l Network: Moody
Format: Christian *Hrs. of News Programming:* News progmg 14 hrs wkly *Target Audience:* 35 plus.
Richard Wheeler, General Manager
John Stanley, General Sales Mgr
Dave Carruthers, Programming Director
Henry Voss, Chief Engineer

WTRH
11-21-1990; 93.3 mhz FM *Hrs Open:* 24; 3 kw; 466 ft.; N39 8 6 W89 6 2
P.O. Box 456, Ramsey, IL 62080 US
(618) 423-2082, *Fax:* (618) 423-2394
wtrh@frontiernet.net
wtrh@frontiernet.net
License: Ramsey, Fayette County, IL held by Countryside Broadcasting Inc.
Arbitron Metro Market: Ramsey, IL *Format:* Oldies, Talk *Hrs. of News Programming:* News progmg 14 hrs wkly *Target Audience:* 35 plus; men & women who love old radio prgms & mus *Adv. Rates:* 11; 11; 11; 11
Dick Wheeler, General Manager and Production Contact
Al Schumacher, Advertising Sales Contact

Rantoul

WKJR
02-01-1963; 1460 khz AM *Hrs Open:* 24; 0.5 kw-D, DA2; 0.065 kw-N, DA2; N40 18 37 W88 12 54
1012 W University, Urbana, IL 61801 US
(217) 893-1460, *Fax:* (217) 893-0884
www.1460sports.com
fanmail@1460sports.com
License: Rantoul, IL held by Ruben's Productions Inc.
Nat'l Network: ESPN Radio
Arbitron Metro Market: Champaign, IL *Format:* Sports *Target Audience:* General. *Adv. Rates:* 20; 20; 20; 20
Rueben Acevero, General Manager
Armando Martinez, Programming Director
Scott Hudson, News Director

WQQB
01-01-1993; 96.1 mhz FM *Hrs Open:* 24; 3.8 kw; 404 ft.; N40 13 27 W88 17 56
P.O. Box 3335, Peoria, IL 61612 US
(217) 367-1195, *Fax:* (217) 367-3291
www.wqqb.com
License: Rantoul, Champaign County, IL held by RadioStar Inc.
Group Owner: RadioStar Inc.; (acq 5-23-2006; grpsl).
Nat'l Reps: McGavren Guild
Arbitron Metro Market: Champaign, IL *Format:* Contemporary Hits/Top 40 *Target Audience:* 18-34; female
Jim Glassman, President
Roxanne Charles, General Manager
Corey Berkemann, General Sales Mgr
Joe McIntyre, Programming Director
Donna Keleher, Office Manager

WJEK(FM)
03-15-1972; 95.3 mhz FM *Hrs Open:* 24; 3 kw; Ant 425 ft; N40 13 05 W88 06 55
2702 Boulder Drive, Urbana, IL 61802
(217) 367-1195, *Fax:* (217) 367-3291
www.myconnectfm.com
Steve.Miller@sjbroadcasting.com
License: Rantoul, Champaign County, IL held by RadioStar Inc.
Group Owner: RadioStar Inc.; (acq 5-23-2006; grpsl)
Nat'l Reps: McGavren Guild
Population Served: 41,518 *Arbitron Metro Market:* Urbana, IL *Format:* Country *No. News Employees:* 1 *Target Audience:* 18-49.
Jim Glassman, President
Roxanne Charles, General Manager
Steve Miller, Sales Manager
Ken Cunningham, Programming Director
Josh Laskowski, Promotions Manager
Jon Hall, Engineering Dir
Donna Keleher, Office Manager
Diane Ducey,Promotions

River Grove

***WRRG**
03-10-1975; 88.9 mhz FM *Hrs Open:* 9 AM-midnight (M-F); 10 AM-midnight; 0.1 kw; 128 ft.; N41 54 56 W87 50 12
2000 N. 5th Avenue, River Grove, IL 60171 US
(708) 583-3110
www.wrrg.org
info@wrrg.org,wrrg@hotmail.com
License: River Grove, Cook County, IL held by Triton College.
Arbitron Metro Market: Chicago *Format:* Alternative, Contemporary Hits/Top 40 *Special Programming:* Jazz 5 hrs, loc 4 hrs, metal 4 hrs, world mus 3 hrs, oldies 11 hrs, classic rock 2 hrs wkly *Target Audience:* 14-40.
Kelli Lynch, Station Manager

Robinson

WTAY
01-09-1956; 1570 khz AM *Hrs Open:* 24; 0.25 kw-D, ND2; 0.188 kw-N, ND2; N39 0 29 W87 46 41
P.O. Box 245, Robinson, IL 62454 US
(618) 544-2191, *Fax:* (618) 544-3621
wtaywtye@yahoo.com
License: Robinson, IL held by Ann Broadcasting Corp.
Nat'l Network: ABC
Format: Adult Contemp *Special Programming:* C&W 12 hrs, farm 3 hrs, polka 3 hrs, big band 10 hrs wkly *Hrs. of News Programming:* news progmg 15 hrs wkly *No. News Employees:* 1 *Adv. Rates:* 10.50; 10.50; 10.50;10.50
Jerry Tye, President
Roy Rice, General Sales Mgr

WTYE
01-04-1963; 101.7 mhz FM; 3.1 kw; 466 ft.; N39 0 29 W87 46 41
PO Box 245, Robinson, IL 62454 US
(618) 544-2191, *Fax:* (618) 544-3621
www.originalcompany.com
License: Robinson, Crawford County, IL
Arbitron Metro Market: Robinson, IL *Adv. Rates:* Same as AM
Mark Lange, President
Jonathan Lange, Operations Dir
Derek Mason, General Sales Mgr
Dave Young, Programming & Sports
Amy Miller, Programming & Sports
Barbara Warren, News Director
Sara Dunn, Traffic Director
Judy Krieg, SalesRepresentative
Saundra Lange, Vice President
Duncan Myers, Sales Director

Rochelle

WRHL
09-16-1966; 1060 khz AM *Hrs Open:* 24; 0.25 kw-D, DA2; 0.05 kw-N, DA2; N41 55 24 W89 3 30
Mailing Address: 400 May Mart Drive, Rochelle, IL 61068 US
Second Address: 400 May Mart Dr., Rochelle, IL 61068
(815) 562-7001, *Fax:* (815) 562-7002
www.wrhl.net
wrhlamfm@rochelle.net
License: Rochelle, IL held by Rochelle Broadcasting Co. Inc.
Nat'l Network: AP Network News *Regional Network:* Ill. Radio Net.; Tribune Radio Networks *Wire Services:* AP
Format: News, News/Talk, 86 *Hrs. of News Programming:* news progmg 140 hrs wkly *No. News Employees:* 2 *Target Audience:* 25-75. *Adv. Rates:* 13; 13; 13; 13
David Van Drew, General Manager
Penny Helm, General Sales Mgr
Greg Saunders, Programming Director
Jeffrey Leon, News Director
Doug White, Chief Engineer
Becky Leininger, Traffic Manager

WRHL-FM
10-05-1973; 102.3 mhz FM *Hrs Open:* 24; 4.6 kw; 180 ft.; N41 55 24 W89 3 30
Mailing Address: Box 177, Rochelle, IL 61068 US
Second Address: 400 May Mart Dr., Rochelle, IL 61068
(815) 562-7001, *Fax:* (815) 562-7002
www.hitsandfavorites.com
jb@wrhl.net
License: Rochelle, Ogle County, IL
Nat'l Network: ABC
Format: Adult Contemp *Hrs. of News Programming:* News progmg one hr wkly *Target Audience:* 25-54; female
Becky Leininger, News Director

Rock Island

*WLKU
10-01-1947; 98.9 mhz FM *Hrs Open:* 24; 39 kw; 922 ft.; N41 19 39 W90 22 46
P.O. Box 705, Mt. Pleasant, SC 29465 US
(916) 251-1600, *Fax:* (916) 251-1650
www.klove.com
License: Rock Island, Rock Island County, IL held by Educational Media Foundation.
Group Owner: EMF Broadcasting; (acq 2-3-2006; $3.5 million).
Nat'l Network: K-Love
Arbitron Metro Market: Quad Cities, IA *Format:* Christian
Mike Novak, President
David Pierce, Programming Director
Ed Lenane, News Director
Sam Wallington, Engineering Dir
Marya Morgan, News Reporter
Richard Hunt, News Reporter

WKBF
02-16-1925; 1270 khz AM *Hrs Open:* 24; 5 kw-D, DAN; 5 kw-N, DAN; N41 29 40 W90 28 0
P.O. Box 705, Mt. Pleasant, SC 29465 US
(888) 321-1270
info@truth1270.com
License: Rock Island, IL held by Quad Cities Media LLC
Arbitron Metro Market: Quad Cities, IA
Randall Melchert, President

*WVIK
02-25-1963; 90.3 mhz FM *Hrs Open:* 24; 31 kw; 1096 ft.; N41 32 49 W90 28 35
639 38th Street, Rock Island, IL 61201 US
(309) 794-7500, *Fax:* (309) 794-1236
www.wvik.org
info@wvik.org
License: Rock Island, Rock Island County, IL held by Augustana College.
Nat'l Network: NPR *Wire Services:* AP
Arbitron Metro Market: Rock Island, IL *Format:* News *Special Programming:* Jazz 9 hrs wkly *Hrs. of News Programming:* news progmg 35 hrs wkly *No. News Employees:* 2 *Target Audience:* General.
David Garner, Operations Dir
Jay Pearce, General Manager
Sonita Oldfield-Carlson, General Sales Mgr
Mindy Heusel, Programming Director
Herb Trix, News Director
Colleen Sibthorp, Business Manager
Jim Peterson, Public AffairsDirector
Jennifer Blohm, Dvelopment Director
Mary McNeil, Underwriting Sales Associate

Rockford

*WFEN
08-25-1991; 88.3 mhz FM; 1 kw horiz, 8.5 kw vert; 574 ft.; N42 21 48 W89 8 6
4700 South Main Street, Rockford, IL 61102 US
(815) 964-9336, *Fax:* (815) 964-0550
www.wfen.org
fred@wfen.org
License: Rockford, Winnebago County, IL held by Faith Center
Arbitron Metro Market: Rockford, IL *Format:* Christian *Special Programming:* Sp one hr wkly *Target Audience:* 35-54.
Fred Tscholl, General Manager
Fred Tscholl, Station Manager
Judy Gors, Manager of Underwriting
Kathy Tscholl, Station Secretary

*WNIU
04-28-1991; 90.5 mhz FM *Hrs Open:* 24; 50 kw; 367 ft.; N42 0 55 W89 0 7
801 North First Street, Dekalb, IL 60115 US
(815) 753-9000, *Fax:* (815) 753-9938
www.northernpublicradio.org
npr@niu.edu
License: Rockford, Winnebago County, IL held by Northern Illinois University.
Nat'l Network: PRI; NPR
Arbitron Metro Market: Rockford, IL *Format:* Classical *Special Programming:* New age 2 hrs, blues 4 hrs wkly *Hrs. of News Programming:* news progmg 52 hrs wkly *No. News Employees:* 2 *Target Audience:* General.
Staci Hoste, General Manager
Jan Kilgard, General Sales Mgr
Bill Drake, Programming Director
Guy Stephens, News Director
Jeff Glass, Chief Engineer

WNTA
12-24-1953; 1330 khz AM *Hrs Open:* 24
Mailing Address: 2830 Sandy Hollow Road, Rockford, IL 61109 US
Second Address: 2830 Sandy Hollow Rd., Rockford, IL 61109
(815) 874-7861, *Fax:* (815) 874-2202
www.funny1330.com
wnta@wnta.com
License: Rockford, IL held by Maverick Media of Rockford License LLC.
Group Owner: Maverick Media LLC; (acq 4-27-2005; grpsl)
Arbitron Metro Market: Rockford, IL *Format:* Comedy *Special Programming:* Gospel 20 hrs wkly *Hrs. of News Programming:* news progmg 2 hrs wkly *No. News Employees:* 2 *Target Audience:* 35 plus.
Gary Rozynek, President
Jay Chapman, General Manager
Ken DeCoster, Programming Director

*WQFL
05-02-1974; 100.9 mhz FM *Hrs Open:* 24; 2.7 kw; 489 ft.; N42 19 20 W89 0 41
Mailing Address: 5375 Pebble Creek Trail, P. O. Box 2730, Rockford, IL 61111 US
Second Address: 5375 Pebble Creek Tr., Loves Park, IL 61111
(815) 654-1200, *Fax:* (815) 282-7779
www.101qfl.com
positive@101qfl.com
License: Rockford, Winnebago County, IL held by Quest for Life Inc.
Arbitron Metro Market: Rockford, IL *Format:* Christian *Hrs. of News Programming:* news progmg one hr wkly *No. News Employees:* 1 *Target Audience:* 25-44; female dominant, educated, upscale & middle class
Ralph Trentadue, General Manager
Rick Hall, Programming Director

WROK
01-01-1923; 1440 khz AM
3901 Brendenwood Road, Rockford, IL 61107 US
(815) 399-2233, *Fax:* (815) 399-8148
www.1440wrok.com
License: Rockford, IL held by Cumulus Licensing Corp.
Group Owner: Cumulus Media Inc.; (acq 10-2-00; grpsl).
Nat'l Network: CBS; Wall Street
Arbitron Metro Market: Rockford, IL *Format:* News, News/Talk, 86 *Target Audience:* P35-64
Scott Maenner, General Sales Mgr
Scot Bertram, Programming Director
Dawn Plock, Promotions Manager
Jan Thorpe, News Director
John Huntley, Chief Engineer

WZOK
01-01-1949; 97.5 mhz FM; 50 kw; 452 ft.; N42 16 45 W89 2 15
3901 Brendenwood Road, Rockford, IL 61107 US
(815) 399-2233, *Fax:* (815) 484-2432
www.97zokonline.com
feedback@97zokonline.com
License: Rockford, Winnebago County, IL
Group Owner: Cumulus Media Inc.
Arbitron Metro Market: Rockford, IL *Format:* Contemporary Hits/Top 40 *Target Audience:* 25-34.
Sweet Lenny, Programming Director
Priscilla Cantu, Promotions Manager
Becky Riojas, Market Manager
Scott Maenner, Sales Manager

Rockton

WGFB
03-01-1963; 103.1 mhz FM *Hrs Open:* 24; 2.4 kw; 525 ft.; N42 22 2 W89 5 13
1884 Plains Avenue, Aurora, IL 60307 US
(815) 874-7861, *Fax:* (815) 874-2202
www.B103fm.com
License: Rockton, Winnebago County, IL held by Maverick Media of Rockford License LLC.
Group Owner: Maverick Media LLC; (acq 4-27-2005; grpsl).
Nat'l Reps: Katz Radio
Arbitron Metro Market: Rockford, IL *Format:* Adult Contemp
Target Audience: 25-54; adult women
Gary Rozynek, President
Jay Chapman, General Manager
Lisa Chatfield, General Sales Mgr
Jim Stone, Programming Director
Michelle Markhan, Promotions Manager
Ken DeCoster, News Director
Chuck Ingle, Chief Engineer
Bill Koch,Sales Manager

Rosemont

*WTZI
88.1 mhz FM; 0.3 kw; 72 ft.; N41 57 20 W87 52 2
US
(847) 524-4619
ccelkgrove@yahoo.com
License: Rosemont, Cook County, IL held by Calvary Chapel of Elk Grove Village.
Arbitron Metro Market: Rosemont, IL
Philipp Ballmaier, President

Rushville

WKXQ
05-01-1985; 92.5 mhz FM *Hrs Open:* 5 AM-midnight; 6 kw; 328 ft.; N40 8 20 W90 39 26
123 N. Liberty Street, P.O. Box 196, Rushville, IL 62681 US
(815) 758-8686, *Fax:* (309) 833-3460
www.radiomacomb.com
wkxq92@frontiernet.net
License: Rushville, Schuyler County, IL held by WPW Broadcasting Inc.
Group Owner: Prairie Radio Communications; (acq 12-6-99; $550,000 with WPWQ(FM) Mount Sterling)
Nat'l Network: CNN Radio
Format: Oldies *Special Programming:* Relg 6 hrs, farm 6 hrs wkly *Hrs. of News Programming:* news progmg 12 hrs wkly *No. News Employees:* 1 *Target Audience:* 18-54.
Don Davis, President
Vanessa Wetterling, General Manager
Michael Weaver, Programming Director

Salem

WJBD
12-16-1956; 1350 khz AM *Hrs Open:* 24; 0.43 kw-D, ND1; 0.059 kw-N, ND1; N38 37 56 W88 55 2
Mailing Address: 980 North Michigan Ave, Suite 1880, Chicago, IL 60611 US
Second Address: 221 E. Broadway, Suite 107, Centralia, IL 62801
(618) 548-2000, *Fax:* (618) 548-2079
www.wjbdradio.com
wjbd@accessus.net
License: Salem, IL held by NRG License Sub. LLC.
Group Owner: NRG Media LLC; (acq 10-31-2005; grpsl)
Format: Country *Special Programming:* Farm 4 hrs, relg 6 hrs wkly *Hrs. of News Programming:* news progmg 30 hrs wkly *No. News Employees:* 3 *Target Audience:* General.
Bruce Kropp, General Manager

WJBD-FM
06-01-1972; 100.1 mhz FM *Hrs Open:* 24; 1.15 kw; 449 ft.; N38 33 45 W88 59 57
Mailing Address: 980 North Michigan Ave, Suite 1880, Chicago, IL 60611 US
Second Address: 310 W. McMackin St., Salem, IL 62881
(618) 548-2000, *Fax:* (618) 548-2079
www.wjbdradio.com
wjbd@accessus.net
License: Salem, Marion County, IL held by NRG License Sub. LLC.
Group Owner: NRG Media LLC
Format: Adult Contemp, News
Matt Tackett, Operations Dir

*WSLE
01-01-2005; 91.3 mhz FM; 0.77 kw; 154 ft.; N38 37 34 W88 56 41
P.O. Drawer 2440, Tupelo, MS 38803 US
(662) 844-8888, *Fax:* (662) 842-6791
www.afa.net
randall@afa.net
License: Salem, Marion County, IL held by American Family Association.
Group Owner: American Family Radio
Arbitron Metro Market: Salem, IL *Format:* Christian
Marvin Sanders, General Manager
John Riley, Programming Director

Sandwich

WAUR
05-01-1986; 930 khz AM *Hrs Open:* 24; 2.5 kw-D, DA2; 4.2 kw-N, DA2; N41 36 26 W88 27 11
8910 University Center Lane, #130, San Diego, CA 92122 US
(312) 461-8540 or (219) 309-9327, *Fax:* (312) 588-0168
www.waur.relevantradio.com
aciabattari@relevantradio.com
License: Sandwich, IL held by Starboard Media Foundation Inc.
Group Owner: Relevant Radio; (acq 5-4-2004; $3.5 million).

Arbitron Metro Market: Hutchinson, MN *Format:* Talk, Christian *Special Programming:* Farm 15 hrs wkly *Target Audience:* 25-54.
Armand Ciabattari, General Manager

Savanna

WCCI
11-07-1971; 100.3 mhz FM *Hrs Open:* 24; 9.6 kw; 515 ft.; N42 7 47 W90 8 24
P.O. Box 310, Savanna, IL 61074 US
(815) 273-7757, *Fax:* (815) 273-2760
www.wcciradio.com
radio@wccilive.com
License: Savanna, Carroll County, IL held by Carroll County Communications Inc.
Nat'l Network: Fox News Radio *Regional Network:* Brownfield
Arbitron Metro Market: Savanna, IL *Format:* Country, News *Hrs. of News Programming:* news progmg 35 hrs wkly *No. News Employees:* 1 *Target Audience:* 25-54. *Adv. Rates:* 9; 9; 9; 9
John Miller, President
Edward Bock, Operations Dir
Brian Reusch, Station Manager
Leslie Smith, Programming Director
Mark Schoening, News Director

Seneca

WJDK-FM
01-01-1993; 95.7 mhz FM; 3 kw; 328 ft.; N41 13 12 W88 32 27
One Broadcast Center, Plano, IL 60545 US
(815) 941-1000, *Fax:* (815) 941-9300
www.wjdkfm.com
License: Seneca, La Salle County, IL held by Grundy County Broadcasters Inc.
Nat'l Network: ABC
Arbitron Metro Market: Chicago, IL *Format:* Adult Contemp *Hrs. of News Programming:* news progmg 14 hrs wkly *No. News Employees:* 1 *Target Audience:* 25-49. *Adv. Rates:* 42; 31; 36; 25
Larry Nelson, President
Mike Williams, Operations Dir
Jack Daly, General Manager

Sheffield

***WPRC**
88.7 mhz FM; 8.5 kw; 417 ft.; N41 36 33.3 W89 40 18.6 US
(309) 692-9242, *Fax:* (309) 692-9241
www.wcicfm.org
wcic@wcicfm.org
License: Sheffield, Bureau County, IL held by Illinois Bible Institute Inc.
Group Owner: Illinois Bible Institute Inc.
Arbitron Metro Market: Sheffield, IL *Format:* Christian, Talk
Dave Brooks, General Manager
Dave Brooks, Station Manager
Jessie Browning, Promotions Manager
Joe Buchanan, Music Director
Katie Post, Office Manager
Trevor Moore, Audio/New Media Producer

Shelbyville

WINU
11-24-1972; 870 khz AM *Hrs Open:* 4:30 AM-7:30 PM
1411 Locust Street, St Louis, MO 63103 US
(314) 421-3020, *Fax:* (314) 421-1702
www.hereshelpnet.org
License: Shelbyville, IL held by New Life Evangelistic Center Inc.
Arbitron Metro Market: Decatur, IL *Format:* Christian *Target Audience:* 25-54.
Gary Scott, General Manager

WEJT
12-31-1969; 105.1 mhz FM *Hrs Open:* 24/7; 13 kw; 466 ft.; N39 35 38 W88 50 45
P.O. Box 150846, Nashville, TN 37215 US
(217) 428-4487, *Fax:* (217) 428-4501
www.wejt.com
cbullock@cromwellradio.com
License: Shelbyville, Shelby County, IL held by Cromwell Group Inc. of Illinois.
Group Owner: The Cromwell Group Inc.; (acq 8-1-89; $320,000 with co-located AM;
Nat'l Reps: Eastman Radio
Arbitron Metro Market: Decatur, IL *Format:* Contemporary Hits/Top 40, Adult Contemp *Target Audience:* 25-54; baby boomers *Adv. Rates:* 30; 28; 30; 20
Tara Nickerson, Operations Dir
Chris Bullock, General Manager
Larry Timmons, Chief Engineer

Sherman

WABZ
05-10-1971; 93.9 mhz FM; 15 kw; 430 ft.; N39 59 25 W89 30 46
3501 Sangamon Avenue, Springfield, IL 62707 US
(217) 753-5400, *Fax:* (217) 753-7902
info@wabz.com
License: Sherman, Sangamon County, IL held by Saga Communications of Illinois LLC.
Group Owner: Saga Communications Inc.; (acq 7-96; grpsl).
Arbitron Metro Market: Sherman, IL *Format:* Classic Rock, Adult Contemp *Target Audience:* 25-54.
Leanne Arndt, General Manager
Kevin Anfield, General Sales Mgr
Bob Parrish, Programming Director
Brandy Moore, Promotions Manager
Michelle Eecles, News Director

Skokie

WTMX
08-18-1961; 101.9 mhz FM *Hrs Open:* 24; 4.2 kw; 1562 ft.; N41 52 44 W87 38 8
P.O. Box 1160, Salt Lake City, UT 84110 US
(312) 946-1019, *Fax:* (312) 946-4747
www.wtmx.com
awicklund@bonnevillechicago.com
License: Skokie, Cook County, IL held by Bonneville International Corp.
Group Owner: Bonneville International Corporation; (acq 8-70)
Nat'l Reps: Katz Radio
Arbitron Metro Market: Chicago, IL *Format:* Adult Contemp *No. News Employees:* 1
Drew Horowitz, President
Barry James, Station Manager
Sara McMurray, General Sales Mgr
Mary Ellen Kachinske, Programming Director
Sandy Patyk, Promotions Manager
Barry Keefe, News Director
Kent Lewin, Chief Engineer
NikkiChuminatto, Music Director
Dave Karwowski, Marketing Director
Dianne Parra, Promotion Manager
Jeff Buti, Digital Media Director
Craig Volpe, Director of Sales
Charmaine Fagan, Vice President - Finance and Administration

Smithboro

***WSWS(FM)**
89.9 mhz FM; 10 kw; Ant 164 ft; N38 56 09 W89 13 56
5210 S.E. Washington Blvd., Bartlesville, OK 74006
(918) 333-8700, *Fax:* (918) 333-3526
License: Smithboro, Bond County, IL held by The Power Foundation
Population Served: 177 *Arbitron Metro Market:* Smithboro, IL
Danny Hester, President

South Beloit

WTJK
05-18-1948; 1380 khz AM *Hrs Open:* 24; 5 kw-D, DAN; 5 kw-N, DAN; N42 27 34 W89 1 43
P.O. Box 27, Beloit, WI 53512 US
(608) 758-9025, *Fax:* (608) 758-9550
www.espn1380.com
aliebetrau@espn1380.com
License: South Beloit, IL held by Good Karma Broadcasting L.L.C.
Group Owner: Good Karma Broadcasting L.L.C.; acq 9-13-00; $235,000)
Nat'l Network: ESPN Radio *Nat'l Reps:* Interep
Arbitron Metro Market: Janesville, WI *Format:* Sports *Target Audience:* 25-54; males *Adv. Rates:* 30; 35; 30; 20
Laurie Clarks, General Manager
Laurie Clarks, General Sales Mgr
Andrew Liebetrau, Programming Director
Hannah Kubiak, Promotions Manager
Warren Jorgensen, Chief Engineer
Brad Fitzke, Sales Executive
Roz McKennon, SalesExecutive
Stacy Todd, Sales Executive
Corey Gloor, Programming Executive
Stephen Johnson, Programming Executive

South Jacksonville

WJVO
09-01-1986; 105.5 mhz FM *Hrs Open:* 24; 6 kw; 328 ft.; N39 43 20 W90 11 43
P.O. Box 1055, Jacksonville, IL 62651 US
(217) 245-5119, *Fax:* (217) 245-1596
wjvofm.com
License: South Jacksonville, Morgan County, IL held by Morgan County Broadcasting Co. Inc.
Nat'l Network: Westwood One; ABC
Format: Country *Hrs. of News Programming:* news progmg 4 hrs wkly *No. News Employees:* 1 *Target Audience:* 25-54.
Sarah Hautala, General Manager

Sparta

WHCO
02-01-1955; 1230 khz AM *Hrs Open:* 24; 1 kw-U, ND1; N38 7 25 W89 43 20
Mailing Address: P.O. Box 255, Sparta, IL 62286 US
Second Address: 47 W. Maine, Mascoutah, IL 62258
(618) 443-2121, *Fax:* (618) 443-2800
www.whcoradio.com
Hoefft@Egyptian.Net
License: Sparta, IL held by Hirsch Communication Engineering Co.
Nat'l Network: CBS; Westwood One *Regional Network:* Brownfield; Ill. Radio Net.
Arbitron Metro Market: St. Louis, MO *Format:* News, News/Talk, 84, Talk *Special Programming:* Pol 2 hrs, farm 20 hrs, relg 10 hrs wkly *Hrs. of News Programming:* news progmg 10 hrs wkly *No. News Employees:* 2*Target Audience:* 25-65.
Jack Scheper Sr., President
Mike Hoeft, News Director

Spring Valley

WIVQ
12-01-1993; 103.3 mhz FM *Hrs Open:* 24; 4.9 kw; 361 ft.; N41 18 9 W89 14 11 *Rebroadcasts:* Rebroadcasts WSTQ 100%
3905 Progress Blvd., Peru, IL 61354 US
(877) 855-2480, *Fax:* (815) 224-2066
qhitmusic.com
q@theradiogroup.net
License: Spring Valley, Bureau County, IL held by Mendota Broadcasting Inc.
Group Owner: Studstill Broadcasting; (acq 7-17-97; $700,000 with WBZG(FM) Peru).
Nat'l Reps: Rgnl Reps *Wire Services:* AP
Arbitron Metro Market: Spring Valley, IL *Format:* Adult Contemp, Contemporary Hits/Top 40 *No. News Employees:* 2 *Target Audience:* 18-44.
Lamar Studstill, Chairman
Owen Studstill, CEO
Cole Studstill, Station Manager
Kim Miller, Promotions Manager
David Kuharski, News Director
Cole Charles Studstill, CFO

***WSOG**
12-01-2002; 88.1 mhz FM *Hrs Open:* 24; 4 kw vert; 262 ft.; N41 17 32 W89 7 59
515 West Minnesota, Spring Valley, IL 61362 US
(815) 220-1929, *Fax:* (815) 220-1929
www.wsogradio.com
wsog881@hotmail.com
License: Spring Valley, Bureau County, IL held by Spirit Education Association Inc.
Arbitron Metro Market: Spring Valley, IL *Format:* Christian
Jim Perona, Sr., General Manager & Founder
Louis Perona, President
Jeremy Caldera, Voicing & Technical Support
Bob Gibson, Programming Planning, Voicing & Logging
Allen Drake, Project Coordinator

Springfield

WDBR
04-01-1948; 103.7 mhz FM; 50 kw; 299 ft.; N39 47 37 W89 36 18
3501 Sangamon Avenue, Springfield, IL 62707 US
(217) 753-5400, *Fax:* (217) 753-7902
www.wdbr.com
msmith@capitolradiogroup.com
License: Springfield, Sangamon County, IL
Group Owner: Saga Communications Inc.
Wire Services: UPI
Arbitron Metro Market: Springfield, IL *Format:* Contemporary Hits/Top 40 *Target Audience:* 18-49; general
Mitch Smith, General Manager
Jason Addams, Programming Director
Scott Lindahl, Promotions Manager

WFMB
01-01-1922; 1450 khz AM *Hrs Open:* 24; 1 kw-U, ND1; N39 45 36 W89 39 5
600 Congress Ave., Suite 1400, Austin, TX 78701 US
(217) 528-3033, *Fax:* (217) 528-5348
www.sportsradio1450.com
sportsradio1450@sportsradio1450.com
License: Springfield, IL held by Neuhoff Family L.P.
Group Owner: Neuhoff Family L.P.; (acq 8-1-2007; grpsl)
Nat'l Network: ESPN Radio; ABC Information & Entertainment
Regional Network: Tribune Radio Networks; Brownfield; RFD Illinois *Nat'l Reps:* Christal
Format: Sports *Hrs. of News Programming:* news progmg 5 hrs wkly *No. News Employees:* 2 *Target Audience:* 25-54; upscale professionals
Kevin O'Dea, General Manager
Kevin Anfield, General Sales Mgr
Danielle Outlaw, Programming Director
Frank Konwinski, Chief Engineer
Jeff Hofmann, News Director
John Price, Program Director

WFMB-FM
07-01-1965; 104.5 mhz FM *Hrs Open:* 24; 43 kw; 430 ft.; N39 45 36 W89 39 5
600 Congress Ave., Suite 1400, Austin, TX 78701 US
(217) 528-3033, *Fax:* (217) 528-5348
www.wfmb.com
wfmb@wfmb.com
License: Springfield, Sangamon County, IL
Group Owner: Neuhoff Family L.P.
Nat'l Network: Motor Racing Net *Nat'l Reps:* Christal
Format: Country *No. News Employees:* 1 *Target Audience:* A 25-54.
Kevin O'Dea, General Manager
Kevin Anfield, General Sales Mgr
Danielle Outlaw, Programming Director
Dave Marsh, Promotions Manager
Kerri Cawley, Information Technology Director
John Spalding, Music Director
Jessica Ross, TrafficManager
Kathy Byerly, Local Sales Manager
Danielle Outlaw, Director of Sales

***WLUJ**
05-24-1995; 89.7 mhz FM; 20 kw; 328 ft.; N39 48 30 W89 37 30
600 West Mason Street, Springfield, IL 62702 US
(217) 528-2300, *Fax:* (217) 528-2400
www.wluj.org
wluj897@ameritech.net
License: Springfield, Sangamon County, IL held by Cornerstone Community Radio Inc.
Nat'l Network: Moody
Format: Christian, Talk *Target Audience:* General.
Arthur Gregg, Operations Dir
Richard Van Zandt, General Manager
John McBride, Station Manager
Richard Beaman, General Sales Mgr
Howard Fouks, Operations Manager
Dick Reed, Vice President

WMAY
10-15-1950; 970 khz AM; 1 kw-D, DA2; 0.5 kw-N, DA2; N39 51 42 W89 32 32
Mailing Address: P.O. Box 460, Springfield, IL 62705 US
Second Address: 1510 N. Third, Riverton, IL 62561
(217) 629-7077, *Fax:* (217) 629-7952
www.wmay.com
wmay@wmay.com
License: Springfield, IL held by Long Nine Inc.
Group Owner: The Mid-West Family Broadcast Group; (acq 12-7-76).
Nat'l Reps: D & R Radio
Arbitron Metro Market: Springfield,IL *Format:* News, News/Talk, 86 *Special Programming:* Big band 5 hrs wkly *Target Audience:* 25-64.
Kevan Kavanough, General Manager
Dave Doetsch, General Sales Mgr
Robb Rose, Programming Director
Amanda Johnson, Promotions Manager
Jim Leach, News Director
Greg Stephens, Chief Engineer

WNNS
11-01-1980; 98.7 mhz FM; 50 kw; 469 ft.; N39 41 59 W89 46 55
P.O. Box 460, Springfield, IL 62705 US
(217) 629-7077, *Fax:* (217) 629-7952
www.wnns.com
wnns@wnns.com
License: Springfield, Sangamon County, IL held by Long Nine Inc.
Group Owner: The Mid-West Family Broadcast Group
Arbitron Metro Market: Springfield, IL *Format:* Adult Contemp
Special Programming: Jazz 6 hrs wkly
Kellie Michaels, Operations Dir
Kavan Kavanough, General Manager
Greg Stephens, Engineering Dir

***WQNA**
08-31-1979; 88.3 mhz FM *Hrs Open:* 24; 0.25 kw; 256 ft.; N39 44 3 W89 38 18
2201 Toronto Road, Springfield, IL 62707 US
(217) 529-5431, *Fax:* (217) 529-7861
www.wqna.org
info@wqna.org
License: Springfield, Sangamon County, IL held by Capital Area Career Center.
Regional Reps: Illinois Student News Network
Format: Variety/Diverse *Special Programming:* Varied *Hrs. of News Programming:* news progmg 6 hrs wkly *No. News Employees:* 1 *Target Audience:* 13-24; student, community, high school & college students
Jim Grimes, General Manager
Jim Pemberton, Programming Director
Kerri Donovan, Engineering Dir

WQQL
11-15-1993; 101.9 mhz FM *Hrs Open:* 24; 50 kw; 272 ft.; N39 42 39 W89 38 42
1030 Durkin Drive, Springfield, IL 62704 US
(217) 753-5400, *Fax:* (217) 753-7902
www.cool1019.com
info@cool1019.com
License: Springfield, Sangamon County, IL held by Saga Communications of Illinois LLC.
Group Owner: Saga Communications Inc.; (acq 9-10-93; $1.44 million;
Nat'l Reps: Katz Radio
Format: Oldies *Hrs. of News Programming:* News progmg 2 hrs wkly *Target Audience:* 25 plus; upscale educated adults
Leanne Arndt, General Manager
Kevin Anfield, General Sales Mgr
Joey Mc Laughlin, Programming Director

***WSCT**
11-01-1993; 90.5 mhz FM *Hrs Open:* 24; 3.8 kw; 410 ft.; N39 38 38 W89 30 51 *Rebroadcasts:* Rebroadcasts WIBI(FM) Carlinville 100%
P.O. Box 140, Carlinville, IL 62626 US
(217) 854-4800, *Fax:* (217) 854-4810
www.wibi.org
wibi@wibi.org
License: Springfield, Sangamon County, IL held by Illinois Bible Institute.
Format: Religious *Hrs. of News Programming:* News progmg 5 hrs wkly *Target Audience:* 25-44; Christian & seeking non-Christians
Melody Miller, Operations Dir
Tom Greene, Station Manager
Rob Regal, Programming Director
G.W. Van Alstine, Promotions Manager
Joe Rother, Engineering Dir

WTAX
01-01-1930; 1240 khz AM; 1 kw-U, ND1; N39 47 36 W89 36 18
PO Box 2759, Springfield, IL 62708 US
(217) 753-5400, *Fax:* (217) 753-7902
www.wtax.com
info@wtax.com
License: Springfield, IL held by Saga Communications of Illinois LLC.
Group Owner: Saga Communications Inc.; (acq 1996).
Nat'l Network: Moody; CBS *Nat'l Reps:* Christal *Wire Services:* UPI
Format: News, News/Talk, 84, Talk *Special Programming:* Farm 16 hrs wkly *Hrs. of News Programming:* news progmg 20, hrs wkly *No. News Employees:* 3 *Target Audience:* 30 plus.
Leanne Arndt, General Manager
Michelle Eccles, News Director

***WUIS**
01-03-1975; 91.9 mhz FM *Hrs Open:* 24; 50 kw; 499 ft.; N39 47 1.1 W89 26 45.9 *Rebroadcasts:* Rebroadcasts WIPA(FM) Pittsfield 100%
Mailing Address: South Sheperd Road, Springfield, IL 62794 US
Second Address: One University Plaza, MS CBM-130, Springfield, IL 62703
(217) 206-9847
www.wuis.org
wuis@wuis.edu
License: Springfield, Sangamon County, IL held by University of Illinois at Springfield.
Nat'l Network: NPR; PRI
Arbitron Metro Market: Springfield, IL *Format:* Jazz, News
Special Programming: NPR entertainment 15 hrs, bluegrass 2 hrs, Singer/ *Hrs. of News Programming:* news progmg 45 hrs wkly *No. News Employees:* 5*Target Audience:* 25-54.
Sinta Seiber, Operations Dir
Bill Wheelhouse, General Manager
Lisa Clemmons-Stott, General Sales Mgr
Sinta Seiber-Lane, Programming Director
Sean Crawford, News Director
Greg Manfroi, Chief Engineer
Sandra McGinnis, BusinessDirector
Randy Eccles, Development Director
Virginia Mitchell, Development Assistant

St. Anne

WXNU
01-01-2006; 106.5 mhz FM; 1.95 kw; 463 ft.; N41 0 20 W87 41 42
US
(815) 935-9555, *Fax:* (815) 935-9593
www.wxnu.com
wlan@starradio.com
License: St. Anne, Kankakee County, IL held by STARadio Corp.
Group Owner: STARadio Corp.
Arbitron Metro Market: Saint Anne, IL *Format:* Country
Brendan Michaels, Operations Dir
Bob Kersmarki, General Manager
Larry Regnier, General Sales Mgr
Phil Reilly, Chief Engineer

St. Joseph

***WGNJ**
01-01-1999; 89.3 mhz FM *Hrs Open:* 24; 50 kw; 459 ft.; N40 5 16 W87 53 42
Mailing Address: P.O. Box 12345, Champaign, IL 61826 US
Second Address: 2421 N. 1450 E. Rd., White Heath, IL 61884
(217) 897-6333
www.greatnewsradio.org
staff@greatnewsradio.org
License: St. Joseph, Champaign County, IL held by Good News Radio Inc.
Nat'l Network: Salem Radio Network
Format: Christian, Religious, 86 *Target Audience:* 35 plus; general
David Herriott, Chairman
Mark Burns, President
Carrie Burns, Operations Dir

Staunton

WAOX
12-01-1999; 105.3 mhz FM *Hrs Open:* 24; 6 kw; 285 ft.; N39 2 37 W89 44 56
P.O. Box 10, Litchfield, IL 62056 US
(618) 635-6000, *Fax:* (217) 532-2431
www.waox.com
waox@waoxradio.com
License: Staunton, Macoupin County, IL held by Talley Broadcasting Corp.
Group Owner: Talley Radio Stations
Nat'l Network: ABC *Nat'l Reps:* Christal *Regional Reps:* Regional 'reps *Wire Services:* AP
Arbitron Metro Market: Staunton, IL. *Format:* Adult Contemp *No. News Employees:* 2 *Target Audience:* 18-54.
Hayward Talley, President
Brian Talley, Operations Dir
Hayward Talley, General Manager
Beth Niehaus, News Director

Sterling

***WNIQ**
91.5 mhz FM *Hrs Open:* 24; 2.4 kw; 328 ft.; N41 53 52 W89 36 20 *Rebroadcasts:* Rebroadcasts WNIJ(FM) De Kalb & WNIU(FM) Rockford 50%
801 North First Street, Dekalb, IL 60115 US
(815) 753-9000, *Fax:* (815) 753-9938
www.northernpublicradio.org
npr@niu.edu
License: Sterling, Whiteside County, IL held by Northern Illinois University.
Nat'l Network: PRI; NPR
Arbitron Metro Market: Freeport, IL *Format:* News, News/Talk, 86 *Hrs. of News Programming:* News progmg 2 hrs wkly *Target Audience:* General.
Staci Hoste, General Manager
Jan Kilgard, General Sales Mgr
Bill Drake, Programming Director
Guy Stephens, News Director

WSDR
08-21-1949; 1240 khz AM *Hrs Open:* 24; 0.5 kw-D, ND1; 1 kw-N, ND1; N41 48 59 W89 40 13
3501 Broadway, P.O. Box 1508, Mount Vernon, IL 62864 US
(815) 625-3400, *Fax:* (815) 625-6940
wsdr1240@theramp.net
License: Sterling, IL held by Withers Broadcasting Co. of Rock River LLC.
Group Owner: Withers Broadcasting Co.; (acq 1-21-98; grpsl).
Nat'l Network: CBS; ABC *Regional Network:* Ill. Radio Net. *Nat'l Reps:* Christal
Format: News, Sports, 86 *Special Programming:* Farm 16 hrs, Sp 4 hrs wkly *Hrs. of News Programming:* news progmg 10 hrs wkly *No. News Employees:* 2 *Target Audience:* 25 plus.
Brian Zschiesche, General Manager
Sherry Smith, General Sales Mgr
Lisa Taylor, Programming Director

WSSQ
08-01-1966; 94.3 mhz FM; 6 kw; 299 ft.; N41 51 6 W89 42 38
3501 Broadway, P.O. Box 1508, Mount Vernon, IL 62864 US
(815) 625-3400, *Fax:* (815) 625-6940
wsdr1240@theramp.net
License: Sterling, Whiteside County, IL
Group Owner: Withers Broadcasting Co.
Nat'l Network: Westwood One; ABC *Nat'l Reps:* Christal
Format: Adult Contemp *Target Audience:* 25-54; women
T.J. Anzvino, General Manager

Streator

WSPL
09-26-1953; 1250 khz AM *Hrs Open:* 24; 0.5 kw-D, DA2; 0.064 kw-N, DA2; N41 9 30 W88 50 13
P. O. Box 377, Streator, IL 61364 US
(815) 672-2947, *Fax:* (815) 673-1833
am1250wspl.com
wspl@theradiogroup.net
License: Streator, IL held by Mendota Broadcasting Inc.
Group Owner: Studstill Broadcasting; (acq 5-30-2000; grpsl)
Arbitron Metro Market: La Salle-Peru, IL *Format:* News, News/Talk, 84, Talk *Hrs. of News Programming:* news progmg 25 hrs wkly *No. News Employees:* 3 *Target Audience:* 35 plus.
Lamar Studstill, Chairman
Owen Studstill, President
Cole Studstill, Operations Dir
Lee Studstill, General Manager
Cheryl Knirlberger, General Sales Mgr
Dave Noesen, News Director
Mark Baker, Chief Engineer

WSTQ
09-15-1964; 97.7 mhz FM *Hrs Open:* 24; 6 kw; 328 ft.; N41 10 49 W88 52 6
P. O. Box 377, Steator, IL 61364 US
(815) 224-2100, *Fax:* (815) 224-2066
qhitmusic.com
q@theradiogroup.net
License: Streator, La Salle County, IL
Group Owner: Studstill Broadcasting
Arbitron Metro Market: La Salle-Peru, IL *Format:* Contemporary Hits/Top 40 *Target Audience:* 18-44.
Cole Studstill, Programming Director

WYYS
01-01-1995; 106.1 mhz FM *Hrs Open:* 24; 2.45 kw; 520 ft.; N41 16 30 W88 57 56
1317 N. 300 East Road, Monticello, IL 61856 US
(815) 224-2100, *Fax:* (815) 224-2066
wyys@theradiogroup.net
License: Streator, La Salle County, IL held by Mendota Broadcasting Inc.
Group Owner: Studstill Broadcasting; (acq 3-8-2000; grpsl)
Nat'l Network: ABC
Arbitron Metro Market: La Salle-Peru, *Format:* Oldies *No. News Employees:* 2 *Target Audience:* 35 plus.
Lamar Studstill, Chairman
Cole Studstill, CFO
Lee Studstill, President

Sugar Grove

***WSRI**
01-01-2005; 88.7 mhz FM *Hrs Open:* 24; 0.6 kw; 338 ft.; N41 42 16 W88 26 2 *Rebroadcasts:* Rebroadcasts KLRD(FM) Yucaipa, CA 100%
1425 N Market Blvd., Suite 9, Sacramento, CA 95834 US
(888) 937-2471, *Fax:* (916) 251-1650
www.air1.com
info@air1.com
License: Sugar Grove, Kane County, IL held by Educational Media Foundation.
Group Owner: EMF Broadcasting
Nat'l Network: Air 1
Arbitron Metro Market: Sugar Grove, IL *Format:* Alternative, Christian *Target Audience:* 25-44; female-Judeo/ Christian
Darrell Chambliss, Chairman
Alan Mason, COO
Mike Novak, President and CEO
David Pierce, Programming Director
Ed Lenane, News Director
Sam Wallington, Engineering Dir
Marya Morgan, News Reporter
Richard Hunt, News Reporter
Larry Moody, Director
Mitch Barnhart, Director
David R. Ferry, Director
Walter Golembeski, Director

Sullivan

WZNX
04-01-1992; 106.7 mhz FM *Hrs Open:* 24; 9.5 kw; 550 ft; N39 36 38 W88 41 32
410 N. Water St., Suite B, Decatur, IL 37215
(217) 428-4487, *Fax:* (217) 428-4501
www.decaturradio.com
cbullock@cromwellradio.com
License: Sullivan, Moultrie County, IL held by WSHY Inc.
Group Owner: The Cromwell Group Inc.; (acq 2-14-97; $750,000)
Nat'l Network: Fox News Network *Nat'l Reps:* Eastman Radio
Population Served: 300,000 *Arbitron Metro Market:* Decatur, IL *Hrs. of News Programming:* 24/7 *No. News Employees:* 1
Target Audience: 25-54; strong men
Tara Nickerson, Operations Dir
Chris Bullock, General Manager
Storm, Programming Director
Larry Timmons, Chief Engineer

Summit

***WARG**
01-01-1976; 88.9 mhz FM *Hrs Open:* 8 AM-10 PM; 0.5 kw horiz, 0.46 kw vert; 82 ft.; N41 46 36 W87 48 17
7329 West 63rd Street, Summit, IL 60501 US
(708) 728-8368, *Fax:* (708) 728-3155
www.warg.argohs.net
info@warg.com
License: Summit, Cook County, IL held by Community High School District No. 217.
Arbitron Metro Market: Summit, IL *Format:* Alternative *Target Audience:* High School Students; alternative subculture
Jennifer Knapp, General Manager

Sycamore

WSQR
06-11-1981; 1180 khz AM
1 Broadcast Center, Plano, IL 60545 US
(630) 552-1000, *Fax:* (630) 552-9300
wspy-news@nelsonmultimedia.net
License: Sycamore, IL held by De kalb County Broadcasters Inc.
Nat'l Network: ABC
Format: Adult Contemp *Special Programming:* Farm 6 hrs wkly
Target Audience: 35-55.
Pam Nelson, CFO
Larry Nelson, President
Beth Pierre, General Manager
Vori Dhabolt, General Sales Mgr

Taylorville

***WIHM**
01-01-1952; 1410 khz AM
9 Cougar Road, Glen Carbon, IL 62034 US
(314) 752-7000
www.covenantnet.net
office@covenantnet.net
License: Taylorville, IL held by Covenant Network
Group Owner: Covenant Network; (acq 7-31-98; $60,000)
Format: Christian, Religious
Tony Holman, President

WQLZ
12-01-1967; 92.7 mhz FM *Hrs Open:* 24; 11.5 kw; 482 ft.; N39 38 38 W89 30 51
Mailing Address: P.O. Box 460, Springfield, IL 62705 US
Second Address: 1510 N. Third, Riverton, IL 62561
(217) 629-7077, *Fax:* (217) 629-7952
www.wqlz.com
wqlz@wqlz.com
License: Taylorville, Christian County, IL held by Long Nine Inc.
Group Owner: Family Stations Inc.; (acq 2-3-93; $1 million;
Format: Rock/AOR *Hrs. of News Programming:* news progmg 3 hrs wkly *No. News Employees:* 4 *Target Audience:* 18-34.
Dave Duetsch, General Sales Mgr
Valerie Knight, Programming Director
Jim Leach, News Director
Greg Stephens, Chief Engineer
Quinn Fagg, Traffic Manager

WTIM-FM
11-13-1997; 97.3 mhz FM *Hrs Open:* 24; 4.6 kw; 374 ft.; N39 27 8 W89 17 10
Mailing Address: 111 West Main Cross, P O Box 169, Taylorville, IL 62568 US
Second Address: 918 E. Park St., Taylorville, IL 62568
(217) 824-3395, *Fax:* (217) 824-3301
www.randyradio.com
License: Taylorville, Christian County, IL held by Miller Communications Inc.
Group Owner: Miller Media Group
Nat'l Network: CNN Radio *Nat'l Reps:* Commercial Media Sales
Arbitron Metro Market: Taylorville, IL *Format:* News, News/Talk, 86 *Special Programming:* Farm 20 hrs, relg 4 hrs wkly *Hrs. of News Programming:* news progmg 25 hrs wkly *No. News Employees:* 1 *Target Audience:* 25 plus.
Randal Miller, President
Kami Payne, General Manager
Brandon Fellows, Programming Director
Steve Butera, News Director

Teutopolis

WKJT
01-01-1994; 102.3 mhz FM *Hrs Open:* 24; 6 kw; 328 ft.; N39 8 30 W88 33 36
1100 Ave. of Mid-America, P.O. Box 566, Effingham, IL 62401 US
(217) 347-5518, *Fax:* (217) 347-5519
www.kjcountry.com
info@kjcountry.com
License: Teutopolis, Effingham County, IL held by Kirby Broadcasting Inc.
Nat'l Network: Fox News Radio
Format: Country
John Kirby, President
Tonya Siner, Operations Dir
Greg Sapp, Station Manager
George Flexter, Programming Director

Thomasboro

WKZS
06-01-1982; 103.3 mhz FM *Hrs Open:* 24; 3 kw; 299 ft.; N40 8 46 W87 27 15
Mailing Address: 820 Railroad St. PO Bx67, Covington, IN 47932 US
Second Address: P.O. Box 67, Covington, IN 47932
(217) 443-4004, *Fax:* (765) 793-4644
www.kisscountryradio.com
info@kisscountryradio.com
License: Thomasboro, Fountain County, IL held by Benton-Weatherford Broadcasting Inc. of Indiana.
Nat'l Network: Jones Radio Networks *Wire Services:* AP
Format: Country *Hrs. of News Programming:* News progmg 10 hrs wkly *No. News Employees:* 1 *Target Audience:* 18-49.
Larry Weatherford, President
Rhea Benton-Weatherford, General Manager
Greg Green, Station Manager
Tara Duncan, Promotions Manager

Tower Hill

WRAN
11-25-1997; 98.3 mhz FM *Hrs Open:* 24; 3.7 kw; 420 ft.; N39 16 48 W88 58 22
111 W. Main Cross, P O Box 169, Taylorville, IL 62568 US
(217) 824-3395, *Fax:* (217) 824-3301
www. randyradio.com
License: Tower Hill, Shelby County, IL held by Kaskaskia Broadcasting Inc.
Group Owner: Miller Media Group
Nat'l Network: CBS *Nat'l Reps:* Commercial Media Sales
Format: Adult Contemp *Special Programming:* Farm 6 hrs, relg 3 hrs wkly *Hrs. of News Programming:* news progmg 25 hrs wkly *No. News Employees:* 1 *Target Audience:* 35—64.
Randal Miller, President
Kami Payne, General Manager
Brandon Fellows, Programming Director
Steve Butera, News Director

Tuscola

WSJK(FM)

09-30-1970; 93.5 mhz FM; 6 kw; 308 ft; N39 54 24 W88 16 35
2702 Boulder Drive, Urbana, IL 61802
(217) 367-1195, *Fax:* (217) 367-3291
www.espncu.com
Steve.Miller@sjbroadcasting.com
License: Tuscola, Douglas County, IL held by RadioStar Inc.
Group Owner: RadioStar Inc.; (acq 5-23-2006; grpsl).
Nat'l Reps: McGavren Guild
Population Served: 81,291 *Arbitron Metro Market:* Champaign, IL *Format:* Alternative *Target Audience:* 18-49; adult professionals & college students
Jim Glassman, President
Roxanne Charles, General Manager
Steve Miller, General Sales Mgr
Ken Cunningham, Programming Director
Josh Laskowski, Promotions Manager
Jon Hail, Engineering Dir
Donna Keleher, Office Manager

Urbana

WBCP

01-01-1948; 1580 khz AM
Unit D, 904 N. 4th St., Champaign, IL 61820 US
(563) 568-3477, *Fax:* (563) 568-3391
knei@kneiradio.com
License: Urbana, IL held by WBCP Inc.
Nat'l Network: American Urban; ABC
Arbitron Metro Market: Anchorage AK *Format:* Oldies
Dr. D.L. Van Voorhis, President
Bill DeGeorge, General Manager

*WILL

03-28-1922; 580 khz AM *Hrs Open:* 24; 5 kw-D, DA2; 0.1 kw-N, DA2; N40 4 53 W88 14 18
300 North Goodwin Ave, Urbana, IL 61801 US
(217) 333-0850, *Fax:* (217) 244-9586
www.will.uiuc.edu
willamfm@uiuc.edu
License: Urbana, IL held by University of Illinois Board of Trustees.
Nat'l Network: NPR; PRI *Wire Services:* AP
Arbitron Metro Market: Champaign, IL *Format:* News, News/Talk, 86, Variety/Diverse *Special Programming:* Farm 7 hrs wkly *Hrs. of News Programming:* news progmg 115 hrs wkly *No. News Employees:* 3 *TargetAudience:* 25-60; educated, upper middle income, professionals
Mike Pritchard, Operations Dir
Mark Leonard, General Manager
Jay Pearce, Station Manager
Kate Dobrovolny, Promotions Manager
Tom Rogers, News Director
Rick Finnie, Chief Engineer
Denise Perry, Traffic Manager

*WILL-FM

09-01-1941; 90.9 mhz FM *Hrs Open:* 24; 105 kw; 850 ft.; N40 2 18 W88 40 10
810 South Wright Street, 228 Gregory Hall, Urbana, IL 61801 US
(217) 333-0850, *Fax:* (217) 244-9586
www.will.uiuc.edu
willamfm@uiuc.edu
License: Urbana, Champaign County, IL held by University of Illinois Board of Trustees.
Wire Services: AP
Arbitron Metro Market: Champaign, IL *TV Affiliate:* *WILL-TV affil *Format:* Variety/Diverse *Hrs. of News Programming:* News progmg 2 hrs wkly *Target Audience:* 35-70.
Jake Schumacher, Programming Director

WCFF

12-04-1967; 92.5 mhz FM *Hrs Open:* 24; 16 kw; 410 ft.; N40 0 45 W88 8 29
504 South Neil Street, Champaign, IL 61820 US
(217) 352-4141, *Fax:* (217) 352-1256
www.925thechief.com
abeck@illiniradio.com
License: Urbana, Champaign County, IL held by Saga Communications of Illinois LLC.
Group Owner: Saga Communications Inc.; (acq 2000; $7 million).
Nat'l Reps: Katz Radio
Arbitron Metro Market: Champaign, IL *Format:* Oldies *Target Audience:* 35-64.
Ed Christian, CEO
Steve Goldstein, President
Jonathan Drake, Operations Dir
Alan Beck, General Manager
Karen Cochrane, General Sales Mgr
Gary Saladino, Promotions Manager
Mike Cation, News Director
Mark Spalding, ChiefEngineer
Ryan Leskis, Promotions Director
Sheila Wetherell, Business Manager

WPGU

04-17-1967; 107.1 mhz FM *Hrs Open:* 24; 3 kw; 236 ft.; N40 6 34 W88 14 6
24 E. Green St., Ste 107, Champaign, IL 61820 US
(217) 337-3100, *Fax:* (217) 337-3162
www.wpgu.com
wpgu@wpgu.com
License: Urbana, Champaign County, IL held by Illini Media Co.
Arbitron Metro Market: Champaign, IL *Format:* Alternative *Hrs. of News Programming:* News progmg 7 hrs wkly *Target Audience:* 18-34.
Mary Cory, General Manager
Scott Downs, General Sales Mgr
Becky Brothman, Programming Director
Beth Rehn, Promotions Manager
Jon Hansen, News Director
Melissa Pasco, Traffic Manager
Rachel Buenting, Traffic Manager

Vandalia

WKRV

05-28-1974; 107.1 mhz FM *Hrs Open:* 24; 6 kw; 328 ft.; N38 59 48 W88 55 44
Mailing Address: 232 South Fourth Street, P.O. Box 100, Vandalia, IL 62471 US
Second Address: 232 S. 4th St., Vandalia, IL 62471
(618) 283-2325, *Fax:* (618) 283-1503
www.vandaliaradio.com
wkrv@sbcglobal.net
License: Vandalia, Fayette County, IL held by Two Petaz Inc.
Group Owner: The Cromwell Group Inc.
Wire Services: Metro Weather Service Inc.
Format: Adult Contemp, Contemporary Hits/Top 40 *Hrs. of News Programming:* news progmg 10 hrs wkly *No. News Employees:* 1 *Target Audience:* 20-45.
Dan Michael, Programming Director

WPMB

12-09-1963; 1500 khz AM *Hrs Open:* 6 AM-sunset
Mailing Address: 232 South Fourth Street, P.O. Box 100, Vandalia, IL 62471 US
Second Address: 232 S. 4th St., Vandalia, IL 62471
(618) 283-2325,(618) 283-2355, *Fax:* (618) 283-1503
wkrv@sbcglobal.net
License: Vandalia, IL held by Two Petaz Inc.
Group Owner: The Cromwell Group Inc.; (acq 2-3-2005; $350,000 with co-located FM).
Wire Services: Metro Weather Service Inc.
Format: Big Band *Special Programming:* Farm 4 hrs, gospel 3 hrs wkly *Hrs. of News Programming:* news progmg 8-10 hrs wkly *No. News Employees:* 2 *Target Audience:* General.
Bayard Walters, President
John Harris, General Manager
Todd Stapleton, Programming Director

*WVNL

10-07-2002; 91.7 mhz FM *Hrs Open:* 24 hrs; 0.1 kw; 164 ft.; N38 56 42 W89 6 10 *Rebroadcasts:* WIBI, Carlinville,IL, 100%
Box 140, Carlinville, IL 62626 US
(217) 854-4800, *Fax:* (217) 854-4810
www.wibi.org
wibi@wibi.org
License: Vandalia, Fayette County, IL held by Illinois Bible Institute Inc.
Arbitron Metro Market: Carlinville, IL *Format:* Christian
Barry Copeland, General Manager
Tom Greene, Station Manager
Rob Regal, Programming Director
G. W. Van Alstine, Promotions Manager
Sally Braundmeier, News Director
Greg Kaurin, Chief Engineer
Joe Buchanan, Music Director
LizEilers, Underwriting Director
Angie Carpenter, Office Manager
Brian Miller, Donor Relations Director
Craig Norrenberns, Promotions Assistant & On-Air Weekends

Vernon Hills

WNVR

03-01-1988; 1030 khz AM
4320 Dundee Road, Northbrook, IL 60062 US
(773) 588-6300, *Fax:* (773) 267-4913
www.polskieradio.com
polskieradio@polskieradio.com
License: Vernon Hills, IL held by Polnet Communications Ltd.
Group Owner: Polnet Communications Ltd.; acq 3-15-91; $495,000;
Wire Services: AP
Arbitron Metro Market: Chicago *TV Affiliate:* Pol *Special Programming:* news progmg 20 hrs wkly *Hrs. of News Programming:* 7 *No. News Employees:* 18-54; Polish speaking au

Virden

WCVS-FM

05-10-1982; 96.7 mhz FM *Hrs Open:* 24; 6 kw; 328 ft.; N39 38 2 W89 48 50
600 Congress Ave., Suite 1400, Austin, TX 78701 US
(217) 528-3033, *Fax:* (217) 528-5348
www.wcvs.com
kevino'dea@neuhoffmedia.com
License: Virden, Macoupin County, IL held by Neuhoff Family L.P.
Group Owner: Neuhoff Family L.P.; (acq 8-1-2007; grpsl)
Nat'l Reps: Christal
Arbitron Metro Market: Springfield, IL *Format:* Rock/AOR *No. News Employees:* 1 *Target Audience:* 18-49; m/p
Kevin O'Dea, General Manager
Kevin Anfield, General Sales Mgr
Danielle Outlaw, Programming Director
Jeff Hofmann, News Director
Frank Konwinski, Chief Engineer
Jeremy Anderson, Program Director
Michelle Mitchell, PromotionsDirector

Virginia

WVIL

02-01-1998; 101.3 mhz FM *Hrs Open:* 24; 4 kw; 390 ft; N40 00 52 W90 19 55
108 E. Main, Beardstown, IL 63105
(217) 323-1790, *Fax:* (217) 323-1705
www.wvilfm.com
lbostwick@mchsi.com
License: Virginia, Cass County, IL held by LB Sports Productions LLC
Nat'l Network: Fox Sports *Regional Network:* Ill. Radio Net.
Population Served: 65,000*Hrs. of News Programming:* news progmg one hr wkly *No. News Employees:* 1 *Target Audience:* 18-65; general
Larry Bostwick, General Manager
Missy DeGroot, Station Manager
Brenda Lawless, General Sales Mgr
Jayneece Bostwick, Programming Director
Gary Glaenzer, Chief Engineer

Warsaw

*WIUW

05-17-1995; 89.5 mhz FM *Hrs Open:* 24; 10.6 kw; 443 ft.; N40 20 44 W91 24 11 *Rebroadcasts:* Rebroadcasts WIUM(FM) Macomb 100%
1 University Circle, Macomb, IL 61455 US
(309) 298-2424, *Fax:* (309) 298-2133
www.tristatesradio.com
publicradio@wiu.edu
License: Warsaw, Hancock County, IL held by Western Illinois University.
Format: News *Hrs. of News Programming:* news progmg 58 hrs wkly *No. News Employees:* 2 *Target Audience:* General.
Ken Thermon, Operations Dir
Dorothy Vallillo, General Manager
Sharon Faust, General Sales Mgr
Rich Egger, News Director

Watseka

WGFA

09-01-1960; 1360 khz AM *Hrs Open:* 6 AM-6 PM; 1 kw-D, DAD; N40 47 37 W87 45 17
Rte 4, P.O. Box 100, Watseka, IL 60970 US
(815) 432-4955, *Fax:* (815) 432-4957
www.wgfaradio.com
info@wgfaradio.com
License: Watseka, IL held by Iroquois County Broadcasting Co.
Nat'l Network: Salem Radio Network *Regional Network:* Ill. Radio Net.
Format: Talk *Hrs. of News Programming:* news progmg 14 hrs wkly *No. News Employees:* 2 *Target Audience:* 30-65; upscale
Justin Kaiser, Operations Dir
Margaret Martin, General Manager
Stacey Smith, Station Manager

WGFA-FM
03-02-1961; 94.1 mhz FM *Hrs Open:* 24; 50 kw; Ant 364 ft; N40 47 37 W87 45 17
1973 E. 1950 North Rd., Watseka, IL 60970
(815) 432-4955, *Fax:* (815) 432-4957
www.wgfaradio.com
941fm@wgfaradio.com
License: Watseka, Iroquois County, IL held by Iroquois County Broadcasting Co.
Nat'l Network: ABC *Nat'l Reps:* Farmakis; Katz Radio
Population Served: 150,000*Special Programming:* Farm 18 hrs, business 2 hrs, sports 18 hrs wkly *Hrs. of News Programming:* news progmg 12 hrs wkly *No. News Employees:* 2 *Target Audience:* 25-54.
Don Elliot, Operations Dir
Margaret Martin, General Manager
Stacey Smith, Station Manager
Carl Gerdovich, News Director
Del Dayton, Chief Engineer
M'Lissa Long, Regional Sales Manager

WKQX
01-01-1948; 95.9 mhz FM *Hrs Open:* 24; 1 kw; 46 ft.; N40 46 17 W87 46 13
Mailing Address: US
Second Address: 230 Merchandise Mart Plaza, Chicago, IL 60654
(312) 527-8348, *Fax:* (312) 527-3620
www.q101.com
info@q101.com
License: Watseka, Cook County, IL held by Emmis Radio License LLC.
Group Owner: Emmis Communications Corp.
Nat'l Reps: D & R Radio
Arbitron Metro Market: Chicago, IL *Format:* Alternative *Target Audience:* 18-34.
Marv Nyren, Operations Dir
Lance Richard, General Sales Mgr
Mike Stern, Programming Director
Jennifer Welch, News Director
Patrick Berger, Chief Engineer

Waukegan

WKRS
09-25-1949; 1220 khz AM *Hrs Open:* 24; 1 kw-D, DA2; 0.09 kw-N, DA2; N42 20 59 W87 52 53
980 N. Michigan Ave., Suite 1880, Chicago, IL 60611 US
(847) 336-7900, *Fax:* (847) 336-1523
www.wkrs.com
License: Waukegan, IL held by NM Licensing LLC.
Group Owner: NextMedia Group Inc.; (acq 11-26-01; grpsl).
Arbitron Metro Market: Chicago, IL *Format:* News, News/Talk, 86 *Hrs. of News Programming:* news progmg 40 hrs wkly *No. News Employees:* 4 *Target Audience:* 25 plus.
Kira La Fond, General Manager
Libby Collins, Programming Director

WXLC
05-01-1963; 102.3 mhz FM; 3 kw; 322 ft.; N42 20 59 W87 52 53
980 N. Michigan Ave., Suite 1880, Chicago, IL 60611 US
(847) 336-7900, *Fax:* (847) 336-1523
www.1023xlc.com
pwenzel@nextmediachicago.com
License: Waukegan, Lake County, IL
Group Owner: NextMedia Group Inc.
Arbitron Metro Market: Waukegan, IL *Format:* Adult Contemp *Target Audience:* 25-44.
Rory Fraley, General Manager
Mike Peof, General Sales Mgr
Haynes Johns, Programming Director
Paul Wenzel, Advertising

West Frankfort

WFRX
05-02-1951; 1300 khz AM; 1 kw-D, ND1; 0.06 kw-N, ND1; N37 53 4 W88 55 44
330 East Kilbourn Ave., Suite 250, Milwaukee, WI 53202 US
(618) 997-8123, *Fax:* (618) 993-2319
License: West Frankfort, IL held by Withers Broadcasting of Southern Illinois LLC.
Group Owner: Withers Broadcasting Co.; (acq 3-17-2008; grpsl)
Nat'l Network: Jones Radio Networks
Arbitron Metro Market: Marion-Carbondale (Southern Illinois) *Format:* Big Band, News *Hrs. of News Programming:* news progmg 20 hrs wkly *No. News Employees:* 2 *Target Audience:* P45+.
Paxton Guy, Operations Dir
Janet Jensen, General Manager
Gina Heern, General Sales Mgr
Stavey Malick, Promotions Manager
Tim Deterding, Chief Engineer

Wheaton

***WETN**
02-27-1962; 88.1 mhz FM *Hrs Open:* 24; 0.25 kw; 141 ft.; N41 52 9 W88 5 56
501 E. College Avenue, Billy Graham Center, Wheaton, IL 60187 US
(630)752-5000, *Fax:* (630) 752-5286
www.wetn.org
wetn@wheaton.edu
License: Wheaton, Du Page County, IL held by Trustees of Wheaton College.
Arbitron Metro Market: Wheaton, IL *Format:* Christian, Classical *Special Programming:* Live sports 5 hrs, live church svcs 3 hrs, live concerts 2 hrs wkly *Hrs. of News Programming:* News progmg 2 hrs wkly *TargetAudience:* 18-49.
Dr. A. Duane Litfin, President
John Rorvik, General Manager
Mark Bartlebaugh, Station Manager

Willow Springs

WCPT
01-01-1941; 820 khz AM *Hrs Open:* Daylight
1436 Auburn Blvd., Sacramento, CA 95815 US
(773) 767-1000, *Fax:* (773) 767-1100
www.chicagoprogressivetalk.com
info@wcpt820.com
License: Willow Springs, IL held by WYPA Inc.
Group Owner: Newsweb Corp.; (acq 2-15-2001; $10.5 million)
Nat'l Network: CNN Radio
Arbitron Metro Market: Chicago *Format:* Alternative, Talk *Target Audience:* 25-64; adults
Harvey Wells, General Manager
Jeff Chardell, General Sales Mgr
Gavin Carroll, Programming Director

Wilmington

WYKT
09-29-1980; 105.5 mhz FM; 1.3 kw; 482 ft.; N41 17 11 W88 14 23
P.O. Box 92, Warrenville, IL 60555 US
(815) 935-9555, *Fax:* (815) 935-9593
www.kat1055.com
wkan@starradio.com
License: Wilmington, Will County, IL held by STARadio Corp.
Group Owner: STARadio Corp.; acq 7-6-98)
Arbitron Metro Market: Wilmington, IL *Format:* Oldies *Special Programming:* Gospel 4 hrs, pub svc 4 hrs, sports 12 hrs wkly *Hrs. of News Programming:* news progmg 4 hrs wkly *No. News Employees:* 1 *TargetAudience:* 25-54.
Robert Kersmarki, Operations Dir
Larry Regnier, General Sales Mgr
Brendan Michaels, Operations Manager

Winnebago

WRTB
01-01-1971; 95.3 mhz FM *Hrs Open:* 24; 1.25 kw; 512 ft.; N42 17 26 W89 9 51
2830 Sandy Hollow Road, Rockford, IL 61109 US
(815) 874-7861, *Fax:* (815) 874-2202
www.953bobfm.com
License: Winnebago, Winnebago County, IL held by Maverick Media of Rockford License LLC.
Group Owner: Maverick Media LLC; (acq 4-27-2005; grpsl)
Nat'l Reps: Katz Radio
Arbitron Metro Market: Rockford, IL *Format:* Contemporary Hits/Top 40, Adult Contemp *Target Audience:* 25-54.
Gary Rozynek, President
Jay Chapman, General Manager
Tim Krull, Programming Director

Winnetka

***WNTH**
12-10-1960; 88.1 mhz FM; 0.1 kw; 82 ft.; N42 5 40 W87 43 7
385 Winnetka Avenue, Winnetka, IL 60093 US
(847) 784-2330, *Fax:* (847) 501-6400
www.wnth.org
License: Winnetka, Cook County, IL held by New Trier Township Board of Education.
Arbitron Metro Market: Cook, IL *Format:* Variety/Diverse
Nina Lynn, Station Manager

Wood River

KFNS
10-05-1961; 590 khz AM; 1 kw-D, DA2; 1 kw-N, DA2; N38 55 43 W90 5 8 *Rebroadcasts:* Simulcast with KFNS-FM Troy, MO 100%
7000 Chippewa Avenue, Suite 200, St. Louis, MO 63119 US
(314) 962-0590, *Fax:* (314) 962-7576
www.kfns.com
License: Wood River, IL held by Big Stick One LLC.
Group Owner: Big League Broadcasting LLC; (acq 7-13-2004; grpsl)
Nat'l Reps: Interep
Arbitron Metro Market: Wood River, IL *Format:* Sports *Target Audience:* 25-54; men
Dave Greene, General Manager
James Oelklaus, General Sales Mgr

Woodlawn

WDML
11-05-1993; 106.9 mhz FM *Hrs Open:* 24; 3 kw; 328 ft.; N38 21 29 W89 5 56
P.O. Box 1591, Mt. Vernon, IL 62864 US
(618) 242-3333, *Fax:* (618) 242-2490
www.wdml.com
wdml@mvn.net
License: Woodlawn, Jefferson County, IL held by Volunteer Broadcasting of Illinois Inc.
Nat'l Network: Westwood One
Arbitron Metro Market: Woodlawn, IL *Format:* Rock/AOR *Special Programming:* Christian rock 3 hrs wkly, House of Blues Radio Hour *Hrs. of News Programming:* everyday 5 3 minute segments *No. News Employees:* 1*Target Audience:* 30 plus; male *Adv. Rates:* 15; 15; 15; 13
David Lister, CEO
Ryan Roddy, COO

Woodstock

WZSR
05-24-1974; 105.5 mhz FM; 1.6 kw; 568 ft.; N42 15 34 W88 21 45
8800 Route 14, Crystal Lake, IL 60012 US
(815) 459-7000, *Fax:* (815) 459-7027
www.star105.com
jobs@star105andy1039.com
License: Woodstock, McHenry County, IL held by NM Licensing LLC.
Group Owner: NextMedia Group Inc.; (acq 11-26-01; grpsl).
Wire Services: UPI
Arbitron Metro Market: Crystal Lake, IL *Format:* Adult Contemp *Special Programming:* Relg one hr wkly *Target Audience:* 25-54; female
Doug Boyd, General Sales Mgr
Steve Cherry, Programming Director
Erica Lorenz, Promotions Manager
Stew Cohen, News Director
Floyd Evans, VP, Regional Manager

***WZKL**
91.7 mhz FM; 6.5 kw vert; 354 ft.; N42 17 56 W88 35 34
600 W. Mason Street, Springfield, IL 62702 US
(916) 251-1600, *Fax:* (916) 251-1650
www.klove.com
License: Woodstock, McHenry County, IL held by Educational Media Foundation.
Group Owner: EMF Broadcasting; (acq 5-22-2008; $32,000 for CP)
Arbitron Metro Market: Woodstock, IL
Darrell Chambliss, Chairman
Alan Mason, CEO/COO
Mike Novak, President
David Pierce, Chief Creative Officer
Alan Mason, Chief Operating Officer
Eric Moser, Chief Financial Officer
Brian Burger, Vice President of Human Resources

Zion

WPJX
09-19-1967; 1500 khz AM *Rebroadcasts:* Simulcast with WEEF(AM) Highland Park 100%
77 West 66th Street, 16th Floor, New York, NY 10023 US
(312) 683-1300, *Fax:* (312) 577-5994
www.musicalatina1500.com
License: Zion, IL held by Polnet Communications Ltd.
Group Owner: Polnet Communications Ltd.; (acq 5-15-2006; $230,000)
Arbitron Metro Market: Lake County, IL *Format:* Ethnic
Sara Vargas, General Manager

WWDV
01-01-1962; 96.9 mhz FM; 50 kw; 500 ft; N42 30 36 W87 53 11
875 N. Michigan Ave., Suite 1510, Chicago, IL 60622
(312) 274-9710, *Fax:* (312) 274-1304
www.wdrv.com
License: Zion, Lake County, IL held by Bonneville Holding Co.
Group Owner: Bonneville International Corporation; (acq 1-25-01; $165 million with WDRV(FM) Chicago).
Population Served: 18,500 *Arbitron Metro Market:* Chicago
Special Programming: Hunnard Broadcasting
Jerry Schnacke, Operations Dir
Greg Solk, Vice President, Operations

Indiana

Anderson

***WBSB**
12-01-1996; 89.5 mhz FM; 0.4 kw vert; 364 ft.; N40 10 38 W85 40 23 *Rebroadcasts:* Rebroadcasts WBST(FM) Muncie 100%
Ad 103, Muncie, IN 47306 US
(765) 285-5888, *Fax:* (765) 285-8937
www.bsu.edu/ipr
info@bsu.edu/ipr
License: Anderson, Madison County, IN held by Ball State University.
Arbitron Metro Market: Muncie, IN *Format:* News *No. News Employees:* 1
Marcus Jackman, General Manager
Pam Coletti, General Sales Mgr
Steven Turpin, Programming Director
Carol Trimmer, Promotions Manager
Dorothy Marvell, News Director
Robert Mittendorf, Chief Engineer
Brian Beaver, News Reporter
Angie Rapp, Marketing Manager
Debbie Webb, Underwriting Adviser

***WGNR**
01-01-1946; 1470 khz AM *Hrs Open:* 12 hrs; 1 kw-D, ND1; 0.036 kw-N, ND1; N40 3 43 W85 42 37
820 North Lasalle Blvd, Chicago, IL 60610 US
(765) 642-2750, *Fax:* (765) 642-4033
www.wgnr.org
wgnr@moody.com
License: Anderson, IN held by Moody Bible Institute of Chicago
Group Owner: The Moody Bible Institute of Chicago
Format: Christian, Talk *Target Audience:* 35-54.
Ray Hashley, General Manager

***WGNR-FM**
09-11-1973; 97.9 mhz FM *Hrs Open:* 24; 50 kw; 489 ft.; N40 3 43 W85 42 34
820 North Lasalle Blvd., Chicago, IL 60610 US
(765) 642-2750, *Fax:* (765) 642-4033
www.wgnr.org
wgnr@moody.edu
License: Anderson, Madison County, IN held by Moody Bible Institute of Chicago
Group Owner: The Moody Bible Institute of Chicago; (acq 12-17-97; $5.5 million with co
Arbitron Metro Market: Indianapolis, IN *Format:* Christian, Religious *No. News Employees:* 1 *Target Audience:* 35-54.
Joe Stowell, President
Ray Hashley, Station Manager
Tom Winn, Programming Director
Sam Sundin, News Director
Jim Wagner, Chief Engineer

WHBU
04-01-1923; 1240 khz AM *Hrs Open:* 24
25 Reliance Drive, Bristol, RI 02809 US
(765) 288-4403, *Fax:* (765) 288-0429
www.1240whbu.com
License: Anderson, IN held by Indiana Sabrecom Inc.
Group Owner: Backyard Broadcasting LLC; (acq 12-1-02; grpsl).
Format: News, News/Talk, 86 *Hrs. of News Programming:* news progmg 40 hrs wkly *No. News Employees:* 1 *Target Audience:* 25-54.
Steve Lindell, Operations Dir
Brett Beshore, Promotions Manager

WQME
11-29-1990; 98.7 mhz FM *Hrs Open:* 0000 - 2400, 24 hours per day, ever; 4.5 kw; 384 ft.; N39 58 59 W85 42 41
1100 East Fifth Street, Anderson, IN 46012 US
(765) 641-4349, *Fax:* (765) 641-3825
www.wqme.com
email@wqme.com
License: Anderson, Madison County, IN held by Anderson University Inc.
Nat'l Network: CNN Radio *Wire Services:* AP
Format: Adult Contemp, Christian *Special Programming:* Relg 9 hrs wkly *Hrs. of News Programming:* News progmg 8 hrs wkly
Target Audience: 25-54. *Adv. Rates:* 20; 20; 20; 20
Donald Boggs, General Manager
Gerald Longenbaugh, General Sales Mgr
Matt Rust, Programming Director
Jill O'Malia, Promotions Manager
Norma Armogum, News Director
Jerry Morton, Engineering Dir

Angola

***WEAX**
09-01-1979; 88.3 mhz FM *Hrs Open:* 24; 0.57 kw; 299 ft.; N41 41 12 W84 59 53
Stewart Hall W. Park St., Angola, IN 46703 US
(260) 665-4288
www.88xradio.com
weaxfm@tristate.edu
License: Angola, Steuben County, IN held by Tri-State University.
Nat'l Network: CNN Radio
Arbitron Metro Market: Angola, IN. *Format:* Alternative *Hrs. of News Programming:* News progmg one hrs wkly *Target Audience:* 18-44.
Josh Hornbacker, Operations Dir

WLKI
07-15-1974; 100.3 mhz FM *Hrs Open:* 24; 4 kw; 394 ft.; N41 40 51 W85 0 5
Mailing Address: P.O. Box 999, Angola, IN 46703 US
Second Address: 2655 State Rd. 127N, Angola, IN 46703
(260) 665-9554, *Fax:* (260) 665-9064
www.wlki.com
wlki@wlki.com
License: Angola, Steuben County, IN held by Lake Cities Broadcasting Corp.
Group Owner: Lake Cities Broadcasting Corp.
Format: Adult Contemp *Target Audience:* 25-49; adults with youthful outlook, skews female *Adv. Rates:* 18.65; 18.65; 18.65; 18.65.
Thomas Andrews, President
Bill Kerner, Operations Dir
Andy St. John, Programming Director
Jim Measel, News Director
Greg Case, Chief Engineer

Attica

WSHP
04-01-1990; 95.7 mhz FM; 3.1 kw; 433 ft.; N40 23 2 W87 7 55
50 East Rivercenter Blvd, Suite 1200, Covington, KY 41011 US
(765) 474-1410, *Fax:* (765) 474-3442
License: Attica, Fountain County, IN held by Artistic Media Partners L.P.
Group Owner: Artistic Media Partners Inc.; (acq 10-3-94; $410,000;
Nat'l Reps: Christal
Arbitron Metro Market: Lafayette, IN *Format:* Classic Rock *Target Audience:* 25-54. *Adv. Rates:* 32; 32; 32; 15
Arthur Angotti, General Manager
Steve Clark, Programming Director
Bob Henning, Chief Engineer

***WFWR**
01-01-2002; 91.5 mhz FM; 0.165 kw vert; 171 ft.; N40 16 47 W87 14 50
909 South McDonald St, Attica, IN 47918 US
(765) 764-1934
www.atticaonline.com/wfwr.htm
WFWR91.5@insightbb.com?subject=Web%20Mail
License: Attica, Fountain County, IN held by Fountain Warren Community Radio Corp.
Arbitron Metro Market: Attica, IN *Format:* Variety/Diverse
Larry Grant, General Manager
Chris W. Gayler, Sales & Graphic Design
David W. Huckleberry, Web Design, Webmaster & Technical Support
A. Troy Sheridan, Sales & Web Design

Auburn

WGBJ
04-10-1967; 102.3 mhz FM *Hrs Open:* 24; 6 kw; 315 ft.; N41 21 7 W85 9 55
2000 Lower Huntington Rd, Fort Wayne, IN 46819 US
(260) 482-4444, *Fax:* (260) 482-4410
www.radiounica1023.com
info@radiounica1023.com
License: Auburn, De Kalb County, IN held by Three Amigo's Broadcasting Inc.
Nat'l Reps: McGavren Guild
Arbitron Metro Market: Fort Wayne, IN
Robert Britt, Operations Dir
Angie Phillips, General Manager

WGLL
09-03-1968; 1570 khz AM *Hrs Open:* 17; 0.5 kw-D, DA2; 0.151 kw-N, DA2; N41 20 1 W85 3 8 *Rebroadcasts:* Rebroadcasts WGL(AM) Fort Wayne 100
2000 Lower Huntington Rd, Fort Wayne, IN 46819 US
(260) 925-4300, *Fax:* (260) 432-0986
License: Auburn, IN held by Kovas Communications of Indiana Inc.
Nat'l Network: CBS *Regional Network:* Network Indiana *Nat'l Reps:* Rgnl Reps
Arbitron Metro Market: Fort Wayne, IN *Format:* Religious *Target Audience:* 25-54.
Raymond Alexander, President

Aurora

WSCH
10-29-1970; 99.3 mhz FM *Hrs Open:* 24; 1.15 kw; 525 ft.; N38 57 55 W84 56 51
6857 Salem Ridge Road, Aurora, IN 47001 US
(812) 537-0944, *Fax:* (812) 537-5735
www.eaglecountryonline.com
info@eaglecountryonline.com
License: Aurora, Dearborn County, IN held by Wagon Wheel Broadcasting LLC.
Group Owner: Wagon Wheel Broadcasting LLC; (acq 2-1-2008; grpsl)
Nat'l Network: ABC; Motor Racing Net *Regional Network:* Brownfield
Arbitron Metro Market: Cincinnati, OH *Format:* Country *Special Programming:* Indiana University Basketball/Football, High Schoo *Hrs. of News Programming:* 12 one-minute newscasts each weekday *No. News Employees:* 1 *Target Audience:* 25-plus. *Adv. Rates:* 16; 16; 16; 16
Melissa Murphy, General Manager
Chelsie Shinkle, Programming Director
Mike Perleberg, News Director
Ted Ryan, Chief Engineer

Austin

WJAA
01-01-1991; 96.3 mhz FM; 3 kw; 328 ft.; N38 50 39 W85 49 26
1531 W. Tipton, Seymour, IN 47274 US
(812) 523-3343, *Fax:* (812) 523-5116
www.wjaa.net
coolbus@wjaa.net
License: Austin, Scott County, IN held by Midland Media Inc.
Nat'l Network: ABC; Westwood One
Arbitron Metro Market: Louisville, KY *Format:* Classic Rock, Rock/AOR *Hrs. of News Programming:* News progmg 5 hrs wkly
Target Audience: 25-54; men & women *Adv. Rates:* 16; 14; 16; 12
Robert Becker, General Manager
Tony Starkey, General Sales Mgr
Shannon Pyle, Programming Director

WXKU-FM
12-01-1993; 92.7 mhz FM *Hrs Open:* 24; 3.6 kw; 423 ft.; N38 49 20 W85 47 38
507 North State Street, North Vernon, IN 47265 US
(812) 346-1927, *Fax:* (812) 346-9722
www.wjcr.org
wjcrfm@yahoo.com
License: Austin, Scott County, IN held by BK Media LLC
Nat'l Network: USA
Arbitron Metro Market: Louisville, KY *Format:* Country *Hrs. of News Programming:* news progmg 21 hrs wkly *No. News Employees:* 1 *Target Audience:* 25-65.
Marty Pieratt, General Manager

Batesville

WRBI
05-14-1977; 103.9 mhz FM *Hrs Open:* 24; 1.95 kw; Ant 360 ft; N39 13 22 W85 15 28
133 S. Main St., Batesville, IN 45215
(812) 934-5111, *Fax:* (812) 934-2765
www.wrbiradio.com
wrbi@wrbiradio.com
License: Batesville, Ripley County, IN held by White River Broadcasting Co. Inc.
Group Owner: The Findlay Publishing Co.; (acq 7-31-97; grpsl).
Nat'l Reps: Rgnl Reps
Population Served: 102,000*Special Programming:* Farm 5 hrs wkly *Hrs. of News Programming:* news progmg 10 hrs wkly *No.*

News Employees: 1 *Target Audience:* General. *Adv. Rates:* 22; 21; 20; 18
Maynard Meyer, CEO
Kris Kuechenmeister, Operations Dir
Ronald Green, General Manager
Caz Burdetter, Programming Director
Mary Mattingly, News Director

Battle Ground

WASK-FM
03-11-1993; 98.7 mhz FM *Hrs Open:* 24; 4.4 kw; 384 ft.; N40 23 26 W86 51 53
Mailing Address: 3575 McCarty Lane, P O Box 7880, Lafayette, IN 47903 US
Second Address: 3575 McCarty Ln., Lafayette, IN 47905
(765) 447-2186, *Fax:* (765) 448-4452
www.wask.com
License: Battle Ground, Tippecanoe County, IN held by WASK Inc.
Group Owner: Schurz Communications Inc.; (acq 3-6-95; $860,000;
Nat'l Reps: Christal *Regional Reps:* Rgnl Reps. *Wire Services:* AP
Arbitron Metro Market: Lafayette, IN *Format:* Oldies *Hrs. of News Programming:* news progmg 20 hrs wkly *No. News Employees:* 4 *Target Audience:* 35 plus; general
John Trent, President
Mark Allen, Operations Dir
Brian Green, General Sales Mgr
Bryan McGarvey, Programming Director
Steve Truex, Chief Engineer

Bedford

WBIW
10-01-1948; 1340 khz AM *Hrs Open:* 24; 1 kw-U, ND1; N38 52 23 W86 28 34
P. O. Box 1307, Bedford, IN 47421 US
(812) 275-7555, *Fax:* (812) 279-8046
www.wbiw.com
comments@wbiw.com
License: Bedford, IN held by Ad-Venture Media Inc.
Nat'l Network: Westwood One; USA *Regional Network:* Network Indiana; Brownfield *Nat'l Reps:* Rgnl Reps
Arbitron Metro Market: Bedford, IN *Format:* News, Sports, 86 *Special Programming:* Sports, weather, farm 3 hrs wkly *Hrs. of News Programming:* news progmg 28 hrs wkly *No. News Employees:* 1 *Target Audience:* 25 plus; general *Adv. Rates:* 22; 17; 22; 16
Dean Spencer, President

WQRK
10-01-1975; 105.5 mhz FM *Hrs Open:* 24; 2 kw; 400 ft.; N38 54 29 W86 28 28
P. O. Box 1307, Bedford, IN 47421 US
(812) 275-7555, *Fax:* (812) 279-8046
www.superoldies.net
oldies105@hpcisp.com
License: Bedford, Lawrence County, IN
Nat'l Network: ABC
Arbitron Metro Market: Indianapolis, I *Format:* Oldies *Hrs. of News Programming:* news progmg 8 hrs wkly *No. News Employees:* 1 *Target Audience:* 35-55; upscale adults
Becky Riopel, General Manager

Beech Grove

WNTS
12-10-1956; 1590 khz AM *Hrs Open:* 24; 5 kw-D, DA2; 0.5 kw-N, DA2; N39 44 21 W86 5 29; N39 44 21 W86 5 26
4800 East Raymond St., Indianapolis, IN 46203 US
(317) 472-7137, *Fax:* (317) 472-7138
License: Beech Grove, IN held by Davidson Media Station WNTS Licensee LLC.
Group Owner: Davidson Media Group LLC; (acq 9-28-2005; $2 million)
Arbitron Metro Market: Indianapolis, IN
Steve Stiegelmeyer, General Manager
Mayra Arroyo, Programming Director

Berne

WZBD
08-27-1993; 92.7 mhz FM *Hrs Open:* 5 AM-10 PM; 4.1 kw; 394 ft.; N40 46 15 W84 56 5
Mailing Address: 935 Sandy Hollow Lane, Portland, IN 47371 US
Second Address: 955 US 27 N., Berne, IN 46711
(260) 726-8729, *Fax:* (260) 726-4311
wpgw@jayco.net
License: Berne, Adams County, IN held by Adams County Radio Inc.
Arbitron Metro Market: Fort Wayne, IN *Format:* Adult Contemp, News *Target Audience:* General.
Rob Weaver, President
Tony Giltner, Operations Dir

Bicknell

WUZR
06-04-1991; 105.7 mhz FM *Hrs Open:* 24; 1.8 kw; 427 ft.; N38 43 47 W87 24 44
1309 Old Orchard Road, Vincennes, IN 47591 US
(812) 882-6060, *Fax:* (812) 885-2604
www.wuzr.com
wuzr@originalcompany.com
License: Bicknell, Knox County, IN held by The Original Co. Inc.
Group Owner: The Original Company Inc.; (acq 4-20-98; $682,000)
Arbitron Metro Market: Vincennes, IN *Format:* Country *Special Programming:* Loc news, high school sports, Univ. of Evansville *Hrs. of News Programming:* news progmg 7 hrs wkly *No. News Employees:* 1 *TargetAudience:* 25-54.
Mark Lange, President
Brad Deetz, Operations Dir
Michelle York, General Sales Mgr
Dave Young, Programming Director
Duncan Myers, Marketing Manager

Bloomington

WBWB
07-17-1978; 96.7 mhz FM *Hrs Open:* 24; 1.65 kw; 440 ft.; N39 9 46 W86 28 21
Mailing Address: 50 East Rivercenter Blvd, Suite 1200, Covington, KY 41011 US
Second Address: 304 State Rd. 446, Bloomington, IN 47401
(812) 336-8000, *Fax:* (812) 336-7000
www.wbwb.com
arthur@artisticradio.com
License: Bloomington, Monroe County, IN held by Artistic Media Partners L.P.
Group Owner: Artistic Media Partners Inc.; (acq 1-89; grpsl;
Nat'l Reps: McGavren Guild *Regional Reps:* Rgnl Reps.
Arbitron Metro Market: Bloomington, IN *Format:* Contemporary Hits/Top 40 *No. News Employees:* 1 *Target Audience:* 18-49.
Arthur Angotti III, CEO/COO
Arthur Angotti III, President
Jim Wodock, General Manager
Jim Wodock, General Sales Mgr
Kevin Stockbridge, Programming Director
Bob Henning, Chief Engineer

***WFHB**
12-01-1992; 91.3 mhz FM *Hrs Open:* 24; 1.6 kw; 390 ft.; N39 1 18 W86 36 5
Mailing Address: P.O. Box 1973, Bloomington, IN 47402 US
Second Address: 108 W. 4th St., Bloomington, IN 47404
(812) 323-1200, *Fax:* (812) 323-0320
www.wfhb.org
volunteer@wfhb.org
License: Bloomington, Monroe County, IN held by Bloomington Community Radio Inc.
Arbitron Metro Market: Bloomington, IN *Format:* News, Variety/Diverse *Special Programming:* Folk 10 hrs, Latin 3 hrs, Finnish 3 hrs wkly *Hrs. of News Programming:* news progmg 5 hrs wkly *No. News Employees:* 1*Target Audience:* General.
Chad Carrothers, General Manager
Alycin Bektesh, News Director
Jeffrey Morris, Chief Engineer
Joe Crawford, Assistant News Director
Jim Manion, Music Director

***WFIU**
09-30-1950; 103.7 mhz FM *Hrs Open:* 24; 29 kw; 646 ft.; N39 8 31 W86 29 43
Indiana University, 1mu Messanine 005, Bloomington, IN 47405 US
(812) 855-1357, *Fax:* (812) 855-5600
www.indianapublicmedia.org
balford@indiana.edu
License: Bloomington, Monroe County, IN held by Trustees of Indiana University.
Nat'l Network: NPR
Arbitron Metro Market: Bloomington, IN *TV Affiliate:* *WTIU(TV) affil. *Format:* Jazz, News *Hrs. of News Programming:* news progmg 7 hrs wkly *No. News Employees:* 1 *Target Audience:* General.
Donna Stroup, CFO
Brad Howard, Director of Engineering and Operations
Christina Kuzmych, Station Manager
Will Murphy, News Director
Bradley Howard, Chief Engineer
Eva Zogorski, Membership Director
John Wright, Computer Networkand Support
Marianne Woodruff, Corporate Development Manager
Scott Witzke, TV Marketing Director
Matt Stonecipher, Computer and Networking Support Analyst
Bill Shaw, News Coordinator

WGCL
03-11-1949; 1370 khz AM *Hrs Open:* 24
P.O. Box 2717, Bloomington, IN 47402 US
(812) 332-3366, *Fax:* (812) 331-4570
www.wgclradio.com
info@wgclradio.com
License: Bloomington, IN held by Sarkes Tarzian Inc.
Group Owner: Sarkes Tarzian Inc.
Nat'l Network: ABC; ESPN Radio *Nat'l Reps:* Christal
Format: News, News/Talk, 86 *Hrs. of News Programming:* news progmg 5 hrs wkly *No. News Employees:* 2 *Target Audience:* 30 plus. *Adv. Rates:* 37; 37; 37; 25
Ron Tarsi, General Manager
Ducan Myers, General Sales Mgr
Don Pratt, Programming Director
Marc Antonetti, Chief Engineer

WTTS
01-07-1960; 92.3 mhz FM *Hrs Open:* 24; 37 kw; 1089 ft.; N39 24 27 W86 8 52
P.O. Box 62, Bloomington, IN 47402 US
(317) 972-9887, *Fax:* (317) 972-9886
www.wttsfm.com
comments@wttsfm.com
License: Bloomington, Monroe County, IN
Group Owner: Sarkes Tarzian Inc.
Nat'l Reps: Christal
Arbitron Metro Market: Indianapolis, IN *Format:* Triple A *Special Programming:* Blues 2 hrs, acoustic show 4 hrs wkly *No. News Employees:* 1 *Target Audience:* 25-54.
Geoff Vargo, VP/General Manager
Daryl McIntire, General Sales Mgr
Brad Holtz, Programming Director
Josh Lantz, Promotions Manager
Laura Duncan, Music Director
Marcie Beasley, Controller
Jake Keebler, Production Director
ErinMasterson, Traffic Director

Boonville

WBNL
09-10-1950; 1540 khz AM *Hrs Open:* 24; 0.25 kw-D, ND2; 0.001 kw-N, ND2; N38 3 58 W87 16 27
Mailing Address: P.O. Box 270, Boonville, IN 47601 US
Second Address: 2177 N. Hwy. 61, Boonville, IN 47601
(812) 897-2080, *Fax:* (812) 897-2130
www.radio1540.net
rturpen@1540.net
License: Boonville, IN held by Turpen Communications LLC
Nat'l Network: USA *Regional Network:* Network Indiana
Arbitron Metro Market: Boonville,IN *Format:* Adult Contemp *Special Programming:* Gospel 5 hrs wkly *Hrs. of News Programming:* news progmg 14 hrs wkly *No. News Employees:* 1 *Target Audience:* 25-54; Women25-54 *Adv. Rates:* 14; 14; 14; na
Ralph Turpen, President

WEJK
12-19-1967; 107.1 mhz FM *Hrs Open:* 24; 1.6 kw; 640 ft.; N37 59 13 W87 16 11
Mailing Address: P. O. Box 270, Boonville, IN 47601 US
Second Address: 1162 Mt. Auburn Rd., Evansville, IN 47720
(812) 424-8284, *Fax:* (812) 421-3273
www.1071jackfm.com/
pbrayfield@southcentralmedia.com
License: Boonville, Warrick County, IN held by Boonville Broadcasting Co. Inc.
Group Owner: South Central Communications Corp.; (acq 8-14-2000; $400,000 for stock
Arbitron Metro Market: Evansville, IN
John Engelbrecht, CEO
Tim Huelsing, Operations Dir
Paul Brayfield, General Sales Mgr
Rsuty James, Programming Director
Chris Myers, Chief Engineer

Brazil

WSDX
01-01-1959; 1130 khz AM *Hrs Open:* 6 AM-2 hrs past sunset; 500 w-D, 20 w-N; N39 30 44 W87 08 18 *Rebroadcasts:* Rebroadcasts WBOW(AM) Terre Haute 9
1301 Ohio St., Terre Haute, IN 47807

(812) 234-9770, *Fax:* (812) 238-1576
espnsportsradio.com
hfarmer@radioworksforme.com
License: Brazil, Clay County, IN held by Crossroads Investments LLC
Group Owner: Crossroads Communications Inc.
Regional Network: Network Indiana *Nat'l Reps:* Roslin *Regional Reps:* Rgnl Reps.
Population Served: 25,000 *Arbitron Metro Market:* Terre Haute, IN *No. News Employees:* 1 *Target Audience:* General; sports fans *Adv. Rates:* 8; 8; 8; 4
Sherri Carlson, Operations Dir

WSDM-FM
11-13-1973; 92.7 mhz FM *Hrs Open:* 24; 6 kw; Ant 298 ft; N39 30 44 W87 08 18
1301 Ohio St., Terre Haute, IN 47807
(812) 234-9770, *Fax:* (812) 238-1576
www.crock927.com
mike@radioworksforme.com
License: Brazil, Clay County, IN held by Crossroads Investments LLC
Group Owner: Crossroads Communications Inc.; (acq 8-1-90; with co-located AM).
Nat'l Reps: Roslin *Regional Reps:* Regional Reps
Population Served: 100,000 *Arbitron Metro Market:* Terre Haute, IN *Hrs. of News Programming:* news progmg 2 hrs wkly *No. News Employees:* 1 *Adv. Rates:* 16; 16; 16; 16
Michael Petersen, General Manager
Marty Combs, Programming Director
Kevin Berlen, Engineering Dir

Bremen

WHPZ
03-01-1993; 96.9 mhz FM; 2 kw; 463 ft.; N41 24 43 W86 1 51
P.O. Box 1538, Marion, IN 46952 US
(574) 291-8200, *Fax:* (574) 291-9043
www.pulsefm.com
info@whpz.com
License: Bremen, Marshall County, IN held by Le Sea Broadcasting Corp.
Group Owner: Le Sea Broadcasting; (acq 1-4-2000; $280,296).
Format: Christian
Tony Hale, CFO
Anna Riblet, Station Manager
Wes Hylton, Chief Engineer

Brookston

WBPE
04-16-1967; 95.3 mhz FM *Hrs Open:* 24; 2.3 kw; 505 ft.; N40 32 48 W86 50 59
5520 East 75th Street, Indianapolis, IN 46250 US
(765) 474-1410, *Fax:* (765) 474-3442
www.wbpefm.com
License: Brookston, White County, IN held by Artistic Media Partners Inc.
Group Owner: Artistic Media Partners Inc.; (acq 9-1-98; $1.8 million)
Arbitron Metro Market: Lafayette, IN *Format:* Adult Contemp *Hrs. of News Programming:* news progmg 14 hrs wkly *No. News Employees:* 1 *Target Audience:* 35 plus; affluent, educated & upscale
Ernie Caldemone, General Manager
Kit Osborne, General Sales Mgr
Jimmy Knight, Programming Director
Bob Henning, Chief Engineer

Brownsburg

***WKLU**
03-23-1992; 101.9 mhz FM *Hrs Open:* 24; 4 kw; 361 ft.; N39 47 13 W86 17 57
733 Green Street, Brownsburg, IN 46112 US
(317) 841-1019, *Fax:* (317) 841-5167
www.wklu.net
bart@wklu.net
License: Brownsburg, Hendricks County, IN held by Indy Radio LLC
Arbitron Metro Market: Indianapolis, IN *Format:* Oldies *Special Programming:* Beetles brunch *No. News Employees:* 2 *Target Audience:* 25-54.
Bart Johnson, General Manager
Libby Zabriskie-Farr, Programming Director
Monica Lephart, Promotions Manager
Aimee McGrath, News Director

Cannelton

WTCJ-FM
05-01-2001; 105.7 mhz FM *Hrs Open:* 24; 2 kw; 584 ft.; N37 47 44 W86 50 58
71 Altdorf Lane, Cannelton, IN 47586 US
(812) 547-2345, *Fax:* (812) 547-2346
www.wtcjfm.com
jcatinna@cromwellradio.com
License: Cannelton, Perry County, IN
Group Owner: The Cromwell Group Inc.
Arbitron Metro Market: Tell CityM IN *Format:* Classic Rock
Jan Catinna, General Manager
Mike Chaney, News Director

Carmel

***WHJE**
09-01-1963; 91.3 mhz FM *Hrs Open:* 24; 0.4 kw; 98 ft.; N39 58 45 W86 7 10
5201 E. 131st Street, Carmel, IN 46032 US
(317) 571-4055, *Fax:* (317) 571-4066
www.whje.com
whje@whje.com
License: Carmel, Hamilton County, IN held by Carmel Clay Schools.
Regional Network: Network Indiana *Wire Services:* UPI
Format: Alternative, Classic Rock *Target Audience:* 12 plus.
Tom Schoeller, General Manager

Centerville

WHON
02-17-1964; 930 khz AM *Hrs Open:* 24
409 Chestnut St #A-154, Chattanooga, TN 37402 US
(765) 962-1595, *Fax:* (765) 966-4824
www.1017thepoint.com
PaulaK@Kicks96.com
License: Centerville, IN held by Brewer Broadcasting Corp.
Group Owner: Brewer Broadcasting Corp.; (acq 11-20-97)
Nat'l Reps: Rgnl Reps
Format: News, News/Talk, 86 *No. News Employees:* 1 *Target Audience:* 35 plus.
Paula Kay King, General Manager
Troy Derengowski, Programming Director
Jeff Lane, News Director
Lindsey Bell, Office Manager
Stacey Chalfant, Traffic Manager
Lottie Jordan, Account Manager

Chandler

WLFW
04-02-1994; 93.5 mhz FM *Hrs Open:* 24; 3.2 kw; 446 ft.; N38 1 27 W87 21 43
Mailing Address: PO Box 3848, Evansville, IN 47736 US
Second Address: 1162 Mt. Auburn Rd., Evansville, IN 47720
(812) 424-8284, *Fax:* (812) 426-7928
www.935thewolf.com
info@935thewolf.com
License: Chandler, Warrick County, IN held by South Central Communications Corp.
Group Owner: South Central Communications Corp.; (acq 1996; $860,000).
Nat'l Network: Westwood One
Arbitron Metro Market: Evansville, IN *Format:* Country *No. News Employees:* 3 *Target Audience:* 35-49.
John Englebrecht, CEO
Craig Jacobus, President
Tim Huelsing, General Manager
Paul Brayfield, General Sales Mgr
Rusty James, Programming Director
James Ashley, Promotions Manager

Charlestown

WAYI
04-07-1998; 104.3 mhz FM *Hrs Open:* 24; 3 kw; Ant 328 ft; N38 28 55 W85 37 33
Box 1043, New Albany, IN 47130
(812) 945-0316, *Fax:* (812) 945-0317
wayi.wayfm.com
supportservices@wayfm.com.
License: Charlestown, Clark County, IN held by Suquehanna Radio Corp
Group Owner: WAY-FM Media Group Inc.; (acq 11-20-2007; $1 million)
Population Served: 36,570 *Arbitron Metro Market:* New Albany, In
Robert Augsburg, President
Matt Hahn, General Manager

Chesterton

***WBEW**
01-01-2001; 89.5 mhz FM; 4 kw; 597 ft.; N41 38 6 W87 2 59
P.O. Box 2011, Jersey City, NJ 07303 US
(312) 948-4632, *Fax:* (312) 948-4837
www.vocalo.org
info@vocalo.org
License: Chesterton, Porter County, IN held by The WBEZ Alliance Inc.
Arbitron Metro Market: Chicago, IL *Format:* Jazz, News, 86
Torey Malatia, President
Greg Salustro, General Sales Mgr

***WDSO**
11-01-1976; 88.3 mhz FM *Hrs Open:* 6 AM Monday through 5 PM Friday; 400 w; 135 ft; N41 36 29 W87 03 37
Chesterton High School, 2125 S. 11th St., Chesterton, IN 46304
(219) 983-3777, *Fax:* (219) 983-3775
www.wdso.org
License: Chesterton, Porter County, IN held by Duneland School Corp.
Regional Network: Network Indiana
Population Served: 149,200 *Arbitron Metro Market:* Chicago
Special Programming: Class one hr, specialty rock 8 hrs wkly
Hrs. of News Programming: News progmg 6 hrs wkly *Target Audience:* General.
Michele Stipanovich, Operations Dir
Matthew Waters, Station Manager

Churubusco

WNHT
08-01-1994; 96.3 mhz FM *Hrs Open:* 24; 6.7 kw; 554 ft.; N41 6 13 W85 10 44
2000 Lower Huntington Rd, Fort Wayne, IN 46819 US
(260) 747-1511, *Fax:* (260) 747-3999
wild963.com
jj@summitcityradio.com
License: Churubusco, Whitley County, IN held by Summit City License Sub, LLC.
Group Owner: Summit City Radio Group; (acq 11-6-2006; grpsl)
Nat'l Reps: Eastman Radio
Arbitron Metro Market: Churubusco, IN. *Format:* Christian *Target Audience:* 18-34; women
J.J. Fabini, Operations Dir
JJ Fabini, General Manager
Dave Reithmiller, General Sales Mgr
Shady Spencer, Programming Director
Katherine Whatley, Promotions Manager

Cicero

***WJCY**
01-01-2005; 91.5 mhz FM; 0.475 kw vert; 194 ft.; N40 11 53 W86 7 44
US
(219) 548-5800, *Fax:* (219) 548-5808
www.calvaryradionetwork.com
info@calvaryradionetwork.com
License: Cicero, Hamilton County, IN held by CSN International.
Group Owner: CSN International
Arbitron Metro Market: Cicero, IN *Format:* Christian
Jim Motshagen, Operations Dir
Kathy Motshagen, Programming Director
Phil Jennings, Chief Engineer
Tom Worthington, VP and Production Servant
Tonya Mandich, Underwriting Specialist

Clarksville

WTFX-FM
01-01-1998; 93.1 mhz FM *Hrs Open:* 24; 4.1 kw; 374 ft.; N38 17 2 W85 54 17
8889 Pelican Bay Boulevard, Suite 1500, Naples, FL 34108 US
(502) 479-2308, *Fax:* (502) 479-2223
www.foxrocks.com
License: Clarksville, Clark County, IN held by CC Licenses LLC.
Group Owner: Clear Channel Communications Inc.
Arbitron Metro Market: Louisville, KY *Format:* Rock/AOR
Charlie Steele, Programming Director
Bill Gentry, Promotions Manager

Clinton

***WPFR-FM**
01-01-1998; 93.7 mhz FM *Hrs Open:* 24; 2.3 kw; 531 ft; N39 33 18 W87 28 40
18889 N. 2350th St., Dennison, IL 62420
(217) 826-9673
wpfr@joink.com
License: Clinton, Vermillion County, IN held by Word Power Inc.

Nat'l Network: Moody
Population Served: 146,605 *Arbitron Metro Market:* Terre Haute, IN *Hrs. of News Programming:* News progmg 17 hrs wkly *Target Audience:* 12 plus. *Adv. Rates:* 30; 30; 30; 30
Paul Ford, President
Eleanor Ford, Operations Dir
Jeff Tucker, Chief Engineer
Dan Watson, Chief of Operations

Cloverdale

*WSPM
01-01-2003; 89.1 mhz FM *Hrs Open:* 24; 0.0115 kw horiz, 22.5 kw vert; 423 ft.; N39 41 19 W86 42 3
6434 La Pas Trail, Indianapolis, IN 46268 US
(317) 870-8400, *Fax:* (317) 870-8404
www.catholicradioindy.org
info@catholicradioindy.org
License: Cloverdale, Putnam County, IN held by Hoosier Broadcasting Corp.
Group Owner: Hoosier Broadcasting Corp.
Arbitron Metro Market: Cloverdale, IN *Format:* Religious
Chuck Cunningham, General Manager
Ed Roehling, General Sales Mgr
Bill Shirk, Programming Director
Jim Ganley, News Director
Marty Hensley, Chief Engineer

Cole

*WHUZ(FM)
88.1 mhz FM; 100 w vert; Ant 121 ft; N40 27 37.5 W85 46 29.4
15 Wood St., Greenfield, IN 46140
(317) 467-1062
License: Cole, Grant County, IN held by Electronic Applications Radio Service Inc.
Group Owner: Electronic Applications Radio Service Inc.
Population Served: 16,042 *Arbitron Metro Market:* Crawfordsville, IN
Patrick Diemer, President

Columbia City

*WJHS
08-12-1985; 91.5 mhz FM *Hrs Open:* 24; 2.65 kw; 220 ft.; N41 10 4 W85 29 41
600 North Whitley Street, Columbia City, IN 46725 US
(260) 248-8915, *Fax:* (260) 244-5610
www.wjhs915.org
wallsll@wjhs915.org
License: Columbia City, Whitley County, IN held by Whitley County Consolidated Schools Board of Contr
Format: Alternative *Target Audience:* Men 25-54; general
Krystal Walker Zoltek, Station Manager
Laurie Walls, Programming Director

Columbus

WCSI
01-01-1950; 1010 khz AM *Hrs Open:* 24; 0.33 kw-D, ND1; 0.018 kw-N, ND1; N39 11 12 W85 57 0
Mailing Address: Box 1789, 3212 Washington St., Columbus, IN 47203 US
Second Address: 3212 Washington St., Columbus, IN 47203
(812) 372-4448, *Fax:* (812) 372-1061
www.wcsi.whiterivernews.com/
news@csiradio.com
License: Columbus, IN held by White River Broadcasting Co.
Group Owner: The Findlay Publishing Co.; (acq 11-1-57)
Regional Reps: Rgnl Reps. *Wire Services:* CBS
Arbitron Metro Market: Columbus, IN *Format:* News, News/Talk, 84, Talk *No. News Employees:* 3 *Target Audience:* 35 plus.
John Foster, Operations Dir
Tasha Mann, General Manager
Kevin Keith, News Director
Chuck Weber, Chief Engineer

WKKG
01-01-1958; 101.5 mhz FM *Hrs Open:* 24; 50 kw; 492 ft.; N39 11 12 W85 57 0
Mailing Address: 3212 Washington Street, Columbus, IN 47202 US
Second Address: 3212 Washington St., Columbus, IN 47203
(812) 372-4448, *Fax:* (812) 372-1061
wkkg.com
wkkg@wkkg.com
License: Columbus, Bartholomew County, IN
Group Owner: The Findlay Publishing Co.
Format: Country *Target Audience:* 25-54.
Scott Michaels, Programming Director
Judy Watkins, News Director
Sam Simmermaker, Sports Director

WINN
01-30-1975; 104.9 mhz FM *Hrs Open:* 24; 6 kw; 299 ft.; N39 11 9 W85 57 37
Mailing Address: 507 North State Street, North Vernon, IN 47265 US
Second Address: 3212 Washington St., Columbus, IN 47203
(812) 372-4448
www.1061theriver.com
riverstudio@1061theriver.com
License: Columbus, Bartholomew County, IN held by White River Broadcasting Co. Inc.
Group Owner: The Findlay Publishing Co.; (acq 1-8-2002)
Arbitron Metro Market: Columbus, IN *Format:* Contemporary Hits/Top 40, Adult Contemp *Target Audience:* 35-54. *Adv. Rates:* 25; 25; 25; 25.
Kurt Kah, President
David Glass, Operations Dir
Tasha Mann, General Manager
Rich Anthony, Programming Director
Barry Wright, News Director
Chuck Weber, Engineering Dir
John Foster, Operations Manager
Sam Simmermaker, SportsDirector

WXCH
11-15-1984; 102.9 mhz FM; 5.1 kw; 318 ft.; N39 11 10 W85 57 29 *Rebroadcasts:* Rebroadcasts WSCH(FM) Aurora 98%
6857 Salem Ridge Road, Aurora, IL 47001 US
(812) 438-2777, *Fax:* (812) 537-5735
wsch@one.net
License: Columbus, Bartholomew County, IN held by Wagon Wheel Broadcasting LLC.
Group Owner: Wagon Wheel Broadcasting LLC; (acq 11-15-2007; grpsl)
Arbitron Metro Market: Columbus, IN *Format:* Country
Dennis Drees, Operations Dir
Marty Pieratt, General Manager
Bob Shannon, News Director

*WKJD
90.3 mhz FM; 3.4 kw vert; 269 ft.; N39 11 10 W85 57 29
1680 Hwy 62 Ne, Corydon, IN 47112 US
(812) 375-9947, *Fax:* (812) 375-2555
www.thebridgefm.org
License: Columbus, Bartholomew County, IN held by Good Samaritan Educational Radio Inc.
Arbitron Metro Market: Columbus, IN
Keith Reising, CEO
Matt Bond, Operations Dir
Melissa Burton, Office Manager

Connersville

WIFE
04-05-1948; 1580 khz AM *Hrs Open:* 24; 0.25 kw-D, ND1; 0.005 kw-N, ND1; N39 38 18 W85 8 54
Mailing Address: 2301 West Main Street, Richmond, IN 47374 US
Second Address: 406 Central Ave., Connersville, IN
(765) 825-6411, *Fax:* (765) 825-2411
www.wifefm.com
john@wifefm.com
License: Connersville, IN held by Rodgers Broadcasting Corp.
Group Owner: Rodgers Broadcasting Corp.; (acq 8-88; grpsl;
Regional Reps: Rgnl Reps.
Arbitron Metro Market: Indianapolis, IN *Format:* Oldies *Special Programming:* Relg 12 hrs wkly *Hrs. of News Programming:* news progmg 3 hrs wkly *No. News Employees:* 2 *Target Audience:* 25-54; affluent,middle-aged country listeners *Adv. Rates:* 19; 19; 19; 19
David Rodgers, President
John Trine, General Manager
John Westover, Station Manager
Ted Cramer, Programming Director
Brett Briscoe, News Director
Mike Peacock, Engineering Dir
Bob Hawkins, Chief Engineer
Barry Welsh, MusicDirector
Kristin Deiwert, News Director
Mike Reese, Programming Director

Corydon

WOCC
05-22-1964; 1550 khz AM; 0.25 kw-D, ND1; 0.006 kw-N, ND1; N38 11 26 W86 8 0
Mailing Address: 211 N Capital Ave, Corydon, IN 47712 US
Second Address: 211 N. Capitol Ave, Corydon, IN 47112
(812) 738-9622, *Fax:* (812) 738-1676
wocc1550@cs.com
License: Corydon, IN held by Richard Lee Brabandt.
Nat'l Network: USA *Regional Network:* Network Indiana *Nat'l Reps:* Rgnl Reps
Arbitron Metro Market: Louisville, KY *TV Affiliate:* Oldies *Special Programming:* news progmg 18 hrs wkly *Hrs. of News Programming:* 1 *No. News Employees:* 34-55; baby boomers

WSFR
01-01-1994; 107.7 mhz FM *Hrs Open:* 24; 8.2 kw; 568 ft.; N38 10 25 W85 54 50
3773 Howard Hughes Pwy, Suite 300n, Las Vegas, NV 89109 US
(502) 589-4800, *Fax:* (502) 583-4820
www.1077sfr.com
License: Corydon, Harrison County, IN held by Cox Radio Inc.
Group Owner: Cox Radio Inc.; (acq 5-99)
Arbitron Metro Market: Louisville, KY *Format:* Rock/AOR *Target Audience:* 25-54.
Shane Collins, Operations Dir
Todd Pitt, General Sales Mgr
Brian Eichenberger, Promotions Manager

Covington

*WFOF
06-17-1984; 90.3 mhz FM *Hrs Open:* 24; 19 kw vert; 266 ft.; N40 9 8 W87 27 58
PO Box 227, Covington, IN 47932 US
(765) 642-2750, *Fax:* (765) 642-4033
www.moodyradioindiana.fm
wgnr@moody.edu
License: Covington, Fountain County, IN held by Doxa Inc.
Format: Religious
Ray McDaniel, President
Ray Hashley, General Manager
Ray Hashley, Station Manager
Tom Winn, Programming Director

Crawfordsville

WCVL
12-12-1964; 1550 khz AM
P. O. Box 1450, Corbin, KY 40702 US
(765) 362-8200, *Fax:* (765) 364-1550
www.wcvlam.com
dapeach@forchtbroadcasting.com
License: Crawfordsville, IN held by C.V.L. Broadcasting Inc.
Group Owner: Key Broadcasting Inc.; (acq 1986)
Nat'l Reps: Rgnl Reps
Arbitron Metro Market: West-Central Indiana *Format:* Oldies *Hrs. of News Programming:* Three Hours per Day *No. News Employees:* 1 *Target Audience:* 45 plus. *Adv. Rates:* $10
Steve Carter, COO
Dave Peach, General Manager
Dustin Zahn, Programming Director
Steven Halsema, News Director

WIMC
06-01-1974; 103.9 mhz FM; 1.35 kw; 495 ft.; N40 8 6 W86 54 14
P.O. Box 1450, Corbin, KY 40702 US
(765) 362-8200, *Fax:* (765) 364-1550
www.crawfordsvilleradio.com
License: Crawfordsville, Montgomery County, IN
Group Owner: Key Broadcasting Inc.
Format: Contemporary Hits/Top 40, Adult Contemp *Target Audience:* 25-49.
Scott Meier, Operations Dir
Stan Parman, Programming Director
Bob Friedle, Chief Engineer
Hal Maas, Music Director

*WNDY
01-01-1997; 91.3 mhz FM *Hrs Open:* 24 hrs; 2.2 kw; 194 ft; N40 03 19 W86 55 57 *Rebroadcasts:* WFRI (PBS Indy) 3am - 5pm
Mailing Address: Box 352, Crawfordsville, IN 47933
Second Address: 301 W. Wabash, Crawfordsville, IN 47933
(765) 361-6240, *Fax:* (765) 361-7004
www.wabash.edu
License: Crawfordsville, Montgomery County, IN held by Wabash College Radio Inc.

Brent Harris, Faculty/Staff Advisor
Michael Brown, General Manager

WCDQ
08-13-1953; 106.3 mhz FM *Hrs Open:* 24; 3.4 kw; 440 ft.; N40 3 19 W86 55 57
Mailing Address: 3800 Victory Parkway, Cincinnati, OH 45207 US
Second Address: 1800 N. 175 W., Crawfordsville, IN 47933
(765) 362-8200, *Fax:* (765) 364-1550
www.wcdqfm.com
dapeach@forchtbroadcasting.com

License: Crawfordsville, Montgomery County, IN held by C.V.L. Broadcasting Inc.
Group Owner: Key Broadcasting Inc.; (acq 12-13-99; $400,000).
Arbitron Metro Market: Crawfordsville, IN *Format:* Country *Hrs. of News Programming:* news progmg 48 hrs wkly *No. News Employees:* 2 *Target Audience:* 25-49; middle & upper class, educated, socially aware
Dave Peach, General Manager
Dustin Zahn, Programming Director
Steven Halsema, News Director
Steve Carter, Chief Engineer

Crothersville

***WOJC**
01-01-2005; 89.7 mhz FM; 0.3 kw vert; 244 ft.; N38 50 39 W85 49 26
3000 W. Macarthur Blvd., Santa Ana, CA 92704 US
(219) 548-5800, *Fax:* (219) 548-5808
www.calvaryradionetwork.com
info@calvaryradionetwork.com
License: Crothersville, Jackson County, IN held by CSN International.
Group Owner: CSN International
Arbitron Metro Market: Crothersville, IN *Format:* Christian
Jim Motshagen, Operations Dir
Kathy Motshagen, Programming Director
Phil Jennings, Chief Engineer
Tom Worthington, VP and Production Servant
Tonya Mandich, Underwriting Specialist

Crown Point

WXRD
11-10-1972; 103.9 mhz FM *Hrs Open:* 24; 1.35 kw; 449 ft.; N41 19 24 W87 21 22
8105 Georgia St, Merrillville, IN 46360 US
(219) 462-6111, *Fax:* (219) 462-4880
www.xrock1039.com
donclark@radiooneindiana.com
License: Crown Point, Lake County, IN held by Porter County Broadcasting Holding Corporation, LL
Group Owner: Porter County Broadcasting Corp.; (acq 2-6-2004; $4.9 million with WZ
Nat'l Network: ABC *Regional Network:* Network Indiana
Arbitron Metro Market: Crown Point, IN *Format:* Classic Rock *Hrs. of News Programming:* news progmg 12 hrs wkly *No. News Employees:* 1 *Target Audience:* 25-54; women
Leigh Ellis, General Manager

***WRTW**
90.5 mhz FM; 3.1 kw; 600 ft.; N41 20 56 W87 24 2
8400 Burr Street, Crown Point, IN 46307 US
(219) 228-2995, *Fax:* (219) 365-2029
www.thekeyfm.com
info@thekeyfm.com
License: Crown Point, Lake County, IN held by Hyles-Anderson College.
Arbitron Metro Market: Crown Point, IN *Format:* Christian
Dan Wolfe, General Manager
Jody McManus, Programming Director
Mike Azinger, Promotions Manager
Bill Flowers, Production Director

Danville

WEDJ
01-10-1975; 107.1 mhz FM *Hrs Open:* 24; 1.8 kw; 604 ft.; N39 48 6 W86 34 24
1800 N. Meridian St., Suite 605, Indianapolis, IN 46202 US
(317) 924-1071, *Fax:* (317) 924-7766
www.wedjfm.com
info@wedjfm.com
License: Danville, Hendricks County, IN held by Continental Broadcast Group Inc.
Nat'l Reps: Univision Radio National Sales
Arbitron Metro Market: Indianapolis, I *Format:* Spanish *Target Audience:* 18-54; hispanic adults *Adv. Rates:* 60; 50; 60; 40.
Martha Miller, Operations Dir
Russ Dodge, General Manager
Manuel Sepulveda, Programming Director
Stephanie Tatay-Myers, Promotions Manager
Phil Alexander, Chief Engineer

Dayton

***WCNB**
91.5 mhz FM; 0.7 kw; 10 ft.; N40 22 27.8 W86 44 25.8
6434 La Pas Trail, Indianapolis, IN 46268 US
(317) 870-8400, *Fax:* (317) 870-8404
www.wjcfradio.org
License: Dayton, Boone County, IN held by Hoosier Broadcasting Corp.
Group Owner: Hoosier Broadcasting Corp.
Arbitron Metro Market: Dayton, IN
William Poorman, President

Decatur

WJZI(AM)
05-22-1964; 1540 khz AM *Hrs Open:* 6:00 am-8:45 pm; 250 w-D; N40 49 14 W84 55 12
Mailing Address: Box 471, Wauchula, FL 33873
Second Address: 133 West Main Street, Peru, IN 46970
(863) 773-9282(863) 773-5008(813) 773-5088, *Fax:* (863) 773-2032
wauc.radiostation@earthlink.net
License: Decatur, Adams County, IN held by Lewis Broadcasting LLC
Nat'l Network: USA *Regional Network:* Network Indiana *Regional Reps:* Indiana Broadcasters Assn
Population Served: 30,000 *Arbitron Metro Market:* Grand Junction CO *Format:* Tejano *Target Audience:* 35-54. *Adv. Rates:* 7.00; 5.00; 6.00; 0.00
Robert Ayala, General Manager

WJZI
1540 khz AM; 0.25 kw-D, NDD; Ant 328 ft; N40 49 14 W84 55 12
P..O. Box 321, 118 South Main Street, Buffton, IN 46714 US
(570) 348-9103
License: Decatur, IN held by The Scranton Times L.P.
Group Owner: Shamrock Communications Inc.
Arbitron Metro Market: Decatur, IN
William Lynett, President

Delphi

WXXB
05-24-1989; 102.9 mhz FM *Hrs Open:* 24; kw
Mailing Address: 200 Monticello Dr, Dyer, IN 46311 US
Second Address: 3575 McCarty Ln., Lafayette, IN 47905
(765) 447-2186, *Fax:* (765) 448-4452
www.b1029.com
logan@b1029.com
License: Delphi, Carroll County, IN held by WASK, Inc.
Group Owner: Schurz Communications Inc.; (acq 10-00; $1 million)
Arbitron Metro Market: Lafayette, IN *Format:* Contemporary Hits/Top 40 *No. News Employees:* 1 *Target Audience:* 18-49.
Robert Rhea, President
Ernie Caldemone, Operations Dir
John Trent, General Manager
John Schurz, General Sales Mgr
Anthony Bannon, Programming Director

Earl Park

WIBN
10-15-1983; 98.1 mhz FM; 25 kw; 328 ft.; N40 34 22 W87 27 12
Box D, Rensselaer, IN 47978 US
(765) 385-2373, *Fax:* (765) 385-2374
www.981wibn.com
wibn@981wibn.com
License: Earl Park, Benton County, IN held by Brothers Broadcasting Corp.
Group Owner: Brothers Broadcasting Corp.; acq 8-95; $100,000).
Format: Oldies
John Balvich, President
John Balvich, General Manager
Jerry Stifle, Programming Director
Ken Stapleton, News Director
Don Kerawac, Chief Engineer

Edinburgh

WYGB
08-24-2000; 100.3 mhz FM *Hrs Open:* 24; 4.9 kw; 361 ft.; N39 21 45 W85 54 23
PO Box 690, Columbus, IN 47202 US
(812) 348-1029, *Fax:* (812) 375-2555
www.korncountry.com
korncountry@korncountry.com
License: Edinburgh, Johnson County, IN held by Edinburgh Radio.
Arbitron Metro Market: Edinburgh, IN *Format:* Country *Target Audience:* 25-54; Bartholomew & Johnson county folks *Adv. Rates:* 23; 20; 24; 9
Keith Reising, CEO

Elkhart

WBYT
04-01-1947; 100.7 mhz FM; 15 kw; 909 ft.; N41 36 58 W86 11 38
237 Edison Road, Suite 200, Mishawaka, IN 46545 US
(574) 258-5483, *Fax:* (574) 258-0930
www.b100.com
bwilliams@federatedmedia.com
License: Elkhart, Elkhart County, IN
Group Owner: Federated Media
Nat'l Reps: Christal
Arbitron Metro Market: Mishawaka, IN *Format:* Country *Special Programming:* Relg 2 hrs wkly *Target Audience:* 25-54. *Adv. Rates:* 65; 65; 65; 45
Brad Williams, General Manager
Stephanie Michel, General Sales Mgr
Jesse Garcia, Programming Director
Greg Trobridge, Chief Engineer

WCMR
03-16-1956; 1270 khz AM *Hrs Open:* 24
Mailing Address: P.O. Box 307, Elkhart, IN 46515 US
Second Address: 25802 County Rd. 26, Elkhart, IN 46515
(574) 875-5166, *Fax:* (574) 875-6662
www.wfrn.com
License: Elkhart, IN held by Progressive Broadcasting System Inc.
Group Owner: Progressive Broadcasting System Inc.
Format: Christian, Talk, 74 *Target Audience:* 30 plus. *Adv. Rates:* 15; 12; 13; 9.
Ed Moore, General Manager
Doug Moore, Programming Director

WFRN-FM
06-10-1963; 104.7 mhz FM *Hrs Open:* 24; 50 kw; 459 ft.; N41 37 18 W85 57 37
Mailing Address: P.O. Box307, Elkhart, IN 46515 US
Second Address: 25802 County Rd. 26, Elkhart, IN 46515
(574) 875-5166, *Fax:* (574) 875-6662
www.wfrn.com
moore@wfrn.com
License: Elkhart, Elkhart County, IN held by Progressive Broadcasting System Inc.
Group Owner: Progressive Broadcasting System Inc.
Nat'l Network: USA *Regional Network:* Network Indiana
Arbitron Metro Market: South Bend, IN *Format:* Christian *No. News Employees:* 1 *Target Audience:* 25-54; families-primarily women *Adv. Rates:* 35; 31; 33; 15.
Edwin Moore, President
Joanne Matthews, News Director
Don Wagner, News Reporter

WTRC
11-18-1931; 1340 khz AM *Hrs Open:* 24; 1 kw-U, ND1; N41 40 28 W85 56 51
P.O. Box 699, Elkhart, IN 46515 US
(574) 389-5100, *Fax:* (574) 389-5101
www.michiananewschannel.com
info@am1340.com
License: Elkhart, IN held by Pathfinder Communications Corp.
Group Owner: Federated Media
Nat'l Network: ABC; Jones Radio Networks *Nat'l Reps:* Christal
Arbitron Metro Market: Elkhart, IN *Format:* News, News/Talk, 86 *Hrs. of News Programming:* news progmg 21 hrs wkly *No. News Employees:* 2 *Target Audience:* 35-64; Elkhart County residents *Adv. Rates:* 55;34; 35; 17
Kathy Uebler, General Manager
Allan Strike, Programming Director
Gary Sieber, News Director

***WVPE**
05-01-1972; 88.1 mhz FM *Hrs Open:* 24; 11.5 kw; 997 ft.; N41 36 49 W86 11 20
2720 California Road, Elkhart, IN 46514 US
(574) 262-5660, *Fax:* (574) 262-5520
www.wvpe.org
wvpe@wvpe.org
License: Elkhart, Elkhart County, IN held by Elkhart Community Schools Corp.
Nat'l Network: PRI; NPR *Wire Services:* UPI
Arbitron Metro Market: South Bend, IN *Format:* Jazz, News, 62, Talk *Special Programming:* Blues 15 hrs, folk 9 hrs wkly *Hrs. of News Programming:* news progmg 13 hrs wkly *No. News Employees:* 1 *TargetAudience:* 25-55.
Anthony Hunt, Station Manager
Lee Burdorf, Programming Director
Kim Macon, Development Director
Linda Picon, Office Manager

Ellettsville

WHCC
01-01-1992; 105.1 mhz FM *Hrs Open:* 24; 1.7 kw; 620 ft.; N39 11 32 W86 41 46
Mailing Address: 5520 East 75th Street, Indianapolis, IN 46250 US
Second Address: 304 State Rd. 446, Bloomington, IN 47401
(812) 336-8000, *Fax:* (812) 336-7000
www.whcc105.com
jim@artisticradio.com
License: Ellettsville, Monroe County, IN held by Artistic Media Partners L.P.
Group Owner: Artistic Media Partners Inc.; (acq 7-96; $675,000).
Nat'l Network: Jones Radio Networks *Regional Reps:* Russ Dodge
Format: Country *No. News Employees:* 2 *Target Audience:* 25-54.
Arthur Angotti III, CEO
Art Angotti, President
Rick Evans, Operations Dir
Jim Wodock, General Manager
Sandy Zehr, Station Manager
Junior Blondell, General Sales Mgr
Bob Henning, Chief Engineer
Shelly Hawkins, BusinessManager
Libby Hiple, Local Sales Manager
Jim Gray, Account Executive
Jane Rubeck, Account Executive
Torry Hamilton, Account Executive

Elwood

WIKL(FM)
07-01-1964; 101.7 mhz FM *Hrs Open:* 24; 6 kw; Ant 328 ft; N40 16 33 W85 51 44 *Rebroadcasts:* Simulcasts WERK(FM) Muncie 80%
Mailing Address: 800 E. 29th St., Muncie, IN 47302
Second Address: 9821 S. 800 W., Daleville, IN 47334
(765) 288-4403, *Fax:* (765) 378-2091
www.werkradio.com
amy.dillon@bybradio.com
License: Elwood, Madison County, IN held by Indiana Sabrecom Inc.
Group Owner: Backyard Broadcasting LLC; (acq 12-1-02; grpsl).
Nat'l Network: ABC *Regional Network:* Network Indiana
Population Served: 70,080 *Arbitron Metro Market:* Muncie, IN *Format:* Oldies *Special Programming:* Gospel 4 hrs wkly *Hrs. of News Programming:* news progmg 2 hrs wkly *No. News Employees:* 1 *TargetAudience:* 25-54; adult buying public *Adv. Rates:* 34; 34; 34; 18
Steve Lindell, General Manager
Jay Garrison, Programming Director
Bret Beshore, Promotions Manager
Sean Mattingly, Chief Engineer
John Seneff, Local Sales Manager
Amy Dillon, VP/Market Manager

Evansville

WABX
01-01-1997; 107.5 mhz FM *Hrs Open:* 24; 2 kw; 561 ft.; N37 59 21 W87 35 48
Mailing Address: 1162 Mt. Auburn Road, Evansville, IN 47736 US
Second Address: 1162 Mount Auburn, Evansville, IN 47720
(312) 204-9900
License: Evansville, Vanderburgh County, IN held by South Central Communications Corp.
Group Owner: South Central Communications Corp.
Nat'l Reps: Katz Radio
Arbitron Metro Market: Mankato-New Ulm-St. Peter MN
Neal Robinson, President

WEOA
01-01-1935; 1400 khz AM *Hrs Open:* 24; 1 kw-U, ND1; N37 56 17 W87 31 51
P. O. Box 3848, Evansville, IN 47736 US
(812) 424-8864, *Fax:* (812) 424-9946
www.1400amweoa.com/
info@weoa.com
License: Evansville, IN held by South Central Communications Corp.
Group Owner: South Central Communications Corp.; acq 11-81)
Nat'l Network: ABC
Arbitron Metro Market: Evansville, IN *Format:* Adult Contemp *Hrs. of News Programming:* Hourly *No. News Employees:* 2 *Target Audience:* 25-49; general
Ed Lander, President
Ed Lander, General Manager
Regina Lander, General Sales Mgr
Jerome Lander, Promotions Manager
Larry Switzer, News Director

WGBF
11-22-1923; 1280 khz AM *Hrs Open:* 24
136 Main Street, #202, Westport, CT 06880 US
(812) 425-4226, *Fax:* (812) 421-0005
License: Evansville, IN
Group Owner: Townsquare Media; (acq 12-3-2003; grpsl).
Nat'l Network: CNN Radio; Westwood One *Nat'l Reps:* Katz Radio
Arbitron Metro Market: Evansville, IN *Format:* News, News/Talk, 86 *Hrs. of News Programming:* news progmg 10 hrs wkly *No. News Employees:* 1 *Target Audience:* 25-54; affluent, mature *Adv. Rates:* 15; 30;25; 5
Mark Thomas, General Manager

WIKY-FM
08-28-1948; 104.1 mhz FM; 39 kw; 571 ft.; N37 59 21 W87 35 48
P.O. Box 3848, Evansville, IN 47736 US
(812) 424-8284, *Fax:* (812) 426-7928
www.wiky.com
info@wiky.com
License: Evansville, Vanderburgh County, IN
Group Owner: South Central Communications Corp.; (Acq 1948)
Arbitron Metro Market: Evansville, IN *Format:* Adult Contemp *Special Programming:* Farm 17 hrs wkly *Target Audience:* 25-54; females, workplace
John Engelbrecht, CEO
Tim Huelsing, Operations Dir
Paul Broyfield, General Sales Mgr
Mark Baker, Programming Director
Nora Mitz, Promotions Manager
Randy Wheeler, News Director
Chris Myers, Chief Engineer
Stephanie Todich,Promotions Manager
Erin Johnson, Traffic Manager

*WNIN-FM
02-01-1982; 88.3 mhz FM *Hrs Open:* 24; 17 kw; 840 ft.; N37 59 1 W87 16 13
405 Carpenter Street, Evansville, IN 47708 US
(812) 423-2973, *Fax:* (812) 428-7548
www.wnin.org
wnin@wnin.org
License: Evansville, Vanderburgh County, IN held by Tri-State Public Teleplex Inc.
Nat'l Network: PRI; NPR
Arbitron Metro Market: Evansville, IN *Format:* News *Hrs. of News Programming:* News progmg 20 hrs wkly *Target Audience:* General.
David Dial, President
Jean Noyes, Station Manager
Daniel Moore, Programming Director

*WPSR
09-01-1957; 90.7 mhz FM *Hrs Open:* 6:45 AM-2:45 PM; 14 kw; 164 ft.; N38 1 44 W87 34 47
5400 First Avenue, Evansville, IN 47710 US
(812) 435-8241, *Fax:* (812) 435-8241
wpsr@907wpsr.com
License: Evansville, Vanderburgh County, IN held by Evansville Vanderburg School Corp.
Regional Network: Network Indiana
Arbitron Metro Market: Evansville, IN *Format:* Variety/Diverse *Hrs. of News Programming:* News progmg 3 hrs wkly *Target Audience:* General.
Michael Reininga, General Manager

*WSWI
08-06-1947; 820 khz AM; 0.25 kw-D, NDD; N37 57 53 W87 40 6
8600 University Blvd., Evansville, IN 47712 US
(812) 465-1665, *Fax:* (812) 461-5261
www.usi.edu/wswi
wswi@usi.edu
License: Evansville, IN held by University of Southern Indiana.
Arbitron Metro Market: Evansville, IN *Format:* Alternative *Hrs. of News Programming:* News progmg 3 hrs wkly *Target Audience:* 18-54; students, faculty & community members
John Morris, General Manager

*WUEV
04-01-1951; 91.5 mhz FM *Hrs Open:* 24; 6.1 kw; 151 ft.; N37 58 24 W87 31 48
1800 Lincoln Ave, Evansville, IN 47722 US
(812) 479-2022, *Fax:* (812) 479-2320
wuev.evansville.edu
wuev@evansville.edu
License: Evansville, Vanderburgh County, IN held by University of Evansville.
Regional Network: Network Indiana *Wire Services:* UPI
Arbitron Metro Market: Evansville, IN *Format:* Jazz, Variety/Diverse *Special Programming:* Children 5 hrs, American Indian one hr wkly *Hrs. of News Programming:* news progmg 10 hrs wkly *No. News Employees:* 3
Mike Crowley, General Manager
Phil Bailey, Chief Engineer

WVHI
10-31-1948; 1330 khz AM; 5 kw-D, DAN; 1 kw-N, DAN; N38 3 12 W87 35 40
3701 Fern Valley Road, Louisville, KY 40219 US
(812) 475-9930, *Fax:* (812) 425-2078
www.wvhi.com
License: Evansville, IN held by Word Broadcasting Network.
Group Owner: Word Broadcasting Network Inc.; (acq 3-17-99).
Arbitron Metro Market: Evansville, IN *Format:* Adult Contemp, Religious *Target Audience:* General.
Krista Denton, General Manager

WJLT
12-22-1964; 105.3 mhz FM *Hrs Open:* 24; 50 kw; 492 ft.; N38 4 45 W87 36 36
136 Main Street, Suite 202, Westport, CT 06880 US
(812) 425-4226, *Fax:* (812) 421-0005
www.lite1053.com
info@lite1053.com
License: Evansville, Vanderburgh County, IN
Group Owner: Townsquare Media; (acq 12-3-2003; grpsl).
Nat'l Network: ABC
Arbitron Metro Market: Evansville, IN *Format:* Oldies *Target Audience:* 25-54. *Adv. Rates:* 30; 30; 30; 20
Mike Sanders, Operations Dir
Mark Thomas, General Manager
Cindy Patrick, Programming Director
Kris Mattingly, Promotions Manager
Rick Crago, Chief Engineer

Ferdinand

WQKZ
11-01-1997; 98.5 mhz FM; 3.6 kw; 423 ft.; N38 10 2 W86 49 49
P.O. Box 167, Jasper, IN 47547 US
(812) 482-2131, *Fax:* (812) 482-9609
wqkz@psci.net
License: Ferdinand, DuBois County, IN held by Gem Communications L.L.P.
Nat'l Network: Jones Radio Networks
Format: Country *Adv. Rates:* 16; 15; 16; 15
G. Earl Metzger, President
Gene Kuntz, General Manager
Gary Hoffman, Programming Director
Chris James, News Director
Frank Hertel, Chief Engineer

Fishers

WFMS
03-17-1957; 95.5 mhz FM *Hrs Open:* 24; 13 kw; 991 ft.; N39 46 3 W86 0 12
140 East Market Street, York, PA 17401 US
(317) 842-9550, *Fax:* (317) 912-1996
www.wfms.com
info@wfms.com
License: Fishers, Marion County, IN held by WFMS Lico Inc.
Group Owner: Cumulus Media Partners LLC; (acq 11-20-72)
Arbitron Metro Market: Indianapolis, IN *Format:* Country
Lisa Juillerat, Programming Director
Christopher Wheat, Promotions Manager
Jake Robinson, Chief Engineer
Karyn Sullyvan, Public Service Announcements

Fort Branch

*WBGW
07-20-1990; 101.5 mhz FM *Hrs Open:* 24; 2.1 kw; 561 ft.; N38 10 45 W87 29 13
Mailing Address: P.O. Box 4164, Evansville, IN 47724 US
Second Address: Box 4463 E. 1200 F, R.R. 2, Haubstadt, IN 47629
(800)264-5550, *Fax:* (812) 768-5552
www.thywordnetwork.org
mail@thyword.org
License: Fort Branch, Gibson County, IN held by Music Ministries Inc.
Nat'l Network: Moody; USA
Arbitron Metro Market: Evansville, IN *Format:* Religious *Hrs. of News Programming:* News progmg 12 hrs wkly *Target Audience:* 35-54.
Floyd Turner, General Manager
Susan Turner, Promotions Manager
Floyd Turner, Chief Engineer
Susan Turner, Financial Secretary

Fort Wayne

WAJI
08-01-1959; 95.1 mhz FM *Hrs Open:* 24; 39 kw; 679 ft.; N41 6 13 W85 11 28
PO Box 62, Bloomington, IN 47402 US
(260) 423-3676, *Fax:* (260) 422-5266
www.waji.com
barb@waji.com
License: Fort Wayne, Allen County, IN held by Sarkes Tarzian Inc.
Group Owner: Sarkes Tarzian Inc.
Nat'l Reps: Katz Radio *Wire Services:* AP
Arbitron Metro Market: Fort Wayne, IN *Format:* Adult Contemp *No. News Employees:* 1 *Target Audience:* 25-54; women
Thomas Tarzian, CEO
Lee Tobin, General Manager
Dan Kennedy, Programming Director
Amy Collins, News Director
Geary Morrill, Chief Engineer
Robert Davis, CFO
Darlene Lee, Controller
Barb Richards, Programming Director

*WBCL
01-08-1976; 90.3 mhz FM *Hrs Open:* 24; 26 kw; 692 ft.; N41 6 13 W85 11 46
1025 W. Rudisill Blvd., Fort Wayne, IN 46807 US
(225) 768-3688, *Fax:* (225) 768-3729
www.jsm.org
kawikfish@yahoo.com
License: Fort Wayne, Allen County, IN held by Taylor University Broadcasting Inc.
David Whitelaw, COO
Jimmy Swaggart, President
John Santiago, Programming Director

*WBOI
06-15-1978; 89.1 mhz FM *Hrs Open:* 24; 34 kw; 604 ft.; N41 6 13 W85 10 44
Mailing Address: P.O. Box 8459, Fort Wayne, IN 46898 US
Second Address: 3204 Clairmont Ct., Fort Wayne, IN 46808
(260) 452-1189, *Fax:* (260) 452-1188
www.wbni.org/
jbrown@nipr.fm
License: Fort Wayne, Allen County, IN held by Northeast Indiana Public Radio Inc.
Nat'l Network: PRI; NPR; AP Radio *Regional Network:* Network Indiana
Arbitron Metro Market: Fort Wayne, IN *Format:* Jazz, News, 62, Talk *Target Audience:* 25 plus.
Will Murphy, President
Katy Anderson, Operations Dir
Will Murphy, General Manager
Karen Fraser, General Sales Mgr
Sean Bueter, News Director
Ed Didier, Chief Engineer
Peggy Gaylord, Director of Underwriting

WFCV
06-17-1968; 1090 khz AM *Hrs Open:* Sunrise-sunset
10550 Barkley, Ste 108, Overland Park, KS 66212 US
(913) 642-7770, *Fax:* (913) 642-1319
www.bottradionetwork.com
comments@bottradionetwork.com
License: Fort Wayne, IN held by Bott Broadcasting.
Group Owner: Bott Radio Network; acq 5-1-80)
Nat'l Network: USA
Arbitron Metro Market: Fort Wayne, IN *Format:* Christian *Target Audience:* 25-54; family oriented
Richard (Dick) Bott, Sr., Founder & Chairman
Tom Holdeman, CFO
Richard (Rich) Bott, II, President/CEO
Eben Fowler, Operations Dir
Dale Gerke, Station Manager
Pat Rulon, Director, National Sales
Rachel Launius, MarketingManager
Jason Potocnik, Director of Traffic Operations
John Beck, Network Development Manager
John Nicholas, Chief Control Room Operator
Candy Green, Program Services Manager
Christopher Murphy, Webmaster

WOWO-FM
03-04-1993; 92.3 mhz FM *Hrs Open:* 24; 2.2 kw; Ant 544 ft; N41 06 39 W85 11 44
2915 Maples Rd., Fort Wayne, IN 46816
(260) 447-5511, *Fax:* (260) 447-7546
www.wowo.com
ghenson@federatedmedia.com
License: Fort Wayne, Allen County, IN held by Pathfinder Communications Corp.
Group Owner: Federated Media; (acq 3-1-97)
Nat'l Network: ABC
Population Served: 380,000 *Arbitron Metro Market:* Fort Wayne, IN *Format:* Classic Rock *Hrs. of News Programming:* news progmg 6 hrs wkly *No. News Employees:* 1 *Target Audience:* 25-54; men and adults
John Dille, President
Jim Allgeier, General Manager
Ben Saurer, General Sales Mgr
Gregg Henson, Programming Director
Brian Sheikn, Promotions Manager
Dave Wheaton, News Director
Mogan David, Engineering Dir
Jack Didier, ChiefEngineer
Kayla Blakeslee, Traffic

WGL
01-24-1924; 1250 khz AM *Hrs Open:* 24
2000 Lower Huntington Rd, Fort Wayne, IN 46819 US
(260) 747-1511, *Fax:* (260) 747-3999
www.1250theriver.com
dave@summitcityradio.com
License: Fort Wayne, IN held by Summit City License Sub, LLC.
Group Owner: Summit City Radio Group; (acq 11-6-2006;. grpsl)
Nat'l Network: CBS
Arbitron Metro Market: Fort Wayne, IN *Format:* Adult Contemp
Hrs. of News Programming: News progmg 2 hrs wkly
J.J. Fabini, Operations Dir
Dave Reithmiller, General Sales Mgr
Scott Howard, Local Sales Manager
Dave Riethmiller, Co-General Manager
J. Fabini, Co-General Manager

WKJG
11-01-1947; 1380 khz AM
2915 Maples Rd., Ft. Wayne, IN 46816 US
(260) 447-5511, *Fax:* (260) 447-7546
www.wise33.com
info@wise33.com
License: Fort Wayne, IN held by Pathfinder Communications Corp.
Group Owner: Federated Media
Nat'l Network: ABC *Nat'l Reps:* Christal
Arbitron Metro Market: Fort Wayne, IN *Format:* Sports
Tony Richards, COO
Mark DePrez, General Manager
Jim Tighe, General Sales Mgr
Jon Zimney, Programming Director
Jack Didion, Engineering Dir
Mogan David, Chief Engineer
Eileen Strickland, Traffic Manager

*WLAB
08-23-1976; 88.3 mhz FM *Hrs Open:* 24; 3.2 kw; 607 ft.; N41 6 13 W85 11 28
1145 South Barr Street, Fort Wayne, IN 46802 US
(260) 483-8236, *Fax:* (260) 482-7707
www.star883.com
don@star883.com
License: Fort Wayne, Allen County, IN held by STAR Educational Media Network (Pending)
Arbitron Metro Market: Fort Wayne, IN *Format:* Adult Contemp, Christian *Target Audience:* 25-54; Christian *Adv. Rates:* 20; 17; 20; 15
Melissa Montana, General Manager
Don Buettner, Programming Director

WLDE
08-24-1970; 101.7 mhz FM *Hrs Open:* 24; 3 kw; 328 ft.; N41 5 2 W85 4 39
PO Box 62, Bloomington, IN 47402 US
(260) 423-3676, *Fax:* (260) 422-5266
www.wlde.com
captainchris@wide.com
License: Fort Wayne, Allen County, IN held by Sarkes Tarzian Inc.
Group Owner: Sarkes Tarzian Inc.; acq 2-16-93;
Nat'l Network: CNN Radio *Nat'l Reps:* Katz Radio *Wire Services:* AP
Arbitron Metro Market: Fort Wayne, IN *Format:* Contemporary Hits/Top 40, Adult Contemp *No. News Employees:* 1 *Target Audience:* Adults 25-54.
Thomas Tarzian, CEO
R. Geoffrey Vargo, President
Lee Tobin, General Manager
Shelly Steckler, Programming Director
Aimee Collins, News Director
Geary Morrill, Chief Engineer
Robert Davis, CFO
Darlene Lee, Controller
ChrisDidier, Program Director

WLYV
03-28-1948; 1450 khz AM *Hrs Open:* 24; 1 kw-D, ND2; 1 kw-N, ND2; N41 4 14 W85 7 10
29200 Vassar Road, Suite 650, Livonia, MI 48152 US
(260) 436-1450, *Fax:* (260) 432-6179
www.redeemerradio.com
Info@redeemerradio.com
License: Fort Wayne, IN held by Fort Wayne Catholic Radio Group Inc.
Nat'l Network: USA
Arbitron Metro Market: Fort Wayne, IN *Format:* Christian, Religious *Special Programming:* Spanish one hr wkly *Target Audience:* 25-54; Christian adults
Chris Langford, President
Jason Garrett, General Manager
Patty Becker, Programming Director

WMEE
02-05-1965; 97.3 mhz FM *Hrs Open:* 24; 26 kw; 689 ft.; N41 6 39 W85 11 44
2915 Maples Road, Fort Wayne, IN 46816 US
(260) 447-5511, *Fax:* (260) 447-7546
www.wmee.com
info@wmee.com
License: Fort Wayne, Allen County, IN held by Pathfinder Communications Corp.
Group Owner: Federated Media
Arbitron Metro Market: Fort Wayne, IN *Format:* Adult Contemp
Hrs. of News Programming: News progmg one hr wkly *Target Audience:* 25-54.
Bob Watson, CFO
John Dille, President
Mark Evans, Operations Dir
Allison Delagrange, General Sales Mgr
Rob Kliey, Programming Director
Brian Sheikh, Promotions Manager
Jack Didier, Engineering Dir
Chris Cage, Music Director

WOWO
03-31-1925; 1190 khz AM *Hrs Open:* 24
P.O. Box 487, Elkhart, IN 46515 US
(260) 447-5511, *Fax:* (260) 447-7546
www.wowo.com
info@wowo.com
License: Fort Wayne, IN held by Pathfinder Communications Corp.
Group Owner: Federated Media
Nat'l Network: CBS *Nat'l Reps:* Christal
Arbitron Metro Market: Fort Wayne, IN *Format:* News, News/Talk, 84, Talk *No. News Employees:* 5 *Target Audience:* 25-54.
Tony Richards, COO
John Dille, President
Jon Zimney, Operations Dir
Mark DePrez, General Manager
Jim Tighe, General Sales Mgr
Andy Ober, News Director
Mogan David, Chief Engineer
Bob Watson, CFO

WXKE
05-06-1976; 103.9 mhz FM *Hrs Open:* 24; 3 kw; 328 ft.; N41 6 32 W85 9 55
2541 Goshen Road, Fort Wayne, IN 46808 US
(260) 747-1511, *Fax:* (260) 747-3999
www.rock104radio.com
jj@summitcityradio.com
License: Fort Wayne, Allen County, IN held by Summit City License Sub, LLC.
Group Owner: Summit City Radio Group; (acq 11-6-2006; grpsl)
Nat'l Reps: Eastman Radio
Arbitron Metro Market: Fort Wayne, IN *Format:* Classic Rock *No. News Employees:* 1
J.J. Fabini, Operations Dir
Dave Reithmiller, General Sales Mgr
Doc West, Programming Director
Katherine Whatley, Promotions Manager

Frankfort

WILO
11-23-1953; 1570 khz AM *Hrs Open:* 5 AM-11 PM; 0.25 kw-D, ND1; 0.25 kw-N, ND1; N40 16 40 W86 29 7
Mailing Address: P.O. Box 545, Frankfort, IN 46041 US
Second Address: 1401 Barner St., Frankfort, IN 46041-1506
(765) 659-3338, *Fax:* (765) 659-3338
www.wilo.us
pddir@kasparradio.com

RADIO - U.S.

License: Frankfort, IN held by Kaspar Broadcasting Co. Inc.
Group Owner: Kaspar Broadcasting Group; (acq 10-1-59).
Nat'l Reps: Rgnl Reps
Format: Oldies *Special Programming:* Farm 12 hrs wkly
Vernon Kaspar, President
Russ Kaspar, Station Manager
Randy Lawson, Programming Director

WSHW
09-14-1962; 99.7 mhz FM; 50 kw; 459 ft.; N40 25 14 W86 24 47
Mailing Address: P. O. Box 545, Frankfort, IN 46041 US
Second Address: 1401 Barner St., Frankfort, IN 46041-1506
(765) 659-3338, *Fax:* (765) 654-3484
www.shine99.com
License: Frankfort, Clinton County, IN held by Kaspar Broadcasting Co. Inc.
Group Owner: Kaspar Broadcasting Group
Arbitron Metro Market: Lafayette, IN *Format:* Adult Contemp
Special Programming: Farm 8 hrs wkly
Russ Kaspar, General Sales Mgr

Franklin

***WFCI**
10-15-1960; 89.5 mhz FM *Hrs Open:* 8 AM-2 AM; 1.15 kw vert; 220 ft.; N39 24 29 W86 8 52
501 E. Monroe St., Franklin, IN 46131 US
(800)852-0232, *Fax:* (317) 738-8233
www.franklincollege.edu
info@franklincollege.edu
License: Franklin, Johnson County, IN held by Franklin College of Indiana.
Arbitron Metro Market: Indianapolis IN *Format:* Contemporary Hits/Top 40 *Target Audience:* 12-24; college & high school students
Harold Camping, General Manager
Joe Papp, Chief Engineer

WFDM-FM
12-15-1961; 95.9 mhz FM; 3.4 kw; 299 ft.; N39 30 49 W86 4 7
54 Monument Circle, Suite 250, Indianapolis, IN 46204 US
(317) 736-4040, *Fax:* (317) 736-4781
www.freedom959.com
License: Franklin, Johnson County, IN held by Pilgrim Communications LLC.
Group Owner: Pilgrim Communications Inc.; (acq 7-2-99)
Nat'l Reps: Rgnl Reps
Arbitron Metro Market: Indianapolis, I *Format:* Talk *Adv. Rates:* 50; 35; 50; 25
Randy Tipmore, Operations Dir
Jeremy Beutel, Programming Director

French Lick

WFLQ
04-12-1983; 100.1 mhz FM *Hrs Open:* 24; 6 kw; 299 ft.; N38 35 41 W86 36 48
P. O. Box 100, French Lick, IN 47432 US
(812) 936-9100, *Fax:* (812) 936-9495
www.wflq.com
wflqfm@smithville.net
License: French Lick, Orange County, IN held by W.G. Willis dba Willtronics Broadcasting.
Nat'l Network: ABC
Format: Country *Special Programming:* Farm 3 hrs, relg 6 hrs, Gospel 4 hrs wkly *Hrs. of News Programming:* news progmg 11 hrs wkly *No. News Employees:* 1 *Target Audience:* 25 plus.
Adv. Rates: 10; 9; 10;9
Catherine Willis, Operations Dir
Col. W.G. Willis, General Manager
Randall Hamm, Programming Director
Joe Randolph, News Director
Bill Willis, Chief Engineer
Charlie Derek, Disc Jockey
Chaz Mixon, Disc Jockey
Kim Stewart, DiscJockey

Gary

***WGVE-FM**
01-01-1954; 88.7 mhz FM; 2.1 kw horiz; 92 ft.; N41 33 15 W87 19 5
620 East Tenth Place, Gary, IN 46402 US
(219) 962-9483, *Fax:* (219) 962-3726
License: Gary, Lake County, IN held by Gary Community School Corp.
Format: Talk *Target Audience:* Northwest Indiana
Sarita Stevens, General Manager
Elizabeth Garcia, Programming Director

WLTH
11-05-1950; 1370 khz AM; 1 kw-D, DAN; 0.5 kw-N, DAN; N41 34 17 W87 19 2; N41 32 22 W87 18 0
2019 Broadway, Gary, IN 46407 US
(219) 794-1370, *Fax:* (219) 794-1377
www.wlth1370.com
info@wlth1370.com
License: Gary, IN held by WLTH Radio Inc.
Nat'l Network: CNN Radio
Arbitron Metro Market: Chicago, IL *Format:* News, News/Talk, 84, Talk *Target Audience:* 30 plus Black
Pluria Marshall Jr., General Manager

WWCA
12-07-1949; 1270 khz AM; 1 kw-U, DA1; N41 31 38 W87 22 36
645 Church St, Suite 400, Norfolk, VA 23510 US
(219) 309-9327
License: Gary, IN held by Starboard Media Foundation Inc.
Group Owner: Relevant Radio; (acq 7-1-2004; $1.5 million).
Arbitron Metro Market: Gary, IN *Format:* Talk
Armand Ciabattari, Station Manager

Goshen

***WGCS**
10-02-1958; 91.1 mhz FM *Hrs Open:* 24; 6 kw; 292 ft.; N41 33 29 W85 51 6
1700 South Main St., Goshen, IN 46526 US
(574) 535-7488, *Fax:* (574) 535-7293
www.globeradio.org
globe@goshen.edu
License: Goshen, Elkhart County, IN held by Goshen College Broadcasting Corp.
Nat'l Network: PRI
Arbitron Metro Market: South Bend, IN *Format:* Variety/Diverse
Special Programming: Sp 8 hrs, news 8 hrs, sports 10 hrs wkly
Hrs. of News Programming: News progmg 8 hrs wkly *Target Audience:* Adults 25-49.
Jason Samuel, General Manager

WKAM
01-01-1954; 1460 khz AM *Hrs Open:* 24; 2.5 kw-D, DAN; 0.5 kw-N, DAN; N41 35 24 W85 48 56
26914 Marcellus Hwy, Dowagiac, MI 49047 US
(574) 533-1460, *Fax:* (574) 534-3698
www.wkam1460.com
License: Goshen, IN held by Fulmer Communications LLC
Nat'l Network: USA *Regional Network:* Network Indiana *Nat'l Reps:* Katz Radio; Rgnl Reps
Format: Adult Contemp *Special Programming:* Southern gospel 6 hrs wkly *Hrs. of News Programming:* news progmg 20 hrs wkly *No. News Employees:* 1 *Target Audience:* 30-65; mature, family oriented, goal oriented*Adv. Rates:* 12; 12; 12; 10
Kent Fulmer, General Manager

WSSM(FM)
01-17-1977; 97.7 mhz FM *Hrs Open:* 24; 3 kw; Ant 482 ft; N41 36 04 W85 55 41
3371 Cleveland Rd., Suite 300, South Bend, IN 46628
(574) 273-9300, *Fax:* (574) 273-9090
www.wzow.com
Jobs@artisticradio.com
License: Goshen, Elkhart County, IN held by Artistic Media Partners Inc.
Group Owner: Artistic Media Partners Inc.; (acq 4-1-2002; $925,000)
Population Served: 101,081 *Arbitron Metro Market:* South Bend, IN *Format:* Classic Rock *Target Audience:* 25-54. *Adv. Rates:* 52; 47; 52; 21
Jack Swart, General Manager
Carrie Jones, General Sales Mgr
Chili Walker, Programming Director
Teresa Holden, Promotions Manager
Rita Kinzie, News Director
Bob Henning, Chief Engineer
Carrie McCaffery, National Sales Manager
Jim Wodock, Bloomington General Manager

Greencastle

***WGRE**
04-25-1949; 91.5 mhz FM *Hrs Open:* 24; 0.8 kw vert; 177 ft.; N39 38 19 W86 51 49
609 So. Locust Street, Greencastle, IN 46135 US
(765) 658-4642, *Fax:* (765) 658-4693
www.wgre.org
newton@depauw.edu
License: Greencastle, Putnam County, IN held by DePauw University.
Nat'l Network: AP Radio *Wire Services:* AP
Format: Alternative *Special Programming:* Jazz 3 hrs, Intl 2 hrs, regl 2 hrs wkly *Hrs. of News Programming:* News progmg 12 hrs wkly *Target Audience:* 18-25; college campus & loc community
Jeff McCall, President
Chris Newton, Operations Dir
Greg Stephan, Chief Engineer

WREB
05-16-1966; 94.3 mhz FM *Hrs Open:* 24; 3 kw horiz; 161 ft.; N39 39 38 W86 53 34
1309 Old Orchard Road, Vincennes, IN 47591 US
(765) 653-9717, *Fax:* (765) 653-6677
www.wrebfm.com
License: Greencastle, Putnam County, IN held by The Original Co.
Group Owner: The Original Company Inc.; (acq 6-22-94; $200,000;
Regional Network: Network Indiana; Brownfield
Format: Country, News, 84 *Special Programming:* Farm 5 hrs wkly *Hrs. of News Programming:* news progmg 37 hrs wkly *No. News Employees:* 1 *Target Audience:* General. *Adv. Rates:* 15; 15; 15; 15
Mark Lange, General Manager
Tonya Sanders, Programming Director

***WQRA**
01-01-2005; 90.5 mhz FM; 8.1 kw; 446 ft.; N39 35 22 W86 33 2
6434 La Pas Trail, Indianapolis, IN 46268 US
(888) 937-2471, *Fax:* (916) 251-1650
www.air1.com
info@air1.com
License: Greencastle, Putnam County, IN held by Educational Media Foundation.
Group Owner: EMF Broadcasting; (acq 11-1-2006; $2 million)
Nat'l Network: Air 1
Arbitron Metro Market: Greencastle, IN *Format:* Alternative, Christian
Darrell Chambliss, Chairman
Alan Mason, COO
Mike Novak, President and CEO
Ed Lenane, News Director
Sam Wallington, Engineering Dir
Dan Antonelli, Chief Business Development Officer
Eric Moser, Chief Financial Officer
BrianBurger, Vice President of Human Resources
D. Kevin Blair, Secretary and General Counsel
Larry Moody, Director
Mitch Barnhart, Director

Greenfield

***WRGF**
01-01-2001; 89.7 mhz FM; 0.75 kw horiz, 2 kw vert; 164 ft.; N39 44 55 W85 40 50
Mailing Address: 110 West North St., Greenfield, IN 46140 US
Second Address: 810 N. Broadway, Greenfield, IN 46140
(317) 462-9211, *Fax:* (317) 467-6755
gcsc.k12.in.us
wrgf@insight66.com
License: Greenfield, Hancock County, IN held by Greenfield Central Community School Corp.
Format: Rock/AOR, Classic Rock
Tim Renshaw, General Manager

WZPL
06-01-1962; 99.5 mhz FM; 19 kw; 774 ft.; N39 45 36 W86 0 22
9245 N Meridian St #300, Indianapolis, IN 46260 US
(317) 816-4000, *Fax:* (317) 816-4080
www.wzpl.com
info@wzpl.com
License: Greenfield, Hancock County, IN held by Entercom Indianapolis License LLC.
Group Owner: Entercom Communications Corp.; (acq 8-26-2004; grpsl).
Nat'l Reps: McGavren Guild
Arbitron Metro Market: Indianapolis, IN *Format:* Adult Contemp
Target Audience: 18-49; women *Adv. Rates:* 200; 200; 200; 100
Steve Hartley, General Sales Mgr
Scott Sands, Programming Director
Toni Williams, Promotions Manager
Gary Hunvnel, News Director
Mike Rabey, Chief Engineer

Greensburg

***WAUZ**
09-01-1998; 89.1 mhz FM *Hrs Open:* 24; 0.8 kw vert; 518 ft.; N39 14 13 W85 34 0
Mailing Address: 1680 Hwy 62 Ne, Corydon, IN 47112 US
Second Address: Box 487, Greensburg, IN 47201

(812) 738-3482, *Fax:* (812) 375-2555
www.wygs.org
ygs@wygs.org
License: Greensburg, Decatur County, IN held by Good Shepherd Radio Inc.
Arbitron Metro Market: Minneapolis-St. Paul, MN *Format:* Christian, Gospel *Target Audience:* 25-40.
Keith Reising, CEO

WRZQ-FM
12-01-1962; 107.3 mhz FM *Hrs Open:* 24; 10.5 kw; 499 ft.; N39 13 35 W85 44 47
825 Washington Street, Columbus, IN 47201 US
(812) 379-1077, *Fax:* (812) 375-2555
www.qmix.com
qmix@qmix.com
License: Greensburg, Decatur County, IN
Format: Adult Contemp *Hrs. of News Programming:* news progmg 4 hrs wkly *No. News Employees:* 1 *Target Audience:* 18-49. *Adv. Rates:* 34; 29; 34; 18
Keith Reising Jr., President
Dave Wineland, Operations Dir
Mike King, General Manager
Mike King, Station Manager
Michelle Hardcastle, General Sales Mgr
C.J. Miller, Programming Director
Sara Beth Clark, Promotions Manager
KeithMaddox, News Director
Jim Burgan, Engineering Dir
Mark Gravely, Disc Jockey
Matt Joyce, Promotions Director

WTRE
07-01-1968; 1330 khz AM *Hrs Open:* 18; 0.5 kw-D, DA2; 0.033 kw-N, DA2; N39 19 41 W85 30 6
825 Washington Street, Columbus, IN 47201 US
(812) 663-3000, *Fax:* (812) 663-8733
www.wtrecommunity.com
sandybiddinger@yahoo.com; ksverseman@hotmail.com
License: Greensburg, IN held by WTRE Inc.
Regional Network: Network Indiana
Arbitron Metro Market: Greensburg, IN *Format:* Country, News, 62, Talk, Variety/Diverse *Special Programming:* Farm 10 hrs, relg 3 hrs wkly *Hrs. of News Programming:* news progmg 24 hrs wkly *No. News Employees:* 1*Target Audience:* 25 plus. *Adv. Rates:* 19; 15; 14; 12
Keith Reising Jr., President
Sandy Biddinger, Sales and News
Mark Gravely, Programming Director
Kathy Verseman, Promotions Manager
Robert Hawkins, Chief Engineer
Gene McCoy, Sales Executive

WTRE(FM)
89.9 mhz FM; 1 kw; 61.65 meters; N39 20 04 W85 35 55
15 Wood Street, Greenfield, IN 46140
(317) 467-1064
License: Greensburg, Decatur County, IN held by Hoosier Public Radio Corp
Martin Hensley, President

Greenwood

WTLC-FM
01-01-1994; 106.7 mhz FM; 6 kw; 325 ft.; N39 42 42 W86 8 45
6264 La Pas Trail, Indianapolis, IN 46268 US
(317) 266-9600, *Fax:* (317) 328-3870
www.tlcnaptown.com/
ibanks@radio-one.com
License: Greenwood, Johnson County, IN held by Radio One of Indiana LLC.
Group Owner: Radio One Inc.; (acq 2-15-01; grpsl).
Arbitron Metro Market: Indianapolis, IN *Format:* Blues, Oldies
Charles Williams, Operations Dir
Brian Wallace, Programming Director
Kay Feenye-Caito, Promotions Manager
Terri Durrett, News Director
Don Payne, Chief Engineer

Hagerstown

***WBSH**
12-01-1996; 91.1 mhz FM; 0.3 kw horiz, 8 kw vert; 200 ft.; N39 56 31 W85 11 41 *Rebroadcasts:* Rebroadcasts WBST(FM) Muncie 100%
Ad 103, Muncie, IN 47306 US
(765) 285-5888, *Fax:* (765) 285-8937
www.bsu.edu/ipr
info@bsu.edu/ipr
License: Hagerstown, Wayne County, IN held by Ball State University.
Arbitron Metro Market: Muncie, IN *Format:* News *Hrs. of News Programming:* news progmg 33 hrs wkly *No. News Employees:* 1 *Target Audience:* General.
Marcus Jackman, General Manager
Pam Coletti, General Sales Mgr
Steven Turpin, Programming Director
Carol Trimmer, Promotions Manager
Dorothy Marvell, News Director
Robert Mittendorf, Chief Engineer
Brian Beaver, News Reporter

Hammond

WJOB
01-01-1928; 1230 khz AM *Hrs Open:* 24
6405 Olcutt Avenue, Hammond, IN 46320 US
(219) 989-8502, *Fax:* (219) 844-6190
www.heyregion.com
debbie@wjpb1230.com
License: Hammond, IN held by Vazquez Development LLC
Arbitron Metro Market: Chicago, IL *Format:* News, News/Talk, 86 *Special Programming:* Sports, Pol 2 hrs, relg 2 hrs, Greek one hr wkly *Hrs. of News Programming:* news progmg 17 hrs wkly *No. News Employees:* 10*Target Audience:* 25-49; general
Michael Stewart, Operations Dir
Debbie Wargo, General Manager
Pat Renwick, General Sales Mgr
Michael Stewart, Programming Director
Ron Perzo, News Director
Tim Saldana, Production
Alexis Vazquez Dedelow, Owner

WPWX
09-14-1959; 92.3 mhz FM *Hrs Open:* 24; 50 kw; 492 ft.; N41 37 50 W87 31 40
P. O. Box 3003, Blue Bell, PA 19422 US
(773) 734-4455, *Fax:* (219) 933-0323
www.power92chicago.com
wpwxinfo@crawfordbroadcasting.com
License: Hammond, Lake County, IN held by Dontron Inc.
Group Owner: Crawford Broadcasting Co.; (acq 9-14-59).
Arbitron Metro Market: Hammound, IN *Format:* Adult Contemp
Target Audience: 18-34; urban
Donald Crawford, President
Taft Harris, General Manager
Jay Allen, Programming Director

Hanna

***WHLP**
01-01-2001; 89.9 mhz FM; 8 kw; 505 ft.; N41 26 9 W86 50 48
3000 W. Macarthur Blvd., Santa Ana, CA 92704 US
(800) 357-4226, *Fax:* (208) 736-1958
www.csnradio.com
csn@csnradio.com
License: Hanna, La Porte County, IN held by CSN International
Group Owner: CSN International
Arbitron Metro Market: South Bend, IN *Format:* Religious
Mike Kestler, President
Daniel Davidson, Operations Dir
Jim Motshagen, General Manager
Kathy Motshagen, Programming Director
Kelly Carlson, Engineering Dir
Jerry Johnson, Engineering Dir
Don Mills, Network Programming Director /Music Director
Ray Gorney, Assistant Director of Engineering
Nolan Mather, Graphics / Website Maintenance
Mike Stocklin, National Underwriting
Austin Morris, Accounting

Hardinsburg

WKLO
01-01-2002; 96.9 mhz FM; 3.5 kw; 433 ft.; N38 28 21 W86 24 39
146 Shelly Court, Mt. Washington, KY 40047 US
(812) 295-9480, *Fax:* (812) 295-4455
www.1080wklo.com
john@1080WKLO.com
License: Hardinsburg, Washington County, IN held by Hembree Communications Inc.
Arbitron Metro Market: Loogootee, IN *Format:* Adult Contemp
Larry Hembree, General Manager
Kim Lozano, General Sales Mgr

Hope

***WYGS**
02-27-2003; 91.1 mhz FM *Hrs Open:* 24; 0.38 kw vert; 328 ft.; N39 13 35 W85 44 47
Mailing Address: 1680 Hwy 62 Ne, Corydon, IN 47112 US
Second Address: 825 Washington St., Columbus, IN 47201
(812) 375-9947, *Fax:* (812) 375-2562
www.wygs.org
jhutson@wygs.org
License: Hope, Bartholomew County, IN held by Good Shepherd Radio Inc.
Arbitron Metro Market: Hope, IN *Format:* Gospel
Keith Reising, Jr., Chairman
Matt Bond, Operations Dir
Mellissa Burton, Office Manager
Jim Hutson
Matt Bond
Keith Reising
Steve Fisher
Melissa Burton

Howe

***WQKO**
01-01-1994; 91.9 mhz FM; 3 kw; 299 ft.; N41 38 59 W85 21 12
3000 W. Macarthur Blvd., Santa Ana, CA 92704 US
(219) 548-5800, *Fax:* (219) 548-5808
www.calvaryradionetwork.com
info@CalvaryRadioNetwork.com
License: Howe, Lagrange County, IN held by CSN International
Group Owner: CSN International; (acq 7-13-98; $80,000).
Format: Christian
Jim Motshag, General Manager
Judy Puente, Programming Director

Huntertown

WQHK-FM
11-08-1966; 105.1 mhz FM; 5.7 kw; 689 ft.; N41 6 39 W85 11 44
2915 Maples Road, Fort Wayne, IN 46816 US
(260) 447-5511, *Fax:* (260) 447-7546
www.k105fm.com
info@k105fm.com
License: Huntertown, Adams County, IN held by Jam Communications Inc.
Group Owner: Federated Media
Arbitron Metro Market: Fort Wayne, IN *Format:* Country
Rob Kelley, Operations Dir
Mark DePrez, General Manager
Mogan David, Chief Engineer

Huntingburg

WBDC
12-22-1975; 100.9 mhz FM *Hrs Open:* 24; 11 kw; 492 ft.; N38 12 31 W86 54 0
Mailing Address: PO Box 1009, Jasper, IN 47547 US
Second Address: Box 330, 501 Old State Rd., Huntingburg, IN 47542-0330
(208) 743-4560, *Fax:* (208) 798-0110
License: Huntingburg, Dubois County, IN held by Dubois County Broadcasting Inc.
Group Owner: DCBroadcasting Inc.
Nat'l Network: CNN Radio; Jones Radio Networks *Regional Network:* Brownfield *Wire Services:* AP
Arbitron Metro Market: Salt Lake City-Ogden-Provo UT *Format:* Jazz, Smooth Jazz *Adv. Rates:* 17; 15; 15; 13
Mark Bolland, President

Huntington

WBZQ
05-25-1957; 1300 khz AM *Hrs Open:* 24; 0.5 kw-D, DA2; 0.019 kw-N, DA2; N40 52 31 W85 28 27
2504 River Park Drive, Fort Wayne, IN 46825 US
(260) 482-8500
License: Huntington, IN held by Larko Communications Inc.
Arbitron Metro Market: Fort Wayne, IN *Format:* Oldies *Target Audience:* 25-65.
Chris Larko, General Manager

WGL-FM
09-01-1965; 102.9 mhz FM *Hrs Open:* 24; 4.7 kw; 299 ft.; N40 55 33 W85 23 15
2541 Goshen Road, Fort Wayne, IN 46808 US
(260) 747-1511, *Fax:* (260) 747-3999
www.1029theriver.com
dave@summitcityradio.com
License: Huntington, Huntington County, IN held by Summit City License Sub, LLC.
Group Owner: Summit City Radio Group; (acq 11-6-2006; grpsl)
Nat'l Network: CBS *Nat'l Reps:* Eastman Radio
Arbitron Metro Market: Huntington, IN *Format:* Adult Contemp
No. News Employees: 1 *Target Audience:* 25-54.
JJ Fabini, Co-General Manager Operations
Dave Riethmiller, Co-General Manager (Sales)
J.J Fabini, Programming Director

RADIO - U.S.

***WVSH**
01-01-1950; 91.9 mhz FM; 0.92 kw horiz; 112 ft.; N40 53 32 W85 30 38
450 McGahn Street, Huntington, IN 46750 US
(260) 356-2019, *Fax:* (260) 358-2210
bwalker@hccsc.k12in.us
License: Huntington, Huntington County, IN held by Huntington County Community School Corp.
Regional Network: Network Indiana
Arbitron Metro Market: Huntington, IN *Format:* Contemporary Hits/Top 40
Bill Walker, General Manager
George Castle, Engineering Dir

Indianapolis

***WBDG**
09-13-1965; 90.9 mhz FM *Hrs Open:* 24; 0.4 kw; 79 ft.; N39 47 5 W86 17 27
1200 N. Girls School Rd., Indianapolis, IN 46224 US
(800) 877-5600, *Fax:* (916) 251-1650
www.klove.com
License: Indianapolis, Marion County, IN held by Metropolitan School District of Wayne Township.
Wire Services: Reuters
Arbitron Metro Market: Tulsa OK *Format:* Christian
Mike Novak, President

WBRI
03-10-1964; 1500 khz AM *Hrs Open:* 6 AM-7 PM; 5 kw-D, DA; N39 52 14 W86 05 17
4802 E. 62nd St., Indianapolis, IN 46220
(317) 255-5484, *Fax:* (317) 255-8592
www.wbrionline.com
wbri@wilkinsradio.com
License: Indianapolis, Marion County, IN held by Heritage Christian Radio Inc.
Group Owner: Wilkins Communications Network Inc.; (acq 7-1-2003; $1.5 million).
Nat'l Network: Salem Radio Network
Population Served: 1,800,000 *Arbitron Metro Market:* Indianapolis, I *Target Audience:* 35 plus. *Adv. Rates:* 35; 35; 35; 35
Bob Wilkins, President
Mitchell Mathis, Operations Dir
Keith Smiley, Station Manager
Tyger Elton, Engineering Dir
LuAnn Wilkins, Executive Vice President
Greg Garrett, Operations Manager

***WEDM**
09-14-1970; 91.1 mhz FM *Hrs Open:* 24; 0.18 kw vert; 217 ft.; N39 47 29 W85 59 53
9301 E. 18th Street, Indianapolis, IN 46229 US
(317) 532-6301, *Fax:* (317) 532-6199
License: Indianapolis, Marion County, IN held by Metropolitan School District of Warren Township.
Arbitron Metro Market: Indianapolis, IN *Format:* Contemporary Hits/Top 40 *Hrs. of News Programming:* News progmg 3 hrs wkly *Target Audience:* General; Warren Township residents
Daniel Henn, Station Manager

WFBQ
11-26-1959; 94.7 mhz FM *Hrs Open:* 24; 58 kw; 804 ft.; N39 53 43 W86 12 4
600 Congress Ave., Suite 1400, Austin, TX 78701 US
(317) 257-7565, *Fax:* (317) 253-6501
www.wfbq.com
info@wfbq.com
License: Indianapolis, Marion County, IN held by Capstar TX LP
Group Owner: Clear Channel Communications Inc.
Nat'l Network: AP Radio
Arbitron Metro Market: Indianapolis, IN *Format:* Classic Rock
Rick Green, General Manager
Buzz Casey, Programming Director
Jim Kendall, Promotions Manager
William Perry, Digital

***WFYI-FM**
10-01-1954; 90.1 mhz FM *Hrs Open:* 24; 10 kw; 561 ft.; N39 53 59 W86 12 1
1401 North Meridian St., Indianapolis, IN 46202 US
(317) 636-2020, *Fax:* (317) 283-6645
www.wfyi.org
captions@wfyi.org
License: Indianapolis, Marion County, IN held by Metropolitan Indianapolis Public Broadcasting Inc.
Nat'l Network: PRI; NPR *Regional Reps:* Indiana Public Broadcasting Station *Wire Services:* AP
Arbitron Metro Market: Indianapolis, IN *TV Affiliate:* *WFYI-TV affil. *Format:* News, News/Talk, 86 *Special Programming:* Black 5 hrs, blues 4 hrs wkly *Hrs. of News Programming:* News progmg 41 hrs wkly *TargetAudience:* 25-64; general
Anthony Lorenz, CFO
Lloyd Wright, President
Theresa Tetrault, General Sales Mgr
Michael Toulouse, Programming Director
Rena Barraclough, Promotions Manager
Steve Jensen, Engineering Dir
Jeanelle Adamak, Executive VicePresident
Alan Cloe, Executive Vice President
Lori Plummer, Promotions Manager

WHHH
10-28-1991; 96.3 mhz FM *Hrs Open:* 24; 3.3 kw; 285 ft.; N39 46 32 W86 9 10
6264 La Pas Trail, Indianapolis, IN 46268 US
(317) 266-9600, *Fax:* (317) 328-3870
www.hot963.com
License: Indianapolis, Marion County, IN held by Radio One of Indiana LLC.
Group Owner: Radio One Inc.; (acq 11-8-01; grpsl).
Nat'l Network: CNN Radio
Arbitron Metro Market: Indianapolis, IN *Format:* Blues *Target Audience:* 18-49.
Alfred Liggins, CEO
Charles Williams, Operations Dir
Michael Davidson, General Sales Mgr
Brian Wallace, Programming Director
Anna Fraser, Promotions Manager
Don Payne, Chief Engineer

WFNI
01-01-1938; 1070 khz AM *Hrs Open:* 24
3500 West Olive Avenue, Suite 300, Burbank, CA 91505 US
(317) 266-9422, *Fax:* (317) 684-2021
www.emmis.com
IR@emmis.com
License: Indianapolis, IN held by Emmis Radio License LLC.
Group Owner: Emmis Communications Corp.; (acq 6-9-94; $26 million with co-lo
Nat'l Network: ESPN Radio *Nat'l Reps:* D & R Radio
Arbitron Metro Market: Indianapolis, IN *Format:* Sports
Jeff Smulyan, CEO
Tom Severino, Operations Dir
Mike Cortese, General Sales Mgr
Kent Sterling, Programming Director
Susan Wells, Promotions Manager
Jeff Dinsmore, Chief Engineer
Patty England, National Sales Manager

***WICR**
08-20-1962; 88.7 mhz FM *Hrs Open:* 24; 8 kw; 685 ft.; N39 53 40 W86 12 21
1400 East Hanna Avenue, Indianapolis, IN 46227 US
(317) 788-3280, *Fax:* (317) 788-3490
wicr.uindy.edu
wicr@uindy.edu
License: Indianapolis, Marion County, IN held by University of Indianapolis.
Nat'l Network: PRI
Arbitron Metro Market: Indianapolis, IN *Format:* Jazz *Hrs. of News Programming:* News progmg 5 hrs wkly *Target Audience:* 35 plus; Educated, Affluent, Older *Adv. Rates:* 50; 40; 50; 40
Beverley Pitts, President
Scott Uecker, General Manager
Russell Maloney, Chief Engineer

***WJEL**
09-03-1975; 89.3 mhz FM *Hrs Open:* 24; 1 kw vert; 115 ft.; N39 54 34 W86 7 39
1901 East 86th Street, Indianapolis, IN 46240 US
(317) 259-5278, *Fax:* (317) 259-5298
www.geocities.com/wjelpower
License: Indianapolis, Marion County, IN held by Metropolitan School District of Washington Townshi
Arbitron Metro Market: Indianapolis, IN *Format:* Variety/Diverse
Tyler Hindman, Operations Dir
John King, General Manager
Robert Hendrix, Programming Director
Mike Rabey, Chief Engineer

WXNT
01-01-1923; 1430 khz AM *Hrs Open:* 24
9245 N Meridian Street, Ste 300, Indianapolis, IN 46260 US
(317) 816-4000, *Fax:* (317) 816-4035
www.newstalk1430.com
info@wxnt.com
License: Indianapolis, IN held by Entercom Indianapolis License LLC
Group Owner: Entercom Communications Corp.
Arbitron Metro Market: Indianapolis, IN *Format:* News, News/Talk, 86 *Special Programming:* Big band 2 hrs wkly *Hrs. of News Programming:* news progmg 18 hrs wkly *No. News Employees:* 1 *Target Audience:* 35-64.
Ben Hoffman, General Sales Mgr
Gary Havens, Programming Director
Alex Keddie, Engineering Dir
Mike Rabey, Chief Engineer

WIBC
12-05-1960; 93.1 mhz FM; 13.5 kw; 991 ft.; N39 46 3 W86 0 12
3500 West Olive Avenue, Suite 300, Burbank, CA 91505 US
(317) 266-9422, *Fax:* (317) 684-2021
www.wibc.com
alan@wibc.com
License: Indianapolis, Marion County, IN held by Emmis Radio License LLC.
Group Owner: Emmis Communications Corp.; (acq 6-9-94; $26 million with co-lo
Arbitron Metro Market: Indianapolis, IN *Format:* News, News/Talk, 86 *No. News Employees:* 12 *Target Audience:* 25-54; white collar, above average income & education
Jeff Smulyan, President
Tom Severino, Operations Dir
Eric Wunnenberg, General Sales Mgr
Alan Furst, Programming Director
Susan Wells, Promotions Manager
Stacy Conrad, News Director
David Hood, Chief Engineer
Jon Quick,Operations Director
Trish Boone, Traffic Manager

WNDE
10-23-1924; 1260 khz AM *Hrs Open:* 24; 5 kw-D, DAN; 5 kw-N, DAN; N39 51 54 W86 3 43
600 Congress Ave., Suite 1400, Austin, TX 78701 US
(317) 257-7565, *Fax:* (317) 254-9619
www.sportsradio1260.com
tomdoran@clearchannel.com
License: Indianapolis, IN held by Capstar TX L.P.
Group Owner: Clear Channel Communications Inc.; (acq 8-30-00; grpsl).
Nat'l Network: AP Radio; ESPN Radio *Nat'l Reps:* Clear Channel
Arbitron Metro Market: Indianapolis, IN *Format:* Sports, Talk
Special Programming: 0 *Target Audience:* 25-54.
Marty Bender, Operations Dir
Rick Green, General Manager
Tom Doran, General Sales Mgr
Buzz Casey, Programming Director
Dan Anderson, Promotions Manager
Debbie Tunny, News Director
Dan Mettler, Engineering Dir
ScottFenstermaker, Chief Engineer
Mark Patrick, Sports Commentator

***WRFT**
06-06-1978; 91.5 mhz FM; 0.13 kw; 180 ft.; N39 40 33 W86 0 56
6141 S. Franklin Road, Indianapolis, IN 46259 US
(317) 803-5552, *Fax:* (317) 862-7262
License: Indianapolis, Marion County, IN held by Franklin Township Community School Corp.
Arbitron Metro Market: Indianapolis, I *Format:* Variety/Diverse *Target Audience:* General.
Steve George, General Manager
Abby Wheeling, Programming Director

WRZX
05-15-1964; 103.3 mhz FM; 18 kw; 850 ft; N39 53 43 W86 12 04
6161 Fall Creek Rd., Indianapolis, IN 78701
(317) 257-7565, *Fax:* (317) 254-9619
www.x103.com
License: Indianapolis, Marion County, IN held by Capstar TX L.P.
Group Owner: Clear Channel Communications Inc.; (acq 8-30-00; grpsl)
Arbitron Metro Market: Indianapolis, I
Buzz Casey, Operations Dir
Rick Green, General Manager
Tom Doran, General Sales Mgr
Buzz Carey, Programming Director
Trish Wicks, Promotions Manager
Scott Fenstermaker, Chief Engineer

WSYW
05-15-1963; 810 khz AM *Hrs Open:* Sunrise-sunset; 0.25 kw-D, NDD; N39 43 32 W86 11 8
1800 N. Meridian St., Suite 605, Indianapolis, IN 46202 US
(317) 924-1071, *Fax:* (317) 924-7766
steph@wedjfm.com
License: Indianapolis, IN held by Continental Broadcast Group Inc.
Nat'l Reps: Univision Radio National Sales
Arbitron Metro Market: Indianapolis, I *Format:* Spanish *Target Audience:* 18+; Hispanic Adults *Adv. Rates:* 60; 50; 60; 40.

Martha Miller, Operations Dir
Russ Dodge, General Manager
Manuel Sepulveda, Programming Director
Stephanie Tatay-Myers, Promotions Manager
Phil Alexander, Chief Engineer

WTLC
07-27-1941; 1310 khz AM *Hrs Open:* 24; 5 kw-D, DAN; 1 kw-N, DAN; N39 43 8 W86 10 33
3500 West Olive Avenue, Suite 300, Burbank, CA 91505 US
(317) 266-9600, *Fax:* (317) 328-3870
www.1310thelight.com
info@1310thelight.com
License: Indianapolis, IN held by Radio One of Indiana LLC.
Group Owner: Radio One Inc.; (acq 11-8-01; grpsl).
Nat'l Network: ABC *Regional Network:* Network Indiana *Nat'l Reps:* Katz Radio
Arbitron Metro Market: Indianapolis, IN *Format:* Gospel, Talk *Hrs. of News Programming:* News progmg one hr wkly *Target Audience:* 35 plus; black females *Adv. Rates:* 60; 50; 50; 30
Charles Williams, Operations Dir
Max Williams, Station Manager
Ian Banks, General Sales Mgr
Khris Raye, Programming Director
Don Payne, Chief Engineer
Brian Harrington, Local Sales Manager
Jason Hunter, Advertising
Amos Brown,PSA Announcements

WYXB
01-22-1968; 105.7 mhz FM *Hrs Open:* 24; 50 kw; 492 ft.; N39 46 3 W86 0 12
950 N. Meridian St., Suite 1200, Indianapolis, IN 46204 US
(317) 266-0100, *Fax:* (317) 684-2021
www.emmis.com
IR@emmis.com
License: Indianapolis, Marion County, IN held by Emmis Radio License LLC.
Group Owner: Emmis Communications Corp.; (acq 9-8-97; with co-located AM).
Nat'l Reps: D & R Radio
Arbitron Metro Market: Indianapolis, IN *Format:* Classic Rock
Special Programming: Gospel 10 hrs wkly *Hrs. of News Programming:* news progmg 3 hrs wkly *No. News Employees:* 1 *Target Audience:* 25-34;adults, (secondary is 25-54)
Jeff Smulyan, President & CEO
Rick Cummings, President
David Edgar, Operations Dir
Tom Severino, General Manager
Mike Cortese, General Sales Mgr
Scott Wheeler, Programming Director
Mary Young, Promotions Manager
Dave Hood,Chief Engineer
Jenni Gray, Regional Sales Manager
Patrick Walsh, EVP,CFO & COO
Scott Enright, EVP, General Counsel
Greg Loewen, Chief Strategy Officer
Paul Brenner, SVP, Chief Technology Officer

WNTR
10-15-1984; 107.9 mhz FM *Hrs Open:* 24; 22 kw; 761 ft.; N39 53 43 W86 12 4
3135 North Meridian Stre, Indianapolis, IN 46204 US
(317) 816-4000, *Fax:* (317) 816-4035
www.1079thetrack.com
info@wntr.com
License: Indianapolis, Marion County, IN held by Entercom Indianapolis License LLC
Group Owner: Entercom Communications Corp.; (acq 8-26-2004; grpsl).
Nat'l Reps: Christal
Arbitron Metro Market: Indianapolis, IN *Format:* Adult Contemp
Special Programming: Jazz 6 hrs wkly *No. News Employees:* 3 *Target Audience:* 25-54.
Amy Dillon, General Sales Mgr
Scott Roddy, Programming Director
Jeff Kuhn, Promotions Manager
Alex Keddie, Engineering Dir
Mike Rabey, Chief Engineer
Jenny Skjodt, VP/Market Manager
Sheri Aquisto, Marketing Manager
MathewAlbro, Imaging Director
Ben Hoffman, Director of Sales

WXLW
08-01-1948; 950 khz AM *Hrs Open:* 24; 5 kw-D, DA2; 0.117 kw-N, DA2; N39 51 5 W86 14 39
54 Monument Circle, #250, Indianapolis, IN 45204 US
(317) 736-4040, *Fax:* (317) 736-4781
www.xl950.com
dave@XL950.com
License: Indianapolis, IN held by Raven Broadcasting Inc.
Nat'l Network: ABC; ESPN Radio
Arbitron Metro Market: Indianapolis, IN *Format:* Sports, Talk
Special Programming: Gospel 5 hrs wkly *Hrs. of News Programming:* News progmg 7 hrs wkly *Target Audience:* 25-54; men, secondary women
Randy Tipmore, General Manager
Dave Grenoble, General Sales Mgr

Jasper

WITZ
07-04-1948; 990 khz AM *Hrs Open:* Sunrise/Sunset; 1 kw-D, ND1; 0.006 kw-N, ND1; N38 21 2 W86 56 26
Mailing Address: P.O. Box 167, Jasper, IN 47546 US
Second Address: 1978 South WITZ Road, Jasper, IN 47546
(812) 482-2131, *Fax:* (812) 482-9609
www.witzamfm.com
witzamfm@psci.net
License: Jasper, IN held by Jasper On The Air Inc.
Jeri Weisheit, News Director

WITZ-FM
11-01-1954; 104.7 mhz FM *Hrs Open:* 24; 50 kw; 390 ft.; N38 21 2 W86 56 26
Mailing Address: P. O. Box 167, Jasper, IN 47546 US
Second Address: 1978 South WITZ Road, Jasper, IN 47546
(812) 482-2131, *Fax:* (812) 482-9609
www.witzamfm.com
witzamfm@psci.net
License: Jasper, Dubois County, IN held by Jasper On The Air Inc.
Nat'l Network: Fox News Radio *Regional Network:* Network Indiana *Nat'l Reps:* Rgnl Reps
Arbitron Metro Market: Evansville, IN *Format:* Adult Contemp *Target Audience:* 18-54.
Earl Metzger, General Manager
Gene Kuntz, General Sales Mgr
Walt Ferber, Programming Director
Brandon Elliott, News Director
Jeri Weisheit, Traffic Manager

***WJPR**
01-01-2006; 91.7 mhz FM; 2.6 kw; 276 ft.; N38 25 23 W86 49 47
1680 Hwy 62ne, Corydon, IN 47112 US
(812) 295-9480, *Fax:* (812) 295-3295
www.wjpr.org
License: Jasper, Dubois County, IN held by Jasper Public Radio Inc.
Arbitron Metro Market: Jasper, IN *Format:* Oldies
Larry Hembree, General Manager

Jeffersonville

WQKC
06-26-1961; 1450 khz AM *Hrs Open:* 24; 1 kw-U; N38 17 41 W85 45 07
PO Box 2098, Omaha, NE 47130
(800) 877-5600, *Fax:* (916) 251-1650
www.klove.com
License: Jeffersonville, Clark County, IN held by Sunnyside Communications Inc.
Group Owner: Cumulus Media Partners LLC; (acq 1-13-2012)
Nat'l Network: ESPN Radio *Regional Reps:* Rgnl Reps.
Population Served: 9,675 *Arbitron Metro Market:* Brownfield TX *Adv. Rates:* 12; 15; 20; 8
Mike Novak, CEO, President
Dr. David R. Ferry, Chief Engineer
Mitch Barnhart, Director
Larry Moody, Director

WQMF
04-25-1974; 95.7 mhz FM; 28.5 kw; 643 ft.; N38 8 16 W85 56 5
200 Concord Plaza, Suite 600, San Antonio, TX 78216 US
(502) 479-2222, *Fax:* (502) 479-2227
www.wqmf.com
License: Jeffersonville, Clark County, IN held by CC Licenses LLC.
Group Owner: Clear Channel Communications Inc.; (acq 1-23-97; $13.5 million)
Arbitron Metro Market: Louisville, KY *Format:* Classic Rock *Target Audience:* 35-54; men
Kevin Hughes, Operations Dir
Bill Gentry, Promotions Manager
Kim Combest, General Sales Manager

Kendallville

WAWK
11-09-1955; 1140 khz AM; 0.25 kw-D, NDD; N41 27 16 W85 15 48
931 N East Avenue, Kendallville, IN 46755 US
(913) 642-7770, *Fax:* (913) 642-1319
www.bottradionetwork.com
License: Kendallville, IN held by Northeast Indiana Broadcasting Inc.
Nat'l Network: USA *Regional Network:* Network Indiana
Format: Christian, Talk *Target Audience:* 25-55. *Adv. Rates:* 16.00; 16.00; 16.00
Trace Thurlby, COO
Richard Bott, President
Richard Bott II, Operations Dir
Pat Rulon, General Sales Mgr
Candy Green, Programming Director
Rachel Moser, Promotions Manager
Jason Potocnik, News Director
Tom Holdeman, CFO
EbenFowler, Operations Director

WBTU
12-16-1964; 93.3 mhz FM *Hrs Open:* 24; 18.5 kw; 384 ft.; N41 12 49 W85 12 4
941 Abbott Road, East Lansing, MT 48823 US
(260) 482-9288, *Fax:* (260) 482-8655
www.us933.us
dave.goode@oasisradiogroup.com
License: Kendallville, Noble County, IN held by Oasis Radio 1 Corp.
Arbitron Metro Market: Fort Wayne, IN *Format:* Country *Target Audience:* 18-54; upscale, young audience
Phil Becker, General Manager
John Buckley, Director of Sales
Scott Roddy, Programming Director
Dave Goode, Promotions Manager
Shelley Hall, News Director
Tami Gatchell, Traffic Manager
Lenny Diana, Content Director

Kentland

WIVR
01-01-2000; 101.7 mhz FM *Hrs Open:* 24; 3.2 kw; 453 ft.; N40 51 52 W87 35 14
1296 Marion Lane, Green Bay, WI 54303 US
(815) 933-9287, *Fax:* (815) 933-8696
www.rivervalleyradio.net
wvliradio@comcast.net
License: Kentland, Newton County, IN held by Milner Broadcasting Enterprises LLC
Group Owner: Milner Broadcasting; (acq 12-11-2000).
Nat'l Network: AP Network News *Wire Services:* AP
Arbitron Metro Market: Watseka, IL *Format:* Country *Hrs. of News Programming:* news progmg 168 bcsts wkly *No. News Employees:* 2 *Target Audience:* 12 plus; anthology country with current & recurrent hits *Adv.Rates:* 20; 20; 20; 15.
Tim Miner, General Manager
Chris Swain, General Sales Mgr
Mickey Milner, Programming Director
Ken Zyre, News Director
Don Kerouac, Chief Engineer
Carla, Traffic Manager
Kathy Gagliano, Vice President/Sales
Gordy McCollum,Public Service Director
Chris Nickles, Production Director
Mike Ruble, Farm Director

Knightstown

***WKPW**
09-07-1993; 90.7 mhz FM; 4.4 kw vert; 180 ft.; N39 46 1 W85 31 0
10892 N. State Road 140, Knightstown, IN 46148 US
(765) 345-9070, *Fax:* (765) 345-7039
www.wkpw.net
wkpw@knightstown.net
License: Knightstown, Rush County, IN held by IN Soldiers' & Sailors' Childrens' HME.
Wire Services: AP
Format: Country *Special Programming:* Gospel *Target Audience:* General.
John Wittkamper, President
Mike York, General Manager
Bob Hawkins, Chief Engineer

Knox

WKVI
06-30-1969; 1520 khz AM; 0.35 kw-C, NDD; 1.8 kw-D, NDD; N41 19 20 W86 36 17
P. O. Box 10, Knox, IN 46534 US
(574) 772-6241, *Fax:* (574) 772-5920
www.wkvi.com
info@spots.com
License: Knox, IN held by Kankakee Valley Broadcasting Co. Inc.

Format: Adult Contemp
Ted Hayes, General Manager
Lo Ann McDaniel, Programming Director
Anita Goodan, News Director

WKVI-FM
07-21-1969; 99.3 mhz FM; 3.3 kw; 299 ft.; N41 19 20 W86 36 17
P. O. Box 10, 400 West Culver Road, Knox, IN 46534 US
(574) 772-6241, *Fax:* (574) 772-5920
www.wkvi.com
info@spots.com
License: Knox, Starke County, IN
Richard Jenkins, President
Kurt Reeder, Operations Dir
Keith Whipple, General Sales Mgr
David Pierce, Programming Director
Ed Lenane, News Director
Sam Wallington, Engineering Dir
Eric Allen, National Sales Manager
MaryaMorgan, News Reporter
Richard Hunt, News Reporter
Karen Johnson, News Reporter

Kokomo

WIOU
07-16-1948; 1350 khz AM *Hrs Open:* 24
Mailing Address: 60 North Wayne Street, Martinsville, IN 46151 US
Second Address: 671 E. 400 S., Kokomo, IN 46902
(765) 453-1212, *Fax:* (765) 455-3882
newsroom.wzwz.wiou@sbcglobal.net
License: Kokomo, IN held by Mid-America Radio Group Inc.
Group Owner: Mid-America Radio Group Inc.; (acq 3-24-93; $1.21 million with co
Nat'l Network: CBS
Format: News, News/Talk, 84, Talk *Hrs. of News Programming:* news progmg 9 hrs wkly *No. News Employees:* 2 *Target Audience:* 25-54.
Steve La Mar, General Manager
Lora Lacy, General Sales Mgr
Allan James, Programming Director

***WIWC**
09-01-1993; 91.7 mhz FM; 2.1 kw; 299 ft.; N40 36 0 W86 18 8
Radio Station Wiwc, 820 North Lasalle Blvd, Kokomo, IN 60610 US
(765) 642-2750, *Fax:* (765) 642-4033
wiwc.mbn.org
wiwc@moody.edu
License: Kokomo, Howard County, IN held by The Moody Bible Institute of Chicago.
Group Owner: The Moody Bible Institute of Chicago
Format: Religious *Target Audience:* 34-55; general
Ray Hashley, General Manager
Tom Winn, Programming Director
Sam Sundin, News Director
Jim Wagner, Chief Engineer

WWKI
10-21-1962; 100.5 mhz FM *Hrs Open:* 24; 50 kw; 480 ft; N40 27 04 W86 02 12
519 N. Main St., Kokomo, IN 85281
(765) 459-4191, *Fax:* (765) 456-1111
www.wwki.com
info@wwki.com
License: Kokomo, Howard County, IN
Group Owner: Cumulus Media Inc.; (acq 6-30-99; grpsl).
Nat'l Network: AP Radio *Nat'l Reps:* Katz Radio *Regional Reps:* Rgnl Reps. *Wire Services:* AP
Population Served: 45,494 *Arbitron Metro Market:* Kokomo, IN *Hrs. of News Programming:* news progmg 13 hrs wkly *No. News Employees:* 2 *Target Audience:* 25-54. *Adv. Rates:* 58; 52; 52; 25
Mike Christopher, General Manager
James Stonecipher, General Sales Mgr
Dave Broman, Programming Director
Robert Longshore, Chief Engineer

WZWZ
11-20-1964; 92.5 mhz FM *Hrs Open:* 24; 6 kw; 325 ft.; N40 28 18 W86 9 52
Mailing Address: 60 North Wayne Street, Martinsville, IN 46151 US
Second Address: 671 E. 400 S., Kokomo, IN 46902
(765) 453-1212, *Fax:* (765) 455-3882
www.z925fm.com
Ernie@Z925fm.com
License: Kokomo, Howard County, IN held by Mid-America Radio Group of Kokomo Inc.
Group Owner: Mid-America Radio Group Inc.
Arbitron Metro Market: Kokomo, IN *Format:* Adult Contemp *Hrs. of News Programming:* News progmg 4 hrs wkly *Target Audience:* 18-49.
Ernie Caldemone, General Manager
Lora Lacy, Sales Manager
Allan James, Programming Director
Carolyn Monroe, Office Manager
Jerry Willis, Sales Representative
Leasa Wilke, Administrative Assistant
Blake Montgomery, SalesRepresentative

La Porte

WCOE
01-23-1964; 96.7 mhz FM *Hrs Open:* 24; 3 kw horiz; 262 ft.; N41 38 0.55 W86 45 32.79
1700 Licolnway Place, Suite 8, Laporte, IN 46350 US
(219) 362-5290, *Fax:* (219) 324-7418
www.wcoefm.com
License: La Porte, La Porte County, IN held by La Porte County Broadcasting Company Inc.
Arbitron Metro Market: La Porte, IN *Format:* Country *Hrs. of News Programming:* news progmg 19 hrs wkly *No. News Employees:* 2 *Target Audience:* 35-54; upper income, middle aged *Adv. Rates:* 23; 21; 23; 21
Donna Eichelberg, Operations Dir
Norma Sabie, General Sales Mgr
Dennis Sidall, Programming Director
Bob Costigan, News Director
Carl Fletcher, Engineering Dir
Kenneth Coe, Advertising Manager
Kate O'Malley, Disc Jockey
DennisSiddall, Disc Jockey
Chip Jones, Sports Commentator

WLOI
01-01-1948; 1540 khz AM *Hrs Open:* Sunrise-sunset
1700 Licolnway Place, Suite 8, Laporte, IN 46350 US
(219) 362-6144, *Fax:* (219) 324-7418
wcoe@csinet.net
License: La Porte, IN held by La Porte County Broadcasting Company Inc.
Nat'l Network: ABC; Westwood One *Regional Network:* Network Indiana; Va. News Net. *Nat'l Reps:* Rgnl Reps
Format: Adult Contemp *Special Programming:* Farm 8 hrs wkly *Hrs. of News Programming:* news progmg 26 hrs wkly *No. News Employees:* 2 *Target Audience:* 35 plus. *Adv. Rates:* 21; 19; 21; 18
Kenneth Coe, President
Norma Sabie, General Sales Mgr
Dennis Siddall, Programming Director
Kate O'Malley, Disc Jockey

Lafayette

WASK
01-01-1942; 1450 khz AM *Hrs Open:* 24; 1 kw-U, ND1; N40 24 8 W86 50 59
Mailing Address: P. O. Box 7880, Lafayette, IN 47903 US
Second Address: 3575 McCarty Ln., Lafayette, IN 47903
(765) 447-2186, *Fax:* (765) 448-4452
www.wask.com
info@wask.com
License: Lafayette, IN held by WASK Inc.
Group Owner: Schurz Communications Inc.; (acq 1-28-91; $8.25 million with co
Nat'l Network: ESPN Radio *Nat'l Reps:* Christal
Arbitron Metro Market: Lafayette, IN *Format:* Sports *Special Programming:* Farm 2 hrs wkly *Hrs. of News Programming:* news progmg 15 hrs wkly *No. News Employees:* 6
John Trent, President
Brian Green, General Sales Mgr
Randy Jones, Programming Director
Steve Truex, Chief Engineer
Bryan McGarvey, Disc Jockey

WSHY
11-28-1959; 1410 khz AM *Hrs Open:* 24; 1 kw-D, DAD; 0.06 kw-N, DA2; N40 21 38 W86 52 38
5520 East 75th Street, Indianapolis, IN 45250 US
(800) 877-5600, *Fax:* (916) 251-1650
www.klove.com
License: Lafayette, IN held by Artistic Media Partners Inc.
Group Owner: Artistic Media Partners Inc.; (acq 9-30-98; $275,000)
Nat'l Network: Fox News Radio; Fox Sports
Arbitron Metro Market: Melbourne AR *Format:* Christian
Mike Novak, President

WAZY-FM
03-01-1965; 96.5 mhz FM *Hrs Open:* 24; 50 kw; 499 ft.; N40 23 2 W87 7 55
5520 W. 75th St., Indianapolis, IN 46250 US
(800) 877-5600, *Fax:* (916) 251-1650
www.klove.com
License: Lafayette, Tippecanoe County, IN held by Artistic Media Partners L.P.
Group Owner: Artistic Media Partners Inc.; (acq 10-86; $2 million;
Nat'l Network: ABC *Regional Network:* Network Indiana *Nat'l Reps:* Christal
Arbitron Metro Market: Inyokern CA *Format:* Christian *Adv. Rates:* 35; 27; 35; 27
Mike Novak, President
David Pierce, Programming Director
Ed Lenane, News Director
Sam Wallington, Engineering Dir
Marya Morgan, News Reporter
Richard Hunt, News Reporter

***WJEF**
02-07-1972; 91.9 mhz FM *Hrs Open:* 24; 0.25 kw; 92 ft.; N40 23 52 W86 52 26
Mailing Address: 1801 South 18th Street, Lafayeytte, IN 47905 US
Second Address: 2300 Cason St., Lafayette, IN 47904
(765) 772-4700
www.jeff92.org
rbrist@lsc.k12.in.us
License: Lafayette, Tippecanoe County, IN held by Lafayette School Corp.
Arbitron Metro Market: Lafayette, IN *Format:* Oldies *Hrs. of News Programming:* News progmg 6 hrs wkly *Target Audience:* General.
Randall Brist, General Manager

WKHY
01-01-1970; 93.5 mhz FM *Hrs Open:* 24; 6 kw; 246 ft.; N40 23 13 W86 58 10
Mailing Address: 711 N. Earl Avenue, Lafayette, IN 47904 US
Second Address: 711 N. Earl Ave., Lafayette, IN 47904
(765) 448-1566, *Fax:* (765) 448-1348
www.wkhy.com
License: Lafayette, Tippecanoe County, IN held by Stay Tuned Broadcasting Corp.
Group Owner: RadioWorks Inc.; (acq 5-12-99; grpsl)
Nat'l Network: AP Radio *Nat'l Reps:* Katz Radio
Arbitron Metro Market: Lafayette, IN *TV Affiliate:* KHY TV
Format: Classic Rock, Rock/AOR *No. News Employees:* 1 *Target Audience:* 25-54; adults that are active, mobile & moderately affluent
John Trent, General Manager
John Schurz, General Sales Mgr
Jeff Strange, Programming Director
Liz Hahn, Promotions Manager
Eric Burch, News Director
Steve Truex, Chief Engineer

WKOA
09-28-1964; 105.3 mhz FM *Hrs Open:* 24; 50 kw; 308 ft.; N40 24 8 W86 50 59
Mailing Address: P. O. Box 7880, Lafayette, IN 47903 US
Second Address: 3575 McCarty Ln., Lafayette, IN 47903
(765) 447-2186, *Fax:* (765) 448-4452
www.wkoa.com
info@wkoa.com
License: Lafayette, Tippecanoe County, IN
Group Owner: Schurz Communications Inc.
Arbitron Metro Market: Lafayette, IN *Format:* Country *Special Programming:* Farm 3 hrs wkly *Hrs. of News Programming:* news progmg 12 hrs wkly *No. News Employees:* 3 *Target Audience:* 25-54.
Skip Davis, General Sales Mgr
Mark Allen, Programming Director
Lindsay Reinert, Promotions Manager
Christine Davis, Disc Jockey
Bob Vizza, Disc Jockey

***WQSG**
01-01-2005; 90.7 mhz FM; 17 kw vert; 328 ft.; N40 22 14 W86 30 32 *Rebroadcasts:* Rebroadcasts WAFR(FM) Tupelo, MS 100%
P.O. Box 106, Roaring Spring, PA 16673 US
(662) 844-8888, *Fax:* (662) 842-6791
www.afr.net
faq@afr.net
License: Lafayette, Tippecanoe County, IN held by American Family Association.
Group Owner: American Family Radio; (acq 7-29-2003).
Arbitron Metro Market: Lafayette, IN *Format:* Christian
Marvin Sanders, General Manager

Lafayette Township

***WCYT**
01-01-1995; 91.1 mhz FM *Hrs Open:* 24; 0.125 kw horiz, 0.12 kw vert; 226 ft.; N40 58 51 W85 16 48
4310 Homestead Rd, Fort Wayne, IN 46804 US
(260) 431-2271, *Fax:* (260) 431-2330
www.wcyt.org
INFO@wcyt.com
License: Lafayette Township, Allen County, IN held by Southwest Allen County Schools.
Arbitron Metro Market: Fort Wayne, IN *Format:* Alternative
Special Programming: Oldies 2 hrs, blues 2 hrs wkly *Target Audience:* General.
Adam Schenkel, General Manager
Adam Schenkel, Station Manager
Joe Asher, Programming Director
Julian Shine, Music Director

Lagrange

WTHD
09-02-1994; 105.5 mhz FM *Hrs Open:* 24; 2.4 kw; 522 ft.; N41 37 24 W85 20 49
206 S. High Street, Lagrange, IN 46761 US
(260) 463-8500, *Fax:* (260) 463-8580
www.wthd.net
wthd@wthd.net
License: Lagrange, Lagrange County, IN held by Lake Cities Broadcasting Corp.
Group Owner: Lake Cities Broadcasting Corp.; (acq 7-14-93;
Nat'l Network: ABC
Arbitron Metro Market: Lagrange, IN *Format:* Country *Hrs. of News Programming:* news progmg 2 hrs wkly *No. News Employees:* 1 *Target Audience:* 25-54.
Penny Mitchell, Operations Dir
Tim Murray, News Director
Thomas Andrews, Chief Engineer
Cheri Murphy, Account Executive
Tom Duke, Account Executive
Carter Snider, Account Executive

Lanesville

WGZB-FM
06-20-1988; 96.5 mhz FM; 1.6 kw; 638 ft.; N38 10 25 W85 54 50
1821 Summit Road, Suite 400, Cincinnati, OH 45237 US
(502) 625-1220, *Fax:* (502) 625-1257
www.b96jams.com
info@b96jams.com
License: Lanesville, Harrison County, IN held by MLB-Louisville IV LLC.
Group Owner: Main Line Broadcasting LLC; (acq 9-12-2007; grpsl)
Arbitron Metro Market: Louisville, KY *Format:* Urban Contemporary
Dale Schafer, General Manager

Lawrence

WRWM(FM)
02-01-1993; 93.9 mhz FM *Hrs Open:* 24; 824 kw; Ant 480 ft; N39 49 39 W85 58 51
6810 N. Shadeland Ave., Indianapolis, IN 46220
(317) 842-9550, *Fax:* (317) 577-3361
www.i94hits.com
License: Lawrence, Marion County, IN held by Indy Lico Inc.
Group Owner: Cumulus Media Partners LLC; (acq 5-5-2006; grpsl)
Population Served: 1,500,000 *Arbitron Metro Market:* Indianapolis, IN
Michele Kiefer, General Sales Mgr
Jeff Andrews, Programming Director
Christopher Wheat, Promotions Manager
Jake Robinson, Chief Engineer

***WRWM(FM)**
93.9 mhz FM; 1 w horiz, 100 w vert; Ant 82 ft; N39 18 27.1 W85 52 11.6
3280 Peachtree Road SW, Atlanta, GA 47203
(404) 949-0700
License: Lawrence, Bartholomew County, IN held by Susquehana Radio Corp
Population Served: 827,609 *Arbitron Metro Market:* Indianapolis, IN
Linda Jerome, President

Lebanon

***WIRE**
01-01-2001; 91.1 mhz FM *Hrs Open:* 24; 3.2 kw vert; 210 ft.; N40 3 48 W86 26 29
6434 La Pas Trail, Indianapolis, IN 46268 US
(317) 870-8400, *Fax:* (317) 870-8404
www.radiomom.fm
cac@hoosierbroadcastingcorp.org
License: Lebanon, Boone County, IN held by Hoosier Broadcasting Corp.
Group Owner: Hoosier Broadcasting Corp.
Format: Adult Contemp *Target Audience:* 25-54; adults *Adv. Rates:* 17; 17; 17; 17
Annie Martin, CFO
William Poorman, President
Chuck Cunningham, Operations Dir

Liberty

***WKWH**
89.7 mhz FM; 300 w vert; Ant 115 ft; N39 39 46.2 W84 55 38
134 Huston St., Connersville, IN
(765) 821-2180
License: Liberty, Union County, IN held by Connersville Apostolic Lighthouse Inc.
Population Served: 2,133 *Arbitron Metro Market:* Liberty, IN
Ira Sult III, CEO

Ligonier

WLEG
06-10-1991; 102.7 mhz FM *Hrs Open:* 24; 2 kw; 394 ft.; N41 27 52 W85 44 40
Mailing Address: 1104 Kings Highway, Winona Lake, IN 46590 US
Second Address: 421 S. 2nd St., Elkhart, IN 46516
(574) 389-5100, *Fax:* (574) 389-5101
www.ilovemyfroggy.com
bwilliams@federatedmedia.com
License: Ligonier, Noble County, IN held by Pathfinder Communications Corp.
Group Owner: Federated Media; (acq 9-26-2002; $550,000).
Format: Adult Contemp
Kathy Uebler, General Manager
Jeff Deweese, Programming Director
George Trobridge, Chief Engineer

Linton

WQTY
09-14-1970; 93.3 mhz FM; 12 kw; 476 ft.; N39 0 46 W87 22 23
Rr #3, Box 1213, Linton, IN 47441 US
(812) 254-4300, *Fax:* (812) 254-4361
www.wqtyfm.com
info@bl.com
License: Linton, Greene County, IN
Group Owner: The Original Company Inc.
Arbitron Metro Market: Terre Haute, IN *Format:* Oldies
Thomas Mandel, President
Dave Johnson, General Manager
Drew Henderson, Programming Director
Mark Biviano, Executive Vice President
Nick Anthony, Executive Vice President

***WYTJ**
89.3 mhz FM; 1 kw; 292 ft.; N39 5 59 W87 10 59
Rr 3 Box 1034, Linton, IN 47441 US
(812) 847-7222
www.wytj893fm.com
wyjt@minerbroadband.com
License: Linton, Greene County, IN held by Bethel Baptist Church.
Arbitron Metro Market: Linton, IN *Format:* Religious
Doug Cassel, General Manager
Harold Smith, Station Manager
Bro Smith

Logansport

WSAL
02-24-1949; 1230 khz AM *Hrs Open:* 24; 1 kw-U, ND1; N40 45 16 W86 18 40
P.O. Box 719, Logansport, IN 46947 US
(574) 722-4000, *Fax:* (574) 722-4010
www.indianasbestradio.com
License: Logansport, IN held by Logansport Radio Corp.
Nat'l Reps: Rgnl Reps
Format: Adult Contemp, News, 62, Talk *Special Programming:* Farm 10 hrs wkly *Hrs. of News Programming:* news progmg 14 hrs wkly *No. News Employees:* 2 *Target Audience:* General.
John Jenkins, CEO
Dan Keister, General Manager
Lisa Downham, General Sales Mgr
Bob Ehle, Jr., News Director
Jeff Smith, Chief Engineer

Loogootee

***WBHW**
09-01-1995; 88.7 mhz FM; 5.3 kw; 479 ft.; N38 34 4.66 W87 12 46.13 *Rebroadcasts:* Rebroadcasts WBGW(FM) Fort Branch 1
P.O. Box 4164, Evansville, IN 47724 US
(800)264-5550, *Fax:* (812) 768-5552
www.thyword.org
mail@thyword.org
License: Loogootee, Martin County, IN held by Music Ministries Inc.
Arbitron Metro Market: Evansville,IN *Format:* Religious
Floyd Turner, General Manager
Floyd Turner, Chief Engineer
Susan Turner, Financial Secretary

WRZR
12-06-1984; 94.5 mhz FM *Hrs Open:* 24; 1.8 kw; 427 ft.; N38 37 9 W86 58 27
Mailing Address: 514 Jfk Avenue, Loogootee, IN 47553 US
Second Address: 514 JFK Ave., Loogootee, IN 47553
(812) 634-9232, *Fax:* (812) 482-3696
www.wrzr.us/
mailbox@wrzr.us
License: Loogootee, Martin County, IN held by Hembree Communications Inc.
Regional Network: Brownfield; Network Indiana *Regional Reps:* Ron Spaulding *Wire Services:* AP
Format: Classic Rock *Special Programming:* Farm 2 hrs wkly *Hrs. of News Programming:* news progmg 2 hrs wkly *No. News Employees:* 1 *Target Audience:* 24-45. *Adv. Rates:* 17; 16; 17; 16
Paul Knies, President
Bill Potter, General Manager
Ron Spaulding, General Sales Mgr
Alan Williams, Programming Director
Mike Carie, News Director
David Ferguson, Chief Engineer

Lowell

WZVN
11-24-1972; 107.1 mhz FM; kw
6405 Olcott Avenue, Hammond, IN 46320 US
(219) 462-6111, *Fax:* (219) 462-4880
www.z1071.com
donclark@radiooneindiana.com
License: Lowell, Lake County, IN held by Porter County Broadcasting Holding Corp. LLC.
Group Owner: Porter County Broadcasting Corp.; (acq 2-6-2004; $4.9 million with WX
Nat'l Network: ABC
Arbitron Metro Market: Valparaiso, IN *Format:* Adult Contemp
Target Audience: 25-54.
Leigh Ellis, President
O.J. Jackson, General Sales Mgr
Scott Wagner, Programming Director
Laura Waluszko, News Director
Carl Fletcher, Chief Engineer
OJ Jackson
Jennifer Finnerty

***WLPR-FM**
01-01-2006; 89.1 mhz FM; 2.4 kw; 253 ft.; N41 19 24 W87 21 22
P O Drawer 2440, Tupelo, MS 38803 US
(219) 756-5656, *Fax:* (219) 755-4312
www.afr.net
License: Lowell, Lake County, IN held by Northwest Indiana Public Broadcasting Inc.
Nat'l Network: NPR
Arbitron Metro Market: Cheney, WA *Format:* News, News/Talk, 86
Thomas Carroll, CEO
Len Clark, Programming Director

Madison

WORX-FM
03-01-1950; 96.7 mhz FM; 1.05 kw; 551 ft.; N38 44 32 W85 21 43
Mailing Address: P. O. Box 1009, Jasper, IN 47547 US
Second Address: 1224 E. Telegraph Hill Rd., Madison, IN 47250
(812) 265-3322, *Fax:* (812) 273-5509
www.worxradio.com
thebestmusic@worxradio.com
License: Madison, Jefferson County, IN held by Dubois County Broadcasting Inc.
Group Owner: DCBroadcasting Inc.
Nat'l Network: Jones Radio Networks *Regional Network:* Network Indiana *Wire Services:* AP

TV Affiliate: Adult contemp *Format:* Agriculture *Special Programming:* news progmg 20 hrs wkly *Hrs. of News Programming:* 1 *Adv. Rates:* 21; 21; 21; 19

WXGO
03-01-1956; 1270 khz AM *Hrs Open:* 24; 1 kw-D, DA2; 0.058 kw-N, DA2; N38 44 28 W85 21 41
Mailing Address: P.O. Box 1009, Jasper, IN 47547 US
Second Address: 1224 E. Telegraph Hill Rd., Madison, IN 47520
(812) 265-3322, *Fax:* (812) 273-5509
www.worxradio.com
manager@worxradio.com
License: Madison, IN held by Dubois County Broadcasting Inc.
Group Owner: DCBroadcasting Inc.
Nat'l Network: USA *Nat'l Reps:* Rgnl Reps
Arbitron Metro Market: Madison, IN *Format:* News, Oldies
Special Programming: Farm 3 hrs, relg 6 hrs wkly *Target Audience:* General.
Paul Knies, President
William Potter, General Manager

***WHMO**
91.1 mhz FM; kw
US
(812) 738-3482, *Fax:* (812) 375-2555
License: Madison, Jefferson County, IN held by Good Samaritan Educational Radio Inc.
Arbitron Metro Market: Madison, IN
Keith Reising, General Manager

Marengo

***WBRO**
01-01-2000; 89.9 mhz FM; 1 kw; 279 ft.; N38 21 49 W86 25 13
1680 Hwy 62 Ne, Corydon, IN 47112 US
(812) 365-9276, *Fax:* (812) 365-2127
www.wbro.org
wbrofm@aol.com
License: Marengo, Crawford County, IN held by Crawford County Community Radio Inc.
Format: Variety/Diverse
Shawn Scott, General Manager

Marion

WBAT
06-07-1947; 1400 khz AM *Hrs Open:* 24; 1 kw-U, ND1; N40 33 40 W85 41 30
Mailing Address: 60 North Wayne Street, Martinsville, IN 46151 US
Second Address: 820 Pennsylvania St., Marion, IN 46953
(208) 734-6633, *Fax:* (208) 736-1958
www.csnradio.com
License: Marion, IN held by Mid-America Radio Group.
Group Owner: Mid-America Radio Group Inc.; (acq 12-88; grpsl;
Nat'l Network: CBS; ESPN Radio *Regional Reps:* Regional Reps
Arbitron Metro Market: Green Forest AR *Format:* Christian *Adv. Rates:* 27; 24; 24; 20
Mike Kestler, President

***WBSW**
01-01-1997; 90.9 mhz FM; 1 kw horiz, 2.4 kw vert; 308 ft.; N40 40 1 W85 37 50 *Rebroadcasts:* Rebroadcasts WBST(FM) Muncie 100%
Ad 103, Muncie, IN 47306 US
(765) 285-5888, *Fax:* (765) 285-8937
www.bsu.edu/ipr
info@bsu.edu/ipr
License: Marion, Grant County, IN held by Ball State University.
Arbitron Metro Market: Muncie, IN *Format:* News *Hrs. of News Programming:* news progmg 33 hrs wkly *No. News Employees:* 1 *Target Audience:* General.
Marcus Jackman, General Manager
Pam Coletti, General Sales Mgr
Steven Turpin, Programming Director
Carol Trimmer, Promotions Manager
Dorothy Marvell, News Director
Robert Mittendorf, Chief Engineer
Brian Beaver, News Reporter

WMRI
05-11-1955; 860 khz AM *Hrs Open:* 24; 1 kw-D, DA2; 0.5 kw-N, DA2; N40 33 12 W85 38 45
Mailing Address: P O Box 1538, Marion, IN 46952 US
Second Address: 820 S. Pennsylvania St., Marion, IN 46953
(765) 664-7396, *Fax:* (765) 668-6767
www.wmri.com
race@wbat.com
License: Marion, IN held by Mid-America Radio of Indiana Inc.
Group Owner: Mid-America Radio Group Inc.; (acq 5-12-2003; with co-located FM)
Nat'l Network: Music of Your Life *Regional Network:* Network Indiana
Format: Oldies *Target Audience:* 35-70. *Adv. Rates:* 12; 10; 12; 8
David Poehler, Operations Dir
Carolyn Bush, General Manager
Gloria Millspaugh, General Sales Mgr
Mike Jenkins, News Director
Vanessa Miller, Operations Manager

WXXC
12-19-1948; 106.9 mhz FM *Hrs Open:* 24; 50 kw; 499 ft.; N40 35 52 W85 39 21
P O Box 1538, Marion, IN 46952 US
(765) 664-7396, *Fax:* (765) 668-6767
www.1069wxxc.com
studio@1069wxxc.com
License: Marion, Grant County, IN held by Mid-America Radio of Indiana Inc.
Group Owner: Mid-America Radio Group Inc.
Nat'l Network: CNN Radio *Regional Network:* Network Indiana
Arbitron Metro Market: Marion, IN *Format:* Contemporary Hits/Top 40, Adult Contemp *Target Audience:* 25-54. *Adv. Rates:* 28; 28; 28; 18
Robert Rhea, President
Vanessa Miller, Operations Dir
Race Ashlyn, General Manager
John Clark, General Sales Mgr
Anthony Bannon, Programming Director
Layla Price, News Director

Martinsville

WCBK-FM
10-15-1968; 102.3 mhz FM; 6 kw; 308 ft.; N39 26 18 W86 27 58
1639 Burton Lane, Martinsville, IN 46151 US
(765) 342-3394, *Fax:* (765) 342-5020
www.wcbk.com
License: Martinsville, Morgan County, IN held by Mid-America Radio Group Inc.
Group Owner: Mid-America Radio Group Inc.
Arbitron Metro Market: Martinsville, IN
Ruth Arney, General Sales Mgr
John Taylor, Programming Director

WMYJ
04-18-1967; 1540 khz AM; 0.25 kw-C, NDD; 0.5 kw-D, NDD; N39 24 31 W86 25 10
Mailing Address: P.O. Box 1970, Martinsville, IN 46151 US
Second Address: 1639 Burton Ln., Martinsville, IN 46151-3004
(765) 342-3394, *Fax:* (765) 342-5020
License: Martinsville, IN held by Mid-America Radio Group Inc.
Group Owner: Mid-America Radio Group Inc.; (acq 8-4-97; with co-located FM)
Nat'l Network: USA
Arbitron Metro Market: Indianapolis, IN *Format:* Gospel *Special Programming:* Farm one hr wkly *Target Audience:* 25-54.
David Keister, General Manager

Michigan City

WEFM
09-15-1966; 95.9 mhz FM *Hrs Open:* 24; 3 kw; 230 ft.; N41 42 58 W86 51 47
1903 Springland Avenue, Michigan City, IN 46360 US
(312) 649-0099, *Fax:* (219) 879-8202
www.us995.cbslocal.com
jeff@cbsradio.com
License: Michigan City, La Porte County, IN held by Michigan City FM Broadcasters Inc.
Nat'l Network: Westwood One; NBC Radio *Regional Network:* Network Indiana
Arbitron Metro Market: Chicago, IL *Format:* Adult Contemp, Oldies *Special Programming:* Farm, relg 4 hrs wkly *No. News Employees:* 1 *Target Audience:* General. *Adv. Rates:* 21; 21; 21; 21
Thomas Burns, President
Ronald Miller, Station Manager
Jim Spevak, General Sales Mgr
Jeff, Programming Director
Tim Volckmann, Chief Engineer

WIMS
08-10-1947; 1420 khz AM *Hrs Open:* 24; 5 kw-D, DA2; 5 kw-N, DA2; N41 40 26 W86 55 58
6405 Olcott Avenue, Hammond, IN 46320 US
(219) 879-9810, *Fax:* (219) 879-9813
www.wimsradio.com
ric@wimsradio.com
License: Michigan City, IN held by Gerard Media LLC
Format: Talk *Special Programming:* Pol 3 hrs wkly *Target Audience:* 30 plus; general *Adv. Rates:* 22; 18; 20; 12
Ric Federighi, General Manager
Johnny Rush, Programming Director

Mitchell

***WMBL**
88.1 mhz FM; 1 kw vert; 400 ft.; N38 45 50 W86 31 15
820 North Lasalle Blvd., Chicago, IL 60610 US
(312) 329-4438
www.mbn.org
moodyradio@moody.edu
License: Mitchell, Lawrence County, IN held by The Moody Bible Institute of Chicago.
Group Owner: The Moody Bible Institute of Chicago
Arbitron Metro Market: Louisville, KY *Format:* Religious
Doug Hastings, General Manager
Denny Nugent, National Program Director
Mark Williames, Engineering Dir
Collin Lambert, Vice-President
Dan Craig, Manager of Programming
Mike Bingham, Manager
Bruce Everhart, Manager, Developmentand Marketing
Chris Segard, Manager, Production Services
Amy Rios, Executive Assistant to Vice President

Monticello

WMRS
03-01-1989; 107.7 mhz FM *Hrs Open:* 24; 2.45 kw; 515 ft.; N40 40 8 W86 41 44
132 N. Main Street, Monticello, IN 47960 US
(574) 583-8121, *Fax:* (574) 583-8933
www.wmrsradio.com
kevinp@wmrsradio.com
License: Monticello, White County, IN held by Monticello Community Radio Inc.
Nat'l Network: USA; Jones Radio Networks
Arbitron Metro Market: Lafayette, IN *Format:* Adult Contemp, Talk, 94 *Special Programming:* Gospel 5 hrs, bluegrass 2 hrs wkly *Hrs. of News Programming:* news progmg 20 hrs wkly *No. News Employees:* 2 *TargetAudience:* 25-60; motivated, intelligent, diverse *Adv. Rates:* 15; 15; 15; 15
Kevin Page, General Manager

Montpelier

***WJCO**
91.3 mhz FM; 0.35 kw vert; 196 ft.; N40 33 21 W85 17 39
US
(219) 548-5800, *Fax:* (219) 548-5808
www.calvaryradionetwork.com
info@calvaryradionetwork.com
License: Montpelier, Blackford County, IN held by CSN International
Group Owner: CSN International
Arbitron Metro Market: Montpelier, IN *Format:* Christian
Jim Motshagen, Operations Dir
Kathy Motshagen, Programming Director
Phil Jennings, Chief Engineer
Tom Worthington, VP and Production Servant
Tonya Mandich, Underwriting Specialist

Morgantown

***WCJL**
01-01-2005; 90.9 mhz FM; 1 kw horiz, 13.5 kw vert; 213 ft.; N39 19 17 W86 31 8
3000 W. Macarthur Blvd., Santa Ana, CA 92704 US
(800) 357-4226, *Fax:* (208) 736-1958
www.csnradio.com
csn@csnradio.com
License: Morgantown, Morgan County, IN held by CSN International.
Group Owner: CSN International
Arbitron Metro Market: Morgantown, IN *Format:* Christian
Mike Kestler, President
Daniel Davidson, Operations Dir
Don Mills, Network Programming Director / Music Director
Kelly Carlson, Engineering Dir
Jerry Johnson, Engineering Dir
Ray Gorney, Assistant Director of Engineering
DustinPamplona, Engineer
Nolan Mather, Graphics / Website Maintenance
Mike Stocklin, National Underwriting
Austin Morris, Accounting
Lois Mills, FCC Applications / Translator Site Manager

Morristown

***WJCF-FM**
01-01-2000; 88.1 mhz FM; 2.7 kw vert; 151 ft.; N39 45 1 W85 33 19

Mailing Address: 7205 Mohawk Lane, Indianapolis, IN 46260 US
Second Address: 15 Wood St., Greenfield, IN 46140-2162
(317) 462-9523, *Fax:* (317) 467-1065
www.wjcfradio.com
wjcfradio@aol.com
License: Morristown, Shelby County, IN held by Indiana Community Radio Corp.
Arbitron Metro Market: Greenfield, IN *Format:* Christian
Jennifer Cox-Hensley, General Manager
Marty Hensley, Programming Director

Mount Vernon

WYFX
08-01-1992; 106.7 mhz FM; 3 kw; 295 ft.; N37 56 3 W87 55 35
1309 Old Orchard Road, Vincennes, IN 47591 US
(812) 882-6060, *Fax:* (812) 838-6434
www.originalcompany.com
marklange@originalcompany.com
License: Mount Vernon, Posey County, IN
Group Owner: The Original Company Inc.
Nat'l Network: ESPN Radio
Arbitron Metro Market: Vincennes, IN *Format:* Sports, Talk
Lowell Davey, President
Paul Montgomery, General Manager
Mark Lange, Owner
Duncan Myers, Marketing Manager
Suzy Duryea, TOC Web Sites

Mt. Vernon

WRCY
08-21-1955; 1590 khz AM; 0.5 kw-D, ND1; 0.035 kw-N, ND1; N37 56 3 W87 55 42
1309 Old Orchard Road, Vincennes, IN 47591 US
(812) 838-4484, *Fax:* (812) 838-6434
www.wyfx.com
espn1067@gmail.com
License: Mt. Vernon, IN held by The Original Co. Inc.
Group Owner: The Original Company Inc.; (acq 1999; $360,000 with co-located
Arbitron Metro Market: Evansville, IN *Format:* Country *Special Programming:* Farm 5 hrs wkly *Target Audience:* 25 plus; loc county
Mark Lange, President
Sean Dulaney, General Manager
Frank Hertel, Chief Engineer

Muncie

***WBST**
09-12-1960; 92.1 mhz FM *Hrs Open:* 24; 3 kw; 299 ft.; N40 12 48 W85 27 36
Ball State University, Ad 103, Muncie, IN 47306 US
(765) 285-5888, *Fax:* (765) 285-8937
www.bsu.edu/ipr
info@bsu.edu/ipr
License: Muncie, Delaware County, IN held by Ball State University.
Nat'l Network: PRI; NPR
Arbitron Metro Market: Muncie, IN *Format:* Classical, News *Hrs. of News Programming:* news progmg 33 hrs wkly *No. News Employees:* 1 *Target Audience:* General.
Marcus Jackman, General Manager
Pam Coletti, General Sales Mgr
Steven Turpin, Programming Director
Carol Trimmer, Promotions Manager
Dorothy Marvell, News Director
Robert Mittendorf, Chief Engineer
Brian Beaver, News Reporter

WERK
01-16-1986; 104.9 mhz FM *Hrs Open:* 24; 6 kw; 328 ft.; N40 9 19 W85 25 48 *Rebroadcasts:* Simulcasts WURK(FM) Elwood 80%
25 Reliance Drive, Bristol, RI 02809 US
(765) 288-4403, *Fax:* (765) 378-2090
www.werkradio.com
amy.dillon@bybradio.com
License: Muncie, Delaware County, IN held by Indiana Sabrecom Inc.
Group Owner: Backyard Broadcasting LLC; (acq 12-1-02; grpsl).
Arbitron Metro Market: Muncie, IN *Format:* Oldies *Adv. Rates:* 34; 34; 34; 18
Steve Lindell, General Manager
John Seneff, Local Sales Manager
Jay Garrison, Assistant Program Director
Bret Beshore, Assistant Program Director
Sean Mattingly, Director of Technical Operations
Amy Dillon, VP/Market Manager

WLBC-FM
10-01-1947; 104.1 mhz FM; 41 kw; 459 ft.; N40 9 40 W85 22 44
800 E. 29th Street, Munice, IN 47302 US
(765) 288-4403
www.wlbc.com
steve@wlbc.com
License: Muncie, Delaware County, IN held by Indiana Sabrecom Inc.
Group Owner: Backyard Broadcasting LLC
Wire Services: AP
Format: News *Hrs. of News Programming:* news progmg 19 hrs wkly *No. News Employees:* 1 *Target Audience:* 18-49; female
Adv. Rates: 39; 37; 37; 29
Steve Lindell, Programming Director
Joanna Black, News Director
Dave Stout, News Reporter

WRFM
02-14-1965; 990 khz AM; 0.25 kw-D, DA2; 0.001 kw-N, DA2; N40 6 54 W85 22 2
1506 S. Parker Dr., Evansville, IN 47714 US
(765) 747-6970, *Fax:* (765) 747-5054
wlhnradio.com
wlhn990@yahoo.com
License: Muncie, IN held by Electronic Applications Radio Service Inc.
Group Owner: Electronic Applications Radio Service Inc.; (acq 3-16-99)
Nat'l Reps: Roslin; Rgnl Reps
Format: Gospel *Target Audience:* 25-54; upscale adults & families, professional & blue collar *Adv. Rates:* 18; 18; 18; 15
Steven Dugger, General Manager

***WWHI**
01-01-1950; 91.3 mhz FM; 0.001 kw horiz, 0.2 kw vert; 233 ft.; N40 11 56 W85 24 49
1601 E. 26th Street, Muncie, IN 47302 US
(765) 747-5339, *Fax:* (765) 747-5325
www.wcrd.iweb.bsu.edu
License: Muncie, Delaware County, IN held by Ball State University
Arbitron Metro Market: Muncie, IN *Format:* Rock/AOR
Ken Wickliffe, General Manager

WXFN
11-01-1926; 1340 khz AM; 1 kw-U, ND1; N40 9 42 W85 22 41
800 E. 29th St, Muncie, IN 47302 US
(765) 288-4403, *Fax:* (765) 288-0429
License: Muncie, IN held by Indiana Sabrecom Inc.
Group Owner: Backyard Broadcasting LLC; (acq 12-1-2002; grpsl).
Nat'l Network: ABC; ESPN Radio; Sporting News Radio Network
Regional Network: Network Indiana *Wire Services:* AP
Arbitron Metro Market: Muncie, IN *Format:* Sports *Special Programming:* Black 3 hrs wkly *Hrs. of News Programming:* news progmg 12 hrs wkly *No. News Employees:* 2 *Target Audience:* 25-54. *Adv. Rates:* 22; 18; 18; 12
Barry Drake, CEO
Steve Lindell, Operations Dir
Joanna Black, News Director
Sean Mattingly, Chief Engineer
Robin Smith, CFO
Jay Garreson, Sports Commentator

***WKMV**
88.3 mhz FM; 0.28 kw; 338 ft.; N40 9 22 W85 25 48
P. O. Box 106, Roaring Spring, PA 16673 US
(800) 877-5600, *Fax:* (916) 251-1650
www.klove.com
License: Muncie, Delaware County, IN held by Educational Media Foundation.
Group Owner: EMF Broadcasting; (acq 3-23-2007; grpsl)
Nat'l Network: K-Love
Format: Christian
Mike Novak, President

Nappanee

WAOR(FM)
12-16-1991; 95.7 mhz FM *Hrs Open:* 24; 1.4 kw; 500 ft; N41 24 43 W86 01 51
237 W. Edison Rd., Mishawaka, IN 46545
(574) 258-5483
www.power957.com
wypw@power957.com
License: Nappanee, Elkhart County, IN held by Talking Stick Communications LLC.
Group Owner: Talking Stick Communications LLC; (acq 8-25-2000).
Nat'l Network: ABC; CBS

Population Served: 600,000*Format:* Adult Contemp *Hrs. of News Programming:* News progmg 10 hrs wkly *Target Audience:* 35-70; secretaries, bankers
Gene Walker, Operations Dir
Abe Thompson, General Manager
Alec Dille, Station Manager
Emily Wideman, General Sales Mgr
Chuck Wright, Programming Director
Greg Trobridge, Chief Engineer

Nashville

WVNI
08-01-1997; 95.1 mhz FM *Hrs Open:* 24; 3.8 kw; 344 ft.; N39 13 52 W86 22 40
Mailing Address: P.O. Box 1970, Martinsville, IN 46151 US
Second Address: 4317 E.3rd St., Bloomington, IN 47401
(812) 335-9500, *Fax:* (812) 335-8880
www.spirit95fm.com
spirit95@spirit95fm.com
License: Nashville, Brown County, IN held by Brown County Broadcasters Inc.
Group Owner: Mid-America Radio Group Inc.; (acq 10-29-97; $20,000 for 51% of s
Nat'l Network: Salem Radio Network
Arbitron Metro Market: Bloomington, IN *Format:* Christian *Target Audience:* 25-54. *Adv. Rates:* 32;22;27;22
Jim Webster, Operations Dir
Diana Nuchols, General Manager
Mark Peterson, Station Manager
Logan Roberson, Production Manager
Ricky House, Account Executive

New Albany

WFIA-FM
01-01-1996; 94.7 mhz FM *Hrs Open:* 24; 3.3 kw; 394 ft.; N38 17 2 W85 54 17
4880 Santa Rosa Road, Suite 300, Camarillo, CA 93012 US
(502) 339-9470, *Fax:* (502) 423-3139
www.salemradiogroup.com
listeners@salemradiogroup.com
License: New Albany, Floyd County, IN held by Salem Media of Kentucky Inc.
Group Owner: Salem Communications Corp.; (acq 1999; $5 million with WRVI(FM) Valley Station, KY)
Nat'l Network: Salem Radio Network *Nat'l Reps:* Salem
Arbitron Metro Market: Louisville, KY *Format:* News, Talk, 74
Target Audience: 30 plus
Tom Hartlage, General Manager
Todd Burns, General Sales Mgr
Carrie Baylor, Promotions Manager
Charlie Strickland, Chief Engineer

***WNAS**
05-28-1949; 88.1 mhz FM; 2.85 kw; 3 ft.; N38 17 56 W85 48 45
618 E. Market St, PO Box 1087, New Albany, IN 47150 US
(812) 981-7625, *Fax:* (812) 949-6926
www.wnas.org
License: New Albany, Floyd County, IN held by New Albany-Floyd County Consolidated School Corp.
Arbitron Metro Market: Louisville, KY *Format:* Contemporary Hits/Top 40
Lee Kelly, General Manager

WNDA
06-15-1949; 1570 khz AM *Hrs Open:* 24; 1.5 kw-D, ND1; 0.233 kw-N, ND1; N38 19 40 W85 46 56
P.O. Box 655, New Albany, IN 47151 US
(812) 949-1570, *Fax:* (812) 949-9623
www.indiana1570.com
news@indiana9.com
License: New Albany, IN held by New Albany Broadcasting Co. Inc.
Nat'l Network: CBS Radio; ESPN Radio
Arbitron Metro Market: Louisville, KY *Format:* News, News/Talk, 86
David Smith, General Manager
Corissa Smith, General Sales Mgr
Ashley Robinson, News Director

New Carlisle

WSMM
07-02-1991; 102.3 mhz FM *Hrs Open:* 24; 2 kw; 397 ft.; N41 43 38 W86 24 30
3371 W. Cleveland Rd., Ext. , Suite 310, South Bend, IN 46628 US
(574) 273-9300, *Fax:* (574) 273-9090
www.wzow.com
michael@wzow.com

License: New Carlisle, St. Joseph County, IN held by Artistic Media Partners Inc.
Group Owner: Artistic Media Partners Inc.; (acq 3-22-2002; $1.5 million)
Arbitron Metro Market: South Bend, IN *Format:* Classic Rock
Adv. Rates: 52; 47; 52; 21
Jack Swart, General Manager
Carrie Jones, General Sales Mgr
Chili Walker, Programming Director
Teresa Holden, Promotions Manager
Rita Kinzie, News Director
Bob Henning, Chief Engineer

New Castle

WLTI(AM)
11-14-1960; 1550 khz AM; 250 w-U, DA-2; N39 55 59 W85 24 26
1134 W. State Rd. 38, Box 690, New Castle, IN 47362
(765) 529-2600, *Fax:* (765) 529-1688
www.wmdh.com
License: New Castle, Henry County, IN
Group Owner: Cumulus Media Inc.; (acq 7-1-99; grpsl).
Regional Network: Network Indiana *Nat'l Reps:* Katz Radio
Population Served: 24,000 *Arbitron Metro Market:* New Castle IN *Format:* Country *Special Programming:* Farm 2 hrs, relg 2 hrs wkly *Target Audience:* 49 plus.
Paulette Lees, General Manager
Pam Price, General Sales Mgr
Jon Sipes, Programming Director

WMDH-FM
08-06-1976; 102.5 mhz FM *Hrs Open:* 24; 50 kw; 499 ft.; N40 3 18 W85 23 5
140 S. Ash Ave., Tempe, AZ 85281 US
(765) 529-2600, *Fax:* (765) 529-1688
www.wmdh.com
License: New Castle, Henry County, IN
Group Owner: Cumulus Media Inc.
Arbitron Metro Market: Muncie, IN *Format:* Country *Special Programming:* Farm one hr wkly *Hrs. of News Programming:* news progmg 2 hrs wkly *No. News Employees:* 1 *Target Audience:* 25-54.
Tom Biolo, General Manager
Norm Grey, General Sales Mgr

New Haven

WJFX
04-01-1990; 107.9 mhz FM *Hrs Open:* 24; 3.2 kw; 453 ft.; N41 1 26 W85 3 51
4840 Sw 80th, Maimi, FL 33143 US
(260) 493-9539, *Fax:* (260) 749-5151
www.hot1079online.com
License: New Haven, Allen County, IN held by Fort Wayne Radio Corp.
Nat'l Reps: Interep
Arbitron Metro Market: Fort Wayne, IN *Format:* Contemporary Hits/Top 40 *Target Audience:* 18-49; adults *Adv. Rates:* 65; 60; 70; 40
Russ Oasis, President
Roger Diehm, Operations Dir
Beth Thornton, General Sales Mgr
Phil Becker, Programming Director

New Washington

***WARA**
01-01-1994; 88.3 mhz FM *Hrs Open:* 24; 0.95 kw; 300 ft.; N38 35 40 W85 28 6 *Rebroadcasts:* Rebroadcasts KLRD(FM) Yucaipa, CA 100%
402 E. Yakim, Suite 1320, Yakim, WA 98901 US
(916) 251-1600, *Fax:* (916) 251-1650
www.air1.com
info@air1.com
License: New Washington, Clark County, IN held by Educational Media Foundation.
Group Owner: EMF Broadcasting; (acq 10-2-2003; grpsl).
Nat'l Network: Air 1
Arbitron Metro Market: Louisville, KY *Format:* Alternative, Christian *No. News Employees:* 3 *Target Audience:* 18-35; Judeo Christian, female
Mike Novak, President
Chip Bailey, Operations Dir

New Whiteland

***WHZN**
88.3 mhz FM; 0.001 kw horiz, 7.8 kw vert; 725 ft.; N39 24 14 W86 8 41
7702 Indian Lake Rd, Indianapolis, IN 46236 US
(815) 939-5330, *Fax:* (815) 939-5087
www.shine.fm
License: New Whiteland, Johnson County, IN held by Horizon Christian Fellowship.
Group Owner: Horizon Christian Fellowship; (acq 3-6-2006)
Arbitron Metro Market: New Whiteland, IN *Format:* Christian
Mike MacIntosh, President
Carl Fletcher, Operations Dir
Justin Knight, General Manager
Brian McIntre, Programming Director
Kurt Wallace, Promotions Manager
Seth Hurd, Digital Media Director
Shannon LaFrance, Impact Advocate
Jeff Enfield, Business Relations Director

Newburgh

WDKS
02-11-1991; 106.1 mhz FM *Hrs Open:* 24; 6 kw; 328 ft.; N37 52 57 W87 32 28
1180 Maple Lane, Newburgh, IN 47630 US
(812) 425-4226, *Fax:* (812) 428-5895
www.1061evansville.com
ryano@1061evansville.com
License: Newburgh, Warrick County, IN
Group Owner: Townsquare Media; (acq 12-3-2003; grpsl).
Nat'l Network: ABC; Westwood One
Arbitron Metro Market: Evansville, IN *Format:* Contemporary Hits/Top 40 *No. News Employees:* 1 *Target Audience:* 18-34; women
LaDonne Craig, General Manager
Angie Ross, Director of Sales
Cat Michaels, Programming Director
Max Powers, Promotions Manager
Gene Stewart, News Director
Rick Crazo, Chief Engineer

WGAB
03-05-1984; 1180 khz AM *Hrs Open:* 24 hrs
1180 Maple Lane, Newburgh, IN 47630 US
(812) 479-5342, *Fax:* (888) 708-8936
www.faith1180.com
info@faith1180.com
License: Newburgh, IN held by Faith Broadcasting LLC
Nat'l Network: ABC; Jones Radio Networks; Salem Radio Network; Westwood One
Arbitron Metro Market: Evansville, IN *Format:* Christian *Target Audience:* 18-54; men & women *Adv. Rates:* 8;12;12;8
Gayle Russ, General Manager

Noblesville

WJJK
09-25-1950; 104.5 mhz FM *Hrs Open:* 24; 50 kw; Ant 492 ft; N39 50 25 W86 10 34
6810 N. Shadeland Ave., Indianapolis, IN 17401
(317) 842-9550, *Fax:* (317) 577-3361
www.1045wjjk.com
info@1045wjjk.com
License: Noblesville, Hamilton County, IN held by Susquehanna Radio Corp
Group Owner: Cumulus Media Partners LLC; (acq 5-5-2006; grpsl)
Population Served: 1,133,200 *Arbitron Metro Market:* Indianapolis, IN *No. News Employees:* 1 *Target Audience:* 25-54.
Michele Kiefer, General Sales Mgr
Anna Fraser, Programming Director
Dan Anderson, Promotions Manager
Jake Robinson, Chief Engineer
Steve Cannon, Programming Director
Karyn Sullyvan, Public Service Announcements Director
RikkiHoughton, Account Executive
Melissa Stoner, Employment and Advertising Contact

North Manchester

***WBKE-FM**
05-01-1967; 89.5 mhz FM *Hrs Open:* 24; 3 kw horiz; 79 ft.; N41 0 40 W85 45 45 *Rebroadcasts:* Rebroadcasts WBNI-FM Ft. Wayne 50%
Box 85, College Ave., N. Manchester, IN 46962 US
(260) 982-5272, *Fax:* (260) 982-5043
www.wbke.manchester.edu
mefetters@manchester.edu
License: North Manchester, Wabash County, IN held by Manchester College.
Arbitron Metro Market: North Manchester, IN *Format:* Variety/Diverse *Special Programming:* Class 10 hrs, Sp one hr, classic rock 6 hrs, AOR *Hrs. of News Programming:* news progmg 10 hrs wkly *No. News Employees:* 1 *Target Audience:* General.
Dan Daggett, General Manager
Alicia Smith, Station Manager
Brandon Curry, Promotions Manager
Michael Paynter, News Director
Les Okeley, Music Director
Mark Zinser, Sports Director

North Vernon

WWWY
03-19-1963; 106.1 mhz FM *Hrs Open:* 24; 50 kw; 486 ft.; N39 4 2 W85 42 10
Mailing Address: P O Box 15435, Cincinnati, OH 45215 US
Second Address: 3212 Washington St., Columbus, IN 47203
(812) 372-4448
www.y106.com
rockme@y106.com
License: North Vernon, Jennings County, IN held by White River Broadcasting Co. Inc.
Group Owner: The Findlay Publishing Co.; (acq 8-1-97; grpsl).
Target Audience: 25-44. *Adv. Rates:* 35;35;35;35
Kurt Kah, President
David Glass, Operations Dir
Tasha Mann, General Manager
Scott Michaels, Programming Director
Kevin Keith, News Director
Chuck Weber, Engineering Dir
John Foster, Operations Manager

WJCP
01-08-1955; 1460 khz AM; 1 kw-D, ND1; 0.092 kw-N, ND1; N38 59 46 W85 39 2
P.O. Box 15435, Cincinnati, OH 45215 US
(812) 346-1927, *Fax:* (812) 346-9722
License: North Vernon, IN held by Columbus Radio Inc.
TV Affiliate: Sports

Notre Dame

***WSND-FM**
09-17-1962; 88.9 mhz FM *Hrs Open:* 7am to 2am M-F; 9am to 2am Sa/Su; 3.4 kw; 361 ft.; N41 36 19 W86 12 45
P O Box 532, Notre Dame, IN 46556 US
Studio (574) 63, *Fax:* (574) 631-3653
www.nd.edu/~wsnd
wsnd@nd.edu
License: Notre Dame, St. Joseph County, IN held by Voice of the Fighting Irish Inc.
Wire Services: UPI
Arbitron Metro Market: South Bend, IN *Format:* Classical *Special Programming:* Jazz, Reggae, Celtic, Blues *Hrs. of News Programming:* 10 *Target Audience:* General public radio.
Laurie McFadden, General Manager
Ed Jaroszewski, Programming Director
Patrick Brown, Student Manager

Oolitic

***WMYJ-FM**
01-01-2005; 88.9 mhz FM; 5.2 kw; 256 ft.; N38 59 14 W86 27 31
1680 Hwy 62 Ne, Corydon, IN 47112 US
(765) 349-1485, *Fax:* (765) 342-3569
License: Oolitic, Lawrence County, IN held by Spirit Educational Radio Inc.
Arbitron Metro Market: Oolitic, IN *Format:* Gospel
David Keister, Chairman
Diana Nuchols, General Manager

Orland

***WCKZ**
02-02-2002; 91.3 mhz FM *Hrs Open:* 24; 2 kw; 299 ft.; N41 44 36 W85 5 48
PO Box 8459, Fort Wayne, IN 46898 US
(260) 452-1189, *Fax:* (260) 452-1188
www.nipr.fm
manager@nipr.fm
License: Orland, Steuben County, IN held by Northeast Indiana Public Radio Inc.
Nat'l Network: NPR
Arbitron Metro Market: Fort Wayne, IN *Format:* Classical
Will Murphy, President / General Manager
Colleen Condron, Operations Dir
Karen Fraser, General Sales Mgr
Sean Bueter, News Director
Ed Didier, Chief Engineer
Janice Furtner, Music Director
Jackie Didier, Traffic Manager
KatyAnderson, Operations Manager
Sarah Delia, Reporter
Lea Denny, Office Manager/Special Events Coordinator
Jennifer DePoy, Finance Manager

Orleans

WPHZ
08-17-1991; 102.5 mhz FM *Hrs Open:* 24; 6 kw; 282 ft.; N38 38 16 W86 27 11
PO Box 1307, Bedford, IN 47421 US
(812) 275-7555, *Fax:* (812) 279-8046
www.wphz.com
info@wphz.com
License: Orleans, Lawrence County, IN held by Mitchell Community Broadcast Co.
Nat'l Network: ABC; Jones Radio Networks *Nat'l Reps:* Rgnl Reps
Arbitron Metro Market: Orleans, IN *Format:* Adult Contemp *Hrs. of News Programming:* news progmg 2 hrs wkly *No. News Employees:* 1 *Target Audience:* General.
Holly Lindsey, General Manager

Paoli

WSEZ
11-07-1963; 1560 khz AM *Hrs Open:* 6 AM-6 PM; 0.25 kw-D, NDD; N38 32 25 W86 28 42
P.O. Box 22, French Lick, IN 47432 US
(812) 723-4484, *Fax:* (812) 723-4966
hitsandfavorites.com
wume@blueriver.net
License: Paoli, IN held by Ironic Broadcasting Inc.
Regional Network: Network Indiana *Nat'l Reps:* Rgnl Reps
Format: Oldies *Special Programming:* Farm 7 hrs wkly *Hrs. of News Programming:* news progmg 7 hrs wkly *No. News Employees:* 1 *Target Audience:* General. *Adv. Rates:* 8; 8; 8; 6
Jerry Wall, General Manager
Jason Archer, Programming Director
Dave Dedrick, News Director
Todd Edwards, Chief Engineer

WUME-FM
09-01-1972; 95.3 mhz FM *Hrs Open:* 24; 3 kw; 299 ft.; N38 32 25 W86 28 42
P.O. Box 22, French Lick, IN 47432 US
(812) 723-4484, *Fax:* (812) 723-4966
hitsandfavorites.com
License: Paoli, Orange County, IN
Nat'l Network: ABC *Regional Reps:* Rgnl Reps
Arbitron Metro Market: Paoli, IN *Format:* Contemporary Hits/Top 40 *Hrs. of News Programming:* news progmg 9 hrs wkly *No. News Employees:* 1 *Target Audience:* General. *Adv. Rates:* 15; 14; 14; 8
Jason Archer, News Director
Neil Barry, Advertising

Pendleton

*WEEM-FM
11-01-1971; 91.7 mhz FM *Hrs Open:* 24; 1.2 kw; 154 ft.; N39 59 52 W85 44 7
201 South East Street, Pendleton, IN 46064 US
(765) 778-2161, *Fax:* (765) 778-0605
www.917weem.org
jpetrey@smadison.k12.in.us
License: Pendleton, Madison County, IN held by South Madison Community School Corp.
Regional Network: Network Indiana
Arbitron Metro Market: Pendleton, IN *Format:* Triple A *Special Programming:* High school sports 10 hrs, acoustic cafe 2 hrs, ed *Target Audience:* Adults 18-45, students 13-18.
Jered Petrey, General Manager
Nick Postlewaite, Programming Director
Madeline May, Promotions Manager
Steve Longenecker, Chief Engineer

Peru

WARU
09-12-1954; 1600 khz AM *Hrs Open:* 24; 1 kw-D, ND2; 0.037 kw-N, ND2; N40 45 53 W86 2 26
Mailing Address: P. O. Box 1970, Martinsville, IN 46151 US
Second Address: 1711 E. Wabash Rd., Peru, IN 46970
(765) 473-4448, *Fax:* (765) 473-4449
www.warufm.com
waru@sbcglobal.net
License: Peru, IN held by Miami County Broadcasting Inc.
Group Owner: Mid-America Radio Group Inc.
Nat'l Network: AP Radio *Nat'l Reps:* Rgnl Reps
Arbitron Metro Market: Peru, IN *Format:* Country *Hrs. of News Programming:* news progmg 20 hrs wkly *No. News Employees:* 1 *Target Audience:* 25-54. *Adv. Rates:* 14; 14; 14; 14
David Keister, President
David Poehler, Operations Dir
Dan Keister, General Manager
Steve Morris, Programming Director

WMYK
04-05-1965; 98.5 mhz FM *Hrs Open:* 24; 6 kw; 328 ft.; N40 37 46 W86 2 30
Mailing Address: P. O. Box 1010, Peru, IN 46970 US
Second Address: 671 E. 400 S., Kokomo, IN 46902
(414)529-2122, *Fax:* (765) 455-3882
www.991themix.com
classicrock985@sbcglobal.net,985rocks@radio.fm
License: Peru, Miami County, IN held by Miami County Broadcasting Inc.
Group Owner: Mid-America Radio Group Inc.; (acq 1996; $360,000 with WARU(AM) P
Nat'l Network: ABC
Arbitron Metro Market: Peru, IN *Format:* Classic Rock *No. News Employees:* 2 *Target Audience:* 25-54.
Allan James, Operations Dir
Steve LaMar, General Manager
Mike Turner, Programming Director
Elise Schrock, News Director
Steve Ross, Chief Engineer

Petersburg

WBTO-FM
10-08-1984; 102.3 mhz FM *Hrs Open:* 24; 3 kw; 322 ft.; N38 30 33 W87 17 28
Mailing Address: PO Box 538, Petersburg, IN 47567 US
Second Address: Box 242, Vincennes, IN 47591
(812) 254-4300, *Fax:* (812) 254-4361
www.wbtofm.com
info@bl.com
License: Petersburg, Pike County, IN held by The Original Co. Inc.
Group Owner: The Original Company Inc.; acq 11-24-99; $400,000)
Nat'l Reps: Rgnl Reps
Format: Classic Rock *Hrs. of News Programming:* News progmg 9 hrs wkly *Target Audience:* General.
Mark Lange, President

Plainfield

WRDZ-FM
07-01-2003; 98.3 mhz FM *Hrs Open:* 24; 3 kw; 299 ft.; N39 45 33 W86 22 30
4802 East 62nd St, Indianapolis, IN 46220 US
(317) 574-2000, *Fax:* (317) 581-1985
www.radiodisney.com
jim.mcconville@disney.com
License: Plainfield, Hendricks County, IN held by Radio Disney Group LLC.
Group Owner: ABC Inc.; (acq 7-1-03; $5.6 million).
Nat'l Network: Radio Disney *Nat'l Reps:* McGavren Guild
Arbitron Metro Market: Indianapolis, IN *Format:* Christian *Target Audience:* W25-44. Kids 4-12 *Adv. Rates:* 75; 75; 75; 75
Jim McCondville, General Manager
Laura Sanchez, Promotions Manager

*WWDL
91.3 mhz FM; 0.2 kw; 141 ft.; N39 40 18 W86 21 30
7700 Indian Lake Rd, Indianapolis, IN 46236 US
(317) 823-2349, *Fax:* (858) 277-1365
License: Plainfield, Boone County, IN held by Horizon Christian Fellowship.
Group Owner: Horizon Christian Fellowship; (acq 3-6-2006).
Arbitron Metro Market: Plainfield, IN
Mike MacIntosh, President

Plymouth

WTCA
08-18-1964; 1050 khz AM *Hrs Open:* 24/7; 0.25 kw-D, DA2; 0.25 kw-N, DA2; N41 19 6 W86 18 41
112 West Washington, Plymouth, IN 46563 US
(574) 936-4096, *Fax:* (574) 936-6776
am1050.com
info@am1050.com
License: Plymouth, IN held by Community Service Broadcasters Inc.
Nat'l Network: Jones Radio Networks *Regional Network:* Brownfield
Arbitron Metro Market: Plymouth, IN *Format:* Contemporary Hits/Top 40, Adult Contemp *Special Programming:* Farm 3 hrs wkly religious 4hrs wkly *Target Audience:* 25-65.
Ken Kunze, General Manager
Kathryn Bottorff, Station Manager
Jim Bottorff, General Sales Mgr
Tony Ross, Programming Director
Kathy Bottorff, News Director
James Kunze, Chief Engineer
Tony Ross, Sports Director

WZOC
07-20-1966; 94.3 mhz FM; 11.5 kw; 492 ft.; N41 31 41 W86 15 53
112 W. Washington Street, Plymouth, IN 46563 US
(574) 233-3141, *Fax:* (574) 289-7382
www.radiomichiana.com/wzoc
bgamble@wsbt.com, tgazzana@wsbt.com
License: Plymouth, Marshall County, IN held by Plymouth Broadcasting Inc.
Arbitron Metro Market: Mishawaka, IN *Format:* Oldies
James Kunze, Station Manager
Tony Gazzana, General Sales Mgr

*WIKV
01-01-2005; 89.3 mhz FM; 1.4 kw; 249 ft.; N41 20 51 W86 20 23
P O Drawer 2440, Tupelo, MS 38803 US
(800) 525-5683, *Fax:* (916) 251-1650
www.klove.com
klove@klove.com
License: Plymouth, Marshall County, IN held by Educational Media Foundation.
Group Owner: EMF Broadcasting; (acq 3-23-2007; grpsl)
Nat'l Network: K-Love
Arbitron Metro Market: Plymouth, IN *Format:* Christian *No. News Employees:* 13
Darrell Chambliss, Chairman
Mike Novak, President and CEO
David Pierce, Chief Creative Officer and Programming Director
Ed Lenane, News Director
Sam Wallington, Engineering Dir
Alan Mason, Chief Operating Officer
Dan Antonelli,Chief Business Development Officer
Eric Moser, Chief Financial Officer
Brian Burger, Vice President of Human Resources
D. Kevin Blair, Secretary and General Counsel
Tim Luttrell, News Reporter

Portage

WNDZ
05-13-1987; 750 khz AM
1436 Auburn Boulevard, Sacramento, CA 95815 US
(773) 792-1121, *Fax:* (773) 792-2904
www.accessradiochicago.com
sales@wsbcradio.com
License: Portage, IN held by WNDZ Inc.
Group Owner: Newsweb Corp.; (acq 3-16-2004; $24 million with WCPQ(FM) Park Forest, IL)
Arbitron Metro Market: Chicago, IL *Format:* Oldies *Target Audience:* General.
Harvey Wells, Operations Dir
Mark Pinski, General Manager
Mike McCarthy, Engineering Dir

Portland

*WBSJ
12-01-1996; 91.7 mhz FM; 2 kw; 220 ft.; N40 24 26 W85 2 15
Rebroadcasts: Rebroadcasts WBST(FM) Muncie 100%
Ad 103, Muncie, IN 47306 US
(765) 285-5888, *Fax:* (765) 285-8937
www.bsu.edu/ipr
info@bsu.edu/ipr
License: Portland, Jay County, IN held by Ball State University.
Arbitron Metro Market: Muncie, IN *Format:* News *Hrs. of News Programming:* news progmg 33 hrs wkly *No. News Employees:* 1 *Target Audience:* General.
Marcus Jackman, General Manager
Pam Coletti, General Sales Mgr
Steven Turpin, Programming Director
Carol Trimmer, Promotions Manager
Dorothy Marvell, News Director
Robert Mittendorf, Chief Engineer
Brian Beaver, News Reporter

WPGW
01-14-1951; 1440 khz AM; 0.5 kw-D, DAD; 0.045 kw-N, DAD; N40 26 10 W85 0 56
P. O. Box 1440, Portland, IN 47371 US
(260) 726-8729, *Fax:* (260) 726-4311
wpgw@jayco.net
License: Portland, IN held by WPGW Inc.
Nat'l Reps: Rgnl Reps
Format: Adult Contemp *Target Audience:* General.
Robert Weaver, President

WPGW-FM
05-19-1975; 100.9 mhz FM; 4.6 kw; 180 ft.; N40 26 10 W85 0 54
P. O. Box 1440, Portland, IN 47371 US

(260) 726-8729, *Fax:* (260) 726-4311
wpgw@jayco.net
License: Portland, Jay County, IN held by WPGW Inc.
Format: Country *Target Audience:* General.
Jeff Overholser, Programming Director
Laurette Horn, News Director

Princeton

WRAY

12-16-1950; 1250 khz AM *Hrs Open:* 24; 1 kw-D, ND1; 0.059 kw-N, ND1; N38 21 25 W87 35 25
P. O. Box 8, Princeton, IN 47670 US
(812) 386-1250, *Fax:* (812) 386-6249
www.wrayradio.com
wray@wrayradio.com
License: Princeton, IN held by Princeton Broadcasting Co. Inc.
Format: News, Talk *No. News Employees:* 3 *Target Audience:* 25-54.
Richard Langford, President
Stephen Langford, General Manager
Lynn Roach, General Sales Mgr
Cliff Ingram, News Director
Floyd Turner, Chief Engineer
Dave Kunkel, Disc Jockey

WRAY-FM

05-15-1960; 98.1 mhz FM *Hrs Open:* 24; 50 kw; 436 ft.; N38 21 25 W87 35 25
P. O. Box 8, Princeton, IN 47670 US
(812) 386-1250, *Fax:* (812) 386-6249
www.wrayradio.com
License: Princeton, Gibson County, IN
Format: Country
Dave Kunkel, Programming Director
Charlene Garrison, News Director
Paul Viton, Disc Jockey

WSJD

10-01-1994; 100.5 mhz FM *Hrs Open:* 24; 6 kw; 328 ft.; N38 23 24 W87 34 23
4314 Cherry Court, Evansville, IN 47714 US
(618) 262-4102, *Fax:* (618) 262-4103
wsjd@midwest.net
License: Princeton, Gibson County, IN held by WSJD Inc.
Group Owner: Southern Wabash Communications Corp.; (acq 8-3-01).
Regional Network: Ill. Radio Net.; Network Indiana; RFD Illinois
Arbitron Metro Market: Evansville, IN *Format:* Oldies *Hrs. of News Programming:* news progmg 20 hrs wkly *No. News Employees:* 1 *Target Audience:* 25 plus. *Adv. Rates:* 15; 12; 15; 5
Randolph Bell, President
Sally Dorgan Potts, Executive Vice President

Rensselaer

WLQI

01-01-1973; 97.7 mhz FM *Hrs Open:* 24; 3.3 kw; 299 ft.; N40 58 14 W87 9 10
Mailing Address: P.O. Box D, Rensselaer, IN 47978 US
Second Address: 560 W. Amster Rd., Rensselaer, IN 47978
(219) 866-5105, *Fax:* (219) 866-4104
www.1560wrin.com
License: Rensselaer, Jasper County, IN
Nat'l Network: Jones Radio Networks *Regional Network:* Tribune Radio Networks
Format: Contemporary Hits/Top 40, Adult Contemp *Hrs. of News Programming:* ndws progmg 10 hrs wkly *No. News Employees:* 1 *Target Audience:* 25 plus. *Adv. Rates:* 18; 13; 13; 7
Serap Jackson, Operations Dir
Michael Meeks, General Manager

*WPUM

09-06-1977; 93.3 mhz FM *Hrs Open:* 24; 0.06 kw; 118 ft.; N40 55 12 W87 9 27
P.O. Box 651, U.S. Highway Route 231, Rensselaer, IN 47978 US
(219) 866-6000
wpum@saintjoe.edu
License: Rensselaer, Jasper County, IN held by St. Joseph's College.
Nat'l Network: Superadio
Special Programming: Country 3 hrs, classical 3 hrs, blues 3 hrs, talk *Hrs. of News Programming:* news progmg 10 hrs wkly *No. News Employees:* 1 *Target Audience:* 18-34; general *Adv. Rates:* 2; 2; 2; 2
Sally Nesselroad, Station Manager

WRIN

09-14-1963; 1560 khz AM; 0.5 kw-C, NDD; 1 kw-D, NDD; N40 57 41 W87 9 7
Mailing Address: P.O. Box D, Rensselaer, IN 47978 US
Second Address: 560 W. Amster Rd., Rensselaer, IN
(219) 866-5105, *Fax:* (219) 866-5106
www.1560wrin.com
License: Rensselaer, IN held by Brothers Broadcasting Corp.
Nat'l Reps: Rgnl Reps
Format: Adult Contemp *Special Programming:* Farm 12 hrs, gospel 2 hrs, relg 10 hrs wkly *Hrs. of News Programming:* news progmg 10 hrs wkly *No. News Employees:* 1 *Target Audience:* 30+.
John Balvich, President
Connie Graham Luthi, General Sales Mgr
Bob Burt, Programming Director
Bob Kurtz, News Director

Richmond

*WECI

09-01-1964; 91.5 mhz FM *Hrs Open:* 6 AM-3 AM; 0.4 kw; 125 ft.; N39 48 29 W84 54 47
Drawer 45, Richmond, IN 47374 US
(765) 983-1246, *Fax:* (765) 983-1641
www.weciradio.org/
Station.manager.weci@gmail.com
License: Richmond, Wayne County, IN held by Earlham College.
Arbitron Metro Market: Richmond, IN *Format:* Country, Variety/Diverse *Special Programming:* Bluegrass/folk 19 hrs, classic rock 16 hrs, progsv
Katie Laushman & Rosa ostrom, Station Manager
Kate Galligan, Programming Director
Krystnell Storr, News Director

WFMG

12-17-1960; 101.3 mhz FM *Hrs Open:* 24; 20.5 kw; 272 ft.; N39 49 41 W84 55 57
2301 West Main Street, Richmond, IN 47374 US
(765) 962-6533, *Fax:* (765) 966-1499
www.g1013.com
info@g1013.com
License: Richmond, Wayne County, IN held by Rodgers Broadcasting Corp.
Group Owner: Rodgers Broadcasting Corp.
Format: Adult Contemp *Special Programming:* Miami University Sports 8 hrs wkly *Hrs. of News Programming:* news progmg 2 hrs wkly *No. News Employees:* 2 *Target Audience:* 18-44. *Adv. Rates:* 22; 22; 22; 11
Rick Duncan, Operations Dir
Rick Duncan, Programming Director
Dave Snow, Promotions Manager
Bob Phillips, News Director
Steve Frey, Advertising
Jessica Leigh, Public Service Announcements
John Rose, Production

WKBV

09-27-1926; 1490 khz AM *Hrs Open:* 24; 1 kw-U; N39 49 30 W84 55 50
Box 1646, 2301 W. Main St., Richmond, IN 47374
(765) 962-6533, *Fax:* (765) 966-1499
License: Richmond, Wayne County, IN held by Rodgers Broadcasting Corp.
Group Owner: Rodgers Broadcasting Corp.; (acq 8-4-97; with co-located FM)
Nat'l Network: ABC; ESPN Radio *Regional Network:* Network Indiana
Population Served: 500,000*Special Programming:* Farm 4 hrs wkly *Hrs. of News Programming:* news progmg 10 hrs wkly *No. News Employees:* 2 *Target Audience:* 25-54. *Adv. Rates:* 16; 16; 16; 8
David Rodgers, President
Steve Frey, Station Manager
Rick Duncan, Programming Director
Bob Phillips, News Director

WQLK

10-15-1973; 96.1 mhz FM *Hrs Open:* 24; 50 kw; 492 ft.; N39 53 33 W84 56 9
PO Box 1647, Richmond, IN 47375 US
(765) 962-1595, *Fax:* (765) 966-4824
www.kicks96.com
License: Richmond, Wayne County, IN held by Brewer Broadcasting Corp.
Group Owner: Brewer Broadcasting Corp.
Arbitron Metro Market: Dayton, OH *Format:* Country *No. News Employees:* 1 *Target Audience:* 25-54.
Steve Baker, Programming Director

Roann

WARU-FM

01-01-2001; 101.9 mhz FM *Hrs Open:* 24; 3.6 kw; 423 ft.; N40 48 30 W85 56 7
P.O. Box 1970, Martinsville, IN 46151 US
(765) 473-4448, *Fax:* (765) 473-4449
www.mitunes1019.com
wade@mitunes1019.com
License: Roann, Wabash County, IN held by Mid-America Radio Group Inc.
Group Owner: Mid-America Radio Group Inc.
Arbitron Metro Market: Peru, IN *Format:* Adult Contemp *Hrs. of News Programming:* news progmg 4 hrs wkly *No. News Employees:* 1 *Adv. Rates:* 18; 18; 18; 18
Andy McCord, Operations Dir
Wade Weaver, General Manager
Scott Norton, General Sales Mgr
Dave Stewart, Programming Director
Jamie Muldrow, Promotions Manager
Brennan Ricks, Sales
Tammy Johnson, Office Manager
Krista Sodervick,Sales
Julie Deniston, Sales

Roanoke

*WBNI-FM

01-01-1991; 94.1 mhz FM *Hrs Open:* 24; 3.4 kw; 328 ft.; N40 58 51 W85 16 48 *Rebroadcasts:* Simulcast with WCKZ(FM) Orland 100%
650 Madison Ave, New York, NY 10022 US
(260) 452-1189, *Fax:* (260) 452-1188
www.nipr.fm
jbrown@nipr.fm
License: Roanoke, Huntington County, IN held by Northeast Indiana Public Radio Inc.
Nat'l Network: NPR
Arbitron Metro Market: Fort Wayne, IN *Format:* Classical
Bruce Haines, General Manager
Karen Fraser, General Sales Mgr
Colleen Condron, Programming Director
Jeanette Dillon, News Director

Rochester

WROI

08-29-1971; 92.1 mhz FM *Hrs Open:* 24; 4.2 kw; 207 ft.; N41 3 14 W86 16 12
110 East 8th Street, Rochester, IN 46975 US
(574) 223-6059, *Fax:* (574) 223-2238
www.wroifm.com
wroi@rtcol.com
License: Rochester, Fulton County, IN held by Bair Communications Inc.
Nat'l Network: ABC Information & Entertainment; Westwood One
Regional Network: Brownfield; Network Indiana *Nat'l Reps:* Rgnl Reps
Format: Oldies *Special Programming:* Farm 10 hrs, relg 6 hrs wkly *Hrs. of News Programming:* news progmg 20 hrs wkly *No. News Employees:* 1 *Target Audience:* General.
Tom Bair, President
Sue Bair, General Sales Mgr
Matt Bair, Programming Director
Baron Imhoof, News Director

*WQKV

01-01-2006; 88.7 mhz FM; 0.25 kw; 162 ft.; N41 3 14 W86 16 12
P O Drawer 240, Tupelo, MS 38801 US
(800) 525-5683, *Fax:* (916) 251-1650
www.klove.com
klove@klove.com
License: Rochester, Fulton County, IN held by Educational Media Foundation.
Group Owner: EMF Broadcasting; (acq 3-23-2007; grpsl)
Nat'l Network: K-Love
Arbitron Metro Market: Rochester, IN *Format:* Christian *No. News Employees:* 13
Darrell Chambliss, Chairman
Mike Novak, President and CEO
David Pierce, Programming Director
Ed Lenane, News Director
Sam Wallington, Engineering Dir
Dan Antonelli, Chief Business Development Officer
Eric Moser, Chief FinancialOfficer
Brian Burger, Vice President of Human Resources
D. Kevin Blair, Secretary and General Counsel
Tim Luttrell, News Reporter

Rockville

WAXI

08-01-1977; 104.9 mhz FM *Hrs Open:* 24; 1.7 kw; 440 ft.; N39 43 44 W87 17 56
1215 Wabash Avenue, Terre Haute, IN 47807 US
(800) 877-5600, *Fax:* (916) 251-1650
www.klove.com

License: Rockville, Parke County, IN held by Crossroads Investments LLC.
Group Owner: Crossroads Communications Inc.; (acq 4-20-98; $485,000).
Nat'l Network: ABC *Regional Network:* Network Indiana *Nat'l Reps:* Rgnl Reps
Arbitron Metro Market: Sulphur LA *Format:* Christian *Adv. Rates:* 13; 13; 13; 10
Darrell Chambliss, Chairman
Mike Novak, President
Chip Bailey, Operations Dir

Royal Center

WHZR
10-16-1989; 103.7 mhz FM *Hrs Open:* 24; 6 kw; 328 ft.; N40 48 43 W86 21 56
Logansport/Peru, Inc., 60 North Wayne Street, Martinsville, IN 46151 US
(574) 732-1037, *Fax:* (574) 739-1037
www.indianasbestradio.com
whzr@verizon.net
License: Royal Center, Cass County, IN held by Mid-America Radio Group of Logansport-Peru Inc.
Group Owner: Mid-America Radio Group Inc.; (acq 5-1-95; $450,000;
Format: Country *Hrs. of News Programming:* news progmg 6 hrs wkly *No. News Employees:* 1 *Target Audience:* 18-49; mass appeal *Adv. Rates:* 15; 15; 15; 15
David Keister, President
Dan Keister, General Manager
Milt Hess, Sports Director
Laurie Novotny, Account Executive
Dale Lowe, Disc Jockey

Rushville

WIFE-FM
08-05-1971; 94.3 mhz FM; 1.05 kw; 561 ft.; N39 42 22 W85 29 41
102 North Perkins Street, Rushville, IN 46173 US
(765) 932-3983, *Fax:* (765) 938-1916
License: Rushville, Rush County, IN held by Rodgers Broadcasting Corp.
Group Owner: Rodgers Broadcasting Corp.; (acq 7-5-2007; $1.5 million)
Nat'l Reps: Christal; Rgnl Reps
Format: Country *Special Programming:* Farm 18 hrs wkly *Target Audience:* 35 plus.
David Rodgers, President
Scott Huber, General Manager
Kevin Stone, General Sales Mgr
Doug Raab, Programming Director
Martha Swain, News Director

*WMUI(FM)
91.9 mhz FM; 225 w; Ant 263 ft; N39 37 10.8 W85 24 24
330 West 8th Street, Rushville, IN 45214
(765) 932-4186
www.wmub.org
License: Rushville, Rush County, IN held by Rush County Schools
Population Served: 6,303 *Arbitron Metro Market:* Rushville, IN
Richard Eiswerth, General Manager

Salem

WNRW(FM)
01-01-1962; 98.9 mhz FM *Hrs Open:* 24; 50 kw; 300 ft; N38 35 59 W86 05 17
4000 # 1 Radio Drive, Louisville, KY 40218-4568
(502) 479-2222, *Fax:* (502) 479-2308
www.kisslouisville.com
jonathanshuford@clearchannel.com
License: Salem, Washington County, IN held by CC Licenses LLC.
Group Owner: Clear Channel Communications Inc.; (acq 12-31-96)
Nat'l Reps: Clear Channel
Population Served: 942,300 *Arbitron Metro Market:* Louisville, KY *Format:* Contemporary Hits/Top 40 *Target Audience:* 18-54; country music listeners
Jonathan Shuford, Programming Director
Bill Gentry, Promotions Manager

WSLM
02-14-1953; 1220 khz AM *Hrs Open:* 18; 5 kw-D, DA2; 0.082 kw-N, DA2; N38 36 55 W86 5 10
Mailing Address: 1308 Hwy 56-E, PO Box 385, Salem, IN 47167 US
Second Address: 1308 Hwy 56 East, Salem, IN 47167
(812) 883-5750, *Fax:* (812) 883-2797
wslmradio.webs.com
wslm@blueriver.net
License: Salem, IN held by Don H. Martin.
Regional Network: Network Indiana; Tribune Radio Networks
Nat'l Reps: Rgnl Reps
Format: Religious *Hrs. of News Programming:* news progmg 12 hrs wkly *No. News Employees:* 5 *Target Audience:* 21-70.
Don Martin, President
J.R. Martin, Station Manager
Rebecca White, Programming Director
Becky White, Advertising Director

WSLM-FM
01-01-1992; 97.9 mhz FM *Hrs Open:* 18; 3 kw; 328 ft.; N38 38 7 W86 10 37
Mailing Address: P.O. Box 385, 1308 Hwy 56-E, Salem, IN 47167 US
Second Address: 1308 Hwy 56 East, Salem, IN 47167
(812) 883-5750, *Fax:* (812) 883-2797
wslmradio.webs.com
wslm@blueriver.net
License: Salem, Washington County, IN held by Rebecca L. White.
Format: Religious *Hrs. of News Programming:* 3 *No. News Employees:* 2 *Target Audience:* 18-65.
Rebecca White, Programming Director
Don Martin, Programming Director

Santa Claus

WAXL
07-30-1996; 103.3 mhz FM *Hrs Open:* 24; 3 kw; 463 ft.; N38 12 31 W86 54 0
Mailing Address: Box 123, Santa Claus, IN 47579 US
Second Address: 501 Old State Rd., Huntingburg, IN 47542
(703) 527-1434
www.whdzx.com
radiobuxton@yahoo.com
License: Santa Claus, Spencer County, IN held by Dubois County Broadcasting Inc.
Group Owner: DCBroadcasting Inc.; (acq 7-25-97)
Nat'l Network: ABC *Regional Network:* Network Indiana; Brownfield *Wire Services:* AP
Adv. Rates: 18; 15; 15; 13
David Wilson, General Manager

Scottsburg

WMPI
12-16-1966; 105.3 mhz FM *Hrs Open:* 24; 2.2 kw; 512 ft.; N38 42 44 W85 41 12
223 N. 820 West, Kokomo, IN 46901 US
(812) 752-5612, *Fax:* (812) 752-2345
www.i1053.com
rrice@i1053.com
License: Scottsburg, Scott County, IN held by D. R. Rice Broadcasting Inc.
Nat'l Reps: Rgnl Reps
Arbitron Metro Market: Louisville, KY *Format:* Country *Hrs. of News Programming:* news progmg 5 hrs wkly *No. News Employees:* 1 *Target Audience:* 25-54.
Donald Rice, President
Raymond Rice, General Manager
Tom Cull, Station Manager
John Ross, Programming Director
Steve Woodruff, Chief Engineer

Seelyville

WXXR(FM)
09-12-1996; 95.9 mhz FM; 4.1 kw; Ant 397 ft; N39 34 29 W87 24 06
824 S. 3rd St., Terre Haute, IN 47807
(812) 232-4161, *Fax:* (812) 234-9999
x959fm.com
License: Seelyville, Vigo County, IN held by Midwest Communications Inc.
Group Owner: Midwest Communications Inc.; (acq 6-13-2005; $3.39 million with
Nat'l Network: Jones Radio Networks *Nat'l Reps:* Christal
Population Served: 60,961 *Arbitron Metro Market:* Terre Haute, IN *Format:* Variety/Diverse, Rock/AOR *Target Audience:* 35-54.
Adv. Rates: 20; 20; 20; 15
Kathleen Walker, General Sales Mgr
Chad Edwards, Programming Director
Karl Wertzler, Promotions Manager
Jerry Arnold, Chief Engineer

Sellersville

WAYI(FM)
02-23-1961; 93.9 mhz FM *Hrs Open:* 24; 2.65 kw; Ant 499 ft; N38 15 21.7 W85 45 29.1
9900 Corporate Campus Way, Louisville, KY 40223
(502) 992-0939
www.classichits939.com
License: Sellersville, Clark County, IN held by S.C.I. Broadcasting Inc.
Group Owner: Cumulus Media Partners LLC; (acq 5-25-2001; grpsl)
Population Served: 500,000 *Arbitron Metro Market:* Louisville, KY *Format:* Contemporary Hits/Top 40, Adult Contemp *Target Audience:* General.
Dugan Ryan, General Manager

Seymour

*WJLR
08-01-1995; 91.5 mhz FM *Hrs Open:* 24; 30 kw; 381 ft.; N38 49 20 W85 47 38
1680 Highway 62 Ne, Corydon, IN 47112 US
(916) 251-1600, *Fax:* (916) 251-1650
www.klove.com
License: Seymour, Jackson County, IN held by Educational Media Foundation.
Group Owner: EMF Broadcasting; (acq 11-9-2004; $150,000).
Nat'l Network: K-Love
Format: Christian *Target Audience:* 30-80; family oriented
Mike Novak, President
Eric Allen, General Sales Mgr
David Pierce, Programming Director
Ed Lenane, News Director
Sam Wallington, Engineering Dir
Marya Morgan, News Reporter
Richard Hunt, News Reporter
Chip Bailey, RegionalManager

WZZB
11-04-1949; 1390 khz AM *Hrs Open:* 24; 1 kw-D, ND1; 0.074 kw-N, ND1; N38 58 33 W85 53 21
Mailing Address: P.O Box 726, Jeffersonville, IN 47131 US
Second Address: 1534 Ewing St., Seymour, IN 47274
(812) 522-1390, *Fax:* (812) 522-9541
www.wzzb1390.com
info@wklo969.com
License: Seymour, IN held by Midnight Hour Broadcasting LLC.
Nat'l Network: USA; Jones Radio Networks *Regional Network:* Network Indiana *Regional Reps:* Rgnl Reps.
Arbitron Metro Market: Seymour, IN *Format:* News, Sports
Special Programming: Farm 2 hrs, relg 6 hrs wkly *Hrs. of News Programming:* news progmg 17 hrs wkly *No. News Employees:* 2 *Target Audience:* 25plus; community oriented
Blair Trask, President
Bud Shippee, Operations Dir
Bob Hawkins, Chief Engineer

Shelbyville

WLHK
11-06-1964; 97.1 mhz FM *Hrs Open:* 24; 23 kw; 732 ft.; N39 40 6 W86 1 44
3500 West Olive Avenue, Suite 300, Burbank, CA 91505 US
(317) 266-9700, *Fax:* (317) 684-2021
www.hankfm.com/
brichards@indy.emmis.com
License: Shelbyville, Shelby County, IN held by Emmis Radio License LLC.
Group Owner: Emmis Communications Corp.; (acq 6-81).
Nat'l Reps: D & R Radio
Arbitron Metro Market: Shelbyville, IN *Format:* Country *No. News Employees:* 1 *Target Audience:* 25-54; female
David Edgar, Operations Dir
Tom Severino, General Manager
Patty England, General Sales Mgr
Bob Richards, Programming Director
Lisa Wall, Promotions Manager
Shelly Grimes, News Director
Dave Hood, Chief Engineer
Kathy Kneer,Local Sales Manager

WSVX
01-14-1961; 1520 khz AM
P. O. Box 15435, Cincinnati, OH 45215 US
(317) 398-2200, *Fax:* (317) 392-3292
www.wsvx.com
info@wsvx.com
License: Shelbyville, IN held by RSE Broadcasting LLC.
Regional Network: Brownfield

Arbitron Metro Market: Indianapolis, I *TV Affiliate:* adult contemp *Special Programming:* news progmg 3 hrs wkly *Hrs. of News Programming:* 1 *No. News Employees:* Shelby County.
Advertising Manager

South Bend

***WETL**
11-17-1958; 91.7 mhz FM; 3 kw; 299 ft.; N41 37 24 W86 14 15
635 South Main Street, South Bend, IN 46623 US
(574) 283-8432, *Fax:* (574) 283-8405
jovermyer@sbcsc.k12.in.us
License: South Bend, St. Joseph County, IN held by South Bend Community School Corp.
Arbitron Metro Market: South Bend, IN *Format:* Talk *Target Audience:* General; student in the South Bend community school and community
Anita Brown, General Manager
John Overmyer, Programming Director
Allen Wujcik, Chief Engineer

WHME
01-01-1968; 103.1 mhz FM *Hrs Open:* 24; 3 kw; 299 ft.; N41 36 11 W86 12 51
61300 South Ironwood Rd, South Bend, IN 46614 US
(574) 291-8200, *Fax:* (574) 291-9043
www.whmefm.com
info@whme.com
License: South Bend, St. Joseph County, IN held by Le Sea Broadcasting Corp.
Group Owner: Le Sea Broadcasting
Arbitron Metro Market: South Bend, IN *TV Affiliate:* WHME-TV affil. *Format:* Adult Contemp, Christian *Hrs. of News Programming:* News progmg 3 hrs wkly *Target Audience:* 24-36; general
Tony Hale, CFO
Anna Riblet, Station Manager
Wes Hylton, Chief Engineer

WHLY
12-22-1947; 1580 khz AM *Hrs Open:* 24; 1 kw-D, DAN; 0.5 kw-N, DAN; N41 41 9 W86 9 53
2010 S. Michigan, South Bend, IN 46613 US
(574) 361-4618
www.holyradio.org
info@holyradio.org
License: South Bend, IN held by Times Communications Inc.
Nat'l Network: EWTN Radio
Arbitron Metro Market: South Bend, IN *Format:* Christian
Robert Liggett, Chairman
James Jenson, President
Lawrence Smith, Operations Dir

WDND
01-01-1944; 1620 khz AM *Hrs Open:* 24
2010 S. Michigan Street, South Bend, IN 46613 US
(574) 273-9300, *Fax:* (574) 273-9090
www.u93.com
License: South Bend, IN held by Artistic Media Partners Inc.
Group Owner: Artistic Media Partners Inc.; (acq 10-22-98; $6,123,180 with co-l
Nat'l Network: ESPN Radio *Nat'l Reps:* McGavren Guild
Arbitron Metro Market: South Bend, IN *Format:* Contemporary Hits/Top 40 *Target Audience:* 25-54.
Arthur Angotti, President
Karen Right, Operations Dir
Jack Swart, General Manager
Mike Sullivan, Station Manager
Pam Homan, General Sales Mgr
Sean Stires, Programming Director

WNDV-FM
01-01-1962; 92.9 mhz FM *Hrs Open:* 24; 12 kw; 879 ft.; N41 36 20 W86 12 46
5520 East 75th Street, Indianapolis, IN 46250 US
(574) 273-9300, *Fax:* (574) 273-9090
www.u93.com
License: South Bend, St. Joseph County, IN
Group Owner: Artistic Media Partners Inc.
Arbitron Metro Market: South Bend, IN *Format:* Contemporary Hits/Top 40 *Target Audience:* 25-44; women
Karen Right, Operations Dir
Pam Homan, General Sales Mgr
Karen Rite, Programming Director

WNSN
08-01-1962; 101.5 mhz FM; 13 kw; 971 ft.; N41 37 0 W86 13 1
300 West Jefferson Blvd., South Bend, IN 46601 US
(574) 233-3241, *Fax:* (574) 289-7382
www.radiomichiana.com
roberts@wsbt.com
License: South Bend, St. Joseph County, IN
Group Owner: Schurz Communications Inc.
Arbitron Metro Market: South Bend, IN *TV Affiliate:* WSBT-TV affil *Format:* Adult Contemp *Hrs. of News Programming:* news progmg 2 hrs wkly *No. News Employees:* 1 *Target Audience:* 25-54; adults
Bill Gamble, Operations Dir
Jim Roberts, Station Manager
Tony Gazzana, General Sales Mgr
Brad King, Promotions Manager

WRBR-FM
01-01-1965; 103.9 mhz FM; 3 kw; 328 ft.; N41 41 53 W86 9 25
237 Edison Road, Suite 200, Mishawaka, IN 46545 US
(574) 258-5483, *Fax:* (574) 258-0930
www.wrbr.com
License: South Bend, St. Joseph County, IN held by Talking Stick Communications L.L.C
Group Owner: Talking Stick Communications LLC; (acq 6-26-2002; $840,879)
Nat'l Reps: Christal
Arbitron Metro Market: South Bend, IN *Format:* Rock/AOR *Target Audience:* 25-54; affluent, older people
Kathy Uebler, General Manager
Tommy Carroll, Programming Director
Greg Trobridge, Chief Engineer

WSBT
04-01-1922; 960 khz AM *Hrs Open:* 24; 5 kw-D, DA2; 5 kw-N, DA2; N41 37 0 W86 13 1
300 West Jefferson Blvd, South Bend, IN 46601 US
(574) 233-3141, *Fax:* (574) 239-4231
www.radiomichiana.com
License: South Bend, IN held by WSBT Inc.
Group Owner: Schurz Communications Inc.
Nat'l Network: Fox News Radio *Nat'l Reps:* Katz Radio
Arbitron Metro Market: South Bend, IN *TV Affiliate:* WSBT-TV affil *Format:* News, News/Talk, 84, Talk *Special Programming:* Relg 2 hrs wkly *Hrs. of News Programming:* news progmg 10 hrs wkly *No. News Employees:* 3 *Target Audience:* 25-54.
Bill Gamble, Operations Dir
Bob Montgomery, Programming Director
Kimberly Crim, Promotions Manager
Jim Roberts, Operations Manager

***WUBS**
01-01-1993; 89.7 mhz FM; 1.5 kw; 79 ft.; N41 40 51 W86 15 34
P.O. Box 3931, South Bend, IN 46619 US
(574) 287-4700, *Fax:* (574) 287-2478
www.wubs.org
broshane@wubs.org
License: South Bend, St. Joseph County, IN held by Interfaith Christian Union Inc.
Arbitron Metro Market: South Bend, IN *TV Affiliate:* UBS-TV *Format:* Religious
Rev. Sylvester Williams Jr., General Manager
Shane Williams, Programming Director
Brian Hoover, Chief Engineer

WUBU
10-01-1992; 106.3 mhz FM *Hrs Open:* 24; 3 kw; 302 ft.; N41 40 35 W86 15 8
515 N. Ridgeland, Oak Park, IL 60302 US
(574) 233-3505, *Fax:* (574) 233-0580
www.wubufm.com
ghegland@wubufm.com
License: South Bend, St. Joseph County, IN held by Partnership Radio LLC
Nat'l Network: Jones Radio Networks *Nat'l Reps:* Interep; McGavren Guild
Arbitron Metro Market: South Bend, IN *Format:* Adult Contemp *Target Audience:* 35-64; adults
Gene Walker, General Manager
Tonya Reed, General Sales Mgr
Greg Trobridge, Chief Engineer
Gary Hegland, Production Manger
Amy Mejer, Business Manager
April Miller, Production Assistant
Ron Moore, Sales Representative

South Whitley

WMYQ
12-02-1992; 101.1 mhz FM *Hrs Open:* 24; 6 kw; 328 ft.; N41 5 58 W85 43 29
P.O.Box 5570, Ft. Wayne, IN 46895 US
(260) 213-4370, *Fax:* (260) 471-4447
www.hotq101.com
info@hotq101.com
License: South Whitley, Whitley County, IN held by Larko Communications Inc.
Nat'l Network: ABC
Arbitron Metro Market: Fort Wayne, IN *Format:* Adult Contemp *Target Audience:* 25-44.
Chris Larko, CEO
Dean Jackson, News Director

Speedway

WNOU
05-28-1967; 100.9 mhz FM *Hrs Open:* 24; 6 kw; 328 ft.; N39 48 1 W86 4 39
6264 La Pas Trail, Indianapolis, IN 46268 US
(317) 266-9600, *Fax:* (317) 328-3870
www.radionowindy.com
License: Speedway, Marion County, IN held by Radio One of Indiana LLC.
Group Owner: Radio One Inc.; (acq 11-8-2001; grpsl)
Nat'l Network: ABC *Nat'l Reps:* Katz Radio
Arbitron Metro Market: Speedway, IN *Format:* Contemporary Hits/Top 40 *Hrs. of News Programming:* news progmg 12 hrs wkly *No. News Employees:* 2 *Target Audience:* 25-54.
Alfred Liggins, President
Charles Williams, Operations Dir
Brian Harrington, General Sales Mgr
Carl Frye, Programming Director

Spencer

WCLS
09-15-1983; 97.7 mhz FM; 6 kw; 328 ft.; N39 13 22 W86 38 40
PO Box 388, Spencer, IN 47460 US
(812) 935-7400, *Fax:* (812) 935-7404
www.wclsfm.com
wclsfm@smithville.net
License: Spencer, Owen County, IN held by Mid-America Radio of Indiana Inc.
Group Owner: Mid-America Radio Group Inc.; (acq 11-13-2002; $321,100).
Nat'l Network: Westwood One
Format: Contemporary Hits/Top 40, Adult Contemp *Special Programming:* Relg 6 hrs wkly
David Bruce, General Manager
David Bruce, General Sales Mgr

Sullivan

WNDI
10-07-1963; 1550 khz AM; 0.25 kw-D, NDD; N39 4 32 W87 23 57
556 East State Road 94, Sullivan, IN 47882 US
(812) 268-6322, *Fax:* (812) 268-6652
License: Sullivan, IN held by JTM Broadcasting Corp.
Arbitron Metro Market: Terre Haute, IN *Format:* Country *Special Programming:* Farm 6 hrs wkly *Target Audience:* 24-54.
John Montgomery, General Manager

WNDI-FM
08-10-1982; 95.3 mhz FM; 6 kw; 328 ft.; N39 9 36 W87 32 32
556 East State Road 54, Sullivan, IN 47882 US
(812) 268-6322, *Fax:* (812) 268-6652
License: Sullivan, Sullivan County, IN held by JTM Broadcasting Corp.
Arbitron Metro Market: Terre Haute, IN
Robert McLimans, Operations Dir
John Schuette, General Sales Mgr
Rick Small, Operations Director

Syracuse

WAWC
05-31-1991; 103.5 mhz FM *Hrs Open:* 24; 3 kw; 328 ft.; N41 22 57 W85 41 35
10129 North 800 East, Syracuse, IN 46567 US
(307) 232-2155
www.kted1005.com
License: Syracuse, Kosciusko County, IN held by Talking Stick Communications LLC.
Group Owner: Talking Stick Communications LLC; (acq 11-1-2006; $600,000)
Nat'l Network: CBS *Regional Network:* Network Indiana
Arbitron Metro Market: Evansville, WY *Adv. Rates:* 15; 15; 15; 5.30
Steven Silberberg, President
Rood Dogg, Programming Director
Courtney Williams, Sales Representative

Tell City

WTCJ
02-01-1948; 1230 khz AM *Hrs Open:* 24
409 Chestnut Street, A-154, Chattanooga, TN 18277 US

(270) 683-5200, *Fax:* (270) 688-0108
www.tellcityradio.com
jcatinna@cromwellradio.com
License: Tell City, IN held by Hancock Communications Inc.
Group Owner: The Cromwell Group Inc.; (acq 12-20-99; $25,000)
Nat'l Network: ABC *Nat'l Reps:* Rgnl Reps
Arbitron Metro Market: Owensboro, KY *Format:* Classic Rock
Special Programming: Gospel 6 hrs wkly *No. News Employees:* 1 *Target Audience:* 25-54; community-oriented listeners *Adv. Rates:* 7.50; 7.50; 7.50;7.50
Bayard Walters, President
Jan Catinna, General Manager
Jeff Morgan, Programming Director
Mike Chaney, News Director

Terre Haute

*WHOJ
01-01-1997; 91.9 mhz FM; 1.5 kw; 46 ft.; N39 28 5 W87 23 59
P.O. Drawer 2440, Tupelo, MS 38803 US
(314) 752-7000
www.covenantnet.net
webmaster@covenantnet.net
License: Terre Haute, Vigo County, IN held by Covenant Network.
Group Owner: Covenant Network; (acq 3-30-2004; $112,500 with KBKC(FM) Moberly, MO)
Arbitron Metro Market: Terre Haute, IN *Format:* Christian, Talk, 74
Tony Holman, General Manager

*WCRT-FM
01-01-1992; 88.5 mhz FM; 550 w; 308 ft; N39 30 14 W87 26 37
2108 W. Springfield, Champaign, IL 62626
(217) 359-8232, *Fax:* (217) 359-7374
www.wbgl.org
wbgl@wbgl.org
License: Terre Haute, Vigo County, IN held by Illinois Bible Institute.
Group Owner: Illinois Bible Institute Inc.
Nat'l Reps: 4101 Fieldstone
Arbitron Metro Market: Terre Haute, IN
Jeff Scott, Station Manager
Ryan Springer, Programming Director
Jennifer Briski, Promotions Manager
Joe Buchanan, Music Director
Zoe Fuller, Underwriting Director

*WISU
09-13-1964; 89.7 mhz FM *Hrs Open:* 11 AM-2 AM; 13.5 kw; 512 ft.; N39 30 26 W87 31 50
217 Dreiser Hall- Isu, Terre Haute, IN 47809 US
(812) 237-3248, *Fax:* (812) 237-8970
wisu.indstate.edu
cmwisufm@ruby.indstate.edu
License: Terre Haute, Vigo County, IN held by Indiana State University Board of Trustees.
Arbitron Metro Market: Terre Haute, IN *Format:* Rock/AOR *Hrs. of News Programming:* News progmg 4 hrs wkly *Target Audience:* 18-25; young professionals, students
Joe Tenerelli, General Manager
David Sabaini, Programming Director
Dan Watson, Chief Engineer

WBOW
05-23-1958; 1300 khz AM *Hrs Open:* 24; 0.5 kw-D, ND1; 0.075 kw-N, ND1; N39 28 1 W87 25 34 *Rebroadcasts:* Rebroadcasts WSDX(AM) Brazil
1215 Wabash Ave., Terre Haute, IN 47807 US
(812) 234-9770, *Fax:* (812) 238-1576
www.espnsportsradio.com
mike@radioworksforme.com
License: Terre Haute, IN held by Crossroads Investments LLC.
Group Owner: Crossroads Communications Inc.; (acq 9-10-97; $57,500 assumption of
Nat'l Network: ESPN Radio *Nat'l Reps:* Roslin *Regional Reps:* Rgnl Reps.
Arbitron Metro Market: Terre Haute, IN *Format:* Sports *Hrs. of News Programming:* News progmg 5 hrs wkly *Target Audience:* 25-64; Sports Fans *Adv. Rates:* 8; 8; 8; 4
Mike Petersen, General Manager
Bill Cook, Programming Director
Kevin Berlen, Chief Engineer

WMGI
06-13-1960; 100.7 mhz FM; 50 kw; 499 ft.; N39 27 22 W87 28 50
824 S. 3rd Street, Terre Haute, IN 47803 US
(812) 232-4161, *Fax:* (812) 234-9999
www.mymixfm.com
chad@1007mixfm.com
License: Terre Haute, Vigo County, IN held by Midwest Communications Inc.
Group Owner: Midwest Communications Inc.; (acq 6-13-2005; $3.39 million with
Nat'l Network: Westwood One *Nat'l Reps:* Christal
Arbitron Metro Market: Terre Haute, IN *Format:* Contemporary Hits/Top 40, Christian *Target Audience:* 18-34. *Adv. Rates:* 43; 43; 43; 28
Kathleen Walker, General Sales Mgr
Chad Edwards, Programming Director
Karl Wertzler, Promotions Manager
Jerry Arnold, Chief Engineer

*WMHD-FM
01-01-1981; 90.7 mhz FM *Hrs Open:* 8 AM-2 AM; 1.4 kw; 230 ft.; N39 30 14 W87 26 37
5500 Wabash Avenue, Terre Haute, IN 47803 US
(812) 872-6923, *Fax:* (812) 872-6926
wmhd@wmhd.rose-hulman.edu
License: Terre Haute, Vigo County, IN held by Rose Hulman Institute of Technology.
Arbitron Metro Market: Terre Haute, IN *Format:* Variety/Diverse
Special Programming: Classical 4 hrs, bluegrass one hr, Jazz 2 hrs, con *Hrs. of News Programming:* News progmg 2 hrs wkly
Target Audience: Loc &college audience
Brooks Borchers, Operations Dir
Brandon Inzego, General Manager
Ben Braun, Programming Director

WPFR
01-06-1948; 1480 khz AM *Hrs Open:* 24; 5 kw-D, 1 kw-N, DA-2; N39 30 02 W87 23 10
18889 N. 23 50th St., Dennison, IL 91505
(217) 826-9673
wpfr@joink.com
License: Terre Haute, Vigo County, IN held by Word Power Inc.
Nat'l Network: Moody
Population Served: 70,286 *Arbitron Metro Market:* Terre Haute, IN *Target Audience:* 12 plus. *Adv. Rates:* 30; 30; 30; 30
Paul Ford, President
Eleanor Ford, Operations Dir
Paul Ford, General Manager
Dan Watson, Chief of Operations

WTHI-FM
10-01-1948; 99.9 mhz FM *Hrs Open:* 24; 50 kw; 489 ft.; N39 27 57 W87 24 12
Mailing Address: 3500 West Olive Avenue, Suite 300, Burbank, CA 91505 US
Second Address: 918 Ohio St., Terre Haute, IN 47808
(812) 917-3901, *Fax:* (812) 234-0089
www.hi99.com
jconner@wthi.emmis.com
License: Terre Haute, Vigo County, IN held by Emmis Radio License LLC.
Group Owner: Emmis Communications Corp.; (acq 1998 grpsl).
Nat'l Network: ABC *Nat'l Reps:* Interep; D & R Radio
Arbitron Metro Market: Terre Haute, IN *Format:* Country *Adv. Rates:* 52; 49; 50; 25
Barry Kent, Operations Dir
James Conner, VP & General Manager
Robert Rhodes, General Sales Mgr
Eric Michaels, Programming Director & Music Director
Holly Burk, Programming Director & Music Director
Chris Perrott, InteractiveAccount Manager
Fred Strohm, Webmaster

Union City

*WJYW
06-01-1999; 88.9 mhz FM *Hrs Open:* 24; 4.1 kw; 285 ft.; N40 11 32 W84 47 58 *Rebroadcasts:* 94.5-Richmond, IN, 97.7-News Paris
Mailing Address: P.O. Box 889, Blacksburg, VA 24063 US
Second Address: 505 S. Division St., Union City, OH 45390
(937) 968-5633, *Fax:* (937) 968-3320
www.889joyfm.com
office@899joyfm.com
License: Union City, Randolph County, IN held by Positive Alternative Radio Inc.
Nat'l Network: Salem Radio Network
Format: Christian *Target Audience:* 25-54; Women
Vernon Baker, CEO
Dan Franks, General Manager

Upland

*WTUR
09-04-1995; 89.7 mhz FM; 0.15 kw; 112 ft.; N40 25 2 W85 29 31
500 West Reade Avenue, Upland, IN 46989 US
(800) 882-3456, *Fax:* (765) 998-4810
www.tayloru.edu/wtur
info@tayloru.edu
License: Upland, Grant County, IN held by Taylor University.
Arbitron Metro Market: Upland, IN *Format:* Christian *Target Audience:* College age.
Dr. Gene B. Habecker, Ph.D., J.D., President
Eric Skala, Operations Dir
Kevin Gehrett, Station Manager
Lauren Matters, Programming Director
Meagan Sather, Promotions Manager
Nick Rodemann, Assistant Station Manager
Doug Walker,Campus Relations
Kathy Bruner, Faculty Advisor
Josh Johnson, Sports Director

Valparaiso

WAKE
11-04-1964; 1500 khz AM *Hrs Open:* 24
2755 Sager Road, Valparaiso, IN 46383 US
(219) 462-6111, *Fax:* (219) 462-4880
www.wakeradio.com
donclark@radiooneindiana.com
License: Valparaiso, IN held by Porter County Broadcasting Holding Corp. LLC.
Group Owner: Porter County Broadcasting Corp.
Nat'l Network: CNN Radio
Arbitron Metro Market: Northwest Indiana *Format:* News *Target Audience:* 30 plus; community oriented, middle to middle-upper class
Leigh Ellis, Chairman
O.J. Jackson, General Sales Mgr
Don Clark, Programming Director
Laura Waluszko, News Director
Carl Fletcher, Chief Engineer
Jennifer Malmquist, Traffic Manager

WLJE
10-06-1967; 105.5 mhz FM; 1.25 kw; 512 ft.; N41 31 28 W87 1 8
2755 Sager Road, Valparaiso, IN 46383 US
(219) 462-8125, *Fax:* (219) 462-4880
www.indiana105.com
donclark@radiooneindiana.com
License: Valparaiso, Porter County, IN
Group Owner: Porter County Broadcasting Corp.
Arbitron Metro Market: Chicago, IL *Format:* Country *Target Audience:* 25-55; family, middle income
Margaret Drake, President
Jonathan Drake, General Manager
Kim Mitchell, General Sales Mgr
Alan Mulford, Chief Engineer

*WVUR-FM
09-25-1966; 95.1 mhz FM *Hrs Open:* 24; 0.036 kw horiz; 125 ft.; N41 27 57 W87 2 29
Office of the Provost, Kretzmann Hall, Valparaiso, IN 46383 US
(219) 464-5383, *Fax:* (219) 464-6742
www.valpo.edu/wvur
wvur@valpo.edu
License: Valparaiso, Porter County, IN held by The Lutheran University Association Inc.
Arbitron Metro Market: Valparaiso, IN *Format:* Variety/Diverse
Special Programming: Class 3 hrs, jazz 3 hrs, urban contemp 3 hrs, meta *Hrs. of News Programming:* news progmg 8 hrs wkly
No. News Employees: 2*Target Audience:* 18-34.
Sam Cain, General Manager
Lauren LaVicka, General Sales Mgr
Raymond Finzel, Programming Director
Kayla Belec, Promotions Manager
Michael Gallenberger, News Director
Nick Schroeder, Chief Engineer
Mary Steele, Traffic Director
Alyssa Mallerdino, Production Director
Joseph Basil, Sports Director
Stephanie O'Sullvan, Assistant Music Director

Van Buren

WCJC
08-28-1989; 99.3 mhz FM *Hrs Open:* 24; 3 kw; 328 ft.; N40 40 1 W85 37 49
60 North Wayne Street, Martinsville, IN 46151 US
(765) 664-6239, *Fax:* (765) 662-0730
www.wcjc.com
bigjohn@wcjc.com
License: Van Buren, Grant County, IN held by Mid-America Radio Group Inc.
Group Owner: Mid-America Radio Group Inc.; acq 12-19-88; grpsl;
Nat'l Network: ABC *Regional Reps:* Regional Reps

RADIO - U.S.

Arbitron Metro Market: Muncie, IN *Format:* Country *Special Programming:* Relg 3 hrs wkly *Hrs. of News Programming:* news progmg 25 hrs wkly *No. News Employees:* 2 *Target Audience:* 25-54; consumer-orientedmodern country fans *Adv. Rates:* 28; 28; 28; 25
David Keister, President
David Poehler, Operations Dir
Race Ashlyn, General Manager
John Clark, Sales Manager
John Morgan, Programming Director
Warren Arnett, Chief Engineer
Tim George, Operations Manager

Veedersburg

WSKL
07-15-1999; 92.9 mhz FM *Hrs Open:* 24; 4.5 kw; 269 ft.; N40 8 46 W87 27 15
1680 Hwy 62 Ne, Corydon, IN 47112 US
(217) 443-4004, *Fax:* (765) 793-4644
www.koololdies.net
fmkool929@aol.com
License: Veedersburg, Fountain County, IN held by Zona Communications Inc.
Nat'l Network: AP Radio; Jones Radio Networks *Wire Services:* AP
Format: Oldies *Hrs. of News Programming:* news progmg 5 hrs wkly *No. News Employees:* 1 *Target Audience:* 35-65.
Rhea Benton-Weatherford, General Manager
Greg Green, Station Manager
J.J. McKay, Programming Director
Tara Duncan, News Director

Versailles

*WKRY
04-11-2003; 88.1 mhz FM *Hrs Open:* 24; 0.5 kw vert; 302 ft.; N39 4 6 W85 15 58
1680 Hwy 62 Ne, Corydon, IN 47112 US
(812) 375-9947, *Fax:* (812) 375-2562
www.wygs.org
jhutson@wygs.org
License: Versailles, Ripley County, IN held by Good Shepherd Radio Inc.
Arbitron Metro Market: Columbus, IN *Format:* Religious
Keith Reising, Jr., Chairman
Keith Reising, CEO
Matt Bond, Operations Dir
Mellissa Burton, Office Manager

Vevay

WKID
09-06-1974; 95.9 mhz FM *Hrs Open:* 24; 2.8 kw; 308 ft.; N38 50 12 W85 1 48
118 West Main Street, Vevay, IN 47043 US
(812) 427-9590, *Fax:* (812) 427-2492
www.k959froggy.com
info@k959froggy.com
License: Vevay, Switzerland County, IN held by Dial Broadcasting Inc.
Nat'l Network: Jones Radio Networks *Regional Network:* Network Indiana *Regional Reps:* Regl Reps *Wire Services:* AP
Format: Country *Hrs. of News Programming:* News progmg 7 hrs wkly *Target Audience:* 25-49; middle-income families *Adv. Rates:* 18; 10; 16; 10
Mike Wigren, Operations Dir
Adam Griffin, General Manager
Helen Peelman, Sales
Susan Benning, Sales
Angie Fay Satterfield, Sales

Vincennes

WAOV
10-22-1940; 1450 khz AM *Hrs Open:* 24; 1 kw-D, ND1; 1 kw-N, ND1; N38 42 26 W87 29 42
1309 Old Orchard Road, Vincennes, IN 47591 US
(812) 882-6060, *Fax:* (812) 885-2604
www.originalcompany.com/pages/7816386.php
waov@originalcompany.com
License: Vincennes, IN held by Old Northwest Broadcasting Inc.
Group Owner: The Original Company Inc.; (acq 9-28-93; $250,000 with WWBL(FM
Nat'l Reps: Rgnl Reps
Arbitron Metro Market: Vincennes, IN *Format:* News, News/Talk, 84, Talk *Hrs. of News Programming:* news progmg 56 hrs wkly *No. News Employees:* 2 *Target Audience:* 25 plus.
Mark Lange, President
Michelle York, General Sales Mgr
Jim Evans, Chief Engineer
Owner, Duncan Myers
Marketing Manager

*WATI
01-01-2002; 89.9 mhz FM; 0.5 kw; 157 ft.; N38 41 47 W87 26 27
P O Drawer 2440, Tupelo, MS 38803 US
(662) 844-8888, *Fax:* (662) 842-6791
www.afr.net
faq@afr.net
License: Vincennes, Knox County, IN held by American Family Association.
Group Owner: American Family Radio
Arbitron Metro Market: Vincennes, IN *Format:* Christian, Religious
Marvin Sanders, General Manager

WFML
05-16-1965; 96.7 mhz FM *Hrs Open:* 24; 2.15 kw; 386 ft.; N38 39 6 W87 28 37
Box 2213, Vincennes, IN 47591 US
(812) 254-6761, *Fax:* (812) 882-2237
www.wfml.net
info@wfml.net
License: Vincennes, Knox County, IN held by The Vincennes University Foundation
Nat'l Network: Fox News Radio *Regional Network:* Network Indiana *Regional Reps:* Rgnl Reps *Wire Services:* AP
Format: Country *Hrs. of News Programming:* news progmg 2 hrs wkly *No. News Employees:* 2 *Target Audience:* 18-54. *Adv. Rates:* 25; 25; 25; 25
Brad Deetz, General Manager
Phil Smith, Station Manager
Beth Davis, General Sales Mgr
Kevin Watson, Programming Director
Dave Folly, Promotions Manager
Dave Foster, News Director
Steve McClure, Chief Engineer
Bob Tester, DiscJockey
Lisa Jackman, Traffic Director
Andy Morrison, Operations Manager
DeWayne Shake, Marketing Executive
Pam Harrawood, Marketing Executive
Amy Schnelle, Marketing Executive

*WVUB
12-07-1970; 91.1 mhz FM; 50 kw; 499 ft.; N38 39 6 W87 28 37
1002 North First Street, Vincennes, IN 47591 US
(812) 888-4357, *Fax:* (812) 882-2237
www.blazer911wvub.com
blazerwvub@hotmail.com
License: Vincennes, Knox County, IN held by Board of Trustees for Vincennes University.
Nat'l Network: PRI
Arbitron Metro Market: Vincennes, IN *TV Affiliate:* WVUT(TV) affil
Format: Adult Contemp *Special Programming:* Class 6 hrs wkly
Phil Smith, Station Manager
Michael Woods, Programming Director
John Szink, News Director
Michael Murphy, Chief Engineer

WZDM
09-01-1988; 92.1 mhz FM *Hrs Open:* 24; 4.1 kw; 400 ft.; N38 41 2 W87 26 8
1309 Old Orchard Road, Vincennes, IN 47591 US
(812) 882-6060, *Fax:* (812) 885-2604
www.wzdm.com
wzdm@originalcompany.com
License: Vincennes, Knox County, IN held by The Original Co. Inc.
Group Owner: The Original Company Inc.
Arbitron Metro Market: Vincennes, IN *Format:* Adult Contemp
Hrs. of News Programming: news progmg 10 hrs wkly *No. News Employees:* 2 *Target Audience:* 25-54; upscale
Mark Lange, President
Michelle York, General Sales Mgr
Dave Young, Programming Director

Wabash

WJOT
11-01-1971; 1510 khz AM; 0.25 kw-D, NDD; N40 47 11 W85 49 19
1360 S. Wabash, Wabash, IN 46992 US
(260) 563-1161, *Fax:* (260) 563-0883
wjot@comtek.com
License: Wabash, IN held by Mid-America Radio of Wabash Inc.
Group Owner: Mid-America Radio Group Inc.
Nat'l Network: Westwood One
Wade Weaver, Promotions Manager

WJOT-FM
07-01-1993; 105.9 mhz FM; 6 kw; 318 ft.; N40 49 54 W85 48 36
1360 S. Wabash, Wabash, IN 46922 US
(260) 563-1161, *Fax:* (260) 563-0883
wjot@comtek.com
License: Wabash, Wabash County, IN held by Mid-America Radio of Wabash Inc.
Group Owner: Mid-America Radio Group Inc.; (acq 7-1-98; $190,000 with co-locat
Nat'l Network: Westwood One *Regional Reps:* Rgnl Reps.
Format: Oldies *Target Audience:* 25-64.
Bill Barrows, Operations Dir
Wade Weaver, General Manager
Jack Elmore, Chief Engineer
Deb Dale, Traffic Manager

WKUZ
04-01-1965; 95.9 mhz FM *Hrs Open:* 24; 4.2 kw; Ant 394 ft; N40 41 54 W85 45 03
Box 342, 1864 S. Wabash St., Wabash, IN 46992
(260) 563-4111, *Fax:* (260) 563-4425
www.wkuz.com
wkuz@kconline.com
License: Wabash, Wabash County, IN held by Upper Wabash Broadcasting Corp.
Nat'l Network: USA *Regional Network:* Brownfield
Population Served: 500,000*Special Programming:* Farm 5 hrs wkly *Hrs. of News Programming:* news progmg 10 hrs wkly *No. News Employees:* 1 *Target Audience:* General. *Adv. Rates:* 10; 10; 10; 10
Toni Adams, President
Charles Adams, General Manager
Paul Adams, Chief Engineer

Wadesville

*WENS
01-01-2005; 90.1 mhz FM; 6 kw vert; 285 ft.; N37 56 3 W87 55 35
Mailing Address: US
Second Address: 15 Wood St., Greenfield, IN 46140-2162
(317) 462-9523, *Fax:* (317) 467-1065
www.wjcfradio.com
wjcfradio@aol.com
License: Wadesville, Posey County, IN held by Indiana Community Radio Corp.
Arbitron Metro Market: Greenfield, IN *Format:* Christian
Jennifer Cox-Hensley, President

Wakarusa

*WYBV
01-01-2006; 89.9 mhz FM; 1.75 kw; 328 ft.; N41 27 50 W85 49 22
8030 Arrowridge Blvd, Charlotte, NC 28273 US
(704) 523-5555, *Fax:* (704) 522-1967
www.bbnradio.org
License: Wakarusa, Elkhart County, IN held by Bible Broadcasting Network Inc.
Group Owner: Bible Broadcasting Network
Arbitron Metro Market: Wakarusa, IN *Format:* Christian
Lowell Davey, President
Marc Pittman, Operations Dir
George Keen, Chief Engineer

Walton

WFRR
01-01-1995; 93.7 mhz FM *Hrs Open:* 24; 6 kw; 328 ft.; N40 43 31 W86 10 33 *Rebroadcasts:* Rebroadcasts WFRN-FM Elkhart 85%
Mailing Address: P.O. Box 307, Elkhart, IN 46515 US
Second Address: 25802 CR 26, Elkhart, IN 46517
(574) 875-5166, *Fax:* (574) 875-6662
www.wfrn.com
moore@wfrn.com
License: Walton, Cass County, IN held by Christian Friends Broadcasting Inc.
Nat'l Network: USA *Regional Network:* Network Indiana *Nat'l Reps:* Salem
Format: Christian *No. News Employees:* 1 *Target Audience:* 25-54; general *Adv. Rates:* 22; 16; 17; 9
Edwin Moore, President
James Carter, Programming Director
Don Wagner, News Director

Wanatah

*WTMK
01-01-2005; 88.5 mhz FM; 1.5 kw; 167 ft.; N41 4 59 W87 10 47
3000 W Macarthur Blvd., Santa Ana, CA 92704 US
(219) 548-5800, *Fax:* (219) 548-5808
www.csnmidwest.com
License: Wanatah, Lake County, IN held by CSN International

Group Owner: CSN International
Arbitron Metro Market: Wanatah, IN *Format:* Religious
Jim Motshagen, General Manager
Kathy Motshagen, Programming Director

Warsaw

WRSW

01-01-1951; 1480 khz AM *Hrs Open:* 24; 1 kw-D, DAN; 0.5 kw-N, DAN; N41 13 21 W85 50 17
1104 Kings Highway, Winona Lake, IN 46590 US
(574) 372-3064, *Fax:* (574) 267-2230
http://espnwarsaw.com/Home.aspx
License: Warsaw, IN held by Talking Stick Communications LLC.
Group Owner: Talking Stick Communications LLC; (acq 12-19-2003; $1.2 million with
Nat'l Network: Westwood One *Regional Network:* Tribune Radio Networks; Network Indiana
Format: Sports *Hrs. of News Programming:* news progmg 18 hrs wkly *No. News Employees:* 1 *Target Audience:* General. *Adv. Rates:* 21; 18; 21; 10.30
Clint Marsh, General Manager
Dan Daggett, General Sales Mgr
Roger Grossman, Programming Director
Jack Didier, Engineering Dir

WRSW-FM

01-01-1948; 107.3 mhz FM; 50 kw; 226 ft.; N41 13 21 W85 50 17
1104 Kings Highway, Winona Lake, IN 46590 US
(574) 372-3064, *Fax:* (574) 267-2230
www.wrsw.net
License: Warsaw, Kosciusko County, IN
Group Owner: Talking Stick Communications LLC
Nat'l Network: Westwood One *Regional Network:* Network Indiana *Nat'l Reps:* Rgnl Reps *Regional Reps:* Rgnl Reps
Format: Contemporary Hits/Top 40, Adult Contemp *Target Audience:* General; affluent adults *Adv. Rates:* 21; 18; 21; 10
Clint Marsh, General Manager
Dan Daggett, General Sales Mgr

Washington

WAMW

01-01-1955; 1580 khz AM *Hrs Open:* Daytime plus FM Translator is 24/7; 0.5 kw-D, DAD; 0.005 kw-N, ND1; N38 38 47 W87 16 48; N38 39 4 W87 9 55 *Rebroadcasts:* 95.9 W240CE 99 watts
102 E. Main Street, Washington, IN 47501 US
(812) 254-6761, *Fax:* (812) 254-3940
www.memories1079.com
wamw@rtccom.net
License: Washington, IN held by DLC Media, Inc.
Nat'l Network: ABC
Arbitron Metro Market: Washington, IN *Format:* Adult Contemp *Special Programming:* The Ed Schultz Show - Agri-Talk -The Dave Crooks S *Hrs. of News Programming:* 25 *No. News Employees:* 2 *Target Audience:* 35 plus
Dave Crooks, President
Andy Morrison, Operations Dir
Brad Deetz, General Manager
Beth Davis, General Sales Mgr
Taylor Brown, Programming Director
Katie Sullivan, Promotions Director

WAMW-FM

11-20-1989; 107.9 mhz FM *Hrs Open:* 24; 3 kw; 328 ft.; N38 38 47 W87 16 47
104 E. Main Street, Washington, IN 47501 US
(812) 254-6761, *Fax:* (812) 254-3940
www.memories1079.com
wamw@rtccom.net
License: Washington, Daviess County, IN held by DLC Media, Inc.
Nat'l Network: ABC Information & Entertainment *Regional Network:* Brownfield; Network Indiana *Wire Services:* AP
Arbitron Metro Market: Washington, IN *Format:* Contemporary Hits/Top 40, Adult Contemp *Special Programming:* Indy Racing League, Notre Dame Football, North Car *Hrs. of News Programming:* 12 *No. News Employees:* 2*Target Audience:* 25-64
Dave Crooks, President
Andy Morrison, Operations Dir
Brad Deetz, General Manager
Beth Davis, General Sales Mgr
Taylor Brown, Programming Director
Katie Sullivan, Promotions Director

WWBL

02-01-1948; 106.5 mhz FM; 50 kw; 341 ft.; N38 39 4 W87 9 55
Mailing Address: 1309 Old Orchard Road, Vincennes, IN 47591 US
Second Address: Box 242, Vincennes, IN 47591-0242
(812) 882-6060
www.wwbl.com
marklange@originalcompany.com
License: Washington, Daviess County, IN held by Old Northwest Broadcasting Inc.
Group Owner: The Original Company Inc.; (acq 10-93; $250,000 with WAOV(AM)
Nat'l Network: ABC *Nat'l Reps:* Rgnl Reps
Arbitron Metro Market: Washington, IN *Format:* Country *Special Programming:* Farm 15 hrs wkly *Hrs. of News Programming:* news progmg 15 hrs wkly *No. News Employees:* 1 *Target Audience:* 18 plus.
Mark Lange, President
Ken Booth, Operations Dir
Duncan Myers, Marketing Director
Jeff Hendershot, Direct Mail

Waynetown

*WSRC(FM)

88.1 mhz FM; 10 kw vert; Ant 410 ft; N39 47 44 W86 48 04
5331 Mount Alifan Dr., Fredonia, NY 92111-2622
(858) 277-4991, *Fax:* (858) 277-1365
License: Waynetown, Hendricks County, IN held by Calvary Chapel of Crawfordsville Inc
Group Owner: Horizon Christian Fellowship
Population Served: 11,194 *Arbitron Metro Market:* Fredonia, NY
Michael MacIntosh, President

West Lafayette

*WKHL

06-15-1992; 106.7 mhz FM *Hrs Open:* 24; 6 kw; 328 ft.; N40 31 20 W86 58 57
2700 -A Kent Avenue, West Lafayette, IN 47906 US
(916) 251-1600, *Fax:* (916) 251-1650
www.klove.com
License: West Lafayette, Tippecanoe County, IN held by Educational Media Foundation.
Group Owner: EMF Broadcasting; (acq 4-17-2008; $1.2 million)
Nat'l Network: K-Love
Arbitron Metro Market: Lafayette, IN *Format:* Christian
Mike Novak, President

*WHPL

09-10-1993; 89.9 mhz FM *Hrs Open:* 24; 2 kw vert; 328 ft.; N40 17 50 W86 54 5
820 North Lasalle Boulevard, Chicago, IL 60610 US
(765) 449-0899, *Fax:* (765) 449-3025
www.moodyradioindiana.fm
WGNR@moddy.edu
License: West Lafayette, Tippecanoe County, IN held by The Moody Bible Institute of Chicago.
Group Owner: The Moody Bible Institute of Chicago; acq 6-20-97)
Nat'l Network: Moody
Arbitron Metro Market: Lafayette, IN *Format:* Religious *Hrs. of News Programming:* News progmg 14 hrs wkly *Target Audience:* 35 plus; relg
Ray Hashley, General Manager

*WBAA

04-04-1922; 920 khz AM; 5 kw-D, DAN; 1 kw-N, DAN; N40 20 29 W86 53 1
1740 Elliott Hall, Rm 11, West Lafayette, IN 47907 US
(765) 494-5920, *Fax:* (765) 496-1542
www.wbaa.org
wbaa@wbaa.org
License: West Lafayette, IN held by Purdue University.
Nat'l Network: NPR; PRI
Arbitron Metro Market: West Lafayette, IN *Format:* Jazz, News, 62, Talk *Hrs. of News Programming:* news progmg 20 hrs wkly *No. News Employees:* 3
Bette Carson Mogridge, Operations Dir
Tim Singleton, General Manager
Greg Kostraba, Programming Director
Mike Loizzo, News Director
Jim Keen, Chief Engineer
Brian Garrity, Corporate Support Manager
Christine Burr, Membership andEvents Manager
Jenny Hood, Traffic Coordinator

*WBAA-FM

02-01-1993; 101.3 mhz FM; 14 kw; 394 ft.; N40 17 50 W86 54 5
1740 Elliott Rm 11, West Lafayette, IN 47907 US
(765) 494-5920, *Fax:* (765) 496-1542
www.wbaa.org
wbaa@wbaa.org
License: West Lafayette, Tippecanoe County, IN held by Purdue University
Nat'l Network: NPR; PRI
Arbitron Metro Market: West Lafayette, IN *Format:* Classical, News *Hrs. of News Programming:* news progmg 20 rs wkly *No. News Employees:* 3
Bette Carson Mogridge, Operations Dir
Tim Singleton, General Manager
Greg Kostraba, Programming Director
Mike Loizzo, News Director
Maurice Mogridge, Engineering Dir
Jim Keen, Chief Engineer
Brian Garrity, Corporate SupportManager
Christine Burr, Membership and Events Manager
Jan Simon, Producer
Jenny Hood, Traffic Coordinator
Kristin Malavenda, News Producer
Pamela Dunn, Corporate Support Manager

West Terre Haute

WWVR

01-20-1967; 105.5 mhz FM *Hrs Open:* 6 AM-2 AM; 3.3 kw; 295 ft.; N39 27 13 W87 28 15
Mailing Address: 3500 West Olive Avenue, Suite 300, Burbank, CA 91505 US
Second Address: 918 Ohio St., Terre Haute, IN 47808
(812) 917-3901, *Fax:* (812) 234-0089
www.1055theriver.com
jconner@wthi.emmis.com
License: West Terre Haute, Vigo County, IN held by Emmis Radio License LLC.
Group Owner: Emmis Communications Corp.
Arbitron Metro Market: Terre Haute, IN *Format:* Classic Rock *Special Programming:* Gospel, news/talk, Black 6 hrs wkly *Hrs. of News Programming:* News progmg 6 hrs wkly *Target Audience:* 35-64.
James Conner, General Manager
James Conner, Station Manager
Barry Kent, Programming Director
Holy Burk, Promotions Manager
Jeff Tucker, Chief Engineer
Fred Strohm, Webmaster
Steve Brown, Music Director
Brian Black,Administrative Assistant
Jerry Felty, Assistant Engineer
Cynthia Gray, Director of Development
Ben Martin, Operations Assistant & Producer/Radio Reading Serv

Wilkinson

*WSMJ(FM)

01-01-2008; 89.1 mhz FM; 150 w vert; Ant 102 ft; N39 52 46.4 W85 38 10.9
15 Wood St., Greenfield, IN 46140
(317) 467-1064
License: Wilkinson, Hancock County, IN held by Hoosier Public Radio Corp.
Population Served: 4,013 *Arbitron Metro Market:* North Wildwood, NJ
Martin Hensley, President

Winamac

WFRI

01-01-1998; 100.1 mhz FM *Hrs Open:* 24; 6 kw; 328 ft.; N41 2 21 W86 30 55 *Rebroadcasts:* Rebroadcasts WFRN-FM Elkhart 80%
P. O. Box 307, Elkhart, IN 46515 US
(574) 875-5166, *Fax:* (219) 875-6662
www.wfrn.com
comments@wfrn.com
License: Winamac, Pulaski County, IN held by Progressive Broadcasting System Inc.
Group Owner: Progressive Broadcasting System Inc.
Nat'l Network: USA *Regional Network:* Network Indiana
Format: Christian *Target Audience:* 25-54. *Adv. Rates:* 13; 11; 12; 7
Edwin Moore, President

Winchester

WZZY

05-01-1967; 98.3 mhz FM *Hrs Open:* 24; 3 kw; 299 ft.; N40 5 23 W84 56 13
P.O. Box 427, Winchester, IN 47394 US
(765) 962-6533, *Fax:* (765) 966-1499
www.todaysmusicmix.com
johnrose@g1013.com
License: Winchester, Randolph County, IN held by Rodgers Broadcasting Corp.
Group Owner: Rodgers Broadcasting Corp.; acq 1-1-00)
Regional Reps: Rgnl Reps.

Arbitron Metro Market: Richmond, IN *Format:* Adult Contemp *Hrs. of News Programming:* news progmg 10 hrs wkly *No. News Employees:* 2 *Target Audience:* 25-54; general
David Rodgers, President
Rick Duncan, Operations Dir
Steve Frey, General Manager
Bob Phillips, News Director
Keith Wade, Disc Jockey

Woodburn

WBYR
10-01-1962; 98.9 mhz FM; 50 kw; 453 ft.; N40 57 14 W84 53 7
421 South Second Street, Elkhart, IN 46516 US
(260) 471-5100, *Fax:* (260) 471-5224
www.989thebear.com
info@wbyrfm.com
License: Woodburn, Van Wert County, IN held by Pathfinder Communications Corp.
Group Owner: Federated Media; (acq 1996; $5.85 million)
Arbitron Metro Market: Fort Wayne, IN *Format:* Rock/AOR *Target Audience:* 18-49; men
Jim Allgeier, General Manager

Zionsville

***WITT**
91.9 mhz FM; 6 kw; 297 ft.; N40 0 14 W86 28 14
6218 Kingsley Drive, Indianapolis, IN 46220 US
(317) 251-3851
www.919witt.org
radio@919witt.org
License: Zionsville, Boone County, IN held by Kids First Inc.
Arbitron Metro Market: Zionsville, IN *Format:* Variety/Diverse
James Walsh, President

Iowa

Adel

***KIHS**
01-01-2004; 88.5 mhz FM; 0.5 kw; 207 ft.; N41 36 9 W94 2 55
3000 West Macarthur Blvd, Santa Ana, CA 92704 US
(800) 357-4226, *Fax:* (208) 736-1958
www.csnradio.com
csn@csnradio.com
License: Adel, Dallas County, IA held by CSN International
Group Owner: CSN International
Arbitron Metro Market: Des Moines, IA *Format:* Christian
Mike Kestler, President
Daniel Davidson, Operations Dir
Ray Garney, General Manager
Kelly Carlson, Engineering Dir
Jerry Johnson, Engineering Dir
Don Mills, Network Programming Director / Music Director
Ray Gorney, AssistantDirector of Engineering
Nolan Mather, Graphics / Website Maintenance
Mike Stocklin, National Underwriting
Austin Morris, Accounting

Albia

KIIC
06-15-1995; 96.7 mhz FM; 10 kw; 463 ft.; N41 0 38 W92 43 47
10 N. Clinton, Albia, IA 52531 US
(641) 932-2112, *Fax:* (641) 932-2113
License: Albia, Monroe County, IA held by Waveguide Communications Inc.
Nat'l Network: AP Network News; Jones Radio Networks
Regional Network: Brownfield
Format: Country *Hrs. of News Programming:* news prgmg 10 hrs wkly *No. News Employees:* 1 *Target Audience:* 25-54.
Joe Milledge, President
Lori McIntire, General Manager

Algona

KLGA
01-01-1956; 1600 khz AM *Hrs Open:* 24
Mailing Address: P. O. Box 160, Algona, IA 50511 US
Second Address: 2102 80th Ave., Algona, IA 50511
(515) 295-2475, *Fax:* (515) 295-3851
www.waittmedia.com
info@waittmedia.com
License: Algona, IA held by NRG License Sub. LLC.
Group Owner: NRG Media LLC; (acq 10-31-2005; grpsl)
Nat'l Network: ABC *Regional Network:* Radio Iowa
Arbitron Metro Market: Mason City, IA *Format:* Adult Contemp
Special Programming: Farm, news, weather *Hrs. of News Programming:* news progmg 44 hrs wkly *No. News Employees:* 1 *Target Audience:* 25-54.
Bob Ketchum, General Manager
Dana Myee, Programming Director

KLGA-FM
08-17-1970; 92.7 mhz FM *Hrs Open:* 6 AM-10:30 PM; 3.5 kw; 449 ft.; N43 4 5 W94 12 8
Mailing Address: P.O. Box 160, Algona, IA 50511 US
Second Address: 2102 80th Ave., Algona, IA 50511
(515) 295-2475, *Fax:* (515) 295-3851
www.waittmedia.com
License: Algona, Kossuth County, IA
Group Owner: NRG Media LLC
Arbitron Metro Market: Mason City, IA
Evan Armstrong, General Manager

Alta

KBVU-FM
01-01-1999; 97.5 mhz FM; 6 kw; 315 ft.; N42 38 5 W95 10 10
610 West 4th Street, Storm Lake, IA 50588 US
(712) 749-1234, *Fax:* (712) 749-1211
edge.bvu.edu
kbvu@bvu.edu
License: Alta, Buena Vista County, IA held by Buena Vista University.
Arbitron Metro Market: Storm Lake, IA *Format:* Alternative *Target Audience:* 18-25; college students
Bruce Ellingson, General Manager

Alton

***KRGO**
91.5 mhz FM; kw*Rebroadcasts:* WJRF/Duluth, MN US
(218) 722-2727, *Fax:* (218) 722-1650
www.refugeradio.com
airstaff@refugeradio.com
License: Alton, Sioux County, IA held by Refuge Media Group.
Arbitron Metro Market: Duluth, MN *Format:* Christian
Daniel Hatifeld, Programming Director

Ames

KASI
01-01-1948; 1430 khz AM *Hrs Open:* 5 AM-midnight; 1 kw-D, ND1; 0.032 kw-N, ND1; N42 2 18 W93 40 53
200 Concord Plaza, Suite 600, San Antonio, TX 78216 US
(515) 232-1430, *Fax:* (515) 232-1439
www.1430kasi.com
info@1430kasi.com
License: Ames, IA held by Citicasters Licenses L.P.
Group Owner: Clear Channel Communications Inc.; (acq 8-24-99; with co-located FM).
Nat'l Network: ABC
Arbitron Metro Market: Ames, IA *Format:* News, News/Talk, 64, Talk *Hrs. of News Programming:* news progmg 25 hrs wkly *No. News Employees:* 2 *Target Audience:* 25 plus.
Joel McCrea, General Manager
Carol Kisling, Station Manager
Tony Calumet, General Sales Mgr
Mel Crippen, Programming Director
Trent Rice, News Director
Mike Stover, Chief Engineer
B.J. Schaben, Sports Commentator
Linda Thede,Traffic Manager

KCCQ
06-20-1968; 105.1 mhz FM *Hrs Open:* 24; 25 kw; 328 ft.; N42 4 38 W93 38 54
200 Concord Plaza, Suite 600, San Antonio, TX 78216 US
(515) 232-1430, *Fax:* (515) 232-1439
www.newrock1051.com
gregchance@newrock1051.com
License: Ames, Story County, IA held by Citicasters Licenses L.P.
Group Owner: Clear Channel Communications Inc.
Arbitron Metro Market: Ames, IA *Format:* Contemporary Hits/Top 40 *Target Audience:* 18-40.
Joel McCrea, General Manager
Linda Thede, News Director
B.J. Schaben, Sports Commentator

KLTI-FM
06-02-1967; 104.1 mhz FM *Hrs Open:* 24; 100 kw; 1010 ft.; N41 54 9 W93 54 15
73 Kercheval Avenue, Grosse Pointe Farms, MI 48236 US
(515) 280-1350, *Fax:* (515) 280-3011
www.lite1041.com
sallen@desmoinesradiogroup.com
License: Ames, Story County, IA held by Saga Communications of Iowa LLC.
Group Owner: Saga Communications Inc.; (acq 1-1-97; $3.2 million)
Nat'l Reps: Katz Radio *Wire Services:* AP
Arbitron Metro Market: Des Moines, IA *Format:* Adult Contemp *Target Audience:* Women; 25-54
Ed Christian, CEO
Scott Allen, Operations Dir
Jeff Delvaux, General Manager
Pam Washington, General Sales Mgr
Scott Allen, Programming Director
Jay Wells, Promotions Manager
Sarah LeVere, Advertising Manager
Pam Washington,Sarah LeVere

***KURE**
04-17-1970; 88.5 mhz FM *Hrs Open:* 24; 0.63 kw; 72 ft.; N42 1 47 W93 38 51
1199 Friley Hall, Ames, IA 50012 US
(515) 294-4332, *Fax:* (515) 294-8093
www.kure885.org
generalmanager@kure885.org
License: Ames, Story County, IA held by Residence Associations Broadcasting Service Inc.
Arbitron Metro Market: Ames, IA *Format:* Variety/Diverse *Hrs. of News Programming:* News progmg 10 hrs wkly *Target Audience:* 18-25; Iowa State Univ students & Ames community
Rezza Rahmoni, Operations Dir
Darren Hushak, General Manager
Kate Derksen, Programming Director
Katherine Beaver, Promotions Manager
Marshall Hilgemann, Chief Engineer
Dax Sunkten, Treasurer
Tabitha Jamerson, UnderwritingDirector
Molly Cleveland, Marketing Director
Louis Hilgemann, External Music Director
Trevin Ward, Internal Music Director
Sam Turner, Sports Director

***WOI**
01-01-1922; 640 khz AM *Hrs Open:* 24; 5 kw-D, 1 kw-N, DA-N; N41 59 34 W93 41 27
2111 Grand Avenue, Suite 100e Univ., Des Moines, IA 50011
(515) 725-1700, *Fax:* (515) 725-1714
www.iowapublicradio.org
License: Ames, Story County, IA held by Iowa State University.
Nat'l Network: NPR; PRI *Wire Services:* AP
Population Served: 3,000,000*Hrs. of News Programming:* news progmg 40 hrs wkly *No. News Employees:* 15 *Target Audience:* General.
Mary Grace Herrington, CEO/COO
Mary Grace Herrington, Programming Director
Steve Schoon, Chief Engineer

***WOI-FM**
07-01-1949; 90.1 mhz FM; 100 kw; 1490 ft.; N41 48 33 W93 36 53
204 Communications Bldg, Ames, IA 50011 US
(515) 294-2025, *Fax:* (515) 294-1544
www.iowapublicradio.org
License: Ames, Story County, IA held by Iowa State University.
Nat'l Network: NPR
TV Affiliate: class *Special Programming:* news progmg 12 hrs wkly *Hrs. of News Programming:* 3 *No. News Employees:* General.
CEO, CEO/COO
Director of Operations, Operations Dir
Director, Fiscal Operations

Ankeny

KPTL
07-01-1991; 106.3 mhz FM *Hrs Open:* 24/7; 25 kw; 328 ft.; N41 40 45 W93 35 46
50 East Rivercenter Blvd, Suite 1200, Covington, KY 41011 US
(515) 245-8900
www.capital1063.com
GregChance@clearchannel.com
License: Ankeny, Polk County, IA held by Citicasters Licenses L.P.
Group Owner: Clear Channel Communications Inc.; (acq 5-4-99; grpsl)
Nat'l Reps: Clear Channel *Wire Services:* AP
Arbitron Metro Market: Des Moines, IA *Format:* Triple A *Target Audience:* 25-54.
Joel McCrea, Operations Dir
Matt Gillon, General Sales Mgr
Greg Chance, Music Director & Promotions
Jim Boyd, News Director
Raleigh Rubenking, Chief Engineer
Molly Pins, Promotions Manager

Asbury

WJOD
03-31-1994; 103.3 mhz FM *Hrs Open:* 24; 6.6 kw; 643 ft.; N42 24 16 W90 34 12
111 East Kilbourn Ave., Suite 2700, Milwaukee, WI 53202 US
(563) 557-1040, *Fax:* (563) 583-4535
www.103wjod.com
info@wjod.com
License: Asbury, Dubuque County, IA held by Cumulus Licensing Corp.
Group Owner: Cumulus Media Inc.; (acq 2-6-98)
Nat'l Network: Jones Radio Networks
Arbitron Metro Market: Dubuque, IA *Format:* Country *Target Audience:* 18-49.
Ken Peiffer, Operations Dir
Scott Lindahl, General Manager

Atlantic

KJAN
09-01-1950; 1220 khz AM *Hrs Open:* 24; 0.178 kw-D, ND1; 0.062 kw-N, ND1; N41 25 2 W95 0 15
1908 East 7th Street, Atlantic, IA 50022 US
(712) 243-3920, *Fax:* (712) 243-3937
www.kjan.com
kjan@metc.net
License: Atlantic, IA held by Wireless Communications Corp.
Nat'l Network: Fox News Radio *Regional Network:* Radio Iowa; Brownfield *Nat'l Reps:* Commercial Media Sales *Wire Services:* AP
Format: Adult Contemp, News *Special Programming:* Farm 12 hrs wkly *Hrs. of News Programming:* news progmg 40 hrs wkly *No. News Employees:* 1 *Target Audience:* 25 plus; general
J.C. Van Ginkel, Chairman
Merlyn Christensen, President
James Field, General Manager

KSWI
07-01-2000; 95.7 mhz FM *Hrs Open:* 24; 20 kw; 358 ft.; N41 26 7 W94 50 0
413 Chestnut Street, Atlantic, IA 50022 US
(712) 243-6885, *Fax:* (712) 243-1691
www.iowasuperstation.com
bill@iowasuperstation.com
License: Atlantic, Cass County, IA held by Meredith Communications L.C.
Nat'l Network: ABC
Arbitron Metro Market: Atlantic, IA *Format:* Contemporary Hits/Top 40, Adult Contemp
Stephen Meredith, President
Bill Saluk, General Manager
Jill Christensen, Programming Director

Audubon

KSOM
08-01-1995; 96.5 mhz FM *Hrs Open:* 24; 100 kw; 528 ft.; N41 26 7 W94 50 0
P O Box 88, Atlantic, IA 50022 US
(712) 243-6885, *Fax:* (712) 243-1691
www.iowasuperstation.com
ksom@mchsi.com
License: Audubon, Audubon County, IA held by Meredith Communications L.C.
Nat'l Network: ABC; Motor Racing Net; Premiere Radio Networks
Arbitron Metro Market: Atlantic, IA *Format:* Country *Hrs. of News Programming:* news progmg 6 hrs wkly *No. News Employees:* 2 *Target Audience:* General; upscale & farmers
Bill Saluk, General Manager
Jill Christensen, Programming Director

Belle Plaine

KZAT-FM
05-30-1997; 95.5 mhz FM *Hrs Open:* 24; 4.4 kw; 384 ft.; N41 56 35 W92 23 51
303 McClellan Street, Tama, IA 52339 US
(641) 484-5958, *Fax:* (641) 484-5962
www.radioz955fm.com
manuel@radioz95fm.com
License: Belle Plaine, Benton County, IA held by Camrory Broadcasting Inc.
Nat'l Network: CBS; Westwood One; ABC *Wire Services:* AP
Arbitron Metro Market: Belle Plaine, IA *Format:* Contemporary Hits/Top 40, Adult Contemp *Special Programming:* Polka 2 hrs Sun am *Hrs. of News Programming:* news progmg 6 hrs wkly *No. News Employees:* 1 *TargetAudience:* 25-54; listeners who are professionals, laborers, commuters, tourists & truckers
Catherine Campbell Currier, President
Jeff Bayer, News Director

Bettendorf

KQCS
07-07-1984; 93.5 mhz FM *Hrs Open:* 24; 6 kw; 318 ft.; N41 36 14 W90 24 43
1229 Brady Street, Davenport, IA 52803 US
(563) 326-2541, *Fax:* (563) 326-0844
www.93rock.net
quadcities.prod@cumulus.com
License: Bettendorf, Scott County, IA held by Cumulus Licensing Corp.
Group Owner: Cumulus Media Inc.; (acq 3-15-00; grpsl).
Arbitron Metro Market: Quad Cities, IA-IL (Davenport-Rock Island-Moline) *Format:* Rock/AOR *Target Audience:* 18-34.
Jack Swart, General Manager
Julie Derrer, General Sales Mgr
Jeff James, Programming Director
Tracy Hall, News Director
Andy Andresen, Chief Engineer

*KNSB(FM)
91.1 mhz FM; 740 w; 116.8 meters; N41 32 43.8 W90 22 23.6
University of Northern Iowa, 324 Communications Arts Center, Cedar Falls, IA 50614-0359
(319) 273-6325
License: Bettendorf, Scott County, IA held by University of Northern Iowa.
Arbitron Metro Market: Quad Cities, IA-IL (Davenport-Rock Island-Moline)
Wayne Jarvis, General Manager

Boone

KFFF(AM)
01-01-1927; 1260 khz AM; 5 kw-D, 33 w-N, DA-D; N42 02 55 W93 53 54
900 8th St., Boone, IA 50036
(515) 432-5014, *Fax:* (515) 432-2092
www.wolfradio933.com
mail@iowanewstalk.com
License: Boone, Boone County, IA held by Boone Biblical Ministries Inc.
Format: Talk
Robert Stumbo, President
Jamie Johnson, General Manager
Bob Pink, Chief Engineer

KFFF-FM
01-01-1950; 99.3 mhz FM; 5.2 kw; Ant 351 ft; N42 02 55 W93 53 54
900 8th St., Boone, IA 50036
(515) 432-5014, *Fax:* (515) 432-2092
mail@iowanewstalk.com
License: Boone, Boone County, IA held by Boone Biblical Ministries Inc.
Format: Religious
Jamie Johnson, Programming Director

KWQW
05-15-1975; 98.3 mhz FM *Hrs Open:* 24; 41 kw; 16.5 meters; N41 49 51 W93 43 54
4143 109th St., Urbandale, IA 02162
(515) 331-9200, *Fax:* (515) 331-9292
www.983wowfm.com
License: Boone, Boone County, IA
Group Owner: Cumulus Media Inc.; (acq 8-29-2003; grpsl).
Nat'l Reps: Christal
Arbitron Metro Market: Des Moines, IA *Hrs. of News Programming:* News progmg 15 hrs wkly *Target Audience:* 25-54.
Jack O'Brien, Operations Dir
Doug Wood, General Sales Mgr
Terry Peters, Promotions Manager

KWBG
01-15-1950; 1590 khz AM *Hrs Open:* 6 AM-11 PM; 1 kw-D, DAN; 0.5 kw-N, DAN; N42 1 22 W93 52 36
P.O. Box 366, Boone, IA 50036 US
(515) 432-2046, *Fax:* (515) 432-1448
www.kwbg.com
ckuster@nrgmedia.com
License: Boone, IA held by NRG License Sub. LLC.
Group Owner: NRG Media LLC; (acq 10-31-2005; grpsl)
Nat'l Network: ABC; ESPN Radio *Regional Network:* Brownfield
Arbitron Metro Market: Boone, IA *Format:* News, News/Talk, 86 *Special Programming:* Farm 15 hrs wkly *Hrs. of News Programming:* news progmg 36 hrs wkly *No. News Employees:* 1 *Target Audience:* 35 plus;Boone County, Iowa residents *Adv. Rates:* 24.90; 24.90; 15.90; 15.90
Brenda Miller, Operations Dir
Carol Kuster, General Manager
Ben Parsons, Webmaster and Sales
Jim Turbes, News Director
Ryan Wendt, Sports Director
Gena Treganza, Billing and Traffic

Britt

KHAM
01-01-2006; 99.5 mhz FM; 0.2 kw; 52 ft.; N43 5 47 W93 48 5
1296 Marian Lane, Green Bay, WI 54304 US
(641) 585-1073, *Fax:* (641) 585-2990
www.kiow.com
kiow@kiow.com
License: Britt, Hancock County, IA held by Coloff Media LLC
Arbitron Metro Market: Britt, IA
Tony Coloff, General Manager

Brooklyn

*KSKB
03-01-1988; 99.1 mhz FM; 44 kw; 525 ft.; N41 41 23 W92 21 31
Mailing Address: 505 Josephine Street, Titusville, FL 32796 US
Second Address: 505 Josephine St., Titusville, FL 32796
(641) 522-7202, *Fax:* (641) 522-7239
noncomradio.net
wpio@gate.net
License: Brooklyn, Poweshiek County, IA held by Florida Public Radio Inc.
Arbitron Metro Market: Brooklyn, IA *Format:* Adult Contemp, Christian *Special Programming:* Ger one hr, Pol one hr wkly *Target Audience:* General.
Bill Korns, General Manager

Burlington

*KAYP
11-01-2000; 89.9 mhz FM; 9 kw vert; 440 ft.; N40 47 59 W91 32 35
P O Drawer 2440, Tupelo, MS 38803 US
(319) 758-6911, *Fax:* (319) 758-6922
www.kayp.afr.net
kayp@mchsi.com
License: Burlington, Des Moines County, IA held by American Family Association.
Group Owner: American Family Radio
Format: Adult Contemp, Christian
Marvin Sanders, General Manager

KBUR
07-01-1941; 1490 khz AM *Hrs Open:* 24; 0.76 kw-U, ND1; N40 49 26 W91 8 33
50 East Rivercenter Blvd, #1200, Covington, KY 41011 US
(319) 752-5402, *Fax:* (319) 752-4715
www.kbur.com
info@kbur.com
License: Burlington, IA held by Pritchard Broadcasting Corp.
Group Owner: Pritchard Broadcasting Corp.; (acq 6-6-2008; with KBKB(AM) Fort Madison)
Regional Network: Radio Iowa
Arbitron Metro Market: Burlington, IA *Format:* Adult Contemp, News, 62, Talk *Special Programming:* Farm 19 hrs wkly *Hrs. of News Programming:* news progmg 28 hrs wkly *No. News Employees:* 3 *Target Audience:* 25 plus; general
John Pritchard, General Manager
Faith Krause, General Sales Mgr

KCPS
07-30-1965; 1150 khz AM *Hrs Open:* 24; 500 w-D, 67 w-N, DA-1; N40 51 11 W91 08 10
Mailing Address: Box 100, W.Burlington, IA 52601
Second Address: 205 S.Gear Av, W.Burlington, IA 52655
(319) 754-6698, *Fax:* (319) 754-8899
www.kcpsradio.com
kcps@aol.com
License: Burlington, Des Moines County, IA held by John Giannettino.
Nat'l Network: Premiere; Dial-Global; TRN *Regional Network:* Chicago Cubs; Chicago Bears; Indy Racing *Nat'l Reps:* Katz Radio
Population Served: 100,000*Special Programming:* Agriculture-business 10 hrs, pro sports 10 hrs wkly *Hrs. of News Programming:* news progmg 7 hrs wkly *No. News Employees:* 1 *Target Audience:* 25-54; middle-aged,upscale & well-informed adults *Adv. Rates:* 10; 10; 10; 8.50
John Giannettino, General Manager
Chip Giannettino, Station Manager
Chip Giannettino, General Sales Mgr
Chip Giannettino, Programming Director
Gary Saunders, News Director
Tracey Rogers, Chief Engineer

KDMG
07-19-1993; 103.1 mhz FM; 12 kw; 476 ft.; N40 44 4 W91 15 15

2850 Mt Pleasant St, Burlington, IA 52601 US
(319) 752-5402, *Fax:* (319) 752-4715
www.bigcountry1031.com
traffic@burlingtonradio.com
License: Burlington, Des Moines County, IA held by Pritchard Broadcasting Corp.
Group Owner: Pritchard Broadcasting Corp.
Nat'l Reps: Katz Radio
Arbitron Metro Market: Burlington, IA *Format:* Country *Hrs. of News Programming:* news progmg 2 hrs wkly *No. News Employees:* 1 *Target Audience:* 25-54. *Adv. Rates:* 24; 24; 24; 12
John Pritchard, President
Joe Bates, Operations Dir
Chet Young, General Sales Mgr

KGRS
11-27-1968; 107.3 mhz FM *Hrs Open:* 24; 100 kw; 430 ft.; N40 49 26 W91 8 33
Mailing Address: 50 East Rivercenter Blvd, #1200, Covington, KY 41011 US
Second Address: 1411 N. Roosevelt Ave., Burlington, IA 52601
(319) 752-2701, *Fax:* (319) 752-5287
www.thenewmix.com
cosmo@thenewmix.com
License: Burlington, Des Moines County, IA held by GAP Broadcasting Burlington License LLC.
Group Owner: GAPWEST Broadcasting; (acq 2-13-2008; grpsl)
Format: Adult Contemp *Hrs. of News Programming:* news progmg 15 hrs wkly *No. News Employees:* 1 *Target Audience:* 18-45
Cosmo Leone, Programming Director
Mark Hempen, News Director
J.K. Martin, Local News Editor

KKMI
10-22-1981; 93.5 mhz FM *Hrs Open:* 24; 6 kw; 305 ft.; N40 49 11 W91 7 2
2850 Mt. Pleasant, Burlington, IA 52601 US
(319) 752-5402, *Fax:* (319) 752-4715
www.935kkmi.com
935kkmi@935kkmi.com
License: Burlington, Des Moines County, IA held by Pritchard Broadcasting Corp.
Group Owner: Pritchard Broadcasting Corp.; (acq 8-5-91)
Nat'l Reps: Katz Radio
Arbitron Metro Market: Davenport, IA *Format:* Adult Contemp *Hrs. of News Programming:* news progmg 2 hrs wkly *No. News Employees:* 2 *Target Audience:* 25-55; upscale *Adv. Rates:* 15; 15; 15; 8
Joe Bates, Operations Dir
John Pritchard, General Manager
Chet Young, General Sales Mgr
Scott Michael, Programming Director

Carroll

KCIM
06-08-1950; 1380 khz AM; 1 kw-D, DA2; 1 kw-N, DA2; N42 2 29 W94 53 6
1119 E. Plaza Drive, Carroll, IA 51401 US
(712) 792-4321, *Fax:* (712) 792-6667
carrollbroadcasting.com
kcimkkrl@win-4-u.net
License: Carroll, IA held by Carroll Broadcasting Co.
Group Owner: Carroll Broadcasting Co.; acq 8-1-85; $1.5 million with co-located FM;
Nat'l Network: CBS *Nat'l Reps:* Katz Radio
Arbitron Metro Market: Carroll, IA *Format:* Oldies
Mary Collison, CEO
Kim Hackett, General Manager/Regional Advertising/National Adve
Lynda Dukes Franey, General Sales Mgr
John Ryan, Programming Director
Bob Grote, Chief Engineer
Deb Lupardus, Sales & Marketing Representative
Rachel Fransen, Sales & Marketing Representative
Pete Collison, Sales & Marketing Representative
Kris Boeckman, Sales & Marketing Representative
Roxanne Aden, Sales & Marketing Representative

KKRL
01-18-1967; 93.7 mhz FM *Hrs Open:* 24; 100 kw; 276 ft.; N42 2 57 W94 53 3
1119 E. Plaza Drive, Carroll, IA 51401 US
(712) 792-4321, *Fax:* (712) 792-6667
carrollbroadcasting.com
kcimkkrl@win-4-u.net
License: Carroll, Carroll County, IA held by Carroll Broadcasting Co.
Group Owner: Carroll Broadcasting Co.
Nat'l Reps: Katz Radio
Arbitron Metro Market: Des Moines, IA *Format:* Oldies *No. News Employees:* 1 *Target Audience:* 18 plus.
John Ryan, Programming Director

*KNSC(FM)
01-01-2004; 90.7 mhz FM *Hrs Open:* 24; 10 kw; Ant 289 ft; N42 07 14 W94 48 49
2022 Communications Bldg. ISU, WOI Radio Group, Ames, IA 50011-3241
(515) 294-2025, *Fax:* (515) 294-1544
www.iowapublicradio.org
woi@iastate.edu
License: Carroll, Carroll County, IA held by Iowa State University of Science and Technology.
Nat'l Network: NPR; PRI
Hrs. of News Programming: News progmg 40 hrs wkly *Target Audience:* General; educated
Mary Grace Herrington, Programming Director
Don Wirth, Director, Fiscal Operations

Castana

*KILV
01-01-2001; 107.5 mhz FM *Hrs Open:* 24; 25 kw; 328 ft.; N42 12 26 W96 7 26
4232 Fowler Ave, Baltimore, MD 21236 US
(916) 251-1600, *Fax:* (916) 251-1650
www.klove.com
klove@klove.com
License: Castana, Monona County, IA held by Educational Media Foundation.
Group Owner: EMF Broadcasting; (acq 10-26-01).
Nat'l Network: K-Love
Format: Christian *No. News Employees:* 3 *Target Audience:* 25-44; female-Judeo/Christian
Mike Novak, President
Glenn Goodwin, Operations Dir
David Pierce, Programming Director
Marya Morgan, News Director
Sam Wallington, Engineering Dir
Richard Hunt, News Reporter

Cedar Falls

KCFI(AM)
02-02-1958; 1250 khz AM *Hrs Open:* 24; 500 w-U, DA-2; N42 32 41 W92 29 16
Box 248, 721 Shirley St., Cedar Falls, IA 50613
(319) 277-1918, *Fax:* (319) 277-5202
www.1650thefan.com
Jesse@1650thefan.com
License: Cedar Falls, Black Hawk County, IA held by Fife Communications L.C.
Population Served: 68,653 *Arbitron Metro Market:* Waterloo, IA *Adv. Rates:* 12; 12; 12; 12
Jim Coloff, President
Tony Coloff, Operations Dir
Jeff Ryant, Station Manager
Sue Coloff, Vice President, Operations

KCNZ
09-01-1998; 1650 khz AM *Hrs Open:* 24
721 Shirley St., Cedar Falls, IA 50613 US
(319) 277-1918, *Fax:* (319) 277-5202
www.1650thefan.com
radio@1650thefan.com
License: Cedar Falls, IA held by Fife Communications Co. LLC.
Nat'l Network: CBS
Arbitron Metro Market: Waterloo-Cedar Falls, IA *Format:* Sports, Talk *Special Programming:* Farm 6 hrs *Hrs. of News Programming:* news progmg 25 hrs wkly *No. News Employees:* 2 *Target Audience:* 25-54;eastern Iowa adults *Adv. Rates:* 22; 18; 14; 10
John Coloff, President
Jim Coloff, General Manager
Doug Petersen, Programming Director
Janelle Rench, Office Manager

*KHKE
04-01-1974; 89.5 mhz FM *Hrs Open:* 24; 10 kw; 417 ft.; N42 23 55 W92 19 34
324 Comm Art Center, Cedar Falls, IA 50614 US
(515) 725-1700, *Fax:* (515) 725-1714
www.iowapublicradio.org
info@iowapublicradio.org
License: Cedar Falls, Black Hawk County, IA held by University of Northern Iowa.
Arbitron Metro Market: Waterloo-Cedar Falls, IA *Format:* Talk *Target Audience:* General.
Mary Grace Herrington, CEO
Kelly Edmister, Station Manager
Al Schares, Programming Director
Steve Schoon, Chief Engineer
Scott Rivers, Director of Network Operations
Al Shares, Music Director

KOEL-FM
01-07-1994; 98.5 mhz FM *Hrs Open:* 24; 15 kw; 423 ft.; N42 26 32 W92 23 48
136 Main Street, Westport, CT 06880 US
(319) 833-4800, *Fax:* (319) 833-4866
www.k985.com
License: Cedar Falls, Black Hawk County, IA held by Cumulus Licensing Corp.
Group Owner: Cumulus Media Inc.; (acq 3-15-00; grpsl).
Arbitron Metro Market: Waterloo, IA *Format:* Country *Hrs. of News Programming:* news progmg one hr wkly *No. News Employees:* 1 *Target Audience:* 18-49; general
Lew Dickey, President
William Hathaway, General Manager

*KUNI
09-15-1960; 90.9 mhz FM *Hrs Open:* 24; 94 kw; 1719 ft.; N42 18 59 W91 51 31
324 Communication Arts, Center, Cedar Falls, IA 50614 US
(515) 725-1700, *Fax:* (515) 725-1714
www.iowapublicradio.org
info@iowapublicradio.org
License: Cedar Falls, Black Hawk County, IA held by University of Northern Iowa.
Nat'l Network: NPR; PRI
Arbitron Metro Market: Cedar Falls, IA *Format:* News, Triple A *Special Programming:* Folk 4 hrs, rhythm and blues 2 hrs wkly *Hrs. of News Programming:* news progmg 74 hrs wkly *No. News Employees:* 3 *TargetAudience:* General.
Mary Grace Herrington, CEO
Al Schares, Programming Director
Steve Schoon, Chief Engineer
Kelly Edmister, Chief Administrative Officer
Scott Rivers, Director of Network Operations
Al Schares, Music Director

Cedar Rapids

*KCCK-FM
09-05-1972; 88.3 mhz FM *Hrs Open:* 24; 10 kw; 420 ft.; N41 54 33 W91 39 17
6301 Kirkwood Blvd.,S.W., Cedar Rapids, IA 52406 US
(319) 398-5446, *Fax:* (319) 398-5492
www.kcck.org
studio@kcck.org
License: Cedar Rapids, Linn County, IA held by Kirkwood Community College.
Nat'l Network: NPR *Wire Services:* AP
Arbitron Metro Market: Cedar Rapids, IA *Format:* Jazz *Special Programming:* Blues 12 hrs, new age 7 hrs wkly *Hrs. of News Programming:* news progmg 2 hrs wkly *No. News Employees:* 1 *Target Audience:* 25-54;educated, affluent, active in community
Kathy Hall, President
George Dorman, Operations Dir
Dennis Green, General Manager
Lisa Baum, General Sales Mgr
Bob Stewart, Programming Director
George Dorman, News Director
Dave Maley, Engineering Dir
Dave Maley, ChiefEngineer

KGYM
12-20-1947; 1600 khz AM *Hrs Open:* 24; 5 kw-U, DA-N; N41 58 15 W91 32 01
1110 26th Ave. S.W., Cedar Rapids, IA 52401
(319) 363-2061, *Fax:* (319) 363-2948
www.kgymradio.com
info@kgymradio.com
License: Cedar Rapids, Linn County, IA held by KZIA Inc.
Nat'l Network: ESPN Radio *Nat'l Reps:* Local Focus Radio *Wire Services:* AP
Population Served: 315,000 *Arbitron Metro Market:* Cedar Rapids, I *Special Programming:* FM translator 106.3 in Iowa City *Hrs. of News Programming:* News progmg one hr wkly *Target Audience:* 18-49.
Rob Norton, President
Greg Runyon, Operations Dir
Julie Hein, General Manager
Joe Drahozal, General Sales Mgr
Scott Unash, Programming Director
Jamie Burks, Promotions Manager
Dorothy Roach, News Director
Robert Norton Jr.,Executive Vice President
Kellie Lala, General Sales Manager

KDAT
05-01-1971; 104.5 mhz FM *Hrs Open:* 24; 100 kw; 551 ft.; N42 4 51 W91 41 45
600 Congress Ave., Suite 1400, Austin, TX 78701 US
(319) 365-9431, *Fax:* (319) 363-8062
www.kdat.com
kdat@kdat.com
License: Cedar Rapids, Linn County, IA held by Cumulus Media Inc.
Group Owner: Cumulus Media Inc.; (acq 8-7-00; grpsl).
Nat'l Reps: Christal
Arbitron Metro Market: Cedar Rapids, IA *Format:* Adult Contemp
Target Audience: 25-54. *Adv. Rates:* Contact Station
Tim Graves, Programming Director
Greg Sher, Promotions Manager

KHAK
07-01-1961; 98.1 mhz FM *Hrs Open:* 24; 100 kw; 459 ft.; N41 55 28 W91 36 55
600 Congress Ave., Suite 1400, Austin, TX 78701 US
(319) 365-9431, *Fax:* (319) 363-8062
www.khak.com
khak@khak.com
License: Cedar Rapids, Linn County, IA held by Cumulus Licensing Corp.
Group Owner: Cumulus Media Inc.; (acq 8-7-00; grpsl).
Regional Network: Brownfield *Nat'l Reps:* Christal
Arbitron Metro Market: Cedar Rapids, IA *Format:* Country *Target Audience:* 25-54; general *Adv. Rates:* Contact Station
Bob James, Programming Director
Greg Sher, Promotions Manager

KMRY
08-01-1949; 1450 khz AM *Hrs Open:* 24; 1 kw-U, ND1; N42 0 25 W91 42 29
1957 Blairs Ferry Rd.,Ne, Cedar Rapids, IA 52402 US
(319) 393-1450, *Fax:* (319) 393-1407
www.kmryradio.com
kmry@kmryradio.com
License: Cedar Rapids, IA held by Sellers Broadcasting Inc.
Nat'l Network: CBS *Wire Services:* AP
Arbitron Metro Market: Cedar Rapids, IA *Format:* Adult Contemp
Special Programming: 50's oldies 3 hrs, polka 3 hrs, big band 2 hrs we *Hrs. of News Programming:* news progmg 20 hrs wkly
No. News Employees: 1*Target Audience:* 40 plus; affluent, upscale adults with large disposable income *Adv. Rates:* 25; 20; 20; 10
Rick Sellers, President
Kevin Alexander, Operations Dir
David Bolt, General Sales Mgr
Eric Christopher, Programming Director
Bob Brooks, News Director
Jim Davies, Chief Engineer
Rick Sampson, Operations Manager

KMJM
07-01-1961; 1360 khz AM *Hrs Open:* 24; 1 kw-D, DA2; 0.124 kw-N, DA2; N41 55 28 W91 36 55
600 Congress Ave., Suite 1400, Austin, TX 78701 US
(319) 395-0530, *Fax:* (319) 393-9600
www.1360kmjm.com/main.html
License: Cedar Rapids, IA held by Capstar TX L.P.
Group Owner: Clear Channel Communications Inc.; (acq 8-30-2000; grpsl).
Arbitron Metro Market: Cedar Rapids, IA *Format:* Sports
JJ Cook, Operations Dir
Jeff Ashcraft, General Manager
Joni Sojka, General Sales Mgr
Randy Lee, Programming Director

KZIA
04-29-1975; 102.9 mhz FM *Hrs Open:* 24; 100 kw; Ant 853 ft; N42 03 25 W91 41 42
1110 26th Ave. S.W., Cedar Rapids, IA 52404
(319) 363-2061, *Fax:* (319) 363-2948
www.kzia.com
kzia@kzia.com
License: Cedar Rapids, Linn County, IA held by KZIA Inc.
Nat'l Reps: Local Focus Radio *Wire Services:* AP
Population Served: 315,000 *Arbitron Metro Market:* Cedar Rapids *Hrs. of News Programming:* news progmg one hr wkly
No. News Employees: 1 *Target Audience:* 18-49.
Rob Norton, President
Greg Runyon, Operations Dir
Julie Hein, General Manager
Joe Drahozal, Station Manager
Greg Runyon, Programming Director
Jamie Burks, Promotions Manager
Scott Schulte, News Director
Rob Norton, ChiefEngineer
Rick Swann, Music Director

WMT
01-01-1922; 600 khz AM *Hrs Open:* 24
50 East Rivercenter Blvd, Suite 1200, Covington, KY 41011 US
(319) 395-0530, *Fax:* (319) 393-0918
www.wmtradio.com
jeffashcraft@clearchannel.com
License: Cedar Rapids, IA held by Citicasters Licenses L.P.
Group Owner: Clear Channel Communications Inc.; (acq 5-4-99; grpsl).
Nat'l Network: CBS
Arbitron Metro Market: Cedar Rapids, IA *Format:* News, News/Talk, 84, Talk *Special Programming:* Farm 19 hrs wkly
Target Audience: 35 plus.
JJ Cook, Operations Dir
Jeff Ashcraft, General Manager
Joni Sojka, General Sales Mgr
Randy Lee, Programming Director
Lisa Pucelik, Promotions Manager
Jeff Schmidt, News Director
Tom Spaight, Chief Engineer
Teisha Welsh,Marketing Director

KKSY-FM
02-14-2008; 96.5 mhz FM; 100 kw; 518 ft.; N42 1 40 W91 38 25
50 East Rivercenter Blvd, Suite 1200, Covington, KY 41011 US
(319) 395-0530, *Fax:* (319) 393-9600
www.965kisscountry.com
License: Cedar Rapids, Jones County, IA held by Citicasters Licenses L.P.
Group Owner: Clear Channel Communications Inc.
Arbitron Metro Market: Cedar Rapids, IA *Format:* Country
JJ Cook, Operations Dir
Jeff Ashcraft, General Manager
Randy Lee, Programming Director
Joni Sojka, Director Of Sales

Centerville

KCOG
03-01-1949; 1400 khz AM *Hrs Open:* 5 AM-midnight; 0.5 kw-D, ND1; 1 kw-N, ND1; N40 44 40 W92 54 32
402 N. 12th Street, Centerville, IA 52544 US
(800) 373-4930
www.kmgo.com
carolyn@kmgo.com
License: Centerville, IA held by KCOG Inc.
Nat'l Network: USA *Regional Network:* Brownfield
Arbitron Metro Market: Centerville, IA *Format:* Adult Contemp
Fred Jenkins, General Manager
Carolyn Jenkins, Sales Manager
Edwin Brand, Programming Director
Russ Ocker, Music Director

KMGO
10-01-1974; 98.7 mhz FM *Hrs Open:* 24; 100 kw; 449 ft.; N40 47 34 W92 52 47
402 N. 12th Street, Centerville, IA 52544 US
(641) 856-3996, *Fax:* (641) 856-3337
www.kmgo.com
kmgofm@lisco.net
License: Centerville, Appanoose County, IA held by KMGO Inc.
Nat'l Network: USA
Format: Country
Larry Stout, Programming Director

Chariton

KEDB
11-15-1979; 105.3 mhz FM *Hrs Open:* 24; 34 kw; 597 ft.; N40 53 23 W93 1 29
C/O Fletcher Heald, 1300 N 17th St, 11th Fl, Arlington, VA 22209 US
(641) 895-7707, *Fax:* (641) 774-8495
www.kedb.fm
brand@kedb.fm
License: Chariton, Lucas County, IA held by Honey Creek Broadcasting LLC
Nat'l Network: Westwood One
Arbitron Metro Market: Chariton, IA *Format:* Adult Contemp
Special Programming: Gosp 5 hrs wkly *Hrs. of News Programming:* news progmg 30 hrs wkly *No. News Employees:* 1 *Target Audience:* 28 plus. *Adv.Rates:* 10; 10; 10; 10
Cindy Spidle, General Sales Mgr
Nick Hoffman, Programming Director
John Johnston, News Director
Fred Jenkins, Engineering Dir
Jill Schull, Local News Editor

Charles City

KCHA
11-01-1949; 1580 khz AM *Hrs Open:* 24; 0.5 kw-D, ND1; 0.01 kw-N, ND1; N43 3 5 W92 40 0
330 East Kilbourn Avenue, Suite 250, Milwaukee, WI 53202 US
(641) 228-1000, *Fax:* (641) 228-1200
www.kchaam.com
KCHA@KCHAAM.com
License: Charles City, IA held by Coloff Media, LLC.
Nat'l Network: ABC News/Talk *Regional Network:* Radio Iowa
Arbitron Metro Market: Charles City - Floyd County, IA *Format:* Adult Contemp *Hrs. of News Programming:* news progmg 7 hrs wkly *No. News Employees:* 1 *Target Audience:* 35 plus.
Jim Coloff, General Manager
Kay Winkelman, General Sales Mgr
Chris Berg, News Director and Program Director
Jeanne Fullard, Account Executive
Tad Barry, Account Executive
Jeanne Fullard, Special Events Coordinator

KCHA-FM
10-01-1971; 95.9 mhz FM *Hrs Open:* 24; 6 kw; 299 ft.; N43 3 5 W92 40 0
330 East Kilbourn Avenue, Suite 250, Milwaukee, WI 53202 US
(641) 228-1000, *Fax:* (641) 228-1200
www.kchafm.com
KCHA@KCHAAM.com
License: Charles City, Floyd County, IA held by Coloff Media, LLC.
Nat'l Network: CNN Radio *Regional Network:* Radio Iowa
Arbitron Metro Market: Charles City - Floyd County, IA *Format:* Adult Contemp *Hrs. of News Programming:* news progmg 7 hrs wkly *No. News Employees:* 1 *Target Audience:* 25-54; adults
Jim Coloff, General Manager
Kay Winkelman, General Sales Mgr
Chris Berg, News Director and Program Director
Jeanne Fullard, Account Executive
Tad Barry, Account Executive
Jeanne Fullard, Special Events Coordinator

Cherokee

KCHE
01-01-1953; 1440 khz AM
201 S. 5th Street, Cherokee, IA 51012 US
(712) 225-2511, *Fax:* (712) 225-2513
www.kcheradio.com
kche1@ncn.net
License: Cherokee, IA held by J & J Radio Corp.
Nat'l Network: ABC *Regional Network:* Radio Iowa
Arbitron Metro Market: Sioux City, IA *Format:* Oldies *Special Programming:* Farm 12 hrs, Sp one hr wkly *Hrs. of News Programming:* news progmg 14 hrs wkly *No. News Employees:* 2 *Target Audience:* 45-80;general *Adv. Rates:* 15; 15; 15; 15
Jeff Fuller, President and Owner
Curt Carlson, Operations Dir
Curt Carlson, General Sales Mgr
Bill Bezoni, Programming Director
Nikki Thunder, News and Promotions Director
Dick Keane, Chief of Operations
Hallie Dessell, TrafficManager
Noel Deering, Computer Tech and Announcer
Keith Crane, Assistant News/ Sport Director
John O'Connor, Sports Director
Andrea McIrvin, Account Executive

KCHE-FM
12-09-1976; 92.1 mhz FM *Hrs Open:* 24; 6 kw; 210 ft.; N42 47 21 W95 33 8
201 South 5th Street, Cherokee, IA 51012 US
(712) 225-2511, *Fax:* (712) 225-2513
www.kcheradio.com
kche1@ncn.net
License: Cherokee, Cherokee County, IA held by J & J Radio Corp.
Nat'l Network: ABC *Regional Network:* Radio Iowa *Nat'l Reps:* Farmakis
Arbitron Metro Market: Cherokee, IA *Format:* Adult Contemp *Hrs. of News Programming:* news progmg 28 hrs wkly *No. News Employees:* 2
Jeff Fuller, President and Owner
Curt Carlson, Operations Dir
Curt Carlson, General Sales Mgr
Bill Bezoni, Programming Director
Nikki Thunder, News and Promotions Director
Dick Keane, Chief of Operations
Hallie Dessell, TrafficManager
Noel Deering, Computer Tech and Announcer
Keith Crane, Assistant News/ Sports Director

RADIO - U.S.

John O'Connor, Sports Director
Andrea McIrvin, Account Executive

Clarinda

KMA-FM

09-25-1990; 99.1 mhz FM *Hrs Open:* 24; 100 kw; 981 ft.; N40 48 4 W94 54 6
209 North Elm Street, Box 960, Shenandoah, IA 51601 US
(712) 246-5270, *Fax:* (712) 246-5275
www.kmaland.com
License: Clarinda, Page County, IA held by KMA Broadcasting L.P.
Nat'l Network: Westwood One; CNN Radio *Wire Services:* AP *Format:* Adult Contemp *Hrs. of News Programming:* news progmg 5 hrs wkly *No. News Employees:* 2 *Target Audience:* 25-44.
Edward May, President
Chuck Morris, Operations Dir
Mark Eno, General Manager
Don Hansen, Station Manager
Sandy Hansen, General Sales Mgr

Clarion

KIAQ

05-18-1964; 96.9 mhz FM *Hrs Open:* 24; 100 kw; 578 ft; N42 40 18 W94 09 11
200 North 10th St., Fort Dodge, IA 50501
(515) 955-5656, *Fax:* (515) 955-5844
www.kiaqfm.com
gbuchanan@threeeagles.com
License: Clarion, Wright County, IA held by Three Eagles of Ft. Dodge Inc.
Group Owner: Three Eagles Communications; (acq 4-22-97; $1,244,117)
Population Served: 304,000*Target Audience:* 25-54.
Rolland Johnson, CEO/COO
Gary Buchanan, President
Jane Morgan, Operations Dir
Greg Wells, General Manager
Barb Dennis, Traffic Manager

Clear Lake

KLKK

02-16-1978; 103.7 mhz FM *Hrs Open:* 24; 25 kw; 328 ft.; N43 7 15 W93 11 36
330 East Kilbourn Avenue, Suite 250, Milwaukee, WI 53202 US
(641) 423-1300, *Fax:* (641) 423-2906
www.klkkfm.com
License: Clear Lake, Cerro Gordo County, IA held by Three Eagles of Lincoln Inc.
Group Owner: Three Eagles Communications; (acq 9-1-2007; grpsl)
Nat'l Reps: Clear Channel
Arbitron Metro Market: Mason City, IA *Format:* Classic Rock *Hrs. of News Programming:* news progmg 42 hrs wkly *No. News Employees:* 1 *Target Audience:* 25-54. *Adv. Rates:* 50; 40; 35; 15
Hal Hofman, General Manager
Drew Kelly, Programming Director
Laurie Gansen, News Director

Clinton

KCLN

12-21-1956; 1390 khz AM *Hrs Open:* 24
P.O. Box 885, Monmouth, IL 61462 US
(563) 243-1390, *Fax:* (563) 242-4567
www.1390kcln.com
kcln@kcln.com
License: Clinton, IA held by WPW Broadcasting Inc.
Group Owner: Prairie Radio Communications; (acq 4-29-99; $800,000 with co-located FM)
Regional Network: Brownfield
Arbitron Metro Market: Davenport, IA *Format:* Big Band *Special Programming:* Farm 10 hrs wkly *Hrs. of News Programming:* news progmg 2 hrs wkly *No. News Employees:* 1 *Target Audience:* 40 plus. *Adv.Rates:* 15; 12; 12; 10.
Don Davis, President
Larry Timpe, General Manager
Chris Streets, Programming Director
Brad Seward, News Director
Aaron Winski, Chief Engineer
Tracie Morgan, Traffic Manager

KMXG

07-01-1974; 96.1 mhz FM *Hrs Open:* 24; 100 kw; 981 ft.; N41 37 58 W90 24 38
1921 Gallows Rd., Suite 850, Vienna, VA 22182 US
(563) 344-7000, *Fax:* (563) 344-7006
www.kmxg.com
License: Clinton, Clinton County, IA held by Citicasters Licenses L.P.
Group Owner: Clear Channel Communications Inc.; (acq 11-15-00; grpsl).
Nat'l Reps: Christal
Arbitron Metro Market: Quad Cities, IA *Format:* Adult Contemp *Special Programming:* Jazz 3 hrs wkly *Hrs. of News Programming:* news progmg 3 hrs wkly *No. News Employees:* 1 *Target Audience:* 25-54; yuppies,baby boomers, upscale professional females *Adv. Rates:* 75; 60; 40; 30
Larry Rosmilso, Operations Dir
Kevin Allensworth, Chief Engineer
Jim O'Hara, Operations Manager

KROS

09-28-1941; 1340 khz AM *Hrs Open:* 5:30 AM-midnight; 1 kw-U, ND1; N41 51 36 W90 12 18
870 13th Ave.N, P.O. Box0518, Clinton, IA 52733 US
(563) 242-1252, *Fax:* (563) 242-4825
www.krosradio.com
contactus@krosradio.com
License: Clinton, IA held by KROS Broadcasting Inc.
Nat'l Network: CNN Radio *Regional Network:* Radio Iowa
Format: Variety/Diverse *Special Programming:* Folk 2 hrs, jazz one hr, blues one hr, gospel one *Hrs. of News Programming:* news progmg 38 hrs wkly *No. News Employees:* 1 *Target Audience:* General; loc audience*Adv. Rates:* 13; 13; 13; 6
Brad Parker, President
Dave Vickers, General Manager
Paul Clark, Programming Director
Dave Vickers, News Director
Tom Messerli, Engineering Dir
Gary Determan, Sports Director

KMCN

12-07-1970; 94.7 mhz FM *Hrs Open:* 24; 3 kw; 328 ft.; N41 54 34 W90 13 28
P.O. Box 885, Monmouth, IL 61462 US
(563) 243-1390, *Fax:* (563) 242-4567
www.947mac.com/
kcln@kcln.com
License: Clinton, Clinton County, IA held by WPW Broadcasting Inc.
Group Owner: Prairie Radio Communications
Arbitron Metro Market: Clinton, IA *Format:* Adult Contemp *Hrs. of News Programming:* news progmg one hr wkly *No. News Employees:* 1 *Target Audience:* 25-54. *Adv. Rates:* 17; 15; 15; 10
Terry Bond, CEO

Council Bluffs

*KIWR

11-23-1981; 89.7 mhz FM *Hrs Open:* 24; 100 kw; 1070 ft.; N41 18 40 W96 1 37
2700 College Road, Council Bluffs, IA 51503 US
(712) 325-3254, *Fax:* (712) 325-3391
www.897theriver.com
sjohn@iwcc.edu
License: Council Bluffs, Pottawattamie County, IA held by Iowa Western Community College.
Arbitron Metro Market: Omaha-Council Bluffs, NE-IA *Format:* Alternative *Special Programming:* Var/div 16 hrs wkly *Hrs. of News Programming:* News progmg 5 hrs wkly *Target Audience:* 18-34; well-educated, upper &middle-upper income *Adv. Rates:* 25; 25; 25; 15
Tom Johnson, CFO
Dan Kinney, President
Sophia John, General Manager

KLNG

01-01-1947; 1560 khz AM *Hrs Open:* 6 AM-sunset
P. O. Box 444, Spartanburg, SC 29304 US
(712) 323-0100, *Fax:* (712) 323-0022
www.wilkinsradio.com
klgn@wilkinsradio.com
License: Council Bluffs, IA held by Wilkins Communications Network Inc.
Group Owner: Wilkins Communications Network Inc.; (acq 4-89; $250,000).
Nat'l Network: Salem Radio Network
Arbitron Metro Market: Omaha, IA *Format:* Christian, Talk *Special Programming:* Sp 10 hrs, Black 6 hrs wkly *Target Audience:* 35 plus. *Adv. Rates:* 35; 35; 35; 35
Bob Wilkins, President
Mitchell Mathis, Operations Dir
Charles Yates, Station Manager
John Bible, Engineering Dir
LuAnn Wilkins, Executive Vice President
Greg Garrett

KQKQ-FM

01-01-1969; 98.5 mhz FM; 100 kw; 1102 ft.; N41 18 25 W96 1 37
1001 Farnam-On-The-Mall, Omaha, NE 68102 US
(402) 342-2000, *Fax:* (402) 346-5748
www.q985fm.com
info@q985fm.com
License: Council Bluffs, Pottawattamie County, IA held by Waitt Omaha LLC.
Group Owner: Waitt Omaha LLC; (acq 1-7-2002; grpsl)
Arbitron Metro Market: Omaha-Council Bluffs, NE-IA *Format:* Adult Contemp *Target Audience:* 18-44.
Mary Quass, CEO
Jim McKernan, General Manager
Rhonda Gerrard, General Sales Mgr
Mark Todd, Programming Director
Brandon Pappas, Promotions Manager
Lori Storz, News Director
Chuck DuCoty, COO
Sam Coughlin, General SalesManager
Nevin Dane, Programming Director

Cresco

KCZQ

04-01-1991; 102.3 mhz FM; 3 kw; 328 ft.; N43 25 47 W92 9 49
116 1st Avenue West, Cresco, IA 52136 US
(563) 547-1000(563) 547-3366, *Fax:* (563) 547-2200
superc@iowatelecom.net
License: Cresco, Howard County, IA held by Mega Media Ltd.
Nat'l Reps: Farmakis *Wire Services:* Agence France-Presse (AFP)
Format: Adult Contemp *Special Programming:* Farm 12 hrs wkly *Target Audience:* General.
James Hebel, President
Debra Lowe, Operations Dir
Jim Bernard, Programming Director
Stan McHenry, Music Director

Creston

KSIB

12-07-1946; 1520 khz AM; 1 kw-D, NDD; N41 2 16 W94 23 38
P.O. Box 426, Creston, IA 50801 US
(641) 782-2155, *Fax:* (641) 782-6963
www.ksibradio.com
License: Creston, IA held by G.O. Radio Ltd.
Nat'l Network: ABC *Regional Network:* Brownfield
Arbitron Metro Market: Creston, IA *Format:* Country *Target Audience:* General.
Dave Rieck, President
Chad Rieck, General Manager
Chad Riek, General Sales Mgr
Ben Walter, Programming Director
Terri Queck-Matzie, News Director
Charlie Maley, Chief Engineer

KSIB-FM

03-01-1966; 101.3 mhz FM *Hrs Open:* 24; 19 kw; 364 ft.; N41 5 41 W94 22 30
P.O. Box 426, Creston, IA 50801 US
(641) 782-2155, *Fax:* (641) 782-6963
www.ksibradio.com
License: Creston, Union County, IA
Regional Network: Brownfield
Arbitron Metro Market: Creston, IA *Format:* Country *Target Audience:* General.
Adam Glenville, Operations Dir
Chad Rieck, General Manager
Kim Tate, Programming Director
Terri Queck-Matzie, News Director
Steve Sandlin, Chief Engineer
Joey Jeffery, Traffic Manager

*KLOX

01-01-2005; 90.9 mhz FM; 0 kw horiz, 4 kw vert; 335 ft.; N41 4 29 W94 22 35
505 Josephine St, Titusville, FL 32796 US
(321) 267-3000, *Fax:* (321) 264-9370
noncomradio.net
wpio@gate.net
License: Creston, Union County, IA held by Florida Public Radio Inc.
Arbitron Metro Market: Titusville, FL *Format:* Adult Contemp, Christian
Randy Henry, President
Archie Shetler, Executive Vice President

Davenport

*KALA
11-04-1967; 88.5 mhz FM *Hrs Open:* 24; 10 kw horiz, 9.33 kw vert; 323 ft.; N41 35 43.8 W90 40 43.7
518 W. Locust St., Davenport, IA 52803 US
(563) 333-6219, *Fax:* (563) 333-6218
web.sau.edu/kala
kala@sau.edu
License: Davenport, Scott County, IA held by St. Ambrose University.
Arbitron Metro Market: Davenport, IA *Format:* Jazz *Special Programming:* Sp 15 hrs, gospel 13 hrs wkly *Hrs. of News Programming:* news progmg 34.5 hrs wkly *No. News Employees:* 1 *Target Audience:* General.
David Baker, Operations Dir

KCQQ
09-01-1996; 106.5 mhz FM *Hrs Open:* 24; 100 kw; 896 ft.; N41 37 58 W90 24 38
Suite 850, 1921 Gallows Road, Vienna, VA 22182 US
(563) 344-7000, *Fax:* (563) 359-8524
www.kcqq106.com
bospates@clearchannel.com
License: Davenport, Scott County, IA held by Citicasters Licenses L.P.
Group Owner: Clear Channel Communications Inc.; (acq 11-15-00; grpsl).
Arbitron Metro Market: Quad Cities, IA-IL (Davenport-Rock Island-Moline) *Format:* Classic Rock *Special Programming:* Relg one hr wkly *Hrs. of News Programming:* news progmg 2 hrs wkly *No. News Employees:* 1*Target Audience:* 25-54. *Adv. Rates:* 125; 90; 60; 30
Gordon Ehler, General Sales Mgr

KJOC
01-01-1947; 1170 khz AM *Hrs Open:* 24; 1 kw-D, DA2; 1 kw-N, DA2; N41 23 21 W90 31 0
136 Main Street, West Port, CT 06880 US
(563) 326-2541, *Fax:* (563) 326-1819
www.kjoc.com
License: Davenport, IA held by Cumulus Licensing Corp.
Group Owner: Cumulus Media Inc.; (acq 3-15-2000; grpsl)
Nat'l Network: CBS
Arbitron Metro Market: Quad Cities, IA-IL (Davenport-Rock Island-Moline) *Format:* Oldies *Target Audience:* 18-49.
Jack Swart, General Manager

WLLR-FM
10-01-1948; 103.7 mhz FM *Hrs Open:* 24; 91 kw; 1191 ft.; N41 32 49 W90 28 35
1921 Gallows Rd., Suite 850, Vienna, VA 22182 US
(563) 359-9557, *Fax:* (563) 344-7016
www.wllr.com
jimohara@clearchannel.com
License: Davenport, Scott County, IA held by Citicasters Licenses L.P.
Group Owner: Clear Channel Communications Inc.
Arbitron Metro Market: Quad Cities, IA *Format:* Country *Hrs. of News Programming:* News progmg 2 hrs wkly *Target Audience:* 25-54.
Mike Weindruch, General Sales Mgr
Jim O'Hara, Programming Director
Carrie Clearman, Promotions Manager
Lorraine Meier, News Director
Kevin Allensworth, Engineering Dir

WOC
02-01-1922; 1420 khz AM; 5 kw-D, DA2; 5 kw-N, DA2; N41 33 0 W90 28 37
1921 Gallows Road, Suite 850, Vienna, VA 22182 US
(563) 344-7000, *Fax:* (563) 344-7065
www.woc1420.com
dankennedy@clearchannel.com
License: Davenport, IA held by Citicasters Licenses L.P.
Group Owner: Clear Channel Communications Inc.; (acq 11-15-2000; grpsl).
Regional Network: Ill. Radio Net.; Radio Iowa *Nat'l Reps:* Christal
Arbitron Metro Market: Quad Cities, IA *TV Affiliate:* Talk *Format:* Agriculture, Variety/Diverse *Hrs. of News Programming:* 5 *No. News Employees:* 35-64; info-oriented adul
Program Director, Programming Director

De Witt

KBOB-FM
01-12-1977; 104.9 mhz FM *Hrs Open:* 24; 12.5 kw; 469 ft.; N41 43 11 W90 34 13
136 Main Street, Westport, CT 06880 US
(563) 326-2541, *Fax:* (563) 326-1819
www.rock1049.net
License: De Witt, Clinton County, IA held by Cumulus Licensing Corp.
Group Owner: Cumulus Media Inc.; (acq 10-2-2000; grpsl)
Arbitron Metro Market: Quad Cities, IA *Format:* Rock/AOR
Jack Swart, General Manager
Julie Derrer, General Sales Mgr
Ryan Chase, Programming Director
Deanna Flynn, News Director
Andy Andresen, Chief Engineer

Decorah

KDEC
05-01-1947; 1240 khz AM *Hrs Open:* 5 AM-10 PM (M-F); 1 kw-U; N43 19 26 W91 47 04
Mailing Address: Box 27, Decorah, IA 52101
Second Address: 110 Highland Dr., Decorah, IA 52101
(563) 382-4251, *Fax:* (563) 382-9540
www.kdecradio.com
kdec@kdecradio.com
License: Decorah, Winneshiek County, IA held by Decorah Broadcasting Inc.
Nat'l Network: Westwood One *Nat'l Reps:* Farmakis
Population Served: 40,000*Hrs. of News Programming:* news progmg 12 hrs wkly *No. News Employees:* 2 *Target Audience:* 35 plus. *Adv. Rates:* 7; 6; 6.50; 4.
Bob Holtan, President
Bob Holtan, General Manager
Jeni Grouws, Station Manager
Jeni Grouwes, Promotions Manager
Darin Svenson, News Director
Eric Papenfuss, Chief Engineer

KDEC-FM
09-02-1986; 100.5 mhz FM *Hrs Open:* 24; 30 kw; Ant 420 ft; N43 19 26 W91 47 04
Mailing Address: Box 27, Decorah, IA 52101
Second Address: 110 Highland Dr., Decorah, IA 52101
(563) 382-4251, *Fax:* (563) 382-9540
www.kdecradio.com
kdec@kdecradio.com
License: Decorah, Winneshiek County, IA held by Decorah Broadcasting Inc.
Population Served: 100,000*Hrs. of News Programming:* news progmg 3 hrs wkly *No. News Employees:* 2 *Target Audience:* 18-54. *Adv. Rates:* 16; 12; 13; 5.50
Bob Holtan, President
Colleen Holtan, Operations Dir
Bob Holtan, General Manager
Jeni Grouws, Station Manager
Jeni Grouws, Programming Director
Darin Svenson, Promotions Manager
Eric Papenfuss, Chief Engineer

*KLCD
07-15-1977; 89.5 mhz FM; 0.1 kw; 180 ft.; N43 18 56 W91 47 18
45 East Seventh St., Saint Paul, MN 55101 US
(507) 282-0910, *Fax:* (507) 282-2107
www.mpr.org
mail@mpr.org
License: Decorah, Winneshiek County, IA held by Minnesota Public Radio Inc.
Nat'l Network: NPR; PRI
Format: Talk *No. News Employees:* 1
John McTaggard, Chairman
Chris Cross, General Manager
Jim McGuinn, Station Manager
Mary Stapek, General Sales Mgr
Timothy Roesler, General Manager of Classical Music
Sea Stachura, News Director
Chris Worthington, ManagingDirector of News

*KLNI
01-01-1993; 88.7 mhz FM *Hrs Open:* 24; 0.1 kw; -36 ft.; N43 18 35 W91 48 30
45 East 7th Street, Saint Paul, MN 55101 US
(507) 282-0910, *Fax:* (507) 282-2107
www.mpr.org
mail@mpr.org
License: Decorah, Winneshiek County, IA held by Minnesota Public Radio
Nat'l Network: NPR
Format: News *No. News Employees:* 1
Chris Cross, General Manager
Mary Stapek, General Sales Mgr
Sea Stachura, News Director

*KWLC
12-01-1926; 1240 khz AM
700 College Drive, Decorah, IA 52101 US
(563) 387-1240, *Fax:* (563) 387-1489
kwlc.luther.edu
kwlcam@luther.edu
License: Decorah, IA held by Luther College.
Arbitron Metro Market: Decorah, IA *Format:* Variety/Diverse
Target Audience: General.
Rhonda Benson-Leach, General Manager
Cindy Ezemack, General Sales Mgr
Kenny Carter, Chief Engineer

Denison

KDSN
04-11-1956; 1530 khz AM *Hrs Open:* 6am-10pm
Mailing Address: P.O. Box 670, Denison, IA 51442 US
Second Address: 1530 Ridge Rd., Denison, IA 51442
(712) 263-3141, *Fax:* (712) 263-2088
www.kdsnradio.com
info@kdsnradio.com
License: Denison, IA held by M & J Radio Corp.
Nat'l Network: ABC *Regional Network:* Radio Iowa *Nat'l Reps:* Farmakis
Arbitron Metro Market: Denison, IA *Format:* Adult Contemp, Country *Special Programming:* Farm 12 hrs, polka 4 hrs, Sp 3 hrs wkly *Hrs. of News Programming:* news progmg 8 hrs wkly *No. News Employees:* 1 *TargetAudience:* General. *Adv. Rates:* 30; 30; 30; 30
Michael Dudding, President
Michael J. Dudding, General Sales Mgr
Deb Nelson, Promotions Manager
Mike Earl, News Director
Phyllis Rohlin, Executive Vice President

KDSN-FM
08-01-1968; 107.1 mhz FM *Hrs Open:* 24; 6 kw; 302 ft.; N42 2 10 W95 19 44
Mailing Address: PO Box 670, Denison, IA 51442 US
Second Address: 1530 Ridge Rd., Denison, IA 51442
(712) 263-3141, *Fax:* (712) 263-2088
www.kdsnradio.com
info@kdsnradio.com
License: Denison, Crawford County, IA held by M & J Radio Corp.
Nat'l Network: ABC *Nat'l Reps:* Farmakis
Arbitron Metro Market: Denison, IA *Format:* Adult Contemp *Hrs. of News Programming:* news progmg 8 hrs wkly *No. News Employees:* 1 *Target Audience:* 21-65 *Adv. Rates:* Same as AM
Deb Nelson, General Manager
Michael J. Dudding, General Sales Mgr
Tom Hamilton, Programming Director
Deb Nelson, Promotions Manager
Mike Earl, News Director
Dick Keane, Engineering Dir
Brian Schmid, Farm Director
Kathy Dudding,Office Manager
Randy Grossman, Sports Commentator
Markita Mujica, Traffic Manager

Des Moines

KBGG
01-01-1998; 1700 khz AM *Hrs Open:* 24; 10 kw-D, ND2; 1 kw-N, ND2; N41 35 30 W93 31 43
2 Newton Executive Park, Newton, MA 02162 US
(515) 331-9200, *Fax:* (515) 331-9292
www.1700thechamp.com
License: Des Moines, IA
Group Owner: Cumulus Media Inc.; (acq 8-29-2003; grpsl)
Nat'l Network: ESPN Radio *Nat'l Reps:* Christal *Wire Services:* UPI
Arbitron Metro Market: Urbandale, IA *Format:* Sports
Terry Peters, Operations Dir
Doug Wood, General Sales Mgr
Jack O'Brien, Operations Manager

*KDFR
03-24-1989; 91.3 mhz FM *Hrs Open:* 24; 32 kw; 446 ft.; N41 36 59 W93 31 36
Mailing Address: 4135 Northgate Blvd #1, Sacramento, CA 95834 US
Second Address: 2350 N.E. 44th Ct., Des Moines, IA 50317
(515) 262-0449
www.familyradio.com
kdfr@familyradio.org
License: Des Moines, Polk County, IA held by Family Stations Inc.
Group Owner: Family Stations Inc.
Arbitron Metro Market: Des Moines, IA *Format:* Religious *Special Programming:* Class 2 hrs wkly *Hrs. of News Programming:*

news progmg 6 hrs wkly *No. News Employees:* 1 *Target Audience:* 25 plus; general
Harold Camping, President
Larry Vavroch, Operations Dir
Mike Destefano, Regional Manager

KXNO
07-21-1921; 1460 khz AM *Hrs Open:* 24; 5 kw-D, DAN; 5 kw-N, DAN; N41 38 45 W93 32 12
600 Congress Avenue, Suite 1400, Austin, TX 78701 US
(515) 245-8900, *Fax:* (515) 245-8906
www.kxno.com
kxno@clearchannel.com
License: Des Moines, IA held by Capstar TX L.P.
Group Owner: Clear Channel Communications Inc.; (acq 8-30-2000; grpsl)
Nat'l Network: Fox Sports
Arbitron Metro Market: Des Moines, IA *Format:* Sports *Target Audience:* 35 plus; 25-54 Male
Geoff Conn, Operations Dir
Joel McCrea, General Manager
Matt Gillon, General Sales Mgr
Van Harden, Programming Director
Jim Boyd, News Director
Raleigh Rubenking, Chief Engineer
Molly Pins, Special Events Coordinator
JulieTraver, Traffic Manager

KGGO
05-31-1964; 94.9 mhz FM *Hrs Open:* 24; 100 kw; 325 meters; N41 37 55 W93 27 27
4143 109th St., Urbandale, IA 78701
(515) 331-9200, *Fax:* (515) 312-9292
www.kggo.com
louspolt@ctcomm.com
License: Des Moines, Polk County, IA
Group Owner: Cumulus Media Inc.; (acq 8-29-03; grpsl).
Nat'l Reps: Christal
Arbitron Metro Market: Des Moines, IA *Special Programming:* Racing 2 hrs wkly
Jack O'Brien, Operations Dir
Doug Wood, General Sales Mgr
Terry Peters, Promotions Manager

KHKI
07-04-1964; 97.3 mhz FM *Hrs Open:* 24; 105 kw; Ant 469 ft; N41 39 46 W93 45 24
4143 109th St., Urbandale, IA 78701
(515) 331-9200, *Fax:* (515) 331-9292
www.973thehawk.com
License: Des Moines, Polk County, IA
Group Owner: Cumulus Media Inc.; (acq 8-29-03; grpsl).
Nat'l Reps: Christal
Population Served: 400,000 *Arbitron Metro Market:* Des Moines, IA *Target Audience:* 18-49.
Jack O'Brien, Operations Dir
Doug Wood, General Sales Mgr
Terry Peters, Promotions Manager

KIOA
09-18-1964; 93.3 mhz FM *Hrs Open:* 24; 82 kw; 1066 ft.; N41 37 55 W93 27 26
73 Kercheval Avenue, Grosse Pointe Farms, MI 48236 US
(515) 280-1350, *Fax:* (515) 280-3011
www.kioa.com
License: Des Moines, Polk County, IA held by Saga Communications of Iowa LLC
Group Owner: Saga Communications Inc.; (acq 4-19-93; $2.7 million with co-located AM;
Arbitron Metro Market: Des Moines, IA *Format:* Oldies *Target Audience:* 25-54.
Jeff Delvaux, General Manager
Pam Washington, General Sales Mgr
Tim Fox, Programming Director
Lindsay Reinert, Promotions Manager
Jay Wells, News Director
Joe Farrington, Chief Engineer
Sarah Levere, Advertising Manager
Lee AnnRose, Traffic Manager

***KJMC**
05-01-1999; 89.3 mhz FM *Hrs Open:* 24; 7.1 kw; 200 ft.; N41 39 21 W93 35 51
1509 Forest Ave., Des Moines, IA 50314 US
(515) 279-1811, *Fax:* (515) 279-1802
io@kjmcfm.com
License: Des Moines, Polk County, IA held by Minority Communications Inc.
Nat'l Network: ABC
Arbitron Metro Market: Des Moines, IA *Format:* Jazz, Oldies
Larry Neville, Operations Dir
Larry Rollins, General Manager
John Farington, Chief of Operations

KKDM
08-22-1995; 107.5 mhz FM *Hrs Open:* 24; 100 kw; 722 ft.; N41 38 38 W93 17 20
200 Concord Plaza, Suite 600, San Antonio, TX 78216 US
(515) 245-8900, *Fax:* (515) 245-8906
www.kiss1075.com
kxno@clearchannel.com
License: Des Moines, Polk County, IA held by Clear Channel Broadcasting Licenses Inc.
Group Owner: Clear Channel Communications Inc.; (acq 9-1-99; $7.35 million)
Nat'l Reps: Clear Channel
Arbitron Metro Market: Des Moines, IA *Format:* Contemporary Hits/Top 40 *Target Audience:* 18-49.
Joel McCrea, General Manager
Matt Gillon, General Sales Mgr
Greg Chance, Programming Director
Daphne Haselhuhn, Promotions Manager
Jay Thomas, Music Director

KDRB
02-01-1948; 100.3 mhz FM *Hrs Open:* 24; 100 kw; 1795 ft.; N41 49 48 W93 36 54
50 East Rivercenter Blvd, Suite 1200, Covington, KY 41011 US
(515) 245-8900, *Fax:* (515) 245-8902
www.thebusfm.com
johnmckeighan@clearchannel.com
License: Des Moines, Polk County, IA held by Citicasters Licenses L.P.
Group Owner: Clear Channel Communications Inc.
Nat'l Reps: Clear Channel *Wire Services:* AP
Arbitron Metro Market: Des Moines, IA *Format:* Variety/Diverse *Target Audience:* 25-54.
Matt Gillon, General Sales Mgr
Jim Boyd, Programming Director
Joel McCrea, Promotions Manager
John McKeighan, Programming Director

KRNT
03-17-1935; 1350 khz AM *Hrs Open:* 24; 5 kw-D, DAN; 5 kw-N, DAN; N41 33 31 W93 34 45
1416 Locust Street, Des Moines, IA 50309 US
(515) 280-1350, *Fax:* (515) 280-3011
www.1350krnt.com
jbrown@desmoinesradiogroup.com
License: Des Moines, IA held by Saga Communications of Iowa LLC
Group Owner: Saga Communications Inc.
Nat'l Network: CBS *Nat'l Reps:* Katz Radio *Wire Services:* AP
Arbitron Metro Market: Des Moines, IA *Format:* Adult Contemp *Target Audience:* 50 plus.
Jeff Delvaux, General Manager
Pam Washington, General Sales Mgr
Jim Brown, Programming Director
Marianne Coppock, Promotions Manager

KSTZ
01-01-1970; 102.5 mhz FM *Hrs Open:* 24; 92 kw; 1260 ft.; N41 48 1 W93 36 27
1416 Locust Street, Des Moines, IA 50309 US
(515) 280-1350, *Fax:* (515) 280-3011
www.star1025.com
sallen@desmoinesradiogroup.com
License: Des Moines, Polk County, IA held by Saga Communications of Iowa LLC
Group Owner: Saga Communications Inc.; (acq 8-88; $3.2 million with co-located AM;
Nat'l Network: CNN Radio *Nat'l Reps:* Katz Radio *Wire Services:* AP
Arbitron Metro Market: Des Moines, IA *Format:* Adult Contemp *Target Audience:* 25-54; emphasis on upscale women
Scott Allen, Operations Dir
Jeff Delvaux, General Manager
Pam Washington, General Sales Mgr
Marianne Coppock, Promotions Manager
Dan Abbuehl, Advertising Manager

KWKY
02-02-1948; 1150 khz AM *Hrs Open:* 24
Mailing Address: 50 East Rivercenter Blvd, Suite 1200, Covington, KY 41011 US
Second Address: 6626 Dubuqe Trail, Norwalk, IA 50211
(515) 223-1150, *Fax:* (515) 981-0840
www.kwky.com
info@kwky.com
License: Des Moines, IA held by Putbrese Communications Ltd.
Nat'l Network: EWTN Radio
Arbitron Metro Market: Norwalk, IA *Format:* Sports, Talk, 20
John Putbrese, President
Matthew Phelps, Operations Dir
Charles Putbrese, General Manager
Dennis Ray, Programming Director
Jon Farrington, Chief Engineer

KPSZ
04-01-1947; 940 khz AM *Hrs Open:* 24; 10 kw-D, DA2; 5 kw-N, DA2; N41 28 35 W93 22 26
1416 Locust Street, Des Moines, IA 50309 US
(515) 280-1350, *Fax:* (515) 280-3011
www.praise940.com
jbrown@desmoinesradiogroup.com
License: Des Moines, IA held by Saga Communications of Iowa LLC
Group Owner: Saga Communications Inc.
Nat'l Network: Salem Radio Network *Nat'l Reps:* Katz Radio *Wire Services:* AP
Arbitron Metro Market: Des Moines, IA *Format:* Christian *Target Audience:* Adult; adult christian, music and program format
Jeff Delvaux, General Manager
Pam Washington, General Sales Mgr
Jim Brown, Programming Director
Pam Washington, Sales Manager
Mark McDowell, Program Coordinator
Shelly Rusch, Account Executive
Mary Sayre, Account Executive
Apiram Raengpradub

WHO
04-10-1924; 1040 khz AM *Hrs Open:* 24
50 East Rivercenter Blvd, Suite 1200, Covington, KY 41011 US
(515) 245-8900, *Fax:* (515) 245-8902
www.whoradio.com
vanharden@clearchannel.com
License: Des Moines, IA held by Citicasters Licenses L.P.
Group Owner: Clear Channel Communications Inc.; (acq 5-4-99; grpsl)
Nat'l Network: Fox News Radio *Nat'l Reps:* Clear Channel *Wire Services:* AP
Arbitron Metro Market: Des Moines, IA *Format:* News, News/Talk, 86 *Special Programming:* Farm 15 hrs wkly *No. News Employees:* 7 *Target Audience:* Adults 25-54
Bonnie Lucas, Operations Dir
Mary Greig, General Sales Mgr
Van Harden, Programming Director
Greg Chance, Promotions Manager
Jim Boyd, News Director
Raleigh RubenKing, Chief Engineer
Joel McCrea, Market Manager
Jim Zabel, SportsDirector
Julie Traver, Traffic Manager
Joel McCrea, Vice President

Dubuque

KATF
06-25-1967; 92.9 mhz FM *Hrs Open:* 24; 89.7 kw; 1014 ft.; N42 31 44 W90 36 58
Mailing Address: 7601 Ganser Wy, Madison, WI 53719 US
Second Address: 346 W. 8th St., Dubuque, IA 52001
(563) 690-0929
www.katfm.com
License: Dubuque, Dubuque County, IA held by Radio Dubuque Inc.
Group Owner: Radio Dubuque Inc.
Wire Services: NWS (National Weather Service)
Arbitron Metro Market: Dubuque, IA *Format:* Adult Contemp *Hrs. of News Programming:* News progmg 3 hrs wkly *Target Audience:* 25-54; adults establishing families, careers & households
Thomas Parsley, General Manager

KDTH
05-04-1941; 1370 khz AM *Hrs Open:* 24; 5 kw-D, DAN; 5 kw-N, DAN; N42 29 6 W90 38 39
Mailing Address: 7601 Ganser Wy, Madison, WI 53719 US
Second Address: 346 W. 8th St., Dubuque, IA 52001
(563) 690-0800, *Fax:* (563) 690-0858
www.kdth.com
kdth@kdth.com
License: Dubuque, IA held by Radio Dubuque Inc.
Group Owner: Radio Dubuque Inc.; (acq 7-1-2000; $3.68 million with co-located FM)
Nat'l Network: CBS *Nat'l Reps:* Katz Radio *Wire Services:* NWS (National Weather Service)
Arbitron Metro Market: Dubuque, IA *Format:* Variety/Diverse *Special Programming:* Farm 17 hrs wkly *Hrs. of News Programming:* news progmg 25 hrs wkly *No. News Employees:*

3 *Target Audience:* 35 plus;responsible adults with established careers & households
Thomas Parsley, Station Manager
Perry Mason, General Sales Mgr
Michael Kaye, Programming Director
Ed Anderson, News Director

KLYV
09-01-1965; 105.3 mhz FM; 50 kw; 330 ft; N42 30 10 W90 42 11
5490 Saratoga Rd., Dubuque, IA 53202
(563) 557-1040, *Fax:* (319) 583-4535
www.y105online.com
License: Dubuque, Dubuque County, IA held by Cumulus Licensing LLC
Group Owner: Cumulus Media Inc.
Population Served: 130,000 *Arbitron Metro Market:* Dubuque, IA *Target Audience:* 18-49.
Scott Thomas, Programming Director

KXGE
03-08-1980; 102.3 mhz FM *Hrs Open:* 24; 2 kw; 308 ft.; N42 35 7 W90 38 50
111 East Kilbourn Avenue, Suite 2700, Milwaukee, WI 53202 US
(563) 557-1040, *Fax:* (563) 583-4535
www.eagle102rocks.com
info@kxge.com
License: Dubuque, Dubuque County, IA held by Cumulus Licensing Corp.
Group Owner: Cumulus Media Inc.; (acq 12-17-98; grpsl)
Nat'l Network: ABC
Arbitron Metro Market: Dubuque, IA *Format:* Classic Rock *Hrs. of News Programming:* news progmg 2 hrs wkly *No. News Employees:* 1 *Target Audience:* 18-49; in high school or college in the 60s & 70s
Dan Sullivan, General Manager
Doris Garius, General Sales Mgr
Scott Thomas, Programming Director
Tom Berryman, News Director

WDBQ
10-30-1933; 1490 khz AM; 1 kw-U, ND1; N42 30 10 W90 42 24
111 East Kilbourn Avenue, Suite 2700, Milwaukee, WI 53202 US
(563) 557-1040, *Fax:* (563) 583-4535
www.wdbqam.com
heather.davis@cumulus.com
License: Dubuque, IA held by Cumulus Licensing Corp.
Group Owner: Cumulus Media Inc.; (acq 12-17-98; grpsl)
Nat'l Network: ABC; Westwood One
Arbitron Metro Market: Dubuque, IA *Format:* News, Sports, 86
Jack Kilcoyne, Programming Director
Mike Field, Disc Jockey
Alan Williams, Traffic Manager

***KNSY(FM)**
01-01-2005; 89.7 mhz FM; 530 w horiz, 2.6 kw vert; Ant 646 ft; N42 36 18 W90 47 57 *Rebroadcasts:* Rebroadcasts KUNI(FM) Cedar Falls 100%
324 Communications Arts Center, Univ. of Northern Iowa, Cedar Falls, IA 50614
(319) 273-6400, *Fax:* (319) 273-2682
www.kuniradio.org
kuni@uni.edu
License: Dubuque, Dubuque County, IA held by University of Northern Iowa.
Arbitron Metro Market: Dubuque, IA *Special Programming:* Blues 5 hrs, folk 4 hrs wkly *Hrs. of News Programming:* news progmg 77 hours *No. News Employees:* 3
Wayne Jarvis, General Manager
Scott Vezdos, Promotions Manager
Greg Shanley, News Director
Steve Schoon, Chief Engineer
Al Shares, Music Director

***KIAD**
01-01-2006; 88.5 mhz FM; 0.75 kw vert; 518 ft.; N42 24 16 W90 34 12 *Rebroadcasts:* Rebroadcasts WAFR(FM) Tupelo, MS 100%
P O Drwaer 2440, Tupelo, MS 38803 US
(662) 844-8888, *Fax:* (662) 842-6791
www.afr.net
faq@afr.net
License: Dubuque, Dubuque County, IA held by American Family Association.
Group Owner: American Family Radio
Arbitron Metro Market: Dubuque, IA *Format:* Christian
Marvin Sanders, General Manager

Dunkerton

KCOO
103.9 mhz FM; 6 kw; 312 ft.; N42 42 23.9 W92 13 3.7 US
(512) 329-5843, *Fax:* (512) 329-5847
www.matineemedia.com
License: Dunkerton, Black Hawk County, IA held by Ace Radio Corp.
Group Owner: Ace Radio Corp.
Arbitron Metro Market: Dunkerton, IA
Stephen Hackerman, President

Dyersville

KDST
08-25-1985; 99.3 mhz FM *Hrs Open:* 24; 3 kw; 299 ft.; N42 25 43 W91 12 50
1931 20th Ave S.E., 600 N. Marquette Rd, Dyersville, IA 53821 US
(563) 875-8193, *Fax:* (563) 875-6001
www.realcountryonline.com
kdst993@iowatelecom.net
License: Dyersville, Dubuque County, IA held by Design Homes Inc.
Nat'l Network: ABC *Regional Network:* Brownfield
Arbitron Metro Market: Dubuque, IA *Format:* Country *Special Programming:* Farm *No. News Employees:* 1 *Target Audience:* 45-60. *Adv. Rates:* 19; 16.50; 16.50; 14.50
Randy Weeks, CEO
Franklin Weeks, President
Doug Langston, Operations Dir
Randy Weeks, General Manager
Doug Langston, Station Manager
Matt Monahan, News Director

Eagle Grove

***KJYL**
02-20-1994; 100.7 mhz FM *Hrs Open:* 24; 25 kw; 328 ft.; N42 39 18 W93 59 24
P.O. Box 72, County Rd 6, Blue Earth, MN 56013 US
(515) 448-4588, *Fax:* (515) 448-5267
www.kjyl.org
License: Eagle Grove, Wright County, IA held by Minn-Iowa Christian Broadcasting Inc.
Group Owner: Minn-Iowa Christian Broadcasting Inc.
Format: Christian *No. News Employees:* 1 *Target Audience:* 30-55.
Jay Rudolph, Operations Dir
Matt Dorfner, General Manager
Mark Bohnett, Chief Engineer

Eddyville

KKSI
07-30-1990; 101.5 mhz FM *Hrs Open:* 24; 49 kw; 499 ft.; N41 7 57 W92 42 12
416 East Main, Ottumwa, IA 52501 US
(641) 684-5563, *Fax:* (641) 684-5832
www.kssclassickrock.com
mail@ottumwaradio.com
License: Eddyville, Wapello County, IA held by O-Town Communications Inc.
Group Owner: O-Town Communications Inc.; (acq 12-10-99; $162,400)
Arbitron Metro Market: Des Moines, IA *Format:* Classic Rock *Hrs. of News Programming:* news progmg 4 hrs wkly *No. News Employees:* 2 *Target Audience:* 25-54. *Adv. Rates:* 29.68;29.68;29.68;27.68
Greg List, President
Bruce Linder, Operations Dir
Mike Buchanan, News Director
Jeff Downing, Operations Director

Eldon

KRKN
01-01-1996; 104.3 mhz FM *Hrs Open:* 24; 23.5 kw; 341 ft.; N40 52 6 W92 18 20
P.O. Box 1420, Mankato, MN 56001 US
(641) 684-5563, *Fax:* (641) 684-5832
www.ottumwaradio.com
mail@ottumwaradio.com
License: Eldon, Wapello County, IA held by O-Town Communications Inc.
Group Owner: O-Town Communications Inc.; (acq 12-10-99; $162,400).
Arbitron Metro Market: Ottumwa *Format:* Country *Hrs. of News Programming:* news progmg 4 hrs wkly *No. News Employees:* 2 *Target Audience:* 18-54. *Adv. Rates:* 29.68; 29.68; 29.68; 27.68
Greg List, President
Bruce Linder, Operations Dir
Mike Buchanan, News Director
Jeff Downing, Operations Manager

Eldora

KDAO-FM
06-01-1992; 99.5 mhz FM *Hrs Open:* 24; 3 kw; 328 ft.; N42 15 49 W93 3 57
Mailing Address: P.O. Box 538, Marshalltown, IA 50158 US
Second Address: 1930 N. Center St., Marshalltown, IA 50158
(641) 752-4122, *Fax:* (641) 752-5121
www.kdao.com
kdao@kdao.com
License: Eldora, Hardin County, IA held by Eldora Broadcasting Co. Inc.
Nat'l Network: Fox News Radio
Arbitron Metro Market: Marshaltown, IA *Format:* Adult Contemp
Target Audience: 25-54.
Mark Osmundson, General Manager

Elkader

KADR
05-15-1983; 1400 khz AM; 1 kw-U, ND1; N42 50 57 W91 24 43
600 N. Marquette Rd., P.O. Box 239, Prairie Du Chien, WI 53821 US
(563) 245-1400, *Fax:* (563) 245-1402
www.am1400online.com
info@hitsandfavorites.com
License: Elkader, IA held by KADR-AM 14, div of Design Homes Inc.
Nat'l Reps: Farmakis
Arbitron Metro Market: Elkader, IA *Format:* Adult Contemp
Troy Thein, Operations Dir
Dan Berns, General Manager

Emmetsburg

KUYY
01-10-1977; 100.1 mhz FM *Hrs Open:* 24; 16 kw; 410 ft.; N43 7 24 W94 51 28
2215 Main Street, P.O. Box 390, Emmetsburg, IA 50536 US
(712) 264-1074, *Fax:* (712) 264-1077
www.y100-fm.com/info/
mspies@nrgmedia.com
License: Emmetsburg, Palo Alto County, IA held by Jim Dandy Broadcasting Inc.
Arbitron Metro Market: Emmetsburg, IA *Format:* Adult Contemp
Target Audience: 25-54. *Adv. Rates:* 14; 12; 12; 10
Stan Calvert, Operations Dir
Marty Spies, General Manager
Stephanie Haviland, General Sales Mgr
Jeff Nixx, Programming Director
Abby Kohlhaas, Promotions Manager
Steve Schwaller, News Director
Steve Heaton, Chief Engineer

Epworth

KGRR
12-10-1994; 97.3 mhz FM *Hrs Open:* 24; 25 kw; 328 ft.; N42 27 29 W90 46 40
Mailing Address: 2115 Jfk Road, Dubuque, IA 52002 US
Second Address: 346 W. 8th St., Dubuque, IA 52004
(563) 690-0800, *Fax:* (563) 588-5688
www.973therock.com
kgrr@kgrr.com
License: Epworth, Dubuque County, IA held by Radio Dubuque Inc.
Group Owner: Radio Dubuque Inc.; acq 7-1-00; $1.5 million).
Nat'l Reps: Katz Radio
Arbitron Metro Market: Dubuque, IA *Format:* Classic Rock, Adult Contemp *Special Programming:* Chop Shop 5 hrs wkly, full metal jackie 2 hrs wkly *Hrs. of News Programming:* news progmg 2 hrs wkly *No. News Employees:* 1 *Target Audience:* 25-54; families
Don Rabbitt, CEO
Thomas Parsley, President
Paul Hemmer, Operations Dir
Perry Mason, Programming Director

Estherville

KILR
12-23-1967; 1070 khz AM *Hrs Open:* 6 AM-2 hrs past sunset
Mailing Address: P.O. Box 453, Estherville, IA 51334 US
Second Address: 3875 150th St., Estherville, IA 51334
(712) 362-2644, *Fax:* (712) 362-5951
kilrradio.com
KILRRADIO@HOTMAIL.COM
License: Estherville, IA held by Jacobson Broadcasting Co. Inc.
Nat'l Network: ABC *Nat'l Reps:* Farmakis
Format: Country *Special Programming:* Farm 9 hrs, relg 11 hrs wkly *Hrs. of News Programming:* news progmg 24 hrs wkly *No.*

News Employees: 1 *Target Audience:* 29-65; loc baby boomers *Adv. Rates:* 20; 20.18; na
Barbara Jacobson, CFO
Roger Jacobson, President
Peggy Zahrt, Operations Dir
Ed Funston, News Director

KILR-FM
10-17-1969; 95.9 mhz FM; 25 kw; 325 ft.; N43 25 45 W94 49 23
P.O. Box 453, Estherville, IA 51334 US
(712) 362-2644, *Fax:* (712) 362-5951
kilrradio.com
KILRRADIO@HOTMAIL.COM
License: Estherville, Emmet County, IA held by Jacobson Broadcasting Co. Inc.
Nat'l Reps: Salem
Format: Country *Target Audience:* 25-54. *Adv. Rates:* 20; 19; 18; 18
Lou Mellini, General Manager

Fairfield

***KHOE**
01-01-1994; 90.5 mhz FM *Hrs Open:* 24; 0.1 kw; 98 ft.; N41 0 59 W91 58 9
1000 N. 4th Street, Fairfield, IA 52557 US
(641) 469-5463
www.khoe.org
khoe@mum.edu
License: Fairfield, Jefferson County, IA held by Fairfield Educational Radio Station.
Format: Classical, Variety/Diverse *Special Programming:* Children 3 hrs, folk 6 hrs, gospel 3 hrs, jazz 2 h *Hrs. of News Programming:* News progmg 2 hrs wkly *Target Audience:* 18-35; University & college audience
Bill Goldstein, CEO
Jeffrey Hedquist, President
Stan Stansberry, General Manager

KKFD-FM
01-01-1977; 95.9 mhz FM *Hrs Open:* 24; 4.1 kw; 400 ft.; N40 58 47 W92 5 45
57- 1/2 S. Court St, P.O. Box 648, Fairfield, IA 52556 US
(641) 472-4191, *Fax:* (641) 472-2071
www.exploreSEiowa.com
License: Fairfield, Jefferson County, IA held by Fairfield License Co. LLC.
Group Owner: GoodRadio.TV
Nat'l Network: ABC
Format: Classic Rock *No. News Employees:* 1 *Target Audience:* Active, affluent adults 30-60
Marie Kiefer, Operations Dir
Tammy Jones, General Manager
Steve Smith, Programming Director
Scott Jackson, News Director
Lee Muntz, Sports Director

KMCD
03-03-1958; 1570 khz AM *Hrs Open:* 24; 0.25 kw-D, ND2; 0.109 kw-N, ND2; N41 0 25 W92 0 50
57- 1/2 S. Court St., P.O. Box 648, Fairfield, IA 52556 US
(641) 472-4191, *Fax:* (641) 472-2071
www.fairfieldiowaradio.com
License: Fairfield, IA held by Fairfield License Co. LLC.
Group Owner: GoodRadio.TV; (acq 6-1-2007; $750,000 with co-located FM)
Nat'l Network: ABC; Jones Radio Networks *Regional Network:* Radio Iowa
Format: Country *No. News Employees:* 1 *Target Audience:* 30 plus; community leaders & Jefferson County
Marie Kiefer, Operations Dir
Tammy Jones, General Manager
Steve Smith, Programming Director
Scott Jackson, News Director
Lee Muntz

Forest City

KIOW
11-08-1978; 107.3 mhz FM *Hrs Open:* 24; 25 kw; 328 ft.; N43 17 2 W93 37 50
Mailing Address: P.O. Box 308, Forest City, IA 50436 US
Second Address: 18643 360th St., Forest City, IA 50436
(641) 585-1073, *Fax:* (641) 585-2990
www.kiow.com
kiow@kiow.com
License: Forest City, Winnebago County, IA held by Pilot Knob Broadcasting Inc.
Nat'l Network: CNN Radio *Regional Network:* Radio Iowa *Nat'l Reps:* Farmakis *Wire Services:* AP
Format: Adult Contemp, Country, 60 *Special Programming:* Farm 15 hrs, contemp hits 19 hrs wkly *Hrs. of News Programming:* news progmg 15 hrs wkly *No. News Employees:* 1 *Target Audience:* General; Adults 25 +*Adv. Rates:* 15.35; 15.35; 15.35; 15.35
Susan Coloff, CFO
Tony Coloff, President

Fort Dodge

***KICB**
09-01-1971; 88.1 mhz FM; 0.2 kw; 131 ft.; N42 29 27 W94 12 1
330 Avenue M, Fort Dodge, IA 50501 US
(515) 576-6049, *Fax:* (515) 576-5656
http://www.iccc.cc.ia.us/kicb
License: Fort Dodge, Webster County, IA held by Iowa Central Community College.
Format: Alternative *Special Programming:* Sports 2 hrs wkly, movies and games 2 hrs wkly, deans list 2 hrs wkly *Target Audience:* 13-34; young men & women with progsv tastes
Robert Paxton, President
Brian Blessman, General Manager
Jeff Nelsen, Chief Engineer

KKEZ
01-01-1966; 94.5 mhz FM *Hrs Open:* 24; 100 kw; 600 ft.; N42 29 43 W94 12 33
200 Concord Plaza, Suite 600, San Antonio, TX 78216 US
(515) 576-7333, *Fax:* (515) 955-4250
www.kkez.com
kkez@clearchannel.com
License: Fort Dodge, Webster County, IA
Group Owner: Three Eagles Communications
Arbitron Metro Market: Des Moines, IA *Format:* Adult Contemp *Hrs. of News Programming:* news progmg 5 hrs wkly *No. News Employees:* 3 *Target Audience:* 18-49.
M. Kent Frandsen, President
Jay Eubanks, General Manager
Jim Davis, Programming Director
Dan Baker, Chief Engineer

***KNSH(FM)**
09-15-1980; 91.1 mhz FM *Hrs Open:* 24; 100 kw; Ant 1,052 ft; N42 49 03 W94 24 41
WOI Radio Group, 2022 Communications Bldg., Ames, IA 50011-3241
(515) 294-2025
www.iowapublicradio.org
woi@iastate.edu
License: Fort Dodge, Webster County, IA held by Iowa State University of Science and Technology.
Nat'l Network: NPR; PRI
Population Served: 17,000*Hrs. of News Programming:* news progmg 41 hrs wkly *No. News Employees:* 1 *Target Audience:* General; educated
Mary Grace Herrington, Programming Director
Don Wirth, Director, Fiscal Operations

KUEL(FM)
07-28-1975; 92.1 mhz FM; 6 kw; Ant 321 ft; N42 28 44 W94 12 10
Box Y, 200 N. 10th St., Fort Dodge, IA 50501
(515) 955-5656, *Fax:* (515) 955-5844
License: Fort Dodge, Webster County, IA held by Three Eagles of Joliet Inc.
Group Owner: Three Eagles Communications; (acq 7-1-2004; grpsl)
Population Served: 206,599 *Arbitron Metro Market:* Des Moines, IA
Rolland Johnson, Chairman
Jay Alexander, Programming Director
Mike Laughter, Engineering Dir

KVFD
12-24-1939; 1400 khz AM *Hrs Open:* 24; 0.85 kw-U, ND1; N42 28 44 W94 12 10
600 N. Kiwanis, Sioux Falls, SD 57104 US
(515) 955-1400, *Fax:* (515) 955-5844
License: Fort Dodge, IA held by Three Eagles of Joliet Inc.
Group Owner: Three Eagles Communications; (acq 7-1-2004; grpsl)
Nat'l Network: ABC *Wire Services:* AP
Arbitron Metro Market: Fort Dodge, IA *Format:* News, Oldies, 84
Gary Buchanan, President
Jay Alexander, Operations Dir
Dennis Martin, General Manager
Mike Laughter, Engineering Dir

KWMT
04-01-1956; 540 khz AM; 5 kw-D, DA2; 0.17 kw-N, DA2; N42 29 45 W94 12 33
200 Concord Plaza, Suite 600, San Antonio, TX 78216 US
(515) 576-5656, *Fax:* (515) 955-5844
www.kwmt.com
info@kwmt.com
License: Fort Dodge, IA held by Three Eagles of Lincoln Inc.
Group Owner: Three Eagles Communications; (acq 9-1-2007; grpsl)
Nat'l Reps: McGavren Guild
Arbitron Metro Market: Fort Dodge, IA *Format:* Country *Special Programming:* Farm *Target Audience:* General.
Ron Revere, General Manager

***KEGR**
01-01-2005; 89.5 mhz FM; 17 kw vert; 364 ft.; N42 40 18 W94 9 11
Mailing Address: 4136 Northgate Blvd., Suite 1, Sacramento, CA 95834 US
Second Address: 4136 Northgate Blvd., Suite 1, Sacramento, IA 95834
(800) 543-1495, *Fax:* (916) 641-8238
www.familyradio.com
info@familyradio.com
License: Fort Dodge, Webster County, IA held by Family Stations Inc.
Group Owner: Family Stations Inc.
Nat'l Network: Family Radio
Arbitron Metro Market: Fort Dodge, IA *Format:* Religious
Harold Camping, President
Pat McMahon, Operations Dir
J.D. Freeman, General Manager

Fort Madison

KBKB
02-06-1948; 1360 khz AM *Hrs Open:* 18; 1 kw-D, ND1; 0.034 kw-N, ND1; N40 39 30 W91 16 20
50 East Rivercenter Blvd, #1200, Covington, KY 41011 US
(319) 752-5402, *Fax:* (319) 752-5287
www.1360kbkb.com
johnp@burlingtonradio.com
License: Fort Madison, IA held by Pritichard Broadcasting Corp.
Group Owner: Pritchard Broadcasting Corp.; (acq 6-6-2008; with KBUR(AM) Burlington)
Arbitron Metro Market: Burlington, IA *Format:* Country
Joe Bates, Operations Dir
John Pritchard, General Manager
Chet Young, General Sales Mgr
Joe Bates, Programming Director

KBKB-FM
06-01-1973; 101.7 mhz FM *Hrs Open:* 24; 50 kw; 466 ft.; N40 43 25 W91 13 49
Mailing Address: 50 East Rivercenter Blvd, #1200, Covington, KY 41011 US
Second Address: 1411 N. Roosevelt Ave., Burlington, IA 52601
(319) 752-2701, *Fax:* (319) 752-5287
www.1017thebull.com
drew@1017thebull.com
License: Fort Madison, Lee County, IA held by GAP Broadcasting Burlington License LLC.
Group Owner: GAPWEST Broadcasting; (acq 2-13-2008; grpsl)
Nat'l Network: ABC
Arbitron Metro Market: Burlington, IA *Format:* Country *Hrs. of News Programming:* news progmg 7 hrs wkly *No. News Employees:* 2
Kosmo Leone, Programming Director
J.K. Martin, News Director

Garnavillo

KCTN
12-06-1982; 100.1 mhz FM *Hrs Open:* 24; 6 kw; 328 ft.; N42 53 6 W91 19 11
P.O. Box 239, 600 N. Marquette Rd, Prairie Du Chien, WI 53821 US
(563) 245-1400, *Fax:* (563) 245-1402
kctn.com
kctn@alpinecom.net
License: Garnavillo, Clayton County, IA held by KCTN-FM 100 div of Design Homes Inc.
Regional Network: Brownfield *Nat'l Reps:* Farmakis
Arbitron Metro Market: Garnavillo, IA *Format:* Country *No. News Employees:* 1 *Target Audience:* 24-55; farmers & rural communities
Randy Weeks, CEO
Dan Berns, General Manager
Troy Thein, Chief of Operations

Glenwood

KXKT
04-08-1966; 103.7 mhz FM *Hrs Open:* 24; 100 kw; 1086 ft.; N41 18 32 W96 1 33

600 Congress Avenue, Suite 1400, Austin, TX 78701 US
(402) 561-2000(402) 962-1037, *Fax:* (402) 551-4315
www.thekat.com
request@thekat.com
License: Glenwood, Mills County, IA held by Capstar TX L.P.
Group Owner: Clear Channel Communications Inc.; (acq 8-30-2000; grpsl).
Arbitron Metro Market: Omaha, NE *Format:* Country *No. News Employees:* 1 *Target Audience:* 18-54; general
Mitch Baker, Operations Dir
Donna Baker, General Manager
Bill Ryan, General Sales Mgr
Tom Goodwin, Programming Director
Brandon Howell, Promotions Manager
Greg Gade, Chief Engineer

Grinnell

KGRN

11-15-1957; 1410 khz AM
909 1/2 Main Street, Grinnell, IA 50112 US
(641) 236-1410, *Fax:* (641) 236-8896
www.http://myiowainfo.com
darin@kcobradio.com
License: Grinnell, IA held by Grinnell License Co. LLC.
Group Owner: GoodRadio.TV; (acq 5-2-2007; $2.25 million)
Nat'l Reps: Farmakis
Format: News, News/Talk, 86 *Hrs. of News Programming:* News progmg 60 hrs wkly *Target Audience:* 25-74
Dean Goodman, President
Ron McCarthy, General Manager

KRTI

05-01-1993; 106.7 mhz FM *Hrs Open:* 24; 50 kw; 492 ft.; N41 48 16 W92 40 9
Mailing Address: P.O. Box 66, 1801 N. 13th Ave. East, Newton, IA 50208 US
Second Address: 1801 N. 13th Ave. E., Newton, IA 50208
(641) 792-5262, *Fax:* (641) 792-8403
www.energy1067.com
info@kcobradio.com
License: Grinnell, Poweshiek County, IA held by Newton License Co. LLC.
Group Owner: GoodRadio.TV; (acq 5-1-2007; grpsl)
Arbitron Metro Market: Grinnell, IA *Format:* Contemporary Hits/Top 40
Tim Graves, Operations Dir
Ron McCarthy, General Manager

Grundy Center

KCRR

10-08-1983; 97.7 mhz FM *Hrs Open:* 24; 16 kw; 407 ft.; N42 23 28 W92 31 57
2003 Elmcrest Drive, Marshalltown, IA 50158 US
(319) 833-4800, *Fax:* (319) 833-4866
www.kcrr.com
kcrr@kcrr.com
License: Grundy Center, Grundy County, IA held by Cumulus Licensing Corp.
Group Owner: Cumulus Media Inc.; (acq 3-15-00; grpsl).
Arbitron Metro Market: Waterloo-Cedar Falls, IA *Format:* Classic Rock *Hrs. of News Programming:* news progmg 3 hrs wkly *No. News Employees:* 2 *Target Audience:* 25-54.
Lew Dickey, CEO
Dick Stadlen, Operations Dir
Greg Sher, General Manager

Hampton

KLMJ

05-16-1983; 104.9 mhz FM *Hrs Open:* 24; 6 kw; 305 ft.; N42 49 52 W93 11 20
Mailing Address: P.O. Box 495, Hampton, IA 50441 US
Second Address: 1509 4th St. N.E., Hampton, IA 50441
(641) 456-5656, *Fax:* (641) 456-5655
www.klmj.com
klmj@klmj.com
License: Hampton, Franklin County, IA held by C.D. Broadcasting Inc.
Nat'l Network: ABC *Regional Network:* Radio Iowa; Brownfield
Nat'l Reps: Farmakis
Arbitron Metro Market: Mason City, IA *Format:* Adult Contemp, Country, 64 *Special Programming:* Iowa State & Univ. of Northern Iowa, farm 8 hrs wk *Hrs. of News Programming:* news progmg 14 hrs wkly *No. NewsEmployees:* 2 *Target Audience:* 25 plus; general *Adv. Rates:* 19; 19; 19; 19
Marlin Burrier, Operations Dir
Craig Donnelly, General Manager

Harlan

KNOD

11-12-1979; 105.3 mhz FM *Hrs Open:* 24; 25 kw; 282 ft.; N41 37 0 W95 16 10
P.O. Box 723, 902 Chatburn Ave, Harlan, IA 51537 US
(712) 755-3883, *Fax:* (712) 755-7511
knodfm.com
knodnews@harlannet.com
License: Harlan, Shelby County, IA held by Wireless Broadcasting L.L.C.
Regional Network: Brownfield
Format: Oldies *Special Programming:* Farm 3 hrs, relg 2 hrs wkly *Hrs. of News Programming:* news progmg 5 hrs wkly *No. News Employees:* 1 *Target Audience:* 25-50. *Adv. Rates:* 12.25; 12.25; 12.25; 12.25.
Richard Keane, Operations Dir
Judy Storm, General Manager
Jason Dinesen, News Director

Hiawatha

*KXGM-FM

01-01-2002; 89.1 mhz FM; 0 kw horiz, 5.8 kw vert; 400 ft.; N42 3 13 W91 44 35
3232 Osage Rd, Waterloo, IA 50703 US
(319) 294-8910
www.891thespirit.com
info@extremegracemedia.org?subject=Information%20EGM
License: Hiawatha, Linn County, IA held by Extreme Grace Media Inc.
Arbitron Metro Market: Cedar Rapids, IA *Format:* Christian
Michael James, Station Manager

Hudson

KCVM

08-27-1997; 93.5 mhz FM *Hrs Open:* 24; 6 kw; 325 ft.; N42 24 47 W92 26 15
506 North Clark Street, Forest City, IA 50436 US
(319) 277-1918(319) 266-6499, *Fax:* (319) 277-5202
www.mix96.net
themix@935themix.com
License: Hudson, Black Hawk County, IA held by Fife Communications Co. L.C.
Arbitron Metro Market: Waterloo-Cedar Falls, IA *Format:* Adult Contemp *Hrs. of News Programming:* news progmg 2 hrs wkly *No. News Employees:* 1 *Target Audience:* 25-54; eastern Iowa adult females *Adv. Rates:* 30; 30; 30; 30
Jim Coloff, President
Tony Coloff, Operations Dir
Jim Coloff, General Manager
Teri Lynn, Programming Director
Jay Rhymer, Promotions Manager
Jesse Gavin, News Director

Humboldt

KHBT

08-05-1970; 97.7 mhz FM *Hrs Open:* 24; 5.8 kw; 276 ft.; N42 43 57 W94 12 23
Mailing Address: 3378 Raccoon Ridge, Adel, IA 50003 US
Second Address: 2196 Montana Ave., Humboldt, IA 50548
(515) 332-4100, *Fax:* (515) 332-2723
www.977thebolt.com
thebolt@waittradio.com
License: Humboldt, Humboldt County, IA held by NRG License Sub. LLC.
Group Owner: NRG Media LLC; (acq 10-31-2005; grpsl)
Wire Services: AP
Format: Adult Contemp *Special Programming:* Farm 10 hrs wkly *Hrs. of News Programming:* news progmg 30 hrs wkly *No. News Employees:* 1 *Target Audience:* 30-65; general
Bob Ketchum, General Manager

Ida Grove

KKIA

09-01-1981; 92.9 mhz FM *Hrs Open:* 24; 25 kw; 328 ft.; N42 29 23 W95 17 40
Mailing Address: 2215 Main Street, P.O. Box 390, Emmetsburg, IA 50536 US
Second Address: P.O. Box 108, Storm Lake, IA 50588
(712) 732-3520, *Fax:* (712) 732-1746
www.stormlakeradio.com
info@stormlakeradio.com
License: Ida Grove, Ida County, IA held by Jim Dandy Broadcasting Inc.
Group Owner: NRG Media LLC; (acq 1-13-2003; $2.5 million with KUYY(FM) Emmetsburg)
Nat'l Network: Fox News Radio *Nat'l Reps:* Farmakis
Format: Country *Special Programming:* Farm 10 hrs wkly *Hrs. of News Programming:* news progmg 5 hrs wkly *No. News Employees:* 1 *Target Audience:* 18-54. *Adv. Rates:* 21; 21; 21; 21
Mary Quass, CEO
Buzz Paterson, General Manager
Chuck DuCoty, COO

Independence

KQMG

12-10-1959; 1220 khz AM; 0.25 kw-D, ND1; 0.134 kw-N, ND1; N42 28 32 W91 52 26
231 1/2 First Street, East, Suite 953, Independence, IA 50644 US
(319) 334-3300, *Fax:* (319) 334-6158
www.lite953.com
kqmg95.3@gmail.com
License: Independence, IA held by KM Radio of Independence L.L.C.
Group Owner: KM Communications Inc.; (acq 10-9-03; $500,000 with co-located FM).
Nat'l Network: ABC
Arbitron Metro Market: Waterloo-Cedar Falls, IA *Format:* Sports, Talk
Noel Showers, Programming Director
Rick Peters, Chief Engineer

KQMG-FM

01-01-1972; 95.3 mhz FM; 2.9 kw; 410 ft.; N42 28 32 W91 52 26
231 1/2 First Street, East, Suite 953, Independence, IA 50644 US
(319) 334-3300, *Fax:* (319) 334-6158
www.lite953.com
kqmgfm@gmail.com
License: Independence, Buchanan County, IA
Group Owner: KM Communications Inc.
Arbitron Metro Market: Waterloo-Cedar Falls, IA *Format:* Sports, Talk
Noel Showers, Programming Director

Indianola

*KSTM

04-15-1994; 88.9 mhz FM; 0.15 kw; 125 ft.; N41 21 49 W93 33 37
701 North C Street, Indianola, IA 50125 US
(515) 961-1747(515) 961-1803, *Fax:* (515) 961-1674
www.889kstm.wordpress.com
KSTM@storm.simpson.edu
License: Indianola, Warren County, IA held by Simpson College.
Arbitron Metro Market: Indianola, IA *Format:* Alternative
Rich Ramos, General Manager

KXLQ

07-22-1963; 1490 khz AM; 0.5 kw-D, ND1; 1 kw-N, ND1; N41 21 24 W93 35 16
810 Main St., Box 228, Pella, IA 50219 US
(248) 557-3500
License: Indianola, IA held by Birach Broadcasting Corp.
Group Owner: Birch Broadcasting Corp.; (acq 8-1-2007; $800,000 with WCXN(AM) Claremont, NC)
Arbitron Metro Market: Indianola, IA
Joe Milledge, Chief Engineer

Iowa City

KCJJ

10-14-1998; 1630 khz AM *Hrs Open:* 24
PO Box 2118, Iowa City, IA 52244 US
(319) 354-1242, *Fax:* (319) 354-1921
www.1630kcjj.com
kcjjam@gmail.com
License: Iowa City, IA held by River City Radio Inc.
Nat'l Network: ABC; CBS *Wire Services:* AP
Arbitron Metro Market: Cedar Rapids, IA *Format:* Talk *No. News Employees:* 4 *Target Audience:* 25-54. *Adv. Rates:* 32; 25; 28; 20
Tom Suter, General Manager
Kurt Means, Senior Account Executive
Deb Kelley-Melsha, Account Executive
Ginny Collins, Board Operator
Jan Soboroff, Business Manager

KKRQ

05-01-1966; 100.7 mhz FM; 100 kw; 531 ft.; N41 45 26 W91 31 31
50 East Rivercenter Blvd, Covington, KY 41011 US
(329) 354-9500, *Fax:* (319) 354-9504
www.thesox.com
License: Iowa City, Johnson County, IA

Group Owner: Clear Channel Communications Inc.
Arbitron Metro Market: Cedar Rapids, IA *Format:* Classic Rock
Richard Jenkins, President
Mike Novak, Operations Dir
Keith Whipple, General Sales Mgr
David Pierce, Programming Director
Ed Lenane, News Director
Sam Wallington, Engineering Dir
Marya Morgan, News Reporter
Richard Hunt, NewsReporter
Marya Morgan, News Reporter
Karen Johnson, Regional Manager
Jared Mitchell

KRNA
10-04-1974; 94.1 mhz FM *Hrs Open:* 24; 100 kw; 981 ft.; N41 45 0 W91 50 16
600 Congress Ave., Suite 1400, Austin, TX 78701 US
(319) 892-3573, *Fax:* (319) 363-8062
www.krna.com
krna@krna.com
License: Iowa City, Johnson County, IA held by Cumulus Licensing Corp.
Group Owner: Cumulus Media Inc.; (acq 2000; grpsl).
Nat'l Reps: Christal
Arbitron Metro Market: Cedar Rapids, IA *Format:* Rock/AOR
Target Audience: 18-49.
Gregg Scharnau, Programming Director
Greg Sher, Promotions Manager

***KRUI-FM**
03-28-1984; 89.7 mhz FM *Hrs Open:* 24; 0.1 kw; 89 ft.; N41 39 29 W91 32 40
129 Grand Avenue Court, Iowa City, IA 52242 US
(319) 335-9525, *Fax:* (319) 335-9526
www.uiowa.edu/~krui
krui@uiowa.edu
License: Iowa City, Johnson County, IA held by Student Broadcasters Inc.
Arbitron Metro Market: Iowa City, IA *Format:* Variety/Diverse *Hrs. of News Programming:* News progmg 7 hrs wkly *Target Audience:* 18-34; Univ
Aaron Roemig, Operations Dir
Nate George, Programming Director
Brian Anstey, Promotions Manager
Bill Penisten, News Director
Adam Erickson, Chief Engineer
Rick Oswavay, News Reporter
Ryal Brier, Sports Commentator

***KSUI**
01-01-1948; 91.7 mhz FM; 100 kw; 1,292 ft; N41 43 15 W91 20 30
710 S. Clinton St. Bldg., Univ . of Iowa, Iowa City, IA 19103
(319) 335-5730, *Fax:* (319) 335-6116
ksui.uiowa.edu
License: Iowa City, Johnson County, IA held by University of Iowa
Nat'l Network: NPR; PRI; BBC

Joan Kjaer, Programming Director
Jim Davies, Engineering Dir

KXIC
06-07-1948; 800 khz AM; 1 kw-D, DA2; 0.199 kw-N, DA2; N41 41 15 W91 32 39
50 East Rivercenter Blvd, Covington, KY 41011 US
(319) 354-9500, *Fax:* (319) 354-9504
www.kxic.com
License: Iowa City, IA held by Citicasters Licenses L.P.
Group Owner: Clear Channel Communications Inc.; (acq 5-4-99; grpsl).
Arbitron Metro Market: Cedar Rapids, IA *Format:* News
John Laton, General Manager
Roy Justis, News Director

***WSUI**
01-01-1919; 910 khz AM
710 Clinton Street Bldg, Iowa City, IA 19103 US
(319) 335-5730, *Fax:* (319) 335-6116
wsui.uiowa.edu
wsui@uiowa.edu
License: Iowa City, IA held by The University of Iowa.
Nat'l Network: NPR
Format: News, News/Talk, 86
John Monick, General Manager
Dennis Reese, Programming Director
Jim Davis, Chief Engineer

Iowa Falls

KIFG
07-22-1962; 1510 khz AM; 0.5 kw-C, NDD; 1 kw-D, NDD; N42 30 49 W93 12 57
P. O. Box 307, Iowa Falls, IA 50126 US
(641) 648-4281, *Fax:* (641) 648-4606
www.kifgradio.com
kifg@iafalls.com
License: Iowa Falls, IA held by Times-Citizen Communications Inc.
Nat'l Network: CNN Radio; Westwood One *Nat'l Reps:* Keystone (unwired net)
Format: Contemporary Hits/Top 40, Adult Contemp *Special Programming:* Farm 5 hrs wkly *No. News Employees:* 1 *Target Audience:* 25 plus.
T.J. Norman, General Manager

KIFG-FM
10-01-1965; 95.3 mhz FM *Hrs Open:* 24; 6 kw; 194 ft.; N42 30 49 W93 12 57
308 1/2 Stevens Street, Iowa Falls, IA 50126 US
(641) 648-4281, *Fax:* (641) 648-4606
www.kifgradio.com
kifg@iafalls.com
License: Iowa Falls, Hardin County, IA held by Times-Citizen Communications Inc.
Format: News, Sports *Special Programming:* School news (during the school year) *No. News Employees:* 1
T.J. Norman, General Manager
Pat Dunn, Programming Director
Ann Denholm, Promotions Manager

Jefferson

KGRA
10-01-1981; 98.9 mhz FM *Hrs Open:* 24; 11 kw; 499 ft.; N41 58 54 W94 31 12
Rr2 Box 106a, Lacrescent, MN 55947 US
(515) 386-2222, *Fax:* (515) 386-2215
kg98@netins.net
License: Jefferson, Greene County, IA held by Coon Valley Communications
Group Owner: Coon Valley Communications Inc.; (acq 1-19-94;
Nat'l Network: ABC
Arbitron Metro Market: Jefferson, IA *Format:* Classic Rock *Hrs. of News Programming:* news progmg 9 hrs wkly *No. News Employees:* 1 *Target Audience:* 25-49; Adults
Patrick Delaney, President
Linda Hass, Operations Dir
Sue Thomsen, General Manager

Keokuk

***KMDY**
01-01-2001; 90.9 mhz FM; 7.7 kw; 197 ft.; N40 30 41 W91 19 50
820 N Lasalle Blvd, Chicago, IL 60610 US
(217) 357-3000, *Fax:* (217) 357-3001
info@kmdyfm.com
License: Keokuk, Lee County, IA held by Cornerstone Community Radio Inc.
Nat'l Network: Moody
Format: Christian
Robert Neff, Operations Dir

KOKX
10-19-1947; 1310 khz AM *Hrs Open:* 24; 1 kw-D, DAN; 0.5 kw-N, DAN; N40 22 50 W91 21 9
P.O. Box 1508, Mount Vernon, IL 62864 US
(319) 524-5410, *Fax:* (319) 524-7275
krnq963@imchsi.com
License: Keokuk, IA held by Withers Broadcasting of Iowa.
Group Owner: Withers Broadcasting Co.; (acq 7-15-81; $900,000 with co-located FM;
Format: News, News/Talk, 84, Talk, Adult Contemp *Special Programming:* Farm 6 hrs wkly *Hrs. of News Programming:* news progmg 25 hrs wkly *No. News Employees:* 2 *Target Audience:* 25-54. *Adv. Rates:* 16;14; 14; 12
W. Russell Withers Jr., President
Gary Folluo, General Manager
Dan Workman, Programming Director
Bill Reed, News Director
Matt Frisbee, News Announcer/Reporter
Preston Hampton, News Director

KOKX-FM
10-15-2000; 95.3 mhz FM *Hrs Open:* 24/7; 100 kw; 804 ft.; N40 24 1 W91 35 9
Mailing Address: P.O. Box No. 1508, Mt. Vernon, IL 62864 US
Second Address: 108 Washington St., Keokuk, IA 52632
(319) 524-5410, *Fax:* (319) 524-7275
krnq963@mchsi.com
License: Keokuk, Lee County, IA held by W. Russell Withers
Group Owner: Withers Broadcasting Co.
Nat'l Network: ABC
Arbitron Metro Market: Quad Cities, IA-IL (Davenport-Rock Island-Moline) *Format:* Oldies *Special Programming:* St. Louis Cardinals Baseball *Hrs. of News Programming:* news progmg 4 hrs wkly *No. News Employees:* 2*Target Audience:* 25-54; women 50% men 50% *Adv. Rates:* 24; 20; 18; 17
Gary M. Folluo, General Manager
Bill Reed, Programming Director
Preston Hampton, News Director
Matt Frisbee, News Reporter
Dan Workman, Program Director

KRNQ
01-01-1999; 96.3 mhz FM *Hrs Open:* 24/7; 19 kw; 804 ft.; N40 24 1 W91 35 9
Post Office Box 1591, Mt. Vernon, IL 62864 US
(319) 524-5410, *Fax:* (319) 524-7275
www.keokukradio.com
gary@keokukradio.com
License: Keokuk, Lee County, IA held by David M. Lister.
Group Owner: Withers Broadcasting Co.; Gary M. Folluo, (319) 524-5410; gmkokx@mchsi.com
Arbitron Metro Market: Keokuk, IA/Burlington, IA/Quincy, IL
Format: Light Rock *Special Programming:* Local Sports *Target Audience:* 18-45; 50/50 male, female *Adv. Rates:* 17; 15; 16; 12.50
Preston Hampton, Operations Dir
Gary Folluo, General Manager
Judy Hall, General Sales Mgr
Preston Hampton, Programming Director
Preston Hampton, News Director
Matt Frisbee, News Anchor
Tara Whitnah, Office Manager
Bill Reed,Sports Director

Knoxville

KNIA
08-30-1960; 1320 khz AM *Hrs Open:* 24; 0.5 kw-D, DA2; 0.222 kw-N, DA2; N41 19 50 W93 6 34
Mailing Address: 1610 N. Lincoln Street, Knoxville, IA 50138 US
Second Address: 1610 N. Lincoln, Knoxville, IA 50138
(641) 842-3161, *Fax:* (641) 842-5606
www.kniakrls.com
kniaakrls@kniakrls.com
License: Knoxville, IA held by M & H Broadcasting Inc.
Regional Network: Radio Iowa
Format: Country *Special Programming:* Relg 18 hrs wkly *Hrs. of News Programming:* news progmg 25 hrs wkly *No. News Employees:* 3 *Target Audience:* 25-54; female *Adv. Rates:* 14.60; 14.60; 14.60; 14.60
Jim Butler, General Manager

KRLS
07-16-1973; 92.1 mhz FM *Hrs Open:* 24; 15.5 kw; 308 ft.; N41 21 40 W93 0 15
Mailing Address: 1610 N. Lincoln Street, PO Box 31, Knoxville, IA 50138 US
Second Address: 1610 N. Lincoln, Knoxville, IA 50138
(641) 842-3161, *Fax:* (641) 842-5606
www.kniakrls.com
License: Knoxville, Marion County, IA
Wire Services: AP
Arbitron Metro Market: Knoxville/Pella, IA *Format:* Adult Contemp *Hrs. of News Programming:* news progmg 25 hrs wkly *No. News Employees:* 3 *Target Audience:* 25-54; primarily female *Adv. Rates:* 17:45;17:45; 17:45; 17:45.
Richard Jenkins, President
Chip Bailey, Operations Dir

Lake City

KIKD
01-01-1997; 106.7 mhz FM *Hrs Open:* 24; 25 kw; 328 ft.; N42 7 14 W94 48 49
Mailing Address: 1119 E. Plaza Drive, Carroll, IA 51401 US
Second Address: 1119 East Plaza Dr., Carroll, IA 51401
(712) 792-4321, *Fax:* (712) 792-6667
www.kick1067.com
License: Lake City, Calhoun County, IA held by Carroll Broadcasting Co.
Group Owner: Carroll Broadcasting Co.; acq 1999; $975,000)
Nat'l Reps: Katz Radio
Format: Country *Hrs. of News Programming:* 2 *Target Audience:* 18-49; contemp country with strong families
Kim Hackett, General Manager
Lynda Dukes-Francy, General Sales Mgr

Lamoni

***KNSL(FM)**
01-01-2000; 97.9 mhz FM *Hrs Open:* 24; 50 kw; Ant 492 ft; N40 48 52 W93 50 15 *Rebroadcasts:* WOI-AM
WOI Radio Group, 2022 Communications Bldg., Ames, IA 50011-3241
(515) 294-2025, *Fax:* (515) 294-1544
www.iowapublicradio.org
woi@iastate.edu
License: Lamoni, Decatur County, IA held by Iowa State University of Science and Technology
Nat'l Network: NPR; PRI
Hrs. of News Programming: 40 hrs wkly *Target Audience:* General; Educated
Don Wirth, Programming Director
Mary Grace Herrington, Director, Iowa Public Radio

Le Mars

KKMA
01-01-1967; 99.5 mhz FM; 100 kw; 791 ft.; N42 28 56 W96 15 30
37 2nd Avenue NW, Box 1410, Le Mars, IA 51031 US
(712) 239-2100, *Fax:* (712) 239-3346
www.kool995.com
License: Le Mars, Plymouth County, IA
Group Owner: Powell Broadcasting Co. Inc.
Regional Reps: REGIONAL REPS
Arbitron Metro Market: Sioux City, IA *Format:* Oldies *Adv. Rates:* 20; 20; 20; 18
Julie Bockholt, Operations Dir
Dennis Bullock, General Manager
Monica Stabile, General Sales Mgr
Scott McKenzie, Programming Director
Justin Barker, Promotions Manager
Tim Guentz, Chief Engineer

KLEM
10-12-1954; 1410 khz AM *Hrs Open:* 24
37-2nd Avenue NW, Box 1410, Le Mars, IA 51031 US
(712) 546-4121, *Fax:* (712) 546-9672
www.klem1410.com
klem@lemarscomm.net
License: Le Mars, IA held by Powell Broadcasting Co Inc.
Group Owner: Powell Broadcasting Co. Inc.; (acq 7-6-99; with co-located FM)
Arbitron Metro Market: Sioux City, IA *Format:* Adult Contemp, News, 84 *Special Programming:* Farm 18 hrs wkly *No. News Employees:* 2
Tom Spies, President
Dennis Bullock, General Manager
Dave Grosenheider, Station Manager
Dave Ruden, Programming Director
Larry Schmitz, News Director
Stan Culley, Chief Engineer
Joanne Glamm, Reporter
Christi Rush

Madrid

***KNWM**
08-21-1997; 96.1 mhz FM *Hrs Open:* 24; 6 kw; 328 ft.; N41 51 5 W93 43 29
2825 East 13th Street, P.O. Box 1750, Ames, IA 50010 US
(515) 327-1071, *Fax:* (515) 327-1073
www.desmoines.fm
knwi@desmoines.fm
License: Madrid, Boone County, IA held by Northwestern College.
Group Owner: Northwestern College & Radio; (acq 12-30-2003; $1.8 million with KNWI(FM) Osceola).
Arbitron Metro Market: Des Moines, IA *Format:* Christian
Richard Whitworth, General Manager
Dave St. John, Programming Director

Manchester

KMCH
12-05-1991; 94.7 mhz FM *Hrs Open:* 24; 6 kw; 328 ft.; N42 31 42 W91 22 53
506 North Clark, Forest City, IA 50436 US
(563) 927-6249, *Fax:* (563) 927-4372
www.kmch.com
kmchradio@iowatelecom.net
License: Manchester, Delaware County, IA held by Coloff Media LLC.
Nat'l Network: CBS
Format: Adult Contemp, Country *Special Programming:* Farm 7 hrs, sports 7 hrs, relg 4 hrs wkly *Hrs. of News Programming:* news progmg 20 hrs wkly *No. News Employees:* 1 *Target Audience:* 25-64; northeast Iowaadults & farm population *Adv. Rates:* 14.50; 14.50; 14.50; 14.50
Anthony Coloff, President
James Coloff, Operations Dir
Jackie Coates, Station Manager
Mike Johnson, Operations Manager

Manson

KXFT
01-01-2007; 99.7 mhz FM; 25 kw; 285 ft.; N42 31 3 W94 20 43 US
(515) 576-7333, *Fax:* (515) 955-4250
kkez@clearchannel.com
License: Manson, Calhoun County, IA held by Three Eagles of Lincoln Inc.
Group Owner: Three Eagles Communications; (acq 9-1-2007; grpsl)
Arbitron Metro Market: Manson, IA *Format:* Contemporary Hits/Top 40
Tracey Williams, General Manager

Maquoketa

KMAQ
08-26-1958; 1320 khz AM *Hrs Open:* 6 AM-10 PM; 0.5 kw-D, ND1; 0.135 kw-N, ND1; N42 5 26 W90 37 43
129 North Main Street, Maquoketa, IA 52060 US
(563) 652-2426, *Fax:* (563) 652-6210
License: Maquoketa, IA held by Maquoketa Broadcasting Co.
Nat'l Network: USA *Regional Network:* Brownfield; Radio Iowa
Nat'l Reps: Farmakis
Format: Country *Special Programming:* Farm 10 hrs, polka 3 hrs wkly *Hrs. of News Programming:* news progmg 28 hrs wkly *No. News Employees:* 1 *Target Audience:* General; adults, high percentage of farmers *Adv.Rates:* 15; 15; 15;15.
Dennis Voy, President
Leighton Hepker, Operations Dir
Tom Messerli, Chief Engineer

KMAQ-FM
09-01-1967; 95.1 mhz FM; 6 kw; 328 ft.; N42 5 26 W90 37 43
129 North Main Street, Maquoketa, IA 52060 US
(563) 652-2426, *Fax:* (563) 652-6210
License: Maquoketa, Jackson County, IA
Regional Network: Radio Iowa *Wire Services:* AP
Hrs. of News Programming: news progmg 28 hrs wkly *No. News Employees:* 1 *Adv. Rates:* 16; 16; 16; 13
Leighton Hepker, General Sales Mgr

Marshalltown

KDAO
12-16-1978; 1190 khz AM *Hrs Open:* 24
Box 538, Marshalltown, IA 50158 US
(641) 752-4122, *Fax:* (641) 752-5121
www.kdao.com
kdao@kdao.com
License: Marshalltown, IA held by MTN Broadcasting Inc.
Arbitron Metro Market: Marshalltown, IA *TV Affiliate:* KDAO-TV affil *Format:* Adult Contemp *Target Audience:* 25-54.
Mark Osmundson, General Manager

KFJB
06-01-1923; 1230 khz AM *Hrs Open:* 24; 1 kw-U, ND1; N42 4 1 W92 58 10
123 W. Main Street, Marshalltown, IA 50158 US
(641) 753-3361, *Fax:* (641) 752-7201
www.1230kfjb.com
office@marshalltownbroadcasting.com
License: Marshalltown, IA held by Marshalltown Broadcasting Inc.
Nat'l Network: ABC *Regional Network:* Brownfield *Nat'l Reps:* Katz Radio *Wire Services:* AP
Arbitron Metro Market: Marshalltown, IW *Format:* News, News/Talk, 86 *Special Programming:* Religious 3 hrs wkly, Sports 40 hrs wkly *Hrs. of News Programming:* news progmg 20 hrs wkly *No. News Employees:* 2*Target Audience:* 35-64. *Adv. Rates:* 35; 30; 33; 18
David Nelson, President
Kyle Martin, Operations Dir
Clark L. Wideman, General Manager
Bill White, Station Manager
Kyle Martin, Programming Director

KXIA
01-01-1968; 101.1 mhz FM *Hrs Open:* 24; 100 kw; 656 ft.; N42 0 19 W92 55 45
Mailing Address: 123 West Main Street, Marshalltown, IA 50158 US
Second Address: 123 W. Main St., Marshalltown, IA 50158
(641) 753-3361, *Fax:* (641) 752-7201
www.kixweb.com
office@marshalltownbroadcasting.com
License: Marshalltown, Marshall County, IA held by Marshalltown Broadcasting Inc.
Nat'l Network: ABC *Regional Network:* Brownfield *Nat'l Reps:* Katz Radio *Wire Services:* AP
Format: Country *Hrs. of News Programming:* news progmg 6 hrs wkly *No. News Employees:* 2 *Target Audience:* 25-54. *Adv. Rates:* 45; 40; 42; 24
Todd Collins, Programming Director

***KRFH**
88.7 mhz FM; 8.3 kw; 95 ft.; N42 4 17 W92 55 19
P O Box 538, Marshalltown, IA 50158 US
(641) 752-4122
License: Marshalltown, Marshall County, IA held by Marshalltown Education Plus Inc.
Arbitron Metro Market: Marshalltown, IA
Brett Gibson, General Manager
David Roble, Programming Director

Mason City

***KBDC**
01-01-2001; 88.5 mhz FM; 68 kw vert; 463 ft.; N43 22 12 W93 16 27
P O Drawer 2440, Tupelo, MS 38803 US
(662) 844-8888, *Fax:* (662) 842-6791
www.afa.net
comments@afa.net
License: Mason City, Cerro Gordo County, IA held by American Family Association.
Group Owner: American Family Radio
Arbitron Metro Market: Tupelo, MS *Format:* Adult Contemp
Marvin Sanders, General Manager

KCMR
05-03-1979; 97.9 mhz FM *Hrs Open:* 24; 6 kw; 315 ft.; N43 7 18 W93 11 50
Mailing Address: P.O. Box 979, 600 First St, NW #101, Mason City, IA 50402 US
Second Address: 600 First St. N.W., Mason City, IA 50401
(641) 424-9300, *Fax:* (641) 423-2221
www.kcmrfm.com
kcmr@kcmronline.org
License: Mason City, Cerro Gordo County, IA held by TLC Broadcasting Corp.
Arbitron Metro Market: Mason City, IA *Format:* Religious *Special Programming:* Class 5 hrs, nostalgia 10 hrs wkly *Target Audience:* Over 30.
Bill Schickel, General Manager
Bob Miller, General Sales Mgr

KGLO
01-17-1937; 1300 khz AM
330 East Kilbourn Avenue, Suite 250, Milwaukee, WI 53202 US
(641) 423-1300, *Fax:* (641) 423-2906
www.rivercitysquare.com
info@rivercitysquare.com
License: Mason City, IA held by Three Eagles of Lincoln Inc.
Group Owner: Three Eagles Communications; (acq 9-1-2007; grpsl)
Nat'l Network: CBS
Arbitron Metro Market: Mason City, IA *Format:* Talk *Special Programming:* Farm 15 hrs wkly *No. News Employees:* 3 *Target Audience:* 25-35; adults *Adv. Rates:* 20; 20; 20; 15.
Tim Fleming, Operations Dir
Charlie Thomas, General Manager
Tim Fleming, Station Manager
Hall Hofman, General Sales Mgr
Tami Ramon, Promotions Manager
Tim Renshaw, News Director
Greg Gade, Chief Engineer
Andy Roat, NationalSales Manager
Jamie Larson, Promotions Director

KIAI
11-01-1985; 93.9 mhz FM; 100 kw; 791 ft.; N43 10 4 W93 6 5
Mailing Address: 330 East Kilbourn Avenue, Suite 250, Milwaukee, WI 53202 US
Second Address: 341 Yorktown Pike, Mason City, IA 50401
(641) 423-1300, *Fax:* (641) 423-2906
www.kiaifm.com
wbowers@masoncity.threeeagles.com
License: Mason City, Cerro Gordo County, IA held by Three Eagles of Lincoln Inc.
Group Owner: Three Eagles Communications
Arbitron Metro Market: Mason City, IA *Format:* Country *Special Programming:* New music nashville 5 hrs wkly *Hrs. of News Programming:* News progmg 2 hrs wkly *Target Audience:* 24-54. *Adv. Rates:* 30; 40;35; 20.
Chris Frenz, General Sales Mgr
J. Brooks, Programming Director

Darcy Piper, News Director
Wolf Bowers, Program Director

KLSS-FM
11-01-1967; 106.1 mhz FM; 100 kw; 315 ft.; N43 8 31 W93 6 40
6900 Van Dorn, Suite 11, Lincoln, NE 68506 US
(641) 423-8634, *Fax:* (641) 423-8206
www.klssradio.com
klss@klssradio.com
License: Mason City, Cerro Gordo County, IA
Nat'l Network: ABC
Arbitron Metro Market: Mason City, IA *Format:* Adult Contemp *Target Audience:* 18-54. *Adv. Rates:* 28; 28; 28; 25
John Swinton, Operations Dir
Pam Dzick, General Sales Mgr
Harry O'Neil, Programming Director
Brenda McWhorter, News Director
Colleen Devine, Disc Jockey
Brian Wilson

KRIB
04-01-1948; 1490 khz AM *Hrs Open:* 24; 1 kw-U, ND1; N43 8 6 W93 12 28
6900 Van Dorn, Suite 11, Lincoln, NE 68506 US
(641) 423-1300, *Fax:* (641) 423-2906
www.discovernorthiowa.com
klss@klssradio.com
License: Mason City, IA held by Three Eagles of Mason City Inc.
Group Owner: Three Eagles Communications; (acq 5-2-97; $3.596 million with co-located FM)
Nat'l Reps: McGavren Guild
Arbitron Metro Market: Mason City, IA *Format:* Oldies *Special Programming:* Relg 5 hrs wkly *Hrs. of News Programming:* news progmg 25 hrs wkly *No. News Employees:* 2 *Target Audience:* 35 plus; marriedup-scale adults, financially secure with two incomes or retired *Adv. Rates:* 23; 23; 23; 20.
Gary Buchanan, President
Christi Lyman, Operations Dir
Dalena Barz, General Manager
Dalena Barz, Station Manager
Jared Allen, Programming Director
Bob Fisher, News Director
Ron Schacts, Chief Engineer

***KRNI**
03-01-1948; 1010 khz AM *Hrs Open:* Sunrise-sunset; 0.76 kw-D, ND1; 0.016 kw-N, ND1; N43 8 31 W93 6 40 *Rebroadcasts:* Rebroadcasts KUNI(FM) Cedar Falls 100%
324 Communications Arts, Center, Cedar Falls, IA 50614 US
(515) 725-1700, *Fax:* (515) 725-1714
www.iowapublicradio.org
info@iowapublicradio.org
License: Mason City, IA held by University of Northern Iowa.
Nat'l Network: PRI; NPR
Arbitron Metro Market: Mason City, IA *Format:* News *Special Programming:* Folk 4 hrs, blues 5 hrs wkly *Hrs. of News Programming:* news progmg 77 hrs wkly *No. News Employees:* 3 *Target Audience:* General.
Wayne Jarvis, General Manager
Scott Vezdan, Promotions Manager
Greg Shanley, News Director
Steve Schoon, Engineering Dir
Jeneane Beck, Local News Editor
Al Schares, Music Director
Pat Blank, Reporter
Tony Dehner, TrafficManager

***KNSM(FM)**
12-15-1987; 91.5 mhz FM *Hrs Open:* 24; 8 kw; 371 ft; N43 09 27 W93 08 11 *Rebroadcasts:* Rebroadcast KUNI (FM) Cedar Falls 100%
c/o KUNI-FM, Univ. of Northern Iowa, Cedar Falls, IA 50614
(319) 273-6400, *Fax:* (319) 273-2682
www.kuniradio.org
kuni@uni.edu
License: Mason City, Cerro Gordo County, IA
Nat'l Network: PRI; NPR
Arbitron Metro Market: Mason City, IA *Hrs. of News Programming:* news progmg 77 hrs wkly *No. News Employees:* 3

Frank Muller, Operations Dir
David Reese, General Manager
Kim Lizny, Programming Director
Joe Sands, Chief Engineer

Milford

KUQQ
10-01-1996; 102.1 mhz FM; 50 kw horiz, 39 kw vert; 420 ft.; N43 24 20 W95 5 1
13906 Gold Circle, Suite 201, Omaha, NE 68144 US
(712) 336-5877, *Fax:* (712) 336-1634
www.kuqqfm.com
mspies@exploreokoboji.com
License: Milford, Dickinson County, IA held by Sorenson Broadcasting Corp.
Group Owner: Sorenson Broadcasting Corp.; (acq 7-1-2004; grpsl)
Arbitron Metro Market: Milford, IA *Format:* Classic Rock *Target Audience:* 18-44.
Neil Lipetzky, CEO
Dean Sorenson, President
Marty Spies, General Manager
Jeff Nixx, Programming Director
Abby Kohlhaas, Promotions Manager
Steve Schwaller, News Director
Steve Heaton, Chief Engineer
Chad Franzen, SportsDirector
Mary Treanor, Music Director
Terry Lowry, Office Manager
Matt Fallon, Production Director
Matt Fallon, Production Director

Mitchellville

***KICJ(FM)**
88.9 mhz FM; 1 kw; Ant 236 ft; N41 40 05 W93 19 43
Rebroadcasts: KUNI-FM,Cedar Falls, IA
2111 Grand Avenue, Suite 100, Des Moines, IA 50312
(800) 861-8000, *Fax:* (515) 725-1714
www.kuniradio.org
info@iowapublicradio.org
License: Mitchellville, Polk County, IA held by University of Northern Iowa.
Population Served: 206,599 *Arbitron Metro Market:* Des Moines, IA *Format:* News, Triple A *Special Programming:* Folk 4hrs, Blues 5 hrs *Hrs. of News Programming:* 77 hrs *No. News Employees:* 3
Wayne Jarvis, General Manager
Scott Vezdos, Promotions Manager
Greg Shanley, News Director
Steve Schoon, Chief Engineer
Al Schares, Music Director

Montezuma

***KRNF**
89.7 mhz FM; 1.6 kw; 346 ft.; N41 43 55 W92 34 1 US
(641) 780-0017
License: Montezuma, Poweshiek County, IA held by American Radio Missions Foundation.
Arbitron Metro Market: Montezuma, IA *Format:* Country
Doug Smiley, General Manager

Mount Pleasant

KILJ
12-01-1974; 1130 khz AM *Hrs Open:* 24
P.O. Box 311, Mt. Pleasant, IA 52641 US
(319) 385-8728, *Fax:* (319) 385-4517
www.kilj.com
kilj@iowatelecom.net
License: Mount Pleasant, IA held by KILJ Inc.
Nat'l Network: ABC *Regional Network:* Brownfield; Radio Iowa
Format: Country *No. News Employees:* 1 *Adv. Rates:* 10; 10; 10; 10
Paul Dennison, President
John Kuhens, Station Manager
Paul Dennison, General Sales Mgr
Theresa Rose, News Director
Paul Dennison, General Sales Manager
Bob Maltocks, Paul Dennison
Lora Roth, Traffic Manager

KILJ-FM
10-01-1970; 105.5 mhz FM *Hrs Open:* 24; 24 kw; 338 ft.; N40 56 55 W91 33 55
P.O. Box 281, Mt. Pleasant, IA 52641 US
(319) 385-8728, *Fax:* (319) 385-4517
www.kilj.com
kiljradio@kilj.com
License: Mount Pleasant, Henry County, IA held by KILJ Inc.
Regional Network: Brownfield; Radio Iowa
Format: Country *No. News Employees:* 1 *Target Audience:* 25-54. *Adv. Rates:* 10; 10; 10; 10
Paul Dennison, President
John Kuhens, General Manager
Paul Dennison, General Sales Mgr
Theresa Rose, News Director

Mount Vernon

***KRNL-FM**
04-01-1948; 89.7 mhz FM *Hrs Open:* Midnight-noon; 0.045 kw; 167 ft.; N41 55 34 W91 25 32
810 Commons Circle, Mt. Vernon, IA 52314 US
(319) 895-4431
www.cornellcollege.edu/krnl/
krnl@cornellcollege.edu
License: Mount Vernon, Linn County, IA held by Cornell College.
Nat'l Network: USA
Format: Talk *Special Programming:* Folk 2 hrs, Ger 2 hrs, jazz 2 hrs, Sp one hr wkly *Target Audience:* 18-25; collegians & those seeking an alternative to coml radio
Jacob Gehl, General Manager
Ji 'Max' Zhang, Station Manager
Josh Boegner, Programming Director
Haley Severance, Promotions Manager

Moville

***KNSX(FM)**
97.1 mhz FM; 5.2 kw; 108.6 meters; N42 32 47.3 W96 01 08.2
Rebroadcasts: KUNI(FM) Cedar Falls 100%
Iowa Public Radio, 2111 Grand Avenue, Suite 100, Des Moines, IA 50312
(515) 725-1700, *Fax:* (515) 725-1714
iowapublicradio.org
License: Moville, Woodbury County, IA held by Iowa State University of Science & Technology

Mary Grace Herrington, CEO

Muscatine

KBEA-FM
02-01-1949; 99.7 mhz FM *Hrs Open:* 24; 100 kw; 869 ft.; N41 36 22 W90 59 35
1229 Brady Street, Davenport, IA 52803 US
(563) 326-2541, *Fax:* (563) 326-1819
License: Muscatine, Muscatine County, IA held by Cumulus Licensing Corp.
Group Owner: Cumulus Media Inc.; (acq 3-15-00; grpsl).
Arbitron Metro Market: Quad Cities, IA-IL (Davenport-Rock Island-Moline) *Format:* Contemporary Hits/Top 40 *No. News Employees:* 1 *Target Audience:* 25-54.
Jack Swart, General Manager
Julie Derrer, General Sales Mgr
Steve Fuller, Programming Director
Tracy Hall, News Director
Andy Andresen, Chief Engineer

KMCS
06-16-1996; 93.1 mhz FM *Hrs Open:* 24; 4.4 kw; 384 ft.; N41 26 34 W91 4 33
3218 Mulberry Avenue, Muscatine, IA 52761 US
(563) 263-2442, *Fax:* (563) 263-9206
www.voiceofmuscatine.com
mail@voiceofmuscatine.com
License: Muscatine, Muscatine County, IA
Group Owner: Prairie Radio Communications
Nat'l Network: USA; AP Radio
Arbitron Metro Market: Muscatine, IA *Format:* Country *Hrs. of News Programming:* News progmg 6 hrs wkly *Target Audience:* 25-54. *Adv. Rates:* Same as AM
Dale Palmer, Operations Dir
Chuck Morgan, General Manager
Julie Williams, Sales Dept.
Shelly Keltner, Sales Dept.
Debbi Hendriks, Sales Dept.
Lisa, Receptionist

KWPC
01-05-1947; 860 khz AM *Hrs Open:* 24; 0.25 kw-D, ND1; 0.008 kw-N, ND1; N41 26 34 W91 4 33
3218 Mulberry Avenue, Muscatine, IA 52761 US
(563) 263-2442, *Fax:* (563) 263-9206
www.voiceofmuscatine.com
mail@voiceofmuscatine.com
License: Muscatine, IA held by WPW Broadcasting Inc.
Group Owner: Prairie Radio Communications; (acq 11-5-99; $2.2 million with co-located FM)
Nat'l Network: USA
Arbitron Metro Market: Muscatine, IA *Format:* Oldies *Hrs. of News Programming:* news progmg 20 hrs wkly *No. News Employees:* 2 *Target Audience:* 25-54. *Adv. Rates:* 17; 17; 17; 17
Terri Forbes, CFO
Don Davis, President
Chuck Morgan, General Manager
Julie Williams, Sales Dept.

Shelly Kltner, Sales Dept.
Debbi Hendricks, Sales Dept.

New Hampton

KCZE

12-01-1992; 95.1 mhz FM; 5.5 kw; 338 ft.; N43 2 46 W92 18 9
330 East Kilbourn Avenue, Suite 250, Milwaukee, WI 53202 US
(641) 228-1000, *Fax:* (641) 228-1200
www.951thebull.com
chrisberg@northiowabroadcasting.com
License: New Hampton, Chickasaw County, IA held by Coloff Media, LLC.
Nat'l Network: CNN Radio *Regional Network:* Radio Iowa
Arbitron Metro Market: New Hampton, IA *Format:* Country
Special Programming: Farm 12 hrs wkly *Target Audience:* General.

Jim Coloff, General Manager
Scott Lane, Station Manager
Chris Berg, Programming Director
Chris Berg, News Director
Chris Berg, News Director

New London

KHDK

10-05-2001; 97.3 mhz FM *Hrs Open:* 24; 3.8 kw; 410 ft.; N40 47 53 W91 26 22
Gammon & Grange, P.C., 8280 Greensboro, 7th Fl., McLean, VA 22102 US
(319) 752-5402, *Fax:* (319) 752-4715
hot973online.com
hot973@hot973online.com
License: New London, Henry County, IA held by Pritchard Broadcasting Corp.
Group Owner: Pritchard Broadcasting Corp.; (acq 12-27-99; $25,000 for CP)
Nat'l Reps: Katz Radio
Arbitron Metro Market: Burlington, IA *Format:* Contemporary Hits/Top 40 *Hrs. of News Programming:* news progmg 1 hrs wkly *No. News Employees:* 1 *Target Audience:* 25-54. *Adv. Rates:* 17; 17; 17; 8

John Pritchard, President
Joe Bates, Operations Dir
John Pritchard, General Manager
Chet Young, General Sales Mgr
Tim Bayless, Programming Director
Joe Bates, Operations Manager/Music Director

New Sharon

KCWN

10-16-1995; 99.9 mhz FM *Hrs Open:* 6 AM-11 PM; 25 kw; 282 ft.; N41 17 32 W92 40 24
Mailing Address: Box 999, Pella, IA 50219 US
Second Address: 304 Oskaloosa St., Pella, IA 50219
(641) 628-9999(888) 506-4562, *Fax:* (641) 628-9229
www.kcwnfm.org
kcwn@kcwnfm.org
License: New Sharon, Mahaska County, IA held by Crown Broadcasting Co.
Arbitron Metro Market: Pella, IA *Format:* Adult Contemp, Christian *Adv. Rates:* 14; 14; 14; 14

Marion Vink, CEO
Beverly DeVries, Station Manager
Sharyl Fosenburg, General Sales Mgr
Nicole Fopma, Traffic Director

Newton

KCOB

09-15-1955; 1280 khz AM; 0.73 kw-D, ND1; 0.019 kw-N, ND1; N41 44 11 W93 1 12
P.O. Box 66, 1801 N. 13th Ave. East, Newton, IA 50208 US
(641) 792-5262, *Fax:* (641) 792-8403
kcobradio.com
info@kcobradio.com
License: Newton, IA held by Newton License Co. LLC.
Group Owner: GoodRadio.TV; (acq 5-1-2007; grpsl)
Arbitron Metro Market: Newton, IA *Format:* Country, News
Special Programming: Farm 2 hrs wkly *Target Audience:* 25-50.

Dean Goodman, CEO
Ron McCarthy, General Manager
Terry Walter, Sports Director and Programming Director
Randy Van, News Director
Phil Benjamin, Chief Engineer

KCOB-FM

01-03-1969; 95.9 mhz FM *Hrs Open:* 18; 5.1 kw; 354 ft.; N41 44 11 W93 1 12
P.O. Box 66, 1801 N. 13th Ave. East, Newton, IA 50208 US
(641) 792-5262, *Fax:* (641) 792-8403
kcobradio.com
info@kcobradio.com
License: Newton, Jasper County, IA held by Newton License Co. LLC.
Group Owner: GoodRadio.TV
Arbitron Metro Market: Newton, IA *Format:* Country

Lamar Marchese, President
Phil Burger, Operations Dir
Melanie Canon, General Sales Mgr
Terry Walter, Sports Director and Programming Director
Randy Van, News Director
Warren Brown, Chief Engineer
Florence Rogers, President
JayBartos, Public Affairs Director

*KKLG

01-01-2005; 88.3 mhz FM; 0.4 kw; 218 ft.; N41 41 33 W93 0 37
Rebroadcasts: Rebroadcasts KLVR(FM) Santa Rosa, CA 100%
188 South Bellevue, Suite 222, Memphis, TN 38104 US
(800) 525-5683, *Fax:* (916) 251-1650
www.klove.com
klove@klove.com
License: Newton, Jasper County, IA held by Educational Media Foundation.
Group Owner: EMF Broadcasting; (acq 9-22-2005; $20,000 for CP)
Nat'l Network: K-Love
Arbitron Metro Market: Newton, IA *Format:* Christian *No. News Employees:* 13

Darrell Chambliss, Chairman
Mike Novak, President and CEO
Glenn Goodwin, General Sales Mgr
David Pierce, Chief Creative Officer and Programming Director
Ed Lenane, News Director
Sam Wallington, Engineering Dir
Marya Morgan, NewsReporter
Richard Hunt, News Reporter
Alan Mason, Chief Operating Officer
Dan Antonelli, Chief Business Development Officer
Eric Moser, Chief Financial Officer
Brian Burger, Vice President of Human Resources

Northwood

KYTC

10-15-1990; 102.7 mhz FM *Hrs Open:* 24; 25 kw; 295 ft.; N43 29 18 W93 14 11
P.O. Box 2837, Mason City, IA 50401 US
(402) 466-1234, *Fax:* (402) 467-4095
www.threeeagles.com
dabarz@masoncity.threeeagles.com
License: Northwood, Worth County, IA held by Three Eagles of Mason City Inc.
Group Owner: Three Eagles Communications; (acq 5-21-99)
Regional Network: Tribune Radio Networks
Arbitron Metro Market: Northwood, IA *Special Programming:* Gospel one hr, relg 2 hrs wkly *Hrs. of News Programming:* news progmg 6 hrs wkly *No. News Employees:* 1 *Target Audience:* 25-64; primary audience men &women 35+ *Adv. Rates:* 23; 23; 23; 19

Rolland Johnson, CEO
Gary Buchanan, President
Henry O'Neil, Operations Dir
Dalena Barz, Station Manager

Oelwein

KOEL

07-23-1950; 950 khz AM *Hrs Open:* 24
136 Main Street, Westport, CT 06880 US
(319) 283-1234, *Fax:* (319) 283-3615
koelam@koel.com
License: Oelwein, IA held by Cumulus Licensing Corp.
Group Owner: Cumulus Media Inc.; (acq 3-15-00; grpsl).
Format: News, News/Talk, 84, Talk *Special Programming:* Farm 16 hrs wkly *Hrs. of News Programming:* news progmg 30 hrs wkly *No. News Employees:* 2 *Target Audience:* 35 plus.

Jeffrey Warshaw, President
Jeff Dientz, Operations Dir
Rob Murthum, General Manager
Craig Friedrich, General Sales Mgr
Rich Calvert, Programming Director
Matt Kelly, Music Director
Bob Fisher, National Sales Manager
DickStadlen, Operations Manager
April Walker, Promotions Manager

KKHQ-FM

12-29-1971; 92.3 mhz FM *Hrs Open:* 24; 100 kw; 1,000 ft; N42 40 53 W91 52 52
Box 720, Blacks Bldg., Waterloo, IA 06880
(319) 833-4800,(800) 923-5635, *Fax:* (319) 833-4866
License: Oelwein, Fayette County, IA held by Cumulus Licensing LLC
Group Owner: Cumulus Media Inc.
Population Served: 150,000 *Arbitron Metro Market:* Waterloo-Cedar Falls, IA *Hrs. of News Programming:* news progmg 2 hrs wkly *No. News Employees:* 1 *Target Audience:* 35 plus.

Mark Anderson, General Sales Mgr
Bill Knight, Programming Director
April Walker, Promotions Manager
Elwin Huffman, News Director
Wes Davis, Chief Engineer

Okoboji

*KOJI

01-01-2002; 90.7 mhz FM *Hrs Open:* 24; 4.5 kw; 371 ft.; N43 9 53 W95 19 29 *Rebroadcasts:* Rebroadcasts KWIT(FM) Sioux City 100%
US
(712) 274-6406, *Fax:* (712) 274-6411
www.kwit-koji.org
gondekg@witcc.edu
License: Okoboji, Dickinson County, IA held by Western Iowa Tech Community College.
Nat'l Network: NPR; PRI *Wire Services:* AP
Arbitron Metro Market: Sioux City, IA *Format:* News, News/Talk, 86 *Special Programming:* Triple A 18 hrs, blues 4 hrs, jazz 17 hrs wkly *Hrs. of News Programming:* news progmg 36 hrs wkly *No. News Employees:* 1

Gretchen Gondek, General Manager
Dennis Semple, Chief Engineer
Duane Kraayenbrink, News Editor
Jake Moreland, Arts Producer
Margaret Holman, Account Executive
Mindy Thompson, Office Assistant
Steve Smith, Operations Manager

Onawa

KQNU(FM)

11-06-1995; 102.3 mhz FM *Hrs Open:* 24; 100 kw; Ant 643 ft; N42 10 29 W96 23 13
2000 Indian Hills Dr., Sioux City, IA 51104
(712) 239-2100, *Fax:* (712) 239-3346
www.jackfm1023.com
License: Onawa, Monona County, IA held by Powell Broadcasting Co. Inc.
Group Owner: Powell Broadcasting Co. Inc.; (acq 5-1-2007; $4.2 million with KKYY(FM) Whiting)
Population Served: 2,997 *Arbitron Metro Market:* Onawa, IA *Format:* Variety/Diverse *Hrs. of News Programming:* One *Target Audience:* 25-54. *Adv. Rates:* 18; 18; 18; 16

Dennis Bullock, General Manager

Osage

KSMA-FM

07-09-1980; 98.7 mhz FM; 25 kw; 328 ft.; N43 21 53 W93 2 53
111 East Kilbourn Ave, Suite 2700, Milwaukee, WI 53202 US
(641) 421-7744, *Fax:* (641) 423-2906
www.kiss987.com
KISS@987KISSCountry.com
License: Osage, Mitchell County, IA held by Three Eagles of Lincoln Inc.
Group Owner: Three Eagles Communications; (acq 9-1-2007; grpsl)
Nat'l Reps: Farmakis
Arbitron Metro Market: Mason City, IA *Format:* Adult Contemp
Target Audience: General; 12-25 *Adv. Rates:* 40; 40; 35; 15

Tim Fleming, Operations Dir
Jim Coloff, General Manager
Dan Maynard, Programming Director
Tami Ramon, Promotions Manager
Laurie Gansen, News Director
J. Brooks, Operations Manager / Program Director
Michelle Horst, BusinessManager
Amber Nuehring, Office Assistant
Jamie Nelson, Marketing Consultants
Tami Ramon, Marketing Consultants
LuAnn Scholbrock, Marketing Consultants

Osceola

***KNWI**
10-04-1982; 107.1 mhz FM *Hrs Open:* 24; 27 kw; 650 ft.; N41 1 34 W93 51 43
4 Catherine Circle, Wilbraham, MA 01095 US
(515) 327-1071, *Fax:* (515) 327-1073
www.desmoines.fm
knwi@desmoines.fm
License: Osceola, Clarke County, IA held by Northwestern College.
Group Owner: Northwestern College & Radio; (acq 12-30-2003; $1.8 million with KNWM(FM) Madrid).
Arbitron Metro Market: Des Moines, IA *Format:* Christian *Target Audience:* 18-44; women
Richard Whitworth, General Manager
Dave St. John, Programming Director

Oskaloosa

KBOE
11-15-1950; 740 khz AM *Hrs Open:* 24; 0.229 kw-D, ND1; 0.01 kw-N, ND1; N41 19 15 W92 38 44
P.O. Box 380, Oskaloosa, IA 52527 US
(515) 673-3493, *Fax:* (515) 673-3495
www.kboeradio.com
kboe@kboeradio.com
License: Oskaloosa, IA held by Jomast Corp.
Regional Network: Brownfield; Radio Iowa
Format: Country *Special Programming:* Gospel 9 hrs wkly *Hrs. of News Programming:* news progmg 15 hrs wkly *No. News Employees:* 1 *Target Audience:* 25-50.
Brad Muhl, President
Glenda Lind-Booy, General Manager
Gary Wilson, Chief Engineer

KBOE-FM
02-07-1964; 104.9 mhz FM *Hrs Open:* 24; 50 kw; 492 ft.; N41 19 15 W92 38 44
P.O. Box 380, Oskaloosa, IA 52577 US
(641) 673-3493, *Fax:* (641) 673-3495
www.kboeradio.com
License: Oskaloosa, Mahaska County, IA held by Jomast Corp.
Nat'l Network: ABC
Format: Country
Glenda Booy, General Manager

***KIGC**
01-01-1975; 88.7 mhz FM *Hrs Open:* 24; 0.23 kw horiz; 121 ft.; N41 18 37 W92 38 49
201 Trueblood Avenue, Oskaloosa, IA 52577 US
(641) 673-1095, *Fax:* (641) 673-1396
License: Oskaloosa, Mahaska County, IA held by William Penn University
Format: Alternative, Black, 64 *Special Programming:* Jazz 12 hrs, gospel 12 hrs wkly *Hrs. of News Programming:* News progmg one hr wkly *Target Audience:* 13-25.
Larz Roberts, General Manager
James Roberts, Programming Director

Ottumwa

KBIZ
01-01-1941; 1240 khz AM; 1 kw-U, ND1; N41 0 0 W92 23 23
209 South Market Street, B/Cast Center, Bx 190, Ottumwa, IA 52501 US
(641) 684-5563, *Fax:* (641) 684-5832
www.kbizam.com
License: Ottumwa, IA held by O-Town Communications Inc.
Group Owner: O-Town Communications Inc.; (acq 10-20-2005; $890,000 with co-located FM).
Nat'l Network: CBS
Arbitron Metro Market: Ottumwa, IA *Format:* News, News/Talk, 86 *Target Audience:* 25-54.
Greg List, President
Jason Van Arkel, Operations Dir
Greg List, General Manager
Mike Buchanan, News Director
Phil Benjamin, Chief Engineer

KLEE
08-01-1954; 1480 khz AM *Hrs Open:* 24
Fletcher, Heald Et Al, 1300 N 17th St, NW 11flr, Washington, DC 22209 US
(641) 682-8711, *Fax:* (641) 682-8482
traffic@kotm.com
License: Ottumwa, IA held by FMC Broadcasting Inc.
Nat'l Network: Westwood One *Regional Network:* Brownfield
Arbitron Metro Market: Des Moines, IA *Format:* Country, News, 62, Talk *Special Programming:* Gospel 6 hrs, polka one hr wkly *Hrs. of News Programming:* news progmg 28 hrs wkly *No. News Employees:* 1 *TargetAudience:* General; people on the move
Thomas Palen, President
Dave Michaels, Programming Director
Marcia Wagner, Promotions Manager
Mike Dixon, News Director
Fred Jenkins, Chief Engineer

KOTM-FM
03-22-1976; 97.7 mhz FM; 19 kw; 367 ft.; N41 1 28 W92 28 56
601 W. Second Street, Ottumwa, IA 52501 US
(641) 682-8711,(641) 682-8712, *Fax:* (641) 682-8482
www.kotm.com
traffic@kotm.com
License: Ottumwa, Wapello County, IA
Nat'l Network: Westwood One
Format: Contemporary Hits/Top 40 *Target Audience:* Teens-50.
Steve Niemeyer, General Manager

KTWA
12-01-1984; 92.7 mhz FM *Hrs Open:* 24; 50 kw; 318 ft.; N41 1 29 W92 28 9
Broadcast Center Box 190, 209 S. Market, Ottumwa, IA 52501 US
(641) 684-5563, *Fax:* (641) 684-5832
www.ktwafm.com
info@ottumwaradio.com
License: Ottumwa, Wapello County, IA held by O-Town Communications Inc.
Group Owner: O-Town Communications Inc.
Arbitron Metro Market: Ottumwa, IA *Format:* Adult Contemp
Greg List, President, General Manager
Greg List, General Manager
Phil Benjamin, Chief Engineer
Margie Stansberry, Sales
Gene Stine, Sales
Lindsey Chapa, Sales
Calynda Argo, Sales
Shea Earlywine, Sales
Sara Jane Douglas,Sales

***KNSZ(FM)**
89.1 mhz FM; 13.5 kw; Ant 449 ft; N40 57 41 W92 22 13
2022 Communications Bldg., Iowa State University, Ames, IA 50011
(515) 294-2025, *Fax:* (515) 294-1544
www.iowapublicradio.org
License: Ottumwa, Wapello County, IA held by Iowa State University of Science and Technology.
Mary Grace Herrington, Programming Director
Don Wirth, Director, Fiscal Operations

Parkersburg

KQCR-FM
10-18-2000; 98.9 mhz FM *Hrs Open:* 24; 6 kw; 328 ft.; N42 33 48 W92 57 22
Mailing Address: 1509 4th Street Ne, P O Box 495, Hampton, IA 50441 US
Second Address: 1509 4th St NE, Hampton, IA 50441-1106
(641) 456-5656, *Fax:* (641) 456-5655
www.kqcr.fm
kqcr@kqcr.fm
License: Parkersburg, Butler County, IA held by CD Broadcasting Inc.
Arbitron Metro Market: Hampton, IA *Format:* Adult Contemp *Hrs. of News Programming:* news progmg 12 hrs wkly *No. News Employees:* 2 *Target Audience:* 25-45; Light, Soft AC 70's, 80's, 90's *Adv. Rates:* 19;19; 19; 19
Marlin Burrier, Operations Dir
Craig Donnelly, General Manager
Duane Carstens, Sales Manager And The Morning Sports Guy
Betsy Roberts, News Director
Steve Daniels, Chief Engineer
Kathy Donnelly, Bookkeeper and Office Manager
MikeBetten, Music Director And Morning Announcer
Mandy Strother, Traffic
Sue Followwill, KLMJ / KQCR Sales Representative and Traffic For K
Gladys Fanny, The Front Desk Receptionist and also Handles the H
Jeff Moss, Sports Director and Play byPlay Voice For KLMJ &

Pella

KAZR
08-01-1976; 103.3 mhz FM *Hrs Open:* 24; 100 kw; 745 ft.; N41 32 18 W93 17 58
73 Kercheval Ave, Crosse Pointe, MI 48236 US
(515) 280-1350, *Fax:* (515) 280-3011
www.lazer1033.com
License: Pella, Marion County, IA held by Saga Communications of Iowa LLC.
Group Owner: Saga Communications Inc.; (acq 9-17-96; $2.7 million)
Nat'l Reps: Katz Radio *Wire Services:* AP
Arbitron Metro Market: Des Moines, IA *Format:* Rock/AOR *Hrs. of News Programming:* news progmg 4 hrs wkly *Target Audience:* 25-44.
Scott Allen, Operations Dir
Jeff Delvaux, General Manager
Pam Washington, General Sales Mgr
Ryan Patrick, Programming Director
Rob Lembke, Promotions Manager
Dan Abbuehl, Advertising Manager
Pam Washington, Sales Director

Perry

KDLS
05-10-1961; 1310 khz AM *Hrs Open:* 6 AM-10 PM; 0.5 kw-D, DA2; 0.3 kw-N, DA2; N41 49 58 W94 2 15
Mailing Address: 2260 141st Drive, P.O. Box 548, Perry, IA 50220 US
Second Address: 2260 141st Drive, Perry, IA 50220
(515) 465-5357, *Fax:* (515) 465-3952
kdls@prairieinet.net
License: Perry, IA held by Coon Valley Communications Inc.
Group Owner: Coon Valley Communications Inc.; (acq 2-15-2006; $300,000)
Nat'l Network: Westwood One; CNN Radio *Nat'l Reps:* Farmakis *Wire Services:* AP
Arbitron Metro Market: Des Moines, IA *Format:* Variety/Diverse *Hrs. of News Programming:* news progmg 25 hrs wkly *No. News Employees:* 1 *Target Audience:* General. *Adv. Rates:* 14; 11; 11; 6
Patrick Delaney, President
Tom Quinlan, Operations Dir
Patrick Graney, General Manager
Bob Pink, Chief Engineer
John Patrick, Operations Director
Marcia Murphy, Traffic Manager

KDLS-FM
02-26-1971; 105.5 mhz FM *Hrs Open:* 6 AM-midnight; 10 kw; 515 ft.; N41 43 35 W93 51 38
P.O. Box 548, 2260 141st Drive, Perry, IA 50220 US
(515) 278-4117, *Fax:* (515) 254-1037
www.laley1055fm.com
info@kdlsfm.com
License: Perry, Dallas County, IA held by Perry Broadcasting Co.
Arbitron Metro Market: Des Moines, IA *Adv. Rates:* 12; 12; 10; 6
Joel Garcia, General Manager

Pleasantville

KICL(FM)
03-12-2008; 96.3 mhz FM; 500 w; Ant 255 ft; N41 21 04 W93 13 58
1513 N. 1st St., Indianola, IA 50125
(515) 961-3338, *Fax:* (515) 961-3338
License: Pleasantville, Marion County, IA held by Iowas State University of Science and Technology
Group Owner: Connoisseur Media LLC
Population Served: 1,695 *Arbitron Metro Market:* Pleasantville, IA *Format:* Country
Rebecca Orr, General Manager

Postville

***KPVL**
01-01-2003; 89.1 mhz FM; 3 kw; 246 ft.; N43 5 20 W91 33 54
116 E. Military Rd, Postville, IA 52162 US
(563) 864-7945, *Fax:* (563) 864-7940
www.kpvlradio.com
info@kpvlradio.com
License: Postville, Allamakee County, IA held by Postville Chamber of Commerce.
Arbitron Metro Market: Postville, IA *Format:* Talk, News
Randy Frank, General Manager

Red Oak

KOAK
08-16-1968; 1080 khz AM *Hrs Open:* Sunrise-sunset
P.O. Box 465, Red Oak, IA 51566 US
(712) 623-2584, *Fax:* (712) 623-2583
kcsifm.com
kcsi@kcsifm.com
License: Red Oak, IA held by Hawkeye Communications Inc.
Nat'l Network: ABC *Regional Network:* Radio Iowa *Wire Services:* AP
Format: Country

Jerry Dietz, President
Melanie West, General Sales Mgr
Marilyn Dietz, News Director

Rock Valley

KIHK
01-01-1998; 106.9 mhz FM *Hrs Open:* 6 AM-6 AM; 25 kw; 328 ft.; N43 20 28 W96 19 3
1039 Radio Drive, Spirit Lake, IA 51360 US
(712) 722-1090, *Fax:* (712) 722-1102
www.ksoufm.com
ksou@waittradio.com
License: Rock Valley, Sioux County, IA held by Sorenson Broadcasting Corp.
Group Owner: Sorenson Broadcasting Corp.; (acq 7-1-2004; grpsl)
Format: Country *Special Programming:* High School sports
Craig Aukes, General Manager
Dan Bonnema, General Sales Mgr
Doug Brock, News Director

Rockford

KYME
01-01-2008; 92.9 mhz FM; 0.375 kw; 33 ft.; N43 3 12 W92 57 15 US
(301) 759-1155
www.cumberlandsmagic.com
psullivan@alleganyradio.com
License: Rockford, Floyd County, IA held by Radioactive LLC.
Group Owner: Radioactive LLC
Arbitron Metro Market: Rockford, IA *Format:* Adult Contemp
Benjamin Homel, President

Sac City

KEWS(FM)
104.7 mhz FM; 6 kw; Ant 159 ft; N42 24 40 W95 00 17
1717 Dixie Hwy., Suite 650, Fort Wright, KY 41011
(859) 331-9100
License: Sac City, Sac County, IA held by Radioactive LLC.
Group Owner: Radioactive LLC
Population Served: 2,197 *Arbitron Metro Market:* Sac City, IA
Benjamin Homel, President

Sageville

KIYX
01-01-1999; 106.1 mhz FM *Hrs Open:* 24; 4.2 kw; 394 ft.; N42 41 27 W90 37 26
7025 Raymond Road, Madison, WI 53744 US
(608) 349-2000, *Fax:* (608) 349-2002
info@kyix.com
License: Sageville, Dubuque County, IA held by Queen B Radio Wisconsin Inc.
Nat'l Network: Westwood One
Format: Contemporary Hits/Top 40 *No. News Employees:* 1 *Adv. Rates:* 8; 6; 6; 6
Dan Sullivan, General Manager

Sanborn

KXIM
98.3 mhz FM; 6 kw; 328 feet; N43 08 31 W95 37 13
6404 South Tomar Road, Sioux Falls, SD
(605) 929-0413
am770radioengineering@gmail.com
License: Sanborn, IA held by AM 770 Radio Engineering
Paul L Heeren, General Manager

Sheldon

KIWA
10-27-1961; 1550 khz AM *Hrs Open:* 24
411 Ninth Street, Sheldon, IA 51201 US
(712) 324-2597, *Fax:* (712) 324-2340
www.kiwaradio.com
newtips@kiwaradio.com
License: Sheldon, IA held by Sheldon Broadcasting Co. Inc.
Nat'l Network: ABC *Regional Network:* Radio Iowa *Nat'l Reps:* Farmakis
Format: News, News/Talk, 86 *Hrs. of News Programming:* news progmg 15 hrs wkly *No. News Employees:* 2 *Target Audience:* General; adult
Walt Pruiksma, General Manager
Wayne Barahona, Programming Director
Tim Torkildson, News Director
Larry Ahrens, Sports Commentator
Jessica DeBoer, Traffic Manager

KIWA-FM
10-01-1971; 105.3 mhz FM *Hrs Open:* 24; 50 kw; Ant 292 ft; N43 11 00 W95 52 05
411 9th St., Sheldon, IA 51201
(712) 324-2597, *Fax:* (712) 324-2340
www.kiwaradio.com
walt@kiwaradio.com
License: Sheldon, Obrien County, IA held by Sheldon Broadcasting Co. Inc.
Nat'l Reps: Farmakis
Population Served: 65,000*Hrs. of News Programming:* news progmg 15 hrs wkly *No. News Employees:* 2 *Target Audience:* General.
Walt Pruiksma, General Manager
Wayne Barahana, Chief Engineer

Shenandoah

KMA
08-12-1925; 960 khz AM *Hrs Open:* 24; 5 kw-D, DAN; 5 kw-N, DAN; N40 46 48 W95 21 23
209 North Elm Street, Shenandoah, IA 51601 US
(712) 246-5270, *Fax:* (712) 246-5275
www.kma960.com
marke@kmakkbz.com
License: Shenandoah, IA held by May Broadcasting Co.
Nat'l Network: ABC
Format: News, News/Talk, 86 *Special Programming:* Farm *Hrs. of News Programming:* news progmg 15 hrs wkly *No. News Employees:* 2 *Target Audience:* 35-54. *Adv. Rates:* 135; 135; 85; 75
Edward May, President
Mark Eno, General Manager
Don Hansen, Station Manager

***KYFR**
01-01-1977; 920 khz AM *Hrs Open:* 24
Mailing Address: 4135 Northgate Blvd, Suite 1, Sacramento, CA 95834 US
Second Address: 700 W. Sheridan Ave., Shenandoah, IA 51601
(712) 246-5151
www.familyradio.com/english
info@familyradio.org
License: Shenandoah, IA held by Family Stations Inc.
Group Owner: Family Stations Inc.; (acq 1976)
Nat'l Network: Family Radio
Arbitron Metro Market: Oakland, CA *Format:* Christian
Harold Camping, President
Mike DeStefano, Station Manager

Sioux Center

***KDCR**
08-16-1968; 88.5 mhz FM; 100 kw; 495 ft.; N43 5 34 W96 9 23
Dordt College Campus, Sioux Center, IA 51250 US
(712) 722-0885, *Fax:* (712) 722-6244
www.kdcrdordt.edu
kdcr@dordt.edu
License: Sioux Center, Sioux County, IA held by Dordt College Inc.
Nat'l Network: USA
Arbitron Metro Market: Sioux Center, IA *Format:* Religious
Special Programming: Farm 2 hrs, Dutch one hr wkly
Dennis DeWaard, General Manager
Denny De Waard, Station Manager
Jim Bolkema, Programming Director
John Slegers, News Director
Ralph Goemaat, Chief Engineer
Jim Bolkema, Music Director
Mike Byker, Sports Director

KSOU
11-17-1969; 1090 khz AM *Hrs Open:* Sunrise-sunset; 0.5 kw-D, DAD; N43 3 22 W96 10 17
P.O. Box 528, Spirit Lake, IA 51360 US
(712) 722-1090(712) 722-1091, *Fax:* (712) 722-1102
www.ksoufm.com
License: Sioux Center, IA held by Sorenson Broadcasting Corp.
Group Owner: Sorenson Broadcasting Corp.; (acq 7-1-2004; grpsl)
Nat'l Reps: Farmakis
Arbitron Metro Market: Sioux Center, IA *Format:* Christian *Hrs. of News Programming:* news progmg 17 hrs wkly *No. News Employees:* 1 *Target Audience:* General.
Shirley Wierda, Operations Dir
Craig Aukes, General Manager
Dan Bonnema, General Sales Mgr
James DeBoer, Programming Director
Doug Broek, News Director
Steve Heaton, Chief Engineer

KSOU-FM
10-17-1974; 93.9 mhz FM *Hrs Open:* 24; 50 kw; 492 ft.; N43 5 1 W96 18 20
P.O. Box 298, Sioux Center, IA 51250 US
(712) 722-1090, *Fax:* (712) 722-1102
www.ksoufm.com
License: Sioux Center, Sioux County, IA
Group Owner: Sorenson Broadcasting Corp.
Nat'l Network: ABC
Arbitron Metro Market: Sioux Center, IA *Format:* Adult Contemp
Steve Heaton, Operations Dir
Scott France, Programming Director
Shirley Wierda, Women's Int Ed

Sioux City

KGLI
03-11-1974; 95.5 mhz FM *Hrs Open:* 24; 100 kw; 899 ft.; N42 30 53 W96 18 13
Mailing Address: P O Box 3009, Sioux City, IA 51102 US
Second Address: 1113 Nebraska St., Sioux City, IA 51105
(712) 258-5595, *Fax:* (712) 252-2430
www.kg95.com
License: Sioux City, Woodbury County, IA
Group Owner: Clear Channel Communications Inc.
Arbitron Metro Market: Sioux City, IA *Format:* Adult Contemp *Target Audience:* 18-49.
Rob Powers, Operations Dir
Mike Newhouse, General Sales Mgr
Ryan Reid, Programming Director
Laura Schiltz, Promotions Manager
Monica Mattoon, News Director
Stan Culley, Chief Engineer
Shirley Dicus, Business Manager
RhondaJohnson, Promotions Manager

KMNS
05-01-1949; 620 khz AM *Hrs Open:* 24
Mailing Address: PO Box 3009, Sioux City, IA 51102 US
Second Address: 1113 Nebraska St., Sioux City, IA 51102
(712) 258-0628, *Fax:* (712) 252-2430
www.620kmns.com
License: Sioux City, IA held by AMFM Radio Licenses LLC.
Group Owner: Clear Channel Communications Inc.; (acq 10-1-2002; grpsl)
Nat'l Reps: Katz Radio
Arbitron Metro Market: Sioux City, IA *Format:* Sports *Target Audience:* 18-54.
Rob Powers, Operations Dir
Rhonda Johnson, General Sales Mgr
Curtis Anderson, Programming Director
Laura Schiltz, Promotions Manager
Monica Mattoon, News Director
Stan Culley, Chief Engineer
Shirley Dicus, Business Manager
MikeNewhouse

***KMSC**
04-01-1978; 92.9 mhz FM; 0.012 kw; 184 ft.; N42 28 28 W96 21 34
1501 Morningside Ave, Sioux City, IA 51106 US
(712) 274-5665, *Fax:* (712) 274-5664
http://kmsc.morningside.edu/
kmsc@morningside.edu
License: Sioux City, Woodbury County, IA held by Morningside College Board of Directors.
Arbitron Metro Market: Sioux City, IA *Format:* Alternative *Target Audience:* General; high school, college students & young professionals
Ron Jorgensen, CFO
John Reinders, President
Dr. Mark Heistad, General Manager
Nick Brincks, Station Manager
Michael Lewis, Promotions Manager
Claire DeRoin, News Director
Bill Deeds, Executive Vice President

KSCJ
01-01-1927; 1360 khz AM *Hrs Open:* 24; 5 kw-D, DAN; 5 kw-N, DAN; N42 33 24 W96 20 12
P.O. Box 788, Baton Rouge, LA 70821 US
(712) 239-2100, *Fax:* (712) 239-3346
www.kscj.com
License: Sioux City, IA held by Powell Broadcasting Co.
Group Owner: Powell Broadcasting Co. Inc.; (acq 1996; $3.8 million with KSUX(FM) Winnebago, NE)
Nat'l Network: ABC *Regional Reps:* REGIONAL REPS
Arbitron Metro Market: Sioux City, IA *Format:* News, News/Talk, 84, Talk *Hrs. of News Programming:* news progmg 42 hrs wkly *No. News Employees:* 2 *Target Audience:* 35-64; educated, higher income, issues-oriented*Adv. Rates:* 20; 20; 20; 15

Dennis Bullock, General Manager
Dave Grossenherder, General Sales Mgr
Steve Arthur, Programming Director
Randy Renshaw, News Director

KSEZ
02-06-1960; 97.9 mhz FM *Hrs Open:* 24; 100 kw; 643 ft.; N42 28 56 W96 15 30
Mailing Address: P.O. Box 3009, Sioux City, IA 51102 US
Second Address: 1113 Nebraska St., Sioux City, IA 51105
(712) 258-5595, *Fax:* (712) 252-2430
www.z98rocks.com
License: Sioux City, Woodbury County, IA
Group Owner: Clear Channel Communications Inc.
Nat'l Network: ABC *Nat'l Reps:* Katz Radio
Arbitron Metro Market: Sioux City, IA *Format:* Classic Rock
Target Audience: 18-49.
Rob Powers, Operations Dir
Rhonda Johnson, General Sales Mgr
Scott Miller, Programming Director
Laura Schiltz, Promotions Manager
Monica Mattoon, News Director
Stan Culley, Chief Engineer
Shirley Dicus, Business Manager
MikeNewhouse, National Sales Manager

***KTFC**
07-01-1965; 103.3 mhz FM *Hrs Open:* 24; 100 kw; 633 ft.; N42 29 5.5 W96 18 18.9
1534 Buchanan Ave, Sioux City, IA 51106 US
(712) 252-4621
www.bottradionetwork.com
kcotter@bottradionetwork.com
License: Sioux City, Woodbury County, IA held by Community Broadcasting Inc.
Group Owner: Bott Radio Network; (acq 12-13-2007; $650,000 with KTFG(FM) Sioux Rapids)
Nat'l Network: USA
Arbitron Metro Market: Sioux City, IA *Format:* Gospel *Special Programming:* Farm one hr, news 10 hrs, children 5 hrs wkly
Richard (Dick) Bott Sr., Chairman
Richard (Rich) Bott, CEO/COO
Richard Bott, President
Eben Fowler, Operations Dir
Donald Swanson, General Manager

***KWIT**
01-31-1978; 90.3 mhz FM *Hrs Open:* 24; 100 kw; 909 ft.; N42 28 56 W96 15 30
4647 Stone Avenue, Sioux City, IA 51102 US
(712) 274-6406, *Fax:* (712) 274-6411
www.kwit-koji.org
gondekg@witcc.edu
License: Sioux City, Woodbury County, IA held by Western Iowa Tech Community College.
Nat'l Network: PRI; NPR
Arbitron Metro Market: Sioux City, IA *Format:* News, News/Talk, 86 *Special Programming:* Blues 2 hrs, Triple A 12 hrs, Sp 20 hrs wkly *Hrs. of News Programming:* news progmg 36 hrs wkly *No. News Employees:* 1 *Target Audience:* 25-54.
Steve Smith, Operations Dir
Gretchen Gondek, General Manager
Duane Kraayenbrink, News Director
Dennis Semple, Chief Engineer
Jake Moreland, Arts Producer
Mindy Thompson, Office Assistant

KWSL
04-01-1938; 1470 khz AM; 5 kw-D, DA2; 5 kw-N, DA2; N42 24 42 W96 25 30
Mailing Address: 4700 S. Lewis Blvd, Sioux City, IA 51106 US
Second Address: 1113 Nebraska St., Sioux City, IA 51105
(712) 255-1470, *Fax:* (712) 252-2430
www.1470kwsl.com
License: Sioux City, IA held by AMFM Radio Licenses LLC.
Group Owner: Clear Channel Communications Inc.; (acq 10-1-2002; grpsl)
Nat'l Reps: Katz Radio
Arbitron Metro Market: Sioux City, IA *Format:* Oldies, Spanish
Target Audience: 25 plus.
Rob Powers, Operations Dir
Mike Newhouse, General Sales Mgr
Curtis Anderson, Programming Director
Laura Schiltz, Promotions Manager
Monica Mattoon, News Director
Stan Culley, Chief Engineer
Magda Orduno, Bilingual Sales
ShirleyDicus, Business Manager
Rhonda Johnson, Promotions Manager

Sioux Rapids

***KTFG**
01-01-1991; 102.9 mhz FM; 49 kw; 495 ft.; N42 54 34.6 W95 9 33.1 *Rebroadcasts:* Rebroadcasts KTFC(FM) Sioux City 100%
Midwest Bible Radio, 1534 Buchanan Ave, Sioux City, IA 51106 US
(712) 252-0327
www.bottradionetwork.com
kcotter@bottradionetwork.com
License: Sioux Rapids, Buena Vista County, IA held by Community Broadcasting Inc.
Group Owner: Bott Radio Network; (acq 12-13-2007; $650,000 with KTFC(FM) Sioux City)
Nat'l Network: USA
Arbitron Metro Market: Sioux City, IA *Format:* Gospel *Special Programming:* Children 5 hrs wkly
Richard (Dick) Bott Sr., Chairman
Richard (Rich) Bott, CEO/COO
Richard(Rich) Bott, President
Eben Fowler, Operations Dir
Donald Swanson, General Manager

Spencer

KICD
12-01-1942; 1240 khz AM *Hrs Open:* 24
Mailing Address: P.O. Box 260, Spencer, IA 51301 US
Second Address: 2600 N. Hwy. Blvd., Spencer, IA 51301
(712) 262-1240, *Fax:* (712) 262-2076
www.kicdam.com
dputnam@spencerradiogroup.com
License: Spencer, IA held by Saga Communications of Iowa LLC.
Group Owner: Saga Communications Inc.; (acq 11-22-99; grpsl)
Nat'l Network: CBS
Format: Talk *Special Programming:* Farm 2 hrs wkly, religious 4 hrs wkly, *Hrs. of News Programming:* news progmg 100 hrs wkly *No. News Employees:* 1 *Target Audience:* 35 plus.
Kevin Tlam, Operations Dir
David Putnam, General Manager
Linda Maske, Station Manager
Brent Palm, News Director
Ryan Long, Engineering Dir
Dan Sketon, Chief Engineer
Troy Leninger, Farm Director
Mark Magnuson, FarmBroadcaster

KICD-FM
09-17-1965; 107.7 mhz FM *Hrs Open:* 24; 100 kw; 285 ft.; N43 9 57 W95 8 46
Mailing Address: P.O. Box 260, Spencer, IA 51301 US
Second Address: 2600 N. Hwy. Blvd., Spencer, IA 51301
(712) 262-1240, *Fax:* (712) 262-2076
www.cd1077fm.com
kicdott@fair.net
License: Spencer, Clay County, IA held by Saga Communications of Iowa LLC.
Group Owner: Saga Communications Inc.
Nat'l Network: CBS
Format: Country *No. News Employees:* 1 *Target Audience:* 25 plus.
David Putman, General Sales Mgr
Rhoda Wedeking, Programming Director

KLLT
02-01-1979; 104.9 mhz FM *Hrs Open:* 24; 25 kw; 279 ft.; N43 17 13 W95 8 34
P.O. Box 260, Spencer, IA 51301 US
(712) 262-1240, *Fax:* (712) 262-2076
www.lite1049.com
dputnam@spencerradiogroup.com;
ktlam@spencerradiogroup.com;
lmaske@spencerradiogroup.com
License: Spencer, Clay County, IA held by Saga Communications of Iowa LLC.
Group Owner: Saga Communications Inc.; (acq 11-22-99; grpsl)
Nat'l Reps: Katz Radio
Format: Light Rock *Hrs. of News Programming:* News progmg one hr wkly *Target Audience:* 25-54.
Edward Christian, CEO
Kevin Tlam, Operations Dir
Dave Putnam, General Manager
Linda Maske, Station Manager
Darby Bishop, Promotions Manager
Ryan Long, News Director

Spirit Lake

KUOO
04-01-1985; 103.9 mhz FM *Hrs Open:* 24; 50 kw; 492 ft.; N43 24 20 W95 5 1
13906 Gold Circle, Suite 201, Omaha, NE 68144 US
(712) 336-5800, *Fax:* (712) 336-1634
www.kuooradio.com
mspies@exploreokoboji.com
License: Spirit Lake, Dickinson County, IA held by Sorenson Broadcasting Corp.
Group Owner: Sorenson Broadcasting Corp.; (acq 7-1-2004; grpsl)
Nat'l Network: Fox News Radio
Arbitron Metro Market: Spirit Lake, IA *Format:* Adult Contemp
Hrs. of News Programming: news progmg 16 hrs wkly *No. News Employees:* 2 *Target Audience:* 25-54.
Neil Lipetzky, CEO
Dean Sorenson, President
Marty Spies, General Manager
Jeff Nixx, Programming Director
Abby Kohlhaas, Promotions Manager
Steve Schwaller, News Director
Steve Heaton, Chief Engineer
Chad Franzen, SportsDirector
Mary Treanor, Music Director
Terry Lowry, Office Manager
Matt Fallon, Production Director
Matt Fallon, Production Director

***KJIA**
01-01-2002; 88.9 mhz FM; 50 kw; 272 ft.; N43 20 34 W95 12 24
Mailing Address: 12089 380th Ave, P O Box 72, Blue Earth, MN 56013 US
Second Address: 7 S. Highway 71, Arnolds Park, IA 51331
(712) 332-2428, *Fax:* (712) 332-2428
www.kjiaradio.com
kjia@kjiaradio.com
License: Spirit Lake, Dickinson County, IA held by Minn-Iowa Christian Broadcasting Inc.
Group Owner: Minn-Iowa Christian Broadcasting Inc.
Arbitron Metro Market: Okoboji, IA *Format:* Christian
Matt Dorfner, General Manager
Steve Ware, Programming Director
Mark Bohnett, Chief Engineer
Matt Dorfner, Executive Director
Lynette Dorfner, Community Relations Representative
Bev Cother, Receptionist

St. Ansgar

***KJCY**
09-01-2001; 95.5 mhz FM *Hrs Open:* 24; 6 kw; 328 ft.; N43 21 52 W92 51 4
1296 Marian Lane, Green Bay, WI 54304 US
(641) 424-5529, *Fax:* (641) 424-5597
www.kjcy.com
kjcy@kjcy.com
License: St. Ansgar, Mitchell County, IA held by Minn-Iowa Christian Broadcasting Inc.
Group Owner: Minn-Iowa Christian Broadcasting Inc.; acq 3-20-01; $200,000).
Format: Christian
Matt Dorfner, President
Matt Donfner, General Manager

State Center

***KTDV**
01-09-2009; 91.9 mhz FM; 22 kw; 307 ft.; N42 15 49 W93 3 57
P. O. Box 538, Marshalltown, IA 50158 US
(641) 752-4122, *Fax:* (641) 752-5121
ktdvradio.com
info@ktdvradio.com
License: State Center, Marshall County, IA held by Marshalltown Education Plus Inc.
Format: Adult Contemp, Christian
Mark Osmundson, General Manager

Storm Lake

KAYL
11-01-1948; 990 khz AM; 0.25 kw-D, ND1; 0.006 kw-N, ND1; N42 38 5 W95 10 10
Mailing Address: 13906 Gold Circle, Suite 201, Omaha, NE 68144 US
Second Address: 606 1/2 Lake Ave., Storm Lake, IA 50588
(712) 732-3520, *Fax:* (712) 732-1746
www.stormlakeradio.com
info@stormlakeradio.com
License: Storm Lake, IA held by Sorenson Broadcasting Corp.
Group Owner: NRG Media LLC; (acq 7-1-2004; grpsl)
Nat'l Network: La Gran D
Arbitron Metro Market: Storm Lake, IA *Adv. Rates:* 22; 22; 22; 22

Mary Quass, CEO
Buzz Paterson, General Manager
Chuck DuCoty, COO

KAYL-FM
02-01-1949; 101.7 mhz FM; 50 kw; 400 ft.; N42 38 5 W95 10 10
13906 Gold Circle, Suite 201, Omaha, NE 68144 US
(712) 732-3520, *Fax:* (712) 732-1746
www.stormlakeradio.com
info@stormlakeradio.com
License: Storm Lake, Buena Vista County, IA held by Sorenson Broadcasting Corp.
Group Owner: NRG Media LLC
Regional Network: Waitt Farm Net.
Arbitron Metro Market: Storm Lake, IA *Format:* Adult Contemp *Hrs. of News Programming:* news progmg 15 hrs wkly *No. News Employees:* 1 *Target Audience:* 25-54; male & female *Adv. Rates:* 28; 28; 28; 28
Mary Quass, CEO
Buzz Paterson, General Manager
Chuck DuCoty, COO

***KOIA**
88.1 mhz FM; kw
US
License: Storm Lake, Buena Vista County, IA held by Ron Elmore Ministries Inc.
Arbitron Metro Market: Storm Lake, IA
Ron Elmore, President

Story City

***KHOI**
89.1 mhz FM; kw
US
(515) 292-2878
www.khoifm.org
khoiradio@gmail.com
License: Story City, Story County, IA held by Unitarian Universalist Fellowship of Ames.
Arbitron Metro Market: Ames, IA *Format:* Talk
Janet Klaas, President

Stuart

KKRF
08-11-1993; 107.9 mhz FM; 9.4 kw; 492 ft.; N41 27 40 W94 29 22
Mailing Address: Rr2 Box 106a, Lacrescent, MN 55947 US
Second Address: 204 S. Division St., Stuart, IA 50250-5021
(515) 465-5357, *Fax:* (515) 465-3952
License: Stuart, Guthrie County, IA held by Coon Valley Communications Inc.
Group Owner: Coon Valley Communications Inc.
Nat'l Network: ABC
Arbitron Metro Market: Des Moines, IA *Format:* Country *Special Programming:* Farm 5 hrs wkly *Hrs. of News Programming:* news progmg 10 hrs wkly *No. News Employees:* 1 *Target Audience:* 25-64; general*Adv. Rates:* 13.50; 13.50; 13.50; 13.50
Pat Delaney, President
John France, Operations Dir
Sue Thomsen, General Manager

Twin Lakes

KTLB
10-05-1975; 105.9 mhz FM *Hrs Open:* 18; 25 kw; 328 ft.; N42 32 9 W94 40 48
6900 Van Dorn, Suite 11, Lincoln, NE 68506 US
(515) 573-5748, *Fax:* (515) 573-3376
License: Twin Lakes, Calhoun County, IA held by Three Eagles of Ft. Dodge Inc.
Group Owner: Three Eagles Communications; (acq 4-22-97; $248,883)
Arbitron Metro Market: Fort Dodge, IA *Format:* Oldies *Special Programming:* Farm 15 hrs, gospel 2 hrs, relg 2 hrs wkly *Hrs. of News Programming:* news progmg 15 hrs wkly *No. News Employees:* 1 *Target Audience:* 35-54; baby boomers
Gary Buchanan, President
Greg Allenson, Operations Dir
Travis Reeves, General Manager
Pat Kolar, General Sales Mgr

Villisca

KCSI
09-01-1979; 95.3 mhz FM *Hrs Open:* 24; 50 kw; 331 ft.; N41 1 35.2 W95 12 2
P.O. Box 465, Red Oak, IA 51566 US
(712) 623-2584, *Fax:* (712) 623-2583
www.kcsifm.com
kcsi@kcsifm.com
License: Villisca, Montgomery County, IA held by Hawkeye Communications Inc.
Nat'l Network: ABC *Regional Network:* Radio Iowa *Wire Services:* AP
Arbitron Metro Market: Villisca, CA *Format:* Country
Jerry Dietz, CEO
Melanie West, General Sales Mgr
Marilyn Dietz, News Director

Vinton

KRQN
01-01-2005; 107.1 mhz FM *Hrs Open:* 24; 4.7 kw; 371 ft.; N42 8 56 W91 52 50
188 South Bellevue, Suite 222, Memphis, TN 38104 US
(319) 365-9431, *Fax:* (319) 363-8062
www.krqn.net
i1071@cumulus.com
License: Vinton, Benton County, IA
Group Owner: Cumulus Media Partners LLC
Nat'l Reps: Christal
Arbitron Metro Market: Cedar Rapids, IA *Format:* Contemporary Hits/Top 40, Adult Contemp *Target Audience:* 35-54 *Adv. Rates:* Contact Station
Tim Graves, Programming Director
Micki Slick, Promotions Manager

Wapello

***KAIP**
01-01-2005; 88.9 mhz FM; 0.001 kw horiz, 13.5 kw vert; 494 ft.; N41 4 59 W91 10 18
US
(888) 937-2471, *Fax:* (916) 251-1650
www.air1.com
info@air1.com
License: Wapello, Louisa County, IA held by Educational Media Foundation.
Group Owner: EMF Broadcasting
Nat'l Network: Air 1
Arbitron Metro Market: Wapello, IA *Format:* Alternative, Christian *No. News Employees:* 3 *Target Audience:* 25-44; Judeo Christian, female
Darrell Chambliss, Chairman
Alan Mason, COO
Mike Novak, President and CEO
Glenn Goodwin, Operations Dir
David Pierce, Programming Director
Ed Lenane, News Director
Sam Wallington, Engineering Dir
Marya Morgan, News Reporter
Richard Hunt, News Reporter
Dan Antonelli, Chief Business Development Officer
Eric Moser, Chief Financial Officer
Brian Burger, Vice President of Human Resources
D. Kevin Blair, Secretary and General Counsel

Washington

KCII
11-12-1961; 1380 khz AM *Hrs Open:* 5 AM-11 PM; 0.5 kw-D, ND1; 0.025 kw-N, ND1; N41 18 18 W91 42 36
P.O. Box 31, 1610 N. Lincoln, Knoxville, IA 50138 US
(319) 653-2113, *Fax:* (319) 653-3500
kciiradio.com
kcii@kciiradio.com
License: Washington, IA held by Home Broadcasting Inc.
Nat'l Network: AP Radio
Arbitron Metro Market: Cedar Rapids, IA *Format:* Adult Contemp, News *Hrs. of News Programming:* news progmg 14 hrs wkly *No. News Employees:* 1 *Target Audience:* 25-54; females *Adv. Rates:* 17.47; 17.47;17.47; 17.47.
Joe Nichols, General Manager
Joe Nichols, General Sales Mgr
Nic Sabatke, Programming Director
Ben Stanton, News Director
Becky Helmick, Traffic Manager

KCII-FM
01-01-1975; 106.1 mhz FM *Hrs Open:* 5 AM-11 PM; 3 kw; 299 ft.; N41 18 18 W91 42 36
P.O. Box 31, 1610 N. Lincoln, Knoxville, IA 50138 US
(319) 653-2113, *Fax:* (319) 653-3500
kciiradio.com
kcii@kciiradio.com
License: Washington, Washington County, IA held by Home Broadcasting Inc.
Arbitron Metro Market: Cedar Rapids, IA *Format:* News, Oldies
Nic Sabatke, Operations Dir
Joe Nichols, General Manager
Ben Stanton, News Director
Dagan Miller, Sports Commentator

Waterloo

***KBBG**
07-26-1978; 88.1 mhz FM *Hrs Open:* 19; 9.5 kw; 154 ft.; N42 30 45 W92 19 24
918 Newell Street, Waterloo, IA 50703 US
(319) 234-1441, *Fax:* (319) 234-6182
www.kbbgfm.org
realmanagement@jbbg.org
License: Waterloo, Black Hawk County, IA held by Afro-American Community Broadcasting Inc.
Nat'l Network: American Urban
Arbitron Metro Market: Waterloo, IA *Format:* Blues, Gospel
Target Audience: General.
Lou Porter, CEO
Lou Porter, President
Beverly Douglas, Station Manager
Lou Lou Porter, General Sales Mgr

KFMW
11-01-1968; 107.9 mhz FM *Hrs Open:* 24; 77 kw; 1804 ft.; N42 24 2 W91 50 36
Mailing Address: Post Office Box 1540, Waterloo, IA 50704 US
Second Address: 514 Jefferson St., Waterloo, IA
(319) 234-2200, *Fax:* (319) 234-0149
www.rock108.com
cross@rock108.com
License: Waterloo, Black Hawk County, IA held by KXEL Broadcasting Co., Inc.
Group Owner: Bahakel Communications
Nat'l Reps: Katz Radio
Arbitron Metro Market: Waterloo-Cedar Falls, IA *Hrs. of News Programming:* news progmg 4 hrs wkly *Target Audience:* 18-34; men
Michael Cross, Operations Dir
Tim Mathews, General Manager

***KNWS**
01-01-1953; 1090 khz AM *Hrs Open:* Sunrise-sunset; 1 kw-D, NDD; N42 26 38 W92 17 58
3003 North Snelling Ave., Roseville, MN 55113 US
(319) 296-1975, *Fax:* (319) 296-1977
www.faith1090.com
info@life1019.com
License: Waterloo, IA held by Northwestern College.
Group Owner: Northwestern College & Radio; (acq 4-2-53).
Nat'l Network: AP Radio
Arbitron Metro Market: Waterloo-Cedar Falls, IA *Format:* Christian, Talk, 74 *Target Audience:* 35 plus.
Paul Virts, President
Doug Smith, Station Manager
Dan Raymond, Programming Director
David Dobes, Chief Engineer

***KNWS-FM**
01-01-1965; 101.9 mhz FM *Hrs Open:* 24; 100 kw; 1572 ft.; N42 24 2 W91 50 36
3003 North Snelling Ave., Roseville, MN 55113 US
(319) 296-1975, *Fax:* (319) 296-1977
www.life1019.com
License: Waterloo, Black Hawk County, IA
Arbitron Metro Market: Waterloo-Cedar Falls, IA *Format:* Adult Contemp, Christian, 74 *Target Audience:* 30-50; women
Doug Smith, Station Manager
Mike Lanser, Programming Director
Dave Dobes, Engineering Dir
Richard Whitworth, Network Director
Brent Manion, Production Director
Dan Raymond, Program Director
Julia Taylor, Promotions Director

KOKZ
11-21-1962; 105.7 mhz FM *Hrs Open:* 24; 100 kw; 1322 ft.; N42 24 35 W92 5 10
514 Jefferson Street, P.O. Box 1540, Waterloo, IA 50704 US
(319) 234-2200, *Fax:* (319) 234-0149
www.cool1057.com
License: Waterloo, Black Hawk County, IA held by KXEL Broadcasting Co., Inc.
Group Owner: Bahakel Communications
Nat'l Reps: Katz Radio
Arbitron Metro Market: Waterloo-Cedar Falls, IA *Format:* Contemporary Hits/Top 40, Adult Contemp *Target Audience:* 25-54.
Tim Mathews, General Manager

KWLO
11-01-1947; 1330 khz AM *Hrs Open:* 24; 5 kw-D, DA2; 5 kw-N, DA2; N42 28 1 W92 15 59
Mailing Address: Post Office Box 1540, Waterloo, IA 50704 US
Second Address: 514 Jefferson St., Waterloo, IA 50704

(319) 234-2200, *Fax:* (319) 234-0149
www.star1330.com
License: Waterloo, IA held by KXEL Broadcasting Co. Inc.
Group Owner: Bahakel Communications; (acq 8-16-96; grpsl)
Nat'l Network: ABC *Nat'l Reps:* Katz Radio
Arbitron Metro Market: Waterloo, IA *Format:* Oldies *Target Audience:* 35 plus.
Beverly Poston, President
Dennis Lowe, Operations Dir
Tim Mathews, General Manager
Amy Mollus, News Director
Mark Schumacher, Chief Engineer

KXEL
07-14-1942; 1540 khz AM *Hrs Open:* 24
514 Jefferson Street, P.O. Box 1540, Waterloo, IA 50704 US
(319) 234-2200, *Fax:* (319) 233-4946
www.kxel.com
bill.wells@wcinet.com
License: Waterloo, IA held by KXEL Broadcasting Co. Inc.
Group Owner: Bahakel Communications; (acq 1-11-58)
Nat'l Network: ABC *Nat'l Reps:* Katz Radio
Arbitron Metro Market: Waterloo-Cedar Falls, IA *Format:* News, News/Talk, 86 *Special Programming:* Relg 20 hrs wkly *Hrs. of News Programming:* news progmg 28 hrs wkly *No. News Employees:* 2 *Target Audience:* 45-65.
Beverly Poston, President
Dennis Lowe, Operations Dir
Bill Wells, General Manager
Cindy Hall, General Sales Mgr
Sarah Chase, Promotions Manager
Mark Schumacher, Chief Engineer
Ken Houser, Account Executive
Ken Hensley, AccountExecutive
Marica Downs, Account Executive

Waukon

KNEI-FM
09-01-1968; 103.5 mhz FM; 37 kw; 574 ft.; N43 18 28 W91 27 18
980 North Michigan Ave, Suite 1880, Chicago, IL 60610 US
(563) 568-3476, *Fax:* (563) 568-3391
knei@kneiradio.com
License: Waukon, Allamakee County, IA held by Wennes Communications Stations Inc.
Nat'l Network: CBS Radio *Regional Network:* Radio Iowa; Brownfield
Format: Country *Hrs. of News Programming:* News progmg one hr wkly *Target Audience:* 25-45.
Greg Wennes, CEO
Chuck Bloxham, General Manager

KHPP(AM)
07-01-1967; 1160 khz AM; 880 w-D, 26 w-N; N43 17 13 W91 28 06
14 W. Main St., Waukon, IA 52172
(563) 568-3477, *Fax:* (563) 568-3391
knei@kneiradio.com
License: Waukon, Allamakee County, IA held by Wennes Communications Stations Inc.
Population Served: 250,000 *Arbitron Metro Market:* Anchorage, AK *Format:* Oldies
Dr. D.L. Van Voorhis, President
Bill DeGeorge, General Manager

Waverly

KWAY
05-06-1958; 1470 khz AM; 1 kw-D, DA2; 0.061 kw-N, DA2; N42 42 13 W92 28 21
P.O. Box 307, 110 29th Ave Sw, Waverly, IA 50677 US
(319) 352-3550, *Fax:* (319) 352-3601
www.kwayradio.com
kwayradio@kwayradio.com
License: Waverly, IA held by Ael Suhr Enterprises Inc.
Arbitron Metro Market: Waverly, IA *Format:* Country
Al Suhr, President
Steven Hatter, Operations Dir

KWAY-FM
12-21-1971; 99.3 mhz FM; 4.6 kw; 180 ft.; N42 42 13 W92 28 21
P.O. Box 307, Waverly, IA 50677 US
(319) 352-3550, *Fax:* (319) 352-3601
www.kwayradio.com
Kwayradio@kwayradio.com
License: Waverly, Bremer County, IA held by Ael Suhr Enterprises Inc.
Arbitron Metro Market: Waverly, IA *Format:* Adult Contemp
Paul Bjornstad, General Manager

***KWVI**
01-01-2006; 88.9 mhz FM; 20 kw vert; 274 ft.; N42 47 21 W92 14 22 *Rebroadcasts:* Rebroadcasts WAFR(FM) Tupelo, MS 100%
P O Drawer 2440, Tupelo, MS 38803 US
(662) 844-8888, *Fax:* (662) 842-6791
www.afr.net
License: Waverly, Bremer County, IA held by American Family Association.
Group Owner: American Family Radio
Format: Christian
Marvin Sanders, General Manager

***KWAR**
01-01-2008; 89.9 mhz FM *Hrs Open:* 24; 0.1 kw; 85 ft.; N42 43 37 W92 29 1
Eight St & First Ave NW, Waverly, IA 50677 US
(319) 352-8209, *Fax:* (319) 352-8610
www.kwar.org
yoursound.kwar@gmail.com
License: Waverly, Bremer County, IA held by Wartburg College.
Arbitron Metro Market: Waverly, IA *Format:* Contemporary Hits/Top 40 *Target Audience:* General.
Andrew Nostvick, Station Manager
Anna Hauskins, Programming Director
Vince Abrahamson, Music Director

Webster City

KQWC
02-05-1950; 1570 khz AM; 250 w-D, 132 w-N; 436 ft; N42 27 45 W93 48 05
Box 550, Webster City, IA 50595
(515) 832-1570, *Fax:* (515) 832-2079
kqradio.com
mharris@nrgmedia.com
License: Webster City, Hamilton County, IA held by NRG License Sub. LLC.
Group Owner: NRG Media LLC; (acq 10-31-2005; grpsl)
Population Served: 50,000*Special Programming:* Farm 8 hrs wkly *Hrs. of News Programming:* news progmg 45 hrs wkly *No. News Employees:* 1 *Target Audience:* 50 plus; affluent with max spendable income *Adv.Rates:* 11; 9; 8; 6
Chuck DuCoty, COO
Mary Quass, CEO/President
Mary Harris, General Manager
Rhonda Martin, Business Manager
Chris Lockwood, Programming Director
Pat Powers, News Director
George Nicholas, Chief Engineer
Chris Lockwood, DiscJockey
Doug Bremer, Sports Director

KQWC-FM
01-01-1969; 95.7 mhz FM; 25 kw; 436 ft; N42 28 04 W93 47 48
P.O. Box 550, Webster City, IA 50595
(515) 832-1570, *Fax:* (515) 832-2079
www.kqradio.com
mharris@nrgmedia.com
License: Webster City, Hamilton County, IA
Group Owner: NRG Media LLC
Nat'l Network: ABC
Hrs. of News Programming: news progmg 35 hrs wkly *No. News Employees:* 1 *Adv. Rates:* 24; 18; 16; 12
Chuck DuCoty, COO
Mary Quass, CEO/President
Mary Harris, General Manager
Rhonda Martin, Business Manager
Chris Lockwood, Programming Director
Pat Powers, News Director
George Nicholas, Chief Engineer
Chris Lockwood, DiscJockey
Doug Bremer, Sports Director

West Des Moines

KJJY
02-04-1978; 92.5 mhz FM *Hrs Open:* 24; 41 kw; Ant 541 ft; N41 39 53 W93 45 25
4143 109th St., Urbandale, IA 02162
(515) 331-9200, *Fax:* (515) 331-9292
www.kjjy.com
License: West Des Moines, Polk County, IA
Group Owner: Cumulus Media Inc.; (acq 8-29-03; grpsl).
Nat'l Reps: Christal
Population Served: 758,000 *Arbitron Metro Market:* Des Moines, IA *Target Audience:* 25-54; general
Jack O'Brien, Operations Dir
Doug Wood, General Sales Mgr
Terry Peters, Promotions Manager

***KWDM**
03-01-1976; 88.7 mhz FM *Hrs Open:* 14; 0.1 kw; 171 ft.; N41 35 25 W93 45 10
1140 35th Street, West Des Moines, IA 50265 US
(515) 226-2660, *Fax:* (515) 226-2609
www.wdm.k12.ia.us/kwdm
kwdmfm@hotmail.com
License: West Des Moines, Polk County, IA held by West Des Moines Community School District.
Arbitron Metro Market: West Des Moines, IA *Format:* Alternative *Special Programming:* Sports 3 hrs wkly *Hrs. of News Programming:* News progmg 3 hrs wkly *Target Audience:* 12-25; educ facility-var progmg
Mack Wzie Carey, Station Manager
Marianne Coppock, General Sales Mgr
Nicole Faust, Promotions Manager

Whiting

KKYY
12-11-1979; 101.3 mhz FM *Hrs Open:* 24; 50 kw; 492 ft.; N42 21 25 W96 8 2
P.O. Box 2307, Newburgh, NY 12550 US
(712) 258-5655
www.y1013.net
License: Whiting, Monona County, IA held by Powell Broadcasting Co. Inc.
Group Owner: Powell Broadcasting Co. Inc.; (acq 5-1-2007; $4.2 million with KZSR(FM) Onawa)
Nat'l Network: Motor Racing Net; Westwood One; ABC
Arbitron Metro Market: Sioux City, IA *Format:* Country *Hrs. of News Programming:* news progmg 20 hrs wkly *No. News Employees:* 1 *Target Audience:* 18-54; adult men & women
Adv. Rates: 15; 15; 15; 12
Jerry Haack, General Manager
Kelli Erickson, General Sales Mgr
Tim Guentz, Programming Director
Pam Guntz, Chief Engineer

Winterset

KPUL
03-01-1994; 99.5 mhz FM *Hrs Open:* 24; 6 kw; 328 ft.; N41 24 2 W93 54 58
5911 Meredith Drive, Ste A, Des Moines, IA 50322 US
(515) 987-9995, *Fax:* (515) 987-9808
www.pulse995.com/
info@pulse995.com
License: Winterset, Madison County, IA held by Positive Impact Media Inc.
Arbitron Metro Market: Des Moines, IA *Format:* Christian *Target Audience:* Families.
David Nadler Jr., General Manager
David St. John, Programming Director

Kansas

Abilene

KABI
04-08-1963; 1560 khz AM *Hrs Open:* 24
Mailing Address: PO Box 1393, McCook, KS 67401 US
Second Address: Box 80, Salina, KS 67402
(785) 823-1111, *Fax:* (785) 823-2034
www.kabiabilene.com
License: Abilene, KS held by MCC Radio LLC.
Group Owner: Morris Radio LLC; (acq 1-30-2004; grpsl).
Nat'l Network: ABC *Regional Network:* Kan. Agriculture
Arbitron Metro Market: Salina, KS *Format:* Adult Contemp
Special Programming: Relg 4 hrs wkly *Hrs. of News Programming:* news progmg 2 hrs wkly *No. News Employees:* 1 *Target Audience:* 35 plus; locresidents of Dickinson County *Adv. Rates:* 12.22; 9.17; 11; 3.67
Robert Protzman, General Manager
Bob Protzman, Station Manager
Mitch Drees, General Sales Mgr
Gary Houser, Programming Director
Clarke Sanders, Promotions Manager
John Anderson, News Director
Mark Beaver, Traffic Manager

KSAJ-FM
12-10-1968; 98.5 mhz FM *Hrs Open:* 24; 100 kw; 440 ft.; N38 47 50 W97 13 1
Mailing Address: P. O. Box 1393, Salina, KS 67402 US
Second Address: 131 N. Santa Fe, Salina, KS 67401
(785) 823-1111, *Fax:* (785) 823-2034
www.ksallink.com
License: Abilene, Dickinson County, KS held by MCC Radio LLC
Group Owner: Morris Radio LLC

Nat'l Network: ABC *Regional Network:* Kan. Info. *Nat'l Reps:* Katz Radio
Arbitron Metro Market: Salina, KS *Format:* Oldies *Hrs. of News Programming:* news progmg 3 hrs wkly *No. News Employees:* 1 *Target Audience:* 35-64; baby boomers *Adv. Rates:* 16.53; 12.39; 14.87; 4.96
Robert Protzman, General Manager
John Anderson, Programming Director
Clarke Sanders, Promotions Manager
Mark Beaver, News Director

Andover

KDGS
11-01-1993; 93.9 mhz FM; 25 kw; 328 ft.; N37 37 0 W97 20 11
331 Lookout Point, Hot Spring, AR 71913 US
(316) 685-2121, *Fax:* (316) 685-3408
www.power939.com
info@power939.com
License: Andover, Butler County, KS held by Entercom Wichita License LLC.
Group Owner: Entercom Communications Corp.; (acq 4-21-00; $3.15 million).
Arbitron Metro Market: Wichita, KS *Format:* Contemporary Hits/Top 40 *Target Audience:* 18-34.
Jackie Wise, General Manager
Mark Yearout, General Sales Mgr
Greg Williams, Programming Director

Arkansas City

*KAXR
01-01-2001; 91.3 mhz FM; 13.5 kw; 322 ft.; N36 55 32 W97 1 34
P O Drawer 2440, Tupelo, MS 38803 US
(662) 844-8888, *Fax:* (662) 842-6791
www.afr.net
comments@afr.net
License: Arkansas City, Cowley County, KS held by American Family Association.
Group Owner: American Family Radio
Arbitron Metro Market: Tupelo, MS *Format:* Christian, Religious
Marvin Sanders, General Manager

KACY
02-01-1999; 102.5 mhz FM *Hrs Open:* 24; 6 kw; 328 ft.; N37 5 1 W96 55 46
P O Box 1704, Stafford, TX 77477 US
(620) 442-1102, *Fax:* (620) 442-8102
www.1025theriver.com
License: Arkansas City, Cowley County, KS held by Third Coast Broadcasting.
Arbitron Metro Market: Wichita, KS *Format:* Rock/AOR, Triple A
Marshall Ice, General Manager

KSOK
01-01-1947; 1280 khz AM *Hrs Open:* 24; 1 kw-D, 100 w-N; N37 05 19 W97 01 56
334 E. Radio Ln., Arkansas City, KS 66762
(620) 442-5400, *Fax:* (620) 442-5401
www.ksokradio.com
ksok@ksokradio.com
License: Arkansas City, Cowley County, KS held by Cowley County Broadcasting Inc.
Nat'l Network: CBS *Regional Network:* Kan. Agriculture
No. News Employees: 1 *Target Audience:* 22-55; blue collar, middle America, people who have children, are still working, & have mortgages *Adv. Rates:* 26; 22; 24; 15
Brian Cunningham, Operations Dir
Marty Mutti, General Manager
Pam Miller, General Sales Mgr
Blake Carter, Promotions Manager
Shawn Wheat, News Director
Christy Bursack, Chief of Operations

KYQQ
11-01-1979; 106.5 mhz FM; 100 kw; 1280 ft.; N37 21 24 W96 57 55
3355 S. Valley View Boulevard, Las Vegas, NV 89102 US
(316) 436-1065, *Fax:* (316) 838-3607
www.radiolobo1065.com
License: Arkansas City, Cowley County, KS held by Journal Broadcast Corp.
Group Owner: Journal Communications Inc.; (acq 6-11-99; grpsl)
Arbitron Metro Market: Arkansas City, KS *Format:* Tejano *Target Audience:* 18-49; Hispanic
Rob Burton, Operations Dir
Eric McCart, General Sales Mgr
Beverlee Brannigan, Programming Director
Manny Cowzinski, Promotions Manager

Arlington

KNZS
09-15-1989; 100.3 mhz FM *Hrs Open:* 24 Hours; 14.5 kw; 443 ft.; N37 55 41 W98 17 58
207 W. 13th Street, N., Wichita, KS 67203 US
(620) 665-5758, *Fax:* (620) 665-6655
production@adastra.kscoxmail.com
License: Arlington, Reno County, KS held by Ad Astra Per Aspera Broadcasting Inc.
Group Owner: Ad Astra Per Aspera Broadcasting Inc.; (acq 12-13-2007; exchange for KIBB(FM) Haven)
Nat'l Network: Jones Radio Networks
Arbitron Metro Market: Hutchinson, KS *Format:* Classic Rock *Hrs. of News Programming:* 2 hours weekly *No. News Employees:* 1 *Target Audience:* Adults 25-64
Aaron West, Operations Dir
Cliff C Shank, General Manager
Mike Hill, General Sales Mgr

Atchison

KAIR
07-28-1939; 1470 khz AM *Hrs Open:* 5 AM-midnight; 1 kw-U, DA1; N39 37 9 W94 59 27
P.O. Box 104, Hiawatha, KS 66434 US
(913) 367-1470, *Fax:* (913) 367-7021
www.kairfm.com
kairradio@gmail.com
License: Atchison, KS held by KNZA Inc.
Group Owner: KNZA Inc.; (acq 8-13-2007 with KAIR-FM Horton)
Nat'l Network: EWTN Radio
Arbitron Metro Market: Atchison, KS *Format:* Christian *Special Programming:* Farm 7 hrs wkly *Target Audience:* General; 25-65 *Adv. Rates:* 16; 14; 16; 10
Greg Buser, President
Mark Oppold, General Manager

Augusta

KFXJ
04-01-1992; 104.5 mhz FM *Hrs Open:* 24; 45 kw; 515 ft.; N37 48 15 W97 15 56
Mailing Address: 3355 S. Valley View Boulevard, Las Vegas, NV 89102 US
Second Address: 4200 N. Old Lawrence Rd., Wichita, KS 67219
(316) 838-9141, *Fax:* (316) 838-3607
www.1045thefox.com
info@104thefox.com
License: Augusta, Butler County, KS held by Journal Broadcast Corp.
Group Owner: Journal Communications Inc.; (acq 6-11-99; grpsl)
Arbitron Metro Market: Wichita, KS *Format:* Classic Rock *Target Audience:* 25-54.
Rob Burton, Operations Dir
Eric McCart, General Sales Mgr
Manny Cowzinski, Promotions Manager
Ray Michaels, Operations Manager
Jason Wituk

KVWF
01-01-2006; 100.5 mhz FM; 25 kw; 276 ft.; N37 44 13 W97 9 25 US
(316) 558-8800, *Fax:* (316) 558-8802
www.wichitawolf.com
kvwf@1005thewolf.com
License: Augusta, Butler County, KS held by Connoisseur Media LLC.
Group Owner: Connoisseur Media LLC
Arbitron Metro Market: Augusta, KS *Format:* Country
Trace Taul, Operations Dir
Doug Downs, General Manager
Ron Allen, Programming Director

Baldwin City

*KNBU
11-29-1965; 89.7 mhz FM; 0.1 kw; 118 ft.; N38 46 45 W95 11 15
PO Box 65, Baldwin City, KS 66006 US
(785) 594-6451, *Fax:* (785) 594-3570
info@knbu.com
License: Baldwin City, Douglas County, KS held by Baker University.
Special Programming: Jazz 15 hrs wkly
Tom Hedrick, General Manager

Baxter Springs

KCAR-FM
06-29-2000; 104.3 mhz FM; 6 kw; 299 ft.; N37 7 34 W94 42 12
C/O Putbrese, Hunsaker, P. O. Box 539, Sterling, VA 20167 US
(417) 781-1313, *Fax:* (417) 781-1316
www.lol1043.com
License: Baxter Springs, Cherokee County, KS held by American Media Investments Inc.
Group Owner: American Media Investments Inc.; (acq 2-17-2009; grpsl)
Arbitron Metro Market: Joplin, MO *Format:* Classic Rock, Oldies
Dave Clemons, General Sales Mgr
Bubba Fontaine, Programming Director
Kathleen Pike, News Director

Belle Plaine

KANR
03-04-1996; 99.7 mhz FM *Hrs Open:* 24; 50 kw; 482 ft.; N37 20 8 W97 27 53
3436 Edgemont, Witchita, KS 67208 US
(316) 652-9275, *Fax:* (316) 683-0818
www.fiesta927.com
fiesta927@gmail.com
License: Belle Plaine, Sumner County, KS held by Daniel D. Smith
Arbitron Metro Market: Witchita, KS
Daniel Smith, President
Joe Roach, Programming Director
Bruce Adamek, News Director

Belleville

KREP
06-26-1984; 92.1 mhz FM *Hrs Open:* 24; 14.5 kw; 276 ft.; N39 45 0 W97 36 48
2307 West Frontage Road, Belleville, KS 66935 US
(785) 527-2266, *Fax:* (785) 527-5919
www.kr92country.com
kr-92@nckcn.com
License: Belleville, Republic County, KS held by First Republic Broadcasting Corp.
Nat'l Network: ABC
Format: Country *Hrs. of News Programming:* news progmg 20 hrs wkly *No. News Employees:* 1 *Target Audience:* 25-55. *Adv. Rates:* 15.00;15.00;15.00;15.00
Deborah Sasser, President
Christine Strutt, General Sales Mgr
Eric Allgood, News Director
Marvin Hoffman, Chief Engineer
Eric Allgood, Sales/Sports Director

Beloit

KVSV
11-21-1979; 1190 khz AM *Hrs Open:* 6 AM-9 PM; 2.3 kw-D, DA1; 0.09 kw-N, DA1; N39 26 53 W98 4 45
PO Box 7, Beloit, KS 67420 US
(785) 738-2206, *Fax:* (785) 738-2208
www.kvsvradio.com
webmaster@kvsvradio.com
License: Beloit, KS held by McGrath Publishing Co.
Regional Network: Kan. Agriculture
Arbitron Metro Market: Beloit, KS *Format:* Adult Contemp *Special Programming:* Farm 9 hrs wkly *Hrs. of News Programming:* news progmg 11 hrs wkly *No. News Employees:* 1 *Target Audience:* General.
John Swanson, Station Manager
Sharon Keister, General Sales Mgr

KVSV-FM
11-11-1980; 105.5 mhz FM *Hrs Open:* 24; 50 kw; 443 ft.; N39 28 9 W98 5 37
P.O. Box 7, Beloit, KS 67420 US
(785) 738-2206, *Fax:* (785) 738-2208
www.kvsvradio.com
webmaster@kvsvradio.com
License: Beloit, Mitchell County, KS
Arbitron Metro Market: Beloit, KS *Format:* Easy Listening
John Swanson, Station Manager
Sharon Keister, General Sales Mgr

Bronson

*KBJQ
01-01-2002; 88.3 mhz FM; 36 kw; 381 ft.; N37 53 56 W95 0 9
P.O. Drawer 2440, Tupelo, MS 38803 US
(662) 844-8888, *Fax:* (662) 842-6791
www.afa.net
License: Bronson, Bourbon County, KS held by American Family Association.
Group Owner: American Family Radio
Arbitron Metro Market: Tupelo, MS *Format:* Religious
Marvin Sanders, General Manager

Burdett

KKDT
93.5 mhz FM; 95 kw; 1000 ft.; N38 36 32 W99 42 11 US
(785) 222-3400, *Fax:* (785) 222-3405
dave935.net
glen.hoyt@postrockradio.com
License: Burdett, Pawnee County, KS held by College Creek Media LLC.
Group Owner: College Creek Media LLC
Arbitron Metro Market: Burdett, KS *Format:* Adult Contemp
Glen Hoyt, General Manager

Burlington

KSNP
06-14-1990; 97.7 mhz FM *Hrs Open:* 6 AM-11 PM; 17.2 kw; 584 ft.; N38 9 57 W95 32 19
250 N. Water, Suite 300, Wichita, KS 67202 US
(620) 364-8807, *Fax:* (620) 364-2047
www.977thedawg.com
ksnp@kans.com
License: Burlington, Coffey County, KS held by Southeast Kansas Broadcasting Co.
Group Owner: My Town Media, Inc.; (acq 1999; $230,000)
Regional Network: Mid-America Ag
Arbitron Metro Market: Burlington, KS *Format:* Country *Special Programming:* Farm 8 hrs, relg 3 hrs wkly *Hrs. of News Programming:* news progmg 5 hrs wkly *No. News Employees:* 1 *Target Audience:* 25-45;industrial employees *Adv. Rates:* 9.25; na; 6; 3.50
Peg Downard, Station Manager
Mindy Ryan, Programming Director
Erin Reece, Sales Manager

Caney

KEOJ
10-15-1992; 101.1 mhz FM *Hrs Open:* 24; 6 kw; 328 ft.; N36 58 19 W95 53 47
P.O. Box 1250, Sapulpa, OK 74067 US
(918) 492-2660, *Fax:* (918) 492-8840
www.kxoj.com
kxoj@kxoj.com
License: Caney, Montgomery County, KS held by KXOJ Inc.
Group Owner: Adonai Radio Group; (acq 4-29-92; grpsl)
Arbitron Metro Market: Tulsa, OK *Format:* Christian *Target Audience:* 18-35; young married Christians
Mike Stephens, President
Joy Stephens, Operations Dir
David Stephens, General Manager
Bob Thornton, Programming Director
Darcy Kimble, News Director
Joe Hancock, Chief Engineer

Carbondale

KMAJ-FM
07-01-1971; 107.7 mhz FM; 53 kw; 772 ft.; N38 57 15 W95 54 43
330 East Kilbourn Ave., Suite 250, Milwaukee, WI 53202 US
(785) 272-2122, *Fax:* (785) 272-6219
www.kmaj.com
info@kmaj.com
License: Carbondale, Shawnee County, KS held by Kansas City Trust LLC, Trustee
Nat'l Network: Westwood One
Arbitron Metro Market: Topeka, KS *Format:* Adult Contemp
John Walker, General Manager
Keith Liefmann, General Sales Mgr
Rich Bowers, Programming Director
Carla Newman, Promotions Manager
Mike Manns, News Director

Cawker City

KZDY
01-01-1999; 96.3 mhz FM *Hrs Open:* 24; 13 kw; 230 ft.; N39 30 29 W98 18 57
P.O. Box 88, Glen Elder, KS 67446 US
(785) 545-3220, *Fax:* (785) 545-3220
www.kdcountry94.com/
info@kzdy.com
License: Cawker City, Mitchell County, KS held by Dierking Communications Inc.
Group Owner: Dierking Communications Inc.; (acq 7-27-2006).
Nat'l Network: Jones Radio Networks; AP Radio
Arbitron Metro Market: Glen Elder, KS *Format:* Adult Contemp *Hrs. of News Programming:* news progmg 6 hrs wkly *No. News Employees:* 1 *Target Audience:* 18-60.
Wade Gerstner, General Manager

Chanute

KKOY
11-17-1952; 1460 khz AM *Hrs Open:* 24
Mailing Address: 250 N. Water, Suite 300, Wichita, KS 67202 US
Second Address: 702 N. Plummer Sts., Chanute, KS 66720
(620) 431-3700, *Fax:* (620) 431-4643
www.kkoy.com
License: Chanute, KS held by Southeast Kansas Broadcasting Co. Inc.
Group Owner: My Town Media, Inc.; (acq 5-21-97; $464,447 with co-located FM)
Nat'l Network: ESPN Radio
Arbitron Metro Market: Joplin, MO *Format:* Sports *Target Audience:* 25-54. *Adv. Rates:* 10.50; 7.50; 7.50; 5.00
Bill Wachter, General Manager
Heather Lee, Programming Director
Rob Strand, News Director

KKOY-FM
01-01-1971; 105.5 mhz FM *Hrs Open:* 24; 8 kw; 584 ft.; N37 35 59 W95 39 10
Mailing Address: 250 N. Water, Suite 300, Wichita, KS 67202 US
Second Address: 702 N. Plummer Sts., Chanute, KS 66720
(620) 431-3700, *Fax:* (620) 431-4643
www.kkoy.com
License: Chanute, Neosho County, KS held by Southeast Kansas Broadcasting Co. Inc.
Group Owner: My Town Media, Inc.
Nat'l Network: ABC
Arbitron Metro Market: Joplin, MO *Format:* Adult Contemp *Adv. Rates:* Same as AM
Chris Kelly, General Manager
Dave Fink, General Sales Mgr

***KANQ**
90.3 mhz FM; 17 kw; Ant 528 ft; N37 35 59 W95 39 10
Box 14, Abilene, KS
(785) 263-7200, *Fax:* (785) 263-3876
www.kjil1057.com
radioforlife@kjil.com
License: Chanute, Neosho County, KS held by Great Plains Christian Radio Inc.
Robert Hughes, CEO

Cimarron

KMML
02-01-2008; 92.9 mhz FM; 32 kw; 610 ft.; N37 56 29.6 W100 18 44.3 *Rebroadcasts:* Rebroadcasts KSMM-FM Liberal 100% US
(620) 225-8080, *Fax:* (620) 624-4606
www.rockingmradio.com
License: Cimarron, Gray County, KS held by Radioactive LLC.
Group Owner: Radioactive LLC
Arbitron Metro Market: Cimarron, KS
Benjamin Homel, President
Enrique Franz, General Manager

Clay Center

KCLY
01-06-1978; 100.9 mhz FM; 35.5 kw; 581 ft.; N39 28 3 W97 3 45
Box 16, Clay Center, KS 67432 US
(785) 632-5661, *Fax:* (785) 632-5662
www.kclyradio.com
rhys@kclyradio.com
License: Clay Center, Clay County, KS held by Taylor Communications.
Nat'l Network: AP Network News *Wire Services:* AP
Arbitron Metro Market: Topeka, KS *Format:* Adult Contemp *Target Audience:* 24-55; general
Kyle Bauer, General Manager
Rocky Downing, Station Manager
Joyce Beck, General Sales Mgr
Jamie Bloom, Programming Director
Michelle Tessaro, News Director
Rod Keen, Engineering Dir
Rhys Baker, Traffic/Billing
Duane Toews, FarmDirector
Susan Carlson, Advertising Consultant
Phil Casper, After Hours Director
Clay Dalquest, Sales Department
Angie Komar, Production Manager

Clearwater

KFH-FM
07-04-1995; 98.7 mhz FM *Hrs Open:* 24; 50 kw; 492 ft.; N37 24 11 W97 35 22
331 Lookout Point, Hot Springs, AR 71913 US
(316) 685-2121, *Fax:* (316) 685-3408
www.kfhradio.com
letters@kfhradio.com
License: Clearwater, Sedgwick County, KS held by Entercom Witicha License LLC.
Group Owner: Entercom Communications Corp.; (acq 5-8-00; $2 million).
Arbitron Metro Market: Wichita, KS *Format:* Sports, Talk *Target Audience:* 18-49; general *Adv. Rates:* 20; 20; 20; 20
Jackie Wise, General Manager
Mark Yearout, General Sales Mgr
Tony Duesing, Programming Director
Jessie Hosning, News Director
Craig Maudlin, Chief Engineer

Coffeyville

KGGF
01-01-1930; 690 khz AM
P.O. Box 4584, Springfield, MO 65808 US
(316) 251-3800, *Fax:* (316) 251-9210
www.radioresultsgroup.com
radioresultsgroup1@sbcglobal.net
License: Coffeyville, KS held by KGGF-KUSN Inc.
Group Owner: Mahaffey Enterprises Inc.; (acq 12-26-90; $750,000 with co-located FM;
Nat'l Network: ABC *Regional Network:* Kan. Agriculture
Arbitron Metro Market: Coffeyville, KS *Format:* News, News/Talk, 84, Talk *Hrs. of News Programming:* news progmg 5 hrs wkly *No. News Employees:* 1 *Target Audience:* 35 plus.
Bill Nolan, CEO
Robert Mahaffey, President
Lance Allred, Operations Dir
Paul Cooper, General Sales Mgr

KKRK
09-01-1983; 98.9 mhz FM *Hrs Open:* 24; 3.2 kw; 453 ft.; N37 6 28 W95 43 22
Mailing Address: Box 4584, Springfield, MO 65808 US
Second Address: 306 W. 8th St., Coffeyville, KS 67337
(620) 251-3800, *Fax:* (620) 251-9210
radioresultsgroup.com
radioresultsgroup1@sbcglobal.net
License: Coffeyville, Montgomery County, KS held by KGGF-KUSN, Inc.
Group Owner: Mahaffey Enterprises Inc.
Arbitron Metro Market: Coffeyville, KS *Format:* Classic Rock *No. News Employees:* 1 *Target Audience:* 35-54.
Bill Nolan, CEO
Robert Mahaffey, President
Ron Lee, Operations Dir
Paul Cooper, General Manager

Colby

KRDQ
09-01-1971; 100.3 mhz FM *Hrs Open:* 24; 100 kw; 610 ft.; N39 28 50 W100 54 34
1660 N. Tyler, Wichita, KS 67212 US
(785) 565-0406, *Fax:* (785) 565-0437
www.rockingmradio.com
cmiller@rockingmradio.com
License: Colby, Thomas County, KS held by Rocking M Radio Inc.
Group Owner: Rocking M Radio Inc.
Nat'l Network: ABC *Regional Network:* Mid-America Ag
Format: Adult Contemp *Target Audience:* 18-49; general
Mike Fell, General Manager
Christopher D. Miller, Vice President

***KTCC**
05-01-1974; 91.9 mhz FM *Hrs Open:* 24; 3 kw; 180 ft.; N39 22 34 W101 3 8
1255 South Range Ave, Colby, KS 67701 US
(785) 462-3984 EXT. 309, *Fax:* (785) 462-4600
www.colbycc.edu
License: Colby, Thomas County, KS held by Colby Community College.
Arbitron Metro Market: Colby, KS *Format:* Contemporary Hits/Top 40 *Special Programming:* Sports 3 hrs, classic rock 3 hrs, hard rock 7 hrs, hip hop 4 hrs wkly *Hrs. of News Programming:* news progmg 14 hrs wkly *No.News Employees:* 1 *Target Audience:* 18-25; young adults
Dr.Stephen M Vacik, President
Corey Sorenson, Station Manager

KWGB
09-01-1998; 97.9 mhz FM *Hrs Open:* 24; 100 kw; 709 ft.; N39 23 24 W101 33 35
Box 569, 3023 West 31st Street, Goodland, KS 67765 US
(785) 899-2309, *Fax:* (785) 899-3062
www.kloe.com

License: Colby, Thomas County, KS held by Melia Communications Inc.
Group Owner: Melia Communications Inc.
Format: Country
Martin Melia, President
Curtis Duncan, Programming Director

KXXX
08-01-1947; 790 khz AM *Hrs Open:* 24; 5 kw-D, ND1; 0.024 kw-N, ND1; N39 23 35 W101 0 6
1660 N. Tyler, Wichita, KS 67212 US
(785) 462-3305, *Fax:* (785) 462-3307
www.nwksradio.com
sacha@rockingmradio.com
License: Colby, KS held by Rocking M Radio Inc.
Group Owner: Rocking M Radio Inc.; (acq 8-31-2007; grpsl)
Nat'l Network: Westwood One *Regional Network:* Mid-America Ag
Arbitron Metro Market: Colby, KS *Format:* Country *Hrs. of News Programming:* news progmg 5 hrs wkly *No. News Employees:* 1 *Target Audience:* 35-55; male, female, city & rural
Melia Clark, Operations Dir
Sacha Sanguinetti, General Manager
Joe Vyzourek, Programming Director
Radonda Buford, Business Manager
Ross Volkmer, Farm Director

Coldwater

***KNJT**
90.3 mhz FM; 1 kw; 128 ft.; N37 16 6 W99 19 33 US
(321) 267-3000, *Fax:* (321) 264-9370
wpio@gate.net
License: Coldwater, Comanche County, KS held by Florida Public Radio Inc.
Arbitron Metro Market: Coldwater, KS
Randy Henry, President
Brian Larson, General Manager

Columbus

KMOQ
12-25-1982; 105.3 mhz FM *Hrs Open:* 24; 13.6 kw; 305 ft.; N37 7 34 W94 42 12
2510 W. 20th Street, Joplin, MO 64804 US
(417) 781-1313, *Fax:* (417) 781-1316
www.kmoq107.com
info@kmoq10.com
License: Columbus, Cherokee County, KS held by American Media Investments Inc.
Group Owner: American Media Investments Inc.; (acq 2-17-2009; grpsl)
Nat'l Network: ABC
Arbitron Metro Market: Joplin, MO *Format:* Contemporary Hits/Top 40 *Target Audience:* 25-54.
Dave Clemons, General Sales Mgr
Chris Stevens, Programming Director
Kathleen Pike, News Director

KJML(FM)
02-01-1980; 107.1 mhz FM; 11.7 kw; Ant 489 ft; N37 14 15 W94 44 15
2510 W. 20th St., Joplin, MO 64804
(417) 781-1313, *Fax:* (417) 781-1316
info@rock105kjml.com
License: Columbus, Cherokee County, KS held by American Media Investments Inc.
Group Owner: American Media Investments Inc.; (acq 2-17-2009; grpsl)
Nat'l Network: ABC
Arbitron Metro Market: Joplin, MO *Hrs. of News Programming:* news progmg 2 hrs wkly *No. News Employees:* 1 *Target Audience:* 18-49; growing families with needs for a wide range of goods & svcs *Adv. Rates:* 10;8; 8; 6
Dave Clemons, General Sales Mgr
Bubba Fontaine, Programming Director
Kathleen Pike, News Director

KJML
107.1 mhz FM; 11.5 kw; 489 ft.; N37 14 15 W94 44 15
2510 W. 20th St., Joplin, MO 64804 US
(213) 494-3377
License: Columbus, Riverside County, KS held by Ether Mining Corp.
Arbitron Metro Market: Columbus, KS
Mark Mueller, Operations Dir

Concordia

KNCK
02-06-1954; 1390 khz AM *Hrs Open:* 24; 0.5 kw-D, ND1; 0.054 kw-N, ND1; N39 33 58 W97 41 4
P.O. Box 629, Concordia, KS 66901 US
(785) 243-1414, *Fax:* (785) 243-1391
License: Concordia, KS held by KNCK Inc.
Format: Country *Special Programming:* Public affrs 2 hrs wkly *Hrs. of News Programming:* news progmg 7 hrs wkly *No. News Employees:* 1 *Target Audience:* 45 plus.
Joe Jindra, President
Marvin Hoffman, Chief Engineer

***KVCO**
05-01-1977; 88.3 mhz FM; 0.125 kw; 75 ft.; N39 33 17 W97 39 48
2221 Campus Drive, Concordia, KS 66901 US
(785) 243-1435(785) 243-4444, *Fax:* (785) 243-1043
www.kvco883.com
kvco@cloud.edu
License: Concordia, Cloud County, KS held by Cloud County Community College.
Nat'l Network: CNN Radio
Arbitron Metro Market: Concordia, KS *Format:* Variety/Diverse *Target Audience:* 16-30 plus; students & young adults
John Chapin, General Manager

Copeland

***KHYM**
12-23-1997; 103.9 mhz FM *Hrs Open:* 24; 100 kw; 751 ft.; N37 28 35 W100 35 59
P.O. Box 991, Meade, KS 67864 US
(620) 873-2991, *Fax:* (620) 873-2755
www.khymfm.org
mike@khym.org; glenn@khym.org; delvin@khym.org; joe@khym.org; steve@khym.org; ele@khym.org; stell@kh
License: Copeland, Gray County, KS held by Great Plains Christian Radio Inc.
Format: Christian, Religious *Hrs. of News Programming:* Family 4 hrs wkly, talk 7 hrs wkly *No. News Employees:* 1 *Target Audience:* 25-54, Christians
Micheal Luskey, President
Jerry Mann, Operations Dir
Glenn Hascoll, Station Manager
Steve Larsen, Chief Engineer

***KJIL**
09-05-1992; 99.1 mhz FM *Hrs Open:* 24; 100 kw; 935 ft.; N37 28 35 W100 35 59
P.O. Box 991, Meade, KS 67864 US
(620) 873-2991, *Fax:* (620) 873-2755
www.kjil.com
kjil@kjil.com
License: Copeland, Gray County, KS held by Great Plains Christian Radio Inc.
Nat'l Network: Moody; USA
Format: Christian, Religious *Target Audience:* 25-60; Evangelical Christians
Don Hughes, President
Michael Luskey, Operations Dir
Delvin Kinser, News Director
Steve Larson, Chief Engineer
Polly Hughes, Traffic Manager

KSKZ
05-01-1994; 98.1 mhz FM *Hrs Open:* 24; 100 kw; 666 ft.; N37 46 48 W100 27 36
C/O Fisher Wayland: Cmc, 2001 Penn. Ave., NW, Washington, DC 20006 US
(620) 276-2366, *Fax:* (620) 276-3568
www.wksradio.com
info@wksradio.com
License: Copeland, Gray County, KS held by Ingstad Broadcasting Inc.
Group Owner: Robert Ingstad Broadcast Properties; (acq 1-27-95;
Arbitron Metro Market: Green City, KS *Format:* Adult Contemp *Target Audience:* 25-54.
Gil Wohler, General Manager
James Janda, Programming Director
Andrew Mahoney, News Director
Tom Dial, Chief Engineer
Rachel Wheet, Traffic Manager

Dearing

KUSN
10-01-1999; 98.1 mhz FM *Hrs Open:* 24 hours daily; 9.7 kw; 495 ft.; N37 6 28 W95 43 22
Mailing Address: P.O. Box 4584, Springfield, MO 65808 US
Second Address: 306 W. 8th St., Coffeyville, KS 67337
(417) 883-9180, *Fax:* (417) 883-9096
License: Dearing, Montgomery County, KS held by KGGF-KUSN Inc.
Group Owner: Mahaffey Enterprises Inc.
Format: Country *Target Audience:* 18-49.
Robert Mahaffey, President
John Leonard, General Manager

Derby

KZCH
01-01-1978; 96.3 mhz FM *Hrs Open:* 24; 50 kw; 492 ft.; N37 43 6 W97 19 5
600 Congress Ave., Suite 1400, Austin, TX 78701 US
(316) 494-6600, *Fax:* (316) 494-6730
www.channel963.com
info@channel963.com
License: Derby, Sedgwick County, KS held by Clear Channel Broadcasting Licenses Inc.
Group Owner: Clear Channel Communications Inc.; (acq 8-30-2000; grpsl).
Nat'l Reps: Clear Channel
Arbitron Metro Market: Wichita, KS *Format:* Contemporary Hits/Top 40 *Target Audience:* 18-34; women
Tom Glade, Operations Dir

Dodge City

KDCC
01-01-1992; 1550 khz AM *Hrs Open:* 7 AM-10 PM; 1 kw-D, DA2; 0.09 kw-N, DA2; N37 47 14 W100 1 55
2500 North 14th Avenue, Dodge City, KS 67801 US
(620) 225-6783(620) 225-6720, *Fax:* (620) 225-0918
License: Dodge City, KS held by Dodge City Community College.
Format: News *Hrs. of News Programming:* News progmg 35 hrs wkly *Target Audience:* 18 plus.
John Ewy, General Manager

KGNO
06-30-1930; 1370 khz AM; 5 kw-D, ND1; 0.23 kw-N, ND1; N37 45 36 W100 5 53
Mailing Address: 1660 North Tyler Road, Wichita, KS 67212 US
Second Address: 106 W Frontview, Dodge City, KS 67801
(620) 225-8080, *Fax:* (620) 225-6655
www.rockingmradio.com
rockswks@sbcgobal.net
License: Dodge City, KS held by Rocking M Radio Inc.
Group Owner: Rocking M Radio Inc.; (acq 8-31-2007; grpsl)
Nat'l Network: ESPN Radio; Fox News Radio *Regional Network:* Mid-America Ag
Format: News, Sports, 86 *Special Programming:* Farm 15 hrs wkly *Target Audience:* 25-54.
Brian Nugen, Operations Dir
Mark Hinca, General Manager
Peggy Burdick, General Sales Mgr
Candace Thomas, News Director

KAHE
05-01-1966; 95.5 mhz FM *Hrs Open:* 24; 100 kw; 577 ft.; N37 38 28 W100 20 40
Mailing Address: 1660 N. Tyler Rd., Wichita, KS 67212 US
Second Address: 106 W Frontview, Dodge City, KS 67801
(620) 225-8080, *Fax:* (620) 225-6655
www.rockingmradio.com
rockswks@global.net
License: Dodge City, Ford County, KS held by Rocking M Radio Inc.
Group Owner: Rocking M Radio Inc.
Nat'l Network: Fox Sports
Format: Oldies *Hrs. of News Programming:* News progmg 5 hrs wkly *Target Audience:* 25-49.
Brian Nugen, General Manager
Peggy Burdick, General Sales Mgr
Candice Thomas, News Director
Mark Hinca, General Manager

***KONQ**
04-26-1978; 91.9 mhz FM; 2.6 kw horiz; 125 ft.; N37 46 33 W100 2 12
2501 North 14th Street, Dodge City, KS 67801 US
(620) 225-6783,(620) 225-6720, *Fax:* (620) 225-0918
www.dodgecitycommunitycollege.com
License: Dodge City, Ford County, KS held by Dodge City Community College.
Format: Adult Contemp, Variety/Diverse *Special Programming:* Black 10 hrs, sports 5 hrs wkly *Hrs. of News Programming:* News progmg 7 hrs wkly
John Ewy, General Manager

KZRD
12-01-1997; 93.9 mhz FM; 100 kw; 807 ft.; N37 55 56 W100 19 2
Mailing Address: 1660 N. Tyler, Wichita, KS 67212 US
Second Address: 106 W Frontview, Dodge City, KS 67801
(785) 565-0406, *Fax:* (785) 565-0437
www.rockingmradio.com
cmiller@rockingmradio.com
License: Dodge City, Ford County, KS held by Rocking M Radio Inc.
Group Owner: Rocking M Radio Inc.; (acq 8-31-2007; grpsl)
Arbitron Metro Market: South West KS
Brian Nugen, Operations Dir
Mark Hinca, General Manager
Peggy Burdick, General Sales Mgr
Candice Thomas, News Director

***KAIG**
01-01-2008; 89.9 mhz FM; 100 kw vert; 696 ft.; N37 55 56 W100 19 2 *Rebroadcasts:* Rebroadcasts KLRD(FM) Yucaipa, CA 100%
1425 N Market Blvd., Suite 9, Sacramento, CA 95834 US
(800) 877-5600, *Fax:* (916) 251-1650
www.air1.com
info@air1.com
License: Dodge City, Ford County, KS held by Educational Media Foundation.
Group Owner: EMF Broadcasting
Nat'l Network: Air 1
Arbitron Metro Market: Centralia, WA *Format:* Alternative, Christian
Mike Novak, President
Crystal Wojteczo, Operations Dir
David Pierce, Programming Director
Ed Lenane, News Director
Sam Wallington, Engineering Dir
Marya Morgan, News Reporter
Richard Hunt, News Reporter

Downs

KDNS
04-11-1994; 94.1 mhz FM *Hrs Open:* 5 AM-1 AM; 28 kw; 292 ft.; N39 30 29 W98 18 57
P.O. Box 88, Glen Elder, KS 67446 US
(785) 545-3220
www.kdcountry94.com
info@kdnsfm.com
License: Downs, Osborne County, KS held by Dierking Communications Inc.
Group Owner: Dierking Communications Inc.; (acq 7-27-2006; $276,000).
Nat'l Network: Jones Radio Networks *Regional Network:* Brownfield
Arbitron Metro Market: Glen Elder, KS *Format:* Country *Special Programming:* Farm 6 hrs, gospel 5 hrs wkly *Hrs. of News Programming:* news progmg 4 hrs wkly *No. News Employees:* 1 *Target Audience:* 25-54.
Wade Gerstner, General Manager

Effingham

KDVB
03-12-2008; 96.9 mhz FM; 0.12 kw; 227 ft.; N39 33 7 W95 25 23 US
(785) 272-2122, *Fax:* (785) 272-6219
www.v100rocks.com
License: Effingham, Atchison County, KS held by Cumulus Licensing LLC.
Group Owner: Cumulus Media Inc.
Arbitron Metro Market: Effingham, KS
Spike Santee, General Manager
Ian, Promotions Manager

El Dorado

***KBTL**
03-01-1998; 88.1 mhz FM; 0.4 kw; 92 ft.; N37 48 16 W96 53 2
901 S. Haverhill Road, El Dorado, KS 67042 US
(316) 321-2222
License: El Dorado, Butler County, KS held by Butler County Community College.
Arbitron Metro Market: El Dorado, KS *Format:* Variety/Diverse
Lance Hayes, General Manager

KAHS
11-16-1953; 1360 khz AM *Hrs Open:* 24; 1 kw-D; N37 48 47 W96 48 44
201 N. Industrial Park Rd., Excelsior Springs, MO 74152
(316) 320-1360
www.1360kahs.com
1360kahs@gmail.com
License: El Dorado, Butler County, KS held by Catholic Radio Network Inc.
Group Owner: Catholic Radio Network Inc.; (acq 12-12-2005; $525,000)
Nat'l Network: CNN Radio; Westwood One
Population Served: 500,000 *Arbitron Metro Market:* Wichita, KS
Special Programming: Jazz 2 hrs wkly *Target Audience:* 35-69.
James O'Laughlin, President

***KTLI**
02-15-1972; 99.1 mhz FM; 100 kw; 617 ft.; N37 56 22 W96 59 20
P.O. Box 1250, Sapulpa, OK 74067 US
(316) 303-9999, *Fax:* (316) 303-9900
k-love.com
info@ktli.com
License: El Dorado, Butler County, KS held by El Dorado Licenses Inc.
Group Owner: EMF Broadcasting; (acq 12-3-2004; $2.95 million).
Arbitron Metro Market: Wichita, KS *Format:* Adult Contemp, Christian *Hrs. of News Programming:* News progmg 25 hrs wkly *Target Audience:* 25-54; women
Crystal Wojtecko, General Sales Mgr

Elk City

KIND-FM
94.9 mhz FM; 6 kw; 272 ft.; N37 15 42 W95 45 59 US
(620)331-6669, *Fax:* (620)331-8008
License: Elk City, KS
Group Owner: Tallgrass Broadcasting LLC
Format: Country

Emporia

KFFX
06-15-1966; 104.9 mhz FM *Hrs Open:* 24; 3 kw; 279 ft.; N38 23 10 W96 10 36
P.O. Box 968, Emporia, KS 66801 US
(620) 342-1400, *Fax:* (620) 342-0804
www.todaysbesthits.com
License: Emporia, Lyon County, KS
Group Owner: Emporia's Radio Stations Inc.
Arbitron Metro Market: Emporia, KS *Format:* Adult Contemp *Hrs. of News Programming:* News progmg 4 hrs wkly *Target Audience:* 20-40.
Steve Rocha, Programming Director
Esther Johnson, News Director

***KJLG**
01-11-1987; 91.9 mhz FM *Hrs Open:* 24; 3 kw; Ant 263 ft; N38 24 35 W96 13 30
Box 506, 815 Graham St., Emporia, KS 66801
(620) 343-9292
kngm@osprey.net
License: Emporia, Lyon County, KS held by Great Plains Christian Radio Inc.
Population Served: 60,000*No. News Employees:* 1 *Target Audience:* Young families and adults.
Robert Hughes, CEO

***KPOR**
06-19-2002; 90.7 mhz FM *Hrs Open:* 24; 2 kw; 328 ft.; N38 26 50 W96 7 42
4135 Northgate Blvd, Suite 1, Sacramento, CA 95834 US
(316) 342-1474
www.familyradio.com
info@familyradio.com
License: Emporia, Lyon County, KS held by Family Stations Inc.
Group Owner: Family Stations Inc.
Arbitron Metro Market: Topeka, KS *Format:* Religious
Harold Camping, General Manager

KANS
04-01-1998; 96.1 mhz FM; 6 kw; 318 ft.; N38 24 21 W96 14 13
1811 6th Avenue, Emporia, KS 66801 US
(620) 343-9393, *Fax:* (620) 342-7617
kans@ksradio.com
License: Emporia, Lyon County, KS held by C&C Consulting Inc.
Arbitron Metro Market: Emporia, KS *Format:* Classic Rock
Marty Hill, General Manager
Lisa Vega, General Sales Mgr
Angie Boden, Programming Director
Brook Reed, News Director

KVOE
01-21-1939; 1400 khz AM; 1 kw-U, ND1; N38 23 10 W96 10 36
P.O. Box 968, Emporia, KS 66801 US
(620) 342-1400, *Fax:* (620) 342-0804
www.kvoe.com
kvoe@kvoe.com
License: Emporia, KS held by Emporia Radio Stations Inc.
Group Owner: Emporia's Radio Stations Inc.; (acq 1-7-87)
Arbitron Metro Market: Emporia, KS *Format:* Adult Contemp, News, 64 *Special Programming:* Sp 3 hrs wkly *Target Audience:* 35-54.
Ron Thomas, General Manager
Erren Harter, Promotions Manager
Jeff O'Dell, News Director
Charlie Allen, Chief Engineer
Greg Rahe, Sports Commentator
Karri Kimberlin, Traffic
Gwen Longbine, Sales
Terry Bontrager,Receptionist/Traffic
Anne Orender, Sales

KVOE-FM
01-16-1985; 101.7 mhz FM *Hrs Open:* 24; 3.2 kw; 299 ft.; N38 21 45 W96 7 0
P.O. Box 968, Emporia, KS 66801 US
(620) 342-1400, *Fax:* (620) 342-0804
www.kvoe.com
kvoe@kvoe.com
License: Emporia, Lyon County, KS held by Emporia Radio Stations Inc.
Group Owner: Emporia's Radio Stations Inc.; (acq 1994)
Arbitron Metro Market: Emporia, KS *Format:* Country *Hrs. of News Programming:* news progmg 7 hrs wkly *No. News Employees:* 2 *Target Audience:* 25-54.
Steve Sauder, CEO
Ron Thomas, General Manager
Erren Harter, Promotions Manager
Jef O'Dell, News Director
Charlie Allen, Chief Engineer
Greg Rahe, Sports Commentator
Karri Kimberlin, Traffic
Gwen Longbine, Sales
TerryBontrager, Receptionist/Traffic
Anne Orender, Sales

***KANH**
01-01-2002; 89.7 mhz FM; 3 kw; 262 ft.; N38 21 45 W96 7 0
Broadcasting Hall, Lawrence, KS 66045 US
(785) 864-4530, *Fax:* (785) 864-5278
www.kpr.ku.edu
kpr@ku.edu
License: Emporia, Lyon County, KS held by University of Kansas.
Nat'l Network: NPR
Arbitron Metro Market: Lawrence, KS *Format:* Jazz
Janet Campbell, General Manager
Darrell Brogdon, Programming Director
Mark Edwards, Promotions Manager
J. Schafer, News Director
Sheri Hamilton, Development Director
Kathleen Harrison, Membership Director
Nicci Banman, BusinessManager
Wendy Huggins, Administrative Associate

Enterprise

***KBMP**
03-06-2002; 90.5 mhz FM *Hrs Open:* 24; 19 kw; 384 ft.; N39 7 53.9 W97 19 58.8 *Rebroadcasts:* Rebroadcasts KSIV-FM Saint Louis, MO 100%
P O Box 1452, Washington, DC 20013 US
(316) 283-4592, *Fax:* (316) 283-3177
www.bottradionetwork.com
comments@bottradionetwork.com
License: Enterprise, Dickinson County, KS held by Community Broadcasting Inc.
Group Owner: Bott Radio Network; (acq 1-26-2006; $30,000 with KARF(FM) Independence)
Format: Christian, Talk *Target Audience:* 25-54; adults
Dan Snell, General Manager

Eureka

KOTE
10-01-1988; 93.5 mhz FM *Hrs Open:* 24; 3 kw; 322 ft.; N37 47 29 W96 17 25
Mailing Address: P.O. Box 331, Eureka, KS 67045 US
Second Address: 1275 P. Rd., Eureka, KS 67045
(620) 583-7414, *Fax:* (620) 583-7233
www.koteinfo.com
steve@kotefm.com
License: Eureka, Greenwood County, KS held by Niemeyer Communications LLC
Format: Classic Rock, Country *No. News Employees:* 1 *Target Audience:* General. *Adv. Rates:* 8; 8; 8; 8
Steve Niemeyer, General Manager

Fairway

KCNW
04-16-1953; 1380 khz AM *Hrs Open:* 24; 2.5 kw-D, ND1; 0.029 kw-N, ND1; N39 4 19 W94 40 58
8910 University Center Lane, #130, San Diego, CA 92122 US
(864) 585-1885, *Fax:* (864) 597-0687
www.wilkinsradio.com
kcnw@wilkinsradio.com
License: Fairway, KS held by Kansas City Radio Inc.
Group Owner: Wilkins Communications Network Inc.; (acq 1-17-2001; $725,000).
Nat'l Network: Westwood One
Arbitron Metro Market: Fairway, KS *Format:* Christian, Talk *No. News Employees:* 1 *Target Audience:* 35 plus; adults involved in community & family *Adv. Rates:* 30; 30; 30; 30
Bob Wilkins, CEO/COO
Mitchell Mathis, President/Chief Operating Officer
Steve Stigall, Operations Dir
Kevin Fears, Station Manager
Kirk Chestnut, Engineering Dir
LuAnn Wilkins, Executive Vice President
Greg Garrett, OperationsManager
Barry Bright, Senior Director, Client Development
Paige Carrick, Network Media Coordinator
Joel Perkins, Director, Client Development
Amy Cleveland, Network Media Coordinator

Fort Scott

KMDO
10-08-1954; 1600 khz AM
Mailing Address: PO Box 12, Fort Scott, KS 66701 US
Second Address: 2 North National Ave, Fort Scott, KS 66701
(620) 223-4500, *Fax:* (620) 223-5662
www.kombfm.com
amy@kombfm.com
License: Fort Scott, KS held by Fort Scott Broadcasting Co.
Nat'l Network: CNN Radio
Arbitron Metro Market: Joplin, MO *Format:* Oldies *Target Audience:* 17+
Tim McKenney, President

KOMB
01-23-1981; 103.9 mhz FM *Hrs Open:* 24 hour; 25 kw; 328 ft.; N37 54 28 W94 46 2
Mailing Address: P.O. Box 72, 2 N. National Ave, Fort Scott, KS 66701 US
Second Address: 2 North Naitonal Ave., PO Box 72, Fort Scott, KS 66701
(620) 223-4500,(620) 223-4501, *Fax:* (620) 223-5662
kombfm.com
tim@kombfm.com
License: Fort Scott, Bourbon County, KS
Nat'l Network: CNN Radio
Arbitron Metro Market: Joplin, MO *Format:* Contemporary Hits/Top 40, Adult Contemp
Timothy McKenney, President
Deb McKenney, General Sales Mgr
Noel Connet, Programming Director
Amy Wood, Promotions Manager
Tom Knight, News Director

*KVCY
11-01-1983; 104.7 mhz FM *Hrs Open:* 24; 16 kw; 410 ft.; N37 52 43 W94 43 24
3434 West Kilbourn Ave., Milwaukee, WI 53208 US
(414) 935-3000, *Fax:* (414) 935-3015
www.vcyamerica.org
vcy@vcyamerica.org
License: Fort Scott, Bourbon County, KS held by VCY America Inc.
Group Owner: VCY America Inc.
Nat'l Network: USA; Moody
Arbitron Metro Market: Milwaukee, WI *TV Affiliate:* KVCX-TV
Format: Christian, Religious
Vic Eliason, Operations Dir
Jim Schneider, Programming Director

Fredonia

KGGF-FM
07-14-1997; 104.1 mhz FM *Hrs Open:* 24/7; 7.3 kw; 535 ft.; N37 22 31 W95 43 41
P.O. Box 4584, Springfield, MO 65808 US
(316) 251-3800, *Fax:* (918) 251-9210
www.radioresultsgroup.com/id7.html
License: Fredonia, Wilson County, KS held by KGGF-KUSN Inc.
Group Owner: Mahaffey Enterprises Inc.
Arbitron Metro Market: Independence, KS *Format:* Oldies *Target Audience:* 45-64
Paul Cooper, General Manager

Galena

KQYX
01-01-1927; 1450 khz AM *Hrs Open:* 24
2702 Iowa Street, Joplin, MO 64804 US
(417) 781-1313, *Fax:* (417) 781-1316
License: Galena, KS held by American Media Investments Inc.
Group Owner: American Media Investments Inc.; (acq 2-17-2009; grpsl)
Arbitron Metro Market: Joplin, MO *Format:* Oldies *Target Audience:* 18-39. *Adv. Rates:* 12; 12; 12; 10
Dave Clemons, General Sales Mgr
Matt Kruger, Programming Director
Kathleen Pike, News Director

Garden City

*KANZ
06-29-1980; 91.1 mhz FM *Hrs Open:* 5 AM-midnight; 100 kw; 959 ft.; N37 46 43 W100 53 43.4 *Rebroadcasts:* Rebroadcasts KZNA(FM) Hill City 100%
201 N. 7th Street, Garden City, KS 67846 US
(620) 275-7444
www.hppr.org
License: Garden City, Finney County, KS held by KANZA Society Inc.
Nat'l Network: PRI; NPR
Arbitron Metro Market: Garden City, KS *Format:* Variety/Diverse *Special Programming:* Jazz 15 hrs, folk 6 hrs, Sp 6 hrs wkly *Hrs. of News Programming:* News progmg 39 hrs wkly *Target Audience:* General.
Don Close, President
Dale Bolton, Operations Dir
Richard Hicks, General Manager
Robert Kirby, Programming Director

KIUL
05-20-1935; 1240 khz AM; 1 kw-U, ND1; N37 59 52 W100 54 25
P.O. Box 364, Pierre, SD 57501 US
(620) 276-3251, *Fax:* (620) 276-3649
www.kiulradio.com
License: Garden City, KS held by Steckline Communications Inc.
Group Owner: Steckline Communications Inc.; (acq 11-28-2006; $550,000 with KYUL(AM) Scott City)
Nat'l Network: CBS; Westwood One
Format: News, News/Talk, 84, Talk *Special Programming:* Farm 5 hrs wkly *Hrs. of News Programming:* news progmg 20 hrs wkly *No. News Employees:* 2 *Target Audience:* 45 plus; upscale adults *Adv. Rates:* 18;16; 18; 14
Danny Havel, Operations Dir
Rick Thomeczek, General Manager

KKJQ
11-20-1962; 97.3 mhz FM *Hrs Open:* 24; 100 kw; 801 ft.; N37 46 48 W100 27 36
P.O. Box 907, Valley City, ND 58072 US
(620) 276-2366, *Fax:* (620) 276-3568
License: Garden City, Finney County, KS held by KBUF Partnership
Group Owner: Robert Ingstad Broadcast Properties
Nat'l Network: ABC
Arbitron Metro Market: Wichita, KS *Format:* Adult Contemp, Country *Target Audience:* 18-49.
Greg Lynn, Programming Director

Girard

KSEK-FM
09-01-1988; 99.1 mhz FM; 6 kw; 325 ft.; N37 29 2 W94 51 8
1612 Woodland Terrace, Pittsburg, KS 66762 US
(620) 232-9912, *Fax:* (620) 232-9915
lynnm@skilonline.com
License: Girard, Crawford County, KS held by Southeast Kansas Independent Living Resource Center Inc.
Group Owner: Southeast Kansas Independent Living Resource Center Inc.; (acq 11-30-2004; $700,000 with KSEK(AM) Pittsburg).
Nat'l Network: AP Network News
Arbitron Metro Market: Pittsburg, KS *Format:* Classic Rock *Hrs. of News Programming:* News progmg 10 hrs wkly *Target Audience:* 25-54; resident adults & univ. students *Adv. Rates:* 150; 120; 120; 120
Lynn Meredith, General Manager

Goodland

KGCR
03-01-1988; 107.7 mhz FM *Hrs Open:* 24; 100 kw; 446 ft.; N39 22 2 W101 26 44
Mailing Address: P.O. Box 8, Aurora, NE 68818 US
Second Address: 3410 Rd. 66, Brewster, KS 67732
(785) 694-2877, *Fax:* (785) 694-2875
www.wordpress.kgcr.org
kgcr@kgcr.com
License: Goodland, Sherman County, KS held by The Praise Network Inc.
Nat'l Network: Moody; USA
Arbitron Metro Market: Goodland, KS *Format:* Christian, Religious, 86 *Special Programming:* Farm 2 hrs wkly *Hrs. of News Programming:* news progmg 30 hrs wkly *No. News Employees:* 1 *Target Audience:* 25-54;Christian families
Lloyd Mintzmyer, CEO
James Claasson, General Manager

KKCI
09-15-1990; 102.5 mhz FM *Hrs Open:* 24; 100 kw; 709 ft.; N39 23 24 W101 33 35
P.O. Box 569, 3023 West 31st, Goodland, KS 67735 US
(785) 899-2309, *Fax:* (785) 899-3062
License: Goodland, Sherman County, KS
Nat'l Network: Jones Radio Networks
Arbitron Metro Market: Wichita, KS *Format:* Adult Contemp, Jazz, 84 *Target Audience:* 25-55.
Steve Wodlinger, General Manager

KLOE
01-01-1947; 730 khz AM *Hrs Open:* 24; 1 kw-D, ND1; 0.02 kw-N, ND1; N39 20 4 W101 45 28
P.O. Box 569, 3023 West 31st, Goodland, KS 67735 US
(785) 899-2309, *Fax:* (785) 899-3062
www.kloe.com
info@kloe.com
License: Goodland, KS held by Melia Communications Inc.
Group Owner: Melia Communications Inc.; acq 1-26-96; $990,000 with co-located FM)
Nat'l Network: CBS *Regional Network:* Kan. Agriculture
Arbitron Metro Market: Wichita, KS *Format:* Country, News, 62, Talk *Target Audience:* General.
Martin Melia, President
Curtis Duncan, Programming Director

Great Bend

*KBDA
01-01-1999; 89.7 mhz FM; 1.4 kw; 112 ft.; N38 20 16 W98 45 48
P O Drawer 2440, Tupelo, MS 38803 US
(662) 844-8888, *Fax:* (662) 842-6791
www.afr.net
comments@afr.net
License: Great Bend, Barton County, KS held by American Family Association.
Group Owner: American Family Radio
Arbitron Metro Market: Tupelo, MS *Format:* Christian, Religious
Marvin Sanders, General Manager

*KHCT
08-03-1992; 90.9 mhz FM; 50 kw; 781 ft.; N38 37 4 W98 56 32
815 N. Walnut, Suite 300, Hutchinson, KS 67501 US
(620) 662-6646
radiokansas.org
rfragoza@radiokansas.org
License: Great Bend, Barton County, KS held by Hutchinson Community College.
Nat'l Network: NPR
Format: News *Target Audience:* General
Geralyn Smith, Operations Dir
Ken Baker, General Manager
Sharon Webb, General Sales Mgr
Ken Baker, Programming Director
Ric Jung, Chief Engineer

KVGB
03-10-1937; 1590 khz AM; 5 kw-D, DAN; 5 kw-N, DAN; N38 18 50 W98 47 35
PO Box 817, Hays, KS 67601 US
(620) 792-3647, *Fax:* (620) 792-3649
www.kvgbam.com
info@eagleradio.net
License: Great Bend, KS held by Eagle Communications Inc.
Group Owner: Eagle Communications Group; (acq 4-95).
Nat'l Network: ABC
Arbitron Metro Market: Great Bend, KS *Format:* News, Sports, 86 *Special Programming:* Farm 7 hrs, relg 2 hrs wkly *Target Audience:* 28 plus.
Rick Nulton, General Manager
Randy Goering, General Sales Mgr

KVGB-FM
01-17-1977; 104.3 mhz FM; 96 kw; 810 ft.; N38 25 54 W98 46 18
PO Box 817, Hays, KS 67601 US
(620) 792-4637, *Fax:* (620) 792-3649
www.b1043.net
info@eagleradio.net

License: Great Bend, Barton County, KS
Group Owner: Eagle Communications Group
Nat'l Network: ABC
Arbitron Metro Market: Great Bend, KS *Format:* Classic Rock
Randy Goering, General Sales Mgr

KZRS
02-03-1986; 107.9 mhz FM *Hrs Open:* 24; 99 kw; 909 ft.; N38 46 16 W98 44 17
1660 N. Tyler, Wichita, KS 67212 US
(620) 792-7108, *Fax:* (620) 792-7051
www.rockingmradio.com/kzrs.htm
kzls@waittradio.com
License: Great Bend, Barton County, KS held by Rocking M Radio Inc.
Group Owner: Rocking M Radio Inc.; (acq 8-31-2007; grpsl)
Regional Network: Mid-America Ag
Arbitron Metro Market: Great Bend, KS *Format:* Adult Contemp *Hrs. of News Programming:* news progmg 5 hrs wkly *No. News Employees:* 1 *Target Audience:* 25-54.
Ken Schwamborn, General Manager
Chris Elson, Programming Director
Rod Rogers, Chief Engineer

***KWBI**
10-10-2001; 91.9 mhz FM *Hrs Open:* 24; 7.4 kw; 259 ft.; N38 20 16 W98 45 48
1425 North Market Blvd., Suite 9, Sacramento, CA 95834 US
(800) 525-5683, *Fax:* (916) 251-1650
www.klove.com
klove@klove.com
License: Great Bend, Barton County, KS held by Educational Media Foundation.
Group Owner: EMF Broadcasting
Nat'l Network: K-Love
Arbitron Metro Market: Omaha, NE *Format:* Christian *No. News Employees:* 13 *Target Audience:* 25-44; Judeo Christian, female
Darrell Chambliss, Chairman
MIke Novak, President & CEO
Crystal Wojteczko, Operations Dir
Eric Allen, General Sales Mgr
David Pierce, Programming Director
Ed Lenane, News Director
Sam Wallington, Engineering Dir
Marya Morgan,News Reporter
Richard Hunt, News Reporter
Laura Daniels, News Reporter
Tim Luttrell, News Reporter
Kenny Noble Cortes, News Reporter
Darren Vinson, News Reporter

***KRTT**
88.1 mhz FM; 0 kw horiz, 0.9 kw vert; 128 ft.; N38 21 46 W98 45 50
US
(321) 267-3000, *Fax:* (321) 264-9370
wpio@gate.net
License: Great Bend, Barton County, KS held by Florida Public Radio Inc.
Arbitron Metro Market: Great Bend, KS
Randy Henry, President

Haven

KIBB
01-01-1998; 97.1 mhz FM; 18.5 kw; 823 ft.; N37 48 0.7 W97 31 29
106 North Main St., Hutchinson, KS 67501 US
(316) 558-8800, *Fax:* (316) 558-8802
www.971bobfm.com
kibb@971bobfm.com
License: Haven, Reno County, KS held by Connoisseur Media of Wichita LLC.
Group Owner: Connoisseur Media LLC; (acq 12-13-2007; exchange for KNZS(FM) Kingman)
Arbitron Metro Market: Wichita, KS *Format:* Adult Contemp
Wichita,KS, General Manager
Kim Kretchmar, General Sales Mgr
Ron Allen, Programming Director

Hays

KAYS
10-15-1948; 1400 khz AM *Hrs Open:* 24; 1 kw-U, ND1; N38 53 29 W99 22 3
Mailing Address: Box 817, Hays, KS 67601 US
Second Address: 2300 Hall St., Hays, KS 67601
(785) 625-2578, *Fax:* (785) 625-3632
www.hayspost.com
License: Hays, KS held by Eagle Communications Inc.
Group Owner: Eagle Communications Group; (Acq 3-20-91; grpsl;
Arbitron Metro Market: Hays, KS *Format:* Oldies *Hrs. of News Programming:* news progmg 6 hrs wkly *No. News Employees:* 1 *Target Audience:* Adults.
Mike Cooper, Programming Director

KHAZ
05-01-1985; 99.5 mhz FM *Hrs Open:* 24; 100 kw; 515 ft; N38 56 29 W99 21 22
Mailing Address: Box 6, Hays, KS 67601
Second Address: 2300 Hall St., Hays, KS 67601
(785) 625-2578, *Fax:* (785) 625-3632
License: Hays, Ellis County, KS held by Cumulus
Group Owner: Eagle Communications Group
Nat'l Network: ABC
Special Programming: Farm 10 hrs, gospel 3 hrs wkly *Hrs. of News Programming:* news progmg 4 hrs wkly *No. News Employees:* 2 *Target Audience:* 25-54.
Scott Boomer, Operations Dir
Todd Lynd, General Manager
Theresa Trapp, Programming Director
Callie Kolacney, News Director
Mark Goff, Chief Engineer

KJLS
06-27-1974; 103.3 mhz FM *Hrs Open:* 24; 100 kw; 994 ft.; N39 1 15 W99 28 12
P.O. Box 597, Hays, KS 67601 US
(785) 625-2578, *Fax:* (785) 625-3632
License: Hays, Ellis County, KS held by Eagle Communications Inc.
Group Owner: Eagle Communications Group; (acq 9-12-00; with KKQY(FM) Hill City).
Format: Adult Contemp *Hrs. of News Programming:* news progmg 8 hrs wkly *No. News Employees:* 1 *Target Audience:* 25-49; 60% female, 40% male
Todd Nelson, General Manager

***KPRD**
01-01-1994; 88.9 mhz FM; 83 kw; 636 ft.; N38 46 16 W98 44 17
P.O. Box 8, Aurora, NE 68818 US
(785) 628-6300, *Fax:* (785) 628-6389
www.kprdradio.org
kprd@kprd.org
License: Hays, Ellis County, KS held by The Praise Network Inc.
Format: Religious *Target Audience:* 20-48.
Lloyd Mintzmyer, CEO
David Breedon, Station Manager

***KZAN**
91.7 mhz FM *Hrs Open:* 24; 7.5 kw; 374 ft.; N38 57 29 W99 21 6.6 *Rebroadcasts:* Rebroadcast KANZ(FM) Garden City 100%
207 N. 7th St., Garden City, KS 67846 US
(620) 274-7444, *Fax:* (620) 275-7496
www.hppr.org
hppr@hppr.org
License: Hays, Ellis County, KS held by Kanza Society Inc.
Nat'l Network: NPR; PRI; AP Radio
Arbitron Metro Market: Hays, Kansas *Format:* News, News/Talk, 86 *Target Audience:* 25-80; educated
Don Close, President
Richard Hicks, General Manager
Diana Gonzales, General Sales Mgr
Bob Kirby, Programming Director
Dale Bolton, Promotions Manager
Chuck Springer, Chief Engineer
Rod Buchele, Vice President
Quentin Hope,Treasurer
Gary Pitner, Secretary
Barb Blevins, Community Donor Relations Assistant
Dean Yates, Texas Underwriting Representative
Deb Oyler, Executive Director

***KHYS**
01-01-2009; 89.7 mhz FM; 0.45 kw; 285 ft.; N38 51 16 W99 22 53 *Rebroadcasts:* Rebroadcasts WAFR(FM) Tupelo, MS 100%
P.O. Box 1458, Washington, DC 20013 US
(662) 844-5036, *Fax:* (662) 842-6791
www.afr.net
contact@afa.net
License: Hays, Ellis County, KS held by American Family Association.
Group Owner: American Family Radio; (acq 6-9-2006)
Nat'l Network: American Family Radio
Arbitron Metro Market: Hays, KS *Format:* Christian
Donald E. Wildmon, Founder
Buster Wilson, General Manager
Jennifer Hagman, Programming Director

KRMR
06-16-2008; 105.7 mhz FM; 20.5 kw; 495 ft.; N38 55 59 W99 19 51
US
(785) 628-6108, *Fax:* (785) 628-1055
License: Hays, Ellis County, KS held by Radioactive LLC.
Group Owner: Radioactive LLC
Nat'l Network: Fox News Radio
Arbitron Metro Market: Hays, KS *Format:* Contemporary Hits/Top 40
Benjamin Homel, President
Corey Sorenson, General Manager

Haysville

KFBZ
08-25-1985; 105.3 mhz FM; 98 kw; 1007 ft.; N37 48 1 W97 31 29
1850 K Street, NW, Suite 900, Washington, DC 20006 US
(316) 685-2121, *Fax:* (316) 685-3408
www.1053thebuzz.com
jwise@entercom.com
License: Haysville, Sedgwick County, KS held by Entercom Wichita License LLC.
Group Owner: Entercom Communications Corp.; (acq 2000; grpsl)
Arbitron Metro Market: Wichita, KS *Format:* Adult Contemp
Special Programming: Relg 2 hrs wkly *Hrs. of News Programming:* News progmg 2 hrs wkly *Target Audience:* 25-54.
Jackie Wise, General Manager
Lisa Crider, General Sales Mgr
Dussty Hayes, Programming Director
Jennifer Lane, Webmaster

Herington

***KJRL**
09-06-1997; 105.7 mhz FM *Hrs Open:* 24; 12.5 kw; 500 ft; N38 37 01 W96 59 09
Box 14, 805 S. Buckeye Avenue, Abilene, KS 67449
(785) 263-7200, *Fax:* (785) 263-3876
www.kjil1057.com
radioforlife@kjil.com
License: Herington, Dickinson County, KS held by Great Plains Christian Radio Inc.
Nat'l Network: Salem Radio Network; Moody *Wire Services:* AP
Population Served: 320,000*Hrs. of News Programming:* news progmg 16 hrs wkly *No. News Employees:* 1 *Target Audience:* 18-54; military & professional including ag, railroad & transportation workers
Frank York, Chairman
Mike Luskey, CEO
Mike Luskey, President
Linda Emig, Operations Dir
Mark Hinca, Station Manager
Deb Hustis, Underwriting Director
Andrea Kunst, IT Director
Jennifer Pooler, Production Director
DelvinKinser, News Director
Steve Larson, Chief Engineer

Hiawatha

KNZA
08-18-1977; 103.9 mhz FM *Hrs Open:* 24; 50 kw; 492 ft.; N39 34 41 W95 33 46
Mailing Address: P.O. Box, Hiawatha, KS 66434 US
Second Address: 1828 Hwy. 73, Hiawatha, KS 66434-0104
(785) 547-3461, *Fax:* (785) 547-9900
knzafm.com
knza@rainbowtel.net
License: Hiawatha, Brown County, KS held by KNZA Inc.
Group Owner: KNZA Inc.; acq 6-83;
Nat'l Network: ABC *Regional Network:* Brownfield *Wire Services:* AP
Format: Country *Special Programming:* Farm 14 hrs wkly *Hrs. of News Programming:* news progmg 10 hrs wkly *No. News Employees:* 1 *Target Audience:* 18-54; general *Adv. Rates:* 19; 15; 15; 13
Robert Hilton, Operations Dir
Greg Buser, General Manager

Hill City

KKQY
08-29-1997; 101.9 mhz FM *Hrs Open:* 24; 97 kw; 994 ft.; N39 1 15 W99 28 12
107 W. 13th Street, P.O. Box 597, Hays, KS 67601 US
(785) 625-2578, *Fax:* (785) 625-3632
www.kkgy.com

License: Hill City, Graham County, KS held by Eagle Communications Inc.
Group Owner: Eagle Communications Group; (acq 9-12-00; with KJLS(FM) Hays).
Arbitron Metro Market: Wichita, KS *Format:* Country *Hrs. of News Programming:* News progmg 5 hrs wkly *Target Audience:* 25-54.
Todd Nelson, General Manager
Todd Lynn, General Sales Mgr
Craig Taylor, Programming Director

***KZNA**
01-01-1986; 90.5 mhz FM *Hrs Open:* 24; 100 kw; 659 ft.; N39 15 57 W99 50 0 *Rebroadcasts:* Rebroadcasts KANZ(FM) Garden City 100%
201 N. 7th Street, Garden City, KS 67846 US
(620) 275-7444, *Fax:* (620) 275-7496
www.hppr.org
hppr@hppr.org
License: Hill City, Graham County, KS held by Kanza Society Inc.
Nat'l Network: PRI; NPR; AP Radio
Arbitron Metro Market: Hill City, KS *Format:* News, News/Talk, 86 *Special Programming:* Jazz 15 hrs, folk 6 hrs, Sp 6 hrs wkly *Hrs. of News Programming:* News progmg 39 hrs wkly *Target Audience:* 25-80; educated
Richard Hicks, General Manager
Bob Kirby, Programming Director
Chuck Springer, Chief Engineer

Hoisington

KHOK
01-01-1978; 100.7 mhz FM *Hrs Open:* 24; 100 kw; 430 ft.; N38 32 49 W98 45 59
P. O. Box 817, Hays, KS 67601 US
(620) 792-3647, *Fax:* (620) 792-3649
www.eagleradio.net
rick.nulton@eagleradio.net
License: Hoisington, Barton County, KS held by Eagle Communications Inc.
Group Owner: Eagle Communications Group; (acq 9-1-86; grpsl; *Format:* Country *Special Programming:* Relg 2 hrs wkly *No. News Employees:* 1 *Target Audience:* 18-44.
Gary Shorman, President
Rick Nulton, General Manager

Holcomb

KBUF
01-01-1948; 1030 khz AM *Hrs Open:* 24
P.O. Box 907, Valley City, ND 58072 US
(620) 276-2366, *Fax:* (620) 276-3568
www.westernkansasnews.com
christaroy@wksradio.com
License: Holcomb, KS held by KBUF Partnership.
Group Owner: Robert Ingstad Broadcast Properties; (acq 11-1-79)
Regional Network: Mid-America Ag *Wire Services:* NWS (National Weather Service); UPI
Arbitron Metro Market: Garden City, KS *Format:* Talk, Country *Special Programming:* Farm 15 hrs wkly *No. News Employees:* 1 *Target Audience:* 25-54; people interested in class country & info progmg *Adv. Rates:* 21.60; 21.60; 21.60; 14.40
Christa Roy, General Manager
James Janda, Programming Director

Horton

KAIR-FM
01-25-1995; 93.7 mhz FM *Hrs Open:* 24; 25 kw; 328 ft.; N39 37 43 W95 18 53
Mailing Address: P.O. Box 104, Hiawatha, KS 66434 US
Second Address: 200 N. 5th St., Atchinson, KS 66002
(913) 367-1470, *Fax:* (913) 367-7021
www.kairfm.com
kairradio@gmail.com
License: Horton, Brown County, KS held by KNZA Inc.
Group Owner: KNZA Inc.; (acq 8-13-2007; with KAIR(AM) Atchison)
Nat'l Network: AP Radio *Wire Services:* AP
Arbitron Metro Market: Atchison, KS *Format:* Country *Hrs. of News Programming:* news progmg 133 hrs wkly *No. News Employees:* 4 *Target Audience:* 25-54. *Adv. Rates:* 16; 14; 16; 8
Greg Buser, President
Mark Oppold, General Manager

Hugoton

KFXX-FM
09-16-1983; 106.7 mhz FM *Hrs Open:* 24; 55 kw; 256 ft.; N37 18 57 W101 20 16
P.O. Box 907, Valley City, ND 58072 US
(503) 223-1441, *Fax:* (503) 223-6909
www.1080thefan.com
jaustin@entercom.com
License: Hugoton, Stevens County, KS held by KBUF Partnership.
Group Owner: Robert Ingstad Broadcast Properties
Arbitron Metro Market: Portland, OR *TV Affiliate:* ESPN *Format:* Sports, Talk *Target Audience:* 18-54, Men
Tim McNamara, General Manager
Jeff Austin, General Sales Mgr

Humboldt

KINZ
09-01-1998; 95.3 mhz FM *Hrs Open:* 24; 24 kw; 335 ft.; N37 44 52 W95 33 39
117 South Grant St., Chanute, KS 66720 US
(620) 431-1333, *Fax:* (620) 431-1943
www.kinz.biz
mike@kinz.biz
License: Humboldt, Allen County, KS held by Sutcliffe Communications LLC.
Nat'l Network: CNN Radio
Format: Classic Rock *Special Programming:* Gospel 3 hrs wkly *Target Audience:* 25-55. *Adv. Rates:* 10; 10; 10; 7
Mike Sutcliffe, CEO
Sheri Sutcliffe, Operations Dir

Hutchinson

***KHCC-FM**
09-11-1972; 90.1 mhz FM *Hrs Open:* 24; 100 kw; 1296 ft.; N38 3 22 W97 44 43
815 N. Walnut, Suite 300, Hutchinson, KS 67501 US
(620) 662-6646
www.radiokansas.org
rfragoza@radiokansas.org
License: Hutchinson, Reno County, KS held by Hutchinson Community College.
Nat'l Network: NPR
Format: News *Special Programming:* Car talk 2 hrs wkly *Hrs. of News Programming:* News progmg 27 hrs wkly
Geralyn Smith, Operations Dir
Ken Baker, General Manager
Sharon Webb, General Sales Mgr
Melody Fisher, Promotions Manager
Ric Jung, Chief Engineer

KHUT
03-15-1972; 102.9 mhz FM; 98 kw; 430 ft.; N38 2 39 W98 0 56
PO Box 817, Hays, KS 67601 US
(620) 662-4486, *Fax:* (620) 662-5357
www.hutchinsonscountrystation.com
randy.mckay@eagleradio.net
License: Hutchinson, Reno County, KS
Group Owner: Eagle Communications Group
Format: Country *Target Audience:* 25-54
Mark Trotman, Operations Dir
Terry Drowhard, General Sales Mgr
Jason Younger, Programming Director
Fred Gough, News Director

KWBW
05-28-1935; 1450 khz AM; 1 kw-U, ND1; N38 4 22 W97 57 53
PO Box 817, Hays, KS 67601 US
(620) 662-4486, *Fax:* (620) 662-5357
www.bwradio.biz/
License: Hutchinson, KS held by Eagle Communications Inc.
Group Owner: Eagle Communications Group; (acq 11-4-91; with co-located FM).
Arbitron Metro Market: Hutchinson, KS *Format:* Sports, Talk *Special Programming:* Black 2 hrs, gospel 11 hrs wkly
Dan Deming, General Manager
John Brennan, General Sales Mgr
Rod Zook, News Director

KZSN
10-07-1968; 102.1 mhz FM *Hrs Open:* 24; 100 kw; 1027 ft.; N37 46 40 W97 30 37
600 Congress Avenue, Suite 1400, Austin, TX 78701 US
(316) 494-6600, *Fax:* (316) 494-6730
www.kzsn.com
info@kzsn.com
License: Hutchinson, Reno County, KS held by Clear Channel Broadcasting Licenses, Inc.
Group Owner: Clear Channel Communications Inc.; (acq 8-30-00; grpsl).
Nat'l Reps: Clear Channel
Arbitron Metro Market: Wichita, KS *Format:* Country *No. News Employees:* 1 *Target Audience:* 25-54; Adults
Lyman James, Operations Dir
Rob Burton, General Manager

KWHK
01-01-2007; 95.9 mhz FM *Hrs Open:* 24; 2.85 kw; 489 ft.; N38 2 57 W98 0 44
US
(620) 665-5758, *Fax:* (620) 665-6655
production@adastra.kscoxmail.com
License: Hutchinson, Reno County, KS held by Ad Astra Per Aspera Broadcasting Inc.
Group Owner: Ad Astra Per Aspera Broadcasting Inc.
Nat'l Network: ABC *Regional Network:* Kan. Info.
Arbitron Metro Market: Dallas-Fort Worth *Format:* Oldies *Hrs. of News Programming:* news progmg 2 hrs wkly *No. News Employees:* 1
Aaron West, Operations Dir
Cliff C Shank, General Manager
Michael Hill, General Sales Mgr
Lucky Kidd, News Director
Susie Deines, Office Manager

Independence

***KARF**
01-01-1997; 91.5 mhz FM; 100 kw vert; 328 ft.; N37 3 55 W95 45 1
P.O. Drawer 2440, Tupelo, MS 38803 US
(913) 642-7770, *Fax:* (913) 642-1319
www.bottradionetwork.com
comments@bottradionetwork.com
License: Independence, Montgomery County, KS held by Community Broadcasting Inc.
Group Owner: Bott Radio Network; (acq 1-26-2006; $30,000 with KBMP(FM) Enterprise)
Nat'l Network: USA
Arbitron Metro Market: Overland Park, KS *Format:* Christian, Talk
Richard Bott II, Operations Dir
Pat Rulon, General Sales Mgr
Candy Green, Programming Director
Rachel Moser, Promotions Manager
Jason Potocnik, News Director

KIND
12-08-1947; 1010 khz AM *Hrs Open:* 24; 0.25 kw-D, ND1; 0.032 kw-N, ND1; N37 13 7 W95 43 30
Po Drawer A, Independence, KS 67301 US
(620) 331-3000, *Fax:* (620) 331-8008
a.bradshaw@tallgrassnation.com
License: Independence, KS held by Tallgrass Broadcasting Inc.
Group Owner: Tallgrass Broadcasting LLC; (acq 10-25-2006; $306,000 with co-located FM)
Nat'l Network: Westwood One *Wire Services:* AP
Format: Adult Contemp *Special Programming:* Big band 2 hrs, class 3 hrs wkly *Target Audience:* 35-65; baby boomers *Adv. Rates:* 18; 18; 18; 18
Joseph Walker, President
Mark Wilson, General Manager

KBIK
05-10-1969; 102.9 mhz FM *Hrs Open:* 24; 25 kw; Ant 272 ft; N37 15 42 W95 45 59
122 W. Myrtle, Independence, KS 67301
(620) 331-3000, *Fax:* (620) 331-8008
a.bradshaw@tallgrassnation.com
License: Independence, Montgomery County, KS held by Tallgrass Broadcasting Inc.
Group Owner: Tallgrass Broadcasting LLC
Nat'l Network: CNN Radio *Wire Services:* AP
Population Served: 65,000*Special Programming:* Alternative 4 hrs, Christian hot adult contemp 2 hrs wkly *Target Audience:* 22-44. *Adv. Rates:* 21; 21; 21; 21
Luis Medina, Operations Dir
Joe Jeldy, Station Manager

***KBQC**
01-01-2002; 88.5 mhz FM; 20 kw vert; 476 ft.; N37 3 11 W96 6 7
P. O. Box 1452, Washington, DC 20013 US
(662) 844-8888, *Fax:* (662) 842-6791
www.afa.net
randall@afa.net
License: Independence, Montgomery County, KS held by American Family Association.
Group Owner: American Family Radio; (acq 12-18-00; buyer paid construction & bcst costs of CP).
Arbitron Metro Market: Tupelo, MS *Format:* Christian
Marvin Sanders, General Manager

Ingalls

KERP

01-01-2001; 96.3 mhz FM *Hrs Open:* 24; 100 kw; 699 ft.; N37 56 30 W100 18 44
Mailing Address: 1776 K Street NW, Washington, DC 20006 US
Second Address: 106 W Frontwiew, Dodge City, KS 67801
(620) 225-8080, *Fax:* (620) 225-6655
www.rockingmradio.com/kerp
rockswks@sbcglobal.net
License: Ingalls, Gray County, KS held by Rocking M Radio Inc.
Group Owner: Rocking M Radio Inc.; (acq 8-31-2007; grpsl)
Nat'l Network: Fox News Radio
Arbitron Metro Market: Dodge City, KS *Format:* Country
Brian Nugen, Operations Dir
Mark Hinca, General Manager
Peggy Burdick, General Sales Mgr
Candace Thomas, News Director

KSSA

07-01-1999; 105.9 mhz FM *Hrs Open:* 24; 100 kw; 666 ft.; N37 46 48 W100 27 36
Box 907, Valley City, ND 58072 US
(620) 276-3251, *Fax:* (620) 276-3568
kssa@wksradio.com
License: Ingalls, Gray County, KS held by KBUF Partnership.
Group Owner: Robert Ingstad Broadcast Properties; (acq 1999; $250,000)
Arbitron Metro Market: Ingalls, KS
G.L. Wohler, General Manager
Rachel Wheet, News Director

Iola

KIOL

07-25-1961; 1370 khz AM *Hrs Open:* 24; 0.5 kw-D, DA2; 0.058 kw-N, DA2; N37 54 7 W95 24 26
P. O. Box 710, Iola, KS 66749 US
(620) 365-3151, *Fax:* (620) 365-5431
www.iolaradio.com
radistation@iolaradio.com
License: Iola, KS held by Iola Broadcasting Inc.
Arbitron Metro Market: Iola, KS *Format:* Oldies
Tom Norris, Station Manager

KIKS-FM

06-09-1977; 101.5 mhz FM *Hrs Open:* 24; 11.5 kw; 289 ft.; N37 54 4 W95 24 4
P. O. Box 710, Iola, KS 66749 US
(620) 365-3151, *Fax:* (620) 365-5431
www.iolaradio.com
radiostation@iolaradio.com
License: Iola, Allen County, KS held by Iola Broadcasting Inc.
Format: Country *Special Programming:* Trading Post 20 hrs wkly
Chelle Hodson, Office Manager

Junction City

KJCK

05-15-1949; 1420 khz AM *Hrs Open:* 24; 1 kw-D, DAN; 0.5 kw-N, DAN; N39 1 33 W96 48 36
PO Box 789, W. Ash & Hwy 77, Junction City, KS 66441 US
(785) 762-5525, *Fax:* (785) 762-5387
www.kjck.com
platinum@kjck.com
License: Junction City, KS held by Platinum Broadcasting Inc.
Group Owner: Platinum Broadcasting Co.; (acq 9-4-86)
Nat'l Network: ABC; Fox News Radio; Sporting News Radio Network *Wire Services:* AP
Format: News, News/Talk, 86 *Hrs. of News Programming:* news progmg 75 hrs wkly *No. News Employees:* 2 *Target Audience:* 35-54. *Adv. Rates:* 14.25; 10.75; 14.25; 10.75
Mark Ediger, General Manager
Ed Klimek, General Sales Mgr
Jerry Brecheisen, Programming Director
Dewey Terrill, News Director
Randy Stewart, Chief Engineer
Jacqueline Petty, News Reporter

KJCK-FM

07-22-1965; 97.5 mhz FM *Hrs Open:* 24; 100 kw; 630 ft.; N39 0 53 W96 52 12
Mailing Address: Post Office Box 789, Junction City, KS 66441 US
Second Address: 1030 Southwind Dr., Junction City, KS 66441
(785) 762-5525, *Fax:* (785) 762-5387
www.kjck.com
platinum@kjck.com
License: Junction City, Geary County, KS held by Platinum Broadcasting Inc.
Group Owner: Platinum Broadcasting Co.
Wire Services: AP
Format: Contemporary Hits/Top 40 *Hrs. of News Programming:* news progmg one hr wkly *No. News Employees:* 2 *Target Audience:* 18-34; young adults
Ed Klimek, Operations Dir
Robert Elfman, Programming Director
Dewey Terrill, News Director
Rodney Baker, Disc Jockey
Matt McBain, Disc Jockey
Erin Voirol, Traffic Manager

Kansas City

KUDL

01-01-2001; 1660 khz AM *Hrs Open:* 24; 10 kw-D, 1 kw-N; N39 06 50 W94 40 45
7000 Squibb Rd, Mission, KS 40509
(913) 677-8998, *Fax:* (913) 677-8061
www.kxtr.com
info@1065thewolf.com
License: Kansas City, Wyandotte County, KS held by Entercom Kansas City License LLC.
Group Owner: Entercom Communications Corp.
Arbitron Metro Market: Kansas City, MO-KS
Herndon Hasty, General Manager
John Verlin, General Sales Mgr
Patrick Nease, Programming Director
Dave Alpert, General Manager

KDTD

01-01-1925; 1340 khz AM *Hrs Open:* 24; 0.2 kw-U, ND1; N38 16 1 W94 30 59
4121 Minnesota Ave., Kansas City, KS 66102 US
(913) 287-1480, *Fax:* (913) 287-5881
www.lagrand1340.com
License: Kansas City, KS held by Davidson Media Station KCKN Licensee LLC.
Group Owner: Davidson Media Group LLC; (acq 10-11-2005; $1.9 million).
Arbitron Metro Market: Kansas City, MO-KS *No. News Employees:* 2
Carlos Mercado, Operations Dir
Dan Perez, General Manager

KFKF-FM

05-28-1963; 94.1 mhz FM; 100 kw; 994 ft.; N39 0 57 W94 30 24
600 New Hampshire Avenue, N.W., Suite 1200, Washington, DC 20037 US
(816) 753-4000, *Fax:* (816) 753-4045
www.kfkf.com
info@kfkf.com
License: Kansas City, Wyandotte County, KS held by Wilks License Co.-Kansas City LLC.
Group Owner: Wilks Broadcast Group LLC; (acq 1-10-2007; grpsl)
Arbitron Metro Market: KS City, MO *Format:* Country *Special Programming:* Country Classics 20 hrs wkly *Target Audience:* 25-54
Mike Rowen, General Manager
Dale Carter, Programming Director
Jillian Gregg, News Director
Ben Weiss, Chief Engineer

KMBZ-FM

10-09-1959; 98.1 mhz FM *Hrs Open:* 24; 100 kw; 994 ft; N39 04 23 W94 29 06
7000 Squibb Rd, Mission, KS 19004
(913) 744-3600, *Fax:* (913) 677-8061
www.kudl.com
info@kudl.com
License: Kansas City, Wyandotte County, KS held by Entercom Kansas City License L.L.C.
Group Owner: Entercom Communications Corp.; (acq 10-17-97; grpsl)
Population Served: 1,500,000 *Arbitron Metro Market:* Kansas City, MO-KS *No. News Employees:* 1 *Target Audience:* 25-44; women
Tom McGinty, Operations Dir
Herndon Hasty, General Manager
Dan Prendiville, General Sales Mgr
Marcy Caldwell, Promotions Manager
Darcie Blake, News Director
Dave Alpert, General Manager

KYYS

01-01-1926; 1250 khz AM; 25 kw-D, DA2; 3.7 kw-N, DA2; N39 11 6 W94 27 28
3270 Blazer Pkwy, Ste 101, Lexington, KY 40509 US
(913) 788-1255, *Fax:* (913) 788-1254
www.lasuperx1250.com
lasuperx1250@lasuperx1250.com
License: Kansas City, KS held by Entercom Kansas City License LLC.
Group Owner: Entercom Communications Corp.; (acq 3-3-99; $2.75 million)
Arbitron Metro Market: Kansas City, MO-KS *Format:* Tejano
Juan C. Ramirez, General Manager

Kingman

*KCVW

12-01-1997; 94.3 mhz FM *Hrs Open:* 24; 50 kw; 492 ft.; N37 48 3 W97 56 49
3405 Shady Bend Drive, Independence, MO 64052 US
(913) 642-7770, *Fax:* (913) 642 1319
www.bottradionetwork.com
comments@bottradionetwork.com
License: Kingman, Kingman County, KS held by Bott Communications Inc.
Group Owner: Bott Radio Network
Nat'l Network: USA
Arbitron Metro Market: Kingman, KS *Format:* Christian, Talk
Target Audience: 25-55.
Richard Bott, Chairman
Richard Bott, CEO/COO
Richard Bott, President
Eben Fowler, Operations Dir
Dan Snell, General Sales Mgr
Jason Potoenik, News Director
Tim Lumpkin, Corporate Controller

Kiowa

KQZQ

01-01-2008; 98.3 mhz FM; 97 kw; 685 ft.; N37 24 9 W98 34 51 US
(620) 231-5620
www.coyotecountry983.com
License: Kiowa, Barber County, KS held by Troy Unruh.
Arbitron Metro Market: Kiowa, KS *Format:* Country
Troy Unruh, General Manager

Larned

KBGL

01-01-2001; 106.9 mhz FM; 100 kw; 486 ft.; N38 27 6 W99 10 3
P.O. Box 597, Hays, KS 67601 US
(620) 792-3647, *Fax:* (620) 792-3649
www.kbglfm.com
info@eagleradio.net
License: Larned, Pawnee County, KS held by Hull Broadcasting Inc.
Arbitron Metro Market: Larned, KS *Format:* Oldies
Phil Grossardt, Operations Dir
Rick Nulton, General Manager
Mike Durler, General Sales Mgr

KSOB

11-01-1965; 96.7 mhz FM; 3 kw; 266 ft.; N38 9 54 W99 6 5
1660 N. Tyler Road, Wichita, KS 67212 US
(620) 792-7108, *Fax:* (620) 792-7051
www.rockingmradio.com
cmiller@rockingmradio.com
License: Larned, Pawnee County, KS
Group Owner: Rocking M Radio Inc.
Format: Oldies *Target Audience:* 30-60; baby boomers with disposable income
Dan Cormack, News Director
Chris Miller, Vice President

KNNS

11-04-1963; 1510 khz AM; 0.5 kw-C, NDD; 1 kw-D, NDD; N38 9 54 W99 6 5
US
(620) 792-7108, *Fax:* (620) 792-7051
kzls@nrgmedia.com
License: Larned, KS held by Rocking M Radio Inc.
Group Owner: Rocking M Radio Inc.; (acq 8-31-2007; grpsl)
Regional Network: Kan. Info.; Kan. Agriculture
Format: Sports *Special Programming:* Farm 10 hrs, gospel 6 hrs, relg 5 hrs wkly *Target Audience:* General; people looking for loc info *Adv. Rates:* 12; 10; 8; 5
Jen Schwamborn, General Manager
Chris Elsen, Programming Director

Lawrence

*KANU

09-15-1952; 91.5 mhz FM *Hrs Open:* 24; 100 kw; 699 ft.; N38 57 14 W95 16 11
226 Strong Hall, Lawrence, KS 66045 US
(785) 864-4530, *Fax:* (785) 864-5278
www.kansaspublicradio.org
kpr@ku.edu

License: Lawrence, Douglas County, KS held by University of Kansas.
Nat'l Network: PRI; NPR
Arbitron Metro Market: Lawrence, KS *Format:* Jazz *Special Programming:* Bluegrass 4 hrs, Celtic 2 hrs, blues 4 hrs wkly *Hrs. of News Programming:* news progmg 35 hrs wkly *No. News Employees:* 3 *TargetAudience:* 25-49; upscale
Janet Campbell, General Manager
Darrell Brogdon, Programming Director
J. Schafer, News Director
Steve Kincaid, Engineering Dir

***KJHK**
01-01-1975; 90.7 mhz FM *Hrs Open:* 24; 2.3 kw; 279 ft.; N38 57 14 W95 16 11
2051 Dole Center, Lawrence, KS 66045 US
(785) 864-4745, *Fax:* (785) 864-5173
www.kjhk.org
kjhk@mail.ku.edu
License: Lawrence, Douglas County, KS held by University of Kansas.
Format: Jazz *Special Programming:* Reggae 3 hrs, blues 2 hrs wkly *Hrs. of News Programming:* News progmg 15 hrs wkly *Target Audience:* 18-34; Univ & community population
Tom Johnson, General Manager
Danielle Basci, Station Manager
Tom Kimmel, Programming Director
Joe Noh, Promotions Manager

KLWN
02-22-1951; 1320 khz AM *Hrs Open:* 24; 0.5 kw-D, ND1; 0.25 kw-N, ND1; N38 56 5 W95 17 12
P.O. Box 1749, Cape Girardeau, MO 63702 US
(785) 843-1320, *Fax:* (785) 841-5941
www.klwn.com
mail@lazer.com
License: Lawrence, KS held by Great Plains Media Inc.
Group Owner: Great Plains Media Inc.; (acq 6-30-2006; with co-located FM)
Format: News, News/Talk, 84, Talk *Special Programming:* Relg 4 hrs wkly *Hrs. of News Programming:* news progmg 10 hrs wkly *No. News Employees:* 2 *Target Audience:* 25-59; adults
John Flood, Programming Director

KKSW
08-20-1963; 105.9 mhz FM *Hrs Open:* 24; 100 kw; 771 ft; N39 02 21 W95 26 59
3125 W. 6th St., Lawrence, KS 63702
(785) 843-1320, *Fax:* (785) 841-5924,(785) 843-4585
www.lazer.com
info@lazer.com
License: Lawrence, Douglas County, KS
Group Owner: Great Plains Media Inc.
Population Served: 100,000 *Arbitron Metro Market:* Topeka, KS *Hrs. of News Programming:* news progmg one hr wkly *No. News Employees:* 2 *Target Audience:* 18-34; young adults
Gary Katz, President
Dennis Carlson, General Manager

Leavenworth

KKLO
01-01-1946; 1410 khz AM
481 Muncie Road, Leavenworth, KS 66048 US
(913) 351-1410, *Fax:* (913) 351-1410
www.hereshelpnet.org
info@kkloam.com
License: Leavenworth, KS held by New Life Evangelistic Center Inc.
Arbitron Metro Market: Kansas City, MO *Format:* Christian *Target Audience:* 25-49; upscale, educated, loyal Christian listeners
Larry Rice, CEO
Saint Johns, General Manager

KQRC-FM
01-01-1962; 98.9 mhz FM; 98.5 kw; 1099 ft.; N39 1 20 W94 30 49
10706 Beaver Dam Road, Cockeysville, MD 21030 US
(913) 744-3600, *Fax:* (913) 677-8061
www.989therock.com
info@989therock.com
License: Leavenworth, Leavenworth County, KS held by Entercom Kansas City License LLC.
Group Owner: Entercom Communications Corp.; (acq 7-14-00; grpsl)
Arbitron Metro Market: Kansas City metro area *Format:* Rock/AOR *Target Audience:* 18-34; above average education & income; upscale professionals
Herndon Hasty, General Manager
John Karpinski, General Sales Mgr
Bob Edwards, Programming Director
Jennifer Morton, Promotions Manager

Dave Alpert, General Manager
Sammy Jo Behrens, Promotions

Leoti

KWKR
11-01-1983; 99.9 mhz FM; 97 kw; 397 ft.; N38 16 39 W101 17 50
Mailing Address: 1309 E. Fulton St., Garden City, KS 67846 US
Second Address: 1402 E. Kansas, Garden City, KS 67846
(620) 276-3251, *Fax:* (620) 276-3568
www.wksradio.com
info@wksradio.com
License: Leoti, Wichita County, KS held by KBUF Partnership.
Group Owner: Robert Ingstad Broadcast Properties; (acq 12-1-97; $841,170).
Nat'l Network: Westwood One
Arbitron Metro Market: Garden City, KS *Format:* Classic Rock *Special Programming:* Sp 3 hrs wkly *Target Audience:* 25-44.
Christa Roy, General Manager
James Janda, Programming Director
Jim Wagoner, News Director

Liberal

KLDG
10-01-1994; 102.7 mhz FM *Hrs Open:* 24; 100 kw; 466 ft.; N37 2 45 W101 6 11
1410 North Western, Liberal, KS 67901 US
(620) 624-3891, *Fax:* (620) 624-7885
www.kscb.net
info@kldgfm.com
License: Liberal, Seward County, KS held by Seward County Broadcasting Co. Inc.
Group Owner: Seward County Broadcasting Co.
Nat'l Network: Jones Radio Networks *Nat'l Reps:* Roslin
Arbitron Metro Market: Wichita, KS *Format:* Country *Hrs. of News Programming:* news progmg 2 hrs wkly *No. News Employees:* 2 *Target Audience:* 18-49; young, mobile & impulsive consumers
John Landon, Chairman
Don Ford, President
Bob Larrabee, Operations Dir
Stuart Melchert, General Manager
Cheryl Collins, General Sales Mgr
Mikki Hofferber, News Director
John Mulhern, Chief Engineer
Mikki Hofferber, TrafficManager

KSCB
07-25-1948; 1270 khz AM *Hrs Open:* 24
1410 North Western, Liberal, KS 67901 US
(620) 624-3891, *Fax:* (620) 624-9472
www.kscb.net
kscb@kscb.net
License: Liberal, KS held by Seward County Broadcasting Co.
Group Owner: Seward County Broadcasting Co.
Nat'l Network: ABC; Westwood One *Regional Network:* Kan. Info. *Nat'l Reps:* Roslin
Arbitron Metro Market: Liberal, KS *Format:* News, News/Talk, 86 *Special Programming:* Farm 6 hrs wkly *No. News Employees:* 3 *Target Audience:* 35 plus.
Terry Miller, Operations Dir
Stuart Melchert, General Manager
Cheryl Collins, General Sales Mgr
Joe Denoyer, News Director
John Mulhurn, Chief Engineer
Brock Kappelmann, News Director
Mikki Hofferber, Traffic Manager

KSCB-FM
07-10-1978; 107.5 mhz FM *Hrs Open:* 24; 100 kw; 466 ft.; N37 2 45 W101 6 11
1410 North Western, Liberal, KS 67901 US
(620) 624-3891, *Fax:* (620) 624-9472
www.kscb.net
kscb@kscb.net
License: Liberal, Seward County, KS held by Seward County Broadcasting Co.
Group Owner: Seward County Broadcasting Co.
Nat'l Network: Jones Radio Networks *Regional Network:* Kan. Info. *Nat'l Reps:* Roslin
Arbitron Metro Market: Liberal, KS *Format:* Adult Contemp *Hrs. of News Programming:* news progmg 7 hrs wkly *No. News Employees:* 2 *Target Audience:* 25-49; young adults
Mikki Hofferber, News Director

KSMM-FM
07-01-1978; 101.5 mhz FM; 100 kw; 541 ft.; N37 3 20 W100 48 40
1660 N. Tyler, Wichita, KS 67212 US
(620) 624-8156, *Fax:* (620) 624-4606
www.rockingmradio.com

License: Liberal, Seward County, KS held by Rocking M Radio Inc.
Group Owner: Rocking M Radio Inc.; (acq 8-31-2007; grpsl)
Arbitron Metro Market: Liberal, KS
Enrique Franz, General Manager
Christopher D. Miller-Vice President

KSMM
09-15-1960; 1470 khz AM
1660 N. Tyler, Wichita, KS 67212 US
(620) 624-8156, *Fax:* (620) 624-4606
www.rockingmradio.com
License: Liberal, KS held by Rocking M Radio Inc.
Group Owner: Rocking M Radio Inc.; (acq 8-31-2007; grpsl)
Regional Network: Mid-America Ag *Nat'l Reps:* McGavren Guild
Arbitron Metro Market: Liberal, KS *Hrs. of News Programming:* News progmg one hr wkly *Target Audience:* 25-54; Spanish speaking
Steve Schiffner, General Manager
Matt Younkin, Programming Director

KZQD
10-01-1997; 105.1 mhz FM; 50 kw; 387 ft.; N37 2 53 W100 54 34
P.O. Box 2636, Liberal, KS 67905 US
(620) 626-8282, *Fax:* (620) 626-8080
www.kzqdradiolibertad.com
radiolibertad@sbglobal.net
License: Liberal, Seward County, KS held by Mario Loredo.
Arbitron Metro Market: Liberal, KS. *Format:* Christian
Mario Loredo, General Manager

Lindsborg

KVOB
10-08-1985; 95.5 mhz FM *Hrs Open:* 24; 15.5 kw; Ant 417 ft; N38 40 00 W97 41 30
641 W. Cloud, Salina, KS 67401
(785) 827-2100, *Fax:* (785) 827-3503
License: Lindsborg, Saline County, KS held by Rocking M Radio Inc.
Group Owner: Rocking M Radio Inc.; (acq 8-31-2007; grpsl)
Population Served: 325,000*Hrs. of News Programming:* News progmg 2 hrs wkly *Target Audience:* 25-49. *Adv. Rates:* 21; 17; 14; 9
James Westling, Operations Dir
Christopher Miller, General Manager
Morgan Lillich, General Sales Mgr
James Westling, Programming Director
Rod Rogers, Chief Engineer

KDJM
01-01-2008; 101.7 mhz FM; 15.5 kw; 410 ft.; N38 40 0 W97 41 30
US
(785) 827-2100, *Fax:* (785) 827-3503
www.salina-radio.com
Mlillich@rockingmradio.com
License: Lindsborg, Saline County, KS held by Radioactive LLC.
Group Owner: Radioactive LLC
Arbitron Metro Market: Lindsborg, KS *Format:* Country
Benjamin Homel, President
James Westling, Operations Dir
Pat Foster, General Manager
Morgan Lillich, Business Manager
Holliegh Henry, Business Development Executives
Russ Litteral, Business Development Executives

Lyons

KXKU
04-10-1970; 106.1 mhz FM *Hrs Open:* 24; 100 kw; 656 ft.; N38 15 47 W97 54 8
106 North Main Street, Hutchinson, KS 67501 US
(620) 665-5758, *Fax:* (620) 665-6655
production@adastra.kscoxmail.com
License: Lyons, Rice County, KS held by Ad Astra Per Aspera Broadcasting Inc.
Group Owner: Ad Astra Per Aspera Broadcasting Inc.; (acq 9-17-86; $366,816;
Nat'l Network: Jones Radio Networks *Regional Network:* Kan. Info.
Arbitron Metro Market: Lyons, KS *Format:* Country *Hrs. of News Programming:* news progmg 2 hrs wkly *No. News Employees:* 1 *Target Audience:* 25-64; listeners throughout central KS
Aaron West, Operations Dir
Cliff C Shank, General Manager
Mike Hill, General Sales Mgr
Lucky Kidd, News Director
Susie Deines, Office Manager

Manhattan

KMAN
06-01-1950; 1350 khz AM *Hrs Open:* 24; 0.5 kw-D, ND1; 0.04 kw-N, ND1; N39 13 0 W96 33 30
Mailing Address: P. O. Box 1350, Manhattan, KS 66502 US
Second Address: 2414 Casement Rd., Manhattan, KS 66502
(785) 776-1350, *Fax:* (785) 539-1000
www.1350kman.com
License: Manhattan, KS held by Manhattan Broadcasting Co.
Group Owner: Seaton Stations
Nat'l Network: CBS; ESPN Radio; Westwood One *Regional Network:* Kan. Info.
Format: News, News/Talk, 84, Talk *Hrs. of News Programming:* news progmg 60 hrs wkly *No. News Employees:* 1 *Target Audience:* 30 plus. *Adv. Rates:* 18; 16; 18; 14
Richard Seaton, Chairman
Richard Wartell, President
Kevin Block, Chief Engineer

KMKF
09-01-1972; 101.5 mhz FM *Hrs Open:* 24; 37 kw; 577 ft.; N39 15 55 W96 27 57
Mailing Address: P. O. Box 1350, Manhattan, KS 66502 US
Second Address: 2414 Casement Rd., Manhattan, KS 66502
(785) 776-1350, *Fax:* (785) 539-1000
www.purerock.com
License: Manhattan, Riley County, KS
Arbitron Metro Market: Topeka, KS *Format:* Rock/AOR *Hrs. of News Programming:* news progmg 2 hrs wkly *No. News Employees:* 1 *Target Audience:* 18-35.
Richard Wartell, General Manager
Corey Dean, Programming Director
Kevin Block, Engineering Dir

*KSDB-FM
01-01-1949; 91.9 mhz FM *Hrs Open:* 24; 1.4 kw; 289 ft.; N39 9 49 W96 31 54
104 Kedzie Hall, Manhattan, KS 66502 US
(785) 532-2971, *Fax:* (785) 532-5484
www.wildcat919.com
radio@ksu.edu
License: Manhattan, Riley County, KS held by Kansas State University.
Arbitron Metro Market: Manhattan, KS *Format:* Alternative, Urban Contemporary *Special Programming:* Black 4 hrs, gospel 3 hrs, jazz 3 hrs wkly *Hrs. of News Programming:* news progmg 12 hrs wkly *No. News Employees:* 1 *Target Audience:* 18-34; young adults *Adv. Rates:* 10; 10; 10; 10
Steve Smethers, COO
Mary Shirk, Operations Dir
Kristin Russell, Station Manager
Jared Clark, Programming Director
Caitlin Whetstone, Promotions Manager
Dan Page, News Director

KXBZ
09-01-1994; 104.7 mhz FM; 50 kw; 488 ft.; N39 15 55 W96 27 59
2414 Casement Rd., Manhattan, KS 66502 US
(785) 776-1350, *Fax:* (785) 539-1000
www.b1047.com
dubs@purerock.com
License: Manhattan, Riley County, KS held by Manhattan Broadcasting Co. Inc.
Group Owner: Seaton Stations; (acq 3-2-99).
Nat'l Network: Westwood One
Arbitron Metro Market: Manhattan, KS *Format:* Country *Target Audience:* 18-35; men & women
Richard Wartell, President

*KGLV
01-01-2008; 88.9 mhz FM; 11 kw; 1047 ft.; N39 0 22 W96 2 57
Rebroadcasts: Rebroadcasts KLVR(FM) Middletown, CA 100%
8030 Arrowridge Blvd, Charlotte, NC 28273 US
(916) 251-1600, *Fax:* (916) 251-1650
www.klove.com
klove@klove.com
License: Manhattan, Riley County, KS held by Educational Media Foundation.
Group Owner: EMF Broadcasting; (acq 10-27-2006; $325,000 for CP)
Nat'l Network: K-Love
Arbitron Metro Market: Manhattan, KS *Format:* Christian
Darrell Chambliss, Chairman
Alan Mason, CEO/COO
Mike Novak, CEO
Crystal Wojteczko, Operations Dir
David Pierce, Chief Creative Officer
Dan Antonelli, Chief Business Development Officer
Eric Moser, Chief Financial Officer
BrianBurger, Vice President of Human Resources
D. Kevin Blair, Secretary and General Counsel

*KJIH
89.9 mhz FM; 11 kw; Ant 230 ft; N39 24 04 W96 25 29
102 Red Branch Ln., Simpsonville, SC
(864) 297-0216, *Fax:* (864) 297-0344
networkofglory.com
info@networkofglory.org
License: Manhattan, Riley County, KS held by Network of Glory Inc.
Lola Richey, President

Marysville

KNDY
07-10-1956; 1570 khz AM *Hrs Open:* 24; 0.25 kw-D, ND2; 0.033 kw-N, ND2; N39 51 2 W96 38 52
1212 11th Road, Marysville, KS 66508 US
(785) 562-2361, *Fax:* (785) 562-2188
License: Marysville, KS held by Dierking Communications Inc.
Group Owner: Dierking Communications Inc.; (acq 9-6-88).
Nat'l Network: ABC *Regional Network:* Mid-America Ag
Format: Country, Agriculture *Hrs. of News Programming:* News progmg 24 hrs wkly *Target Audience:* General.
Bruce Dierking, President

KNDY-FM
07-23-1974; 95.5 mhz FM *Hrs Open:* 24; 25 kw; 328 ft.; N39 57 36 W96 44 5
1212 11th Road, Marysville, KS 66508 US
(785) 562-2361, *Fax:* (785) 562-2188
License: Marysville, Marshall County, KS
Group Owner: Dierking Communications Inc.
Nat'l Network: ABC *Regional Network:* Mid-America Ag
Format: Country
Larry Steckline, General Sales Mgr
Myron Nolind, Chief Engineer

*KMLL
91.7 mhz FM; 0.6 kw; 285 ft.; N39 52 12 W96 44 45 US
(662) 844-8888, *Fax:* (662) 842-6791
www.afr.net
License: Marysville, Marshall County, KS held by American Family Association.
Group Owner: American Family Radio
Arbitron Metro Market: Marysville, KS *Format:* Christian
Donald Wildmon, Chairman

McPherson

KBBE
01-12-1974; 96.7 mhz FM *Hrs Open:* 24; 6 kw; 246 ft.; N38 20 30 W97 40 12
P.O. Box 1069, McPherson, KS 67460 US
(620) 241-1504, *Fax:* (620) 241-3196
midkansasradio.com
oldies96.7@midkansasradio.com
License: McPherson, McPherson County, KS
Nat'l Network: ABC
Arbitron Metro Market: McPherson, KS *Format:* Oldies *No. News Employees:* 1
Joe Johnston, General Manager

KNGL
01-04-1949; 1540 khz AM; 0.25 kw-D, ND2; 0.002 kw-N, ND2; N38 20 30 W97 40 12
P.O. Box 1069, McPherson, KS 67460 US
(620) 241-1504, *Fax:* (620) 241-3196
midkansasradio.com
talkradio1540@midkansasradio.com
License: McPherson, KS held by Davies Communications Inc.
Nat'l Network: ABC *Regional Network:* Kan. Info.; Kan. Agriculture
Format: Talk *Special Programming:* Relg 5 hrs wkly *No. News Employees:* 1 *Target Audience:* 25-54. *Adv. Rates:* 14; 11; 11; 8
Jerry Davies, President
Mark Ekeland, Operations Dir
Joe Johnston, General Manager
Scott Seirer, General Sales Mgr
Shawn White, Chief Engineer
Diane Davies, Executive Vice President
Nick Gosnell, Diane Davies

Medicine Lodge

*KREJ
01-01-1990; 101.7 mhz FM *Hrs Open:* 24; 50 kw; 476 ft.; N37 14 0 W98 39 44
505 Josephine Street, Titusville, FL 32796 US
(620) 886-3537, *Fax:* (321) 264-9370
www.krejksns.org
License: Medicine Lodge, Barber County, KS held by Florida Public Radio Inc.
Nat'l Network: Moody
Format: Religious *Target Audience:* General.
Mike Henry, Operations Dir
Mike Henry, General Manager
Randy Henry, Chief Engineer

*KSNS
04-01-1999; 91.5 mhz FM; 96 kw vert; 463 ft.; N37 14 2 W98 39 55
Mailing Address: 505 Josephine St, Titusville, FL 32796 US
Second Address: 505 Josephine St., Titusville, FL 32796
(620) 886-3537
License: Medicine Lodge, Barber County, KS held by Florida Public Radio Inc.
Format: Christian
Mike Henry, General Manager

Minneapolis

KZUH
02-24-1993; 92.7 mhz FM *Hrs Open:* 24; 50 kw; 492 ft; N39 00 52 W97 37 42
641 W. Cloud, Salina, KS 67212
(785) 827-2100, *Fax:* (785) 827-3503
License: Minneapolis, Ottawa County, KS held by Rocking M Radio Inc.
Group Owner: Rocking M Radio Inc.; (acq 8-31-2007; grpsl)
Population Served: 150,000*Target Audience:* 18-54.
Darren Irwin, General Manager
James Wiley, Operations Manager

Mission

KCZZ
10-01-1957; 1480 khz AM *Hrs Open:* 24; 1 kw-D, DA2; 0.5 kw-N, DA2; N39 4 5 W94 42 9
10706 Beaver Dam Road, Cockeysville, MD 21030 US
(913) 287-1480, *Fax:* (913) 287-5881
License: Mission, KS held by Davidson Media Station KCZZ Licensee LLC.
Group Owner: Davidson Media Group LLC; (acq 1-28-2005; $3.9 million with KAKS(FM) Huntsville, AR).
Nat'l Reps: Lotus Entravision Reps LLC
Arbitron Metro Market: Mission, KS *Target Audience:* 18-49; adults *Adv. Rates:* 40; 40; 40; 15
Carlos Mercado, Operations Dir
Dan Perez, General Manager

Ness City

KXNC
104.7 mhz FM; 16.5 kw; 896 ft.; N38 36 32 W99 42 11 US
(785) 222-3400, *Fax:* (785) 222-3405
kiss1047.net
glen.hoyt@postrockradio.com
License: Ness City, Ness County, KS held by College Creek Media LLC.
Group Owner: College Creek Media LLC
Arbitron Metro Market: Ness City, KS *Format:* Contemporary Hits/Top 40
Christopher Devine, General Manager
Glen Hoyt, General Sales Mgr
Chris Elsen, Programming Director

Newton

KJRG
05-24-1953; 950 khz AM
P. O. Box 567, Newton, KS 67114 US
(316) 283-4592, *Fax:* (316) 283-3177
www.bottradionetwork.com
comments@bottradionetwork.com
License: Newton, KS held by Community Broadcasting Inc.
Group Owner: Bott Radio Network; (acq 6-20-2006; $650,000)
Nat'l Network: USA
Arbitron Metro Market: Wichita, KS *Format:* Christian, Talk *Target Audience:* 25-54.
Richard Bott, Sr., Chairman
Richard Bott, II, CEO
Richard Bott, II, President
Eben Fowler, Operations Dir
Richard Bott, General Manager
Pat Rulon, General Sales Mgr
Candy Green, Programming Director
Jason Potocnik, NewsDirector
Ken Monroe, Corporate Production Director
John Dale, Director of Marketing

Jason Potocnik, Director of Traffic
Rachel Launius, Marketing Manager

KFTI-FM
01-01-1959; 92.3 mhz FM *Hrs Open:* 24; 100 kw; 640 ft.; N38 1 12 W97 23 4
Mailing Address: P. O. Box 567, Newton, KS 67114 US
Second Address: 4200 N. Old Lawrence Rd., Wichita, KS 67219
(316) 838-9141, *Fax:* (316) 838-3607
www.classiccountry923.com
info@classiccountry923.com
License: Newton, Harvey County, KS held by Journal Broadcast Corp.
Group Owner: Journal Communications Inc.; (acq 3-20-2000; $4.25 million)
Arbitron Metro Market: Wichita, KS *Format:* Country
Rob Burton, Operations Dir
Eric McCart, General Sales Mgr
Ray Micheals, Programming Director
Manny Cowzinski, Promotions Manager

North Fort Riley

KBLS
01-01-1993; 102.5 mhz FM; 100 kw; 492 ft.; N38 57 5 W96 47 45
PO Box 1393, McCook, KS 67402 US
(785) 823-1111, *Fax:* (785) 823-2034
www.sunny1025.com
angie.reed@sunny1025.com
License: North Fort Riley, Geary County, KS held by MCC Radio LLC.
Group Owner: Morris Radio LLC; (acq 1-14-2004; grpsl).
Arbitron Metro Market: Salina, KS *Format:* Adult Contemp *Hrs. of News Programming:* news progmg 2 hrs wkly *No. News Employees:* 3 *Target Audience:* 25-54; women *Adv. Rates:* 18.84; 14.13; 16.96; 5.65
William Morris IV, President
Robert Protzman, General Manager
Bob Protzman, Station Manager
Mitch Drees, General Sales Mgr
John Anderson, Programming Director
Clarke Sanders, Promotions Manager
Mark Beaver, News Director

North Newton

***KBCU**
04-06-1989; 88.1 mhz FM *Hrs Open:* 24 (T-Su); 8 AM-midnight (M); 0.15 kw; 56 ft.; N38 4 26 W97 20 35
300 East 27th, North Newton, KS 67117 US
(316) 284-5228, *Fax:* (316) 284-5286
www.bethelks.edu/kbu
kbcu@bethelks.edu
License: North Newton, Harvey County, KS held by Bethel College.
Regional Network: Kan. Info.
Arbitron Metro Market: North Newton, KS *Format:* Variety/Diverse *Special Programming:* Sp 2 hrs wkly *Hrs. of News Programming:* News progmg 5 hrs wkly *Target Audience:* General; college students & Harvey County
Christine Crouse-Dick, General Manager

Norton

KQNK
10-30-1963; 1530 khz AM; 1 kw-D, NDD; N39 49 37 W99 52 8
P.O. Box 220, Norton, KS 67654 US
(785) 877-3378, *Fax:* (785) 877-3379
www.kqnk.com
kqnk@ruraltel.net
License: Norton, KS held by Dierking Communications Inc.
Group Owner: Dierking Communications Inc.; (acq 7-13-99; $165,000 with co-located FM).
Nat'l Reps: Keystone (unwired net)
Format: Contemporary Hits/Top 40
Bruce Dierking, President
Marvin Matchett, General Manager
Mandi Fick, General Sales Mgr
Deena Wente, Programming Director

KQNK-FM
03-01-1993; 106.7 mhz FM; 21 kw; 358 ft.; N39 47 51 W99 53 29
P.O. Box 220, Norton, KS 67654 US
(785) 877-3378, *Fax:* (785) 877-3379
www.kqnk.com
License: Norton, Norton County, KS
Group Owner: Dierking Communications Inc.
Format: Contemporary Hits/Top 40
John Detz, President
Ron Wiley, Operations Dir

***KSNB**
91.5 mhz FM; 0.25 kw; 171 ft.; N39 47 51 W99 53 29
US
(662) 844-8888, *Fax:* (662) 842-6791
www.afr.net
License: Norton, Norton County, KS held by American Family Association.
Group Owner: American Family Radio
Arbitron Metro Market: Norton, KS *Format:* Christian
Donald Wildmon, Chairman

Oberlin

KFNF
07-01-1977; 101.1 mhz FM *Hrs Open:* 24; 100 kw; 443 ft.; N39 49 38 W100 38 48
1660 N. Tyler, Wichita, KS 67212 US
(785) 475-2225, *Fax:* (785) 475-2510
kfnf@highplainsradio.net
License: Oberlin, Decatur County, KS held by Armada Media - McCook Inc.
Group Owner: Armada Media Corp.; (acq 3-31-2007; grpsl)
Nat'l Network: ABC *Regional Network:* Mid-America Ag
Arbitron Metro Market: Oberlin, KS *Format:* Country *Special Programming:* Gospel 3 hrs wkly *Target Audience:* 25-65; farmers *Adv. Rates:* 13; 13; 13; na
Adam Kadavy, Operations Dir
Bryan Loker, General Manager

***KRLE**
01-01-2009; 89.7 mhz FM; 0.27 kw; 115 ft.; N39 48 11 W100 31 43 *Rebroadcasts:* Rebroadcasts KLVR(FM) Middletown, CA 100%
P O Box 1458, Washington, DC 20013 US
(916) 251-1600, *Fax:* (916) 251-1650
www.klove.com
klove@klove.com
License: Oberlin, Decatur County, KS held by Educational Media Foundation.
Group Owner: EMF Broadcasting; (acq 3-23-2007; grpsl)
Nat'l Network: K-Love
Arbitron Metro Market: Oberlin, KS *Format:* Christian
Darrell Chambliss, Chairman
Alan Mason, CEO/COO
Mike Novak, CEO
David Pierce, Chief Creative Officer
Dan Antonelli, Chief Business Development Officer
Eric Moser, Chief Financial Officer
Brian Burger, Vice President of HumanResources
D. Kevin Blair, Secretary and General Counsel

Ogden

KQLA
02-14-1986; 103.5 mhz FM *Hrs Open:* 24; 41 kw; 312 ft.; N39 9 21 W96 36 44
Mailing Address: P.O. Box 789 West Ash, Highway 77, Junction City, KS 66441 US
Second Address: 122 S. 4th, Suite A, Manhattan, KS 66502
(785) 587-0103, *Fax:* (785) 776-0110
www.kqla.com
robert.elfman@eagleradio.net
License: Ogden, Riley County, KS held by Platinum Broadcasting Co.
Group Owner: Platinum Broadcasting Co.; (acq 9-24-97; $650,000)
Nat'l Network: ABC *Regional Reps:* Regional Rep Corp
Format: Adult Contemp *Hrs. of News Programming:* news progmg 10 hrs wkly *No. News Employees:* 1 *Target Audience:* 18-44; mobile, educated persons with quality income *Adv. Rates:* 15; 12; 15; 12
Ed Klimek, President
Mark Ediger, General Manager
Robert Elfman, Programming Director

Oketo

***KOKN**
88.7 mhz FM; kw
US
License: Oketo, Marshall County, KS held by Ron Elmore Ministries Inc.
Arbitron Metro Market: Hobs, MN
Ron Elmore, President

Olathe

KCCV-FM
12-01-1993; 92.3 mhz FM *Hrs Open:* 24; 8.3 kw; 564 ft.; N38 56 10 W94 50 41
10550 Barkley, Ste 108, Overland Park, KS 66212 US
(913) 642-7600, *Fax:* (913) 642-1319
www.bottradionetwork.com
kccv@bottradionetwork.com
License: Olathe, Johnson County, KS held by Bott Broadcasting Co.
Group Owner: Bott Radio Network; acq 7-1-92; $537,500;
Nat'l Network: USA
Arbitron Metro Market: Overland Park, KS *Format:* Christian, Talk
Target Audience: 25-54; family oriented
Trace Thurlby, COO
Richard Bott, President
Eben Fowler, Operations Dir
Pat Rulon, General Sales Mgr
Rachel Moser, Promotions Manager
Jason Potocnik, News Director
Tom Holdeman, CFO
Richard Bott II, Executive Vice President
Dan Shell, Regional Manager

Olpe

KEKS
103.1 mhz FM; 2.45 kw; 315 ft.; N38 17 37 W96 13 3
US
(620) 343-6144, *Fax:* (620) 343-6844
kiss1031.net
info@keksfm.com
License: Olpe, Lyon County, KS held by Andrew A. Wachter.
Arbitron Metro Market: Emporia, KS
Andrew Wachter, General Manager

Olsburg

***KANV**
01-01-2003; 91.3 mhz FM; 6 kw; 328 ft.; N39 0 55 W96 53 55
Broadcasting Hall, Lawrence, KS 66045 US
(785) 864-4530, *Fax:* (785) 864-5278
www.kpr.ku.edu
kpr@ku.edu
License: Olsburg, Pottawatomie County, KS held by The University of Kansas.
Nat'l Network: NPR
Arbitron Metro Market: Topeka, KS *Format:* Jazz *No. News Employees:* 5
Cordelia Brown, Operations Dir
Janet Campbell, General Manager
Darrell Brogdon, Programming Director
J. Schafer, News Director
Steve Kincaid, Engineering Dir
Bruce Mensie, Chief Engineer
Nicci Banman, Business Manager
WendyHuggins, Administrative Associate
Mark Edwards, Music Director/Classical Announcer
Laura Lorson, All Things Considered Host/Producer
Bryan Thompson, Health Reporter
Stephen Koranda, Statehouse Reporter

Osage City

KMXN
07-26-1982; 92.9 mhz FM *Hrs Open:* 24; 7.9 kw; Ant 538 ft; N38 48 21 W95 42 58
3125 W. 6th St., Lawrence, KS 66801
(785) 843-1320, *Fax:* (785) 841-5924
License: Osage City, Osage County, KS held by Great Plains Media Inc.
Group Owner: Great Plains Media Inc.; (acq 6-30-2006)
Arbitron Metro Market: Topeka, KS
Jay Wachs, General Manager
Amber Lee, Programming Director
Morgan Grammer, Chief Engineer

Ottawa

KCHZ
03-01-1962; 95.7 mhz FM; 96 kw; Ant 981 ft; N39 00 45 W95 01 46
5800 Foxridge Dr., Suite 600, Mission, KS 20910
(913) 514-3000, *Fax:* (913) 262-3946
www.957thevibe.com
License: Ottawa, Franklin County, KS held by A R Licensing LLC
Group Owner: Cumulus Media Partners LLC; (acq 5-3-2006; grpsl)
Population Served: 11,036 *Arbitron Metro Market:* Kansas City, MO-KS
Maurice DeVoe, Operations Dir
Tim Robisch, General Manager
Pat Gibbs, General Sales Mgr
Jamie Cox, Promotions Manager

KOFO
09-24-1949; 1220 khz AM *Hrs Open:* 24; 250 w-D, 40 w-N; N38 35 04 W95 15 57
320 E. Radio Rd., Box 16, Ottawa, KS 66067
(785) 242-1220, *Fax:* (785) 242-1442
www.kofo.com
kofo@kofo.com
License: Ottawa, Franklin County, KS held by Brandy Communications Inc.
Nat'l Network: ABC *Regional Network:* Kan. Agriculture
Population Served: 55,000 *Arbitron Metro Market:* Kansas City, MO *Special Programming:* Farm 2 hrs wkly *Hrs. of News Programming:* news progmg 7 hrs wkly *No. News Employees:* 1 *Target Audience:* 25-54; Male& Female
Brad Howard, President

***KRBW**
01-01-1997; 90.5 mhz FM; 0.43 kw; 187 ft.; N38 35 4 W95 15 56
P.O Box 2440, Tupelo, MS 38803 US
(785) 242-9050, *Fax:* (662) 842-6791
www.internet4christ.com/krbw/
krbw9050@hometc.com
License: Ottawa, Franklin County, KS held by American Family Association
Group Owner: American Family Radio; (acq 1-24-97)
Format: Christian
Marvin Sanders, General Manager

***KTJO-FM**
05-01-1951; 88.9 mhz FM *Hrs Open:* 7 AM-midnight; 0.145 kw; 66 ft.; N38 36 16 W95 15 49
1001 South Cedar Street, Ottawa, KS 66067 US
(785) 242-5200, *Fax:* (785) 242-7429
info@ktjo.com
License: Ottawa, Franklin County, KS held by Ottawa University.
Arbitron Metro Market: Ottawa, KS *Format:* Christian, Variety/Diverse *Hrs. of News Programming:* News progmg 5 hrs wkly *Target Audience:* General; Ottawa Univ community & City of Ottawa, KS
Bradley Howard, CEO
Ben Weiss, Engineering Dir

Overland Park

KCCV
01-01-1962; 760 khz AM *Hrs Open:* Sunrise-sunset
10550 Barkley, Ste 108, Overland Park, KS 66212 US
(913) 642-7600, *Fax:* (913) 642-1319
www.bottradionetwork.com
kccv@bottradionetwork.com
License: Overland Park, KS held by Bott Broadcasting Co.
Group Owner: Bott Radio Network; (acq 1962)
Nat'l Network: USA
Arbitron Metro Market: Overland Park, KS *Format:* Christian, Talk, 74 *Target Audience:* 25-54; family-oriented
Trace Thurlby, COO
Richard Bolt, President
Eben Fowler, Operations Dir
Pat Rulon, General Sales Mgr
Rachel Moser, Promotions Manager
Jason Potocnik, News Director
Tom Holdeman, CFO
Richard Bott II, Executive Vice President
Dan Shell, Regional Manager

Parsons

KLKC
01-01-1948; 1540 khz AM; 0.25 kw-D, ND2; 0.001 kw-N, ND2; N37 20 35 W95 13 55
PO Box 853, Parsons, KS 67357 US
(620) 421-6400, *Fax:* (620) 421-5570
klkc.com
lynnm@skilonline.com
License: Parsons, KS held by Southeast Kansas Independent Living Resource Center Inc.
Group Owner: Southeast Kansas Independent Living Resource Center Inc.; (acq 12-6-2005; $334,932 with co-located FM)
Arbitron Metro Market: Joplin, MO *Format:* Sports, Talk *Special Programming:* Farm 2 hrs, relg 2 hrs, big band 3 hrs wkly *Hrs. of News Programming:* News progmg 28 hrs wkly *Target Audience:* 12-60; general*Adv. Rates:* 12.65; 9.90; 9.90; 9.90
Lynn Meredith, General Manager
Colt Smith, General Sales Mgr
Steve Lardy, Programming Director
Annette Tucker, News Director
Terry Blackburn, Music Director
Ed Hernandez

KLKC-FM
10-01-1978; 93.5 mhz FM *Hrs Open:* 6 AM-11 PM; 3 kw; 266 ft.; N37 20 35 W95 13 55
PO Box 853, Parsons, KS 67357 US
(620) 421-6400, *Fax:* (620) 421-5570
lynnm@skilonline.com
License: Parsons, Labette County, KS
Arbitron Metro Market: Joplin, MO *Format:* Oldies *Adv. Rates:* Same as AM
James Auel, General Manager

Phillipsburg

KKAN
12-31-1959; 1490 khz AM *Hrs Open:* 24; 1 kw-U, ND1; N39 47 32 W99 19 55
205 F Street, P.O. Box 548, Phillipsburg, KS 67661 US
(785) 543-2151, *Fax:* (785) 543-2152
www.kkankqma.com
radio@kkankqma.com
License: Phillipsburg, KS held by Walter C. Seidel.
Regional Network: Kan. Info.
Format: News, Variety/Diverse *Special Programming:* Farm 10 hrs, gospel 12 hrs wkly *Target Audience:* General; rural population & small towns
Bob Yates, General Manager
Tad Felts, News Director
Robert Yates III, Systems Administrator

KQMA
07-14-1984; 92.5 mhz FM; 100 kw; 512 ft.; N39 37 2 W99 17 55
205 F Street, P.O. Box 548, Phillipsburg, KS 67661 US
(785) 543-2151, *Fax:* (785) 543-2152
www.kkankqma.com
License: Phillipsburg, Phillips County, KS held by Walter C. Seidel
Format: Variety/Diverse
Bob Yates, General Manager
Tad Felts, News Director
Tad Felts, Sports Director

Pittsburg

KKOW
10-11-1937; 860 khz AM *Hrs Open:* 24; 10 kw-D, DAN; 5 kw-N, DAN; N37 24 46 W94 38 16
1162 E Hwy 126, Pittsburg, KS 66762 US
(620) 231-7200, *Fax:* (620) 231-3321
www.kkowam.com
kkow@kkowradio.com
License: Pittsburg, KS held by American Media Investment Inc.
Nat'l Network: CBS *Nat'l Reps:* McGavren Guild
Arbitron Metro Market: Joplin, MO *Format:* Country *Hrs. of News Programming:* news progmg 5 hrs wkly *No. News Employees:* 2 *Target Audience:* General.
Chris Kelly, General Manager

KKOW-FM
04-20-1975; 96.9 mhz FM; 100 kw; 912 ft.; N37 18 44 W94 48 58
1162 E. Hwy 126, Pittsburg, KS 66762 US
(620) 231-7200, *Fax:* (620) 231-3321
www.kkowfm.com
kkow@kkowradio.com
License: Pittsburg, Crawford County, KS held by American Media Investments Inc.
Arbitron Metro Market: Joplin, MO *Format:* Country
Chris Kelly, General Manager
Dave Fink, General Sales Mgr

***KRPS**
04-29-1988; 89.9 mhz FM *Hrs Open:* 24; 100 kw; 1001 ft.; N37 18 44 W94 48 58
1701 South Broadway, Pittsburg, KS 66762 US
(620) 235-4288, *Fax:* 620(235-4290)
www.krps.org
krps@pittstate.edu
License: Pittsburg, Crawford County, KS held by Pittsburg State University.
Nat'l Network: NPR; PRI
Arbitron Metro Market: Four State area *Special Programming:* Folk 3 hrs *Hrs. of News Programming:* News progmg 39 hrs wkly
Matt Larson, Operations Dir
Missi Kelly, General Manager
Vicki Pritchett, General Sales Mgr
Tim Metcalf, Programming Director

KSEK
01-01-1948; 1340 khz AM; 1 kw-U, ND1; N37 23 44 W94 40 42
1604 E. Quincy, P.O. Box 383, Pittsburg, KS 66762 US
(620) 232-9912, *Fax:* (620) 232-9915
lynnm@skilonline.com
License: Pittsburg, KS held by Southeast Kansas Independent Living Resource Center Inc.
Group Owner: Southeast Kansas Independent Living Resource Center Inc.; (acq 11-30-2004; $700,000 with KSEK-FM Girard).
Nat'l Network: ESPN Radio; AP Network News
Arbitron Metro Market: Pittsburg, KS *Format:* Sports *Special Programming:* High school basketball & football *Hrs. of News Programming:* News progmg 10 hrs wkly *Target Audience:* 25 plus. *Adv. Rates:* 120;120; 120; 120
Lynn Meredith, General Manager

Plainville

KFIX
05-11-1998; 96.9 mhz FM *Hrs Open:* 24; 10.5 kw; 876 ft.; N39 1 15 W99 28 12
Mailing Address: P.O. Box 597, Hays, KS 67601 US
Second Address: 2300 Hall, Hays, KS 67601
(785) 628-1064, *Fax:* (785) 628-1822
studio@kfix.com
License: Plainville, Rooks County, KS held by Hull Broadcasting Inc.
Arbitron Metro Market: Hays, KS *Format:* Rock/AOR *Target Audience:* 25-64.
Richard Hull, President
Nancy Baumrucker, General Manager
Cameron Perry, Programming Director
Callie Kolacny, News Director
Kristy Pfeifer, Traffic Manager

Pleasanton

***KPIO-FM**
93.7 mhz FM; 25 kw; 328 ft.; N38 14 23 W94 56 36 US
(816) 630-1090
www.thecatholicradionetwork.com
info@thecatholicradionetwork.com
License: Pleasanton, Linn County, KS held by Kansas City Catholic Network Inc.
Arbitron Metro Market: Pleasanton, KS *Format:* Christian
James O'Laughlin, President

Pratt

KHMY
07-01-1965; 93.1 mhz FM *Hrs Open:* 24; 100 kw; 991 ft.; N37 55 43 W98 18 36
1660 North Tyler Road, Wichita, KS 67212 US
(620) 662-5900, *Fax:* (620) 662-5797
www.khmyfm.com/?nc=1347475603258.43
info@khmtfm.com
License: Pratt, Pratt County, KS held by Eagle Communications Inc.
Group Owner: Eagle Communications Group; (acq 3-17-03; swap for KSSH(FM) Ingalls).
Nat'l Reps: McGavren Guild
Arbitron Metro Market: Pratt, KS *Format:* Adult Contemp
Casey Osburn, Operations Dir
Mark Trotman, General Manager
Terry Drouhard, General Sales Mgr
Casey Osburn, Programming Director
Fred Gough, News Director

KMMM
09-19-1963; 1290 khz AM *Hrs Open:* 24; 5 kw-D, DA2; 0.5 kw-N, DA2; N37 38 34 W98 40 39
1660 N. Tyler, Wichita, KS 67212 US
(620) 672-5581, *Fax:* (620) 672-5583
www.superhits129.com
kwls@rocking.com
License: Pratt, KS held by Rocking M Radio Inc.
Group Owner: Rocking M Radio Inc.; (acq 8-31-2007; grpsl)
Regional Network: Mid-America Ag *Nat'l Reps:* McGavren Guild
Arbitron Metro Market: Pratt, KS *Format:* Oldies *Hrs. of News Programming:* news progmg 3 hrs wkly *No. News Employees:* 1 *Target Audience:* 25 plus; rural
Eric Strobel, General Manager
Lisa Coss, Station Manager
Carl Raida, Programming Director

Riley

KACZ
09-16-2003; 96.3 mhz FM; 12.5 kw; 476 ft.; N39 13 34 W96 37 0
12249 S. Mullen, Olathe, KS 66062 US
(785) 776-1350, *Fax:* (785) 539-1000
www.z963.com
Danielle@1350kman.com
License: Riley, Riley County, KS held by Manhattan Broadcasting Co. Inc.
Group Owner: Seaton Stations

Wire Services: AP
Arbitron Metro Market: Topeka, KS *Format:* Contemporary Hits/Top 40 *Hrs. of News Programming:* news progmg 4 hrs wkly *No. News Employees:* 3 *Target Audience:* 18-59; woman *Adv. Rates:* 18; 16; 18; 14
Richard Wartell, President

Rozel

KKCV
01-01-2007; 102.5 mhz FM *Hrs Open:* 24; 100 kw; Ant 488 ft; N37 57 28 W99 25 45.2
10550 Barkley, Suite 100, Overland Park, KS
(913) 642-7770, *Fax:* (913) 642-1319
www.bottradionetwork.com
License: Rozel, Pawnee County, KS held by Bott Communications Inc.
Group Owner: Bott Radio Network
Nat'l Network: USA
Target Audience: 25-55.
Richard Bott II, President
Pat Rulon, General Sales Mgr
Candy Green, Programming Director
John Dale, Director of Marketing
Jason Potocnik, News Director
Tom Holdeman, CFO
Eben Fowler, Operations Director

Russell

KRSL-FM
07-01-1965; 95.9 mhz FM; 1.35 kw; 486 ft.; N38 54 22 W98 51 39
P. O. Box 666, Russell, KS 67665 US
(785) 483-3121, *Fax:* (785) 483-6511
www.krsl.com
comments@krsl.com
License: Russell, Russell County, KS held by White Communications L.L.C.
Arbitron Metro Market: Russell, KS *Format:* Contemporary Hits/Top 40, Adult Contemp *Adv. Rates:* $13; 11; 11
Larry Calvery, General Manager
Mike McKenna, Station Manager
David Elliott, News Director

KRSL
01-11-1956; 990 khz AM; 0.25 kw-D, ND1; 0.03 kw-N, ND1; N38 54 22 W98 51 39
P. O. Box 666, Russell, KS 67665 US
(785) 483-3121, *Fax:* (785) 483-6511
www.krsl.com
Comments@krsl.com
License: Russell, KS held by White Communications L.L.C.
Arbitron Metro Market: Russell ,KS *Format:* Contemporary Hits/Top 40, Adult Contemp *Special Programming:* Polka 4 hrs, farm 2 hrs wkly *Target Audience:* 24 plus; general *Adv. Rates:* 13; 11; 11
Larry Calvery, General Manager
Mike McKenna, Station Manager
Brenda Calvery, General Sales Mgr
David Elliott, News Director

Saint Marys

KTOP-FM
12-04-1994; 102.9 mhz FM; 50 kw; 320 ft; N39 05 34 W95 47 05
825 S. Kansas Ave., Topeka, KS 12550
(785) 272-2122, *Fax:* (785) 272-6219
www.cumulus.com
oldieskqtp@aol.com
License: Saint Marys, Pottawatomie County, KS held by Cumulus Licensing Corp.
Group Owner: Cumulus Media Inc.; (acq 4-13-01; with KWIC(FM) Topeka).
Target Audience: 35-54.
John Walker, General Manager
Keith Liefmann, General Sales Mgr
Rich Bowers, Programming Director
Carla Newman, Promotions Manager
Mike Manns, News Director

Salina

*KAKA
01-01-2002; 88.5 mhz FM; 46 kw; 394 ft.; N39 4 12 W97 51 14
P O Drawer 2440, Tupelo, MS 38803 US
(662) 844-8888, *Fax:* (662) 842-6791
www.afr.net
License: Salina, Saline County, KS held by American Family Association.
Group Owner: American Family Radio
Arbitron Metro Market: Tupelo, MS *Format:* Religious
Marvin Sanders, Station Manager

*KCVS
01-01-1994; 91.7 mhz FM *Hrs Open:* 24; 11.5 kw; 748 ft.; N38 39 58 W97 41 30
3434 West Kilbourn Avenue, Milwaukee, WI 53208 US
(414) 935-3000, *Fax:* (414) 935-3015
www.vcyamerica.org
vcy@vcyamerica.org
License: Salina, Saline County, KS held by VCY/America Inc.
Group Owner: VCY America Inc.; (acq 7-2-97).
Nat'l Network: Moody; USA
Arbitron Metro Market: Milwaukee, WI *Format:* Christian
Vic Eliason, Operations Dir
Jim Schneider, Programming Director

KFRM
01-01-1947; 550 khz AM *Hrs Open:* sun up to sun down
P. O. Box 16, Clay Center, KS 67432 US
(785) 632-5661, *Fax:* (785) 632-5662
www.kfrm.com
webmaster@kfrm.com
License: Salina, KS held by Taylor Communications Inc.
Nat'l Network: AP Network News *Wire Services:* AP
Arbitron Metro Market: Clay Center, KA *Format:* Talk *Special Programming:* Gospel 5 hrs wkly *Hrs. of News Programming:* news progmg 6 hrs wkly *No. News Employees:* 2 *Target Audience:* 25-55; agricultural*Adv. Rates:* 120; 120;100; 25
Rod Keen, Operations Dir
Kyle Bauer, General Manager
Michelle Tessaro, News Director
Duane Toews, Farm Director
Rocky Downing, Sports Commentator
Joe Woodward, Traffic Manager
Phil Kasper, Weekend/Evening Manager

*KHCD
01-28-1988; 89.5 mhz FM *Hrs Open:* 24; 100 kw; 902 ft.; N39 6 16 W97 23 15 *Rebroadcasts:* Rebroadcasts KHCC-FM Hutchinson 100%
815 N. Walnut, Suite 300, Hutchinson, KS 67501 US
(620) 662-6646
www.radiokansas.org
rfragoza@radiokansas.org
License: Salina, Saline County, KS held by Hutchinson Community College.
Nat'l Network: NPR
Format: News *Special Programming:* Car talk 2 hrs wkly *Hrs. of News Programming:* News progmg 27 hrs wkly
Geralyn Smith, Operations Dir
Ken Baker, General Manager
Sharon Webb, General Sales Mgr
Ric Jung, Chief Engineer

KINA
04-20-1964; 910 khz AM *Hrs Open:* 24 hrs; 0.5 kw-D, DA2; 0.029 kw-N, DA2; N38 45 52 W97 32 30
PO Box 817, Hays, KS 67601 US
(785) 825-4631, *Fax:* (785) 825-4600
License: Salina, KS held by Eagle Communications Inc.
Group Owner: Eagle Communications Group; (Acq 11-1-95; $235,000)
Nat'l Network: Fox News Radio *Wire Services:* AP
Format: News, News/Talk, 84, Talk *Target Audience:* 45 plus; middle to upper income adults
Scott Woodson, Operations Dir
Jerry Hinrikus, General Manager
Larry Avery, General Sales Mgr

KSAL
05-18-1937; 1150 khz AM *Hrs Open:* 24
Mailing Address: PO Box 1393, Salina, KS 67402 US
Second Address: 131 N. Santa Fe, Salina, KS 67401
(785) 823-1111, *Fax:* (785) 823-2034
www.ksallink.com
License: Salina, KS held by MCC Radio LLC.
Group Owner: Morris Radio LLC; (acq 1-30-2004; grpsl).
Nat'l Network: ABC *Regional Network:* Kan. Agriculture; Kan. Info. *Nat'l Reps:* Katz Radio *Wire Services:* AP
Arbitron Metro Market: Salina, KS *Format:* News, News/Talk, 86 *Special Programming:* Farm 3 hrs wkly *Hrs. of News Programming:* news progmg 20 hrs wkly *No. News Employees:* 3 *Target Audience:* 35-64.*Adv. Rates:* 27.50; 20.63; 24.75; 8..25
Bill Ray, Operations Dir
Robert Protzman, General Manager
Rich Alexander, Programming Director
Clarke Sanders, Promotions Manager
Todd Pittenger, News Director

KSKG
01-01-1961; 99.9 mhz FM *Hrs Open:* 24; 100 kw; 571 ft.; N38 47 36 W97 31 33
PO Box 817, Hays, KS 67601 US
(785) 827-4631, *Fax:* (785) 825-4600
www.999kskg.com
License: Salina, Saline County, KS held by Eagle Communications Inc.
Group Owner: Eagle Communications Group
Arbitron Metro Market: Salina, KS *Format:* Country *Special Programming:* Gospel 3 hrs wkly *Target Audience:* 25-54; 51% female, 49% male (baby boomers)
Gary Shorman, President
Scott Carroll, Operations Dir
Jerry Hinrikus, General Manager
Randy Picking, News Director
Mark Goff, Chief Engineer
Cher Richards, Traffic Manager

KYEZ
05-01-1975; 93.7 mhz FM *Hrs Open:* 24; 100 kw; 509 ft.; N38 57 14 W97 36 29
Mailing Address: PO Box 1393, Salina, KS 67402 US
Second Address: 131 N. Santa Fe, Salina, KS 67401
(785) 823-1111, *Fax:* (785) 823-2034
www.y937.com
License: Salina, Saline County, KS
Group Owner: Morris Radio LLC
Nat'l Reps: Katz Radio
Arbitron Metro Market: Salina, KS *Format:* Country *Hrs. of News Programming:* news progmg 2 hrs wkly *No. News Employees:* 3 *Target Audience:* 25-54. *Adv. Rates:* 25.40; 19.05; 22.86; 7.62
Bill Ray, Operations Dir
Robert Protzman, General Manager
Bob Portzman, Station Manager
Mitch Drees, General Sales Mgr
Chad Allen, Programming Director
Clarke Sanders, Promotions Manager

KSAL-FM
10-01-1988; 104.9 mhz FM; 14 kw; 440 ft.; N38 52 36 W97 43 15
Mailing Address: 1825 South Ohio Street, McCook, KS 67401 US
Second Address: 131 N.Santa Fe, Salina, KS 67401
(785) 823-1111, *Fax:* (785) 823-2034
www.1049classichits.com/
billray@1049classichits.com
License: Salina, Saline County, KS held by MCC Radio LLC.
Group Owner: Morris Radio LLC; (acq 1-14-2004; grpsl).
Nat'l Reps: Katz Radio
Arbitron Metro Market: Salina, KS *Format:* Contemporary Hits/Top 40 *Hrs. of News Programming:* news progmg 5 hrs wky *No. News Employees:* 3 *Target Audience:* 18-44. *Adv. Rates:* 21.20; 15.90; 19.08; 6.36
Bill Ray, Operations Dir
Robert Protzman, General Manager
Bob Protzman, Station Manager
Mitch Drees, General Sales Mgr
Kevin Taylor, Programming Director
Clarke Sanders, Promotions Manager
Mark Beaver, News Director

Scott City

KYUL
10-13-1962; 1310 khz AM; 0.5 kw-D, ND1; 0.147 kw-N, ND1; N38 31 35 W100 54 42
P.O. Box 931, Huron, SD 57350 US
(620) 872-5345, *Fax:* (620) 872-5422
www.kiulradio.com
License: Scott City, KS held by Steckline Communications Inc.
Group Owner: Steckline Communications Inc.; (acq 11-28-2006; $550,000 with KIUL(AM) Garden City)
Regional Network: Kan. Info.; Kan. Agriculture
Arbitron Metro Market: Garden City, KS *Format:* News, News/Talk, 86 *Special Programming:* Farm 5 hrs wkly, health 5 hrs wkly *Hrs. of News Programming:* news prgomg 140 hrs wkly *Target Audience:* 35-64
Rick Everett, General Manager
Alex Mayer, Programming Director

KSKL
11-09-1964; 94.5 mhz FM; 100 kw; 351 ft.; N38 31 35 W100 54 42
P.O. Box 907, Valley City, ND 58072 US
(620) 872-5345, *Fax:* (620) 872-5422
www.wksradio.com
info@wksradio.com
License: Scott City, Scott County, KS held by Western Kansas Wireless Inc.

Group Owner: Robert Ingstad Broadcast Properties; (acq 3-26-93; $175,000 with co-located AM;
Regional Network: Kan. Info.
Arbitron Metro Market: Scott City, KS *Format:* Oldies
Christa Roy, General Manager
Bob Dale, Station Manager
James Janda, Programming Director
Jim Wagoner, News Director

*KJLJ
88.5 mhz FM; 25 kw; 292 ft.; N38 32 55 W100 57 37 US
(620) 873-2991, *Fax:* (620) 873-2755
www.kjil.com
kjil@kjil.com
License: Scott City, Scott County, KS held by Great Plains Christian Radio Inc.
Arbitron Metro Market: Scott City, KS *Format:* Christian
Robert Hughes, CEO

Seneca

KMZA
10-15-1992; 92.1 mhz FM *Hrs Open:* 24; 4 kw; 404 ft.; N39 49 34 W96 1 45 *Rebroadcasts:* Rebroadcasts KNZA(FM) Hiawatha 90%
P.O. Box 104, Hiawatha, KS 66434 US
(785) 336-6166, *Fax:* (785) 336-3600
www.kmzafm.com
kmzafm@bbwi.net
License: Seneca, Nemaha County, KS held by KNZA Inc.
Group Owner: KNZA Inc.
Format: Country *Special Programming:* Farm 7 hrs wkly *Hrs. of News Programming:* news progmg 10 hrs wkly *No. News Employees:* 1 *Target Audience:* General. *Adv. Rates:* 19; 15; 15; 13
Greg Buser, President
Robert Hilton, Operations Dir
L.J. Trant, Programming Director
Heidi Wolfgang, News Director

Shawnee

KCMO-FM
05-04-1948; 94.9 mhz FM *Hrs Open:* 24; 100 kw; 1119 ft.; N39 5 26 W94 28 18
401 City Avenue, Suite 409, Bala Cynwyd, PA 19004 US
(913) 514-3000, *Fax:* (913) 514-3004
www.710kcmo.com
bill.ryan@cumulus.com
License: Shawnee, Jackson County, KS held by Susquehanna Kansas City Partnership.
Group Owner: Cumulus Media Partners LLC
Nat'l Reps: Katz Radio
Arbitron Metro Market: Shawnee, KS *Format:* Oldies *Hrs. of News Programming:* news progmg 2 hrs wkly *No. News Employees:* 1 *Target Audience:* 25-54.
Mark Sullivan, Senior Vice President, General Manager
Bill Ryan, General Sales Mgr
Don Daniels, Programming Director
Tom Bamford, Producer / PSA Director
Brian Goeke, Director of Marketing & Online
John Gallagher, Vice President ofSales

Silver Lake

KCVT
01-01-1996; 92.5 mhz FM *Hrs Open:* 24; 6.7 kw; 387 ft.; N39 8 42 W95 55 37
11974 Connell, Overland Park, KS 66213 US
(913) 642-7770, *Fax:* (913) 642 1319
www.bottradionetwork.com
comments@bottradionetwork.com
License: Silver Lake, Shawnee County, KS held by Richard P. Bott II.
Group Owner: Bott Radio Network
Nat'l Network: USA
Arbitron Metro Market: Silver Lake, KS *Format:* Christian, Talk
Richard Bott, Chairman
Richard Bott, CEO/COO
Richard Bott, President
Eben Fowler, Operations Dir
Candy Green, Programming Director
Tim Lumpkin, Corporate Controller

Sterling

KSKU
06-12-1995; 94.7 mhz FM *Hrs Open:* 24; 50 kw; 486 ft.; N38 13 50 W98 18 53
106 N. Main Street, Hutchinson, KS 67501 US
(620) 665-5758, *Fax:* (620) 665-6655
http://www.adastraradio.net
ksku@adastra.kscoxmail.com
License: Sterling, Rice County, KS held by Ad Astra Per Aspera Broadcasting Inc.
Group Owner: Ad Astra Per Aspera Broadcasting Inc.
Nat'l Network: Jones Radio Networks
Format: Contemporary Hits/Top 40 *Hrs. of News Programming:* news progmg 2 hrs wkly *No. News Employees:* 1 *Target Audience:* 18-54; general
Mike Hill, Operations Dir
Cliff C Shank, General Manager
Lucky Kidd, Programming Director
Susie Deines, Office Manager
Aaron West, Operations Manager

Topeka

*KBUZ
01-01-1994; 90.3 mhz FM; 11 kw; 840 ft.; N39 0 19 W96 2 58
Po Drawer 2440, Tupelo, MS 38803 US
(316) 436-1065, *Fax:* (316) 838-3607
www.radiolobo1065.com
License: Topeka, Shawnee County, KS held by American Family Association.
Group Owner: American Family Radio; (acq 12-30-94;
Arbitron Metro Market: Wichita, KS *Format:* Spanish
Bob Faulkner, Station Manager
Jennie Crable, Promotions Manager
George McGurk, Chief Engineer

KDVV
05-29-1960; 100.3 mhz FM; 100 kw; 984 ft.; N38 57 15 W95 54 43
330 East Kilbourn Ave., Suite 250, Milwaukee, WI 53202 US
(785) 272-2122, *Fax:* (785) 272-6219
www.v100rocks.com
info@v100rocks.com
License: Topeka, Shawnee County, KS held by Cumulus Licensing LLC.
Group Owner: Cumulus Media Inc.
Nat'l Network: Westwood One
Arbitron Metro Market: Topeka, KS *Format:* Rock/AOR *Target Audience:* 18-54.
Benjamin Johnson, General Manager
David Nguyen, General Sales Mgr
Erik Magnuson, Programming Director
Lindsay Schrupp, News Director
Rich Lusch, Chief Engineer
A.J. Ramirez, Music Director
Sean Johannessen, Music Director
BryceFsch, Programming Director

*KJTY
08-31-1985; 88.1 mhz FM *Hrs Open:* 24; 35 kw; 584 ft.; N38 53 23 W95 17 17
341 S. Washington, Lancaster, WI 53813 US
(785) 357-8888, *Fax:* (785) 357-0100
www.myflr.org
info@kjtyfm.com
License: Topeka, Shawnee County, KS held by Family Life Broadcasting Inc.
Group Owner: Family Life Communications Inc.; (acq 5-23-2007; grpsl)
Nat'l Network: USA
Arbitron Metro Market: Topeka, KS *Format:* Religious *Special Programming:* Children 5 hrs wkly *Hrs. of News Programming:* News progmg 15 hrs wkly *Target Audience:* 25-49.
Randy Carlson, President
Adam Nash, Programming Director

KMAJ
07-01-1947; 1440 khz AM
330 East Kilbourn Ave., Suite 250, Milwaukee, WI 53202 US
(785) 272-2122, *Fax:* (785) 272-6219
www.kmaj.com
info@kmaj.com
License: Topeka, KS held by Cumulus Licensing Corp.
Group Owner: Cumulus Media Inc.; (acq 7-31-98; grpsl)
Nat'l Network: ABC; ESPN Radio; Westwood One
Arbitron Metro Market: Topeka, KS *Format:* News, News/Talk, 84, Talk *Target Audience:* General.
John Walker, General Manager
Keith Liefmann, General Sales Mgr
Rose Diehl, Programming Director
Carla Newman, Promotions Manager
Mike Manns, News Director

KTOP
07-01-1947; 1490 khz AM; 1 kw-U, ND1; N39 4 39 W95 40 46
330 East Kilbourn Ave., Suite 250, Milwaukee, WI 53202 US
(785) 272-2122, *Fax:* (785) 272-6219
www.ktop1490.com
License: Topeka, KS held by Cumulus Licensing Corp.
Group Owner: Cumulus Media Inc.; (acq 7-31-98; grpsl)
Nat'l Network: ESPN Radio
Arbitron Metro Market: Topeka, KS *Format:* Sports
Kevin Klein, General Manager
Forrest Smithkors, Programming Director

KTPK
11-25-1974; 106.9 mhz FM *Hrs Open:* 24; 100 kw; 1211 ft.; N39 1 34 W95 55 1
222 Pasadena Place, Orlando, FL 32803 US
(785) 273-1069(785) 297-1069, *Fax:* (785) 273-0123
www.countrylegends1069.com
Jallangm@countrylegends1069.com
License: Topeka, Shawnee County, KS held by JMJ Broadcasting Co. Inc.
Nat'l Reps: Katz Radio
Arbitron Metro Market: Topeka, KS *Format:* Country *Hrs. of News Programming:* news progmg 6 hrs wkly *No. News Employees:* 2 *Target Audience:* 25-64; mobile, family-oriented, high-income professional adults*Adv. Rates:* 29; 26; 26; 8
Herbert McCord, President
Jim Allan, General Manager
Greg Ball, General Sales Mgr
Robb Rose, Programming Director
Megan Kirkwood, Promotions Manager
Megan Kirkwood, News Director
Roy Baum, Engineering Dir
Trevor Kirkwood, MusicDirector

KWIC
10-15-1993; 99.3 mhz FM *Hrs Open:* 24; 6.8 kw; 538 ft.; N39 3 50 W95 45 49
P.O. Box 2307, Newburgh, NY 12550 US
(785) 272-2122, *Fax:* (785) 272-6219
www.eagle993.com
info@eagle993.com
License: Topeka, Shawnee County, KS held by Cumulus Licensing Corp.
Group Owner: Cumulus Media Inc.; (acq 4-13-01; with KQTP(FM) Saint Marys).
Arbitron Metro Market: Topeka, KS *Format:* Contemporary Hits/Top 40, Adult Contemp
John Walker, General Manager
Keith Liefmann, General Sales Mgr
Les Glenn, Programming Director
Carla Newman, Promotions Manager
Mike Manns, News Director

WIBW
05-08-1927; 580 khz AM *Hrs Open:* 24
725 Broad Street, P.O. Box 936, Augusta, GA 30903 US
(785) 272-3456, *Fax:* (785) 228-7282
www.580wibw.com
larry.riggins@morris.com
License: Topeka, KS held by Morris Communications Corp.
Group Owner: Morris Radio LLC; (acq 12-22-97; grpsl)
Nat'l Network: ABC *Regional Network:* Kan. Agriculture; Kan. Info. *Nat'l Reps:* Katz Radio *Wire Services:* AP
Arbitron Metro Market: Topeka, KS *Format:* News, News/Talk, 84, Talk *Hrs. of News Programming:* news progmg 15 hrs wkly *No. News Employees:* 4 *Target Audience:* Adults 25+.
Michael Osterhaut, Operations Dir
Larry Riggins, General Manager
Jeremy Lamb, General Sales Mgr
Keith Montgomery, Programming Director
Kala Davis, Promotions Manager
Mark Willis, News Director
Roy Baum, Chief Engineer
JakeLebahn, Sports Director
Kelly Lenz, Agriculture Director

WIBW-FM
09-01-1961; 94.5 mhz FM *Hrs Open:* 24; 98.4 kw; 1152 ft.; N39 0 22 W96 2 57
725 Broad Street, P.O. Box 936, Augusta, GA 30903 US
(785) 272-3456, *Fax:* (785) 228-7282
www.94country.com
larry.riggins@morris.com
License: Topeka, Shawnee County, KS held by Morris Communications Corp.
Group Owner: Morris Radio LLC
Regional Network: Kan. Info.; Kan. Agriculture *Nat'l Reps:* Katz Radio
Arbitron Metro Market: Topeka, KS *Format:* Country *Hrs. of News Programming:* news progmg 4 hrs wkly *No. News Employees:* 4 *Target Audience:* Adults 25-54.
Michael Osterhout, Operations Dir
Larry Riggins, General Manager

Jeremy Lamb, General Sales Mgr
Keith Montgomery, Programming Director
Kala Davis, Promotions Manager
Jan Lundsford, News Director
Roy Baum, Chief Engineer
JakeJacobson, Radioworks
Stephanie Lynn, Music Director
Devin Walker, Director of Digital Operations

Ulysses

KULY

03-01-1965; 1420 khz AM *Hrs Open:* 24; 1 kw-D, DA2; 0.5 kw-N, DA2; N37 32 53 W101 21 49
P.O. Box 907, Valley City, ND 58072 US
(620) 276-2366, *Fax:* (620) 356-3635
www.wksradio.com
christaroy@wksradio.com
License: Ulysses, KS held by KBUF Partnership.
Group Owner: Robert Ingstad Broadcast Properties
Nat'l Network: Westwood One *Regional Network:* Kan. Info.; Kan. Agriculture
Arbitron Metro Market: Ulysses, KS *Format:* Country *Special Programming:* Farm 12 hrs, Sp 3 hrs wkly *Hrs. of News Programming:* news progmg 24 hrs wkly *No. News Employees:* 1 *Target Audience:* 21-65; middleto upper class workers, farmers & housewives
Christa Roy, General Manager
Bob Dale, Station Manager
James Janda, Programming Director
Jim Wagoner, News Director
Jerry Jones, Sports Director
Lory Williams, Farm Director

Wamego

KHCA

03-06-1986; 95.3 mhz FM *Hrs Open:* 24; 6 kw; 325 ft.; N39 12 35 W96 21 5
Mailing Address: 103 North 3rd Street, Box 1471, Manhattan, KS 66502 US
Second Address: 103 N. 3rd, Manhattan, KS 66502
(785) 537-9595, *Fax:* (785) 537-2955
www.angel95fm.com
angel95@hotmail.com
License: Wamego, Pottawatomie County, KS held by KHCA Inc.
Nat'l Network: Salem Radio Network
Format: Adult Contemp, Christian *Special Programming:* Alternative 20 hrs wkly *No. News Employees:* 1 *Target Audience:* Christian, 18-54
Jerry Hutchinson, President

Wellington

KLEY

11-19-1966; 1130 khz AM *Hrs Open:* 24; 0.25 kw-D, DA2; 0.001 kw-N, DA2; N37 14 28 W97 24 4
P.O. Box 707, Wellington, KS 67152 US
(620) 326-3341, *Fax:* (620) 326-8512
kley@sutv.com
License: Wellington, KS held by Johnson Enterprises Inc.
Group Owner: Johnson Enterprises Inc.; (acq 5-1-89; $575,000 with co-located FM;
Nat'l Network: USA *Regional Network:* Kan. Info.; Kan. Agriculture
Arbitron Metro Market: Wichita, KS *Format:* News, Talk *Special Programming:* Farm 10 hrs, relg 4 hrs wkly *Hrs. of News Programming:* news progmg 20 hrs wkly *No. News Employees:* 1 *Target Audience:* General.*Adv. Rates:* 7; 7; 7; 7
E. Gordon Johnson, President
Travis Turner, Operations Dir
Larry Waggoner, Chief Engineer

KWME

08-27-1979; 92.7 mhz FM *Hrs Open:* 24; 14 kw; 427 ft.; N37 20 8 W97 27 53
338 South Kley Drive, Wellington, KS 67152 US
(620) 326-3341, *Fax:* (620) 326-8512
www.kwme.com/
kley@sutv.com
License: Wellington, Sumner County, KS
Group Owner: Johnson Enterprises Inc.
Nat'l Network: USA
Arbitron Metro Market: Wellington. KS *Format:* Oldies *No. News Employees:* 1 *Target Audience:* 35-64. *Adv. Rates:* 7; 7; 7; 7
Travis Turner, Programming Director

Wichita

*KCFN

04-23-1978; 91.1 mhz FM *Hrs Open:* 24; 100 kw; 486 ft.; N38 1 9 W97 23 1
P.O. Drawer 2440, Tupelo, MS 38803 US
(316) 831-9111, *Fax:* (316) 831-9119
www.kcfn.net
INFO@AFR.NET
License: Wichita, Sedgwick County, KS held by American Family Association
Group Owner: American Family Radio; (acq 5-94)
Arbitron Metro Market: Wichita, KS *Format:* Christian *Special Programming:* Relg, news/talk *Hrs. of News Programming:* News progmg 2 hrs wkly *Target Audience:* 35-65; general
Don Wildmon, Chairman
Tim Widmon, President
Cindy Kreyer, General Manager

KEYN-FM

10-01-1968; 103.7 mhz FM *Hrs Open:* 24; 98 kw; 1007 ft.; N37 48 1 W97 31 29
1850 K Street, NW, Suite 900, Washington, DC 20006 US
(316) 685-2121, *Fax:* (316) 685-3408
www.keyn.com
info@keyn.com
License: Wichita, Sedgwick County, KS held by Entercom Wichita License LLC.
Group Owner: Entercom Communications Corp.; (acq 2000; grpsl)
Nat'l Network: ABC
Arbitron Metro Market: Wichita, KS *Format:* Oldies *Special Programming:* Dr. Demento 2 hrs wkly *Hrs. of News Programming:* News progmg 5 hrs wkly *Target Audience:* 25-54; baby boomers
Jackie Wise, General Manager
Lisa Crider, General Sales Mgr

KLIO

09-01-1923; 1070 khz AM *Hrs Open:* 24; 10 kw-D, 1 kw-N, DA-N; N37 42 47 W97 19 59
Mailing Address: Box 1402, Wichita, KS 89102
Second Address: 4200 N. Old Lawrence Rd., Wichita, KS 67219
(316) 838-9141, *Fax:* (316) 838-3607
www.kfdi.com
info@kfdi.com
License: Wichita, Sedgwick County, KS held by Journal Broadcast Corp.
Group Owner: Journal Communications Inc.; (acq 6-11-99; grpsl)
Nat'l Network: ABC
Population Served: 411,000 *Arbitron Metro Market:* Wichita, KS *No. News Employees:* 7 *Target Audience:* 25-54.
Beverlee Brannigan, Programming Director
Dan Dillon, News Director
Orin Friesen, Disc Jockey
Johnny Western, Disc Jockey
Dugg Collins, Disc Jockey
Krysti Bradford, Traffic Manager

KFDI-FM

06-06-1963; 101.3 mhz FM; 100 kw; 1138 ft.; N37 47 47 W97 31 59
Mailing Address: 3355 S. Valley View Boulevard, Las Vegas, NV 89102 US
Second Address: 4200 N. Old Lawrence Rd., Wichita, KS 67219
(316) 838-9141, *Fax:* (316) 838-3607
www.kfdi.com
License: Wichita, Sedgwick County, KS held by Journal Broadcast Corp.
Group Owner: Journal Communications Inc.
Arbitron Metro Market: Wichita, KS *Format:* Country *Target Audience:* 25-54; adults
Dugg Collins, Programming Director
Johnny Western, Disc Jockey
Orin Friesen, Disc Jockey

KNSS

05-26-1922; 1330 khz AM *Hrs Open:* 24; 5 kw-D, DAN; 5 kw-N, DAN; N37 42 47 W97 14 51
US
(316) 685-2121, *Fax:* (316) 685-3408
www.knssradio.com
info@knssradio.com
License: Wichita, KS held by Entercom Wichita License LLC.
Group Owner: Entercom Communications Corp.; (acq 2000; grpsl).
Nat'l Network: CBS *Wire Services:* Weather Wire
Arbitron Metro Market: Wichita, KS *Format:* News, News/Talk, 86 *Target Audience:* 25-54.
Jackie Wise, General Manager
Lisa Crider, General Sales Mgr
Tony Duesing, Programming Director
Steve McIntosh, News Director

KICT-FM

04-28-1972; 95.1 mhz FM *Hrs Open:* 24; 100 kw; 899 ft.; N37 47 58 W97 31 58
3355 S. Valley View Boulevard, Las Vegas, NV 89102 US
(316) 838-9141, *Fax:* (316) 838-3607
www.t95.com
emmcar@journalbroadcastinggroup.com;
lfetter@journalbroadcastinggroup.com;
jwilson@journalbroadcasti
License: Wichita, Sedgwick County, KS held by Journal Broadcast Corp.
Group Owner: Journal Communications Inc.; (acq 6-14-99; grpsl)
Arbitron Metro Market: Wichita, KS *Format:* Rock/AOR *Special Programming:* Dee Snider 2 hrs wkly *Hrs. of News Programming:* news progmg 15 hrs wkly *No. News Employees:* 2 *Target Audience:* 18-44.
Eric McCart, General Manager
Lisa Fetter, General Sales Mgr
Ray Michaels, Programming Director
Manny Cowzinski, Promotions Manager
Jason Wilson, Local Sales Manager

KTHR

04-17-1967; 107.3 mhz FM *Hrs Open:* 24; 100 kw; 843 ft.; N37 46 40 W97 30 37
600 Congress Ave., Suite 1400, Austin, TX 78701 US
(316) 494-6600, *Fax:* (316) 494-6730
www.1073theroad.com
info@1073theroad.com
License: Wichita, Sedgwick County, KS held by Clear Channel Broadcasting Licenses, Inc.
Group Owner: Clear Channel Communications Inc.; (acq 8-30-2000; grpsl).
Nat'l Reps: Clear Channel *Wire Services:* UPI
Arbitron Metro Market: Wichita, KS *Format:* Classic Rock *Target Audience:* 25-54; Males
Tom Glade, Operations Dir

*KMUW

04-26-1949; 89.1 mhz FM *Hrs Open:* 24; 100 kw; 911 ft.; N37 46 26 W97 30 51.8
3317 E. 17th St. N., Wichita, KS 67208 US
(316) 978-6789, *Fax:* (316) 978-3946
www.kmuw.org
info@kmuw.org
License: Wichita, Sedgwick County, KS held by Wichita State University.
Nat'l Network: NPR; PRI *Regional Network:* Kan. Info. *Wire Services:* AP
Arbitron Metro Market: Wichita, KS *Format:* Jazz, News, 90 *Special Programming:* Gospel 2 hrs, jazz 14 hrs, folk/world 5 hrs, AAA 1 *Hrs. of News Programming:* news progmg 121 hrs wkly *No. News Employees:* 2*Target Audience:* General.
Pat Hayes, Operations Dir
Mark McCain, General Manager
Larry Bennett, Programming Director
Lu Stephens, Promotions Manager
Jon Cyphers, Engineering Dir

KGSO

01-01-1950; 1410 khz AM *Hrs Open:* 24; 5 kw-D, DA2; 1 kw-N, DA2; N37 44 5 W97 21 6
3337 W. Central, Wichita, KS 67203 US
(316) 721-4407, *Fax:* (316) 721-8276
www.kgso.com
License: Wichita, KS held by Steckline Communications Inc.
Group Owner: Steckline Communications Inc.; (acq 7-1-2005; $1.3 million)
Nat'l Network: ESPN Radio; NBC Radio; USA *Regional Network:* Mid-America Ag
Arbitron Metro Market: Wichita, KS *Format:* Sports *Target Audience:* Men 25-54.
Todd Johnson, General Manager

KFH

10-28-1947; 1240 khz AM; 0.63 kw-U, ND1; N37 43 6 W97 19 5
600 Congress Ave., Suite 1400, Austin, TX 78701 US
(316) 685-2121, *Fax:* (316) 685-3408
www.kfhradio.com
letters@kfhradio.com
License: Wichita, KS held by Entercom Wichita License L.L.C.
Group Owner: Entercom Communications Corp.; (acq 2000; grpsl).
Nat'l Network: CBS *Nat'l Reps:* D & R Radio
Arbitron Metro Market: Wichita, KS *Format:* Sports, Talk *Target Audience:* 35 plus; professionals
Jackie Wise, General Manager

KQAM

01-01-1936; 1480 khz AM; 5 kw-D, DA2; 1 kw-N, DA2; N37 44 21 W97 16 14
1850 K Street, NW, Suite 900, Washington, DC 20006 US
(316) 685-2121, *Fax:* (316) 685-3408
www.kqamradio.com
License: Wichita, KS held by Radio Disney Group LLC.

Group Owner: ABC Inc.; (acq 7-29-02; $2 million).
Nat'l Network: Radio Disney
Arbitron Metro Market: Wichita, KS *Format:* News, News/Talk, 86
Greg Steckline, President

KRBB
09-19-1948; 97.9 mhz FM *Hrs Open:* 24; 100 kw; 1027 ft.; N37 46 40 W97 30 37
600 Congress Avenue, Suite 1400, Austin, TX 78701 US
(316) 494-6600, *Fax:* (316) 494-6730
www.b98fm.com
info@b98fm.com
License: Wichita, Sedgwick County, KS held by Capstar TX L.P.
Group Owner: Clear Channel Communications Inc.; (acq 8-30-00; grpsl)
Nat'l Reps: Clear Channel
Arbitron Metro Market: Wichita, KS *Format:* Adult Contemp
Special Programming: Jazz 2 hrs, Sp 3 hrs, love songs 18 hrs wkly *No. News Employees:* 1 *Target Audience:* W 25-54; a 25-54; working & family oriented
Lyman James, Operations Dir
Rob Burton, General Manager
Frank Flores, General Sales Mgr
Austin Henry, Promotions Manager

KSGL
08-01-1957; 900 khz AM; 0.25 kw-D, DA2; 0.028 kw-N, DA2; N37 41 33 W97 22 54
3337 West Central, Wichita, KS 67203 US
(316) 942-3231, *Fax:* (316) 942-9314
www.ksgl.com
info@ksgl.com
License: Wichita, KS held by Agape Communications Inc.
Nat'l Network: USA
Arbitron Metro Market: Wichita, KS *Format:* Religious
Don Clifford, President
Norbert Atherton, Operations Dir
Terry Atherton, General Manager

***KYFW**
09-24-1988; 88.3 mhz FM *Hrs Open:* 24; 17 kw; 141 ft.; N37 40 22 W97 20 8
8030 Arrowridge Blvd, Charlotte, NC 28273 US
(704) 523-5555, *Fax:* (316) 788-7883
www.bbnradio.org
kyfw@bbnradio.org
License: Wichita, Sedgwick County, KS held by Bible Broadcasting Network.
Group Owner: Bible Broadcasting Network; acq 6-26-89)
Arbitron Metro Market: Charlotte, NC *Format:* Christian *Target Audience:* General.
Lowell Davey, President
Matt Johnson, General Manager

***KYWA**
06-17-2004; 90.7 mhz FM *Hrs Open:* 24; 70 kw horiz, 67.5 kw vert; 472 ft.; N37 28 37 W97 4 28
3811 North Meridian, Wichita, KS 67204 US
(316) 831-0907, *Fax:* (316) 831-0910
www.kwya.wayfm.com
supportservices@wayfm.com
License: Wichita, Sedgwick County, KS held by WAY-FM Media Group Inc.
Group Owner: WAY-FM Media Group Inc.; (acq 4-12-2004; $485,000)
Arbitron Metro Market: Wichita, KS *Format:* Christian *Target Audience:* 25-44; Females
Dave Conour, Operations Dir
Paul Anthony, Station Manager

Winfield

KSOK-FM
01-01-1996; 95.9 mhz FM *Hrs Open:* 24; 15.2 kw; Ant 420 ft; N37 04 32 W96 56 13
334 E. Radio Ln., Arkansas City, KS 66762
(620) 442-5400, *Fax:* (620) 442-5401
www.ksokradio.com
ksok@ksokradio.com
License: Winfield, Cowley County, KS held by Cowley County Broadcasting Inc.
Nat'l Network: CBS *Regional Network:* Kan. Agriculture
Population Served: 40,000*No. News Employees:* 1 *Target Audience:* 22-55; blue collar, middle America, people who have children, are still working, & have mortgages *Adv. Rates:* 26; 22; 24; 15
Brian Cunningham, Operations Dir
Marty Mutti, General Manager
Pam Miller, Station Manager
Pam Miller, General Sales Mgr
Marty Mutti, Programming Director
Blake Carter, Promotions Manager
Shawn Wheat, News Director
BrianCunningham, Engineering Dir
Brian Cunningham, Chief Engineer

***KBDD**
01-01-2000; 91.9 mhz FM; 48 kw; 492 ft.; N37 22 56 W96 57 20
Mailing Address: P O Drawer 2440, Tupelo, MS 38803 US
Second Address: 8919 World Ministry Ave., Baton Rouge, LA 70810
(225) 768-3688, *Fax:* (225) 768-3724
www.jsm.org
kawikfish@yahoo.com
License: Winfield, Cowley County, KS held by Family Worship Center Church Inc.
Group Owner: Family Worship Center Church Inc.; acq 6-10-2004; $1.15 million).
Format: Christian
David Whitelaw, COO
Jimmy Swaggart, President
John Santiago, Programming Director

KKLE
08-19-1963; 1550 khz AM *Rebroadcasts:* Rebroadcasts KLEY(AM) Wellington 98%
P. O. Box 707,Kley Drive, Wellington, KS 67152 US
(620) 221-3341, *Fax:* (620) 326-8512
www.kkle.com
kley@sutv.com
License: Winfield, KS held by Johnson Enterprises Inc.
Group Owner: Johnson Enterprises Inc.; (acq 1990)
Nat'l Network: ESPN Radio; USA
Arbitron Metro Market: Wichita, KS *Format:* Sports *Target Audience:* General. *Adv. Rates:* 7; 7; 7; 7
Gordon Johnson, President
Gordon Johnson, General Manager

KWLS
01-01-1980; 107.9 mhz FM *Hrs Open:* 24; 50 kw; 492 ft.; N37 15 46 W96 53 42
1604 E. Quincy, Pittsburgh, KS 66762 US
(316) 776-9530, *Fax:* (316) 612-1077
www.kwlsradio.com
License: Winfield, Cowley County, KS held by Mid-America Ag Network Inc.
Nat'l Reps: McGavren Guild
Arbitron Metro Market: Wichita, KS *Format:* Country *Adv. Rates:* 16; 12; 12; 9.60
Larry Steckline, President
Chris Carter, Operations Dir
Denise Sherman, General Sales Mgr
Michael Carter, Promotions Manager

***KSWC**
11-01-1967; 100.3 mhz FM; 0.009 kw horiz; 43 ft.; N37 14 45 W96 58 15
100 College Street, Winfield, KS 67156 US
(620) 229-6263
www.scdigital.org/stream/
License: Winfield, Cowley County, KS held by Southwestern College.
Arbitron Metro Market: Winfield, KS *Format:* Talk *Target Audience:* 21 & younger.
Tom Jacobs, General Manager

Kentucky

Albany

WANY
10-25-1958; 1390 khz AM; 1 kw-D, NDD; N36 41 54 W85 9 0
P. O. Box 400, Albany, KY 42602 US
(606) 387-5186, *Fax:* (606) 387-6595
mix1063@hotmail.com
License: Albany, KY held by Pamela Allred dba Albany Broadcasting Co.
Nat'l Reps: Keystone (unwired net)
Arbitron Metro Market: Albany, KY *Format:* Country *Special Programming:* Farm 2 hrs, gospel 6 hrs wkly
Randy Speck, General Manager
Larry Nelson, Chief Engineer

WANY-FM
04-18-1966; 106.3 mhz FM; 2.7 kw horiz; 154 ft.; N36 41 54 W85 9 0
P. O. Box 400, Albany, KY 42602 US
(606) 387-5186, *Fax:* (606) 387-6595
License: Albany, Clinton County, KY
Arbitron Metro Market: Albany, KY *Format:* Country
Terry Forcht, CEO
Trevor Grigsby, General Manager

Allen

WMDJ-FM
09-01-1984; 100.1 mhz FM; 2.6 kw; 492 ft.; N37 35 12 W82 42 57
Mailing Address: P. O. Box 530, Martin, KY 41649 US
Second Address: Old Hwy. Rt. 80, Martin, KY 41649
(606) 874-8005, *Fax:* (606) 874-0057
www.wmdjfm.com
fm100wmdj@mikrotec.com
License: Allen, Floyd County, KY held by Floyd County Broadcasting Co. Inc.
Nat'l Reps: Katz Radio
Arbitron Metro Market: Martin, KY *Format:* Country, Oldies
Target Audience: 25-65.
Dale McKinney, General Manager
Jamie Johnson, Station Manager
Mona Dingus, General Sales Mgr

Annville

WANV
01-01-2006; 96.7 mhz FM; 1.85 kw; 499 ft.; N37 13 24 W84 2 1 US
(606) 864-2148, *Fax:* (606) 528-9824
www.967wanv.com
info@wanvfm.com
License: Annville, Jackson County, KY held by F.T.G. Broadcasting Inc.
Group Owner: Key Broadcasting Inc.
Arbitron Metro Market: Annville, KY *Format:* Contemporary Hits/Top 40, Adult Contemp
Terry Forcht, CEO
Trevor Grigsby, General Manager

Ashland

WCMI
01-01-1935; 1340 khz AM *Hrs Open:* 24; 1 kw-U; N38 28 02 W82 35 50
401 11th St., Suite 200, Huntington, WV 25701
(304) 523-8401, *Fax:* (304) 523-4848
www.wcmi.am
License: Ashland, Boyd County, KY held by Fifth Avenue Broadcasting Co. Inc.
Group Owner: Kindred Communications Inc.; (acq 1-26-98; with WCMI-FM Catletts
Nat'l Network: NBC/ESPN
Population Served: 24,000 *Arbitron Metro Market:* Huntington-Ashl
Mike Kirtner, President
Reeves Kirtner, Operations Dir

WDGG
01-01-1948; 93.7 mhz FM *Hrs Open:* 24; 100 kw; 741 ft.; N38 23 14 W82 39 45
401 11th T, Ste 200, Huntington, WV 25701 US
(304) 523-8401, *Fax:* (304) 523-4848
www.937thedawg.com
sales@937thedawg.com
License: Ashland, Boyd County, KY held by Fifth Avenue Broadcasting Co. Inc.
Group Owner: Kindred Communications Inc.; (acq 1988).
Nat'l Network: Jones Radio Networks; Motor Racing Net
Regional Network: W. Va. MetroNews Network *Nat'l Reps:* McGavren Guild *Wire Services:* Accu-Weather; AP
Arbitron Metro Market: Huntington-Ashland, WV-KY *Format:* Country *Hrs. of News Programming:* news progmg 2 hrs wkly
No. News Employees: 1 *Target Audience:* 25-49; male
Tom Wolf, CEO
Mike Kirtner, President
Rae Ann Parsons, General Sales Mgr
Cameron Smith, Engineering Dir

***WKAO**
91.1 mhz FM; 7 kw; 354 ft.; N38 25 11 W82 24 6
PO Box 889, Blacksburg, VA 24063 US
(540) 961-2377, *Fax:* (540) 951-5282
www.parfm.com
License: Ashland, Boyd County, KY held by Positive Alternative Radio Inc.
Group Owner: Positive Alternative Radio Inc.
Arbitron Metro Market: Ashland, KY
Edward Baker, President

Auburn

WBVR-FM
05-01-1965; 96.7 mhz FM *Hrs Open:* 24; 45 kw; 423 ft.; N36 50 35 W86 15 30
PO Box 298, Russellville, KY 42276 US

(270) 843-3333, *Fax:* (270) 843-0454
www.beaverfm.com
travislee@beaverfm.com
License: Auburn, Logan County, KY held by Forever Communications Inc.
Group Owner: Forever Communications Inc.; (acq 1984)
Nat'l Reps: Christal
Arbitron Metro Market: Bowling Green, KY *Format:* Country
Target Audience: 18-54. *Adv. Rates:* 60; 60; 50; 25
Christine Hillard, President
Mark Mackey, General Manager
Myla Thomas, Programming Director

***WAYD**
01-01-2005; 88.1 mhz FM; 1 kw; 371 ft.; N36 57 37 W86 32 49
P.O. Box 887, Brentwood, TN 37024 US
(888) 339-2936, *Fax:* (615) 261-3967
www.waym.wayfm.com
supportservices@wayfm.com
License: Auburn, Logan County, KY held by WAY-FM Media Group Inc.
Group Owner: WAY-FM Media Group Inc.
Format: Christian
Matt Austin, General Manager
Teresa White, General Sales Mgr
Jeff Brown, Programming Director
Bob Augsburg, Founder

Barbourville

WYWY
12-13-1955; 950 khz AM; 1 kw-D, ND2; N36 50 26 W83 52 16
222 Daniel Boone Dr., Barbourville, KY 40906 US
(606) 546-4128, *Fax:* (606) 546-4138
wkkqproduction@yahoo.com
License: Barbourville, KY held by Barbourville Community Broadcasting Co.
Arbitron Metro Market: Barbourville, KY *Format:* Gospel, Religious
Mildred Engle, President
Chad Engle, General Manager
Sherry Moore, General Sales Mgr
Pat Jordan, News Director
Orville Burnett, Chief Engineer

WKKQ
10-02-1974; 96.1 mhz FM; 25 kw; 328 ft.; N36 51 59 W83 54 0
222 Daniel Boone Drive, Barbourville, KY 40906 US
, *Fax:* (606) 546-4138
wkkqproduction@yahoo.com
License: Barbourville, Knox County, KY held by Barbourville Commuity Broadcasting Co.
Arbitron Metro Market: Barbourville, KY *Format:* Adult Contemp
Target Audience: 25-34.
Randy Brock, General Sales Mgr
Sean Terrell, Programming Director

Bardstown

WBRT
12-01-1954; 1320 khz AM; 1 kw-D; N37 49 09 W85 29 10
106 S. 3rd St., Bardstown, KY 42141
(502) 348-3943, *Fax:* (502) 348-4043
www.wbrtcountry.com
info@wbrtcountry.com
License: Bardstown, Nelson County, KY held by Bardstown Radio Team, LLC
Nat'l Reps: Rgnl Reps
Population Served: 11,839 *Arbitron Metro Market:* Bardstown, Ky *Special Programming:* Farm 10 hrs wkly *Target Audience:* 20 plus.
Kenny Fogle, General Manager

Beattyville

WLJC
05-12-1965; 102.1 mhz FM; 1.5 kw; 656 ft.; N37 36 47 W83 40 18
219 Radio Station Loop, Beattyville, KY 41311 US
(606) 464-3600, *Fax:* (606) 464-5021
www.wljc.com
wljc@wljc.com
License: Beattyville, Lee County, KY held by Hour of Harvest Inc.
Nat'l Reps: Rgnl Reps
Format: Adult Contemp
Margaret Drake, President
Jonathan Drake, General Manager
Kim Mitchell, General Sales Mgr
Alan Mulford, Chief Engineer

Benton

***WAAJ**
01-01-1996; 89.7 mhz FM; 6 kw vert; 299 ft.; N36 48 31 W88 13 26
Mailing Address: P O Box 281, Hardin, KY 42048 US
Second Address: 219 College St., Harding, KY 42048
(270) 437-4095, *Fax:* (270) 437-4098
www.hmiradio.com
info@hmiradio.com
License: Benton, Marshall County, KY held by Heartland Ministries.
Arbitron Metro Market: Benton, KY *Format:* Gospel
Darrell Gibson, President
Adam Tarnowski, Operations Dir
Eddie Sheridan, General Manager

WCBL
12-13-1954; 1290 khz AM *Hrs Open:* 24; 5 kw-D, ND1; 0.053 kw-N, ND1; N36 51 31 W88 20 11
1039 Egner's Ferry Rd, P.O. Box 387, Benton, KY 42025 US
(270) 527-3102, *Fax:* (270) 527-5606
www.thelakecurrent.com
wcbl@freelandbroadcasting.com
License: Benton, KY held by Jim W. Freeland.
Group Owner: Freeland Broadcasting Stations; (acq 11-17-98; with co-located FM)
Format: Sports, Talk *Hrs. of News Programming:* news progmg 7 hrs wkly *No. News Employees:* 1 *Target Audience:* General. *Adv. Rates:* 15; 15; 15; 15
Sherry Rickman, Operations Dir
Chris Freeland, General Manager
Gregg Leath, Programming Director
Sam Rickmon, News Director
Shane Freeland, Disc Jockey

***WTRT**
12-01-1998; 88.1 mhz FM *Hrs Open:* 24; 0.6 kw vert; 253 ft.; N36 47 53 W88 20 50
Mailing Address: P.O. Box 281, Hardin, KY 42048 US
Second Address: 219 College St., Harding, KY 42048
(270) 437-4095, *Fax:* (270) 437-4098
www.hmiradio.com
info@hmiradio.com
License: Benton, Marshall County, KY held by Heartland Ministries
Arbitron Metro Market: Benton, KY *Format:* Adult Contemp, Christian
Darrell Gibson, President
Eddie Sheridan, General Manager
Jeremy Johnson, Programming Director
Adam Tarnowski, Operations Coordinator

***WVHM**
06-01-1989; 90.5 mhz FM; 16.5 kw; 335 ft.; N36 48 31 W88 13 26
Mailing Address: P.O. Box 281, Hardin, KY 42048 US
Second Address: 219 College St., Hardin, KY 42048
(270) 437-4095, *Fax:* (270) 437-4098
www.hmiradio.com
info@hmiradio.com
License: Benton, Marshall County, KY held by Heartland Ministries.
Nat'l Network: USA
Arbitron Metro Market: Hardin, KY *Format:* Gospel *Target Audience:* 18-49.
Darrell Gibson, President
Eddie Sheridan, General Manager
Cecil Glass, Station Manager
Jeremy Johnson, Programming Director
Adam Tarnowski, Operations Coordinator

Berea

WKXO
07-18-1971; 1500 khz AM *Hrs Open:* 6 AM-7 PM; 0.25 kw-D, NDD; N37 35 12 W84 18 4
1030 Winchester Road, Irvine, KY 40336 US
(859) 623-1389, *Fax:* (859) 623-1341
www.wbairforce.com/weky
coyote@wcyofm.com
License: Berea, KY held by Wallingford Communications LLC.
Group Owner: Wallingford Broadcasting Co.; (acq 1999; grpsl)
Nat'l Network: Jones Radio Networks
Arbitron Metro Market: Lexington-Fayette, KY *Format:* News, News/Talk, 86 *Hrs. of News Programming:* news progmg 3 hrs wkly *No. News Employees:* 1 *Target Audience:* 21 plus.
Kelly Wallingford, General Manager
Ray White, Programming Director

WLFX
09-27-1990; 106.7 mhz FM *Hrs Open:* 24; 3.3 kw; 420 ft.; N37 39 40 W84 8 55
1030 Winchester Road, Irvine, KY 40336 US
(859) 623-1389, *Fax:* (859) 623-1341
www.wbairforce.com/weky
coyote@wcyofm.com
License: Berea, Madison County, KY
Group Owner: Wallingford Broadcasting Co.
Arbitron Metro Market: Lexington-Fayette, KY *Format:* Classic Rock *Special Programming:* Gospel 12 hrs wkly
John Englebrecht, CEO
Craig Jacobus, President
Tim Huelsing, General Manager
Paul Brayfield, General Sales Mgr
Rusty James, Programming Director
James Ashley, Promotions Manager

Bowling Green

WBGN
11-24-1959; 1340 khz AM *Hrs Open:* 24; 1 kw-U, ND1; N37 0 34 W86 27 9
P.O. Box 900, Bowling Green, KY 42102 US
(270) 843-3333, *Fax:* (270) 783-0454
www.1340wbgn.com
joneal@forevercomm.com
License: Bowling Green, KY held by Forever Communications Inc.
Group Owner: Forever Communications Inc.; (acq 2001)
Nat'l Network: ABC; ESPN Radio *Regional Network:* Ky. News Net *Nat'l Reps:* Christal
Arbitron Metro Market: Bowling Green, KY *Format:* Sports *Target Audience:* 35-54. *Adv. Rates:* 20; 20; 15; 10
Mark Mackey, General Manager
Joe O'Neal, General Sales Mgr
Chris Idle, Programming Director

***WCVK**
04-22-1986; 90.7 mhz FM; 14 kw; 449 ft.; N37 0 18 W86 31 19
Mailing Address: 1403 Scottsville Rd., Bowling Green, KY 42104 US
Second Address: 1407 Scottsville Rd., Bowling Green, KY 42104
(270) 781-7326, *Fax:* (270) 781-8005
www.christianfamilyradio.com
mike@christianfamilyradio.com
License: Bowling Green, Warren County, KY held by Bowling Green Community Broadcasting Inc.
Nat'l Network: Salem Radio Network
Arbitron Metro Market: Bowling Green, KY *Format:* Adult Contemp, Christian *Special Programming:* Christian Rock 10hrs weekly *Target Audience:* 25-54; Christian men & women
Mike Wilson, General Manager
Susan ""West"" Woodard, Programming Director
Derek Gregory, Promotions Manager

WDNS
03-12-1973; 93.3 mhz FM *Hrs Open:* 24; 12 kw; 472 ft.; N36 56 39 W86 15 11
P. O. Box 930, Bowling Green, KY 42102 US
(270) 781-2121, *Fax:* (270) 842-0232
www.wdnsfm.com
info@wdnsfm.com
License: Bowling Green, Warren County, KY held by Daily News Broadcasting Co.
Arbitron Metro Market: Bowling Green, KY *Format:* Classic Rock *Hrs. of News Programming:* news progmg 7 hrs wkly *No. News Employees:* 1 *Target Audience:* 18-54.
Sean Sheenan, Operations Dir
Art Kalemkarian, General Manager
Bryan Locke, Programming Director
John Blazek, Chief Engineer

WGGC
06-23-1961; 95.1 mhz FM *Hrs Open:* 24; 100 kw; 988 ft.; N36 54 43 W86 11 21
245 West Dixie Ave., P.O. Box 517, Elizabethtown, KY 42701 US
(270) 783-8730, *Fax:* (270) 783-8665
www.wggc.com
darrin@wggc.com
License: Bowling Green, Warren County, KY held by Heritage Communications Inc.
Arbitron Metro Market: Bowling Green, KY *Format:* Country
Bill Evans, General Manager
Darrin Evans, Station Manager
Dan Callahan, Disc Jockey
Maxwell P. Murphy, Disc Jockey

WKCT
11-01-1947; 930 khz AM *Hrs Open:* 24; 5 kw-D, DAN; 0.5 kw-N, DAN; N37 1 53 W86 26 18

RADIO - U.S.

Mailing Address: P. O. Box 930, Bowling Green, KY 42101 US
Second Address: 804 College St., Bowling Green, KY 42101
(270) 781-2121, *Fax:* (270) 842-0232
www.93wkct.com
alan@wdnsfm.com
License: Bowling Green, KY held by Daily News Broadcasting Co.
Nat'l Network: CBS
Arbitron Metro Market: Bowling Green, KY *Format:* News, News/Talk, 86 *Hrs. of News Programming:* news progmg 25 hrs wkly *No. News Employees:* 1 *Target Audience:* 25 plus.
Alan Cooper, General Manager
Chad Young, Programming Director

***WKYU-FM**
11-01-1980; 88.9 mhz FM *Hrs Open:* 24; 98 kw; 719 ft.; N37 5 23 W86 38 5
1 Big Red Way, Bowling Green, KY 42101 US
(270) 745-5489, *Fax:* (270) 745-6272
www.wkyu.org
wkyufm@wku.edu
License: Bowling Green, Warren County, KY held by Western Kentucky University.
Nat'l Network: NPR; PRI
Arbitron Metro Market: Bowling Green, KY *TV Affiliate:* *WKYU-TV affil *Format:* News *Hrs. of News Programming:* news progmg 35 hrs wkly *No. News Employees:* 3 *Target Audience:* General.
Peter Bryant, General Manager

***WWHR**
08-18-1988; 91.7 mhz FM *Hrs Open:* 24; 1.3 kw; 374 ft.; N37 0 19 W86 31 23
College Heights, 1 Big Red Way, Bowling Green, KY 42101 US
(270) 745-5439, *Fax:* (270) 745-5835
www.revolution.fm
gm@revolution.fm
License: Bowling Green, Warren County, KY held by Western Kentucky University.
Arbitron Metro Market: Bowling Green, KY *Format:* Variety/Diverse *Special Programming:* Soul 2 hrs, punk 2 hrs, gothic 2 hrs, loc 2 hrs, e *Hrs. of News Programming:* news progmg 5 hrs wkly *No. News Employees:* 2*Target Audience:* Adults 18-34.
Dr. Marjorie Yambor, General Manager
Nash Gumm, Station Manager
Savannah Burke, Programming Director
Nathan Smith, Production Director
Angela Conway, Public Relations Director
Salena Lisner, Human Resources Director
Sean Strain,Internet Director
Nick Lough, Underwriting Director

Brandenburg

WMMG
07-01-1984; 1140 khz AM
Mailing Address: 1715 Bypass Road, P.O. Box 309, Bradenburg, KY 40108 US
Second Address: 1715 Bypass Rd., Brandenburg, KY 40108
(270) 422-4440, *Fax:* (270) 422-3464
www.wmmgradio.com
wmmg935@bbtel.com
License: Brandenburg, KY held by Meade County Communications Inc.
Nat'l Reps: Rgnl Reps
Arbitron Metro Market: Brandenburg, KY *Format:* Country
Special Programming: Relg 8 hrs wkly *Adv. Rates:* 12; 12; 9; 12
Gwen Blevins, General Manager

WMMG-FM
08-23-1972; 93.5 mhz FM; 3.4 kw; 289 ft.; N37 59 5 W86 9 24
1715 Bypass Road, Brandenburg, KY 40108 US
(270) 422-4440, *Fax:* (270) 422-3464
www.wmmgradio.com
wmmg935@bbtel.com
License: Brandenburg, Meade County, KY held by Meade County Communications Inc.
Nat'l Reps: Rgnl Reps
Arbitron Metro Market: Brandenburg, KY *Target Audience:* 18-65. *Adv. Rates:* Same as AM
J. Spangler, President
Lori Spangler, Operations Dir

Brownsville

WKLX
01-01-2000; 100.7 mhz FM; 8 kw; 584 ft.; N37 9 19 W86 19 33
1519 Euclid Avenue, Bowling Green, KY 42103 US
(270) 651-6050, *Fax:* (270) 651-7666
www.bowlinggreensam.com
License: Brownsville, Edmonson County, KY held by Charles M. Anderson.
Arbitron Metro Market: Bowling Green, OH *Format:* Adult Contemp
Darron Steenbergen, General Manager

Buffalo

WXAM
11-26-1974; 1430 khz AM; 1 kw-D, ND1; 0.042 kw-N, ND1; N37 31 49 W85 42 49
P.O. Box 177, Hodgenville, KY 42748 US
(270) 763-0800, *Fax:* (270) 769-6349
License: Buffalo, KY held by Mark Goodman Productions Inc.
Nat'l Network: ESPN Radio
Arbitron Metro Market: Buffalo, KY *Format:* Sports, Talk
Roth Stratton, General Manager

Burgin

WKYB
105.9 mhz FM; 3 kw; 141 m; N37 48 49 W84 39 28
8686 Michael Lane, Fairfield, OH
(513) 829-7700
License: Burgin, Mercer County, KY held by Vernon R. Baldwin Inc.
Group Owner: Vernon R Baldwin Inc; (acq 12/14/2011; grpsl)

Marcella Baldwin, President

Burkesville

WKYR-FM
10-01-1988; 107.9 mhz FM *Hrs Open:* 24; 6 kw; 312 ft.; N36 47 26 W85 22 47
Mailing Address: P.O. Box 340, Burkesville, KY 42717 US
Second Address: Hwy. 90 E., Burkesville, KY 42717
(270) 433-7191, *Fax:* (270) 433-7195
wkyr@mchsi.com
License: Burkesville, Cumberland County, KY held by Cumberland Broadcasting LLC
Nat'l Network: ABC; Jones Radio Networks *Regional Network:* Ky. News Net
Format: Country
Jessie Crabtree, General Manager

Burnside

WSFE
02-28-1984; 910 khz AM *Hrs Open:* 24
Mailing Address: P.O. Box 740, Somerset, KY 42501 US
Second Address: 101 First Radio Ln., Somerset, KY 42503
(606) 678-5151, *Fax:* (606) 678-2026
www.wsfeam.com
License: Burnside, KY held by Capstar TX L.P.
Group Owner: Clear Channel Communications Inc.; (acq 12-8-2000; grpsl).
Format: Talk *Hrs. of News Programming:* news progmg 5 hrs wkly *No. News Employees:* 1 *Target Audience:* 25-54.
Richard Dills, General Manager
Jo-Ella Shelly, General Sales Mgr
Rod Zimmerman, Programming Director
Jim Mercer, Chief Engineer

WSEK
08-17-1985; 93.9 mhz FM; 50 kw; 492 ft.; N37 9 15 W84 27 35
Mailing Address: P.O. Box 740, Somerset, KY 42502 US
Second Address: 101 First Radio Ln., Burnside, KY 42503
(606_ 678-5151, *Fax:* (606) 678-2026
www.wsfeam.com
wsek@clearchannel.com
License: Burnside, Pulaski County, KY
Group Owner: Clear Channel Communications Inc.
Arbitron Metro Market: Burnside, KY *Format:* Country
Dr. Kenneth Lindow, President
Joy Clark, General Manager
Roger Johnson, Programming Director

Cadiz

WKDZ
04-08-1966; 1110 khz AM *Hrs Open:* 24; 1 kw-D; N36 52 57 W87 50 44
Mailing Address: Box 1900, Cadiz, KY 42211
Second Address: 19 Wooldridge Ln., Cadiz, KY 42211-0316
(270) 522-3232, *Fax:* (270) 522-1110
www.oldies1480.com
bmann@wkdzradio.com
License: Cadiz, Trigg County, KY held by Ham Broadcasting Co. Inc.
Nat'l Network: Fox News
Population Served: 100,000*Special Programming:* Farm 2 hrs wkly *Hrs. of News Programming:* news progmg 18 hrs wkly *No. News Employees:* 6 *Target Audience:* 25-54.
D.J. Everett III, President
Beth Mann, General Manager
Alan Watts, News Director

WKDZ-FM
05-18-1972; 106.5 mhz FM *Hrs Open:* 24; 13.4 kw; 449 ft.; N36 48 29 W87 38 9
1487 Will Jackson Road, Cadiz, KY 42211 US
(270) 522-3232, *Fax:* (270) 522-1110
wkdzradio.com
wkdz@wkdzradio.com
License: Cadiz, Trigg County, KY held by Ham Broadcasting Co. Inc.
Format: Country *Hrs. of News Programming:* news progmg 20 hrs wkly *No. News Employees:* 2 *Target Audience:* 35-64.
Ryan McIntyre, Operations Dir
Evan Caposerri, General Manager
Casey Ross, Programming Director
Jim Cavanaugh, Chief Engineer

Calvert City

WCCK
01-01-1993; 95.7 mhz FM *Hrs Open:* 24; 3.5 kw; 341 ft.; N37 6 47 W88 21 34
2 Aspen Street, Calvert City, KY 42029 US
(270) 395-5133, *Fax:* (270) 395-5231
www.thelakecurrent.com
wcck@freelandbroadcasting.com
License: Calvert City, Marshall County, KY held by Jim Freeland DBA Freeland Broadcasting.
Group Owner: Freeland Broadcasting Stations
Nat'l Network: AP Radio
Arbitron Metro Market: Calvert City,ky *Format:* Country *Hrs. of News Programming:* News progmg 10 hrs wkly *Target Audience:* 30 plus; professionals and retired *Adv. Rates:* 15; 13; 14; 10
Jim Freeland, CEO
Sherry Darnall, Operations Dir
Greg Leath, Programming Director
Brad Hosford, Chief Engineer

Campbellsville

***WAPD**
01-01-1996; 91.7 mhz FM; 2.323 kw vert; 217 ft.; N37 19 59 W85 19 53
P.O. Drawer 2440, Tupelo, MS 38803 US
(662) 844-8888(662) 844-6191
www.afr.net
faq@afr.net
License: Campbellsville, Taylor County, KY held by American Family Association.
Group Owner: American Family Radio
Arbitron Metro Market: Campbellsville, KY *Format:* Christian
Linda Collins, General Manager

WCKQ
12-01-1964; 104.1 mhz FM *Hrs Open:* 24; 17 kw; 394 ft.; N37 20 7 W85 22 33
Mailing Address: P.O. Box 1505, Glasgow, KY 42141 US
Second Address: Box 1053, Campbellsville, KY 42719
(270) 789-2401, *Fax:* (270) 789-1450
www.myq104.com
wckq@commonwealthbroadcasting.com
License: Campbellsville, Taylor County, KY held by CBC of Marion and Taylor Counties Inc.
Group Owner: Commonwealth Broadcasting Corp.; (acq 6-30-97; $720,000 with co-located AM)
Nat'l Network: ABC; Jones Radio Networks *Nat'l Reps:* Rgnl Reps
Arbitron Metro Market: Campbellsville, KY *Format:* Adult Contemp *Hrs. of News Programming:* news progmg 7 hrs wkly *No. News Employees:* 1 *Target Audience:* 18-44. *Adv. Rates:* 12; 12; 12; na
Steve Newberry, President
Marty Bagby, Operations Dir
Barb Smith, General Manager
Barb Smith, Station Manager
Greg Gribbins, General Sales Mgr
Rob Collins, Promotions Manager
Mike Graham, Chief Engineer

WTCO
03-01-1948; 1450 khz AM *Hrs Open:* 24; 1 kw-U, ND1; N37 20 7 W85 22 33
Mailing Address: P.O. Box 1505, Glasgow, KY 42142 US
Second Address: Box 1053, Campbellsville, KY 42718

(270) 469-9826
www.wtcosports.com
License: Campbellsville, KY held by CBC of Marion and Taylor Counties Inc.
Group Owner: Commonwealth Broadcasting Corp.
Nat'l Network: ESPN Radio
Arbitron Metro Market: Campbellsville, KY *Format:* Sports *No. News Employees:* 1 *Target Audience:* 25-64. *Adv. Rates:* 6; 6; 6; na

*WLCU

88.7 mhz FM; 0.8 kw; 207 ft.; N37 20 39 W85 21 34 US
(270) 789-5008
www.campbellsville.edu
License: Campbellsville, Taylor County, KY held by Campbellsville University.
Arbitron Metro Market: Campbellsville, KY
J. Alvin Hardy, General Manager
Benji Kelly, Vice President for Development
Patricia Daugherty, Donor Relations Coordinator
Paula Smith, Director of Alumni Relations
Natalie Burdette, Director of Annual Giving
Joe Walters, SeniorCampaign Officer
Kaleb Chowning, Research and Communications Coordinator

Campton

WCBJ

01-01-1999; 103.7 mhz FM; 4.1 kw; 397 ft.; N37 39 3 W83 26 21
129 College Street, West Liberty, KY 41472 US
(606) 668-9225, *Fax:* (606) 743-9557
License: Campton, Wolfe County, KY held by Morgan County Industries Inc.
Group Owner: Morgan County Industries Inc.
Format: Classic Rock
Tina Moore, General Manager
Dewey Blevins, General Sales Mgr
Paul Lyons, Chief Engineer

Cannonsburg

WYHY

12-01-1987; 1080 khz AM *Rebroadcasts:* Simulcast with WOKU(AM) Hurricane, WV 100%
P.O. Box 889, Blackburg, VA 24060 US
606-928-3778, *Fax:* 606-928-1659
info@i64country.com
License: Cannonsburg, KY held by Big River Radio Inc.
Group Owner: Baker Family Stations
Arbitron Metro Market: Huntington-Ashl *TV Affiliate:* Relg *No. News Employees:* General.
General Manager, Jeremy Wolfe
Station Manager, Station Manager

Carlisle

WBVX

12-01-1994; 92.1 mhz FM *Hrs Open:* 24; 32 kw; 610 ft.; N38 11 19 W84 22 13
3270 Blazer Parkway, Suite 101, Lexington, KY 40509 US
(859) 233-1515, *Fax:* (859) 233-1517
www.b92fm.com
License: Carlisle, Nicholas County, KY held by L.M. Communications of Kentucky LLC.
Group Owner: L M Communications Inc.; (acq 8-17-01; $4.8 million).
Nat'l Reps: Katz Radio
Arbitron Metro Market: Lexington-Fayette, KY *Format:* Contemporary Hits/Top 40, Adult Contemp *Hrs. of News Programming:* News progmg one hr wkly *Target Audience:* General.
Lynn Martin, President
James MacFarlane, General Manager

Carrollton

WIKI

04-12-1968; 95.3 mhz FM *Hrs Open:* 24; 1.8 kw; 423 ft.; N38 39 58 W85 16 51
507 North State Street, North Vernon, IN 47265 US
(812) 346-1927, *Fax:* (812) 346-9722
License: Carrollton, Carroll County, KY held by Wagon Wheel Broadcastiing LLC.
Group Owner: Wagon Wheel Broadcasting LLC; (acq 11-14-2007; grpsl)
Nat'l Network: Jones Radio Networks; CNN Radio *Nat'l Reps:* Rgnl Reps
Format: Country *Hrs. of News Programming:* News progmg 10 hrs wkly *Target Audience:* 10-90; general
Marty Pieratt, General Manager

Catlettsburg

WCMI-FM

01-19-1972; 92.7 mhz FM *Hrs Open:* 24; 2.35 kw; 531 ft.; N38 28 2 W82 35 50
401 11th Street, Suite 200, Huntington, WV 25701 US
(304) 523-8401, *Fax:* (304) 523-4848
www.planet927.com
reeves@kindredcom.net
License: Catlettsburg, Boyd County, KY held by Fifth Avenue Broadcasting Co. Inc.
Group Owner: Kindred Communications Inc.; (acq 7-7-98; with WCMI(AM) Ashland).
Regional Network: Ky. News Net *Nat'l Reps:* McGavren Guild
Wire Services: Accu-Weather; AP
Arbitron Metro Market: Huntington-Ashl *Format:* Rock/AOR *Hrs. of News Programming:* news progrmg 5 hrs wkly *No. News Employees:* 1
Mke Kirtner, CEO
Mike Kirtner, President
Reeves Kirtner, Operations Dir
Rich Myhrwold, General Sales Mgr
Reeves Kirtner, Programming Director
Jim Kowalski, Engineering Dir
Rich Mhyrwold, Regional Sales Manager

Cave City

WHHT(FM)

09-02-1988; 103.7 mhz FM *Hrs Open:* 24; 13.5 kw; 449 ft.; N36 57 34 W86 0 8
Mailing Address: P.O. Box 1505, Glasgow, KY 42142 US
Second Address: 113 W. Public Sq., Suite 400, Glasgow, KY 42141
(270) 651-6060, *Fax:* (270) 651-7666
www.1037thepoint.net
wptq@commonwealthbroadcasting.com
License: Cave City, Barren County, KY held by Commonwealth Broadcasting Corp.
Group Owner: Commonwealth Broadcasting Corp.; (acq 11-25-97)
Nat'l Network: Westwood One
Arbitron Metro Market: Bowling Green, KY *Format:* Classic Rock *Hrs. of News Programming:* news progmg 7 hrs wkly *No. News Employees:* 1 *Target Audience:* 25-44.
Kellie Wood, Operations Dir
Darren Steenbergen, General Manager

Central City

WMTA

02-19-1955; 1380 khz AM *Hrs Open:* 24; 0.5 kw-D, ND1; 0.023 kw-N, ND1; N37 16 34 W87 8 39
One Wmta Drive, P.O. Box 973, Central City, KY 42330 US
(812) 479-5342, *Fax:* (812) 474-0483
www.faith1180.com
info@faith1180.com
License: Central City, KY held by Faith Broadcasting Company
Arbitron Metro Market: Central City, IN *Format:* Religious *Hrs. of News Programming:* News progmg 20 hrs wkly *Target Audience:* General.
Gayle Russ, CEO
Jonathan Williams, Engineering Dir

WNES

01-01-1955; 1050 khz AM; 1 kw-D, ND1; 0.172 kw-N, ND1; N37 16 9 W87 8 32
P. O. Box 471, Central City, KY 42330 US
(270) 754-3000, *Fax:* (270) 754-9484
License: Central City, KY held by Starlight Broadcasting.
Nat'l Network: CBS
Arbitron Metro Market: Central City, KY *Format:* Sports, Talk
Special Programming: Farm 7 hrs wkly
Andy Anderson, CEO
Jowanna Bandy, General Manager
Stan Barnett, Programming Director

WQXQ

12-18-1956; 101.9 mhz FM; 100 kw; 669 ft.; N37 35 3 W86 59 29
P.O. Box 471, Central City, KY 42330 US
(270) 754-3000, *Fax:* (270) 754-9484
www.q1019.com
wqxq@ocdirect.net
License: Central City, Muhlenberg County, KY held by Starlight Broadcasting
Format: Adult Contemp
Brian Schimmel, General Manager

Clinton

WQQR

11-02-1955; 94.7 mhz FM *Hrs Open:* 24; 50 kw; 472 ft.; N36 45 19 W88 39 36.6
Mailing Address: 1715 Nashville Street, P.O. Box 298, Russellville, KY 42276 US
Second Address: 6000 Bristol Drive, Paducah, KY 42003
(270) 554-8255, *Fax:* (270) 554-5468
www.wqqr.com
License: Clinton, Graves County, KY held by Bristol Broadcasting Co. Inc.
Group Owner: Bristol Broadcasting Co. Inc.
Regional Reps: Rgnl Reps.
Format: Classic Rock *No. News Employees:* 1 *Target Audience:* 25 plus. *Adv. Rates:* 26; 19; 26; 16
Nick Black, Programming Director

Coal Run

WPKE-FM

09-21-1974; 103.1 mhz FM *Hrs Open:* 24; 1.2 kw; 741 ft.; N37 27 57 W82 33 4
Mailing Address: 250 East Elkhorn Street, Elkhorn City, KY 41522 US
Second Address: 1240 Radio Dr., Pikeville, KY 41501
(606) 437-4051, *Fax:* (606) 432-2809
www.ekbradio.com
wdhr@wdhr.com
License: Coal Run, Pike County, KY held by East Kentucky Broadcasting Corp.
Group Owner: East Kentucky Broadcasting Corp.; acq 6-94; $480,000 with WBPA(AM) Elkhorn City).
Nat'l Network: ABC *Regional Reps:* Rgnl Reps
No. News Employees: 1 *Target Audience:* General.
Keith Casebolt, General Manager

Columbia

WAIN

08-01-1951; 1270 khz AM *Hrs Open:* 24
Mailing Address: P. O . Box 1450, Corbin, KY 40702 US
Second Address: 1521 Liberty Rd., Columbia, KY 42728
(270) 384-2135, *Fax:* (270) 384-6722
www.1270wain.com
wain@forchtbroadcasting.com
License: Columbia, KY held by Tri-County Radio Broadcasting Corp.
Group Owner: Key Broadcasting Inc.
Regional Network: Ky. News Net *Nat'l Reps:* Rgnl Reps *Regional Reps:* Rgnl Reps
Arbitron Metro Market: Columbia, KY *Format:* Oldies *Special Programming:* Farm 2 hrs *Hrs. of News Programming:* news progmg 8 hrs wkly *No. News Employees:* 1 *Target Audience:* 16-65. *Adv. Rates:* 14;13; 14; 10
Gary Phelps, General Manager
Louise Wooten, General Sales Mgr

WAIN-FM

03-01-1968; 93.5 mhz FM *Hrs Open:* 24; 4.6 kw; 199 ft.; N37 6 26 W85 16 42
Mailing Address: P.O. Box 1450, Corbin, KY 40702 US
Second Address: 1521 Liberty Rd., Columbia, KY 42728
(270) 384-2135, *Fax:* (270) 384-6722
935wain.com
wain@forchtbroadcasting.com
License: Columbia, Adair County, KY
Group Owner: Key Broadcasting Inc.
Nat'l Network: ABC
Arbitron Metro Market: Columbia, KY *Format:* Country *No. News Employees:* 1 *Target Audience:* 16-65. *Adv. Rates:* Same as AM
Lisa Fisher, News Director
Delno Salmon, Disc Jockey

Corbin

WCTT

05-09-1947; 680 khz AM *Hrs Open:* 5 AM-midnight
Mailing Address: 701 South Main Street, Corbin, KY 40701 US
Second Address: 821 Adams Rd., Corbin, KY 40701
(606) 528-4717, *Fax:* (606) 528-4487
www.wctt.com
pdir@wkdp.com
License: Corbin, KY held by Encore Communications Inc.
Nat'l Network: ABC *Nat'l Reps:* Rgnl Reps
Arbitron Metro Market: Corbin, KY *Format:* Adult Contemp, News, 62, Oldies, Talk *No. News Employees:* 1
Stephanie Mullins, General Manager
Lindsay Peterson, Programming Director
Leslie Fields, News Director

WCTT-FM
06-01-1967; 107.3 mhz FM *Hrs Open:* 24; 50 kw; 492 ft.; N36 54 9 W84 4 55
Mailing Address: 701 South Main Street, Corbin, KY 40701 US
Second Address: 821 Adams Rd., Corbin, KY 40701
(606) 528-4717, *Fax:* (606) 528-4487
www.wctt.com
pdir@wkdp.com
License: Corbin, Whitley County, KY
Nat'l Reps: Rgnl Reps
Arbitron Metro Market: Corbin, KY *Format:* Adult Contemp *Hrs. of News Programming:* News progmg one hr wkly *Target Audience:* 18-54.
Mark Wilson, Operations Dir
Lindsay Peterson, Programming Director
Leslie Fields, News Director
Matt Howell, Engineering Dir
Heidi Decker, Disc Jockey
Sammi Austin, Disc Jockey
Maverick Johnson, Disc Jockey
Tracy Black, PublicAffairs Director

WKDP
11-23-1961; 1330 khz AM; 5 kw-D, DA2; 0.016 kw-N, DA2; N36 56 20 W84 4 44
Mailing Address: 701 South Main Street, Corbin, KY 40701 US
Second Address: 821 Adams Rd., Corbin, KY 40701
(606) 528-6617, *Fax:* (606) 528-4487
www.wkdp.com
swaggoner@wkdp.com
License: Corbin, KY held by Eubanks Broadcasting Inc.
Nat'l Reps: Rgnl Reps
Format: News, News/Talk, 86, Religious *Target Audience:* 30-64.
Dallas Eubanks, President
Stephanie Mullins, General Manager
Derek Eubanks, Chief Engineer

WKDP-FM
01-01-1967; 99.5 mhz FM; 25 kw; 709 ft.; N36 57 14 W83 58 41
701 Main Street, Corbin, KY 40701 US
(606) 528-6617, *Fax:* (606) 528-4487
www.wkdp.com
swaggoner@wkdp.com
License: Corbin, Whitley County, KY held by Eubanks Broadcasting Inc.
Nat'l Network: ABC
Format: Country *Target Audience:* General.
Rich Archut, Operations Dir

WRSL
11-01-1961; 1600 khz AM *Hrs Open:* Sunrise-sunset; 2 kw-D, 27 w-N; N37 01 06 W84 05 58
1100 S. Main St., London, KY 40484
(606) 878-1600, *Fax:* (606) 878-1116
License: Corbin, Whitley County, KY held by Lincoln-Garrard Broadcasting Co. Inc.
Population Served: 70,000
Johnathan Smith, President
Dave Colvin, General Manager

***WEKF**
06-24-2003; 88.5 mhz FM *Hrs Open:* 24; 21 kw vert; 499 ft.; N37 1 13 W84 23 41 *Rebroadcasts:* Rebroadcasts WEKU(FM) Richmond 100%
521 Lancaster Ave, Richmond, KY 40475 US
(800) 621-8890, *Fax:* (859) 622-6276
www.weku.fm
weku@eku.edu
License: Corbin, Whitley County, KY held by Eastern Kentucky University.
Nat'l Network: NPR; PRI *Wire Services:* AP
Arbitron Metro Market: Corbin, KY *Format:* Classical, News *Hrs. of News Programming:* news progmg 35 hrs wkly *No. News Employees:* 3 *Target Audience:* General.
Mary Ellyn Cain, Operations Dir
Tim Singleton, General Manager
Carol Siler, General Sales Mgr
Laura Allen, Programming Director
Charles Compton, News Director
Bill Browning, Chief Engineer

Covington

WCVG
10-29-1965; 1320 khz AM *Hrs Open:* 24; 0.5 kw-D, DA2; 0.43 kw-N, DA2; N39 2 44 W84 30 30
35 Island Drive, Eastpoint, FL 32328 US
(866) 305-1570, *Fax:* (859) 655-4345
www.gospel1320.com
info@wcvg.com
License: Covington, KY held by Davidson Media Station WCVG Licensee LLC.
Group Owner: Davidson Media Group LLC; (acq 11-2-2006; $1.9 million)
Arbitron Metro Market: Cincinnati, OH *Format:* Gospel *Adv. Rates:* 40; 40; 40; 35
Jeff Eldred, Operations Dir
Simon Cipriano, General Manager
John Jones, Programming Director
Mayra Arroyo, Promotions Manager
Avery Corbin, Promotions Manager

Crab Orchard

WPBK
01-01-2008; 102.9 mhz FM *Hrs Open:* 24; 2.75 kw; 361 ft.; N37 25 39 W84 39 21
US
(606) 365-2126
www.wpbkfm.com
renee@wpbkfm.com
License: Crab Orchard, Lincoln County, KY held by Radioactive LLC.
Group Owner: Radioactive LLC
Arbitron Metro Market: Crab Orchard, KY
Jonathan L. Smith, President
Renee Knies, Station Manager
David Smith, Chief Engineer

Cumberland

WCPM
10-01-1951; 1280 khz AM *Hrs Open:* 24 hrs a day; 1 kw-D, ND1; 0.115 kw-N, ND1; N36 58 25 W82 59 15
101 Keller Street, Cumberland, KY 40823 US
(606) 589-4623
www.wcpmradio.com
wcpmradio@windstream.net
License: Cumberland, KY held by Cumberland City Broadcasting Inc.
Nat'l Network: Jones Radio Networks; AP Radio
Arbitron Metro Market: Cumberland,KY *Format:* Country, News, 74 *Special Programming:* Black one hr, farm one hr wkly *Hrs. of News Programming:* News progmg 9 hrs wkly *Target Audience:* 18-49; general *Adv.Rates:* 6; 5; 6; 5
Susan Burton, General Manager
Susan Burton, Station Manager
Laura Hewitt, News Director

Cynthiana

WCYN
09-01-1956; 1400 khz AM; 0.5 kw-D, ND1; 1 kw-N, ND1; N38 24 20 W84 17 32
10 Court Street, Cynthiana, KY 41031 US
(859) 234-1400, *Fax:* (859) 234-1425
www.wcyn.com
chris.winkle@wcyn.com
License: Cynthiana, KY held by WCYN Broadcasting Inc.
Nat'l Reps: Keystone (unwired net); Rgnl Reps
Arbitron Metro Market: Lexington, KY *Format:* Oldies *Target Audience:* General.
Chris Winkle, President
Chris Winkle, General Manager
Blake Bishop, News Director

WCYN-FM
06-01-1970; 102.3 mhz FM; 3.4 kw; 400 ft.; N38 24 39 W84 19 7
Rebroadcasts: Rebroadcasts WLXX(FM) Lexington 100%
10 Court Street, PO Box 398, Cynthiana, KY 41031 US
(859) 253-5900, *Fax:* (859) 253-5940
www.wvlkfm.net
License: Cynthiana, Harrison County, KY held by Cumulus Licensing LLC.
Group Owner: Cumulus Media Inc.; (acq 11-26-2002)
Arbitron Metro Market: Lexington, KY *Format:* Country
Ken Fearnow, General Manager

Danville

***WDFB-FM**
09-01-1992; 88.1 mhz FM *Hrs Open:* 24; 170 w; 328 ft; N37 35 46 W84 50 19
Mailing Address: Box 106, Danville, KY 40423
Second Address: 3596 Alum Springs Rd., Danville, KY 40422
(859) 236-9333, *Fax:* (859) 236-3348
www.wdfb.com
wdfb@wdfb.org
License: Danville, Boyle County, KY held by Alum Springs Educational Corp.
Nat'l Network: USA
Target Audience: General. *Adv. Rates:* 6; 6; 5
Mildred Drake, President
Mildred Drake, General Sales Mgr
Cindy Pike, News Director

WHIR
10-27-1947; 1230 khz AM *Hrs Open:* 24; 1 kw-U, ND1; N37 40 28 W84 46 6
324 West Main Street, Danville, KY 40422 US
(859) 236-2711, *Fax:* (859) 236-1461
www.hometownlive.net
hometownradio@bellsouth.net
License: Danville, KY held by Hometown Broadcasting of Danville Inc.
Nat'l Network: Westwood One; Motor Racing Net; Sporting News Radio Network; Talk Radio Network *Nat'l Reps:* Rgnl Reps
Arbitron Metro Market: Lexington-Fayette, KY *Format:* News, News/Talk, 86 *Hrs. of News Programming:* news progmg 2 hrs wkly *No. News Employees:* 1 *Target Audience:* 25-54; business owners, sports fans, housewives
Bruce Leslie, President
Jim Parman, Operations Dir
Robert Wagner, General Manager
Vicki Hyde, News Director

Drakesboro

WNTC
01-01-2001; 103.9 mhz FM; 1.95 kw; 407 ft.; N37 6 50 W87 3 52
4314 Cherry Court, Evansville, IN 47714 US
(615) 844-1039, *Fax:* (615) 777-2284
www.wnsr.com
info@wnsr.com
License: Drakesboro, Muhlenberg County, KY held by Nashville's SportsRadio Inc.
Group Owner: Southern Wabash Communications Corp.; (acq 10-17-01).
Arbitron Metro Market: Nashville, TN *Format:* Sports
Randolph Bell, President
Wayne DeSylvia, Station Manager

Edmonton

WHSX
04-05-1990; 99.1 mhz FM *Hrs Open:* 24; 6 kw; 328 ft.; N37 1 33 W85 33 14
P.O. Box 377, Edmonton, KY 42129 US
(270) 786-1000, *Fax:* (270) 786-4402
www.thehoss.com
991@scrtc.com
License: Edmonton, Metcalfe County, KY held by Hart County Communications Inc.
Arbitron Metro Market: Bowling Green, KY *Format:* Country
Special Programming: Farm 15 hrs wkly *Hrs. of News Programming:* news progmg 10 hrs wkly *No. News Employees:* 1 *Target Audience:* 25-54. *Adv.Rates:* 10; 10; 10; na
Dewayne Forbis, General Manager

Elizabethtown

WIEL
10-01-1950; 1400 khz AM *Hrs Open:* 24; 1 kw-U, ND1; N37 41 11 W85 52 19
406 South Mulberry St, Elizabethtown, KY 42701 US
(270) 763-0800, *Fax:* (270) 769-6349
License: Elizabethtown, KY held by Elizabethtown CBC Inc.
Group Owner: Commonwealth Broadcasting Corp.; (acq 5-12-00; grpsl)
Nat'l Network: ABC *Nat'l Reps:* Rgnl Reps *Wire Services:* AP
Format: Sports *Hrs. of News Programming:* news progmg one hr wkly *No. News Employees:* 1 *Target Audience:* 24-54; upscale adult *Adv. Rates:* 10; 8; 10; 4.50
Dan Michaels, Operations Dir
Roth Stratton, General Manager
Holli Lee, News Director
Misty Monroe, News

***WKUE**
10-15-1990; 90.9 mhz FM *Hrs Open:* 24; 5.2 kw; 633 ft.; N37 44 46 W85 53 18 *Rebroadcasts:* Rebroadcasts WKYU-FM Bowling Green 100%
College Heights, 1 Big Red Way, Bowling Green, KY 42101 US
(270) 745-5489, *Fax:* (270) 745-6272
www.wkufm.org
wkyufm@wku.edu
License: Elizabethtown, Hardin County, KY held by Western Kentucky University.
Nat'l Network: NPR; PRI
Format: News *Special Programming:* Jazz 15 hrs, folk 5 hrs wkly *Hrs. of News Programming:* news progmg 30 hrs wkly *No. News Employees:* 3 *Target Audience:* General.
Peter Bryant, General Manager

WQXE
11-24-1969; 98.3 mhz FM; 8.5 kw; 531 ft.; N37 43 18 W86 2 10
P. O. Box 517, Elizabethtown, KY 42702 US
(270) 737-8000, *Fax:* (270) 737-7229
www.wqxe.com
bill@wqxe.com
License: Elizabethtown, Hardin County, KY held by Skytower Communications E'town Inc.
Nat'l Network: Westwood One
Format: Adult Contemp *Target Audience:* 25-54; upscale, dual income families *Adv. Rates:* 31; 29; 31; 25
Bill Evans, President

Elkhorn City

WEKB
11-24-1979; 1460 khz AM *Hrs Open:* 24; 5 kw-D, ND1; 0.114 kw-N, ND1; N37 18 25 W82 19 53 *Rebroadcasts:* Simulcast with WPKE(AM) Pikeville 100%
Mailing Address: PO Box 2200, 1240 Radio Drive, Pikeville, KY 41502 US
Second Address: 1240 Radio Dr., Pikeville, KY 41501
(606) 437-4051, *Fax:* (606) 432-2809
www.myoldiesradio.com
wdhr@wdhr.com
License: Elkhorn City, KY held by East Kentucky Broadcasting Corp.
Group Owner: East Kentucky Broadcasting Corp.; (acq 6-94; $480,000 with co-located FM).
Nat'l Network: ABC *Regional Reps:* Rgnl Reps
Arbitron Metro Market: Pikeville,KY *Format:* Oldies *Target Audience:* 25-49.
Walter E. May, CEO/COO
Cindy May Johnson, President
Cindy May Johnson, General Manager
Dan P'Pool, Director of Sales
Paul Manuel, Chief Engineer

Elkton

WEKT
07-21-1977; 1070 khz AM
P.O. Box 577, Elkton, KY 42220 US
(270) 265-5636, *Fax:* (270) 265-5637
www.wektgospelradio.com/
wektan1070@yahoo.com
License: Elkton, KY held by M&R Broadcasting Inc.
Nat'l Network: USA
Arbitron Metro Market: Elkton, KY *Format:* Gospel
Marshall Sidebottom, General Manager
Nick Reed, Owner

Eminence

WLUE
06-01-1956; 1600 khz AM; 500 w-D, 48 w-N; N38 21 02 W85 11 11
111 S. First St., La Grange, KY 40019
(502) 222-9171, *Fax:* (502) 222-9173
www.latina1600.com
License: Eminence, Henry County, KY held by Metro East CBC Inc.
Group Owner: Commonwealth Broadcasting Corp.; (acq 4-13-00; $600,000 with WTSZ-FM Eminence).
Population Served: 16,000 *Arbitron Metro Market:* Louisville, KY *Target Audience:* 25-54.
Dugan Ryan, General Manager

WTUV-FM
07-04-1988; 105.7 mhz FM; 3 kw; 328 ft.; N38 21 9 W85 11 9
P.O. Box 655, New Albany, IN 47151 US
(502) 671-8407, *Fax:* (502) 671-8743
www.lacalienteradio.com
info@lacalienteradio.com
License: Eminence, Henry County, KY held by Davidson Media Station WTSZ Licensee LLC.
Group Owner: Davidson Media Group LLC; (acq 5-3-2006; $500,000)
Arbitron Metro Market: Louisville, KY
Catalina Ibarra, Station Manager
Paul Dendy, General Sales Mgr
Dennis Mendez, Programming Director
Jenny Sanchez, Traffic Manager

Erlanger

WIZF
09-22-1965; 101.1 mhz FM; 2.5 kw; 509 ft.; N39 6 18 W84 33 25
1821 Summit Road, Suite 400, Cincinnati, OH 45237 US
(513) 679-6000, *Fax:* (513) 679-6014
wiznation.com
stharris@radio-one.com
License: Erlanger, Kenton County, KY held by Blue Chip Broadcasting Licenses Ltd.
Group Owner: Radio One Inc.; (acq 4-30-2001; grpsl).
Arbitron Metro Market: Cincinnati, OH *Format:* Adult Contemp *Target Audience:* 18-54.
Alfred Wiggins, CEO
Barry Mayo, President
Lisa Thal, General Manager
Sharon McCormick, General Sales Mgr
Stephen Harris, Programming Director

Falmouth

WIOK
06-01-1981; 107.5 mhz FM *Hrs Open:* 24; 1.35 kw; 696 ft.; N38 35 13 W84 21 40
13297 Green Road, Walton, KY 41094 US
(859) 472-1075, *Fax:* (859) 472-2875
wiok@fuse.net
License: Falmouth, Pendleton County, KY held by Hammond Broadcasting Inc.
Nat'l Network: USA *Nat'l Reps:* Rgnl Reps
Arbitron Metro Market: Cincinnati, OH *Format:* Gospel *Hrs. of News Programming:* News progmg 12 hrs wkly *Target Audience:* 25-64; women *Adv. Rates:* 144; 108; 144; 120
Jan Hammond, Operations Dir
Jamie Porter, General Sales Mgr

Fearsville

***WYJZ**
91.7 mhz FM; kw
US
(317) 467-1062
License: Fearsville, Christian County, KY held by Electronic Applications Radio Service Inc.
Group Owner: Electronic Applications Radio Service Inc.
Arbitron Metro Market: Lebanon, IN
Patrick Diemer, President

Flemingsburg

WFLE
11-01-1981; 1060 khz AM; 0.5 kw-D, DAD; N38 27 1 W83 44 6
Route 3, #1 Radio Drive, Flemingsbury, KY 41041 US
(606) 849-4433, *Fax:* (606) 845-9353
License: Flemingsburg, KY held by DreamCatcher Communications Inc.
Group Owner: DreamCatcher Communications Inc.; acq 5-23-02; $607,491 with co-located FM).
Format: Country, Gospel *Target Audience:* 25-54.
Don Bowles, President
Carl Haight, General Manager
Kim Hester, General Sales Mgr
Eddie Plummer, Promotions Manager

WFLE-FM
02-01-1993; 95.1 mhz FM; 1.61 kw; 449 ft; N38 24 42 W83 34 41
334 Recreation Park Rd., Flemingsburg, KY 41041
(606) 849-4433, *Fax:* (606) 845-9353
License: Flemingsburg, Fleming County, KY held by Dreamcatcher Communications
Group Owner: Donald Venita Bawles; 09/20/2004

Donald Bawles, President
Kim Hester, Station Manager
Kim Hester, General Sales Mgr
Eddie Plummer, Programming Director
Eddie Plummer, News Director
Tyrone Henry, Chief Engineer

Florence

WDJO(AM)
09-01-1984; 1160 khz AM *Hrs Open:* 24; 5 kw-D, 990 w-N, DA-2; N38 58 09 W84 40 56
635 W. 7th St., Suite 400, Cincinnati, OH 45203
(513) 421-1480, *Fax:* (513) 421-1486
www.oldies1480.net
mikegavin@oldies1480.net
License: Florence, Boone County, KY held by Christian Broadcasting System Ltd.
Group Owner: Christian Broadcasting System Ltd.; (acq 2-10-2006; swap of WDJO(AM) and WCVX(AM) Cincinnati, OH plus $6.75 million cash for WLQV(AM) Detroit, MI).
Population Served: 296,223 *Arbitron Metro Market:* Cincinnati, OH *Format:* Oldies *Hrs. of News Programming:* News progmg 6 hrs wkly *Target Audience:* 25-54; 35-64; adults *Adv. Rates:* 50; 45; 50; 15
Jon Yinger, President
Rodger Kay, Operations Dir
Brian Kauffman, General Manager
Gary Stephens, Station Manager
Michael Gavin, General Sales Mgr
Dusty Rhodes, Programming Director
Ben Clinkenbeard, Account Executive
AndreaTaylor, Office Manager

Fort Campbell

WEGI
07-27-1963; 1370 khz AM *Hrs Open:* 24; 1 kw-D, ND1; 0.053 kw-N, ND1; N36 38 28 W87 26 1
P.O. Box 2249, Clarksville, TN 37042 US
(320) 252-6200, *Fax:* (320) 252-9367
www.wmin1010.com
License: Fort Campbell, KY held by Saga Communications of Tuckessee L.L.C.
Group Owner: Saga Communications Inc.; (acq 2-1-2001; grpsl)
Arbitron Metro Market: Evanston WY *Format:* Adult Contemp
Herb Hoppe, General Manager
Doug Kertz, General Sales Mgr
Gary Moore, Programming Director

WCVQ
08-01-1969; 107.9 mhz FM *Hrs Open:* 24; 100 kw; 902 ft.; N36 32 23 W87 39 45
P.O. Box 2249, Clarksville, TN 37042 US
(931) 648-7720, *Fax:* (931) 648-7769
www.q108.com
Ryan@Q108.com
License: Fort Campbell, Christian County, KY held by Saga Communications of Tuckessee LLC.
Group Owner: Saga Communications Inc.; (acq 2-1-2001; grpsl)
Arbitron Metro Market: Clarksville-Hopkinsville, TN *Format:* Adult Contemp *Hrs. of News Programming:* news progmg 2 hrs wkly *No. News Employees:* 1 *Target Audience:* 25-40.
Scott Chase, Operations Dir
Katie Gambill, General Manager

Fort Knox

WLVK
10-01-1967; 105.5 mhz FM *Hrs Open:* 24; 3.2 kw; 456 ft.; N37 46 57 W85 54 38
Mailing Address: P.O. Box 2481, Elizabethtown, KY 42701 US
Second Address: 519 N. Miles St., Elizabethtown, KY 42702
(270) 766-1035, *Fax:* (270) 769-1052
www.bigcat1055.com
wlvk@bigcat1055.com
License: Fort Knox, Hardin County, KY held by W & B Broadcasting Co. Inc.
Arbitron Metro Market: Fort Knox, KY *Format:* Country *Special Programming:* Lou Helton Country Countdown *Hrs. of News Programming:* 4 hrs wkly *No. News Employees:* 14 *Target Audience:* 25-49; young & middleage country fans *Adv. Rates:* 32; 32; 32; 8
Bill Walters, President
Cale Tharp, Operations Dir
Rene Bell, General Manager

Fort Thomas

WYGY
01-01-1925; 97.3 mhz FM *Hrs Open:* 24; 2.55 kw; 509 ft.; N39 12 1 W84 31 22
600 New Hampshire Ave., N.W., Suite 1200, Washington, DC 20037 US
(513) 699-5959, *Fax:* (513) 699-5000
theworldwidewolf.com
rjames@theworldwidewolf.com
License: Fort Thomas, Butler County, KY held by Bonneville Holding Co.
Group Owner: Bonneville International Corporation; (acq 3-14-2008; grpsl)
Arbitron Metro Market: Cincinnati, OH *Format:* Country *Hrs. of News Programming:* News progmg 8 hrs wkly
Mike Fredrick, General Manager
Christine Mello, General Sales Mgr
Travis Moon, Programming Director

WYGY(FM)
04-18-1994; 97.3 mhz FM *Hrs Open:* 24; 2.55 kw; Ant 508 ft; N39 12 01 W84 31 22
2060 Reading Rd., Cincinnati, OH 45202
(513) 699-5959, *Fax:* (513) 699-5000
www.973thesound.com
License: Fort Thomas, Campbell County, KY held by Bonneville Holding Co.
Group Owner: Bonneville International Corporation; (acq 3-14-2008; grpsl)
Population Served: 395,000 *Arbitron Metro Market:* Cincinnati, OH *Format:* Alternative *Hrs. of News Programming:* News progmg 4 hrs wkly

Jim Bryant, Operations Dir
Rory Flynn, General Sales Mgr
Jay Kruz, Programming Director

Frankfort

WKYW
02-01-1946; 1490 khz AM *Hrs Open:* 24
P.O. Box 1505, Glasgow, KY 42142 US
(502) 875-1130, *Fax:* (502) 875-1225
License: Frankfort, KY held by Forever South Licenses LLC.
Group Owner: Forever Communications Inc.; (acq 11-1-2007; grpsl)
Nat'l Network: Westwood One *Nat'l Reps:* Rgnl Reps
Format: Oldies *Hrs. of News Programming:* news progmg 12 hrs wkly *No. News Employees:* 2 *Target Audience:* 25-55. *Adv. Rates:* 28; 16; 18; 14
Brian Sands, General Manager

WSTV-FM
04-15-1991; 103.7 mhz FM *Hrs Open:* 24; 2.5 kw; 358 ft.; N38 13 17 W84 54 52
P.O. Box 1505, Glasgow, KY 42142 US
(502) 875-1130, *Fax:* (502) 875-1225
www.star1037.com
License: Frankfort, Franklin County, KY held by Forever South Licenses LLC.
Group Owner: Forever Communications Inc.; (acq 11-1-2007; grpsl)
Nat'l Network: Westwood One
Format: Adult Contemp *Hrs. of News Programming:* news progmg 4 hrs wkly *No. News Employees:* 2 *Target Audience:* 25-54.
Brian Sands, General Manager

WFKY
01-01-1967; 104.9 mhz FM *Hrs Open:* 24; 3.4 kw; 282 ft.; N38 13 18 W84 54 54
P.O. Box 1505, Glasgow, KY 42142 US
(502) 875-1130, *Fax:* (502) 875-1225
www.myfroggyville.com
gator@capcityradio.com
License: Frankfort, Franklin County, KY
Group Owner: Forever Communications Inc.
Format: Country *Hrs. of News Programming:* news progmg 168 hrs wkly *No. News Employees:* 2 *Target Audience:* 25-54. *Adv. Rates:* 18; 18; 18; 18
Brian Sands, General Manager
Jim Beam, Disc Jockey
Sally Mander, Disc Jockey
James Pond, Disc Jockey

Franklin

WFKN
04-25-1954; 1220 khz AM *Hrs Open:* 24; 0.25 kw-D, ND1; 0.09 kw-N, ND1; N36 44 20 W86 34 42
400 South Record Street, Dallas, TX 75202 US
(270) 586-4481, *Fax:* (270) 586-6031
www.franklinfavorite.com
wfkn@franklinfavorite.com
License: Franklin, KY held by WFKN LLC
Nat'l Reps: Rgnl Reps
Format: Country *Special Programming:* Relg, farm 6 hrs wkly *Hrs. of News Programming:* news progmg 16 hrs wkly *No. News Employees:* 2 *Target Audience:* General.
Kendra Holt, CFO
Jamie Johnson, General Manager
Brownie Bennett, General Sales Mgr
Shelly Jent, News Director
James Mooneyhan, Sports Announcer
Charlie Portmann, News and Sports Editor

Fulton

WWKF
09-01-1954; 99.3 mhz FM *Hrs Open:* 24; 3 kw; 299 ft.; N36 27 59 W88 56 47
1729 Nailing Drive, Union City, TN 38261 US
(731) 885-1240, *Fax:* (731) 885-3405
www.kf99kq105.com
acetj@acetj.com
License: Fulton, Fulton County, KY held by WENK of Union City Inc.
Group Owner: WENK of Union City Inc.; (acq 10-1-82; $473,131; *Nat'l Reps:* Rgnl Reps
Arbitron Metro Market: Fulton, KY *Format:* Contemporary Hits/Top 40 *No. News Employees:* 1 *Target Audience:* 18-34.
Terry Hailey, President & General Manager
Jerry McCain, Traffic Manager
JimAdcock, Sales Rep
Lorrie Matlock, Sales Rep
Brent Hinson, Website Enquiry

***WKMT**
89.5 mhz FM; 4.5 kw; 353 ft.; N36 34 10 W88 50 13 US
(270) 809-4745, *Fax:* (270) 809-4667
www.wkms.org
License: Fulton, Fulton County, KY held by Board of Regents, Murray State University.
Arbitron Metro Market: Fulton, KY *Format:* Variety/Diverse
Randy Dunn, President
Kate Lochte, Station Manager

Garrison

WOKE
09-07-1998; 98.3 mhz FM; 5.2 kw; 351 ft.; N38 36 26 W83 2 33
P.O. Box 889, Blacksburg, VA 24063 US
(606) 932-2223, *Fax:* (606) 932-6132
www.wokejoyfm.org
info@wokejoyfm.org
License: Garrison, Lewis County, KY held by Big River Radio Inc.
TV Affiliate: Relg

Georgetown

***WKVO**
10-01-1963; 89.9 mhz FM *Hrs Open:* 24; 50 kw; 410 ft.; N38 12 15 W84 32 51
400 E College St, Georgetown, KY 40324 US
(916) 251-1600
www.klove.com
klove@klove.com
License: Georgetown, Scott County, KY held by Educational Media Foundation.
Group Owner: EMF Broadcasting; (acq 3-12-2004; $1.7 million).
Nat'l Network: K-Love
Arbitron Metro Market: Lexington-Fayet *Format:* Religious
Darrell Chambliss, Chairman
Alan Mason, COO
Mike Novak, President
Chip Bailey, Operations Dir
David Pierce, Programming Director
Ed Lenane, News Director
Sam Wallington, Engineering Dir
Marya Morgan, News Reporter
RichardHunt, News Reporter
Tracy Butler, Traffic Manager

WWTF
09-06-1957; 1580 khz AM; 10 kw-D, DA2; 0.045 kw-N, DA2; N38 10 5 W84 35 37
50 East Rivercenter Blvd, Covington, KY 41011 US
(859) 422-1000, *Fax:* (859) 422-1071
www.groovin1580.com
Christyshaw@clearchannel.com
License: Georgetown, KY held by Citicasters Licenses L.P.
Group Owner: Clear Channel Communications Inc.; (acq 6-30-97; grpsl)
Nat'l Reps: Christal
Arbitron Metro Market: Lexington, KY *Format:* Urban Contemporary *Hrs. of News Programming:* News progmg 2 hrs wkly *Adv. Rates:* 12; 12; 12; 4
Gene Guinn, General Manager

WXZZ
09-10-1973; 103.3 mhz FM; 6 kw; 328 ft.; N38 3 56 W84 29 13
111 East Kilbourn Avenue, Suite 2700, Milwaukee, WI 53202 US
(859) 253-5900, *Fax:* (859) 253-5940
www.zrock103.com
john.lewis@cumulus.com
License: Georgetown, Scott County, KY held by Cumulus Licensing Corp.
Group Owner: Cumulus Media Inc.; (acq 7-22-99; grpsl)
Arbitron Metro Market: Lexington, KY *No. News Employees:* 3 *Target Audience:* 18-34. *Adv. Rates:* 30; 30; 30; 15
John Lewis, General Manager
Scott Frazier, General Sales Mgr
Mario Anderson, Promotions Manager

Glasgow

WCLU
09-25-1946; 1490 khz AM
PO Box 1628, Glasgow, KY 42142 US
(270) 651-9149, *Fax:* (270) 651-9222
www.wcluradio.com
emilyrose@wcluradio.com
License: Glasgow, KY held by Royse Radio Inc.
Nat'l Network: CBS
Arbitron Metro Market: Bowling Green, KY *Format:* Variety/Diverse *Target Audience:* 30 plus; listeners with disposable income
Henry Royse, President
Henry Royse, General Manager

WLYE-FM
01-01-1997; 94.1 mhz FM *Hrs Open:* 24; 4.5 kw; 299 ft.; N36 59 2 W85 52 20
P.O. Box 1628, Glasgow, KY 42142 US
(270) 843-3333, *Fax:* (270) 843-0454
mark@forevercom.com
License: Glasgow, Barren County, KY held by Forever Communications Inc.
Group Owner: Forever Communications Inc.; acq 9-3-03).
Nat'l Reps: Christal
Arbitron Metro Market: Bowling Green, KY *Format:* Country *Hrs. of News Programming:* news progmg 6 hrs wkly *No. News Employees:* 1 *Target Audience:* 25-54; adults, serving southern central Kentucky *Adv. Rates:* 20; 20; 20; 10
Christine Hillard, President
Mark Mackey, General Manager

WOVO
07-14-1972; 105.3 mhz FM; 15 kw; 433 ft.; N36 58 50 W86 6 10
Mailing Address: P.O. Box 1505, Glasgow, KY 42142 US
Second Address: 113 W. Public Sq., Suite 400, Glasgow, KY 42141
(270) 651-6050, *Fax:* (270) 651-7666
www.my1053.com
wovo@cbcradio.net
License: Glasgow, Barren County, KY held by Newberry Broadcasting Inc.
Group Owner: Commonwealth Broadcasting Corp.; (acq 11-25-97; grpsl)
Arbitron Metro Market: Bowling Green, KY *Format:* Oldies
Derron Steenbergen, General Manager
Kelly McKay, Programming Director

***WSGP**
01-01-2002; 88.3 mhz FM; 13 kw; 299 ft.; N36 49 5 W85 41 30
Mailing Address: 93 Rainbow Terrace Rd., Somerset, KY 42503 US
Second Address: 93 Rainbow Terr., Glasgow, KY
(800) 408-8888, *Fax:* (606) 679-1342
www.kingofkingsradio.net
dcradio@alltel.net
License: Glasgow, Barren County, KY held by Somerset Educational Broadcasting Foundation.
Arbitron Metro Market: Somerset, KY *Format:* Religious
David Carr, General Manager
Carolyn Jones, Programming Director
Marvin Whitaker, Chief Engineer

WCDS
01-01-2007; 1230 khz AM
Mailing Address: US
Second Address: 113 W Public Sq., Suite 400, Glasgow, KY 42141
(270) 651-6050, *Fax:* (270) 651-7666
License: Glasgow, KY held by Anderson Communications LLC.
Nat'l Network: ESPN Radio
Arbitron Metro Market: Glasgow, KY *Format:* Sports
Charles Anderson, General Manager

Grand Rivers

WCBL-FM
03-03-1966; 99.1 mhz FM; 16 kw; 417 ft.; N37 6 47 W88 21 34
P.O. Box 387, 1039 Egner's Ferry Road, Benton, KY 42025 US
(270) 527-3102, *Fax:* (270) 527-5606
www.thelakecurrent.com
wcbl@freelandbroadcasting.com
License: Grand Rivers, Marshall County, KY
Group Owner: Freeland Broadcasting Stations
Format: Oldies *Adv. Rates:* Same as AM
Chad Winstead, Programming Director

Grayson

WGOH
06-01-1959; 1370 khz AM *Hrs Open:* 6 AM-2 hrs past sunset; 5 kw-D, ND1; 0.021 kw-N, ND1; N38 19 44 W82 58 33
PO Box 487, Grayson, KY 41143 US
(606) 474-5144, *Fax:* (606) 474-7777
www.wgohwugo.com
mail @wgohwugo.com
License: Grayson, KY held by Carter County Broadcasting Co.
Nat'l Network: CBS *Regional Network:* Ky. News Net *Nat'l Reps:* Rgnl Reps *Wire Services:* AP
Arbitron Metro Market: Huntington-Ashland, WV-KY *Format:* Country *Special Programming:* Bluegrass *Hrs. of News*

Programming: news progmg 30 hrs wkly *No. News Employees:* 1 *Target Audience:* 35-65. *Adv.Rates:* 5; 4; 4; na
Jeff Roe, Operations Dir
Francis Nash, General Manager
Mike Phillips, Programming Director
Jim Phillips, News Director
William Craig, Engineering Dir
Melodie Carter, Traffic Manager

WUGO
02-01-1967; 102.3 mhz FM *Hrs Open:* 24; 4.8 kw; 360 ft; N38 19 44 W82 58 33
Box 487, 150 Radio Tower Dr., Grayson, KY 41143
(606) 474-5144, *Fax:* (606) 474-7777
www.wgohwugo.com
License: Grayson, Carter County, KY held by Carter County Broadcasting Co. Inc.
Nat'l Reps: Rgnl Reps *Wire Services:* AP
Arbitron Metro Market: Huntington-Ashland, WV-KY *Hrs. of News Programming:* News progmg 30 hrs wkly *Target Audience:* 25-54. *Adv. Rates:* 8; 6; 6; na
Francis Nash, General Manager

Greensburg

WGRK-FM
12-15-1977; 105.7 mhz FM *Hrs Open:* 24; 5.1 kw; 358 ft.; N37 15 34 W85 30 57
Mailing Address: P.O. Box 457, Glasgow, KY 42141 US
Second Address: 50 Friendship Pike, Greensburg, KY 42719
(270) 932-7401, *Fax:* (270) 789-1450
www.kcountry1057.com
wgrk@commonwealthbroadcasting.com
License: Greensburg, Green County, KY held by Green County CBC, Inc.
Group Owner: Commonwealth Broadcasting Corp.
Format: Country *No. News Employees:* 1
Steve Newberry, President
Marty Bagby, Operations Dir
Barb Smith, General Manager
Greg Gribbins, General Sales Mgr
Trent Ford, Programming Director

Greenup

WLGC
04-01-1985; 1520 khz AM; 5 kw-D; N38 35 44 W82 51 20
1401 Winchester Ave., Ashland, KY 41144
(606) 920-9565, *Fax:* (606) 920-9523
License: Greenup, Greenup County, KY held by Greenup County Broadcasting Inc.
Nat'l Network: Sporting News Radio Network
Arbitron Metro Market: Huntington-Ashl *No. News Employees:* 1
Mark Justice, Operations Dir
Bobby Hall, General Manager
Scott Martin, Station Manager
Jim Forest, General Sales Mgr
Fred Francis, Chief Engineer

WLGC-FM
09-01-1982; 105.7 mhz FM; 12.5 kw; 466 ft.; N38 35 44 W82 51 22
P.O. Box 685, Greenup, KY 41144 US
(606) 920-9565, *Fax:* (606) 920-9523
www.wlgcradio.com
wlgc@inet99.net
License: Greenup, Greenup County, KY held by Greenup County Broadcasting Inc.
Regional Network: Ky. News Net *Wire Services:* AP
Arbitron Metro Market: Huntington-Ashland, WV-KY *Format:* Country *Hrs. of News Programming:* news progmg 3 hrs wkly *No. News Employees:* 1 *Target Audience:* 25-54; middle income listeners *Adv. Rates:* 15;13; 14; 10
Bob Hall, General Manager
Scott Martin, General Sales Mgr
Mark Justice, Programming Director

Greenville

WKYA
12-11-1981; 105.5 mhz FM; 3 kw horiz, 2.6 kw vert; 299 ft.; N37 11 45 W87 12 38
Highway 63 West, Box 471, Central City, KY 42330 US
(270) 338-6655, *Fax:* (270) 338-7388
License: Greenville, Muhlenberg County, KY held by Starlight Broadcasting Co.
Group Owner: Starlight Broadcasting Co.; acq 1996; grpsl).
Format: Oldies *Target Audience:* 18-40.
Andy Anderson, CEO
Richard Neathamer, Operations Dir
Stan Barnett, General Manager

Hardinsburg

WULF
07-09-1970; 94.3 mhz FM; 40 kw; 525 ft.; N37 52 18 W86 16 4
P.O. Box 1450, Corbin, KY 40702 US
(270) 765-0943, *Fax:* (270) 737-7229
943wulf.com
jodie@wqxe.com
License: Hardinsburg, Breckinridge County, KY held by Skytower Communications - 94.3 LLC
Arbitron Metro Market: Hardinsburg, KY *Format:* Country
Bill Evans, President

WXBC
08-15-1992; 104.3 mhz FM *Hrs Open:* 24; 2.3 kw; 377 ft.; N37 46 14 W86 26 7
Mailing Address: P.O. Box 104, Hardinsburg, KY 42301 US
Second Address: 110 S. Main St., Hardinsburg, KY 40143
(270) 756-1043, *Fax:* (270) 756-1086
wxbc1043.com
wxbc@bbtel.com
License: Hardinsburg, Breckinridge County, KY held by Breckinridge Broadcasting Co. Inc.
Nat'l Network: Fox News Radio
Arbitron Metro Market: Hardinsburg, KY *Format:* Country *Hrs. of News Programming:* news progmg 15 hrs wkly *No. News Employees:* 1 *Target Audience:* 25-55. *Adv. Rates:* 10;10;10;10
Jo Ann Keenan, CEO
Dennis Day, Operations Dir
Ken Thornhill, News Director
Amanda Zimmer, Office Manager
Terry Henning Hopfer, Advertising Sales Manager

Harlan

WFSR
04-01-1976; 970 khz AM; 5 kw-D, ND1; 0.024 kw-N, ND1; N36 52 2 W83 19 36
Mailing Address: PO Box 818, 125 S. Main St, Harlan, KY 40831 US
Second Address: 125 S. Main, Harlan, KY 40831
(606) 573-1470, *Fax:* (606) 573-1473
wtuk-wfsr@harlanonline.net
License: Harlan, KY held by Eastern Broadcasting Co.
Format: Gospel *Target Audience:* 25-54; adult purchasers
Jeff Capps, General Manager

WHLN
05-30-1941; 1410 khz AM; 5 kw-D, 94 w-N; N36 52 02 W83 19 36
Mailing Address: Box 898, Harlan, KY 40831
Second Address: 100 Eversole St., Suite 1, Harlan, KY 40831
(606) 573-2540, *Fax:* (606) 573-7557
whln@harlanonline.net
License: Harlan, Harlan County, KY held by Radio Harlan Inc.
Nat'l Network: ABC *Nat'l Reps:* Rgnl Reps *Wire Services:* AP
Population Served: 200,000*Target Audience:* 25-54. *Adv. Rates:* 14; 14; 14; 14
James O. Morgan, President
James O. Morgan, General Manager

WTUK
06-26-1991; 105.1 mhz FM; 0.53 kw; 1037 ft.; N36 54 9 W83 18 1
Mailing Address: P.O. Box 818, Harlan, KY 40831 US
Second Address: 125 S. Main, Harlan, KY 40831
(606) 573-1470, *Fax:* (606) 573-1473
www.wtuk1051.com
info@wtuk1051.com
License: Harlan, Harlan County, KY
Arbitron Metro Market: Harlan, KY *Format:* Country *Special Programming:* Sports, news *Hrs. of News Programming:* News prgmg every hour
Jeff Capps, Station Manager
Charles Anthony, Programming Director

Harold

WXLR
01-01-1994; 104.9 mhz FM; 0.37 kw; 922 ft.; N37 31 59 W82 29 40
Us Hwy 23 Main Street, Paulsboro Row, Harold, KY 41635 US
(606) 478-1200, *Fax:* (606) 478-4202
License: Harold, Floyd County, KY held by Adam D. Gearheart.
Arbitron Metro Market: Pikeville, KY *Format:* Country
Adam Gearheart, President

Harrodsburg

WHBN
06-25-1955; 1420 khz AM *Hrs Open:* 24; 1 kw-D, ND1; 0.046 kw-N, ND1; N37 44 3 W84 48 50
3270 Blazer Parkway, Suite 101, Lexington, KY 40509 US
(859) 236-2711, *Fax:* (859) 236-1461
www.hometownlive.net
hometownradio@bellsouth.net
License: Harrodsburg, KY held by Hometown Broadcasting of Harrodsburg Inc.
Nat'l Network: Jones Radio Networks; AP Radio *Regional Network:* Ky. News Net *Nat'l Reps:* Rgnl Reps *Regional Reps:* Rgnl Reps.
Arbitron Metro Market: Lexington-Fayette, KY *Format:* Country, Gospel *Hrs. of News Programming:* news progmg 21 hrs wkly *No. News Employees:* 1 *Target Audience:* General; residents of Mercer county *Adv. Rates:* Call
Jim Parman, Operations Dir
Robert Wagner, General Manager
Vicki Hyde, News Director

Hartford

WXMZ
05-18-1972; 99.9 mhz FM *Hrs Open:* 16; 6 kw; 328 ft; N37 26 36 W86 53 57 *Rebroadcasts:* Rebroadcasts WKYA(FM) Greenville 100%
Box 106, Hartford, KY 42330
(270) 298-3268, *Fax:* (270) 298-9326
www.wxmzfm.com
info@wxmzfm.com
License: Hartford, Ohio County, KY held by Starlight Broadcasting Co Inc
Population Served: 2,700 *Arbitron Metro Market:* Hartford, KY
Sherri Sawyer, General Manager
Dan Baron, General Sales Mgr
Michael Webb, Programming Director
Paula Davis, Promotions Manager
Gennora Reed, General Sales Manager

Hawesville

WKCM
11-07-1972; 1160 khz AM *Hrs Open:* 24; 2.5 kw-D, DAN; 1 kw-N, DAN; N37 54 20 W86 45 30
PO Box 150846, Nashville, TN 37215 US
(270) 683-5200, *Fax:* (270) 688-0108
www.owensbororadio.com
dpowers@cromwellradio.com
License: Hawesville, KY held by Hancock Communications Inc.
Group Owner: The Cromwell Group Inc.
Format: Country *Special Programming:* Farm 3 hrs, sports 6 hrs wkly *Hrs. of News Programming:* news progmg 10 hrs wkly *No. News Employees:* 1 *Target Audience:* 25-54; general *Adv. Rates:* 5; 5; 5; 3.50
Bayard Walters, President
Dale Powers, General Manager
Jeff Nalley, General Sales Mgr
Jeff Morgan, Programming Director
Amy Spalding, News Director

Hazard

***WEKH**
02-01-1985; 90.9 mhz FM *Hrs Open:* 24; 31 kw; 1063 ft.; N37 11 35 W83 11 17 *Rebroadcasts:* Rebroadcasts WEKU-FM Richmond 100%
102 Perkins Building, Richmond, KY 40475 US
(859) 622-1660, *Fax:* (859) 622-6276
www.weku.fm
wekunews@eku.edu
License: Hazard, Perry County, KY held by Board of Regents, Eastern Kentucky University.
Nat'l Network: NPR; PRI *Wire Services:* AP
Arbitron Metro Market: Hazard, KY *Format:* News *Hrs. of News Programming:* news progmg 35 hrs wkly *No. News Employees:* 3 *Target Audience:* General.
Mary Ellyn Cain, Operations Dir
Tim Singleton, General Manager
Carol Siler, General Sales Mgr
Laura Allen, Programming Director
Charles Compton, News Director
Bill Browning, Chief Engineer

WJMD
07-26-1989; 104.7 mhz FM *Hrs Open:* 24; 0.48 kw; 1135 ft.; N37 11 36 W83 11 4
Mailing Address: P.O. Box 7001, Hazard, KY 41702 US
Second Address: 516 Main Street, Hazard, KY 41701
(606) 439-3358, *Fax:* (606) 439-3371
www.reason.kzoo.edu/wjmd
wjmd@windstream.net
License: Hazard, Perry County, KY held by Hazard Broadcasting Services
Nat'l Network: Salem Radio Network

Format: Religious *Hrs. of News Programming:* news progmg 7 hrs wkly *No. News Employees:* 2 *Target Audience:* General.
Michael Barnett, General Manager

WKIC(AM)
11-23-1947; 1390 khz AM; 5 kw-D; N37 14 19 W83 12 41
Mailing Address: Box 7428, Hazard, KY 41702
Second Address: 516 Main St., Hazard, KY 41701
(606) 436-2121, *Fax:* (606) 436-4172
wsgsfm@alltel.net
License: Hazard, Perry County, KY held by Mountain Broadcasting Service Inc.
Nat'l Network: Westwood One *Nat'l Reps:* Rgnl Reps
Population Served: 5,459
Faron Sparkman, General Manager

WQXY
03-01-1988; 1560 khz AM; 0.5 kw-C, NDD; 1 kw-D, NDD; N37 16 27 W83 11 29
PO Box 1981, Hazard, KY 41701 US
(606) 785-6129, *Fax:* (606) 785-0106
info@wqmg.com
License: Hazard, KY held by Black Gold Broadcasting.
Nat'l Network: Jones Radio Networks; AP Radio; CNN Radio
Format: Oldies *Target Audience:* 25-54; educated, mobile, child-rearing couples in suburbs, blue collar workers
Randy Thompson, General Manager

WSGS
02-03-1959; 101.1 mhz FM; 100 kw horiz, 88 kw vert; 1463 ft.; N37 11 38 W83 10 52
P.O. Box 7898, Hazard, KY 41701 US
(606) 436-2121, *Fax:* (606) 436-4172
www.wsgs.com
wsgsfm@alltel.net
License: Hazard, Perry County, KY held by Mountain Broadcasting Service Inc.
Nat'l Network: ABC *Regional Network:* Ky. News Net
Format: Country
John Hill, General Manager

Henderson

WGBF-FM
12-01-1971; 103.1 mhz FM *Hrs Open:* 24; 3.2 kw; 453 ft.; N37 46 54 W87 37 24
136 Main St, Suite 202, Westport, CT 06880 US
(812) 425-4226, *Fax:* (812) 421-0005
www.103gbfrocks.com
info@103gbfrocks.com
License: Henderson, Henderson County, KY
Group Owner: Townsquare Media; (acq 12-3-2003; grpsl).
Nat'l Network: ABC
Arbitron Metro Market: Evansville, IN *Format:* Rock/AOR *No. News Employees:* 1 *Target Audience:* 18-49. *Adv. Rates:* 60; 45; 50; 20
Mark Thomas, General Manager
Mike Sanders, Programming Director
Bobby Gates, Promotions Manager

WKDQ
01-01-1947; 99.5 mhz FM *Hrs Open:* 24; 98 kw; 984 ft.; N37 52 57 W87 32 28
P.O. Box 3353, Evansville, IN 47732 US
(812) 425-4226
www.wkdq.com
info@wkdq.com
License: Henderson, Henderson County, KY
Group Owner: Townsquare Media; (acq 2-25-03; grpsl).
Nat'l Reps: Christal
Arbitron Metro Market: Evansville, IN *Format:* Country *No. News Employees:* 2 *Target Audience:* 25-54.
Jon Prell, Programming Director
Lori Tevault, Promotions Manager

***WKPB**
04-01-1990; 89.5 mhz FM *Hrs Open:* 24; 43 kw; 377 ft.; N37 51 6 W87 19 43 *Rebroadcasts:* Rebroadcasts WKYU-FM Bowling Green 100%
1 Big Red Way, Bowling Green, KY 42101 US
(270) 745-5489, *Fax:* (270) 745-6272
www.wkyufm.org
wkyufm@wku.edu
License: Henderson, Henderson County, KY held by Western Kentucky University.
Nat'l Network: NPR; PRI
Arbitron Metro Market: Evansville, IN *Format:* News *Hrs. of News Programming:* news progmg 35 hrs wkly *No. News Employees:* 3 *Target Audience:* General.
Peter Bryant, General Manager

WSON
12-17-1941; 860 khz AM *Hrs Open:* 24; 0.5 kw-D, DAN; 0.5 kw-N, DAN; N37 51 11 W87 32 12
Mailing Address: P. O. Box 418 ., 230 Second St., Henderson, KY 42420 US
Second Address: 230 2nd St., Henderson, KY 42420
(270) 826-3923, *Fax:* (270) 826-7572
www.wsonradio.com
License: Henderson, KY held by Henson Media of Henderson, CO
Nat'l Network: ABC *Nat'l Reps:* Rgnl Reps *Wire Services:* AP
Arbitron Metro Market: Evansville, IN *Format:* Adult Contemp
Special Programming: Farm 2 hrs wkly *Hrs. of News Programming:* news progmg 8 hrs wkly *No. News Employees:* 1 *Target Audience:* 35+. *Adv.Rates:* 16; 14; 14; 12
Ed Henson, President
Darlene Hawkins, Operations Dir
Ed Henson, General Manager
Bill Stephens, News Director

Highland Heights

***WNKU**
04-29-1985; 89.7 mhz FM *Hrs Open:* 21 (M-F); 20 (S); 19 (Su); 12 kw horiz, 9.9 kw vert; 318 ft.; N39 2 21 W84 27 57
P.O. Box 337, Highland Heights, KY 41076 US
(859) 572-6500, *Fax:* (859) 572-6604
www.wnku.org
radio@wnku.org
License: Highland Heights, Campbell County, KY held by Northern Kentucky University.
Nat'l Network: PRI; NPR
Arbitron Metro Market: Cincinnati, OH *Format:* News, Triple A *Hrs. of News Programming:* news progmg 40 hrs wkly *No. News Employees:* 2 *Target Audience:* 35-49.
Grady Kirkpatrick, General Manager
Aaron Sharpe, General Sales Mgr

Hindman

WKCB
01-26-1971; 1340 khz AM; 1 kw-U, ND1; N37 19 45 W83 0 17
Mailing Address: P.O. Box 864, Hindman, KY 41822 US
Second Address: 1517 Hwy. 550 W., Hindman, KY 41822
(606) 785-3129, *Fax:* (606) 785-0106
www.wkcb.com
request@wkcb.com
License: Hindman, KY held by Hindman Broadcasting Corp.
Nat'l Reps: Rgnl Reps
Format: Christian
Randy Thompson, General Manager
Paul Hoskins, Programming Director

WKCB-FM
12-13-1974; 107.1 mhz FM; 1.55 kw; 650 ft.; N37 19 56 W82 56 52
Rt 550 West, Hindman, KY 41822 US
(606) 785-3129, *Fax:* (606) 785-0106
www.wkcb.com
request@wkcb.com
License: Hindman, Knott County, KY held by Hindman Broadcasting Corp.
Format: Rock/AOR
Hays McMakin, President
Tom McMakin, Operations Dir
Jeff Ray, General Manager
Robert Haydon, General Sales Mgr
Becky Black, Programming Director
Carol Lynn, Promotions Manager
Doug Walker, Chief Engineer
Chris Conkright,Information Technology
Ron Caudill, Sales Manager

Hodgenville

WRZI
03-01-1974; 107.3 mhz FM; 3.8 kw; Ant 420 ft; N37 40 21 W85 44 34
611 W. Poplar St., Suite C2, Elizabethtown, KY 42701
(270) 763-0800, *Fax:* (270) 769-6349
www.etownstar.com
info@etownstar.com
License: Hodgenville, Larue County, KY held by Elizabethtown CBC Inc.
Group Owner: Commonwealth Broadcasting Corp.; (acq 7-1-2000; grpsl)
Nat'l Reps: Keystone (unwired net); Rgnl Reps
Population Served: 98,000*Special Programming:* Farm 2 hrs wkly *Target Audience:* 18-44; females
Steve Newberry, President
Dale Thornhill, Operations Dir
Roth Stratton, General Manager

Hopkinsville

WHOP
01-08-1940; 1230 khz AM *Hrs Open:* 24; 1 kw-U, ND1; N36 52 54 W87 30 44
Mailing Address: PO Box 709, Hopkinsville, KY 42240 US
Second Address: 220 Dink Embry's Buttermilk Rd., Hopkinsville, KY 42240-8802
(270) 885-5331, *Fax:* (270) 885-2688
www.lite987whop.com
whopamfm@bellsouth.net
License: Hopkinsville, KY held by Hop Broadcasting Inc.
Group Owner: Key Broadcasting Inc.; (acq 10-28-99; with co-located FM)
Nat'l Network: CBS *Regional Network:* Ky. News Net *Nat'l Reps:* Rgnl Reps
Arbitron Metro Market: Clarksville-Hopkinsville, TN-KY *Format:* News, News/Talk, 86 *No. News Employees:* 2 *Target Audience:* 30 plus. *Adv. Rates:* 16; 16; 16; 12
Mike Chadwell, General Manager

WHOP-FM
05-01-1948; 98.7 mhz FM *Hrs Open:* 24; 100 kw; Ant 620 ft; N36 55 41 W87 32 50
Mailing Address: Box 709, Hopkinsville, KY 42241
Second Address: 220 Buttermilk Rd., Hopkinsville, KY 42240-8802
(270) 885-5331, *Fax:* (270) 885-2688
www.lite987whop.com
License: Hopkinsville, Christian County, KY held by Hop Broadcasting Inc.
Group Owner: Key Broadcasting Inc.
Nat'l Reps: Rgnl Reps
Population Served: 300,000 *Arbitron Metro Market:* Clarksville-Hopkinsville, TN-KY *Hrs. of News Programming:* news progmg 15 hrs wkly *No. News Employees:* 2 *Target Audience:* 18-54. *Adv. Rates:* 30; 22; 22;15
Mike Tarter, CEO/COO
Mike Chadwell, General Manager
Traci Mason, General Sales Mgr
Jeff Sisk, Programming Director
Adam May, News Director
Rick Crago, Engineering Dir

***WNKJ**
08-03-1981; 89.3 mhz FM *Hrs Open:* 24; 12 kw; 330 ft; N36 48 34 W87 24 20
Mailing Address: Box 1029, Hopkinsville, KY 42240
Second Address: 1100 E. 18th St., Hopkinsville, KY 42240
(270) 886-9655, *Fax:* (270) 885-7210
www.wnkj.org
wnkj@wnkj.org
License: Hopkinsville, Christian County, KY held by Pennyrile Christian Community Inc.
Nat'l Network: Moody
Arbitron Metro Market: Clarksville-Hopkinsville, TN-KY *Special Programming:* Black 4.5 hrs, Korean 1/2 hr, Sp 3/4 hr wkly *Hrs. of News Programming:* News progmg 12 hrs wkly *Target Audience:* General.
Jim Dozier Adams, General Manager
Donald Griffey, Chief Engineer

WHVO
09-19-1954; 1480 khz AM *Hrs Open:* 24; 1 kw-D, ND1; 0.024 kw-N, ND1; N36 52 15 W87 30 43
400 Hammond Plaza, Hopkinsville, KY 42240 US
(270) 886-1480, *Fax:* (270) 886-6286
www.oldies1480.com
oldies@oldies1480.com
License: Hopkinsville, KY held by Ham Broadcasting Inc.
Nat'l Network: AP Network News; Jones Radio Networks; Fox News Radio *Regional Network:* Ky. News Net *Nat'l Reps:* Rgnl Reps
Arbitron Metro Market: Clarksville-Hopkinsville, TN-KY *Format:* Oldies *Special Programming:* Relg 6 hrs, gospel 3 hrs wkly *Hrs. of News Programming:* news progmg 3 hrs wkly *No. News Employees:* 2 *TargetAudience:* 35-54; Upscale Baby-boomers
D.J. Everett, President
Bill Booth, Operations Dir
Beth Mann, General Manager
Amy Berry, General Sales Mgr
Alan Watts, News Director

WVVR
07-01-1960; 100.3 mhz FM *Hrs Open:* 24; 100 kw; 1001 ft.; N36 56 58 W87 40 18
1700 Dawson Springs Road, Hopkinsville, KY 42240 US

(931) 648-7720, *Fax:* (931) 648-7769
www.thebeaver.com
License: Hopkinsville, Christian County, KY held by Saga Communications of Tuckessee LLC.
Group Owner: Saga Communications Inc.; (acq 11-27-2000; $7 million)
Regional Reps: Rgnl Reps.
Arbitron Metro Market: Hopkinsville, KY *Format:* Country *Hrs. of News Programming:* news progmg 7 hrs wkly *No. News Employees:* 1 *Target Audience:* 18-54; working class *Adv. Rates:* 56; 48; 52; 32
Katie Gambill, General Manager

WZZP
02-28-2001; 97.5 mhz FM; 6 kw; 328 ft.; N36 45 47 W87 26 59
P O Box 2249, Clarksville, TN 37042 US
(931) 648-7720, *Fax:* (931) 648-7769
www.z975.com
courtney@z975.com
License: Hopkinsville, Christian County, KY held by Saga Communications of Tuckessee L.L.C.
Group Owner: Saga Communications Inc.; (acq 2-1-01; grpsl).
Arbitron Metro Market: Clarksville, TN
Scott Chase, Operations Dir
Katie Gambill, General Manager
Sande Cox, Sales Manager
Jared Mims, Programming Director

Horse Cave

WHHT
09-19-1994; 106.5 mhz FM; 3 kw; 476 ft.; N37 13 57 W85 52 6
Mailing Address: P.O. Box 1505, Glasgow, KY 42142 US
Second Address: 113 W. Public Sq., Suite 400, Glasgow, KY 42141
(270) 651-6050, *Fax:* (270) 651-7666
License: Horse Cave, Hart County, KY held by Commonwealth Broadcasting Corp.
Group Owner: Commonwealth Broadcasting Corp.; (acq 11-25-97; grpsl)
Nat'l Network: Westwood One
Arbitron Metro Market: Bowling Green, KY *Format:* Adult Contemp
Kellie Wood, Operations Dir
Derron Steenbergen, General Manager

Hyden

WKIC
11-07-1988; 97.9 mhz FM; 1.75 kw; Ant 1,207 ft; N37 11 36 W83 11 04
Mailing Address: Box 7280, Hazard, KY 41749
Second Address: 516 Main St., Hazard, KY 41701
(606) 436-9898, *Fax:* (606) 436-4172
wzqq@alltel.net
License: Hyden, Leslie County, KY held by Leslie County Broadcasting Inc.
Nat'l Network: ABC
Target Audience: General.
Stuart Sparkman, CEO
Mike Reeves, General Manager
Bob Hale, Chief Engineer

Irvine

WCYO
08-01-1991; 100.7 mhz FM *Hrs Open:* 24; 9.2 kw; 505 ft.; N37 39 40 W84 8 55
P. O. Box 281, Irvine, KY 40336 US
(859) 623-1386, *Fax:* (859) 623-1241
www.wcyofm.com
License: Irvine, Estill County, KY held by Kentucky River Broadcasting Co. Inc.
Group Owner: Wallingford Broadcasting Co.
Arbitron Metro Market: Richmond -Lexington, KY *Format:* Country
Sean Hamilton, General Manager
Trizdon Reynolds, General Sales Mgr
Karl Shannon, Programming Director
Ron Lykins, News Director

WIRV
07-02-1960; 1550 khz AM; 1 kw-D, ND1; 0.005 kw-N, ND1; N37 42 57 W83 58 29
PO Box 281, Irvine, KY 40336 US
(859) 623-1386, *Fax:* (859) 623-1241
www.wbairforce.com
License: Irvine, KY held by Kentucky River Broadcasting Co Inc.
Group Owner: Wallingford Broadcasting Co.
Nat'l Reps: Rgnl Reps
Format: Oldies
Kelly Wallingford, General Manager
Ray White, Programming Director

Jackson

WEKG
03-07-1969; 810 khz AM; 5 kw-D, NDD; N37 34 41 W83 24 19
1024 College Avenuee, Jackson, KY 41339 US
(606) 666-7531, *Fax:* (606) 666-4946
kdavidson@wjsn.com
License: Jackson, KY held by Intermountain Broadcasting Co.
Arbitron Metro Market: Jackson, KY *Format:* Gospel
Gloria Hay, CEO
Gloria Hay, General Manager
Doug Neace, General Sales Mgr

WJSN-FM
01-01-1979; 97.3 mhz FM; 19 kw; 814 ft.; N37 40 19 W83 24 21
1024 College Avenue, Jackson, KY 41339 US
(606) 666-7531, *Fax:* (606) 666-4946
wjsn.awardspace.com
kdavidson@wjsn.com
License: Jackson, Breathitt County, KY
Format: Country
Hap Ritchey, Programming Director
Bill Reed, News Director
Larry Walters, Disc Jockey
Nicole Lewis, Disc Jockey
Deborah Walters, News Reporter
William Reed, Reporter
Cheryl Walters, Women's Int Ed

***WYLC**
89.7 mhz FM; 0.45 kw; 240 ft.; N37 35 8 W83 14 59
Mailing Address: US
Second Address: 3019 Hwy. 30 W., Jackson, KY 41339
(606) 295-3225
License: Jackson, Breathitt County, KY held by Breathitt Listeners Choice Radio Inc.
Arbitron Metro Market: Jackson, NY *Format:* Children
Earl Lovely, Chairman

Jamestown

WJKY
09-03-1967; 1060 khz AM; 1 kw-D, NDD; N37 1 31 W85 4 23
Mailing Address: P.O. Box 800, Jamestown, KY 42629 US
Second Address: 2804 South US Hwy 127, Russell Springs, KY 42642
(270) 866-3487, *Fax:* (270) 866-2060
www.lakercountry.com
License: Jamestown, KY held by Lake Cumberland Broadcasters
Format: Country
Mae Hoover, General Manager
Kem Bell, Advertising Manager
Greg Hammond, Sport Commentator
Audie Hammond, Sport Commentator

WJRS
09-03-1966; 104.9 mhz FM; 2 kw; 361 ft.; N37 1 31 W85 4 23
Mailing Address: P.O. Box 800, Jamestown, KY 42629 US
Second Address: 2804 South US Hwy 127, Russell Springs, KY 42642
(270) 866-3487, *Fax:* (270) 866-2060
www.lakercountry.com
License: Jamestown, Russell County, KY held by Lake Cumberland Broadcasters.
Wire Services: NWS (National Weather Service)
Format: Country
Linda Byrd, General Manager
Aaron Miller, General Sales Mgr
Chris Kampmeier, Programming Director
Rick Everett, Promotions Manager
Pat Lynch, Programming Director
Josh Egolf, Promotions Manager

Jeffersontown

WGRK
03-15-1972; 1200 khz AM; 0.5 kw-C, NDD; 1 kw-D, NDD; N37 15 34 W85 30 57
Mailing Address: P.O. Box 457, Glasgow, KY 42141 US
Second Address: 50 Friendship Pike, Campbellsville, KY 42719
(270) 932-7401(270) 789-1464, *Fax:* (888) 531-6397
www.kcountry1057.com
wgrk@commonwealthbroadcasting.com
License: Jeffersontown, KY held by Green County CBC Inc.
Group Owner: Commonwealth Broadcasting Corp.; (acq 10-30-97; $600,000 with co-located FM)
Nat'l Network: ABC; Jones Radio Networks *Nat'l Reps:* Rgnl Reps
Arbitron Metro Market: Jeffersontown, KY *Format:* Country *Hrs. of News Programming:* news progmg 7 hrs wkly *No. News Employees:* 1 *Target Audience:* 25-54.
Steve Newberry, President
Marty Bagby, Operations Dir
Barb Smith, General Manager
Barb Smith, Station Manager
Greg Gribbins, General Sales Mgr
Kevin Johnson, Programming Director
Bill Sanders, News Director
Mike Graham, ChiefEngineer

WMJM
12-01-1978; 101.3 mhz FM; 2 kw; 194 ft.; N38 13 42 W85 38 22
1821 Summit Road, Suite 400, Cincinnati, OH 45237 US
(502) 625-1220, *Fax:* (502) 625-1259
www.1013online.com
License: Jeffersontown, Jefferson County, KY held by MLB-Louisville IV LLC.
Group Owner: Main Line Broadcasting LLC; (acq 9-12-2007; grpsl)
Arbitron Metro Market: Louisville, KY *Format:* Adult Contemp
Dale Schaefer, General Manager

Jenkins

WIFX-FM
05-10-1975; 94.3 mhz FM *Hrs Open:* 24; 6.3 kw horiz, 6.24 kw vert; 1345 ft.; N37 9 59 W82 37 13
P.O. Box 1123, Jenkins, KY 41537 US
(606) 478-1200, *Fax:* (606) 478-4202
www.foxy943.com
wifx@foxy943.com
License: Jenkins, Letcher County, KY held by AJSPD LLC
Format: Rock/AOR *Hrs. of News Programming:* News progmg 2 hrs wkly *Target Audience:* 25-45.
Adam Gearheart, General Manager

WKVG
02-01-1970; 1000 khz AM *Hrs Open:* 7:30 AM- 6 PM; 1 kw-D, NDD; N37 9 59 W82 37 13
Mailing Address: P. O. Box 613, Pound, VA 24279 US
Second Address: Box 1474, Jenkins, KY 41537
(606) 832-4655, *Fax:* (606) 832-4656
License: Jenkins, KY held by Martins and Assoc. Inc.
Format: Gospel, Religious *Hrs. of News Programming:* News progmg 9 hrs wkly *Target Audience:* General. *Adv. Rates:* 4.75; 4.75; 4.75; N/A
Emma Martin, General Manager

Junction City

WDFB
05-20-1985; 1170 khz AM *Hrs Open:* Sunrise-sunset; 1 kw-D, DAD; N37 35 46 W84 50 19
Mailing Address: 3596 Alum Springs Road, Danvillle, KY 40422 US
Second Address: 3596 Alum Springs Rd., Danville, KY 40422
(859) 236-9333, *Fax:* (859) 236-3348
www.wdfb.com
wdfb@searnet.com
License: Junction City, KY held by Alum Springs Vision and Outreach Corp.
Nat'l Network: USA
Arbitron Metro Market: Junction City, KY *Format:* Religious
Target Audience: General. *Adv. Rates:* 6; 6; 6; 6
Donald Drake, President
Cindy Pike, News Director
Mildred Drake, Executive Vice President

Keavy

***WVCT**
01-01-1984; 91.5 mhz FM *Hrs Open:* 24; 0.1 kw horiz, 2.4 kw vert; 381 ft.; N36 59 1 W84 8 1
968 W. City Dam Road, Keavy, KY 40737 US
(606) 528-4671, *Fax:* (606) 526-0589
www.thegospeleagle.com
csivley@bellsouth.net
License: Keavy, Laurel County, KY held by Victory Training School Corp.
Arbitron Metro Market: Keavy, KY *Format:* Gospel
Brenda Sivley, President
Charles Sivley, General Manager

Keene

WJMM-FM
12-09-1969; 99.1 mhz FM *Hrs Open:* 24; 2.1 kw; 558 ft.; N38 3 56 W84 29 13
3270 Blazer Parkway, Suite 101, Lexington, KY 40509 US

(859) 264-9700, *Fax:* (859) 264-9705
www.wjmm.com
wjmm@ckcradio.com
License: Keene, Jessamine County, KY held by Christian Broadcasting System Ltd.
Group Owner: Christian Broadcasting System Ltd.; (acq 7-1-2006; grpsl).
Format: Christian, Religious
Benson Gregory, General Manager
Benson Gregory, Station Manager
Ed Wright, Programming Director
Jessica Rice, Promotions Manager
Dennis Blais, Chief Engineer
John Wells, Public Service Director
Tracy Adkisson, BusinessManager
Bruse Edwards, Music Director
Ronnie Hupp, Disc Jockey
Mike Duncan, Account Executive

La Center

WRJJ

01-01-2008; 104.3 mhz FM; 4 kw; 125 ft.; N37 4 30 W88 58 22 US
(618) 967-3704
License: La Center, Ballard County, KY held by Janet Jensen.
Arbitron Metro Market: La Center, KY
Janet Jensen, General Manager

Lancaster

WRNZ

10-01-1988; 105.1 mhz FM *Hrs Open:* 24; 3 kw; 325 ft; N37 36 06 W84 34 27
2063 Shakertown Rd., Danville, KY 41144
(859) 236-2711, *Fax:* (859) 236-1461
www.hometownLIVE.net
hometownradio@bellsouth.net
License: Lancaster, Garrard County, KY held by Hometown Broadcasting of Lancaster Inc.
Nat'l Reps: Rgnl Reps *Regional Reps:* Rgnl Reps
Population Served: 200,000 *Arbitron Metro Market:* Lexington-Fayet *Special Programming:* Relg 4 hrs wkly *Hrs. of News Programming:* news progmg 2 hrs wkly *No. News Employees:* 1 *Target Audience:* 25-54;upscale, white collar, baby boomers, business owners *Adv. Rates:* Call
Jim Parman, Operations Dir
Robert Wagner, General Manager
Vicki Hyde, News Director

Lawrenceburg

WKYL

05-11-1993; 102.1 mhz FM *Hrs Open:* 24; 6 kw; 328 ft.; N38 1 37 W84 52 59
1030 Burlington Lane, Frankfort, KY 40601 US
(502) 839-1021
www.weku.fm
License: Lawrenceburg, Anderson County, KY held by Davenport Broadcasting Inc.
Nat'l Network: Jones Radio Networks
Format: Jazz, Smooth Jazz *Special Programming:* Relg 2 hrs wkly *Target Audience:* 30-50; higher income; especially at-work listeners
C. Michael Davenport, General Manager

Lebanon

WLBN

10-01-1954; 1590 khz AM *Hrs Open:* 24; 1 kw-D, ND1; 0.024 kw-N, ND1; N37 35 55 W85 14 47
P.O Box 457, Glasgow, KY 42141 US
(270) 692-3126, *Fax:* (270) 692-6003
www.1590wlbn.com
License: Lebanon, KY held by CBC of Marion County Inc.
Group Owner: Commonwealth Broadcasting Corp.; (acq 7-3-97; $360,000 with co-located FM).
Nat'l Network: Jones Radio Networks *Nat'l Reps:* Rgnl Reps
Format: Oldies *Special Programming:* Gospel 5 hrs, open mike 5 hrs wkly *Hrs. of News Programming:* news progmg 13 hrs wkly *No. News Employees:* 1 *Target Audience:* 35-64. *Adv. Rates:* 8; 8; 8; 6
Andy Colley, Operations Dir
Lisa Kearnes, General Manager
Patty Brown, News Director
Mike Graham, Chief Engineer

WLSK

10-01-1979; 100.9 mhz FM *Hrs Open:* 24; 6.6 kw; 413 ft.; N37 41 43 W85 19 6
P.O Box 457, Glasgow, KY 42141 US
(2700 692-3126, *Fax:* (270) 692-6003
www.lebanonmike.com
wlsk@commonwealthbroadcasting.com
License: Lebanon, Marion County, KY
Group Owner: Commonwealth Broadcasting Corp.
Format: Variety/Diverse *Hrs. of News Programming:* news progmg 9 hrs wkly *No. News Employees:* 1 *Target Audience:* 30-49. *Adv. Rates:* 12; 12; 12; 12.
Andy Colley, Operations Dir
Lisa Kearnes, General Manager
Patty Brown, News Director

Lebanon Junction

WKMO

10-01-1979; 99.3 mhz FM; 6 kw; 312 ft.; N37 44 26 W85 49 28
PO Box 457, Glasgow, KY 42141 US
502-769-0800, *Fax:* 502-769-6349
info@1063thebear.com
License: Lebanon Junction, Bullittt County, KY held by Elizabethtown CBC Inc.
Group Owner: Commonwealth Broadcasting Corp.; (acq 12-23-2002; $900,000)
Nat'l Reps: Rgnl Reps
TV Affiliate: Country *Special Programming:* news progmg one hr wkly *Hrs. of News Programming:* 1 *Adv. Rates:* 22; 18; 22; 15
CEO, CEO/COO
Operations Manager

Ledbetter

*WKYP

01-01-2004; 90.1 mhz FM; 1 kw vert; Ant 328 ft; N37 06 10 W88 24 15
Mailing Address: Box 281, Hardin, KY 42048
Second Address: 219 College St., Harding, KY 42048
(270) 437-4095, *Fax:* (270) 437-4098
www.hmiradio.com
info@hmiradio.com
License: Ledbetter, Livingston County, KY held by Heartland Ministries Inc.

Darrell Gibson, President
Jeremy Johnson, Programming Director

Leitchfield

WKHG

10-29-1967; 104.9 mhz FM; 3.5 kw; 272 ft.; N37 30 40 W86 17 15
2160 Brandenburg Road, Leitchfield, KY 42754 US
(270) 259-5692, *Fax:* (270) 259-5692
www.k105.com
news@k105.com
License: Leitchfield, Grayson County, KY held by Heritage Media of Kentucky Inc.
Format: Adult Contemp
Mike Novak, Operations Dir

WMTL

01-17-1959; 870 khz AM; 0.5 kw-D, NDD; N37 30 40 W86 17 15
2160 Branderburg Road, Leitchfield, KY 42754 US
(270) 259-3165, *Fax:* (270) 259-5693
news@k105.com
License: Leitchfield, KY held by Heritage Media of Kentucky Inc.
Arbitron Metro Market: Leitchfield, KY *Format:* Country
Mark Buckles, President
Ed Thomas, Chief Engineer

Lerose

*WEBF

03-01-1999; 88.3 mhz FM *Hrs Open:* 3 PM-9 PM (M-F); 1 kw; Ant 321 ft; N37 36 23 W83 41 16
Owsley County High School, Hwy. 28/ E. Shepherd Ln., Booneville, KY 41314
(606) 593-5185, *Fax:* (606) 593-6312
www.owsley.kyschools.us
tburns@owsley.k12.ky.us
License: Lerose, Owsley County, KY held by Board of Regents - Morehead State University
Population Served: 15,000*Target Audience:* 12-35; poor & uneducated in need of information
Diana Gross, Chairman
Stephen Jackson, CEO
Dan Conti, General Manager
Bill Hodges, Programming Director
Jerry McIntosh, CFO

Lewisport

WLME

07-01-1990; 102.7 mhz FM *Hrs Open:* 24; 2.25 kw; 545 ft.; N37 47 44 W86 50 58
P.O. Box 150846, Nashville, TN 37215 US
(270) 683-5200, *Fax:* (270) 688-0108
spots@wrioradio.com
License: Lewisport, Perry County, KY held by WLME Inc.
Group Owner: The Cromwell Group Inc.
Nat'l Network: Jones Radio Networks *Nat'l Reps:* Rgnl Reps
Format: Adult Contemp *Special Programming:* Sports 6 hrs wkly *Hrs. of News Programming:* news progmg 3 hrs wkly *No. News Employees:* 1 *Target Audience:* 25-54; general
Bayard Walters, President
Kevin Riecke, General Manager

Lexington

WBUL-FM

07-15-1969; 98.1 mhz FM; 100 kw; 561 ft.; N38 2 7 W84 27 2
50 East Rivercenter Blvd, Covington, KY 41011 US
(859) 422-1000, *Fax:* (859) 422-1038
www.wbul.com
michaeljordan@clearchannel.com
License: Lexington, Fayette County, KY held by Citicasters Licenses L.P.
Group Owner: Clear Channel Communications Inc.; (acq 5-4-99; grpsl).
Arbitron Metro Market: Lexington, KY *Format:* Country *Target Audience:* 25-49; baby boomers who grew up with Stones & Beatles
Michael Jordan, Operations Dir
Gene Guinn, General Manager
Mandy Daugherty, Programming Director
JB Sprinkle, Online Content Director

WLAP

09-01-1922; 630 khz AM *Hrs Open:* 24; 5 kw-D, DA2; 1 kw-N, DA2; N38 7 25 W84 26 45
50 East Rivercenter Blvd, Suite 1200, Covington, KY 41011 US
(859) 422- 1000, *Fax:* (859) 422- 1038
www.wlap.com
info@wlap.com
License: Lexington, KY held by Citicasters Licenses L.P.
Group Owner: Clear Channel Communications Inc.
Nat'l Network: CBS *Nat'l Reps:* Christal
Arbitron Metro Market: Lexington-Fayette, KY *Format:* News *No. News Employees:* 1 *Target Audience:* 18-49; men
Kevin Bell, Programming Director

WLXG

01-01-1946; 1300 khz AM; 2.5 kw-D, 1 kw-N, DA-N; N38 05 50 W84 31 45
401 W. Main St., Suite 301, Lexington, KY 40578
(859) 233-1515, *Fax:* (859) 233-1517
www.wlxg.com
jmac@lmcomm.com
License: Lexington, Fayette County, KY held by L.M. Communications Inc.
Group Owner: L M Communications Inc.; (acq 7-1-84)
Nat'l Network: ESPN Radio *Nat'l Reps:* Katz Radio
Population Served: 190,000 *Arbitron Metro Market:* Lexington-Fayet *Hrs. of News Programming:* News progmg 5 hrs wkly *Target Audience:* 25-54; adults
Lynn Martin, President
James MacFarlane, General Manager

WMXL

01-01-1940; 94.5 mhz FM *Hrs Open:* 24; 85 kw; 636 ft.; N38 7 24 W84 26 37
50 East Rivercenter Blvdsuite 1200, Covington, KY 41011 US
(859) 422-1000, *Fax:* (859) 422-1038
www.mymix945.com
info@wmxl.com
License: Lexington, Fayette County, KY held by Citicasters Licenses L.P.
Group Owner: Clear Channel Communications Inc.; (acq 5-4-99; grpsl).
Arbitron Metro Market: Lexington, KY *Format:* Adult Contemp *Hrs. of News Programming:* News progmg 3 hrs wkly *Target Audience:* 25-54; women
Michael Jordan, Operations Dir
Gene Guinn, General Manager
Dale O'Brien, Programming Director
Mandy Daugherty, Promotions Manager
Karyn Czar, News Director
Gerry Westerberg, Chief Engineer

*WRFL

03-03-1988; 88.1 mhz FM; 7.9 kw; 285 ft.; N38 2 19 W84 30 16
026 Grehan Journalism Bl, Lexington, KY 40506 US

(859) 257-4636,(859) 257-9735, *Fax:* (859) 323-1039
gm@wrfl881.org
License: Lexington, Fayette County, KY held by Radio Free Lexington Inc.
Arbitron Metro Market: Lexington-Fayette, KY *Format:* Variety/Diverse
John Clark, General Manager

*WUKY
03-13-1941; 91.3 mhz FM *Hrs Open:* 24; 100 kw; 779 ft.; N37 52 45 W84 19 33
340 McVey Hall, Lexington, KY 40506 US
(859) 257-3221, *Fax:* (859) 257-6291
wuky.org
npr.rocks@email.uky.edu
License: Lexington, Fayette County, KY held by University of Kentucky
Nat'l Network: NPR; PRI *Wire Services:* AP
Arbitron Metro Market: Lexington, KY *Format:* News, Triple A *Hrs. of News Programming:* news progmg 62 hrs wkly *No. News Employees:* 25 *Target Audience:* 25-54 *Adv. Rates:* non-commercial
John Lumagui, Operations Dir
Tom Godell, General Manager
Rusty Sharp, Programming Director
Gail Bennett, Promotions Manager
Alan Lytle, News Director
John Lumagui, Engineering Dir
Lori Horine, Business Manager
Mike Graves,Music Director

WVLK
10-01-1947; 590 khz AM *Hrs Open:* 24
111 East Kilbourn Avenue, Suite 2700, Milwaukee, WI 53202 US
(859) 253-5959, *Fax:* (859) 253-5940
www.wvlkam.com
License: Lexington, KY held by Cumulus Licensing Corp.
Group Owner: Cumulus Media Inc.; (acq 7-22-99; grpsl).
Nat'l Network: CBS
Arbitron Metro Market: Lexington, KY *Format:* News, News/Talk, 84, Talk *No. News Employees:* 5 *Target Audience:* 25-54.
Robert Lindsey, Operations Dir
Ken Fearnow, General Manager

WLXX
02-01-1962; 92.9 mhz FM *Hrs Open:* 24; 100 kw; 850 ft.; N38 2 22 W84 24 11
111 East Kilbourn Avenue, Suite 2700, Milwaukee, WI 53202 US
(859) 253-5900, *Fax:* (859) 253-5940
www.wlxxthebear.com
License: Lexington, Fayette County, KY
Arbitron Metro Market: Lexington, KY *Format:* Country
John Lewis, General Manager
Scott Frazier, General Sales Mgr
Marshall Stewark, Programming Director
Mario Anderson, Promotions Manager

Lexington-Fayette

WLKT
07-30-1992; 104.5 mhz FM; 50 kw; 466 ft.; N38 4 9 W84 18 44
50 East Rivercenter Blvd., Suite 1200, Covington, KY 41011 US
(859) 422-1000, *Fax:* (859) 422-1038
www.wlkt.com
info@wlkt.com
License: Lexington-Fayette, Fayette County, KY held by Citicasters Licenses L.P.
Group Owner: Clear Channel Communications Inc.; (acq 5-4-99; grpsl).
Arbitron Metro Market: Lexington-Fayette, KY *Format:* Contemporary Hits/Top 40
Gene Guinn, General Manager

Liberty

WKDO
11-01-1963; 1560 khz AM; 1 kw-D, NDD; N37 18 22 W84 55 2
Mailing Address: P. O. Box 990, Liberty, KY 42539 US
Second Address: 988 Dry Ridge Rd., Liberty, KY 42539
(606) 787-7331, *Fax:* (606) 787-2166
License: Liberty, KY held by Radio Station WKDO.
Nat'l Network: USA
Format: Country *Target Audience:* 18-49.
Carlos Wesley, President
David Smith, Chief Engineer

WKDO-FM
01-01-1977; 98.7 mhz FM *Hrs Open:* 16; 25 kw; 240 ft.; N37 18 22 W84 55 2
P.O. Box 990, Liberty, KY 42539 US
(606) 787-7331, *Fax:* (606) 787-2166
License: Liberty, Casey County, KY held by Radio Station WKDO.
Hrs. of News Programming: news progmg 21 hrs wkly *No. News Employees:* 3 *Target Audience:* 15-35.
Rich Archut, Operations Dir

London

WFTG
09-01-1955; 1400 khz AM *Hrs Open:* 24
Mailing Address: P. O. Box 1450, Corbin, KY 40702 US
Second Address: 534 Tobacco Rd., London, KY 40741
(606) 864-2148, *Fax:* (606) 864-0645
www,wftgam.com
trgrigsby@broadcasting.net
License: London, KY held by F.T.G. Broadcasting Inc.
Group Owner: Key Broadcasting Inc.; (acq 8-5-92; $410,000;
Regional Network: Ky. News Net
Format: Talk *No. News Employees:* 1 *Target Audience:* 40 plus.
Mike Tarter, President
Brisgett Gambret, General Manager
Travis Stevens, Programming Director
Phillip Fraley, Chief Engineer

WGWM
08-08-1981; 980 khz AM *Hrs Open:* 24
568 Old Richmond Road, London, KY 40741 US
(606) 878-0980, *Fax:* (606) 878-0980
License: London, KY held by WGWM Broadcasting Inc.
Format: Gospel *Hrs. of News Programming:* News progmg 5 hrs wkly *Target Audience:* 25-54; male/female
Elmer Oakley, General Manager

WWEL
09-15-1970; 103.9 mhz FM *Hrs Open:* 24; 5.4 kw; 348 ft.; N37 8 30 W84 4 45
Mailing Address: P. O. Box 1450, Corbin, KY 40702 US
Second Address: 534 Tobacco Rd., London, KY 40741
(606) 864-2148, *Fax:* (606) 864-0645
www.sam1039.com
License: London, Laurel County, KY
Group Owner: Key Broadcasting Inc.
Nat'l Network: NBC Radio *Regional Network:* Ky. News Net
Arbitron Metro Market: London, KY *Format:* Classic Rock *Hrs. of News Programming:* news progmg 21 hrs wkly *No. News Employees:* 1 *Target Audience:* 18-40. *Adv. Rates:* 1; 10
Mike Tarter, President
Bridgett Gambrel, General Manager
Terry Harris, Programming Director
Brian Sizemore, News Director
Frances Wilhoit, Account Executive
Ashley Butt, Account Executive

WYGE
01-01-1994; 92.3 mhz FM *Hrs Open:* 24; 23.5 kw; 732 ft.; N37 9 1 W83 59 32
201 East Second St, London, KY 40741 US
(606) 877-1326, *Fax:* (606) 883-6424
www.good-news-outreach.org
wygeradio@yahoo.com
License: London, Laurel County, KY held by Ethel Huff Broadcasting LLC.
Nat'l Network: Salem Radio Network; USA
Arbitron Metro Market: London, KY *Format:* Religious *Adv. Rates:* 10; 9; 10; 7
Ethel Huff, Chairman
Gene Huff, General Manager

Louisa

WZAQ
05-17-1991; 92.3 mhz FM; 4.5 kw; 377 ft.; N38 10 33 W82 37 39
P.O. Box 176, Louisa, KY 41230 US
(606) 244-0130, *Fax:* (606) 244-0130
www.wzaqfm.com
info@wzaqfm.com
License: Louisa, Lawrence County, KY held by Louisa Communications Inc.
Arbitron Metro Market: Huntington-Ashl *Format:* Country
Harold Britton, President
Marti Fairchild, General Manager

Louisville

WAMZ
09-01-1966; 97.5 mhz FM *Hrs Open:* 24; 100 kw; 673 ft.; N38 3 50 W85 43 52
8889 Pelican Bay Boulevard, Suite 1500, Naples, FL 34108 US
(502) 479-2222, *Fax:* (502) 479-2308
www.wamz.com
karenpaschal@clearchannel.com
License: Louisville, Jefferson County, KY held by CC Licenses LLC.
Group Owner: Clear Channel Communications Inc.
Arbitron Metro Market: Louisville, KY *Format:* Country
Coyote Calhoun, Programming Director

WDJX
08-01-1963; 99.7 mhz FM; 24 kw; 715 ft.; N38 21 53 W85 50 18
50 East Rivercenter Blvd, Suite 1200, Covington, KY 41011 US
(502) 625-1220, *Fax:* (502) 625-1256
www.wdjx.com
benandkellyshow@gmail.com
License: Louisville, Jefferson County, KY held by MLB-Louisville IV LLC.
Group Owner: Main Line Broadcasting LLC; (acq 9-12-2007; grpsl)
Arbitron Metro Market: Louisville, KY *Format:* Christian
Dale Schaefer, General Manager

WFIA
03-01-1947; 900 khz AM *Hrs Open:* 24
50 East Rivercenter Blvd, Suite 1200, Covington, KY 41011 US
(502) 339-9470, *Fax:* (502) 423-3139
www.salemradiogroup.com
pcopass@salemradiolouisville.com
License: Louisville, KY held by Salem Media Group LLC.
Group Owner: Salem Communications Corp.; (acq 1-24-2001; $1.75 million)
Nat'l Reps: Salem
Arbitron Metro Market: Louisville, KY *Format:* Christian, Talk *Hrs. of News Programming:* News progmg 2 hrs wkly *Target Audience:* 30 plus; general
Tim Hartlage, General Manager
Todd Burns, Sales Manager
Dave Reichel, Programming Director
Carrie Baylor, Promotions Manager
Gregg Kramer, Accounting/Traffic
Patty Copass, Human Resources/Business Office
Jessica Wilder, AccountExecutive
Lance Kohler, Account Executive
Michael Booth, Account Executive
Bob Battoe, Account Executive

*WFPK
10-04-1954; 91.9 mhz FM *Hrs Open:* 24; 6.8 kw; 774 ft.; N38 21 55 W85 50 24
301 York St., Louisville, KY 40203 US
(502) 814-6500, *Fax:* (502) 814-6599
www.wfpk.org
dreynolds@louisvillepublicmedia.org
License: Louisville, Jefferson County, KY held by Kentucky Public Radio Inc.
Nat'l Network: PRI; NPR
Arbitron Metro Market: Louisville, KY *Format:* Alternative *Target Audience:* 25 plus.
Donovan Reynolds, General Manager
Stacy Owen, Programming Director

*WFPL
02-20-1950; 89.3 mhz FM *Hrs Open:* 24; 21 kw; 774 ft.; N38 21 55 W85 50 24
301 York St., Louisville, KY 40203 US
(502) 814-6500, *Fax:* (502) 814-6599
www.wfpl.org
tmundt@louisvillepublicmedia.org
License: Louisville, Jefferson County, KY held by Kentucky Public Radio Inc.
Nat'l Network: NPR; PRI
Arbitron Metro Market: Louisville, KY *Format:* News, News/Talk, 86 *Hrs. of News Programming:* news progmg 124 hrs wkly *No. News Employees:* 3 *Target Audience:* General.
Donovan Reynolds, General Manager
Rick Howlett, Programming Director

WHAS
07-18-1922; 840 khz AM *Hrs Open:* 24; 50 kw-U, ND1; N38 15 40 W85 25 43
8889 Pelican Bay Boulevard, Suite 1500, Naples, FL 34108 US
(502) 479-2222, *Fax:* (502) 479-2308
www.whas.com
info@whas.com
License: Louisville, KY held by CC Licenses LLC.
Group Owner: Clear Channel Communications Inc.; (acq 8-86; with co-located FM)
Nat'l Reps: Clear Channel
Arbitron Metro Market: Louisville, KY *Format:* News, News/Talk, 86 *Hrs. of News Programming:* news progmg 14 hrs wkly *No. News Employees:* 12 *Target Audience:* 25-54.
Kevin Hughes, General Manager
Doug Wethington, General Sales Mgr
Kelly Carls, Programming Director
Kirk Wesley, Chief Engineer

WKJK
11-01-1948; 1080 khz AM *Hrs Open:* 24; 10 kw-D, DA2; 1 kw-N, DA2; N38 18 29 W85 49 45; N38 18 28 W85 49 45
8889 Pelican Bay Boulevard, Suite 1500, Naples, FL 34108 US
(502) 479-2222, *Fax:* (502) 479-2308
www.talkradio1080.com
jimfenn@clearchannel.com
License: Louisville, KY held by CC Licenses LLC.
Group Owner: Clear Channel Communications Inc.; (acq 9-13-96; $1 million with intellectual property of WSFR(FM) Corydon, IN)
Nat'l Network: CBS Radio *Nat'l Reps:* Clear Channel
Arbitron Metro Market: Louisville, KY *Format:* Talk *Target Audience:* 35-64; men
Jim Fenn, Programming Director
Bill Gentry, Promotions Manager

WGTK
12-30-1933; 970 khz AM *Hrs Open:* 24; 5 kw-D, DA2; 5 kw-N, DA2; N38 19 5 W85 44 39
888 - 7th Avenue, New York, NY 10106 US
(502) 339-9470, *Fax:* (502) 423-3139
www.970wgtk.com
License: Louisville, KY held by Salem Media of Kentucky Inc.
Group Owner: Salem Communications Corp.; (acq 10-4-2000)
Arbitron Metro Market: Louisville, KY *Format:* News, News/Talk, 86 *Hrs. of News Programming:* news progmg 21 hrs wkly *No. News Employees:* 1 *Target Audience:* 35 plus; people with most discretionary incomes
CC Matthews, Operations Dir
Tim Hartlage, General Manager

WLLV
06-01-1940; 1240 khz AM; 1 kw-U, ND1; N38 14 49 W85 42 19
3270 Blazer Pkwy S101, Lexington, KY 40509 US
(502) 776-1240, *Fax:* (502) 776-1250
wlouwllv@davidsonmedicgroup.com
License: Louisville, KY held by Davidson Media Station WLLV Licensee LLC.
Group Owner: Davidson Media Group LLC; (acq 4-12-2006; $2.65 million with WLOU(AM) Louisville).
Arbitron Metro Market: Louisville, KY *Format:* Black, Gospel
Vivien Ogburn, Station Manager

WLOU
01-01-1948; 1350 khz AM; 2.2 kw-D, DAN; 0.5 kw-N, DAN; N38 13 52 W85 49 22
3270 Blazer Pkwy, Suite 101, Lexington, KY 40509 US
(502) 776-1240, *Fax:* (502) 776-1250
www.wlouonline.com
wlouwllv@davidsonmediagroup.com
License: Louisville, KY held by Davidson Media Station WLOU Licensee LLC.
Group Owner: Davidson Media Group LLC; (acq 4-12-2006; $2.65 million with WLLV(AM) Louisville).
Nat'l Network: American Urban
Arbitron Metro Market: Louisville, KY *Format:* Gospel *Target Audience:* 25-54; mature adults
Vivien Ogburn, Station Manager

WXMA
10-01-1964; 102.3 mhz FM *Hrs Open:* 24; 6 kw; 285 ft.; N38 14 37 W85 45 34
50 East Rivercenter Blvd., Suite 1200, Covington, KY 41011 US
(502) 625-1220, *Fax:* (502) 625-1258
www.themaxfm.com
info@wxma.com
License: Louisville, Jefferson County, KY held by MLB-Louisville IV LLC.
Group Owner: Main Line Broadcasting LLC; (acq 9-12-2007; grpsl)
Arbitron Metro Market: Louisville, KY *Format:* Adult Contemp *Target Audience:* 25-49; young adults who enjoy modern/alternative rock *Adv. Rates:* 110; 100; 110; 80
Dale Schaefer, General Manager

WRKA
01-01-1974; 103.9 mhz FM *Hrs Open:* 24; 1.35 kw; 489 ft.; N38 15 22 W85 45 29
6358 Limewood Circle, Louisville, KY 40222 US
(502) 589-4800, *Fax:* 502-561-2988
www.countrylegends1039.com
Shane.Collins@coxinc.com
License: Louisville, Jefferson County, KY held by Cox Radio Inc.
Group Owner: Cox Radio Inc.; (acq 8-26-99; $1.77 million)
Nat'l Reps: Christal *Wire Services:* AP
Arbitron Metro Market: Louisville, KY *Format:* Country *Hrs. of News Programming:* News progmg one hr wkly *Target Audience:* 25-54; emphasis on 25-44
Shane Collins, Operations Dir
Todd Pitt, General Sales Mgr
Matt Killion, Programming Director
Brian Eichenberger, Promotions Manager
Amy Torres, General Sales Manager/Internet Sales

WLGX
06-07-1993; 100.5 mhz FM *Hrs Open:* 24; 37.4 kw; Ant 554 ft; N38 03 49 W85 43 52
4000 #1 Radio Dr., Louisville, KY 34108
(502) 479-2222, *Fax:* (502) 479-2308
www.louieonline.com
louie@louieonline.com
License: Louisville, Jefferson County, KY held by Clear Channel Broadcasting Licenses Inc.
Group Owner: Clear Channel Communications Inc.; (acq 9-13-96; $6.9 million with co-located AM).
Nat'l Reps: Clear Channel
Arbitron Metro Market: Louisville, KY *Hrs. of News Programming:* News progmg 3 hrs wkly *Target Audience:* 18-49; general
Bill Gentry, General Manager

WTUV
08-20-1958; 620 khz AM *Hrs Open:* 24; 0.5 kw-D, DA2; 0.5 kw-N, DA2; N38 18 59 W85 42 8
162 W. Broadway, Louisville, KY 40202 US
(502) 583-6200, *Fax:* (502) 473-7500
www.lapoderosaky.com
info@coronmediagroup.com
License: Louisville, KY held by Davidson Media Station WTMT Licensee LLC.
Group Owner: Davidson Media Group LLC; (acq 6-30-2006; $1 million).
Arbitron Metro Market: Louisville, KY
Paul Dendy, General Manager
Catalina Ibarra, Station Manager
Dennis Mendez, Programming Director
Jenny Sanchez, Traffic Manager

***WUOL-FM**
12-20-1976; 90.5 mhz FM *Hrs Open:* 24; 21 kw; 774 ft.; N38 21 55 W85 50 24
2301 South 3rd Street, Louisville, KY 40292 US
(502) 814-6500, *Fax:* (502) 814-6599
www.wuol.org
dgilliam@louisvillepublicmedia.org
License: Louisville, Jefferson County, KY held by Kentucky Public Radio Inc.
Arbitron Metro Market: Louisville, KY *Format:* Talk *Hrs. of News Programming:* News progmg 2 hrs wkly *Target Audience:* General; those interested in quality music & info
Donovan Reynolds, General Manager
Daniel Gilliam, Programming Director
Gray Smith, Underwriting

WKRD
01-01-1936; 790 khz AM *Hrs Open:* 24; 5 kw-D, DA2; 1 kw-N, DA2; N38 11 34 W85 31 14 *Rebroadcasts:* Simulcast with WKRD-FM Shelbyville 100%
8889 Pelican Bay Boulevard, Suite 1500, Naples, FL 34108 US
(502) 479-2222, *Fax:* (502) 479-2308
www.790wkrd.com
jimfenn@clearchannel.com
License: Louisville, KY held by Clear Channel Broadcasting Licenses Inc.
Group Owner: Clear Channel Communications Inc.; (acq 1996)
Nat'l Network: Fox Sports; Premiere Radio Networks *Nat'l Reps:* Clear Channel
Arbitron Metro Market: Louisville, KY *Format:* Sports *Hrs. of News Programming:* News progmg 2 hrs wkly *Target Audience:* 25-54.
Buddy Peterson, General Sales Mgr
Jim Fenn, Programming Director

Lyndon

WQNU
10-19-1964; 103.1 mhz FM *Hrs Open:* 24; 23 kw; 554 ft.; N38 19 28 W85 33 0
3773 Howard Hughes Pwy, Suite 300n, Las Vegas, NV 89109 US
(502) 589-4800
newcountryq1031.com
License: Lyndon, Jefferson County, KY held by Cox Radio Inc.
Group Owner: Cox Radio Inc.
Nat'l Reps: Christal *Wire Services:* AP
Arbitron Metro Market: Louisville, KY *Format:* Country *Target Audience:* 35-54
Kitty Malone, General Sales Mgr
Matt Killion, Programming Director
Todd Schumacher, Promotions Manager
Amy Torres, General Sales Manager/Internet Sales

Madisonville

WFMW
01-01-1947; 730 khz AM *Hrs Open:* 24
Mailing Address: 2380 North Main Street, Madisonville, KY 42431 US
Second Address: 2380 N. Main St., Madisonville, KY 42431
(270) 821-4096, *Fax:* (270) 821-5954
www.wfmw.net
wfmw@wfmw.net
License: Madisonville, KY held by Sound Broadcasters Inc.
Nat'l Network: CNN Radio *Nat'l Reps:* Rgnl Reps *Wire Services:* AP
Format: Country *Hrs. of News Programming:* news progmg 13 hrs wkly *No. News Employees:* 1 *Target Audience:* 18 plus. *Adv. Rates:* 15; 15; 15; 15
Robert Kelley, President
Danny Koeber, Programming Director
Chris Gardener, News Director
Chris Meyers, Chief Engineer
Steven Strait, Disc Jockey
Rick Stevens, Disc Jockey

WKTG
04-19-1949; 93.9 mhz FM *Hrs Open:* 24; 35 kw; 584 ft.; N37 31 26 W87 24 11
Mailing Address: P. O. Box 338, Madisonville, KY 42431 US
Second Address: 2380 N. Main St., Madisonville, KY 42431
(270) 821-1156
www.wktg.com
wktg@wktg.com
License: Madisonville, Hopkins County, KY
Nat'l Network: USA
Format: Rock/AOR *Hrs. of News Programming:* news progmg 3 hrs wkly *No. News Employees:* 1 *Target Audience:* 20-45. *Adv. Rates:* 18; 18; 18; 18
Robert Kelley, Station Manager
Bill McClone, Programming Director
Kevin O'Connor, Disc Jockey
Erin Grant, Disc Jockey

***WSOF-FM**
02-01-1977; 89.9 mhz FM; 39 kw; 282 ft.; N37 21 26 W87 28 41
1415 Island Ford Rd, Madisonville, KY 42431 US
(270) 825-3004
www.wsof.org
comments@wsof.org
License: Madisonville, Hopkins County, KY held by Temple Broadcasting Co.
Nat'l Network: USA
Format: Christian *Target Audience:* General; Christian
Gary Hall, General Manager

WTTL
09-16-1956; 1310 khz AM *Hrs Open:* 24; 1.5 kw-D, DAN; 0.5 kw-N, DAN; N37 20 12 W87 32 41
Mailing Address: 265 South Main Street, Madisonville, KY 42431 US
Second Address: 265 S. Main St., Madisonville, KY 42431
(270) 821-1310, *Fax:* (270) 825-3260
License: Madisonville, KY held by Madisonville CBC Inc.
Group Owner: Commonwealth Broadcasting Corp.; (acq 2-8-2000; $1.31 million with co-located FM)
Arbitron Metro Market: Madisonville, KY *Format:* News, Sports, 86 *Target Audience:* 25-54.
Tom Rogers, General Manager
Lee Ann Oliver, General Sales Mgr
Stephanie Vandygraiff, News Director

WTTL-FM
09-07-1992; 106.9 mhz FM *Hrs Open:* 24; 2 kw; 528 ft; N37 22 51 W87 28 04
Mailing Address: Box 1310, Madisonville, KY 42431
Second Address: 265 S. Main St., Madisonville, KY 42431
(270) 825-1079, *Fax:* (270) 825-3260
License: Madisonville, Hopkins County, KY
Group Owner: Commonwealth Broadcasting Corp.
Nat'l Network: ABC; Jones Radio Networks
Target Audience: 25-34.
Dex Gage, General Manager
Ed Wilhelm, Chief Engineer

***WKMD**
90.9 mhz FM; 20.5 kw; 400 ft.; N37 21 47 W87 30 56
2108 University Station, Murray, KY 42071 US
(270) 809-4359, *Fax:* (270) 809-4667
www.wkms.org
msu.wkms@murraystate.edu
License: Madisonville, Hopkins County, KY held by Board of Regents, Murray State University.
Arbitron Metro Market: Madisonville, KY

Kate Lochte, Station Manager
Tracy Ross, Programming Director

Manchester

WKLB
09-26-1981; 1290 khz AM *Hrs Open:* 24; 5 kw-D, ND1; 0.034 kw-N, ND1; N37 8 15 W83 46 50
Mailing Address: P. O. Box 448, Manchester, KY 40962 US
Second Address: 106 Richmond Rd., Manchester, KY 40962
(606) 598-2445, *Fax:* (606) 598-2653
www.wklb.com
wklb1stchoice@yahoo.com
License: Manchester, KY held by Barker Broadcasting Co.
Nat'l Reps: Rgnl Reps *Regional Reps:* Barker Broadcasting
Format: Country *Hrs. of News Programming:* news progmg 8 hrs wkly *No. News Employees:* 1 *Target Audience:* 24-65; working people
Larry Barker, President

WTBK
10-01-1989; 105.7 mhz FM *Hrs Open:* 19; 5 kw; 715 ft.; N37 8 59 W83 45 8
Mailing Address: PO Box 453, Manchester, KY 40962 US
Second Address: 107 Dickerson St., Manchester, KY 40962
(606) 598-7588, *Fax:* (606) 598-7598
wtbkradio@yahoo.com
License: Manchester, Clay County, KY held by Manchester Communications Inc.
Nat'l Network: Westwood One; ABC
Format: Classic Rock *Special Programming:* Talk 8 hrs wkly *Hrs. of News Programming:* news progmg 10 hrs wkly *No. News Employees:* 1 *Target Audience:* General; 18 plus in the morning, 16-45 at night
Tim Finley, General Manager

WWLT
08-09-1967; 103.1 mhz FM *Hrs Open:* 24; 2.1 kw; 564 ft.; N37 4 30 W83 49 14
100 Thompson-Poynter Rd., London, KY 40741 US
(513) 829-7700
www.klove.com
License: Manchester, Clay County, KY held by Wilderness Hills Broadcasting Co.
Group Owner: Vernon R Baldwin Inc.; (acq 1956)
Nat'l Network: K-Love
Arbitron Metro Market: Manchester, KY *Format:* Christian
Vernon Baldwin, President

WWXL
01-01-1956; 1450 khz AM *Hrs Open:* 24 Hours; 1 kw-U, ND1; N37 9 4 W83 45 45
4260 East Laurel Road, London, KY 40741 US
(606) 598-9995, *Fax:* (606) 598-9995
License: Manchester, KY held by Juanita H. Nolan
Arbitron Metro Market: Manchester, KY *Format:* Sports, Talk *Hrs. of News Programming:* news progmg 3 hrs wkly *No. News Employees:* 1 *Target Audience:* 35-54; programmed for adults 35-54 *Adv. Rates:* 20,20,20,10
Jonathan Dobson, General Manager
Juanita Nolan, Owner

Mannsville

WVLC
12-31-1994; 99.9 mhz FM *Hrs Open:* 24; 11 kw; 492 ft.; N37 10 4 W85 11 26
Mailing Address: P.O. Box 4190, Campbellsville, KY 42719 US
Second Address: 101 East Main St., Campbellsville, KY 42719
(270) 789-4998, *Fax:* (270) 789-4584
www.wvlc.com
bigdawg@wvlc.com
License: Mannsville, Taylor County, KY held by Patricia Rodgers.
Nat'l Network: Jones Radio Networks; CNN Radio
Arbitron Metro Market: Campbellsville, KY *Format:* Country *No. News Employees:* 2 *Target Audience:* General.
Lash Franklin, Operations Dir
Jan Royce, General Manager
Chase McBridge, News Director
Mike Wilson, News Reporter
Tammy Sexton, Office Manager
Brent Thompson, Sales Rep
Teresa Schwoebel, Sales Rep

Marion

WMJL
07-10-1968; 1500 khz AM *Hrs Open:* 6 AM-sunset; 0.175 kw-D, NDD; N37 20 16 W88 4 3
Mailing Address: P. O. Box 68, Marion, KY 42064 US
Second Address: 251 Club Dr., Marion, KY 42064
(270) 965-2271, *Fax:* (270) 965-4464
License: Marion, KY held by Joe Myers Production Inc.
Nat'l Reps: Rgnl Reps
Arbitron Metro Market: Marion, KY *Hrs. of News Programming:* news progmg 12 hrs wkly *No. News Employees:* 1 *Target Audience:* General.
Joe Myers, President

WMJL-FM
06-01-1993; 102.7 mhz FM *Hrs Open:* 24; 6 kw; 328 ft.; N37 20 16 W88 4 3
P.O. Box 68, Marion, KY 42064 US
(270) 965-2271, *Fax:* (270) 965-4464
License: Marion, Crittenden County, KY held by Joe Myers Production Inc.
Arbitron Metro Market: Marion, KY *Format:* Oldies
Randy Hugg, Operations Dir
Lisa Rich, General Manager
Todd Lewis, General Sales Mgr
Steve Shoffner, News Director
Gary Homza, Chief Engineer

Mayfield

WLLE
01-01-1997; 102.1 mhz FM; 50 kw; 472 ft.; N36 45 57.8 W88 38 49.8
Mailing Address: P O Box 900, Bowling Green, KY 42102 US
Second Address: 1176 State Rt. 45 N., Mayfield, KY 42066
(270) 554-0093, *Fax:* (270) 554-4613
www.willieradio.com
jamiefutrell@wkyq.com
License: Mayfield, Hickman County, KY held by Bristol Broadcasting Co. Inc.
Group Owner: Bristol Broadcasting Co. Inc.; (acq 3-15-2004; grpsl)
Arbitron Metro Market: Mayfield, Ky *Format:* Country *No. News Employees:* 1
Gary Morse, General Manager

WNGO
01-07-1947; 1320 khz AM *Hrs Open:* 5 AM-10 PM; 1 kw-D, ND1; 0.097 kw-N, ND1; N36 45 37 W88 38 20 *Rebroadcasts:* Rebroadcasts WKYX(AM) Paducah 90%
Mailing Address: 1715 Nashville Street, P.O. Box 298, Russellville, KY 42276 US
Second Address: 6000 Bristol Dr., Paducah, KY 42003
(270) 554-8255, *Fax:* (270) 554-5468
www.wkyx.com
License: Mayfield, KY held by Bristol Broadcasting Co. Inc.
Group Owner: Bristol Broadcasting Co. Inc.; acq 2-20-2004; grpsl).
Format: News, News/Talk, 86 *Hrs. of News Programming:* news progmg 12 hrs wkly *No. News Employees:* 1 *Target Audience:* 24-54.
Gary Morse, General Manager
Jamie Futrell, General Sales Mgr
Greg Dunker, Programming Director
Greg Walker, Chief Engineer

WYMC
10-18-1976; 1430 khz AM *Hrs Open:* 24; 1 kw-D, DAN; 1 kw-N, DAN; N36 47 12 W88 39 16
Mailing Address: P. O. Box V, 197 Wymc Road, Mayfield, KY 42066 US
Second Address: 197 WYMC Rd., Mayfield, KY 42066
(270) 247-1430, *Fax:* (270) 247-1825
radio@wymcradio.com
License: Mayfield, KY held by JDM Communications Inc.
Arbitron Metro Market: Mayfield, KY *Format:* Adult Contemp *No. News Employees:* 1 *Target Audience:* 35-64; affluent, business oriented *Adv. Rates:* 20; 9; 12; 8.10
Jim Moore, General Manager

Maysville

WFTM
01-01-1948; 1240 khz AM *Hrs Open:* 6 AM-11 PM; 1 kw-U, ND1; N38 38 10 W83 45 38
626 Forest Ave., Maysville, KY 41056 US
(606) 564-3361, *Fax:* (606) 564-4291
www.wftm.net
wftmnews@maysvilleky.net
License: Maysville, KY held by Standard Tobacco Co.
Nat'l Reps: Keystone (unwired net); Rgnl Reps
Format: Contemporary Hits/Top 40 *Special Programming:* Farm 6 hrs, gospel 5 hrs, relg 5 hrs wkly *Hrs. of News Programming:* news progmg 10 hrs wkly *No. News Employees:* 1 *Target Audience:* 50-70.
J.A. Finch, President
Jeff Cracraft, Operations Dir
Doug McGill, General Manager
Dave Gray, News Director

WFTM-FM
10-26-1965; 95.9 mhz FM *Hrs Open:* 24; 3 kw; 308 ft.; N38 38 35 W83 46 47
626 Forest Avenue, Maysville, KY 41056 US
(606) 564-3361, *Fax:* (606) 564-4291
www.wftm.net
wftmsales@maysvilleky.net
License: Maysville, Mason County, KY
Nat'l Network: AP Radio
Format: Classic Rock *No. News Employees:* 1 *Target Audience:* 18-55.
Danny Weddle, General Sales Mgr
Philip Hay, Sales

McDaniels

*WBFI
09-07-1987; 91.5 mhz FM *Hrs Open:* 24; 5 kw; 328 ft.; N37 36 6 W86 22 13
P.O. Box 2, McDaniels, KY 40152 US
(270) 257-2689(888) 333-9234, *Fax:* (270) 257-8344
www.wbfiradio.com
License: McDaniels, Breckenridge County, KY held by Bethel Fellowship Inc.
Nat'l Network: USA
Format: Adult Contemp, Christian *Hrs. of News Programming:* News progmg 20 hrs wkly *Target Audience:* General; Christians
Ronald Miller, President
Roger Goostree, General Manager
Daryl Cook, Programming Director

McKee

WWAG
11-01-1990; 107.9 mhz FM *Hrs Open:* 24; 3.9 kw; 410 ft.; N37 23 39 W83 54 27
Star Route; Box 16, Sand Gap, KY 40481 US
(606) 287-9924
www.wwagfm.com
License: McKee, Jackson County, KY held by Dandy Broadcasting Inc.
Nat'l Network: ABC *Nat'l Reps:* Rgnl Reps
Arbitron Metro Market: Jackson County, KY *Format:* Country *Special Programming:* Bluegrass 9 hrs wkly, gospel 8 hrs on Sunday *Hrs. of News Programming:* news progmg 10 hrs wkly *No. News Employees:* 1 *TargetAudience:* General. *Adv. Rates:* 10; 8; 10; 6.25
Dan Brockman, President
Sherry Brockman, General Manager

*KYAI
01-01-2008; 89.3 mhz FM; 50 kw; 165 m; N33 10 30 W102 17 20
Rebroadcasts: Rebroadcasts KLVR(FM) Middletown, CA 100%
2351 Sunset Blvd., Suite 170-218, Rocklin, CA 38104
(916) 251-1600, *Fax:* (916) 251-1650
www.klove.com
License: McKee, Terry County, KY held by Educational Media Foundation.
Group Owner: EMF Broadcasting; (acq 11-1-2006; grpsl)
Nat'l Network: K-Love
Mike Novak, President

Middlesboro

WFXY
03-01-1969; 1490 khz AM *Hrs Open:* 24; 1 kw-U, ND1; N36 36 47 W83 42 34
Mailing Address: PO Box 999, Middlesboro, KY 40965 US
Second Address: 2118 Cumberland Ave., Middlesboro, KY 40965
(606) 248-8993, *Fax:* (606) 248-6397
www.1490wfxy.com
katcountry@gmail.com
License: Middlesboro, KY held by Country-Wide Broadcasters Inc.
Nat'l Network: Jones Radio Networks *Regional Network:* Tenn. Radio Net. *Nat'l Reps:* Rgnl Reps
Format: Adult Contemp *Special Programming:* Black 2 hrs, gospel 3 hrs, relg 3 hrs wkly *Hrs. of News Programming:* news progmg 20 hrs wkly *No. News Employees:* 2 *Target Audience:* 25-54; community-oriented
Frank Smith, Operations Dir
Brian O'Brien, General Manager
Penny Smith, General Sales Mgr

WMIK
11-15-1948; 560 khz AM; 2.5 kw-D, ND1; 0.088 kw-N, ND1; N36 37 38 W83 42 52
Mailing Address: P. O. Box 608, Middlesboro, KY 40965 US
Second Address: N. 19th St., Middlesboro, KY 40965

(606) 248-5842, *Fax:* (606) 248-7660
www.wmikradio.com/
wmikradio@bellsouth.net
License: Middlesboro, KY held by Gateway Broadcasting Inc.
Arbitron Metro Market: Middlesboro, KY *Format:* Gospel *Special Programming:* Farm one hr, gospel 2 hrs wkly
Roy Shotten, General Manager
Chuck Owens, Chief Engineer

WMIK-FM
06-04-1971; 92.7 mhz FM; 0.35 kw; 1345 ft.; N36 35 39 W83 47 42
P.O. Box 608, Middlesboro, KY 40965 US
(606) 248-5842, *Fax:* (606) 248-7660
www.wmikradio.com/
wmikradio@bellsouth.net
License: Middlesboro, Bell County, KY held by Gateway Broadcasting Inc.
Regional Network: Tenn. Radio Net.
Arbitron Metro Market: Middlesboro, KY *Format:* Religious
Raymond Kassis, President
Paul Esposito, General Manager
Jim Conn, Programming Director
Jan Ferguson, Chief Engineer

Midway

WBTF
01-01-1998; 107.9 mhz FM; 6 kw; 328 ft.; N38 11 41 W84 38 25
101 Venture, Lexington, KY 40510 US
(859) 233-1515, *Fax:* (859) 233-1517
www.1079thebeat.com
License: Midway, Woodford County, KY held by L.M. Communications of Kentucky L.L.C.
Group Owner: L M Communications Inc.; (acq 4-10-01).
Nat'l Reps: Katz Radio
Arbitron Metro Market: Lexington-Fayette, KY *Format:* Urban Contemporary, Christian *Hrs. of News Programming:* News progmg 24 hrs wkly *Target Audience:* 18-49; adults
Lynn Martin, President
James MacFarlane, General Manager
James McFarlane, Promotions Manager

Monticello

WFLW
05-19-1955; 1360 khz AM *Hrs Open:* 6 AM-6 PM
P. O. Box 427, Monticello, KY 42633 US
(606) 348-8427, *Fax:* (606) 348-3867
License: Monticello, KY held by Stephen Staples Jr.
Nat'l Reps: Rgnl Reps
Format: Gospel *Special Programming:* Farm 5 hrs, news/talk 10 hrs wkly *No. News Employees:* 1 *Target Audience:* General.
Stephen Staples Jr., General Manager
Debbie Brown, Programming Director
Bruce Correll, Chief Engineer

WKYM
12-19-1965; 101.7 mhz FM *Hrs Open:* 24; 1.75 kw; 617 ft.; N36 48 36 W84 50 49
P.O. Box 427, Monticello, KY 42633 US
(606) 348-8427
www.wkym.com
wkymmail@wkym.com
License: Monticello, Wayne County, KY
Nat'l Reps: Rgnl Reps
Format: Classic Rock *Target Audience:* 18-50; baby boomers
Stephen Staples Jr., Programming Director

WMKZ
06-01-1990; 93.1 mhz FM *Hrs Open:* 24; 1.45 kw; 676 ft.; N36 48 29 W84 50 46
183 Old Hwy 90, Monticello, KY 42633 US
(606) 348-3393, *Fax:* (606) 348-3330
www.wmkz.com
studio@z93cantry.com
License: Monticello, Wayne County, KY held by Monticello-Wayne County Media Inc.
Nat'l Network: USA
Arbitron Metro Market: Monticello, KY *Format:* Country *Hrs. of News Programming:* News progmg 9 hrs wkly *Target Audience:* 24-55; general
Joel Catron, General Manager

Morehead

***WBMK**
01-01-2002; 88.5 mhz FM; 0.6 kw; 522 ft.; N38 10 38 W83 24 24
P O Box 1452, Washington, DC 20013 US
(662) 844-8888, *Fax:* (666) 842-6791
www.afa.net/Radio/
info@afr.net
License: Morehead, Rowan County, KY held by American Family Association.
Group Owner: American Family Radio; (acq 11-26-99)
Arbitron Metro Market: Morehead, KY *Format:* Christian
Marvin Sanders, General Manager

WIVY
07-01-1994; 96.3 mhz FM *Hrs Open:* 24; 2.15 kw; 518 ft.; N38 10 33 W83 24 28
Mailing Address: P.O. Box 1010, Owingsville, KY 40360 US
Second Address: 123 East First St., Morehead, KY 40351
(606) 784-9966, *Fax:* (606) 674-6700
www.wivyradio.com
info@wivyradio.com
License: Morehead, Rowan County, KY held by Gateway Radio Works Inc.
Group Owner: Gateway Radio Works Inc.
Nat'l Network: ABC
Arbitron Metro Market: Lexington-Fayette, KY *Format:* Oldies *No. News Employees:* 2 *Target Audience:* 25 plus; affluent, well educ, mature adult, higher spendable income *Adv. Rates:* 18; 14; 18; 10
Hays McMakin, President
Tom McMakin, Operations Dir
Jeff Ray, General Manager
Robert Haydon, General Sales Mgr
Becky Black, Programming Director
Carol Lynn, Promotions Manager
Dan Manley, News Director
Doug Walker, ChiefEngineer
Chris Conkright, Information Technology
Ron Caudill, Senior Sales Executive

***WMKY**
06-01-1965; 90.3 mhz FM *Hrs Open:* 24; 37 kw; 904 ft.; N38 10 38 W83 24 17
Upo Box 903, Morehead, KY 40351 US
(606) 783-2001, *Fax:* (606) 783-2335
www.msuradio.com
wmky@moreheadstate.edu
License: Morehead, Rowan County, KY held by Morehead State University
Nat'l Network: PRI; NPR *Regional Network:* Ky. News Net *Wire Services:* AP
Arbitron Metro Market: Lexington, KY *Format:* Variety/Diverse *Special Programming:* Bluegrass, Blues, Jazz, Storytelling *No. News Employees:* 10 *Target Audience:* 25-54
Greg Jenkins, Operations Dir
Paul Hitchcock, General Manager
Chuck Mraz, News Director

WMOR
02-18-1955; 1330 khz AM
129 College Street, Wet Liberty, KY 41472 US
(606) 784-4141, *Fax:* (606) 743-9557
License: Morehead, KY held by Morgan County Industries Inc.
Group Owner: Morgan County Industries Inc.; acq 3-16-99; $300,000 with co-located FM)
Nat'l Network: Moody
Arbitron Metro Market: Morehead, KY *Format:* Country
C.C. Smith, President

WMOR-FM
06-15-1965; 106.1 mhz FM; 19.5 kw; 374 ft.; N38 10 56 W83 26 56
129 College Street, West Liberty, KY 41472 US
(606) 784-4141, *Fax:* (606) 743-9557
http://www.wqxxonline.com/
info@wqxxonline.com
License: Morehead, Rowan County, KY held by Morgan County Industries Inc.
Group Owner: Morgan County Industries Inc.
Arbitron Metro Market: Morehead, KY
B.R. Anderson, Sr, President
David Malcolm, General Manager

Morganfield

***WKVN**
08-08-1967; 95.3 mhz FM; 25 kw; 269 ft.; N37 46 38 W87 37 26
P. O. Box 369, Morganfield, KY 42437 US
(916) 251-1600, *Fax:* (916) 251-1650
www.klove.com
License: Morganfield, Union County, KY held by Educational Media Foundation.
Group Owner: EMF Broadcasting; (acq 1-21-2009)
Nat'l Network: K-Love
Arbitron Metro Market: Morganfield, CA *Format:* Christian *Target Audience:* 25-64; general
Mike Novak, President

WMSK
11-21-1960; 1550 khz AM *Hrs Open:* 24; 250 w-D; N37 40 00 W87 55 40
Mailing Address: Box 369, Morganfield, KY 42437
Second Address: 1339 US 60 W., Morganfield, KY 42437
(270) 389-1550, *Fax:* (270) 389-1553
wmsk@bellsouth.net
License: Morganfield, Union County, KY held by Henson Media Inc.
Nat'l Network: Jones Radio Networks *Regional Network:* Ky. News Net *Nat'l Reps:* Rgnl Reps *Wire Services:* AP
Population Served: 50,000*Hrs. of News Programming:* News progmg 20 hrs wkly *Target Audience:* General; adults 25-64
Adv. Rates: 6.25; 6.25; 6.25; 6.25
Edward Henson, President
Bob Hite, Operations Dir
John Robinson, General Manager
Don Sheridan, General Sales Mgr
Rhonda Gibson, Traffic Manager

***WBOO**
90.3 mhz FM; 1 kw vert; 108 ft.; N37 36 41.8 W87 57 19.1 US
(317) 467-1062
License: Morganfield, Union County, KY held by Electronic Applications Radio Service Inc.
Group Owner: Electronic Applications Radio Service Inc.
Arbitron Metro Market: Morganfield, KY
Patrick Diemer, President

***WEUC**
12-29-2008; 88.7 mhz FM; 0 kw horiz, 3 kw vert; 259 ft.; N37 44 9 W87 59 45
US
(270) 389-4281, *Fax:* (270) 389-3581
www.weuc.org
License: Morganfield, Union County, KY held by Saint Ann Radio Group Inc.
Nat'l Network: EWTN Radio
Arbitron Metro Market: Morganfield, KY *Format:* Christian
Richard A Nally, President
Ed Thomas, Chief Engineer
Dr Darrell R French, Vice President

Morgantown

WLBQ
01-01-1976; 1570 khz AM *Hrs Open:* 6 AM-10 PM
P. O. Box 130, Morgantown, KY 42261 US
(270) 526-3321, *Fax:* (270) 526-5393
info@wlbqam.com
License: Morgantown, KY held by Butler County Broadcasting Co.
Nat'l Network: ABC
Format: Country *Hrs. of News Programming:* news progmg 8 hrs wkly *No. News Employees:* 1 *Target Audience:* General; residents of Morgantown & Butler County, KY
Charles Black, President
Jan Embry, Operations Dir
Howard Phelps, Station Manager

WWKN
99.1 mhz FM; 0.65 kw; 226 ft.; N37 13 38 W86 41 54
US
(469) 619-1001
License: Morgantown, Butler County, KY held by Independence Media Holdings LLC.
Group Owner: Independence Media Holdings LLC
Arbitron Metro Market: Morgantown, KY
David Jacobs, CEO

Mount Sterling

***WAXG**
01-01-1998; 88.1 mhz FM; 0.3 kw; 174 ft.; N38 3 39 W83 57 20
P O Drawer 2440, Tupelo, MS 38803 US
(800) 877-5600, *Fax:* (916) 251-1650
www.klove.com
License: Mount Sterling, Montgomery County, KY held by American Family Association.
Group Owner: American Family Radio
Arbitron Metro Market: Jackson WY *Format:* Christian
Darrell Chambliss, Chairman
Mike Novak, President

Mount Vernon

WRVK
04-30-1957; 1460 khz AM *Hrs Open:* 6 AM-9 PM
P.O. Box 1288, Mt. Vernon, KY 40456 US

(606) 256-2146, *Fax:* (606) 256-9146
www.wrvk1460.com
manager@wrvk1460.com
License: Mount Vernon, KY held by Saylor Broadcasting Inc.
Format: Country, Gospel *Target Audience:* General. *Adv. Rates:* 9:50; 9:50; na; 9:50
Charles Saylor, President
Charles Saylor, Station Manager
Charles Napier, General Sales Mgr

Mt Washington

WLCR
10-29-1955; 1040 khz AM
3600 Goldsmith Lane, Louisville, KY 40220 US
(502) 451-9527, *Fax:* (502) 451-9527
www.wlcr.net
wlcr@wlcr.net
License: Mt Washington, KY held by LCR Partners L.P.
Arbitron Metro Market: Louisville, KY *Format:* Religious *Target Audience:* General; Those interested in the existance of God
Vince Heuser, General Manager

Mt. Sterling

WMST
10-17-1957; 1150 khz AM *Hrs Open:* 24
645 Lakeshore Drive, Lexington, KY 40502 US
(859) 498-5608, *Fax:* (859) 498-7930
www.wmstradio.com
info@wmstradio.com
License: Mt. Sterling, KY held by Gateway Radio Works Inc.
Group Owner: Gateway Radio Works Inc.; Acq. Jan-1-00
Nat'l Network: CBS Radio *Regional Reps:* Rgnl. Reps.
Arbitron Metro Market: Lexington, KY *Format:* News, News/Talk, 86 *Special Programming:* Farm 2 hrs wkly *Hrs. of News Programming:* 37 hrs wkly *No. News Employees:* 2 *Target Audience:* 25 plus; affluent,mature adult, high spendalbe income, well educated *Adv. Rates:* 18; 14; 18; 10
Hays McMakin, President
Tom McMakin, Operations Dir
Jeff Ray, General Manager
Vernice Taylor, Station Manager
Robert Haydon, General Sales Mgr
Tom Byron, Promotions Manager
Dan Manley, News Director
Doug Walker, ChiefEngineer
Bill Hardin, Account Services
Frances Denney, Senior Administrative Executive

WWRW
05-28-1968; 105.5 mhz FM; 3 kw; 300 ft; N38 05 36 W83 56 39
2601 Nicholasville Rd., Lexington, KY 40502
(859) 422-1000, *Fax:* (859) 422-1038
www.wmkj.com
info@wmkj.com
License: Mt. Sterling, Montgomery County, KY held by Aloha Station Trust LLC
Population Served: 28,000
Gene Guinn, General Manager

Munfordville

WCLU-FM
08-01-1964; 102.3 mhz FM; 2.8 kw; 410 ft.; N37 10 41 W85 55 15
P.O. Box 1628, Glasgow, KY 42142 US
(270) 651-9149, *Fax:* (270) 651-9222
www.wcluradio.com
emilyrose@wcluradio.com
License: Munfordville, Hart County, KY held by Royse Radio Inc.
Arbitron Metro Market: Bowling Green, KY *Format:* Adult Contemp
Henry Royse, President
Henry Royse, General Manager

WLOC
02-01-1993; 1150 khz AM *Hrs Open:* 24
Mailing Address: P.O. Box 1628, Glasgow, KY 42142 US
Second Address: 1130 South Dixie, Horse Cave, KY 42749
(270) 786-4400, *Fax:* (270) 786-4402
www.wloconline.com
wloc@scrtc.com
License: Munfordville, KY held by Forbis Communications Inc.
Arbitron Metro Market: Bowling Green, KY *Format:* Country, Gospel *Target Audience:* 25 plus; serve entire area
DeWayne Forbis, President
Dewayne Forbis, General Manager
Chris Jessie, Programming Director
Joe Berry, News Director

Murray

WFGS
06-23-1967; 103.7 mhz FM *Hrs Open:* 24; 100 kw; 659 ft.; N36 32 58 W88 19 52
1715 Nashville Street, Russellville, KY 42276 US
(270) 753-2400, *Fax:* (270) 753-9434
www.froggy103.com
scott@forevercomm.com
License: Murray, Calloway County, KY held by Forever Communications Inc.
Group Owner: Forever Communications Inc.
Nat'l Network: Westwood One
Arbitron Metro Market: Murray, KY *Format:* Country *Hrs. of News Programming:* news progmg 4 hrs wkly *No. News Employees:* 1 *Target Audience:* 18-45. *Adv. Rates:* 23; 19; 16; 13
Scotts Swalls, General Manager
Tony Doolin, Programming Director
Neal Bradley, Sports Director

*WKMS-FM
05-11-1970; 91.3 mhz FM *Hrs Open:* 24; 100 kw; 600 ft.; N36 55 17 W88 5 48
2018 University Station, Murray, KY 42071 US
(800) 599-4737, *Fax:* (270) 809-4667
www.wkms.org
wkms@murraystate.edu
License: Murray, Calloway County, KY held by Board of Regents, Murray State University.
Nat'l Network: NPR; PRI *Wire Services:* AP
Format: News, Variety/Diverse *Special Programming:* Class 15 hrs, folk & bluegrass 3 hrs, AAA 3 hrs, u *Hrs. of News Programming:* news progmg 82 hrs wkly *No. News Employees:* 2 *Target Audience:* 35 plus; lifelong learners
Tracy Ross, Operations Dir
Kate Lochte, Station Manager
Ronda Gibson, General Sales Mgr
Mark Welch, Programming Director
Chad Lampe, News Director
Allen Fowler, Chief Engineer

WNBS
07-01-1948; 1340 khz AM *Hrs Open:* 24; 1 kw-U, ND1; N36 37 42 W88 18 4
1715 Nashville Street, Russellville, KY 42276 US
(270) 753-2400, *Fax:* (270) 753-9434
www.1340wnbs.com
License: Murray, KY held by Forever Communications Inc.
Group Owner: Forever Communications Inc.; acq 12-31-02; grpsl).
Nat'l Network: ESPN Radio; CBS Radio *Regional Network:* Ky. News Net *Regional Reps:* Rgnl Reps.
Arbitron Metro Market: Murray, KY *Format:* News, Sports, 86 *Hrs. of News Programming:* news progmg 10 hrs wkly *No. News Employees:* 1 *Target Audience:* 25-55.
Debbie Howard, General Manager
Neal Bradley, Programming Director
Candi Freeland, News Director

WOFC
09-12-1978; 1130 khz AM *Hrs Open:* 24
1715 Nashville Street, Russellville, KY 42276 US
(270) 753-2400, *Fax:* (270) 753-9434
www.1130theoffice.com
License: Murray, KY held by Forever Communications Inc.
Group Owner: Forever Communications Inc.; (acq 12-31-2002; grpsl)
Nat'l Network: ESPN Radio *Regional Reps:* Rgnl reps.
Format: Sports *Adv. Rates:* 12; 11; 10; 9
Scott Swalls, General Manager
Neal Bradley, Programming Director
Adam Bittel, Chief Engineer

Neon

WIZD
08-31-1956; 1480 khz AM *Hrs Open:* 12; 5 kw-D; N37 11 54 W82 42 42
486 Lakeside Dr., Jenkins, KY 41829
(606) 634-9430
License: Neon, Letcher County, KY held by Letcher County Broadcasting Inc.
Population Served: 150,000*Target Audience:* 24-60; general
Ernestine Kincer, President
G.C. Kincer, General Manager

Newburg

WHBE
01-01-1992; 680 khz AM *Hrs Open:* 24; 1.3 kw-D, 450 w-N, DA-2; N38 05 31 W85 40 56
11700 Commonwealth Dr., Suite 800, Louisville, KY 40219
(502) 240-0602, *Fax:* (502) 240-0940
www.radiodisney.com
john.salzman@disney.com
License: Newburg, Breckinridge County, KY held by Radio Disney Group LLC.
Group Owner: ABC Inc.; (acq 2-14-02; $1.92 million).
Arbitron Metro Market: Louisville, KY *Target Audience:* Age 25-44 mothers of children; Mothers of children younger than 15
John Salzman, Station Manager

Newport

WNOP
08-21-1948; 740 khz AM *Hrs Open:* 24
1518 Dalton Street, Cincinnati, OH 45214 US
(513) 731-7740, *Fax:* (513) 731-6465
www.sacredheartradio.com
info@sacredheartradio.com
License: Newport, KY held by Sacred Heart Radio, Inc.
Arbitron Metro Market: Cincinnati, OH *Format:* Talk, Christian
Bill Levitt, Station Manager

Nicholasville

WCGW
09-15-1986; 770 khz AM; 1 kw-D, NDD; N37 53 7 W84 31 46
3270 Blazer Pkwy, Suite 101, Lexington, KY 40509 US
(859) 873-8844, *Fax:* (859) 873-1318
www.wcgwam.com
770AM@CKCRadio.com
License: Nicholasville, KY held by Christian Broadcasting System Ltd.
Group Owner: Christian Broadcasting System Ltd.; (acq 7-1-2006; grpsl).
Nat'l Network: USA
Arbitron Metro Market: Versailles, KY *Format:* Gospel *Target Audience:* 25-54; above average in educ, family size, income *Adv. Rates:* 20; 20; 20; na
Benson Gregory, Station Manager
Dennis Blais, Chief Engineer

WLTO
08-29-1988; 102.5 mhz FM *Hrs Open:* 24; 4.6 kw; 373 ft.; N37 57 37 W84 32 42
111 East Kilbourn Avenue, Suite 2700, Milwaukee, WI 53202 US
(859) 253-5900, *Fax:* (859) 253-5940
www.hot102.net
steve.bearance@cumulus.com
License: Nicholasville, Jessamine County, KY held by Cumulus Licensing Corp.
Group Owner: Cumulus Media Inc.; (acq 7-22-99; grpsl)
Arbitron Metro Market: Lexington, KY *Format:* Contemporary Hits/Top 40 *Target Audience:* 18-44
Ken Fearnow, General Manager
Scott Frazier, General Sales Mgr
Tabatha Levrault, Programming Director

WMJR
10-19-1954; 1380 khz AM *Hrs Open:* 24
2909 Richmond Road, Suite 5, Lexington, KY 40509 US
(859) 278-0894, *Fax:* (859) 278-0426
www.wmjr.net
info@wmjr.net
License: Nicholasville, KY held by Thy Kingdom Come Network Inc.
Arbitron Metro Market: Lexington, KY *Format:* Religious *Target Audience:* 35-64.
Leo Brown, President

North Corbin

WKFC
01-01-2008; 101.9 mhz FM; 6 kw; 328 ft.; N37 2 9 W84 5 5 US
(606) 878-9532, *Fax:* (606) 878-1116
www.wkfcfm.com
License: North Corbin, Laurel County, KY held by Radioactive LLC.
Group Owner: Radioactive LLC
Arbitron Metro Market: North Corbin, KY *Format:* Country
Benjamin Homel, President
Dave Colvin, General Manager

Oak Grove

WEGI-FM
08-31-1964; 94.3 mhz FM *Hrs Open:* 24; 6 kw; 256 ft.; N36 38 28 W87 26 1
401 Church St., Nashville, TN 37219 US
(931) 648-7720, *Fax:* (931) 648-7769
eagle943.com

RADIO - U.S.

License: Oak Grove, Christian County, KY held by Saga Communications of Tuckessee LLC.
Group Owner: Saga Communications Inc.; (acq 10-4-2002; $1.5 million with co-located AM)
Arbitron Metro Market: Clarksville-Hopkinsville, TN-KY *Format:* Contemporary Hits/Top 40, Adult Contemp *Hrs. of News Programming:* news progmg 5 hrs wkly *No. News Employees:* 1 *Target Audience:* 25-54.
Scott Chase, Operations Dir
Katie Gambill, Sales Manager
J.T. Daniels, Programming Director
Lee Erwin, News Director

Okolona

*WJIE-FM
01-01-1988; 88.5 mhz FM *Hrs Open:* 24; 24.5 kw horiz, 18.5 kw vert; 623 ft.; N38 1 59 W85 45 16
Mailing Address: 5400 Minors Lane, Louisville, KY 40219 US
Second Address: 5400 Minors Ln., Louisville, KY 40219
(502) 968-1220, *Fax:* (502) 962-3143
www.wjie.org
jimfraser@wjie.org
License: Okolona, Jefferson County, KY held by Evangel Schools Inc.
Nat'l Network: Moody
Format: Christian *Hrs. of News Programming:* News progmg 7 hrs wkly *Target Audience:* 25-49; Christian adults *Adv. Rates:* 25; 20; 25; 10
Jim Fraser, General Manager
Jim Galipeau, Programming Director
Christin Ray, Disc Jockey
Chris Crain, Assistant Program Director
Ceci Labarge, Disc Jockey
Jason Brock, Disc Jockey
Bill Lawson, Disc Jockey
Randy Ollis, StaffMeterologist

Owensboro

WBKR
01-01-1948; 92.5 mhz FM *Hrs Open:* 24; 91 kw; 1050 ft.; N37 36 29 W87 3 15
P.O Box 3353, Evansville, IN 47732 US
(800)-666-1031, *Fax:* (270) 683-2128
wbkr.com
moon@wbkr.com
License: Owensboro, Daviess County, KY
Group Owner: Townsquare Media
Arbitron Metro Market: Owensboro, KY *Format:* Country *Special Programming:* Farm 2 hrs wkly *No. News Employees:* 2 *Target Audience:* 25-54.
LaDonne Craig, General Manager
Traci Davis, Director of Sales
Moon Mullins, Programming Director
Cathy Carton, News Director
Rick Crago, Engineering Dir
Dave Spenser, Music Director
Michael Owns, Traffic Manager

*WKWC
01-21-1983; 90.3 mhz FM *Hrs Open:* 24; 5 kw; 82 ft.; N37 44 32 W87 7 27
3000 Frederica St., Owensboro, KY 42301 US
(270) 852-3601, *Fax:* (270) 852-3599
kwcweb.kwc.edu/wkwc/pantherradio
patherradio@kwc.edu
License: Owensboro, Daviess County, KY held by Kentucky Wesleyan College.
Format: Triple A *Hrs. of News Programming:* News progmg 2 hrs wkly *Target Audience:* 12 plus.
Derik Hancock, General Manager

WOMI
03-07-1938; 1490 khz AM; 0.83 kw-U, ND1; N37 44 29 W87 6 58
C/O Brill Media Co, PO Box 3353, Evansville, IN 47708 US
(270) 683-1558, *Fax:* (270) 683-2128
www.1490womi.com
License: Owensboro, KY
Group Owner: Townsquare Media; (acq 2-25-03; with co-located FM).
Nat'l Reps: Christal
TV Affiliate: Talk *Hrs. of News Programming:* 2 *No. News Employees:* 35-64.
General Manager, General Manager

WSTO
06-07-1948; 96.1 mhz FM *Hrs Open:* 24; 100 kw; 1001 ft.; N37 46 20 W87 21 27
Mailing Address: P.O. Box 3353, Evansville, IN 47732 US
Second Address: 1162 Mt. Auburn Rd., Evansville, KY 47720
(812) 424-8284, *Fax:* (812) 463-7911
www.hot96.com
License: Owensboro, Daviess County, KY held by South Central Communications Corp.
Group Owner: South Central Communications Corp.; (acq 12-30-2003; $13 million).
Arbitron Metro Market: Evansville, IN *Format:* Contemporary Hits/Top 40 *Hrs. of News Programming:* news progmg one hr wkly *No. News Employees:* 4 *Target Audience:* 18-34.
Robert Shirel, CFO
Tim Huelsing, Operations Dir
Jaleigh Burger, General Sales Mgr
Jason Addams, Programming Director
Falen Bonsett, Promotions Manager

WVJS
11-26-1947; 1420 khz AM *Hrs Open:* 24
P.O. Box 3353, Evansville, IN 47732 US
(270) 683-5200, *Fax:* (270) 688-0108
www.oldiesowensboro.com
jcatinna@cromwellradio.com
License: Owensboro, KY held by Cromwell Group Inc. of Kentucky.
Group Owner: The Cromwell Group Inc.; (acq 11-20-02; $300,000).
Nat'l Network: ABC *Nat'l Reps:* Rgnl Reps
Arbitron Metro Market: Owensboro, KY *Format:* News, Sports *Special Programming:* Farm one hr wkly *Hrs. of News Programming:* One *No. News Employees:* 1 *Target Audience:* 35-54.
Bayard Walters, President
Jan Catinna, General Manager
Mike Chaney, News Director

*WJVK
01-01-2004; 91.7 mhz FM; 0.1 kw; 174 ft.; N37 44 48 W87 6 58
Rebroadcasts: WCVK(FM)
Mailing Address: 1407 Scottsville Rd, Bowling Green, KY 42104 US
Second Address: 1407 Scottsville Rd., Bowling Green, KY 42104
(270) 781-7326, *Fax:* (270) 781-8005
www.christianfamilyradio.com
mike@christianfamilyradio.com
License: Owensboro, Daviess County, KY held by Bowling Green Community Broadcasting Inc.
Arbitron Metro Market: Owensboro, KY *Format:* Christian
Ken Burns, Operations Dir
Mike Wilson, General Manager
Susan ""West"" Woodard, Programming Director
Derek Gregory, Promotions Manager
Donna Brown, Office Manager/Bookkeeper
Mary Beth Warren, Administrative Assistant
DaleMcCubbins, Production Manager

Owingsville

WKYN
12-01-1983; 107.7 mhz FM *Hrs Open:* 24; 6 kw; 328 ft.; N38 6 8 W83 50 12
Mailing Address: P.O. Box 1010, Owingsville, KY 40360 US
Second Address: , Winchester, KY 40391
(859) 498-1077, *Fax:* (859) 498-7930
www.wkynradio.com
info@wkynradio.com
License: Owingsville, Bath County, KY held by Gateway Radio Works Inc.
Group Owner: Gateway Radio Works Inc.
Nat'l Network: NBC Radio
Arbitron Metro Market: Lexington-Fayette, KY *Format:* Country *Hrs. of News Programming:* 10 hrs wkly *No. News Employees:* 2 *Adv. Rates:* 18; 14; 18; 10
Hays McMakin, President
Tom McMakin, Operations Dir
Jeff Ray, General Manager
Vernice Taylor, Station Manager
Bill Hardin, General Sales Mgr
Tom Byron, Promotions Manager
Frances Denney, News Director
Doug Walker, ChiefEngineer
Robert Haydon, Account Services
Dan Manley, News/Programming Director

Paducah

WDDJ
11-26-1946; 96.9 mhz FM *Hrs Open:* 24; 100 kw; 778 ft.; N37 2 56 W88 36 52
Mailing Address: 901 East Valley Drive, Bristol, VA 24201 US
Second Address: 6000 Bristol Dr., Paducah, KY 42003
(270) 534-9690, *Fax:* (270) 554-5468
www.electric969.com
pd@electric969.com
License: Paducah, McCracken County, KY held by Bristol Broadcasting Co. Inc.
Group Owner: Bristol Broadcasting Co. Inc.; (acq 6-24-97; $2.7 million with co-located AM).
Arbitron Metro Market: Paducah, KY *Format:* Contemporary Hits/Top 40 *Hrs. of News Programming:* news progmg 2 hrs wkly *No. News Employees:* 2 *Target Audience:* 18-49; active, white & blue collar adults *Adv.Rates:* 75; 75; 75; 40
Gary Morse, General Manager
Jamie Futrell, General Sales Mgr
Mark Summer, Programming Director
Greg Walker, Chief Engineer

WDXR
12-24-1957; 1450 khz AM *Hrs Open:* 24; 1 kw-U, ND1; N37 5 55 W88 37 19
Mailing Address: P.O. Box 900, 948 Fairview Avenue, Bowling Green, KY 42102 US
Second Address: 1176 Stat Rt. 45 N., Paducah, KY
(270) 247-5122, *Fax:* (270) 554-5468
License: Paducah, KY held by Bristol Broadcasting Co. Inc.
Group Owner: Bristol Broadcasting Co. Inc.; (acq 3-15-2004; grpsl)
Nat'l Network: ABC
Arbitron Metro Market: Paducah, KY *Format:* Urban Contemporary *Hrs. of News Programming:* news progmg 5 hrs wkly *No. News Employees:* 1 *Target Audience:* 30-65.
Gary Morse, General Manager

*WGCF
12-01-1996; 89.3 mhz FM *Hrs Open:* 24; 12 kw; 492 ft.; N37 11 31 W88 58 41
P.O. Box 189, Bowling Green, KY 42102 US
(270) 462-3020, *Fax:* (270) 462-3024
License: Paducah, McCracken County, KY held by American Family Association.
Group Owner: American Family Radio; (acq 11-25-2003; $200,000).
Format: Adult Contemp
Bill Hughes, General Manager

WKYQ
01-01-1947; 93.3 mhz FM *Hrs Open:* 24; 100 kw; 915 ft.; N37 2 56 W88 36 52
Mailing Address: P.O. Box 1389, Bristol, VA 24203 US
Second Address: 6000 Bristol Drive, Paducah, KY 42003
(270) 554-8255, *Fax:* (270) 554-5468
www.wkyq.com
production@wkyq.com
License: Paducah, McCracken County, KY
Group Owner: Bristol Broadcasting Co. Inc.
Format: Country *No. News Employees:* 3 *Target Audience:* 25-54. *Adv. Rates:* 85; 85; 85; 45
Bobby Cook, Operations Dir
Gary Morse, General Manager
Jamie Futrell, General Sales Mgr
Jeff Lawrence, Programming Director
Donna Groves, News Director
Greg Walker, Engineering Dir

WKYX
01-01-1946; 570 khz AM *Hrs Open:* 24; 1 kw-D, DA2; 0.5 kw-N, DA2; N37 0 53 W88 36 46 *Rebroadcasts:* Simulcast with WKYX-FM Golconda, IL 100%
Mailing Address: P. O. Box 1389, Bristol, VA 24203 US
Second Address: 6000 Bristol Dr., Paducah, KY 42003
(270) 554-8255, *Fax:* (270) 554-5468
www.wkyx.com
License: Paducah, KY held by Bristol Broadcasting Co. Inc.
Group Owner: Bristol Broadcasting Co. Inc.; (acq 11-23-71)
Nat'l Reps: Christal
Format: News, News/Talk, 86 *Hrs. of News Programming:* news progmg 20 hrs wkly *No. News Employees:* 3 *Target Audience:* 25-54; middle to upper income *Adv. Rates:* 35; 35; 35; 15
Gary Morse, General Manager
Jamie Futrell, General Sales Mgr
Greg Dunker, Programming Director
Donna Groves, News Director

WPAD
08-23-1930; 1560 khz AM *Hrs Open:* 24; 10 kw-D, DA3; 1 kw-N, DA3; DA3; 5 kw-N; N37 3 8 W88 36 3
Mailing Address: 901 East Valley Drive, Bristol, VA 24201 US
Second Address: 6000 Bristol Dr., Paducah, KY 42003
(270) 534-9690, *Fax:* (270) 554-4613
www.electric969.com
info@electric969.com
License: Paducah, KY held by Bristol Broadcasting Co. Inc.
Group Owner: Bristol Broadcasting Co. Inc.

Nat'l Network: Westwood One
Format: Sports *Hrs. of News Programming:* news progmg 22 hrs wkly *No. News Employees:* 2 *Target Audience:* 35-64; upscale, white-collar *Adv. Rates:* Same as FM
Alfonso Gimenez-Porrata, CEO
Alfonso Gimenez-Lucchetti, Operations Dir
Sayda Ortiz, General Sales Mgr
Maria Luisa Gimenez-Lucchetti, Vice President, Operations

***WNFC**
91.7 mhz FM; 15 kw; 297 ft.; N37 3 41.4 W88 50 25.7 US
(270) 369-8614, *Fax:* (270) 369-7402
www.wjcr.org
donjrwjcr@yahoo.com
License: Paducah, McCracken County, KY held by FM 90.1 Inc.
Arbitron Metro Market: Paducah, KY
Don Powell, General Manager

Paintsville

WKYH
03-18-1985; 600 khz AM
P.O. Box 1407, Ste 6 Woodland Place, Paintsville, KY 41240 US
(606) 789-3333, *Fax:* (859) 402-0260
ckbelhasen@belsouth.net
License: Paintsville, KY held by Highlands Broadcasting Corp.
Nat'l Network: Westwood One
Format: News, News/Talk, 84, Talk *Target Audience:* 25-49; middle to upper class adults
Charles K. Belhasen, President
Charles Belhasen, General Manager

WKLW-FM
06-18-1993; 94.7 mhz FM *Hrs Open:* 24; 4.9 kw; 732 ft.; N37 47 42 W82 48 3
Mailing Address: P.O. Drawer 1407, Ste Six Woodland Pl, Paintsville, KY 41240 US
Second Address: 865 S. Mayo Tr., Paintsville, KY 41240
(606) 789-6664, *Fax:* (606) 789-6669
www.wklw.com
wklwfm@belsouth.net
License: Paintsville, Johnson County, KY held by B & G Broadcasting Inc.
Format: Adult Contemp
Alan Burton, General Manager

WSIP
04-24-1949; 1490 khz AM; 1 kw-U, ND1; N37 48 21 W82 46 1
Mailing Address: P.O. Box 1450, Corbin, KY 40702 US
Second Address: 127 Main St., Paintsville, KY 41240
(606) 789-5311, *Fax:* (606) 789-7200
www.wsipam.com
wsipradio@bellsouth.net
License: Paintsville, KY held by S.I.P. Broadcasting Inc.
Group Owner: Key Broadcasting Inc.; (acq 2-84)
Nat'l Reps: Rgnl Reps
Format: Oldies *Target Audience:* General.
Spike Berkhimer, General Manager

WSIP-FM
01-12-1965; 98.9 mhz FM *Hrs Open:* 24; 100 kw; 627 ft.; N37 51 30 W82 47 41
Mailing Address: P. O. Box 1450, Corbin, KY 40702 US
Second Address: 127 Main St., Paintsville, KY 41240
(606) 789-5311, *Fax:* (606) 789-7200
www.wsipfm.com
wsipradio@bellsouth.net
License: Paintsville, Johnson County, KY
Group Owner: Key Broadcasting Inc.
Format: Country
Harold Miller Jr., CEO
Theresa Miller, Operations Dir
Dave Baker, Vice President, Operations

Paris

WGKS
06-05-1968; 96.9 mhz FM; 50 kw; 492 ft.; N38 7 32 W84 21 12
1300 Greendale Road, Lexington, KY 40511 US
(859) 233-1515, *Fax:* (859) 233-1517
www.969kissfm.com
jmac@lmcomm.com
License: Paris, Bourbon County, KY held by L.M. Communications Inc.
Group Owner: L M Communications Inc.
Nat'l Network: ABC *Nat'l Reps:* Katz Radio
Arbitron Metro Market: Lexington-Fayette, KY *Format:* Adult Contemp *Hrs. of News Programming:* news progmg 10 hrs wkly *No. News Employees:* 1
Lynn Martin, President
James MacFarlane, General Manager
Skip Eliot, Programming Director

WYGH
01-01-1993; 1440 khz AM *Hrs Open:* 24
13297 Green Road, Walton, KY 41094 US
(859) 472-1075, *Fax:* (859) 472-2875
wiok@fuse.net
License: Paris, KY held by Hammond Broadcasting Inc.
Arbitron Metro Market: Lexington-Fayet *Format:* Gospel
Jan Hammond, General Manager

***WPTJ**
08-01-2003; 90.7 mhz FM *Hrs Open:* 24; 10 kw; 315 ft.; N38 19 40 W84 7 44
Mailing Address: 1811 Cynthiana, Millersburg Rd, Paris, KY 40361 US
Second Address: Lay Witness Broadcasting, Box 7, Paris, KY 40362-0007
(859) 484-9691
jsmith@wptj.org
License: Paris, Bourbon County, KY held by Lay Witness Outreach Inc.
Arbitron Metro Market: Paris, KY *Format:* Religious *Adv. Rates:* 150; 120; 150; 100
John Smith, General Manager
John Brett, Programming Director

Philpot

WBIO
11-18-1993; 94.7 mhz FM *Hrs Open:* 24; 3 kw; 328 ft.; N37 41 50 W86 59 28
P. O. Box 150846, Nashville, TN 37215 US
(270) 683-5200, *Fax:* (270) 688-0108
www.wbio.com
jcatinna@cromwellradio.com
License: Philpot, Daviess County, KY held by Hancock Communications Inc.
Group Owner: The Cromwell Group Inc.; (acq 6-17-93; $90,565;
Nat'l Network: ABC *Nat'l Reps:* Rgnl Reps
Arbitron Metro Market: Owensboro, Ky *Format:* Country *Hrs. of News Programming:* news progmg 4 hrs wkly *No. News Employees:* 1 *Target Audience:* 25-54. *Adv. Rates:* 20; 20; 20; 12
Bayard Walters, CEO
Jan Catinna, General Manager
Mike Chaney, News Director

Pikeville

WDHR
03-25-1966; 93.1 mhz FM *Hrs Open:* 24; 22 kw; 758 ft.; N37 27 57 W82 33 4
P.O. Box 2200, Pikeville, KY 41501 US
(606) 437-4051, *Fax:* (606) 432-2809
www.wdhr.com
wdhr@wdhr.com
License: Pikeville, Pike County, KY held by East Kentucky Broadcasting Corp.
Group Owner: East Kentucky Broadcasting Corp.
Nat'l Network: ABC
Arbitron Metro Market: Pikeville, KY *Format:* Country *No. News Employees:* 2
Cindy May Johnson, GM
George Wells, General Manager

***WJSO**
04-01-1989; 90.1 mhz FM *Hrs Open:* 24; 3.8 kw; 456 ft.; N37 27 52 W82 32 45
820 N. Lasalle Blvd., Chicago, IL 60610 US
(606) 432-0351, *Fax:* (312) 329-8980
wjso.mbn.org
wjso@moody.edu
License: Pikeville, Pike County, KY held by Moody Bible Institute of Chicago.
Group Owner: The Moody Bible Institute of Chicago; acq 12-18-91; donation;
Nat'l Network: Moody
Format: Religious *Hrs. of News Programming:* News progmg 15 hrs wkly *Target Audience:* 35-55.
Scott Keegan, General Manager

WLSI
01-20-1949; 900 khz AM *Hrs Open:* 24*Rebroadcasts:* Simulcast with WPRT(AM) Prestonburg 100%
Mailing Address: P.O. Box 2347, Pikeville, KY 41501 US
Second Address: 1240 Radio Dr., Pikeville, KY 41501
(606) 437-4051, *Fax:* (606) 432-2809
www.ekbradio.com
wdhr@wdhr.com
License: Pikeville, KY held by East Kentucky Broadcasting Corp.
Group Owner: East Kentucky Broadcasting Corp.; (acq 5-14-2003; $531,273 with WZLK(FM) Virgie)
Nat'l Network: CNN Radio; NBC Radio; Sporting News Radio Network
Format: Talk *Hrs. of News Programming:* news progmg 21 hrs wkly *No. News Employees:* 1 *Target Audience:* 25-49.
Keith Casebolt, General Manager

WPKE
07-31-1949; 1240 khz AM *Hrs Open:* 24*Rebroadcasts:* Rebroadcasts WBPA(AM) Elkhorn City 100%
Mailing Address: 1240 Radio Drive, Pikeville, KY 41502 US
Second Address: 1240 Radio Dr., Pikeville, KY 41501
(606) 437-4051, *Fax:* (606) 432-2809
www.wdhr.com
wdhr@wdhr.com
License: Pikeville, KY held by East Kentucky Broadcasting Corp.
Group Owner: East Kentucky Broadcasting Corp.; acq 1962).
Nat'l Reps: Rgnl Reps *Regional Reps:* Rgnl Reps
Format: Oldies *Hrs. of News Programming:* news progmg 5 hrs wkly *No. News Employees:* 1 *Target Audience:* General.
Keith Casebolt, General Manager
Randy Jones, Programming Director
Walter Dingus, Chief Engineer

Pineville

WANO
03-16-1957; 1230 khz AM; 1 kw-U, ND1; N36 46 7 W83 42 59
P.O. Box 999, Middlesboro, KY 40965 US
(606) 248-8993, *Fax:* (606) 248-6397
www.1230wano.com
katcountryky@gmail.com
License: Pineville, KY held by Cumberland Media Group Inc.
Arbitron Metro Market: Pineville, KY. *Format:* Oldies
Brian O'Brien, Operations Dir

WRIL
02-24-1973; 106.3 mhz FM; 1.15 kw; 748 ft.; N36 45 16 W83 42 12
Mailing Address: P.O. Box 693, Pineville, KY 40977 US
Second Address: 25 E. Log Mountain, Pineville, KY 40977
(606) 337-5202, *Fax:* (606) 337-8020
wrilcountry@yahoo.com
License: Pineville, Bell County, KY held by Pine Hills Broadcasting Inc.
Format: Country
Gayle McPherson, General Manager

Pippa Passes

***WWJD**
11-01-1986; 91.7 mhz FM *Hrs Open:* 24; 7.3 kw; 545 ft.; N37 19 45 W82 52 30
100 Purpose Road, Pippa Passes, KY 41844 US
(606) 368-6131, *Fax:* (606) 368-6017
wwjd@alc.edu
License: Pippa Passes, Knott County, KY held by Alice Lloyd College.
Arbitron Metro Market: Pippa Passes, KY *Format:* Adult Contemp, Christian *Target Audience:* 13-25.
Jason Stowers, General Manager

Plum Springs

WWKU
10-01-1962; 1450 khz AM
Mailing Address: P.O. Box 457, Glasgow, KY 42141 US
Second Address: 113 W. Public Sq., Suite 400, Glasgow, KY 42141
(270-651-6050, *Fax:* (270-651-7666
www.espn1450.net/
License: Plum Springs, KY held by Newberry Broadcasting Inc.
Group Owner: Commonwealth Broadcasting Corp.
Arbitron Metro Market: Glasgow,KY *Format:* Sports
Anthony Lee, Station Manager

Prestonsburg

WDOC
11-01-1957; 1310 khz AM *Hrs Open:* Sunrise-sunset
P.O. Box 307, Prestonsburg, KY 41653 US
(606) 886-2338(606) 886-8409, *Fax:* (606) 263-4923
www.q95fm.net
gorm.collins@wdocinc.com
License: Prestonsburg, KY held by WDOC Inc.
Nat'l Reps: Rgnl Reps
Arbitron Metro Market: Prestonsburg, KY *Format:* Gospel *Target Audience:* 25-64. *Adv. Rates:* 7; 5; 6; na
Gormon Collins Jr., President
Gormon Collins, Jr., General Manager

Samantha Osborne, General Sales Mgr
Jamie Howell, News Director

WPRT
12-05-1952; 960 khz AM *Rebroadcasts:* Simulcast with WLSI(AM) Pikeville 100%
Mailing Address: Us Highway 23, Main Street, Paulboro Row, Harold, KY 41635 US
Second Address: 1240 Radio Dr., Pikesville, KY 41501
(606) 437-4051, *Fax:* (606) 432-2809
www.900wlsi.com
wdhr@wdhrcom
License: Prestonsburg, KY held by East Kentucky Radio Network Inc.
Group Owner: East Kentucky Radio Network Inc.; (acq 10-26-2001)
Nat'l Network: CNN Radio; NBC Radio; Sporting News Radio Network
Format: Talk
Keith Casebolt, General Manager

WQHY
02-11-1968; 95.5 mhz FM *Hrs Open:* 24; 100 kw; 1001 ft.; N37 41 45 W82 45 24
University Drive, P.O. Box 309, Prestonsburg, KY 41653 US
(606) 886-2338,(606) 886-8409, *Fax:* (606) 886-1026
www.q95fm.net
q95prod@bellsouth.net
License: Prestonsburg, Floyd County, KY held by WDOC, Inc.
Nat'l Network: ABC *Nat'l Reps:* Rgnl Reps
Format: Contemporary Hits/Top 40 *Hrs. of News Programming:* news progmg 2 hrs wkly *No. News Employees:* 1 *Target Audience:* 18-34. *Adv. Rates:* 24; 20; 22; 14
Gormon Collins, Jr., General Manager
Samantha Osborne, General Sales Mgr
Jessica Sparks, Programming Director
Carla Hughes, News Director
Russ Lafforty, Chief Engineer

WXKZ-FM
02-10-1967; 105.3 mhz FM; 4.7 kw; 371 ft.; N37 39 24 W82 45 58
P.O. Box 1049, Harold, KY 41635 US
(606) 478-1200, *Fax:* (606) 478-4202
www.thedoublex.com
wifx@foxy943.com
License: Prestonsburg, Floyd County, KY held by Adam Gearheart dba WXLR-FM
Format: Oldies
Barry Boyd, General Manager
Mel Stevens, Programming Director

Princeton

WAVJ
04-01-1969; 104.9 mhz FM *Hrs Open:* 24; 6 kw; 174 ft.; N37 7 14 W87 51 31
Mailing Address: P.O. Box 1505, Glasgow, KY 42142 US
Second Address: 108 W. Main St., Princeton, KY 42445
(877) 702-9293, *Fax:* (303) 702-9293
www.wayfm.com
supportservices@wayfm.com
License: Princeton, Caldwell County, KY held by Caldwell County CBC Inc.
Group Owner: Commonwealth Broadcasting Corp.
Arbitron Metro Market: Brush CO *Format:* Christian
Robert Augsburg, President

WPKY
03-15-1950; 1580 khz AM *Hrs Open:* 24; 0.25 kw-D, ND1; 0.009 kw-N, ND1; N37 7 14 W87 51 31
Mailing Address: P.O. Box 1505, Glasgow, KY 42142 US
Second Address: 108 W. Main St., Princeton, KY 42445
(270) 365-2072, *Fax:* (270) 365-2073
wavj@commonwealthbroadcasting.com
License: Princeton, KY held by Caldwell County CBC Inc.
Group Owner: Commonwealth Broadcasting Corp.; (acq 6-25-98; $362,000 with co-located FM)
Nat'l Network: ESPN Radio
Format: Sports *Hrs. of News Programming:* news progmg 11 hrs wkly *No. News Employees:* 1 *Target Audience:* General.
Tom Rogers, General Manager
LeeAnn Oliver, General Sales Mgr
Ed Thomas, Chief Engineer

Providence

WWKY
04-09-1976; 97.7 mhz FM *Hrs Open:* 24; 6 kw; 328 ft.; N37 24 52 W87 34 23
Mailing Address: P.O. Box 1505, Glasgow, KY 42142 US
Second Address: 265 S. Main St., Madisonville, KY 42431
(270) 825-9779, *Fax:* (270) 825-3260
wwky@commonwealthbroadcasting.com
License: Providence, Webster County, KY held by Hopkins-Webster CBC Inc.
Group Owner: Commonwealth Broadcasting Corp.; (acq 5-21-98; $425,000).
Nat'l Network: CNN Radio *Regional Network:* Ky. News Net
Format: Oldies *Hrs. of News Programming:* news progmg 21 hrs wkly *No. News Employees:* 2 *Target Audience:* 25-54.
Tom Rogers, General Manager
Lee Oliver, General Sales Mgr
Stephanie Vandygraiff, News Director

Radcliff

WAKY
07-25-1995; 103.5 mhz FM *Hrs Open:* 24; 3.5 kw; Ant 761 ft; N37 52 45 W85 43 03
Mailing Address: Box 2087, Elizabethtown, KY 42702
Second Address: 519 N. Miles, Elizabethtown, KY 42701
(270) 766-1035, *Fax:* (270) 769-1052
www.waky1035.com
rbell@waky1035.com
License: Radcliff, Hardin County, KY held by W & B Broadcasting Inc.
Group Owner: W & B Broadcasting Inc.
Nat'l Network: ABC
Population Served: 513,878*Hrs. of News Programming:* news progmg 4 hrs wkly *No. News Employees:* 14 *Target Audience:* 25-54; baby boomers *Adv. Rates:* 32; 32; 32; 8
Bill Walters, President
Cale Tharp, Operations Dir
Rene Bell, General Manager
Les Cook, Programming Director
Al Mayo, News Director
Cayce Happel, Engineering Dir

Reidland

WZZL
10-01-1992; 106.7 mhz FM *Hrs Open:* 24; 4.7 kw; 371 ft.; N37 5 55 W88 37 19
3501 Broadway, P.O. Box 1508, Mount Vernon, IL 62864 US
(270) 538-5251, *Fax:* (270) 415-0599
www.wzzl.com
rlambert@withersradio.net
License: Reidland, McCracken County, KY held by Withers Broadcasting Co. of Paducah LLC.
Group Owner: Withers Broadcasting Co.; (acq 9-11-97; grpsl).
Arbitron Metro Market: Paducah, KY *Format:* Rock/AOR *Target Audience:* 18-49.
Rick Lambert, General Manager
Jolie Birchfield, Sales Manager
Melanie Shepherd, Account Executive
Shane Hook, Account Executive
Priscilla Thompson, Account Executive
Jana Adams, Account Executive

Richmond

WCBR
03-01-1969; 1110 khz AM *Hrs Open:* Sunrise-sunset; 0.25 kw-D, NDD; N37 44 9 W84 16 5
Mailing Address: PO Box 570, Richmond, KY 40476 US
Second Address: 509 Leighway Dr., Richmond, KY 40475
(859) 623-1235, *Fax:* (859) 623-7094
wcbr1110.com
wcbrradio@bellsouth.net
License: Richmond, KY held by WCBR Inc.
Nat'l Network: USA
Arbitron Metro Market: Richmond,KY *Format:* Gospel *Special Programming:* Loc talk shows, news, sports & relg talk 35 hrs wkly *Hrs. of News Programming:* News progmg 5 hrs wkly *Target Audience:* 35 plus; olderadult listener *Adv. Rates:* 8.50; 8.50; 8.50; 8.50
Bill Robbins, President
Malissa Blair, News Director
David Humes, Executive Vice President

***WEKU**
09-01-1968; 88.9 mhz FM *Hrs Open:* 24; 50 kw; 719 ft.; N37 52 45 W84 19 33
102 Perkins Building, Richmond, KY 40475 US
(859) 622-1660, *Fax:* (859) 622-6276
www.weku.fm
weku@eku.edu
License: Richmond, Madison County, KY held by Board of Regents, Eastern Kentucky University.
Nat'l Network: NPR; PRI *Wire Services:* AP
Arbitron Metro Market: Richmond, KY *Format:* News *Hrs. of News Programming:* news progmg 35 hrs wkly *No. News Employees:* 3 *Target Audience:* General.
Mary Ellyn Cain, Operations Dir
Tim Singleton, General Manager
Carol Siler, General Sales Mgr
Laura Allen, Programming Director
Charles Compton, News Director
Bill Browning, Chief Engineer

WEKY
10-17-1953; 1340 khz AM *Hrs Open:* 24; 1 kw-U, ND1; N37 43 0 W84 18 25
1030 Winchester Road, Irvine, KY 40336 US
(859) 623-1386, *Fax:* (859) 623-1341
www.wekyam.com
coyote@wcyofm.com
License: Richmond, KY held by Wallingford Communications Inc.
Group Owner: Wallingford Broadcasting Co.; (acq 1999; grpsl)
Regional Network: Ky. News Net *Nat'l Reps:* Rgnl Reps
Arbitron Metro Market: Richmond, KY *Format:* News, News/Talk, 86 *Special Programming:* Black 12 hrs, relg 6 hrs wkly *Hrs. of News Programming:* news progmg 3 hrs wkly *No. News Employees:* 1 *Target Audience:* 25-54.
Kelly Wallingford, General Manager
Ray White, Programming Director

WVLK-FM
05-12-1972; 101.5 mhz FM *Hrs Open:* 24; 9 kw; 541 ft.; N37 52 45 W84 19 33
111 East Kilbourn Avenue, Suite 2700, Milwaukee, WI 53202 US
(859) 253-5900, *Fax:* (859) 253-5940
www.wvlkam.com
License: Richmond, Madison County, KY held by Cumulus Licensing Corp.
Group Owner: Cumulus Media Inc.; (acq 10-5-99; grpsl)
Arbitron Metro Market: Lexington-Fayette, KY *Format:* Sports, Talk *Hrs. of News Programming:* news progmg 6 hrs wkly *No. News Employees:* 1
Anread Ayers, General Manager
Ken Fearnow, General Manager

Russell Springs

WHVE
01-01-1993; 92.7 mhz FM; 6 kw; 328 ft.; N37 4 40 W85 10 28
Mailing Address: PO Box 927, Columbia, KY 42728 US
Second Address: 7955 Russell Springs Rd., Russell Springs, KY 42642
(270) 384-7979, *Fax:* (270) 384-6244
www.ridingthewave.com
thewave@ridingthewave.com
License: Russell Springs, Russell County, KY held by Shoreline Communications Inc.
Format: Adult Contemp
Alan Reed, CEO
Don Salmon, Operations Dir
Jan Royse, General Manager
Ted Beckman, General Sales Mgr
Larry Smith, Programming Director

WIDS
10-14-1982; 570 khz AM *Hrs Open:* 24
13297 Green Road, Walton, KY 41094 US
(859) 472-1075, *Fax:* (859) 472-2875
www.tri-stategospel.org
wiok@fuse.net
License: Russell Springs, KY held by Hammond Broadcasting Inc.
Format: Gospel
Jan Hammond, General Manager

Russellville

WUBT
03-28-1965; 101.1 mhz FM *Hrs Open:* 24; 47 kw; 1289 ft.; N36 31 36 W86 41 14
600 Congress Avenue, Suite 1400, Austin, TX 78701 US
(615) 664-2400, *Fax:* (615) 664-2457
www.101thebeat.com
info@101thebeat.com
License: Russellville, Logan County, KY held by Capstar TX L.P.
Group Owner: Clear Channel Communications Inc.; (acq 8-30-00; grpsl).
Arbitron Metro Market: Nashville, TN *Format:* Urban Contemporary
David Alpert, General Manager
Bill Reed, General Sales Mgr
Keith Kaufman, Promotions Manager

WRUS
08-28-1953; 610 khz AM *Hrs Open:* 24; 1.8 kw-D, ND1; 0.059 kw-N, ND1; N36 50 40 W86 55 21
1715 Nashville Street, P.O. Box 298, Russellville, KY 42276 US

(270) 726-6100, *Fax:* (270) 726-3095
www.wrusam.com
wrus@bellsouth.net
License: Russellville, KY held by Logan Radio Inc.
Format: Variety/Diverse
Chris McGinnis, General Manager

Salt Lick

WKCA
04-19-1976; 97.7 mhz FM *Hrs Open:* 24; 3 kw; 469 ft.; N38 10 33 W83 24 28
Mailing Address: 35 Island Drive, Eastpoint, FL 32328 US
Second Address: 123 East First St., Morehead, KY 40351
(308) 381-1430, *Fax:* (308) 382-6701
www.2dayfm1031.com
info@familyradio.com
License: Salt Lick, Bath County, KY held by Gateway Radio Works Inc.
Group Owner: Gateway Radio Works Inc.; (acq 9-7-2007)
Nat'l Network: CBS Radio
Arbitron Metro Market: Ravenna NE *Format:* Rock/AOR *Adv. Rates:* 18;14;18;10
Donald Wilks, President
Alan Usher, General Manager

Salyersville

WRLV
09-01-1979; 1140 khz AM *Hrs Open:* 12; 1 kw-D, NDD; N37 44 58 W83 5 19
Mailing Address: 1030 Winchester Rd., Irvine, KY 40336 US
Second Address: 225 S. Church St., Salyersville, KY 41465
(606) 349-6125,(606) 349-6126, *Fax:* (606) 349-6129
www.wrlvradio.com
coyote2@foothills.net
License: Salyersville, KY held by Morgan County Industires Inc.
Group Owner: Morgan County Industries Inc.; (acq 7-5-2007; $460,000 with co-located FM)
Nat'l Reps: Rgnl Reps
Format: Country *Hrs. of News Programming:* news progmg 5 hrs wkly *No. News Employees:* 2 *Target Audience:* 35-65; middle age to elderly *Adv. Rates:* 3.50; 3.50; 3.50; na
C.C. Smith, President
Kathy Puckett, General Manager
Teresa Witten, Programming Director
Sanford Baca, Local News Editor
Bryan Russell, Promotions Director

WRLV-FM
08-25-1989; 106.5 mhz FM *Hrs Open:* 24; 5.9 kw; 331 ft.; N37 45 27 W83 3 50
Mailing Address: 1030 Winchester Road, Irvine, KY 40336 US
Second Address: 225 S. Church St., Salyersville, KY 41465
(606) 349-6125, *Fax:* (606) 349-6129
www.wrlvradio.com
License: Salyersville, Magoffin County, KY
Group Owner: Morgan County Industries Inc.
Nat'l Reps: Rgnl Reps
Format: Country *Hrs. of News Programming:* news progmg 5 hrs wkly *No. News Employees:* 2 *Target Audience:* 18-80; young to elderly *Adv. Rates:* 8.75; 8.75; 8.75; 8.75
Kathy Puckett, General Sales Mgr
Bryan Russell, Programming Director
Teresa Witten, News Director
Sanford Baca, Local News Editor
Terry Lykins, Religion Ed
Hershall Wright, Religion Ed
Scott Ratliff, Sports Commentator

Science Hill

WYKY
01-01-2008; 106.1 mhz FM; 1.95 kw; 584 ft.; N37 7 53 W84 32 21
US
(606) 678-8151, *Fax:* (606) 678-8152
www.somerset106.com
License: Science Hill, Pulaski County, KY held by F.T.G. Broadcasting Inc.
Group Owner: Key Broadcasting Inc.
Arbitron Metro Market: Science Hill, KY *Format:* Adult Contemp
Terry Forcht, President
Bryan McFarland, General Manager
Trevor Grigsby, Programming Director

Scottsville

WLCK
02-27-1958; 1250 khz AM *Hrs Open:* 6 AM-9 PM; 0.86 kw-D, ND1; 0.076 kw-N, ND1; N36 44 25 W86 10 31
Mailing Address: P.O. Box 158, Scottsville, KY 42164 US
Second Address: 104 1/2 Public Sq., Scottsville, KY 42164
(270) 237-3148, *Fax:* (270) 237-3533
www.wvleradio.com
wlckwvle@nctc.com
License: Scottsville, KY held by Skytower Communications Group LLC
Nat'l Network: USA
Arbitron Metro Market: Bowling Green, KY *Format:* Religious *Hrs. of News Programming:* news progmg 12 hrs wkly *No. News Employees:* 1 *Target Audience:* General.
Darrin Evans, President
Chris Nelson, General Manager
Max Murphy, Chief Engineer

WVLE
02-26-1967; 99.3 mhz FM; 6 kw; 328 ft.; N36 44 25 W86 10 31
Mailing Address: P.O. Box 158, Scottsville, KY 42164 US
Second Address: 104 1/2 Public Sq., Scottsville, KY 42164
(270) 237-3148, *Fax:* (270) 237-3533
www.wvle.net
License: Scottsville, Allen County, KY
Arbitron Metro Market: Bowling Green, KY *Format:* Country
Greg Gribbins, General Manager

Shelbyville

WCND
06-03-1964; 940 khz AM; 0.25 kw-D, ND2; 0.01 kw-N, ND2; N38 12 48 W85 10 16
P.O. Box 1505, Glasgow, KY 42142 US
(248) 557-3500, *Fax:* (248) 557-2950
www.birach.com
sima@BIRACH.Com
License: Shelbyville, KY held by Birach Broadcasting Corp.
Group Owner: Birach Broadcasting Corp.
Arbitron Metro Market: Louisville, KY *Format:* Oldies *Hrs. of News Programming:* news progmg one hr wkly *No. News Employees:* 1 *Target Audience:* 35-64; upscale, white collar
Rick Loesch, President
Cuervo Curtis, Operations Dir
Tom Charity, General Sales Mgr
Sam Walker, Programming Director

WVKY(FM)
09-30-1989; 101.7 mhz FM *Hrs Open:* 24; 6 kw; Ant 328 ft; N38 12 48 W85 10 16 *Rebroadcasts:* Simulcasts WKRD(AM) Louisville 100%
4000 Radio Drive, Louisville, KY 40218
(502) 479-2222, *Fax:* (502) 479-2308
www.790wkrd.com
License: Shelbyville, Shelby County, KY held by CC Licenses LLC.
Group Owner: Clear Channel Communications Inc.; (acq 2-1-2002; with co-located AM)
Nat'l Network: Fox Sports
Population Served: 750,000 *Arbitron Metro Market:* Louisville, KY
Jim Fenn, Programming Director
Bill Gentry, Promotions Manager

WVKY
12-01-1962; 101.7 mhz FM *Hrs Open:* 24; 6 kw; 328 ft.; N38 12 48 W85 10 16
P.O. Box 1505, Glasgow, KY 42142 US
(859) 264-9700, *Fax:* (859) 264-9705
www.wvky.com
License: Shelbyville, Jessamine County, KY held by Christian Broadcasting System Ltd.
Group Owner: Christian Broadcasting System Ltd.; (acq 7-1-2006; grpsl).
Arbitron Metro Market: Lexington, KY *Format:* News, News/Talk, 86
Jonathon Yinger, President
Benson Gregory, General Manager

Shepherdsville

WLRS
01-01-1993; 105.1 mhz FM; 1.9 kw; 591 ft.; N38 4 55 W85 47 6
P.O Box 655, New Albany, IN 47151 US
(502) 625-1220, *Fax:* (502) 584-1051
www.wlrs.com
info@wlrs.com
License: Shepherdsville, Bullitt County, KY held by MLB-Louisville IV LLC.
Group Owner: Main Line Broadcasting LLC; (acq 9-12-2007; grpsl)
Arbitron Metro Market: Louisville, KY *Format:* Rock/AOR
Dale Schaeffer, VP/Market Manager
George Lindsey, Operations Dir
Holly Bussey, Director of Sales
Tommy Lee Gudding, Programming Director

Smiths Grove

WUHU
12-01-1986; 107.1 mhz FM *Hrs Open:* 24; 50 kw; 492 ft.; N36 50 35 W86 15 30
P. O. Box 900, Bowling Green, KY 42102 US
(270) 843-3333, *Fax:* (270) 843-0454
www.allhitwuhu107.com
joneal@forevercomm.com
License: Smiths Grove, Warren County, KY held by Forever Communications Inc.
Group Owner: Forever Communications Inc.; (acq 2001)
Nat'l Reps: Christal
Arbitron Metro Market: Bowling Green, KY *Format:* Adult Contemp *Target Audience:* 18-49. *Adv. Rates:* 40; 35; 35; 20
Christine Hillard, President
Joe O'Neal, General Sales Mgr
Brooke Summers, Programming Director
Executive VP of Sales

***WBFK**
91.1 mhz FM; 750 watts; 190 meters; N37 06 39 W89 58 44
PO Box 7441, Amarillo, TX
(806) 353-1488, *Fax:* (806) 353-1542
www.calvaryamarillo.org
License: Smiths Grove, KY held by Grace Community Church of Amarillo
William Gehm, President

Somerset

***WDCL-FM**
07-01-1985; 89.7 mhz FM *Hrs Open:* 24; 100 kw; 571 ft.; N37 9 29 W85 9 50 *Rebroadcasts:* Rebroadcasts WKYU-FM Bowling Green 100%
1 Big Red Way, Bowling Green, KY 42101 US
(270) 745-5489(800) 599-9598, *Fax:* (270) 745-6272
www.wkyufm.org
wkyufm@wku.edu
License: Somerset, Pulaski County, KY held by Western Kentucky University.
Nat'l Network: PRI; NPR
Arbitron Metro Market: Somerset, KY *Format:* News *Special Programming:* Folk 5 hrs, jazz 15 hrs wkly *Hrs. of News Programming:* news progmg 35 hrs wkly *No. News Employees:* 3 *Target Audience:* General.
John Campbell, Operations Dir
Peter Bryant, General Manager
Peter Bryant, Station Manager
Dan Modlin, News Director
Don Eastman, Chief Engineer
Lee Stott, Music Director

WLLK-FM
08-14-1989; 102.3 mhz FM *Hrs Open:* 24; 6 kw; 328 ft.; N37 4 41 W84 40 39
Mailing Address: Post Office Box 3404, Somerset, KY 42564 US
Second Address: 101 First Radio Ln., Somerset, KY 42503
(606) 678-5151, *Fax:* (606) 678-2026
www.somersetradio.com
wsek@clearchannel.com
License: Somerset, Pulaski County, KY held by Capstar TX L.P.
Group Owner: Clear Channel Communications Inc.; (acq 12-8-2000; grpsl).
Format: Adult Contemp *Hrs. of News Programming:* news progmg 6 hrs wkly *No. News Employees:* 1 *Target Audience:* 25-54. *Adv. Rates:* 20; 15; 18; 10
Richard Dills, General Manager

WKEQ
09-01-1964; 97.1 mhz FM; 27.5 kw; 659 ft.; N36 57 40 W84 34 7
Mailing Address: P.O. Box 740, Somerset, KY 42501 US
Second Address: 101 First Radio Ln., Somerset, KY 42503
(606) 678-5151, *Fax:* (606) 678-2026
www.wsfcam.com
License: Somerset, Pulaski County, KY
Group Owner: Clear Channel Communications Inc.
Wire Services: NOAA Weather
Format: Contemporary Hits/Top 40, Adult Contemp
Rod Zimmerman, Operations Dir
Bruce Welker, General Manager
Wynona Padgett, Promotions Manager
Jim Mercer, Chief Engineer

WSFC
12-14-1947; 1240 khz AM *Hrs Open:* 24; 0.79 kw-U, ND1; N37 7 3 W84 36 42
Mailing Address: P.O.Box 740, Somerset, KY 42501 US
Second Address: 101 First Radio Ln., Somerset, KY 42503

(606) 678-5151, *Fax:* (606) 678-2026
www.wsfcam.com
License: Somerset, KY held by Capstar TX L.P.
Group Owner: Clear Channel Communications Inc.; (acq 12-8-2000; grpsl).
Nat'l Reps: Rgnl Reps *Wire Services:* NOAA Weather
Format: Talk *Hrs. of News Programming:* news progmg 15 hrs wkly *No. News Employees:* 1 *Target Audience:* General.
Rod Zimmerman, Operations Dir
Bruce Welker, General Manager
Rod Zimmerman, Programming Director
Wynona Padgett, Promotions Manager
Mike Murphy, Production Manager

***WTHL**
07-16-1987; 90.5 mhz FM; 50 kw; 591 ft.; N37 7 52 W84 33 15
Mailing Address: 93 Rainbow Terrace Road, Somerset, KY 42503 US
Second Address: 93 Rainbow Terr., Somerset, KY 42503
(606) 679-6300, *Fax:* (606) 679-1342
www.kingofkingsradio.net
dcradio@alltel.net
License: Somerset, Pulaski County, KY held by Somerset Educational Broadcasting Foundation.
Nat'l Network: Moody
Arbitron Metro Market: Somerset,KY *Format:* Religious *Special Programming:* Gospel under 20 hrs wkly *Target Audience:* 40 plus; people with conservative, traditional & relg values & interests
David Carr, General Manager
Carolyn Jones, Programming Director
Marvin Whitaker, Chief Engineer

WTLO
11-01-1958; 1480 khz AM
Mailing Address: P.O. Box 1480, P.O. Drawer, Somerset, KY 42501 US
Second Address: 290 WTLO Rd., Somerset, KY 42503
(606) 678-8151, *Fax:* (606) 678-8152
www.wtloam.com
wtlo@usa.com
License: Somerset, KY held by F.T.G. Broadcasting Inc.
Group Owner: Key Broadcasting Inc.; (acq 2-4-2008; $300,000)
Nat'l Network: ABC
Arbitron Metro Market: Somerset, KY *Format:* Oldies *Special Programming:* Farm one hr, relg 4 hrs wkly *Target Audience:* 45 plus; upscale & highly mobile
Mike Tarter, General Manager
Dave Childders, General Sales Mgr
Josh Good, Programming Director
Kevin Wilson, Account Executive
Amy Stroud, Digital Media Coordinator
Greg Moore, Production

***WKVY**
01-01-2004; 88.1 mhz FM *Hrs Open:* 24; 4 kw vert; 526 ft.; N37 4 36 W84 48 39
1425 N Market Blvd., Suite 9, Sacramento, CA 95834 US
(800) 525-5683, *Fax:* (916) 251-1650
www.klove.com
klove@klove.com
License: Somerset, Pulaski County, KY held by Educational Media Foundation.
Group Owner: EMF Broadcasting
Nat'l Network: K-Love
Arbitron Metro Market: Somerset, KY *Format:* Christian *No. News Employees:* 13 *Target Audience:* 25-44; Judeo Christian, female
Darrell Chambliss, Chairman
Mike Novak, President and CEO
Chip Bailey, Operations Dir
David Pierce, Chief Creative Officer and Programming Director
Ed Lenane, News Director
Sam Wallington, Engineering Dir
Marya Morgan, NewsReporter
Richard Hunt, News Reporter
Alan Mason, Chief Operating Officer
Dan Antonelli, Chief Business Development Officer
Eric Moser, Chief Financial Officer
Brian Burger, Vice President of Human Resources

Springfield

WYSB
02-17-1989; 102.7 mhz FM *Hrs Open:* 24; 4 kw; 354 ft.; N37 41 43 W85 19 6
P.O. Box 1505, Glasgow, KY 42142 US
(502) 350-4482, *Fax:* (888) 531-6397
www.1027wysb.com
info@1027wysb.com
License: Springfield, Washington County, KY held by Washington County CBC Inc.
Group Owner: Commonwealth Broadcasting Corp.; (acq 10-30-97; $350,000).
Nat'l Network: ABC *Regional Network:* Ky. News Net
Arbitron Metro Market: Springfield, KY *Format:* Adult Contemp
Special Programming: Sports 12 hrs, farm 10 hrs wkly *Hrs. of News Programming:* news progmg 20 hrs wkly *No. News Employees:* 1 *Target Audience:* 25-55.
Jim Parker, Operations Dir
Lisa Kearnes, General Manager
Tom Redmon, News Director
Kenny Fogle, Advertising Director

St. Matthews

WVEZ
04-01-1967; 106.9 mhz FM; 24.5 kw; 669 ft.; N38 22 19 W85 49 33
3773 Howard Hughes Pwy, Suite 300n, Las Vegas, NV 89109 US
(502) 589-4800, *Fax:* (502) 583-4820
www.lite1069.com
info@lite1069.com
License: St. Matthews, Jefferson County, KY held by Cox Radio Inc.
Group Owner: Cox Radio Inc.; (acq 5-99)
Arbitron Metro Market: Louisville, KY *Format:* Adult Contemp
Special Programming: Delilah *Target Audience:* 24-54; upper-scale, working women
Shane Collins, Operations Dir
Todd Pitt, General Sales Mgr
Don Nordin, Programming Director
Brian Eichenberger, Promotions Manager

Stamping Ground

WLXO
12-15-1994; 96.1 mhz FM; 6 kw; 328 ft.; N38 12 15 W84 32 51
1821 Summit Road, Suite 400, Cincinnati, OH 45237 US
(859) 294-0961, *Fax:* (859) 233-1517
www.hank961.com
info@hank961.com
License: Stamping Ground, Scott County, KY held by Clarity Communications Inc.
Nat'l Network: Talk Radio Network *Nat'l Reps:* Katz Radio
Arbitron Metro Market: Lexington-Fayette, KY *Format:* Talk *Hrs. of News Programming:* News progmg 20 hrs wkly
Charlie Cohn, President
James MacFarlane, General Sales Mgr

Stanford

***WXKY-FM**
05-22-1967; 96.3 mhz FM; 4.9 kw; 732 ft.; N37 31 27 W84 52 12
P. O. Box 300, Stanford, KY 40484 US
(916) 251-1600, *Fax:* (916) 251-1650
www.klove.com
License: Stanford, Lincoln County, KY held by Educational Media Foundation.
Group Owner: EMF Broadcasting; (acq 10-20-2004; $800,000).
Nat'l Network: K-Love
Format: Christian
Mike Novak, President
Chip Bailey, Operations Dir
David Pierce, Programming Director
Ed Lenane, News Director
Sam Wallington, Engineering Dir
Marya Morgan, News Reporter
Richard Hunt, News Reporter

Stanton

WBFC
06-21-1975; 1470 khz AM
Mailing Address: P.O. Box 577, Stanton, KY 40380 US
Second Address: 2401 Paint Creek Rd., Stanton, KY 40380
(606) 663-6631, *Fax:* (606) 663-2267
www.wbfcam.com
beverly@wbfcam.com
License: Stanton, KY held by Combs Broadcasting Inc.
Arbitron Metro Market: Stanton,KY *Format:* Gospel
James H. Combs, CEO/COO
James Harold Combs, President
Beverly Combs, General Manager
Daniel Morton, Vice President
Beverly Combs, Secretary and Treasurer
Jerarld Faulkne, Board of Directors
Geff Combs, Board of Directors
LannyRogers, Board of Directors
F.M Sponcil, Board of Directors

WSKV-FM
08-10-1974; 104.9 mhz FM *Hrs Open:* 24; 720 w; 680 ft; N37 45 43 W83 50 36
Mailing Address: Box 610, Stanton, KY 40380
Second Address: 28 W. Hall's Rd., Stanton, KY 40380
(606) 663-2811, *Fax:* (606) 663-2895
www.wskvfm.com
License: Stanton, Powell County, KY held by Moore Country 104 LLC
Nat'l Network: KNN
Population Served: 120,000*Hrs. of News Programming:* 6 hrs per week *Target Audience:* General.
A.C. Moore, Owner
Ethan Moore, General Manager
Ethan Moore, General Sales Mgr
Mary Moore, Programming Director
Ethan Moore, Promotions Manager
Ethan Moore, Chief Engineer

Sturgis

WMSK-FM
11-21-1960; 101.3 mhz FM *Hrs Open:* 24; 6 kw; N37 40 00 W87 55 40
Mailing Address: P.O. Box 369, Morganfield, KY
Second Address: 1339 US 60 W., Morganfield, KY 42437
(270) 389-1550, *Fax:* (270) 389-1553
wmsk@bellsouth.net
License: Sturgis, Union County, KY held by Henson Media Inc.
Nat'l Network: Jones Radio Networks *Regional Network:* Ky. News Net *Nat'l Reps:* Rgnl Reps *Wire Services:* AP
Hrs. of News Programming: News progmg 20 hrs wkly *Target Audience:* General; adults 25-64 *Adv. Rates:* 7.00; 7.00; 7.00; 7.00
Edward Henson, President
Bob Hite, Operations Dir
John Robinson, General Manager
Don Sheridan, General Sales Mgr
Rhonda Gibson, Traffic Manager

Tompkinsville

WTKY
05-28-1960; 1370 khz AM *Hrs Open:* daytimer; 2.1 kw-D, NDD; N36 43 27 W85 40 53
352 Radio Station Road, Tompkinsville, KY 42167 US
(270) 487-6119, *Fax:* (270) 487-8462
kixcountry@scrtc.com
License: Tompkinsville, KY held by Whittimore Enterprises Inc.
Nat'l Network: USA *Nat'l Reps:* Rgnl Reps
Arbitron Metro Market: Tompkinsville, KY *Format:* Country
Special Programming: gospel/religious & bluegrass *Hrs. of News Programming:* progmg 4 hrs wkly *No. News Employees:* 2 *Target Audience:* 55+.*Adv. Rates:* 35; 28; 32; 28
Rebecca Brown, General Manager

WTKY-FM
01-20-1972; 92.1 mhz FM *Hrs Open:* 6AM-11PM; 5.3 kw; 351 ft.; N36 49 7 W85 39 32
352 Radio Station Road, Tompkinsville, KY 42167 US
(270) 487-6119, *Fax:* (270) 487-8462
kixcountry@scrtc.com
License: Tompkinsville, Monroe County, KY held by Whittimore Enterprises Inc.
Nat'l Network: USA *Nat'l Reps:* Rgnl Reps
Arbitron Metro Market: Tompkinsville, KY *Format:* Country *Hrs. of News Programming:* news progmg 2 hrs wkly *No. News Employees:* 2 *Target Audience:* Female 18-45. *Adv. Rates:* 35; 28; 32; 28
Rebecca Brown, General Manager

WKWY
01-01-2003; 102.7 mhz FM *Hrs Open:* 6AM - 11PM; 6 kw; 315 ft.; N36 43 27 W85 40 53
470 Adams Lane, Lafayette, TN 37083 US
(270) 487-6119, *Fax:* (270) 487-8462
kixcountry@scrtc.com
License: Tompkinsville, Monroe County, KY held by Whittimore Enterprises
Nat'l Network: USA *Nat'l Reps:* Rgnl Reps
Arbitron Metro Market: Tompkinsville, KY *Format:* Country *Hrs. of News Programming:* news progmg 2 wkly *No. News Employees:* 2 *Adv. Rates:* 35; 28; 32; 28
Rebecca Brown, General Manager

Upton

***WJCR-FM**
02-01-1990; 90.1 mhz FM *Hrs Open:* 24; 100 kw; 384 ft.; N37 25 57 W86 1 50
Mailing Address: P.O. Box 91, Upton, KY 42784 US
Second Address: 13101 Raider Hollow Rd., Upton, KY 42784

(270) 369-8614, *Fax:* (270) 369-7402
www.wjcr.org
wjcrfm@yahoo.com
License: Upton, Hardin County, KY held by FM 90.1 Inc.
Format: Gospel *Special Programming:* 5 hrs live prayline wkly
Target Audience: General.
Lauree K. Powell, CFO
Don Powell, President
Gary Richardson, Station Manager
Larry Baysinger, Chief Engineer

Valley Station

WSYI
01-01-1982; 105.9 mhz FM; 1.9 kw; 413 ft; N38 08 16 W85 56 06
9960 Corporate Campus Dr., Suite 3600, Louisville, KY 93012
(502) 339-9470, *Fax:* (502) 423-3139
www.salemradiogroup.com
License: Valley Station, Jefferson County, KY held by WAY Media Group Inc.
Group Owner: WAY Media Group Inc.; (acq 10-2-2008; $3 million)
Nat'l Network: Salem Radio Network *Nat'l Reps:* Salem
Arbitron Metro Market: Louisville, KY
CC Matthews, Operations Dir
Tim Hartlage, General Manager

Vanceburg

WKKS
06-01-1958; 1570 khz AM; 1 kw-D, NDD; N38 35 50 W83 20 50
1106 Fairlane Drive, Vanceburg, KY 41179 US
(606) 796-3031, *Fax:* (606) 796-6186
License: Vanceburg, KY held by Brown Communications Inc.
Format: Country
Dennis Brown, President

WKKS-FM
01-01-1983; 104.9 mhz FM; 3 kw; 299 ft.; N38 36 19 W83 19 57
1106 Fairlane Drive, P.O. Box 10, Vanceburg, KY 41179 US
(606) 796-3031, *Fax:* (606) 796-6186
License: Vanceburg, Lewis County, KY held by Brown Communications Inc.
Format: Contemporary Hits/Top 40
Frank Osborn, President
Sandy Mathews, General Sales Mgr
Bill Morgan, Programming Director
Ruth Law, Promotions Manager

Vancleve

WMTC
06-01-1948; 730 khz AM *Hrs Open:* 6 AM-sunset; 5 kw-D, DA2; 0.05 kw-N, DA2; N37 36 12 W83 26 39
Box 2, 75 Mill Creek, Lawson Road, Vancleve, KY 41385 US
(606) 666-5006, *Fax:* (606) 666-7534
www.mountaingospel.org
studio@mountaingospel.org
License: Vancleve, KY held by Kentucky Mountain Holiness Assn.
Nat'l Network: Salem Radio Network
Arbitron Metro Market: Vancleve, KY *Format:* Christian, Religious
Special Programming: Farm one hr wkly *Hrs. of News Programming:* News progmg 14 hrs wkly
Philip Speas, President
Jennifer Cox, General Manager
Anna Marshall, Programming Director
Kenneth Amspaugh, Chief Engineer

WMTC-FM
01-01-1991; 99.9 mhz FM *Hrs Open:* 24; 6 kw; 328 ft.; N37 36 23 W83 26 48
Box 2, 75 Mill Creek - Lawson R, Vancleve, KY 41385 US
(606) 666-5006, *Fax:* (606) 666-7534
www.mountaingospel.org
studio@mountaingospel.org
License: Vancleve, Breathitt County, KY held by Kentucky Mountain Holiness Assn.
Arbitron Metro Market: Vancleve, KY *Format:* Christian, Religious
Special Programming: Farm one hr wkly *Adv. Rates:* 3; 3; 3; 3
Seldon Short, Operations Dir
Seldon Short, General Manager
Jennifer Cox, Programming Director
Theresa Kerley, Disc Jockey
Gordon Sampsel, Music Director

Versailles

WCDA
07-16-1973; 106.3 mhz FM *Hrs Open:* 24; 3.7 kw; 420 ft.; N38 2 51 W84 29 57
P.O. Box 11788, Lexington, KY 40578 US
(859) 280-1063, *Fax:* (859) 233-1517
www.your1063.com
License: Versailles, Woodford County, KY held by L.M. Communications Inc.
Group Owner: L M Communications Inc.; acq 9-3-98).
Nat'l Reps: Katz Radio
Arbitron Metro Market: Lexington, KY *Format:* Adult Contemp
Hrs. of News Programming: news progmg 2 hrs wkly *No. News Employees:* 1 *Target Audience:* 25-49; female
Lynn Martin, President
James MacFarlane, General Manager
James McFarlane, Promotions Manager

Vine Grove

WTHX
10-05-1993; 101.5 mhz FM *Hrs Open:* 24; 6 kw; 328 ft; N37 35 07 W85 50 20
611 W. Poplar St., Suite C2, Elizabethtown, KY 42701
(270) 763-0800, *Fax:* (270) 769-6349
etownpoint.com
info@etownpoint.com
License: Vine Grove, Hardin County, KY held by Elizabethtown CBC Inc.
Group Owner: Commonwealth Broadcasting Corp.; (acq 7-1-00; grpsl).
Regional Reps: Rgnl Reps.
Population Served: 200,000*Hrs. of News Programming:* news progmg 3 hrs wkly *No. News Employees:* 1 *Target Audience:* 25-45; males *Adv. Rates:* 18; 18; 18; 10
Steve Newberry, President
Dan Diaz, Operations Dir
Roth Stratton, General Manager
Misty Russell, Programming Director
Holli Lee, News Director
Mike Graham, Engineering Dir

Virgie

WZLK
11-15-1992; 107.5 mhz FM; 1.45 kw; 679 ft.; N37 27 57 W82 33 4
Mailing Address: P.O. Box 2347, Pikeville, KY 41501 US
Second Address: 1240 Radio Dr., Pikesville, KY 41502
(606) 437-4051, *Fax:* (606) 432-2809
www.ekbradio.com
dppool@ekbradio.com, waltmay@ekbradio.com
License: Virgie, Pike County, KY held by East Kentucky Broadcasting Corp.
Group Owner: East Kentucky Broadcasting Corp.; (acq 5-14-2003; $531,273 with WLSI(AM) Pikeville).
Arbitron Metro Market: Virgie, KY *Format:* Contemporary Hits/Top 40, Light Rock
Keith Casebolt, General Manager
Dan P'Pool, General Sales Mgr
Walt May II, Programming Director

Warfield

*WNON
91.3 mhz FM; kw
US
(606) 395-6831
License: Warfield, Martin County, KY held by Calvery Temple Community Church.
Regional Network: ABN Radio
Arbitron Metro Market: Lebanon, IN
Arnold Damron, President

West Liberty

WLKS
07-25-1965; 1450 khz AM *Hrs Open:* 24; 1 kw-U, ND1; N37 55 36 W83 16 41
129 College Street, West Liberty, KY 41472 US
(606) 743-3145, *Fax:* (606) 743-9557
License: West Liberty, KY held by Morgan County Industries Inc.
Group Owner: Morgan County Industries Inc.
Nat'l Reps: Rgnl Reps
Format: Oldies *Special Programming:* Farm 5 hrs wkly *Hrs. of News Programming:* news progmg 35 hrs wkly *No. News Employees:* 1 *Target Audience:* General. *Adv. Rates:* 4; 4; 4; 4
Paul Lyons, General Manager

WLKS-FM
01-01-1994; 102.9 mhz FM *Hrs Open:* 24; 6 kw; 328 ft.; N38 2 16 W83 20 18
129 College Street, West Liberty, KY 41472 US
(606) 743-1029, *Fax:* (606) 743-9557
License: West Liberty, Morgan County, KY held by Morgan County Industries Inc.
Group Owner: Morgan County Industries Inc.
Format: Country
Carol Walters, Operations Dir
Tim Kelly, Programming Director
Mike Jeffries, News Director
Scott Truxel, Local News Editor

Whitesburg

*WMMT
11-01-1985; 88.7 mhz FM *Hrs Open:* 24; 1 kw horiz, 15 kw vert; 1470 ft.; N37 6 38 W82 44 15
306 Madison Street, Whitesburg, KY 41858 US
(606) 633-0108, *Fax:* (606) 633-1009
www.appalshop.org
wmmtfm@appalshop.org
License: Whitesburg, Letcher County, KY held by Appalshop Inc.
Regional Network: Kentucky Educational Television
Arbitron Metro Market: Whitesburg, KY *Format:* Variety/Diverse
Target Audience: General.
Cheryl Marshall, General Manager

WTCW
02-19-1953; 920 khz AM; 4.2 kw-D, ND1; 0.043 kw-N, ND1; N37 8 46 W82 46 1
P.O. Box 1450, Corbin, KY 40702 US
(606) 633-2711, *Fax:* (606) 633-4445
www.wtcwam.com
wxkq@yahoo.com
License: Whitesburg, KY held by T.C.W. Broadcasting Co. Inc.
Group Owner: Key Broadcasting Inc.; (acq 1-1-86; $765,000 with co-located FM;
Nat'l Network: CBS *Nat'l Reps:* Rgnl Reps
Arbitron Metro Market: Whitesburg, KY *Format:* Country *Target Audience:* 30 plus.
Kevin Day, General Manager
Bob Scott, On-Air and Production Director
Lisa Elkins, Account Executive

WXKQ-FM
11-25-1964; 103.9 mhz FM; 0.28 kw; 1500 ft.; N37 6 38 W82 44 15
P.O. Box 1450, Corbin, KY 40702 US
(606) 633-2711, *Fax:* (606) 633-4445
www.1039thebulldog.com
License: Whitesburg, Letcher County, KY
Group Owner: Key Broadcasting Inc.
Arbitron Metro Market: Whitesburg, KY *Format:* Contemporary Hits/Top 40
J.J. Fabini, Operations Dir
Kevin Day, General Manager, Program Director, Account Executi
Rob Livergood, General Sales Mgr
Doc West, Programming Director
Bob Scott, Production Director
Lisa Elkins, Account Executive

Whitesville

WXCM
05-01-1993; 97.1 mhz FM; 4 kw; 404 ft.; N37 41 50 W86 59 28
P.O. Box 150846, Nashville, TN 37215 US
(270) 683-5200, *Fax:* (270) 688-0108
www.owensbororadio.com
spots@wrioradio.com
License: Whitesville, Daviess County, KY held by The Cromwell Group Inc. of Kentucky.
Group Owner: The Cromwell Group Inc.; (acq 1993; $170,000;
Arbitron Metro Market: Whitesville, KY *No. News Employees:* 1 *Target Audience:* Males in 30's. *Adv. Rates:* 20; 20; 20; 15
Bayard Walters, CEO
Kevin Riecke, Operations Dir
Jan Catinna, General Manager
Jeff Nalley, General Sales Mgr
Mike Chaney, News Director

Whitley City

WHAY
12-01-1990; 98.3 mhz FM *Hrs Open:* 24; 5.1 kw; 354 ft.; N36 39 40 W84 26 53
Box 69, Whitley City, KY 42653 US
(606) 376-2218, *Fax:* (606) 376-5146
www.hay98.com
whayradio@highland.net
License: Whitley City, McCreary County, KY held by Tim Lavender.
Format: Triple A *Hrs. of News Programming:* News progmg 5 hrs wkly *Target Audience:* 30 plus.
Dave Shelley, General Manager

Wickliffe

WBCE
01-04-1981; 1200 khz AM; 1 kw-D, NDD; N36 58 54 W89 4 39
Mailing Address: P. O. Box 128, Wickliffe, KY 42087 US
Second Address: 1136 Barlow Rd., Wickliffe, KY 42087
(740) 548-5919, *Fax:* (740) 548-5911
License: Wickliffe, KY held by WBCE Inc.
Format: Christian
Holly Casagrande, General Manager
Margaret Litton, Programming Director

WGKY
01-01-1987; 95.9 mhz FM *Hrs Open:* 24; 2.45 kw; 361 ft.; N36 56 17 W88 58 1
930 Wickliffe Road, P.O. Box 500, Wickliffe, KY 42087 US
(270) 538-5251, *Fax:* (270) 415-0599
www.959wgky.com
cbell@withersradio.net
License: Wickliffe, Ballard County, KY held by W. Russell Withers Jr.
Group Owner: Withers Broadcasting Co.; (acq 2-21-2006; $400,000)
Nat'l Network: Jones Radio Networks *Regional Network:* Brownfield *Regional Reps:* Rgnl Reps.
Format: Oldies *Hrs. of News Programming:* News progmg 5 hrs wkly *Target Audience:* 24-54; rural homeowners, farmers
Clay Reed, Operations Dir
Rick Lambert, General Manager
Kathy Duncan, Station Manager

Williamsburg

WEKC
09-21-1981; 710 khz AM; 4.2 kw-D, NDD; N36 46 28 W84 10 5
Mailing Address: Rt 550 West, Hindman, KY 41822 US
Second Address: 402 Main St., Williamsburg, KY 40769
(606) 549-3000, *Fax:* (606) 539-0916
www.wekc.net
wekc@wekc.net
License: Williamsburg, KY held by Gerald Parks
Nat'l Network: USA
Arbitron Metro Market: Williamsburg, KY *Format:* Gospel, Religious *Hrs. of News Programming:* News progmg 5 hrs wkly *Target Audience:* General; young adults, All ages, race & creed *Adv. Rates:* 10, 10, 10, 6
Kay Parks, Station Manager

*WCWC
03-07-1959; 1430 khz AM *Hrs Open:* Daylight
C/O Fletcher, Heald Esq, 1300 N 17th Sr, 11th Flr, Arlington, VA 22209 US
radiowcwc@bellsouth.net
License: Williamsburg, KY held by Whitley County Board of Education
Arbitron Metro Market: Williamsburg, KY
Lonnie Anderson, General Manager
Jill Roaden, Station Manager

WEZJ-FM
11-01-1990; 104.3 mhz FM; 6.2 kw; 656 ft.; N36 44 43 W84 11 24
522 Main Street, Williamsburg, KY 40769 US
(606) 549-2285, *Fax:* (606) 549-5565
License: Williamsburg, Whitley County, KY held by Whitley Broadcasting Co. Inc.
Nat'l Reps: Rgnl Reps
Arbitron Metro Market: Williamsburg, KY *Format:* Country
David Estes, General Manager
Rick Campbell, Programming Director
Frank Folson, Chief Engineer

Williamstown

WNKR
04-01-1992; 106.7 mhz FM *Hrs Open:* 24; 1.8 kw; 607 ft.; N38 41 19 W84 35 7
11 N Main Street, Dry Ridge, KY 41035 US
(859) 824-9106, *Fax:* (859) 824-9835
www.1067wnkr.com
wnkrproduction@fuse.net
License: Williamstown, Grant County, KY held by Grant County Broadcasters Inc.
Regional Network: Ky. News Net *Nat'l Reps:* Rgnl Reps
Arbitron Metro Market: Cincinnati, OH *Format:* Country *Hrs. of News Programming:* news progmg 6 hrs wkly *No. News Employees:* 1 *Target Audience:* 35-54; adults *Adv. Rates:* 60;60; 60; 50
Robert Wallace, President
Jay Anthony, Operations Dir
Jeffrey Ziesmann, General Manager
Laura Eisenmenger, General Sales Mgr
Katherine Marshall, News Director
Jim Stitt, Chief Engineer

Wilmore

*WLAI
10-27-1969; 107.1 mhz FM *Hrs Open:* 24; 3.6 kw; 128 m; N37 40 28 W84 46 06 *Rebroadcasts:* Rebroadcasts KLRD(FM) Yucaipa, CA 100%
2351 Sunset Blvd., Suite 170-218, Rocklin, CA 41144
(916) 251-1600, *Fax:* (916) 251-1650
www.air1.com
info@air1.com
License: Wilmore, Boyle County, KY held by Educational Media Foundation.
Group Owner: EMF Broadcasting; (acq 5-20-2005; $1 million).
Nat'l Network: Air 1
Population Served: 200,000 *Arbitron Metro Market:* Lexington, KY
Mike Novak, President
Chip Bailey, Operations Dir
David Pierce, Programming Director
Ed Lenane, News Director
Sam Wallington, Engineering Dir
Marya Morgan, News Reporter
Richard Hunt, News Reporter

WVRB
09-18-1995; 95.3 mhz FM *Hrs Open:* 24; 4.1 kw; 397 ft.; N37 57 37 W84 32 42
8686 Michael Lane, Fairfield, OH 45014 US
(707) 528-9236, *Fax:* (916) 251-1650
www.air1.com
info@air1.com
License: Wilmore, Jessamine County, KY held by Vernon R. Baldwin Inc.
Group Owner: Vernon R Baldwin Inc.; acq 7-26-94;
Nat'l Network: Air 1
Arbitron Metro Market: Lexington, KY *Format:* Alternative, Christian *Target Audience:* 20-45; Christians baby boomers
Mike Novak, President

Winchester

WKQQ
01-01-1974; 100.1 mhz FM *Hrs Open:* 24; 20 kw; 636 ft.; N38 7 24 W84 26 37
50 East Rivercenter Blvd, Suite 1200, Covington, KY 41011 US
(859) 422-1000, *Fax:* (859) 422-1038
www.wkqq.com
info@wkqq.com
License: Winchester, Clark County, KY held by Citicasters Licenses L.P.
Group Owner: Clear Channel Communications Inc.; (acq 5-4-99; grpsl).
Arbitron Metro Market: Lexington-Fayette, KY *Format:* Classic Rock *Hrs. of News Programming:* news progmg 3 hrs wkly *No. News Employees:* 1 *Target Audience:* 18-49; women
Gene Guinn, General Manager

Louisiana

Abbeville

KFTE
06-01-1974; 105.1 mhz FM *Hrs Open:* 24; 25 kw; 300 ft; N30 00 40 W92 07 21
1749 Bertrand Dr., Lafayette, LA 70510
(337) 233-6000, *Fax:* (337) 234-7360
www.kpel1051news.com
info@kpel1051news.com
License: Abbeville, Vermilion County, LA
Group Owner: Townsquare Media
Arbitron Metro Market: Lafayette, LA *Adv. Rates:* 25; 22; 25; 17
Bernadette Lee, Programming Director

KROF
07-09-1948; 960 khz AM *Hrs Open:* 24; 1 kw-D, ND1; 0.095 kw-N, ND1; N30 0 40 W92 7 21
9525 U.S. Highway 167, Abbeville, LA 70510 US
(337) 233-6000, *Fax:* (337) 234-7360
www.talkradio960.com
info@talkradio960.com
License: Abbeville, LA
Group Owner: Townsquare Media; (acq 12-7-2001; grpsl)
Arbitron Metro Market: Lafayette, LA *Format:* Talk *Adv. Rates:* 22; 15; 15; na
Mike Grimsley, General Manager
Frank Malambri, General Sales Mgr
Jeremy Lawrence, Programming Director
Kyle Vidrine, Chief Engineer

Alexandria

*KAPM
06-01-1998; 91.7 mhz FM; 1 kw; 128 ft.; N31 16 4 W92 26 24
P O Drawer 2440, Tupelo, MS 38803 US
(662) 844-8888, *Fax:* (662) 842-6791
www.afr.net
License: Alexandria, Rapides County, LA held by American Family Association.
Group Owner: American Family Radio
Arbitron Metro Market: Tupelo, MO *Format:* Christian, Religious
Marvin Sanders, General Manager

KDBS
12-01-1953; 1410 khz AM *Hrs Open:* 24
600 Congress Avenue, Suite 1400, Austin, TX 78701 US
(318) 443-7454(318) 445-1234, *Fax:* (318) 445-7231
www.kdixie.com
daveg@kswl.com
License: Alexandria, LA held by Cenla Broadcasting Licensing Co. LLC.
Group Owner: Cenla Broadcasting Co. Inc.; (acq 11-13-2006; grpsl)
Nat'l Network: ESPN Radio
Arbitron Metro Market: Alexandria, LA *Format:* Sports
Charlie Sopraz, Operations Dir
Taylor Thompson, General Manager
Tish Robertson, General Sales Mgr
Dave Grachien, Programming Director
Sybil Ford, News Director
Linnie Dupree, Chief Engineer

KEDG
01-01-2001; 106.9 mhz FM; 6 kw; 328 ft.; N31 18 26 W92 23 56
Mailing Address: 188 South Bellevue, Suite 222, Memphis, TN 38104 US
Second Address: 1115 Texas Ave, Alexandria, LA 71301
(318) 445-1234(318) 487-1035, *Fax:* (318) 473-1960
www.sunny1069fm.com/pages/5618403.php
License: Alexandria, Rapides County, LA held by Flinn Broadcasting Corp.
Arbitron Metro Market: Alexandria, LA *Format:* Urban Contemporary
Taylor Thompson, General Manager
Randy James, Programming Director

KMXH
02-01-1993; 93.9 mhz FM; 6 kw; 328 ft.; N31 16 4 W92 26 24
P O Box 5504, Alexandria, LA 71307 US
(318) 445-0800, *Fax:* (318) 445-1445
License: Alexandria, Rapides County, LA held by FM Broadcasting Corp.
Arbitron Metro Market: Alexandria, LA *Format:* Urban Contemporary
Cathy Rogers, CFO
Kevin Wagner, President
Bruce Pattani, General Sales Mgr
Cheron Holland, News Director
Charles Washam, Local Sales Manager

KJMJ
09-21-1935; 580 khz AM *Hrs Open:* 24
6420 Richmond Ave, Ste 620, Houston, TX 77057 US
(318) 561-6145, *Fax:* (318) 449-9954
www.radiomaria.us
info.usa@radiomaria.org
License: Alexandria, LA held by Radio Maria Inc.
Group Owner: Radio Maria Inc.; acq 9-20-99).
Arbitron Metro Market: Alexandria, LA *Format:* Christian, Talk, 74 *Hrs. of News Programming:* News progmg 8 hrs wkly *Target Audience:* Homebound, prisoners & sick
Dale DePerrodill, General Sales Mgr
Duane Stenzel, Programming Director
Danny Brou, Chief Engineer

*KLSA
01-01-1987; 90.7 mhz FM *Hrs Open:* 24; 100 kw; 1243 ft.; N31 33 56 W92 32 50 *Rebroadcasts:* Rebroadcasts KDAQ(FM) Shreveport 100%
99 Lakeshore Drive, Baton Rouge, LA 70805 US
(318) 797-5150, *Fax:* (318) 797-5265
www.redriverradio.org
listenermail@redriverradio.com
License: Alexandria, Rapides County, LA held by Board of Supervisors Louisiana State University & Agricultural Mechanical College.
Nat'l Network: NPR; PRI
Arbitron Metro Market: Alexandria, LA *Format:* Classical, Jazz, 60 *Hrs. of News Programming:* Nws progmg 40 hrs wkly
Rick Shelton, Operations Dir
Kermit Poling, General Manager

***KLXA**
11-01-1998; 89.9 mhz FM *Hrs Open:* 24; 3 kw; 328 ft.; N31 22 40 W92 28 27
6652 North Club Dr., Shreveport, LA 71107 US
(916) 251-1600, *Fax:* (916) 251-1650
www.klove.com
klov@klove.com
License: Alexandria, Rapides County, LA held by Educational Media Foundation.
Group Owner: EMF Broadcasting; (acq 12-1-03; $125,000).
Nat'l Network: K-Love
Arbitron Metro Market: Alexandria, LA *Format:* Christian *No. News Employees:* 3 *Target Audience:* 25-44; Judeo Christian, female
Mike Novak, President
Chip Bailey, Operations Dir
David Pierce, Programming Director
Ed Lenane, News Director
Sam Wallington, Engineering Dir
Marya Morgan, News Reporter
Richard Hunt, News Reporter
Tracy Butler, TrafficManager

KQID-FM
09-17-1978; 93.1 mhz FM; 97 kw; 1522 ft.; N31 38 20 W92 12 18
Mailing Address: 1115 Texas Avenue, Alexandria, LA 71301 US
Second Address: 1115 Texas Ave., Alexandria, LA 71306
(318) 445-1234, *Fax:* (318) 473-1960
www.q93fm.com
info@q93fm.com
License: Alexandria, Rapides County, LA
Group Owner: Cenla Broadcasting Co. Inc.
Arbitron Metro Market: Alexandria, LA *Format:* Contemporary Hits/Top 40
MaryElin Macht, Programming Director

KRRV-FM
05-11-1969; 100.3 mhz FM *Hrs Open:* 24; 98 kw; 1053 ft.; N31 1 59 W92 30 8
600 Congress Avenue, Suite 1400, Austin, TX 78701 US
(318) 445-1234, *Fax:* (318) 473-1960
www.krrvonline.com
hollywood@cenlabroadcasting.com
License: Alexandria, Rapides County, LA held by Cenla Broadcasting Licensing Co. LLC.
Group Owner: Cenla Broadcasting Co. Inc.
Arbitron Metro Market: Alexandria area *Format:* Country
Hollywood Harrison, Programming Director

KSYL
04-01-1947; 970 khz AM; 1 kw-D, DAN; 1 kw-N, DAN; N31 19 33 W92 29 17
Mailing Address: 1115 Texas Avenue, Alexandria, LA 71301 US
Second Address: 1115 Texas Ave., Alexandria, LA 71301
(318) 445-1234, *Fax:* (318) 442-8255
www.ksyl.com
info@ksyl.com
License: Alexandria, LA held by Cenla Broadcasting Inc.
Group Owner: Cenla Broadcasting Co. Inc.; (acq 8-1-80)
Arbitron Metro Market: Alexandria, LA *Format:* Talk
Taylor Thompson, President
Dave Graichen, Programming Director

KZMZ
01-01-1947; 96.9 mhz FM *Hrs Open:* 24; 98 kw; Ant 1,053 ft; N31 01 59 W92 30 08
1115 Texas Ave, Alexandria, LA 78701
(318) 445-1234, *Fax:* (318) 445-7231
chad@cenlabroadcasting.com
License: Alexandria, Rapides County, LA held by Cenla Broadcasting Licensing Co. LLC.
Group Owner: Cenla Broadcasting Co. Inc.; (acq 11-13-2006; grpsl)
Population Served: 475,000 *Arbitron Metro Market:* Alexandria, LA *Hrs. of News Programming:* news progmg 2 hrs wkly *No. News Employees:* 1 *Target Audience:* Adults 25-54
Taylor Thompson, General Manager
Chad Soprano, General Sales Mgr

Amite

WABL
01-01-1956; 1570 khz AM *Hrs Open:* 12; 0.5 kw-D, ND2; 0.015 kw-N, ND2; N30 42 31 W90 31 31
Mailing Address: 12515 Bankston Road, Amite, LA 70422 US
Second Address: 12515 Bankston Rd., Amite, LA 70422
(780) 672-9822, *Fax:* (780) 672-4678
www.981camfm.com
License: Amite, LA held by Spotlight Broadcasting LLC
Group Owner: Spotlight Broadcasting LLC; acq 6-8-01; $70,000).
Arbitron Metro Market: Norfolk NE *Format:* Contemporary Hits/Top 40, Adult Contemp
David Gilmore, General Sales Mgr

WTGG
03-03-1997; 96.5 mhz FM *Hrs Open:* 24; 6 kw; 328 ft.; N30 37 24 W90 24 19
215 East Bay St., Magnolia, MS 39652 US
(985) 345-0060, *Fax:* (985) 542-9377
kajun107.com
License: Amite, Tangipahoa County, LA held by Southwest Broadcasting Inc.
Group Owner: Southwest Broadcasting Inc.; acq 4-8-98; $650,000)
Nat'l Network: Westwood One *Regional Network:* La. Net.
Arbitron Metro Market: Baton Rouge, LA *Format:* Oldies *Hrs. of News Programming:* news progmg one hr wkly *No. News Employees:* 1 *Target Audience:* 25-54; women
Charles Dowdy, CEO
Eloise Dowdy, General Manager
Ben Bickham, Chief Engineer

Angola

***KLSP**
08-12-1986; 91.7 mhz FM; 0.105 kw; 52 ft.; N30 57 17 W91 35 45
La. State Penitentiary, Angola, LA 70712 US
(225) 655-2281, *Fax:* (225) 655-2273
www.corrections.state.la.us/lsp/klsp.htm
info@klspfm.com
License: Angola, West Feliciana County, LA held by Angola Educational Foundation Inc.
Arbitron Metro Market: Baton Rouge, LA *Format:* Variety/Diverse *Special Programming:* Black 10 hrs, C&W 6 hrs, jazz 7 hrs, poets corner *Target Audience:* General.
Burl Cain, General Manager
Maurice Rabalais, Station Manager

Arcadia

***KHCL**
01-20-2001; 92.5 mhz FM *Hrs Open:* 24; 6 kw; 328 ft.; N32 27 27 W92 59 38 *Rebroadcasts:* Rebroadcasts KHCB-FM Houston, TX 95%
1004 Elm St, Minden, LA 71055 US
(713) 520-5200
www.khcb.org
email@khcb.org
License: Arcadia, Bienville County, LA held by Houston Christian Broadcasters Inc.
Group Owner: Houston Christian Broadcasters Inc.
Nat'l Network: Moody
Arbitron Metro Market: Houston, TX *Format:* Christian
Bruce Munsterman, General Manager
Dan Wales, Chief Engineer
Bonnie BeMent, Assistant General Manager

Atlanta

KCIJ
01-01-2002; 106.5 mhz FM *Hrs Open:* 24; 25 kw; 328 ft.; N31 48 29 W92 48 22
Dba Coochie Brake B/G Co, 3712 Cornell Drive, Shreveport, LA 71107 US
(318) 354-4000, *Fax:* (318) 352-9598
www.106kcij.com
License: Atlanta, Winn County, LA held by North Face Broadcasting L.L.C.
Arbitron Metro Market: Alexandria, LA *Format:* Contemporary Hits/Top 40, Adult Contemp *Target Audience:* 25-54; general
John Brewer, Operations Dir
Bill Vance, Station Manager

Baker

WBRP
06-16-1994; 107.3 mhz FM *Hrs Open:* 24; 4.6 kw; 328 ft; N30 37 24 W91 09 50
Mailing Address: Box 2231, Baton Rouge, LA 70802
Second Address: 929-B Government St., Baton Rouge, LA 70802
(225) 388-9898, *Fax:* (225) 383-3700
www.countrylegends1073.com
owen.weber@gbcradio.com
License: Baker, East Baton Rouge County, LA held by Guaranty Broadcasting Co. of Baton Rouge LLC.
Group Owner: Guaranty Broadcasting Co. of Baton Rouge, LLC; (acq 2-5-97).
Population Served: 750,000 *Arbitron Metro Market:* Baton Rouge, LA *Special Programming:* LSU WOMEN'S BASKETBALL *Target Audience:* Adults 25-54;
George Foster Jr., Chairman
Bridger Eglin, President
Owen Weber, Operations Dir
Dave Dunaway, Operations Manager

Ball

KBKK
09-01-1998; 105.5 mhz FM *Hrs Open:* 24; 6 kw; 318 ft.; N31 25 39 W92 24 18
92 West Shamrock, Pineville, LA 71360 US
(318) 487-1035, *Fax:* (318) 487-4419
www.1055kbuck.com
License: Ball, Rapides County, LA held by Opus Broadcasting Alexandria LLC.
Group Owner: Opus Media Holdings LLC; (acq 9-30-2004; $3.38 million with KLAA-FM Tioga).
Nat'l Reps: Christal *Wire Services:* AP
Arbitron Metro Market: Alexandria, LA *Format:* Country *Special Programming:* Nascar *Target Audience:* 50 plus.
Kim Jones, President

KWDF
01-01-1986; 840 khz AM; 8 kw-D, NDD; N31 22 40 W92 28 27
3712 Cornell Dr., Shreveport, LA 71107 US
(318) 640-4373, *Fax:* (318) 640-5971
www.wilkinsradio.com/article.asp?id=2126295
janet@wilknsradio.com
License: Ball, LA held by NWLA Broadcasting L.L.C.
Nat'l Network: USA
Arbitron Metro Market: Pineville, LA *Format:* Gospel *Adv. Rates:* 6; 6; 6; na
Al Moore, President
Jimmy Bryant, Operations Dir
Sharon Thorne, General Manager
John Ponthier, Station Manager
Jimmy Bryant, Programming Director
Tommy Moore, Chief Engineer

Basile

KYBG
05-04-1990; 102.1 mhz FM *Hrs Open:* 24; 3 kw; Ant 328 ft; N30 28 52 W92 35 50
Box 60571, Lafeyette, LA 70526
(337) 783-2521, *Fax:* (337) 783-5744
www.kqis.com
License: Basile, Evangeline County, LA held by Third Partner Broadcasting Inc.
Nat'l Network: ABC
Arbitron Metro Market: Lafayette, LA *Hrs. of News Programming:* News progmg 3 hrs wkly *Target Audience:* 25-55; middle-income
Phil Lizotte, General Manager
Jimmy Cole, General Sales Mgr
Hans Nelson, Programming Director

Bastrop

***KAXV**
01-01-2000; 91.9 mhz FM; 12 kw; 456 ft.; N32 49 22 W92 7 28
P O Drawer 2440, Tupelo, MS 38803 US
(662) 844-8888, *Fax:* (662) 842-6791
www.afr.net
comments@afr.net
License: Bastrop, Morehouse County, LA held by American Family Radio.
Group Owner: American Family Radio
Arbitron Metro Market: Tupelo, MS *Format:* Christian, Religious
Marvin Sanders, General Manager

KJMG
01-01-1996; 97.3 mhz FM *Hrs Open:* 24; 5.9 kw; 328 ft.; N32 40 20 W91 55 6
Mailing Address: 5021 - 6th Place, Meridian, LA 39305 US
Second Address: Box 4808, Monroe, LA 71211
(318) 388-2323, *Fax:* (318) 388-0569
www.majic97.com
License: Bastrop, Morehouse County, LA held by Holladay Broadcasting of Louisiana LLC
Group Owner: Holladay Broadcasting of Louisiana LLC; acq 9-30-98; $700,000).
Nat'l Network: ABC *Nat'l Reps:* McGavren Guild
Arbitron Metro Market: Monroe, LA *Format:* Adult Contemp
Special Programming: Blues 12 hrs wkly *Target Audience:* 25-54.
Bob Holladay, President

KRVV
01-01-1977; 100.1 mhz FM *Hrs Open:* 24; 50 kw; 492 ft.; N32 40 20 W91 55 6
Mailing Address: 1108 Hudson Lane, Monroe, LA 71211 US
Second Address: 1109 Hudson Ln., Monroe, LA 71201

(318) 388-2323, *Fax:* (318) 388-0569
www.thebeat.net
krvv@bayou.com
License: Bastrop, Morehouse County, LA held by Holladay Broadcasting of Louisiana LLC
Group Owner: Holladay Broadcasting of Louisiana LLC; acq 10-15-91; $1 million;
Nat'l Network: ABC *Nat'l Reps:* McGavren Guild
Arbitron Metro Market: Monroe, LA *Format:* Urban Contemporary
Special Programming: Gospel 4 hrs wkly *Target Audience:* 18-49.
Bob Holladay, President

Baton Rouge

KBRH

01-01-1953; 1260 khz AM *Hrs Open:* 24; 5 kw-D, ND1; 0.127 kw-N, ND1; N30 27 38 W91 14 37
1050 South Foster Drive, Baton Rouge, LA 70806 US
(225) 383-3243, *Fax:* (225) 379-7685
License: Baton Rouge, LA held by East Baton Rouge Parish School Board
Arbitron Metro Market: Baton Rouge, LA *Format:* Blues *Target Audience:* 35 plus.
Jerry Papenfuss, CEO
Greg Brady, Operations Dir
Doug Gray, General Manager
Brian Lokken, News Director

*KLSU

10-01-1981; 91.1 mhz FM *Hrs Open:* 24; 5.7 kw; 161 ft.; N30 24 37 W91 10 37
B-39 Hodges, Lsu, Baton Rouge, LA 70803 US
(225) 578-8688, *Fax:* (225) 388-1698
www.klsu.fm
info@klsufm.com
License: Baton Rouge, East Baton Rouge County, LA held by Louisiana State University.
Nat'l Reps: Rgnl Reps
Arbitron Metro Market: Baton Rouge, LA *Format:* Variety/Diverse *Hrs. of News Programming:* News progmg one hr wkly *Target Audience:* 18-25; university students & college age listeners
Peyton Juneau, Station Manager

*WBRH

09-01-1977; 90.3 mhz FM *Hrs Open:* 24; 3.5 kw; 478 ft.; N30 26 36.31 W91 10 53.61
1050 South Foster Drive, Baton Rouge, LA 70806 US
(225) 388-9030, *Fax:* (225) 379-7685
www.baton-rouge.com/wbrh/
License: Baton Rouge, East Baton Rouge County, LA held by East Baton Rouge Parish School Board
Nat'l Network: NPR
Arbitron Metro Market: Baton Rouge, LA *Format:* Jazz *Target Audience:* 25-54; men
Larry Davis, Station Manager
Lyn Kenyon, General Sales Mgr
Rob Payer, Programming Director

WDGL

10-01-1968; 98.1 mhz FM *Hrs Open:* 24; 95 kw; 1499 ft.; N30 21 58 W91 12 47
Mailing Address: P.O. Box 2231, Baton Rouge, LA 70821 US
Second Address: 929-B Government St., Baton Rouge, LA 70802
(225) 388-9898, *Fax:* (225) 383-3700
www.eagle981.com
gordy.rush@gbcradio.com
License: Baton Rouge, East Baton Rouge County, LA held by Guaranty Broadcasting Co. of Baton Rouge LLC.
Group Owner: Guaranty Broadcasting Co. of Baton Rouge, LLC
Wire Services: AP
Arbitron Metro Market: Baton Rouge, LA *Format:* Classic Rock
Special Programming: LSU FOOTBALL AND BASEBALL PLAY BY PLAY BROADCASTS; Don Dubuc Fishing *Target Audience:* Adults 25-54
George Foster Jr., Chairman
Bridger Eglin, President
Owen Weber, Operations Dir
Dave Dunaway, OM
Dave Dunaway, Operations Manager

WPYR

01-01-1956; 1380 khz AM
600 Congress Ave., Suite 1400, Austin, TX 78701 US
(225) 448-3754, *Fax:* (226) 231-1879
www.brcatholicradio.com
info@brcatholicradio.com
License: Baton Rouge, LA held by Davidson Media Station WPYR Licensee LLC.
Group Owner: Davidson Media Group LLC; (acq 9-16-2008; exchange for WBZK(AM) York, SC)
Arbitron Metro Market: Baton Rouge, LA *Format:* Christian, Talk, 74 *Adv. Rates:* 25; 25; 25; na
Mark Kennedy, Programming Director

WIBR

07-18-1948; 1300 khz AM; 5 kw-D, 1 kw-N, DA-2; N30 28 25 W91 13 34
650 Wooddale Blvd., Baton Rouge, LA 85281
(225) 926-1106, *Fax:* (225) 928-1606
License: Baton Rouge, East Baton Rouge County, LA
Group Owner: Cumulus Media Inc.; (acq 1999; grpsl).
Nat'l Network: ABC *Regional Network:* La. Net. *Nat'l Reps:* McGavren Guild *Wire Services:* UPI
Population Served: 245,752 *Arbitron Metro Market:* Baton Rouge, LA *Target Audience:* 25-50.
Greg Benefield, General Manager

WJBO

12-11-1934; 1150 khz AM; 5 kw-U, DA1; N30 27 47 W91 16 10
600 Congress Ave., Suite 1400, Austin, TX 78701 US
(225) 231-1860, *Fax:* (225) 231-1873
www.wjbo.com
info@wjbo.com
License: Baton Rouge, LA held by Capstar TX L.P.
Group Owner: Clear Channel Communications Inc.; (acq 8-30-2000; grpsl)
Nat'l Network: CBS; Westwood One
Arbitron Metro Market: Baton Rouge, LA *Format:* News, Sports, 86 *Target Audience:* 20 plus.
Donnie Picou, Operations Dir

*WJFM

06-01-1995; 88.5 mhz FM *Hrs Open:* 24; 25.5 kw; 279 ft.; N30 23 6 W91 5 23
Mailing Address: P. O. Box 262550, Baton Rouge, LA 70826 US
Second Address: 8919 World Ministry Ave., Baton Rouge, LA 70810
(225) 768-3688, *Fax:* (225) 768-3729
www.jsm.org
kawikfish@yahoo.com
License: Baton Rouge, East Baton Rouge County, LA held by Family Worship Center Church Inc.
Group Owner: Family Worship Center Church Inc.; (acq 12-15-99).
Arbitron Metro Market: Baton Rouge, LA *Format:* Christian *Hrs. of News Programming:* news progmg 2 hrs wkly *No. News Employees:* 1 *Target Audience:* 25-54; full gospel Christians & anyone searching for hope
David Whitelaw, COO
Jimmy Swaggart, President
John Santiago, Programming Director

WFMF

01-01-1941; 102.5 mhz FM; 96 kw; 1499 ft.; N30 19 34 W91 16 36
600 Congress Ave., Suite 1400, Austin, TX 78701 US
(225) 231-1860, *Fax:* (225) 231-1873
www.wfmf.com
jimcallow@baycitiesradio.net
License: Baton Rouge, East Baton Rouge County, LA held by Capstar TX L.P.
Group Owner: Clear Channel Communications Inc.
Arbitron Metro Market: Baton Rouge, LA *Format:* Contemporary Hits/Top 40 *Target Audience:* 18-34; female
Harold Camping, President
Jason Frentses, Operations Dir
Charles Menut, Station Manager
Bob Murphey, Programming Director

WUBR

11-01-1946; 910 khz AM
3000 Tecumseh Street, Baton Rouge, LA 70805 US
(517) 351-3333
License: Baton Rouge, LA held by Communications Capital Co. III LLC.
Group Owner: Communications Capital Managers LLC; (acq 2-17-2006; $75,000)
Arbitron Metro Market: Baton Rouge, LA *Target Audience:* 18-59.
Michael Oesterle, CEO
Sandra Pate, General Manager

WPFC

01-01-1963; 1550 khz AM *Hrs Open:* Sunrise-sunset; 5 kw-D, ND2; 0.042 kw-N, ND2; N30 30 7 W91 12 39
6940 Harry Drive, Baton Rouge, LA 70806 US
(225) 926-1506, *Fax:* (225) 926-4974
www.1550wpfc.com
License: Baton Rouge, LA held by Victory and Power Ministries Inc.
Nat'l Network: USA
Arbitron Metro Market: Baton Rouge, LA *Format:* Gospel, Religious *Hrs. of News Programming:* news progmg 3 hrs wkly *No. News Employees:* 2 *Target Audience:* 35-59; middle-class female
Pastor Moore, CEO
Keith Richard, Station Manager

*WRKF

01-18-1980; 89.3 mhz FM *Hrs Open:* 24; 28 kw; 935 ft.; N30 22 22 W91 12 16
3050 Valley Creek Drive, Baton Rouge, LA 70808 US
(225) 926-3050, *Fax:* (225) 926-3105
www.wrkf.org
License: Baton Rouge, East Baton Rouge County, LA held by Public Radio Inc.
Nat'l Network: NPR; PRI
Arbitron Metro Market: Baton Rouge, LA *Format:* News, News/Talk, 86 *Hrs. of News Programming:* news progmg 35 hrs wkly *No. News Employees:* 1 *Target Audience:* General.
Blythe Earl, General Manager
Malcolm Robinson, General Sales Mgr

WTGE

09-10-1966; 100.7 mhz FM *Hrs Open:* 24; 97 kw; 1,499 ft; N30 19 35 W91 16 36
Mailing Address: Box 2231, Baton Rouge, LA 70802
Second Address: 929-B Government St., Baton Rouge, LA 70802
(225) 388-9898, *Fax:* (225) 383-3700
www.newcountry1007.com
owen.weber@gbcradio.com
License: Baton Rouge, East Baton Rouge County, LA held by Guaranty Broadcasting Co. of Baton Rouge LLC.
Group Owner: Guaranty Broadcasting Co. of Baton Rouge, LLC; (acq 1996; $5.5 million).
Population Served: 750,000 *Arbitron Metro Market:* Baton Rouge, LA *Special Programming:* NEW ORLEANS SAINTS FOOTBALL PLAY BY PLAY and LSU MEN'S BASKETBALL
Target Audience: Adults 25-54
George Foster Jr., Chairman
Bridger Eglin, President
Owen Weber, Operations Dir
Dave Dunaway, Operations Manager

WYNK-FM

12-07-1968; 101.5 mhz FM *Hrs Open:* 24; 97 kw; 1499 ft.; N30 19 34 W91 16 36
600 Congress Ave., Suite 1400, Austin, TX 78701 US
(225) 231-1860, *Fax:* (225) 231-1873
www.wynk.com
info@wynk.com
License: Baton Rouge, East Baton Rouge County, LA held by Capstar TX L.P.
Group Owner: Clear Channel Communications Inc.; (acq 8-30-2000; grpsl)
Arbitron Metro Market: Baton Rouge, LA *Format:* Country *No. News Employees:* 2 *Target Audience:* 18-54.
Donnie Picou, General Manager
Bob Murphy, Programming Director

Bayou Vista

KQKI-FM

12-31-1976; 95.3 mhz FM; 16.5 kw; 400 ft.; N29 39 28 W91 17 41
P. O. Box 847, Morgan City, LA 70381 US
(985) 395-2853, *Fax:* (985) 395-5094
www.quickiecountry.com
jaboyne@cox.net
License: Bayou Vista, St. Mary County, LA held by Teche Broadcasting Corp.
Nat'l Network: ABC *Regional Network:* La. Net.
Format: Country *Hrs. of News Programming:* news progmg 17 hrs wkly *No. News Employees:* 1 *Target Audience:* 30 plus; general *Adv. Rates:* 18; 17; 17.50; 15
Paul Cook/Owner, CEO/COO
Julie Boyne, General Manager
Ernest Dean Polk, Station Manager
Julie Boyne, General Sales Mgr
J. J. Starbuck, Programming Director

Belle Chasse

KKND

03-01-1990; 102.9 mhz FM; 4.7 kw; Ant 604 ft; N29 57 14 W89 56 58
201 St. Charles Ave., Suite 201, New Orleans, LA 27103
(504) 581-7002, *Fax:* (504) 566-4857
www.power1029.com
lbj.kmez@citcomm.com
License: Belle Chasse, Plaquemines County, LA
Group Owner: Cumulus Media Inc.; (acq 8-29-2003; grpsl)

Population Served: 2,965,100 *Arbitron Metro Market:* New Orleans, LA *Target Audience:* 35-54; female
Dave Siebert, General Manager
LeBron Joseph, Programming Director

Benton

KSYR
01-01-1981; 92.1 mhz FM *Hrs Open:* 24; 6 kw; 322 ft.; N32 39 19 W93 41 36
3712 Cornell Drive, Shreveport, LA 71107 US
(318) 222-3122, *Fax:* (318) 459-1493
License: Benton, Bossier County, LA held by Access. 1 Louisiana Holding Co. LLC.
Group Owner: Access.1 Communications Corp.; (acq 5-5-00; grpsl).
Nat'l Network: ABC
Arbitron Metro Market: Shreveport, LA *No. News Employees:* 1
Target Audience: 35 plus; upper income, upwardly mobile
Cary Camp, President
Don Zimmerman, General Sales Mgr

Berwick

KBZE
07-04-1990; 105.9 mhz FM; 4 kw; 404 ft.; N29 45 27 W91 10 25
Mailing Address: Po Drawer N, Morgan City, LA 70380 US
Second Address: 1320 Victor II Blvd., Morgan City, LA 70380
(985) 385-6266, *Fax:* (985) 385-6268
ww.kbze.com
kbze@petronet.net
License: Berwick, St. Mary County, LA held by HubCast Broadcasting Inc.
Nat'l Network: ABC
Arbitron Metro Market: Morgan City, La *Format:* Adult Contemp, Sports, 74 *Hrs. of News Programming:* news progmg 10 hrs wkly *No. News Employees:* 1 *Target Audience:* 24-54; middle to upper income
Howard Castay Jr., President
Darlene Castay, Operations Dir

Blanchard

KDKS-FM
10-19-1998; 102.1 mhz FM *Hrs Open:* 24; 20 kw; 367 ft.; N32 35 57 W93 54 1
208 N. Thomas Drive, Shreveport, LA 71107 US
(318) 222-3122, *Fax:* (318) 320-0102
www.kdks.fm
info@kdks.fm
License: Blanchard, Caddo County, LA held by Access. 1 Louisiana Holding Co. LLC.
Group Owner: Access.1 Communications Corp.; (acq 6-30-00; $7.9 million with KLKL(FM) Minden).
Arbitron Metro Market: Shreveport, LA *Format:* Adult Contemp *No. News Employees:* 1 *Target Audience:* 25-54.
Cary Camp, General Manager
Quinn Echols, Programming Director
Cary Camp, Market Manager
Johnette Robinson, Digital Marketing Manager

*KFLO-FM
01-01-2006; 89.1 mhz FM; 38 kw; 406 ft.; N32 18 28 W93 58 34
Mailing Address: P.O. Box 6505, Shreveport, LA 71136 US
Second Address: 2097 N. Hearne Ave., Shreveport, LA 71107
(318) 550-2000, *Fax:* 318-550-2002
miracle891.org
info@miracle891.org
License: Blanchard, Caddo County, LA held by Family Life Educational Foundation
Arbitron Metro Market: Dallas-Fort Worth *Format:* Religious
A.T. Moore, President
Dan Perkins, Operations Dir
Donna Cole, General Manager
Joe Miot, Programming Director

Bogalusa

WBOX
03-01-1954; 920 khz AM; 1 kw-D, NDD; N30 50 29 W89 50 6
Mailing Address: P. O. Box 351, Columbia, MS 39429 US
Second Address: 22037 Hwy. 436, Bogalusa, LA 70427
(504) 732-4288
info@wbox(am/fm).com
License: Bogalusa, LA held by Best Country Broadcasting LLC
Arbitron Metro Market: Columbia, MS *Format:* Country
Ben Strickland, President

Bossier City

KBCL
09-01-1957; 1070 khz AM; 0.25 kw-D, NDD; N32 32 14 W93 43 28
316-B Gregg Street, Shreveport, LA 71104 US
(318) 861-1070
www.kbclthebridge.org
kbcl_radio@bellsouth.net
License: Bossier City, LA held by Barnabas Center Ministries
Arbitron Metro Market: Shreveport, LA *Format:* Christian, Talk
Leon McKee, General Manager
Jean McKee, Programming Director

Boyce

KBCE
03-29-1982; 102.3 mhz FM; 21 kw; 289 ft.; N31 22 21 W92 38 9
2826 Lee Street, Suite 6, Alexandria, LA 71409 US
(318) 445-0800, *Fax:* (318) 445-1445
License: Boyce, Rapides County, LA held by Trinity Broadcasting Corp.
Nat'l Network: American Urban *Nat'l Reps:* D & R Radio
Arbitron Metro Market: Alexandria, LA *Format:* Urban Contemporary *No. News Employees:* 2 *Target Audience:* General.
Kevin Wagner, President
Bruce Pattani, General Sales Mgr
Cheron Holland, News Director

Breaux Bridge

KPEL-FM
05-01-1993; 96.5 mhz FM *Hrs Open:* 24; 22.5 kw; 328 ft; N30 06 09 W91 59 30
1749 Bertrand Dr., Lafayette, LA 70505
(337) 233-6000, *Fax:* (337) 234-7360
www.planet1051.com
tard@planet965.com
License: Breaux Bridge, St. Martin County, LA
Group Owner: Townsquare Media; (acq 12-7-2001; grpsl)
Arbitron Metro Market: Lafayette, LA *Special Programming:* Local 1 hr wkly *Target Audience:* 18-35
Mike Grimsley, General Manager
Scott Pessin, Programming Director

Broussard

*WHFG
01-01-2008; 91.3 mhz FM; 6 kw; 367 ft.; N29 58 4 W91 55 31
516 South 4th St, Las Vegas, NV 89101 US
(817) 641-3495
License: Broussard, Lafayette County, LA held by Mary V. Harris Foundation.
Arbitron Metro Market: Windom, MN
Linda De Romanett, President

Brusly

KRVE
09-09-1989; 96.1 mhz FM *Hrs Open:* 24; 50 kw; 449 ft.; N30 29 37 W91 0 19
600 Congress Ave., Suite 1400, Austin, TX 78701 US
(225) 231-1860, *Fax:* (225) 231-1869
www.961theriver.com
info@murphysamandjodi.com
License: Brusly, West Baton Rouge County, LA held by Capstar TX L.P.
Group Owner: Clear Channel Communications Inc.; (acq 8-30-00; grpsl).
Arbitron Metro Market: Baton Rouge, LA *Format:* Adult Contemp *No. News Employees:* 3 *Target Audience:* 25-54; women
Dick Lewis, General Manager
Bob Murphy, Programming Director
Libby Davis, Promotions Manager

Bunkie

KEZP
01-01-1993; 104.3 mhz FM *Hrs Open:* 24; 19.2 kw; 374 ft.; N31 5 14 W92 21 34
1605 Murray Street, Suite 120, Alexandria, LA 71301 US
(318) 487-1035, *Fax:* (318) 487-1045
www.red1043.com
info@kezp.com
License: Bunkie, Avoyelles County, LA held by Opus Broadcasting Alexandria LLC.
Group Owner: Opus Media Holdings LLC; (acq 9-30-2004; $1.83 million)
Nat'l Network: Westwood One
Arbitron Metro Market: Alexandria, LA *Format:* Rock/AOR *No. News Employees:* 1 *Target Audience:* 35-64.
Mark Jones, General Manager

Buras

*KMRL
04-22-1995; 91.9 mhz FM; 11.5 kw; 787 ft.; N29 33 45 W89 49 46
P.O. Box 1307, Buras, LA 70041 US
(504) 362-3379
License: Buras, Plaquemines County, LA held by New Orleans Quality Radio Inc.
Target Audience: General.
W. Christopher Beary, President

Church Point

*KCKR
01-01-2007; 91.9 mhz FM; 12.5 kw horiz, 12.4 kw vert; 466 ft.; N30 19 47 W92 5 6
Mailing Address: 17967 Brownsferry Road, Athens, AL 35611 US
Second Address: 8919 World Ministry Ave., Baton Rouge, LA 70810
(225) 768-3102
www.jsm.org
License: Church Point, Acadia County, LA held by Family Worship Center Church Inc.
Group Owner: Family Worship Center Church Inc.; (acq 10-22-2007; $3.6 million)
Arbitron Metro Market: Fayetteville (Northwest Arkansas), AR
Format: Religious
Jimmy Swaggart, President

Clinton

*WBKL
09-23-1981; 92.7 mhz FM *Hrs Open:* 24; 32 kw; 604 ft.; N30 51 3 W91 4 31 *Rebroadcasts:* Rebroadcasts KLVR(FM) Santa Rosa, CA 100%.
13855 Plank Road, Baker, LA 70714 US
(916) 251-1600, *Fax:* (916) 251-1650
www.klove.com
License: Clinton, East Feliciana County, LA held by Educational Media Foundation.
Group Owner: EMF Broadcasting; (acq 7-1-2005; $3.2 million)
Nat'l Network: K-Love
Arbitron Metro Market: Baton Rouge, LA *Format:* Christian
Mike Novak, President
Chip Bailey, Operations Dir
David Pierce, Programming Director
Ed Lenane, News Director
Sam Wallington, Engineering Dir
Marya Morgan, News Reporter
Richard Hunt, News Reporter

*WWRA
01-01-2008; 91.9 mhz FM; 5 kw; 269 ft.; N30 49 0 W90 48 42 US
(225) 791-1429
www.amorradio.org
License: Clinton, East Feliciana County, LA held by Victory Harvest Church.
Arbitron Metro Market: Clinton, LA *Format:* Religious
Dulio Canossa, General Manager

Columbia

KQLQ
01-21-1980; 103.1 mhz FM *Hrs Open:* 24; 25 kw; 328 ft.; N32 11 44 W92 9 48
350 Park Aven, 20th Floor, New York, NY 10022 US
(318) 387-3922, *Fax:* (318) 322-4585
1031theparty.com
hot1031@opusbroadcasting.com
License: Columbia, Caldwell County, LA held by Opus Broadcasting Monroe L.L.C.
Group Owner: Opus Media Holdings LLC; (acq 7-19-2004; grpsl).
Arbitron Metro Market: Columbia, LA *Format:* Urban Contemporary
Chris Zimmerman, General Manager

Coushatta

KSBH
11-15-1992; 94.9 mhz FM *Hrs Open:* 24; 25 kw; 328 ft.; N31 51 34 W93 13 0
505 Royal St., Suite B, Natchitoches, LA 71547 US
(318) 354-4000, *Fax:* (318) 352-9598
License: Coushatta, Red River County, LA held by KSBH L.L.C.
Arbitron Metro Market: Natchitoches, LA *Format:* Country *Target Audience:* 18-54.

John Brewer, Operations Dir
Bill Vance, Station Manager
Shane Evath, News Director

KRRP
05-01-1981; 950 khz AM *Hrs Open:* 24; 0.5 kw-D, DA2; 0.209 kw-N, DA2; N31 56 49 W93 20 13
P.O. Box 1362, 1519 Ringgold Avenue, Coushatta, LA 71019 US
(318) 932-6704, *Fax:* (318) 932-9700
krrp@cp-tel.net
License: Coushatta, LA held by Roberto Feliz
Nat'l Network: ESPN Radio
Arbitron Metro Market: Coushatta, LA *Format:* Sports *Hrs. of News Programming:* news progmg 20 hrs wkly *No. News Employees:* 1 *Target Audience:* 35 plus; mature, educated, affluent listeners *Adv. Rates:* 15; 15; 15; 12
Chris Boyd, General Manager
George Moore, Programming Director
Robert Abrahams, Chief Engineer

Crowley

KAJN-FM
10-01-1977; 102.9 mhz FM *Hrs Open:* 24; 95 kw; 1499 ft.; N30 2 19 W92 22 15
Mailing Address: P.O. Box 1469, Crowley, LA 70527 US
Second Address: 110 W. 3rd St., Crowley, LA 70526
(337) 783-1560, *Fax:* (337) 783-1674
www.kajn.com
License: Crowley, Acadia County, LA held by Agape Broadcasters Inc.
Nat'l Network: USA *Wire Services:* AP
Arbitron Metro Market: Crowley, LA *Format:* Religious *Special Programming:* Black 2 hrs wkly *Hrs. of News Programming:* news progmg 3 hrs wkly *No. News Employees:* 1 *Target Audience:* 25-44; female, familyoriented *Adv. Rates:* 40.56; 36.30; 36.36; 30.65
Barry Thompson, CEO
Annette Thompson, Operations Dir
Bryan Rivera, General Sales Mgr
Craig Thompson, Programming Director
Steve Cook, News Director

KSIG
05-01-1947; 1450 khz AM; 1 kw-U, ND1; N30 13 45 W92 20 59
Mailing Address: 320 North Parkerson Ave., Crowley, LA 70526 US
Second Address: 320 N. Parkerson Ave., Crowley, LA 70527
(337) 783-2520, *Fax:* (337) 783-5744
www.ksig.com
License: Crowley, LA held by Acadia Broadcast Partners Inc.
Arbitron Metro Market: Crowley, LA *Format:* Oldies *Special Programming:* Fr 18 hrs, farm 5 hrs wkly
Chris Afiesh, President
Jimmy Cole, General Sales Mgr
Hans Nelson, Programming Director
Tony Evans, Chief Engineer

De Quincy

KTSR
11-01-1985; 92.1 mhz FM *Hrs Open:* 24; 13.5 kw; 448 ft.; N30 13 16 W93 18 40
P.O. Box 1180, De Ridder, LA 70634 US
(337) 433-1641, *Fax:* (337) 433-2999
www.kissfm921.com
License: De Quincy, Calcasieu County, LA held by GAP Broadcasting Lake Charles License LLC.
Group Owner: GAP Broadcasting LLC; (acq 2-6-2008; grpsl)
Arbitron Metro Market: Lake Charles metro area *Format:* Contemporary Hits/Top 40
Mike Grimsley, General Manager
Aaron Turner, General Sales Mgr
Erik Tee, Programming Director
Dave Chimeno, Chief Engineer

De Ridder

***KBAN**
01-01-2001; 91.5 mhz FM; 20.5 kw; 361 ft.; N30 38 10 W93 2 33
Mailing Address: P O Drawer 2440, Tupelo, MS 38803 US
Second Address: Quicken Ministries %AFR, 1411 Parish Rd., Lake Charles, LA 70611
(662) 844-8888, *Fax:* (662) 842-6791
www.afr.net
comments@myafr.com
License: De Ridder, Beauregard County, LA held by American Family Association.
Group Owner: American Family Radio
Arbitron Metro Market: Tupelo, MS *Format:* Christian, Religious
Marvin Sanders, General Manager
Elizabeth Arrington, Station Manager

KDLA
11-11-1950; 1010 khz AM *Hrs Open:* Sunrise-sunset; 1 kw-D, ND1; 0.04 kw-N, ND1; N30 52 43 W93 17 25
645 Church Street, Sutie 400, Norfolk, VA 23510 US
(318) 462-1000, *Fax:* (318) 462-1000
License: De Ridder, LA held by Christian Broadcasting of De Ridder Inc.
Group Owner: Willis Broadcasting Corp.; (acq 2-18-98; $150,000).
Nat'l Network: Reach Satellite
Format: Gospel *Target Audience:* 18-54.
Guy Giuliano, President
Dawson Austin, Operations Dir

KQLK
09-06-1991; 97.9 mhz FM *Hrs Open:* 24; 50 kw; 492 ft.; N30 36 57 W93 13 31
P.O. Box 19090, Lake Charles, LA 70616 US
(337) 439-3300, *Fax:* (337) 433-7278
www.kqlk.com
info@kqlk.com
License: De Ridder, Beauregard County, LA held by Cumulus Licensing LLC.
Group Owner: Cumulus Media Inc.; (acq 12-6-2004; $3 million with KAOK(AM) Lake Charles).
Arbitron Metro Market: Lake Charles, LA *Format:* Adult Contemp
Eric Nielson, Operations Dir
Jimmie Cole, General Manager
Jill Moore, General Sales Mgr
Crash Kelley, Programming Director
Chanel County, Promotions Manager
Richard Rhodes, Chief Engineer

Delhi

KGGM
09-01-1991; 93.5 mhz FM; 6 kw; 328 ft.; N32 27 45 W91 33 13
Box 426, Delhi, LA 71232 US
(318) 878-8255, *Fax:* (318) 728-3571
License: Delhi, Richland County, LA held by Kenneth W. Diebel
Format: Gospel
Ken Diebel, President

Denham Springs

WLRO
04-15-1959; 1210 khz AM *Hrs Open:* 18; 10 kw-D, 1 kw-N, DA-N; N30 31 20 W90 58 15
5555 Hilton Ave., Suite 500, Baton Rouge, LA 78701
(225) 231-1860, *Fax:* (225) 231-1869
www.thescore1210.com
License: Denham Springs, Livingston County, LA held by Capstar TX LLC
Group Owner: Clear Channel Communications Inc.; (acq 8-30-00; grpsl)
Nat'l Network: Westwood One
Population Served: 750,000 *Arbitron Metro Market:* Baton Rouge, LA *No. News Employees:* 2 *Target Audience:* 25-54.
Bob Murphy, Operations Dir
Dick Lewis, General Manager
Mike Scott, General Sales Mgr
Libby Davis, Promotions Manager

Donaldsonville

KYPY
01-01-1972; 104.9 mhz FM *Hrs Open:* 24; 6 kw; Ant 299 ft; N30 05 57 W91 00 13 *Rebroadcasts:* Rebroadcasts WNXX(FM) Jackson 100%
Mailing Address: Box 2231, Baton Rouge, LA 70346
Second Address: 929 B Government St., Baton Rouge, LA 70802-6033
(225) 388-9898 ext 148, *Fax:* (225) 499-9800
www.104thex.com
owen.weber@98radio.com
License: Donaldsonville, Ascension County, LA held by Guaranty Broadcasting Co. of Baton Rouge LLC.
Group Owner: Guaranty Broadcasting Co. of Baton Rouge, LLC; (acq 2-18-2000; $1.2 million).
Nat'l Reps: McGavren Guild
Population Served: 150,000 *Arbitron Metro Market:* Baton Rouge, LA *Hrs. of News Programming:* News progmg 2 hrs wkly *Target Audience:* 18-34. *Adv. Rates:* 18.40; 18.40; 18.40; 18.40
George Foster Jr., Chairman
Bridger Eglin, President
Owen Weber, Operations Dir
Dave Dunaway, Operations Manager

Dry Prong

***KVDP**
08-13-1985; 89.1 mhz FM; 4.5 kw; 295 ft.; N31 35 20 W92 30 59
Mailing Address: P. O. Box 214, Dry Prong, LA 71423 US
Second Address: 160 Bud Walker Rd., Dry Prong, LA 71423
(318) 899-5837, *Fax:* (318) 899-7624
License: Dry Prong, Grant County, LA held by Dry Prong Educational Broadcasting Foundation Inc.
Nat'l Network: USA
Arbitron Metro Market: Dry Prong, LA *Format:* Christian, Religious
Donna Clina, General Manager
Darris Cline, Chief Engineer

Dubach

KNBB
06-04-1984; 97.7 mhz FM *Hrs Open:* 5 AM-11 PM; 50 kw; 464 ft.; N32 40 9 W92 37 58
Mailing Address: P.O. Box 977, Ruston, LA 71273 US
Second Address: 500 N. Monroe St., Ruston, LA 71270
(318) 255-5000, *Fax:* (318) 255-5084
www.espn977.com
seanfox@espn977.com
License: Dubach, Lincoln County, LA held by Communications Capital Co. II of Louisiana LLC.
Group Owner: Communications Capital Managers LLC; (acq 5-27-2003; $1.5 million)
Nat'l Network: ESPN Radio
Arbitron Metro Market: Monroe, LA *Format:* Sports, Talk *Target Audience:* 25-44; men
Gary McKenney, General Manager
Sean Fox, Programming Director

Empire

KWMZ-FM
06-01-2001; 104.5 mhz FM; 7.8 kw; Ant 850 ft; N29 33 45 W89 49 46
c/o Hartman Leito & Bolt LLP, 6100 Southwest Blvd., Suite 500, Fort Worth, TX 29564
(817) 738-2400
License: Empire, Plaquemines County, LA held by On Top Communications of Louisiana LLC, Debtor-in-Possession
Bryan Rice, General Manager

Erath

KHXT
04-01-1992; 107.9 mhz FM *Hrs Open:* 24; 25 kw; 328 ft; N30 02 54 W91 59 49
1749 Bertrand Dr., Lafayette, LA 70505
(337) 233-6000, *Fax:* (337) 234-7360
www.1079ishot.com
info@1079ishot.com
License: Erath, Vermilion County, LA
Group Owner: Townsquare Media; (acq 12-7-2001; grpsl)
Regional Network: La. Net. *Nat'l Reps:* Katz Radio
Population Served: 300,000 *Arbitron Metro Market:* Lafayette, LA *Hrs. of News Programming:* News progmg 25 hrs wkly *Target Audience:* 12-34.
Mike Grimsley, General Manager
Chris Logan, Programming Director

Erwinville

***KPAE**
09-30-1985; 91.5 mhz FM *Hrs Open:* 24; 10 kw; 164 ft.; N30 32 9 W91 24 52 *Rebroadcasts:* Rebroadcasts WPAE (FM) Centreville, MS 75%
Mailing Address: 13028 Us Hwy 190 West, Erwinville, LA 70767 US
Second Address: 122 E. Main St., Centreville, MS 39631
(601) 645-6515, *Fax:* (225) 627-4970,(601) 645-9122
www.soundradio.org
wpaefm@telepak.net
License: Erwinville, West Baton Rouge County, LA held by Port Allen Educational Broadcasting Foundation.
Nat'l Network: Moody
Format: Religious *Target Audience:* General.
Willie Kennedy, President

Eunice

KEUN
10-01-1952; 1490 khz AM *Hrs Open:* 24; 1 kw-U, ND1; 150 ft.; N30 28 17 W92 24 51
P. O. Box 1049, Eunice, LA 70535 US
(337) 457-3041, *Fax:* (337) 457-3081
www.keunworldwide.com
spots@keunworldwide.com
License: Eunice, LA held by Tri-Parish Broadcasting Co. Inc.
Nat'l Network: Radio America *Regional Network:* La. Net.
Arbitron Metro Market: Lafayette, LA *Format:* News, News/Talk, 86 *Special Programming:* Cajun one hr wkly *Hrs. of News*

Programming: news progmg 6 min every hr *No. News Employees:* 1 *Target Audience:* 25plus. *Adv. Rates:* 8; 8; 8; 3
Rick Nesbitt, General Manager
Tony Evans, Chief Engineer

KEUN-FM
10-22-1981; 105.5 mhz FM *Hrs Open:* 24; 1 kw; 486 ft.; N30 26 16 W92 26 49
PO Box 1049, 330 West Laurel Ave, Eunice, LA 70535 US
(337) 457-3041, *Fax:* (337) 457-3081
www.keunworldwide.com
spots@keunworldwide.com
License: Eunice, St. Landry County, LA held by Tri-Parish Broadcasting Co. Inc.
Nat'l Network: ABC
Arbitron Metro Market: Lafayette, LA *Format:* Country *Special Programming:* Cajun music 12 hrs wkly *Hrs. of News Programming:* Local news progmg one hr wkly *No. News Employees:* 1 *Target Audience:* P 25-54.*Adv. Rates:* 18; 17; 18; 15
Rick Nesbitt, General Manager

Farmerville

KBYO-FM
04-19-1979; 92.7 mhz FM *Hrs Open:* 24; 6 kw; 328 ft.; N32 40 31 W92 19 10
Po Drawer 399, 408 Cedar, Farmerville, LA 71241 US
(318) 516-3033, *Fax:* (318) 323-3719
www.fun927fm.com/
License: Farmerville, Union County, LA held by Union Broadcasting Co. Inc.
Arbitron Metro Market: Monroe, LA *Format:* Adult Contemp *Target Audience:* 24-65; adult audience with incomes to buy
Lee Fletcher, General Manager

Ferriday

KFNV-FM
10-01-1971; 107.1 mhz FM *Hrs Open:* 24; 18.5 kw; 233 ft.; N31 36 8 W91 32 27
Mailing Address: P.O. Box 1319, Columbia, LA 71418 US
Second Address: 917 S. EE Wallace Blvd., Ferriday, LA 71334
(800) 784-1071, *Fax:* (318) 757-7689
www.kfnvfm.com
License: Ferriday, Concordia County, LA held by Tom D. Gay
Group Owner: The Radio Group
Arbitron Metro Market: Ferriday LA *Format:* Contemporary Hits/Top 40, Adult Contemp *Hrs. of News Programming:* News progmg 2 hrs wkly *Target Audience:* 25-55; baby boomers *Adv. Rates:* 9; 8; 8; 5
Desiree Smith, General Manager

Folsom

WJSH
03-01-1996; 104.7 mhz FM *Hrs Open:* 24; 6 kw; 328 ft.; N30 39 55 W90 4 49
7106 Laird, #201, Panama City Beach, FL 32408 US
(985) 542-0060, *Fax:* (985) 542-9377
License: Folsom, St. Tammany County, LA held by Southwest Broadcasting.
Group Owner: Southwest Broadcasting Inc.; (acq 11-17-2000).
Arbitron Metro Market: Folsom, LA *Format:* Jazz, Smooth Jazz
Charles Dowdy, CEO
Eloise Dowdy, General Manager
Ben Bickham, Chief Engineer

Franklin

KDDK
05-09-1975; 105.5 mhz FM; 3 kw; Ant 300 ft; N29 50 14 W91 32 22 *Rebroadcasts:* Rebroadcasts KJCB(AM) Lafayette 100%
5047 Hwy. 1148, Plaquemine, LA 23261
(225) 687-2882
www.kddkfm.com
kddk@bellsouth.net
License: Franklin, St. Mary County, LA held by Radio & Investments Inc.
Population Served: 100,000
Ken Noble, General Manager

KFRA
06-04-1961; 1390 khz AM; 0.5 kw-D, ND1; 0.244 kw-N, ND1; N29 50 14 W91 32 22
P.O. Box 27224, Richmond, VA 23261 US
(337) 924-7100
http://www.1390kfra.com/
kbze.kfra@gmail.com
License: Franklin, LA held by Castay Media Inc.
Arbitron Metro Market: Franklin, LA
Howard Castay, President

Franklinton

WOMN
12-05-1966; 1110 khz AM *Hrs Open:* Sunrise-sunset; 1 kw-D, NDD; N30 51 34 W90 9 57
P.O.Box 604, Franklinton, LA 70438 US
(985) 624-9452, *Fax:* (985) 624-9559
mpittman@pittmanbroadcasting.com
License: Franklinton, LA held by Pittman Broadcasting Services LLC.
Group Owner: Pittman Broadcasting Services LLC; (acq 6-4-2002; with co-located FM)
Arbitron Metro Market: New Orleans, LA *Format:* Country *Target Audience:* General.
Mike Mitchell, General Sales Mgr
Tony Evans, Chief Engineer

WUUU
03-03-1997; 98.9 mhz FM *Hrs Open:* 24; 6 kw; 108 ft.; N30 51 34 W90 9 57
P O Box 604, Franklinton, LA 70438 US
(985) 624-9452, *Fax:* (985) 624-9559
mpittman@pittmanbroadcasting.com
License: Franklinton, Washington County, LA held by Pittman Broadcasting Services LLC.
Group Owner: Pittman Broadcasting Services LLC
Arbitron Metro Market: New Orleans, LA
Joe Mule, General Manager
Dale Mitchell, Programming Director

Galliano

WTIX-FM
11-16-1975; 94.3 mhz FM *Hrs Open:* 24; 100 kw; 981 ft.; N29 33 45 W89 49 46
1206 Decatur Street, New Orleans, LA 70116 US
(504) 454-9000, *Fax:* (504) 454-9002
wtixfm.com
info@wtixfm.com
License: Galliano, Lafourche County, LA held by Fleur de Lis Broadcasting Inc.
Nat'l Network: ABC
Arbitron Metro Market: New Orleans, LA *Format:* Oldies *Hrs. of News Programming:* News progmg 4 hrs wkly *Target Audience:* 25-54. *Adv. Rates:* 35; 35; 35; 20
George Buck, President
Michael Costello, General Manager

Garyville

***WCKW**
12-22-1970; 1010 khz AM *Hrs Open:* 24
3501 North Causeway Blvd, Ste 700, Metairie, LA 70002 US
(314) 752-7000, *Fax:* (314) 752-7702
www.covenantnet.net
License: Garyville, LA held by Covenant Network
Group Owner: Covenant Network; (acq 10-17-2006)
Arbitron Metro Market: River Parishes *Format:* Religious *Target Audience:* 18-54.
John Anthony Holman, President

Gibsland

KBEF
05-23-2001; 104.5 mhz FM; 6 kw; 328 ft.; N32 31 59 W93 11 34
P.O. Box 218, Dubberly, LA 71024 US
(318) 377-1240, *Fax:* (318) 377-4619
www.kbef.com
kaso1240@yahoo.com
License: Gibsland, Bienville County, LA held by Amistad Communications Inc.
Group Owner: Amistad Communications Inc.; (acq 7-12-2000; $375,000 for CP with KASO(AM) Minden).
Arbitron Metro Market: Minden, LA *Format:* Christian
Mike Griffith, General Manager

Golden Meadow

KLEB
05-13-1963; 1600 khz AM *Hrs Open:* 24; 5 kw-D, DA2; 0.25 kw-N, DA2; N29 23 43 W90 16 1
P.O. Drawer 1350, Larose, LA 70373 US
(985) 798-7792, *Fax:* (985) 798-7793
www.klrzfm.com
klrz@mobiletel.com
License: Golden Meadow, LA held by Coastal Broadcasting of Larose Inc.
Arbitron Metro Market: New Orleans, LA *Format:* Oldies, Country *Target Audience:* 25 plus; general *Adv. Rates:* 20; 15; 20; 10
Andrea Galjour, Operations Dir
Jerry Gisclair, General Manager

***KUHN**
88.9 mhz FM; 1 kw; 75 ft.; N29 20 53 W90 14 55 US
(985) 475-6640, *Fax:* (985) 475-7109
www.unitedhoumanation.org
License: Golden Meadow, Lafourche County, LA held by United Houma Nation Inc.
Arbitron Metro Market: Golden Meadow, LA
Brenda Robichaux, General Manager

Grambling

***KGRM**
01-01-1974; 91.5 mhz FM *Hrs Open:* 24; 50 kw; 492 ft.; N32 30 56 W92 43 27
Mailing Address: P.O. Box 417, Grambling, LA 71245 US
Second Address: Washington Johnson Complex 2nd Fl., 403 Main St., Grambling, LA 71245
(318) 274-6343, *Fax:* (318) 274-3245
www.gram.edu/kgrm
evansjb@gram.edu
License: Grambling, Lincoln County, LA held by Grambling State University.
Format: Gospel *Special Programming:* Jazz 56 hrs wkly, blues 9 hrs wkly *Target Audience:* Black community.
Joyce Evans, General Manager

Gray

KCIL
08-01-1967; 96.7 mhz FM *Hrs Open:* 24; 12 kw; Ant 476 ft; N29 41 39 W90 59 58
Mailing Address: Box 2068, Houma, LA 70802
Second Address: 120 Prevost Dr., Houma, LA 70364
(985) 851-1020, *Fax:* (985) 872-4403
www.mix967.net
info@mix967.net
License: Gray, St. Mary County, LA held by Sunburst Media-Louisiana LLC.
Group Owner: Sunburst Media-Louisiana LLC; (acq 1-23-2007; grpsl)
Nat'l Network: Jones Radio Networks
Hrs. of News Programming: News progmg 2 hrs wkly *Target Audience:* 18-34; majority women
John Delise, Operations Dir
Danny Fletcher, General Manager

Gretna

KGLA
01-06-1969; 1540 khz AM; 1 kw-D, NDD; N29 53 15 W90 5 3
PO Box 428, Marrero, LA 70072 US
(504) 347-1540, *Fax:* (504) 340-4737
www.tropical1540.com
info@kgla.tv
License: Gretna, LA held by Crocodile Broadcasting Corp.
Arbitron Metro Market: New Orleans, LA *Format:* Spanish
Ernesto Schweikert, General Manager
Miriam Danilov, General Sales Mgr
Mario Raul Zavala, Programming Director

KKNO
09-10-1989; 750 khz AM *Hrs Open:* Sunrise-sunset; 0.25 kw-D, NDD; N29 53 15 W90 5 3
P.O. Box 641403, Kenner, LA 70064 US
(504) 347-7775, *Fax:* (504) 347-7440
kkno750am@aol.com
License: Gretna, LA held by Robert C. Blakes Enterprises Inc.
Arbitron Metro Market: New Orleans, LA *Format:* Christian, Gospel, 74 *Hrs. of News Programming:* News progmg 10 hrs wkly *Target Audience:* General. *Adv. Rates:* 18.00; 18.00; 18.00; na
Robert Blakes Sr., President
Lois Blakes, General Manager
Stacey Blakes, General Sales Mgr

Hammond

***KSLU**
11-11-1974; 90.9 mhz FM *Hrs Open:* 24; 3 kw; 141 ft.; N30 30 53 W90 27 59
Slu Bx 783, University Station, Hammond, LA 70402 US
(985) 549-2330, *Fax:* (985) 549-3960
www.kslu.org
kslu@selu.edu
License: Hammond, Tangipahoa County, LA held by Southeastern Louisiana University.
Nat'l Network: PRI
Arbitron Metro Market: Hammond, LA *Format:* Alternative *Hrs. of News Programming:* news progmg 30 hrs wkly *No. News Employees:* 1 *Target Audience:* General. *Adv. Rates:* 15; 10; 10; 8

Todd Delaney, General Manager
Don Ellzey, News Director
Steve Portier, Chief Engineer

WRQQ(FM)
04-03-1965; 103.3 mhz FM *Hrs Open:* 24; 100 kw; Ant 1,004 ft; N30 24 06 W90 50 43
650 Wooddale Blvd., Baton Rouge, LA 70806-2930
(225) 926-1106, *Fax:* (225) 928-1606
www.sunny1033.com
wcdv.fm@citcomm.com
License: Hammond, Tangipahoa County, LA
Group Owner: Cumulus Media Inc.; (acq 1999; grpsl).
Nat'l Network: ABC *Regional Network:* La. Net. *Nat'l Reps:* McGavren Guild
Arbitron Metro Market: Baton Rouge, LA *Hrs. of News Programming:* news progmg 3 hrs wkly *No. News Employees:* 1 *Target Audience:* 25-54.
Greg Benefield, General Manager

WFPR
11-15-1947; 1400 khz AM *Hrs Open:* 24; 1 kw-U, ND1; N30 30 31 W90 30 18
PO Box 1829, Hammond, LA 70404 US
(985) 345-0060, *Fax:* (985) 542-9377
swapshop@nsbradiobroadcasting.com
License: Hammond, LA held by North Shore Broadcasting Co. Inc.
Nat'l Network: CBS
Format: Country *Special Programming:* Farm one hr, gospel 12 hrs wkly *Hrs. of News Programming:* news progmg 7 hrs wkly *No. News Employees:* 1 *Target Audience:* 35-64. *Adv. Rates:* 20; 15; 15; 10
Wayne Dowdy, President
Eloise Dowdy, General Manager
Ben Bickham, Programming Director

WHMD
08-26-1974; 107.1 mhz FM; 6 kw; 328 ft.; N30 25 32 W90 17 1
929 Government Street, Baton Rouge, LA 70821 US
(985) 345-0060, *Fax:* (985) 542-9377
License: Hammond, Tangipahoa County, LA
Format: Country *Adv. Rates:* 25; 20; 20; 15
Moss Bresnahan, President
John Gasque, Programming Director
Tom Holloway, Underwriting Director

Haughton

KBTT
01-01-1993; 103.7 mhz FM *Hrs Open:* 24; 6 kw; 328 ft.; N32 33 11 W93 34 56
P.O. Box 103, Shreveport, LA 71161 US
(318) 222-3122, *Fax:* (318) 459-1493
www.1037thabeat.fm
License: Haughton, Bossier County, LA held by Access. 1 Louisiana Holding Co. LLC.
Group Owner: Access.1 Communications Corp.; (acq 5-10-00; grpsl).
Arbitron Metro Market: Shreveport, LA *Format:* Urban Contemporary *No. News Employees:* 1 *Target Audience:* 18-34.
Cary Camp, General Manager

Hodge

KRLQ
08-15-2007; 94.1 mhz FM; 47 kw; 507 ft.; N32 24 35 W92 53 49
Mailing Address: US
Second Address: 1319 N. Vienna, Ruston, LA 71270
(318) 255-7941, *Fax:* (318) 255-8211
krlq941fm@bellsouth.net
License: Hodge, Jackson County, LA held by William W. Brown.
Nat'l Network: ABC *Regional Network:* La. Net.
Arbitron Metro Market: Hodge, LA *Format:* Country, Sports, 86
William Brown, General Manager

Homer

***KYLA**
03-01-1998; 106.7 mhz FM; 50 kw; 459 ft.; N32 44 39 W93 22 52
3712 Cornell Drive, Shreveport, LA 71107 US
(916) 251-1600, *Fax:* (916) 251-1650
www.klove.com
License: Homer, Claiborne County, LA held by Educational Media Foundation.
Group Owner: EMF Broadcasting; (acq 5-30-2006).
Nat'l Network: K-Love
Format: Christian
Mike Novak, President
Chip Bailey, Operations Dir
David Pierce, Programming Director
Ed Lenane, News Director
Sam Wallington, Engineering Dir
Marya Morgan, News Reporter
Richard Hunt, News Reporter

Houma

KJIN
04-01-1946; 1490 khz AM *Hrs Open:* 24; 1 kw-U, ND1; N29 34 14 W90 43 42
Mailing Address: P.O Box 2068, Houma, LA 70360 US
Second Address: 120 Prevost Dr., Houma, LA 70364
(985) 851-1020, *Fax:* (985) 872-4403
info@mix967.net
License: Houma, LA held by Sunburst Media-Louisiana LLC.
Group Owner: Sunburst Media-Louisiana LLC; (acq 1-23-2007; grpsl)
Nat'l Network: ABC *Nat'l Reps:* Roslin
Format: Sports *Hrs. of News Programming:* news progmg 3 hrs wkly *No. News Employees:* 1 *Target Audience:* 35 plus. *Adv. Rates:* 15; 15; 15; 10
John Delise, Operations Dir
Danny Fletcher, General Manager
Cade Voison, Programming Director
Bo Hoover, Chief Engineer

KVDU
11-15-1968; 104.1 mhz FM *Hrs Open:* 24; 100 kw; Ant 1,945 ft; N29 57 13 W90 43 25
929 Howard Ave., New Orleans, LA 70360
(504) 679-7300, *Fax:* (504) 679-7358
www.kissneworleans.com
info@kyrk.com
License: Houma, Terrebonne County, LA held by Clear Channel Broadcasting Licenses Inc.
Group Owner: Clear Channel Communications Inc.; (acq 1-27-2009; with WJRR(FM) Cocoa Beach, FL)
Nat'l Reps: Clear Channel
Population Served: 2,500,000 *Arbitron Metro Market:* New Orleans, LA *Hrs. of News Programming:* news progmg 2 hrs wkly *No. News Employees:* 1 *Target Audience:* 25-54.
Dick Lewis, General Manager
Michael Scott, General Sales Mgr
Mike Kramer, Programming Director
Tom Courtney, Chief Engineer

Iota

***KITA**
01-01-2008; 89.5 mhz FM; 19 kw vert; 433 ft.; N30 11 17 W92 37 55 *Rebroadcasts:* Rebroadcasts KLRD(FM) Yucaipa, CA 100%
188 South Bellevue, Suite 222, Memphis, TN 38104 US
(888) 937-2471, *Fax:* (916) 251-1650
www.air1.com
info@air1.com
License: Iota, Acadia County, LA held by Educational Media Foundation.
Group Owner: EMF Broadcasting; (acq 11-1-2006; grpsl)
Nat'l Network: Air 1
Arbitron Metro Market: Iota, LA *Format:* Alternative, Christian
Darrell Chambliss, Chairman
Alan Mason, COO
Mike Novak, President and CEO
Chip Bailey, Operations Dir
Ed Lenane, News Director
Sam Wallington, Engineering Dir
Eric Moser, Chief Financial Officer
Brian Burger, Vice President ofHuman Resources
D. Kevin Blair, Secretary and General Counsel
Larry Moody, Director
Mitch Barnhart, Director

Jackson

WNXX
10-17-2001; 104.5 mhz FM *Hrs Open:* 24; 3 kw; 472 ft.; N30 44 44 W91 7 32 *Rebroadcasts:* Rebroadcasts KNXX(FM) Donaldsonville 100%
Mailing Address: 729 Champagne Drive, Kenner, LA 70065 US
Second Address: 929-B Government St., Baton Rouge, LA 70802
(225) 388-9898, *Fax:* (225) 383-3700
www.1045espn.com
cindy.manzella@gbcradio.com
License: Jackson, East Feliciana County, LA held by Guaranty Broadcasting Co. of Baton Rouge LLC.
Group Owner: Guaranty Broadcasting Co. of Baton Rouge, LLC; (acq 10-5-2000; $1.044 million)
Arbitron Metro Market: Baton Rouge, LA *Format:* Alternative *Target Audience:* Adults 18-49.
George Foster Jr., Chairman
Bridger Eglin, President
Owen Weber, Operations Dir
Dave Dunaway, Operations Manager
Charles Hanagriff, Sports Director
James Gilmore, Online Marketing Manager
Gordy Rush, Market Manager

Jean Lafitte

KXMG
12-31-1965; 107.5 mhz FM; 69 kw; Ant 650 ft; N29 26 48 W90 44 34
Mailing Address: Box 2068, Houma, LA 70802
Second Address: 120 Prevost Dr., Houma, LA 70364
(985) 851-1020, *Fax:* (985) 872-4403
www.1075kcil.net
info@1075kcil.net
License: Jean Lafitte, Terrebonne County, LA held by Sunburst Media-Louisiana LLC.
Group Owner: Sunburst Media-Louisiana LLC
Population Served: 250,000 *Arbitron Metro Market:* New Orleans, LA *Hrs. of News Programming:* news progmg 2 hrs wkly *No. News Employees:* 1 *Target Audience:* Adults; 25-54
Adv. Rates: 55; 55; 45; 25
John Brewer, Operations Dir
Bill Vance, Station Manager
Shane Evath, News Director

Jena

***KAYT**
01-01-2001; 88.1 mhz FM; 15.5 kw horiz, 70 kw vert; 1007 ft.; N31 33 55 W92 33 0
2721 East Erwin Street, Tyler, TX 75708 US
(318) 484-2500, *Fax:* (318) 487-0909
www.kaytfm.com
kayt88@suddenlink.mail.com
License: Jena, La Salle County, LA held by Black Media Works Inc.
Group Owner: Black Media Works Inc.
Arbitron Metro Market: Alexandria, LA *Format:* Religious
Raymond Kassis, General Manager
Jocelyn Jacob, Station Manager

KJNA-FM
11-01-1976; 102.7 mhz FM *Hrs Open:* 24; 6 kw; 299 ft.; N31 41 51 W92 5 43
Mailing Address: 2nd and Elm Street, Jena, LA 71342 US
Second Address: 1791 N. 2nd St., Jena, LA 71342
(318) 992-4155, *Fax:* (318) 992-4479
kjnafm@hotmail.com
License: Jena, La Salle County, LA held by Little River Radio Co.
Group Owner: The Radio Group
Format: Country *Hrs. of News Programming:* news progmg 20 hrs wkly *No. News Employees:* 1 *Target Audience:* 25-54.
Larry Evans, General Manager

Jennings

KJEF
11-01-1950; 1290 khz AM *Hrs Open:* 24; 1 kw-D, ND1; 0.28 kw-N, ND1; N30 12 38 W92 39 55
1215 S. Lake Arthur Ave., Jennings, LA 70546 US
(337) 433-1641, *Fax:* (337) 433-2999
www.cajunradio.net
License: Jennings, LA held by GAP Broadcasting Lake Charles License LLC.
Group Owner: GAP Broadcasting LLC; (acq 2-6-2008; grpsl)
Regional Network: La. Net.
Format: Ethnic *Target Audience:* General.
Sara Cormier, General Manager
Aaron Turner, General Sales Mgr
Mike Soileau, Programming Director
Dave Chimeno, Chief Engineer

KHLA
01-01-1963; 92.9 mhz FM *Hrs Open:* 24; 30 kw; 640 ft.; N30 10 48 W93 1 52
1215 S. Lake Arthur Ave., Jennings, LA 70546 US
(337) 433-1641, *Fax:* (337) 433-2999
www.929thelake.com
License: Jennings, Jefferson Davis County, LA held by GAP Broadcasting Lake Charles License LLC.
Group Owner: GAP Broadcasting LLC; (acq 2-6-2008; grpsl)
Format: Contemporary Hits/Top 40, Adult Contemp
Sara Cormier, Station Manager
Aaron Turner, General Sales Mgr
Gary Shannon, Programming Director

Jonesboro

***KTOC-FM**
10-01-1967; 104.9 mhz FM; 25 kw; 236 ft.; N32 13 28 W92 43 27

Mailing Address: 3712 Cornell Dr., Shreveport, LA 71107 US
Second Address: 8919 World Ministry Ave., Baton Rouge, LA 70810
(225) 768-3688(225) 768-8300, *Fax:* (225) 768-3729
www.jsm.org
kawikfish@yahoo.com
License: Jonesboro, Jackson County, LA held by Family Worship Center Church Inc.
Group Owner: Family Worship Center Church Inc.; (acq 9-25-2002; $200,000 with co-located AM).
Arbitron Metro Market: Baton Rouge, LA *Format:* Christian
David Whitelaw, COO
Jimmy Swaggart, President
John Santiago, Programming Director

Jonesville

KZKR
01-01-2001; 105.1 mhz FM; 6 kw; Ant 315 ft; N31 36 21 W91 50 06
Mailing Address: Box 768, Natchez, MS 39711
Second Address: 2 Oferrall St., Natchez, LA 39120-3000
(601) 442-4895, *Fax:* (601) 446-8260
License: Jonesville, Catahoula County, LA held by First Natchez Corp.
Group Owner: First Natchez Radio Group; (acq 8-30-99; $150,000).
Margaret Perkins, General Manager
Mickey Alexander, Programming Director
Brenda Green, News Director
Keith Sanders, Chief Engineer

Kaplan

KMDL
08-01-1981; 97.3 mhz FM *Hrs Open:* 24; 38 kw; 561 ft.; N30 2 54 W91 59 49
P.O. Box 53708, Lafayette, LA 70505 US
(337) 233-6000, *Fax:* (337) 234-7360
www.973thedawg.com
info@973thedawg.com
License: Kaplan, Vermilion County, LA
Group Owner: Townsquare Media; (acq 12-7-2001; grpsl)
Nat'l Network: AP Radio
Arbitron Metro Market: Lafayette, LA *Format:* Country *Hrs. of News Programming:* News progmg 7 hrs wkly *Target Audience:* 25-54.
Mike Grimsley, General Manager
Scott Bryant, Programming Director

Kenner

WWL-FM
09-08-1970; 105.3 mhz FM; 96 kw; 1004 ft.; N29 58 57 W89 57 9
3525 N. Causeway Blvd, #1053, Metairie, LA 70002 US
(504) 260-1870, *Fax:* (504) 593-2187
www.wwl.com
info@wwl.com
License: Kenner, Jefferson County, LA held by Entercom New Orleans License LLC.
Group Owner: Entercom Communications Corp.; (acq 12-13-99; grpsl).
Arbitron Metro Market: New Orleans, LA *Format:* News, Talk
Ken Beck, General Manager
Patrick Galloway, General Sales Mgr
Diane Newman, Programming Director
Dave Cohen, News Director
Joe Pollet, Chief Engineer
Mark Broudreaux, General Sales Manager

Kentwood

WEMX
12-14-1967; 94.1 mhz FM *Hrs Open:* 24; 100 kw; 981 ft; N30 51 18 W90 39 59
140 South Ash Ave, Tempe, AZ 85281
(225) 926-1106, *Fax:* (225) 928-1606
www.max94one.com
wemx.fm@citcomm.com
License: Kentwood, Tangipahoe County, LA
Group Owner: Cumulus Media Inc.; (acq 1-14-99; grpsl).
Population Served: 2,225 *Arbitron Metro Market:* Kentwood, LA
Greg Benefield, General Manager

*WPEF
91.5 mhz FM; 6 kw; 292 ft.; N31 2 2 W90 25 27 US
(504) 816-8000, *Fax:* (504) 816-8580
License: Kentwood, Tangipahoe County, LA held by Providence Educational Foundation Inc.
Arbitron Metro Market: Kentwood, LA
Clay Corvin, General Manager

LaPlace

WDVW(FM)
01-10-1966; 92.3 mhz FM *Hrs Open:* 24; 100 kw; Ant 1,945 ft; N29 57 10 W90 43 26
P.O. BOX 488, Humboldt, TN 38343
(504) 581-7002, *Fax:* (504) 566-4857
www.diva923.com
License: LaPlace, St. John the Baptist County, LA
Group Owner: Cumulus Media Inc.; (acq 1-30-2004; $14.25 million).
Nat'l Reps: Christal *Regional Reps:* Christal Radio
Population Served: 65,187 *Arbitron Metro Market:* Jackson, TN
Dave Siebert, General Manager
John McQueen, Programming Director

Lacombe

WYLK
03-01-1996; 94.7 mhz FM *Hrs Open:* 24; 2.9 kw; 479 ft.; N30 23 8 W89 55 33
7106 Laird, #201, Panama City Beach, FL 32408 US
(985) 867-5990, *Fax:* (985) 867-9530
www.lake947.net
License: Lacombe, St. Tammany County, LA held by North Shore Broadcasting Inc.
Arbitron Metro Market: Lacombe, LA *Format:* Christian *Hrs. of News Programming:* news progmg 2 hrs wkly *No. News Employees:* 1 *Target Audience:* 25-54; general
Vicki Hays, General Manager

Lafayette

KFXZ
11-15-1960; 1520 khz AM *Hrs Open:* 24
8641 United Plaza Blvd., Suite 300, Baton Rouge, LA 70809 US
(337) 993-5500, *Fax:* (337) 993-5510
fsr1520.com
info@fsr1520.com
License: Lafayette, LA held by Pittman Broadcasting Services LLC
Group Owner: Pittman Broadcasting Services LLC; (acq 1-28-2004; grpsl)
Arbitron Metro Market: Lafayette, LA *Format:* Sports, Talk
Charles Sagona, General Manager

KJCB
04-09-1982; 770 khz AM; 1 kw-D, DAN; 0.5 kw-N, DAN; N30 17 55 W91 59 30
413 Jefferson Street, Lafayette, LA 70501 US
(337) 233-4262, *Fax:* (337) 235-9681
www.blackaction.net
License: Lafayette, LA held by R & M Broadcasting Inc.
Arbitron Metro Market: Lafayette, LA *Format:* Gospel *Target Audience:* 25-54.
Jenelle Schargios, General Manager

KPEL
01-02-1950; 1420 khz AM; 1 kw-D, DAN; 0.75 kw-N, DAN; N30 16 38 W92 3 51
P.O. Box 53708, Lafayette, LA 70505 US
(337) 233-6000, *Fax:* (337) 234-7360
www.espn1420.com
info@espn1420.com
License: Lafayette, LA
Group Owner: Townsquare Media; (acq 12-7-2001; grpsl)
Regional Network: La. Net. *Nat'l Reps:* Christal
Arbitron Metro Market: Lafayette, LA *Format:* Sports *Target Audience:* 35-54; male
Mike Grimsley, General Manager
Chuck Wood, General Sales Mgr
Kyle Vidrine, Chief Engineer

KRRQ
01-01-1996; 95.5 mhz FM; 50 kw; 443 ft; N30 21 08 W92 10 51
202 Galbert Rd., Lafayette, LA 85281
(337) 232-1311, *Fax:* (337) 233-3779
www.krrq.com
krrq@krrq.com
License: Lafayette, Lafayette County, LA
Group Owner: Cumulus Media Inc.; (acq 1-14-99; grpsl).
Arbitron Metro Market: Lafayette Metro area
Jim Beard, General Manager

*KRVS
01-01-1962; 88.7 mhz FM; 27.5 kw horiz, 100 kw vert; 1243 ft.; N30 19 20 W92 22 40
Mailing Address: Usl Box 42171, Lafayette, LA 70504 US
Second Address: 231 Hebrard Blvd., Lafayette, LA 70503
(337) 482-5787, *Fax:* (337) 482-6101
www.krvs.org
krvs@louisiana.edu
License: Lafayette, Lafayette County, LA held by University of Southwestern Louisiana.
Nat'l Network: NPR
Arbitron Metro Market: Lafayette, LA *Format:* Blues, Jazz *Target Audience:* General.
James Hebert, Operations Dir
Dave Spizale, General Manager
Judith Meriwether, General Sales Mgr
Kim Richard, Promotions Manager
Karl Fontenot, Chief Engineer
Kim Neustrom, Marketing Director

*KIKL
02-07-1988; 90.9 mhz FM *Hrs Open:* 24; 8.2 kw; 377 ft.; N30 17 5 W92 4 3
107 Parkgate Drive, Tupelo, MS 38803 US
(916) 251-1600, *Fax:* (916) 251-1650
www.klove.com
:klove@klove.com
License: Lafayette, Lafayette County, LA held by Educational Media Foundation.
Group Owner: EMF Broadcasting; (acq 4-25-2005; $1.5 million).
Nat'l Network: K-Love
Arbitron Metro Market: Rocklin, CA *Format:* Christian
Darrell Chambliss, Chairman
Mike Novak, CEO/COO
Mike Novak, President
Chip Bailey, Operations Dir
David Pierce, Programming Director
Ed Lenane, News Director
Sam Wallington, Engineering Dir
Marya Morgan, News Reporter
RichardHunt, News Reporter

KSMB
01-01-1964; 94.5 mhz FM; 100 kw; Ant 1,079 ft; N30 21 44 W92 12 53
202 Galbert Road, Lafayette, LA 70809
(337) 232-1311, *Fax:* (337) 233-3779
www.ksmb.com
License: Lafayette, Lafayette County, LA
Group Owner: Cumulus Media Inc.; (acq 4-26-01; grpsl).
Population Served: 122,130 *Arbitron Metro Market:* Lafayette, LA *Target Audience:* 18-49; active on-the-go adults
Jim Beard, General Manager

KTDY
09-15-1966; 99.9 mhz FM; 100 kw; 984 ft.; N30 12 6 W91 46 37
C/O Fletcher, Heald, 1300 North 17th Street, Arlington, VA 22209 US
(337) 237-5839, *Fax:* (337) 233-6000
www.999ktdy.com
info@999ktdy.com
License: Lafayette, Lafayette County, LA
Group Owner: Townsquare Media
Arbitron Metro Market: Lafayette, LA *Format:* Adult Contemp *Target Audience:* 25-54; female
Mike Grimsley, General Manager
Pam Begnaud, General Sales Mgr
C.J. Clements, Programming Director

KVOL
05-18-1935; 1330 khz AM; 5 kw-D, DAN; 1 kw-N, DAN; N30 14 29 W92 3 31
P.O. Box 788, Baton Rouge, LA 70821 US
(337) 993-5500, *Fax:* (337) 993-5510
www.kvol1330.com
kvol@pittmanbroadcasting.com
License: Lafayette, LA held by Pittman Broadcasting Services LLC
Group Owner: Pittman Broadcasting Services LLC; acq 1-28-2004; grpsl).
Nat'l Network: Westwood One
Arbitron Metro Market: Lafayette, LA *Format:* News, Talk *Target Audience:* 25-54; middle & upper income
Charles Sagona, General Manager

Lake Arthur

KJMH
08-01-1998; 107.5 mhz FM *Hrs Open:* 24; 50 kw; 463 ft.; N30 12 7 W92 56 47
P.O. Box 3067, Lake Charles, LA 70602 US
(337) 433-1641, *Fax:* (337) 433-2999
www.107jamz.com
License: Lake Arthur, Jefferson Davis County, LA held by GAP Broadcasting Lake Charles License LLC.
Group Owner: GAP Broadcasting LLC; (acq 2-6-2008; grpsl)
Nat'l Reps: Christal
Arbitron Metro Market: Lake Charles metro area *Format:* Urban Contemporary *No. News Employees:* 1 *Target Audience:* 25-54.

George Francis, General Manager
Aaron Turner, General Sales Mgr
Erik Tee, Programming Director
Dave Chimeno, Chief Engineer

Lake Charles

KAOK
05-10-1947; 1400 khz AM *Hrs Open:* 24; 1 kw-D, ND1; 1 kw-N, ND1; N30 14 10 W93 10 2
307 S. Jefferson, Covington, LA 70433 US
(337) 439-3300, *Fax:* (337) 433-7278
www.kaok.com
eric.nielson@cumulus.com
License: Lake Charles, LA held by Cumulus Licensing LLC.
Group Owner: Cumulus Media Inc.; (acq 12-6-2004; $3 million with KQLK(FM) De Ridder).
Nat'l Network: CBS *Regional Network:* La. Net.
Arbitron Metro Market: Lake Charles, LA *Format:* News, News/Talk, 86 *Hrs. of News Programming:* news progmg 168 hrs wkly *No. News Employees:* 1 *Target Audience:* 24 plus; baby boomers
Lewis Dickey Jr., President
Eric Nielson, Operations Dir
Jimmie Cole, General Sales Mgr
Eric Nielson, Programming Director
Chanel County, Promotions Manager
Richard Rhodes, Chief Engineer

KBIU
12-01-1976; 103.3 mhz FM *Hrs Open:* 24; 35 kw; 479 ft.; N30 14 41 W93 20 37
111 East Kilbourn Avenue, Suite 2700, Milwaukee, WI 53202 US
(337) 439-3300, *Fax:* (337) 433-7701
www.kbiu.com
cj.jones@cumulus.com
License: Lake Charles, Calcasieu County, LA held by Cumulus Licensing Corp.
Group Owner: Cumulus Media Inc.; (acq 12-17-98; grpsl)
Nat'l Reps: Katz Radio
Arbitron Metro Market: Lake Charles, LA *Format:* Adult Contemp
Target Audience: 25-54; adult
Eric Nielson, Operations Dir
Lance Knoll, General Sales Mgr
C.C. Jones, Promotions Manager
Holly Fontenot, News Director
Richard Rhodes, Chief Engineer
Jill Moore, General Sales Manager

KNGT
11-08-1965; 99.5 mhz FM; 100 kw; 1171 ft.; N30 17 26 W93 34 35
P.O. Box 3067, Lake Charles, LA 70602 US
(337) 433-1641, *Fax:* (337) 433-2999
www.gator995.com
georgefrancis@townsquaremedia.com
License: Lake Charles, Calcasieu County, LA held by GAP Broadcasting Lake Charles License LLC
Group Owner: GAP Broadcasting LLC; (acq 2-6-2008; grpsl)
Nat'l Reps: Christal
Arbitron Metro Market: Lake Charles, LA *Format:* Country
Special Programming: Local 20 hours wkly *Target Audience:* 25-54.
George Francis, General Manager
Aaron Turner, General Sales Mgr
Todd Stone, Programming Director
Dave Chimeno, Chief Engineer
Don Rivers, Program Director

KLCL
05-12-1935; 1470 khz AM; 5 kw-D, ND1; 0.5 kw-N, ND1; N30 15 31 W93 16 7
P.O. Box 3067, Lake Charles, LA 70502 US
(337) 433-1641, *Fax:* (337) 433-2999
www.cajunradio.net
License: Lake Charles, LA held by GAP Broadcasting Lake Charles License LLC
Group Owner: GAP Broadcasting LLC; (acq 2-6-2008; grpsl)
Regional Network: La. Net.
Arbitron Metro Market: Lake Charles, L *Format:* Ethnic *Target Audience:* 18-64.
Sara Cormier, General Manager
Mike Soileau, Programming Director

*KOJO
01-01-1990; 91.1 mhz FM *Hrs Open:* 24; 4 kw horiz, 14 kw vert; 387 ft.; N30 12 7 W92 56 47 *Rebroadcasts:* Rebroadcasts KJMJ(AM) Alexandria
7355 North Oracle Rd., Tucson, AZ 85704 US
(318) 561-6145, *Fax:* (318) 449-9954
www.radiomaria.us
info.usa@radiomaria.org
License: Lake Charles, Calcasieu County, LA held by Radio Maria Inc.
Group Owner: Radio Maria Inc.; acq 10-13-99).
Arbitron Metro Market: Lake Charles, LA *Format:* Christian, Talk, 74 *Target Audience:* General; Christians seeking training & encouragement through Bible teaching programs
Duane Stenzel, General Manager
Dale DePerrodell, General Sales Mgr
Danny Brou, Chief Engineer

KXZZ
01-01-1947; 1580 khz AM *Hrs Open:* 24; 1 kw-D, DAN; 1 kw-N, DAN; N30 15 28 W93 11 55
111 East Kilbourn Avenue, Suite 2700, Milwaukee, WI 53202 US
(337) 439-3300, *Fax:* (337) 433-7701
www.kxzz1580am.com
License: Lake Charles, LA held by Cumulus Licensing Corp.
Group Owner: Cumulus Media Inc.
Nat'l Network: American Urban *Nat'l Reps:* Katz Radio
Arbitron Metro Market: Lake Charles, LA *Format:* Black *Target Audience:* 25-54; adult
Eric Nielson, Operations Dir
CJ Jones, General Manager
Jimmie Cole, General Sales Mgr
Chanel County, Promotions Manager

KYKZ
01-01-1976; 96.1 mhz FM *Hrs Open:* 24; 100 kw; 479 ft.; N30 14 41 W93 20 37
111 East Kilbourn Avenue, Suite 2700, Milwaukee, WI 53202 US
(337) 439-3300, *Fax:* (337) 436-7278
www.kykz.com
info@kykz.com
License: Lake Charles, Calcasieu County, LA held by Cumulus Licensing Corp.
Group Owner: Cumulus Media Inc.; (acq 12-17-98; grpsl)
Arbitron Metro Market: Lake Charles, LA *Format:* Country *Hrs. of News Programming:* news progmg 8 hrs wkly *No. News Employees:* 3 *Target Audience:* General.
Jill Moore, General Sales Mgr
Eric Nielson, Programming Director
Chanel County, Promotions Manager
Richard Rhodes, Chief Engineer

*KYLC
01-01-2001; 90.3 mhz FM; 80 kw vert; 469 ft.; N30 38 10 W93 2 33
P O Box 106, Roaring Springs, PA 16673 US
(662) 844-8888, *Fax:* (662) 842-6791
www.afr.net
faq@afr.net
License: Lake Charles, Calcasieu County, LA held by American Family Association.
Group Owner: American Family Radio; (acq 3-14-01).
Arbitron Metro Market: Tupelo, MS *Format:* Christian, Religious
Marvin Sanders, General Manager

Lake Providence

KLPL(AM)
06-27-1957; 1050 khz AM; 250 w-D, 22 w-N; N32 48 59 W91 12 22
645 Church St., Willis Broadcasting Corp., Norfolk, VA 23510
(757) 622-4600, *Fax:* (757) 624-6515
License: Lake Providence, East Carroll County, LA held by Willis Broadcasting Corp.
Group Owner: Willis Broadcasting Corp.; acq 4-21-98; $120,000 with co-located FM).
Population Served: 10,300*Target Audience:* General.
Robert Dominguez, General Manager
Toya Hall, Programming Director

KLPL(FM)
01-28-1975; 92.7 mhz FM; 3 kw; Ant 154 ft; N32 48 59 W91 12 22
645 Church St., Willis Broadcasting Corp., Norfolk, LA 23510
(757) 622-4600, *Fax:* (757) 624-6515
License: Lake Providence, East Carroll County, LA
Population Served: 10,300
Angela Carter, General Manager
Chris Hertlein, Programming Director

Larose

KLRZ
03-29-1993; 100.3 mhz FM *Hrs Open:* 24; 89 kw; 586 ft.; N29 33 1 W90 21 4
P.O. Drawer 1350, Larose, LA 70373 US
(985) 798-7792, *Fax:* (985) 798-7793
www.klrzfm.com
klrz@mobilete.com
License: Larose, Lafourche County, LA held by Coastal Broadcasting of Larose Inc.
Nat'l Network: Westwood One
Arbitron Metro Market: New Orleans, LA *Format:* Ethnic *Hrs. of News Programming:* news progmg 22 hrs wkly *No. News Employees:* 1 *Target Audience:* 25-54; professionals
Andrea Galjour, Operations Dir
Jerry Gisclair, General Manager

Leesville

KJAE
10-01-1979; 93.5 mhz FM; 7.5 kw; 328 ft.; N31 8 28 W93 17 44
Mailing Address: PO Box 1323 ., 101 Lees Lane, Leesville, LA 71466 US
Second Address: 101 Lees Ln., Leesville, LA 71446
(337) 239-3402, *Fax:* (337) 238-9283
www.kjae935.com
info@kjae935.com
License: Leesville, Vernon County, LA
Format: Country
Timothy Brown, General Manager
Roger Tighe, Chief Engineer

KLLA
09-01-1956; 1570 khz AM
Mailing Address: 101 Lees Lane, PO Box 1323, Leesville, LA 71446 US
Second Address: 101 Lees Ln., Leesville, LA 71446
(337) 239-3402, *Fax:* (337) 238-9283
www.kjae935.com
info@kjae935.com
License: Leesville, LA held by Pene Broadcasting Co.
Arbitron Metro Market: Alexandria, LA *Format:* Country
Penny Scogin, General Manager
Peggy Merritt, General Sales Mgr
Tony Evans, Chief Engineer

KVVP
01-20-1977; 105.7 mhz FM *Hrs Open:* 24; 13.5 kw; 449 ft.; N31 0 19 W93 16 42
P.O. Drawer K, Leesville, LA 71496 US
(337) 537-5887, *Fax:* (337) 537-4152
www.kvvp.com
kvvp@kvvp.com
License: Leesville, Vernon County, LA held by Stannard Broadcasting Co. Inc.
Arbitron Metro Market: Leesville, LA *Format:* Country *Special Programming:* Relg 9 hrs wkly *Hrs. of News Programming:* news progmg 15 hrs wkly *No. News Employees:* 1 *Target Audience:* 18-54; adults withspending power
Alan Taylor, CFO
Doug Stannard, President

KBDV
01-01-2008; 92.7 mhz FM *Hrs Open:* 24 hours; 6 kw; 328 ft.; N31 7 7 W93 11 12
US
(318) 256-5924, *Fax:* (318) 256-0950
www.bdcradio.com
eagle92.7@suddenlinkmail.com
License: Leesville, Vernon County, LA held by Baldridge-Dumas Communications Inc.
Group Owner: Baldridge-Dumas Communications Inc.
Arbitron Metro Market: Leesville, LA *Format:* Adult Contemp
Michael Parker, Operations Dir
Rhonda Leach, General Manager
Cindy Ezernack, Station Manager
Jenny Hodge, General Sales Mgr

Mamou

KBON
06-01-1997; 101.1 mhz FM *Hrs Open:* 24; 25 kw; 328 ft.; N30 29 50 W92 15 59
1601 Poinciana, Mamou, LA 70554 US
(337) 546-0007, *Fax:* (337) 546-0097
www.kbon.com
101.1@kbon.com
License: Mamou, Evangeline County, LA held by Rose Ann Marx.
Format: Country
Paul Marx, General Manager

Mansfield

KJVC
09-01-1976; 92.7 mhz FM *Hrs Open:* 24; 3 kw; 299 ft.; N32 1 18 W93 44 18
3801 Skillern Blvd., Flower Mound, TX 75028 US
(318) 697-4000, *Fax:* (318) 697-4004

License: Mansfield, De Soto County, LA held by Metropolitan Radio Group Inc.
Group Owner: Metropolitan Radio Group Inc.; acq 10-97; $85,000)
Format: Country *Adv. Rates:* 6; 6; 6; 6
David Grahams, General Manager

***KHMD**
05-01-1994; 104.7 mhz FM *Hrs Open:* 24; 25 kw; 328 ft.; N31 57 49 W93 53 58
3801 Skillern Blvd, Flower Mound, TX 75028 US
(713) 520-5200
www.khcb.org
License: Mansfield, De Soto County, LA held by Houston Christian Broadcasters Inc.
Group Owner: Houston Christian Broadcasters Inc.; (acq 12-30-2008; $150,000)
Arbitron Metro Market: Shreveport, LA *Format:* Christian
Bruce Munsterman, General Manager

***KMSL**
01-01-2006; 91.7 mhz FM; 12 kw vert; 339 ft.; N32 10 39 W93 55 2 *Rebroadcasts:* Rebroadcasts WAFR(FM) Tupelo, MS 100% US
(662) 844-8888, *Fax:* (662) 842-6791
www.afr.net
License: Mansfield, De Soto County, LA held by American Family Association.
Nat'l Network: American Family Radio
Arbitron Metro Market: El Dorado, AR *Format:* Christian
Marvin Sanders, General Manager

Mansura

KZLG
07-01-2000; 95.9 mhz FM *Hrs Open:* 24; 6 kw; 322 ft.; N31 2 49 W91 59 41
Mailing Address: P O Box 493, Moreauville, LA 71355 US
Second Address: 10586 Hwy. 1, Moreauville, LA 71355
(928) 522-8282, *Fax:* (318) 985-2995
www.eaglerocksonline.com
Jim@EagleRocksOnline.com
License: Mansura, Avoyelles County, LA held by Amy M. Coco.
Nat'l Network: AP Radio *Regional Network:* La. Net.
Arbitron Metro Market: Flagstaff, AZ *Format:* Adult Contemp *Hrs. of News Programming:* 3 hrs *Target Audience:* 25 plus. *Adv. Rates:* 8; 8; 8; 8
Louis Coco, Jr, General Manager
Jim Seemiller, Director, Digital and National Sales

Many

***KAVK**
06-01-1998; 89.3 mhz FM; 12 kw; 427 ft.; N31 32 5 W93 25 21
Po Drawer 2440, Tupelo, MS 38803 US
(662) 844-8888, *Fax:* (662) 842-6791
www.afr.net
comments@afr.net
License: Many, Sabine County, LA held by American Family Association.
Group Owner: American Family Radio
Arbitron Metro Market: Tupelo, MS *Format:* Christian, Religious
Marvin Sanders, General Manager

KWLV
11-12-1977; 107.1 mhz FM; 25 kw; 253 ft.; N31 36 27 W93 24 5
595 San Antonio Avenue, Many, LA 71449 US
(318) 256-5177, *Fax:* (318) 256-0950
www.bdcradio.com
kwlv@bellsouth.net
License: Many, Sabine County, LA
Arbitron Metro Market: Many, LA *Format:* Country *Target Audience:* 20 plus.
Rhonda Benson Leach, General Manager
Cindy Ezernack, Station Manager
Cindy Ezernack, General Sales Mgr
Gordon Rivert, News Director
Kenny Carter, Chief Engineer
Brenda Springer, Traffic Director/ Offive Manager

Marksville

KAPB-FM
08-14-1971; 97.7 mhz FM; 6 kw; 328 ft.; N31 7 27 W92 4 40
Mailing Address: P. O. Box 1319, Columbia, LA 71418 US
Second Address: 520 Chester, Marksville, LA 71351
(318) 253-5272, *Fax:* (318) 253-5262
kapbfm@yahoo.com
License: Marksville, Avoyelles County, LA held by Three Rivers Radio Co.
Group Owner: The Radio Group
Arbitron Metro Market: Alexandria, LA *Format:* Country
Pamela Couvillion, General Manager
Larry Young, Chief Engineer

Maurice

KYMK-FM
06-13-1985; 106.3 mhz FM; 2.6 kw; 495 ft.; N30 4 16 W92 11 53
140 South Ash Avenue, Tempe, AZ 85281 US
(337) 993-5500, *Fax:* (337) 993-5510
License: Maurice, Vermilion County, LA held by Pittman Broadcasting Services LLC.
Group Owner: Pittman Broadcasting Services LLC; (acq 1-28-2004; grpsl)
Arbitron Metro Market: Maurice, LA *Format:* Adult Contemp
Charles Sagona, General Manager

Minden

KASO
04-01-1952; 1240 khz AM *Hrs Open:* 24; 1 kw-U, ND1; N32 37 50 W93 16 56
Post Office Box 1240, Minden, LA 71058 US
(318) 377-1240, *Fax:* (318) 377-461
www.kbef.com
kaso1240@yahoo.com
License: Minden, LA held by Amistad Communications Inc.
Group Owner: Amistad Communications Inc.; (acq 10-2000; $375,000 with CP for KBEF(FM) Gibsland).
Nat'l Network: Jones Radio Networks *Regional Network:* La. Net.
Arbitron Metro Market: Minden, LA *Format:* Adult Contemp *Hrs. of News Programming:* News progmg 102 hrs wkly *Target Audience:* 35-64; male & female *Adv. Rates:* 33; 16; 16; 16
Fred Caldwell, President
Mike Griffith, General Manager
Mark Cheesne, Programming Director

KLKL
07-01-1978; 95.7 mhz FM *Hrs Open:* 24; 50 kw; 469 ft.; N32 33 16 W93 31 47
7308 Old River Road, Shreveport, LA 71105 US
(318) 222-3122, *Fax:* (318) 459-1493
www.klkl.fm
info@oldies957.fm
License: Minden, Webster County, LA held by Access. 1 Louisiana Holding Co. LLC.
Group Owner: Access.1 Communications Corp.; (acq 6-30-00; $7.9 million with KDKS-FM Blanchard).
Arbitron Metro Market: Shreveport, LA *Format:* Oldies *No. News Employees:* 1 *Target Audience:* 25-54.
Cary Camp, General Manager

Monroe

KRJO
05-01-2001; 1680 khz AM *Hrs Open:* 24
Mailing Address: 3436 Hwy 45 North, Meridan, MS 39302 US
Second Address: 1109 Hudson Ln., Monroe, LA 71201
License: Monroe, LA held by Holladay Broadcasting of Louisiana LLC
Group Owner: Holladay Broadcasting of Louisiana LLC; acq 11-21-2003; grpsl).
Nat'l Reps: McGavren Guild

***KBMQ**
08-15-1999; 88.7 mhz FM *Hrs Open:* 24; 25 kw horiz, 24.5 kw vert; 458 ft.; N32 24 15 W92 2 7
1700 Parkview Drive, Monroe, LA 71202 US
(318) 387-1230, *Fax:* (318) 387-8856
www.887fm.org
info@887fm.org
License: Monroe, Ouachita County, LA held by Media Ministries Inc.
Arbitron Metro Market: Monroe, LA *Format:* Christian *Hrs. of News Programming:* News progmg one hr wkly *Target Audience:* 25-54; women *Adv. Rates:* 25; 25; 25; 20
Phillip Brooks, Programming Director
Susan Peacock, Promotions Manager

***KEDM**
04-23-1991; 90.3 mhz FM *Hrs Open:* 24; 100 kw; 856 ft.; N32 39 38 W91 59 28
150 Riverside Mall, Baton Rouge, LA 70801 US
(318) 342-5556, *Fax:* (318) 342-5570
www.kedm.org
License: Monroe, Ouachita County, LA held by University of Louisiana at Monroe
Nat'l Network: NPR *Regional Network:* La. Net. *Wire Services:* AP
Arbitron Metro Market: Monroe, LA *Format:* Classical, Jazz, 60
Jay Curtis, Programming Director
Bob Lenox, News Director
Kenneth Sanders, Chief Engineer
Susan Allain, Development Director
Sunny Merriwether, News Director
Jay Curtis, Program Director

KJLO-FM
07-01-1946; 104.1 mhz FM *Hrs Open:* 24; 97 kw; 1017 ft.; N32 39 36 W92 5 15
Mailing Address: C/O Donald A. Fishman, 1001 Penn Ave, N.W. 1300, Washington, DC 20004 US
Second Address: 1109 Hudson Ln., Monroe, LA 71201
(318) 388-2323, *Fax:* (318) 388-0569
www.kjlo.com
License: Monroe, Ouachita County, LA held by Holladay Broadcasting of Louisiana LLC.
Group Owner: Holladay Broadcasting of Louisiana LLC; (acq 10-1-2006; $500,000)
Nat'l Reps: McGavren Guild
Arbitron Metro Market: Monroe, LA *Format:* Country *Special Programming:* Gospel 4 hrs wkly *No. News Employees:* 1 *Target Audience:* 25-54.
Robert Holladay, President

KLIP
04-01-1993; 105.3 mhz FM *Hrs Open:* 24; 50 kw; 433 ft.; N32 33 8 W92 8 33
Mailing Address: 3436 Highway 45 North, Meredian, MS 39301 US
Second Address: 1109 Hudson Ln., Monroe, LA 71201
(318) 388-2323, *Fax:* (318) 388-0569
www.la105.com
la105@bayou.com
License: Monroe, Ouachita County, LA held by Holladay Broadcasting of Louisiana LLC
Group Owner: Holladay Broadcasting of Louisiana LLC; acq 11-21-2003; grpsl).
Nat'l Network: ABC *Nat'l Reps:* McGavren Guild
Arbitron Metro Market: Monroe, LA *Format:* Contemporary Hits/Top 40, Adult Contemp *Hrs. of News Programming:* News progmg 2 hrs wkly *Target Audience:* 25-54.
Bob Holladay, President

KXRR
11-15-1965; 106.1 mhz FM; 97 kw; 1017 ft.; N32 39 36 W92 5 15
350 Park Avenue, 20th Floor, New York, NY 10022 US
(318) 387-3922, *Fax:* (318) 322-4585
rock106kxrr.com
License: Monroe, Ouachita County, LA held by Opus Broadcasting Monroe L.L.C.
Group Owner: Opus Media Holdings LLC; (acq 7-19-2004; grpsl).
Nat'l Reps: Christal
Arbitron Metro Market: Monroe, LA *Target Audience:* 25-49.
Chris Zimmerman, General Manager

***KXUL**
05-09-1973; 91.1 mhz FM *Hrs Open:* 24; 8.5 kw; 715 ft.; N32 39 38 W91 59 28
128 Stubbs Hall, Monroe, LA 71209 US
(318) 342-5985
www.kxul.com
License: Monroe, Ouachita County, LA held by University of Lousiana at Monroe.
Arbitron Metro Market: Monroe, LA *Format:* Alternative *Target Audience:* 12-34.
Joel Willer, Programming Director

KMLB
07-01-1931; 540 khz AM
Mailing Address: 1400 Oliver Road, Monroe, LA 71201 US
Second Address: 1109 Hudson Ln., Monroe, LA 71201
(318) 388-2323, *Fax:* (318) 388-0569
www.kmlb.com
talk540@bayou.com
License: Monroe, LA held by Holliday Broadcasting of Louisiana LLC.
Group Owner: Holladay Broadcasting of Louisiana LLC; (acq 3-4-2008; $150,000)
Nat'l Network: ABC; ABC Information & Entertainment; Fox News Radio; Premiere Radio Networks; Talk Radio Network *Regional Network:* La. Net.; La. Agri-News; Yancey AG Network; Agri-Net
Nat'l Reps: Eastman Radio
Arbitron Metro Market: Monroe, LA *Format:* News, Talk *Special Programming:* New Orleans Saints/LSU *Hrs. of News Programming:* 3hrs / day *No. News Employees:* 1 *Target Audience:* 25 plus.
Bob Holladay, General Manager
Cory Crowe, Programming Director

KNOE-FM
01-29-1967; 101.9 mhz FM; 97 kw horiz, 96 kw vert; 1516 ft.; N32 11 50 W92 4 14
PO Box 4067, Monroe, LA 71211 US

(318) 807-3285, *Fax:* (318) 325-9466
www.starradiomonroe.com
License: Monroe, Ouachita County, LA held by Radio Monroe LLC
Arbitron Metro Market: Monroe, LA *Format:* Contemporary Hits/Top 40
Bobby Richards, Programming Director

*KYFL
10-08-1992; 89.5 mhz FM *Hrs Open:* 24; 25 kw; 377 ft.; N32 33 8 W92 8 33
8030 Arrowridge Blvd., Charlotte, NC 28273 US
(704) 523-5555
www.bbnradio.org
bbn@bbnradio.org
License: Monroe, Ouachita County, LA held by Bible Broadcasting Network Inc.
Group Owner: Bible Broadcasting Network
Arbitron Metro Market: Charlotte, NC *Format:* Christian *Hrs. of News Programming:* News progmg 3 hrs wkly *Target Audience:* General.
Michael Thomson, General Manager

Moreauville

KLIL
07-25-1980; 92.1 mhz FM; 6 kw; 299 ft.; N31 2 53 W91 59 47
Mailing Address: P.O. Box 365, Moreauville, LA 71355 US
Second Address: 10586 Hwy. 1, Moreauville, LA 71355
(318) 985-2929, *Fax:* (318) 985-2995
klil@kricket.net
License: Moreauville, Avoyelles County, LA held by Cajun Broadcasting Inc.
Nat'l Network: AP Radio *Regional Network:* La. Net.
Arbitron Metro Market: Alexandria, LA *Format:* Oldies *Target Audience:* 20 plus; working adults *Adv. Rates:* 7; 7; 7; 7
Louis Coco Jr., President

Morgan City

KMRC
04-01-1954; 1430 khz AM *Hrs Open:* 24; 0.5 kw-D, NDD; N29 45 3 W91 10 24
409 Duke Street, Morgan City, LA 70380 US
(985) 384-1430, *Fax:* (985) 384-2351
www.kmrc1430.com
kmrc@kmrc1430.com
License: Morgan City, LA held by Spotlight Broadcasting L.L.C.
Group Owner: Spotlight Broadcasting LLC; acq 2-1-00; $109,000).
Format: Adult Contemp *Hrs. of News Programming:* news progmg 5 hrs wkly *No. News Employees:* 1 *Target Audience:* 25-54; middle to upper income *Adv. Rates:* 12; 10; 10; 6.
Patrick Andras, CEO
John Stork, General Manager

Moss Bluff

KZWA
08-12-1994; 104.9 mhz FM; 25 kw; 328 ft.; N30 27 15 W93 8 20
P. O. Box 699, Lake Charles, LA 70602 US
(337) 491-9955, *Fax:* (337) 433-8097
www.kzwafm.com/
info@kzwa.com
License: Moss Bluff, Calcasieu County, LA held by B & C Broadcasting Inc.
Arbitron Metro Market: Moss Bluff, LA. *Format:* Urban Contemporary *Target Audience:* 18-34.
Faye Brown-Blackwell, CEO
Faye B. Blackwell, Owner

Natchitoches

*KBIO
07-02-2002; 89.7 mhz FM; 0.1 kw; 295 ft.; N31 47 13 W93 7 52
Rebroadcasts: Rebroadcasts KJMJ(AM) Alexandria
P O Drawer 2440, Tupelo, MS 38803 US
(318) 561-6145, *Fax:* (318) 449-9954
www.radiomaria.us
info.usa@radiomaria.org
License: Natchitoches, Natchitoches County, LA held by Radio Maria Inc.
Group Owner: Radio Maria Inc.; (acq 9-6-2001)
Arbitron Metro Market: Alexandria, LA *Format:* Christian, Talk, 74
Duane Stenzel, General Manager
Dale DePerrodil, General Sales Mgr
Danny Brou, Chief Engineer

KDBH-FM
07-01-1965; 97.5 mhz FM; 6 kw; 220 ft.; N31 48 17 W93 1 27
720 Front Street, PO Box 607, Natchitoches, LA 71457 US
(318) 352-9696, *Fax:* (318) 357-9595
www.bdcradio.com/index.php/stations/kdbh-975-fm/
kdbh@suddenlinkmail.com
License: Natchitoches, Natchitoches County, LA held by Baldridge-Dumas Communications Inc.
Group Owner: Baldridge-Dumas Communications Inc.; acq 5-14-01; $340,000 with co-located AM including two-year noncompete agreement).
Nat'l Network: Jones Radio Networks *Regional Network:* La. Net.
Arbitron Metro Market: Many, LA *Format:* Country
Rhonda Benson, General Manager
Rhonda Benson, Station Manager
Gordon Rivet, News Director
Kenny Carter, Chief Engineer

KNOC
05-01-1947; 1450 khz AM *Hrs Open:* 24; 1 kw-U, ND1; N31 45 47 W93 3 47
PO Box 607, Natchitoches, LA 71458 US
(318) 354-4000, *Fax:* (318) 352-9598
License: Natchitoches, LA held by North Face Broadcasting L.L.C.
Nat'l Network: ABC
Format: News, News/Talk, 86 *Hrs. of News Programming:* news progmg 20 hrs wkly *No. News Employees:* 1 *Target Audience:* 35 plus; upper-middle class *Adv. Rates:* 20; 20; 20; 10
John Brewer, Operations Dir
Bill Vance, Station Manager
Shane Erath, News Director

*KNWD
09-01-1975; 91.7 mhz FM *Hrs Open:* 24; 0.255 kw horiz; 164 ft.; N31 44 51 W93 5 47
P. O. Box 3038, Natchitoches, LA 71457 US
(318) 357-4180, *Fax:* (318) 357-4398
www.nsula.edu/thedemon
knwd917@yahoo.com
License: Natchitoches, Natchitoches County, LA held by Northwestern State University of Louisiana.
Format: Variety/Diverse *Hrs. of News Programming:* news progmg 3 hrs wkly *No. News Employees:* 1 *Target Audience:* 18-25.
Elliot Westphal, Station Manager

KZBL
10-08-1985; 100.7 mhz FM *Hrs Open:* 24; 25 kw; 276 ft.; N31 48 17 W93 1 27
1115 Washington Street, Natchitoches, LA 71457 US
(318) 357-1007, *Fax:* (318) 357-9595
www.kzblradio.com/
kzbl@suddenlinkmail.com
License: Natchitoches, Natchitoches County, LA held by Baldridge-Dumas Communications Inc.
Group Owner: Baldridge-Dumas Communications Inc.; acq 6-21-99; $400,000).
Nat'l Network: Jones Radio Networks
Arbitron Metro Market: Natchitoches, LA *Format:* Oldies *Hrs. of News Programming:* News progmg 10 hrs wkly *Target Audience:* 25-50. *Adv. Rates:* 16; 12; 12; 10
Rhonda Benson, Station Manager

New Iberia

KANE
08-01-1946; 1240 khz AM *Hrs Open:* 24; 1 kw-U, ND1; N30 1 3 W91 50 10
2316 E. Main St., New Iberia, LA 70560 US
(337) 365-3434, *Fax:* (337) 365-9117
www.kane1240.com
kane@kane1240.com
License: New Iberia, LA held by Coastal Broadcasting of Lafourche L.L.C.
Regional Network: La. Net.
Arbitron Metro Market: New Iberia, LA *Format:* Ethnic *Hrs. of News Programming:* News progmg 30 hrs wkly *Target Audience:* 25-54. *Adv. Rates:* 21; 16; 19; 14
Jerry Gisclair, General Manager

KNIR
06-01-1951; 1360 khz AM *Hrs Open:* 24
145 W Main Street, New Iberia, LA 70560 US
(318) 561-6145, *Fax:* (318) 449-9954
www.radiomaria.us
info.usa@radiomaria.org
License: New Iberia, LA held by Radio Maria Inc.
Group Owner: Radio Maria Inc.; (acq 6-10-2003; $45,000).
Arbitron Metro Market: Lafayette, LA *Format:* Christian
Father Stenzel, General Manager

KRDJ
01-01-1991; 93.7 mhz FM *Hrs Open:* 24; 100 kw; Ant 971 ft; N30 20 19 W91 31 23
20 Galbert Rd., Lafayette, LA 70821
(337) 232-1311
www.red937.com
krdj.fm@citcomm.com
License: New Iberia, Iberia County, LA
Group Owner: Cumulus Media Inc.; (acq 10-8-99; $9.5 million)
Population Served: 500,000 *Arbitron Metro Market:* Baton Rouge, LA *Target Audience:* 18-44; men
Mary Galyean, General Manager

KXKC
01-01-1969; 99.1 mhz FM *Hrs Open:* 24; 100 kw; 1,039 ft; N30 12 06 W91 46 37
202 Galbert Rd., Lafayette, LA 70560
(337) 232-1311
www.kxkc.com
info@kxkc.com
License: New Iberia, Iberia County, LA
Group Owner: Cumulus Media Inc.; (acq 12-5-2003; $7.6 million).
Population Served: 122,130 *Arbitron Metro Market:* Lafayette, LA *Target Audience:* 18-49.
Mary Galyean, General Manager

New Orleans

WBOK
02-01-1951; 1230 khz AM; 1 kw-U, ND1; N29 59 18 W90 2 45
645 Church St, Suite 400, Norfolk, VA 23510 US
(504) 942-0106, *Fax:* (291) 291-6804
www.wbok1230am.com
Cheryl@WBOK1230am.com
License: New Orleans, LA held by Bakewell Media of Louisiana LLC.
Arbitron Metro Market: New Orleans, LA *Format:* Gospel *Target Audience:* 25 plus.
Danny Bakewell Sr., General Manager

*WBSN-FM
02-05-1979; 89.1 mhz FM *Hrs Open:* 24; 11 kw; 440 ft.; N29 55 11 W90 1 29
3939 Gentilly Blvd., New Orleans, LA 70126 US
(504) 816-8000, *Fax:* (504) 816-8580
www.lifesongs.com
onair@lifesongs.com
License: New Orleans, Orleans County, LA held by Providence Educational Foundation.
Arbitron Metro Market: New Orleans, LA *Format:* Christian *Target Audience:* 25-49; active, Christian oriented families
Stan Watts, General Manager

WEZB
09-01-1945; 97.1 mhz FM; 99 kw; 984 ft.; N29 55 11 W90 1 29
10706 Beaver Dam Road, Cockeysville, MD 21030 US
(504) 260-9797, *Fax:* (504) 593-2205
www.b97.com
ino@b97.com
License: New Orleans, Orleans County, LA held by Entercom New Orleans License LLC.
Group Owner: Entercom Communications Corp.; (acq 12-13-99; grpsl)
Arbitron Metro Market: New Orleans, LA *Format:* Contemporary Hits/Top 40 *Target Audience:* 18-34; females
Ken Beck, General Manager
Patrick Galloway, General Sales Mgr
Mike Kaplan, Programming Director
Joe Pollet, Chief Engineer

WGSO
01-27-1946; 990 khz AM *Hrs Open:* 24; 1 kw-D, ND1; 0.4 kw-N, ND1; N29 57 24 W90 4 34
110 Veterans Blvd., Suite 300, Metairie, LA 70005 US
(985) 639-3820, *Fax:* (985) 639-3869
www.wgso.com
info@wgso.com
License: New Orleans, LA held by Northshore Radio LLC
Arbitron Metro Market: New Orleans, LA *Format:* News, News/Talk, 86
Mike Starr, General Manager

WLMG
03-15-1970; 101.9 mhz FM *Hrs Open:* 24; 99 kw; 984 ft.; N29 55 11 W90 1 29
10706 Beaver Dam Road, Cockeysville, MD 21030 US
(504) 593-6376, *Fax:* (504) 593-1850
www.magic1019.com
info@magic1019.com
License: New Orleans, Orleans County, LA
Group Owner: Entercom Communications Corp.
Arbitron Metro Market: New Orleans, LA *Format:* Adult Contemp
Patrick Galloway, General Sales Mgr
Andy Holt, Programming Director

WLNO
05-26-1995; 1060 khz AM *Hrs Open:* 24
4100 E. Mississippi Ave, Suite 1750, Denver, CO 80222 US
(504) 362-9800, *Fax:* (504) 362-5541
www.wlno.com
wlno@i-55.com
License: New Orleans, LA held by Communicom Co. of Louisiana L.P.
Arbitron Metro Market: New Orleans, LA *Format:* Christian, Religious *Target Audience:* General.
Carl DiMaria, CEO
Richard Kylberg, President

WNOE-FM
09-15-1968; 101.1 mhz FM *Hrs Open:* 24; 100 kw; 1004 ft.; N29 58 57 W89 57 9
929 Howard Ave., New Orleans, LA 70113 US
(504) 679-7300, *Fax:* (504) 679-7343
www.wnoe.com
ProgramDirector@WNOE.com
License: New Orleans, Orleans County, LA held by Clear Channel Communications Inc.
Group Owner: Clear Channel Communications Inc.; acq 1996; grpsl)
Nat'l Network: ABC; Westwood One *Nat'l Reps:* Clear Channel
Arbitron Metro Market: New Orleans, LA *Format:* Country *No. News Employees:* 1 *Target Audience:* 25-54.
Dick Lewis, General Manager
Mike Scott, General Sales Mgr
Sam McGuire, Programming Director
Richard Atwood, Chief Engineer

WODT
07-23-1923; 1280 khz AM; 5 kw-U, DA1; N29 53 43 W90 0 16
3305 W. Mountain Rd. #60, Las Vegas, NV 89102 US
(504) 679-7300, *Fax:* (504) 679-7345
darnettamahaffy@clearchannel.com
License: New Orleans, LA held by Clear Channel Radio Licenses Inc.
Group Owner: Clear Channel Communications Inc.; (acq 7-24-92)
Nat'l Reps: Clear Channel
Arbitron Metro Market: New Orleans, LA *TV Affiliate:* Urban Gospel *Special Programming:* News progmg one hr wkly *No. News Employees:* 35 plus; general

WQUE-FM
01-01-1949; 93.3 mhz FM *Hrs Open:* 24; 98.8 kw; 984 ft.; N29 55 11 W90 1 29
3305 W. Mountain Rd, #60, Las Vegas, NV 89102 US
(504) 679-7300, *Fax:* (504) 679-7345
www.Q93.com
webmaster@Q93.com
License: New Orleans, Orleans County, LA held by Clear Channel Radio Licenses Inc.
Group Owner: Clear Channel Communications Inc.
Nat'l Network: Premiere Radio Networks *Nat'l Reps:* Clear Channel
Arbitron Metro Market: New Orleans, LA *Format:* Urban Contemporary *Hrs. of News Programming:* 2 *No. News Employees:* 1
Mike Scott, General Sales Mgr
Derrick Corbett, Programming Director
Richard Atwood, Chief Engineer

***WRBH**
01-01-1980; 88.3 mhz FM *Hrs Open:* 24; 51 kw; 623 ft.; N29 56 59 W89 57 28
3606 Magazine Street, New Orleans, LA 70115 US
(504) 899-1144, *Fax:* (504) 899-1165
www.wrbh.org
Natalia@WRBH.ORG
License: New Orleans, Orleans County, LA held by Radio for the Blind and Print Handicapped Inc.
Arbitron Metro Market: New Orleans, LA *Format:* News *Hrs. of News Programming:* News progmg 28 hrs wkly *Target Audience:* Blind & print handicapped.
Natalia Gonzales, Operations Dir
Jackie Bullock, Programming Director
Ernie Kain, Chief Engineer

WRNO-FM
10-17-1967; 99.5 mhz FM; 100 kw; 1004 ft.; N29 58 57 W89 57 9
3825 Forrestgate Drive, Suite 100, Winston-Salem, NC 27103 US
(504) 679-7300, *Fax:* (504) 679-7345
www.wrno.com
License: New Orleans, Orleans County, LA held by Clear Channel Broadcasting Licenses Inc.
Group Owner: Clear Channel Communications Inc.; (acq 8-8-2002; swap for KKND(FM) Port Sulphur).
Nat'l Network: Premiere Radio Networks; ABC; Fox News Radio; Westwood One
Arbitron Metro Market: New Orleans, LA *Format:* News, News/Talk, 86 *No. News Employees:* 3
Dick Lewis, Operations Dir
Mike Scott, General Sales Mgr
Jim Fisher, Programming Director
Bob Christopher, News Director
Richard Atwood, Chief Engineer

WSHO
01-01-1926; 800 khz AM; 1 kw-D, DA2; 0.233 kw-N, DA2; N29 50 42 W90 6 39
1001 Howard Avenue, Suite 4304, New Orleans, LA 70113 US
(504) 527-0800, *Fax:* (504) 527-0881
www.wsho.com
whso@wsho.com
License: New Orleans, LA held by Shadowlands Communications L.L.C.
Nat'l Network: Salem Radio Network
Arbitron Metro Market: New Orleans, LA *Format:* Religious *Target Audience:* 25-54.
William Ainsworth, President
Mike Patton, Chief Engineer

WWWL
04-21-1925; 1350 khz AM *Hrs Open:* 24; 5 kw-D, DAN; 5 kw-N, DAN; N29 55 27 W90 2 4
2000 West 41st St., Baltimore, MD 21211 US
(504) 593-6376, *Fax:* (504) 593-1850
www.1350espn.com
License: New Orleans, LA held by Entercom New Orleans License LLC.
Group Owner: Entercom Communications Corp.; (acq 12-13-99; grpsl)
Nat'l Network: ESPN Radio
Arbitron Metro Market: New Orleans, LA *Format:* Sports
Ken Beck, General Manager
Malcolm Pelham, General Sales Mgr
Diane Newman, Programming Director
Joe Pollet, Chief Engineer
Mark Broudreaux, General Sales Manager

WIST
01-01-1948; 690 khz AM *Hrs Open:* 24; 10 kw-D, DA2; 5 kw-N, DA2; N29 57 53 W89 57 31
1206 Decatur Street, New Orleans, LA 70116 US
(504) 552-2412, *Fax:* (504) 552-2430
www.wistradio.com
feedback@wistradio.com
License: New Orleans, LA held by WTIX Inc.
Group Owner: GHB Radio Group; (acq 2-12-92; $800,000;
Arbitron Metro Market: New Orleans, LA *Format:* Oldies, Talk *Hrs. of News Programming:* News progmg 30 hrs wkly *Target Audience:* 25 plus; affluent, educated, professional *Adv. Rates:* 50; 40; 40; 50
Daniel Frazier, General Manager
John Bradley, Sales Representative

WKBU
02-01-1953; 95.7 mhz FM; 99.5 kw; 984 ft.; N29 55 11 W90 1 29
3525 N.Causewy Blvd#1053, Metairie, LA 70002 US
(504) 593-6376, *Fax:* (504) 593-1850
bayou957.com
mail@entercom.com
License: New Orleans, Orleans County, LA held by Entercom New Orleans License LLC.
Group Owner: Entercom Communications Corp.; (acq 12-13-99; grpsl)
Arbitron Metro Market: New Orleans, LA *Format:* Classic Rock *Target Audience:* 25-54.
Patrick Galloway, General Sales Mgr
Mike Kaplan, Programming Director
Dave Cohen, News Director
Joe Pollet, Chief Engineer

***WTUL**
11-14-1974; 91.5 mhz FM *Hrs Open:* 24; 1.5 kw; 161 ft.; N29 56 18 W90 7 7
Tulane University Center, 6823 St. Charles Ave., New Orlans, LA 70118 US
(504) 865-5887
www.wtul.fm
wtul@tulane.edu
License: New Orleans, Orleans County, LA held by Tulane Educational Fund.
Arbitron Metro Market: New Orleans, LA *Format:* Alternative *Hrs. of News Programming:* News progmg 3 hrs wkly *Target Audience:* General.
Sarah Gersten, General Manager
Chelsea O'Lansen, Programming Director
Fred Schaefer, Promotions Manager
Andy Zellinger, Office Manager
Judah Lea, Head Music Director
Hunter King, Technical Director
Ruth Vernotico, Director ofDevelopment and Special Projects
Matt Handsfield, Assistant General Manager
Nicole Harvey, Social Media Director

WVOG
04-23-1964; 600 khz AM *Hrs Open:* 5:30 AM-8:30 PM; 1 kw-D, ND2; 0.031 kw-N, ND1; N29 57 25 W90 9 33
2730 Loumor Ave, Matairie, LA 70001 US
(504) 831-6941, *Fax:* (504) 831-2647
www.wwcr.com
License: New Orleans, LA held by F.W. Robbert Broadcasting Co. Inc.
Group Owner: F W Robbert Broadcasting Co. Inc.; acq 6-28-74).
Arbitron Metro Market: New Orleans, LA *Format:* Christian, Talk *Hrs. of News Programming:* News progmg 2 hrs wkly *Target Audience:* 30 plus. *Adv. Rates:* 9; 9; 9; na
Fred P. Westenberger, President
Eric Westenberger, Station Manager
Eric Martin, Programming Director
Earnie Harvey, Chief Engineer
Gina Marino, Secretary

WWL
03-31-1922; 870 khz AM *Hrs Open:* 24; 50 kw-U, DA1; N29 50 14 W90 7 55
10706 Beaver Dam Road, Cockeysville, MD 21030 US
(504) 593-6376, *Fax:* (504) 593-1850
www.wwl.com
info@wwl.com
License: New Orleans, LA held by Entercom New Orleans License LLC.
Group Owner: Entercom Communications Corp.; (acq 12-13-99; grpsl)
Nat'l Network: CBS *Nat'l Reps:* D & R Radio
Arbitron Metro Market: New Orleans, LA *Format:* News, News/Talk, 84, Talk
Diane Newman, Operations & Program Director
Chris Claus, Vice President/General Manager
Malcolm Pelham, General Sales Mgr
Helen Centanni, Promotions Manager
Joe Pollet, Chief Engineer
Steve Geller, Producer/Sports
Donnie Picou,Director of Sales
Jay Vise, Digital Content Manager
Scott Colomb, Web Developer

***WWNO**
02-20-1972; 89.9 mhz FM *Hrs Open:* 24; 35 kw; 984 ft.; N29 55 11 W90 1 29
U. New Orleans-Lakefront, 2000 Lakeshore Drive, New Orleans, LA 70148 US
(504) 280-7000, *Fax:* (504) 280-6061
www.wwno.org
info@wwno.org
License: New Orleans, Orleans County, LA held by Louisiana State University.
Nat'l Network: PRI; NPR *Wire Services:* AP
Arbitron Metro Market: New Orleans, LA *Format:* Jazz, News *Hrs. of News Programming:* News progmg 39 hrs wkly *Target Audience:* 35 plus; well-educated professionals, mgrs, artists & art patrons
Ron Curtis, Operations Dir
Chuck Miller, General Manager
Karen Anklam, General Sales Mgr
Fred Kasten, Programming Director
Eileen Fleming, News Reporter
Ron Biava, Development and Marketing Manager
Jameeta Youngblood, BusinessManager
Jenni Lawson, Production Manager

***WWOZ**
12-06-1980; 90.7 mhz FM *Hrs Open:* 24; 4 kw; 509 ft.; N29 57 24 W90 4 31
Mailing Address: P.O. Box 51840, New Orleans, LA 70151 US
Second Address: 1008 N. Peters, New Orleans, LA 70116
(504) 568-1239, *Fax:* (504) 558-9332
www.wwoz.org
wwoz@wwoz.org
License: New Orleans, Orleans County, LA held by Friends of WWOZ Inc.
Arbitron Metro Market: New Orleans, LA *Format:* Blues, Jazz *Hrs. of News Programming:* News progmg 5 hrs wkly *Target Audience:* 35-55; upscale & educated males
Jorge Fuentes, Operations Dir
David Freedman, General Manager
Dwayne Breashears, Programming Director
Damond Jacob, Chief Engineer
Tony Guillory, IT Manager

Scott Borne, Music Director
Beau Royster, Chief Financial and BusinessDevelopment Officer
Crystal Gross, Development Director
Molly Cobb, Membership Director

WYLD
01-01-1949; 940 khz AM *Hrs Open:* 24
200 Concord Plaza, San Antonio, TX 78216 US
(504) 679-7300, *Fax:* (504) 679-7343
www.am940.com
info@am940.com
License: New Orleans, LA held by Clear Channel Radio Licenses Inc.
Group Owner: Clear Channel Communications Inc.; (acq 3-25-93;
Nat'l Network: ABC; Westwood One *Nat'l Reps:* Clear Channel
Arbitron Metro Market: New Orleans, LA *Format:* Gospel *Target Audience:* 25-54.
Dick Lewis, General Manager

WYLD-FM
01-01-1971; 98.5 mhz FM *Hrs Open:* 24; 97.8 kw; 984 ft.; N29 55 11 W90 1 29
3305 W. Mountain Road, #60, Las Vegas, NV 89102 US

www.wyldfm.com
License: New Orleans, Orleans County, LA held by Clear Channel Radio Licenses Inc.
Group Owner: Clear Channel Communications Inc.
Arbitron Metro Market: New Orleans, LA *Format:* Adult Contemp *Hrs. of News Programming:* news progmg 5 hrs wkly *No. News Employees:* 2
Earl Lovely, Chairman

New Roads

KQXL-FM
10-01-1979; 106.5 mhz FM *Hrs Open:* 24; 50 kw; Ant 485 ft; N30 37 24 W91 09 50
650 Wooddale Blvd., Baton Rouge, LA 85281
(225) 926-1106, *Fax:* (225) 928-1606
www.q106dot5.com
kqxl.fm@citcomm.com
License: New Roads, Pointe Coupee County, LA
Group Owner: Cumulus Media Inc.; (acq 1-14-99; grpsl).
Nat'l Network: CBS
Population Served: 600,000 *Arbitron Metro Market:* Baton Rouge, LA *No. News Employees:* 1 *Target Audience:* 18-54; Black adults
Greg Capogna, General Manager
Denise Johnson, General Sales Mgr
J'Michael, Programming Director
Deontray Alexander, Promotions Manager

***KPCP**
88.3 mhz FM; 6 kw horiz, 5.53 kw vert; 299 ft.; N30 43 20.4 W91 35 45.6
US
(225) 638-6822, *Fax:* (225) 638-6822
www.kpcp883.com
rgremillion@bellsouth.net

License: New Roads, Pointe Coupee County, LA held by Stop the Violence/Save the Children Inc.
Arbitron Metro Market: New Roads, LA *Format:* Adult Contemp
Roosevelt Gremillion, President
Joseph R. Gremillion III, Board Operator
Nickolas Gremillion, Music Director
Patricia Johnson, Secretary

KCLF
08-19-1964; 1500 khz AM; 1 kw-D, ND1; N30 44 8 W91 24 58
P.O. Box 9, New Roads, LA 70760 US
(225) 638-6822, *Fax:* (225) 638-6882
www.kclf1500am.com
rgremillion@bellsouth.net
License: New Roads, LA held by New World Broadcasting Co. Inc.
Arbitron Metro Market: New Roads, LA *Format:* Urban Contemporary
Roosevelt Gremillion, General Manager

Norco

WFNO
01-01-1987; 830 khz AM; 5 kw-D, DA2; 0.75 kw-N, DA2; N30 3 0 W90 22 41
110 Veterans Blvd., Ste 300, Metairie, LA 70005 US
(504) 832-3555, *Fax:* (504) 838-7700
License: Norco, LA held by Davidson Media Station WFNO Licensee LLC.
Group Owner: Davidson Media Group LLC; (acq 1-11-2007; $2 million)
Wire Services: AP
Arbitron Metro Market: New Orleans, LA *Format:* Spanish *Hrs. of News Programming:* news progmg 12 hrs wkly *No. News Employees:* 2 *Target Audience:* 18-44.
Yadira Hernandez, General Manager
Jose Hidalgo, Programming Director

***WNKV**
01-01-2007; 91.1 mhz FM; 4.7 kw vert; 230 ft.; N29 48 34 W90 25 17 *Rebroadcasts:* Rebroadcasts KLVR(FM) Middletown, CA 100%
188 South Bellevue, Suite 222, Memphis, TN 38104 US
(800) 525-5683, *Fax:* (916) 251-1650
www.klove.com
klove@klove.com
License: Norco, St. Charles County, LA held by Educational Media Foundation.
Group Owner: EMF Broadcasting; (acq 11-1-2006; grpsl)
Nat'l Network: K-Love
Arbitron Metro Market: Norco, LA *Format:* Christian *No. News Employees:* 13
Darrell Chambliss, Chairman
Mike Novak, President and CEO
Chip Bailey, Operations Dir
David Pierce, Programming Director
Ed Lenane, News Director
Sam Wallington, Engineering Dir
Dan Antonelli, Chief Business DevelopmentOfficer
Eric Moser, Chief Financial Officer
Brian Burger, Vice President of Human Resources
D. Kevin Blair, Secretary and General Counsel
Tim Luttrell, News Reporter

North Fort Polk

KUMX
05-10-1995; 106.7 mhz FM *Hrs Open:* 24; 6 kw; 315 ft.; N31 3 5 W93 16 41
421 Tilley Road, Leesville, LA 71446 US
(337) 537-9000, *Fax:* (337) 537-4152
www.kumxfm.com
info@kumxfm.com
License: North Fort Polk, Vernon County, LA held by West Central Broadcasting Co. Inc.
Nat'l Network: ABC
Arbitron Metro Market: Leesville, LA *Format:* Adult Contemp, Christian *Special Programming:* Tom Joiner *Hrs. of News Programming:* 12pm, 5pm *No. News Employees:* 12 *Target Audience:* 22-42. *Adv. Rates:* 78; 78; 78; 78
Alan Taylor, CFO
Doug Stannard, General Manager

Oak Grove

KWCL-FM
01-30-1973; 96.7 mhz FM *Hrs Open:* 24; 23 kw; 341 ft.; N32 51 32 W91 21 22
Mailing Address: P. O. Box 260, 8612 Hwy Two, Oak Grove, LA 71263 US
Second Address: 230 E. Main St., Oak Grove, LA 71263
(318) 428-9670, *Fax:* (318) 428-2476
kwcl@bellsouth.net
License: Oak Grove, West Carroll County, LA held by KWCL-FM Broadcasting Co. Inc.
Nat'l Network: ABC; Jones Radio Networks
Arbitron Metro Market: Oak Grove, LA *Format:* Oldies *Hrs. of News Programming:* news progmg 17 hrs wkly *No. News Employees:* 1 *Target Audience:* General. *Adv. Rates:* 8; 8; 8; 6
Irene Robinson, President
Kelley Lovell, Programming Director

Oakdale

KKST
01-01-1972; 98.7 mhz FM *Hrs Open:* 24; 48 kw; Ant 1,053 ft; N31 01 59 W92 30 08
1115 Texas Ave., Alexandria, LA 78701
(318) 445-1234, *Fax:* (318) 445-7231
www.cenlabroadcasting.com
chad@cenlabroadcasting.com
License: Oakdale, Allen County, LA held by Cenla Broadcasting Licensing Co. LLC.
Group Owner: Cenla Broadcasting Co. Inc.; (acq 11-13-2006; grpsl)
Population Served: 150,000 *Arbitron Metro Market:* Alexandria, LA *Hrs. of News Programming:* news progmg 20 hrs wkly *No. News Employees:* 1 *Target Audience:* 18-49; women
Taylor Thompson, General Manager
Chad Soprano, General Sales Mgr

Oil City

KRMD-FM
08-01-1948; 101.1 mhz FM; 97.7 kw; 345.7 meters; N32 41 08 W93 56 00
270 Plaza Loop, PO Box 5459, Bossier City, LA 78701
(318) 549-8500, *Fax:* (318) 549-8505
www.krmd.com
krmd@cumulus.com
License: Oil City, Caddo County, LA held by Cumulus Licensing Corp.
Group Owner: Cumulus Media Inc.; (acq 8-7-2000; grpsl)
Nat'l Reps: Christal
Population Served: 369,800 *Arbitron Metro Market:* Shreveport, LA *No. News Employees:* 2 *Target Audience:* 25-54. *Adv. Rates:* 100; 85; 95; 45
Phil Robkin, General Manager
Chuck Redden, General Sales Mgr
James Anthony, Programming Director
Gary Robinson, Promotions Manager
Rick Taylor, News Director
Jasen Bragg, Engineering Dir
Margie Bueche, General Sales Manager

Opelousas

KOGM
06-18-1965; 107.1 mhz FM *Hrs Open:* 24; 0.75 kw; 933 ft.; N30 20 32 W91 57 46
Mailing Address: P. O. Box 1150, Opelousas, LA 70570 US
Second Address: 216 N. Court St., Opelousas, LA 70570
(337) 942-2633, *Fax:* (337) 942-2635
kslokogm@bellsouth.net
License: Opelousas, St. Landry County, LA held by KSLO Broadcasting Company
Group Owner: Delta Media Corp.
Nat'l Network: ABC Music Radio *Regional Network:* La. Net.
Arbitron Metro Market: Lafayette, LA *Format:* Adult Contemp *Hrs. of News Programming:* 1 hour per week *No. News Employees:* 1 *Target Audience:* 25 plus.
Penny Smith, CEO
Kristi Castille, Operations Dir
Chris Lamke, General Manager
Missy Benoit, Programming Director
Kyle Vidrine, Engineering Dir
Bea Pefferkorn, Office Manager
Justin Duren, Production Director

KSLO
09-01-1947; 1230 khz AM *Hrs Open:* 24
Mailing Address: P. O. Box 1150, Opelousas, LA 70571 US
Second Address: 216 N. Court St., Opelousas, LA 70570
(337) 942-2633, *Fax:* (337) 942-2635
www.ksloradio.com
kslokogm@bellsouth.net
License: Opelousas, LA held by KSLO Broadcasting Co. Inc.
Group Owner: Delta Media Corp.
Nat'l Network: ABC *Regional Network:* La. Agri-News; La. Net.
Arbitron Metro Market: Opelousas, LA *Format:* Country, News *Hrs. of News Programming:* 10 hrs. per week *No. News Employees:* 1 *Adv. Rates:* 15.55; 15.55; 15.55; 15.55
Penny Smith, CEO
Chris Lamke, General Manager
Missy Benoit, Programming Director
Kyle Vidrine, Engineering Dir
Justin Duren, Music Director
Bea Pefferkorn, Office Manager

KFXZ-FM
08-03-1989; 105.9 mhz FM; 3.4 kw; 433 ft.; N30 27 59 W92 4 31
202 Galbert Rd., Lafayette, LA 70506 US
(337) 993-5500, *Fax:* (337) 993-5510
www.z1059.com
kfxz@pittmanbroadcasting.com
License: Opelousas, St. Landry County, LA held by Pittman Broadcasting Services LLC
Group Owner: Pittman Broadcasting Services LLC; (acq 1-28-2004; grpsl)
Arbitron Metro Market: Lafayette, LA *Format:* Urban Contemporary
Charles Sagona, General Manager

Pineville

KTTP
09-13-1974; 1110 khz AM; 2 kw-D, NDD; N31 21 52 W92 27 15
34-D Macarthur Drive, Alexandria, LA 71303 US
(318) 473-4388, *Fax:* (318) 449-1779
kttpam1110@aol.com
License: Pineville, LA held by Benjamin-Dane LLC
Arbitron Metro Market: Alexandria, LA *Format:* Gospel *Target Audience:* 25-70. *Adv. Rates:* 120; 120; 120; na

Ronald Reeves, President
Carolyn Frazier, Station Manager
Dave Grayso, Engineering Dir

Plaquemine

***KPAQ**
88.1 mhz FM; 2.9 kw vert; 308 ft.; N30 15 41 W91 18 40
P O Drawer 2440, Tupelo, MS 38803 US
(662) 844-8888, *Fax:* (662) 842-6791
www.afa.net
randall@afa.net
License: Plaquemine, Iberville County, LA held by American Family Association.
Group Owner: American Family Radio
Arbitron Metro Market: Plaquemine, LA *Format:* Christian
Marvin Sanders, General Manager

Port Allen

WXOK
02-01-1953; 1460 khz AM *Hrs Open:* 24; 4.7 kw-D, 290 w-N; N30 28 08 W91 12 24
650 Wooddale Blvd., Baton Rouge, LA 85281
(225) 926-1106, *Fax:* (225) 928-1606
www.heaven1460.com
wxok.am@citcomm.com
License: Port Allen, East Baton Rouge County, LA
Group Owner: Cumulus Media Inc.; (acq 1-14-99).
Nat'l Network: ABC
Population Served: 230,139 *Arbitron Metro Market:* Baton Rouge, LA *Target Audience:* 18 plus.
Greg Benefield, General Manager

Port Sulphur

KAGY
08-17-1966; 1510 khz AM *Hrs Open:* 6 AM-6 PM; 1 kw-D, NDD; N29 29 3 W89 42 15
P.O. Box 1307, Buras, LA 70041 US
(985) 384-1430, *Fax:* (985) 384-2351
www.kmrcradio.com
kmrc@kmrc1430.com
License: Port Sulphur, LA held by Spotlight Broadcasting of New Orleans LLC
Group Owner: Spotlight Broadcasting LLC; (acq 12-30-2002; $250,000).
Arbitron Metro Market: Metairie, LA *Format:* Adult Contemp
Target Audience: 24-54; general *Adv. Rates:* 12; 12; 12; 12
Patrick Andras, CEO
John Stork, General Manager

KMEZ
07-04-1989; 106.7 mhz FM *Hrs Open:* 24; 100 kw; Ant 981 ft; N29 48 30 W89 45 42
201 St. Charles Ave., Suite 201, New Orleans, LA 78216
(504) 581-7002, *Fax:* (504) 566-4857
www.oldschool1067.com
trapper.john@citcomm.com
License: Port Sulphur, Plaquemines County, LA
Group Owner: Cumulus Media Inc.; (acq 8-29-2003; grpsl)
Nat'l Reps: Clear Channel
Arbitron Metro Market: New Orleans, LA *No. News Employees:* 1 *Target Audience:* 25-54.
Dave Siebert, General Manager
Trapper John, Programming Director

***KSUL**
91.5 mhz FM; kw
P O Drawer 2440, Tupelo, MS 38803 US
(845) 794-9898, *Fax:* (845) 794-0125
www.wsul.com
office@wsul.com
License: Port Sulphur, Plaquemines County, LA held by American Family Association.
Group Owner: American Family Radio
Arbitron Metro Market: New York, NY

Rayne

KLEJ
01-01-1993; 106.7 mhz FM; 3 kw; Ant 328 ft; N30 18 17 W92 20 47
Mailing Address: Box 228, Crowley, LA 70527
Second Address: 320 N. Parkerson Ave., Crowley, LA 70526
(337) 783-2520, *Fax:* (337) 783-5744
www.countrylegends1067.com
License: Rayne, Acadia County, LA held by Broadcast Partners Inc.
Arbitron Metro Market: Lafayette, LA
Phil Lizotte, President
Jimmy Cole, General Sales Mgr
Hans Nelson, Programming Director
Tony Evans, Chief Engineer

Rayville

KMYY
09-01-1984; 92.3 mhz FM *Hrs Open:* 16; 11.5 kw; 486 ft.; N32 29 1 W91 54 10
1207 Louisa Street, Rayville, LA 71269 US
(318) 387-3922, *Fax:* (318) 322-4585
www.realcountry923.com
923thewolf@gmail.com
License: Rayville, Richland County, LA held by Opus Broadcasting Monroe L.L.C.
Group Owner: Opus Media Holdings LLC; (acq 7-19-2004; grpsl).
Arbitron Metro Market: Monroe, LA *Format:* Country
Chris Zimmerman, General Manager

Reserve

WPRF
08-01-1991; 94.9 mhz FM *Hrs Open:* 24; 50 kw; Ant 482 ft; N29 43 48 W90 43 37
770 N. Jefferson St., Milwaukee, WI 70068
(414) 273-3776, *Fax:* (414) 291-3776
www.wauksportsradio@msn.com
License: Reserve, St. John the Baptist County, LA held by Southeastern Broadcasting Inc.
Population Served: 156,929 *Arbitron Metro Market:* Eugene-Springfield OR
Craig Karmazin, President
C.J. Knee, Operations Dir
Bill Johnson, Programming Director
Warren Jorgenson, News Director

Richwood

KHLL
03-01-1995; 100.9 mhz FM; 25 kw; 328 ft.; N32 24 25 W92 4 13
217 Gilliland Rd, West Monroe, LA 71291 US
(318) 323-5994, *Fax:* (318) 323-6680
www.hillradio.com
mail@hillradio.com
License: Richwood, Ouachita County, LA held by Dan Gilliland.
Format: Christian
Rick Godley, General Manager

KLIC
01-01-1950; 1230 khz AM *Hrs Open:* 24; 1 kw-U; N32 25 43 W92 04 43
130 N 2nd St. Ste C, Monroe, LA 71211
(318) 387-1230, *Fax:* (318) 387-8856
www.am1230thesource.com
phillip@887fm.org
License: Richwood, Ouachita County, LA held by Media Ministries Inc.
Nat'l Network: Salem Radio Network
Population Served: 150,000 *Arbitron Metro Market:* Monroe, LA
Hrs. of News Programming: News progmg 14 hrs wkly *Target Audience:* 25-54; Adults 35 + *Adv. Rates:* 14; 13; 14; 9
Tony Davis, President
Mike Downhour, General Manager
Diane Osborne, General Sales Mgr
Naomi Thompson, News Director
Ernie Sandidge, Engineering Dir
Mark Kemp, Traffic Manager

Ruston

***KAPI**
02-01-1998; 88.3 mhz FM; 0.3 kw; 197 ft.; N32 33 8 W92 39 21
P.O. Drawer 2440, Tupelo, MS 38803 US
(662) 844-8888, *Fax:* (662) 842-6791
www.afr.net
comments@afr.net
License: Ruston, Lincoln County, LA held by American Family Association.
Group Owner: American Family Radio
Arbitron Metro Market: Tupelo, MO *Format:* Christian, Religious
Marvin Sanders, General Manager

***KLPI**
01-01-1973; 89.1 mhz FM; 4 kw; 285 ft.; N32 31 41 W92 38 50
Mailing Address: 900 Gilman, Ruston, LA 71270 US
Second Address: Union Bldg., 101 Wysteria St., Ruston, LA 71272
(318) 257-4851, *Fax:* (318) 257-5073
www.891klpi.org
general@891klpi.org
License: Ruston, Lincoln County, LA held by Louisiana Tech University.
Arbitron Metro Market: Monroe, LA *Format:* Alternative *No. News Employees:* 2 *Target Audience:* 18-24; college students
Angela Carter, General Manager
Chris Hertlein, Programming Director

KPCH
01-01-1999; 99.3 mhz FM *Hrs Open:* 24; 24.5 kw; 331 ft.; N32 28 53 W92 40 34
Mailing Address: 109 Llanfair Drive, Ruston, LA 71270 US
Second Address: 500 N. Monroe St., Ruston, LA 71270
(318) 255-5000, *Fax:* (318) 255-5084
thepeach@bayou.com
License: Ruston, Lincoln County, LA held by Communications Capital Co. II of Louisiana LLC.
Group Owner: Communications Capital Managers LLC; (acq 3-4-2002; grpsl)
Regional Network: La. Net.
Arbitron Metro Market: Monroe, LA *Format:* Oldies *Adv. Rates:* 19; 19; 19; 19
Gary McKenney, General Manager
Tommy Gray, Chief Engineer

KRUS
11-07-1947; 1490 khz AM; 1 kw-U, ND1; N32 30 48 W92 39 56
Mailing Address: P. O. Box 430, Ruston, LA 71270 US
Second Address: 500 N. Monroe St., Ruston, LA 71270
(318) 255-5000
z1075fm@bayou.com
License: Ruston, LA held by Communications Capital Co. II of Louisiana LLC.
Group Owner: Communications Capital Managers LLC; (acq 3-4-2002; grpsl)
Arbitron Metro Market: Ruston, LA *Format:* Black, Gospel *Target Audience:* 25-55; Black
Gary McKenney, General Manager
James Cooper, Programming Director
Tommy Gray, Chief Engineer

KXKZ
06-29-1966; 107.5 mhz FM *Hrs Open:* 24; 100 kw; 1066 ft.; N32 26 37 W92 42 43
Mailing Address: 500 N. Monroe, P.O. Box 430, Ruston, LA 71270 US
Second Address: 500 N. Monroe St., Ruston, LA 71270
(318) 255-5000
www.z1075fm.com
License: Ruston, Lincoln County, LA
Group Owner: Communications Capital Managers LLC
Nat'l Network: ABC *Wire Services:* ESSA Weather Service
Arbitron Metro Market: Ruston, LA *Format:* Country *Hrs. of News Programming:* news progmg 7 hrs wkly *No. News Employees:* 1
Target Audience: 25-54.
Matt McKenney, Programming Director

Shreveport

KVMA-FM
01-01-2001; 102.9 mhz FM *Hrs Open:* 24; 42 kw; 535 ft.; N32 29 36 W93 45 55
600 Congress Avenue, Suite 1400, Austin, TX 78701 US
(318) 549-8500, *Fax:* (318) 549-8505
magic1029fm.com
cumulus.shreveport@cumulus.com
License: Shreveport, Caddo County, LA held by Cumulus Licensing Corp.
Group Owner: Cumulus Media Inc.; (acq 10-23-2000)
Wire Services: AP
Arbitron Metro Market: Bossier City, LA *Format:* Urban Contemporary
Phil Robkin, General Manager
Paul Farnharn, General Sales Mgr
Rashon Vance, Programming Director
Jasen Bragg, Chief Engineer

***KDAQ**
12-21-1984; 89.9 mhz FM *Hrs Open:* 24; 100 kw; 932 ft.; N32 40 40 W93 55 30
Mailing Address: One University Place, Shreveport, LA 71115 US
Second Address: One University Pl., Shreveport, LA 71115
(318) 797-5150(800) 552-8502, *Fax:* (318) 797-5265
www.redriverradio.org
listenermail@redriverradio.com
License: Shreveport, Caddo County, LA held by Louisiana State University Board of Supervisors.
Nat'l Network: NPR; PRI
Arbitron Metro Market: Shreveport, LA *Format:* Classical, Jazz, 60 *Hrs. of News Programming:* News progmg 40 hrs wkly *Target Audience:* General.
Rick Shelton, Operations Dir
Kermit Poling, General Manager
Bill Beckett, Programming Director

KEEL
01-01-1922; 710 khz AM *Hrs Open:* 24; 50 kw-D, DA2; 5 kw-N, DA2; N32 40 35 W93 51 35
50 East Rivercenter Boulevard, #1200, Covington, KY 41011 US
(318) 688-1130, *Fax:* (318) 687-8574
www.710keel.com
info@710keel.com
License: Shreveport, LA held by GAP Broadcasting Shreveport License LLC.
Group Owner: GAP Broadcasting LLC; (acq 8-3-2007; grpsl)
Regional Network: La. Net. *Nat'l Reps:* D & R Radio
Arbitron Metro Market: Shreveport, LA *Format:* News, Talk *Hrs. of News Programming:* news progmg 6 hrs wkly *No. News Employees:* 5 *Target Audience:* 25-54; men
Lisa Janes, General Manager
Casey Ryan, General Sales Mgr
Erin McCarty, Programming Director
Craig Westbrook, Chief Engineer

KSYB
07-10-1975; 1300 khz AM *Hrs Open:* 24; 5 kw-D, ND1; 0.03 kw-N, ND1; N32 31 48 W93 48 16
Mailing Address: 3712 Cornell Dr., Shreveport, LA 71107 US
Second Address: 1526 Corporate Dr., Shreveport, LA 71107
(318) 222-2744, *Fax:* (318) 425-7507
ksyb@amistadradiogroup.com
License: Shreveport, LA held by Amistad Communications Inc.
Group Owner: Amistad Communications Inc.; (acq 10-26-2000; $900,000).
Arbitron Metro Market: Shreveport, LA *Format:* Christian, Gospel
Special Programming: Sports 10 hrs wkly *Target Audience:* Christian families *Adv. Rates:* 16; 16; 16; 16
Fred Caldwell, CEO
Rhonda Phillips-Sanders, General Manager
James W. Lane Jr., General Sales Mgr
Tawanna Gadson, Programming Director

KIOU
01-01-1950; 1480 khz AM *Hrs Open:* 6 AM-6 PM; 1 kw-D, ND2; 0.129 kw-N, ND2; N32 34 18 W93 44 39
3801 Skillern, Blvd., Flower Mound, TX 75028 US
(318) 222-0272, *Fax:* (318) 222-0271
License: Shreveport, LA held by Metropolitan Radio Group Inc.
Group Owner: Metropolitan Radio Group Inc.; acq 10-97; $70,500)
Arbitron Metro Market: Shreveport, LA *Format:* Gospel *Target Audience:* General.
Ernest Pickens, General Manager

KXKS-FM
05-17-1968; 93.7 mhz FM; 95 kw; 1010 ft.; N32 40 39 W93 55 41
50 East Rivercenter Boulevard, #1200, Covington, KY 41011 US
(318) 688-1130, *Fax:* (318) 687-8574
www.kisscountry937.com
info@kisscountry937.com
License: Shreveport, Caddo County, LA held by GAP Broadcasting Shreveport License LLC.
Group Owner: GAP Broadcasting LLC
Arbitron Metro Market: Shreveport, LA *Format:* Country *Target Audience:* 25-54; 30 yr old female
Chris Evans, Programming Director

KMJJ-FM
12-05-1976; 99.7 mhz FM; 23.5 kw; 533 ft.; N32 29 36 W93 45 55
600 Congress Avenue, Suite 1400, Austin, TX 78701 US
(318) 549-8500, *Fax:* (318) 549-8505
www.997kmjj.com
cumulus.shreveport@cumulus.com
License: Shreveport, Caddo County, LA held by Cumulus Licensing Corp.
Group Owner: Cumulus Media Inc.; (acq 8-7-00; grpsl).
Arbitron Metro Market: Shreveport, LA *Format:* Urban Contemporary *Hrs. of News Programming:* News progmg one hr wkly *Target Audience:* 18-49; African American & general *Adv. Rates:* 75; 65; 75; 35
Phil Robkin, General Manager
Paul Farnham, General Sales Mgr
Jay Tek, Programming Director
Gary Robinson, Promotions Manager
Jasen Bragg, Chief Engineer

KOKA
08-01-1954; 980 khz AM *Hrs Open:* 24; 5 kw-D, ND2; 0.079 kw-N, ND2; N32 31 30 W93 48 30
1315 Milam Street, P.O. Box 103, Shreveport, LA 71107 US
(318) 222-3122, *Fax:* (318) 459-1493
www.koka.am
info@koka.am
License: Shreveport, LA held by Access. 1 Louisiana Holding Co. LLC.
Group Owner: Access.1 Communications Corp.; (acq 12-20-02; grpsl).
Nat'l Reps: D & R Radio
Arbitron Metro Market: Shreveport, LA *Format:* Gospel *No. News Employees:* 1 *Target Audience:* 25-64; middle-aged, middle class, Black adults
Cary Camp, General Manager
Don Zimmerman, General Sales Mgr
Eddie Giles, Programming Director

KRMD
06-01-1928; 1340 khz AM *Hrs Open:* 24; 1 kw-U, ND1; N32 29 36 W93 45 55
600 Congress Ave., Suite 1400, Austin, TX 78701 US
(318) 549-8500, *Fax:* (318) 549-8505
www.supertalk1340.com
krmd@cumulus.com
License: Shreveport, LA held by Cumulus Licensing Corp.
Group Owner: Cumulus Media Inc.
Arbitron Metro Market: Shreveport, LA *Format:* Talk
John Sherman, Programming Director

KRUF
11-05-1948; 94.5 mhz FM *Hrs Open:* 24; 99 kw; 1096 ft.; N32 40 13 W93 55 59
50 East Rivercenter Boulevard, #1200, Covington, KY 41011 US
(318) 688-1130, *Fax:* (318) 687-8574
www.k945.com
info@k945.com
License: Shreveport, Caddo County, LA
Group Owner: GAP Broadcasting LLC
Arbitron Metro Market: Shreveport, LA *Format:* Contemporary Hits/Top 40
Erin Bristol, Programming Director

***KSCL**
03-11-1976; 91.3 mhz FM *Hrs Open:* 24; 2.6 kw; 184 ft.; N32 28 51.4 W93 43 51.1
2911 Centenary Blvd, PO Box 41188, Shreveport, LA 71134 US
(318) 869-5296, *Fax:* (318) 869-5294
www.centenary.edu
kscl@centenary.edu
License: Shreveport, Caddo County, LA held by Centenary College of Louisiana.
Arbitron Metro Market: Shreveport, LA *Format:* Alternative *Hrs. of News Programming:* news progmg 4 hrs wkly *No. News Employees:* 1 *Target Audience:* General; college students & adults interested in div music
David Rowe, CEO/COO
John Schleass, Station Manager
Alyson Escude, Programming Director
Tyler Davis, Music Director
Jon Schleuss, Station Manager

KVKI-FM
05-01-1959; 96.5 mhz FM *Hrs Open:* 24; 95 kw; 797 ft.; N32 35 38 W93 51 39
50 East Rivercenter Boulevard, #1200, Covington, KY 41011 US
(318) 688-1130, *Fax:* (318) 688-9839
www.965kvki.com
License: Shreveport, Caddo County, LA held by GAP Broadcasting Shreveport License LLC.
Group Owner: GAP Broadcasting LLC; (acq 8-3-2007; grpsl)
Nat'l Reps: D & R Radio
Arbitron Metro Market: Shreveport, LA *Format:* Adult Contemp *No. News Employees:* 1 *Target Audience:* 25-54; female
Lisa Janes, General Manager
Steve King, Programming Director
Casey Ryan, Director of Sales

KWKH
09-01-1925; 1130 khz AM *Hrs Open:* 24
50 East Rivercenter Boulevard, #1200, Covington, KY 41011 US
(318) 688-1130, *Fax:* (318) 687-8574
www.kwkhonline.com
info@kwkhonline.com
License: Shreveport, LA held by GAP Broadcasting Shreveport License LLC.
Group Owner: GAP Broadcasting LLC; (acq 8-3-2007; grpsl)
Nat'l Reps: D & R Radio
Arbitron Metro Market: Shreveport, LA *Format:* Country *Hrs. of News Programming:* news progmg 18 hrs wkly *No. News Employees:* 4 *Target Audience:* Male 25-54.
Lisa Janes, General Manager
Elaine McLemore, Programming Director
Craig Westbrook, Chief Engineer
Casey Ryan, Director of Sales

Simmesport

KSLO-FM
01-01-2008; 105.3 mhz FM; 190 w; Ant 205 ft; N30 59 32 W91 50 53
3501 Northwest Evangeline Thruway, Carencro, LA
(337) 896-1600, *Fax:* (337) 896-2695
License: Simmesport, Avoyelles County, LA held by Delta Media Corp.
Eddie Blanchard, General Manager

Slidell

WSLA
12-05-1963; 1560 khz AM *Hrs Open:* Daytime; 1 kw-D, NDD; N30 15 0 W89 45 46
Mailing Address: P.O. Box 1175, Slidell, LA 70459 US
Second Address: 38230 Coast Blvd., Slidell, LA 70458
(985) 643-1560, *Fax:* (985) 649-9822
1560@bellsouth.net
License: Slidell, LA held by MAPA Broadcasting L.L.C.
Nat'l Network: USA *Regional Network:* La. Net.
Arbitron Metro Market: New Orleans, LA *Format:* Sports *Target Audience:* 25 plus; news intensive audience & sports fans *Adv. Rates:* 35; 15; 25
George Mayoral, General Manager
Jim Sommers, Programming Director

South Fort Polk

KROK
02-22-2003; 95.7 mhz FM *Hrs Open:* 24hrs; 25 kw; 294 ft.; N31 3 5 W93 16 41
595 San Antonio Ave, Many, LA 71449 US
(337) 537-9292, *Fax:* (337) 537-4152
www.krok.com
krok@krok.com
License: South Fort Polk, Vernon County, LA held by West Central Broadcasting Co. Inc.
Arbitron Metro Market: South Fort Polk, LA *Format:* Alternative *Target Audience:* 18-54.
Alan Taylor, CFO
Doug Stannard, President

Springhill

KTKC
06-30-1954; 1460 khz AM *Hrs Open:* Sunrise-sunset; 1 kw-D, 220 w-N; N33 00 02 W93 28 43
541 S. Main St., Springhill, LA 75028
(318) 539-4616, *Fax:* (318) 539-2356
License: Springhill, Webster County, LA held by The RAFTT Corp.
Group Owner: The RAFTT Corp.; (acq 4-6-2009; $55,000)
Population Served: 25,000 *Arbitron Metro Market:* Shreveport, LA
Earnest Pickens, General Manager

KTKC-FM
09-05-1975; 92.9 mhz FM *Hrs Open:* 24; 40 kw horiz, 13.3 kw vert; 548 ft.; N33 0 30 W93 28 38
3801 Skillern Blvd., Flower Mound, TX 75028 US
(318) 539-4616, *Fax:* (318) 539-2356
www.ktkcfm.com
License: Springhill, Webster County, LA held by Metropolitan Radio Group Inc.
Group Owner: Metropolitan Radio Group Inc.; acq 6-97; with co-located AM)
Nat'l Network: ABC
Arbitron Metro Market: Shreveport, LA *Format:* Black, Gospel *Target Audience:* 35-54.
Earnest Pickens, General Manager
Rudy Johnson, Chief Engineer

St. Martinville

***KSJY**
01-01-2005; 89.9 mhz FM; 30 kw; 466 ft.; N30 8 3 W91 51 46
P.O. Drawer 2440, Tupelo, MS 38803 US
(662) 844-8888, *Fax:* (662) 842-6791
www.afr.net
comments@afr.net
License: St. Martinville, St. Martin County, LA held by American Family Association.
Group Owner: American Family Radio
Arbitron Metro Market: Tupelo, MO *Format:* Christian, Religious
Marvin Sanders, General Manager

Sulphur

KEZM
01-01-1955; 1310 khz AM *Hrs Open:* 24; 0.5 kw-D, DA2; 0.05 kw-N, DA2; N30 13 27 W93 22 44
101 West Napoleon Street, Sulphur, LA 70663 US
(337) 527-3611, *Fax:* (337) 527-0213
www.kezmonline.com
License: Sulphur, LA held by Merchant Broadcasting Inc.
Nat'l Network: Sporting News Radio Network
Arbitron Metro Market: Lake Charles, LA *Format:* Sports *Hrs. of News Programming:* news progmg 5 hrs wkly *No. News Employees:* 1 *Target Audience:* 18-63; upscale baby-boomers
Adv. Rates: 4; 4; 4; 3
Bruce Merchant, President
Kathy Soileau, General Sales Mgr

KKGB
12-17-1977; 101.3 mhz FM *Hrs Open:* 24; 12 kw; 479 ft.; N30 14 41 W93 20 37
111 East Kilbourn Avenue, Suite 2700, Milwaukee, WI 53202 US
(337) 439-3300, *Fax:* (337) 436-7278
www.kkgb.com
info@kkgb.com
License: Sulphur, Calcasieu County, LA held by Cumulus Licensing Corp.
Group Owner: Cumulus Media Inc.; (acq 12-17-98; grpsl)
Nat'l Reps: Christal
Arbitron Metro Market: Lake Charles, L *Format:* Classic Rock *No. News Employees:* 1 *Target Audience:* General; baby boomers
Eric Nielson, Operations Dir
Jill Moore, General Sales Mgr
Jim Vidler, Promotions Manager

***KRLR**
01-01-2007; 89.1 mhz FM; 0.001 kw horiz, 16 kw vert; 394 ft.; N30 21 6 W93 23 49 *Rebroadcasts:* Rebroadcasts KLVR(FM) Santa Rosa, CA 100%
188 S. Bellevue, Suite 222, Memphis, TN 38104 US
(800) 877-5600, *Fax:* (916) 251-1650
www.klove.com
License: Sulphur, Calcasieu County, LA held by Educational Media Foundation.
Group Owner: EMF Broadcasting; (acq 11-1-2006; grpsl)
Nat'l Network: K-Love
Arbitron Metro Market: Sulphur, LA *Format:* Christian
Darrell Chambliss, Chairman
Mike Novak, President
Chip Bailey, Operations Dir

Tallulah

KBYO
09-04-1954; 1360 khz AM; 0.5 kw-D, ND2; 0.131 kw-N, ND2; N32 25 37 W91 13 15
Mailing Address: 3046 Indiana Ave, Suite 231, Vicksburg, MS 39180 US
Second Address: 1109 Hudson Ln., Monroe, LA 71201
(318) 388-2323, *Fax:* (318) 388-0569
License: Tallulah, LA held by Holladay Broadcasting of Louisiana LLC.
Group Owner: Holladay Broadcasting of Louisiana LLC; (acq 1-10-2003; $450,000 with co-located FM)
Arbitron Metro Market: Monroe, LA
Robert Holladay, President
Russell Kendrick, Chief Engineer

KLSM
04-29-1983; 104.5 mhz FM; 25 kw; 328 ft.; N32 22 13 W91 7 39
3046 Indiana Ave, Suite 231, Vicksburg, MS 39180 US
(601) 636-2340, *Fax:* (601) 638-0869
spots@river101.com
License: Tallulah, Madison County, LA held by Holladay Broadcasting of Louisiana LLC.
Group Owner: Holladay Broadcasting of Louisiana LLC
Arbitron Metro Market: Vicksburg, MS *Format:* Adult Contemp *Target Audience:* 25-54.
Bob Holladay, General Manager

KTJZ
01-01-2008; 97.5 mhz FM; 6 kw; 308 ft.; N32 25 42 W91 18 47 US
(225) 334-7490, *Fax:* (225) 334-7491
lanaapc1@juno.com
License: Tallulah, Madison County, LA held by Mid South Communications Co. Inc.
Arbitron Metro Market: Tallulah, LA *Format:* Blues, Gospel
Ernest Johnson, Chairman

Thibodaux

***KNSU**
02-15-1972; 91.5 mhz FM *Hrs Open:* 10 AM-2 AM (M-F); noon-2 AM (S, Su); 0.25 kw vert; 148 ft.; N29 47 29 W90 48 7
P. O. Box 2664, Thibodaux, LA 70310 US
(985) 448-4586, *Fax:* (985) 449-7106
www.nicholls.edu/knsu
lance.arnold@nicholls.edu
License: Thibodaux, Lafourche County, LA held by Board of Trustees, Nicholls State University.
Format: Alternative *Hrs. of News Programming:* News progmg 10 hrs wkly *Target Audience:* 18 plus.
Katie Kingdon, Station Manager
Jonathan DeSilvie, Programming Director

KTIB
12-24-1953; 640 khz AM *Hrs Open:* 24; 5 kw-D, DA2; 1 kw-N, DA2; N29 51 5 W90 54 48
108 Green Street, P.O. Box 682, Thibodaux, LA 70301 US
(985) 447-6404, *Fax:* (985) 447-6464
www.ktib640.com
ktib@charter.net
License: Thibodaux, LA held by Gap Broadcasting LLC
Nat'l Network: Jones Radio Networks; Premiere Radio Networks; Talk Radio Network *Regional Network:* La. Net. *Nat'l Reps:* Commercial Media Sales
Arbitron Metro Market: Thibodaux, LA
George Laughlin, CEO
Linda Bellanger, General Manager

***KTLN**
05-01-1995; 90.5 mhz FM *Hrs Open:* 24; 0.2 kw vert; 358 ft.; N29 43 18 W90 46 33 *Rebroadcasts:* Rebroadcasts WWNO(FM) New Orleans 100%
Library Building Rm 450, 2000 Lakeshore Drive, New Orleans, LA 70148 US
(504) 280-7000, *Fax:* (504) 280-6061
www.wwno.org
info@wwno.org
License: Thibodaux, Lafourche County, LA held by Board of Supervisors of Louisiana State University and Agricultural and Mechanical College, University of New Orleans.
Nat'l Network: NPR; PRI
Arbitron Metro Market: New Orleans, LA *Format:* Jazz, News *Hrs. of News Programming:* News progmg 39 hrs wkly *Target Audience:* 35-70; well educated professionals, managers, artists & arts patrons
Ronald Curtis, Operations Dir
Chuck Miller, General Manager
Karen Anklam, General Sales Mgr
Fred Kasten, Programming Director
Robert Carroll, Chief Engineer

KXOR-FM
05-01-1966; 106.3 mhz FM *Hrs Open:* 24; 25 kw; 328 ft.; N29 38 52 W90 41 34
Mailing Address: 929-B Government Street, Baton Rouge, LA 70802 US
Second Address: 120 Prevost Dr., Houma, LA 70364
(985) 851-1020, *Fax:* (985) 872-4403
www.rock1063.net
info@rock1063.net
License: Thibodaux, Lafourche County, LA held by Sunburst Media-Louisiana LLC.
Group Owner: Sunburst Media-Louisiana LLC; (acq 1-23-2007; grpsl)
Regional Network: La. Agri-News
Hrs. of News Programming: News progmg 20 hrs wkly *Target Audience:* 18-54. *Adv. Rates:* 25; 20; 25; 15
John Delise, Operations Dir
Danny Fletcher, General Manager

Tioga

KLAA-FM
05-25-1984; 103.5 mhz FM *Hrs Open:* 24; 50 kw; 476 ft.; N31 25 39 W92 24 18
92 West Shamrock Street, Pineville, LA 71360 US
(318) 487-1035, *Fax:* (318) 487-4419
www.la103.com
License: Tioga, Rapides County, LA held by Opus Broadcasting Alexandria LLC.
Group Owner: Opus Media Holdings LLC; (acq 9-30-2004; $3.38 million with KBKK(FM) Ball).
Nat'l Reps: Christal *Wire Services:* AP
Arbitron Metro Market: Alexandria, LA *Format:* Country *Hrs. of News Programming:* news progmg 4 hrs wkly *No. News Employees:* 1 *Target Audience:* 25-54; working people, upscale professionals
Kim Jones, President

Varnado

WBOX-FM
11-01-1985; 92.9 mhz FM; 3 kw; 322 ft.; N30 54 10 W89 57 36
Mailing Address: P. O. Box 351, Columbia, MS 39429 US
Second Address: 22037 Hwy.436, Bogalusa, LA 70427
(504) 732-4288, *Fax:* (985) 732-4288
License: Varnado, Washington County, LA held by Best Country Broadcasting LLC
Arbitron Metro Market: Columbia, MS *Format:* Country
Ben Strickland, President

Vidalia

KWTG
01-01-1994; 104.7 mhz FM; 3 kw; 266 ft.; N31 35 5 W91 23 18
Mailing Address: 381 John R. Junkin Drive, Natchez, MS 39120 US
Second Address: 917 S.E.E. Wallace Blvd., Ferriday, LA 71334
(318) 757-4200, *Fax:* (318) 757-7689
www.kwtgfm.com
License: Vidalia, Concordia County, LA held by Tom D. Gay.
Group Owner: The Radio Group
Arbitron Metro Market: Vidalia, LA *Format:* Country
Desiree Smith, General Manager

Ville Platte

KVPI
11-01-1953; 1050 khz AM *Hrs Open:* 6 AM-midnight; 250 w-D, 10 w-N; N30 41 39 W92 18 46
Mailing Address: Box J, Ville Platte, LA 73586
Second Address: 809 W. LaSalle St., Ville Platte, LA 70586
(337) 363-2124, *Fax:* (337) 363-3574
Kvpionline.com
kvpiamfm@gmail.com
License: Ville Platte, Evangeline County, LA held by Ville Platte Broadcsting Co.
Regional Network: La. Net.
Population Served: 79,692*Special Programming:* Cajun 12 hrs wkly *Hrs. of News Programming:* news progmg 12 hrs wkly *No. News Employees:* 1 *Target Audience:* 32-65.
Rhonda Fink Pucheu, President
Mark Layne, General Manager
Mark Layne, General Sales Mgr
Randy Guillory, News Director
Dave Graichen, Chief Engineer
Bonnie Fontenot, Office Manager

KVPI-FM
02-26-1967; 92.5 mhz FM *Hrs Open:* 24; 3.9 kw horiz; Ant 220 ft; N30 41 39 W92 18 46
Mailing Address: Box J, Ville Platte, LA 70586
Second Address: 809 W. LaSalle St., Ville Platte, LA 70586
(337) 363-2124, *Fax:* (337) 363-3574
www.oldies925.com
kvpiamfm@gmail.com
License: Ville Platte, Evangeline County, LA held by Ville Platte Broadcasting Co.
Nat'l Network: NBC Radio *Wire Services:* AP
Population Served: 72,940*Special Programming:* Cajun French 6 hrs wkly. *Hrs. of News Programming:* news progmg 12 hrs wkly *No. News Employees:* 1 *Target Audience:* 32-65.
Rhonda Pucheu, President
Mark Layne, General Manager
Mark Layne, General Sales Mgr
Danny Poullard, Programming Director
Cheryl DeBallion, News Director
Bonnie Fontenot, Office Manager
Randy Guillory, Sports Commentator

Vivian

KNCB
04-09-1966; 1320 khz AM *Hrs Open:* Sunrise-sunset; 5 kw-D, ND1; 0.057 kw-N, ND1; N32 54 7 W93 58 58
Mailing Address: P. O. Box 1072, Vivian, LA 71082 US
Second Address: 17525 Hwy. 1 N., Vivian, LA 71082
(318) 375-3278, *Fax:* (318) 375-3329
rjc1072@cs.com
License: Vivian, LA held by North Caddo Broadcasting Co.
Arbitron Metro Market: Shreveport, LA *Format:* Country, Gospel, 60, News/Talk, Talk *Target Audience:* General. *Adv. Rates:* 16; 14; 10; 8.15
Ruby Collins, General Manager
Rudy Johnson, Chief Engineer

KNCB-FM
09-28-1996; 105.3 mhz FM *Hrs Open:* 24; 3.2 kw; 449 ft.; N32 55 54 W93 54 22
Mailing Address: P.O. Box 1072, Vivian, LA 71082 US
Second Address: 17525 Hwy. 1 N., Vivian, LA 71082

(318) 375-3278, *Fax:* (318) 375-3329
rjc1072@cs.com
License: Vivian, Caddo County, LA
Nat'l Network: ABC
Arbitron Metro Market: Shreveport, LA *Format:* Country *Adv. Rates:* 16; 14; 10; 8.15
Ronald Kramer, CEO
Bryon Lambert, Operations Dir
Paul Westhelle, General Sales Mgr
Mitchell Christian, CFO

Washington

KNEK
08-18-1980; 1190 khz AM; 250 w-D; N30 35 09 W92 04 00
202 Galbert Rd., Lafayette, LA 85281
(337) 232-1311, *Fax:* (337) 233-3779
www.knek.com
License: Washington, St. Landry County, LA
Group Owner: Cumulus Media Inc.; (acq 1-14-99; grpsl)
Regional Network: La. Net.
Arbitron Metro Market: Lafayette, LA *Target Audience:* 25-54.
Jim Beard, General Manager

KNEK-FM
01-01-1989; 104.7 mhz FM *Hrs Open:* 24; 25 kw; 328 ft.; N30 25 17 W92 6 50
140 South Ash Avenue, Tempe, AZ 85281 US
(337) 232-1311, *Fax:* (337) 233-3779
www.knek.com
License: Washington, St. Landry County, LA
Group Owner: Cumulus Media Inc.
Arbitron Metro Market: Lafayette, LA *Format:* Adult Contemp
Jim Beard, General Manager
Deidre Williams, Programming Director
Jared Verrett, Chief Engineer

West Monroe

KMBS
08-01-1956; 1310 khz AM; 5 kw-D, ND1; 0.049 kw-N, ND1; N32 29 2 W92 9 10
613 N 5th Street, P.O. Box 547, West Monroe, LA 71291 US
(318) 323-1310
License: West Monroe, LA held by Red Bear Broadcasting
Nat'l Network: ABC
Arbitron Metro Market: Monroe, LA *Format:* Sports
Chuck Redden, General Manager

KZRZ
08-01-1967; 98.3 mhz FM *Hrs Open:* 24; 50 kw; 492 ft.; N32 39 38 W91 59 28
350 Park Avenue, 20th Floor, New York, NY 10022 US
(318) 387-3922, *Fax:* (318) 322-4585
www.sunny983.com
sunny983@comcast.net
License: West Monroe, Ouachita County, LA held by Opus Broadcasting Monroe L.L.C.
Group Owner: Opus Media Holdings LLC; (acq 7-19-2004; grpsl).
Arbitron Metro Market: Monroe, LA *Format:* Adult Contemp
Target Audience: 18-54; mid to upper income
Chris Zimmerman, General Manager
Mike Dawnhour, General Sales Mgr

White Castle

KKAY
11-01-1976; 1590 khz AM *Hrs Open:* 24; 1 kw-D, ND1; 0.067 kw-N, ND1; N30 11 1 W91 6 27
3365 Hwy - 1 South, Donaldsonville, LA 70346 US
(225) 473-6397, *Fax:* (225) 473-5764
www.kkay1590.com
www.globalradokkay.com
License: White Castle, LA held by Cactus Communications LLC.
Arbitron Metro Market: Baton Rouge, LA *Format:* Variety/Diverse
Adv. Rates: 13.25; 13.25; 13.25; na
David Dawson, General Manager

Winnfield

KVCL-FM
11-03-1966; 92.1 mhz FM *Hrs Open:* 24; 6 kw; 210 ft.; N31 56 54 W92 37 37
P. O. Box 548, Winnfield, LA 71483 US
(318) 628-5822, *Fax:* (318) 628-7355
License: Winnfield, Winn County, LA held by Baldridge-Dumas Communications Inc.
Group Owner: Baldridge-Dumas Communications Inc.; (acq 12-28-2006; $300,000 with co-located AM)
Arbitron Metro Market: Alexandria LA *Format:* Country *Hrs. of News Programming:* news progmg 22 hrs wkly *No. News Employees:* 2
Ted Dumas, General Manager

Winnsboro

KMAR-FM
08-01-1969; 95.9 mhz FM *Hrs Open:* 24; 6 kw; 178 ft.; N32 11 2 W91 44 51
Mailing Address: P. O. Box 1319, Columbia, LA 71418 US
Second Address: 1823 Hwy. 618, Winnsboro, LA 71295
(318) 435-5141, *Fax:* (318) 435-5749
www.kmarfm.com
kmarfm@bellsouth.net
License: Winnsboro, Franklin County, LA held by Boeuf River Broadcasting Co.
Group Owner: The Radio Group; (acq 11-89; $200,000 with co-located AM;
Nat'l Network: ABC *Wire Services:* UPI
Format: Country *Hrs. of News Programming:* news progmg 20 hrs wkly *No. News Employees:* 1 *Target Audience:* 30-60; adults *Adv. Rates:* 12; 12; 12; 12
Rene Johnston, General Manager

Zwolle

KTEZ
07-04-2002; 99.9 mhz FM *Hrs Open:* 24 hours; 6 kw; 328 ft.; N31 39 17 W93 29 4
P O Box 11196, College Station, TX 77842 US
(318) 256-5924, *Fax:* (318) 256-0950
www.bdcradio.com
kwlv@bellsouth.net
License: Zwolle, Sabine County, LA held by Baldridge-Dumas Communications Inc.
Group Owner: Baldridge-Dumas Communications Inc.; (acq 2-25-2002).
Format: Adult Contemp
Tedd Dumas, Operations Dir
Rhonda Leach, General Manager
Cindy Ezernack, Station Manager

Maine

Auburn

WTHT
02-01-1977; 99.9 mhz FM *Hrs Open:* 24; 28.5 kw; 643 ft.; N43 57 7 W70 17 46
912 Washington Street, Auburn, ME 04210 US
(207) 797-0780, *Fax:* (207) 797-0368
www.999thewolf.com
info@999thewolf.com
License: Auburn, Androscoggin County, ME held by Nassau Broadcasting III L.L.C.
Group Owner: Nassau Broadcasting Partners L.P.; (acq 4-6-2004; grpsl).
Arbitron Metro Market: Portland, ME *Format:* Country *Target Audience:* Women 18-34, women 25-54; Maine's kiss 99.9
Stan Manning, Operations Dir
Pat Collins, General Manager
Tim Gatz, General Sales Mgr
Stann Bennett, Programming Director
Corey Garrison, Promotions Manager
Bill Ryall, Chief Engineer

Augusta

WJZN
02-23-1932; 1400 khz AM *Hrs Open:* 24; 1 kw-U; N44 17 30 W69 46 27 *Rebroadcasts:* Rebroadcasts WTVL(AM) Waterville 100%
56 Western Avenue, Suite 13, Augusta, ME 13203
(207) 623-4735, *Fax:* (207) 626-5948
www.1400and1490.com
augusta@catomm.com
License: Augusta, Kennebec County, ME
Group Owner: Cumulus Media Inc.; (acq 4-26-2001; grpsl).
Nat'l Reps: D & R Radio
Population Served: 19,103 *Arbitron Metro Market:* Augusta, ME
No. News Employees: 1 *Target Audience:* 20-40; young adults
Al Perry, General Manager
Julie Beaulieu, General Sales Mgr
Renee Nelson, News Director
Bob Perry, Chief Engineer

WVQM
07-01-1961; 101.3 mhz FM; 41 kw; 371 ft.; N44 18 36 W69 49 51
Rebroadcasts: Simulcast with WVOM(FM) Howland 100%
330 East Kilbourn Avenue, Suite 250, Milwaukee, WI 53202 US
(207) 623-9000, *Fax:* (207) 623-9007
www.wvomfm.com
kellyslater@clearchannel.com
License: Augusta, Kennebec County, ME held by Blueberry Broadcasting LLC.
Group Owner: Blueberry Broadcasting LLC; (acq 7-29-2008; grpsl)
Arbitron Metro Market: Augusta-Waterville, ME *Format:* News, News/Talk, 86
Steve Smith, Operations Dir
Kelly Slater, General Manager
Rick Dugal, General Sales Mgr

*WMDR
10-02-1946; 1340 khz AM *Hrs Open:* 24
160 Bangor Street, Augusta, ME 04330 US
(207) 622-1340, *Fax:* (207) 623-2874
www.worshipradionetwork.org
denise@worshipradionetwork.org
License: Augusta, ME held by Light of Life Ministries Inc.
Arbitron Metro Market: Augusta, ME *Format:* Religious *Special Programming:* stories *Hrs. of News Programming:* News progmg 5 hrs wkly *Target Audience:* General.
Denise LaFountain, General Manager
Frank Speed, Programming Director

WMME-FM
01-14-1981; 92.3 mhz FM; 50 kw; 499 ft.; N44 20 7 W69 41 1
1064 James Street, Syracuse, NY 13203 US
(207) 623-4735, *Fax:* (207) 626-5948
www.92moose.fm
License: Augusta, Kennebec County, ME
Group Owner: Cumulus Media Inc.
Arbitron Metro Market: Augusta, ME *Format:* Contemporary Hits/Top 40 *Target Audience:* General
J. Spangler, President
Lori Spangler, Operations Dir

Bangor

WAEI
01-01-1924; 910 khz AM *Hrs Open:* 18
27 State Street, 6th Flr, Bangor, ME 04401 US
(858) 277-4991, *Fax:* (858) 277-1365
www.ksrdradio.com
License: Bangor, ME held by Blueberry Broadcasting LLC.
Group Owner: Blueberry Broadcasting LLC; (acq 7-29-2008; grpsl)
Arbitron Metro Market: Portland OR *Adv. Rates:* 25; 20; 22; 10
Mike MacIntosh, President
Brian KC Jones, General Manager

WEZQ
06-09-1976; 92.9 mhz FM *Hrs Open:* 24; 20 kw; 787 ft; N44 45 35 W68 33 55
49 Acme Road, Brewer, ME 53202
(207) 989-5631, *Fax:* (207) 989-5685
www.wezq-fm.com
info@wezq-fm.com
License: Bangor, Penobscot County, ME held by Townsquare Media Bangor License LLC
Group Owner: Cumulus Media Inc.; (acq 3-1-99; grpsl)
Nat'l Reps: D & R Radio
Population Served: 33,011 *Arbitron Metro Market:* Bangor, ME
No. News Employees: 1 *Target Audience:* 25-54.
Paul Dupuis, Operations Dir
Tom Preble, General Manager
Dorian Daniels, Programming Director

*WHCF
08-10-1981; 88.5 mhz FM *Hrs Open:* 24; 35 kw; 1621 ft.; N45 7 46 W68 21 28
Mailing Address: 1476 Broadway, Bangor, ME 04401 US
Second Address: 1476 Broadway, Bangor, ME 4401
(207) 947-2751, *Fax:* (207) 947-0010
whcffm.com
contact@whcffm.com
License: Bangor, Penobscot County, ME held by Bangor Baptist Church
Nat'l Network: Salem Radio Network
Arbitron Metro Market: Bangor, ME *Format:* Christian, Gospel, 74
Special Programming: Children 2 hours wkly *Hrs. of News Programming:* 2 Min. hourly *Target Audience:* 35-55; Adults
Scott Stewart, Chairman
Jerry Mick, President
Tim Collins, Operations Dir
Marc Tischart, General Manager
Joe Polek, Programming Director
Stacey Brann, Chief Engineer

*WHSN
09-01-1974; 89.3 mhz FM *Hrs Open:* 24; 3 kw; 85 ft.; N44 49 46 W68 47 39
1 College Circle, Bangor, ME 04401 US

(207) 941-7116, *Fax:* (207) 947-3987
www.whsn-fm.com
whsn@nescom.edu
License: Bangor, Penobscot County, ME held by Husson University Board of Trustees.
Wire Services: AP
Arbitron Metro Market: Bangor, ME *Format:* Alternative *Hrs. of News Programming:* news progmg 7 hrs wkly *No. News Employees:* 1 *Target Audience:* 12-35; high school & college students
Ben Haskell, General Manager
Mark Nason, Programming Director
Susan Patten, News Director
David MacLaughlin, Engineering Dir

*WMEH
09-14-1970; 90.9 mhz FM *Hrs Open:* 24; 13.5 kw; 807 ft.; N44 45 45 W68 33 58
Mailing Address: 1450 Lisbon Street, Lewiston, ME 04240 US
Second Address: 1450 Lisbon St., Lewiston, ME 4240
(207) 783-9101, *Fax:* (207) 942-2857
www.mpbn.net
cbeck@mpbn.net
License: Bangor, Penobscot County, ME held by Maine Public Broadcasting Corp.
Nat'l Network: NPR; PRI
Arbitron Metro Market: Bangor, ME *Format:* Jazz, News
Mark Vogelzang, CEO
Alexander G. Maxwell, Operations Dir
Mary Mayo, General Sales Mgr
Charles Beck, Programming Director
Keith Shortall, News Director
Christopher Amann, CFO
Alexander G. Maxwell,Jr., COO

WBFB
03-15-1961; 97.1 mhz FM *Hrs Open:* 24; 5 kw; Ant 1,230 ft; N44 42 13 W69 04 07
184 Target Industrial Cir., Bangor, ME 04401
(207) 947-9100, *Fax:* (207) 942-8039
www.weei.com
License: Bangor, Penobscot County, ME held by Blueberry Broadcasting LLC.
Group Owner: Blueberry Broadcasting LLC; (acq 7-29-2008; grpsl)
Population Served: 200,000 *Arbitron Metro Market:* Bangor, ME *Target Audience:* General. *Adv. Rates:* 22; 18; 20; 10
Holly Rae, Programming Director

WZON
12-01-1926; 620 khz AM *Hrs Open:* 24; 5 kw-D, DAN; 5 kw-N, DAN; N44 49 44 W68 47 8
P.O. Box 1929, Bangor, ME 04402 US
(207) 990-2800, *Fax:* (207) 990-2444
www.zoneradio.com
wzon@zoneradio.com
License: Bangor, ME held by The Zone Corp.
Group Owner: The Zone Corp.; acq 9-1-93; $236,200;
Arbitron Metro Market: Bangor, ME *Format:* Sports, Talk *Hrs. of News Programming:* news progmg 18 hrs wkly *No. News Employees:* 1 *Target Audience:* General; info & entertainment seekers *Adv. Rates:* 20; 15;20; 14
Stephen King, President
Bobby Russell, Station Manager
Ken Wood, General Sales Mgr
Dale Duff, Programming Director

Bar Harbor

WLKE
06-01-1992; 99.1 mhz FM *Hrs Open:* 24; 45 kw; 397 ft.; N44 26 41 W68 1 22
P.O. Box 9494, Ellsworth, ME 04605 US
(207) 947-9100, *Fax:* (207) 942-8039
www.971thebear.com
pauldupuis@blueberrybroadcasting.com
License: Bar Harbor, Hancock County, ME held by Blueberry Broadcasting LLC.
Group Owner: Blueberry Broadcasting LLC; (acq 7-29-2008; grpsl)
Nat'l Network: ABC *Nat'l Reps:* Christal
Format: Country *No. News Employees:* 1 *Target Audience:* General.
Jack O'Brien, Operations Dir
Josh Scroggins, General Manager
Bruce Biette, General Sales Mgr
Paul Dupuis, Programming Director

WBQI
05-06-1995; 107.7 mhz FM *Hrs Open:* 24; 11.5 kw; 489 ft.; N44 33 13 W68 5 40 *Rebroadcasts:* Rebroadcasts WBQQ (FM) Kennebunk 90%
P.O. Box 6111, Bar Harbor, ME 04609 US
(207) 667-9800, *Fax:* (207) 967-8671
www.wbachradio.com
License: Bar Harbor, Hancock County, ME held by Nassau Broadcasting III L.L.C.
Group Owner: Nassau Broadcasting Partners L.P.; (acq 4-6-2004; grpsl).
Nat'l Network: CBS; Westwood One
Arbitron Metro Market: Bar Harbor, ME *Format:* Talk *Special Programming:* Blues 15 hrs wkly *Hrs. of News Programming:* news progmg 6 hrs wkly *No. News Employees:* 1 *Target Audience:* 25-54; baby boomers
Pat Collins, General Manager

Bath

WBCI
06-01-1971; 105.9 mhz FM; 50 kw; 499 ft.; N44 4 9 W69 55 28
Mailing Address: 122 Main Street, Topsham, MA 04086 US
Second Address: 122 Main St., Topsham, ME 4086
(239) 263-7700, *Fax:* (239) 263-0998
License: Bath, Sagadahoc County, ME held by Blount Communications Inc.
Group Owner: Blount Communications Group; (acq 4-20-95; $375,000)
Nat'l Network: Salem Radio Network *Nat'l Reps:* Salem
Arbitron Metro Market: Arlington TX *Adv. Rates:* 16; 16; 16; 16
David Budd, General Manager

WJTO
09-30-1957; 730 khz AM *Hrs Open:* 24; 1 kw-D, ND2; 0.006 kw-N, ND2; N43 52 39 W69 50 49
P.O. Box 474, Rowley, MA 01969 US
(207) 443-6671
www.wjto.com
License: Bath, ME held by Blue Jey Broadcasting Co.
Arbitron Metro Market: Portland, ME *Format:* Adult Contemp *Hrs. of News Programming:* News progmg 2 hrs wkly *Target Audience:* 35 plus; adults along the Maine coastline
Bob Bittner, General Manager

Belfast

WBAK
03-07-1986; 104.7 mhz FM *Hrs Open:* 24; 10 kw; 1,099 ft; N44 34 51 W68 53 51
184 Target Industrial Circle, Bangor, ME 04605
(207) 947-9100, *Fax:* (207) 942-8039
www.1047the bear.com
info@1074the bear.com
License: Belfast, Waldo County, ME held by Blueberry Broadcasting LLC.
Group Owner: Blueberry Broadcasting LLC; (acq 7-29-2008; grpsl)
Population Served: 300,000 *Arbitron Metro Market:* Bangor, ME *No. News Employees:* 2 *Target Audience:* 18-49.
Josh Scroggins, General Manager

Benedicta

*WRPB
89.3 mhz FM; 0.145 kw; 207 ft.; N45 47 11 W68 24 44 US
(207) 622-1340, *Fax:* (207) 623-2874
www.worshipradionetwork.org
info@worshipradionetwork.org
License: Benedicta, Aroostook County, ME held by Light of Life Ministries Inc.
Arbitron Metro Market: Augusta, ME *Format:* Christian
Denise La Fountain, General Manager
Nan Parsons, Sales Manager
Brad Taylor, Current Business & Church Sponsorship
Nan Parsons, Sponsor Worship-FM
Samantha Heyns, Individual Sponsorships & Pledge
Brad Taylor, Event/Concert
KarenRossignol, Volunteer Questions

Biddeford

WCYY
08-01-1972; 94.3 mhz FM *Hrs Open:* 24; 11.5 kw; 482 ft.; N43 32 39 W70 24 16
7201 W. Lake Mead Blvd., Suite 400, Las Vegas, NV 89128 US
(207) 774-6364, *Fax:* (207) 774-8707
www.wcyy.com
License: Biddeford, York County, ME
Group Owner: Cumulus Media Inc.; (acq 7-7-99; grpsl).
Nat'l Reps: Christal
Arbitron Metro Market: Portland, ME *Format:* Rock/AOR *No. News Employees:* 1 *Target Audience:* 25-44; educated, affluent
Michael Sambrook, General Manager
Mike Marcello, General Sales Mgr
Herb Ivy, Programming Director

WVAE
01-01-1948; 1400 khz AM *Hrs Open:* 24; 1 kw-U, ND1; N43 28 52 W70 29 8
110 Main St Ste 1102, Saco, ME 04072 US
(207) 774-4561, *Fax:* (207) 774-3788
www.ilovethebay.com
info@ilovethebay.com
License: Biddeford, ME held by Saga Communications of New England LLC.
Group Owner: Saga Communications Inc.; (acq 11-17-03; $350,000).
Nat'l Network: Jones Radio Networks
Format: Adult Contemp *Special Programming:* Relg 2 hrs wkly *No. News Employees:* 1 *Target Audience:* 35 plus; upscale professional
Harry Nelson, Station Manager

Blue Hill

*WERU-FM
06-01-1988; 89.9 mhz FM *Hrs Open:* 6 AM-1 AM; 11.5 kw; 856 ft.; N44 26 4 W68 35 25
Mailing Address: 1186 Acadia Hwy, East Orland, ME 04431 US
Second Address: 1186 Acadia Hwy., East Orland, ME 4431
(207) 469-6600, *Fax:* (207) 469-8961
www.weru.org
amy@weru.org
License: Blue Hill, Hancock County, ME held by Salt Pond Community Broadcasting Co.
Arbitron Metro Market: Blue Hill, ME *Format:* Variety/Diverse *Target Audience:* General.
Joel Mann, Operations Dir
Matt Murphy, General Manager
Amy Browne, News & Public Affairs Manager
Bruce Clark, Chief Engineer
Chris Stark, Office Manager & Volunteer Cordinator
Caren Mulford, Development Manager
Sylvia Smith,Central Database Manager
Willie Marquart, Finance Manager
Denis Howard, Music Director

Boothbay Harbor

WTQX
04-01-1984; 96.7 mhz FM *Hrs Open:* 24; 15.5 kw; 417 ft.; N44 1 31 W69 34 17 *Rebroadcasts:* Simulcast with WTOS-FM Skowhegan 100%
330 East Kilbourn Avenue, Suite 250, Milwaukee, WI 53202 US
(207) 623-9000, *Fax:* (207) 623-9007
www.wtosfm.com
jackobrien@blueberrybroadcasting.com
License: Boothbay Harbor, Lincoln County, ME held by Blueberry Broadcasting LLC.
Group Owner: Blueberry Broadcasting LLC; (acq 7-29-2008; grpsl)
Arbitron Metro Market: Lincoln County, Maine *Target Audience:* 25-49.
Don Shields, Operations Dir
Kelly Slater, General Manager
Rick Dougal, General Sales Mgr
Steve Smith, Programming Director

Brewer

WKIT-FM
02-14-1979; 100.3 mhz FM *Hrs Open:* 24; 16 kw; 883 ft.; N44 40 39 W68 45 15
PO Box 1929, Bangor, ME 04402 US
(207) 990-2800, *Fax:* (207) 990-2444
www.zoneradio.com
wkit@zoneradio.com
License: Brewer, Penobscot County, ME held by The Zone Corp.
Group Owner: The Zone Corp.; acq 9-95; $800,000 with co-located AM)
Arbitron Metro Market: Bangor, ME *Format:* Classic Rock *No. News Employees:* 2 *Target Audience:* 18-49.
Stephen King, CEO
Bobby Russell, General Manager
Ken Wood, General Sales Mgr

WQCB
01-20-1986; 106.5 mhz FM *Hrs Open:* 24; 98 kw; 1079 ft.; N45 3 26 W69 11 27
Mailing Address: 330 East Kilbourn Ave, Suite 250, Milwaukee, WI 53202 US
Second Address: 49 Acme Rd., Brewer, ME 4412

(207) 989-5631, *Fax:* (207) 989-5685
www.wqcb-fm.com
q1065@midmaine.com
License: Brewer, Penobscot County, ME held by Cumulus Licensing Corp.
Group Owner: Cumulus Media Inc.; (acq 2-20-98; $6.4 million with WBZN(FM) Old Town)
Nat'l Reps: McGavren Guild
Arbitron Metro Market: Bangor, ME *Format:* Country *Hrs. of News Programming:* news progmg 4 hrs wkly *No. News Employees:* 2 *Target Audience:* 25-54; general
Paul Dupuis, Operations Dir
Tom Preble, General Manager
Darin Ingersoll, Programming Director

Brunswick

*WBOR
04-01-1957; 91.1 mhz FM *Hrs Open:* 7 AM-2 AM; 0.3 kw horiz; 154 ft.; N43 54 34 W69 57 43
1 College Street, Brunswick, ME 04011 US
(207) 725-3210 (207) 725-3250, *Fax:* (207) 725-3510
www.wbor.org
wbor@bowdoin.edu
License: Brunswick, Cumberland County, ME held by Trustees of Bowdoin College.
Format: Variety/Diverse *Target Audience:* General.
Adam Paltrineri, Station Manager

WCME(AM)
12-01-1955; 900 khz AM *Hrs Open:* 24; 1 kw-D, 66 w-N; N43 55 40 W69 59 43 *Rebroadcasts:* Simulcasts WJAE(AM) Westbrook
Atlantic Coast Radio, 779 Warren Ave., Portland, ME 04103-1007
(207) 773-9695, *Fax:* (207) 761-4406
www.thebigjab.com
shoe@thebigjab.com
License: Brunswick, Cumberland County, ME held by Blue Jey Broadcasting Co. Inc.
Nat'l Reps: McGavren Guild
Population Served: 35,000 *Arbitron Metro Market:* Portland, ME *Format:* Sports, Talk *Hrs. of News Programming:* news progmg 4 hrs wkly *No. News Employees:* 2 *Target Audience:* 25-54.
Adv. Rates: 30;25; 20; 15.
Jon Van Hoogenstyn, General Manager
David Shumacher, Programming Director

Calais

*WMED
11-01-1983; 89.7 mhz FM; 30 kw; 525 ft.; N45 1 45 W67 19 26
Rebroadcasts: Rebroadcasts WMEH(FM) Bangor 100%
Mailing Address: 1450 Lisbon Street, Lewiston, ME 04240 US
Second Address: 1450 Lisbon St., Lewiston, ME 4240
(207) 783-9101, *Fax:* (207) 942-2857
www.mpbn.net
cbeck@mpbn.net
License: Calais, Washington County, ME held by Maine Public Broadcasting Corp.
Nat'l Network: NPR; PRI
Arbitron Metro Market: Calais, ME *Format:* Jazz, News
P. James Dowe, Jr, CEO
Mary Mayo, General Sales Mgr
Charles Beck, Programming Director
Christopher Amann, CFO
Alexander G. Maxwell, Jr, COO

WQDY-FM
01-14-1976; 92.7 mhz FM *Hrs Open:* 24; 3 kw; 299 ft.; N45 10 2 W67 16 38
P.O. Box 403, Calais, ME 04619 US
(207) 454-7545, *Fax:* (207) 454-3062
www.wqdy.fm
wqdy@wqdy.fm
License: Calais, Washington County, ME held by WQDY Inc.
Nat'l Network: Jones Radio Networks; ABC *Wire Services:* AP
Format: Classic Rock *No. News Employees:* 1
Bill McVicar, President
Roger Holst, Chief Engineer

Camden

WQSS
05-01-1988; 102.5 mhz FM *Hrs Open:* 24; 7.9 kw; 1201 ft.; N44 12 40 W69 9 6
20 South Street, Bangor, ME 04401 US
(207) 623-9000, *Fax:* (207) 623-9007
License: Camden, Knox County, ME held by Blueberry Broadcasting LLC.
Group Owner: Blueberry Broadcasting LLC; (acq 7-29-2008; grpsl)
Format: Adult Contemp
Bruce Biette, Operations Dir

*WMEP
10-01-2002; 90.5 mhz FM; 0 kw horiz, 2 kw vert; 1217 ft.; N44 12 40 W69 9 6 *Rebroadcasts:* Rebroadcasts WMEH(FM) Bangor 100%
Mailing Address: 65 Texas Avenue, Bangor, ME 04401 US
Second Address: 1450 Lisbon St., Lewiston, ME 4240
(800) 884-1717, *Fax:* (207) 942-2857
www.mpbn.net
csweet@mpbn.net
License: Camden, Knox County, ME held by Maine Public Broadcasting Corp.
Nat'l Network: NPR; PRI
Arbitron Metro Market: Bangor, ME *Format:* Jazz, News
Mark Vogelzang, President & CEO
Mary Mayo, General Sales Mgr
Charles Beck, Programming Director
Keith Shortall, News & Public Affairs Director
Christopher Amann, CFO
Alexander G. Maxwell, Jr, COO
Charles Beck, V.P. , Director ofRadio & Television
Jennifer Foley, V.P. Development: Philanthropic Giving
Gil Maxwell, V.P. Technology & Chief Technology Officer
Pam Smart, Membership Director

Caribou

WCXU
11-15-1986; 97.7 mhz FM *Hrs Open:* 24; 20 kw; 318 ft.; N46 47 26 W67 55 7
152 East Green Ridge Rd., Caribou, ME 04736 US
(207) 473-7513, *Fax:* (207) 472-3221
www.channelxradio.com
channelxradio@yahoo.com
License: Caribou, Aroostook County, ME held by The Canxus Broadcasting Corp.
Group Owner: Canxus Broadcasting Corp.
Regional Reps: Cyr Associates.
Arbitron Metro Market: Aroostook County, ME *Format:* Adult Contemp, News, 64 *Hrs. of News Programming:* news progmg 21 hrs wkly *No. News Employees:* 1 *Target Audience:* 25-54; educated, div occupations, affluent
Dennis Curley, CEO
Dennis Curley, President
Richard Chandler, General Manager
Richard Chandler, Station Manager
Phil Shaw, Programming Director
Douglas Christensen, News Director

*WFST
07-15-1956; 600 khz AM *Hrs Open:* 24; 5 kw-D, ND1; 0.127 kw-N, ND1; N46 53 12 W68 2 44
Mailing Address: P.O. Box 600, Rt. 161 New Sweden Rd, Cariboo, ME 04736 US
Second Address: 670 Sweden Rd., Caribou, ME 4736
(207) 492-6000, *Fax:* (207) 493-3268
www.wfst.net
wfst@maine.rr.com
License: Caribou, ME held by Northern Broadcast Ministries Inc.
Nat'l Network: Moody; Salem Radio Network
Format: Christian, Gospel, 74 *Target Audience:* General.
Donald Flewelling, President
Tom Hale, Operations Dir
John Stephenson, General Manager
Dick Waugh, Programming Director
Dick Waugh, Music Director
Linda Waugh, Secretary

Corinth

*WXBP
90.3 mhz FM; 2 kw; 902 ft.; N45 3 26 W69 11 27
US

www.thepresence.fm
info@thepresence.fm
License: Corinth, ME held by The Presence Radio Network Inc.
Group Owner: The Presence Radio Network Inc.
Format: Religious
Cynthia Nickless, Executive Director
Josh Houde, Production Assistant
Richard Hyatt, Engineering Consultant

Dennysville

WCRQ
05-01-1998; 102.9 mhz FM *Hrs Open:* 24; 100 kw; 456 ft.; N45 1 44 W67 19 25
1064 James Street, Syracuse, NY 13203 US
(207) 454-7545, *Fax:* (207) 454-3062
www.wcrqfm.com
onair@wcrqfm.com
License: Dennysville, Washington County, ME held by WQDY Inc.
Arbitron Metro Market: St. Stephen, Dennysville,ME *Format:* Adult Contemp *Hrs. of News Programming:* News progmg 6 hrs wkly *Target Audience:* 18-49; mass appeal
Bill McVicar, President
Bill Conley, Programming Director

Dexter

*WKVZ
01-01-1993; 102.1 mhz FM *Hrs Open:* 24; 23 kw; 673 ft.; N45 2 40 W69 15 1
378 Main Street, Dexter, ME 04930 US
(916) 251-1600, *Fax:* (916) 251-1650
www.klove.com
License: Dexter, Penobscot County, ME held by Educational Media Foundation.
Group Owner: EMF Broadcasting; (acq 4-6-2009; $550,000 with WFZX(FM) Searsport)
Nat'l Network: K-Love
Arbitron Metro Market: Bangor, ME *Format:* Christian
Mike Novak, President

Eastport

*WSHD
04-01-1984; 91.7 mhz FM; 0.012 kw; 115 ft.; N44 54 30 W66 59 24
89 High Street, Eastport, ME 04631 US
(207) 853-6254, *Fax:* (207) 853-2919
www.shead.org
License: Eastport, Washington County, ME held by Shead High School.
Format: Variety/Diverse *Target Audience:* General.
Rafi Hopkins, Chief Engineer

Ellsworth

WDEA
12-13-1958; 1370 khz AM; 5 kw-U, DA-2; N44 28 00 W68 28 11
Mailing Address: 49 Acme Road, Brewer, ME 53202
Second Address: 49 Acme Rd., Brewer, ME 4412
(207) 989-5631, *Fax:* (207) 989-5685
www.am1370wdea.com
q1065@midmaine.com
License: Ellsworth, Hancock County, ME held by Townsquare Media Bangor License LLC
Group Owner: Cumulus Media Inc.; (acq 1999; grpsl)
Nat'l Network: CBS *Nat'l Reps:* D & R Radio
Population Served: 54,578 *Arbitron Metro Market:* Hancock County, ME *Target Audience:* 35 plus.
Tom Preble, General Manager
Dan Groshon, Director of Sales
Fred Miller, Programming Director
Michael O'Hara, Promotions Manager
Jodi Hersey, News Director
Richard Hyatt, Chief Engineer
Fred Mille, Brand Manager:

WKSQ
05-27-1982; 94.5 mhz FM *Hrs Open:* 24; 11.5 kw; 1027 ft.; N44 39 31 W68 36 17
P.O. Box 9494, Ellsworth, ME 04605 US
(207) 947-9100, *Fax:* (207) 942-8039
www.kiss945.com
info@kiss945.com
License: Ellsworth, Hancock County, ME held by Blueberry Broadcasting LLC.
Group Owner: Blueberry Broadcasting LLC; (acq 7-29-2008; grpsl)
Nat'l Reps: Christal
Arbitron Metro Market: Bangor, ME *Format:* Adult Contemp *Hrs. of News Programming:* news progmg 7 hrs wkly *No. News Employees:* 3 *Target Audience:* 25-54.
Jon Shields, Operations Dir
Josh Scroggins, General Sales Mgr

WWMJ
12-27-1965; 95.7 mhz FM; 11.5 kw; 1030 ft.; N44 39 31 W68 36 20
Mailing Address: 111 East Kilbourn Avenue, Suite 2700, Milwaukee, WI 53202 US
Second Address: 49 Acme Rd., Ellsworth, ME 4412
(207) 989-5631, *Fax:* (207) 989-5685
www.wwmj-fm.com
q1065@midmaine.com
License: Ellsworth, Hancock County, ME

Arbitron Metro Market: Bangor, ME *Format:* Contemporary Hits/Top 40, Adult Contemp *Target Audience:* 25-54.
Michael Long, Operations Dir
Tom Preble, General Manager
Alberta Jackson, General Sales Mgr
Darryl Elliott, Programming Director
Nikita Pogue, Promotions Manager
Dan Groshon, Director of Sales
Fred Miller, Brand Manager

Fairfield

WCTB
11-01-1993; 93.5 mhz FM; 10.5 kw; 499 ft.; N44 44 42 W69 41 32
P.O. Box 159, Skowhegan, ME 04976 US
(207) 660-4888, *Fax:* (207) 660-4889
www.935trueoldies.com
License: Fairfield, Somerset County, ME held by Mountain Wireless Inc.
Group Owner: Mountain Wireless Inc.; acq 4-20-94; $60,000
Arbitron Metro Market: Augusta-Waterville, ME *Format:* Classic Rock
Jay Hanson, General Manager

Farmington

WKTJ-FM
08-21-1973; 99.3 mhz FM *Hrs Open:* 24; 1.5 kw; 400 ft.; N44 39 22 W70 11 48
Voter Hill Road, Farmington, ME 04938 US
(207) 778-3400, *Fax:* (207) 778-3000
www.wktj.com
wktj@wktj.com
License: Farmington, Franklin County, ME held by Franklin Broadcasting Corp.
Format: Oldies *Hrs. of News Programming:* News progmg 12 hrs wkly *Target Audience:* 25-54. *Adv. Rates:* 20; 16; 20; 12
Rick Davis, General Manager
Steve Bull, General Sales Mgr
Kathy Shrewsbury, News Director

Fort Kent

*WMEF
03-01-1994; 106.5 mhz FM; 7.4 kw; 302 ft.; N47 15 30 W68 33 30 *Rebroadcasts:* Rebroadcasts WMEH(FM) Bangor 100%.
Mailing Address: 1450 Lisbon Street, Lewiston, ME 04240 US
Second Address: 1450 Lisbon St., Lewiston, ME 4240
(207) 783-9101, *Fax:* (207) 942-2857
www.mpbn.net
cbeck@mpbn.net
License: Fort Kent, Aroostook County, ME held by Maine Public Broadcasting Corp.
Nat'l Network: PRI; NPR
Arbitron Metro Market: Fort Kent, ME *Format:* Jazz, News *Target Audience:* General
Mark Vogelzang, CEO
Mary Mayo, General Sales Mgr
Charles Beck, Programming Director
Keith Shortall, News Director
Christopher Amann, CFO
Alexander Maxwell Jr., COO
Joe Riley, Vice President, Media Services

Freeport

*WMSJ
12-01-1997; 89.3 mhz FM; 7.5 kw vert; 505 ft.; N43 45 45 W70 19 30
P O Box 432, Freeport, ME 04032 US
(207) 865-3448, *Fax:* (207) 865-1763
www.positive.fm
info@positive.fm
License: Freeport, Cumberland County, ME held by The Positive Radio Network.
Arbitron Metro Market: Freeport, ME *Format:* Christian *Target Audience:* 25-48.
John Libby, Chairman
Marc Tischart, Operations Dir
Suzanne Happs, General Manager
Kenny Robinson, Programming Director
Chris Scotland, Promotions Manager
Mark Marston, Office Manager
Shawn Katzbeck, Business DevelopmentDirector
Joseph Standish, Technical Support

Gardiner

WABK-FM
04-01-1974; 104.3 mhz FM; 50 kw; 371 ft.; N44 18 36 W69 49 51
330 East Kilbourn Avenue, Suite 250, Milwaukee, WI 53202 US
(403) 362-3418, *Fax:* (403) 362-8168
1011thefox@mewcap.ca
License: Gardiner, Kennebec County, ME held by Blueberry Broadcasting LLC.
Group Owner: Blueberry Broadcasting LLC; (acq 7-29-2008; grpsl)
Arbitron Metro Market: Portland OR *Format:* Adult Contemp
Douglas Kirk, Chairman
Thomas Pippy, CFO
Steve Kassay, Operations Dir
Simon Constam, General Sales Mgr
Cathy Philippo, News Director

WFAU
09-23-1968; 1280 khz AM *Hrs Open:* 24; 5 kw-D, DAN; 5 kw-N, DAN; N44 14 53 W69 48 51 *Rebroadcasts:* Simulcasts with WRKD(AM) Rockland 100%
330 East Kilbourn Avenue, Suite 250, Milwaukee, WI 53202 US
(207) 623-9000, *Fax:* (207) 623-9007
www.foxsportsmaine.com
License: Gardiner, ME held by Blueberry Broadcasting LLC.
Group Owner: Blueberry Broadcasting LLC; (acq 7-29-2008; grpsl)
Arbitron Metro Market: Gardiner, ME *Format:* Sports *Hrs. of News Programming:* news progmg 34 hrs wkly *No. News Employees:* 1 *Target Audience:* 25-54.
Kelly Slater, General Manager
Sharon Griffith, News Director

Gorham

WLVP
03-03-1980; 870 khz AM; 10 kw-D, DA2; 1 kw-N, DA2; N43 39 46 W70 29 41 *Rebroadcasts:* Simulcasts WLAM(AM) Lewiston 100%
912 Washington St, Auburn, ME 04240 US
(207) 797-0780, *Fax:* (207) 797-0368
License: Gorham, ME held by Nassau Broadcasting III L.L.C.
Group Owner: Nassau Broadcasting Partners L.P.; (acq 4-6-2004; grpsl)
Arbitron Metro Market: Portland, ME *Format:* Oldies
Stan Manning, Operations Dir
Patrick Collins, General Manager
Tim Gatz, General Sales Mgr
Sean Baker, Programming Director
Bill Ryall, Chief Engineer

*WMPG
09-01-1973; 90.9 mhz FM *Hrs Open:* 24; 4.5 kw; 640 ft.; N43 44 37.7 W70 20 0.8
107 Main St., Bangor, ME 04401 US
(207) 780-4943, *Fax:* (207) 780-4590
www.wmpg.org
stationmanager@wmpg.org
License: Gorham, Cumberland County, ME held by Trustees University of Maine.
Arbitron Metro Market: Gorham, ME *Format:* Variety/Diverse *Special Programming:* Sp 4 hrs, Balkan 2 hrs, Cambodian 2 hrs, African *Hrs. of News Programming:* News progmg 10 hrs wkly *Target Audience:* General; anygroup currently underserved by other loc stns
Dave Wade, Chairman
Kelsey Perchinski, General Manager
James Rand, Station Manager
Lisa Bunker, Programming Director
Brian Dyer, Chief Engineer
Ron Raymond, Music Director
Joel Lamer, Technical Director

Gray

WJJB-FM
11-15-1975; 96.3 mhz FM; 40 kw; Ant 1,410 ft; N44 15 03 W70 25 16
779 Warren Ave., Portland, ME 02116
(207) 773-9695, *Fax:* (207) 761-4406
www.thebigjab.com
shoe@thebigjab.com
License: Gray, Cumberland County, ME held by Atlantic Coast Radio L.L.C.
Group Owner: Atlantic Coast Radio L.L.C.; (acq 9-8-2000; grpsl)
Nat'l Network: Sporting News Radio Network *Nat'l Reps:* McGavren Guild
Population Served: 950,000 *Arbitron Metro Market:* Portland, ME
Jon Van Hoogenstyn, General Manager

Hampden

WRME
750 khz AM
US
(908) 730-7959
License: Hampden, ME held by Charles A. Hecht and Alfredo Alonso.
Group Owner: Charles A. Hecht and Alfredo Alonso Stns
Arbitron Metro Market: Hampden, ME
Charles Hecht, General Manager

Harpswell

*WYFP
07-08-1993; 91.9 mhz FM *Hrs Open:* 24; 6 kw; 144 ft.; N43 44 14 W69 59 39
8030 Arrowridge Boulevard, Charlotte, NC 28273 US
(704) 523-5555, *Fax:* (704) 522-1967
www.bbnradio.org
bbn@bbnradio.org
License: Harpswell, Cumberland County, ME held by Bible Broadcasting Network Inc.
Group Owner: Bible Broadcasting Network; acq 9-30-97; $150,000)
Nat'l Network: USA
Arbitron Metro Market: Harpswell, ME *Format:* Religious *Special Programming:* Christian rock 4 hrs, praise & worship 3 hrs wkly *Target Audience:* 25-49.
Dennis Gast, Operations Dir
T. A. Smith, General Manager
Teddi Wilson, Programming Director

Houlton

WHOU-FM
01-13-1976; 100.1 mhz FM *Hrs Open:* 24; 9.6 kw; 525 ft.; N46 8 35 W68 6 50
Mailing Address: 39 Court Street, P.O. Box 40, Houlton, ME 04730 US
Second Address: 39 Court St., Suite 215, Houlton, ME 4730
(207) 532-3600, *Fax:* (207) 521-0056
www.whoufm.com
sales@whoufm.com
License: Houlton, Aroostook County, ME held by County Communications Inc.
Nat'l Network: ABC
Format: Adult Contemp *Special Programming:* Sacred one hr wkly *Hrs. of News Programming:* News progmg 8 hrs wkly *Target Audience:* 25-54.
David Moore, President
Jacqueline Spencer, Operations Dir
Fred Grant, General Manager
JoLene Ledger, Station Manager
Ken Holck, General Sales Mgr
George Kelley, Programming Director
Barrett Quinn, Chief Engineer
Susan Hamel,Traffic Manager and Production
Mike Folsom, Account Executive and Sports Director
Linnwood Hersey, Sales Account Executive
Ian Small, Web Development and Graphic Artist
Zach Goodwin, Disc Jockey
Ryan Hill, Disc Jockey

Howland

WVOM
06-01-1993; 103.9 mhz FM; 90 kw; 1509 ft.; N45 7 46 W68 21 28 *Rebroadcasts:* Rebroadcasts WBYA(FM) Searsport 80%
263 State Street, Bangor, ME 04401 US
(207) 947-9100, *Fax:* (207) 942-8039
www.thevoicemaine.com
License: Howland, Penobscot County, ME held by Blueberry Broadcasting LLC.
Group Owner: Blueberry Broadcasting LLC; (acq 7-29-2008; grpsl)
Nat'l Network: CBS; Westwood One
Arbitron Metro Market: Bangor, ME *Format:* News, News/Talk, 86 *Target Audience:* 25-64; upper income, professional, managerial
Jon Shields, Operations Dir
Josh Scroggins, General Manager
Katrina Walls, Programming Director

Islesboro

WBYA
01-01-1999; 105.5 mhz FM; 25 kw; 305 ft.; N44 18 58 W68 58 12
20 South Street, Bangor, ME 04401 US
(702) 736-6161
License: Islesboro, Waldo County, ME held by Nassau Broadcasting III L.L.C.
Group Owner: Nassau Broadcasting Partners L.P.; (acq 4-6-2004; grpsl).
Arbitron Metro Market: Payson AZ
Will Kemp, President

RADIO - U.S.

Kennebunk

WBQQ

11-01-1991; 99.3 mhz FM *Hrs Open:* 24; 3 kw; 328 ft.; N43 24 16 W70 26 15
169 Port Road, Kennebunk, ME 04043 US
(207) 797-0780, *Fax:* (207) 967-8671
www.999thewolf.com/
License: Kennebunk, York County, ME held by Nassau Broadcasting III L.L.C.
Group Owner: Nassau Broadcasting Partners L.P.; (acq 4-6-2004; grpsl)
Nat'l Network: ABC
Format: Talk *Target Audience:* 35-64; upscale
Pat Collins, Operations Dir
Patrick Collins, General Manager
Tim Gatz, General Sales Mgr
Stan Bennett, Programming Director
Corey Garrison, Promotions Manager
Stan Manning, Operations Director

Kennebunkport

WBQW

12-01-1994; 104.7 mhz FM; 6 kw; Ant 292 ft; N43 26 36 W70 26 38 *Rebroadcasts:* Rebroadcasts WBQQ(FM) Kennebunk 90%
169 Port Rd., Kennebunk, ME 04043
(207) 797-0780, *Fax:* (207) 967-8671
www.wbachradio.com
License: Kennebunkport, York County, ME held by Nassau Broadcasting III L.L.C.
Group Owner: Nassau Broadcasting Partners L.P.; (acq 4-6-2004; grpsl)
Nat'l Network: AP Radio
Special Programming: Jazz 5 hrs wkly *Target Audience:* 25-54; upscale, affluent, management, professionals
Pat Collins, Operations Dir
Scott Hooper, Programming Director
Stan Manning, Operations Director

*WMEK

88.3 mhz FM; 250 w; Ant 138 ft; N43 24 16 W70 26 15
17 Varney St., Lebanon, ME
(603) 767-5994
License: Kennebunkport, York County, ME held by New Life Media.
Ford Bishop, President

Kittery

WSHK

10-01-1992; 105.3 mhz FM *Hrs Open:* 24; 2.2 kw; 371 ft; N43 10 28 W70 46 50 *Rebroadcasts:* Rebroadcasts WSAK(FM) Hampton, NH 100%
Mailing Address: Box 576, Dover, NH 01950
Second Address: 292 Middle Rd., Dover, NH 03820-4901
(603) 749-9750, *Fax:* (603) 749-1459
www.shark1053.com
info@wokq.com
License: Kittery, York County, ME
Group Owner: Cumulus Media Inc.; (acq 7-7-99; grpsl).
Nat'l Network: CNN Radio *Nat'l Reps:* Christal *Wire Services:* AP
Population Served: 9,543 *Arbitron Metro Market:* Kittery, ME *No. News Employees:* 2 *Target Audience:* 25-54.
Farid Suleman, CEO
Judy Ellis, President
Mark Ericson, Operations Dir
Marty Lessard, General Manager
Jonathan Smith, Programming Director

Lewiston

*WARX

02-29-1948; 93.9 mhz FM *Hrs Open:* 24; 27.5 kw; 633 ft.; N44 8 40 W70 1 22
Post Office Box 820, Newburyport, MA 01950 US
(888) 937-2471, *Fax:* (916) 251-1650
www.air1.com
License: Lewiston, Androscoggin County, ME held by Educational Media Foundation.
Group Owner: EMF Broadcasting; (acq 6-5-2008; $1 million)
Nat'l Network: Air 1
Arbitron Metro Market: Lewiston-Auburn, ME *Format:* Christian
Alan Mason, COO
Mike Novak, President

*WRBC

10-06-1958; 91.5 mhz FM *Hrs Open:* 24; 0.12 kw; 16 ft.; N44 6 18 W70 12 32
121 Lane Hall, Lewiston, ME 04240 US
(207) 777-7532, *Fax:* (207) 795-8793
www.bates.edu/wrbc
mgraham3@bates.edu
License: Lewiston, Androscoggin County, ME held by President and Trustees of Bates College.
Format: Christian *Target Audience:* General; anyone searching for something different
Ky Windborn, General Manager

WFNK

03-01-1973; 107.5 mhz FM; 100 kw; 928 ft.; N44 0 12 W70 25 24
P.O. Box 929, Lewiston, ME 04240 US
(207) 797-0780, *Fax:* (207) 797-0368
www.1075frank.com
info@1075frank.com
License: Lewiston, Androscoggin County, ME held by Nassau Broadcasting III L.L.C.
Group Owner: Nassau Broadcasting Partners L.P.; (acq 4-6-2004; grpsl).
Nat'l Reps: D & R Radio
Arbitron Metro Market: Portland, ME *Format:* Classic Rock
Pat Collins, General Manager
Tim Gatz, General Sales Mgr
Stan Bennett, Programming Director
Corey Garrison, Promotions Manager
Stan Manning, Operations Director
Amy Ryan, Production Director

WEZR

08-21-1938; 1240 khz AM *Hrs Open:* 24; 1 kw-U; N44 06 55 W70 14 56
555 Center St., Auburn, ME 04268
(207) 784-4700, *Fax:* (207) 784-4700
www.ez1240.com
dickgleason@gmail.com
License: Lewiston, Androscoggin County, ME held by Mountain Valley Broadcasting Inc.
Group Owner: Gleason Radio Group; (acq 11-28-90)
Nat'l Network: USA *Nat'l Reps:* CYR Associates *Regional Reps:* CYR Associates
Population Served: 100,000 *Arbitron Metro Market:* Lewiston-Auburn, ME *Hrs. of News Programming:* Top & bottom of each hour *No. News Employees:* 3 *Target Audience:* General. *Adv. Rates:* 20; 20; 20; 20
Richard Gleason, President
Richard Gleason, General Manager
Bonnie McHugh, Station Manager
Jeremy Rush, Programming Director
Dave Alpert, News Director
Bob Perry, Chief Engineer

WLAM

09-04-1947; 1470 khz AM; 5 kw-U, DA1; N44 3 47 W70 15 0
P.O. Box 929, Lewiston, ME 04240 US
(207) 797-0780, *Fax:* (207) 797-0368
License: Lewiston, ME held by Nassau Broadcasting III L.L.C.
Group Owner: Nassau Broadcasting Partners L.P.; (acq 4-6-2004; grpsl).
Nat'l Reps: D & R Radio
Arbitron Metro Market: Portland, ME *Format:* Oldies
Tim Gatz, General Sales Mgr
Stan Manning, Operations Director

Lincoln

*WHMX

04-01-1975; 105.7 mhz FM *Hrs Open:* 24; 48 kw; 466 ft.; N45 20 38 W68 30 24
Mailing Address: 1746 Broadway, Bangor, ME 04401 US
Second Address: 1476 Broadway, Bangor, ME 4401
(207) 947-2751, *Fax:* (207) 947-0010
www.solutionfm.com
contact@solutionfm.com
License: Lincoln, Penobscot County, ME held by Bangor Baptist Church.
Arbitron Metro Market: Bangor, ME *Format:* Christian *Target Audience:* 18-35.
Pencil Boone, General Manager
Tim Collins, Programming Director
Jolie Littlefield, Promotions Manager
Morgan Smith, Music Director

*WWLN

90.5 mhz FM; 0.065 kw; 492 ft.; N45 20 41 W68 30 30 US
(207) 622-1340, *Fax:* (207) 623-2874
www.godscountry.lightoflife.info
License: Lincoln, Penobscot County, ME held by Light of Life Ministries Inc.
Arbitron Metro Market: Lincoln, ME
Ryan Gagne, Operations Dir
Raymond Bouchard, General Manager
Roger Jackson, Programming Director

Machias

WALZ-FM

11-25-1978; 95.3 mhz FM *Hrs Open:* 24; 3 kw; 220 ft.; N44 44 8 W67 30 11 *Rebroadcasts:* Rebroadcasts WQDY-FM Calais 100%
P.O. Box 403, Calais, ME 04619 US
(207) 454-7545, *Fax:* (207) 454-3062
www.wqdy.fm
wqdy@wqdy.fm
License: Machias, Washington County, ME held by William McVicar & Roger Holst, general partnership
Nat'l Network: ABC; Jones Radio Networks *Wire Services:* AP
Arbitron Metro Market: Calais, ME *Format:* Contemporary Hits/Top 40, Adult Contemp *Special Programming:* Boston Red Sox *No. News Employees:* 1
Roger Holst, Operations Dir
William McVicar, General Manager

*WUMM

01-01-2008; 91.7 mhz FM; 0.1 kw; 72 ft.; N44 42 33 W67 27 29 US
(207) 255-1200
www.umm.maine.edu/wumm
wumm@maine.edu
License: Machias, Washington County, ME held by University of Maine System.
Arbitron Metro Market: Machias, ME *Format:* Variety/Diverse
Tom Boutureira, Chairman
Daniel Swain, General Manager
Blaine Jones, Vice Chairman

Madawaska

WCXX

01-30-1988; 102.3 mhz FM *Hrs Open:* 24; 1.2 kw; 423 ft.; N47 19 51 W68 20 26 *Rebroadcasts:* Rebroadcasts WCXU(FM) Caribou 50%
152 E. Green Ridge Rd, Caribou, ME 04736 US
(207) 473-7513, *Fax:* (207) 472-3221
www.channelxradio.com
channelxradio@yahoo.com
License: Madawaska, Aroostook County, ME held by Canxus Broadcasting Corp.
Group Owner: Canxus Broadcasting Corp.
Nat'l Network: CNN Radio *Regional Reps:* Cyr Associates.
Arbitron Metro Market: Aroostook County, ME *Format:* Adult Contemp, News, 64 *Hrs. of News Programming:* news progmg 16 hrs wkly *No. News Employees:* 1 *Target Audience:* 18-54.
Adv. Rates: 20; 15; 18; 12
Dennis Curley, President
Richard Chandler, General Manager
Richard Chandler, Station Manager
Douglas Christensen, News Director

Madison

WIGY

01-01-1995; 97.5 mhz FM *Hrs Open:* 24; 6 kw; 328 ft.; N44 47 32 W69 58 10
330 East Kilbourn Avenue, Suite 250, Milwaukee, WI 53202 US
(207) 623-9000, *Fax:* (207) 623-9007
www.foxsportsmaine.com
donaldshields@clearchannel.com
License: Madison, Somerset County, ME held by Blueberry Broadcasting LLC.
Group Owner: Blueberry Broadcasting LLC; (acq 7-29-2008; grpsl)
Regional Reps: Cyr Associates.
Format: Sports *Target Audience:* 25-54.
Kelly Slater, General Manager
Rick Dugal, General Sales Mgr
Donald Shield, Programming Director

Mexico

WTBM

09-15-1988; 100.7 mhz FM *Hrs Open:* 24; 0.85 kw; 1273 ft.; N44 34 56 W70 37 59 *Rebroadcasts:* Simulcast with WOXO-FM Norway 99%
P.O. Box 72, Norway, ME 04268 US
(207) 743-5911, *Fax:* (207) 743-5913
www.woxo.com
info@oxocountry.com
License: Mexico, Oxford County, ME held by Mountain Valley Broadcasting Inc.
Group Owner: Gleason Radio Group; (acq 12-90;
Nat'l Network: USA *Nat'l Reps:* CYR Associates

Arbitron Metro Market: Portland, ME *Format:* Country, Sports *Special Programming:* Financial Advise 3 hrs *Hrs. of News Programming:* news progmg 12 hrs wkly *No. News Employees:* 2 *Target Audience:* General.*Adv. Rates:* 20; 20; 20; 20
Dick Gleason, President/General Manager
Jeremy Rush, Operations Dir
Vic Hodgkins, Station Manager
Scott Garnett, News Director
Dawn Dunn, Traffic Manager

Milbridge

WRMO
01-01-2005; 93.7 mhz FM *Hrs Open:* 24 hours; 22.5 kw; 669 ft.; N44 38 33 W68 10 18
1750 Freedom Road, Little Chute, WI 54140 US
(207) 546-7510
info@937wrmo.com
License: Milbridge, Washington County, ME held by Steven A. Roy, Personal Representative, Estate of Lyle Evans
Nat'l Reps: Rgnl Reps
Arbitron Metro Market: Milbridge, ME *Format:* Adult Contemp *Hrs. of News Programming:* 5am, 6am, 7am, 8am, 9am, 12pm, 5pm *Target Audience:* 35+ *Adv. Rates:* 15; 15; 10; 8
Mike McSorley, General Manager

Millinocket

WSYY
12-07-1963; 1240 khz AM *Hrs Open:* 24; 1 kw-U, ND1; N45 40 24 W68 43 7
Lake Road, PO Box 1240, Millinocket, ME 04462 US
(207) 723-9657, *Fax:* (207) 723-5900
www.themountain949.com
calendar@themountain949.com
License: Millinocket, ME held by Katahdin Communications Inc.
Nat'l Network: ESPN Radio *Regional Reps:* Cyr Associates.
Arbitron Metro Market: Bangor, ME *Format:* Sports *Target Audience:* General. *Adv. Rates:* 6; 6; 6; 6
James Talbot, President
Dave Keys, News Director

WSYY-FM
04-12-1978; 94.9 mhz FM *Hrs Open:* 24; 23.5 kw; 692 ft.; N45 42 58 W68 47 54
P.O. Box 1240, Lake Rd., Millinocket, ME 04462 US
(207) 723-9657, *Fax:* (207) 723-5900
www.themountain949.com
License: Millinocket, Penobscot County, ME
Nat'l Network: CBS Radio
Arbitron Metro Market: Bangor, ME *Format:* Variety/Diverse *Target Audience:* 20-45.
Mike Michaels, Operations Dir
John Hunt, General Manager
Andrew Bednar, Promotions Manager

Monticello

WXME
09-02-1981; 780 khz AM
1010 North Broadway, Yonkers, NY 10701 US
(207) 538-9180
License: Monticello, ME held by Allan H. Weiner
Format: Talk
Allan Weiner, President

WBCQ-FM
09-01-2008; 94.7 mhz FM; 6 kw; 312 ft.; N46 20 30 W67 49 4 US
(207) 532-3600, *Fax:* (207) 521-0056
www.wbcqfm.com
License: Monticello, Aroostook County, ME held by Allan H. Weiner & Barbara A. Weiner dba WBCQ Radio.
Arbitron Metro Market: Monticello, ME *Format:* Country
David Moore, General Manager

North Windham

WXTP
01-01-1996; 106.7 mhz FM *Hrs Open:* 24; 810 w; Ant 623 ft; N43 51 06 W70 19 40
Mailing Address: 477 Congress St., 3rd Fl. Annex, Portland, ME 04242
Second Address: 99 Danville Corner Rd., North Windham, ME 4210
(207) 797-0780, *Fax:* (207) 797-0368
www.boneradio.com
info@boneradio.com
License: North Windham, Cumberland County, ME held by Nassau Broadcasting III L.L.C.
Group Owner: Nassau Broadcasting Partners L.P.; (acq 4-6-2004; grpsl).
Nat'l Network: AP Radio
Arbitron Metro Market: Portland, ME *Target Audience:* 35 plus; general
Patrick Collins, General Manager
Tim Gatz, General Sales Mgr
Sean Baker, Programming Director
Bill Ryall, Chief Engineer
Jennifer Bachelder, Traffic Manager

North Yarmouth

WCLZ
04-11-1965; 98.9 mhz FM; 48 kw; 400 ft.; N43 55 40 W69 59 42
P.O. Box 820, Newburyport, MA 01950 US
(207)774-4561
www.989wclz.com
ethan@989wclz.com.
License: North Yarmouth, Cumberland County, ME held by Saga Communications of New England LLC.
Group Owner: Saga Communications Inc.; (acq 10-15-2007; $3.5 million)
Nat'l Reps: Christal
Arbitron Metro Market: Portland, ME *Format:* Triple A
Larry Julius, General Sales Mgr
Ethan Minton, Programming Director

Norway

WOXO-FM
12-12-1970; 92.7 mhz FM *Hrs Open:* 24; 5.2 kw; 735 ft.; N44 17 47 W70 37 5 *Rebroadcasts:* Rebroadcasts WTBM(FM) Mexico 99%
P.O. Box 72, Norway, ME 04268 US
(207) 743-5911, *Fax:* (207) 743-5913
www.woxo.com
info@woxo.com
License: Norway, Oxford County, ME held by Mountain Valley Broadcasting Inc.
Group Owner: Gleason Radio Group; (acq 12-12-75).
Nat'l Network: USA *Nat'l Reps:* CYR Associates
Arbitron Metro Market: Portland, ME *Format:* Country, Sports *Hrs. of News Programming:* news progmg 12 hrs wkly *No. News Employees:* 2 *Target Audience:* General. *Adv. Rates:* 20; 20; 20; 20
Richard Gleason, President
Jeremy Rush, Operations Dir
Vic Hodgkins, Station Manager
Jay Philips, Programming Director

Oakland

***WMDR-FM**
01-01-2006; 88.9 mhz FM *Hrs Open:* 24; 100 kw; 1283 ft.; N44 14 58 W70 25 25
160 Bangor Street, Augusta, ME 04330 US
(207) 622-1340, *Fax:* (207) 623-2874
www.worshipradionetwork.org
denise@lworshipradionetwork.org
License: Oakland, Kennebec County, ME held by Light of Life Ministries Inc.
Arbitron Metro Market: Oakland, ME *Format:* Christian, Country *Hrs. of News Programming:* News progmg one hr wkly
Ray Bouchard, CEO/COO
Ryan Gagne, Operations Dir
Denise Lafountain, General Manager
Roger Jackson, Programming Director

Old Town

WBZN
01-01-1995; 107.3 mhz FM; 50 kw; 308 ft; N45 02 06 W68 40 57
Mailing Address: 49 Acme Road, Brewer, ME 53202
Second Address: 49 Acme Rd., Brewer, ME 4412
(207) 989-5631, *Fax:* (207) 989-5685
www.wbzn-fm.com
z1073@midmaine.com
License: Old Town, Penobscot County, ME held by Townsquare Media Bangor License LLC
Group Owner: Cumulus Media Inc.; (acq 2-20-98; $6.4 million with WQCB(FM) Brewer)
Population Served: 9,474 *Arbitron Metro Market:* Brewer, ME
Paul Dupuis, Operations Dir
Tom Preble, General Manager
Dick Hyatt, Chief Engineer

Orono

***WMEB-FM**
04-01-1963; 91.9 mhz FM *Hrs Open:* 24; 10 kw; 171 ft.; N44 55 8 W68 40 0
107 Main Street, Bangor, ME 04401 US
(207) 581-4340, *Fax:* (207) 581-4343
www.wmeb.fm
wmeb919@hotmail.com
License: Orono, Penobscot County, ME held by Board of Trustees, University of Maine.
Arbitron Metro Market: Orono, ME *Format:* Variety/Diverse *Target Audience:* General.
Thomas Grucza, Station Manager

Pittsfield

***WJCX**
12-01-1993; 99.5 mhz FM; 6 kw; 328 ft.; N44 48 11 W69 10 6
3000 W. Macarthur Blvd, Santa Ana, CA 92704 US
(207) 884-6052, *Fax:* (207) 884-6052
www.calvarychapel.com
wjcx@calvarychapel.com
License: Pittsfield, Somerset County, ME held by CSN International.
Group Owner: CSN International; (acq 1996; $87,500)
Format: Christian, News, 62, Talk, Religious *Target Audience:* 18-34; young adults
Mike Archer, General Manager

Pittston Farm

***WHPF**
88.1 mhz FM; 0.25 kw; -240 ft.; N45 53 38 W69 57 54 US
(207) 622-1340, *Fax:* (207) 623-2874
www.worshipradionetwork.org
info@worshipradionetwork.org
License: Pittston Farm, Somerset County, ME held by Light of Life Ministries Inc.
Arbitron Metro Market: Augusta, ME *Format:* Christian
Denise LaFountain, General Manager
Nan Parsons, Sales Manager
Brad Taylor, Current Business & Church Sponsorship
Nan Parsons, Sponsor Worship-FM
Samantha Heyns, Individual Sponsorships & Pledge
Brad Taylor, Event/Concert
KarenRossignol, Volunteer Questions

Portland

WBAE
03-01-1946; 1490 khz AM *Hrs Open:* 24
420 Western Ave, South Portland, MI 48236 US
(801) 359-3147, *Fax:* (801) 359-8112
www.familyradio.com
info@familyradio.com
License: Portland, ME held by Saga Communications of New England LLC.
Group Owner: Saga Communications Inc.; (acq 1996; $10 million with co-located FM).
Nat'l Network: CNN Radio
Arbitron Metro Market: Newport OR *Format:* Christian, Religious
Harold Camping, General Manager

WBLM
02-01-1966; 102.9 mhz FM; 100 kw; 1,460 ft; N43 55 28 W70 29 28
One City Ctr., Portland, ME 01950
(207) 774-6364, *Fax:* (207) 774-8707
www.wblm.com
Kris.Currier@citcomm.com
License: Portland, Cumberland County, ME
Group Owner: Cumulus Media Inc.; (acq 7-7-99; grpsl).
Nat'l Reps: Christal
Population Served: 593,820 *Arbitron Metro Market:* Portland, ME *Target Audience:* 25-54; active, involved, fun-loving
Michael Sambrook, General Manager
Mike Marcello, General Sales Mgr

WGAN
08-03-1938; 560 khz AM
420 Western Ave, South Portland, ME 04106 US
(207) 774-4561, *Fax:* (207) 774-3788
www.560wgan.com
wgan@560wgan.com
License: Portland, ME held by Saga Communications of New England LLC.
Group Owner: Saga Communications Inc.; (acq 6-2-92; grpsl, including co-located FM).
Nat'l Network: CNN Radio
Arbitron Metro Market: Portland, ME *Format:* News, News/Talk, 86 *Hrs. of News Programming:* news progmg 20 hrs plus wkly
Cary Pahigian, President
Jeff Wade, Programming Director
Victoria Foley, Promotions Manager
Jeff Wade, News Director

WJBQ
06-01-1960; 97.9 mhz FM; 16 kw; 889 ft; N43 51 06 W70 19 40
One City Center, Portland, ME 01950
(207) 774-6364, *Fax:* (207) 774-8087
www.wjbq.com
wjbq@wjbq.com
License: Portland, Cumberland County, ME
Group Owner: Cumulus Media Inc.; (acq 7-7-99; grpsl).
Nat'l Reps: Christal
Population Served: 150,000 *Arbitron Metro Market:* Portland, ME *Target Audience:* 25-44; female listeners
Michael Sambrook, General Manager
Tim Moore, Programming Director

WLOB
02-02-1957; 1310 khz AM *Hrs Open:* 24; 5 kw-U, DA-2; N43 41 22 W70 20 06 *Rebroadcasts:* Simulcast with WLOB-FM Topsham 100%
779 Warren Ave., Portland, ME 02116
(207) 773-9695, *Fax:* (207) 761-4406
newstalkWLOB@yahoo.com
License: Portland, Cumberland County, ME held by Atlantic Coast Radio L.L.C.
Group Owner: Atlantic Coast Radio L.L.C.; (acq 9-8-00; grpsl).
Nat'l Network: Fox News Radio *Nat'l Reps:* McGavren Guild
Population Served: 250,000 *Arbitron Metro Market:* Portland, ME *Hrs. of News Programming:* News progmg 17 hrs wkly *Target Audience:* General.
J.J. Jeffrey, President
Richard Ringenback, Operations Dir
Jon Van Hoogenstyn, General Manager
Morgan Grumbach, General Sales Mgr
Devin Terwilleger, Chief Engineer

***WMEA**
04-01-1974; 90.1 mhz FM *Hrs Open:* 24; 24.5 kw; 1896 ft.; N43 51 30 W70 42 41 *Rebroadcasts:* Rebroadcasts WMEH(FM) Bangor 100%
Mailing Address: 1450 Lisbon Street, Lewiston, ME 04240 US
Second Address: 1450 Libson St., Lewiston, ME 4240
(800) 884-1717, *Fax:* (207) 942-2857
www.mpbn.net
cbeck@mpbn.net
License: Portland, Cumberland County, ME held by Maine Public Broadcasting Corp.
Nat'l Network: NPR; PRI
Arbitron Metro Market: Portland, ME *Format:* News, Triple A *Hrs. of News Programming:* news progmg 20 hrs wkly *No. News Employees:* 8 *Target Audience:* 25-64.
Alexander G. Maxwell Jr., COO
P. James Dowe, Jr., President
Alexander G. Maxwell, Jr., Operations Dir
Mary Mayo, General Sales Mgr
Charles Beck, Programming Director
Christopher Amann, CFO

WMGX
06-10-1977; 93.1 mhz FM; 50 kw; 443 ft.; N43 41 17 W70 15 27
420 Western Ave, South Portland, ME 04106 US
(207) 774-4561, *Fax:* (207) 774-3788
www.coast931.com
info@coast931.com
License: Portland, Cumberland County, ME
Group Owner: Saga Communications Inc.
Arbitron Metro Market: Portland, ME *Format:* Adult Contemp
Bruce Simel, General Manager
Colleen Jackson, Programming Director

WPOR
10-31-1967; 101.9 mhz FM *Hrs Open:* 24; 32 kw; 610 ft.; N43 45 33 W70 19 15
420 Western Ave, South Portland, ME 04106 US
(207) 774-4561, *Fax:* (207) 774-3788
www.wpor.com
wpor@wpor.com
License: Portland, Cumberland County, ME
Group Owner: Saga Communications Inc.
Arbitron Metro Market: Portland, ME *Format:* Country
Howard Tuuri, Operations Dir
Bernadette Osdal, General Sales Mgr
Gerry Brauer, Promotions Manager
Tom Paleveda, Operations Manager

WZAN
07-13-1925; 970 khz AM; 5 kw-D, DAN; 5 kw-N, DAN; N43 36 19 W70 19 18
420 Western Ave, South Portland, ME 04106 US
(207) 774-4561, *Fax:* (207) 774-3788
www.970wzan.com
feedback@970wzan.com
License: Portland, ME held by Saga Communications of New England LLC.
Group Owner: Saga Communications Inc.; (acq 6-23-93; $350,000 with WYNZ-FM Westbrook;
Nat'l Network: CBS; CNN Radio *Nat'l Reps:* Katz Radio
Arbitron Metro Market: Portland, ME *Format:* Talk *Target Audience:* 25-54 Males.
Cary Pahigian, President
Chris McGorrill, Operations Dir

Presque Isle

WBPW
09-01-1973; 96.9 mhz FM *Hrs Open:* 24; 100 kw; 440 ft; N46 45 52 W67 59 23
551 Main St., Presque Isle, ME 13203
(207) 769-6600, *Fax:* (207) 764-5274
www.bigcountry969.com
chris.obrien@townsquaremedia.com
License: Presque Isle, Aroostook County, ME
Group Owner: Cumulus Media Inc.; (acq 4-26-00; grpsl).
Nat'l Network: ABC *Nat'l Reps:* Katz Radio
Population Served: 9,641 *Arbitron Metro Market:* Presque Isle, ME *Special Programming:* NASCAR, American Country Countdown *Hrs. of News Programming:* news progmg 2 hrs wkly *No. News Employees:* 1 *TargetAudience:* 25-54. *Adv. Rates:* 34; 30; 34; 18
Lisa Miles, General Manager
Lisa Miles, Director of Sales
Chris O'Brien, Programming Director
Mark Shaw, News Director

WEGP
06-24-1960; 1390 khz AM *Hrs Open:* 24
3 State Street Place, Presque Isle, ME 04769 US
(207) 762-6700, *Fax:* (207) 762-3319
www.wegp.net
sandy@wegp.net
License: Presque Isle, ME held by Decelles/Smith Media Inc.
Nat'l Network: Fox News Radio; Premiere Radio Networks; Talk Radio Network; Westwood One
Arbitron Metro Market: Presque Isle, ME. *Format:* News, Talk *Target Audience:* Adults; mature listeners over age 29
Paul Decelles, President
Patrick Patterson, Operations Dir
Bonnie Pack, General Sales Mgr

***WMEM**
01-01-1975; 106.1 mhz FM; 100 kw; 1073 ft.; N46 33 6 W67 48 38 *Rebroadcasts:* Rebroadcasts WMEH(FM) Bangor 100%
Mailing Address: 1450 Lisbon Street, Lewiston, ME 04240 US
Second Address: 1450 Lisbon St., Lewiston, ME 4240
(207) 783-9101, *Fax:* (207) 942-2857
www.mpbn.net
cbeck@mpbn.net
License: Presque Isle, Aroostook County, ME held by Maine Public Broadcasting Corp.
Nat'l Network: NPR; PRI
Arbitron Metro Market: Presque Isle, ME *Format:* Jazz, News
Mark Vogelzang, CEO
Mary Mayo, General Sales Mgr
Charles Beck, Programming Director
Keith Shortall, News Director
Christopher Amann, CFO
Alexander G. Maxwell, Jr, COO

WOZI
02-02-1981; 101.9 mhz FM *Hrs Open:* 24; 7.9 kw; Ant 1,207 ft; N46 32 51 W67 48 35
551 Main St., Presque Isle, ME 13203
(207) 769-6600, *Fax:* (207) 764-5274
www.102therock.com
wozi.radio@citcomm.com
License: Presque Isle, Aroostook County, ME
Group Owner: Cumulus Media Inc.; (acq 4-26-01; grpsl).
Nat'l Network: Westwood One *Nat'l Reps:* Katz Radio
Population Served: 150,000*Hrs. of News Programming:* news progmg one hr wkly *No. News Employees:* 1 *Target Audience:* 25-54. *Adv. Rates:* 15; 12; 13; 6
Lisa Miles, General Manager
Chris O' Brien, Programming Director

WQHR
01-01-1981; 96.1 mhz FM *Hrs Open:* 24; 95 kw; 1,309 ft; N46 32 55 W67 48 35
551 Main St., Presque Isle, ME 13203
(207) 769-6600, *Fax:* (207) 764-5274
www.HitMusicQ96.com
wqhr.radio@citcomm.com
License: Presque Isle, Aroostook County, ME
Group Owner: Cumulus Media Inc.; (acq 4-26-01; grpsl).
Nat'l Network: ABC *Nat'l Reps:* Katz Radio
Population Served: 250,000*Hrs. of News Programming:* news progmg 2 hrs wkly *No. News Employees:* 1 *Target Audience:* 18-49. *Adv. Rates:* 34; 30; 34; 18
Lisa Miles, General Manager
Mark Shaw, Programming Director

***WUPI**
07-26-1973; 92.1 mhz FM *Hrs Open:* 24; 0.017 kw horiz; -39 ft.; N46 40 15 W68 1 0
107 Main Street, Bangor, ME 04401 US
(207) 768-9741, *Fax:* (207) 768-9742
www.umpi.maine.edu
meg@wupifm.com
License: Presque Isle, Aroostook County, ME held by University of Maine Trustees.
Arbitron Metro Market: Presque Isle, ME *Format:* Variety/Diverse *Hrs. of News Programming:* news progmg 5 hrs wkly *No. News Employees:* 2 *Target Audience:* 16-35.
Dr. Don Zillman, President
Marjorie McNamara, General Manager
Larry French, Station Manager
Laura Mooney, General Sales Mgr
Meg Medlinskas, Programming Director
Jeffery Carmicheal, Engineering Dir

Rockland

WMCM
04-16-1968; 103.3 mhz FM *Hrs Open:* 24; 16 kw; 771 ft.; N44 7 35 W69 8 18
15 Payne Ave., Rt #1 South, Rockland, ME 04841 US
(207) 623-9000, *Fax:* (207) 623-9007
License: Rockland, Knox County, ME held by Blueberry Broadcasting LLC.
Arbitron Metro Market: Rockland, ME *Format:* Country *No. News Employees:* 1 *Target Audience:* General. *Adv. Rates:* 30; 25; 25; 15
Sharon Griffith, News Director
Matt Thompson, Local News Editor
Don Shields, Political Ed

WRKD
10-01-1952; 1450 khz AM *Hrs Open:* 24; 1 kw-U, ND1; N44 7 34 W69 8 19
15 Payne Ave., Rt #1 South, Rockland, ME 04841 US
(207) 623-9000, *Fax:* (207) 623-9007
www.foxsportsmaine.com
License: Rockland, ME held by Blueberry Broadcasting LLC.
Group Owner: Blueberry Broadcasting LLC; (acq 7-29-2008; grpsl)
Nat'l Network: Westwood One *Nat'l Reps:* CYR Associates
Format: Sports *Hrs. of News Programming:* news progmg 11 hrs wkly *No. News Employees:* 1 *Target Audience:* 35 plus. *Adv. Rates:* 30; 25; 25; 15
Kelly Slater, General Manager
Rick Dugal, General Sales Mgr
Don Shields, Programming Director

Rumford

WTME
08-21-1953; 780 khz AM *Rebroadcasts:* Simulcast with WKTQ(AM) South Paris 100%
20 Park Plaza, Suite 720, Boston, MA 02116 US
(207) 743-5911, *Fax:* (207) 743-5913
www.wtme.com
info@woxo.com
License: Rumford, ME held by Mountain Valley Broadcasting Inc.
Group Owner: Gleason Radio Group; (acq 11-2-2000; $50,000)
Nat'l Network: USA; USA *Nat'l Reps:* CYR Associates
Format: Talk *Hrs. of News Programming:* Top of each hour *No. News Employees:* 1 *Target Audience:* General. *Adv. Rates:* 10; 10; 10; 10
Richard Gleason, President
Jeremy Rush, Operations Dir

Saco

WPEI
07-18-1982; 95.9 mhz FM *Hrs Open:* 24; 4.1 kw; 397 ft.; N43 32 33 W70 24 17
583 Warren Avenue, Portland, ME 04103 US
(207) 773-9695, *Fax:* (207) 761-4406
www.weei.com
License: Saco, York County, ME held by Atlantic Coast Radio L.L.C.
Group Owner: Atlantic Coast Radio L.L.C.; acq 7-12-99; $1.15 million)
Nat'l Network: Westwood One *Nat'l Reps:* McGavren Guild *Wire Services:* AP
Arbitron Metro Market: Portland, ME *Format:* Sports *Target Audience:* 18-34. *Adv. Rates:* 50; 45; 45; 45

Lisa Menconi, CFO
J.J. Jeffrey, President
Buzz Bradley, Operations Dir
Jon Van Hoogenstyn, General Manager
Morgan Grumbach, General Sales Mgr
Linda Petrin, News Director
Gene Terwilliger, Chief Engineer

Sanford

WXEX-FM

10-10-1975; 92.1 mhz FM *Hrs Open:* 24; 1.2 kw; 525 ft; N43 35 24 W70 22 20
One Washington St., Dover, NH 20036
(603) 749-5900, *Fax:* (603) 749-0088
www.fnxradio.com
info@fnxradio.com
License: Sanford, York County, ME held by FNX Broadcasting LLC.
Group Owner: Phoenix Media Communications Group
Nat'l Reps: McGavren Guild
Arbitron Metro Market: Portsmouth-Dover-Rochester, NH *Special Programming:* Jazz 6 hrs, talk 2 hrs wkly *No. News Employees:* 1 *Target Audience:* General.
Gary Kurtz, General Manager
Keith Dakin, Programming Director
Michael Snow, Promotions Manager
Chris Hall, Chief Engineer

*WSEW

03-02-1992; 88.7 mhz FM; 10 kw; 564 ft.; N43 25 5 W70 48 4
P.O. Box 6336, East Rochester, NH 03868 US
(603) 859-9170, *Fax:* (603) 859-8172
www.wsew.org
wsew@wsew.org
License: Sanford, York County, ME held by Word-Radio Educational Foundation.
Nat'l Network: Moody
Format: Religious
Sharon Malone, Operations Dir
Ronald Malone, General Manager

WWSF

11-09-1957; 1220 khz AM *Hrs Open:* 24; 1 kw-D, 234 w-N; N43 25 53 W70 45 44
One Washington St., Dover, NH 20036
(603) 749-5900, *Fax:* (603) 749-0088
fnxradio.com
info@fnxradio.com
License: Sanford, York County, ME held by FNX Broadcasting LLC.
Group Owner: Phoenix Media Communications Group; (acq 5-17-99; $1.025 million with co-located FM).
Population Served: 20,000
Sam Pseifle, General Manager

Scarborough

WHXR

01-01-1960; 106.3 mhz FM; 3 kw; Ant 299 ft; N43 35 24 W70 22 20
477 Congress St., Suite 3 A, 3rd Fl. Annex, Portland, ME 04043
(207) 797-0780, *Fax:* (207) 797-0368
www.boneradio.com
info@boneradio.com
License: Scarborough, Cumberland County, ME held by Nassau Broadcasting III L.L.C.
Group Owner: Nassau Broadcasting Partners L.P.; (acq 4-6-2004; grpsl)
Population Served: 200,000 *Arbitron Metro Market:* Portland, ME
Pat Collins, Operations Dir
Stan Manning, Operations Director

Searsport

*WKVV

10-10-1994; 101.7 mhz FM *Hrs Open:* 6 AM-midnight; 2.65 kw; 1004 ft.; N44 34 51 W68 53 47
263 State St., Bangor, ME 04401 US
(916) 251-1600, *Fax:* (916) 251-1650
www.klove.com
License: Searsport, Waldo County, ME held by Educational Media Foundation.
Group Owner: EMF Broadcasting; (acq 4-6-2009; $550,000 with WGUY(FM) Dexter)
Nat'l Network: K-Love
Format: Christian
Mike Novak, President

Skowhegan

WFMX

09-01-1989; 107.9 mhz FM; 22 kw; 387 ft.; N44 37 1 W69 37 31
P.O. Box 274, No. Marshfield, MA 02059 US
(207) 474-5171, *Fax:* (207) 474-3299
www.mixmaine.com
maine.radio@verizon.net
License: Skowhegan, Somerset County, ME held by Mountain Wireless Inc.
Group Owner: Mountain Wireless Inc.; (acq 11-20-97; $222,355)
Arbitron Metro Market: Augusta-Waterville, ME *Format:* Adult Contemp *Target Audience:* 25-54; baby boomers who grew up with Top-40 radio
Jay Hanson, General Manager

WSKW

01-01-1956; 1160 khz AM; 10 kw-D, ND1; 0.73 kw-N, ND1; N44 44 43 W69 41 36; N44 44 42 W69 41 32
Mailing Address: P.O. Box 159, Skowhegan, ME 04976 US
Second Address: 208 Middle Rd., Skowhegan, ME 4976
(207) 474-5171, *Fax:* (207) 474-3299
maine.radio@verizon.net
License: Skowhegan, ME held by Mountain Wireless Inc.
Group Owner: Mountain Wireless Inc.; (acq 1999; $1.6 million with WCTB(FM) Fairfield)
Nat'l Network: ESPN Radio
Arbitron Metro Market: Augusta-Watervi *Format:* Country *Target Audience:* 12 plus; loc sports fans
Jay Hanson, General Manager

WTOS-FM

11-13-1969; 105.1 mhz FM *Hrs Open:* 24; 57 kw; 2451 ft.; N45 1 54 W70 18 50
330 East Kilbourn Ave., Suite 250, Milwaukee, WI 53202 US
(207) 623-9000, *Fax:* (207) 623-9007
www.wtosfm.com
reverend@clearchannel.com
License: Skowhegan, Somerset County, ME held by Blueberry Broadcasting LLC.
Group Owner: Blueberry Broadcasting LLC; (acq 7-29-2008; grpsl)
Arbitron Metro Market: Augusta, ME *Format:* Rock/AOR *Hrs. of News Programming:* news progmg 3 hrs wkly *No. News Employees:* 1 *Target Audience:* 18-49.
Kelly Slater, General Manager
Steve Smith, Programming Director

South Paris

WKTQ

10-28-1955; 1450 khz AM *Hrs Open:* 24; 1 kw-U, ND1; N44 13 16 W70 31 43 *Rebroadcasts:* Simulcast with WTME(AM) Rumford 100%
P.O. Box 72, Norway, ME 04268 US
(207) 743-5911, *Fax:* (207) 743-5913
www.wtme.com
dick@gleasonmedia.com,info@woxo.com
License: South Paris, ME held by Mountain Valley Broadcasting Inc.
Group Owner: Gleason Radio Group; (acq 7-27-76).
Nat'l Network: USA; USA *Nat'l Reps:* CYR Associates
Format: Talk *Hrs. of News Programming:* Top of each hour *No. News Employees:* 1 *Target Audience:* General. *Adv. Rates:* 20; 20; 20; 20
Richard Gleason, President
Jeremy Rush, Operations Dir
Victor Hodgkins, Station Manager

South Portland

WYNZ

02-01-1976; 100.9 mhz FM; 25 kw; Ant 305 ft; N43 41 26 W70 19 05
420 Western Ave., South Portland, ME 04106
(207) 774-4561, *Fax:* (207) 774-3788
www.y1009.com
bighits@y1009.com
License: South Portland, Cumberland County, ME held by Saga Communications of New England LLC.
Group Owner: Saga Communications Inc.; (acq 6-23-93; $350,000 with WYNZ(AM) Portland;
Nat'l Network: CNN Radio *Nat'l Reps:* Katz Radio
Arbitron Metro Market: Portland, ME *Target Audience:* 25-54.
Cary Pahigian, President
Chris McGorrill, Operations Dir
Tina Segerstrom, General Sales Mgr
Randi Kirshbaun, Programming Director
Jeffrey Wade, News Director
Andy Armstrong, Engineering Dir
Tina Seuerstrom, General SalesManager

Thomaston

WBQX

05-29-1992; 106.9 mhz FM *Hrs Open:* 24; 29.5 kw; 633 ft.; N44 6 30 W69 9 28 *Rebroadcasts:* Rebroadcasts WBQQ(FM) Kennebunk 100%
169 Port Road, Kennebunk, ME 04043 US
(207) 594-9283, *Fax:* (207) 594-1620
www.wbachradio.com
pcollins@nassaubroadcasting.com
License: Thomaston, Knox County, ME held by Nassau Broadcasting III L.L.C.
Group Owner: Nassau Broadcasting Partners L.P.; (acq 4-6-2004; grpsl).
Regional Reps: Kettell-Carter.
Arbitron Metro Market: Rockland, ME *Format:* Talk *Special Programming:* Jazz 2 hrs, children one hr wkly *Hrs. of News Programming:* News progmg 4 hrs wkly *Target Audience:* 35 plus; affluent, upscale adults
Louis Mercatanti, CEO
Pat Collins, Operations Dir
Scott Hooper, Programming Director

Topsham

WPPI

01-01-1993; 95.5 mhz FM *Hrs Open:* 24; 6 kw; Ant 456 ft; N43 54 12 W70 02 13 *Rebroadcasts:* Simulcasts with WEEI(AM) Boston, MA
779 Warren Ave., Portland, ME 04011
(207) 773-9695, *Fax:* (207) 761-4406
License: Topsham, Sagadahoc County, ME held by Atlantic Coast Radio L.L.C.
Group Owner: Atlantic Coast Radio L.L.C.; (acq 9-30-99)
Nat'l Network: ESPN *Nat'l Reps:* McGavren Guild
Population Served: 700,000*Target Audience:* 25-49; middle class, active lifestyle with discretionary income *Adv. Rates:* 125; 70; 60; 20
J.J. Jeffrey, President
David Schumacher, Operations Dir
Jon Van Hoogenstyn, General Manager
Morgan Grumbach, General Sales Mgr
Devon Terwilliger, Chief Engineer

Van Buren

WCXV

98.1 mhz FM; 6 kw; 3 ft.; N47 10 4 W67 57 43 *Rebroadcasts:* Rebroadcasts WCXU (FM) Caribou 100%
Rural Route 2, Box 2100, Caribou, ME 04736 US
(207) 473-7513, *Fax:* (207) 472-3221
www.channelxradio.com
channelxradio@yahoo.com
License: Van Buren, Aroostook County, ME held by Canxus Broadcasting Corp.
Group Owner: Canxus Broadcasting Corp.
Arbitron Metro Market: Van Buren, ME *Format:* Adult Contemp, News, 64
Dennis Curley, President
Richard Chandler, Vice President
Douglas Christensen, News Director
Phillip Shaw Neal, Music Director / Production Directo
Pamela Curley, Traffic Director
Cheryl LaFrance, Continuity Director
StaceySkinner, Advertising Sales Representatives
Greg Beidelman, Advertising Sales Representatives

Veazie

WNZS

08-01-2002; 1340 khz AM *Hrs Open:* 24
Mailing Address: US
Second Address: 379 Riverside Dr, Eddington, ME 4428
(207) 947-9697, *Fax:* (207) 989-5251
License: Veazie, ME held by Waterfront Communications Inc.
Nat'l Network: Salem Radio Network; Talk Radio Network; ABC Information & Entertainment *Nat'l Reps:* Commercial Media Sales *Regional Reps:* Cyr Association
Arbitron Metro Market: Bangor, ME *Format:* News, News/Talk, 86 *Hrs. of News Programming:* news progmg 15 hrs wkly *No. News Employees:* 2 *Target Audience:* 25-54; 35-64; adults in metro Banger area *Adv. Rates:* 10; 7; 8; 5.
Jocelynn Priestley, Station Manager

WWNZ

08-01-2004; 1400 khz AM *Hrs Open:* 24; 1 kw-D, 810 w-N; N44 50 50 W68 40 48
Mailing Address: Box 8526, Bangor, ME
Second Address: 379 Riverside Dr., Eddington, ME 4428
(207) 947-9697, *Fax:* (207) 989-5251
wnzproduction@aol.com

License: Veazie, Penobscot County, ME held by Waterfront Communications Inc.
Nat'l Network: USA; Fox News Radio; Wall Street *Nat'l Reps:* Commercial Media Sales *Regional Reps:* Cyr Associates
Population Served: 150,000 *Arbitron Metro Market:* Bangor, ME *Target Audience:* 25-54; 35-64; Banger metro area adults 25 plus *Adv. Rates:* 10; 7; 8; 5
Daniel Priestley, President
Jocelynn Priestley, Station Manager

Waterville

WEBB
03-26-1968; 98.5 mhz FM *Hrs Open:* 24; 61 kw; 305 ft; N44 33 52 W69 36 39
Mailing Address: 56 Western Avenue, Suite 13, Augusta, ME 13203
Second Address: 56 Western Ave. Suite 13, Augusta, ME 4330
(207) 623-4735, *Fax:* (207) 626-5948
www.b985.fm
Al.Perry@townsquaremedia.com
License: Waterville, Kennebec County, ME
Group Owner: Cumulus Media Inc.
Population Served: 15,697 *Arbitron Metro Market:* Waterville, ME *No. News Employees:* 1
Dean O'Neal, Operations Dir
Al Perry, General Manager
Julie Beaulieu, Director of Sales

***WMEW**
11-01-1983; 91.3 mhz FM *Hrs Open:* 24; 3 kw; 299 ft.; N44 29 23 W69 39 5 *Rebroadcasts:* Rebroadcasts WMEH(FM) Bangor 100%
Mailing Address: 1450 Lisbon Street, Lewiston, ME 04240 US
Second Address: 1450 Lisbon St., Lewiston, ME 4240
(207) 783-9101, *Fax:* (207) 942-2857
www.mpbn.net
cbeck@mpbn.net
License: Waterville, Kennebec County, ME held by Maine Public Broadcasting Corp.
Nat'l Network: NPR; PRI
Arbitron Metro Market: Waterville, ME *Format:* Jazz, News *Hrs. of News Programming:* news progmg 20 hrs wkly *No. News Employees:* 8 *Target Audience:* 25-64.
Mark Vogelzang, CEO
Mary Mayo, General Sales Mgr
Charles Beck, Programming Director
Keith Shortall, News Director
Christopher Amann, CFO
Alexander G. Maxwell, Jr, COO

***WMHB**
10-01-1974; 89.7 mhz FM *Hrs Open:* 6 AM-12 AM; 0.11 kw vert; 105 ft.; N44 33 57 W69 39 49
Mayflower Hill Drive, Colby College, Waterville, ME 04901 US
(207) 859-5454
www.wmhb.org
info@wmhb.org
License: Waterville, Kennebec County, ME held by Mayflower Hill Broadcasting Corp.
Arbitron Metro Market: Augusta, ME *Format:* Variety/Diverse
Special Programming: Indie, Folk, Hip-hop, Jazz, World, Rock, Loud Rock *Hrs. of News Programming:* News progmg 2.5 hrs wkly *Target Audience:* 5-100; wecater to everyone
Benjy Ogden, President
Dan Echt, Operations Dir
Kathleen Fallon, General Manager
Kelly Wharton, General Sales Mgr
Luke Bowe, Programming Director
Jeffrey Oakes, Programming Director

WTVL
06-19-1946; 1490 khz AM; 1 kw-U, ND1; N44 33 52 W69 36 39
Mailing Address: 1064 James Street, Syracuse, NY 13203 US
Second Address: 52 Western Ave., Augusta, ME 4330
(207) 623-4735, *Fax:* (207) 626-5948
www.1400and1490.com
mac.dickson@townsquaremedia.com
License: Waterville, ME
Group Owner: Cumulus Media Inc.; (acq 4-26-2001; grpsl).
Arbitron Metro Market: Augusta, ME *Format:* Oldies *Target Audience:* 25-54.
Farid Suleman, CEO
Julie Beaulieu, General Manager
Al Perry, General Sales Mgr
Mac Dickson, Programming Director
Renee Nelson, News Director
Bob Perry, Chief Engineer
Al Perry, Regional Sales Manager

Westbrook

WRED
11-08-1959; 1440 khz AM; 5 kw-D, DAN; 5 kw-N, DAN; N43 40 50 W70 22 47
583 Warren Avenue, Portland, ME 04103 US
(207) 773-9695, *Fax:* (207) 761-4406
www.thebigjab.com
shoe@thebigjab.com
License: Westbrook, ME held by Atlantic Coast Radio L.L.C.
Group Owner: Atlantic Coast Radio L.L.C.; (acq 9-99)
Nat'l Network: Sporting News Radio Network *Nat'l Reps:* McGavren Guild
Arbitron Metro Market: Portland, ME *Format:* Sports, Talk *Target Audience:* General; male
Dave Schumacher, Operations Dir
Jon Van Hoogenstyn, General Manager

***WRKJ**
88.5 mhz FM; 2 kw; 354 ft.; N43 41 10 W70 30 30 US
(207) 591-4651
www.885wrkj.org
ron.wrkj@gmail.com
License: Westbrook, Cumberland County, ME held by Calvary Chapel of Portland.
Arbitron Metro Market: Westbrook, ME
Vincent Magowan, CEO

Winslow

***WWWA**
04-23-1999; 95.3 mhz FM *Hrs Open:* 24; 12 kw; 673 ft.; N44 42 48 W69 43 39
P.O. Box 332, Litchfield, ME 04330 US
(207) 622-1340, *Fax:* (207) 623-2874
www.worshipradionetwork.org
denise@worshipradionetwork.org
License: Winslow, Kennebec County, ME held by Light of Life Ministries Inc.
Arbitron Metro Market: Winslow, ME *Format:* Christian
Denise LaFountain, Station Manager
Brad Taylor, Programming Director

Winter Harbor

WNSX
01-01-1999; 97.7 mhz FM; 50 kw; 489 ft.; N44 33 13 W68 5 40
53 Main St. Suite 202, Bar Harbor, ME 04609 US
(207) 667-0002, *Fax:* (207) 667-0627
www.wnsxradio.com
billd@wnsx.net
License: Winter Harbor, Hancock County, ME held by Stony Creek Broadcasting LLC
Wire Services: AP
Arbitron Metro Market: Hancock County, ME *Format:* Classic Rock *Hrs. of News Programming:* News progmg 4 hrs. wkly *No. News Employees:* 1 *Target Audience:* Adults; 25+
Bill Da Butler, Operations Dir
Mark Osborne, General Manager
Irene Hafford, General Sales Mgr
Bill Ducharme, Chief Engineer
Natalie Knox, Sales

Yarmouth

***WYAR**
11-16-1998; 88.3 mhz FM *Hrs Open:* 24; 1 kw horiz; 79 ft.; N43 45 56 W70 8 27
219 Cousins Street, Yarmouth, ME 04096 US
(207) 847-3169
www.wyar.org
wyar@maine.rr.com
License: Yarmouth, Cumberland County, ME held by Heritage Radio Society Inc.
Arbitron Metro Market: Yarmouth, ME *Format:* Big Band, Oldies
Target Audience: General; senior citizens & young people
Gary King Sr., CEO
James Brown, Operations Dir

York Center

WSKX
06-01-1987; 95.3 mhz FM *Hrs Open:* 24; 1.45 kw; 676 ft.; N43 13 25 W70 41 37
600 Congress Avenue, Suite 1400, Austin, TX 78701 US
(603) 436-7300, *Fax:* (603) 430-9415
www.wubbfm.com
ianhorne@clearchannel.com
License: York Center, York County, ME held by Capstar TX L.P.
Group Owner: Clear Channel Communications Inc.; (acq 8-30-2000; grpsl)
Nat'l Reps: Katz Radio
Arbitron Metro Market: Portsmouth, NH *Format:* Contemporary Hits/Top 40 *Hrs. of News Programming:* news progmg 7 hrs wkly *No. News Employees:* 1 *Target Audience:* 18-34. 60% females
Jeff Pierce, Programming Director
Elizabeth Tretter, Promotions Manager

Maryland

Aberdeen

WAMD
05-01-1957; 970 khz AM *Hrs Open:* 24
P.O. Box 970, Aberdeen, MD 21001 US
(410) 306-6270, *Fax:* (410) 575-6890
www.khztv.com
HitMe@khztv.com
License: Aberdeen, MD held by First Broadcasting Investment Partners LLC
Group Owner: First Broadcasting Operating Inc.; (acq 6-13-2005; grpsl)
Nat'l Network: ABC
Arbitron Metro Market: Aberdeen, MD *Format:* Oldies *Hrs. of News Programming:* News progmg 24 hrs wkly *Target Audience:* 35+; primarily female
John Meadows, Operations Dir
Heather Frye, General Manager
Carol Powel, News Director

Annapolis

WLZL
05-16-1960; 107.9 mhz FM *Hrs Open:* 24; 50 kw; Ant 500 ft; N38 59 45 W76 39 27
918 Chesapeake Ave., Annapolis, MD 95834
(410) 268-6200, *Fax:* (410) 268-0931
www.familyradio.com
License: Annapolis, Anne Arundel County, MD held by Family Stations Inc.
Group Owner: Family Stations Inc.; (acq 1-7-72)
Nat'l Network: Family Radio
Harold Camping, General Manager

WNAV
01-01-1949; 1430 khz AM; 5 kw-D, DAN; 1 kw-N, DAN; N38 59 0 W76 31 21
236 Admiral Drive, Annapolis, MD 21401 US
(410) 263-1430, *Fax:* (410) 268-5360
www.1430wnav.com
stevehopp@wnav.com
License: Annapolis, MD held by Sajak Broadcasting Corp.
Nat'l Network: CBS Radio; Westwood One
Arbitron Metro Market: Baltimore, MD *Format:* Adult Contemp
Special Programming: Baltimore Orioles baseball, Naval Academy sports *No. News Employees:* 2 *Target Audience:* 35 plus.
Patrick Sajak, President
Steve Hopp, General Manager
Dan O'Neil, General Sales Mgr
Bill Lusby, Programming Director
Barbara Cox, News Director

WYRE
01-01-1946; 810 khz AM *Hrs Open:* Sunrise-Sunset; 0.25 kw-D, NDD; N38 58 13 W76 30 28
112 Main Street, 3rd Floor, Annapolis, MD 21401 US
301-879-2422, *Fax:* 301-879-2562
License: Annapolis, MD held by Bay Broadcasting Corp.
Arbitron Metro Market: Baltimore, MD
Richard Dent, President
Raul Lopez Bastidas, General Manager

Baltimore

WBAL
11-02-1925; 1090 khz AM *Hrs Open:* 24; 50 kw-U, DA-N; N39 22 33 W76 46 21
3800 Hooper Ave., Baltimore, MD 10019
(410) 467-3000, *Fax:* (410) 338-6675
www.wbal.com
news@wbal.com
License: Baltimore, Baltimore County, MD held by WBAL Div., The Hearst Corp.
Nat'l Network: CBS Radio *Nat'l Reps:* Eastman
Population Served: 2,100,000 *Arbitron Metro Market:* Baltimore, MD *Target Audience:* 25-54.
Edward Kiernan, General Manager
Bob Cecil, General Sales Mgr
Dave Hill, Programming Director
Lori Smyth, Promotions Manager

Merrie Street, News Director
Kerry Plackmeyer, Chief Engineer
Steve Hartman, National Sales Manager
Dave Koenig, Traffic Manager
John Brunnett, Business Manager

WFSI
07-27-1955; 860 khz AM; 2.5 kw-D, 66 w-N, DA-2; N39 18 43 W76 29 26
600 Washington Ave., Towson, MD 20037
(410) 825-7700
www.familyradio.com
info@familyradio.com
License: Baltimore, Baltimore County, MD held by Family Stations Inc.
Group Owner: Family Stations Inc.; (acq 3-2-2005; $7.5 million with WBMD(AM) Baltimore)
Population Served: 905,759 *Arbitron Metro Market:* Baltimore, MD *Target Audience:* 18-49.
Harold Camping, General Manager
Bill Sadlier, General Sales Mgr

***WBJC**
04-06-1951; 91.5 mhz FM; 50 kw; 499 ft.; N39 23 11 W76 43 52
2901 Liberty Heights Ave, Baltimore, MD 21215 US
(410) 580-5800, *Fax:* (410) 580-5858
www.wbjc.com
wbjcinformation@wbjc.com
License: Baltimore, Baltimore County, MD held by Baltimore City Community College
Nat'l Network: PRI
Arbitron Metro Market: Baltimore, MD *Format:* Classical
Kati Harrison, Operations Dir
Joseph M. Hutchins, General Manager
Jim Ward, General Sales Mgr
Jonathan Palevsky, Programming Director

WBMD
12-07-1947; 750 khz AM *Hrs Open:* Sunrise-sunset; 0.73 kw-D, NDD; N39 19 26 W76 32 56
600 New Hampshire Avenue, NW, Suite 1200, Washington, DC 20037 US
1(800)543-1495, *Fax:* (410) 268-0931
www.familyradio.com
familyradio@familyradio.org
License: Baltimore, MD held by Family Stations Inc.
Group Owner: Family Stations Inc.; (acq 3-2-2005; $7.5 million with WBGR(AM) Baltimore)
Arbitron Metro Market: Oakland, CA *Format:* Religious *Target Audience:* 12 plus.
Harold Camping, General Manager
Bill Sadlier, General Sales Mgr

WCAO
05-08-1922; 600 khz AM; 5 kw-U, DA1; N39 25 47 W76 45 42
50 East Rivercenter Boulevard, Suite 1200, Covington, KY 41011 US
(410) 366-7600, *Fax:* (410) 467-0011
www.heaven600.com
baltimorepsa@clearchannel.com
License: Baltimore, MD held by Citicasters Licenses L.P.
Group Owner: Clear Channel Communications Inc.; (acq 5-99; grpsl).
Arbitron Metro Market: Baltimore, MD *Format:* Black, Gospel
Kevin Friedman, General Manager
Bill Hopkinson, General Sales Mgr
Lee Michaels, Programming Director
Donna Jean, Promotions Manager

WCBM
01-01-1924; 680 khz AM *Hrs Open:* 24
1205 York Rd-Penthouse, Lutherville, MD 21093 US
(410) 580-6800, *Fax:* (410) 580-6810
www.wcbm.com
bpettit@wcbm.com
License: Baltimore, MD held by M-10 Broadcasting
Nat'l Network: CBS
Arbitron Metro Market: Baltimore, MD *Format:* Talk *Hrs. of News Programming:* news progmg 11 hrs wkly *No. News Employees:* 3 *Target Audience:* 25-54; informed adults with major purchasing power
Nick Mangione Jr., Operations Dir
Bob Pettit, General Manager
Marc Beavin, General Sales Mgr
Sean Casey, Programming Director
Eddie Applefeld, Promotions Manager

***WEAA**
01-10-1977; 88.9 mhz FM *Hrs Open:* 24; 12.5 kw; 220 ft.; N39 20 31 W76 35 13
Hillen Road & Coldspring, Baltimore, MD 21239 US
(443) 885-3564, *Fax:* (443) 885-8206
www.weaa.org
weaa@moac.morgan.edu
License: Baltimore, Baltimore County, MD held by Morgan State University.
Nat'l Network: NPR *Wire Services:* AP
Arbitron Metro Market: Baltimore, MD *Format:* Jazz, News, 62, Talk *Special Programming:* Urban oldies 5 hrs, Caribbean 7 hrs, Africian world 4 hrs, gospel 13 hrs, hip hop 5 hrs wkly *Hrs. of News Programming:* newsprogmg 10 hrs wkly *No. News Employees:* 1 *Target Audience:* 25-54 *Adv. Rates:* 65; 65; 65; 55
LaFontaine Oliver, General Manager
Sandi Mallony, Programming Director

WERQ-FM
01-01-1960; 92.3 mhz FM *Hrs Open:* 24; 37 kw; 571 ft.; N39 20 20 W76 40 2
5900 Princess Grdn Pkwy, 7th Floor, Lanham, MD 20706 US
(410) 332-8200, *Fax:* (410) 944-7182
www.92q.com
hmazer@radio-one.com
License: Baltimore, Baltimore County, MD held by Radio One Licenses LLC
Group Owner: Radio One Inc.; (acq 6-21-93; $9 million with co-located AM;
Arbitron Metro Market: Baltimore, MD *Format:* Urban Contemporary *Target Audience:* 18-34; young adults
Alfred Liggins, CEO
Howard Mazer, General Manager
Dave Willner, Sales Manager
Al Payne, Programming Director
David McCallister, Promotions Manager
Karl Goehring, Chief Engineer
Ki Ki Brown, Assistant Promotions Director
NamonJones, Regional Digital Sales Manager
Glenn Lipman, Business Manager
Ajaya "AJ" Smith, Imaging Director
LeVardis "Black" McLaughin, Production Director
Earlene Korchi, Traffic Director

WRBS
03-01-1941; 1230 khz AM *Hrs Open:* 24; 1 kw-U; N39 18 58 W76 36 03
3500 Commerce Dr., Baltimore, MD 93012
(410) 247-4100, *Fax:* (410) 247-4533
www.wrbsam.com
info@wrbs.com
License: Baltimore, Baltimore County, MD held by WRBS-AM LLC
Population Served: 8,000,000 *Arbitron Metro Market:* Baltimore, MD
Joe Norris, Operations Dir

WIYY
12-07-1958; 97.9 mhz FM; 13.5 kw; 945 ft.; N39 20 5 W76 39 3
3800 Hooper Avenue, Baltimore, MD 21211 US
(410) 467-3000, *Fax:* (410) 338-6483
www.classic98rock.com
classic98rock@hearst.com
License: Baltimore, Baltimore County, MD
Arbitron Metro Market: Baltimore, MD *Format:* Rock/AOR *Target Audience:* 18-49.
Hugues Jean, General Sales Mgr
Dave Hill, Programming Director
Lori Smyth, Promotions Manager
Steve Hartman, Regional Sales Manager

WJZ
06-08-1922; 1300 khz AM *Hrs Open:* 24; 5 kw-D, DA2; 5 kw-N, DA2; N39 20 0 W76 46 13 *Rebroadcasts:* Rebroadcasts WJFK-FM Manassas, VA 77%
600 New Hampshire Ave, Suite 1200, Washington, DC 20037 US
(410) 825-1000, *Fax:* (410) 821-5482
www.espn1300.com
www.baltimore.cbslocal.com/category/sports
License: Baltimore, MD held by CBS Radio WLIF-AM Inc.
Group Owner: CBS Radio; (acq 5-29-89; $32 million with co-located FM;
Nat'l Network: ESPN Radio *Nat'l Reps:* CBS Radio
Arbitron Metro Market: Baltimore, MD *Format:* Sports, Talk *Target Audience:* 18-49; men
Dan Mason, President
Bob Philips, Operations Dir

***WYPR**
05-23-1979; 88.1 mhz FM; 15.5 kw; 425 ft.; N39 19 53 W76 39 28
2216 N. Charles Street, Baltimore, MD 21218 US
(410) 235-1660, *Fax:* (410) 235-1161
www.wypr.org
tbrandon@wypr.org
License: Baltimore, Baltimore County, MD held by WYPR License Holding LLC
Nat'l Network: NPR; PRI
Arbitron Metro Market: Baltimore, MD *Format:* Jazz, News, 62, Talk
Anthony Brandon, President
Andy Bienstock, Programming Director

WLIF
12-24-1970; 101.9 mhz FM; 13.5 kw; 961 ft.; N39 25 2 W76 33 23
600 New Hampshire, N.W., Suite 1200, Washington, DC 20037 US
(410) 825-1000, *Fax:* (410) 296-9543
www.1019litefm.com
info@1019litefm.com
License: Baltimore, Baltimore County, MD held by CBS Radio WLIF-AM Inc.
Group Owner: CBS Radio
Arbitron Metro Market: Baltimore, MD *Format:* Adult Contemp
Special Programming: Jazz 8 hrs wkly
Sharon Johnson, President

WZFT
01-01-1949; 104.3 mhz FM; 13 kw; Ant 964 ft; N39 20 10 W76 38 59
711 W. 40th St., Suite 350, Baltimore, MD 41011
(410) 366-7600, *Fax:* (410) 467-0011
www.channel1043.com
License: Baltimore, Baltimore County, MD held by Citicasters Licenses L.P.
Group Owner: Clear Channel Communications Inc.; (acq 5-4-99; grpsl)
Nat'l Reps: Katz Radio
Population Served: 1,300,000 *Arbitron Metro Market:* Baltimore, MD *Target Audience:* 25-44.
Kevin Friedman, General Manager

WOLB
11-25-1947; 1010 khz AM
5900 Princess Garden Pky, 7th Floor, Lanham, MD 2O706 US
(410) 332-8200, *Fax:* 410-547-8783
www.wolb1010.com
License: Baltimore, MD held by Radio One Licenses LLC
Group Owner: Radio One Inc.
Nat'l Reps: Katz Radio
Arbitron Metro Market: Baltimore, MD *TV Affiliate:* Talk *Format:* Religious *Special Programming:* News progmg 5 hrs wkly *No. News Employees:* 35 plus; African American

WPOC
01-01-1959; 93.1 mhz FM; 16 kw; 866 ft.; N39 17 13 W76 45 16
50 East Rivercenter Boulevard, Suite 1200, Covington, KY 41011 US
(410) 366-7600, *Fax:* (410) 235-3899
www.wpoc.com
megstevens@wpoc.com
License: Baltimore, Baltimore County, MD held by Citicasters Licenses L.P.
Group Owner: Clear Channel Communications Inc.; (acq 4-29-99; grpsl).
Arbitron Metro Market: Baltimore, MD *Format:* Country
Kevin Friedman, General Manager
Meg Stevens, Programming Director

WRBS-FM
08-01-1964; 95.1 mhz FM *Hrs Open:* 24; 50 kw; 499 ft; N39 15 21 W76 40 29
3500 Commerce Drive, Baltimore, MD 21227
(410) 247-4100, *Fax:* (410) 247-4533
www.951shinefm.com
info@wrbs.com
License: Baltimore, Baltimore County, MD held by Peter and John Radio Fellowship Inc.
Population Served: 200,000 *Arbitron Metro Market:* Baltimore, MD *Hrs. of News Programming:* news progmg 6 hrs wkly *No. News Employees:* 1
Steven Lawhon, General Manager
David Paul, Programming Director

WWIN
01-01-1951; 1400 khz AM *Hrs Open:* 24
5900 Princess Garden Pky, Baltimore, MD 20706 US
(410) 332-8200, *Fax:* (410) 944-1047
www.spirit1400.com
License: Baltimore, MD held by Radio One Licenses LLC.
Group Owner: Radio One Inc.; (acq 1-23-92; $7.5 million with WWIN-FM Glen Burnie)
Nat'l Reps: Katz Radio
Arbitron Metro Market: Baltimore, MD *Format:* Gospel *Hrs. of News Programming:* news progmg one hr wkly *No. News Employees:* 1 *Target Audience:* 25-54; Black, relg

Al Payne, Operations Dir
Howard Mazer, General Manager
Dave Willner, General Sales Mgr
Kelly Wynder, Programming Director
Karl Goehring, Chief Engineer
Earlene Korchi, Traffic Director
Ajaya Smith, Imaging Director
GlennLipman, Business Manager
Tia Johnson, Assistant Promotions Director
Mike Roberts, Programming Assistant

WWMX
01-01-1960; 106.5 mhz FM *Hrs Open:* 24; 8.3 kw; 1138 ft.; N39 20 10 W76 38 59
600 New Hamphire Ave, Suite 1200, Washington, DC 20037 US
(410) 825-1065, *Fax:* (410) 321-4548
www.mix1065.fm
dave.labrozzi@infinitybroadcasting.com
License: Baltimore, Baltimore County, MD held by CBS Radio Stations Inc.
Group Owner: CBS Radio
Arbitron Metro Market: Baltimore, MD *TV Affiliate:* WJZ-TV
Format: Adult Contemp *Target Audience:* 25-54.
Tracy Brandys, General Sales Mgr
Dave Labrozzi, Programming Director
Dave Burgess, Promotions Manager
Digital Sales Manager, News Director

WQSR
12-15-1947; 102.7 mhz FM; 50 kw; 436 ft.; N39 23 11 W76 43 52
600 New Hampshire Ave., Suite 1200, Washington, DC 20037 US
(410) 366-7600, *Fax:* (240) 747-3747
www.1027jackfm.com
info@wqsr.com
License: Baltimore, Baltimore County, MD held by Citicasters Licenses Inc.
Group Owner: Clear Channel Communications Inc.; (acq 4-1-2009; grpsl)
Arbitron Metro Market: Baltimore, MD *Format:* Variety/Diverse
Hartley Adkins, General Manager
James Howard, Programming Director
Sheila Silverstein, Promotions Manager
Heather O'Malley, Website
Paul Krakovsky, Online Sales

Bel Air

***WHFC**
01-01-1972; 91.1 mhz FM *Hrs Open:* 24; 1.1 kw; 226 ft.; N39 33 22 W76 16 48
401 Thomas Run Road, Bel Air, MD 21014 US
(410) 836-4151, *Fax:* (410) 836-4180
www.whfc911.org
whfc@harford.edu
License: Bel Air, Harford County, MD held by Harford Community College.
Arbitron Metro Market: Baltimore, MD *Format:* Variety/Diverse
Special Programming: AAA 15 hrs, class 18 hr, jazz 18 hrs, Christian 6 *Target Audience:* 24-42; upwardly mobile professionals
Gary Helton, General Manager

Berlin

WOCQ
06-25-1981; 103.9 mhz FM; 6 kw; 328 ft.; N38 22 58 W75 18 58
224 Maugers Mill Road, Pottstown, PA 19464 US
, *Fax:* (302) 856-7633
www.oc104.com
License: Berlin, Worcester County, MD held by Great Scott Broadcasting.
Group Owner: Great Scott Broadcasting; acq 11-7-97; $2.775 million)
Arbitron Metro Market: Salisbury-Ocean *TV Affiliate:* Hip Hop
Special Programming: news progmg 4 hrs wkly *Hrs. of News Programming:* 1 *No. News Employees:* 18-49.

Bethesda

WIAD
10-01-1959; 94.7 mhz FM *Hrs Open:* 24; 20.5 kw; Ant 771 ft; N38 57 49 W77 06 18
8403 Colesville Rd., Ste. 1500, Silver Spring, MD 20037
(301) 683-0947, *Fax:* (301) 881-8746
www.947freshfm.com
License: Bethesda, Montgomery County, MD held by CBS Radio East Inc.
Group Owner: CBS Radio; (acq 8-1-85; grpsl;
Nat'l Network: CNN Radio *Nat'l Reps:* CBS Radio
Arbitron Metro Market: Washington, DC *Target Audience:* 25-49.
Michael Hughes, General Manager
Greg Dunkin, Programming Director

WMMJ
11-12-1961; 102.3 mhz FM; 2.9 kw; 479 ft.; N38 56 10 W77 5 33
5900 Princess Grdn Pkwy, 8th Floor, Lanham, MD 20706 US
(301) 306-1111, *Fax:* (301) 918-3901
www.mymajicdc.com
mymajicdc@interactiveone.com
License: Bethesda, Montgomery County, MD held by Radio One Licenses LLC.
Group Owner: Radio One Inc.; (acq 11-8-01; grpsl).
Arbitron Metro Market: Washington, DC *Format:* Adult Contemp
Target Audience: 25-54
Catherine Hughes, Chairman
Alfred Liggins, CEO
Michele Wiliams, General Manager
Dion Burkett-Lewis, Programming Director
Sherise Malachi, Promotions Manager
Scott Royster, CFO

Bowie

WNEW(FM)
01-01-1947; 99.1 mhz FM *Hrs Open:* 24; 45 kw; 157 m; N38 59 46 W76 39 26
4200 Parliament Pl., Suite 300, Lanham, MD 20706
(301) 306-0991, *Fax:* (301) 731-0431
www.elzolradio.com
License: Bowie, Anne Arundel County, MD held by CBS Radio East Inc.
Group Owner: CBS Radio; (acq 11-13-98; grpsl)
Nat'l Reps: CBS Radio
Population Served: 5,000,000 *Arbitron Metro Market:* Washington, DC *Hrs. of News Programming:* news progmg 5 hrs wkly *No. News Employees:* 1 *Target Audience:* Adults 18-49; upscale professionals
Michael Hughes, General Manager
Areacely Rivera, Programming Director

Braddock Heights

WTLP
04-08-1972; 103.9 mhz FM *Hrs Open:* 24; 0.35 kw; 958 ft.; N39 27 50 W77 29 44 *Rebroadcasts:* Rebroadcasts WTOP-FM Washington, DC 100%
P.O. Box 1160, Salt Lake City, UT 84110 US
(202) 895-5000, *Fax:* (202) 895-5103
www.wtopnews.com
newsroom@wtopnews.com
License: Braddock Heights, Frederick County, MD held by Bonneville Holding Co.
Group Owner: Bonneville International Corporation; (acq 1996; grpsl)
Nat'l Network: CBS Radio *Nat'l Reps:* Katz Radio
Arbitron Metro Market: Washington, DC *Format:* News *No. News Employees:* 4 *Target Audience:* General.
Joel Oxley, General Manager
Mitch Miller, Asst. News and Program Director
Mike McMearty, News Director
Jim Battagliese, Director of Traffic and Transit Operations
Darci Marchese, Managing Editor/Reporter
Jim Farley, V.P. of News &Programming

Brunswick

WTRI
10-02-1966; 1520 khz AM
P.O. Box 123, Crownsville, MD 21032 US
(301) 834-9000, *Fax:* (301) 834-6944
www.radioearl.com
earl@radioearl.com
License: Brunswick, MD held by WTRI Holding LLC
Arbitron Metro Market: Brunswick, MD *Format:* Country
Martin Sheehan, General Manager
Buddy Rizer, Programming Director
Fred Rohner, News Director

California

WKIK-FM
12-01-1994; 102.9 mhz FM *Hrs Open:* 24; 4 kw; 394 ft.; N38 22 3 W76 36 55 *Rebroadcasts:* Simulcast with WKIK(AM) La Plata 100%
5940 Waldorf-Leonardtown, Morgan Bldg., S.R. 5, Mechanicsville, MD 20659 US
(301) 884-5550, *Fax:* (301) 884-0280
www.wkik.com
wsmdfm@aol.com
License: California, St. Marys County, MD held by Somar Communications Inc.
Group Owner: Somar Communications Inc.; acq 1993; $130,000;
Format: Country *Target Audience:* 25-54.
Roy Robertson, President
Terrell Soellner, Operations Dir
Sharon Robertson, General Sales Mgr

Cambridge

WCEM
01-01-1947; 1240 khz AM *Hrs Open:* 24
2 Bay St., P.O. Box 237, Cambridge, MD 21613 US
(410) 228-4800, *Fax:* (410) 228-0130
www.mtslive.com
espn@intercom.net
License: Cambridge, MD held by MTS Broadcasting L.C.
Group Owner: MTS Broadcasting; (acq 6-20-93; $1.8 million with co-located FM;
Nat'l Network: Westwood One; ESPN Radio
Format: Sports *Special Programming:* Relg 5 hrs wkly *No. News Employees:* 1 *Target Audience:* 25-54.
Shane Walker, Operations Dir
Troy Hill, General Manager
Shan Shariff, Programming Director
Al Ackerman, News Director
Bryan Harz, Engineering Dir
Dwight Cromwell, Reporter

WCEM-FM
01-29-1968; 106.3 mhz FM; 6 kw; 325 ft.; N38 35 3 W76 4 54
Mailing Address: P.O. Box 237, Cambridge, MD 21613 US
Second Address: Box 237, Cambridge, MD 21613
(410) 228-4800, *Fax:* (410) 228-0130
www.mtslive.com
theheat@intercom.net
License: Cambridge, Dorchester County, MD
Format: Adult Contemp *Target Audience:* 18-49.
Troy D. Hill, General Manager
Kirsten Strohmer, General Sales Mgr
Al Ackerman, News Director
Shane Walker, Office Manager
Shan Shariff, Sports Commentator

Catonsville

WJZ-FM
11-22-1963; 105.7 mhz FM *Hrs Open:* 24; 50 kw; 492 ft.; N39 19 26 W76 32 56
116 Huntington Ave., Boston, MA 02116 US
(410) 825-1000, *Fax:* (410) 821-8256
www.1057thefan.com
License: Catonsville, Baltimore County, MD held by CBS Radio Stations Inc.
Group Owner: CBS Radio; (acq 11-13-98; grpsl)
Nat'l Reps: Christal
Arbitron Metro Market: Baltimore, MD *Format:* Sports *No. News Employees:* 1 *Target Audience:* 25-54.
Robert Philips, Operations Dir

Chestertown

WCTR
06-16-1963; 1530 khz AM; 0.27 kw-C, NDD; 1 kw-D, NDD; N39 13 35 W76 5 20
Mailing Address: P.O. Box 700, Chestertown, MD 21620 US
Second Address: 231 Flatland Rd., Chestertown, MD 21620
(410) 778-1530, *Fax:* (410) 778-4800
www.wctr.com
info@wctr.com
License: Chestertown, MD held by WCTR Broadcasting LLC
Nat'l Network: ABC *Regional Reps:* Rgnl Reps
Arbitron Metro Market: Kent County, MD *Format:* Oldies *Hrs. of News Programming:* News progmg 10 hrs wkly *Target Audience:* 35 plus.
Richard Gelfman, President
Keith Thompson, Operations Dir
Ken Collins, General Manager
Sean Hall, News Director

College Park

***WMUC-FM**
09-10-1979; 88.1 mhz FM *Hrs Open:* 24; 0.01 kw; 3 ft.; N38 58 59 W76 56 37
3130 S Campus Dining Hal, College Park, MD 20742 US
(301) 314-7867, *Fax:* (301) 314-7879
www.wmucradio.com
general@wmucradio.com
License: College Park, Prince Georges County, MD held by University of Maryland.
Arbitron Metro Market: Washington, DC *Format:* Variety/Diverse
Target Audience: College students.
Christina Gatte, Operations Dir
Scott Kornberg, General Manager

Lealin Queen, Programming Director
Adam Rosenfeld, Promotions Manager
Liz Lane, News Director

Crisfield

WBEY-FM
07-01-1995; 97.9 mhz FM; 4.3 kw; 379 ft.; N38 1 45 W75 45 5
Mailing Address: 2802 Lomax Court, Waldorf, MD 20602 US
Second Address: 1637 Dunn Swamp Rd., Pocomoke City, MD 21851
(410) 968-9696, *Fax:* (410) 957-6080
www.easternshoreradio.com
bay979@gmail.com
License: Crisfield, Somerset County, MD held by Bay Broadcasting.
Arbitron Metro Market: Crisfield, MD *Format:* Country
Michael Powell, General Manager
Adam Riggin, Programming Director

Cumberland

WCBC
06-24-1953; 1270 khz AM; 5 kw-D, DA2; 1 kw-N, DA2; N39 40 28 W78 46 48
P.O. Box 290, Cumberland, MD 21502 US
(301) 724-5000, *Fax:* (301) 722-8336
www.wcbcradio.com
News@WCBCRadio.com
License: Cumberland, MD held by Cumberland Broadcasting Co. Inc.
Nat'l Network: ABC; Westwood One
Arbitron Metro Market: Cumberland, MD *Format:* News, News/Talk, 86 *Hrs. of News Programming:* news progmg 3 hrs wkly *No. News Employees:* 2 *Target Audience:* 25 plus. *Adv. Rates:* 19.50; 19.50; 19.50; 19.50
David Aydelotte Sr., President
Mary Clites, General Manager
Jim Robey, Station Manager

WKGO
04-01-1962; 106.1 mhz FM *Hrs Open:* 24; 5.4 kw; 1411 ft.; N39 34 54 W78 53 58
Mailing Address: 350 Byrd Avenue, Cumberland, MD 21502 US
Second Address: 350 Byrd Ave., Cumberland, MD 21502
(301) 722-6666, *Fax:* (301) 722-0945
www.go106.com
go106@go106.com
License: Cumberland, Allegany County, MD held by WTBO-WKGO Corp. L.L.C.
Group Owner: Wooster Republican Printing Co.
Nat'l Network: Westwood One
Format: Classic Rock *Hrs. of News Programming:* news progmg one hr wkly *No. News Employees:* 1 *Target Audience:* 25-54.
Richard Cornwell, General Sales Mgr
Tim Martin, Programming Director
Jim Van, News Director
Mark St. John, Disc Jockey
Ray Wagner, Disc Jockey

WCMD
01-01-1948; 1230 khz AM *Hrs Open:* 24
15 Campbell Street, Luray, VA 22835 US
(301) 759-1005, *Fax:* (301) 777-5404
www.1230espnam.com
jenna.smith@alleganyradio.com
License: Cumberland, MD held by Broadcast Communications Inc.
Group Owner: Broadcast Communications Inc.
Arbitron Metro Market: Cumberland, MD *Format:* Sports *Hrs. of News Programming:* news progmg 20 hrs wkly *No. News Employees:* 2 *Target Audience:* 25-54.
Gary Fisher, President
Jim MacMillan, Programming Director

WTBO
12-13-1928; 1450 khz AM *Hrs Open:* 24; 1 kw-U, ND1; N39 38 43 W78 45 5
Mailing Address: P.O. Box 1644, Cumberland, MD 21502 US
Second Address: 350 Byrd Ave., Cumberland, MD 21502
(301) 722-6666, *Fax:* (301) 722-0945
www.wtboam.com
License: Cumberland, MD held by WTBO-WKGO Corp. LLC.
Group Owner: Wooster Republican Printing Co.; (acq 11-1-77).
Nat'l Network: CSN
Arbitron Metro Market: Cumberland, MD *Format:* Oldies *Hrs. of News Programming:* news progmg 20 hrs wkly *No. News Employees:* 1 *Target Audience:* 40 plus. *Adv. Rates:* 18; 14; 18; 12
G. Dix II, President
Linda Ward, Operations Dir
Richard Cornwell, General Manager
Tim Martin, Promotions Manager
Jim Van, News Director
Mark Workman, Chief Engineer
R. DiBuono, Traffic Manager

Denton

WKDI
12-27-1988; 840 khz AM *Hrs Open:* Sunrise-sunset; 1 kw-D, DAD; N38 53 53 W75 51 10
Mailing Address: P.O. Obx 889, Blacksburg, VA 24063 US
Second Address: 24580 Station Rd., Denton, MD 21629
(410) 479-2288, *Fax:* (410) 479-5188
wkdi@broadcast.net
License: Denton, MD held by Bayshore Communications Inc.
Format: Christian, Talk *Hrs. of News Programming:* News progmg 12 hrs wkly *Target Audience:* 25-49; middle-income Christians
Edward Baker, CEO
Michael McCoy, General Manager

Easton

WKHZ
09-29-1960; 1460 khz AM; 1 kw-D, 500 w-N, DA-2; N38 46 13 W76 04 55
306 Port St., Easton, MD 22901
(410) 822-3301, *Fax:* (410) 822-0576
stacie@wceiradio.com
License: Easton, Talbot County, MD held by First Media Radio L.L.C.
Group Owner: First Media Radio LLC; (acq 11-30-99; $4 million with co-located FM)
Nat'l Network: Jones Radio Networks
Population Served: 70,000*Target Audience:* 45 plus; mature adults
Matt Spence, Programming Director

WCEI-FM
05-14-1975; 96.7 mhz FM *Hrs Open:* 24; 12.5 kw; 463 ft.; N38 57 21.8 W76 5 35.6
1150 Pepsi Place, Suite 300, Charlottesville, VA 22901 US
(410) 822-3301, *Fax:* (410) 822-0576
www.wceiradio.com
stacie@wceiradio.com
License: Easton, Talbot County, MD
Group Owner: First Media Radio LLC
Arbitron Metro Market: Easton,MD *Format:* Adult Contemp *No. News Employees:* 1 *Target Audience:* 25-54.
Alex Kolbieski, CEO
Stacie Monz, General Manager
Julie Johnson, News Director
Don Bumpus, Local News Editor

Elkton

*WOEL-FM
09-01-1978; 89.9 mhz FM; 3 kw; 259 ft.; N39 35 35 W75 51 49
Mailing Address: P. O. Box 246, Elkton, MD 21921 US
Second Address: 3141 Old Elk Neck Rd., Elkton, MD 21922
410-392-3225, *Fax:* 410-392-3229
apd.saved@juno.com
License: Elkton, Cecil County, MD held by Maryland Baptist Bible College.
Nat'l Network: USA
TV Affiliate: Relg

WSRY
08-22-1963; 1550 khz AM; 1 kw-D, DA2; 0.001 kw-N, DA2; N39 35 45 W75 47 50
179 Stanton Christiana Road, Christiana, DE 19702 US
(302) 731-7270, *Fax:* (302) 738-3090
www.myreachradio.com
listenercare@myreachradio.com
License: Elkton, MD held by Priority Radio Inc.
Group Owner: Priority Radio Inc.; (acq 12-10-99)
Nat'l Network: ESPN Radio
Arbitron Metro Market: Wilmington, DE *Format:* Religious *Special Programming:* Relg 3 hrs, farm one hr wkly *Target Audience:* 25-64. *Adv. Rates:* 21; 17; 19; 13
Dan Edwards, General Manager

Emmitsburg

*WMTB-FM
10-01-1977; 89.9 mhz FM *Hrs Open:* Noon-3 PM; 0.1 kw; 144 ft.; N39 41 2 W77 21 25
Radio Station Wmtb-Fm, Emmitsburg, MD 21727 US
(301) 447-5240
www.msmary.edu/wmtb
License: Emmitsburg, Frederick County, MD held by Mount Saint Mary's College.
Arbitron Metro Market: Emmitsburg, MD *Format:* Alternative
Special Programming: Folk one hr, gospel one hr, relg 4 hrs wkly *Hrs. of News Programming:* News progmg 2 hrs wkly
Target Audience: General; college &community
Randy Gray, General Manager

Federalsburg

WTDK
12-02-1978; 107.1 mhz FM *Hrs Open:* 24; 3.9 kw; 407 ft.; N38 46 2 W75 44 46
P.O. Box 237, Cambridge, MD 21613 US
(410) 288-4800, *Fax:* (410) 228-0130
www.mtslive.com
theduck@mtslive.com
License: Federalsburg, Caroline County, MD held by MTS Broadcasting.
Group Owner: MTS Broadcasting; acq 1-30-97)
Nat'l Network: USA; Westwood One
Arbitron Metro Market: Federalsburg, MD *Format:* Oldies *Hrs. of News Programming:* News progmg 4 hrs wkly *Target Audience:* 25-54; affluent listeners
Thomas Mulitz, President
Shane Walker, Operations Dir
Troy Hill, General Manager
Kirsten Strohmer, General Sales Mgr
Al Ackerman, News Director

Frederick

WFMD
01-01-1936; 930 khz AM *Hrs Open:* 24; 5 kw-D, DA2; 2.5 kw-N, DA2; N39 24 55 W77 27 41
600 Congress Avenue, Suite 1400, Austin, TX 78701 US
(301) 663-4181, *Fax:* (301) 682-8018
www.wfmd.com
info@wfmd.com
License: Frederick, MD held by Aloha Station Trust LLC
Nat'l Network: ABC *Wire Services:* AP
Arbitron Metro Market: Frederick, MD *Format:* News, News/Talk, 84, Talk *Hrs. of News Programming:* news pogmg 20 hrs wkly *No. News Employees:* 3 *Target Audience:* 35-64.
Frank Mitchell, Production Director
Doug Hillard, General Manager
Josh Brooks, General Sales Mgr
Frank Mitchell, Programming Director
Jessica Mitko, Promotions Manager
Dianah Gibson, News Director
Linda Beaulieu, Director ofSales
Phyliss Betson, Human Resources
April Simerly, Public Service Announcements
Patrick Mendonca, Webmaster
Kevin McManus, News Reporter
Robert Dacey, News Reporter

WFRE
02-19-1961; 99.9 mhz FM *Hrs Open:* 24; 7.6 kw; 1165 ft.; N39 30 0 W77 29 58
600 Congress Avenue, Suite 1400, Austin, TX 78701 US
(301) 663-4181, *Fax:* (301) 682-8018
www.wfre.com
JessicaMitko2@clearchannel.com
License: Frederick, Frederick County, MD held by Aloha Station Trust LLC
Nat'l Reps: Clear Channel *Wire Services:* AP
Arbitron Metro Market: Frederick, MD *Format:* Country *Hrs. of News Programming:* news progmg one hr wkly *No. News Employees:* 3 *Target Audience:* 25-54.
Doug Hillard, General Manager
Troy Skinner, General Sales Mgr
Jessica Mitko, Promotions Manager
Dianah Gibson, News Director
Linda Beaulieu, Director of Sales
Josh Brooks, National Sales Manager
Frank Mitchell, ProductionManager
Phyliss Betson, Human Resources
April Simerly, Public Service Announcements
Patrick Mendonca, Webmaster

*WYPF
05-01-1991; 88.1 mhz FM *Hrs Open:* 24; 1 kw; 1115 ft.; N39 29 31 W77 30 0
P.O. Box 205, Braddock Heights, MD 21714 US
(410) 235-1660, *Fax:* (410) 235-1161
www.wypr.org
frontdesk@wypr.org
License: Frederick, Frederick County, MD held by Your Public Radio Corp.
Nat'l Network: NPR; PRI
Format: News, News/Talk, 86 *Target Audience:* General.

Anthony Brandon, President
Anthony Brandon, General Manager
Brian Crompwell, Business Manager
Paul Hollis, Public Information Assistant
Kristin Beno, Director of Membership
Alexandra Price, Director of Development
Kyle Leslie,Director of New Media
Ami Dougherty, Traffic Assistant

WWFD
12-15-1960; 820 khz AM *Hrs Open:* 24; 4.3 kw-D, DAN; 0.43 kw-N, DAN; N39 24 42 W77 28 20 *Rebroadcasts:* Rebroadcasts WFED(AM) Washington, DC 100%
PO Box 1160, Salt Lake City, UT 84110 US
(202) 895-5000, *Fax:* (202) 895-5144
www.federalnewsradio.com
License: Frederick, MD held by Bonneville Holding Co.
Group Owner: Bonneville International Corporation; (acq 1996; grpsl)
Nat'l Reps: Katz Radio
Arbitron Metro Market: Washington, DC *Format:* News *Target Audience:* General.
Joel Oxley, General Manager
Lisa Wolfe, Programming Director

Frostburg

WFRB
12-20-1958; 560 khz AM *Hrs Open:* 24; 5 kw-D, ND1; 0.055 kw-N, ND1; N39 41 2 W78 57 57
350 Byrd Avenue, Cumberland, MD 21502 US
(301) 689-8871, *Fax:* (301) 689-8880
www.talkradio560.com
wfrb@wfrb.com
License: Frostburg, MD held by WTBO-WKGO Corp. L.L.C.
Group Owner: Wooster Republican Printing Co.; (acq 6-1-97; $3.5 million with co-located FM).
Format: Talk *Hrs. of News Programming:* news progmg 10 hrs wkly *No. News Employees:* 1 *Target Audience:* 40 plus; those gainfully employed in the market for goods & svcs *Adv. Rates:* 18; 14; 18; 12
G. Charles Dix II, President
Richard Cornwell, General Manager
Tim Martin, Programming Director
Hannah Ford, Promotions Manager
Jim Van, News Director
Mark Workman, Engineering Dir
Carson Yoder, Programming Director
ChrisBagley, Traffic Manager

WFRB-FM
10-01-1965; 105.3 mhz FM *Hrs Open:* 24; 13.5 kw; 958 ft.; N39 41 2 W78 57 57
350 Byrd Avenue, Cumberland, MD 21502 US
(301) 689-8871, *Fax:* (301) 689-8880
www.wfrb.com
wfrb@wfrb.com
License: Frostburg, Allegany County, MD
Group Owner: Wooster Republican Printing Co.
Format: Country *Hrs. of News Programming:* news progmg 5 hrs wkly *No. News Employees:* 2
David Miller, Operations Dir
Chuck Peterson, General Manager
Marcella Vance, General Sales Mgr
Justin Maglione, Promotions Manager
Krissy Golden, News Director
Mark Kesner, Chief Engineer
Elwood King, Disc Jockey
Max James,Disc Jockey
Ben Gates, Public Affairs Director

***WFWM**
04-01-1986; 91.9 mhz FM *Hrs Open:* 24; 0.255 kw horiz, 1.3 kw vert; 1424 ft.; N39 34 54 W78 53 53
Room 025, Compton Hall, Frostburg, MD 21532 US
(301) 687-4143, *Fax:* (301) 687-7040
www.wfwm.org
wfwm@frostburg.edu
License: Frostburg, Allegany County, MD held by Frostburg State University.
Nat'l Network: NPR *Wire Services:* AP
Format: Classical, Jazz *Special Programming:* Educ 11 hrs wkly *Hrs. of News Programming:* news progmg 2 hrs wkly *No. News Employees:* 1 *Target Audience:* General.
Chuck Dicken, General Manager
Chuck Dicken, Station Manager
Chuck Dicken, Programming Director
Jeff Rosedale, News Director
Jeff Rosendale, Production

***WLIC**
10-01-1989; 97.1 mhz FM *Hrs Open:* 24; 0.15 kw; 1355 ft.; N39 34 54 W78 53 58 *Rebroadcasts:* Rebroadcasts WAIJ(FM) Grantsville 100%
Mailing Address: 34 Springs Road, P.O. Box 540, Frostburg, MD 21532 US
Second Address: He's Alive Corp. Offices, 34 Springs Rd., Grantsville, MD 21536
(301) 895-3292, *Fax:* (301) 895-3293
www.hesalive.net
hesalive@hesalive.net
License: Frostburg, Alleghany County, MD held by He's Alive Inc.
Group Owner: He's Alive Inc.
Nat'l Network: USA
Format: Adult Contemp, Christian, 44 *Target Audience:* 18-35.
Sharon Johnson, President

Fruitland

WKHI
01-01-1972; 107.7 mhz FM *Hrs Open:* 24; 5.3 kw; 348 ft.; N38 23 0 W75 24 53
224 Maugers Mill Road, Pottstown, PA 19464 US
(302) 856-2567, *Fax:* (302) 856-7633
www.1077joefm.com
sue@greatscottbroadcasting.com
License: Fruitland, Wicomico County, MD held by Great Scott Broadcasting.
Group Owner: Great Scott Broadcasting; (acq 7-16-99; $700,000 with WXSH(FM) Pocomoke City, MD)
Nat'l Network: NBC
Arbitron Metro Market: Salisbury-Ocean City, MD *Format:* Country *Special Programming:* Black 5 hrs, gospel 5 hrs wkly *Target Audience:* 25-54.
Faye Scott, President
Sue Timmons, General Manager
Adam Davis, Programming Director
Tracy Baker, News Director

Gaithersburg

WMET
01-31-1983; 1160 khz AM *Hrs Open:* 24
8945 N. Westland Drive, Ste 302, Gaithersburg, MD 20877 US
(877) 636-1160, *Fax:* (301) 585-1682
www.gmonline.info/
ylevin@wmet1160.com
License: Gaithersburg, MD held by Beltway Acquisition Corp.
Nat'l Network: NBC Radio
Arbitron Metro Market: Gaithersburg, MD *Format:* Religious *Target Audience:* 25 plus.
Irene Lagan, General Manager

Glen Burnie

WFBR
05-15-1963; 1590 khz AM; 1 kw-U, DA-2; N39 10 36 W76 37 20
159 8th Ave. N.W., Glen Burnie, MD 21061
(410) 761-1590, *Fax:* (410) 761-9220
License: Glen Burnie, Anne Arundel County, MD held by Way Broadcasting Licensee LLC
Population Served: 1,300,000 *Arbitron Metro Market:* Baltimore, MD
Arthur Liu, President
Libby Parris, General Manager
Jean Alston, Programming Director

WWIN-FM
09-15-1964; 95.9 mhz FM *Hrs Open:* 24; 3 kw horiz, 3 kw vert; 299 ft; N39 12 16 W76 34 07
1705 Whitehead Rd., Baltimore, MD 20706
(410) 332-8200, *Fax:* (410) 944-1282
www.magic959.com
License: Glen Burnie, Anne Arundel County, MD held by Radio One Licenses LLC.
Group Owner: Radio One Inc.; (acq 1-23-92; $7.5 million with WWI
Nat'l Network: ABC *Nat'l Reps:* Christal
Population Served: 915,800 *Arbitron Metro Market:* Baltimore, MD *Hrs. of News Programming:* news progmg one hr wkly *No. News Employees:* 1 *Target Audience:* 25-54; Black adult
Al Payne, Operations Dir
Howard Mazer, General Manager
Jack McCarty, General Sales Mgr
Al Payne, Programming Director

Grantsville

***WAIJ**
10-01-1984; 90.3 mhz FM *Hrs Open:* 19; 10 kw horiz, 8.8 kw vert; 561 ft.; N39 42 14 W79 5 31
Mailing Address: 34 Springs Road, P.O. Box 540, Grantsville, MD 21536 US
Second Address: He's Alive Corp. Offices, 34 Springs Rd., Grantsville, MD 21536
(301) 895-3292, *Fax:* (301) 895-3293
www.hesalive.net
info@hesalive.net
License: Grantsville, Garrett County, MD held by He's Alive Inc.
Group Owner: He's Alive Inc.
Nat'l Network: USA
Arbitron Metro Market: Oakland, MD *Format:* Christian, Gospel *Target Audience:* 18-35.
Sharon Johnson, President
Melissa Flores, General Manager
Tim Eutin, Programming Director

Grasonville

WRNR-FM
04-01-1980; 103.1 mhz FM; 6 kw; 328 ft.; N38 56 37 W76 10 43
8317 Front Beach Rd., Suite 21, Panama City, FL 32407 US
(410) 626-0103, *Fax:* (410) 267-7634
www.wrnr.com
info@wrnr.com
License: Grasonville, Queen Annes County, MD held by Empire Broadcasting System Inc.
Nat'l Network: CBS Radio
Arbitron Metro Market: Baltimore, MD *Format:* Alternative, Variety/Diverse *Hrs. of News Programming:* news progmg 2 hrs wkly *No. News Employees:* 1 *Target Audience:* 25-54; adults
Bob Waugh, Operations Dir
Judy Buddensick, General Sales Mgr

Hagerstown

WARK
07-20-1947; 1490 khz AM *Hrs Open:* 24; 1 kw-U, ND1; N39 37 35 W77 42 40 *Rebroadcasts:* Rebroadcasts WAFY(FM) Middletown 20-30%
880 Commonwealth Ave., Hagerstown, MD 21740 US
(301) 733-4500, *Fax:* (301) 733-0040
webmaster@wark.am
License: Hagerstown, MD held by Nassau Broadcasting III L.L.C.
Group Owner: Nassau Broadcasting Partners L.P.; (acq 2-25-2005; $18 million with co-located FM).
Arbitron Metro Market: Hagerstown, MD *Format:* Talk *Special Programming:* Jazz 2 hrs wkly *Hrs. of News Programming:* news progmg 8 hrs wkly *No. News Employees:* 2 *Target Audience:* 25-54.
Rick Mussleman, General Manager
Marcia Cason, General Sales Mgr
Caroline Henneberger, News Director
Bill McCarrey, Engineering Dir

***WGMS**
06-15-1993; 89.1 mhz FM *Hrs Open:* 24; 0.9 kw; 1339 ft.; N39 41 47 W77 30 50 *Rebroadcasts:* Rebroadcasts WETA-FM Washington 100%
P.O. Box 2626, Washington, DC 20013 US
(703) 998-2600, *Fax:* (703) 824-7288
www.weta.org/fm
radio@weta.com
License: Hagerstown, Washington County, MD held by Greater Washington Education Telecommunication Association.
Nat'l Network: NPR; PRI
Arbitron Metro Market: Hagerstown, MD *Format:* Talk *Target Audience:* General; educated adults
Timothy C. Coughlin, Chairman
Sharon Percy Rockefeller, President and Chief Executive Officer
Dan De Vany, General Manager
Mike Byrnes, Chief Engineer
Joseph B. Bruns, Executive Vice President and Chief Operating Offic
DaltonDelan, Executive Vice President and Chief Programming Off
Polly Povejsil Heath, Senior Vice President and Chief Financial Officer

WJEJ
10-01-1932; 1240 khz AM *Hrs Open:* 24; 1 kw-U, ND1; N39 40 0 W77 43 30
1135 Haven Road, Hagerstown, MD 21740 US
(301) 739-2323, *Fax:* (301) 797-7408
www.wjejradio.com
wjej@myactv.net
License: Hagerstown, MD held by Hagerstown Broadcasting Co. Inc.
Nat'l Network: CBS *Wire Services:* Metro Weather Service Inc.
Arbitron Metro Market: Hagerstown-Chambersburg-Waynesboro, MD-PA *Format:* Easy Listening *Hrs. of News Programming:*

news progmg 24 hrs wkly *No. News Employees:* 1 *Target Audience:* 35 plus.
John Staub, President
Joanna Staub, Operations Dir
Louis Scally, Programming Director
Tom Bradley, News Director
Jackie Hall, Traffic Manager

WAYZ
01-01-1946; 104.7 mhz FM *Hrs Open:* 24; 8.3 kw; 1378 ft.; N39 41 47 W77 30 47
1135 Haven Road, Hagerstown, MD 21740 US
(717) 597-9200, *Fax:* (717) 597-9210
www.wayz.com
info@wayz.com
License: Hagerstown, Washington County, MD held by H.J.V. L.P.
Group Owner: VerStandig Broadcasting; (acq 8-28-2000; $2.5 million and WWMD(FM) Waynesboro, PA).
Wire Services: UPI
Arbitron Metro Market: Hagerstown, MD *Format:* Country *Special Programming:* Relg 3 hrs wkly *Target Audience:* 25-54.
Dottie Hedglin, General Manager
Blake Truman, General Sales Mgr
Chris Maestle, Programming Director
Toni Anderson, Music Director

***WZXH**
01-01-2009; 91.7 mhz FM; 900 w; Ant 423 ft; N39 27 39 W77 41 58 *Rebroadcasts:* Rebroadcasts WBYO(FM) Sellersville, PA 100%
Box 186, Sellersville, PA
(215) 721-2141, *Fax:* (215) 721-9811
www.wordfm.org
License: Hagerstown, Washington County, MD held by Four Rivers Community Broadcasting Corp.
Arbitron Metro Market: Hagerstown-Chambersburg-Waynesboro, MD-PA
Charles Loughery, President
Meg Sabulsky, Operations Dir
David Baker, General Manager
Meg Sabulsky, Programming Director
William Dunn, Promotions Manager
Charles Doughery, Engineering Dir

Halfway

WHAG
06-09-1962; 1410 khz AM *Hrs Open:* 6 AM-7 PM
1250 Maryland Ave, Hagerstown, MD 21740 US
(301) 797-7300, *Fax:* (301) 797-2659
License: Halfway, MD held by MLB-Hagerstown-Chambersburg IV LLC.
Group Owner: Main Line Broadcasting LLC; (acq 7-20-2005; grpsl).
Arbitron Metro Market: Hagerstown-Chambersburg-Waynesboro, MD-PA *Format:* News, News/Talk, 86 *Hrs. of News Programming:* news progmg 7 hrs wkly *No. News Employees:* 2 *Target Audience:* 25-64.
Rich Bateman, General Manager

WDLD
01-01-1965; 96.7 mhz FM; 4.8 kw; 164 ft.; N39 37 3 W77 44 17
1250 Maryland Avenue, Hagerstown, MD 21740 US
(301) 797-7300, *Fax:* (301) 797-2659
www.wild967.fm
info@wild967.fm.com
License: Halfway, Washington County, MD
Group Owner: Main Line Broadcasting LLC
Nat'l Network: ABC
Arbitron Metro Market: Hagerstown-Chambersburg-Waynesboro, MD-PA *Format:* Classic Rock, Rock/AOR *Target Audience:* 18-54; adults, young families
Brian Cleary, Operations Dir
Frank Hamilton, General Manager
Dixie Penner, Promotions Manager
Marie Merrill, News Director

Havre De Grace

WJSS
05-15-1948; 1330 khz AM *Hrs Open:* 24; 5 kw-D, DAN; 0.5 kw-N, DAN; N39 33 55 W76 7 8
1205 York Road, Lutherville, MD 21093 US
(410) 939-0800, *Fax:* (410) 939-2156
www.wjss1330.com
info@wjss.com
License: Havre De Grace, MD held by Benjamin-Dane LLC
Arbitron Metro Market: Havre de Grace, MD *Format:* News, News/Talk, 86 *Target Audience:* General.
Ronald Reeves, President

WXCY
06-19-1960; 103.7 mhz FM *Hrs Open:* 24; 37 kw; 551 ft.; N39 33 52 W76 6 7
2727 Shipley Rd., P.O. Box 7492, Wilmington, DE 19803 US
(410) 939-1100, *Fax:* (410) 939-1104
www.wxcyfm.com
wxcy@wxcyfm.com
License: Havre De Grace, Harford County, MD held by Delmarva Broadcasting Co.
Group Owner: Delmarva Broadcasting Co.
Wire Services: Metro Weather Service Inc.
Arbitron Metro Market: Wilmington, DE *Format:* Country *Special Programming:* Relg 2 hrs, NASCAR info updates on race day 6 hrs *No. News Employees:* 2 *Target Audience:* 25-54. *Adv. Rates:* 70; 60; 70; 50
Willis Schenk, Chairman
Pete Booker, CEO
Bob Mercer, Operations Dir
Bob Bloom, General Manager

Hurlock

WAAI
06-01-1989; 100.9 mhz FM *Hrs Open:* 24; 1.3 kw; 502 ft.; N38 37 28 W75 53 20
Mailing Address: P.O. Box 237, Cambridge, MD 21613 US
Second Address: 2 Bay St., Cambridge, MD 21613
(410) 228-4800, *Fax:* (410) 228-0130
www.mtslive.com
waai@mtslive.com
License: Hurlock, Dorchester County, MD held by MTS Broadcasting.
Group Owner: MTS Broadcasting; acq 1-30-97)
Nat'l Network: ABC *Nat'l Reps:* Rgnl Reps *Wire Services:* ABC
Arbitron Metro Market: Hurlock, MD *Format:* Country *Special Programming:* Gospel 4 hrs wkly *Hrs. of News Programming:* news progmg 6 hrs wkly *No. News Employees:* 4 *Target Audience:* 25-54; general
Thomas Mulitz, President
Shane Walker, Operations Dir
Troy Hill, General Manager
Kirsten Strohmor, General Sales Mgr
Bryan Harz, Chief Engineer

Indian Head

WWGB
06-01-1986; 1030 khz AM *Hrs Open:* Sunrise-sunset; 50 kw-D, DAD; N38 33 53 W76 49 1
3270 Blazer Pkwy, Ste. 101, Lexington, KY 40509 US
(301) 899-1444, *Fax:* (301) 899-7244
www.wwgb.com
radio@wwgb.com
License: Indian Head, MD held by Good Body Media LLC.
Group Owner: Mountain Broadcasting Corp.; (acq 7-15-2002).
Arbitron Metro Market: Indian Head, MD *Format:* Christian
Ruth Salmeron, Station Manager

La Plata

WKIK
10-01-1965; 1560 khz AM *Hrs Open:* 12; 0.25 kw-C, NDD; 1 kw-D, NDD; N38 32 36 W76 59 37
P.O. Box 2470, La Plata, MD 20646 US
(301) 884-5550, *Fax:* (301) 884-0280
www.wkik.com
wsmdfm@aol.com
License: La Plata, MD held by Somar Communications Inc.
Group Owner: Somar Communications Inc.; acq 4-12-91; $65,000;
Nat'l Network: ABC
Arbitron Metro Market: Washington, DC *Format:* Country *Special Programming:* Local news, Baltimore Ravens football *Hrs. of News Programming:* News progmg 5 hrs wkly *Target Audience:* 25-54.
Terrell Soellner, Operations Dir
Roy Robertson, General Manager

Laurel

WILC
12-23-1965; 900 khz AM *Hrs Open:* 5 AM-4 AM; 1.9 kw-D, DA2; 0.5 kw-N, DA2; N39 4 57 W76 50 19
1550 Hemlock Street, N.W, Washington, DC 20012 US
(301) 419-2122, *Fax:* (301) 419-2409
www.radiovivc900.com
viva900@tvcontacto.net
License: Laurel, MD held by ZGS Radio Inc.
Nat'l Network: CNN Radio *Nat'l Reps:* Univision Radio National Sales
Arbitron Metro Market: Washington, DC *Format:* Adult Contemp *Hrs. of News Programming:* News progmg 10 hrs wkly *Target Audience:* General. *Adv. Rates:* 100; 80; 80; 70
Patricia Omana, General Manager
Sergio Uriola, Programming Director
Mavi Raez, News Director

Lexington Park

WPTX
07-01-1998; 1690 khz AM
1930 Isaac Newton Square, Suite 207, Reston, VA 20190 US
(301) 870-5550
wsmdfm@aol.com
License: Lexington Park, MD held by Somar Communications Inc.
Group Owner: Somar Communications Inc.; (acq 2-12-2001; $2.25 million with WMDM(FM) Lexington Park including three-year, $100,000 noncompete agreement)
Arbitron Metro Market: Lexington Park, MD *Format:* News, News/Talk, 86
Terrell Soellner, Operations Dir
Roy Robertson, General Manager
Sharon Robertson, General Sales Mgr

WMDM
12-16-1976; 97.7 mhz FM; 6 kw; 328 ft.; N38 16 58 W76 33 39
P.O.Box 600, Lexington Park, MD 20653 US
(301) 884-5550, *Fax:* (301) 884-0280
www.977therocket.com
License: Lexington Park, St. Marys County, MD held by Somar Communications Inc.
Group Owner: Somar Communications Inc.; (acq 2-12-2001; $2.25 million with WPTX(AM) Lexington Park including three-year, $100,000 noncompete agreement)
Arbitron Metro Market: Lexington, MD *Format:* Light Rock *Target Audience:* 25-54.
Sharon Robertson, Operations Dir
Roy Robertson, General Manager
Patrick Wood, News Director

Maugansville

***WHGT**
12-05-2006; 1590 khz AM *Hrs Open:* 24
4850 Connecticut Ave NW, Washington, DC 20008 US
(301) 582-0378, *Fax:* (301) 582-1620
www.aheartforhagerstown.com
office@aheartforhagerstown.com
License: Maugansville, MD held by Emmanuel Baptist Temple
Arbitron Metro Market: Maugansville, MD *Format:* Christian *Special Programming:* Church worship svc one hr wkly *Hrs. of News Programming:* News progmg 14 hrs wkly *Target Audience:* Conservative Christian
Dr. Larry Aikens Jr., General Manager
Ed Hampton, Interim Senior Pastor
Cliff Mowen, Bus/Visitation/Hospital Pastor
David Zyskowski, Director of Children's Ministries

Mechanicsville

WSMD-FM
09-01-1988; 98.3 mhz FM *Hrs Open:* 24; 3 kw; 328 ft.; N38 24 49 W76 46 31
Post Office Box 2470, Laplata, MD 20646 US
(301) 870-5550
wsmdfm@aol.com
License: Mechanicsville, St. Marys County, MD held by Somar Communications Inc.
Group Owner: Somar Communications Inc.
Nat'l Network: ABC
Format: Adult Contemp *Special Programming:* Local news *Hrs. of News Programming:* news progmg 6 hrs wkly *No. News Employees:* 1 *Target Audience:* 25-54.
Roy Robertson, President
Terrell Soellner, Operations Dir
Sharon Robertson, General Sales Mgr

Middletown

WAFY
05-07-1990; 103.1 mhz FM *Hrs Open:* 24; 1 kw; 571 ft.; N39 25 5 W77 30 3
5742 Industry Lane, Frederick, MD 21704 US
(301) 620-7700(301) 620-1031, *Fax:* (301) 696-0509
www.key103radio.com
lveihmeyer@nassaubroadcasting.com
License: Middletown, Frederick County, MD held by Nassau Broadcasting III L.L.C.
Group Owner: Nassau Broadcasting Partners L.P.; (acq 2-14-2005; $15.7 million).
Nat'l Reps: Katz Radio

Arbitron Metro Market: Frederick, MD *Format:* Adult Contemp *No. News Employees:* 2 *Target Audience:* 25-54; upscale, well-educated, great radio commitment
Rick Musselman, COO
Larry Veihmeyer, Director of Sales
Tom Shinn, Programming Director
Brian Corson, Promotions Manager
Mick Rapeer, Chief Engineer
Rona Mensah, Disc Jockey
Marc Richards, Disc Jockey
Dan Stevens, DiscJockey
Larry Veihmeyer, DOS

Midland

WDZN
08-29-1988; 99.5 mhz FM *Hrs Open:* 24; 1.05 kw; 787 ft.; N39 40 29.5 W78 57 43.3
US
(301) 724-6000, *Fax:* (301) 724-0617
www.radiodisney.com
License: Midland, Hampshire County, MD held by Charter Equities Inc.
Group Owner: West Virginia
Nat'l Network: Jones Radio Networks
Arbitron Metro Market: Midland, MD *Format:* Children *Hrs. of News Programming:* news progmg 15 hrs wkly *No. News Employees:* 1 *Target Audience:* 25-54; adult decision makers
Adv. Rates: 18; 18; 18; 13
Warren Gregory, President
Travis Medcalf, Operations Dir
Rick Williams, Chief Engineer

*WLVV
88.3 mhz FM; 2 w vert; Ant 1,351 ft; N39 34 51 W78 54 01
4271 Muncy-Exchange Rd., Turbotville, PA
(570) 412-6295
License: Midland, Allegany County, MD held by Muncy Hills Broadcasting Inc.
Van Michael, President

Morningside

WNEW
10-01-1954; 1580 khz AM *Hrs Open:* 24; 50 kw-D, 250 w-N, DA; N38 52 07 W76 53 48
4200 Parliament Place, Suite 300, Lanham, MD 20037
(301) 918-0955, *Fax:* (301) 459-9509
www.bigtalker1580.com
License: Morningside, Prince Georges County, MD held by CBS Radio WPGC(AM) Inc.
Group Owner: CBS Radio; (acq 1994; with co-located FM)
Population Served: 756,510 *Arbitron Metro Market:* Washington, DC *Target Audience:* 18-54.
Sam Rogers, General Manager

WPGC-FM
02-01-1959; 95.5 mhz FM *Hrs Open:* 24; 50 kw; 486 ft.; N38 51 49 W76 54 40
600 New Hampshire Ave., Suite 1200, Washington, DC 20037 US
(301) 918-0955, *Fax:* (301) 459-9509
www.wpgc955.com
License: Morningside, Prince Georges County, MD held by CBS Radio Inc. of Maryland.
Group Owner: CBS Radio
Arbitron Metro Market: Washington, DC *Format:* Contemporary Hits/Top 40 *Target Audience:* 18-54.
John Rohm, Operations Dir
Fred Traynor, General Sales Mgr
Jay Bohannon, Programming Director

Mountain Lake Park

WKHJ
07-09-1990; 104.5 mhz FM *Hrs Open:* 24; 1.5 kw; 663 ft.; N39 24 37 W79 17 15
P.O. Box 2337, Mtn. Lake Park, MD 21550 US
(301) 334-4272, *Fax:* (301) 334-2152
www.wkhj.com
wkhj@verizon.net
License: Mountain Lake Park, Garrett County, MD held by Southern Highlands Inc.
Nat'l Network: CNN Radio
Format: Adult Contemp *Hrs. of News Programming:* news progmg 12 hrs wkly *No. News Employees:* 1 *Target Audience:* 18-49. *Adv. Rates:* 24; 18; 24; 18
Terry King, General Manager
Pam Trickett, Promotions Manager
James Shaffer, News Director
Paul Mullan, Chief Engineer

Myersville

WWEG
03-01-1957; 106.9 mhz FM *Hrs Open:* 24; 15.5 kw; 853 ft.; N39 29 57 W77 36 42
880 Commonwealth Ave., Hagerstown, MD 21740 US
(301) 733-4500, *Fax:* (301) 733-0040
www.1069theeagle.com
info@1069theeagle.com
License: Myersville, Washington County, MD
Group Owner: Nassau Broadcasting Partners L.P.
Nat'l Network: Westwood One
Arbitron Metro Market: Hagerstown,MD *Format:* Contemporary Hits/Top 40, Adult Contemp *No. News Employees:* 2
Peter Stover, President
Kym McKay, Programming Director

Oakland

WMSG
05-19-1963; 1050 khz AM; 1 kw-D, ND1; 0.075 kw-N, ND1; N39 23 32 W79 23 54
P.O. Box 449, Oakland, MD 21550 US
(301) 334-3800, *Fax:* (301) 334-2152
www.wmsg.com
office@wkhj.com
License: Oakland, MD held by Oakland Media Group Inc.
Nat'l Network: CBS
Arbitron Metro Market: Oakland, MD *Format:* Oldies *Target Audience:* General.
Paul Mullan, General Manager

WWHC
01-01-1966; 92.3 mhz FM; 1.4 kw; 689 ft.; N39 26 41 W79 31 42
P.O. Box 449, Oakland, MD 21550 US
(301) 334-3800, *Fax:* (301) 334-2152
www.traincountry.com
office@wkhj.com
License: Oakland, Garrett County, MD held by Oakland Media Group
Nat'l Network: ABC
Arbitron Metro Market: Oakland, MD *Format:* Country
Paul Mullen, Operations Dir
Paul Mullen, General Manager

Ocean City

WAMS(AM)
07-01-1960; 1590 khz AM *Hrs Open:* 24; 1 kw-D, 500 w-N, DA-2; N38 24 16 W75 07 37
Mailing Address: 11500 Coastal Hwy., Sea Watch Suite #1, Ocean City, MD 21842
Second Address: 12216 Parklawn Dr., Suite 203, Rockville, MD 20852
(410) 723-9100
khzradio.com
wkhz1590@aol.com
License: Ocean City, Worcester County, MD held by Radio Broadcast Communications Inc.
Population Served: 550,000 *Arbitron Metro Market:* Salisbury-Ocean City, MD *Hrs. of News Programming:* News progmg 2 hrs wkly *Target Audience:* 25-54; active, thinking, responsive, affluent adults, with high disposableincome
Bill Parris, President

*WYPO
04-15-1994; 106.9 mhz FM; 4.5 kw; 384 ft.; N38 19 39 W75 11 50
#39 Thistle Lane/Bethany Meadows, Frankford, DE 19945 US
(410) 235-1660, *Fax:* (410) 235-1161
www.wypr.org
tbrandon@wypr.org
License: Ocean City, Worcester County, MD held by WYPR License Holding LLC
Nat'l Network: NPR; PRI
Arbitron Metro Market: Salisbury-Ocean *Format:* Jazz, News, 62, Talk
Anthony Brandon, President
Anthony Brandon, General Manager
Carol Madow, Promotions Manager

*WSDL
02-13-1998; 90.7 mhz FM *Hrs Open:* 24; 18.5 kw; 331 ft.; N38 30 6 W75 10 7
P O Box 2596, Salisbury, MD 21802 US
(410) 543-6895, *Fax:* (410) 548-3000
www.publicradiodelmarva.net
prd@salisbury.edu
License: Ocean City, Worcester County, MD held by Salisbury State University Foundation Inc.
Nat'l Network: NPR; PRI
Arbitron Metro Market: Salisbury-Ocean *Format:* News *Hrs. of News Programming:* news progmg 24 hrs wkly *No. News Employees:* 1 *Target Audience:* General.
Mike Dunn, General Manager
Chris Ranck, Programming Director
Don Rush, News Director

WWFG
06-30-1978; 99.9 mhz FM; 38 kw; 469 ft.; N38 25 20 W75 8 23
330 East Kilbourn Ave, Suite 250, Milwaukee, WI 53202 US
(410) 742-1923, *Fax:* (410) 742-2329
www.froggy999 .com
froggyemail@yahoo.com
License: Ocean City, Worcester County, MD held by Capstar TX L.P.
Group Owner: Clear Channel Communications Inc.; (acq 8-7-00; grpsl).
Nat'l Reps: Clear Channel
Arbitron Metro Market: Ocean City, MD *Format:* Country *Target Audience:* 25-54; affluent, upwardly mobile
Brian Cleary, Operations Dir
Frank Hamilton, General Manager
Paul Burton, General Sales Mgr
Josh Wolff, Programming Director
Dixie Penner, Promotions Manager
Marie Merrill, News Director
Steve Moore, Web Content Director
ChrisWalus, Market Manager
Matt Derrick, Operations Manager

*WRAU
88.3 mhz FM; 50 kw; 492 ft.; N38 23 12 W75 17 27
4400 Massachusetts Ave., NW, Washington, DC 20016 US
(202) 885-1200, *Fax:* (202) 885-1269
www.wamu.org
License: Ocean City, Worcester County, MD held by Exec. Comm. of Bd. of Trustees of American University.
Arbitron Metro Market: Ocean City, MD
Caryn Mathes, General Manager

Ocean City-Salisbury

WQHQ
07-31-1965; 104.7 mhz FM; 33 kw; 610 ft.; N38 23 15 W75 17 30
111 East Kilbourn, Suite 2700, Milwaukee, WI 53202 US
(410) 742-1923, *Fax:* (410) 742-2329
www.q105fm.com
License: Ocean City-Salisbury, Worcester County, MD
Arbitron Metro Market: Salisbury-Ocean City, MD *Format:* Adult Contemp *Target Audience:* 25-54.
Rob Kelley, Operations Dir
Mark DePrez, General Manager
Mogan David, Chief Engineer

Ocean Pines

WAVD
03-01-1994; 97.1 mhz FM *Hrs Open:* 24; 4.6 kw; 374 ft; N38 22 75 W75 10 32
Mailing Address: Box 909, Salisbury, MD 19803
Second Address: 919 Ellegood St., Salisbury, MD 21801
(410) 219-3500, *Fax:* (410) 548-1543
www.wqjz.com
wqjz@radiocenter.com
License: Ocean Pines, Worcester County, MD held by Delmarva Broadcasting Co.
Group Owner: Delmarva Broadcasting Co.; acq 6-26-97; grpsl)
Nat'l Reps: Katz Radio *Wire Services:* AP
Arbitron Metro Market: Salisbury-Ocean City, MD *No. News Employees:* 1 *Target Audience:* 30-60.
Joe Edwards, Operations Dir
Joe Beall, General Manager
Jeff Twilley, Chief Engineer

Pikesville

WQAL(AM)
04-05-1955; 1370 khz AM; 50 kw-D, 7.7 kw-N, DA-2; N39 26 23 W76 21 20
Hilton Plaza, 1726 Reisterstown, Baltimore, MD 21208
(410) 580-6800, *Fax:* (410) 580-6810
www.v1370.com
bcarl@wcbm.com
License: Pikesville, Baltimore County, MD held by M-10 Broadcasting Inc.
Nat'l Network: Fox Sports
Population Served: 619,493 *Arbitron Metro Market:* Baltimore, MD *Format:* Sports
Nick Mangione Jr., Operations Dir
Bob Pettit, General Manager
Marc Beavin, General Sales Mgr

Eddie Applefeld, Promotions Manager
Terry Trouyet, Operations Director

Pocomoke City

WGOP
08-01-1955; 540 khz AM; 0.5 kw-D, ND1; 0.243 kw-N, ND1; N38 3 11 W75 34 11
7 Fifth Street, Crisfield, MD 21817 US
(410) 957- 6081, *Fax:* (410) 457- 6080
www.birach.com
sima@BIRACH.Com
License: Pocomoke City, MD held by Birach Broadcasting Corp.
Group Owner: Birach Broadcasting Corp.; acq 11-25-92; $127,500;
Arbitron Metro Market: Pocomoke City, MD *Format:* Adult Contemp
Mike Powell, Operations Dir
Michael Powell, General Manager

WXSH
05-01-1992; 106.1 mhz FM; 4 kw; 341 ft.; N38 4 36 W75 32 18
1508 Market Street, Pocomoke City, MD 21851 US
(410) 957-6081, *Fax:* (410) 957-6080
www.maxima90zero.com
bay979@gmail.com
License: Pocomoke City, Worcester County, MD held by Great Scott Broadcasting.
Group Owner: Great Scott Broadcasting; (acq 7-16-99; $700,000 with WKHI(FM) Fruitland)
Arbitron Metro Market: Salisbury-Ocean City, MD *Format:* Urban Contemporary
Michael Powell, General Manager

WICO-FM
10-01-2000; 92.5 mhz FM; 2.95 kw; 472 ft.; N38 8 35 W75 39 53
6107 Elmendorf Drive, Suitland, MD 20746 US
(410) 219-3500, *Fax:* (410) 548-1543
www.wicotalk.com
wico@wicoam.com
License: Pocomoke City, Worcester County, MD held by Delmarva Broadcasting Co.
Group Owner: Delmarva Broadcasting Co.; acq 7-10-2000; $425,000)
Nat'l Network: CBS *Nat'l Reps:* Katz Radio *Wire Services:* AP
Arbitron Metro Market: Salisbury, MD *Format:* Talk *Hrs. of News Programming:* news progmg 2 hrs wkly *No. News Employees:* 1 *Target Audience:* Adults 35-54; baby boomers
Joe Edwards, Operations Dir
Joe Beail, General Manager
Bill Reddish, News Director
Jeff Twilley, Chief Engineer
Mike Kazala, Regional General Manager

Potomac-Cabin John

WCTN
01-01-1965; 950 khz AM *Hrs Open:* 24
7825 Tuckerman Lane, Potomac, MD 20854 US
(301) 879-2422, *Fax:* (301) 879-2562
www.radiolajefa.com
hernan@radiolajefa.com
License: Potomac-Cabin John, MD held by Win Radio Broadcasting Corp.
Arbitron Metro Market: Washington, DC *Format:* Oldies
Richard Yoon, President
Mauricio Rosales, General Manager

Prince Frederick

WWXT
08-01-1971; 92.7 mhz FM *Hrs Open:* 24; 2.85 kw; 476 ft.; N38 40 26 W76 35 41
P. O. Box 547, Prince Frederick, MD 20678 US
(301) 230-3500, *Fax:* (240) 430-2675
www.espn980.com
License: Prince Frederick, Calvert County, MD held by Red Zebra Broadcasting Licensee LLC.
Group Owner: Red Zebra Holdings LLC; (acq 5-9-2006; grpsl).
Nat'l Network: ESPN Radio
Arbitron Metro Market: Washington, DC *Format:* Sports
Bruce Gilbert, CEO

Princess Anne

*WESM
03-29-1987; 91.3 mhz FM *Hrs Open:* 24; 45 kw; 299 ft.; N38 12 37 W75 40 56
Backbone Road, Princess Anne, MD 21853 US
(410) 651-8001, *Fax:* (410) 651-8005
www.wesm913.org
wesm913@umes.edu
License: Princess Anne, Somerset County, MD held by University of Maryland Eastern Shore.
Nat'l Network: NPR; PRI
Arbitron Metro Market: Princess Anne, MD *Format:* Blues, Jazz *Special Programming:* Blues 5 hrs, reggae 2 hrs, big band 10 hrs, gospel 20 hrs wkly *Hrs. of News Programming:* news progmg 15 hrs wkly *No. NewsEmployees:* 1 *Target Audience:* General.
Dr. Thelma Thompson, President
Angel Resto Jr., Operations Dir
Stephen Williams, General Manager
Yancy Carrigan, Programming Director
Brian Daniels, Webmaster
Daphne Chatham, Administrative Assistant
Yancy Carrigan, MusicDirector

WOLC
12-24-1976; 102.5 mhz FM; 50 kw; 499 ft.; N38 6 43 W75 39 14
P. O. Box 130, Princess Anne, MD 21853 US
(410) 543-9652, *Fax:* (410) 651-9652
www.wolc.org
wolc@wolc.org
License: Princess Anne, Somerset County, MD held by Maranatha Inc.
Arbitron Metro Market: Salisbury-Ocean *TV Affiliate:* Relg *No. News Employees:* 25-64.

Rockville

WLXE
11-01-1951; 1600 khz AM *Hrs Open:* 24; 1 kw-D, 500 w-N, DA-N; N39 05 51 W77 09 07
13321 New Hampshire Ave, Suite 207, Silver Spring, MD 10153
(301) 879-2422, *Fax:* (301) 879-9070
License: Rockville, Montgomery County, MD held by Multicultural Radio Broadcasting Licensee LLC.
Group Owner: Multicultural Radio Broadcasting Inc.; (acq 7-31-01; $800,000).
Population Served: 4,000,000 *Arbitron Metro Market:* Washington, DC
Bill Parris, General Manager
Raul Lopez, Station Manager
Raul Lopez, General Sales Mgr
Raul Lopez, Programming Director

Salisbury

*WDIH
06-01-1990; 90.3 mhz FM; 0.38 kw; 180 ft.; N38 24 28 W75 36 16
P.O. Box 186, Salisbury, MD 21801 US
(443) 736-4257, *Fax:* (410) 713-4371
www.wdihradio90-3.org
wdihradio@comcast.net
License: Salisbury, Wicomico County, MD held by Salisbury Educational Broadcasting Foundation.
Arbitron Metro Market: Salisbury, MD *Format:* Christian
Bishop Dr. George Copeland, General Manager

WICO
09-01-1957; 1320 khz AM *Hrs Open:* 24; 1 kw-D, ND1; 0.028 kw-N, ND1; N38 21 39 W75 37 0
Mailing Address: 2727 Shipley Rd., P.O. Box 7492, Wilmington, DE 19803 US
Second Address: 919 Ellegood St., Salisbury, MD 21801
(410) 219-3500, *Fax:* (410) 548-1543
www.wicoam.com
wico@radiocenter.com
License: Salisbury, MD held by Delmarva Broadcasting Co.
Group Owner: Delmarva Broadcasting Co.; (acq 6-26-97; grpsl)
Nat'l Network: CBS Radio *Nat'l Reps:* Katz Radio *Wire Services:* AP
Arbitron Metro Market: Salisbury-Ocean City, MD *Format:* News, News/Talk, 84, Talk *Special Programming:* Farm one hr wkly *Hrs. of News Programming:* news progmg 18 hrs wkly *No. News Employees:* 2 *TargetAudience:* 35-64.
Joe Edwards, Operations Dir
Joe Beail, General Manager
Bill Reddish, News Director
Jeff Twilley, Chief Engineer

WKTT
09-03-1969; 97.5 mhz FM *Hrs Open:* 24; 4.5 kw; 299 ft.; N38 21 39 W75 37 0 *Rebroadcasts:* Rebroadcasts WZKT(FM) Lewes, DE 100%
Mailing Address: 2727 Shipley Rd., P.O. Box 7492, Wilmington, DE 19803 US
Second Address: 919 Ellegood St., Salisbury, MD 21801
(410) 219-3500, *Fax:* (410) 548-1543
www.catcountryradio.com
catcountry@radiocenter.com
License: Salisbury, Wicomico County, MD held by Delmarva Broadcasting Co.
Group Owner: Delmarva Broadcasting Co.; 1997
Nat'l Network: Motor Racing Net *Nat'l Reps:* Katz Radio *Wire Services:* AP
Arbitron Metro Market: Salisbury-Ocean City, MD *Format:* Country *Hrs. of News Programming:* news progmg 3 hrs wkly *No. News Employees:* 1 *Target Audience:* 25-54.
Joe Edwards, Operations Dir
Joe Beail, General Manager
E.J. Foxx, Programming Director
Brian Hall, Promotions Manager
Jeff Twiley, Chief Engineer

WJDY
03-14-1958; 1470 khz AM *Hrs Open:* 6 AM-midnight; 5 kw-D, DAD; 0.043 kw-N, DA2; N38 23 30 W75 38 48
111 East Kilbourn Ave., Suite 2700, Milwaukee, WI 53202 US
(410) 742-1923, *Fax:* (410) 742-2329
www.wjdy.com
billbaker@clearchannel.com
License: Salisbury, MD held by Capstar TX L.P.
Group Owner: Clear Channel Communications Inc.
Arbitron Metro Market: Salisbury-Ocean City, MD *Format:* Oldies *Target Audience:* 04-12.
John Thomas-Mason, News Director

*WLVW
07-25-1982; 105.5 mhz FM; 2.1 kw; Ant 384 ft; N38 24 26 W75 35 57
Gateway Crossing, 351 Tilghman Rd., Salisbury, MD 53202
(410) 742-1923, *Fax:* (410) 742-2329
www.kiss1055.com
kissfm@kiss1055.com
License: Salisbury, Wicomico County, MD held by Aloha Station Trust LLC
Nat'l Reps: Clear Channel
Arbitron Metro Market: Salisbury-Ocean City, MD *No. News Employees:* 1 *Target Audience:* 18-44.
Brian Cleary, Operations Dir
Frank Hamilton, General Manager
Dixie Penner, Promotions Manager
Marie Merrill, News Director

WSBY-FM
12-13-1989; 98.9 mhz FM *Hrs Open:* 24; 6 kw; 325 ft.; N38 18 0 W75 37 41
111 East Kilbourn Ave., Suite 2700, Milwaukee, WI 53202 US
(410) 742-1923, *Fax:* (410) 742-2329
www.wsby.com
delmarvapsa@clearchannel.com
License: Salisbury, Wicomico County, MD held by Capstar TX L.P.
Group Owner: Clear Channel Communications Inc.; (acq 8-7-00; grpsl).
Arbitron Metro Market: Salisbury-Ocean *Format:* Urban Contemporary *No. News Employees:* 1 *Target Audience:* 25-54.
Matt Derrick, Operations Dir
Frank Hamilton, General Manager
Paul Burton, General Sales Mgr
Bill Baker, Programming Director
Kenny Love, Chief Engineer
Marie Merrill, Traffic Manager

*WSCL
05-29-1987; 89.5 mhz FM *Hrs Open:* 24; 33 kw; 584 ft.; N38 39 15 W75 36 42
Mailing Address: P.O. Box 2596, Salisbury, MD 21802 US
Second Address: S. Salisbury Blvd., Salisbury, MD 21802
(410) 543-6895, *Fax:* (410) 548-3000
www.delmarvapublicradio.net
dpr@salisbury.edu
License: Salisbury, Wicomico County, MD held by Salisbury State University Foundation Inc.
Nat'l Network: NPR; PRI; AP Radio
Arbitron Metro Market: Salisbury-Ocean *Format:* Talk *Hrs. of News Programming:* news progmg 29 hrs wkly *No. News Employees:* 1 *Target Audience:* General.
Bill Bukowski, Operations Dir
Mike Dunn, General Manager
Chris Ranck, Programming Director
Don Rush, News Director

WTGM
09-13-1940; 960 khz AM *Hrs Open:* 24; 5 kw-D, DA2; 5 kw-N, DA2; N38 25 44 W75 37 26
111 East Kilbourn Ave., Suite 2700, Milwaukee, WI 53202 US
(410) 742-1923, *Fax:* (410) 742-2329
www.sportstalk960.com
delmarvapsa@clearchannel.com
License: Salisbury, MD held by Capstar TX L.P.

RADIO - U.S.

Group Owner: Clear Channel Communications Inc.; (acq 8-7-00; grpsl).
Arbitron Metro Market: Salisbury, MD *Format:* Sports *No. News Employees:* 1 *Target Audience:* 25-64.
Matt Derrick, Operations Dir
Frank Hamilton, General Manager
Paul Burton, General Sales Mgr
Randy Scott, Programming Director
John Thomas-Mason, News Director
Steve Moore, Web Content Director
Chris Walus, Market Manager

Silver Spring

WBQH(AM)
12-07-1946; 1050 khz AM *Hrs Open:* 24; 1 kw-D, 44 w-N; N39 00 50 W77 01 46 *Rebroadcasts:* Rebroadcasts WTOP-FM Washington, DC 100%
3400 Idaho Ave. N.W., Washington, DC 20016
(202) 895-5000, *Fax:* (202) 895-5016
www.wtopnews.com
info@wtopnews.com
License: Silver Spring, Montgomery County, MD held by Bonneville Holding Co.
Group Owner: Bonneville International Corporation; (acq 12-13-2004; $4 million)
Nat'l Network: CBS Radio *Wire Services:* AP
Population Served: 3,500,000 *Arbitron Metro Market:* Washington, DC *Format:* News
Bruce Reese, President
Joel Oxley, General Manager
Jim Farley, Programming Director

WBQH
12-07-1946; 1050 khz AM
8121 Georgia Ave 10th Fl, Silver Spring, MD 20910 US
(202)450-1508
www.lameramera1050.com
License: Silver Spring, MD held by Washington DC FCC License Sub LLC
Group Owner: Hubbard Broadcasting
Format: Spanish
Carlos Navarro, General Manager
Ruby Ramirez, Sales & Finance Director
Ismael Quintana, Programming Director

Snow Hill

WAMS-FM
02-01-2004; 101.1 mhz FM *Hrs Open:* 24; 1.2 kw; Ant 489 ft; N38 12 57 W75 19 21
Snow Hill Broadcasting L.L.C., 7200 Coastal Hwy., Ocean City, MD 21817
(410) 524-6862, *Fax:* (410) 524-6808
www.wqmr.com
kevin@wqmr.com
License: Snow Hill, Worcester County, MD held by Snow Hill Broadcasting L.L.C.
Population Served: 296,100 *Arbitron Metro Market:* Salisbury-Ocean City, MD *Special Programming:* Power Talk(local) Travel Show/Car Doc/Garison Show/ Tasting Room/ Satellite Sisters *Target Audience:* 18-64 Persons.*Adv. Rates:* 20; 20; 20; 20
Jack Gillen, President
Kevin Brenahan, Operations Dir
R.J. Shingleton, General Sales Mgr
Corey Duices, Programming Director
Heather Shingleton, News Director

St. Mary's City

***WGWS**
88.1 mhz FM; 1.1 kw; 174 ft.; N38 8 43 W76 22 22 US
(301) 862-4435
License: St. Mary's City, Saint Mary's County, MD held by Calvary Baptist Church of Lexington Park Inc.
Arbitron Metro Market: Saint Mary'S City, MD
William Ruckman, Chairman

St. Michaels

WINX-FM
01-01-2000; 94.3 mhz FM; 4.6 kw; 361 ft.; N38 37 49 W76 3 25
35 Oldsolomons Island Rd, Annapolis, MD 21401 US
(410) 822-3301, *Fax:* (410) 822-0576
www.winxfm.com
requests@winxfm.com
License: St. Michaels, Talbot County, MD held by First Media Radio LLC
Arbitron Metro Market: Saint Michaels, MD *Format:* Country
Matt Spence, Operations Dir
Stacie Monz, General Manager
Bill Parris, Station Manager
Cheryl Baynard, General Sales Mgr
Don O'Brien, Programming Director
Tina Saddler, Office Manager

Takoma Park

***WGTS**
05-08-1957; 91.9 mhz FM *Hrs Open:* 24; kw
7600 Flower Avenue, Takoma Park, MD 20912 US
(301) 891-4200, *Fax:* (301) 270-9191
www.wgts919.com
wgts@wgts919.com
License: Takoma Park, Montgomery County, MD held by Columbia Union College Broadcasting Inc.
Arbitron Metro Market: Washington, DC *Format:* Religious *Target Audience:* General.
Gerry Fuller, Chairman
John Konrad, General Manager
Becky Wilson Ali Gray, Programming Director

Thurmont

WTHU
06-12-1967; 1450 khz AM *Hrs Open:* 24; 0.5 kw-D, ND1; 0.4 kw-N, ND1; N39 37 37 W77 24 11
10 Radio Lane, Thurmont, MD 21788 US
(310) 637-6736, *Fax:* (240) 288-8337
www.wthu.org
License: Thurmont, MD held by Christian Radio Coalition Inc.
Arbitron Metro Market: Thurmont, MD *Format:* Talk
Michael Betteridge, General Manager
Foxglove Zayuri, News Director
Elizabeth lawrence, Production Manager
Rick Brown, Account Executive
William Warren, Director of IT Services

Towson

WNST
10-27-1955; 1570 khz AM; 5 kw-D, ND1; 0.237 kw-N, ND1; N39 25 4 W76 33 23
3248 Rittenhouse St NW, Washington, DC 20015 US
(410) 821-9678, *Fax:* (410) 828-4698
www.wnst.net
info@wnst.net
License: Towson, MD held by Nasty 1570 Sports LLC.
Arbitron Metro Market: Baltimore, MD *Format:* Sports
Paul Kopelke, General Manager
Steve Hennessey, General Sales Mgr

***WTMD**
02-12-1976; 89.7 mhz FM *Hrs Open:* 24; 10 kw; 236 ft.; N39 23 45 W76 36 29
Towson University, 8000 York Road, Towson, MD 21252 US
(410) 704-8938, *Fax:* (410) 704-2609
www.wtmd.org
wtmd@towson.edu
License: Towson, Baltimore County, MD held by Towson University.
Arbitron Metro Market: Towson, MD *Format:* Triple A *Hrs. of News Programming:* News progmg 6 hrs wkly *Target Audience:* 25-64.
Ryan Glaeser, Operations Dir
Stephen Yasko, General Manager
Scott Mullins, Programming Director
Tyler Laporte, Music Director
Sam Gallant, Producer
Kristin Bachran, Membership Manager
Chris Hawkins, Underwriting and SponsorshipManager
Megan Amoss, Traffic Coordinator

Waldorf

WPRS-FM
02-01-1965; 104.1 mhz FM *Hrs Open:* 24; 20 kw; 801 ft.; N38 37 7.4 W76 50 39
C/O David K Redd, P.O. Box 1160, Salt Lake City, UT 84110 US
(301) 306-1111
www.praise1041.com
info@praise1041.com
License: Waldorf, Charles County, MD held by Radio One Licenses LLC.
Group Owner: Radio One Inc.; (acq 9-5-2007)
Arbitron Metro Market: Waldorf, MD *Format:* Black, Gospel
Chris Wegmann, General Manager
Ron Thompson, Programming Director
Sherise Malachi, Promotions Manager
Sheila Stewart, News Director/Community Events/Public Affairs
Pharoh Martin, Online Editor
Yolanda Adams, Executive Producer

Walkersville

WDMV
12-01-1994; 700 khz AM; 5 kw-D, DAD; N39 27 27 W77 19 27
21700 Northwestern Hwy, Tower 14, Ste 1190, Southfield, MI 48075 US
(703) 272-7600, *Fax:* (703) 272-7604
www.birach.com
sima@birach.com
License: Walkersville, MD held by Birach Broadcasting Corp.
Group Owner: Birach Broadcasting Corp.; (acq 9-95).
Arbitron Metro Market: Walkersville, MD
Sima Birach, President

Westernport

WWPN
10-01-1993; 101.1 mhz FM; 0.32 kw; 1368 ft.; N39 22 58 W79 4 43
Box 3382, Lavale, MD 21502 US
(301) 463-5100
www.spirit101.com
License: Westernport, Allegany County, MD held by Ernest F. Santmyire.
Arbitron Metro Market: Westernport, MD *Format:* Christian, Religious *Target Audience:* 18-45; working class
Ernest Santmyire, CEO

Westminster

WZBA
11-01-1959; 100.7 mhz FM *Hrs Open:* 24; 25 kw; 689 ft.; N39 26 50 W76 46 48
149 Penn Avenue, Scranton, PA 18505 US
(410) 771-8484, *Fax:* (410) 771-1616
www.thebayonline.com
jlaird@thebayonline.com
License: Westminster, Carroll County, MD held by Shamrock Communications Inc.
Group Owner: Shamrock Communications Inc.; (acq 4-7-81; $1.74 million with co-located AM;
Arbitron Metro Market: Baltimore, MD *Format:* Classic Rock *Hrs. of News Programming:* News progmg one hr wkly *Target Audience:* 25-49; men & women active in the country life group
Jeff Laird, General Manager
Lynn Pollvoy, General Sales Mgr
Jon McGann, Programming Director
Laura Sigler, News Director
Dave Schmidt, Chief Engineer

WTTR
07-01-1953; 1470 khz AM *Hrs Open:* 24; 1 kw-D, DAN; 1 kw-N, DAN; N39 34 37 W77 1 21
149 Penn Avenue, Scranton, PA 18503 US
(410) 876-1515, *Fax:* (410) 876-5095
www.wttr.com
info@wttr.com
License: Westminster, MD held by Sajak Broadcasting Corp.
Arbitron Metro Market: Baltimore, MD *Format:* Contemporary Hits/Top 40, Adult Contemp *Special Programming:* Farm 4 hrs wkly *Hrs. of News Programming:* news progmg 12 hrs wkly *No. News Employees:* 1 *TargetAudience:* 35-64.
Pat Sajak, CEO
Steve Hopp, General Manager
Dwight Dingle, Station Manager
Mark Woodworth, News Director

Wheaton

WACA
01-01-1954; 1540 khz AM; 1 kw-C, NDD; 5 kw-D, NDD; N39 0 50 W77 1 46
2000 K St., N.W., Suite 600, Washington, DC 20006 US
(512) 467-0643
License: Wheaton, MD held by Entravision Holdings LLC.
Group Owner: Entravision Communications Corp.; (acq 3-14-00; grpsl)
Arbitron Metro Market: Monterey-Salinas-Santa Cruz CA
Robert Walker, President

Williamsport

***WCRH**
07-24-1976; 90.5 mhz FM *Hrs Open:* 24; 10 kw; 879 ft.; N39 39 34 W77 57 56
Mailing Address: P.O. Box 439, Williamsport, MD 21795 US
Second Address: 12146 Cedar Ridge Rd., Williamsport, MD 21795

(301) 582-0285, *Fax:* (301) 582-2707
www.wcrh.org
wcrh@wcrh.org
License: Williamsport, Washington County, MD held by Cedar Ridge Children's Home and School Inc.
Nat'l Network: Moody
Arbitron Metro Market: Hagerstown, MD *Format:* Religious *Hrs. of News Programming:* news progmg 9 hrs wkly *No. News Employees:* 1 *Target Audience:* 25-45.
David Swacina, CEO
Jeff Ward, Operations Dir

WICL
11-15-1972; 95.9 mhz FM *Hrs Open:* 24; 3.3 kw; 299 ft.; N39 36 18 W77 46 49
5393 Royal Mile Boulevard, Salisbury, MD 21801 US
(304) 263-8868, *Fax:* (304) 263-8906
959.grapesoda.com
License: Williamsport, Washington County, MD held by Prettyman Broadcasting Co.
Group Owner: Prettyman Broadcasting Co.; (acq 3-10-98; $1.05 million).
Arbitron Metro Market: Williamsport, MD *Format:* Oldies *Hrs. of News Programming:* News progmg 15 hrs wkly *Target Audience:* 35-64.
Norm Slemenda, General Manager

Worton

*WKHS
03-28-1974; 90.5 mhz FM; 17.5 kw; 217 ft.; N39 16 55 W76 5 26
Mailing Address: Washington Avenue, Chestertown, MD 21620 US
Second Address: Rts. 297 & 298, Worton, MD 21678
(410) 778-4249, *Fax:* (410) 778-3802
www.wkhsradio.org
wkhsradio@gmail.com
License: Worton, Kent County, MD held by Board of Education of Kent County.
Format: Variety/Diverse *Special Programming:* Oldies 6 hrs, children 5 hrs, country 2 hrs, big b *Target Audience:* 12 plus.
Steve Kramarck, General Manager
Chris Singleton, Station Manager

Massachusetts

Acton

*WHAB
08-01-1979; 89.1 mhz FM *Hrs Open:* 10 AM-5:30 PM (M-F); 0.008 kw; 26 ft.; N42 28 48 W71 27 28
96 Hayward Road, Acton, MA 01720 US
(978) 264-4700
www.quadphonic.com
License: Acton, Middlesex County, MA held by Acton-Boxborough Regional School District.
Format: News, Variety/Diverse
Dan Drinkwater, General Manager

Amherst

*WAMH
01-01-1955; 89.3 mhz FM *Hrs Open:* 24; 0.15 kw; 719 ft.; N42 21 51 W72 25 24
Box 1808, P.O. Box 5000, Amherst, MA 01002 US
(413) 542-2224(413) 542-2288
www.amherst.edu/~wamh
wamh@amherst.edu
License: Amherst, Hampshire County, MA held by Trustees of Amherst College.
Arbitron Metro Market: Amherst, MA *Format:* Variety/Diverse *Hrs. of News Programming:* News progmg 2 hrs wkly *Target Audience:* 16-32; youth of today
Ashley Hogan, General Manager
Chris Spaide, Programming Director
Dan Correia, Chief Engineer

*WFCR
05-06-1961; 88.5 mhz FM *Hrs Open:* 24; 13 kw; Ant 895 ft; N42 21 49 W72 25 24
131 County Circle, Hampshire House, Amherst, MA 01003
(413) 545-0100, *Fax:* (413) 545-2546
www.nepr.net
radio@nepr.net
License: Amherst, Hampshire County, MA held by University of Massachusetts.
Nat'l Network: PRI; NPR *Wire Services:* AP
Population Served: 1,183,119 *Arbitron Metro Market:* Springfield, MA *Special Programming:* Sp 2 hrs wkly *Hrs. of News Programming:* news progmg 40 hrs wkly *No. News Employees:* 6 *Target Audience:* General.
Martin Miller, General Manager

*WMUA
01-01-1949; 91.1 mhz FM *Hrs Open:* 24; 0.45 kw; 128 ft.; N42 23 37 W72 31 21
102 Campus Center, Amherst, MA 01003 US
(413) 545-2876, *Fax:* (413) 545-0682
www.wmua.org
manager@wmua.org
License: Amherst, Hampshire County, MA held by Board of Trustees of University of Massachusetts.
Arbitron Metro Market: Hampshire, MA *Format:* Variety/Diverse *Hrs. of News Programming:* News progmg 3 hrs wkly *Target Audience:* General; Univ
Kevin Eglitis, General Manager
Nick Russo, Programming Director
Ben Axelson, News Director
Dan Ferreira, Chief Engineer
Corey Charron, Music Director

WRNX
11-12-1990; 100.9 mhz FM; kw
98 Lower Westfield Road, Holyoke, MA 01040 US
(413) 781-1011, *Fax:* (413) 734-4434
www.wrnx.com
License: Amherst, Hampshire County, MA held by CC Licenses LLC.
Group Owner: Clear Channel Communications Inc.; (acq 4-1-2007; grpsl)
Arbitron Metro Market: Springfield, MA *Format:* Triple A
Sean Davey, General Manager

WPNI
04-02-1963; 1430 khz AM *Hrs Open:* 6 AM-midnight; 5 kw-D, DA2; 0.011 kw-N, DA2; N42 21 25 W72 29 13
98 Lower Westfield Rd, Holyoke, MA 01040 US
(413) 536-1105, *Fax:* (413) 536-1153
License: Amherst, MA held by 6 Johnson Road Licenses Inc.
Group Owner: Pamal Broadcasting Ltd.; (acq 5-29-2003; $8 million with co-located FM)
Arbitron Metro Market: Springfield, MA *Format:* News, News/Talk, 86
Fred Caruso, Operations Dir
Jeff Fisher, General Manager
Jess Levitan, General Sales Mgr
Amy Bates, News Director
Cathy Keizer, Traffic Manager

Andover

WXRV
06-01-1959; 92.5 mhz FM *Hrs Open:* 24; 25 kw; 712 ft.; N42 46 23 W71 6 1
288 South River Road, Bedford, NH 03110 US
(978) 374-4733, *Fax:* (978) 373-8023
www.wxrv.com
info@wxrv.com
License: Andover, Essex County, MA held by Beanpot License Corp.
Group Owner: Northeast Broadcasting Company Inc.; (acq 1981).
Arbitron Metro Market: Andover, MA *Format:* Adult Contemp, Triple A *Target Audience:* 25-54.
Terry Lieberman, General Manager
Steve Young, General Sales Mgr
Ron Bowen, Programming Director
John Mullett, Promotions Manager
AJ Crozby, Production Director
Rita Cary, Air Staff
Carolyn Morrell, Air Staff
Matt Phipps, AirStaff
Irene Collins, Air Staff

Ashland

WSRO
05-01-1967; 650 khz AM
22942 Captain Kidd Lane, Cudjoe Key, FL 33042 US
(508) 424-2568, *Fax:* (508) 820-2473
www.wsro.com
wsroam650@yahoo.com
License: Ashland, MA held by Langer Broadcasting Group L.L.C.
Group Owner: Langer Broadcasting Group L.L.C.; acq 1996; $10,000).
Arbitron Metro Market: Boston *Format:* Talk, Religious *Target Audience:* 20-80; general
Carl Abrams, General Manager

Athol

WXRG
12-04-1989; 99.9 mhz FM *Hrs Open:* 24; 1.85 kw; 407 ft.; N42 35 39 W72 12 2
P.O. Box 1230, Claremont, NH 03743 US
(978) 374-4733, *Fax:* 978-373-8023
www.wxrv.com
info@wxrv.com
License: Athol, Worcester County, MA held by County Broadcasting Co. LLC.
Group Owner: Northeast Broadcasting Company Inc.; (acq 10-6-2003; $650,000 with WJOE(AM) Orange-Athol).
Nat'l Network: ABC
Arbitron Metro Market: Haverhill, Ma *Format:* Classic Rock
Glenn Cardinal, General Manager
Spencer Marshall, Programming Director
John Mullett, Promotions Manager
AJ Crozby, Production Director

Attleboro

WARL
10-08-1950; 1320 khz AM; 5 kw-D, DA2; 5 kw-N, DA2; N41 57 33 W71 19 37
100 Bedford Street, New Bedford, MA 02719 US
(508) 989-5013, *Fax:* (401) 521-5878
www.1320thedrive.com
scott@spojo.com
License: Attleboro, MA held by The ADD Radio Group Inc.
Arbitron Metro Market: Providence-Warwick-Pawtucket, RI *Format:* News, News/Talk, 84, Talk *Target Audience:* 18 plus; middle to upper middle class
Scott MacPherson, General Manager

Baptist Village

*WWQZ
89.5 mhz FM; 40 w horiz, 35 w vert; Ant 384 ft; N42 05 01 W72 24 51
52 New Hartford Rd., Barkhamsted, CT
(860) 379-3365, *Fax:* (860) 828-6109
www.junctionradio.org
License: Baptist Village, Hampden County, MA held by Morgan Brook Chirstian Radio Inc.
G. Thomas Palmer, President

Barnstable

WQRC
07-20-1970; 99.9 mhz FM *Hrs Open:* 24; 50 kw; 381 ft.; N41 41 19 W70 20 49
737 Westmain Street, Hyannis, MA 02601 US
(508) 771-1224, *Fax:* (508) 775-2605
www.wqrc.com
wqrc@wqrc.com
License: Barnstable, Barnstable County, MA held by Sandab Communications Limited Partnership II
Group Owner: Sandab Communications L.P. II; acq 4-16-92; grpsl;
Nat'l Network: AP Radio *Nat'l Reps:* Clear Channel *Wire Services:* AP
Arbitron Metro Market: Cape Cod, MA *Format:* Adult Contemp *Hrs. of News Programming:* news progmg 32 hrs wkly *No. News Employees:* 4 *Target Audience:* Adults/women; 25-54
Wayne W. White, Operations Dir
Gregory D. Bone, General Manager
Stephen M. Colella, General Sales Mgr
Michelle Lorraine, Promotions Manager
Donna Credit, News Director
Judy Crocker, Sales Manager

Bayview

*WPMW
88.5 mhz FM; 0.14 kw; 177 ft.; N41 38 22.6 W70 58 4.9 US
(508) 996-1039, *Fax:* (508) 996-8296
www.radiocormariae.com
webmaster@radiocormariae.com
License: Bayview, Bristol County, MA held by Academy of the Immaculate Inc.
Nat'l Network: EWTN Radio
Arbitron Metro Market: New Bedford, MA *Format:* Christian
Louis Maximilian Smith, General Manager
John Mary Risse, Webmaster

Beverly

WNSH
12-23-1963; 1570 khz AM *Hrs Open:* 24
Longmeadow Way, Box 403, Hamilton, MA 01936 US

(978) 921-1570, *Fax:* (978) 468-1954
www.viva1570.com
jackwhite@wnsh.com
License: Beverly, MA held by Willow Farm Inc.
Arbitron Metro Market: Boston, MA *Format:* Talk *Hrs. of News Programming:* news progmg 15 hrs wkly *No. News Employees:* 2 *Target Audience:* 35 plus.
Jack White, General Manager

Boston

WBMX
01-01-1948; 104.1 mhz FM *Hrs Open:* 24; 21 kw; 771 ft.; N42 20 50 W71 4 59
600 New Hampshire Ave., Suite 1200, Washington, DC 20037 US
(617) 746-1300, *Fax:* (617) 779-2002
www.mix1041.cbslocal.com/
mmullaney@mix1041.com
License: Boston, Suffolk County, MA held by CBS Radio Stations Inc.
Group Owner: CBS Radio; (acq 6-5-98; grpsl)
Nat'l Network: CBS *Nat'l Reps:* Christal
Arbitron Metro Market: Boston, MA *Format:* Adult Contemp
Barbara Jean Scannell, General Manager
Doreen Wong, General Sales Mgr
Steve Salhany, Programming Director
Dana Zabilski, Promotions Manager
Mike Mullaney, Music Director/APD

*WBUR-FM
03-01-1950; 90.9 mhz FM *Hrs Open:* 24; 12 kw; 1001 ft.; N42 18 27 W71 13 27
890 Commonwealth Avenue, Boston, MA 02215 US
(617) 353-0909, *Fax:* (617) 353-4747
www.wbur.org
info@wbur.org
License: Boston, Suffolk County, MA held by The Executive Committee of Trustees of The Boston University.
Nat'l Network: NPR; PRI
Arbitron Metro Market: Boston, MA *Format:* News, Talk *Target Audience:* 25-54; intelligent adults interested in news natl, internatl & local
Jean Wong, CFO
Paul LaCamera, General Manager
Corey Lewis, Station Manager
Sam Fleming, Programming Director
John Davidow, News Director
Jeff Hutton, Engineering Dir

WBZ
09-19-1921; 1030 khz AM *Hrs Open:* 24; 50 kw-U, DA1; N42 16 44 W70 52 34
600 New Hampshire Avenue, NW, Suite 1200, Washington, DC 20037 US
(617) 787-7000, *Fax:* (617) 787-5969
www.boston.cbslocal.com/
License: Boston, MA held by CBS Radio East Inc.
Group Owner: CBS Radio
Nat'l Network: ABC; CBS *Nat'l Reps:* CBS Radio
Arbitron Metro Market: Boston,MA *Format:* News, News/Talk, 86 *Target Audience:* 25-54.
Ted Jordan, General Manager
Peter Casey, Programming Director

WEEI
12-01-1926; 850 khz AM *Hrs Open:* 24
401 City Avenue, Suite 409, Bala Cynwyd, PA 19004 US
(617) 779-3500, *Fax:* (617) 779-3557
www.weei.com
info@weei.com
License: Boston, MA held by Entercom Boston License L.L.C.
Group Owner: Entercom Communications Corp.; (acq 10-15-98; $82 million with WRKO(AM) Boston)
Nat'l Network: CBS
Arbitron Metro Market: Boston, MA *Format:* Sports, Talk *No. News Employees:* 6 *Target Audience:* 25-54.
Julie Kahn, General Manager
Jim Rushton, General Sales Mgr
Jason Wolfe, Programming Director

*WERS
11-14-1949; 88.9 mhz FM *Hrs Open:* 24; 4 kw; 610 ft.; N42 21 8 W71 3 25
100 Beacon Street, Boston, MA 02116 US
(617) 824-8890, *Fax:* (617) 824-8804
www.wers.org
info@wers.org
License: Boston, Suffolk County, MA held by Emerson College.
Wire Services: AP
Arbitron Metro Market: Boston, MA *Format:* Variety/Diverse *Hrs. of News Programming:* news progmg 3.5 hrs wkly *No. News Employees:* 6
Howard D. Simpson, Operations Dir
Dr. Jack Casey, General Manager
Mariel Wade, Programming Director
Jen Gasbarro, Promotions Manager
Alyssa Edes, News Director
R. J. Perkins, Engineering Dir
Andrew Kessler, MembershipCoordinator
Peter Kirchoff, Underwriting Director
Sara Morgan, Marketing Director
Bentley Holt, Assistant Program Director - Daytime Programming
Kendall Stewart, Daytime Music Director
Kathleen St. Fleur, Music Director - UrbanProgramming

WEZE
590 khz AM *Hrs Open:* 24; 5 kw-U, DA1; N42 24 24 W71 5 14
4880 Santa Rosa Road, Suite 300, Camarillo, CA 93012 US
(617) 691-2574, *Fax:* (617) 328-0375
www.wezeradio.com
contactus@salemradioboston.com
License: Boston, MA held by Pennsylvania Media Associates Inc.
Group Owner: Salem Communications Corp.; (acq 1-31-97; $6 million)
Arbitron Metro Market: Boston, MA *Format:* Talk, Religious *Hrs. of News Programming:* News progmg 5 hrs wkly *Target Audience:* 25 plus.
Edward Atsinger III, President
Tim Szymanski, Operations Dir
Pat Ryan, General Manager
Patricia Ryan, General Sales Mgr
Frank Kelley, Chief Engineer
Basil Yarde, Director of Church Relations
Pauline Rockwell, Business Manager
Carole Howley-Simmons, Account Executive
Veronica Navarro, Traffic Coordinator
Carol Austin, Production Director
Christie Reading, Administrative Assistant/ Web & Graphics Personnel

*WGBH(FM)
10-06-1951; 89.7 mhz FM *Hrs Open:* 24; 98 kw; 650 ft; N42 12 42 W71 06 51
1 Guest St., Brighton, MA 2135
(617) 300-2000, *Fax:* (617) 300-5400
www.wgbh.org
wgbh@wgbh.org
License: Boston, Suffolk County, MA held by WGBH Educational Foundation.
Nat'l Network: PRI; NPR
Population Served: 330,000 *Arbitron Metro Market:* Boston *TV Affiliate:* *WGBH-TV, *WGBX-TV affils *Format:* Jazz, News
Special Programming: Folk 10 hrs, blues 8 hrs, Irish 2 hrs, cultural 3 *Hrs. of NewsProgramming:* News progmg 22 hrs wkly
Target Audience: General.
John Abbott, President
Marita Rivero, General Manager

WILD
01-01-1946; 1090 khz AM
90 Warren Street, Boston, MA 02119 US
(617) 471-0618, *Fax:* (617) 471-4289
www.wild949.com
randerson@radio-one.com
License: Boston, MA held by Radio One of Boston Licenses LLC.
Group Owner: Radio One Inc.; (acq 12-20-2000; $5 million in cash & stock merger)
Nat'l Network: ABC *Nat'l Reps:* Roslin
Arbitron Metro Market: Boston *Format:* News, News/Talk, 86
Target Audience: General.
Rick Anderson, General Manager

WJMN
03-31-1948; 94.5 mhz FM; 9.2 kw; 1158 ft.; N42 18 27 W71 13 27
433 E. Las Colinas Blvd, #1130, Irving, TX 75039 US
(781) 663-2500, *Fax:* (781) 290-0722
www.jamn945.com
management@jamn945.com
License: Boston, Suffolk County, MA held by AMFM Radio Licenses L.L.C.
Group Owner: Clear Channel Communications Inc.; (acq 8-30-00; grpsl)
Nat'l Reps: Katz Radio
Arbitron Metro Market: Boston *Format:* Contemporary Hits/Top 40 *Target Audience:* 12-44. *Adv. Rates:* 400; 400; 450; 300
Tom McConnell, General Manager

WMJX
01-06-1982; 106.7 mhz FM; 21.5 kw; 771 ft.; N42 20 50 W71 4 59
Two Kennedy Boulevard, East Brunswick, NJ 08816 US
(617) 822-6420, *Fax:* (617) 822-6571
dkelley@magic1067.com
License: Boston, Suffolk County, MA held by Greater Boston Radio Inc.
Group Owner: Greater Media Inc.; (acq 2-85)
Nat'l Reps: Katz Radio
Arbitron Metro Market: Boston, MA *Format:* Adult Contemp
Phil Redo, General Manager
Jackie Laudry, General Sales Mgr
Don Kelley, Programming Director

WWDJ
02-04-2008; 1150 khz AM *Hrs Open:* 24
8121 Georgia Ave, Silver Spring, MD 20910 US
(617) 328-0880, *Fax:* (617) 328-0375
www.radioluzboston.com
DanyP@SalemRadioBoston.com
License: Boston, MA held by Pennsylvania Media Associates Inc.
Group Owner: Salem Communications Corp.; (acq 10-31-2003; $8.6 million)
Arbitron Metro Market: Boston, MA *Format:* Christian
Dany Perez, Station Manager
Patricia Ryan, General Sales Mgr

WWZN
01-01-1934; 1510 khz AM; 50 kw-U, DA-2; N42 23 10 W71 12 01
1 Van De Graaff Dr., Suite 300, Burlington, MA 60062
(781) 221-7878, *Fax:* (781) 221-7877
www.1510thezone.com
wwzn@1510thezone.com
License: Boston, Suffolk County, MA held by Blackstrap Broadcasting LLC
Group Owner: Rose City Radio Corp.
Nat'l Network: Sporting News Radio Network
Population Served: 535,000 *Arbitron Metro Market:* Boston
Target Audience: 25-54.
Anthony Pepe, General Manager
Brian Uluski, General Sales Mgr
Jon Anik, Programming Director
Brad Parsons, Chief Engineer

WODS
01-01-1948; 103.3 mhz FM; 8.7 kw; 1152 ft.; N42 18 27.4 W71 13 26.7
600 New Hampshire Avenue, NW, Suite 1200, Washington, DC 20037 US
(617) 787-7500, *Fax:* (617) 787-7523
www.oldies1033.com
murley.tina@cbsradio.com
License: Boston, Suffolk County, MA held by CBS Radio East Inc.
Group Owner: CBS Radio; (acq 11-13-98; grpsl)
Nat'l Reps: CBS Radio
Arbitron Metro Market: Boston *TV Affiliate:* Top 40
General Manager, General Manager

WMKI
01-01-1922; 1260 khz AM
866 2nd Ave., 2nd Fl, New York, NY 10017 US
(617) 787-0146, *Fax:* (617) 787-1236
www.disney.com
License: Boston, MA held by Radio Disney Group LLC.
Group Owner: ABC Inc.; (acq 8-22-00; grpsl).
Nat'l Network: USA
Arbitron Metro Market: Boston *Format:* Children *Target Audience:* 6-14. *Adv. Rates:* 100; 100; 100; 40
Michael Kellogg, Station Manager

*WRBB
10-01-1970; 104.9 mhz FM *Hrs Open:* 24; 0.019 kw; 89 ft.; N42 20 19 W71 5 28
360 Huntington Avenue, Boston, MA 02115 US
(617) 373-4338, *Fax:* (617) 373-5095
www.wrbbradio.org
License: Boston, Suffolk County, MA held by Northeastern University.
Arbitron Metro Market: Boston *Format:* Variety/Diverse *Hrs. of News Programming:* news progmg 2 hrs wkly *No. News Employees:* 1 *Target Audience:* 12-35; college, urban
Emily Rodrigues, General Manager
Michelle Bablo, Programming Director
Ryan Scianino, Engineering Dir

WRKO
01-01-1922; 680 khz AM; 50 kw-D, DA2; 50 kw-N, DA2; N42 29 25 W71 13 5
401 City Avenue, Suite 409, Bala Cynwyd, PA 19004 US

(617) 779-3400, *Fax:* (617) 779-3467
www.wrko.com
License: Boston, MA held by Entercom Boston License L.L.C.
Group Owner: Entercom Communications Corp.; (acq 10-15-98; $82 million with WEEI(AM) Boston)
Nat'l Network: ABC
Arbitron Metro Market: Boston *Format:* Talk *Target Audience:* 25-54.
Julie Kahn, General Manager
Jim Rushton, General Sales Mgr
Christina Andres, Promotions Manager

WROL
10-08-1950; 950 khz AM *Hrs Open:* 24; 5 kw-D, NDD; 0.09 kw-N, ND1; N42 26 15 W70 59 40
20 Park Plaza, Suite 720, Boston, MA 02116 US
(617) 328-0880, *Fax:* (617) 328-0375
www.wrolboston.com
PatR@SalemRadioBoston.com
License: Boston, MA held by Salem Media Group LLC.
Group Owner: Salem Communications Corp.; (acq 3-2-2001; $11 million)
Arbitron Metro Market: Boston *Format:* Christian *Special Programming:* Irish music programming; Car Doctor *Target Audience:* Adults.
Patricia Ryan, General Sales Mgr

WTKK
01-01-1945; 96.9 mhz FM; 22.5 kw; 735 ft.; N42 20 50 W71 4 59
P.O. Box 1059, East Brunswick, NJ 08816 US
(617) 822-9600, *Fax:* (617) 822-6871
www.wtkk.com
License: Boston, Suffolk County, MA held by Greater Boston Radio Inc.
Group Owner: Greater Media Inc.; (acq 3-31-93; $11.65 million;
Nat'l Reps: Katz Radio
Arbitron Metro Market: Boston *Format:* Talk
Nika Desautels, General Sales Mgr
Grace Blazer, Programming Director
Hisham Fayed, Promotions Manager

***WUMB-FM**
09-19-1982; 91.9 mhz FM *Hrs Open:* 24; 0.66 kw; 207 ft.; N42 15 27 W71 1 44
Harbor Campus, Boston, MA 02125 US
(617) 287-6900, *Fax:* (617) 287-6916
www.wumb.org
wumb@umb.edu
License: Boston, Suffolk County, MA held by The University of Massachusetts.
Nat'l Network: PRI; NPR
Arbitron Metro Market: Boston, MA *Format:* Variety/Diverse *Hrs. of News Programming:* News progmg 5 hrs wkly *Target Audience:* 25-40.
Patricia Monteith, General Manager
Patty Domeniconi, Station Manager
Brian Quinn, Programming Director
Grady Moates, Engineering Dir
Anita Lee, Membership Coordinator
Jay Moberg, Music Director

WZLX
01-01-1979; 100.7 mhz FM; 21.5 kw; 771 ft.; N42 20 50 W71 4 59
600 New Hampshire Ave., Suite 1200, Washington, DC 20037 US
(617) 746-5100, *Fax:* (617) 746-5105
www.wzlx.com
mikethomas@wzlx.com
License: Boston, Suffolk County, MA held by CBS Radio Inc. of Boston.
Group Owner: CBS Radio; (acq 11-13-98; grpsl)
Nat'l Network: CBS *Nat'l Reps:* CBS Radio
Arbitron Metro Market: Boston, MA *Format:* Classic Rock *Target Audience:* 25-54; males
Mark Hannon, General Manager
David Place, General Sales Mgr
Mike Thomas, Programming Director
Joe Soucise, Chief Engineer
Carter Alan, Music Director/APD
Cha Chi Loprete, Marketing Director
Adam Luciano, PromotionsCoordinator
Dan Baptiste, Local Sales Manager
Kevin Brown, Digital Sales Manager
Tim Staskiewicz, Digital Director

Boxford

***WBMT**
01-30-1978; 88.3 mhz FM *Hrs Open:* 2:30 PM-9 PM(M-F); 10 AM-6 PM(S,Su); 0.66 kw; 33 ft.; N42 37 38 W70 58 32
20 Endicott Road, Topsfield/Boxford, MA 01983 US
(978) 887-8830
www.masconomet.org
wbmtradio@masconomet.org
License: Boxford, Essex County, MA held by Masconomet Regional High School System.
Arbitron Metro Market: Topsfieldboxford, MA *Format:* Rock/AOR
Joseph Czarnecki, General Manager

Brewster

***WZAI**
01-01-2006; 94.3 mhz FM; 4.7 kw; Ant 372 ft; N41 46 36 W70 00 40 *Rebroadcasts:* Rebroadcasts WCAI-FM Woods Hole 100%
Mailing Address: Box 82, Woods Hole, MA
Second Address: 3 Water St, Woods Hole, MA 2543
(508) 548-9600, *Fax:* (508) 548-5517
www.capeandislands.org
cainan@wgbh.org
License: Brewster, Barnstable County, MA held by WGBH Educational Foundation.
Nat'l Network: NPR
John Voci, Station Manager

Bridgewater

***WBIM-FM**
11-01-1972; 91.5 mhz FM *Hrs Open:* 24; 0.18 kw; 72 ft.; N41 59 15 W70 58 21
Rondileau Campus Center, Bridgewater, MA 02325 US
(508) 531-2858, *Fax:* (508) 531-1786
www.bridgew.edu/wbim
wbim@bridgew.edu
License: Bridgewater, Plymouth County, MA held by Bridgewater State College.
Arbitron Metro Market: Bridgewater, MA *Format:* Variety/Diverse *Hrs. of News Programming:* news progmg 14 hrs wkly *No. News Employees:* 1 *Target Audience:* 18-35; college students & loc residents
Mariela Herrarte, General Manager
Tom Hanley, Programming Director
Paul Lantieri, Promotions Manager
Melinda Garcia, Music Director

Brockton

WXBR
11-27-1946; 1460 khz AM; 5 kw-D, DAN; 1 kw-N, DAN; N42 2 54 W71 3 20
211 Jason Street, Pittsfield, MA 02101 US
(508) 587-2400, *Fax:* (508) 587-4786
www.1460wxbr.com
License: Brockton, MA held by BTR Boston Inc.
Group Owner: BusinessTalkRadio.Net Inc.; (acq 11-13-2006; $1 million)
Arbitron Metro Market: Brockton, MA *Format:* News, News/Talk, 84, Talk *Target Audience:* 35 plus; general *Adv. Rates:* 16; 12; 9; 6
Richard Muserlian, General Manager
Richard Muserlian, Marketing Specialist

WKAF
07-21-1948; 97.7 mhz FM; 2.05 kw; 568 ft.; N42 12 42 W71 6 51
Rebroadcasts: simulcasts WAAF (FM) Westborough 100%
211 Jason Street, Pittsfield, MA 02101 US
(617) 779-5400
www.waaf.com
License: Brockton, Plymouth County, MA held by Entercom Boston License L.L.C.
Group Owner: Entercom Communications Corp.; (acq 12-27-2006; $30 million)
Arbitron Metro Market: Boston, Ma *Format:* Rock/AOR *Adv. Rates:* 16; 16; 13; 6
Julie Kahn, General Manager

WMSX
07-17-1961; 1410 khz AM; 1 kw-D, DA2; 0.156 kw-N, DA2; N42 3 30 W71 2 40
288 Linwood Street, Brockton, MA 02401 US
(508) 587-5454, *Fax:* (508) 537-1903
info@kingdomchurch.net
License: Brockton, MA held by Kingdom Church
Arbitron Metro Market: Boston, MA *Format:* Spanish
Alex Hurt, President

Brookline

WBOS
01-01-1955; 92.9 mhz FM *Hrs Open:* 24; 18.5 kw; 735 ft.; N42 20 50 W71 4 59
P. O. Box 1059, East Brunswick, NJ 08816 US
(617) 822-9600, *Fax:* (617) 822-6771
www.myradio929.com/
kwest@myradio929.com
License: Brookline, Norfolk County, MA held by Greater Los Angeles Radio Inc.
Group Owner: Greater Media Inc.; (acq 7-23-97)
Nat'l Reps: Katz Radio
Arbitron Metro Market: Boston, MA *Format:* Triple A *Hrs. of News Programming:* news progmg 3 hrs wkly *No. News Employees:* 1 *Target Audience:* 25-49; baby boomers seeking diverse quality music
Rob Williams, General Manager
Jonathan Finn, General Sales Mgr
Ken West, Programming Director
Jason Rossi, Promotions Manager
Crystal Margolis, Marketing Director

WUNR
01-01-1947; 1600 khz AM
160 N. Washington St., Boston, MA 02114 US
(617) 367-9003, *Fax:* (617) 367-2265
wunr.com
info@wunr.com
License: Brookline, MA held by Champion Broadcasting System Inc.
Arbitron Metro Market: Boston, MA *Format:* Ethnic
Steve Lalli, General Manager
Velma May, Programming Director
Samantha Edwards, Public Service Director

Cambridge

WHRB
05-01-1957; 95.3 mhz FM *Hrs Open:* 24; 1.45 kw; 607 ft.; N42 21 8 W71 3 25
389 Harvard Street, Cambridge, MA 02138 US
(617) 495-8138, *Fax:* (617) 496-3990
www.whrb.org
mail@whrb.org
License: Cambridge, Middlesex County, MA held by Harvard Radio Broadcasting Co. Inc.
Arbitron Metro Market: Boston *Format:* Jazz, Rock/AOR *Hrs. of News Programming:* News progmg 4 hrs wkly *Adv. Rates:* 36; 32; 36; 32
Anna Roth, President
Charlie Hobbs, General Manager
Garrett Kingman, Programming Director
Ben Philipson, Chief Engineer
Allan Hsiao, Sales Director
Nikhil Mehra, Business Director
Vipul Shekhawat, Chief Studio Engineer
RachelHorn, PSA Director

WJIB
01-01-1948; 740 khz AM *Hrs Open:* 24; 0.25 kw-D, ND1; 0.005 kw-N, ND1; N42 23 13 W71 8 21
P.O. Box 747, Rowley, MA 01969 US
(617) 868-7400
www.wjib740.com
License: Cambridge, MA held by Bob Bittner Broadcasting Inc.
Arbitron Metro Market: Boston *Format:* Adult Contemp *Special Programming:* French 10 hrs, gospel 4 hrs wkly *Hrs. of News Programming:* News progmg 3 hrs wkly *Target Audience:* 40-75; locally-programmed for thoseenjoying good adult mus
Bob Bittner, President

***WMBR**
04-10-1961; 88.1 mhz FM *Hrs Open:* 6 AM-2 AM; 0.72 kw; 295 ft.; N42 21 42 W71 5 3
C/O Wmbr, 3 Ames Street, Cambridge, MA 02142 US
(617) 253-4000, *Fax:* (617) 232-1384
www.wmbr.mit.edu
info@wmbr.mit.edu
License: Cambridge, Middlesex County, MA held by Technology Broadcasting Corp.
Arbitron Metro Market: Boston, MA *Format:* Variety/Diverse *Target Audience:* General.
Gloria Apolinario, General Manager
Christopher Bobko, Station Manager
Dugan Hayes, General Manager

Charlton

***WYCM**
01-01-1976; 90.1 mhz FM *Hrs Open:* 24; 0.1 kw; 390 ft.; N42 8 1 W71 57 26
57 Muggett Hill Rd, Charlton, MA 01507 US
(508) 248-0049, *Fax:* (508) 248-4518
www.wycm.com
stationmanager@wycm.com
License: Charlton, Worcester County, MA held by Christian Mix Radio Inc.

RADIO - U.S.

Arbitron Metro Market: Charlton, MA *Format:* Christian
Stephen Binley, Station Manager
Judy Pelletier, Promotions Manager

Chatham

WFCC-FM

03-24-1987; 107.5 mhz FM *Hrs Open:* 24; 50 kw; 341 ft.; N41 44 14 W70 0 40
750 South Street, Waltham, MA 02154 US
(508) 771-1224, *Fax:* (508)775-2065
www.wfcc.com
info@capecodbroadcasting.com
License: Chatham, Barnstable County, MA held by Cape Cod Broadcasting License I LLC
Group Owner: Sandab Communications L.P. II; (acq 1-31-2008; $7.5 million with WOCN-FM Orleans)
Arbitron Metro Market: Chatham, MA *Format:* Classical *Hrs. of News Programming:* News progmg 2 hrs wkly *No. News Employees:* 2 *Target Audience:* 25 plus; upscale, affluent, educated adults
Wayne White, Operations Dir
Greg Bone, General Manager

Chicopee

WACE

12-01-1946; 730 khz AM *Hrs Open:* 24; 5 kw-D, ND1; 0.008 kw-N, ND1; N42 10 2 W72 37 31
Mailing Address: 20 Park Plaza, Suite 720, Boston, MA 02116 US
Second Address: 326 Chicopee St., Chicopee, MA 1013
(956) 487-8015
License: Chicopee, MA held by Carter Broadcasting Corp.
Arbitron Metro Market: Las Vegas NV
Eloy Vera, General Manager

Concord

WBNW

08-28-1989; 1120 khz AM *Hrs Open:* 5 AM-10 PM; 5 kw-D, DA2; 1 kw-N, DA2; N42 26 54 W71 25 39
4 Deerfield Drive, Medfield, MA 02052 US
(781) 474-5180, *Fax:* (781) 433-0002
www.moneymattersboston.com
info@wbnw.com
License: Concord, MA held by Money Matters Radio Inc.
Regional Reps: New England.
Arbitron Metro Market: Needham, MA *Format:* News, Talk *Hrs. of News Programming:* News progmg 17 hrs wkly *Target Audience:* 35 plus; upscale, suburban families
Barry Armstrong, President
David Cullinane, General Manager
Josh Brickman, General Sales Mgr
Kate Davey, Marketing Assistant

*WIQH

12-01-1971; 88.3 mhz FM *Hrs Open:* 1-9:30 PM (M-F); 10 AM-10 PM (S); 0.1 kw horiz; 23 ft.; N42 26 48 W71 20 49
500 Walden Street, Concord, MA 01742 US
(978) 318-1400
www.wiqh.org
wiqh@colonial.net
License: Concord, Middlesex County, MA held by Concord-Carlisle Regional School District.
Arbitron Metro Market: Boston *Format:* Rock/AOR *Target Audience:* 12-21; teenagers
Daniel Roberts, Pilar Broggi, General Manager
Ned Roos, Station Manager
Cole Heywood, Elise Meltaus, Programming Director
Mike McCormack, News Director
Joe Jacobs, News Director
Noah Bromberg, News Director
Daniel Moore, MusicDirector
Connor Gushue, Training Director
Kaylin Two Feathers, Publicity Director
Orin Robichaud, Technology Directors

Dedham

WAMG

06-01-2005; 890 khz AM *Hrs Open:* 24
767 Fifth Avenue, 50th Floor, New York, NY 10153 US
(508) 791-2111
www.megaboston.com/
igois@goisbroadcasting.com
License: Dedham, MA held by J Sports Licensee LLC
Nat'l Network: ESPN Radio *Nat'l Reps:* McGavren Guild
Arbitron Metro Market: Worcester, MA *Format:* Sports *Target Audience:* 18 plus; males
Jessamy Tang, General Manager
Neil Kelleter, General Sales Mgr

Len Weiner, Programming Director
Kara Lachance, Promotions Manager

Deerfield

*WNNZ-FM

05-01-1982; 91.7 mhz FM *Hrs Open:* 7 AM-8 PM (M-F); 4 AM-11 PM (S); 7; 100 w; 314 ft; N42 32 05 W72 35 32
Deerfield Academy, Deerfield, MA 01342
(413) 774-1539, *Fax:* (413) 772-1100
License: Deerfield, Franklin County, MA held by Trustees of Deerfield Academy.
Population Served: 150,000*Target Audience:* 10-20; teens, young adults, pre-teens
Christopher Stacy, General Manager

Dennis

WEII

06-15-1981; 96.3 mhz FM *Hrs Open:* 24; 25 kw; 297 ft.; N41 43 44 W70 10 2
154 Barnstable Rd., Hyannis, MA 02601 US
(617) 779-3500, *Fax:* (617) 779-3500
www.963weei.com
License: Dennis, Barnstable County, MA held by Qantum of Cape Cod License Co. LLC.
Group Owner: Qantum Communications Corp.; (acq 6-11-2003; grpsl)
Nat'l Reps: Eastman Radio
Arbitron Metro Market: Cape Cod, MA *Format:* Sports
Steve McVie Solomon, Operations Dir
Allison Makkay, General Manager

Dudley

*WXRB

01-01-1975; 95.1 mhz FM *Hrs Open:* 24; 0.014 kw horiz; 125 ft.; N42 2 40 W71 55 52
125 Center Road, P.O. Box 5000, Dudley, MA 01571 US
(508) 213-2138
www.wxrbfm.com
wxrbfm@yahoo.com
License: Dudley, Worcester County, MA held by WXRB-FM Educational Broadcasting Inc.
Arbitron Metro Market: Whitman, MA *Format:* Oldies *Special Programming:* Nichols College sports *Target Audience:* 18 plus.
Peter Q. George, Station Manager

East Longmeadow

WHNP

01-01-1947; 1600 khz AM *Hrs Open:* daytime only; 2.5 kw-D, NDD; N42 4 25 W72 31 28 *Rebroadcasts:* simulcast of WHMP (AM) Northampton
45 Fisher Avenue, East Longmeadow, MA 01028 US
(413) 586-7400, *Fax:* (413) 585-0927
www.whmp.com
License: East Longmeadow, MA held by Saga Communications of New England LLC.
Group Owner: Saga Communications Inc.; (acq 6-2-92; grpsl).
Nat'l Network: CBS Radio *Wire Services:* AP
Arbitron Metro Market: Springfield, MA *Format:* News, News/Talk, 86 *Target Audience:* 18-49; upscale young adults
Barbara Kuschka, Operations Dir
Sean O'Mealy, General Manager
Chris Collins, News Director
Howard Frost, Chief Engineer

Easthampton

WWEI

10-01-1967; 105.5 mhz FM *Hrs Open:* 24; 720 w horiz, 706 w vert; Ant 918 ft; N42 14 29 W72 38 57 *Rebroadcasts:* Simulcast with WEEI (AM) Boston 100%
Mailing Address: 01202
Second Address: 1350 Main St., Suite 1206, Easthampton, MA
(413) 594-6585, *Fax:* (413) 592-1891
www.wveifm.com
License: Easthampton, Hampshire County, MA held by Entercom Springfield License LLC.
Group Owner: Entercom Communications Corp.; (acq 9-5-2007; $5.75 million)
Nat'l Network: Fox Sports; Westwood One *Nat'l Reps:* D & R Radio; Interep
Population Served: 139,000 *Arbitron Metro Market:* Springfield, MA *Target Audience:* 25-54; men; adults
Julie Kahn, Operations Dir
Stephen Paul Garsh, General Manager

Easton

*WSHL-FM

01-01-1973; 91.3 mhz FM *Hrs Open:* 24; 0.1 kw; 66 ft.; N42 3 27 W71 4 47
320 Washington Street, Easton, MA 02356 US
(508) 565-1000, *Fax:* (508) 565-1974
www.stonehill.edu
wshl@stonehill.edu
License: Easton, Bristol County, MA held by Stonehill College.
Wire Services: UPI
Format: Variety/Diverse *Target Audience:* 19-30.
Ryan Delehunt, General Manager
Peter George, Chief Engineer

Everett

WKOX

01-20-1952; 1430 khz AM *Hrs Open:* 24; 5 kw-D, 1 kw-N, DA-N; N42 24 11 W71 04 29
99 Revere Beach Pkwy., Medford, MA 75039
(781) 396-1430, *Fax:* (781) 391-3064
www.1200rumba.com
License: Everett, Middlesex County, MA held by AMFM Radio Licenses L.L.C.
Group Owner: Clear Channel Communications Inc.; (acq 8-30-2000; grpsl)
Population Served: 743,900 *Arbitron Metro Market:* Boston
Jake Karger, General Manager

Fairhaven

WFHN

03-01-1989; 107.1 mhz FM *Hrs Open:* 24; 5.4 kw; 344 ft.; N41 38 25 W70 55 3
1750 Rockville Pike, Suite 20, Rockville, MD 20852 US
(508) 999-6690, *Fax:* (508) 999-1420
www.fun107.com
jr.reitz@townsquaremedia.com
License: Fairhaven, Bristol County, MA
Group Owner: Cumulus Media Inc.; (acq 2-23-00; grpsl).
Nat'l Reps: McGavren Guild
Arbitron Metro Market: Fairhaven, MA *Format:* Contemporary Hits/Top 40 *Target Audience:* 18-49.
Wayne Leland, President
Gail Leblanc, General Manager and Director of Sales
JR Reitz, Brand Manager

Fall River

WHTB

05-13-1948; 1400 khz AM *Hrs Open:* 5 AM-11 PM; 1 kw-U, ND1; N41 41 23 W71 8 43
456 Rock Street, Fall River, MA 02722 US
(508) 678-9727, *Fax:* (508) 673-0310
License: Fall River, MA held by SNE Broadcasting Ltd.
Nat'l Reps: McGavren Guild
Arbitron Metro Market: Providence-Warwick-Pawtucket, RI
Format: Ethnic, Talk *Special Programming:* English 10 hrs, Pol one hr, Cambodian one hr, Fr o *Target Audience:* 25-64; Portuguese (ethnic) *Adv. Rates:* 24;22; 20; 18
Robert Karam, President
Hector Gauthier, Station Manager

WSAR

01-01-1921; 1480 khz AM; 5 kw-U, DA1; N41 43 26 W71 11 21
456 Rock Street, Fall River, MA 02722 US
(508) 678-9727, *Fax:* (508) 673-0310
www.wsar.com
hector@wsar.com
License: Fall River, MA held by Bristol County Broadcasting Inc.
Arbitron Metro Market: Providence-Warw *Format:* News, News/Talk, 84, Talk *Special Programming:* Por 3 hrs wkly *Target Audience:* 25 plus.
Keri Rodrigues, Operations Dir
Paul Giammarco, General Manager
Carole Mailloux, General Sales Mgr

Falmouth

WCIB

01-01-1970; 101.9 mhz FM; 50 kw; 479 ft.; N41 33 31 W70 35 46
154 Barnstable Road, Hyannis, MA 02601 US
(508) 778-2888, *Fax:* (508) 778-9651
www.cool102.com
kevin@qantumcapecod.com
License: Falmouth, Barnstable County, MA held by Qantum of Cape Cod License Co. LLC.
Group Owner: Qantum Communications Corp.; (acq 6-11-03; grpsl).
Nat'l Reps: Eastman Radio

Arbitron Metro Market: Cape Cod, MA *Format:* Contemporary Hits/Top 40, Adult Contemp *Target Audience:* 25-54.
Kevin Matthews, Operations Manager:
Allison Makkay Davis, General Manager

***WFPB-FM**
01-01-1996; 91.9 mhz FM; 0.3 kw horiz, 6 kw vert; 250 ft.; N41 36 50 W70 35 56 *Rebroadcasts:* Rebroadcasts WUMB-FM Boston 100%
100 Morrissey Blvd., Boston, MA 02125 US
(617) 287-6900, *Fax:* (617) 287-6916
www.wumb.org
wumb@umb.edu
License: Falmouth, Barnstable County, MA held by University of Massachusetts.
Nat'l Network: NPR
Format: Variety/Diverse
Patricia Monteith, General Manager
Danielle Knight, General Sales Mgr
Brian Quinn, Programming Director

Fitchburg

WPKZ
10-06-1941; 1280 khz AM *Hrs Open:* 24; 5 kw-D, DA2; 1 kw-N, DA2; N42 35 40 W71 50 12
P. O. Box 727, Fitchburg, MA 04120 US
(978) 343-3766, *Fax:* (978) 345-6397
www.wpkz.net/
radio@i1280.com
License: Fitchburg, MA held by Central Broadcasting Co. LLC
Nat'l Network: ABC
Arbitron Metro Market: Fitchburg, MA *Format:* Sports, Talk *Hrs. of News Programming:* news progmg 10 hrs wkly *No. News Employees:* 2 *Target Audience:* 28 plus; loc listeners in the heart of New England *Adv.Rates:* 30; 20; 30; 10
Ray C, Operations Dir
William Macek, General Manager
Ben Parker, Station Manager
John Speeney, General Sales Mgr
Anne Bisbee, Office Manager

WFGL
02-01-1950; 960 khz AM *Hrs Open:* 24; 2.5 kw-D, DA2; 1 kw-N, DA2; N42 35 24 W71 49 43 *Rebroadcasts:* Rebroadcasts KAWZ(FM) Twin Falls, ID 50%
3000 W. Macarthur Blvd., Santa Ana, CA 92704 US
(978) 342-5025
www.wfgl.org
mail@wfgl.org
License: Fitchburg, MA held by CSN International.
Group Owner: CSN International; acq 1993)
Arbitron Metro Market: Fitchburg, MA *Format:* Christian *Target Audience:* 25-54; college & career age, young families
Jim Mottshager, General Manager
Pete Cesnoia, Station Manager

WXLO
08-01-1960; 104.5 mhz FM *Hrs Open:* 24; 37 kw; 564 ft.; N42 30 27 W71 49 37
250 Commercial St. #530, Worceser, MA 01608 US
(508) 752-1045, *Fax:* (508) 793-0824
www.wxlo.com
License: Fitchburg, Worcester County, MA
Group Owner: Cumulus Media Inc.
Nat'l Reps: McGavren Guild
Arbitron Metro Market: Worcester, MA *Format:* Adult Contemp *Special Programming:* 70s mus 5 hrs wkly *Hrs. of News Programming:* News progmg 5 hrs wkly *Target Audience:* 25-54.
Bonnie Gomes, General Manager
JayBeau Jones, Programming Director

***WXPL**
08-01-1985; 91.3 mhz FM; 0.1 kw; -135 ft.; N42 35 18 W71 47 26
160 Pearl Street, Fitchburg, MA 01420 US
(978) 665-3163, *Fax:* (978) 665-3693
wxpl@fsc.edu
License: Fitchburg, Worcester County, MA held by Fitchburg State College.
Arbitron Metro Market: Fitchburg, MA *Format:* Triple A *Target Audience:* 16-25.
Sherry Horeanopoulos, General Manager

Framingham

***WDJM-FM**
01-01-1973; 91.3 mhz FM; 0.1 kw; 89 ft.; N42 17 44 W71 26 18
100 State Street, Framingham, MA 01701 US
(508) 626-4622, *Fax:* (508) 626-4939
www.wdjm913.org
wdjmfm@gmail.com
License: Framingham, Middlesex County, MA held by Framingham State College.
Arbitron Metro Market: Boston, MA *Format:* Alternative *Target Audience:* 15-35; college, surrounding community & commuters
Jason Harrington, General Manager

WROR-FM
01-01-1959; 105.7 mhz FM; 23 kw; 735 ft.; N42 20 50 W71 4 59
P. O. Box 1059, East Brunswick, NJ 08816 US
(617) 822-9600, *Fax:* (617) 822-6471
www.wror.com
License: Framingham, Middlesex County, MA held by Greater Boston Radio Inc.
Group Owner: Greater Media Inc.; (acq 10-11-96)
Arbitron Metro Market: Boston *Format:* Contemporary Hits/Top 40, Adult Contemp *Target Audience:* 25-54.
Phil Redo, General Manager
Chris Paquin, General Sales Mgr

Franklin

***WGAO**
01-01-1975; 88.3 mhz FM; 0.175 kw; 190 ft.; N42 5 8 W71 23 54
99 Main Street, Franklin, MA 02038 US
(508) 528-4210, *Fax:* (508) 528-7846
www.dean.edu
License: Franklin, Norfolk County, MA held by Dean College.
Nat'l Network: AP Radio
Arbitron Metro Market: Boston *Format:* Classic Rock *Special Programming:* Relg 8 hrs wkly *Target Audience:* 15-25.
Vic Michaels, General Manager

Gardner

WGAW
01-01-1946; 1340 khz AM; 1 kw-U, ND1; N42 35 33 W71 59 20
Green St. PO Box 87, Gardner, MA 01440 US
(978) 632-1340, *Fax:* (978) 632-1332
www.wgaw1340.com
License: Gardner, MA held by County Broadcasting Co. LLC.
Group Owner: Northeast Broadcasting Company Inc.; (acq 12-2-2003; $235,000).
Nat'l Network: ABC
Format: News, News/Talk, 86
William Curtis, Operations Dir
Chris Thompson, General Manager
Chuck Wright, Programming Director
Kevin Kistler, News Director

***WJWT**
01-01-2006; 91.7 mhz FM; 0.85 kw; 276 ft.; N42 33 29 W72 3 6 US
(714) 825-9663, *Fax:* (714) 825-9661
www.renewfm.org
License: Gardner, Worcester County, MA held by CSN International
Group Owner: CSN International
Arbitron Metro Market: Gardner, MA *Format:* Religious
George Small, General Manager
Terry LeTourneau, Station Manager
Donna Carvella, Underwriting Development Associate
Dan Barnes, Partner Relationship Manager

Gloucester

WBOQ
09-14-1964; 104.9 mhz FM *Hrs Open:* 24; 3.2 kw; 446 ft.; N42 35 36 W70 43 28
32 Fairfield Street, Boston, MA 02116 US
(978) 927-1049, *Fax:* (978) 921-2635
www.northshore1049.com
promo@northshore1049.com
License: Gloucester, Essex County, MA held by Westport Communications L.P.
Arbitron Metro Market: Beverly, MA *Format:* News, Sports *Hrs. of News Programming:* News progmg 3 hrs wkly *Target Audience:* 25-54; mass appeal classical favorites
Todd Tanger, General Manager
Charlie Curtis, Programming Director

Great Barrington

***WAMQ**
11-01-1988; 105.1 mhz FM *Hrs Open:* 24; 0.73 kw; 919 ft.; N42 9 36 W73 28 48 *Rebroadcasts:* Rebroadcasts WAMC-FM Albany, N.Y. 100%
318 Central Avenue, Albany, NY 12206 US
(518) 465-5233, *Fax:* (518) 432-6974
www.wamc.org
mail@wamc.org
License: Great Barrington, Berkshire County, MA held by WAMC.
Group Owner: WAMC/Northeast Public Radio; (acq 3-5-93; $325,000;
Nat'l Network: NPR; PRI *Wire Services:* AP
Arbitron Metro Market: Great Barrington, MA *Format:* News, News/Talk, 86 *Special Programming:* Folk 7 hrs, jazz 13 wkly *Target Audience:* General.
Alan Chartock, CEO
Selma Kaplan, Operations Dir
Dona Frank, General Sales Mgr
David Galletly, Vice President

WSBS
12-01-1956; 860 khz AM *Hrs Open:* 24
466 Curran Highway, P.O. Box 707, North Adam, MA 01247 US
(413) 528-0860, *Fax:* (413) 528-2162
www.wsbs.com
fun@wsbs.com
License: Great Barrington, MA held by Vox Communications Group LLC.
Group Owner: Vox Communications; (acq 5-10-2004; grpsl).
Nat'l Network: AP Radio *Nat'l Reps:* D & R Radio *Wire Services:* AP
Format: Adult Contemp *Hrs. of News Programming:* news progmg 10 hrs wkly *No. News Employees:* 3 *Target Audience:* 25 plus; general
David Isby, General Manager
Dave Isby, General Sales Mgr
Jesse Stewart, Programming Director
Peter Berry, Promotions Manager
Tom Conklin, News Director

Greenfield

WIZZ
08-26-1980; 1520 khz AM; 10 kw-D, DAD; N42 36 12 W72 36 21
Mailing Address: P. O. Box 1230, Claremont, NH 03743 US
Second Address: 369 S. Shelburne Rd., Greenfield, MA 1370
(413) 774-5757, *Fax:* (413) 625-8274
www.wizzradio.com
phild@wizzradio.com
License: Greenfield, MA held by P. & M. Radio LLC
Nat'l Network: AP Network News
Format: Oldies
Phillip Drumheller, President
Phil D., Owner and General Manager
Diane H. Kanzier, Office Manager
Dan Ferriera, Chief Engineer
Laura D., Administrative Assistant
Lynn Langevin, Sales Associate
Al Sax, Sales Associate
John Merz,Sales Associate

WHMQ
05-15-1938; 1240 khz AM *Hrs Open:* 24; 1 kw-U; N42 35 21 W72 37 08 *Rebroadcasts:* Rebroadcasts WHMP(AM) Northampton 100%
15 Hampton Ave., Northampton, MA 01301
(413) 586-7400, *Fax:* (413) 585-0927
www.whmp.com
License: Greenfield, Franklin County, MA held by Saga Communications of New England LLC.
Group Owner: Saga Communications Inc.; (acq 4-1-2001; $2.2 million with co-located FM)
Nat'l Network: CBS Radio *Wire Services:* AP
Population Served: 65,000*Hrs. of News Programming:* news progmg 20 hrs wkly *No. News Employees:* 2 *Target Audience:* 35 plus. *Adv. Rates:* 40; 28; 34; 23
Barbara Kuschka, Operations Dir
David Musante, General Manager
David Musante, General Sales Mgr
Denise Uozella, News Director
Howard Frost, Chief Engineer

WHAI
05-15-1948; 98.3 mhz FM *Hrs Open:* 24; 2 kw; 404 ft.; N42 34 15 W72 38 42
P. O. Box 32, 81 Woodard Rd, Greenfield, MA 01302 US
(413) 774-4301, *Fax:* (413) 773-5637
whai.com
info@whai.com
License: Greenfield, Franklin County, MA held by Saga Communications of New England LLC.
Group Owner: Saga Communications Inc.
Format: Adult Contemp *No. News Employees:* 1 *Target Audience:* 25-54. *Adv. Rates:* 40; 32; 32; 20
Dan Guin, General Manager
Nick Danjer, Programming Director

WPVQ
07-26-1981; 95.3 mhz FM *Hrs Open:* 24; 0.57 kw; 761 ft.; N42 41 50 W72 36 20
P. O. Box 1230, Claremont, NH 03743 US

RADIO - U.S.

(413) 774-4301, *Fax:* (413) 773-5637
www.bear953.com
info@whai.com
License: Greenfield, Franklin County, MA held by Saga Communications of New England LLC.
Group Owner: Saga Communications Inc.; (acq 2-13-2004; grpsl).
Format: Country *Target Audience:* 18-45.
Dan Guin, General Manager

Haverhill

WCEC

01-01-1947; 1490 khz AM *Hrs Open:* 24; 1 kw-U, ND1; N42 46 22 W71 6 1
462 Merrimack Street, Methuen, MA 01844 US
(978) 683-7171, *Fax:* (978) 687-1180
www.1490wcec.com
traffic@1110wccmam.com
License: Haverhill, MA held by Costa-Eagle Radio Ventures L.P.
Group Owner: Costa-Eagle Radio Ventures L.P.; (acq 1998)
Nat'l Reps: Roslin
Arbitron Metro Market: Boston *Format:* Talk *Target Audience:* Sp speaking.
Luis Reyes, Operations Dir
Patrick Costa, General Manager

Holliston

*WHHB

04-17-1979; 99.9 mhz FM; 0.017 kw; 203 ft.; N42 12 42 W71 26 36
370 Hollis Street, Holliston, MA 01746 US
(508) 429-0677, *Fax:* (508) 429-8225
www.whhbfm.com
requests@whhbfm.com
License: Holliston, Middlesex County, MA held by Holliston High School.
Format: Variety/Diverse
Christopher Murphy, General Manager

Holyoke

*WCCH

01-01-1977; 103.5 mhz FM *Hrs Open:* 6 AM-11 PM; 0.009 kw; 259 ft.; N42 11 55 W72 38 27
303 Homestead Avenue, Holyoke, MA 01040 US
(413) 552-2488(413) 538-7060
wcchradio@hotmail.com,info@wcch.com
License: Holyoke, Hampden County, MA held by Holyoke Community College.
Arbitron Metro Market: Springfield, MA *Format:* Variety/Diverse
Joanne Kostides, General Manager

Hyannis

WCOD-FM

06-02-1967; 106.1 mhz FM *Hrs Open:* 24; 50 kw; 430 ft.; N41 43 44 W70 10 2
278 South Sea Ave, West Yarmouth, MA 02673 US
(508) 778-2888, *Fax:* (508) 778-9651
www.106wcod.com
news@95wxtk.com
License: Hyannis, Barnstable County, MA held by Qantum of Cape Cod License Co. LLC.
Group Owner: Qantum Communications Corp.; (acq 4-11-2005; grpsl).
Nat'l Reps: Eastman Radio
Arbitron Metro Market: Cape Cod, MA *Format:* Adult Contemp *No. News Employees:* 2 *Target Audience:* 25-54.
Allison Makkay, General Manager
Kevin Matthews, Programming Director

WPXC

01-09-1987; 102.9 mhz FM *Hrs Open:* 24; 3.1 kw; 463 ft.; N41 41 20 W70 20 49
154 Barnstable Road, Hyannis, MA 02601 US
(508) 775-5678, *Fax:* (508) 862-6329
www.pixy103.com
info@pixy103.com
License: Hyannis, Barnstable County, MA
Group Owner: Codcomm Inc.; (acq 11-8-2005; grpsl)
Nat'l Reps: McGavren Guild
Arbitron Metro Market: Cape Cod, MA *Hrs. of News Programming:* news progmg 4 hrs wkly *No. News Employees:* 3 *Target Audience:* General.
Jake Demmin, General Manager
Suzanne Tonaire, Programming Director

Lawrence

WNNW

08-01-1947; 800 khz AM *Hrs Open:* 24
462 Merrimack St., Methuen, MA 01844 US
(978) 688-8000, *Fax:* (978) 687-1180
www.power800am.com
traffic@1110wccmam.com
License: Lawrence, MA held by Costa-Eagle Radio Ventures L.P.
Group Owner: Costa-Eagle Radio Ventures L.P.; acq 3-27-98; $405,000).
Nat'l Network: CNN Radio *Nat'l Reps:* Lotus Entravision Reps LLC *Wire Services:* AP
Arbitron Metro Market: Methuen, MA *Hrs. of News Programming:* news progmg 10 hrs wkly *No. News Employees:* 2 *Target Audience:* 35-64; general *Adv. Rates:* 100; 75; 100; 35
Patrick Costa, General Manager
Johnny McKenzie, Programming Director

WEEI(FM)

04-01-1960; 93.7 mhz FM *Hrs Open:* 24; 50 kw; 430 ft; N42 40 26 W71 11 26
Entercom Boston, 20 Guest St., 3rd Fl., Brighton, MA 2135
(617) 779-5300, *Fax:* (617) 931-7827
www.937mikefm.com
info@937mikefm.com
License: Lawrence, Essex County, MA held by Entercom Boston II License L.L.C.
Group Owner: Entercom Communications Corp.; (acq 10-15-98; grpsl)
Population Served: 300,000 *Arbitron Metro Market:* Boston *Target Audience:* 25-54.
Julie Kahn, General Manager
Christina Anders, Promotions Manager

WEEI-FM

10-17-1967; 93.7 mhz FM *Hrs Open:* 24; 34 kw; 584 ft.; N42 31 53 W70 59 12
401 City Avenue, Suite 409, Bala Cynwyd, PA 19004 US
(401) 751-9334, *Fax:* (401) 351-8109
www.weei.com/weei/
info@weei.com
License: Lawrence, Washington County, MA held by Entercom Providence License LLC.
Group Owner: Entercom Communications Corp.; (acq 6-15-2004; $14.5 million).
Nat'l Network: Westwood One
Arbitron Metro Market: Providence, RI *Format:* Sports, Talk *No. News Employees:* 1 *Target Audience:* 25-49.
Joseph Field, Chairman
David Field, CEO
Joseph Harrington, Station Manager
Rod Morrison, Promotions Manager

Leicester

WVNE

06-19-1991; 760 khz AM *Hrs Open:* Sunrise-sunset; 8.6 kw-C, NDD; 25 kw-D, NDD; N42 14 57 W72 4 41
70 James Street, Suite 201, Worcester, MA 01603 US
(508) 831-9863, *Fax:* (508) 831-7964
www.wvne.net
info@wvne.net
License: Leicester, MA held by Blount Masscom Inc.
Group Owner: Blount Communications Group; (acq 5-15-90;
Nat'l Network: Salem Radio Network
Arbitron Metro Market: Leicester, MA *Format:* Christian, Religious *Target Audience:* 25-54. *Adv. Rates:* 25.20; 15.30; 25.20; na
William Blount, President
David Young, Operations Dir
Emanuel DaCunha, Station Manager
Deborah Blount, Executive Vice President
Randolph Berkson, Operations Manager

Leominster

WCMX

11-13-1967; 1000 khz AM *Hrs Open:* 6 AM-2 hrs past sundown; 1 kw-D, NDD; N42 31 25 W71 44 7
194 Electric Avenue, Lunenburg, MA 01462 US
(978) 582-8282, *Fax:* (978) 582-4978
www.hope1000.net
nburke@hope1000.net
License: Leominster, MA held by Twin City Baptist Temple Inc.
Nat'l Network: Salem Radio Network
Arbitron Metro Market: Lunenburg, MA *Format:* Christian *Hrs. of News Programming:* News progmg 7 hrs wkly *Target Audience:* 35-54 women. *Adv. Rates:* 12; 10; 12; 8
Pastor Erven Burke, General Manager
Nathan Burke, Station Manager

Lowell

WCAP

06-10-1951; 980 khz AM *Hrs Open:* 24; 5 kw-D, DA2; 5 kw-N, DA2; N42 39 16 W71 21 43
243 Central Street, Lowell, MA 01852 US
(978) 454-0404, *Fax:* (978) 458-9124
www.980wcap.com
sam@980wcap.com
License: Lowell, MA held by Merrimack Valley Radio LLC
Nat'l Network: ABC *Regional Reps:* LOCAL *Wire Services:* AP
Arbitron Metro Market: Lowell, Ma *Format:* News, Talk *Hrs. of News Programming:* News progmg 20 hrs wkly *Target Audience:* 25 plus; business people, professionals, factory workers, housewives *Adv. Rates:* 60; 40;60; 40
Ryan Johnston, Operations Dir
Clark Smidt, General Sales Mgr
Dean Johnson, Programming Director
Stuart Steller, Promotions Manager
Bernice Corpuz, News Director
Sam Poulten, Partner
Mary Treen, Business Manager

*WUML

11-06-1967; 91.5 mhz FM *Hrs Open:* 18; 1.4 kw; 207 ft.; N42 39 7 W71 19 15
61 Wilder Street, Lowell, MA 01854 US
(978) 934-4975, *Fax:* (978) 934-3031
www.wuml.org
wuml@wuml.org
License: Lowell, Middlesex County, MA held by University of Massachusetts-Lowell Board of Trustees.
Arbitron Metro Market: Boston *Format:* Variety/Diverse *Target Audience:* 16-25.
Nate Osit, General Manager
Joe Keefe, Programming Director

WCRB

01-01-1947; 99.5 mhz FM; 27 kw; 653 ft.; N42 39 14 W71 13 2
P.O. 1059, East Brunswick, NJ 08816 US
(781) 893-7080, *Fax:* (781) 893-0038
www.wcrb.com
wcrb@wcrb.com
License: Lowell, Middlesex County, MA held by Nassau Broadcasting II L.L.C.
Group Owner: Nassau Broadcasting Partners L.P.; (acq 11-15-2006; exchange for WNUW(FM) Burlington, NJ)
Arbitron Metro Market: Boston *Format:* Classical *Target Audience:* 30-64; adults
Nancy Dieterich, General Manager
Mark Edwards, Programming Director
Tim Neill, Promotions Manager

WLLH

06-01-2005; 1400 khz AM *Hrs Open:* 24; 1 kw-U, ND1; N42 42 27 W71 9 51
8121 Georgia Avenue, 10th Floor, Silver Spring, MD 20910 US
(617) 830-1000
www.890espn.com
laura.wareck@espnboston.com
License: Lowell, MA held by J Sports Licensee LLC
Nat'l Network: ESPN Radio *Nat'l Reps:* McGavren Guild
Arbitron Metro Market: Boston *Format:* Sports *Target Audience:* Males 18+.
Jessamy Tang, General Manager
Neil Kelleher, General Sales Mgr
Kara Lachance, Programming Director
Len Weiner, Programming Director

Lynn

WHBA

08-05-1963; 101.7 mhz FM *Hrs Open:* 24; 1.7 kw; 626 ft; N42 21 08 W71 03 25
25 Exchange St., Lynn, MA 02215
(781) 595-6200, *Fax:* (781) 595-3810
www.fnxradio.com
fnxradio@fnxradio.com
License: Lynn, Essex County, MA held by MCC Broadcasting Inc.
Group Owner: Phoenix Media Communications Group; (acq 11-10-82;
Nat'l Reps: McGavren Guild *Wire Services:* AP
Population Served: 3,880,000 *Arbitron Metro Market:* Boston *Special Programming:* Jazz 8 hrs, loc music 2 hrs wkly *Hrs. of News Programming:* news progmg 2 hrs wkly *No. News Employees:* 1 *Target Audience:* 18-49; well-educated, affluent & socially active trend setters
Brad Mindich, Chairman
Stephen Mindich, CEO
Gary Kurtz, General Manager

Jordi Chapdelaine, General Sales Mgr
Keith Dakin, Programming Director
Christopher Hall, Chief Engineer
Rick Gallagher, CFO

WLYN
11-01-1947; 1360 khz AM *Hrs Open:* 24; 700 w-D, 76 w-N; N42 27 17 W70 58 44
500 W. Cummings Park, Suite 2600, Woburn, MA 02818
(781) 938-0869, *Fax:* (781) 938-0933
www.peace.str3am.com:6660/wlyn
jeffk@mrbi.net
License: Lynn, Essex County, MA held by Multicultural Radio Broadcasting Licensee LLC.
Group Owner: Multicultural Radio Broadcasting Inc.; (acq 8-7-2002; $1.78 million)
Population Served: 3,000,000 *Arbitron Metro Market:* Boston
Target Audience: Hispanic (Spanish & Portuguese) *Adv. Rates:* 50; 50; 50; 50
Jeff Kline, General Manager

Marion

***WWTA**
01-01-1996; 88.5 mhz FM; 0.1 kw; 52 ft.; N41 42 32 W70 45 57
Front Street, Marion, MA 02738 US
(508) 748-2000, *Fax:* (508) 291-6666
www.taboracademy.org
kkistler@taboracademy.org
License: Marion, Plymouth County, MA held by Tabor Academy.
Arbitron Metro Market: Marion, MA *Format:* Variety/Diverse
Karl Kistler, General Manager

Marshfield

WATD-FM
12-05-1977; 95.9 mhz FM *Hrs Open:* 24; 1.6 kw; 469 ft.; N42 6 39 W70 42 17
130 Enterprise Drive, Marshfield, MA 02050 US
(781) 837-1166, *Fax:* (781) 837-1978
www.959watd.com
news@959watd.com
License: Marshfield, Plymouth County, MA held by Marshfield Broadcasting Co.
Arbitron Metro Market: Boston.MA *Format:* Adult Contemp, Blues, 64 *Hrs. of News Programming:* news progmg 10 hrs wkly *No. News Employees:* 2 *Target Audience:* 25-64; South Shore residents
Edward Perry, Jr, President

Mashpee

WHYA(FM)
02-12-1987; 101.1 mhz FM *Hrs Open:* 24; 3.7 kw; Ant 253 ft; N41 36 50 W70 35 56 *Rebroadcasts:* Rebroadcasts WFQR(FM) Harwich Port 100%
278 South Sea Ave., West Yarmouth, MA 2673
(508) 775-5678, *Fax:* (508) 862-6329
www.frankplaysitall.com
License: Mashpee, Barnstable County, MA held by Codcomm Inc
Group Owner: Codcomm Inc.; (acq 11-7-2005; grpsl)
Nat'l Reps: Katz Radio
Arbitron Metro Market: Cape Cod, MA *No. News Employees:* 1
Target Audience: 35-64.
Terri Gamble, General Manager

Maynard

***WAVM**
04-01-1973; 91.7 mhz FM *Hrs Open:* 24; 0.5 kw horiz; 77 ft.; N42 25 17 W71 27 10
Wavm - 1 Tiger Drive, Maynard, MA 01754 US
(307) 638-8921, *Fax:* (307) 638-8922
www.wavm.org
License: Maynard, Middlesex County, MA held by Maynard Public Schools.
Format: Oldies
Steven Silberberg, President
Roger Ingram, General Manager

Medford

***WMFO**
03-01-1971; 91.5 mhz FM; 0.125 kw; 135 ft.; N42 24 27 W71 7 15
Mailing Address: 44 Professors Row, Room 110, Medford, MA 02155 US
Second Address: 474 Boston Ave., Medford, MA 2155
(617) 625-0800, *Fax:* (617) 625-6072
www.wmfo.org
wmfo@wmfo.org
License: Medford, Middlesex County, MA held by Tufts University.
Arbitron Metro Market: Boston, MA *Format:* Variety/Diverse
Annie Ross, General Manager

WXKS-FM
09-01-1960; 107.9 mhz FM *Hrs Open:* 24; 20.5 kw; 771 ft.; N42 20 50 W71 4 59
433 E. Las Colinas Blvd, #1130, Irving, TX 75039 US
(781) 663-2500, *Fax:* (781) 290-0722
www.kiss108.com
License: Medford, Middlesex County, MA held by AMFM Radio Licenses L.L.C.
Group Owner: Clear Channel Communications Inc.
Arbitron Metro Market: Medford, MA *Format:* Christian *Target Audience:* 25-54.
Tom McConnell, General Manager

Middleborough Center

WVBF
01-01-1993; 1530 khz AM *Hrs Open:* 24
Mailing Address: P.O. Box 329, Middleboro, MA 02346 US
Second Address: 130 Enterprise Dr., Marshfield, MA 2050
(508) 822-1106
www.hometowntalkradio.com
WVBF1530@hotmail.com
License: Middleborough Center, MA held by Steven J. Callahan.
Nat'l Network: Westwood One; NBC Radio
Arbitron Metro Market: Taunton, MA *Format:* Public Affairs, News
Tony Lopes, General Manager

Milford

WMRC
10-06-1956; 1490 khz AM *Hrs Open:* 24; 1 kw-U, ND1; N42 8 12 W71 30 50
Mailing Address: 258 Main Street, Ste 301, Milford, MA 01757 US
Second Address: 258 Main St., Milford, MA 1757
(508) 473-1490, *Fax:* (508) 478-2200
www.wmrcdailynews.com
wmrc@wmrcdailnews.com
License: Milford, MA held by First Class Radio Corp.
Arbitron Metro Market: Worcester, MA *Format:* Adult Contemp
Hrs. of News Programming: news progmg 32 hrs wkly *No. News Employees:* 2 *Target Audience:* 25-54. *Adv. Rates:* 36; 24; 36; 24
Thomas McAuliffe Sr., President
Rick Michaels, Operations Dir
Thomas McAuliffe II, General Manager
Ray Auger, Promotions Manager
Ed Thompson, News Director

Milton

***WMLN-FM**
04-01-1975; 91.5 mhz FM *Hrs Open:* 24; 0.17 kw; 95 ft.; N42 14 28 W71 6 52
1071 Blue Hill Avenue, Milton, MA 02186 US
(617) 333-0311, *Fax:* (617) 333-2123
www.cumy.edu:8080/student/wmln/wmln
afrank@curry.edu
License: Milton, Norfolk County, MA held by Curry College.
Nat'l Network: CNN Radio *Wire Services:* AP
Arbitron Metro Market: Boston, MA *Format:* Adult Contemp, News, 62, Talk, Variety/Diverse *Hrs. of News Programming:* News progmg 15 hrs wkly *Target Audience:* General.
Alan Frank, General Manager

Nahant

WESX
01-01-1939; 1230 khz AM
P. O. Box 130, Quincy, MA 02169 US
(617) 884-4500, *Fax:* (617) 884-4515
www.wesx1230am.com
info@wesx1230am.com
License: Nahant, MA held by North Shore Broadcasting Corp.
Nat'l Network: ABC; Westwood One *Wire Services:* AP
Arbitron Metro Market: Nahant, MA *Format:* Ethnic *Special Programming:* Auto repair 2 hrs, gardening 2 hrs, home improvement 2 hrs, restaurant/dining 2 hrs, Pol 2 hrs wkly *Hrs. of News Programming:* news progmg 25 hrswkly *No. News Employees:* 2 *Target Audience:* 35 plus; general *Adv. Rates:* 55; 31; 55; 17
Charles Banta, General Manager

Nantucket

***WNAN**
03-15-2000; 91.1 mhz FM; 2.3 kw vert; 210 ft.; N41 17 6 W70 8 39 *Rebroadcasts:* Rebroadcasts WCAI-FM Woods Hole 100%
Mailing Address: 125 Western Avenue, Boston, MA 02134 US
Second Address: 3 Water St., Woods Hole, MA 2543
(508) 548-9600, *Fax:* (508) 548-5517
www.wgbh.org
cainan@wgbh.org
License: Nantucket, Nantucket County, MA held by WGBH Educational Foundation.
Nat'l Network: NPR
Arbitron Metro Market: Nantucket, MA *Format:* News, News/Talk, 86
John Voci, Station Manager

***WNCK**
06-28-2002; 89.5 mhz FM *Hrs Open:* 24; 0.078 kw horiz, 0.5 kw vert; 118 ft.; N41 17 6 W70 8 39 *Rebroadcasts:* Rebroadcasts WGBH(FM) Boston 100%
57 Pocomo Road, Nantucket, MA 02554 US
(617) 300-2000, *Fax:* (617) 300-1025
www.wgbh.org
ClosedCaptioningConcerns@wgbh.org
License: Nantucket, Nantucket County, MA held by Nantucket Public Radio Inc.
Arbitron Metro Market: Boston, MA *Format:* Variety/Diverse
Target Audience: 40 plus.
Benjamin Godley, COO
Jonathan C. Abbott, President and Chief Executive Officer
David Bernstein, Vice President and General Manager
Winifred Lenihan, Promotions Manager
Michael Foti, Engineering Dir
Margaret Drain, Vice Presidentfor National Programming
Jeanne M. Hopkins, Vice President, Communications and Government Rela
Joseph M. Igoe, Vice President and Chief Technology Officer
Susan L. Kantrowitz, Vice President and General Counsel
Vinay Mehra, Chief FinancialOfficer, Vice President for Financ

WAZK
06-13-2012; 97.7 mhz; 1750 w; 236 ft; N41 17 06 W70 08 25
19 Old South Road, Nantucket, MA
(508)228-9770
www.ackfm.com
info@ackfm.com
License: Nantucket, MA
Group Owner: Vertical Resources LLC
Jeff Shapiro, Bob Shapiro
Justin Tyler, Operations Dir
Jennifer McAllister, Business Manager
Lauren Sleeth, General Sales Mgr

Natick

WQOM
11-01-1972; 1060 khz AM *Hrs Open:* 24; 40 kw-D, 2.5 kw-N, 22 kw-CH, DA-3; N42 17 17 W71 25 55
100 Mount Wayte St., 100 Summer St., Framingham, MA 33042
(508) 820-2430
www.wbix.com
alex@wbix.com
License: Natick, Middlesex County, MA held by WBIX Corp.
Group Owner: Langer Broadcasting Group L.L.C.; (acq 11-29-2005).
Population Served: 2,900,000 *Arbitron Metro Market:* Boston
Alex Langer, General Manager
Jim Harris, General Sales Mgr

New Bedford

WBSM
07-17-1949; 1420 khz AM; 5 kw-D, DA2; 1 kw-N, DA2; N41 39 2 W70 54 58
1750 Rockville Pike, Suite 20, Rockville, MD 20852 US
(508) 999-6690, *Fax:* (508) 999-1420
www.wbsm.com
pete.braley@townsquaremedia.com
License: New Bedford, MA
Group Owner: Cumulus Media Inc.; (acq 4-26-2001; grpsl)
Nat'l Reps: Christal
Arbitron Metro Market: Fairhaven, MA *Format:* News, News/Talk, 84, Talk
Gail Le Blanc, General Manager
Gail LeBlanc, Director of Sales
Pete Braley, Programming Director
Deborah Aguiar, Promotions Manager

WCTK
12-09-1946; 98.1 mhz FM *Hrs Open:* 24; 47.3 kw; 508 ft; N41 37 21 W70 55 07

75 Oxford St., Providence, RI 17604
(401) 467-4366, *Fax:* (401) 941-2795
www.wctk.com
twall@hallradio.com
License: New Bedford, Bristol County, MA held by Hall Communications Inc.
Group Owner: Hall Communications Inc.
Nat'l Reps: Eastman Radio
Population Served: 1,594,300 *Arbitron Metro Market:* Providence-Warwick-Pawtucket, RI *Target Audience:* 25-54.
Adv. Rates: 140; 130; 130; 50
Bonnie Rowbotham, CEO
Arthur Rowbotham, President
Tom Wall, General Sales Mgr
Bob Walker, Programming Director
Briget D'Antonio, Promotions Manager
Craig Healy, Engineering Dir
Tom Wall, Vice President

WJFD-FM
02-22-1949; 97.3 mhz FM *Hrs Open:* 24; 50 kw; 499 ft.; N41 38 20 W70 52 27
270 Union Street, New Bedford, MA 02740 US
(508) 997-2929, *Fax:* (508) 990-3893
www.wjfd.com
claudia@wjfd.com
License: New Bedford, Bristol County, MA held by Edmund Dinis, trustee
Arbitron Metro Market: Providence-Warwick-Pawtucket, RI
Format: Ethnic *Target Audience:* General; Portuguese-speaking community
Edmund Dinis, President

WNBH
05-21-1921; 1340 khz AM *Hrs Open:* 24; 1 kw-U, ND1; N41 37 21 W70 55 7 *Rebroadcasts:* Simulcast with WLKW(AM) West Warwick, RI
P.O. Box 4368, Lancaster, PA 17604 US
(508) 979-8003, *Fax:* (508) 979-8009
www.wnbhradio.com
twall@hallradio.com
License: New Bedford, MA held by Hall Communications Inc.
Group Owner: Hall Communications Inc.; (acq 10-1-66)
Nat'l Network: ESPN Radio *Nat'l Reps:* Eastman Radio
Arbitron Metro Market: Providence,RI *Format:* Sports *Special Programming:* Pol 2 hrs wkly *Hrs. of News Programming:* News progmg 3 hrs wkly *Target Audience:* Men 25-54 *Adv. Rates:* 30; 20; 20; 10
Bonnie Rowbotham, Chairman
Arthur Rowbotham, President
Tom Wall, Operations Dir

***WFHL**
01-01-2003; 88.1 mhz FM; 0.3 kw; 135 ft.; N41 38 15 W70 52 19
Mailing Address: P.O. Box 3025, New Bedford, MA 02741 US
Second Address: 71 William, New Bedford, MA 2740
(508) 991-7600
www.radiowfhl.com
radio@radiowfhl.com
License: New Bedford, Bristol County, MA held by New Bedford Christian Radio Inc.
Arbitron Metro Market: New Bedford, MA *Format:* Portugese
Manuel Pereira, General Manager

Newburyport

WNBP
03-10-1957; 1450 khz AM *Hrs Open:* 24; 1 kw-U, ND1; N42 49 23 W70 51 42
44 Merrimac St., Second Floor East, Newburyport, MA 01950 US
(978) 462-1450, *Fax:* (978) 462-0333
www.wnbp.com
info@wnbp.com
License: Newburyport, MA held by Port Broadcasting LLC
Nat'l Network: AP Radio *Wire Services:* AP
Arbitron Metro Market: Boston, MA *Format:* Adult Contemp
Special Programming: Irish 4 hrs wkly *Hrs. of News Programming:* news progmg 5 hrs wkly *No. News Employees:* 1
Target Audience: 25-54.
Peter Falconi, Operations Dir
Carl Strube, General Manager
Ted Brouse, General Sales Mgr
Charlie Curtis, Programming Director

***WNEF**
91.7 mhz FM; 0.001 kw horiz, 1 kw vert; 328 ft.; N42 51 56 W70 56 17 *Rebroadcasts:* Rebroadcasts WUMB-FM Boston 100%
100 Morrissey Blvd., Boston, MA 02125 US
(617) 287-6900, *Fax:* (617) 287-6916
www.wumb.org
wumb@umb.edu
License: Newburyport, Essex County, MA held by University of Massachusetts.
Arbitron Metro Market: Boston, MA *Format:* Variety/Diverse
Patricia Monteith, General Manager
Danielle Knight, General Sales Mgr
Brian Quinn, Programming Director

Newton

WXKS
04-01-1947; 1200 khz AM *Hrs Open:* 24; 50 kw-U, DA-2; N42 17 20 W71 11 21
99 Revase Beach Pkwy., Medford, MA 33407
(781) 396-1430, *Fax:* (781) 391-3064
www.1200rumba.com
License: Newton, Middlesex County, MA held by Capstar TX L.P.
Group Owner: Clear Channel Communications Inc.; (acq 2-15-2001; $10 million)
Population Served: 1,700,000 *Arbitron Metro Market:* Boston
Tom McConnell, General Manager

WNTN
04-01-1968; 1550 khz AM; 10 kw-D, ND2; 0.003 kw-N, ND2; N42 21 27 W71 14 30
134 Rumford Ave, Newton, MA 02446 US
(617) 969-1550
www.wntn.com
info@wntn.com
License: Newton, MA held by Colt Communications LLC.
Arbitron Metro Market: Boston, MA *Format:* Greek *Special Programming:* Irish 6 hrs, Indian 2 hrs wkly *Target Audience:* 40 plus.
Paul Roberts, Operations Dir
Rob Rudnick, General Manager
John Frassica, General Sales Mgr
Leo Sullivan, Chief Engineer

***WZBC**
04-01-1974; 90.3 mhz FM *Hrs Open:* 24; 1 kw; 220 ft.; N42 20 5 W71 10 31
140 Commonwealth Avenue, Chestnut Hill, MA 02167 US
(617) 552-3511, *Fax:* (617) 552-1738
www.wzbc.org
info@wzbc.org
License: Newton, Middlesex County, MA held by Trustees of Boston College.
Arbitron Metro Market: Boston *Format:* Alternative *Target Audience:* 18-34.
Maddie Hall, General Manager

Norfolk

WDIS
03-20-1978; 1170 khz AM *Hrs Open:* Day Time
226 Montello Street, Brockton, MA 02301 US
(508) 384-8255, *Fax:* (508) 384-1530
www.wdisam.com
info@wdisam.com
License: Norfolk, MA held by Discussion Radio Inc.
Nat'l Network: Salem Radio Network
Arbitron Metro Market: Boston, MA *Format:* News, News/Talk, 86
Hrs. of News Programming: news progmg 6 hrs wkly *No. News Employees:* 1 *Target Audience:* 35-64. *Adv. Rates:* 24; 24; 24; 24.
Corine Slade, General Manager
Dan Collier, Programming Director

North Adams

***WJJW**
09-05-1973; 91.1 mhz FM; 0.423 kw; -830 ft.; N42 41 27 W73 6 16
375 Church Street, North Adams, MA 01247 US
(413) 662-5405
www.mcla.edu
webmaster@mcla.edu
License: North Adams, Berkshire County, MA held by Massachusetts College of Liberal Arts.
Harris Elder, General Manager
Nick Strassel, Programming Director
Paul Wiley, Chief Engineer

WUPE-FM
07-12-1964; 100.1 mhz FM; 1.3 kw; 502 ft.; N42 41 51 W73 3 52
466 Curran Highway, North Adams, MA 01247 US
(413) 663-6567, *Fax:* (413) 662-2143
www.wupe.com
info@wupe.com
License: North Adams, Berkshire County, MA held by Vox Communications Group LLC
Group Owner: Vox Communications
Arbitron Metro Market: North Adams, MA *Format:* Oldies *Target Audience:* 35 plus.
Dick Savage, General Sales Mgr

WNAW
11-23-1947; 1230 khz AM; 1 kw-U, ND1; N42 41 3 W73 6 23
PO Box 707, North Adams, MA 01247 US
(413) 663-6567, *Fax:* (413) 662-2143
www.wnaw.com
wnaw@wnaw.com
License: North Adams, MA held by Vox Communications Group LLC.
Group Owner: Vox Communications; (acq 5-10-2004; grpsl).
Nat'l Reps: McGavren Guild
Arbitron Metro Market: Baltimore, MD *Format:* Adult Contemp
No. News Employees: 2 *Target Audience:* Adults.
Earl Ingalls, General Manager
Peter Barry, Promotions Manager
Ken Jones, Chief Engineer

North Dartmouth

***WTKL**
09-01-1973; 91.1 mhz FM; 1.2 kw; 299 ft.; N41 37 43 W71 0 24
285 Old Westport Road, North Dartmouth, MA 02747 US
(916) 251-1600, *Fax:* (916) 251-1650
www.klove.com
License: North Dartmouth, Bristol County, MA held by Educational Media Foundation.
Group Owner: EMF Broadcasting; (acq 6-30-2006; $725,000).
Nat'l Network: K-Love
Format: Christian
Mike Novak, President
Glenn Goodwin, Operations Dir

***WUMD**
06-10-2006; 89.3 mhz FM *Hrs Open:* 24; 0.096 kw horiz, 9.6 kw vert; 305 ft.; N41 37 43 W71 0 24
285 Old Westport Road, North Dartmouth, MA 02747 US
(508) 999-8149
www.893wumd.org
wumd@umassd.edu
License: North Dartmouth, Bristol County, MA held by University of Massachusetts.
Arbitron Metro Market: North Dartmouth, MA *Format:* Variety/Diverse *Target Audience:* 13-60; general, high school, college, community
Jennifer Mulcare-Sullivan, Station Manager

Northampton

WEIB
01-01-2001; 106.3 mhz FM *Hrs Open:* 24; 3 kw; 289 ft.; N42 22 25 W72 40 26
6 Wilkin Drive, Longmeadow, MA 01106 US
(413) 585-1112, *Fax:* (413) 585-9138
www.weibfm.com
weibfm@aol.com
License: Northampton, Hampshire County, MA held by Cutting Edge Broadcasting Inc.
Arbitron Metro Market: Northampton, MA *Format:* Jazz, Smooth Jazz
Carol Cutting, President
Drew Dawson, Programming Director

WHMP
12-01-1950; 1400 khz AM *Hrs Open:* 24; 1 kw-U; N42 19 36 W72 39 28
15 Hampton Ave., Northampton, MA 78701
(413) 586-7400, *Fax:* (413) 585-0927
www.whmp.com
License: Northampton, Hampshire County, MA held by Saga Communications of New England LLC.
Group Owner: Saga Communications Inc.; (acq 2000; $12 million with co-loca
Nat'l Network: CBS Radio *Nat'l Reps:* Katz Radio *Wire Services:* AP
Population Served: 100,000 *Arbitron Metro Market:* Springfield, MA *Special Programming:* Pol 3 hrs wkly *Hrs. of News Programming:* news progmg 40 hrs wkly *No. News Employees:* 2 *Target Audience:* 35 plus;upscale, well educated
David Musante, General Manager
David Musante, General Sales Mgr
Chris Belmonte, Programming Director
Denise Vozella, News Director
Howard Frost, Chief Engineer

WLZX
11-01-1956; 99.3 mhz FM *Hrs Open:* 24; 5.8 kw; 331 ft.; N42 22 25 W72 40 26
600 Congress Ave, Suite 1400, Austin, TX 78701 US

(413) 525-4141, *Fax:* (413) 525-4334
www.lazer993.com
info@lazer993.com
License: Northampton, Hampshire County, MA held by Saga Communications of New England LLC.
Group Owner: Saga Communications Inc.; (acq 2000; $12 million with co-located AM).
Arbitron Metro Market: Springfield, MA *Format:* Rock/AOR *No. News Employees:* 2 *Target Audience:* 18-34; male
Gary Zenobi, General Manager
Bill Buller, General Sales Mgr
Courtney Quinn, Programming Director
Kristin McCauley, News Director
Tina Shotwell, Traffic Manager

*WOZQ
01-01-1981; 91.9 mhz FM *Hrs Open:* 6 AM-2 AM; 0.2 kw horiz, 0.175 kw vert; -115 ft.; N42 19 13 W72 38 14
College Hall, Northampton, MA 01063 US
(413) 585-4956,(413) 585-4977, *Fax:* (413) 585-4166
www.smith.edu/wozq
wozq@email.smith.edu
License: Northampton, Hampshire County, MA held by Trustees of Smith College.
Format: Variety/Diverse *Target Audience:* 15 plus; college students & area businesses
Dana Feldesman, Station Manager
Patrick Connelly, General Sales Mgr
Mary Nastasi, Programming Director
Matthea Doughtry, News Director
Elizabeth Willis, Chief Engineer
Carolyn Cunha, Music Director

Orange

WJDF
01-01-1995; 97.3 mhz FM; 5.8 kw; 82 ft.; N42 36 3 W72 23 1
P.O. Box 973, Orange, MA 01364 US
(978) 544-5335, *Fax:* (978) 544-2131
www.wjdf.com
info@wjdf.com
License: Orange, Franklin County, MA held by Deane Brothers Broadcasting Corp.
Format: Adult Contemp
Donn Deane, General Manager
Chad Songer, General Sales Mgr
Jay Deane, Programming Director

Orleans

WFPB
04-10-1970; 1170 khz AM *Hrs Open:* 24; 1 kw-D, DAD; N41 46 48 W70 0 36 *Rebroadcasts:* Rebroadcasts WUMB-FM Boston 100%
100 Morrissey Boulevard, Boston, MA 02125 US
(617) 287-6900, *Fax:* (617) 287-6916
www.wumb.org
wumb@umb.edu
License: Orleans, MA held by University of Massachusetts.
Arbitron Metro Market: Cape Cod, MA *Format:* Variety/Diverse
Patricia Monteith, General Manager
Danielle Knight, General Sales Mgr
Brian Quinn, Programming Director

WOCN-FM
07-25-1974; 104.7 mhz FM *Hrs Open:* 24; 50 kw horiz, 36 kw vert; 459 ft.; N41 46 48 W70 0 36
750 South Street, Waltham, MA 02154 US
(508) 771-1224, *Fax:* (508) 775-2605
www.ocean1047.com
wocn@ocean1047.com
License: Orleans, Barnstable County, MA held by Cape Cod Broadcasting License II LLC.
Group Owner: Sandab Communications L.P. II; (acq 7-10-2007; $7.5 million with WFCC-FM Chatham)
Nat'l Network: AP Radio *Nat'l Reps:* Clear Channel *Wire Services:* AP
Arbitron Metro Market: Cape Cod, MA *Format:* Variety/Diverse, Classic Rock *Hrs. of News Programming:* news progmg 32 hrs wkly *No. News Employees:* 4 *Target Audience:* Adults 25-64.
Wayne W. White, Operations Dir
Gregory D. Bone, General Manager
Stephen M. Colella, General Sales Mgr
Michelle Lorraine, Promotions Manager
Shai Jackson, News Director
Judy Crocker, Sales Manager

*WFMR
91.3 mhz FM; 1.15 kw; 282 ft.; N41 46 36 W70 0 40
14 Center Street, Provicetown, MA 02657 US
(508) 487-2619, *Fax:* (508) 487-5524
www.womr.org
info@womr.org
License: Orleans, Barnstable County, MA held by Lower Cape Communications Inc.
Arbitron Metro Market: Orleans, MA *Format:* Public Affairs
Tina Lynde, President

Petersham

*WNGB
91.3 mhz FM; 0.6 kw; -174 ft.; N42 31 30 W72 16 42
US
(518) 686-0975, *Fax:* (518) 686-0975
www.wngn.org
wngn@wngn.org
License: Petersham, Worcester County, MA held by Northeast Gospel Broadcasting Inc.
Arbitron Metro Market: Petersham, MA *Format:* Christian, Gospel
Brian Larson, General Manager
Bill Dagle, Vice President

Pittsfield

WBEC
03-01-1947; 1420 khz AM *Hrs Open:* 24; 1 kw-D, DAN; 1 kw-N, DAN; N42 26 40 W73 16 43
21 Chastellux Avenue, Newport, RI 02840 US
(800) 877-5600, *Fax:* (916) 251-1650
www.klove.com
License: Pittsfield, MA held by Vox Communications Group LLC.
Group Owner: Vox Communications; (acq 9-13-2002; grpsl).
Arbitron Metro Market: Odessa-Midland TX *Format:* Christian
Mike Novak, President

WBRK
02-20-1938; 1340 khz AM *Hrs Open:* 24; 1 kw-U, ND1; N42 27 0 W73 12 55
100 North Street, Pittsfield, MA 01201 US
(413) 442-1553, *Fax:* (413) 445-5294
www.wbrk.com
WBRK@WBRK.COM
License: Pittsfield, MA held by WBRK Inc.
Nat'l Network: CBS; Westwood One *Regional Reps:* interep loca focus
Arbitron Metro Market: PITTSFIELD MA *Format:* Variety/Diverse *Special Programming:* Pol 2 hrs, Irish one hr, relg 2 hrs wkly *No. News Employees:* 2 *Target Audience:* 35 plus.
Willard Hodgkins III, CEO
Willard Chip Hodgkins, President
Michael Bunn, Operations Dir
Robert Shade, VP Sales
Rick Beltaire, Programming Director
Cheryl Tripp, Promotions Manager
John Campoli, Executive Vice President

WBRK-FM
10-10-1970; 101.7 mhz FM *Hrs Open:* 24; 3 kw; 144 ft.; N42 28 31 W73 16 7
100 North Street, Pittsfield, MA 01201 US
(413) 442-1553, *Fax:* (413) 445-5294
www.wbrk.com
WBRK@WBRK.COM
License: Pittsfield, Berkshire County, MA
Nat'l Network: ABC
Arbitron Metro Market: PITTSFIELD MA *Format:* Adult Contemp *Target Audience:* 25-54.
Willard "Chip" Hodgkins, President
Larry Davis, Station Manager
Robert Shade, VP Sales
Rob Payer, Programming Director

WUPE
09-09-1971; 1110 khz AM *Hrs Open:* 24; 5 kw-D, DAD; N42 26 22 W73 17 30
P.O. Box 1265, Pittsfield, MA 01202 US
(413) 499-3333, *Fax:* (413) 442-1590
www.wupe.com
wupe@wupe.com
License: Pittsfield, MA held by Vox Communications Group LLC.
Group Owner: Vox Communications; (acq 12-8-2003; $2.83 million with co-located FM)
Nat'l Network: ABC *Nat'l Reps:* D & R Radio
Arbitron Metro Market: Pittsfield, MA *Format:* Oldies *Hrs. of News Programming:* news progmg 14 hrs wkly *No. News Employees:* 1 *Target Audience:* 25-54; baby boomers *Adv. Rates:* 17; 14; 17; na
Mike Patrick, Operations Dir
Earl Ingalls, General Sales Mgr
Larry Kratka, News Director
Ken Jones, Chief Engineer
Victoria Spencer, Local Sales Manager
Peter Barry, VP/Market Manager

WBEC-FM
01-01-1975; 95.9 mhz FM *Hrs Open:* 24; 1 kw; 558 ft.; N42 24 44 W73 17 5
P.O. Box 1265, 501 East St., Pittsfield, MA 01202 US
(413) 499-3333, *Fax:* (413) 442-1590
live959.com
info@959.com
License: Pittsfield, Berkshire County, MA
Group Owner: Vox Communications
Nat'l Network: Westwood One
Arbitron Metro Market: Pittsfield, MA *Format:* Adult Contemp *Hrs. of News Programming:* news progmg 28 hrs wkly *No. News Employees:* 1 *Target Audience:* 25-54; young adults with families *Adv. Rates:* 25;22; 25; 20
Todd Lee, Operations Dir
Victoria Spencer, General Sales Mgr
Cheryl Adams, Promotions Manager
Larry Kratka, Network News
Peter Barry, VP/Market Manager

Plymouth

WPLM
08-08-1955; 1390 khz AM; 5 kw-D, DA2; 5 kw-N, DA2; N41 58 5 W70 42 6
P.O. Box 1390, North Plymouth, MA 02362 US
(508) 746-1390, *Fax:* (508) 830-1128
alana@991.com
License: Plymouth, MA held by Plymouth Rock Broadcasting Co. Inc.
Nat'l Reps: Roslin
Arbitron Metro Market: Boston *Format:* Adult Contemp, Talk
Dr. Laurie Campbell, President
Alan Anderson, General Manager
Sean Casey, Promotions Manager
Chip Morgan, Chief Engineer
Pat Carroll, Public Service Director

WPLM-FM
06-25-1961; 99.1 mhz FM; 50 kw; 430 ft.; N41 58 2 W70 42 4
P.O. Box 1390, North Plymouth, MA 02362 US
(508) 746-1390, *Fax:* (508) 830-1128
alana@991.com
License: Plymouth, Plymouth County, MA held by Plymouth Rock Broadcasting Co. Inc.
Arbitron Metro Market: Boston *Format:* Adult Contemp
Tom Cuddy, Operations Dir
Steven Borneman, Station Manager
Scott Shannon, Programming Director
Theresa Angela, Promotions Manager
Patty Steele, News Director
Kevin Plumb, Engineering Dir
Tony Mascaro, Music Director

Provincetown

*WOMR
03-21-1982; 92.1 mhz FM; 6 kw; 161 ft.; N42 3 54 W70 9 31
P.O. Box 975, Provincetown, MA 02657 US
508-487-2619, *Fax:* (508) 487-5524
www.womr.org
info@womr.org
License: Provincetown, Barnstable County, MA held by Lower Cape Communications Inc.
Arbitron Metro Market: Cape Cod, MA *TV Affiliate:* Variety *Format:* Black *Special Programming:* News progmg 5.5 hrs wkly *No. News Employees:* General; div *Adv. Rates:* 12; 12; 12; 12
Operations Manager, Operations Dir
Station Manager, Dave Meyer
Operations Manager

Quincy

WJDA
09-13-1947; 1300 khz AM *Hrs Open:* 24; 1 kw-D, ND1; 0.072 kw-N, ND1; N42 15 35 W70 58 36
P. O. Box 130, Quincy, MA 02169 US
(617) 884-4500, *Fax:* (617) 884-4515
www.wjda1300am.com
info@wjda1300am.com
License: Quincy, MA held by South Shore Broadcasting Co.
Nat'l Network: ABC
Arbitron Metro Market: Boston *Format:* Ethnic *Special Programming:* Cantonese 3 hrs wkly *Hrs. of News Programming:* news progmg 10 hrs wkly *No. News Employees:* 2 *Target Audience:* 35 plus. *Adv. Rates:* 40; 32
Charles Banta, President
Mike Logan, News Director

Rockland

*WRPS
02-08-1974; 88.3 mhz FM *Hrs Open:* 24; 0.105 kw; 138 ft.; N42 7 43 W70 55 1
34 Goddard Avenue, Rockland, MA 02370 US
(781) 871-0724, *Fax:* (781) 982-1483
wrps883@yahoo.com
License: Rockland, Plymouth County, MA held by Rockland Public Schools.
Arbitron Metro Market: Boston *Format:* Adult Contemp *Target Audience:* General.
David Cable-Murphy, General Manager
Robert Mulligan, Chief Engineer

Salem

*WMWM
01-01-1976; 91.7 mhz FM *Hrs Open:* 7 AM-midnight; 0.13 kw; 79 ft.; N42 30 14 W70 53 26
Salem State College, Salem, MA 01970 US
(978) 219-9170, *Fax:* (978) 542-8307
www.wmwm.freehostia.com
wmwmsalem@gmail.com
License: Salem, Essex County, MA held by Salem State College.
Arbitron Metro Market: Boston, MA *Format:* Variety/Diverse *Target Audience:* General.
Eric Roberts, General Manager
Dan Rockwood, Programming Director
Paul Collins, Chief Engineer

Sandwich

*WSDH
01-01-1976; 91.5 mhz FM *Hrs Open:* 10 AM-4 PM (M-F); 0.31 kw; 151 ft.; N41 44 6 W70 27 35
Quaker Meetinghouse Road, East Sandwich, MA 02537 US
(508) 888-0420, *Fax:* (508) 833-8392
License: Sandwich, Barnstable County, MA held by Sandwich Public Schools.
Format: Variety/Diverse *Hrs. of News Programming:* News progmg 4 hrs wkly *Target Audience:* 12-40.
Chip Hill, General Manager

Scituate

*WSMA
05-01-2006; 90.5 mhz FM; 0.005 kw horiz, 7.7 kw vert; 492 ft.; N41 56 2 W70 35 10
US
(800) 357-4226, *Fax:* (208) 736-1958
www.csnradio.com
csn@csnradio.com
License: Scituate, Plymouth County, MA held by CSN International.
Group Owner: CSN International
Arbitron Metro Market: Scituate, MA *Format:* Christian, Gospel
Mike Kestler, President
Daniel Davidson, Operations Dir
Ellen Rocco, General Manager
Don Mills, Network Programming Director / Music Director
Kelly Carlson, Engineering Dir
Jerry Johnson, Engineering Dir
Ray Gorney, AssistantDirector of Engineering
Dustin Pamplona, Engineer
Nolan Mather, Graphics / Website Maintenance
Mike Stocklin, National Underwriting
Austin Morris, Accounting
Lois Mills, FCC Applications / Translator Site Manager

Sheffield

*WBSL-FM
09-01-1973; 91.7 mhz FM; 0.23 kw horiz; -75 ft.; N42 6 57 W73 25 0
245 N. Undermountain Rd., Sheffield, MA 01257 US
(413) 229-8511(413) 229-1927, *Fax:* (413) 229-1229
www.berkshireschool.org
bclough@berkshireschool.org
License: Sheffield, Berkshire County, MA held by Berkshire School Inc.
Format: Variety/Diverse *Special Programming:* Jazz 15 hrs, Black 2 hrs, folk 2 hrs, Sp 2 hrs, Pol one hr wkly *Target Audience:* General.
John Weinner, Station Manager
Thomas Jaworski, Engineering Dir
Coleen Cox, Station Advisor
James Harris, Station Advisor
Vickie Sheppard, Station Manager

South Hadley

*WMHC
05-14-1957; 91.5 mhz FM; 0.1 kw; -16 ft.; N42 15 12 W72 34 40
3 Carr Lab, South Hadley, MA 01075 US
(413) 538-2044, *Fax:* (413) 538-2431
www.mtholyoke.edu/org/wmhc
amlewis@mtholyoke.edu
License: South Hadley, Hampshire County, MA held by President & Trustees of Mount Holyoke College.
Nat'l Network: AP Radio
Arbitron Metro Market: South Hadley, MA *Format:* Rock/AOR *Target Audience:* General; Mount Holyoke College Community
Catherine Moldonado, Programming Director

South Yarmouth

WKPE-FM
08-01-1994; 103.9 mhz FM; 5.5 kw; 341 ft.; N41 41 26 W70 11 21
2201 Old Court Road, Baltimore, MD 21208 US
(508) 771-1224, *Fax:* (508) 775-2605
www.capecountry104.\com
wkpe@capecountry104.com
License: South Yarmouth, Barnstable County, MA held by Sandab Communications L.P. II.
Group Owner: Sandab Communications L.P. II; acq 6-19-98; $1.2 million)
Nat'l Reps: Clear Channel
Arbitron Metro Market: Cape Cod, MA *TV Affiliate:* Country *No. News Employees:* P 18 - 54
Sales Manager

Southbridge

WESO
03-20-1955; 970 khz AM *Hrs Open:* 24; 1 kw-D, ND1; 0.021 kw-N, ND1; N42 3 59 W71 59 28
16 Walker Avenue, Westfield, MA 01085 US
(508) 909-0970, *Fax:* (508) 764-2682
thespirit970.com
info@weso970am.com
License: Southbridge, MA held by Money Matters Inc.
Arbitron Metro Market: Southbridge, MA *Format:* Country, News, 62, Sports, Talk *Special Programming:* Pol 3 hrs *Hrs. of News Programming:* news progmg 30 hrs wkly *No. News Employees:* 2 *Target Audience:* 34-59. *Adv. Rates:* 24; 20; 24; 18
Dick Vaughan, COO
Lia Zaido, Operations Dir
Camie Luke, Promotions Manager
J.P. Ellery, News Director

WWFX
11-01-1968; 100.1 mhz FM *Hrs Open:* 24; 2.85 kw; 479 ft.; N42 13 28 W71 52 51
Mailing Address: 295 Bridle Trail Road, Needham, MA 02192 US
Second Address: WBA Inc., 295 Bridle Trail Rd, Needham, MA 2192
(508) 752-1045, *Fax:* (508) 793-0824
www.thefoxfm.com
License: Southbridge, Worcester County, MA
Group Owner: Cumulus Media Inc.; (acq 4-26-01; grpsl).
Nat'l Network: Jones Radio Networks *Nat'l Reps:* D & R Radio
Arbitron Metro Market: Worcester, MA *Format:* Rock/AOR *Hrs. of News Programming:* news progmg 10 hrs wkly *No. News Employees:* 2 *Target Audience:* 25-54.
JayBeau Jones, Operations Dir
Bonnie Gomes, General Manager
Tim Brennan, Promotions Manager

Springfield

*WAIC
02-01-1967; 91.9 mhz FM; 0.23 kw horiz; 66 ft.; N42 6 44 W72 33 29
1000 State Street, Springfield, MA 01109 US
(860) 278-5310, *Fax:* (413) 205-3943
www.cpbn.org/
events@cptv.org
License: Springfield, Hampden County, MA held by American International College.
Arbitron Metro Market: Springfield, MA *Format:* Variety/Diverse *Special Programming:* Gospel *Target Audience:* 16-40.
Will Hughes, CEO
Jean Paul, Operations Dir
Doc Holiday, General Manager
Christopher Flynn, Director of Major Gifts & Planned Giving

WAQY
12-17-1966; 102.1 mhz FM *Hrs Open:* 24; 17 kw; 781 ft.; N42 5 0 W72 42 16
45 Fisher Ave, East Longmeadow, MA 01028 US
(413) 525-4141, *Fax:* (413) 525-4334
www.rock102.com
rcressman@lazer993.com
License: Springfield, Hampden County, MA held by Saga Communications of New England LLC.
Group Owner: Saga Communications Inc.; (acq 6-2-92; grpsl).
Nat'l Reps: Katz Radio
Arbitron Metro Market: Springfield, MA *Format:* Classic Rock *Target Audience:* General; upscale young adults with high income
Gary Zenobi, General Manager
Rob Cressman, Programming Director
Alex Byrne, Promotions Manager
Kristin McCauley, News Director

WHYN
01-01-1941; 560 khz AM *Hrs Open:* 24
3305 West Spring Mt Rd, Suite 60, Las Vegas, NV 89102 US
(413) 781-1011, *Fax:* (413) 734-4434
www.whynam560.com
promotions@whyn.com
License: Springfield, MA held by CC Licenses LLC.
Group Owner: Clear Channel Communications Inc.; (acq 1996; grpsl)
Arbitron Metro Market: Springfield, MA *Format:* News, News/Talk, 86 *No. News Employees:* 6 *Target Audience:* General.
Pat McKay, Operations Dir
Sean Davey, General Manager

WHYN-FM
01-01-1946; 93.1 mhz FM; 8.6 kw; 1001 ft.; N42 14 28 W72 38 56
3305 W. Spring Mount. Rd, Ste 60, Las Vegas, NV 89102 US
(413) 781-1011, *Fax:* (413) 734-4434
www.mix931.com
fm@mix931.com
License: Springfield, Hampden County, MA held by CC Licenses LLC.
Group Owner: Clear Channel Communications Inc.
Arbitron Metro Market: Springfield, MA *Format:* Adult Contemp *Target Audience:* 25-54.
David D'Dugenio, General Sales Mgr

WHLL
09-01-1932; 1450 khz AM; 1 kw-U, ND1; N42 6 32 W72 36 44
Mailing Address: 101 West Street, Springfield, MA 01104 US
Second Address: 101 West St., Springfield, MA 1104
(413) 737-1414, *Fax:* (413) 737-1488
www.1450whll.com
info@947wmas.com
License: Springfield, MA
Group Owner: Cumulus Media Inc.; (acq 6-3-2004; $22 million with co-located FM)
Nat'l Network: ABC
Arbitron Metro Market: Springfield, MA *Format:* Sports *Special Programming:* Black one hr, relg 2 hrs wkly
Susan Van Stone, Operations Dir
Craig Swim, General Sales Mgr
Rob Anthony, Programming Director
Lucie Grondin, Promotions Manager
Frank Connolly, News Director
Richard Kenadek, Chief Engineer

*WNEK-FM
02-17-1976; 105.1 mhz FM; 0.013 kw; -23 ft.; N42 6 55 W72 31 5
1215 Wilbraham Road, Springfield, MA 01119 US
(413) 782-1582, *Fax:* (413) 796-2008
www.wnek.wneclubs.org/
License: Springfield, Hampden County, MA held by Trustees of Western New England College.
Arbitron Metro Market: Springfield, MA *Format:* Variety/Diverse *Target Audience:* 15-35; college community, greater Springfield area
Specer Bracco, Operations Dir
Ian Martin, General Manager

*WSCB
03-01-1958; 89.9 mhz FM; 0.1 kw; 36 ft.; N42 5 59 W72 33 30
263 Alden Street, Springfield, MA 01109 US
(413) 748-3000, *Fax:* (413) 748-3153
www.spfldcol.edu
License: Springfield, Hampden County, MA held by President & Trustees of Springfield College.
Arbitron Metro Market: Springfield, MA *Format:* Variety/Diverse
Dr. Richard Flynn, President
Shazz Wilson, Station Manager
Hunter Golden, Programming Director
Greg Antonelli, News Director

WSPR
06-01-1936; 1270 khz AM; 5 kw-D, DA2; 1 kw-N, DA2; N42 5 24 W72 36 11
270 Union Street, New Bedford, MA 02740 US
(413) 781-5200, *Fax:* (413) 734-2240
www.wspr1270.com
msanchez@davidsonmediagroup.com
License: Springfield, MA held by Davidson Media Station WSPR Licensee LLC.
Group Owner: Davidson Media Group LLC; (acq 5-16-2005; $6.8 million with WACM(AM) West Springfield)
Arbitron Metro Market: Springfield, MA
Paul Gois, General Manager

***WTCC**
08-19-1971; 90.7 mhz FM; 4 kw; 92 ft.; N42 6 32 W72 34 45
Mailing Address: #1 Armory Square, Springfield, MA 01105 US
Second Address: One Armory Sq., Springfield, MA 1105
(413) 746-9822, *Fax:* (413) 781-3747
www.wtccfm.org
fkrampits@stcc.edu
License: Springfield, Hampden County, MA held by Springfield Technical Community College.
Arbitron Metro Market: Springfield, MA *Format:* Variety/Diverse *Target Audience:* General.
Denise Stewart, Station Manager
Mark Leak, Programming Director
Beverly Showell, News Director
Fred Krampito, Chief Engineer

Sudbury

***WYAJ**
09-01-1980; 97.7 mhz FM; 0.004 kw; 220 ft.; N42 22 30 W71 24 28
390 Lincoln Rd., Sudbury, MA 01776 US
(978) 443-9961, *Fax:* (978) 443-8824
www.lsrhs.net
contact.us@lsrhs.net
License: Sudbury, Middlesex County, MA held by Lincoln-Sudbury Regional School District.
Arbitron Metro Market: Sudbury, MA *Format:* Variety/Diverse *Special Programming:* Black 6 hrs, class 3 hrs, jazz 5 hrs, loc rock art *Target Audience:* General.
Paul Sarapas, General Manager

Taunton

WSNE-FM
01-26-1966; 93.3 mhz FM; 31 kw; 591 ft.; N41 51 56 W71 17 22
600 Congress Ave., Suite 1400, Austin, TX 78701 US
(401) 781-9979,(401) 224-1933, *Fax:* (401) 781-9329
www.933coastfm.com
feedback@933coastfm.com
License: Taunton, Bristol County, MA held by Capstar TX L.P.
Group Owner: Clear Channel Communications Inc.; (acq 8-30-00; grpsl).
Nat'l Network: AP Radio; Premiere Radio Networks *Nat'l Reps:* Clear Channel
Arbitron Metro Market: Providence-Warwick-Pawtucket, RI *Format:* Adult Contemp *Special Programming:* Pub affrs 4 hrs wkly *Target Audience:* 25-54; mostly women
James Corwin, General Manager
Mark Coffey, General Sales Mgr
Rick Everett, Programming Director
Melissa Bowler, Promotions Manager

Tisbury

WMVY
06-01-1981; 92.7 mhz FM *Hrs Open:* 21; 3 kw; 315 ft.; N41 26 16 W70 36 51
Mailing Address: P.O. Box 958, 211 Jason St., Pittsfield, MA 01202 US
Second Address: 57 Carrolls Way, Vineyard Haven, MA 2568
(508) 693-5000, *Fax:* (508) 693-8211
www.mvyradio.com
gorcutt@mvyradio.com
License: Tisbury, Dukes County, MA held by Aritaur Communications Inc.
Nat'l Network: Moody; AP Radio *Nat'l Reps:* McGavren Guild
Arbitron Metro Market: Cape Cod, MA *Format:* Rock/AOR *Special Programming:* Class 4 hrs, jazz 4 hrs wkly *No. News Employees:* 1 *Target Audience:* 25-49; upper income, active consumer group
Joseph Gallagher, President
Greg Orcutt, General Manager
P.J. Finn, Programming Director
Nick Ward, Promotions Manager

Truro

WGTX
01-01-2000; 102.3 mhz FM; 2.15 kw; 266 ft.; N42 1 20 W70 4 28
246 Walnut Street, Suite C, Newton, MA 02160 US
(617) 254-6333, *Fax:* (617) 254-2234
karl@karlnurse.com
License: Truro, Barnstable County, MA held by Dunes 102FM LLC
Arbitron Metro Market: Provincetown, MA *Format:* News, News/Talk, 86
Karl Nurse, General Manager
Ron Barnes, Chief Engineer

Turners Falls

WRSI
07-01-1984; 93.9 mhz FM *Hrs Open:* 24; 2.5 kw; 358 ft.; N42 32 1 W72 35 34
424 State Road, Whately, MA 01373 US
(413) 586-7400, *Fax:* (413) 585-0927
www.wrsi.com
License: Turners Falls, Franklin County, MA held by Saga Communications of New England LLC.
Group Owner: Saga Communications Inc.; (acq 2-13-2004; grpsl).
Nat'l Network: CBS Radio
Arbitron Metro Market: Springfield, MA *Format:* Triple A *Hrs. of News Programming:* News progmg 9 hrs wkly *Target Audience:* 18-54; young, educated, spend money *Adv. Rates:* 35; 25; 30; 15
Sean O'Mealy, General Manager
Chris Belmonte, Programming Director
Howard Frost, Chief Engineer

Waltham

***WBRS**
02-05-1968; 100.1 mhz FM *Hrs Open:* 24; 0.025 kw; 151 ft.; N42 22 9 W71 15 28
415 South Street, Waltham, MA 02254 US
(781) 736-5277
www.wbrs.org
gm@wbrs.org
License: Waltham, Middlesex County, MA held by Brandeis University.
Wire Services: UPI
Arbitron Metro Market: Waltham, MA *Format:* Variety/Diverse *Hrs. of News Programming:* News progmg 5 hrs wkly *Target Audience:* General.
Jesse Manning, General Manager
Abby Vigderman, Programming Director
Jeremy Berman, News Director

WKLB-FM
01-01-1948; 102.5 mhz FM *Hrs Open:* 24; 14 kw; 906 ft.; N42 18 37 W71 14 14
750 South Street, Box 9173, Waltham, MA 02154 US
(617) 822-6880, *Fax:* (617) 822-6659
www.wklb.com
mbrophey@wklb.com
License: Waltham, Middlesex County, MA held by Charles River Broadcasting WCRB License Corp.
Group Owner: Greater Media Inc.; (acq 11-15-2006)
Nat'l Reps: Katz Radio
Arbitron Metro Market: Boston,MA *Format:* Country *Target Audience:* 25-54.
Phil Redo, General Manager
Mark Keaney, General Sales Mgr
Mike Brophey, Programming Director
Dawn Santolucito, Promotions Manager

Ware

WARE
07-11-1948; 1250 khz AM
67 Lakeview Drive, Sandy Hook, CT 06482 US
(413) 289-2300, *Fax:* (413) 289-2323
www.realoldies1250.net
manager@realoldies1250.net
License: Ware, MA held by Success Signal Broadcasting Inc.
Nat'l Network: Fox News Radio *Nat'l Reps:* Rgnl Reps
Arbitron Metro Market: Springfield, MA *Format:* Oldies *Special Programming:* Pol 4 hrs wkly *No. News Employees:* 3 *Target Audience:* 30 plus.
Marshall Sanft, President

Watertown

WRCA
01-01-1948; 1330 khz AM *Hrs Open:* 24
P.O. Box 1306, East Greenwich, RI 02818 US
(617) 492-3330, *Fax:* (617) 492-2800
1330wrca.com
License: Watertown, MA held by WAEC License LP.
Group Owner: Beasley Broadcast Group Inc.; (acq 5-2000; $6 million)
Arbitron Metro Market: Boston *Format:* Ethnic *Hrs. of News Programming:* News progmg 10 hrs wkly *Target Audience:* General. *Adv. Rates:* 35; 35; 35; 35
Stu Fink, General Manager

WAZN
01-01-1958; 1470 khz AM *Hrs Open:* 24; 1.4 kw-D, 3.4 kw-N, DA-2; N42 24 49 W71 12 40 *Rebroadcasts:* Rebroadcasts WLYN(AM) Lynn (partial
500 W. Cummings Park, Suite 2600, Woburn, MA 33042
(781) 938-0869, *Fax:* (781) 938-0933
www.peace.str3am.com:6660/wazn
Jeffk@mrbi.net
License: Watertown, Middlesex County, MA held by Multicultural Radio Broadcasting Licensee LLC.
Group Owner: Multicultural Radio Broadcasting Inc.; (acq 12-11-2002; $1.8 million)
Population Served: 2,000,000 *Arbitron Metro Market:* Boston *Target Audience:* Russian, Hispanic (Sp & Portuguese) *Adv. Rates:* 50; 50; 50; 50
Jeff Kline, General Manager

Webster

WGFP
04-01-1980; 940 khz AM *Hrs Open:* 24; 1 kw-D, ND2; 0.004 kw-N, ND2; N42 3 17 W71 50 0
445 Pennsylvania Avenue, Suite 125, Ft. Washington, PA 19034 US
(508) 943-9400, *Fax:* (508) 943-0405
www.coolcountry940.com
barry@coolcountry940.com
License: Webster, MA held by Just Because Inc.
Arbitron Metro Market: Worcester, MA *Format:* Country *Special Programming:* live high school sports *Hrs. of News Programming:* News progmg 25 hrs wkly *Target Audience:* 25-54.
Barry Sims, CEO

WORC-FM
04-08-1994; 98.9 mhz FM; 1.87 kw; 410 ft.; N42 2 11 W71 59 22
250 Commercial Street, Suite 530, Worcester, MA 06108 US
(508) 752-1045, *Fax:* (508) 793-0824
www.oldies989.com
jaybeau.jones@citcomm.com
License: Webster, Worcester County, MA
Group Owner: Cumulus Media Inc.; (acq 6-8-99; $3.5 million).
Nat'l Network: Westwood One; ABC
Arbitron Metro Market: Worcester, MA *TV Affiliate:* Oldies *Format:* Variety/Diverse, Ethnic *Special Programming:* News progmg 8 hrs wkly *No. News Employees:* 25-49.

Wellesley

***WZLY**
09-20-1976; 91.5 mhz FM; 0.007 kw; 154 ft.; N42 17 35 W71 18 21
106 Central Street, Wellesley, MA 02181 US
(781) 283-2690
www.wzly.net
gm@wzly.net
License: Wellesley, Norfolk County, MA held by Wellesley College.
Arbitron Metro Market: Wellesley, MA *Format:* Variety/Diverse *Target Audience:* General; Wellesley town and college community
Hannah Allen, General Manager
Tildy Banker-Johnson, Programming Director
Krista Douglass, Promotions Manager
Samaa Ahmed, News Director
Kelly Waters, Music Director
Michelle Surka, Music Director
Hallie Santo, Secretary
SophieJohnson, Special-Events Coordinator
Karin Robinson, Special-Events Coordinator
Esther Gonzalez, Record Librarian

Wellfleet

***WRYP**
01-01-2006; 90.1 mhz FM; 2.5 kw vert; 80 ft.; N42 1 53 W70 5 26 US
(888) 310-7729
www.renewfm.com
info@renewfm.org
License: Wellfleet, Barnstable County, MA held by Horizon Christian Fellowship

Group Owner: Horizon Christian Fellowship; (acq 3-24-2006; $150,000 for CP).
Arbitron Metro Market: Wellfleet, MA *Format:* Christian
George Small, General Manager
Terry LeTourneau, Station Manager
Donna Carvella, Underwriting Development Associate
Dan Barnes, Partner Relationship Manager

West Barnstable

***WKKL**
09-19-1977; 90.7 mhz FM *Hrs Open:* 24; 0.205 kw; 125 ft.; N41 41 31 W70 20 16
Route 132, West Barnstable, MA 02668 US
(508) 375-4030, *Fax:* (508) 375-4020
www.geocities.com/wkkl247
wkkl247@yahoo.com
License: West Barnstable, Barnstable County, MA held by Board of Trustees Cape Cod Community Colleges.
Arbitron Metro Market: Cape Cod, MA *Format:* Alternative
Lisa Zinsius, General Manager

West Springfield

WACM
08-28-1949; 1490 khz AM; 0.47 kw-U, ND1; N42 5 55 W72 37 45
34 Sylvan Street, W. Springfield, MA 01089 US
License: West Springfield, MA held by Davidson Media Station WACM Licensee LLC.
Group Owner: Davidson Media Group LLC; (acq 5-16-2005; $6.8 million with WSPR(AM) Springfield)
Raul Ortiz, President

West Yarmouth

***WBUR**
10-01-1940; 1240 khz AM *Hrs Open:* 24; 1 kw-U, ND1; N41 38 7 W70 14 6 *Rebroadcasts:* Rebroadcasts WBUR-FM Boston 98%
890 Commonwealth Ave, Attn. Gm C/O Wbur, Boston, MA 02215 US
(617) 353-0909, *Fax:* (617) 353-4747
www.wbur.org
info@wbur.org
License: West Yarmouth, MA held by The Executive Committee of Trustees of The Boston University
Arbitron Metro Market: Boston, MA *Format:* News, News/Talk, 86 *Special Programming:* Sp 5 hrs wkly *Hrs. of News Programming:* News progmg 78 hrs wkly *Target Audience:* 25-54; intelligent adults interested in news& politics
Jean Wong, CFO
Paul LaCamera, General Manager
Corey Lewis, Station Manager
Sam Fleming, Programming Director
John Davidson, News Director
Jeffrey Hutton, Engineering Dir

WXTK
12-30-1948; 95.1 mhz FM; 50 kw; 262 ft.; N41 38 8 W70 14 6
278 South Sea Avenue, West Yarmouth, MA 02673 US
(508) 778-2888, *Fax:* (508) 778-9651
www.95wxtk.com
info@95wxtk.com
License: West Yarmouth, Barnstable County, MA held by Qantum of Cape Cod License Co. LLC.
Group Owner: Qantum Communications Corp.; (acq 2005; grpsl).
Nat'l Network: ABC *Nat'l Reps:* Eastman Radio
Arbitron Metro Market: Cape Cod, MA *Format:* News, News/Talk, 84, Talk *No. News Employees:* 1 *Target Audience:* 25 plus.
Kevin Matthews, Operations Dir
Allison Makkay, General Manager
Steve McVie Solomon, Programming Director
Matt Pitta, News Director

Westborough

WAAF
06-15-1961; 107.3 mhz FM; 9.6 kw; 1099 ft.; N42 20 9 W71 42 57
401 City Avenue, Suite 409, Bala Cynwyd, PA 19004 US
(617) 779-5400, *Fax:* (617) 931-1073
www.waaf.com
rvaleri@entercom.com
License: Westborough, Worcester County, MA
Group Owner: Entercom Communications Corp.
Arbitron Metro Market: Westborough, MA *Format:* Rock/AOR *Target Audience:* 25-54.
Julie Kahn, General Manager

Westfield

WNNZ
07-08-1987; 640 khz AM *Hrs Open:* 24
200 Concord Plaza, Suite 600, San Antonio, TX 78216 US
(413) 545-0100, *Fax:* (413) 545-2546
www.nepr.net
radio@nepr.net
License: Westfield, MA held by CC Licenses LLC.
Group Owner: Clear Channel Communications Inc.; (acq 11-24-98; $1.2 million)
Nat'l Network: NPR
Arbitron Metro Market: Springfield, MA *Format:* News *Target Audience:* 25-54; upscale adults
Martin Miller, CEO/COO
Bart Rankin, Operations Dir
Sean Davey, General Manager
Helen Barrington, Programming Director
Fred Bever, News Director
Charles Dube, Chief Engineer

***WSKB**
10-01-1974; 89.5 mhz FM; 0.1 kw; -217 ft.; N42 7 55 W72 47 51
605 Loomis St, Westfield, MA 01085 US
(413) 572-5427, *Fax:* (413) 572-5625
www.wsc.ma.edu/wskb
License: Westfield, Hampden County, MA held by Westfield State College.
Format: Variety/Diverse *Target Audience:* General.
Andrew Johnson, General Manager
Brendan Mehu, Programming Director
Karen Renda, Promotions Manager

Williamstown

***WCFM**
09-08-1958; 91.9 mhz FM; 0.44 kw; -837 ft.; N42 42 38 W73 12 6
Hopkins Hall Williams Co, Williamstown, MA 01267 US
(413) 597-3265, *Fax:* (413) 597-2259
wcfm.williams.edu
wcfmbd@wso.williams.edu
License: Williamstown, Berkshire County, MA held by The President & Trustees of Williams College.
Arbitron Metro Market: Twin Falls, ID
Adam Ain, General Manager

Winchendon

***WKMY**
01-01-2006; 91.1 mhz FM; 0.06 kw; 450 ft.; N42 42 9 W72 2 18
Rebroadcasts: Rebroadcasts KLVR(FM) Middletown, CA 100%
Falls Road, Toccoa Falls, GA 30598 US
(800) 877-5600, *Fax:* (916) 251-1650
www.klove.com
License: Winchendon, Worcester County, MA held by Educational Media Foundation.
Group Owner: EMF Broadcasting; (acq 6-30-2005; $15,000 for CP)
Nat'l Network: K-Love
Arbitron Metro Market: Winchendon, MA *Format:* Christian
Darrell Chambliss, Chairman
Mike Novak, President
Glenn Goodwin, Operations Dir

Woods Hole

***WCAI**
09-25-2000; 90.1 mhz FM; 1.3 kw vert; 249 ft.; N41 26 16 W70 36 51
Mailing Address: 125 Western Avenue, Boston, MA 02134 US
Second Address: 3 Water St., Woods Hole, MA 2543
(508) 548-9600, *Fax:* (508) 548-5517
wwe.wgbh.org
cainan@wgbh.org
License: Woods Hole, Barnstable County, MA held by WGBH Educational Foundation
Nat'l Network: NPR
Arbitron Metro Market: Woods Hole, MA *Format:* News, News/Talk, 86
John Voci, Station Manager
Susan Loucks, General Sales Mgr
Steve Young, Programming Director

Worcester

***WBPR**
01-01-1994; 91.9 mhz FM; 0.37 kw; 699 ft.; N42 18 11 W71 53 52 *Rebroadcasts:* Rebroadcasts WUMB-FM Boston 100%
100 Morrissey Boulevard, Boston, MA 02125 US
(617) 287-6900, *Fax:* (617) 287-6916
www.wumb.org
wumb@umb.edu
License: Worcester, Worcester County, MA held by University of Massachusetts.
Arbitron Metro Market: Boston, MA *Format:* Variety/Diverse *No. News Employees:* 25 *Target Audience:* 25-45.
Patricia Monteith, General Manager
Danielle Knight, General Sales Mgr
Brian Quinn, Programming Director

***WCHC**
09-12-1977; 88.1 mhz FM *Hrs Open:* 7 AM-2 AM; 0.1 kw vert; -7 ft.; N42 14 15 W71 48 31
PO Box 4a, Worcester, MA 01610 US
(508) 793-2475, *Fax:* (508) 793-2471
www.college.holycross.edu/wchc
wchc@holycross.edu
License: Worcester, Worcester County, MA held by Trustees of the College of the Holy Cross.
Arbitron Metro Market: Worcester, MA *Format:* Alternative *Special Programming:* Black 8 hrs, class 6 hrs, jazz 6 hrs, metal 6 hrs, funk 3 hrs wkly *Hrs. of News Programming:* News progmg 5 hrs wkly *Target Audience:* 12-35; adventurous
Andrew Rhoades, General Manager

WCRN
12-05-1994; 830 khz AM
20 Park Plaza, Suite 720, Boston, MA 02116 US
(508) 438-0965, *Fax:* (508) 770-0659
www.wcrnradio.com
chris@wcrnradio.com
License: Worcester, MA held by Carter Broadcasting Corp.
Arbitron Metro Market: Worcester, MA *Format:* Talk *Target Audience:* 25-54.
Ken Carter, President
Tony Chavez, Operations Dir
Kurt Carberry, General Manager
Art Dufault, Station Manager
Chris Thompson, General Sales Mgr

***WCUW**
12-04-1973; 91.3 mhz FM *Hrs Open:* 24; 0.63 kw; 144 ft.; N42 15 46 W71 47 59
910 Main Street, Worcester, MA 01610 US
(508) 753-1012
www.wcuw.org
wcuw@wcuw.org
License: Worcester, Worcester County, MA held by WCUW Inc.
Arbitron Metro Market: Worcester, MA *Format:* Variety/Diverse *Special Programming:* Fr 2 hrs, Sp 19 hrs, Ger 2 hrs, Pol 6 hrs, ethnic 10 hrs wkly *Hrs. of News Programming:* News progmg one hr wkly *Target Audience:* General.
Joe Cutroni, General Manager

***WICN**
11-21-1969; 90.5 mhz FM *Hrs Open:* 24; 1.1 kw; 810 ft.; N42 18 11 W71 53 52
6 Chatham Street, Worcester, MA 01609 US
(508) 752-0700, *Fax:* (508) 752-7518
www.wicn.org
webmaster@wicn.org
License: Worcester, Worcester County, MA held by WICN Public Radio Inc.
Nat'l Network: NPR
Arbitron Metro Market: Worcester, MA *Format:* Big Band, Jazz *Hrs. of News Programming:* News progmg 12 hrs wkly *Target Audience:* 35 plus; high education, high income *Adv. Rates:* 30-40 a spot
Mike Gorman, President
Thomas Kenney, Operations Dir
Brian Barlow, General Manager
Tyra Penn, General Sales Mgr
Kyle Warren, Operations Director

WNEB
12-18-1946; 1230 khz AM *Hrs Open:* 24; 1 kw-U, ND1; N42 16 23 W71 49 23
100 Mt Wayte Avenue, Framingham, MA 01702 US
(508) 767-1230, *Fax:* (508) 831-7964
www.1230radio.com
info@1230radio.com
License: Worcester, MA held by Blount Masscom Inc.
Group Owner: Blount Communications Group
Arbitron Metro Market: Worcester, MA *Format:* Religious *Target Audience:* 25-54. *Adv. Rates:* 20; 20; 20; 10
William Blount, President
David Young, Operations Dir
Emanuel DaCunha, Station Manager
Randolph Berkson, Operations Manager

WORC
02-01-1925; 1310 khz AM; 5 kw-D, DA2; 1 kw-N, DA2; N42 13 19 W71 49 2
455 Pennsylvania Ave., Suite 125, Ft. Washington, PA 19034 US
(508) 791-2111, *Fax:* (508) 752-6897
www.megaworcester.com/
info@power1310.com
License: Worcester, MA held by Antonio F. Gois.

Nat'l Network: Westwood One
Arbitron Metro Market: Worcester, MA *TV Affiliate:* Sp *Format:* Sports *Hrs. of News Programming:* 1 *No. News Employees:* 29-54; Latinos

WSRS
06-17-1940; 96.1 mhz FM *Hrs Open:* 24; 16.5 kw; 863 ft.; N42 18 34 W71 54 13
600 Congress Avenue, Suite 1400, Austin, TX 78701 US
(508) 757-9696, *Fax:* (508) 757-1779
www.wsrs.com
info@wsrs.com
License: Worcester, Worcester County, MA
Group Owner: Clear Channel Communications Inc.
Nat'l Network: ABC
Arbitron Metro Market: Worcester, MA *Format:* Adult Contemp *Hrs. of News Programming:* news progmg 5 hrs wkly *No. News Employees:* 1 *Target Audience:* 25-54.
Tom Holt, Programming Director
Bruce Palmer, Promotions Manager
George Brown, News Director
Lanie Brown, Traffic Manager

WTAG
05-01-1924; 580 khz AM *Hrs Open:* 24; 5 kw-D, DA2; 5 kw-N, DA2; N42 20 13 W71 49 15
600 Congress Avenue, Suite 1400, Austin, TX 78701 US
(508) 795-0580,(508) 757-9696, *Fax:* (508) 757-1779
www.wtag.com
info@wsrs.com
License: Worcester, MA held by Capstar TX L.P.
Group Owner: Clear Channel Communications Inc.; (acq 8-30-2000; grpsl).
Nat'l Network: CBS
Arbitron Metro Market: Worcester, MA *Format:* News, News/Talk, 86 *Special Programming:* Sports *Hrs. of News Programming:* news progmg 40 hrs wkly *No. News Employees:* 6 *Target Audience:* 25-54.
Greg Byrne, Operations Dir
Michael Schaus, General Manager
Susan Remkiewicz, General Sales Mgr
George Brown, Programming Director
Bruce Palmer, Promotions Manager
Dan Kelleher, Chief Engineer

WVEI
01-01-1926; 1440 khz AM *Hrs Open:* 24; 5 kw-D, DAN; 5 kw-N, DAN; N42 17 25 W71 50 47 *Rebroadcasts:* Simulcast with WEEI(AM) Boston 100%
401 City Avenue, Suite 409, Bala Cynwyd, PA 19004 US
(508) 752-5611, *Fax:* (508) 752-1006
www.weei.com
jsheridan@entercom.com
License: Worcester, MA held by Entercom Boston II License LLC.
Group Owner: Entercom Communications Corp.; (acq 10-15-98; grpsl)
Nat'l Reps: CBS Radio
Arbitron Metro Market: Worcester, MA *Format:* Sports
Julie Kahn, Station Manager
Jack Sheridan, General Sales Mgr
Eric Fitch, Chief Engineer

Mexico

Tijuana

XETRA
01-01-1934; 690 khz AM *Hrs Open:* 24
MX
(818) 972-4200, *Fax:* (818) 972-4210
www.wradio690.com
License: Tijuana, BN held by Clear Channel Communications Inc.
Nat'l Network: ABC
Arbitron Metro Market: Burbank, CA *Format:* Adult Contemp *Target Audience:* 25-54; men
Kevin McCarthy, President
Dan Weiner, General Sales Mgr

XETRAFM
01-01-1978; 91.1 mhz FM *Hrs Open:* 24; kw
MX
(858) 535-2500
www.91x.com
gwolfson@lmasandiego.com
License: Tijuana, BN held by Clear Channel Communications Inc.
Arbitron Metro Market: San Diego, CA *Format:* Alternative *No. News Employees:* 1 *Target Audience:* 18-49; very active, college educated, above market average income, single
Mike Glickenhaus, President
Tim Dukes, Operations Dir
Gregg Wolfson, VP/General Manager
Bill Lipis, Station Manager
Christy Taylor, Programming Director
Josh Hammond, Promotions Manager
Lisa Minjares, Director, Digital Media

XHRMFM
01-01-1981; 92.5 mhz FM *Hrs Open:* 24; kw
MX
(619) 570-1925, *Fax:* 858) 522-5717
www.magic925.com
gwolfson@lmasandiego.com
License: Tijuana, BN held by The Rivas Kaloyan Family.
Arbitron Metro Market: San Diego, CA *Format:* Adult Contemp, Oldies *Target Audience:* 18-49.
Mike Glickenhouse, General Manager

Michigan

Ada

WPRR
01-01-1998; 1680 khz AM *Hrs Open:* 24
4417 Broadmoor S.E., Kentwood, MI 49512 US
(616) 554-5958, *Fax:* (616) 656-9326
www.publicrealityradio.org
info@publicrealityradio.org
License: Ada, MI held by Goodrich Radio L.L.C.
Arbitron Metro Market: Grand Rapids, MI *Format:* Talk *No. News Employees:* 1 *Adv. Rates:* 26; 21; 21; 15
Robert Goodrich, Chairman
Robert Goodrich, President
Ross Pettinga, Station Manager
David Fletcher, Programming Director

Adrian

WABJ
11-13-1946; 1490 khz AM *Hrs Open:* 24; 1 kw-U, ND1; N41 54 2 W84 0 51
121 W. Maumec, Adrian, MI 49221 US
(219) 756-5656, *Fax:* (219) 755-4312
www.afr.net
License: Adrian, MI held by Friends Communications of Michigan Inc.
Group Owner: Friends Communications Inc.; (acq 10-1-90; grpsl;
Regional Network: Mich. Farm *Regional Reps:* Michigan.
Arbitron Metro Market: Cheney WA *Format:* News, News/Talk, 86
Thomas Carroll, CEO
Len Clark, Programming Director

WLEN
06-09-1965; 103.9 mhz FM *Hrs Open:* 24; 3 kw; 299 ft; N41 54 11 W83 59 13
Mailing Address: Box 687, Adrian, MI 49221
Second Address: 242 W. Maumee St., Adrian, MI 49221
(517) 263-1039, *Fax:* (517) 265-5362
www.wlen.com
License: Adrian, Lenawee County, MI held by Lenawee Broadcasting Co.
Nat'l Network: CBC News Radio
Special Programming: Sp 4 hrs wkly *No. News Employees:* 1 *Target Audience:* 25-54.
Julie Koehn, President
Julie Koehn, General Manager
Julie Koehn, Station Manager
Pat Hayes, General Sales Mgr
Dale Gaertner, Programming Director
Dominic Fracassa, News Director
Tom Peterson, Engineering Dir
Tom Peterson, ChiefEngineer

WQTE
09-01-1976; 95.3 mhz FM *Hrs Open:* 24; 3 kw; 299 ft.; N41 48 15 W84 5 25
121 West Maunee Street, Adrian, MI 49221 US
(517) 265-1500, *Fax:* (517) 263-4525
friends@tc3net.com
License: Adrian, Lenawee County, MI held by Friends Communications of Michigan Inc.
Group Owner: Friends Communications Inc.; (acq 10-1-90; grpsl;
Format: Country *Hrs. of News Programming:* News progmg 2 hrs wkly *Target Audience:* 25-54.
Larry Augustine, General Manager
Patricia Wendt, News Director
Harry Bingaman, Chief Engineer

***WVAC-FM**
02-13-1967; 107.9 mhz FM; 0.087 kw; 84 ft.; N41 53 49 W84 3 40
110 S. Madison, Adrian, MI 49221 US
(517) 265-5161, *Fax:* (517) 264-3331
www.adrian.edu
License: Adrian, Lenawee County, MI held by Adrian College Board of Trustees.
Arbitron Metro Market: Adrian, MI *Format:* Variety/Diverse *Target Audience:* 18-23; those affiliated to the college lifestyle
Stephen Shehan, Operations Dir

Albion

***WUFN**
04-01-1971; 96.7 mhz FM *Hrs Open:* 24; 3.2 kw; 456 ft.; N42 15 56 W84 38 43
7335 N. Oracle, Ste. 200, Tucson, AZ 85704 US
(520) 742-6976, *Fax:* (520) 469-7312
www.myflr.org
dphelps@flc.org
License: Albion, Calhoun County, MI held by Family Life Broadcasting System.
Group Owner: Family Life Communications Inc.
Nat'l Network: USA; AP Radio
Arbitron Metro Market: Battle Creek, MI *Format:* Christian, Religious *Hrs. of News Programming:* News progmg 1.5 hrs wkly *Target Audience:* 25-54; Christian families
Randy Carlson, President
Dawn Bumstead, General Manager

Allendale

***WGVU-FM**
07-15-1983; 88.5 mhz FM *Hrs Open:* 24; 4 kw; 295 ft.; N43 3 24 W85 57 37
301 West Fulton Street, Grand Rapids, MI 49504 US
(616) 331-6666, *Fax:* (616) 331-6625
www.wgvu.org
wgvu@gvsu.edu
License: Allendale, Ottawa County, MI held by Board of Control of Grand Valley State University.
Nat'l Network: NPR; AP Radio
Format: Jazz, News *Hrs. of News Programming:* news progmg 26 hrs wkly *No. News Employees:* 5 *Target Audience:* 25 plus; mid to upper educ & income levels
Ken Kolbe, Operations Dir
Michael Walenta, General Manager
Gary Hunt, Programming Director
Pamela Holtz, Promotions Manager
Fred Martino, News Director

Alma

WFYC
08-17-1948; 1280 khz AM *Hrs Open:* 24
PO Box 669, Alma, MI 48801 US
(989) 463-3175, *Fax:* (989) 463-6674
www.wqbxradio.com
wqbx@cmsinter.net
License: Alma, MI held by Jacom Inc.
Format: Sports *Special Programming:* Farm 4 hrs wkly *Target Audience:* 25-50. *Adv. Rates:* 10.50; 10.50; 10.50; 9
James Sommerville, President
Susan Sommerville, Promotions Manager

***WQAC**
03-27-1993; 90.9 mhz FM *Hrs Open:* 7 AM-2 AM (M-F); noon-2 AM (S, Su); 0.1 kw; 66 ft.; N43 22 46 W84 40 25
614 West Superior Street, Alma, MI 48801 US
(989) 463-7095, *Fax:* (989) 463-7277
students.alma.edu/organizations/wqac
wqaccharts@blazemail.com
License: Alma, Gratiot County, MI held by Alma College.
Format: Alternative *Target Audience:* 13-24; high school & college students
Steven Best, General Manager

Alpena

WATZ
01-01-1946; 1450 khz AM *Hrs Open:* 20; 1 kw-U, ND1; N45 3 58 W83 29 6
Mailing Address: 123 Prentiss Street, Alpena, MI 49707 US
Second Address: 123 Prentiss, Alpena, MI 49707
(989) 354-8400, *Fax:* (989) 354-3436
www.watz.com
watz@watz.com
License: Alpena, MI held by WATZ Radio Inc.
Group Owner: Midwestern Broadcasting Co.
Regional Network: Mich. Farm

Arbitron Metro Market: Alpena, MI *Format:* Talk *Special Programming:* Farm 3 hrs, Ger 2 hrs, Pol 2 hrs, relg 2 hrs wkly *Hrs. of News Programming:* news progmg 31 hrs wkly *No. News Employees:* 2 *TargetAudience:* 35-64.
Steve Wright, Operations Dir
Mike Centala, General Manager
Bruce Johnson, News Director

WATZ-FM
01-01-1967; 99.3 mhz FM *Hrs Open:* 20; 17 kw; 843 ft.; N44 51 25 W83 32 34
Mailing Address: 314 E. Front St., Traverse City, MI 49684 US
Second Address: 123 Prentiss, Alpena, MI 49707
(989) 354-8400, *Fax:* (989) 354-3436
www.watz.com
License: Alpena, Alpena County, MI
Group Owner: Midwestern Broadcasting Co.
Arbitron Metro Market: Alpena, MI *Format:* Country *Target Audience:* 25-54.
Suzie Martin, Programming Director

***WCML-FM**
04-24-1978; 91.7 mhz FM *Hrs Open:* 24; 92 kw; 1194 ft.; N45 8 17.3 W84 9 43.6 *Rebroadcasts:* Rebroadcasts WCMU-FM Mount Pleasant 100%
3965 E Broomfield Road, Mt. Pleasant, MI 48859 US
(989) 774-3105, *Fax:* (989) 774-4427
www.wcmu.org
schud1ra@cmich.edu
License: Alpena, Alpena County, MI held by Central Michigan University.
Nat'l Network: NPR; PRI *Wire Services:* AP
Arbitron Metro Market: Michigan, Upper Peninsula,MS *TV Affiliate:* *WCML(TV) affil *Format:* Jazz, News *Hrs. of News Programming:* news progmg 45 hrs wkly *No. News Employees:* 2 *Target Audience:* General.
Edward Grant, General Manager
Ray Ford, Programming Director

WHSB
05-01-1965; 107.7 mhz FM; 100 kw; 610 ft.; N45 3 46 W83 42 56
1491 M-32 West, Alpena, MI 49707 US
(989) 354-4611, *Fax:* (989) 354-4014
www.alpenanow.com
tnrn@charterinternet.com
License: Alpena, Alpena County, MI held by Edwards Communications LC.
Group Owner: Edwards Communications L.C.; (acq 12-21-2004; grpsl).
Nat'l Reps: Michigan Spot Sales *Wire Services:* UPI
Format: Adult Contemp *Target Audience:* 25-54.
Jerry Edwards, President
Tim Allen, Operations Dir
Darrel Kelly, Programming Director
Michael Leland, News Director
Steve Johnston, Engineering Dir
Mike Crane, Director of Radio
Sarah Jacobs, Audience Service Manager
Mary KayDadisman, Director of Development
Sheryl Gasser, Talk Director
Jeffrey Potter, Marketing Director
Kathy Beringer, Membership Service Manger

Ann Arbor

WAAM
10-01-1947; 1600 khz AM *Hrs Open:* 24; 5 kw-D, DA2; 5 kw-N, DA2; N42 11 32 W83 41 9
4230 Packard Road, Ann Arbor, MI 48108 US
(225) 768-3102, *Fax:* (225) 768-3729
www.jsm.org
kawikfish@yahoo.com
License: Ann Arbor, MI held by Ann Arbor First Ventures L.P.
Nat'l Network: Westwood One
Arbitron Metro Market: El Dorado AR *Format:* Christian, Religious *Adv. Rates:* 38; 38; 34; 20
David Whitelaw, COO

***WCBN-FM**
01-23-1972; 88.3 mhz FM *Hrs Open:* 24; 0.2 kw vert; 177 ft.; N42 16 37 W83 44 7
5000 Ls & a Bldg, 5th Flr, Ann Arbor, MI 48109 US
(734) 647-4122(734) 763-3535
www.wcbn.org
fm@wcbn.org
License: Ann Arbor, Washtenaw County, MI held by Regents of the University of Michigan.
Arbitron Metro Market: Ann Arbor, MI *Format:* Variety/Diverse *Target Audience:* 18-49.
Rob Goldey, General Manager
Kristin Sumrall, Programming Director
Alex Sergay, Chief Engineer

WWWW-FM
03-01-1962; 102.9 mhz FM *Hrs Open:* 24; 50 kw; 440 ft.; N42 14 46 W83 50 58
111 East Kilbourn Ave., Suite 2700, Milwaukee, WI 53202 US
(734) 302-8100, *Fax:* (734) 213-7508
www.w4country.com
programming@w4country.com
License: Ann Arbor, Washtenaw County, MI held by Capstar TX L.P.
Group Owner: Clear Channel Communications Inc.; (acq 8-7-2000; grpsl).
Nat'l Reps: Cumulus Radio Sales
Arbitron Metro Market: Ann Arbor, MI *Format:* Country
Bob Bolak, General Manager
Brent Dingman, General Sales Mgr
Brian Cowan, Programming Director

WQKL
02-14-1967; 107.1 mhz FM; 3 kw; 289 ft.; N42 16 41 W83 44 32
111 East Kilbourn Ave., Suite 2700, Milwaukee, WI 53202 US
(734) 302-8100, *Fax:* (734) 213-7508
www.annarbors107one.com
License: Ann Arbor, Washtenaw County, MI
Nat'l Reps: Cumulus Radio Sales
Arbitron Metro Market: Ann Arbor, MI *Format:* Triple A *Hrs. of News Programming:* news progmg 4 hrs wkly *No. News Employees:* 1 *Target Audience:* 25-50; women
Brent Dingman, General Sales Mgr
Chris Ammel, Programming Director
Chris Wachner, Promotions Manager
Brian Larsen, News Director

WTKA
04-26-1945; 1050 khz AM; 10 kw-D, DA2; 0.5 kw-N, DA2; N42 8 46 W83 39 36
111 East Kilbourn Ave., Suite 2700, Milwaukee, WI 53202 US
(734) 302-8100, *Fax:* (734) 213-7508
www.wtka.com
studio@wtka.com
License: Ann Arbor, MI held by Capstar TX L.P.
Group Owner: Clear Channel Communications Inc.; (acq 8-7-00; grpsl).
Nat'l Network: ESPN Radio *Nat'l Reps:* Cumulus Radio Sales
Arbitron Metro Market: Ann Arbor, MI *Format:* Sports *No. News Employees:* 1 *Target Audience:* 18-34; male
Jessica Husted, General Sales Mgr
Ira Weintraub, Programming Director
Ryan Albig, Promotions Manager
Brian Laren, News Director
Sam Webb, AM Local Show
Andy Evans, AM Local Show
Scott Meier, Market Manager
Tyler Crawford,Production Director

***WUOM**
01-01-1948; 91.7 mhz FM *Hrs Open:* 24; 93 kw; 778 ft.; N42 24 27 W83 54 50
5000 Lsa Building, 5th Floor, Ann Arbor, MI 48109 US
(734) 764-9210, *Fax:* (734) 647-3488
www.michiganradio.org
michigan.radio@umich.edu
License: Ann Arbor, Washtenaw County, MI held by The Regents of University of Michigan.
Nat'l Network: NPR; PRI *Wire Services:* AP
Arbitron Metro Market: Ann Arbor, MI *Format:* News, News/Talk, 86 *Hrs. of News Programming:* news progmg 140 hrs wkly *No. News Employees:* 7
Peggy Watson, Operations Dir
Tamar Charney, Programming Director
Vincent Duffy, News Director
Larry Jonas, Director of Development
Steve Chrypinski, Marketing Director
Kathy Agosta, Director of Corporate Support

Ashley

WJSZ
03-14-1994; 92.5 mhz FM *Hrs Open:* 24; 4 kw; 400 ft.; N43 10 56 W84 27 3
1907 W-M-21, Owosso, MI 48867 US
(989) 725-1925, *Fax:* (989) 725-7925
www.z925.com
rodk@voyager.net
License: Ashley, Gratiot County, MI held by Krol Communications Inc.
Regional Network: Mich. Farm
Format: Adult Contemp *Hrs. of News Programming:* 90 mins wkly *Target Audience:* 25-54; general *Adv. Rates:* 30; 24; 24; 15
Rob Krol, President
Angie Bucsf, General Manager

Atlanta

WFDX
10-20-1988; 92.5 mhz FM *Hrs Open:* 24; 100 kw; 869 ft.; N45 1 0 W84 21 10
2215 Oak Indust. Dr. N.E, Grand Rapids, MI 49505 US
(231) 947-5396, *Fax:* (231) 947-7002
www.943thefoxfm.com
charlie@wklt.com
License: Atlanta, Montmorency County, MI held by Northern Michigan Radio Inc.
Nat'l Reps: Christal
Arbitron Metro Market: Traverse City, MI *Format:* Contemporary Hits/Top 40, Adult Contemp *No. News Employees:* 1 *Target Audience:* 25-54.
Charlie Ferguson, General Manager
Greg Marsh, General Sales Mgr
Dennis Winslow, Programming Director
Kristal Flateau, News Director

Auburn Hills

***WAHS**
01-01-1975; 89.5 mhz FM; 0.1 kw; 141 ft.; N42 37 42 W83 13 56
2800 Waukegan, Auburn Hills, MI 48326 US
(248) 852-9247, *Fax:* (248) 852-0595
License: Auburn Hills, Oakland County, MI held by Avondale School District.
Arbitron Metro Market: Auburn Hills, MI *Format:* Contemporary Hits/Top 40
Rick Kreinbring, General Manager

***WXOU**
08-01-1995; 88.3 mhz FM *Hrs Open:* 24; 0.11 kw; 256 ft.; N42 42 35 W83 13 50
49 Oakland Center, Auburn Hills, MI 48309 US
(248) 370-4273, *Fax:* (248) 370-2846
www.wxou.org
wxou@wxou.org
License: Auburn Hills, Oakland County, MI held by Oakland University.
Arbitron Metro Market: Auburn Hills, MI *Format:* Variety/Diverse *Hrs. of News Programming:* 8 hrs wkly *No. News Employees:* 5 *Target Audience:* General; univ & loc community not serviced by coml media
Sean Varicalli, General Manager
Christine Stover, General Sales Mgr
Christina Venditti, Programming Director
Josh Nagy, Promotions Manager
Ashley Allison, News Director
Patrick Cymbalski, Assistant Program Director
Matt Pocket,Sports Director
Joe Iaconis, IT Director

Bad Axe

WLEW
01-01-1950; 1340 khz AM *Hrs Open:* 24; 1 kw-D, DAD; 1 kw-N, DAD; N43 48 3 W83 1 23
935 South Van Dyke Rd, Bad Axe, MI 48413 US
(989) 269-9931, *Fax:* (989) 269-7702
www.thumbnet.net
info@thumbnet.net
License: Bad Axe, MI held by Thumb Broadcasting Inc.
Format: Country *Hrs. of News Programming:* news progmg 19 hrs wkly *No. News Employees:* 2 *Target Audience:* 18-50.
Richard Aymen, General Manager

WLEW-FM
01-01-1956; 102.1 mhz FM *Hrs Open:* 24; 50 kw; Ant 492 ft; N43 53 28 W83 07 26
935 S. Van Dyke Rd., Bad Axe, MI 48413
(989) 269-9931, *Fax:* (989) 269-7702
License: Bad Axe, Huron County, MI held by Thumb Broadcasting Inc.
Population Served: 620,000*Target Audience:* 25-50.
Richard Aymen, Operations Dir
Matthew Aymen, General Sales Mgr
Craig Routzhan, News Director
Jerry Stocker, Chief Engineer
Tina Hind, Traffic Manager

Baraga

***WVCN**
01-01-1998; 104.3 mhz FM *Hrs Open:* 24; 100 kw; 860 ft.; N46 39 50 W88 23 6
3434 W Kilbourn Ave, Milwaukee, WI 53208 US
(414) 935-3000, *Fax:* (414) 935-3015
www.vcyamerica.org
wvcn@vcyamerica.org

License: Baraga, Baraga County, MI held by Keweenaw Bay Broadcasting Inc.
Group Owner: VCY America Inc.; (acq 7-8-99)
Format: Christian
Dr. Randall Melchert, President
Vic Eliason, Operations Dir
Jim Schneider, Programming Director
Gordon Morris, News Director
Andy Eliason, Chief Engineer
Tom Schlueter, Music Director

Battle Creek

WBCK

07-09-1948; 930 khz AM; 5 kw-D, 1 kw-N, DA-2; N42 17 40 W85 11 00
390 Golden Ave., Battle Creek, MI 78701
(269) 963-5555, *Fax:* (269) 963-5185
License: Battle Creek, Calhoun County, MI held by Stratus Radio LLC
Population Served: 170,000 *Arbitron Metro Market:* Battle Creek, M
Tim Collins, General Manager

WBCK-FM

02-28-1975; 95.3 mhz FM; 3 kw; 269 ft.; N42 17 17 W85 9 54
600 Congress Ave., Suite 1400, Austin, TX 78701 US
(269) 963-5555, *Fax:* (269) 963-5185
www.wbckfm.com
tim.collins@cumulus.com
License: Battle Creek, Calhoun County, MI held by Capstar TX L.P.
Group Owner: Clear Channel Communications Inc.; (acq 8-30-2000; grpsl)
Arbitron Metro Market: Battle Creek, MI *Format:* News, News/Talk, 86 *Target Audience:* 25-54.
Tim Collins, Operations Dir
Steve Stoimenoff, General Manager
Tim Collins, Promotions Manager
Robert Nelson, News/Production
Walker Sisson, Chief Engineer

WKFR-FM

06-11-1963; 103.3 mhz FM *Hrs Open:* 24; 50 kw; 482 ft.; N42 21 20 W85 20 28
330 East Kilbourn Ave., Suite 250, Milwaukee, WI 53202 US
(269) 344-0111, *Fax:* (269) 344-4223
www.wkfr.com
radio@wkfr.com
License: Battle Creek, Calhoun County, MI held by Cumulus Licensing Corp.
Group Owner: Cumulus Media Inc.; (acq 5-26-98; grpsl)
Arbitron Metro Market: Kalamazoo, MI *Format:* Contemporary Hits/Top 40 *Hrs. of News Programming:* news progmg 3 hrs wkly *No. News Employees:* 1 *Target Audience:* 25-54.
Lew Dickey, CEO
Mike McKelly, Operations Dir
Ken Evans, Programming Director
Martin Gausvik, CFO
John Pinch, COO

WBFN

07-01-1993; 1400 khz AM
600 Congress Ave., Suite 1400, Austin, TX 78701 US
(520) 742-6976, *Fax:* (520) 742-6979
www.flc.org
License: Battle Creek, MI held by Aloha Station Trust LLC
Arbitron Metro Market: Battle Creek, MI *Format:* Christian
Randy Carlson, President

Bay City

*WCHW-FM

09-01-1973; 91.3 mhz FM; 0.11 kw horiz; 125 ft.; N43 35 19 W83 52 28
1624 Columbus Avenue, Bay City, MI 48708 US
(989) 892-1741(989) 892-5533, *Fax:* (989) 892-7946
www.wchwonline.freewebspace.com
wchwonline@fnmail.com
License: Bay City, Bay County, MI held by School District Bay City.
Arbitron Metro Market: Bay City, MI *Format:* Rock/AOR
Jeremy Powers, General Manager

WHNN

01-01-1947; 96.1 mhz FM *Hrs Open:* 24; 100 kw; 1020 ft.; N43 33 10 W83 41 24
3420 Pine Tree Road, Lansing, MI 48911 US
(989) 298-9466, *Fax:* (989) 754-9600
www.whnn.com
License: Bay City, Bay County, MI
Group Owner: Cumulus Media Inc.; (acq 4-26-01; grpsl).
Arbitron Metro Market: Saginaw-Bay City-Midland, MI *Format:* Oldies *Hrs. of News Programming:* news progmg 6 hrs wkly *No. News Employees:* 1 *Target Audience:* 25-54.
Scott Meier, General Manager
Scott Stein, Programming Director

WIOG

09-01-1969; 102.5 mhz FM *Hrs Open:* 24; 86 kw; 801 ft.; N43 28 24 W83 50 40
140 South Ash Avenue, Tempe, AZ 85281 US
(989) 776-2100, *Fax:* (989) 754-5990
www.wiog.com
info@wiog.com
License: Bay City, Bay County, MI
Group Owner: Cumulus Media Inc.; (acq 2-8-99; grpsl).
Nat'l Network: ABC *Nat'l Reps:* McGavren Guild
Arbitron Metro Market: Saginaw-Bay City-Midland, MI *Format:* Adult Contemp *Hrs. of News Programming:* news progmg 5 hrs wkly *No. News Employees:* 1 *Target Audience:* 25-54.
Chris Monk, General Manager
Matt Bing, General Sales Mgr
Nate Rose, Programming Director
Rachel Geddes, Promotions Manager
Tom Clark, General Sales Manager

WMAX

06-05-1925; 1440 khz AM *Hrs Open:* 24; 5 kw-D, DA2; 2.5 kw-N, DA2; N43 31 27 W83 57 58 *Rebroadcasts:* WDEO(AM) Ypsilanti 97%
321 Rivard Blvd., Grosse Points, MI 48230 US
(734) 930-5200, *Fax:* (989) 930-3101
www.avemariaradio.net
mjones@avemariaradio.net
License: Bay City, MI held by 990 Investors L.L.C.
Nat'l Network: EWTN Radio
Arbitron Metro Market: Saginaw, MI *Format:* Talk, Christian *Hrs. of News Programming:* news progmg 14 hrs wkly *No. News Employees:* 2 *Target Audience:* 25-54; adult Christian *Adv. Rates:* 25; 25; 45; 25
Al Kresta, CEO
Michael Jones, President

*WLKB

07-25-1993; 89.1 mhz FM *Hrs Open:* 24; 50 kw vert; 371 ft.; N43 33 42 W83 58 52 *Rebroadcasts:* Rebroadcasts KLVR(FM) Santa Rosa, CA 100%
919 29th St., Bay City, MI 48708 US
(916) 251-1600, *Fax:* (916) 251-1650
www.klove.com
klove@klove.com
License: Bay City, Bay County, MI held by Educational Media Foundation.
Group Owner: EMF Broadcasting; (acq 8-8-2006; $800,000)
Nat'l Network: K-Love
Arbitron Metro Market: Rocklin, CA *Format:* Christian *No. News Employees:* 3 *Target Audience:* 25-44; female-Judeo Christian
Darrell Chambliss, Chairman
Mike Novak, CEO
Mike Novak, President
Pam Patrick-Thompson, Operations Dir
David Pierce, Programming Director
Ed Lenane, News Director
Sam Wallington, Engineering Dir
Marya Morgan, News Reporter
Richard Hunt, News Reporter
Mitch Barnhart, Director
Larry Moody, Director
Dr.David.R.Ferry, Director

*WUCX-FM

09-01-1989; 90.1 mhz FM; 30 kw; 479 ft.; N43 33 10 W83 41 24
3965 E. Broomfield Rd., Mt. Pleasant, MI 48859 US
(989) 686-9292, *Fax:* (989) 686-0155
www.delta.edu/broadcasting
wucx@delta.edu
License: Bay City, Bay County, MI held by Central Michigan University.
Nat'l Network: NPR; PRI
Arbitron Metro Market: Bay City, MI *Format:* Blues, Jazz, 60 *Target Audience:* General.
Barry Baker, General Manager
Howard Sharper, Production/Program Director
Tom Bennett, Chief Engineer
Mary Male, Development Manager
Chas Eldridge, Traffic & Website Coordinator
Lee Monday, Production Coordinator
Joe Yezak,Program Manager

Bear Creek Township

*WTLI

09-16-1998; 89.3 mhz FM; 17 kw vert; 1024 ft.; N45 10 12 W84 45 4 *Rebroadcasts:* rebroadcast of WLGH(FM) Leroy Township
3302 N. Van Dyke Rd., Imlay City, MI 48444 US
(888) 887-7139, *Fax:* (877) 850-0881
www.positivehits.com
411@smile.fm
License: Bear Creek Township, Emmet County, MI held by Superior Communications.
Group Owner: Superior Communications
Arbitron Metro Market: Petoskey, MI *Format:* Christian
Jenn Czelada, General Manager
Ed Czelada, Programming Director

Bear Lake

WCUZ

11-02-1987; 100.1 mhz FM; 2.05 kw; 564 ft.; N44 30 54 W86 6 53 *Rebroadcasts:* Simulcasts WLDR-FM Traverse City 100%
Mailing Address: P.O. Box 262, Bear Lake, MI 49617 US
Second Address: 1532 Forrester Rd, Frankfort, MI 49635
(231) 947-3220, *Fax:* (231) 947-7201
www.wldr.com
License: Bear Lake, Manistee County, MI held by Roy E. Henderson.
Group Owner: Fort Bend Broadcasting Co.; (acq 9-27-2000; $590,000 with WOUF(FM) Beulah)
Format: Country
Roy Henderson, General Manager

Beaverton

WMRX-FM

09-15-1980; 97.7 mhz FM; 4.1 kw; 400 ft.; N43 53 16 W84 31 45 *Rebroadcasts:* Rebroadcasts WMPX(FM) Midland 100%
Mailing Address: 1510 Bayliss Street, Midland, MI 48640 US
Second Address: 1510 Bayliss St., Midland, MI 48640
989-631-1490, *Fax:* (989) 631-6357
www.wmpxwmrx.com
admin@wmpxwmrx.com
License: Beaverton, Gladwin County, MI held by Steel Broadcasting Inc.
Nat'l Network: ABC
Arbitron Metro Market: Saginaw, MI *Format:* Oldies, Adult Contemp *Special Programming:* Sounds of Sinatra 2 hrs wkly *Hrs. of News Programming:* News progmg 8 hrs wkly *No. News Employees:* 1 *Target Audience:* General; 35+
Thomas Steel, President
Jon Walding, General Sales Mgr
Brad Morgan, Programming Director
Tom Steel, News Director

Belding

*WSLI

01-01-2009; 90.9 mhz FM; 11.5 kw vert; 240 ft.; N43 5 12 W85 18 59 *Rebroadcasts:* Rebroadcasts WLGH(FM) Leroy Township 100%
3302 N Van Dyke, Imlay City, MI 48444 US
(888) 887-7139
www.smile.fm
411@smile.fm
License: Belding, Ionia County, MI held by Smile FM.
Group Owner: Superior Communications
Arbitron Metro Market: Belding, MI *Format:* Christian
Edward Czelada, President
Jenn Czelada, General Manager
Dale Mazzoline, Feature Production
Ed Czelada, Administration, Programming & Engineering
Clayton Hewitt, Administration and Engineering
Aaron Burrell, Administration

Benton Harbor

WSJM-FM

06-15-1998; 94.9 mhz FM *Hrs Open:* 24; 2.2 kw; 381 ft.; N42 4 19 W86 22 14
Mailing Address: P O Box 107, St. Joseph, MI 49085 US
Second Address: 580 E. Napier Ave., Benton Harbor, MI 49022
(269) 925-1111, *Fax:* (269) 925-1011
www.wsjm.com
news@wsjm.com
License: Benton Harbor, Berrien County, MI held by WSJM Inc.
Group Owner: The Mid-West Family Broadcast Group
Regional Reps: Michigan Spot Sales
Arbitron Metro Market: St. Joseph,MI *Format:* News, News/Talk, 86
Gayle Olson, President
Joe Daguanno, Operations Dir
Dave Doetsch, General Manager

Bob Bucholtz, General Sales Mgr
Sue Patzen, Promotions Manager
Jim Gifford, Operations Director

WHFB-FM
10-10-1947; 99.9 mhz FM; 50 kw; 407 ft.; N41 57 42 W86 21 2
2100 Fairplain Avenue, Benton Harbor, MI 49022 US
(269) 925-9300, *Fax:* (269) 925-0065
www.catcountry999.com
info@catcountry999.com
License: Benton Harbor, Berrien County, MI held by WHFB Broadcast Associates L.P.
Format: Country *Target Audience:* 25-54.
Mike Sullivan, General Sales Mgr
Jim Roberts, Programming Director

***WAYO**
89.9 mhz FM; 0.25 kw; 335 ft.; N42 4 19 W86 22 14
1159 E Beltline Ave Ne, Grand Rapids, MI 49505 US
(888) 525-8830, *Fax:* (616) 942-7078
www.way.fm
License: Benton Harbor, Berrien County, MI held by Cornerstone University.
Arbitron Metro Market: Benton Harbor, MI *Format:* Christian *Target Audience:* Teens, young adults.
Rich Anderson, General Manager

Benton Harbor-St. Jo

WHFB
09-22-1947; 1060 khz AM; 2.5 kw-C, ND1; 5 kw-D, ND1; ND1; 0.0013; N42 4 44 W86 28 1; N42 4 44 W86 28 0
2100 Fairplain Avenue, Benton Harbor, MI 49022 US
(269) 925-9300, *Fax:* (269) 925-0065
www.whfbam.com
whfbam@whfbam.com
License: Benton Harbor-St. Jo, MI held by WHFB Broadcast Associates L.P.
Regional Network: Mich. Farm
Format: News, News/Talk, 86 *No. News Employees:* 1 *Target Audience:* General.
Bill Stanley, General Manager
Jill Ferraro, General Sales Mgr

Berrien Springs

***WAUS**
01-01-1971; 90.7 mhz FM *Hrs Open:* 24; 50 kw; 492 ft.; N41 57 42 W86 21 2
Waus, Andrews University, Berrien Springs, MI 49104 US
(269) 471-3400, *Fax:* (269) 471-3804
www.waus.org
waus@andrews.edu
License: Berrien Springs, Berrien County, MI held by Andrews Broadcasting Corp.
Nat'l Network: PRI
Arbitron Metro Market: Tyler-Longview, TX *Format:* Talk *Special Programming:* Relg 10 hrs wkly *Hrs. of News Programming:* News progmg 3 hrs wkly *Target Audience:* 35 plus; listeners with interest in classicalmusic
Niels-Erik Andreasen, Chairman
Sharon Dudgeon, General Manager
Bill Brent, Programming Director

Beulah

WOUF
01-01-1998; 99.3 mhz FM; 50 kw horiz; 430 ft.; N44 36 38 W86 9 38
1532 Forrester Road, Frankfort, MI 49635 US
(231) 947-3220, *Fax:* (231) 947-7201
www.wouffm.com
License: Beulah, Benzie County, MI held by Roy E. Henderson.
Group Owner: Fort Bend Broadcasting Co.; acq 9-27-2000; $590,000 with WCUZ(FM) Bear Lake)
Arbitron Metro Market: Traverse City,MI *Format:* Country *Target Audience:* 18-54; male
Roy Henderson, General Manager

Big Rapids

WBRN
01-06-1953; 1460 khz AM *Hrs Open:* 24
17964 River's Edge Dr., Big Rapids, MI 49307 US
(231) 796-7000, *Fax:* (231) 796-7951
www.wbrn.com
news@bigrapidsradionetwork.com
License: Big Rapids, MI held by Mentor Partners Inc.
Group Owner: Mentor Partners Inc.; (acq 6-21-2005; $850,000 with co-located FM).
Nat'l Network: ESPN Radio *Regional Network:* Minn. News Net.
Nat'l Reps: Michigan Spot Sales
Arbitron Metro Market: Big Rapids, MI *Format:* News, News/Talk, 84, Talk *Hrs. of News Programming:* news progmg 12 hrs wkly *No. News Employees:* 1 *Target Audience:* 35 plus; adults *Adv. Rates:* 8.35; 8.35;8.35; 8.35
Jeffrey Scarpelli, President
Brian Goodenow, Operations Dir
Jeff Scarpelli, General Manager
Brian Goodenow, Programming Director
Steve Gove, News Director
Mark Wittkoski, Chief Engineer

WWBR
09-01-1964; 100.9 mhz FM *Hrs Open:* 24; 6 kw; 318 ft.; N43 39 49 W85 28 54
17964 River's Edge Dr., Big Rapids, MI 49307 US
(231) 796-7000, *Fax:* (231) 796-7951
www.wwbr.com
news@bigrapidsradionetwork.com
License: Big Rapids, Mecosta County, MI
Group Owner: Mentor Partners Inc.
Regional Network: Mich. Radio *Wire Services:* AP
Arbitron Metro Market: Big Rapids, MI *Format:* Country *Hrs. of News Programming:* news progmg 10 hrs wkly *No. News Employees:* 1 *Target Audience:* 25-54. *Adv. Rates:* 24;20;22;18
Jeff Scarpelli, President
Marc Pittman, Operations Dir
Jeff Scarpelli, General Manager
Brian Goodenow, Programming Director
Steve Gove, News Director
Mark Wittkoski, Chief Engineer

WODJ
10-21-1959; 1590 khz AM *Hrs Open:* 24
US
(231) 830-0176, *Fax:* (231) 830-0194
wodj-am.fimc.net
License: Big Rapids, MI
Group Owner: Cumulus Media Inc.; (acq 9-28-2005; grpsl).
Arbitron Metro Market: Muskegon, MI *Format:* Talk
Jeff Morton, General Manager

WYBR
06-30-1982; 102.3 mhz FM *Hrs Open:* 24; 10.5 kw; 436 ft.; N43 41 1 W85 34 56
40 Pearl NW, Grand Rapids, MI 49503 US
(231) 796-7000, *Fax:* (231) 796-7951
www.wybr.com
License: Big Rapids, Mecosta County, MI held by Mentor Partners Inc.
Group Owner: Mentor Partners Inc.; (acq 8-10-98).
Arbitron Metro Market: Big Rapids, MI *Format:* Adult Contemp *Special Programming:* Relg one hr wkly *Hrs. of News Programming:* news progmg 8 hrs wkly *No. News Employees:* 2 *Target Audience:* 25-49. *Adv.Rates:* 22; 19; 20; 16
Jeffrey Scarpelli, General Manager
Diane Scarpelli, General Sales Mgr
Brian Goodenow, Programming Director
Steve Gove, News Director
Mark Wittkoski, Chief Engineer

Birmingham

WCSX
03-14-1987; 94.7 mhz FM *Hrs Open:* 24; 13.5 kw; 951 ft.; N42 27 13 W83 9 50
P.O. Box 1059, East Brunswick, NJ 08816 US
(248) 398-9470, *Fax:* (248) 541-9279
www.wcsx.com
promotions@wcsx.com
License: Birmingham, Oakland County, MI held by Greater Michigan Radio Inc.
Group Owner: Greater Media Inc.; (acq 7-3-73)
Nat'l Reps: McGavren Guild
Arbitron Metro Market: Detroit,MI *Format:* Classic Rock *Target Audience:* 25-54; males
Tom Bender, Operations Dir

Bloomfield Hills

***WBFH**
10-01-1976; 88.1 mhz FM *Hrs Open:* 24; 0.36 kw; 180 ft.; N42 34 42 W83 17 10
4175 Andover Road, Bloomfield Hills, MI 48302 US
(248)-341-9234, *Fax:* (248) 341-5679
www.wbfh.fm
thebiff@Radio.fm
License: Bloomfield Hills, Oakland County, MI held by Board of Education of Bloomfield Hills School District.
Arbitron Metro Market: Bloomfield Hills, MI *Format:* Sports, Talk *Special Programming:* Prep sports 6 hrs wkly *Target Audience:* 12-34.
Justin Lopas, Operations Dir
Pete Bowers, General Manager
Paul Stewart, Station Manager
Paul Stewart, Programming Director
Grace McIlhon & Sean Shepard, Promotions Manager
Eric Bloom, News Director
Randy Carr, Engineering Dir
Danny Harwood, Production Director
Jeremy Fishman, Music Director
Bryan Furlong, Video Department Director
Michael Blumenthal, Sports Director
Joshua Lumsden, Public Affairs Director

Bluffton

WGZR
06-22-1988; 106.9 mhz FM *Hrs Open:* 24; 100 kw; Ant 800 ft; N32 13 36 W80 50 53
401 Mall Blvd., Suite 101 D, Savannah, GA
(912) 351-9830, *Fax:* (912) 352-4821
luckydogcountry1069.com
mhalverson@adventureradio.fm
License: Bluffton, Beaufort County, SC held by Monterey Licenses LLC.
Group Owner: Triad Broadcasting Co. L.L.C.; (acq 8-8-2000; grpsl)
Nat'l Reps: Christal
Population Served: 500,000 *Arbitron Metro Market:* Savannah, GA *No. News Employees:* 1 *Target Audience:* 18-54 *Adv. Rates:* 60; 60; 60; 60
Mark Halverson, General Manager

Boyne City

WBCM
04-10-1978; 93.5 mhz FM *Hrs Open:* 24; 14 kw; 928 ft.; N45 19 27 W84 52 44 *Rebroadcasts:* Simulcast of WTCM-FM Traverse City
314 East Front Street, Traverse City, MI 49684 US
(505) 758-4491, *Fax:* (505) 758-4452
www.radiotaos.com
production@kxmt.com
License: Boyne City, Charlevoix County, MI held by Biederman Investments Inc.
Group Owner: Midwestern Broadcasting Co.; (acq 9-6-90; $250,000;
Nat'l Reps: Katz Radio
Format: Adult Contemp
Jeff Singer, Operations Dir
Pattee Brown, General Sales Mgr
Jennifer Trujillo, News Director

Bridgeport

WNEM
11-26-1956; 1250 khz AM *Hrs Open:* 24; 5 kw-D, 1.1 kw-N, DA-2; N43 20 31 W83 53 57
Mailing Address: Box 531, Saginaw, MI 48734
Second Address: 107 N. Franklin St., Saginaw, MI 48607
(989) 755-8191, *Fax:* (989) 758-2110
www.wnem.com
wnem@wnem.com
License: Bridgeport, Saginaw County, MI held by Meredith Corp.
Group Owner: Meredith Broadcasting Group, Meredith Corp.; (acq 5-18-2004; $1.1 million).
Arbitron Metro Market: Saginaw-Bay City-Midland, MI
Al Blinke, General Manager
Jeff Guilbert, General Sales Mgr
Karen Frey, Programming Director
Ian Rubin, News Director
Mike Miller, Chief Engineer

Bridgman

WYTZ
03-01-1993; 97.5 mhz FM *Hrs Open:* 24; 3.8 kw; 413 ft.; N41 59 19 W86 31 46
P O Box 107, St. Joseph, MI 49085 US
(269) 925-1111, *Fax:* (269) 925-1011
robb@975country.com
License: Bridgman, Berrien County, MI held by WSJM Inc.
Group Owner: The Mid-West Family Broadcast Group; (acq 1996; grpsl)
Nat'l Reps: Christal
Arbitron Metro Market: Bridgman, MI *Format:* Country *No. News Employees:* 5 *Target Audience:* 25-54.
Joe Daguanno, Operations Dir
Gayle Olson, General Manager
Bob Bucholtz, General Sales Mgr
Robb Rose, Programming Director
Sue Patzer, Promotions Manager
Jim Gifford, Operations Manager

Bronson

*WCVM
01-01-1998; 94.7 mhz FM *Hrs Open:* 24; 4 kw; 404 ft.; N41 44 32 W85 14 34
3000 W. Macarthur Blvd., Santa Ana, CA 92704 US
(260) 745-0576, *Fax:* (260) 745-2001
www.wbcl.org/
wqko@wqko.com,info@calvaryradionetwork.com
License: Bronson, Branch County, MI held by CSN International.
Group Owner: CSN International; acq 12-1-98; $80,000)
Arbitron Metro Market: Bronson, MI *Format:* Christian *Target Audience:* Teen-young adult.
Jim Motshagen, General Manager
Jill Johnston, Promotions Manager

Brooklyn

WKHM-FM
01-01-1994; 105.3 mhz FM *Hrs Open:* 24; 2.2 kw; 377 ft.; N42 9 14 W84 24 7
915 Riverside Avenue, Adrian, MI 49221 US
(517) 787-9546, *Fax:* (517) 787-7517
www.k1053.com
mdaly@wkhm.com
License: Brooklyn, Jackson County, MI held by Jackson Radio Works Inc.
Group Owner: Jackson Radio Works Inc.; (acq 12-8-97; grpsl).
Regional Reps: Michigan Spot Sls
Format: Adult Contemp *No. News Employees:* 2 *Target Audience:* 18-49.
Bruce Goldsen, President
Sue Goldsen, Operations Dir
Jamie McKibbin, Station Manager
Michael Bradford, Chief Engineer

Buchanan

WSMK
01-01-1991; 99.1 mhz FM *Hrs Open:* 24; 3 kw; 328 ft.; N41 52 51 W86 18 13
7606 Harold Avenue, Gary, IN 46403 US
(269) 683-4343, *Fax:* (269) 683-7759
www.wsmkradio.com
sales@wsmkradio.com
License: Buchanan, Berrien County, MI held by Marion R. Williams.
Group Owner: Marion R. Williams Stns
Arbitron Metro Market: South Bend, IN *Format:* Adult Contemp *Target Audience:* 25 - 44; females
Marion Williams, General Manager

Burton

*WTAC
01-01-2002; 89.7 mhz FM; 15 kw vert; 361 ft.; N42 44 56 W83 42 59 *Rebroadcasts:* simulcasts WLGH (FM) Leroy Township 100%
601 Savidge St, Reed City, MI 49677 US
(888) 887-7139, *Fax:* (877) 850-0881
www.smile.fm
411@smile.fm
License: Burton, Genesee County, MI held by Superior Communications.
Group Owner: Superior Communications
Arbitron Metro Market: Burton, MI *Format:* Christian
Edward Czelada, President
Dale Mazzoline, Feature Production
Ed Czelada, Administration, Programming & Engineering
Clayton Hewitt, Administration and Engineering
Aaron Burrell, Administration

Cadillac

WATT
09-01-1945; 1240 khz AM *Hrs Open:* 24; 1 kw-U; N44 13 27 W85 24 06
Mailing Address: Box 520, Cadillac, MI 49770
Second Address: 7825 S. Mackinaw Tr., Cadillac, MI 49601
(231) 775-1263, *Fax:* (231) 779-2844
www.watt1240.com
License: Cadillac, Wexford County, MI held by MacDonald Garber Broadcasting Inc.
Group Owner: MacDonald Garber Broadcasting Co.; (acq 11-17-98; grpsl)
Nat'l Network: Fox News Radio; Radio America *Nat'l Reps:* Eastman *Regional Reps:* Eastman
Population Served: 11,500*Target Audience:* General. *Adv. Rates:* 18; 18; 18; 18
Trish Garber, President
Kerry Davis, General Manager
Bill Michaels, Programming Director
Rich Spicer, News Director
Brian Brachel, Engineering Dir

WCKC
09-15-1985; 107.1 mhz FM; 2.75 kw; 482 ft.; N44 10 16 W85 20 13 *Rebroadcasts:* WGFM-FM Cheboygan 100%
232 Front Street, No. 2, Traverse City, MI 49684 US
(231) 627-2341, *Fax:* (231) 627-7000
www.classicrockthebear.com
info@classicrockthebear.com
License: Cadillac, Wexford County, MI held by Northern Star Broadcasting L.L.C.
Group Owner: Northern Star Broadcasting L.L.C.; (acq 9-11-98; grpsl)
Arbitron Metro Market: Northern Michigan and Upper Peninsula *Format:* Classic Rock *Target Audience:* 25-54.
Palmer Pyle, President
April Hurley-Rose, Operations Dir

WLJW
03-15-2004; 1370 khz AM *Hrs Open:* 24; 5 kw-D, DA2; 1 kw-N, DA2; N44 13 54 W85 24 45 *Rebroadcasts:* Simulcast with WLJN(AM) Elmwood Township
314 E Front Street, Traverse City, MI 49684 US
(231) 946-1400, *Fax:* (231) 946-3959
www.wljn.com
info@wljn.com
License: Cadillac, MI held by Good News Media Inc.
Group Owner: Good News Media Inc.; acq 3-5-2004; $85,001).
Nat'l Network: Moody; Salem Radio Network *Nat'l Reps:* Katz Radio *Wire Services:* AP
Format: Christian, Talk, 74 *Target Audience:* General.
D.C. Cavender, Operations Dir
Brian Harcey, General Manager
Pete Lathrop, Programming Director
Don Parker, Chief Engineer
Jane Cavender, Disc Jockey
Carla Wanlass, Business Administrator
Lisa Lempke, Administrator to theExecutive Director
Dave Stockfish, Disc Jockey

WJZQ
10-15-1961; 92.9 mhz FM *Hrs Open:* 24; 100 kw; 912 ft.; N44 35 41 W85 11 53
314 E Front Street, Traverse City, MI 49684 US
(231) 947-7675, *Fax:* (231) 929-3988
www.929thebreeze.com
wjzq@929thebreeze.com
License: Cadillac, Wexford County, MI held by WKJF Radio Inc.
Group Owner: Midwestern Broadcasting Co.; (acq 10-29-2001; with co-located AM).
Nat'l Reps: Katz Radio
Arbitron Metro Market: Traverse City-Petoskey, MI *Format:* Jazz, Smooth Jazz *Hrs. of News Programming:* news progmg 2 hrs wkly *No. News Employees:* 1 *Target Audience:* 35-64; affluent adults *Adv. Rates:* 20; 20; 20; 20
John Dew, General Manager
Joel Franck, News Director
Eric Send, Chief Engineer
Barbara Kanarek, Traffic Manager

WLXV
07-07-1974; 96.7 mhz FM; 7.2 kw; 604 ft.; N44 22 51 W85 33 24
Mailing Address: P.O. Box 286, Petosky, MI 49770 US
Second Address: 7825 S. Mackinaw Tr., Cadillac, MI 49601
(231) 775-1263, *Fax:* (231) 779-2844
www.mix96cadillac.com
rich@mix96cadillac.com
License: Cadillac, Wexford County, MI
Group Owner: MacDonald Garber Broadcasting Co.
Arbitron Metro Market: Traverse City, MI *Format:* Adult Contemp *Hrs. of News Programming:* news progmg one hr wkly *No. News Employees:* 1 *Adv. Rates:* 28; 28; 28; 28
Rich Spicer, Programming Director

*WOLW
05-26-1988; 91.1 mhz FM; 50 kw horiz, 28 kw vert; 699 ft.; N44 16 33 W85 42 49 *Rebroadcasts:* Rebroadcasts WPHN(FM) Gaylord 100%
Mailing Address: P.O. Box 695, Gaylord, MI 49735 US
Second Address: 1511 M-32 E., Gaylord, MI 49735
(989) 732-6274, *Fax:* (989) 732-8171
www.ncradio.org
ncr@ncradio.org
License: Cadillac, Wexford County, MI held by Northern Christian Radio Inc.
Group Owner: Northern Christian Radio Inc.
Nat'l Network: Moody
TV Affiliate: Relg *Special Programming:* News progmg 10 hrs wkly *No. News Employees:* 35-54. *Target Audience:* Joe Sereno
CEO, CEO/COO

*WGCP
91.9 mhz FM; 2.1 kw; 144 ft.; N44 17 8 W85 29 20
US
(231) 468-2087
License: Cadillac, Wexford County, MI held by West Central Michigan Media Ministries.
Arbitron Metro Market: Cadillac, MI *Format:* Religious
David Bolduc, President

Caro

WIDL
10-16-1974; 92.1 mhz FM; 6 kw; 318 ft.; N43 28 51 W83 20 31
125 Eagles Nest Drive, Seneca, SC 29678 US
(989) 672-1360, *Fax:* (989) 673-0256
www.tuscolatoday.com
studio@mix921.com
License: Caro, Tuscola County, MI
Group Owner: Edwards Communications L.C.
Format: Adult Contemp
Tim Murphy, General Manager
Stacey Linn, Programming Director

WKYO
05-19-1962; 1360 khz AM; 1 kw-D, DA2; 1 kw-N, DA2; N43 27 32 W83 23 39
125 Eagles Nest Drive, Seneca, SC 29678 US
(989) 672-1360, *Fax:* (989) 673-0256
www.tuscolatoday.com
studio@mix921.com
License: Caro, MI held by Edwards Communications L.C.
Group Owner: Edwards Communications L.C.; (acq 2-25-98; with co-located FM).
Format: Oldies
Tim Murphy, General Manager
Stacey Linn, Programming Director

Carrollton

WSGW-FM
03-11-1991; 100.5 mhz FM *Hrs Open:* 24; 6 kw; 328 ft.; N43 33 42 W83 58 52
3420 Pine Tree Road, Lansing, MI 48911 US
(989) 752-3456, *Fax:* (989) 754-5046
www.fmtalk1005.com
info@fmtalk1005.com
License: Carrollton, Saginaw County, MI held by NM Licensing LLC.
Group Owner: NextMedia Group Inc.; (acq 12-30-2002; grpsl)
Wire Services: Metro Weather Service Inc.
Arbitron Metro Market: Saginaw, MI *Format:* Talk *No. News Employees:* 1 *Target Audience:* 18-49; women & teens
David Mauer, Programming Director
Ben Dietzel, Advertising
Shannone Dunlap, VP

Cassopolis

WGTO
08-01-1988; 910 khz AM *Hrs Open:* 24; 1 kw-D, DA2; 0.035 kw-N, DA2; N41 57 14 W86 0 59
Mailing Address: 6036 S. Bishop St, Chicago, IL 60636 US
Second Address: 58176 O'Keefe Rd, Cassopolis, MI 49031
(269) 782-9010, *Fax:* (269) 782-5107
www.wgtoradio.com
License: Cassopolis, MI held by Larry Langford Jr.
Arbitron Metro Market: South Bend, IN *Format:* Oldies *Special Programming:* Blues 4 hrs, gospel 10 hrs wkly *Target Audience:* 25-49; middle class Black adults
Larry Langford, President
Chris Cole, Station Manager

Charlevoix

WKHQ-FM
05-16-1980; 105.9 mhz FM *Hrs Open:* 24; 100 kw; 892 ft.; N45 10 49 W85 5 50
Mailing Address: P.O. Box 286, Petosky, MI 49770 US
Second Address: 2095 U.S. 131 S., Petoskey, MI 49770
(231) 347-8713, *Fax:* (231) 347-8782
www.106khq.com
info@106khq.com
License: Charlevoix, Charlevoix County, MI held by MacDonald Garber Broadcasting Co.
Group Owner: MacDonald Garber Broadcasting Co.; acq 11-17-98; grpsl)
Nat'l Network: ABC *Nat'l Reps:* McGavren Guild
Arbitron Metro Market: Traverse City-Petoskey, MI *Format:* Contemporary Hits/Top 40 *No. News Employees:* 1 *Target Audience:* 18-34.
Trish MacDonald-Garder, General Manager
Tom Clemens, General Sales Mgr

Luke Spencer, Programming Director
Bob Sheen, News Director
Bob White, Chief Engineer

WMKT
07-20-1974; 1270 khz AM *Hrs Open:* 24
Mailing Address: P.O. Box 286, Petosky, MI 49770 US
Second Address: 2095 U.S. 131 S., Petoskey, MI 49770
(866) 371-1270
www.wmktthetalkstation.com
bill.michaels@106khq.com
License: Charlevoix, MI held by MacDonald Garber Broadcasting Co.
Group Owner: MacDonald Garber Broadcasting Co.
Arbitron Metro Market: Traverse City, MI *Format:* News, News/Talk, 86 *Target Audience:* 35 plus; listeners with spendable income
Bill Michaels, Operations Dir
Eric Michaels, Programming Director

WCZW
01-31-2003; 107.9 mhz FM *Hrs Open:* 24; 5 kw; Ant 164 ft; N45 20 00 W85 14 47 *Rebroadcasts:* Rebroadcasts WCCW-FM Traverse City
300 E. Front St., Suite 450, Traverse City, MI 49684
(231) 946-6211, *Fax:* (231) 946-1914
www.wccwi.com
License: Charlevoix, Charlevoix County, MI held by WCCW Radio Inc.
Group Owner: Midwestern Broadcasting Co.
Nat'l Network: ABC *Nat'l Reps:* Katz Radio
Target Audience: 35 plus; baby boomers *Adv. Rates:* 12; 12; 12; 12
Brian Hale, Operations Dir
Hal Payne, General Manager
Dave Gauthier, Programming Director
Wendy Sobeck, News Director
Eric Send, Chief Engineer

***WTCK**
01-01-2006; 90.9 mhz FM *Hrs Open:* all; 5.5 kw; 996 ft.; N45 30 5.2 W85 1 48.7
US
(231) 238-0811, *Fax:* (231) 238-0803
www.baragabroadcasting.com
Christine@baragamail.com
License: Charlevoix, Charlevoix County, MI held by Baraga Broadcasting Inc.
Arbitron Metro Market: Charlevoix, MI *Format:* Christian
Harry Speckman, Operations Dir
Christine Schicker, Station Manager
Rocky Stammer, IT
Brian Brachel, Chief Engineer
Tom McMahon, Marketing
Bob Frasier, Controller
Irene Morrison, Fundraising & Data-Base
Suzanne Herpel,Secretary

Charlotte

WJXQ
05-30-1976; 106.1 mhz FM *Hrs Open:* 24; 49 kw; 489 ft; N42 23 28 W84 37 22
2495 N. Cedar, Suite 106, Holt, MI 48823
(517) 699-0111, *Fax:* (517) 699-1880
www.q106fm.com
License: Charlotte, Jackson County, MI held by Midwest Communications Inc.
Group Owner: Rubber City Radio Group Inc.; (acq 7-1-2010; grpsl).
Nat'l Network: Jones Radio Networks *Nat'l Reps:* Katz Radio
Wire Services: AP
Population Served: 500,000 *Arbitron Metro Market:* Lansing-East Lansing, MI *Hrs. of News Programming:* news progmg one hr wkly *No. News Employees:* 1 *Target Audience:* 25-44; baby boomers with an inclination forrock and roll
Paul Cashin, Operations Dir
Dave Johnson, General Manager
Scott Truman, General Sales Mgr
Sheri Vegas, Programming Director

Cheboygan

WCBY
10-28-1954; 1240 khz AM; 1 kw-U, ND1; N45 39 38 W84 29 26
232 Front Street, No. 2, Traverse City, MI 49684 US
(231) 627-2341, *Fax:* (231) 627-7000
www.wcbyradio.com/
mary@nsbroadcasting.com
License: Cheboygan, MI held by Northern Star Broadcasting L.L.C.
Group Owner: Northern Star Broadcasting L.L.C.; (acq 12-12-2005; grpsl)
Nat'l Reps: Michigan Spot Sales
Arbitron Metro Market: Cheboygan, MI *Format:* Big Band, Oldies
Target Audience: 35-64.
Palmer Pyle, President
April Hurley-Rose, Operations Dir
Mark Belanger, General Sales Mgr

WGFM
08-15-1968; 105.1 mhz FM; 43 kw; 968 ft.; N45 10 12 W84 45 4
232 Front Street, No. 2, Traverse City, MI 49684 US
(231) 627-2341, *Fax:* (231) 627-7000
www.classicrockthebear.com
info@classicrockthebear.com
License: Cheboygan, Cheboygan County, MI
Group Owner: Northern Star Broadcasting L.L.C.
Arbitron Metro Market: Traverse City-Petoskey, MI *Format:* Classic Rock
Harold Miller Jr., President
Russ Fender, Operations Dir
Theresa Miller, General Manager

Chocolay Township

WUPZ
01-01-2008; 94.9 mhz FM; 100 kw; 512 ft.; N46 30 51.7 W87 28 40.2
US
(906) 255-0656, *Fax:* (906) 255-0607
www.949thebay.com
949thebay@radioeagle.com
License: Chocolay Township, Iron County, MI held by Radioactive LLC.
Group Owner: Radioactive LLC
Arbitron Metro Market: Chocolay Township, MI *Format:* Contemporary Hits/Top 40
Benjamin Homel, President

Clare

WCFX
06-28-1967; 95.3 mhz FM *Hrs Open:* 24; 6 kw; 328 ft.; N43 44 41 W84 48 9
5847 Venture Way, Mt. Pleasant, MI 48858 US
(989) 772-4173, *Fax:* (989) 773-1236
www.wcfx.com
kent@wcfx.com
License: Clare, Clare County, MI held by Grenax Broadcasting LLC
Group Owner: Grenax Broadcasting LLC; (acq 2-5-2004).
Arbitron Metro Market: Mount Pleasant,MI *Format:* Christian
Target Audience: 18-49. *Adv. Rates:* 28; 30; 28; 20
Greg Dinetz, President
Kent Bergstrom, Operations Dir
Jim Spangenberg, General Manager
Rob Ryan, Promotions Manager

Clyde Township

***WXPZ**
90.1 mhz FM; 0.02 kw horiz, 1.5 kw vert; 243 ft.; N42 33 57 W86 12 26
US
(616) 726-0193
License: Clyde Township, Allegan County, MI held by Tim Woodson Ministries Inc.
Arbitron Metro Market: Scottsdale, AZ
Timothy Woodson, Chairman

Coldwater

WNWN-FM
11-11-1950; 98.5 mhz FM; 50 kw; 469 ft.; N42 3 28 W84 59 51
P O Box 2048, Wausau, WI 54402 US
(269) 968-1991, *Fax:* (269) 968-1881
www.wincountry.com
License: Coldwater, Branch County, MI held by Midwest Communications Inc.
Group Owner: Midwest Communications Inc.; acq 6-1-95; grpsl)
Nat'l Reps: Christal *Wire Services:* Accu-Weather
Arbitron Metro Market: Kalamazoo, MI *TV Affiliate:* Country
Special Programming: news progmg 5 hrs wkly *Hrs. of News Programming:* 3 *No. News Employees:* 25-54.

WTVB
08-07-1949; 1590 khz AM *Hrs Open:* 24; 5 kw-D, DAN; 1 kw-N, DAN; N41 54 34 W85 0 21
P O Box 2048, Wausau, WI 54402 US
(517) 279-1590, *Fax:* (517) 279-4695
wtvbam.com
wtvb@wtvbam.com
License: Coldwater, MI held by Midwest Communications Inc.
Group Owner: Midwest Communications Inc.; acq 6-1-95; grpsl)
Nat'l Reps: Christal *Wire Services:* NOAA Weather
Arbitron Metro Market: Coldwater, MI *Format:* Oldies *Special Programming:* Farm 6 hrs wkly *Hrs. of News Programming:* news progmg 10 hrs wkly *No. News Employees:* 2
D.E. Wright, President
Peter Tanz, General Manager
Ken Delaney, Station Manager

***WYBA**
07-15-2008; 90.1 mhz FM; 250 w vert; Ant 62 ft; N41 56 24 W85 02 47
Mailing Address: Box 220, Coldwater, MI
Second Address: 385 Airport Dr., Coldwater, MI 49036
(517) 278-7339, *Fax:* (517) 278-6973
www.bbnradio.org
bbn@bbnradio.org
License: Coldwater, Branch County, MI held by Michiana Christian Broadcasters Inc.
Nat'l Network: Bible Bcstg Net

Wayne Reese, President

Coleman

***WPRJ**
12-07-1992; 101.7 mhz FM *Hrs Open:* 24; 4.6 kw; 374 ft.; N43 48 39 W84 27 50
5444 N. Coleman Rd., P,O, Box 236, Coleman, MI 48618 US
(989) 465-9775, *Fax:* (989) 465-1060
www.wprj.org
1017thefuse@1017thefuse.com
License: Coleman, Midland County, MI held by Come Together Ministries Inc.
Arbitron Metro Market: Saginaw-Bay City-Midland, MI *Format:* Adult Contemp, Christian *Target Audience:* 18 plus; youth, young singles & married
Gary Bugh, President
Connie Wieber, Station Manager

Coopersville

WHTS
09-14-1983; 105.3 mhz FM; 20 kw; 794 ft.; N43 18 35 W85 54 45
1883 Eloise Drive, Muskegon, MI 49444 US
(616) 774-8461, *Fax:* (616) 774-2491
1053hotfm.com
beau.derek@cumulus.com
License: Coopersville, Ottawa County, MI
Group Owner: Cumulus Media Inc.; (acq 11-29-2005; $4.1 million)
Arbitron Metro Market: Grand Rapids, MI *Format:* Contemporary Hits/Top 40 *Target Audience:* 25-54; adult women
Brent Alberts, Operations Dir
Scott Meier, General Manager
Kate Conley, General Sales Mgr

Crystal Falls

WOBE
06-01-2000; 100.7 mhz FM; 100 kw; 653 ft.; N45 49 16 W88 2 34
2450 Crooks Ave., Kaukauna, WI 54130 US
(906) 774-5731, *Fax:* (906) 774-4542
www.classichitsb100fm.com
peterson.trisha@gmail.com
License: Crystal Falls, Iron County, MI held by Results Broadcasting of Iron Mountain Inc.
Group Owner: Results Broadcasting; (acq 11-1-2001; $800,000).
Nat'l Network: ABC
TV Affiliate: Classic hits *Hrs. of News Programming:* 1 *No. News Employees:* 25-65.
General Manager, General Manager

Dearborn

***WHFR**
12-20-1985; 89.3 mhz FM *Hrs Open:* 24; 270 w; 98 ft; N42 19 26 W83 14 09
Henry Ford Community College, 5101 Evergreen Rd., Dearborn, MI 48128
(313) 845-9676,(313) 845-9842, *Fax:* (313) 317-4034
www.whfr.fm
whfr@hfcc.edu
License: Dearborn, Wayne County, MI held by Henry Ford Community College.
Nat'l Network: PRI
Population Served: 800,000 *Arbitron Metro Market:* Detroit
Special Programming: Jazz 10 hrs, world mus 2 hrs, big band 6 hrs, blues 12 hrs wkly *Hrs. of News Programming:* News progmg one hr wkly *Target Audience:* General.

Lara Hrycaj, Operations Dir
Susan McGraw, General Manager

WNIC
12-01-1946; 100.3 mhz FM *Hrs Open:* 24; 32 kw; 600 ft.; N42 23 22 W83 8 53
433 E. Las Colinas Blvd, #1130, Irving, TX 75039 US
(248) 324-5800, *Fax:* (248) 848-0179
www.fresh100.com
License: Dearborn, Wayne County, MI held by AMFM Radio Licenses L.L.C.
Group Owner: Clear Channel Communications Inc.; (acq 8-30-00; grpsl).
Arbitron Metro Market: Detroit, MI *Format:* Adult Contemp *Hrs. of News Programming:* news progmg 2 hrs wkly *No. News Employees:* 1 *Target Audience:* 25-54; female
Liz Walterhouse, General Sales Mgr
Don Gosselin, Programming Director
Rebecca Falk, Promotions Manager

WDTW
12-29-1946; 1310 khz AM *Hrs Open:* 24; 5 kw-D, DA2; 5 kw-N, DA2; N42 15 50 W83 15 14
433 E. Las Colinas Blvd, #1130, Irving, TX 75039 US
(248) 324-5800, *Fax:* (248) 848-0396
www.1310wdtw.com
elliotlerner@clearchannel.com
License: Dearborn, MI held by AMFM Radio Licenses L.L.C.
Group Owner: Clear Channel Communications Inc.; (acq 8-30-2000; grpsl).
Nat'l Network: Westwood One
Arbitron Metro Market: Detroit *Format:* Alternative, Talk *Hrs. of News Programming:* news progmg 27 hrs wkly *No. News Employees:* 4 *Target Audience:* 25-54; men 25-54
Dom Theodore, Operations Dir
Til Levesque, General Manager

Dearborn Heights

WNZK
10-12-1985; 690 khz AM; 2.5 kw-D, DA2; 2.5 kw-N, DA2; N42 5 55 W83 19 48
21700 Northwestern Hwy, Ste 1190, Tower 14, Southfield, MI 48075 US
(248) 557-3500, *Fax:* (248) 557-2950
www.birach.com
sima@birach.com
License: Dearborn Heights, MI held by Birach Broadcasting Corp.
Group Owner: Birach Broadcasting Corp.; (acq 1984).
Arbitron Metro Market: Detroit *TV Affiliate:* Ethnic *No. News Employees:* General.
President and CEO, CEO/COO

Detroit

***WDET-FM**
02-13-1949; 101.9 mhz FM *Hrs Open:* 24; 48 kw; 554 ft.; N42 21 6 W83 3 48
4600 Cass Avenue, Detroit, MI 48201 US
(313) 577-4146, *Fax:* (313) 577-1300
www.wdetfm.org
wdetfm@wdetfm.org
License: Detroit, Wayne County, MI held by Wayne State University.
Nat'l Network: NPR
Arbitron Metro Market: Detroit, MI *Format:* News *Special Programming:* Jazz 15 hrs, folk 3 hrs, bluegrass 2 hrs, gospel 2 hrs, blues 3 hrs, reggae 2 hrs wkly *Hrs. of News Programming:* news progmg 118 hrs wkly *No.News Employees:* 6 *Target Audience:* 35-64; public radio & news consumers
Yolanda Dunn, CFO
J.Mikel Ellcessor, General Manager
Tim Hygh, Station Manager
Ron Jones, Programming Director
Jerome Vaughn, News Director
Jerome Vaughn, News/Programming Director

WDFN
12-17-1939; 1130 khz AM; 50 kw-D, DA2; 10 kw-N, DA2; N42 6 39 W83 11 52
433 E. Las Colinas Blvd, #1130, Irving, TX 75039 US
(248) 324-5800, *Fax:* (248) 848-0396
www.wdfn.com
JonelleCriscuolo@clearchannel.com
License: Detroit, MI held by AMFM Radio Licenses L.L.C.
Group Owner: Clear Channel Communications Inc.; (acq 8-30-2000; grpsl).
Nat'l Network: Westwood One
Arbitron Metro Market: Detroit, MI *Format:* Sports, Talk *Target Audience:* 25-54.
Til Levesque, General Manager
Elliot Lerner, General Sales Mgr

WDRQ
07-09-1947; 93.1 mhz FM *Hrs Open:* 24; 26.5 kw; 669 ft.; N42 28 16 W83 12 3
77 West 66th Street, 16th Fl, New York, NY 10023 US
(313) 871-9300, *Fax:* (313) 872-0190
www.931dougfm.com
lori.bennett@cumulus.com
License: Detroit, Wayne County, MI
Group Owner: Cumulus Media Inc.; (acq 6-12-2007; grpsl)
Nat'l Reps: ABC Radio Sales *Wire Services:* AP
Arbitron Metro Market: Detroit, MI *Format:* Adult Contemp *Hrs. of News Programming:* 3 per day *No. News Employees:* 1 *Target Audience:* Persons 25-54 *Adv. Rates:* Contact
Steve Kosbau, President
Byron ""Ron"" Harrell, Operations Dir
Matt Spatafora, Programming Director
Kevin Hawley, Chief Engineer
Julie Law, Director of Marketing

WDMK
05-26-1960; 105.9 mhz FM; 20 kw; 725 ft.; N42 28 16 W83 12 3
5900 Princess Garden Pkwy, 8th Floor, Lanham, MD 20706 US
(313) 259-2000, *Fax:* (313) 259-7011
www.kissdetroit.com
kyoung@radio-one.com
License: Detroit, Wayne County, MI held by Radio One of Detroit LLC.
Group Owner: Radio One Inc.; (acq 11-8-2001; grpsl).
Arbitron Metro Market: Detroit, MI *Format:* Blues *Special Programming:* Sports 2 hrs, entertainment guide 2 hrs wkly
Target Audience: 25-49.
Alfred Liggins, President
Carol Lawrence-Dobrusin, General Manager
Benita Gray, Programming Director

***WRCJ-FM**
02-05-1948; 90.9 mhz FM *Hrs Open:* Midnight-noon; 42 kw horiz, 38 kw vert; 541 ft.; N42 22 25 W83 6 50
9345 Lawton, Detroit, MI 48206 US
(313)494-6400, *Fax:* (313) 494-6087
www.wrcjfm.org/
90.9@dptv.org
License: Detroit, Wayne County, MI held by Board of Education, City of Detroit.
Arbitron Metro Market: Detroit, MI *Format:* Jazz *No. News Employees:* 15 *Target Audience:* General; intergenerational-urban/suburban
Donald Walker, Operations Dir
Robert Scott, General Manager
Dave Wagner, Programming Director
Ken Sands, Promotions Manager
Steve Johnson, Chief Engineer

WGPR
01-01-1961; 107.5 mhz FM *Hrs Open:* 24; 50 kw; Ant 405 ft; N42 21 28 W83 03 55
3146 Jefferson E., Detroit, MI 48207
(313) 259-8862, *Fax:* (313) 259-6662
www.wgprdetroit.com
wgprvp@aol.com
License: Detroit, Wayne County, MI held by WGPR Inc.
Population Served: 151,148 *Arbitron Metro Market:* Detroit *TV Affiliate:* WGPR-TV affil *Target Audience:* 25-54
James Dogan, CEO
Kenneth Hollowell, Operations Dir
Carolyn James, Programming Director
Fernando Green, Operations Manager

WJLB
01-01-1926; 97.9 mhz FM; 50 kw; 489 ft.; N42 24 22 W83 6 44
Penobscot Bldg , 645 Gri, Suite 633, Detroit, MI 48226 US
(313) 965-2000, *Fax:* (313) 965-3965
www.fm98wjlb.com
brianboettcher@clearchannel.com
License: Detroit, Wayne County, MI held by AMFM Radio Licenses L.L.C.
Group Owner: Clear Channel Communications Inc.; (acq 8-30-00; grpsl)
Arbitron Metro Market: Detroit *Format:* Urban Contemporary
Target Audience: 18-49; Black adults
Til Levesque, General Manager
David Crumb, General Sales Mgr
K. J. Holiday, Programming Director
Charles Pugh, News Director
Thomas Christie, Chief Engineer
Brian Boettcher, General Sales Manager
Cheron Mans, Music Director

WJR
05-04-1922; 760 khz AM; 50 kw-U, ND1; N42 10 5 W83 12 54
77 West 66th St. 16th Fl, New York, NY 10023 US
(313) 875-4440, *Fax:* (313) 875-9022
www.wjr.net
info@wjr.net
License: Detroit, MI
Group Owner: Cumulus Media Inc.; (acq 6-12-2007; grpsl)
Nat'l Reps: ABC Radio Sales
Arbitron Metro Market: Detroit *Format:* News, News/Talk, 86
Target Audience: 12 plus.
Mike Fezzey, President
Tom O'Brien, General Sales Mgr
Dick Haefner, News Director

WKQI
02-12-1949; 95.5 mhz FM *Hrs Open:* 24; 100 kw; 427 ft.; N42 28 23 W83 11 59
15401 West Ten Mile Road, Oak Park, MI 48326 US
(248) 324-5800, *Fax:* (248) 848-0272
www.channel955.com
programing@channel955.com
License: Detroit, Wayne County, MI held by AMFM Radio Licenses L.L.C.
Group Owner: Clear Channel Communications Inc.; (acq 8-30-00; grpsl).
Nat'l Network: Premiere Radio Networks
Arbitron Metro Market: Detroit *Format:* Contemporary Hits/Top 40
Target Audience: 18-49; active, upscale women
Til Levesque, General Manager
Dom Theodore, Programming Director
Rebecca Falk, Promotions Manager
Beau Daniels, Music Director

WXYT-FM
05-09-1941; 97.1 mhz FM; 15 kw; 892 ft.; N42 28 58 W83 12 19
Mailing Address: 600 New Hampshire Avenue, NW, Suite 1200, Washington, DC 20037 US
Second Address: 31555.14 Mile Rd Farnubgtion Hill, Detroit, MI 48334
(248) 855-5100, *Fax:* (248) 455-7369
www.1270sports.com
wxyt@wxyt.com
License: Detroit, Wayne County, MI held by CBS Radio East Inc.
Group Owner: CBS Radio; (acq 3-9-89;
Nat'l Network: ESPN Radio; Westwood One
Arbitron Metro Market: Detroit *Format:* Sports *No. News Employees:* 3
Kevin Murphy, Operations Dir
Dan Zampillo, Programming Director

WLQV
01-01-1925; 1500 khz AM *Hrs Open:* 24; 50 kw-D, 10 kw-N, DA-2; N42 13 52 W83 11 58
Two Radio Plaza, Ferndale, MI 48152
(248) 581-1234, *Fax:* (248) 581-1231
www.faithtalk1500.com
License: Detroit, Wayne County, MI held by Caron Broadcasting Inc.
Group Owner: Salem Communications Corp.; (acq 2-10-2006; swap for WDJO(AM) Florence, KY and WCVX(AM) Cincinnati, OH plus $6.75 million cash)
Nat'l Network: Salem Radio Network
Arbitron Metro Market: Detroit *Hrs. of News Programming:* news progmg 2 hrs wkly *No. News Employees:* 1 *Target Audience:* 25-65 plus; middle class
Steve Dealy, Operations Dir
Chris MacCourtney, General Manager
Brad Smith, General Sales Mgr

WMUZ
11-11-1958; 103.5 mhz FM; 50 kw; 466 ft.; N42 22 40 W83 14 32
P. O. Box 3003, Blue Bell, PA 19422 US
(313) 272-3434, *Fax:* (313) 272-5045
www.wmuz.com
station@wumz.com
License: Detroit, Wayne County, MI held by WMUZ Radio Inc.
Group Owner: Crawford Broadcasting Co.
Arbitron Metro Market: Detroit, MI *Format:* Christian
Donald Crawford, President
Rich Hanovich, Operations Dir
Frank Franciosi, General Manager

WMXD
12-08-1964; 92.3 mhz FM; 45 kw; 479 ft.; N42 19 55 W83 2 42
Penobscot Bldg. 645 Gris, Suite 633, Detroit, MI 48226 US
(248) 324-5800, *Fax:* (313) 965-3965
www.mix923fm.com
contact@mix923fm.com
License: Detroit, Wayne County, MI held by AMFM Radio Licenses L.L.C.
Group Owner: Clear Channel Communications Inc.; (acq 8-30-00; grpsl).
Arbitron Metro Market: Detroit, MI *Format:* Adult Contemp

RADIO - U.S.

Til Levesque, General Manager
Gayle Lewkow, General Sales Mgr
Jamillah Muhammad, Programming Director
Randy Auerbach, Chief Engineer

WOMC

03-05-1948; 104.3 mhz FM; 190 kw; 361 ft.; N42 28 10 W83 6 54
600 New Hampshire Ave., Suite 1200, Washington, DC 20037 US
(248) 581-2200, *Fax:* (248) 546-5446
www.womc.com
kpmurphy@cbs.com
License: Detroit, Wayne County, MI held by CBS Radio Inc. of Michigan.
Group Owner: CBS Radio; (acq 4-28-88)
Nat'l Network: Westwood One
Arbitron Metro Market: Detroit *TV Affiliate:* Oldies *Special Programming:* news progmg 4 hrs wkly *Hrs. of News Programming:* 1 *No. News Employees:* 25-54; upscale
Program Director, Programming Director

WDVD

06-01-1948; 96.3 mhz FM; 20 kw; 787 ft.; N42 27 13 W83 9 50
77 West 66th Street, 16th Fl, New York, NY 10023 US
(313) 871-3030, *Fax:* (313) 875-9636
www.963wdvd.com
License: Detroit, Wayne County, MI
Group Owner: Cumulus Media Inc.
Arbitron Metro Market: Detroit *Format:* Adult Contemp
Steve Kosbau, President
Ron Harrell, Programming Director
Lisa Jesswein, News Director

WDTK

01-01-1926; 1400 khz AM; 1 kw-U, ND1; N42 24 22 W83 6 44
645 Griswold, Suite 2050, Detroit, MI 48226 US
(248) 581-1234, *Fax:* (248) 581-1231
www.wdtkam.com
zaron@wdtkam.com
License: Detroit, MI held by Pennsylvania Media Associates Inc.
Group Owner: Salem Communications Corp.; (acq 9-30-2004; $4.75 million).
Nat'l Reps: Salem
Arbitron Metro Market: Detroit *Format:* News, News/Talk, 86
Steve Dealy, Operations Dir
Christian MacCourtney, General Manager
Brad Smith, General Sales Mgr

WRIF

01-01-1948; 101.1 mhz FM *Hrs Open:* 24; 27 kw; 879 ft.; N42 28 14 W83 15 1
P O Box 1059, E. Brunswick, NJ 08816 US
(248) 547-0101, *Fax:* (248) 542-8800
wrif.com
License: Detroit, Wayne County, MI held by Greater Media Inc.
Group Owner: Greater Media Inc.; acq 12-15-87)
Nat'l Reps: Katz Radio
Arbitron Metro Market: Detroit *Format:* Rock/AOR *Target Audience:* 18-49; men
Tom Bender, General Manager

WDZH

01-01-1961; 98.7 mhz FM; 50 kw; 462 ft; N42 23 42 W83 08 58
26495 American Dr., Southfield, MI 20037
(248) 455-7350, *Fax:* (248) 855-1302
www.wvmv.com
License: Detroit, Wayne County, MI held by CBS Radio East Inc.
Group Owner: CBS Radio; (acq 12-89; grpsl;
Population Served: 3,500,000 *Arbitron Metro Market:* Detroit
Debbie Kenyon, Operations Dir
Sheryl Coyne, General Sales Mgr
Tom Sleeker, Operations Manager

WWJ

08-20-1920; 950 khz AM *Hrs Open:* 24; 5 kw-U, DA-N; N42 26 47 W83 10 23
26495 American Dr., Southfield, MI 20037
(248) 455-7200, *Fax:* (248) 304-4970
www.wwj.com
wwjnewsroom@cbsradio.com
License: Detroit, Wayne County, MI held by CBS Radio East Inc.
Group Owner: CBS Radio; (acq 3-9-89;
Nat'l Network: CBS
Population Served: 7,065,585 *Arbitron Metro Market:* Detroit, MI *TV Affiliate:* WWJ-TV affil *No. News Employees:* 32 *Target Audience:* General.
Kevin Murphy, General Manager
Pete Kowalski, General Sales Mgr
Rob Davidek, Programming Director
Debbie Spatafora, Promotions Manager
Ralph Hunt, Chief Engineer
Florence Walton, News Reporter
Vickie Thomas, News Reporter
JeffGilbert, News Reporter
Tim Skubick, Political Ed

WMGC-FM

03-06-1960; 105.1 mhz FM; 50 kw; 492 ft.; N42 27 13 W83 9 50
P.O. Box 1059, 2 Kennedy Blvd., East Brunswick, NJ 08816 US
(248) 414-5600, *Fax:* (248) 542-7700
www.detroitmagic.com
info@detroitmagic.com
License: Detroit, Wayne County, MI held by Greater Boston Radio Inc.
Group Owner: Greater Media Inc.; (acq 12-5-96)
Arbitron Metro Market: Detroit, MI *Format:* Adult Contemp *Target Audience:* General; professional, upscale, educated
Peter Smyth, President
Tom Bender, General Manager

WXYT

10-10-1925; 1270 khz AM *Hrs Open:* 24
Mailing Address: 600 New Hampshire Ave, Suite 1200, Washington, DC 20037 US
Second Address: 31555. 14 Mille Rd., Farminhtion Hill, MI 48334
(248) 855-5100, *Fax:* (248) 455-7369
www.1270sports.com
971@theticket.com
License: Detroit, MI held by CBS Radio Inc. of Detroit
Group Owner: CBS Radio; (acq 11-13-98; grpsl)
Arbitron Metro Market: Detroit, MI *Target Audience:* 25-54.
Kevin Murphy, General Manager
Steve Wright, Station Manager
Jennifer Vanvallis, General Sales Mgr
Dan Zampillo, Programming Director

WYCD

05-04-1960; 99.5 mhz FM; 17.5 kw; 787 ft.; N42 27 13 W83 9 50
600 New Hampshire Ave., Suite 1200, Washington, DC 20037 US
(248) 581-2200, *Fax:* (248) 546-5446
www.wycd.cbslocal.com
stephen.schram@infinitybroadcasting.com
License: Detroit, Wayne County, MI held by CBS Radio Inc. of Michigan.
Group Owner: CBS Radio; (acq 1-96; grpsl)
Arbitron Metro Market: Southfield, MI *Format:* Country *Target Audience:* 12-34.
Debbie Kenyon, General Manager
Jay Jennings, General Sales Mgr
Tim Roberts, Programming Director
Maureen Barkume, Promotions Manager

WDTW-FM

10-16-1960; 106.7 mhz FM; 61 kw; 509 ft.; N42 19 55 W83 2 42
Suite 600, 300 Crescent Court, Dallas, TX 75201 US
(248) 324-5800, *Fax:* (248) 848-0396
www.foxspacelive.com
License: Detroit, Wayne County, MI held by AMFM Radio Licenses L.L.C.
Group Owner: Clear Channel Communications Inc.
Arbitron Metro Market: Farmington Hills, MI *Format:* Country
Til Levesque, General Manager
David Crumb, General Sales Mgr

Dewitt

WQHH

01-01-1991; 96.5 mhz FM; 6 kw; 322 ft.; N42 50 58 W84 40 4
1011 Northcrest Road, Suite 4, Lansing, MI 48910 US
(517) 393-1320, *Fax:* (517) 393-0882
www.power965fm.com
License: Dewitt, Clinton County, MI held by The MacDonald Broadcasting Co.
Group Owner: MacDonald Broadcasting Co.; (acq 10-3-2006; $3.65 million with WXLA(AM) Dimondale)
Nat'l Reps: D & R Radio
Arbitron Metro Market: Lansing-East Lansing, MI *Format:* Urban Contemporary *Target Audience:* 18-49. *Adv. Rates:* 25; 25; 25; 25
Kenneth MacDonald Jr., CEO
Cindy Tuck, General Manager
Sharon Crane, General Sales Mgr

Dimondale

WXLA

09-20-1982; 1180 khz AM *Hrs Open:* 12; 1 kw-D, DA; N42 39 01 W84 34 49
600 W. Cavanaugh, Lansing, MI 48906
(517) 393-1320, *Fax:* (517) 393-0882
License: Dimondale, Eaton County, MI held by The MacDonald Broadcasting Co.
Group Owner: MacDonald Broadcasting Co.; (acq 10-3-2006; $3.65 million)
Nat'l Reps: D & R Radio
Population Served: 1,237 *Arbitron Metro Market:* Dimondale, MI
Kenneth MacDonald Jr., CEO
Cindy Tuck, General Manager
Sharon Crane, General Sales Mgr

Dowagiac

WHPD

01-01-1971; 92.1 mhz FM *Hrs Open:* 24; 3.3 kw; 299 ft.; N41 59 52 W86 3 14 *Rebroadcasts:* Simulcast with WHPZ(FM) Bremen, IN
Mailing Address: 68455 Riverview Drive, South Haven, MI 49090 US
Second Address: 26914 Marcellus Hwy., Dowagiac, MI 49047
(574) 291-8200, *Fax:* (574) 291-9043
www.pulsefm.com
info@whpd.com
License: Dowagiac, Cass County, MI held by LeSea Broadcasting Corp.
Group Owner: Le Sea Broadcasting; (acq 4-12-2005; $950,000 with co-lo
Nat'l Reps: Michigan Spot Sales
Arbitron Metro Market: South Bend, IN *Format:* Christian *Target Audience:* 25-64. *Adv. Rates:* 15; 12; 12; 8
Pete Sumrall, General Manager
Tom Scott, Programming Director

Eagle

*WJOM

01-01-2006; 88.5 mhz FM; 4.3 kw vert; 131 ft.; N42 48 25 W84 47 18
US
(888) 887-7141
www.smile.fm
Jennc@smile.fm
License: Eagle, Clinton County, MI held by Michigan Community Radio.
Arbitron Metro Market: Eagle, MI *Format:* Christian
Ed Czelada, President
Ed Czelada, Administration, Programming & Engineering
Clayton Hewitt, Administration and Engineering
Aaron Burrell, Administration
Dale Mazzoline, Production

East Jordan

*WICV

06-25-1989; 100.9 mhz FM *Hrs Open:* 24; 2.8 kw; 489 ft.; N45 10 40 W85 5 57 *Rebroadcasts:* Rebroadcasts WIAA(FM) Interlochen 100%
P.O. Box 199, Interlochen, MI 49643 US
(231) 276-4400, *Fax:* (231) 276-4417
www.interlochen.org/ipr
ipr@interlochen.org
License: East Jordan, Charlevoix County, MI held by Interlochen Center for the Arts
Nat'l Network: NPR; PRI; ABC *Regional Network:* Mich. Radio *Format:* Classical, News *Target Audience:* 35-80; upper income, arts-oriented, civic-minded professionals
Thom Paulson, Operations Dir

East Lansing

*WDBM

02-24-1989; 88.9 mhz FM *Hrs Open:* 24; 2 kw; 279 ft.; N42 42 20 W84 28 30
G-4 Holden Hall, East Lansing, MI 48824 US
(517) 353-4414
www.impact89fm.org
manager@impact89fm.org
License: East Lansing, Ingham County, MI held by Board of Trustees of Michigan State University.
Arbitron Metro Market: East Lansing, MI *Format:* Alternative *Special Programming:* Blues 4 hrs, jazz 5 hrs, heavy metal 4 hrs, progsv country 4 hrs, Christian rock 4 hrs wkly *Hrs. of News Programming:* News progmg 10hrs wkly *Target Audience:* 18-34; students of MSU
Gary Reid, General Manager
Aaron Young, Station Manager
Aiman Farooq, Programming Director
Devin Culham & Sam Riddle, Promotions Manager
Emanuele Berry, News Director
Josh Rickert, Production Director

WFMK

07-16-1959; 99.1 mhz FM *Hrs Open:* 24; 28 kw; 600 ft.; N42 40 33 W84 30 0

Mailing Address: 3420 Pine Tree Road, Lansing, MI 48911 US
Second Address: 3420 Pine Tree Rd., Lansing, MI 48911
(517) 394-3999, *Fax:* (517) 394-3391
www.99wfmk.com
wfmk@acd.net
License: East Lansing, Ingham County, MI
Group Owner: Cumulus Media Inc.; (acq 2000; grpsl).
Nat'l Reps: Christal
Arbitron Metro Market: Lansing-East Lansing, MI *Format:* Adult Contemp *Hrs. of News Programming:* news progmg 2 hrs wkly *No. News Employees:* 1 *Target Audience:* 25-54.
Brent Alberts, Operations Dir
Matt Hanlon, General Manager
Josh Strickland, Programming Director
Jordan Lee, Promotions Manager

***WKAR**
08-18-1922; 870 khz AM; 10 kw-D, DAD; N42 42 19 W84 28 30
84 Wilson Road, East Lansing, MI 48824 US
(517) 432-9527, *Fax:* (517) 353-7124
www.wkar.org
mail@wkar.org
License: East Lansing, MI held by Board of Trustees of Michigan State University.
Nat'l Network: NPR; PRI
Arbitron Metro Market: Lansing-East Lansing, MI *Format:* News, News/Talk, 86 *Special Programming:* Sp 3 hrs wkly *Hrs. of News Programming:* news progmg 25 hrs wkly *No. News Employees:* 5
Gene Purdum, Operations Dir
DeAnne Hamilton, General Manager
Cindy Herfindahl, General Sales Mgr
Curt Gilleo, Programming Director
Diane Hutchens, Promotions Manager
Kevin Laveny, News Director
Gary Blievernicht, EngineeringDir

***WKAR-FM**
10-10-1948; 90.5 mhz FM; 85 kw; 884 ft.; N42 42 7 W84 24 48
84 Wilson Road, East Lansing, MI 48824 US
(517) 432-9527, *Fax:* (517) 353-7124
www.wkar.org
mail@wkar.org
License: East Lansing, Ingham County, MI held by Board of Trustees of Michigan State University.
Arbitron Metro Market: Lansing-East Lansing, MI *TV Affiliate:* *WKAR-TV affil *Format:* News *Special Programming:* Jazz 7 hrs wkly
Huberto Biaggi, President
Raul Muxo, General Sales Mgr
Carlos Gonzalez, Programming Director

WMMQ
11-16-1963; 94.9 mhz FM; 50 kw; 492 ft.; N42 38 45 W84 33 38
3420 Pine Tree Road, Lansing, MI 48911 US
(517) 394-7272, *Fax:* (517) 394-3391
www.wmmq.com
brent.alberts@citcomm.com
License: East Lansing, Ingham County, MI
Group Owner: Cumulus Media Inc.; 2000
Arbitron Metro Market: Lansing, MI *Format:* Classic Rock *No. News Employees:* 1 *Target Audience:* 18-49 adults
Farid Suleman, Chairman
Matt Hanlon, General Manager
Brent Alberts, Programming Director
Deb Hart, News Director

WVFN
09-01-1964; 730 khz AM *Hrs Open:* 24; 0.5 kw-D, DAD; 0.05 kw-N, DAD; N42 38 45 W84 33 39; N42 38 45 W84 33 38
3420 Pine Tree Rd, Lansing, MI 48911 US
(517) 394-7272, *Fax:* (517) 394-3391
www.thegame730am.com
info@thegame730am.com
License: East Lansing, MI
Group Owner: Cumulus Media Inc.; (acq 2000; grpsl).
Nat'l Network: ESPN Radio *Nat'l Reps:* Christal
Arbitron Metro Market: Lansing, MI *Format:* Sports, Talk *Target Audience:* 25-54.
Farid Suleman, CEO
Brent Alberts, Operations Dir
Matt Hanlon, General Manager
Steve Goupil, News Director
Tim Nester, AM Operations Manager
Tim Staudt, Sports Commentator

East Tawas

***WRQC(FM)**
01-01-2008; 91.3 mhz FM; 20 kw vert; Ant 269 ft; N44 16 25 W83 39 48 *Rebroadcasts:* Rebroadcasts WPHN(FM) Gaylord 100%
Box 695, Gaylord, MI 49734-0695
(989) 732-6274, *Fax:* (989) 732-8171
www.ncradio.org
ncr@ncradio.org
License: East Tawas, Iosco County, MI held by Northern Christian Radio Inc.
Group Owner: Northern Christian Radio Inc.
Population Served: 352,428 *Arbitron Metro Market:* Bakersfield, CA *Format:* Christian, Religious
George Lake Jr., General Manager

Elmwood Township

***WLJN**
12-23-1982; 1400 khz AM *Hrs Open:* 24; 0.64 kw-U, ND1; N44 46 36 W85 39 43 *Rebroadcasts:* Simulcast with WLJW(AM) Cadillac
Mailing Address: PO Box 1400, Traverse City, MI 49685 US
Second Address: 1101 Cass St., Traverse City, MI 49684
(231) 946-1400, *Fax:* (231) 946-3959
www.wljn.com
info@wljn.com
License: Elmwood Township, MI held by Good News Media Inc.
Group Owner: Good News Media Inc.
Format: Talk, Religious *Hrs. of News Programming:* News progmg 4 hrs wkly *Target Audience:* General.
Brian Harcey, General Manager
Pete Lathrop, Programming Director

Escanaba

WCHT
12-01-1958; 600 khz AM; 0.57 kw-D, DA1; 0.134 kw-N, DA1; N45 48 19 W87 10 13
524 Ludington St., #300, Escanaba, MI 49829 US
(906) 789-9700, *Fax:* (906) 789-9701
www.wchtradio.com
rrnnews@radioresultsnetwork.com
License: Escanaba, MI held by Lakes Radio Inc.
Group Owner: Lakes Radio Inc.
Nat'l Network: CBS Radio *Nat'l Reps:* Christal
Arbitron Metro Market: Escanaba, MI *Format:* News, News/Talk, 86 *Special Programming:* Farm one hr, forestry one hr wkly *Hrs. of News Programming:* 24 *No. News Employees:* 4 *Target Audience:* 25-54.
Rick Duerson, General Manager

WDBC
09-04-1941; 680 khz AM *Hrs Open:* 24; 10 kw-D, DA2; 1 kw-N, DA2; N45 45 53 W87 5 48
604 Ludington Street, Escanaba, MI 49829 US
(906) 786-3804, *Fax:* (906) 789-9959
www.kmbbroadcasting.com/wdbc/
wykxinfo@yahoo.com
License: Escanaba, MI held by KMB Broadcasting Co. Inc.
Nat'l Network: ABC *Regional Network:* Mich. Radio *Nat'l Reps:* Katz Radio *Wire Services:* AP
Arbitron Metro Market: Escanaba, MI *Format:* Oldies *Special Programming:* Relg 4 hrs, children one hr wkly *Hrs. of News Programming:* news progmg 12 hrs wkly *No. News Employees:* 1 *Target Audience:* 25-54.
Betsy Cooke, President
Alice Sabuco, General Manager
Kim Rabitoy, General Sales Mgr
Erik Adams, News Director

WGLQ
09-11-1976; 97.1 mhz FM; 100 kw; 1070 ft.; N46 8 4 W86 56 52
524 Ludinton St., #300, Escanaba, MI 49829 US
(906) 228-9700, *Fax:* (906) 789-9700
www.wglqradio.com
info@radioresultsnetwork.com
License: Escanaba, Delta County, MI held by Lakes Radio, Inc.
Nat'l Network: NBC *Nat'l Reps:* Christal
Format: Adult Contemp *No. News Employees:* 4
Rick Duerson, General Manager

WYKX
12-22-1977; 104.7 mhz FM *Hrs Open:* 24; 100 kw; 351 ft.; N45 55 41 W87 16 0
604 Ludington Street, Escanaba, MI 49829 US
(906) 786-3800, *Fax:* (906) 789-9959
www.kmbbroadcasting.com/wykx
wdbcam@charterinternet.com
License: Escanaba, Delta County, MI
Nat'l Network: ABC; Jones Radio Networks *Wire Services:* AP
Arbitron Metro Market: Escanaba, MI *Format:* Country *Hrs. of News Programming:* news progmg 4 hrs wkly *No. News Employees:* 1 *Target Audience:* General; 25-54
Alice Sabuco, General Manager
Kim Rabitoy, General Sales Mgr
Allen Gibbs, Programming Director
Erik Adams, News Director
Wayne Nault, Music Director

***WUPJ**
90.9 mhz FM; 100 kw vert; 66 meters; N34 41 15 W82 59 13
409 Rainbow Circle, Kingsport, TN
(423) 963-9548
License: Escanaba, MI held by Clean Air Broadcasting Corp
David Purin, President

Essexville

WMJO
01-01-1992; 97.3 mhz FM *Hrs Open:* 24; 3 kw; 328 ft.; N43 30 51 W83 45 51
Mailing Address: P.O. Box 1776, Saginaw, MI 48605 US
Second Address: 2000 Whittier St., Saginaw, MI 48601
(989) 752-8161, *Fax:* (989) 752-8102
www.973joefm.com
admin@973joefm.com
License: Essexville, Bay County, MI held by The MacDonald Broadcasting Co.
Group Owner: MacDonald Broadcasting Co.; (acq 12-20-2001; grpsl).
Nat'l Reps: Eastman Radio *Regional Reps:* Eastman Radio *Wire Services:* AP
Arbitron Metro Market: Saginaw, MI *Format:* Adult Contemp *No. News Employees:* 1 *Target Audience:* 25-54; Women with families
Kenneth MacDonald Jr., CEO
Duane Alverson, President
Jim Kramer, Operations Dir
Mary Yearham, General Sales Mgr
Cindy Tuck, Vice President

Farmington Hills

WFDF
05-25-1922; 910 khz AM *Hrs Open:* 24
One East First St., Genesse Towers, Ste 1830, Flint, MI 48502 US
(305) 823-0990, *Fax:* (305) 823-9322
www.radiodisney.com/detroit
kimberly.r.munoz@disney.com
License: Farmington Hills, MI held by Radio Disney Group LLC.
Group Owner: ABC Inc.; (acq 8-15-2002; $3 million).
Nat'l Network: Radio Disney *Nat'l Reps:* McGavren Guild
Arbitron Metro Market: Farmington Hills, MI *Format:* Children *Target Audience:* M/F 6-16, F25-49
Rich Padgen, General Manager
Brian Christy, Promotions Manager
Elise Bennett, Promotions Manager

Fenton

WCXI
11-15-1985; 1160 khz AM; 1 kw-U, DA1; N42 48 30 W83 43 50
15130 North Road, Fenton, MI 48430 US
(810) 750-1911, *Fax:* (810) 750-9028
www.birach.com
sima@birach.com
License: Fenton, MI held by Birach Broadcasting Corp.
Group Owner: Birach Broadcasting Corp.; acq 9-13-99; $708,000)
Nat'l Network: American Urban
Arbitron Metro Market: Flint, MI *Format:* Country *Target Audience:* General; average age 35, primarily female, average income $35,000
Sima Birach, President & CEO
Brenda Charette, Operations Dir
John Morris, Programming Director

Flint

WCRZ
11-04-1961; 107.9 mhz FM; 50 kw; 331 ft.; N42 58 49 W83 34 40
Mr. John Risher, Gm, G-33387 E. Bristol Road, Flint, MI 48501 US
(810) 743-1080, *Fax:* (810) 742-5170
www.wcrz.com
jaypatrick@wcrz.com
License: Flint, Genesee County, MI
Arbitron Metro Market: Flint, MI *Format:* Adult Contemp
Kelly Quinn, General Manager
Kelly Quinn, General Sales Mgr

WDZZ-FM
09-29-1979; 92.7 mhz FM; 3 kw; 328 ft.; N43 2 29 W83 41 28
One East First St. #1830, Flint, MI 48502 US
(810) 238-7300, *Fax:* (810) 743-2500
www.wdzz.com
jeff.wade@cumulus.com

License: Flint, Genesee County, MI held by Cumulus Licensing Corp.
Group Owner: Cumulus Media Inc.; (acq 3-15-00; grpsl).
Arbitron Metro Market: Flint, MI *Format:* Urban Contemporary *Special Programming:* Gospel 8 hrs, teen talk one hr, concerned pastors one hr wkly *Target Audience:* Adults.
Jeff Wade, Operations Dir
Scott Meier, General Manager

WFBE
10-05-1953; 95.1 mhz FM *Hrs Open:* 5 AM-1 AM; 50 kw; 243 ft; N43 01 13 W83 40 40
G 4511 Miller Rd., Flint, MI 48911
(810) 720-9510, *Fax:* (810) 720-9513
www.b95.fm
chris.monk@cumulus.com
License: Flint, Genesee County, MI
Group Owner: Cumulus Media Inc.; (acq 4-26-01; grpsl).
Nat'l Network: PRI
Population Served: 15,000 *Arbitron Metro Market:* Flint, MI *Hrs. of News Programming:* News progmg 3 hrs wkly *Target Audience:* General; country music listeners
Chris Monk, General Manager
Greg Bryant, General Sales Mgr
April Hurley Rose, Programming Director
Matt Hanlon, Regional President

WFLT
12-05-1955; 1420 khz AM *Hrs Open:* 24
718 Beach Street, Flint, MI 48502 US
(810) 239-5733, *Fax:* (810) 239-7134
wflt1420am@aol.com
License: Flint, MI held by C.E.B.A.
Arbitron Metro Market: Flint, MI *Format:* Black, Gospel *Hrs. of News Programming:* news progrmg 6 hrs wkly *No. News Employees:* 2 *Target Audience:* Adults 35+ *Adv. Rates:* $20.00
Sammie L. Jordan Jr., General Manager

WFNT
04-10-1953; 1470 khz AM *Hrs Open:* 24; 5 kw-D, DA2; 1 kw-N, DA2; N42 58 22 W83 38 24
John Risher/Gen. Manager, G-33387 E. Bristol Road, Flint, MI 48501 US
(810) 743-8255, *Fax:* (810) 742-5170
www.wfnt.com
info@wfnt.com
License: Flint, MI
Group Owner: Townsquare Media; (acq 8-13-98; grpsl).
Arbitron Metro Market: Flint, MI *Format:* Oldies *No. News Employees:* 3
Kelly Quinn, General Manager
Dan Foley, Programming Director
Carolyn Gerace, Promotions Manager
Chris Pavelich, News Director
Mike Hutchens, Chief Engineer
Dan Foley, Director of Sales

***WFUM(FM)**
08-23-1985; 91.1 mhz FM *Hrs Open:* 24; 18 kw; 489 ft; N42 53 57 W83 27 42 *Rebroadcasts:* Rebroadcasts WUOM(FM) Ann Arbor 100%
535 W. William St., Suite 110, Ann Arbor, MI 48103
(734) 764-9210, *Fax:* (734) 647-3488
michiganradio.org
michigan.radio@umich.edu
License: Flint, Genesee County, MI held by Regents of the University of Michigan.
Nat'l Network: NPR
Arbitron Metro Market: Flint, MI *TV Affiliate:* *WFUM-TV affil
Peggy Watson, Operations Dir
Michael Leland, News Director

***WAKL**
09-01-1997; 88.9 mhz FM *Hrs Open:* 24; 0.38 kw vert; 263 ft.; N42 58 49 W83 34 40
503 Wood St., Fenton, MI 48430 US
(916) 251-1600, *Fax:* (916) 251-1650
www.klove.com
klove@klove.com
License: Flint, Genesee County, MI held by Educational Media Foundation.
Group Owner: EMF Broadcasting; (acq 11-19-01; $450,000).
Nat'l Network: K-Love
Arbitron Metro Market: Flint, MI *Format:* Christian *No. News Employees:* 3 *Target Audience:* 25-44; female-Judeo Christian
Mike Novak, President
David Pierce, Programming Director
Ed Lenane, News Director
Sam Wallington, Engineering Dir
Marya Morgan, News Reporter
Richard Hunt, News Reporter

WSNL
04-26-1946; 600 khz AM *Hrs Open:* 24
6171 S. Center Road, Grand Blanc, MI 48439 US
(810) 694-4146, *Fax:* (810) 694-0661
www.cbsl.biz
License: Flint, MI held by Christian Broadcasting System Ltd.
Group Owner: Christian Broadcasting System Ltd.; (acq 1-22-93; $400,000;
Arbitron Metro Market: Flint, MI *Format:* Christian, Talk *Target Audience:* 25-54; 35+.
Jon Yinger, President
Evelyn Shaw, Operations Dir
Graham Parker, Operations Manager

WTRX
10-01-1947; 1330 khz AM; 5 kw-D, DA2; 1 kw-N, DA2; N42 58 24 W83 39 2
Suite 100, 3071 Bay Rd., Saginaw, MI 48603 US
(810) 238-7300, *Fax:* (810) 424-3595
www.wtrxsports.com
License: Flint, MI
Group Owner: Cumulus Media Inc.; (acq 10-6-00; $180,000).
Arbitron Metro Market: Flint, MI *Format:* Sports, Talk *Target Audience:* 18-49 Males
Chris Monk, General Manager
Greg Bryant, General Sales Mgr
April Rose, Programming Director
Matt Hanlon, Regional President

WWCK
11-11-1946; 1570 khz AM; 1 kw-D, ND1; 0.179 kw-N, ND1; N43 0 39 W83 39 3
136 Main Street, Suite 202, Westport, CT 06880 US
(810) 238-7300, *Fax:* (810) 238-7310
www.1570supertalk.com
info@1570supertalk.com
License: Flint, MI held by Cumulus Licensing Corp.
Group Owner: Cumulus Media Inc.; (acq 3-15-00; grpsl).
Nat'l Network: Westwood One
Arbitron Metro Market: Flint, MI *Format:* News, News/Talk, 86 *Target Audience:* 18-34.
Scott Meier, General Manager
Ed Leick, General Sales Mgr
Nikki Bednarski, Promotions Manager
Les Root, News Director
Dan Greer, Chief Engineer
Pam Cantar, Traffic Director

WWCK-FM
09-01-1964; 105.5 mhz FM; 25 kw; 328 ft.; N43 0 39 W83 39 4
136 Main Street, Suite 202, Westport, CT 06880 US
(810) 238-7300, *Fax:* (810) 238-7310
www.wwck.com
info@wwck.com
License: Flint, Genesee County, MI
Arbitron Metro Market: Flint, MI *Format:* Contemporary Hits/Top 40
Peter Fretwell, General Manager
Ed Leick, General Sales Mgr
Nikki Bednarski, Promotions Manager
Pam Cantar, Traffic Director

Fowler

WQBX
11-01-1964; 104.7 mhz FM *Hrs Open:* 24; 6 kw; 328 ft.; N43 22 8 W84 36 19
PO Box 669, Alma, MI 48801 US
(989) 463-3175, *Fax:* (989) 463-6674
www.wqbxradio.com
License: Fowler, Gratiot County, MI
Nat'l Network: ABC
Format: Adult Contemp *Adv. Rates:* 15.25; 15.25; 15.25; 13
Randy Wanek, General Sales Mgr
Jeff Lynn, Programming Director

Frankenmuth

WRCL
01-01-2001; 93.7 mhz FM *Hrs Open:* 24; 3.5 kw; 436 ft.; N43 18 19.4 W83 33 5.4
2134 Fox Ridge Drive, Howell, MI 48843 US
(810) 251-5937, *Fax:* (810) 742-5170
www.club937.com
clay@club937.com
License: Frankenmuth, Saginaw County, MI
Group Owner: Townsquare Media; (acq 11-9-01; $7 million with WFGR(FM) Grand Rapids).
Nat'l Network: CNN Radio; Westwood One
Arbitron Metro Market: Burton, MI *Format:* Christian *Target Audience:* 12-34; children & adults
J. Patrick, Operations Dir
Kelly Quinn, General Manager
Clay Church, Programming Director
Clay Church, Music Director
Pete Clinton, Director of Sales
Molly Baade, Digital Sales Manager

Frankfort

WBNZ
10-02-1978; 92.3 mhz FM *Hrs Open:* 24; 50 kw; 446 ft.; N44 36 38 W86 9 38
Mailing Address: 3105 S. M L King Jr., Blvd., Suite 169, Lansing, MI 48910 US
Second Address: 1532 Forrester Rd, Frankfort, MI 49635
(231) 352-6374, *Fax:* (231) 352-4335
www.wbnz.com
traffic@wldrradio.com
License: Frankfort, Benzie County, MI held by The Kalil Holding Group LLC.
Nat'l Reps: Patt
Arbitron Metro Market: Traverse City-Petoskey, MI *Format:* Classic Rock *Special Programming:* Folk 2 hrs, big band 2 hrs wkly *Hrs. of News Programming:* news progmg 3 hrs wkly *No. News Employees:* 1 *TargetAudience:* 25-54. *Adv. Rates:* 14; 12; 14; 8
Roy Henderson, General Manager

Freeland

***WTRK**
01-01-2005; 90.9 mhz FM; 0.43 kw; 324 ft.; N43 33 42 W83 58 52
P.O. Drawer 2440, Tupelo, MS 38803 US
(888) 937-2471, *Fax:* (916) 251-1650
www.air1.com
info@air1.com
License: Freeland, Saginaw County, MI held by Educational Media Foundation.
Group Owner: EMF Broadcasting; (acq 6-29-2005; $75,000)
Nat'l Network: Air 1
Arbitron Metro Market: Freeland, MI *Format:* Alternative, Christian
Darrell Chambliss, Chairman
Alan Mason, COO
Mike Novak, President and CEO
David Pierce, Programming Director
Ed Lenane, News Director
Sam Wallington, Engineering Dir
Marya Morgan, News Reporter
Richard Hunt, News Reporter
Tracy Butler, Traffic Manager
Mitch Barnhart, Director
David R. Ferry, Director
Walter Golembeski, Director

Gagetown

***WCTP**
01-01-2006; 88.5 mhz FM *Hrs Open:* 24; 6 kw; 328 ft.; N43 45 36 W83 5 45
4330 Farver Road, Gagetown, MI 48735 US
(989) 315-8043, *Fax:* (989) 872-3700
www.wctpradiofm.com
info@wctpradiofm.com
License: Gagetown, Tuscola County, MI held by Plonta Broadcasting Inc.
Arbitron Metro Market: Gagetown, MI *Format:* Gospel *No. News Employees:* 3
Duane Plonta, President

Gaylord

***WBLW**
01-01-2000; 88.1 mhz FM *Hrs Open:* 24 hours; 5 kw vert; 853 ft.; N45 10 12 W84 45 4
Mailing Address: 232 South Townline Rd, Gaylord, MI 49735 US
Second Address: 232 S. Townline Rd., Gaylord, MI 49735
(989) 705-7464, *Fax:* (989) 731-1122
www.wblwradio.com
info@wblwradio.com
License: Gaylord, Otsego County, MI held by Gaylord Baptist Christian School.
Nat'l Network: USA
Arbitron Metro Market: Gaylord, MI, *Format:* Christian
Jay Towne, General Manager
Bro. Tim Ramsey, Station Manager
Tim Ramsey, Programming Director
Bro. Dominic Garrisi, Assistant Chief Engineer

WSRT
11-18-1972; 106.7 mhz FM *Hrs Open:* 24; 100 kw; 581 ft.; N45 2 44 W84 50 46
2215 Oak Industrial Dr., Grand Rapids, MI 49505 US
(231) 947-0003, *Fax:* (231) 947-7002
License: Gaylord, Otsego County, MI held by Northern Radio of Gaylord Inc.
Nat'l Reps: Christal
Arbitron Metro Market: Traverse City-Petoskey, MI *Format:* Adult Contemp *Target Audience:* 18-49; rgnl orientation including Traverse City, Petoskey, Cheboygan-active life style
Charlie Ferguson, General Manager
Greg Marsh, General Sales Mgr
Dennis Winslow, Programming Director
Kristal Flateau, News Director
Dennis Murray, Chief Engineer

WMJZ-FM
01-01-1984; 101.5 mhz FM; 50 kw; 492 ft.; N45 1 10 W84 24 28
Mailing Address: P. O. Box 25, 650 East Main Street, Gaylord, MI 49735 US
Second Address: 3687 Old US Hwy. 27 S., Gaylord, MI 49735
(989) 732-2341, *Fax:* (989) 732-6202
www.radioeaglegaylord.com
License: Gaylord, Ostego County, MI held by Darby Advertising Inc.
Group Owner: Darby Advertising Inc.; (acq 1-1-98; with co-located AM)
Nat'l Network: Motor Racing Net
Arbitron Metro Market: Gaylod, MI *Format:* Variety/Diverse
Target Audience: 25-54. *Adv. Rates:* 25; 25; 25; 25
Kent Smith, President
Mike Reling, Operations Dir
Kent Smith, General Manager
Rosemary Smith, General Sales Mgr
Chip Aledge, Programming Director

***WPHN**
04-07-1985; 90.5 mhz FM *Hrs Open:* 24; 100 kw; 1001 ft.; N45 8 17 W84 9 44
Mailing Address: 1511 M-32 East/PO Bx 695, Gaylord, MI 49735 US
Second Address: 1511 M-32 E., Gaylord, MI 49735
(989) 732-6274, *Fax:* (989) 732-8171
www.ncradio.org
ncr@ncradio.org
License: Gaylord, Otsego County, MI held by Northern Christian Radio Inc.
Group Owner: Northern Christian Radio Inc.
Nat'l Network: Moody; USA
Format: Christian, Religious *Hrs. of News Programming:* News progmg 10 hrs wkly *Target Audience:* 25-55.
Joe Sereno, Chairman
George Lake Jr., CEO

Gladstone

WGKL
02-15-1999; 105.5 mhz FM; 10 kw; 377 ft.; N45 48 17 W87 10 15
2001 Pennsylvania Ave., N.W., Suite 400, Washington, DC 20006 US
(906) 789-9700, *Fax:* (906) 789-9700
www.radioresultsnetwork.com
rick@radioresultsnetwork.com
License: Gladstone, Delta County, MI held by Lakes Radio Inc.
Group Owner: Lakes Radio Inc.
Nat'l Network: ABC *Nat'l Reps:* Christal
Format: Oldies *No. News Employees:* 4 *Target Audience:* adults 25-64
Rick Duerson, General Manager

Gladwin

WGDN
12-07-1974; 1350 khz AM
3601 W. Woods Rd, Gladwin, MI 48624 US
(989) 426-1031, *Fax:* (989) 426-9436
www.103country.com
steve@103country.com
License: Gladwin, MI held by Apple Broadcasting Co. Inc.
Format: Religious *Target Audience:* 35 plus.
Steve Coston, General Manager

WGDN-FM
02-07-1978; 103.1 mhz FM; 11.5 kw; 486 ft.; N43 57 17 W84 32 59
3601 West Woods Road, Gladwin, MI 48624 US
(989) 426-1031, *Fax:* (989) 426-9436
www.103country.com
steve@103country.com
License: Gladwin, Gladwin County, MI
Nat'l Network: Westwood One
Format: Country
George Jones, Chairman
Marlon Kiser, CEO
Steve Coston, General Manager
Winnette Jessup, General Sales Mgr
Corey Pratt, Production
Winnette Jessup, Traffic Manager

Glen Arbor

WGFN
02-01-1991; 98.1 mhz FM *Hrs Open:* 24; 21 kw; 738 ft.; N44 49 16 W85 59 47 *Rebroadcasts:* WGFN-FM Cheboygan 100%
232 Front Street, No. 2, Traverse City, MI 49684 US
(231) 627-2341, *Fax:* (231) 627-7000
www.classicrockthebear.com
info@classicrockthebear.com
License: Glen Arbor, Leelanau County, MI held by Northern Star Broadcasting L.L.C.
Group Owner: Northern Star Broadcasting L.L.C.; (acq 12-12-2005; grpsl)
Arbitron Metro Market: Traverse City-Petoskey, MI *Format:* Classic Rock *No. News Employees:* 1
Palmer Pyle, President
April Hurley-Rose, Operations Dir

WJZJ
09-01-1997; 95.5 mhz FM *Hrs Open:* 24; 21 kw; 738 ft.; N44 49 16 W85 59 47
232 Front Street, No. 2, Traverse City, MI 49684 US
(231) 627-2341, *Fax:* (231) 627-7000
www.modernrockthezone.com
info@modernrockthezone.com
License: Glen Arbor, Leelanau County, MI held by Northern Star Broadcasting L.L.C.
Group Owner: Northern Star Broadcasting L.L.C.; (acq 12-12-2005; grpsl)
Arbitron Metro Market: Traverse City-Petoskey, MI *Format:* Rock/AOR
Palmer Pyle, President
April Hurley-Rose, General Manager

Good Hart

***WJOG**
01-01-2006; 91.3 mhz FM; 6 kw vert; 623 ft.; N45 30 33 W85 2 11 *Rebroadcasts:* simulcasts WJOM (FM) Eagle 100%
US
(888) 887-7139
www.smile.fm
Jennc@smile.fm
License: Good Hart, Emmet County, MI held by Michigan Community Radio.
Arbitron Metro Market: Jackson, TN *Format:* Gospel
Ed Czelada, President
Ed Czelada, Administration, Programming & Engineering
Clayton Hewitt, Administration and Engineering
Aaron Burrell, Administration
Dale Mazzoline, Production

Goodland Township

***WHYT**
01-01-2004; 88.1 mhz FM; 0.4 kw vert; 581 ft.; N43 10 30 W83 4 2
601 Savidge St, Reed City, MI 49677 US
(888) 887-7139, *Fax:* (877) 850-0881
www.smile.fm
Jennc@smile.fm
License: Goodland Township, Lapeer County, MI held by Smile FM.
Group Owner: Superior Communications
Arbitron Metro Market: Goodland Township, MI *Format:* Christian
Ed Czelada, President
Jenn Czelada, General Manager
Ed Czelada, Administration, Programming & Engineering
Clayton Hewitt, Administration and Engineering
Aaron Burrell, Administration
Dale Mazzoline, Production

Grand Haven

WGHN
07-16-1956; 1370 khz AM *Hrs Open:* 24; 500 w-D, 22 w-N; N43 02 17 W86 13 46
Box 330, One S. Harbor, Grand Haven, MI 49417
(616) 842-8110, *Fax:* (616) 842-4350
www.sportsradio1370.com
License: Grand Haven, Ottawa County, MI held by WGHN Inc.
Nat'l Network: ESPN Radio *Nat'l Reps:* Patt
Population Served: 120,000 *Arbitron Metro Market:* Grand Rapids, M *Adv. Rates:* 18; 15; 17; 10
Will Tieman, President
Eric Kaelin, General Manager

WGHN-FM
01-28-1969; 92.1 mhz FM *Hrs Open:* 24; 6 kw; 213 ft.; N43 3 25 W86 14 28
One South Harbor, Box 330, Grand Haven, MI 49417 US
(616) 842-8110, *Fax:* (616) 842-4350
www.wghn.com
eric@wghn.com
License: Grand Haven, Ottawa County, MI
Nat'l Network: CBS Radio *Regional Network:* Mich. Farm
Arbitron Metro Market: Grand Rapids, MII *Format:* Adult Contemp *Special Programming:* Farm 5 hrs wkly *Hrs. of News Programming:* news progmg 30 hrs wkly *No. News Employees:* 2 *Target Audience:* 25-54.
Eric Kaelin, General Manager
Jesse Bruce, Programming Director
Walt Zerlaut, News Director
Vicki Coulson, Traffic Manager
Leslie Cassis Withun, Sales Executive
John Roberts, Disc Jockey

Grand Rapids

***WAYG**
05-18-1978; 89.9 mhz FM *Hrs Open:* 24; 4.9 kw; 207 ft.; N42 58 40 W85 35 44 *Rebroadcasts:* Rebroadcasts WAYK(FM) Kalamazoo 75%
1159 East Beltline, Grand Rapids, MI 49525 US
(307) 638-8921, *Fax:* (307) 638-8922
1049krrr.com
License: Grand Rapids, Kent County, MI held by Cornerstone University
Arbitron Metro Market: Guernsey WY *Format:* Oldies
Steven Silberberg, President
Roger Ingram, General Manager

WBCT
10-01-1951; 93.7 mhz FM *Hrs Open:* 24; 320 kw; 781 ft.; N42 37 56 W85 32 16
3305 W. Spring Mtn., Rd., Las Vegas, NV 89102 US
(520) 797-4434
License: Grand Rapids, Kent County, MI held by CC Licenses LLC.
Group Owner: Clear Channel Communications Inc.; (acq 1996; grpsl)
Nat'l Reps: Clear Channel
Arbitron Metro Market: Houston-Galveston
Ted Tucker, General Manager

***WBLU-FM**
08-18-1979; 88.9 mhz FM; 0.65 kw; 400 ft.; N42 59 15 W85 37 26 *Rebroadcasts:* Rebroadcasts WBLV(FM) Twin Lake 100%
Route 2, Twin Lake, MI 49457 US
(231) 894-2616(231) 458-9258, *Fax:* (231) 893-2457
www.bluelake.org
radio@bluelake.org
License: Grand Rapids, Kent County, MI held by Blue Lake Fine Arts Camp.
Nat'l Network: PRI; NPR
Arbitron Metro Market: Twin Lake, MI *Format:* Jazz, News
Special Programming: Folk 5 hrs wkly *Target Audience:* Adults.
Gordon Christensen, Operations Dir
Dave Myers, General Manager
Steve Albert, Programming Director
Don Hoogeboom, Chief Engineer
Bonnie Bierma, Music Director

***WCSG**
06-09-1973; 91.3 mhz FM; 37 kw; 571 ft.; N42 47 46 W85 38 58
1159 E. Beltline Avenue, Northeast, Grand Rapids, MI 49505 US
(616) 942-1500, *Fax:* (616) 942-7078
www.wcsg.org
wcsg@wcsg.org
License: Grand Rapids, Kent County, MI held by Cornerstone University.
Nat'l Network: AP Radio
Arbitron Metro Market: Grand Rapids, MI *Format:* Christian *Hrs. of News Programming:* news progmg 2 hrs wkly *No. News Employees:* 2 *Target Audience:* 35-49.
Dr. Joseph Stowell, President
Lee Geysbeek, Operations Dir
Chris Lemke, General Manager
Patty Riva, Promotions Manager
Tom Bosscher, Chief Engineer

WBFX
01-01-1965; 101.3 mhz FM *Hrs Open:* 24; 50 kw; 420 ft.; N43 2 28 W85 21 28

200 Concord Plaza, Suite 600, San Antonio, TX 78216 US
(616) 459-1919, *Fax:* (616) 242-6599
www.101thefoxrocks.com
timfeagan@clearchannel.com
License: Grand Rapids, Kent County, MI
Group Owner: Clear Channel Communications Inc.
Arbitron Metro Market: Grand Rapids, MI *Format:* Classic Rock
Rich Berry, General Sales Mgr
Doug Montgomery, Programming Director

WFGR

08-09-1992; 98.7 mhz FM; 2.75 kw; 492 ft.; N43 1 57 W85 41 47
220 Lyon St, NW Ste 425, Grand Rapids, MI 49503 US
(616) 451-4800, *Fax:* (616) 451-4225
www.wfgr.com
jerry.tarrants@townsquaremedia.com
License: Grand Rapids, Kent County, MI
Group Owner: Townsquare Media; (acq 9-25-01; $3.9 million for stock).
Arbitron Metro Market: Grand Rapids, MI *Format:* Oldies *Target Audience:* 25 plus; affluent, well-educated professionals
Terry Jacobs, President
Russ Hines, General Manager
Tim Huston, Director of Sales
Jerry Tarrants, Brand Manager

WFUR

11-01-1947; 1570 khz AM *Hrs Open:* 24; 1 kw-D, ND1; 0.307 kw-N, ND1; N42 57 14 W85 41 52
Mailing Address: PO Box 1808, Grand Rapids, MI 49501 US
Second Address: 399 Garfield Ave. S.W., Grand Rapids, MI 49504
(616) 451-9387, *Fax:* (616) 451-8460
www.wfuramfm.com
wfuramfm@cbcglobal.net
License: Grand Rapids, MI held by Furniture City Broadcasting Corp.
Group Owner: Kuiper Stns; (acq 3-10-50)
Nat'l Network: USA
Arbitron Metro Market: Grand Rapids, MII *Format:* Religious *Hrs. of News Programming:* News progmg 5 hrs wkly *Target Audience:* 35 plus; 60% female, 30% male
William Kuiper Sr., President
Steven Kuiper, Operations Dir
Dave Kuiper, News Director
Bill Kuiper Jr., Chief Engineer
Pat Deja, Public Affairs Director

WFUR-FM

09-01-1960; 102.9 mhz FM *Hrs Open:* 24; 50 kw; 492 ft.; N42 57 13 W85 41 55
Mailing Address: PO Box 1808, Grand Rapids, MI 49501 US
Second Address: 399 Garfield Ave. S.W., Grand Rapids, MI 49504
(616) 451-9387, *Fax:* (616) 451-8460
www.wfuramfm.com
wfuramfm@cbcglobal.net
License: Grand Rapids, Kent County, MI
Nat'l Network: USA
Arbitron Metro Market: Grand Rapids, MII *Format:* Religious *Hrs. of News Programming:* News progmg 5 hrs wkly *Target Audience:* 35-64; Christian family music listeners & homeowners
Pat Deja, Programming Director
Doug Wentworth, News Director
Dave Kuiper, Disc Jockey

WGRD-FM

08-01-1962; 97.9 mhz FM *Hrs Open:* 24; 13 kw; 591 ft.; N42 47 46 W85 38 58
600 Congress Ave., Suite 1400, Austin, TX 78701 US
(616) 451-4800, *Fax:* (616) 451-0113
www.wgrd.com
License: Grand Rapids, Kent County, MI
Group Owner: Townsquare Media; (acq 8-7-00; grpsl).
Nat'l Reps: Katz Radio
Arbitron Metro Market: Grand Rapids, MII *Format:* Alternative *Hrs. of News Programming:* news progmg 3 hrs wkly *No. News Employees:* 1 *Target Audience:* 18-49.
Phil Catlett, General Manager
Paul Boscarino, General Sales Mgr

WLAV-FM

01-01-1947; 96.9 mhz FM *Hrs Open:* 24; 50 kw; 489 ft.; N43 2 1 W85 31 15
P.O. Box 8, Bloomington, IL 61702 US
(616) 774-8461, *Fax:* (616) 774-2491
www.wlav.com
info@wlav.com
License: Grand Rapids, Kent County, MI
Group Owner: Cumulus Media Inc.; (acq 5-30-00; grpsl).
Nat'l Network: ABC
Arbitron Metro Market: Grand Rapids, MI *Format:* Classic Rock *Target Audience:* 25-49.
Matthew Hanlon, President
Brent Alberts, Operations Dir
Matt Hanlon, General Manager
Kim Lozano, General Sales Mgr
Rob Brant, Programming Director
Melissa Bosvich, News Director
John Alan, Chief Engineer

WLHT-FM

02-28-1962; 95.7 mhz FM; 40 kw; 551 ft.; N43 1 57 W85 41 47
600 Congress Ave., Suite 1400, Austin, TX 78701 US
(616) 451-4855, *Fax:* (616) 451-9595
www.wlht.com
billb@wlht.com
License: Grand Rapids, Kent County, MI held by Regent Broadcasting of Grand Rapids Inc.
Arbitron Metro Market: Grand Rapids, MI *Format:* Adult Contemp *Target Audience:* 25-54.
Terry Jacobs, President
Bill Bailey, Programming Director

WNWZ

11-01-1947; 1410 khz AM; 1 kw-D, ND1; 0.048 kw-N, ND1; N42 59 14 W85 37 26
600 Congress Ave., Suite 1400, Austin, TX 78701 US
616-451-4800, *Fax:* (616) 451-9595
http://funny1410am.com/help/
Russ.Hines@townsquaremedia.com
License: Grand Rapids, MI
Group Owner: Townsquare Media; (acq 8-7-00; grpsl).
Nat'l Network: Jones Radio Networks
Arbitron Metro Market: Grand Rapids, M *TV Affiliate:* Comedy *No. News Employees:* 35 plus; professionals
General Manager, General Manager
Director of Sales, General Sales Mgr
Brand Manager

WOOD

01-01-1924; 1300 khz AM
3305 W. Spring Mtn., Rd., Las Vegas, NV 89102 US
(616) 459-1919, *Fax:* (616) 723-3303
www.woodradio.com
info@woodradio.com
License: Grand Rapids, MI held by CC Licenses LLC.
Group Owner: Clear Channel Communications Inc.; (acq 5-10-96; grpsl)
Nat'l Network: ABC *Nat'l Reps:* Clear Channel
Arbitron Metro Market: Grand Rapids, M *TV Affiliate:* Talk *Special Programming:* news progmg 24 hrs wkly *Hrs. of News Programming:* 6 *No. News Employees:* 35-54.
Operations Manager, Operations Dir
General Sales Manager, General Sales Mgr

WSRW-FM

01-01-1962; 105.7 mhz FM *Hrs Open:* 24; 265 kw; Ant 810 ft; N42 41 13 W85 30 35
77 Monroe Cir., Suite 1000, Grand Rapids, MI 49503
(616) 459-1919, *Fax:* (616) 242-6599
www.woodfm.com
info@woodfm.com
License: Grand Rapids, Kent County, MI held by CC Licenses LLC.
Group Owner: Clear Channel Communications Inc.
Arbitron Metro Market: Grand Rapids, MI *Hrs. of News Programming:* News progmg 10 hrs wkly
Doug Montgomery, Operations Dir
Tim Kiesling, Programming Director
Glenn Del Vecchio, Promotions Manager
David Messner, News Director

WTKG

02-01-1945; 1230 khz AM *Hrs Open:* 24; 1 kw-D, ND2; 1 kw-N, ND2; N42 59 42 W85 40 36
200 Concord Plaza, Suite 600, San Antonio, TX 78216 US
(616) 459-1919, *Fax:* (616) 723-3303
www.wtkg.com
info@wtkg.com
License: Grand Rapids, MI held by CC Licenses LLC.
Group Owner: Clear Channel Communications Inc.; (acq 1996; grpsl).
Nat'l Reps: Clear Channel
Arbitron Metro Market: Grand Rapids, MI *Format:* Talk *Hrs. of News Programming:* news progmg 7 hrs wkly *No. News Employees:* 2 *Target Audience:* 25-54; conservative
Skip Essick, Operations Dir
Tim Feagan, General Manager
Henry Capogna, General Sales Mgr
Phil Tower, Programming Director
Kristen Everhart, Promotions Manager
Rob St. Mary, News Director
Don Missad, Chief Engineer
Bruce Law,Director of Sales
Doug Montgomery, Operations Manager
Michele Johnson, Business Manager

*WVGR

12-07-1961; 104.1 mhz FM *Hrs Open:* 24; 96 kw; 725 ft.; N42 39 17 W85 31 38 *Rebroadcasts:* Rebroadcasts WUOM(FM) Ann Arbor 100%
5000 Ls&A Building, 5th Floor, Ann Arbor, MI 48109 US
(734) 764-9210, *Fax:* (734) 647-3488
www.michiganradio.org
michigan.radio@umich.edu
License: Grand Rapids, Kent County, MI held by Regents of the University of Michigan.
Nat'l Network: NPR; PRI
Arbitron Metro Market: Grand Rapids, MI *Format:* News, News/Talk, 86 *Hrs. of News Programming:* news progmg 140 hrs wkly *No. News Employees:* 12
Peggy Watson, Operations Dir
Vincent Duffey, News Director
Bob Skon, Chief Engineer
Sarah Hulett, Assistant News Director
Jennifer Guerra, Reporter/Producer
Lester Graham, Investigative Reporter

Grayling

WGRY

08-01-1970; 1230 khz AM *Hrs Open:* 24; 0.75 kw-U, ND1; N44 39 5 W84 44 18
6514 Old Lake Road, Grayling, MI 49738 US
(989) 348-6171, *Fax:* (989) 348-6181
www.gannonbroadcasting.com
radio@i2k.net
License: Grayling, MI held by Gannon Broadcasting.
Nat'l Reps: Michigan Spot Sales
Format: Contemporary Hits/Top 40 *Hrs. of News Programming:* news progmg 16 hrs wkly *No. News Employees:* 1 *Target Audience:* 25 plus.
William Gannon, President
Pete Michaels, Operations Dir

WGRY-FM

06-16-1977; 100.3 mhz FM; 60 kw; 430 ft.; N44 34 15 W84 41 33
6514 Old Lake Rd., Grayling, MI 49738 US
(989) 348-6171, *Fax:* (989) 348-6181
www.gannonbroadcasting.com
radio@i2k.net
License: Grayling, Crawford County, MI held by Gannon Broadcasting Systems Inc.
Nat'l Network: ABC *Nat'l Reps:* Patt
Format: Country *Target Audience:* 25-54.
William Gannon, President
Pete Michaels, Operations Dir

Greenville

WGLM

05-19-1960; 1380 khz AM
Mailing Address: 9181 S. Greenville Road, Greenville, MI 48838 US
Second Address: 9181 S. Greenville Rd., Greenville, MI
(616) 754-3656, *Fax:* (616) 754-2390
wscgradio@chartermi.net
License: Greenville, MI held by Packer Radio Greenville Inc.
Format: News, Sports, 86
Chris Loiselle, CFO
Bruce Bentley, Operations Dir
John Clark, General Manager
Ralph Haines, Chief Engineer

*WDPW

91.9 mhz FM; 4 kw vert; 207 ft.; N43 5 12 W85 18 59 US
(616) 698-1831
License: Greenville, Montcalm County, MI held by Larlen Communications Inc.
Arbitron Metro Market: Polson, MT
P.R. Frank, Operations Dir
Ken Kreitzer, General Manager
Christopher Hartley, Programming Director
Tom Nornhold, Chief Engineer
Jennifer Bryant, Assistant Music Director

Gulliver

WCMM

01-01-1982; 102.5 mhz FM; 100 kw; 814 ft.; N45 58 1 W86 29 18
101 Huron Court, Negaunee, MI 49866 US

(906) 789-9700, *Fax:* (906) 789-9701
www.wcmmradio.com
rnnews@radioresultsnetwork.com
License: Gulliver, Schoolcraft County, MI held by Lakes Radio Inc.
Group Owner: Lakes Radio Inc.; acq 11-30-99; grpsl)
Nat'l Network: ABC *Nat'l Reps:* Christal
Arbitron Metro Market: Gulliver, MI *Format:* Country *No. News Employees:* 4 *Target Audience:* 18-54; younger, contemp, mobile adult workers
Rick Duerson, General Manager

Gwinn

WUPT
01-01-2008; 100.3 mhz FM; 100 kw; 512 ft.; N46 30 51.7 W87 28 40.2
US
(906) 255-0656, *Fax:* (906) 255-0607
www.1003thepoint.com
License: Gwinn, Marquette County, MI held by Radioactive LLC.
Group Owner: Radioactive LLC
Arbitron Metro Market: Gwinn, MI *Format:* Contemporary Hits/Top 40, Adult Contemp
Benjamin Homel, President
Kent Smith, General Manager
Rosemary Smith, General Sales Mgr
Ryan Beckman, Sports Director
Chip Arledge, Director Of Commotion & Product Development

Hancock

WMPL
03-02-1957; 920 khz AM; 1 kw-D, ND1; 0.206 kw-N, ND1; N47 6 5 W88 35 26
326 Quincy Street, Hancock, MI 49930 US
(906) 482-3700, *Fax:* (906) 482-1540
www.wmpl920.com
rick@wmpl920.com
License: Hancock, MI held by J & J Broadcasting Inc.
Nat'l Network: USA *Nat'l Reps:* Michigan Spot Sales
Arbitron Metro Market: Hancock, MI *Format:* News, Sports, 86 *Hrs. of News Programming:* news progmg 15 hrs wkly *No. News Employees:* 1 *Target Audience:* General. *Adv. Rates:* 10; 8; 8; 5
Jerry Hackman, President
Jay Nix, Operations Dir
Ken Waldrop, General Manager
Mariann Schulze, General Sales Mgr
Mitchell Lake, News Director
Ted Franz, Chief Engineer
Josh Ylitalo, Traffic Manager

WKMJ-FM
01-01-1968; 93.5 mhz FM; 13.5 kw; 456 ft.; N47 6 6 W88 34 11
326 Quincy Street, Hancock, MI 49930 US
(906) 482-3700, *Fax:* (906) 482-1540
www.themix93.com
rick@wmpl920.com
License: Hancock, Houghton County, MI held by J & J Broadcasting Inc.
Nat'l Network: Jones Radio Networks
Arbitron Metro Market: Hancock, MI *Format:* Adult Contemp, Sports *No. News Employees:* 1 *Target Audience:* 18-45. *Adv. Rates:* 14; 13; 13; 9
Kate Lochte, Station Manager

WGLI
02-11-2003; 98.7 mhz FM *Hrs Open:* 24; 100 kw; 522 ft.; N47 6 13 W88 34 4
1296 Marian Lane, Green Bay, WI 54304 US
(906) 353-9287, *Fax:* (906) 483-4910
www.keepitintheup.com
eagleadmin@up.net
License: Hancock, Houghton County, MI held by Keweenaw Bay Indian Community
Nat'l Network: Jones Radio Networks
Arbitron Metro Market: Traverse City, MI *Format:* Classic Rock
Special Programming: Loc talk 5 hrs wkly
Ed Janisse, General Manager
John Preston, General Sales Mgr
Brian Keinath, Program/Music Director
Deborah Hilscher, Office Manager

Hanover

*WJKZ
90.9 mhz FM; kw
US
(517) 999-3737
www.foundationradio.org
License: Hanover, Jackson County, MI held by Saidnewsfoundation.
Arbitron Metro Market: Hanover, MI
David Schaberg, General Manager

Harbor Beach

*WSMB
03-01-1925; 89.3 mhz FM; kw
US
(901) 767-0104, *Fax:* (901) 767-0582
License: Harbor Beach, Shelby County, MI held by Entercom Memphis License LLC.
Group Owner: Entercom Communications Corp.; (acq 12-13-99; grpsl)
Nat'l Network: Fox Sports
Arbitron Metro Market: Memphis, TN *Format:* Sports
Dan Barron, Operations Dir
Kory Myers, General Sales Mgr
Dennis Fuller, Programming Director
Rondi Atkinson, Promotions Manager
Mike Schwartz, Chief Engineer

WCZE
01-01-2005; 103.7 mhz FM; 43 kw; 528 ft.; N43 41 10 W82 59 40
6940 Armstrong Rd #N, Imlay City, MI 48444 US
(888) 887-7139, *Fax:* (877) 850-0881
www..smile.fm
jennc@smile.FM
License: Harbor Beach, Huron County, MI held by Jennifer & Edward Czelada.
Format: Christian
Jenn Czelada, General Manager
Ed Czelada, Programming Director
Aaron Burrell, Administration
Clayton Hewitt, Administration and Engineering
Ed Czelada, Administration, Programming & Engineering
Dale Mazzoline, Production

Harbor Springs

*WCMW-FM
08-15-1988; 103.9 mhz FM *Hrs Open:* 24; 12 kw; 1001 ft.; N45 30 8 W85 1 44 *Rebroadcasts:* Rebroadcasts WCMU-FM Mount Pleasant 100%
3965 East Broomfield Rd., Mt Pleasant, MI 48859 US
(989) 774-3105, *Fax:* (989) 774-4427
www.wcmu.org
schud1ra@cmich.edu
License: Harbor Springs, Emmet County, MI held by Central Michigan University.
Nat'l Network: NPR; PRI *Wire Services:* AP
Arbitron Metro Market: Michigan, Upper Peninsula, MS *Format:* Jazz, News *Hrs. of News Programming:* news progmg 45 hrs wkly *No. News Employees:* 2
Ed Grant, General Manager

*WHBP
90.1 mhz FM; 1.2 kw; 1004 ft.; N45 30 8 W85 1 44
US
(231) 276-4400, *Fax:* (231) 276-4417
www.interlochen.org/ipr
License: Harbor Springs, Emmet County, MI held by Interlochen Center for the Arts.
Arbitron Metro Market: Harbor Springs, MI
Thom Paulson, General Manager

Harrietta

WKAD
01-01-2003; 93.7 mhz FM; 4.3 kw; Ant 390 ft; N44 16 41 W85 35 28
Box 520, Cadillac, MI 49412
(231) 775-1263, *Fax:* (231) 779-2844
www.cadillacoldies.com
License: Harrietta, Wexford County, MI held by Cadillac Broadcasting LLC
Population Served: 14,894 *Arbitron Metro Market:* Traverse City, MI
Trish Garber, CEO
Rich Spicer, Programming Director

Harrison

*WBHL
90.7 mhz FM; 100 w; Ant 98 ft; N44 01 02 W84 47 56
Box 549, Harrison, MI
(989) 539-7105
License: Harrison, Clare County, MI held by The Country King Inc.
David Carmine, President

Harrisville

*WSFP
01-01-2006; 88.1 mhz FM; 0.48 kw; 472 ft.; N45 3 50 W83 42 57 *Rebroadcasts:* Simulcasts WJOM(FM) Eagle 100%
US
(888) 887-7139
www.smile.fm
411@smile.fm
License: Harrisville, Montmorency County, MI held by Michigan Community Radio.
Arbitron Metro Market: Harrisville, MI *Format:* Christian
Edward Czelada, President
Dale Mazzoline, Feature Production
Ed Czelada, Administration, Programming & Engineering
Clayton Hewitt, Administration and Engineering
Aaron Burrell, Administration

Hart

WWKR
07-01-1995; 94.1 mhz FM *Hrs Open:* 24; 5 kw; 682 ft.; N43 40 34 W86 14 20
P O Box 855, Ludington, MI 49431 US
(231) 843-0941, *Fax:* (231) 843-9411
www.94k-rock.com
License: Hart, Oceana County, MI held by Synergy Media Inc.
Nat'l Network: AP Network News *Nat'l Reps:* Michigan Spot Sales *Regional Reps:* Michigan Spot Sales
Arbitron Metro Market: Mason, MI *Format:* Classic Rock *Hrs. of News Programming:* news progmg 2 hrs wkly *Target Audience:* 25-54; baby boomers
Todd Mohr, President
Stacy Johnson, Operations Dir
Tom Green, Chief Engineer

Hartford

WCXT
10-31-1981; 98.3 mhz FM; 3.7 kw; 427 ft.; N42 15 14 W86 20 9
Mailing Address: P O Box 107, St. Joseph, MI 49085 US
Second Address: 580 E. Napier Ave., Benton Harbor, MI 49022
(269) 925-1111, *Fax:* (269) 925-1011
www.thecoast.fm
paul@975ycountry.com
License: Hartford, Van Buren County, MI held by WSJM Inc.
Group Owner: The Mid-West Family Broadcast Group; (acq 10-95; with WCSY(AM) South Haven)
Arbitron Metro Market: Hartford, MI *Format:* Adult Contemp
Gayle Olson, President
Paul Layendecker, Operations Dir
Dave Doetsch, General Manager
Bob Bucholtz, General Sales Mgr
Mark Durocher, Programming Director
Sue Patzer, Promotions Manager
Jim Gifford, News Director

Hastings

WBCH
11-01-1957; 1220 khz AM *Hrs Open:* 24
Mailing Address: P. O. Box 88, 119 W. State Street, Hastings, MI 49058 US
Second Address: 119 W. State St., Hastings, MI 49058
(301) 759-1005, *Fax:* (301) 759-3124
www.cumberlandsmagic.com
License: Hastings, MI held by Barry Broadcasting Co.
Regional Network: Mich. Farm *Regional Reps:* Patt. *Wire Services:* NOAA Weather
Arbitron Metro Market: Spencer IA *Format:* Adult Contemp *Adv. Rates:* 18; 14; 18; 10
Dale Miller, President
Jerry Hannahs, Promotions Manager

WBCH-FM
12-01-1967; 100.1 mhz FM *Hrs Open:* 24; 3 kw; 295 ft.; N42 37 34 W85 16 41
P. O. Box 88, 119 W State Street, Hastings, MI 49058 US
(970) 920-9600, *Fax:* (970) 544-5239
www.aspenglenwood.com
sales@aspenglenwood.com
License: Hastings, Barry County, MI
Nat'l Network: ABC *Wire Services:* NOAA Weather
Arbitron Metro Market: Billings MT *Format:* Easy Listening
Marcos Rodriguez, General Manager

Hemlock

WCEN-FM
08-08-1963; 94.5 mhz FM; 100 kw; 981 ft.; N43 43 36 W84 36 16
2929 S. Isabella Rd., Mt. Pleasant, MI 48858 US

(989) 752-3456, *Fax:* (989) 754-5046
www.945themoose.com
info@945themoose.com
License: Hemlock, Saginaw County, MI held by NM Licensing LLC.
Group Owner: NextMedia Group Inc.; (acq 12-30-02; grpsl).
Wire Services: Metro Weather Service Inc.
Arbitron Metro Market: Saginaw-Bay City-Midland, MI *Format:* Country *Target Audience:* 25-54; medium income, rural & urban
Shannone Dunlap, Operations Dir
Joby Phyllis, Programming Director

Highland Park

*WHPR-FM
05-21-1954; 88.1 mhz FM *Hrs Open:* 24; 0.012 kw; 105 ft.; N42 24 29 W83 5 30
15851 Woodward Avenue, Highland Park, MI 48203 US
(313) 868-6612, *Fax:* (313) 868-8725
www.whprradio.com
tv68whpr@aol.com
License: Highland Park, Wayne County, MI held by R.J.s Late Night Entertainment Corp.
Format: Oldies, Talk *Target Audience:* 21 & over; African Americans 40 plus politically aware & motivated
R. J. Watkins, Operations Dir
Henry Tyler, Vice President

Hillman

WKJZ
12-01-1993; 94.9 mhz FM; 50 kw; 492 ft.; N45 1 15 W83 55 21
Rebroadcasts: Rebroadcasts WQLB(FM) Tawas City 85%
P.O. Box 549, Tawas City, MI 48764 US
(989) 362-3417, *Fax:* (989) 362-4544
www.wkjc.com
wkjc@wkjc.com
License: Hillman, Montmorency County, MI held by Carroll Enterprises Inc.
Group Owner: Carroll Enterprises Inc.; acq 6-29-92;
Format: Classic Rock
John Carroll Jr., General Manager

Hillsdale

WCSR
05-21-1959; 1340 khz AM; 0.5 kw-D, ND1; 0.25 kw-N, ND1; N41 55 41 W84 38 10 *Rebroadcasts:* Simulcast with WCSR-FM Hillsdale 98%
Mailing Address: 170 North West Street, Hillsdale, MI 49242 US
Second Address: 170 N. West St., Hillsdale, MI 49242
(517) 437-4444, *Fax:* (517) 437-7461
www.radiohillsdale.com
wcsrinc@comcast.net
License: Hillsdale, MI held by WCSR Inc.
Regional Network: Mich. Farm
Arbitron Metro Market: Hillsdale, MI *Format:* Adult Contemp
Special Programming: Farm 3 hrs, relg 10 hrs wkly *Target Audience:* 25 plus; county-wide
Anthony Flynn, President
Michael Flynn, General Manager

WCSR-FM
05-19-1973; 92.1 mhz FM; 6 kw; 243 ft.; N41 55 41 W84 38 10
Mailing Address: 170 N. West St, Box 273, Hillsdale, MI 49242 US
Second Address: 170 N. West St., Hillsdale, MI 49242
(517) 437-4444, *Fax:* 517) 437-7461
www.radiohillsdale.com
wcsrinc@comcast.net
License: Hillsdale, Hillsdale County, MI
Arbitron Metro Market: Hillsdale, MI
Brian Lamb, CEO
Kate Mills, General Manager

Holland

WHTC
07-31-1948; 1450 khz AM *Hrs Open:* 24; 1 kw-U, ND1; N42 47 41 W86 6 22
87 Central Ave., Holland, MI 49423 US
(616) 392-3121, *Fax:* (616) 392-8066
www.whtc.com
whtc@whtc.com
License: Holland, MI held by Midwest Communications Inc.
Group Owner: Midwest Communications Inc.; (acq 8-1-00; grpsl).
Nat'l Network: CBS *Nat'l Reps:* Christal
Arbitron Metro Market: Grand Rapids, MI *Format:* News, News/Talk, 86 *Special Programming:* Sp 3 hrs wkly *Hrs. of News Programming:* news progmg 15 hrs wkly *No. News Employees:* 1 *Target Audience:* 35 plus.*Adv. Rates:* 25; 20; 20; 15
Duke Wright, President
Peter Tanz, General Manager
Kevin Oswald, General Sales Mgr
Brent Alan, Programming Director
Gary Stevens, News Director

WTNR
03-21-1961; 94.5 mhz FM *Hrs Open:* 24; 50 kw; 499 ft.; N42 51 20 W85 57 45
P.O. Box 8, Bloomington, IL 61702 US
(616) 774-8461, *Fax:* (616) 774-2491
www.thunder945.com
info@thunder945.com
License: Holland, Ottawa County, MI
Group Owner: Cumulus Media Inc.; (acq 4-26-2001; grpsl).
Nat'l Network: ABC *Nat'l Reps:* Katz Radio
Arbitron Metro Market: Grand Rapids, MI *Format:* Country *Target Audience:* 18-34; men
Matt Hanlon, General Manager
Jeff Morton, General Sales Mgr
Kate Conley, General Sales Manager

*WTHS
10-15-1984; 89.9 mhz FM *Hrs Open:* 24; 1 kw; 154 ft; N42 47 16 W86 06 02
Box 9000, Hope College, Holland, MI 49423
(616) 395-7878,(616) 395-7880, *Fax:* (616) 395-7958
http://wths.hope.edu
wths@hope.edu
License: Holland, Ottawa County, MI held by Hope College Board of Trustees.
Hrs. of News Programming: News progmg 7 hrs wkly *Target Audience:* 15-30; students & adults
Richard Forrest Dodson, General Manager
Matt Costello, Program Director/Co-Music Director
Sara Sanchez, Co-Music Director
Christopher Rodriguez, Co-Music Director
Michael Kroneman, Business & Underwriting Director
Carolyn Wermuth,Business & Underwriting Director
Christopher Beaudoin, Web Director
Carter Jones, Co-News Director
Tom Zahari, Co-News Director
William DeBoer, Production Director

WMAX-FM
09-01-1962; 96.1 mhz FM *Hrs Open:* 24; 50 kw horiz, 45 kw vert; 492 ft.; N42 49 10 W85 52 9
200 Concord Plaza, Suite 600, San Antonio, TX 78216 US
(616) 459-1919, *Fax:* (616) 235-9600
www.961maxfm.com
brucelaw@clearchannel.com
License: Holland, Ottawa County, MI held by CC Licenses LLC.
Group Owner: Clear Channel Communications Inc.; (acq 1-27-2009)
Nat'l Reps: Clear Channel
Arbitron Metro Market: Grand Rapids, MI *Format:* Adult Contemp
Target Audience: 25-34; women
Skip Essick, Operations Dir
Tim Feagan, General Manager
Henry Capogna, General Sales Mgr
Tony Brooks, Programming Director
Doug Montgomery, Operations Manager
Michele Johnson, Business Manager
Bruce Law, Director of Sales

Holt

WLCM
08-25-1956; 1390 khz AM *Hrs Open:* 24 Hours; 5 kw-D, 4.5 kw-N, DA-D; N42 34 02 W84 51 58 (day), N42 33 07 W84 33 05 (night)
Mailing Address: Box 338, Charlotte, MI 48439
Second Address: 1613 W. Lawrence, Charlotte, MI 48813
(517) 543-8200, *Fax:* (517) 543-7779
www.wlcmradio.com
jeff.frank@cbslradio.com
License: Holt, Ingham County, MI held by Christian Broadcasting System Ltd.
Group Owner: Christian Broadcasting System Ltd.; (acq 1-5-93; assumption of land contract;
Population Served: 700,000 *Arbitron Metro Market:* Lansing-East Lansing, MI *Special Programming:* Gospel 3 hrs wkly *Hrs. of News Programming:* News progmg 2 hrs wkly
Target Audience: 25-55; general
Jon Yinger, CEO
Evelyn Shaw, Operations Dir
Jeff Frank, General Manager

Holton

WVIB
01-01-1971; 100.1 mhz FM; 2.9 kw; 472 ft.; N43 18 50 W86 9 17
517 North Beebe Street, Fremont, MI 49412 US
(231) 830-0176, *Fax:* (231) 830-0194
www.v100fm.com
License: Holton, Muskegon County, MI
Group Owner: Cumulus Media Inc.; (acq 9-28-2005)
Arbitron Metro Market: Muskegon, MI *Format:* Urban Contemporary
Jon Russell, Operations Dir
Rich Berry, General Sales Mgr
Scott Meier, Market Manager

Honor

WSRJ
01-01-2002; 105.5 mhz FM; 17 kw; 367 ft.; N44 39 41 W85 48 53
Rebroadcasts: Rebroadcasts WSRT(FM) Gaylord 75%
2215 Oak Indust. Dr. Ne, Grand Rapids, MI 49505 US
(231) 947-0003, *Fax:* (231) 947-7002
ww.itm2057.com
programming@1067wsrt.com
License: Honor, Benzie County, MI held by Northern Radio of Michigan Inc.
Arbitron Metro Market: Grand Rapids, MI *Format:* Classic Rock
Charlie Ferguson, General Manager

Houghton

WCCY
01-01-1929; 1400 khz AM *Hrs Open:* 24; 1 kw-U, ND1; N47 8 6 W88 33 53
313 Montezuma Avenue, Houghton, MI 49931 US
(906) 482-7700, *Fax:* (906) 482-7751
www.wccy.com
jharju@up.net
License: Houghton, MI held by Heartland Comm. Houghton License LLC.
Group Owner: Heartland Communications Group LLC; (acq 1-6-2005; grpsl).
Nat'l Network: ABC; ESPN Radio; Jones Radio Networks
Regional Network: Mich. Radio *Nat'l Reps:* Michigan Spot Sales
Arbitron Metro Market: Houghton, MI *Format:* Sports, Adult Contemp *Special Programming:* Relg one hr, pub affrs one hr wkly *Hrs. of News Programming:* news progmg 18 hrs wkly *No. News Employees:* 1 *TargetAudience:* 35+.
Chuck Sebastian, Operations Dir
Jeff Harju, General Manager

*WGGL-FM
02-01-1982; 91.1 mhz FM *Hrs Open:* 24; 100 kw; 860 ft.; N47 2 8 W88 41 43
45 East 7th Street, Saint Paul, MN 55101 US
(651) 290-1500, *Fax:* (651) 290-1224
www.minnesota.publicradio.org
info@minnesota.publicradio.org
License: Houghton, Houghton County, MI held by Minnesota Public Radio Inc.
Nat'l Network: PRI; NPR *Regional Network:* Minn. Pub. Radio
Format: News *No. News Employees:* 1 *Target Audience:* General.
William Kling, President
Erik Nycklemoe, Operations Dir
Larissa Anderson, Assistant Producer
Sasha Aslanian, Producer/Reporter
Elizabeth Baier, Reporter

WHKB
09-01-1989; 102.3 mhz FM; 6 kw; 548 ft.; N47 8 6 W88 33 53
815-12 Marlowe Road, Raleigh, NC 27609 US
(906) 482-7700, *Fax:* (906) 482-7751
www.kbear102.com
License: Houghton, Houghton County, MI held by Heartland Comm. Houghton License LLC.
Group Owner: Heartland Communications Group LLC; (acq 1-6-2005; grpsl).
Nat'l Network: ABC; Jones Radio Networks *Regional Network:* Mich. Radio *Nat'l Reps:* Michigan Spot Sales
Format: Country *Hrs. of News Programming:* news progmg 18 hrs/week *No. News Employees:* 1 *Target Audience:* 25-54.
Chuck Sebastian, Operations Dir
John Speeney, General Manager
Betsy Ely, News Director

*WMTU-FM
01-26-1994; 91.9 mhz FM; 0 kw horiz, 4.4 kw vert; 479 ft.; N47 8 27 W88 32 26
West Wadsworth Hall Mtu, Houghton, MI 49931 US
(906) 487-2333, *Fax:* (906) 487-3016
www.wmtu.mtu.edu
wmtu@mtu.edu
License: Houghton, Houghton County, MI held by Michigan Technological University.
Arbitron Metro Market: Houghton, MI *Format:* Variety/Diverse

George Olszewski, General Manager
Lindsay Worden, Station Manager
Matt Derucki, Programming Director
Dea Occhietti, Promotions Manager
Josh Martin, Chief Engineer

WOLV
03-07-1980; 97.7 mhz FM; 6.5 kw; 591 ft.; N47 8 6 W88 33 53
313 Montezuma Ave., Houghton, MI 49931 US
(906) 482-7700, *Fax:* (906) 482-7751
www.thewolf.com
License: Houghton, Houghton County, MI
Group Owner: Heartland Communications Group LLC
Nat'l Network: ABC; Jones Radio Networks *Regional Network:* Mich. Radio *Nat'l Reps:* Michigan Spot Sales
TV Affiliate: Classic Hits *Special Programming:* news prgmg 18 hrs/week *Hrs. of News Programming:* 1 *No. News Employees:* 25-54.
General Manager, General Manager
Programming Director, Programming Director

Houghton Lake

WTWS
03-26-1975; 92.1 mhz FM *Hrs Open:* 24; 0.92 kw; 748 ft.; N44 17 21 W84 44 32
209 E. Spruce St., PO Box 549, Harrison, MI 48625 US
(989) 366-5364, *Fax:* (989) 366-6200
www.921thetwister.com
License: Houghton Lake, Clare County, MI held by Coltrace Communications Inc.
Format: Country
Michael Jay, General Manager

WUPS
07-01-1961; 98.5 mhz FM *Hrs Open:* 24; 100 kw; Ant 981 ft; N44 17 18 W84 44 30
Box 468, Prudenville, MI 48651
(989) 366-5364, *Fax:* (989) 366-6200
www.wups.com
wupsfm@yahoo.com
License: Houghton Lake, Roscommon County, MI held by Coltrace Communications Inc.
Nat'l Network: ABC *Nat'l Reps:* Rgnl Reps
Population Served: 200,000*Hrs. of News Programming:* news progmg 6 hrs wkly *No. News Employees:* 1 *Target Audience:* 25-54; general
Sindy Fuller, President
Sindy Fuller, Operations Dir
Tammy Thompson, Station Manager
Sindy Fuller, General Sales Mgr
Michael Bonomo, Programming Director
Michael Bonomo, Promotions Manager
Michael Bonomo, News Director
CraigBowman, Engineering Dir
Craig Bowman, Chief Engineer

Howell

WHMI-FM
09-01-1977; 93.5 mhz FM *Hrs Open:* 24; 5.2 kw; 354 ft.; N42 39 47 W83 56 23
Mailing Address: P.O. Box 935, Howell, MI 48844 US
Second Address: 1277 Parkway Dr., Howell, MI 48843
(517) 546-0860, *Fax:* (517) 546-1758
www.whmi.com
whmi@whmi.com
License: Howell, Livingston County, MI held by The Livingston Radio Co.
Nat'l Network: CNN Radio *Nat'l Reps:* Michigan Spot Sales
Arbitron Metro Market: Detroit *Format:* Contemporary Hits/Top 40, Adult Contemp *Hrs. of News Programming:* news progmg 10 hrs wkly *No. News Employees:* 3 *Target Audience:* 25-64.
Marcia Jablonski, CEO
Reed Kittredge, Operations Dir
Greg Jablonski, General Manager
Debbie Platt, General Sales Mgr

Hudson

WBZV
03-01-1995; 102.5 mhz FM *Hrs Open:* 24; 6 kw; 328 ft.; N41 53 3 W84 31 24
121 W. Maumee Street, Adrian, MI 49221 US
(517) 265-9500, *Fax:* (517) 263-4525
friends@tc3net.com
License: Hudson, Lenawee County, MI held by Friends Communications of Hudson Inc.
Group Owner: Friends Communications Inc.
Nat'l Network: ABC *Nat'l Reps:* Michigan Spot Sales
Arbitron Metro Market: Hudson, MI *Format:* Classic Rock *Hrs. of News Programming:* news progmg 6 hrs wkly *No. News Employees:* 1 *Target Audience:* 25-54.
Bob Elliot, Chairman

Imlay City

***WDTR**
12-01-2000; 89.1 mhz FM; 1.5 kw; Ant 171 ft; N43 03 42 W83 05 44
Michigan Community Radio, Box 388, Williamston, MI 48444
(810) 721-0891, *Fax:* (413) 410-9708
www.positivehits.com
info@joyfm.net
License: Imlay City, Lapeer County, MI held by Michigan Community Radio.
Jenn Czelada, General Manager
Ed Czelada, Programming Director

Indian River

WMKC
02-08-1982; 102.9 mhz FM; 100 kw; 1102 ft.; N45 30 8 W85 1 44
232 Front Street, No. 2, Traverse City, MI 49684 US
(231) 627-2341, *Fax:* (231) 627-7000
www.1029bigcountry.com
License: Indian River, Mackinac County, MI
Group Owner: Northern Star Broadcasting L.L.C.
Arbitron Metro Market: Traverse City, MI *Format:* Country
Chris Monk, Operations Dir

Inkster

WDRJ
11-01-1956; 1440 khz AM *Hrs Open:* 24
1514 East Jefferson Ave, Detroit, MI 48207 US
(313) 871-1440, *Fax:* (313) 871-6088
www.1440wdrj.com
1440@communicom.com
License: Inkster, MI held by Davidson Media Station WMKM Licensee LLC.
Group Owner: Davidson Media Group LLC; (acq 5-28-2004; $5.75 million)
Arbitron Metro Market: Detroit, MI *Format:* Religious *Target Audience:* 35 plus; adult Black church audience
Rich Kylberg, President
Raymond Burkhart, General Manager
Carl Dimaria, General Sales Mgr

Interlochen

***WIAA**
07-22-1963; 88.7 mhz FM *Hrs Open:* 24; 100 kw; 1033 ft.; N44 16 33 W85 42 49
Mailing Address: PO Box 199, Interlochen, MI 49643 US
Second Address: One Lyon St., Interlochen, MI 49643
(231) 276-4400, *Fax:* (231) 276-4417
www.interlochen.org/ipr
ipr@interlochen.org
License: Interlochen, Grand Traverse County, MI held by Interlochen Center for the Arts.
Nat'l Network: NPR; PRI
Arbitron Metro Market: Traverse City-Petoskey, MI *Format:* Classical, News *Target Audience:* 35-80; professional, arts-oriented, upper-income
Thom Paulson, Operations Dir

Ionia

WION
02-01-1953; 1430 khz AM *Hrs Open:* 24
12110 Wabash Road, 12110 Wabash Road, Milan, MI 48160 US
(616) 527-9466, *Fax:* (616) 775-5908
www.i1430.com
office@i1430.com
License: Ionia, MI held by Packer Radio WION LLC
Nat'l Network: CNN Radio; Sporting News Radio Network
Regional Network: Mich. Radio
Arbitron Metro Market: Grand Rapids, MI *Format:* Variety/Diverse *No. News Employees:* 1
Jim ""Carlyle"" Angus, CEO
Jim Carlyle, General Manager
Jim Aaron, Programming Director
Jim Aaron, Co-owner and Disc Jockey
Garry Osborn, Disc Jockey
Phil Cloud, Disc Jokcey and Account Representative
Dan Ferguson, SalesRepresentative
Scott Beetman, Engineer

Iron Mountain

WIMK
12-27-1981; 93.1 mhz FM *Hrs Open:* 24; 100 kw; 591 ft.; N45 49 16 W88 2 28 *Rebroadcasts:* Rebroadcasts WUPK-FM Marquette 100%
980 North Michigan Ave, Suite 1880, Chicago, IL 60611 US
(906) 774-4321, *Fax:* (906) 774-7799
rockthebear.com
thebear@uplogon.com
License: Iron Mountain, Dickinson County, MI held by Northern Star Broadcasting L.L.C.
Group Owner: Northern Star Broadcasting L.L.C.; acq 11-5-01; grpsl).
Format: Classic Rock, Rock/AOR *No. News Employees:* 1
Target Audience: 25-54. *Adv. Rates:* 20; 17.50; 15; 10
Steve Ponchaud, Operations Dir
Veronica Roberts, General Manager
Tom Hill, News Director
Coral Howe, Chief Engineer
Michelle Ellsworth, Traffic Manager

WJNR-FM
08-17-1972; 101.5 mhz FM; 100 kw; 614 ft.; N45 49 16 W88 2 34
PO Box 1062, Iron Mountain, MI 49801 US
(906) 774-5731, *Fax:* (906) 774-4542
www.frogcountry.com
peterson.trisha@gmail.com
License: Iron Mountain, Dickinson County, MI held by Results Broadcasting of Michigan Inc.
Group Owner: Results Broadcasting; (acq 6-5-97).
Nat'l Network: ABC
Format: Country *Target Audience:* 25-54.
Bruce Grassman, President
Keith Huotari, Operations Dir
Trisha Peterson, General Manager
Aaron Harper, News Director
Walt Baldwin, Chief Engineer

WMIQ
01-01-1947; 1450 khz AM *Hrs Open:* 24; 1 kw-U, ND1; N45 49 16 W88 3 16
980 North Michigan Ave, Suite 1880, Chicago, IL 60611 US
(906) 774-4321, *Fax:* (906) 774-7799
talk1450wmiq@uplogon.com
License: Iron Mountain, MI held by Northern Star Broadcasting L.L.C.
Group Owner: Northern Star Broadcasting L.L.C.
Nat'l Network: USA *Nat'l Reps:* Patt
Arbitron Metro Market: Iron Mountain, MI *Format:* News, News/Talk, 84, Talk *Hrs. of News Programming:* news progmg 24 hrs wkly *No. News Employees:* 1 *Target Audience:* 35-64; educated, middle to upper incomelisteners *Adv. Rates:* Same as FM
Kevin Richtig, Programming Director

***WVCM**
91.5 mhz FM *Hrs Open:* 24; 0.5 kw vert; 600 ft.; N45 49 15 W88 2 25
3434 West Kilbourn Ave, Milwaukee, WI 53208 US
(414) 935-3000, *Fax:* (414) 935-3015
www.vcyamerica.org
vcy@vcyamerica.org
License: Iron Mountain, Dickinson County, MI held by VCY America Inc.
Group Owner: VCY America Inc.
Arbitron Metro Market: Milwaukee, WI *Format:* Christian
Randall Melchert, President
Vic Eliason, Operations Dir
Jim Schneider, Programming Director

WHTO
01-01-2003; 106.7 mhz FM; 6.1 kw; 676 ft.; N45 49 16 W88 2 34
400 East Maple, Fremont, MI 49412 US
(906) 774-5731, *Fax:* (906) 774-4542
www.1067themountain.com
peterson.trisha@gmail.com
License: Iron Mountain, Dickinson County, MI held by Results Broadcasting of Iron Mountain Inc.
Group Owner: Results Broadcasting; (acq 6-29-2005; $650,000)
Nat'l Network: ABC
Arbitron Metro Market: Iron Mountain, MI *Format:* Oldies
Trisha Peterson, General Manager

Iron River

WFER
11-18-1949; 1230 khz AM *Hrs Open:* 5 AM-11 PM; 1 kw-U; N46 03 55 W88 38 17
Box AC, 809 W. Genesee St., Iron River, MI 49935
(906) 265-5104, *Fax:* (906) 265-3486
wikb@sbcglobal.net

License: Iron River, Iron County, MI held by Heartland Communications License LLC.
Group Owner: Heartland Communications Group LLC; (acq 5-10-2004; $1.25 million with co-located FM)
Nat'l Reps: Roslin
Population Served: 20,000*Hrs. of News Programming:* news progmg 15 hrs wkly *No. News Employees:* 1 *Target Audience:* General.
Jay Barry, General Manager
Margaret Henschel, General Sales Mgr
Jeff Bonno, Chief Engineer

WIKB-FM
09-25-1981; 99.1 mhz FM *Hrs Open:* 5 AM-11 PM; 60 kw; 492 ft.; N46 6 3 W88 32 23
Mailing Address: P. O. Box Ac, Iron River, MI 49935 US
Second Address: 809 W. Genesee St., Iron River, MI 49935
(906) 265-5104, *Fax:* (906) 265-3486
www.wikb.com
wikb@sbcglobal.net
License: Iron River, Iron County, MI held by Heartland Communications License LLC.
Group Owner: Heartland Communications Group LLC
Format: Adult Contemp
Kirk Tollett, General Manager
Scott Humphrey, News Director
Jennifer Tollett, Traffic Manager

Ironwood

WIMI
03-01-1976; 99.7 mhz FM; 100 kw; 561 ft.; N46 25 25 W90 14 53
120 S, Mill Street, Merrill, WI 54452 US
(906) 932-2411, *Fax:* (906) 932-2485
www.wimifm.com
wimi@broadcast.net
License: Ironwood, Gogebic County, MI held by Magellan Broadcasting LLC.
Format: Adult Contemp
Scott Meier, Operations Dir
Stan Parman, Programming Director
Bob Friedle, Chief Engineer
Hal Maas, Music Director

WJMS
11-03-1931; 590 khz AM *Hrs Open:* 24; 5 kw-D, DAN; 1 kw-N, DAN; N46 25 25 W90 12 30
120 S. Mill Street, Merrill, WI 54452 US
(906) 932-2411, *Fax:* (906) 932-2485
www.wjmsam.com
wimi@broadcast.net
License: Ironwood, MI held by Magellan Broadcasting LLC.
Nat'l Network: CBS *Nat'l Reps:* D & R Radio
Format: Country, Talk *No. News Employees:* 1 *Target Audience:* 25 plus.
David Winters, President
Frede Falls, Programming Director

WUPM
10-17-1977; 106.9 mhz FM; 53 kw; 495 ft.; N46 28 18 W90 0 43
209 Harrison Street, Ironwood, MI 49938 US
(906) 932-5234, *Fax:* (906) 932-1548
www.wupm-whry.com
License: Ironwood, Gogebic County, MI held by Big G Little O Inc.
Nat'l Network: ABC
Arbitron Metro Market: Ironwood, MI *Format:* Adult Contemp
Charles Gervasio, President
Laura Keller, Programming Director

***WKIW**
01-01-2008; 88.3 mhz FM; 300 w vert; Ant 515 ft; N46 26 28 W90 11 26 *Rebroadcasts:* Rebroadcasts KLVR(FM) Middletown, CA 100%
2351 Sunset Blvd., Suite 170-218, Rocklin, CA 38104
(916) 251-1600, *Fax:* (916) 251-1650
www.klove.com
License: Ironwood, Gogebic County, MI held by Educational Media Foundation.
Group Owner: EMF Broadcasting; (acq 7-23-2007; grpsl)
Nat'l Network: K-Love
Mike Novak, President

Ishpeming

WIAN
01-01-1947; 1240 khz AM
980 North Michigan Avenue, Suite 1880, Chicago, IL 60611 US
(906) 225-1313, *Fax:* (906) 225-1324
info@wjpd.com
License: Ishpeming, MI held by Northern Star Broadcasting L.L.C.
Group Owner: Northern Star Broadcasting L.L.C.; (acq 11-5-2001; grpsl)
Format: News, News/Talk, 86
Tammy Johnson, General Manager
Ariane Kachmarsky, Programming Director
John Focke, News Director
Coral Howe, Chief Engineer

WJPD
05-15-1975; 92.3 mhz FM; 100 kw; 509 ft.; N46 30 51 W87 28 58
980 North Michigan Avenue, Suite 1880, Chicago, IL 60611 US
(906) 225-1313, *Fax:* (906) 225-1324
www.wjpd.com
info@wjpd.com
License: Ishpeming, Marquette County, MI held by Northern Star Broadcasting L.L.C.
Group Owner: Northern Star Broadcasting L.L.C.
Wire Services: UPI
Format: Country
Austin Davis, Programming Director
Sherry Flick, News Director
Jill Gleeson, Disc Jockey
Kenny Marks, Disc Jockey
Laura Mack, Disc Jockey
Tor Michaels, News Reporter

WMQT-FM
01-26-1974; 107.7 mhz FM *Hrs Open:* 24; 98 kw; 639 ft.; N46 30 8 W87 38 52
P.O. Box 467, Ishpeming, MI 49849 US
(906) 225-9100, *Fax:* (906) 225-5577
www.wmqt.com
tom@wmqt.com
License: Ishpeming, Marquette County, MI held by Taconite Broadcasting Inc.
Arbitron Metro Market: Ishpeming, MI *Format:* Adult Contemp
No. News Employees: 1 *Target Audience:* 18-49.
Tom Mogush, General Manager
Carol Keast, News Director
Casey Ford, Sports Commentator

WZAM
06-26-1959; 970 khz AM *Hrs Open:* 24; 5 kw-D, ND2; 0.062 kw-N, ND2; N46 30 20 W87 32 24
PO Box467, Ishpeming, MI 49849 US
(906) 225-9100, *Fax:* (906) 225-5577
www.espn970.com
tom@wmqt.com
License: Ishpeming, MI held by Taconite Broadcasting Inc.
Nat'l Network: ESPN Radio
Arbitron Metro Market: Ishpeming, MI *Format:* Sports, Talk *No. News Employees:* 1 *Target Audience:* 25-54.
Tom Mogush, General Manager
Jim Koski, Programming Director
Casey Ford, News Director

Jackson

WIBM
01-01-1925; 1450 khz AM *Hrs Open:* 24
915 Riverside Avenue, Adrian, MI 49221 US
(517) 787-9546, *Fax:* (517) 787-7517
www.espnradio1450.com
mdaly@wkhm.com
License: Jackson, MI held by Jackson Radio Works Inc.
Group Owner: Jackson Radio Works Inc.; acq 11-14-97; grpsl)
Nat'l Network: ESPN Radio *Regional Reps:* Michigan Spot Sales
Format: Sports *Special Programming:* Polish, Spanish *Hrs. of News Programming:* news progmg one hr wkly *No. News Employees:* 2 *Target Audience:* 18-49; sports enthusiasts
Bruce Goldsen, President
Sue Goldsen, Operations Dir
Jamie McKibbin, Station Manager
Marc Daly, Programming Director
Michael Bradford, Chief Engineer

***WJKN**
01-01-1962; 1510 khz AM; 5 kw-D, DAD; N42 11 10 W84 22 39
P.O. Box 468, Prudenville, MI 48651 US
(517) 750-9723, *Fax:* (517) 750-6619
info@home.fm
License: Jackson, MI held by Spring Arbor University
Nat'l Network: CBS; Westwood One *Nat'l Reps:* Patt
Arbitron Metro Market: Lansing-East Lansing, MI *Format:* Religious
Carl Fletcher, General Manager
Dave Benson, Chief Engineer

WKHM
12-07-1951; 970 khz AM *Hrs Open:* 24; 1 kw-D, DA2; 1 kw-N, DA2; N42 11 39 W84 25 50
915 Riverside Avenue, Adrian, MI 49221 US
(517) 787-9546, *Fax:* (517) 787-7517
www.wkhm.com
mdaly@wkhm.com
License: Jackson, MI held by Jackson Radio Works Inc.
Group Owner: Jackson Radio Works Inc.; acq 12-8-97; grpsl).
Nat'l Network: ABC *Regional Network:* Mich. Radio *Regional Reps:* Mich. Spot Sales
Format: News, News/Talk, 86 *Hrs. of News Programming:* news progmg 15 hrs wkly *No. News Employees:* 1 *Target Audience:* 25-64.
Bruce Goldsen, President
Sue Goldsen, Operations Dir
Jamie McKibbin, Station Manager
Marc Daly, Programming Director
Kathy Beauchamp, News Director
Michael Bradford, Chief Engineer
Deanna Stocker, Sales Director

WVIC
01-01-1955; 94.1 mhz FM; 40 kw; Ant 551 ft; N42 23 32 W84 40 00
2495 N. Cedar, Holt, MI 48823
(517) 699-0111, *Fax:* (517) 699-1880
www.wvic.net
License: Jackson, Jackson County, MI held by Midwest Communications Inc.
Group Owner: Rubber City Radio Group Inc.; (acq 7-1-2010; grpsl)
Nat'l Reps: Katz Radio *Wire Services:* AP
Population Served: 864,300 *Arbitron Metro Market:* Lansing-East Lansing, MI *Hrs. of News Programming:* news progmg 17.5 hrs wkly *No. News Employees:* 1 *Target Audience:* 25-54; female 25-49 *Adv. Rates:* 50;50; 50; 30
Paul Cashin, Operations Dir
Dave Johnson, General Manager
Scott Truman, General Sales Mgr

Kalamazoo

***WAYK**
02-03-1997; 88.3 mhz FM *Hrs Open:* 24; 10 kw vert; 397 ft.; N42 18 23 W85 39 25
1001 E. Beltline Ave. Ne, Grand Rapids, MI 49505 US
(877) 702-9293, *Fax:* (719) 278-4339
www.kxwy.wayfm.com
supportservices@wayfm.com
License: Kalamazoo, Kalamazoo County, MI held by Cornerstone University.
Arbitron Metro Market: Rye CO *Format:* Christian
Robert Augsburg, President

***WIDR**
07-07-1975; 89.1 mhz FM *Hrs Open:* 24; 0.1 kw; 187 ft.; N42 16 55 W85 37 5
West Michigan Avenue, Kalamazoo, MI 49008 US
(269) 387-6301, *Fax:* (269) 387-2839
www.widr.org
info@widr.org
License: Kalamazoo, Kalamazoo County, MI held by Western Michigan University Board of Trustees.
Arbitron Metro Market: Kalamazoo, MI *Format:* Variety/Diverse *Hrs. of News Programming:* News progmg 7 hrs wkly *Target Audience:* 18-25; college students
Andrew Grabowski, General Manager
Mallory Dowd, Programming Director

***WKDS**
10-01-1982; 89.9 mhz FM *Hrs Open:* 24; 0.14 kw; 125 ft.; N42 14 36 W85 34 19
606 East Kilgore Road, Kalamazoo, MI 49001 US
(269) 343-2211, *Fax:* (269) 343-3710
www.wkds.4t.com
operations@cactv.org
License: Kalamazoo, Kalamazoo County, MI held by Kalamazoo Board of Education.
Arbitron Metro Market: Kalamazoo, MI *Format:* Variety/Diverse *Hrs. of News Programming:* News progmg 3 hrs wkly *Target Audience:* High school & college students.
Mark Monk, Operations Dir

WKMI
08-01-1947; 1360 khz AM *Hrs Open:* 24
330 East Kilbourn Ave., Suite 250, Milwaukee, WI 53202 US
(269) 344-0111, *Fax:* (269) 344-4223
www.wkmi.com
radio@wkmi.com
License: Kalamazoo, MI held by Cumulus Licensing Corp.
Group Owner: Cumulus Media Inc.; (acq 5-26-98; grpsl)
Arbitron Metro Market: Kalamazoo, MI *Format:* News, News/Talk, 86 *Special Programming:* Sports *Hrs. of News Programming:* news progmg 30 hrs wkly *No. News Employees:* 1 *Target Audience:* 25 plus.

Lew Dickey, CEO
Mike McKelly, Operations Dir
Rob Wagley, General Manager
Bill Anthony, Programming Director
Martin Gausvik, CFO
Jon Pinch, COO

WKPR
10-20-1960; 1440 khz AM *Hrs Open:* 6 AM-sunset
Box 50867, Kalamazoo, MI 49005 US
(269) 381-1420
www.wfuramfm.com
wfuramfm@sbcglobal.net
License: Kalamazoo, MI held by Kalamazoo Broadcasting Co.
Group Owner: Kuiper Stns
Nat'l Network: USA
Arbitron Metro Market: Kalamazoo, MI *Format:* Religious *Target Audience:* 25 plus.
William Kuiper Sr., President
Stan Gebben, Station Manager
William Kuiper Jr., Chief Engineer

WKZO
09-10-1931; 590 khz AM *Hrs Open:* 24
4200 W. Main St, Kalamazoo, MI 49006 US
(269) 345-7121, *Fax:* (269) 345-1436
www.wkzo.com
License: Kalamazoo, MI held by Midwest Communications Inc.
Group Owner: Midwest Communications Inc.; (acq 5-1-2006; grpsl).
Nat'l Network: CBS *Nat'l Reps:* Christal
Arbitron Metro Market: Kalamazoo, MI *Format:* News, News/Talk, 86 *Special Programming:* Farm 10 hrs, relg 5 hrs wkly *No. News Employees:* 5 *Target Audience:* 25 plus; upscale, 60% male, 40% female
Duey Wright, President
Peter Tanz, General Manager
Michael Klein, General Sales Mgr
Jay Morris, Programming Director
Walker Sisson, Chief Engineer

***WMUK**
01-08-1951; 102.1 mhz FM *Hrs Open:* 24; 50 kw; 489 ft.; N42 25 3 W85 31 55
Western Michigan Univ., Kalamazoo, MI 49008 US
(269) 387-5715, *Fax:* (269) 387-4630
www.wmuk.org
wmukfm@wmich.edu
License: Kalamazoo, Kalamazoo County, MI held by Western Michigan University Board of Trustees.
Nat'l Network: NPR; PRI *Regional Network:* Minn. Pub. Radio
Arbitron Metro Market: Kalamazoo, MI *Format:* Jazz, News *Special Programming:* Bluegrass 4 hrs wkly *Hrs. of News Programming:* news progmg 38 hrs wkly *No. News Employees:* 3 *Target Audience:* General;educated adults
Gordon Bolar, General Manager
Gordon Bolar, General Sales Mgr
Klayton Woodworth, Programming Director
Andrew Robins, News Director
Michael Hahn, Advertising Manager

WVFM
06-19-1964; 106.5 mhz FM; 33 kw; 600 ft.; N42 28 35 W85 29 5
4200 West Main Street, Kalamazoo, MI 49006 US
(269) 345-7121, *Fax:* (269) 345-1436
www.wvfm.com
License: Kalamazoo, Kalamazoo County, MI held by Midwest Communications Inc.
Group Owner: Midwest Communications Inc.; (acq 5-1-2006; grpsl)
Nat'l Reps: Christal
Arbitron Metro Market: Kalamazoo, MI *Format:* Adult Contemp *No. News Employees:* 4 *Target Audience:* 25-54; women
D. E. Wright, President
Mike Klein, General Sales Mgr
Ken Lanphear, Programming Director
Peter Tanz, Promotions Manager
John McNeill, News Director
Walker Sisson, Engineering Dir

Kalkaska

WKLT
04-08-1979; 97.5 mhz FM *Hrs Open:* 24; 32 kw; 617 ft.; N44 47 29 W85 14 20
1020 Hastings Street, Traverse City, MI 49686 US
(231) 947-0003, *Fax:* (231) 947-7002
www.wklt.com
License: Kalkaska, Kalkaska County, MI held by Northern Radio of Michigan
Nat'l Reps: Christal
Arbitron Metro Market: Traverse City-Petoskey, MI *Format:* Rock/AOR *Special Programming:* Sunday night classics, blues 2 hrs wkly *Hrs. of News Programming:* News progmg 2 hrs wkly *Target Audience:* 25-54; babyboomers & young adults
Charlie Ferguson, General Manager
Greg Marsh, General Sales Mgr
Terri Ray, Programming Director
Kristal Flateau, News Director
Dennis Murray, Chief Engineer

Kentwood

***WGVU**
12-25-1954; 1480 khz AM *Hrs Open:* 24
301 W. Fulton, Grand Rapids, MI 49504 US
(616) 331-6666, *Fax:* (616) 331-6625
www.wgvu.org
wgvu@gvsu.edu
License: Kentwood, MI held by Grand Valley State Univ.
Nat'l Network: NPR; PRI
Arbitron Metro Market: Grand Rapids, MI *Format:* News *Hrs. of News Programming:* news progmg 89 hrs wkly *No. News Employees:* 3 *Target Audience:* 35-44; college-educated men with average income
Ken Kolbe, Operations Dir
Michael Walenta, General Manager
Pamela Holtz, Promotions Manager
Fred Martino, News Director
Bob Lumbert, Chief Engineer
Jim Rademaker, Special Events Coordinator
Ed Spier, Traffic Manager

WVHF
09-18-1978; 1140 khz AM *Hrs Open:* 15 hrs; 5 kw-D, DA; N42 56 13 W85 27 20
1919 Eastern Ave. S.E., Grand Rapids, MI 49512
(616) 475-4299 Ext. 11, *Fax:* (616) 475-4335
www.wjnz.com
mjs@wjnz.com
License: Kentwood, Kent County, MI held by WJNZ Radio L.L.C.
Nat'l Network: ABC; Premiere Radio Networks
Population Served: 703,400 *Arbitron Metro Market:* Grand Rapids, MI *Special Programming:* Jazz 6 hrs, gospel 4 hrs *Hrs. of News Programming:* Top of the hour 6a-7p *Target Audience:* 25-54; Baby Boomers *Adv.Rates:* 25; 23; 26; 17
Mike St. Cyr, President
Selina James, Office Manager

Kingsford

***WEUL**
02-11-1990; 98.1 mhz FM; 1 kw; 466 ft.; N45 49 58 W88 4 57
Rebroadcasts: Simulcast with WHWL(FM) Marquette, WHWG(FM) Trout Lake
130 Carmen Drive, Marquette, MI 49855 US
(906) 249-1423, *Fax:* (906) 249-4042
www.whwl.net
whwl@whwl.net
License: Kingsford, Dickinson County, MI held by Gospel Opportunities Inc.
Arbitron Metro Market: Kingsford, MI *Format:* Religious *No. News Employees:* 3
W. Curtis Marker, General Manager
Andy Larsen, News Director
Curt Marker, Manager
Beth Marker, Part-time Bookkeeper
Kathy Kantola, Executive Assistant

Kingsley

WJNL
04-17-1947; 1210 khz AM; 2.5 kw-C, NDD; 50 kw-D, NDD; N44 33 34 W85 35 37
Mailing Address: 5900 Princess Garden Pkwy, 8th Floor, Lanham, MD 20706 US
Second Address: 310 West Front St., Traverse City, MI 49684
(231) 947-1210
www.wjml.com
talk@wjnl.com
License: Kingsley, MI held by Stone Communications Inc.
Nat'l Network: CBS Radio *Regional Network:* Mich. Talk
Format: News, Sports, 86 *Hrs. of News Programming:* News progmg 72 hrs wkly *Target Audience:* 25 plus. *Adv. Rates:* 25; 25; 25; 18.
Richard Stone, President
Philip Clever, Station Manager

L'Anse

WCUP
01-01-1998; 105.7 mhz FM *Hrs Open:* 24; 51 kw; 856 ft.; N46 39 50 W88 23 6
1300 N 17th St., 11th Floor, Rosslyn, VA 22209 US
(906) 353-9287, *Fax:* (906) 353-9200
www.keepitintheup.com
eagleadmin@up.net
License: L'Anse, Baraga County, MI held by Keweenaw Bay Indian Community
Nat'l Network: ABC
Arbitron Metro Market: L'anse, MI *Format:* Country *Special Programming:* American Indian 2 hrs; polka 2 hrs wkly *Hrs. of News Programming:* News progrmg one hr wkly *Target Audience:* 18 plus.
Ed Janisse, General Manager
John Preston, General Sales Mgr
Brian Keinath-, Programming Director

Lake City

***WAIR**
104.9 mhz FM; 1.6 kw; 489 ft.; N44 14 56 W85 18 48
3302 N. Van Dyke, Imlay City, MI 48444 US
(888) 887-7139, *Fax:* (877) 850-0881
www.positivehits.com
jennc@smile.FM
License: Lake City, Missaukee County, MI held by Superior Communications.
Group Owner: Superior Communications
Arbitron Metro Market: Lake City, MI *Format:* Christian
Jenn Czelada, General Manager
Ed Czelada, Programming Director
Aaron Burrell, Administration
Clayton Hewitt, Administration and Engineering
Ed Czelada, Administration, Programming & Engineering
Dale Mazzoline, Production

Lake Isabella

WRAX
98.9 mhz FM; 6 kw; Ant 328 ft; N43 52 51 W86 13 04
1717 Dixie Hwy., Suite 650, Fort Wright, KY
(859) 331-9100
License: Lake Isabella, Mason County, MI held by Radioactive LLC.
Group Owner: Radioactive LLC
Benjamin Homel, President

Lakeview

WGLM-FM
11-01-1989; 106.3 mhz FM; 3 kw; 328 ft.; N43 24 33 W85 15 53
Mailing Address: P.O. Box 578, Greenville, MI 48838 US
Second Address: 9181 S. Greenville Rd., Greenville, MI 48838
(616) 754-3656, *Fax:* (616) 754-2390
wscgradio@chartermi.net
License: Lakeview, Montcalm County, MI held by Packer Radio Greenville Inc.
Format: Country
Bruce Bentley, Operations Dir
John Clark, General Manager

Lansing

WHZZ
01-01-1967; 101.7 mhz FM *Hrs Open:* 24; 4.1 kw; 397 ft.; N42 41 29 W84 33 29
600 West Cavanaugh Rd., Lansing, MI 48910 US
(517) 393-1320, *Fax:* (517) 393-0882
www.1017fm.com
License: Lansing, Ingham County, MI held by MacDonald Broadcasting Co.
Group Owner: MacDonald Broadcasting Co.
Nat'l Reps: D & R Radio *Wire Services:* AP
Arbitron Metro Market: Lansing-East Lansing, MI *Format:* Adult Contemp *Target Audience:* 25-54; upscale adults *Adv. Rates:* 45; 45; 45; 30
Sharon Crane, General Sales Mgr
Shane Pitman, News Director
Gary Harding, Chief Engineer

WILS
07-17-1947; 1320 khz AM
2000 Whittier, Saginaw, MI 48601 US
(517) 393-1320, *Fax:* (517) 393-0882
www.1320wils.com
cindytuck@macdonaldbroadcasting.com
License: Lansing, MI held by MacDonald Broadcasting Co.
Group Owner: MacDonald Broadcasting Co.; (acq 12-20-2001; grpsl)
Nat'l Network: Fox News Radio *Nat'l Reps:* D & R Radio
Arbitron Metro Market: Lansing-East Lansing, MI *Format:* News, News/Talk, 86 *Adv. Rates:* 45; 45; 45; 30
Cindy Tuck, General Manager
Sharon Crane, General Sales Mgr

Scott Holliday, Programming Director
Lee Cohen, Sales
Dave Horski, Traffic Director
Mark Pruchniewski, Production Director

WITL-FM
04-15-1964; 100.7 mhz FM; 26.5 kw; 643 ft.; N42 40 33 W84 30 0
3420 Pine Tree Road, Lansing, MI 48911 US
(517) 393-1010, *Fax:* (517) 394-3391
www.witl.com
rick.sarata@cumulus.com
License: Lansing, Ingham County, MI
Group Owner: Cumulus Media Inc.; (acq 2000; grpsl).
Nat'l Reps: Christal
Arbitron Metro Market: Lansing-East Lansing, MI *Format:* Country *No. News Employees:* 1 *Target Audience:* 25-54.
Farid Suleman, Chairman
Brent Alberts, Operations Dir
Matt Hanlon, General Manager
Kelly Norton, General Sales Mgr
Chris Tyler, Programming Director
Jordan Lee, Promotions Manager
Steve Goupil, News Director
Rick Housley, ChiefEngineer
Chris Potter, Regional Sales Manager
AJ Wilson, Disc Jockey
Chris Tyler, Disc Jockey
Jordan Lee, Disc Jockey

WJIM
01-01-1934; 1240 khz AM *Hrs Open:* 24
3420 Pine Tree Road, Lansing, MI 48911 US
(517) 394-7272, *Fax:* (517) 394-3391
www.wjimam.com
tim.nester@citcomm.com
License: Lansing, MI
Group Owner: Cumulus Media Inc.; (acq 2000; grpsl)
Nat'l Network: Westwood One; ABC *Nat'l Reps:* Christal
Arbitron Metro Market: Lansing-East Lansing, MI *Format:* News, Talk *Hrs. of News Programming:* news progmg 4 hrs wkly *No. News Employees:* 1 *Target Audience:* 25-54.
Farid Suleman, CEO
Brent Alberts, Operations Dir
Matt Hanlon, General Manager
Steve Goupil, News Director
Tim Nester, AM Operations Manager

WJIM-FM
06-01-1960; 97.5 mhz FM *Hrs Open:* 24; 45 kw; 512 ft.; N42 40 33 W84 30 0
3420 Pine Tree Road, Lansing, MI 48911 US
(517) 394-7272, *Fax:* (517) 394-3391
www.new975.com
info@new975.com
License: Lansing, Ingham County, MI
Group Owner: Cumulus Media Inc.
Arbitron Metro Market: Lansing-East Lansing, MI *Format:* Contemporary Hits/Top 40 *Hrs. of News Programming:* news progmg 2 hrs wkly *No. News Employees:* 1
Farid Suleman, Chairman
Brent Alberts, Operations Dir
Matt Hanlon, General Manager
Josh Strickland, Programming Director

***WLNZ**
02-11-1994; 89.7 mhz FM; 0 kw horiz, 0.42 kw vert; 98 ft.; N42 44 15 W84 33 12
PO Box 40010, Lansing, MI 48933 US
(517) 483-1710, *Fax:* (517) 483-1894
www.wlnz.org
info@wlnz.org
License: Lansing, Ingham County, MI held by Lansing Community College.
Nat'l Network: PRI; NPR
Arbitron Metro Market: Lansing-East Lansing, MI *Format:* Blues, Jazz, 90 *Special Programming:* Reggae 4 hrs, big band 3 hrs, folk 3 hrs, Sp 4 hrs
Dave Downing, General Manager
Lyn Peraino, Programming Director
Lyle Laylin, Chief Engineer
Dae Lowry, Music Director

Lapeer

WLCO
11-16-1962; 1530 khz AM; 5 kw-D, DAD; N43 1 35 W83 17 12
286 W. Nepessing Street, Lapeer, MI 48446 US
(810) 743-1080, *Fax:* (810) 742-5170
info@wlco.com
License: Lapeer, MI
Group Owner: Townsquare Media; (acq 7-18-2002; $1.3 million with co-located FM)
Nat'l Network: ABC *Nat'l Reps:* Patt
Arbitron Metro Market: Flint, MI *Format:* Country *Target Audience:* 35 plus. *Adv. Rates:* 20; 25; 20; na
Zoe Burdine-Fly, General Manager

***WMPC**
12-06-1926; 1230 khz AM *Hrs Open:* 24; 1 kw-U, ND1; N43 4 46 W83 18 35
P. O. Box 104, Lapeer, MI 48446 US
(810) 664-6211, *Fax:* (810) 664-5361
wmpc@chartermi.net
License: Lapeer, MI held by The Calvary Bible Church of Lapeer Inc.
Nat'l Network: Moody *Wire Services:* AP
Arbitron Metro Market: Detroit, MI *Format:* Religious *Hrs. of News Programming:* news progmg 24 hrs wkly *No. News Employees:* 1 *Target Audience:* General.
Bob Baldwin, General Manager

WQUS
02-06-1968; 103.1 mhz FM; 2.6 kw; 341 ft.; N43 4 43 W83 11 24
286 W. Nepessing Street, Lapeer, MI 48446 US
(810) 743-1080, *Fax:* (810) 742-5170
www.us103.com
info@us103.com
License: Lapeer, Lapeer County, MI
Group Owner: Townsquare Media
Arbitron Metro Market: Flint, MI *Format:* Rock/AOR *Special Programming:* AOR, gospel, blues *Target Audience:* 25-40; college educated men & women *Adv. Rates:* 50; 35; 45; 30
Kelly Quinn, General Manager
Pete Clinton, General Sales Mgr
Brian Beddow, Programming Director
Tony LaBrie, Music Director

Leland

WFCX
08-09-1991; 94.3 mhz FM *Hrs Open:* 24; 20.5 kw; 764 ft.; N44 46 19 W85 40 58 *Rebroadcasts:* Rebroadcasts WFDX(FM) Atlanta 100%
2215 Oak Indust. Dr. N.E, Grand Rapids, MI 49505 US
(231) 947-5396, *Fax:* (231) 947-7002
License: Leland, Leelanau County, MI held by Northern Michigan Radio Inc.
Nat'l Reps: Christal
Arbitron Metro Market: Traverse City, MI *Format:* Contemporary Hits/Top 40, Adult Contemp *Special Programming:* Relg one hr wkly *Hrs. of News Programming:* news progmg 7 hrs wkly *No. News Employees:* 1 *TargetAudience:* 25-54.
Charlie Ferguson, General Manager
Dennis Winslow, Programming Director

Leroy Township

***WLGH**
12-01-1996; 88.1 mhz FM; 0.001 kw horiz, 6.7 kw vert; 571 ft.; N42 42 20 W84 21 27
601 Savidge St, Reed City, MI 49677 US
(517) 381-0573, *Fax:* (877) 850-0881
www.positivehits.com
info@positivehits.com
License: Leroy Township, Osceola County, MI held by Superior Communications.
Group Owner: Superior Communications
Format: Christian
Jenn Czelada, General Manager
Ed Czelada, Programming Director

Lexington

WBTI
07-13-1991; 96.9 mhz FM *Hrs Open:* 24; 3 kw; 328 ft.; N43 12 34 W82 32 10
2379 Miltary Street, Port Huron, MI 48060 US
(810)982-9000, *Fax:* (810) 987-9380
www.wbti.com
sshigley@radiofirst.net
License: Lexington, Sanilac County, MI held by Liggett Communications L.L.C
Group Owner: Liggett Communications L.L.C.
Arbitron Metro Market: Port Huron, Mi *Format:* Adult Contemp *Target Audience:* 18-34.
Scott Shigley, Director of Sales
Ben Coburn, Programming Director

Linwood

WSAG
11-01-2002; 104.1 mhz FM; 4.6 kw; 325 ft.; N43 43 30 W83 56 50
Mailing Address: 125 North Mable, Pinconning, MI 48650 US
Second Address: 2000 Whittier Street, Saginaw, MI 48601
(989) 752-8161, *Fax:* 989-752-8102
thebay104fm.com
License: Linwood, Bay County, MI held by MacDonald Boadcasting Co.
Group Owner: MacDonald Broadcasting Co.; (acq 6-30-2005)
Nat'l Reps: Eastman Radio *Regional Reps:* Eastman Radio *Wire Services:* AP
Arbitron Metro Market: Saginaw, MI *Format:* Classic Rock *No. News Employees:* 1
Ken MacDonald, Jr., CEO
Duane Alverson, President
Jim Kramer, Operations Dir
Mary Yearham, General Sales Mgr
Cindy Tuck, Vice President

Livonia

WCAR
10-23-1963; 1090 khz AM; 0.25 kw-D, DA2; 0.5 kw-N, DA2; N42 19 46 W83 21 43
724 First Street North, 4th Floor, Minneapolis, MN 55401 US
(734) 525-1111, *Fax:* (734) 525-3608
www.espn1090.com/
info@espn1090.com
License: Livonia, MI held by 1090 Investments L.L.C.
Arbitron Metro Market: Garden City,MI *Format:* Christian *Special Programming:* Ethnic *Target Audience:* 25 plus.
John Browne, President

Ludington

WKLA
10-09-1944; 1450 khz AM *Hrs Open:* 24; 1 kw-U, ND1; N43 57 5 W86 25 28
215 Harbor Drive, Ludington, MI 49431 US
(231) 843-3438, *Fax:* (231) 843-1886
License: Ludington, MI held by Lake Michigan Broadcasting Inc.
Group Owner: Lake Michigan Broadcasting Inc.; (acq 9-20-96; grpsl).
Format: News, News/Talk, 86 *Hrs. of News Programming:* news progmg 4 hrs wkly *No. News Employees:* 1 *Target Audience:* 40 plus; mature adults
Jason Wilder, Operations Dir
Lynn Baerwolf, General Manager
Richard Young, General Sales Mgr
Alan Neushwander, News Director

WKLA-FM
05-01-1971; 106.3 mhz FM; 4.9 kw; 361 ft.; N44 3 27 W86 24 58
215 Harbor Drive, Ludington, MI 49431 US
(231) 843-3438, *Fax:* (231) 843-1886
License: Ludington, Mason County, MI held by Lake Michigan Broadcasting Inc.
Group Owner: Lake Michigan Broadcasting Inc.
Nat'l Network: ABC *Regional Reps:* Patt Media
Format: Adult Contemp *Hrs. of News Programming:* news progmg 3 hrs wkly *No. News Employees:* 2 *Target Audience:* 25-50. *Adv. Rates:* 24; 20; 22; 14
Richard Young, Promotions Manager
Rod Beckman, News Director

Luna Pier

WMIM
07-16-1967; 98.3 mhz FM *Hrs Open:* 24; 3.4 kw; Ant 443 ft; N41 40 05 W83 27 11
14930 Laplaisance Rd. Suite 113, Monroe, MI 53202
(734) 242-6600, *Fax:* (734) 242-6599
www.tower983.com
info@tower983.com
License: Luna Pier, Monroe County, MI held by Cumulus Licensing Corp
Group Owner: Cumulus Media Inc.; (acq 7-98; $2.8 million)
Nat'l Reps: Michigan Spot Sales
Population Served: 300,000 *Arbitron Metro Market:* Toledo, OH *Special Programming:* Relg 3 hrs wkly *Hrs. of News Programming:* news progmg 3 hrs wkly *No. News Employees:* 1 *Target Audience:* 25-54.
Skip Schmidt, General Manager
Sherri Borer, General Sales Mgr
Steve Marshall, Programming Director
London Mitchell, News Director

Mackinaw City

***WIAB**
10-01-2000; 88.5 mhz FM; 0.001 kw horiz, 20 kw vert; 430 ft.; N45 40 0 W84 38 5 *Rebroadcasts:* Simulcast with WIAA(FM) Interlochen 100%
P O Box 334, Stanwood, MI 49346 US
(616) 726-0193
License: Mackinaw City, Cheboygan County, MI held by Interlochen Center for the Arts
Arbitron Metro Market: Scottsdale AZ
Timothy Woodson, Chairman

WLJZ
09-06-1989; 94.5 mhz FM; 50 kw; 361 ft.; N45 40 0 W84 38 5
232 Front Street, No. 2, Traverse City, MI 49684 US
(231) 627-2341, *Fax:* (231) 627-7000
www.nsbroadcasting.com
info@nsbroadcasting.com
License: Mackinaw City, Cheboygan County, MI held by Northern Star Broadcasting L.L.C.
Group Owner: Northern Star Broadcasting L.L.C.; (acq 12-12-2005; grpsl)
Arbitron Metro Market: Traverse City-Petoskey, MI *Format:* Country
Palmer Pyle, President
April Hurley-Rose, Operations Dir

Manistee

WMTE
06-07-1951; 1340 khz AM *Hrs Open:* 24; 1 kw-U, ND1; N44 14 7 W86 19 5
359 River St., Manistee, MI 49660 US
(231) 352-9603, *Fax:* (231) 352-7877
License: Manistee, MI held by Lake Michigan Broadcasting Inc.
Group Owner: Lake Michigan Broadcasting Inc.; (acq 9-20-96; grpsl).
Nat'l Network: ABC *Nat'l Reps:* Michigan Spot Sales
Arbitron Metro Market: Manistee, MI *Format:* News, News/Talk, 86 *No. News Employees:* 1 *Target Audience:* General. *Adv. Rates:* 12; 12; 12; 7.
Jason Wilder, Operations Dir
Judith Ouvry, Station Manager
Richard Young, General Sales Mgr
Alan Neushwander, News Director
Mike Baerwolf, Chief Engineer
Ben Failor, Regional Sales Manager

WMLQ
08-01-1970; 97.7 mhz FM *Hrs Open:* 24; 2.5 kw; 515 ft.; N44 12 40 W86 17 53
3800 Victory Parkway, Cincinnati, OH 45207 US
(213) 843-0941, *Fax:* (231) 843-9411
www.97-coastfm.com
License: Manistee, Manistee County, MI held by Synergy Media Inc.
Regional Network: Mich. Farm *Nat'l Reps:* Michigan Spot Sales
Regional Reps: Michigan Spot Sales
Arbitron Metro Market: Manistee, MI *Format:* Adult Contemp
Target Audience: 35-64; Adults
Stacy Johnson, Operations Dir
Todd Mohr, General Manager
Tom Green, Chief Engineer

WMTE-FM
06-22-1994; 101.5 mhz FM *Hrs Open:* 24; 6 kw; 262 ft.; N44 12 41 W86 17 53
P.O. Box 727, Manistee, MI 49660 US
(607) 749-9942, *Fax:* (607) 749-2374
judy@wkla.com
License: Manistee, Manistee County, MI held by Lake Michigan Broadcasting Inc.
Group Owner: Lake Michigan Broadcasting Inc.; (acq 2000; $300,000).
Regional Reps: Patt Media
Arbitron Metro Market: Manistee, MI *Format:* Oldies *Special Programming:* Pol 6 hrs, relg 2 hrs wkly *No. News Employees:* 1 *Adv. Rates:* 18; 16; 17; 9.
Judith Ouvry, Station Manager
Richard Young, General Sales Mgr
Mike Baerwolf, Programming Director
Alan Neushwander, News Director
Jason Wilder, Operations Manager
Ben Failor, Regional Sales Manager

***WLMN**
89.7 mhz FM; 15 kw; 282 ft.; N44 6 18 W86 15 1
US
(231) 276-4400, *Fax:* (231) 276-4417
www.interlochen.org/ipr
License: Manistee, Manistee County, MI held by Interlochen Center for the Arts.
Arbitron Metro Market: Manistee, MI *Format:* News
Thom Paulson, General Manager

Manistique

WTIQ
02-11-1968; 1490 khz AM; 1 kw-U, ND1; N45 57 51 W86 16 37
101 Huron Court, Negaunee, MI 49866 US
(906) 341-1490, *Fax:* (906) 341-9717
www.wtiqradio.com
rrnnews@radioresultsnetwork.com
License: Manistique, MI held by Lakes Radio Inc.
Group Owner: Lakes Radio Inc.; acq 11-30-99; grpsl)
Regional Network: MNN
Arbitron Metro Market: Manistique, MI *Format:* Oldies *Target Audience:* 25-54; blue & white collar
Rick Duerson, General Manager
L. David Vaughan, Station Manager

WPIQ
01-01-2005; 92.7 mhz FM; 24.5 kw; 713 ft.; N45 58 0 W86 29 17
101 Huron Court, Negaunee, MI 49866 US
(906)228-6800, *Fax:* (906) 228-8128
www.wpiqradio.com
wpiq@greatlakesradio.org
License: Manistique, Schoolcraft County, MI held by Todd Stuart Noordyk.
Group Owner: Great Lakes Radio Inc.
Nat'l Network: Premiere Radio Networks; ABC
Arbitron Metro Market: Traverse City, MI *Format:* News, News/Talk, 86 *No. News Employees:* 2 *Adv. Rates:* 13; 13; 13; 10
Todd Noordyk, General Manager
Devin Lawrence, Station Manager
Bill Tibor, General Sales Mgr
Walt Lindala, News Director
Staci Zanetti, Traffic Manager

Marine City

WHLX
12-10-1951; 1590 khz AM *Hrs Open:* 24; 1 kw-D, DA2; 0.102 kw-N, DA2; N42 43 42 W82 31 15 *Rebroadcasts:* Rebroadcasts WHLS (AM) Port Huron 100%.
2379 Military Street, Port Huron, MI 48060 US
(810) 982-9000, *Fax:* (810) 987-9380
License: Marine City, MI held by Liggett Communications LLC.
Group Owner: Liggett Communications L.L.C.; (acq 5-1-2000).
Nat'l Network: ABC
Arbitron Metro Market: Detroit *Format:* Adult Contemp, Oldies
Target Audience: 25-54.
Robert Liggett, Chairman
James Jenson, President
Lawrence Smith, Operations Dir

Marlette

WBGV
07-25-1999; 92.5 mhz FM *Hrs Open:* 24; 3 kw; 328 ft.; N43 17 10 W82 58 17
Mailing Address: 309 George Vth Avenue, Croswell, MI 48422 US
Second Address: 19 S. Elk St., Sandusky, MI 48422
(810) 648-2700, *Fax:* (810) 648-3242
www.sanilacbroadcasting.com
boba@sanilacbroadcasting.com
License: Marlette, Sanilac County, MI held by GB Broadcasting Co.
Nat'l Network: ABC
Arbitron Metro Market: Sandusky, MI *Format:* Country *Hrs. of News Programming:* news progmg 2 hrs wkly *No. News Employees:* 1 *Target Audience:* General. *Adv. Rates:* 13; 13; 13; 13
George Benko, President
Bob Armstrong, General Manager
Stan Grabitz, Programming Director
Renae Davis, News Director

Marquette

WDMJ
07-01-1931; 1320 khz AM
980 North Michigan Avenue, Suite 1880, Chicago, IL 60611 US
(906) 225-1313, *Fax:* (906) 225-1324
www.wjpd.com
wjpd@wjpd.com
License: Marquette, MI held by Northern Star Broadcasting L.L.C.
Group Owner: Northern Star Broadcasting L.L.C.; acq 11-5-01; grpsl).
Nat'l Reps: Michigan Spot Sales
Arbitron Metro Market: Marquette, MI *Format:* News, News/Talk, 86 *Target Audience:* 25-54.
Bill Curtis, General Manager
Joseph Dexter, News Director

WFXD
04-06-1974; 103.3 mhz FM *Hrs Open:* 24; 100 kw; 938 ft.; N46 36 14 W87 37 15
307 South Front St., Marquette, MI 49855 US
(906) 227-8888, *Fax:* (906) 228-8128
www.wfxd.com
toddn@greatlakesradio.org
License: Marquette, Marquette County, MI held by Great Lakes Radio Inc.
Group Owner: Great Lakes Radio Inc.; (acq 11-30-99; grpsl)
Format: Country *Target Audience:* 25-54.
Todd Noordyk, General Manager
Walt Lindala, News Director
Staci Zanetti, Traffic Manager

***WHWL**
12-16-1965; 95.7 mhz FM; 100 kw; 531 ft.; N46 29 52 W87 24 59
130 Carmen Drive, Marquette, MI 49855 US
(906) 249-1423, *Fax:* (906) 249-4042
www.whwl.net
whwl@whwl.net
License: Marquette, Marquette County, MI held by Gospel Opportunities Inc.
Format: Religious
W. Curtis Marker, General Manager

***WNMU-FM**
08-01-1963; 90.1 mhz FM *Hrs Open:* 24; 100 kw; 928 ft.; N46 21 9 W87 51 32
Radio Station Wnmu-Fm, Marquette, MI 49855 US
(906) 227-2600, *Fax:* (906) 227-2905
www.nmu.edu/wnmufm
esmith@nmu.edu
License: Marquette, Marquette County, MI held by Board of Trustees of Northern Michigan University.
Nat'l Network: NPR; PRI *Wire Services:* AP
Arbitron Metro Market: Marquette, MI *TV Affiliate:* *WNMU-TV affil *Format:* Jazz, News *Special Programming:* Educ *Hrs. of News Programming:* News progmg 31 hrs wkly
Eric Smith, General Manager
Evelyn Massaro, Station Manager
Stan Wright, Programming Director
Nicole Walton, News Director
Mike Perucco, Chief Engineer

WUPK
05-01-1992; 94.1 mhz FM *Hrs Open:* 24; 4.4 kw; 381 ft.; N46 30 51 W87 28 58 *Rebroadcasts:* Rebroadcasts WIMK(FM) Iron Mountain 100%
980 North Michigan Ave, Suite 1880, Chicago, IL 60611 US
(906) 225-1313, *Fax:* (906) 225-1324
www.rockthebear.com
prodguy@uplogon.com
License: Marquette, Marquette County, MI held by Northern Star Broadcasting L.L.C.
Group Owner: Northern Star Broadcasting L.L.C.; acq 11-5-01; grpsl).
Nat'l Reps: Patt
Arbitron Metro Market: Marquette, MI *Format:* Classic Rock, Rock/AOR *Hrs. of News Programming:* news progmg 3 hrs wkly *No. News Employees:* 1 *Target Audience:* 25-54; baby boomers
Chris Monk, Operations Dir
Tammy Johnson, General Manager

***WUPX**
01-01-1994; 91.5 mhz FM *Hrs Open:* 24; 1.7 kw; 436 ft.; N46 30 52 W87 29 7
Office of the Dean, 1401 Presque Isle Ave, Marquette, MI 49855 US
(906) 227-2348, *Fax:* (906) 227-2344
www.wupx.com
wupx@nmu.edu
License: Marquette, Marquette County, MI held by Board of Control of Northern Michigan University.
Arbitron Metro Market: Marquette, MI *TV Affiliate:* *WNMU-TV affil *Format:* Alternative *Special Programming:* Black 6 hrs, jazz 2 hrs wkly *Target Audience:* College.
Marcela Godoy, General Manager
Adam Holloway, Station Manager
Jeffrey Matthias, Programming Director
Jacob Stipe, Promotions Manager
Marcus Davenport, Station Engineer
Will Getts, Production Director
Jack Meeks, MusicDirector
Vanesa Taylor, Public Affairs Coordinator

RADIO - U.S.

Marshall

WBXX
10-01-1968; 104.9 mhz FM; 6 kw; 328 ft.; N42 18 47 W84 55 46
600 Congress Ave., Suite 1400, Austin, TX 78701 US
(269) 963-5555, *Fax:* (269) 963-5185
www.wbxx.ils-bc.com
jeff.jennings@cumulus.com
License: Marshall, Calhoun County, MI held by Capstar TX L.P.
Group Owner: Clear Channel Communications Inc.
Arbitron Metro Market: Battle Creek, MI *Format:* Adult Contemp
Target Audience: 18-49.
Steve Stoimenoff, General Manager
Jeff Jennings, Programming Director
Nathan Adams, Production Coordinator/Sports Director/News

Mason

***WUNN**
05-11-1967; 1110 khz AM *Hrs Open:* Sunrise-sunset; 1 kw-D, DAD; N42 33 4 W84 24 15
7355 N. Oracle Road #200, Tucson, AZ 85704 US
(800) 776-1070, *Fax:* (520) 469-7312
www.967flr.org
wunn@flc.org
License: Mason, MI held by Family Life Broadcasting System.
Group Owner: Family Life Communications Inc.; (acq 1-1-69).
Arbitron Metro Market: Albion, MI *Format:* Gospel *Hrs. of News Programming:* News progmg 1.5 hrs wkly *Target Audience:* 25-54; Christian families
Randy Carlson, President
Dawn Bumstead, General Manager
Bob Wolfe, Chief Engineer

Mattawan

WZUU
04-01-1991; 92.5 mhz FM *Hrs Open:* 24; 6000 w; 1000 ft; N42 34 52 W85 45 17
Box 80, 706 E. Allegan St., Otsego, MI 49078
(269) 343-1717, *Fax:* (269) 692-6861
www.wzuu.com
tflynn@wqxc.com
License: Mattawan, Van Buren County, MI held by Forum Communications Inc.
Group Owner: Forum Communications Co.; (acq 6-1-97)
Regional Reps: Michigan Spot Sales
Population Served: 500,000 *Arbitron Metro Market:* Kalamazoo, MI *Special Programming:* Bob and Tom, NASCAR Sprint Cup *Hrs. of News Programming:* news progmg 1 hr wkly *No. News Employees:* 1 *Target Audience:* 25-54 *Adv. Rates:* On request
Robert Brink, President
Tom Flynn, General Manager
Tim Bontrager, General Sales Mgr
Todd Overhuel, Programming Director
Jeff Cassidy, Promotions Manager
Bill Mitchell, News Director
Walker Sisson, Chief Engineer

McMillan

WMJT
01-01-2006; 96.7 mhz FM; 50 kw; 413 ft.; N46 32 2 W85 35 24
Mailing Address: US
Second Address: 210 W. John St., Newberry, MI 49868-1125
(906) 293-1400, *Fax:* (906) 293-5161
www.radioeagle.com
teri@radioeagle.com
License: McMillan, Luce County, MI held by David L. Smith.
Arbitron Metro Market: McMillan, MI *Format:* Adult Contemp
Dave Smith, President
Mike Reling, Operations Dir
Chip Arledge, Programming Director
Teri Petrie, General Manager and General Sales Manager

Menominee

WAGN
11-14-1952; 1340 khz AM *Hrs Open:* 24; 1 kw-U; N45 06 27 W87 36 25
413 10th Ave., Menominee, MI 49858
(906) 863-5551, *Fax:* (906) 863-5679
baycitiesradio.net
License: Menominee, Menominee County, MI held by Armada Media - Menominee Inc.
Group Owner: Armada Media Corp.; (acq 12-19-2006; grpsl)
Nat'l Network: CBS Radio; Marketwatch *Regional Network:* Wisconsin Radio Net.; Michigan Radio Network *Wire Services:* AP
Population Served: 55,000*Hrs. of News Programming:* news progmg 15 hrs wkly *No. News Employees:* 1 *Target Audience:* 30 plus; older, affluent adults
Jim Callow, Operations Dir
Chris Bernier, General Manager
Barb Vandehei, General Sales Mgr
Jim Callow, Programming Director
Ken Conners, News Director
Jim Callow, Chief Engineer

WHYB
10-24-1984; 103.7 mhz FM *Hrs Open:* 24; 7 kw; 299 ft.; N45 4 0 W87 39 55
413 10th Ave., Menominee, MI 49858 US
(906) 863-5551, *Fax:* (906) 863-5679
www.baycitiesradio.net
jimcallow@baycitiesradio.net
License: Menominee, Menominee County, MI held by Armada Media-Menominee Inc.
Group Owner: Armada Media Corp.
Nat'l Network: CBS Radio *Regional Network:* Wisconsin Radio Net. *Wire Services:* AP
Format: Oldies *Hrs. of News Programming:* news progmg 5 hrs wkly *No. News Employees:* 1 *Target Audience:* 35+
Jim Callow, Operations Dir
Mike Peot, General Manager
Ken Conners, News Director
Chris Johnson, Sports Director
Nicole Kelsey, Account Executive

Michigamme

***WKPK**
01-01-2009; 88.3 mhz FM; 15 kw vert; 827 ft.; N46 36 14 W87 37 15
2628 Howard Rd, Petdskey, MI 49770 US
(517) 381-0573
www.smile.fm
License: Michigamme, Marquette County, MI held by Northland Community Broadcasters.
Arbitron Metro Market: Anchorage, AK *Format:* Christian
Edward Czelada, President
Jennifer Czelada, General Manager

Midland

WKQZ
12-14-1976; 93.3 mhz FM; 39 kw; 554 ft.; N43 50 46 W84 5 32
140 South Ash Avenue, Tempe, AZ 85281 US
(989) 776-2100, *Fax:* (989) 754-5990
www.z93kqz.fm
info@z93kqz.fm
License: Midland, Midland County, MI
Group Owner: Cumulus Media Inc.; (acq 2-8-99; grpsl).
Nat'l Reps: McGavren Guild
Arbitron Metro Market: Saginaw-Bay City-Midland, MI *Target Audience:* 25-44; males
Chris Monk, General Manager
Tom Clark, General Sales Mgr
Stan Parman, Programming Director
Hal Maas, News Director
Bob Friedle, Chief Engineer

WMPX
09-11-1948; 1490 khz AM *Hrs Open:* 24; 1 kw-U, ND1; N43 36 48 W84 13 17
Mailing Address: 1510 Bayliss Street, Midland, MI 48640 US
Second Address: 1510 Bayliss St., Midland, MI 48640
(989) 631-1490, *Fax:* (989) 631-6357
www.wmpxwmrx.com
admin@wmpxwmrx.com
License: Midland, MI held by Steel Broadcasting Inc.
Nat'l Network: ABC *Nat'l Reps:* Patt
Arbitron Metro Market: Saginaw-Bay City-Midland, MI *Format:* Oldies, Adult Contemp *Special Programming:* Sounds of Sinatra 2 hrs wkly, relg 3 hrs wkly *Hrs. of News Programming:* news progmg 9 hrs wkly *No. NewsEmployees:* 1 *Target Audience:* General.
Thomas Steel, President
Jon Walding, General Sales Mgr

***WUGN**
12-02-1973; 99.7 mhz FM; 100 kw; 997 ft.; N43 30 56 W84 32 49
7355 N. Oracle, #200, Tucson, AZ 85704 US
(989) 631-7060, *Fax:* (989) 631-4825
www.997.org
997@997.org
License: Midland, Midland County, MI held by Family Life Communications System.
Group Owner: Family Life Communications Inc.; (acq 1996).
Nat'l Network: Salem Radio Network
Arbitron Metro Market: Midland, MI *Format:* Christian *Hrs. of News Programming:* News progmg 8 hrs wkly *Target Audience:* 35-54; female with young children
Peter Brooks, General Manager

Mio

WAVC
10-01-1994; 93.9 mhz FM; 50 kw; 433 ft.; N44 43 40 W84 21 35
Rebroadcasts: Rebroadcasts WMKC(FM) Saint Ignace 100%
232 Front Street, No. 2, Traverse City, MI 49684 US
(870) 425-4971, *Fax:* (870) 424-9717
www.mountaintalk97.com
License: Mio, Oscoda County, MI held by Northern Star Broadcasting L.L.C.
Group Owner: Northern Star Broadcasting L.L.C.; (acq 9-11-98; grpsl)
Arbitron Metro Market: Calico Rock AR *Format:* News, News/Talk, 86 *Hrs. of News Programming:* news progmg 29 hrs/week *No. News Employees:* 1
Scott Gray, CEO, General Manager
Kim Szecksi, News Director
Mike Wiseman, Engineering Dir
Dale Hoffman, Host, Producer
Roy Roane, Sales Representative

Monroe

***WYDM**
11-01-1978; 97.5 mhz FM; 0.049 kw; 135 ft.; N41 55 7 W83 26 12
1275 Macomb Street, Monroe, MI 48161 US
(734) 265-3550
www.monroeccc.edu
mbeaudr@monroeccc.edu
License: Monroe, Monroe County, MI held by Monroe Public Schools
Arbitron Metro Market: Monroe, MI *Format:* Variety/Diverse
Target Audience: 15-24.
Mike Brandt, General Manager
Wendy Sherrod, General Sales Mgr

WRDT
07-12-1956; 560 khz AM *Hrs Open:* 24
P.O. Box 3003, Blue Bell, PA 19422 US
(313) 272-3434
www.wrdt560.com
station@wmuz.com
License: Monroe, MI held by WMUZ Radio Inc.
Group Owner: Crawford Broadcasting Co.; (acq 6-16-97; $3.15 million).
Nat'l Reps: McGavren Guild
Arbitron Metro Market: Detroit *Format:* Christian
Rich Hanovich, Operations Dir
Frank Franciosi, General Manager

***WSMF**
01-01-2003; 88.1 mhz FM; 910 w; Ant 144 ft; N41 55 08 W83 22 34 *Rebroadcasts:* rebroadcast of WHYT(FM) Imlay city 100%
Box 388, Williamston, MI 49770
(810) 721-0891, *Fax:* (413) 410-9708
www.joyfm.net
info@joyfm.net
License: Monroe, Monroe County, MI held by Northland Community Broadcasters.
Jenn Czelada, General Manager

Mount Clemens

WPZR
11-06-1960; 102.7 mhz FM *Hrs Open:* 24; 50 kw; 499 ft; N42 32 39 W82 54 09
3250 Franklin, Detroit, MI 20706
(313) 259-2000, *Fax:* (313) 259-7011
www.kissdetroit.com
License: Mount Clemens, Macomb County, MI held by Radio One of Detroit LLC.
Group Owner: Radio One Inc.; (acq 1999; $27 million).
Nat'l Network: ABC *Nat'l Reps:* D & R Radio
Arbitron Metro Market: Detroit *Target Audience:* 25-49; rock and rollers of all ages
Carol Lawrence-Dobrusin, General Manager

Mount Pleasant

***WCMU-FM**
04-06-1964; 89.5 mhz FM *Hrs Open:* 24; 100 kw; 420 ft.; N43 34 24 W84 46 21
3965 Broomfield Road, Mt. Pleasant, MI 48859 US
(989) 774-3105, *Fax:* (989) 774-4427
www.wcmu.org
schud1ra@cmich.edu
License: Mount Pleasant, Isabella County, MI held by Central Michigan University.
Nat'l Network: NPR; PRI
Arbitron Metro Market: Michigan, Upper Peninsula, MS *TV Affiliate:* *WCMU-TV affil *Format:* Jazz, News *Hrs. of News*

Programming: news progmg 30 hrs wkly *No. News Employees:* 2 *Target Audience:* General.
Ed Grant, General Manager

WCZY-FM
08-20-1991; 104.3 mhz FM *Hrs Open:* 24; 3 kw; 328 ft.; N43 35 39 W84 49 26
4065 E. Wing Rd, Mt. Pleasant, MI 48858 US
(989) 772-9664, *Fax:* (989) 773-5000
www.wczy.net
steve@wczy.net
License: Mount Pleasant, Isabella County, MI held by Central Michigan Communications Inc.
Nat'l Network: Jones Radio Networks *Nat'l Reps:* Michigan Spot Sales *Regional Reps:* Patt.
Arbitron Metro Market: Mt. Pleasant, MI *Format:* Adult Contemp, Easy Listening *Hrs. of News Programming:* news progmg 6 hrs wkly *No. News Employees:* 1 *Target Audience:* 25-54. *Adv. Rates:* 18; 18; 18; 18
Mike Carey, President
Bob Peters, General Sales Mgr
Tina Sawyer, News Director
Lisa Johnson, Traffic Manager

***WMHW-FM**
11-20-1972; 91.5 mhz FM *Hrs Open:* 24; 9.1 kw; 538 ft.; N43 34 33 W84 46 29
US
(989) 774-7287, *Fax:* (989) 774-2426
www.wmhw.org
wmhw@mail.cmich.edu
License: Mount Pleasant, Isabella County, MI held by Board of Trustees, Central Michigan University.
Regional Network: Mich. Radio
Arbitron Metro Market: Mount Pleasant, MI *Format:* Alternative *Hrs. of News Programming:* News progmg 10 wkly *Target Audience:* 12-34.
Chad Roberts, Operations Dir
Peter Orlik, General Manager
Randy Kapenga, Chief Engineer

Munising

***WAZP**
01-01-2000; 89.7 mhz FM *Hrs Open:* 24; kw
US
(506) 646-5161
License: Munising, Northampton County, MI held by Delmarva Educational Association.
Nat'l Network: K-Love
Arbitron Metro Market: Saint John NB *Format:* News, News/Talk, 86
Rael Merson, President
Jim Hamm, General Manager

WQXO
09-20-1955; 1400 khz AM *Hrs Open:* 24; 1 kw-U, ND1; N46 24 30 W86 38 22
309 South Front St., Marquette, MI 49855 US
(906) 228-6800, *Fax:* (906) 228-8128
wqxo.com
toddn@greatlakesradio.org
License: Munising, MI held by Great Lakes Radio Inc.
Group Owner: Great Lakes Radio Inc.; (acq 11-30-99; grpsl).
Nat'l Reps: Patt
Format: Oldies *Target Audience:* 25-54.
Todd Noordyk, General Manager
Bill Tibor, General Sales Mgr
Joel Polkinghorne, Programming Director
Walt Lindala, News Director

Muskegon

WGVS
01-01-1926; 850 khz AM *Hrs Open:* 24; 1 kw-U, DA1; N43 8 5 W86 15 41 *Rebroadcasts:* Rebroadcasts WGVU(AM) Kentwood 100%
301 West Fulton, Grand Rapids, MI 49504 US
(616) 331-6666, *Fax:* (616) 331-6625
www.wgvu.org
wgvu@gvsu.edu
License: Muskegon, MI held by Grand Valley State University.
Nat'l Network: NPR; PRI
Arbitron Metro Market: Muskegon, MI *Format:* News
Ken Kolbe, Operations Dir
Michael Walenta, General Manager
Gary Hunt, General Sales Mgr
Scott Vander Werf, Programming Director
Pamela Holtz, Promotions Manager
Fred Martino, News Director
Bob Lumbert, Engineering Dir
Ed Spier,Traffic Manager

WKBZ
06-15-1947; 1090 khz AM *Hrs Open:* 6 AM-2 hrs past sunset
136 Main St., Suite 202, Westport, CT 06880 US
(231) 733-2600, *Fax:* (231) 733-7461
www.newstalk1090.com
timfeagan@clearchannel.com
License: Muskegon, MI held by CC Licenses LLC.
Group Owner: Clear Channel Communications Inc.; (acq 1-17-2001; grpsl).
Nat'l Reps: D & R Radio
Arbitron Metro Market: Muskegon, MI *Format:* News, Talk *No. News Employees:* 1 *Target Audience:* 25-54 primary; 35-64 secondary
Doug Montgomery, Operations Dir
Tim Feagan, General Manager
Amanda Alexander, General Sales Mgr
Mark Dixon, Programming Director
Christy Mack, Promotions Manager
Ron Steenwyk, Promotions Director

WOOD-FM
01-01-1962; 106.9 mhz FM *Hrs Open:* 24; 50 kw; Ant 479 ft; N43 13 48 W86 05 03
3565 Green St., Muskegon, MI 06880
(231) 733-2600, *Fax:* (231) 733-7461
www.107mus.com
License: Muskegon, Muskegon County, MI held by CC Licenses LLC.
Group Owner: Clear Channel Communications Inc.
Population Served: 160,000 *Arbitron Metro Market:* Muskegon, MI
Mark Dixon, Programming Director

WMUS
02-01-1990; 107.9 mhz FM *Hrs Open:* 24; 15 kw; 348 ft; N43 17 41 W86 13 12
3565 Green St., Muskegon, MI 49512
(231) 733-2600, *Fax:* (231) 739-9037,(213) 733-7461
www.star108.com
License: Muskegon, Muskegon County, MI held by CC Licenses LLC.
Group Owner: Clear Channel Communications Inc.; (acq 1-17-2001; grpsl).
Population Served: 350,000 *Arbitron Metro Market:* Muskegon, MI *Target Audience:* 18-49.
David Taff, Operations Dir
Bart Brandmiller, General Manager
John Bouwhuis, General Sales Mgr
Don Beno, Programming Director
Christy Mack, Promotions Manager

WSNX-FM
11-18-1971; 104.5 mhz FM *Hrs Open:* 24; 32 kw; 620 ft.; N43 12 16 W86 1 45
4417 Broadmoor S.E., Kentwood, MI 49512 US
(616) 459-1919, *Fax:* (616) 235-9104
www.wsnx.com
info@wsnx.com
License: Muskegon, Muskegon County, MI held by CC Licenses LLC.
Group Owner: Clear Channel Communications Inc.; (acq 9-30-99)
Nat'l Network: ABC *Nat'l Reps:* Clear Channel
Arbitron Metro Market: Grand Rapids, MI *Format:* Urban Contemporary, Contemporary Hits/Top 40 *Hrs. of News Programming:* news progrmg one hr wkly *No. News Employees:* 1 *Target Audience:* 18-34; women
Skip Essick, Operations Dir

***WMCQ**
03-31-2005; 91.7 mhz FM; 6 kw; 328 ft.; N43 18 37 W85 54 44
P.O. Box 334, Stanwood, MI 49346 US
(662) 844-8888, *Fax:* (662) 842-6791
www.afa.net
faq@afr.net
License: Muskegon, Muskegon County, MI held by American Family Association.
Group Owner: American Family Radio; (acq 12-20-2002).
Arbitron Metro Market: Tupelo, MS *Format:* Christian
Marvin Sanders, General Manager

Muskegon Heights

WMRR
03-29-1974; 101.7 mhz FM *Hrs Open:* 24; 12 kw; 476 ft.; N43 16 38 W86 20 5
4417 Broadmoor S.E., Kentwood, MI 49512 US
(231) 733-2600, *Fax:* (231) 733-7461
www.rock1017fm.com
timfeagan@clearchannel.com
License: Muskegon Heights, Muskegon County, MI held by CC Licenses LLC.
Group Owner: Clear Channel Communications Inc.; (acq 1-17-2001; grpsl).
Nat'l Network: Westwood One *Wire Services:* UPI
Arbitron Metro Market: Grand Rapids, MII *Format:* Light Rock
Target Audience: 25-54; male
Doug Montgomery, Operations Dir
Tim Feagan, General Manager
Amanda Alexander, General Sales Mgr
Andy O'Riley, Programming Director
Emily Pearce, Promotions Manager

Negaunee

WKQS-FM
01-05-1998; 101.9 mhz FM; 13 kw; 938 ft.; N46 36 14 W87 37 15
101 Huron Court, Negaunee, MI 49866 US
(906) 228-6800, *Fax:* (906) 228-8128
www.wkqsfm.com
toddn@greatlakesradio.org
License: Negaunee, Marquette County, MI held by Great Lakes Radio Inc.
Group Owner: Great Lakes Radio Inc.
Format: Contemporary Hits/Top 40, Oldies
Todd Noordyk, General Manager
Walt Lindala, News Director
Staci Zanetti, Traffic Manager

WNGE
01-01-2001; 99.5 mhz FM; 3.6 kw; 430 ft.; N46 30 51 W87 28 58
980 North Michigan Avenue, Suite 1880, Chicago, IL 60611 US
(906) 225-1313, *Fax:* (906) 225-1324
info@wjpd.com
License: Negaunee, Marquette County, MI held by Northern Star Broadcasting L.L.C.
Group Owner: Northern Star Broadcasting L.L.C.; acq 11-5-01; grpsl).
Arbitron Metro Market: Negaunee, MI *Format:* Oldies
Tammy Johnson, General Manager

Newaygo

WLAW
08-15-2005; 92.5 mhz FM; 2.25 kw; 541 ft.; N43 18 35 W85 54 45
400 East Maple, Fremont, MI 49412 US
(231) 830-0176, *Fax:* (616) 774-2491
www.925fmtheoutlaw.com
info@924fmtheoutlaw.com
License: Newaygo, Newaygo County, MI
Group Owner: Cumulus Media Inc.; (acq 7-8-2005).
Arbitron Metro Market: Newaygo, MI *Format:* Country
Matt Hanlon, General Manager
Rich Berry, General Sales Mgr
Rick Hickman, Senior Account Executive

Newberry

***WIHC**
04-24-1989; 97.9 mhz FM *Hrs Open:* 24; 50 kw; 492 ft.; N46 26 58 W85 6 4 *Rebroadcasts:* WGFM-FM Cheboygan 75%
980 North Michigan Ave., Suite 1880, Chicago, IL 60611 US
(231) 627-2341, *Fax:* (231) 627-7000
www.classicrockthebear.com
info@classicrockthebear.com
License: Newberry, Luce County, MI held by Northern Star Broadcasting L.L.C.
Group Owner: Northern Star Broadcasting L.L.C.; (acq 9-11-98; grpsl).
Format: Classic Rock *Target Audience:* 18-44.
Palmer Pyle, President
April Hurley-Rose, Operations Dir

WNBY
05-16-1966; 1450 khz AM
Mailing Address: P.O. Box 501, Newberry, MI 49868 US
Second Address: Hwy. S. M-123, Newberry, MI 49868
(906) 293-3221, *Fax:* (906) 293-8275
www.wnby.net/
wnby@up.net
License: Newberry, MI held by Sovereign Communications LLC
Nat'l Reps: Patt
Arbitron Metro Market: Newberry, MI *Format:* Country *Special Programming:* Polka 2 hrs wkly *Target Audience:* 35 plus.
Travis Freeman, General Manager
Linda Peters, General Sales Mgr
Sarah Price, Programming Director

WNBY-FM
01-01-1977; 93.9 mhz FM; 50 kw; 443 ft.; N46 26 58 W85 6 4
P.O. Box 501, Newberry, MI 49868 US

RADIO - U.S.

(906) 293-3221, *Fax:* (906) 293-8275
www.oldies93fm.com/
theresa@rock101.net
License: Newberry, Luce County, MI held by Sovereign Communications LLC
Arbitron Metro Market: Newberry, MI *Format:* Oldies *Target Audience:* 25-45.
John Dash, President
Harriett Dash, Station Manager

***WUMI**
90.3 mhz FM; kw
US
(231) 420-1325
License: Newberry, Luce County, MI held by Korkee Inc.
Arbitron Metro Market: Newberry, MI
Robert Naismith, General Manager

Niles

WTRC-FM
09-13-1968; 95.3 mhz FM *Hrs Open:* 24; 3.3 kw; 298 ft; N41 49 22 W86 17 03
237 Edison Rd., Mishawaka, IN 46515
(574) 258-5483, *Fax:* (574) 258-0930
www.waor.com
waor@waor.com
License: Niles, Berrien County, MI held by Pathfinder Communications Corp.
Group Owner: Federated Media
Nat'l Reps: Christal
Population Served: 500,000 *Arbitron Metro Market:* South Bend, IN *Hrs. of News Programming:* News progmg 5 hrs wkly *Target Audience:* 25-54; predominantly male, socially active, economically secure *Adv. Rates:* 70; 70; 70; 70
Brad Williams, General Manager
Mike Ragozino, Promotions Manager

WNIL
12-06-1956; 1290 khz AM *Hrs Open:* 24; 0.5 kw-D, ND2; 0.044 kw-N, ND2; N41 49 22 W86 17 3
P.O. Box 487, Elkhart, IN 46515 US
(574) 258-5483, *Fax:* (574) 258-0930
www.mighty1290.com
cmarsh@b100.com
License: Niles, MI held by Pathfinder Communications Corp.
Group Owner: Federated Media; (acq 7-21-99; $2 million with co-lo
Nat'l Network: Salem Radio Network
Arbitron Metro Market: Berrien, IN *Format:* Religious, Talk
Special Programming: Relg 6 hrs wkly *Hrs. of News Programming:* News progmg 5 hrs wkly *Target Audience:* 35-54; adult, pro-active, community-involvedpeople *Adv. Rates:* 15; 15; 15; 15
Clint Marsh, Operations Dir
Brad Williams, General Manager

North Muskegon

WLCS
11-01-1983; 98.3 mhz FM *Hrs Open:* 24; 1.6 kw; 456 ft.; N43 18 50 W86 9 17
1802 S. Fernandez Ave, Arlington Heights, IL 60005 US
(231) 830-0176, *Fax:* (231) 830-0194
www4.ncsu.edu
License: North Muskegon, Muskegon County, MI
Group Owner: Cumulus Media Inc.; (acq 9-28-2005; grpsl).
Format: Oldies *Hrs. of News Programming:* News progmg one hr wkly *Target Audience:* 35-54; general
John Russell, Operations Dir
Jeff Morton, General Manager
Renee Dudek, General Sales Mgr

***WHEY**
88.9 mhz FM; 1 kw; 157 ft.; N43 16 45 W86 20 32
US
(231) 744-6940
License: North Muskegon, Muskegon County, MI held by Muskegon Community Radio Broadcast Co.
Arbitron Metro Market: North Muskegon, MI *Format:* Christian
William Erickson, President

Norway

WZNL
03-15-1990; 94.3 mhz FM; 2.4 kw; 650 ft.; N45 49 15 W88 2 25
980 North Michigan Ave, Suite 1880, Chicago, IL 60611 US
(906) 774-4321, *Fax:* (906) 774-7799
www.wznl.tripod.com
star943@uplogon.com
License: Norway, Dickinson County, MI held by Northern Star Broadcasting L.L.C.
Group Owner: Northern Star Broadcasting L.L.C.; acq 11-5-01; grpsl).
Nat'l Network: Westwood One
Arbitron Metro Market: Iron Mountain, MI *Format:* Adult Contemp *Target Audience:* 18-54.
Tom Hill, Operations Dir
Veronica Roberts, General Manager

Novi

***WOVI**
09-04-1978; 89.5 mhz FM *Hrs Open:* 24; 0.1 kw; 105 ft.; N42 27 49 W83 29 28
25345 Taft Road, Novi, MI 48375 US
(248) 449-1526, *Fax:* (248) 449-1519
License: Novi, Oakland County, MI held by Board of Education Novi School District.
Format: Alternative, Classic Rock *Target Audience:* General.
Dave Legg, General Manager

Okemos

***KTGG**
08-15-1985; 1540 khz AM *Hrs Open:* Sunrise-sunset; 0.185 kw-C, NDD; 0.45 kw-D, NDD; N42 9 13 W84 32 57
106 E. Main Street, Spring Arbor, MI 49283 US
(517) 750-6540, *Fax:* (517) 750-6619
www.home.fm
info@home.fm
License: Okemos, MI held by Spring Arbor University.
Format: Religious *Target Audience:* 18-49; rural to urban
Hal Munn, President
Carl Fletcher, General Manager
Rachel Buchanan, Programming Director

Olivet

***WOCR**
04-22-1975; 89.1 mhz FM; 0.5 kw; 82 ft.; N42 26 31 W84 55 30
320 S. Main St, Olivet, MI 49076 US
(269) 749-7598, *Fax:* (269) 749-7695
wocr@olivetcollege.edu
License: Olivet, Eaton County, MI held by Olivet College.
TV Affiliate: CHR *Special Programming:* News progmg one hr wkly *No. News Employees:* College; high school and

Ontonagon

***WOAS**
11-15-1978; 88.5 mhz FM *Hrs Open:* 8 AM-10 PM (M-F); 10 w; 124 ft; N46 52 30 W89 18 00
701 Parker, Ontonagon, MI 49953
(906) 884-4433, *Fax:* (906) 884-2742
www.woas-fm.org
ken@oasd.k12.mi.us
License: Ontonagon, Ontonagon County, MI held by Ontonagon Area School District.
Population Served: 1,000*Target Audience:* General; local residents of the area
Ken Raisanen, General Manager

WUPY
01-01-1987; 101.1 mhz FM *Hrs Open:* 24; 100 kw; 696 ft.; N46 45 1.4 W89 10 46.2
1300 N 17th Street, 11th Floor, Arlington, VA 22209 US
(906) 884-9668, *Fax:* (906) 884-4985
www.wupy101.com
wupy@jamadots.com
License: Ontonagon, Ontonagon County, MI held by SNRN Broadcasting Inc.
Nat'l Network: ABC
Arbitron Metro Market: Ontonagon, MI *Format:* Country *Special Programming:* relg 3 hrs, polka 1 hr wkly *Hrs. of News Programming:* news progmg 13 hrs wkly *No. News Employees:* 2 *Target Audience:* 25 plus.
Kenny Lee, General Manager
Jay Nix, General Sales Mgr
Jackie Dobbins, Programming Director
Ted.K.Frantz, Chief Engineer
Bob Peltola, Sports Director

Orchard Lake

***WBLD**
05-28-1974; 89.3 mhz FM *Hrs Open:* 2; 0.015 kw horiz; 161 ft.; N42 33 56 W83 21 32
4925 Orchard Lake Road, West Bloomfield, MI 48323 US
(248) 865-6754, *Fax:* (248) 865-6756
www.wbldradio.tripod.com/
wbld_fm@hotmail.com
License: Orchard Lake, Oakland County, MI held by West Bloomfield Board of Education.
Arbitron Metro Market: West Bloomfield, MI *Format:* Variety/Diverse
Paul Townley, Station Manager
Randy Long, Chief Engineer

Oscoda

WWTH
08-29-1992; 100.7 mhz FM *Hrs Open:* 24; 20.5 kw; 361 ft.; N44 34 42 W83 22 40
12730 Newberry Drive, Grand Ledge, MI 48837 US
(989) 354-4611, *Fax:* (989) 354-4014
www.alpenanow.com
thebay@truenorthradionetwork.com
License: Oscoda, Iosco County, MI held by Edwards Communications LC.
Group Owner: Edwards Communications L.C.; (acq 12-21-2004; grpsl).
Nat'l Reps: Roslin *Regional Reps:* Michigan.
Arbitron Metro Market: Alpena, MI *Format:* Adult Contemp *Hrs. of News Programming:* news progmg 4 hrs wkly *No. News Employees:* 1 *Target Audience:* 25-54. *Adv. Rates:* 15; 15; 15; 10
Tony Calumet, General Manager
Darrel Kelly, General Sales Mgr

***WCMB-FM**
06-01-1998; 95.7 mhz FM *Hrs Open:* 24; 25 kw; 699 ft.; N44 40 29 W83 31 6 *Rebroadcasts:* Rebroadcasts WCMU-FM Mount Pleasant 100%
3965 E. Broomfield Road, Mt. Pleasant, MI 48859 US
(989) 774-3105, *Fax:* (989) 774-4427
www.wcmu.org
schud1ra@cmich.edu
License: Oscoda, Iosco County, MI held by Central Michigan University.
Nat'l Network: NPR; PRI *Regional Network:* Mich. Radio *Wire Services:* AP
Arbitron Metro Market: Michigan, Upper Peninsula, MS *Format:* Jazz, News *Hrs. of News Programming:* news progmg 45 hrs wkly *No. News Employees:* 2
Edward Grant, General Manager
Kim Walters, General Sales Mgr
Ray Ford, Programming Director
Art Curtis, Promotions Manager
David Nicholas, News Director
Randy Kapenga, Chief Engineer

Otsego

WAKV
01-01-1958; 980 khz AM *Hrs Open:* 24; 1 kw-D; N42 27 33 W85 43 58
213 Gilkey St., Plainwell, MI 49080
(269) 685-2438
980am@net-link.net
License: Otsego, Allegan County, MI held by Vintage Radio Enterprises L.L.C.
Wire Services: AP
Population Served: 300,000 *Arbitron Metro Market:* Kalamazoo, MI *Target Audience:* 50 plus; adults
Jim Higgs, President
Jim Higgs, General Manager
Jim Higgs, News Director

WQXC-FM
04-17-1981; 100.9 mhz FM; 3 kw; 299 ft; N42 30 31 W85 46 08
Mailing Address: Box 80, Otsego, MI 49078
Second Address: 706 E. Allegan St., Otsego, MI 49078
(269) 692-6851, *Fax:* (269) 692-6861
www.wqxc.com
tflynn@wqxc.com
License: Otsego, Allegan County, MI held by Forum Communications Inc.
Population Served: 300,000 *Arbitron Metro Market:* Kalamazoo, MI
Deb Whiteman, CFO
Robert Brink, President
Tom Flynn, General Manager
Tim Bontrager, General Sales Mgr
Todd Overhaul, Programming Director
Bill Mitchell, News Director
Walker Sisson, Chief Engineer

Ovid-Elsie

***WOES**
03-21-1978; 91.3 mhz FM; 0.55 kw horiz; 171 ft.; N43 2 44 W84 23 14
8989 Colony Road, Elsie, MI 48831 US
517-371-2642, *Fax:* 517-862-4463

License: Ovid-Elsie, Clinton County, MI held by Ovid-Elsie Area Schools.
TV Affiliate: Variety

Owosso

WOAP
01-01-1948; 1080 khz AM; 1 kw-D, NDD; N43 1 51 W84 10 41
2391 Briarwood Dr., Owosso, MI 48867 US
989-472-4104, *Fax:* 989-472-4106
License: Owosso, MI held by 1090 Investments L.L.C.
TV Affiliate: Hits of the 40s, 50s & 60s

WRSR
12-02-1965; 103.9 mhz FM; 2.85 kw; 482 ft.; N42 59 44 W83 59 33
136 Main Street, Suite 202, Westport, CT 06880 US
(810) 238-7300, *Fax:* (810) 238-7310
www.classicfox.com
info@classicfox.com
License: Owosso, Shiawassee County, MI held by Cumulus Licensing Corp.
Group Owner: Cumulus Media Inc.; (acq 3-15-00; grpsl).
Arbitron Metro Market: Flint, MI *Format:* Classic Rock *Special Programming:* Class one hr, relg one hr, sports 4 hrs wkly
Target Audience: 25-54.
Scott Meier, General Manager
Jeff Wade, Programming Director
Les Root, News Director
Dan Greer, Chief Engineer

Palmer

WRUP
06-21-1974; 98.3 mhz FM *Hrs Open:* 24; 2.6 kw; 1018 ft.; N46 36 14 W87 37 15
309 South Front St., Marquette, MI 49855 US
(906) 228-6800, *Fax:* (906) 228-8128
wrup.com
toddn@greatlakesradio.org
License: Palmer, Alger County, MI
Group Owner: Great Lakes Radio Inc.
Nat'l Network: Westwood One *Nat'l Reps:* Patt
Format: Classic Rock *Target Audience:* 18-54.
Yolanda Zabala, General Manager

Paradise

WUPN
95.1 mhz FM; 25 kw; 233 ft.; N46 27 57.6 W84 43 9.9 US
(989) 732-2341, *Fax:* (989) 732-6202
License: Paradise, Chippewa County, MI held by Darby Advertising Inc.
Group Owner: Darby Advertising Inc.
Arbitron Metro Market: Paradise, MI
Kent Smith, President

Pentwater

WMOM
09-26-1999; 102.7 mhz FM; 6 kw; 328 ft.; N43 52 10 W86 21 32
4359 South Howell Ave, Suite 106, Milwaukee, WI 53207 US
(231) 845-9666, *Fax:* (231) 845-9322
www.wmom.fm
news@wmom.fm; sales@wmom.fm
License: Pentwater, Oceana County, MI held by Bay View Broadcasting Inc.
Arbitron Metro Market: Pentwater, MI *Format:* Adult Contemp
Patrick Lopeman, General Manager
Brian Renchler, News Director

Petoskey

WJML
12-06-1966; 1110 khz AM *Hrs Open:* 24; 10 kw-D, DA; N45 20 05 W84 55 34
2175 Click Rd., Petoskey, MI 49770
(231) 348-5000
www.wjml.com
talk@wjml.com
License: Petoskey, Emmet County, MI held by Stone Communications Inc.
Nat'l Network: CBS *Regional Network:* Mich. Talk
Population Served: 415,627 *Arbitron Metro Market:* Traverse City-Petoskey, MI *Special Programming:* Loc professional and college sports, relg 4 hrs wkly *Hrs. of News Programming:* news progmg 72 hrs wkly *No. NewsEmployees:* 1 *Target Audience:* 25 plus. *Adv. Rates:* 20; 20; 20; 18
Richard Stone, President
Philip Clever, Station Manager

WARD
06-16-2000; 750 khz AM *Hrs Open:* 24*Rebroadcasts:* Rebroadcasts WLDR-FM Traverse City 100%
2175 Click Road, Petoskey, MI 49770 US
(231) 947-3220, *Fax:* (231) 947-7201
www.wldrradio.com
License: Petoskey, MI held by Roy E. Henderson.
Group Owner: Fort Bend Broadcasting Co.; (acq 4-25-2007; swap with WJNL(AM) Kingsley)
Arbitron Metro Market: Traverse City-Petoskey, MI *Format:* Country
Roy Henderson, General Manager

WKLZ-FM
12-07-1965; 98.9 mhz FM *Hrs Open:* 24; 100 kw; 801 ft.; N45 28 40 W84 57 4 *Rebroadcasts:* Rebroadcasts WKLT(FM) Kalkaska 85%
2215 Oak Indust. Dr. N.E, Grand Rapids, MI 49505 US
(231 947-0003, *Fax:* (231) 947-7002
www.wklt.com
License: Petoskey, Emmet County, MI held by Northern Radio of Petoskey Inc.
Nat'l Network: ABC *Nat'l Reps:* Christal
Arbitron Metro Market: Traverse City-Petoskey, MI *Format:* Rock/AOR *Hrs. of News Programming:* News progmg 2 hrs wkly
Target Audience: 18-49; baby boomers
Charlie Ferguson, General Manager
Greg Marsh, General Sales Mgr
Terri Ray, Programming Director
Kristal Flateau, News Director
Dennis Murray, Chief Engineer

WLXT
01-01-1967; 96.3 mhz FM; 100 kw; 981 ft.; N45 19 17 W84 52 33
P.O. Box 286, Petosky, MI 49770 US
(231) 347-8713, *Fax:* (231) 347-8782
www.lite96.com
info@lite96.com
License: Petoskey, Emmet County, MI held by MacDonald Garber Broadcasting Inc
Group Owner: MacDonald Garber Broadcasting Co.
Arbitron Metro Market: Traverse City, MI *Format:* Adult Contemp
No. News Employees: 4
Heather Leigh, Programming Director

WMBN
05-01-1946; 1340 khz AM *Hrs Open:* 24; 1 kw-U, ND1; N45 20 50 W84 58 1
Mailing Address: P.O. Box 286, Petosky, MI 49770 US
Second Address: 2095 U.S. 131 S., Petoskey, MI 49770
(231) 347-8713, *Fax:* (231) 347-8782
www.1340amwmbn.com
License: Petoskey, MI held by MacDonald Garber Broadcasting Inc.
Group Owner: MacDonald Garber Broadcasting Co.; acq 11-17-98; grpsl).
Nat'l Reps: D & R Radio
Arbitron Metro Market: Traverse City, MI *Format:* Sports *Hrs. of News Programming:* news progmg 2 hrs wkly *No. News Employees:* 2 *Target Audience:* 35 plus.
Trish MacDonald-Garber, General Manager
Kerry Davis, General Sales Mgr
Greg Marshall, Programming Director
Bob White, News Director
Brian Brachel, Chief Engineer

Pickford

WMKD
12-22-2000; 105.5 mhz FM; 100 kw; 253 ft.; N46 23 48 W84 23 52
5605 Chisolm Road, Johns Island, SC 29455 US
(231) 922-4981, *Fax:* (231) 922-3633
www.nsbroadcasting.com
mary@nsbroadcasting.com
License: Pickford, Chippewa County, MI held by Northern Star Broadcasting LLC.
Group Owner: Northern Star Broadcasting L.L.C.; (acq 10-21-2005; $900,000).
Arbitron Metro Market: Pickford, MI *Format:* Religious
Mary Reynolds, General Sales Mgr

Pinconning

WLUN
11-15-1983; 100.9 mhz FM *Hrs Open:* 24; 2.6 kw; 495 ft.; N43 50 46 W84 5 32
140 South Ash Avenue, Tempe, AZ 85281 US
(989) 837-6126, *Fax:* (989) 837-8780
License: Pinconning, Bay County, MI held by The Last Bastion Station Trust LLC, as Trustee
Nat'l Network: ESPN Radio
Arbitron Metro Market: Pinconning, MI *Format:* Sports, Talk
Target Audience: 25-54; general
Paul Barbeau, General Manager
Brad Golder, Programming Director

Pittsford

*WPCJ
10-23-1985; 91.1 mhz FM *Hrs Open:* 16; 0.27 kw; 184 ft.; N41 53 4 W84 28 15
9400 Beecher Road, Pittsford, MI 49271 US
(517) 523-3427, *Fax:* (517) 523-3427
www.freedomfarm.info
wpcj@freedomfarm.info
License: Pittsford, Hillsdale County, MI held by Pittsford Educational Broadcasting Foundation.
Nat'l Network: Moody
Format: Christian, Religious *Hrs. of News Programming:* News progmg 10 hrs wkly *Target Audience:* General; rural
Tim Neinas, Station Manager
Ed Trombley, Chief Engineer

Plymouth

*WSDP
02-14-1972; 88.1 mhz FM *Hrs Open:* 24; 0.2 kw; 72 ft.; N42 20 50 W83 29 51
46181 Joy Road, Canton, MI 48187 US
(734) 416-7732, *Fax:* (734) 416-7732
www.881theescape.com
881ThePark@gmail.com
License: Plymouth, Wayne County, MI held by Plymouth Canton Community Schools.
Arbitron Metro Market: Detroit *Format:* Contemporary Hits/Top 40 *Hrs. of News Programming:* News progmg 2 hrs wkly *Target Audience:* General.
Bill Keith, Station Manager
Dallas Haselhuhn, Programming Director
Lillian Thompson, Promotions Manager
Archana Sondor, News Director

Port Huron

WGRT
12-01-1991; 102.3 mhz FM *Hrs Open:* 24; 3 kw; 318 ft; N43 04 08 W82 28 48
624 Grand River Ave., Port Huron, MI 48060
(810) 987-3200, *Fax:* (810) 987-3325
www.wgrt.com
wgrtoffice@sbcglobal.net
License: Port Huron, St. Clair County, MI held by Port Huron Family Radio Inc.
Nat'l Network: ABC
Population Served: 200,000 *Arbitron Metro Market:* Detroit *No. News Employees:* 1 *Target Audience:* General.
Martin Doorn, President
Martin Doorn, General Manager
Bruce Peterson, General Sales Mgr
Cathie Martin, News Director
Susan Doorm, Promotions/Sales Manager
George Van Camp, Production Manager
Martha Van Camp, Client ServicesManager

WHLS
08-08-1938; 1450 khz AM *Hrs Open:* 24; 1 kw-U, ND1; N42 58 37 W82 27 52
Mailing Address: 808 Huron Avenue, Port Huron, MI 48060 US
Second Address: 808 Huron Ave., Port Huron, MI 48060
(810) 982-9000, *Fax:* (810) 987-9380
www.whls.net
whls@whls.net
License: Port Huron, MI held by Liggett Communications L.L.C.
Nat'l Reps: Michigan Spot Sales
Arbitron Metro Market: Detroit *Format:* Oldies *Special Programming:* Black one hr, Sp one hr wkly *Target Audience:* 18-50; middle class
Robert Liggett, Chairman
James Jensen, President
Lawrence Smith, General Manager
Kristine Sikkema, General Sales Mgr
Jim McKenzie, Programming Director
Bill Gilmer, News Director
Craig Bowman, Chief Engineer
Dennis Stuckey,Sports Commentator
Staci O'Brien, Traffic Manager

*WNFA
05-15-1986; 88.3 mhz FM *Hrs Open:* 24; 1.3 kw; 200 ft.; N42 59 36 W82 28 6 *Rebroadcasts:* Rebroadcasts WNFR(FM) Sandusky 100%
2865 Maywood Drive, Port Huron, MI 48060 US

(810) 985-3260, *Fax:* (810) 985-7712
www.power883.com
info@power883.com
License: Port Huron, St. Clair County, MI held by Ross Bible Church.
Nat'l Network: Moody; USA
Arbitron Metro Market: Port Huron, MI *Format:* Religious *Hrs. of News Programming:* News progmg 14 hrs wkly *Target Audience:* 25-44; females
Lori McNaughton, Operations Dir
Brian Smith, Programming Director
Ellyn Davey, Music Director

***WORW**
05-31-1973; 91.9 mhz FM; 0.18 kw horiz; 20 ft.; N43 1 30 W82 26 10
1799 Krafft Road, Port Huron, MI 48060 US
(810) 984-2675, *Fax:* (810) 984-2747
www.port-huron.k12.mi.us/ourschools/highschools/phn/actclubs/worwradiostation/
License: Port Huron, St. Clair County, MI held by Port Huron Area School District.
TV Affiliate: var

WPHM
12-06-1947; 1380 khz AM *Hrs Open:* 24; 5 kw-D, DA2; 5 kw-N, DA2; N42 51 50 W82 29 40
2379 Military Street, Port Huron, MI 48060 US
(810) 982-9000, *Fax:* (810) 987-9380
www.wphm.net
info@wphmam.net
License: Port Huron, MI held by Liggett Communications L.L.C.
Group Owner: Liggett Communications L.L.C.; acq 5-1-2000; grpsl).
Nat'l Reps: Michigan Spot Sales *Wire Services:* NWS (National Weather Service)
Arbitron Metro Market: Detroit *Format:* News, News/Talk, 86 *Hrs. of News Programming:* News progmg 40 hrs wkly *Target Audience:* 25-54.
Robert Liggett, Chairman
James Jewsen, President
Lawrence Smith, General Manager
Kristine Sikkema, General Sales Mgr
Paul Miller, Programming Director
Craig Bowman, Engineering Dir

WSAQ
08-07-1964; 107.1 mhz FM *Hrs Open:* 24; 6 kw; 299 ft.; N42 58 37 W82 27 52
Mailing Address: 808 Huron Avenue, Port Huron, MI 48061 US
Second Address: 808 Huron Ave., Port Huron, MI 48060
(810) 982-9000, *Fax:* (810) 987-9380
www.wsaq.net
License: Port Huron, St. Clair County, MI held by Liggett Communications L.L.C.
Arbitron Metro Market: Detroit *Format:* Country *Target Audience:* 25-55.
Farid Suleman, CEO
Judy Ellis, President
Mark Ericson, Operations Dir
Marty Lessard, General Manager
Scott Shigley, General Sales Mgr
Chuck Santoni, Programming Director

***WSGR-FM**
10-01-1971; 91.3 mhz FM; 0.12 kw; 43 ft.; N42 58 43 W82 25 45
323 Erie Street, P.O. Box 5015, Port Huron, MI 48061 US
(313) 989-5646, *Fax:* (313) 984-2852
License: Port Huron, St. Clair County, MI held by St. Clair County Community College.
Format: Jazz *Special Programming:* Metal-hard rock 12 hrs, urban 6 hrs wkly *Target Audience:* General; all age groups
John Hill, General Manager

Portage

WKZO-FM
06-01-1992; 96.5 mhz FM; 3 kw; Ant 321 ft; N42 12 55 W85 36 37
4200 W. Main St., Kalamazoo, MI 54403
(269) 345-7121, *Fax:* (269) 345-1436
www.y965country.com
License: Portage, Kalamazoo County, MI held by Midwest Communications Inc.
Group Owner: Midwest Communications Inc.
Nat'l Reps: Christal
Arbitron Metro Market: Kalamazoo, MI *No. News Employees:* 4 *Target Audience:* 25-49.
D.J. Wright, President
Mike Klein, General Sales Mgr
P.J. Lacey, Programming Director
Peter Tanz, Promotions Manager
Walker Sisson, Engineering Dir

WNWN
07-25-1986; 1560 khz AM; 4.1 kw-D, DAD; N42 10 59 W85 35 30
P. O. Box 2048, Wausau, WI 54402 US
(269) 345-7121, *Fax:* (269) 345-1436
www.1560radio.com
License: Portage, MI held by Midwest Communications Inc.
Group Owner: Midwest Communications Inc.; acq 1995; grpsl)
Nat'l Reps: Christal
Arbitron Metro Market: Kalamazoo, MI *TV Affiliate:* Urban contemp *Format:* Blues *Special Programming:* news progmg 5 hrs wkly *Hrs. of News Programming:* 2 *No. News Employees:* 25-54; emphasis on 35-50

WYZO-FM
06-01-1992; 96.5 mhz FM; 3 kw; Ant 321 ft; N42 12 55 W85 36 37
4200 W. Main St., Kalamazoo, MI 49006
(269) 345-7121, *Fax:* (269) 345-1436
www.y965country.com
License: Portage, Kalamazoo County, MI held by Midwest Communications Inc.
Group Owner: Midwest Communications Inc.
Nat'l Reps: Christal
Arbitron Metro Market: Kalamazoo, MI *Format:* Country *No. News Employees:* 4 *Target Audience:* 25-49.
D.J. Wright, President
Mike Klein, General Sales Mgr
P.J. Lacey, Programming Director
Peter Tanz, Promotions Manager
Walker Sisson, Engineering Dir

WRKR
10-13-1988; 107.7 mhz FM *Hrs Open:* 24; 50 kw; 486 ft.; N42 7 44 W85 20 22
330 East Kilbourn Ave., Suite 250, Milwaukee, WI 53202 US
(269) 344-0111, *Fax:* (269) 344-4223
www.wrkr.com
radio@wrkr.com
License: Portage, Kalamazoo County, MI held by Cumulus Licensing Corp.
Group Owner: Cumulus Media Inc.; (acq 5-26-98; grpsl)
Arbitron Metro Market: Kalamazoo, MI *Format:* Classic Rock, Rock/AOR *Special Programming:* Blues 5 hrs, jazz 4 hrs wkly *Hrs. of News Programming:* news progmg 4 hrs wkly *No. News Employees:* 2 *Target Audience:* 25-54.
Lew Dickey, CEO
Mike McKelly, Operations Dir
Jay Deacon, Programming Director
Dale Schiesser, Chief Engineer
Martin Gausvik, CFO
John Pinch, COO

Powers

WUPF
01-01-2008; 107.3 mhz FM; 50 kw; 318 ft.; N45 42 39 W87 20 49 US
(906) 233-0279, *Fax:* (906) 233-0282
www.radioeagleescanaba.com
kent@radioeagle.com
License: Powers, Menominee County, MI held by Radioactive LLC.
Group Owner: Radioactive LLC
Arbitron Metro Market: Powers, MI *Format:* Classic Rock
Benjamin Homel, President
Kent Smith, General Manager
Rosemary Smith, General Sales Mgr
Chip Arledge, Programming Director
Lisa Glish, Senior Account Executive

Raco

***WJOH**
01-01-2006; 91.5 mhz FM; 5.5 kw; 328 ft.; N46 23 28 W84 27 52
Rebroadcasts: simulcasts WJOM (FM) Eagle 100%
US
(888) 887-7140
www.smile.fm
Jennc@smile.fm
License: Raco, Chippewa County, MI held by Michigan Community Radio.
Arbitron Metro Market: Raco, MI *Format:* Christian
Ed Czelada, President
Ed Czelada, Administration, Programming & Engineering
Clayton Hewitt, Administration and Engineering
Aaron Burrell, Administration
Dale Mazzoline, Production

Reed City

WDEE-FM
08-16-1997; 97.3 mhz FM; 2.85 kw; 479 ft.; N43 46 53 W85 36 58
101 S. Higbee, Reed City, MI 49677 US
(231)796-9730, *Fax:* (231) 796-9738
www.sunny973.com
sunny@sunny973.com
License: Reed City, Osceola County, MI held by Steven V. Beilfuss.
Arbitron Metro Market: Reed City, MI *Format:* Oldies *Target Audience:* 35 plus; anyone who likes oldies
Steven Beilfuss, General Manager
Scott Roman, News Director

Republic

WUPG
01-01-2008; 96.7 mhz FM; 50 kw; 351 ft.; N46 30 29.2 W87 58 6.5
US
(906) 485-4313, *Fax:* (906) 485-4313
www.radioeaglemarquette.com
License: Republic, Marquette County, MI held by Radioactive LLC.
Group Owner: Radioactive LLC
Arbitron Metro Market: Republic, MI
Benjamin Homel, President
Kent Smith, General Manager
Sally Mitchell, General Sales Mgr
Chip Arledge, Programming Director

Richland

***WMJC**
01-01-2008; 91.9 mhz FM; 6 kw vert; Ant 221 ft; N42 27 13 W85 20 39
5331 Mt. Alifan Dr., San Diego, CA
(858) 277-4991, *Fax:* (858) 277-1365
www.ksrdradio.com
License: Richland, Kalamazoo County, MI held by Horizon Christian Fellowship.
Group Owner: Horizon Christian Fellowship; (acq 2-3-2006; $250,000 for CP)

Mike MacIntosh, President
Brian KC Jones, General Manager

Riverside

***WSIS**
01-01-2008; 88.7 mhz FM; 6 kw; 384 ft.; N42 15 14 W86 20 9
Rebroadcasts: Rebroadcasts WHYT(FM) Goodland Township 100%
3302 N Van Dyke, Imlay City, MI 48444 US
(517) 381-0573, *Fax:* (877) 850-0881
www.smile.fm
411@smile.fm
License: Riverside, Missaukee County, MI held by Smile FM.
Group Owner: Superior Communications
Arbitron Metro Market: Riverside, MI *Format:* Christian
Jenn Czelada, General Manager
Aaron Burrell, Administration
Clayton Hewitt, Administration and Engineering
Ed Czelada, Administration, Programming & Engineering
Dale Mazzoline, Production

Rockford

WMJH
01-01-1965; 810 khz AM; 3.6 kw-D, NDD; N43 7 5 W85 34 46
6272 28th Street, S.E., Grand Rapids, MI 49546 US
(616) 451-0551, *Fax:* (616) 451-0565
www.birach.com/
elprimo_e@yahoo.com
License: Rockford, MI held by Birach Broadcasting Corp.
Group Owner: Birach Broadcasting Corp.; (acq 11-6-2001; $1.9 million with WMFN(AM) Zeeland).
Nat'l Network: CBS; Westwood One
Arbitron Metro Market: Grand Rapids, MI| *Target Audience:* 30 plus.
Efraim Cano, General Manager

Rogers City

WHAK
05-01-1949; 960 khz AM; 5 kw-D, ND1; 0.136 kw-N, ND1; N45 23 53 W83 55 19
1491 M -32, West, Alpena, MI 49707 US

(989) 354-4611, *Fax:* (989) 354-4014
www.1007theundercountry.com
tnrn@charterinternet.com
License: Rogers City, MI held by Edwards Communications LC
Group Owner: Edwards Communications L.C.
Nat'l Reps: Michigan Spot Sales
Format: Country *Target Audience:* 18-75.
Darrell Kelly, Programming Director
Mary Garrow, News Director

WHAK-FM
04-01-1994; 99.9 mhz FM; 50 kw; 476 ft.; N45 23 53 W83 55 19
1491 M-32 West, Alpena, MI 49707 US
(989) 354-4611, *Fax:* (989) 354-4014
www.999thewave.com
tnrn@charterinternet.com
License: Rogers City, Presque Isle County, MI held by Edwards Communications LC
Group Owner: Edwards Communications L.C.; (acq 12-21-2004; grpsl).
Format: Oldies
Tony Calumet, General Manager
Danny Stann, Programming Director
Phil Heimerl, News Director
Darrel Kelly, Chief Engineer
Mary Garrow, Traffic Manager

WRGZ
06-16-1984; 96.7 mhz FM; 42 kw; 531 ft.; N45 21 2 W83 46 59
Rebroadcasts: Simulcast with WATZ-FM Alpena 100%
Mailing Address: 3800 Victory Parkway, Cincinnati, OH 45207 US
Second Address: 123 Prentiss St., Alpena, MI 49707
(989) 354-8400, *Fax:* (989) 354-3436
www.watz.com
watz@watz.com
License: Rogers City, Presque Isle County, MI held by WATZ Radio Inc.
Group Owner: Midwestern Broadcasting Co.; (acq 5-26-2006; $411,000).
Arbitron Metro Market: Alpena, MI *Format:* Country *No. News Employees:* 1
Mike Centala, General Manager
Bruce Johnson, News Director
Mark Nowak, Chief Engineer
Phil Wenzel, Music Director
Sheryl Wright, Traffic Coordinator
Steven J. Wright, Operations

Roscommon

WQON
03-01-1990; 101.1 mhz FM *Hrs Open:* 24; 3.4 kw; 443 ft.; N44 34 15 W84 41 33
6514 Old Lake Rd., Grayling, MI 49738 US
(989) 348-6171, *Fax:* (989) 348-6181
www.gannonbroadcasting.com
radio@i2k.net
License: Roscommon, Roscommon County, MI held by Gannon Broadcasting Systems Inc.
Nat'l Reps: Michigan Spot Sales
Format: Adult Contemp *Hrs. of News Programming:* news progmg 16 hrs wkly *No. News Employees:* 1 *Target Audience:* 25 plus.
Pete Michaels, Operations Dir
William Gannon, General Manager

Rose Township

***WMSD**
08-11-2000; 90.9 mhz FM *Hrs Open:* 24; 5 kw vert; Ant 69 ft; N44 25 58 W84 00 33
2906 E Heath Rd., Lupton, MI 48635
(989) 473-4616
www.wmsdradio.com
wmsd@M33access.com
License: Rose Township, Ogemaw County, MI held by Bible Baptist Church.
Population Served: 90,000
Paul Heaton, President
Paul Heaton, Programming Director
Dan Karbginsky, Chief Engineer
Tony Madaj, Assistant Programming Director
Kim Landenberg, Office Manager

Royal Oak

WEXL
10-01-1923; 1340 khz AM *Hrs Open:* 24; 1 kw-D, DAD; 1 kw-N, DAD; N42 28 10 W83 6 54
P.O. Box 3003, Blue Bell, PA 19422 US
(313) 272 -1340, *Fax:* (313) 272-5045
www.wexl1340.com
station@wmuz.com
License: Royal Oak, MI held by WMUZ Radio Inc.
Group Owner: Crawford Broadcasting Co.; (acq 4-18-97; $3.5 million)
Arbitron Metro Market: Royal Oak, MI *Format:* Gospel *Target Audience:* General.
Rich Hanovich, Operations Dir
Frank Franciosi, General Manager

Rust Township

***WJOJ**
12-01-2001; 89.7 mhz FM; 0.001 kw horiz, 31 kw vert; 469 ft.; N44 42 12 W83 31 27
2628 Howard Road, Petoskey, MI 49770 US
(810) 721-0891
411@smile.fm.com
License: Rust Township, Alcona County, MI held by Northland Community Broadcasters.
Arbitron Metro Market: Harrisville, MI *Format:* Christian
Jenn Czelada, General Manager
Ed Czelada, Programming Director

Saginaw

WGER
02-19-1969; 106.3 mhz FM; 4.4 kw; 381 ft.; N43 28 36 W83 57 6
140 South Ash Avenue, Tempe, AZ 85281 US
(989) 752-3456, *Fax:* (989)754-5046
www.mix1063fm.com
License: Saginaw, Saginaw County, MI
Arbitron Metro Market: Saginaw-Bay City-Midland, MI *Format:* Adult Contemp *Target Audience:* 25-54; upscale, mid/high level income
Brian Fig Figula, Programming Director

WILZ
01-01-1992; 104.5 mhz FM; 2.9 kw; 413 ft.; N43 23 34 W83 55 27
140 South Ash Avenue, Tempe, AZ 85281 US
(989) 776-2100, *Fax:* (989) 754-5990
www.wheelz.fm
info@wheelz.fm
License: Saginaw, Saginaw County, MI
Group Owner: Cumulus Media Inc.; (acq 2-8-99).
Nat'l Reps: McGavren Guild
Arbitron Metro Market: Saginaw-Bay City-Midland, MI *Format:* Classic Rock *Target Audience:* 35-54; adults
Scott Meier, Operations Dir
Stan Parman, Programming Director
Bob Friedle, Chief Engineer
Hal Maas, Music Director

WKCQ
01-01-1947; 98.1 mhz FM; 50 kw; 492 ft.; N43 25 4 W83 55 6
Mailing Address: P.O. Box 1776, Saginaw, MI 48605 US
Second Address: 2000 Whittier Street, Saginaw, MI 48601
(989) 752-8161, *Fax:* (989) 752-8102
www.98fmkcq.com
License: Saginaw, Saginaw County, MI
Group Owner: MacDonald Broadcasting Co.
Nat'l Reps: Eastman Radio *Regional Reps:* Eastman Radio *Wire Services:* AP
Arbitron Metro Market: Saginaw-Bay City-Midland, MI *Format:* Country *No. News Employees:* 1
Ken MacDonald, Jr., CEO
Duane Alverson, President
Cindy Tuck, Operations Dir
Mary Yearham, General Sales Mgr
Jim Kramer, Operations Manager

WSAM
01-01-1940; 1400 khz AM; 1 kw-U, ND1; N43 25 0 W83 55 5
Mailing Address: P.O. Box 1776, Saginaw, MI 48605 US
Second Address: 2000 Whittier Street, Saginaw, MI 48605
(989) 752-8161, *Fax:* (989) 752-8102
thebay104fm.com
License: Saginaw, MI held by MacDonald Broadcasting Co.
Group Owner: MacDonald Broadcasting Co.; acq 12-20-2001; grpsl).
Nat'l Reps: Eastman Radio *Regional Reps:* Eastman Radio
Arbitron Metro Market: Saginaw-Bay Cit *Format:* Easy Listening *No. News Employees:* 1 *Target Audience:* 25 plus.
Ken MacDonald, Jr., CEO
Duane Alverson, President
Jim Kramer, Operations Dir
Mary Yearham, General Sales Mgr
Cindy Tuck, Vice President

WSGW
08-11-1950; 790 khz AM *Hrs Open:* 24; 5 kw-D, DA2; 1 kw-N, DA2; N43 27 40 W83 48 48
140 South Ash Avenue, Tempe, AZ 85281 US
(989) 752-6111, *Fax:* (989) 754-5046
www.wsgw.com
info@wsgw.com
License: Saginaw, MI held by NM Licensing LLC.
Group Owner: NextMedia Group Inc.; (acq 12-30-2002; grpsl).
Nat'l Network: CBS *Regional Network:* Mich. Farm
Arbitron Metro Market: Saginaw-Bay Cit *Format:* News, News/Talk, 86 *Special Programming:* Farm 10 hrs wkly *Hrs. of News Programming:* news progmg 40 hrs wkly *No. News Employees:* 5 *Target Audience:* 35-54;general
Dave Maurer, Operations Dir
Shannone Dunlap, General Manager
Terry Henne, General Sales Mgr
Doug Brinks, Chief Engineer

WTLZ
11-15-1968; 107.1 mhz FM *Hrs Open:* 24; 4.9 kw; 361 ft.; N43 21 14 W83 55 6
P.O. Box 690, New Castle, IN 47362 US
(989) 921-7107, *Fax:* (989) 754-5046
www.kisswtlz.com
License: Saginaw, Saginaw County, MI held by NM Licensing LLC.
Group Owner: NextMedia Group Inc.; (acq 12-30-02).
Nat'l Network: American Urban
Arbitron Metro Market: Saginaw, MI *Format:* Blues *Special Programming:* Gospel 6 hrs wkly *Hrs. of News Programming:* News progmg 6 hrs wkly *Target Audience:* 18-49; upscale, Blacks, women
Shannone Dunlap, General Manager
Yvonne Daniels, Programming Director

Saint Johns

WQTX
07-15-1972; 92.1 mhz FM *Hrs Open:* 24; 6 kw; Ant 400 ft; N42 53 29 W84 34 27
2495 N. Cedar, Holt, MI 48823
(517) 699-0111, *Fax:* (517) 699-1880
www.wqtx.net
wqtx@wqtx.net
License: Saint Johns, Clinton County, MI held by Midwest Communications Inc.
Group Owner: Rubber City Radio Group Inc.; (acq 7-1-2010; grpsl)
Nat'l Network: Jones Radio Networks *Nat'l Reps:* Katz Radio
Wire Services: AP
Population Served: 397,000 *Arbitron Metro Market:* Lansing-East Lansing, MI *Hrs. of News Programming:* news progmg 8 hrs wkly *No. News Employees:* 1 *Target Audience:* 35 plus. *Adv. Rates:* 35; 35; 35; 25
Thomas Mandel, President
Dave Johnson, General Manager
Drew Henderson, Programming Director
Mark Biviano, Executive Vice President
Nick Anthony, Executive Vice President

Salem Township

WSDS
01-01-1962; 1480 khz AM *Hrs Open:* 24; 0.75 kw-D, DA2; 3.8 kw-N, DA2; N42 15 42 W83 37 10
580 West Clark Road, Ypsilanti, MI 48197 US
(734) 484-1480, *Fax:* (734) 484-5313
wsds@wsds1480.com
License: Salem Township, MI held by Birach Broadcasting Corp.
Group Owner: Birach Broadcasting Corp.; (acq 1-25-2005; $1.5 million).
Arbitron Metro Market: Ann Arbor, MI *Special Programming:* Mexican Regional Music and Latin *Hrs. of News Programming:* top at hour 8am-8pm *No. News Employees:* 1 *Target Audience:* 25 plus. *Adv. Rates:* 55x60sec - 45x30sec
Jose Vazquez, President
Carmen Perez, Operations Dir
Alex Resendez, General Manager
Francisco Urrutia, General Sales Mgr
Miguel Vega, Programming Director
Ivonne Machado, Promotions Manager
Ralph Hines, Chief Engineer

Saline

WLBY
01-01-1958; 1290 khz AM *Hrs Open:* Sunrise-sunset; 0.5 kw-D, DA2; 0.026 kw-N, DA2; N42 12 17 W83 47 19
330 East Kilbourn Ave., Suite 250, Milwaukee, WI 53202 US

(734) 302-8100, *Fax:* (734) 213-7508
www.1290wlby.com
programming@1290wlby.com
License: Saline, MI held by Capstar TX L.P.
Group Owner: Clear Channel Communications Inc.; (acq 8-7-2000; grpsl)
Nat'l Reps: Cumulus Radio Sales *Wire Services:* AP
Arbitron Metro Market: Ann Arbor, MI *Format:* Talk *Hrs. of News Programming:* news progmg 15 hrs wkly *No. News Employees:* 1
Scott Meier, General Manager
Jessica Husted, General Sales Mgr
Chris Ammel, Programming Director
Ryan Albig, Promotions Manager
Doug Gondek, Local Sales Manager

Sandusky

WMIC
06-27-1968; 660 khz AM; 1 kw-D, DAD; N43 23 34 W82 49 57
19 South Elk Street, Sandusky, MI 48471 US
(810) 648-2700, *Fax:* (810) 648-3242
www.sanilacbroadcasting.com
wmic@avc1.net
License: Sandusky, MI held by Sanilac Broadcasting Co.
Regional Network: Mich. Farm
Arbitron Metro Market: Sandusky, MI *Format:* Country, News, 62, Talk *Special Programming:* Farm 12 hrs, Pol 5 wkly *Hrs. of News Programming:* news progmg 20 hrs wkly *No. News Employees:* 2 *Target Audience:* 25 plus; general *Adv. Rates:* 13; 13; 13; 13
George Benko, President
Robert Benko, Operations Dir
Bob Armstrong, General Manager
Stan Grabitz, Programming Director
Renae Davis, News Director
Kevin Larke, Chief Engineer

*WNFR
02-14-1994; 90.7 mhz FM; 42 kw; 492 ft.; N43 10 27 W82 36 1
Rebroadcasts: Rebroadcasts WNFA(FM) Port Huron 100%
2865 Maywood Drive, Port Huron, MI 48060 US
(810) 985-3260, *Fax:* (810) 985-7712
www.wnradio.com
License: Sandusky, Sanilac County, MI held by Ross Bible Church.
Nat'l Network: Moody; USA
Arbitron Metro Market: Sandusky, MI *Format:* Religious *Target Audience:* 25-44; females
Lori McNaughton, Operations Dir
Brian Smith, Station Manager
Ellyn Davey, Programming Director
Jana Simpson, News Director
Ed Czelada, Chief Engineer

WTGV-FM
08-16-1971; 97.7 mhz FM *Hrs Open:* 24; 3 kw; 325 ft.; N43 23 34 W82 50 6
19 South Elk Street, Sandusky, MI 48471 US
(810) 648-2700, *Fax:* (810) 648-3242
www.sanilacbroadcasting.com
boba@sanilacbroadcasting.com
License: Sandusky, Sanilac County, MI held by Sanilac Broadcasting Co
Arbitron Metro Market: Sandusky, MI *Format:* Adult Contemp *Adv. Rates:* 13; 13; 13; 13
Bob Armstrong, General Manager
Stan Grabiitz, Programming Director
Renae Davis, News Director
George Benko, Founder
Robert Benko, Founder

Saugatuck

WYVN
07-04-1987; 92.7 mhz FM *Hrs Open:* 24; 3.3 kw; 374 ft.; N42 41 10 W86 10 5
P.O. Bx 927 403 Water St, Saugatuck, MI 49453 US
(616) 392-3121, *Fax:* (616) 392-8066
www.927thevan.com
esther.gillis@mwcradio.com
License: Saugatuck, Allegan County, MI held by Midwest Communications Inc.
Group Owner: Midwest Communications Inc.; (acq 9-5-2001)
Nat'l Reps: Christal
Arbitron Metro Market: Saugatuck, MI *Format:* Contemporary Hits/Top 40, Adult Contemp *Hrs. of News Programming:* news progmg one hr wkly *No. News Employees:* 1 *Target Audience:* 25-54.
D.E. Wright, President
Kevin Oswald, General Sales Mgr

Brent Alan, Programming Director
Peter Tanz, Promotions Manager
Gary Stevens, News Director

Sault Sainte Marie

WKNW
08-25-1990; 1400 khz AM *Hrs Open:* 24; 1 kw-D, ND1; 0.95 kw-N, ND1; N46 29 18 W84 19 45
980 North Michigan Ave., Suite 1880, Chicago, IL 60611 US
(906) 635-0995, *Fax:* (906) 635-1216
License: Sault Sainte Marie, MI held by Northern Star Broadcasting L.L.C.
Group Owner: Northern Star Broadcasting L.L.C.
Format: News, News/Talk, 84, Talk
Paul Van Wagner, Programming Director

Sault Ste. Marie

*WCMZ-FM
07-13-1990; 98.3 mhz FM *Hrs Open:* 24; 25 kw; 328 ft.; N46 29 10 W84 13 49 *Rebroadcasts:* Rebroadcasts WCMU-FM Mount Pleasant 100%
3965 E. Broomfield Road, Mt. Pleasant, MI 48859 US
(989) 774-3105, *Fax:* (989) 774-4427
www.wcmu.org
schud1ra@cmich.edu
License: Sault Ste. Marie, Chippewa County, MI held by Central Michigan University.
Nat'l Network: NPR; PRI *Regional Network:* Mich. Radio *Wire Services:* AP
Arbitron Metro Market: Michigan, Upper Peninsula,MS *Format:* Jazz, News *Hrs. of News Programming:* news progmg 45 hrs wkly *No. News Employees:* 2 *Target Audience:* General.
Ed Grant, General Manager
Ann Blatte, General Sales Mgr
Ray Ford, Programming Director
Art Curtis, Promotions Manager
Randy Kapenga, Chief Engineer

*WLSO
01-01-1995; 90.1 mhz FM; 0.1 kw; 98 ft.; N46 29 31 W84 21 48
1000 College Drive, Sault Sainte Marie, MI 49783 US
(906) 635-2107, *Fax:* (906) 635-2111
www.lssu.edu/wlso
wlso@gw.lssu.edu
License: Sault Ste. Marie, Chippewa County, MI held by Lake Superior State University.
Format: Variety/Diverse
Scott Korb, General Sales Mgr

WSOO
06-01-1940; 1230 khz AM; 1 kw-U, ND1; N46 26 16 W84 22 42
1219 North Mission Rd., Mt. Pleasant, MI 48858 US
(906) 632-2231, *Fax:* (906) 632-4411
License: Sault Ste. Marie, MI held by Sovereign Communications LLC
Nat'l Network: ABC; ESPN Radio *Nat'l Reps:* Michigan Spot Sales
Format: Adult Contemp
Tom Ewing, General Manager
Linda Peters, General Sales Mgr
Mark Sanangelo, Programming Director
John Bell, News Director

WSUE
01-01-1978; 101.3 mhz FM; 100 kw; 220 ft.; N46 26 16 W84 22 42
P.O. Box 1230, Sault Ste. Marie, MI 49783 US
(906) 632-2231, *Fax:* (906) 632-4411
License: Sault Ste. Marie, Chippewa County, MI
Format: Classic Rock
Peter Johams, General Manager

WYSS
07-12-1972; 99.5 mhz FM; 100 kw; 253 ft.; N46 23 48 W84 23 52
980 North Michigan Ave., Suite 1880, Chicago, IL 60611 US
(906) 635-0995, *Fax:* (906) 635-1216
www.995yesfm.com
License: Sault Ste. Marie, Chippewa County, MI held by Northern Star Broadcasting L.L.C.
Group Owner: Northern Star Broadcasting L.L.C.; acq 11-5-01; grpsl).
Nat'l Network: Westwood One
Arbitron Metro Market: Altoona, PA *Format:* Contemporary Hits/Top 40 *Target Audience:* 18-49.
Keith Neve, General Manager
Tim Ellis, Programming Director
Brian Larson, News Director
Carol Howe, Chief Engineer
Renee Peterson, Traffic Manager

*WTHN
01-29-2005; 102.3 mhz FM *Hrs Open:* 24; 22.5 kw; 344 ft.; N46 29 8 W84 13 49 *Rebroadcasts:* WPHN (FM) Gaylord 100%
1511 M-32 East, Gaylord, MI 49735 US
(989) 732-6274, *Fax:* (989) 732-8171
www.ncradio.org
ncr@ncradio.org
License: Sault Ste. Marie, Chippewa County, MI held by Northern Christian Radio Inc.
Group Owner: Northern Christian Radio Inc.
Arbitron Metro Market: Gaylord, MI *Format:* Christian, Religious
George Lake Jr., CEO

Schoolcraft

*WOFR
05-01-2003; 89.5 mhz FM *Hrs Open:* 24; 10 kw; 138 ft.; N42 6 38 W85 37 57
Mailing Address: 4135 Northgate Blvd, Suite 1, Sacramento, CA 95834 US
Second Address: 290 Hegenberger Rd., Oakland, CA 94621
(800) 543-1495, *Fax:* (916) 641-8238
www.familyradio.com
international@familyradio.com
License: Schoolcraft, Kalamazoo County, MI held by Family Stations Inc.
Group Owner: Family Stations Inc.
Arbitron Metro Market: Oakland, CA *Format:* Christian, Religious
John Rorvik, Operations Dir
Harold Camping, General Manager
Craig Hulsebos, Programming Director

Scottville

WKZC
02-16-1983; 94.9 mhz FM *Hrs Open:* 24; 17 kw; 400 ft.; N44 3 27 W86 24 58
215 Harbor Drive, Ludington, MI 49431 US
(231) 843-3438, *Fax:* (231) 843-1886
www.yourcountryz95.com
mike@wkla.com.com
License: Scottville, Mason County, MI held by Lake Michigan Broadcasting Inc.
Group Owner: Lake Michigan Broadcasting Inc.; (acq 9-20-96; grpsl).
Nat'l Network: ABC *Nat'l Reps:* Patt
Format: Country *Hrs. of News Programming:* news progmg 5 hrs wkly *No. News Employees:* 1 *Target Audience:* 25-54. *Adv. Rates:* 22; 18; 20; 10
Lynn Baerwolf, President
Jason Wilder, Operations Dir

Shepherd

WMMI
02-02-1987; 830 khz AM *Hrs Open:* Daytime; 1 kw-D, NDD; N43 33 42 W84 45 0
4065 East Wing Rd, Mount Pleasant, MI 48858 US
(989) 772-9664, *Fax:* (989) 773-5000
www.wczy.net
wczy@wczy.net
License: Shepherd, MI held by Central Michigan Communications Inc.
Regional Network: Mich. Talk *Nat'l Reps:* Michigan Spot Sales
Regional Reps: Patt. *Wire Services:* AP
Arbitron Metro Market: Shepherd, MI *Format:* Talk *Hrs. of News Programming:* news progmg 6 hrs wkly *No. News Employees:* 1 *Target Audience:* 25-54; general *Adv. Rates:* 18; 18; 18; N/A
Mike Carey, President
John Sebastian, Programming Director
Tina Sawyer, News Director
Lisa Johnson, Traffic Manager

South Haven

WCSY-FM
03-01-1996; 103.7 mhz FM *Hrs Open:* 24; 3 kw; 328 ft.; N42 18 2 W86 15 3
P O Box 107, St. Joseph, MI 49085 US
(269) 637-6397, *Fax:* (269) 637-2675
www.wcsy.com
spencer@wcsy.com
License: South Haven, Van Buren County, MI held by WSJM Inc.
Group Owner: The Mid-West Family Broadcast Group; (acq 4-96; grpsl)
Nat'l Network: ABC *Nat'l Reps:* Rgnl Reps *Wire Services:* AP
Arbitron Metro Market: South Haven, MI *Format:* Oldies *Special Programming:* The Daily Buzz with Paul Layendecker - Weekdays at 9am and Noon, TejanoMex SUPERSHOW - Sunday 6-10PM

Gayle Olson, President
Dave Doetsch, Vice President / General Manager:
Joe Jason, Station Manager
Bob Bucholtz, General Sales Mgr
Sue Patzen, Promotions Manager
Annette Weston, News Director
Terry Green, Chief Engineer
SpencerRivers, Content Director
Paul Layendecker, Operations Manager
Zack East, Assistant Operations Manager

Southfield

***WSHJ**
02-28-1967; 88.3 mhz FM *Hrs Open:* 7:30 AM-10 PM; 0.105 kw; 69 ft.; N42 28 12 W83 15 51
24675 Lahser Road, Southfield, MI 48034 US
(248) 746-8500
www.southfield.k12.mi.us
License: Southfield, Oakland County, MI held by Board of Education Southfield Public Schools.
Arbitron Metro Market: Detroit *Format:* Oldies *Target Audience:* General; students & families
Jamie Rudolph, General Manager

Spring Arbor

***WJKN-FM**
01-01-2005; 89.3 mhz FM; 2.5 kw vert; 272 ft.; N42 9 13 W84 32 57
106 E Main Street, Spring Arbor, MI 49283 US
(517) 750-6540, *Fax:* (517) 750-6619
www.893themessage.com
info@893themessage.com
License: Spring Arbor, Jackson County, MI held by Spring Arbor University.
Arbitron Metro Market: Spring Arbor, MI *Format:* Christian
Malachi Crane, General Manager
Tonya Hernandez, Programming Director
Rachel Ryder, Promotions Manager
Dave Benson, Chief Engineer
Malachi Crane, Executive Director

Springfield

***WCFG**
90.9 mhz FM *Hrs Open:* 24; 0.7 kw; 351 ft.; N42 21 20 W85 20 28
1159 E Beltline Ave Ne, Grand Rapids, MI 49505 US
(616) 942-1500, *Fax:* (616) 942-7078
www.wcsg.org
wcsg@wcsg.org
License: Springfield, Calhoun County, MI held by Cornerstone University.
Arbitron Metro Market: Springfield, MI *Format:* Christian *Target Audience:* 35-49.
Chris Lemke, General Manager

St. Ignace

WIDG
06-07-1966; 940 khz AM *Hrs Open:* Sunrise-sunset
232 Front Street, No. 2, Traverse City, MI 49684 US
(231) 238-0811, *Fax:* (231) 238-0803
www.baragabroadcasting.com
Christine@baragamail.com
License: St. Ignace, MI held by Baraga Broadcasting Inc.
Format: Christian
Harry Speckman, General Manager
Christine Schicker, Station Manager
Brian Brachel, Chief Engineer
Fr. Harry Speckman, Advisor
Tom McMahon, Marketing
Bob Fraiser, Controller
Irene Morrison, Fundraising and Data-Base
SuzanneHerpel, Secretary

St. Johns

WWSJ
09-23-1959; 1580 khz AM *Hrs Open:* 24; 1 kw-D, DA2; 0.003 kw-N, DA2; N42 58 14 W84 32 59
815 Maryland Ne, Grand Rapids, MI 49505 US
(989) 224-7911, *Fax:* (989) 224-4683
www.wwsj.com
info@wwsj.com
License: St. Johns, MI held by L. Harp, H. Harp, W. Hill, Elmira Hill.
Nat'l Network: American Urban
Arbitron Metro Market: Lansing, MI *Format:* Gospel *Adv. Rates:* 20; 20; 20; 10
Larry Harp, President
Helen Harp, Programming Director
Danielle Beckley, Promotions Manager
Ed Czelada, Chief Engineer
Dione Harp, Music Director

St. Joseph

WIRX
06-20-1966; 107.1 mhz FM *Hrs Open:* 24; 1.2 kw; 499 ft.; N42 4 19 W86 22 14
Mailing Address: P.O. Box 107, St. Joseph, MI 49085 US
Second Address: 580 E. Napier, Saint Joseph, MI 49022
(269) 925-1111, *Fax:* (269) 925-1011
wirx.com
info@wirx.com
License: St. Joseph, Berrien County, MI
Group Owner: The Mid-West Family Broadcast Group
Wire Services: AP
Target Audience: 18-49.
Bob Bucholtz, General Sales Mgr

WSJM
11-18-1956; 1400 khz AM *Hrs Open:* 24; 0.88 kw-U, ND1; N42 5 12 W86 26 40
Mailing Address: Box 107, St Joseph, MI 49085 US
Second Address: 580 E. Napier, Benton Harbor, MI 49022
(269) 925-1111, *Fax:* (269) 925-1011
www.wsjm.com
info@wsjm.com
License: St. Joseph, MI held by WSJM Inc.
Group Owner: The Mid-West Family Broadcast Group; (acq 1-1-59)
Nat'l Network: ABC *Regional Network:* Mich. Talk *Wire Services:* AP
Format: News, News/Talk, 86 *Special Programming:* Black 5 hrs wkly *Hrs. of News Programming:* news progmg 30 hrs wkly *No. News Employees:* 4 *Target Audience:* 35 plus.
Gayle Olson, President
Joe Daguanno, Operations Dir
Annette Weston, News Director
Jim Gifford, Operations Director
Bob Bucholtz, Sales

St. Louis

WMLM
12-15-1977; 1520 khz AM *Hrs Open:* 24
Mailing Address: P.O. Box 17, St. Louis, MI 48880 US
Second Address: 4170 N. State Rd., Alma, MI 48801
(989) 463-4013, *Fax:* (989) 463-4014
wmlm@cmsinter.net
License: St. Louis, MI held by Siefker Broadcasting Corp.
Nat'l Network: ABC
Format: Country *Special Programming:* Farm 5 hrs, gospel 2 hrs wkly *Target Audience:* 35 plus. *Adv. Rates:* 12.50; 11.00; 12.50.
Gregory Siefker, President

Standish

***WWCM**
01-01-1990; 96.9 mhz FM *Hrs Open:* 24; 3 kw; 328 ft.; N44 2 8 W84 0 31 *Rebroadcasts:* Rebroadcasts WCMU-FM Mount Pleasant 100%
7585 Pigeon Road, Pigeon, MI 48755 US
(989) 774-3105, *Fax:* (989) 774-4427
www.wcmu.org
cmuradio@radio.cmich.edu
License: Standish, Arenac County, MI held by Central Michigan University
Format: Jazz, News *Target Audience:* General.
Ed Grant, General Manager

Stephenson

WMXG
01-01-1999; 106.3 mhz FM; 50 kw; 492 ft.; N45 38 36 W87 22 37
1101c Ludington St., Escanaba, WI 49829 US
(906) 786-0060, *Fax:* (906) 786-2990
www.wmxg.com
mix106@chartermi.net
License: Stephenson, Menominee County, MI held by Pacer Radio of the Near-North.
Arbitron Metro Market: Stephenson, MI *Format:* Contemporary Hits/Top 40
Mike DuBord, General Manager

Sterling Heights

***WUFL**
10-26-1988; 1030 khz AM *Hrs Open:* Daytime
Mailing Address: 7355 N. Oracle, #200, Tucson, AZ 85740 US
Second Address: 42669 Garfield Rd., Suite 328, Clinton Township, MI 48038
(586) 263-1030, *Fax:* (586) 228-1030
www.myflr.org
License: Sterling Heights, MI held by Family Life Broadcasting System.
Group Owner: Family Life Communications Inc.; acq 10-25-88)
Nat'l Network: USA
Arbitron Metro Market: Detroit, MI *Format:* Christian, Religious *Hrs. of News Programming:* 45 min news progmg wkly *Target Audience:* 35-54; Women
Dr. Randy L.Carlson, President
Adam Nash, Programming Director
Alonzo Williams, Evan Carlson
Executive Director of Marketing and Community Tran, Rod Robison
Vice President of Development

Sturgis

WBET
01-01-1951; 1230 khz AM; 1 kw-U, DA-1; N41 46 11 W85 25 09
Mailing Address: Box 7080, Sturgis, MI 46703
Second Address: 70808 S. Nottawa Rd., Sturgis, MI 49091
(269) 651-2383,(269) 651-2384, *Fax:* (269) 659-1111
www.wmshradio.com
wmsh@wmshradio.com
License: Sturgis, St. Joseph County, MI held by Lake Cities Broadcasting Corp.
Group Owner: Lake Cities Broadcasting Corp.; acq 1-12-98; $600,000 with co-located FM)
Nat'l Network: ABC; ESPN Radio *Nat'l Reps:* Michigan Spot Sales
Population Served: 100,000*Target Audience:* 25-54.
Carter Snider, General Manager
Mike Stiles, News Director

WBET-FM
01-01-1951; 99.3 mhz FM; 2.15 kw; Ant 390 ft; N41 46 11 W85 25 09
Box 7080, Sturgis, MI 46703
(269) 651-2383, *Fax:* (269) 659-1111
www.wmshradio.com
License: Sturgis, St. Joseph County, MI held by Lake Cities Broadcasting Corp.
Group Owner: Lake Cities Broadcasting Corp.
Tom Crawford, General Manager

Tawas City

***WHST**
11-01-1972; 106.1 mhz FM *Hrs Open:* 24; 25 kw; 305 ft.; N44 16 25 W83 39 48 *Rebroadcasts:* Rebroadcasts WPHN(FM) Gaylord 100%
1491 M-32 West, Alpena, MI 49707 US
(989) 732-6274, *Fax:* (989) 732-8171
www.ncradio.org
ncr@ncradio.org
License: Tawas City, Iosco County, MI held by Northern Christian Radio Inc.
Group Owner: Northern Christian Radio Inc.; acq 7-19-01).
Format: Christian, Religious *Target Audience:* 25-54.
George Lake Jr., General Manager

WKJC
10-01-1979; 104.7 mhz FM; 50 kw; 492 ft.; N44 24 48 W83 37 14
Mailing Address: P.O. Box 549, Tawas City, MI 48764 US
Second Address: 523 Meadow Rd., Tawas City, MI 48763
(989) 362-3417, *Fax:* (989) 362-4544
www.wkjc.com
wkjc@wkjc.com
License: Tawas City, Iosco County, MI held by Carroll Enterprises Inc.
Group Owner: Carroll Enterprises Inc.
Format: Country
Jeffrey Smith, President

WQLB
07-01-1997; 103.3 mhz FM; 15 kw; 423 ft.; N44 24 48 W83 37 14
P.O. Box 549, Tawas City, MI 48764 US
(989) 362-3417, *Fax:* (989) 362-4544
www.wkjc.com
wkjc@wkjc.com
License: Tawas City, Iosco County, MI held by Carroll Broadcasting Inc.
Regional Network: Minn. News Net.
Format: Classic Rock
John Carroll Jr., General Manager
Tim Carroll, General Sales Mgr
Deb Michaels, Programming Director

Mary Hill, News Director
Marvin Walther, Chief Engineer

Tawas City-East Tawa

WIOS

09-27-1958; 1480 khz AM; 1 kw-D, DAD; 0.109 kw-N, DA2; N44 15 48 W83 32 42
Mailing Address: P.O. Box 549, 523 Meadow Road, Tawas City, MI 48763 US
Second Address: 523 Meadow Rd., Tawas City, MI 48763
(989) 362-3417, *Fax:* (989) 362-4544
www.wiosradio.com
wkjc@wkjc.com
License: Tawas City-East Tawa, MI held by Carroll Enterprises Inc.
Group Owner: Carroll Enterprises Inc.; (acq 5-1-69)
Regional Network: Mich. Farm *Nat'l Reps:* Michigan Spot Sales
Format: Talk *Special Programming:* Big band 6 hrs wkly *Target Audience:* 25 plus; general
John Carroll Sr., Chairman
John Carroll Jr., CEO
Tim Carroll, General Sales Mgr

Taylor

WCHB

01-01-1990; 1200 khz AM
5900 Princess Garden Pkwy, 8th Floor, Lanham, MD 20706 US
(313) 259-2000, *Fax:* (313) 259-7011
www.wchbnewsdetroit.com
License: Taylor, MI held by Radio One of Detroit LLC.
Group Owner: Radio One Inc.; (acq 6-19-98; $34.2 million with WDTJ(FM) Detroit)
Arbitron Metro Market: Detroit,MI *Format:* Gospel *Target Audience:* Adults 25-54.
Alfred Liggins, President
Dr. Wendell Cox, Operations Dir
Carol Lawrence-Dobrusin, General Manager

Three Rivers

WRCI

05-03-1962; 1520 khz AM *Hrs Open:* 24
59750 Constantine Road, Three Rivers, MI 49093 US
(269) 278-1815, *Fax:* (269) 273-7975
www.wlkm.com
info@wlkm.com
License: Three Rivers, MI held by Impact Radio LLC
Group Owner: Impact Radio LLC; (acq 8-1-2002; grpsl)
Nat'l Network: AP Radio; Jones Radio Networks *Regional Network:* Mich. Radio *Regional Reps:* Patt Media Sales
Format: Country *Hrs. of News Programming:* news progmg 14 hrs wkly *No. News Employees:* 1 *Target Audience:* General.
Dennis Rumsey, President
Pat Holtz, Operations Dir
Kathy Loker, General Sales Mgr
Walker Sisson, Engineering Dir

WLKM-FM

03-01-1975; 95.9 mhz FM *Hrs Open:* 24; 3.6 kw; 425 ft.; N41 53 51 W85 33 51
59750 Constantine Road, Three Rivers, MI 49093 US
(269) 278-1815, *Fax:* (269) 273-7975
www.wlkm.com
info@wlkm.com
License: Three Rivers, St. Joseph County, MI held by Impact Radio LLC
Group Owner: Impact Radio LLC
Nat'l Network: CNN Radio *Regional Reps:* Patt Media Sales *Wire Services:* AP
Format: Contemporary Hits/Top 40, Adult Contemp *Hrs. of News Programming:* news progmg 2 hrs wkly *No. News Employees:* 1 *Target Audience:* 25-54.
Pat Holtz, Operations Dir
Dennis Rumsey, General Manager
Kathy Loker, General Sales Mgr
Walker Sisson, Engineering Dir

Traverse City

WCCW

07-15-1960; 1310 khz AM
314 East Front Street, Traverse City, MI 49684 US
(231) 946-6211, *Fax:* (231) 946-1914
www.wccwi.com
License: Traverse City, MI held by Midwestern Broadcasting Co.
Group Owner: Midwestern Broadcasting Co.; (acq 9-16-96; $2.2 million with co-located FM)
Nat'l Reps: Michigan Spot Sales; Katz Radio
Arbitron Metro Market: Traverse City-Petoskey, MI *Format:* Sports
Hal Payne, General Sales Mgr
Dave Gauthier, Programming Director
John Patrick, National Sales Manager

WCCW-FM

11-08-1967; 107.5 mhz FM; 50 kw; 492 ft.; N44 46 2 W85 41 26
314 East Front Street, Traverse City, MI 49684 US
(231) 946-6211, *Fax:* (231) 946-1914
www.wccwi.com
georgeb@wccw.fm
License: Traverse City, Grand Traverse County, MI
Arbitron Metro Market: Traverse City-Petoskey, MI *Format:* Oldies
Ross Biederman, CEO/COO
Ross Biederman, President
Howard Tuten, General Manager

*WICA

09-13-2000; 91.5 mhz FM *Hrs Open:* 24; 4 kw; 748 ft.; N44 45 22 W85 40 42
P O Box 199, Interlocen, MI 49643 US
(231) 276-4400, *Fax:* (231) 276-4417
www.interlochen.org/ipr
ipr@interlochen.org
License: Traverse City, Grand Traverse County, MI held by Interlochen Center for the Arts.
Wire Services: AP
Arbitron Metro Market: Traverse City-Petoskey, MI *Format:* News, Talk *Hrs. of News Programming:* news progmg 168 hrs wkly *No. News Employees:* 4 *Target Audience:* 25-80.
Thom Paulson, Operations Dir

WLDR-FM

07-17-1966; 101.9 mhz FM *Hrs Open:* 24; 100 kw; 630 ft.; N44 46 13 W85 41 43
118 South Union Street, Traverse City, MI 49684 US
(231) 352-9603, *Fax:* (231) 352-7877
www.wldr.com
wldr@wldr.com
License: Traverse City, Grand Traverse County, MI held by Great Northern Broadcasting System Inc.
Group Owner: Fort Bend Broadcasting Co.; (acq 4-10-2001; $3.6 million for stock)
Arbitron Metro Market: Traverse City-Petoskey, MI *Format:* Country *No. News Employees:* 1 *Target Audience:* 25-54. *Adv. Rates:* 25; 30; 25; 14
Roy Henderson, CEO
Steve Smith, CFO

*WLJN-FM

10-01-1989; 89.9 mhz FM *Hrs Open:* 24; 39 kw vert; 554 ft.; N44 46 36 W85 39 43
Mailing Address: P.O. Box 1400, Traverse City, MI 49685 US
Second Address: 1101 Cass St., Traverse, MI 49684
(231) 946-1400, *Fax:* (231) 946-3959
www.wljn.com
info@wljn.com
License: Traverse City, Grand Traverse County, MI held by Good News Media Inc.
Group Owner: Good News Media Inc.
Arbitron Metro Market: Traverse City-Petoskey, MI *Format:* Christian, Religious *Hrs. of News Programming:* News progmg 4 hrs wkly *Target Audience:* General.
Brian Harcey, General Manager
Pete Lathrop, Programming Director

*WNMC-FM

10-01-1967; 90.7 mhz FM *Hrs Open:* 8 AM-2 AM; 0.6 kw; 538 ft.; N44 46 36 W85 41 2
1701 E, Front St., Traverse City, MI 49686 US
(231) 995-2562, *Fax:* (231) 922-8963
www.wnmc.org
License: Traverse City, Grand Traverse County, MI held by Northwestern Michigan College.
Arbitron Metro Market: Traverse City, MI *Format:* Blues, Jazz, 94 *Special Programming:* American Indian one hr, Black 20 hrs, folk 11 hrs,
Eric Hines, Station Manager

WTCM

01-01-1941; 580 khz AM *Hrs Open:* 24
314 East Front Street, Traverse City, MI 49684 US
(231) 947-7675, *Fax:* (231) 929-3988
www.wtcmi.com
wtcm@wtcmradio.com
License: Traverse City, MI held by WTCM Radio Inc.
Group Owner: Midwestern Broadcasting Co.
Arbitron Metro Market: Traverse City, MI *Format:* News, News/Talk, 86 *Special Programming:* Farm 5 hrs wkly *Hrs. of News Programming:* news progmg 12 hrs wkly *No. News Employees:* 4 *Target Audience:* 25-54.
Ross Biederman, President
Chris Warren, General Manager
Paul Binsfeld, General Sales Mgr
Jack O'Malley, Programming Director
David Barr, Promotions Manager
Joel Frank, News Director

WTCM-FM

12-13-1965; 103.5 mhz FM *Hrs Open:* 24; 100 kw; 991 ft.; N44 27 31 W85 42 2
314 East Front Street, Traverse City, MI 49684 US
(231) 947-7675, *Fax:* (231) 929-3988
www.wtcmi.com
wtcm@wtcmradio.com
License: Traverse City, Grand Traverse County, MI
Arbitron Metro Market: Traverse City, MI *Format:* Country *Target Audience:* 25-54.
Ross Biederman, President
Harry Speckman, Operations Dir
Chris Warren, General Manager
Paul Binsfeld, General Sales Mgr
Jack O'Malley, Programming Director
David Barr, Promotions Manager
Joel Frank, News Director

Trout Lake

*WHWG

01-01-1999; 89.9 mhz FM; 1 kw; 390 ft.; N46 11 17 W84 56 46
Rebroadcasts: Rebroadcasts WHWL(FM) Marquette 100%
130 Carmen Drive, Marquette, MI 49855 US
(906) 249-1423, *Fax:* (906) 249-4042
www.whwl.net
whwl@whwl.net
License: Trout Lake, Chippewa County, MI held by Gospel Opportunities Inc.
Format: Religious
W. Curtis Marker, General Manager

Tuscarora Township

WWSS

95.3 mhz FM; 3.3 kw; Ant 447 ft; N44 52 43 W84 40 50
Box 1766, Gaylord, MI
(989) 732-2341, *Fax:* (989) 732-6202
License: Tuscarora Township, Crawford County, MI held by Darby Advertising Inc.
Group Owner: Darby Advertising Inc.
Kent Smith, President

Tuscola

WWBN

09-14-1987; 101.5 mhz FM *Hrs Open:* 24; 1.8 kw; 489 ft.; N43 12 0 W83 33 30
G-3338 East Bristol Road, Burton, MI 48529 US
(810) 742-1470, *Fax:* (810) 742-5170
www.banana1015.com
info@banana1015.com
License: Tuscola, Tuscola County, MI
Group Owner: Townsquare Media; (acq 12-19-97; grpsl).
Nat'l Reps: Katz Radio
Arbitron Metro Market: Flint, MI *Format:* Rock/AOR *Hrs. of News Programming:* news progmg 20 hrs wkly *No. News Employees:* 1 *Target Audience:* 18-49; men *Adv. Rates:* 50; 50; 50; 50
Bill Stakelin, President
Fred Murr, Operations Dir
Kelly Quinn, General Manager
Pete Clinton, Director of Sales
Brian Beddow, Programming Director
J. Patrick, Operations Manager
Tony LaBrie, Brand Manager

Twin Lake

*WBLV

07-03-1982; 90.3 mhz FM *Hrs Open:* 24; 100 kw; 607 ft.; N43 33 0 W86 2 34 *Rebroadcasts:* Rebroadcasts WBLU-FM Grand Rapids 100%
Route #2, Twin Lake, MI 49457 US
(231) 894-1966, *Fax:* (231) 893-2457
www.bluelake.org
radio@bluelake.org
License: Twin Lake, Muskegon County, MI held by Blue Lake Fine Arts Camp.
Nat'l Network: PRI; NPR *Regional Network:* Minn. Pub. Radio
Arbitron Metro Market: Twin Lake, MI *Format:* Jazz, News
Special Programming: Folk 5 hrs wkly *Hrs. of News Programming:* News progmg 20 hrs wkly *Target Audience:* Adult.
Dave Myers, General Manager
Steve Albert, Programming Director

Vassar

WOWE
07-01-1990; 98.9 mhz FM; 3 kw; 328 ft.; N43 17 56 W83 30 34
107 South Main Street, Vassar, MI 48768 US
(810) 234-4335, *Fax:* (810) 234-7286
wowe@sbcglobal.net
License: Vassar, Tuscola County, MI held by Praestantia Broadcasting Inc.
Arbitron Metro Market: Flint, MI *Format:* Urban Contemporary
Michael Shumpert, President

Walker

WTRV
06-15-1993; 100.5 mhz FM *Hrs Open:* 24; 3 kw; 328 ft.; N43 0 59 W85 44 24
600 Congress Ave., Suite 1400, Austin, TX 78701 US
(616) 451-4800, *Fax:* (616) 451-0113
www.theriver-fm.com
Tom.Cook@townsquaremedia.com
License: Walker, Kent County, MI
Group Owner: Townsquare Media; (acq 8-7-00; grpsl).
Nat'l Reps: Katz Radio
Arbitron Metro Market: Grand Rapids, MI *Format:* Adult Contemp *Target Audience:* 35-64.
Russ Hines, General Manager
Tim Huston, Sales Director
Tom Cook, Programming Director
Digital Sales Manager

Walled Lake

WPON
12-01-1954; 1460 khz AM *Hrs Open:* 24; 1 kw-D, DA2; 0.76 kw-N, DA2; N42 32 38 W83 29 58
2222 Franklin, Bloomfield Hills, MI 48302 US
(248) 557-3500, *Fax:* (248) 557-4321
www.wpon.com
wpon@wpon.com
License: Walled Lake, MI held by Birach Broadcasting Corp.
Group Owner: Birach Broadcasting Corp.; acq 5-25-2004; $800,000).
Arbitron Metro Market: Detroit *Format:* Oldies, Talk *Target Audience:* 35-65; 35 and above *Adv. Rates:* 40; 40; 40; 40
Jimmie James, Operations Dir
Sima Birach, General Manager

Warren

***WPHS**
03-20-1964; 89.1 mhz FM *Hrs Open:* 6:30 AM-8:30 PM; 0.1 kw; 98 ft.; N42 31 0 W83 0 36
Mailing Address: 31300 Anita, Warren, MI 48093 US
Second Address: Warren Consolidated Schools, 31300 Anita, Warren, MI 48093
(586) 698-4501
www.wphs.com
wphs@wphs.com
License: Warren, Macomb County, MI held by Warren Consolidated Schools.
Format: Urban Contemporary *Special Programming:* Blues 3 hrs, Pol 2 hrs, news 5 hrs, country 4 hrs, Christian rock 4 hrs wkly *Hrs. of News Programming:* news progmg 10 hrs wkly *No. News Employees:* 2 *TargetAudience:* 12-27; males
Jenny Stanczyk, General Manager

West Branch

WBMI
11-07-1977; 105.5 mhz FM; 6 kw; 299 ft.; N44 17 57 W84 15 54
1491m - 32 West, Alpena, MI 49707 US
(989) 345-4269, *Fax:* (989) 345-3996
License: West Branch, Ogemaw County, MI held by Peggy R. Warner
Nat'l Network: Jones Radio Networks
Format: Oldies *Special Programming:* Pol 6 hrs wkly *Target Audience:* 25-54.
Charlie Cobb, General Manager
Mike McCall, Programming Director

White Star

***WEJC**
07-01-2001; 88.3 mhz FM; 0.001 kw horiz, 55 kw vert; 374 ft.; N43 41 40 W84 5 3
3302 N Van Dyke, Imlay City, MI 48444 US
(517) 381-0573, *Fax:* (877) 850-0881
www.positivehits.com
info@positivehits.com
License: White Star, Gladwin County, MI held by Superior Communications.
Group Owner: Superior Communications
Arbitron Metro Market: White Star, MI *Format:* Christian
Jenn Czelada, General Manager
Ed Czelada, Programming Director

Whitehall

WWSN
04-01-1991; 97.5 mhz FM *Hrs Open:* 24; 1.7 kw; Ant 426 ft; N43 23 04 W86 19 30
3375 Merriam St, Suite 201, Muskegon Heights, MS 60005
(616) 774-8461, *Fax:* (616) 774-2491
www.975thechamp.com
info@975thechamp.com
License: Whitehall, Muskegon County, MI held by Radio License Holding CBC LLC
Nat'l Network: Westwood One
Hrs. of News Programming: News progmg one hr wkly *Target Audience:* 25-49; male and female
Jon Russell, Operations Dir
Jeff Morton, General Manager
Renee Dudek, General Sales Mgr
John Alan, Chief Engineer

WGVS-FM
01-01-1975; 95.3 mhz FM; 2 kw; 361 ft.; N43 21 14 W86 19 38
Rebroadcasts: Rebroadcasts WGVU-FM Allendale 100%
301 West Fulton, Grand Rapids, MI 49504 US
(616) 331-6666, *Fax:* (616) 331-6625
www.wgvu.edu
wgva@gvsu.edu
License: Whitehall, Muskegon County, MI
Arbitron Metro Market: Muskegon, MI *Format:* Jazz, News
Ed Spier, News Director

WKLQ
10-01-1989; 1490 khz AM; 1 kw-U, ND1; Ant 492 ft; N43 23 4 W86 19 30
1802 S. Fernandez, Arlington Heights, IL 60005 US
(616) 774-8461, *Fax:* (616) 774-2491
info@wklq.com
License: Whitehall, MI
Group Owner: Cumulus Media Inc.; (acq 5-30-2000; grpsl).
Nat'l Network: Westwood One *Nat'l Reps:* D & R Radio
Arbitron Metro Market: Grand Rapids, M *TV Affiliate:* Active rock
Hrs. of News Programming: 1 *No. News Employees:* 25-54.

Wixom

***WSHM**
88.3 mhz FM; kw
US
(313) 755-5163
License: Wixom, Oakland County, MI held by By Grace Through Faith.
Arbitron Metro Market: Wixom, MI
Mark Ramseyer, General Manager

Wyoming

***WYCE**
11-01-1983; 88.1 mhz FM *Hrs Open:* 24; 10 kw; 164 ft.; N42 54 43 W85 41 0
711 Bridge Street, NW, Grand Rapids, MI 49504 US
(616) 742-9923, *Fax:* (616) 742-0599
www.grcmc.org
comment@wyce.org
License: Wyoming, Kent County, MI held by Grand Rapids Cable Access Center Inc.
Arbitron Metro Market: Wyoming, MI *Format:* Alternative *Special Programming:* Folk one hr, Sp 10 hrs *Target Audience:* 25-54; general *Adv. Rates:* 25; 18; 25; 15
Kevin Murphy, Station Manager
Pete Bruinsma, Programming Director

WYGR
11-14-1964; 1530 khz AM; 0.25 kw-C, NDD; 0.5 kw-D, NDD; N42 55 38 W85 44 50
P. O. Box 9591, Wyoming, MI 49509 US
(616) 452-8589, *Fax:* (616) 248-0176
www.wygr.net
License: Wyoming, MI held by WYGR Broadcasting.
Nat'l Reps: Patt
Arbitron Metro Market: Wyoming, MI *Format:* Spanish *Special Programming:* Polka pops 3 hrs wkly *Target Audience:* Sp speaking Hispanics.
Roland Rusticus, Station Manager
Scott Richards, Programming Director
Robert Van Prooyen, Chief Engineer

Ypsilanti

***WEMU**
12-08-1965; 89.1 mhz FM *Hrs Open:* 24; 15.5 kw; 289 ft.; N42 15 48 W83 37 34
Mailing Address: 426 King Hall, Ypsilanti, MI 48197 US
Second Address: Eastern Michigan Univ., 426 King Hall, Ypsilanti, MI 48197
(734) 487-2229(734) 487-8936, *Fax:* (734) 487-1015
www.wemu.org
wemu@emich.edu
License: Ypsilanti, Washtenaw County, MI held by Eastern Michigan University.
Nat'l Network: NPR *Wire Services:* AP
Arbitron Metro Market: Ypsilanti, MI *Format:* Blues, Jazz, 60 *Hrs. of News Programming:* news progmg 39 hrs wkly *No. News Employees:* 4 *Target Audience:* General.
Michael Jewett, Operations Dir
Mary Motherwell, General Manager
Mary Motherwell, General Sales Mgr
Clark Smith, Programming Director
Ray Cryderman, Chief Engineer
Linda Yohn, Music Director

WDEO
11-16-1962; 990 khz AM *Hrs Open:* 24; 9.2 kw-D, DA2; 0.25 kw-N, DA2; N42 15 53 W83 36 47; N42 15 55 W83 36 42
Box 1520, Ypsilanti, MI 48197 US
(734) 930-5200, *Fax:* (734) 930-3179
www.avemariaradio.net
hroot@wdeo.net
License: Ypsilanti, MI held by Word Broadcasters Inc.
Arbitron Metro Market: Ann Arbor, MI *Format:* Christian, Talk
Hrs. of News Programming: News progmg 9 hrs wkly *Target Audience:* 21 plus; adult Christian *Adv. Rates:* 45; 45; 65; 45
Al Kresta, CEO
Steve Clarke, Operations Dir
Michael Jones, General Manager

Zeeland

***WGNB**
01-21-1989; 89.3 mhz FM *Hrs Open:* 24; 30 kw; 499 ft.; N42 50 14 W85 59 17
Of Chicago, 820 N Lasalle Blvd, Chicago, IL 60610 US
(616) 772-7300, *Fax:* (616) 772-9663
www.wgnb.fm
wgnb@moody.edu
License: Zeeland, Ottawa County, MI held by The Moody Bible Institute of Chicago Inc.
Group Owner: The Moody Bible Institute of Chicago; acq 2-5-91;
Nat'l Network: Salem Radio Network; Moody
Arbitron Metro Market: Grand Rapids, MII *Format:* Religious *Hrs. of News Programming:* News progmg 15 hrs wkly *Target Audience:* 35-54; Evangelical Christians
Dr. Paul Nyquist, President
Scott Curtis, Operations Dir
Jack Haveman, Station Manager
Tom Bosscher, Chief Engineer

WJQK
08-23-1971; 99.3 mhz FM *Hrs Open:* 24; 4.7 kw; 371 ft.; N42 48 59 W85 57 24
5658 143rd Avenue, Holland, MI 49423 US
(616) 931-9930, *Fax:* (616) 931-1280
www.jq99.com
traffic@jq99.com
License: Zeeland, Ottawa County, MI held by Lanser Broadcasting Corp.
Nat'l Network: Fox News Radio *Nat'l Reps:* Salem *Regional Reps:* Mich Spot Sales *Wire Services:* Metro Weather Service Inc.
Arbitron Metro Market: Grand Rapids, MI *Format:* Christian *Hrs. of News Programming:* News progmg 7 hrs wkly *Target Audience:* 25-49. *Adv. Rates:* 49; 42; 49; 42
Les Lanser, President
Brad Lanser, Operations Dir
Troy West, Station Manager

WMFN
02-01-1990; 640 khz AM *Hrs Open:* 24; 1.2 kw-D, ND1; 0.23 kw-N, ND1; N42 48 59 W85 57 24
2422 Burton, S.E., Grand Rapids, MI 49546 US
(616) 949-8585, *Fax:* (616) 949-9262
production@hottalk640.com
License: Zeeland, MI held by Birach Broadcasting Corp.
Group Owner: Birach Broadcasting Corp.; acq 11-6-01; $1.9 million with WMJH(AM) Rockford).
Nat'l Network: CBS
Arbitron Metro Market: Grand Rapids, MII *Format:* Tejano *Target Audience:* 25-54.

Tyrone Bynum, General Manager

WPNW
11-02-1956; 1260 khz AM *Hrs Open:* 24; 10 kw-D, DA2; 1 kw-N, DA2; N42 43 56 W86 6 6
5658 143rd Ave., Holland, MI 49423 US
(616) 931-6620, *Fax:* (616) 931-1280
www.1260thepledge.com
traffic@jq99.com
License: Zeeland, MI held by Lanser Broadcasting Corp.
Nat'l Network: CNN Radio *Nat'l Reps:* Salem
Arbitron Metro Market: Zeeland, MI *Format:* News, Talk *Special Programming:* Sp 2 hrs, farm one hr wkly *Hrs. of News Programming:* news progmg 9 hrs wkly *No. News Employees:* 1 *Target Audience:* 35 plus;mature adults *Adv. Rates:* 18; 18; 18; 18
Leslie Lanser, President
Troy West, Station Manager
Chad Millard, General Sales Mgr
Jason Cramer, Programming Director
Bradley Lanser, Executive Vice President

Minnesota

Ada

KRJB
09-01-1985; 106.5 mhz FM; 100 kw; 452 ft.; N47 18 41 W96 31 13
312 West Main Street, Ada, MN 56510 US
(218) 784-2844, *Fax:* (218) 784-3749
www.krjbradio.com
krjbada@loretel.net
License: Ada, Norman County, MN held by R & J Broadcasting.
Regional Network: MNN
Arbitron Metro Market: Fargo-Moorhead *Format:* Country *Adv. Rates:* 18; 18; 17; 10
Jim Birkemeyer, General Manager
Woody Roux, Programming Director
Heather Krogstadt, Traffic Manager

Aitkin

KKIN
06-01-1961; 930 khz AM *Hrs Open:* 24; 2.5 kw-D, ND1; 0.36 kw-N, ND1; N46 32 26 W93 39 22
Mailing Address: 702 Poplar Ave., Cloquet, MN 55720 US
Second Address: 37208 U.S. Hwy. 169, Aitkin, MN 56431
(218) 927-2100, *Fax:* (218) 927-4090
www.kkinradio.com
kkinamradio@embargmail.com
License: Aitkin, MN held by Red Rock Radio Corp.
Group Owner: Red Rock Radio Corp.; (acq 9-1-2006; grpsl)
Nat'l Network: Jones Radio Networks
Arbitron Metro Market: Saint Cloud, MN *Format:* Contemporary Hits/Top 40 *No. News Employees:* 1 *Target Audience:* General. *Adv. Rates:* 9.50; 9.50; 9.50; 9.50
Ro Grignon, President
Terry D. Modl, General Manager
Boyd Brenner, General Sales Mgr
Terry D. Modl, Programming Director

KKIN-FM
01-03-1972; 94.3 mhz FM *Hrs Open:* 24; 14 kw; 436 ft.; N46 41 18 W93 35 58
Mailing Address: 702 Poplar Ave., Cloquet, MN 55720 US
Second Address: 37208 U.S. Hwy. 169, Aitkin, MN 56431
(218) 927-2100, *Fax:* (218) 927-4090
www.kkinradio.com
kkinradio@embargmail.com
License: Aitkin, Aitkin County, MN held by Red Rock Radio Corp.
Group Owner: Red Rock Radio Corp.
Arbitron Metro Market: Duluth, MN *Format:* Country *Hrs. of News Programming:* news progmg 5 hrs wkly *No. News Employees:* 1 *Target Audience:* 35 plus. *Adv. Rates:* Same as AM
Ro Grignon, President
Terry D. Modl, General Manager
Dewey Moede, Station Manager
Boyd Brenner, General Sales Mgr
Terry D. Modl, Programming Director

Albany

KASM
11-20-1950; 1150 khz AM; 2.1 kw-D, ND1; 0.021 kw-N, ND1; N45 37 53 W94 36 0
Mailing Address: 1986 Julep Road, St. Cloud, MN 56301 US
Second Address: 35223 238th Ave., Albany, MN
(320) 845-2184, *Fax:* (320) 845-2187
www.kasmwqpm.com
studio@kasmradionetwork.com
License: Albany, MN held by Starcom LLC
Regional Reps: Hyett/Ramsland.
Arbitron Metro Market: Albany, MN *Format:* Country, News, 66 *Special Programming:* Oldies, Ger mus 2 hrs, farm 6 hrs wkly *Hrs. of News Programming:* news progmg 2 hrs wkly *No. News Employees:* 1 *TargetAudience:* 36 plus.
Randy Rothstein, General Manager
Mark Sprint, Programming Director

KDDG
10-01-1993; 105.5 mhz FM; 6 kw; 328 ft.; N45 37 53 W94 36 0
1986 Julep Road, St. Cloud, MN 56301 US
(320) 845-2184, *Fax:* (320) 845-2187
kddg1150fm@albanytel.com
License: Albany, Stearns County, MN held by Starcom LLC
Arbitron Metro Market: St. Cloud, MN *Format:* Adult Contemp
Steve Bayless, Operations Dir
Kandi Bray, General Manager
Ali Allison, News Director
Stephen White, Chief Engineer

Albert Lea

KATE
10-01-1937; 1450 khz AM *Hrs Open:* 24; 1 kw-U, ND1; N43 38 0 W93 22 15
Highway 16, Luverne, MN 56156 US
(507) 373-2338, *Fax:* (507) 373-4736
www.albertlearadio.com
news@albertlearadio.com
License: Albert Lea, MN held by Three Eagles of Luverne Inc.
Group Owner: Three Eagles Communications; (acq 5-21-99; with co-located FM)
Regional Network: Minn. News Net.; Minn. Farm *Nat'l Reps:* McGavren Guild *Regional Reps:* Midwest Radio. *Wire Services:* AP
Arbitron Metro Market: Albert Lea, MN *Format:* Adult Contemp, News, 62, Talk *Special Programming:* Farm 18 hrs, Sp 2 hrs wkly *Hrs. of News Programming:* news progmg 30 hrs wkly *No. News Employees:* 3 *TargetAudience:* 12 plus; general *Adv. Rates:* 22; 22; 22; 22
Gary Buchanan, President
Bob Mithuen, General Manager
Courtnay Doyle, General Sales Mgr
Steve Oman, News Director

KCPI
07-01-1974; 94.9 mhz FM *Hrs Open:* 24; 5 kw; 295 ft.; N43 38 0 W93 22 15
Highway 16, Luverne, MN 56156 US
(507) 373-2338, *Fax:* (507) 373-4736
copy@albertlearadio.com
License: Albert Lea, Freeborn County, MN held by Three Eagles of Luverne Inc.
Group Owner: Three Eagles Communications; (Acq 8-1-99)
Nat'l Network: ABC
Arbitron Metro Market: Albert Lea, MN *Format:* Adult Contemp *Hrs. of News Programming:* news progmg 12 hrs wkly *No. News Employees:* 1 *Target Audience:* 25-54. *Adv. Rates:* 16; 16; 16; 16
Bruce Munsterman, President

KQPR
08-14-1990; 96.1 mhz FM *Hrs Open:* 24; 25 kw; 308 ft.; N43 36 58 W93 12 47
330 East Kilbourn Avenue, Suite 250, Milwaukee, WI 53202 US
(507) 373-9401, *Fax:* (507) 373-9045
www.power96rocker.com
kqpr@power96rocker.com
License: Albert Lea, Freeborn County, MN held by Hometown Broadcasting Inc.
Nat'l Network: Jones Radio Networks *Regional Network:* Linder Farm *Nat'l Reps:* Hyett/Ramsland
Arbitron Metro Market: Albert Lea-Austin *Format:* Light Rock *No. News Employees:* 1 *Target Audience:* General.
Greg Jensen, CEO
Anna Rahn, General Manager
Ron Hunter, Programming Director
Jim Pilgrim, News Director
Marv Olson, Chief Engineer
Stephen Helleksen, Information Technology
Kristi Swalve, Traffic Manager

Alexandria

***KBHG**
89.5 mhz FM; kw
515 Pike Street East, Osakis, MN 56360 US
(320) 859-3000, *Fax:* (320) 859-3010
david@praisefm.org
License: Alexandria, Douglas County, MN held by Christian Heritage Broadcasting Inc.
Arbitron Metro Market: Alexandria, MN *Format:* Christian
David McIver, General Manager

KULO
01-01-1976; 94.3 mhz FM *Hrs Open:* 24; 12 kw; 466 ft.; N45 56 25 W95 28 3
Mailing Address: PO Box 241, 105 2nd Ave Ne, Glenwood, MN 56334 US
Second Address: 604 Third Ave. W., Alexandria, MN 56308
(320) 762-2154, *Fax:* (320) 762-2156
cool943.com
100.7@kikvfm.com
License: Alexandria, Douglas County, MN held by BDI Broadcasting Inc.
Group Owner: Omni Broadcasting Co.; (acq 12-31-2001; $700,000).
Nat'l Network: ABC
Format: Oldies *Hrs. of News Programming:* news progmg 12 hrs wkly *No. News Employees:* 1 *Target Audience:* 35-64; adults
Lou Buron, CEO
Dave Vagle, General Manager
Trudy Blanshan, General Sales Mgr
Johnny Rocket, Programming Director
Jim Rohn, News Director
Mary Campbell, CFO

KXRZ
04-02-1984; 99.3 mhz FM *Hrs Open:* 24; 6 kw; Ant 285 ft; N45 52 47 W95 18 35
Mailing Address: 1312 Broadway, Alexandria, MN 56334
Second Address: Box 69, Alexandria, MN 56308
(320) 763-3131, *Fax:* (320) 763-5641
www.z99radio.com
thefolks@kxra.com
License: Alexandria, Douglas County, MN held by Paradis Broadcasting of Alexandria Inc.
Group Owner: Paradis Broadcasting of Alexandria Inc.; acq 5-1-00; $900,000).
Nat'l Network: Dial Global Hot AC *Regional Reps:* Midwest Radio.
Population Served: 40,000*Special Programming:* Relg 3 hrs wkly *Hrs. of News Programming:* news progmg 5 hrs wkly *No. News Employees:* 1 *Target Audience:* 18-40; young adults *Adv. Rates:* 20; 18; 20; 10.
Brett Paradis, President
Brett Paradis, General Manager
Bruce McKirdy, General Sales Mgr

KXRA
07-27-1949; 1490 khz AM *Hrs Open:* 24; 1 kw-U; N45 52 05 W95 21 47
Box 69, 1312 Broadway, Alexandria, MN 56308
(320) 763-3131, *Fax:* (320) 763-5641
www.kxra.com
thefolks@kxra.com
License: Alexandria, Douglas County, MN held by Paradis Broadcasting of Alexandria Inc.
Group Owner: Paradis Broadcasting of Alexandria Inc.; (acq 10-1-88).
Nat'l Network: NBC Radio *Regional Network:* MNN *Regional Reps:* Midwest Radio.
Population Served: 40,000*Special Programming:* Farm 5 hrs, relg 2 hrs wkly *Hrs. of News Programming:* news progmg 25 hrs wkly *No. News Employees:* 1 *Target Audience:* 35-64. *Adv. Rates:* 20; 18; 15; 12
Mel Paradis, Chairman
Brett Paradis, President
Brett Paradis, General Manager
Bruce McKirdy, General Sales Mgr

KXRA-FM
05-01-1968; 92.3 mhz FM *Hrs Open:* 24; 13.5 kw; 446 ft; N45 52 30 W95 21 30
Box 69, 1312 Broadway, Alexandria, MN 56308
(320) 763-5131, *Fax:* (320) 763-5641
www.kxra.com
License: Alexandria, Douglas County, MN
Group Owner: Paradis Broadcasting of Alexandria Inc.
Population Served: 50,000*Hrs. of News Programming:* news progmg 5 hrs wkly *No. News Employees:* 1 *Target Audience:* 25-45; young adults, dual income households *Adv. Rates:* 20; 18; 20; 15
Brett Paradis, President
Bruce McKirdy, General Sales Mgr

Anoka

KQQL
08-01-1968; 107.9 mhz FM; 96 kw; 1093 ft.; N45 20 20 W93 23 27
60 South 6th Street, Suite 930, Minneapolis, MN 55402 US

(952) 417-3000, *Fax:* (952) 417-3001
www.kool108.com
info@kqql.com
License: Anoka, Anoka County, MN held by AMFM Broadcasting Licenses LLC.
Group Owner: Clear Channel Communications Inc.; (acq 8-30-2000; grpsl).
Nat'l Reps: Clear Channel
Arbitron Metro Market: Minneapolis-St. Paul *Format:* Adult Contemp *Target Audience:* 25-54.
Mick Anselmo, President

Appleton

*KRSU
02-01-1997; 88.5 mhz FM; 100 kw; 984 ft; N45 10 03 W96 00 02
Saint Johns University, Box 7711, Collegeville, MN 55101
(320) 363-7702, (651) 290-1500, *Fax:* (320) 363-4948
kncm@mpr.org,mail@mpr.org
License: Appleton, Swift County, MN held by Minnesota Public Radio.
William Kling, CEO
Steve Griffith, Operations Dir
Jon Gossett, General Sales Mgr
Eric Nycklemoe, Programming Director
Bill Wareham, News Director
Mark Alfuth, CFO
Dianne Krizan, Development Director
Deborah Brown, DevelopmentDirector
Thomas Kigin, Executive Vice President

*KNCM
10-25-1989; 91.3 mhz FM *Hrs Open:* 24; 75 kw; 1,158 ft; N45 10 03 W96 00 02 *Rebroadcasts:* Rebroadcast of KSJN(FM) Minneapolis-St. Paul
480 Cedar St., St. Paul, MN 55101
(800) 228-7123,(651) 290-1500, *Fax:* (651) 290-1224
www.mpr.org
info@mpr.org
License: Appleton, Swift County, MN held by Minnesota Public Radio Inc.
Nat'l Network: NPR; PRI *Regional Network:* Minn. Pub. Radio
John McTaggard, Chairman
William Kling, President
Jim McGuinn, Station Manager
Timothy Roesler, General Manager of Classical Music
Chris Worthington, News Director

Atwater

KKLN
11-26-1988; 94.1 mhz FM *Hrs Open:* 24; 6 kw; 328 ft.; N45 4 24 W94 45 19
1986 Julep Road, St. Cloud, MN 56301 US
(320) 235-1194, *Fax:* (320) 235-6894
www.kkln.com
info@kkln.com
License: Atwater, Kandiyohi County, MN held by Flagship Broadcasting.
Arbitron Metro Market: Saint Cloud, MN *Format:* Rock/AOR *Special Programming:* NASCAR Sprint Cup Races *No. News Employees:* 1 *Target Audience:* General. *Adv. Rates:* 20; 15; 15; 10
John Jennings, President
Nate Thomas, Operations Dir
Melanie Eckhart, News Director
Justin Klinghagen, Operating Partner

Austin

KAUS
05-30-1948; 1480 khz AM *Hrs Open:* 24; 1 kw-D, DA2; 1 kw-N, DA2; N43 37 20 W92 59 26
P.O. Box 159, Austin, MN 55912 US
(507) 437-7666, *Fax:* (507) 437-7669
www.kaus.com
kaus@kaus.com
License: Austin, MN held by Three Eagles of Luverne Inc.
Group Owner: Three Eagles Communications; (acq 4-1-00; grpsl)
Nat'l Network: NBC *Regional Network:* MNN
Arbitron Metro Market: Austin, MN *Format:* Adult Contemp, News, 62, Oldies, Talk *Hrs. of News Programming:* news progmg 20 hrs wkly *No. News Employees:* 2 *Target Audience:* 25-54.
Rolland Johnson, Chairman
Gary Buchanan, President
Bob Mithuen, General Manager
Joyce Marshall, General Sales Mgr
John Schramek, Programming Director
Ron Schat, Engineering Dir

KAUS-FM
01-01-1963; 99.9 mhz FM *Hrs Open:* 24; 100 kw; 928 ft.; N43 37 42 W93 9 12
P.O. Box 159, Austin, MN 55912 US
(507) 437-7666, *Fax:* (507) 437-7669
www.kaus.com
kaus@kaus.com
License: Austin, Mower County, MN held by Three Eagles of Luverne Inc.
Group Owner: Three Eagles Communications
Arbitron Metro Market: Austin, MN *Format:* Country *Hrs. of News Programming:* news progmg 12 hrs wkly *No. News Employees:* 2 *Target Audience:* 25-54.
Scott Soderberg, Programming Director
Tim Allen, Promotions Manager

*KMSK
01-12-1981; 91.3 mhz FM *Hrs Open:* 24; 0.135 kw; 194 ft.; N43 40 39 W93 0 4 *Rebroadcasts:* Rebroadcasts KMSU(FM) Mankato 100%
Msu 153, P. O. Box 8400, Mankato, MN 56002 US
(507) 389-5678, *Fax:* (507) 389-1705
www.kmsu.org
info@kmsu.org
License: Austin, Mower County, MN held by Mankato State University.
Nat'l Network: NPR
Format: Public Affairs *Special Programming:* Drama 3 hrs, folk/ethnic 5 hrs, new age 5 hrs wkly *Hrs. of News Programming:* news progmg 50 hrs wkly *No. News Employees:* 1 *Target Audience:* General; upscale,educated
Karen Wright, Operations Dir
Jim Gullickson, General Manager

KQAQ
04-16-1960; 970 khz AM *Hrs Open:* 5 AM-midnight; 5 kw-D, DA2; 0.5 kw-N, DA2; N43 42 27 W92 56 45
330 East Kilbourn Avenue, Suite 250, Milwaukee, WI 53202 US
(507) 373-9600, *Fax:* (507) 373-9045
www.classiccountrylegends.com
kqar@classiccountrylegends.com
License: Austin, MN held by Hometown Broadcasting Inc.
Nat'l Network: Fox News Radio; Motor Racing Net; Jones Radio Networks *Regional Network:* Linder Farm
Format: Country
Anna Rahn, General Manager

*KNSE
90.1 mhz FM *Hrs Open:* summer 2003; 6 kw; 318 ft.; N43 38 27 W93 8 51
45 East Seventh Street, Saint Paul, MN 55101 US
(651) 290-1500, *Fax:* (651) 290-1224
www.mpr.org
newsroom@mpr.org
License: Austin, Mower County, MN held by Minnesota Public Radio.
Arbitron Metro Market: Mason City, IA *Format:* News
Ian R Friendly, Chairman
Jon McTaggart, President
Jon Gossett, General Sales Mgr
Erik Nycklemoe, Programming Director
Bill Wareham, News Director
Randy Hogan, Vice Chair
Bradbury H Anderson, Secretary

Babbitt

KAOD
01-01-1999; 106.7 mhz FM; 33 kw; 430 ft.; N47 41 18 W91 54 21 *Rebroadcasts:* Rebroadcast of KQDS-FM Duluth 100%
111 Marquette Ave.#100, Minneapolis, MN 55401 US
(218) 728-9500, *Fax:* (218) 723-1499
www.95kqds.com
kqds@95kdqs.com
License: Babbitt, St. Louis County, MN held by Red Rock Radio Corp.
Group Owner: Red Rock Radio Corp.; acq 1-10-00; grpsl).
Arbitron Metro Market: Duluth, MN *Format:* Classic Rock
Shawn Skramstad, General Manager
Jim Payne, General Sales Mgr
Bill Jones, Programming Director
Jason Manning, News Director

Bagley

KKCQ-FM
10-01-1997; 96.7 mhz FM *Hrs Open:* 24; 25 kw; 328 ft.; N47 36 12 W95 32 40
P.O. Box 606, Fosston, NM 56542 US
(218) 435-1071, *Fax:* (218) 435-1480
www.kkcqradio.com
License: Bagley, Clearwater County, MN held by Pine to Prairie Broadcasting Inc.
Nat'l Network: ABC
Arbitron Metro Market: Grand Forks, ND *Format:* Country *Special Programming:* Farm 10 hrs, relg 9 hrs wkly *No. News Employees:* 1 *Adv. Rates:* 14; 11; 12.50; 9
Phil Ehlke, General Manager
Don Brinkman, General Sales Mgr
Laura Hamilton, News Director
Jim Offerdahl, Chief Engineer
Jamie Nesvold, Music Director
Karen Bingham, Office Manager
Tom Lano, Sports Director

Barnesville

KBVB
01-02-1976; 95.1 mhz FM *Hrs Open:* 24; 100 kw; 384 ft.; N46 49 9 W96 45 56
Mailing Address: 1020 25th Street South, Fargo, ND 58108 US
Second Address: Box 10097, Fargo, ND 58106
(701) 237-5346, *Fax:* (701) 237-0980
www.bob95fm.com
studio@bob95fm.com
License: Barnesville, Clay County, MN held by Radio Fargo-Moorhead Inc.
Group Owner: Radio Fargo-Moorhead Inc.; (acq 1-19-2007; grpsl)
Nat'l Reps: Eastman Radio
Arbitron Metro Market: Fargo-Moorhead, ND-MN *Format:* Country *Target Audience:* Adults 18 - 54
Nancy Odney, COO
John Austin, Operations Dir

Baxter

WWWI
08-29-1987; 1270 khz AM *Hrs Open:* 24; 5 kw-D, DAN; 5 kw-N, DAN; N46 17 55 W94 16 42
305 West Washington St, PO Box 783, Brainerd, MN 56401 US
(218) 828-9994, *Fax:* (218) 828-8327
www.3wiradio.com
talk@3wiradio.com
License: Baxter, MN held by Tower Broadcasting Corp.
Nat'l Network: CBS
Arbitron Metro Market: Baxter, MN *Format:* News, News/Talk, 86 *Target Audience:* 25 plus. *Adv. Rates:* 12; 12; 12; 12
James Pryor, President
Lon Schmidt, News Director
Mary Pryor, Office Manager/Co-Owner
Steve Foy, Sales Executive
Stephanie Palmer, Office Assistant

Bemidji

KBHP
08-03-1972; 101.1 mhz FM *Hrs Open:* 24; 100 kw; 522 ft.; N47 22 11 W94 52 54
C/O Haley Bader, P O Box 1656, Bemidji, MN 56619 US
(218) 444-1500, *Fax:* (218) 759-0345
www.kb101fm.com
phanson@pbbroadcasting.com
License: Bemidji, Beltrami County, MN held by Paul Bunyan Broadcasting Co.
Group Owner: Omni Broadcasting Co.
Nat'l Network: ABC *Regional Network:* MNN
Arbitron Metro Market: Bemidji, MN *Format:* Country *Hrs. of News Programming:* news progmg 12 hrs wkly *No. News Employees:* 1 *Target Audience:* 25-54.
Mary Campbell, CFO
Todd Haugen, Operations Dir
Lou Buron, General Manager
Peggy Hanson, General Sales Mgr
Mardy Karger, News Director
Mark Anderson, Chief Engineer

*KBSB
01-19-1970; 89.7 mhz FM *Hrs Open:* 24; 0.12 kw horiz; 125 ft.; N47 29 0 W94 52 27
1500 Birchmont Dr, Bemidji, MN 56601 US
(218) 755-4120, *Fax:* (218) 755-4119
www.fm90.org
License: Bemidji, Beltrami County, MN held by Bemidji State University.
Format: Contemporary Hits/Top 40 *Special Programming:* American Indian 3 hrs, folk 3 hrs wkly *Target Audience:* 12-28; teens to young adults *Adv. Rates:* 3; 3; 3; 3
Nick Stroltman, Station Manager

KBUN
01-01-1946; 1450 khz AM *Hrs Open:* 24

RADIO - U.S.

Mailing Address: P.O. Box 1656, Bemidji, MN 56619 US
Second Address: 502 Beltrami Ave. N.W., Bemidji, MN 56601
(218) 444-1500, *Fax:* (218) 751-8091
phanson@pbbroadcasting.com
License: Bemidji, MN held by Paul Bunyan Broadcasting Co.
Group Owner: Omni Broadcasting Co.; (acq 6-22-89;
Nat'l Network: ESPN Radio; Westwood One *Regional Network:* MNN
Format: Sports, Talk *Hrs. of News Programming:* news progmg 12 hrs wkly *No. News Employees:* 1 *Target Audience:* 18-54.
Lou Buron, CEO
Peggy Hanson, General Sales Mgr
Mardy Karger, News Director
Mary Campbell, CFO
Kevin Jackson, Operations Manager

*KCRB-FM
12-22-1982; 88.5 mhz FM *Hrs Open:* 24; 83 kw; 988 ft.; N47 42 21 W94 29 9 *Rebroadcasts:* Rebroadcast of KSJN(FM) Minneapolis-St. Paul
45 East Seventh Street, Saint Paul, MN 55101 US
(651) 290-1500, *Fax:* (651) 290-1224
www.mpr.org
info@mpr.org
License: Bemidji, Beltrami County, MN held by Minnesota Public Radio Inc.
Nat'l Network: PRI; NPR *Regional Network:* Minn. Pub. Radio
Arbitron Metro Market: St. Paul, MN *Format:* Talk *Hrs. of News Programming:* news progmg 25 hrs wkly *No. News Employees:* 1
Ian R Friendly, Chairman
Jon MacTaggart, President
Randy Hogan, Vice Chair
Bradbury H. Anderson, Secretary

KKBJ
10-31-1977; 1360 khz AM *Hrs Open:* 24; 5 kw-D, DAN; 2.5 kw-N, DAN; N47 26 32 W94 51 57
2115 Washington Avenue, Bemidji, MN 56601 US
(218) 751-7777, *Fax:* (218) 759-0658
www.kkbj.com
License: Bemidji, MN held by R.P. Broadcasting Corp.
Nat'l Network: AP Radio *Wire Services:* AP
Arbitron Metro Market: Fargo, ND *Format:* Talk *Hrs. of News Programming:* news progmg 15 hrs wkly *No. News Employees:* 1 *Target Audience:* 25-54.
Roger Paskvan, President
Daniel Voss, General Manager
Chuck Sebastian, Programming Director
Rocky Coffin, Religion Ed

KKBJ-FM
08-08-1983; 103.7 mhz FM *Hrs Open:* 24; 100 kw; 479 ft.; N47 33 21 W94 48 4
3516 Mill St., Bemidji, MN 56601 US
(218)751-7777, *Fax:* (218) 759-0658
www.kkbj.com
License: Bemidji, Beltrami County, MN held by R.P. Broadcasting Corp.
Wire Services: AP
Arbitron Metro Market: Fargo, ND *Format:* Adult Contemp *Hrs. of News Programming:* news progmg 20 hrs wkly *No. News Employees:* 1 *Target Audience:* 18-49; 40% male & 60% female
Adv. Rates: 21; 21; 21; 18
Daniel Voss, General Sales Mgr
Tracy Bailey, Promotions Manager

KKZY
05-07-1999; 95.5 mhz FM *Hrs Open:* 24; 100 kw; 423 ft.; N47 22 12 W94 52 54
Mailing Address: 4350n Fairfax Dr, Suite 900, Arlington, VA 22205 US
Second Address: 502 Beltrami Ave. N.W., Bemidji, MN 56601
(218) 444-1500, *Fax:* (218) 751-8091
www.kzyfm955.com
License: Bemidji, Beltrami County, MN held by BG Broadcasting Inc.
Group Owner: Omni Broadcasting Co.; (acq 6-22-98)
Nat'l Network: ABC
Arbitron Metro Market: Fargo, MD *Format:* Adult Contemp *Hrs. of News Programming:* news progmg 12 hrs wkly *No. News Employees:* 1 *Target Audience:* 25-54; adults
Lou Buron, CEO
Peggy Hanson, General Sales Mgr
Kevin Jackson, Programming Director
Mardy Karger, News Director
Mary Campbell, CFO

*KNBJ
07-01-1994; 91.3 mhz FM *Hrs Open:* 24; 65 kw; 988 ft.; N47 42 21 W94 29 9 *Rebroadcasts:* Rebroadcasts KNOW-FM Minneapolis-St. Paul 90%
45 East Seventh Street, Saint Paul, MN 55101 US
(651) 290-1500, *Fax:* (651) 290-1224
www.mpr.org
License: Bemidji, Beltrami County, MN held by Minnesota Public Radio.
Nat'l Network: PRI; NPR *Regional Network:* Minn. Pub. Radio
Format: News
John McTaggard, Chairman
William Kling, General Manager
Jim McGuinn, Station Manager
Timothy Roesler, General Manager of Classical Music
Chris Worthington, News Director

Benson

KBMO
12-01-1956; 1290 khz AM *Hrs Open:* 24
105 13th Street, N, Benson, MN 56215 US
(320) 843-3290, *Fax:* (320) 843-3955
kscr@info-link.net
License: Benson, MN held by Quest Broadcasting Inc.
Nat'l Network: Jones Radio Networks *Regional Network:* MNN
Arbitron Metro Market: Benson, MN *Format:* Contemporary Hits/Top 40 *Special Programming:* Farm 10 hrs wkly *Hrs. of News Programming:* news progmg 25 hrs wkly *No. News Employees:* 1 *Target Audience:* 40plus.
Paul Estenson, President
Allison McGeary, General Sales Mgr
Jason Brandt, Programming Director
Maynard Meyer, Chief Engineer
Jeremy Goucet, Traffic Manager

KSCR-FM
04-26-1968; 93.5 mhz FM *Hrs Open:* 24; 25 kw; 328 ft.; N45 19 6 W95 33 48
105 13th Street, N., Benson, MN 56215 US
(320) 843-3290, *Fax:* (320) 843-3955
License: Benson, Swift County, MN held by Quest Broadcasting Inc.
Arbitron Metro Market: Benson, MN *Format:* Contemporary Hits/Top 40, Adult Contemp *Target Audience:* 18-54.
Sabrina Pack, General Manager
Ted Tucker, Programming Director

Blackduck

WBJI
01-01-1991; 98.3 mhz FM *Hrs Open:* 24; 100 kw; 479 ft.; N47 33 21 W94 48 4
102 Lincoln Ave., S.E., Bemidji, MN 56601 US
(218) 751-7777, *Fax:* (218) 759-0658
www.wbji.com
wbji@paulbunyon.net
License: Blackduck, Beltrami County, MN held by R.P. Broadcasting Inc.
Nat'l Network: ABC
Arbitron Metro Market: Bemidji, MN *Format:* Sports *Special Programming:* NASCAR 4 hrs wkly *Hrs. of News Programming:* news progmg 8 hrs wkly *No. News Employees:* 1 *Target Audience:* 35-64; adults with aboveaverage income
Roger Paskvan, CEO
Marla Weckman, President
Dan Voss, General Manager
Jeff Halverson, General Sales Mgr
Mark Ricci, Programming Director
Tracy Bailey, Promotions Manager
Brian Schultz, News Director
Tracy Bailey, TrafficManager
Marla Weckman, Business Manager

WMIS-FM
01-01-2007; 92.1 mhz FM; 36 kw; 577 ft.; N47 33 26 W94 48 4 US
(218) 751-7777
www.wmisfm.com
License: Blackduck, Beltrami County, MN held by Paskvan Media Inc.
Arbitron Metro Market: Blackduck, MN *Format:* Rock/AOR
Troy Paskvan, President

WQXJ
01-01-2008; 104.5 mhz FM; 8.5 kw; 486 ft.; N47 33 26 W94 48 4 US
(218) 444-1500, *Fax:* (218) 751-8091
www.trueoldies1045.com
phanson@pbbroadcasting.com
License: Blackduck, Beltrami County, MN held by BG Broadcasting Inc.
Group Owner: Omni Broadcasting Co.
Nat'l Network: ABC
Arbitron Metro Market: Blackduck, MN *Format:* Oldies
Mary Campbell, CFO
Kev Jackson, Operations Dir
Lou Buron, General Manager
Peggy Hanson, General Sales Mgr
Mardy Karger, News Director
Mark Anderson, Chief Engineer

*WYNJ
89.5 mhz FM; 0.8 kw; 328 ft.; N47 44 21 W94 41 10 US
(800) 775-4673
www.lifetalk.net
License: Blackduck, Beltrami County, MN held by We Have This Hope Christian Radio Inc.
Arbitron Metro Market: Blackduck, MN *Format:* Christian
Vern Erickson, President
John Geli, Program Manager
Marcelo Vallado, Chief Engineer
Debby Wade, Administration/Station Relations Director
Deloris Trujillo, HR Director

Blooming Prairie

KOWZ-FM
09-01-1995; 100.9 mhz FM; 100 kw; 620 ft.; N44 2 44 W93 23 2
1929 Cedar Ave., South, Owatonna, MN 55060 US
(507) 444-9224, *Fax:* (507) 444-9080
License: Blooming Prairie, Steele County, MN held by Blooming Prairie Farm Radio Inc.
Group Owner: Linder Broadcasting Group
Format: Adult Contemp
Jeff Seaton, General Manager

Blue Earth

KBEW
08-29-1963; 1560 khz AM; 1 kw-D; N43 38 48 W95 33 48
Box 278, Blue Earth, MN 55987
(507) 526-2181, *Fax:* (507) 526-7468
kbew@bevcomm.net
License: Blue Earth, Faribault County, MN held by KBEW Radio Inc.
Group Owner: The Result Radio Group; (acq 2-1-81)
Nat'l Network: CBS *Regional Network:* Linder Farm *Nat'l Reps:* Katz Radio *Wire Services:* AP
Population Served: 50,000*Special Programming:* Farm 15 hrs wkly *Hrs. of News Programming:* news progmg 17 hrs wkly *No. News Employees:* 1 *Target Audience:* Farming community. *Adv. Rates:* 15.30; 13.50;15.30; 13.50
Jerry Papenfuss, President
Kevin Benson, Station Manager
Randy Allen, Programming Director
Norm Hall, News Director
Jeff Vriesen, Chief Engineer

KBEW-FM
01-01-1993; 98.1 mhz FM *Hrs Open:* 24; 25 kw; 328 ft; N43 38 44 W94 05 33
Box 278, Blue Earth, MN 55987
(507) 526-2181, *Fax:* (507) 526-7468
kbew@bevcomm.net
License: Blue Earth, Faribault County, MN held by KBEW Radio Inc.
Group Owner: The Result Radio Group
Regional Network: Linder Farm *Nat'l Reps:* Katz Radio *Wire Services:* AP
Population Served: 50,000*Hrs. of News Programming:* news progmg 3 hrs wkly *No. News Employees:* 1 *Target Audience:* 18-54. *Adv. Rates:* Same as AM
Kevin Benson, General Manager
Randy Allen, Programming Director
Norm Hall, News Director
Jeff Vriesen, Chief Engineer

*KJLY
11-01-1983; 104.5 mhz FM; 50 kw; 492 ft.; N43 54 38 W94 3 9
Mailing Address: P.O. Box 72, Blue Earth, MN 56013 US
Second Address: 12089 380th Ave., Blue Earth, MN 56013
(507) 526-3233, *Fax:* (507) 526-3235
www.kjly.com
kjly@kjly.com
License: Blue Earth, Faribault County, MN held by Minn-Iowa Christian Broadcasting Inc.
Group Owner: Minn-Iowa Christian Broadcasting Inc.
Nat'l Network: Moody; Salem Radio Network
Format: Religious *Special Programming:* Farm 5 hrs, children 4 hrs wkly *Hrs. of News Programming:* News progmg 21 hrs wkly *Target Audience:* 45-65.
Maurice Schwen, President
Eugene Stallkang, Operations Dir
Matt Dorfner, General Manager

Steve Ware, Programming Director
Mark Croom, Chief Engineer

Brainerd

*KBPR

02-01-1988; 90.7 mhz FM *Hrs Open:* 24; 34 kw; 679 ft.; N46 25 21 W94 27 41 *Rebroadcasts:* Rebroadcast of KSJN(FM) Minneapolis-St. Paul
45 East Seventh Street, St. Paul, MN 55101 US
(651) 290-1500, *Fax:* (651) 290-1224
www.mpr.org
info@mpr.org
License: Brainerd, Crow Wing County, MN held by Minnesota Public Radio.
Nat'l Network: PRI; NPR *Regional Network:* Minn. Pub. Radio *Format:* Talk *No. News Employees:* 2 *Target Audience:* General.
William Kling, President
Erik Nycklemoe, Operations Dir

KUAL-FM

06-03-1994; 103.5 mhz FM; 20 kw; 279 ft.; N46 19 56 W94 10 26
300 North Lake Avenue, Pasadena, CA 91101 US
(218) 828-1244, *Fax:* (218) 828-1119
www.cool1035.com
production@branerd.net
License: Brainerd, Crow Wing County, MN
Group Owner: Omni Broadcasting Co.
Nat'l Network: ABC
Arbitron Metro Market: Brainerd, MN *Format:* Oldies *Hrs. of News Programming:* news progmg 12 hrs wkly *No. News Employees:* 1 *Target Audience:* 25-54; adults
Tess Taylor, Operations Dir
Billy Holiday, Programming Director

KLIZ

08-06-1946; 1380 khz AM *Hrs Open:* 24; 5 kw-D, DAN; 5 kw-N, DAN; N46 19 55 W94 10 26
Mailing Address: 602 Laurel Street, Brainerd, MN 56401 US
Second Address: 13225 Dogwood Dr., Baxter, MN 56425-8613
(218) 828-1244, *Fax:* (218) 828-1119
brainerdradio.net
production@brainerd.net
License: Brainerd, MN held by BL Broadcasting Inc.
Group Owner: Omni Broadcasting Co.; (acq 4-1-2004; grpsl).
Nat'l Network: Sporting News Radio Network
Arbitron Metro Market: Saint Cloud, MN *Format:* Sports, Talk *Hrs. of News Programming:* news progmg 12 hrs wkly *No. News Employees:* 1 *Target Audience:* 25-64; adults
Lou Buron, CEO
G. Michael Boen, General Manager
Jeff Hilborn, General Sales Mgr
Tess Taylor, News Director
Mary Campbell, CFO
Danny Wild

KLIZ-FM

05-23-1960; 107.5 mhz FM; 100 kw; 351 ft.; N46 19 56 W94 10 26
Mailing Address: P.O. Box 980, Brainerd, MN 56401 US
Second Address: 13225 Dogwood Dr., Baxter, MN 56425
(218) 828-1244, *Fax:* (218) 828-1119
production@branerd.net
License: Brainerd, Crow Wing County, MN
Group Owner: Omni Broadcasting Co.
Nat'l Network: ABC *Regional Network:* Minn. News Net.
Arbitron Metro Market: Saint Cloud, MN *Format:* Classic Rock *Hrs. of News Programming:* news progmg 12 hrs wkly *No. News Employees:* 1 *Target Audience:* 18-54; adults
Brad Hollstrom, Operations Dir
Janice Degner, General Sales Mgr
Kelly Klaas, Farm Director

KVBR

05-16-1964; 1340 khz AM *Hrs Open:* 24; 1 kw-U, ND1; N46 20 51 W94 10 52
Mailing Address: P.O. Box 980, Brainerd, MN 56401 US
Second Address: 13225 Dogwood Dr., Baxter, MN 56425-8613
(218) 828-1244, *Fax:* (218) 828-1119
brainerdradio.net
production@brainerd.net
License: Brainerd, MN held by BL Broadcasting Inc.
Group Owner: Omni Broadcasting Co.; (acq 4-1-2004; grpsl).
Nat'l Network: ABC; USA; Westwood One *Regional Network:* MNN
Arbitron Metro Market: Brainerd, MN *Format:* Sports *Hrs. of News Programming:* news progmg 12 hrs wkly *No. News Employees:* 1 *Target Audience:* 25-54; adults
Lou Buron, CEO
G. Michael Boen, General Manager
Jeff Hilborn, General Sales Mgr
Tess Taylor, News Director
Mary Campbell, CFO
Danny Wild, Operations Director

WJJY-FM

07-21-1978; 106.7 mhz FM *Hrs Open:* 24; 100 kw; 558 ft.; N46 26 34 W94 22 55
Mailing Address: C/O Haley, Bader & Potts, 4350 N. Fairfax Dr, #900, Arlington, VA 22203 US
Second Address: 13225 Dogwood Dr., Baxter, MN 56425-8613
(218) 828-1244, *Fax:* (218) 828-1119
brainerdradio.net
production@brainerd.net
License: Brainerd, Crow Wing County, MN held by BL Broadcasting Inc.
Group Owner: Omni Broadcasting Co.; (acq 3-2-94; $900,000;
Nat'l Network: ABC
Format: Adult Contemp *Hrs. of News Programming:* news progmg 20 hrs wkly *No. News Employees:* 1 *Target Audience:* 25-54; adults
Lou Buron, CEO
G. Michael Boen, General Manager
Jeff Hillborn, General Sales Mgr
Tess Taylor, News Director
Mary Campbell, CFO
Mark Hegstrom, Operations Manager

*KBPN

07-01-2003; 88.3 mhz FM *Hrs Open:* 24; 5 kw; 669 ft.; N46 25 21 W94 27 41
Mailing Address: 45 East Seventh Street, Saint Paul, MN 55101 US
Second Address: Minnesota Public Radio, 45 E. 7th St., Saint Paul, MN 55101
(218) 829-1072, *Fax:* (218) 751-8640
www.mpr.org
kbooth@mpr.org
License: Brainerd, Crow Wing County, MN held by Minnesota Public Radio.
Arbitron Metro Market: Bemidji, MN *Format:* News
Kristi Booth, Station Manager
Barb Treat, General Sales Mgr
Tim Post, News Director
Kristi Booth, Regional Network Director
Tom Robertson, Reporter
Natalie Grosfield, Regional Office Coordinator
Barb Treat, Account Executive
Tom Robertson, Reporter

Breckenridge

KBMW

08-28-1948; 1450 khz AM
605 Dakota Avenue, Wahpeton, ND 58075 US
(701) 642-8747, *Fax:* (701) 642-9501
www.kbmwam.com
studio@kbmwam.com
License: Breckenridge, MN held by Monterey Licenses LLC.
Group Owner: Triad Broadcasting Co. L.L.C.; (acq 1-31-03; $1.2 million).
Format: Country *Hrs. of News Programming:* news progmg 18 hrs wkly *No. News Employees:* 1 *Target Audience:* 25-54; general
Bill Dadlow, Station Manager

KLTA

02-17-1970; 105.1 mhz FM *Hrs Open:* Monday- Friday 8-5pm; 100 kw; 659 ft.; N46 32 46 W96 37 39
Mailing Address: Post Office Box 1248, Minnetonka, MN 55345 US
Second Address: 2720 7th Ave. S., Fargo, ND 58103
(701) 237-4500, *Fax:* (701) 235-9082
www.fm1051.net
studio@fm.105.net
License: Breckenridge, Wilkin County, MN held by Monterey Licenses LLC.
Group Owner: Triad Broadcasting Co. L.L.C.; (acq 10-99; grpsl).
Nat'l Reps: Christal *Wire Services:* AP
Arbitron Metro Market: Fargo *Format:* Variety/Diverse *Target Audience:* 25-54; skews female
Tom Douglas, CEO
David Benjamin, President
Nancy Odney, General Manager
Jessica Benson, General Sales Mgr

Breezy Point

WZFJ(FM)

06-14-1984; 104.3 mhz FM *Hrs Open:* 24; 50 kw; 492 ft.; N46 36 13 W94 15 4
Mailing Address: P.O. Box 300, Breezy Point, MN 56472 US
Second Address: 7170 Ski Chatet Dr., Breezy Point, MN 56472
(218) 562-4884, *Fax:* (218) 562-4058
www.klks.com
klakes@uslink.net
License: Breezy Point, Crow Wing County, MN held by Lakes Broadcasting Group Inc.
Arbitron Metro Market: Saint Cloud, MN *Format:* Big Band, Adult Contemp *Hrs. of News Programming:* news progmg 25 hrs wkly *No. News Employees:* 2 *Target Audience:* 40 plus.
Allen Gray, Chairman
Bob Bundgaard, CEO
Marj Bundgaard, General Manager
Thomas Kenow, General Sales Mgr
David Pundt, News Director
Diane Anderson, CFO
Carol Bundgaard

Brooklyn Park

KMNQ

04-15-1956; 1470 khz AM *Hrs Open:* 24; 5 kw-D, DA2; 5 kw-N, DA2; N45 5 17 W93 22 59
444 Cedar St. Suite 1900, St. Paul, MN 55101 US
(612) 729-5900, *Fax:* (612) 729-5999
www.lainvasora1400.com
lainvasora1400@lainvasora1400.com
License: Brooklyn Park, MN held by Davidson Media Station KLBP Licensee LLC.
Group Owner: Davidson Media Group LLC; (acq 9-7-2005; $5.2 million with KMNV(AM) Saint Paul)
Nat'l Network: Westwood One *Regional Network:* MNN
Arbitron Metro Market: Minneapolis-St. Paul, MN
Marian Sanchez, General Manager

Browerville

KXDL

05-15-1992; 99.7 mhz FM *Hrs Open:* 24; 6 kw; 312 ft.; N46 3 12 W94 50 46
221 South Lake Street, Long Prairie, MN 56347 US
(320) 732-2164, *Fax:* (320) 732-2284
kxdlhotrodradio.com
License: Browerville, Todd County, MN held by Prairie Broadcasting Co.
Regional Reps: O'Malley.
Format: Adult Contemp *Special Programming:* Sports 2 hrs wkly *Hrs. of News Programming:* News progmg 4 hrs wkly *Target Audience:* 18-44; female
Gene Sullivan, President
Clif Cline, Operations Dir
Todd Jensen, General Sales Mgr

Buffalo

KRWC

11-16-1971; 1360 khz AM *Hrs Open:* 24; 0.5 kw-D, ND1; 0.027 kw-N, ND1; N45 10 0 W93 55 11
Mailing Address: PO Box 267, Buffalo, MN 55313 US
Second Address: 1472 10th St. N.W., Buffalo, MN 55313
(763) 682-4444, *Fax:* (763) 682-3542
www.krwc1360.com
info@krwc1360.com
License: Buffalo, MN held by Donnell Inc.
Nat'l Network: CNN Radio *Regional Network:* MNN
Arbitron Metro Market: Buffalo, MN *Format:* Adult Contemp, Country, 60, News/Talk, Oldies, Talk *Hrs. of News Programming:* news progmg 16 hrs wkly *No. News Employees:* 1 *Target Audience:* 25 plus.
Joe Carlson, President
Tim Matthews, Operations Dir
John George, Chief Engineer

Buhl

*WIRN

01-01-1997; 92.5 mhz FM; 26 kw; 558 ft.; N47 29 46 W92 47 5
45 East Seventh St, Saint Paul, MN 55101 US
(651) 291-1500, *Fax:* (651) 222-7795
www.mpr.org
info@mpr.org
License: Buhl, St. Louis County, MN held by Minnesota Public Radio.
Regional Network: Minn. Pub. Radio
Format: News
William Kling, President
Kat Eldred, General Manager
Cynthia Johnson, General Sales Mgr
Bob Kelleher, News Director
Doug Thompson, Engineering Dir

Caledonia

KCLH

11-14-1994; 94.7 mhz FM *Hrs Open:* 24; 2.1 kw; 561 ft.; N43 41 24 W91 30 9
980 North Michigan Ave., Suite 1880, Chicago, IL 60611 US
(608) 782-1230, *Fax:* (608) 782-1170
www.classichits947.com
License: Caledonia, Houston County, MN held by Family Radio Inc.
Group Owner: The Mid-West Family Broadcast Group; (acq 7-19-01; grpsl).
Wire Services: AP
Arbitron Metro Market: La Crosse, WI *Format:* Contemporary Hits/Top 40, Adult Contemp *Hrs. of News Programming:* news progmg one hr wkly *No. News Employees:* 4 *Target Audience:* General; 25-54 *Adv. Rates:* 72; 39; 42; 3 0
Dick Record, President
Brian Michaels, Operations Dir
Samantha Strong, Programming Director
Stephanie Paige, Promotions Manager

Cambridge

WGVY

05-05-1973; 105.3 mhz FM *Hrs Open:* 24; 25 kw; 299 ft.; N45 34 40 W93 12 56 *Rebroadcasts:* Rebroadcasts WGVX(FM) Lakeville
917 North Lilac Drive, Minneapolis, MN 55422 US
(612) 617-4000, *Fax:* (612) 623-9105
www.love105.fm
email@love105.fm
License: Cambridge, Isanti County, MN
Group Owner: Cumulus Media Inc.; (acq 6-12-2007; grpsl)
Nat'l Network: ABC *Nat'l Reps:* Interep
Arbitron Metro Market: Minneapolis, MN *Format:* Oldies *Special Programming:* Farm 8 hrs wkly
Marc Kalman, President
Dave Hamilton, Operations Dir
Pete Frisch, General Sales Mgr
Chris Rahn, Programming Director
Brook Johnson, Promotions Manager
Susan Larkin, General Sales Manager
Ben Gnam, Music Director
LeslieHeinemann, National Sales Manager
Shelley Miller, Promotions Director

Cass Lake

*KOJB

90.1 mhz FM; 18 kw; 459 ft.; N47 20 4 W94 12 43
US
(218) 339-5652, *Fax:* (218) 335-7288
www.kojb.org
brad.walhof@llojibwe.org
License: Cass Lake, Cass County, MN held by Leech Lake Band of Ojibwe.
Nat'l Network: NPR
Arbitron Metro Market: Cass Lake, MN *Format:* Native American
Arthur La Rose, Chairman
Brad Walhof, Station Manager
Marie Rock, Program Manager
Tracy O'Brien, Office Manager

Chatfield

KFIL-FM

09-01-1970; 103.1 mhz FM; 3.5 kw; 522 ft.; N43 43 59 W92 5 8
Mailing Address: P. O. Box 370, Preston, MN 55965 US
Second Address: 300 St. Paul St. S.W., Preston, MN 55965
(507) 765-3856, *Fax:* (507) 765-2738
License: Chatfield, Fillmore County, MN held by KFIL Inc.
Group Owner: Cumulus Media Inc.
Arbitron Metro Market: Preston, MN *Format:* Country
Robin Wade, Programming Director

Cloquet

WKLK

01-31-1950; 1230 khz AM *Hrs Open:* 24; 0.72 kw-U, ND1; N46 44 58 W92 25 17
1104 Cloquet Avenue, Cloquet, MN 55720 US
(218) 879-4534, *Fax:* (218) 879-1962
www.wklkradio.com
info@wklkradio.com
License: Cloquet, MN held by QB Broadcasting Ltd.
Group Owner: Quarnstrom Media Group LLC; (acq 5-12-92; $200,000 with co-located FM;
Format: Contemporary Hits/Top 40 *Hrs. of News Programming:* news progmg 16 hrs wkly *No. News Employees:* 1 *Target Audience:* Community oriented.
Mark Senarighi, General Manager
Jake Kachinske, Programming Director
Bill Meyes, Chief Engineer

WKLK-FM

04-30-1992; 96.5 mhz FM *Hrs Open:* 24; 25 kw; 315 ft.; N46 44 58 W92 25 17
1104 Cloquet Avenue, Cloquet, MN 55720 US
(218) 879-4534, *Fax:* (218) 879-1962
www.wklkradio.com
info@wklkradio.com
License: Cloquet, Carlton County, MN held by QB Broadcasting Ltd.
Group Owner: Quarnstrom Media Group LLC
Format: Adult Contemp
Kevin Callahan, Operations Dir
Dan Austin, General Manager
Suzette Anthony, General Sales Mgr
Jay Scott, Programming Director
Jillian Shuhart, Promotions Manager
Mike Carey, News Director

*WSCN

11-17-1975; 100.5 mhz FM *Hrs Open:* 24; 97 kw; 876 ft.; N46 47 21 W92 6 51
45 East 7th Street, St. Paul, MN 55101 US
(651) 290-1500, *Fax:* (651) 290-1295
www.minnesotapublicradio.org
info@minnesotapublicradio.org
License: Cloquet, Carlton County, MN held by Minnesota Public Radio.
Nat'l Network: PRI; NPR *Regional Network:* Minn. Pub. Radio
Format: News
Ian R Friendly, Chairman
Randall J Hogan, CEO
Jon McTaggart, President

*WGZS

89.1 mhz FM; 50 kw; 443 ft.; N46 50 11 W92 42 8
US
(218) 878-7292
www.wgzs89.net
WGZS@fdlrez.com
License: Cloquet, Carlton County, MN held by Fond du Lac Band of Lake Superior Chippewa.
Arbitron Metro Market: Cloquet, MN
Dan Huculak, Operations Dir
Karen Diver, General Manager
Pam Belgarde, Station Manager

Cold Spring

KMXK

08-30-1968; 94.9 mhz FM *Hrs Open:* 24; 50 kw; 492 ft.; N45 23 53 W94 25 15
50 E. Rivercenter Blvd., Suite 180, Covington, KY 14011 US
(320) 251-4422, *Fax:* (320) 251-1855
www.mix949.com
studio@kiss96.com
License: Cold Spring, Stearns County, MN
Group Owner: Townsquare Media; (acq 5-1-99; grpsl)
Arbitron Metro Market: St. Cloud, MN *Format:* Adult Contemp
Target Audience: 35-54.
Terry Jacobs, CEO
Bill Stakelin, President
Fred Murr, Operations Dir
David Engberg, General Manager
John Schroeder, General Sales Mgr
Mike Dylan, Programming Director
Lee Voss, News Director
Mark Young, Chief Engineer
DonBurggraff, Traffic Manager

Coleraine

KGPZ

07-01-1995; 96.1 mhz FM *Hrs Open:* 24; 100 kw; 577 ft.; N47 19 31 W93 16 18
5732 Eagle View Drive, Duluth, MN 55803 US
(218) 327-3339, *Fax:* (218) 327-3425
www.kgpzfm.com
kgpz@paulbunyan.net
License: Coleraine, Itasca County, MN held by Latto Northland Broadcasting Inc.
Group Owner: Lew Latto Group of Northland Radio Stations
Nat'l Network: ABC
Format: Country *Target Audience:* 35-64.
Lew Latto, President
Dennis Yourczek, Operations Dir

Collegeville

*KNSR

08-29-1988; 88.9 mhz FM *Hrs Open:* 24; 100 kw; 728 ft.; N45 29 52 W94 32 14
45 East Seventh Street, St. Paul, MN 55101 US
(320) 363-7702, *Fax:* (320) 363-4948
www.minnesotapublicradio.org
knsr@mpr.org,mail@mpr.org
License: Collegeville, Stearns County, MN held by Minnesota Public Radio.
Nat'l Network: PRI; NPR *Regional Network:* Minn. Pub. Radio
Format: News *No. News Employees:* 2 *Target Audience:* General.
William Kling, President
Kat Eldred, General Manager

*KSJR-FM

01-21-1967; 90.1 mhz FM *Hrs Open:* 24; 100 kw; 846 ft.; N45 29 52 W94 32 14 *Rebroadcasts:* Rebroadcast of KSJN(FM) Minneapolis
45 East Seventh Street, St. Paul, MN 55101 US
(651) 290-1500, *Fax:* (651) 290-1224
www.mpr.org
info@mpr.org
License: Collegeville, Stearns County, MN held by Minnesota Public Radio.
Nat'l Network: PRI *Regional Network:* Minn. Pub. Radio
Arbitron Metro Market: St. Paul, MN *Format:* Talk *No. News Employees:* 2 *Target Audience:* General.
Ian R Friendly, Chairman
John Mc Taggart, President

Cook

*WQRN

88.9 mhz FM; 16 kw; 230 ft.; N47 53 9 W92 39 47
US
(414) 935-3000, *Fax:* (414) 935-3015
www.vcyamerica.org
vcy@vcyamerica.org
License: Cook, St. Louis County, MN held by VCY America Inc.
Group Owner: VCY America Inc.
Arbitron Metro Market: Cook, MN *Format:* Christian
Jeff Fitzgerald, Operations Dir
Vic Eliason, General Manager
Wayne Fisk, Programming Director
Andrew Kalb, Executive Director, Programming

Coon Rapids

KTMY

12-24-1979; 107.1 mhz FM *Hrs Open:* 24; 22 kw; 587 ft.; N45 3 45 W93 8 21
125 East Third Street, New Richmond, WI 54017 US
(651) 647-1500, *Fax:* (801) 908-1569
www.1500espn.com
info@ktmy.com
License: Coon Rapids, Davis County, MN held by Citicasters Licenses L.P.
Group Owner: Clear Channel Communications Inc.; (acq 5-3-2004; $22 million with KOSY-FM Spanish Fork)
Nat'l Reps: Clear Channel; Katz Radio
Arbitron Metro Market: Coon Rapids, MN *Target Audience:* 25-54; adults *Adv. Rates:* 100; 125; 125; 50
Bill Betts, Operations Dir
Stu Stanek, General Manager
Bill Matthews, General Sales Mgr
Brad Lane, Programming Director
Ryan Barnholdt, Promotions Manager
Kimberly Dickerson, General Sales Manager
John Soucheray, Sales
BernieLaur, Online Sales

WTMY(FM)

09-01-1968; 107.1 mhz FM *Hrs Open:* 24; 22 kw; Ant 587 ft; N45 03 45 W93 08 21
3415 University Ave., Minneapolis, MN 55414
(651) 642-4107, *Fax:* (651) 647-2932
www.fm107.fm
info@fm107.fm
License: Coon Rapids, Anoka County, MN held by WFMP-FM LLC.
Group Owner: Hubbard Broadcasting Inc.; (acq 12-21-2000; $27 million)
Nat'l Reps: Christal *Wire Services:* Wheeler News Service
Arbitron Metro Market: Minneapolis-St. Paul, MN
Dan Seeman, General Manager

Crookston

KQHT
03-01-1986; 96.1 mhz FM; 100 kw; 413 ft.; N47 50 43 W96 50 22
4701 East Lake Harriet Pkwy, Minneapolis, NM 55409 US
(701) 746-1417, *Fax:* (701) 746-1410
www.961thefox.com
patmclean@clearchannel.com
License: Crookston, Polk County, MN held by Citicasters Licenses L.P.
Group Owner: Clear Channel Communications Inc.; (acq 10-26-99; grpsl).
Regional Reps: Hyett/Ramsland.
Arbitron Metro Market: Grand Forks, ND *Format:* Contemporary Hits/Top 40 *Target Audience:* 18-49.
Pat McLean, General Manager
Kathy Loff, General Sales Mgr
Brian Lee Rivers, Programming Director
Dave Schroeder, Chief Engineer

KROX
04-01-1948; 1260 khz AM *Hrs Open:* 5:30 AM To midnight; 1 kw-D, 500 w-N, DA-N; N47 47 20 W96 35 40
208 S. Main St., P.O. Box 620, Crookston, MN 56716
(218) 281-1140, *Fax:* (218) 281-5036
www.kroxam.com
krox@rrv.net
License: Crookston, Polk County, MN held by Gopher Communications Co.
Nat'l Network: CNN Radio *Regional Network:* MNN *Wire Services:* AP
Arbitron Metro Market: Grand Forks, ND-MN *Special Programming:* Farm 10 hrs wkly *Hrs. of News Programming:* one. *No. News Employees:* 1 *Target Audience:* 35 plus; general
Chris Fee, President
Jeanette Fee, Operations Dir
Chris Fee, Station Manager
Chris Fee, General Sales Mgr
Chris Fee, Programming Director
Maryann Simmons, News Director
Stan Mueller, Chief Engineer
Jacob Fee, Music Director

KYCK
03-04-1980; 97.1 mhz FM *Hrs Open:* 24; 100 kw; 372 ft.; N47 49 20 W96 49 13
Old Belmont Road South, Grand Forks, ND 58201 US
(701) 775-4611, *Fax:* (701) 772-0540
www.97kyck.com
live@97kyck.com
License: Crookston, Polk County, MN held by Leighton Enterprises Inc.
Group Owner: Leighton Enterprises Inc.
Arbitron Metro Market: Thompson, ND *No. News Employees:* 2
Jarrod Thomas, Operations Dir
Jack Hansen, General Manager
Phil O'Reilley, Programming Director

Crosby

KFGI
10-10-1990; 101.5 mhz FM; 25 kw; 328 ft.; N46 33 52 W93 57 3
PO Box 1656, Bemidji, MN 56619 US
(218) 927-2100, *Fax:* (218) 927-4090
kkinradio.com
License: Crosby, Crow Wing County, MN held by Red Rock Radio Corp.
Group Owner: Red Rock Radio Corp.; (acq 9-1-2006; grpsl)
Nat'l Network: Jones Radio Networks
Arbitron Metro Market: Aitkin, MN *Format:* Classic Rock
Terry Dee, General Manager
Rick Skog, Programming Director
Tom Martin, News Director
Marcy Daun, Traffic Manager

Dassel

KARP-FM
06-06-1968; 106.9 mhz FM *Hrs Open:* 24; 7 kw; 554 ft.; N45 2 43 W94 33 32
20132 Highway 15 North, Hutchinson, MN 55350 US
(320) 587-2140, *Fax:* (320) 587-5158
www.karpradio.com
info@karpfmradio.com
License: Dassel, Meeker County, MN held by Iowa City Broadcasting Co. Inc.
Group Owner: Tom Ingstad Broadcasting Group
Wire Services: AP
Arbitron Metro Market: Saint Cloud, MN *Format:* Country *Hrs. of News Programming:* news progmg 3 hrs wkly *No. News Employees:* 2 *Target Audience:* 18 plus.
Mike Novak, President
Dale Koktan, General Manager
Darla Kramer, Office Manager
Randy Asplund, Administrative Assistant

Deer River

KBAJ
01-01-2000; 105.5 mhz FM; 100 kw; 509 ft.; N47 20 22 W93 23 48 *Rebroadcasts:* Rebroadcasts KQDS-FM Duluth 100%
Suite 100, 111 Marquette Avenue, S., Minneapolis, MN 55401 US
(218) 728-9500, *Fax:* (218) 723-1499
www.96kqds.com
kqds@95kqds.com
License: Deer River, Itasca County, MN held by Red Rock Radio Corp.
Group Owner: Red Rock Radio Corp.; acq 1-10-00; grpsl).
Arbitron Metro Market: Duluth, MN *Format:* Adult Contemp
Shawn Skramstad, General Manager
Jim Payne, General Sales Mgr
Bill Jones, Programming Director
Jason Manning, News Director

Detroit Lakes

KDLM
10-01-1951; 1340 khz AM *Hrs Open:* 24; 1 kw-U, ND1; N46 50 14 W95 50 17
P. O. Box 1458, St. Cloud, MN 56302 US
(218) 847-5624, *Fax:* (218) 847-7657
www.1340kdlm.com
kdlmkbot@lakesnet.net
License: Detroit Lakes, MN held by Leighton Enterprises Inc.
Group Owner: Leighton Enterprises Inc.
Nat'l Network: CBS *Regional Network:* MNN *Wire Services:* AP
Arbitron Metro Market: Detroit Lakes, MN *Format:* Adult Contemp, News, 62, Sports, Talk *Special Programming:* Farm one hr, relg 8 hrs wkly *Hrs. of News Programming:* news progmg 10 hrs wkly *No. News Employees:* 1*Target Audience:* 30 plus.
Adv. Rates: 19.50; 19.50; 19.50; 19.50
Alver Leighton, Chairman
John Sowada, President
Denny Niess, Operations Dir
Jeff Leighton, General Manager
Andy Lia, Operations Manager

KRCQ
07-04-1994; 102.3 mhz FM *Hrs Open:* 24; 50 kw; 413 ft.; N46 43 19 W95 50 37
Suite 615, 227 West 1st Street, Duluth, MN 55802 US
(218) 847-5624, *Fax:* (218) 847-2271
www.realcountry102.com
krcq@lakesnet.net
License: Detroit Lakes, Becker County, MN held by Detroit Lakes Broadcasting Co. Inc.
Wire Services: AP
Format: Country *Hrs. of News Programming:* news progmg 10 hrs wkly *No. News Employees:* 1 *Target Audience:* General.
Adv. Rates: 15; 14; 15; 14
Jeff Leighton, General Manager
Deb Olson, General Sales Mgr
Travis McGinnis, Webmaster

Dilworth

WZFG
01-01-2007; 1100 khz AM
Mailing Address: US
Second Address: 64 Broadway, Fargo, ND 58102
(701) 664-3322, *Fax:* (701) 356-5111
www.am1100.tv/
License: Dilworth, MN held by SMAHH Communications Inc.
Arbitron Metro Market: Dilworth, MN *Format:* Talk
J. Scott Hennen, President
Jill Renee Helm, Operations Dir
Greg Burd, General Sales Mgr
Dustin Moore, Programming Director

Duluth

KDAL
11-26-1936; 610 khz AM; 5 kw-D, DAN; 5 kw-N, DAN; N46 43 14 W92 10 36
5727 Tokay Blvd., Madison, WI 53719 US
(218) 722-4321, *Fax:* (218) 722-5423
www.kdal610.com
info@kdal.com
License: Duluth, MN held by Midwest Communications Inc.
Group Owner: Midwest Communications Inc.; (acq 8-1-2001; grpsl)
Nat'l Network: CBS; Westwood One; Jones Radio Networks
Regional Network: MNN *Regional Reps:* Hyett/Ramsland. *Wire Services:* AP
Arbitron Metro Market: Duluth-Superior, MN-WI *Format:* News, News/Talk, 86, Variety/Diverse *No. News Employees:* 3 *Target Audience:* 35-64. *Adv. Rates:* 30; 22; 22; 18.
Duke Wright, CEO
Jack Lawson, Operations Dir
Mike Rasmusson, General Sales Mgr
Bruce Ciskie, Programming Director
John Talcott, Chief Engineer

KDAL-FM
07-01-1985; 95.7 mhz FM; 100 kw; 725 ft.; N46 47 15 W92 7 21
5727 Tokay Blvd., Madison, WI 53719 US
(218) 722-4321, *Fax:* (218) 722-5423
www.kdal610.com
tr@957thebridge.com
License: Duluth, St. Louis County, MN held by Midwest Communications Inc.
Group Owner: Midwest Communications Inc.
Wire Services: AP
Arbitron Metro Market: Duluth-Superior, MN-WI *Format:* Alternative *Target Audience:* 25-49.
Duke Wright, CEO
Jack Lawson, Operations Dir
Mike Rasmusson, General Sales Mgr
John Talcott, Chief Engineer

*KDNI
04-16-1983; 90.5 mhz FM *Hrs Open:* 24; 2 kw; 728 ft.; N46 47 21 W92 6 51
Mailing Address: 3003 North Snelling Ave, St. Paul, MN 55113 US
Second Address: Northwestern College, 3003 N. Snelling Ave. N., Roseville, MN 55811
(218) 722-6700, *Fax:* (218) 722-1092
www.kdnw.fm
kdnw@kdnw.fm.org
License: Duluth, St. Louis County, MN held by Northwestern College Radio Network.
Group Owner: Northwestern College & Radio; (acq 12-18-92).
Nat'l Network: AP Radio *Wire Services:* AP
Arbitron Metro Market: Duluth-Superior, MN-WI *Format:* Talk *Hrs. of News Programming:* News progmg 5 hrs wkly *Target Audience:* 25-54; baby boomers
Paul Virts, Operations Dir
Paul Harkness, Station Manager

*KDNW
12-01-1993; 97.3 mhz FM *Hrs Open:* 24; 72 kw; 551 ft.; N46 47 20 W92 7 4
3003 North Sneeling Ave, St. Paul, MN 55113 US
(218) 722-6700, *Fax:* (218) 722-1092
www.kdnw.fm
kdnw@kdnw.fm
License: Duluth, St. Louis County, MN held by Northwestern College.
Group Owner: Northwestern College & Radio; (acq 12-4-91; $20,000;
Nat'l Network: AP Radio *Wire Services:* AP
Arbitron Metro Market: Duluth-Superior, MN-WI *Format:* Christian *Target Audience:* 25-54.
Paul Virts, Operations Dir
Paul Harkness, Station Manager

KKCB
01-01-1966; 105.1 mhz FM; 100 kw; Ant 789 ft; N46 47 21 W92 06 51
14 E. Central Entrance, Duluth, MN 47732
(218) 727-4500, *Fax:* (218) 727-9356
www.kkcb.com
License: Duluth, St. Louis County, MN held by Townsquare Media
Arbitron Metro Market: Duluth-Superior, MN-WI *Target Audience:* General.
David Drew, Operations Dir
Merry Wallin, General Manager
Derek Falter, General Sales Mgr
Kimberly Carr, Promotions Manager

KLDJ
01-01-1994; 101.7 mhz FM *Hrs Open:* 24; 18.5 kw; 823 ft.; N46 47 13 W92 7 17
C/O Brill Media Co., P. O. Box 3353, Evansville, IN 47732 US
(218) 727-4500, *Fax:* (218) 727-9356
www.kool1017.com
License: Duluth, St. Louis County, MN held by GAP Broadcasting Duluth License LLC.
Group Owner: GAPWEST Broadcasting; (acq 2-13-2008; grpsl)
Nat'l Reps: Christal

Arbitron Metro Market: Duluth, MN *Format:* Oldies *Target Audience:* 25-54; general
Merry Wallin, Operations Dir
Debbi Passo, General Sales Mgr
Karina Bite, Promotions Manager
Mark Marette, News Director
David Drew, Operations Manager

KQDS
03-11-1963; 1490 khz AM *Hrs Open:* 24
4015 Ninth Avenue, Sw, Fargo, SD 58103 US
(218) 728-9500, *Fax:* (218) 723-1499
www.fan1490.com
thefan@fan1490.com
License: Duluth, MN held by Red Rock Radio Corp.
Group Owner: Red River Broadcast Co. L.L.C.
Nat'l Network: Fox Sports
Arbitron Metro Market: Duluth-Superior, MN-WI *Format:* Sports
Dave Reed, General Manager

KQDS-FM
04-01-1976; 94.9 mhz FM *Hrs Open:* 24; 100 kw; 846 ft.; N46 47 37 W92 7 3
4015 Ninth Avenue, Sw, Fargo, SD 58103 US
(218) 728-9500, *Fax:* (218) 723-1499
www.fan1490.com
thefan@fan1490.com
License: Duluth, St. Louis County, MN held by Red Rock Radio Corp.
Group Owner: Red Rock Radio Corp.; (acq 1-10-2000; grpsl)
Nat'l Reps: McGavren Guild *Regional Reps:* O'Malley.
Arbitron Metro Market: Duluth-Superior, MN-WI *Format:* Light Rock *Target Audience:* 25-54. *Adv. Rates:* 40; 56; 40; 20
Shawn Skramstad, General Manager
Jim Payne, General Sales Mgr
Bill Jones, Programming Director
Carlene Burstad, Traffic Manager

KTCO
06-14-1972; 98.9 mhz FM *Hrs Open:* 24; 100 kw; 600 ft.; N46 47 27 W92 6 59
5727 Tokay Blvd., Madison, WI 53719 US
(218) 722-4321, *Fax:* (218) 722-5423
wwwktcofm.com/.ktco.fm
david@ktco.fm.net
License: Duluth, St. Louis County, MN held by Midwest Communications Inc.
Group Owner: Midwest Communications Inc.; acq 8-1-01; grpsl).
Regional Reps: Hyett/Ramsland.
Arbitron Metro Market: Duluth-Superior, MN-WI *Format:* Country *Target Audience:* 25-49.
Duke Wright, President
Jack Lawson, Operations Dir
Mike Rasmusson, General Sales Mgr
Jayson McQueary, Programming Director
John Talcott, Chief Engineer

***KUMD-FM**
05-26-1971; 103.3 mhz FM *Hrs Open:* 5 AM-3 AM (M-F); 6 AM-11 PM (Su); 95 kw; 820 ft.; N46 47 31 W92 7 21
10 University Drive, Duluth, MN 55812 US
(218) 726-7181, *Fax:* (218) 726-6571
www.kumd.org
kumd@kumd.org
License: Duluth, St. Louis County, MN held by Board of Regents of University of Minnesota.
Nat'l Network: PRI
Arbitron Metro Market: Duluth, MN *Format:* Triple A *Hrs. of News Programming:* News progmg 12 hrs wkly *Target Audience:* 25-45.
Vicki Jacoba, Station Manager
Paul Damberg, General Sales Mgr
Maija Jenson, Programming Director
Kirk Kersten, Chief Engineer
Christine Dean, Music Director/Webmaster
Donna Neveau, Office Administrator
Christopher Harwood,Production Director
Erik Carlson, College Music Director
Sam, Marketing/Event Coordinator

WEBC
06-01-1924; 560 khz AM; 5 kw-D, DA2; 5 kw-N, DA2; N46 38 37 W91 59 9
P.O. Box 3355, Evansville, IN 47732 US
(218) 727-4500, *Fax:* (218) 727-9356
www.560webc.com
merrywallin@townsquaremedia.com
License: Duluth, MN held by GAP Broadcasting Duluth License LLC.
Group Owner: GAPWEST Broadcasting; (acq 2-13-2008; grpsl)
Nat'l Network: ESPN Radio *Nat'l Reps:* Christal
Arbitron Metro Market: Duluth, MN *Format:* News, News/Talk, 84, Talk
Erik Hellum, President
Merry Wallin, Operations Dir
Merry Wallin, General Manager
Kristine Jensen, Director of Sales
Corey Carter, Programming Director
Randy Wabik, Chief Engineer
David Drew, Operations Manager

***WJRF**
10-22-1982; 89.5 mhz FM *Hrs Open:* 24; 0 kw horiz, 2.85 kw vert; 512 ft.; N46 47 21 W92 7 9
425 West Superior Street, Suite 300, Duluth, MN 55802 US
(218) 722-2727, *Fax:* (218) 722-1650
www.refugeradio.com
airstaff@refugeradio.com
License: Duluth, St. Louis County, MN held by Refuge Media Group.
Arbitron Metro Market: Duluth, MN *Format:* Christian *Target Audience:* 18-34; female
Mike Morrone, President
Paulette Kutzler, General Manager

***WSCD-FM**
01-01-1975; 92.9 mhz FM; 70 kw; 607 ft.; N46 47 20 W92 7 4
45 East Seventh Street, Saint Paul, MN 55101 US
(218) 722-9411, *Fax:* (218) 720-4900
www.mpr.org
info@mpr.org
License: Duluth, St. Louis County, MN held by Minnesota Public Radio.
Regional Network: Minn. Pub. Radio
Arbitron Metro Market: Duluth-Superior, MN-WI *Format:* Classical
Jim McTaggard, Chairman
William Kling, President
Kat Eldred, General Manager
John McGuinn, Station Manager
Timothy Roesler, General Manager of Classical Music
Chris Worthington, News Director

WWJC
04-26-1963; 850 khz AM; 10 kw-D; N46 39 19 W92 12 40
1120 E. McCuen St., Duluth, MN 55808
(218) 626-2738, *Fax:* (603) 907-7881
www.wwjc.com
radio@wwjc.com
License: Duluth, St. Louis County, MN held by WWJC Inc.
Nat'l Network: USA
Population Served: 225,000 *Arbitron Metro Market:* Duluth-Superior
Ted Elm, General Manager
Taylor Elm, Traffic Manager

Eagle Lake

KXLP
01-01-2007; 94.1 mhz FM; 3.7 kw; 397 ft.; N44 8 31 W94 0 5 US
(507) 345-4537, *Fax:* (507) 345-5364
www.94kxlp.com
chrispainter@radiomankato.com
License: Eagle Lake, Blue Earth County, MN held by Radioactive LLC.
Group Owner: Radioactive LLC
Arbitron Metro Market: Eagle Lake, MN *Format:* Classic Rock
Special Programming: Oldies 15 hrs wkly *Target Audience:* 25-54.
Benjamin Homel, President
Jo Bailey, Operations Dir
JO Guck Bailey, General Sales Manager

East Grand Forks

KGFK
08-14-1959; 1590 khz AM *Hrs Open:* 24; 5 kw-D, 1 kw-N, DA-2; N47 52 41 W97 00 24
Mailing Address: Box 13638, Grand Forks, ND 58201
Second Address: 1185 9th St. N.E., Thompson, ND 58278
(701) 772-2204, *Fax:* (701) 772-0540
www.leightonbroadcasting.com
general@kcnn.com
License: East Grand Forks, Polk County, MN held by Leighton Enterprises Inc.
Group Owner: Leighton Enterprises Inc.; (acq 11-14-2003;. $2.5 million)
Nat'l Network: CBS; CNN Radio *Wire Services:* AP
Population Served: 100,000 *Arbitron Metro Market:* Grand Forks, ND-MN *Special Programming:* Farm 6 hrs wkly *Hrs. of News Programming:* 2 *Target Audience:* 25-60.
Jarrod Thomas, Operations Dir
Jeff Hoberg, General Manager
Linn Hodgson, General Sales Mgr
Doug Barrett, News Director

KZLT-FM
04-01-1975; 104.3 mhz FM; 100 kw; 458 ft.; N47 48 49 W96 55 48
667 Demers Avenue, Grand Forks, ND 58201 US
(701) 775-4611, *Fax:* (701) 772-0540
www.1043kzlt.com
k.smith@literock1043.com
License: East Grand Forks, Polk County, MN held by Leighton Enterprises Inc.
Group Owner: Leighton Enterprises Inc.
Arbitron Metro Market: Grand Forks, ND-MN *Format:* Adult Contemp
Matt Opsahl, Programming Director

Eden Prarie

WGVZ
03-01-1993; 105.7 mhz FM *Hrs Open:* 24; 0.95 kw; 833 ft.; N44 58 34 W93 16 20 *Rebroadcasts:* Rebroadcasts WGVX(FM) Lakeville
917 North Lilac Drive, Minneapolis, MN 55422 US
(612) 617-4000, *Fax:* (612) 623-9105
www.love105.fm
License: Eden Prarie, Hennepin County, MN
Group Owner: Cumulus Media Inc.; (acq 6-12-2007; grpsl)
Nat'l Network: ABC *Nat'l Reps:* Katz Radio
Arbitron Metro Market: Minneapolis, MN *Format:* Oldies *Adv. Rates:* 85; 70; 70; 30
Marc Kalman, President
Dave Hamilton, Operations Dir
Pete Frisch, General Sales Mgr
Chris Rahn, Programming Director
Brook Johnson, Promotions Manager
Shelley Malecha Wilkes, General Sales Manager
Jeremy Stone, Music Director
Leslie Heinemann, National Sales Manager
Joni Schmidt, Promotions Manager

Edina

KTWN-FM
09-23-1993; 96.3 mhz FM *Hrs Open:* 24; 100 kw; Ant 577 ft; N44 56 25 W93 55 43
5300 Edina Industrial Blvd., Suite 200, Edina, MN 56001
(952) 842-7200, *Fax:* (952) 842-1048
www.b96online.com
info@kttbfm.com,info@kttb.com
License: Edina, McLeod County, MN held by Northern Lights Broadcasting LLC
No. News Employees: 1 *Target Audience:* 18-34; adults *Adv. Rates:* 19; 15; 19; 12.50
Steve Woodbury, Operations Dir
John McMonagle, General Sales Mgr

Elk River

KLCI
12-01-1974; 106.1 mhz FM *Hrs Open:* 24; 9.1 kw; 538 ft.; N45 14 20 W93 41 14
Mailing Address: 1986 Julep Road, St. Cloud, MN 56301 US
Second Address: 32215 124th St., Elk River, MN 55271
(763) 389-1300, *Fax:* (763) 389-1359
License: Elk River, Sherburne County, MN
Arbitron Metro Market: Minneapolis, MN *Format:* Country *Hrs. of News Programming:* News progmg 7 hrs wkly
George Pelletier, Operations Dir
Don Kliewer, General Manager
Jim Alan, News Director
Mike Laughter, Chief Engineer
Tom Hughes, Operations Director

Ely

WELY
10-02-1954; 1450 khz AM
904 South Central Ave, Ely, MN 55731 US
(218) 365-4444, *Fax:* (218) 365-3657
www.wely.com
wely@spacestar.net
License: Ely, MN held by Bois Forte Tribal Council
Arbitron Metro Market: Ely, MN *Format:* Variety/Diverse *Target Audience:* General; senior citizens
Bill Roloff, General Manager
Brett Ross, Programming Director
Joany Haag, News Director

WELY-FM
07-25-1992; 94.5 mhz FM; 6 kw; 328 ft.; N47 53 40 W91 51 50
18 East 41st Street, 10th Floor, New York, NY 10017 US

(218) 365-4444, *Fax:* (218) 365-3657
www.wely.com
welydj@wely.com
License: Ely, St. Louis County, MN
Arbitron Metro Market: Ely, MN
Anthony Gonzales, Programming Director

***WIRC**
89.3 mhz FM; 18.5 kw; 381 ft.; N47 53 1 W91 50 31
US
(651) 290-1500, *Fax:* (651) 290-1243
www.mpr.org
info@mpr.org
License: Ely, St. Louis County, MN held by Minnesota Public Radio.
Arbitron Metro Market: Ely, MN *Format:* News
Ian R Friendly, Chairman
Jon McTaggart, President
William Kling, General Manager
Daniel Gilliam, Programming Director
Mike Edgerly, News Director
Valerie Arganbright, Managing Director, Membership
Eugene Cha, AssociateProducer
JJ Yore, Vice President, Programming
Randy Hogan, Vice Chairman

Eveleth

KRBT
12-01-1948; 1340 khz AM *Hrs Open:* 24; 1 kw-U, ND1; N47 28 40 W92 32 0
5732 Eagle View Drive, Duluth, MN 55803 US
(218) 741-5922, *Fax:* (218) 741-7302
www.krbtam.com
weve@spacestar.net
License: Eveleth, MN held by Iron Range Broadcasting Inc.
Group Owner: Lew Latto Group of Northland Radio Stations; (acq 5-1-78)
Arbitron Metro Market: Iron Range *Format:* Sports *Special Programming:* Finnish one hr, polka 3 hrs wkly *Target Audience:* 25-54. *Adv. Rates:* 12; 10; 10; 10
Lew Latto, President
Jerry Sylvester, VP
Mike Edwards, Programming Director
Steve Carlson, News Director

WEVE-FM
06-26-1978; 97.9 mhz FM *Hrs Open:* 24; 100 kw; 518 ft.; N47 35 53 W92 13 26
P.O. Box 650, Eveleth, MN 55734 US
(218) 741-5922, *Fax:* (218) 741-7302
www.wevefm.com
weve@wevefm.com
License: Eveleth, St. Louis County, MN
Group Owner: Lew Latto Group of Northland Radio Stations
Arbitron Metro Market: Eveleth, MN *Format:* Adult Contemp *Hrs. of News Programming:* news progmg one hr wkly *No. News Employees:* 1 *Adv. Rates:* 18; 18; 15; 15
Lew Latto, President/Owner
Dennis Jerrold, Vice President/General Manager
Nancy Grummett, Sales Manager
Steve Carlson, News & Weather Director
Office/Traffic, Dawn Hoyt
Office/Traffic, Bob Phillips
Advertising Executive, MikeKoenigsberg
Advertising Executive, Sue Grummett
Advertising Executive

Eyota

KDCZ
01-01-2008; 103.9 mhz FM; 1.3 kw; Ant 566 ft; N44 02 25 W92 13 05
122 4th St. S.W., Rochester, MN
(507) 286-1010, *Fax:* (507) 286-9370
www.klcxfm.com
info@klcxfm.com
License: Eyota, Olmsted County, MN held by Cumulus Licensing LLC.
Group Owner: Cumulus Media Inc.
Nat'l Network: Westwood One *Nat'l Reps:* Christal *Wire Services:* AP
Arbitron Metro Market: Rochester, MN *Hrs. of News Programming:* news progmg 2 hrs wkly *No. News Employees:* 1 *Target Audience:* 25-49.
Shannon Knoepke, General Manager
Terry Lee, General Sales Mgr
Jeff Cecil, Programming Director
Kim David, News Director
Bill Davis, Chief Engineer

Fairmont

KFMC-FM
07-31-1978; 106.5 mhz FM *Hrs Open:* 24; 100 kw; 371 ft.; N43 37 45 W94 29 0
Mailing Address: 1371 W. Lair Rd. Box 491, Fairmont, MT 56031 US
Second Address: 1371 W. Lair Rd., Fairmont, MN 56031
(507) 235-5595, *Fax:* (507) 235-5973
www.ksum.com
classic@kfmc.com
License: Fairmont, Martin County, MN
Arbitron Metro Market: Fairmont, MN *Format:* Classic Rock
Special Programming: 2 hrs agriculture wkly *No. News Employees:* 1 *Target Audience:* 25-54.
Dan Brookens, Programming Director
Rob Halvorsen, News Director
Lynn Yuen, Research Director

KSUM
01-01-1949; 1370 khz AM; 1 kw-D, DA2; 1 kw-N, DA2; N43 37 45 W94 29 0
Mailing Address: P.O. Box 491, 1371 W. Lair Road, Fairmont, MN 56031 US
Second Address: 1371 W. Lair Rd., Fairmont, MN 56031
(507) 235-5595, *Fax:* (507) 235-5973
www.ksum.com
classics@kfmc.com
License: Fairmont, MN held by Woodward Broadcasting Inc.
Nat'l Reps: Hyett/Ramsland
Arbitron Metro Market: Fairmont, MN *Format:* Agriculture, News, 84 *Target Audience:* General.
Charles Woodward, General Manager
Stan Brookens, Programming Director
Rod Halverson, News Director
Ethan V-production director

***KRLP**
01-01-2008; 88.1 mhz FM; 0.04 kw; 387 ft.; N43 53 3 W95 10 56
Rebroadcasts: Rebroadcasts KLVR(FM) Middletown, CA 100%
P. O. Box 1452, Washington, DC 20013 US
(916) 251-1600, *Fax:* (916) 251-1650
www.klove.com
klove@klove.com
License: Fairmont, Cottonwood County, MN held by Educational Media Foundation.
Group Owner: EMF Broadcasting; (acq 3-23-2007; grpsl)
Nat'l Network: K-Love
Arbitron Metro Market: Fairmont, MN *Format:* Christian
Darrell Chambliss, Chairman
Alan Mason, CEO/COO
Mike Novak, CEO
David Pierce, Chief Creative Officer
Dan Antonelli, Chief Business Development Officer
Eric Moser, Chief Financial Officer
Brian Burger, Vice President of HumanResources
D. Kevin Blair, Secretary and General Counsel

Faribault

KBGY
10-01-2001; 107.5 mhz FM *Hrs Open:* 24; 48 kw; 394 ft.; N44 12 42 W93 20 18
Fisher Wayland Ste-400, 2001 Pennsylvania Ave NW, Washington, DC 20006 US
(952) 435-5777, *Fax:* (952) 435-3181
License: Faribault, Rice County, MN held by Milestone Radio II LLC
Arbitron Metro Market: Fairbault, MN *Format:* Christian *Hrs. of News Programming:* news progmg 10 hrs wkly *No. News Employees:* 1 *Target Audience:* General; 25-54
Tom Payne, General Manager

KDHL
01-10-1948; 920 khz AM *Hrs Open:* 24; 5 kw-D, DA2; 5 kw-N, DA2; N44 15 47 W93 16 29
330 East Kilbourn Avenue, Suite 250, Milwaukee, WI 53202 US
(507) 334-0061, *Fax:* (507) 334-7057
www.kdhlradio.com
info@kdhlradio.com
License: Faribault, MN held by Cumulus Licensing Corp.
Group Owner: Cumulus Media Inc.; (acq 7-21-98; grpsl)
Regional Network: MNN
Arbitron Metro Market: Faribault, MN *Format:* News, Sports *Hrs. of News Programming:* news progmg 8 hrs wkly *No. News Employees:* 1 *Target Audience:* 35 plus.
Gary Foss, General Manager
John Anderson, Programming Director
Gordy Kosfeld, News Director
Shannon Knoepke, Market Manager
Paul Benzick, Business Manager

KQCL
01-10-1968; 95.9 mhz FM; 3 kw; 328 ft.; N44 21 25 W93 11 31
330 East Kilbourn Avenue, Suite 250, Milwaukee, WI 53202 US
(507) 334-0061, *Fax:* (507) 334-7057
www.power96radio.com
License: Faribault, Rice County, MN held by Cumulus Licensing Corp.
Group Owner: Cumulus Media Inc.
Format: Light Rock *Target Audience:* 18-49.
Paul Benzick, Operations Dir
Mike Eiler, Programming Director
Shannon Knoepke, Promotions Manager

Fergus Falls

KBRF
10-20-1926; 1250 khz AM *Hrs Open:* 24; 5 kw-D, DAN; 2.2 kw-N, DAN; N46 16 22 W96 2 41
Mailing Address: P.O. Box 767, Winona, MN 55987 US
Second Address: 728 Western Ave. N., Fergus Falls, MN 56537
(218) 736-7596, *Fax:* (218) 736-2836
www.lakesradio.net
lakesradio@lakesradio.net
License: Fergus Falls, MN held by Result Radio Inc.
Group Owner: The Result Radio Group; (acq 1-30-78).
Nat'l Network: Westwood One *Nat'l Reps:* Hyett/Ramsland *Wire Services:* AP
Format: News, News/Talk, 86 *Special Programming:* Farm 15 hrs, relg 5 hrs wkly *Hrs. of News Programming:* news progmg 20 hrs wkly *No. News Employees:* 2 *Target Audience:* Adults 35+. *Adv. Rates:* 33; 30;33; 25
Jerry Papenfuss, CEO
Greg Brady, Operations Dir
Doug Gray, General Manager
Brian Lokken, News Director

KJJK
12-01-1986; 1020 khz AM *Hrs Open:* 24; 2 kw-D, DAN; 0.37 kw-N, DAN; N46 14 43 W95 58 46
Mailing Address: P.O. Box 5767, Winona, MN 55987 US
Second Address: 728 Western Ave. N., Fergus Falls, MN 56537
(218) 736-7596, *Fax:* (218) 736-2836
www.lakesradio.net
lakesradio@lakesradio.net
License: Fergus Falls, MN held by Result Radio Inc.
Group Owner: The Result Radio Group; (acq 3-27-97; $1.1 million with co-located FM)
Nat'l Network: ABC; Westwood One *Nat'l Reps:* Hyett/Ramsland
Format: Oldies *Special Programming:* Relg 3 hrs wkly *Hrs. of News Programming:* news progmg one hr wkly *No. News Employees:* 2 *Target Audience:* 35 plus; family, home owners, execs, mgrs, dual house income*Adv. Rates:* 16; 12; 12; 7.50
Jerry Papenfuss, CEO
Greg Brady, Operations Dir
Doug Gray, General Manager
Jeff Swedberg, Programming Director
Brian Lokken, News Director

KJJK-FM
10-14-1981; 96.5 mhz FM *Hrs Open:* 24; 100 kw; 561 ft.; N46 14 43 W95 58 46
Mailing Address: P.O. Box 5767, Winona, MN 55982 US
Second Address: 728 Western Ave. N., Fergus Falls, MN 56537
(218) 736-7596, *Fax:* (218) 736-2836
www.lakesradio.net
lakesradio@lakesradio.net
License: Fergus Falls, Otter Tail County, MN held by Result Radio Inc.
Group Owner: The Result Radio Group
Nat'l Network: ABC *Nat'l Reps:* Hyett/Ramsland
Format: Country *Hrs. of News Programming:* news progmg 3 hrs wkly *No. News Employees:* 2 *Target Audience:* 21-54; today's country music fans *Adv. Rates:* 32.00; 23.00; 23.00; 17.50
Jerry Papenfuss, CEO
Greg Brady, Operations Dir
Doug Gray, General Manager
Jeff Swedberg, Programming Director

KZCR
01-19-1968; 103.3 mhz FM *Hrs Open:* 24; 100 kw; 650 ft.; N46 28 6 W96 11 54
Mailing Address: Box 767, Winona, MN 55987 US
Second Address: 728 Western Ave, Fergus Falls, MN 56537
(218) 736-7596, *Fax:* (218) 736-2836
www.lakesradio.net
lakesradio@lakesradio.net
License: Fergus Falls, Otter Tail County, MN held by Result Radio Inc.
Group Owner: The Result Radio Group
Nat'l Reps: Hyett/Ramsland *Regional Reps:* Hyett/Ramsland

RADIO - U.S.

Arbitron Metro Market: Fergus Falls, MN *Hrs. of News Programming:* news progmg 10 hrs wkly *No. News Employees:* 2 *Target Audience:* Adults 25-49. *Adv. Rates:* 27.00; 21.00; 21.00; 12.50

Jerry Papenfuss, CEO
Susan Kay, Operations Dir
Doug Gray, General Manager
Greg Brady, Programming Director

***KNWF**

04-01-2003; 91.5 mhz FM; 2.7 kw; 217 ft.; N46 19 12 W96 5 32
Rebroadcasts: Rebroadcast of KNOW-FM Minneapolis-St. Paul
45 East Seventh Street, Saint Paul, MN 55101 US
(651) 290-1500, *Fax:* (651) 290-1224
www.mpr.org
newsroom@mpr.org
License: Fergus Falls, Otter Tail County, MN held by Minnesota Public Radio.
Arbitron Metro Market: St. Paul, MN *Format:* News

William Kling, General Manager
Mike Edgerly, News Director
Larissa Anderson, Assistant Producer
Valerie Arganbright, Managing Director, Membership
Sarah Ashworth, Producer, MPR Morning Edition
Sasha Aslanian, Producer/Reporter
Robert Boos, Associate Editor, Online News
Linda Fantin, Director, Public Insight Journalism

***KCMF**

06-06-2003; 89.7 mhz FM; 2.7 kw; 217 ft.; N46 19 12 W96 5 32
Rebroadcasts: Rebroadcasts KSJN(FM) Minneapolis
45 East Seventh Street, Saint Paul, MN 55101 US
(651) 290-1500, *Fax:* (651) 290-1224
www.mpr.org
newsroom@mpr.org
License: Fergus Falls, Otter Tail County, MN held by Minnesota Public Radio.
Arbitron Metro Market: St. Paul, MN *Format:* Talk

William Kling, General Manager
Mike Edgerly, News Director
Larissa Anderson, Assistant Producer
Valerie Arganbright, Managing Director, Membership
Sarah Ashworth, Producer, MPR Morning Edition
Sasha Aslanian, Producer/Reporter
Robert Boos, Associate Editor, Online News
Linda Fantin, Director, Public Insight Journalism

Fisher

KSNR

05-01-1976; 100.3 mhz FM *Hrs Open:* 24; 100 kw; 564 ft.; N47 58 38 W96 36 42
P.O. Box 1248, Minnetonka, MN 55345 US
(701) 746-1417, *Fax:* (701) 746-1410
www.ksnrfm100.com
patmclean@clearchannel.com
License: Fisher, Pennington County, MN held by Citicasters Licenses L.P.
Group Owner: Clear Channel Communications Inc.; (acq 10-26-99; grpsl).
Arbitron Metro Market: Grand Forks, ND *Format:* Country *Special Programming:* Farm one hr wkly *Hrs. of News Programming:* news progmg 10 hrs wkly *No. News Employees:* 1 *Target Audience:* 25-54; boomers &kids

Ken Morgan, Operations Dir
Pat McLean, General Manager
David Andrews, Programming Director
Susie Johnson, Promotions Manager
Shannon Stone, News Director
Dave Schroeder, Engineering Dir
Josh Jones, Disc Jockey

Forest Lake

WLKX-FM

10-28-1978; 95.9 mhz FM *Hrs Open:* 24; 3 kw; 299 ft.; N45 17 40 W93 4 22
15226 West Freeway Drive, Forest Lake, MN 55025 US
(651) 464-6796, *Fax:* (651) 464-3638
www.spirit.fm
tom@spirit.net
License: Forest Lake, Washington County, MN held by Lakes Broadcasting Co. Inc.
Arbitron Metro Market: Minneapolis-St. Paul, MN *Format:* Adult Contemp, Christian *Special Programming:* Auction show 9 hrs, relg 6 hrs wkly *Hrs. of News Programming:* news progmg 20 hrs wkly *No. News Employees:* 1 *Target Audience:* 25-54; general

Gary Kastner, General Manager

Fosston

KKCQ

12-12-1966; 1480 khz AM *Hrs Open:* 24
Mailing Address: P. O. Box 606, Fosston, MN 56542 US
Second Address: 35006 Hwy. 2 E., Fosston, MN 56542
(218) 435-1919, *Fax:* (218) 435-1480
www.kkcqradio.com
License: Fosston, MN held by Pine to Prairie Broadcasting Inc.
Regional Network: MNN
Arbitron Metro Market: Grand Forks, ND *Format:* Oldies, Talk
Special Programming: Farm 5 hrs, relg 4 hrs wkly *Hrs. of News Programming:* news progmg 4 hrs wkly *No. News Employees:* 1
Target Audience: 25-54; family-oriented adults

Bob Overmoe, President
Phil Ehlke, General Manager
Don Brinkman, General Sales Mgr
Laura Hamilton, News Director
Jim Offerdahl, Chief Engineer
Jamie Nesvold, Music Director
Karen Bingham, Office Manager
Tom Lano, SportsDirector

Glencoe

KTWN

08-05-1957; 1310 khz AM *Hrs Open:* 24; 1 kw-D, 343 w-N, DA-1; N44 19 51 W93 58 19
5300 Edina Industrial Blvd., Suite 200, Edina, MN 56082
(952) 842-7200, *Fax:* (952) 842-1048
License: Glencoe, Nicollet County, MN held by Northern Lights Broadcasting LLC.
Population Served: 71,000 *Arbitron Metro Market:* Mankato-New Ulm-St. Peter, MN

Steve Woodbury, General Manager

Glenwood

KMGK

03-11-1983; 107.1 mhz FM *Hrs Open:* 24; 3.3 kw; 299 ft.; N45 36 53 W95 23 28
PO Box 241, 105 2nd Ave, Ne, Glenwood, MN 56334 US
(320) 634-5358, *Fax:* (320) 634-5359
www.kmgk1071.com
traffic@kmgk1071.com
License: Glenwood, Pope County, MN held by Branstock Communications Inc.
Regional Network: Minn. News Net.
Arbitron Metro Market: St. Cloud, MN *Format:* Classic Rock *Hrs. of News Programming:* news progmg 13 wkly *No. News Employees:* 1 *Target Audience:* 25-54. *Adv. Rates:* 12; 12; 12; 12

Steven Nestor, CEO
Paul Rykhus, General Sales Mgr
Dave McClurg, Promotions Manager
Rockland DeBoer, News Director

***KRFG**

90.5 mhz FM; kw*Rebroadcasts:* WJRF/Duluth, MN
US
(218) 722-2727, *Fax:* (218) 722-1650
www.refugeradio.com
airstaff@refugeradio.com
License: Glenwood, Pope County, MN held by Refuge Media Group.
Arbitron Metro Market: Duluth, MN *Format:* Christian *Target Audience:* 18-34 female

Daniel Hatifeld, Programming Director

Golden Valley

KDIZ

05-13-1948; 1440 khz AM *Hrs Open:* 24; 5 kw-D, DAN; 0.5 kw-N, DAN; N44 59 20 W93 21 6
917 North Lilac Drive, Minneapolis, MN 55422 US
(612) 617-4000, *Fax:* (612) 676-8292
www.disney.com
License: Golden Valley, MN held by RD Minneapolis Assets LLC.
Group Owner: ABC Inc.; (Acq 6-30-86)
Nat'l Reps: ABC Radio Sales
Arbitron Metro Market: Minneapolis-St. Paul, MN *Format:* Children *Hrs. of News Programming:* news progmg 5 hrs wkly
No. News Employees: 1 *Target Audience:* 18-49; baby boomers/Generation X

Beth Muschel, Programming Director
Kevin McCarthy, Promotions Manager

KQRS-FM

09-01-1963; 92.5 mhz FM *Hrs Open:* 24; 100 kw; 1033 ft.; N45 3 30 W93 7 27
917 North Lilac Drive, Golden Valley, MN 55422 US
(612) 617-4000, *Fax:* (612) 623-9292
www.92kqrs.com
mail@92kqrs.com
License: Golden Valley, Hennepin County, MN
Group Owner: Cumulus Media Inc.; (acq 6-12-2007; grpsl)
Nat'l Network: ABC *Nat'l Reps:* ABC Radio Sales
Arbitron Metro Market: Minneapolis-St. Paul *Format:* Adult Contemp

Marc Kalman, President
Pete Frisch, General Sales Mgr
Dave Hamilton, Programming Director
Brent Wilcox, Promotions Manager
Carolyn Kuhrke, News Director
David Szaflarski, Chief Engineer
Reed Endersbe, Music Director

KYCR

10-27-1961; 1570 khz AM *Hrs Open:* 24; 3.8 kw-D, ND1; 0.23 kw-N, ND1; N44 57 39 W93 21 25
4880 Santa Rosa Road, Suite 300, Camarillo, CA 93012 US
(651) 405-8800, *Fax:* (651) 405-8222
www.kycr.com
comments@business1570.com
License: Golden Valley, MN held by Common Ground Broadcasting Co. Inc.
Group Owner: Salem Communications Corp.; (acq 7-2-98; $2.7 million with KTEK(AM) Alvin, TX)
Arbitron Metro Market: Eagan, MN *Format:* Religious, Talk
Special Programming: Sp 14 hrs wkly *Hrs. of News Programming:* News progmg 6 hrs wkly *Target Audience:* 25-49; 60% female, 40% male

Lee Michaels, Operations Dir
Ron Stone, General Manager
Brian Acker, General Sales Mgr
Nick Novak, Programming Director
Kate Fisher, Promotions Manager
Scott Todd, Chief Engineer
Nic Anderson, General Sales Manager
Cindy Bohm,Traffic Director
Ross Brendel, Producer
Eric Emery, Productionn/ Imaging Director
Steve Smit, Engineer
Mike Murphy, Account Executive

Grand Marais

***WTIP**

07-01-1998; 90.7 mhz FM *Hrs Open:* 5 AM-3 AM; 25 kw; 584 ft.; N47 46 9 W90 20 49 *Rebroadcasts:* Rebroadcasts KUMD-FM Duluth 70%
Mailing Address: P.O. Box 1005, Grand Marais, MN 55604 US
Second Address: 55 W. 5th St., Grand Marais, MN 55604
(218) 387-1070, *Fax:* (218) 387-1120
www.wtip.org
info@wtip.org
License: Grand Marais, Cook County, MN held by Cook County Community Radio Corp.
Arbitron Metro Market: Grand Marais, MN *Format:* Adult Contemp, Triple A *Special Programming:* Blues 15 hrs, AOR 15 hrs, progsv rock 15 hrs wkly *Hrs. of News Programming:* News progmg 15 hrs wkly *Target Audience:* General.

Ann Possis, President
Deb Benedict, Station Manager
Kristy Johnson, Programming Director
Barbara Jean Meyers, News Director
Jeff Nemitz, Engineering Dir
Mike Raymond, Executive Vice President
Cathy Quinn, Music Director
JanaKokemiller-Berka, Development Assistant
Melanie Steele, Development Director

WXXZ

01-01-1999; 95.3 mhz FM; 63 kw; 686 ft.; N47 39 55 W90 42 22
Rebroadcasts: Rebroadcasts KQDS-FM Duluth 100%
Suite 100, 111 Marquette Avenue, Minneapolis, MN 55401 US
(218) 722-0921, *Fax:* (218) 723-1499
License: Grand Marais, Cook County, MN held by Red Rock Radio Corp.
Group Owner: Red Rock Radio Corp.; acq 1-10-00; grpsl).
Arbitron Metro Market: Grand Marais, MN *Format:* Classic Rock

Shawn Skramstad, General Manager
Jim Payne, General Sales Mgr
Bill Jones, Programming Director
Jason Manning, News Director

***WLSN**

01-01-2005; 89.7 mhz FM; 6 kw; 636 ft.; N47 46 4 W90 20 47
45 East Seventh Street, Saint Paul, MN 55101 US
(651) 290-1500, *Fax:* (651) 290-1224
www.mpr.org
newsroom@mpr.org

License: Grand Marais, Cook County, MN held by Minnesota Public Radio.
Regional Network: Minn. Pub. Radio
Arbitron Metro Market: St. Paul, MN *Format:* News
William Kling, President
Kat Eldred, General Manager
Mike Edgerly, News Director
Larissa Anderson, Assistant Producer
Valerie Arganbright, Managing Director, Membership
Sarah Ashworth, Producer, MPR Morning Edition
SashaAslanian, Producer/Reporter
Robert Boos, Associate Editor, Online News
Linda Fantin, Director, Public Insight Journalism

***WMLS**
88.7 mhz FM; 6 kw; 636 ft.; N47 46 4 W90 20 47
45 East Seventh Street, Saint Paul, MN 55101 US
(651) 290-1500, *Fax:* (651) 290-1224
www.mpr.org
newsroom@mpr.org
License: Grand Marais, Cook County, MN held by Minnesota Public Radio.
Regional Network: Minn. Pub. Radio
Arbitron Metro Market: St. Paul, MN *Format:* Classical
William Kling, President
Kat Eldred, General Manager
Cynthia Johnson, General Sales Mgr
Mike Edgerly, News Director
Doug Thompson, Engineering Dir
Larissa Anderson, Assistant Producer
Valerie Arganbright, Managing Director,Membership
Sarah Ashworth, Producer, MPR Morning Edition
Sasha Aslanian, Producer/Reporter
Robert Boos, Associate Editor, Online News
Linda Fantin, Director, Public Insight Journalism

Grand Rapids

***KAXE**
04-23-1976; 91.7 mhz FM; kw
1841 E. Hwy. 169, Grand Rapids, MN 55744 US
(218) 326-1234, *Fax:* (218) 326-1235
www.kaxe.org
kaxe@kaxe.org
License: Grand Rapids, Itasca County, MN held by Northern Community Radio Inc.
Nat'l Network: NPR; PRI
Arbitron Metro Market: Grand Rapids, MN *Format:* Variety/Diverse *Target Audience:* General.
Sandy Roggenjamp, President
Maggie Montgomery, General Manager
John Bauer, General Sales Mgr
Heidi Holtan, Programming Director
Dan Houg, Engineering Dir

KMFY
12-05-1975; 96.9 mhz FM *Hrs Open:* 24; 100 kw; 479 ft.; N47 15 17 W93 26 3
Mailing Address: 507 Southeast 11th St, P O Box 597, Grand Rapids, MN 55744 US
Second Address: 507 11th St. S.E., Grand Rapids, MN 55744
(218) 999-5639, *Fax:* (218) 990-5609
License: Grand Rapids, Itasca County, MN
Arbitron Metro Market: Duluth, MN *Format:* Adult Contemp *No. News Employees:* 1 *Target Audience:* 35-54.
Bob Fox, General Manager

KOZY
01-29-1948; 1320 khz AM *Hrs Open:* 24; 5 kw-D, DAN; 5 kw-N, DAN; N47 10 22 W93 27 10
Mailing Address: P.O. Box 597, Grand Rapids, MN 55744 US
Second Address: 507 11th St. S.E., Grand Rapids, MN 55744
(218) 999-5699, *Fax:* (218) 990-5609
kozykmfy@mchsi.com
License: Grand Rapids, MN held by Itasca Broadcasting Inc.
Nat'l Network: ABC *Regional Network:* MNN
Format: Classic Rock *No. News Employees:* 1 *Adv. Rates:* 12.75; 12.75; 12.75; 12.75
Mike Iaizzo, President

***KGRP**
01-01-2007; 89.7 mhz FM; kw
US
(707) 528-4434, *Fax:* (707) 527-8216
www.k1063.fm
License: Grand Rapids, Sonoma County, MN held by Redwood Empire Stereocasters.
Group Owner: Redwood Empire Stereocasters; (acq 11-15-2007; $2.9 million)
Nat'l Reps: McGavren Guild *Wire Services:* AP
Arbitron Metro Market: Cazadero, CA *Format:* Country
Gordon Zlot, President

Granite Falls

KKRC
10-05-1993; 93.9 mhz FM *Hrs Open:* 24; 6 kw; 262 ft.; N44 51 24 W95 37 46
4701 East Lake Harriet Pkwy, Minneapolis, MN 55409 US
(320) 269-8815, *Fax:* (320) 269-8449
License: Granite Falls, Yellow Medicine County, MN held by Iowa City Broadcasting Co.
Group Owner: Tom Ingstad Broadcasting Group
Nat'l Network: ABC *Regional Network:* Minn. News Net. *Nat'l Reps:* Katz Radio
Arbitron Metro Market: Saint Cloud, MN *Format:* Oldies *Adv. Rates:* 20; 16; 16; 12
Dwight Mulder, Operations Dir
Roberta Kuno, General Manager
Roger Hill, General Sales Mgr

Gunflint Lake

***WKEK**
06-28-2011; 89.1 mhz FM; 1000 w; 259 ft; N48 04 40 W90 45 34
1712 W. Highway 61, PO Box 1005, Grand Marais, MN
(218)387-1070, *Fax:* (218)387-1120
www.wtip.org
wtip@boreal.org
License: Gunflint Lake, Cook County, MN held by Cook County Community Radio Corporation

Ann Possis, President
Greg Tofte, Vice Chair
Molly Hicken, Secretary
Executive Director, General Sales Mgr
Barbara Jean Johnson, News Director

Hastings

KDWA
10-24-1963; 1460 khz AM *Hrs Open:* 24
514 Vermillion Street, PO Box 215, Hastings, MN 55033 US
(651) 437-1460, *Fax:* (651) 438-3042
www.kdwa.com
dan@kdwa.com
License: Hastings, MN held by K & M Broadcasting Inc.
Nat'l Network: CNN Radio *Regional Network:* MNN
Arbitron Metro Market: Minneapolis-St. Paul, MN *Format:* News, Sports, 86 *Hrs. of News Programming:* news progmg 18 hrs wkly *No. News Employees:* 15 *Target Audience:* 25-65; general
Dan Massman, General Manager

Hermantown

WWAX
06-17-1996; 92.1 mhz FM; 5.4 kw; 705 ft.; N46 47 41 W92 7 5
Suite 1501, 111 Marquette Ave. South, Minneapolis, MN 55401 US
(218) 728-9500, *Fax:* (218) 723-1499
www.nu92.fm
NU92@NU92.fm
License: Hermantown, St. Louis County, MN held by Red Rock Radio Corp.
Group Owner: Red Rock Radio Corp.; acq 1-10-00; grpsl).
Arbitron Metro Market: Duluth, MN *Format:* Adult Contemp *Target Audience:* 18-35; general
Shawn Skramstad, General Manager
Jim Payne, General Sales Mgr
Bill Jones, Programming Director
Jason Manning, News Director

Hibbing

WMFG
01-01-1935; 1240 khz AM *Hrs Open:* 24; 1 kw-U; N47 24 30 W92 57 04
807 W. 37th St., Hibbing, MN 55720
(218) 263-7531, *Fax:* (218) 263-6112
lindas@mwcradio.com
License: Hibbing, St. Louis County, MN held by Midwest Communications Inc.
Group Owner: Midwest Communications Inc.; (acq 5-10-2004; grpsl).
Regional Network: MNN
Population Served: 70,000*Special Programming:* Folk, relg 4 hrs, polka 4 hrs wkly *Hrs. of News Programming:* news progmg 13 hrs wkly *No. News Employees:* 2 *Target Audience:* 25-55; men
Kristi Garrity, General Manager
Doug Diedrich, Programming Director
Craig Holgate, News Director
Dan Klaysmat, Engineering Dir

WMFG-FM
01-01-1971; 106.3 mhz FM *Hrs Open:* 24; 25 kw; 253 ft.; N47 24 30 W92 57 5
702 Poplar Street, Cloquet, MN 55720 US
(218) 263-7531, *Fax:* (218) 263-6112
www.mwcradio.com
lindas@mwcradio.com
License: Hibbing, St. Louis County, MN held by Midwest Communications Inc.
Group Owner: Midwest Communications Inc.
Arbitron Metro Market: Hibbing, MN *Format:* Contemporary Hits/Top 40, Adult Contemp *Target Audience:* 25-54.
Duke Wright, CEO/COO
Jose Fajardo, President
Jeff Wright, General Sales Mgr

WTBX
12-31-1980; 93.9 mhz FM; 100 kw; 531 ft.; N47 22 24 W93 0 48
645 North Michigan Ave., Chicago, IL 60601 US
(218) 263-7531, *Fax:* (218) 263-6112
www.wtbx.com
lindas@mwcradio.com
License: Hibbing, St. Louis County, MN held by Midwest Communications Inc.
Group Owner: Midwest Communications Inc.
Arbitron Metro Market: Hibbing, MN *Format:* Contemporary Hits/Top 40 *Target Audience:* 18-40.
Richard Gleason, President
Jeremy Rush, Operations Dir
Vic Hodgkins, Station Manager

***KADU**
07-18-1994; 90.1 mhz FM; 1.5 kw; 338 ft.; N47 24 10 W92 57 50
Rebroadcasts: Simulcast with KBHW(FM) International Falls 100%
12104 Old Highway 169, Hibbing, MN 55746 US
(218) 285-7398
www.psalm995.org
connect@psalm995.org
License: Hibbing, St. Louis County, MN held by Heartland Christian Broadcasters Inc.
Group Owner: Heartland Christian Broadcasters Inc.; (acq 4-22-2005; $30,000).
Arbitron Metro Market: Hibbing, MN *Format:* Christian
Bruce Christopherson, Station Manager
Gene Gee, Programming Director

Hinckley

***WGRH**
88.5 mhz FM; 3.8 kw; 422 ft.; N46 1 28.2 W93 1 21.3
US
(651) 290-1500, *Fax:* (651) 290-1243
www.mpr.org
info@mpr.org
License: Hinckley, Pine County, MN held by Minnesota Public Radio.
Arbitron Metro Market: Hinckley, MN *Format:* News
Ian R Friendly, Chairman
Jon McTaggart, President
William Kling, General Manager
Daniel Gilliam, Programming Director
Mike Edgerly, News Director
Valerie Arganbright, Managing Director, Membership
Eugene Cha, AssociateProducer
JJ Yore, Vice President, Programming
Randy Hogan, Vice Chairman

Hutchinson

KDUZ
09-16-1953; 1260 khz AM *Hrs Open:* 24; 1 kw-D, ND1; 0.064 kw-N, ND1; N44 54 24 W94 21 59
20132 Hwy 15 North, Hutchinson, MN 55350 US
(320) 587-2140, *Fax:* (320) 587-5158
www.kduz.com
info@kduz.com
License: Hutchinson, MN held by Iowa City Broadcasting Co. Inc.
Group Owner: Tom Ingstad Broadcasting Group; (acq 4-1-2000; grpsl)
Regional Network: Minn. News Net.; Minn. Farm *Regional Reps:* Hyett/Ramsland. *Wire Services:* AP
Arbitron Metro Market: Hutchinson, MN *Format:* News, Oldies, 84 *Special Programming:* Farm 18 hrs, gospel 3 hrs, polka 8 hrs, Sp one hr wkly *Hrs. of News Programming:* news progmg 21 hrs wkly *No. News Employees:* 2 *Target Audience:* 30 plus; general *Adv. Rates:* 37; 31; 37; 20
Tom Ingstag, Chairman
John Mons, Operations Dir
Dale Koktan, General Manager
Jim Ohnstad, Programming Director

Mark Wodarczyk, News Director
Duane Wawyrzniak, Chief Engineer
Darla Kramer, Office Manager
Randy Asplund,Administrative Assistant

International Falls

*KBHW

01-04-1983; 99.5 mhz FM *Hrs Open:* 24; 100 kw; 561 ft.; N48 33 45 W93 49 21
Mailing Address: P. O. Box 409, Pequot Lakes, MN 56472 US
Second Address: 4090 Hwy.11, International Falls, MN 56649
(218) 285-7398, *Fax:* (218) 285-7419
www.psalm995.org
connect@psalmfm.org
License: International Falls, Koochiching County, MN held by Heartland Christian Broadcasters.
Group Owner: Heartland Christian Broadcasters Inc.; (acq 7-23-99; $1 with KXBR(FM) International Falls)
Nat'l Network: USA; Moody
Arbitron Metro Market: International Falls, MN *Format:* Christian *Hrs. of News Programming:* News progmg 15 hrs wkly *Target Audience:* General.
Gene Gee, Operations Dir
Bruce Christopherson, General Manager

*KXBR

06-01-2000; 91.9 mhz FM; 1.5 kw; 128 ft.; N48 34 15 W93 26 19
P O Box 409, 100 Brunes Street, Pequot Lakes, MN 56472 US
(218) 285-9190, *Fax:* (218) 285-7419
www.edge919.com
dj@edge919.com
License: International Falls, Koochching County, MN held by Heartland Christian Broadcasters.
Group Owner: Heartland Christian Broadcasters Inc.; (acq 7-23-99; $1 with KBHW(FM) International Falls)
Format: Christian
Gene Gee, Operations Dir
Bruce Christopherson, General Manager

KGHS

09-01-1959; 1230 khz AM *Hrs Open:* 24; 0.46 kw-D, ND2; 0.23 kw-N, ND2; N48 35 29 W93 22 54
P.O. Box 591, Int'l Falls, MN 56649 US
(218) 283-3481, *Fax:* (218) 283-3087
www.ksdmradio.com
kghsksdm@northwinds.net
License: International Falls, MN held by Red Rock Radio Corp.
Group Owner: Red Rock Radio Corp.; (acq 9-1-2006; grpsl)
Nat'l Network: Jones Radio Networks *Regional Network:* MNN
Format: Oldies *Hrs. of News Programming:* news progmg 10 hrs wkly *No. News Employees:* 1 *Adv. Rates:* 19; 18; 16; 10
Ro Grignon, President
Dennis Martin, General Manager
Jerry Franzen, Programming Director
Bill Meys, Chief Engineer

KSDM

03-17-1979; 104.1 mhz FM *Hrs Open:* 24; 8.5 kw; Ant 200 ft; N48 35 39 W93 22 56
519 3rd St., International Falls, MN 56649
(218) 283-2622, *Fax:* (218) 283-3087
www.ksdmradio.com
License: International Falls, Koochching County, MN held by Red Rock Radio Corp.
Group Owner: Red Rock Radio Corp.
Nat'l Network: AP
Population Served: 30,000*Hrs. of News Programming:* news progmg 20 hrs wkly *No. News Employees:* 1 *Adv. Rates:* 19; 18; 16; 10
Dennis Martin, General Manager
Dennis Martin, General Sales Mgr
Jerry Franzen, News Director

*KITF

88.3 mhz FM; 5.75 kw; Ant 154 ft; N48 28 24 W93 20 00
480 Cedar St., Saint Paul, MN
(651) 290-1259
www.mpr.org
License: International Falls, Koochching County, MN held by Minnesota Public Radio.
Regional Network: Minn. Pub. Radio
John McTaggard, Chairman
Thomas Kigin, President
Jim McGuinn, Station Manager
Timothy Roesler, General Manager of Classical Music
Chris Worthington, News Director

Jackson

KKOJ

07-10-1980; 1190 khz AM *Hrs Open:* Sunrise-sunset; 5 kw-D, DAD; N43 31 45 W95 0 5
Mailing Address: P.O. Box 29, Jackson, MN 56143 US
Second Address: 71991 US Hwy. 71, Jackson, MN 56143
(507) 847-5400, *Fax:* (507) 847-5745
www.kkoj.com
info@kkoj.com
License: Jackson, MN held by Kleven Broadcasting Co. of Minnesota.
Regional Network: Linder Farm *Wire Services:* AP
Arbitron Metro Market: Mankato, MN *Format:* Country *Special Programming:* Farm 15 hrs wkly *Hrs. of News Programming:* news progmg 20 hrs wkly *No. News Employees:* 1 *Target Audience:* General. *Adv. Rates:* 19.80; 19.80; 19.80; 13.50
Doug Johnson, President
Dave Maschoff, News Director
Lee Larson, Sports Commentator
Jerrie Johnson, Traffic Manager
Lee Larson

KRAQ

04-25-1994; 105.7 mhz FM *Hrs Open:* 24; 25 kw; 328 ft.; N43 36 54 W94 57 48
Mailing Address: Post Office Box 29, Jackson, MN 56143 US
Second Address: 71991 US Hwy. 71, Jackson, MN 56143
(507) 847-5400, *Fax:* (507) 847-5745
www.kkoj.com
info@kkoj.com
License: Jackson, Jackson County, MN held by Kleven Broadcasting Co. of Minnesota.
Nat'l Network: AP Radio *Wire Services:* AP
Format: Oldies *Hrs. of News Programming:* new progmg 18 hrs wkly *No. News Employees:* 1 *Adv. Rates:* 18.90; 18.90; 18.90; 13.50
Doug Johnson, President
Dave Maschoff, News Director
Jerrie Johnson, Traffic Manager

Kelliher

KKWB

01-01-2008; 102.5 mhz FM; 50 kw; 472 ft.; N47 44 21 W94 41 10
Mailing Address: US
Second Address: 324 Beltrami Ave. N.W., Bemidji, MN 56601-3105
(218) 732-3306, *Fax:* (218) 732-3307
www.coyote102.com
kprmkdk@unitelc.com
License: Kelliher, Beltrami County, MN held by Bemidji Radio Inc.
Arbitron Metro Market: Kelliher, MN *Format:* Country
Edward De La Hunt, General Manager

La Crescent

KQEG

04-05-1989; 102.7 mhz FM *Hrs Open:* 24; 4 kw; 702 ft.; N43 43 17 W91 17 24
505 King Street, Ste 221, La Crosse, WI 54601 US
(608) 782-8335, *Fax:* (608) 782-8340
www.eagle1027.com
License: La Crescent, Houston County, MN held by White Eagle Broadcasting Inc.
Group Owner: La Crosse Radio Group; (acq 2-4-2000; $2 million).
Regional Reps: O'Malley.
Arbitron Metro Market: La Crosse, WI *Format:* Oldies *Hrs. of News Programming:* News progmg 4 hrs wkly *Target Audience:* 25-54.
Pat Smith, General Manager

*KXLC

11-24-1991; 91.1 mhz FM *Hrs Open:* 24; 0.23 kw; 843 ft.; N43 48 16.1 W91 22 19.3
45 East 7th Street, St. Paul, MN 55101 US
(507) 282-0910, *Fax:* (507) 282-2107
www.mpr.org
License: La Crescent, Houston County, MN held by Minnesota Public Radio.
Nat'l Network: NPR; PRI *Regional Network:* Minn. Pub. Radio
Arbitron Metro Market: Rochester, MN *Format:* News *Hrs. of News Programming:* news progmg 24 hrs wkly *No. News Employees:* 1 *Target Audience:* General.
Chris Cross, General Manager
Mary Stapek, General Sales Mgr
Sea Stachura, News Director

Lake City

KMFX-FM

02-14-1991; 102.5 mhz FM; 9.4 kw; 528 ft.; N44 16 45 W92 23 38
330 East Kilbourn Avenue, Suite 250, Milwaukee, WI 53202 US
(507) 288-3888, *Fax:* (507) 288-7815
License: Lake City, Wabasha County, MN held by CC Licenses LLC.
Group Owner: Clear Channel Communications Inc.; (acq 10-2000; grpsl).
Nat'l Reps: D & R Radio
Format: Country
Bob Fox, General Manager

KLCH

12-01-2001; 94.9 mhz FM *Hrs Open:* 24; 5 kw; 328 ft.; N44 29 15 W92 13 55
122 Sw Forth Street, Rochester, MN 55901 US
(651) 388-7151, *Fax:* (651) 388-7153
www.lakehits95.com
news@kwng.com
License: Lake City, Wabasha County, MN held by Q Media Group LLC
Arbitron Metro Market: Rochester, MN *Format:* Adult Contemp *No. News Employees:* 2 *Target Audience:* 25-54. *Adv. Rates:* 23.50; 19.50; 23.50; 19.50
Tom Hughes, Operations Dir
Don Kliewer, General Manager
Ronnie Stockwell, Business Manager
Erika Duxbury, Traffic Manager
Tom Hughes, Operations Manager
Jack Colwell, Sports Director
Dawn Laffey, Account Executive
JodieSchultz, Account Executive

Lake Crystal

KMKO-FM

01-01-2005; 95.7 mhz FM; 6 kw; Ant 328 ft; N44 03 06 W94 17 59
1807 Lee Blvd, North Mankato, MN
(507) 345-4646, *Fax:* (507) 345-3299
www.957theblaze.com
dsturgeon@mankato.threeeagles.com
License: Lake Crystal, Blue Earth County, MN held by Three Eagles of Luverne Inc.
Group Owner: Three Eagles Communications; (acq 9-12-2005; $620,000 for CP)
Nat'l Reps: Katz Radio
No. News Employees: 1
Larry LeBlanc, Operations Dir
Dave Sturgeon, General Manager
Jen Jones, General Sales Mgr
Jeff Spence, Programming Director
Mike Schoen, Promotions Manager
Randall Harder, News Director
Jill Mason, Business Manager
Al Clennon,Local Sales Manager

Lakeville

WGVX

02-01-1993; 105.1 mhz FM *Hrs Open:* 24; 2.6 kw; 499 ft.; N44 42 5 W93 9 2
917 North Lilac Drive, Minneapolis, MN 55422 US
(612) 617-4000, *Fax:* (612) 623-9105
www.love105.fm
email@love105.fm
License: Lakeville, Dakota County, MN
Group Owner: Cumulus Media Inc.; (acq 6-12-2007; grpsl)
Nat'l Network: ABC *Nat'l Reps:* Interep
Arbitron Metro Market: Minneapolis, MN *Format:* Oldies
Marc Kalman, President
Dave Hamilton, Operations Dir
Pete Frisch, General Sales Mgr
Chris Rahn, Programming Director
Brook Johnson, Promotions Manager
Susan Larkin, General Sales Manager
Ben Gnam, Music Director
LeslieHeinemann, National Sales Manager
Joni Schmidt, Promotions Director

Litchfield

KLFD

01-02-1959; 1410 khz AM *Hrs Open:* 24; 0.5 kw-D, ND1; 0.045 kw-N, ND1; N45 7 2 W94 33 13
234 N. Sibley Avenue, Litchfield, MN 55355 US
(320) 693-3281, *Fax:* (320) 693-3283
www.klfd1410.com
info@klfd1410.com

License: Litchfield, MN held by Mid-Minnesota Broadcasting Co. *Arbitron Metro Market:* Saint Cloud, MN *Format:* Variety/Diverse *Special Programming:* Farm 20 hrs, relg 3 hrs wkly *Hrs. of News Programming:* news progmg 10 hrs wkly *No. News Employees:* 1 *Target Audience:* 25-54.

Steve Gretsch, President
Jennifer Flynn, General Sales Mgr
Aaron Imholte, Programming Director
Tim Bergstrom, News Director

Little Falls

KFML

11-01-1988; 94.1 mhz FM *Hrs Open:* 24; 6 kw; 328 ft.; N46 0 15 W94 19 40
70 N.E. First Avenue, Little Falls, MN 56345 US
(320) 632-2992, *Fax:* (320) 632-2571
www.fallsradio.com
License: Little Falls, Morrison County, MN held by Little Falls Radio Corp.
Group Owner: Little Falls Radio Corp.; (acq 6-28-2004)
Nat'l Network: CNN Radio *Regional Network:* Minn. News Net.
Arbitron Metro Market: Little Falls, MN *Format:* Adult Contemp *Hrs. of News Programming:* news progmg 3 hrs wkly *No. News Employees:* 1 *Target Audience:* 25-54.

Tim McCoy, General Manager
Belinda Beninger, General Sales Mgr
Steve Sunshine, Programming Director

KLTF

10-01-1950; 960 khz AM *Hrs Open:* 24; 5 kw-D, ND1; 0.038 kw-N, ND1; N46 0 16 W94 19 42
70 Northeast 1st Avenue, Little Falls, MN 56345 US
(320) 632-2992, *Fax:* (320) 632-2571
www.fallsradio.com
ads@fallsradio.com
License: Little Falls, MN held by Little Falls Radio Corp.
Group Owner: Little Falls Radio Corp.; acq 6-28-2004; grpsl).
Nat'l Network: Fox News Radio; ABC; Fox Sports; Westwood One *Regional Network:* MNN; Linder Farm
Arbitron Metro Market: Morrison County, MN *Format:* News, News/Talk, 86 *Special Programming:* Farm 8 hrs, relg 4 hrs, polka 2 hrs, party line 5 *Hrs. of News Programming:* news progmg 24 hrs wkly *No. News Employees:* 1 *Target Audience:* 35-65; loc audience who listen for news & info

Rod Grams, President
Chris Grams, General Manager
Melanie Lintner, General Sales Mgr
Lacey Welle, News Director
Al Windsperger, Sports Commentator

WYRQ-FM

05-19-1980; 92.1 mhz FM *Hrs Open:* 24; 3 kw; 299 ft; N45 56 57 W94 17 48
16405 Haven Rd., Little Falls, MN 56345
(320) 632-2992, *Fax:* (320) 632-2571
www.fallsradio.com
License: Little Falls, Morrison County, MN held by Little Falls Radio Corp.
Group Owner: Little Falls Radio Corp.; acq 6-28-2004; grpsl).
Nat'l Network: NBC *Regional Network:* MNN; Minn. Farm *Wire Services:* UPI
Population Served: 50,000*Hrs. of News Programming:* news progmg 20 hrs wkly *No. News Employees:* 1 *Target Audience:* 25-54; farmers & working people

Rod Grams, President
Chris Grams, General Manager
Rod Grams, Station Manager
Chris Grams, General Sales Mgr
Al Windsperger, Programming Director
Larry Bargardt, Promotions Manager
Corey Fink, News Director
Doug Thompson, ChiefEngineer

Long Prairie

KEYL

09-15-1959; 1400 khz AM *Hrs Open:* 24; 1 kw-U, ND1; N45 57 45 W94 52 9
P.O. Box 187, Long Prairie, MN 56347 US
(320) 732-2164, *Fax:* (320) 732-2284
www.kxdlhotrodradio.com/keyl_1400am.htm
keyl@keylrealcountry.com
License: Long Prairie, MN held by Prairie Broadcasting Co.
Nat'l Network: ABC
Arbitron Metro Market: Long Prairie, MN *Format:* Country *Special Programming:* Farm 5 hrs, sports 10 hrs, relg 4 hrs wkly *Hrs. of News Programming:* News progmg 15 hrs wkly *Target Audience:* 25 plus.

Gene Sullivan, President
Todd Jensen, General Sales Mgr

Luverne

KLQL

11-24-1971; 101.1 mhz FM *Hrs Open:* 24; 100 kw; 531 ft.; N43 48 24 W96 12 23
Hwy 16 East, Luverne, MN 56156 US
(507) 283-4444, *Fax:* (507) 283-4445
License: Luverne, Rock County, MN
Arbitron Metro Market: Mankato, MN *Format:* Country *Special Programming:* Farm 10 hrs, gospel 4 hrs wkly *Hrs. of News Programming:* News progmg 4 hrs wkly *Target Audience:* 25-54.

Matt Crosby, General Sales Mgr
Bruce Thalhuber, Programming Director

KQAD

03-01-1971; 800 khz AM *Hrs Open:* 24; 0.5 kw-D, DA2; 0.08 kw-N, DA2; N43 39 1 W96 10 19
Hwy 16 East, Luverne, MN 56156 US
(507) 283-4444, *Fax:* (507) 283-4445
www.oursiouxland.com
info@luverne.threeeagles.com
License: Luverne, MN held by Three Eagles Communications, Luverne.
Group Owner: Three Eagles Communications; (acq 1996; grpsl)
Nat'l Reps: Hyett/Ramsland
Arbitron Metro Market: Luverene-Rock Rapids *Format:* Adult Contemp *Special Programming:* Relg 5 hrs wkly *Hrs. of News Programming:* news progmg 5 hrs wkly *No. News Employees:* 1 *Target Audience:* 50 plus.

Steve Graphenteen, General Manager

Madison

KLQP

01-31-1983; 92.1 mhz FM *Hrs Open:* 24; 25 kw; 300 ft; N45 01 37 W96 11 15
Box 70, 623 W. 3rd St., Madison, MN 56256
(320) 598-7301, *Fax:* (320) 598-7955
www.klqpfm.com
klqpfm@farmerstel.net
License: Madison, Lac Qui Parle County, MN held by Lac Qui Parle Broadcasting Co. Inc.
Nat'l Network: CNN Radio *Regional Network:* Minn. News Net.
Population Served: 40,000*Special Programming:* Farm 5 hrs wkly *Hrs. of News Programming:* News progmg 18 hrs wkly *Target Audience:* General. *Adv. Rates:* 7; 7; 7; 3.50

Don Grose, General Manager
Don Grose, Station Manager
Don Grose, General Sales Mgr
Trent Allen, Programming Director
Ashley Crewe, Promotions Manager
Wallis Snowden, News Director

Mahnomen

KRJM

08-27-2001; 101.5 mhz FM *Hrs Open:* 24; 25 kw; 328 ft.; N47 27 23 W96 7 57
312 West Main Street, Ada, MN 56510 US
(218) 935-5355, *Fax:* (218) 935-9020
www.krjmradio.com
krjm@arvig.net
License: Mahnomen, Mahnomen County, MN held by R & J Broadcasting.
Arbitron Metro Market: Mahnomen, MN *Format:* Oldies

Jim Birkemeyer, General Manager

Mankato

KEEZ-FM

04-01-1968; 99.1 mhz FM *Hrs Open:* 24; 100 kw; 784 ft.; N44 3 6 W94 17 59 *Rebroadcasts:* 101.7FM
PO Box 3345, Mankato, MN 56002 US
(507) 345-4646, *Fax:* (507) 345-3299
www.myz99.com
dsturgeon@mankato.threeeagles.com
License: Mankato, Blue Earth County, MN held by Three Eagles of Luverne Inc.
Group Owner: Three Eagles Communications; (acq 6-19-00; grpsl)
Nat'l Network: Westwood One *Nat'l Reps:* Katz Radio
Arbitron Metro Market: Mankato-New Ulm-St. Peter, MN *Format:* Adult Contemp *No. News Employees:* 1 *Target Audience:* 18-49 *Adv. Rates:* 25; 30; 25; 18

Larry LeBlanc, Operations Dir
Brad Leggett, General Manager
Kathy Varva, General Sales Mgr
Brad Steele, Programming Director
Mike Schoen, Promotions Manager
Randall Harder, News Director
Ron Schacht, Chief Engineer
Kathy Varva,Local Sales Manager
Randall Harder, News Director

*KMSU

01-07-1963; 89.7 mhz FM *Hrs Open:* 24; 17 kw; 436 ft.; N44 8 31 W94 0 6
Msu 153, P.O. Box 8400, Mankato, MN 56002 US
(507) 389-5678, *Fax:* (507) 389-1705
www.kmsu.org
info@kmsu.org
License: Mankato, Blue Earth County, MN held by Mankato State University.
Nat'l Network: PRI
Arbitron Metro Market: Mankato, MN *Format:* Public Affairs *Special Programming:* Drama 3 hrs, folk/ethnic 5 hrs, new age 5 hrs wkly *Hrs. of News Programming:* news progmg 50 hrs wkly *No. News Employees:* 1*Target Audience:* General; upscale, educated

Karen Wright, Operations Dir
Jim Gullickson, General Manager

KTOE

01-01-1950; 1420 khz AM *Hrs Open:* 24; 5 kw-D, DAN; 5 kw-N, DAN; N44 10 6 W93 54 37
Box 1420, Mankato, MN 56002 US
(507) 345-4537, *Fax:* (507) 345-5364
www.ktoe.com
info@ktoe.com
License: Mankato, MN held by Minnesota Valley Broadcasting Co.
Group Owner: Linder Broadcasting Group
Arbitron Metro Market: Mankato-New Ulm-St. Peter, MN *Format:* News, News/Talk, 86 *Hrs. of News Programming:* news progmg 21 hrs wkly *No. News Employees:* 3 *Target Audience:* 25-54.

John Linder, CEO
Jo Bailey, Operations Dir
Jo Guck Bailey, General Manager
Jo Guck Bailey, General Sales Mgr

KYSM

07-25-1938; 1230 khz AM *Hrs Open:* 24
330 East Kilbourn Avenue, Suite 250, Milwaukee, WI 53202 US
(507) 388-2900, *Fax:* (507) 345-4657
www.thefan1230.com/
License: Mankato, MN held by Minnesota Valley Broadcasting Co.
Group Owner: Linder Broadcasting Group; (acq 12-31-2007; $700,000)
Arbitron Metro Market: Mankato, MN *Format:* Sports, Talk

Jo Bailey, Operations Dir

KYSM-FM

04-01-1948; 103.5 mhz FM *Hrs Open:* 24; 100 kw; 541 ft.; N44 10 20 W94 2 23
330 East Kilbourn Avenue, Suite 250, Milwaukee, WI 53202 US
(507) 345-4646, *Fax:* (507) 345-4675
country103.com
dsturgeon@mankato.threeeagles.com
License: Mankato, Blue Earth County, MN held by Three Eagles of Lincoln Inc.
Group Owner: Three Eagles Communications; (acq 6-8-2007; grpsl)
Nat'l Reps: Katz Radio *Wire Services:* AP
Arbitron Metro Market: Mankato, MN *Format:* Country *Special Programming:* Sp one hr wkly *Hrs. of News Programming:* news progmg one hr wkly *No. News Employees:* 2 *Target Audience:* 25-54. *Adv. Rates:* 75; 75; 75; 25

Brad Leggett, General Manager
Kathy Varva, General Sales Mgr
Larry LeBlanc, Programming Director
Mike Schoen, Promotions Manager
Randall Harder, News Director
Al Clennon, Local Sales Manager

Maplewood

WCTS

08-01-1964; 1030 khz AM *Hrs Open:* 24; 50 kw-D, DA2; 1 kw-N, DA2; N44 52 1 W92 54 2
1250 West Broadway, Minneapolis, MN 55411 US
(763) 417-8270, *Fax:* (763) 417-8278
www.wctsradio.com
info@wctsradio.com
License: Maplewood, MN held by Central Baptist Theological Seminary of Plymouth.
Nat'l Network: Moody *Wire Services:* AP
Arbitron Metro Market: Minneapolis-Saint Paul, MN *Format:* Christian, Religious *Hrs. of News Programming:* News progmg 3 hrs wkly *Target Audience:* 30 plus; Christian

Stephen Davis, Operations Dir
Kimball Cummings Jr., General Manager

RADIO - U.S.

Marshall

KARZ
07-07-1985; 107.5 mhz FM; 15 kw; 430 ft.; N44 19 32 W95 52 19
Mailing Address: P.O. Box 1420, Mankato, MN 56002 US
Second Address: 1414 E. College Dr., Marshall, MN 56258
(507) 532-2282, *Fax:* (507) 532-3739
www.marshallradio.net
info@marshallradio.net
License: Marshall, Lyon County, MN held by KMHL Broadcasting Co. Inc.
Group Owner: Linder Broadcasting Group; (acq 5-6-97; $450,000)
Arbitron Metro Market: Marshall, MN *Format:* Classic Rock
Target Audience: 25-54. *Adv. Rates:* 10.50; 10.50; 10.50; 8.25
Keith Petermeier, Operations Dir
Brad Strootman, General Manager
Scott Schmeling, Chief Engineer

KKCK
12-13-1967; 99.7 mhz FM *Hrs Open:* 24; 100 kw; 925 ft.; N44 16 56 W96 19 5
P.O. Box 1420, Mankato, MN 56001 US
(507) 532-2282, *Fax:* (507) 532-3739
marshallradio.net
info@marshallradio.net
License: Marshall, Lyon County, MN
Arbitron Metro Market: Mankato, MN *Format:* Adult Contemp *Hrs. of News Programming:* news progmg 8 hrs wkly *No. News Employees:* 1 *Target Audience:* 21-39. *Adv. Rates:* 19.50; 16.25; 16.25; 12
Brad Stoutman, General Sales Mgr
Russ Berreth, Programming Director
Keith Petermierer, Promotions Manager
Val Braun, News Director
Aaron Ziemer, Local News Editor

KMHL
11-30-1946; 1400 khz AM *Hrs Open:* 24; 1 kw-U, ND1; N44 26 59 W95 45 43
Box 1420, Mankato, MN 56002 US
(507) 532-2282, *Fax:* (507) 532-3739
www.marshallradio.com
License: Marshall, MN held by KMHL Broadcasting Co.
Group Owner: Linder Broadcasting Group
Nat'l Network: ABC *Regional Network:* Linder Farm; MNN *Nat'l Reps:* Katz Radio
Format: News, News/Talk, 86 *Special Programming:* Relg 7 hrs wkly *Hrs. of News Programming:* news progmg 20 hrs wkly *No. News Employees:* 1 *Target Audience:* 27 plus. *Adv. Rates:* 23; 13.50; 13.50; 11.25
Donald Linder, President
John Linder, Operations Dir
Brad Strootman, General Manager
Justin Thordsen, Programming Director
Val Braun, News Director
Scott Schmelling, Chief Engineer
Keith Petermeier, Chief of Operations
LynnKettelson, Keith Petermeier
Aaron Ziemer, Public Affairs Director

*KOMH
90.7 mhz FM; kw
US
(910) 368-1581
License: Marshall, Lyon County, MN held by Shining Light Ministries.
Arbitron Metro Market: Marshall, MN
Joshua Hawkins, President

*KRGM
89.9 mhz FM; 4 kw; 535 ft.; N44 29 3 W95 29 27
US
(218) 722-2727, *Fax:* (218) 279-5010
www.refugeradio.com
License: Marshall, Lyon County, MN held by Refuge Media Group.
Arbitron Metro Market: Duluth, MN
Mike Marrone, President
Paulette Kutzler, General Manager

Minneapolis

*KBEM-FM
10-04-1970; 88.5 mhz FM *Hrs Open:* 24; 2.9 kw; 479 ft.; N44 59 54 W93 11 18
807 N E Broadway, Minneapolis, MN 55413 US
(612) 668-1735, *Fax:* (612) 668-1766
jazz88.mpls.k12.mn.us
studio@jazz88fm.com
License: Minneapolis, Hennepin County, MN held by Special School District No. 1, Board of Education.
Nat'l Network: PRI
Arbitron Metro Market: Minneapolis, MN *Format:* Jazz *Special Programming:* Bluegrass 4 hrs, Sp 4 hrs wkly *Hrs. of News Programming:* news progmg 14 hrs wkly *No. News Employees:* 1 *Target Audience:* 35 plus;jazz/progsv adults, club/audiophiles
Michele McKenzie, Station Manager
Ted Allison, General Sales Mgr
Kevin O'Connor, Programming Director
Ed Jones, News Director
Michael Jamnick, Engineering Dir

*KFAI
05-01-1978; 90.3 mhz FM *Hrs Open:* 24; 0.9 kw; 791 ft.; N44 58 34 W93 16 21
1808 Riverside Avenue, Minneapolis, MN 55454 US
(612) 341-3144, *Fax:* (612) 341-4281
www.kfai.org
janislaneewart@kfai.org
License: Minneapolis, Hennepin County, MN held by Fresh Air Inc.
Arbitron Metro Market: Minneapolis-St. Paul, MN *Format:* Variety/Diverse *Special Programming:* Black 10 hrs, folk 6 hrs, Fr 2 hrs, jazz 12 hrs, Sp 8 hrs wkly *Hrs. of News Programming:* news progmg 7 hrs wkly *No.News Employees:* 1 *Target Audience:* General; underserved, under-represented communities
Janis Lane-Ewart, General Manager
Diane Wanner, General Sales Mgr
Dan Richmond, Programming Director
Jackson Buck, Promotions Manager
Lauretta Dawolo, News Director
Dan Zimmerman, Chief Engineer

KTCN
01-01-1923; 1130 khz AM *Hrs Open:* 24; 50 kw-D, 25 kw-N, DA-2; N44 38 48 W93 23 31
1600 Utica Ave. S., Suite 400, Minneapolis, MN 55431
(952) 417-3000, *Fax:* (612) 417-3001
www.kfan.com
info@k102.com
License: Minneapolis, Hennepin County, MN held by AMFM Broadcasting Licenses LLC.
Group Owner: Clear Channel Communications Inc.; (acq 8-30-2000; grpsl)
Nat'l Reps: Clear Channel
Arbitron Metro Market: Minneapolis-St. Paul, MN *Hrs. of News Programming:* news progmg 20 hrs wkly *No. News Employees:* 40 *Target Audience:* 25-54; males
Mick Anselmo, Operations Dir
Todd Kalman, General Sales Mgr
Chad Abbott, Programming Director
Matt Tell, Promotions Manager
Cathy Maness, News Director
Dan Motler, Engineering Dir
Jess Meyer, Engineering Director
Jeff Framke,National Sales Manager
Lisa Sanderson, Promotions Director
John Jansen, Public Affairs Director

KFXN
04-05-1962; 690 khz AM; 0.5 kw-D, DA2; 0.004 kw-N, DA2; N45 1 25 W93 22 58
100 North Sixth Street, Suite 306c, Minneapolis, MN 55403 US
(952) 417-3000, *Fax:* (952) 417-3001
www.hmongradioam690.com/
info@kdwb.com
License: Minneapolis, MN held by AMFM Broadcasting Licenses LLC.
Group Owner: Clear Channel Communications Inc.; (acq 8-30-2000; grpsl)
Arbitron Metro Market: Minneapolis, MN *Format:* Japanese, Korean, 18 *Special Programming:* Cultural Talk 10 hrs wkly
Target Audience: 25-54, Asian Adults
Mick Anselmo, President
Todd Kalman, General Sales Mgr
Chad Abbott, Programming Director
Jess Meyer, Chief Engineer

*KMOJ
09-15-1978; 89.9 mhz FM *Hrs Open:* 24; 6.2 kw; 394 ft.; N45 4 7 W93 10 34
501 Bryant Avenue North, Minneapolis, MN 55405 US
(612) 377-0594, *Fax:* (612) 377-3990
in fo@kmojfm.com
License: Minneapolis, Hennepin County, MN held by Center for Communication & Development.
Arbitron Metro Market: Minneapolis, MN *Format:* Urban Contemporary *Hrs. of News Programming:* news progmg 4 hrs wkly *No. News Employees:* 2 *Target Audience:* General.
Kelvin Quarles, General Manager

KSJN
01-01-1956; 99.5 mhz FM; 100 kw; 1033 ft.; N45 3 30 W93 7 27
45 East 7th Street, St. Paul, MN 55101 US
(651) 290-1500, *Fax:* (651) 290-1224
www.mpr.org
info@mpr.org
License: Minneapolis, Hennepin County, MN held by Minnesota Public Radio Inc.
Wire Services: Reuters
Arbitron Metro Market: St. Paul, MN *Format:* Talk
William Kling, President
Erik Nycklemoe, Operations Dir
Jon Gossett, General Sales Mgr
Mary Ladner, Promotions Manager
Bill Wareham, News Director

KTCZ-FM
01-01-1956; 97.1 mhz FM *Hrs Open:* 24; 100 kw; 1033 ft.; N45 3 30 W93 7 27
100 N Sixth St, Suite 306c, Minneapolis, MN 55403 US
(952) 417-3000, *Fax:* (952) 417-3001
cities97.com
info@cities97.com
License: Minneapolis, Hennepin County, MN held by AMFM Broadcasting Licenses LLC.
Group Owner: Clear Channel Communications Inc.
Arbitron Metro Market: Minneapolis-St. Paul, MN *Format:* Adult Contemp
Mick Anselmo, President
Erik Christopherson, General Sales Mgr
Lauren MacLeash, Programming Director
Dave Sheets, Promotions Manager

*KTIS
02-07-1949; 900 khz AM *Hrs Open:* 24
3003 North Snelling Ave, Roseville, MN 55113 US
(651) 631-5000, *Fax:* (651) 631-5084
www.ktis.fm
info@ktis.fm
License: Minneapolis, MN held by Northwestern College.
Group Owner: Northwestern College & Radio
Arbitron Metro Market: Minneapolis-St. Paul, MN *Format:* Christian, News, 74 *Hrs. of News Programming:* news progmg 20 hrs wkly *No. News Employees:* 2 *Target Audience:* 35-45.
Paul Virts, President
Marilyn Ryan, Operations Dir
Jason Sharp, Station Manager

*KTIS-FM
05-01-1949; 98.5 mhz FM *Hrs Open:* 24; 100 kw; 1033 ft.; N45 3 30 W93 7 27
3003 North Snelling Ave, St. Paul, MN 55113 US
(651) 631-5000, *Fax:* (651) 631-5084
www.ktis.fm
info@ktis.fm
License: Minneapolis, Hennepin County, MN held by Northwestern College.
Group Owner: Northwestern College & Radio
Nat'l Network: AP Network News
Arbitron Metro Market: Minneapolis-St. Paul, MN *Format:* Religious *Hrs. of News Programming:* news progmg 20 hrs wkly *No. News Employees:* 1 *Target Audience:* 25-45.
Alan Cureton, President
Harv Hendrickson, Operations Dir
Jason Sharp, Station Manager
Dr. Paul Virts, Executive Vice President

*KUOM
01-13-1922; 770 khz AM *Hrs Open:* Sunrise-sunset; 5 kw-D, NDD; N44 59 54 W93 11 18
330 21st. Avenue, South, Minneapolis, MN 55455 US
(612) 625-3500, *Fax:* (612) 625-2112
www.radiok.org
request@radiok.org
License: Minneapolis, MN held by University of Minnesota
Wire Services: AP
Arbitron Metro Market: Minneapolis, MN *Format:* Rock/AOR
Target Audience: 18-34
Sara Miller, Station Manager
Caleigh Souhan, Programming Director
Larry Oberg, Chief Engineer
Amy Daml, Program Coach
Chase Mathey, Music Director
Sarah Lemanczyk, Programming Advisor
Greg Sakowski, Production Director
StuartSanders, Development Director
Brody Howard, Studio K Producer

KXXR
01-06-1961; 93.7 mhz FM *Hrs Open:* 24; 100 kw; 1033 ft.; N45 3 30 W93 7 27

917 North Lilac Drive, Minneapolis, MN 55422 US
(612) 617-4000, *Fax:* (612) 676-8293
www.93x.com
mail@93x.com
License: Minneapolis, Hennepin County, MN
Group Owner: Cumulus Media Inc.; (acq 6-12-2007; grpsl)
Nat'l Reps: Interep
Arbitron Metro Market: Minneapolis-St. Paul, MN *Format:* Rock/AOR *Target Audience:* 18-54.
Marc Kalman, Station Manager
Shelly M. Wilkes, General Sales Mgr
Wade Linder, Programming Director
Wendy Ellis, Promotions Manager

WCCO
10-02-1924; 830 khz AM *Hrs Open:* 24; 50 kw-U, ND1; N45 10 40 W93 20 55
600 New Hampshire Avenue, NW, Suite 1200, Washington, DC 20037 US
(612) 370-0611, *Fax:* (612) 370-0159
www.minnesota.cbslocal.com/station/830-wcco/
newstips@wccoradio.com
License: Minneapolis, MN held by Infinity Media Corp.
Group Owner: CBS Radio; (acq 11-13-98; grpsl).
Nat'l Network: CBS *Nat'l Reps:* Interep
Arbitron Metro Market: Minneapolis-St. Paul, MN *Format:* News, News/Talk, 86 *Hrs. of News Programming:* news progmg 25 hrs wkly *No. News Employees:* 7 *Target Audience:* General.
Mary Niemeyer, General Sales Mgr
Wendy Paulson, Programming Director
Amy Mauzy, Promotions Manager
Craig Walters, Chief Engineer
Sue Hemmeke, National Sales Manager

KMNB
08-27-1973; 102.9 mhz FM *Hrs Open:* 24; 100 kw; 1,033 ft; N45 03 30 W93 07 27
625 2nd Ave. S., Minneapolis, MN 20037
(612) 339-1029,(612) 339-1083, *Fax:* (612) 339-5653
www.wlte.com
info@wlte.com
License: Minneapolis, Hennepin County, MN
Arbitron Metro Market: Minneapolis-St. Paul, MN *Hrs. of News Programming:* News progmg 5 hrs wkly *Target Audience:* 25-54.
Chris Kalis, Promotions Manager

WLOL
01-01-1939; 1330 khz AM *Hrs Open:* 24; 9.7 kw-D, DA2; 5.1 kw-N, DA2; N44 47 2 W93 20 38
45 East Seveveth Street, Saint Paul, MN 55101 US
(612)643-4119, *Fax:* (763)546-4444
www.relevantradio.com
info@relevantradio.com
License: Minneapolis, MN held by Starboard Media Foundation Inc.
Group Owner: Relevant Radio; (acq 3-16-2004; $6.75 million)
Arbitron Metro Market: Minneapolis, MN *Format:* Christian *Hrs. of News Programming:* 3 hrs news progmg wkly
Thomas Vorpahl, Chairman
Trish Leurck, CEO
Paul Sadek, Station Manager
Bob Benes, General Sales Mgr
Mike Kendall, Programming Director

KFXN-FM
06-26-1965; 100.3 mhz FM *Hrs Open:* 24; 97 kw; 905 ft; N45 20 12 W93 23 28
1600 Utica Ave. S., Suite 400, Minneapolis, MN 55403
(952) 417-3000, *Fax:* (952) 417-3001
www.kjzi.com
info@kjzi.com
License: Minneapolis, Hennepin County, MN held by AMFM Broadcasting Licenses LLC.
Group Owner: Clear Channel Communications Inc.; (acq 8-30-2000; grpsl).
Nat'l Network: Fox News Radio *Nat'l Reps:* Clear Channel
Population Served: 2,500,000 *Arbitron Metro Market:* Minneapolis-St. Paul, MN *No. News Employees:* 3 *Target Audience:* Adults 25-54; adults
Mick Anselmo, President

WWTC
08-10-1925; 1280 khz AM
8910 University Center Lane, #130, San Diego, CA 92122 US
(651) 405-8800, *Fax:* (651) 405-8222
www.am1280thepatriot.com
comments@am1280thepatriot.com
License: Minneapolis, MN held by Salem Media Group LLC.
Group Owner: Salem Communications Corp.; (acq 12-18-2000; $7 million with WAUK(AM) Jackson, WI)
Arbitron Metro Market: Egan, MN *Format:* News, News/Talk, 86
Target Audience: 18-54. *Adv. Rates:* 100; 75; 100; 50
Lee Michaels, Operations Dir
Ron Stone, General Manager
Nic Anderson, General Sales Mgr
Nick Novak, Programming Director
Zech Hipp, Promotions Manager
Steve Smit, Chief Engineer
Cindy Bohm, Traffic Director
Eric Emery,Production/Imaging Director
Desta Kraft, Administrative Assistant
Laurie Krier, Business Manager
Kirsten Aura, Account Executive

Minneapolis-St. Paul

*KNOW-FM
07-01-1967; 91.1 mhz FM; 100 kw; 1275 ft.; N45 3 44 W93 8 21
45 East Seventh Street, St. Paul, MN 55101 US
(651) 290-1500, *Fax:* (651) 290-1224
www.mpr.org
info@mpr.org
License: Minneapolis-St. Paul, Hennepin County, MN held by Minnesota Public Radio.
Wire Services: Reuters
Arbitron Metro Market: Minneapolis-St. Paul, MN *Format:* News
John McTaggard, Chairman
William Kling, President
Erik Nycklemoe, Operations Dir
Jim McGuinn, Station Manager
Timothy Roesler, General Manager of Classsical Music
Chris Worthington, News Director

Montevideo

*KBPG
07-01-2002; 89.5 mhz FM; 0.5 kw; 151 ft.; N44 54 50 W95 44 10
P.O. Box 1458, Washington, DC 20013 US
(662) 844-8888, *Fax:* (662) 842-6791
www.afr.net
License: Montevideo, Chippewa County, MN held by American Family Association.
Group Owner: American Family Radio; (acq 11-26-99).
Nat'l Network: USA
Format: Religious
Don Wildman, General Manager

KDMA
12-21-1951; 1460 khz AM *Hrs Open:* 24
4701 East Lake Harriet Parkway, Minneapolis, MN 55409 US
(320) 269-8815(320) 269-5131, *Fax:* (320) 269-8449
kdmaprod@charterinternet.com
License: Montevideo, MN held by Iowa City Broadcasting Co.
Group Owner: Tom Ingstad Broadcasting Group; (acq 10-21-97; grpsl)
Regional Network: Linder Farm *Regional Reps:* O'Malley. *Wire Services:* Weather Wire
Format: Country *Special Programming:* Farm 7 hrs wkly *No. News Employees:* 1 *Adv. Rates:* 19.25; 15.75; 15.75; 12
Dwight Mulder, Operations Dir
Roberta Kuno, Station Manager
Roger Hill, General Sales Mgr
Lynn Ketelson, Farm Director

KMGM
10-01-1982; 105.5 mhz FM *Hrs Open:* 24; 3 kw; 295 ft.; N44 51 24 W95 37 46
4701 East Lake Harriet Parkway, Minneapolis, MN 55409 US
(320) 269-8815, *Fax:* (320) 269-8449
License: Montevideo, Chippewa County, MN held by Iowa City Broadcasting Co.
Group Owner: Tom Ingstad Broadcasting Group
Wire Services: Weather Wire
Format: Classic Rock *Target Audience:* 25-54.
Roberta Kuno, General Manager
Roger Hill, General Sales Mgr

Moorhead

*KCCD
06-01-1992; 90.3 mhz FM *Hrs Open:* 24; 100 kw vert; 495 ft.; N46 45 35 W96 36 26
45 East 7th Street, Saint Paul, MN 55101 US
(651) 290-1500
www.minnesota.publicradio.org
License: Moorhead, Clay County, MN held by Minnesota Public Radio.
Nat'l Network: NPR; PRI *Regional Network:* Minn. Pub. Radio
Arbitron Metro Market: Saint Paul, MN *Format:* News *No. News Employees:* 2 *Target Audience:* General.
William Kling, President
Vern Goodin, General Manager
Julia Beaton, General Sales Mgr

*KCCM-FM
10-23-1971; 91.1 mhz FM *Hrs Open:* 24; 67 kw; 659 ft.; N46 45 35 W96 36 26
45 East Seventh Street, St. Paul, MN 55101 US
(651) 290-1500, *Fax:* (218) 299-3418
www.minnesota.publicradio.org
License: Moorhead, Clay County, MN held by Minnesota Public Radio Inc.
Nat'l Network: NPR; PRI *Regional Network:* Minn. Pub. Radio
Arbitron Metro Market: Saint Paul, MN *Format:* Ethnic *Hrs. of News Programming:* news progmg one hr wkly *No. News Employees:* 2 *Target Audience:* General.
William Kling, President
Vern Goodin, General Manager
Julia Beaton, General Sales Mgr

KQWB-FM
11-01-1966; 98.7 mhz FM; 100 kw; 581 ft.; N46 45 35 W96 36 26
Mailing Address: 301 8th Street South, Fargo, ND 58103 US
Second Address: 2720 7th Ave. S., Fargo, ND 58103
(701) 237-4500, *Fax:* (701) 235-9082
www.q98.com
studio@q98.com
License: Moorhead, Clay County, MN held by Monterey Licenses LLC.
Group Owner: Triad Broadcasting Co. L.L.C.; (acq 10-99; grpsl)
Nat'l Reps: Christal
Arbitron Metro Market: Fargo-Moorhead, ND-MN *Format:* Classic Rock *Target Audience:* 18-49; men
Nancy Odney, Operations Dir
John Austin, Operations Director
Anne Phibian, Operations Manager

KVXR
11-30-1937; 1280 khz AM *Hrs Open:* 24
1020 25th Street South, Fargo, ND 58108 US
(701) 866-2606
bob@am1280thevoice.com
License: Moorhead, MN held by Voice of Reason Radio
Arbitron Metro Market: Fargo-Moorhead, ND-MN *Format:* Christian
Robert Schumacher, President

KVOX-FM
11-30-1966; 99.9 mhz FM *Hrs Open:* 24; 100 kw; 381 ft.; N46 49 9 W96 45 56
Mailing Address: 1020 25th Street South, Fargo, ND 58108 US
Second Address: 2720 7th Ave. St., Fargo, ND 58103
(701) 237-4500, *Fax:* (701) 235-9082
www.froggyweb.com
studio@froggyweb.com
License: Moorhead, Clay County, MN held by Monterey Licenses L.L.C.
Group Owner: Triad Broadcasting Co. L.L.C.
Nat'l Reps: Christal *Wire Services:* AP
Arbitron Metro Market: Fargo-Moorhead, ND-MN *Format:* Country *Hrs. of News Programming:* News progmg 7 hrs wkly
Target Audience: 25-54; female skew
David Benjamin, President
Nancy Odney, General Manager
Jessica Benson, General Sales Mgr
Shawn Reed, Programming Director
Brianne Thompson, Promotions Manager
Michael Brooks, VP/ Market Manager

Moose Lake

WMOZ
01-01-2001; 106.9 mhz FM; 6 kw; 164 ft.; N46 30 20 W92 40 45
1104 Cloquet Avenue, Cloquest, MN 55720 US
(218) 879-4534, *Fax:* (218) 879-1962
License: Moose Lake, Carlton County, MN held by QB Broadcasting Ltd.
Group Owner: Quarnstrom Media Group LLC
Arbitron Metro Market: Moose Lake, MN *Format:* Oldies
Mark Senarighi, General Manager

Mora

KBEK
05-12-1995; 95.5 mhz FM *Hrs Open:* 24; 25 kw; 328 ft.; N45 44 33 W93 22 48
PO Box 136, 1947 Dennis Road, Mora, MN 55051 US
(320) 679-6955, *Fax:* (320) 679-2348
www.kbek.com
kbek@besttimes.com
License: Mora, Kanabec County, MN held by Colleen McKinney, personal representative

Arbitron Metro Market: Mora, MN *Format:* Oldies *Hrs. of News Programming:* News progmg 8 hrs wkly *Target Audience:* General.
Colleen McKinney, General Manager
Scott McKenney, Programming Director
Diana Wilson, Promotions Manager
Ty Laugerman, News Director

Morris

KKOK-FM
09-16-1976; 95.7 mhz FM; 100 kw; 361 ft.; N45 36 11 W95 53 14
1020 25th Street South, Fargo, ND 58108 US
(320) 589-3131, *Fax:* (320) 589-2715
www.kmrskkok.com
kmrskkok@fedtel.net
License: Morris, Stevens County, MN
Arbitron Metro Market: Saint Cloud, MN *Format:* Country
Deborah Driggins-Mattheis, General Manager
Bill Eckersen, Programming Director
Katie McKenzie, News Director
Paul McDonald, Sports Director
Krystal Dohlen, Marketing Consultant
Aileen Sperr, Marketing Consultant
Milissa Bjorge,Traffic Manager

KMRS
09-16-1956; 1230 khz AM *Hrs Open:* 19; 1 kw-U, ND1; N45 36 11 W95 53 14
1020 25th Street South, Fargo, ND 58108 US
(320) 589-3131, *Fax:* (320) 589-2715
www.kmrskkok.com
kmrskkok@fedtel.net
License: Morris, MN held by Iowa City Broadcasting Co.
Group Owner: Tom Ingstad Broadcasting Group; (acq 1-11-2000; with co-located FM).
Nat'l Reps: McGavren Guild
Format: Adult Contemp, News, 62, Talk *Hrs. of News Programming:* news progmg 80 hrs wkly *No. News Employees:* 1 *Target Audience:* 35-64; farmers & agri-business people
Deb Mattheis, General Manager
Deb Mattheis, General Sales Mgr
Bill Eckersen, Programming Director
Katie McKenzie, News Director
Ken Bartz, Chief Engineer

*KUMM
09-17-1970; 89.7 mhz FM *Hrs Open:* 24; 0.7 kw; 125 ft.; N45 35 11 W95 53 57
E. 4th St & College Ave, Morris, MN 56267 US
(320) 589-6076, *Fax:* (320) 589-6084
www.kumm.org
bark0293@morris.umn.edu
License: Morris, Stevens County, MN held by University of Minnesota.
Wire Services: AP
Arbitron Metro Market: Morris, MN *Format:* Alternative *Hrs. of News Programming:* News progmg 3 hrs wkly *Target Audience:* 18-30; primarily college students *Adv. Rates:* 6; 4; 6; 3.
Mike Doucette, General Manager
Taylor Barker, Station Manager
Gerard Van Wijk, Programming Director
Kevin Klawitter, News Director
Sonia Ellison, Music Director
Isaac Johnson, Music Director
Teague Goodsky, Publicity Director
Becky Wielenberg, Training Director

Nashwauk

WNMT
06-02-1975; 650 khz AM; 10 kw-D, DAN; 1 kw-N, DAN; N47 22 31 W93 0 56
645 North Michigan Ave., Chicago, IL 60601 US
(218) 263-7531, *Fax:* (218) 263-6112
www.wnmtradio.com
lindas@mwcradio.com
License: Nashwauk, MN held by Midwest Communications Inc.
Group Owner: Midwest Communications Inc.; acq 5-10-2004; grpsl).
Arbitron Metro Market: Hibbing, MN *Format:* News, News/Talk, 86 *Special Programming:* Pol 2 hrs wkly *Target Audience:* 35 plus.
Kristi Garrity, General Manager
Craig Holgate, Programming Director
Danny Klaysmat, Chief Engineer

KMFG
10-01-1997; 102.9 mhz FM; 25 kw; 253 ft.; N47 24 30 W92 57 5
1104 Cloquet Avenus, Cloquet, MN 55720 US
(218) 263-7531, *Fax:* (218) 263-6112
www.kmfgfm.com
webmaster.mwcradio@mwcradio.com
License: Nashwauk, Itasca County, MN held by Midwest Communications Inc.
Group Owner: Midwest Communications Inc.; acq 5-10-2004; grpsl).
Nat'l Network: ABC
Arbitron Metro Market: Hibbing, MN *Format:* Classic Rock *Target Audience:* 24-55.
Duke Wright, President CEO
Kristi Garrity, General Manager
Doug Diedrich, Programming Director
Mary Kay Wright, Vice President Marketing and Research & Developmen
Michael Wright, Senior Vice President
Esther Gillis, Director ofHuman Resources
Jeff Wright, Vice President Sales
Paul Rahmlow, Chief Financial Officer
Jeff McCarthy, Vice President Programming

New Prague

KCHK
09-22-1969; 1350 khz AM *Hrs Open:* 24; 0.5 kw-D, DA2; 0.07 kw-N, DA2; N44 34 39 W93 30 16
Mailing Address: 207 Textile Bldg., 119 North 4th Street, Minneapolis, MN 55401 US
Second Address: 25821 Langford Ave., New Prague, MN 56071
(952) 758-2571, *Fax:* (952) 758-3170
www.kchkradio.net
kchkamfm@beucomm.net
License: New Prague, MN held by Ingstad Brothers Broadcasting LLC
Group Owner: Ingstad Brothers Broadcasting LLC; acq 5-1-2004; grpsl).
Nat'l Network: ABC *Regional Network:* MNN *Wire Services:* NWS (National Weather Service)
Arbitron Metro Market: Minneapolis-St. Paul, MN *Format:* News, News/Talk, 86 *Special Programming:* Sp. 6 hrs, Pol, Czch, Ger 40 hrs wkly *Hrs. of News Programming:* News progmg 50 hrs wkly *Target Audience:* 35-59.*Adv. Rates:* 10; 10; 10; 10
Ned Newberg, General Manager
Dave Douglas, Engineering Dir

KRDS-FM
12-01-1990; 95.5 mhz FM *Hrs Open:* 24; 6 kw; 328 ft.; N44 27 40 W93 35 8
207 Textile Bldg., 119 North 4th Street, Minneapolis, MN 55401 US
(952) 758-2571, *Fax:* (952) 758-3170
www.kchkradio.net
kchkamfm@beucomm.net
License: New Prague, Le Sueur County, MN held by Ingstad Brothers Broadcasting LLC
Group Owner: Ingstad Brothers Broadcasting LLC
Wire Services: NWS (National Weather Service)
Arbitron Metro Market: Minneapolis-St. Paul, MN *Format:* Oldies *Hrs. of News Programming:* news progmg 7 hrs wkly *No. News Employees:* 3 *Target Audience:* 25-64; general
Mike Nolen, General Manager
Lynn Nolen, Station Manager

New Ulm

KNUJ
05-01-1949; 860 khz AM *Hrs Open:* 24; 1 kw-D, ND1; 0.005 kw-N, ND1; N44 17 10 W94 25 50
330 East Kilbourn Avenue, Suite 250, Milwaukee, WI 53202 US
(507) 359-2921, *Fax:* (507) 359-4520
www.knuj.net
knuj@knuj.net
License: New Ulm, MN held by Ingstad Brothers Broadcasting LLC
Group Owner: Ingstad Brothers Broadcasting LLC; acq 5-1-2004; grpsl).
Arbitron Metro Market: Mankato-New Ulm *Format:* Country *Special Programming:* Old-time 8 hrs wkly *Hrs. of News Programming:* news progmg 30 hrs wkly *No. News Employees:* 2 *Target Audience:* 30 plus.
Jim Bartels, Operations Dir

KATO-FM
11-21-1966; 93.1 mhz FM; 100 kw; 489 ft.; N44 7 44 W94 11 15
330 East Kilbourn Avenue, Suite 250, Milwaukee, WI 53202 US
(507) 345-4537, *Fax:* (507) 345-5364
www.minnesota93.com/
License: New Ulm, Brown County, MN held by Minnesota Valley Broadcasting Co.
Group Owner: Linder Broadcasting Group; (acq 9-1-2007; $3.13 million)
Arbitron Metro Market: Mankato, MN *Format:* Country
Jo Bailey, Operations Dir

Nisswa

KBLB
01-01-2002; 93.3 mhz FM *Hrs Open:* 24; 100 kw; 558 ft.; N46 26 34 W94 22 55
Mailing Address: P.O. Box 1656, Bemidji, MN 56619 US
Second Address: 13225 Dogwood Dr., Baxter, MN 56425-8613
(218) 828-1244, *Fax:* (218) 828-1119
brainerdradio.net
production@brainerd.net
License: Nisswa, Crow Wing County, MN held by BL Broadcasting Inc.
Group Owner: Omni Broadcasting Co.; (acq 12-11-2000).
Nat'l Network: ABC *Regional Network:* Minn. News Net.
Format: Country *Hrs. of News Programming:* news progmg 12 hrs wkly *No. News Employees:* 1 *Target Audience:* 25-54; adults
Lou Buron, CEO
G. Michael Boen, General Manager
Al Davison, Programming Director
Tess Taylor, News Director
David Cox, Chief Engineer
Mary Campbell, CFO

North Branch

*KMKL
10-06-2001; 90.3 mhz FM *Hrs Open:* 24; 15 kw vert; 397 ft.; N45 32 36 W92 58 24
US
(800) 525-5683, *Fax:* (916) 251-1650
www.klove.com
klove@klove.com
License: North Branch, Chisago County, MN held by Educational Media Foundation.
Group Owner: EMF Broadcasting
Nat'l Network: K-Love
Arbitron Metro Market: North Branch, MN *Format:* Christian *No. News Employees:* 3 *Target Audience:* 25-44; Judeo Christian, female
Darrell Chambliss, Chairman
Mike Novak, President and CEO
John Clements, Operations Dir
David Pierce, Programming Director
Ed Lenane, News Director
Sam Wallington, Engineering Dir
Scott Smith, Music Director
Marya Morgan, NewsReporter
Richard Hunt, News Reporter
Tracy Butler, Traffic Manager
Laura Daniels, News Reporter
Tim Luttrell, News Reporter

North Mankato

KDOG
04-01-1985; 96.7 mhz FM; 4 kw; 650 ft.; N44 13 20 W94 7 3
P.O. Box 1420, Mankato, MN 56001 US
(507) 345-4537, *Fax:* (507) 345-5364
www.katoinfo.com
License: North Mankato, Blue Earth County, MN held by Minnesota Valley Broadcasting Co.
Group Owner: Linder Broadcasting Group
Arbitron Metro Market: Mankato-New Ulm-St. Peter, MN *Format:* Adult Contemp *Hrs. of News Programming:* news progmg 4 hrs wkly *No. News Employees:* 1
Jo Bailey, Operations Dir

Northfield

*KRLX
01-25-1975; 88.1 mhz FM; 0.1 kw; 16 ft.; N44 27 39 W93 9 21
300 North College Street, Northfield, MN 55057 US
(507) 646-4102
krlxweb.carleton.edu
License: Northfield, Rice County, MN held by Carleton College.
Arbitron Metro Market: Northfield, MN *Format:* Talk *Target Audience:* General; college-associated people and rural
Mary Henke-Haney, Station Manager
Ben Blink, Programming Director
Brandon Walker, News Director

KYMN
09-27-1968; 1080 khz AM *Hrs Open:* 24; 1 kw-D; N44 29 12 W93 06 20
200 Division Street, Suite 260, Northfield, MN 55057
(507) 645-5695, *Fax:* (507) 645-9768
contact@kymnradio.net

License: Northfield, Rice County, MN held by Northfield Media LLC
Nat'l Network: NBC News Radio *Regional Network:* Minnesota Twins Radio Network
Population Served: 100,000*Special Programming:* Eclectic Music, Local Talk shows 10hrs, relg 2 hrs, *Hrs. of News Programming:* news progmg 72 hrs wkly *No. News Employees:* 1 *Target Audience:* 35-54; parentswith school-age children, well-educated *Adv. Rates:* 18; 16; 14; 10
Jeff Johnson, President
Tim Freeland, General Sales Mgr

*KCMP
04-04-1968; 89.3 mhz FM *Hrs Open:* 24; 97.6 kw; 768 ft.; N44 41 21 W93 4 21
1520 St. Olaf Avenue, Northfield, MN 55057 US
(651) 290-1500, *Fax:* (651) 290-1295
www.minnesota.publicradio.org
License: Northfield, Rice County, MN held by Minnesota Public Radio
Arbitron Metro Market: Saint Paul, MN *Format:* Triple A
William Kling, President
Jon Gossett, General Sales Mgr
Bill Wareham, News Director

Olivia

KOLV
06-27-1983; 100.1 mhz FM; 50 kw; 466 ft.; N44 58 14 W95 14 59
P.O. Box 838, Willmar, MN 56201 US
(320) 523-1017, *Fax:* (320) 523-1018
www.k100realcountry.com
askusa@kwlm.com
License: Olivia, Renville County, MN held by Bold Radio Inc.
Group Owner: Linder Broadcasting Group; (acq 3-18-98; $335,000).
Regional Network: Linder Farm *Nat'l Reps:* Keystone (unwired net)
Format: Country, Variety/Diverse *Special Programming:* Big band, adult contemp, oldies, Top-40
Steve Linder, President
Doug Loy, General Manager
Maryelin Macht, Programming Director

Ortonville

*KCGN-FM
09-23-1983; 101.5 mhz FM *Hrs Open:* 24; 98 kw; 1001 ft.; N45 22 29 W97 2 20
14747 482nd Avenue, P.O. Box 101, Milbank, SD 57252 US
(320) 859-3000, *Fax:* (320) 859-3010
www.praisefm.org
info@praisefm.org
License: Ortonville, Big Stone County, MN held by Praise Broadcasting Inc.
Format: Adult Contemp, Christian *Target Audience:* 25-44; middle-aged women *Adv. Rates:* 14; 11; 14; 11
David McIver, General Manager
Jack Zitzmann, Programming Director
Steve Kneprath, Chief Engineer
Sherrie McIver, Music Director
Michelle Anderson, Traffic Manager

KDIO
07-23-1956; 1350 khz AM
232 Third Street, Ne, Valley City, ND 58072 US
(320) 839-2581, *Fax:* (320) 839-2571
bigstoneradio.com
kdio@bigstoneradio.com
License: Ortonville, MN held by Armada Media-Watertown Inc.
Group Owner: Armada Media Corp.; (acq 8-3-2007; grpsl)
Nat'l Network: ABC *Regional Network:* Linder Farm; Minn. News Net.
Arbitron Metro Market: Ortonville, MN *Format:* Country *Special Programming:* Farm 18 hrs, relg 5 hrs wkly
Jeff Kurtz, President
Joan Lien, General Sales Mgr
Julie Anne French, Programming Director

KPHR
01-01-1996; 106.3 mhz FM; 100 kw; 955 ft.; N45 6 17 W96 59 17
232 Third Street, Ne, Valley City, ND 58072 US
(605) 884-1000, *Fax:* (605) 884-3549
www.bigstoneradio.com
power106@iw.net; jeffkurtz@bigstoneradio.com
License: Ortonville, Big Stone County, MN held by Armada Media-Watertown Inc.
Group Owner: Armada Media Corp.
Arbitron Metro Market: Watertown, SD *Format:* Classic Rock
Jeff Kurtz, Operations Dir
Kim Krause, News Director

Osakis

*KBHL
03-11-1985; 103.9 mhz FM; 6 kw; 328 ft.; N45 50 24 W95 5 56
515 Pike St. E., Osakis, MN 56360 US
(320) 859-3000, *Fax:* (320) 859-3010
www.praisefm.org
mail@praisefm.org
License: Osakis, Douglas County, MN held by Christian Heritage Broadcasting Inc.
Nat'l Network: Moody
Arbitron Metro Market: Osakis, MN *Format:* Christian
Dave Hartman, Operations Dir
David McIver, General Manager

Owatonna

KRFO
01-01-1950; 1390 khz AM *Hrs Open:* 5 AM-midnight; 0.5 kw-D, ND1; 0.094 kw-N, ND1; N44 4 29 W93 10 46
330 East Kilbourn Avenue, Suite 250, Milwaukee, WI 53202 US
(507) 451-2250, *Fax:* (507) 451-8837
www.krforadio.com
License: Owatonna, MN held by Cumulus Licensing Corp.
Group Owner: Cumulus Media Inc.; (acq 7-21-98; grpsl)
Format: Oldies *Special Programming:* Sp 2 hrs wkly *Hrs. of News Programming:* news progmg 18 hrs wkly *No. News Employees:* 1 *Target Audience:* 35 plus.
Gary Foss, General Manager
John Connor, General Sales Mgr
Loren Hart, Programming Director
Bill Dahlstrom, Chief Engineer

KRFO-FM
12-29-1966; 104.9 mhz FM *Hrs Open:* 18; 4.7 kw; 174 ft.; N44 4 29 W93 10 46
330 East Kilbourn Avenue, Suite 250, Milwaukee, WI 53202 US
(507) 451-2250, *Fax:* (507) 451-8837
www.krforadio.com
info@krfonews.com
License: Owatonna, Steele County, MN
Format: Country *Hrs. of News Programming:* news progmg 12 hrs wkly *No. News Employees:* 1 *Target Audience:* 25-54.
Thomas Kigin, President

Park Rapids

KDKK
12-01-1967; 97.5 mhz FM; 100 kw; 636 ft.; N46 55 51 W95 0 27
P.O. Box 49, Highway 34 East, Park Rapids, MN 65470 US
(218) 732-3306
www.kkradionetwork.com
License: Park Rapids, Hubbard County, MN
Wire Services: Weather Wire
Arbitron Metro Market: Park Rapids, MN *Format:* Contemporary Hits/Top 40 *Target Audience:* 40 plus.
E.P. De La Hunt, General Manager
Bernie Schumacher, Women's Int Ed

KPRM
12-01-1962; 870 khz AM; 25 kw-D, DAN; 1 kw-N, DAN; N46 55 42 W95 0 22; N46 54 18 W95 1 4
P.O. Box 49, Highway 34 East, Park Rapids, MN 56470 US
(218) 732-3306, *Fax:* (218) 732-3307
www.kkradionetwork.com
kprmkdkk@unitelc.com
License: Park Rapids, MN held by De La Hunt Broadcasting Corp.
Nat'l Network: CBS
Format: Country *Target Audience:* 25 plus.
Ed DeLa Hunt, General Manager
Bernie Schumacher, General Sales Mgr
David De La Hunt, Chief Engineer

KXKK
01-01-1998; 92.5 mhz FM; 10 kw; 584 ft.; N46 55 51 W95 0 27
Rt. 4, Box 430a, Park Rapids, MN 56470 US
(218) 732-3306, *Fax:* (218) 732-3307
License: Park Rapids, Hubbard County, MN held by Bernadine A. Schumacher.
Arbitron Metro Market: Park Rapids, MN *Format:* Country
Bernadine Schumacher, General Manager

Paynesville

KZPK
12-01-1995; 98.9 mhz FM *Hrs Open:* 24; 47 kw; 499 ft.; N45 34 3 W94 30 43
22184 Fairmont Road, St. Cloud, MN 56301 US
(320) 251-1450, *Fax:* (320) 251-8952
www.wildcountry99.com
info@wildcountry989.com
License: Paynesville, Stearns County, MN held by Leighton Enterprises Inc.
Group Owner: Leighton Enterprises Inc.; acq 4-15-97; $1 million)
Arbitron Metro Market: St. Cloud, MN *Format:* Country
Al Leighton, CEO
Matt Senne, Operations Dir
John Sowada, General Manager
Denny Niess, General Sales Mgr
Matt Senne, Programming Director
Melissa Malat, Promotions Manager
Cassie Hart, News Director
Dale Daley, ChiefEngineer
Denise Prozinski, General Sales Manager
Kathy Carton, Traffic Manager
Cindy Niess, Traffic Manager

Pelican Rapids

KBOT
06-01-1994; 104.1 mhz FM *Hrs Open:* 24; 50 kw; 456 ft.; N46 43 19 W95 50 37
Mailing Address: P.O. Box 746, Detroit Lakes, MN 56302 US
Second Address: 128 Junius Ave. W., Fergus Falls, MN 56537
(218) 847-5624, *Fax:* (218) 847-7657
www.wild1041.com
kdlmkbot@lakesnet.net
License: Pelican Rapids, Otter Tail County, MN held by Leighton Enterprises Inc.
Group Owner: Leighton Enterprises Inc.; (acq 9-24-96; $700,000).
Regional Reps: O'Malley.
Arbitron Metro Market: Fargo-Moorhead, ND-MN *Format:* Country *Hrs. of News Programming:* news progmg one hr wkly *No. News Employees:* 1 *Target Audience:* 25-54; Fargo-Moorhead, metro & TSA listeners *Adv.Rates:* 19.50; 19.50; 19.50; 19.50
Alver Leighton, CEO
John Sowada, President
Denny Niess, Operations Dir
Jeff Leighton, General Manager
Kevin Flynn, Programming Director
Andy Lia, Operations Manager

Pequot Lakes

*KTIG
04-30-1978; 102.7 mhz FM *Hrs Open:* 24; 40 kw; 541 ft.; N46 40 48 W94 25 2
P.O. Box 409, Pequot Lakes, MN 56472 US
(218) 568-4422, *Fax:* (218) 568-5950
theword.mn/
License: Pequot Lakes, Crow Wing County, MN held by Minnesota Christian Broadcasters Inc.
Nat'l Network: Moody; USA
Arbitron Metro Market: Minneapolis-St. Paul, MN *Format:* Religious *Target Audience:* 35-55; general
Mike Heuberger, General Manager
Phil Kvamme, Programming Director
Randy Kennedy, News Director
Aaron Pearson, Chief Engineer

KLKS
01-01-2002; 100.1 mhz FM; 3.9 kw; Ant 407 ft; N46 40 48 W94 25 02
Box 409, Pequot Lakes, MN 56472
(866) 568-4422, *Fax:* (218) 568-5950
License: Pequot Lakes, Crow Wing County, MN held by Minnesota Christian Broadcasters Inc.
Nat'l Network: Moody; USA

Mike Heuberger, General Manager
Tim Norman, Programming Director
Aaron Pearson, News Director
Dwayne Walker, Chief Engineer

Perham

KPRW
08-26-1996; 99.5 mhz FM *Hrs Open:* 24; 6 kw; 328 ft.; N46 33 16 W95 27 24
PO Box 767, Winona, MN 55987 US
(218) 346-4800, *Fax:* (218) 346-7595
www.lakes995.com EXPIRED?
lakesradio@lakesradio.net
License: Perham, Otter Tail County, MN held by Jerry Papenfuss.
Group Owner: The Result Radio Group
Nat'l Reps: Hyett/Ramsland
Arbitron Metro Market: Perham, MN, Fergus Falls, Detroit Lakes
Format: Triple A *Hrs. of News Programming:* news progmg 10 hrs wkly *No. News Employees:* 1 *Target Audience:* 25-54. *Adv. Rates:* 24; 18; 18;12

RADIO - U.S.

Jerry Pappenfuss, CEO
Doug Gray, General Manager
David Howey, Programming Director

Pillager

WWWI-FM

01-01-2000; 95.9 mhz FM; 6 kw; 240 ft.; N46 15 3 W94 19 30
11 S.E. Bryant Ave., Wadena, MN 56482 US
(218) 828-9994, *Fax:* (218) 828-8327
www.3wiradio.com
talK@3wiradio.com
License: Pillager, Cass County, MN held by Tower Broadcasting Corp.
Arbitron Metro Market: Brainerd, MN *Format:* News, News/Talk, 86
James Pryor, General Manager
Lon Schmidt, News Director

Pine City

WCMP

06-13-1957; 1350 khz AM *Hrs Open:* 24; 1 kw-D, ND1; 0.052 kw-N, ND1; N45 49 10 W92 59 45
Rr Two Box 257f, Pine City, MN 55063 US
(715)-825-4240, *Fax:* (715)-825-4244
www.redrockonair.com
jesselogan@redrockonair.com.
License: Pine City, MN held by Quarnstrom Media Group LLC
Group Owner: Quarnstrom Media Group LLC; acq 9-22-03).
Regional Network: MNN
Arbitron Metro Market: Sebring, FL *Format:* News *Special Programming:* Farm 6 hrs wkly *Hrs. of News Programming:* News progmg 25 hrs wkly *Target Audience:* 30 plus; farmers, commuters, homemakers *Adv. Rates:* 25; 20; 25; 15
Al Quarstrom, President
Mike Hughes, General Manager
Matt Born, Programming Director
Paula Butterfield, News Director
Bill Mayes, Chief Engineer

WCMP-FM

10-15-1977; 100.9 mhz FM *Hrs Open:* 24; 25 kw; 276 ft.; N45 54 7 W92 57 25
Rural Route 2, Box 257-F, Pine City, MN 55063 US
(715)-825-4240, *Fax:* (715)-825-4244
www.redrockonair.com
jesselogan@redrockonair.com.
License: Pine City, Pine County, MN held by Quarnstrom Media Group LLC
Group Owner: Quarnstrom Media Group LLC; acq 8-23-01; $1.2 million with co-located AM including five-year noncompete agreement).
Arbitron Metro Market: Sebring, FL *Format:* News, Sports *Target Audience:* 18 plus; commuters, working adults with families
Mike Hughes, General Manager

Pipestone

KISD

11-20-1968; 98.7 mhz FM *Hrs Open:* 24; 100 kw; 1014 ft.; N43 53 52 W95 56 50
Mailing Address: West Highway 30, Box 456, Pipestone, MN 56164 US
Second Address: 608 W. Hwy. 30, Pipestone, MN 56164
(507) 825-4282, *Fax:* (507) 825-3364
kisdradio.com
kloh@klohradio.com
License: Pipestone, Pipestone County, MN
Nat'l Network: ABC *Wire Services:* AP
Format: Oldies *Target Audience:* 18-65. *Adv. Rates:* Same as AM
Rob Harder, Programming Director
Ian Richards, Disc Jockey
John Chrisopher Kowsky, Disc Jockey
Dawn Marcel, Disc Jockey
Stormy Morgan, Disc Jockey
Mark Holman, Disc Jockey

KLOH

06-01-1955; 1050 khz AM *Hrs Open:* 24
Mailing Address: West Highay 30, Box 456, Pipestone, MN 56164 US
Second Address: 608 W. Hwy. 30, Pipestone, MN 56164
(507) 825-4282, *Fax:* (507) 825-3364
www.klohradio.com
kloh@klohradio.com
License: Pipestone, MN held by Wallace Christensen.
Nat'l Network: ABC *Regional Network:* Linder Farm *Wire Services:* AP
Arbitron Metro Market: Mankato, MN *Format:* News, Talk *Special Programming:* Relg 5 hrs, Sp 2 hrs wkly *Adv. Rates:* 18; 18; 18; 15
Diane Carlson, Operations Dir
Collin Christensen, General Manager
Carmen Christensen, General Sales Mgr
Mylan Ray, Programming Director
Bernie Wieme, News Director
Honee Longstreet, Traffic Manager

Preston

KFIL

05-21-1966; 1060 khz AM
P. O. Box 370, Preston, MN 55965 US
(507) 765-3856, *Fax:* (507) 765-2738
License: Preston, MN held by KFIL Inc.
Group Owner: Cumulus Media Inc.; (acq 3-30-2004; grpsl)
Regional Network: MNN
Arbitron Metro Market: Preston, MN *Format:* Country
Bruce Fishbaugher, General Manager
Bruce Fishbaugher, General Sales Mgr
John Milne, Programming Director
John Milne, News Director
Bill Davis, Chief Engineer

Princeton

WQPM

02-01-1967; 1300 khz AM *Hrs Open:* 24
Mailing Address: 1986 Julep Road, St. Cloud, MN 56301 US
Second Address: 32215 124th St., Princeton, MN 55271
(763) 389-1300, *Fax:* (763) 389-1359
www.bob106radio.com
License: Princeton, MN held by Milestone Radio L.L.C.
Nat'l Network: ABC *Regional Network:* Minn. Pub. Radio
Format: Country *Special Programming:* Farm 2 hrs wkly *Hrs. of News Programming:* news progmg 20 hrs wkly *No. News Employees:* 1 *Target Audience:* 25-54.
Dennis Carpenter, President
Neil Freeman, General Manager
Howard Johnson, General Sales Mgr
Neil Freedman, Programming Director

*KPCS

04-23-2010; 89.7 mhz FM; 50 kw vert; Ant 105 ft; N45 35 54 W93 33 18
Box 18000, Pensacola, FL 32523
(850) 479-6570, *Fax:* (850) 969-1638
www.rejoice.org
License: Princeton, Mille Lacs County, MN held by Pensacola Christian College Inc.
Troy Shoemaker, President
Caleb Keener, Station Manager
Tonita Ohman, Promotions Manager

Proctor

KBMX

01-01-1994; 107.7 mhz FM *Hrs Open:* 24; 7.7 kw; 912 ft.; N46 47 13 W92 7 17
100 Elizabeth Street, Duluth, MN 55803 US
(218) 727-4500, *Fax:* (218) 727-9356
www.mix108.com
MerryWallin@townsquaremedia.com
License: Proctor, St. Louis County, MN held by GAP Broadcasting Duluth License LLC.
Group Owner: GAPWEST Broadcasting; (acq 2-13-2008; grpsl)
Arbitron Metro Market: Proctor, MN *Format:* Adult Contemp *Hrs. of News Programming:* News progmg one hr wkly *Target Audience:* 25-54; working adults & families
Merry Wallin, Operations Dir
Merry Wallin, General Manager
Kristine Jensen, Digital Sales Manager
Laura Peterson, Programming Director
Kariana Bite, Promotions Manager
Randy Wabik, Chief Engineer
David Drew, OperationsManager
Derek Falter, Director of Sales

Red Wing

KCUE

01-29-1949; 1250 khz AM *Hrs Open:* 24; 1 kw-D, ND1; 0.11 kw-N, ND1; N44 32 14 W92 31 21
600 N. Kiwanis Plaza, Sioux Falls, SD 57104 US
(651) 388-7151, *Fax:* (651) 388-7153
www.1250kcue.com
news@kwng.com
License: Red Wing, MN held by Q-Media.
Group Owner: Quarnstrom Media Group LLC; (acq 6-81; $1.1 million with co-located FM;
Regional Network: MNN
Arbitron Metro Market: Red Wing, MN *Format:* Country *Hrs. of News Programming:* news progmg 7 hrs wkly *No. News Employees:* 2 *Target Audience:* 35 plus; information consumer *Adv. Rates:* 33; 29; 33; 29
Tom Hughes, Operations Dir
Donald Kliewer, General Manager
Jack Colwell, News Director

KWNG

08-26-1965; 105.9 mhz FM *Hrs Open:* 24; 12 kw; 328 ft.; N44 32 14 W92 31 21
600 N. Kiwanis Avenue, Sioux Falls, SD 57104 US
(651) 388-7151, *Fax:* (651) 388-7153
www.kwng.com
news@kwng.com
License: Red Wing, Goodhue County, MN held by Q-Media.
Group Owner: Quarnstrom Media Group LLC
Nat'l Network: ABC Information & Entertainment
Arbitron Metro Market: Red Wing, MN *Format:* Contemporary Hits/Top 40, Adult Contemp *Hrs. of News Programming:* news progmg one hr wkly *No. News Employees:* 2 *Target Audience:* 25-44; family & yuppie *Adv.Rates:* 33; 29; 33; 29
Alan Quarnstrom, CEO
Tom Hughes, Operations Dir
Donald Kliewer, General Manager
Ronnie Stockwell, Business Manager
Erika Duxbury, Triffic Manager
Jack Colwell, Sports Director
Dawn Laffey, Account Executive
Jodie Schultz,Account Executive
Craig Livingstone, Account Executive

Redwood Falls

KLGR

11-01-1954; 1490 khz AM; 1 kw-U, ND1; N44 32 33 W95 7 57
1077 Meadow Lane, Fond Du Lac, WI 54935 US
(507) 637-2989, *Fax:* (507) 637-5347
www.myklgr.com
klgr@mchsi.com
License: Redwood Falls, MN held by Three Eagles of Luverne Inc.
Group Owner: Three Eagles Communications; (acq 12-13-99; with co-located FM).
Regional Network: MNN
Arbitron Metro Market: Mankato, MN *Format:* Country *Target Audience:* General.
Mike Neudecker, General Manager
Laura Olson, Programming Director
Randy Clausen, Sports Director
Joel Goche, Account Manager
Tara Anderson, Account Manager
Karlene Rose, Account Manager

*KRFI

88.1 mhz FM; 0.36 kw; 168 ft.; N44 32 28 W95 10 58 US
(651) 290-1259
www.mpr.org
License: Redwood Falls, Redwood County, MN held by Minnesota Public Radio.
Regional Network: Minn. Pub. Radio
Arbitron Metro Market: Redwood Falls, MN *Format:* News
Thomas Kigin, President
Hear Bill Buzenberg, Senior Vice President News Broadcast Editor, Deputy News Editor
Hear Melanie Sommer, Online News Editor

Richfield

KDWB-FM

01-01-1969; 101.3 mhz FM *Hrs Open:* 24; 100 kw; 1033 ft.; N45 3 30 W93 7 27
100 N Sixth St, Suite 306c, Minneapolis, MN 55403 US
(952) 417-3000, *Fax:* (952) 417-3001
www.kdwb.com
info@kdwb.com
License: Richfield, Hennepin County, MN held by AMFM Radio Licenses LLC.
Group Owner: Clear Channel Communications Inc.; (acq 8-30-00; grpsl).
Nat'l Reps: Clear Channel
Arbitron Metro Market: Minneapolis-St. Paul, MN *Format:* Contemporary Hits/Top 40 *No. News Employees:* 1 *Target Audience:* 18-34; women
Mick Anselmo, President

KKMS

10-18-1949; 980 khz AM *Hrs Open:* 24
4880 Santa Rosa Road, Suite 300, Camarillo, CA 93012 US

(651) 405-8800, *Fax:* (651) 405-8222
www.kkms.com
License: Richfield, MN held by Common Ground Broadcasting Inc.
Group Owner: Salem Communications Corp.; (acq 9-27-96; $3 million)
Arbitron Metro Market: Minneapolis, MN *Format:* Christian, Talk *Target Audience:* 18-50. *Adv. Rates:* 73; 58; 73
Lee Michaels, Operations Dir
John Hunt, General Manager
Brian Acker, General Sales Mgr
Nick Novak, Programming Director
Kate Fisher, Promotions Manager
Scott Todd, Chief Engineer

Rochester

*KFSI
04-28-1981; 92.9 mhz FM; 6 kw; 318 ft.; N44 1 27 W92 32 36
4016 28th Street, S.E., Rochester, MN 55904 US
(507) 289-8585, *Fax:* (507) 529-4017
www.kfsi.org
shine@kfsi.org
License: Rochester, Olmsted County, MN held by Faith Sound Inc.
Nat'l Network: Moody
Arbitron Metro Market: Rochester, MN *Format:* Adult Contemp, Christian *Special Programming:* Youth 2 hrs wkly
Ray Logan, President
Paul Logan, Operations Dir
Steve Schuh, Engineering Dir
Mike Anderson, Music Director

*KZSE
12-17-1974; 91.7 mhz FM *Hrs Open:* 24; 100 kw; Ant 953 ft; N44 02 26 W92 20 28
206 S. Broadway, Suite 735, Rochester, MN 55101
(507) 282-0910, *Fax:* (507) 282-2107
www.mpr.org
License: Rochester, Olmsted County, MN held by Minnesota Public Radio Inc.
Nat'l Network: NPR; PRI *Regional Network:* Minn. Pub. Radio
Population Served: 463,000 *Arbitron Metro Market:* Rochester, MN *No. News Employees:* 1
John McTaggard, Chairman
Jim McGuinn, General Manager
Chris Cross, Station Manager
Mary Stapek, General Sales Mgr
Timothy Roesler, General Manager of Classical Music
Sea Stachura, News Director
Chris Worthington, ManagingDirector of News

*KMSE
08-01-1998; 88.7 mhz FM *Hrs Open:* 24; 0.85 kw; 561 ft.; N44 2 28.1 W92 20 25.4
1520 Olaf Ave., Northfield, MN 55057 US
(507) 282-0910, *Fax:* (507) 282-2107
www.mpr.org
License: Rochester, Olmsted County, MN held by Minnesota Public Radio
Arbitron Metro Market: Rochester, MN *Format:* Triple A *No. News Employees:* 1
John McTaggard, Chairman
Chris Cross, General Manager
Jim McGuinn, Station Manager
Mary Stapek, General Sales Mgr
Steve Nelson, Programming Director
Timothy Roesler, General Manager of Classical Music
Chris Worthington, NewsDirector

KNXR
12-24-1965; 97.5 mhz FM; 100 kw; 1,040 ft; N44 02 28 W92 20 25
1620 Greenview Dr. S.W., Rochester, MN 55902
(507) 288-7700, *Fax:* (507) 288-4531
www.knxr.com
License: Rochester, Olmsted County, MN held by United Audio Corp.
Nat'l Network: CBS; Wall Street *Nat'l Reps:* McGavren Guild
Wire Services: AP
Population Served: 225,000 *Arbitron Metro Market:* Rochester, MN *Special Programming:* Class 4 hrs, talk 2 hrs wkly *Target Audience:* 35 plus.
Thomas Jones, President

KOLM
11-01-1963; 1520 khz AM *Hrs Open:* 24
1220 4th Ave., S.W., Rochester, MN 55902 US
(507) 286-1010, *Fax:* (507) 286-9370
www.1520theticket.com
info@1520theticket.com
License: Rochester, MN held by Cumulus Licensing LLC.
Group Owner: Cumulus Media Inc.; (acq 3-31-2004; grpsl)
Nat'l Network: Westwood One *Regional Network:* Linder Farm
Nat'l Reps: Christal
Arbitron Metro Market: Rochester, MN *Format:* Sports *Hrs. of News Programming:* news progmg 3 hrs wkly *No. News Employees:* 2 *Target Audience:* 35-64; male 55%, female 45%
Shannon Knoepke, General Manager
Terry Lee, General Sales Mgr
Brent Ackerman, Programming Director
Kim David, News Director
Bill Davis, Chief Engineer

KRCH
01-01-1972; 101.7 mhz FM *Hrs Open:* 24; 39 kw; 554 ft.; N44 6 59 W92 41 22
330 East Kilbourn Avenue, Suite 250, Milwaukee, WI 53202 US
(507) 288-3888, *Fax:* (507) 288-7815
www.laser1017.net
info@laser1017.net
License: Rochester, Olmsted County, MN
Group Owner: Clear Channel Communications Inc.
Arbitron Metro Market: Rochester, MN *Format:* Classic Rock *Target Audience:* 25-54.
Bob Fox, General Manager

KROC
10-01-1935; 1340 khz AM *Hrs Open:* 24; 1 kw-U, ND1; N44 1 47 W92 29 31
122 Sw 4th Street, Rochester, MN 55902 US
(507) 286-1010, *Fax:* (507) 280-0000
www.krocam.com
brent@kroc.com
License: Rochester, MN held by Cumulus Licensing LLC.
Group Owner: Cumulus Media Inc.; (acq 3-29-2004; grpsl)
Nat'l Reps: Hyett/Ramsland
Arbitron Metro Market: Rochester, MN *Format:* News, News/Talk, 86 *Special Programming:* Farm 12 hrs wkly *Hrs. of News Programming:* news progmg 42 hrs wkly *No. News Employees:* 3 *Target Audience:* 30-64.
Rosanne Rybak, General Manager
Perry Lee, General Sales Mgr
Brent Ackerman, Programming Director
Kim David, News Director
Bill Davis, Chief Engineer

KROC-FM
07-01-1965; 106.9 mhz FM; 100 kw; 1109 ft.; N43 34 15 W92 25 37
122 Sw 4th Street, Rochester, MN 55902 US
(507) 286-1010, *Fax:* (507) 280-0000
www.kroc.com
brent@kroc.com
License: Rochester, Olmsted County, MN
Group Owner: Cumulus Media Inc.
Arbitron Metro Market: Rochester-Austin-Mason City *Format:* Contemporary Hits/Top 40 *Target Audience:* 18-54.
Dr. James Eckman, President
Gordon Wheeler, Station Manager
Taryn Julane, Programming Director

*KRPR
01-01-1976; 89.9 mhz FM *Hrs Open:* 24; 3.2 kw; Ant 590 ft; N44 02 28 W92 20 25
Rochester Public Radio, 1620 Greenview Dr. S.W., Rochester, MN 55902
(507) 288-2376, *Fax:* (507) 288-4531
www.krpr.org
License: Rochester, Olmsted County, MN held by Rochester Public Radio
Nat'l Network: USA
Population Served: 100,000 *Arbitron Metro Market:* Rochester, MN *Target Audience:* General.
Thomas Jones, President
Todd Brakke, General Manager
Aaron Manthei, Chief Engineer

KFAN
11-27-1957; 1270 khz AM; 5 kw-D, 1 kw-N, DA-2; N43 58 47 W92 26 51
1530 Greenview Dr. S.W., Suite 200, Rochester, MN 53202
(507) 288-3888, *Fax:* (507) 288-7815
www.laser1017.net
info@laser1017.net
License: Rochester, Olmsted County, MN held by CC Licenses LLC.
Group Owner: Clear Channel Communications Inc.; (acq 9-25-2000; grpsl).
Nat'l Network: CBS *Regional Network:* MNN *Nat'l Reps:* D & R Radio
Population Served: 75,000 *Arbitron Metro Market:* Rochester, MN *Target Audience:* Men.
Bob Fox, General Manager
Mary Anne Nonn, General Sales Mgr
Mark Clark, Promotions Manager
Craig Erpestad, Chief Engineer

KWWK
07-04-1967; 96.5 mhz FM *Hrs Open:* 24; 43 kw; 528 ft.; N44 1 59 W92 36 10
1220 4th Ave., S.W., Rochester, MN 55902 US
(507) 286-1010, *Fax:* (507) 286-9370
www.quickcountry.com
info@quickcountry.com
License: Rochester, Olmsted County, MN
Group Owner: Cumulus Media Inc.
Nat'l Reps: Christal
Arbitron Metro Market: Rochester, MN *Format:* Country *Hrs. of News Programming:* News progmg 2 hrs wkly *Target Audience:* 25-54; male & female 18-49, 25-54, 35-54
Shannon Knoepke, General Manager
Brent Ackerman, Programming Director
Bill Davis, Chief Engineer

*KLSE
02-01-1989; 90.7 mhz FM *Hrs Open:* 24; 1.38 kw; Ant 259 ft; N44 02 26 W92 20 28
206 S. Broadway, Suite 735, Rochester, MN 55101
(507) 282-0910, *Fax:* (507) 282-2107
www.mpr.org
License: Rochester, Olmsted County, MN held by Minnesota Public Radio Inc.
Nat'l Network: NPR; PRI *Regional Network:* Minn. Pub. Radio
Arbitron Metro Market: Rochester, MN *No. News Employees:* 1
John McTaggard, Chairman
Chris Cross, General Manager
John McGuinn, Station Manager
Mary Stapek, General Sales Mgr
Timothy Roesler, General Manager of Classical Music
Sea Stachura, News Director
Chris Worthington, ManagingDirector of News

Rockville

KYES
1180 khz AM
Mailing Address: US
Second Address: 1310 2nd St. N., Sauk Rapids, MN 56379-2532
(320) 257-9700, *Fax:* (320) 257-1624
www.kyesradio.com
friends@KYESRadio.com
License: Rockville, MN held by Throw Fire Project.
Arbitron Metro Market: Sauk Rapids, MN *Format:* Christian
Andrew Hilger, President
Deb Huschle, General Manager
Mike Van Vooren, Programming Coordinator
Todd Manske, Business Development

Roseau

KCAJ-FM
06-01-1996; 102.1 mhz FM *Hrs Open:* 24; 50 kw; 285 ft.; N48 38 50 W95 44 10
P.O.B. 358, 407 - 3rd Street N.W., Roseau, MN 56751 US
(218) 463-3360, *Fax:* (218) 463-1977
wild102fm.com
info@wild102fm.com
License: Roseau, Roseau County, MN held by Jack J. Swanson.
Nat'l Network: CNN Radio *Regional Network:* Minn. News Net.
Arbitron Metro Market: Roseau, MN *Format:* Contemporary Hits/Top 40 *Hrs. of News Programming:* news progmg 10 hrs wkly *No. News Employees:* 1 *Target Audience:* General.
Jack Swanson, General Manager
Jack McDonald, General Sales Mgr
Justin Gallo, Promotions Manager

KRWB
04-05-1963; 1410 khz AM *Hrs Open:* 24
Route 5, Box 9, Langdon, ND 58249 US
(218) 463-1410, *Fax:* (218) 463-3778
www.1410krwb.com
agency@kq92.com
License: Roseau, MN held by Border Broadcasting L.P.
Nat'l Network: ABC
Arbitron Metro Market: Warraod, MN *Format:* Classic Rock *No. News Employees:* 1 *Target Audience:* 25-54; general *Adv. Rates:* 15; 13; 10; 8
Mike Pederson, General Manager

*KRXW
01-01-2008; 103.5 mhz FM; 48 kw; 493 ft.; N48 54 10 W95 22 38.1
US

(651) 290-1500, *Fax:* (651) 290-1224
www.mpr.org
License: Roseau, Roseau County, MN held by Minnesota Public Radio.
Arbitron Metro Market: Roseau, MN *Format:* News
David Kansas, CEO/COO
Judy McAlpine, Senior Vice President
Daniel Gilliam, Programming Director
Mike Edgerly, News Director
Valerie Arganbright, Managing Director
Tom Kigin, Executive Vice President
Mary Pat Ladner, VicePresident, Marketing
Mary Nease, Senior Vice President, Human Resources

Rushford

KWNO-FM
12-18-1991; 99.3 mhz FM *Hrs Open:* 24; 11 kw; 495 ft.; N43 56 32 W91 43 9
Mailing Address: Box 767, 752 Bluffview Cir., Winona, MN 55947 US
Second Address: 752 Bluffview Cir., Winona, MN 55987
(507) 452-4000; (800) 584-6782, *Fax:* (507) 452-9494
www.winonaradio.com
jristow@winonaradio.com
License: Rushford, Fillmore County, MN held by KAGE Inc.
Group Owner: The Result Radio Group; (acq 6-19-95; $1 million with KWNO(AM) Winona)
Wire Services: AP
Arbitron Metro Market: Winona, MN *Format:* Country *Hrs. of News Programming:* news progmg one hr wkly *No. News Employees:* 1 *Target Audience:* 18-49; active young students & working persons
Jerry Papenfuss, CEO
Pat Papenfuss, President
Les Guderian, General Sales Mgr
Aaron Taylor, Programming Director
Darryl Smelser, News Director
Bob Sebo, Public Affairs Director

Saint Peter

*KNGA
03-29-1985; 90.5 mhz FM *Hrs Open:* 24; 75 kw; 708 ft; N44 13 20 W94 07 03
Minnesota Public Radio Inc., 480 Cedar St., St. Paul, MN 55101
(651) 290-1500, *Fax:* (651) 290-1224
www.mpr.org
mail@mpr.org
License: Saint Peter, Nicollet County, MN held by Minnesota Public Radio Inc.
Nat'l Network: PRI *Regional Network:* Minn. Pub. Radio
Population Served: 200,000 *Arbitron Metro Market:* Mankato-New Ulm-St. Peter, MN *Special Programming:* Folk var 17 hrs wkly *No. News Employees:* 2 *Target Audience:* General.
John Taggard, Chairman
William Kling, President
Jim McGuinn, General Manager
Timothy Roesler, General Manager of Classical Music
Chris Worthington, News Director

*KGAC
03-01-1992; 91.5 mhz FM *Hrs Open:* 24; 8.5 kw; 600 ft; N44 13 20 W94 07 03 *Rebroadcasts:* Rebroadcasts KNOW-FM Minneapolis-St. Paul
Minnesota Public Radio, 480 Cedar St., Saint Paul, MN 55101
(800) 228-7123, *Fax:* (507) 651-1295
www.mpr.org
mail@mpr.org
License: Saint Peter, Nicollet County, MN held by Minnesota Public Radio.
Nat'l Network: NPR; PRI *Regional Network:* Minn. Pub. Radio
Population Served: 150,000 *Arbitron Metro Market:* Mankato-New Ulm-St. Peter, MN *No. News Employees:* 2
Target Audience: General.
John McTaggard, Chairman
William Kling, General Manager
Jim McGuinn, Station Manager
Jon Gossett, General Sales Mgr
Erik Nycklemoe, Programming Director
Mary Ladner, Promotions Manager
Bill Wareham, News Director
ChrisWorthington, Managing Director of News
Timothy Roesler, Managing Director of News

Sartell

KZRV
08-26-1988; 96.7 mhz FM *Hrs Open:* 24; 50 kw; 453 ft.; N45 46 3 W94 8 4
1986 Julep Road, St. Cloud, MN 56301 US
(320) 251-4422, *Fax:* (320) 251-1855
www.kiss96.com
studio@kiss96.com
License: Sartell, Stearns County, MN
Group Owner: Townsquare Media; (acq 5-8-2001; grpsl)
Arbitron Metro Market: St. Cloud, MN *Format:* Rock/AOR *No. News Employees:* 1
Dave Engberg, General Manager
Lee Voss, News Director
Mark Young, Chief Engineer

Sauk Centre

KIKV-FM
12-25-1970; 100.7 mhz FM *Hrs Open:* 24; 100 kw; 791 ft.; N45 41 10 W95 8 3
Mailing Address: P.O. Box 1656, Bemidji, MN 56619 US
Second Address: 604 Third Ave. W., Alexandria, MN 56308
(320) 762-2154, *Fax:* (320) 762-2156
kikvradio.com
100.7@kikvfm.com
License: Sauk Centre, Douglas County, MN held by BDI Broadcasting Inc.
Group Owner: Omni Broadcasting Co.; (acq 9-25-89; $855,000;
Nat'l Network: ABC *Regional Network:* Linder Farm
Format: Country *Special Programming:* Farm 20 hrs wkly *Hrs. of News Programming:* news progmg 12 hrs wkly *No. News Employees:* 1 *Target Audience:* 25-54; adults
Lou Buron, CEO
Dave Vagle, General Manager
Trudy Blanshan, General Sales Mgr
Rick Blanshan, Programming Director
Jim Rohn, News Director
Mary Campbell, CFO
Paul Sorum, Mary Campbell

Sauk Rapids

WBHR
08-03-1963; 660 khz AM *Hrs Open:* 24
Golden Spike Rd, Bx 366, Sauk Rapids, MN 56079 US
(320) 257-6403, *Fax:* (320) 252-9367
www.660wbhr.com
mail@660wbhr.com
License: Sauk Rapids, MN held by Tri-County Broadcasting Inc.
Group Owner: Tri-County Broadcasting Inc.
Nat'l Network: Radio Disney
Arbitron Metro Market: Sauk Rapids, MN *Format:* Sports
Herb Hoppe, President
Gary Hoppe, Operations Dir
Doug Kurtz, General Sales Mgr

WHMH-FM
10-31-1975; 101.7 mhz FM *Hrs Open:* 24; 50 kw; 476 ft.; N45 30 2 W94 14 31
1010 2nd St. N., Box 366, Sauk Rapids, MN 56379 US
(320) 252-6200, *Fax:* (320) 252-9367
www.rockin101.com
mail@rockkin101.com
License: Sauk Rapids, Benton County, MN
Group Owner: Tri-County Broadcasting Inc.
Arbitron Metro Market: St. Cloud, MN
Leonard Moore, President

WVAL
03-01-1999; 800 khz AM; 2.6 kw-D, DA2; 0.85 kw-N, DA2; N45 36 18 W94 8 21
Mailing Address: 1010 2nd St South, PO Box 366, Sauk Rapids, MN 56379 US
Second Address: 1010 2nd St. N., Sauk Rapids, MN 56379
(320) 252-6200, *Fax:* (320) 252-9367
www.800wval.com
original@800wval.com
License: Sauk Rapids, MN held by Tri-County Broadcasting Inc.
Group Owner: Tri-County Broadcasting Inc.
Arbitron Metro Market: Sauk Rapids, MN *Format:* Classical, Country
Herb Hoppe, General Manager
Doug Kertz, General Sales Mgr
Kevin Lange, Programming Director

WMIN
01-01-2008; 1010 khz AM
US
(320) 252-6200, *Fax:* (320) 252-9367
www.wmin1010.com
License: Sauk Rapids, MN held by Herbert M. Hoppe.
Arbitron Metro Market: Evanston, WY *Format:* Adult Contemp
Herb Hoppe, General Manager
Doug Kertz, General Sales Mgr
Gary Moore, Programming Director

WXYG
540 khz AM; 250 w-U, DA-2; N45 36 18 W94 08 21
Box 366, Sauk Rapids, MN
(320) 252-6200, *Fax:* (320) 252-9367
License: Sauk Rapids, Benton County, MN held by Herbert M. Hoppe.

Herbert Hoppe, General Manager

Sebeka

*KOPJ
89.3 mhz FM *Hrs Open:* 24; 100 kw; Ant 872 ft; N46 40 35.9 W94 43 02
PO Box 481, Park Rapids, MN 98901
(218) 237-4673
www.wehavethishoperadio.net
sserickson@hotmail.com
License: Sebeka, Menahga County, MN held by We Have This Hope Inc.
Nat'l Network: LifeTalk Radio Network
Sharon Erickson, President
Sharon Erickson, General Manager

Shakopee

KQSP
10-06-1963; 1530 khz AM *Hrs Open:* 24; 8.6 kw-D, DA2; 0.01 kw-N, DA2; N44 48 26 W93 33 25
1107 Hazeltine Boulevard, Suite 520, Chaska, MN 55318 US
(847) 687-6550
www.magic1530.com
License: Shakopee, MN held by Broadcast One Inc.
Yong Kim, President

Slayton

KJOE
01-01-1993; 106.1 mhz FM *Hrs Open:* 24; 13 kw; 971 ft.; N43 53 52 W95 56 50
West Highway 30, Pipestone, MN 56164 US
(507) 836-6125,(507) 836-6126, *Fax:* (507) 836-6537
www.kjoeradio.com
kjoe@kjoeradio.com
License: Slayton, Murray County, MN held by Wallace Christensen.
Format: Country
Wallace Christensen, President
Diane Marie, Operations Dir
Collin Christensen, General Manager
Carmen Christensen, General Sales Mgr
Mylan Ray, Programming Director
Bernard Wieme, Promotions Manager
Joel Herrig, News Director
Honee Longstreet, Traffic Manager

Sleepy Eye

KNUJ-FM
06-01-1995; 107.3 mhz FM *Hrs Open:* 24; 4 kw; 407 ft.; N44 19 38 W94 43 41 *Rebroadcasts:* Rebroadcasts KNUJ(AM) New Ulm 70%
330 East Kilbourn Avenue, Suite 250, Milwaukee, WI 53202 US
(507) 359-2921, *Fax:* (507) 359-4520
www.knuj.net
knuj@knuj.net
License: Sleepy Eye, Brown County, MN held by Ingstad Brothers Broadcasting LLC
Group Owner: Ingstad Brothers Broadcasting LLC; acq 5-1-2004; grpsl).
Format: Adult Contemp *Hrs. of News Programming:* news progmg 20 hrs wkly *No. News Employees:* 1 *Target Audience:* 18-49; slightly more females than males
Jim Bartels, Operations Dir
Janine Enter, General Sales Mgr
Brian Filzen, Programming Director
Mike Lemmer, News Director
Greg Brandt, Chief Engineer

Spring Grove

KQYB
08-02-1980; 98.3 mhz FM *Hrs Open:* 24; 33 kw; 607 ft.; N43 40 53 W91 45 28
980 North Michigan Ave., Suite 1880, Chicago, IL 60611 US
(608) 782-1230, *Fax:* (608) 782-1170
www.kq98.com
email@kq98.com
License: Spring Grove, Houston County, MN held by Family Radio Inc.
Group Owner: The Mid-West Family Broadcast Group; (acq 7-19-01; grpsl).

Wire Services: AP
Arbitron Metro Market: LaCrosse, WI *Format:* Country *Hrs. of News Programming:* news progmg one hr wkly *No. News Employees:* 1 *Target Audience:* General. *Adv. Rates:* 50; 45; 47; 35
Dick Record, CEO

Spring Valley

KVGO
01-01-1993; 104.3 mhz FM; 10 kw; 512 ft.; N43 38 23 W92 38 30
P.O. Box 370, Preston, Mn, MN 55965 US
(507) 765-3856, *Fax:* (507) 765-2738
License: Spring Valley, Fillmore County, MN held by KVGO Inc.
Group Owner: Cumulus Media Inc.; (acq 3-30-2004; grpsl).
Nat'l Reps: D & R Radio
Arbitron Metro Market: Preston, MN *Format:* Oldies
Bruce Fishbaugher, General Manager
John Milne, Programming Director

*KVCS
89.1 mhz FM; 12 kw; Ant 138 meters; N43 38 34 W92 31 35
3434 W. Kilbourn Ave., Milwaukee, WI
(414) 935-3000, *Fax:* (414) 935-3015
www.vcyamerica.org
KVCS@vcyamerica.org
License: Spring Valley, Fillmore County, MN held by VCY America Inc.
Group Owner: VCY America Inc.

Vic Eliason, General Manager
Jim Schneider, Programming Director
Andy Eliason, Chief Engineer

Springfield

KNSG
01-01-1995; 94.7 mhz FM *Hrs Open:* 24; 50 kw; 472 ft.; N44 21 54 W95 19 27
330 East Kilbourn Avenue, Suite 250, Milwaukee, WI 53202 US
(507) 532-2282, *Fax:* (507) 532-3739
marshallradio.net
info@marshallradio.net
License: Springfield, Brown County, MN held by Springfield Radio Inc.
Nat'l Network: Westwood One *Regional Network:* Linder Farm; Minn. News Net. *Nat'l Reps:* Katz Radio *Wire Services:* AP
Format: Adult Contemp *Special Programming:* Farm 15 hrs, women 3 hrs wkly *Target Audience:* 30 plus; women *Adv. Rates:* 10.50; 10.50; 10.50; 8.25
Heath Radke, Operations Dir
Brad Strootman, General Manager

St. Charles

KDZZ
04-18-1998; 107.7 mhz FM *Hrs Open:* 24; 1.95 kw; 571 ft.; N44 2 25 W92 13 5
1220 4th Avenue Sw, Rochester, MN 55902 US
(507) 286-1010, *Fax:* (507) 286-9370
www.zrock1077.com
License: St. Charles, Winona County, MN held by Cumulus Licensing LLC.
Group Owner: Cumulus Media Inc.; (acq 3-31-2004; grpsl)
Nat'l Reps: Christal
Arbitron Metro Market: Rochester, MN
Shannon Knoepke, General Manager

St. Cloud

*KCFB
11-17-1986; 91.5 mhz FM *Hrs Open:* 24; 15 kw; 348 ft.; N45 30 2 W94 14 31 *Rebroadcasts:* Rebroadcasts KTIG(FM) Pequot Lakes 100%
P.O. Box 409, Pequot Lakes, MN 56472 US
(320) 252-4214, *Fax:* (218) 568-5950
License: St. Cloud, Stearns County, MN held by Minnesota Christian Broadcasters Inc.
Nat'l Network: Moody *Wire Services:* AP
Arbitron Metro Market: St. Cloud, MN *Format:* Religious *Hrs. of News Programming:* news progmg 14 hrs wkly *No. News Employees:* 1 *Target Audience:* General.
Mike Heuberger, General Manager
Jim Park, Programming Director

KCLD-FM
05-01-1948; 104.7 mhz FM; 100 kw; 984 ft.; N45 34 3 W94 30 43
Mailing Address: P. O. Box 1458, St. Cloud, MN 56302 US
Second Address: 619 W. St. Germain St., Saint Cloud, MN 56302
(320) 251-1047, *Fax:* (320) 251-8952
www.1047kcld.com
jjholiday@1047kcld.com
License: St. Cloud, Stearns County, MN held by Leighton Enterprises Inc.
Group Owner: Leighton Enterprises Inc.
Arbitron Metro Market: St. Cloud, MN *Format:* Contemporary Hits/Top 40
Bob Leighton, General Sales Mgr
J.J. Holiday, Programming Director
Tamo, Music Director
Travis McGinnis, Web Master

KNSI
06-01-1938; 1450 khz AM; 1 kw-U, ND1; N45 32 21 W94 10 5
Mailing Address: P. O. Box 1458, St. Cloud, MN 56302 US
Second Address: 619 W. St. Germain St., Saint Cloud, MN 56302
(320) 251-1450, *Fax:* (320) 251-8952
www.1450knsi.com
info@1450knsi.com
License: St. Cloud, MN held by Leighton Enterprises Inc.
Group Owner: Leighton Enterprises Inc.; acq 9-15-75)
Regional Reps: O'Malley.
Arbitron Metro Market: St. Cloud, MN *Format:* News, News/Talk, 86 *Target Audience:* 35 plus; males
John Sowada, President
Denny Niess, General Sales Mgr
Matt Senne, Programming Director
Kathy Carton, News Director
Dale Daley, Chief Engineer
Denise Prozinski, Sales Director

*KVSC
05-10-1967; 88.1 mhz FM *Hrs Open:* 20-24; 16.5 kw vert; 446 ft.; N45 31 0 W94 13 52
720 Fourth Avenue South, 27 Stewart Hall, St. Cloud, MN 56301 US
(320) 308-5872, *Fax:* (320) 308-5337
www.kvsc.org
info@kvsc.org
License: St. Cloud, Stearns County, MN held by St. Cloud State University.
Nat'l Network: PRI *Wire Services:* AP
Arbitron Metro Market: St. Cloud, MN *Format:* Alternative *Special Programming:* jazz, indie, folk, americana, MN music *Hrs. of News Programming:* news progmg 12 hrs wkly *No. News Employees:* 2.5 *TargetAudience:* 17-60; educated, progsv *Adv. Rates:* 15; 15; 15; 15
Jim Grey, Operations Dir
Roya Majid, General Manager
Jo McMullen-Boyer, Station Manager
Cheyenne Malcolm, Programming Director
Amelia Rowland, News Director
Jett Carmack, Arts and Cultural Heritage Producer
Alex Hartman, ProjectAnalyst
Conrad Magalis, Marketing / Sales Director
James Tollefson, Music Director
Nick Hendrickson, Production Director
Dave Overlund, Sports Director

WJON
09-01-1950; 1240 khz AM *Hrs Open:* 24
50 E. Rivercenter Blvd., Suite 180, Covington, KY 14011 US
(320) 251-4422
www.wjon.com
info@wjon.com
License: St. Cloud, MN
Group Owner: Townsquare Media; (acq 5-1-99; grpsl)
Nat'l Network: CBS *Regional Network:* MNN
Arbitron Metro Market: St. Cloud, MN *Format:* News, News/Talk, 86 *Hrs. of News Programming:* news progmg 30 hrs wkly *No. News Employees:* 3 *Target Audience:* 25 plus.
Mike Dylan, Operations Dir
Dave Engberg, General Manager
Bob Hughes, Programming Director
Lee Voss, News Director
Mark Young, Chief Engineer

WWJO
01-01-1975; 98.1 mhz FM; 97 kw; 1001 ft.; N45 48 52 W94 1 38
50 E. Rivercenter Blvd., Suite 180, Covington, KY 14011 US
(320) 251-4422
www.98country.com
License: St. Cloud, Stearns County, MN
Group Owner: Townsquare Media
Arbitron Metro Market: St. Cloud, MN *Format:* Country *Target Audience:* 18 plus.
Terry Jacobs, CEO
Bill Stakelin, President
Fred Murr, Operations Dir
David Engberg, General Manager
Steve Lahr, Director of Sales
Bill Fink, Programming Director
Lynn Larson, Promotions Manager
Sandi Davis, Assistant MusicDirector
Dave McCord, Brand Manager

St. James

KRRW
07-24-1983; 101.5 mhz FM *Hrs Open:* 24; 14 kw; 446 ft.; N43 52 27 W94 36 0
P.O. Box 1420, Mankato, MN 56001 US
(507) 345-4537, *Fax:* (507) 345-5364
krrw@linderradio.com
License: St. James, Watonwan County, MN held by Minnesota Valley Broadcasting Co.
Group Owner: Linder Broadcasting Group; (acq 1996; $800,000 with KXAC(FM) St)
Regional Network: Linder Farm
Format: Country *Special Programming:* Sp one hr wkly *Hrs. of News Programming:* news progmg 16 hrs wkly *No. News Employees:* 1 *Target Audience:* 25-54.
Jo Bailey, Operations Dir

KXAC
11-01-1992; 100.5 mhz FM *Hrs Open:* 24; 34 kw; 591 ft.; N43 57 3 W94 23 25
P.O. Box 1420, Mankato, MN 56001 US
(507) 345-4537, *Fax:* (507) 345-5364
kxac@linderradio.com
License: St. James, Watonwan County, MN held by Minnesota Valley Broadcasting Co.
Group Owner: Linder Broadcasting Group; (acq 1996; $800,000 with KXAX(FM) St)
Regional Network: MNN
Format: Oldies *Target Audience:* 25-58.
Jo Bailey, Operations Dir

St. Joseph

KCML
01-01-1998; 99.9 mhz FM; 2.9 kw; 476 ft.; N45 32 21 W94 10 5
Mailing Address: P O Box 1458, St. Cloud, MN 56302 US
Second Address: 619 W. Saint Germain St., St. Cloud, MN 56301
(320) 251-1450, *Fax:* (320) 251-8952
www.lite999.com
info@lite999.com
License: St. Joseph, Stearns County, MN held by Leighton Enterprises Inc.
Group Owner: Leighton Enterprises Inc.
Arbitron Metro Market: St. Cloud, MN *Format:* Contemporary Hits/Top 40
Al Leighton, CEO
John Sowada, General Manager
Denny Niess, General Sales Mgr
Ron Linder, Programming Director
Cindy Niess, News Director
Dale Daley, Chief Engineer
Denise Prozinski, General Sales Manager

KKJM
05-07-1996; 92.9 mhz FM *Hrs Open:* 24; 25 kw; 328 ft.; N45 38 19 W94 22 23
640 Lincoln Ave., Se, Box 220, St. Cloud, MN 56302 US
(320) 251-1780, *Fax:* (320) 257-1624
www.spirit929.com
friends@spirit929.com
License: St. Joseph, Stearns County, MN held by Gabriel Communications Co., St. Cloud.
Wire Services: AP
Arbitron Metro Market: St. Cloud, MN *Format:* Adult Contemp, Christian *Hrs. of News Programming:* News progmg 5 hrs wkly *Target Audience:* 25-54; females *Adv. Rates:* 18; 18; 18; 18
Deb Huschle, General Manager
Diana Madsen, Programming Director
Michelle Crabb, News Director

St. Louis Park

*KDXL
03-17-1977; 106.5 mhz FM *Hrs Open:* 7:30 AM-10 PM (M-F); 0.008 kw; 85 ft.; N44 56 36 W93 21 39
6425 W. 33rd Street, St. Louis Park, MN 55426 US
(952) 928-6000, *Fax:* (952) 928-6208
License: St. Louis Park, Hennepin County, MN held by Independent School District 283.
Arbitron Metro Market: Minneapolis-St. Paul, MN *Format:* Classic Rock, Rock/AOR *Target Audience:* 15-30; high school students & loc residents
Charlie Fiss, Station Manager

KTNF
05-13-1958; 950 khz AM *Hrs Open:* 24; 1 kw-D, DA2; 1 kw-N, DA2; N44 52 8 W93 25 11
600 New Hampshire Ave., N.W., Suite 1200, Washington, DC 20037 US
(952) 946-8885, *Fax:* (952) 946-0888
www.am950ktnf.com
traffic@am950ktnf.com
License: St. Louis Park, MN held by JR Broadcasting LLC
Nat'l Network: Air America; CNN Radio; Jones Radio Networks
Wire Services: AP
Arbitron Metro Market: Eden Prair, MN *Format:* Talk *Target Audience:* 35+.
Janet Robert, President

KZJK
07-01-1962; 104.1 mhz FM; 100 kw; 1033 ft.; N45 3 30 W93 7 27
600 New Hampshire Ave., N.W., Suite 1200, Washington, DC 20037 US
(612) 370-0611
www.1041jackfm.com
drmonfre@wcco.com
License: St. Louis Park, Hennepin County, MN held by The Audio House Inc.
Group Owner: CBS Radio
Arbitron Metro Market: Saint Louis Park, MN *Format:* Oldies
Mary Neimeyer, Operations Dir
Rob Berrell, General Manager
Patrick Stelzner, General Sales Mgr
John Lassman, Programming Director
Kris Cegla, Promotions Manager
Sean Johnson, Web Administrator
Dan Monfre, Digital SalesManager

***KUOM-FM**
02-17-2003; 106.5 mhz FM *Hrs Open:* 4:30 PM-8 AM M-F; 24 S-S; 0.006 kw; 208 ft.; N44 56 47.4 W93 19 24.1 *Rebroadcasts:* Rebroadcasts KUOM(AM) Minneapolis 100%
US
(612) 625-3500, *Fax:* (612) 625-2112
www.radiok.org
request@radiok.org
License: St. Louis Park, Hennepin County, MN held by Regents of the University of Minnesota.
Wire Services: AP
Arbitron Metro Market: Saint Louis Park, MN *Format:* Rock/AOR *Target Audience:* 18-34
Sara Miller, Station Manager
Caleigh Souhan, Programming Director
Morgan Luther, Promotions Manager
Larry Oberg, Chief Engineer
Amy Daml, Program Coach
Chase Mathey, Music Director
Sarah Lemanczyk, Programming Advisor
GregSakowski, Production Director
Stuart Sanders, Development Director
Brody Howard, Studio K Producer

St. Paul

KEEY-FM
06-01-1969; 102.1 mhz FM *Hrs Open:* 24; 100 kw; 1033 ft.; N45 3 30 W93 7 27
7900 Xerxes Avenue South, Suite 102, Bloomington, MN 55431 US
(952) 417-3000, *Fax:* (612) 417-3001
www.k102.com
info@keey.com
License: St. Paul, Ramsey County, MN held by AMFM Broadcasting Licenses LLC.
Group Owner: Clear Channel Communications Inc.
Nat'l Reps: Clear Channel
Arbitron Metro Market: Minneapolis-St. Paul, MN *Format:* Country *Hrs. of News Programming:* news progmg 2 hrs wkly *No. News Employees:* 40 *Target Audience:* 25-54; women
Mike Anselmo, President
Rob Berrell, General Sales Mgr
Gregg Swedberg, Programming Director
Matt Tell, Promotions Manager
Cathy Maness, News Director
Mary Gallas, Music Director

KMNV
01-01-1936; 1400 khz AM *Hrs Open:* 24; 1 kw-U, ND1; N44 57 28 W93 12 23
611 Frontenac Place, St. Paul, MN 55104 US
(612) 729-5900, *Fax:* (612) 729-5999
info@kmnvam.com
License: St. Paul, MN held by Davidson Media Station KLBB Licensee LLC.
Group Owner: Davidson Media Group LLC; (acq 9-7-2005; $5.2 million with KMNQ(AM) Brooklyn Park)
Regional Network: ABN Radio
Arbitron Metro Market: Minneapolis, MN
Tim Dennis, General Manager

KNOF
04-10-1960; 95.3 mhz FM *Hrs Open:* 6 AM-10 PM; 6 kw; 249 ft.; N44 56 48 W93 9 26
1347 Selby Avenue, St. Paul, MN 55104 US
(651) 645-8271, *Fax:* (651) 645-4593
License: St. Paul, Ramsey County, MN held by Selby Gospel Broadcasting Co.
Nat'l Network: Salem Radio Network
Arbitron Metro Market: Minneapolis, MN *Format:* Gospel *Special Programming:* Black 5 hrs, Sp one hr, Russian one hr wkly *Hrs. of News Programming:* News progmg 2 hrs wkly *Target Audience:* All ages.
Paul Freitag, President
Phil Mullen, Operations Dir

KSTP
04-01-1924; 1500 khz AM
3415 University Ave, St. Paul, MN 55114 US
(651) 647-1500, *Fax:* (651) 649-1515
www.am1500.com
info@kstp.com
License: St. Paul, MN held by KSTP-AM L.L.C., a Delaware L.L.C.
Group Owner: Hubbard Broadcasting Inc.
Nat'l Reps: Christal *Wire Services:* AP
Arbitron Metro Market: Minneapolis-St. Paul, MN *TV Affiliate:* KSTP-TV affil. *Format:* Talk *Hrs. of News Programming:* news progmg 5 hrs wkly *No. News Employees:* 3 *Target Audience:* 25-54; adults
Stanley Hubbard, CEO
Virginia Morris, President
Todd Fisher, Operations Dir
John Soucheray, General Sales Mgr
Brad Lane, Programming Director
Ryan barnholdt, Promotions Manager

KSTP-FM
11-01-1965; 94.5 mhz FM; 95 kw; 1220 ft.; N45 3 45 W93 8 22
3415 University Avenue, St Paul, MN 55114 US
(651) 642-4141, *Fax:* (651) 642-4239
www.ks95.com
info@kstp.com
License: St. Paul, Ramsey County, MN held by KSTP-FM L.L.C. a Delaware L.L.C.
Group Owner: Hubbard Broadcasting Inc.
Nat'l Network: ABC *Nat'l Reps:* Christal *Wire Services:* AP
Arbitron Metro Market: Minneapolis-St. Paul, MN *TV Affiliate:* KSTP-TV affil *Format:* Adult Contemp *No. News Employees:* 1 *Target Audience:* 25-54; female
Dave Bestler, Operations Dir
John Gonzales, General Sales Mgr
Leighton Peck, Programming Director

WREY
09-19-1959; 630 khz AM
PO Box 25555, St. Paul, MN 55125 US
(612) 729-3776, *Fax:* (612) 724-0437
www.radiorey630am.com
lupe@radiorey630am.com
License: St. Paul, MN held by 630 Radio Inc.
Arbitron Metro Market: Minneapolis-St. Paul, MN *Format:* Spanish
Felicia Ortega, COO
Guadalupe Gonzales, President
Manuel Robles, General Manager
Enrique Levien, Programming Director

***WMCN**
09-15-1979; 91.7 mhz FM *Hrs Open:* 8 AM-4 AM (M-F); 11 AM-4 AM (S, Su); 0.005 kw; 161 ft.; N44 56 19 W93 10 4
1600 Grand Ave, St. Paul, MN 55105 US
(651) 696-6082, *Fax:* (651) 696-6689
www.macalester.edu/wmcn
wmcn@macalester.edu
License: St. Paul, Ramsey County, MN held by Macalester College.
Arbitron Metro Market: Minneapolis, MN *Format:* Variety/Diverse *Special Programming:* Country 2 hrs, Latin 6 hrs, multicultural 10 hrs, *Target Audience:* General, students
Patrick McGrath, General Manager
Ethan Torrey, Chief Engineer

St. Peter

KRBI-FM
09-01-1966; 105.5 mhz FM *Hrs Open:* 24; 25 kw; 222 ft.; N44 10 20 W94 2 23
1031 West Grace, St. Peter, MN 56082 US
(507) 345-4646, *Fax:* (507) 345-3299
www.river105.com
License: St. Peter, Nicollet County, MN held by Three Eagles Communications LLC.
Group Owner: Three Eagles Communications; (acq 7-16-2003; $3.2 million with co-located AM)
Nat'l Reps: Katz Radio
Arbitron Metro Market: Mankato, MN *Format:* Adult Contemp *Hrs. of News Programming:* news progmg one hr wkly *No. News Employees:* 1 *Target Audience:* 25-54; people liking classic hits, 70s-90s & small amounts ofnews, weather, & sports *Adv. Rates:* 26; 26; 26; 26
Larry LeBlanc, Operations Dir
Brad Leggett, General Manager
Jen Jones, General Sales Mgr
Mike Schoen, Programming Director
Randall Harder, News Director
Ron Schacht, Chief Engineer
Jill Mason, Business Manager
Kathy Varva,Local Sales Manager

Staples

KNSP
06-03-1982; 1430 khz AM *Hrs Open:* 24; 1 kw-D, ND1; 0.199 kw-N, ND1; N46 21 34 W94 46 55
Mailing Address: 602 Laurel Street, Brainerd, MN 56401 US
Second Address: 201 1/2 Jefferson St. S., Wadena, MN 56482
(218) 631-1803, *Fax:* (218) 631-4557
kwadknsp.net
kwadkkws@arvig.net
License: Staples, MN held by BL Broadcasting Inc.
Group Owner: Omni Broadcasting Co.; (acq 4-1-2004; grpsl).
Nat'l Network: ABC *Regional Network:* Minn. Farm; Minn. News Net.
Format: Country *Special Programming:* Farm 10 hrs wkly *Hrs. of News Programming:* news progmg 20 hrs wkly *No. News Employees:* 1 *Target Audience:* 25-54; adults
Lou Buron, CEO
Rick Youngbauer, General Manager
Kyle Gylsen, Programming Director
Sherry Linnes, Promotions Manager
Mary Campbell, CFO

KSKK
08-01-1994; 94.7 mhz FM *Hrs Open:* 24; 50 kw; 469 ft; N46 33 08 W94 39 03
11 S.E. Bryant Ave., Wadena, MN 56470
(218) 631-3441, *Fax:* (218) 631-3414
kskk@eot.com
License: Staples, Todd County, MN held by NorMin Broadcasting Co.
Nat'l Network: CBS
Hrs. of News Programming: News progmg 20 hrs wkly *Target Audience:* 30 plus. *Adv. Rates:* 12; 12; 12; 12
David De LaHunt, CEO
Joleen De LaHunt, Operations Dir
Gene Marie Kanten, General Manager
Heidi Hutson, General Sales Mgr

Starbuck

KRVY-FM
01-01-2001; 97.3 mhz FM *Hrs Open:* 24; 50 kw; 492 ft.; N45 31 42 W95 32 52
Mailing Address: 752 Bluff View Circle, Winona, MN 55989 US
Second Address: 730 N.E. Hwy. 71, Willmar, MN 56201
(320) 231-1600, *Fax:* (320) 235-7010
www.k-musicradio.com
License: Starbuck, Pope County, MN held by Iowa City Broadcasting Co.
Group Owner: Tom Ingstad Broadcasting Group; (acq 7-19-99; $200,000 for stock).
Wire Services: UPI
Format: Adult Contemp, Light Rock *Hrs. of News Programming:* news progmg 8 hrs wkly *No. News Employees:* 1 *Target Audience:* 25-54; male & female *Adv. Rates:* 16.25; 16.25; 16.25; 16.25
Doug Hanson, General Manager
Rob Ryan, Programming Director
Beverly Ahlquist, News Director

Stewartville

KYBA
02-01-1993; 105.3 mhz FM; 50 kw; 492 ft.; N43 40 23 W92 41 54

1901 First Ave N W, Stewartville, MN 55976 US
(507) 286-1010, *Fax:* (507) 286-9370
www.y105fm.com
shannon.knoepke@cumulus.com
License: Stewartville, Olmsted County, MN held by Cumulus Licensing LLC
Group Owner: Cumulus Media Inc.; (acq 3-29-2004; grpsl).
Nat'l Network: ABC *Nat'l Reps:* Christal *Regional Reps:* Christal Radio
Arbitron Metro Market: Rochester, MN *Format:* Adult Contemp
Target Audience: 25-54. *Adv. Rates:* 26; 26; 26; 22
Brent Ackerman, Operations Dir
Shannon Knoepke, General Manager
Terry Lee, Advertising
Tom Garrett, Program Diretor
Kim David, News Director
Bill Davis, Chief Engineer

Stillwater

KLBB
03-13-1949; 1220 khz AM *Hrs Open:* 24; 5 kw-D, ND1; 0.254 kw-N, ND1; N45 3 15 W92 49 42
125 East Third Ave, New Richmond, WI 54017 US
(651) 439-5006, *Fax:* (651) 439-5015
www.klbbradio.com
dan@mighty1220.com
License: Stillwater, MN held by Endurance Broadcasting LLC
Nat'l Network: ABC; Westwood One *Regional Network:* Minn. News Net.
Arbitron Metro Market: Stillwater, MN *Format:* Adult Contemp *No. News Employees:* 1 *Target Audience:* 35-64. *Adv. Rates:* 25; 20; 25; 15
Daniel Smith, CEO
Scott Murray, General Manager
Reed Hagen, Programming Director

Sunburg

KLFN
01-01-2003; 106.5 mhz FM; 6 kw; 328 ft.; N45 22 14 W95 8 28
601 15th Avenue Ne, Waseca, MN 56093 US
(320) 235-1342, *Fax:* (320) 235-9111
www.kwlm.com
askus@kwlm.com
License: Sunburg, Kandiyohi County, MN held by Lakeland Broadcasting Co.
Arbitron Metro Market: Willmar, MN *Format:* Classic Rock
Doug Loy, General Manager
Maryelin Macht, Programming Director
J.P. Cola, News Director

Thief River Falls

KKAQ
11-02-1979; 1460 khz AM *Hrs Open:* 24; 2.5 kw-D, ND1; 0.15 kw-N, ND1; N48 7 25 W96 8 31
P.O. Box 218, Thief River Falls, MN 56701 US
(218) 681-4900, *Fax:* (218) 681-3717
www.trfradio.com
info@trradio.com
License: Thief River Falls, MN held by Iowa City Broadcasting Co. Inc.
Group Owner: Tom Ingstad Broadcasting Group; (acq 11-19-99; $620,000 with co-located FM).
Arbitron Metro Market: Grand Forks, ND *Format:* News, Sports *No. News Employees:* 1 *Target Audience:* 25-54.
John Praska, General Manager
Mark Stromstodt, Programming Director
Key Teeters, News Director
Stan Mueller, Chief Engineer
Sheila Strange, Traffic Manager

KKDQ
11-01-1989; 99.3 mhz FM *Hrs Open:* 24; 18 kw; 387 ft.; N48 3 22 W96 22 23
P. O. Box 218, Thief River Falls, MN 56701 US
(218) 681-4900, *Fax:* (218) 681-3717
www.trfradio.com
info@trradio.com
License: Thief River Falls, Pennington County, MN held by Iowa City Broadcasting Co. Inc.
Arbitron Metro Market: Grand Forks, ND *Format:* Country, Sports
Joel McCrea, General Manager
Matt Gillon, General Sales Mgr
Greg Chance, Programming Director
Sean Cage, Music Director

KNTN
12-13-1991; 102.7 mhz FM *Hrs Open:* 24; 100 kw; 538 ft.; N47 58 38 W96 36 32
45 East Seventh Street, St. Paul, MN 55101 US
(218) 299-3666, *Fax:* (218) 299-3418
www.mpr.org
License: Thief River Falls, Pennington County, MN held by Minnesota Public Radio Inc.
Nat'l Network: NPR; PRI *Regional Network:* Minn. Pub. Radio *Format:* News *No. News Employees:* 2 *Target Audience:* General.
John McTaggard, Chairman
William Kling, President
Vern Goodin, General Manager
Jim McGuinn, Station Manager
Julia Beaton, General Sales Mgr
Timothy Roesler, General Manager of Classical Music
Chris Worthington, News Director

*KQMN
11-26-1990; 91.5 mhz FM *Hrs Open:* 24; 84 kw; 653 ft.; N47 58 38 W96 36 32
45 East 7th Street, St. Paul, MN 55101 US
(651) 290-1500, *Fax:* (218) 299-3418
www.minnesota.publicradio.org
License: Thief River Falls, Pennington County, MN held by Minnesota Public Radio.
Nat'l Network: NPR; PRI
Arbitron Metro Market: Grand Forks, ND *Format:* News/Talk, Classical *No. News Employees:* 2
Ian R. Friendly, Chairman
David W. Kansas, COO
Jon McTaggart, President

*KSRQ
11-15-1971; 90.1 mhz FM *Hrs Open:* 24; 24 kw; 335 ft.; N48 1 19 W96 22 12
1101 Hwy One East, Thief River Falls, MN 56701 US
(218) 681-0791(800) 959-6282, *Fax:* (218) 681-0774
www.pioneer90.org
travis.ryder@northlandcollege.edu
License: Thief River Falls, Pennington County, MN held by Northland Community & Technical College
Regional Reps: Jim Lowe; Independent Community Media *Wire Services:* AP
Arbitron Metro Market: Thief River Falls, MN *Format:* Alternative, Triple A *Special Programming:* Sp one hr, adult standards 5 hrs wkly *Hrs. of News Programming:* News progmg 10 hrs wkly *Target Audience:* 18-54;professionals *Adv. Rates:* 10; 10; 10; 10
Anne Temte, President
Ben Kosharek, Operations Dir
Travis Ryder, General Manager
Stan Mueller, Chief Engineer

KTRF
01-30-1947; 1230 khz AM *Hrs Open:* 24; 1 kw-U, ND1; N48 7 47 W96 11 11
P.O. Box 1248, Minnetonka, MN 55345 US
(218) 681-4900, *Fax:* (218) 681-3717
www.trfradio.com
ktrf@mncable.net
License: Thief River Falls, MN held by Iowa City Broadcasting Co.
Nat'l Network: CBS *Regional Network:* MNN
Arbitron Metro Market: Thief River Falls, MN *Format:* Adult Contemp, News *Special Programming:* Farm 12 hrs wkly *Hrs. of News Programming:* news progmg 35 hrs wkly *No. News Employees:* 2 *Target Audience:* General; 25 plus
Jon Praska, General Manager
Mark Allen, Programming Director
Key Teters, News Director

Tracy

KARL
07-19-1994; 105.1 mhz FM *Hrs Open:* 24; 45 kw; 502 ft.; N44 19 32 W95 52 19
Mailing Address: P.O. Box 1420, Mankato, MN 56001 US
Second Address: 1414 E. College Dr., Marshall, MN 56258
(507) 629-3355, *Fax:* (507) 532-3739
www.1051karl.com
License: Tracy, Lyon County, MN held by KMHL Broadcasting Co.
Group Owner: Linder Broadcasting Group; (acq 12-17-92; $22,100;
Nat'l Network: ABC *Regional Network:* Linder Farm
Arbitron Metro Market: Tracy, MN *Format:* Country *Special Programming:* Farm 15 hrs wkly *Hrs. of News Programming:* News progmg 3 hrs wkly *Target Audience:* General. *Adv. Rates:* 12.75; 12.75; 12.75; 9.25
Donald Linder, President
John Linder, Operations Dir
Brad Strootman, General Manager
Justin Thordson, Operations Manager

Two Harbors

KZIO
09-01-1995; 104.3 mhz FM; 50 kw; 397 ft.; N46 56 28 W91 58 58
111 Marquette Avenue, #100, Minneapolis, MN 55401 US
(218) 723-1043, *Fax:* (218) 723-1499
www.94xrocks.com
License: Two Harbors, Lake County, MN held by Red Rock Radio Corp.
Group Owner: Red Rock Radio Corp.; acq 1-10-00; grpsl).
Arbitron Metro Market: Two Harbors, MN *Format:* Rock/AOR
Sean Skramstad, General Manager
Jim Payne, General Sales Mgr
Bill Jones, Programming Director
Jason Manning, News Director

Verndale

KVKK
01-01-2005; 1070 khz AM
US
(218) 732-3306, *Fax:* (218) 732-3307
License: Verndale, MN held by DJ Broadcasting Corp.
Arbitron Metro Market: Verndale, MN *Format:* Country
Edward DeLaHunt Sr., General Manager

Virginia

WUSZ
06-02-1971; 99.9 mhz FM *Hrs Open:* 24; 100 kw; 531 ft.; N47 22 24 W93 0 48
South 17th Street &, Sixth Ave., Virginia, MN 55792 US
(218) 263-7531, *Fax:* (218) 263-6112
www.radiousa.com
kristi@mwcradio.com
License: Virginia, St. Louis County, MN held by Midwest Communications Inc.
Group Owner: Midwest Communications Inc.; acq 5-10-2004; grpsl).
Nat'l Network: USA *Regional Network:* MNN
Arbitron Metro Market: Hibbing, MN *Format:* Country *Hrs. of News Programming:* News progmg one hr wkly *Target Audience:* 25-49; blue and white collar workers and families
Kristi Garrity, General Manager

Virginia-Hibbing

*WIRR
12-01-1985; 90.9 mhz FM *Hrs Open:* 24; 21 kw; 551 ft.; N47 29 46 W92 47 5
45 E. Seventh St, Saint Paul, MN 55101 US
(218) 722-9411, *Fax:* (218) 720-4900
www.mpr.org
info@mpr.org
License: Virginia-Hibbing, St. Louis County, MN held by Minnesota Public Radio Inc.
Nat'l Network: PRI; NPR *Regional Network:* Minn. Pub. Radio *Format:* Talk *No. News Employees:* 3 *Target Audience:* General.
William Kling, President
Kat Eldred, General Manager

Wabasha

WBHA
04-01-1976; 1190 khz AM *Hrs Open:* 6 AM-sunset; 1 kw-D; N44 20 44 W91 58 28 *Rebroadcasts:* Rebroadcasts KMFX-FM Lake City 90%
1530 Greenview Dr. S.W., Rochester, MN 53202
(507) 288-3888, *Fax:* (507) 288-7815
www.1025thefox.com
License: Wabasha, Wabasha County, MN held by CC Licenses LLC.
Group Owner: Clear Channel Communications Inc.; (acq 9-25-2000; grpsl).
Regional Network: MNN
Target Audience: 18-54.
Craig Erpestad, Operations Dir
Bob Fox, General Manager
Mary Anne Nons, General Sales Mgr

Wadena

KKWS
09-23-1968; 105.9 mhz FM *Hrs Open:* 24; 100 kw; 561 ft.; N46 35 59 W94 54 4
Mailing Address: P.O. Box 980, Brainerd, MN 56401 US
Second Address: 201 1/2 Jefferson St. S., Wadena, MN 56482
(218) 631-1803, *Fax:* (218) 631-4557
www.superstationk106.com
info@superstationk106.com
License: Wadena, Wadena County, MN

Group Owner: Omni Broadcasting Co.
Nat'l Network: ABC
Arbitron Metro Market: Saint Cloud, MN *Format:* Country *Hrs. of News Programming:* news progmg 12 hrs wkly *No. News Employees:* 1 *Target Audience:* 25-54; adults
Danny Wild, Programming Director

KWAD
04-24-1948; 920 khz AM *Hrs Open:* 24
Mailing Address: P.O. Box 980, Brainerd, MN 56401 US
Second Address: 201 1/2 Jefferson St. S., Wadena, MN 56482
(218) 631-1803, *Fax:* (218) 631-4557
www.superstationk106.com/kwad.htm
kwadkkws@arvig.net
License: Wadena, MN held by BL Broadcasting Inc.
Group Owner: Omni Broadcasting Co.; (acq 4-1-2004; grpsl).
Nat'l Network: ABC *Regional Network:* Minn. Farm; Minn. News Net.
Format: Country *Special Programming:* Farm 10 hrs wkly *Hrs. of News Programming:* news progmg 20 hrs wkly *No. News Employees:* 1 *Target Audience:* 25-54; adults
Lou Buron, CEO
Rick Youngbauer, General Manager
Kyle Gylsen, Programming Director
Sherry Linnes, Promotions Manager
Mary Campbell, CFO

Waite Park

KLZZ
07-01-1989; 103.7 mhz FM; 9 kw; 413 ft.; N45 30 2 W94 14 31
1986 Julep Road, St. Cloud, MN 56301 US
(320) 251-4422, *Fax:* (320) 251-1855
www.1037theloon.com
License: Waite Park, Stearns County, MN
Group Owner: Townsquare Media
Arbitron Metro Market: St. Cloud, MN *Format:* Classic Rock
Don Monson, Programming Director

KXSS
01-01-1981; 1390 khz AM; 2.5 kw-D, DA2; 1 kw-N, DA2; N45 32 31 W94 15 41
1986 Julep Road, St. Cloud, MN 56301 US
(320) 251-4422, *Fax:* (320) 251-1855
www.1390thefan.com
studio@kiss96.com
License: Waite Park, MN
Group Owner: Townsquare Media; (acq 5-8-2001; grpsl).
Arbitron Metro Market: St. Cloud, MN *Format:* Sports *Target Audience:* 18-49.
William Stakelin, President
David Engberg, General Manager
Dick Nelson, Programming Director
Lee Voss, News Director
Mark Young, Chief Engineer
Steve Lahr, Director of Sales
Jay Cladwell, Brand Manager

Walker

KAKK
07-11-1970; 1570 khz AM *Hrs Open:* 24
P.O. Box 980, Brainerd, MN 56401 US
(218) 732-3306, *Fax:* (218) 547-4001
License: Walker, MN held by Edward De La Hunt
Regional Network: MNN
Arbitron Metro Market: Fargo, MD *Format:* Oldies *Target Audience:* General.
Brad Walhof, General Manager
Marcus Mitchell, News Director

KLLZ-FM
05-06-1984; 99.1 mhz FM *Hrs Open:* 24; 100 kw; 505 ft.; N47 12 52 W94 55 18
Mailing Address: P.O. Box 980, Brainerd, MN 56401 US
Second Address: 502 Beltrami Ave. N.W., Bemidji, MN 56601
(218) 444-1500, *Fax:* (218) 751-8091
phanson@pbbroadcasting.com
License: Walker, Cass County, MN held by BG Broadcasting Inc.
Group Owner: Omni Broadcasting Co.; (acq 10-24-2000).
Nat'l Network: ABC
Arbitron Metro Market: Fargo, MD *Format:* Classic Rock *Hrs. of News Programming:* news progmg 12 hrs wkly *No. News Employees:* 1 *Target Audience:* 25-54; adults
Lou Buron, CEO
Peggy Hanson, General Sales Mgr
Mardy Karger, News Director
Mary Campbell, CFO
Jack Hicks

KQKK
05-01-1999; 101.9 mhz FM *Hrs Open:* 5:30 AM-Midday; 50 kw; 390 ft.; N47 3 14 W94 15 32
P.O. Box 49, Hwy 34 East, Park Rapids, MN 56470 US
(218) 547-4000, *Fax:* (218) 547-4001
www.kkradionetwork.com
kqkkkakk@eot.com
License: Walker, Cass County, MN held by CJ Broadcasting.
Nat'l Network: CBS Radio *Wire Services:* AP
Format: Adult Contemp
Bradley Walhof, General Manager
Marcu Mitchell, News Director

Warroad

KKWQ
08-01-1989; 92.5 mhz FM *Hrs Open:* 24; 100 kw; 463 ft.; N48 49 41 W95 23 16
501 East Lake Street, Box 69, Warroad, MN 56763 US
(218) 386-3024, *Fax:* (218) 386-3090
www.kq92.com
info@kkwqfm.com
License: Warroad, Roseau County, MN held by Border Broadcasting LP
Nat'l Network: ABC; Jones Radio Networks *Regional Network:* Minn. News Net.
Arbitron Metro Market: Grand Forks, ND *Format:* Country *Target Audience:* 25-54. *Adv. Rates:* 24; 24; 24; 24
Mike Pederson, President

*KOLJ-FM
91.7 mhz FM; 0.25 kw; -230 ft.; N48 54 26 W95 18 58
US
(940) 663-5711, *Fax:* (940) 663-2125
www.radio1150.net
john@radio1150.net
License: Warroad, Roseau County, MN held by We Have This Hope Christian Radio Inc.
Arbitron Metro Market: Warroad, MN
Vern Erickson, President

Waseca

KRUE
12-22-1971; 1170 khz AM *Hrs Open:* 24; 2.5 kw-D, 60 w-N, 1 kw-CH; N44 02 45 W93 23 08 (D), N44 04 45 W93 30 24 (N)
255 Cedarale Dr. S.E., Owatonna, MN 58106
(507) 444-9224, *Fax:* (507) 444-9080
License: Waseca, Waseca County, MN held by Main Street Broadcasting Inc.
Group Owner: Linder Broadcasting Group; (acq 12-26-01; with co-located FM).
Regional Network: MNN
Population Served: 65,000*Hrs. of News Programming:* news progmg 12 hrs wkly *No. News Employees:* 2 *Target Audience:* 30-65; general, farm
Jeff Seaton, General Manager

KKOR
06-01-1972; 92.1 mhz FM *Hrs Open:* 24; 25 kw; 286 ft; N44 02 45 W93 23 08
58106
(507) 444-9224, *Fax:* (507) 444-9080
www.star92radio.com
License: Waseca, Waseca County, MN
Group Owner: Linder Broadcasting Group
Nat'l Network: ABC
Hrs. of News Programming: news progmg 4 hrs wkly *No. News Employees:* 1 *Target Audience:* 25-54.
Jeff Seaton, General Manager

Watertown

KPNP
05-16-1996; 1600 khz AM *Hrs Open:* 24; 5 kw-U, DA1; N44 55 23 W93 46 56
P.O. Box 1420, Mankato, MN 56001 US
(763) 585-1600
www.kpnp1600.com
peter@kpnp1600.com
License: Watertown, MN held by Self Retire Inc.
Arbitron Metro Market: Brooklyn Center, MN *Format:* Ethnic
Peter Phia Xiong, General Manager

Willmar

*KBHZ
02-16-1996; 91.9 mhz FM; 25 kw; 328 ft.; N45 0 40 W94 53 56
515 Pike Street East, Osakis, MN 56360 US
(320) 859-3000, *Fax:* (320) 859-3010
www.praisefm.org
mail@praisefm.org
License: Willmar, Kandiyohi County, MN held by Christian Heritage Broadcasting Inc.
Arbitron Metro Market: Osakis, MN *Format:* Religious
Dave Hartman, Operations Dir
David McIver, General Manager

KDJS
03-02-1981; 1590 khz AM *Hrs Open:* 24; 1 kw-D, 89 w-N, DA-2; N45 05 07 W95 00 19
Mailing Address: Box 380, Willmar, MN 56201
Second Address: 730 N.E. Hwy. 71, Willmar, MN 56201
(320) 231-1600, *Fax:* (320) 235-7010
www.k-musicradio.com
spots@k-musicradio.com
License: Willmar, Kandiyohi County, MN held by Iowa City Broadcasting Inc.
Population Served: 100,000*Special Programming:* Farm 5 hrs wkly *No. News Employees:* 1 *Target Audience:* 25-54. *Adv. Rates:* 10; 10; 10; 2
Doug Hanson, General Manager
Doug Hanson, General Sales Mgr
Rob Ryan, Programming Director
Bev Ahlquist, News Director
Steve Youngberg, Chief Engineer
Jeremy Goulet, Traffic Manager

KDJS-FM
05-17-1993; 95.3 mhz FM *Hrs Open:* 24; 50 kw; 436 ft; N45 01 23 W95 15 57
Mailing Address: Box 380, Willmar, MN 56201
Second Address: 730 N.E. Hwy. 71, Willmar, MN 56201
(320) 231-1600, *Fax:* (320) 235-7010
www.k-musicradio.com
spots@k-musicradio.com
License: Willmar, Kandiyohi County, MN held by Iowa City Broadcasting Inc.
Regional Reps: Tacher
Population Served: 100,000*No. News Employees:* 1
Doug Hanson, General Manager
Doug Hanson, General Sales Mgr
Bob Ryan, Programming Director
Bev Alquist, News Director
Steve Youngberg, Engineering Dir
Steve Youngberg, Chief Engineer

KQIC
07-01-1965; 102.5 mhz FM; 100 kw; 830 ft.; N45 11 40 W95 5 1
Mailing Address: P. O. Box 838, Willmar, MN 56201 US
Second Address: 1340 N. 7th St., Willmar, MN 56201
(320) 235-3535, *Fax:* (320) 235-1340
www.1025fm.com
License: Willmar, Kandiyohi County, MN
Format: Adult Contemp *Target Audience:* 18-49. *Adv. Rates:* 31.25; 30; 31.25; 25
MaryElin Macht, Programming Director

KWLM
01-01-1940; 1340 khz AM *Hrs Open:* 24; 1 kw-U, ND1; N45 8 0 W95 2 35
Mailing Address: P. O. Box 838, Willmar, MN 56201 US
Second Address: 1340 N. 7th St., Willmar, MN 56201
(320) 235-1340, *Fax:* (320) 235-9111
www.kwlm.com
askus@kwlm.com
License: Willmar, MN held by Steven W. Linder.
Regional Network: Linder Farm
Arbitron Metro Market: Willmar, MN *Format:* News, News/Talk, 86 *Special Programming:* Farm 8 hrs wkly *Hrs. of News Programming:* news progmg 30 hrs wkly *No. News Employees:* 3 *Target Audience:* General.*Adv. Rates:* 30.50; 29; 30.50; 24.50
Doug Loy, General Sales Mgr
J.P. Cola, News Director
Pete Hoagland, Chief Engineer
Mary Overman, Traffic Manager

*KKLW
01-29-2004; 90.9 mhz FM *Hrs Open:* 24; 0.4 kw; 423 ft.; N45 11 52 W94 56 58
1425 N. Market Blvd, Suite 9, Sacramento, CA 95834 US
(800) 525-5683, *Fax:* (916) 251-1650
www.klove.com
klove@klove.com
License: Willmar, Kandiyohi County, MN held by Educational Media Foundation.
Group Owner: EMF Broadcasting
Nat'l Network: K-Love
Arbitron Metro Market: Willmar, MN *Format:* Christian *No. News Employees:* 3 *Target Audience:* 25-44; Judeo Christian, female
Darrell Chambliss, Chairman
Mike Novak, President and CEO
John Clements, Operations Dir
David Pierce, Programming Director

Ed Lenane, News Director
Sam Wallington, Engineering Dir
Marya Morgan, News Reporter
Richard Hunt, NewsReporter
Laura Daniels, News Reporter
Tim Luttrell, News Reporter
Kenny Noble Cortes, News Reporter
Darren Vinson, News Reporter

Wilton

WBKK
820 khz AM; 15 kw-D, 750 w-N, DA-2; N47 23 29 W95 04 40
Box 49, Park Rapids, MN
(218) 732-3306
License: Wilton, Beltrami County, MN held by Bemidji Radio Inc
Edward De La Hunt Sr., General Manager

Windom

KDOM
12-28-1958; 1580 khz AM *Hrs Open:* 24; 1 kw-D, DA2; 0.002 kw-N, DA2; N43 51 41 W95 5 50
Box 218, Windom, MN 56101 US
(507) 831-3908, *Fax:* (507) 831-3913
www.kdomradio.com
kdomnew@windomnet.com
License: Windom, MN held by Windom Radio Inc.
Group Owner: The Result Radio Group; (acq 4-89; with co-located FM;
Regional Network: MNN
Arbitron Metro Market: Windom, MN *Format:* Country, News, 62, Sports, Talk *Hrs. of News Programming:* news progmg 21 hrs wkly *No. News Employees:* 1 *Target Audience:* General; farm audience, housewives, businessowners & laborers *Adv. Rates:* 31; 31; 27; 27
Dave Cory, General Manager
Judi Cory, General Sales Mgr
Dirk Abraham, News Director

KDOM-FM
12-08-1976; 94.3 mhz FM *Hrs Open:* 6 AM-midnight; 5.7 kw; 335 ft.; N43 53 6 W95 10 56
Box 218, Windom, MN 56101 US
(507) 831-3908, *Fax:* (507) 831-3913
www.kdomradio.com
kdomnew@windomnet.com
License: Windom, Cottonwood County, MN held by Windom Radio Inc.
Group Owner: The Result Radio Group
Arbitron Metro Market: Windom, MN *Format:* Country, News, 62, Sports, Talk *Adv. Rates:* 31; 31; 27; 27
Jo Bailey, Operations Dir
Dave Cory, General Manager
Judi Cory, General Sales Mgr

*KQRB
02-01-2003; 89.9 mhz FM; 0.25 kw; 171 ft.; N43 51 15 W95 7 30
88 Casey Jones Blvd., Jackson, TN 38305 US
(662) 844-8888, *Fax:* (662) 842-6791
www.afr.net
faq@afr.net
License: Windom, Winona County, MN held by American Family Association.
Group Owner: American Family Radio
Nat'l Network: USA
Arbitron Metro Market: Tupelo, MS *Format:* Christian
Roy Willoff, General Manager

*KJWR
01-01-2008; 90.9 mhz FM *Hrs Open:* 24; 25 kw; 328 ft.; N44 0 22 W95 12 9 *Rebroadcasts:* Rebroadcasts KJIA(FM) Spirit Lake, IA 100%
12089 380th Ave., P O Box 72, Blue Earth, MN 56013 US
(800) 810-5559, *Fax:* (712) 332-2428
www.kjwrradio.com
kjwr@kjwrradio.com
License: Windom, Cottonwood County, MN held by Minn-Iowa Christian Broadcasting Inc.
Group Owner: Minn-Iowa Christian Broadcasting Inc.
Arbitron Metro Market: Windom, MN *Format:* Christian
Eugene Stallkamp, President
Matt Dorfner, General Manager
Steve Ware, Programming Director
Mark Bohnett, Chief Engineer
Matt Dorfner, Executive Director
Doug Johnson, Program Coordinator

Winona

KAGE
02-17-1957; 1380 khz AM *Hrs Open:* Sunrise-sunset
P.O. Box 767, Winona, MN 55987 US
(507) 452-4000, *Fax:* (507) 452-9494
www.winonaradio.com
jpapenfuss@winonradio.com
License: Winona, MN held by KAGE Inc.
Group Owner: The Result Radio Group; (acq 1-73)
Wire Services: AP
Arbitron Metro Market: Winona, MN *Format:* Country *Special Programming:* Farm, relg *Hrs. of News Programming:* news progmg 7 hrs wkly *No. News Employees:* 1 *Target Audience:* 35 plus; general
Pat Papenfuss, President
Jerry Papenfuss, General Manager
Les Guderian, General Sales Mgr
Darryl Smelser, News Director
Steve Schuh, Chief Engineer
Paul Van Beck, Sports Commentator

KAGE-FM
08-14-1971; 95.3 mhz FM *Hrs Open:* 24; 11 kw; 495 ft.; N44 2 31 W91 40 47
Box 767, Winona, MN 55987 US
(507) 452-4000, *Fax:* (507) 452-9494
www.winonaradio.com
jristow@winonaradio.com
License: Winona, Winona County, MN held by KAGE Inc.
Group Owner: The Result Radio Group
Wire Services: AP
Arbitron Metro Market: Winona, MN *Format:* Adult Contemp *Hrs. of News Programming:* news progmg 14 hrs wkly *No. News Employees:* 1 *Target Audience:* 25-54.
Jerry Papenfuss, CEO
Aaron Taylor, Programming Director

KHME
06-04-1992; 101.1 mhz FM *Hrs Open:* 24; 5 kw; 741 ft.; N44 4 26 W91 34 38
Mailing Address: 980 North Michigan Ave., Suite 1880, Chicago, IL 60611 US
Second Address: 752 Bluffview Cir., Winona, MN 55987
(507) 452-4000, *Fax:* (507) 452-9494
www.winonaradio.com
jristow@winonaradio.com
License: Winona, Winona County, MN held by KAGE Inc.
Group Owner: The Result Radio Group; (acq 10-19-01; $1 million).
Wire Services: AP
Format: Classic Rock *Hrs. of News Programming:* news progmg 20 hrs wkly *No. News Employees:* 2 *Target Audience:* 25-54; women
Pat Papenfuss, Operations Dir
Jerry Papenfuss, General Manager
Les Guderian, General Sales Mgr

*KQAL
12-12-1975; 89.5 mhz FM *Hrs Open:* 24; 2.5 kw; 690 ft.; N44 4 26 W91 34 38
Mailing Address: P.O. Box 5838, Winona, MN 55987 US
Second Address: 175 W. Mark St., Winona, MN 55987
(507) 453-2222, *Fax:* (507) 457-5226
www.kqal.org
kqal@kqal.org
License: Winona, Winona County, MN held by Winona State University.
Nat'l Network: AP Radio *Wire Services:* AP
Format: Variety/Diverse *Special Programming:* Class 14 hrs, pub affrs 10 hrs wkly *Hrs. of News Programming:* News progmg 5 hrs wkly *Target Audience:* General.
Mike Martin, Operations Dir
Mike Martin, General Manager
Doug Westerman, General Sales Mgr
Teri Tenseth, Programming Director
Nate Siems, News Director

*KSMR
11-01-1978; 92.5 mhz FM; 0.004 kw; -141 ft.; N44 2 47 W91 41 43
700 Terrace Heights, Box 29, Winona, MN 55987 US
(507) 457-1613, *Fax:* (507) 457-1439
www.smumn.edu
info@ksmr.com
License: Winona, Winona County, MN held by St. Mary's University
Arbitron Metro Market: Winona, MN *Format:* Rock/AOR *Target Audience:* 18-24.
Dean Beckman, General Manager

KWNO
01-01-1938; 1230 khz AM *Hrs Open:* 24
216 Center Street, Winona, MN 55987 US
(507) 452-4000; (800) 584-6782, *Fax:* (507) 452-9494
www.winonaradio.com
jristow@winonaradio.com
License: Winona, MN held by KAGE Inc.
Group Owner: The Result Radio Group; (acq 6-19-95; $1 million with KWNO-FM Rushford)
Regional Network: MNN *Wire Services:* AP
Arbitron Metro Market: Winona, MN *Format:* News, News/Talk, 64, Sports, Talk *Special Programming:* Polka 5 hrs wkly *Hrs. of News Programming:* news progmg 21 hrs wkly *No. News Employees:* 1 *Target Audience:* 35 plus; Sports fans
Pat Papenfuss, Chairman
Jerry Papenfuss, CEO

Winthrop

KHRS
07-01-2008; 105.9 mhz FM; 23 kw; 344 ft.; N44 28 25 W94 28 15
Rebroadcasts: Simulcast with KXLP(FM) Eagle Lake 100% US
(507) 345-4537, *Fax:* (507) 345-5364
License: Winthrop, Sibley County, MN held by Ketelsen Radio Inc.
Arbitron Metro Market: Winthrop, MN *Format:* Classic Rock
Jo Bailey, Operations Dir

Worthington

KITN
11-01-1994; 93.5 mhz FM *Hrs Open:* 24; 50 kw; 466 ft.; N43 31 31 W95 24 47
P.O. Box 1420, Mankato, MN 56001 US
(507) 376-6165, *Fax:* (507) 376-5071
www.935thebreeze.com
contactus@935thebreeze.com
License: Worthington, Nobles County, MN held by Three Eagles of Luverne Inc.
Group Owner: Three Eagles Communications; (acq 12-23-99; grpsl)
Regional Network: MNN
Format: Adult Contemp
Gary Buchanan, CFO
Tom Mulso, General Manager
Jerry Mason, Programming Director
Darrell Stitt, News Director
Bob Cook, Chief Engineer

*KRSW
12-01-1973; 89.3 mhz FM; 100 kw; 554 ft.; N43 53 1 W95 55 44
45 East Seventh Street, Saint Paul, MN 55101 US
(605) 335-6666(651) 290-1259, *Fax:* (605) 335-1259
License: Worthington, Nobles County, MN held by Minnesota Public Radio Inc.
Nat'l Network: PRI; NPR
Arbitron Metro Market: St.Paul,MN *Format:* Talk
William Kling, President

KWOA
10-11-1947; 730 khz AM *Hrs Open:* 24; 1 kw-D, ND1; 0.159 kw-N, ND1; N43 37 48 W95 40 32
1077 Meadow Lane, Fond Du Lac, WI 54935 US
(507) 376-6165, *Fax:* (507) 376-5071
www.kwoa.com
contactus@935thebreeze.com
License: Worthington, MN held by Three Eagles of Luverne Inc.
Group Owner: Three Eagles Communications; (acq 12-23-99; grpsl)
Nat'l Network: CBS; Fox Sports *Nat'l Reps:* Hyett/Ramsland
Regional Reps: Midwest Radio.
Arbitron Metro Market: Worthington, MN *Format:* News, News/Talk, 86 *Special Programming:* Farm *Hrs. of News Programming:* news progmg 18 hrs wkly *No. News Employees:* 2 *Target Audience:* 35 plus.
Jerry Mason, Operations Dir
Tom Mulso, General Manager
Tony Winter, Programming Director
Darrell Stitt, News Director

KUSQ-FM
05-03-1961; 95.1 mhz FM *Hrs Open:* 20; 100 kw; Ant 660 ft; N43 37 48 W95 40 32
28779 County Hwy. 35, Worthington, MN 56187
(507) 376-6165, *Fax:* (507) 376-5071
951theeagle.com
contactus@935thebreeze.com
License: Worthington, Nobles County, MN
Group Owner: Three Eagles Communications
Population Served: 103,500*Hrs. of News Programming:* news progmg 10 hrs wkly *No. News Employees:* 1
Jay Kelly, Programming Director
Tony Winter, Music Director

KUSQ
01-01-2008; 95.1 mhz FM; 100 kw; 650 ft.; N43 37 48 W95 40 32
1077 Meadow Lane, Fond Du Lac, WI 54935 US
(507) 376-6165, *Fax:* (507) 376-5071
www.951theeagle.com
contactus@951theeagle.com
License: Worthington, Osceola County, MN held by Absolute Communications L.L.C.
Arbitron Metro Market: Worthington, MN *Format:* Christian
Todd Mejia, General Manager

Worthington-Marshall

***KNSW**
01-01-1979; 91.7 mhz FM; 99 kw; 797 ft.; N43 53 1 W95 55 44
45 East Seventh Street, St. Paul, MN 55101 US
(651) 290-1500, *Fax:* (651) 290-1224
www.mpr.org
newsroom@mpr.org
License: Worthington-Marshall, Nobles County, MN held by Minnesota Public Radio.
Arbitron Metro Market: Worthington, MN *Format:* News, News/Talk, 86
Ian R Friendly, Chairman
Jon McTaggart, President
William Kling, General Manager

Mississippi

Aberdeen

WWZQ
02-01-1952; 1240 khz AM; 1 kw-U, ND1; N33 48 32 W88 32 33
402 S. Matubba Street, Aberdeen, MI 39730 US
(662) 256-9726, *Fax:* (662) 256-9725
www.fm95radio.com
fm95@fm95radio.com
License: Aberdeen, MS held by Stanford Communications Inc.
Group Owner: Stanford Communications Inc.; acq 12-2-99; $51,000)
Nat'l Network: USA
Arbitron Metro Market: Tupelo, MS *Format:* Oldies *Special Programming:* Gospel 8 hrs wkly
Ed Stanford, General Manager

Ackerman

WFCA
01-01-1986; 107.9 mhz FM *Hrs Open:* 24; 100 kw; 1,007 ft; N33 25 25 W89 24 13
40 Mecklin Ave., French Camp, MS 39745
(662) 547-6414, *Fax:* (662) 547-9451
www.wfcafm108.com
sales@wfcafm108.com
License: Ackerman, Choctaw County, MS held by French Camp Radio Inc.
Regional Network: Miss. News Net.
Target Audience: General.
Carol Prewiit, Operations Dir
Charles Carroll, Station Manager
H Glen Barlow, General Sales Mgr
Ron Linkins, Programming Director

Amory

WAFM
01-01-1974; 95.7 mhz FM *Hrs Open:* 24; 6 kw; 274 ft.; N33 58 33 W88 29 29
Mailing Address: P.O. Box 458, Amory, MS 38821 US
Second Address: 521 Hwy.278 W., Amory, MS 38821
(662) 256-9726, *Fax:* (662) 256-9725
www.fm95radio.com
fm95@fm95radio.com
License: Amory, Monroe County, MS held by Stanford Communications Inc.
Group Owner: Stanford Communications Inc.; 9/21/1992
Nat'l Network: ABC
Arbitron Metro Market: Amory-Monroe County, MS *Format:* Oldies *Special Programming:* Relg 2 hrs wkly
Ed Stanford, General Manager
Ken Wardlaw, Programming Director
Clara Kennedy, News Director
Olen Booth, Engineering Dir

WAMY
10-23-1955; 1580 khz AM *Hrs Open:* 6 AM-10PM; 1 kw-D, ND1; 0.018 kw-N, ND1; N33 58 33 W88 29 29 *Rebroadcasts:* Rebroadcasts WWZQ(AM) Aberdeen 75%
Mailing Address: P.O. Box 458, Amory, MS 38821 US
Second Address: 521 Hwy.278 W., Amory, MS 38821
(662) 256-9726, *Fax:* (662) 256-9725
fm95radio.com
fm95radio@fm95radio.com
License: Amory, MS held by Stanford Communications Inc.
Group Owner: Stanford Communications Inc.; acq 9-21-92; $85,000 with co-located FM;
Nat'l Network: USA
Arbitron Metro Market: Tupelo, MS *Format:* News, Sports, 86
Special Programming: Relg 6 hrs, Gospel 6 hrs wkly *No. News Employees:* 1 *Target Audience:* Genral.
Ed Stanford, CEO
Teresa Stanford, Operations Dir
Olen Booth, Chief Engineer
Ken Wardlaw, Operations Manager
Clara Kennedy, Traffic Manager

Artesia

WSMS
01-01-1985; 99.9 mhz FM *Hrs Open:* 24; 47 kw; 505 ft.; N33 39 14 W88 37 15
P.O Box 8950, Columbus, MS 39701 US
(662) 327-1183, *Fax:* (662) 654-6510
www.999thefoxrocks.com
info@999thefoxrocks.com
License: Artesia, Lowndes County, MS held by Cumulus Licensing Corp.
Group Owner: Cumulus Media Inc.; (acq 9-99; grpsl).
Arbitron Metro Market: Artesia, MS *Format:* Rock/AOR *Target Audience:* 18-49.
Cole Evans, General Sales Mgr
C. S. Jones, Promotions Manager

Baldwyn

WESE
10-01-1980; 92.5 mhz FM *Hrs Open:* 24; 12 kw; 472 ft.; N34 21 46 W88 35 28
Mailing Address: 111 East Kilbourn Avenue, Suite 2700, Milwaukee, WI 53202 US
Second Address: 5026 Cliff Gookin Blvd., Tupelo, MS 38801
(601) 842-1067, *Fax:* (601) 842-0725
www.925jamz.com
License: Baldwyn, Lee County, MS held by Clear Channel Broadcasting Licenses Inc.
Group Owner: Clear Channel Communications Inc.; (acq 12-19-2000; grpsl)
Nat'l Network: ABC *Nat'l Reps:* Interep
Arbitron Metro Market: Baldwyn, MS *Format:* Urban Contemporary *Special Programming:* Gospel 6 hrs, Blues 6 hrs wkly *Target Audience:* 18-54.
Rick Stevens, Operations Dir
Mark Maharrey, General Manager

Batesville

WBLE
08-01-1978; 100.5 mhz FM; 50 kw; 492 ft.; N34 22 44 W89 45 57
P.O. Box 1528, Batesville, MS 38606 US
(662) 563-4664, *Fax:* (662) 563-9002
www.wble101.com/
advertising@wble101.com
License: Batesville, Panola County, MS held by Batesville Broadcasting Co. Inc.
Arbitron Metro Market: Batesville, MS *Format:* Country *Target Audience:* 25 plus.
J. Boyd Ingram, General Manager

WJBI
06-19-1953; 1290 khz AM; 0.73 kw-D, ND1; 0.091 kw-N, ND1; N34 18 13 W89 58 59
P. O. Box 1528, Batesville, MS 38606 US
(662) 563-1290, *Fax:* (662) 563-9002
License: Batesville, MS held by Batesville Broadcasting Co. Inc.
Format: Adult Contemp *Target Audience:* 30 plus.
J. Boyd Ingram, General Manager

Bay Springs

WIZK
1570 khz AM *Hrs Open:* 12; 3.2 kw-D, NDD; N31 57 56 W89 18 3
645 Church Street, Suite 400, Norfolk, VA 23510 US
(601) 764-9888, *Fax:* (601) 764-9887
mitchhughey@hughes.net
License: Bay Springs, MS held by M. Jerome Hughey
Arbitron Metro Market: Laurel-Hattiesburg, MS *Format:* Country *Target Audience:* 25-54; baby boomers & older consumers *Adv. Rates:* 25; 20; 25; na
Mitchell Hughey, CEO
Tom Diaz, Chief Engineer

Bay St. Louis

WZKX
02-14-1966; 107.9 mhz FM; 100 kw; 1526 ft.; N30 45 5 W89 3 24
PO Box 2639, Gulfport, MS 39505 US
(228) 896-5500, *Fax:* (228) 896-0458
www.kicker108.com
rhodes@kicker108.com
License: Bay St. Louis, Hancock County, MS
Arbitron Metro Market: Bay Saint Louis, MS *Format:* Country
Morgan Dowdy, General Manager
Steve Spillmann, General Sales Mgr
Dennis Warren, Local Sales Manager
Bryan Rhodes, Operations Manager

Belzoni

WBYP
01-01-1986; 107.1 mhz FM *Hrs Open:* 24; 9.4 kw; 531 ft.; N33 3 4 W90 37 51
Mailing Address: P.O. Box 130, Yazoo City, MS 39194 US
Second Address: 611 Center Park Ln., Yazoo City, MS 39194
(662) 746-7676, *Fax:* (662) 746-1525
www.power107.org
power107@power107.org
License: Belzoni, Humphreys County, MS held by Zoo-Bel Broadcasting LLC.
Nat'l Network: ABC *Regional Network:* Miss. News Net. *Nat'l Reps:* Rgnl Reps
Arbitron Metro Market: Yazoo City, MS *Format:* Country, Gospel
Hrs. of News Programming: news progmg 18 hrs wkly *No. News Employees:* 3 *Target Audience:* 18-65; Adults
Colon Johnston, General Manager
Brenda Johnston, News Director

WELZ
01-01-1959; 1460 khz AM; 1 kw-D, NDD; N33 10 24 W90 28 51
Mailing Address: 8 Southwood Blvd., Clinton, MS 39056 US
Second Address: 204 Church St., Belzoni, MS 39038
(662) 746-7676, *Fax:* (662) 746-1525
www.power107.org
power107@power107.org
License: Belzoni, MS held by Zoo-Bel Broadcasting LLC.
Regional Network: Miss. News Net.
Arbitron Metro Market: Belzoni, MS *Format:* Black, Blues, 44 *Hrs. of News Programming:* 5 Hours Per Week *No. News Employees:* 1 *Target Audience:* 25 - 65
Colon Johnston, General Manager

Benton

WXTN
10-23-1959; 1000 khz AM
100 Radio Rd., PO Box 369, Lexington, MS 39095 US
(662) 834-1025, *Fax:* (662) 834-1254
class102@cablesouthmedia.net
License: Benton, MS held by Brad Maurice Cothran
Arbitron Metro Market: Lexington, MS *Format:* Christian, Gospel
Brad Cothran, General Manager

***WYAD**
88.3 mhz FM; 0.1 kw; 33 ft.; N32 50 37 W90 14 26
US
(662) 571-2987
License: Benton, Yazoo County, MS held by Bountiful Blessings Broadcasting Inc.
Arbitron Metro Market: Benton, MS
Joseph Thomas, General Manager

Bentonia

***WJNS-FM**
12-13-1968; 92.1 mhz FM; 4.8 kw; 365 ft.; N32 33 25 W90 20 14
645 Church St, Ste 400, Norfolk, VA 23510 US
(662) 746-5921, *Fax:* (662) 746-5996
License: Bentonia, Yazoo County, MS held by Family Worship Center Church Inc.
Group Owner: Family Worship Center Church Inc.; acq 6-16-2004; $350,000).
Format: Religious *Special Programming:* Farm 16 hrs, weather 16 hrs wkly *Target Audience:* 25-54.
Bruce Grassman, President
Keith Huotari, Operations Dir
Trisha Peterson, General Manager
Aaron Harper, News Director
Walt Baldwin, Chief Engineer

Biloxi

***WMAH-FM**
12-01-1983; 90.3 mhz FM *Hrs Open:* 24; 100 kw; 1414 ft.; N30 45 18 W88 56 44

3825 Ridgewood Road, Jackson, MS 39211 US
(601) 432-6565, *Fax:* (601) 432-6806
www.mpbonline.org
License: Biloxi, Harrison County, MS held by Mississippi Authority for Educational Television.
Nat'l Network: PRI; NPR *Wire Services:* AP
Arbitron Metro Market: Biloxi, MI *TV Affiliate:* WMAH-TV *Format:* News *Hrs. of News Programming:* news progmg 100 hrs wkly *No. News Employees:* 7 *Target Audience:* General.
Jason Klein, Operations Dir
Jay Woods, General Manager
Ty Warren, General Sales Mgr
Mari Irby, Promotions Manager
Teresa Colier, News Director
Bob Buie, Engineering Dir
Karen Hearn, Music Director
Beverly Belding, RegionalSales Manager
LaSharne Patton, Traffic Manager

WMJY
07-11-1966; 93.7 mhz FM *Hrs Open:* 24; 100 kw horiz, 98.3 kw vert; 984 ft.; N30 29 9 W88 42 53
600 Congress Ave., Suite 1400, Austin, TX 78701 US
(228) 388-2323, *Fax:* (228) 388-2362
www.magic937.com
reggiebates@clearchannel.com
License: Biloxi, Harrison County, MS held by CC Licenses LLC.
Group Owner: Clear Channel Communications Inc.; (acq 2-2-2004; grpsl).
Nat'l Reps: Clear Channel *Wire Services:* AP
Arbitron Metro Market: Biloxi, MS *Format:* Adult Contemp *Hrs. of News Programming:* news progmg 5 hrs wkly *No. News Employees:* 1 *Target Audience:* 25-54.
Reggie Bates, General Manager
Richard Hinshaw, General Sales Mgr
Walter Brown, Programming Director
Kristan Saucier, Promotions Manager

WXBD
05-01-1948; 1490 khz AM *Hrs Open:* 24; 1 kw-U, ND1; N30 23 38 W88 59 58
2511 Garden Road, Building A, Suite 104, Monterey, CA 93940 US
(228) 388-2001, *Fax:* (228) 896-9736
wxbd@sportsradiowxbd.com
License: Biloxi, MS held by Monterey Licenses LLC.
Group Owner: Triad Broadcasting Co. L.L.C.; (acq 6-30-99; grpsl)
Arbitron Metro Market: Biloxi, MS *Format:* Sports
Jay Taylor, Operations Dir

WTNI
01-01-2003; 1640 khz AM
100 22nd Ave., South, Ste A, Meridian, MS 39301 US
(228) 388-2001, *Fax:* (228) 896-9736
www.967thechamp.com
License: Biloxi, MS held by Monterey Licenses LLC.
Group Owner: Triad Broadcasting Co. L.L.C.; (acq 5-16-00).
Nat'l Network: ABC *Wire Services:* AP
Arbitron Metro Market: Gulfport, MS *Format:* News, News/Talk, 86
Steve Fehder, General Manager

Booneville

WBIP
09-01-1950; 1400 khz AM *Hrs Open:* 24; 1 kw-U; N34 38 21 W88 34 33
Mailing Address: Box 356, Booneville, MS 38829
Second Address: 1100 So. Second St., Booneville, MS 38829-2572
(662) 728-0200, *Fax:* (662) 728-2572
WBIPAM@YAHOO.COM
License: Booneville, Prentiss County, MS held by Community Broadcasting Services of Mississippi Inc
Regional Network: Miss. News Net.
Population Served: 50,000 *Arbitron Metro Market:* Tupelo, MS *Hrs. of News Programming:* News progmg 7 hrs wkly *Target Audience:* 24-54. *Adv. Rates:* 5; 5; 5; 5
Larry Melton, President
Jerry Thornton, Operations Dir
Larry Hill, General Manager
Marty Williams, Station Manager

***WMAE-FM**
12-01-1983; 89.5 mhz FM *Hrs Open:* 24; 85 kw; 653 ft.; N34 40 0 W88 45 5
3825 Ridgewood Road, Jackson, MS 39211 US
(601) 432-6565, *Fax:* (601) 432-6806
www.mpbonline.org
License: Booneville, Prentiss County, MS held by Mississippi Authority for Educational Television.
Nat'l Network: PRI; NPR *Wire Services:* AP
Arbitron Metro Market: Tupelo, MS *TV Affiliate:* WMAE-TV *Format:* News *Hrs. of News Programming:* news progmg 100 hrs wkly *No. News Employees:* 7 *Target Audience:* General.
Jason Klein, Operations Dir
Jay Woods, General Manager
Marie Antoon, General Sales Mgr

Brandon

WRBJ-FM
12-01-1974; 97.7 mhz FM *Hrs Open:* 24; 6 kw; 328 ft.; N32 10 31 W89 56 10
P.O. Box 145, Brandon, MS 39043 US
(601) 974-5700, *Fax:* (601) 974-5711
www.cw34jackson.com/997fm
License: Brandon, Rankin County, MS held by Roberts Radio Broadcasting LLC
Arbitron Metro Market: Jackson, MS *Format:* Urban Contemporary *Target Audience:* 18-34.
Keith Smith, General Manager

WFQY
06-01-1967; 970 khz AM; 1 kw-D, DA; N32 17 20 W89 59 50
209 Commerce Dr., Suite D, Brandon, MS 39043
(601) 825-2970, *Fax:* (601) 825-0339
www.thefan970.com
License: Brandon, Rankin County, MS held by Jackson Radio LLC
Population Served: 500,000 *Arbitron Metro Market:* Jackson, MS
Max Howell, General Manager

Brookhaven

WBKN
07-29-1976; 92.1 mhz FM *Hrs Open:* 24; 3.4 kw; 302 ft.; N31 33 48 W90 26 27
Mailing Address: P.O. Box 711, Brookhaven, MS 39601 US
Second Address: 911 Hwy. 550, Brookhaven, MS 39602
(601) 833-9210, *Fax:* (601) 833-6221
brookhavenbroadcast@yahoo.com
License: Brookhaven, Lincoln County, MS held by Brookhaven Broadcasting Inc.
Regional Network: Miss. News Net.
Arbitron Metro Market: Brookhaven, MS *Format:* Country *Special Programming:* Gospel 3 hrs wkly *Hrs. of News Programming:* News progmg 5 hrs wkly *Target Audience:* 25-54. *Adv. Rates:* 13.85; 13.85; 13.85;13.85
C. Wayne Dowdy, President
Tyler Bridge, Operations Dir
Ken Hollingsworth, General Manager
Robbie Hamilton, General Sales Mgr
Gaye Laird, Programming Director
Jamey Lambert, Min Affairs Director

WCHJ
08-15-1955; 1470 khz AM *Hrs Open:* 24 hrs
Mailing Address: 210 West Corut St., Brookhaven, MS 39601 US
Second Address: 983 Sawmill Ln., Brookhaven, MS 39601
(601) 823-9006, *Fax:* (601) 823-0503
www.victory1470wchj.com
victory1470wchj@birch.net
License: Brookhaven, MS held by Tillman Broadcasting Network Inc.
Nat'l Network: USA
Arbitron Metro Market: Brookhaven, MS *Format:* Black, Gospel *Hrs. of News Programming:* News progmg one hr wkly *Target Audience:* 25-54. *Adv. Rates:* 10; 10; 10; 10 (60 sec spot)
Charles Tillman, CEO
Joe Segura, Assistant Operations Director

Brooksville

WAJV
08-01-1995; 98.9 mhz FM *Hrs Open:* 24; 5.8 kw; 676 ft.; N33 20 40 W88 32 47
P.O. Box 707, Columbus, MS 39703 US
(662) 338-5424, *Fax:* (662) 338-5436
www.joy989.com
wmsuproduction@urbanradio.fm
License: Brooksville, Noxubee County, MS held by Urban Radio Licenses LLC
Group Owner: Urban Radio Licenses LLC; (acq 4-20-2001).
Arbitron Metro Market: Columbus, MS *Format:* Gospel *Hrs. of News Programming:* News progmg 14 hrs wkly *Target Audience:* General.
Kevin Wagner, President
James Alexander, Operations Dir
Ron Davis, Programming Director

Bude

***WMAU-FM**
12-01-1983; 88.9 mhz FM *Hrs Open:* 24; 100 kw; 961 ft.; N31 22 22 W90 45 4
3825 Ridgewood Road, Jackson, MS 39211 US
(601) 432-6565, *Fax:* (601) 432-6806
www.mpbonline.org
License: Bude, Franklin County, MS held by Mississippi Authority for Educational Television.
Nat'l Network: NPR; PRI *Wire Services:* AP
Arbitron Metro Market: Bude, MS *TV Affiliate:* WMAU-TV *Format:* News *Hrs. of News Programming:* news progmg 100 hrs wkly *No. News Employees:* 7 *Target Audience:* General.
Jason Klein, Operations Dir
Jay Woods, General Manager
Marie Antoon, General Sales Mgr

WMJU
08-30-1999; 104.3 mhz FM *Hrs Open:* 24; 25 kw; 328 ft.; N31 33 33 W90 40 26
Mailing Address: D-3, 736 N. Jackson Street, Brookhaven, MS 39601 US
Second Address: 911 Hwy. 550, Brookhaven, MS 39601
(601) 833-9210, *Fax:* (601) 833-6221
brookhavenbroadcast@yahoo.com
License: Bude, Franklin County, MS held by Brookhaven Broadcasting Inc.
Arbitron Metro Market: Bude, MS *Format:* Adult Contemp *Hrs. of News Programming:* news progmg 10 hrs wkly *No. News Employees:* 1 *Target Audience:* 25-49; adults who are middle income & above
C. Wayne Dowdy, President
Ken Hollingsworth, General Manager
Robbie Hamilton, General Sales Mgr
Gaye Laird, Programming Director

Burnsville

***WOWL**
01-01-2000; 91.9 mhz FM; 18 kw; 548 ft.; N34 55 47 W88 24 37
#17 County Road 404, Luka, MS 38852 US
(662) 423-9919, *Fax:* (662) 423-9333
License: Burnsville, Tishomingo County, MS held by Southern Community Services Inc.
Nat'l Reps: Rgnl Reps
Format: Adult Contemp
Derrick Robinson, General Manager

Byhalia

***WMSB**
01-04-1971; 88.9 mhz FM *Hrs Open:* 24; 52 kw vert; 476 ft.; N34 39 30 W89 37 32
P.O. Box 241880, Memphis, TN 38124 US
(662) 844-5036, *Fax:* (662) 842-7798
www.afr.net
info@afa.net
License: Byhalia, Tate County, MS held by American Family Association.
Group Owner: American Family Radio; (acq 4-13-2007; $2 million)
Nat'l Network: American Family Radio
Format: Christian
Donald Wildmon, Chairman

Canton

WMGO
12-09-1954; 1370 khz AM *Hrs Open:* 24; 1 kw-D, ND1; 0.028 kw-N, ND1; N32 37 36 W90 1 47
360 North Liberty Street, Canton, MS 39046 US
(601) 859-2373, *Fax:* (601) 859-2664
www.wmgoradio.com
admin@wmgo.com
License: Canton, MS held by WMGO Broadcasting Corp. Inc.
Regional Network: Miss. News Net.
Arbitron Metro Market: Jackson, MS *Format:* Variety/Diverse *Hrs. of News Programming:* news progmg 12 hrs wkly *No. News Employees:* 1 *Target Audience:* 25-54; upscale & involved adults *Adv. Rates:* 14.50;9.50; 10.50; 3.50
Jerry Lousteau, President
John Woods, Programming Director

WONG
04-01-1989; 1150 khz AM; 0.5 kw-D, ND1; 0.019 kw-N, ND1; N32 32 35 W90 3 36
111 Reece Park Lane, Tallahassee, FL 32301 US
(601) 855-2035, *Fax:* (601) 855-2094
wong1150am@cs.com
License: Canton, MS held by Marion R. Williams.
Group Owner: Marion R. Williams Stns; (acq 7-26-99; $50,000)

Nat'l Network: American Urban
Arbitron Metro Market: Jackson, MS *TV Affiliate:* Gospel, blues
No. News Employees: 25 plus.

Carthage

WKOZ-FM
04-01-1979; 98.3 mhz FM; 20 kw; Ant 328 ft; N32 43 29 W89 32 44
Mailing Address: Box 1700, Kosciusko, MS 39051
Second Address: 1 Golf Course Rd., Kosciusko, MS 39039
(662) 289-1340, *Fax:* (662) 289-7907
www.kicks98.com
info@kicks98.com
License: Carthage, Leake County, MS held by Johnny Boswell Radio LLC
Nat'l Network: USA *Wire Services:* NOAA Weather
Johnny Boswell, CEO
Eric Matthews, Operations Dir
Lora Bain, General Manager

Centreville

*WPAE
01-01-1997; 89.7 mhz FM *Hrs Open:* 24; 70 kw; 298 ft; N31 05 56 W91 02 27 *Rebroadcasts:* Rebroadcasts KPAE(FM) Erwinville, L
Mailing Address: Box 1390, Centreville, MS 70767
Second Address: 122 E. Main St., Centreville, MS 39631
(601) 645-6515, *Fax:* (601) 645-9122
License: Centreville, Amite County, MS held by Port Allen Educational Broadcasting Foundation.
Nat'l Network: Moody
Population Served: 1,000,000*Special Programming:* Children 5 hrs, Gospel 15 hrs wkly *Adv. Rates:* none
Willie Kennedy, General Manager
Willie Kennedy, Station Manager
Willie Kennedy, Programming Director
Willie Kennedy, Promotions Manager
Bo Hoover, Chief Engineer

WKJN
11-21-1977; 104.9 mhz FM; 3 kw; 299 ft.; N31 6 7 W91 2 27
215 East Bay Street, Magnolia, MS 39652 US
(601) 684-4116, *Fax:* (601) 684-4654
License: Centreville, Amite County, MS held by Southwest Broadcasting.
Group Owner: Southwest Broadcasting Inc.
Arbitron Metro Market: Centreville, MS *Format:* Country
Charles Dowdy, General Manager

Charleston

*WTGY
04-01-1986; 95.7 mhz FM *Hrs Open:* 18; 6 kw; 328 ft.; N33 53 28 W90 3 9
PO Box 9, Charleston, MS 38921 US
(225) 768-8300, *Fax:* (225) 768-3729
sonlifetv.com
License: Charleston, Tallahatchie County, MS held by Family Worship Center Church Inc.
Group Owner: Family Worship Center Church Inc.; acq 7-15-02; $300,000).
Arbitron Metro Market: Charleston, MS *Format:* Religious
David Whitelaw, COO
Jimmy Swaggart, President
John Santiago, Programming Director

Clarksdale

WAID
07-01-1978; 106.5 mhz FM *Hrs Open:* 24; 50 kw; 295 ft.; N34 9 22 W90 37 52
P.O. Box 780, Cleveland, MS 38732 US
(662) 627-2281, *Fax:* (662) 624-2900
www.missradio.com
License: Clarksdale, Coahoma County, MS held by Radio Cleveland Inc.
Group Owner: Radio Cleveland Inc.; acq 8-2-83; $185,000;
Nat'l Network: USA
Arbitron Metro Market: Cleveland, MS *Format:* Urban Contemporary *Hrs. of News Programming:* news progmg 2 hrs wkly *No. News Employees:* 1 *Target Audience:* General.
Clint Webster, General Manager
Greg Shurden, General Sales Mgr
Jim Thomas, Programming Director
Houston McDavid, Chief Engineer

WKDJ-FM
11-01-1988; 96.5 mhz FM; 6 kw; 328 ft.; N34 9 22 W90 37 52
P.O. Box 780, Cleveland, MS 38732 US
(662) 627-2281, *Fax:* (662) 624-2900
www.missradio.com
License: Clarksdale, Coahoma County, MS held by Clint Webster.
Format: Country *Target Audience:* 25-55.
Clint Webster, General Manager
Greg Shurden, Station Manager
Jim Thomas, Programming Director

WROX
01-01-1944; 1450 khz AM *Hrs Open:* 24; 1 kw-U; N34 12 40 W90 34 42
628 Desoto Avenue, Clarksdale, MS 38732
(662) 627-1450, *Fax:* (662) 621-1176
License: Clarksdale, Coahoma County, MS held by LL James Medua LLC
Group Owner: Contemporary Communications
Population Served: 65,000*Special Programming:* Blues Saturday nights *Hrs. of News Programming:* news progmg 3 hrs wkly *No. News Employees:* 1 *Target Audience:* General *Adv. Rates:* 6; 5; 5.50; 4.50
Paul Wilson, Co-Owner
Bobbie Wilson, Co-Owner

Cleveland

WCLD
01-01-1949; 1490 khz AM *Hrs Open:* 24; 1 kw-U, ND1; N33 44 1 W90 42 50
Mailing Address: P.O. Box 780, Cleveland, MS 38732 US
Second Address: Drawer 780, Cleveland, MS
(601)843-4091, *Fax:* (601)843-9805
www.missradio.com
wcld@tecinfo.com
License: Cleveland, MS held by Radio Cleveland Inc.
Group Owner: Radio Cleveland Inc.; acq 1957)
Arbitron Metro Market: Cleveland, MS *Format:* Black, Gospel
Target Audience: 18 plus.
Jim Thomas, Operations Dir
Clint Webster, General Manager
Kevin Cox, General Sales Mgr
Houston McDavitt, Chief Engineer
Vicky Lowry, Traffic Manager

WCLD-FM
01-01-1972; 103.9 mhz FM *Hrs Open:* 24; 24.5 kw; 315 ft.; N33 44 1 W90 42 50
Mailing Address: P. O. Box 780, Cleveland, MS 38732 US
Second Address: Drawer 780, Cleveland, MS 38732
(601)843-4091, *Fax:* (601)843-9805
www.missradio.com
License: Cleveland, Bolivar County, MS
Arbitron Metro Market: Cleveland, MS *Format:* Urban Contemporary *Target Audience:* 18 plus.
Vicky Lowry, News Director

*WDFX
01-01-1993; 98.3 mhz FM; 25 kw; 328 ft.; N33 52 47 W90 42 32
P.O. Box 2440, Tupelo, MS 38803 US
(662) 844-8888, *Fax:* (662) 840-3187
www.afr.net
faq@afr.net
License: Cleveland, Bolivar County, MS held by American Family Association Inc.
Nat'l Network: USA
Arbitron Metro Market: Cleveland, MS *Format:* Christian
Don Wildman, General Manager

Clinton

WHJT
01-01-1974; 93.5 mhz FM *Hrs Open:* 24; 6 kw; 328 ft.; N32 20 15 W90 19 47
Mailing Address: 100 S. Jefferson Street, Clinton, MS 39058 US
Second Address: 100 S. Jefferson, Clinton, MS 39058
(601) 925-3458, *Fax:* (601) 925-3337
www.star93fm.com
Sales@Star93FM.com
License: Clinton, Hinds County, MS held by Mississippi College.
Wire Services: NOAA Weather
Arbitron Metro Market: Jackson, MS *Format:* Contemporary Hits/Top 40 *Special Programming:* Relg 6 hrs wkly *Hrs. of News Programming:* News progmg 7 hrs wkly *Target Audience:* 18-54; upper & middle class Christianlisteners
Billy Lytal, President
Russ Robinson, Station Manager

WTWZ
10-10-1982; 1120 khz AM *Hrs Open:* Sunrise-sunset
P. O. Box 7094, Jackson, MS 39282 US
(601) 346-0074, *Fax:* (601) 346-0896
am1120@wtwzradio.com
License: Clinton, MS held by Terry E. Wood.
Nat'l Network: USA *Regional Network:* Miss. News Net.
Arbitron Metro Market: Jackson, MS *Format:* Blues *Hrs. of News Programming:* News progmg 7 hrs wkly *Target Audience:* 18-50; 50% men & 50% women *Adv. Rates:* 10; 10; 10; 10
Terry Wood, President

Coldwater

WVIM-FM
01-01-1976; 95.3 mhz FM *Hrs Open:* 24; 3.4 kw; 440 ft.; N34 48 22 W89 59 47
5555 McCracken Road, Hernando, MS 38632 US
(662) 349-0826, *Fax:* (662) 349-9255
ppesce@comcast.net
License: Coldwater, Tate County, MS held by Memphis First Ventures L.P.
Arbitron Metro Market: Southaven, MS *Format:* Country *Target Audience:* 25-54. *Adv. Rates:* 25; 25; 25; 15
Chip Miller, President
Paul Pesce, Station Manager

Collins

*WLVZ
08-15-1978; 107.1 mhz FM *Hrs Open:* 24; 2.25 kw; 541 ft.; N31 31 47 W89 30 30 *Rebroadcasts:* Rebroadcasts KLVR(FM) Middletown, CA 100%
37 South High Ave, Columbia, MS 39429 US
(916) 251-1600, *Fax:* (916) 251-1650
www.klove.com
License: Collins, Covington County, MS held by Educational Media Foundation.
Group Owner: EMF Broadcasting; (acq 7-15-2005; $700,000)
Nat'l Network: K-Love
Arbitron Metro Market: Laurel-Hattiesburg, MS *Format:* Christian
Mike Novak, President

Collinsville

WZKR
01-01-2001; 103.3 mhz FM *Hrs Open:* 24; 13 kw; 347 ft.; N32 20 39 W88 42 40
100 22nd Avenue South, Suite A, Meridian, MS 39301 US
(601) 693-1103, *Fax:* (601) 693-9949
B103@comcast.net
License: Collinsville, Newton County, MS held by Morning Star Media LLC
Nat'l Network: Salem Radio Network *Nat'l Reps:* Salem
Arbitron Metro Market: Collinsville, MS *Format:* Country *Target Audience:* 25-54.
Ron Harper, General Manager

Columbia

WCJU
12-20-1946; 1450 khz AM *Hrs Open:* 24; 1 kw-U, ND1; N31 14 14 W89 50 24
P. O. Box 472, Columbia, MS 39429 US
(601) 736-2616, *Fax:* (601) 736-2617
www.wcjuam.com
wcju@wcjufm.com
License: Columbia, MS held by WCJU Inc.
Nat'l Network: ABC *Nat'l Reps:* Keystone (unwired net)
Arbitron Metro Market: Columbia, MS *Format:* News, News/Talk, 84, Talk *Special Programming:* Gospel 4 hrs wkly *Hrs. of News Programming:* news progmg 30 hrs wkly *No. News Employees:* 2 *Target Audience:* 18-54.
T. McDaniel, President
Steve Mercier, Operations Dir
John Pittman Jr., Programming Director
Pam Ball, Regional Sales Manager

WFFF
04-14-1961; 1360 khz AM *Hrs Open:* 24; 1 kw-D, ND1; 0.159 kw-N, ND1; N31 15 44 W89 50 41
PO Box 550, Columbia, MS 39429 US
(601) 736-1360, *Fax:* (601) 736-1361
wfffradio@zzip.cc
License: Columbia, MS held by Haddox Enterprises Inc.
Nat'l Network: ABC *Regional Network:* Miss. News Net.
Arbitron Metro Market: Columbia, MS *Format:* Gospel, Country *Hrs. of News Programming:* news progmg 8 hrs wkly *No. News Employees:* 4 *Target Audience:* General.
Ronnie Geiger, President
Terri Geiger, Operations Dir

WFFF-FM
10-01-1966; 96.7 mhz FM *Hrs Open:* 24; 6 kw; 299 ft.; N31 15 44 W89 50 41
PO Box 550, Columbia, MS 39429 US

(601) 736-1360, *Fax:* (601) 736-1361
wfffradio@zzip.cc
License: Columbia, Marion County, MS
Regional Network: Miss. News Net.
Arbitron Metro Market: Columbia, MS *Format:* Adult Contemp *Hrs. of News Programming:* news progmg 8 hrs wkly *No. News Employees:* 4 *Target Audience:* 25-54.
Ronnie Geiger, Operations Dir
Terri Geiger, News Director

***WPRG**
89.5 mhz FM; 0.25 kw; 207 ft.; N31 15 44 W89 51 41
P. O. Box 1452, Washington, DC 20013 US
(662) 844-8888, *Fax:* (662) 842-6791
www.afr.net
faq@afr.net
License: Columbia, Marion County, MS held by American Family Association.
Group Owner: American Family Radio; (acq 10-1-01).
Nat'l Network: USA
Arbitron Metro Market: Tupelo, MS *Format:* Christian
Marvin Sanders, General Manager

Columbus

WTWG
01-01-1950; 1050 khz AM; 1 kw-D, ND1; 0.048 kw-N, ND1; N33 30 36 W88 24 46
Mailing Address: 1910 14th Ave, N., Columbus, MS 39701 US
Second Address: 1910 14th Ave. N., Columbus, MS 39703
(250) 248-4211, *Fax:* (250) 248-4210
www.thelounge999.com
info@thelounge999.com
License: Columbus, MS held by T & W Communications Inc.
Arbitron Metro Market: Paragould AR *Format:* Adult Contemp *No. News Employees:* 1 *Target Audience:* 45 plus; adults
Rob Bye, General Manager
Marlow Weldon, News Director
Pam Doherty, Traffic Manager

WJWF
11-01-1969; 1400 khz AM; 1 kw-U, ND1; N33 29 30 W88 24 14
420 20th Street North, Suite 1600, Birmingham, AL 35203 US
(662) 327-1183, *Fax:* (662) 328-1122
License: Columbus, MS held by Cumulus Licensing Corp.
Group Owner: Cumulus Media Inc.; (acq 2-14-2002; with co-located FM)
Nat'l Network: ESPN Radio
Arbitron Metro Market: Columbus-Starkville-West Point, MS
Format: Sports
C.J. Jones, Operations Dir

WKOR-FM
12-16-1992; 94.9 mhz FM *Hrs Open:* 24; 50 kw; 492 ft.; N33 28 38 W88 16 25
P.O. Box 1076, Columbus, MS 98703 US
(662) 327-1183, *Fax:* (662) 328-1122
www.k949.net
info@k949.net
License: Columbus, Lowndes County, MS held by Cumulus Licensing Corp.
Group Owner: Cumulus Media Inc.; (acq 2-14-02; grpsl).
Nat'l Network: ABC
Arbitron Metro Market: Columbus-Starkville-West Point, MS
Format: Country *Target Audience:* 18-54.
Cole Evans, General Sales Mgr
C. J. Jones, Promotions Manager

WNMQ
11-01-1969; 103.1 mhz FM; 22 kw; 755 ft.; N33 20 40 W88 32 47
420 20th Street North, Suite 1600, Birmingham, AL 35203 US
(662) 327-1183, *Fax:* 662-328-1122
www.1031theteam.com/
greg.benefield@cumulus.com
License: Columbus, Lowndes County, MS held by Cumulus Licensing LLC.
Group Owner: Cumulus Media Inc.
Arbitron Metro Market: Columbus, MS *Format:* Sports
Cheryl Kinderman, General Manager

***WCSO**
01-01-2006; 90.5 mhz FM; 10 kw vert; 530 ft.; N33 20 44 W88 14 6 *Rebroadcasts:* Rebroadcasts WAFR(FM) Tupelo 100%
P.O. Drawer 2440, Tupelo, MS 38803 US
(662) 844-8888, *Fax:* (662) 842-6791
www.afr.net
faq@afr.net
License: Columbus, Lowndes County, MS held by American Family Association.
Group Owner: American Family Radio
Arbitron Metro Market: Columbus, MS *Format:* Christian
Marvin Sanders, General Manager

***WMUW**
02-22-2008; 88.5 mhz FM *Hrs Open:* 24/7; 1,000 w EH Rad; Ant 89 ft; N33 29 23 W88 25 18
Mississippi University for Women, 1100 College St. - MUW - 1619, Columbus, MS 39701
(662) 329-7255, *Fax:* (662) 329-7250
www.muw.edu/wmuw
wmuw@muw.edu
License: Columbus, Lowndes County, MS held by Mississippi University for Women.
Population Served: 30,000 *Arbitron Metro Market:* Columbus-Starkv *Hrs. of News Programming:* News progmg 2.5 hrs wkly *Target Audience:* College students and those that like music
Timothy Etheridge, Operations Dir
Eric Harlan, General Manager
Timothy Etheridge, Programming Director
Hilary Jasain, Music Director
Alonzo Bouldin, Music Director

Columbus Afb

WACR-FM
06-01-1975; 105.3 mhz FM; 50 kw; 352 ft.; N33 40 9 W88 40 8
4307 Highway 39n, Meridian, MS 39301 US
(662) 338-5424, *Fax:* (662) 338-5436
www.wacr1053.com
wmsuproduction@urbanradio.fm
License: Columbus Afb, Lowndes County, MS held by Urban Radio Licenses LLC.
Group Owner: Urban Radio Licenses LLC; (acq 7-13-2005; $1.1 million)
Arbitron Metro Market: Aberdeen, MS *Format:* Black, Blues
Pamela Hancock, General Manager
Aubra Turner, Advertising Contact

Como

WRBO
09-28-1966; 103.5 mhz FM *Hrs Open:* 24; 100 kw; 587 ft.; N34 51 44 W89 52 42
Two Newton Executive Park, Newton, MA 02162 US
(901) 682-1106
www.soulclassics.com
License: Como, Panola County, MS
Group Owner: Cumulus Media Inc.; (acq 3-23-2004; grpsl).
Nat'l Network: ABC; Westwood One *Nat'l Reps:* Katz Radio
Arbitron Metro Market: Memphis, TN *Format:* Black *Target Audience:* 25-54.
Sherri Sawyer, General Manager
Amy Goodman, General Sales Mgr
Henry Nelson, Programming Director
Marvin Emilien, Promotions Manager

Corinth

WADI
10-26-1968; 95.3 mhz FM; 2.6 kw; 472 ft.; N34 55 47 W88 24 37
1608 Johns Street, Corinth, MS 38834 US
(304) 556-4900, *Fax:* (304) 556-4981
www.wvpubcast.org
feedback@wvpubcast.org
License: Corinth, Alcorn County, MS held by Power Valley Communications Inc.
Arbitron Metro Market: Dubuque IA *Format:* News
Rita Ray, General Manager
Marilyn DeVita, General Sales Mgr
James Muhammad, Programming Director
Greg Collard, News Director
Jack Wells, Chief Engineer
Teresa Wills, Traffic Manager

WTKN
03-01-1946; 1230 khz AM; 1 kw-U, ND1; N34 57 27 W88 31 17
1608 John Street, Corinth, MS 38834 US
(662) 423-9533, *Fax:* (662) 423-9333
www.newstalkam1230.com
License: Corinth, MS held by Perihelion Global Inc.
Arbitron Metro Market: Corinth, MS
Rick Biddle, General Manager

WKCU
10-24-1965; 1350 khz AM *Hrs Open:* 24
P.O. Box 1471, Corinth, MS 38834 US
(662) 286-8451, *Fax:* (662) 286-8452
wxrz@earthlink.net
License: Corinth, MS held by TeleSouth Communications Inc.
Group Owner: TeleSouth Communications Inc.; acq 12-20-02; $350,000 with co-located FM).
Regional Network: Miss. News Net. *Wire Services:* NWS (National Weather Service)
Format: Christian *Special Programming:* Black 2 hrs wkly *Hrs. of News Programming:* News progmg 12 hrs wkly *Target Audience:* 25-54; female *Adv. Rates:* 5; 5; 5; 3
James Anderson, General Manager

WXRZ
01-01-1967; 94.3 mhz FM *Hrs Open:* 24; 25 kw; 328 ft.; N34 48 36 W88 34 45
P.O. Box 1471, Corinth, MS 38834 US
(662) 286-8451, *Fax:* (662) 286-8452
wxrz@earthlink.net
License: Corinth, Alcorn County, MS held by TeleSouth Communications Inc.
Group Owner: TeleSouth Communications Inc.
Wire Services: NWS (National Weather Service)
Arbitron Metro Market: Corinth, MS *Format:* Talk *Adv. Rates:* 7; 7; 7; 6
James Anderson, Station Manager

Crenshaw

WHKL
03-01-1997; 106.9 mhz FM; 6 kw; 328 ft.; N34 26 51 W90 6 25
P.O. Box 1528, Batesville, MS 38606 US
(662) 563-4664, *Fax:* (662) 563-9008
www.whkl107.com
country101radio@yahoo.com
License: Crenshaw, Panola County, MS held by Batesville Broadcasting Co. Inc.
Format: Oldies
John Ingram, General Manager

De Kalb

WJXM
01-01-1999; 105.7 mhz FM; 50 kw; 384 ft.; N32 38 37 W88 40 29
P.O. Box 1699, Meridian, MS 39302 US
(601) 693-2661, *Fax:* (601) 483-0826
www.1057thebeat.com
wjxm@wokk.com
License: De Kalb, Kemper County, MS held by Mississippi Broadcasters L.L.C.
Group Owner: Mississippi Broadcasters L.L.C.
Arbitron Metro Market: Meridian, MS *Format:* Urban Contemporary
Scott Stevens, Operations Dir
Clay Holladay, General Manager

Decatur

***WSQH**
01-01-2005; 91.7 mhz FM; 18 kw; 476 ft.; N32 23 57 W89 5 2
P.O. Box 1458, Washington, DC 20013 US
(662) 844-8888, *Fax:* (662) 842-6791
www.afr.net
faq@afr.net
License: Decatur, Scott County, MS held by Salt & Light Communications Inc.
Nat'l Network: USA
Arbitron Metro Market: Decatur, MS *Format:* Christian
Marvin Sanders, General Manager

Duck Hill

***WAUM**
01-01-1998; 91.9 mhz FM; 2.5 kw; 512 ft.; N33 38 34 W89 29 59
P O Drawer 2440, Tupelo, MS 38803 US
(662) 844-8888, *Fax:* (662) 842-6791
www.afr.net
License: Duck Hill, Montgomery County, MS held by American Family Association.
Group Owner: American Family Radio
Nat'l Network: USA
Format: Gospel
Marvin Sanders, General Manager

Durant

WLIN-FM
01-01-1997; 101.1 mhz FM; 4.8 kw horiz, 4.6 kw vert; 371 ft.; N33 3 51 W89 36 12
P.O. Box A, Kosciusko, MS 39090 US
(662) 289-1050, *Fax:* (662) 289-7907
www.breezynews.com
breezy@boswellmedia.net
License: Durant, Holmes County, MS held by Boswell Radio LLC.
Format: Adult Contemp
Johnny Boswell, General Manager
Ann Steen, Station Manager
Jerry Price, General Sales Mgr
Eric Matthews, Programming Director

Ellisville

WJKX
10-05-1973; 102.5 mhz FM *Hrs Open:* 24; 50 kw; 492 ft.; N31 46 5 W89 10 12
2018 Highway 15 North, Laurel, MS 39441 US
(601) 296-9800, *Fax:* (601) 296-9838
www.102jkx.com
mailto:contact@102jkx.com
License: Ellisville, Jones County, MS held by CC Licenses LLC.
Group Owner: Clear Channel Communications Inc.; (acq 12-19-2000; grpsl)
Arbitron Metro Market: Laurel-Hattiesburg, MS *Format:* Urban Contemporary
Mike Comfort, General Manager

Eupora

WLZA
09-01-1978; 96.1 mhz FM *Hrs Open:* 24; 50 kw; 500 ft; N33 28 18 W89 13 36
Box 884, 1105 A Stark Rd, Starkville, MS 38803
(662) 324-9601, *Fax:* (662) 324-7400
wlza@961wlza.com
License: Eupora, Webster County, MS held by Metro Radio.
Group Owner: Air South Radio Inc.
Arbitron Metro Market: Columbus-Starkville-West Point, MS *Target Audience:* General.
Olvie Sisk, President
Carolyn Jackson, General Manager
Carolyn Jackson, Station Manager
Bill Thunlow, General Sales Mgr
Bill Thunlow, Programming Director
Greg Magy, Traffic Manager

Fayette

WTYJ
10-17-1983; 97.7 mhz FM; 6 kw; 500 ft; N31 40 32 W91 06 18
20 E. Franklin St., Natchez, MS 39120
(601) 442-2522, *Fax:* (601) 446-9918
wmiswtyj@bellsouth.net
License: Fayette, Jefferson County, MS held by Natchez Broadcasting Inc.
Nat'l Network: American Urban *Regional Network:* Miss. News Net.
Population Served: 100,000*Target Audience:* Black.
James Nutter, President
Calvin Butler, Operations Dir
LlJuna Weir, Station Manager
Diana Nutter, Secretary/Treasurer

Flora

WFMN
07-07-1997; 97.3 mhz FM *Hrs Open:* 24; 19.5 kw; 367 ft.; N32 27 21 W90 15 32
6310 I-55 North, Jackson, MS 32911 US
(601) 957-1700, *Fax:* (601) 956-5228
www.supertalkms.com
bwallace@telesouth.com
License: Flora, Madison County, MS held by TeleSouth Communications Inc.
Group Owner: TeleSouth Communications Inc.; acq 9-8-97; $700,000)
Nat'l Network: ABC
Arbitron Metro Market: Jackson, MS *Format:* Sports, Talk *Adv. Rates:* 25; 20; 22; 16
Steve Davenport, President
John Winfield, Operations Dir
Paul Gallo, General Manager

WYAB
08-01-1997; 103.9 mhz FM *Hrs Open:* 24; 5 kw; 325 ft.; N32 26 49 W90 18 8
157 Avondale Road, Box 182, Canton, MI 39046 US
(601) 879-0093, *Fax:* (601) 427-0088
www.wyab.com
matt@wyab.com
License: Flora, Madison County, MS held by SSR Communications Inc.
Arbitron Metro Market: Flora, MS *Format:* Talk *No. News Employees:* 1 *Target Audience:* 25-64. *Adv. Rates:* 17.50; 12.50; 15.50; 8.50
Matthew Wesolowski, CEO

Flowood

WPBQ
01-01-1995; 1240 khz AM *Hrs Open:* 24; 0.88 kw-U, ND1; N32 18 3 W90 8 12
1240 Old Pearl Levy Road, Flowood, MS 39209 US
(601) 355-1240, *Fax:* (601) 355-1069
www.espnradio1240.com
License: Flowood, MS held by PDB Corp.
Arbitron Metro Market: Jackson, MS *Format:* Sports *Target Audience:* 25-54.
Derrel Palmer, General Manager

Forest

***WMBU**
10-03-1997; 89.1 mhz FM *Hrs Open:* 24; 10 kw horiz, 100 kw vert; 640 ft.; N32 18 54 W89 21 12 *Rebroadcasts:* Rebroadcasts WMBV(FM) Dixon's Mills, AL 95%
Mailing Address: 820 North Lasalle Blvd., Chicago, IL 60610 US
Second Address: Box 91, Dixons Mills, AL 36736
(601) 775-3100, *Fax:* (601) 775-3400
www.moodyradiosouth.fm
wmbu@radiosouth.edu
License: Forest, Scott County, MS held by The Moody Bible Institute of Chicago.
Group Owner: The Moody Bible Institute of Chicago
Nat'l Network: Moody *Wire Services:* AP
Arbitron Metro Market: Lake, MS *Format:* Christian *Special Programming:* Children 2 hrs wkly *Target Audience:* 35-54.
Rob Moore, General Manager
John Roger, Programming Director

WQST
09-01-1955; 850 khz AM *Hrs Open:* Daylight; 10 kw-D, DAD; N32 21 46 W89 25 9 *Rebroadcasts:* website streaming audio @ www. 850amwqst.com
1017 N. State Street, Jackson, MS 39201 US
(601) 469-1960, *Fax:* (601) 469-1366
www.850amwqst.com
wqstgospel@aol.com
License: Forest, MS held by Ace Broadcasting Inc.
Regional Network: Miss. News Net.
Arbitron Metro Market: Jackson, MS *Format:* Gospel *Hrs. of News Programming:* News progmg 12 hrs per day *Target Audience:* 35+; Adults *Adv. Rates:* 8 per 60 sec
Frank Edmondson, General Manager
Dan Davis, Programming Director

***WQST-FM**
09-01-1962; 92.5 mhz FM; 97 kw; 991 ft.; N32 21 48 W89 25 29
P.O. Drawer 2440, Tupelo, MS 38803 US
(601) 362-4277, *Fax:* (601) 362-1994
www.afr.net
info@afr.net
License: Forest, Scott County, MS held by American Family Association Inc.
Group Owner: American Family Radio
Nat'l Network: USA
Format: Christian
Jim Thorn, General Manager

Friar's Point

***WWUN-FM**
01-01-1973; 101.5 mhz FM; 14 kw; 395 ft.; N34 34 2 W90 37 37
P.O. Box 1475, Clarksdale, MS 38614 US
(870) 572-3677
wwun@csnradio.com
License: Friar's Point, Coahoma County, MS held by CSN International.
Group Owner: CSN International; (acq 8-27-2001)
Arbitron Metro Market: Clarksdale, MS *Format:* Christian, Religious
Charles Smith, President
Jeffrey Smith, Operations Dir
Clayton Collier, Station Manager

Friars Point

WNEV
98.7 mhz FM; 6 kw; 328 ft.; N34 21 56 W90 38 14 US
(870) 572-9506, *Fax:* (870) 572-1845
www.force3radio.com
force2@sbcglobal.net
License: Friars Point, Coahoma County, MS held by L.T. Simes II & Raymond Simes.
Arbitron Metro Market: Friars Point, MS *Format:* Blues, Gospel
Raymond Simes, General Manager
Elaine Simes, Advertising Manager
Earnest Simes, Music Director

Fulton

WFTA
08-19-1976; 101.9 mhz FM *Hrs Open:* 24; 50 kw; 479 ft.; N34 15 46 W88 32 24
Mailing Address: P.O. Box 2116, Tupelo, MS 38803 US
Second Address: 1241 Cliff Gookin Blvd., Radio Bldg., Tupelo, MS 38801
(662) 842-7625, *Fax:* (662) 842-9568
no station wensite
License: Fulton, Itawamba County, MS held by Air South Radio Inc.
Group Owner: Air South Radio Inc.
Arbitron Metro Market: Tupelo, MS *Format:* Adult Contemp *Hrs. of News Programming:* News progmg 4 hrs wkly *Target Audience:* 14-44.
Gene Sisk, President
Olvie Sisk, General Manager
Fred Blalock, Station Manager

Gluckstadt

WYOY
01-07-1976; 101.7 mhz FM *Hrs Open:* 24; 50 kw; 456 ft.; N32 25 36 W90 12 20
3436 Highway 45 North, Meridian, MS 39301 US
(601) 956-0102, *Fax:* (601) 978-3980
www.y101.com
frontdesk@us963.com
License: Gluckstadt, Madison County, MS held by New South Radio Inc.
Group Owner: New South Communications Inc.; (acq 11-10-94; $750,000 with WLRM(AM) Ridgeland;
Nat'l Reps: McGavren Guild
Arbitron Metro Market: Jackson, MS *Format:* Contemporary Hits/Top 40 *Target Audience:* 18-49.
Gwen Rakestraw, General Manager

Greenville

WLTM
05-01-1970; 97.9 mhz FM *Hrs Open:* 5:30 AM-midnight; 48 kw horiz; Ant 502 ft; N33 23 51 W91 00 35
Mailing Address: Box 1816, Greenville, MS 38702
Second Address: 800 Hwy 1 South, Delta Plaza, Ste #39, Greenville, MS 38701
(662) 378-2617, *Fax:* (662) 378-8341
info@wbaq.com
License: Greenville, Washington County, MS held by Debut Broadcasting Mississippi Inc.
Group Owner: Debut Broadcasting Corp. Inc.; (acq 6-19-2007; grpsl)
Nat'l Network: ABC *Regional Network:* Miss. News Net.
Population Served: 75,000*Special Programming:* Farm one hr, btfl sacred music 4 hrs wkly *Hrs. of News Programming:* News progmg 14 hrs wkly *Target Audience:* 25-54; quality-conscious adults with spendable income
Linda mcKee, Operations Dir
James Karr, General Manager
Margaret Karr, General Sales Mgr

WDMS
12-01-1967; 100.7 mhz FM; 100 kw; 443 ft.; N33 25 20 W91 1 41
P.O. Box 1438, Greenville, MS 38701 US
(662) 334-4559, *Fax:* (662) 332-1315
www.wdms.fm
wdms@bellsouth.net
License: Greenville, Washington County, MS
Regional Network: Miss. News Net.
Arbitron Metro Market: Greenville, MI *Format:* Country
Linda Tackett, News Director

WGVM
01-01-1948; 1260 khz AM; 2.4 kw-D, NDD; N33 25 20 W91 1 41
Mailing Address: P. O. Box 1438, Greenville, MS 38701 US
Second Address: 1383 Pickett St., Greenville, MS 38701
(662) 334-4550, *Fax:* (662) 332-1315
wdms@bellsouth.net
License: Greenville, MS held by WDMS Inc.
Target Audience: General.
George Kimble, President
Alan Bishop, Operations Dir
Paula Triplett, General Sales Mgr
Mike Smith, Programming Director
Ted Baker, News Director

WNIX
08-01-1937; 1330 khz AM *Hrs Open:* 24; 1 kw-D, DAN; 0.5 kw-N, DAN; N33 24 36 W91 1 3
Mailing Address: P.O. Box 1816, Greenville, MS 38701 US
Second Address: Unit 39 Delta Plaza Mall, 800 Hwy. 1 S., Greenville, MS 38701
(662) 378-2617, *Fax:* (888) 704-4762
www.wnixradio.com
info@deltaradio.net
License: Greenville, MS held by Debut Broadcasting Mississippi Inc.

Group Owner: Debut Broadcasting Corp. Inc.; (acq 6-19-2007; grpsl)
Arbitron Metro Market: Greenville, MS *Format:* Oldies
James Karr Jr., General Manager

***WLRK**
01-01-2006; 91.5 mhz FM; 50 kw vert; 322 ft.; N33 32 25 W91 22 39
US
(800) 525-5683, *Fax:* (916) 251-1650
www.klove.com
klove@klove.com
License: Greenville, Washington County, MS held by Educational Media Foundation.
Group Owner: EMF Broadcasting; (acq 1-23-2008; $320,000 with KAKV(FM) El Dorado, AR)
Nat'l Network: K-Love
Arbitron Metro Market: Greenville, MS *Format:* Christian *No. News Employees:* 13
Darrell Chambliss, Chairman
Mike Novak, President and CEO
Chip Bailey, Operations Dir
David Pierce, Chief Creative Officer and Programming Director
Ed Lenane, News Director
Sam Wallington, Engineering Dir
Alan Mason, ChiefOperating Officer
Dan Antonelli, Chief Business Development Officer
Eric Moser, Chief Financial Officer
Brian Burger, Vice President of Human Resources
D. Kevin Blair, Secretary and General Counsel
Tim Luttrell, News Reporter

WJIW
104.7 mhz FM; 31 kw; 620 ft.; N33 28 10 W90 50 30
204 Moore Street, Helena, AR 72342 US
(662) 332-5701, *Fax:* (870) 334-9049
www.wjiwfm.com
em@lordradio.com
License: Greenville, Washington County, MS held by Mondy-Burke Broadcasting Network.
Arbitron Metro Market: Grenville, MS *Format:* Gospel
April Mondy, Operations Dir
Elijah Mondy, General Manager
Belinda Mondy, General Sales Mgr
Elijah Mondy Jr., Co-Owner
Darren Smith, Co-Owner
Kirkland Burke, Co-Owner
Belinda Mondy, Exec. Administrator
Glenda Smith, Exec.Administrator
Zipporah Mondy, Sales/Music Director

***WDSV**
91.9 mhz FM; 1.5 kw horiz, 1.35 kw vert; 344 ft.; N33 24 21 W90 59 30
US
(662) 537-4939, *Fax:* (662) 335-5295
www.wdsv919fm.org
contact@wdsv919fm.org
License: Greenville, Washington County, MS held by Delta Foundation Inc.
Arbitron Metro Market: Greenville, MS *Format:* Talk
Cindy Ayers, CEO
Navine J. Bell, Programming Director
Mashaeiba Minor, News Director
Ethel Bryant, Production Coordination Director
Theresa Brewer, Public Service Announcements Producer
Anthony Adams, Chief Operations Officer

Greenwood

WABG
02-01-1950; 960 khz AM *Hrs Open:* 6 AM-1 PM
Mailing Address: 2001 Garrard Avenue, Greenwood, MS 38930 US
Second Address: Box 408, Greenwood, MS 38935-0408
(281) 446-5725, *Fax:* (281 540-2198
www.ksbj.org
License: Greenwood, MS held by SPB LLC
Arbitron Metro Market: Benton AR *Format:* Christian
Tim McDermott, General Manager

WGNL
12-01-1989; 104.3 mhz FM *Hrs Open:* 24; 50 kw; 299 ft.; N33 40 45 W90 4 7
Mailing Address: Box 1801, 503 Ione St., Greenwood, MS 38930 US
Second Address: 503 Ione St., Greenwood, MS 38930
(662) 453-1646, *Fax:* (662) 453-7002
www.broadcasturban.net
wgnlbooth@bellsouth.net
License: Greenwood, Leflore County, MS held by Team Broadcasting Co. Inc.
Nat'l Reps: Dora-Clayton
Format: Adult Contemp *Special Programming:* Jazz 6 hrs wkly *Hrs. of News Programming:* news progmg 12 hrs wkly *No. News Employees:* 1 *Target Audience:* 18 plus.
Maxine Hughes, Operations Dir
Ruben Hughes, General Manager

WGRM
01-01-1937; 1240 khz AM; 0.72 kw-U, ND1; N33 32 2 W90 11 42
645 Church Street, Suite 400, Norfolk, VA 23510 US
(662) 453-1240, *Fax:* (662) 453-1241
wgrmradiostation@bellsouth.net
License: Greenwood, MS held by Christian Broadcasting of Greenwood Inc.
Group Owner: Willis Broadcasting Corp.; (acq 2-22-99; $500,000 with co-located FM)
Format: Gospel *Special Programming:* Black 2 hrs wkly *Target Audience:* 25-45.
Lee Hall, General Manager
Gwen Riley, Music Director
Gwen Rilley, Traffic Manager

WGRM-FM
07-17-1989; 93.9 mhz FM *Hrs Open:* 24; 12 kw; 295 ft.; N33 32 2 W90 11 42
645 Church Street, Suite 400, Norfolk, VA 23510 US
(662) 453-1240, *Fax:* (662) 453-1241
wgrmradiostation@bellsouth.net
License: Greenwood, Leflore County, MS
Group Owner: Willis Broadcasting Corp.
Format: Gospel
Kent Smith, President

WKXG
01-01-1987; 1540 khz AM *Hrs Open:* 6 AM-10 PM
Mailing Address: 6310 I-55 North, Jackson, MS 39211 US
Second Address: 3192 Browning Rd., Greenwood, MS 38935
(662) 453-2174, *Fax:* (662) 455-5733
License: Greenwood, MS held by TeleSouth Communications Inc.
Group Owner: TeleSouth Communications Inc.; (acq 8-1-88)
Charlotte Michael, General Manager

***WMAO-FM**
12-01-1983; 90.9 mhz FM *Hrs Open:* 24; 100 kw; 879 ft.; N33 22 34 W90 32 32
3825 Ridgewood Road, Jackson, MS 39211 US
(601) 432-6119, *Fax:* (601) 432-6806
www.mpbonline.org
License: Greenwood, Leflore County, MS held by Mississippi Authority for Educational Television.
Nat'l Network: PRI; NPR *Wire Services:* AP
Arbitron Metro Market: Greenwood, MS *TV Affiliate:* WMAO-TV
Format: News *Hrs. of News Programming:* news progmg 100 hrs wkly *No. News Employees:* 7 *Target Audience:* General.
Jason Klein, Operations Dir
Jay Woods, General Manager
Ty Warren, General Sales Mgr
Mari Irby, Promotions Manager
Teresa Collier, News Director
Bob Buie, Engineering Dir
Karen Hearn, Music Director
Bill Ellison, Regional SalesManager
LaSharne Patton, Traffic Manager

WYMX
06-15-1965; 99.1 mhz FM *Hrs Open:* 24/7; 100 kw; Ant 1,029 ft; N33 31 12 W90 08 28
Box 1686, Greenwood, MS 39211
(662) 453-2174, *Fax:* (662) 455-5733
License: Greenwood, Leflore County, MS held by TeleSouth Communications Inc.
Group Owner: TeleSouth Communications Inc.
Population Served: 315,000*Adv. Rates:* Call for rate information
Jim Chick, General Manager
Stacy McClain, Programming Director
Rea Edwards, News Director

WBZL(FM)
103.3 mhz FM; 6 kw; Ant 328 ft; N33 32 21 W90 02 08
6311 Ridgewood Road, Jackson, MS 38935-1686
(662) 453-2174, *Fax:* (662) 455-5733
License: Greenwood, Leflore County, MS held by TeleSouth Communications Inc.
Group Owner: TeleSouth Communications Inc.
Population Served: 6,639 *Arbitron Metro Market:* Mount Vernon, IN
Charlotte Michael, General Manager

Grenada

WQXB
10-16-1970; 100.1 mhz FM; 48 kw; 503 ft.; N33 51 24 W89 55 15
P.O. Box 946, Grenada, MS 38901 US
License: Grenada, Grenada County, MS held by Chatterbox Inc.
Format: Country
Bob Adams, General Manager

WOHT
01-01-2003; 92.3 mhz FM; 4.1 kw; 397 ft.; N33 51 33 W89 55 13
P.O. Box 1438, Cleveland, MS 38732 US
(662) 226-3133, *Fax:* (662) 226-3233
star92@star92fm.com
License: Grenada, Grenada County, MS held by Century Broadcasting L.L.C.
Format: Oldies
Will Stammerjohan, General Manager

WMUT
01-01-2004; 101.3 mhz FM; 6 kw; 328 ft.; N33 49 20 W89 55 40
Mailing Address: 188 South Bellevue, Suite 222, Memphis, TN 28104 US
Second Address: 157 Dowdle Rd., Grenada, MS 38901
(662) 832-8023, *Fax:* (662) 226-3233
www.rebsportsradio.com
License: Grenada, Grenada County, MS held by George S. Flinn Jr.
Nat'l Network: CNN Radio; Westwood One
Arbitron Metro Market: Tupelo, MS *Format:* Sports, Talk *Target Audience:* 18-54. *Adv. Rates:* 180; 180; 180; 120
Will Stammerjohan, General Manager
Connie Stammerjohan, General Sales Mgr

Gulfport

***WAOY**
01-01-1999; 91.7 mhz FM; 78 kw; 1089 ft.; N30 42 29 W89 5 6
Rebroadcasts: Rebroadcasts WAFR(FM) Tupelo 80%
P.O. Drawer 2440, Tupelo, MS 38803 US
(601) 844-8888, *Fax:* (601) 842-6791
www.afr.net
faq@afr.net
License: Gulfport, Harrison County, MS held by American Family Association Inc.
Group Owner: American Family Radio
Nat'l Network: USA
Arbitron Metro Market: Gulfport, MS *Format:* Christian *Target Audience:* General.
Marvin Sanders, General Manager

WGCM
01-01-1928; 1240 khz AM *Hrs Open:* 24; 1 kw-U, ND1; N30 25 45 W89 1 10
P.O. Box 2639, Gulfport, MS 39505 US
(228) 896-5500, *Fax:* (228) 896-0458
www.coast102.com
pat@coast102.com
License: Gulfport, MS held by JMD Inc.
Arbitron Metro Market: Biloxi-Gulfport-Pascagoula, MS *Format:* Country *Target Audience:* 35 plus.
Morgan Dowdy, President
Bryan Rhodes, Operations Dir
Steve Spillman, General Sales Mgr
Pat McGowan, Programming Director
Gwen Wilson, News Director
Dave Melton, Chief Engineer

WGCM-FM
11-14-1969; 102.3 mhz FM *Hrs Open:* 24; 50 kw; 394 ft.; N30 20 44 W89 11 47
P.O. Box 2639, Gulfport, MS 39505 US
(228) 896-5500, *Fax:* (228) 896-0458
www.coast102.com
pat@coast102.com
License: Gulfport, Harrison County, MS
Arbitron Metro Market: Biloxi-Gulfport-Pascagoula, MS *Format:* Easy Listening *Target Audience:* 25-54.
Buddy Baylor, General Sales Mgr
Pat McGowan, Programming Director

WUJM
07-13-1977; 96.7 mhz FM *Hrs Open:* 24; 4.3 kw; 390 ft.; N30 27 31 W89 4 46
2511 Garden Road, Building A, Suite 104, Monterey, CA 93940 US
(228) 388-2001, *Fax:* (228) 896-9736
www.molly967.com
molly967@molly967.com
License: Gulfport, Harrison County, MS held by Monterey Licenses LLC.

Group Owner: Triad Broadcasting Co. L.L.C.; (acq 7-14-99; grpsl)
Arbitron Metro Market: Biloxi-Gulfport-Pascagoula, MS *Format:* Adult Contemp
Buddy Burch, Operations Dir
Jay Taylor, Operations Director

WQFX
05-07-1975; 1130 khz AM
336 Rodenberg Avd, Biloxi, MS 39531 US
(228) 374-9739, *Fax:* (228) 374-9739
www.wqfx.net
wqfxradio@aol.com
License: Gulfport, MS held by Walking by Faith Ministries Inc.
Group Owner: Walking by Faith Ministries Inc.; (acq 1994)
Arbitron Metro Market: Biloxi-Gulfport-Pascagoula, MS *Format:* Gospel
James Black, General Manager

WROA
02-27-1955; 1390 khz AM; 5 kw-D, DA2; 5 kw-N, DA2; N30 27 30 W89 4 45
P.O.Box 2639, Gulfport, MS 39503 US
(228) 896-5500, *Fax:* (228) 896-0458
www.morgan@kiker108.com
License: Gulfport, MS held by Dowdy & Dowdy Partnership.
Arbitron Metro Market: Biloxi-Gulfport-Pascagoula, MS *Format:* Contemporary Hits/Top 40 *Special Programming:* Farm one hr wkly
Charles Dowdy, President
Morgan Dowdy, General Manager

WXYK
01-01-1964; 107.1 mhz FM *Hrs Open:* 24; 2.8 kw; 400 ft.; N30 27 31 W89 4 46
2511 Garden Road, Building A, Suite 104, Monterey, CA 93940 US
(228) 388-2001, *Fax:* (228) 896-9736
www.1071themonkey.net
wxyk@monkeyradio.com
License: Gulfport, Harrison County, MS held by Monterey Licenses LLC.
Group Owner: Triad Broadcasting Co. L.L.C.; (acq 7-14-99; grpsl)
Nat'l Network: ABC
Arbitron Metro Market: Gulfport, MS *Format:* Contemporary Hits/Top 40
Kenny West, Operations Dir
Ricky Mitchell, General Sales Mgr
Mindy Patton, Promotions Manager
Bill West, V.P./Market Manager
Michelle Shortridge, HR Director

Guntown

WBVV
01-15-1976; 99.3 mhz FM *Hrs Open:* 24; 15.5 kw; 420 ft.; N34 21 46 W88 35 28
P.O. Box 356, Booneville, MS 38829 US
License: Guntown, Lee County, MS held by CC Licenses LLC.
Group Owner: Clear Channel Communications Inc.; (acq 9-27-2001; $700,000 including 5-year noncompete agreement)
Nat'l Network: USA; Reach Satellite *Regional Network:* Miss. News Net.
Arbitron Metro Market: Booneville, MS *Format:* Religious
Mark Maharrey, General Manager

Hattiesburg

***WAII**
01-01-1998; 89.3 mhz FM; 1 kw; 269 ft.; N31 16 59 W89 21 1
Po Drawer 2440, Tupelo, MS 38803 US
(662) 844-8888, *Fax:* (662) 842-6791
www.afr.net
faq@afr.net
License: Hattiesburg, Forrest County, MS held by American Family Association.
Group Owner: American Family Radio
Nat'l Network: USA
Arbitron Metro Market: Laurel, MS *Format:* Religious
Marvin Sanders, General Manager

WHSY
09-01-1954; 950 khz AM *Hrs Open:* 24; 5 kw-D, ND2; 0.064 kw-N, ND2; N31 22 33 W89 19 49
PO Box 15216, Hattiesburg, MS 39401 US
(601) 582-7078, *Fax:* (601) 582-7122
www.whsy950.com
whsy950@yahoo.com
License: Hattiesburg, MS held by Gulf South Communications LLC
Nat'l Network: CBS Radio
Arbitron Metro Market: Laurel-Hattiesburg, MS *Format:* News, Talk
Charlie Holt, President

WFOR
05-01-1924; 1400 khz AM *Hrs Open:* 24
111 East Kilboirn Avenue, Suite 2700, Milwaukee, WI 53202 US
(601) 296-9800, *Fax:* (601) 296-9838
License: Hattiesburg, MS held by CC Licenses LLC.
Group Owner: Clear Channel Communications Inc.; (acq 12-19-2000; grpsl).
Arbitron Metro Market: Laurel-Hattiesburg, MS *Format:* Sports *Target Audience:* 35 plus.
Mike Comfort, General Manager
Jackson Walker, Programming Director
Glen Musgrove, Chief Engineer

WJMG
05-10-1982; 92.1 mhz FM *Hrs Open:* 24; 6 kw; 299 ft.; N31 20 33 W89 17 53
1204 Graveline Street, Hattiesburg, MS 39401 US
(601) 544-1941, *Fax:* (601) 544-1947
License: Hattiesburg, Forrest County, MS held by Vernon C. Floyd dba Circuit Broadcasting of Hattiesburg
Arbitron Metro Market: Laurel-Hattiesburg, MS *Format:* Urban Contemporary
Vernon Floyd, General Manager

WORV
06-07-1969; 1580 khz AM; 1 kw-D, ND1; 0.088 kw-N, ND1; N31 20 33 W89 17 53
1204 Graveline St., Hattiesburg, MS 39401 US
(601) 544-1941, *Fax:* (601) 544-1947
License: Hattiesburg, MS held by Vernon C. Floyd dba Circuit Broadcasting of Hattiesburg.
Nat'l Network: American Urban *Nat'l Reps:* Dora-Clayton
Arbitron Metro Market: Laurel-Hattiesb *TV Affiliate:* Relg

***WUSM-FM**
05-10-1973; 88.5 mhz FM; 3 kw; 424 ft.; N31 18 25.6 W89 24 47.2
Box 10045 S. Station, Hattiesburg, MS 39406 US
(601) 266-4287
www.wusm.usm.edu
wusm@usm.edu
License: Hattiesburg, Forrest County, MS held by University of Southern Mississippi.
Arbitron Metro Market: Hattiesburg, MS *Format:* Triple A, Variety/Diverse *Hrs. of News Programming:* news progmg 22 hrs wkly *No. News Employees:* 4 *Target Audience:* General; college students & upper income univ& community listeners
Audrey.K.Lucas, President
Jeff Rassier, General Manager
Chris Campbell, Programming Director

WFFX
07-01-1966; 103.7 mhz FM *Hrs Open:* 24; 100 kw; Ant 1,056 ft; N31 31 37 W89 08 07
6555 Hwy. 98 W., Suite 8, Hattiesburg, MS 53202
(601) 296-9800, *Fax:* (601) 296-9838
www.thefoxrocks1037.com
License: Hattiesburg, Forrest County, MS held by CC Licenses LLC.
Group Owner: Clear Channel Communications Inc.
Population Served: 500,000 *Arbitron Metro Market:* Laurel-Hattiesburg, MS *Target Audience:* 25-54.
Mike Comfort, General Manager

WXRR
07-01-1967; 104.5 mhz FM *Hrs Open:* 24; 100 kw; 981 ft.; N31 25 52 W89 8 51
P.O. Box 6408, Laurel, MS 39441 US
(601) 544-0095, *Fax:* (601) 649-8199
www.rock104fm.com
rock104fm@rock104fm.com
License: Hattiesburg, Forrest County, MS held by Blakeney Communications Inc.
Group Owner: Blakeney Communications Inc.; acq 8-30-94; $450,000 with co-located AM;
Arbitron Metro Market: Hattiesburg, MS *Format:* Classic Rock *Target Audience:* General.
Larry Blakeney, President

Hazlehurst

WDXO
12-24-1970; 92.9 mhz FM *Hrs Open:* 24; 2.7 kw; 497 ft.; N31 53 33 W90 24 8
Post Office Box 2016, Monticello, MS 39654 US
(601) 587-7625, *Fax:* (601) 587-9401
License: Hazlehurst, Copiah County, MS held by TeleSouth Communications Inc.
Group Owner: TeleSouth Communications Inc.
Nat'l Network: ABC
Arbitron Metro Market: Hazlehurst, MS *Format:* Sports *Target Audience:* 18-50.
Rusty O'Neal, General Manager

WOEG
06-01-1953; 1220 khz AM
Post Office Box 2016, Monticello, MS 39654 US
(601) 587-9363, *Fax:* (601) 587-7625
License: Hazlehurst, MS held by TeleSouth Communications Inc.
Group Owner: TeleSouth Communications Inc.; (acq 6-20-2006; grpsl).
TV Affiliate: Black *No. News Employees:* General; Black

Heidelberg

WLAU
05-01-1980; 99.3 mhz FM *Hrs Open:* 24; 50 kw; 492 ft; N31 49 17 W89 18 37
6555 Hwy. 98 W., Suite 8, Hattiesburg, MS 53202
(601) 296-9800, *Fax:* (601) 296-9838
www.eagle99.com
contact@eagle99.com
License: Heidelberg, Jasper County, MS held by CC Licenses LLC.
Group Owner: Clear Channel Communications Inc.; (acq 12-19-2000; grpsl).
Regional Network: Miss. News Net.
Population Served: 350,000 *Arbitron Metro Market:* Laurel-Hattiesburg, MS *Target Audience:* General.
Jackson Walker, Operations Dir
Mike Comfort, General Manager
Glenn Musgrove, Chief Engineer

Holly Springs

WKRA
09-02-1966; 1110 khz AM *Hrs Open:* Sunrise-sunset; 1 kw-D, NDD; N34 47 11 W89 25 0
Mailing Address: 145 Memphis St, Holly Springs, MS 38635 US
Second Address: 1400 Hwy 4 E, Ste C, Holly Springs, MS 38635
(662) 252-1110, *Fax:* (662) 252-2739
power927fm.com
wkraradio@gmail.com
License: Holly Springs, MS held by Bill Autry.
Regional Network: Miss. News Net.
Arbitron Metro Market: Memphis, TN *Format:* Ethnic *Special Programming:* Gospel 12 hrs wkly *Hrs. of News Programming:* news progmg 9 hrs wkly *No. News Employees:* 1 *Target Audience:* 25-55.
Deirdra Autry, General Manager

WKRA-FM
06-30-1976; 92.7 mhz FM *Hrs Open:* 24; 3 kw; 299 ft.; N34 47 11 W89 25 0
Mailing Address: 145 Memphis St, Holly Springs, MS 38635 US
Second Address: 1400 Hwy 4 E, Ste C, Holly Springs, MS 58635
(662) 252-6692, *Fax:* (662) 252-2739
power927fm.com
power927@gmail.com
License: Holly Springs, Marshall County, MS
Arbitron Metro Market: Memphis, TN *Format:* Adult Contemp *No. News Employees:* 1 *Target Audience:* General; Black community
Deirdra Autry, Operations Dir

***WURC**
10-14-1988; 88.1 mhz FM; 3 kw; 272 ft.; N34 46 53 W89 26 49
150 Rust Avenue, Holly Springs, MS 38635 US
(662) 252-5881, *Fax:* (662) 252-8869
www.wurc.org
wurc@wurc.org
License: Holly Springs, Marshall County, MS held by Rust College Inc.
Nat'l Network: NPR
Arbitron Metro Market: Holly Springs, MS *Format:* Blues, Gospel, 52, News, News/Talk, Talk *Target Audience:* General; alternative seekers and minority listeners
David Beckley, President
Debayo Moyo, General Manager
Wayne.A.Fiddis, Station Manager
Learline Rayford, Secretary/Traffic Coordinator
Jerald White, Broadcast Engineer
Sharron Goodman-Hill, Instructor & Music Director

Horn Lake

WHAL-FM
07-26-1994; 95.7 mhz FM *Hrs Open:* 24; 6 kw; 289 ft.; N35 8 9 W89 58 17
200 Concord Plaza, Suite 600, San Antonio, TX 78216 US

(901) 259-1300, *Fax:* (901) 259-6451
www.hallelujahfm.com
info@halleujahfm.com
License: Horn Lake, DeSoto County, MS held by CC Licenses LLC.
Group Owner: Clear Channel Communications Inc.; (acq 1996; grpsl).
Nat'l Reps: Clear Channel
Arbitron Metro Market: Memphis, TN *Format:* Gospel *Hrs. of News Programming:* News progmg 3 hrs wkly *Target Audience:* 35-54; baby boomers
Tim Davies, General Manager
Ralph Salierno, General Sales Mgr
Eileen Collier, Programming Director
Frank Gilbert, Promotions Manager

Houston

WCPC
10-21-1955; 940 khz AM *Hrs Open:* 5 AM-9:15 PM
1189 Highway 15, North, Houston, MS 38851 US
(662) 456-3071, *Fax:* (662) 456-3072
License: Houston, MS held by Cajun Radio Corp.
Group Owner: Wilkins Communications Network Inc.; (acq 6-1-2007; $200,000)
Nat'l Network: USA *Regional Network:* Miss. News Net.
Arbitron Metro Market: Tupelo, MS *Format:* Black, Christian, 30, Gospel *Hrs. of News Programming:* news progmg 14 hrs wkly *No. News Employees:* 1 *Target Audience:* Adults *Adv. Rates:* 7; 7; 7; 7
Robert Wilkins, President
Melanie Mathis Munlin, Operations Dir
Robin Mathis, General Manager
Don Tallent, News Director

WSYE
09-19-1968; 93.3 mhz FM *Hrs Open:* 24; 100 kw; 1804 ft.; N33 45 6 W88 52 40
Mailing Address: 3436 Highway 45 North, Meridian, MS 39301 US
Second Address: 2214 S. Gloster, Tupelo, MS 38802
(662) 842-7658, *Fax:* (662) 842-0197
www.sunny93fm.net
License: Houston, Chickasaw County, MS held by JMD Inc.
Nat'l Reps: Christal
Arbitron Metro Market: Tupelo, MS *Format:* Adult Contemp *Hrs. of News Programming:* news progmg 2 hrs wkly *No. News Employees:* 1 *Target Audience:* 25-54. *Adv. Rates:* 36; 36; 36; 28
Steve Drunam, Operations Dir
Brenda Bebout, Station Manager
Scott Bebout, Promotions Manager

Indianola

WNLA
05-01-1953; 1380 khz AM *Hrs Open:* 12; 0.5 kw-D, ND1; 0.044 kw-N, ND1; N33 28 41 W90 38 28; N33 27 32 W90 37 45
P.O. Box 667, Indianola, MS 38751 US
(662) 887-1380, *Fax:* (662) 887-6006
www.wnlaradio.com
wnlaamfm@bellsouth.net
License: Indianola, MS held by Debut Broadcasting Mississippi Inc.
Group Owner: Debut Broadcasting Corp. Inc.; (acq 6-7-2007; $300,000 with co-located FM)
Regional Network: Miss. News Net.
Arbitron Metro Market: Greenville, MS *Format:* Black, Gospel *Target Audience:* 21-55; Black
Robert Marquitz, President
Erin Ely, General Manager
Gerry Brophy, General Sales Mgr
Bob Taylor, Chief Engineer

WIBT
09-01-1969; 105.5 mhz FM *Hrs Open:* 24; 4.4 kw; 200 ft; N33 28 41 W90 38 28
Box 667, Hwy. 448, Indianola, MS 38751
(662) 887-1380, *Fax:* (662) 887-1396
wnlaamfm@bellsouth.net
License: Indianola, Sunflower County, MS held by Debut Broadcasting Mississippi Inc.
Group Owner: Debut Broadcasting Corp. Inc.
Hrs. of News Programming: News progmg 21 hrs wkly *Target Audience:* 21-55. *Adv. Rates:* 8; 8; 8; na
Ben Smith, General Manager
Cindi McCarty, General Sales Mgr
Kevin Fitzgerald, Engineering Dir

WTCD
05-01-1990; 96.9 mhz FM *Hrs Open:* 24; 40 kw; 548 ft.; N33 34 34 W90 22 33
6310 I-55 North, Jackson, MS 39211 US
(662) 453-2174, *Fax:* (662) 455-5733
www.supertalkms.com
License: Indianola, Sunflower County, MS held by TeleSouth Communications Inc.
Group Owner: TeleSouth Communications Inc.; acq 5-28-97; $325,000)
Nat'l Network: USA *Regional Network:* Miss. News Net.
Arbitron Metro Market: Indianola, MS *Format:* News, News/Talk, 86 *Special Programming:* Farm 5 hrs, relg 11 hrs, talk 10 hrs wkly *Hrs. of News Programming:* news progmg 20 hrs wkly *No. News Employees:* 1*Target Audience:* 35-64; strong family orientation, middle to upper incomes
Steve Davenport, CEO & Owner
Jim Chick, General Manager
Debbie Smothers, Station Manager
MikeBernsen, CFO

*WYTF
08-26-2004; 88.7 mhz FM; 100 kw vert; 636 ft.; N33 35 3 W90 36 13
P.O. Drawer 2440, Tupelo, MS 38803 US
(662) 844-8888, *Fax:* (662) 842-6791
www.afr.net
faq@afr.net
License: Indianola, Sunflower County, MS held by American Family Association.
Group Owner: American Family Radio
Nat'l Network: USA
Arbitron Metro Market: Indianola, MS *Format:* Christian
Don Wildman, General Manager

Itta Bena

*WVSD
06-23-1991; 91.7 mhz FM *Hrs Open:* 6 AM-midnight; 3 kw; 292 ft.; N33 31 5 W90 20 38
14000 Hwy 82, Box 7221, Itta Bena, MS 38941 US
(662) 254-3612, *Fax:* (662) 254-3611
License: Itta Bena, Leflore County, MS held by Mississippi Valley State University.
Arbitron Metro Market: Itta Bena, MS *Format:* Gospel, Jazz
Special Programming: Oldies 10 hrs, reggae/Latin 3 hrs, comedy 2 hrs wk
Dr. Lester Newman, President
Larz Roberts, General Manager
Debra Harmon, Programming Director

Iuka

WKZU
11-05-1970; 104.9 mhz FM *Hrs Open:* 24/7; 50 kw; 443 ft.; N34 46 35 W88 23 40
311 W. Eastport, St. Iuka, MS 38852 US
(662) 837-1023, *Fax:* (662) 837-2994
www.ClassicRadioFM.com
classicradiofm@aol.com
License: Iuka, Tishomingo County, MS held by Kudzu Communications Inc.
Arbitron Metro Market: Tupelo, MS *Format:* Country *Special Programming:* Bluegrass, Bluegrass Gospel *Target Audience:* 25-54; 50% men & 50% women
Scott Peters, General Manager
Lisa Yates, General Sales Mgr
Froggy McAllister, Programming Director

Jackson

WJDX
01-01-1929; 620 khz AM *Hrs Open:* 24; 5 kw-D, DAN; 1 kw-N, DAN; N32 22 56 W90 11 26
Mailing Address: 600 Congress Ave., Suite 1400, Austin, TX 78701 US
Second Address: 1375 Beasley Rd., Jackson, MS 39206
(601) 982-1062, *Fax:* (601) 362-1905
www.wjdx.com
info@wjdx.com
License: Jackson, MS held by Capstar TX L.P.
Group Owner: Clear Channel Communications Inc.; (acq 8-30-2000; grpsl)
Nat'l Reps: McGavren Guild
Arbitron Metro Market: Jackson, MS *Format:* Sports, Talk *Special Programming:* Farm 2 hrs wkly *Hrs. of News Programming:* news progmg 10 hrs wkly *No. News Employees:* 1 *Target Audience:* 25-54; middle toupper income contemp adults
Kenneth Windham, General Manager
Mary Kirby, General Sales Mgr
Randy Bell, Programming Director
Jason Black, Chief Engineer
Theresa Banks, Traffic Manager

WJMI
01-01-1967; 99.7 mhz FM *Hrs Open:* 24; 98 kw; 1060 ft.; N32 12 28 W90 24 50
200 Concord Plaza, Suite 600, San Antonio, TX 78216 US
(601) 957-1300, *Fax:* (601) 956-0516
www.wjmi.com
production@wjmi.com
License: Jackson, Hinds County, MS held by Urban Radio II L.L.C.
Group Owner: Inner City Broadcasting
Arbitron Metro Market: Jackson, MS *Format:* Adult Contemp *No. News Employees:* 1 *Target Audience:* 18-49.
Stan Branson, Programming Director

*WJSU-FM
08-01-1975; 88.5 mhz FM; 24.5 kw; 200 ft.; N32 17 47 W90 12 23
P.O. Box 18450, Jackson, MS 39217 US
(601) 979-2285, *Fax:* (601) 979-2878
www.wjsu.com
wjsufm@jsums.edu
License: Jackson, Hinds County, MS held by Jackson State University.
Nat'l Network: NPR
Arbitron Metro Market: Jackson, MS *Format:* Jazz, News *Hrs. of News Programming:* news prgmg 36 hrs wkly *No. News Employees:* 2 *Target Audience:* 25-54; middle-class multiracial who prefer jazz
Gina Carter-Simmers, General Manager

WHLH
11-19-1973; 95.5 mhz FM; 100 kw; 1480 ft.; N32 14 26 W90 24 15
600 Congress Ave., Suite 1400, Austin, TX 78701 US
(601) 982-1062, *Fax:* (601) 362-1905
www.hallelujah955.com
info@hallelujah955.com
License: Jackson, Hinds County, MS held by Capstar TX L.P.
Group Owner: Clear Channel Communications Inc.; (acq 8-30-00; grpsl).
Nat'l Network: CBS *Nat'l Reps:* D & R Radio
Arbitron Metro Market: Jackson, MS *Format:* Gospel *Target Audience:* 18-34; female
Jenell Roberts, Programming Director

WJQS
01-01-1947; 1400 khz AM *Hrs Open:* 24; 1 kw-U, ND1; N32 19 12 W90 11 25
200 Concord Plaza, Suite 600, San Antonio, TX 78216 US
(601) 965-2001, *Fax:* (601) 961-3042
www.1400wjqs.com
info@1400wjqs.com
License: Jackson, MS held by Urban Radio II L.L.C.
Group Owner: Inner City Broadcasting; (acq 8-25-2000; grpsl)
Arbitron Metro Market: Jackson, MS *Format:* News
Gary Michiels, General Manager

*WMPN-FM
11-01-1984; 91.3 mhz FM *Hrs Open:* 24; 45 kw; 1388 ft.; N32 11 29 W90 24 22
US
(601) 432-6565, *Fax:* (601) 432-6806
www.mpbonline.org
communications@mpbonline.org.
License: Jackson, Hinds County, MS held by Mississippi Authority for Educational Television.
Nat'l Network: PRI; NPR *Wire Services:* AP
Arbitron Metro Market: Jackson, MS *Format:* News *Hrs. of News Programming:* news progmg 100 hrs wkly *No. News Employees:* 7 *Target Audience:* General.
Robert Sawyer, Chairman
Jason Holland, Operations Dir
Jay Woods, General Manager
Marie Antoon, General Sales Mgr
Mari Irby, Promotions Manager

*WMPR
01-01-1983; 90.1 mhz FM; 100 kw; 449 ft.; N32 11 33 W90 5 28
1018 Pecan Park Circle, Jackson, MS 39209 US
(601) 948-5835, *Fax:* (601) 948-6162
www.wmpr901.com
wmpr@wmpr901.com
License: Jackson, Hinds County, MS held by J.C. Maxwell Broadcasting Group Inc.
Arbitron Metro Market: Jackson, MS *Format:* Variety/Diverse
Charles Evers, General Manager

WMSI-FM
01-01-1948; 102.9 mhz FM *Hrs Open:* 24; 100 kw; 1886 ft.; N32 12 49 W90 22 56

RADIO - U.S.

Mailing Address: 600 Congress Ave., Suite 1400, Austin, TX 78701 US
Second Address: 1375 Beasley Rd., Jackson, MS 39206
(601) 982-1062, *Fax:* (601) 362-1905
www.miss103.com
info@miss103.com
License: Jackson, Hinds County, MS held by Capstar TX L.P.
Group Owner: Clear Channel Communications Inc.
Arbitron Metro Market: Jackson, MS *Format:* Country *Special Programming:* Farm one hr wkly *Hrs. of News Programming:* News progmg 4 hrs wkly *Target Audience:* 25 plus.
Steve Kelly, Operations Dir
Kenny Windham, General Manager
Doug Jones, General Sales Mgr
Rick Adams, Programming Director
Diana Bass, News Director
Marshall Stewart, Music Director

WOAD

01-01-1929; 1300 khz AM; 5 kw-D, ND1; 1 kw-N, ND1; N32 23 12 W90 9 47
200 Concord Plaza, Suite 600, San Antonio, TX 78216 US
(601) 957-1300, *Fax:* (601) 956-0516
www.woad.com
production@wjmi.com
License: Jackson, MS held by Urban Radio II L.L.C.
Group Owner: Inner City Broadcasting; (acq 8-25-2000; grpsl).
Nat'l Network: American Urban; ABC *Wire Services:* Weather Wire
Arbitron Metro Market: Jackson, MS *TV Affiliate:* Gospel *No. News Employees:* 25-54.

WSFZ

09-01-1938; 930 khz AM *Hrs Open:* 24
Mailing Address: 301 Congress Ave, Suite 410, Austin, TX 78701 US
Second Address: 574 Highway 51 North, Suite F, Ridgeland, MS 39157
(601) 605-6656, *Fax:* (601) 605-6646
www.supersport930.com
eubie@supersport930.com
License: Jackson, MS held by Sportsrad Inc.
Nat'l Network: Westwood One; Sporting News Radio Network
Arbitron Metro Market: Jackson, MS *Format:* Sports
Bryan Eubank, General Manager
Bo Bounds, General Sales Mgr

*WJLV

08-10-1971; 94.7 mhz FM *Hrs Open:* 24; 100 kw; 1,168 ft; N32 16 53 W90 17 41
222 Beasley Rd., Jackson, MS 39205
(601) 957-3000, *Fax:* (601) 956-0370
www.947jackfm.com
jack@947jackfm.com
License: Jackson, Hinds County, MS held by Backyard Broadcasting Mississippi Licensee LLC
Group Owner: Backyard Broadcasting LLC; (acq 5-31-2002; $4,830,000 with WRXW(FM) Pearl)
Nat'l Reps: Christal
Population Served: 330,000 *Arbitron Metro Market:* Jackson, MS *Hrs. of News Programming:* news progmg one hr wkly *No. News Employees:* 1 *Target Audience:* 25-54. *Adv. Rates:* 50; 45; 45; 25
Barry Drake, President
Jason Williams, General Manager
Don Wayne, Programming Director

Kosciusko

WJDX-FM

06-25-1965; 105.1 mhz FM *Hrs Open:* 24; 100 kw; 981 ft; N32 41 25 W89 52 06
Box 31999, Jackson, MS 78701
(601) 982-1062, *Fax:* (601) 362-8270
www.q1051.com
stancebinghan@clearchannel.com
License: Kosciusko, Attala County, MS held by Capstar TX L.P.
Group Owner: Clear Channel Communications Inc.; (acq 8-30-00; grpsl)
Population Served: 450,000 *Arbitron Metro Market:* Jackson, MS *Target Audience:* 35-64. *Adv. Rates:* 18; 15; 18; 15
Steve Kelly, Operations Dir
Kenneth Windham, General Manager

Laurel

WAML

10-20-1932; 1340 khz AM *Hrs Open:* 24; 1 kw-U, ND1; N31 40 1 W89 8 59
318 West 5th Street, Laurel, MS 39440 US
(601) 425-0011, *Fax:* (601) 425-0016
License: Laurel, MS held by Walking by Faith Ministries Inc.
Group Owner: Walking by Faith Ministries Inc.; (acq 10-1-99)
Arbitron Metro Market: Laurel, MS *Format:* Sports, Talk *Target Audience:* General.
James Black, General Manager

*WATP

01-01-1998; 90.9 mhz FM; 69 kw; 723 ft.; N31 52 39 W88 52 44
P O Drawer 2440, Tupelo, MS 38803 US
(662) 844-8888, *Fax:* (662) 842-6791
www.afr.net
faq@afr.net
License: Laurel, Jones County, MS held by American Family Association.
Group Owner: American Family Radio
Nat'l Network: USA
Arbitron Metro Market: Laurel, MS *Format:* Religious
Marvin Sanders, General Manager

WHJA

02-27-1957; 890 khz AM *Hrs Open:* Sunrise-sunset; 10 kw-C, NDD; 10 kw-D, NDD; N31 31 29 W89 14 31
3201 Sheffield Drive, Emmaus, PA 18049 US
(601) 296-9800, *Fax:* (601) 296-9838
License: Laurel, MS held by CC Licenses LLC.
Group Owner: Clear Channel Communications Inc.; (acq 12-19-2000; grpsl)
Arbitron Metro Market: Laurel, MS *Format:* Blues *Hrs. of News Programming:* news progmg 4 hrs wkly *No. News Employees:* 1 *Target Audience:* General.
Jackson Walker, Operations Dir
Mike Comfort, General Manager
James Harris, General Sales Mgr
Denise Brooks, Programming Director
Terri Hudson, News Director
Glen Musgrove, Chief Engineer

WMXI

04-01-1989; 98.1 mhz FM; 2.55 kw; 512 ft.; N31 33 22 W89 9 9
Mailing Address: 100 22nd Ave., South Suite A, Meridian, MS 39301 US
Second Address: 7501 U.S. Hwy. 49, Hattiesburg, MS 39403
(601) 264-0443, *Fax:* (601) 264-5733
www.wmxi.com
zoo107@bellsouth.net
License: Laurel, Jones County, MS held by Rainey Broadcasting Inc.
Nat'l Network: Premiere Radio Networks
Arbitron Metro Market: Laurel, MS *Format:* News, News/Talk, 86 *Special Programming:* sports *Hrs. of News Programming:* 24 *Target Audience:* adults 25 plus *Adv. Rates:* $25.00
Ted Tibbett, General Manager

WNSL

03-10-1959; 100.3 mhz FM; 100 kw; 1063 ft.; N31 31 37 W89 8 7
3201 Sheffield Drive, Emmaus, PA 18049 US
(601) 296-9800, *Fax:* (601) 296-9838
www.sl100.com
contact@sl100.com
License: Laurel, Jones County, MS
Group Owner: Clear Channel Communications Inc.
Nat'l Network: ABC
Arbitron Metro Market: Laurel, MS *Format:* Contemporary Hits/Top 40 *Target Audience:* 18-49. *Adv. Rates:* 42; 42; 42; 28
Don King, Programming Director

Leland

WBAD

01-01-1973; 94.3 mhz FM *Hrs Open:* 19; 50 kw; 289 ft.; N33 24 55 W90 59 18
Mailing Address: P.O. Box 4426, Greenville, MS 38701 US
Second Address: 126 Seven Oaks Rd., Greenville, MS 38701
, *Fax:* (208) 734-6633
www.csnradio.com
License: Leland, Washington County, MS held by Interchange Communications Inc.
Nat'l Network: American Urban
Arbitron Metro Market: Junction City OR *Format:* Christian
Mike Stocklin, General Manager

WESY

04-08-1957; 1580 khz AM *Hrs Open:* 24; 1 kw-D, ND1; 0.048 kw-N, ND1; N33 22 46 W90 55 47
Mailing Address: P.O. Box 4426, Greenville, MS 38701 US
Second Address: 126 Seven Oaks Rd., Greenville, MS 38701
(662) 335-9265, *Fax:* (662) 335-5538
wbad@tecinfo.com
License: Leland, MS held by East Delta Communications Inc.
Nat'l Network: American Urban
Arbitron Metro Market: Leland, MS *Format:* Blues, Gospel, 74 *Target Audience:* 18-54.
William Jackson, President
Stanley Sherman, Executive Vice President

WIQQ

09-01-1985; 102.3 mhz FM *Hrs Open:* 24; 1.65 kw; 446 ft.; N33 23 51 W91 0 35
Mailing Address: P.O. Box 1816, Greenville, MS 38702 US
Second Address: Unit 39, 800 Hwy. 1 S., Greenville, MS 38702
(662) 378-2617, *Fax:* (662) 378-8341
wiqq@sellsouth.net
License: Leland, Washington County, MS held by Debut Broadcasting Mississippi Inc.
Group Owner: Debut Broadcasting Corp. Inc.; (acq 6-19-2007; grpsl)
Nat'l Network: USA; Jones Radio Networks *Regional Network:* Ark. Radio Net. *Nat'l Reps:* McGavren Guild
Format: Adult Contemp *Special Programming:* Farm 6 hrs, relg 6 hrs wkly *Hrs. of News Programming:* news progmg 4 hrs wkly *No. News Employees:* 1 *Target Audience:* 18-49; multi-paycheck & spendable income
Robert Marquitz, President
James Karr Jr., Operations Dir
Percy Kuhn, Chief Engineer
Linda McKee, Operations Manager

Lexington

WAGR-FM

06-01-1990; 102.5 mhz FM; 6 kw; 328 ft.; N33 9 6 W90 7 45
100 Radio Rd, PO Box 369, Lexington, MS 39095 US
(662) 834-1025(662) 834-1254, *Fax:* (662) 834-1254
class102@cablesouthmedia.net
License: Lexington, Holmes County, MS held by Brad Maurice Cothran
Arbitron Metro Market: Lexington, MS *Format:* Country, Oldies
Brad Cothran, General Manager

Liberty

WAZA

01-01-1998; 107.7 mhz FM; 25 kw; 328 ft.; N31 17 12 W90 47 53
215 East Bay Street, Magnolia, MS 39652 US
(800) 877-5600, *Fax:* (916) 251-1650
www.klove.com
License: Liberty, Amite County, MS held by Southwest Broadcasting Inc.
Group Owner: Southwest Broadcasting Inc.
Arbitron Metro Market: East Wenatchee WA *Format:* Christian
Michael Novak, President

Long Beach

WJZD-FM

03-20-1994; 94.5 mhz FM *Hrs Open:* 24; 6 kw; 322 ft.; N30 26 0 W89 2 10
Mailing Address: P. O. Box 6216, Gulfport, MS 39506 US
Second Address: 10211 Southpark Dr., Gulfport, MS 39503
(228) 896-5307, *Fax:* (228) 896-5703
www.wjzd.com
info@wjzd.com
License: Long Beach, Harrison County, MS held by WJZD Inc.
Nat'l Network: ABC *Wire Services:* AP
Arbitron Metro Market: Biloxi-Gulfport-Pascagoula, MS *Format:* Adult Contemp, News, 62, Talk *Special Programming:* American Blues Network *Hrs. of News Programming:* news progmg 2 hrs wkly *No. News Employees:* 2*Target Audience:* P 18-54 *Adv. Rates:* 75; 60; 60; 50
Rip Daniels, CEO
Danielle Jewett, Operations Dir

Lorman

*WPRL

10-12-1987; 91.7 mhz FM *Hrs Open:* 6 AM-2 AM (M-F); 6 AM-midnight (S,; 3 kw; 299 ft.; N31 53 37 W91 8 54
Mailing Address: 1000 Asu Drive, Box #269, Lorman, MS 39096 US
Second Address: Alcorn State Univ., 1000 Alcorn Dr., Lorman, MS 39096
(601) 877-6290,(601) 877-6613, *Fax:* (601) 877-2213
alconstateuniv.edu
lljunag@hotmail.com
License: Lorman, Jefferson County, MS held by Alcorn State University.
Nat'l Network: PRI; NPR; AP Radio
Format: Variety/Diverse *Hrs. of News Programming:* news progmg 23 hrs wkly *No. News Employees:* 1 *Target Audience:* General; African-American, rural, University faculty & students
Lijuana Weir, Operations Dir

Louisville

WLSM-FM
04-22-1966; 107.1 mhz FM *Hrs Open:* 24; 12.5 kw; 466 ft.; N33 7 20 W89 1 7
Mailing Address: P.O Box 279, Louisville, MS 39339 US
Second Address: 2142 Hwy. 14 E., Louisville, MS 39339
(662) 773-3481, *Fax:* (662) 773-3482
majic107@dixie-net.com
License: Louisville, Winston County, MS held by Harrison Communications Inc.
Nat'l Network: ABC; Jones Radio Networks *Regional Network:* Miss. News Net.
Format: Adult Contemp *Target Audience:* 18-54.
Phillip Harrison, President
Stacy Harrison, Station Manager

***KOUI**
90.7 mhz FM; kw
US
License: Louisville, Winston County, MS held by Ron Elmore Ministries Inc.
Arbitron Metro Market: Louisville, MS
Ron Elmore, President

Lucedale

WVGG
09-03-1960; 1440 khz AM; 5 kw-D; N30 56 00 W88 36 20
Mailing Address: Box 827, Lucedale, MS 39355
Second Address: 3276 Hwy. 198 W., Lucedale, MS 39452
(601) 947-8151, *Fax:* (601) 947-8152
jdl@datasync.com
License: Lucedale, George County, MS held by JDL Corp.
Nat'l Reps: Dora-Clayton; Keystone (unwired net)
Population Served: 35,000*Target Audience:* General.
Larry Shirley, President
Lillian Hodgel, General Sales Mgr
Bob Bonnell, Farm Director

WRBE-FM
04-01-1993; 106.9 mhz FM; 6 kw; 259 ft.; N30 55 58 W88 36 21
Mailing Address: 129 Long Blvd., Quitman, MS 39355 US
Second Address: 3276 Hwy. 198 W., Lucedale, MS 39452
(601) 947-8151, *Fax:* (601) 947-8152
License: Lucedale, George County, MS held by JDL Corp.
Nat'l Network: Jones Radio Networks; Westwood One *Regional Network:* Miss. News Net.
Format: Country
Larry Shirley, General Manager
Anthony Pugh, General Sales Mgr
Bob Bonnell, Farm Director

Lumberton

WZNF
12-10-1983; 95.3 mhz FM *Hrs Open:* 24; 100 kw; 1426 ft.; N30 45 5 W89 3 24
522 D., Mitchell Self Mem. Drive, Muscle Shoals, AL 35662 US
(228) 896-5500, *Fax:* (228) 896-0458
www.z95fm.com
patty@z95fm.com
License: Lumberton, Lamar County, MS held by JMD Inc.
Arbitron Metro Market: Biloxi-Gulfport-Pascagoula, MS *Format:* Classic Rock
Morgan Dowdy, CEO
Buddy Baylor, General Manager

Madison

WUSJ
09-16-1966; 96.3 mhz FM; 100 kw; 1284 ft.; N32 11 29 W90 24 22
No. 1 Golfcourse Rd., Kosciusko, MS 39090 US
(601) 956-0102, *Fax:* (601) 978-3890
www.us963.com
gwenr@radiopeople.net
License: Madison, Madison County, MS held by New South Communications Inc.
Group Owner: New South Communications Inc.; acq 8-24-99; $5 million)
Arbitron Metro Market: Jackson, MS *Format:* Country
Gwen Rakestraw, General Manager

***WQVI**
07-20-2004; 90.5 mhz FM; 60 kw vert; 430 ft.; N32 42 51 W89 49 19
P. O. Box 2440, Tupelo, MS 38803 US
(662) 844-8888, *Fax:* (662) 842-6791
www.afr.net
faq@afr.net
License: Madison, Scott County, MS held by American Family Association.
Group Owner: American Family Radio
Nat'l Network: USA
Arbitron Metro Market: Madison, MS *Format:* Christian
Marvin Sanders, General Manager

Magee

WKXI-FM
04-11-1970; 107.5 mhz FM; 98 kw; 951 ft.; N32 15 29 W89 47 22
200 Concord Plaza, Suite 600, San Antonio, TX 78216 US
(601) 957-1300, *Fax:* (601) 956-0516
www.kixie107.com
production@wjmi.com
License: Magee, Simpson County, MS held by Urban Radio II L.L.C.
Group Owner: Inner City Broadcasting; (acq 8-25-2000; grpsl).
Arbitron Metro Market: Jackson, MS *Format:* Urban Contemporary *Target Audience:* 25-54.
Kevin Webb, Operations Dir
Stan Branson, Operations Manager

WSJC
07-05-1957; 810 khz AM; 50 kw-D, DAN; 0.5 kw-N, DAN; N31 52 0 W89 41 35
P.O. Box 1177, Jackson, MS 39205 US
(601) 849-5838, *Fax:* (601) 849-5838
wsjcradio.com
License: Magee, MS held by Witko Broadcasting L.L.C.
Format: Religious
Norm Wick, General Manager

Mantee

WKBB
04-14-1974; 100.9 mhz FM; 47 kw; 510 ft.; N33 40 43 W88 48 18
PO Box 1336, 413 North Forrest Street, West Point, MS 39773 US
(662) 494-1450, *Fax:* (662) 494-9762
www.supertalk.fm
License: Mantee, Clay County, MS
Arbitron Metro Market: Columbus-Starkville-West Point, MS
Format: News, News/Talk, 86 *Target Audience:* 35-54.
William Miller, General Manager

Marietta

WXWX
01-01-2008; 96.3 mhz FM; 3.9 kw; 410 ft.; N34 24 33 W88 32 24 US
(662) 680-1606
License: Marietta, Prentiss County, MS held by George S. Flinn Jr.
Nat'l Network: ESPN Radio
Arbitron Metro Market: Marietta, MS *Format:* Sports
Russ Wilson, General Manager

Marion

WKZB
03-15-1990; 95.1 mhz FM; 50 kw; 606 ft; N32 26 08 W88 36 24
4307 Hwy. 39 N., Meridian, MS 39301
(601) 693-2381, *Fax:* (601) 485-2972
License: Marion, Lauderdale County, MS held by CC Licenses LLC.
Group Owner: Clear Channel Communications Inc.; (acq 3-16-2001; grpsl).
Population Served: 45,083 *Arbitron Metro Market:* Meridian, MS *Target Audience:* 25-54.
Mark Maharrey, General Manager
Ann Burton, Programming Director
Jeff McDermott, Assistant Programming Director

McComb

WAKH
10-15-1978; 105.7 mhz FM *Hrs Open:* 24; 100 kw; 489 ft; N31 16 50 W90 27 05
Mailing Address: Box 1649, McComb, MS 39503
Second Address: 206 N. Front, McComb, MS 39649
(601) 648-4116, *Fax:* (601) 684-4654
k106.net
spats@k106.net
License: McComb, Pike County, MS
Group Owner: Southwest Broadcasting Inc.
Target Audience: General.
Charles Dowdy, General Manager
Robbie Hamilton, General Sales Mgr
Dave Hughes, Programming Director

WAPF
04-25-1975; 1140 khz AM; 1 kw-D, NDD; N31 14 51 W90 25 14
Mailing Address: P.O.B 2639, Gulfport, MS 39503 US
Second Address: 206 N. Front, McComb, MS 39648
(601) 684-4116, *Fax:* (601) 684-4654
License: McComb, MS held by Southwest Broadcasting Inc.
Group Owner: Southwest Broadcasting Inc.; (acq 8-5-93; $600,000;
Regional Network: Miss. News Net.
Arbitron Metro Market: Baton Rouge LA *Format:* Sports *Target Audience:* General.
Charles Dowdy, General Manager

WAKK
04-18-1948; 980 khz AM; 5 kw-D, ND1; 0.152 kw-N, ND1; N31 12 51 W90 27 42
Mailing Address: P. O. Drawer 1056, Oxford, MS 39655 US
Second Address: Drawer 1649, McComb, MS 39648
(601) 684-4116, *Fax:* (601) 684-4654
License: McComb, MS held by Southwest Broadcasting Inc.
Group Owner: Southwest Broadcasting Inc.; (acq 9-86; $600,000 with co-located FM;
Nat'l Network: ABC
Arbitron Metro Market: Mccomb, MS *Format:* Gospel *Target Audience:* General.
Wayne Dowdy, President
Charles Dowdy, General Manager
David Hughes, Programming Director

***WAQL**
01-01-1999; 90.5 mhz FM; 30 kw; 534 ft.; N31 26 1 W90 34 45
Po Drawer 2440, Tupelo, MS 38803 US
(662) 844-8888, *Fax:* (662) 842-6791
www.afr.net
faq@afr.net
License: McComb, Pike County, MS held by American Family Association.
Group Owner: American Family Radio
Nat'l Network: USA
Arbitron Metro Market: McComb, MS *Format:* Religious
Marvin Sanders, General Manager

Meridian

WALT
01-01-1946; 910 khz AM *Hrs Open:* 24; 5 kw-D, ND1; 1 kw-N, ND1; N32 23 37 W88 40 8
3436 Highway 45n, Meridian, MS 39301 US
(601) 693-2661, *Fax:* (601) 483-0826
michelle@910talkradio.com
License: Meridian, MS held by New South Communications Inc.
Group Owner: New South Communications Inc.; acq 4-1-57)
Nat'l Reps: McGavren Guild
Arbitron Metro Market: Meridian, MS *Format:* News, News/Talk, 86 *Target Audience:* 35-64. *Adv. Rates:* 12; 12; 12; 8
F.E. Holladay, President
Paul Bucurel, General Manager

WYHL
12-01-1957; 1450 khz AM *Hrs Open:* 24/7; 1 kw-U, ND1; N32 23 9 W88 41 36
4307 Highway 39 North, Meridian, MS 39301 US
(601) 693-2381, *Fax:* (601) 485-2972
License: Meridian, MS held by CC Licenses LLC.
Group Owner: Clear Channel Communications Inc.; (acq 3-16-2001; grpsl)
Arbitron Metro Market: Meridian, MS *Format:* Gospel
Mark Maharrey, General Manager
Ann Burton, Programming Director
Sam Weaver, Program Director

WJDQ
02-01-1968; 101.3 mhz FM; 99 kw; Ant 581 ft; N32 18 43 W88 41 33
4307 Hwy. 39 N., Meridian, MS 39301
(601) 693-2381, *Fax:* (601) 485-2972
License: Meridian, Lauderdale County, MS held by CC Licenses LLC.
Group Owner: Clear Channel Communications Inc.; (acq 3-16-2001; grpsl).
Population Served: 101,300 *Arbitron Metro Market:* Meridian, MS
Mark Maharrey, General Manager
Ann Burton, Programming Director
Jack Edwards, Program Director

***WMAW-FM**
12-01-1983; 88.1 mhz FM *Hrs Open:* 24; 100 kw; 1050 ft.; N32 8 18 W89 5 36
3825 Ridgewood Road, Jackson, MS 39211 US

(601) 432-6565, *Fax:* (601) 432-6806
www.mpbonline.org
License: Meridian, Lauderdale County, MS held by Mississippi Authority for Educational Television.
Nat'l Network: PRI; NPR *Wire Services:* AP
Arbitron Metro Market: Meridian, MS *TV Affiliate:* WMAW-TV
Format: News *Hrs. of News Programming:* news progmg 100 hrs wkly *No. News Employees:* 7 *Target Audience:* General.
Jason Klein, Operations Dir
Jay Woods, General Manager
Marie Antoon, General Sales Mgr

WMER
10-16-1973; 1390 khz AM *Hrs Open:* 19; 5 kw-D, ND1; 0.101 kw-N, ND1; N32 20 41 W88 41 32
1413 Rubush Avenue, Meridian, MS 39301 US
(601) 693-9637, *Fax:* (601) 693-9637
License: Meridian, MS held by Michael H. Glass.
Nat'l Network: USA
Arbitron Metro Market: Meridian, MS *Format:* Gospel *Target Audience:* 25-54; upscale, young families, non-working mothers
Mike Cushman, Operations Dir
Rick Hencley, General Manager
Steve Potter, General Sales Mgr
Paul Orth, Chief Engineer

WALT-FM
01-01-1994; 102.1 mhz FM; 800 w; Ant 610 ft; N32 21 51 W88 38 34
3436 Hwy. 45 N., Meridian, MS 39302
(601) 693-2661, *Fax:* (601) 483-0826
wmmz@wokk.com
License: Meridian, Lauderdale County, MS held by Mississippi Broadcasters L.L.C.
Group Owner: Mississippi Broadcasters L.L.C.; (acq 2-26-93; $243,500;
Arbitron Metro Market: Meridian, MS
Clay Holladay, President
Scott Stevens, Operations Dir
Karen Bostick, General Sales Mgr
Scott Shepperd, Chief Engineer

WMOX
12-01-1945; 1010 khz AM *Hrs Open:* 24; 10 kw-D, DA2; 1 kw-N, DA2; N32 23 42 W88 39 28
PO Box 5184, Meridian, MS 39302 US
(601) 693-1891, *Fax:* (601) 483-1010
www.wmox.net
wmoxradio@wmox.net
License: Meridian, MS held by Magnolia State Broadcasting Inc.
Regional Network: Miss. News Net. *Nat'l Reps:* Dora-Clayton
Arbitron Metro Market: Meridian, MS *Format:* News, Sports, 86
Special Programming: Relg 8 hrs wkly *No. News Employees:* 1
Target Audience: 25 plus; College educated with 30k plus annual income *Adv. Rates:* 20; 16; 16; 10
Eddie Smith, President
William Smith, Operations Dir

WNBN
11-01-1987; 1290 khz AM *Hrs Open:* 18
1290 Hawkins Crossing Rd, Meridian, MS 39301 US
(601) 286-7030, *Fax:* (601) 286-3070
License: Meridian, MS held by Frank Rackley Jr.
Arbitron Metro Market: Meridian, MS *Format:* Blues, Gospel
Special Programming: Black, women's, business, inspirational
Hrs. of News Programming: News progmg 61 hrs wkly *Target Audience:* 18-54. *Adv. Rates:* 10; 10; 10; 9.50.
Frank Rackley Jr., General Manager

WOKK
08-01-1967; 97.1 mhz FM; 100 kw; 600 ft.; N32 19 30 W88 41 17
3436 Highway 45n, Meridian, MS 39301 US
601-693-2661, *Fax:* (601) 693-3439
www.wokk.com
michelle@910talkradio.com
License: Meridian, Lauderdale County, MS
Arbitron Metro Market: Meridian, MS *TV Affiliate:* Country *No. News Employees:* 25-54.
Program Director/ Operations manager, Programming Director
Operations Manager

Merigold

WKXY
01-01-2003; 92.1 mhz FM; 6 kw; 328 ft.; N33 52 49 W90 42 24
607 Frederick Drive, Cleveland, MS 38732 US
(662) 843-3392, *Fax:* (888) 704-4762
www.kix921.com
License: Merigold, Bolivar County, MS held by Delta Radio LLC.
Group Owner: Contemporary Communications
Arbitron Metro Market: Merigold, MS *Format:* Country
Shawn McIntire, General Manager
Dan Hawthorne, News Director

Mississippi State

***WMAB-FM**
12-01-1983; 89.9 mhz FM *Hrs Open:* 24; 64.3 kw; 1061 ft.; N33 21 14 W89 9 0
3825 Ridgewood Road, Jackson, MS 39211 US
(601) 432-6565, *Fax:* (601) 432-6806
www.mpbonline.org
communications@mpbonline.org
License: Mississippi State, Oktibbeha County, MS held by Mississippi Authority for Educational Television.
Nat'l Network: PRI; NPR *Wire Services:* AP
Arbitron Metro Market: MS State, MS *TV Affiliate:* WMAB-TV
Format: News *Hrs. of News Programming:* news progmg 100 hrs wkly *No. News Employees:* 7 *Target Audience:* General.
Marie Antoon, Chairman
Jay Woods, General Manager
Jason Klein, Programming Director

Monticello

WRQO
11-19-1990; 102.1 mhz FM *Hrs Open:* 24; 50 kw; 433 ft.; N31 36 13 W90 12 26
Mailing Address: P.O. Box 2016, Monticello, MS 39654 US
Second Address: Box 1084, Monticello, MS 39654
(601) 587-9363,(601) 587-7625, *Fax:* (601) 587-9401,(601) 835-5005
country@wrqo-q102.com
License: Monticello, Lawrence County, MS held by TeleSouth Communications Inc.
Group Owner: TeleSouth Communications Inc.; (acq 6-20-2006; grpsl).
Nat'l Network: CBS *Regional Network:* Miss. News Net.
Format: Talk *Special Programming:* Farm one hr, relg 10 hrs wkly *Hrs. of News Programming:* News progmg 15 hrs wkly *Target Audience:* 25-54.
Stephen Davenport, President
Randy Bullock, Operations Dir
Marcus Rusty O'Neal, General Manager

WMLC
01-01-1969; 1270 khz AM; 1 kw-D, ND2; 0.053 kw-N, ND2; N31 33 24 W90 8 6
Rt.1, Box 293, Monticello, MS 39654 US
(601) 587-1270, *Fax:* (601) 587-2119
wmlc@bellsouth.net
License: Monticello, MS held by Walking by Faith Ministries Inc.
Group Owner: Walking by Faith Ministries Inc.; (acq 6-28-2006; $50,000)
Nat'l Network: ESPN Radio
Arbitron Metro Market: Monticello, MS *Format:* Sports
Will Watson, General Manager

Moss Point

WBUV
06-01-1964; 104.9 mhz FM *Hrs Open:* 24; 16 kw; 879 ft.; N30 29 9 W88 42 53
200 Concord Plaza, Suite 600, San Antonio, TX 78216 US
(228) 388-2323, *Fax:* (228) 388-2362
www.newsradio1049fm.com
reggiebates@clearchannel.com
License: Moss Point, Jackson County, MS held by CC Licenses LLC.
Group Owner: Clear Channel Communications Inc.; (acq 12-7-98; $1.4 million swap with WYOK(FM) Atmore, AL).
Nat'l Network: Fox News Radio; Fox Sports; Premiere Radio Networks *Nat'l Reps:* Clear Channel *Wire Services:* AP
Arbitron Metro Market: Moss Point, MS *Format:* News, News/Talk, 86 *No. News Employees:* 4 *Target Audience:* 25-54; men
Reggie Bates, General Manager
Richard Hinshaw, General Sales Mgr
Walter Brown, Programming Director
Kristan Saucier, Promotions Manager
Kelly Bennett, News Director
Sheila Taylor, Traffic Manager

Natchez

***WASM**
01-01-2001; 91.1 mhz FM; 1 kw; 193 ft.; N31 33 24 W91 23 0
P.O. Drawer 2440, Tupelo, MS 38803 US
(662) 844-8888, *Fax:* (662) 842-6791
www.afr.net
faq@afr.net
License: Natchez, Adams County, MS held by American Family Association.
Group Owner: American Family Radio
Nat'l Network: USA
Arbitron Metro Market: Natchez, MS *Format:* Religious
Marvin Sanders, General Manager

WMIS
05-18-1941; 1240 khz AM *Hrs Open:* 24; 1 kw-U; N31 31 14 W91 23 09
Mailing Address: Box 1248, Natchez, MS 39121
Second Address: 20 E. Franklin St., Natchez, MS 39120
(601) 442-2522, *Fax:* (601) 446-9918
wmiswtyj@bellsouth.net
License: Natchez, Adams County, MS held by Natchez Broadcasting Co.
Nat'l Network: American Urban *Regional Network:* Miss. News Net.
Population Served: 100,000 *Arbitron Metro Market:* Jackson, MS
Target Audience: General; Black *Adv. Rates:* 16; 16; 16; 16
Diana Nutter, President
Calvin Butler, Operations Dir
James Nutter, General Manager
Lijuna Weir, Station Manager

WNAT
12-04-1949; 1450 khz AM *Hrs Open:* 24; 1 kw-U, ND1; N31 33 33 W91 23 30
Mailing Address: P.O. Box 768, #2 O'Ferrall Street, Natchez, MS 39121 US
Second Address: 2 O'Ferral St., Natchez, MS 39121
(601) 442-4895, *Fax:* (601) 446-8260
www.listenupyall.com
License: Natchez, MS held by First Natchez Corp.
Group Owner: First Natchez Radio Group; (acq 11-28-58).
Regional Network: Miss. News Net.
Arbitron Metro Market: Natchez, MS *Format:* News, News/Talk, 84, Talk *Special Programming:* Gospel 18 hrs wkly *No. News Employees:* 2 *Target Audience:* 25-54. *Adv. Rates:* 16; 18; 16; 10
Marie Perkins, President
Margaret Perkins, General Manager
Mickey Alexander, Programming Director
Keith Sanders, News Director
Brenda Green, Traffic Manager

WQNZ
03-01-1968; 95.1 mhz FM *Hrs Open:* 24; 100 kw; 719 ft.; N31 30 33.4 W91 24 18.6
Post Office Drawer 768, Natchez, MS 39121 US
(601) 442-4895, *Fax:* (601) 446-8260
www.wnat1450.com
License: Natchez, Adams County, MS held by First Natchez Corp.
Group Owner: First Natchez Radio Group
Regional Network: La. Net.
Format: Country *Hrs. of News Programming:* news progmg 7 hrs wkly *No. News Employees:* 2 *Target Audience:* 25 plus. *Adv. Rates:* 18.50; 16.50; 18.50; 16.50
Chris Allinger, Programming Director

WKSO
03-01-1993; 97.3 mhz FM; 1.45 kw; 686 ft.; N31 30 33 W91 24 19
Mailing Address: P.O. Box 2057, Natchez, MS 39121 US
Second Address: 2 O'Ferrall St., Natchez, MS 39420
(601) 442-4895, *Fax:* (601) 446-8260
listenupyall.com
License: Natchez, Adams County, MS held by Will Perk Broadcasting.
Group Owner: First Natchez Radio Group; (acq 8-31-92; $36,000;
Nat'l Network: ABC
Arbitron Metro Market: Natchez, MS *Format:* Adult Contemp *Adv. Rates:* 8; 7; 8; 7
Margaret Perkins, General Manager

New Albany

WNAU
03-27-1955; 1470 khz AM
PO Box 808, New Albany, MS 38652 US
(662) 534-8133, *Fax:* (662) 538-4183
www.wnau1470.com
info@wnau1470.com
License: New Albany, MS held by MPM Investment Group
Regional Network: Miss. News Net.
Arbitron Metro Market: Tupelo, MS *Format:* News, Oldies, 84
Special Programming: Gospel *Target Audience:* 25-54.
Terry Cook, President
Ricky McCollum, Executive Vice President

WWZD-FM
03-03-1986; 106.7 mhz FM *Hrs Open:* 24; 28 kw; 656 ft.; N34 29 6 W88 54 2
Mailing Address: 111 East Kilbourn Avenue, Suite 2700, Milwaukee, WI 53202 US
Second Address: 5026 Cliff Gookin Blvd., Tupelo, MS 38803
(662) 842-1067, *Fax:* (662) 842-0725
www.wizard106.com
markmaharrey@urbanradio.fm
License: New Albany, Union County, MS held by Clear Channel Broadcasting Licenses Inc.
Group Owner: Clear Channel Communications Inc.; (acq 12-19-00; grpsl)
Nat'l Network: ABC *Nat'l Reps:* Interep
Arbitron Metro Market: Tupelo, MS *Format:* Country *Special Programming:* Southern gospel 4 hrs wkly *No. News Employees:* 1 *Target Audience:* 25-54.
Rick Stevens, Operations Dir
Mark Maharrey, General Manager
Bill Hughes, Programming Director

WTPO
101.5 mhz FM; kw
US
(512) 329-5843
www.matineemedia.com
License: New Albany, Union County, MS held by Ace Radio Corp.
Group Owner: Ace Radio Corp.
Arbitron Metro Market: New Albany, MS
Stephen Hackerman, President

New Augusta

WZHL
101.7 mhz FM; 5 kw; 312 ft.; N31 13 0.5 W89 10 56.8
US
(713) 528-2517
License: New Augusta, Perry County, MS held by Ace Radio Corp.
Group Owner: Ace Radio Corp.
Arbitron Metro Market: New Augusta, MS
Stephen Hackerman, President

New Hebron

***WSMP**
91.9 mhz FM; 0.75 kw; 194 ft.; N31 40 36 W89 52 36
US
(601) 849-9111, *Fax:* (601) 849-0582
info@churchalive.net
License: New Hebron, Lawrence County, MS held by Church Alive Inc.
Arbitron Metro Market: New Hebron, MS
Gene Amason II, General Manager

Newton

WUCL
04-17-1975; 97.9 mhz FM *Hrs Open:* 24; 11 kw; Ant 492 ft; N32 29 16 W89 01 23
4307 Hwy. 39 N., Meridian, MS 39301
(601) 693-2381, *Fax:* (601) 485-2972
License: Newton, Newton County, MS held by CC Licenses LLC.
Group Owner: Clear Channel Communications Inc.; (acq 3-16-2001; grpsl)
Mark Maharrey, General Manager
Ann Burton, Programming Director
Sam Weaver, Program Director

Ocean Springs

WOSM
02-12-1971; 103.1 mhz FM *Hrs Open:* 24; 50 kw; 459 ft.; N30 24 34 W88 42 23
4720 Radio Road, Ocean Springs, MS 39564 US
(228) 875-9031, *Fax:* (228) 875-6461
wosm@wosmradio.com
License: Ocean Springs, Jackson County, MS held by Charles H. Cooper.
Nat'l Network: AP Radio; Salem Radio Network *Wire Services:* AP
Arbitron Metro Market: Biloxi-Gulfport-Pascagoula, MS *Format:* Gospel *Hrs. of News Programming:* News progmg 14 hrs wkly *Target Audience:* 18-54; family
Phil Moss, Operations Dir
Charles Cooper, General Manager
Margaret Cooper, Programming Director

WQYZ
09-01-1992; 92.5 mhz FM *Hrs Open:* 24; 6 kw; 322 ft.; N30 27 9 W88 51 21
P.O. Box 4779, Biloxi, MS 39535 US
(228) 388-2323, *Fax:* (228) 388-2362
www.925fmthebeat.com
License: Ocean Springs, Jackson County, MS held by Capstar TX L.P.
Group Owner: Clear Channel Communications Inc.; (acq 7-5-2005; $1,287,200)
Nat'l Reps: Clear Channel *Wire Services:* AP
Arbitron Metro Market: Biloxi-Gulfport-Pascagoula, MS *Format:* Blues *Hrs. of News Programming:* News progmg one hr wkly *Target Audience:* 28-42; adult families/singles *Adv. Rates:* 20; 20; 20; 10
Walter Brown, Operations Dir
Reggie Bates, General Manager
Ron Hill, General Sales Mgr
Kelly Bennett, News Director
Sheila Taylor, Traffic Manager

Okolona

WWKZ
12-15-1978; 103.9 mhz FM *Hrs Open:* 24; 50 kw; 394 ft.; N34 12 18 W88 41 49
1910 14th Avenue North, Columbus, MS 39701 US
(435) 637-1167, *Fax:* (435) 637-1177
koal@emerytelcom.net
License: Okolona, Lowndes County, MS held by Citicasters Licenses L.P.
Group Owner: Clear Channel Communications Inc.; (acq 7-13-2005; $2.2 million)
Nat'l Network: American Urban
Arbitron Metro Market: San Antonio TX *Format:* Light Rock
Neal Robinson, President
Tom Anderson, General Manager

Olive Branch

KJMS
03-10-1965; 101.1 mhz FM *Hrs Open:* 24; 100 kw; 561 ft.; N35 13 22 W90 2 36
200 Concord Plaza, Suite 600, San Antonio, TX 78216 US
(901) 259-1300, *Fax:* (901) 259-6449
www.v10ll.com
jeffreyjones@clearchannel.com
License: Olive Branch, De Soto County, MS held by CC Licenses LLC.
Group Owner: Clear Channel Communications Inc.
Arbitron Metro Market: Memphis, TN *Format:* Urban Contemporary *Target Audience:* 18-49.
Tim Davies, Operations Dir
Ralph Salierno, General Sales Mgr
Eileen Collier, Programming Director
Franklin Gilbert Jr., Promotions Manager
Alonzo Pendleton, Chief Engineer

Oxford

***WAVI**
01-01-2002; 91.5 mhz FM; 8.13 kw vert; 574 ft.; N34 11 57 W89 49 9
P.O. Drawer 2440, Tupelo, MS 38803 US
(801) 363-1818, *Fax:* (801) 533-9136
www.afr.net
License: Oxford, Lafayette County, MS held by American Family Association.
Group Owner: American Family Radio
Nat'l Network: USA
Donna Maldonado, General Manager

***WMAV-FM**
12-01-1983; 90.3 mhz FM *Hrs Open:* 24; 100 kw vert; 1240 ft.; N34 17 28 W89 42 21
3825 Ridgewood Road, Jackson, MS 39211 US
(601) 432-6565, *Fax:* (601) 432-6806
www.mpbonile.org
License: Oxford, Lafayette County, MS held by Mississippi Authority for Educational Television.
Nat'l Network: PRI; NPR *Wire Services:* AP
Arbitron Metro Market: Oxford, MS *TV Affiliate:* WMAV-TV
Format: News *Hrs. of News Programming:* news progmg 100 hrs wkly *No. News Employees:* 7 *Target Audience:* General.
Jason Klein, Operations Dir
Jay Woods, General Manager
Ty Warren, General Sales Mgr
Marie Antoon, Executive Director

WOXD
10-01-1988; 95.5 mhz FM *Hrs Open:* 24; 6 kw; 328 ft.; N34 18 10 W89 31 25
302 Highway 7, South, Oxford, MS 38655 US
(662) 533-4487,(662) 234-9631, *Fax:* (662) 236-5390
www.bullseye955.com
production@bullseye955.com
License: Oxford, Lafayette County, MS held by Taylor Communications.
Nat'l Reps: Rgnl Reps
Format: Contemporary Hits/Top 40, Adult Contemp *Special Programming:* Gospel 12 hrs wkly *Target Audience:* 25-54. *Adv. Rates:* 14; 14; 14; 14
Jason Plunk, President
Ron Cox, General Manager

WQLJ
12-31-1984; 93.7 mhz FM *Hrs Open:* 24; 13 kw; 456 ft.; N34 20 5 W89 43 29
Mailing Address: 307 South Lamar, Oxford, MS 38655 US
Second Address: 461 Hwy. 6 W., Oxford, MS 38655
(662) 236-0093, *Fax:* (662) 234-5155
www.wqlj.com
q937@exceedtech.net
License: Oxford, Lafayette County, MS held by TeleSouth Communications Inc.
Group Owner: TeleSouth Communications Inc.; acq 11-30-99; $1.4 million)
Regional Network: Miss. News Net.
Format: Adult Contemp *Special Programming:* Contemp Christian 9 hrs wkly *Hrs. of News Programming:* news progmg one hrs wkly *No. News Employees:* 1 *Target Audience:* 18-45. *Adv. Rates:* 19; 19; 19; 10
Steve Davenport, CEO
Jim Martin, Operations Dir
Rick Mize, General Manager
Bryan Hadley, News Director
Judy McCormick, Traffic Manager

WWMS
01-01-1969; 97.5 mhz FM; 100 kw; 981 ft.; N34 10 5 W89 9 23
Mailing Address: P.O. Box 2639, Gulfport, MS 39505 US
Second Address: 2214 S. Gloster St., Tupelo, MS 38801
(662) 842-7658, *Fax:* (662) 842-0197
www.miss98.net
License: Oxford, Lafayette County, MS held by San-Dow Broadcasting Inc.
Arbitron Metro Market: Tupelo, MS *Format:* Country *Special Programming:* Farm 2 hrs wkly *Target Audience:* General.
Brenda Bebout, General Manager
Scott Bebout, Promotions Manager

Pascagoula

WKNN-FM
12-01-1964; 99.1 mhz FM *Hrs Open:* 24; 99 kw horiz, 97.3 kw vert; 984 ft.; N30 29 9 W88 42 53
600 Congress Ave., Suite 1400, Austin, TX 78701 US
(228) 388-2323, *Fax:* (228) 388-2362
www.k99fm.com
License: Pascagoula, Jackson County, MS held by CC Licenses LLC.
Group Owner: Clear Channel Communications Inc.; (acq 2-2-2004; grpsl).
Nat'l Reps: Clear Channel *Wire Services:* AP
Arbitron Metro Market: Biloxi-Gulfport-Pascagoula, MS *Format:* Country *Hrs. of News Programming:* news progmg 6 hrs wkly *No. News Employees:* 1 *Target Audience:* 25-54.
Walter Brown, Operations Dir
Reggie Bates, General Manager
Ron Hill, General Sales Mgr
Kelly Bennett, News Director
Sheila Taylor, Traffic Manager

***WPAS**
03-25-2004; 89.1 mhz FM; 60 kw; 574 ft.; N30 33 3 W88 27 6
P O Drawer 2440 107, Parkgate, MS 33880 US
(662) 844-8888, *Fax:* (662) 842-6791
www.afr.net
faq@afr.net
License: Pascagoula, Jackson County, MS held by American Family Association.
Group Owner: American Family Radio
Nat'l Network: USA
Arbitron Metro Market: Pascagoula, MS *Format:* Christian
Marvin Sanders, General Manager

Pascagoula-Moss Point

WPMO
09-01-1951; 1580 khz AM *Hrs Open:* 24; 5 kw-D, 51 w-N, DA-2; N30 23 01 W88 32 07
5115 Telephone Rd., Pascagoula, MS 39567
(228) 762-5683, *Fax:* (228) 762-1222
License: Pascagoula-Moss Point, Jackson County, MS held by Flagship Radio Group Inc.

Arbitron Metro Market: Biloxi-Gulfport-Pascagoula, MS
Henry Hoot, General Manager

Pearl

WJNT
10-28-1980; 1180 khz AM *Hrs Open:* 24; 10 kw-C, DAN; 50 kw-D, DAN; DAN; 0.5 kw-; N32 17 43 W90 6 54
Box 1248, Jackson, MS 39215 US
(601) 957-1300, *Fax:* (601) 956-0516
www.wjnt.com
contactus@wjnt.com
License: Pearl, MS held by Urban Radio II L.L.C.
Group Owner: Inner City Broadcasting; (acq 10-23-2006; $1.65 million)
Nat'l Network: Premiere Radio Networks; ABC; Talk Radio Network; Westwood One *Nat'l Reps:* D & R Radio
Arbitron Metro Market: Jackson, MS *Format:* News, News/Talk, 86 *Hrs. of News Programming:* news progmg 28 hrs wkly *Target Audience:* 35 plus; high income, college educated, home owners
Charles Warfield, President
Stan Carter, Operations Dir
Kevin Webb, General Manager

*WJAI
11-07-1994; 93.9 mhz FM *Hrs Open:* 24; 6 kw; 328 ft; N32 17 52 W89 59 56
222 Beasley Rd., Jackson, MS 39206
(601) 957-3000, *Fax:* (601) 956-0370
www.rock939.com
brad.stevens@bybradio.com
License: Pearl, Rankin County, MS held by Backyard Broadcasting Mississippi LLC
Group Owner: Backyard Broadcasting LLC; (acq 5-31-2002; $4,830,000 with WWJK(FM) Jackson).
Nat'l Network: ABC; Westwood One *Regional Reps:* Christal.
Population Served: 250,000 *Arbitron Metro Market:* Jackson, MS *Hrs. of News Programming:* news progmg one hr wkly *No. News Employees:* 1 *Target Audience:* 35 plus. *Adv. Rates:* 30; 30; 30; 20
Barry Drake, President
Jason Williams, General Manager
Brad Stevens, Programming Director

Petal

WZLD
01-01-1986; 106.3 mhz FM *Hrs Open:* 24; 10.5 kw; 1063 ft.; N31 31 37 W89 8 7
2571 Old Richton Road, Petal, MS 39465 US
(601) 296-9800, *Fax:* (601) 296-9838
www.wild1063.com
contact@wizldfm.com
License: Petal, Forrest County, MS held by CC Licenses LLC.
Group Owner: Clear Channel Communications Inc.; (acq 12-19-2000; grpsl)
Nat'l Network: CNN Radio *Regional Network:* Miss. News Net.
Arbitron Metro Market: Hattiesburg, MI *Format:* Urban Contemporary *Special Programming:* Sports 3 hrs wkly *Hrs. of News Programming:* News progmg 4 hrs wkly *Target Audience:* 25-54; upscale, educated &professional
Jackson Walker, Operations Dir
Michael Comfort, General Manager
Kahilla Hakimzadeh, General Sales Mgr

Philadelphia

WHOC
07-31-1948; 1490 khz AM; 1 kw-U, ND1; N32 45 52 W89 7 48
1016 West Beacon Street, Philadelphia, MS 39350 US
(601) 656-1490, *Fax:* (601) 656-1491
wwslfm@yahoo.com
License: Philadelphia, MS held by WHOC Inc.
Regional Network: Miss. News Net.
Format: Talk, Adult Contemp *Special Programming:* Farm 2 hrs wkly *Target Audience:* General.
Joe Vines, Operations Dir
Leah Jarrell, General Manager
Rex Smith, Chief Engineer

WWSL
01-01-1981; 102.3 mhz FM; 4.9 kw; 364 ft.; N32 43 35 W89 5 56
Mailing Address: P.O. Box 26, Philadelphia, MS 39350 US
Second Address: 1016 W. Beacon St., Philadelphia, MS 39350
(601) 656-7102, *Fax:* (601) 656-1491
License: Philadelphia, Neshoba County, MS held by H & GC Inc.
Nat'l Network: Westwood One *Regional Network:* Miss. News Net.
Arbitron Metro Market: Philadelphia, MS *Format:* Adult Contemp, Classical
Nick Ferrara, General Manager

Picayune

WMTI
11-01-1973; 106.1 mhz FM *Hrs Open:* 24; 28 kw; 659 ft.; N30 31 17 W90 1 12
929 Government Street, Baton Rouge, LA 70802 US
(504) 581-7002, *Fax:* (504)-566-4857
License: Picayune, Pearl River County, MS
Group Owner: Cumulus Media Inc.; (acq 1-3-2006; $7 million)
Arbitron Metro Market: New Orleans, LA *Format:* Oldies *Hrs. of News Programming:* news progmg 2 hrs wkly *No. News Employees:* 2 *Target Audience:* 18-45; young professionals
Adv. Rates: 45; 35; 40; 25.
Dave Siebert, General Manager
Steven Kline, General Sales Mgr
Jim Hanzo, Programming Director
Bill Major, Chief Engineer

WRJW
10-01-1949; 1320 khz AM *Hrs Open:* 5a-10p; 5 kw-D, 75 kw-N; N30 31 06 W89 38 41
Mailing Address: Box 907, Picayune, MS 39466
Second Address: 2438 Hwy. 43 S., Picayune, MS 39466
(601) 798-4835, *Fax:* (601) 798-9755
www.wrjwradio.com
wrjw@bellsouth.net
License: Picayune, Pearl River County, MS held by Pearl River Communications Inc.
Nat'l Network: ABC *Regional Network:* Miss. News Net.
Population Served: 48,000*Special Programming:* Black 8 hrs, farm 6 hrs, relg 16 hrs, sports 4 hrs *Hrs. of News Programming:* news progmg 10 hrs wkly *No. News Employees:* 2 *Target Audience:* 18-54; contempcountry listeners
Denise Wilson, Operations Dir
Delores Wood, General Manager
Roy Bunales, Programming Director
Dusty Dearman, News Director
Phil Moss, Music Director

Pickens

WRKS
105.9 mhz FM; 23000 w; 735 ft; N32 38 53 W89 59 20
731 South Pear Orchard Road, Suite 27, Ridgeland, MS 78216
(212)352-5761, *Fax:* (212)929-1814
www.thezone1059.com
info@thezone1059.com
License: Pickens, Holmes County, MS
Group Owner: Urban Radio II LLC

Pontotoc

WSEL
11-30-1962; 1440 khz AM; 1 kw-D, ND1; 0.066 kw-N, ND1; N34 15 10 W88 57 36
P.O. Box 3788, Tupelo, MS 38803 US
(662) 489-0297, *Fax:* (662) 488-9735
License: Pontotoc, MS held by Ollie Collins Jr.
Arbitron Metro Market: Tupelo, MS *Format:* Religious
Ollie Collins Jr., General Manager
Jerry Campbell, Chief Engineer

WSEL-FM
01-01-1966; 96.7 mhz FM; 3 kw horiz; 299 ft.; N34 15 10 W88 57 36
P.O. Box 3788, Tupelo, MS 38803 US
(662) 489-0297, *Fax:* (662) 488-9735
License: Pontotoc, Pontotoc County, MS
Arbitron Metro Market: Tupelo, MS *Format:* Religious
Ollie Collins, Jr., General Manager

Poplarville

WRPM
01-01-1963; 1170 khz AM *Hrs Open:* 6 AM-6 PM; 1 kw-C, NDD; N30 48 55 W89 30 24
P.O. Box 2639, Gulfport, MS 39505 US
(601) 795-4900, *Fax:* (601) 795-0277
wrpm@wrpm.com
License: Poplarville, MS held by Dowdy & Dowdy Partnership
Thomas Vaughn, General Manager

Port Gibson

*WATU
01-01-1999; 89.3 mhz FM; 24.5 kw; 384 ft.; N32 7 56 W90 45 29
Po Drawer 2440, Tupelo, MS 38803 US
(662) 844-8888, *Fax:* (662) 842-6791
www.afr.net
License: Port Gibson, Claiborne County, MS held by American Family Association.
Group Owner: American Family Radio
Nat'l Network: USA
Arbitron Metro Market: Port Gibson, MS *Format:* Religious
Marvin Sanders, General Manager

Potts Camp

WCNA
10-01-1995; 95.9 mhz FM *Hrs Open:* 24; 14 kw; 436 ft.; N34 35 51 W89 6 12
P.O. Box 2116, Tupelo, MS 38803 US
(662) 842-9595, *Fax:* (662) 842-9568
License: Potts Camp, Marshall County, MS held by Olvie E. Sisk.
Group Owner: Air South Radio Inc.
Arbitron Metro Market: Tupelo, MS *Format:* Classic Rock *Hrs. of News Programming:* News progmg 14 hrs wkly
Gene Sisk, President
Ivous Sisk, Operations Dir
Fred Blalock, Station Manager

Prentiss

WCJU-FM
01-01-2002; 104.9 mhz FM; 2.8 kw; Ant 436 ft; N31 31 56 W89 56 17
Box 472, Columbia, MS 39429
(601) 736-8889, *Fax:* (601) 736-2617
wcju@wcjufm.com
License: Prentiss, Jefferson Davis County, MS held by Sunbelt Broadcasting Corp.
Group Owner: Sunbelt Broadcasting Corp.

Steve Mercier, Operations Dir
Tommy McDaniel, General Manager

WJDR
06-01-1982; 98.3 mhz FM *Hrs Open:* 24; 6 kw; 328 ft.; N31 29 37 W89 53 33
P.O. Box 351, Columbia, MS 39429 US
(601) 731-2298, *Fax:* (601) 792-2057
www.wagsradio.com
wagsradio@sc.rr.com
License: Prentiss, Jefferson Davis County, MS held by Sunbelt Broadcasting Corp.
Group Owner: Sunbelt Broadcasting Corp.; acq 12-1-85)
Nat'l Network: ABC *Regional Network:* Miss. News Net.
Format: Country *Special Programming:* Black 5 hrs wkly *Hrs. of News Programming:* News progmg 20 hrs wkly *Target Audience:* 25-54.
Thomas McDaniel, President
Jody Fortenberry, Station Manager

Quitman

WQMS
02-02-1968; 1500 khz AM; 1 kw-D, NDD; N32 3 51 W88 43 27
Po Drawer 70, Quitman, MS 39355 US
(601) 557-4710
www.wqmsradio.com
info@wqmsradio.com
License: Quitman, MS held by Stephen C. Hellinger
Arbitron Metro Market: Quitman, MS *Format:* Sports
Simcha Hellinger, General Manager

*WMSO
07-31-1981; 98.9 mhz FM *Hrs Open:* 24; 25 kw; Ant 315 ft; N32 03 51 W88 43 27 *Rebroadcasts:* Rebroadcasts KLVR(FM) Santa Rosa, CA 100%
2351 Sunset Blvd., Suite 170-218, Rocklin, CA 39355
(916) 251-1600, *Fax:* (916) 251-1650
www.klove.com
License: Quitman, Clarke County, MS held by Educational Media Foundation.
Group Owner: EMF Broadcasting; (acq 4-29-2005; $500,000)
Nat'l Network: K-Love

Mike Novak, President
Chip Bailey, Operations Dir
David Pierce, Programming Director
Ed Lenane, News Director
Sam Wallington, Engineering Dir
Marya Morgan, News Reporter
Richard Hunt, News Reporter

Redwood

WVBG-FM
01-01-2005; 105.5 mhz FM; 1.95 kw; 430 ft.; N32 23 22 W90 48 34
US
(601) 883-0848
www.vicksburgv105.com
mark@vicksburgv105.com

License: Redwood, Warren County, MS held by Lendsi Radio LLC.
Arbitron Metro Market: Redwood, MS *Format:* Oldies
Darrell Chambliss, Chairman
Mark Jones, CEO/COO
Dailon Huskey, Operations Dir
Lina Jones, General Manager
Stephen Donnovan, Engineering Dir

Richton

WXHB
01-01-1995; 96.5 mhz FM; 5.7 kw; 574 ft.; N31 28 9 W88 45 53
1315 25th Avenue, Gulfport, MS 39501 US
(601) 649-0095, *Fax:* (601) 649-8199
www.wxhbfm.com
wxhb@wxhbfm.com
License: Richton, Perry County, MS held by Blakeney Communications Inc.
Group Owner: Blakeney Communications Inc.; acq 3-27-03; $650,000).
Arbitron Metro Market: Richton, MS *Format:* Gospel
Larry Blakeney, President
Andy Webb, Operations Dir
Debbie Blakeney, General Manager
Melissa Johnson, Account Executive
Nicki Hudson, Account Executive
Jan Baird, Traffic & Billing
Jessica Lamar, Traffic & Billing
JeanHolifield, Accounting

Ridgeland

WIIN
12-01-1984; 780 khz AM *Hrs Open:* Sunrise-sunset; 5 kw-D, NDD; N32 25 36 W90 12 19
3436 Highway 45 North, Meridan, MS 39302 US
(601) 956-0102, *Fax:* (601) 978-3980
frontdesk@us963.com
License: Ridgeland, MS held by New South Radio Inc.
Group Owner: New South Communications Inc.; (acq 11-10-94; $750,000 with WLIN(FM) Gluckstadt;
Nat'l Reps: McGavren Guild
Arbitron Metro Market: Jackson, MS *Format:* Oldies *Target Audience:* General; Adult professionals
Mark McCoy, Operations Dir
Gwen Rakestraw, General Manager
Bill Rakestraw, General Sales Mgr

Ripley

WCSA
01-01-1995; 1260 khz AM; 0.5 kw-D, NDD; N34 43 15 W88 56 40
4598 Appleville Street, Memphis, TN 38109 US
(601) 837-2816
License: Ripley, MS held by Keyboard Broadcasting Communication.
Arbitron Metro Market: Memphis, TN
Michael Powell, General Manager

WSKK
06-01-1979; 102.3 mhz FM *Hrs Open:* 24; 3.5 kw; 433 ft.; N34 42 35 W88 50 36
107 East Spring Street, P O Box 572, Ripley, MS 38663 US
(662) 837-1023, *Fax:* (662) 837-2994
classicradiofm@aol.com
License: Ripley, Tippah County, MS held by Kudzu Communications Inc.
Arbitron Metro Market: Tupelo, MS *Format:* Contemporary Hits/Top 40, Adult Contemp *Special Programming:* Religious 1 hrs, gospel 3 hrs, bluegrass 3 hrs wkl *Hrs. of News Programming:* News programming 1 hrs wkly*Target Audience:* 25-54 male/felmale
Scott Peters, President

Rosedale

WMJW
01-01-1993; 107.5 mhz FM *Hrs Open:* 24; 25 kw; 328 ft.; N33 56 48 W90 50 58
P.O. Box 780, Cleveland, MO 38732 US
(662) 843-4091, *Fax:* (662) 843-9805
License: Rosedale, Bolivar County, MS held by Radio Cleveland Inc.
Group Owner: Radio Cleveland Inc.; acq 7-18-95).
Arbitron Metro Market: Cleavland, MS *Format:* Country *Hrs. of News Programming:* News progmg 8 hrs wkly *Target Audience:* 25-54; adults
Clint Webster, President
Kevin Cox, Operations Dir
Vickie Lowery, News Director
Jim Thomas, Operations Manager
Jim Gregory, Public Affairs Director

Saltillo

WWMR
01-01-2008; 102.9 mhz FM; 12.5 kw; 466 ft.; N34 24 33 W88 32 24
US
(601) 957-1700, *Fax:* (601) 956-5228
www.supertalk.fm
License: Saltillo, Lee County, MS held by George S. Flinn III.
Arbitron Metro Market: Saltillo, MS *Format:* Talk
Russ Wilson, General Manager

Sandersville

WKZW
07-07-1975; 94.3 mhz FM; 50 kw; 492 ft.; N31 25 50 W89 8 51
Mailing Address: P.O. Box 6408, Laurel, MS 39441 US
Second Address: Box 16596, Hattiesburg, MS 39404
(601) 649-0095, *Fax:* (601) 649-8199
www.kz94.com
kz94@kz94.com
License: Sandersville, Jasper County, MS held by Blakeney Communications Inc.
Group Owner: Blakeney Communications Inc.; acq 3-25-98; $553,000 for stock)
Arbitron Metro Market: Laurel-Hattiesburg, MS *Format:* Adult Contemp *Target Audience:* 18-60; average working people *Adv. Rates:* 28; 26; 26; 24
Larry Blakeney, President
Randy Blakeney, General Manager
Stephen St. James, Programming Director

Sardis

KBUD
01-01-2005; 102.1 mhz FM; 4 kw; 404 ft.; N34 22 33 W89 45 52
Rebroadcasts: Simulcast with WHBQ-FM Germantown, TN 100%
188 S Belleveue, Suite 222, Memphis, TN 98104 US
(901) 375-9324, *Fax:* (901) 375-0041
www.flinn.com
mail@flinn.com
License: Sardis, Panola County, MS held by George S. Flinn Jr.
Arbitron Metro Market: Memphis, TN *Format:* Contemporary Hits/Top 40
Keith Parnell, General Manager
Edrick Kearney, Station Manager

Senatobia

WSAO
08-08-1962; 1140 khz AM *Hrs Open:* 5 AM-5 PM; 5 kw-D, NDD; N34 36 56 W89 56 9
Mailing Address: PO Box 190, Senatobia, MS 38668 US
Second Address: 15763 Hwy. 4 E., Senatobia, MS 38668
(662) 562-4445, *Fax:* (662) 562-4445
License: Senatobia, MS held by Jesse C. Ross and Earnestine A. Ross.
Regional Network: Miss. News Net.
Format: Religious *No. News Employees:* 1 *Target Audience:* General.
Jesse Ross, General Manager

Sharon

WRTM-FM
07-16-1999; 100.5 mhz FM *Hrs Open:* 24; 6 kw; Ant 328 ft.; N31 31 20 W90 04 36
Mailing Address: Box 9734, Jackson, MS 39286
Second Address: 855 S. Pear Orchard Dr., Suite 204, Ridgeland, MS 39157
(601) 856-1932, *Fax:* (601) 856-1937
www.smoothsoul1005.com
smoothsoul1005@bellsouth.net
License: Sharon, Madison County, MS held by Commander Communications Corp.
Arbitron Metro Market: Jackson, MS *Target Audience:* 25-54.
Marty Hart, Operations Dir
Carl Haynes, General Manager
Carl Haynes, General Sales Mgr
Emmette Rushing, Chief Engineer

Southaven

WAVN
06-04-1990; 1240 khz AM *Hrs Open:* 24; 0.58 kw-U, ND1; N34 58 57 W90 0 45
6080 Mt. Moriah, Memphis, TN 38115 US
(601) 393-8056, *Fax:* (601) 393-8066
License: Southaven, MS held by Arlington Broadcasting Co. Inc.
Regional Network: Miss. News Net.
Format: Oldies
Colleen Barill, General Manager

Starkville

***WJZB**
01-01-1999; 88.7 mhz FM; 1 kw; 243 ft.; N33 27 47 W88 49 1
P.O. Drawer 2440, Tupelo, MS 38803 US
(662) 844-8888, *Fax:* (662) 842-6791
www.afr.net
License: Starkville, Oktibbeha County, MS held by American Family Association Inc.
Group Owner: American Family Radio; (acq 10-8-97)
Nat'l Network: USA
Arbitron Metro Market: Columbus-Starkville-West Point, MS
Format: Religious
Marvin Sanders, General Manager

WKOR
07-05-1968; 980 khz AM; 1 kw-D, NDD; N33 28 44 W88 44 40
P.O.B 1076 - 2nd Ave N., Court Sq. Tower Ste. 601, Columbus, MS 39701 US
(662) 327-1183, *Fax:* (662) 328-1122
k949.net
info@K949.net
License: Starkville, MS held by Cumulus Licensing Corp.
Group Owner: Cumulus Media Inc.; (acq 2-14-02).
Arbitron Metro Market: Columbus-Starkville-West Point, MS
Format: Sports *Target Audience:* General; business professionals
Cole Evans, General Sales Mgr
CJ Jones, Promotions Manager

WMSU
09-13-1979; 92.1 mhz FM; 1.1 kw; 499 ft.; N33 25 49 W88 45 17
P.O.B. 1076-2nd Ave. N., Court Sq. Tower Ste. 601, Columbus, MS 39701 US
(662) 338-5424, *Fax:* (662) 338-5436
www.power92jamz.net
wmsuproduction@urbanradio.fm
License: Starkville, Oktibbeha County, MS held by Urban Radio Licenses LLC.
Group Owner: Urban Radio Licenses LLC; (acq 12-7-2000).
Arbitron Metro Market: Columbus, MS *Format:* Urban Contemporary *Target Audience:* 25-54.
Kevin Wagner, President
James Alexander, Operations Dir

***WMSV**
03-01-1994; 91.1 mhz FM; 14 kw; 456 ft.; N33 25 56 W88 45 0
P.O. Box 6101, Mississippi State, MS 39762 US
(662) 325-8034, *Fax:* (662) 325-8037
www.wmsv.msstate.edu
wmsv@msstate.edu
License: Starkville, Oktibbeha County, MS held by Mississippi State University.
Arbitron Metro Market: Columbus, MS *Format:* Alternative
Steve Ellis, General Manager

WMXU
07-15-1968; 106.1 mhz FM *Hrs Open:* 24; 40 kw; 502 ft.; N33 17 38 W88 39 27
P.O. Box 1076, Columbus, MS 98703 US
(662) 327-1183, *Fax:* (662) 328-1122
www.mix1061.com
greg.benefield@cumulus.com
License: Starkville, Oktibbeha County, MS
Group Owner: Cumulus Media Inc.
Arbitron Metro Market: Columbus, MS *Format:* Urban Contemporary
Bobby Holiday, Programming Director

WSSO
11-08-1948; 1230 khz AM; 1 kw-U, ND1; N33 27 9 W88 49 15
P.O. Box 1076, Columbus, MS 38703 US
(662) 327-1183, *Fax:* (662) 328-1122
License: Starkville, MS held by Cumulus Licensing Corp.
Group Owner: Cumulus Media Inc.; (acq 1998; grpsl)
Regional Network: Miss. News Net. *Nat'l Reps:* Keystone (unwired net) *Regional Reps:* Allied Radio Partners.
Arbitron Metro Market: Columbus-Starkville-West Point, MS
Format: Sports *Special Programming:* Black 12 hrs wkly
C.J. Jones, Operations Dir

State College

WQJB
104.5 mhz FM; 12 kw; 476 ft.; N33 22 4 W88 41 39
188 South Bellevue, Suite 222, Memphis, TN 38104 US

RADIO - U.S.

(901) 375-9324, *Fax:* (901) 375-0041
www.flinn.com
mail@flinn.com
License: State College, Oktibbeha County, MS held by George S. Flinn Jr.
Arbitron Metro Market: Memphis, TN *Format:* Country
Melanie Henkin-Booth, General Manager

Stonewall

WEXR
01-01-1998; 106.9 mhz FM *Hrs Open:* 24; 2.55 kw; 508 ft; N32 10 48 W88 40 22
Box 5797, Meridian, MS 39302
(601) 693-2661, *Fax:* (601) 483-0826
wmlv@wokk.com
License: Stonewall, Clarke County, MS held by Mississippi Broadcasters L.L.C.
Group Owner: Mississippi Broadcasters L.L.C.
Arbitron Metro Market: Meridian, MS *Target Audience:* 25-54.
Clay Holladay, President
Scott Stevens, Operations Dir
Karen Bostick, General Sales Mgr
Van Mac, News Director
Scott Shepperd, Chief Engineer

Strasburg

WZEC
01-01-1987; 104.9 mhz FM *Hrs Open:* 24; 3 kw; Ant 219 ft; N39 01 22 W78 25 35 *Rebroadcasts:* Simulcast with WWRE(FM) Berryville 100%
Mailing Address: Box 3300, Winchester, VA
Second Address: 520 N. Pleasant Valley Rd., Winchester, VA 22601
(540) 667-2224, *Fax:* (540) 722-3295
www.everythingthatrocks.fm
License: Strasburg, Shenandoah County, VA held by Mid Atlantic Network Inc.
Group Owner: Mid Atlantic Network; (acq 7-8-97; $850,000 with WWRE(FM) Berryville).
Arbitron Metro Market: Winchester, VA *Target Audience:* 18 plus.
Allen Shaw, President
Jeff Adams, Operations Dir
Kathie Flerx, General Manager
Ron Baker, Programming Director
Robert Allen, News Director

Sumrall

WFMM
01-01-1998; 97.3 mhz FM; 6 kw; 328 ft.; N31 21 18 W89 31 19
Rebroadcasts: Rebroadcasts WFMN(FM) Flora 100%.
6310 I-55 North, Jackson, MS 39211 US
(601) 957-1700, *Fax:* (601) 956-5228
www.supertalkms.com
apeterson@telesouth.com
License: Sumrall, Lamar County, MS held by TeleSouth Communications Inc.
Group Owner: TeleSouth Communications Inc.; acq 1999; $200,000)
Format: News, News/Talk, 86
Paul Gallo, General Manager

WGDQ
01-01-2005; 93.1 mhz FM; 25 kw; 302 ft.; N31 22 58 W89 23 43
619 McInnis Spring Road, Hattiesburg, MS 39401 US
(601) 544-1941, *Fax:* (601) 544-1947
License: Sumrall, Lamar County, MS held by Unity Broadcasters.
Arbitron Metro Market: Hattiesburg, MS *Format:* Oldies
Victor Floyd, General Manager

Taylorsville

WBBN
03-20-1985; 95.9 mhz FM; 100 kw; 732 ft.; N31 38 3 W89 28 35
P.O. Box 6408, Laurel, MS 39441 US
(800) 877-5600, *Fax:* (916) 251-1650
www.godscountryradionetwork.com
info@happyjubilee.com
License: Taylorsville, Smith County, MS held by Blakeney Communications Inc.
Group Owner: Blakeney Communications Inc.
Arbitron Metro Market: Eureka CA *Format:* Country, Gospel
Mike Novak, President

Tchula

WGNG
01-01-2001; 106.3 mhz FM; 7.1 kw; 499 ft.; N33 18 6 W90 7 31
503 Ione Street, Greenwood, MS 38930 US
(662) 453-1646, *Fax:* (662) 453-7002
wgnlbooth@bellsouth.net
License: Tchula, Holmes County, MS held by Team Broadcasting Co. Inc.
Format: Urban Contemporary
Reuben Hughes, General Manager

Tunica

WIVG
01-01-1998; 96.1 mhz FM; 4.1 kw; 807 ft.; N34 43 36 W90 9 43
2307 Princess Anne St, Greensboro, NC 27408 US
(901) 454-9948, *Fax:* (901) 454-1027
www.q1075.com/
License: Tunica, Tunica County, MS held by Flinn Broadcasting Corp.
Arbitron Metro Market: Memphis, TN *Format:* Contemporary Hits/Top 40
Carmen Reyes, General Manager

Tupelo

*WAFR
08-31-1991; 88.3 mhz FM *Hrs Open:* 24; 75 kw; 492 ft.; N34 28 28 W88 43 41
P. O. Drawer 2440, 107 Parkgate, Tupelo, MS 38803 US
(662) 844-8888(662) 844-8893, *Fax:* (662) 842-6791
www.afr.net
faq@afr.net
License: Tupelo, Lee County, MS held by American Family Association.
Nat'l Network: American Family Radio
Arbitron Metro Market: Tupelo, MS *Format:* Christian *Hrs. of News Programming:* news progmg 3 hrs wkly *No. News Employees:* 1 *Target Audience:* 30-60; conservative Christian
Don Wildmon, General Manager

*WAJS
01-01-1996; 91.7 mhz FM; 23 kw; 505 ft.; N33 55 35 W88 39 46
Po Drawer 2440, Tupelo, MS 38803 US
(662) 844-8888, *Fax:* (662) 842-6791
www.afr.net
faq@afr.net
License: Tupelo, Lee County, MS held by American Family Association.
Group Owner: American Family Radio
Nat'l Network: USA
Arbitron Metro Market: Tupelo, MS. *Format:* Christian
Marvin Sanders, General Manager

*WAQB
01-01-1997; 90.9 mhz FM; 35 kw; 427 ft.; N34 28 28 W88 43 41
P.O. Box 2440, Tupelo, MS 38803 US
(662) 844-8888, *Fax:* (662) 842-6791
www.afr.net
faq@afr.net
License: Tupelo, Lee County, MS held by American Family Association.
Group Owner: American Family Radio
Nat'l Network: USA
Arbitron Metro Market: Tupelo, MS *Format:* Gospel
Don Wildmon, General Manager

WELO
05-15-1944; 580 khz AM *Hrs Open:* 24
P.O. Box 2639, Gulfport, MS 39503 US
(662) 842-7658, *Fax:* (662) 842-0197
msradiogroup.com/
License: Tupelo, MS held by JMD Inc.
Arbitron Metro Market: Tupelo, MS *Format:* Big Band *Special Programming:* Farm one hr wkly *Target Audience:* 45 plus.
Dave Dunaway, Operations Dir
Brenda Bebout, General Manager
Scott Kelly, Programming Director
Cathy Williams, News Director

WKMQ
08-25-1972; 1060 khz AM *Hrs Open:* 24
Mailing Address: 111 East Kilbourn Avenue, Suite 2700, Milwaukee, WI 53202 US
Second Address: 5026 Cliff Gookin Blvd., Tupelo, MS 38801
(662) 842-1067, *Fax:* (662) 842-0725
rickstevens@clearchannel.com
License: Tupelo, MS held by Capstar TX L.P.
Group Owner: Clear Channel Communications Inc.; (acq 12-19-2000; grpsl)
Arbitron Metro Market: Tupelo, MS *Format:* Talk *Target Audience:* 35-54.
Rick Stevens, Operations Dir
Mark Maharrey, General Manager
Cynthia South, General Sales Mgr
Jerry Mathis, Chief Engineer

WTUP
10-01-1953; 1490 khz AM *Hrs Open:* 24
Mailing Address: 111 East Kilbourn Avenue, Suite 2700, Milwaukee, WI 53202 US
Second Address: 5026 Cliff Gookin Blvd., Tupelo, MS 38801
(662) 842-1067, *Fax:* (662) 842-0725
urbanradio.fm
License: Tupelo, MS held by Capstar TX L.P.
Group Owner: Clear Channel Communications Inc.; (acq 12-19-2000; grpsl)
Regional Network: Miss. News Net. *Nat'l Reps:* Interep
Arbitron Metro Market: Tupelo, MS *Format:* Sports *Hrs. of News Programming:* news progmg 12 hrs wkly *No. News Employees:* 1 *Target Audience:* 25-54; men
Rick Stevens, Operations Dir
Rebecca Yarbrough, Sales Director
Mark Maharrey, Market Manager

WZLQ
09-01-1968; 98.5 mhz FM; 100 kw; 981 ft.; N34 10 5 W89 9 23
P.O. Box 1056, Oxford, MS 38655 US
(662) 842-7658, *Fax:* (662) 842-0197
www.z985.net
License: Tupelo, Lee County, MS
Arbitron Metro Market: Tupelo, MS *Format:* Adult Contemp *Target Audience:* 25-54.
Steve Drumm, Programming Director

Tylertown

WTYL
02-08-1969; 1290 khz AM *Hrs Open:* 11; 1 kw-D, NDD; N31 7 50 W90 8 13
930 Union Road, Tylertown, MS 39667 US
(601) 876-2105, *Fax:* (601) 876-9551
License: Tylertown, MS held by Tylertown Broadcasting Co.
Arbitron Metro Market: Tylertown, MS *Format:* Country *Special Programming:* Farm 6 hrs wkly
Carolyn Dillon, President
Gail Ratcliff, Programming Director

WTYL-FM
04-09-1970; 97.7 mhz FM *Hrs Open:* 24; 3 kw; 144 ft.; N31 7 50 W90 8 13
930 Union Road, Tylertown, MS 39667 US
(601) 876-2105, *Fax:* (601) 876-9551
License: Tylertown, Walthall County, MS
Arbitron Metro Market: Tylertown, MS
Gail Ratcliff, News Director

WFCG
01-01-2005; 107.3 mhz FM; 3.2 kw; Ant 457 ft; N31 04 39 W90 04 46
Box 1649, McComb, MS
(985) 839-3782, *Fax:* (985) 839-3783
License: Tylertown, Walthall County, MS held by Southwest Broadcasting Inc.
Group Owner: Southwest Broadcasting Inc.

C. Wayne Dowdy, President
William Giles, General Manager

Union

WZKS
10-01-1995; 104.1 mhz FM; 19 kw; 535 ft.; N32 29 53 W88 53 20
4307 Highway 39 N, Meridian, MS 39301 US
(601) 693-2381, *Fax:* (601) 485-2972
www.1041kissfm.com
License: Union, Walthall County, MS held by CC Licenses LLC.
Group Owner: Clear Channel Communications Inc.; (acq 3-16-2001; grpsl).
Arbitron Metro Market: Union, MS *Format:* Urban Contemporary
Mark Maharrey, General Manager
Ann Burton, Programming Director
Sam Weaver, Program Director

University

WUMS
04-10-1989; 92.1 mhz FM *Hrs Open:* 24; 2.9 kw; 476 ft.; N34 24 12 W89 24 13
Farley Hall, Room 231, University, MS 38677 US
(662) 915-5503, *Fax:* (662) 915-5703
myrebelradio.com/
manager@myrebelradio.com
License: University, Lafayette County, MS held by Student Media Center of the University of Mississippi.
Nat'l Network: Premiere Radio Networks; CNN Radio *Wire Services:* AP
Arbitron Metro Market: Oxford, MS *Format:* Adult Contemp, Alternative *Special Programming:* International 2 hrs, women

one hr, the 80s 2 hrs wkly *Hrs. of News Programming:* News progmg 2 hrs wkly *Target Audience:* 18-24.
Jason Caviness, General Manager
Stephen Goforth, Programming Director

Utica

WJXN-FM
08-28-1990; 100.9 mhz FM *Hrs Open:* 24; 39 kw; 551 ft.; N32 3 13 W90 20 23
645 Church Street, Suite 400, Norfolk, VA 23510 US
(800) 434-8400, *Fax:* (800) 372-0888
www.klove.com
License: Utica, Hinds County, MS held by Flinn Broadcasting Corp.
Nat'l Network: USA *Wire Services:* NWS (National Weather Service)
Arbitron Metro Market: Jackson, MS *Format:* Christian *Target Audience:* 25 plus.
George Flinn, President
Karen Porter, Station Manager
Steve Poston, Programming Director

Vicksburg

WBBV
08-21-1989; 101.3 mhz FM; 13 kw; 394 ft.; N32 20 42 W90 52 55
1601 E North Frontage Rd, Vicksburg, MS 39180 US
(416) 213-1035, *Fax:* (416) 233-8617
z103halifax.com
info@z103halifax.com
License: Vicksburg, Warren County, MS held by Debut Broadcasting Mississippi Inc.
Group Owner: Debut Broadcasting Corp. Inc.; (acq 8-27-2008; $900,000)
Arbitron Metro Market: San Angelo TX *Format:* Contemporary Hits/Top 40 *Adv. Rates:* 20; 17; 17; 14
Al Erickson, President
Ray Lawson, Station Manager

WJKK
03-19-1966; 98.7 mhz FM *Hrs Open:* 24; 52 kw; 1284 ft.; N32 11 29 W90 24 22
265 High Point Drive, Jackson, MS 39123 US
(601) 956-0102, *Fax:* (601) 978-3980
www.mix987.com
frontdesk@us963.com
License: Vicksburg, Warren County, MS held by New South Radio Inc.
Group Owner: New South Communications Inc.; (acq 1-89; $1.1 million;
Arbitron Metro Market: Jackson, MS *Format:* Adult Contemp *Hrs. of News Programming:* news progmg one hr wkly *No. News Employees:* 1 *Target Audience:* 18-49; upper income & educ
Gwen Rakestraw, General Manager

WQBC
01-01-1931; 1420 khz AM *Hrs Open:* 24; 1 kw-D, ND1; 0.5 kw-N, ND1; N32 19 56 W90 51 0
Mailing Address: P.O.Box 8082, Vicksburg, MS 39181 US
Second Address: Box 820483, Vicksburg, MS 39182
(601) 636-1108, *Fax:* (601) 631-0087
License: Vicksburg, MS held by Grace Media International LLC
Nat'l Network: ESPN Radio
Format: Sports, Talk
Mike Corley, President
Jerry Rushins, General Manager

WVBG
01-01-1948; 1490 khz AM *Hrs Open:* 24
P.O. Box 31235, Jackson, MS 31235 US
(601) 883-0848
www.vicksburgv105.com/index.html
mark@vicksburgv105.com
License: Vicksburg, MS held by Commander Communications Corp.
Format: Contemporary Hits/Top 40, Adult Contemp *Hrs. of News Programming:* 168 hrs. News progmg wkly *Target Audience:* 25 plus.
Dailon Huskey, Operations Dir
Mark Jones, General Manager
Stephen Donovan, Engineering Dir

WSTZ-FM
06-01-1968; 106.7 mhz FM; 85 kw; 1886 ft.; N32 12 49 W90 22 56
Mailing Address: 600 Congress Ave., Suite 1400, Austin, TX 78701 US
Second Address: 1375 Beasley Rd., Jackson, MS 39206
(601) 982-1062, *Fax:* (601) 362-1905
www.z106.com
dougjones@clearchannel.com
License: Vicksburg, Warren County, MS held by Capstar TX L.P.
Group Owner: Clear Channel Communications Inc.; (acq 8-30-00; grpsl).
Nat'l Reps: D & R Radio
Arbitron Metro Market: Jackson, MS *Format:* Classic Rock *Target Audience:* 25-54.
Kenneth Windham, General Manager

Walnut

WLRC
06-21-1982; 850 khz AM; 0.94 kw-D, NDD; N34 56 46 W88 52 44
Mailing Address: 190 Luna Street, P.O. Box 142, Walnut, MS 38683 US
Second Address: 7760 Hwy. 72 E., Walnut, MS 38683
(662) 223-4071, *Fax:* (662) 223-4072
www.wlrcradio.com
info@wlrc.com
License: Walnut, MS held by B.R. & Martha S. Clayton.
Regional Network: Miss. News Net.
Format: Christian *Hrs. of News Programming:* News progmg 14 hrs wkly
Don Davis, President
Mike Weaver, Operations Dir
Vanessa Wetterling, General Manager
Mike Weave, Programming Director

Washington

WWUU
103.9 mhz FM; 450 watts; 175 meters; N31 30 16 W91 21 06
740 Highway 49 North, Suite R, Flora, MS
(601) 201-2789, *Fax:* (601) 427-0088
License: Washington, Adams County, MS held by SSR Communications Inc

Brad Hunstable, President

Water Valley

WTNM
08-01-1996; 105.5 mhz FM *Hrs Open:* 24; 4.7 kw; 371 ft.; N34 12 45 W89 44 49
Mailing Address: P.O. Box 1528, Batesville, MS 38606 US
Second Address: 461 Hwy. 6 W., Oxford, MS 38655
(662) 236-0073, *Fax:* (662) 234-5155
www.supertalkms.com
supertalk1055@exceedtech.net
License: Water Valley, Yalobusha County, MS held by TeleSouth Communications Inc.
Group Owner: TeleSouth Communications Inc.; acq 3-17-00).
Regional Network: Miss. News Net.
Format: Talk *Special Programming:* Christian, contemp 4 hrs wkly *Hrs. of News Programming:* news progmg 3 hrs wkly *No. News Employees:* 1 *Target Audience:* 25 plus. *Adv. Rates:* 10; 10; 10; 5
Steve Davenport, CEO
Jim Martin, Operations Dir
Rick Mize, General Manager

Waynesboro

WABO
09-11-1954; 990 khz AM; 1 kw-D, ND2; 0.1 kw-N, ND2; N31 40 48 W88 40 34
Mailing Address: P. O. Box 507, Waynesboro, MS 39367 US
Second Address: 6746 Hwy. 184 W., Waynesboro, MS 39367
(604) 299-8863, *Fax:* (604) 299-3088
www.rj1200.com
info@rj1200.com
License: Waynesboro, MS held by Martin Broadcasting Inc.
Arbitron Metro Market: Albuquerque NM *Format:* Ethnic
Shushma Datt, CEO
Sudhir Datta, General Manager

WABO-FM
06-13-1973; 105.5 mhz FM; 6 kw; 144 ft.; N31 40 40 W88 40 13
Mailing Address: P. O. Box 507, Waynesboro, MS 39367 US
Second Address: 6746 Hwy. 184 W., Waynesboro, MS 39367
(800) 877-5600, *Fax:* (916) 251-1650
www.air1.com
info@air1.com
License: Waynesboro, Wayne County, MS
Arbitron Metro Market: Belcourt ND *Format:* Alternative, Christian
Mike Novak, President

***WZKM**
89.7 mhz FM; 67 kw; 581 ft.; N31 50 9 W88 52 21
1425 N Market Blvd, Suite 9, Sacramento, CA 95843 US
(662) 844-8888, *Fax:* (662) 842-6791
www.afr.net
faq@afr.net
License: Waynesboro, Wayne County, MS held by American Family Association.
Group Owner: American Family Radio; (acq 1-24-03).
Nat'l Network: USA
Arbitron Metro Market: Tupelo, MS *Format:* Religious
Don Wildmon, General Manager

Wiggins

WCPR-FM
12-01-1992; 97.9 mhz FM *Hrs Open:* 24; 50 kw; 466 ft.; N30 36 59 W89 8 3
2511 Garden Road, Building A, Suite 104, Monterey, CA 93940 US
(228) 388-2001(228) 388-2771 (request line), *Fax:* (228) 896-9736
www.979cprrocks.com
bwest@msmediaradio.com
License: Wiggins, Stone County, MS held by Monterey Licenses LLC.
Group Owner: Triad Broadcasting Co. L.L.C.; (acq 7-14-99; grpsl)
Nat'l Network: ABC
Arbitron Metro Market: Biloxi MS *Format:* Alternative, Rock/AOR
Buddy Burch, Operations Dir
Jay Taylor, Operations Director

Winona

WONA
10-25-1958; 1570 khz AM; 1 kw-D, ND1; 0.025 kw-N, ND1; N33 27 52 W89 44 11
P. O. Box 746, Winona, MS 38967 US
(601) 283-1570, *Fax:* (601) 283-1571
hawg95@cablesouthmedia.net
License: Winona, MS held by Southern Electronics Co.
TV Affiliate: Country
Operations Manager

WONA-FM
01-04-1976; 95.1 mhz FM; 10 kw; 515 ft.; N33 34 56 W89 44 52
P. O. Box 746, Winona, MS 38967 US
(662) 283-1570, *Fax:* (662) 283-1520
http://www.hawg95.com/
hawg95@cablesouthmedia.net
License: Winona, Montgomery County, MS held by Southern Electronics Co.
TV Affiliate: Country

Yazoo City

***WYAZ**
01-01-2005; 89.5 mhz FM; 85 kw; 531 ft.; N32 48 4 W89 56 32
P O Box 1458, Washington, DC 20013 US
(662) 844-8888, *Fax:* (662) 842-6791
www.afa.net
randall@afa.net
License: Yazoo City, Yazoo County, MS held by American Family Association.
Group Owner: American Family Radio; (acq 5-13-2004).
Arbitron Metro Market: Yazoo City, MS *Format:* Christian
Marvin Sanders, General Manager

Missouri

Adrian

***KYLF**
05-11-2012; 88.9 mhz FM; 30 kw; 452 ft; N38 12 04 W94 16 12
10550 Barkley, Overland Park, KS
(913)642-7770, *Fax:* (913)642-1319
www.bottradionetwork.com
comments@bottradionetwork.com
License: Adrian, Bates County, MO
Group Owner: Community Broadcasting Inc.

Richard Bott Sr, Chairman
Richard Bott II, President/CEO
Tom Holdeman, CFO
Tim Lumpkin, Corporate Controller
Eben Fowler, Director of Operations
Pat Rulon, Director of National Sales

Albany

***KGTR**
89.9 mhz FM; kw
US
(580) 653-2777

License: Albany, Gentry County, MO held by Ron Elmore Ministries Inc.
Arbitron Metro Market: Larned, KS
Ron Elmore, President

Arcadia

KTNX
01-01-2006; 103.9 mhz FM; 0.45 kw; 932 ft.; N37 34 23 W90 41 35
US
(573) 701-9590, *Fax:* (573) 701-9696
License: Arcadia, Iron County, MO held by Southern Star Broadcasting of Missouri LLC.
Group Owner: Southern Star Broadcasting of Missouri LLC; (acq 5-8-2008; grpsl)
Arbitron Metro Market: Arcadia, MO *Format:* Contemporary Hits/Top 40
Chip Miller, President
Joel Jordan, Operations Dir

Arnold

*KGNA-FM
03-26-1987; 89.9 mhz FM *Hrs Open:* 24; 0.15 kw horiz, 0.084 kw vert; 131 ft.; N38 26 14 W90 23 24 *Rebroadcasts:* Rebroadcasts KGNV(FM) Washington 100%
1770 Missouri State Road, Arnold, MO 63010 US
(636) 239-0400, *Fax:* (636) 239-4448
www.goodnewsvoice.org
info@goodnewsvoice.org
License: Arnold, Jefferson County, MO held by Missouri River Christian Broadcasting Inc.
Group Owner: Missouri River Christian Broadcasting Inc.; (acq 10-5-99).
Nat'l Network: Moody; Salem Radio Network
Arbitron Metro Market: Arnold, MO *Format:* Gospel, News, 62, Religious, Talk *Hrs. of News Programming:* News progmg 14 hrs wkly *Target Audience:* 20-70:; inquisitive, conservative, liberal, philosophical *Adv. Rates:* 8; 8; 8; 8
James C. Goggan, President
James Goggan, General Manager
Marilyn Goggan, Programming Director

Asbury

KWXD
10-01-1993; 103.5 mhz FM; 16 kw; 413 ft.; N37 23 44 W94 40 42
P.O. Box 383, Pittsburg, KS 66762 US
(620) 232-5993, *Fax:* (620) 232-5550
www.1035x.net
License: Asbury, Jasper County, MO held by Southeast Kansas Broadcasting Co. Inc.
Group Owner: My Town Media, Inc.
Arbitron Metro Market: Pittsburg, KS *Format:* Rock/AOR *Adv. Rates:* 100; 80; 80; 80
Lance Sayler, President

Ash Grove

KSGF-FM
03-01-1994; 104.1 mhz FM; 21.5 kw; 354 ft.; N37 15 22 W93 41 14
5850 Highway 93 South, Whitefish, MT 59937 US
(417) 865-6614, *Fax:* (417) 865-9643
www.ksgf.com
nreed@jrn.com
License: Ash Grove, Greene County, MO held by Journal Broadcast Corp.
Group Owner: Journal Communications Inc.; (acq 11-26-2003; $5 million with KZRQ-FM Mount Vernon).
Arbitron Metro Market: Ash Grove, MO *Format:* News, Talk
Chris Cannon, Operations Dir
Rex Hansen, General Manager

Ashland

KOQL
10-01-1993; 106.1 mhz FM *Hrs Open:* 24; 69 kw; 958 ft.; N38 45 1 W92 33 31
503 Old Hwy. 63 North, Columbia, MO 65201 US
(573) 449-4141, *Fax:* (573) 449-7770
www.q1061.com
info@q1061.com
License: Ashland, Boone County, MO held by Cumulus Licensing LLC.
Group Owner: Cumulus Media Inc.; (acq 4-26-2004; grpsl).
Nat'l Reps: Katz Radio
Arbitron Metro Market: Columbia, MO *Format:* Contemporary Hits/Top 40
D. Larimer, Programming Director

Aurora

KSWF
02-19-1968; 100.5 mhz FM; 33 kw; 600 ft.; N37 5 39 W93 31 5
1350 One Galleria Tower, 13355 Noel Road, Dallas, TX 75240 US
(417) 890-5555, *Fax:* (417) 890-5050
www.1005thewolf.com
studio@1005thewolf.com
License: Aurora, Lawrence County, MO held by Clear Channel Broadcasting Licenses Inc.
Group Owner: Clear Channel Communications Inc.; (acq 10-10-2000; grpsl).
Arbitron Metro Market: Springfield, MO *Format:* Country *Special Programming:* discover and uncover 2 hrs wkly *Target Audience:* 18-54; general
Paul Kelley, Operations Dir
Keith Lisemann, General Manager
Megan Staurt Annis, Station Manager
Kelli Presley, General Sales Mgr
Kat Morgan Gaines, Production Director
Mary Brown, Traffic Manager
Lynne Strickland, Web

KSWM
10-19-1961; 940 khz AM *Hrs Open:* 24; 1 kw-D, ND2; 0.025 kw-N, NDD; N36 59 39 W93 42 58
P.O. Box 492, Sulphur Springs, TX 75483 US
(417) 678-0416, *Fax:* (417) 678-4111
www.talonbroadcasting.com
kswm@radiotalon.com
License: Aurora, MO held by Falcon Broadcasting Inc.
Nat'l Network: CNN Radio; USA *Regional Network:* Missourinet
Arbitron Metro Market: Aurora, MO *Format:* News, News/Talk, 86 *Hrs. of News Programming:* news progmg 168 hrs wkly *No. News Employees:* 2 *Target Audience:* General.
Bill Lewis, Operations Dir
DeWayne Gandy, General Manager
Lance Matlock, General Sales Mgr
Dan Kesterson, Programming Director

Ava

KKOZ
01-01-1968; 1430 khz AM; 0.5 kw-D, ND1; 0.02 kw-N, ND1; N36 55 48 W92 39 19
P.O. Box 386, Ava, MO 65608 US
(417) 683-4191
www.kkoz.com
news@kkoz.com
License: Ava, MO held by Corum Industries Inc.
Arbitron Metro Market: Springfield, MO
Art Corum, Operations Dir
Joe Corum, General Manager
Chantelle Emmerson, General Sales Mgr
Heather Lee, Programming Director
Rob Strand, News Director
Jeanette Gooden, Office Manager
Vickie Corum, Bids for Bargains Mgr
TimLandsdown, Sports

KKOZ-FM
01-01-1990; 92.1 mhz FM *Hrs Open:* 6 AM-10 PM; 4.5 kw; 381 ft.; N36 55 48 W92 39 19
P. O. Box 386, Ava, MO 65608 US
(417) 683-4191
www.kkoz.com
news@kkoz.com
License: Ava, Douglas County, MO held by Corum Industries Inc.
Regional Network: Missourinet
Arbitron Metro Market: Springfield, MO *Format:* News, News/Talk, 86 *Hrs. of News Programming:* News progmg 15 hrs wkly *Target Audience:* 45 plus; farm oriented
Art Corum, Operations Dir
Joe Corum, General Manager
Chantelle Emmerson, General Sales Mgr
Vickie Corum, News Director
Jeanette Gooden, Office Manager
Vickie Corum, Bids for Bargains Mgr
Tim Landsdown, Sports

Ballwin

*KGNX
02-01-1978; 89.7 mhz FM; 120 w; Ant 171 ft; N38 37 23 W90 32 01
Box 4038, 16464 Burkhardt Pl., Chesterfield, MO 63006
(636) 532-6515,(636) 532-3100, *Fax:* (636) 530-7928
ymcastlouis.org
nhall@ymcastlouis.org
License: Ballwin, St. Louis County, MO held by YMCA of Greater St. Louis-W. County Branch.
Arbitron Metro Market: St. Louis, MO
Kent Frandsen, President
Jay Eubanks, General Manager
Lori Gill, News Director
Paul Anderson, Chief Engineer

Bethany

KAAN
12-03-1983; 870 khz AM *Hrs Open:* Sunrise-sunset; 0.93 kw-D, NDD; N40 15 23 W94 9 23
300 W. Reed, Moberly, MO 65270 US
(660) 425-6380, *Fax:* (660) 425-8148
www.northwestmoinfo.com
stuartj@regionalradio.com
License: Bethany, MO held by Cameron/Bethany License Co. LLC.
Group Owner: GoodRadio.TV; (acq 8-8-2007; grpsl)
Regional Network: Missourinet
Arbitron Metro Market: Bethany, MO *Format:* Country, News *Special Programming:* Farm 10 hrs, relg one hr wkly *Hrs. of News Programming:* news progmg 10 hrs wkly *No. News Employees:* 3 *Target Audience:* 25plus. *Adv. Rates:* 25; 21; 19; 18
Connie Querry, Operations Dir
Doug Schmitz, General Manager
Mike Mattson, Station Manager
Denise Fritzel, General Sales Mgr
Stuart Johnson, Programming Director
Stuart Johnson, News Director
Gregg Richwine, Engineering Dir

KAAN-FM
10-27-1978; 95.5 mhz FM *Hrs Open:* 19; 50 kw; 354 ft.; N40 15 23 W94 9 23
300 W. Reed, Moberly, MO 65270 US
(660) 425-6380, *Fax:* (660) 425-8148
www.northwestmoinfo.com
stuartj@regionalradio.com
License: Bethany, Harrison County, MO held by Cameron/Bethany License Co. LLC
Group Owner: GoodRadio.TV
Arbitron Metro Market: Bethany, MO *No. News Employees:* 3
Doug Schmitz, General Manager

Birch Tree

KBMV-FM
01-01-1983; 107.1 mhz FM *Hrs Open:* 24; 25 kw; 328 ft.; N36 56 3 W91 43 7
204 East Washington, Doniphan, MO 63935 US
(417) 255-0427, *Fax:* (417) 255-2907
www.threeriversdailynews.com
thepoint@centurytel.net
License: Birch Tree, Shannon County, MO held by Three Rivers Communications, LLC
Regional Reps: True Media; Regional Reps
Format: Adult Contemp *No. News Employees:* 1 *Target Audience:* 18-54
Connie Feifer, General Manager

Bismarck

KHCR
01-01-2005; 99.5 mhz FM; 4.2 kw; 798 ft.; N37 38 52 W90 37 33
627 Stte Highway 47, Bonne Terre, MO 63628 US
(314) 909-8569, *Fax:* (314) 835-9739
www.joyfmonline.org
sandi@joyfmonline.org
License: Bismarck, St. Francois County, MO held by Joseph W. & Donna M. Bollinger.
Arbitron Metro Market: Bismarck, MO *Format:* Christian, Religious
Sandi Brown, General Manager
Nick Spiniolas, Promotions Manager
Kelly Corday, News & Traffic Director
Greg Cassidy, Music Director
Kim Underwood, Social Media Director
Ryan Wiggins, Production Director
Jill Willis,Concerts/Events Manager
Jill Holt, Bookkeeper
Amy Strong, Donor Relations

Bloomfield

*KAIA
91.5 mhz FM; 49 kw vert; 417 ft.; N36 40 31 W89 46 19
P O Drawer 2440, Tupelo, MS 28803 US
(888) 937-2471, *Fax:* (916) 251-1650
www.air1.com
info@air1.com

License: Bloomfield, Stoddard County, MO held by Educational Media Foundation.
Group Owner: EMF Broadcasting; (acq 3-23-2007; grpsl)
Nat'l Network: Air 1
Arbitron Metro Market: Bloomfield, MO *Format:* Alternative, Christian
Darrell Chambliss, Chairman
Alan Mason, COO
Mike Novak, President and CEO
Ed Lenane, News Director
Sam Wallington, Engineering Dir
Dan Antonelli, Chief Business Development Officer
Eric Moser, Chief Financial Officer
BrianBurger, Vice President of Human Resources
D. Kevin Blair, Secretary and General Counsel
Larry Moody, Director
Mitch Barnhart, Director

Blue Springs

KCWJ
02-02-1984; 1030 khz AM *Hrs Open:* 24; 200 ft. haat
9734 Wornall Road, Suite 101, Kansas City, MO 64116 US
(816) 313-0049, *Fax:* (816) 313-1036
www.kcwj.org
info@kcwj.org
License: Blue Springs, MO held by KCWJ Inc./dba Christian Broadcasting Associates L.P.
Nat'l Network: Salem Radio Network *Nat'l Reps:* Salem *Regional Reps:* PioneerSports Sales *Wire Services:* Metro Weather Service Inc.
Arbitron Metro Market: Kansas City, MO-KS *Format:* Christian, Gospel *Special Programming:* local and regional sports *Hrs. of News Programming:* News progmg 5 hrs wkly *Target Audience:* 18-49; family orientedChristian audience *Adv. Rates:* 60;25 60;25 60;25 60;25
Ken Ball, General Manager
Jason Friedline, General Sales Mgr
Ed Treese, Chief Engineer
Jeff Henderson, Sales Account Executive
Willie Williams, Public Relations and Sales

Bolivar

KYOO
11-01-1961; 1200 khz AM; 1 kw-D, NDD; N37 37 16 W93 24 6
304 E. Jackson, Bolivar, MO 65613 US
(417) 326-5259(417) 326-5257, *Fax:* (417) 326-5900
www.kyooradio.com/
kyooradio@aol.com
License: Bolivar, MO held by KYOO Communications
Nat'l Network: ABC *Wire Services:* NWS (National Weather Service)
Arbitron Metro Market: Bolivar, MO *Format:* Country, News *Special Programming:* Farm 3 hrs, gospel 2 hrs wkly *Hrs. of News Programming:* news progmg 12 hrs. wkly *No. News Employees:* 1 *Target Audience:* 10-72 yrs. *Adv. Rates:* 22.50; 9; 6
Stephen Paris, President
Ann Paris, Operations Dir

Bonne Terre

KDBB
09-01-1989; 104.3 mhz FM *Hrs Open:* 24; 1.65 kw; 663 ft.; N37 48 1 W90 33 47
P O Box 36, Park Hills, MO 63601 US
(573) 431-1000, *Fax:* (573) 431-0850
www.b104fm.com
radio@b104fm.com
License: Bonne Terre, St. Francois County, MO held by MKS Broadcasting Inc.
Nat'l Network: Westwood One
Arbitron Metro Market: Park Hills, MO *Hrs. of News Programming:* news progmg 20 hrs wkly *No. News Employees:* 1 *Target Audience:* 25-55.
M.L. Steinmetz, President
Larry D. Joseph, General Manager
Kelly Valle, General Sales Mgr
Jason Loughary, Programming Director
Erik Hanson, News Director

Boonville

KWJK
09-15-1999; 93.1 mhz FM *Hrs Open:* 24; 7.2 kw; 413 ft.; N38 56 31 W92 34 32
1600 Radio Hill Road, Boonville, MO 65233 US
(573) 441-9310, *Fax:* (660) 882-6688
www.931jack.fm
kwrt@classicnet.net
License: Boonville, Cooper County, MO held by Bittersweet Broadcasting Inc.
Arbitron Metro Market: Columbia, MO *Format:* Adult Contemp
William Glynn Jr., President

KCLR-FM
10-01-1974; 99.3 mhz FM *Hrs Open:* 24; 33 kw; 591 ft.; N38 46 34 W92 32 45
P.O. Box 1749, Cape Girardeau, MO 63702 US
(573) 875-1099, *Fax:* (573) 875-2439
www.clear99.com
cynthias@zrgmail.com
License: Boonville, Cooper County, MO held by Zimmer Broadcasting Co.
Group Owner: Zimmer Radio Inc.
Nat'l Reps: Christal
Arbitron Metro Market: Columbia, MO *Format:* Country *Hrs. of News Programming:* news progmg 3 hrs wkly *No. News Employees:* 3 *Target Audience:* 25-54.
Jennifer Herrin, Operations Dir
Carla Lieble, General Manager
Cynthia Schreen, General Sales Mgr
Teresa Davis, Programming Director
Shelley Tucker, News Director
Drew Haines, Chief Engineer

KWRT
08-11-1953; 1370 khz AM *Hrs Open:* 24; 1 kw-D, ND1; 0.084 kw-N, ND1; N38 56 44 W92 46 14
1600 Radio Hill Rd, Boonville, MO 65233 US
(660) 882-6686, *Fax:* (660) 882-6688
www.1370kwrt.com
kwrt@classicnet.net
License: Boonville, MO held by Big Country of Missouri Inc.
Nat'l Network: Jones Radio Networks *Regional Network:* Missourinet
Arbitron Metro Market: Boonville, MO *Format:* Country *Special Programming:* Farm 5 hrs wkly *Hrs. of News Programming:* news progmg 5 hrs wkly *No. News Employees:* 1 *Target Audience:* 35 plus; general
Dick Billings, President
Pat Billings, Operations Dir
Matt Billings, General Manager
Ted Bleil, News Director
Mike Mcgowan, Chief Engineer
Sharon Korte, Sports Commentator

Bourbon

KZOC
94.1 mhz FM; 6 kw; 328 feet; N38 05 00 W91 15 00
1282 Smallwood Drive, Suite 372, Waldorf, MD
(202) 251-7589
License: Bourbon, MO held by Alma Corporation

Dennis Wallace, President

Bowling Green

KPVR
08-01-1975; 94.1 mhz FM *Hrs Open:* 24; 7.5 kw; 592 ft.; N39 15 45 W91 4 9
11388 Pike 133, Lousiana, MO 63353 US
(314) 909-8569, *Fax:* (314) 835-9739
www.joyfmonline.org
info@joyfmonline.org
License: Bowling Green, Pike County, MO held by Four Him Enterprises L.L.C.
Format: Christian
Sandi Brown, General Manager
Greg Cassidy, Programming Director

Branson

*KLFC
07-01-1988; 88.1 mhz FM *Hrs Open:* 24; 1.8 kw; Ant 390 ft; N36 33 06 W93 14 17
205 W. Atlantic, Branson, MO 65615
(417) 334-5532, *Fax:* (417) 335-2437
www.klfcradio.com
881fm@klfcradio.com
License: Branson, Taney County, MO held by Mountaintop Broadcasting Inc.
Nat'l Network: USA
Population Served: 100,000*Hrs. of News Programming:* news progmg 7 hrs wkly *No. News Employees:* 1 *Target Audience:* Adults 25-50.
Herb Smith, President
Vicky Smith, Operations Dir
Darin Ahrends, Station Manager
Herb Smith, Promotions Manager
Darin Ahrends, News Director

KOMC
12-21-1956; 1220 khz AM *Hrs Open:* 24; 1 kw-D, 53 w-N; N36 37 12 W93 12 40 *Rebroadcasts:* Rebroadcasts KDMC-FM Kimberling City 95%
202 Courtney St., Branson, MO 65616
(417) 334-6003,(417) 334-6012, *Fax:* (417) 334-7141
www.hometownradioonline.com
krzk@krzk.com
License: Branson, Taney County, MO held by KOMC-KRZX LLC.
Group Owner: Earls Broadcasting Co.; (acq 11-21-86; $335,000).
Nat'l Network: CBS *Regional Network:* Missourinet
Population Served: 42,000*Hrs. of News Programming:* news progmg 10 hrs wkly *No. News Employees:* 3 *Target Audience:* 40 plus. *Adv. Rates:* 17; 13; 16; 11
Charles Earls, President
Scottie Earls, General Manager
Steve Willoughby, Station Manager
Scott McCaulley, Programming Director
Kristen Clemmens, Promotions Manager
Sally Kaucher, News Director
Greg Pyron, Chief Engineer

*KOZO
01-01-1998; 89.7 mhz FM *Hrs Open:* 24; 0.15 kw horiz, 20 kw vert; 427 ft.; N36 33 4 W93 14 36
P.O. Box 1924, Tulsa, OK 74101 US
(918) 455-5693,(417) 339-3388, *Fax:* (417) 339-3410
www.oasisnetwork.org
mail@oasisnetwork.org
License: Branson, Taney County, MO held by Creative Educational Media Corp. Inc.
Nat'l Network: USA *Regional Reps:* Rgnl Reps
Format: Religious *Target Audience:* General.
David Ingles, President

KRZK
03-01-1971; 106.3 mhz FM *Hrs Open:* 24; 5.7 kw; 672 ft; N36 43 52 W93 10 03
202 Courtney St., Branson, MO 65616
(417) 334-6003,(417) 334-6012, *Fax:* (417) 334-7141
hometowndailynews.com
krzk@krzk.com
License: Branson, Taney County, MO
Group Owner: Earls Broadcasting Co.
Nat'l Network: ABC
Hrs. of News Programming: news progmg 7 hrs wkly *No. News Employees:* 3 *Target Audience:* 25-54; Branson & loc tourists
Adv. Rates: 40; 30; 40; 20
Charles Earles, CEO
Scottie Earles, General Manager
Steve Willoughby, Station Manager
Kristen Clemmens, Programming Director
Greg Pyron, Chief Engineer

Bridgeton

KBWX
11-15-2010; 100.3 mhz; 17000 w; 150 m; N38 41 07 W90 22 54
50 East Rivercenter Blvd, Suite 1200, Covington, KY 41011

www.brewstlouis.com
License: Bridgeton, St. Louis County, MO
Group Owner: Citicasters Licenses Inc.

Brookfield

KFMZ
02-14-1956; 1470 khz AM *Hrs Open:* 24; 0.5 kw-D, DA2; 0.02 kw-N, DA2; N39 50 26 W93 4 52 *Rebroadcasts:* Rebroadcasts KZBK-FM Brookfield
107 South Main, Brookfield, MO 64628 US
(660) 258-3383, *Fax:* (660) 258-7307
www.bestbroadcastgroup.com/kfmz.htm
kfmz@bestbroadcastgroup.com
License: Brookfield, MO held by Best Broadcasting Inc.
Group Owner: Best Broadcast Group; (acq 6-14-93; $70,000 with co-located FM;
Nat'l Network: ABC
Arbitron Metro Market: Brookfield, MO *Format:* Adult Contemp
Hrs. of News Programming: News progmg 4 hrs wkly *Target Audience:* 18-49; men & women with spendable income
Phillip Chirillo, President
Dale Palmer, Operations Dir

KZBK
09-01-1981; 96.9 mhz FM *Hrs Open:* 24; 50 kw; 492 ft.; N39 54 32 W93 4 34
PO Box 219, Brookfield, MO 64628 US
(660) 258-3383, *Fax:* (660) 258-7307
www.kzbkradio.com/
kzbk@shighway.com

License: Brookfield, Linn County, MO held by Best Broadcasting Inc.
Group Owner: Best Broadcast Group
Arbitron Metro Market: Brookfield, MO *Format:* Adult Contemp
Phil Chirillo, President
Dale A. Palmer, Operations Dir

KFMZ(AM)
02-14-1956; 1470 khz AM *Hrs Open:* 24; 500 w-D, 20 w-N, DA; N39 50 26 W93 04 52 *Rebroadcasts:* Rebroadcasts KZBK-FM Brookfield
107 S. Main, Brookfield, MO 64628
(660) 258-3383, *Fax:* (660) 258-7307
www.bestbroadcastgroup.com/kfmz.htm
kfmz@bestbroadcastgroup.com
License: Brookfield, Linn County, MO held by Best Broadcasting Inc.
Group Owner: Best Broadcast Group; (acq 6-14-93; $70,000 with co-located FM;
Nat'l Network: ABC
Population Served: 4,474 *Arbitron Metro Market:* Brookfield, MO *Hrs. of News Programming:* News progmg 4 hrs wkly *Target Audience:* 18-49; men & women with spendable income
Phillip Chirillo, President
Dale Palmer, Operations Dir

Brookline

KQRA
05-28-2002; 102.1 mhz FM *Hrs Open:* 24; 4.9 kw; 361 ft.; N37 12 39 W93 13 42
C/O Fisher Wayland #400, 2001 Pennsylvania Ave NW, Washington, DC 20006 US
(417) 447-1021, *Fax:* (417) 886-2155
www.q1021.fm
kbergman@mwfmarketing.fm
License: Brookline, Greene County, MO held by MW SpringMo Inc.
Group Owner: The Mid-West Family Broadcast Group
Nat'l Reps: Eastman Radio
Arbitron Metro Market: Springfield, MO *Target Audience:* 18-49; active adults *Adv. Rates:* 40; 45; 45; 25
Rick McCoy, President
Mary Fleenor, Operations Dir
Malcolm Hukriede, General Sales Mgr
Kristen Bergman, Programming Director
Nichole Buckner, News Director
Jeanne Guittar, Business Manager
Shadow Williams, Music Director
KeithAbercrombie, Regional Sales Manager

Buffalo

KBFL-FM
01-01-1965; 99.9 mhz FM *Hrs Open:* 24; 3.1 kw; 476 ft.; N37 31 14 W93 6 14
Mailing Address: P.O. Box 492, Sulphur Springs, TX 75483 US
Second Address: 304 S. Pine, Buffalo, MO 65622
(417) 862-3751, *Fax:* (417) 869-7675
www.kbflfm.com
manager@radiospringfield.com
License: Buffalo, Dallas County, MO held by Meyer-Baldridge Inc.
Group Owner: Meyer Communications Inc.; (acq 6-1-2000; $550,000).
Nat'l Network: NBC Radio *Regional Network:* Missourinet
Arbitron Metro Market: Springfield, MO *Format:* News, News/Talk, 64, Sports, Talk *Special Programming:* Gospel 3 hrs wkly *Hrs. of News Programming:* news progmg 15 hrs wkly *No. News Employees:* 1 *TargetAudience:* 34-54; male-female adults
Kenneth Meyer, President
Bill Jones, General Manager
Rob Evans, Programming Director
R.J. McCalister, News Director
Dale Blankenship, Chief Engineer

Butler

KMAM
05-11-1962; 1530 khz AM *Hrs Open:* 16; 0.5 kw-D, NDD; N38 14 56 W94 19 18
Mailing Address: 800 East Nursery Street, Butler, MO 64730 US
Second Address: none, none, none, none
(660) 679-4191, *Fax:* (660) 679-4193
www.921kmoe.com
news@fm92radio.com
License: Butler, MO held by Bates County Broadcasting Co.
Nat'l Network: ABC *Regional Network:* Brownfield
Format: Country *Special Programming:* Farm/Abc World News/ Local News *Hrs. of News Programming:* news progmg 15 hrs wkly *No. News Employees:* 1 *Target Audience:* General; family *Adv. Rates:* 16; 16; 16; 16
Melody Thornton, President

KMOE
01-15-1975; 92.1 mhz FM *Hrs Open:* 16; 4.7 kw; 148 ft.; N38 14 56 W94 19 18
800 East Nursery Street, Butler, MO 64730 US
(660) 679-4191, *Fax:* (660) 679-4193
www.921knoe.com
License: Butler, Bates County, MO
Keith Sanderson, Station Manager
Daniel Boyd, Programming Director
Delvin Kinser, News Director

Cabool

KOZX
05-01-1978; 98.1 mhz FM; 3 kw; 220 ft.; N37 7 58 W92 8 3
P.O. Box 514, Cabool, MO 65689 US
(417) 926-4650, *Fax:* (417) 926-7604
License: Cabool, Texas County, MO held by Ozark Media Inc.
Group Owner: Ozark Media Inc.; (acq 5-1-2007; $625,000 with KELE-FM Mountain Grove)
Format: Contemporary Hits/Top 40, Adult Contemp *Special Programming:* Farm 2 hrs wkly
Tracy O'Quinn, General Sales Mgr
Shawn Anthony, Programming Director
Jim Morris, News Director
Tonya Shannon, Traffic Manager

***KCVY**
01-01-2003; 89.9 mhz FM *Hrs Open:* 24; 10.5 kw; 495 ft.; N37 5 32 W92 3 10 *Rebroadcasts:* Rebroadcasts KCVO-FM Camdenton 100%.
P O Drawer 2440, Tupelo, MS 38803 US
(573) 346-3200, *Fax:* (573) 346-1010
www.spiritfm.org
License: Cabool, Texas County, MO held by Lake Area Educational Broadcasting Foundation.
Nat'l Network: Salem Radio Network
Arbitron Metro Market: Camdenton, MO *Format:* Christian *Hrs. of News Programming:* News progmg one hr wkly *Target Audience:* 25-45.
James McDermott, President

***KZGM**
01-01-2009; 88.1 mhz FM; 12.5 kw vert; 443 ft.; N37 7 15 W92 0 9
US
(417) 200-0522, *Fax:* (206) 202-1735
www.kz88.org
radio@kz88.org
License: Cabool, Texas County, MO held by Real Community Radio Network Inc.
Arbitron Metro Market: Cabool, MO *Format:* Talk
Kazie Perkins, Operations Dir
Gene Colliflower, News Director

California

KATI
07-27-1984; 94.3 mhz FM *Hrs Open:* 19; 50 kw; 492 ft.; N38 31 25 W92 24 25
P. O. Box 3353, Evansville, IN 47732 US
(573) 893-5696, *Fax:* (573) 893-4137
www.kat943.com
kati@zrgmail.com
License: California, Moniteau County, MO held by Zimmer Radio of Mid-Missouri Inc.
Arbitron Metro Market: Jefferson City, MT *Format:* Country
Ron Covert, General Manager

KRLL
07-27-1984; 1420 khz AM *Hrs Open:* 18; 0.5 kw-D, ND1; 0.225 kw-N, ND1; N38 38 12 W92 35 0
P.O. Box 307, 100 a E Buchanan, California, MO 65018 US
(573) 796-3139, *Fax:* (573) 796-4131
krll01@embarqmail.com
License: California, MO held by Moniteau Communications Inc.
Format: Country *Special Programming:* Farm 5 hrs, gospel 3 hrs wkly *Hrs. of News Programming:* news progmg 19 hrs wkly *No. News Employees:* 1 *Target Audience:* 20 plus.
Jeffrey Shackleford, President

Camdenton

***KCVO-FM**
09-23-1985; 91.7 mhz FM *Hrs Open:* 24; 10 kw; 436 ft.; N38 1 13 W92 45 27
Mailing Address: P.O. Box 800, Camdenton, MO 65020 US
Second Address: 128 Possom Hollow Dr, Camdenton, MO 65020
(573) 346-3200, *Fax:* (573) 346-1010
www.spiritfm.org
License: Camdenton, Camden County, MO held by Lake Area Educational Broadcasting Foundation.
Nat'l Network: Salem Radio Network
Arbitron Metro Market: Camdenton, MO *Format:* Christian *Hrs. of News Programming:* News progmg one hr wkly *Target Audience:* 25-45.
Alice McDermott, CFO
James McDermott, President
Jim McDermott, General Manager
Alice McDermott, Financial Director

Cameron

KMRN
02-01-1971; 1360 khz AM *Hrs Open:* 5:30 AM-7 PM; 500 w-D, 25 w-N; N39 41 05 W94 14 22
607 E. Platte Clay Way, P.O. Box 643, Cameron, MO 65279
(816) 632-6661, *Fax:* (816) 632-1334
www.northwestmoinfo.com
dschmitz@regionalradio.com
License: Cameron, Clinton County, MO held by Cameron/Bethany License Co. LLC.
Group Owner: GoodRadio.TV; (acq 8-8-2007; grpsl)
Nat'l Network: Fox News Radio *Regional Network:* Missourinet; Brownfield
Population Served: 50,000 *Arbitron Metro Market:* Kansas City, MO-KS *Special Programming:* Local News, Talk & Farm *Hrs. of News Programming:* 5 hrs *No. News Employees:* 9 *Target Audience:* General. *Adv.Rates:* 12; 10; 11; na
Dean Goodman, Chairman
George Pelletier Jr, CEO/COO
Doug Schmitz, General Manager
Chris Ward, Programming Director
Chris Ward, Promotions Manager
Chris Ward, News Director
Lloyd Collins, Engineering Dir
Gregg Richwine, ChiefEngineer

KKWK
04-05-1995; 100.1 mhz FM; 50 kw; 492 ft.; N39 57 28 W94 06 55
607 E. Platte Clay Way, P.O. Box 643, Cameron, MO 65279
(816) 632-6661, *Fax:* (816) 632-1334
www.northwestmoinfo.com
License: Cameron, Clinton County, MO
Group Owner: GoodRadio.TV
Nat'l Network: Fox News Radio *Regional Network:* Brownfield
Population Served: 250,000*Special Programming:* Community Affairs *No. News Employees:* 2 *Target Audience:* 25-49. *Adv. Rates:* 29.50; 23; 23; 14
Dean Goodman, Chairman
George Pelletier Jr, CEO/COO
Doug Schmitz, General Manager
Doug Schmitz, Station Manager
Doug Schmitz, General Sales Mgr
Chris Ward, News Director
Gregg Richwine, Engineering Dir
Lloyd Collins, ChiefEngineer
Ruth Hammontree, Traffic Manager

***WRVX**
91.7 mhz FM; 20 kw; Ant 321 ft; N39 52 42 W94 05 33
219 Dodd Rd., Ringgold, GA
(706) 965-2355, *Fax:* (706) 965-3755
License: Cameron, Clinton County, MO held by Victor Broadcasting Inc.
James Price III, President

Campbell

KFEB
10-01-1998; 107.5 mhz FM; 17.5 kw; 390 ft.; N36 29 55 W89 51 16
Rt. 13, Box 44, Poplar Bluff, MO 63901 US
(573) 686-3700, *Fax:* (573) 686-1713
info@foxradionetwork.com
License: Campbell, Dunklin County, MO held by Eagle Bluff Enterprises.
Group Owner: Eagle Bluff Enterprises
Arbitron Metro Market: Poplar Bluff, MO *Format:* Rock/AOR
Steven Fuchs, General Manager

Canton

KRRY
05-04-1971; 100.9 mhz FM *Hrs Open:* 24; 28 kw; 656 ft.; N39 53 9 W91 36 38
119 North 3rd St, Box 711, Hannibal, MO 63401 US
(217) 223-5292, *Fax:* (217) 223-5299
www.y101radio.com
Ed.Foxall@townsquaremedia.com

License: Canton, Lewis County, MO held by Double O Radio of Missouri
Group Owner: Double O Radio L.L.C.; 02.09.2010
Nat'l Reps: McGavren Guild
Arbitron Metro Market: Quincy, IL-Hannibal, MO *Format:* Contemporary Hits/Top 40 *Adv. Rates:* 19.52; 16.51; 18.02; 7.50
Ed Foxall, General Manager
Jeff Asmussen, General Sales Mgr
Dennis Oliver, Programming Director
Ed Foxall, Promotions Manager
Gary Glaenzer, Chief Engineer

Cape Girardeau

KAPE
01-01-1951; 1550 khz AM
Mailing Address: P.O. Box 1508, Mount Vernon, IL 62864 US
Second Address: 901 S. Kings Hwy., Cape Girardeau, MO 63703
(573) 339-7000, *Fax:* (573) 651-4100
www.kaperadio1550.com
lambert@withersradio.net
License: Cape Girardeau, MO held by Withers Broadcasting Co. of Missouri LLC.
Group Owner: Withers Broadcasting Co.; (acq 6-72).
Nat'l Network: Westwood One; Fox Sports *Nat'l Reps:* Katz Radio *Wire Services:* AP
Arbitron Metro Market: Cape-Girardeau, MT *Format:* News, Sports, 86 *Target Audience:* 25-54; active, aware adults
W. Russell Withers Jr., President
Rick Lambert, General Manager
Kevin Casey, Programming Director
Smokey King, Chief Engineer

KEZS-FM
12-10-1970; 102.9 mhz FM *Hrs Open:* 24; 100 kw; 948 ft.; N37 24 23 W89 33 44
P.O. Box 1749, Cape Girardeau, MO 63702 US
(573) 335-8291, *Fax:* (573) 335-4806
www.k103fm.com
k103@zrgmail.com
License: Cape Girardeau, Cape Girardeau County, MO held by MRR License LLC
Group Owner: MAX Media L.L.C.; (acq 6-2-2004; grpsl).
Arbitron Metro Market: Cape Girardeau, MO *Format:* Country *No. News Employees:* 1 *Target Audience:* 25-54.
Whitney Thomas, Programming Director

KGIR
06-10-1966; 1220 khz AM *Hrs Open:* 24; 0.25 kw-D, ND1; 0.137 kw-N, ND1; N37 18 3 W89 29 27
P.O. Box 1749, Cape Girardeau, MO 63702 US
(573) 335-8291, *Fax:* (573) 335-4806
www.espn1220.com
kgir@kgir.com
License: Cape Girardeau, MO held by MRR License LLC.
Group Owner: MAX Media L.L.C.; (acq 6-2-2004; grpsl)
Nat'l Network: ESPN Radio
TV Affiliate: ESPN *Format:* Sports, Talk *Target Audience:* 18 plus; men
Cristy Benton, General Manager
Meg Davis, General Sales Mgr
Erik Sean, Programming Director
Faume Riggin, News Director
Sherry Crider, Traffic Manager

KGMO
03-17-1969; 100.7 mhz FM; 100 kw; 991 ft.; N37 21 45 W89 31 19
P.O. Box 1508, Mount Vernon, IL 62864 US
(573) 651-4100
www.kgmo.com
rlambert@withersradio.net
License: Cape Girardeau, Cape Girardeau County, MO held by Withers Broadcasting Co. of Missouri LLC
Group Owner: Withers Broadcasting Co.
Nat'l Reps: Katz Radio
Format: Classic Rock *Hrs. of News Programming:* news progmg 10 hrs wkly *Target Audience:* 25-54
Rick Lambert, General Manager
Kevin Casey, Station Manager
Chris Cook, Promotions Manager
Jared Smith, Production Director

*KRCU
03-03-1976; 90.9 mhz FM; 6.5 kw vert; 696 ft.; N37 24 17 W89 34 6
One University Plaza, Cape Girardeau, MO 63701 US
(573) 651-5070, *Fax:* (573) 651-5071
www.semo.edu
comments@krcu.org
License: Cape Girardeau, Cape Girardeau County, MO held by Board of Regents of Southeast Missouri State University.
Nat'l Network: NPR; PRI
Arbitron Metro Market: Cape Girardeau, Sikeston/MO's Parkland
Format: Classical, Jazz, 60 *Target Audience:* General.
Jason Brown, Operations Dir
Dan Woods, General Manager
Amanda Lincoln, General Sales Mgr
Jacob McCleland, Programming Director
Allen Lane, Chief Engineer

KZIM
01-01-1925; 960 khz AM *Hrs Open:* 24; 5 kw-D, DAN; 0.5 kw-N, DAN; N37 18 59 W89 29 6
P.O. Box 1749, Cape Girardeau, MO 63702 US
(573) 355-8291, *Fax:* (573) 355-4806
www.960kzim.com
kzim@zrgmail.com
License: Cape Girardeau, MO held by MRR License LLC
Group Owner: MAX Media L.L.C.
Nat'l Network: CBS
Arbitron Metro Market: Cape Girardeau, MO *Format:* News, News/Talk, 86 *Target Audience:* 35-64.
Faume Riggin, Programming Director

Carrollton

KAOL
04-18-1959; 1430 khz AM *Hrs Open:* 24; 0.5 kw-D, ND1; 0.027 kw-N, ND1; N39 19 58 W93 32 15
102 North Mason, Carrollton, MO 64633 US
(660) 542-0404, *Fax:* (660) 542-0420
www.kmzu.com
kmzu@carolnet.com
License: Carrollton, MO held by Kanza Inc.
Nat'l Reps: McGavren Guild
Arbitron Metro Market: Carrollton, MT *Format:* Country *Special Programming:* Sp 3 hrs wkly *Hrs. of News Programming:* news progmg 10 hrs wkly *No. News Employees:* 2 *Target Audience:* 25-54; farm families &those with agricultural backgrounds
Miles Carter, General Manager
Rick Barton, General Sales Mgr
Scott Powell, Programming Director
Chastity Anderson, News Director
Jim Woods, Music Director
Sue Lightfoot, Traffic Manager

KMZU
07-13-1962; 100.7 mhz FM; 99 kw; 991 ft.; N39 21 59 W93 24 12
Rebroadcasts: Rebroadcasts WHB(AM) Kansas City 95%
102 North Mason, Box 279, Carrollton, MO 64633 US
(660) 542-0404, *Fax:* (660) 542-0420
www.kmzu.com
License: Carrollton, Carroll County, MO held by Kanza Inc.
Don Sibley, Programming Director

Carthage

KDMO
06-03-1947; 1490 khz AM *Hrs Open:* 24; 1 kw-U; N37 10 58 W94 21 43
Mailing Address: Box 426, Carthage, MO 64836
Second Address: 221 E. 4th St.
(417) 358-6054,
modulation45@yahoo.com
License: Carthage, Jasper County, MO held by Ronald L. Petersen
Nat'l Network: NBC News Radio *Nat'l Reps:* In house
Population Served: 397,000 *Arbitron Metro Market:* Joplin, MO
Special Programming: Sp 10 hrs wkly *Hrs. of News Programming:* news progmg 10 hrs wkly *No. News Employees:* 1 *Target Audience:* 55 plus.
Ronald Petersen, President

KMXL
01-10-1972; 95.1 mhz FM *Hrs Open:* 24; 50 kw; 472 ft; N37 10 58 W94 21 35
Mailing Address: Box 426, Carthage, MO 64836
Second Address: 221 E. 4th St., Carthage, MO 64836
(417) 358-6054,
www.951mikefm.com
modulation45@yahoo.com
License: Carthage, Jasper County, MO held by Ronald L. Petersen Sr.
Nat'l Network: NBC Radio *Nat'l Reps:* In house
Population Served: 775,000 *Arbitron Metro Market:* Joplin, MO *Hrs. of News Programming:* news progmg one hr wkly *No. News Employees:* 1 *Target Audience:* 25-54; young adults & baby-boomers
Ronald Petersen Sr., President
Ronald Petersen Jr., Station Manager

Caruthersville

KCRV
02-22-1950; 1370 khz AM; 1 kw-D, ND1; 0.063 kw-N, ND1; N36 12 50 W89 41 25
Mailing Address: P.O. Box 1927, Cape Girardeau, MO 63702 US
Second Address: 1303 Southwest Dr., Kennett, MO 63857
(573) 888-4616, *Fax:* (573) 888-4991
www.kcrvradio.com
info@kcrvradio.com
License: Caruthersville, MO held by Pollack Broadcasting Co.
Group Owner: Pollack Broadcasting Co.; (acq 9-21-99; with co-located FM)
Nat'l Network: Moody *Regional Network:* Brownfield
Arbitron Metro Market: Caruthersville, MO *Format:* Country
Special Programming: Relg 20 hrs wkly *Target Audience:* General; residents of Pemiscot county
Anita Phillips, President
Lory Phillips, General Manager
David Phillips, Station Manager
Rick Neurauter, Advertising Director

KCRV-FM
04-28-1975; 105.1 mhz FM; 4.8 kw; 328 ft.; N36 12 50 W89 41 25
Mailing Address: P.O. Box 909, Caruthersville, MO 63830 US
Second Address: 1303 Southwest Dr., Kennett, MO 63857
(573) 888-4616, *Fax:* (573) 888-4991
info@kcrvradio.com
License: Caruthersville, Pemiscot County, MO held by Pollack Broadcasting Co.
Group Owner: Pollack Broadcasting Co.
Arbitron Metro Market: Jonesboro, AR *Format:* Oldies
Mike Newport, Operations Dir
Ruth Seymour, General Manager
Jennifer Ferro, Station Manager
David Kleinbart, General Sales Mgr
Ariana Morgenstern, Programming Director
Steve Herbert, Chief Engineer

Cassville

KRMO
08-01-1950; 990 khz AM *Hrs Open:* 24; 2.5 kw-D, ND1; 0.047 kw-N, ND1; N36 56 15 W93 55 30
1569 North Central, Monett, MO 65708 US
(417) 235-6041, *Fax:* (417) 235-6388
www.krmo.com
kkbl@talonbroadcasting.com
License: Cassville, MO held by Eagle Broadcasting Inc.
Regional Network: Brownfield; Missourinet
Arbitron Metro Market: Joplin, MO *Format:* Country *Hrs. of News Programming:* news progmg 10 hrs wkly *No. News Employees:* 1 *Target Audience:* 35 plus; business professionals, farmers, elderly *Adv. Rates:* 12; 12; 12; 12
Duane Gandy, President
Bill Lewis, Operations Dir
Janet Gandy, General Manager
Lance Mettlach, General Sales Mgr
Dan Kesterson, Programming Director
Sam Clapper, News Director

Cedar Hill

*KNLH
10-01-1998; 89.5 mhz FM; 0.068 kw; 699 ft.; N38 21 40 W90 32 54
1411 Locust Street, St. Louis, MO 63103 US
(314) 436-2424, *Fax:* (314) 436-2434
www.hereshelpnet.org
larryr@hereshelpnet.org
License: Cedar Hill, Jefferson County, MO held by New Life Evangelistic Center Inc.
Format: Adult Contemp, Gospel, 86
Victor Anderson, General Manager

Centralia

KMFC
02-03-1986; 92.1 mhz FM *Hrs Open:* 24; 1.85 kw; Ant 418 ft; N39 09 58 W92 09 52
1249 E. Hwy. 22, Centralia, MO 65240
(573) 682-5525, *Fax:* (573) 682-2744
www.kmfc.com
info@kmfc.com
License: Centralia, Boone County, MO held by Clair Broadcasting Co.
Nat'l Network: USA
Population Served: 260,000 *Arbitron Metro Market:* Columbia, MO *Special Programming:* Black 3 hrs, gospel 2 hrs, Sp one hr wkly *Target Audience:* 25-50. *Adv. Rates:* 15; 11.25; 14.25; 8.25

Jerry Clair, General Manager
Sharon Dollens, Station Manager
Tonya Beamer, General Sales Mgr
Deanna Arnold, Promotions Manager
Sharon Dollens, News Director

Chaffee

KREZ

07-01-1990; 104.7 mhz FM; 7.7 kw; 585 ft.; N37 9 46 W89 28 59
P.O. Box 818, C/O Station Wqrl, Benton, IL 62812 US
(573) 339-7000, *Fax:* (573) 651-4100
www.softrock1047.com
rlambert@withersradio.net
License: Chaffee, Scott County, MO held by Dana R. Withers
Nat'l Reps: Katz Radio
Arbitron Metro Market: Cape Girardeau, MO *Format:* Adult Contemp *Target Audience:* 18-49.
Rick Lambert, General Manager
Steve Thomas, Programming Director
Rebecca Thomas, Promotions Manager

Charleston

KCHR

01-01-1953; 1350 khz AM *Hrs Open:* 24; 1 kw-D, ND1; 0.079 kw-N, ND1; N36 55 30 W89 17 45
P. O. Box 432, Charleston, MO 63834 US
(573) 683-6044
License: Charleston, MO held by South Missouri Broadcasting Co. Inc.
Arbitron Metro Market: Charleston, MO *Format:* Oldies, Talk *Special Programming:* Oldies about 3 hrs *Hrs. of News Programming:* News progmg 21 hr per day *Target Audience:* General.
James Byrd, III, President
Danny Adams, General Manager
Pam Haws, Programming Director
Charlie Lampe, Chief Engineer

KWKZ

02-01-1993; 106.1 mhz FM *Hrs Open:* 24; 34 kw; 584 ft.; N37 3 38 W89 37 27
753 Enterprise, Cape Girardeau, MO 63703 US
(573) 334-7800, *Fax:* (573) 334-7440
www.kwkz.com
License: Charleston, Mississippi County, MO held by Anderson Broadcasting Co. Inc.
Arbitron Metro Market: Cape Giradeau, MO *Format:* Country *Target Audience:* 18-44; 35-55 male, 30-45 female
Ann Anderson, Chairman
Bill Anderson, CEO
Susan Bell, Programming Director
Palmer Johnson, Engineering Dir

Chillicothe

KCHI

03-03-1950; 1010 khz AM; 0.25 kw-D, ND1; 0.037 kw-N, ND1; N39 45 51 W93 33 21
PO Box 227, Chillicothe, MO 64601 US
(660) 646-4173, *Fax:* (660) 646-2868
www.kchi.com
kchi@greenhills.net
License: Chillicothe, MO held by Livingston Broadcasting Inc.
Regional Network: Missourinet
Arbitron Metro Market: Chillicothe, MO *Format:* News *Target Audience:* 35-49.
Dan Leatherman, Owner, General Manager
Randy Dean, Programming Director
Tom Tingerthal, News Director
Jessica Frizzell, Traffic Manager
Michelle, Office Manager
Rosina, Account Executive

KCHI-FM

10-01-1976; 98.5 mhz FM; 3.2 kw; 453 ft.; N39 44 50 W93 38 38
P.O. Box 227, Chillicothe, MO 64601 US
(660) 646-4173, *Fax:* (660) 646-2868
www.kchi.com
kchi@greenhills.net
License: Chillicothe, Livingston County, MO held by Livingston Broadcasting Inc.
Arbitron Metro Market: Chillicothe, MO
Joe Carroll, President
Dan Leatherman, Owner, General Manager
Randy Dean, Programming Director
Tom Tingerthal, News Director
Jessica Frizzell, Traffic Manager
Michelle, Office Manager
Rosina, Account Executive

*KRNW

08-30-1993; 88.9 mhz FM *Hrs Open:* 24; 38 kw; 512 ft.; N39 48 48 W93 35 26
800 University Drive, Maryville, MO 64468 US
(660) 562-1163, *Fax:* (660) 562-1832
www.kxcv.org
kxcv@nwmissouri.edu
License: Chillicothe, Livingston County, MO held by Northwest Missouri State University.
Format: News, News/Talk, 86 *Hrs. of News Programming:* news progmg 39 hrs wkly *No. News Employees:* 2 *Target Audience:* General.
John Jasinski, President
Patty Andrews Holley, Operations Dir
Rodney Harris, General Manager
Patty Holley, Programming Director
Darren Perkins, Chief Engineer
John Coffey, Sports Director

*KLWL

88.1 mhz FM; 50 kw vert; 75 m; N39 54 35 W93 21 42
Box 391, Twin Falls, ID
(208)733-3133, *Fax:* (208) 736-1958
www.csnradio.com
License: Chillicothe, Livingston County, MO held by Calvary Chapel of Twin Falls Inc
Micheal Kestler, President

Clayton

*KFUO

12-14-1924; 850 khz AM *Hrs Open:* Sunrise-sunset; 5 kw-D, NDD; N38 38 20 W90 18 57
85 Founders Lane, St. Louis, MO 63105 US
(314) 505-7800, *Fax:* (314) 725-3801
www.kfuo.org
worldwide@kfuo.org
License: Clayton, MO held by Lutheran Church-Missouri Synod
Nat'l Network: AP Network News
Arbitron Metro Market: St. Louis, MO *Format:* Religious, Talk *Target Audience:* General.
Gary Duncan, Operations Dir
Dennis Stortz, General Manager
Paul Clayton, Programming Director
Chuck Rathert, Promotions Manager

KLJY

01-01-1948; 99.1 mhz FM *Hrs Open:* 24; 100 kw; 1,026 ft; N38 39 08 W90 17 03
85 Founders Ln., St. Louis, MO 63105
(314) 725-0099, *Fax:* (314) 725-3801
www.classic99.com
dstortz@classic99.com
License: Clayton, St. Louis County, MO held by Lutheran Church-Missouri Synod
Nat'l Network: Wall Street; CNN Radio *Nat'l Reps:* McGavren Guild
Arbitron Metro Market: St. Louis, MO *Special Programming:* Metropolitan Opera *Target Audience:* General; upscale, educated
Dennis Stortz, General Manager
Oliver Trittler, General Sales Mgr
Jim Connett, Programming Director

KSIV

1320 khz AM *Hrs Open:* 24; 4.6 kw-D, DAN; 0.27 kw-N, DAN; N38 36 26 W90 21 14
10550 Barkley, Ste 108, Overland Park, KS 66212 US
(314) 961-1320, *Fax:* (314) 961-7562
www.bottradionetwork.com
info@bottradionetwork.com
License: Clayton, MO held by Bott Broadcasting.
Group Owner: Bott Radio Network; acq 2-25-82;
Nat'l Network: USA
Arbitron Metro Market: St. Louis, MO *Format:* Christian *Target Audience:* 25-54; family-oriented
Richard Bott II, CEO/COO
Richard Bott, President
Richard Bott II, Operations Dir
Michael McHardy, General Manager
Pat Rulon, General Sales Mgr

*KWUR

07-04-1976; 90.3 mhz FM *Hrs Open:* 24; 0.009 kw; 95 ft.; N38 38 55 W90 18 28
1 Brookings Drive, Campus Box 1205, Clayton, MO 63130 US
(314) 935-5952, *Fax:* (314) 935-8833
www.kwur.com
License: Clayton, St. Louis County, MO held by Washington University.
Arbitron Metro Market: St. Louis, MO *Format:* Alternative, Variety/Diverse *Target Audience:* 18 plus; those seeking alternative radio
Mickey Bradford, General Manager
Aaron Fleischauer, Station Manager
Eden Lewis, Promotions Manager
TBA, Chief Engineer
Hana Toribara, Music Director
Taryn Sirias, Treasurer
Matt Callahan, 0
Noah Rowlett, Webmaster
SeanCotton, Audio Service
Rici Wittkugel, Promotions

Cleveland

KCTO

11-08-2007; 1160 khz AM
US
(816) 792-1140, *Fax:* (816) 792-8258
www.kcxl.com
davekcxl@yahoo.com
License: Cleveland, MO held by Alpine Broadcasting Corp.
Nat'l Network: AP Network News
Arbitron Metro Market: Cleveland, MO *Format:* Talk *Adv. Rates:* 30; 30; 25; 20
Peter Schartel, President
David Brewer, Station Manager
Jonne Santoli, Programming Director

Clinton

KDKD

01-01-1951; 1280 khz AM *Hrs Open:* 24
Mailing Address: P.O. Box 448, Clinton, MO 64735 US
Second Address: 2201 N. Antioch Rd., Clinton, MO 64735
(660) 885-6141, *Fax:* (660) 885-4801
www.mykdkd.com
bob@kdkd.net
License: Clinton, MO held by GoodRadio.TV
Group Owner: GoodRadio.TV; (acq 10-7-2003; with co-located FM)
Nat'l Network: ABC Information & Entertainment *Regional Network:* Missourinet *Nat'l Reps:* Rgnl Reps
Arbitron Metro Market: Clinton, MO *Format:* Oldies *Hrs. of News Programming:* news progmg 10 hrs wkly *No. News Employees:* 1 *Target Audience:* 25-55.
Bob May, General Manager
Bob May, General Sales Mgr
Dave Young, Programming Director
David Lee, News Director
Jennifer Schlagle, Traffic Manager

KDKD-FM

01-01-1975; 95.3 mhz FM *Hrs Open:* 24; 14.5 kw; 433 ft.; N38 22 18 W93 55 6
Mailing Address: P.O. Box 448, Clinton, MO 64735 US
Second Address: 2201 N. Antioch Rd., Clinton, MO 64735
(660) 885-6141, *Fax:* (660) 885-4801
www.kdkd.net
bob@kdkd.com
License: Clinton, Henry County, MO held by GoodRadio.TV
Group Owner: GoodRadio.TV; (acq 5-28-1985)
Nat'l Network: Fox News Radio; Motor Racing Net *Regional Network:* Missourinet *Nat'l Reps:* Rgnl Reps
Arbitron Metro Market: Clinton, MO *Format:* Country *Special Programming:* NASCAR - MRN + PRN *Hrs. of News Programming:* 10+ *No. News Employees:* 1 *Target Audience:* 25-55.
Jennifer Schlagle, Operations Dir
Bob May, General Manager
Bob May, General Sales Mgr
Dave Young, Programming Director
David Lee, News Director
Barry Wilson, Engineering Dir
David Lee, News Director

*KLRQ

10-05-1990; 96.1 mhz FM *Hrs Open:* 24; 100 kw; 988 ft.; N38 28 27 W93 30 28 *Rebroadcasts:* Rebroadcasts KLVR(FM) Santa Rosa, CA 100%
702 E. Ohio, Box 446, Clinton, MO 64735 US
(916) 251-1600, *Fax:* (916) 251-1650
www.klove.com
License: Clinton, Henry County, MO held by Educational Media Foundation.
Group Owner: EMF Broadcasting; (acq 12-23-2003; $1.9 million).
Nat'l Network: K-Love
Format: Christian
Mike Novak, President
Glenn Goodwin, Operations Dir

Eric Allen, General Sales Mgr
David Pierce, Programming Director
Ed Lenane, News Director
Sam Wallington, Engineering Dir
Scott Smith, Music Director
Marya Morgan, ScottSmith
Richard Hunt, News Reporter
Tracy Butler, Traffic Manager

Columbia

*KBIA

01-01-1972; 91.3 mhz FM *Hrs Open:* 24; 100 kw; 610 ft.; N38 53 16 W92 15 48
409 Jesse Hall, Columbia, MO 65211 US
(573) 882-3431, *Fax:* (573) 882-2636
www.kbia.org
kbia@kbia.org
License: Columbia, Boone County, MO held by Board of Curators, University of Missouri.
Group Owner: The Curators of the University of Missouri
Nat'l Network: NPR; PRI
Arbitron Metro Market: Columbia, MO *Format:* News *Hrs. of News Programming:* news progmg 55 hrs wkly *No. News Employees:* 2 *Target Audience:* 25-64. *Adv. Rates:* 30; 20; 30; 10
Karen Walker Seeger, Operations Dir
Michael Dunn, General Manager
Roger Karwoski, Station Manager
Robert Wells, General Sales Mgr
Kyle Felling, Programming Director
Janet Saidi, News Director

KBXR

11-11-1994; 102.3 mhz FM *Hrs Open:* 24; 3.5 kw; 856 ft.; N39 0 52 W92 16 32
503 Old Highway 63 North, Columbia, MO 65201 US
(573) 874-1023, *Fax:* (573) 449-7770
www.bxr.com
1023bxr@gmail.com
License: Columbia, Boone County, MO held by Cumulus Licensing LLC.
Group Owner: Cumulus Media Inc.; (acq 4-26-2004; grpsl).
Nat'l Reps: Katz Radio
Arbitron Metro Market: Columbia, MO *Format:* Rock/AOR *Hrs. of News Programming:* news progmg one hr wkly *No. News Employees:* 3 *Target Audience:* 29-59; educated professional/technical
Greg DeRue, General Manager
Liz Mozzocco, Programming Director
Dan Claxton, News Director
Tom Holmes, Chief Engineer
Mary Kelley, Traffic Manager

KCMQ

12-03-1967; 96.7 mhz FM *Hrs Open:* 24; 99.1 kw; 912 ft.; N38 41 30 W92 5 44
P.O. Box 1749, Cape Girardeau, MO 63702 US
(573) 875-1099, *Fax:* (573) 875-2439
www.kcmq.com
License: Columbia, Boone County, MO held by Zimmer Radio of Mid-Missouri Inc.
Arbitron Metro Market: Columbia, MO *Format:* Rock/AOR *Hrs. of News Programming:* News progmg one hr wkly *Target Audience:* 25-54; male
John Zimmer, Chairman
Carla Leible, General Manager
Dave Wisniewski, General Sales Mgr
Nicci Garmon, Programming Director
Shelley Tucker, News Director
Drew Haigh, Chief Engineer

*KCOU

10-31-1973; 88.1 mhz FM *Hrs Open:* 24; 0.43 kw; 144 ft.; N38 56 24 W92 19 16
227 University Hall, Columbia, MO 65211 US
(573) 882-7820, *Fax:* (573) 882-6262
www.kcou.mu.org
comments@kcou.fm
License: Columbia, Boone County, MO held by The Curators of the University of Missouri.
Arbitron Metro Market: Columbia, MO *Format:* Alternative, Rock/AOR *Target Audience:* 18-22; students & community members
Matt Brown, General Manager
Nick Holder, Programming Director
Jill Ornitz, Promotions Manager
Kate Masters, News Director
John Constance, Chief Engineer
Elle Hoffman, Music Director
Nathan Frey, Production Director
DrewBrackett, Sports Director
Nick Holder, Recruitment Director

KFRU

10-10-1925; 1400 khz AM *Hrs Open:* 24
503 Old 63 North, Columbia, MO 65201 US
(573) 449-4141, *Fax:* (573) 449-7770
www.kfru.com
kevin.joyce@cumulus.com; greg.renoe@cumulus.com; chris.kellog@cumulus.com
License: Columbia, MO held by Cumulus Licensing LLC.
Group Owner: Cumulus Media Inc.; (acq 4-26-2004; grpsl).
Regional Network: Missourinet
Arbitron Metro Market: Columbia, MO *Format:* News, News/Talk, 86 *Special Programming:* The Woman show 2 hrs wkly, pets 1 hr wkly, gardening 1 hr wkly *Hrs. of News Programming:* news progmg 140 hrs wkly *No. NewsEmployees:* 9 *Target Audience:* General.
Greg Renoe, General Sales Mgr
Chris Kellogg, Programming Director
Kevin Joyce, Marketing Director

*KOPN

03-01-1973; 89.5 mhz FM *Hrs Open:* 24; 36 kw; 236 ft.; N38 59 53 W92 11 48
915 E. Broadway, Columbia, MO 65201 US
(573) 874-1139, *Fax:* (573) 499-1662
www.kopn.org
mail@kopn.org
License: Columbia, Boone County, MO held by New Wave Corp.
Nat'l Network: NPR; PRI
Arbitron Metro Market: Columbia, MO *Format:* News, News/Talk, 86 *Special Programming:* Blues 13 hrs, Black 10 hrs, AAA 10 hrs, Grateful Dead 6 hrs, jazz 4 hrs, gospel 3 hrs, bluegrass 6 hrs, folk 2 hrs wkly *Hrs. of NewsProgramming:* News progmg 40 hrs wkly *Target Audience:* 25-54; well educated, upwardly mobile
David Owens, General Manager
Julie Baka, General Sales Mgr
Steve Jerrett, Programming Director
Rich Winkel, Chief Engineer

KPLA

02-23-1983; 101.5 mhz FM *Hrs Open:* 24; 41 kw; 1063 ft.; N39 0 52 W92 16 32
603 Old Highway 63 North, Columbia, MO 65201 US
(573) 449-4141, *Fax:* (573) 449-7770
www.kpla.com
studio@kpla.com
License: Columbia, Boone County, MO held by Cumulus Licensing LLC.
Group Owner: Cumulus Media Inc.; (acq 4-26-2004; grpsl).
Arbitron Metro Market: Columbia, MO *Format:* Adult Contemp *Hrs. of News Programming:* news progmg one hr wkly *No. News Employees:* 2 *Target Audience:* 25-54.
Chris Kellogg, Programming Director

KTGR

01-01-1955; 1580 khz AM
P.O. Box 1749, Cape Girardeau, MO 63702 US
(573) 875-1099, *Fax:* (573) 875-2439
ktgr.com
License: Columbia, MO held by Zimmer Radio of Mid-Missouri Inc.
Nat'l Network: ABC; ESPN Radio
Arbitron Metro Market: Columbia, MO *Format:* Sports *Target Audience:* 18-34; male
David Guttormson, General Manager

*KWWC-FM

02-02-1965; 90.5 mhz FM *Hrs Open:* 24; 1.25 kw; 131 ft.; N38 57 12 W92 19 5
East Broadway At Ripley, Columbia, MO 65201 US
(800) 876-7207, *Fax:* (573) 876-2330
www.stephens.edu/campuslife/kwwc/
info@stephens.edu
License: Columbia, Boone County, MO held by Stephens College.
Arbitron Metro Market: Columbia, MO *Format:* Jazz, Oldies *Target Audience:* 25-60; college educated, professional or retired with middle upper income
Jonna Wiseman, General Manager
Max Ornles, Chief Engineer

Concordia

*KYRV

01-01-1998; 88.1 mhz FM; 1 kw vert; 213 ft.; N38 52 10 W93 32 58
712 Chaucer Lane, Warrensburg, MO 64093 US
(660) 747-4155, *Fax:* (660) 747-4155
License: Concordia, Lafayette County, MO held by Full Smile Inc.
Arbitron Metro Market: Concordia, MO *Format:* Gospel
Jim McCollum, General Manager

Country Club

*KJCV-FM

01-01-2005; 89.7 mhz FM; 3.9 kw; Ant 548 ft; N39 42 35 W95 02 33
Bott Radio Network, 10550 Barkley, Overland Park, KS 64052
(913) 642-2424, *Fax:* (913) 642-1319
www.bottradionetwork.com
License: Country Club, Andrew County, MO held by Community Broadcasting Inc.
Group Owner: Bott Radio Network
Nat'l Network: USA
Rich Bott, President
Dan Snell, General Sales Mgr
Candy Green, Programming Director
Rachel Moser, Promotions Manager
Jason Potocnik, News Director
Pat Rulon, National Sales Manager

Crestwood

KSHE

02-11-1961; 94.7 mhz FM *Hrs Open:* 24; 100 kw; 1027 ft.; N38 34 24 W90 19 30
950 N. Meridian St., Suite 1200, Indianapolis, IN 46204 US
(314) 621-0095, *Fax:* (314) 621-3428
www.kshe95.com
info@kshe95.com
License: Crestwood, St. Louis County, MO held by Emmis Radio License LLC.
Group Owner: Emmis Communications Corp.; (acq 3-19-84; grpsl;
Nat'l Reps: D & R Radio
Arbitron Metro Market: St. Louis, MO *Format:* Classic Rock, Rock/AOR *Hrs. of News Programming:* news progmg one hr wkly *No. News Employees:* 1 *Target Audience:* 18-40.
John Beck Jr., General Manager
Mike Peterson, General Sales Mgr
Kyle Guderian, Promotions Manager

Cuba

*KGNN-FM

01-26-1997; 90.3 mhz FM *Hrs Open:* 24; 6.3 kw; 325 ft.; N38 5 11 W91 18 30 *Rebroadcasts:* Rebroadcasts KGNV(FM) Washington 100%
P.O. Box 87, Washington, MO 63090 US
(636) 385-3787, *Fax:* (636) 239-4448
goodnewsvoice.org
info@goodnewsvoice.org
License: Cuba, Crawford County, MO held by Missouri River Christian Broadcasting Inc.
Group Owner: Missouri River Christian Broadcasting Inc.
Nat'l Network: Moody; Salem Radio Network
Format: Gospel, News, 62, Talk *Special Programming:* Children 7 hrs wkly *Hrs. of News Programming:* News progmg 14 hrs wkly *Target Audience:* 20-70; inquisitive, conservative, philosophical, liberal *Adv. Rates:* 8; 8; 8; 8
James Goggan, President
Charles Sachse, General Manager
Rob Allyn, Engineering Dir
Marilyn Goggan, Program Director

*KNLQ

01-01-2004; 91.9 mhz FM; 5 kw; 249 ft.; N38 2 14 W91 23 4
1411 Locust Street, St. Louis, MO 63103 US
(314) 421-3020, *Fax:* (314) 421-1702
www.hereshelpnet.org
License: Cuba, Crawford County, MO held by New Life Evangelistic Center Inc.
Arbitron Metro Market: Cuba, MO *Format:* Gospel
Rick Jesse, Station Manager

De Soto

*KDJR

01-29-1991; 100.1 mhz FM; 2 kw; 348 ft.; N38 1 25 W90 34 2
Mailing Address: 513 Rockhill Road, Columbia, MO 65201 US
Second Address: 8919 World Ministry Ave., Baton Rouge, LA 70810
(225) 768-3688(225) 766-8300, *Fax:* (225) 768-3729
www.jsm.org
kawikfish@yahoo.com
License: De Soto, Jefferson County, MO held by Family Worship Center Church Inc.
Group Owner: Family Worship Center Church Inc.; (acq 9-27-2005; $1.25 million).
Arbitron Metro Market: St. Louis, MO *Format:* Religious

David Whitelaw, COO
Jimmy Swaggart, President
John Santiago, Programming Director

Dexter

KDEX

02-01-1956; 1590 khz AM *Hrs Open:* 5 AM-midnight; 0.62 kw-D, NDD; N36 47 20 W89 54 28
Mailing Address: P.O. Box 249, Dexter, MO 63841 US
Second Address: 20487 State Hwy 114, Dexter, MO 63841
(573) 624-3545, *Fax:* (573) 624-9926
www.kdexfm.com
kdex1@dexter.net
License: Dexter, MO
Nat'l Network: ABC; Jones Radio Networks
Arbitron Metro Market: Dexter, MO *Format:* Country
Tony James, Operations Dir
Walter Turner, General Manager
Joeli Barbour, Station Manager
Walt Turner, General Sales Mgr
Dave Obergoenner, Chief Engineer

KDEX-FM

07-17-1969; 102.3 mhz FM *Hrs Open:* 24; 5.9 kw; 279 ft.; N36 47 20 W89 54 28
P.O. Box 249, Dexter, MO 63841 US
(573) 624-3545, *Fax:* (573) 624-9926
www.kdexfm.com
kdex1@dexter.net
License: Dexter, Stoddard County, MO held by Dexter Broadcasting Inc.
Regional Network: Yancey AG Network
Arbitron Metro Market: Dexter, MO *Format:* Country *Hrs. of News Programming:* news progmg 5 hrs wkly *No. News Employees:* 2 *Target Audience:* 25-54.
Tony James, Operations Dir
Walt Turner, General Manager
Dave Obergoenner, Chief Engineer
Joeli Barbour, National Sales Manager

Dixon

*KCVZ

05-01-2003; 92.1 mhz FM *Hrs Open:* 24; 6 kw; 328 ft.; N37 57 59 W92 10 3 *Rebroadcasts:* Rebroadcasts KCVO-FM Camdenton 100%
4359 South Howell Ave., Suite 106, Milwaukee, WI 53207 US
(573) 346-3200, *Fax:* (573) 346-1010
www.spiritfm.org
License: Dixon, Pulaski County, MO held by Lake Area Educational Broadcasting Foundation
Nat'l Network: Salem Radio Network
Arbitron Metro Market: Camdenton, MO *Format:* Christian *Hrs. of News Programming:* News progmg one hr wkly *Target Audience:* 25-45.
Alice McDermott, CFO
James McDermott, President
Jim McDermott, General Manager
Alice McDermott, Financial Director

Doniphan

KDFN

02-04-1963; 1500 khz AM
204 East Washington St, Doniphan, MO 63935 US
(573) 686-3700, *Fax:* (573) 686-1713
info@foxradionetwork.com
License: Doniphan, MO held by Eagle Bluff Enterprises.
Group Owner: Eagle Bluff Enterprises; (acq 9-8-99; grpsl)
Regional Network: Missourinet
Format: Oldies *Special Programming:* Farm 5 hrs wkly *Target Audience:* General.
Steven Fuchs, General Manager
Shelley Fuchs, Programming Director
Ken Hosler, News Director
Maria Tillman, Traffic Manager

KOEA

04-11-1975; 97.5 mhz FM; 40 kw; 577 ft.; N36 35 20 W90 49 10
204 E. Washington St., Doniphan, MO 63935 US
(573) 686-3700, *Fax:* (573) 686-1713
info@foxradionetwork.com
License: Doniphan, Ripley County, MO held by Eagle Bluff Enterprises.
Group Owner: Eagle Bluff Enterprises
Format: Country
Steven Fuchs, General Sales Mgr
Skeet Collins, Programming Director
Tammy Jameson, Promotions Manager

Doolittle

KUMR

104.5 mhz FM; 3.9 kw; 407 ft.; N37 56 21.3 W91 56 44.9 US
(573) 308-1045, *Fax:* (573) 341-3443
www.mysunny1045.com
License: Doolittle, Phelps County, MO held by Alma Corp.
Group Owner: Alma Corp.
Arbitron Metro Market: Doolittle, MO *Format:* Easy Listening
Dennis Wallace, President
Keith Stephenson, General Manager

East Prairie

KYMO

11-15-1965; 1080 khz AM; 0.5 kw-D, NDD; N36 47 49 W89 21 19
Mailing Address: P.O. Box 130, East Prairie, MO 63845 US
Second Address: 390 S. Hwy. 102, East Prairie, MO 63845
(573) 649-3597, *Fax:* (573) 649-3983
kymo@bootheel.net
License: East Prairie, MO held by Usher Broadcasting Inc.
Arbitron Metro Market: Marion IL *Format:* Easy Listening
Barney Webster, President
Michael Bennett, Operations Dir
Reid Howell, Programming Director

El Dorado Springs

KESM-FM

06-01-1965; 105.5 mhz FM; 6 kw; 187 ft.; N37 51 51 W94 0 54
200 Radio Lane, El Dorado Springs, MO 64744 US
(417) 876-2741, *Fax:* (417) 876-2743
www.kesmradio.com
kesm@kesmradio.com
License: El Dorado Springs, Cedar County, MO held by Wildwood Communications Inc.
Arbitron Metro Market: El Dorado, AR
Andy Taylor, President

Eldon

KLOZ

07-01-1979; 92.7 mhz FM *Hrs Open:* 24; 31 kw; 620 ft.; N38 20 27 W92 35 33
209 East Second Street, Eldon, MO 65026 US
(573) 348-1958, *Fax:* (573) 348-1923
www.todaysbesthits.com
mike@mix927.com
License: Eldon, Miller County, MO held by Benne Broadcasting Co. L.L.C.
Nat'l Network: ABC
Arbitron Metro Market: Columbia, MO *Format:* Adult Contemp *Target Audience:* 25-54; 70% female/30% male with average or above income
Denny Benne, General Manager
Greg Sullens, Station Manager
Mike Clayton, Programming Director
Dan Yeager, Engineering Dir

KZWV

01-01-2006; 101.9 mhz FM *Hrs Open:* 24; 43 kw; 528 ft.; N38 16 46 W92 35 6 US
(573) 746-7873, *Fax:* (573) 746-7874
www.1019thewave.com
thewave@1019thewave.com
License: Eldon, Miller County, MO held by Randall C. Wright.
Arbitron Metro Market: Osage Beach, MO *Format:* Adult Contemp, Jazz, 80 *Target Audience:* 25 plus; affluent adults
John Caran, General Manager
Steve Richards, Programming Director
Stacy Johnson, News Director
Jessica Brink, Traffic Manager

Eldorado Springs

KESM

07-18-1961; 1580 khz AM; 0.5 kw-D, ND1; 0.032 kw-N, ND1; N37 51 51 W94 0 54
200 Radio Lane, El Dorado Springs, MO 64744 US
(417) 876-2741, *Fax:* (417) 876-2743
www.kesmradio.com
kesm@kesmradio.com
License: Eldorado Springs, MO held by Wildwood Communications Inc.
Arbitron Metro Market: El Dorado, AR *Format:* Oldies, Country *Target Audience:* General.
Donald Kohn, President
Jena Worthington, Station Manager

Ellington

KDKN

01-01-1999; 106.7 mhz FM; 3 kw; 298 ft; N37 13 58 W90 51 08
1411 Locust St., St. Louis, MO 63103
(314) 421-3020, *Fax:* (314) 436-2434
www.hereshelpnet.org
larryr@hereshelpnet.org
License: Ellington, Reynolds County, MO held by New Life Evangelistic Center.

Larry Rice, General Manager
Judy Redlich, General Sales Mgr

Excelsior Springs

*KEXS

08-01-1968; 1090 khz AM
201 Industrial Park Road, Excelsior Springs, MO 64024 US
(816) 630-1090
www.thecatholicradionetwork.com
kccatholic@aol.com
License: Excelsior Springs, MO held by Catholic Radio Network Inc.
Group Owner: Catholic Radio Network Inc.; (acq 5-17-2004; $825,000)
Nat'l Network: USA
Arbitron Metro Market: Excelsior Springs, MO *Format:* Christian *Target Audience:* 25-54.
James O'Laughlin, General Manager

Fairview Heights

KQQZ

11-01-1968; 1190 khz AM *Hrs Open:* Sunrise-sunset; 10 kw-D, 22 w-N, DA-2; N38 42 25 W90 03 10
8045 Big Bend Blvd., St. Louis, MO 65201
(314) 962-0590, *Fax:* (314) 962-7576
www.kfns.com
License: Fairview Heights, St. Clair County, IL held by Big Stick Three LLC.
Group Owner: Big League Broadcasting LLC; (acq 7-13-2004; grpsl).
Nat'l Network: ESPN Radio
Arbitron Metro Market: St. Louis, MO *Target Audience:* 25-64; sports fans, men 25-54
Mike Phares, General Manager

Farmington

KREI

12-07-1947; 800 khz AM *Hrs Open:* 24; 1 kw-D, ND2; 0.15 kw-N, ND2; N37 47 32 W90 24 36
Mailing Address: Box 461, Farmington, MO 63640 US
Second Address: 1401 KREI Blvd., Farmington, MO 63640
(573) 756-6476, *Fax:* (573) 756-1110
www.myMOinfo.com
j98@j98.com
License: Farmington, MO held by Festus/Farmington License Co. LLC.
Group Owner: GoodRadio.TV; (acq 8-8-2007; grpsl)
Nat'l Network: ABC; Premiere Radio Networks; Talk Radio Network; Westwood One; NBC Radio *Regional Network:* Missourinet
Format: News, News/Talk, 86 *Hrs. of News Programming:* news progmg 40 hrs wkly *No. News Employees:* 12 *Target Audience:* General.
Dean Goodman, President
Richard Womack, General Manager
Kimberly Long, Station Manager
Scott Kubala, Programming Director
Kevin Brooks, Chief Engineer

KTJJ

06-05-1977; 98.5 mhz FM *Hrs Open:* 24; 100 kw; 1040 ft.; N37 43 7 W90 33 1
Mailing Address: Krei Blvd., P.O. Box 461, Farmington, MO 63640 US
Second Address: 1401 KREI Blvd., Farmington, MO 63640
(573) 756-6476, *Fax:* (573) 756-1110
www.myMOinfo.com
j98@j98.com
License: Farmington, St. Francois County, MO held by Festus/Farmington License Co. LLC.
Group Owner: GoodRadio.TV
Nat'l Network: ABC
Arbitron Metro Market: Farmington, MO *Format:* Country *Hrs. of News Programming:* news progmg 16 hrs wkly *No. News Employees:* 12 *Target Audience:* General.
Dean Goodman, President
Richard Womack, General Manager
Kim Long, Station Manager

Scott Kubala, Programming Director
Kevin Brooks, Chief Engineer
Tami Propst, Office Manager

Fayette

KSSZ

07-15-1994; 93.9 mhz FM *Hrs Open:* 24; 25 kw; 328 ft.; N39 3 28 W92 28 49
P.O. Box 1749, Cape Girardeau, MO 63702 US
(573) 875-1099, *Fax:* (573) 875-2439
www.939theeagle.com
eagle939@zrgmail.com
License: Fayette, Howard County, MO held by Zimmer Radio of Mid-Missouri Inc.
Nat'l Network: ABC; Jones Radio Networks; Westwood One *Wire Services:* AP
Arbitron Metro Market: Columbia, MO *Format:* News, News/Talk, 86 *Hrs. of News Programming:* news progmg 4 hrs wkly *No. News Employees:* 2 *Target Audience:* 25-54; adults
Jennifer Herrin, Operations Dir
Carla Lieble, General Manager
Cynthia Schreen, General Sales Mgr
Nicci Garmon, Programming Director
Shelley Tucker, News Director
Drew Haines, Chief Engineer

Ferguson

*KCFV

04-17-1972; 89.5 mhz FM *Hrs Open:* 16; 0.1 kw; 161 ft.; N38 46 7 W90 17 16
3400 Pershall Road, Ferguson, MO 63135 US
(314) 513-4472,(314) 513-4478, *Fax:* (314) 513-4217
www.stlcc.edu/fv/kcfv
tgorry@stlcc.edu
License: Ferguson, St. Louis County, MO held by St. Louis Community College District.
Arbitron Metro Market: St. Louis, MO *Format:* Adult Contemp *Special Programming:* Jazz 8 hrs, Black 4 hrs, hard rock 4 hrs wkly *Hrs. of News Programming:* News progmg 2 hrs wkly *Target Audience:* General.
Dianna Kirby, General Manager
Tim Croskey, Chief Engineer

Festus

KJFF

05-10-1951; 1400 khz AM *Hrs Open:* 24; 1 kw-U, ND1; N38 13 56 W90 23 50
P.O. Box 461, Farmington, MO 63640 US
(636) 937-7642, *Fax:* (636) 937-3636
www.kjff.com
kjff@k98.com
License: Festus, MO held by Festus/Farmington License Co. LLC.
Group Owner: GoodRadio.TV; (acq 8-8-2007; grpsl)
Nat'l Network: ABC *Regional Network:* Missourinet
Arbitron Metro Market: St. Louis, MO *Format:* News, News/Talk, 86 *Hrs. of News Programming:* news progmg 30 hrs wkly *No. News Employees:* 4 *Target Audience:* General.
Dean Goodman, President
Dick Womack, General Manager
Kirk Mooney, Station Manager
Matt West, Programming Director
Kevin Brooks, Chief Engineer

*KTBJ

01-01-1998; 89.3 mhz FM; 25 kw; 371 ft.; N38 9 16 W90 2 7
3000 West Macarthur, Third Floor, Santa Ana, CA 92704 US
(636) 937-5222, *Fax:* (636) 937-5224
www.csnradio.com
info@ktbj.com
License: Festus, Jefferson County, MO held by CSN International
Group Owner: CSN International; acq 6-17-98; $100,000).
Arbitron Metro Market: Festus, MO *Format:* Christian, Talk
Mike Kestler, President
Scott Parker, Station Manager
Don Mills, Programming Director
Kelly Carlson, Engineering Dir

Florissant

KFTK

04-15-1977; 97.1 mhz FM *Hrs Open:* 24; 100 kw; 561 ft.; N38 46 45 W90 43 43
200 West 41st Street, Baltimore, MD 21211 US
(314) 231-9710, *Fax:* (314) 621-3000
www.971talk.com
stl.ms@emies.com
License: Florissant, St. Louis County, MO held by Emmis Radio License LLC.
Group Owner: Emmis Communications Corp.; (acq 9-26-2000; grpsl).
Nat'l Reps: McGavren Guild
Arbitron Metro Market: St. Louis, MO *Format:* Talk
John Beck, Operations Dir
John Beck, Station Manager
Karen Kelly, General Sales Mgr
Jeff Allen, Programming Director
Tony Colombo, Promotions Manager
Karen Kelly, Sales
Annie Frey, Webmaster
Jim Modglin, Assistant ProgramDirector

Fredericktown

KYLS

06-29-1963; 1450 khz AM *Hrs Open:* 24; 1 kw-U, ND1; N37 35 0 W90 17 31
Mailing Address: 2413 East Malone Avenue, Sikeston, MO 63801 US
Second Address: 900 East Karsch Blvd., Farmington, MO
(573) 701-9590, *Fax:* (573) 701-9696
www.froggy96.com
License: Fredericktown, MO held by Southern Star Broadcasting of Missouri LLC.
Group Owner: Southern Star Broadcasting of Missouri LLC; (acq 5-8-2008; grpsl)
Nat'l Network: ESPN Radio
Arbitron Metro Market: Farmington, MO *Format:* Sports *Target Audience:* 24-55; Men
Chip Miller, President
Joel Jordan, Operations Dir

Fulton

KFAL

11-14-1950; 900 khz AM *Hrs Open:* 19; 1 kw-D, ND1; 0.135 kw-N, ND1; N38 51 58 W91 57 15
3000 East Chestnut Expwy, Springfield, MO 65802 US
(573) 642-3341(573) 875-1099, *Fax:* (573) 642-3343
www.kfalthebig900.com/?page_id=3
License: Fulton, MO held by Zimmer Radio of Mid-Missouri Inc.
Nat'l Network: Motor Racing Net *Regional Network:* Missourinet
Arbitron Metro Market: Columbia, MO *Format:* Country *Special Programming:* Other 6 hrs wkly *Hrs. of News Programming:* news progmg 3 hrs wkly *No. News Employees:* 1 *Target Audience:* 35 plus. *Adv. Rates:* 14; 14; 14; 12
John Zimmer, Chairman
Jerry Zimmer, CEO
Don Zimmer, President
Jeremiah Washington, General Manager
Steve Mallinkrott, General Sales Mgr

KTGR-FM

01-01-1970; 100.5 mhz FM *Hrs Open:* 24; 6 kw; Ant 300 ft; N38 51 58 W91 57 15
1805 Westminster, Jefferson City, MO 65802
(573) 642-3341,(573) 875-1099, *Fax:* (573) 642-3343
License: Fulton, Callaway County, MO held by Zimmer Radio of Mid-Missouri Inc.
Nat'l Network: ABC; Westwood One; Jones Radio Networks
Population Served: 12,248*Hrs. of News Programming:* news progmg 2 hrs wkly *No. News Employees:* 1 *Target Audience:* 25-54. *Adv. Rates:* 13; 13; 13; 5
Howard Kalmenson, President
Mike Ginsburg, General Manager

Gainesville

KMAC

03-17-1994; 99.7 mhz FM *Hrs Open:* 24; 50 kw; Ant 492 ft; N36 36 06 W92 25 48
100 Bluebird St., Harrison, AR 23225
(870) 743-1157, *Fax:* (870) 743-1168
kmac997@hotmail.com
License: Gainesville, Ozark County, MO held by KTLO LLC
Group Owner: KTLO LLC; (acq 12-19-94; $150,000;
Target Audience: General.
David Fransen, General Manager

Gallatin

KGOZ

06-01-1994; 101.7 mhz FM *Hrs Open:* 24; 15 kw; 423 ft.; N39 53 14 W93 43 24
P.O. Box 217, Trenton, MO 64683 US
(660) 359-2727, *Fax:* (660) 359-4126
http://www.parbroadcastgroup.com/kgoz.htm
john@kttn.com
License: Gallatin, Daviess County, MO held by PAR Broadcasting Co. Inc.
Nat'l Network: Jones Radio Networks *Nat'l Reps:* Rgnl Reps
Format: Country *Hrs. of News Programming:* News progmg 2 hrs wkly *No. News Employees:* 1 *Target Audience:* 14-50. *Adv. Rates:* 25; 20; 15; 15
John Ausberger, President
John Anthony, General Manager
Jeanette Houck, General Sales Mgr
Dave Counsell, News Director

Garden City

KCJK

01-01-2001; 105.1 mhz FM *Hrs Open:* 24; kw
4301 West 129th Street, Suite 130, Overland Park, KS 66213 US
(913) 514-3000, *Fax:* (913) 514-3002
www.1051jackfm.com
jared.robb@cumulus.com
License: Garden City, Cass County, MO held by CMP Houston-KC LLC.
Group Owner: Cumulus Media Partners LLC; (acq 5-3-2006; grpsl).
Nat'l Reps: Katz Radio
Arbitron Metro Market: KS City, MO *Format:* Adult Contemp *Hrs. of News Programming:* News progmg 10.5 hrs wkly *Target Audience:* 25-54.
Chris Hoffman, Operations Dir
Mark Sullivan, General Manager
Jared Robb, General Sales Mgr
Bryan Truta, Programming Director
Nycki Pace, Promotions Manager

Gideon

KGLU

103.9 mhz FM; 2.5 kw; 400 ft.; N36 25 31 W89 41 29 US
(901) 685-0882
www.1039thebuzz.com
License: Gideon, New Madrid County, MO held by Pollack Steel Supply Inc.
Arbitron Metro Market: Gideon, MO *Format:* Adult Contemp
Sydney Pollack, President

Gladstone

KGGN

11-18-1996; 890 khz AM; 0.96 kw-D, DAD; N39 11 4 W94 27 28
3270 Blazer Pkwy Ste 101, Lexington, KY 40509 US
(816) 333-0092, *Fax:* (816) 363-8120
www.kggnam.com
kggnproduction@aol.com
License: Gladstone, MO held by Mortenson Broadcasting Co.
Group Owner: Mortenson Broadcasting Co.; acq 12-24-96; $450,000)
Arbitron Metro Market: KS City, MO *Format:* Gospel *Special Programming:* Ministry 5 hrs wkly *Target Audience:* 25-54, Christian
Rita Berry, General Manager
Reggie Brown, Programming Director

Gordonville

KCGQ-FM

01-01-1978; 99.3 mhz FM *Hrs Open:* 24; 5 kw; 358 ft.; N37 21 34 W89 37 16
P.O. Box 1749, Cape Girardeau, MO 63702 US
(573) 335-8291, *Fax:* (573) 335-4806
www.realrock993.com
License: Gordonville, Cape Girardeau County, MO held by MRR License LLC.
Group Owner: MAX Media L.L.C.
Format: Rock/AOR *Target Audience:* 18-49; general
Scott Hartline, Programming Director

Grandin

KCBW

104.5 mhz FM; 6 kw; 328 feet; N36 48 15 W90 43 12
932 County Road 448, Poplar Bluff, MO
(573) 686-3700, *Fax:* (573) 686-1713
www.foxradionetwork.com
License: Grandin, MO held by Fox Radio Network LLC
Steve Fuchs, President

Half Way

KYOO-FM

04-01-1995; 99.1 mhz FM; 25 kw; 328 ft.; N37 45 41 W93 15 42
304 E. Jackson, Bolivar, MO 65613 US

RADIO - U.S.

(417) 326-5259(417) 326-5257, *Fax:* (417) 326-5900
www.kyooradio.com/
kyooradio@aol.com
License: Half Way, Polk County, MO held by KYOO Communications.
Nat'l Network: ABC
Arbitron Metro Market: Bolivar, MO *Format:* Adult Contemp *Hrs. of News Programming:* news progmg 5 hrs wkly *No. News Employees:* 1 *Target Audience:* 10-72. *Adv. Rates:* 20.50; 9; 6; na
Stephen Paris, President
Ann Paris, Operations Dir

Hannibal

KGRC
11-28-1968; 92.9 mhz FM; 100 kw; 502 ft.; N39 43 48 W91 24 19
2 Dearborn Square, Kankakee, IL 60901 US
(217) 224-4102, *Fax:* (217) 224-4133
www.real929.com
jbates@staradio.com
License: Hannibal, Marion County, MO held by STARadio Corp.
Group Owner: STARadio Corp.; acq 12-2-98; $2.1 million with KZZK(FM) New London)
Nat'l Network: Westwood One *Nat'l Reps:* Katz Radio
Format: Contemporary Hits/Top 40 *Hrs. of News Programming:* news progmg one hr wkly *No. News Employees:* 1 *Target Audience:* 18-49; women
Howard Doss, President
Michael Moyers, Operations Dir
Brenda Park, Programming Director
Phil Reilly, Chief Engineer
Samantha Barnes, Music/Production Director

KHMO
04-01-1941; 1070 khz AM *Hrs Open:* 24
119 N. Third St. Box 711, Hannibal, MO 63401 US
(573) 221-3450, *Fax:* (573) 221-5331
www.khmoradio.com
harold.smith@townsquaremedia.com
License: Hannibal, MO held by Bick Broadcasting.
Group Owner: Bick Broadcasting Co.; (acq 8-1-85; $1.35 million;
Nat'l Reps: McGavren Guild *Wire Services:* Weather Wire
Format: News, News/Talk, 84, Talk *Special Programming:* Agriculture 5 hrs wkly *Hrs. of News Programming:* news progmg 100 hrs wkly *No. News Employees:* 2
Ed Foxall, General Manager
Jeff Asmussen, General Sales Mgr
Jeff Dorsey, Programming Director
John Hanvelt, News Director
Gary Glaenzer, Chief Engineer
Harold Smith, Program Director

***KJIR**
04-01-2000; 91.7 mhz FM *Hrs Open:* 24; 12 kw; 570 ft.; N39 41 54 W91 29 48
222 North 6th Street, Quincy, IL 62301 US
(217) 221-9410, *Fax:* (217) 228-0966
thecross@kjir.org
License: Hannibal, Marion County, MO held by Believers Broadcasting Corp.
Format: Gospel *Hrs. of News Programming:* News progmg 7.5 hrs wkly *Target Audience:* Christian; 30-70
I. Carl Geisendorfer, General Manager
Michael Wartman, Programming Director

Harrisonville

KCFX
07-19-1974; 101.1 mhz FM; 97 kw; 1099 ft.; N39 1 20 W94 30 49
10706 Beaver Dam Road, Cockeysville, MD 21030 US
(913) 514-3000, *Fax:* (913) 514-3001
www.101thefox.net
info@kcfxfm.com
License: Harrisonville, Cass County, MO held by Susquehanna Kansas City Partnership.
Group Owner: Cumulus Media Partners LLC; (acq 7-14-00; grpsl)
Nat'l Reps: Katz Radio
Arbitron Metro Market: Kansas City, MO-KS *Format:* Classic Rock *Target Audience:* 25-54; baby boomers
Dave Alpert, Operations Dir
Jeanna White, General Sales Mgr
Chris Hoffman, Operations Manager

Hayti

***WGCQ**
01-01-1993; 98.7 mhz FM; 6 kw; 220 ft.; N36 19 6 W89 42 1
PO Box 3404, Somerset, KY 42564 US
(916) 251-1600, *Fax:* (916) 251-1650
www.godscountryradionetwork.com
info@happyjubilee.com
License: Hayti, Pemiscot County, MO held by Educational Media Foundation.
Group Owner: EMF Broadcasting; (acq 1-25-2001; $450,000)
Format: Country, Gospel *Target Audience:* 18-50.
Mike Novak, President

Hazelwood

WHHL
10-10-1967; 104.1 mhz FM *Hrs Open:* 24; 50 kw; 459 ft.; N38 39 8 W90 17 3
3500 West Olive Avenue, Suite 300, Burbank, CA 91505 US
(314) 989-9550, *Fax:* (314) 989-1041
www.red1041.com
stl.ms@emies.com
License: Hazelwood, Jersey County, MO held by Radio One Licenses LLC.
Group Owner: Radio One Inc.; (acq 12-19-2005; $20 million).
Arbitron Metro Market: St. Louis, MO *Format:* Urban Contemporary *Special Programming:* Heartland issues one hr, today's issues one hr, pu *Hrs. of News Programming:* news progmg 2 hrs wkly *No. News Employees:* 1*Target Audience:* 25-54; families with children, singles
John Beck, Operations Dir
Lisa Sesti, Station Manager
Nate Dixon, General Sales Mgr
Boogie D, Programming Director
Sparkl West, Promotions Manager
Gary Benett, Chief Engineer
Darla Harper, Business Manager
Jeff Laramie,National Sales Manager

Hermann

KQQX
09-01-1985; 93.3 mhz FM; 10.25 kw; 1050 ft.; N38 6 16 W91 2 30
3418 Douglas Road, Florissant, MO 63034 US
(314) 921-9330
www.knsx.com
93x@knsx.com
License: Hermann, Gasconade County, MO held by Broadcast Communications Inc.
Format: Alternative
Ruth Choate, General Manager

High Point

***KMCV**
01-01-2001; 89.9 mhz FM; 50 kw; 316 ft.; N38 35 48 W92 32 17
P O Drawer 2440, Tupelo, MS 38803 US
(573) 893-8990, *Fax:* (573) 893-8991
www.bottradionetwork.com
kmcv@bottradionetwork.com
License: High Point, Moniteau County, MO held by Community Broadcasting Inc.
Group Owner: Bott Radio Network; (acq 2-7-01; $1.25 million with KSCV(FM) Springfield).
Nat'l Network: USA
Format: Christian, Talk
Richard Bott II, President
Sue Stoltz, General Manager
Pat Rulon, General Sales Mgr
Candy Green, Programming Director
Rachel Moser, Promotions Manager
Jason Potocnik, News Director

Hollister

KBCV
01-01-2004; 1570 khz AM
US
(913) 642-7770, *Fax:* (913) 642-1319
www.bottradionetwork.com
comments@bottradionetwork.com
License: Hollister, MO held by Bott Communications Inc.
Group Owner: Bott Radio Network
Nat'l Network: USA
Format: Christian, Talk
Richard Bott, Sr., Founder & Chairman
Tom Holdeman, CFO
Richard Bott, II, President/CEO
Eben Fowler, Operations Dir
Monna Stafford, General Manager
Pat Rulon, General Sales Mgr
Candy Green, Programming Director
Rachel Moser,Promotions Manager
Jason Potocnik, News Director
Tim Lumpkin, Corporate Controller
Pat Rulon, National Sales Manager
Ken Monroe, Corporate Production
Larry Ross, Assistant Production
John Dale, Director of Marketing
Lindsey Filby,Graphics Manager

Houston

KBTC
06-28-1962; 1250 khz AM; 1 kw-D, ND1; 0.051 kw-N, ND1; N37 19 45 W91 53 55
PO Box 30, Houston, MO 65483 US
(417) 967-3353, *Fax:* (417) 967-2281
www.bigcountry99.com
rocky@mediaprofessionalsinc.com
License: Houston, MO held by Metropolitan Radio Group Inc.
Group Owner: Metropolitan Radio Group Inc.
Arbitron Metro Market: Houston, TX
Rob Grace, President
Gary Bridgman, General Manager
Ben Johnson, Programming Director
Dale Johnson, Chief Engineer

KUNQ
05-01-1965; 99.3 mhz FM *Hrs Open:* 24; 30 kw; 604 ft.; N37 5 32 W92 3 10
P.O. Box 30, Houston, MO 65483 US
(417) 967-3353, *Fax:* (417) 967-2281
www.bigcountry99.com
kunq@kunq.net
License: Houston, Texas County, MO held by Metropolitan Radio Group Inc.
Group Owner: Metropolitan Radio Group Inc.; (acq 6-22-2000; $150,000 with co-located AM)
Arbitron Metro Market: Houston, MO *Format:* Country *Special Programming:* Farm 2 hrs, gospel 10 hrs wkly *Hrs. of News Programming:* news progmg 12 hrs wkly *No. News Employees:* 1 *Target Audience:* 25-69;blue collar
Rick Vermillion, General Manager
Shelly Adams, Station Manager
Max Owens, General Sales Mgr
Cynthia Spratt, News Director
Bob Moore, Chief Engineer
Marilou Candela, General Sales Manager

Independence

KCTE
01-01-1947; 1510 khz AM *Hrs Open:* Sunrise-sunset; 10 kw-D, DAD; N39 4 14 W94 26 58
20285 Mission Road, Stilwell, KS 66085 US
(913) 344-1500, *Fax:* (913) 344-1599
www.1510.com
License: Independence, MO held by Union Broadcasting Inc.
Nat'l Network: CBS Radio; ESPN Radio; Sporting News Radio Network
Arbitron Metro Market: Independence, MO *Format:* Sports, Talk *No. News Employees:* 2 *Target Audience:* Adults.
Nick McCabe, Operations Dir
Chad Boeger, General Manager
Gary Hailes, General Sales Mgr
Dennis Rooney, News Director

Ironton

KYLS-FM
01-06-1984; 95.9 mhz FM *Hrs Open:* 24; 3.1 kw; 650 ft.; N37 40 2 W90 34 38
1242 Highway Oo, Fredericktown, MO 63645 US
(573) 701-9590, *Fax:* (573) 701-9696
www.froggy96.com
joel.jordan@southernstarbroadcasting.com
License: Ironton, Iron County, MO held by Southern Star Broadcasting of Missouri LLC.
Group Owner: Southern Star Broadcasting of Missouri LLC; (acq 5-8-2008; grpsl)
Arbitron Metro Market: Farmington, MO *Format:* Country *Target Audience:* 18-54.
Chip Miller, President
Joel Jordan, Operations Dir
Jeremy Martin, Programming Director
Wanda Emert, News Director

Jackson

KJXX
03-01-1972; 1170 khz AM *Hrs Open:* 24
P.O. Box 546, Jackson, MO 63755 US
(573) 339-7000, *Fax:* (573) 651-4100
www.1170kjxx.com
rlambert@withersradio.net
License: Jackson, MO held by W. Russell Withers Jr.

Group Owner: Withers Broadcasting Co.; (acq 6-28-2005; $150,000)
Nat'l Network: Fox News Radio
Arbitron Metro Market: Jackson, MO *Format:* Religious *Special Programming:* Parenting and family talk *Target Audience:* General.
Rick Lambert, General Manager
Steve Thomas, Operations Manager and Program Director

***KHIS**
07-19-2010; 89.9 mhz FM; 12500 w; 466 ft; N37 22 40 W89 56 05
318 Monroe Avenue, Belton, MO 64012

www.khisradio.org
License: Jackson, Cape Girardeau County, MO
Group Owner: Pure Word Communications
Glen Cantrell, Music Director

Jefferson City

***KJLU**
08-01-1973; 88.9 mhz FM *Hrs Open:* 6 AM-midnight; 29.5 kw; 604 ft.; N38 27 29 W92 13 32
820 Chestnut Street, Jefferson City, MO 65102 US
(573) 681-5301,(573) 681-5296, *Fax:* (573) 681-5299
www.lincolnu.edu/~kjlu/
info@kjlu.com
License: Jefferson City, Cole County, MO held by Board of Curators of Lincoln University.
Format: Jazz *Target Audience:* 18-54.
Michael Downey, General Manager
Dan Turner, Programming Director
LaVaughn Wilson, Promotions Manager
Leslie Cross, News Director

KBBM
01-01-1974; 100.1 mhz FM *Hrs Open:* 24; 33 kw; 600 ft.; N38 31 25 W92 24 25
P.O. Box 1749, Cape Girardeau, MO 63702 US
(573) 893- 5100, *Fax:* (573) 893-8330
www.buzz.fm
buzz@buzz.fm
License: Jefferson City, Cole County, MO
Group Owner: Cumulus Media Inc.
Format: Rock/AOR *No. News Employees:* 2 *Target Audience:* 18-34.
T. Miller, Programming Director

KWOS
02-01-1954; 950 khz AM; 5 kw-D, DAN; 0.5 kw-N, DAN; N38 31 13 W92 10 42
P.O. Box 3353, Evansville, IN 47732 US
(573) 893-5696, *Fax:* (573) 893-4137
www.kwos.com
kati@zrgmail.com
License: Jefferson City, MO held by Zimmer Radio of Mid-Missouri Inc.
Arbitron Metro Market: Columbia, MO *Format:* News, News/Talk, 86 *Special Programming:* Farm 12 hrs wkly
John Zimmer, Chairman
Carla Leible, General Manager
Russ Davis, General Sales Mgr
Warren Krech, Programming Director
John Marsh, News Director
Jeff Studley, Chief Engineer

KTXY
12-01-1969; 106.9 mhz FM; 96 kw; 1250 ft.; N38 38 16 W92 29 34
Brill Media Co, PO Box 3353, Evansville, IN 47732 US
(573) 875-1099, *Fax:* (573) 875-2439
www.y107.com
y107@zrgmail.com
License: Jefferson City, Cole County, MO
Arbitron Metro Market: Jefferson City, MO *Format:* Adult Contemp
Dave Wisniewski, General Sales Mgr

KLIK
01-01-1937; 1240 khz AM *Hrs Open:* 24; 1 kw-U, ND1; N38 33 50 W92 11 21
P.O. Box 1749, Cape Girardeau, MO 63702 US
(573) 893-5100, *Fax:* (573) 893-8330
www.klik1240.com
info@klik1240.com
License: Jefferson City, MO held by Cumulus Licensing LLC.
Group Owner: Cumulus Media Inc.; (acq 4-26-2004; grpsl).
Arbitron Metro Market: Jefferson City, MO *Format:* News, News/Talk, 86 *Hrs. of News Programming:* news progmg 39 hrs wkly *No. News Employees:* 4 *Target Audience:* 35 plus; mid to upper income-well informed
Lew Dickey, President
Kevin Joyce, VP/ General Manager
Darryl Burnett, General Sales Mgr
Brian Wilson, Programming Director
Nick Snyder, Promotions Manager
0, News Director
Chris Kellogg, KLIK Programming

KZJF
01-01-2000; 104.1 mhz FM *Hrs Open:* 24; 5.3 kw; 348 ft.; N38 33 50 W92 11 21
Post Office Box 34, Cape Girardeau, MO 63702 US
(573) 893-5100, *Fax:* (573) 893-8330
www.jeffcountry.com
Kevin.Joyce@cumulus.com?subject=JEFF%20Website%20Feedback
License: Jefferson City, Cole County, MO held by Cumulus Licensing LLC.
Group Owner: Cumulus Media Inc.; (acq 4-26-2004; grpsl).
Nat'l Reps: Katz Radio
Arbitron Metro Market: Jefferson City, MO *Format:* Country
Kevin Joyce, VP/General Manager
Darryl Burnett, General Sales Mgr
Mike Alan, Programming Director
C.J. Engle, Promotions Manager
Dean Morgan, News Director
Tim Murphy, KZJF Programming
Nick Snyder, KZJF Promotions/Webmaster

Joplin

KIXQ
11-01-1974; 102.5 mhz FM *Hrs Open:* 24; 100 kw; 912 ft.; N37 5 49 W94 34 25
PO Box 1749, Cape Girardeau, MO 63702 US
(417) 624-1025, *Fax:* (417) 781-6842
www.kix1025.com
chade@zrgmail.com
License: Joplin, Jasper County, MO held by Zimmer Radio Inc.
Group Owner: Zimmer Radio Inc.; (acq 6-30-97; grpsl).
Nat'l Reps: Christal
Arbitron Metro Market: Joplin, MO *Format:* Country *Special Programming:* Class 3 hrs wkly *No. News Employees:* 4 *Target Audience:* 25-54.
James Zimmer, President
Chad Elliot, Operations Dir
Kara Marxer, Programming Director
Mel Williams, Engineering Dir
Rob Meyer, Program Director
Jennifer Barns, PSA Director
Terry Hester, Vice President

***KOBC**
03-17-1969; 90.7 mhz FM *Hrs Open:* 18; 60 kw; 495 ft.; N37 3 8 W94 23 20
1111 N. Main Street, Joplin, MO 64801 US
(916) 251-1600, *Fax:* (916) 251-1650
www.klove.com
License: Joplin, Jasper County, MO held by Educational Media Foundation.
Group Owner: EMF Broadcasting; (acq 10-1-2008; $1 million)
Nat'l Network: K-Love
Arbitron Metro Market: Joplin, MO *Format:* Christian
Mike Novak, President

KZRG
11-21-1948; 1310 khz AM *Hrs Open:* 24 hrs; 5 kw-D, 1 kw-N, DA-2; N37 07 03 W94 32 41
2702 E. 32nd St., Joplin, MO 64801
(417) 624-1025, *Fax:* (417) 781-6842
www.newstalkKZRG.com
chade@zrgmail.com
License: Joplin, Jasper County, MO held by Zimmer Radio Inc.
Group Owner: Zimmer Radio Inc.; (acq 11-15-2005; $350,100)
Nat'l Network: Fox News Radio *Regional Network:* Missourinet
Nat'l Reps: Christal *Wire Services:* AP
Arbitron Metro Market: Joplin, MO *Hrs. of News Programming:* 5 *No. News Employees:* 4
James Zimmer, CEO
Chad Elliot, Operations Dir
Larry Boyd, General Manager
Carol Daley, General Sales Mgr
Chad Elliott, Programming Director
Josh Marsh, News Director
Mel Williams, Chief Engineer
Kara Marxer, News Director

WMBH
05-25-1962; 1560 khz AM *Hrs Open:* 6 AM-9 PM; 0.25 kw-D, ND1; 0.009 kw-N, ND1; N37 4 10 W94 32 49
2510 West 20th Street, Joplin, MO 64804 US
(417) 781-1313, *Fax:* (417) 781-1316
License: Joplin, MO held by Hardman Broadcasting Inc.
Arbitron Metro Market: Joplin, MO *Format:* Urban Contemporary
Dave Clemons, General Sales Mgr

KSYN
12-19-1960; 92.5 mhz FM *Hrs Open:* 24 hrs; 100 kw; 984 ft.; N37 5 49 W94 34 25
Post Office Box 1749, Cape Girardeau, MO 63702 US
(417) 624-1025, *Fax:* (417) 781-6842
www.ksyn925.com
License: Joplin, Jasper County, MO held by Zimmer Radio Inc.
Group Owner: Zimmer Radio Inc.; (acq 6-30-97; grpsl).
Arbitron Metro Market: Joplin, MO *Format:* Contemporary Hits/Top 40 *Target Audience:* 18-34.
Chad Elliot, Operations Dir
Steve Kraus, Programming Director
Larry Boyd, Promotions Manager
Mel Williams, Chief Engineer
Kara Marxer, News Director

KZYM
06-01-1946; 1230 khz AM *Hrs Open:* 24; 1 kw-U, ND1; N37 4 48 W94 33 10
1411 Locust Street, St. Louis, MO 63103 US
(417) 624-1025, *Fax:* (417) 781-6842
www.1230thetalker.com
chade@zrgmail.com
License: Joplin, MO held by Zimmer Radio Inc.
Group Owner: Zimmer Radio Inc.; (acq 9-30-2005; $300,000)
Nat'l Network: Salem Radio Network *Regional Network:* Missourinet *Nat'l Reps:* Christal *Wire Services:* AP
Arbitron Metro Market: Joplin, MO *Format:* Talk *Hrs. of News Programming:* news hourly *No. News Employees:* 30 *Target Audience:* General.
James Zimmer, President
Chad Elliot, Operations Dir
Carol Daily, General Sales Mgr
Brett James, Programming Director
Mel Williams, Directorr Of It/ Engineering
Rob Meyer, Assistant Operations Manager
Larry Boyd, MarketManager
Christie Ogle, Business Office Manager

***KXMS**
04-05-1986; 88.7 mhz FM; 10 kw vert; 184 ft.; N37 5 57 W94 27 46
3650 E. Newman Rd., Joplin, MO 64801 US
(417) 625-9356, *Fax:* (417) 625-9742
www.kxms.org
kxms@mssc.edu
License: Joplin, Jasper County, MO held by Board of Governors— Missouri Southern State College
Arbitron Metro Market: Joplin, MO *Format:* Variety/Diverse
Special Programming: Big band 2 hrs wkly
Jeffrey Skibbe, General Manager
Jeffrey Scibbe, Programming Director

Kansas City

KBEQ-FM
11-01-1960; 104.3 mhz FM *Hrs Open:* 24; 99 kw; 988 ft.; N39 4 59 W94 28 49
600 New Hampshire Avenue, N.W., Suite 1200, Washington, DC 20037 US
(816) 753-4000, *Fax:* (816) 753-4045
www.q104kc.com
License: Kansas City, Jackson County, MO held by Wilks License Co.-Kansas City LLC.
Group Owner: Wilks Broadcast Group LLC; (acq 1-10-2007; grpsl)
Arbitron Metro Market: KS City, MO *Format:* Country *Hrs. of News Programming:* news progmg 6 hrs wkly *No. News Employees:* 1 *Target Audience:* 18-54; women
Mike Rowen, General Manager
Ted Ivey, General Sales Mgr
Mike Kennedy, Programming Director
Jillian Gregg, News Director
Ben Weiss, Chief Engineer

KCMO
03-01-1922; 710 khz AM *Hrs Open:* 24; 10 kw-D, DA2; 5 kw-N, DA2; N39 19 8 W94 29 48
401 City Avenue, Suite 409, Bala Cynwyd, PA 19004 US
(913) 514-3000, *Fax:* (913) 514-3004
www.710kcmo.com
bill.ryan@cumulus.com
License: Kansas City, MO held by Susquehanna Kansas City Partnership.
Group Owner: Cumulus Media Partners LLC; (acq 7-14-2000; grpsl).
Nat'l Reps: Katz Radio

Arbitron Metro Market: Kansas City, MO *Format:* Talk *Special Programming:* Pub affrs one hrs wkly *Hrs. of News Programming:* news progmg 30 hrs wkly *No. News Employees:* 3 *Target Audience:* 35-64.
Dave Alpert, Operations Dir
Mark Sullivan, Senior Vice President, General Manager
Bill Ryan, General Sales Mgr
Chris Hoffman, Programming Director
Tom Bamford, Producer / PSA Director
Brian Goeke, Director of Marketing & Online
John Gallagher, Vice President of Sales

*KCUR-FM
10-01-1957; 89.3 mhz FM *Hrs Open:* 24; 100 kw; 820 ft.; N39 4 59 W94 28 49
4825 Troost, Ste 202, Kansas City, MO 64110 US
(816) 235-1551, *Fax:* (816) 235-2864
www.kcur.org
kcur@umkc.edu
License: Kansas City, Jackson County, MO held by Curators of the University of Missouri.
Group Owner: The Curators of the University of Missouri
Nat'l Network: NPR; PRI
Arbitron Metro Market: Kansas City, MO-KS *Format:* News *Special Programming:* Sp 2 hrs wkly *Hrs. of News Programming:* news progmg 50 hrs wkly *No. News Employees:* 3 *Target Audience:* General; educated
Nico Leone, General Manager
Parker Van Hecke, General Sales Mgr
Bill Anderson, Programming Director
Frank Morris, News Director
Robin Cross, Engineering Dir
Robert Moore, Music Director
Steve Bell, Reporter

*KKFI
02-28-1988; 90.1 mhz FM *Hrs Open:* 24; 100 kw; 423 ft.; N39 5 5 W94 28 47
Mailing Address: PO Box 32250, Kansas City, MO 64171 US
Second Address: 900 1/2 Westport Rd., Kansas City, MO 64111
(816) 931-3122, *Fax:* (816) 931-7870
www.kkfi.org
info@kkfi.org
License: Kansas City, Jackson County, MO held by Mid-Coast Radio Project Inc.
Arbitron Metro Market: Kansas City, MO *Format:* News, Talk *Special Programming:* Jazz 10 hrs, blues 9 hrs, Sp 16 hrs, folk 4 hrs, A *Hrs. of News Programming:* News progmg 10 hrs wkly *Target Audience:* General;women & minorities *Adv. Rates:* 32.50; 28.50; 32.50; 12.50
Dorothy Hawkins, General Manager

*KLJC
08-09-1970; 88.5 mhz FM *Hrs Open:* 24; 100 kw; 745 ft.; N39 4 24 W94 29 6
15800 Calvary Road, Kansas City, MO 64147 US
(816) 331-8700, *Fax:* (816) 331-3497
www.kljc.org
kljc@kljc.org
License: Kansas City, Jackson County, MO held by Calvary Bible College.
Nat'l Network: Salem Radio Network
Arbitron Metro Market: Kansas City, MO *Format:* Christian *Hrs. of News Programming:* News progmg 6 hrs wkly *Target Audience:* 25-54.
Elwood Chipchase, President
Michael Griman, Programming Director
Glenn Williams, Chief Engineer

KMBZ
01-01-1921; 980 khz AM; 5 kw-D, DAN; 5 kw-N, DAN; N39 2 17 W94 36 55
401 City Avenue, Suite 409, Bala Cynwyd, PA 19004 US
(913) 677-8998, *Fax:* (913) 677-8901
www.kmbz.com
info@kmbzam.com
License: Kansas City, MO held by Entercom Kansas City News License L.L.C.
Group Owner: Entercom Communications Corp.; (acq 3-6-97; grpsl)
Arbitron Metro Market: Kansas City, MO *Format:* News
Rich Deutsch, General Sales Mgr
Neil Larrimore, Programming Director
Nicole Teich, News Director
Mike Cooney, Chief Engineer
Megan Wilson, Traffic Manager

KMXV
03-03-1958; 93.3 mhz FM *Hrs Open:* 24; 100 kw; 1066 ft.; N39 0 57 W94 30 24
Mailing Address: 600 New Hampshire Ave., N.W. Suite 1200, Washington, DC 20037 US
Second Address: 508 West Port Road, Suite 202, Kansas City, MO 64111
(816) 756-5698, *Fax:* (816) 931-8540
www.mix93.com
info@mix93.com
License: Kansas City, Jackson County, MO held by Wilks License Co.-Kansas City LLC.
Group Owner: Wilks Broadcast Group LLC; (acq 1-10-2007; grpsl)
Arbitron Metro Market: Kansas City, MO *Format:* Contemporary Hits/Top 40 *No. News Employees:* 1 *Target Audience:* 18-49; women
Mike Kennedy, Operations Dir
Mike Rowen, General Manager
Mark Herrell, General Sales Mgr
Teresa Maxwell, News Director
Ben Weiss, Chief Engineer

KPHN
09-01-1971; 1190 khz AM *Hrs Open:* 24
1212 Baltimore, Kansas City, KS 64105 US
(816) 421-1900, *Fax:* (816) 471-1320
www.radiodisney.com
mark.t.ballard@abc.com
License: Kansas City, MO held by Radio Disney Group LLC.
Group Owner: ABC Inc.; (acq 7-19-2002; $3.8 million)
Nat'l Network: Radio Disney
Arbitron Metro Market: KS City, MO *Format:* Children
Robert Hill, Promotions Manager
Sean Cocchia, Sr. VP & General Mngr
Ray de la Garza, VP Programming
Phil Guerini, VP Marketing

KPRS
01-01-1963; 103.3 mhz FM *Hrs Open:* 24; 100 kw; 994 ft.; N39 0 57 W94 30 24
11131 Colorado Ave, Kansas City, MO 64137 US
(816) 763-2040, *Fax:* (816) 966-1055
www.kprs.com
License: Kansas City, Jackson County, MO held by Carter Broadcast Group Inc.
Group Owner: Carter Broadcast Group Inc.
Nat'l Reps: Eastman Radio
Arbitron Metro Market: Kansas City, MO-KS *Format:* Urban Contemporary *Hrs. of News Programming:* News progmg one hr wkly *Target Audience:* 18-34 and 25-54; mid-upper income
Myron Fears, Operations Dir
Michael L. Carter, General Manager
Todd Fries, General Sales Mgr
Myron Fears, Programming Director
Rich McCauley, Promotions Manager
Mark Leaver, Chief Engineer

KPRT
01-01-1950; 1590 khz AM *Hrs Open:* 24; 1 kw-D, ND1; 0.047 kw-N, ND1; N39 4 5 W94 32 10
11131 Colorado Ave, Kansas City, MO 64137 US
(816) 763-2040, *Fax:* (816) 966-1055
www.kprs.com/KPRT.aspx
License: Kansas City, MO held by Carter Broadcast Group Inc.
Group Owner: Carter Broadcast Group Inc.
Nat'l Reps: Eastman Radio
Arbitron Metro Market: Kansas City, MO-KS *Format:* Gospel *Target Audience:* 25-54
Myron Fears, Operations Dir
Michael Carter, General Manager
Todd Fries, General Sales Mgr
Myron Fears, Programming Director
Rich McCauley, Promotions Manager
Mark Leaver, Chief Engineer

KCKC
03-05-1961; 102.1 mhz FM; 100 kw; 1119 ft.; N39 5 26 W94 28 18
600 New Hampshire Ave NW, Suite 1200, Washington, DC 20037 US
(816) 576-7102, *Fax:* (816) 531-6547
www.star102.com
info@ksrh.com
License: Kansas City, Jackson County, MO held by Wilks License Co.-Kansas City LLC.
Group Owner: Wilks Broadcast Group LLC; (acq 1-10-2007; grpsl)
Wire Services: UPI
Arbitron Metro Market: Kansas City, MO-KS *Format:* Adult Contemp
Mike Rowen, General Manager
Tony DeMarco, General Sales Mgr
Heather Fischer, Promotions Manager

KRBZ
01-01-1959; 96.5 mhz FM *Hrs Open:* 24; 98.5 kw; 1099 ft.; N39 1 20 W94 30 49
10706 Beaver Dam Road, Cockeysville, MD 21030 US
(913) 576-7965, *Fax:* (913) 677-7520
www.965thebuzz.com
bedwards@entercom.com
License: Kansas City, Jackson County, MO held by Entercom Kansas City License L.L.C.
Group Owner: Entercom Communications Corp.; (acq 7-14-00; grpsl)
Arbitron Metro Market: Mission, KS *Format:* Rock/AOR *Target Audience:* 25 plus; adults with above-average disposable income
Cindy Schloss, General Manager
Nic Merenda, General Sales Mgr

KZPT
10-01-1962; 99.7 mhz FM; 100 kw; Ant 1,010 ft; N39 05 01 W94 30 57
7000 Squibb Rd., Mission, KS 19004
(913) 744-3600
www.997theboulevard.com
gberg@enentercom.com
License: Kansas City, Jackson County, MO held by Entercom Kansas City License L.L.C.
Group Owner: Entercom Communications Corp.
Arbitron Metro Market: Kansas City, MO-KS
Kevin Klein, General Sales Mgr
Greg Bergen, Programming Director

KCSP
02-16-1922; 610 khz AM *Hrs Open:* 24
401 City Avenue, Suite 409, Bala Cynwyd, PA 19004 US
(913) 744-3624, *Fax:* (913) 677-8061
www.610sports.com
rmaguire@entercom.com
License: Kansas City, MO held by Entercom Kansas City License L.L.C.
Group Owner: Entercom Communications Corp.; (acq 10-17-97; grpsl).
Nat'l Network: Sporting News Radio Network *Nat'l Reps:* D & R Radio
Arbitron Metro Market: Kansas City, MO *Format:* Country *Hrs. of News Programming:* News progmg 8 hrs wkly *Target Audience:* 25-54; general
Herndon Hasty, General Manager
Wayne WalkerParks, General Sales Mgr
Ryan Maguire., Programming Director
Dustin Boehm, Promotions Manager
Dave Alpert, General Manager

WHB
06-10-1936; 810 khz AM *Hrs Open:* 24; 50 kw-D, DAN; 5 kw-N, DAN; N39 18 21 W94 34 30
102 North Mason, Carrollton, MO 64633 US
(913) 344-1500, *Fax:* (913) 344-1599
License: Kansas City, MO held by Union Broadcasting Inc.
Nat'l Network: ESPN Radio; Sporting News Radio Network
Arbitron Metro Market: KS City, MO *Format:* Sports, Talk *Special Programming:* Sp 2 hrs wkly *Hrs. of News Programming:* news progmg 19 hrs wkly *No. News Employees:* 2 *Target Audience:* Males: 18 plus.
Nick McCabe, Operations Dir
Chad Boeger, General Manager
Sandy Cohen, General Sales Mgr
Gabe Boucher, Promotions Manager
Ed Treese, Chief Engineer

Kennett

*KAUF
06-01-1998; 89.9 mhz FM; 1 kw; 164 ft.; N36 14 32 W90 3 54
P O Drawer 2440, Tupelo, MS 38803 US
(662) 844-8888, *Fax:* (662) 842-6791
www.afr.net
License: Kennett, Dunklin County, MO held by American Family Association.
Group Owner: American Family Radio
Arbitron Metro Market: Tupelo, MS *Format:* Christian, Religious
Marvin Sanders, General Manager

KBOA
01-01-1963; 1540 khz AM; 0.5 kw-C, ND3; 1 kw-D, ND3; ND3; 0.001 k; N36 15 11 W90 2 56
342 River Oaks Road, Memphis, TN 38120 US
(573) 888-4616, *Fax:* (573) 888-4890
License: Kennett, MO held by Pollack Broadcasting Co.
Group Owner: Pollack Broadcasting Co.; acq 9-25-98; $450,000 with KBOA-FM Piggott, AR)

Format: Contemporary Hits/Top 40 *Special Programming:* Farm 5 hrs wkly
Perry Jones, General Manager
Monte Lyons, Programming Director
Charles Isbell, News Director
Palmer Johnson, Chief Engineer

KXOQ
12-13-1995; 104.3 mhz FM; 6 kw; 328 ft.; N36 21 58 W90 5 36
Mailing Address: Hc 1 Box 14, Williamsville, MO 63967 US
Second Address: 700 N. Bypass, Kennett, MO 63857
(573) 686-3700, *Fax:* (573) 686-6116
www.foxradionetwork.com
kotc@sheltonbbs.com
License: Kennett, Dunklin County, MO
Format: Oldies
Blake Brewer, President
Gabe Ednay, Chief Engineer

Kimberling City

KOMC-FM
01-01-1992; 100.1 mhz FM *Hrs Open:* 24; 36 kw; Ant 577 ft; N36 31 58 W93 19 43
202 Courtney St., Branson, MO 65616
(417) 334-6003, *Fax:* (417) 334-7141
www.komc.com
krzk@krzk.com
License: Kimberling City, Stone County, MO held by KOMC-KRZK LLC.
Group Owner: Earls Broadcasting Co.; (acq 6-27-97; $1,064,919).
Nat'l Network: ABC; CBS
Population Served: 70,000*Hrs. of News Programming:* news progmg 11 hrs wkly *No. News Employees:* 2 *Target Audience:* 45 plus; Branson & local tourists *Adv. Rates:* 40; 36; 38; 22
Charles Earls, President
Scottie Earls, General Manager
Steve Willoughby, Station Manager
Eric Marshall, Programming Director
Kristen Clemmens, Promotions Manager
Sally Kaucher, News Director
Greg Pyron, Chief Engineer

Kirksville

***KKTR**
01-01-2002; 89.7 mhz FM; 3.5 kw; Ant 197 ft; N40 10 40 W92 34 40
409 Jesse Hall, Columbia, MO 63501
(573) 882-3431, *Fax:* (573) 882-2636
www.kbia.org
License: Kirksville, Adair County, MO held by Truman State University.
Mike Dunn, General Manager
Sally Jameson, Station Manager
Robert Wells, General Sales Mgr
Kyle Felling, Programming Director
Roger Karowski, Chief Engineer

***KVSR**
10-06-1997; 90.7 mhz FM *Hrs Open:* 24; 32.5 kw; 325 ft; N40 13 46 W92 32 38
Mailing Address: Box 500, Kirksville, MO 63501
Second Address: RR5, Box 14AB, Kirksville, MO 63501
(660) 665-0466, *Fax:* (660) 665-7304
www.khgn.org
khgn@kvmo.net
License: Kirksville, Adair County, MO held by Care Broadcasting Inc.
Nat'l Network: Moody
Target Audience: 30 plus; general
Dennis Phelps, President
Tom Lloyd, Chief Engineer

KIRX
10-17-1947; 1450 khz AM *Hrs Open:* 24; 1 kw-U, ND1; N40 12 24 W92 34 31
P.O.Box 130, 1308 N. Baltimore St., Kirksville, MO 63501 US
(660) 665-3781, *Fax:* (660) 665-0711
www.1450kirx.com
kirx@cableone.net
License: Kirksville, MO held by KIRX Inc.
Regional Network: Brownfield
Format: Oldies *Special Programming:* Farm 10 hrs wkly *Hrs. of News Programming:* news progmg 40 hrs wkly *No. News Employees:* 2 *Target Audience:* 25-54; general
David Nelson, President
Steven Lloyd, Executive Vice President

KLTE
05-20-1991; 107.9 mhz FM *Hrs Open:* 24; 97 kw; 981 ft.; N39 57 23 W92 58 29
#3 Crown Dr, Suite 100, Kirksville, MO 63501 US
(660) 627-5583, *Fax:* (660) 665-8900
www.bottradionetwork.com
comments@bottradionetwork.com
License: Kirksville, Adair County, MO held by Bott Communications Inc.
Group Owner: Bott Radio Network
Nat'l Network: USA *Nat'l Reps:* Salem
Arbitron Metro Market: Columbia, MO *Format:* Christian *Hrs. of News Programming:* News progmg 3 hrs wkly *Target Audience:* 35 plus. *Adv. Rates:* 204; 168; 180; 84
Richard Bott II, Chairman
Dick Bott Sr., CEO
Paul Shipman, General Sales Mgr
Candy Green, Programming Director
Tom Holdeman, CFO
Trace Thurlby, Tom Holdeman

KRXL
09-01-1967; 94.5 mhz FM *Hrs Open:* 24; 90 kw; 1010 ft.; N40 14 34 W92 25 42
Mailing Address: P.O. Box 130, Kirksville, MO 63501 US
Second Address: 1308 N. Baltimore, Kirksville, MO 63501
(660) 665-9828, *Fax:* (660) 665-0711
www.945thex.com
krxl@cableone.net
License: Kirksville, Adair County, MO held by KIRX Inc.
Nat'l Network: ABC
Arbitron Metro Market: Kirksville, MO *Format:* Classic Rock *Hrs. of News Programming:* News progmg 2 hrs wkly *Target Audience:* 25-54.
Steve Lloyd, General Manager

***KTRM**
02-10-1998; 88.7 mhz FM *Hrs Open:* 7 AM-2 AM; 3.5 kw; 197 ft.; N40 10 40 W92 34 40
East Normal Street, Kirksville, MO 63501 US
(660) 785-4000, *Fax:* (660)785-4506
ktrm.truman.edu
ktrmtheedge@hotmail.com
License: Kirksville, Adair County, MO held by Truman State University.
Arbitron Metro Market: Kirksville, MO *Format:* Alternative *Hrs. of News Programming:* News progmg 3 hrs wkly
Geoffrey Woehlk, Station Manager
Brooke Giddens, Programming Director
Jessica McMichael, News Director

KTUF
02-14-1983; 93.7 mhz FM *Hrs Open:* 24; 50 kw; 492 ft.; N40 11 16 W92 31 32
Mailing Address: P.O. Box 130, 1308 N. Baltimore, Kirksville, MO 63501 US
Second Address: 1308 N. Baltimore Rd., Kirksville, MO 63501
(660) 627-5883, *Fax:* (660) 665-0711
www.937ktuf.com
ktuf@cableone.net
License: Kirksville, Adair County, MO held by KIRX Inc.
Nat'l Network: ABC
Arbitron Metro Market: Kirksville, MO *Format:* Country *Hrs. of News Programming:* news progmg 40 hrs wkly *No. News Employees:* 2 *Target Audience:* 18-44.
David Nelson, President
Duncan Miller, Operations Dir
Steve Lloyd, General Manager
Steven Lloyd, Executive Vice President

***KCKV**
91.9 mhz FM *Hrs Open:* 24; 1 kw; 308 ft.; N40 13 46 W92 32 38
P O Box 467, Quincy, IL 62306 US
(573) 346-3200, *Fax:* (573) 346-1010
www.lifechangingradio.org
License: Kirksville, Adair County, MO held by Lake Area Educational Broadcasting Foundation
Arbitron Metro Market: Kirksville, MO *Format:* Religious *Target Audience:* 45+
Alice McDermott, CFO
James McDermott, President

Knob Noster

***KCVQ**
07-01-1998; 89.7 mhz FM *Hrs Open:* 24; 7.7 kw; 230 ft.; N38 52 10 W93 32 58 *Rebroadcasts:* Rebroadcasts KCVO-FM Camdenton 100%
P.O. Box 800, Camdenton, MO 65020 US
(573) 346-3200, *Fax:* (573) 346-1010
www.spiritfm.org
email@spiritfm.org
License: Knob Noster, Johnson County, MO held by Lake Area Educational Broadcasting Foundation.
Nat'l Network: Salem Radio Network
Arbitron Metro Market: Camdenton, MO *Format:* Christian *Hrs. of News Programming:* One *Target Audience:* 25-45.
Alice McDermott, CFO
James McDermott, President
Jim McDermott, General Manager
Alice McDermott, Financial Director

KXKX
06-24-1983; 105.7 mhz FM *Hrs Open:* 24; 38 kw; 446 ft.; N38 45 34 W93 25 32
119 N. Third St, Box 711, Hannibal, MO 63401 US
(660) 826-1050, *Fax:* (660) 827-5072
www.kxkx.com
info@kxkx.com
License: Knob Noster, Johnson County, MO held by Bick Broadcasting Co.
Group Owner: Bick Broadcasting Co.; (acq 7-19-89; $185,000;
Arbitron Metro Market: Sedalia, MO *Format:* Country *Hrs. of News Programming:* news progmg 5 hrs wkly *No. News Employees:* 1 *Target Audience:* 25-54.
Dennis Polk, General Manager
Doug Sokolowski, Programming Director
Danny Hampton, News Director
Carl Zimmerschied, Chief Engineer
Dee Johnson, Traffic Manager

La Monte

KPOW-FM
11-18-1998; 97.7 mhz FM *Hrs Open:* 24; 100 kw; 981 ft.; N39 3 10 W93 16 1
P. O. Box 1546, 906 Thompson Blvd., Sedalia, MO 65302 US
(660) 826-5005, *Fax:* (660) 826-5557
www.power977.com
sales@bennemedia.com
License: La Monte, Pettis County, MO held by Sedalia Investment Group L.L.C.
Nat'l Network: CNN Radio
Arbitron Metro Market: Columbia, MO, parts of KS City *Format:* Talk *Special Programming:* Blues 6 hrs wkly *Hrs. of News Programming:* news progmg 2 hrs wkly *No. News Employees:* 1 *Target Audience:* 25-54.*Adv. Rates:* 19.55; 16.24; 19.55; 9.83
Stuart Steinmetz, General Manager
Sally Altena, General Sales Mgr

Lake Ozark

KQUL
05-09-1994; 102.7 mhz FM *Hrs Open:* 24; 6 kw; 328 ft.; N38 2 6 W92 34 31
209 E. 2nd Street, Eldon, MO 65026 US
(573) 348-1958, *Fax:* (573) 348-1923
mike@mix927.com
License: Lake Ozark, Camden County, MO held by Benne Broadcasting of Lake Ozark Inc.
Format: Oldies *Target Audience:* 35-60.
Denny Benne, General Manager
Greg Sullens, Station Manager
Mike Clayton, Programming Director

Lamar

KHST
05-01-1992; 101.7 mhz FM; 22 kw; 328 ft.; N37 25 27 W94 16 11
Mailing Address: P.O. Box 383, Pittsburg, KS 66762 US
Second Address: 412 Locust St., Pittsburg, KS 66762
(620) 232-5993, *Fax:* (620) 232-5550
www.mycountry1017.com
info@hometownstation.com
License: Lamar, Barton County, MO held by Southeast Kansas Broadcasting Co. Inc.
Group Owner: My Town Media, Inc.; (acq 9-22-98; $330,000)
Arbitron Metro Market: Joplin, MO *Format:* Country *Target Audience:* 25-54. *Adv. Rates:* 100; 80; 80; 80
Lance Sayler, President
Dave Lee, Operations Dir

Lebanon

KBNN
10-20-1973; 750 khz AM *Hrs Open:* 6 AM-sunset
P.O.Box 1112, Lebanon, MO 65536 US
(417) 532-9111, *Fax:* (417) 532-3989
www.regionalradio.com
kjel@regionalradio.com

License: Lebanon, MO held by Waynesville/Lebanon License Co. LLC.
Group Owner: GoodRadio.TV; (acq 8-8-2007; grpsl)
Regional Network: Missourinet
Format: Talk *Special Programming:* News, farm 8 hrs wkly *Hrs. of News Programming:* news progmg 35 hrs wkly *No. News Employees:* 5 *Target Audience:* 35-64; middle America *Adv. Rates:* 40; 38; 24; 24
Theresa Nixon, Operations Dir
Mike Edwards, General Manager
Marcy Todd, News Director

KCLQ
05-18-1979; 107.9 mhz FM *Hrs Open:* 24; 19 kw; 669 ft.; N37 48 11 W92 33 1
18785 Finch Rd, Lebanon, MO 65536 US
(417) 532-2962, *Fax:* (417) 532-5184
www.1079thecoyote.com
kclq@kclq.com
License: Lebanon, Laclede County, MO
Arbitron Metro Market: Lebanon, MO *Format:* Country *Hrs. of News Programming:* news progmg 3 hrs wkly *No. News Employees:* 3 *Target Audience:* 25-54; female *Adv. Rates:* 23.25; 20.25; 21.75; 11.25
Wilburn Luna, CFO
Fred Key, President
Audrey Luna, General Manager
Doug Smith, General Sales Mgr
Juan Vela, Programming Director
Freddy Maskill, Promotions Manager
Jeff Rottman, News Director

KJEL
10-20-1973; 103.7 mhz FM *Hrs Open:* 24; 100 kw; 984 ft.; N37 49 10 W92 44 51
P.O. Box 430, Moberly, MO 65270 US
(417) 532-9111, *Fax:* (417) 532-3989
www.regionalradio.com
License: Lebanon, Laclede County, MO held by Waynesville/Lebanon License Co. LLC.
Group Owner: GoodRadio.TV
Nat'l Network: ABC
Format: Country *Hrs. of News Programming:* news progmg 45 hrs wkly *No. News Employees:* 5 *Target Audience:* 25-65; equal Male/Female *Adv. Rates:* 44; 38; 28; 25
Teresa Nixon, Operations Dir
Mike Edwards, General Manager
Mary Todd, News Director
Bob Moore, Chief Engineer
Marcy Todd, Office Manager

KLWT
07-04-1948; 1230 khz AM *Hrs Open:* 24; 1 kw-U, ND1; N37 40 40 W92 41 16
18785 Finch Road, Lebanon, MO 65536 US
(417) 532-2962, *Fax:* (417) 532-5184
www.klwt1230.com
klwt@klwt1230.com
License: Lebanon, MO held by Pearson Broadcasting of Lebanon Inc.
Format: Country, News, 62, Sports, Talk *Hrs. of News Programming:* news progmg 10 hrs wkly *No. News Employees:* 3 *Target Audience:* 30 plus; adults *Adv. Rates:* 15.75; 12.75; 14.25; 9
Kit Caldwell, Operations Dir
Dan Caldwell, General Manager
Brian McClendon, General Sales Mgr
Jannise Restivo, News Director

*KTTK
01-01-1992; 90.7 mhz FM *Hrs Open:* 5 AM-midnight; 11 kw; 476 ft.; N37 37 58 W92 45 22
221 East Commercial St., Lebanon, MO 65536 US
(417) 588-1435, *Fax:* (417) 532-3055
License: Lebanon, Laclede County, MO held by Lebanon Educational Broadcasting Foundation.
Nat'l Network: USA
Arbitron Metro Market: Lebanon, MO *Format:* Christian *Special Programming:* Gospel 7 hrs wkly
Max Rhoades, General Manager
Dave Hutton, Programming Director

Lee's Summit

*KLRX
01-01-1998; 97.3 mhz FM; 55 kw; 1171 ft.; N39 5 26 W94 28 18
P.O. Box 219, Moberly, MO 65270 US
(913) 344-1500, *Fax:* (913) 344-1599
www.klove.com
info@klove.com
License: Lee's Summit, Jackson County, MO held by Union First Broadcasting LLC
Nat'l Network: K-Love
Arbitron Metro Market: Kansas City, MO-KS *Format:* Christian
Chad Boeger, General Manager

Lexington

KLEX
04-19-1956; 1570 khz AM *Hrs Open:* 24; 250 w-D, 58 w-N; N39 11 14 W93 50 03 *Rebroadcasts:* Rebroadcasts KAYX(FM) Richmond 100%
111 W. Main St., Richmond, MO 66212
(816) 470-9925, *Fax:* (816) 470-8925
www.bottradionetwork.com
comments@bottradionetwork.com
License: Lexington, Lafayette County, MO held by Bott Communications Inc.
Group Owner: Bott Radio Network; (acq 1994; with KAYX(FM) Richmond)
Nat'l Network: USA
Population Served: 50,000 *Arbitron Metro Market:* Kansas City, MO *Target Audience:* 25-54.
Richard Bott II, President
Eben Fowler, Operations Dir
Pat Rulon, General Sales Mgr
Candy Green, Programming Director
John Dale, Promotions Manager
Jason Potochik, News Director
Tom Holdeman, CFO
Ed Treese, Engineer

Liberty

WDAF-FM
11-09-1979; 106.5 mhz FM; 100 kw; 981 ft.; N39 4 24 W94 29 6
10706 Beaver Dam Road, Cockeysville, MD 21030 US
(913) 677-8998, *Fax:* (913) 677-8061
www.1065thewolf.com
info@1065thewolf.com
License: Liberty, Clay County, MO held by Entercom Kansas City License LLC.
Group Owner: Entercom Communications Corp.; (acq 7-14-00; grpsl).
Nat'l Reps: D & R Radio
Arbitron Metro Market: Kansas City, MO *Format:* Jazz, Smooth Jazz *Target Audience:* 18-34.
Herndon Hasty, General Manager
Joanne Raines, General Sales Mgr
Wes Poe, Program Director and Music Director
Natalie Puhr, Program Director and Music Director
Kelsey Nelson, Promotions Coordinator
Justin Neighbor, PromotionsAssistant

KCXL
02-14-1967; 1140 khz AM
310 South La Frenz Road, Liberty, MO 64068 US
(816) 792-1140, *Fax:* (816) 792-8258
www.kcxl.com
kcxl11140@yahoo.com
License: Liberty, MO held by Alpine Broadcasting Corp.
Nat'l Network: AP Network News; Jones Radio Networks
Arbitron Metro Market: Liberty, MO *Format:* Adult Contemp, Talk *Special Programming:* News 4 hrs, Sp 5 hrs, relg 3 hrs, health 17 hrs wkly *Target Audience:* 25-54; baby boomers *Adv. Rates:* 25; 20; 25; 15
Peter Schartel, President
David Brewer, Operations Dir
David Brewer, Station Manager
Jonne Santoli, General Sales Mgr
John Christopher, Chief Engineer

*KWJC
04-14-1974; 91.9 mhz FM *Hrs Open:* 24; 7 kw; 623 ft.; N39 7 23 W94 23 24
Div/DBA: Dpeartment of Communication
Dept. of Communication, 500 College Hill, Liberty, MO 64068 US
(816) 415-7594, *Fax:* (816) 415-5027
www.air1.com
License: Liberty, Clay County, MO held by William Jewell College.
Arbitron Metro Market: Kansas City, MO-KS *Format:* Contemporary Hits/Top 40 *Special Programming:* Class 10 hrs, Christian 10 hrs wkly *Hrs. of News Programming:* News progmg 5 hrs wkly *Target Audience:* 12-34; men& women *Adv. Rates:* 10; 10; 10; 8
Paul Worstell, General Manager

Licking

*KIKG
91.1 mhz FM; kw
US
License: Licking, Texas County, MO held by Ron Elmore Ministries Inc.
Arbitron Metro Market: Licking, MO
Ron Elmore, President

Linn

KJMO
01-01-2006; 97.5 mhz FM; 6 kw; 328 ft.; N38 29 56.9 W91 53 0.4 US
(573) 893-5100, *Fax:* (573) 893-8330
www.kjmo.com
info@kjmo.com
License: Linn, Osage County, MO held by Cumulus Licensing LLC.
Group Owner: Cumulus Media Inc.
Arbitron Metro Market: Jefferson City, MO *Format:* Oldies
Kevin Joyce, VP
Darryl Burnett, General Sales Mgr
Chris Kellogg, Programming Director
Nick Snyder, Promotions Manager

Louisiana

KJFM
09-04-1984; 102.1 mhz FM; 3.7 kw; 387 ft.; N39 26 29 W91 2 19
Mailing Address: P.O. Box 438, Louisiana, MO 63353 US
Second Address: 615 Georgia St., Louisiana, MO 63353
(573) 754-5102, *Fax:* (573) 754-5544
kjfmradio@yahoo.com
License: Louisiana, Pike County, MO held by Foxfire Communications Inc.
Nat'l Network: ABC Information & Entertainment *Regional Network:* Missourinet
Format: Country *Hrs. of News Programming:* 27 hrs news progmg wkly *Target Audience:* 25-54. *Adv. Rates:* 22.5; 20; 20; 17.50
Marianne Everhart, Operations Dir
Thom T. Sanders, General Manager

Lutesville

KMHM
08-04-1995; 104.1 mhz FM *Hrs Open:* 24; 2.5 kw; 509 ft.; N37 22 40 W89 56 4
9077 Ava Road, Ava, IL 62907 US
(573) 238-1041, *Fax:* (573) 238-0104
www.kmhm.net
kmhm1041@clas.net
License: Lutesville, Bollinger County, MO held by Southern Gospetality LLC.
Nat'l Network: Salem Radio Network
Format: Gospel *Hrs. of News Programming:* News progmg 14 hrs wkly *Target Audience:* 30-55; Christians and family-oriented listeners *Adv. Rates:* 12; 11:50; 12; 11:50
Harold Lawder, CEO
Will Stephens, General Manager
Glen Augur, Station Manager
Joy Duprey, Programming Director
Tom Beattie, Chief Engineer
Sheila Kirkpatrick, Music Director

Macon

KIRK
01-01-1998; 99.9 mhz FM *Hrs Open:* 24; 12.5 kw; 463 ft.; N39 36 2 W92 34 24
Mailing Address: 300 West Reed Street, P.O Box 619, Moberly, MO 65270 US
Second Address: 300 W. Reed St., Moberly, MO 65270
(660) 263-6999, *Fax:* (660) 263-2300
regionalradio.com
License: Macon, Macon County, MO held by Moberly/Macon License Co. LLC.
Group Owner: GoodRadio.TV; (acq 8-8-2007; grpsl)
Format: Adult Contemp
Terry Strickland, General Manager

KLTI
01-30-1966; 1560 khz AM *Hrs Open:* 24
408 W. Reed, PO Box 219, Moberly, MO 65270 US
(660) 385-1560, *Fax:* (660) 385-7090
www.kltiradio.com
klti@kltiradio.com
License: Macon, MO held by Chirillo Electronics Inc.
Group Owner: Best Broadcast Group
Format: Country *Target Audience:* 25-44.
Dale Palmer, General Manager

Madison

KTCM

97.3 mhz FM; 25 kw; Ant 328 ft; N39 28 52 W92 10 13
525 S. Flagler Dr., # 21-A, West Palm Beach, FL
(561) 515-6142
License: Madison, Monroe County, MO held by Christine Radio LLC.
Group Owner: GoodRadio.TV; (acq 10-4-2007)
Trace Michaels, General Manager
Brad Elliott, Programming Director
Chris Andrews, Chief Engineer

Malden

KLSC

11-23-1979; 92.9 mhz FM *Hrs Open:* 6 AM-midnight; 50 kw; 476 ft.; N36 40 31 W89 46 19
P.O. Box 1749, Cape Girardeau, MO 63702 US
(573) 471-1400, *Fax:* (573) 471-1402
License: Malden, Dunklin County, MO
Group Owner: MAX Media L.L.C.
Format: Adult Contemp *Hrs. of News Programming:* news progmg 30 hrs wkly *No. News Employees:* 2 *Target Audience:* General.
Mike Renick, Programming Director

KMAL

09-15-1954; 1470 khz AM *Hrs Open:* 6 AM-sunset; 1 kw-D, NDD; N36 33 8 W89 58 42 *Rebroadcasts:* Simulcasts KSIM (Sikeston)
P.O. Box 1749, Cape Girardeau, MO 63702 US
(573) 471-1400, *Fax:* (573) 471-1402
www.1400ksim.com
License: Malden, MO held by MRR License LLC.
Group Owner: MAX Media L.L.C.; (acq 6-2-2004; grpsl).
Arbitron Metro Market: Girardeau, MO *Format:* News, News/Talk, 86 *No. News Employees:* 3 *Target Audience:* 35 plus.
Christy Benton, General Manager
Meg Davis, General Sales Mgr
Tyler Morrison, Programming Director
Mike Coffey, Chief Engineer
Sherry Crider, Traffic Manager

Malta Bend

KRLI

10-28-1996; 103.9 mhz FM *Hrs Open:* 24; 12 kw; 879 ft.; N39 21 59 W93 24 12
203 North Mason Street, Carrollton, MO 64633 US
(660) 542-0404, *Fax:* (660) 542-3152
www.krli.net
advertise@krli.net
License: Malta Bend, Saline County, MO held by Kanza Inc.
Format: Big Band, Jazz, 64 *Hrs. of News Programming:* news progmg 6 hrs wkly *No. News Employees:* 2 *Target Audience:* 45 plus; baby boomers *Adv. Rates:* 96; 96; 96; 42
Miles Carter, CEO

Mansfield

KTRI-FM

01-01-1978; 95.9 mhz FM *Hrs Open:* 24; 8.9 kw; 541 ft.; N37 17 10 W92 36 55
7450 Midlothian Pike, Richmond, VA 23225 US
(417) 235-6041, *Fax:* (417) 235-6388
www.buzz959.com/index.php?option=com_content&view=article&id=52&Itemid=43
License: Mansfield, Wright County, MO held by Thirteen Forty Productions Inc.
Arbitron Metro Market: Monett, MO *Format:* Adult Contemp
Gary Snadon, President

Marble Hill

KYRX

12-01-1999; 97.3 mhz FM; 3.6 kw; 427 ft.; N37 22 49 W90 4 49
P O Box 818, Benton, IL 62812 US
(573) 339-7000, *Fax:* (573) 651-4100
License: Marble Hill, Bollinger County, MO held by Dana R. Withers.
Nat'l Reps: Katz Radio
Format: Oldies
Rick Lambert, General Manager

Marshall

KMMO

05-29-1949; 1300 khz AM *Hrs Open:* 24; 1 kw-D, ND1; 0.068 kw-N, ND1; N39 8 3 W93 13 19
P. O. Box 128, Marshall, MO 63540 US
(660) 886-7422, *Fax:* (660) 886-6291
License: Marshall, MO held by Missouri Valley Broadcasting Inc.
Eric Strobel, General Manager
Carl Raida, Programming Director

KMMO-FM

12-01-1968; 102.9 mhz FM *Hrs Open:* 24; 100 kw; 381 ft.; N39 8 3 W93 13 19
P. O. Box 128, Marshall, MO 65340 US
(660) 886-7422, *Fax:* (660) 886-6291
License: Marshall, Saline County, MO held by Missouri Valley Broadcasting Inc.
Nat'l Network: CBS
Format: Country *Target Audience:* General. *Adv. Rates:* 30; 28; 30; 20
John Wilson, General Manager
Peter Hollabaugh, General Sales Mgr
Ken Lewellen, News Director

*KMVC

11-01-1968; 91.7 mhz FM *Hrs Open:* 7 AM-11 PM (M-F); 9 AM-11 PM (S); n; 0.1 kw vert; 62 ft.; N39 6 31 W93 11 29
500 East College Street, Marshall, MO 65340 US
(660) 831-4193, *Fax:* (660) 886-9818
kmvc@moval.edu
License: Marshall, Saline County, MO held by Missouri Valley College.
Format: Alternative, Blues *Special Programming:* Black 10 hrs, progsv 10 hrs, relg 16 hrs, classic *Hrs. of News Programming:* News progmg 3 hrs wkly *Target Audience:* 17-26; pre-, current & post-college age
Brent Foster, General Manager
Josh Branch, Station Manager

Marshfield

KKLH

06-01-1982; 104.7 mhz FM *Hrs Open:* 24; 34 kw; 594 ft.; N37 12 21 W92 54 20
C/O Fisher Wayland: Jsr, 2001 Penn. Ave, NW #400, Washington, DC 20006 US
(417) 886-5677, *Fax:* (417) 886-2155
www.1047thecave.com
info@1047thecave.com
License: Marshfield, Webster County, MO held by MW SpringMo Inc.
Group Owner: The Mid-West Family Broadcast Group; (acq 1996; $1.8 million).
Nat'l Reps: Eastman Radio
Arbitron Metro Market: Springfield, MO *Format:* Classic Rock *Target Audience:* 35-54. *Adv. Rates:* 30; 35; 35; 15
Rick McCoy, President
Mary Fleenor, Operations Dir
Malcolm Hurriede, General Sales Mgr
John Kimmons, Programming Director
Jeanne Guittar, Business Manager
Keith Abercrombie, Regional Sales Manager
Jeanne Guittar, TrafficManager
Nichole Buckner

KMRF

11-01-1969; 1510 khz AM *Hrs Open:* Sunrise-sunset
1411 Locust Street, St Louis, MO 63103 US
(417) 468-6188, *Fax:* (417) 859-2916
License: Marshfield, MO held by New Life Evangelistic Center Inc.
Nat'l Network: USA *Regional Network:* Missourinet; Brownfield
Arbitron Metro Market: Springfield, MO *Format:* Gospel *Hrs. of News Programming:* news progmg 6 hrs wkly *No. News Employees:* 1 *Target Audience:* General.
Larry Rice, President
Ed Moore, Operations Dir
Hank Zenicwicz, Programming Director

*KNLM

91.9 mhz FM; 1.75 kw; 249 ft.; N37 19 1 W92 57 51
Rebroadcasts: Rebroadcasts KNLG(FM) New Bloomfield 100%
1411 Locust Street, St. Louis, MO 63103 US
(417) 468-6188, *Fax:* (417) 859-2916
License: Marshfield, Webster County, MO
Format: Christian *Target Audience:* General.
Marvin Sanders, General Manager

Maryville

KNIM

01-01-1953; 1580 khz AM *Hrs Open:* 24; 0.7 kw-D, ND1; 0.007 kw-N, ND1; N40 19 3 W94 52 14
Mailing Address: P.O. Box 278, Maryville, MO 64468 US
Second Address: 1618 S. Main, Maryville, MO 64468
(660) 582-2151, *Fax:* (660) 582-3211
knimmaryville.com
knim@knimmaryville.com
License: Maryville, MO held by Nodaway Broadcasting Corp.
Nat'l Network: CNN Radio *Nat'l Reps:* Keystone (unwired net)
Format: News, Sports *Special Programming:* Farm 5 hrs wkly *No. News Employees:* 1 *Target Audience:* 25-54.
Joyce Cronin, President
Jim Cronin, Executive Vice President

KVVL

09-01-1972; 97.1 mhz FM *Hrs Open:* 24; 21.5 kw; Ant 354 ft; N40 23 31 W94 58 04
Mailing Address: Box 278, Maryville, MO 64468
Second Address: 1618 S. Main, Maryville, MO 64468
(660) 582-2151, *Fax:* (660) 582-3211
www.knimmaryville.com
License: Maryville, Nodaway County, MO
Wire Services: AP
Population Served: 120,000*Hrs. of News Programming:* news progmg 25 hrs wkly *No. News Employees:* 1
Mike Robbins, General Manager
Dan Thomas, Programming Director

*KXCV

01-01-1971; 90.5 mhz FM *Hrs Open:* 24; 100 kw; 634 ft.; N40 24 9 W94 53 16
800 University Drive, Maryville, MO 64468 US
(660) 562-1163(660) 562-1164, *Fax:* (660) 562-1832
www.kxcv.org
kxcv@nwmissouri.edu
License: Maryville, Nodaway County, MO held by Northwest Missouri State University.
Nat'l Network: NPR; PRI
Arbitron Metro Market: Maryville, MO *Format:* Jazz, News *Hrs. of News Programming:* news progmg 39 hrs wkly *No. News Employees:* 2 *Target Audience:* General.
John Jasinski, President
Patty Holley, Operations Dir
Rodney Harris, General Manager
Patty Andrews Holley, Programming Director
Venus Brown, Promotions Manager
Kirk Wayman, News Director
Darren Perkins, Chief Engineer
JohnCoffey, Sports Director
Marcia Fish, Traffic Manager
Venus Brown, Membership Development/ Events Coordinator

Memphis

KMEM-FM

03-29-1982; 100.5 mhz FM *Hrs Open:* 24; 25 kw; 299 ft.; N40 29 59 W92 9 58
Mailing Address: P.O. Box 121, Memphis, MO 63555 US
Second Address: 650 N. Clay, Memphis, MO 63555
(660) 465-7225, *Fax:* (660) 465-2626
www.kmemfm.com
mdenney@kmemfm.com
License: Memphis, Scotland County, MO held by Boyer Broadcasting Co. Inc.
Regional Network: Missourinet; Brownfield
Format: Country *Special Programming:* Farm 8 hrs, relg 4 hrs wkly *Hrs. of News Programming:* news progmg 15 hrs wkly *No. News Employees:* 1 *Target Audience:* General; adult audience 30+ *Adv. Rates:* 16.50;16.50; 16.50; 12.50
Mark McVey, President
Karen McVey, Operations Dir
Mark Denney, General Manager

Mexico

*KJAB-FM

10-09-1985; 88.3 mhz FM *Hrs Open:* 24; 4.8 kw vert; 272 ft.; N39 6 13 W91 53 35
621 West Monroe, Mexico, MO 65265 US
(573) 581-8606, *Fax:* (573) 581-9655
www.kjab.com
kjab@kjab.com
License: Mexico, Audrain County, MO held by Mexico Educational Broadcasting Foundation.
Nat'l Network: USA
Format: Gospel *Special Programming:* Gospel 20 hrs, relg 20 hrs wkly *Hrs. of News Programming:* news progmg 2 hrs wkly *No. News Employees:* 1 *Target Audience:* General.
Kevin Weber, President
Daniel Taylor, Programming Director
Tim Knight, Underwriting Director

KWWR

12-14-1966; 95.7 mhz FM *Hrs Open:* 24; 91 kw; 1181 ft.; N39 15 49 W92 8 6
Mailing Address: 1705 E. Liberty, P.O. Box 475, Mexico, MO 65265 US
Second Address: 1705 E. Liberty St., Mexico, MO 65265-3537

(573) 581-5500, *Fax:* (573) 581-1801
info.kwwr.com
production@radiogetsresults.net
License: Mexico, Audrain County, MO held by KXEO Radio Inc.
Nat'l Network: CNN Radio; Westwood One *Wire Services:* NWS (National Weather Service); AP
Arbitron Metro Market: Mexico, MO *Format:* Country *Special Programming:* Farm, News, Sports *No. News Employees:* 21
Target Audience: 24-54. *Adv. Rates:* 57; 45; 57; 29
Anne Johnson, President
Gary Leonard, Operations Dir
Michael Daugherty, General Manager
David Moser, General Sales Mgr
Matt Bingham, Programming Director
Chris Newbrough, News Director
Penny Daugherty, Traffic Manager

KXEO
12-03-1948; 1340 khz AM *Hrs Open:* 24
Mailing Address: P.O. Box 475, Mexico, MO 65265 US
Second Address: 1705 E. Liberty St., Mexico, MO 65265-0475
(573) 581-5500, *Fax:* (573) 581-1801
www.kxeo.com
kxeo@radiogetsresults.net
License: Mexico, MO held by KXEO Radio Inc.
Nat'l Network: CNN Radio; Westwood One *Regional Network:* Missourinet; Brownfield *Wire Services:* AP
Arbitron Metro Market: Mexico, MO *Format:* Adult Contemp, News, 84 *Hrs. of News Programming:* News progmg 4 hrs wkly
Target Audience: 25-54. *Adv. Rates:* 24; 20; 24; 20
Gary Leonard, General Manager
Chris Newbrough, News Director

***KAUD**
90.5 mhz FM; 0.45 kw; 158 ft.; N39 10 36 W91 47 41.9 US
(573) 882-3431, *Fax:* (573) 882-2636
www.kbia.org
kbia@kbia.org
License: Mexico, Audrain County, MO held by The Curators of the University of Missouri.
Group Owner: The Curators of the University of Missouri
Nat'l Network: NPR; PRI
Arbitron Metro Market: Columbia, MO *Format:* Classical
Karen Walker Seeger, Operations and Music Director
Mike Dunn, General Manager
Robert Wells, General Sales Mgr
Kyle Felling, Programming Director
Janet Saidi, News Director
Roger Karwoski, Chief Engineer
Sally Jameson, BusinessManager
Ryan Famuliner, Asst. News Director
Nathan Anderson, Development
Shannon Watkins, Membership Coordinator
Tracy Borengasser, Box Office Manager
Anne French, Box Office Asst. and Outreach Coordinator

Miner

KBHI
01-01-2001; 107.1 mhz FM; 3.7 kw; 420 ft.; N36 56 33 W89 41 47
P O Box 818, Benton, IL 62812 US
(573) 471-2000, *Fax:* (573) 471-8525
www.star1071.com
License: Miner, Scott County, MO held by Dana R. Withers.
Nat'l Reps: Katz Radio
Arbitron Metro Market: Sikeston, MO *Format:* Oldies
Rick Lambert, General Manager
Joe Bill Davis, Station Manager
C.J. Cruze, Programming Director

Moberly

***KBKC**
01-01-2004; 90.1 mhz FM; 0.33 kw; 253 ft.; N39 24 39 W92 26 46
P O Drawer 2440, Tupelo, MS 38803 US
(314) 752-7000
www.covenantnet.net
covenantnetwork@juno.com
License: Moberly, Randolph County, MO held by Covenant Network.
Group Owner: Covenant Network; (acq 3-30-2004; $112,500 with WHOJ(FM) Terre Haute, IN)
Arbitron Metro Market: St. Louis, MO *Format:* Christian
Tony Holman, General Manager
Jim Schaper, Programming Director

KRES
10-01-1966; 104.7 mhz FM; 100 kw; 1020 ft.; N39 27 35 W92 42 7
Mailing Address: P.O. Box 619, Moberly, MO 65270 US
Second Address: 300 West Reed, Moberly, MO 65270
(660) 263-1600, *Fax:* (660) 269-8811
www.centralmoinfo.com
kresnews@regionalradio.com
License: Moberly, Randolph County, MO
Group Owner: GoodRadio.TV
Nat'l Network: ABC
Format: Country
George Pelletier, COO
Dean Goodman, President
Stephanie Ross, Operations Dir
Terry Strickland, General Manager
Brad Boyer, Programming Director
Mike Lear, News Director

KWIX
06-17-1950; 1230 khz AM *Hrs Open:* 24; 0.49 kw-D, ND1; 1 kw-N, ND1; N39 24 11 W92 25 57
Mailing Address: 300 West Reed Street, Moberly, MO 65270 US
Second Address: 300 West Reed, Moberly, MO 65270
(660) 263-1600, *Fax:* (660) 269-8811
www.centralmoinfo.com
kresnews@regionalradio.com
License: Moberly, MO held by Moberly/Macon License Co. LLC.
Group Owner: GoodRadio.TV; (acq 8-8-2007; grpsl)
Nat'l Network: CBS *Wire Services:* NOAA Weather
Arbitron Metro Market: Moberly, Mo *Format:* Talk *Hrs. of News Programming:* news progmg 30 hrs wkly *No. News Employees:* 4 *Target Audience:* General.
George Pelletier, COO
Terry Strickland, General Manager
Brad Boyer, Programming Director
Mike Lear, News Director
Lloyd Collins, Chief Engineer
Stephanie Ross, Webmaster

KZZT
04-10-1987; 105.5 mhz FM *Hrs Open:* 24; 50 kw; 492 ft.; N39 26 2 W92 14 24
Mailing Address: P. O. Box 128, Highway 63 & Route Ee, Moberly, MO 65270 US
Second Address: 1037 County Rd., Moberly, MO 65270
(660) 263-9390, *Fax:* (660) 263-8800
www.kzztradio.com
kzzt@mcmsys.com
License: Moberly, Randolph County, MO held by FM 105 Inc.
Group Owner: Best Broadcast Group; (acq 7-9-97; $200,000 for 43%).
Nat'l Network: ABC
Arbitron Metro Market: Columbia, MO *Format:* Contemporary Hits/Top 40, Adult Contemp *Hrs. of News Programming:* News progmg 5 hrs wkly *Target Audience:* 25-54; men & women with spendable income
Phil Chirillo, President
Dale Palmer, Operations Dir

***KSDQ**
88.7 mhz FM; 17 kw vert; 187 ft.; N39 14 40 W92 12 40 US
(573) 682-5887
www.ksdqradio.net
KSDQradio@sunnydale.org
License: Moberly, Randolph County, MO held by Sunnydale Seventh-Day Adventist Church.
Arbitron Metro Market: Moberly, MO
Micky Burkett, Operations Dir
Erving Bales, General Manager

Monett

KKBL
12-01-1977; 95.9 mhz FM *Hrs Open:* 24; 6 kw; 269 ft.; N36 56 15 W93 55 30
1569 N. Central St., Monett, MO 65708 US
(417) 235-6041, *Fax:* (417) 235-6388
www.buzz959.com
info@buzz959.com
License: Monett, Barry County, MO
Arbitron Metro Market: Joplin, MO *Format:* Rock/AOR *Hrs. of News Programming:* news progmg 4 hrs wkly *No. News Employees:* 1 *Target Audience:* General; young, adults, families
Adv. Rates: 12; 12; 12; 12
Daniel Voss, General Sales Mgr
Tracy Bailey, Promotions Manager

Monroe City

KWBZ
07-04-1981; 107.5 mhz FM; 10 kw; 328 ft.; N39 35 12 W91 47 57
3642 Flora Place, St. Louis, MO 63110 US
(217) 885-3222(217) 224-4653, *Fax:* (217) 885-3233
www.oldiessuperstation.com
wpwq106@adams.net
License: Monroe City, Monroe County, MO held by WPW Broadcasting Inc.
Group Owner: Prairie Radio Communications; (acq 8-17-2000)
Arbitron Metro Market: Quincy, IL *Format:* Oldies
Phil Alexander, General Manager

Montgomery City

KMCR
08-15-1977; 103.9 mhz FM *Hrs Open:* 24; 6 kw; 299 ft.; N38 59 10 W91 30 39
107 South Main, Brookfield, MO 64628 US
(573) 564-2275, *Fax:* (573) 564-8036
www.bestbroadcastgroup.com
kmcr@socket.net
License: Montgomery City, Montgomery County, MO held by Chirillo Electronics Inc.
Group Owner: Best Broadcast Group; (acq 1994).
Regional Network: Missourinet
Format: Adult Contemp *Special Programming:* Farm 2 hrs, relg 2 hrs wkly *Hrs. of News Programming:* news progmg 3 hrs wkly
No. News Employees: 1 *Target Audience:* 25-60; male/female
Dale Palmer, Operations Dir

Mount Vernon

KRVI
07-29-1993; 106.7 mhz FM; 25 kw; 328 ft; N37 09 16 W93 36 58
2330 W. Grand St., Springfield, MO 59937
(417) 865-6614, *Fax:* (417) 865-9643
www.2rocks.com
ccannon@journalbroadcastgroup.com
License: Mount Vernon, Lawrence County, MO held by Journal Broadcast Corp.
Group Owner: Journal Communications Inc.; (acq 11-26-2003; $5 million with KSGF-FM Ash Grove).
Chris Cannon, Operations Dir
Rex Hansen, General Manager
Janelle Carter, General Sales Mgr

Mountain Grove

KELE
11-16-1954; 1360 khz AM *Hrs Open:* 24; 1 kw-D, NDD; 0.06 kw-N, ND1; N37 8 7 W92 14 59
800 North Hubbard, Mountain Grove, MO 65711 US
(417) 926-4650, *Fax:* (417) 926-7604
tonya@925thegrove.com
License: Mountain Grove, MO held by Quorum Radio Partners Inc.
Nat'l Network: USA *Regional Network:* Brownfield
Format: Country *Hrs. of News Programming:* news progmg 10 hrs wkly *No. News Employees:* 1 *Adv. Rates:* 5; 5; 5; 5
Tracy O'Quinn, General Manager
Shaun Anthony, Programming Director
Jim Morris, News Director
Terry Dobson, Sports Commentator
Perry Dobson, Sports Commentator
Tonya Shannon, Traffic Manager

KELE-FM
01-01-1977; 92.5 mhz FM; 3 kw; 300 ft.; N37 8 7 W92 14 59
800 N. Hubbard, Mountain Grove, MO 65711 US
(417) 926-4650, *Fax:* (417) 926-7604
tonya@925thegrove.com
License: Mountain Grove, Wright County, MO held by Ozark Media Inc.
Group Owner: Ozark Media Inc.; (acq 5-1-2007; $625,000 with KOZX(FM) Cabool)
Format: Country *Special Programming:* Relg 3 hrs wkly *Hrs. of News Programming:* news progmg 8 hrs wkly *No. News Employees:* 1 *Target Audience:* 24-59; general *Adv. Rates:* 13.75; 9.25; 11.75; 8
Tracy O'Quinn, General Manager
Shaun Anthony, Programming Director
Jim Morris, News Director
Perry Dobson, Sports Commentator
Terry Dobson, Sports Commentator
Tonya Shannon, Traffic Manager

Mountain View

KUPH
07-31-1998; 96.9 mhz FM *Hrs Open:* 24; 50 kw; 492 ft.; N36 59 29 W91 47 41
983 East U.W. Hwy 160, West Plains, MO 65775 US
(417) 967-3353, *Fax:* (417) 967-2281
www.thefox969.com
Traffic@MediaProfessionalsInc.com

License: Mountain View, Howell County, MO held by Central Ozark Radio Network Inc.
Arbitron Metro Market: Mountain View, MO *Format:* Adult Contemp *Hrs. of News Programming:* News progmg 2 hrs wkly *Target Audience:* 25-54; upscale, mature individuals *Adv. Rates:* 10.50; 10.50; 10.50; na
Tom Marhefka, CEO
Bob Eckman, General Manager
Jonathon Bergman, General Sales Mgr
Gary Lee, Programming Director
Mike Robertson, News Director
Jim White, Chief Engineer

Naylor

KZMA
01-01-2005; 99.9 mhz FM; 4.2 kw; 387 ft.; N36 39 43 W90 29 16
20001 Pa Ave NW, Suite 400, Washington, DC 20006 US
(573) 778-0142, *Fax:* (573) 686-2377
www.kzmafm.com
jhborders@yahoo.com
License: Naylor, Ripley County, MO held by Daniel S. Stratemeyer
Arbitron Metro Market: Naylor, MO *Format:* Adult Contemp
Jim Borders, General Manager

Neosho

KBTN
02-01-1954; 1420 khz AM *Hrs Open:* 5 AM-midnight; 1 kw-D, DAN; 0.5 kw-N, DAN; N36 50 52 W94 19 12
Mailing Address: P. O. Box K, Neosho, MO 64850 US
Second Address: 216 W. Spring, Neosho, MO 64850
(417) 781-1313, *Fax:* (417) 781-1316
www.kbtnradio.com
License: Neosho, MO held by American Media Investments Inc.
Group Owner: American Media Investments Inc.; (acq 2-17-2009; grpsl)
Nat'l Network: ABC; CNN Radio
Arbitron Metro Market: Joplin, MO *Format:* Country *Special Programming:* Farm 6 hrs wkly *Hrs. of News Programming:* news progmg 14 hrs wkly *No. News Employees:* 2 *Target Audience:* 18-54.
Gail Johnson, General Manager
Monica Blain, Programming Director
David Horvath, News Director
Art Morris, Chief Engineer

KBTN-FM
01-01-1995; 99.7 mhz FM *Hrs Open:* 24; 16.5 kw; 404 ft.; N36 54 33 W94 27 40
P.O. Box K, Neosho, MO 64850 US
(417) 781-1313, *Fax:* (417)781-1316
www.kbtnradio.com
info@997kbtn.com
License: Neosho, Newton County, MO held by American Media Investments Inc.
Group Owner: American Media Investments Inc.; (acq 2-17-2009; grpsl)
Arbitron Metro Market: Joplin, MO *Format:* Country *Hrs. of News Programming:* news progmg 9 hrs wkly *No. News Employees:* 2 *Target Audience:* 18 plus.
Warren McDonald, Operations Dir
Jennifer Isom, General Manager
Dave Clemons, General Sales Mgr
Steve Smith, Programming Director

*KNEO
10-01-1986; 91.7 mhz FM *Hrs Open:* 24; 14.0 kw; 374 ft; N36 52 49 W94 26 59
10827 E. Hwy. 86, Neosho, MO 64850
(417) 451-5636, *Fax:* (417) 451-1891
www.kneo.org
kneo@kneo.org
License: Neosho, Newton County, MO held by Sky High Broadcasting Corp.
Nat'l Network: USA; Moody
Population Served: 650,000*Hrs. of News Programming:* News progmg 10 hrs wkly *Target Audience:* 30-65. *Adv. Rates:* Sponsorship rates available
Mark Taylor, President
Adam Winkler, Operations Dir
Mark Taylor, General Manager
Mark Taylor, Programming Director
Andy Farmer, Production Director
Clark Matthews, Website Development

Nevada

KNEM
01-01-1949; 1240 khz AM *Hrs Open:* 24; 0.5 kw-U, ND1; N37 51 37 W94 22 54
P.O. Box 447, Nevada, MO 64772 US
(417) 667-3113, *Fax:* (417) 667-9797
www.knemknmo.com
mharbit@knemknmo.com
License: Nevada, MO held by Harbit Communications Inc.
Regional Network: Brownfield; Missourinet
Format: Country *Special Programming:* Farm one hr, Christian 5 hrs wkly *Hrs. of News Programming:* news progmg 30 hrs wkly *No. News Employees:* 1 *Target Audience:* General. *Adv. Rates:* 15.19; 14; 15.19;10
Mike Harbit, President
Russ Warren, News Director
Daryl Nickolaus, Chief Engineer

KNMO-FM
09-10-1984; 97.5 mhz FM *Hrs Open:* 24; 6 kw; 281 ft.; N37 52 45 W94 20 15
P.O. Box 447, Nevada, MO 64772 US
(417) 667-3113, *Fax:* (417) 667-9797
www.knemknmo.com
License: Nevada, Vernon County, MO
Adv. Rates: Same as AM
Darren Nez, General Manager

New Bloomfield

*KNLG
07-20-1997; 90.3 mhz FM *Hrs Open:* 24; 0.15 kw; 217 ft.; N38 42 16 W92 5 20
1411 Locust Street, St Louis, MO 63103 US
(573) 896-5945, *Fax:* (573) 896-4376
www.heresshelpnet.org
License: New Bloomfield, Callaway County, MO held by New Life Evangelistic Center Inc.
Format: Gospel *Hrs. of News Programming:* News progmg 9 hrs wkly *Target Audience:* General.
Rev. Larry Rice, President
John Shepard, Programming Director

New London

KZZK
04-01-1996; 105.9 mhz FM *Hrs Open:* 24; 10 kw; 515 ft.; N39 43 48 W91 24 19
2 Dearborn Square, Kankakee, IL 60901 US
(217) 224-4102, *Fax:* (217) 224-4133
www.kzzk.com
kzzk@staradio.com
License: New London, Ralls County, MO held by STARadio Corp.
Group Owner: STARadio Corp.; acq 12-2-98; $2.1 million with KGRC(FM) Hannibal)
Arbitron Metro Market: New London, MO *Format:* Alternative, Classic Rock *Hrs. of News Programming:* News progmg 2 hrs wkly *Target Audience:* 18-49; skews male
Howard Doss, President
Mike Moyers, General Manager
Brenda Park, General Sales Mgr
Quaid, Programming Director
Phil Reilly, Chief Engineer

New Madrid

KTMO
01-31-1976; 106.5 mhz FM *Hrs Open:* 24; 50 kw; 469 ft.; N36 25 31 W89 41 29
Mailing Address: 1600 Southtrust Tower, Birmingham, AL 35203 US
Second Address: 12323 Jefferson Ave., New Madrid, MO 63857 , *Fax:* (573) 888-4890
License: New Madrid, New Madrid County, MO
Group Owner: Pollack Broadcasting Co.
Nat'l Network: ABC
Format: Country *No. News Employees:* 1 *Target Audience:* 18-49 adults; males
Lynn Carmichael, General Manager

Nixa

KGBX-FM
12-01-1989; 105.9 mhz FM *Hrs Open:* 24; 38 kw; 558 ft.; N37 17 41 W93 9 10
1350 One Galleria Tower, 13355 Noel Road, Dallas, TX 75240 US
(417) 890-5555, *Fax:* (417) 823-8504
www.kgbx.com
kgbx@kgbx.com
License: Nixa, Christian County, MO held by Clear Channel Broadcasting Licenses Inc.
Group Owner: Clear Channel Communications Inc.
Arbitron Metro Market: Springfield, MO *Format:* Adult Contemp *Special Programming:* 70's Saturday *Hrs. of News Programming:* news progmg 5 hrs wkly *No. News Employees:* 1 *Target Audience:* 25-54; educated,high income, women
Keith Liesmann, General Manager
Megan Staurt Annis, Station Manager
Kelli Presley, General Sales Mgr
Brian Edwards, Programming Director
Sarah Green, Promotions Manager
Paul Kelly, Programming Director
Traffic Manager, MaryBrown

North Kansas City

KMJK
09-11-1969; 107.3 mhz FM *Hrs Open:* 24; 100 kw; 299 meters; N39 02 15 W93 55 48
5800 Foxridge Dr, Suite 600, Mission, KS 64133
(913) 514-3000, *Fax:* (816) 353-2300
magic@1073.com
License: North Kansas City, Lafayette County, MO held by A R Licensing LLC.
Group Owner: Cumulus Media Partners LLC; (acq 5-3-2006; grpsl)
Population Served: 2,000,000 *Arbitron Metro Market:* Kansas City, MO-KS *Hrs. of News Programming:* news progmg 5 hrs wkly *No. News Employees:* 1 *Target Audience:* 25-54.
Lewis Dickey, CEO
Tim Robisch, General Manager
Page Olson, General Sales Mgr
Jerold Jackson, Programming Director
John Groves, Promotions Manager
Dennis Ebersoll, Chief Engineer

Oran

*KCGR
01-01-2008; 90.5 mhz FM; 2.1 kw; 241 ft.; N36 59 52 W89 38 52
Rebroadcasts: Rebroadcasts KSIV-FM Saint Louis 100%
US
(913) 642-7770, *Fax:* (913) 642-1319
www.bottradionetwork.com
comments@bottradionetwork.com
License: Oran, Scott County, MO held by Community Broadcasting Inc.
Group Owner: Bott Radio Network
Arbitron Metro Market: Oran, MO *Format:* Christian
Michael McHardy, General Manager

Osage Beach

KRMS
12-01-1952; 1150 khz AM *Hrs Open:* 24
P.O.Box 225, Osage Beach, MO 65065 US
(573) 348-2772, *Fax:* (573) 348-2779
www.krmsradio.com
info@krmsradio.com
License: Osage Beach, MO held by Viper Communications Inc.
Group Owner: Viper Communications Broadcast Group; (acq 11-97; $500,000 with co-located FM).
Nat'l Network: CBS *Regional Network:* Missourinet
Arbitron Metro Market: Lake of the Ozarks *Format:* News, News/Talk, 86
Ken Kuenzie, President
Dennis Klautzer, Operations Dir
Paul Hannigan, News Director
Tammy Pitts, Traffic Manager

KMYK
04-12-1964; 93.5 mhz FM; 39 kw; 551 ft.; N38 9 52 W92 36 12
P. O. Box 225, 5715 West Highway 54, Osage Beach, MO 65065 US
(573) 348-2772, *Fax:* (573) 348-2779
www.935rocksthelake.com
info@krmsradio.com
License: Osage Beach, Camden County, MO
Group Owner: Viper Communications Broadcast Group
Arbitron Metro Market: Lake of the Ozarks *Format:* Light Rock
Jim Richards, Operations Dir
Bob Bolinger, General Manager
Jimmy Steele, Programming Director
Kristin Ferguson, Promotions Manager

*KIRL
89.3 mhz FM; 0 kw horiz, 0.3 kw vert; 210 ft.; N38 7 20 W92 40 42
US
(660) 238-1024
License: Osage Beach, Camden County, MO held by Full Smile Inc.
Arbitron Metro Market: Osage Beach, MO
Joey Anderson, Operations Dir

Osceola

*KCVJ

06-29-1990; 100.3 mhz FM *Hrs Open:* 24; 6 kw; 282 ft.; N38 3 43 W93 33 24 *Rebroadcasts:* Rebroadcasts KCVO-FM Camdenton 100%
P.O. Box 800, Camdenton, MO 65020 US
(573) 346-3200, *Fax:* (573) 346-1010
www.spiritfm.org
License: Osceola, St. Clair County, MO held by Lake Area Educational Broadcasting Foundation
Nat'l Network: Salem Radio Network
Arbitron Metro Market: Osceola, MO *Format:* Christian *Hrs. of News Programming:* 1 *Target Audience:* 25-45.
Alice McDermott, CFO
James McDermott, President
Jim McDermott, General Manager
Alice McDermott, Financial Director

Otterville

*KCVK

01-01-2001; 107.7 mhz FM *Hrs Open:* 24; 3.7 kw; 410 ft.; N38 40 26 W92 51 44 *Rebroadcasts:* Rebroadcasts KCVO-FM Camdenton 100%
185 Commerce Center, Greenville, SC 29615 US
(573) 346-3200, *Fax:* (573) 346 1010
www.spiritfm.org
License: Otterville, Cooper County, MO held by Lake Area Educational Broadcasting Foundation
Nat'l Network: Salem Radio Network
Format: Christian *Hrs. of News Programming:* News progmg one hr wkly *Target Audience:* 25-45.
Alice McDermott, CFO
James McDermott, President
James McDermott, Programming Director

Overland

*KRHS

11-07-1977; 90.1 mhz FM; 0.014 kw horiz; 144 ft.; N38 42 38 W90 21 22
2420 Woodson, Overland, MO 63114 US
(314) 429-7111, *Fax:* (314) 429-6725
http://www.edline.net/pages/Ritenour_High_School/News___Media/KRHS_90_1_FM_Radioactiv
License: Overland, St. Louis County, MO held by Ritenour Consolidated School District.
Target Audience: General.
Jane Bannester, General Manager

Owensville

KXMO-FM

01-01-2001; 95.3 mhz FM *Hrs Open:* 24; 37 kw; 564 ft.; N38 8 6 W91 23 59
P.O. Box 4584, Springfield, MO 65808 US
(573) 364-2525, *Fax:* (573) 364-5161
www.resultsradioonline.com
miket.resultsradio@sbcglobal.net
License: Owensville, MO held by KTTR-KZNN Inc.
Arbitron Metro Market: Rolla, MO *Format:* Oldies *Target Audience:* 35-64; male & female
John Mahaffey, Chairman
Robert Mahaffey, President
Steve Gigstad, Operations Dir
Michael Thompson, General Manager/Sales Manager
Kathy Bogart, Office Manager
Becky Johnson, Traffic Manager
Production Department, ProductionDepartment
Tonya Bramel, Account Executive
Anna Poling, Account Executive

Ozark

KOSP

01-01-1995; 92.9 mhz FM *Hrs Open:* 24; 50 kw; Ant 492 ft; N36 58 26 W93 25 37
319 E. Battlefield, Suite B, Springfield, MO 65613
(417) 886-5677, *Fax:* (417) 886-2155
www.basscountry.fm
info@basscountry.fm
License: Ozark, Christian County, MO held by MW Springmo Inc.
Group Owner: The Mid-West Family Broadcast Group; (acq 12-15-99).
Nat'l Network: NBC Radio *Nat'l Reps:* Eastman Radio
Population Served: 295,300 *Arbitron Metro Market:* Springfield, MO *Target Audience:* 30-50. *Adv. Rates:* 30; 33; 33; 15.
Rick McCoy, President
Mary Fleenor, Operations Dir
Malcolm Hukriede, General Sales Mgr
Charlie Mason, Promotions Manager
Jeanne Guittar, Business Manager
Keith Abercrombie, Regional Sales Manager
Nicole Buckner, TrafficManager

Palmyra

KICK-FM

09-01-1981; 97.9 mhz FM *Hrs Open:* 24; 43 kw; 531 ft.; N39 45 26 W91 29 58
P.O. Box 711, 119 North 3rd, Hannibal, MO 63401 US
(217) 223-5292, *Fax:* (573) 221-5331
www.979kickfm.com
Doc.Holliday@townsquaremedia.com;
Ed.Foxall@townsquaremedia.com;
Jeff.Asmussen@townsquaremedia.com
License: Palmyra, Marion County, MO held by Bick Broadcasting Co.
Group Owner: Bick Broadcasting Co.
Nat'l Reps: McGavren Guild
Format: Country *No. News Employees:* 2 *Target Audience:* 25-54; mainstream adults
Ed Foxall, General Manager
Jeff Asmussen, General Sales Mgr
Jeff Dorsey, Programming Director
John Hanvelt, News Director
Gary Glaenzer, Chief Engineer
Jeff Holliday, Program Director

Park Hills

*KBGM

01-01-2001; 91.1 mhz FM; 8 kw; 620 ft.; N37 48 4 W90 33 51
Po Drawer 2440, Tupelo, MS 38803 US
(662) 844-8888, *Fax:* (662) 842-6791
www.afr.net
License: Park Hills, St. Francois County, MO held by American Family Association.
Group Owner: American Family Radio
Arbitron Metro Market: Park Hills, MO *Format:* Christian, Religious
Marvin Sanders, General Manager

KFMO

07-01-1947; 1240 khz AM; 1 kw-U, ND1; N37 51 10 W90 31 13
Mailing Address: P.O. Box 36, Park Hills, MO 63601 US
Second Address: 804 St. Joe Dr., Park Hills, MO 63601
(573) 431-2000, *Fax:* (573) 431-0850
www.kfmo.com
License: Park Hills, MO held by MKS Broadcasting Inc.
Nat'l Network: Westwood One
Arbitron Metro Market: Flat River, MO *Format:* News, News/Talk, 84, Talk *Hrs. of News Programming:* news progmg 150 hrs wkly *Target Audience:* 25-54
M.L. Steinmetz, President
Larry Joseph, Operations Dir
Kelly Valle, General Sales Mgr
Greg Camp, Programming Director
Gib Collins, News Director

Parkville

*KGSP

04-01-1972; 90.5 mhz FM *Hrs Open:* 6 AM-midnight (M-F); 9 AM-midnight; 0.099 kw; 59 ft.; N39 11 24 W94 40 49
Box 2 8700 River Park Dr, Parkville, MO 64152 US
(816) 741-2000, *Fax:* (816) 741-4911
www.kgsp.park.edu
kgsp@park.edu
License: Parkville, Platte County, MO held by Board of Trustees of Park College.
Format: Alternative *Special Programming:* Jazz 14 hrs, gospel 3 hrs, blues 12 hrs wkly *Hrs. of News Programming:* News progmg 6 hrs wkly *Target Audience:* General; college students
Steve Youngblood, General Manager

Perryville

KBDZ

01-30-1990; 93.1 mhz FM *Hrs Open:* 24; 1.6 kw; 623 ft.; N37 38 56 W89 56 21
Mailing Address: P.O. Box 428, Ste. Genevieve, MO 63670 US
Second Address: Box 428, Radio Hill, Ste. Genevieve, MO 63670
(573) 547-8005, *Fax:* (573) 883-2866
www.kbdx931.com
License: Perryville, Perry County, MO held by Donze Communications Inc.
Arbitron Metro Market: Perryville, MO *Format:* Country, News *Special Programming:* Sports 5 hrs, relg 5 hrs, farm 2 hrs wkly *Hrs. of News Programming:* news progmg 5 hrs wkly *No. News Employees:* 3 *TargetAudience:* 25-54.
Elmo Donze, President
Bob Scott, General Sales Mgr
Don Pritchard, News Director
Brian Snider, Reporter

Piedmont

KPWB

05-16-1966; 1140 khz AM; 1 kw-D, NDD; N37 8 29 W90 42 11
204 Washington, Doniphan, MO 63935 US
(573) 223-4218, *Fax:* (573) 223-2351
License: Piedmont, MO held by Southern Star Broadcasting of Missouri LLC.
Group Owner: Southern Star Broadcasting of Missouri LLC; (acq 5-8-2008; grpsl)
Nat'l Network: USA *Regional Network:* Missourinet
Format: Gospel *Target Audience:* 18 plus; Christians *Adv. Rates:* 3.60; 3; 3; na
Wanda Emert, General Manager

KPWB-FM

09-05-1985; 104.9 mhz FM; 3.7 kw; 856 ft.; N37 11 35 W90 39 49
204 East Washington, Doniphan, MO 63935 US
(573) 223-4218, *Fax:* (573) 223-2351
License: Piedmont, Wayne County, MO held by Southern Star Broadcasting of Missouri LLC.
Group Owner: Southern Star Broadcasting of Missouri LLC; (acq 5-8-2008; grpsl)
Nat'l Network: USA
Format: Country *Target Audience:* General. *Adv. Rates:* 7; 7; 7; 7
Wanda Emert, Operations Dir
Fred Dockins, Chief Engineer

Pleasant Hope

KTOZ-FM

05-01-1993; 95.5 mhz FM; 44 kw; 522 ft.; N37 13 25 W93 14 30
1856 South Glenstone, Springfield, MO 65804 US
(417) 890-5555, *Fax:* (417) 890-5050
www.alice955.com
alice955@alice955.com
License: Pleasant Hope, Polk County, MO held by Clear Channel Broadcasting Licenses Inc.
Group Owner: Clear Channel Communications Inc.; (acq 10-10-00; grpsl).
Arbitron Metro Market: Springfield, MO *Format:* Adult Contemp *Target Audience:* 18-34; young adults, 60/40 female/male split
Paul Kelley, Operations Dir
Keith Liesmann, General Manager
Kelli Presley, General Sales Mgr
Sarah Green, Promotions Manager

Point Lookout

*KCOZ

01-01-1995; 91.7 mhz FM; 0.2 kw; 187 ft.; N36 36 39 W93 14 23
College of the Ozarks, Point Lookout, MO 65726 US
(417) 334-6411, *Fax:* (417) 335-2618
www.cofo.edu
info@kcozfm.com
License: Point Lookout, Taney County, MO held by College of the Ozarks.
Nat'l Network: PRI; NPR
Arbitron Metro Market: Point Lookout, MO *Format:* Blues, Jazz, 60, News/Talk, Talk *Special Programming:* Folk 10 hrs, new age 10 hrs wkly *Target Audience:* Older & educated.
Jae Jones, General Manager

*KSMS-FM

02-12-1962; 90.5 mhz FM; 8.5 kw; 771 ft.; N36 33 44 W93 15 35
Rebroadcasts: Rebroadcasts KSMU(FM) Springfield 100%
901 S. National Ave, Springfield, MO 65804 US
(417) 836-5878, *Fax:* (417) 836-5889
www.ksmu.org
ksmu@missouristate
License: Point Lookout, Taney County, MO held by Board of Governors, Southwest Missouri State University
Arbitron Metro Market: Springfield, MO *Format:* Classical, News *Target Audience:* 25-54.
Tammy Wiley, General Manager

Poplar Bluff

KAHR

03-03-1985; 96.7 mhz FM; 6 kw; 328 ft.; N36 45 59 W90 28 52
Hc 1 Box 14, Williamsville, MO 63967 US
(573) 686-3700, *Fax:* (573) 686-1713
www.foxradionetwork.com
info@foxradionetwork.com

License: Poplar Bluff, Butler County, MO held by Eagle Bluff Enterprises
Arbitron Metro Market: Poplar Bluff, MT *Format:* Adult Contemp *Target Audience:* 18-54; listeners living in the middle-class strata
Steven Fuchs, General Manager

KJEZ
08-20-1977; 95.5 mhz FM *Hrs Open:* 24; 100 kw; 410 ft.; N36 50 50 W90 19 52
P.O. Box 1749, Girardeau, MO 63702 US
(573) 785-0881, *Fax:* (573) 785-0646
www.kjez.com
Ajohnr@riverradio.net
License: Poplar Bluff, Butler County, MO held by MRR License LLC.
Group Owner: MAX Media L.L.C.; (acq 6-2-2004; grpsl).
Nat'l Network: Westwood One
Format: Classic Rock *Hrs. of News Programming:* News progmg 10 hrs wkly *Target Audience:* 18-49; general
John Rice, General Manager
Katie Wylie, General Sales Mgr
Randy Bailey, Programming Director
Charlie Lampe, Chief Engineer

KKLR-FM
01-01-1952; 94.5 mhz FM *Hrs Open:* 24; 100 kw; 807 ft.; N36 45 46 W90 26 3
P.O. Box 1749, Cape Girardeau, MO 63701 US
(573) 785-0881, *Fax:* (573) 785-0646
www.clear94.com
clear94@riverradio.net
License: Poplar Bluff, Butler County, MO
Group Owner: MAX Media L.L.C.
Arbitron Metro Market: Jonesboro, AR *Format:* Country *Target Audience:* 18-49.
John Rice, General Manager
John Rice, Station Manager
Galen Stevens, Programming Director

KLID
05-22-1961; 1340 khz AM *Hrs Open:* 24; 1 kw-U, ND1; N36 46 3 W90 22 11
102 N. 11th Street, Poplar Bluff, MO 63901 US
(573) 686-1600, *Fax:* (573) 785-9844
info@klidam.com
License: Poplar Bluff, MO held by Browning Skidmore Broadcasting Inc.
Arbitron Metro Market: Jonesboro, AR *Format:* Oldies, Sports, 86
Special Programming: Relg 2 hrs, Black 2 hrs wkly *Hrs. of News Programming:* News progmg 15 hrs wkly *Target Audience:* 18-54; upper class,professionals *Adv. Rates:* 9; 7; 9; 6
Chris Browning, President
Dolores Skidmore, General Manager
Palmer Johnson, Chief Engineer
Paul White, Disc Jockey
Alverna Skidmore, Paul White
Nick Novak, Sports Commentator

***KLUH**
10-08-1988; 90.3 mhz FM *Hrs Open:* Monday- Friday 9-5pm; 25 kw; 253 ft.; N36 43 8 W90 23 48
Kluh Radio Lone Star Rd, Route 8 Box 14, Poplar Bluff, MO 63901 US
(573) 686-1663, *Fax:* (573) 686-7703
www.dcmliferadio.org
info@dcmliferadio.org
License: Poplar Bluff, Butler County, MO held by David Craig Ministries
Format: Religious *Target Audience:* General.
David Craig, General Manager
Harriet Craig, General Sales Mgr
John Moore, Programming Director

***KOKS**
10-02-1988; 89.5 mhz FM *Hrs Open:* 24; 100 kw; 423 ft; N36 48 40 W90 27 50
2773 Barron Road, Poplar Bluff, MO 63901
(573) 686-5080, *Fax:* (573) 686-5544
koksradio@mycitycable.com
License: Poplar Bluff, Butler County, MO held by Calvary Educational Broadcasting Network
Population Served: 1,000,000*Hrs. of News Programming:* News progmg 14 hrs wkly *Target Audience:* General.
Nina Stewart, Station Manager
Charley Lampe, Chief Engineer
Ben Stewart, Music Director

KWOC
05-10-1938; 930 khz AM *Hrs Open:* 24; 5 kw-D, DAN; 0.5 kw-N, DAN; N36 43 15 W90 22 4
P.O. Box 1749, Cape Girardeau, MO 63701 US
(573) 785-0881, *Fax:* (573) 785-0646
www.kwoc.com
clear94@riverradio.net
License: Poplar Bluff, MO held by MRR License LLC.
Group Owner: MAX Media L.L.C.; (acq 6-2-2004; grpsl).
Regional Network: Missourinet; Brownfield
Arbitron Metro Market: Poplar Bluff, MO *Format:* News, News/Talk, 86 *Hrs. of News Programming:* news progmg 5 hrs wkly *No. News Employees:* 2 *Target Audience:* 25-54; adults with middle to upper income
Rick Sinclair, Operations Dir
Roger Hager, General Manager
Katie Wylie, General Sales Mgr
Rick Carl, Programming Director
Bill Steiger, News Director
Charlie Lampe, Chief Engineer
Pam Gray, Traffic Manager
Rick Carl PublicService Director

KLUE
01-01-1995; 103.5 mhz FM *Hrs Open:* 24; 50 kw; 325 ft.; N36 50 50 W90 19 52
P.O. Box 558, Metropolis, IL 62960 US
(618) 564-9836, *Fax:* (618) 564-3202
klue1035.bizland.com/
jhborders@yahoo.com
License: Poplar Bluff, Butler County, MO held by Benjamin Stratemeyer
Arbitron Metro Market: Poplar Bluff, MO *Format:* Variety/Diverse
Willie Kerns, Operations Dir
Samuel Stratemeyer, General Manager

KPPL
01-01-2003; 92.5 mhz FM; 25 kw; 328 ft.; N36 50 59 W90 22 20
Route #2, Box 496, Portageville, MO 63873 US
(573) 686-3700, *Fax:* (573) 686-1713
info@foxradionetwork.com
License: Poplar Bluff, Butler County, MO held by George S. Flinn Jr.
Arbitron Metro Market: Poplar Bluff, MO *Format:* Country
Steven Fuchs, General Manager
Shelly Fuchs, Programming Director
Palmer Johnson, Chief Engineer

***KPBR**
03-15-2006; 91.7 mhz FM *Hrs Open:* 24; 1.9 kw; 249 ft.; N36 49 2.7 W90 27 20.2
US
(406) 248-7777
www.1059thebar.com
License: Poplar Bluff, Carbon County, MO held by Connoisseur Media LLC.
Group Owner: Connoisseur Media LLC
Arbitron Metro Market: Poplar Bluff, MO *Format:* Country
Cam Maxwell, General Manager
Willy Tyler, Programming Director

Portageville

KMIS
09-01-1960; 1050 khz AM *Hrs Open:* 24; 0.6 kw-D, NDD; N36 25 31 W89 41 29
Mailing Address: 1600 Southtrust Tower, Birmingham, AL 35203 US
Second Address: 1303 Southwest Dr., Kennett, MO 63857 , *Fax:* (573) 888-4890
ktme@il.net
License: Portageville, MO held by Pollack Broadcasting Co.
Group Owner: Pollack Broadcasting Co.; (acq 5-7-2001; with KTMO(FM) New Madrid).
Regional Network: Missourinet
Format: News, Sports *Special Programming:* Relg gospel 5 hrs wkly *No. News Employees:* 1 *Target Audience:* General.
Bill Pollack, President
Monte Lyons, Operations Dir
Perry Jones, General Manager
Charles Isabell, News Director
P.J. Johnson, Chief Engineer

Potosi

KHZR
04-17-1997; 97.7 mhz FM *Hrs Open:* 24; 26.5 kw; 679 ft.; N37 57 31 W90 45 47
1800 State Hwy. 47, Bonne Terre, MO 63628 US
(314) 909-8569, *Fax:* (314) 835-9739
www.joyfmonline.org
info@joyfmonline.org
License: Potosi, Washington County, MO held by Four Him Enterprises L.L.C.
Format: Christian *Target Audience:* Christian Adults
Sandi Brown, General Manager
Brenda Pacini, Office Assistant

***KNLP**
04-01-1998; 89.7 mhz FM; 2.3 kw; 262 ft.; N37 55 42 W90 46 2
1411 Locust Street, St. Louis, MO 63103 US
(314) 436-2424, *Fax:* (314) 436-2434
www.hereshelpnet.org
larryr@hereshelpnet.org
License: Potosi, Washington County, MO held by New Life Evangelistic Center Inc.
Format: Adult Contemp, Gospel, 86
Larry Rice, General Manager

Ravenwood

***KEXS-FM**
01-01-2008; 106.1 mhz FM; 50 kw; 423 ft.; N40 25 15 W94 43 20 US
(816) 630-1090
www.thecatholicradionetwork.com
catholicradionetwork@gmail.com
License: Ravenwood, Nodaway County, MO held by Catholic Radio Network Inc.
Group Owner: Catholic Radio Network Inc.
Arbitron Metro Market: Excelsior Springs, MO *Format:* Religious
James O'Laughlin, General Manager

Republic

KADI-FM
06-18-1990; 99.5 mhz FM *Hrs Open:* 24; 6 kw; 328 ft.; N37 9 54 W93 23 44
1601 W Sunshine Rd # P, Springfield, MO 65807 US
(417) 831-0995, *Fax:* (417) 831-4026
www.99hitfm.com
info@99hitfm.com
License: Republic, Greene County, MO held by Vision Communications Inc.
Arbitron Metro Market: Brookline Station, MT *Format:* Adult Contemp, Christian *Hrs. of News Programming:* News progmg 8 hrs wkly *Target Audience:* General; adults in their mid 30s
R.C. Amer, General Manager
Mark Hill, General Sales Mgr
Rod Kettleman, Programming Director

Richmond

KAYX
08-01-1990; 92.5 mhz FM; 2.35 kw; 535 ft.; N39 11 14 W93 50 3
Rebroadcasts: Rebroadcasts KCCV(AM) Overland Park, KS 85%
10550 Barkley, Overland Park, KS 66212 US
(816) 470-9925, *Fax:* (816) 470-8925
www.bottradionetwork.com
kayx@bottradionetwork.com
License: Richmond, Ray County, MO held by Bott Communications, Inc.
Group Owner: Bott Radio Network; (acq 1996)
Nat'l Network: USA
Arbitron Metro Market: KS City, MO *Format:* Christian, Talk
Richard Bott Sr., President
Richard Bott II, Operations Dir
Pat Rulon, General Sales Mgr
Candy Green, Programming Director
Rachel Launius, Promotions Manager
Jason Potocnik, News Director

Rolla

KDAA
11-20-1964; 103.1 mhz FM *Hrs Open:* 24; 2.05 kw; 571 ft.; N37 52 39 W91 44 45
901 Pine Street, Rolla, MO 65401 US
(573) 364-2525, *Fax:* (573) 364-5161
www.resultsradioonline.com
License: Rolla, Phelps County, MO held by KDAA-KMOZ LLC.
Group Owner: Mahaffey Enterprises Inc.; (acq 9-28-2001; $418,000 assumption of debt for 50% with co-located AM).
Arbitron Metro Market: Rolla, MO *Format:* Contemporary Hits/Top 40, Adult Contemp *Target Audience:* 18-44.
Steve Gigstad, Operations Dir
Michael Thompson, General Manager
Steve Ryan, Programming Director
Tracy Weber, News Director
Kathy Bogart, Office Manager
Becky Johnson, Traffic Manager

***KMNR**
01-01-1974; 89.7 mhz FM; 0.45 kw; 325 ft.; N37 57 7 W91 46 12
Univ. of Mo.-Rolla, University Ctr West, Rolla, MO 65409 US

(573) 341-4272
//kmnr.org
kmnr@mst.edu
License: Rolla, Phelps County, MO held by Curators of the University of Missouri.
Group Owner: The Curators of the University of Missouri
Nat'l Network: AP Radio
Format: Variety/Diverse *Target Audience:* 18-25; college community
Patrick Turley, General Manager

KMOZ
08-19-1960; 1590 khz AM; 1 kw-D, 88 w-N; N37 56 41 W91 48 40
1701 N. Bishop, Suite 15, Rolla, MO 65401
(573) 647-6285, *Fax:* (573) 426-4450
www.bottradionetwork.com
comments@bottradionetwork.com
License: Rolla, Phelps County, MO held by Community Broadcasting Inc.
Group Owner: Bott Radio Network; (acq 5-5-2006; $40,000).
Nat'l Network: USA
Target Audience: 50 plus; mature adults
Richard Bott II, Operations Dir
Eben Fowler, General Manager
Pat Rulon, General Sales Mgr
Candy Green, Programming Director
John Dale r, Promotions Manager
Jason Potocnik, News Director
Tom Holdeman, CFO
Bob Moore, Engineer

KTTR
09-30-1947; 1490 khz AM *Hrs Open:* 24; 1 kw-U, ND1; N37 56 42 W91 44 46
Mailing Address: Box 4584, Springfield, MO 65808 US
Second Address: 1505 Soest Rd., Rolla, MO 65401
(573) 364-2525, *Fax:* (573) 364-5161
License: Rolla, MO held by KTTR-KZNN Inc.
Group Owner: Mahaffey Enterprises Inc.; (acq 6-1-84; with co-located FM;
Regional Network: Missourinet
Arbitron Metro Market: Columbia, MO *Format:* News, News/Talk, 84, Talk *No. News Employees:* 1 *Target Audience:* General. *Adv. Rates:* 39; 31; 37; 28
John Mahaffey, Chairman
Robert Mahaffey, President
Mike Thompson, General Manager
Steve Gidstad, Programming Director
Lee Buhr, News Director
Bob Moore, Chief Engineer

***KMST**
01-01-1964; 88.5 mhz FM *Hrs Open:* 24; 100 kw; 479 ft.; N37 47 56 W91 43 28
Univ. of Mo.- Rolla, Library Building Roomg-6, Rolla, MO 65409 US
(573) 341-4386, *Fax:* (573) 341-4889
www.kmst.org
kmst@mst.edu
License: Rolla, Phelps County, MO held by The Curators of the University of Missouri.
Group Owner: The Curators of the University of Missouri
Nat'l Network: NPR; PRI *Wire Services:* AP
Arbitron Metro Market: Rolla, MO *TV Affiliate:* *KOMU-TV affil.
Format: News, Variety/Diverse *Special Programming:* Bluegrass 5 hrs, jazz 3 hrs, folk 5 hrs wkly *Hrs. of News Programming:* News progmg 35 hrs wkly*Target Audience:* General.
Wayne Bledsoe, General Manager
John Francis, Programming Director
Tricia Crout, Promotions Manager
Charles Knapp, Chief Engineer
Joel Goodridge, Marketing Manager
Norm Movitz, Producer
Jim Graham, Underwriting Coordinator
SandyCrouch, Administrative Assistant
Katie Lacewell, Secretary

KZNN
02-12-1973; 105.3 mhz FM; 100 kw; 630 ft.; N37 52 39 W91 44 45
Mailing Address: Box 4584, Springfield, MO 65808 US
Second Address: 1505 Soest Rd., Rolla, MO 65401
(573) 364-2525, *Fax:* (573) 364-5161
www.resultsradioonline.com
License: Rolla, Phelps County, MO
Group Owner: Mahaffey Enterprises Inc.
Nat'l Network: ABC *Regional Network:* Brownfield
Arbitron Metro Market: Rolla, MO *Format:* Country
Wayne Jarvis, General Manager

Saint Joseph

KSFT(AM)
06-01-1946; 1550 khz AM *Hrs Open:* 24; 5 kw-U, DA-N; N39 42 23 W94 44 36
Mailing Address: Box 8550, Saint Joseph, MO 64508
Second Address: 4104 Country Ln., Saint Joseph, MO 64506
(816) 233-8881, *Fax:* (816) 279-8280
www.stjoeradio.com
License: Saint Joseph, Buchanan County, MO held by Eagle Communications Inc.
Group Owner: Eagle Communications Group; (acq 3-1-99; $4 million with co-located FM).
Population Served: 150,000 *Arbitron Metro Market:* Saint Jose, MO *Format:* Oldies *Hrs. of News Programming:* News progmg 5 hrs wkly *Target Audience:* 45-64. *Adv. Rates:* 15; 14; 15; 11
Gary Shorman, CEO
Kevin Wagner, Operations Dir
Gary Exline, General Manager
Teresa Hetz, Promotions Manager
Barry Birr, News Director
Ed Jurich, Engineering Dir
Mark Vail, COO
Georgia Roades, Traffic Manager

***KSJI**
91.1 mhz FM; 50 kw; Ant 492 ft; N39 40 51 W94 46 47
2414 S. Leonard Rd., Saint Joseph, MO 64503
(816) 233-2577, *Fax:* (816) 233-2374
License: Saint Joseph, Buchanan County, MO held by Good News Ministries Inc.
Chris Meikel, General Manager
Chris Meikel, General Sales Mgr
James Schumaker, Programming Director
Jeff Landers, Engineering Dir
Jeff Landers, Chief Engineer

Saint Louis

***KDHX**
10-14-1987; 88.1 mhz FM *Hrs Open:* 24; 42 kw; 738 ft.; N38 25 1 W90 25 59
3504 Magnolia, St Louis, MO 63113 US
(314) 664-3955, *Fax:* (314) 664-1020
www.kdhx.org
ljweir@kdhx.org
License: Saint Louis, St. Louis County, MO held by Double Helix Corp.
Nat'l Network: PRI
Arbitron Metro Market: St. Louis, MO *Format:* Variety/Diverse *Target Audience:* General.
Paul Dever, President
Larry Weir, Operations Dir
Tim Yeaglin, Treasurer
Matthew Potter, Secretary

KXFN
01-01-1927; 1380 khz AM *Hrs Open:* 24; 5 kw-D, 1 kw-N, DA-3; N38 31 27 W90 14 17
22 Morgan St, Saint Louis, MO 63108
(314) 969-1380,(314) 436-3283, *Fax:* (314) 367-8647
www.1380espn.com
License: Saint Louis, St. Louis County, MO held by Simmons Austin, LS LLC.
Group Owner: Simmons Media Group; (acq 7-29-2004; $2.05 million)
Nat'l Network: ESPN Radio
Population Served: 504,000 *Arbitron Metro Market:* St. Louis, MO *Hrs. of News Programming:* News progmg 168 hrs wkly *Target Audience:* 25-54; men and women *Adv. Rates:* 45; 30; 45; 25
John Helmkamp, General Manager
Mike Brownsher, Programming Director

Salem

KKID
01-01-1971; 92.9 mhz FM *Hrs Open:* 6 AM-midnight; 21 kw; 361 ft.; N37 43 45 W91 28 23
P.O. Box 650, Salem, MO 65560 US
(573) 364-4433, *Fax:* (573) 364-8385
www.kkid929fm
929fm@kkid929fm.com
License: Salem, Dent County, MO held by Ultra-Sonic Broadcast Stations Inc.
Nat'l Network: USA
Arbitron Metro Market: Columbia, MO *Format:* Country *Hrs. of News Programming:* news progmg 20 hrs wkly *No. News Employees:* 1 *Target Audience:* 30-49.
David Wheeler, President
Steve Wheeler, General Sales Mgr
Al Martia, Programming Director

KSMO
11-01-1953; 1340 khz AM *Hrs Open:* 24; 1 kw-U, ND1; N37 37 36 W91 32 9
800 South Main, P.O. Box 229, Salem, MO 65560 US
(573) 729-6117, *Fax:* (573) 729-7337
www.ksmoradio.com
ksl340@fidnet.com
License: Salem, MO held by KSMO Enterprises.
Nat'l Network: AP Network News *Regional Network:* Missourinet; Brownfield *Nat'l Reps:* Commercial Media Sales *Wire Services:* The Sports Network; AP
Arbitron Metro Market: Salem. MO *Format:* Country, News, 62, Sports, Talk *Special Programming:* Farm 18 hrs wkly *Hrs. of News Programming:* news progmg 40 hrs wkly *No. News Employees:* 1 *Target Audience:* General; middle class *Adv. Rates:* 16; 13; 15; 10
Stanley Podorski, President
Stan Podorski, General Manager
Melba Hendrick, General Sales Mgr
Stan Stevens, News Director

***KCVX**
02-01-2004; 91.7 mhz FM *Hrs Open:* 24; 40 kw; 210 ft.; N37 36 16 W91 32 46 *Rebroadcasts:* Rebroadcasts KCVO(FM) Campenton 100%
Hc 82 Box 118, Salem, MO 65560 US
(573) 346-3200, *Fax:* (573) 346-1010
www.spiritfm.org
License: Salem, Dent County, MO held by Lake Area Educational Broadcasting Foundation
Nat'l Network: Salem Radio Network
Arbitron Metro Market: Camdenton, MO *Format:* Christian *Hrs. of News Programming:* News progmg one hr wkly *Target Audience:* 25-45; primarily females, married with children
Alice McDermott, CFO
James McDermott, President

Sarcoxie

***KCKJ**
89.5 mhz FM; 31 kw; Ant 328 ft; N37 04 34 W93 55 27
4899 E. 7th St., Joplin, MO
(417) 782-2141, *Fax:* (417) 782-9141
License: Sarcoxie, Jasper County, MO held by Calvary Chapel of Joplin.
Jeffery Kingery, President

Savannah

KSJQ
09-01-1991; 92.7 mhz FM *Hrs Open:* 24; 50 kw; 492 ft.; N39 58 34 W94 58 37
Mailing Address: P.O. Box 817, 2703 Hall Street, Hays, KS 67601 US
Second Address: 4104 Country Ln., St. Joseph, MO 64506
(816) 233-8881, *Fax:* (816) 279-8280
www.stjoeradio.com
License: Savannah, Andrew County, MO held by Eagle Communications Inc.
Group Owner: Eagle Communications Group; (acq 1993; $450,000;
Nat'l Reps: Katz Radio *Wire Services:* AP
Arbitron Metro Market: St. Joseph, MO *Format:* Country *Hrs. of News Programming:* news progmg 3 hrs wkly *No. News Employees:* 2 *Adv. Rates:* 29; 24; 26; 20
Gary Shorman, CEO
Gary Exline, Operations Dir
Brent Harmon, Programming Director
Teresa Hetz, Promotions Manager
Barry Birr, News Director
Mark Vail, COO
Kevin Wagner, Operations Director
Shannon Diggs, Traffic Manager

Scott City

KGKS
01-01-1998; 93.9 mhz FM; 16.5 kw; 407 ft.; N37 21 34 W89 37 16
P.O. Box 1749, Cape Girardeau, MO 63702 US
(573) 335-8291, *Fax:* (573) 335-4806
www.kiss939.com
kiss@riverradio.net
License: Scott City, Scott County, MO held by MRR License LLC.
Group Owner: MAX Media L.L.C.; (acq 6-2-2004; grpsl).
Format: Adult Contemp
Christy Benton, General Manager
Meg Davis, General Sales Mgr
Whitney Thomas, Programming Director
Nicole Arnzen, Promotions Manager
Mike Cossey, Chief Engineer

Sedalia

KDRO
09-13-1939; 1490 khz AM *Hrs Open:* 24; 0.78 kw-U, ND1; N38 40 35 W93 15 18
301 S. Ohio St., Sedalia, MO 65301 US
(660) 826-5005, *Fax:* (660) 826-5557
www.kdro.com
1490@kdro.com
License: Sedalia, MO held by Mathewson Broadcasting Co.
Nat'l Network: CBS *Regional Network:* Brownfield; Missourinet
Arbitron Metro Market: Sedalia, MO *Format:* Country *Special Programming:* Farm 6 hrs, Black one hr, relg 3 hrs wkly *Hrs. of News Programming:* news progmg 11 hrs wkly *No. News Employees:* 2 *Target Audience:* General. *Adv. Rates:* 19.55; 16.24; 19.55; 9.83
Stu Steinmetz, General Manager
Stu Steinmetz, Station Manager
Tom Upton, Programming Director
Jeff Spalding, News Director
Susan Daniels, Traffic Manager

KSDL
05-11-1964; 92.3 mhz FM *Hrs Open:* 24; 6 kw; 292 ft.; N38 44 3 W93 13 31
119 North 3rd, Box 711, Hannibal, MO 63401 US
(660) 826-1050, *Fax:* (660) 827-5072
www.ksdl.com
radio92@ksdl.com
License: Sedalia, Pettis County, MO
Group Owner: Bick Broadcasting Co.
Wire Services: U.S. Weather Service
Arbitron Metro Market: Sedalia, MO *Format:* Adult Contemp *No. News Employees:* 2 *Target Audience:* 12-40; women
Peggy Gordon-Miller, President
Jay Buchholz, General Manager

KSIS
02-18-1954; 1050 khz AM *Hrs Open:* 24
119 North 3rd, Box 711, Hannibal, MO 63401 US
(660) 826-1050, *Fax:* (660) 827-5072
www.ksisradio.com
ksis@bickbroadcasting.com
License: Sedalia, MO held by Bick Broadcasting Co.
Group Owner: Bick Broadcasting Co.; (acq 1-1-87)
Wire Services: U.S. Weather Service
Arbitron Metro Market: Sedalia, MO *Format:* News, News/Talk, 86 *No. News Employees:* 2 *Target Audience:* 25-54.
Dennis Polk, General Manager
Dennis Polk, General Sales Mgr

Seligman

KIGL
08-01-1986; 93.3 mhz FM *Hrs Open:* 24; 100 kw; 492 ft.; N36 28 3 W94 10 25
Mailing Address: 600 Congress Ave., Suite 1400, Austin, TX 78701 US
Second Address: 2049 E Joyce Blvd, Suite, Fayetteville, AR 72703
(479) 973-9339, *Fax:* (479) 582-5302
www.933theeagle.com,magic1079.com
License: Seligman, Barry County, MO held by Capstar TX L.P.
Group Owner: Clear Channel Communications Inc.; (acq 8-30-00; grpsl).
Nat'l Network: USA
Arbitron Metro Market: Fayetteville (Northwest Arkansas), AR *Format:* Classic Rock *Hrs. of News Programming:* news progmg 7 hrs wkly *No. News Employees:* 1 *Target Audience:* 35 plus; mature, upscale professionals*Adv. Rates:* 55; 50; 50; 25
Tony Beringer, General Manager
Dave Ashcroft, Programming Director
Jess Smith, News Director

Shelbina

*KKWW
03-16-2012; 89.1 mhz FM; 12.5 kw; 325 ft; N39 40 21 W91 58 34
1411 Locust Street, St. Louis, MO
License: Shelbina, Shelby County, MO
Group Owner: New Life Evangelistic Center Inc.
Lawrence W. Rice Jr, Chairman

Shell Knob

KQMO
07-16-1999; 97.7 mhz FM *Hrs Open:* 24; 2.1 kw; 558 ft.; N36 44 55 W93 39 32
P.O. Box 648, Aurora, MO 65605 US
(417) 235-6041, *Fax:* (417) 235-6388
www.kqmo977.com
kqmo@radiotalon.com
License: Shell Knob, Barry County, MO held by Falcon Broadcasting Inc.
Format: News *Hrs. of News Programming:* news progmg 21 hrs wkly *No. News Employees:* 1 *Target Audience:* Mexican-Hispanic.
Dewayne Gandy, General Manager

Sikeston

KBXB
09-12-1968; 97.9 mhz FM *Hrs Open:* 24; 50 kw; 469 ft.; N36 59 52 W89 38 52
P.O. Box 1508, Mount Vernon, IL 62864 US
(573) 471-2000, *Fax:* (573) 471-8525
www.b979.net
cjcruze@withersradio.net
License: Sikeston, Scott County, MO
Group Owner: Withers Broadcasting Co.
Nat'l Reps: Katz Radio
Arbitron Metro Market: Sikeston, MO *Format:* Country *Target Audience:* 18-49.
Hugh Robinson, General Sales Mgr

KRHW
03-17-1966; 1520 khz AM
P.O. Box 1508, Mount Vernon, IL 62864 US
(573) 471-2000, *Fax:* (573) 471-8525
License: Sikeston, MO held by Withers Broadcasting Co. of Southeast Missouri LLC.
Group Owner: Withers Broadcasting Co.; (acq 4-96; with co-located FM).
Arbitron Metro Market: MO Bootheel *Format:* Country *Special Programming:* Farm 6 hrs wkly *Target Audience:* 45 plus.
Rick Lambert, General Manager
Joe Bill Davis, General Sales Mgr
Kidd Manning, Programming Director
John Steeke, News Director
Smokey King, Chief Engineer

KSIM
07-17-1948; 1400 khz AM; 1 kw-U, ND1; N36 52 12 W89 36 32
P.O. Box 1749, Cape Girardeau, MO 63702 US
(573) 335-8291, *Fax:* (573) 335-4806
www.1400ksim.com
Ksim@riverradio.net
License: Sikeston, MO held by MRR License LLC.
Group Owner: MAX Media L.L.C.; (acq 6-2-2004; grpsl)
Nat'l Reps: Christal
Arbitron Metro Market: Cape Girardeau, MO *Format:* News, News/Talk, 86 *Special Programming:* Loc sports, news, Paul Harvey, various features *No. News Employees:* 4 *Target Audience:* 25-54.
Whitney Thomas, Operations Dir
Steve Stephenson, General Manager
Meg Davis, General Sales Mgr
Faune Riggin, Programming Director
Faune Riggin, News Director

Sparta

KSPW
03-01-1989; 96.5 mhz FM *Hrs Open:* 24; 50 kw; 492 ft.; N36 57 16 W93 17 22
Mailing Address: 3355 S. Valley View Boulevard, Las Vegas, NV 89102 US
Second Address: 2330 W. Grand St., Springfield, MO 65802
(417) 865-6614, *Fax:* (417) 865-9643
www.power965.com
License: Sparta, Christian County, MO held by Journal Broadcast Corp.
Group Owner: Journal Communications Inc.; (acq 6-11-99; grpsl)
Nat'l Reps: Christal
Arbitron Metro Market: Springfield, MO *Format:* Contemporary Hits/Top 40 *No. News Employees:* 6 *Target Audience:* 18-34; young active adults *Adv. Rates:* 20; 25; 30; 20
Steven Smith, CEO
Doug Kiel, President
Valorie Knight, Operations Dir
Rex Hansen, General Manager
Janelle Carter, General Sales Mgr
Simon Nytes, Programming Director
Carl Gardner, Executive Vice President

Springfield

*KSCV
04-03-2001; 90.1 mhz FM *Hrs Open:* 24; 9 kw; 492 ft.; N37 17 41 W93 9 10 *Rebroadcasts:* Rebroadcasts KCCV(FM) Overland Park, KS 90%
P.O. Drawer 2440, Tupelo, MS 38803 US
(417) 864-0901, *Fax:* (417) 862-7263
bottradionetwork.com
kscv@bottradionetwork.com
License: Springfield, Greene County, MO held by Community Broadcasting Inc.
Group Owner: Bott Radio Network; (acq 2-7-01; 1.25 million with KMCV(FM) High Point).
Nat'l Network: USA
Arbitron Metro Market: Springfield, MO *Format:* Christian, Talk *Hrs. of News Programming:* News progmg 4 hrs wkly *Target Audience:* 25-54 plus; women 60%, men 40% *Adv. Rates:* 19; 17; 18; 10
Paul Schneider, Operations Dir
Monna Stafford, General Sales Mgr

KGMY
10-31-1926; 1400 khz AM; 1 kw-U, ND1; N37 11 46 W93 19 21
1350 One Galleria Tower, 13355 Noel Road, Dallas, TX 75240 US
(417) 890-5555, *Fax:* (417) 890-5050
www.espn1400.com
studio@espn1400.com
License: Springfield, MO held by Clear Channel Broadcasting Licenses Inc.
Group Owner: Clear Channel Communications Inc.; (acq 10-10-2000; grpsl)
Arbitron Metro Market: Springfield, MO *Format:* Sports *Target Audience:* 35 plus; affluent, educated white-collar skewing 35 plus year olds
Paul Kelley, Operations Dir
Paul Windisch, General Manager
Eldon Combs, General Sales Mgr
Sarah Green, Promotions Manager
Mary Brown, News Director
Shawn Baker, Chief Engineer
Kelli Presley, National Sales Manager

KADI
07-29-1949; 1340 khz AM
Attn: Kent Emmons, 166 Eagle Pointe Drive, Branson, MO 65616 US
(417) 831-0995, *Fax:* (417) 831-4026
www.1039bigtalker.com
License: Springfield, MO held by Vision Communications Inc.
Arbitron Metro Market: Springfield, MO *Format:* Talk *Special Programming:* Shopping 6 hrs wkly, local business 2 hr wkly *Hrs. of News Programming:* news progmg 120 hrs wkly
R.C. Amer, General Manager
Mark Hill, General Sales Mgr
Jason Worth, Programming Director

KLFJ
11-01-1974; 1550 khz AM *Hrs Open:* 24; 5 kw-D, ND1; 0.028 kw-N, ND1; N37 11 45 W93 19 7
430-C Highway 165 South, Branson, MO 65616 US
(417) 831-1550
sobrien@kgrandcrowneresorts.com
License: Springfield, MO held by 127 Inc.
Arbitron Metro Market: Springfield, MO *Format:* News *Adv. Rates:* 20; 18; 15; 8
Kent Emmons, General Manager
Shelly O'Brien, Station Manager
Patricia Pugh, Promotions Manager

*KSMU
05-07-1974; 91.1 mhz FM *Hrs Open:* 24; 40 kw; 410 ft.; N37 10 14 W93 19 25
901 South National, Springfield, MO 65804 US
(417) 836-5878, *Fax:* (417) 836-5889
www.ksmu.org
ksmu@missouristate
License: Springfield, Greene County, MO held by Board of Governors, Southwest Missouri State University
Nat'l Network: NPR
Arbitron Metro Market: Springfield, MO *Format:* Classical, News *Special Programming:* Jazz 10 hrs wkly *Hrs. of News Programming:* news progmg 54 hrs wkly *No. News Employees:* 1 *Target Audience:* 25-54.
Tammy Wiley, General Manager

KBFL
01-01-1972; 1060 khz AM *Hrs Open:* 6 AM-sunset + 2 hrs
610 W. College, Springfield, MO 65806 US
(417) 862-3751, *Fax:* (417) 869-7675
www.ktozam.com
ktozam@pcis.net
License: Springfield, MO held by Meyer-Baldridge Inc.
Group Owner: Meyer Communications Inc.; (acq 2-27-2006; $275,000)
Arbitron Metro Market: Springfield, MO *Format:* Adult Contemp, Big Band, 64 *Special Programming:* Jazz 12 hrs, blues 4 hrs,

RADIO - U.S.

50s mus 4 hrs wkly *Target Audience:* General. *Adv. Rates:* 21.00; 21.00; 21.00; 21.00
Kenneth Meyer, President
Bonnie Bell, General Sales Mgr
Jamie Turner, Programming Director
R.J. McAlister, News Director

KSGF
01-01-1926; 1260 khz AM *Hrs Open:* 24; 5 kw-D, DAN; 5 kw-N, DAN; N37 15 51 W93 19 4 *Rebroadcasts:* Rebroadcast KSGF-FM Ash Grove
Mailing Address: 3355 S. Valley View Boulevard, Las Vegas, NV 89102 US
Second Address: 2330 W. Grand, Springfield, MO 65802
(417) 865-6614, *Fax:* (417) 865-9643
www.ksgf.com
nreed@jrn.com
License: Springfield, MO held by Journal Broadcast Corp.
Group Owner: Journal Communications Inc.; (acq 6-11-99; grpsl).
Regional Network: Missourinet *Nat'l Reps:* Christal
Arbitron Metro Market: Springfield, MO *Format:* News, News/Talk, 86 *Hrs. of News Programming:* news progmg 30 hrs wkly *No. News Employees:* 4 *Target Audience:* 35-54. *Adv. Rates:* 25; 30; 35; 10
Steven Smith, CEO
Doug Kiel, President
Rex Hansen, Operations Dir
Nick Reed, Programming Director
Kris Addison, Promotions Manager
Carl Gardner, Executive Vice President
Karen Campbell, National Sales Manager
Chris Cannon,Operations Manager
Kortni Tucker, Assist. Program Director/ Producer for KSGF Mornin
Jason Rima, Traffic for KSGF Mornings
Keith Marion, Producer for KSGF Weekends

KTTS-FM
08-01-1948; 94.7 mhz FM *Hrs Open:* 24; 98 kw; 1102 ft.; N37 10 30 W93 2 35
3355 S. Valley View Boulevard, Las Vegas, NV 89102 US
(417) 865-6614, *Fax:* (417) 865-9643
www.ktts.com
news@ktts.com
License: Springfield, Greene County, MO held by Journal Broadcast Corp.
Group Owner: Journal Communications Inc.
Nat'l Reps: Christal
Arbitron Metro Market: Springfield, MO *Format:* Country *Hrs. of News Programming:* news progmg 5 hrs wkly *No. News Employees:* 4 *Target Audience:* 25-54; adults *Adv. Rates:* 140; 130; 120; 30
Rex Hansen, General Manager
Chris Michaels, Programming Director

KTXR
06-12-1962; 101.3 mhz FM *Hrs Open:* 24; 97.8 kw; 1489 ft.; N37 11 41 W92 56 7
Mailing Address: 3000 E.Chestnut Expreswy, Springfield, MO 65802 US
Second Address: Box 3925, Springfield, MO 65802
(417) 862-3751, *Fax:* (417) 869-7675
www.radiospringfield.com
manager@radiospringfield.com
License: Springfield, Greene County, MO held by Stereo Broadcasting Inc.
Group Owner: Meyer Communications Inc.
Arbitron Metro Market: Springfield, MO *Format:* Easy Listening *Special Programming:* MSU Bears sports, St. Louis Cardinals baseball *Hrs. of News Programming:* 21 *No. News Employees:* 2 *Target Audience:* 35plus; female
Kenneth E. Meyer, President
Bonnie Bell, General Sales Mgr
Jamie Turner, Programming Director
Pat Willis, News Director
Dale Blankenship, Chief Engineer

***KWFC**
04-17-1985; 89.1 mhz FM *Hrs Open:* 24; 98 kw; 1122 ft.; N37 12 6 W92 56 33
Mailing Address: P.O. Box 8900, Springfield, MO 65801 US
Second Address: 2316 N. Benton, Springfield, MO 65801
(417) 869-0891, *Fax:* (417) 866-7525
www.kwfc.org
info@kwfc.org
License: Springfield, Greene County, MO held by Baptist Bible College Inc.
Nat'l Network: USA *Wire Services:* AP
Arbitron Metro Market: Springfield, MO *Format:* Christian, Religious *Hrs. of News Programming:* news progmg 17 hrs wkly *No. News Employees:* 1 *Target Audience:* General; conservative, church-oriented *Adv.Rates:* 216; 216; 216; 216;
Gary Longstaff, General Manager
Kyle Dowden, Programming Director
Brady Shoemaker, News Director
Vickie Hawkins, Traffic Manager

***KWND**
07-12-1993; 88.3 mhz FM *Hrs Open:* 24; 35 kw horiz, 34.9 kw vert; 633 ft.; N37 10 30 W93 2 35
5015 South Florida Ave, Suite 104, Lakeland, FL 33813 US
(417) 889-0883, *Fax:* (417) 886-8656
www.88.3thewind.com
883@883thewind.com
License: Springfield, Greene County, MO held by The Radio Training Network.
Arbitron Metro Market: Springfield, MO *Format:* Adult Contemp, Christian *Special Programming:* Gospel 3 hrs wkly *Target Audience:* 25-49.
Ben Birdsong, General Manager
Chalmer Harper, Station Manager
Jeremy Morris, Programming Director
Johanna Antes, Director Of Support
Kathleen Birdsong, Office Manager
Keith Stafford, Underwriter
Lowell Hamilton, BusinessRepresentative
Mike Russel, Program Director
Sue Bowen, Administrative Assistant

KWTO
12-25-1933; 560 khz AM; 5 kw-D, DA2; 4 kw-N, DA2; N36 56 40 W93 13 17
Mailing Address: 3000 E Chestnut Exp Way, Springfield, MO 65802 US
Second Address: 3000 E. Chestnut Expwy., Springfield, MO 65808
(417) 862-3751, *Fax:* (417) 869-7675
www.radiospringfield.com
manager@radiospringfield.com
License: Springfield, MO held by KWTO Inc.
Group Owner: Meyer Communications Inc.; (acq 3-20-95; $1.88 million with co-located FM;
Arbitron Metro Market: Springfield, MO *Format:* News, News/Talk, 84, Talk *Special Programming:* Farm 20 hrs, relg one hr wkly *Hrs. of News Programming:* News progmg one hr wkly *Target Audience:* 25-55; male
Kenneth Meyer, President
Bonnie Bell, General Sales Mgr
Dan Vaughn, Programming Director
Susie Proffitt, News Director
Dale Blankenship, Chief Engineer
Lewis Miller, Farm Director
R.J. McAllister, News Reporter

KWTO-FM
11-23-1967; 98.7 mhz FM *Hrs Open:* 24; 96 kw; 551 ft.; N37 4 6 W93 18 31
Mailing Address: 3000 E. Chestnut Exprway, Springfield, MO 65808 US
Second Address: 3000 E. Chestnut Expwy., Springfield, MO 65808
(417) 862-3751, *Fax:* (417) 869-7675
www.radiospringfield.com
manager@radiospringfield.com
License: Springfield, Greene County, MO
Group Owner: Meyer Communications Inc.
Arbitron Metro Market: Springfield, MO *Format:* Sports, Talk *Target Audience:* 25-45; male dominant middle class
Bonnie Bell, Operations Dir
Lewis Miller, General Sales Mgr
Susie Proffitt, News Director
R.J. McAllister, Reporter

KXUS
04-17-1969; 97.3 mhz FM *Hrs Open:* 24; 100 kw; 581 ft.; N37 11 10 W93 1 23
1350 Galleria Tower, 13355 Noel Road, Dallas, TX 75240 US
(417) 890-5555, *Fax:* (417) 823-8506
www.us97.com
us97@us97.com
License: Springfield, Greene County, MO held by Clear Channel Broadcasting Licenses Inc.
Group Owner: Clear Channel Communications Inc.; (acq 10-10-00; grpsl).
Arbitron Metro Market: Springfield, MO *Format:* Classic Rock *Hrs. of News Programming:* news progmg 5 hrs wkly *No. News Employees:* 1 *Target Audience:* 25-54; males -75%
Paul Kelley, Operations Dir
Keith Liesmann, General Manager
Dave Hines, Program Director/ Music Director
Sarah Green, Program Director/ Music Director
Mary Brown, News Director
Shawn Baker, Chief Engineer
Kelli Presley, Directorof Sales
Kat Morgan Gaines, Production Director
Megan Stuart Annis, Business Manager

St. Louis

WEW
04-26-1921; 770 khz AM *Hrs Open:* 2 hrs past sunset (pssa)
Mailing Address: 3801 Skillern Blvd., Flower Mound, TX 75028 US
Second Address: 21700 Northwestern Hwy, Tower 14, Ste 1190, Southfield, MI 48075
(314) 781-9397(314) 969-7700, *Fax:* (314) 781-8545
www.wewradio.com
WEWRadio@aol.com
License: St. Louis, MO held by Birach Broadcasting Corp.
Group Owner: Birach Broadcasting Corp.; acq 1-6-2004; $1.35 million).
Nat'l Network: CBS Radio; CNN Radio
Arbitron Metro Market: St. Louis, MO *Format:* Ethnic *Special Programming:* Ger 2 hrs, Pol 2 hrs wkly *Target Audience:* 35-64; Mature audience/older *Adv. Rates:* 20; 20; 20; 15
Sima Birach, CEO
Rich Vannoy, Operations Dir

St. Charles

***KCLC**
10-01-1968; 89.1 mhz FM *Hrs Open:* 24; 50 kw; 239 ft.; N38 47 13.5 W90 30 27.9
209 S. Kingshighway, St. Charles, MO 63301 US
(636) 949-4891, *Fax:* (636) 949-4111
www.891thewood.com
fm891@lindenwood.edu
License: St. Charles, St. Charles County, MO held by Lindenwood University.
Arbitron Metro Market: St. Louis, MO *Format:* Triple A *Target Audience:* 18-34; young adults
Mike Wall, General Manager

KHOJ
04-13-1958; 1460 khz AM
3713 Highway 94 North, St. Charles, MO 63366 US
(314) 752-7000
www.covenantnet.net
covenantnetwork@juno.com
License: St. Charles, MO held by Covenant Network.
Group Owner: Covenant Network; (acq 5-13-2005; $730,000)
Arbitron Metro Market: St. Louis, MO
Tony Holman, General Manager
Jim Schaper, Programming Director

St. James

KTTR-FM
01-01-1994; 99.7 mhz FM *Hrs Open:* 24; 12 kw; 472 ft.; N38 4 14 W91 39 53 *Rebroadcasts:* Rebroadcasts KTTR(AM) Rolla 90%.
Mailing Address: Box 4584, Springfield, MO 65808 US
Second Address: 1505 Soest Rd., Rolla, MO 65808
(573) 364-2525, *Fax:* (573) 364-5161
License: St. James, Phelps County, MO held by KTTR-KZNN Inc.
Group Owner: Mahaffey Enterprises Inc.
Regional Network: Missourinet
Arbitron Metro Market: Columbia, MO *Format:* News, News/Talk, 86 *Hrs. of News Programming:* news progmg 20 hrs wkly *No. News Employees:* 1 *Target Audience:* 25-54.
John Mahaffey, Chairman
Robert B. Mahaffey, President

St. Joseph

KFEQ
02-16-1926; 680 khz AM *Hrs Open:* 24
Mailing Address: P.O. Box 817, 2703 Hall Street, Hays, KS 67601 US
Second Address: 4104 Country Ln., Saint Joseph, MO 64506
(816) 233-8881, *Fax:* (816) 279-8280
www.stjoeradio.com
garyexline@eagleradio.net
License: St. Joseph, MO held by Eagle Communications Inc.
Group Owner: Eagle Communications Group; (acq 3-20-69; grpsl;
Nat'l Network: ABC *Nat'l Reps:* Katz Radio *Wire Services:* AP
Arbitron Metro Market: Saint Joseph, MO *Format:* News, News/Talk, 84, Talk *Special Programming:* Farm 20 hrs wkly *Hrs. of News Programming:* news progmg 50 hrs wkly *No. News Employees:* 4 *Target Audience:* 18 plus; adults *Adv. Rates:* 65, 26, 28, 23

Gary Shorman, CEO
Gary Exline, Operations Dir
Kevin Wagner, Operations Director

KGNM
11-01-1985; 1270 khz AM *Hrs Open:* 24; 1 kw-D, ND1; 0.036 kw-N, ND1; N39 44 39 W94 47 16
2414s. Leonard Road, St. Joseph, MO 64503 US
(816) 233-2577, *Fax:* (816) 233-2374
kgnmradio.com
kgnm@stjoelive.com
License: St. Joseph, MO held by Orama Inc.
Nat'l Network: USA
Format: Adult Contemp, Christian *Target Audience:* 30-55; conservative *Adv. Rates:* $12 per :60/$10 per; 30
Rory Pullen, President
Greg Glauser, Operations Dir
Chris Meikel, General Manager
Marci Meikel, Programming Director

KKJO-FM
09-01-1962; 105.5 mhz FM *Hrs Open:* 24; 100 kw; 981 ft.; N39 42 35 W95 2 33
2703 Hall, P.O. Box 817, Hays, KS 67601 US
(816) 233-8881, *Fax:* (816) 279-8280
www.kjo1055.com
License: St. Joseph, Buchanan County, MO
Arbitron Metro Market: Kansas City, MO *Format:* Adult Contemp *Hrs. of News Programming:* news progmg 2 hrs wkly *No. News Employees:* 2 *Target Audience:* 18-49. *Adv. Rates:* 37; 32; 35; 29
Greg Lynn, Programming Director

***KSRD**
01-01-2004; 91.9 mhz FM; 10 kw; 492 ft.; N39 42 35 W95 2 33
1215 Jules Street, St. Joseph, MO 64501 US
(816) 233-5773, *Fax:* (816) 233-5777
www.air1.com
info@ksrdradio.com
License: St. Joseph, Buchanan County, MO held by Horizon Christian Fellowship.
Group Owner: Horizon Christian Fellowship; (acq 8-26-2004; $10,600)
Arbitron Metro Market: Kansas City, KS *Format:* Christian
Brian Jones, General Manager

St. Louis

KATZ
01-03-1955; 1600 khz AM *Hrs Open:* 24
50 East Rivercenter Blvd, Suite 1200, Covington, KY 41011 US
(314) 333-8000, *Fax:* (314) 333-8311
www.gospel1600.com
License: St. Louis, MO held by Citicasters Licenses L.P.
Group Owner: Clear Channel Communications Inc.; (acq 5-4-99; grpsl).
Nat'l Network: American Urban
Arbitron Metro Market: St. Louis, MO *Format:* Gospel *Target Audience:* 25-54; Adults
Tommy Austin, Operations Dir
Dennis Lamme, General Manager
Beth Davis, General Sales Mgr
Pierre Troupe, General Sales Manager

KEZK-FM
09-01-1968; 102.5 mhz FM *Hrs Open:* 24; kw
600 New Hampshire Ave, Suite 1200, Washington, DC 20037 US
(314) 531-0000, *Fax:* (314) 969-7638
www.kezk.com
info@kezk.com
License: St. Louis, St. Louis County, MO held by CBS Radio Holdings Inc.
Group Owner: CBS Radio; (acq 11-13-98; grpsl)
Arbitron Metro Market: St. Louis, MO *Format:* Adult Contemp *Target Audience:* 25-54; high average household income
Beth Davis, General Manager

KIHT
12-22-1959; 96.3 mhz FM; 80 kw; 1027 ft.; N38 34 24 W90 19 30
10706 Beaver Dam Road, Cockeysville, MD 21030 US
(314) 621-4106, *Fax:* (314) 621-3000
www.k-hits.com
john@stl.emmis.com
License: St. Louis, St. Louis County, MO held by Emmis Radio License LLC.
Group Owner: Emmis Communications Corp.; (acq 9-26-2000; grpsl).
Arbitron Metro Market: St. Louis, MO *Format:* Contemporary Hits/Top 40, Adult Contemp *Target Audience:* 25-54.
John Beck, Operations Dir
Lois Sampson-Hooker, General Manager
Steve Williams, General Sales Mgr

Jeff Allen, Programming Director
Kyle Guderian, Promotions Manager
John Beck, Senior Vice President
Rick Balis, Program Director

KJSL
09-19-1938; 630 khz AM *Hrs Open:* 24; 5 kw-D, DA2; 5 kw-N, DA2; N38 40 18 W90 6 52
P.O. 3003, Blue Bell, PA 19422 US
(314) 878-3600, *Fax:* (314) 656-3608
www.truthtalk630.com
License: St. Louis, MO held by WMUZ Radio Inc.
Group Owner: Crawford Broadcasting Co.; (acq 1994; $1.57 million)
Arbitron Metro Market: St. Louis, MO *Format:* Christian, Talk *Target Audience:* 30-60.
Laura Scotti, General Manager
Beth Kreminski, Station Manager

KLOU
11-01-1962; 103.3 mhz FM *Hrs Open:* 24; 90 kw; 1027 ft.; N38 34 24 W90 19 30
50 East Rivercenter Boulevard, Suite 1200, Covington, KY 41011 US
(314) 333-8000, *Fax:* (314) 333-8314
www.playwhatiwant.com
License: St. Louis, St. Louis County, MO held by Citicasters Licenses L.P.
Group Owner: Clear Channel Communications Inc.; (acq 5-4-99; grpsl)
Arbitron Metro Market: St. Louis, MO *Format:* Oldies *No. News Employees:* 1 *Target Audience:* 25-54.
Tommy Austin, Operations Dir
Dennis Lamme, General Manager
Beth Davis, General Sales Mgr
John Helmkamp, Promotions Manager
Al Fox, General Sales Manager

KMOX
12-24-1925; 1120 khz AM *Hrs Open:* 24
600 New Hampshire Avenue, NW, Suite 1200, Washington, DC 20037 US
(314) 621-2345, *Fax:* (314) 444-1860
www.kmox.com
kmox@kmox.com
License: St. Louis, MO held by CBS Radio East Inc.
Group Owner: CBS Radio; (acq 11-13-98; grpsl)
Nat'l Network: CBS
Arbitron Metro Market: St. Louis, MO *Format:* News, News/Talk, 84, Talk *Special Programming:* Jazz 4 hrs, relg one hr wkly *Hrs. of News Programming:* news progmg 60 hrs wkly *No. News Employees:* 16 *TargetAudience:* 25 plus.
Ron Korb, General Manager
Melissa Horton, General Sales Mgr
Skip Walters, Programming Director
Ken Eklund, Chief Engineer
Angie Depping, Research Director

KSD
11-01-1954; 93.7 mhz FM *Hrs Open:* 24; 74 kw; 1027 ft.; N38 34 24 W90 19 30
50 East Rivercenter Boulevard, Suite 1200, Covington, KY 41011 US
(314) 333-8000, *Fax:* (314) 333-8332
thebullrocks.com
License: St. Louis, St. Louis County, MO held by Citicasters Licenses L.P.
Group Owner: Clear Channel Communications Inc.; (acq 5-4-99; grpsl).
Arbitron Metro Market: St. Louis, MO *Format:* Country *No. News Employees:* 1 *Target Audience:* 18-34; adults
Tommy Austin, Operations Dir
Dennis Lamme, General Manager
Beth Davis, General Sales Mgr
John Helmkamp, Promotions Manager
Aaron Hyland, General Sales Manager

***KSIV-FM**
04-13-1950; 91.5 mhz FM; kw
3405 Shady Bend Dr., Independence, MO 64052 US
(314) 961-1320, *Fax:* (314) 961-7562
www.bottradionetwork.com
info@bottradionework.com
License: St. Louis, St. Louis County, MO held by Community Broadcasting Inc.
Group Owner: Bott Radio Network; (acq 1996; $1.625 million)
Arbitron Metro Market: Saint Louis, MO *Format:* Christian, Religious
Richard Bott II, CEO/COO
Richard Bott, President
Michael McHardy, General Manager
Pat Rulon, General Sales Mgr

KSLZ
09-28-1972; 107.7 mhz FM *Hrs Open:* 24; 100 kw; 1027 ft.; N38 34 24 W90 19 30
50 East Rivercenter Blvd, Suite 1200, Covington, KY 41011 US
(314) 333-8000, *Fax:* (314) 333-8312
www.z1077.com
License: St. Louis, St. Louis County, MO held by Citicasters Licenses L.P.
Group Owner: Clear Channel Communications Inc.; (acq 5-4-99; grpsl).
Arbitron Metro Market: St. Louis, MO *Format:* Contemporary Hits/Top 40 *Target Audience:* 18-34; adults
Tommy Austin, Operations Dir
Dennis Lamme, General Manager
Beth Davis, General Sales Mgr
John Helmkamp, Promotions Manager
Scott Adamec, General Sales Manager

KSTL
01-01-1948; 690 khz AM *Hrs Open:* 18; 1 kw-D, ND1; 0.0179 kw-N, ND1; N38 37 1 W90 10 17
P.O. Box 3003, Blue Bell, PA 19422 US
(314) 878-3600(618) 874-5785, *Fax:* (314) 656-3608
www.shine690.com
bethk@crawfordbroadcasting.com
License: St. Louis, MO held by WMUZ Radio Inc.
Group Owner: Crawford Broadcasting Co.; (acq 1994)
Arbitron Metro Market: Creve Coeur, MO *Format:* Gospel *Adv. Rates:* 420; 420; 420; na
Donald Crawford, President
Beth Kriminski, Station Manager

KTRS
02-14-1922; 550 khz AM *Hrs Open:* 24
638 West Port Plaza, St Louis, MO 63146 US
(314) 453-5500, *Fax:* (314) 453-9704
www.ktrs.com
info@ktrs.com
License: St. Louis, MO held by KTRS-AM License L.L.C.
Nat'l Network: ABC *Nat'l Reps:* Christal *Wire Services:* AP
Arbitron Metro Market: St. Louis, MO *Format:* News, News/Talk, 84, Talk *No. News Employees:* 40 *Target Audience:* 35-64.
Tim Dorsey, President
Geoff Witt, General Sales Mgr

***KWMU**
06-02-1972; 90.7 mhz FM; 100 kw; 948 ft.; N38 34 50 W90 19 45
8001 Natural Bridge Road, St. Louis, MO 63121 US
(314) 516-5968, *Fax:* (314) 516-5993
www.kwmu.org
kwmu@kwmu.org
License: St. Louis, St. Louis County, MO held by The Curators of the University of Missouri.
Group Owner: The Curators of the University of Missouri
Nat'l Network: NPR; PRI *Wire Services:* AP
Arbitron Metro Market: St. Louis, MO *Format:* News *Hrs. of News Programming:* news progmg 40 hrs wkly *No. News Employees:* 5 *Target Audience:* 27-45; upscale
Patricia Wente, General Manager
Shelly Kerley, Station Manager
Shelley Kerley, General Sales Mgr
Mike Schrand, Programming Director
Phil Donato, Promotions Manager
Bill Raack, News Director

KXEN
05-10-1951; 1010 khz AM *Hrs Open:* 24
PO Box 8085, Mitchell, IL 62040 US
(314) 454-0400, *Fax:* (618) 797-2293
www.kxen1010.com
info@kxen1010.com
License: St. Louis, MO held by BDJ Radio Enterprises LLC
Arbitron Metro Market: St. Louis, MO *Format:* Religious
Dirk Hallemeier, General Manager
Jay Madas, Programming Director

KYKY
01-01-1960; 98.1 mhz FM *Hrs Open:* 24; kw
600 New Hampshire Ave.NW, Suite 1200, Washington, DC 20037 US
(314) 531-0000, *Fax:* (314) 531-9855
www.y98.com
eeleavy@stl.cbs.com
License: St. Louis, St. Louis County, MO held by CBS Radio Holdings Inc.
Group Owner: CBS Radio; (acq 11-13-98; grpsl)
Nat'l Network: Westwood One
Arbitron Metro Market: St. Louis, MO *Format:* Adult Contemp *Target Audience:* 25-54.
John Sheean, Senior Vice President
Beth Davis, General Manager

Marty Link, Programming Director
Sharie Levingston, Local Sales Manager
Lindsey Wright, Marketing Director
Lisa Letterman, Digital Sales Manager
Ashley Long, WebAdministrator

WIL-FM
07-15-1962; 92.3 mhz FM; 99 kw; 984 ft.; N38 28 56 W90 23 53
10706 Beaver Dam Road, Cockeysville, MD 21030 US
(314) 983-6000, *Fax:* (314) 994-9421
www.wil92.com
info@wil92.com
License: St. Louis, St. Louis County, MO held by Bonneville Holding Co.
Group Owner: Bonneville International Corporation
Arbitron Metro Market: St. Louis, MO *Format:* Country
W. Grant Hafley, CEO
Dave Wilson, Operations Dir
Joel Losego, General Manager

KZQZ
02-09-1922; 1430 khz AM *Hrs Open:* 24; 5 kw-D, DA2; 5 kw-N, DA2; N38 32 9 W90 11 26
10706 Beaver Dam Road, Cockeysville, MD 21030 US
(314) 983-6000, *Fax:* (314) 994-9421
kzqz1430am.com
info@kzqz1430am.com
License: St. Louis, MO held by Entertainment Media Trust, Dennis J. Watkins, trustee
Nat'l Network: Westwood One
Arbitron Metro Market: St. Louis, MO *Format:* Oldies *No. News Employees:* 1 *Target Audience:* 35 plus; affluent, mature baby boomers
John Kijowski, General Manager
Keith Kraus, General Sales Mgr
Greg Mozingo, Programming Director
Tom Ennis, News Director
Marshall Rice, Chief Engineer

St. Robert

KFLW
03-22-1994; 98.9 mhz FM *Hrs Open:* 24; 6.7 kw; 627 ft.; N37 52 42 W92 1 4
P.O. Box 209, Waynesville, MO 65583 US
(573) 336-5359, *Fax:* (573) 336-7619
www.kflw989.com
License: St. Robert, Pulaski County, MO held by Ozark Media Inc.
Group Owner: Ozark Media Inc.; (acq 2-21-2002; $575,000)
Arbitron Metro Market: Saint Robert, MO *Format:* Adult Contemp *Hrs. of News Programming:* News progmg 3 hrs wkly *Target Audience:* 25-55.
Dalton Wright, President
Tracey O'Quinn, General Manager

Ste. Genevieve

***KSEF**
09-14-2006; 88.9 mhz FM; 20 kw vert; 673 ft.; N37 47 58 W90 33 44 *Rebroadcasts:* Rebroadcasts KRCU(FM) Cape Girardeau 100%
One University Plaza, Cape Girardeau, MO 63701 US
(573) 651-5070, *Fax:* (573) 651-5071
www.southeastpublicradio.org
comments@krcu.org
License: Ste. Genevieve, St. Francois County, MO held by Board of Regents, Southeast Missouri State University.
Nat'l Network: NPR; PRI
Arbitron Metro Market: Sainte Genevieve, MO *Format:* Classical, Jazz, 60
Jason Brown, Operations Dir
Dan Woods, General Manager
Amanda Lincoln, General Sales Mgr
Jacob McCleland, Programming Director
Allen Lane, Chief Engineer
Sean Kenney, Radio Producer
Samantha Power, Web Producer/Reporter
Jeanette Lawson, Administrative Assistant

Steelville

KLPW-FM
08-01-1966; 107.3 mhz FM *Hrs Open:* 24; 6.7 kw; 627 ft.; N37 55 17 W91 26 36
Mailing Address: 3333 S. Atlantic Ave., #1404, Daytona Beach Shores, FL 32118 US
Second Address: 6531 Hwy. BB, Washington, MO 63090
(636) 583-5155, *Fax:* (636) 583-1644
License: Steelville, Lincoln County, MO held by Marathon Media Group L.L.C.
Arbitron Metro Market: St. Louis, MO *Format:* Country *Hrs. of News Programming:* news progmg 16.5 hrs wkly *No. News Employees:* 2 *Target Audience:* 18-49.
Tim McDonald, General Manager
Steve Leslie, Programming Director
Marcy Frankenberg, News Director
John Covington, Local News Editor

Stockton

KRWP
01-20-1999; 107.7 mhz FM *Hrs Open:* 24; 11.7 kw; Ant 479 ft; N37 31 24 W93 52 40
Box 1070, 1225 South St., Suite B, Stockton, MO 65785
(417) 276-5253, *Fax:* (417) 276-2255
License: Stockton, Cedar County, MO held by Cumulus Licensing LLC.
Group Owner: Cumulus Media Inc.; (acq 4-27-2004; $825,000).
Nat'l Network: Jones Radio Networks *Regional Network:* Missourinet
Population Served: 79,000*Special Programming:* Local news, weather, farm 8 hrs wkly *Hrs. of News Programming:* News progmg 16 hrs wkly *Target Audience:* 25-54; male & female
Lance Beamer, General Manager
Ed Koca, Programming Director
Ed Koka, News Director
Lee Reisinger, Chief Engineer

Sullivan

KTUI
02-14-1966; 1560 khz AM *Hrs Open:* 6 AM-sunset; 1 kw-D, NDD; N38 11 42 W91 11 12
4045 N. Serv. Rd, West #, Sullivan, MO 63080 US
(573) 468-5101, *Fax:* (573) 468-5440
www.ktui.com
custserv@fidelitycommunications.com
License: Sullivan, MO held by Fidelity Broadcasting Inc.
Regional Network: Missourinet
Arbitron Metro Market: St. Louis, MO *Format:* News, News/Talk, 86 *No. News Employees:* 1 *Target Audience:* General.
John Rice, General Manager
Sam Scott, Programming Director
Wilma Scott, Traffic Manager

KTUI-FM
01-01-1981; 102.1 mhz FM; 6 kw; 276 ft.; N38 11 42 W91 11 12
P. O. Box 99, 4045 N Service Rd, W. #1, Sullivan, MO 63080 US
(573) 468-5101, *Fax:* (573) 468-5440
www.ktui.com
custserv@fidelitycommunications.com
License: Sullivan, Franklin County, MO held by Fidelity Broadcasting Inc.
Regional Network: Missourinet
Arbitron Metro Market: St. Louis, MO *Format:* Country, Sports *Target Audience:* General.
John Rice, Operations Dir

Sunrise Beach

***KCRL**
09-01-1998; 90.3 mhz FM *Hrs Open:* 24; 4.5 kw vert; 197 ft.; N38 14 22 W92 45 56
Mailing Address: 10550 Barkley, Suite 108, Overland Park, KS 66212 US
Second Address: 30690 Gray Eagle Rd., Gravois Mills, MO 65037
(913) 642-7770, *Fax:* (913) 642 1319
www.bottradionetwork.com
comments@bottradionetwork.com
License: Sunrise Beach, Camden County, MO held by Community Broadcasting Inc.
Group Owner: Bott Radio Network
Nat'l Network: USA
Arbitron Metro Market: Overland Park,KS *Format:* Christian, Talk *Target Audience:* 25-55.
Richard Bott, Chairman
Richard Bott, CEO
Richard Bott, President
Eben Fowler, Operations Dir
Tom Holdeman, CFO
Tim Lumpkin, Corporate Controller

Tarkio

KRSS
08-22-1977; 93.5 mhz FM *Hrs Open:* 24; 11 kw; 489 ft.; N40 31 11 W95 11 3
3000 West Macarthur Blvd, 3rd Floor, Santa Ana, CA 92704 US
(660) 736-4321, *Fax:* (660) 736-5789
www.krss.me/index.php?option=com_contact&view=category&catid=0&Itemid=56
License: Tarkio, Atchison County, MO held by CSN International
Group Owner: CSN International
Arbitron Metro Market: Tarkio,MO *Format:* Christian *Target Audience:* General.
Mick Miller, General Manager

Thayer

KALM
12-11-1953; 1290 khz AM *Hrs Open:* 6 AM-sunset
P.O. Box 15, Thayer, MO 65791 US
(417) 264-7211, *Fax:* (417) 264-7212
www.AM1290TheGift.com
peggy@kkountry.com
License: Thayer, MO held by E-Communications LLC
Regional Network: Brownfield; Missourinet *Regional Reps:* Regional Reps
Arbitron Metro Market: Thayer, MO *Format:* Gospel *Hrs. of News Programming:* news progmg 70 hrs wkly *No. News Employees:* 1 *Target Audience:* 18 plus; farmers, ranchers, rural families
Adv. Rates: :60-$14.00—:30-$12.25
Robert Eckman, President

KSAR
92.3 mhz FM *Hrs Open:* 24; 50 kw; 427 ft.; N36 21 58 W91 28 35
Mailing Address: P O Box 458, Salem, AR 72576 US
Second Address: 352 Hwy. 62/412, Salem, AR 72576
(870) 856-3240, *Fax:* (870) 856-4408
www.myhometownradiostations.com/ksar___92_3_fm
hometownradio@centurytel.net
License: Thayer, Oregon County, MO held by Bragg Broadcasting Corp.
Regional Network: Ark. Radio Net.
Arbitron Metro Market: Cherokee Village, AR *Format:* Country, News, 84 *Special Programming:* Farm 4 hrs wkly *Target Audience:* 25-54.
James Bragg, General Manager

Trenton

KTTN
04-17-1955; 1600 khz AM *Hrs Open:* 24; 0.5 kw-D, ND1; 0.033 kw-N, ND1; N40 5 0 W93 33 30
Mailing Address: 804 Main Street, Box 307, Trenton, MO 64683 US
Second Address: 804 Main St., Trenton, MO 64683
(660) 359-2261, *Fax:* (660) 359-4126
www.kttn.com
john@kttn.com
License: Trenton, MO held by Luehrs Broadcasting Co.
Nat'l Network: AP Radio; Jones Radio Networks
Arbitron Metro Market: Trenton, MO *Format:* Adult Contemp *Hrs. of News Programming:* News progmg 8 hrs wkly *Target Audience:* 35 plus; general *Adv. Rates:* 5; 4; 4; na
David Pridemore, General Manager
Ken Berry, Station Manager
Traffic Director, Michelle Shaw
Sales account executives, Jerry Shirley
Sales account executives

KTTN-FM
09-15-1978; 92.3 mhz FM *Hrs Open:* 24; 18.5 kw; 381 ft.; N40 5 0 W93 33 30
Mailing Address: 804 Main Street, Trenton, MO 64683 US
Second Address: 804 Main St., Trenton, MO 64683
(660) 359-2261, *Fax:* (660) 359-4126
www.kttn.com
john@kttn.com
License: Trenton, Grundy County, MO held by Luehrs Broadcasting Co.
Nat'l Network: AP Radio *Regional Network:* Brownfield; Missourinet *Regional Reps:* Rgnl Reps
Arbitron Metro Market: Trenton, MO *Format:* Country, News, 84 *Special Programming:* Gospel 6 hrs wkly *Hrs. of News Programming:* news progmg 15 hrs wkly *No. News Employees:* 2 *Target Audience:* General.*Adv. Rates:* 25; 20; 15; 15
John Ausberger, President
John Anthony, General Manager
Traffic Director, Michelle Shaw
Sales account executives, Jerry Shirley
Sales account executives

Troy

KYRO
02-22-1959; 1280 khz AM *Hrs Open:* 24; 660 w-D, 45 w-N; N37 58 28 W90 45 44
P.O. Box 280, Potosi, MO 63664
news@kyro.com
License: Troy, Lincoln County, MO held by JLF Communications LLP.

Group Owner: The RAFTT Corp.
Nat'l Network: ABC *Regional Network:* Missourinet
Population Served: 30,000*Hrs. of News Programming:* news progmg 12 hrs wkly *No. News Employees:* 1 *Target Audience:* 25 plus; general *Adv. Rates:* 9; 8; 9; 7
James Porter, President
Debra Porter, Operations Dir

KFNS-FM
11-29-1993; 100.7 mhz FM; 6 kw; 328 ft.; N39 3 13 W90 59 47
Rebroadcasts: Simulcast with KFNS(AM) Wood River, IL 100%
8045 Big Bend Boulevard, St. Louis, MO 63119 US
(636) 356-4487, *Fax:* (636) 356-4363
www.westplexradio.com/
kfns@kfns.com
License: Troy, Lincoln County, MO held by Big Stick Two LLC.
Group Owner: Big League Broadcasting LLC; (acq 7-13-2004; grpsl).
Arbitron Metro Market: Troy, MO *Format:* Sports
Dave Greene, General Manager
James Oelklaus, General Sales Mgr

Union

KLPW
08-18-1954; 1220 khz AM *Hrs Open:* 24; 1 kw-D, ND1; 0.126 kw-N, ND1; N38 28 57 W91 2 39
980 North Michigan Avenue, Suite 1880, Chicago, IL 60611 US
(636) 583-5155, *Fax:* (636) 583-1644
www.klpwam.com
klpwam@klpw.com
License: Union, MO held by Broadcast Properties Inc.
Arbitron Metro Market: St. Louis, MO *Format:* Talk *Special Programming:* Relg 6 hrs wkly *Hrs. of News Programming:* news progmg 40 hrs wkly *No. News Employees:* 2 *Target Audience:* 25-54; male
Ray Heller, Operations Dir
Tim McDonald, General Manager
Dee Coppeans, General Sales Mgr
Greg Marshall, Programming Director
Diana Stanley, Promotions Manager
John Covington, News Director
Tom Lyons, Chief Engineer
MarcyFrankenberg, Traffic Manager

Van Buren

*KBIY
01-01-2001; 91.3 mhz FM; 100 kw horiz, 98 kw vert; 492 ft.; N37 6 25 W90 59 30
1411 Locust Street, St. Louis, MO 63103 US
(314) 421-3020, *Fax:* (314) 421-1702
www.hereshelpnet.org
larryr@hereshelpnet.org
License: Van Buren, Carter County, MO held by New Life Evangelistic Center Inc.
Arbitron Metro Market: Saint Louis, MO *Format:* Adult Contemp, Gospel
Larry Rice, President

Vandalia

KKAC
104.3 mhz FM; 11.38 kw; 486 ft.; N39 25 4 W91 27 26
3418 Douglas Rd, Florissant, MO 63034 US
(573) 594-6000, *Fax:* (314) 594-2100
www.actioncountry.com
kkacfm@vandaliamo.net
License: Vandalia, Lincoln County, MO held by Broadcast Associates Inc.
Arbitron Metro Market: Vandalia, MO *Format:* Country
Joe Baker, Operations Dir
Chuck Branstetter, General Sales Mgr

Versailles

KTKS
06-16-1989; 95.1 mhz FM *Hrs Open:* 24; 12.5 kw; 463 ft.; N38 24 32 W92 45 42
Mailing Address: P. O. Box 409, Versailles, MO 65084 US
Second Address: 16875 Hwy 52, Barnett, MO 65011
(573) 378-5669, *Fax:* (573) 378-6640
lakeradio.com
jay@lakeradio.net
License: Versailles, Morgan County, MO held by Twin Lakes Communications Inc.
Nat'l Network: CNN Radio *Wire Services:* AP
Arbitron Metro Market: Versailles, MO *Format:* Country *Special Programming:* Farm 2 hrs, relg 3 hrs wkly *Hrs. of News Programming:* news progmg 23 hrs wkly *No. News Employees:* 1 *Target Audience:* 25-54;loc rural audience & transient tourist population

Douglas Fisher, Chairman
James Fisher, President
Sheryl Lehman, General Sales Mgr
J.T. Gerlt, Programming Director

Vienna

*KNLN
90.9 mhz FM; 10 kw; 328 ft.; N38 11 27 W92 7 22
1411 Locust Street, St. Louis, MO 63103 US
(314) 421-3020, *Fax:* (314) 421-1702
www.hereshelpnet.org
larryr@hereshelpnet.org
License: Vienna, Maries County, MO held by New Life Evangelistic Center Inc.
Arbitron Metro Market: St. Louis, MO *Format:* Religious
Larry Rice, General Manager
Larry Rice, Founder and Director

Warrensburg

*KTBG
04-01-1962; 90.9 mhz FM; 97 kw; 443 ft.; N38 55 54 W93 49 6
Wood 11, Office of Broadcast Serv, Warrensburg, MO 64093 US
(660) 543-4130, *Fax:* (660) 543-8863
www.ktbg.fm
jhart@ktbg.fm
License: Warrensburg, Johnson County, MO held by Central Missouri State University Board of Regents.
Nat'l Network: NPR; PRI
Arbitron Metro Market: Warrensburg, MO *Format:* Triple A *Target Audience:* General.
Donald Peterson, General Manager
Jon Hart, Music & Programming
Byron Johnson, Music & Programming
Mark Pearce, Underwriting
Andy Stanley, Underwriting
Clint Bradt, Underwriting

KOKO
12-01-1953; 1450 khz AM *Hrs Open:* 24; 1 kw-U, ND1; N38 46 32 W93 43 12
119 North Third Street, Hannibal, MO 63401 US
(660) 747-9191, *Fax:* (660) 747-5611
www.warrensburgradio.com
License: Warrensburg, MO held by D & H Media L.L.C.
Nat'l Network: ABC *Regional Network:* Missourinet
Format: Oldies, Sports *Hrs. of News Programming:* news progmg 20 hrs wkly *No. News Employees:* 1 *Target Audience:* 25-54; educated-mainly female & sports enthusiasts *Adv. Rates:* 13; 12; 13; 12
Vance Delozier, President
Greg Hassler, General Manager

Warrenton

KFAV
11-01-1991; 99.9 mhz FM *Hrs Open:* 24; 10.5 kw; 512 ft.; N38 50 20 W91 2 40
P. O. Box 545, Frankfort, IN 46041 US
(636) 456-3311, *Fax:* (636) 978-4710
www.kfav.com
kwreksava@socket.net
License: Warrenton, Warren County, MO
Group Owner: Kaspar Broadcasting Group
Arbitron Metro Market: St. Louis, MO *Format:* Country *Hrs. of News Programming:* news progmg 2 hrs wkly *No. News Employees:* 3 *Target Audience:* 20-49; general *Adv. Rates:* Same as AM
Pete Benedetti, CEO
Tom Oakes, General Manager
McConnell Adams, Programming Director
Trila Bumstead, CFO

KWRE
03-09-1949; 730 khz AM *Hrs Open:* 5 AM-11 PM; 1 kw-D, ND1; 0.12 kw-N, ND1; N38 49 20 W91 8 15
P.O. Box 545, Frankfort, IN 46041 US
(636) 377-2300, *Fax:* (636) 456-8767
www.kwre.com
kwrekfav@socket.net
License: Warrenton, MO held by Kaspar Broadcasting Co.
Group Owner: Kaspar Broadcasting Group
Arbitron Metro Market: Warrenton, MO *Format:* Country *Special Programming:* Farm one hr wkly *Hrs. of News Programming:* news progmg 3 hrs wkly *No. News Employees:* 3 *Target Audience:* 35 plus. *Adv.Rates:* 36; 19.50; 24; 7.50
V.J. Kaspar, President
Mike Thomas, Operations Dir
Mark Becker, General Sales Mgr

Warsaw

KAYQ
03-10-1980; 97.1 mhz FM *Hrs Open:* 24; 6 kw; 240 ft.; N38 17 19 W93 18 32
Mailing Address: Box 1420, Warsaw, MO 65355 US
Second Address: Truman Hills Mall, Suite 6, Warsaw, MO
(660) 438-7343, *Fax:* (660) 438-7159
kayqtraffic@embarqmail.com
License: Warsaw, Benton County, MO held by Valkyrie Broadcasting Co. Inc.
Nat'l Network: AP Radio
Arbitron Metro Market: Warsaw, MO *Format:* Country *Hrs. of News Programming:* news progmg 5 hrs wkly *No. News Employees:* 1
Jim McCollum, President
Joey Anderson, General Manager
Glenna Thrasher, News Director

Washington

*KGNV
12-25-1990; 89.9 mhz FM *Hrs Open:* 24; 1 kw; 213 ft.; N38 35 49 W91 6 17
P. O. Box 87, Washington, MO 63090 US
(636) 385-3787, *Fax:* (636) 293-4448
goodnewsvoice.org
License: Washington, Franklin County, MO held by Missouri River Christian Broadcasting Inc.
Group Owner: Missouri River Christian Broadcasting Inc.
Nat'l Network: Moody; Salem Radio Network
Format: Gospel, News, 62, Talk *Special Programming:* Class 5 hrs, children 6 hrs, teen 5 hrs wkly *Hrs. of News Programming:* News progmg 14 hrs wkly *Target Audience:* 20-70; inquisitive, conservative, liberal,philosophical *Adv. Rates:* 8; 8; 8; 8
James Goggan, President
Charles Sachse, Station Manager

KSLQ-FM
11-21-1989; 104.5 mhz FM *Hrs Open:* 24; 3 kw; 328 ft.; N38 36 3 W90 56 4
8604 Hedgebur, St. Louis, MO 63114 US
(636) 239-6800, *Fax:* (636) 239-0364
www.kslq.co
License: Washington, Franklin County, MO held by Y2K Inc.
Nat'l Network: USA *Regional Network:* Missourinet
Arbitron Metro Market: Washington, MO *Format:* Adult Contemp *Target Audience:* 25-54.
Robert Eurich, President

KWMO
10-19-1985; 1350 khz AM; 0.5 kw-D, DA2; 0.084 kw-N, DA2; N38 34 44 W90 59 57
8604 Hedgebur, St. Louis, MO 63114 US
(636) 239-5432, *Fax:* (636) 239-0364
www.themouth.info
License: Washington, MO held by Computraffic Inc.
Nat'l Network: USA *Regional Network:* Missourinet
Arbitron Metro Market: Washington, MO *Format:* Talk *Target Audience:* 35-54.
Waldo Zimarskie, General Manager
Chris Dieckhause, News Director

Waynesville

KFBD-FM
12-09-1964; 97.9 mhz FM *Hrs Open:* 5 AM-midnight; 10 kw; 515 ft.; N37 56 50 W92 21 18
PO Box 583, 104 Peggy Ave, Waynesville, MO 65583 US
(573) 336-4913, *Fax:* (573) 336-2222
www.myozarksonline.com
License: Waynesville, Pulaski County, MO
Group Owner: GoodRadio.TV
Arbitron Metro Market: Waynesville, MO *Format:* Adult Contemp
Mike Edwards, General Manager
Sue Jones, Business Manager

KJPW
04-03-1962; 1390 khz AM *Hrs Open:* 19; 5 kw-D, ND1; 0.111 kw-N, ND1; N37 49 9 W92 9 6
Mailing Address: P. O. Box D, Waynesville, MO 65583 US
Second Address: 313 Old Rte 66, St. Robert, MO 65583-0480
(573) 336-4913, *Fax:* (573) 336-2222
www.myozarksonline.com
kjpw@regionalradio.com
License: Waynesville, MO held by Waynesville/Lebanon License Co. LLC.
Group Owner: GoodRadio.TV; (acq 8-8-2007; grpsl)
Nat'l Network: Fox News Radio *Regional Network:* Missourinet
Format: Talk *Special Programming:* Relg 2 hrs wkly *Hrs. of News Programming:* news progmg 14 hrs wkly *No. News*

Employees: 1 *Target Audience:* General. *Adv. Rates:* 22; 18; 16; 13.
Mike Edwards, General Manager
Gary Knehans, Station Manager
Warren Goforth, News Director
Bob Moore, Chief Engineer
Sue Jones, Business Manager

KOZQ-FM
05-02-1968; 102.3 mhz FM *Hrs Open:* 19; 2.65 kw; Ant 492 ft; N37 49 09 W92 09 06
Box D, Waynesville, MO 65583
(573) 336-4913,(573) 336-4450, *Fax:* (573) 336-2222
kjpw@regionalradio.com
License: Waynesville, Pulaski County, MO held by Waynesville/Lebanon License Co. LLC.
Group Owner: GoodRadio.TV
Nat'l Network: Fox News Radio
Population Served: 60,000*Hrs. of News Programming:* news progmg 7 hrs wkly *No. News Employees:* 1 *Target Audience:* General. *Adv. Rates:* 17; 13; 17; 13
Gary Knehans, Operations Dir
Mike Edwards, General Manager
Mke Edwards, General Sales Mgr
Warren Goforth, News Director
Dan Boucher, Engineering Dir
Dave Howlett, Local Sales Manager

KIIK
05-09-1968; 1270 khz AM; 500 w-D; N37 49 42 W92 10 27
Mailing Address: Box D, Waynesville, MO 65583
Second Address: 313 Old Rte. 66, Waynesville, MO 65584
(573) 336-4913, *Fax:* (573) 336-2222
License: Waynesville, Pulaski County, MO held by Waynesville/Lebanon License Co. LLC.
Group Owner: GoodRadio.TV; (acq 8-8-2007; grpsl)
Population Served: 100,000*Target Audience:* 40 plus.
Mike Edwards, General Manager

Webb City

KJMK
09-10-1985; 93.9 mhz FM *Hrs Open:* 24 hrs; 48 kw; 505 ft; N37 14 34 W94 30 21
2702 E. 32nd, Joplin, MO 63702
(417) 624-1025, *Fax:* (417) 781-6842
www.939literock.com
chade@zrgmail.com
License: Webb City, Jasper County, MO held by Zimmer Radio Inc.
Group Owner: Zimmer Radio Inc.; (acq 6-17-97; grpsl)
Nat'l Reps: Christal
Arbitron Metro Market: Joplin, MO *Target Audience:* 25-54.
James Zimmer, CEO
Chad Elliott, Operations Dir
Larry Boyd, General Manager
Carol Daily, General Sales Mgr
Rob Meyer, Programming Director
Jesse White, Promotions Manager
Josh Marsh, News Director
Mel Williams, Chief Engineer

KKLL
03-10-1984; 1100 khz AM; 2.5 kw-C, NDD; 5 kw-D, NDD; N37 6 23 W94 16 50
1411 Locust Street, St. Louis, MO 63103 US
(417) 781-1100, *Fax:* (417) 781-1100
info@kkllam.com
License: Webb City, MO held by New Life Evangelistic Center Inc.
Arbitron Metro Market: Joplin, MO *Format:* Christian
Charlie Hale, Operations Dir

KXDG
09-01-1988; 97.9 mhz FM *Hrs Open:* 24; 15.5 kw; 417 ft.; N37 14 34 W94 30 21
P.O. Box 1749, Cape Girardeau, MO 63702 US
(417) 624-1025, *Fax:* (417) 781-6842
www.bigdog979.com
License: Webb City, Jasper County, MO held by Zimmer Radio Inc.
Group Owner: Zimmer Radio Inc.; (acq 6-17-97; grpsl).
Nat'l Reps: Christal
Arbitron Metro Market: Joplin, MO *Format:* Classic Rock *No. News Employees:* 4 *Target Audience:* General.
James Zimmer, President
Chad Elliott, Operations Dir
Carol Daily, General Sales Mgr
Chris Hayes, Programming Director
Mel Williams, Chief Engineer
Kara Marxer, News Director
Rob Meyer, Assistant Operations Manager
Chris Hayes,Program Director
Christe Ogle, Business Office Manager
Larry Boyd, Market Manager

West Plains

KKDY
03-31-1984; 102.5 mhz FM *Hrs Open:* 24; 50 kw; 486 ft.; N36 41 22 W91 53 45
983 East Us Highway 160, West Plains, MO 65775 US
(417) 256-1025, *Fax:* (417) 256-2208
www.kkdy.com
news@ozarkradionetwork.com
License: West Plains, Howell County, MO held by Central Ozark Radio Network Inc.
Nat'l Network: CNN Radio
Arbitron Metro Market: Springfield, MO *Format:* Country *Special Programming:* Contemp Christian 3 hrs wkly *Hrs. of News Programming:* news progmg 10 hrs wkly *No. News Employees:* 2 *Target Audience:* 18-49.
Tom Marhefka, President
Bob Eckman, Operations Dir
Jonathan Bergman, General Sales Mgr
Bobby Helm, News Director
Bill Martin, Chief Engineer
Chuck Boone, Operations Director
Crystal Cook, Traffic Manager

KSPQ
01-01-1951; 93.9 mhz FM; 100 kw; 650 ft.; N37 0 12 W91 54 24
983 Us Hwy 160 East, West Plains, MO 65775 US
(417) 256-2322, *Fax:* (417) 256-2208
www.ozarkareanetwork.com
hotcountrykdy@kkdy.com
License: West Plains, Howell County, MO
Arbitron Metro Market: West Plains, MO *Format:* Classic Rock *Target Audience:* 45-65 plus.
Jonathan Bergman, General Sales Mgr
Mike Crase, Programming Director

KWPM
01-01-1947; 1450 khz AM *Hrs Open:* 24; 1 kw-U, ND1; N36 44 28 W91 50 1
983 Us Hwy. 160 E., West Plains, MO 65775 US
(417) 256-1025, *Fax:* (417) 256-2208
www.ozarkradionetwork.com
news@ozarkradionetwork.com
License: West Plains, MO held by Missouri Ozarks Radio Network.
Regional Network: Brownfield; Missourinet
Arbitron Metro Market: West Plains, MO *Format:* News, News/Talk, 86 *No. News Employees:* 4 *Target Audience:* 25-54.
Tom Marheska, Operations Dir
Gerry Elan, General Manager
Jonathan Bergman, General Sales Mgr
Bobby Helm, News Director
Bill Martin, Chief Engineer
Crystal Cook, Traffic Manager

***KSMW**
90.3 mhz FM; 0.8 kw; 394 ft.; N36 44 48.4 W91 49 55.8
901 South National Ave, Springfield, MO 65804 US
(417) 836-5878, *Fax:* (417) 836-5889
www.ksmu.org
ksmu@missouristate
License: West Plains, Howell County, MO held by Board of Governors, Southwest Missouri State University.
Arbitron Metro Market: Springfield, MO *Format:* News
Tammy Wiley, General Manager
Missy Shelton, News Director
Doug Waugh, Chief Engineer
Rachel Knight, Assistant to the General Manager
Lori Street, Membership Manager
Sue Camp, Membership Coordinator
Jamie Miller, MembershipCoordinator
Liz Malarkey, Traffic Coordinator
Barb McMeekin, Corporate Support Manager

Wheeling

KULH
05-03-1999; 105.9 mhz FM *Hrs Open:* 24; 6 kw; 328 ft.; N39 54 25 W93 20 28
Box 217, Trenton, MO 64683 US
(877) 639-1059, *Fax:* (660) 646-2242
www.1059thewave.com
ean1059@sbcglobal.net
License: Wheeling, Livingston County, MO held by Resources Management Unlimited, Inc.
Nat'l Network: USA
Arbitron Metro Market: Wheeling, MO *Format:* Adult Contemp, Christian *Target Audience:* General. *Adv. Rates:* 15; 15; 15; 15
Ean Leppin, General Manager
Holly Mosier, Traffic Manager
Rod Tompkins, Sports Director and Sales Rep.

Willard

KOMG
08-15-1992; 105.1 mhz FM; 50 kw; Ant 492 ft; N37 01 01 W93 30 31
319-B E. Battlefield, Springfield, MO 65807
(417) 886-5677, *Fax:* (417) 886-2155
www.star1051.fm
info@star1051.fm
License: Willard, Greene County, MO held by MW SpringMo Inc.
Group Owner: The Mid-West Family Broadcast Group
Nat'l Network: NBC Radio *Nat'l Reps:* Eastman Radio
Population Served: 295,300 *Arbitron Metro Market:* Springfield, MO *Target Audience:* 35-64. *Adv. Rates:* 30; 35; 35; 35; 15
Rick McCoy, President
Mary Fleenor, Operations Dir
Malcolm Hukriede, General Sales Mgr
Summer Stevens, Promotions Manager
Jeanne Guittar, Business Manager
Keith Abercrombie, Regional Sales Manager
Nichole Buckner, TrafficManager

Willow Springs

KUKU
10-01-1957; 1330 khz AM *Hrs Open:* Sunrise-sunset; 1 kw-D, ND1; 0.052 kw-N, ND1; N36 58 47 W91 59 29 *Rebroadcasts:* Rebroadcasts KWPM(AM) West Plains 100%
Box 250, Willow Springs, MO 65793 US
(417) 469-2500, *Fax:* (417) 934-2565
www.ozarknewstalkradio.com
gto@kuku.com
License: Willow Springs, MO held by Missouri Ozarks Radio Network.
Nat'l Network: ABC
Arbitron Metro Market: Willow Springs, MO *Format:* News, News/Talk, 86
Tove Sorensen, Operations Dir
Roe Edmons, Production Director

KUKU-FM
06-15-1985; 100.3 mhz FM *Hrs Open:* 24; 50 kw; 492 ft.; N37 3 49 W92 1 39
Box 250, Willow Springs, MO 65793 US
(417) 469-2500, *Fax:* (417) 934-2565
www.ozarknewstalkradio.com
License: Willow Springs, Howell County, MO
Arbitron Metro Market: Willow Springs, MO *Format:* Oldies *Hrs. of News Programming:* news progmg 27 hrs wkly *No. News Employees:* 2 *Target Audience:* 29 plus.
Gary Taylor, Programming Director
Harlin Hutchinson, News Director

Windsor

KWKJ
02-21-2002; 98.5 mhz FM *Hrs Open:* 24; 9 kw; 535 ft.; N38 35 37 W93 31 26
P. O. Box 4584, Springfield, MO 65808 US
(660) 747-9191, *Fax:* (660) 747-5611
www.warrensburgradio.com
ghassler@kwkj.com
License: Windsor, Henry County, MO held by D & H Media LLC
Wire Services: AP
Arbitron Metro Market: Warrensburg, MO *Format:* Country *Hrs. of News Programming:* news progmg 1 hr wkly *No. News Employees:* 1 *Target Audience:* Students; Central MO State Univ. Students and like age group*Adv. Rates:* 14;13;14;13
Vance DeLozier, President
Greg Hassler, Operations Dir

Montana

Alberton

KOYT(FM)
105.5 mhz FM; 1.1 kw; Ant 787 ft; N47 02 05 W114 41 11
Box 4106, Missoula, MT 59806
(406) 728-5000, *Fax:* (406) 721-3020
License: Alberton, Mineral County, MT held by CCR-Missoula IV LLC.
Group Owner: Cherry Creek Radio LLC; (acq 10-31-2006; grpsl)
Population Served: 1,359,758 *Arbitron Metro Market:* San Antonio, TX
Chad Parrish, General Manager

Anaconda

KGLM-FM
01-18-1974; 97.7 mhz FM *Hrs Open:* 24; 2.75 kw; 984 ft.; N46 6 4 W112 56 59
P.O. Box 811, Deer Lodge, MT 59722 US
(406) 563-8011, *Fax:* (406) 563-8259
www.magic97.net
mail@magic97.mobi
License: Anaconda, Deer Lodge County, MT held by Butte Broadcasting Inc.
Format: Adult Contemp *Target Audience:* 18 plus.
Ron Davis, President
Joe Frankland, Operations Dir
Paula Carriger, General Manager

KANA
08-01-1947; 580 khz AM *Hrs Open:* 24
P.O. Box 580, Anaconda, MT 59711 US
(406) 563-8011, *Fax:* (406) 563-8259
mail@magic97.mobi
License: Anaconda, MT held by Butte Broadcasting Inc.
Nat'l Network: ABC
Arbitron Metro Market: Great Falls, MT *Format:* Oldies *Hrs. of News Programming:* News progmg one hr wkly *Target Audience:* 40+.
Ron Davis, President
Joe Frankland, Operations Dir
Paula Carriger, General Manager

Arlee

*KJFT
01-01-2007; 90.3 mhz FM; 0.4 kw; 1906 ft.; N47 1 4 W114 0 49
3000 W. Macarthur Blvd., Santa Ana, CA 92704 US
(800) 357-4226, *Fax:* (208) 736-1958
www.csnradio.com
csn@csnradio.com
License: Arlee, Lake County, MT held by CSN International
Group Owner: CSN International
Arbitron Metro Market: Arlee, MT *Format:* Christian
Mike Kestler, President
Daniel Davidson, Operations Dir
Jason Pace, General Manager
Don Mills, Network Programming Director / Music Director
Kelly Carlson, Engineering Dir
Jerry Johnson, Engineering Dir
Ray Gorney, AssistantDirector of Engineering
Dustin Pamplona, Engineer
Nolan Mather, Graphics / Website Maintenance
Mike Stocklin, National Underwriting
Austin Morris, Accounting
Lois Mills, FCC Applications / Translator Site Manager

Baker

KFLN
07-14-1964; 960 khz AM; 5 kw-D, ND1; 0.091 kw-N, ND1; N46 22 31 W104 16 25
P. O. Box 790, Baker, MT 59313 US
(406) 778-3371, *Fax:* (406) 778-3373
http://www.newellbroadcasting.com/
kfln@midrivers.com
License: Baker, MT held by Newell Broadcasting Corp.
Nat'l Network: ABC *Regional Network:* Agrinet *Wire Services:* AP
Arbitron Metro Market: Baker, MT *Format:* Classic Rock *Special Programming:* Farm 5 hrs wkly, Sports 5 hrs wkly *Hrs. of News Programming:* news progmg 10 hrs wkly *Target Audience:* 18-64
Russ Newell, President
Devin Bannister, General Sales Mgr
Russ Newell

KJJM
05-26-2001; 100.5 mhz FM *Hrs Open:* 24; 7.4 kw; 610 ft.; N46 30 20 W104 12 36
Mailing Address: P O Box 790, Baker, MT 59313 US
Second Address: 3600 Hwy. 7, Baker, MT 59313
(406) 778-3371, *Fax:* (406) 778-3373
License: Baker, Fallon County, MT held by Newell Broadcasting Corp.
Format: Classic Rock
Russ Newell, General Manager
Vaughn Zenko, Programming Director

Belgrade

KGVW
02-01-1959; 640 khz AM *Hrs Open:* 24; 10 kw-D, DA2; 1 kw-N, DA2; N45 46 15 W111 13 26
2050 Amsterdam Road, Belgrade, MT 59714 US
(406) 388-4281, *Fax:* (406) 388-1700
http://www.kcmmtheone.com/
License: Belgrade, MT held by Gallatin Valley Witness Inc.
Nat'l Network: USA
Format: News, News/Talk, 86, Religious *Hrs. of News Programming:* news progmg 16 hrs wkly *No. News Employees:* 1 *Target Audience:* 35-64; business people, farmers & housewives *Adv. Rates:* 10; 10; 10; 10
Mark Brashear, President
Bryan Brucks, Operations Dir
C.J. Swoboda, Programming Director
Dale Heidner, Chief Engineer

KISN
11-01-1963; 96.7 mhz FM; 18.5 kw; 814 ft.; N45 40 24 W110 52 2
101 West Grand Avenue, Chicago, IL 60610 US
(406) 586-2343, *Fax:* (406) 587-2202
www.bozemanskissfm.com
License: Belgrade, Gallatin County, MT held by GAP Broadcasting Bozeman License LLC.
Group Owner: GAPWEST Broadcasting; (acq 2-13-2008; grpsl)
Arbitron Metro Market: Bozeman, MT *Format:* Contemporary Hits/Top 40 *Target Audience:* 25-54; women
Sylvia Drain, General Manager
Sammy Suarez, Programming Director

KCMM
01-01-2001; 99.1 mhz FM; 25 kw; 203 ft.; N45 46 15 W111 13 26
2050 Amsterdam Road, Belgrade, MT 59714 US
(406) 388-4281, *Fax:* (406) 388-1700
www.kcmmtheone.com
info@kcmmtheone.com
License: Belgrade, Gallatin County, MT held by Gallatin Valley Witness Inc.
Arbitron Metro Market: Belgrade, MT *Format:* Christian
Phil Lang, CFO
Bryan Brucks, General Manager
Mark Brashear, General Sales Mgr
Dale Heidner, Chief Engineer

*KGCM
01-01-2006; 90.9 mhz FM; 5.5 kw vert; 623 ft.; N45 57 25 W111 22 11
US
(800) 877-5600, *Fax:* (916) 251-1650
www.godscountryradionetwork.com
info@happyjubilee.com
License: Belgrade, Gallatin County, MT held by Educational Media Foundation.
Group Owner: EMF Broadcasting
Arbitron Metro Market: Eureka, CA *Format:* Country, Gospel
Mike Novak, President

Belt

*KGFJ
88.1 mhz FM; 0.25 kw; 1960 ft.; N47 9 34 W111 0 39
US
(800) 357-4226, *Fax:* (208) 736-1958
www.csnradio.com
License: Belt, Cascade County, MT held by Calvary Chapel of Twin Falls Inc.
Group Owner: CSN International
Arbitron Metro Market: Belt, MT
Michael Kestler, President
Daniel Davidson, Operations Dir
Don Mills, Music director
Kelly Carlson, Engineering Dir
Ray Gorney, Assistant Director of Engineering
Lois Mills, Translator Site Manager

Big Sky

KBZM
07-31-1998; 104.7 mhz FM *Hrs Open:* 24; 5 kw; 3337 ft.; N45 16 41 W111 26 57 *Rebroadcasts:* Simulcast on KKQX(FM) Manhattan
47520 Gallatin Road, Suite 1d, Gallatin Gateway, MT 59730 US
(406) 582-1045, *Fax:* (406) 582-0388
www.montanassuperstation.com
jbalding@kbzm.com
License: Big Sky, Gallatin County, MT held by Orion Media LLC.
Nat'l Reps: Interep *Regional Reps:* Local Focus 310-441-8188
Arbitron Metro Market: Bozeman, MT *Format:* Classic Rock
Special Programming: 6a-10a; 3p-6p *No. News Employees:* 2
Target Audience: Adults; 25-54
Jeff Balding, General Manager
Susan Balding, General Sales Mgr
Colter Langan, Programming Director

Big Timber

*KYPB
89.3 mhz FM; 0.5 kw; 413 ft.; N45 45 1 W109 57 16
US
(406) 657-2941, *Fax:* (406) 657-2977
www.yellowstonepublicradio.org
mail@ypradio.org
License: Big Timber, Sweet Grass County, MT held by Montana State University - Billings.
Arbitron Metro Market: Big Timber, MT *Format:* Variety/Diverse
Dennis Hall, President
Ken Siebert, General Manager / Media Services Director
Jackie Yamanaka, News Director
Jim Nichols, Chief Engineer
Barbara Bernheim, Development and Listener Support Manager
Alicia Lee, Underwriting Manager /Public Information Manager
Ana Henrickson, Business & Finance Manager
Art Hooker, Control Room Operator / Production Assistant
Merry Ann Peters, Control Room Operator
Wesley Jessen, Media Services Assistant / Control Room Operator

Bigfork

KIBG
01-01-2001; 100.7 mhz FM; 85 kw; 2119 ft.; N47 46 25 W114 16 4
P O Box 2158, Ketchum, ID 83340 US
(406) 883-5255, *Fax:* (406) 883-4441
www.thebig100.com
info@750kerr.com
License: Bigfork, Flathead County, MT held by Anderson Radio Broadcasting Inc.
Group Owner: Anderson Radio Broadcasting Inc.; (acq 9-22-2003; grpsl)
Arbitron Metro Market: Polson, MT
Dennis Anderson, General Manager
Gary Meili, General Sales Mgr
Dean August, Programming Director
Jeff Smith, News Director
Tony Mulligan, Chief Engineer

Billings

KBBB(FM)
12-06-1987; 103.7 mhz FM *Hrs Open:* 24; 100 kw; 480 ft; N45 46 00 W108 27 27
27 N. 27th St., 23rd Fl. Crowne Plaza, Billings, MT 59101
(406) 248-7827, *Fax:* (406) 252-9577
www.kmhk.com
bobfreeman@townsquaremedia.com
License: Billings, Yellowstone County, MT held by GAP Broadcasting Billings License LLC.
Group Owner: GAPWEST Broadcasting; (acq 2-13-2008; grpsl)
Nat'l Reps: Tacher
Arbitron Metro Market: Billings, MT *Format:* Adult Contemp
Target Audience: 25-54; general
Roy Brown, Operations Dir
Bob Freeman, General Manager
Larry Wilson, Programming Director

KYSX(FM)
12-01-1998; 105.1 mhz FM *Hrs Open:* 24; 6 kw; Ant 233 ft; N45 45 57 W108 27 17
222 N. 32nd St., 10th Floor, Billings, MT 59101
(406) 238-1000, *Fax:* (406) 238-1038
License: Billings, Yellowstone County, MT
Group Owner: Benedetti Media Group LLC; (acq 10-26-99; grpsl).
Nat'l Network: ESPN Radio
Arbitron Metro Market: Billings, MT *Format:* Sports *Target Audience:* 25-54. *Adv. Rates:* 15; 15; 15; 5
Pete Benedetti, CEO
Kyle McCoy, General Manager

KBLG
09-25-1955; 910 khz AM *Hrs Open:* 24
North 1212 Washington, Suite 307, Spokane, WA 99201 US
(406) 248-7777, *Fax:* (406) 652-4899
www.kblg910.com
License: Billings, MT held by CCR-Billings IV LLC
Group Owner: Cherry Creek Radio LLC
Nat'l Network: CBS
Arbitron Metro Market: Billings, MT *Format:* News, News/Talk, 84, Talk *Hrs. of News Programming:* news progmg 46 hrs wkly *No. News Employees:* 1 *Target Audience:* 35-64; upscale executives
Cal Hunter, General Manager

KBUL
03-20-1951; 970 khz AM *Hrs Open:* 24
Mailing Address: City Center West, 7201 W. Lake Mead Blvd, Las Vegas, NV 89128 US
Second Address: 27 N. 27th St., 23rd Fl., Billings, MT 59101
(406) 294-0970, *Fax:* (406) 252-9577
www.newsradio970.com
bobfreeman@townsquaremedia.com
License: Billings, MT held by GAP Broadcasting Billings License LLC.
Group Owner: GAPWEST Broadcasting; (acq 2-13-2008; grpsl)
Nat'l Reps: Christal
Arbitron Metro Market: Billings, MT *Format:* News *Hrs. of News Programming:* news progmg 2 hrs wkly *No. News Employees:* 1 *Target Audience:* 25-54.
Dennis Coffman, President
Bob Freeman, General Manager
Roy Brown, General Sales Mgr
Pat Stinson, Programming Director
Stacy Ulstad, News Director
Dick Jones, Chief Engineer

KRZN
01-01-1998; 96.3 mhz FM; 100 kw; 696 ft.; N45 45 37 W108 27 9
N. 1212 Washington, Suite 307, Spokane, WA 99201 US
(406) 248-7777, *Fax:* (406) 652-4899
www.thezone963.com
License: Billings, Yellowstone County, MT held by CCR-Billings IV LLC.
Group Owner: Cherry Creek Radio LLC; (acq 10-31-2006; grpsl)
Arbitron Metro Market: Billings, MT *Format:* Rock/AOR
Cam Maxwell, General Manager
Dan Reese, Station Manager
Scott Fredricks, Sales Manager

KCTR-FM
08-14-1979; 102.9 mhz FM; 100 kw; 499 ft.; N45 45 59 W108 27 19
Mailing Address: City Center West, 7201 W. Lake Mead Blvd, Las Vegas, NV 89128 US
Second Address: 27 N. 27th St., 23rd Fl., Billings, MT 59101
(406) 248-7827, *Fax:* (406) 252-9577
www.kctr.com
License: Billings, Yellowstone County, MT held by GAP Broadcasting Billings License LLC.
Group Owner: GAPWEST Broadcasting; (acq 2-13-2008; grpsl)
Arbitron Metro Market: Billings, MT *Format:* Country
Don Oylear, General Manager
Tammie Torren, Programming Director

***KEMC**
04-25-1973; 91.7 mhz FM *Hrs Open:* 24; 100 kw; 518 ft.; N45 39 31 W108 34 14
1500 North 30th Street, Billings, MT 59101 US
(406) 657-2941, *Fax:* (406) 657-2977
www.yellowstonepublicradio.org
mail@yellowstonepublicradio.org
License: Billings, Yellowstone County, MT held by Montana State University/Billings.
Nat'l Network: NPR; AP Radio
Arbitron Metro Market: Billings, MT *Format:* Jazz, News *Special Programming:* Folk 5 hrs wkly *Hrs. of News Programming:* news progmg 24 hrs wkly *No. News Employees:* 1 *Target Audience:* General.
Dennis Hall, President
Ken Siebert, General Manager
Jackie Yamanaka, News Director
Jim Nichols, Chief Engineer

***KBZR**
05-02-1965; 88.5 mhz FM; kw
US
(402) 571-0200, *Fax:* (402) 571-0833
www.kvss.com
kvss@kvss.com
License: Billings, Lancaster County, MT held by VSS Catholic Communications Inc.
Arbitron Metro Market: Billings, NE *Format:* Christian *Special Programming:* Live Mass 2 hrs wkly, business 1 hr wkly *Target Audience:* Christian Families
John Soukup, Station Manager
Mark Voris, Chief Engineer

KGHL
06-08-1928; 790 khz AM *Hrs Open:* 24; 5 kw-U, DA-N; N45 43 34 W108 36 35
222 N. 32nd St., Billings, MT 60611
(406) 238-1000, *Fax:* (406) 238-1038
www.mighty790.com
nick.tyler@benedettimedia.com
License: Billings, Yellowstone County, MT held by KGHL Radio LLC
Group Owner: New Northwest Broadcasters LLC; (acq 8-10-99; grpsl)
Nat'l Network: CBS *Wire Services:* AP
Population Served: 165,500 *Arbitron Metro Market:* Billings, MT *Hrs. of News Programming:* news progmg 4 hrs wkly *No. News Employees:* 1 *Target Audience:* 25-54.
Kyle McCoy, General Manager
Nick Tyler, Programming Director
Denise Tysver, News Director
Connor Powers, Chief Engineer

KGHL(FM)
08-01-1978; 98.5 mhz FM; 85 kw; Ant 370 ft; N45 45 51 W108 27 18
222 N. 32nd St., Billings, MT 59101
(406) 238-1000, *Fax:* (406) 238-1038
www.985thewolf.com
streaming@benedettimedia.com
License: Billings, Yellowstone County, MT held by BMG Billings, LLC
Group Owner: New Northwest Broadcasters LLC
Population Served: 192,800 *Arbitron Metro Market:* Billings, MT *Format:* Country *Target Audience:* 18-54.
Pete Benedetti, CEO
Kyle McCoy, Operations Dir
Emily Petroff, General Sales Mgr
Nick Tyler, Programming Director
Scott Phillips, Program Director

KKBR
12-17-1963; 97.1 mhz FM *Hrs Open:* 24; 28 kw; 400 ft.; N45 45 59 W108 27 19
City Center West, 7201 W. Lake Mead Blvd, Las Vegas, NV 89128 US
(406) 248-7827, *Fax:* (406) 252-9577
www.kbear.com
License: Billings, Yellowstone County, MT held by GAP Broadcasting Billings License LLC.
Group Owner: GAPWEST Broadcasting; (acq 2-13-2008; grpsl)
Arbitron Metro Market: Billings, MT *Format:* Oldies
Don Oylear, General Manager
Larry Wilson, Programming Director

KMHK
01-01-1975; 103.7 mhz FM; 100 kw; 479 ft.; N45 46 0 W108 27 27
City Center West, 7201 W. Lake Mead Blvd., Las Vegas, NV 89128 US
(406) 248-7827, *Fax:* (406) 252-9577
www.kmhk.com
License: Billings, Big Horn County, MT held by GAP Broadcasting Billings License LLC.
Group Owner: GAPWEST Broadcasting; (acq 2-13-2008; grpsl)
Arbitron Metro Market: Billings, MT *Target Audience:* 18-34; general
Dennis Koffman, General Manager
Jay Branden, Promotions Manager

KRKX
07-01-1989; 94.1 mhz FM *Hrs Open:* 24; 100 kw; 591 ft.; N45 45 37 W108 27 9
North 1212 Washington, Suite 124, Spokane, WA 99201 US
(406) 248-7777, *Fax:* (406) 652-4899
www.941ksky.com
License: Billings, Yellowstone County, MT held by CCR-Billings IV LLC
Group Owner: Cherry Creek Radio LLC; (acq 10-31-2006; grpsl)
Arbitron Metro Market: Billings Metro area *Format:* Country *Target Audience:* 25-54; affluent *Adv. Rates:* 60; 60; 60; 60
Terry Keys, Operations Dir
Debbie Sundberg, General Manager
Augie Aga, General Sales Mgr

KURL
10-15-1959; 730 khz AM *Hrs Open:* 24; 5 kw-D, 236 w-N; N45 45 29 W108 29 53
Mailing Address: Box 30315, Billings, MT 99201
Second Address: 636 Haugen, Billings, MT 59101
(406) 245-3121, *Fax:* (406) 245-0822
www.kurlradio.com
genmgr@kurlradio.com
License: Billings, Yellowstone County, MT held by Elenbaas Media Inc.
Nat'l Network: Salem
Population Served: 125,000 *Arbitron Metro Market:* Billings, MT *Target Audience:* 35-64.
Herm Elenbaas, President

KURL(FM)
04-05-1969; 93.3 mhz FM *Hrs Open:* 24; 100 kw; 700 ft; N45 45 37 W108 27 09
2075 Central Ave., PO Box 31038, Billings, MT 59102
(406) 652-8400, *Fax:* (406) 652-4899
www.newstalk730.com
y930@y93.com
License: Billings, Yellowstone County, MT held by CCR-Billings IV LLC.
Group Owner: Cherry Creek Radio LLC; (acq 10-31-2006; grpsl)
Nat'l Network: ABC
Population Served: 105,636 *Arbitron Metro Market:* Billings, MT *Format:* Classic Rock *Hrs. of News Programming:* news progmg 2 hrs wkly *No. News Employees:* 1 *Target Audience:* 18-49; women *Adv. Rates:* 35; 35; 30; 25
Steve Aga, General Manager
Dave Wood, Programming Director
Michael Lyon, News Director
Bruce Faulkner, Chief Engineer

KRPM
01-01-2001; 107.5 mhz FM; 100 kw; 446 ft.; N45 45 48 W108 27 20
218 N Wolcott, Casper, WY 82601 US
(406) 238-1000, *Fax:* (406) 238-1038
www.magic1075fm.com
kyle.mccoy@benedettimedia.com
License: Billings, Yellowstone County, MT held by BMG Billings, LLC
Group Owner: Benedetti Media Group LLC; (acq 10-26-99)
Arbitron Metro Market: Billings, MT *Target Audience:* 25-54.
Pete Benedetti, CEO
Kyle McCoy, General Manager

***KBLW**
08-01-2002; 90.1 mhz FM *Hrs Open:* 24; 0.45 kw; 449 ft.; N45 45 37 W108 27 9 *Rebroadcasts:* Rebroadcasts KXEI(FM) Havre 100%.
Mailing Address: P O Drawer 2440, Tupelo, MS 38803 US
Second Address: 317 First St., Havre, MT 59501
(406) 265-5845, *Fax:* (406) 265-8860
www.ynopradio.org
ynop@ynopradio.org
License: Billings, Yellowstone County, MT held by Hi-Line Radio Fellowship Inc.
Nat'l Network: Moody; Salem Radio Network *Wire Services:* AP
Arbitron Metro Market: Billings, MT *Format:* Religious *Target Audience:* General; those looking for Christian inspirational music & progmg
Brenda Boyum, KXEI Station Manager
Clark Berg, KALS Sales Manager
David Brown, YNOP Program Director
Nicholas Tobiason, Music/IT Director
Ron Huckeby, Chief Engineer
Crystal MacInnes, Production Assistant
Elizabeth McClenahan,Office Manager at KXEI/Webmaster
Joe McGee, KALS Account Executive
Carlene Prince, YNOP Associate Network Manager
Dan Shepherd, KALS Account Executive

***KLMT**
12-18-2002; 89.3 mhz FM *Hrs Open:* 24; 0.35 kw horiz, 0.98 kw vert; 528 ft.; N45 45 48 W108 27 20
6363 Highway 50 East, Carson City, NV 89701 US
(775) 883-5647
www.pilgrimradio.com
info@pilgrimradio.com
License: Billings, Yellowstone County, MT held by Western Inspirational Broadcasters Inc.
Arbitron Metro Market: Billings, MT *Format:* Christian *No. News Employees:* 1
Tim Weidemann, Operations Dir
Tom Hesse, General Manager
Bill Feltner, Programming Director
Patrick Herman, Music Director

***KLRV**
01-01-2005; 90.9 mhz FM; 7.5 kw vert; 593 ft.; N45 45 54 W108 27 19 *Rebroadcasts:* Rebroadcasts KLVR(FM) Santa Rosa, CA).
188 South Bellevue, Suite 222, Memphis, TN 38104 US
(800) 525-5683, *Fax:* (916) 251-1650
www.klove.com
klove@klove.com
License: Billings, Yellowstone County, MT held by Educational Media Foundation.
Group Owner: EMF Broadcasting; (acq 12-8-2004; $100,000 for CP with CP for KLWC(FM) Casper, WY).
Nat'l Network: K-Love
Arbitron Metro Market: Billings, MT *Format:* Christian

Darrell Chambliss, Chairman
Mike Novak, President and CEO
Mike Lee, Operations Dir
David Pierce, Programming Director
Ed Lenane, News Director
Sam Wallington, Engineering Dir
Marya Morgan, News Reporter
Richard Hunt, NewsReporter
Tracy Butler, Traffic Manager
Laura Daniels, News Reporter
Tim Luttrell, News Reporter
Kenny Noble Cortes, News Reporter

Bozeman

*KBMC
10-01-1991; 102.1 mhz FM; 20.5 kw; 728 ft.; N45 38 18 W111 16 5 *Rebroadcasts:* Rebroadcasts KEMC(FM) Billings 100%
1500 North 30th Street, Billings, MT 59101 US
(406) 657-2941, *Fax:* (406) 657-2977
www.ypradio.org
License: Bozeman, Gallatin County, MT held by Montana State University/Billings.
Arbitron Metro Market: Billings, MT *Format:* Jazz, News
Lois Bent, General Manager

KBOZ
12-19-1975; 1090 khz AM; 5 kw-D, DAN; 5 kw-N, DAN; N45 36 58 W111 5 16
Mailing Address: P.O. Box 519, Bozeman, MT 59771 US
Second Address: 5445 Johnson Rd., Bozeman, MT 59715
(406) 587-9999, *Fax:* (406) 587-5855
less@kboz.com
License: Bozeman, MT held by Reier Broadcasting Co. Inc.
Group Owner: Reier Broadcasting Co. Inc.; acq 10-18-96; grpsl).
Nat'l Network: CBS; Jones Radio Networks
Format: Talk *Target Audience:* 25-64.
Bill Reier, General Manager
Eric Reier, General Sales Mgr
Brian Bennett, Programming Director
Les Clay, News Director
Dick Jones, Chief Engineer
Diane Stovall, Traffic Manager

*KGLT
12-01-1963; 91.9 mhz FM; 12000 kw; 365 ft; N45 41 35 W110 59 00
Montana State Univ., Rm. 376, Bozeman, MT 59717
(406) 994-3001, *Fax:* (406) 994-1987
License: Bozeman, Gallatin County, MT held by Montana State University.
Population Served: 67,000*Target Audience:* General.
Ellen King Rodgers, General Manager
Jim Kehoe, Programming Director
John Campbell, Chief Engineer

KMMS
10-15-1939; 1450 khz AM
125 W. Mendenhall, Bozeman, IL 59715 US
(406) 586-2343, *Fax:* (406) 587-2202
www.kmmsam.com
License: Bozeman, MT held by GAP Broadcasting Bozeman License LLC.
Group Owner: GAPWEST Broadcasting; (acq 2-13-2008; grpsl)
Nat'l Network: ABC *Nat'l Reps:* Clear Channel
Format: News, News/Talk, 84, Talk *Hrs. of News Programming:* News progmg one hr wkly *Target Audience:* 35-64.
Samuel Weller, President
Sylvia Drain, General Manager
Kay Ruh, General Sales Mgr
George Carter, Programming Director
Mary Atkins, Promotions Manager
John Russell, News Director
Dennis Mountford, Chief Engineer
Lenny Jones,Traffic Manager

KMMS-FM
08-14-1986; 95.1 mhz FM *Hrs Open:* 24; 94 kw; 781 ft.; N45 40 24 W110 52 2
101 West Grand Avenue, Chicago, IL 60610 US
(406) 586-2343, *Fax:* (406) 587-2202
www.mooseradio.com
License: Bozeman, Gallatin County, MT held by GAP Broadcasting Bozeman License LLC.
Group Owner: GAPWEST Broadcasting; (acq 2-13-2008; grpsl)
Format: Triple A *Adv. Rates:* 33; 30; 32; 22
Michelle Wolfe, Programming Director

KOBB
05-22-1950; 1230 khz AM *Hrs Open:* 24; 1 kw-U, ND1; N45 39 33 W111 3 22
Mailing Address: PO Box 20, Bozeman, MT 59715 US
Second Address: 5445 Johnson Rd., Bozeman, MT 59718
(406) 587-9999, *Fax:* (406) 587-5855
reier@bigsky.net
License: Bozeman, MT held by Reier Broadcasting Co. Inc.
Group Owner: Reier Broadcasting Co. Inc.; (acq 2-19-93; $125,000;
Nat'l Network: ABC *Regional Network:* Agrinet *Regional Reps:* Tacher.
Format: Adult Contemp *Hrs. of News Programming:* News progmg 15 hrs wkly *Target Audience:* 30 plus; affluent adults
William Reier Sr., President
Eric Reier, General Sales Mgr
Diane Stovall, News Director
Dick Jones, Chief Engineer

KOBB-FM
11-01-1980; 93.7 mhz FM; 51 kw; -128 ft.; N45 36 58 W111 5 16
P.O. Box 20, Bozeman, MT 59715 US
(406) 587-9999, *Fax:* (406) 587-5855
less@kboz.com
License: Bozeman, Gallatin County, MT held by Reier Broadcasting Co. Inc.
Group Owner: Reier Broadcasting Co. Inc.
Format: Oldies *Target Audience:* 25-54.
Tuck Reier, Operations Dir
Dave Visscher, Programming Director

KBOZ-FM
01-01-1983; 99.9 mhz FM; 19 kw; -184 ft.; N45 36 58 W111 5 16
Mailing Address: P.O. Box 20, Bozeman, MT 59715 US
Second Address: 5445 Johnson Rd., Bozeman, MT 59718
(406) 587-9999, *Fax:* (406) 587-5855
www.kboz.com/
less@kboz.com
License: Bozeman, Gallatin County, MT
Group Owner: Reier Broadcasting Co. Inc.
Arbitron Metro Market: Bozeman, MT *Format:* Country
Terry Michaels, Programming Director
Diane Stovall, News Director

KZMY
01-01-2004; 103.5 mhz FM *Hrs Open:* 24; 100 kw; 948 ft.; N45 57 25 W111 22 11
3610 Broadwater Street, Bozeman, MT 59715 US
(406) 556-0123, *Fax:* (406) 587-2202
my1035.com
erinphillips@townsquarmedia.com
License: Bozeman, Gallatin County, MT held by GAP Broadcasting Bozeman License LLC.
Group Owner: GAPWEST Broadcasting; (acq 2-13-2008; grpsl)
Arbitron Metro Market: Great Falls, MT *Format:* Adult Contemp
Dick Loughney, General Manager
Erin Phillips, Brand Manager
Dick Loughney, Director of Sales

*KLBZ
01-01-2007; 89.3 mhz FM; 7 kw vert; 679 ft.; N45 57 25 W111 22 11 *Rebroadcasts:* Rebroadcasts KLVR(FM) Middletown, CA 100%
1425 N Market Blvd., Suite 9, Sacramento, CA 95834 US
(800) 877-5600, *Fax:* (916) 251-1650
www.klove.com
License: Bozeman, Gallatin County, MT held by Educational Media Foundation.
Group Owner: EMF Broadcasting
Nat'l Network: K-Love
Arbitron Metro Market: Bozeman, MT *Format:* Christian
Darrell Chambliss, Chairman
Mike Novak, CEO, President
Mike Lee, Operations Dir
Dr. David R. Ferry, Chief Engineer
Mitch Barnhart, Director
Larry Moody, Director

Butte

KAAR
11-01-1988; 92.5 mhz FM *Hrs Open:* 24; 4.5 kw; 1804 ft.; N46 0 29 W112 26 30
Mailing Address: N. 1212 Washington, Suite 307, Spokane, WA 99201 US
Second Address: Box 3788, Butte, MT 59702
(406) 494-1030, *Fax:* (406) 494-6020
jgray@cherrycreekradio.com
License: Butte, Silver Bow County, MT held by CCR-Butte IV LLC.
Group Owner: Cherry Creek Radio LLC; (acq 10-31-2006; grpsl)
Nat'l Reps: McGavren Guild
Arbitron Metro Market: Butte, MT *Format:* Country *Hrs. of News Programming:* News progmg 8 hrs wkly *Target Audience:* General.
Jeff Gray, Operations Dir
Chris Ackerman, General Manager
Rene Wimberley, General Sales Mgr

*KAPC
01-01-1999; 91.3 mhz FM; 0.8 kw; 1873 ft.; N46 0 27 W112 26 30
Partv Building, Rm 180, Missoula, MT 59812 US
(406) 243-4931, *Fax:* (406) 243-3299
www.kufm.org
License: Butte, Silver Bow County, MT held by University of Montana.
Nat'l Network: NPR *Wire Services:* AP
Arbitron Metro Market: Missoula, MT *Format:* Classical, Jazz, 60 *Hrs. of News Programming:* News progmg 2 hrs wkly
William Marcus, General Manager

KBOW
02-14-1947; 550 khz AM; 5 kw-D, DAN; 1 kw-N, DAN; N45 58 30 W112 34 18
Mailing Address: 190 Kossuth, Butte, MT 59701 US
Second Address: 660 Dewey Blvd., Butte, MT 59702
(406) 494-7777, *Fax:* (406) 494-5534
mail@kbow&kopr.com
License: Butte, MT held by Butte Broadcasting Inc.
Nat'l Network: CBS
Format: Sports *Special Programming:* Farm 5 hrs, relg 2 hrs wkly *Target Audience:* 25 plus; general
Ron Davis, President
Fran Workman, Operations Dir
Paul Panisko, Programming Director
Mike Beckworth, Promotions Manager
Pat Schulte, News Director
Chuck Beardslee, Engineering Dir
Araka Williams, Traffic Manager

KMBR
02-07-1980; 95.5 mhz FM; 50 kw; 1821 ft.; N46 0 29 W112 26 30
Mailing Address: N 1212 Washington, Suite 307, Spokane, WA 99201 US
Second Address: 750 Dewey Blvd., Butte, MT 59702
(406) 494-5895, *Fax:* (406) 494-6020
www.955kmbr.com
jgray@cherrycreekradio.com
License: Butte, Silver Bow County, MT
Group Owner: Cherry Creek Radio LLC
Nat'l Reps: McGavren Guild
Format: Classic Rock
John Klapperich, CEO
Terri Bush, General Sales Mgr
Roxi Lennox, Programming Director
Van Craft, Chief Engineer

*KMSM-FM
01-01-1975; 103.9 mhz FM *Hrs Open:* 24; 0.74 kw; -223 ft.; N46 0 44 W112 33 26
Kmsm-Fm/Montana Tech, 1300 West Park Street, Butte, MT 59701 US
(406) 496-4601
www.mtech.edu/kmsm
kmsm@mtech.edu
License: Butte, Silver Bow County, MT held by Associated Students of Montanta Tech.
Arbitron Metro Market: Great Falls, MT *Format:* Alternative, Variety/Diverse *Special Programming:* Jazz 5 hrs, relg 3 hrs, class 2 hrs wkly *Hrs. of News Programming:* News progmg 2 hrs wkly *Target Audience:* General; very diversified group
Wendy Dyer, General Manager
Ben Carter, Station Manager

KOPR
10-26-1972; 94.1 mhz FM *Hrs Open:* 24; 58 kw; 1857 ft.; N46 0 23 W112 26 28
P.O. Box 3389, Butte, MT 59702 US
(406) 494-7777, *Fax:* (406) 494-5534
mail@kbow&kopr.com
License: Butte, Silver Bow County, MT held by Butte Broadcasting Inc.
Format: Adult Contemp *Hrs. of News Programming:* news progmg 5 hrs wkly *No. News Employees:* 2 *Target Audience:* 25-45; women
Fran Workman, Operations Dir

KXTL
01-01-1927; 1370 khz AM *Hrs Open:* 24
Mailing Address: North 1212 Washington, Suite 307, Spokane, WA 99201 US
Second Address: North 1212 Washington, Suite 307, Spokane, WA 99201
(406) 494-4442, *Fax:* (406) 494-6020
www.kxtl.com
jgray@cherrycreekradio.com

License: Butte, MT held by CCR-Butte IV LLC.
Group Owner: Cherry Creek Radio LLC; (acq 10-31-2006; grpsl)
Nat'l Reps: McGavren Guild
Format: Oldies *Special Programming:* Relg one hr wkly *Hrs. of News Programming:* News progmg 14 hrs wkly *Target Audience:* 25-54.
Jeff Gray, Operations Dir
Chris Ackerman, General Manager
Roger Bennett, Chief Engineer
Tammy Gordon, Traffic Manager

***KEDR(FM)**
01-01-2003; 88.1 mhz FM; 850 w vert; Ant 1,729 ft; N46 00 27 W112 26 30 *Rebroadcasts:* Rebroadcasts KUFR(FM) Salt Lake City, UT 100%
Family Stations Inc., 290 Hegenberger Rd., Oakland, CA 94621
(800) 543-1495, *Fax:* (916) 641-8238
www.familyradio.com
info@familyradio.com
License: Butte, Silver Bow County, MT held by Family Stations Inc.
Group Owner: Family Stations Inc.
Nat'l Network: Family Radio
Population Served: 17,663 *Arbitron Metro Market:* Bay City, TX
Format: Christian, Religious
Harold Camping, President
Harold Camping, General Manager

***KFRD**
01-01-2006; 88.9 mhz FM; 2.8 kw vert; 1729 ft.; N46 0 27 W112 26 30 *Rebroadcasts:* Rebroadcasts KUFR(FM) Salt Lake City, UT 100%
4135 Northgate Blvd, Suite 1, Sacramento, CA 95834 US
1-800-543-1495, *Fax:* (801) 359-8112
www.familyradio.com
info@familyradio.com
License: Butte, Silver Bow County, MT held by Family Stations Inc.
Group Owner: Family Stations Inc.
Arbitron Metro Market: Butte, MT *Format:* Christian, Religious
Harold Camping, General Manager

***KJLF**
01-01-2008; 90.5 mhz FM; 1 kw vert; 1739 ft.; N46 0 22 W112 26 33 *Rebroadcasts:* Rebroadcasts KXEI(FM) Havre 100%
P.O. Box 2426, Havre, MT 59501 US
(406) 265-5845, *Fax:* (406) 265-8860
www.ynopradio.org
info@ynopradio.org
License: Butte, Silver Bow County, MT held by Hi-Line Radio Fellowship Inc.
Nat'l Network: Salem Radio Network
Arbitron Metro Market: Butte, MT *Format:* Christian, Religious
Target Audience: General; those looking for inspirational Christian music & programming
Roger Lonnquist, General Manager
Brenda Boyum, Station Manager
Clark Berg, General Sales Mgr
David Brown, Programming Director
Ron Huckeby, Chief Engineer

Cascade

KIKF
01-01-2002; 104.9 mhz FM; 94 kw; 2037 ft.; N47 9 34 W111 0 39
409 S Beach Road, Hobe Sound, FL 33455 US
(406) 761-2800, *Fax:* (406) 727-7218
www.1049wolf.com
tjlee@mykikfm.com
License: Cascade, Cascade County, MT held by Fisher Radio Regional Group Inc.
Group Owner: Fisher Communications Inc.; (acq 3-12-01).
Nat'l Reps: McGavren Guild
Arbitron Metro Market: Great Falls, MT *Format:* Country
Jim Senst, General Manager
Tonya Jorgensen, General Sales Mgr
T.J. Lee, Operations Manager and Programn Director

Chinook

KRYK
11-19-1983; 101.3 mhz FM *Hrs Open:* 5 a.m. - midnight; 100 kw; 679 ft.; N48 23 29 W109 17 50
P.O. Box 7000, Havre, MT 59501 US
(406) 265-7841, *Fax:* (406) 265-8855
www.kryk.com
nmb@nmbi.com
License: Chinook, Blaine County, MT held by New Media Broadcasters Inc.
Group Owner: New Media Broadcasters Inc.; (acq 12-30-2002: grpl)
Nat'l Network: ABC
Arbitron Metro Market: Havre, MT *Format:* Adult Contemp *Hrs. of News Programming:* News progmg 10 hrs wkly *No. News Employees:* 3 *Target Audience:* 18-49.
C. David Leeds, President
Marlys Flathers, General Manager
Geoff Cole, Programming Director
Kyke Leeds, Promotions Manager
Justin Krezelak, News Director
Bruce Faulkner, Engineering Dir
Ron Bruschi, Sports Director

Choteau

***KUDI**
88.7 mhz FM; 0.11 kw; -118 ft.; N47 48 24 W112 10 43
Mailing Address: US
Second Address: 414 S. Main St., Choteau, MT 59422
(406) 467-2303
License: Choteau, Teton County, MT held by New Life Assembly Church.
Arbitron Metro Market: Choteau, MT *Format:* Christian
Mike Manuel, President

Circle

***KMGT**
90.3 mhz FM; kw
Mailing Address: US
Second Address: 1105 F Ave., Circle, MT 59215
(406) 696-8555, *Fax:* (406) 485-2332
License: Circle, McCone County, MT held by Circle Community Radio Association.
Arbitron Metro Market: Circle, MT
Jerrod Williams, General Manager

Colstrip

***KMCJ**
08-01-2001; 99.5 mhz FM *Hrs Open:* 24; 100 kw; 801 ft.; N46 10 32 W106 24 21 *Rebroadcasts:* Rebroadcasts KXEI(FM) Havre 100%
Mailing Address: 433 Driftwood Ave, Apt. #4, Estes Park, CO 80517 US
Second Address: 317 First St., Havre, MT 59501
(406) 265-5845, *Fax:* (406) 265-8860
www.ynopradio.org
info@ynop.org
License: Colstrip, Rosebud County, MT held by Hi-Line Radio Fellowship Inc.
Nat'l Network: Salem Radio Network *Wire Services:* AP
Arbitron Metro Market: Havre, MT *Format:* Christian, Religious
Target Audience: General:; those looking for inspirational Christian music & programming
Roger Lonnquist, YNOP General Manager
Brenda Boyum, KXEI Station Manager
Clark Berg, KALS Sales Manager
David Brown, YNOP Program Director
Ron Huckeby, Chief Engineer
MarySue Amundgaard, KALS Office Staff
Joanna Baer,Announcer/Office Assistant
Earl Houtz, Announcer
Dave Kirby, Announcer
Crystal MacInnes, Production Assistant
Elizabeth McClenahan, Office Manager at KXEI/Webmaster

***KYPC**
89.9 mhz FM; 3.5 kw; 1171 ft.; N45 50 17 W106 54 16
US
(406) 657-2941, *Fax:* (406) 657-2977
www.yellowstonepublicradio.org
mail@ypradio.org
License: Colstrip, Rosebud County, MT held by Montana State University - Billings.
Arbitron Metro Market: Colstrip, MT *Format:* Variety/Diverse
Dennis Hall, President
Ken Siebert, General Manager / Media Services Director
Jackie Yamanaka, News Director
Jim Nichols, Chief Engineer
Barbara Bernheim, Development and Listener Support Manager
Alicia Lee, Underwriting Manager /Public Information Manager
Ana Henrickson, Business & Finance Manager
Art Hooker, Control Room Operator / Production Assistant
Merry Ann Peters, Control Room Operator
Wesley Jessen, Media Services Assistant / Control Room Operator

Columbia Falls

KHNK
11-17-1998; 95.9 mhz FM *Hrs Open:* 24; 55 kw horiz, 5.6 kw vert; 2287 ft.; N48 30 42 W114 22 16
Box 5409, Kalispell, MT 59903 US
(406) 755-8700, *Fax:* (406) 755-8770
www.beebroadcasting.com
kkmt@beebroadcasting.com
License: Columbia Falls, Flathead County, MT held by Bee Broadcasting Inc.
Group Owner: Bee Broadcasting Inc.; (acq 12-31-97; $337,500)
Format: Country
Mark Wagner, General Manager

KRVO
01-01-2006; 103.1 mhz FM; 8 kw; 2362 ft.; N48 30 43 W114 22 13
US
(406) 755-8700, *Fax:* (406) 755-8770
www.beebroadcasting.com
kdbr@beebroadcasting.com
License: Columbia Falls, Flathead County, MT held by Cathleen R. Bee.
Arbitron Metro Market: Columbia Falls, MT *Format:* Alternative
Cathleen Bee, General Manager

Conrad

KTZZ
07-01-1997; 93.7 mhz FM *Hrs Open:* 24; 100 kw; 558 ft.; N47 49 13 W111 47 56
Mailing Address: P. O. Box F, Black Eagle, MT 59414 US
Second Address: 3313 15th St. N.E., PO Box F, Black Eagle, MT 59414
(406) 761-1310, *Fax:* (406) 454-3775
License: Conrad, Pondera County, MT held by Jeannine M. Mason.
Nat'l Network: ABC
Format: Classic Rock *Hrs. of News Programming:* news progmg 5 hrs wkly *No. News Employees:* 1 *Target Audience:* 25-54; general
Steven Dow, President
Laurie Vosberg, General Sales Mgr

Darby

KHDV
01-01-2007; 107.9 mhz FM; 14 kw; 361 ft.; N46 13 46 W114 14 1
US
(406) 542-1025, *Fax:* (406) 721-1036
www.moclub.com
info@mtnbdc.com
License: Darby, Ravalli County, MT held by Sheila Callahan and Friends Inc.
Group Owner: Sheila Callahan and Friends Inc.
Arbitron Metro Market: Darby, MT
Sheila Callahan, General Manager
Kris Hardy, Traffic Director
Marsha Davis, Executive Assistant

Deer Lodge

KBCK
01-01-1963; 1400 khz AM
P. O. Box 580, Anaconda, MT 59711 US
License: Deer Lodge, MT held by Robert Cummings Toole
Target Audience: 18 plus.
Chuck Schwartz, General Manager

KQRV
07-04-1997; 96.9 mhz FM; 20 kw; 984 ft.; N46 6 3 W112 57 0
774 Eastside Road, Deer Lodge, MT 59722 US
(406) 846-1100, *Fax:* (406) 846-1100
riverradio@bresnan.net
License: Deer Lodge, Powell County, MT held by Robert Cummings Toole.
Arbitron Metro Market: Butte, MT *Format:* Country
Robert Toole, General Manager
Karen Toole, General Sales Mgr

Dillon

KBEV-FM
08-01-1972; 98.3 mhz FM; 10.5 kw; 495 ft; N45 14 22 W112 40 03
610 N. Montana St., Dillon, MT 69725
(406) 683-2800, *Fax:* (406) 683-9480
License: Dillon, Beaverhead County, MT held by Dead-Air Broadcasting Co. Inc.
Jo Ann Juliano, President
Jo Ann Juliano, Owner
John B Schuyler, Jr, Programming Director
Ron Huckeby, Chief Engineer

KDBM
01-01-1957; 1490 khz AM

P.O. Box 546, Dillon, MT 69725 US
(406) 683-2800(406) 683-6171, *Fax:* (406) 683-9480
www.kdbmkbev.com
License: Dillon, MT held by Dead-Air Broadcasting Co. Inc.
Arbitron Metro Market: Dillon, MT *Format:* Country
Jo Ann Juliano, President
Kathy Wise, General Manager
Kasey Briggs, General Sales Mgr
John Schuyler, Programming Director
Ron Huckaby, Chief Engineer
Jo An Juliano, Owner
John Schuyler, Vice President
Rick Kuntz, SportsTeam
John Jorey, Sports Team

***KDWG**
90.9 mhz FM *Hrs Open:* 24; 0.85 kw; -236 ft.; N45 12 33 W112 38 14
Campus Box 119, 710 S Atlantic St, Dillion, MT 59725 US
(406) 683-7331
www.my.umwestern.edu/kdwg
kdwg@umwestern.edu
License: Dillon, Beaverhead County, MT held by Western Montana College University of Montana.
Arbitron Metro Market: Dillon, MT *Format:* Rock/AOR
Cory Craden, Programming Director

Dutton

KVVR
08-07-2001; 97.9 mhz FM; 100 kw; 715 ft.; N47 36 52 W111 20 51
409 Cardiff Lane, Manchester, MO 63021 US
(406) 761-7600, *Fax:* (406) 761-5511
License: Dutton, Teton County, MT held by CCR-Great Falls IV LLC.
Group Owner: Cherry Creek Radio LLC; (acq 12-19-2003; grpsl)
Arbitron Metro Market: Great Falls, MT *Format:* Adult Contemp
Ron Korb, General Manager

East Helena

KHKR-FM
04-13-1989; 104.1 mhz FM; 5 kw; 653 ft.; N46 46 11 W112 1 25
P.O. Box 4111, Helena, MT 59604 US
(406) 442-4490, *Fax:* (406) 442-7356
www.khkr.com
info@khkr.com
License: East Helena, Lewis and Clark County, MT held by CCR-Helena IV LLC.
Group Owner: Cherry Creek Radio LLC; (acq 2-3-2004; grpsl).
Format: Country *Target Audience:* 25-54.
Dewey Bruce, General Manager

KKGR
05-26-1988; 680 khz AM
1400 Eleventh Avenue, Helena, MT 59601 US
(406) 443-5237
info@kkgram.com
License: East Helena, MT held by KKGR Inc.
Arbitron Metro Market: Great Falls, MT *Format:* Oldies
Jim Schaffer, General Manager
Ron Davidson, General Manager

East Missoula

KMPT
06-27-1959; 930 khz AM *Hrs Open:* 24; 5 kw-D, DAN; 1 kw-N, DAN; N46 51 57 W114 4 57
980 North Michigan Ave., Suite 1880, Chicago, IL 60611 US
(406) 728-9300, *Fax:* (406) 542-2329
www.klcy930.com
License: East Missoula, MT held by GAP Broadcasting Missoula License LLC.
Group Owner: GAPWEST Broadcasting; (acq 2-13-2008; grpsl)
Format: Alternative, Talk *Hrs. of News Programming:* News progmg 14 hrs wkly *Target Audience:* 35-54; adult spenders
Gene Peterson, General Manager
Jim Colter, General Sales Mgr
Kirk Patrick, Programming Director
Pete Denault, News Director
Todd Clark, Chief Engineer

Eureka

KZXT
93.5 mhz FM; 2 kw; -689 ft.; N48 54 0.7 W115 1 20.7
US
(406) 883-5255, *Fax:* (406) 883-4441
License: Eureka, Lincoln County, MT held by Anderson Radio Broadcasting Inc.
Group Owner: Anderson Radio Broadcasting Inc.; (acq 6-6-2008; $140,406 for CP)
Arbitron Metro Market: Eureka, MT
Dennis Anderson, President

Evergreen

KQJZ
01-01-2008; 1340 khz AM
US
(406) 257-9430, *Fax:* (406) 752-0313
www.smoothkqjz.com
License: Evergreen, MT held by Anderson Radio Broadcasting Inc.
Group Owner: Anderson Radio Broadcasting Inc.; (acq 2-29-2008; $200,000)
Arbitron Metro Market: Evergreen, MT *Format:* Jazz, Smooth Jazz
Dennis Anderson, President
Dan Snyder, Account Executive
Mike Hodges, Account Executive

Fairfield

KINX
02-04-2002; 102.7 mhz FM; 93.3 kw horiz, 62.2 kw vert; 896 ft.; N47 36 24 W111 21 31
US
(406) 452-1073, *Fax:* (406) 727-7218
www.sam1073.com
mail@1073.com
License: Fairfield, Cascade County, MT held by Fisher Radio Regional Group Inc.
Group Owner: Fisher Communications Inc.
Nat'l Reps: McGavren Guild
Arbitron Metro Market: Fairfield, MT *Format:* Variety/Diverse
Target Audience: 25-54.
Terry Strickland, General Manager
Troy Mellinger, Programming Director
Courteney McKinnon, Asst. Program Director

Florence

KDTR
01-01-2005; 103.3 mhz FM; 1.84 kw; 2083 ft.; N46 48 6 W113 58 22
US
(406) 721-6800, *Fax:* (406) 329-1850
www.trail1033.com
rharsell@simmonsmedia.com
License: Florence, Ravalli County, MT held by Spanish Peaks Broadcasting Inc.
Group Owner: Spanish Peaks Broadcasting Inc.
Nat'l Reps: Interep
Arbitron Metro Market: Florence, MT *Format:* Triple A *No. News Employees:* 1 *Target Audience:* 25-54; adults *Adv. Rates:* 27; 24; 27; 15
Rod Harsell, General Manager
Robert Chase, Programming Director

Forsyth

KIKC
10-10-1975; 1250 khz AM *Hrs Open:* 24; 5 kw-D, ND2; 0.132 kw-N, ND2; N46 15 30 W106 41 21
Mailing Address: P.O. Box 1140, Forsyth, MT 59327 US
Second Address: 210 W. Front St., Forsyth, MT 59327
(406) 346-2711, *Fax:* (406) 346-2712
www.kikcradio.com
kikc@rangeweb.net
License: Forsyth, MT held by Mile City, Forsyth Broadcasting Inc.
Wire Services: AP
Format: Oldies *Target Audience:* 18-35; general *Adv. Rates:* 9; 9; 9; 9
Stephen Marks, President

KIKC-FM
09-01-1980; 101.3 mhz FM *Hrs Open:* 24; 100 kw; 1010 ft.; N46 10 32 W106 24 21
Mailing Address: P.O. Box 1140, Forsyth, MT 59327 US
Second Address: 210 W. Front St., Forsyth, MT 59327
(406) 346-2711, *Fax:* (406) 346-2712
www.kikcradio.com
kikc@rangeweb.net
License: Forsyth, Rosebud County, MT held by Miles City, Forsyth Broadcasting Inc.
Nat'l Network: CNN Radio *Nat'l Reps:* Interep *Regional Reps:* Allied Radio Partners *Wire Services:* AP
Format: Country *Hrs. of News Programming:* News progmg 4 hrs wkly *Target Audience:* 18 plus; general *Adv. Rates:* 18; 18; 18; 18
Steve Marks, CEO
Dick Haugen, Operations Dir
Grant West, Programming Director
Patti Haugen, Operations Manager

Fort Belknap Agency

***KGVA**
10-01-1996; 88.1 mhz FM; 95 kw; 797 ft.; N48 11 18 W108 42 36
P.O. Box 159, Harlem, MT 59526 US
(406) 353-4656, *Fax:* (406) 353-2898
www.kgvafm.org
kgvaradiostation@yahoo.com
License: Fort Belknap Agency, Blaine County, MT held by Fort Belknap College.
Nat'l Network: NPR
Format: News, News/Talk, 86 *Special Programming:* American Indian 60 hrs wkly *Target Audience:* General.
Gerald Stiffarm, Operations Dir
Will Gray Jr., General Manager

Fort Benton

KJCD
01-01-2008; 95.9 mhz FM; 0.1 kw horiz; 13 ft.; N47 50 8 W110 39 10
US
(406) 442-2655
License: Fort Benton, Chouteau County, MT held by Montana Christian Radio Association
Arbitron Metro Market: Fort Benton, MT *Format:* Adult Contemp
Roger Lonnquist, President

Four Corners

KSCY
03-01-2008; 106.9 mhz FM; 4 kw; 646 ft.; N45 38 20 W111 15 56
US
(406) 582-1045, *Fax:* (406) 582-0388
License: Four Corners, Gallatin County, MT held by Radick Construction Inc.
Arbitron Metro Market: Dallas-Fort Worth *Format:* Country
Jeff Balding, General Manager

Frenchtown

KGVO-FM
01-01-2007; 101.5 mhz FM; 3.4 kw; Ant 2,089 ft; N46 48 08 W113 58 21
3250 S. Reserve St., Suite 200, Missoula, MT 59801-8236
(406) 721-4749, *Fax:* (406) 542-2329
www.1015theview.com
dannyd@townsquaremedia.com
License: Frenchtown, Missoula County, MT held by Townsquare Media Missoula License LLC
Group Owner: GAPWEST Broadcasting; (acq 2-13-2008; $500,000)
Population Served: 67,290 *Arbitron Metro Market:* Missoula, MT
Format: Classic Rock
Dave Cowan, General Manager
Shawna Batt, General Sales Mgr
Erik O'Connor, Programming Director
Shawna Batt, Director of Sales
Danny D, Brand Manager

Glasgow

KLAN
03-01-1983; 93.5 mhz FM; 3 kw; 299 ft.; N48 5 42 W106 37 8
P.O. 671, Glasgow, MT 59230 US
(406) 228-9336, *Fax:* (406) 228-9338
www.kltz.com
kltz@kltz.com
License: Glasgow, Valley County, MT held by Glasgow Broadcasting Corp.
Arbitron Metro Market: Billings, MT *Format:* Adult Contemp
Shirley Trang, General Manager
Leila J., General Sales Mgr
Tim Phillips, Programming Director
Stan Ozark, News Director
Lori Mason, Music Director
Gwen Page, Traffic Manager
Annette Vegge, Office Manager
Mary Nyquist,Production

KLTZ
08-14-1954; 1240 khz AM; 1 kw-U, ND1; N48 13 9 W106 38 54
P.O. Box 671, Glasgow, MT 59230 US
(406) 228-9336, *Fax:* (406) 228-9338
www.kltz.com
kltz@kltz.com
License: Glasgow, MT held by Glasgow Broadcasting Inc.

Regional Network: Agrinet
Format: Country *Target Audience:* 25 plus.
Shirley Trang, General Manager
Tim Phillips, Programming Director
Stan Ozark, News Director
Gwen Page, Traffic Manager
Annette Vegge, Office Manager

Glendive

KDZN
12-21-1969; 96.5 mhz FM *Hrs Open:* 24; 90 kw horiz; 489 ft.; N47 5 15 W104 48 4
210 South Douglas, Glendive, MT 59330 US
(406) 377-3377, *Fax:* (406) 365-2181
www.kxgn.com
kxgnkdzn@midrivers.com
License: Glendive, Dawson County, MT held by Magic Air Communications Co.
Nat'l Network: CBS Radio; Westwood One *Wire Services:* AP
Arbitron Metro Market: Glendive, MT *Format:* Country *Hrs. of News Programming:* News progmg 4 hrs wkly *Target Audience:* 25-54.
Steven Marks, President
Paul Sturlaugson, General Manager
Marcy Copp, Programming Director
Ed Agre, News Director

KGLE
08-22-1962; 590 khz AM *Hrs Open:* 24; 1 kw-D, ND2; 0.111 kw-N, ND2; N47 5 50 W104 47 9
86 Seven Mile Road, P.O. Box 1169, Glendive, MT 59330 US
(406) 377-3331, *Fax:* (406) 377-3332
www.kgle.org
kgle@midrivers.com
License: Glendive, MT held by Friends of Christian Radio Inc.
Nat'l Network: Salem Radio Network *Wire Services:* AP
Format: Religious *Hrs. of News Programming:* news 20 hrs wkly *Target Audience:* 35-64; general *Adv. Rates:* 6; 6; 6; 6
Tom Fatzinger, President
Jim McBride, General Manager
Diane Odenbach, Station Manager

KXGN
09-23-1948; 1400 khz AM *Hrs Open:* 24; 1 kw-U, ND1; N47 5 40 W104 42 50
210 South Douglas, Glendive, MT 59330 US
(406) 377-3377, *Fax:* (406) 365-2181
www.glendivebroadcasting.com
kxgnkdzn@midrivers.com
License: Glendive, MT held by Glendive Broadcasting Corp.
Nat'l Network: ABC *Wire Services:* NWS (National Weather Service)
TV Affiliate: KXGN-TV affil *Format:* Adult Contemp, Oldies
Special Programming: Derry Brownfield 5 hrs, farm 2 hrs wkly
Hrs. of News Programming: news progmg 6 hrs wkly *No. News Employees:* 1 *Adv. Rates:* 15.50; 15.50; 5.50; na
Stephen Marks, President
Paul Sturlaugson, General Manager
Paul Strulaugson, Executive Vice President

Great Falls

KAAK
06-19-1972; 98.9 mhz FM *Hrs Open:* 24; 100 kw; 482 ft.; N47 32 23 W111 17 6
N. 1212 Washington, Suite 307, Spokane, WA 99201 US
(406) 761-7600, *Fax:* (406) 761-5511
License: Great Falls, Cascade County, MT held by CCR-Great Falls IV LLC.
Group Owner: Cherry Creek Radio LLC; (acq 5-31-2007; grpsl)
Arbitron Metro Market: Great Falls, MT *Format:* Adult Contemp *Target Audience:* 25-44.
Ron Korb, General Manager

KEIN
07-01-1922; 1310 khz AM *Hrs Open:* 24; 5 kw-D, ND2; 1 kw-N, ND2; N47 31 20 W111 23 18
Mailing Address: 3313 15th Street N.E., Box F, Black Eagle, MT 59414 US
Second Address: 3313 15th St. N.E., Black Eagle, MT 59414
(406) 761-1310, *Fax:* (406) 454-3775
License: Great Falls, MT held by Munson Radio Inc.
Format: Adult Contemp *Hrs. of News Programming:* news progmg 5 hrs wkly *No. News Employees:* 1 *Target Audience:* 35 plus. *Adv. Rates:* 17.50; 17.50; 16.50; 15.00
Steven Dow, President

*KGFC
01-01-1996; 88.9 mhz FM *Hrs Open:* 24; 6 kw; 243 ft.; N47 27 52.4 W111 21 17.8 *Rebroadcasts:* Rebroadcasts KXEI(FM) Havre 100%.
P.O. Box 2426, Havre, MT 59501 US
1 (800) 442-9222, *Fax:* (406) 265-8860
www.ynop.org
info@ynop.org
License: Great Falls, Cascade County, MT held by Hi-Line Radio Fellowship Inc.
Wire Services: AP
Format: Christian, Religious *Target Audience:* General; those looking for inspirational Christian music & progmg
Roger Lonnquist, General Manager
Brenda Boyum, Station Manager
David Brown, Programming Director
Nicholas Tobiason, Music/IT Director

*KGPR
04-01-1984; 89.9 mhz FM *Hrs Open:* 24; 9.5 kw; 295 ft.; N47 32 23 W111 17 6 *Rebroadcasts:* Rebroadcasts KUFM(FM) Missoula 100%
Mailing Address: P.O. Box 3343, Great Falls, MT 59403 US
Second Address: Box 6010, 2100 16th Ave. S., Great Falls, MT 59406-6010
(406) 268-3739, *Fax:* (406) 268-3736
www.kgpr.org
info@kgpr.org
License: Great Falls, Cascade County, MT held by Great Falls Public Radio Association.
Nat'l Network: PRI; NPR
Format: News *Hrs. of News Programming:* News progmg 44 hrs wkly *Target Audience:* General.
Joseph Duffy, President
Bill Tacke, Operations Dir
Tom Halverson, Station Manager
Carol Spahr, General Sales Mgr

KLFM
02-14-1982; 92.9 mhz FM *Hrs Open:* 24; 98 kw; 410 ft.; N47 32 19 W111 15 41
Mailing Address: P.O. Box 3309, Great Falls, MT 59403 US
Second Address: 20 3rd St. N., Great Falls, MT 59403
(406) 761-7600, *Fax:* (406) 761-5511
License: Great Falls, Cascade County, MT held by CCR-Great Falls IV LLC.
Group Owner: Cherry Creek Radio LLC; (acq 12-19-2003; grpsl).
Arbitron Metro Market: Great Falls, MT *Format:* Oldies *Target Audience:* 25-54.
Ron Korb, General Manager

KMON
05-30-1947; 560 khz AM *Hrs Open:* 24
20 3rd Street N., Great Falls, MT 59401 US
(406) 761-7600, *Fax:* (406) 761-5511
www.kmon.com
560@kmon.com
License: Great Falls, MT held by CCR-Great Falls IV LLC.
Group Owner: Cherry Creek Radio LLC; (acq 12-19-2003; grpsl)
Format: Country *Special Programming:* Sports 5 hrs wkly *Hrs. of News Programming:* news progmg 20 hrs wkly *No. News Employees:* 1 *Target Audience:* 35-64.
Ron Korb, General Manager
Melissa Horton, General Sales Mgr
Skip Walters, Programming Director
Ken Eklund, Chief Engineer
Angie Depping, Research Director

KMON-FM
10-01-1972; 94.5 mhz FM *Hrs Open:* 24; 98 kw; 495 ft.; N47 32 19 W111 15 41
P.O. Box 3309, Great Falls, MT 59403 US
(406) 761-7600, *Fax:* (406) 761-5511
www.kmonfm.com
License: Great Falls, Cascade County, MT
Group Owner: Cherry Creek Radio LLC
Wire Services: U.S. Weather Service
Format: Country *Hrs. of News Programming:* news progmg 5 hrs wkly *No. News Employees:* 1 *Target Audience:* 25-54.
Ron Korb, General Sales Mgr
Scott Hershey, Programming Director

KQDI
01-01-1955; 1450 khz AM; 0.72 kw-U, ND1; N47 27 56 W111 19 22
N. 1212 Washington, Suite 307, Spokane, WA 99201 US
(406) 761-2800, *Fax:* (406) 727-7218
www.newstalk1450.com
License: Great Falls, MT held by Fisher Radio Regional Group Inc.
Group Owner: Fisher Communications Inc.; (acq 9-27-95; with co-located FM).
Nat'l Reps: Christal
Arbitron Metro Market: Great Falls area *Format:* News, News/Talk, 86 *Target Audience:* 25-54.
Dave France, Operations Dir
Terry Strickland, General Manager
Anna Palagi, General Sales Mgr
Pam Bennett, News Director
Joe Bower, Chief Engineer

KQDI-FM
12-31-1963; 106.1 mhz FM; 100 kw; 276 ft; N47 31 57 W111 16 41
Box 3129, Great Falls, MT 99201
(406) 761-2800, *Fax:* (406) 727-7218
License: Great Falls, Cascade County, MT
Group Owner: Fisher Communications Inc.
Population Served: 65,000*Target Audience:* 18-49.
Howard Doss, President
T J Lee, Operations Dir
Jim Senst, General Manager
Tonya Jorgensen, General Sales Mgr
Jared Walker, Programming Director
Greg Miller, Chief Engineer

KXGF
01-01-1987; 1400 khz AM; 1 kw-U; N47 27 56 W111 20 22
Mailing Address: Box 3129, Great Falls, MT 99201
Second Address: 1300 Central Ave. W., Great Falls, MT 59403
(406) 761-2800, *Fax:* (406) 727-7218
License: Great Falls, Cascade County, MT held by Staradio Corp
Group Owner: Staradio Corp; (acq 12-28-94; grpsl, including co-
Nat'l Reps: Katz
Population Served: 86,000*Special Programming:* Farm 2 hrs wkly *Target Audience:* 35-64.
Jim Senst, Vice President
T.S. Lee, Operations Dir
Jim Senst, General Manager
Tonya Jorgensen, General Sales Mgr
Troy Mellinger, Programming Director
Troy Mellinger, News Director
Greg Muir, Chief Engineer

KLSK
01-01-2003; 100.3 mhz FM; 100 kw; 495 ft.; N47 15 57 W111 8 39
188 South Bellevue, Suite 222, Memphis, TN 38104 US
(800) 525-5683, *Fax:* (916) 251-1650
www.klove.com
klove@klove.com
License: Great Falls, Cascade County, MT held by Flinn Broadcasting Corp.
Arbitron Metro Market: Great Falls, MT *Format:* Urban Contemporary
Darrell Chambliss, Chairman
Mike Novak, President and CEO
Karen Wheatley, General Manager
David Pierce, Programming Director
Ed Lenane, News Director
Sam Wallington, Engineering Dir
Scott Smith, Music Director
Marya Morgan,News Reporter
Richard Hunt, News Reporter
Tracy Butler, Traffic Manager
Laura Daniels, News Reporter
Tim Luttrell, News Reporter

*KGFA
01-01-2006; 90.7 mhz FM; 2.3 kw; 299 ft.; N47 31 57 W111 16 38
P.O. Drawer 2440, Tupelo, MS 38803 US
(888) 937-2471, *Fax:* (916) 251-1650
www.air1.com
info@air1.com
License: Great Falls, Cascade County, MT held by Educational Media Foundation.
Group Owner: EMF Broadcasting; (acq 3-23-2007; grpsl)
Nat'l Network: Air 1
Arbitron Metro Market: Great Falls, MT *Format:* Alternative, Christian
Darrell Chambliss, Chairman
Alan Mason, COO
Mike Novak, President and CEO
Ed Lenane, News Director
Sam Wallington, Engineering Dir
Eric Moser, Chief Financial Officer
Brian Burger, Vice President of Human Resources
D. KevinBlair, Secretary and General Counsel
Larry Moody, Director
Mitch Barnhart, Director

*KFRW
01-01-2007; 91.9 mhz FM; 50 kw; 466 ft.; N47 49 13 W111 47 56
Rebroadcasts: Rebroadcasts KUFR(FM) Salt Lake City, UT 100%
4135 Northgate Blvd., Suite 1, Sacramento, CA 95834 US

(800) 543-1495, *Fax:* (916) 641-8238
www.familyradio.com
info@familyradio.com
License: Great Falls, Cascade County, MT held by Family Stations Inc.
Group Owner: Family Stations Inc.
Arbitron Metro Market: Great Falls, MT *Format:* Christian, Religious
Harold Camping, General Manager

***KAFH**
01-01-2006; 91.5 mhz FM; 1 kw; 298 ft.; N47 31 57 W111 16 38
Rebroadcasts: Rebroadcasts WAFR(FM) Tupelo, MS 100%
P O Drawer 2440, Tupelo, MS 38803 US
(662) 844-8888, *Fax:* (662) 842-6791
www.afa.net
License: Great Falls, Cascade County, MT held by American Family Association.
Group Owner: American Family Radio
Arbitron Metro Market: Great Falls, MT *Format:* Christian
Marvin Sanders, General Manager

Hamilton

KBAZ
02-11-1969; 96.3 mhz FM *Hrs Open:* 24; 50 kw; 2090 ft.; N46 48 8 W113 58 21
101 West Grand, Suite 600, Chicago, IL 60610 US
(406) 728-9300, *Fax:* (406) 542-2329
www.963theblaze.com
License: Hamilton, Ravalli County, MT held by GAP Broadcasting Missoula License LLC.
Group Owner: GAPWEST Broadcasting; (acq 2-13-2008; grpsl)
Format: Alternative
Angel Hughes, Operations Dir
Dave Cowan, General Manager

KLYQ
02-03-1961; 1240 khz AM *Hrs Open:* 5:30 AM-midnight; 1 kw-U, ND1; N46 15 22 W114 9 45
101 West Grand, Suite 600, Chicago, IL 60610 US
(406) 363-3010, *Fax:* (406) 363-6436
www.klyq.com
contact@klyq.com
License: Hamilton, MT held by GAP Broadcasting Missoula License LLC.
Group Owner: GAPWEST Broadcasting; (acq 2-13-2008; grpsl)
Arbitron Metro Market: Great Falls, MT *Format:* News, News/Talk, 86 *Hrs. of News Programming:* news progmg 25 hrs wkly *No. News Employees:* 1 *Target Audience:* 25-54; adults
Steve Fullerton, Operations Dir
Gene Peterson, General Manager
Jim Coulter, General Sales Mgr
Mike Daniels, Chief Engineer
Don Davis, Sports Commentator

***KUFN**
10-01-1998; 91.9 mhz FM; 0.9 kw; 427 ft.; N46 13 46 W114 14 1
Broadcast Media Center, Missoula, MT 59812 US
(406) 243-4931, *Fax:* (406) 243-3299
www.kufm.org
License: Hamilton, Ravalli County, MT held by The University of Montana.
Nat'l Network: NPR *Wire Services:* AP
Arbitron Metro Market: Hamilton, MT *Format:* Classical, Jazz, 60 *Hrs. of News Programming:* News progmg 2 hrs wkly
William Marcus, General Manager
Michael Marsolek, Programming Director
Sally Mauk, News Director
Saxon Holbrook, Technical Director
William Marcus, Director of UM Broadcast Media Center
Sue Ginn, Accounting Associate
JerriBalsam, Administrative Associate
Edward F. O'Brien, Assistant News Director
Linda Talbott, Associate Director
Kathy Woodford, Director of Corporate Support

***KMZO**
90.7 mhz FM *Hrs Open:* 24; 5 kw; 331 ft.; N46 13 46 W114 14 1
2201 South 6th St., Las Vegas, NV 89104 US
(208) 734-5777, *Fax:* (702) 731-1992
www.sosradio.net
scott@sosradio.net
License: Hamilton, Ravalli County, MT held by Faith Communications Corp.
Group Owner: Faith Communications Corp.
Arbitron Metro Market: Great Falls, MT *Format:* Christian *Hrs. of News Programming:* News progmg 5 hrs wkly
Jack French, CEO
Brad Staley, President and General Manager
Scott Herrold, Programming Director
Chris Staley, Promotions Manager
Tim Hunt, Network Director of Engineering
Gary Thompson, Creative Services Director
Mike Mead, DonorRelations
Marney Domeraski, Donor Relations
Dawn Vincent, Listener Services
Rick Hall, Music Director
Chris Staley, Vice-President of Programming & Administration

Hardin

KHDN
12-28-1962; 1230 khz AM *Hrs Open:* 24; 1 kw-U, ND1; N45 42 55 W107 35 59
PO Box 230, Hardin, MT 59034 US
(406) 665-2828, *Fax:* (406) 665-2131
www.bigskyradio.net
rich@bigskyradio.net
License: Hardin, MT held by Sun Mountain Inc.
Group Owner: Sun Mountain Inc.; (acq 11-30-2000)
Nat'l Network: ABC
Format: Adult Contemp, News *Hrs. of News Programming:* News progmg 24 hrs wkly *Target Audience:* 25-54.
Richard Solberg, President

Havre

***KNMC**
02-01-1979; 90.1 mhz FM; 0.38 kw; -112 ft.; N48 32 31 W109 41 17
Cowan Hall, Cowan Drive, Havre, MT 59501 US
(406) 657-2941, *Fax:* (406) 657-2977
License: Havre, Hill County, MT held by Montana State University-Northern.
Format: Jazz *Special Programming:* Class 10 hrs wkly
Marvin Granger, General Manager

KOJM
10-31-1947; 610 khz AM *Hrs Open:* 5 a.m.-midnight; 1 kw-D, DA2; 1 kw-N, DA2; N48 34 48 W109 38 54
P.O. Box 7000, Havre, MT 59501 US
(406) 265-7841, *Fax:* (406) 265-8855
www.kojm.com
nmb@nmbi.com
License: Havre, MT held by New Media Broadcasters Inc.
Group Owner: New Media Broadcasters Inc.; (acq 12-30-2002; grpsl)
Nat'l Network: ABC *Wire Services:* AP
Format: Adult Contemp *Special Programming:* Agriculture 4 hrs wkly *Hrs. of News Programming:* news progmg 20 wkly *No. News Employees:* 3 *Target Audience:* 30-64; boomer generation
C. David Leeds, President
Marlys Flathers, General Manager
Geoff Cole, Programming Director
Kyle Leeds, Promotions Manager
Justin Krezelak, News Director
Bruce Faulkner, Chief Engineer
Ron Bruschi, Sports Director

KPQX
03-08-1975; 92.5 mhz FM *Hrs Open:* 5 a.m.-midnight; 96 kw; 1788 ft.; N48 10 55 W109 41 1
P.O. Box 7000, Havre, MT 59501 US
(406) 265-7841, *Fax:* (406) 265-8855
www.kpqx.com
nmb@nmbi.com
License: Havre, Hill County, MT held by New Media Broadcasters Inc.
Group Owner: New Media Broadcasters Inc.; (acq 12-30-2002; grpsl)
Nat'l Network: ABC *Wire Services:* AP
Format: Country *Special Programming:* Farm 10 hrs wkly *Hrs. of News Programming:* News progmg 20 hrs wkly *No. News Employees:* 3 *Target Audience:* 25-54.
C. David Leeds, President
Marlys Flathers, General Manager
Geoff Cole, Programming Director
Kyle Leeds, Promotions Manager
Justin Krezelak, News Director
Bruce Faulkner, Chief Engineer
Ron Bruschi, Sports Director

***KXEI**
07-28-1983; 95.1 mhz FM *Hrs Open:* 24; 98 kw; 1699 ft.; N48 10 42 W109 41 21
Mailing Address: P.O. Box 2426, Havre, MT 59501 US
Second Address: 317 First St., Havre, MT 59501
(406) 265-5845, *Fax:* (406) 265-8860
www.ynopradio.org
info@ynop.org
License: Havre, Hill County, MT held by Hi-Line Radio Fellowship Inc.
Nat'l Network: Moody; Salem Radio Network *Wire Services:* AP
Arbitron Metro Market: Havre, MT *Format:* Christian, Religious
Special Programming: C&W one hr, farm one hr wkly *Target Audience:* General; those looking for Christian inspirational music & progmg
Roger Lonnquist, General Manager
Brenda Boyum, Station Manager
Brian Jackson, Programming Director
Elizabeth McClenahan, Office Manager

Helena

KBLL
09-01-1937; 1240 khz AM
Mailing Address: 1400 11th Avenue, Helena, MT 59601 US
Second Address: 110 E. Broadway St., Helena, MT 59601
(406) 442-4490, *Fax:* (406) 442-6161
www.kbllradio.com
License: Helena, MT held by CCR-Helena IV LLC
Group Owner: Cherry Creek Radio LLC; (acq 6-30-2004; $2.8 million with co-located FM)
Arbitron Metro Market: Helena, MT *Format:* News, News/Talk, 86
Target Audience: 29-54; high buying power
Dewey Bruce, General Manager
Chris McCarthy, General Sales Mgr
Stan Evans, Programming Director
Cato Butler, News Director
Ken Eklund, Chief Engineer
Michele McAlister, Traffic Manager

KBLL-FM
08-01-1979; 99.5 mhz FM; 12 kw; 1932 ft.; N46 44 51.8 W112 19 47.6
1400 11th Avenue, Helena, MT 59601 US
(406) 442-4490, *Fax:* (406) 442-6161
www.kbllradio.com
kbllam@cherrycreekradio.com
License: Helena, Lewis and Clark County, MT held by CCR-Helena IV LLC.
Group Owner: Cherry Creek Radio LLC
Arbitron Metro Market: Helena, MT *Format:* Country
Kurt Kittelson, Programming Director

KCAP
10-01-1949; 1340 khz AM; 1 kw-U, ND1; N46 36 43 W112 3 13
Mailing Address: 110 Broadway St., Helena, MT 59601 US
Second Address: 110 E. Broadway St., Helena, MT 59601
(406) 442-4490, *Fax:* (406) 442-7356
www.cherrycreekradio.com
dbruce@cherrycreekradio.com
License: Helena, MT held by CCR-Helena IV LLC.
Group Owner: Cherry Creek Radio LLC; (acq 2-3-2004; grpsl)
Nat'l Network: CBS; Moody; Fox Sports
Arbitron Metro Market: Helena, MT *Format:* News, News/Talk, 84, Talk *Target Audience:* 25-54.
Dewey Bruce, General Manager
Jim Willard, General Sales Mgr
Stan Evans, Programming Director
Cato Butler, News Director
Ken Eklund, Chief Engineer
Michele McAlister, Traffic Manager

KMTX
11-01-1976; 950 khz AM *Hrs Open:* 25.?A?; 5 kw-D, DAN; 5 kw-N, DAN; N46 40 28 W112 1 5
Mailing Address: 1300 North 17th Street, 11th Floor, Rosslyn, VA 22209 US
Second Address: 516 Fuller, Helena, MT 59601
(406) 442-0400, *Fax:* (406) 442-0491
License: Helena, MT held by KMTX LLC.
Nat'l Network: AP Radio
Format: Oldies
James O'Connell, President
Kevin Skaalure, General Manager

KMTX-FM
01-19-1985; 105.3 mhz FM; 87 kw horiz, 58 kw vert; 1946 ft.; N46 44 52 W112 19 47
Mailing Address: 1300 North 17th Street, 11th Floor, Rosslyn, VA 22209 US
Second Address: 516 Fuller, Helena, MT 59601
(406) 443-1053
License: Helena, Lewis and Clark County, MT
Nat'l Network: ABC
Format: Adult Contemp
Kevin Skaalure, General Manager
Steve Phillips, Promotions Manager
Karen Feldner, News Director
Shawn Ketchum, Chief Engineer

RADIO - U.S.

***KUHM**
01-01-2000; 91.7 mhz FM; 0.91 kw; 761 ft.; N46 46 11 W112 1 22 *Rebroadcasts:* Rebroadcasts KUFM(FM) Missoula 100%
Partv Building, Room 180, Missoula, MT 59812 US
(406) 243-4931, *Fax:* (406) 243-3299
www.kufm.org
License: Helena, Lewis and Clark County, MT held by The University of Montana.
Nat'l Network: NPR *Wire Services:* AP
Arbitron Metro Market: Helena, MT *Format:* Classical, Jazz, 60 *No. News Employees:* 2
William Marcus, General Manager
Michael Marsolek, Programming Director
Sally Mauk, News Director
Saxon Holbrook, Technical Director
William Marcus, Director of UM Broadcast Media Center
Sue Ginn, Accounting Associate
JerriBalsam, Administrative Associate
Edward F. O'Brien, Assistant News Director
Linda Talbott, Associate Director
Kathy Woodford, Director of Corporate Support

***KVCM**
08-02-1993; 103.1 mhz FM *Hrs Open:* 24; 30 kw; 771 ft.; N46 46 7 W112 1 21 *Rebroadcasts:* Rebroadcasts KXEI(FM) Havre 100%.
PO Box 2426, Havre, MT 59501 US
(406) 265-5845, *Fax:* (406) 265-8860
www.ynopradio.org
info@ynop.org
License: Helena, Lewis and Clark County, MT held by Hi-Line Radio Fellowship Inc.
Nat'l Network: Moody; Salem Radio Network *Wire Services:* AP
Arbitron Metro Market: Helena, MT *Format:* Christian, Religious
Target Audience: General:; those looking for inspirational Christian music & progmg
Roger Lonnquist, General Manager
Brenda Boyum, Station Manager
Brian Jackson, Programming Director
Nicholas Tobiason, Music/IT Director
Ron Huckeby, Chief Engineer
Joanna Baer, Office Assistant
Crystal MacInnes, ProductionAssistant

KZMT
01-01-1975; 101.1 mhz FM; 90.5 kw; 1991 ft.; N46 44 51.8 W112 19 47.6
101 West Grand, Chicago, IL 60610 US
(406) 442-4490, *Fax:* (406) 442-7356
www.kzmt.com
kbllfm@cherrycreekradio.com
License: Helena, Lewis and Clark County, MT held by CCR-Helena IV LLC.
Group Owner: Cherry Creek Radio LLC
Arbitron Metro Market: Helena, MT *Format:* Classic Rock *Target Audience:* 18-54; upscale, entrepreneurial, adults
Michele McAlister, News Director

***KHLV**
01-01-2005; 90.1 mhz FM *Hrs Open:* 24; 0.001 kw horiz, 3.5 kw vert; 662 ft.; N46 46 7 W112 1 21 *Rebroadcasts:* Rebroadcasts KLVR(FM) Santa Rosa, CA 100%
1425 N Market Blvd., Suite 9, Sacramento, CA 95834 US
(800) 525-5683, *Fax:* (916) 251-1650
www.klove.com
klove@klove.com
License: Helena, Lewis and Clark County, MT held by Educational Media Foundation.
Group Owner: EMF Broadcasting
Nat'l Network: K-Love
Arbitron Metro Market: Helena, MT *Format:* Christian *No. News Employees:* 13 *Target Audience:* 25-44; Judeo Christian, female
Darrell Chambliss, Chairman
Mike Novak, President and CEO
Mike Lee, Operations Dir
David Pierce, Chief Creative Officer and Programming Director
Ed Lenane, News Director
Sam Wallington, Engineering Dir
Marya Morgan, NewsReporter
Richard Hunt, News Reporter
Alan Mason, Chief Operating Officer
Dan Antonelli, Chief Business Development Officer
Eric Moser, Chief Financial Officer
Brian Burger, Vice President of Human Resources

Helena Valley N

KMXM(FM)
01-01-2008; 101.7 mhz FM; 100 kw; Ant 895 ft; N47 36 24 W111 21 31
118 6th St. S., Great Falls, MT 59401-3625
(406) 761-8816, *Fax:* (406) 454-3484
License: Helena Valley N, Chouteau County, MT held by The Montana Radio Company LLC
Group Owner: College Creek Media LLC
Population Served: 189 *Arbitron Metro Market:* Highwood, MT
Format: Contemporary Hits/Top 40
Neal Robinson, President
Darnell Washington, General Manager

Joliet

KWMY
02-15-2006; 105.9 mhz FM *Hrs Open:* 24; 100 kw; 440 ft.; N45 39 31 W108 34 14
US
(406) 248-7777, *Fax:* (406) 248-857
www.my925fm.com
planet@planet1067.com
License: Joliet, Stillwater County, MT held by Chaparral Broadcasting Inc.
Group Owner: Chaparral Communications; (acq 11-30-92; $215,000 with KPOW(AM) Powell, WY;
Arbitron Metro Market: Billings, MT *Format:* Contemporary Hits/Top 40, Adult Contemp
Cam Maxwell, General Manager

Kalispell

KALS
11-01-1974; 97.1 mhz FM; 26.5 kw; 2487 ft.; N48 0 48 W114 21 55
PO Box 9710, Kalispell, MT 59904 US
(406) 752-5257, *Fax:* (406) 752-3416
www.kals.com
kals@kals.com
License: Kalispell, Flathead County, MT held by Kalispell Christian Radio Fellowship Inc.
Arbitron Metro Market: Kalispell, MT *Format:* Adult Contemp, Christian *Special Programming:* Class one hr wkly *Target Audience:* 25-54
Brad Rauch, General Manager

KBBZ
09-12-1983; 98.5 mhz FM; 61 kw horiz, 6.1 kw vert; 2379 ft.; N48 30 42 W114 22 14
P.O. Box 5409, Kalispell, MT 59903 US
(406) 755-8700, *Fax:* (406) 755-8770
www.kbbz.com
kbbz@beebroadcasting.com
License: Kalispell, Flathead County, MT held by Bee Broadcasting Inc.
Group Owner: Bee Broadcasting Inc.; acq 6-12-83; $315,000;
Arbitron Metro Market: Kalispell, MT *Format:* Adult Contemp
Benny Bee, President
Benny Bee Jr., Operations Dir
Mark Wagner, General Manager

KDBR
11-01-1993; 106.3 mhz FM; 59 kw horiz, 5.9 kw vert; 2365 ft.; N48 30 42 W114 22 16
Box 5409, Kalispell, MT 59903 US
(406) 257-5327(406) 755-8700, *Fax:* (406) 755-8770
www.kdbr.com
kdbr@beebroadcasting.com
License: Kalispell, Flathead County, MT held by Bee Broadcasting Inc.
Group Owner: Bee Broadcasting Inc.
Arbitron Metro Market: Kalispell, MT *Format:* Country
Benny Bee, President
Mark Wagner, General Manager

KGEZ
03-24-1927; 600 khz AM *Hrs Open:* 24; 5 kw-D, DA2; 1 kw-N, DA2; N48 9 40 W114 16 51
P. O. Box 169, Kalispell, MT 59903 US
(406) 752-2600, *Fax:* (406) 257-0459
www.z600.com
stokes@z600.com
License: Kalispell, MT held by Skyline Broadcasters Inc.
Nat'l Network: USA
Format: News, News/Talk, 84, Talk *Target Audience:* 25-60. *Adv. Rates:* 18; 18; 18; 18
John Stokes, General Manager

KOFI
11-11-1955; 1180 khz AM *Hrs Open:* 24; 50 kw-D, DAN; 10 kw-N, DAN; N48 11 52 W114 15 3
Mailing Address: 317 First Avenue, East, Kalispell, MT 59901 US
Second Address: 317 First Ave. E., Kalispell, MT 59901
(406) 755-6690, *Fax:* (406) 752-5078
www.kofi.com
kofi@kofi.radio.com
License: Kalispell, MT held by KOFI Inc.
Nat'l Network: ABC; CNN Radio
Format: News, News/Talk, 64, Talk *Hrs. of News Programming:* news progmg 35 hrs wkly *No. News Employees:* 2 *Target Audience:* 25-54. *Adv. Rates:* 26.50; 21.50; 26.50; 21.50
Dave Rae, General Manager

KZMN
06-10-1988; 103.9 mhz FM *Hrs Open:* 24; 100 kw horiz, 43 kw vert; 571 ft.; N48 5 39 W114 16 11
Mailing Address: P.O. Box 608, Kalispell, MT 59903 US
Second Address: 317 First Ave. E., Kalispell, MT 59901
(406) 755-6690,(406) 752-5078
www.kzmn.com
kofi@kofiradio.com
License: Kalispell, Flathead County, MT
Nat'l Network: CNN Radio
Format: Classic Rock *Hrs. of News Programming:* News progmg 3 hrs wkly *Target Audience:* 18-49.
Dave Rae, President
Mike Jorgensen, Operations Dir

***KSPL**
02-01-1997; 90.9 mhz FM *Hrs Open:* 24 hours; 250 w; 2,529 ft; N48 30 22 W114 20 49 *Rebroadcasts:* Rebroadcasts KMBI-FM Spokane, WA 100%
c/o KMBI-FM, 5408 S. Freya, Spokane, WA 60610
(509) 448-2555, *Fax:* (509) 448-6855
www.moodyradionw.fm
kmbi@moody.edu
License: Kalispell, Flathead County, MT held by Moody Bible Institute of Chicago.
Group Owner: The Moody Bible Institute of Chicago
Target Audience: 35-54; Christian men & women
Richard Monteith, General Manager
Chris Wright, Programming Director
Gordon Canady (Spokane), Engineering Dir
Scott Richardson (KSPL only), Chief Engineer
Dee Marie, Afternoon Announcer
Jane Frazer, Part Time Announcer
ShellyHogeweide, Part Time Announcer
Gary Leonard, Part Time Announcer

***KUKL**
10-01-1998; 90.1 mhz FM; 1.83 kw; 2579 ft.; N48 30 22 W114 20 49
Broadcast Media Center, Partv Building, Room 180, Missoula, MT 59812 US
(406) 243-4931, *Fax:* (406) 243-3299
www.mtpr.org
License: Kalispell, Flathead County, MT held by University of Montana.
Nat'l Network: NPR *Wire Services:* AP
Arbitron Metro Market: Kalispell, MT *Format:* Classical, Jazz, 60
Hrs. of News Programming: News progmg 2 hrs wkly
William Marcus, General Manager
Michael Marsolek, Programming Director
Sally Mauk, News Director
Saxon Holbrook, Technical Director
William Marcus, Director of UM Broadcast Media Center
Sue Ginn, Accounting Associate
JerriBalsam, Administrative Associate
Edward F. O'Brien, Assistant News Director
Linda Talbott, Associate Director
Kathy Woodford, Director of Corporate Support

***KLKM**
01-01-2006; 88.7 mhz FM; 3.3 kw; 2575 ft.; N48 0 48 W114 21 55 *Rebroadcasts:* Rebroadcasts KLVR(FM) Santa Rosa, CA 100%
188 S. Bellevue, Suite 222, Memphis, TN 38104 US
(800) 525-5683, *Fax:* (916) 251-1650
www.klove.com
klove@klove.com
License: Kalispell, Flathead County, MT held by Educational Media Foundation.
Group Owner: EMF Broadcasting; (acq 1-11-2005; $95,000 for CP).
Nat'l Network: K-Love
Arbitron Metro Market: Kalispell, MT *Format:* Christian *No. News Employees:* 13
Darrell Chambliss, Chairman
Mike Novak, President and CEO

Mike Lee, Operations Dir
Eric Allen, General Sales Mgr
David Pierce, Chief Creative Officer and Programming Director
Ed Lenane, News Director
Sam Wallington, EngineeringDir
Marya Morgan, News Reporter
Richard Hunt, News Reporter
Alan Mason, Chief Operating Officer
Dan Antonelli, Chief Business Development Officer
Eric Moser, Chief Financial Officer
Brian Burger, Vice President of Human Resources

Laurel

KBSR
09-01-1979; 1490 khz AM *Hrs Open:* 24; 1 kw-U, ND1; N45 39 11 W108 45 9
PO Box 230, Hardin, MT 59034 US
(406) 665-2828, *Fax:* (406) 665-2131
www.bigskyradio.net
rich@bigskyradio.net
License: Laurel, MT held by Sun Mountain Inc.
Group Owner: Sun Mountain Inc.; (acq 11-30-2000)
Nat'l Network: ABC
Arbitron Metro Market: Billings, MT *Format:* News, Talk *Hrs. of News Programming:* News prgmg 24 hrs wkly *Target Audience:* 35 plus; professional, business people
Richard Solberg, President

KRSQ
06-09-1994; 101.9 mhz FM; 100 kw; 367 ft.; N45 45 48 W108 27 20
101 West Grand, Chicago, IL 60610 US
(406) 238-1000, *Fax:* (406) 238-1038
www.hot1019.com
kyle.mccoy@benedettimedia.com
License: Laurel, Yellowstone County, MT held by BMG Billings, LLC
Group Owner: Benedetti Media Group LLC; acq 8-10-99; grpsl).
Arbitron Metro Market: Billings, MT *Format:* Contemporary Hits/Top 40 *Target Audience:* 18-49.
Pete Benedetti, CEO
Terry Strickland, General Manager
Emily Petroff, General Sales Mgr
Kyle McCoy, Programming Director

Lewistown

KLCM
04-01-1975; 95.9 mhz FM; 3 kw; -230 ft.; N47 4 16 W109 24 32
P.O. Box 620, Lewistown, MT 59457 US
(406) 707-5275, *Fax:* (406) 538-3495
www.kxlo-klcm.com
info@kxlo-klcm.com
License: Lewistown, Fergus County, MT held by Montana Broadcast Communications Inc.
Arbitron Metro Market: Great Falls, MT *Format:* Contemporary Hits/Top 40, Adult Contemp *Target Audience:* 18-54.
George Pelletier, Operations Dir
Don Kliewer, General Manager
Jim Alan, News Director
Mike Laughter, Chief Engineer
Tom Hughes, Operations Director

KXLO
01-01-1947; 1230 khz AM
P. O. Box 620, Lewistown, MT 59457 US
(406) 707-5275, *Fax:* (406) 538-3495
www.kxlo-klcm.com
kxlo@lewistown.net
License: Lewistown, MT held by KXLO Broadcast Inc.
Nat'l Network: CBS
Arbitron Metro Market: Lewistown, MT *Format:* Country *Special Programming:* Farm *Target Audience:* General.
Fred Lark, Owner/President
Fred Lark, General Manager
Phyllis, Station Manager
Bethany Lark, Programming Director
Jay Gordon, Sports Director

*KLEU
10-21-2003; 91.1 mhz FM *Hrs Open:* 24; 4 kw; 1877 ft.; N47 10 39.4 W109 32 5.6 *Rebroadcasts:* Rebroadcasts KXEI(FM) Havre 100%
131 Erik Drive, Bozeman, MT 59715 US
(406) 265-5845, *Fax:* (406) 265-8860
www.ynopradio.org
info@ynop.org
License: Lewistown, Fergus County, MT held by Hi-Line Radio Fellowship Inc.
Nat'l Network: Moody; Salem Radio Network *Wire Services:* AP
Arbitron Metro Market: Havre, MT *Format:* Christian, Religious
Roger Lonnquist, YNOP General Manager
Brenda Boyum, KXEI Station Manager
Clark Berg, KALS Sales Manager
David Brown, YNOP Program Director
Ron Huckeby, Chief Engineer
MarySue Amundgaard, KALS Office Staff
Joanna Baer,Announcer/Office Assistant
Earl Houtz, Announcer
Dave Kirby, Announcer
Crystal MacInnes, Production Assistant
Elizabeth McClenahan, Office Manager at KXEI/Webmaster

Libby

KLCB
12-23-1950; 1230 khz AM *Hrs Open:* 16; 1 kw-U, ND1; N48 22 14 W115 32 19
Mailing Address: 251 West Cedar Street, PO Box 730, Libby, MT 59923 US
Second Address: 251 W. Cedar St., Libby, MT 59923
(406) 293-6234, *Fax:* (406) 293-6235
License: Libby, MT held by Lincoln County Broadcasters Inc.
Nat'l Network: ABC
Arbitron Metro Market: Great Falls, MT *Format:* Country *Hrs. of News Programming:* news progmg 13 hrs wkly *No. News Employees:* 1 *Target Audience:* 25-54.
Duane Williams, CEO

KTNY
04-05-1986; 101.7 mhz FM *Hrs Open:* 16; 3 kw; -1017 ft.; N48 22 14 W115 32 19
Mailing Address: P.O. Box 730, 251 West Cedar Street, Libby, MT 59923 US
Second Address: 251 W. Cedar St., Libby, MT 59923
(406) 293-6234, *Fax:* (406) 293-6235
License: Libby, Lincoln County, MT held by Lincoln County Broadcasters Inc.
Nat'l Network: ABC
Arbitron Metro Market: Libby, MT *Format:* Oldies *Hrs. of News Programming:* news progmg 16 hrs wkly *No. News Employees:* 1 *Target Audience:* 35-54.
Duane Williams, CEO

*KVRZ
88.9 mhz FM; 0.085 kw; 1247 ft.; N48 29 13 W115 47 39 US
(406) 293-6551
www.kvrz.net
License: Libby, Lincoln County, MT held by Troy Fine Arts Council.
Arbitron Metro Market: Libby, MT
Scott Curry, President
Brian Sherry, Station Manager
John Herrmann, Vice President

*KUFL
90.5 mhz FM; 1 kw; -1043 ft.; N48 22 45 W115 33 29 US
(406) 243-4931, *Fax:* (406) 243-3299
www.mtpr.org
License: Libby, Lincoln County, MT held by The University of Montana.
Arbitron Metro Market: Libby, MT *Format:* Public Affairs *No. News Employees:* 6
William Marcus, General Manager
Michael Marsolek, Programming Director
Sally Mauk, News Director
Doug Drader, Chief Engineer
Beth Anne Austein, Production
Anne Hosler, Membership Manager
Kathy Woodford, Director of CorporateSupport
Jeff Croonenberghs, Chief Operator
Saxon Holbrook, Technical Director

Livingston

KOZB
12-01-1977; 97.5 mhz FM *Hrs Open:* 24; 100 kw; 246 ft.; N45 39 26 W110 58 22
P.O. Box 20, Bozeman, MT 59715 US
(406) 587-9999, *Fax:* (406) 587-5855
reier@bigsky.net
License: Livingston, Park County, MT held by Reier Broadcasting Co. Inc.
Group Owner: Reier Broadcasting Co. Inc.; acq 10-18-96; grpsl).
Arbitron Metro Market: Bozemon, MT *Format:* Classic Rock *No. News Employees:* 2 *Target Audience:* 18-44.
Bill Reier, General Manager

KPRK
01-10-1947; 1340 khz AM *Hrs Open:* 5:30 AM-midnight; 1 kw-U, ND1; N45 40 21 W110 32 21
980 North Michigan Ave, Suite 1880, Chicago, IL 60611 US
(406) 222-2841, *Fax:* (406) 222-1341
kprkam@mooseradio.com
License: Livingston, MT held by GAP Broadcasting Bozeman License LLC.
Group Owner: GAPWEST Broadcasting; (acq 2-13-2008; grpsl)
Nat'l Network: AP Radio
Arbitron Metro Market: Bozemon, MT *Format:* Talk *Special Programming:* Oldies 5 hrs, big band 4 hrs wkly *Hrs. of News Programming:* News progmg 15 hrs wkly *Target Audience:* 25-64; general
Dave Cowan, General Manager
Courtney Lehman, Station Manager
Kaye Rugh, General Sales Mgr
Gary Weiss, News Director
Ron Huckeby, Chief Engineer

KXLB
100.7 mhz FM; 94 kw; 814 ft.; N45 40 24 W110 52 2
980 Norht Michigan Avenue, Suite 1880, Chicago, IL 60611 US
(406) 586-2343
www.xlcountry.com
colleenoquinn@townsquaremedia.com
License: Livingston, Park County, MT held by GAP Broadcasting Bozeman License LLC.
Group Owner: GAPWEST Broadcasting; (acq 2-13-2008; grpsl)
Arbitron Metro Market: Bozeman, MT *Format:* Country
Dick Loughney, General Manager/Director of Sales
Colleen O'Quinn, Programming Director

*KYPM
90.1 mhz FM; 0.44 kw; 869 ft.; N45 35 51 W110 32 45 US
(406) 657-2941, *Fax:* (406) 657-2977
www.yellowstonepublicradio.org
License: Livingston, Park County, MT held by Montana State University -Billings.
Arbitron Metro Market: Livingston, MT
Dennis Hall, President
Ken Siebert, Media Services Director
Jackie Yamanaka, News Director
Jim Nichols, Chief Engineer
Barbara Bernheim, Development and Listener Support Manager
Alicia Lee, Underwriting Manager / Public InformationManager
Ana Henrickson, Business & Finance Manager
Brad Edwards Jazz, Programmer / Announcer
Wesley Jessen, Media Services Assistant / Control Room Operator

Lockwood

*KYWH
01-01-2006; 88.9 mhz FM; 1.9 kw vert; Ant 452 ft; N45 51 12 W108 45 50
2121 South 48th St. West, Billings, MT 92706
(406) 254-1944, *Fax:* (406) 294-1946
www.calvarychapel.com/billings
License: Lockwood, Yellowstone County, MT held by CSN International
Group Owner: CSN International
Wayne Hathaway, General Manager

KYLW
01-01-2005; 1450 khz AM *Hrs Open:* 24 US
(406) 665-2828, *Fax:* (406) 665-2131
www.bigskyradio.net
rich@bigskyradio.net
License: Lockwood, MT held by Sun Mountain Inc.
Group Owner: Sun Mountain Inc.; (acq 7-7-2005; $26,000 for CP)
Nat'l Network: ABC
Arbitron Metro Market: Lockwood, MT *Target Audience:* General.
Richard Solberg, General Manager

KPLN
03-01-2006; 106.7 mhz FM; 100 kw; 512 ft.; N45 45 54 W108 27 19
US
(406) 248-7777, *Fax:* (406) 248-8577
www.planet1067.com
License: Lockwood, Yellowstone County, MT held by Connoisseur Media LLC.
Group Owner: Connoisseur Media LLC
Arbitron Metro Market: Lockwood, MT *Format:* Adult Contemp, Contemporary Hits/Top 40

Cam Maxwell, General Manager

Lolo

KDXT
01-01-2008; 97.9 mhz FM; 10 kw; 417 ft.; N46 30 37 W113 58 48 US
(406) 541-1071, *Fax:* (406) 721-1036
www.107theranch.com
License: Lolo, Missoula County, MT held by Sheila Callahan and Friends Inc.
Group Owner: Sheila Callahan and Friends Inc.
Arbitron Metro Market: Lolo, MT *Format:* Country
Sheila Callahan, General Manager

Malta

KMMR
09-09-1980; 100.1 mhz FM *Hrs Open:* 6 AM-11 PM; 2.25 kw; 377 ft.; N48 15 17 W107 49 18
PO Box 1073, Malta, MT 59538 US
(406) 654-2472, *Fax:* (406) 654-2506
www.kmmrfm.com
License: Malta, Phillips County, MT held by KMMR Radio Inc.
Nat'l Network: ABC
Format: Adult Contemp, Country *Hrs. of News Programming:* news progmg 3 hrs wkly *No. News Employees:* 1 *Target Audience:* 18-65; general, rural *Adv. Rates:* 7.50; 7.50; 7.50; 7.50
Gregory Kielb, President
Claudette Kielb, Operations Dir
Valene Kielb, Programming Director
Joyce Robinson, Operations Director

Manhattan

KKQX
11-01-2005; 105.7 mhz FM *Hrs Open:* 24; 12.3 kw; 682 ft.; N45 38 16 W111 16 5 *Rebroadcasts:* Simulcast on KBZM (FM) Big Sky
US
(406) 582-1045, *Fax:* (406) 582-0388
www.kbzm.com
sbalding@kbzm.com
License: Manhattan, Gallatin County, MT held by Radick Construction Inc.
Regional Reps: Local Focus 310-441-8188
Arbitron Metro Market: Rocklin, CA *Format:* Classic Rock, Adult Contemp *No. News Employees:* 2 *Target Audience:* 25-54.
John Radick, President

Miles City

KATL
09-04-1941; 770 khz AM *Hrs Open:* 24; 10 kw-D, DAN; 1 kw-N, DAN; N46 23 46 W105 46 44
Mailing Address: P. O. Box 700, Miles City, MT 59301 US
Second Address: 818 Main St., Miles City, MT 59301
(406) 234-7700, *Fax:* (406) 234-7783
www.katlradio.com
katlradio@katlradio.com
License: Miles City, MT held by Star Printing Co.
Nat'l Network: Westwood One; ABC *Wire Services:* AP
Arbitron Metro Market: Miles City, MT *Format:* Adult Contemp *Hrs. of News Programming:* news progmg 17 hrs wkly *No. News Employees:* 8 *Target Audience:* 25-54; Adults *Adv. Rates:* 12.50, 12.50; 12.50
John Sullivan, President
Donald Richard, General Manager
Mark Waddington, General Sales Mgr

*KYPR
11-17-1988; 90.7 mhz FM *Hrs Open:* 24; 0.5 kw; 502 ft.; N46 23 22 W105 45 22 *Rebroadcasts:* Rebroadcasts KEMC(FM) Billings 100%
1500 N. 30th Street, Billings, MT 59101 US
(406) 657-2941, *Fax:* (406) 657-2977
www.yellowstonepublicradio.org
License: Miles City, Custer County, MT held by Montana State University-Billings.
Nat'l Network: NPR; PRI
Arbitron Metro Market: Billings, MT *Format:* Variety/Diverse *Hrs. of News Programming:* News progmg 39 hrs wkly *Target Audience:* General.
Dennis Hall, President
Ken Siebert, General Manager
Jackie Yamanaka, News Director
Jim Nichols, Chief Engineer

KYUS-FM
11-08-1984; 92.3 mhz FM *Hrs Open:* 24; 100 kw; 984 ft.; N46 24 4 W105 39 6
Mailing Address: 508 Main Street, Room 200, Miles City, MT 59301 US
Second Address: 508 Main St., Rm. 200, Miles City, MT 53901
(406) 234-5626, *Fax:* (406)-874-7000
terry@kyuskmta.com
License: Miles City, Custer County, MT held by Marks Radio Group.
Nat'l Network: USA
Arbitron Metro Market: Billings, MT *Format:* Adult Contemp *Special Programming:* Farm one hr wkly *Hrs. of News Programming:* news progmg 3 hrs wkly *No. News Employees:* 1 *Target Audience:* 18-54; programmedfor general audience appeal
Terry Virag, General Manager
Lee Akers, News Director
Paul Grutkowski, Chief Engineer
C.W. Wilcox, Sports Commentator
Charice Virag, Traffic Manager

KMTA
10-01-1986; 1050 khz AM *Hrs Open:* 24; 10 kw-D, ND2; 0.136 kw-N, ND2; N46 24 4 W105 39 6
Mailing Address: PO Box 1426, Miles City, MT 59301 US
Second Address: 508 Main St., Rm. 200, Miles City, MT 59301
(406) 234-5626, *Fax:* (406) 874-7000
License: Miles City, MT held by Marks Radio Group.
Nat'l Network: USA
Format: Classic Rock *Hrs. of News Programming:* news progmg 6 hrs wkly *No. News Employees:* 1 *Target Audience:* 25-54.

Missoula

*KBGA
08-24-1996; 89.9 mhz FM; 1 kw; -262 ft.; N46 52 56 W113 59 8
Office of President, University Hall, Missoula, MT 59812 US
(406) 243-6758, *Fax:* (406) 243-6428
www.kbga.org
gm@kbga.org
License: Missoula, Missoula County, MT held by The University of Montana.
Arbitron Metro Market: Missoula, MT *Format:* Talk *Hrs. of News Programming:* 10 *No. News Employees:* 2
Chris Justice, General Manager

KGGL
04-29-1977; 93.3 mhz FM; 43 kw; 2549 ft.; N47 1 57 W113 59 31
Mailing Address: N. 1212 Washington, Suite 307, Spokane, WA 99201 US
Second Address: 1600 N. Ave. W., Missoula, MT 59801
(406) 728-9399, *Fax:* (406) 721-3020
www.eagle93.com
License: Missoula, Missoula County, MT held by CCR-Missoula IV LLC.
Group Owner: Cherry Creek Radio LLC
Nat'l Reps: McGavren Guild
Arbitron Metro Market: Missoula, MT *Format:* Country *Target Audience:* 25-54.
Scott Richards, Operations Dir
Chad Parrish, General Manager
Bill McPherson, General Sales Mgr
Samantha Honold, News Director
Joe Bowers, Chief Engineer
Michelle Weber, Business Manager

KGRZ
01-01-1947; 1450 khz AM *Hrs Open:* 24; 1 kw-U, ND1; N46 52 39 W114 2 36
Mailing Address: N. 1212 Washington, Suite 307, Spokane, WA 99201 US
Second Address: 1600 N. Ave. W., Missoula, MT 59801
(406) 728-1450, *Fax:* (406) 721-3020
License: Missoula, MT held by CCR-Missoula IV LLC.
Group Owner: Cherry Creek Radio LLC; (acq 10-31-2006; grpsl)
Nat'l Reps: McGavren Guild
Format: Sports, Talk *Target Audience:* 25-54; male, sports orientated
Scott Richards, Operations Dir
Chad Parrish, General Manager
Bill McPherson, General Sales Mgr
Samantha Honold, News Director
Joe Bowers, Chief Engineer
Michelle Weber, Business Manager

KGVO
01-18-1931; 1290 khz AM; 5 kw-U, DA-N; N46 49 47 W114 04 45
3250 S. Reserve St., Suite 200, Missoula, MT 60611
(406) 728-9300, *Fax:* (406) 542-2329
www.kgvo1290.com
License: Missoula, Missoula County, MT held by Townsquare Media
Group Owner: GAPWEST Broadcasting; (acq 2-13-2008; grpsl)
Nat'l Network: Fox News Radio
Population Served: 90,000*Target Audience:* General.
Scott Shannon, Operations Dir
Shawne Bott, General Manager
Scott Shannon, Programming Director
Carl Severo, Engineering Dir

KMSO
02-09-1985; 102.5 mhz FM *Hrs Open:* 24; 29 kw; 1752 ft.; N46 48 30 W113 58 38
Mailing Address: P.O. Box 309, Missoula, MT 59806 US
Second Address: 725 Strand Ave., Missoula, MT 59801
(406) 542-1025, *Fax:* (406) 721-1036
www.moclub.com
info@kmso.com
License: Missoula, Missoula County, MT held by Sheila Callahan & Friends Inc.
Group Owner: Sheila Callahan and Friends Inc.
Nat'l Network: AP Radio *Regional Reps:* Tacher; Portland *Wire Services:* AP
Format: Adult Contemp *Special Programming:* Relg one hr wkly *Hrs. of News Programming:* News progmg 6 hrs wkly *Target Audience:* 25-54; upscale professional, well-educated mgmt level *Adv. Rates:* 34; 34; 34; 22
Sheila Callahan, General Manager
Diana Helms, General Sales Mgr
Dale Desmond, Programming Director
Kris Hardy, News Director

*KMZL
01-01-1998; 91.1 mhz FM *Hrs Open:* 24; 2.2 kw; 2054 ft.; N46 48 9 W113 58 21
2201 South 6th Street, Las Vegas, NV 89104 US
(800) 804-5452
sosradio.net
info@sosradio.net
License: Missoula, Missoula County, MT held by Faith Communications Corp.
Group Owner: Faith Communications Corp.
Format: Adult Contemp, Christian *Hrs. of News Programming:* News progmg 5 hrs wkly *Target Audience:* 25-44.
Jack French, CEO
Brad Staley, General Manager
Chris Staley, Programming Director

*KUFM
01-31-1965; 89.1 mhz FM; 14.5 kw; 2474 ft.; N47 1 58 W113 59 29
Broadcast Media Center, Partv Building, Room 180, Missoula, MT 59812 US
(406) 243-4931, *Fax:* (406) 243-3299
www.mtpr.org
License: Missoula, Missoula County, MT held by University of Montana.
Nat'l Network: NPR *Wire Services:* AP
Arbitron Metro Market: Missoula, MT *Format:* Jazz *No. News Employees:* 2
William Marcus, General Manager
Michael Marsolek, Programming Director
Sally Mauk, News Director
Saxon Holbrook, Technical Director
William Marcus, Director of UM Broadcast Media Center
Sue Ginn, Accounting Associate
JerriBalsam, Administrative Associate
Edward F. O'Brien, Assistant News Director
Linda Talbott, Associate Director
Kathy Woodford, Director of Corporate Support

KYLT
07-15-1955; 1340 khz AM *Hrs Open:* 24; 1 kw-U, ND1; N46 52 56 W113 59 8
Mailing Address: N. 1212 Washington, Suite 307, Spokane, WA 99201 US
Second Address: 1600 North Ave. W., Suite 101, Missoula, MT 59801-5500
(406) 721-9300, *Fax:* (406) 721-3020
www.1340kylt.com
kylt@1340kylt.com
License: Missoula, MT held by CCR-Missoula IV LLC.
Group Owner: Cherry Creek Radio LLC; (acq 10-31-2006; grpsl)
Nat'l Network: Fox Sports *Nat'l Reps:* McGavren Guild
Arbitron Metro Market: Missoula, MT *Format:* Sports *Target Audience:* 35-55.
Scott Richards, Operations Dir
Chad Parrish, General Manager
Bill McPherson, General Sales Mgr
Samantha Honold, News Director
Joe Bowers, Chief Engineer
Michelle Weber, Business Manager

KYSS-FM
05-11-1969; 94.9 mhz FM *Hrs Open:* 24; 63 kw; 2392 ft.; N47 1 57 W113 59 30
980 North Michigan Ave., Suite 1880, Chicago, IL 60611 US
(406) 543-9500, *Fax:* (406) 542-2329
www.kyssfm.com
shawnabatt@townsquaremedia.com
License: Missoula, Missoula County, MT held by GAP Broadcasting Missoula License LLC.
Group Owner: GAPWEST Broadcasting; (acq 2-13-2008; grpsl)
Arbitron Metro Market: Missoula,MT *Format:* Country *Hrs. of News Programming:* News progmg 12 hrs wkly *Target Audience:* 25-54; adults
Shawna Batt, Director of Sales
Craig Johnson, Programming Director

KZOQ-FM
07-29-1974; 100.1 mhz FM *Hrs Open:* 24; 13.5 kw; Ant 2,102 ft; N46 48 09 W113 58 21
Box 4106, 1600 North Ave. W., Missoula, MT 99201
(406) 728-5000, *Fax:* (406) 721-3020
License: Missoula, Missoula County, MT
Group Owner: Cherry Creek Radio LLC
Nat'l Reps: Tacher
Target Audience: 25-54.
Tom Anthony, Operations Dir
Bob Breck, General Manager
Dan Buchta, General Sales Mgr
Eric Wolfermann, Programming Director
Angel Hughes, Promotions Manager
Lauri Pulley, News Director
Joe Bowers, Chief Engineer
Rose Ramer,Business Manager

KYJK
07-01-2005; 105.9 mhz FM *Hrs Open:* 25.?Â ?; 1.84 kw; 2083 ft.; N46 48 6 W113 58 22
US
(406) 721-6800, *Fax:* (406) 329-1850
www.jackfmmissoula.com
rharsell@simmonsmedia.com
License: Missoula, Missoula County, MT held by Spanish Peaks Broadcasting Inc.
Group Owner: Spanish Peaks Broadcasting Inc.
Nat'l Reps: Interep
Arbitron Metro Market: Missoula, MT *Format:* Adult Contemp *Target Audience:* 25-54; adults *Adv. Rates:* 18; 15; 18; 9
Rod Harsell, General Manager

***KJCG**
88.3 mhz FM; 1 kw vert; 2034 ft.; N46 48 6 W113 58 22
820 North Lasalle Blvd., Chicago, IL 60610 US
(406) 265-5845, *Fax:* (406) 265-8860
www.ynop.org
info@ynop.org
License: Missoula, Missoula County, MT held by The Moody Bible Institute of Chicago.
Group Owner: The Moody Bible Institute of Chicago
Arbitron Metro Market: Missoula, MT
Roger Lonnquist, General Manager
Brenda Boyum, Station Manager
Clark Berg, General Sales Mgr
David Brown, Programming Director
Ron Huckeby, Chief Engineer
Announcer/Office Assistant

Montana City

KOYT(FM)
01-01-2007; 98.5 mhz FM; 6 kw; Ant -108 ft; N46 33 25.8 W111 55 01.4
501 South Cherry Street, Suite 480, Denver, CO 59604
License: Montana City, Jefferson County, MT held by Cherry Creek Radio LLC.
Group Owner: Cherry Creek Radio LLC
Population Served: 28,592 *Arbitron Metro Market:* Helena, MT
Dewey Bruce, General Manager

Pablo

KKMT
01-01-2006; 99.7 mhz FM; 1.8 kw; 2113 ft.; N47 46 25 W114 16 4
US
(406) 883-5255, *Fax:* (406) 883-4411
www.star99hits.com
info@kkmtfm.com
License: Pablo, Lake County, MT held by Anderson Radio Broadcasting Inc.
Group Owner: Anderson Radio Broadcasting Inc.
Arbitron Metro Market: Pablo, MT *Format:* Adult Contemp, Contemporary Hits/Top 40
Dennis Anderson, President

Park City

***KBIL**
01-01-2006; 89.7 mhz FM *Hrs Open:* 24; 2.7 kw vert; 525 ft.; N45 51 12 W108 45 50 *Rebroadcasts:* Rebroadcasts KLRD(FM) Yucaipa, CA 100%
16075 W Belleview Ave, Morrison, CO 80465 US
(888) 937-2471, *Fax:* (916) 251-1650
www.air1.com
info@air1.com
License: Park City, Stillwater County, MT held by Educational Media Foundation.
Group Owner: EMF Broadcasting; (acq 10-2-2003; grpsl).
Nat'l Network: Air 1
Arbitron Metro Market: Billings, MT *Format:* Alternative, Christian *No. News Employees:* 3 *Target Audience:* 25-44; Judeo Christian female
Darrell Chambliss, Chairman
Alan Mason, COO
Mike Novak, President and CEO
Mike Lee, Operations Dir
David Pierce, Programming Director
Ed Lenane, News Director
Sam Wallington, Engineering Dir
Marya Morgan, News Reporter
Richard Hunt, News Reporter
Larry Moody, Director
Mitch Barnhart, Director
David R. Ferry, Director
Walter Golembeski, Director

Pinesdale

KXDR
07-16-1999; 106.7 mhz FM *Hrs Open:* 24; 38 kw; 2090 ft.; N46 48 9 W113 58 19
3565 Standish Avenue, Santa Rosa, CA 95407 US
(406) 728-5000, *Fax:* (406) 721-3020
www.starfm.net
License: Pinesdale, Ravalli County, MT held by CCR-Missoula IV LLC.
Group Owner: Cherry Creek Radio LLC; (acq 10-31-2006; grpsl)
Nat'l Reps: McGavren Guild
Arbitron Metro Market: Missoula, MT *Format:* Contemporary Hits/Top 40
Scott Richards, Operations Dir
Chad Parrish, General Manager
Bill McPherson, General Sales Mgr
Samantha Honold, News Director
Michelle Weber, Business Manager

KXDR(FM)
01-01-2003; 106.7 mhz FM; 13 kw; Ant 2,089 ft; N46 48 09 W113 58 19
Cherry Creek Radio, 1600 North Ave., Missoula, MT 59801
(406) 728-5000, *Fax:* (406) 721-3020
License: Pinesdale, Ravalli County, MT held by CCR-Missoula IV LLC.
Group Owner: Cherry Creek Radio LLC; (acq 10-31-2006; grpsl)
Nat'l Reps: McGavren Guild
Population Served: 58,950 *Arbitron Metro Market:* Great Falls, MT *Format:* Oldies
Scott Richards, Operations Dir
Chad Parrish, General Manager
Bill McPherson, General Sales Mgr
Samantha Honold, News Director
Joe Bowers, Chief Engineer
Michelle Weber, Business Manager

Plains

***KPLG**
01-01-1998; 91.5 mhz FM *Hrs Open:* 24; 1.8 kw; 4042 ft.; N47 22 22 W114 51 31 *Rebroadcasts:* Rebroadcasts KXEI(FM) Havre 100%
P O Box 2426, Havre, MT 59501 US
(406) 265-5845, *Fax:* (406) 265-8860
www.ynop.org
ynop@ynop.org
License: Plains, Sanders County, MT held by Hi Line Radio Fellowship Inc.
Nat'l Network: Moody; Salem Radio Network *Wire Services:* AP
Format: Religious *Target Audience:* General; those who are looking for Christian progmg
Roger Lonnquist, General Manager
Brenda Boyum, Station Manager
Clark Berg, General Sales Mgr
David Brown, Programming Director
Ron Huckeby, Chief Engineer

Plentywood

KATQ
09-14-1979; 1070 khz AM *Hrs Open:* 6 AM-6 PM
112 Third Ave., East, Plentywood, MT 59254 US
(406) 765-1480, *Fax:* (406) 765-2357
www.katqradio.com
katq@nemont.net
License: Plentywood, MT held by Radio International-KATQ Broadcast Association Inc.
Arbitron Metro Market: Plentywood, MT *Format:* Country *Special Programming:* Top-40, farm 5 hrs, relg 6 hrs wkly *Target Audience:* 18-54. *Adv. Rates:* 9.50; 9; 8.50; na
Myrna Kampen, President
Bruce Lapke, Operations Dir
Casandra Syme, General Manager
Art Gehnert, Chief Engineer

KATQ-FM
06-01-1962; 100.1 mhz FM *Hrs Open:* 24; 3 kw horiz; 33 ft.; N48 47 6 W104 32 0
112 Third Ave., East, Plentywood, MT 59254 US
(406) 765-1480, *Fax:* (406) 765-2357
www.katqradio.com
katq@nemont.net
License: Plentywood, Sheridan County, MT held by Radio International-KATQ Broadcast Association Inc.
Nat'l Network: ABC; AP Radio
Arbitron Metro Market: Plentywood, MT *Format:* Country *Adv. Rates:* Same as AM
Grant Lindsey, News Director

Polson

KERR
03-22-1976; 750 khz AM; 50 kw-D, DAN; 1 kw-N, DAN; N47 38 34 W114 7 25
PO Box 1233, Bismarck, ND 58502 US
(406) 883-5255, *Fax:* (406) 883-4441
www.750kerr.com
info@750kerr.com
License: Polson, MT held by Anderson Radio Broadcasting Inc.
Group Owner: Anderson Radio Broadcasting Inc.; acq 9-22-2003; grpsl).
Arbitron Metro Market: Polson, MT *Format:* Country *Target Audience:* General.
Dennis Anderson, President

***KPJH**
89.5 mhz FM; 0.13 kw; 1870 ft.; N47 46 25 W114 16 5
US
(406) 243-4931, *Fax:* (406) 243-3299
www.mtpr.org
License: Polson, Lake County, MT held by The University of Montana.
Nat'l Network: NPR
Arbitron Metro Market: Polson, MT *Format:* Public Affairs *No. News Employees:* 6
William Marcus, General Manager
Michael Marsolek, Programming Director
Sally Mauk, News Director
Doug Drader, Chief Engineer
Beth Anne Austein, Production
Anne Hosler, Membership Manager
Kathy Woodford, Director of CorporateSupport
Jeff Croonenberghs, Chief Operator
Saxon Holbrook, Technical Director

***KMBM**
90.7 mhz FM; 1.95 kw; 135 ft.; N47 40 37 W114 8 33
US
(406) 883-7252
License: Polson, Lake County, MT held by Divine Mercy Apostolate.
Nat'l Network: EWTN Radio
Arbitron Metro Market: Polson, MT *Format:* Religious
Jeffrey Devlin, President

Pryor

***KPGB**
88.3 mhz FM; 0.1 kw vert; -325 ft.; N45 26 6 W108 32 9
P O Box 24, Pryor, MT 59066 US
(406) 255-0994, *Fax:* (406) 255-8688
www.kpgbfaithbaptistchurch.com
ronvicky01@hughes.net
License: Pryor, Big Horn County, MT held by Faith Baptist Church.
Arbitron Metro Market: Pryor, MT *Format:* Religious

Ronnie Henderson, General Manager

Red Lodge

KMXE-FM
01-24-1994; 99.3 mhz FM *Hrs Open:* 24; 30 kw; 1211 ft.; N45 11 39 W109 20 30
P.O. Box 1678, Red Lodge, MT 59068 US
(406) 446-1199, *Fax:* (406) 446-9178
fm99mtn@starband.net
License: Red Lodge, Carbon County, MT held by Silver Rock Communications Inc.
Format: Oldies *Hrs. of News Programming:* news progmg one hr wkly *No. News Employees:* 1 *Target Audience:* 25-49; upwardly mobile *Adv. Rates:* 15; 15; 15; 15
Leslie Brent-Oliphant, President
Jeffrey Oliphant, Executive Vice President

Rocky Boy's Reserv.

***KHEW**
88.5 mhz FM; 16 kw; 1579 ft.; N48 10 42 W109 41 21
US
(406) 395-4396, *Fax:* (406) 395-4497
www.rockyboy.org
License: Rocky Boy's Reserv., Hill County, MT held by Chippewa Cree Tribe of the Rocky Boy's Reservation.
Arbitron Metro Market: Rocky Boy's Reservation, MT *Format:* Native American
Dustin White, Programming Director

Ronan

KQRK
10-04-1981; 92.3 mhz FM *Hrs Open:* 24; 60 kw; 2320 ft.; N47 46 25 W114 16 4
P. O. Box 1233, Bismarck, ND 58501 US
(406) 883-5255, *Fax:* (406) 883-4441
www.qcountry923.com
info@750kerr.com
License: Ronan, Lake County, MT held by Anderson Radio Broadcasting Inc.
Group Owner: Anderson Radio Broadcasting Inc.; (acq 9-22-2003; grpsl).
Arbitron Metro Market: Kalispell-Flathead Valley, MT *Format:* Rock/AOR *Target Audience:* 25-49.
A.L. Anderson, President
Dennis Anderson, General Manager

Roundup

***KLMB**
88.3 mhz FM; 0.25 kw vert; 79 ft.; N46 27 58 W108 33 20
US
(406) 323-1861
License: Roundup, Musselshell County, MT held by Roundup Community Radio Association.
Arbitron Metro Market: Roundup, MT
Bill Edwards, President

Scobey

KCGM
06-21-1971; 95.7 mhz FM *Hrs Open:* 16; 52 kw; 659 ft.; N48 48 3 W105 21 0
20 Main St. PO Bx 220, Scobey, MT 59263 US
(406) 487-2293, *Fax:* (406) 487-5923
info@kcgm.com
License: Scobey, Daniels County, MT held by Prairie Communications Inc.
Nat'l Network: USA *Regional Reps:* Taylor Brown *Wire Services:* AP
Format: Country *Special Programming:* Farm 6 hrs wkly *Hrs. of News Programming:* news progmg 8 hrs wkly *No. News Employees:* 2 *Adv. Rates:* 8.60; 8.60; 8.60; 8.60
Dixie Halverson, CEO

Shelby

KSEN
08-11-1947; 1150 khz AM *Hrs Open:* 19
830 Oilfield Ave, Shelby, MT 59474 US
(406) 434-5241, *Fax:* (406) 434-2122
www.ksenam.com/help/
ksen@shelby.mt.us
License: Shelby, MT held by Capstar TX L.P.
Group Owner: Clear Channel Communications Inc.; (acq 2-21-01; grpsl).
Arbitron Metro Market: Shelby, MT *Format:* Oldies *Special Programming:* Farm 8 hrs wkly *Hrs. of News Programming:* news progmg 15 hrs wkly *No. News Employees:* 1 *Target Audience:* 25-59.
Lowrey Maya, CEO
Jim Sargent, Operations Dir
Julie Martin, General Manager
Julie Martin, General Sales Mgr
Mark Daniels, News Director
Tony Mulligan, Chief Engineer
Anne James, Public Affairs Director
Jim Sargent, TrafficManager

KZIN-FM
12-09-1978; 96.7 mhz FM *Hrs Open:* 24; 100 kw; 551 ft.; N48 19 42 W112 2 3
830 Oilfield Avenue, Shelby, MT 59474 US
(406) 434-5241, *Fax:* (406) 434-2122
k96fm.com/
License: Shelby, Toole County, MT
Group Owner: Clear Channel Communications Inc.
Arbitron Metro Market: Shelby, MT *Format:* Country *Hrs. of News Programming:* news progmg 6 hrs wkly *No. News Employees:* 1 *Target Audience:* 18-49.
Julie Martin, Director of Sales
Anne Weins, Programming Director

Sidney

KTHC
12-01-1996; 95.1 mhz FM; 100 kw; 719 ft.; N48 2 52 W103 59 1
Mailing Address: P.O. Box 3309, Great Falls, MT 59403 US
Second Address: Box 2048, Williston, ND 58802
(406) 433-5090(701) 572-5371, *Fax:* (406) 433-5095(701) 572-7511
power95@midrivers.com
License: Sidney, Richland County, MT held by CCR-Williston IV LLC.
Group Owner: Cherry Creek Radio LLC; (acq 12-19-2003; grpsl).
Arbitron Metro Market: Sidney, MT *Format:* Adult Contemp *Target Audience:* General.
Larry Timpe, Operations Dir

KGCX
06-01-2004; 93.1 mhz FM *Hrs Open:* 24; 55 kw; Ant 499 ft; N47 45 02 W104 18 22
213 2nd Ave. S.W., Sidney, MT 85377
(406) 433-5429, *Fax:* (406) 433-5430
www.kgcx.com
kgcxeagle@midrivers.com
License: Sidney, Richland County, MT held by Sidney Community Broadcasting Corp.
Nat'l Network: Fox News Radio *Nat'l Reps:* The Teacher Company
Hrs. of News Programming: News progmg 15 hrs wkly *Adv. Rates:* 7.50; 7.50; 7.50; 6.50
Stephen Marks, President
Andrew Sturlaugson, Operations Manager
Paul Sturlaugson, Vice President/General Manager
Paul Sturlaugson, Vice President/General Manager
Melissa Quilling, Sales Manager
Andrew Sturlaugson, ProgrammingDirector
Andrew Sturlaugson, Promotions Manager
Emilie Boyles, News Director
Wayne Harbig, Engineering Dir
Wayne Harbig, Chief Engineer
Staci Smith, Office Manager

Somers

***KFLF**
91.3 mhz FM; 1 kw; 259 ft.; N48 4 7 W114 2 20
US
(703) 812-0415
www.freshliferadio.com
License: Somers, Flathead County, MT held by Fresh Life Church Inc.
Arbitron Metro Market: Somers, MT
Levi Lusko, President

St. Regis

KZJZ
99.1 mhz FM; 0.93 kw; 2844 ft.; N47 22 20 W114 51 28
US
(406) 883-5255, *Fax:* (406) 883-4441
www.991theriver.com
License: St. Regis, Mineral County, MT held by Anderson Radio Broadcasting Inc.
Group Owner: Anderson Radio Broadcasting Inc.; (acq 6-6-2008; $75,000 for CP)
Arbitron Metro Market: Saint Regis, MT *Format:* Easy Listening
Dennis Anderson, President

Stanford

***KYPF**
89.5 mhz FM; 4 kw; 1890 ft.; N47 10 39 W109 32 9
US
(406) 657-2941, *Fax:* (406) 657-2977
www.yellowstonepublicradio.org
mail@ypradio.org
License: Stanford, Judith Basin County, MT held by Montana State University - Billings.
Arbitron Metro Market: Standford/Lewistown, MT *Format:* News
Dennis Hall, President
Ken Siebert, General Manager / Media Services Director
Jackie Yamanaka, News Director
Jim Nichols, Chief Engineer
Barbara Bernheim, Development and Listener Support Manager
Alicia Lee, Underwriting Manager /Public Information Manager
Ana Henrickson, Business & Finance Manager
Art Hooker, Control Room Operator / Production Assistant
Merry Ann Peters, Control Room Operator
Wesley Jessen, Media Services Assistant / Control Room Operator

Stevensville

KKVU
07-16-2005; 104.5 mhz FM; 14.15 kw; 2083 ft.; N46 48 6 W113 58 22
US
(406) 721-6800, *Fax:* (406) 329-1850
www.u1045.com
tanthony@simmonsmedia.com
License: Stevensville, Ravalli County, MT held by Spanish Peaks Broadcasting Inc.
Group Owner: Spanish Peaks Broadcasting Inc.
Nat'l Reps: Interep
Arbitron Metro Market: Stevensville, MT *Format:* Adult Contemp *No. News Employees:* 1 *Target Audience:* Adults 18-49. *Adv. Rates:* 18; 15; 18; 9
Rod Harsell, General Manager

Superior

KENR
10-01-1999; 107.5 mhz FM; 100 kw horiz; 945 ft.; N47 1 45 W114 41 18
6807 Foxglove Drive, Cheyenne, WY 82009 US
(406) 728-9300, *Fax:* (406) 542-2329
www.1075zoofm.com
shawnabatt@townsquaremedia.com
License: Superior, Mineral County, MT held by GAP Broadcasting Missoula License LLC.
Group Owner: GAPWEST Broadcasting; (acq 2-13-2008; grpsl)
Arbitron Metro Market: Missoula, MT *Format:* Contemporary Hits/Top 40
Dave Cowan, General Manager
Kathy Anderson, General Sales Mgr
Aaron Traylor, Programming Director

Three Forks

KMTZ
107.7 mhz FM; 23 kw; 846 ft.; N45 38 20 W111 15 56
US
(406) 542-1025, *Fax:* (406) 721-1036
License: Three Forks, Gallatin County, MT held by Sheila Callahan and Friends Inc.
Group Owner: Sheila Callahan and Friends Inc.
Arbitron Metro Market: Three Forks, MT
M. Sheila Murphy, President

West Yellowstone

KEZQ
06-01-1996; 92.9 mhz FM; 46 kw; 2733 ft.; N44 33 41 W111 26 32
4350 N. Fairfax Drive, Suite 900, Arlington, VA 22203 US
(203) 912-3761
License: West Yellowstone, Gallatin County, MT held by Resurgence Development LLC
Arbitron Metro Market: Westport, CT *Format:* Adult Contemp
Scott Parker, General Manager

KWYS
12-20-1967; 920 khz AM; 1 kw-D, ND2; 0.038 kw-N, ND2; N44 38 56 W111 5 50
P.O. Box 2158, Ketchum, ID 83340 US
(406) 646-7361
www.kwys920.com
License: West Yellowstone, MT held by Chaparral Broadcasting Inc.

Group Owner: Chaparral Communications
Nat'l Network: CNN Radio
Arbitron Metro Market: West Yellowstone *Format:* Oldies
Scott Anderson, General Manager

Whitefish

KJJR
02-14-1979; 880 khz AM; 10 kw-D, ND1; 0.5 kw-N, ND1; N48 23 44 W114 19 11
P.O. Box 5409, Kalispell, MT 59903 US
(406) 755-8700, *Fax:* (406) 755-8770
www.beebroadcasting.com
KJJR@beebroadcasting.com
License: Whitefish, MT held by Bee Broadcasting Inc.
Group Owner: Bee Broadcasting Inc.
Format: News, News/Talk, 86
Benny Bee, President
Mark Wagner, General Manager

KWOL-FM
01-01-2005; 105.1 mhz FM; 62 kw; 2405 ft.; N48 30 43 W114 22 13
US
(406) 755-8700, *Fax:* (406) 755-8770
www.1051cool.com
info@1051cool.com
License: Whitefish, Flathead County, MT held by Cathleen R. Bee dba Rose Communications.
Arbitron Metro Market: Whitefish, MT *Format:* Oldies
Cassie Bee, General Manager

KSAM
01-01-2006; 1240 khz AM
US
(406) 755-8700, *Fax:* (406) 755-8770
www.beebroadcasting.com
kdbr@beebroadcasting.com
License: Whitefish, MT held by Bee Broadcasting Inc.
Group Owner: Bee Broadcasting Inc.
Arbitron Metro Market: Whitefish, MT *Format:* Alternative
Benny Bee, President
Mark Wagner, General Manager

Whitehall

***KQLR**
01-01-2007; 89.7 mhz FM; 1.45 kw vert; 1795 ft.; N46 0 22 W112 26 33 *Rebroadcasts:* Rebroadcasts KLVR(FM) Santa Rosa, CA 100%
16075 West Bellveiw Ave, Morrison, CO 80465 US
(800) 877-5600, *Fax:* (916) 251-1650
www.klove.com
License: Whitehall, Jefferson County, MT held by Educational Media Foundation.
Group Owner: EMF Broadcasting; (acq 12-2-2005; $28,450 for CP)
Nat'l Network: K-Love
Arbitron Metro Market: Whitehall, MT *Format:* Christian
Mike Novak, President
Mike Lee, Operations Dir

Wolf Point

KVCK
09-01-1957; 1450 khz AM *Hrs Open:* 24; 1 kw-U, ND1; N48 5 18 W105 39 22
324 Main Street, Wolf Point, MI 59201 US
(406) 653-1900, *Fax:* (406) 653-1909
www.wolfpoint.com
2wolftwn@nemontel.net
License: Wolf Point, MT held by Wolf Town Wireless Inc.
Nat'l Network: ABC
Arbitron Metro Market: Wolf Point, MT *Format:* Oldies *Special Programming:* Farm 6 hrs wkly *Hrs. of News Programming:* News progmg 15 hrs wkly *Target Audience:* General.
Larry Corns, Programming Director

KVCK-FM
09-01-1981; 92.7 mhz FM *Hrs Open:* 24; 11.5 kw; 499 ft.; N48 11 9 W105 40 8
324 Main Street, Wolf Point, MI 59201 US
(406) 653-1900, *Fax:* (406) 653-1909
www.wolfpoint.com
2wolftwn@nemontel.net
License: Wolf Point, Roosevelt County, MT
Arbitron Metro Market: Wolf Point, MT *Format:* Country *Special Programming:* Farm 6 hrs wkly *Hrs. of News Programming:* News progmg 15 hrs wkly
Susan Allmer, General Manager

***KYPW**
88.3 mhz FM; 0.73 kw; 194 ft.; N48 2 8 W105 31 13
US
(406) 657-2941, *Fax:* (406) 657-2977
www.yellowstonepublicradio.org
mail@ypradio.org
License: Wolf Point, Roosevelt County, MT held by Montana State University - Billings.
Arbitron Metro Market: Wolf Point, MT
Dennis Hall, President
Ken Siebert, General Manager / Media Services Director
Jackie Yamanaka, News Director
Jim Nichols, Chief Engineer
Barbara Bernheim, Development and Listener Support Manager
Alicia Lee, Underwriting Manager /Public Information Manager
Ana Henrickson, Business & Finance Manager
Art Hooker, Control Room Operator / Production Assistant
Merry Ann Peters, Control Room Operator
Wesley Jessen, Media Services Assistant / Control Room Operator

Wyola

***KZXZ**
90.9 mhz FM; kw
US
(479) 646-6700, *Fax:* (479) 646-1373
www.kzkzfm.com
kzkzfm@kzkzfm.com
License: Wyola, Big Horn County, MT held by 1 A Chord Inc.
Arbitron Metro Market: Wyola, MT
Mary Fay Jackson, President

Nebraska

Ainsworth

KBRB
02-06-1968; 1400 khz AM *Hrs Open:* 24; 1 kw-U, ND1; N42 33 16 W99 49 52
122 East 2nd Street, PO Box 285, Ainsworth, NE 69210 US
(402) 387-1400, *Fax:* (402) 387-2624
kbrbradio.com
kbrb@sscg.net
License: Ainsworth, NE held by K.B.R. Broadcasting Co.
Nat'l Network: ABC *Regional Network:* Brownfield *Wire Services:* AP
Format: Adult Contemp, Country *Hrs. of News Programming:* News progmg 30 hrs wkly *Target Audience:* General. *Adv. Rates:* 8.25; 8.25; 8.25; 8.25
Lorris Rice, President
Cody Goochey, Programming Director
Angie Von Heeder, Promotions Manager
Renee Adkisson, News Director
Randy Brudigan, Chief Engineer

KBRB-FM
05-30-1983; 92.7 mhz FM; 4.5 kw; 331 ft.; N42 33 16 W99 49 52
122 East Second St., PO Box 285, Ainsworth, NE 69210 US
(402) 387-1400, *Fax:* (402) 387-2624
License: Ainsworth, Brown County, NE held by K.B.R. Broadcasting Co.
Nat'l Network: ABC *Regional Network:* Brownfield *Wire Services:* AP
Format: Adult Contemp *Adv. Rates:* Same as AM
Renee Adkisson, News Director

Albion

KUSO
05-10-2000; 92.7 mhz FM *Hrs Open:* 24; 50 kw; 492 ft.; N41 49 50 W97 41 12
Mailing Address: P.O. Box 144, West Point, NE 68788 US
Second Address: 214 N. 7th St., Norfolk, NE 68701
(402) 371-0100, *Fax:* (402) 371-0050
www.us92.com
dave@us92.com
License: Albion, Boone County, NE held by Flood Communications L.L.C.
Arbitron Metro Market: Norfolk, NE *Format:* Country *Special Programming:* Farm 10 hrs wkly *Hrs. of News Programming:* news progmg 3 hrs wkly *No. News Employees:* 1 *Target Audience:* General. *Adv. Rates:* 264; 225; 264; 216
Michael Flood, President
Dave Amick, Operations Dir
Mike Flood, General Manager
Angie Stenger, Sales Manager
Dave Amick, Programming Director
Lydee Jo Krueger, Promotions Manager
Brian Masters, Operations Manager/NewsDirector
Lee Terry, Chief Engineer
Ann Neilsen, Traffic Manager
Kristi Green, Music Director
Jay Johnson, Public Service Director
Eric McKay, News Associates/Sports Director
Jill Austin, Account Executive
Laura Alder, OfficeAssistant

Allen

KHSK
100.9 mhz FM; 10 kw horiz, 0 kw vert; N42 30 29 W96 56 1
US
(312) 204-9900
License: Allen, Dixon County, NE held by College Creek Media LLC.
Group Owner: College Creek Media LLC
Arbitron Metro Market: Allen, NE
Neal Robinson, President

Alliance

KAAQ
09-30-1985; 105.9 mhz FM *Hrs Open:* 24; 100 kw; 705 ft.; N41 50 29 W103 5 7
P.O. Box 817, 2703 Hall Street, Hays, KS 67601 US
(308)762-1400, *Fax:* (308) 762-7804
www.doubleqcountry.com
kcow@bbc.net
License: Alliance, Box Butte County, NE held by Eagle Communications Inc.
Group Owner: Eagle Communications Group
Nat'l Network: ABC Information & Entertainment; ABC Music Radio *Nat'l Reps:* Interep *Wire Services:* NWS (National Weather Service); AP
Arbitron Metro Market: Denver-Boulder, CO *Format:* Country *Special Programming:* Farm 4 hrs wkly *Hrs. of News Programming:* news progmg 15 hrs wkly *No. News Employees:* 2 *Target Audience:* 18-54. *Adv.Rates:* 45; 45; 45; 30.
Mark Vail, Operations Dir
Mike Fell, General Manager
John Jones, General Sales Mgr
Kevin Horn, Programming Director
Mike Glesinger, Operations Manager
Jason Wentworth, Production Director

KCOW
02-15-1949; 1400 khz AM *Hrs Open:* 24 (M-S); 1 kw-U, ND1; N42 6 26 W102 53 15
P.O. Box 817, 2703 Hall Street, Hays, KS 67601 US
(308) 762-1400, *Fax:* (308) 762-7804
www.kcowradio.com
kcow@bbc.net
License: Alliance, NE held by Eagle Communications Inc.
Group Owner: Eagle Communications Group; (acq 1965)
Nat'l Network: ABC Information & Entertainment; ABC Music Radio *Nat'l Reps:* Interep *Wire Services:* NWS (National Weather Service); AP
Arbitron Metro Market: Alliance, NE *Format:* News, News/Talk, 64, Talk *Special Programming:* Farm 18 hrs wkly *Hrs. of News Programming:* news progmg 22 hrs wkly *No. News Employees:* 2 *Target Audience:* 25-54. *Adv. Rates:* 27.50; 27.50; 15; 15
Gary Shorman, CEO
Mark Vail, President
Jason Wentworth, Operations Dir
Terri Friesen, General Manager
John Jones, General Sales Mgr
Jason Wentworth, Programming Director
Mike Glesinger, Operations Manager
Jennifer Schmid,Traffic Director
Terri Friesen, Billing & Bookkeeping
Cory Sorenson, Market Director
Helen Iossi, Account Executive

***KPNY**
01-01-1978; 102.1 mhz FM *Hrs Open:* 24; 100 kw; 522 ft.; N42 7 1 W103 7 9
P.O. Box 1153, Scottsbluff, NE 69361 US
(402) 845-6595
www.missionnebraska.org
email@mybridgeradio.net
License: Alliance, Box Butte County, NE held by Mission Nebraska Inc.
Group Owner: Mission Nebraska Inc.; (acq 2-5-2007; $360,000)
Format: Religious *Target Audience:* 18-35.
Stan Parker, General Manager

***KTNE-FM**
05-01-1990; 91.1 mhz FM *Hrs Open:* 24; 92 kw; Ant 1,325 ft; N41 50 24 W103 03 18 *Rebroadcasts:* Rebroadcasts KUCV(FM) Lincoln 100%

Mailing Address: 68501
Second Address: 1800 N. 33rd St., Lincoln, NE 68503
(402) 472-3611, *Fax:* (402) 472-2403
netnebraska.org/radio
radio@netnebraska.org
License: Alliance, Box Butte County, NE held by Nebraska Educational Telecommunications Commission
Nat'l Network: NPR; APM; PRI *Regional Network:* NET Radio
Hrs. of News Programming: news prgmg 45 hrs wkly *No. News Employees:* 8 *Target Audience:* 35 plus; general
Rod Bates, General Manager
Nancy Finken, Station Manager
Susan Dinsmore, General Sales Mgr
Nancy Finken, Programming Director
Mary Jane Winquest, Promotions Manager
Stacey Decker, News Director
William Stibor, Music Director
Jeff Smith, Operations

Auburn

KNCY-FM
09-18-1981; 103.1 mhz FM *Hrs Open:* 24; 14 kw; 436 ft.; N40 27 57 W95 45 38
4301 W 129th St., Suite 130, Overland Park, KS 66213 US
(402) 873-3348, *Fax:* (402) 873-7882
kncycountry.com
kncy@kncycountry.com
License: Auburn, Nemaha County, NE held by Riverfront Broadcasting LLC
Nat'l Network: ABC *Wire Services:* AP
Format: Country, News *Hrs. of News Programming:* news progmg 30 hrs wkly *No. News Employees:* 2 *Adv. Rates:* 19; 19; 19; 19
Scott Kooistra, General Manager
Chris Yates, General Sales Mgr
Doug Jennings, Programming Director

Aurora

KRGY
03-01-1980; 97.3 mhz FM *Hrs Open:* 24; 50 kw; 348 ft.; N40 52 44 W98 5 36
Mailing Address: P.O. Box 404, Shenandoah, IA 51601 US
Second Address: Box 4907, Aurora, NE 68802
(308) 381-1430, *Fax:* (308) 382-6701
www.gifamilyradio.com/STAR/star.htm
info@gifamilyradio.com
License: Aurora, Hamilton County, NE held by Legacy Communications LLC
Group Owner: Legacy Communications LLC; (acq 5-17-2004; grpsl).
Nat'l Network: ABC
Arbitron Metro Market: Lincoln, NE *Format:* Adult Contemp *Hrs. of News Programming:* news progmg 2 hrs wkly *No. News Employees:* 2 *Target Audience:* 18-49.
Jim Davis, Operations Dir
Lyle Nelson, General Manager

*KJGS
10-12-2011; 91.9 mhz FM; kw
US
(760)375-2355
ejwitzel@mchsi.com
License: Aurora, Hamilton County, NE
Group Owner: Radio 74 Internationale
Format: Religious
Ron Myers, Founder

Bassett

*KMNE-FM
06-01-1991; 90.3 mhz FM *Hrs Open:* 24; 92.3 kw; 1,292 ft; N42 20 05 W99 29 01 *Rebroadcasts:* Simulcasts KUCV(FM) Lincoln 100%
1800 N. 33rd St., Lincoln, NE 68501
(402) 472-3611, *Fax:* (402) 472-2403
netnebraska.org/radio
radio@netnebraska.org
License: Bassett, Rock County, NE held by Nebraska Educational Telecommunications Commission
Nat'l Network: NPR; APM; PRI *Regional Network:* NET Radio
Hrs. of News Programming: news progmg 45 hrs wkly *No. News Employees:* 8 *Target Audience:* General.
Rod Bates, General Manager
Nancy Finken, Station Manager
Susan Dinsmore, General Sales Mgr
Nancy Finken, Programming Director
Mary Jane Winquest, Promotions Manager
Dennis Kellogg, News Director
Stacey Decker, Engineering Dir
William Stibor, Music Director
Jeff Smith, Operations

Beatrice

KTGL
11-26-1962; 92.9 mhz FM *Hrs Open:* 24; 100 kw; 810 ft.; N40 31 6 W96 46 7
600 Congress Avenue, Suite 1400, Austin, TX 78701 US
(402) 466-1234, *Fax:* (402) 467-4095
www.ktgl.com
License: Beatrice, Gage County, NE held by Three Eagles of Lincoln Inc.
Group Owner: Three Eagles Communications; (acq 4-10-2007; grpsl)
Arbitron Metro Market: Lincoln, NE *Format:* Classic Rock *Hrs. of News Programming:* news progmg 3 hrs wkly *No. News Employees:* 1 *Target Audience:* 18-49.
James Keck, General Manager

KWBE
06-12-1949; 1450 khz AM *Hrs Open:* 24; 0.53 kw-U, ND1; N40 15 49 W96 46 27
P. O. Box 30181, Lincoln, NE 68503 US
(402) 228-5923, *Fax:* (402) 228-3704
www.kwbe.com
kwbe@broadcasthouse.com
License: Beatrice, NE held by NRG License Sub. LLC.
Group Owner: NRG Media LLC; (acq 12-28-2007; grpsl)
Nat'l Network: CBS; Westwood One *Regional Reps:* Howard Anderson.
Arbitron Metro Market: Beatrice, NE *Format:* Adult Contemp, News, 62, Talk *Special Programming:* Farm 14 hrs wkly *Hrs. of News Programming:* news progmg 25 hrs wkly *No. News Employees:* 1 *Target Audience:* 24-54; mature, affluent adults
Adv. Rates: 17.50; 16.50; 17.50; 15.50
Jay Stalder, General Manager
Rick Siebert, Owner, Station Manager
Charlie Brogan, General Sales Mgr
Nichole Scholl, Promotions Manager
Doug Kennedy, News Director
Tom Russell, Engineer
Bryan Cook, Sports Director
Laurie Leners,Office Manager
Ashley Mantgen, Marketing
Tracy Shew, Marketing
Phil Rogge, On Air Staff

*KNBE
01-01-2008; 88.9 mhz FM; 7.5 kw vert; 479 ft.; N40 33 3 W96 38 45
US
(225) 768-3102, *Fax:* (225) 768-3729
www.jsm.org
kawikfish@yahoo.com
License: Beatrice, Gage County, NE held by Family Worship Center Church Inc.
Group Owner: Family Worship Center Church Inc.; (acq 10-12-2006; grpsl)
Arbitron Metro Market: El Dorado, AR *Format:* Christian, Religious
David Whitelaw, COO

Bellevue

KOZN
06-01-1999; 1620 khz AM *Hrs Open:* 24
1001 Farnam-On-The-Mall, Omaha, NE 68102 US
(402) 342-2000, *Fax:* (402) 346-5748
www.1620thezone.com
nnelkin@nrgmedia.com
License: Bellevue, NE held by Waitt Omaha LLC.
Group Owner: Waitt Omaha LLC; (acq 1-7-2002; grpsl)
Nat'l Network: ESPN Radio; Westwood One *Nat'l Reps:* Katz Radio
Arbitron Metro Market: Omaha, NB *Format:* Sports *Target Audience:* 25-54; men
Mark Todd, Operations Dir
Jim McKernan, General Manager
Rhonda Gerrard, General Sales Mgr
Neil Nelkin, Programming Director
Brandon Pappas, Promotions Manager
Lori Storz, News Director
Tim Marshall, Sales Manager

KZOT
03-19-1987; 1180 khz AM *Hrs Open:* 24; 25 kw-D, 1 kw-N, DA-2; N41 16 12 W95 47 10
5011 Capitol Ave., Omaha, NE 68102
(402) 342-2000, *Fax:* (402) 346-5748
1180labonita.com
info@1180labonita.com
License: Bellevue, Sarpy County, NE held by Waitt Omaha LLC.
Group Owner: Waitt Omaha LLC; (acq 1-7-2002; grpsl)
Population Served: 350,000 *Arbitron Metro Market:* Omaha-Council Bluffs, NE-IA *Target Audience:* 18+; General
Mark Todd, Operations Dir
Jim McKernan, General Manager
Rhonda Gerrard, General Sales Mgr
Neil Nelkin, Programming Director
Lyn Farhenbruch, News Director
Darwin Stinton, Chief Engineer
Tim Marshall, Sales Manager

Bennington

KFFF
06-10-1991; 93.3 mhz FM; 6 kw; Ant 350 ft; N41 22 57 W96 07 57
5010 Underwood Ave., Omaha, NE 78701
(402) 561-2000, *Fax:* (402) 556-8937,(402) 551-9333
www.krrk.com,www.us933.com
michellematthews@clearchannel.com
License: Bennington, Douglas County, NE held by Capstar TX L.P.
Group Owner: Clear Channel Communications Inc.; (acq 8-30-2000; grpsl)
Arbitron Metro Market: Omaha-Council Bluffs, NE-IA
Taylor Walet, General Manager
Jean St. James, General Sales Mgr
Erik Johnson, Programming Director

Blair

*KDCV-FM
10-01-1972; 88.7 mhz FM *Hrs Open:* 24; 0.006 kw horiz; 89 ft.; N41 33 7 W96 9 20
2848 College Drive, Blair, NE 68008 US
(402) 426-7322, *Fax:* (402) 426-7382
www.huntel.net/kdcv
kdcv@dana.edu
License: Blair, Washington County, NE held by Dana College.
Arbitron Metro Market: Blair, NE *Format:* Variety/Diverse *Target Audience:* 25-54; community, 18-34 college community
Vern Wirka, General Manager

KBLR-FM
09-10-2002; 97.3 mhz FM; 25 kw horiz, 24.5 kw vert; 302 ft.; N41 38 21 W96 12 31
1001 Farnam on the Mall, Omaha, NE 68102 US
(402) 721-1340, *Fax:* (402) 721-5023
www.kblr-fm.com
breker@myradiofremont.com
License: Blair, Washington County, NE held by Waitt Omaha LLC.
Group Owner: Waitt Omaha LLC; (acq 1-7-2002; grpsl)
Arbitron Metro Market: Omaha, NE *Format:* Country
Chris Walz, Operations Dir
Del Meyer, General Manager
Berry C. Reker, Sales & Promotion Manager
Chris Walz, Sr. Account Executive
Earnie Parker, Advertising Consultant

Bridgeport

KOZY-FM
01-01-2001; 101.3 mhz FM; 100 kw; Ant 1,112 ft; N41 50 23 W103 49 36
Box 1263, Scottsbluff, NE 69363
(308) 632-5667, *Fax:* (308) 635-1905
www.kozy1013.com
info@hometownfamilyradio.com
License: Bridgeport, Morrill County, NE held by Legacy Communications LLC.
Group Owner: Legacy Communications LLC; (acq 12-13-2007; grpsl)
No. News Employees: 2 *Target Audience:* 25-54; general
Alan Usher, CEO/COO

Broken Bow

KBBN-FM
06-15-1982; 95.3 mhz FM *Hrs Open:* 6 AM-11 PM; 30 kw; 574 ft.; N41 23 14 W99 49 15
P. O. Box 409, Broken Bow, NE 68822 US
(308) 872-5881, *Fax:* (308) 872-3284
www.kbbn.com
info@sandhillexpress.com
License: Broken Bow, Custer County, NE held by Custer County Broadcasting Co.
Arbitron Metro Market: Broken Bow, NB *Format:* Classic Rock *Hrs. of News Programming:* news progmg 10 hrs wkly *No. News Employees:* 1 *Target Audience:* 24-45; baby boomers & on either edge of age breakdown

David Birnie, General Manager
Jeff Bailey, Programming Director

KCNI
09-28-1949; 1280 khz AM *Hrs Open:* 6 AM-6 PM; 1 kw-D, NDD; N41 24 31 W99 40 28
Box 409, Broken Bow, NE 68822 US
(308) 872-5881, *Fax:* (308) 872-3284
www.kbbn.com
info@sandhillexpress.com
License: Broken Bow, NE held by Custer County Broadcasting Co.
Arbitron Metro Market: Broken Bow, NE *Format:* Country *Hrs. of News Programming:* news progmg 24 hrs wkly *No. News Employees:* 1 *Target Audience:* 25-65; focus on rural audience
David Birnie, Operations Dir
David Birnie, Owner, General Manager, Sales Manager, KBBN Progra
Jeff Bailey, Programming Director
Julie Toline, News Director
Val Lane, Chief Engineer
Bob Bowles, Copy Writer, Commerical Production
Cynthia Huhman, Office Manager, Commerical Traffic Manager, and Sa
Tamie Thurn, Sales Executive
Colleen Warwick, Sales Executive
Brandon Peoples, Sports Director
Pat Lindner, Studio Engineer

Central City

KZEN
07-22-1985; 100.3 mhz FM *Hrs Open:* 24; 100 kw; 1844 ft.; N41 32 28 W97 40 45
6900 Van Dorn, Suite 11, Lincoln, NE 68506 US
(402) 466-1234, *Fax:* (402) 467-4095
www.threeeagles.com
sgossweiler@threeeagles.com
License: Central City, Merrick County, NE held by Three Eagles of Columbus Inc.
Group Owner: Three Eagles Communications; (acq 9-5-97; grpsl)
Nat'l Network: ABC; AP Radio *Nat'l Reps:* Interep *Wire Services:* AP
Arbitron Metro Market: Columbus, NE *Format:* Country *Special Programming:* Relg 5 hrs, farm 20 hrs wkly *Hrs. of News Programming:* news progmg 18 hrs wkly *No. News Employees:* 2 *Target Audience:* 25-54;rgnl, rural & small town audience
Rolland Johnson, CEO
Gary Buchanan, President
Dean Johnson, Operations Dir
Greg Wells, General Manager
Cindy Harris, CFO

Chadron

***KCNE-FM**
08-29-1991; 91.9 mhz FM *Hrs Open:* 24; 8.4 kw; 338 ft; N42 48 47 W103 00 22 *Rebroadcasts:* Rebroadcasts KUCV(FM) Lincoln 100%
Mailing Address: 68501
Second Address: 1800 N. 33rd St., Lincoln, NE 68503
(402) 472-3611, *Fax:* (402) 472-2403
netnebraska.org/radio
radio@netnebraska.org
License: Chadron, Dawes County, NE held by Nebraska Educational Telecommunications Commission
Nat'l Network: NPR; APM; PRI *Regional Network:* NET Radio *Hrs. of News Programming:* news progmg 45 hrs wkly *No. News Employees:* 8 *Target Audience:* General.
Rod Bates, General Manager
Nancy Finken, Station Manager
Susan Dinsmore, General Sales Mgr
Nancy Finken, Programming Director
Mary Jane Winquest, Promotions Manager
Dennis Kellogg, News Director
William Stibor, Music Director
Jeff Smith, Operations

KCSR
05-09-1954; 610 khz AM *Hrs Open:* 24; 1 kw-D, ND1; 0.118 kw-N, ND1; N42 49 56 W103 1 0
226 Bordeaux St, Chadron, NE 69337 US
(308) 432-5545(308) 432-2233, *Fax:* (308) 432-5601
www.chadrad.com
kcsr@chadrad.com
License: Chadron, NE held by Chadrad Communications Inc.
Nat'l Network: AP Radio *Regional Network:* Mid-America Ag; Brownfield *Wire Services:* AP
Arbitron Metro Market: Chadron, NE *Format:* Country *Special Programming:* Farm 6 hrs wkly *Hrs. of News Programming:* news progmg 20 hrs wkly *No. News Employees:* 2 *Target Audience:* 25-54; people in theranch, farm & agricultural industry
Adv. Rates: 18; 18; 18; 8
Dennis Brown, President
Duanne Ekwall, Operations Dir
Kathi Brown, General Sales Mgr
J.J. Archer, Programming Director
Chris Faukhauser, News Director
Brian Taylor, Chief Engineer
Joe Lowery, Music Director
Greg Mahaco, SportsCommentator

KQSK
06-01-1983; 97.5 mhz FM *Hrs Open:* 24; 100 kw; Ant 840 ft; N42 38 06 W103 06 12 *Rebroadcasts:* Simulcast with KAAQ(FM) Alliance 95%
1210 West 10th St., P.O. Box 600, Alliance, NE 67601
(308) 762-1400, *Fax:* (308) 762-7804
www.doubleqcountry.com
kcow@bbc.net
License: Chadron, Dawes County, NE held by Eagle Communications Inc.
Group Owner: Eagle Communications Group; (acq 6-13-91; $125,000;
Nat'l Network: ABC Information & Entertainment; ABC Music Radio *Nat'l Reps:* Regional Reps *Wire Services:* AP; NWS (National Weather Service)
Population Served: 65,000*Special Programming:* Farm 4 hrs wkly *Hrs. of News Programming:* news progmg 15 hrs wkly *No. News Employees:* 2 *Target Audience:* 18-54. *Adv. Rates:* 45; 45; 45; 30
Michael Glesinger, Operations Dir
Terri Friesen, General Manager
Jason Wentworth, Programming Director
John Axtell, News Director
Tony Cuesto, Chief Engineer
Christie Marsh, Office Manager

KCNB
02-28-2008; 94.7 mhz FM *Hrs Open:* 24; 100 kw; 472 ft.; N42 39 5.1 W102 41 49.3
Mailing Address: US
Second Address: 331 Main St., Chadron, NE 69337
(308) 432-2060, *Fax:* (308) 432-2059
www.b947.com
License: Chadron, Dawes County, NE held by Eagle Communications Inc.
Group Owner: Eagle Communications Group
Arbitron Metro Market: Chadron, NE *Format:* Adult Contemp *No. News Employees:* 1 *Target Audience:* 18-54.
Gary Shorman, CEO
Mark Vail, President
Mike Fell, General Manager
Corey Sorenson, Market Director
Cassie Pappas, Account Executive
John Axtell, News & Sports

Columbus

KJSK
04-28-1948; 900 khz AM *Hrs Open:* 24; 1 kw-D, ND1; 0.065 kw-N, ND1; N41 26 12 W97 23 47
P.O. Box 99, Attn: Ann Robertson, Columbus, NE 68602 US
(402) 564-2891, *Fax:* (402) 564-1999
www.kjsk.com
production@columbus.threeeagles.com
License: Columbus, NE held by Three Eagles of Columbus Inc.
Group Owner: Three Eagles Communications; (acq 8-23-01; $2.7 million with co-located FM including five-year noncompete agreement).
Nat'l Network: CBS Radio *Wire Services:* AP
Arbitron Metro Market: Lincoln, NE *Format:* News, News/Talk, 86 *Special Programming:* Pol 4 hrs, Sp 6 hrs, relg 20 hrs wkly *Hrs. of News Programming:* news prgmg one hour/week *No. News Employees:* 1 *TargetAudience:* General.
Tim Barrett, Operations Dir
Steve Gossweiler, General Manager
Lisa Cherry, General Sales Mgr
James Nickel, Programming Director
Jamie Afrank, Promotions Manager
Gina Jackson, News Director
Bob Cook, Chief Engineer

KKOT
11-25-1969; 93.5 mhz FM *Hrs Open:* 24; 100 kw; 981 ft.; N41 32 28 W97 40 45
1367 33rd Avenue, Columbus, NE 68601 US
(402) 564-2866, *Fax:* (402) 564-2867
www.mycentralnebraska.com
production@columbus.threeeagles.com
License: Columbus, Platte County, NE
Nat'l Reps: McGavren Guild
Arbitron Metro Market: Lincoln, NE *Format:* Classic Rock *Special Programming:* Farm 8 hrs wkly *Hrs. of News Programming:* news progmg 15 hrs wkly *No. News Employees:* 2 *Target Audience:* 18-49; youngfamilies
Gary Buchanan, COO
Susan Littlefield, General Sales Mgr
Dean Johnson, Programming Director
Bobbie Freeborn, News Director

KLIR
08-01-1964; 101.1 mhz FM; 100 kw; 761 ft.; N41 16 55 W97 24 30
P.O. Box 99, Attn: Ann Robertson, Columbus, NE 68602 US
(402) 564-2866, *Fax:* (402) 564-1999
www.klir.net
klirnet@megavision.com
License: Columbus, Platte County, NE held by Three Eagles of Columbus Inc.
Group Owner: Three Eagles Communications
Nat'l Network: CNN Radio *Wire Services:* AP
Arbitron Metro Market: Lincoln, NE *Format:* Adult Contemp
Special Programming: Oldies 12 hrs wkly *No. News Employees:* 1 *Target Audience:* General.
Tim Barrett, Operations Dir
Steve Gossweiler, General Manager
Lisa Cherry, General Sales Mgr
Riley Scott, Programming Director
Jamie Afrank, Promotions Manager
Tony Correa, News Director
Rob Hadland, Production Manager
GinaJackson

***KTLX**
07-01-1974; 91.9 mhz FM; 0.1 kw; 52 ft.; N41 26 26 W97 21 14
2200 - 25th Street, Columbus, NE 68601 US
(402) 564-8548, *Fax:* (402) 562-6003
www.ktlx.org
ktlx@megavision.com
License: Columbus, Platte County, NE held by TLC Educational Corp.
Arbitron Metro Market: Columbus, NE *Format:* Religious
Gary Spuit, President
Russ Rote, General Manager

KTTT
12-02-1962; 1510 khz AM; 0.5 kw-D, NDD; N41 27 14 W97 24 20
1418 25th St., Columbus, NE 68601 US
(402) 564-1510, *Fax:* (402) 564-2867
License: Columbus, NE held by Three Eagles Communications Inc.
Group Owner: Three Eagles Communications; acq 1996)
Nat'l Reps: McGavren Guild
Arbitron Metro Market: Columbus, NE *Format:* Talk *Special Programming:* Polka, farm 5 hrs, Ger 5 hrs, Pol 5 hrs wkly *Hrs. of News Programming:* news progmg 10 hrs wkly *No. News Employees:* 1 *Target Audience:* 25-65.
Rolland Johnson, CEO
Gary Buchanan, President
Dean Johnson, Operations Dir
Greg Wells, General Manager
Melissa Sanford, General Sales Mgr
Jim Dolezel, Programming Director
Bobbie Freeborn, News Director
Bob Cook, ChiefEngineer
Cindy Harris, CFO
Susan Littlefield, Farm Director

Cozad

***KAMI**
11-01-1965; 1580 khz AM *Hrs Open:* 8 AM-5 PM
835 Meridan Street, Cozad, NE 69130 US
(402) 465-8850, *Fax:* (402) 465-8852
www.bottradionetwork.com
kcvn@bottradionetwork.com
License: Cozad, NE held by Community Broadcasting Inc.
Group Owner: Bott Radio Network
Nat'l Network: USA
Arbitron Metro Market: Lincoln, NB *Format:* Christian, Talk *Target Audience:* 25-54; adults
Rich Bott, President
Tom Millett, General Manager
Pat Rulon, General Sales Mgr
Candy Green, Programming Director
Jason Potocnik, News Director

***KCVN**
08-04-1983; 104.5 mhz FM *Hrs Open:* 24; 100 kw; 985 ft.; N40 41 48 W99 47 18
835 Meridan Street, Cozad, NE 69130 US

(402) 465-8850, *Fax:* (402) 465-8852
www.bottradionetwork.com
kcvn@bottradionetwork.com
License: Cozad, Dawson County, NE held by Community Broadcasting Inc.
Group Owner: Bott Radio Network; (acq 7-9-2004; $365,000 with co-located AM).
Nat'l Network: USA
Arbitron Metro Market: Lincoln, NB *Format:* Christian, Talk *Target Audience:* 25-54; adults
Dick Bott, Sr., Chairman
Rich Bott, II, CEO
Rich Bott, II, President
Eben Fowler, Operations Dir
Tom Millett, General Manager
Pat Rulon, General Sales Mgr
Candy Green, Programming Director
Jason Potocnik, News Director

Crawford

*KCFD
88.1 mhz FM; 1.5 kw; 659 ft.; N42 45 38 W103 39 26
US
(256) 497-4502
southcultural@yahoo.com
License: Crawford, Dawes County, NE held by Southern Cultural Foundation.
Arbitron Metro Market: Crawford, NE *Format:* Classic Rock
Richard Dabney, General Manager

Crete

*KDNE
08-30-1993; 91.9 mhz FM; 0.2 kw; 66 ft.; N40 37 16 W96 57 4
1014 Boswell Avenue, Crete, NE 68333 US
(402) 826-8677, *Fax:* (402) 826-8634
www.doaneline.com/kdne/
kdne@doane.edu
License: Crete, Saline County, NE held by Doane College Board of Trustees.
Arbitron Metro Market: Crete, NE *Format:* Alternative *Target Audience:* General; males & females between the ages of 12 to 34
Jonathan Brand, President
Lee Thomas, General Manager
John Thayer, Station Manager
Corey Rotschafer, Programming Director
Tyler Weihe, Editor In Chief
Erin Bell, Managing Director
Alyssa Bouc, News Editor
Richard Creeger,Sports Editor

KIBZ
08-20-1976; 104.1 mhz FM *Hrs Open:* 24; 31 kw; 614 ft.; N40 31 6 W96 46 7
600 Congress Avenue, Suite 1400, Austin, TX 78701 US
(402) 466-1234, *Fax:* (402) 467-4095
www.kibz.com
License: Crete, Saline County, NE held by Three Eagles of Lincoln Inc.
Group Owner: Three Eagles Communications; (acq 4-10-2007; grpsl)
Arbitron Metro Market: Lincoln, NE *Format:* Rock/AOR *No. News Employees:* 1 *Target Audience:* 18-34.
James Keck, General Manager

Crookston

KINI
01-01-1978; 96.1 mhz FM *Hrs Open:* 24; 90 kw; 499 ft.; N43 7 50 W100 54 2
P.O. Box 419, St. Francis, SD 57572 US
(605) 747-2291, *Fax:* (605) 747-5791
www.gwtc.net/~kinifm
kinifm@gwtc.net
License: Crookston, Cherry County, NE held by Rosebud Educational Society Inc.
Wire Services: AP
Format: Adult Contemp, Native American *Special Programming:* American Indian 15 hrs, gospel 6 hrs, relg 6 hrs wkly *Hrs. of News Programming:* news progmg 12 hrs wkly *No. News Employees:* 1 *Target Audience:* General; Indian & white
Fr. John Hatcher, President
Richard Iyotte, Station Manager
Marcy VanWinkle, Executive Vice President

Dakota City

KTFJ
01-01-1991; 1250 khz AM *Hrs Open:* 24; 0.5 kw-D, DA2; 0.7 kw-N, DA2; N42 26 33 W96 15 41 *Rebroadcasts:* Rebroadcasts KTFC(FM) Sioux City, IA.
1534 Buchanan Ave, Sioux City, IA 51106 US
(712) 252-4621
www.bottradionetwork.com
License: Dakota City, NE held by Donald A. Swanson.
Nat'l Network: USA
Arbitron Metro Market: Sioux City, IA *Format:* Gospel
Richard (Dick) Bott Sr., Chairman
Richard (Rich) Bott, CEO/COO
Richard(Rich) Bott, President
Eben Fowler, Operations Dir
Kim Cotter, General Manager

Emerson

KCTY
10-19-1975; 104.9 mhz FM *Hrs Open:* 24; 25 kw; 302 ft.; N42 14 4 W97 3 20
300 Madison Avenue, Norfolk, NE 68701 US
(509) 783-0783, *Fax:* (509) 735-8627
www.ktch.com
info@ktch.com
License: Emerson, Wayne County, NE held by Wayne Radio Work LLC.
Arbitron Metro Market: Wayne, NE *Format:* Oldies *No. News Employees:* 1 *Target Audience:* General.
David Kelly, General Manager
Mick Kemp, General Sales Mgr
Dan Baddorf, Programming Director
Joel Janecek, News Director
Tony Wortman, Chief Engineer

Fairbury

KGMT
06-13-1960; 1310 khz AM *Hrs Open:* 6 AM-6 PM; 0.5 kw-D, ND2; 0.095 kw-N, ND2; N40 6 58 W97 9 5
414 Fourth St., Fairbury, NE 68352 US
(402) 729-3382, *Fax:* (402) 729-3446
www.kutt95.com
kutt@diodecom.net
License: Fairbury, NE held by Siebert Communications Inc.
Nat'l Reps: Farmakis
Format: News, Oldies *Special Programming:* Farm 18 hrs wkly *Hrs. of News Programming:* News progmg 10 hrs wkly *No. News Employees:* 2 *Target Audience:* 25-52.
Rick Siebert, President
Randy Bauer, General Manager
Laurie Lenders, Station Manager
Brad Achtemeier, General Sales Mgr
Randy Bauer, Program Director

Falls City

KLZA
07-07-1998; 101.3 mhz FM; 25 kw; 328 ft.; N40 6 54 W95 39 6
P.O. Box 104, Hiawatha, KS 66434 US
(402) 245-6010, *Fax:* (402) 245-6040
sunny1013fm@hotmail.com
License: Falls City, Richardson County, NE held by KNZA Inc.
Group Owner: KNZA Inc.
Format: Classic Rock *No. News Employees:* 3
Robert Hilton, Operations Dir
Mike Gilmore, Station Manager
Mike Slocum, Chief Engineer

KTNC
08-03-1957; 1230 khz AM *Hrs Open:* 24; 0.5 kw-D, ND1; 1 kw-N, ND1; N40 3 57 W95 36 55
PO Box 589, 1602 Stone Street, Falls City, NE 68355 US
(402) 245-2453, *Fax:* (402) 245-5862
www.ktncradio.com
ktnc@sentco.net
License: Falls City, NE held by KNZA Inc.
Group Owner: KNZA Inc.; (acq 9-7-2007; $330,000)
Nat'l Network: ABC *Regional Network:* Brownfield
Arbitron Metro Market: Falls City, NE *Format:* Oldies *Special Programming:* Christian mus one hr wkly *Hrs. of News Programming:* news progmg 23 hrs wkly *No. News Employees:* 1 *Target Audience:* 25 plus;farmers, businessmen, employees, retirees *Adv. Rates:* 15; 14.70; 15; 14.40
Gregory Buser, President
Robert Hilton, Operations Dir
Aaron Wisdom, General Sales Mgr
Gerald Hopp, News Director
Jackie Johnson, Traffic Manager

Firth

KNTK
93.7 mhz FM; 6 kw; Ant 226 ft; N40 34 57.4 W96 37 15.2
5829 N. 60th St., Omaha, NE
(402) 571-0200, *Fax:* (402) 571-0833
License: Firth, Lancaster County, NE held by VSS Catholic Communications Inc.
Arbitron Metro Market: Lincoln, NE
Jim Carroll, General Manager

Fremont

KFMT-FM
07-01-1972; 105.5 mhz FM *Hrs Open:* 5 AM-midnight; 1.2 kw; 449 ft.; N41 24 40 W96 31 53
1001 Farnam-On-The-Mall, Omaha, NE 68102 US
(402) 721-1340, *Fax:* (402) 721-5023
www.kfmt.com
kfmt@midia.com
License: Fremont, Dodge County, NE held by NRG Media LLC.
Group Owner: NRG Media LLC
Arbitron Metro Market: Fremont, NE *Format:* Classic Rock *Target Audience:* 25-54.
Del Meyer, General Manager
Barry C. Reker, General Sales Mgr

KHUB
12-01-1939; 1340 khz AM *Hrs Open:* 5 AM-midnight; 0.5 kw-D, ND1; 0.25 kw-N, ND1; N41 25 58 W96 27 16
1001 Farnam-On-The-Mall, Omaha, NE 68102 US
(402) 721-1340, *Fax:* (402) 721-5023
www.khubradio.com
VMarshall@nrgmedia.com
License: Fremont, NE held by NRG Media LLC.
Group Owner: NRG Media LLC; (acq 10-31-2005; grpsl)
Format: News, News/Talk, 86 *Special Programming:* Farm 6 hrs wkly *Hrs. of News Programming:* news progmg 25 hrs wkly *No. News Employees:* 1 *Target Audience:* 35 plus; mature adults
Chris Walz, Operations Dir
Del Meyer, General Manager
Virginia Marshall, Station Manager
Barry Reker, General Sales Mgr
Jessica Meistrell, News Director
Barry Reker, General Sales Manager

Gering

KMOR
08-01-1996; 93.3 mhz FM; 100 kw; Ant 1,020 ft; N41 50 23 W103 49 36
Box 1263, Scottsbluff, NE 69363
(308) 632-5667, *Fax:* (308) 635-1905
www.kmorfm.com
info@hometownfamilyradio.com
License: Gering, Scotts Bluff County, NE held by Legacy Communications LLC.
Group Owner: Legacy Communications LLC; (acq 12-13-2007; grpsl)
Population Served: 125,000
Alan Usher, CEO/COO

Gibbon

KMTY
10-01-1970; 97.7 mhz FM *Hrs Open:* 24; 55 kw; 253 ft.; N40 26 26 W99 23 59
Mailing Address: P.O. Box 465, Holdrege, NE 68949 US
Second Address: 613 4th Ave., Holdrege, NE 68949
(308) 995-4020, *Fax:* (308) 995-2202
kmtyfm.com
License: Gibbon, Phelps County, NE held by Armada Media-McCook Inc.
Group Owner: Armada Media Corp.; (acq 5-16-2008; grpsl)
Nat'l Network: ABC
Format: Adult Contemp *Target Audience:* 20-45.
Bryan Loker, General Manager
Kris Shaver, General Sales Mgr

Gordon

KSDZ
05-19-1979; 95.5 mhz FM *Hrs Open:* 24; 60 kw; 312 ft.; N42 47 56 W102 15 40
616 North Ash Street, Gordon, NE 69343 US
(308) 282-2500, *Fax:* (308) 282-0061
www.ksdzfm.com
thetwister@ksdzfm.com
License: Gordon, Sheridan County, NE held by DJ Broadcasting Inc.
Nat'l Network: ABC *Wire Services:* AP

Arbitron Metro Market: Gordon, NE *Format:* Oldies, Country *Target Audience:* 25-54. *Adv. Rates:* 35; 35; 35; 35
Jim Lambley, President

Grand Island

KMMJ
11-01-1925; 750 khz AM *Hrs Open:* Sunrise-sunset
Mailing Address: P.O. Box 404, Shenandoah, IA 51601 US
Second Address: Box 4907, Grand Island, NE 68802
(308) 382-2800, *Fax:* (308) 382-6701
missionnebraska.org/thebridge/
ausher@krgi.com
License: Grand Island, NE held by Mission Nebraska Inc.
Group Owner: Mission Nebraska Inc.; (acq 5-1-2006; $825,000)
Format: Christian
Alan Usher, Operations Dir
Jim Davis, Programming Director

KRGI
04-01-1953; 1430 khz AM; 5 kw-D, DAN; 1 kw-N, DAN; N40 52 17 W98 16 27
Mailing Address: P.O. Box 404, Shenandoah, IA 51601 US
Second Address: 3205 W. N. Front St., Grand Island, NE 68803
(308) 381-1430, *Fax:* (308) 382-6701
www.krgi.com
krgi@krgi.com
License: Grand Island, NE held by Legacy Communications LLC.
Group Owner: Legacy Communications LLC; (acq 5-17-2004; grpsl).
Nat'l Reps: Christal
Arbitron Metro Market: Grand Island-Kearney *Format:* News, News/Talk, 86 *Target Audience:* 25-54.
Chris Loghry, Operations Dir
Alan Usher, General Manager
Rob Fossberg, News Director
Chuck Walker, Chief Engineer
Alie Schlachter, Traffic Manager

KRGI-FM
10-30-1975; 96.5 mhz FM *Hrs Open:* 24; 100 kw; 420 ft.; N40 51 53 W98 23 47
Mailing Address: P.O. Box 404, Shenandoah, IA 51601 US
Second Address: 3205 W. N. Front St., Grand Island, NE 68803
(308) 381-1430, *Fax:* (308) 382-6701
www.nebraskasbestcountry.com
ausher@krgi.com
License: Grand Island, Hall County, NE
Group Owner: Legacy Communications LLC
Nat'l Network: ABC
Arbitron Metro Market: Grand Island-Kearney *Format:* Country
Alie Schlachter, News Director

*KROA
08-11-1967; 95.7 mhz FM *Hrs Open:* 24; 100 kw; 459 ft.; N40 47 11 W98 22 0
P.O. Box 495, Doniphan, NE 68832 US
(402) 845-6595, *Fax:* (402) 845-6597
www.mybridgeradio.net
email@mybridgeradio.net
License: Grand Island, Hall County, NE held by Mission Nebraska Inc.
Group Owner: Mission Nebraska Inc.; (acq 11-25-2003; $1.5 million)
Nat'l Network: Moody
Arbitron Metro Market: Grand Island-Kearney *Format:* Religious
Dave Chally, Chairman
Dr. James Eckman, President
Gordon Wheeler, Station Manager
Taryn Julane, Programming Director

KSYZ-FM
11-01-1982; 107.7 mhz FM *Hrs Open:* 24; 100 kw; 899 ft; N40 51 53 W98 23 47
Mailing Address: 3532 W. Captial Ave., Grand Island, NE 68508
Second Address: Box 5108, Grand Island, NE 68802
(308) 381-1077, *Fax:* (308) 384-8900
www.ksyz.com
ksyzprod@nrgmedia.com
License: Grand Island, Hall County, NE held by NRG Media LLC.
Group Owner: NRG Media LLC; (acq 10-31-2005; $5.28 million)
Target Audience: 25-49; adults *Adv. Rates:* 30; 25; 25; 16
Jim Cartwright, Operations Dir
Tim Marshall, General Manager

*KLNB
01-01-2005; 88.3 mhz FM *Hrs Open:* 24; 1.7 kw; 147 ft.; N40 54 50 W98 23 52
P. O. Box Drawer 2440, Tupelo, MS 38803 US
(800) 525-5683, *Fax:* (916) 251-1650
www.klove.com
klove@klove.com
License: Grand Island, Hall County, NE held by Educational Media Foundation.
Group Owner: EMF Broadcasting; (acq 3-11-2003; grpsl).
Nat'l Network: K-Love
Arbitron Metro Market: Grand Island, NE *Format:* Christian *No. News Employees:* 13 *Target Audience:* 25-44; Judeo Christian, female
Darrell Chambliss, Chairman
Mike Novak, President and CEO
Jennifer Lohman, Operations Dir
David Pierce, Chief Creative Officer and Programming Director
Ed Lenane, News Director
Sam Wallington, Engineering Dir
Marya Morgan, NewsReporter
Richard Hunt, News Reporter
Alan Mason, Chief Operating Officer
Dan Antonelli, Chief Business Development Officer
Eric Moser, Chief Financial Officer
Brian Burger, Vice President of Human Resources

*KNFA
01-01-2008; 90.7 mhz FM; 1.3 kw; 191 ft.; N40 54 50 W98 23 52
Mailing Address: P O Box 1452, Washington, DC 20013 US
Second Address: 8919 World Ministry Ave., Baton Rouge, NE 70810
(225) 768-3102, *Fax:* (225) 768-3729
www.jsm.org
kawikfish@yahoo.com
License: Grand Island, Hall County, NE held by Family Worship Center Church Inc..
Group Owner: Family Worship Center Church Inc.; (acq 10-12-2006; grpsl)
Arbitron Metro Market: Grand Island, NE *Format:* Christian, Religious
David Whitelaw, COO

Hastings

KLIQ
01-01-2001; 94.5 mhz FM *Hrs Open:* 24; 97.7 kw; 948 ft.; N40 36 8 W98 50 21
1001 Farnum-On-The-Mall, Omaha, NE 68102 US
(402) 461-4922, *Fax:* (402) 461-3866
www.kliqfm.com
thebreeze@kliqfm.com
License: Hastings, Adams County, NE held by Platte River Radio Inc.
Group Owner: Platte River Radio Inc.; (acq 2-1-2006; $700,000).
Nat'l Network: ABC *Wire Services:* AP
Arbitron Metro Market: Hastings, NB *Format:* Adult Contemp *Special Programming:* News & special community interest *No. News Employees:* 1 *Target Audience:* 25-54.
Jim Stevens, Operations Dir
Craig Eckert, General Manager
Brad Beahm, Programming Director
Kevin Michaelson, News Director

*KCNT
02-22-1971; 88.1 mhz FM *Hrs Open:* 24; 2.3 kw horiz; 180 ft.; N40 34 52 W98 19 58
P.O. Box 1024, Hastings, NE 68902 US
(402) 463-9811, *Fax:* (402) 461-2454
www.cccneb.edu/programs/mart/kcnt/index.html
rglenn@cccneb.edu
License: Hastings, Adams County, NE held by Central Community College.
Arbitron Metro Market: Hastings, NE *Format:* Contemporary Hits/Top 40
John Brooks, General Manager
Dr. Deb Brennan, Executive Vice President
Marni Nelson-Snyde, Grants Manager
Heidi Farrall, Grants Development Coordinator
Michelle Setlik, Grants Compliance Officer
Christopher Waddle, JD, ExecutiveDirector
Tom Peters, ITS Manager

*KFKX
90.1 mhz FM; 0.78 kw vert; 223 ft.; N40 34 27 W98 22 19
700 Turner Street, Hastings, NE 68901 US
(402) 461-7367, *Fax:* (402) 461-7442
kfkx@hastings.edu
License: Hastings, Adams County, NE held by Hastings College.
Wire Services: AP
Arbitron Metro Market: Hastings, NE *Format:* Urban Contemporary *Target Audience:* General.
Phillip Dudley, President
Bart Jones, Operations Dir
Sharon Behl Brooks, General Manager
Stefan Welsh, Station Manager

KHAS
09-30-1940; 1230 khz AM *Hrs Open:* 24; 1 kw-U, ND1; N40 34 40 W98 24 17
Mailing Address: 902 W. 2nd St, # 200, Hastings, NE 68901 US
Second Address: 500 East J St., Hastings, NE 68901
(402) 462-5101, *Fax:* (402) 461-3866
hastingslink.com
khaskics@windstream.net
License: Hastings, NE held by Platte River Radio Inc.
Group Owner: Platte River Radio Inc.; (acq 2-1-2006; $560,000 with KICS(AM) Hastings).
Nat'l Network: CBS *Regional Network:* Brownfield *Regional Reps:* Howard Anderson *Wire Services:* AP
Format: Adult Contemp *Special Programming:* Farm 2 hrs, class 2 hrs wkly *Hrs. of News Programming:* news progmg 20 hrs wkly *No. News Employees:* 1 *Target Audience:* 35 plus; general
David Oldfather, President
Craig Eckert, General Manager
Jim Stevens, Station Manager
Tyson Havraneck, Programming Director
Mike Smithson, News Director
Mike Will, Sports Director

*KHNE-FM
06-01-1990; 89.1 mhz FM *Hrs Open:* 24; 64.3 kw; 328 ft; N40 46 17 W98 05 22 *Rebroadcasts:* Rebroadcasts KUCV(FM) Lincoln 100%.
1800 N. 33rd St., Lincoln, NE 68501
(402) 472-3611, *Fax:* (402) 472-2403
netnebraska.org/radio
radio@netnebraska.org
License: Hastings, Adams County, NE held by Nebraska Educational Telecommunications Commission
Nat'l Network: NPR; APM; PRI *Regional Network:* Net Radio
Hrs. of News Programming: news progmg 45 hrs wkly *No. News Employees:* 8 *Target Audience:* General.
Rod Bates, General Manager
Nancy Finken, Station Manager
Susan Dinsmore, General Sales Mgr
Nancy Finken, Programming Director
Mary Jane Winquest, Promotions Manager
Dennis Kellogg, News Director
Stacey Decker, Engineering Dir
William Stibor, Music Director
Jeff Smith, Operations

KICS
04-15-1964; 1550 khz AM *Hrs Open:* 24; 0.5 kw-D, ND1; 0.027 kw-N, ND1; N40 34 3 W98 22 31
906 West 2nd Street, Suite 200, Hastings, NE 68901 US
(402) 462-5101, *Fax:* (402) 461-3866
www.khasradio.com
generalmanager@espnsupersation.com
License: Hastings, NE held by Platte River Radio Inc.
Group Owner: Platte River Radio Inc.; (acq 2-1-2006; $560,000 with KHAS(AM) Hastings).
Nat'l Network: ESPN Radio *Regional Reps:* Howard Anderson
TV Affiliate: ESPN *Format:* Sports *Special Programming:* College football 8 hrs wkly *Hrs. of News Programming:* news progmg 12 hrs wkly *No. News Employees:* 1 *Target Audience:* 18-54; males
David Oldfather, President
Wayne Specht, General Manager
Jim Stevens, Station Manager

KROR
02-01-1965; 101.5 mhz FM *Hrs Open:* 24; 100 kw; Ant 1,004 ft; N40 39 28 W98 52 04
3532 W. Capital Ave., Grand Island, NE 68506
(308) 381-1077, *Fax:* (308) 384-8900
www.rock1015.com
ksyzprod@nrgmedia.com
License: Hastings, Adams County, NE held by NRG License Sub LLC.
Group Owner: NRG Media LLC; (acq 1-31-2006; swap for KLIQ(FM) Hastings)
Population Served: 250,000*Target Audience:* 25-54. *Adv. Rates:* 30; 24; 24; 16
Jim Cartwright, Operations Dir
Tim Marshall, General Manager

Hershey

KNPQ
01-01-2008; 107.3 mhz FM *Hrs Open:* 24; 25 kw; 226 ft.; N41 9 14 W100 46 22.4
Mailing Address: US
Second Address: 1301 E. 4th St., North Platte, NE 69101
(308) 532-1120, *Fax:* (308) 532-0458
knpqcountry.com
chuck.schwartz@eagleradio.net

RADIO - U.S.

License: Hershey, Lincoln County, NE held by Eagle Communications Inc.
Group Owner: Eagle Communications Group
Arbitron Metro Market: Hershey, NE *Format:* Country *Hrs. of News Programming:* news prgmg one hour wkly *No. News Employees:* 1 *Target Audience:* 18-44. *Adv. Rates:* same as KOOQ
Gary Shorman, President
Dave Lee, Operations Dir
Jerome Gilg, General Manager
Scott Olesky, General Sales Mgr
David Fudge, Programming Director
Dianne Morales, Promotions Manager
Kris Allen, News Director
Tony Cuesta, ChiefEngineer
Dan Lucero, Sports Director
Chris Nelson, Office Manager
Dixon Powers, Account Executive
Olivia Brown, Account Executive
Connie Jurgens, Account Executive

Holdrege

KUVR
10-20-1956; 1380 khz AM
Mailing Address: 613 4th Avenue, Holdrege, NE 68949 US
Second Address: 613 4th Ave., Holdrege, NE 68949
(308) 345-5400, *Fax:* (308) 345-4720
www.plainsreporter.com
bryan@highplainsradio.net?subject=Email%20for%20further%20details%20here
License: Holdrege, NE held by Armada Media-McCook Inc.
Group Owner: Armada Media Corp.; (acq 5-16-2008; grpsl)
Arbitron Metro Market: Holdrege, NE *Format:* Oldies *Special Programming:* Farm 5 hrs, big band 5 hrs, contemp gospel 5 hrs wkly *Target Audience:* 35-54.
Andrew Stossmeister, Operations Dir
Bryan Loker, General Manager
Jim Conner, General Sales Mgr
Val Lane, Chief Engineer
Randy Issler, Music Director

Hubbard

*KAYA
01-01-1998; 91.3 mhz FM; 5.1 kw; 377 ft.; N42 21 10 W96 31 32
Mailing Address: P O Drawer 2440, Tupelo, MS 38803 US
Second Address: 1211 Tri-View, Sioux City, IA 51103
(662) 844-8888, *Fax:* (662) 842-6791
www.afr.net
comments@afr.net
License: Hubbard, Dakota County, NE held by American Family Association.
Group Owner: American Family Radio
Arbitron Metro Market: Tupelo, MS *Format:* Christian, Religious
Marvin Sanders, General Manager

Humboldt

*KNIT
90.1 mhz FM; 6.1 kw horiz; Ant 607 ft; N40 13 11 W95 39 55
Box 94, Stonewall, OK
(580) 265-9475
License: Humboldt, Richardson County, NE held by Union Valley Baptist Church Inc.
Steve Vandegrift, General Manager

Imperial

KADL
01-01-2003; 102.9 mhz FM; 300 w; Ant 223 ft; N40 30 45 W101 38 39
Mailing Address: PO Box 333, McCook, NE 69001
Second Address: 824 Douglas St., Imperial, NE 69033
(308) 345-5400,(308) 882-4209, *Fax:* (308) 345-4720,(308) 882-4319
www.kadlimperial.com
bryan@highplainsradio.net
License: Imperial, Chase County, NE held by Armada Media - McCook Inc.
Group Owner: Armada Media Corp.; (acq 1-17-2007; grpsl)
Bryan Loker, General Manager
Bryan Loker, General Sales Mgr
Andrew Stossmeister, Programming Director

Kearney

KGFW
01-01-1927; 1340 khz AM *Hrs Open:* 24
Mailing Address: 1001 Farnam-On-The-Mall, Omaha, NE 68114 US
Second Address: 2223 Central Ave., Kearney, NE 68847
(308) 698-2131, *Fax:* (308) 237-0312
www.kgfw.com
swhite@nrgmedia.com
License: Kearney, NE held by NRG License Sub. LLC.
Group Owner: NRG Media LLC; (acq 10-31-2005; grpsl)
Nat'l Network: Westwood One *Regional Network:* Waitt Farm Net.; Brownfield *Nat'l Reps:* Christal *Wire Services:* AP
Format: News, News/Talk, 86 *Special Programming:* Farm 8 hrs, sports 10 hrs wkly *Hrs. of News Programming:* news progmg 25 hrs wkly *No. News Employees:* 2 *Target Audience:* 25 plus; adults in central Nebraska
Mary Quass, President
Mark Reid, Operations Dir
Andrew Mihm, Programming Director

KXPN
12-05-1956; 1460 khz AM *Hrs Open:* 24; 5 kw-D, ND1; 0.056 kw-N, ND1; N40 42 45 W99 10 15
Mailing Address: 403 East 25th St, Kearney, NE 68847 US
Second Address: 403 E. 25th St., Kearney, NE 68848
(308) 236-9900, *Fax:* (308) 234-6781
www.espnsuperstation.com
generalmanager@espnsuperstation.com
License: Kearney, NE held by Platte River Radio Inc.
Group Owner: Platte River Radio Inc.; (acq 1-1-94; $750,000 with co-located FM;
Nat'l Network: ESPN Radio
Arbitron Metro Market: Lincoln, NE *Format:* Sports *Hrs. of News Programming:* news progmg 2 hrs wkly *No. News Employees:* 1 *Target Audience:* 25-54; men *Adv. Rates:* 27; 19; 27; 12
David Oldfather, President
Craig Eckert, General Manager
Dan Beck, Programming Director

KKPR-FM
11-01-1962; 98.9 mhz FM *Hrs Open:* 24; 100 kw; 627 ft.; N40 48 53 W98 46 12
PO Box 130, Kearney, NE 68848 US
(308) 236-9900, *Fax:* (308) 234-6781
www.kkpr.com
generalmanager@kkpr.com
License: Kearney, Buffalo County, NE
Group Owner: Platte River Radio Inc.
Arbitron Metro Market: Lincoln, NE *Format:* Oldies *Hrs. of News Programming:* news progmg 3 hrs wkly *No. News Employees:* 1 *Target Audience:* 35-64. *Adv. Rates:* 27; 19; 27; 12.
Dan Beck, Programming Director
Johnnie McCann, General Sales Mgr

*KLPR
03-08-1968; 91.1 mhz FM *Hrs Open:* 6 AM-midnight; 1 kw; 102 ft.; N40 42 30 W99 5 45
109 Thomas Hall, Kearney, NE 68849 US
(308) 865-8217
klpr.unk.edu
License: Kearney, Buffalo County, NE held by University of Nebraska at Kearney.
Arbitron Metro Market: Lincoln, NE *Format:* Jazz, Rock/AOR
Special Programming: Class 18 hrs wkly
Roy Hyatte, General Manager

KQKY
10-01-1979; 105.9 mhz FM *Hrs Open:* 24; 97.6 kw; 1204 ft.; N40 36 8 W98 50 21
Mailing Address: 1001 Farnam-On-The-Mall, Omaha, NE 68102 US
Second Address: 2223 Central Ave., Kearney, NE 68847
(308) 698-2100, *Fax:* (308) 237-0312
www.kqky.com
License: Kearney, Buffalo County, NE held by NRG License Sub. LLC.
Group Owner: NRG Media LLC
Nat'l Network: Fox News Radio; Superadio *Nat'l Reps:* Christal *Wire Services:* AP
Arbitron Metro Market: Grand Island-Kearney *Format:* Contemporary Hits/Top 40 *Target Audience:* 18-49.
Mary Quass, President
Mark Reid, Operations Dir
John McDonald, General Manager
Sharon White, Station Manager
Jason Murphy, Programming Director

KRNY
01-01-1987; 102.3 mhz FM *Hrs Open:* 24; 77.1 kw; 1086 ft.; N40 36 8 W98 50 21
Mailing Address: 2202 Central Avenue, Suite 300, Kearney, NE 68847 US
Second Address: 2223 Central Ave., Kearney, NE 68847
(308) 698-2100, *Fax:* (308) 237-0312
www.krny.com
License: Kearney, Buffalo County, NE held by NRG License Sub. LLC.
Group Owner: NRG Media LLC; (acq 10-31-2005; grpsl)
Nat'l Network: Fox News Radio; Premiere Radio Networks *Nat'l Reps:* Christal *Wire Services:* AP
Arbitron Metro Market: Tri Cities, NB (Kearney, Grand Island, Hastings) *Format:* Country *Hrs. of News Programming:* News progmg 2 hrs wkly *Target Audience:* 25 plus.
Mary Quass, President
Mark Reid, Operations Dir
John McDonald, General Manager
Sharon White, Station Manager
Scott O'Rourke, Programming Director
Dave Jenner, Sports Director

Kimball

KIMB
01-01-1958; 1260 khz AM; 1 kw-D, ND1; 0.112 kw-N, ND1; N41 15 42 W103 40 6
213 S. Chestnut St., Kimball, NE 69145 US
(970) 867-7271, *Fax:* (970) 867-2676
License: Kimball, NE held by Main Street Communications, LLC
Target Audience: General.
Alec Creighton, General Manager

*KVAM
88.3 mhz FM; 510 w; Ant 282 ft; N41 11 36 W103 31 45
6139 Franklin Park Rd., McLean, VA
(703) 761-5013
License: Kimball, Kimball County, NE held by Cedar Cove Broadcasting Inc.
A. Wray Fitch III, President

La Vista

KOOO
06-22-1958; 101.9 mhz FM *Hrs Open:* 24; 100 kw; Ant 1,132 ft; N40 47 09 W96 23 07
5011 Capitol Ave., Omaha, NE 68102
(402) 342-2000, *Fax:* (402) 346-5748
thebigo1019.com
info@thebigo1019.com
License: La Vista, Sarpy County, NE held by Waitt Omaha LLC.
Group Owner: Waitt Omaha LLC; (acq 1-7-2002; grpsl)
Nat'l Reps: Katz Radio
Population Served: 2,120,000 *Arbitron Metro Market:* Omaha-Council Bluffs, NE-IA *Target Audience:* 25-54; general
Mark Todd, Operations Dir
Jim McKernan, General Manager
Rhonda Gerrard, General Sales Mgr
Billy Shears, Programming Director
Chris Pflaum, Promotions Manager
Cynthia Wallace, News Director
Sam Coughlin, General Sales Manager

Lexington

*KLNE-FM
05-04-1990; 88.7 mhz FM *Hrs Open:* 24; 43.8 kw; 938 ft; N40 23 05 W99 27 30 *Rebroadcasts:* Rebroadcasts KUCV(FM) Lincoln 100%
1800 N. 33rd St., Lincoln, NE 68501
(402) 472-3611, *Fax:* (402) 472-2403
netnebraska.org/radio
radio@netnebraska.org
License: Lexington, Dawson County, NE held by Nebraska Educational Telecommunications Commission
Nat'l Network: NPR; APM; PRI *Regional Network:* Nebraska Public Radio
Hrs. of News Programming: news progmg 45 hrs wkly *No. News Employees:* 8 *Target Audience:* General
Rod Bates, General Manager
Nancy Finken, Station Manager
Susan Dinsmore, General Sales Mgr
Nancy Finken, Programming Director
Mary Jane Winquest, Promotions Manager
Dennis Kellogg, News Director
Stacey Decker, Engineering Dir
William Stibor, Music Director
Jeff Smith, Operations

KRVN
02-01-1951; 880 khz AM *Hrs Open:* 24; 50 kw-U, DA-N; N40 31 03 W99 23 20
Box 880, 1007 Plum Creek Pkwy., Lexington, NE 68850
(308) 324-2371, *Fax:* (308) 324-5786
www.krvn.com
krvnam@krvn.com
License: Lexington, Dawson County, NE held by Nebraska Rural Radio Assn.
Group Owner: Nebraska Rural Radio Association; (acq 2-1-51)
Nat'l Network: Fox News Radio *Nat'l Reps:* Katz Radio *Wire Services:* AP

Special Programming: Relg 12 hrs wkly *Hrs. of News Programming:* news progmg 30 hrs wkly *No. News Employees:* 4 *Target Audience:* General; Nebraska farm/ranch families & consumers *Adv. Rates:* 230; 230; 136; 90

Craig Larson, General Manager
Dwight Lane, Station Manager
Amy Biehl-Owens, General Sales Mgr
Adam Smith, Programming Director
Beth Rogers, Promotions Manager
Frank Snyder, News Director
Rod Zeigler, Engineering Dir
MikeLePorte, Farm Director

KRVN-FM
11-01-1962; 93.1 mhz FM *Hrs Open:* 24; 100 kw; 890 ft; N40 41 48 W99 47 18
Box 880, 1007 Plum Creek Pkwy., Lexington, NE 22203
(308) 324-2371, *Fax:* (308) 324-5786
www.krvnfm.com
krvnam@kryp.com
License: Lexington, Dawson County, NE
Group Owner: Nebraska Rural Radio Association
Nat'l Network: Fox News Radio *Nat'l Reps:* Katz Radio
Population Served: 125,000*Special Programming:* Farm 10 hrs wkly *Hrs. of News Programming:* news prog 20 hrs wkly *No. News Employees:* 1 *Target Audience:* Contemp young adults *Adv. Rates:* 50; 50; 35; 25

Craig Larson, General Manager
Dwight Lane, Station Manager
Amy Biehl-Owens, General Sales Mgr
Adam Smith, Programming Director
Beth Rogers, Promotions Manager
Frank Snyder, News Director
Rod Zeigler, Engineering Dir
MikeLePorte, Farm Director

Lincoln

KBBK
09-01-1968; 107.3 mhz FM *Hrs Open:* 24; 100 kw; 551 ft.; N40 43 38 W96 36 51
P. O. Box 30181, Lincoln, NE 68503 US
(402) 475-4567, *Fax:* (402) 479-1411
www.b1073.com
news@broadcasthouse.com
License: Lincoln, Lancaster County, NE held by NRG License Sub. LLC.
Group Owner: NRG Media LLC; (acq 12-28-2007; grpsl)
Arbitron Metro Market: Lincoln, NE *Format:* Adult Contemp
Target Audience: 25-54; middle-to-upper income, households, in-office & in-store lstng

Ami Graham, General Manager
Tina Segerstrom, General Sales Mgr
Steve Albertsen, Programming Director

KFOR
03-04-1924; 1240 khz AM *Hrs Open:* 24; 1 kw-U, ND1; N40 49 12 W96 39 29
6900 Van Dorn, Suite 11, Lincoln, NE 68501 US
(402) 466-1234, *Fax:* (402) 467-4095
www.kfor1240.com
kfor@threeeagles.com
License: Lincoln, NE held by Coloff Broadcasting.
Group Owner: Three Eagles Communications; (acq 1996; $5.3 million with co-located FM)
Arbitron Metro Market: Lincoln, NE *Format:* News, News/Talk, 86
Special Programming: Problems and solutions 7 hrs wkly, art link 2 hrs wkly *Hrs. of News Programming:* news progmg 20 hrs wkly *No. News Employees:* 6 *Target Audience:* 25-54.

Roland Johnson, CEO
James Keck, Station Manager
Joy Patton, General Sales Mgr
Mark Taylor, Programming Director
Dale Johnson, News Director
Cindy Harris, CFO
Gary Buchanan, COO

KFRX
02-23-1973; 106.3 mhz FM *Hrs Open:* 24; 100 kw; 702 ft.; N40 43 40 W96 36 50
600 Congress Avenue, Suite 1400, Austin, TX 78701 US
(402) 466-1234, *Fax:* (402) 467-4095
www.kfrxfm.com
lindsey@kfrxfm.com; matt@kfrxfm.com; chi@kfrxfm.com
License: Lincoln, Lancaster County, NE held by Three Eagles of Lincoln Inc.
Group Owner: Three Eagles Communications; (acq 4-10-2007; grpsl)
Arbitron Metro Market: Lincoln, NE *Format:* Contemporary Hits/Top 40

James Keck, General Manager
Matt McKay, Programming Director

KLNC
01-01-1992; 105.3 mhz FM; 3.2 kw; 453 ft.; N40 43 38 W96 36 51
P.O. Box 30181, Lincoln, NE 68503 US
(402) 475-4567, *Fax:* (402) 479-1411
1053wow.com
news@broadcasthouse.com
License: Lincoln, Lancaster County, NE held by NRG License Sub. LLC.
Group Owner: NRG Media LLC; (acq 12-28-2007; grpsl)
Arbitron Metro Market: Lincoln, NE *Format:* Oldies

Mark Halverson, Operations Dir
Ami Graham, General Sales Mgr
E.J. Marshall, Programming Director
Steve Looney, Chief Engineer
J. Pat Miller, Operations Manager

***KLCV**
01-01-1996; 88.5 mhz FM *Hrs Open:* 8 AM-5 PM (M-F); 46 kw; 1255 ft.; N40 47 10 W96 23 10
10550 Barkley, Suite 108, Overland Park, KS 66212 US
(402) 465-8850, *Fax:* (402) 465-8852
klcv@bottradionetwork.com
License: Lincoln, Lancaster County, NE held by Community Broadcasting Inc.
Group Owner: Bott Radio Network
Nat'l Network: USA
Arbitron Metro Market: Lincoln, NE *Format:* Christian, Talk *Target Audience:* 25 plus; Christian families

Richard Bott Sr., President
Tom Millett, General Manager
Pat Rulon, General Sales Mgr
Candy Green, Programming Director

KLIN
08-01-1947; 1400 khz AM *Hrs Open:* 24
P.O. Box 30181, Lincoln, NE 68503 US
(402) 475-4567, *Fax:* (402) 479-1411
www.klin.com
news@broadcasthouse.com
License: Lincoln, NE held by NRG License Sub. LLC.
Group Owner: NRG Media LLC; (acq 12-28-2007; grpsl)
Nat'l Network: Fox News Radio
Arbitron Metro Market: Lincoln, NE *Format:* News, News/Talk, 86 *Hrs. of News Programming:* news progmg 80 hrs wkly *No. News Employees:* 4 *Target Audience:* 35-64; upper income, business owner, educated with highdisposable income

Mark Halverson, General Manager
John Bishop, Programming Director
Greg Jackson, News Director
Bill Frost, Chief Engineer

KLMS
10-01-1949; 1480 khz AM; 1 kw-D, DA2; 0.75 kw-N, DA2; N40 47 47 W96 34 56
6900 Van Dorn, Suite 11, Lincoln, NE 68506 US
(402) 466-1234, *Fax:* (402) 467-4095
www.espn1480.com
License: Lincoln, NE held by Coloff Broadcasting.
Group Owner: Three Eagles Communications; (acq 1996; grpsl)
Arbitron Metro Market: Lincoln, NE *Format:* Sports

Roland Johnson, CEO
Mark Taylor, Operations Dir
Bill Doleman, Programming Director
Vicki Marker, Promotions Manager
Terri Hutchinson, News Director
Bob Cook, Chief Engineer
Cindy Harris, CFO
Gary Buchanan, Dale Johnson
LocalNews Editor

***KRNU**
02-23-1970; 90.3 mhz FM *Hrs Open:* 24; 0.1 kw; 125 ft.; N40 49 11 W96 42 11
206 Avery Hall, Lincoln, NE 68508 US
(402) 472-3054, *Fax:* (402) 472-8403
www.krnu.unl.edu
krnu@unl.edu
License: Lincoln, Lancaster County, NE held by University of Nebraska.
Nat'l Network: ABC
Arbitron Metro Market: Lincoln, NE *TV Affiliate:* *KUON-TV affil.
Format: Rock/AOR *Special Programming:* Hip-hop 2 hrs, electronic 4 hrs, gospel 2 hrs, ja *Hrs. of News Programming:* News progmg 5 hrs wkly

Rick Alloway, General Manager
Barney McCoy, News Director
Vance Payne, Chief Engineer

***KUCV**
01-01-1968; 91.1 mhz FM *Hrs Open:* 24; 19.5 kw horiz, 100 kw ver; Ant 689 ft; N40 31 06 W96 46 06
1800 N. 33rd St., Lincoln, NE 68501
(402) 472-3611, *Fax:* (402) 472-2403
netnebraska.org/radio
radio@netnebraska.org
License: Lincoln, Lancaster County, NE held by Nebraska Educational Telecommunications Commission
Nat'l Network: NPR; APM; PRI *Regional Network:* NET Radio
Population Served: 1,100,000 *Arbitron Metro Market:* Lincoln, NE *Hrs. of News Programming:* news progmg 45 hrs wkly *No. News Employees:* 8 *Target Audience:* General.

Rod Bates, General Manager
Nancy Finken, Station Manager
Susan Dinsmore, General Sales Mgr
Nancy Finken, Programming Director
Mary Jane Winquest, Promotions Manager
Dennis Kellogg, News Director
Stacey Decker, Engineering Dir
William Stibor, Music Director
Jeff Smith, Operations

***KZUM**
01-01-1978; 89.3 mhz FM *Hrs Open:* 6 AM-2 AM; 1.5 kw; 102 ft.; N40 48 47 W96 42 24
941 O Street, Suite 1025, Lincoln, NE 68508 US
(402) 474-5086, *Fax:* (402) 474-5091
www.kzum.org
gm@kzum.org
License: Lincoln, Lancaster County, NE held by Sunrise Communications Inc.
Arbitron Metro Market: Lincoln, NE *Format:* Jazz, Variety/Diverse
Special Programming: Sp 4 hrs, rock/progsv 15 hrs, new age 8 hrs, blues 13 hrs, folk 8 hrs, gospel 3 hrs wkly *Hrs. of News Programming:* News progmg 11hrs wkly *Target Audience:* General; the unserved & underserved population *Adv. Rates:* 15; 15; 15; 15

Alisa Kushner, Operations Dir
Cathy Behrns, General Manager
James Terry, General Sales Mgr
Ryan Evans, Programming Director
Barry Reutzel, Webmaster

Loup City

***KSRC**
88.1 mhz FM; kw
US
(918) 333-8700
License: Loup City, Sherman County, NE held by Pearl Communications Group.
Arbitron Metro Market: Kansas City, MO *Format:* Adult Contemp

Danny Hester, President

Maxwell

KHAQ
01-01-2000; 98.5 mhz FM *Hrs Open:* 24; 85 kw; Ant 371 ft; N41 12 49 W100 43 49
Mailing Address: Box 333, McCook, NE 69001
Second Address: 1811 W. O St., McCook, NE 69001
(308) 345-5400, *Fax:* (308) 345-4720
www.kicx.net
bryan@highplainsradio.net
License: Maxwell, Lincoln County, NE held by Armada Media - McCook Inc.
Group Owner: Armada Media Corp.; (acq 3-31-2007; grpsl)
Population Served: 40,000*Target Audience:* 18-54.

Rob Mandeville, General Manager
Dalene Skates, General Sales Mgr

McCook

KBRL
09-26-1947; 1300 khz AM; 5 kw-D, DA2; 0.136 kw-N, DA2; N40 11 31 W100 39 6
Mailing Address: 802 West C Street, McCook, NE 69001 US
Second Address: 1811 W. O St., McCook, NE 699001
(308) 345-5400, *Fax:* (308) 345-4720
www.kicx.net
bryan@highplainsradio.net
License: McCook, NE held by Armada Media - McCook Inc.
Group Owner: Armada Media Corp.; (acq 3-31-2007; grpsl)
Format: Oldies *Target Audience:* 35-64.

Clint Bradbury, Operations Dir
Bryan Loker, General Manager
Rich Barnett, News Director
Ron Fritz, Chief Engineer

KICX-FM
01-31-1979; 96.1 mhz FM *Hrs Open:* 24; 55 kw; 295 ft.; N40 10 17 W100 41 4
802 West C Street, McCook, NE 69001 US
(705) 722-5429, *Fax:* (308) 345-4720
www.kicx106.com
mora.austin@larchecom.com; jlatimer@kicxfm.com; jennifer.bertucci@larchecom.com
License: McCook, Red Willow County, NE held by Armada Media - McCook Inc.
Group Owner: Armada Media Corp.; (acq 3-31-2007; grpsl)
Nat'l Network: ABC
Format: Country *No. News Employees:* 1 *Target Audience:* 25-64.
Paul Larche, President
Mora Austin, General Manager
Jennifer Bertucci, Station Manager
Martin Vanderwoude, Programming Director
Ted Roop, Promotions Manager

KIOD
05-01-1981; 105.3 mhz FM *Hrs Open:* 24; 100 kw; Ant 591 ft; N40 11 27 W100 48 29
Mailing Address: Box 939, McCook, NE 69001
Second Address: 106 W. 8th St., McCook, NE 69001
(308) 345-1981, *Fax:* (308) 345-7202
coyote105.com
info@hometownfamilyradio.com
License: McCook, Red Willow County, NE held by Legacy Communications LLC.
Group Owner: Legacy Communications LLC; (acq 10-13-2005; $1.3 million with
Population Served: 40,000*Special Programming:* Sports 10 hrs, farm 6 hrs wkly *Hrs. of News Programming:* news progmg 5 hrs wkly *No. News Employees:* 1 *Target Audience:* 25-54. *Adv. Rates:* 15; 15; 15; 8
Alan Usher, CEO/COO
Jesse Stevens, Programming Director
Ann Doyle, News Director
Derek Beck, Music Director

***KNGN**
06-23-1961; 1360 khz AM *Hrs Open:* 6 AM-2 hrs past sunset
1333 S. Kirkwood Rd, St. Louis, MO 63122 US
(308) 345-2006, *Fax:* (308) 345-2052
www.kngn.org
goodnews@mccooknet.com
License: McCook, NE held by Kansas Nebraska Good News Broadcasting Corp.
Format: Religious *Hrs. of News Programming:* News progmg 7 hrs wkly *Target Audience:* 35 plus; family oriented
Greg Stuekwiseh, President
Mike Nielsen, General Manager

KSWN
09-17-1998; 93.9 mhz FM *Hrs Open:* 24; 50 kw; 492 ft.; N40 11 27 W100 48 29
P O Box 939, 106 Wesst 8th St, McCook, NE 69001 US
(308) 345-1100, *Fax:* (308) 345-7202
mccookfamilyradio.gifamilyradio.com/us939.htm
jay@coyote105.com
License: McCook, Red Willow County, NE held by Legacy Communications LLC.
Group Owner: Legacy Communications LLC; (acq 10-13-2005; $1.3 million with KIOD(FM) McCook)
Nat'l Network: ESPN Radio
Arbitron Metro Market: McCook, NE *Format:* Adult Contemp, Sports *Target Audience:* 25-54. *Adv. Rates:* 10; 10; 10; 6.50
Eileen Austin, Operations Dir
Jay Austin, General Manager
Jesse Stevens, Programming Director

KNAX
700 khz AM
US
(308) 345-5400, *Fax:* (308) 345-4720
License: McCook, NE held by McCook Radio Group L.L.C.
Arbitron Metro Market: McCook, NE
David Stout, General Manager
Connie Stout, General Sales Mgr
Rich Barnett, News Director

KZMC
10-25-2006; 102.1 mhz FM; 100 kw; Ant 590 ft; N40 11 27 W100 48 29
Mailing Address: Box 939, McCook, NE
Second Address: 106 W. 8th St., McCook, NE 69001-3508
(308) 345-1981, *Fax:* (308) 345-7202
www.hometownfamilyradio.com/Z/index.php
info@hometownfamilyradio.com
License: McCook, Red Willow County, NE held by Legacy Communications LLC.
Group Owner: Legacy Communications LLC
Alan Usher, Operations Dir
Jesse Stevens, Operations Manager

KQHK
01-01-2008; 103.9 mhz FM; 50 kw; 371 ft.; N40 10 19 W100 41 5 US
(308) 345-5400, *Fax:* (308) 345-4720
www.kicx.net
License: McCook, Red Willow County, NE held by Armada Media - McCook Inc.
Group Owner: Armada Media Corp.; (acq 3-31-2007; grpsl)
Arbitron Metro Market: McCook, NE *Format:* Classic Rock
Andrew Stossmeister, Operations Dir
Bryan Loker, General Manager

Merriman

***KRNE-FM**
08-29-1991; 91.5 mhz FM *Hrs Open:* 24; 92 kw; 964 ft; N42 40 38 W101 42 36 *Rebroadcasts:* Rebroadcasts KUCV(FM) Lincoln 100%
1800 N. 33rd St., Lincoln, NE 68501
(402) 472-3611, *Fax:* (402) 472-2403
netnebraska.org/radio
radio@netnebraska.org
License: Merriman, Cherry County, NE held by Nebraska Educational Telecommunications Commission
Nat'l Network: NPR; APM; PRI *Regional Network:* NET Radio
Hrs. of News Programming: news progmg 45 hrs wkly *No. News Employees:* 8 *Target Audience:* General.
Rod Bates, General Manager
Nancy Finken, Station Manager
Susan Dinsmore, General Sales Mgr
Nancy Finken, Programming Director
Mary Jane Winquest, Promotions Manager
Dennis Kellogg, News Director
Stacey Decker, Engineering Dir
Bill Stibor, Music Director
Jeff Smith, Operations

Milford

KFGE
01-01-1996; 98.1 mhz FM; 100 kw; 981 ft.; N40 51 52 W97 16 14
4343 O St., Lincoln, NE 68510 US
(402) 475-4567, *Fax:* (402) 479-1411
www.froggy981.com
news@broadcasthouse.com
License: Milford, Seward County, NE held by NRG License Sub. LLC.
Group Owner: NRG Media LLC; (acq 12-28-2007; grpsl)
Arbitron Metro Market: Lincoln, NE *Format:* Country
Mark Halverson, Operations Dir
Ami Graham, General Sales Mgr
Steve Albertson, Programming Director
Steve Looney, Chief Engineer
J. Pat Miller, Operations Manager

Minatare

KHYY
01-01-2008; 106.9 mhz FM; 25 kw; 92 ft.; N41 51 50 W103 42 20
Mailing Address: US
Second Address: 2002 Char Ave., Scottsbluff, NE 69361
(308) 632-5667, *Fax:* (308) 635-1905
License: Minatare, Scotts Bluff County, NE held by Legacy Communications LLC.
Group Owner: Legacy Communications LLC; (acq 2-19-2008; $200,000 with KETT(FM) Mitchell)
Arbitron Metro Market: Centennial, CO *Format:* Country
Julie Marshall, General Manager

Mitchell

KETT
01-01-2008; 99.3 mhz FM; 0.95 kw; 817 ft.; N41 50 23 W103 49 35
Mailing Address: US
Second Address: 2002 Char Ave., Scottsbluff, NE 69361
(308) 632-5667, *Fax:* (308) 635-1905
License: Mitchell, Scotts Bluff County, NE held by Legacy Communications LLC.
Group Owner: Legacy Communications LLC; (acq 2-19-2008; $200,000 with KHYY(FM) Minatare)
Arbitron Metro Market: Glen Elder, KS
Julie Marshall, General Manager

Nebraska City

KNCY
06-29-1959; 1600 khz AM *Hrs Open:* 24; 0.5 kw-D, DA2; 0.031 kw-N, DA2; N40 40 27 W95 53 8
7301 West 129 Th St., Suite 130, Overland Park, KS 66213 US
(402) 873-3348, *Fax:* (402) 873-7882
www.kncycountry.com
kncy@kncycountry.com
License: Nebraska City, NE held by Riverfront Broadcasting LLC
Nat'l Network: ABC
Format: Variety/Diverse *Special Programming:* Farm 3 hrs, sports 6 hrs wkly *Hrs. of News Programming:* news progmg 21 hrs wkly *No. News Employees:* 2 *Target Audience:* 18-80; local residents, farmers, businessowners, workers, students *Adv. Rates:* 10; 10; 10; 5
Scott Kooistra, General Manager
Chris Yates, General Sales Mgr

KBBX-FM
02-01-1995; 97.7 mhz FM *Hrs Open:* 24; 99 kw; 978 ft.; N40 53 27 W96 9 11
P.O. Box 693, Milwaukee, WI 53201 US
(402) 884-0968, *Fax:* (402) 884-4754
www.radiolobo977.com
info@z92.com
License: Nebraska City, Otoe County, NE held by Connoisseur Media of Omaha LLC..
Group Owner: Connoisseur Media LLC; (acq 9-25-2006; $7.5 million).
Nat'l Network: ABC *Regional Network:* Southwest Agri-Radio
Arbitron Metro Market: Omaha-Lincoln *Format:* Tejano *Target Audience:* 25-54.
Tom Land, Operations Dir
Steve Wexler, General Manager
Jim Timm, General Sales Mgr
Kurt Owens, Programming Director
RosAnna Salcido, Promotions Manager
Bill Jensen, News Director

New Castle

***KTUN(FM)**
74.5 mhz FM; 3 kw; Ant 328 ft; N40 59 52 W97 16 02
1201 18th Street, Suite 250, Denver, CO 75063
License: New Castle, CO held by Wildcat Communications LLC
Population Served: 860 *Arbitron Metro Market:* Utica, NE
I. Johnson, President

Norfolk

KQKX
08-01-1971; 106.7 mhz FM *Hrs Open:* 24; 100 kw; Ant 1,027 ft; N41 55 59 W97 40 49
Mailing Address: Box 789, Norfolk, NE 68701
Second Address: 309 Braasch Ave., Norfolk, NE 68701
(402) 371-0780, *Fax:* (402) 371-6303
www.kexl.com
bhughes@kexl.com
License: Norfolk, Madison County, NE held by WJAG Inc.
Group Owner: WJAG Inc.
Nat'l Network: Fox News Radio; Westwood One *Wire Services:* AP
Population Served: 100,000*Hrs. of News Programming:* news progmg 6 hrs wkly *No. News Employees:* 2 *Target Audience:* 18-49; full service FM adults *Adv. Rates:* 25; 23; 25; 20
Bradley Hughes, Operations Dir
Sally Lewis, General Sales Mgr
Michael Nissen, Programming Director
Jim Curry, News Director
Susan Risinger, Farm Director
Jeffrey Steffen, Operations Manager
Joe Tjaden, Sports Commentator
DeniseReikofski, Traffic Manager

KNEN
04-06-1979; 94.7 mhz FM; 100 kw; 539 ft.; N41 55 28 W97 36 22
Box 937, 300 Madison Ave, Norfolk, NE 68702 US
(402) 371-0100, *Fax:* (402) 371-0050
www.knenfm.com
License: Norfolk, Madison County, NE held by Red Beacon Communications LLC.
Format: Classic Rock *Special Programming:* Farm 10 hrs wkly *Hrs. of News Programming:* news progmg 15 hrs wkly *No. News Employees:* 2 *Target Audience:* 25-54; young to middle-aged *Adv. Rates:* 19.50;19.50; 19.50; 18.50
Andy Stenger, General Manager

***KPNO**
09-23-1992; 90.9 mhz FM *Hrs Open:* 24; 100 kw; 338 ft.; N42 6 16 W97 20 11

Box 8, Aurora, NE 68818 US
(402) 379-3677, *Fax:* (402) 379-3662
www.goodnewsgreatmusic.com
email@goodnewsgreatmusic.com
License: Norfolk, Madison County, NE held by The Praise Network Inc.
Nat'l Network: Moody; USA
Format: Religious *Hrs. of News Programming:* News progmg 14 hrs wkly *Target Audience:* 25-54; family-oriented adults
Herb Roszhart Jr., CEO
Jon Shipman, General Manager
Brian Gall, Station Manager

***KXNE-FM**
05-29-1990; 89.3 mhz FM *Hrs Open:* 24; 42.3 kw; 984 ft; N42 14 15 W97 16 41 *Rebroadcasts:* Rebroadcasts KUCV(FM) Lincoln 100%
1800 N. 33rd St., Lincoln, NE 68501
(402) 472-3611, *Fax:* (402) 472-2403
netnebraska.org/radio
radio@netnebraska.org
License: Norfolk, Madison County, NE held by Nebraska Educational Telecommunications Commission
Nat'l Network: NPR; APM; PRI *Regional Network:* NET Radio *Hrs. of News Programming:* news progmg 45 hrs wkly *No. News Employees:* 8 *Target Audience:* General.
Rod Bates, General Manager
Nancy Finken, Station Manager
Susan Dinsmore, General Sales Mgr
Nancy Finken, Programming Director
Mary Jane Winquest, Promotions Manager
Dennis Kellogg, News Director
Stacey Decker, Engineering Dir
William Stibor, Music Director
Jeff Smith, Operations

WJAG
07-27-1922; 780 khz AM *Hrs Open:* Sunrise-sunset; 1 kw-D, NDD; N42 1 54 W97 29 47
Mailing Address: P. O. Box 789, 309 Braasch Avenue, Norfolk, NE 68701 US
Second Address: 309 Braasch Ave., Norfolk, NE 68701
(402) 371-0780, *Fax:* (402) 371-6303
www.wjag.com
bhughes@wjag.com
License: Norfolk, NE held by WJAG Inc.
Group Owner: WJAG Inc.
Nat'l Network: ABC; ESPN Radio *Wire Services:* AP
Format: News, News/Talk, 84, Talk *Hrs. of News Programming:* news progmg 10 hrs wkly *No. News Employees:* 2 *Target Audience:* 35-64; info-oriented
Bradley Hughes, Operations Dir
Sally Lewis, General Sales Mgr
Michael Nissen, Programming Director
Stephanie Hoff, Promotions Manager
Jim Curry, News Director
Susan Risinger, Farm Director
Jeffrey Steffen, Operations Manager
Joe Tjaden, Sports Commentator

***KLSB**
91.7 mhz FM; 8 kw; Ant 454 ft; N42 04 54 W97 48 55
Box 159, Rural Hall, NC
(605) 868-0525
License: Norfolk, Madison County, NE held by Church Planters of America.
Danny Hawkins, President

North Platte

KELN
02-01-1979; 97.1 mhz FM *Hrs Open:* 24; 100 kw; 459 ft.; N41 14 20 W100 41 43
Mailing Address: P.O. Box 817, 2703 Hall Street, Hays, KS 67601 US
Second Address: 1301 E. 4th St., North Platte, NE 69103
(308) 532-1120, *Fax:* (308) 532-0458
mix97one.com
License: North Platte, Lincoln County, NE held by Eagle Communications Inc.
Group Owner: Eagle Communications Group; (acq 1982)
Wire Services: AP
Arbitron Metro Market: North Platte, NE *Format:* Adult Contemp *Hrs. of News Programming:* news progmg one hr wkly *No. News Employees:* 1 *Target Audience:* 21-44; Young adults *Adv. Rates:* same as KOOQ
Gary Shorman, President
Dave Lee, Operations Dir
Jerome Gilg, General Manager
Scott Olesky, General Sales Mgr
David Fudge, Programming Director
Dianne Morales, Promotions Manager
Kris Allen, News Director
Tony Cuesta,Engineering Dir

***KJLT**
07-01-1957; 970 khz AM *Hrs Open:* Sunrise-sunset
Mailing Address: P. O. Box 709, North Platte, NE 69103 US
Second Address: 201 S. Bailey Ave., North Platte, NE 69101
(308) 532-5515
www.kjlt.org
kjlt@kjlt.org
License: North Platte, NE held by Tri-State Broadcasting Assn. Inc.
Nat'l Network: Moody; Salem Radio Network *Wire Services:* NOAA Weather; AP
Format: Christian *Special Programming:* Sp one hr wkly *Target Audience:* General; families
John Townsend, President
John L. Townsend, Programming Director
Gary Hofer, Chief Engineer

***KJLT-FM**
09-24-1979; 94.9 mhz FM *Hrs Open:* 24; 100 kw; 755 ft.; N40 59 49 W100 52 47
Mailing Address: P.O. Box 709, North Platte, NE 69103 US
Second Address: 201 S. Bailey Ave., North Platte, NE 69101
(308) 532-5515
www.kjlt.org
License: North Platte, Lincoln County, NE held by Tri-State Broadcasting Assn. Inc.
Nat'l Network: Moody; Salem Radio Network *Wire Services:* AP
Format: Adult Contemp, Gospel, 74 *Target Audience:* General; young adults
Todd Nelson, General Manager

KODY
07-05-1930; 1240 khz AM; 1 kw-U, ND1; N41 9 14 W100 46 23
1001 Farnum-On-The-Mall, Omaha, NE 69102 US
(308) 532-3344, *Fax:* (308) 534-6651
www.kodyradio.com
info@kodyradio.com
License: North Platte, NE held by Armada Media-McCook Inc.
Group Owner: Armada Media Corp.; (acq 5-16-2008; grpsl)
Nat'l Network: CBS; Moody; Westwood One *Nat'l Reps:* Katz Radio
Format: News, News/Talk, 86 *Target Audience:* 25 plus; middle to upper income
Tony Lama, Operations Dir
Rob Mandeville, General Manager
Rob Mandeville, General Sales Mgr
George Keltz, News Director
Lisa Arent, Traffic Manager

KOOQ
01-01-1966; 1410 khz AM *Hrs Open:* 24; 5 kw-D, DAN; 0.5 kw-N, DAN; N41 10 30 W100 45 7
Mailing Address: P.O. Box 817, 2703 Hall Street, Hays, KS 67601 US
Second Address: 1301 E. 4th St., North Platte, NE 69103
(308) 532-1120, *Fax:* (308) 532-0458
1410amespn.com
chuck.schwartz@eagleradio.net
License: North Platte, NE held by Eagle Communications Inc.
Group Owner: Eagle Communications Group
Nat'l Network: ESPN Radio
Format: Sports *Hrs. of News Programming:* news prmrg one hour/week *No. News Employees:* 1 *Target Audience:* 18-45; males *Adv. Rates:* 16; 15; 15; 12
Gary Shorman, President
Chuck Schwartz, General Manager
Jerome Gilg, General Sales Mgr
David Fudge, Programming Director
Dianne Morales, Promotions Manager
Tony Cuesta, Chief Engineer

***KPNE-FM**
07-01-1991; 91.7 mhz FM *Hrs Open:* 24; 16.5 kw horiz, 81 kw vert; 843 ft; N41 01 21 W101 09 13 *Rebroadcasts:* Rebroadcasts KUCV(FM) Lincoln 100%
Mailing Address: 1800 N. 33rd St., Lincoln, NE 68501
Second Address: NE
(402) 472-3611, *Fax:* (402) 472-2403
netnebraska.org
radio@netnebraska.org
License: North Platte, Lincoln County, NE held by Nebraska Educational Telecommunications Commission
Nat'l Network: NPR; APM; PRI *Regional Network:* NET Radio *Hrs. of News Programming:* 45 hrs wkly *No. News Employees:* 8 *Target Audience:* General
Rod Bates, General Manager
Nancy Finken, Station Manager
Susan Dinsmore, General Sales Mgr
Nancy Finken, Programming Director
Mary Jane Winquest, Promotions Manager
Dennis Kellogg, News Director
Stacey Decker, Engineering Dir
William Stibor, Music Director
Jeff Smith, Operations

KXNP
06-07-1982; 103.5 mhz FM *Hrs Open:* 24; 100 kw; 479 ft.; N41 12 49 W100 43 48
1001 Farnam-On-The-Mall, Omaha, NE 68102 US
(308) 532-3344, *Fax:* (308) 534-6651
www.tlama.com
info@kodyradio.com
License: North Platte, Lincoln County, NE held by Armada Media-McCook Inc.
Group Owner: Armada Media Corp.; (acq 5-16-2008; grpsl)
Nat'l Network: Jones Radio Networks
Arbitron Metro Market: North Platte, NE *Format:* Country
Lisa Arent, News Director

***KFJS**
07-16-2012; 90.1 mhz FM; 1400 w; 421 ft; N41 12 13 W100 43 58
13326 A Street, Omaha, NE
(402) 571-0200
www.spiritcatholicradio.com
kvss@kvss.com
License: North Platte, Lincoln County, NE
Group Owner: Vss Catholic Communications
Jim Carroll, Executive Director
Bruce McGregor, Program Director
Bernie Schaefer, Development Director

O'Neill

KBRX
11-01-1955; 1350 khz AM *Hrs Open:* 24; 1 kw-D, ND2; 0.044 kw-N, ND2; N42 27 34 W98 39 23
Mailing Address: 250 North Jefferson St., PO Box 150, O'Neill, NE 68763 US
Second Address: 251 N. Jefferson St., O'Neill, NE
(402) 336-1612, *Fax:* (402) 336-3585
www.kbrx.com
Gil@kbrx,com
License: O'Neill, NE held by Ranchland Broadcasting Co. Inc.
Nat'l Network: ABC *Regional Network:* Brownfield *Wire Services:* AP
Format: Classic Rock *Special Programming:* Farm 12 hrs, Ger 6 hrs wkly *Hrs. of News Programming:* news progmg 25 hrs wkly *No. News Employees:* 1 *Target Audience:* 25-65. *Adv. Rates:* 14; 14; 14; 14
Gilbert Poese, President
Scott Poese, General Manager

KBRX-FM
12-01-1973; 102.9 mhz FM *Hrs Open:* 24; 100 kw; Ant 500 ft; N42 26 06 W98 33 39
Box 150, 251 N. Jefferson, O'Neill, NE 68763
(402) 336-1612, *Fax:* (402) 336-3585
www.kbrx.com
scott@kbrx.com
License: O'Neill, Holt County, NE held by Ranchland Broadcasting Co. Inc.
Nat'l Network: ABC *Regional Network:* Brownfield *Wire Services:* AP
Population Served: 45,000*No. News Employees:* 1 *Target Audience:* 25-60. *Adv. Rates:* 17; 17; 17; 13
Gil Poese, President
Scott Poese, General Manager
Scott Poese, General Sales Mgr

Ogallala

KMCX-FM
01-01-1975; 106.5 mhz FM *Hrs Open:* 24; 100 kw; 315 ft.; N41 8 2 W101 41 42
600 Congress Avenue, Suite 1400, Austin, TX 78701 US
(308) 284-3633, *Fax:* (308) 284-3517
www.4koga.com,www.kmcx.com
License: Ogallala, Keith County, NE held by Capstar TX L.P.
Group Owner: Clear Channel Communications Inc.; (acq 8-30-2000; grpsl).
Format: Country *Special Programming:* Farm 2 hrs wkly *Hrs. of News Programming:* news progmg 10 hrs wkly *No. News Employees:* 1 *Target Audience:* 25-54; general
Corey Andersen, Operations Dir
Katrina Twomey, General Manager
John Brandt, General Sales Mgr
Susan Jones, News Director
Dave Geho, Chief Engineer

KOGA
01-23-1955; 930 khz AM; 5 kw-D, DA2; 0.5 kw-N, DA2; N41 8 32 W101 42 48
Mailing Address: 600 Congress Avenue, Suite 1400, Austin, TX 78701 US
Second Address: 113 W. 4th St., Ogallala, NE 69153
(308) 284-3633, *Fax:* (308) 284-3517
www.4koga.com
thelake@lakemac.net
License: Ogallala, NE held by Capstar TX L.P.
Group Owner: Clear Channel Communications Inc.; (acq 8-30-00; grpsl).
Format: Oldies *Special Programming:* Farm 10 hrs wkly
Corey Anderson, Operations Dir
Katrina Twomby, General Manager
John Brandt, General Sales Mgr
Tracey Knapp, Programming Director
Greg Holl, News Director
Dave Geho, Chief Engineer

KOGA-FM
11-01-1978; 99.7 mhz FM *Hrs Open:* 24; 100 kw; 804 ft.; N41 3 50 W101 20 16
Mailing Address: 600 Congress Avenue, Suite 1400, Austin, TX 78701 US
Second Address: 113 W. 4th St., Ogallala, NE 69153
(308) 284-3633, *Fax:* (308) 284-3517
997thelake.com
License: Ogallala, Keith County, NE
Group Owner: Clear Channel Communications Inc.
Format: Rock/AOR
Greg Hill, News Director

Omaha

KOTK
03-02-1957; 1420 khz AM; 1 kw-D, DA2; 0.33 kw-N, DA2; N41 11 59 W95 54 34
P.O. Box 693, Milwaukee, WI 53201 US
(402) 422-1600, *Fax:* (402) 422-1602
www.1420kotk.com
anunez@salemomaha.com
License: Omaha, NE held by Pennsylvania Media Associates Inc.
Group Owner: Salem Communications Corp.; (acq 12-7-2005; $900,000)
Nat'l Reps: Salem
Arbitron Metro Market: Omaha, NB *Format:* Religious
Mike Shane, Operations Dir
Greg Vogt, General Manager
Jim Leedham, Chief Engineer

KCRO
03-01-1922; 660 khz AM
3615 Dodge Street, Omaha, NE 68131 US
(402) 422-1600, *Fax:* (402) 422-1602
www.kcro.com
License: Omaha, NE held by Salem Media of Illinois LLC.
Group Owner: Salem Communications Corp.; (acq 9-1-2005; $3.1 million).
Nat'l Network: Salem Radio Network *Nat'l Reps:* Salem
Arbitron Metro Market: Omaha-Council Bluffs, NE-IA *Format:* Christian, Talk
Greg Vogt, General Manager
Sue Garrett, General Sales Mgr
Jim Leedham, Chief Engineer
Peggy Holzapfel, Business Manager

KISO
10-21-1983; 96.1 mhz FM *Hrs Open:* 24; 100 kw; Ant 1,414 ft; N41 04 14 W96 13 33
5010 Underwood Avenue, Omaha, NE 68132
(402) 561-2000, *Fax:* (402) 558-8937
www.961thebrew.com
info@kqbw.com
License: Omaha, Douglas County, NE held by Clear Channel Broadcasting Licenses Inc.
Group Owner: Clear Channel Communications Inc.; (acq 10-9-2003; $10.5 million).
Population Served: 537,700 *Arbitron Metro Market:* Omaha-Council Bluffs, NE-IA *Hrs. of News Programming:* news progmg one hr wkly *No. News Employees:* 1
Donna Baker, General Manager
Jean St. James, General Sales Mgr
Tom Stanton, Promotions Manager
Greg Grade, Chief Engineer

KEZO-FM
05-15-1961; 92.3 mhz FM; 95 kw; 1184 ft.; N41 18 16 W96 1 41
11128 John Galt Blvd., Suite 192, Omaha, NE 68137 US
(402) 592-5300, *Fax:* (402) 592-6605
www.z92.com
info@z92.com
License: Omaha, Douglas County, NE held by Journal Broadcast Corp.
Group Owner: Journal Communications Inc.; (acq 11-29-94; $9 million with co-located AM;
Arbitron Metro Market: Omaha-Council Bluffs, NE-IA *Format:* Rock/AOR
Rob Burton, General Manager
Jim Spector, Programming Director
Brian Delehant, Promotions Manager
Susie Copenhaver, News Director

KFAB
01-01-1924; 1110 khz AM *Hrs Open:* 24; 50 kw-D, DAN; 50 kw-N, DAN; N41 7 11 W96 0 6
600 Congress Avenue, Suite 1400, Austin, TX 78701 US
(402) 561-2000, *Fax:* (402) 556-8937
www.kfab.org
License: Omaha, NE held by Capstar TX L.P.
Group Owner: Clear Channel Communications Inc.; (acq 8-30-2000; grpsl)
Nat'l Network: ABC *Nat'l Reps:* Christal
Arbitron Metro Market: Omaha-Council Bluffs, NE-IA *Format:* News, News/Talk, 86 *Special Programming:* Farm 5 hrs wkly *Hrs. of News Programming:* news progmg 6 hrs wkly *No. News Employees:* 3 *Target Audience:* 35-64.
Michelle Matthews, Operations Dir
Taylor Walet, General Manager
Marnie Simpson, General Sales Mgr
Gary Sadlemyer, Programming Director
Kevin Simonson, Promotions Manager
Tom Stanton, News Director
Greg Gade, Chief Engineer
RichDenison, News Reporter
Jim Rose, Sports Commentator
Sarah McCabe, Traffic Manager

KGBI-FM
05-17-1966; 100.7 mhz FM *Hrs Open:* 24; 100 kw; 1014 ft.; N41 18 40 W96 1 37
1311 South 9th Street, Omaha, NE 68108 US
(402) 422-1600, *Fax:* (402) 422-1602
www.kgbifm.com
kgbi@kgbifm.com
License: Omaha, Douglas County, NE held by Pennsylvania Media Associates Inc.
Group Owner: Salem Communications Corp.; (acq 1-31-2005; $8 million).
Nat'l Reps: Salem
Arbitron Metro Market: Omaha,NE *Format:* Christian *Hrs. of News Programming:* news progmg 28 hrs wkly *No. News Employees:* 1 *Target Audience:* 25-54; conservative, Evangelical
Mike Shane, Operations Dir
Greg Vogt, General Manager
Jim Leedham, Chief Engineer

KGOR
01-01-1959; 99.9 mhz FM *Hrs Open:* 24; 110 kw; 1214 ft.; N41 18 29 W96 1 36
600 Congress Avenue, Suite 1400, Austin, TX 78701 US
(402) 561-2000, *Fax:* (402) 556-8937
www.kgor.com
annmariekrahulec@clearchannel.com
License: Omaha, Douglas County, NE held by Capstar TX L.P.
Group Owner: Clear Channel Communications Inc.
Arbitron Metro Market: Omaha-Council, NE *Format:* Contemporary Hits/Top 40 *No. News Employees:* 1 *Target Audience:* 35-54.
Meg Delone, General Sales Mgr
Lester St. James, Programming Director
Tom Stanton, News Director

***KIOS-FM**
09-15-1969; 91.5 mhz FM; 55 kw; 554 ft.; N41 17 15 W95 59 37
3230 Burt Street, Omaha, NE 68131 US
(402) 557-2777, *Fax:* (402) 557-2559
www.kios.org
edward.mcgrath@ops.org,listener@kios.org
License: Omaha, Douglas County, NE held by Douglas County School District 001.
Nat'l Network: NPR; PRI *Wire Services:* AP
Arbitron Metro Market: Omaha-Council Bluffs, NE-IA *Format:* Jazz, News *Special Programming:* Local Jazz 15 hrs wkly *No. News Employees:* 1
Molly Nicklin, Operations Dir
Bob Coate, Station Manager
Edward McGrath, General Sales Mgr
Katie Knapp, News Director
Richard Dennis, Chief Engineer
Mike Jacobs, Music Director

KOIL
03-01-1925; 1290 khz AM *Hrs Open:* 24; 5 kw-U, DA-N; N41 11 20 W96 00 21
5011 Capitol Ave., Omaha, NE 68102
(402) 342-2000, *Fax:* (402) 346-5748
www.1290kkar.com
info@1290kkar.com
License: Omaha, Douglas County, NE held by Waitt Omaha LLC.
Group Owner: Waitt Omaha LLC; (acq 1-7-2002; grpsl)
Nat'l Network: ABC; Fox News Radio; Jones Radio Networks; Premiere Radio Networks; Talk Radio Network *Nat'l Reps:* Katz Radio
Population Served: 346,929 *Arbitron Metro Market:* Omaha-Council Bluffs, NE-IA *Target Audience:* General. *Adv. Rates:* 100; 100; 100; 45
Mark Todd, Operations Dir
Jim McKernan, General Manager
Rhonda Gerrard, General Sales Mgr
Neil Nelkin, Programming Director
Terry Leahy, News Director
Darwin Stinton, Chief Engineer
Tim Marshall, Sales Manager
Lori Storz,Traffic Manager

KKCD
08-11-1990; 105.9 mhz FM *Hrs Open:* 24; 50 kw; 479 ft.; N41 12 4 W95 57 12
11128 John Galt Blvd., Suite 192, Omaha, NE 68137 US
(402) 592-5300, *Fax:* (402) 331-1348
www.cd1059.com
info@cd1059.com
License: Omaha, Douglas County, NE held by Journal Broadcast Corp.
Group Owner: Journal Communications Inc.; (acq 2-95; $3.55 million;
Nat'l Network: AP Network News
Arbitron Metro Market: Omaha, NE *Format:* Classic Rock *Special Programming:* Jazz 4 hrs, blues one hr, reggae one hr wkly *Hrs. of News Programming:* news progmg 10 hrs wkly *No. News Employees:* 1 *TargetAudience:* 25-54.
Steve Wexler, Operations Dir
Ros Mercio, General Sales Mgr
Jim Spector, Programming Director
Brian Delehant, Promotions Manager
Bill Jensen, News Director
John Gaeta, Chief Engineer

KOMJ
03-01-1942; 1490 khz AM *Hrs Open:* 24
P.O. Box 693, Milwaukee, WI 53201 US
(402) 592-5300,(402) 898-5300, *Fax:* (402) 331-1348
License: Omaha, NE held by Cochise Broadcasting LLC.
Group Owner: Cochise Broadcasting LLC; (acq 3-27-2007; $500,000)
Arbitron Metro Market: Omaha-Council Bluffs, NE-IA *Format:* Adult Contemp *No. News Employees:* 1 *Target Audience:* 18-49.
Tom Land, Operations Dir
Kathy Hedstrom, General Sales Mgr
Kurt Owens, Programming Director
Heath Hedstrom, Promotions Manager
Bill Jensen, News Director
John Gaeta, Chief Engineer
Cheryl Brye, Traffic Manager

KSRZ
05-12-1972; 104.5 mhz FM; 98 kw; 1088 ft.; N41 18 16 W96 1 41
P.O. Box 693, Milwaukee, WI 53201 US
(402) 592-5300, *Fax:* (402) 592-6605
www.104star.com
info@104star.com
License: Omaha, Douglas County, NE held by Journal Broadcast Corp.
Group Owner: Journal Communications Inc.; (acq 1-98; $5.475 million with co-located AM)
Arbitron Metro Market: Omaha, NE *Format:* Adult Contemp
Tom Land, Operations Dir
Steve Wexler, General Manager
Jim Timm, Station Manager
Kris Christiansen, General Sales Mgr
Kurt Owens, Programming Director
Stephanie Chandler, Promotions Manager
Kathi Knutson, News Director
JohnGaeta, Chief Engineer
Jill Butler, General Sales Manager
Dave Swan, Music Director

***KVNO**
08-27-1972; 90.7 mhz FM *Hrs Open:* 24; 8.9 kw; 646 ft.; N41 18 25 W96 1 37
60th and Dodge Street, Engg 202, Omaha, NE 68182 US
(402) 559-5866, *Fax:* (402) 554-2440
www.kvno.org
info@kvno.com
License: Omaha, Douglas County, NE held by University of Nebraska Board of Regents.
Arbitron Metro Market: Omaha-Council Bluffs, NE-IA *Format:* Talk *Hrs. of News Programming:* news progmg 2.5 hrs wkly *No. News Employees:* 1 *Target Audience:* General.
Dana Buckingham, Operations Dir
Robert Franklin, General Manager
James Arey, Programming Director
Anne Hellbusch, Promotions Manager
Robyn Wisch, News Director
Frank Vacek, Engineering Dir
Dave Kline, Engineering Dir
DanaBuckingham, Assistant General Manager
Frank Vacek, Engineering Services Manager
Anne Hellbusch, Marketing Mnager
Robyn Wisch, News Director
Lindsey Petersson, News Reporters

***KVSS**
01-09-1999; 102.7 mhz FM *Hrs Open:* 24; 1 kw; 380 ft; N41 18 40 W96 01 37
Mailing Address: 68506
Second Address: 5829 N. 60th St., Omaha, NE 68104
(402) 571-0200, *Fax:* (402) 571-0833
www.bbnradio.org
kvss@kvss.com
License: Omaha, NE held by Bible Broadcasting Network Inc.
Group Owner: Bible Broadcasting Network; (acq 3-4-2009; $825,000)
Arbitron Metro Market: Omaha-Council Bluffs, NE-IA *Target Audience:* General.
Jim Taphorn, CFO
Lowell Davey, President
Mike Delich, Operations Dir
Jim Carroll, General Manager
Vicki Sempek, General Sales Mgr
Bruce McGregor, Programming Director
T. Scott Marr, News Director
Chuck Ramold, ChiefEngineer
Mary Beth Jorgensen, General Sales Manager
D. Ann Yeoman, Operations Manager

KXSP
04-02-1923; 590 khz AM *Hrs Open:* 24; 5 kw-U, ND1; N41 19 0 W95 59 52
3355 S. Valley View Blvd., Las Vegas, NV 89102 US
(402) 592-5300, *Fax:* (402) 331-1348
www.bigsports590.com
info@bigsports590.com
License: Omaha, NE held by Journal Broadcast Corp.
Group Owner: Journal Communications Inc.; (acq 10-26-98 with co-located FM).
Arbitron Metro Market: Omaha-Council Bluffs, NE-IA *Format:* Sports *No. News Employees:* 4 *Target Audience:* General.
Tom Land, Operations Dir
Steve Wexler, General Manager
Jim Timm, General Sales Mgr
Bill Jensen, News Director
John Gaeta, Chief Engineer
Cheryl Brye, Traffic Manager

KQCH
01-01-1959; 94.1 mhz FM *Hrs Open:* 24; 95 kw; 1184 ft.; N41 18 16 W96 1 41
3355 S. Valley View Blvd., Las Vegas, NV 89102 US
(402) 592-5300, *Fax:* (402) 331-1348
License: Omaha, Douglas County, NE
Group Owner: Journal Communications Inc.
Wire Services: Weather Wire; Reuters
Arbitron Metro Market: Omaha-Council Bluffs, NE-IA *Format:* Adult Contemp *Target Audience:* 25-54.
Jill Butler, General Sales Mgr
Erik Johnson, Programming Director
Larkin Cavanaugh, Promotions Manager
Kathi Knutson, News Director
Peter Shinn, Farm Director
Bill Jensen, News Reporter

Orchard

***KGRD**
06-14-1987; 105.3 mhz FM *Hrs Open:* 24; 100 kw; 502 ft.; N42 20 45 W98 25 5
P.O. Box 8, Aurora, NE 68818 US
(402) 336-3886
www.kgrd.org
email@goodnewsmusic.org
License: Orchard, Antelope County, NE held by The Praise Network Inc.
Nat'l Network: Salem Radio Network *Wire Services:* AP
Format: Christian, Religious *Hrs. of News Programming:* News progmg 10 hrs wkly *Target Audience:* 35-54.
Lloyd Mintzmeyer, President
Todd Gunnarson, Station Manager
Bill Taylor, Programming Director

Ord

KNLV
07-15-1965; 1060 khz AM *Hrs Open:* 24
205 South 16th Street, Ord, NE 68862 US
(308) 728-3263, *Fax:* (308) 728-3264
knlv@yahoo.com
License: Ord, NE held by Sandhills Advertising Corp.
Nat'l Network: ABC *Wire Services:* AP
Format: Oldies *Special Programming:* Farm 8 hrs, Pol/Czeck/Bohemian 4 hrs wkly *Target Audience:* 25-64.
Johnnie James, General Manager
Gene McCoy, General Sales Mgr
Jeannie Neidhardt, Promotions Manager
Johnnie James, News Director
Randy Faaborg, Chief Engineer
Kristen Miller, Traffic Manager

KNLV-FM
07-10-1981; 103.9 mhz FM *Hrs Open:* 24; 30 kw; Ant 638 ft; N41 34 17 W98 55 21
205 S. 16th St., Ord, NE 68862
(308) 728-3263, *Fax:* (308) 728-3264
License: Ord, Valley County, NE held by Sandhills Advertising Corp.
Nat'l Network: ABC *Wire Services:* AP
Population Served: 7,200*Special Programming:* Farm 8 hours
Target Audience: 18-54. *Adv. Rates:* 14; 14; 13; 6
Johnnie James, Station Manager
Gene McCoy, General Sales Mgr
Johnnie James rdt, Promotions Manager
Val Lane, Chief Engineer
Amber Whited, Traffic Manager

Overton

***KHZY**
01-01-2007; 99.3 mhz FM; 100 kw; 751 ft.; N40 41 49 W99 47 16
Rebroadcasts: Rebroadcasts KSRD(FM) Saint Joseph, MO 100%
US
(816) 233-5773, *Fax:* (816) 233-5777
www.ksrdradio.com
License: Overton, Dawson County, NE held by Horizon Christian Fellowship.
Group Owner: Horizon Christian Fellowship; (acq 2-9-2006; grpsl)
Arbitron Metro Market: Overton, NE *Format:* Christian
Mike MacIntosh, President
Brian KC Jones, General Manager

Paxton

KZTL
01-01-2007; 93.5 mhz FM; 100 kw; 753 ft.; N41 3 50 W101 20 16 US
(308) 532-5767, *Fax:* (308) 535-9100
www.wildcountry935.com
License: Paxton, Keith County, NE held by Legacy Communications LLC.
Group Owner: Legacy Communications LLC; (acq 8-14-2007; $475,000 for CP with CP for KRNP(FM) Sutherland)
Arbitron Metro Market: Paxton, NE *Format:* Country
Alan Usher, General Manager

Pierce

KEXL
11-05-2009; 97.5 mhz FM; 6.5 kw; 463 ft.; N42 19 17 W97 25 40 US
(402)371-0780, *Fax:* (402)371-6303
www.literock97.com
License: Pierce, Pierce County, NE held by WJAG Inc
Group Owner: WJAG Inc.
Format: Light Rock
Bradley Hughes, General Manager

Plattsmouth

KMMQ
10-26-1970; 1020 khz AM *Hrs Open:* Sunrise-sunset
625 First Avenue, Plattsmouth, NE 68048 US
(402) 342-2000, *Fax:* (402) 346-5748
www.radiodisney.com
info@radiodisney.com
License: Plattsmouth, NE held by Waitt Omaha LLC.
Group Owner: Waitt Omaha LLC; (acq 1-17-2001; $750,000)
Nat'l Network: Radio Disney
Arbitron Metro Market: Omaha-Council Bluffs, NE-IA *Format:* Children
Mark Todd, Operations Dir
Jim Kernan, General Manager
Rhonda Gerrard, General Sales Mgr
Neil Nelkin, Programming Director
Terry Leahy, News Director
Darwin Stinton, Chief Engineer
Tim Marshall, Sales Manager
Cynthia Wallace,Traffic Manager

KOPW
07-01-1993; 106.9 mhz FM *Hrs Open:* 24; 25 kw; 328 ft.; N41 9 18 W95 45 42
13906 Gold Circle, Omaha, NE 68144 US
(402) 342-2000, *Fax:* (402) 346-5748
power1069fm.com
info@power1069fm.com
License: Plattsmouth, Cass County, NE held by Platte Broadcasting Co. Inc.
Group Owner: Waitt Omaha LLC
Nat'l Reps: Katz Radio
Arbitron Metro Market: Omaha-Council Bluffs, NE-IA *Format:* Contemporary Hits/Top 40 *Target Audience:* 18-34; gen
Mark Todd, Operations Dir
Jim McKernan, General Manager
Rhonda Gerrard, General Sales Mgr
Bryant McCain, Programming Director
Marcey Gibson, Promotions Manager
Cynthia Wallace, News Director
Sam Coughlin, General Sales Manager

Ponca

***KFHC**
01-01-2008; 88.1 mhz FM; 2.28 kw horiz, 8.8 kw vert; 417 ft.; N42 27 48 W96 37 1.9
P O Box 2140, Northside Station, Sioux City, IA 81104 US
(712) 224-5342, *Fax:* (712) 224-5345
www.fhcradio.com
fhradio@fhradio.com
License: Ponca, Dixon County, NE held by St. Gabriel Communications Ltd.
Nat'l Network: EWTN Radio
Arbitron Metro Market: Sioux City, IA *Format:* Christian
John Fitzsimmons, President
James Cameron, Operations Dir
Ted Warren, General Manager
Renee Gonzalez, General Sales Mgr
John Wolpert, Vice-President
Paul Wolpert, Treasurer/Secretary

Ralston

***KMLV**
07-21-2001; 88.1 mhz FM *Hrs Open:* 24; 59 kw; 1280 ft.; N41 18 40 W96 1 37 *Rebroadcasts:* Rebroadcasts KLVR(FM) Middletown, CA 100%
1425 N. Market Blvd, Suite 9, Sacramento, CA 95834 US
(916) 251-1600, *Fax:* (916) 251-1650
www.klove.com
klove@klove.com
License: Ralston, Douglas County, NE held by Educational Media Foundation.
Group Owner: EMF Broadcasting
Nat'l Network: K-Love
Arbitron Metro Market: Omaha, NE *Format:* Christian *Target Audience:* 25-44; Judeo Christian, female
Mike Novak, President
Jennifer Lohman, Operations Dir

Ravenna

KKJK
06-01-2006; 103.1 mhz FM; 100 kw; 640 ft.; N40 48 57 W98 46 18
Mailing Address: US
Second Address: 3205 W. North Front St., Grand Island, NE 68803

RADIO - U.S.

(308) 381-1430, *Fax:* (308) 382-6701
www.2dayfm1031.com
info@familyradio.com
License: Ravenna, Buffalo County, NE held by Community Radio Inc.
Arbitron Metro Market: Ravenna, NE *Format:* Rock/AOR
Donald Wilks, President
Alan Usher, General Manager

Sargent

KHZZ
01-01-2008; 92.1 mhz FM; 0.11 kw; 52 ft.; N41 38 29 W99 22 12 US
(402) 845-6595, *Fax:* (858) 277-1365
License: Sargent, Custer County, NE held by Horizon Christian Fellowship.
Group Owner: Horizon Christian Fellowship; (acq 2-9-2006; grpsl)
Arbitron Metro Market: Sargent, NE *Format:* Christian
Mike MacIntosh, President

Scottsbluff

KNEB
01-01-1948; 960 khz AM *Hrs Open:* 5 AM-1 AM
P.O. Box 239, Scottsbluff, NE 69363 US
(308) 632-7121, *Fax:* (308) 635-1079
www.kneb.com
kneb@actcom.net
License: Scottsbluff, NE held by Nebraska Rural Radio Association.
Group Owner: Nebraska Rural Radio Association; (acq 8-1-84)
Format: News, News/Talk, 86, Country *Special Programming:* Farm 18 hrs, Sp 5 hrs wkly *No. News Employees:* 2 *Target Audience:* 18 plus. *Adv. Rates:* 70; 70; 50; 25
Larry Hudkins, President
Craig Larson, Station Manager
Kendra Feather, General Sales Mgr
Dennis Ernest, Programming Director

KNEB-FM
12-25-1960; 94.1 mhz FM *Hrs Open:* 5 AM-1 AM; 100 kw; 679 ft.; N41 42 4 W103 40 49
P.O. Box 239, Scottsbluff, NE 69363 US
(308) 632-7121, *Fax:* (308) 635-1079
License: Scottsbluff, Scotts Bluff County, NE
Group Owner: Nebraska Rural Radio Association
Format: Country, Agriculture *Adv. Rates:* Same as AM
Craig Larson, Station Manager
Kendra Feather, General Sales Mgr
Dennis Ernest, Programming Director

KOLT
02-15-1930; 1320 khz AM *Hrs Open:* 24; 5 kw-D, 1 kw-N, DA-N; N41 51 37 W103 41 53
Mailing Address: Box 1263, Scottsbluff, NE 69363
Second Address: 2002 Char Ave., Scottsbluff, NE 69361
(308) 632-5667, *Fax:* (308) 635-1905
www.koltam.com
info@hometownfamilyradio.com
License: Scottsbluff, Scotts Bluff County, NE held by Legacy Communications LLC.
Group Owner: Legacy Communications LLC; (acq 12-13-2007; grpsl)
Nat'l Network: ESPN Radio
Population Served: 15,000
Alan Usher, CEO/COO

*KLJV
02-20-2003; 88.3 mhz FM *Hrs Open:* 24; 0.39 kw; 781 ft.; N41 50 21 W103 49 53
US
(800) 525-5683, *Fax:* (916) 251-1650
www.klove.com
klove@klove.com
License: Scottsbluff, Scotts Bluff County, NE held by Educational Media Foundation.
Group Owner: EMF Broadcasting
Nat'l Network: K-Love
Arbitron Metro Market: Scottsbluff, NE *Format:* Christian *No. News Employees:* 13 *Target Audience:* 25-44.
Darrell Chambliss, Chairman
Mike Novak, President and CEO
Jennifer Lohman, Operations Dir
David Pierce, Chief Creative Officer and Programming Director
Ed Lenane, News Director
Sam Wallington, Engineering Dir
Marya Morgan, NewsReporter
Richard Hunt, News Reporter
Alan Mason, Chief Operating Officer
Dan Antonelli, Chief Business Development Officer
Eric Moser, Chief Financial Officer
Brian Burger, Vice President of Human Resources

*KDAI
01-01-2008; 89.1 mhz FM; 1.4 kw; 781 ft.; N41 50 21 W103 49 53 *Rebroadcasts:* Rebroadcasts KLRD(FM) Yucaipa, CA 100% US
(800) 877-5600, *Fax:* (916) 251-1650
www.air1.com
info@air1.com
License: Scottsbluff, Scotts Bluff County, NE held by Educational Media Foundation.
Group Owner: EMF Broadcasting; (acq 7-23-2007; grpsl)
Nat'l Network: Air 1
Arbitron Metro Market: Scottsbluff, NE *Format:* Alternative, Christian
Mike Novak, President

Seward

KZKX
11-12-1976; 96.9 mhz FM; 100 kw; 610 ft; N41 07 26 W96 50 03
3800 Cornhusker Hwy., Lincoln, NE 78701
(402) 466-1234, *Fax:* (402) 467-4095
www.threeeagles.com
jpatten@threeeagles.com
License: Seward, Seward County, NE held by Three Eagles of Lincoln Inc.
Group Owner: Three Eagles Communications; (acq 4-10-2007; grpsl)
Population Served: 262,341 *Arbitron Metro Market:* Lincoln, NE *Target Audience:* 25-54.
James Keck, General Manager

Shubert

*KSSH
91.3 mhz FM; kw
US
(620) 225-8080, *Fax:* (620) 225-6655
License: Shubert, Richardson County, NE held by Ron Elmore Ministries Inc.
Arbitron Metro Market: Dodge City, KS
Ron Elmore, President

Sidney

KSID
06-02-1952; 1340 khz AM *Hrs Open:* 24; 1 kw-U, ND1; N41 7 50 W102 58 15
P. O. Box 37, Sidney, NE 69162 US
(308) 254-5803, *Fax:* (308) 254-5901
www.ksibradio.com
License: Sidney, NE held by KSID Radio Inc.
Arbitron Metro Market: Sidney, NE *Format:* Country *Special Programming:* Farm 5 hrs wkly *Target Audience:* General. *Adv. Rates:* 15; 15; 15; na
Elizabeth Young, President
Suzy Ernest, General Manager
Lana Butts, General Sales Mgr
Hunter Arterburn, Programming Director
Dave Collins, News Director
Dennis Brothers, Chief Engineer
Jean Spruckmeyer, Traffic Manager

KSID-FM
09-13-1974; 98.7 mhz FM; 62 kw; 371 ft.; N41 11 3 W103 11 37
P. O. Box 37, Sidney, NE 69162 US
(308) 254-5803, *Fax:* (308) 254-5901
www.ksibradio.com
License: Sidney, Cheyenne County, NE
Arbitron Metro Market: Sidney, NE *Format:* Adult Contemp
Suzy Ernest, General Manager
Lana Butts, General Sales Mgr
Hunter Arterburn, Programming Director
Dave Collins, News Director

South Sioux City

KSFT-FM
01-01-1997; 107.1 mhz FM *Hrs Open:* 24; 2.3 kw; 325 ft.; N42 32 16 W96 26 58
Mailing Address: P.O. Box 3009, Sioux City, IA 51102 US
Second Address: 1113 Nebraska St., Sioux City, IA 51102
(712) 258-6740, *Fax:* (712) 252-2430
www.kiss107siouxcity.com
License: South Sioux City, Dakota County, NE held by AMFM Radio Licenses LLC.
Group Owner: Clear Channel Communications Inc.; (acq 10-1-2002; grpsl)
Nat'l Reps: Katz Radio
Arbitron Metro Market: Sioux City, IA *Format:* Oldies *Target Audience:* 12-35.
Rob Powers, Operations Dir
Mike Newhouse, General Sales Mgr
Rob Powers, Programming Director
Laura Schiltz, Promotions Manager
Monica Mattoon, News Director
Stan Culley, Chief Engineer
Shirley Dicus, Business Manager
RhondaJohnson, Promotions Manager

Superior

KRFS
03-17-1959; 1600 khz AM *Hrs Open:* 6 AM-sunset; 0.5 kw-D, ND1; 0.044 kw-N, ND1; N40 1 30 W98 4 38
Route 2 Box 149, Superior, NE 68978 US
(402) 879-4741, *Fax:* (402) 879-4741
www.krfsfm.com
krfsfm@yahoo.com
License: Superior, NE held by CK Broadcasting Inc.
Regional Network: Brownfield
Format: Adult Contemp *Special Programming:* Farm 5 hrs, gospel 3 hrs, relg 3 hrs wkly *Hrs. of News Programming:* News progmg 11 hrs wkly *Target Audience:* 25-55; general *Adv. Rates:* 6; 6; 6; na
Cory Kopsa, General Manager
Marvin Hoffman, Chief Engineer

KRFS-FM
02-25-1977; 103.9 mhz FM *Hrs Open:* 24; 6 kw; 220 ft.; N40 6 20 W98 6 20
Route 2, Box 149, Superior, NE 68978 US
(402) 879-4741, *Fax:* (402) 879-4741
www.krfsfm.com
krfs@yahoo.com
License: Superior, Nuckolls County, NE
Regional Network: Brownfield
Format: Country
Cory Kopsa, News Director

Sutherland

KRNP
01-01-2007; 100.7 mhz FM; 100 kw; 753 ft.; N41 3 50 W101 20 16
US
(308) 532-5767, *Fax:* (308) 535-9100
www.rock100fm.com
License: Sutherland, Lincoln County, NE held by Legacy Communications LLC.
Group Owner: Legacy Communications LLC; (acq 8-14-2007; $475,000 for CP with CP for KZTL(FM) Paxton)
Arbitron Metro Market: Sutherland, NE
Alan Usher, General Manager

Terrytown

KCMI
03-01-1981; 96.9 mhz FM *Hrs Open:* 24; 100 kw; 692 ft.; N41 42 8 W103 41 0
P. O. Box 401, Scottsbluff, NE 69361 US
(308) 632-5264, *Fax:* (308) 635-0104
www.kcmifm.com
info@kcmifm.com
License: Terrytown, Scotts Bluff County, NE held by Christian Media Inc.
Nat'l Network: USA *Regional Network:* Brownfield
Arbitron Metro Market: Terrytown, NE *Format:* Religious *Special Programming:* Class 4 hrs wkly *Hrs. of News Programming:* News progmg 12 hrs wkly *Target Audience:* 25 plus. *Adv. Rates:* 9; 9; 9; 9
Glenn Hascall, General Manager
Gary Almquist, General Sales Mgr
Lorraine Brown, News Director
Sherry Kaiser, Clerk/librarian, Cross Times content editor and co
Lorraine Brown, Office Staff
Elnora Bauer, Office Staff

KOAQ
06-15-1961; 690 khz AM *Hrs Open:* 24; 1 kw-D, DA2; 0.065 kw-N, DA2; N41 50 55 W103 40 2
Mailing Address: P.O. Box 532, Scottsbluff, NE 69363 US
Second Address: 2002 Char Ave., Scottsbluff, NE 69361
(308) 632-5667, *Fax:* (308) 635-1905
www.koaqam.com
info@hometownfamilyradio.com
License: Terrytown, NE held by Legacy Communications LLC.
Group Owner: Legacy Communications LLC; (acq 12-13-2007; grpsl)
Format: Oldies *Target Audience:* 25-54; Baby Boomers

Julie Marshall, General Manager
Mandi Adams, Promotions Manager

Valentine

KVSH
03-06-1961; 940 khz AM *Hrs Open:* 16; 5 kw-D, ND1; 0.019 kw-N, ND1; N42 51 54 W100 31 7
126 W. 3rd Street, Valentine, NE 69201 US
(402) 376-2400, *Fax:* (402) 376-2402
www.kvsh.com
info@kvsh.com
License: Valentine, NE held by Heart City Radio Corp.
Wire Services: AP
Arbitron Metro Market: Valentine, NE *Format:* Country *Hrs. of News Programming:* news progmg 24 hrs wkly *No. News Employees:* 1 *Target Audience:* 35-60; general
Dave Otradovsky, President
Zach Dean, General Sales Mgr
Mike Burge, Programming Director
Kerri, Traffic

***KKNL**
89.3 mhz FM; 0.25 kw; 184 ft.; N42 53 22 W100 33 15 US
(662) 844-5036, *Fax:* (662) 842-7798
www.afr.net
contact@afa.net
License: Valentine, Cherry County, NE held by American Family Association.
Group Owner: American Family Radio
Arbitron Metro Market: Valentine, NE *Format:* Christian
Donald E. Wildmon, Founder
Buster Wilson, General Manager
Jennifer Hagman, Programming Director

***KMBV**
90.7 mhz FM; 0.68 kw; 105 ft.; N42 53 17 W100 33 11 US
(402) 477-1090
www.missionnebraska.org
License: Valentine, Cherry County, NE held by Mission Nebraska Inc.
Group Owner: Mission Nebraska Inc.
Arbitron Metro Market: Valentine, NE *Format:* Country
Stanley Parker, General Manager

Waverly

***KRKR**
03-06-1975; 95.1 mhz FM *Hrs Open:* 24; 50 kw; 276 ft.; N40 58 48 W96 41 46
6900 Van Dorn, Suite 11, Lincoln, NE 68506 US
(402) 466-1234, *Fax:* (402) 467-4095
License: Waverly, Douglas County, NE held by Chapin Enterprises LLC
Arbitron Metro Market: Lincoln, NE *Format:* Adult Contemp, Christian *Hrs. of News Programming:* news progmg 2 hrs wkly *No. News Employees:* 1 *Target Audience:* 25-54.
Mark Taylor, Operations Dir
Scott Kaye, Programming Director
Vicki Marker, Promotions Manager
Dale Johnson, News Director
Bob Cook, Chief Engineer
Teri Hutchinson, Traffic Manager

Wayne

KTCH
03-18-1968; 1590 khz AM *Hrs Open:* 24; 2.5 kw-D, 47 w-N, DA-2; N42 14 03 W97 03 19
Mailing Address: Box 413, W. Hwy. 35, Wayne, NE 68701
Second Address: 85592 574th Avenue, Wayne, NE 68787
(402) 375-3700, *Fax:* (402) 375-5402
www.waynedailynews.com
ktch@ktch.com
License: Wayne, Wayne County, NE held by Wayne Radio Works LLC.
Group Owner: David M. Kelly; (acq 5-30-2008; $450,000 with KCTY(FM) Wayne)
Nat'l Network: CBS *Regional Network:* Brownfield *Nat'l Reps:* Regional Reps *Wire Services:* AP
Population Served: 40,000*Special Programming:* Farm 20 hrs wkly *Hrs. of News Programming:* news progmg 15 hrs wkly *No. News Employees:* 1 *Target Audience:* 30-64. *Adv. Rates:* 8; 8; 8; 7
David M. Kelly, Owner
David M. Kelly, General Manager
Mick Kemp, General Sales Mgr
Dan Baddorf, Programming Director
Joel Janecek, News Director
Tony Wortman, Chief Engineer

***KWSC**
10-13-1971; 91.9 mhz FM; 0.32 kw horiz; 95 ft.; N42 14 30 W97 0 48
1111 Main Street, Wayne, NE 68787 US
(402) 375-7536(402) 375-7426
www.wsc.edu/k92
k92radio@hotmail.com
License: Wayne, Wayne County, NE held by Wayne State College.
Nat'l Network: Westwood One
Format: Alternative, Rock/AOR *Special Programming:* Black 4 hrs, jazz 2 hrs, heavy metal 2 hrs, blues 2 hrs wkly *Target Audience:* 18 plus.
Frank Venturo, General Manager

West Point

KTIC
03-17-1985; 840 khz AM *Hrs Open:* Sunrise-sunset; 5 kw-D, NDD; N41 47 6 W96 40 39
P.O.Box 880, Lexington, NE 68850 US
(402) 372-5423, *Fax:* (402) 372-5425
www.kticam.com
dlane@kticradio.com
License: West Point, NE held by Nebraska Rural Radio Association.
Group Owner: Nebraska Rural Radio Association; (acq 8-1-97; $1.5 million with co-located FM)
Nat'l Network: ABC *Regional Network:* Nebraska Public Radio
Nat'l Reps: Katz Radio *Regional Reps:* Neb. Pub. *Wire Services:* AP
Arbitron Metro Market: West Point, NE *Format:* Country, News *Hrs. of News Programming:* news progmg 20 hrs wkly *No. News Employees:* 1 *Target Audience:* General; farmers, ranchers, stockmen and all involved inagri-business *Adv. Rates:* 70; 70; 70; na
Charlie Brogan, General Manager
Jay Thouvenell, Station Manager
Judy Mauch, General Sales Mgr
Bob Flittie, News Director
Rod Zeigler, Engineering Dir
Vern Killion, Chief Engineer
Randy Koenen, Farm Director
Judy Mauch, GeneralSales Manager
Richard Sterling, Music Director
Tom McMahon, Sports Commentator
Tammie Harrington, Traffic Manager

KTIC-FM
08-01-1988; 107.9 mhz FM *Hrs Open:* 18; 33 kw; 597 ft.; N41 52 53 W97 0 58
P.O.Box 880, Lexington, NE 68850 US
(402) 372-5423, *Fax:* (402) 372-5425
www.kticradio.com
dlane@kticradio.com
License: West Point, Cuming County, NE
Group Owner: Nebraska Rural Radio Association; (Acq 1997)
Nat'l Network: ABC
Arbitron Metro Market: West Point, NE *Format:* Country *Special Programming:* Farm 10 hrs wkly *Hrs. of News Programming:* news progmg 12 hrs wkly *No. News Employees:* 1 *Target Audience:* 25-49; generalaudience, adults *Adv. Rates:* 21; 21; 21; 8
Jay Thouvenell, Station Manager
Randy Koenen, General Sales Mgr
Richard Sterling, Programming Director
Karen Benne, News Director
Rod Zeigler, Engineering Dir
Tom McMahon, Sports Commentator
Karen Benne, FM Traffic Director,Receptionist
Jodi Frye, Am Traffic Director , Receptionist
Judy Mauch, Sales Manager
Tom Goodwin, Production/ Continuity Dirretor
Tom McMahon, Sports Director

Wilber

***KFLV**
03-01-2001; 89.9 mhz FM *Hrs Open:* 24; 5.8 kw; 515 ft.; N40 31 6 W96 46 6
1425 N Market Blvd., Suite 9, Sacramento, CA 95834 US
(707) 538-9236, *Fax:* (707) 538-9246
www.klove.com
klove@klove.com
License: Wilber, Saline County, NE held by Educational Media Foundation.
Group Owner: EMF Broadcasting
Nat'l Network: K-Love
Arbitron Metro Market: Wilber, NE *Format:* Christian *No. News Employees:* 2 *Target Audience:* 25-44; Judeo-Christian, female
Mike Novak, CEO/COO
Mike Novak, President
Jennifer Lohman, Operations Dir
Eric Allen, General Sales Mgr
David Pierce, Programming Director
Ed Lenane, News Director
Sam Wallington, Engineering Dir
Marya Morgan, News Reporter
Richard Hunt, News Reporter

Winnebago

KSUX
06-01-1990; 105.7 mhz FM *Hrs Open:* 24; 50 kw; 463 ft.; N42 20 33 W96 31 13
8641 United Plaza Blvd, Suite 300, Baton Rouge, LA 70809 US
(712) 239-2100, *Fax:* (712) 239-3346
www.ksux.com
License: Winnebago, Thurston County, NE held by Powell Broadcasting Co.
Group Owner: Powell Broadcasting Co. Inc.; (acq 1996; $3.8 million with KSCJ(AM) Sioux City, IA)
Arbitron Metro Market: Sioux City, IA *Format:* Country *No. News Employees:* 2 *Target Audience:* 25-54; female average to above average income, secondary male *Adv. Rates:* 30; 30; 30; 25
Dennis Bullock, General Manager
Dave Grosenheider, General Sales Mgr
Tony Michaels, Programming Director
Tony Michaels, Promotions Manager

York

KAWL
09-01-1954; 1370 khz AM *Hrs Open:* 24; 0.5 kw-D, ND1; 0.176 kw-N, ND1; N40 50 30 W97 35 16
Rr4, Box 121a, York, NE 68467 US
(402) 362-4433, *Fax:* (402) 362-6501
www.kawlam.com
kawl@alltel.net
License: York, NE held by MWB Broadcasting LLC
Nat'l Network: ABC *Regional Network:* Mid-America Ag *Nat'l Reps:* Interep *Wire Services:* AP
Arbitron Metro Market: York, NB *Format:* Oldies, Talk *Special Programming:* Farm 7 hrs, women 3 hrs wkly *Hrs. of News Programming:* news progmg 10 hrs wkly *No. News Employees:* 1 *Target Audience:* 20 plus;general *Adv. Rates:* 20; 16; 18; 10
Mark Jensen, General Manager
Donna Panritz, General Sales Mgr
Bob Bedient, News Director
Linda Korbelik, Sales
Brenda Janzen, Traffic Manager

KTMX
09-01-1970; 104.9 mhz FM *Hrs Open:* 24; 13 kw; 974 ft.; N40 45 7 W97 27 4
Route 4, Box 121a, York, NE 68467 US
(402) 362-4433, *Fax:* (402) 362-6501
hitsandfavorites.com
ktmx@alltel.net
License: York, York County, NE held by MWB Broadcasting LLC
Nat'l Network: ABC *Nat'l Reps:* McGavren Guild
Arbitron Metro Market: York, NE *Format:* Adult Contemp *Hrs. of News Programming:* news progmg 3 hrs wkly *No. News Employees:* 1 *Target Audience:* 25-54; general *Adv. Rates:* Same as AM
Mary Fay Jackson, President

***KEIS**
90.3 mhz FM; 1.6 kw; 217 ft.; N40 49 41.8 W97 42 59.1 US
(864) 297-0216, *Fax:* (864) 297-0344
networkofglory.com
info@networkofglory.org
License: York, York County, NE held by Network of Glory Inc.
Arbitron Metro Market: York, NE *Format:* Christian, Gospel
Lola Richey, President

Nevada

Alamo

***KQLN**
91.3 mhz FM; 0.5 kw vert; -919 ft.; N37 23 1 W115 10 41 US
(775) 751-2579
www.kqln.org
kqlnradio@Yahoo.com
License: Alamo, Lincoln County, NV held by Talk Radio of Pahrump Inc.
Arbitron Metro Market: Alamo, NV
Geraldine Ahrens, President

Amargosa Valley

KPKK
01-01-2003; 101.1 mhz FM; 51 kw horiz; -49 ft.; N36 38 33 W116 23 53
2570 S Eastern Avenue, Las Vegas, NV 89109 US
(312) 204-9900, *Fax:* (312) 587-9466
License: Amargosa Valley, Nye County, NV held by Sky Media L.L.C.
Arbitron Metro Market: Chicago, IL
Bruce Buzil, General Manager

Battle Mountain

*KCWW
91.9 mhz FM; 45 kw; 693 m; N40 37 15 W116 41 18
6363 Highway 50 East, Carson City, NV
(775) 883-5647
www.kpcw.org
paullierman@pilgrimradio.com
License: Battle Mountain, Lander County, NV held by Western Inspirational Broadcasters Inc.
Group Owner: Western Inspirational Broadcasters Inc.
Larry Warren, General Manager
Jan Williams, Programming Director
Leslie Thatcher, News Director

Boulder City

KCYE
04-01-1989; 102.7 mhz FM *Hrs Open:* 24; 96 kw; 1978 ft.; N35 56 46 W115 2 34
3825 Forrestgate Drive, Suite 100, Winston-Salem, NC 27103 US
(702) 730-0300, *Fax:* (702) 736-8447
www.1027thecoyote.com
kcyefm@kcyefm.com
License: Boulder City, Clark County, NV held by KJUL License LLC.
Group Owner: Beasley Broadcast Group Inc.; (acq 1-31-2001; grpsl).
Arbitron Metro Market: Las Vegas, NV *Format:* Country *Hrs. of News Programming:* News progmg one hr wkly *Target Audience:* 35-64. *Adv. Rates:* 100; 110; 100; 75
Justin Chase, Operations Dir
Tom Humm, General Manager
Lee Grau, General Sales Mgr
Justin Chase, Programming Director
Lamar Smith, Engineering Dir
Stephen Rutherford, Chief Engineer
Cory Cuddeback, National Sales Manager
Courtney Smith, Marketing Director
Rick Bruno, Station Photographer

Bunkerville

KYLI
96.7 mhz FM; 93 kw; Ant 1,886 ft; N36 49 53 W114 26 12
980 N. Michigan Ave., Suite 1880, Chicago, IL
(312) 204-9900
License: Bunkerville, Clark County, NV held by College Creek Media LLC.
Group Owner: College Creek Media LLC
Arbitron Metro Market: Las Vegas, NV
Bruce Buzil, General Manager

Cal-Nev-Ari

KVAL
01-01-2008; 104.9 mhz FM; 0.1 kw; 2372 ft.; N35 15 8 W114 44 58
US
(928) 855-1051, *Fax:* (928) 855-7996
www.maddogwireless.net
License: Cal-Nev-Ari, Clark County, NV held by Smoke and Mirrors LLC.
Group Owner: Smoke and Mirrors LLC
Arbitron Metro Market: Cal-Nev-Ari, NV *Format:* Adult Contemp
Rick Murphy, General Manager

Carlin

KHIX
03-01-2001; 96.7 mhz FM *Hrs Open:* 24; 12.6 kw; 1598 ft.; N40 55 18 W115 50 58
3325 Conservanlane, Middleton, WI 53562 US
(775) 777-1196, *Fax:* (775) 777-9587
www.mix96.fm
ken@rubyradio.fm
License: Carlin, Elko County, NV held by Ruby Radio Corp.
Group Owner: Ruby Radio Corp.; (acq 6-15-2003; $475,000 for CP)
Format: Adult Contemp
Ken Sutherland, President
Alene Sutherland, Vice President

Carson City

KBUL-FM
11-30-1984; 98.1 mhz FM *Hrs Open:* 24; 72 kw; 2293 ft.; N39 15 32 W119 42 6
City Center West, 7201 W. Lake Mead Blvd, Las Vegas, NV 89128 US
(775) 789-6700, *Fax:* (775) 789-6767
www.kbul.com
License: Carson City, Carson City County, NV
Group Owner: Cumulus Media Inc.; (acq 5-29-92).
Arbitron Metro Market: Reno, Nevada *Format:* Country *Hrs. of News Programming:* news progmg 4 hrs wkly *No. News Employees:* 1 *Target Audience:* 25-54.
Andrew Perini, General Manager
Jennifer Odom, General Sales Mgr
Brad Hensen, Programming Director
Derek Gunn, Promotions Manager
Rick Worthington, News Director

*KNIS
10-15-1989; 91.3 mhz FM *Hrs Open:* 24; 67 kw; 2165 ft.; N39 15 30 W119 42 36
6363 Highway 50 East, Carson City, NV 89701 US
(775) 883-5647, *Fax:* 775-883-5704
License: Carson City, Carson City County, NV held by Western Inspirational Broadcasters Inc.
Arbitron Metro Market: Reno, NV *Format:* Christian, Talk *No. News Employees:* 1
Tim Weidemann, Operations Dir
Tom Hesse, General Manager
Bill Feltner, Programming Director
Patrick Herman, Music Director

KCMY
05-14-1955; 1300 khz AM; 5 kw-D, DAN; 0.5 kw-N, DAN; N39 9 59 W119 43 37
1960 Idaho Street, Carson City, NV 89701 US
(775) 884-8000, *Fax:* (775) 882-3961
License: Carson City, NV held by The Evans Broadcast Co. Inc.
Nat'l Network: Fox News Radio
Arbitron Metro Market: Carson City *Format:* Country *Hrs. of News Programming:* news progmg 16 hrs wkly *No. News Employees:* 2 *Target Audience:* 35-54. *Adv. Rates:* 18; 16; 18; 8
Jerry Evans, General Manager

KSGG
06-27-1972; 97.3 mhz FM *Hrs Open:* 24; 87 kw; 2,112 ft; N39 15 21 W119 42 37
961 Matley Ln., Suite 120, Reno, NV 90067
(775) 829-1964, *Fax:* (775) 825-3183
www.973bobfm.com
License: Carson City, Carson City County, NV held by Americom Las Vegas L.P.
Group Owner: Americom; (acq 4-27-98; grpsl).
Population Served: 285,000 *Arbitron Metro Market:* Reno, NV *Hrs. of News Programming:* news progmg 2 hrs wkly *No. News Employees:* 1 *Target Audience:* 18-34; women
Tom Quinn, President
Daniel Cook, General Manager
Greg Cobb, General Sales Mgr
Sandy Vance, News Director
Steve Webber, Chief Engineer

Crystal

KHWG-FM
100.1 mhz FM; 4 kw; Ant 827 ft; N36 27 45 W116 03 33
250 W. Nopah Vista Ave., Pahrump, NV 89060
License: Crystal, Nye County, NV held by President of the Liberty Church and His Successors
Population Served: 8,777 *Arbitron Metro Market:* Crystal, NV
Keily Miller, General Manager

Dayton

KTHX-FM
06-10-1983; 100.1 mhz FM *Hrs Open:* 24; 12 kw; 2162 ft.; N39 15 34 W119 42 21
7087 North Traverse, Clovis, CA 93611 US
(775) 333-0123, *Fax:* (775) 322-7361
www.kthxfm.com
info@ktjxfm.com
License: Dayton, Lyon County, NV held by Wilks License Co.-Reno LLC.
Group Owner: Wilks Broadcast Group LLC; (acq 9-29-2005; grpsl).
Nat'l Network: ABC
Arbitron Metro Market: Reno, NV *Format:* Triple A *Hrs. of News Programming:* News progmg 2 hrs wkly *Target Audience:* 18-49; upscale, high income & educated
Rob Brooks, Operations Dir
Andrew Perini, General Manager
Rob Brooks, Programming Director
Jay Davis, News Director

Elko

KELK
12-07-1948; 1240 khz AM *Hrs Open:* 24; 1 kw-U, ND1; N40 50 37 W115 44 58
PO Box 5566, Elko, NV 89802 US
(775) 738-1240, *Fax:* (775) 753-5556
elkoradio.com
elkoradio@elkoradio.com
License: Elko, NV held by Elko Broadcasting Co.
Arbitron Metro Market: Elko, NV *Format:* Adult Contemp *Hrs. of News Programming:* news progmg 25 hrs wkly *No. News Employees:* 1 *Target Audience:* 25-54; upscale, family oriented, white collar workforce *Adv.Rates:* 18; 18; 18; 18
Paul Gardner, President
Tyler Gunter, General Manager

KLKO
05-01-1982; 93.7 mhz FM; 4.5 kw; Ant 1,538 ft; N40 55 20 W115 50 56
1800 Idaho St., Elko, NV 89802
(775) 738-1240, *Fax:* (775) 753-5556
elkoradio.com
License: Elko, Elko County, NV held by Elko Broadcasting Co.
Population Served: 35,000*Hrs. of News Programming:* news progmg 5 hrs wkly *No. News Employees:* 1 *Adv. Rates:* 20; 20; 20; na
Paul Gardner, President
Lori Gilbert, News Director
Eric Allen, National Sales Manager
Marya Morgan, News Reporter
Richard Hunt, News Reporter
Karen Johnson, News Reporter

*KNCC
01-01-1992; 91.5 mhz FM *Hrs Open:* 24; 0.054 kw; 2041 ft.; N40 53 41 W115 37 44 *Rebroadcasts:* Rebroadcasts *KUNR(FM) Reno
University of Nv, Reno, Kunr, Mail Stop 294, Reno, NV 89557 US
(775) 327-5867, *Fax:* (775) 738-8771
carl@gbcnv.edu
License: Elko, Elko County, NV held by Great Basin College.
Format: Big Band, Jazz, 60 *Special Programming:* Public radio
Carl Diekhans, General Manager

KRJC
10-01-1981; 95.3 mhz FM *Hrs Open:* 24; 25 kw; 774 ft.; N40 54 35 W115 49 5
1859 Manzanita Drive, Elko, NV 89801 US
(775) 738-9895, *Fax:* (775) 753-8085
www.krjc.com
krjc@krjc.com
License: Elko, Elko County, NV held by Holiday Broadcasting of Elko.
Group Owner: Carlson Communications International
Nat'l Network: AP Network News *Wire Services:* AP
Format: Country *Hrs. of News Programming:* news progmg 4 hrs wkly *No. News Employees:* 1 *Target Audience:* 25-54. *Adv. Rates:* 15; 15; 15; 13
Ralph J. Carlson, President
Stacey Sawyer, General Manager
Jennifer Sprout, Station Manager
Kristi Agenbroad, General Sales Mgr
Julie Hughes, Programming Director

KTSN
11-01-1996; 1340 khz AM; 1 kw-U, ND1; N40 52 8 W115 43 9
1859 Manzanita Drive, Elko, NV 89801 US
(775) 738-9895, *Fax:* (775) 753-9895
www.ktsn1340.com
License: Elko, NV held by Humboldt Broadcasting LLC.
Group Owner: Carlson Communications International
Arbitron Metro Market: Elko, NV *Format:* News, Sports, 86
Jennifer Sprout, Station Manager
Kristi Agenbroad, General Sales Mgr

KZBI
01-01-2005; 94.5 mhz FM; 36 kw; Ant 1,519 ft; N40 55 18 W115 50 58
1750 Manzanita Drive, Suite 1, Elko, NV
(775) 777-1196, *Fax:* (775) 777-9587

License: Elko, Elko County, NV held by Ruby Radio Corp.
Group Owner: Ruby Radio Corp.; (acq 10-25-2005; exchange for KCLS)
Ken Sutherland, President
Alene Sutherland, Operations Dir
Ken Sutherland, General Manager
Ken Sutherland, Programming Director

KPHD
97.5 mhz FM; 85 kw horiz; 1558 ft.; N40 55 18 W115 50 58
US
(312) 204-9900
License: Elko, Elko County, NV held by College Creek Media LLC.
Group Owner: College Creek Media LLC
Arbitron Metro Market: Elko, NV
Neal Robinson, President

***KTQQ**
88.1 mhz FM; 230 w; 1811 ft; N40 42 01 W115 54 07
PO Box 716, Ridgecrest, CA
(760)375-2355
www.radio74.net
ejwitzel@mchsi.com
License: Elko, Elko County, NV held by Radio 74 Internationale
Ron Myers, Founder

Ely

KDSS
12-22-1984; 92.7 mhz FM *Hrs Open:* 24; 32 kw; 961 ft.; N39 14 46 W114 55 39
501 Aultman St., # 208, Ely, NV 89301 US
(775) 289-6474, *Fax:* (775) 289-6531
kdss@wpis.net
License: Ely, White Pine County, NV held by Coates Broadcasting Inc.
Nat'l Network: Jones Radio Networks
Format: Country *Special Programming:* Nashville News, fishing, outdoor *Hrs. of News Programming:* News progmg 10 hrs wkly *Target Audience:* 18-64; older demographics, new & classic C&W listeners
Samantha Coates, President
Karen Livingston, General Manager
Jim Liebsack, Chief Engineer

KELY
07-08-1950; 1230 khz AM *Hrs Open:* 24; 0.25 kw-U, ND1; N39 15 45 W114 51 46
807 Avenue F, Ely, NV 89301 US
(775) 289-2077, *Fax:* (775) 289-6997
www.kely1230.com
License: Ely, NV held by Ely Radio LLC.
Group Owner: Ely Radio LLC; (acq 3-21-2006; $140,000)
Arbitron Metro Market: Ely, NV *Format:* Talk *Special Programming:* Local High School Sports *Hrs. of News Programming:* 5 *No. News Employees:* 1 *Target Audience:* 35 plus. *Adv. Rates:* 20; 10; 10; 11
Wyatt Cox, General Manager

Fallon

KRNG
07-04-1997; 101.3 mhz FM *Hrs Open:* 24; 1.65 kw; Ant 2,207 ft; N39 42 30 W119 10 16
Mailing Address: Box 490, Wadsworth, NV 89442
Second Address: 360 Pyramid St., Wadsworth, NV 89442
(775) 575-7777, *Fax:* (775) 575-7737
www.renegaderadio.org
email@renegaderadio.org
License: Fallon, Churchill County, NV held by Sierra Nevada Christian Music Association Inc.
Nat'l Reps: McGavren Guild
Population Served: 200,000 *Arbitron Metro Market:* Reno, NV *Target Audience:* 12-35; youth, young adults *Adv. Rates:* 9.33; 9.33; 9.33; 5
Rev. Karry Crites, President
William Bauer PhD., Operations Dir

KVLV
05-09-1957; 980 khz AM *Hrs Open:* 6 AM-sunset; 5 kw-D, NDD; N39 29 47 W118 48 50
1155 Gummow Drive, Fallon, NV 89406 US
(702) 423-2243, *Fax:* (702) 423-8889
www.kvlvradio.com
kvlv@phonewave.net
License: Fallon, NV held by Lahontan Valley Broadcasting LLC.
Nat'l Network: ABC
Arbitron Metro Market: Fallon, NV *Format:* Country *Hrs. of News Programming:* News progmg 10 hrs wkly *Target Audience:* 25 plus. *Adv. Rates:* 15; 15; 15; na.
Mike McGinness, General Manager

KKTV
11-26-1966; 99.5 mhz FM *Hrs Open:* 24; 6 kw; Ant 250 ft; N39 29 47 W118 48 50
1155 Gummow Dr., Fallon, NV 89406
(775) 423-2243, *Fax:* (775) 423-8889
License: Fallon, Churchill County, NV held by Lahontan Valley Broadcasting LLC.
Nat'l Network: AP Radio
Population Served: 40,000*Hrs. of News Programming:* News progmg 10 hrs wkly *Adv. Rates:* 15; 15; 15; 15
Mike McGinness, General Manager
Lynn Pearce, Chief Operator

KHWG
06-01-2005; 750 khz AM
US
(775) 428-1764, *Fax:* (775) 428-1765
www.khwgclassiccountry.com
khwg@ccomm.net
License: Fallon, NV held by Media Enterprises Inc.
Arbitron Metro Market: Fallon, NV *Format:* Country
Keily Miller, President
Dee Gregory, General Manager
Bill Kling, Station/Production Manager
Lisa DeWitt, Sales Manager
Dizzy Don Roberts, Music Director

***KQNV**
89.9 mhz FM; 0.6 kw; 33 ft.; N39 27 42 W118 42 38
US
(702) 731-5588, *Fax:* (702) 731-5851
License: Fallon, Churchill County, NV held by American Educational Broadcasting Inc.
Arbitron Metro Market: Fallon, NV
Carl Auel, President

KKTU-FM
99.3 mhz FM; 6000 w; 249 ft; N39 29 26 W118 49 08
1155 Gummow Drive, Fallon, NV 89406
(775) 423-2243
License: Fallon, Churchill County, NV
Group Owner: Lahontan Valley Broadcasting Company LLC

Gardnerville-Minden

KKFT
09-19-1985; 99.1 mhz FM *Hrs Open:* 24; 410 w; Ant 2,006 ft; N39 15 34 W119 42 21
1960 Idaho St., Carson City, NV 89423
(775) 884-8000, *Fax:* (775) 882-3961
www.991fmtalk.com
jerry@991fmtalk.com
License: Gardnerville-Minden, Douglas County, NV held by Jerry Evans
Nat'l Network: Fox News Radio
Population Served: 600,000*Hrs. of News Programming:* news progmg 24 hrs wkly *No. News Employees:* 2 *Target Audience:* 25-54; btfl people *Adv. Rates:* 32; 30; 32; 14
Jerry Evans, CEO
David Reichert, General Sales Mgr
Jen Austin, Assistant

Gerlach

***KLAP**
89.5 mhz FM; 0.13 kw; -325 ft.; N40 39 6 W119 21 14
US
(775) 279-6677
openskyradio.org
klap@klap.fm
License: Gerlach, Washoe County, NV held by OpenSkyRadio Corp.
Arbitron Metro Market: Gerlach, NV *Format:* Country
Jeffrey Cotton, General Manager

***KFBR**
01-20-2011; 91.5 mhz FM; 600 w; 46 ft; N40 39 07 W119 21 25
320 Main Street, Gerlach, NV
(775)557-2900
www.blackrockdesert.org
License: Gerlach, Washoe County, NV
Group Owner: Friends Of Black Rock High Rock Inc.
Deborah Lassiter, President
Karen Dallett, Executive Director
Michael Black, Coordinator

Hawthorne

***KQMC**
90.1 mhz FM; 0.48 kw vert; 3140 ft.; N38 27 28 W118 45 52
1601 Belvedere Rd, 204 East, West Palm Beach, FL 33406 US
(702) 731-5588
www.kqmc.com
License: Hawthorne, Mineral County, NV held by American Educational Broadcasting Inc.
Arbitron Metro Market: Hawthorne, NV *Format:* Classical
Lee Amundsen, General Manager

***KAVB**
12-01-2007; 98.7 mhz FM *Hrs Open:* 24; 0.1 kw; -853 ft.; N38 31 26.6 W118 37 18
US
(213) 627-8711, *Fax:* (213) 627-8712
www.almavision.com
info@almavision.com
License: Hawthorne, Mineral County, NV held by Alma Vision Hispanic Network Inc.
Arbitron Metro Market: Hawthorne, NV *Format:* Spanish
Juan Caamano, President

***KELC**
91.9 mhz FM; 0.5 kw; -853 ft.; N38 31 26.6 W118 37 18
US
(702) 731-5588, *Fax:* (702) 731-5851
License: Hawthorne, Mineral County, NV held by American Educational Broadcasting Inc.
Arbitron Metro Market: Hawthorne, NV
Carl Auel, President

Henderson

KQLL
05-01-1956; 1280 khz AM *Hrs Open:* 24; 5 kw-D, 28 w-N; N36 03 13 W114 58 30
150 Spectrum Blvd., Las Vegas, NV 89104
(702) 258-0285, *Fax:* (702) 732-3060
www.1280talk.com
info@kdoxam.com
License: Henderson, Clark County, NV held by S & R Broadcasting Inc.
Nat'l Reps: Lotus Entravision Reps LLC
Population Served: 160,000 *Arbitron Metro Market:* Las Vegas, NV *Target Audience:* General; Hispanic, above-average income, high home ownership *Adv. Rates:* 40; 40; 40; 40
Paul Ruttan, President
Scott Gentry, General Manager
Ellen Walker, General Sales Mgr
Roberto Ibarra, Programming Director
Warren Brown, Chief Engineer

KMXB
02-10-1970; 94.1 mhz FM *Hrs Open:* 24; 100 kw; 1161 ft.; N36 0 30 W115 0 20
600 New Hampshire Ave., N.W., Suite 1200, Washington, DC 20037 US
(702) 889-5100, *Fax:* (702) 257-2936
www.mix941.fm
justin@mix941.fm
License: Henderson, Clark County, NV held by CBS Radio Stations Inc.
Group Owner: CBS Radio; (acq 11-13-98; grpsl)
Nat'l Network: CBS Radio
Arbitron Metro Market: Las Vegas, NV *Format:* Adult Contemp *No. News Employees:* 1 *Target Audience:* 18-49; female *Adv. Rates:* 300; 275; 260; 100
John Sykes, CEO
Tom Humm, Operations Dir
Lorene Malis, General Sales Mgr
Jennifer DiFazio, Promotions Manager
Jacques Tortoli, CFO
John Fullam, Jacques Tortoli
Lori Heeren, Regional Sales Manager

KXNT-FM
11-28-1982; 100.5 mhz FM *Hrs Open:* 24; 100 kw; 1,105 ft; N36 00 28 W115 00 20
6655 W. Sahara Ave., Suite C 216, Las Vegas, NV 20037
(702) 889-5100, *Fax:* (702) 257-2936
www.jackbaby.com
jack@jackbaby.com
License: Henderson, Clark County, NV held by Infinity Radio Inc.
Group Owner: CBS Radio; (acq 11-13-98; grpsl).
Nat'l Network: CBS Radio *Nat'l Reps:* Katz Radio
Arbitron Metro Market: Las Vegas, NV *Hrs. of News Programming:* News progmg one hr wkly *Target Audience:* 25-54. *Adv. Rates:* 180; 180; 180; 65
Joel Hollander, CEO
John Sykes, President
Tom Humm, Operations Dir
Craig Powers, Programming Director
Sam Ballenger, Promotions Manager
Lorene Malis, National Sales Manager
Herb Perry, Public Affairs Director

KWNR
07-18-1972; 95.5 mhz FM; 92 kw; 1161 ft.; N36 0 31 W115 0 22
50 East Rivercenter Blvd, Suite 1200, Covington, KY 41011 US
(702) 238-7300, *Fax:* (702) 732-4890
www.kwnr.com
info@kwnr.com
License: Henderson, Clark County, NV held by Citicasters Licenses L.P.
Group Owner: Clear Channel Communications Inc.; (acq 1999; grpsl).
Arbitron Metro Market: Henderson, NV *Format:* Country *Target Audience:* 18-54.
Brandy Newman, Operations Dir
Sean Cassidy, General Sales Mgr
Brooks O'Brien, Programming Director
Bill Lubitz, Promotions Manager
Mitch Kelly, News Director
Greg Benson, Chief Engineer

Incline Village

KRNO
07-01-1974; 106.9 mhz FM *Hrs Open:* 24; 35 kw; 2989 ft.; N39 18 38 W119 53 1
1900 Avenue of the Stars, Suite 1880, Los Angeles, CA 90067 US
(775) 829-1964, *Fax:* (775) 825-3183
www.sunny1069.com
webmaster@sunny1069.com
License: Incline Village, Washoe County, NV held by Americom Las Vegas L.P.
Group Owner: Americom; (acq 4-16-98; grpsl).
Arbitron Metro Market: Reno, NV *Format:* Adult Contemp *Hrs. of News Programming:* news progmg 18 hrs wkly *No. News Employees:* 1 *Target Audience:* 25-54; women *Adv. Rates:* 12; 12; 12; na
Tom Quinn, President
Daniel Cook, General Manager
Greg Cobb, General Sales Mgr
Dan Fritz, Programming Director
Sandy Vance, News Director
Steve Weber, Chief Engineer

Indian Springs

KRGT
11-22-2002; 99.3 mhz FM *Hrs Open:* 24; 31 kw; 2264 ft.; N36 19 28 W115 33 58
Plaza Hotel, #1 Main St, Las Vegas, NV 89101 US
(702) 284-6400, *Fax:* (702) 284-6403
lakallelasvegas.univision.com/
License: Indian Springs, Clark County, NV held by Univision Radio License Corp.
Group Owner: Univision Radio; (acq 9-22-2003; grpsl).
Arbitron Metro Market: Las Vegas Valley *Format:* Spanish
Dana Demerjian, Operations Dir
Cristina Valarezo, General Sales Mgr
Ratael Miramontes, Programming Director
Zulema Santacruz, Promotions Manager
Glocia Salvador, News Director
Manny Garcia, Chief Engineer
Brent Berger, LocalSales Manager
Joe Reynolds, National Sales Manager

KURR
01-01-2007; 103.1 mhz FM; 100 kw; 1952 ft.; N36 50 49 W113 29 28
US
(801) 524-2600, *Fax:* (801) 524-6002
License: Indian Springs, Washington County, NV held by Western Broadcasting, LS LLC.
Group Owner: Simmons Media Group
Arbitron Metro Market: Hurricane, UT
Bret Leifson, General Manager

Jackpot

***KBSJ**
91.3 mhz FM; 3.7 kw; 2464 ft.; N41 47 8 W114 50 22
1910 University Dirve, Boise, ID 83725 US
(208) 426-3663, *Fax:* (208) 344-6631
www.boisestatepublicradio.org
boisestatepublicradio@boisestate.edu
License: Jackpot, Elko County, NV held by Idaho State Board of Education.
Arbitron Metro Market: Boise, OD *Format:* Classical, Jazz
Erik Jones, Operations Dir
John Hess, General Manager
Hy Kloc, General Sales Mgr
Ele Ellis, Programming Director
Sadie Babits, News Director
Tom Taylor, Engineering Dir
Betsy Micone, Business Director
Brad Campbell, OperationsManager
Adrienne Zachary, Marketing & Special Events Coordinator
Arthur Balinger, Producer/ Program Host
Carol Wilke, Membership Assistant
Craig Morgan, Web & Graphic Designer

Las Vegas

KBAD
06-01-1953; 920 khz AM
6290 Sunset Blvd, Ste 1600, Los Angeles, CA 90028 US
(702) 876-1460, *Fax:* (702) 876-6685
www.werlv.com
lotussignup@yahoo.com
License: Las Vegas, NV held by Lotus Broadcasting Corp.
Group Owner: Lotus Communications Corp.; (acq 11-4-92; $1.42 million with co-located FM;
Nat'l Network: Fox Sports *Nat'l Reps:* Interep
Arbitron Metro Market: Las Vegas, NV *Format:* Sports *Target Audience:* 18 plus.
Tony Bonnici, General Manager
Jesse Leeds, General Sales Mgr
Mitch Moss, Programming Director

***KCEP**
10-01-1973; 88.1 mhz FM *Hrs Open:* 24; 9.8 kw; 1194 ft.; N36 0 31 W115 0 22
2228 Comstock Drive, Las Vegas, NV 89030 US
(702) 648-0104, *Fax:* (702) 647-0803
www.power881v.com
cknight@power881v.com
License: Las Vegas, Clark County, NV held by Economic Opportunity Board of Clark County.
Arbitron Metro Market: Las Vegas, NV *Format:* Black, Blues
Special Programming: Gospel 14 hrs, Jazz 12 hrs wkly *Hrs. of News Programming:* News progmg 11 hrs wkly *Target Audience:* 12-55; African-Americans
Craig Knight, Programming Director

KDWN
04-07-1975; 720 khz AM *Hrs Open:* 24
No. 1 Main Street, Plaza Hotel, Las Vegas, NV 89101 US
(702) 730-0300, *Fax:* (702) 736-8447
www.kdwn.com
kdwn@kdwn.com
License: Las Vegas, NV held by KDWN License L.P.
Group Owner: Beasley Broadcast Group Inc.; (acq 8-7-2006; $17 million).
Nat'l Network: Fox News Radio
Arbitron Metro Market: Las Vegas, NV *TV Affiliate:* . *Format:* News, News/Talk, 86 *Target Audience:* 35-54. *Adv. Rates:* 39; 33; 39; 22
Tom Davis, General Manager
Mark Warlaumont, General Sales Mgr
John Shaffer, Programming Director
John Shaffer, News Director
Stephen Rutherford, Chief Engineer
Angie Rush, Technical Operator
Quintin Allen, Technical Operator

KENO
01-01-1940; 1460 khz AM; 10 kw-D, DA2; 0.62 kw-N, DA2; N36 11 25 W115 10 35
6290 Sunset Blvd, #1600, Hollywood, CA 90028 US
(702) 876-1460, *Fax:* (702) 876-6685
License: Las Vegas, NV held by Lotus Broadcasting Corp.
Group Owner: Lotus Communications Corp.; (acq 6-1-65)
Nat'l Network: ESPN Deportes *Nat'l Reps:* Interep
Arbitron Metro Market: Las Vegas, NV *Format:* Sports
Tony Bonnici, General Manager
Jesse Leeds, General Sales Mgr
Alvaro Puentes, Programming Director

KWID
03-22-1963; 101.9 mhz FM; 47 kw; 1900 ft.; N35 56 44 W115 2 31
50 East Rivercenter Blvd, Suite 1200, Covington, KY 41011 US
(702) 238-7300, *Fax:* (702) 792-9018
info@kwidfm.com
License: Las Vegas, Clark County, NV held by Texas Lotus Corp.
Group Owner: Lotus Communications Corp.; (acq 7-29-2008; with KVMX(FM) Bakersfield, CA in exchange for KZEP-FM San Antonio, TX)
Arbitron Metro Market: Las Vegas, NV *Format:* Spanish *Target Audience:* 25-49.
Brandy Newman, Operations Dir
Kelly Kibler, General Manager
Sam Loya, General Sales Mgr
Benjamin Acevedo, Promotions Manager
Greg Benson, Chief Engineer

***KSOS**
07-18-1972; 90.5 mhz FM *Hrs Open:* 24; 100 kw; 1270 ft.; N36 0 29 W115 0 20
2201 South 6th Street, Las Vegas, NV 89103 US
(702) 731-5452, *Fax:* (702) 731-1992
www.sosradio.net
info@sosradio.net
License: Las Vegas, Clark County, NV held by Faith Communications Corp.
Group Owner: Faith Communications Corp.; (acq 12-31-71).
Arbitron Metro Market: Las Vegas, NV *Format:* Religious *Hrs. of News Programming:* News progmg 5 hrs wkly *Target Audience:* 25-44; young families
Brad Staley, CEO
Brad Staley, General Manager
Duane Luchsinger, Station Manager
Scott Herrold, Programming Director

KISF
03-01-1989; 103.5 mhz FM; 100 kw; 1158 ft.; N36 0 29 W115 0 20
3102 Oak Lawn Avenue, Suite 215, Dallas, TX 75219 US
(702) 284-6400, *Fax:* (702) 284-6403
www.univision.com
License: Las Vegas, Clark County, NV held by HBC License Corp.
Group Owner: Univision Radio; (acq 9-22-2003; grpsl).
Arbitron Metro Market: Las Vegas, NV
Dana Demerjian, Operations Dir
Cristina Valarelo, General Sales Mgr
Roberto Warling, Programming Director
Zulema Santacruz, Promotions Manager
Gloria Salvador, News Director
Manny Garcia, Chief Engineer
Joe Reynolds, NationalSales Manager
Brent Berger, Regional Sales Manager

KKLZ
01-26-1984; 96.3 mhz FM *Hrs Open:* 24; 100 kw; 1175 ft.; N36 0 29 W115 0 20
3825 Forrestgate Drive, Suite 100, Winston-Salem, NC 27103 US
(702) 739-9600, *Fax:* (702) 736-8447
www.963kklz.com
kklzfm@kklzfm.com
License: Las Vegas, Clark County, NV held by Beasley Broadcasting of NV LLC.
Group Owner: Beasley Broadcast Group Inc.; (acq 2-1-2001; grpsl)
Arbitron Metro Market: Las Vegas, NV *Format:* Contemporary Hits/Top 40, Adult Contemp *No. News Employees:* 1 *Target Audience:* 25-44; baby boomers
Mark Warlaumont, General Sales Mgr
Dan Hallett, Programming Director
Brian Shapiro, News Director
Stephen Rutherford, Chief Engineer
Al Mollet, General Sales Manager
Dan Lea, Music Director
Al Mollet, News Director
DennisMitchell

KKVV
05-01-1990; 1060 khz AM *Hrs Open:* 24; 5 kw-D, ND1; 0.043 kw-N, ND1; N36 9 22 W115 15 24
1601 Belvedere Rd, 204 E, West Palm Beach, FL 33406 US
(702) 731-5588, *Fax:* (702) 731-5851
www.kkvv.com
kkvv@kkvv.com,kkvvradio@aol.com
License: Las Vegas, NV held by Las Vegas Broadcasters Inc.
Nat'l Network: Salem Radio Network *Nat'l Reps:* Salem
Arbitron Metro Market: Las Vegas, NV *Format:* Adult Contemp, Talk, 74 *Special Programming:* Sp christian 20 hrs wkly *Hrs. of News Programming:* 2 hrs news progmg wkly min *No. News Employees:* 2 *TargetAudience:* General; General *Adv. Rates:* 18; 18; 18; 18
Carl Auel, President
Jane Filler, Operations Dir
Fred Hodges, General Manager

KLAV
06-01-1947; 1230 khz AM *Hrs Open:* 24
1000 Olde Doubloon Drive, Vero Beach, FL 32963 US
(702) 796-1230, *Fax:* (702) 853-2599
www.klav1230am.com
patriceburker@broadcasting.com
License: Las Vegas, NV held by Burken Broadcasting LLC
Arbitron Metro Market: Las Vegas, NV *Format:* Sports, Talk
Special Programming: Relg 3 hrs, Indian one hr, Hawaiian 4 hrs, Arabic *Target Audience:* 25-54.

Patrice Donley, Operations Dir
Peggy Merrill, Station Manager
Jon Lindquist, Operations Manager

KLUC-FM
01-01-1956; 98.5 mhz FM *Hrs Open:* 24; 97 kw; 1181 ft.; N36 0 29 W115 0 20
600 New Hampshire Avenue, N.W, Suite 1200, Washington, DC 20037 US
(702) 253-9800, *Fax:* (702) 889-7373
www.kluc.cbslocal.com
info@kluc.com
License: Las Vegas, Clark County, NV held by Infinity Radio Inc.
Group Owner: CBS Radio; (acq 12-14-00; grpsl).
Arbitron Metro Market: Las Vegas, NV *Format:* Contemporary Hits/Top 40 *No. News Employees:* 1 *Target Audience:* 18-34.
Marty Basch, General Manager
Frank Feder, General Sales Mgr
Cat Thomas, Programming Director
Kyle Helmic, Promotions Manager
Theresa Dunbar, News Director
Tracy Teagarden, Chief Engineer

***KCNV**
03-24-1980; 89.5 mhz FM *Hrs Open:* 24; 98 kw; Ant 1,532 ft; N35 56 50 W115 03 01
1289 S. Torrey Pines, Las Vegas, NV 89146
(702) 258-9895, *Fax:* (702) 258-5646
www.knpr.org
info@knpr.org
License: Las Vegas, Clark County, NV held by Nevada Public Radio Corp.
Population Served: 1,200,000 *Arbitron Metro Market:* Las Vegas, NV *Target Audience:* 35-54.
Flo Rogers, President
Phil Burger, Operations Dir
Melanie Canon, General Sales Mgr
Joe Sands, Chief Engineer
Jay Bartos, Public Affairs Director

KOMP
09-01-1966; 92.3 mhz FM; 25 kw; 3688 ft.; N35 57 57 W115 30 3
6290 Sunset Boulevard, Suite 1600, Los Angeles, CA 90028 US
(702) 876-1460, *Fax:* (702) 876-6685
www.wearelv.com
License: Las Vegas, Clark County, NV held by Lotus Broadcasting Corp.
Group Owner: Lotus Communications Corp.
Nat'l Reps: Interep *Wire Services:* UPI
Arbitron Metro Market: Las Vegas, NV *Format:* Rock/AOR
Jesse Leeds, General Sales Mgr
John Griffin, Programming Director

KPLV
09-01-1977; 93.1 mhz FM; 24 kw; 3743 ft.; N35 58 2 W115 30 6
50 East Rivercenter Blvd, Ste 1200, Covington, KY 41011 US
(702) 238-7300, *Fax:* (702) 732-4890
www.my931vegas.com
info@931theparty.com
License: Las Vegas, Clark County, NV held by Citicasters Licenses L.P.
Group Owner: Clear Channel Communications Inc.; (acq 1999)
Arbitron Metro Market: Las Vegas, NV *Format:* Contemporary Hits/Top 40
Tom Chase, Operations Dir
Brandy Newman, General Manager
Aaron Crowley, General Sales Mgr
Chris Pickett, Programming Director
Mitch Kelly, News Director
Greg Benson, Chief Engineer
Bryan Shaw, Web Services

KRLV
01-01-1947; 1340 khz AM *Hrs Open:* 24; 1 kw-U, ND1; N36 9 22 W115 15 24
P.O. Box 1270, Tulsa, OK 74101 US
(702) 796-1230, *Fax:* (702) 853-2597
www.krlv1340am.com
generalmanager@krlv.net
License: Las Vegas, NV held by Burken Broadcasting LLC
Arbitron Metro Market: Las Vegas Valley *Format:* Tejano *Hrs. of News Programming:* news progmg 12 hrs wkly *No. News Employees:* 3 *Target Audience:* 25-54. *Adv. Rates:* 30; 30; 25; 25
Jon Lindquist, Operations Dir
Alcides Vicente, General Manager
Peggy Merrill, Station Manager
Bruce Garrett, General Sales Mgr
John Lindquist, Programming Director

KSNE-FM
08-18-1987; 106.5 mhz FM *Hrs Open:* 24; 100 kw; 1155 ft.; N36 0 30 W115 0 20
50 East Rivercenter Blvd, Suite 1200, Covington, KY 41011 US
(702) 238-7300, *Fax:* (702) 732-4597
www.ksne.com/main.html
License: Las Vegas, Clark County, NV held by Citicasters Licenses L.P.
Group Owner: Clear Channel Communications Inc.; (acq 1999; grpsl).
Arbitron Metro Market: Las Vegas, NV *Format:* Adult Contemp
Special Programming: Relg one hr, pub affrs one hr wkly *Hrs. of News Programming:* News progmg 4 hrs wkly *Target Audience:* 25-54; emphasis on women
Jamal Parker, General Sales Mgr
Tom Chase, Programming Director
Mitch Kelly, News Director
Tree Lee, Engineering Dir

***KUNV**
04-21-1981; 91.5 mhz FM *Hrs Open:* 24; 15 kw; 1099 ft.; N36 0 28 W115 0 20
2601 Enterprise Road, Reno, NV 89512 US
(702) 895-0065, *Fax:* (702) 895-0068
www.kunv.org
frank.mueller@kunv.org
License: Las Vegas, Clark County, NV held by University of Nevada Board of Regents.
Nat'l Network: NPR
Arbitron Metro Market: Las Vegas, NV *Format:* Jazz *Special Programming:* Sp 5 hrs, electronic 2 hrs, community affrs 4 hrs, Ger one hr wkly *Target Audience:* General. *Adv. Rates:* 50; 50; 50; 50
Frank Muller, Operations Dir
Frank Mueller, General Manager
Kim Lizny, Programming Director
Ryan 'RT' Thorp, News and Community Partnership Manager
Joe Sands, Chief Engineer
Dave Nourse, Operations Manager
Kim Linzy, MusicDirector & Asst. Operations Manager
Gretchen Rexroad, Business Manager
Steven Zeller, Production Engineer

KQRT
01-01-1993; 105.1 mhz FM *Hrs Open:* 24; 50 kw; 62 ft.; N36 20 0 W115 21 41
103 Entrance Drive, Suite 1, Livingston, TX 77351 US
(702) 434-0015, *Fax:* (702) 507-1081
www.tricolor1051.com
License: Las Vegas, Clark County, NV held by Entravision Holdings LLC.
Group Owner: Entravision Communications Corp.; (acq 3-14-2000; grpsl).
Nat'l Reps: Lotus Entravision Reps LLC
Arbitron Metro Market: Las Vegas, NV *TV Affiliate:* KINC(TV) *Format:* Spanish, Christian *Target Audience:* Spanish; young *Adv. Rates:* 80; 70; 80; 50
Walter Ulloa, CEO
Chris Roman, General Manager
Jr Desamours, General Sales Mgr
Gerry Fernandez, Promotions Manager
Erin Thomas, News Director
David Ferran, Radio Sales Manager
Mike Scanlon, TV Sales Manager

KXPT
11-29-1961; 97.1 mhz FM; 25 kw; 3675 ft.; N35 58 2 W115 30 6
6290 Sunset Blvd., Suite 1600, Los Angeles, CA 90028 US
(702) 876-1460, *Fax:* (702) 876-6685
www.wearelv.com
LOTUSSIGNUP@YAHOO.COM
License: Las Vegas, Clark County, NV held by Lotus Broadcasting Corp.
Group Owner: Lotus Communications Corp.
Nat'l Reps: Interep
Arbitron Metro Market: Las Vegas, NV *Format:* Contemporary Hits/Top 40, Adult Contemp *Target Audience:* 35-49.
John Griffin, Operations Dir
Jesse Leeds, General Sales Mgr

***KNPR**
10-31-2003; 88.9 mhz FM; 24.5 kw; Ant 3,680 ft; N35 58 02 W115 30 06
1289 S. Torrey Pines Dr., Las Vegas, NV 89122
(702) 258-9895, *Fax:* (702) 258-5646
www.knpr.org
info@knpr.org
License: Las Vegas, Clark County, NV held by Nevada Public Radio.
Nat'l Network: NPR; PRI
Population Served: 1,800,000 *Arbitron Metro Market:* Las Vegas, NV
Flo Rogers, President/General Manager
Phil Burger, Operations Dir
Christine Kiely, General Sales Mgr
Dave Becker, Programming Director
Adam Burke, News Director
Joe Sands, Chief Engineer

KWWN
01-01-2007; 1100 khz AM
US
(702) 876-1460, *Fax:* (702) 876-6685
www.wearelv.com
info@espn1100.com
License: Las Vegas, NV held by Lotus Broadcasting Corp.
Group Owner: Lotus Communications Corp.
Nat'l Network: ESPN Radio *Nat'l Reps:* Interep
Arbitron Metro Market: Las Vegas, NV *Format:* Sports
Tony Bonnici, General Manager
Jessee Leeds, General Sales Mgr
Mitch Moss, Programming Director
Andy Kaye, News Director

***KVKL**
01-01-2006; 91.1 mhz FM; 41 kw; 1066 ft.; N35 37 41 W115 16 24
1601 Belvedere Rd, 204 E, West Palm Beach, FL 33406 US
(702) 731-5588
License: Las Vegas, Clark County, NV held by Southern Nevada Educational Broadcasters.
Arbitron Metro Market: Farmington, NM
Carl Auel, CEO
Fred Hodges, General Manager

KMZQ
01-01-2008; 670 khz AM
US
(702) 736-6161, *Fax:* (702) 385-6001
www.670theq.com
License: Las Vegas, NV held by Kemp Communications Inc.
Group Owner: Kemp Communications Inc.
Arbitron Metro Market: Las Vegas, NV *Format:* Talk
Will Kemp, President
Gary Cox, General Manager

Laughlin

KJJJ
05-24-1994; 102.3 mhz FM; 17 kw; 1890 ft.; N35 1 58 W114 21 57
P.O. Box 2009, Lake Havasu City, AZ 86405 US
(928) 855-9336, *Fax:* (928) 855-9333
www.kjjjfm.com
steve@kjjjfm.com
License: Laughlin, Mohave County, NV held by Steven M. Greeley.
Format: Country
Steve Greeley, CEO
Traceye Jones, General Manager

Logandale

KADD
09-01-1997; 93.5 mhz FM; 93 kw horiz; 2090 ft.; N36 38 7 W114 7 18
P.O. Box 67, Santa Clara, CA 95052 US
(928) 855-4560, *Fax:* (928) 855-7996
www.maddog.net
epress@maddog.net
License: Logandale, Clark County, NV held by M&M Broadcasting LLC
Arbitron Metro Market: Las Vegas, NV *Format:* Adult Contemp
Chris Rolando, General Manager

Lovelock

KWNZ
01-01-2008; 106.3 mhz FM; 3 kw horiz; Ant 2,106 ft; N40 07 05.2 W118 43 35.5
149 Penn Ave., Scranton, PA
(570) 348-9103, *Fax:* (570) 348-9109
License: Lovelock, Pershing County, NV held by Shamrock Communications Inc.
Group Owner: Shamrock Communications Inc.; (acq 9-19-2007; $500,000 for CP)
William Lynett, President

Lund

*KWPR

09-01-2000; 88.7 mhz FM *Hrs Open:* 24; 3 kw; 2201 ft.; N39 18 54 W115 5 19 *Rebroadcasts:* Rebroadcasts KNPR(FM) Las Vegas 100%
1289 S. Torrey Pines Dr., Las Vegas, NV 89146 US
(702) 258-9895, *Fax:* (702) 258-5646
www.nevadapublicradio.org
reception@knpr.org
License: Lund, White Pine County, NV held by Nevada Public Radio.
Arbitron Metro Market: Henderson, NV *Format:* News, Variety/Diverse
Lamar Marchese, General Manager

Mesquite

KVEG

07-23-2001; 97.5 mhz FM *Hrs Open:* 24; 100 kw; 1969 ft.; N36 35 6 W114 36 1
300 South Fourth St., Las Vegas, NV 89101 US
(702) 736-6161, *Fax:* (702) 736-2986
www.kvegas.com
lapablaza@kvegas.com
License: Mesquite, Clark County, NV held by Kemp Broadcasting Inc.
Group Owner: Kemp Communications Inc.
Arbitron Metro Market: Las Vegas, NV *Format:* Contemporary Hits/Top 40 *Target Audience:* 25-39.
Gary Cox, Operations Dir
Sherita Salisbury, Programming Director

*KAIZ

01-01-2005; 90.9 mhz FM *Hrs Open:* 24; 0.5 kw; 761 ft.; N36 53 48 W114 17 23 *Rebroadcasts:* Rebroadcasts KLRD(FM) Yucaipa, CA 100%
US
(888) 937-2471, *Fax:* (916) 251-1650
www.air1.com
info@air1.com
License: Mesquite, Clark County, NV held by Educational Media Foundation.
Group Owner: EMF Broadcasting
Nat'l Network: Air 1
Arbitron Metro Market: Mesquite, NV *Format:* Alternative, Christian *No. News Employees:* 3 *Target Audience:* 18-35; Judeo-Christian, female
Darrell Chambliss, Chairman
Alan Mason, COO
Mike Novak, President and CEO
Dan Beck, Operations Dir
Eric Allen, General Sales Mgr
David Pierce, Programming Director
Ed Lenane, News Director
Sam Wallington, Engineering Dir
Larry Moody, Director
Mitch Barnhart, Director
David R. Ferry, Director
Walter Golembeski, Director
David Pierce, Chief Creative Officer

*KAER

01-01-2006; 89.3 mhz FM *Hrs Open:* 24; 0.74 kw; 784 ft.; N36 53 48 W114 17 23 *Rebroadcasts:* Rebroadcasts KLRD(FM) Yucaipa, CA 100%
1425 N. Market Blvd., Suite 9, Sacramento, CA 95834 US
(888) 937-2471, *Fax:* (916) 251-1650
www.air1.com
info@air1.com
License: Mesquite, Washington County, NV held by Educational Media Foundation.
Group Owner: EMF Broadcasting
Nat'l Network: Air 1
Arbitron Metro Market: Mesquite, NV *Format:* Alternative, Christian *No. News Employees:* 3 *Target Audience:* 19-35; Judeo Christian female
Darrell Chambliss, Chairman
Alan Mason, COO
Mike Novak, President and CEO
Mike Lee, Operations Dir
Eric Allen, General Sales Mgr
David Pierce, Programming Director
Ed Lenane, News Director
Sam Wallington, Engineering Dir

*KEKL

01-01-2005; 88.5 mhz FM; 20.5 kw; 489 ft.; N36 41 0 W114 30 48
1601 Belverdera Rd, 204 E., West Palm Beach, FL 33406 US
(800) 525-5683, *Fax:* (916) 251-1650
www.klove.com
klove@klove.com
License: Mesquite, Clark County, NV held by Southern Nevada Educational Broadcasters.
Arbitron Metro Market: Mesquite, NV *Format:* Christian, Gospel
No. News Employees: 13
Darrell Chambliss, Chairman
Carl Auel, CEO
Mike Novak, President and CEO
Fred Hodges, General Manager
David Pierce, Programming Director
Ed Lenane, News Director
Sam Wallington, Engineering Dir
Dan Antonelli, Chief BusinessDevelopment Officer
Eric Moser, Chief Financial Officer
Brian Burger, Vice President of Human Resources
D. Kevin Blair, Secretary and General Counsel
Tim Luttrell, News Reporter

Moapa

KXLI

01-01-2008; 94.5 mhz FM; 93 kw horiz; Ant 2,089 ft; N36 38 07 W114 07 18
7251 W. Lake Mead Blvd., Suite 300, Las Vegas, NV
(702) 655-1249, *Fax:* (702) 655-6175
www.vibevegas.com
License: Moapa, Clark County, NV held by Aurora Media LLC.
Arbitron Metro Market: Las Vegas, NV
Scott Mahalick, General Manager

Moapa Valley

KJUL

07-01-2001; 104.7 mhz FM *Hrs Open:* 24; 100 kw; 604 ft.; N36 41 0 W114 30 48
7032 Valley Nails Lane, Las Vegas, NV 89110 US
(702) 258-0285, *Fax:* (702) 258-7570
www.kjul1047.com
scott@smiradio.com
License: Moapa Valley, Clark County, NV held by Summit American Inc.
Wire Services: AP
Arbitron Metro Market: Las Vegas, NV *Format:* Adult Contemp, Country *Target Audience:* 25-54. *Adv. Rates:* 5; 5; 5; na
Scott Gentry, General Manager
Kurt Gentry, Station Manager
Scott Gentry, Programming Director

KRRN

11-01-1990; 92.7 mhz FM; 100 kw horiz; 1926 ft.; N36 36 4 W114 35 6
1955 Casino Drive #101, Laughlin, NV 89029 US
(702) 434-0015, *Fax:* (323) 900-6108
www.elgato9278.com
License: Moapa Valley, Mohave County, NV held by Entravision Holdings LLC.
Group Owner: Entravision Communications Corp.; (acq 8-29-02; $12.43 million).
Nat'l Network: ABC
Arbitron Metro Market: Moapa Valley-Las Vegas, NV Dolan Springs, AZ *Format:* Tejano
Rick Murphy, Operations Dir
David Ferran, General Sales Mgr

North Las Vegas

KYDZ

01-01-1956; 1140 khz AM *Hrs Open:* 24 hrs
600 New Hampshire Ave., N.W., Suite 1200, Washington, DC 20037 US
(702) 253-9800, *Fax:* (702) 889-7373
www.kydzradiolv.com
License: North Las Vegas, NV held by CBS Radio Stations Inc.
Group Owner: CBS Radio
Arbitron Metro Market: Las Vegas, NV *Format:* Children
Leah Hovig, Operations Dir
Frank Feder, General Sales Mgr
Cat Thomas, Programming Director
Juicy Balaoro, Promotions Manager
Mike Weaver, Chief Engineer
Lori Heeren, General Sales Manager

KSHP

01-01-1954; 1400 khz AM *Hrs Open:* 24
14 Douglas Avenue, Elgin, IL 60120 US
(702) 221-1200, *Fax:* (702) 221-2285
www.kshp.com/
info@kshp.com
License: North Las Vegas, NV held by Las Vegas Radio Co.
Group Owner: McNaughton-Jakle Stations; (acq 9-20-96; $600,000).
Arbitron Metro Market: Las Vegas, NV *Format:* Sports *Adv. Rates:* 40; 25; 40; 25
K. Richard Jakle, President
Brett Grant, Operations Dir
Brett Grant, General Manager
Renee Reed, General Sales Mgr
Joe Sands, Chief Engineer

KFRH

09-01-1982; 104.3 mhz FM *Hrs Open:* 24; 24.5 kw; 3701 ft.; N35 58 2 W115 30 6
3825 Forrestgate Drive, Suite 100, Winston-Salem, NC 27103 US
(702) 730-0300, *Fax:* (702) 736-8447
www.1027fresh.fm
kfrhfm@kfrhfm.com
License: North Las Vegas, Clark County, NV held by KJUL License LLC.
Group Owner: Beasley Broadcast Group Inc.; (acq 9-6-2000; grpsl)
Arbitron Metro Market: Las Vegas, NV *Format:* Adult Contemp
Tom Davis, General Manager
Mark Warlaumont, General Sales Mgr
Don Hallett, Programming Director
Courtney Smith, Promotions Manager
Patti Mills, General Sales Manager

KXNT

01-01-1986; 840 khz AM *Hrs Open:* 24
600 New Hampshire Avenue, N.W., Suite 1200, Washington, DC 20037 US
(702) 364-8400, *Fax:* (702) 889-7384
www.kxnt.com
info@kxnt.com
License: North Las Vegas, NV held by Infinity Radio Inc.
Group Owner: CBS Radio; (acq 11-13-98; grpsl).
Nat'l Network: CBS Radio
Arbitron Metro Market: Las Vegas, NV *Format:* News, News/Talk, 86 *Target Audience:* 35-64; upscale adults *Adv. Rates:* 140; 175;140; 20
Tom Humm, General Manager
Dan Larson, General Sales Mgr
Jack Landreth, Programming Director
Tracy Teagarden, Engineering Dir

Overton

KVGQ

106.9 mhz FM; 92 kw; Ant 2,043 ft; N36 50 55 W114 28 23
Wells Fargo Tower, 17th Fl., 3800 Howard Hughes Pkwy., Las Vegas, NV
, *Fax:* (702) 736-2986
License: Overton, Clark County, NV held by Kemp Communications Inc.
Group Owner: Kemp Communications Inc.
Arbitron Metro Market: Las Vegas, NV
Will Kemp, President

Pahrump

KXTE

01-01-1989; 107.5 mhz FM *Hrs Open:* 24; 24.5 kw; 3730 ft.; N35 57 57 W115 30 3
600 New Hampshire Ave NW, Suite 1200, Washington, DC 20037 US
(702) 257-1075, *Fax:* (702) 889-7575
www.xtremeradio.fm
License: Pahrump, Nye County, NV held by Infinity Radio Inc.
Group Owner: CBS Radio; (acq 11-13-98; grpsl).
Arbitron Metro Market: Las Vegas, NV *Format:* Alternative, Talk *Target Audience:* 18-49.
Frank Feder, General Manager
Frank Feder, General Sales Mgr
Chris Ripley, Programming Director
Tracy Teagarden, Chief Engineer
Jerry McKenna, Market Manager

KNYE

11-19-2001; 95.1 mhz FM *Hrs Open:* 24; 6 kw; -93 ft.; N36 11 52 W116 2 8
Hc 65 Box 71885, Pahrump, NV 89041 US
(775) 751-6100, *Fax:* (775) 751-6193
www.knye.com
karen@knye.com
License: Pahrump, Nye County, NV held by Pahrump Radio Inc.
Arbitron Metro Market: Las Vegas, NV *Format:* Oldies
Karen Jackson, President
Joe Sands, Chief Engineer

Panaca

*KLNR

05-01-1989; 91.7 mhz FM *Hrs Open:* 24; 1 kw; 3425 ft.; N37 53 38 W114 34 40 *Rebroadcasts:* Rebroadcasts KNPR(FM) Las Vegas 100%
1289 S. Torrey Pines Dr., Las Vegas, NV 89102 US
(702) 258-9895, *Fax:* (702) 258-5646
reception@knpr.org
License: Panaca, Lincoln County, NV held by Nevada Public Radio.
Nat'l Network: NPR
Arbitron Metro Market: Las Vegas, NV *Format:* News
Lamar Marchese, General Manager

Paradise

KNUU

02-21-1962; 970 khz AM *Hrs Open:* 24
4800 North Central Ave, Phoenix, AZ 85012 US
(702) 735-8644, *Fax:* (702) 734-4755
www.knews970.com
License: Paradise, NV held by BTR West Inc.
Group Owner: BusinessTalkRadio.Net Inc.; (acq 11-13-2006; $3.9 million)
Nat'l Network: Wall Street; ABC; CNN Radio
Arbitron Metro Market: Las Vegas, NV *Format:* News, News/Talk, 86 *Hrs. of News Programming:* news progmg 154 hrs wkly *No. News Employees:* 8 *Target Audience:* 35 plus.
Michael Metter, President
Jim Servino, General Manager

Reno

KJFK

10-30-1963; 1230 khz AM *Hrs Open:* 24; 0.82 kw-U, ND1; N39 30 41 W119 42 51
1900 Avenue of the Stars, Suite 1880, Los Angeles, CA 90067 US
(775) 829-1964, *Fax:* (775) 825-3183
www.1230kjfk.com
info@1230kjfk.com
License: Reno, NV held by Americom Las Vegas L.P.
Group Owner: Americom
Arbitron Metro Market: Reno, Nevada *Format:* Alternative, Talk *Target Audience:* 35 plus.
Tom Quinn, President
Daniel Cook, General Manager
Dan Fritz, Programming Director
Steve Weber, Chief Engineer

KDOT

10-12-1966; 104.5 mhz FM *Hrs Open:* 24; 25 kw; 2930 ft.; N39 18 48 W119 52 59
6290 Sunset Blvd., Hollywood, CA 90028 US
(775) 329-9261, *Fax:* (775) 323-1450
www.kdot.com
javet@kdot.com
License: Reno, Washoe County, NV held by Lotus Radio Corp.
Group Owner: Lotus Communications Corp.; (acq 3-30-93; $600,000 with KIRS(AM) Sun Valley;
Nat'l Reps: D & R Radio
Arbitron Metro Market: Reno, NV *Format:* Rock/AOR *Hrs. of News Programming:* news progmg 3 hrs wkly *No. News Employees:* 1 *Target Audience:* 18-49; young active adults that like today's lifestyle
Jave Patterson, Operations Dir
Dane Wilt, General Manager
Chip Cooper, General Sales Mgr
Jack Landreth, Programming Director
Derek Sante, Promotions Manager
Joanne Silvernail, News Director

KHIT

01-29-1955; 1450 khz AM *Hrs Open:* 24
C/O Jerome S. Boros, Esq, 1290 Ave of the Americas, New York, NY 10104 US
(775) 329-9261, *Fax:* (775) 323-1450
kena@kozzradio.com
License: Reno, NV held by Lotus Radio Corp.
Group Owner: Lotus Communications Corp.; (acq 9-67)
Nat'l Network: Fox Sports *Nat'l Reps:* D & R Radio
Arbitron Metro Market: Reno, NV *TV Affiliate:* ESPN *Format:* Sports *Target Audience:* 25-49.
Jim McClain, Operations Dir
Dane Wilt, General Manager
Raina Weathers, General Sales Mgr
Ken Allen, Promotions Manager
Steve Diamond, News Director
Mike Weaver, Chief Engineer
Dawn Keeble, Traffic Manager

*KIHM

01-01-1984; 920 khz AM *Hrs Open:* 24
605 West Lake Boulevard, Suite 5, Tahoe City, CA 96145 US
(916) 535-0500, *Fax:* (916) 535-0504
www.ihradio.org
License: Reno, NV held by IHR Educational Broadcasting
Group Owner: IHR Educational Broadcasting; acq 8-24-2000).
Arbitron Metro Market: Reno, NV *Format:* Christian
Doug Pearson, Station Manager

KKOH

10-13-1970; 780 khz AM *Hrs Open:* 24; 50 kw-D, DAN; 50 kw-N, DAN; N39 40 41 W119 48 6
City Center West, 7201 W. Lake Mead Blvd, Las Vegas, NV 89128 US
(775) 789-6700, *Fax:* (775) 789-6767
www.kkoh.com
dan.mason@citcomm.com
License: Reno, NV
Group Owner: Cumulus Media Inc.; (acq 5-18-92; $12.5 million; grpsl;
Nat'l Reps: McGavren Guild
Arbitron Metro Market: Reno, NV *Format:* News, News/Talk, 86 *Special Programming:* Sports, Sp 2 hrs wkly *Hrs. of News Programming:* news progmg 28 hrs wkly *No. News Employees:* 4 *Target Audience:* 35-64.
Andrew Perini, General Manager
Jerry Juskiw, General Sales Mgr
Dan Mason, Programming Director

KNEV

12-25-1953; 95.5 mhz FM; 60 kw; 2280 ft.; N39 15 34 W119 42 16
City Center West, 7201 W. Lake Mead Blvd, Las Vegas, NV 89128 US
(775) 789-6700, *Fax:* (775) 789-6767
www.magic95.com
License: Reno, Washoe County, NV
Group Owner: Cumulus Media Inc.; (acq 4-13-93; $500,000;
Arbitron Metro Market: Reno, NV *Format:* Adult Contemp *Special Programming:* Jazz 2 hrs, relg one hr, pub affrs one hr wkly *Target Audience:* General.
Andrew Perini, General Manager
Kathy Williams, General Sales Mgr
Nick Elliott, Programming Director
Rick Worthington, News Director
Martin Stabbert, Chief Engineer

KURK

11-01-1994; 92.9 mhz FM; 48 kw; 502 ft.; N39 35 3 W119 48 6
City Center West, 7201 W. Lake Mead Blvd, Las Vegas, NV 89128 US
(775) 333-0123, *Fax:* (775) 322-7361
www.kurkfm.com
info@kurkfm.com
License: Reno, Washoe County, NV held by Wilks License Co.-Reno LLC.
Group Owner: Wilks Broadcast Group LLC; (acq 9-29-2005; grpsl)
Arbitron Metro Market: Reno, NV *Format:* Classic Rock
Raina Malone, General Manager
Chuck Reeves, Programming Director
Jay Davis, News Director

KOZZ-FM

09-01-1969; 105.7 mhz FM *Hrs Open:* 24; 25 kw; 2930 ft.; N39 18 48 W119 52 59
Mailing Address: 6290 Sunset Blvd., Los Angeles, CA 90028 US
Second Address: 2900 Sutro St., Reno, NV 89512
(775) 329-9261, *Fax:* (775) 323-1450
www.kozzradio.com
License: Reno, Washoe County, NV held by Lotus Radio Corp.
Group Owner: Lotus Communications Corp.; (acq 1-1-78)
Arbitron Metro Market: Reno, NV *Format:* Classic Rock
Bill Shriftman, CFO
Rick Carter, Programming Director
Dawn Keeble, News Director

KPLY

10-25-1928; 630 khz AM
6290 Sunset Blvd, Suite 1600, Hollywood, CA 90028 US
(775) 329-9261, *Fax:* (775) 323-1450
www.espn945.com
dane@lotusradio.com
License: Reno, NV held by Lotus Radio Corp.
Group Owner: Lotus Communications Corp.; (Acq 1995; $325,000)
Arbitron Metro Market: Reno, NV *Format:* Sports *Target Audience:* 25-54.
Jave Patterson, Operations Dir
Dane Wilt, General Manager
Chip Cooper, General Sales Mgr
Ken Allen, Programming Director

KRNV-FM

08-12-1986; 102.1 mhz FM *Hrs Open:* 24; 11 kw; 492 ft.; N39 35 3 W119 47 52
1500 Foremaster Lane, #2, Las Vegas, NV 89101 US
(775) 333-1017, *Fax:* (775) 333-9046
www.entravision.com; www.tricolor1021.com
License: Reno, Washoe County, NV held by Entravision Holdings LLC.
Group Owner: Entravision Communications Corp.; (acq 3-14-00; grpsl).
Arbitron Metro Market: Reno, NV *Format:* Tejano *Target Audience:* 18-49; adults
Walter Ulloa, Chairman
Walter Ulloa, CEO
Jeff Liberman, President
Jeffery A. Liberman, Operations Dir
Viola Cody, General Sales Mgr
Julio Cisneros, Programming Director
Christopher T. Young, Exec. VP, Treasurer & CFO

*KUNR

10-07-1963; 88.7 mhz FM; 20 kw; 2169 ft.; N39 15 34 W119 42 16
Kunr, Mail Stop 294, Reno, NV 89557 US
(775) 327-5867, *Fax:* (775) 784-1381
www.kunr.org
feedback@kunr.org
License: Reno, Washoe County, NV held by University of Nevada Board of Regents.
Nat'l Network: NPR; PRI
Arbitron Metro Market: Reno, NV *Format:* Jazz, News *Special Programming:* Folk 2 hrs, ethnic 9 hrs wkly *Target Audience:* General.
Steven Zink, President
Terry Joy, Operations Dir
David Stipech, General Manager
Albert ""AJ"" Kenneson, Office Manager / Program Officer
Shannon Graves, Chief Engineer
Theresa Reilly, Business Sponsorships
M'Lissa Wilkins,Business Office Support

KXEQ

07-01-1946; 1340 khz AM; 0.9774 kw-U, ND1; N39 31 5 W119 44 29
323 East San Joaquin St., Tulare, CA 93274 US
(775) 827-1111(775) 827-1313, *Fax:* (775) 827-2082
kxeq@scbglobal.net
License: Reno, NV held by Azteca Broadcasting Corp.
Group Owner: Azteca Broadcasting Corp.; acq 10-16-91; $30,000;
Nat'l Network: AP Radio
Arbitron Metro Market: Reno, NV
Jose Mares, General Manager
Jose Arriaga, Programming Director

KXTO

01-01-1991; 1550 khz AM *Hrs Open:* 24; 2.5 kw-D, ND1; 0.094 kw-N, ND1; N39 34 39 W119 50 52
4604 Hurford Terrace, Encino, CA 91436 US
(775) 248-3257, *Fax:* (775) 284-3259
www.lavozcristiana.com
radio@lavozcristiana.com
License: Reno, NV held by First Broadcasting of Nevada Inc.
Arbitron Metro Market: Reno, NV *Format:* Religious *Hrs. of News Programming:* News progmg 10 hrs wkly *Target Audience:* Hispanics. *Adv. Rates:* 24; 20; 24; 16
Yolanda Amaya, General Manager

*KJIV

89.5 mhz FM; kw
Meadows Community Colleg, 7000 Dandini Blvd., Reno, NV 89512 US
(775) 824-8611
www.tmcc.edu
License: Reno, Washoe County, NV held by Board of Regents of the Nevada System of Higher Education.
Arbitron Metro Market: Reno, NV
Michael Rainey, General Manager

Smith

KSVL

01-01-1999; 92.3 mhz FM; 0.49 kw; 2073 ft.; N38 41 6 W119 11 4
P.O. Box 123, Smith, NV 89430 US
(775) 465-2200
www.ksvl92.com
ksvl92@yahoo.com
License: Smith, Lyon County, NV held by Donegal Enterprises.

Arbitron Metro Market: Smith, NV *Format:* Talk
Wayne Donegal, General Manager

Sparks

KBZZ
08-09-1960; 1270 khz AM *Hrs Open:* 24
1900 Avenue of the Stars, Suite 1880, Los Angeles, CA 90067 US
(775) 829-1964, *Fax:* (775) 825-3183
www.kbzz.com
info@kbzz.com
License: Sparks, NV held by Americom Las Vegas L.P.
Group Owner: Americom; (acq 1996; grpsl)
Nat'l Network: CBS; Westwood One
Arbitron Metro Market: Reno, NV *Format:* News, News/Talk, 84, Talk *Target Audience:* 25-54; primarily men who are interested in sports
Tom Quinn, President
Daniel Cook, General Manager
Dan Fritz, Programming Director
Steve Webber, Chief Engineer

KMXW
07-01-1983; 100.9 mhz FM *Hrs Open:* 24; 2.9 kw; 203 ft; N39 22 04 W119 47 07
300 E. 2nd St. 14th Floor, Reno, NV 89512
(775) 333-0123, *Fax:* (775) 333-0110
License: Sparks, Washoe County, NV held by Wilks License Co.-Reno LLC.
Group Owner: Wilks Broadcast Group LLC; (acq 9-29-2005; grpsl).
Nat'l Network: ABC
Arbitron Metro Market: Reno, NV *Target Audience:* 18-54; general
Raina Malone, General Manager
Jeremy Smith, Programming Director
Lori Quinn, News Director
Matt Bates, Music Director

KWFP
01-01-1993; 92.1 mhz FM *Hrs Open:* 24; 8.9 kw; Ant 502 ft; N39 35 03 W119 48 06
300 E. Second St. 14 th Fl., Reno, NV 89502
(775) 333-0123
www.smoothjazzreno.com
info@smoothjazzreno.com
License: Sparks, Washoe County, NV held by Wilks License Co.-Reno LLC.
Group Owner: Wilks Broadcast Group LLC; (acq 9-29-2005; grpsl).
Population Served: 300,000 *Arbitron Metro Market:* Reno, NV
Reina Malone, General Manager
Jay Davis, Programming Director
Jay Davis, News Director

KNNR
01-01-2002; 1400 khz AM; 600 w-U; N39 34 10 W119 45 03
1085 E. 2nd St., Suite 1, Reno, NV 38104
(775) 348-5852, *Fax:* (775) 348-5865
www.mega1400.com
mega@lameganet.com
License: Sparks, Washoe County, NV held by George S. Flinn Jr.
Ruben Villalobos, General Manager
Nora Breton, General Sales Mgr

*KLRH
88.3 mhz FM; 2.95 kw; 2877 ft.; N39 45 38 W119 27 59
US
(800) 525-5683, *Fax:* (916) 251-1650
www.klove.com
klove@klove.com
License: Sparks, Washoe County, NV held by Educational Media Foundation.
Group Owner: EMF Broadcasting
Nat'l Network: K-Love
Arbitron Metro Market: Sparks, NV *Format:* Christian *No. News Employees:* 13 *Target Audience:* 25-44; Judeo Christian female
Darrell Chambliss, Chairman
Mike Novak, President and CEO
Dan Beck, Operations Dir
David Pierce, Programming Director
Ed Lenane, News Director
Sam Wallington, Engineering Dir
Richard Hunt, News Reporter
Marya Morgan, NewsReporter
Dan Antonelli, Chief Business Development Officer
Eric Moser, Chief Financial Officer
Brian Burger, Vice President of Human Resources
D. Kevin Blair, Secretary and General Counsel

Spring Creek

KBGZ
11-18-2007; 103.9 mhz FM; 12.6 kw; Ant 1,597 ft; N40 55 18 W115 50 58
c/o Ruby Radio Corp., 1750 Manzanita, Suite 1, Elko, NV
(775) 777-1196, *Fax:* (775) 777-9587
License: Spring Creek, Elko County, NV held by Ruby Radio Corp.
Group Owner: Ruby Radio Corp.
Population Served: 25,000 *Target Audience:* 18-54; men & women
Ken Sutherland, President
Alene Sutherland, Operations Dir
Mike Allen, News Director

Sun Valley

KZTQ
01-01-2002; 93.7 mhz FM; 3.6 kw; Ant 423 ft; N39 35 02 W119 47 54
595 E. Plumb Ln., Reno, NV 38104
(775) 789-6700, *Fax:* (775) 789-6767
wild937.com
angel.garcia@citcomm.com
License: Sun Valley, Washoe County, NV held by Flinn Broadcasting Corp.
Arbitron Metro Market: Reno, NV
Dana Johnson, General Manager

KUUB
01-01-1999; 94.5 mhz FM; 50 kw; 459 ft.; N39 35 2 W119 47 53
6290 Sunset Blvd, Suite 1600, Los Angeles, CA 90028 US
(775) 329-9261, *Fax:* (775) 323-1450
www.945themountain.com
License: Sun Valley, Washoe County, NV held by Lotus Radio Corp.
Group Owner: Lotus Communications Corp.
Arbitron Metro Market: Reno, NV *TV Affiliate:* ESPN *Format:* Sports, Talk
Dane Wilt, General Manager
Chip Cooper, General Sales Mgr
Chuck Short, News Director
Mike Weaver, Chief Engineer

KQLO
01-01-1946; 1590 khz AM; 5 kw-D, ND1; 0.067 kw-N, ND1; N39 24 57 W119 42 51
3550 Chinee Way, Suite B, Reno, NV 89511 US
(775) 827-1589, *Fax:* (775) 284-2092
www.radio1590.com
ragrcia@radio1590.com
License: Sun Valley, NV held by Universal Broadcasting Inc.
Nat'l Reps: Interep
Arbitron Metro Market: Reno, NV *Format:* News, Spanish, 86
Target Audience: General. *Adv. Rates:* 21; 21; 21; 18
Lee Chavez, General Manager
Ricardo Garcia, General Sales Mgr
Sonya Saz, Programming Director

*KXNV
89.1 mhz FM; kw
US
(775) 348-7557, *Fax:* (775) 348-7707
www.planevada.org
info@planevada.org
License: Sun Valley, NV held by Progressive Leadership Alliance of Nevada
Bob Fulkerson, Station Manager

Tonopah

KHWK
07-29-1982; 92.7 mhz FM; 0.29 kw; 971 ft.; N38 4 22 W117 13 16
P.O. Box 1669, Tonopah, NV 89049 US
(888) 288-4199, *Fax:* (435) 628-6636
www.alienradio.us
requests@alienradio.fm
License: Tonopah, Nye County, NV held by Donald W. Kaminiski Jr.
Format: Alternative *Special Programming:* Talk 20 hours wkly
Target Audience: Paranormal Enthusiasts
Don Kaminski, CEO

*KTPH
10-01-1988; 91.7 mhz FM *Hrs Open:* 24; 1 kw; 1411 ft.; N38 3 7 W117 13 30 *Rebroadcasts:* Rebroadcasts KNPR(FM) Las Vegas 100%
1289 S. Torrey Pines Dr., Las Vegas, NV 89102 US
(702) 258-9895, *Fax:* (702) 258-5646
www.knpr.org
reception@knpr.org
License: Tonopah, Nye County, NV held by Nevada Public Radio.
Nat'l Network: NPR
Arbitron Metro Market: Las Vegas, NV *Format:* Classical, News
Florence Rogers, President
Florence Rogers, General Manager
Dave Becker, Programming Director
Adam Burke, News Director

Wendover

KVUW
01-01-2006; 102.3 mhz FM; 3 kw; 26 ft.; N40 44 30 W114 2 10
218 N Wolcott, Casper, WY 82601 US
(435) 665-0600, *Fax:* (435) 665-0600
License: Wendover, Elko County, NV held by Murray Grey Broadcasting Inc.
Group Owner: Northeast Broadcasting Company Inc.; (acq 12-21-2005; $750,000 with KRQU(FM) Laramie, WY)
Arbitron Metro Market: Wendover, NV
Steven Silberberg, President

Whitney

KLSQ
08-15-1986; 870 khz AM *Hrs Open:* 24
3102 Oak Lawn Ave., Suite 215, Dallas, TX 75219 US
(702) 284-6400, *Fax:* (702) 284-6403
www.univision.com
License: Whitney, NV held by HBC-Las Vegas Inc.
Group Owner: Univision Radio; (acq 9-22-2003; grpsl).
Arbitron Metro Market: Las Vegas, NV *Target Audience:* 35 plus.
Dana Demerjiah, Operations Dir
Dana Demerjian, General Manager
Cristina Valarezo, General Sales Mgr
Jose Santos, Programming Director
Gloria Salvador, News Director
Manny Garcia, Chief Engineer

Winnemucca

KWNA
01-28-1955; 1400 khz AM *Hrs Open:* 24; 1 kw-U, ND1; N40 57 23 W117 42 48
Mailing Address: P. O. Box 1400, Winnemucca, NV 89445 US
Second Address: 335 West 4th Street, Winnemucca, NV 89445
(775) 623-5203, *Fax:* (775) 625-1011
BOBBOLTON1@AOL.com
License: Winnemucca, NV held by Ely Radio LLC.
Group Owner: Ely Radio LLC; (acq 11-6-2006; $500,000 with co-located FM)
Nat'l Network: ABC
Arbitron Metro Market: Winnemucca, NV *Format:* News, News/Talk, 86 *Special Programming:* Farm 2 hrs wkly *Hrs. of News Programming:* news progmg 12 hrs wkly *No. News Employees:* 2 *Target Audience:* General.
Bob Bolton, General Manager
Rodd Stowell, Programming Director
Rachael Marie, News Director
Sandy Crownover, Traffic Manager

KWNA-FM
04-03-1982; 92.7 mhz FM *Hrs Open:* 24; 0.47 kw; 2116 ft.; N41 0 40 W117 45 59
Mailing Address: P.O. Box 1400, Winnemucca, NV 89446 US
Second Address: 335 West 4th Street, Winnemucca, NV 89445
(775) 623-5203, *Fax:* (775) 625-1011
BOBBOLTON1@AOL.com
License: Winnemucca, Humboldt County, NV
Group Owner: Ely Radio LLC
Nat'l Network: ABC
Arbitron Metro Market: Winnemucca, NV *Format:* Country *Target Audience:* 25-54.
Sandy Crownover, Operations Dir
Bob Bolton, General Manager
Rodd Stowell, Programming Director

*KWNM
89.7 mhz FM; kw
US
(615) 469-5122, *Fax:* (615) 216-7266
www.lifetalk.net
License: Winnemucca, Humboldt County, NV held by Life Talk Radio Inc.
Arbitron Metro Market: Hurley, NM
Don Schneider, President

New Hampshire

Bedford

WMLL
06-01-1996; 96.5 mhz FM; 0.73 kw; 935 ft.; N42 59 2 W71 35 22
73 Kercheval Avenue, Grosse Pointe Farms, MI 48236 US
(603) 669-7979,(603) 669-5777, *Fax:* (603) 669-4641
www.965themill.com
License: Bedford, Hillsborough County, NH held by Saga Communications of New England LLC.
Group Owner: Saga Communications Inc.; (acq 9-29-97; $3.3 million).
Nat'l Reps: Katz Radio
Arbitron Metro Market: Manchester, NH *Format:* Classic Rock
Target Audience: 35-54; baby boomers
Edward Christian, CEO
Raymond Garon, President
J.C. Haze, Operations Dir
Samuel Bush, CFO

Belmont

WNHW
05-08-1994; 93.3 mhz FM; 0.3 kw; 1020 ft.; N43 23 52 W71 33 3
P.O. Box 1923, Concord, NH 03302 US
(603) 224-8486, *Fax:* (603) 528-5185
www.933thewolf.com
adukette@nassaubroadcasting.com
License: Belmont, Belknap County, NH held by Nassau Broadcasting III L.L.C.
Group Owner: Nassau Broadcasting Partners L.P.; (acq 10-1-2004; $8 million with WJYY(FM) Concord).
Arbitron Metro Market: Concord, NH *Format:* Country
Brit Johnson, General Manager
Pete DeTone, General Sales Mgr
AJ Dukette, Programming Director
Kim Terbrack, Promotions Manager
Steve Ordinetz, Engineering Dir

Berlin

WMOU
01-01-1947; 1230 khz AM *Hrs Open:* 24
38 Glen Avenue, Box 489, Berlin, NH 03570 US
(603) 752-1230, *Fax:* (603) 788-3536
wmou@ncia.net
License: Berlin, NH held by Barry P. Lunderville.
Group Owner: Barry P. Lunderville Stns; (acq 11-11-2003; $75,000)
Nat'l Network: Westwood One
Arbitron Metro Market: Berlin, NH *Format:* Adult Contemp
Special Programming: Fr 3 hrs, talk 2 hrs, swap shop 3 hrs wkly *Hrs. of News Programming:* news progmg 6 hrs wkly *No. News Employees:* 1 *TargetAudience:* 25-54; local residents of northern New Hampshire
Barry Lunderville, President
Bob Barbin, Operations Dir
Randy Frank, General Sales Mgr
Brian Lunderville, Chief Engineer

WKDR
1490 khz AM
US
(603) 752-1230, *Fax:* (603) 752-3117
License: Berlin, NH held by Barry P. Lunderville.
Group Owner: Barry P. Lunderville Stns
Arbitron Metro Market: Berlin, NH *Format:* Adult Contemp
Barry Lunderville, General Manager

Campton

WLKC
01-01-1997; 105.7 mhz FM *Hrs Open:* 24; 4.1 kw; 390 ft.; N43 45 45 W71 39 0 *Rebroadcasts:* Rebroadcasts WXRU(FM) Wolfeboro 100%
288 South River Road, Bedford, NH 03110 US
(802) 288-1033, *Fax:* (802) 288-8134
www.92.5theriver.com
nebco231@hotmail.com
License: Campton, Grafton County, NH held by Devon Broadcasting Co. Inc.
Format: Triple A *Target Audience:* 25-54.
Steve Young, General Manager
Dana Marshall, Programming Director
Stephanie Battaglia, News Director
Lou Muise, Chief Engineer

Claremont

WHDQ
01-01-1948; 106.1 mhz FM; 1.6 kw; 2247 ft.; N43 26 15 W72 27 8
Box 1230, Claremont, NH 03743 US
(603) 298-0332, *Fax:* (603) 727-0134
www.q106rock.com
info@q106rock.com
License: Claremont, Sullivan County, NH
Group Owner: Nassau Broadcasting Partners L.P.
Format: Classic Rock
Gene Purcell, General Manager
Phil Corrivean, Station Manager

WTSV
01-01-1948; 1230 khz AM; 1 kw-U, ND1; N43 22 15 W72 19 42
P. O. Box 1230, Claremont, NH 03743 US
(603) 542-7735, *Fax:* (603) 542-8721
License: Claremont, NH held by Nassau Broadcasting III L.L.C.
Group Owner: Nassau Broadcasting Partners L.P.; (acq 8-2-2004; grpsl).
Nat'l Network: ABC; ESPN Radio *Regional Reps:* Roslin.
Arbitron Metro Market: Lebanon, NH *Format:* Sports *Target Audience:* 35 plus.
Jeffrey Shapiro, President
Shirley Clark, General Manager

Concord

***WEVO(FM)**
08-04-1981; 89.1 mhz FM *Hrs Open:* 24; 50 kw; 380 ft; N43 12 53 W71 34 28
2 Pillsbury Street, 6th Floor, Concord, NH 3301
(603) 228-8910, *Fax:* (603) 224-6052
www.nhpr.org
admin@nhpr.org
License: Concord, Merrimack County, NH held by New Hampshire Public Radio Inc.
Nat'l Network: NPR; PRI *Wire Services:* AP
Population Served: 42,733 *Arbitron Metro Market:* Concord, NH *Format:* News, News/Talk, 86 *Special Programming:* Folk 3 hrs wkly *Hrs. of News Programming:* news progmg 42 hrs wkly *No. News Employees:* 9*Target Audience:* 25-54; well educated adults
Elizabeth Gardella, President & CEO
Sarah Ashworth, News Director
John Huntley, Engineering Dir
Todd Mayo, Treasurer
Todd Bookman, Health Reporter
Michael D. Redmond, Secretary
Janet Prince, Vice Chair
Emily Corwin, StateImpactNH Reporter
Chris Jensen, North Country Reporter

WJYY
09-15-1983; 105.5 mhz FM *Hrs Open:* 24; 1.55 kw; 456 ft.; N43 16 46 W71 30 15
P.O. Box 1923, Concord, NH 03302 US
(603) 225-1160, *Fax:* (603) 224-7280
www.wjyy.com
License: Concord, Merrimack County, NH held by Nassau Broadcasting III L.L.C.
Group Owner: Nassau Broadcasting Partners L.P.; (acq 10-1-2004; $8 million with WNHW(FM) Belmont).
Format: Contemporary Hits/Top 40 *Hrs. of News Programming:* news progmg 6 hrs wkly *No. News Employees:* 1 *Target Audience:* 25-54.
Brit Johnson, General Manager
Pete DeTone, General Sales Mgr
Joe Dukette, Programming Director
Dawn Parris, General Sales Manager

WKXL
06-15-1946; 1450 khz AM *Hrs Open:* 24; 1 kw-U, ND1; N43 11 39 W71 33 17
P. O. Box 875, Concord, NH 03301 US
(603) 225-5521, *Fax:* (603) 224-6404
www.wkxl1450.com
info@wkxl1450.com
License: Concord, NH held by New Hampshire Family Radio LLC
Nat'l Network: AP Radio *Wire Services:* AP
Arbitron Metro Market: Concord (Lake Regions), NH *Format:* News, News/Talk, 86 *Hrs. of News Programming:* news progmg 36 hrs wkly *No. News Employees:* 2 *Target Audience:* 35 plus; adults in Concord, Hillsboro,Manchester & contiguous towns *Adv. Rates:* 15; 7.50; 15; 5
Anthony Schilella, Station Manager

WWHK
03-07-1972; 102.3 mhz FM *Hrs Open:* 24; 3 kw; 285 ft.; N43 13 0 W71 34 34
P. O. Box 875, Concord, NH 03301 US
(603) 225-1160, *Fax:* (603) 225-8935
www.thehawkrocks.com
jfronk@nassaubroadcasting.com
License: Concord, Merrimack County, NH held by Capitol Broadcasting Corp. Inc.
Group Owner: Vox Communications; (acq 8-12-99)
Target Audience: 25-54; adult audience in Merrimack county - south central NH
Brid Johnson, General Manager

***WSPS**
01-01-1974; 90.5 mhz FM *Hrs Open:* 24; 0.2 kw; -59 ft.; N43 11 37 W71 34 29
325 Pleasant Street, Concord, NH 03301 US
(603) 228-4810,(603) 230-5810, *Fax:* (603) 229-4891
www.wsps.sps.edu
wsps@sps.edu
License: Concord, Merrimack County, NH held by St. Paul's School.
Format: Variety/Diverse *Target Audience:* General.
David Harvey, General Manager
Glenn Reider, Station Manager

***WVNH**
03-07-1999; 91.1 mhz FM; 0.65 kw vert; 331 ft.; N43 23 54 W71 25 24
PO Box 40, Concord, NH 03302 US
(603) 227-0911
www.nhgr.org
info@nhgr.org
License: Concord, Merrimack County, NH held by New Hampshire Gospel Radio Inc.
Arbitron Metro Market: Concord, NH *Format:* Christian
Peter Stohrer, Station Manager & President
John Loker, Vice President
George Dyksta, Treasurer
Janice Cyr, Office Administrator

***WEVO**
08-04-1981; 89.1 mhz FM *Hrs Open:* 24; 50 kw; 381 ft; N43 12 53 W71 34 28 *Rebroadcasts:* Rebroadcasts WEVO(FM) Concord 100%
2 Pillsbury St., 6th Floor, Concord, NH 03301
(603) 228-8910, *Fax:* (603) 224-6052
www.nhpr.org
admin@nhpr.org
License: Concord, Merrimack County, NH held by New Hampshire Public Radio Inc.
Nat'l Network: NPR; PRI; APM *Wire Services:* AP
Special Programming: Folk 3 hrs wkly *Hrs. of News Programming:* news progmg 42 hrs wkly *No. News Employees:* 9 *Target Audience:* 25-54.
Elizabeth Gardella, President & CEO
Scott McPherson, Vice President, Operations & Finance
Jim McCann, Director of Corporate Support
Abby Goldstein, Vice President, Programming
Sarah Ashworth, News Director
Michael Saffell, Directorof Technology

Conway

WBNC
12-21-1955; 1050 khz AM; 1 kw-D, ND1; 0.063 kw-N, ND1; N43 58 48 W71 6 36
Mailing Address: P. O. Box 2008, Conway, NH 03818 US
Second Address: 2 Common Court, Unit A30, North Conway, NH 3860
(603) 356-8870, *Fax:* (603) 356-8875
www.conwaymagic.com/
lucia@wmwv.com
License: Conway, NH held by Mt. Washington Radio & Gramophone L.L.C.
Group Owner: Mt. Washington Radio & Gramophone L.L.C.
Arbitron Metro Market: Conway, NH *Format:* Adult Contemp
Greg Frizzell, General Manager
Christoper McNevich, VP of Sales/Marketing
Gair MacKenzie, News Director

WVMJ
10-23-1995; 104.5 mhz FM *Hrs Open:* 24; 1.85 kw; 429 ft.; N43 56 48 W71 8 24
Mailing Address: P.O. Box 2008, Conway, NH 03818 US
Second Address: 2 Common Court, Unit A30, N. Conway, NH 3860
(603) 356-8870, *Fax:* (603) 356-8875
www.conwaymagic.com
lucia@wmwv.com
License: Conway, Carroll County, NH held by Mt. Washington Radio & Gramophone L.L.C.
Group Owner: Mt. Washington Radio & Gramophone L.L.C.; acq 10-15-01; grpsl).

RADIO - U.S.

Arbitron Metro Market: Conway, NH *Format:* Adult Contemp *Adv. Rates:* 25; 25; 25; 17.50
Greg Frizzell, General Manager
Christoper McNevich, VP of Sales/Marketing
Cooper Fox, Programming Director
Gair MacKenzie, News Director

WMWV
06-23-1967; 93.5 mhz FM; 1.85 kw; 423 ft.; N43 56 48 W71 8 24
Mailing Address: P. O. Box 2008, Conway, NH 03818 US
Second Address: 2 Common Court, Unit A30, North Conway, NH 3860
(603) 356-8870, *Fax:* (603) 356-8875
www.wmwv.com
office@wmwv.com
License: Conway, Carroll County, NH held by Mt. Washington Radio & Gramophone L.L.C.
Group Owner: Mt. Washington Radio & Gramophone L.L.C.; acq 9-27-01; grpsl).
Nat'l Reps: Roslin
Arbitron Metro Market: Conway, NH *Format:* Triple A
Lucia Seavey, Operations Dir
Greg Frizzell, General Manager
Mark Johnson, Programming Director
Gair MacKenzie, News Director

Derry

WDER
10-01-1983; 1320 khz AM *Hrs Open:* 24; 10 kw-D, DA2; 1 kw-N, DA2; N42 51 59 W71 17 14
8 Lawrence Rd., Derry, NH 03038 US
(603) 437-9337(603) 434-9302, *Fax:* (603) 434-1035
www.wder.com
wderam1320@aol.com
License: Derry, NH held by Blount Communications Inc. of NH.
Group Owner: Blount Communications Group; (acq 9-5-00; $793,000)
Nat'l Network: Salem Radio Network
Arbitron Metro Market: Manchester, NH *Format:* Talk, Religious *Target Audience:* 25-54; male & female
William Blount, President
David Young, Operations Dir
Steve Sobozenski, Operations Manager

Dover

WOKQ
08-01-1970; 97.5 mhz FM; 50 kw; 492 ft.; N43 13 26 W70 58 18
Mailing Address: Post Office Box 820, Newburyport, MA 01950 US
Second Address: 292 Middle Rd., Dover, NH 03820-4901
(603) 749-9750, *Fax:* (603) 749-1459
www.wokq.com
info@wokq.com
License: Dover, Strafford County, NH
Group Owner: Cumulus Media Inc.; (acq 9-1-99; grpsl).
Nat'l Network: CNN Radio *Nat'l Reps:* Christal *Wire Services:* AP
Arbitron Metro Market: Portsmouth-Dove *TV Affiliate:* Country *Hrs. of News Programming:* 2 *No. News Employees:* 25-54; general
CEO, Judy Ellis

WTSN
08-01-1956; 1270 khz AM *Hrs Open:* 24; 5 kw-D, DA2; 5 kw-N, DA2; N43 11 1 W70 51 14
P. O. Box 400, Back Rd., Dover, NH 03820 US
(603) 742-0987, *Fax:* (603) 742-0448
www.987thebay.com
susan@987thebay.com
License: Dover, NH held by Garrison City Broadcasting Inc.
Nat'l Reps: McGavren Guild
Arbitron Metro Market: Dover, NH *Format:* News, News/Talk, 84, Talk *No. News Employees:* 3 *Target Audience:* 35-64; very affluent *Adv. Rates:* 50, 40, 40, 20
Bob Demers, CEO
Susan Demers Weigold, Senior Vice President
Sarah Sullivan, Operations Dir
Rick Bean, General Manager
Carole Lanctat, Business Manager

Durham

***WUNH**
07-15-1963; 91.3 mhz FM *Hrs Open:* 24; 1.45 kw horiz, 6 kw vert; 256 ft.; N43 9 23 W70 56 26
Memorial Union Building, Durham, NH 03824 US
(603) 862-2541, *Fax:* (603) 862-2543
www.wunh.unh.edu
gm@wunh.unh.edu
License: Durham, Strafford County, NH held by University of New Hampshire.
Nat'l Network: AP Radio
Arbitron Metro Market: Dover, NH *Format:* Alternative *Special Programming:* Black 4 hrs, blues 3 hrs, jazz 5 hrs, Pol 2 hrs, *Hrs. of News Programming:* News progmg 7 hrs wkly *Target Audience:* Diverse.
Ian Chase, General Manager
Charlie MacCall, Programming Director
Travis Harsin, Promotions Manager
Daniel Day, News Director
Peter Geremia, Chief Engineer
Hannah DeBenedictis, Production Director
Scott Higgins, BusinessManager
Matt Walsh, Sports Director
Garrett Marker, Music Director
Amanda Mead, Secretary

Exeter

WERZ
09-21-1972; 107.1 mhz FM; 5.2 kw; 348 ft.; N43 1 38 W70 52 51
600 Congress Avenue, Suite 1400, Austin, TX 78701 US
(603) 436-7300, *Fax:* (603) 430-9415
www.werz.com
info@werz.com
License: Exeter, Rockingham County, NH
Group Owner: Clear Channel Communications Inc.
Arbitron Metro Market: Exeter, NH *Format:* Contemporary Hits/Top 40
Michael O'Donnell, Programming Director
Beth La Rocque, News Director

WXEX
06-04-1966; 1540 khz AM; 2.5 kw-C, ND3; 5 kw-D, ND3; ND3; 0.003 k; N42 59 23 W70 56 14
600 Congress Avenue, Suite 1400, Austin, TX 78701 US
(603) 583-4767, *Fax:* (603) 430-9415
www.1540wxex.com
comments@WXEXradio.com
License: Exeter, NH held by Aruba Capital Holdings LLC
Nat'l Reps: McGavren Guild
Arbitron Metro Market: Portsmouth-Dover-Rochester, NH
Format: News, News/Talk, 84, Talk
Dan Pierce, Operations Dir
Robert Greer, General Manager
Judy Figliulo, General Sales Mgr
Jennifer McElreavy, Promotions Manager
Kelly Brown, News Director
Ken Neeman, Chief Engineer
Roger Wood, News Director
Beth LaRocque,Traffic Manager

***WPEA**
01-01-1964; 90.5 mhz FM; 0.1 kw; 33 ft.; N42 58 44 W70 57 0
20 Main Street, Exeter, NH 03833 US
(603) 777-4414
WPEA@exeter.edu
License: Exeter, Rockingham County, NH held by Trustees of Phillips Exeter Academy.
Format: Variety/Diverse *Target Audience:* General; students
Alex Snipes, General Manager
Tersa Haire, General Sales Mgr
Tony Gee, Programming Director

Farmington

***WNHI**
07-09-1999; 106.5 mhz FM *Hrs Open:* 24; 2.9 kw; 486 ft.; N43 24 1 W71 9 27 *Rebroadcasts:* Rebroadcasts KLVR(FM) Middletown, CA 100%
19 Boas Lane, Wilton, CT 06897 US
(916) 251-1600, *Fax:* (916) 251-1650
www.klove.com
License: Farmington, Strafford County, NH held by Educational Media Foundation.
Group Owner: EMF Broadcasting; (acq 6-2-2008; $1 million)
Nat'l Network: Air 1
Arbitron Metro Market: Portsmouth-Dove *Format:* Christian
Mike Novak, President

Fitzwilliam Depot

WZNH
870 khz AM
US
(845) 356-9613
License: Fitzwilliam Depot, NH held by Steven Wendell.
Arbitron Metro Market: Fitzwilliam Depot, NH
Steven Wendell, General Manager

Franklin

WFTN
10-30-1966; 1240 khz AM; 1 kw-U, ND1; N43 27 16 W71 38 33
PO Box 99, Babbit Rd, Franklin, NH 03235 US
(603) 934-2500, *Fax:* (603) 934-2933
License: Franklin, NH held by Northeast Communications Corp.
Group Owner: Northeast Communications Corp.; acq 9-30-74)
Format: Contemporary Hits/Top 40
Jeff Fisher, President
Fred Caruso, Operations Dir
Jeff Levitan, General Sales Mgr
Rick Ganley, Promotions Manager
Amy Bates, News Director
Gary Ford, Music Director
Cathy Keyser, Traffic Manager

WFTN-FM
04-10-1987; 94.1 mhz FM; 6 kw; 328 ft.; N43 28 23 W71 36 20
P.O.Box 99, Franklin, NH 03235 US
(603) 934-2500, *Fax:* (603) 934-2933
License: Franklin, Merrimack County, NH
Format: Adult Contemp
Danny Weddle, General Sales Mgr
Philip Hay, Sales

Hampton

WSAK
08-01-1992; 102.1 mhz FM *Hrs Open:* 24; 3 kw; 328 ft.; N42 53 51 W70 53 2 *Rebroadcasts:* Rebroadcasts WSHK(FM) Kittery, ME 100%
Mailing Address: Post Office Box 820, Newburyport, MA 01950 US
Second Address: 292 Middle Rd., Dover, NH 03820-4901
(603) 749-9750, *Fax:* (603) 749-1459
www.shark1053.com
info@wokq.com
License: Hampton, Rockingham County, NH
Group Owner: Cumulus Media Inc.; (acq 7-7-99; grpsl).
Nat'l Network: CNN Radio *Nat'l Reps:* Christal *Wire Services:* AP
Arbitron Metro Market: Hampton, NH *Format:* Contemporary Hits/Top 40, Adult Contemp *No. News Employees:* 2 *Target Audience:* 25-49.
Farid Suleman, CEO
Judy Ellis, President
Mark Ericson, Operations Dir
Marty Lessard, General Manager
Ken Hoffman, General Sales Mgr
Jonathan Smith, Programming Director

Hanover

***WEVH**
10-01-1993; 91.3 mhz FM; 0.175 kw; 1181 ft.; N43 42 30 W72 9 16 *Rebroadcasts:* Rebroadcasts WEVO(FM) Concord 100%
207 North Main Street, Concord, NH 03301 US
(603) 228-8910, *Fax:* (603) 224-6052
www.nhpr.org
License: Hanover, Grafton County, NH held by New Hampshire Public Radio Inc.
Nat'l Network: NPR; PRI *Wire Services:* AP
Arbitron Metro Market: Hanover, NH *Format:* News, News/Talk, 86 *Special Programming:* Folk 3 hrs wkly *Hrs. of News Programming:* news progmg 42 hrs wkly *No. News Employees:* 9 *Target Audience:* 25-54.
Barbara J. Couch, Chairman
Elizabeth Gardella, President & CEO
Sarah Ashworth, News Director
Todd Mayo, Treasurer
Todd Bookman, Health Reporter
Michael D. Redmond, Secretary
Janet Prince, Vice Chair
Emily Corwin, StateImpact NHReporter
Chris Jensen, North Country Reporter

WFRD
02-19-1976; 99.3 mhz FM *Hrs Open:* 24; 6 kw; Ant 328 ft; N43 39 14 W72 17 44.2
Mailing Address: Box 957, Hanover, NH 03755
Second Address: 3rd Fl., Robinson Hall, Dartmouth College, Hanover, NH 3826
(603) 646-3313,(603) 646-3826, *Fax:* (603) 643-7655
www.wfrd.com
License: Hanover, Grafton County, NH
Population Served: 150,000*No. News Employees:* 2 *Target Audience:* 18-45.
Heath Cole, Operations Dir
Heath Cole, General Manager
Heath Cole, Station Manager
Geanette Foster, General Sales Mgr
Geanette Foster, Programming Director

Mirkeood Gorup LLC, Engineering Dir
Gary2 Savoie, Chief Engineer

WGXL
01-12-1987; 92.3 mhz FM; 6 kw; 325 ft.; N43 39 17 W72 17 41
31 Hanover St, Suite 4, Lebanon, NH 03766 US
(603) 448-1400, *Fax:* (603) 448-1755
www.wgxl.com
info@wgxl.com
License: Hanover, Grafton County, NH held by Great Eastern Radio LLC.
Group Owner: Great Eastern Radio LLC; (acq 10-30-2007; grpsl)
Format: Adult Contemp *Target Audience:* 25-49.
Melissa Dubbin, President
Galen Joseph-Hunter, General Manager
Tom Roe, Programming Director

WTSL
10-01-1950; 1400 khz AM *Hrs Open:* 24; 1 kw-U, ND1; N43 41 3 W72 17 46
31 Hanover Street, Suite 4, Lebanon, NH 03766 US
(603) 448-1400, *Fax:* (603) 448-1755
www.wtsl.com
License: Hanover, NH held by Great Eastern Radio LLC.
Group Owner: Great Eastern Radio LLC; (acq 10-30-2007; grpsl)
Nat'l Network: CBS
Arbitron Metro Market: Lebanon, NH *Format:* News, News/Talk, 84, Talk *Hrs. of News Programming:* news progmg 25 hrs wkly *No. News Employees:* 2 *Target Audience:* 35 plus.
Michael Barrett, Operations Dir
Tim Plant, General Manager
Gary Laperle, Chief Engineer
Christopher Olsen, General Manager

Haverhill

WYKR-FM
02-19-1990; 101.3 mhz FM *Hrs Open:* 6 AM-10 PM; 3 kw; 39 ft.; N44 6 49 W71 58 54
Mailing Address: P.O. Box 11oo, Wells River, VT 05081 US
Second Address: Box 1013, Woodsville, NH 3785
(802) 757-2773, *Fax:* (802) 757-2774
www.wykr.com
wykr@kingcon.com
License: Haverhill, Grafton County, NH held by Puffer Broadcasting Inc.
Nat'l Network: Westwood One; NBC; Jones Radio Networks *Nat'l Reps:* Roslin
Arbitron Metro Market: Haverhill, NH *Format:* Country *Target Audience:* 25 plus.
Stephen Puffer, President
Teresa Puffer, Operations Dir
Don Smith, Chief Engineer

Henniker

***WNEC-FM**
02-09-1971; 91.7 mhz FM *Hrs Open:* 17; 0.12 kw; -210 ft.; N43 10 34 W71 49 22
23 Bridge Street, Simon Center, Henniker, NH 03242 US
(603) 428-2278, *Fax:* (603) 428-7230
www.nec.edu/necradio
wnec@nec.edu
License: Henniker, Merrimack County, NH held by New England College.
Arbitron Metro Market: Henniker, NH *Format:* Adult Contemp, Black, 52 *Special Programming:* Blues 4 hrs, country 3 hrs, American Indian 18 hrs *Hrs. of News Programming:* News progmg one hr wkly *Target Audience:* 18-25; college students
Ambrose Metzegen, CEO
Meghan Stone, Station Manager
Justin McDougall, Programming Director
Dale Carlow, Engineering Dir
Kristen Westhoven, Music Director

WNNH
11-17-1989; 99.1 mhz FM *Hrs Open:* 24; 2.8 kw; 479 ft.; N43 12 49 W71 41 19
501 South Street, Concord, NH 03304 US
(603)224-8486, *Fax:* (603) 528-5185
www.wjyy.com
adukette@nassaubroadcasting.com
License: Henniker, Merrimack County, NH held by Nassau Broadcasting III L.L.C.
Group Owner: Nassau Broadcasting Partners L.P.; (acq 3-16-2004; grpsl)
Nat'l Reps: McGavren Guild
Arbitron Metro Market: Henniker, NH *Format:* Talk *Hrs. of News Programming:* news progmg 20 hrs wkly *No. News Employees:* 2 *Target Audience:* 25-54; mass appeal
Andy Mack, Operations Dir
Rob Fulmer, General Manager
Pete DeTone, General Sales Mgr
AJ Dukette, Programming Director
Kim Terbrack, Promotions Manager
Ken Cail, News Director

Hillsboro

WTPL
10-01-1989; 107.7 mhz FM *Hrs Open:* 24; 1.25 kw horiz, 1.22 kw vert; 712 ft.; N43 9 17 W71 47 44
P.O. Box 1923, Concord, NH 03302 US
(603) 545-0777, *Fax:* (603) 545-0781
www.wtplfm.com
License: Hillsboro, Hillsborough County, NH held by Great Eastern Radio LLC.
Group Owner: Great Eastern Radio LLC; (acq 6-3-2004; $1.5 million)
Nat'l Network: CBS Radio; ESPN Radio
Arbitron Metro Market: Manchester, NH *Format:* News, News/Talk, 84, Talk *Hrs. of News Programming:* news progmg 50 hrs wkly *No. News Employees:* 2 *Target Audience:* 35 plus; adult audience in Merrimack &Hillsborough counties
Bob Lipman, Operations Dir
Mike Johnson, General Manager
Jim Whedon, General Sales Mgr

Hinsdale

WYRY
06-30-1987; 104.9 mhz FM *Hrs Open:* 24; 4.1 kw; 400 ft.; N42 46 33 W72 27 17
30-10 Warwick Rd., Winchester, NH 03470 US
(603) 239-8200, *Fax:* (603) 239-6203
www.wyry.com
License: Hinsdale, Cheshire County, NH held by Tri-Valley Broadcasting Corp.
Nat'l Network: Jones Radio Networks
Arbitron Metro Market: Hinsdale, NH *Format:* Country *Hrs. of News Programming:* news progmg 10 hrs wkly *No. News Employees:* 3 *Target Audience:* 25-49; upscale adults & business decision makers
Brian McCormick, Operations Dir
Sean Patrik, Programming Director
Dan Guy, Chief Engineer

Jackson

***WEVJ**
08-02-2009; 99.5 mhz FM *Hrs Open:* 24; 4.7 kw; 171 ft.; N44 10 30 W71 10 7 *Rebroadcasts:* Rebroadcasts WEVO(FM) Concord 100%
207 N Main Street, Concord, NH 03301 US
(603) 228-8910, *Fax:* (603) 224-6052
www.nhpr.org
admin@nhpr .org
License: Jackson, Carroll County, NH held by New Hampshire Public Radio.
Nat'l Network: NPR; PRI *Wire Services:* AP
Arbitron Metro Market: Lewiston, ME *Format:* News, News/Talk, 86 *No. News Employees:* 9 *Target Audience:* 25-54.
Betsy Gardela, President
Elizabeth Gardella, General Manager
Mark Bevis, News Director
John Huntley, Engineering Dir

Jaffrey

WXNH
540 khz AM
US
(845) 356-9613
License: Jaffrey, NH held by Steven Wendell.
Arbitron Metro Market: Nanuet, NY
Steven Wendell, General Manager

Keene

***WEVN**
04-01-1994; 90.7 mhz FM *Hrs Open:* 24; 1.5 kw; 938 ft.; N43 2 0 W72 22 4 *Rebroadcasts:* Rebroadcasts WEVO(FM) Concord 100%
207 North Main Street, Concord, NH 03301 US
(603) 228-8910, *Fax:* (603) 224-6052
www.nhpr.org
admin@nhpr.org
License: Keene, Cheshire County, NH held by New Hampshire Public Radio Inc.
Nat'l Network: NPR; PRI *Wire Services:* AP
Arbitron Metro Market: Keene, NH *Format:* News, News/Talk, 86 *Special Programming:* Folk 3 hrs wkly *Hrs. of News Programming:* news progmg 42 hrs wkly *No. News Employees:* 9 *Target Audience:* 25-54.
Elizabeth Gardella, President & CEO
Sarah Ashworth, News Director
John Huntley, Engineering Dir
Todd Mayo, Treasurer
Todd Bookman, Health Reporter
Michael D. Redmond, Secretary
Janet Prince, Vice Chair
Emily Corwin, StateImpactNH Reporter
Chris Jensen, North Country Reporter

WSNI
01-01-1983; 97.7 mhz FM *Hrs Open:* 24; 2.15 kw; 554 ft.; N42 54 57 W72 19 53
227 Concord Street, Haverhill, MA 01830 US
(603) 352-9230, *Fax:* (603) 357-3926
www.sunnykeene.com
License: Keene, Cheshire County, NH held by Saga Communications of New England LLC.
Group Owner: Saga Communications Inc.; (acq 4-1-2003; $400,000)
Nat'l Network: ABC
Format: Adult Contemp *Hrs. of News Programming:* news progmg 7 hrs wkly *No. News Employees:* 2 *Target Audience:* 25-54; 60% female, 40% male *Adv. Rates:* 30; 20; 30; 12
Robert Cox, Operations Dir
Vicki Lenanan, Promotions Manager
Steve Hamel, Operations Manager

WZBK
05-01-1959; 1220 khz AM
13 Lamson Street, P.O. Box 707, Keene, NH 03431 US
(603) 352-9230, *Fax:* (603) 357-3926
www.wkbkradio.com
www.wkbkam.com
info@wkbkam.com
License: Keene, NH held by Saga Communications of New Hampshire LLC.
Group Owner: Saga Communications Inc.; (acq 7-1-2002; $2.63 million with WOQL(FM) Winchester)
Format: News, News/Talk, 86 *Target Audience:* 25-54; general
Bruce Lyons, Station Manager
Susan Wells, General Sales Mgr
Steve Hamill, Programming Director
Paul Schering, News Director
Ira Wilner, Chief Engineer
Jen Bond, Traffic Manager

WKBK
06-02-1927; 1290 khz AM
Mailing Address: P.O. Box 466, Keene, NH 03431 US
Second Address: 69 Stanhope Ave., Keene, NH 3431
(603) 352-9230, *Fax:* (603) 357-3926
www.wkbkam.com
info@wkbk.com
License: Keene, NH held by Saga Communications of New England LLC.
Group Owner: Saga Communications Inc.; (acq 5-1-02; grpsl).
Nat'l Network: CBS *Nat'l Reps:* McGavren Guild
Format: News, Talk *Target Audience:* 25 plus.
Stephen Hamel, Operations Dir
Bruce Lyons, General Manager
Dan Mitchell, Programming Director
Vicky Lenahan, Promotions Manager
Paul Scheuring, News Director
Ira Wilner, Chief Engineer
Jennifer Bond, Traffic Manager

WKNE
05-01-1964; 103.7 mhz FM; 12 kw; 991 ft.; N43 2 0 W72 22 4
P.O. Box 466, Keene, NH 03431 US
(603) 352-9230, *Fax:* (603) 357-3926
www.wkne.com
info@wkne.com
License: Keene, Cheshire County, NH held by Saga Communications of New England LLC.
Group Owner: Saga Communications Inc.
Format: Contemporary Hits/Top 40, Adult Contemp *Target Audience:* 18-49.
Jennifer Bond, News Director

***WKNH**
11-01-1975; 91.3 mhz FM *Hrs Open:* 24; 0.275 kw; -387 ft.; N42 55 36 W72 16 54
229 Main Street, Keene, NH 03435 US
(603) 358-2420, *Fax:* (603) 358-2417
www.jumblue.com/wknh
wknhinfo@aol.com
License: Keene, Cheshire County, NH held by Board of Trustees University System of New Hampshire.
Format: Alternative *Special Programming:* Class 4 hrs, folk 6 hrs, jazz 3 hrs, blues 3 hrs, *Hrs. of News Programming:* news progmg 3 hrs wkly *No. News Employees:* 2 *Target Audience:* General.

RADIO - U.S.

James McCluskey, General Manager

Laconia

WEMJ
04-09-1961; 1490 khz AM; 1 kw-U, ND1; N43 32 29 W71 27 45
1921 Gallows Rd, #850, Vienna, VA 22182 US
(603) 524-1323, *Fax:* (603) 528-5185
www.1490wemj.com/
pkelly@nassaubroadcasting.com
License: Laconia, NH held by Nassau Broadcasting III L.L.C.
Group Owner: Nassau Broadcasting Partners L.P.
Nat'l Network: CBS *Nat'l Reps:* D & R Radio
Arbitron Metro Market: Laconia, NH *Format:* Talk
Marc Taub, General Manager
Uriel Rendon, General Sales Mgr
Maria Pilar, Programming Director

WEZS
08-22-1922; 1350 khz AM; 5 kw-D, ND1; 0.112 kw-N, ND1; N43 30 27 W71 31 0
266 Union Avenue, Laconia, NH 03246 US
(603) 524-6288, *Fax:* (603) 528-1638
www.wezs.com
staff@wezs.com
License: Laconia, NH held by Gary W. Hammond.
Nat'l Network: USA
Arbitron Metro Market: Laconia, NH *Format:* Oldies *Target Audience:* 45 plus. *Adv. Rates:* 15; 14; 14; 6
Gary Hammond, General Manager

WLNH-FM
11-22-1965; 98.3 mhz FM *Hrs Open:* 24 hrs; 15.5 kw; 407 ft.; N43 35 46 W71 29 55
1921 Gallows Rd. #850, Vienna, VA 22182 US
(603) 524-1323, *Fax:* (603) 528-5185
www.wlnh.com
info@wlnh.com
License: Laconia, Belknap County, NH held by Nassau Broadcasting III L.L.C.
Group Owner: Nassau Broadcasting Partners L.P.; (acq 4-7-2004; grpsl).
Format: Adult Contemp *Target Audience:* 25-54.
Chris Ialuna, Programming Director
Molly King, Promotions Manager

Lancaster

WXXS
01-01-1998; 102.3 mhz FM *Hrs Open:* 24; 1.5 kw; 965 ft.; N44 23 39 W71 39 20
Mailing Address: 20 Middle Street, Lancaster, NH 03584 US
Second Address: 195 Main St., Lancaster, NH 3584
(603) 444-4102, *Fax:* (603) 788-3536
kiss102@together.net
License: Lancaster, Coos County, NH held by Radio New England Broadcasting LLC
Group Owner: Barry P. Lunderville Stns
Nat'l Network: CBS
Arbitron Metro Market: Lancaster, NH *Format:* Adult Contemp
Brian Lunderville, Operations Dir
Barry Lunderville, General Manager
Danielle Corbiel, News Director

Lebanon

WXXK
12-18-1990; 100.5 mhz FM *Hrs Open:* 24; 22 kw; 325 ft.; N43 39 18 W72 17 42
31 Hanover Street, Suite 4, Lebanon, NH 03766 US
(603) 448-1400, *Fax:* (603) 448-1755
www.kixx.com
JTYLER@GREATEASTERNRADIO.COM
License: Lebanon, Grafton County, NH held by Great Eastern Radio LLC.
Group Owner: Great Eastern Radio LLC; (acq 10-30-2007; grpsl)
Nat'l Network: Westwood One; CNN Radio
Arbitron Metro Market: Lebanon, NH *Format:* Country *Hrs. of News Programming:* news progmg 20 hrs wkly *No. News Employees:* 3 *Target Audience:* 25-54.
Cheryl Frisch, CFO
Kenny Michaels, Operations Dir
Wally Caswell, General Manager
Justin Tyler, Programming Director
Matt Cross, News Director
Lori Richardson, Traffic Director

*WVFA
02-06-2004; 90.5 mhz FM *Hrs Open:* 24; 0.012 kw; 614 ft.; N43 36 56 W72 10 24
Mailing Address: PO Box 126, Hartford, VT 05047 US
Second Address: 48 Wescott Rd., Enfield, NH 3748
(802) 295-9683, *Fax:* (802) 295-9683
www.wvfaradio.com
vtpreacher@aol.com
License: Lebanon, Grafton County, NH held by Green Mountain Educational Fellowship Inc.
Wire Services: AP
Arbitron Metro Market: Hartford, VT *Format:* Religious *Hrs. of News Programming:* News progmg 11 hrs wkly *Target Audience:* 25-49; primary
William Wittik, President
Betsy Murray, Operations Dir
Elmer Murray, Operations Manager

WUVR
01-01-2004; 1490 khz AM
US
(603) 448-0500, *Fax:* (603) 448-6601
www.wntk.com
info@wntk.com
License: Lebanon, NH held by KOOR Communications Inc.
Group Owner: KOOR Communications Inc.
Arbitron Metro Market: Lebanon, NH *Format:* News, News/Talk, 86
Robert Vinikoor, General Manager
Dave Shurtleff, News Director
Russ McCallister, Chief Engineer

Lisbon

WLTN-FM
09-01-1991; 96.7 mhz FM *Hrs Open:* 24; 6 kw; 295 ft.; N44 13 11 W71 52 7
15 Main Street, Littleton, NH 03561 US
(603) 444-3911, *Fax:* (603) 444-7186
mix967@roadrunner.com
License: Lisbon, Grafton County, NH held by Barry P. Lunderville L.L.C.
Group Owner: Barry P. Lunderville Stns
Nat'l Network: Westwood One
Arbitron Metro Market: Littleton, NH *Format:* Adult Contemp *Hrs. of News Programming:* news progmg 7 hrs wkly *No. News Employees:* 1 *Target Audience:* 25-54. *Adv. Rates:* Same as AM
Danielle Corbiel, News Director

Littleton

WLTN
10-10-1963; 1400 khz AM *Hrs Open:* 24; 1 kw-U, ND1; N44 18 47 W71 46 8
15 Main Street, Littleton, NH 03561 US
(603) 444-3911, *Fax:* (603) 444-7186
mix967@roadrunner.com
License: Littleton, NH held by Barry P. Lunderville L.L.C.
Group Owner: Barry P. Lunderville Stns; (acq 6-30-2005; with WLTN-FM Lisbon)
Arbitron Metro Market: Littleton, NH *Format:* Oldies *Hrs. of News Programming:* news progmg 40 hrs wkly *No. News Employees:* 1 *Target Audience:* 21-65. *Adv. Rates:* 21; 14; 14; 14
Barry Lunderville, General Manager
Christina Brooks, General Sales Mgr
Phil Rivera, Programming Director
Jim Clothey, News Director
Brian Lunderville, Chief Engineer
Danielle Corbiel, Traffic Manager

WMTK
02-23-1985; 106.3 mhz FM *Hrs Open:* 24; 0.39 kw; 1257 ft.; N44 21 14 W71 44 23
PO Box 106, Littleton, NH 03561 US
(603) 444-5106, *Fax:* (603) 444-1205
www.notchfm.com
info@notchfm.com
License: Littleton, Grafton County, NH held by Vermont Broadcast Associates Inc.
Group Owner: Vermont Broadcast Associates Inc.; (acq 8-2000; $250,000)
Arbitron Metro Market: Littleton, NH *Format:* Contemporary Hits/Top 40 *No. News Employees:* 1 *Target Audience:* 30-50; slightly more males, active lifestyles *Adv. Rates:* 30; 30; 30; 20
Bruce James, General Manager
Steve Nichols, General Sales Mgr
Todd Wellington, News Director
Don Smith, Chief Engineer

Madbury

WWNH
05-20-1989; 1340 khz AM *Hrs Open:* 24
Mailing Address: P.O.Box 69, Dover, NH 03820 US
Second Address: 284 Rt. 155, Dover, NH 3821
(603) 742-8575, *Fax:* (603) 743-6444
www.loveradio.net
info@loveradio.net
License: Madbury, NH held by Harvest Broadcasting.
Nat'l Network: USA
Arbitron Metro Market: Portsmouth-Dove *Format:* Adult Contemp *Special Programming:* Family 24 hrs wkly *Hrs. of News Programming:* News progmg 3 hrs wkly *Target Audience:* General; 29 plus
Patti Smith, CEO
Ernie Jenkins, Operations Dir
Steve Donnell, Chief Engineer

Manchester

WFEA
03-08-1932; 1370 khz AM
500 Commercial Street, Manchester, NH 03101 US
(603) 669-5777, *Fax:* (603) 669-4641
www.wfea1370.com
raydionh@wzid.com
License: Manchester, NH held by Saga Communications of New England LLC.
Group Owner: Saga Communications Inc.; (acq 6-2-92; grpsl, including co-located FM).
Regional Reps: Katz.
Arbitron Metro Market: Manchester, NH *Format:* Adult Contemp *Special Programming:* Fr 3 hrs, Sp 2 hrs wkly *Target Audience:* 50 plus; Modern Maturity market
Ray Garon, President/General Manager
Ray Garon, General Manager
Andy Orcutt, Director of Sales
Pat Mckay, Operations Manager & Program Director
Shannon Stephens, Operations Manager & Program Director
Peter Stohrer, EngineeringDir

WGIR
10-01-1941; 610 khz AM *Hrs Open:* 24; 5 kw-D, DA2; 1 kw-N, DA2; N43 0 57 W71 28 48
600 Congress Avenue, Suite 1400, Austin, TX 78701 US
(603) 625-6915, *Fax:* (603) 625-9255
www.wgiram.com
info@wgiram.com
License: Manchester, NH held by Capstar TX L.P.
Group Owner: Clear Channel Communications Inc.; (acq 8-30-00; grpsl)
Nat'l Network: Fox News Radio; Westwood One
Format: News, News/Talk, 84, Talk *Hrs. of News Programming:* news progmg 38 hrs wkly *No. News Employees:* 2 *Target Audience:* 35-54.
Joseph Graham, General Manager

WGIR-FM
06-05-1963; 101.1 mhz FM; 11.5 kw; 1027 ft.; N42 58 54 W71 35 21
600 Congress Avenue, Suite 1400, Austin, TX 78701 US
(603) 625-6915, *Fax:* (603) 669-0610
www.rock101fm.com
info@rock101fm.com
License: Manchester, Hillsborough County, NH
Group Owner: Clear Channel Communications Inc.
Format: Rock/AOR
Marty McFly, Programming Director
Helen Daniels, News Director

WGAM
10-01-1946; 1250 khz AM *Hrs Open:* 5 AM-11 PM; 5 kw-D, DA2; 5 kw-N, DA2; N43 0 40 W71 30 19
288 South River Road, Bedford, NH 03110 US
(603) 880-9001, *Fax:* (603) 577-8682
www.wgamradio.com
info@wgamradio.com
License: Manchester, NH held by Absolute Broadcasting LLC.
Group Owner: Absolute Broadcasting LLC; (acq 11-21-2006; $1.6 million)
Nat'l Network: Fox Sports
Arbitron Metro Market: Manchester, NH *Format:* Sports
Jerry DiGrezio, General Manager

*WLMW
09-01-1997; 90.7 mhz FM *Hrs Open:* 24; 15 w; 869 ft; N42 58 59 W71 35 25
Mailing Address: Box 366, Auburn, NH 03060
Second Address: 134 Hollis Rd., Amherst, NH 3031
(603) 672-0573, *Fax:* (603) 672-0573
www.nhfamilyradio.org
jim@nhfamilyradio.org
License: Manchester, Hillsborough County, NH held by Knowledge For Life.

Jim Phelan, General Manager
Jim Phelan, Station Manager

WZID
01-01-1948; 95.7 mhz FM; 14.5 kw; 925 ft.; N42 59 2 W71 35 22
500 Commercial Ave, Manchester, NH 03101 US
(603) 669-5777, *Fax:* (603) 669-4641
www.wzid.com
radionh@wzid.com
License: Manchester, Hillsborough County, NH
Group Owner: Saga Communications Inc.
Arbitron Metro Market: Manchester, NH *Format:* Adult Contemp
Target Audience: 25-54.
Ray Garon, General Manager
Andy Orcutt, General Sales Mgr
Bob Bronson, Programming Director

WGAM(AM)
1250 khz AM; 1 kw-D, 670 w-N; N44 30 00 W71 33 50
Mailing Address: 141 Main Street, Nashua, NH 3561
Second Address: 195 Main St., Lancaster, NH 03060
(603) 444-4102, *Fax:* (603) 788-3536
kiss102@together.net
License: Manchester, Coos County, NH held by Absolute Broadcasting
Group Owner: Barry P. Lunderville Stns
Population Served: 109,830 *Arbitron Metro Market:* Manchester, NH
Pete Hamel, General Manager

Meredith

WWHQ
11-16-1988; 101.5 mhz FM; 6 kw; 328 ft.; N43 35 46 W71 29 55
1921 Gallows Road Suite, Vienna, VA 22182 US
(603) 524-1323, *Fax:* (603) 528-5185
www.thehawkrocks.com
Zack@TheHawkRocks.com
License: Meredith, Belknap County, NH held by Nassau Broadcasting III L.L.C.
Group Owner: Nassau Broadcasting Partners L.P.; (acq 4-7-2004; grpsl)
Arbitron Metro Market: Gilford, NH *Format:* Classic Rock
Louis Mercatanti, President
Dominic Biello, Operations Dir
Jim Adams, General Manager
Zack Derby, Programming Director
Kim Terbrack, Promotions Manager

***WANH**
91.5 mhz FM; 1.7 kw horiz; 26 ft.; N43 41 25 W71 22 34 US
(603) 227-0911
www.wvnh.org
License: Meredith, Belknap County, NH held by New Hampshire Gospel Radio Inc.
Arbitron Metro Market: Meredith, NH
Peter Stohrer, General Manager

Moultonborough

WSCY
05-31-1993; 106.9 mhz FM; 0.13 kw; 2096 ft.; N43 46 9 W71 18 52
P.O. Box 99, Franklin, NH 03235 US
(603) 253-8080, *Fax:* (603) 934-2933
www.wscy.com
info@mix941fm.com
License: Moultonborough, Carroll County, NH held by Northeast Communications Corp.
Group Owner: Northeast Communications Corp.; acq 5-4-93; $399,072;
Format: Country
Jeff Fisher, President
Jeff Fisher, General Manager
Jeff Levitan, General Sales Mgr
Amy Bates, News Director
Jeff Levitan, Vice President

Mount Washington

WHOM
07-09-1958; 94.9 mhz FM; 48 kw; 3743 ft.; N44 16 11 W71 18 15
Post Office Box 820, Newburyport, MA 01950 US
(207) 774-6364, *Fax:* (207) 774-8707
www.whom949.com
whom@whom949.com
License: Mount Washington, Coos County, NH
Group Owner: Cumulus Media Inc.; (acq 7-7-99; grpsl).
Nat'l Reps: Christal
Arbitron Metro Market: Portland, ME *Format:* Adult Contemp, Light Rock *Target Audience:* 35-64; professionals with active lifestyles
Mike Sambrook, General Manager
Barbara Cole, General Sales Mgr
Tim Moore, Programming Director

Nashua

WFNQ
10-19-1987; 106.3 mhz FM *Hrs Open:* 24; 0.95 kw; 541 ft.; N42 44 7 W71 23 37
55 Lake Street, Nashua, NH 03060 US
(603) 889-1063, *Fax:* (603) 882-0688
www.1063frankfm.com
jfronk@nassaubroadcasting.com
License: Nashua, Hillsborough County, NH held by Nassau Broadcasting III L.L.C.
Group Owner: Nassau Broadcasting Partners L.P.; (acq 3-16-2004; grpsl)
Format: Adult Contemp *Hrs. of News Programming:* news progmg 5 hrs wkly *No. News Employees:* 1 *Target Audience:* 18-49.
Louis Mercatanti, President
Andy Mack, Operations Dir
Pete Detone, General Manager
Phyllis Knight, General Sales Mgr
Jim Fronk, Programming Director
Dirk Nadon, Chief Engineer

WGHM
01-01-1991; 900 khz AM *Hrs Open:* 6 AM-6 PM (Oct-Apr); 6 AM-10 PM (Ma
Longmeadow Way, Box 403, Hamilton, MA 01936 US
(603) 880-9001, *Fax:* (603) 577-8682
www.wgamradio.com
info@wgamradio.com
License: Nashua, NH held by Absolute Broadcasting LLC.
Group Owner: Absolute Broadcasting LLC; (acq 11-2-2005; $925,000)
Nat'l Network: Fox Sports
Arbitron Metro Market: Nashua, NH *Format:* Sports *Target Audience:* 35 plus.
Jerry DiGrezio, General Manager
Marty Terrell, General Sales Mgr
John Kosian, Programming Director
Paul Hust, News Director

WSMN
03-09-1958; 1590 khz AM *Hrs Open:* 18; 5 kw-U, DA1; N42 44 40 W71 29 52
502 West Hollis St., P.O. Box 548, Nashua, NH 03061 US
(603) 880-9001, *Fax:* (603) 577-8682
www.wsmnradio.com
info@wgamradio.com
License: Nashua, NH held by Absolute Broadcasting LLC.
Group Owner: Absolute Broadcasting LLC; (acq 11-10-2005; $250,000)
Nat'l Network: ESPN Radio
Format: News, News/Talk, 84, Talk
Jerry DiGrezio, General Manager

***WEVS**
01-01-2005; 88.3 mhz FM; 3.5 kw horiz, 5 kw vert; 69 ft.; N42 45 0 W71 28 47 *Rebroadcasts:* Rebroadcasts WEVO(FM) Concord 100%
207 N. Main St., Concord, NH 03301 US
(603) 228-8910, *Fax:* (603) 224-6052
www.nhpr.org
License: Nashua, Hillsborough County, NH held by New Hampshire Public Radio Inc.
Nat'l Network: NPR; PRI
Arbitron Metro Market: Nashua, NH *Format:* News, News/Talk, 86
Barbara J. Couch, Chairman
Elizabeth (Betsy) Gardella, President & CEO
Mark Bevis, News Director
John Huntley, Engineering Dir
Todd Mayo, Treasurer
Janet Prince, Vice Chair
Michael D. Redmond, Secretary

New London

WNTK-FM
11-30-1992; 99.7 mhz FM *Hrs Open:* 24; 1.45 kw; 676 ft.; N43 26 52 W72 2 4 *Rebroadcasts:* Rebroadcasts WNTK(AM) Newport 50%
Mailing Address: 297 Beaver Meadow Road, Norwich, VT 05055 US
Second Address: 103 Hanover St., Lebanon, NH 3766
(603) 448-0500, *Fax:* (603) 448-6601
www.wntk.com
info@wntk.com
License: New London, Merrimack County, NH held by Koor Communications Inc.
Group Owner: KOOR Communications Inc.
Arbitron Metro Market: Newport, NH *Format:* News, Talk *No. News Employees:* 2 *Target Audience:* 24-54. *Adv. Rates:* 19; 19; 19; 19
Robert Vinikoor, CEO
Sheila Vinikoor, President
Dave Shurtleff, News Director
Russ McCallister, Chief Engineer

***WSCS**
02-01-1996; 90.9 mhz FM; 0.063 kw horiz, 0.25 kw vert; 299 ft.; N43 24 41 W71 58 33
100 Main Street, New London, NH 03257 US
(603) 526-3493, *Fax:* (603) 526-3452
www.colby-sawyer.edu/wscs
wscs@colby-sawyer.edu
License: New London, Merrimack County, NH held by Colby-Sawyer College.
Pat Gamble, Station Manager

Newport

WCNL
08-11-1960; 1010 khz AM *Hrs Open:* 24
P.O. Box 2295, New London, NH 03257 US
(603) 863-0080, *Fax:* (603) 448-6601
www.country1010.com
bob@wntk.com
License: Newport, NH held by KOOR Communications.
Group Owner: KOOR Communications Inc.; (acq 8-88; $250,000;
Arbitron Metro Market: Newport, NH *Format:* Country *Target Audience:* 25-54; informed adults
Robert Vinikoor, President
Sheila Vinikoor, News Director

North Conway

WPKQ
10-01-1952; 103.7 mhz FM *Hrs Open:* 24; 21.5 kw; 3802 ft.; N44 16 13 W71 18 17 *Rebroadcasts:* Rebroadcasts WOKQ(FM) Dover 80%
Mailing Address: 7201 W. Lake Mead Blvd., Suite 400, Las Vegas, NV 89128 US
Second Address: 2617 White Mountain Hwy., North Conway, NH 3860
(603) 749-9750, *Fax:* (603) 749-6589
www.wpkq.com
mail@wokq.com
License: North Conway, Carroll County, NH
Group Owner: Cumulus Media Inc.; (acq 7-7-99; grpsl).
Nat'l Network: CNN Radio *Nat'l Reps:* Christal *Wire Services:* AP
Arbitron Metro Market: Concord (Lake Regions), NH *Format:* Country *No. News Employees:* 2 *Target Audience:* 25-54; New England residents
Farid Suleman, CEO
Judy Ellis, President
Mark Ericson, Operations Dir
Martin Lessard, General Manager
Ken Hoffman, General Sales Mgr
Mark Jennings, Programming Director

Peterborough

WDER-FM
06-01-1971; 92.1 mhz FM *Hrs Open:* 24; 180 w; Ant 1,332 ft; N42 51 42 W71 52 46 *Rebroadcasts:* Rebroadcasts WFNX(FM) Lynn, MA 80%
Mailing Address: 25 Exchange St., Lynn, MA 03302
Second Address: 32 Technology Way 2W8, Nashua, NH 3060
(603) 882-9210, *Fax:* (603) 578-9210
www.fnxradio.com
fnxradio@fnxradio.com
License: Peterborough, Hillsborough County, NH held by FNX Broadcasting of New Hampshire LLC.
Group Owner: Phoenix Media Communications Group; (acq 11-29-99).
Wire Services: AP
Population Served: 511,000 *Arbitron Metro Market:* Boston
Special Programming: Gay talk 2 hrs, jazz 6 hrs wkly *Hrs. of News Programming:* news progmg 2 hrs wkly *No. News Employees:* 1 *Target Audience:* Adults 18-44; young, educated white collar professionals with extremely active lifestyles
Stephen Mindich, CEO
Gary Kurtz, General Manager
Peter Cawley, General Sales Mgr
Keith Dakin, Programming Director
Chris Hall, Chief Engineer

Pittsburgh

***WKST-FM**
91.1 mhz FM; 1.1 kw horiz, 3 kw vert; Ant 358 ft; N43 56 48 W71 08 24
2625 South Memorial Drive, Suite A, Tulsa, OK 4027
(918) 664-4581
License: Pittsburgh, PA held by Capstar Texas LLC
Population Served: 5,083 *Arbitron Metro Market:* Lebanon, ME
Ford Bishop, President

Plymouth

***WPCR-FM**
09-29-1974; 91.7 mhz FM *Hrs Open:* 24; 0.215 kw; -377 ft.; N43 45 25 W71 41 23
P. O. Box 189, Plymouth, NH 03264 US
(603) 535-2242 (office),(603) 536-5000 (univ. swit, *Fax:* (603) 535-2783
wpcr.plymouth.edu
genmgr@wpcr.plymouth.edu
License: Plymouth, Grafton County, NH held by Plymouth State College.
Nat'l Network: AP Radio
Format: Rock/AOR *Special Programming:* Class 3 hrs, jazz 3 hrs, reggae 3 hrs, blues 3 hrs, comedy 3 hrs wkly *Target Audience:* 15-35; college students & those interested in progressive alternative music
Randy Parson, General Manager

WPNH
11-10-1965; 1300 khz AM *Hrs Open:* 24; 5 kw-D, NDD; 0.082 kw-N, ND1; N43 46 32 W71 42 20
Mailing Address: 110 Babbitt Road, Franklin, NH 03235 US
Second Address: 110 Babbitt Rd., Franklin, NH 3235
(603) 536-2500,(603) 536-2501, *Fax:* (603) 934-2933
info@mix941fm.com
License: Plymouth, NH held by Northeast Communications Corp.
Group Owner: Northeast Communications Corp.; acq 2-9-99; with co-located FM)
Format: Big Band *Special Programming:* Breakfast with the bands 6 hrs wkly *Target Audience:* 35 plus. *Adv. Rates:* 118; 18; 18; 18
Fred Caruso, Operations Dir
Jeff Fisher, General Manager
Jess Levitan, General Sales Mgr
Amy Bates, News Director
Cathy Keizer, Traffic Manager

WPNH-FM
10-01-1975; 100.1 mhz FM; 0.41 kw; 1234 ft.; N43 44 21 W71 47 27
Mailing Address: Box 99, Franklin, NH 03235 US
Second Address: 110 Babbitt Rd., Franklin, NH 3235
(603) 536-2500,(603) 536-2501, *Fax:* (603) 934-2933
www.wpnhfm.com
info@mix941fm.com
License: Plymouth, Grafton County, NH held by Northeast Communications Corp.
Format: Alternative
Rick Ganley, Programming Director
Cathy Keizer, News Director
Mark Decker, Disc Jockey
Derek Lavoy, Disc Jockey
Mark Servente, Disc Jockey
Terry Hughes, Disc Jockey
Bob Moulton, Disc Jockey

Portsmouth

WHEB
01-14-1964; 100.3 mhz FM; 50 kw; 459 ft.; N43 3 11 W70 46 4
600 Congress Avenue, Suite 1400, Austin, TX 78701 US
(603) 436-7300, *Fax:* (603) 430-9415
www.wheb.com
info@wheb.com
License: Portsmouth, Rockingham County, NH held by Capstar TX L.P.
Group Owner: Clear Channel Communications Inc.; (acq 8-30-00; grpsl).
Arbitron Metro Market: Portsmouth-Dover-Rochester, NH
Format: Rock/AOR *Target Audience:* 18-49.
Christopher Garrett, Operations Dir
Robert Greer, General Manager
Christine Sieks, General Sales Mgr
Kelly Brown, News Director
Kenneth Neelan, Chief Engineer
Greg Kretschmar, Disc Jockey
Sandy Nagle, Traffic Manager

WMYF
12-05-1960; 1380 khz AM *Hrs Open:* 24; 1 kw-D, DAN; 1 kw-N, DAN; N43 3 48 W70 47 9
600 Congress Avenue, Suite 1400, Austin, TX 78701 US
(603) 436-7300, *Fax:* (603) 430-9415
www.sportsanimalnh.com
License: Portsmouth, NH held by Capstar TX L.P.
Group Owner: Clear Channel Communications Inc.
Arbitron Metro Market: Portsmouth, NH *Format:* Sports *Target Audience:* 25-54.
Judy Figliulo, General Sales Mgr
Michael O'Donnell, Programming Director
Heather Salisbury, News Director

Rochester

WPKX(AM)
01-01-1947; 930 khz AM *Hrs Open:* 24; 5 kw-U, DA-N; N43 17 13 W70 56 55
815 Lafayette Rd., Portsmouth, NH 3801
(603) 436-7300, *Fax:* (603) 430-9415
www.sportsanimalnh.com
License: Rochester, Strafford County, NH held by Capstar TX L.P.
Group Owner: Clear Channel Communications Inc.
Population Served: 310,000 *Arbitron Metro Market:* Portsmouth-Dover-Rochester, NH *Format:* News, News/Talk, 84, Talk *Target Audience:* 25-64; decision-makers, heads of businesses, households
Dan Pierce, Programming Director
Roger Wood, News Director
Kelly Brown, News Director
Beth LaRocque, Traffic Manager

WQSO
10-21-1979; 96.7 mhz FM *Hrs Open:* 24; 3 kw; 328 ft.; N43 17 14 W70 56 49
600 Congress Avenue, Suite 1400, Austin, TX 78701 US
(603) 436-7300, *Fax:* (603) 430-9415
License: Rochester, Strafford County, NH held by Capstar TX L.P.
Group Owner: Clear Channel Communications Inc.; (acq 8-30-00; grpsl).
Arbitron Metro Market: Portsmouth-Dover-Rochester, NH
Format: Oldies *Hrs. of News Programming:* news progmg 12 hrs wkly *No. News Employees:* 3 *Target Audience:* 25-54.
Robert Greer, General Manager

Salem

WCCM
01-10-1977; 1110 khz AM; 5 kw-D, DAD; N42 45 42 W71 16 13
462 Merrimack St., Methuen, MA 01344 US
(978) 683-7171, *Fax:* (978) 687-1180
www.1110wccm.com
info@1110wccmam.com
License: Salem, NH held by Costa-Eagle Radio Ventures L.P.
Group Owner: Costa-Eagle Radio Ventures L.P.; (acq 1996)
Nat'l Reps: Roslin
Arbitron Metro Market: Portsmouth, MA *Format:* News, News/Talk, 86 *Hrs. of News Programming:* news progmg 25 hrs wkly *No. News Employees:* 2 *Target Audience:* General.
Pat Costa, General Manager
John Bassett, Station Manager
Bruce Arnold, Programming Director

Somersworth

WBYY
01-25-1995; 98.7 mhz FM *Hrs Open:* 24; 6 kw; 315 ft.; N43 14 11 W70 53 37
P.O. Box 400, Dover, NH 03820 US
(603) 742-0987, *Fax:* (603) 742-0448
www.987thebay.com
susan@987thebay.com
License: Somersworth, Strafford County, NH held by Garrison City Broadcasting Inc.
Arbitron Metro Market: Dover, NH *Format:* Adult Contemp *No. News Employees:* 2 *Target Audience:* 25-54. *Adv. Rates:* 60; 50; 50; 30
Bob Demers Sr., CEO
Sarah Sullivan, Operations Dir
Michael L. Dafoe, General Manager
Mike Pomp, News Director
Jeff Rosenberg, Chief Engineer
Julie Michalik, Traffic Manager
Susan Demers Weigold, Senior Vice President

Swanzey

WEEY
01-01-1972; 93.5 mhz FM; 2 kw; 574 ft.; N42 54 57 W72 19 52
52 Main Street, West Lebanon, NH 03784 US
(617) 779-3500, *Fax:* (617) 779-3557
www.weei.com
License: Swanzey, Windsor County, NH held by Great Eastern Radio LLC.
Group Owner: Great Eastern Radio LLC; (acq 10-30-2007; grpsl)
Arbitron Metro Market: Brighton, MA *Format:* Sports *Target Audience:* 25-54.
Michael Barrett, Operations Dir
Tim Plante, General Manager
Chris Olsen, General Sales Mgr

Walpole

WFYX
11-01-2000; 96.3 mhz FM; 0.32 kw; 407 ft.; N43 8 14 W72 25 59
Rebroadcasts: Rebroadcasts WWOD(FM) Hartford, VT 100%
50 Park Avenue, Claremont, NH 03743 US
(603) 298-0332, *Fax:* (603) 727-0134
www.bestoldies104.com

mtrombly@nassaubroadcasting.com
License: Walpole, Cheshire County, NH held by Nassau Broadcasting III L.L.C.
Group Owner: Nassau Broadcasting Partners L.P.; (acq 8-13-2004; grpsl)
Arbitron Metro Market: Walpole, NH *Format:* Oldies
Mike Trombly, General Manager
Matt Houseman, Programming Director
Brett Franklin, Public Service Director

Whitefield

WNYN-FM
01-01-2007; 99.1 mhz FM; 0.46 kw; 1135 ft.; N44 21 10 W71 44 15
US
(802) 223-2396, *Fax:* (802) 223-1520
www.free991.com
License: Whitefield, Coos County, NH held by White Park Broadcasting Inc.
Group Owner: Northeast Broadcasting Company Inc.
Arbitron Metro Market: Whitefield, NH *Format:* Adult Contemp
Steven Silberberg, President
Ed Flanagan, General Manager

Winchester

WINQ
10-15-1991; 98.7 mhz FM *Hrs Open:* 24; 2.15 kw; 554 ft.; N42 54 57 W72 19 53
13 Lamson Street, Keene, NH 03431 US
(603) 352-9230, *Fax:* (603) 357-3926
www.987wink.com
License: Winchester, Cheshire County, NH held by Saga Communications of New Hampshire LLC.
Group Owner: Saga Communications Inc.; (acq 7-1-2002; $2.63 million with WZBK(AM) Keene).
Nat'l Network: ABC; Jones Radio Networks
Arbitron Metro Market: Winchester, NH *Format:* Country *Hrs. of News Programming:* news progmg 8 hrs wkly *No. News Employees:* 4 *Target Audience:* 25-54.
Robert Cox, Operations Dir
Bob Cox, General Manager
Susan Wells, General Sales Mgr
Mark Heasley, Programming Director
Vicki Lenahan, Promotions Manager

Wolfeboro

WASR
04-01-1970; 1420 khz AM *Hrs Open:* 5 AM-8 PM
Mailing Address: P. O. Box 900, Wolfeboro, NH 03894 US
Second Address: 73 Varney Rd., Wolfeboro, NH 03894-0900
(603) 569-1420, *Fax:* (603) 569-1900
www.wasr.net
mail@wasr.net
License: Wolfeboro, NH held by Winnipesaukee Network Inc.
Arbitron Metro Market: Wolfeboro, NH *Format:* Adult Contemp, News *Hrs. of News Programming:* news progmg 35 hrs wkly *No. News Employees:* 4 *Target Audience:* 25-54.
Grant Hatch, President
Gary Hammond, Engineering Dir

WLKZ
02-01-1985; 104.9 mhz FM *Hrs Open:* 24; 0.56 kw; 1065 ft.; N43 32 45.3 W71 22 42.8
Mailing Address: 21 Production Place, #15, Gilford, NH 03246 US
Second Address: 25 Country Club Rd., Bldg. One, Gilford, NH 3249

(603) 524-1323, *Fax:* (603) 528-5185
www.franknh.com
wlkz@metroczst.net
License: Wolfeboro, Carroll County, NH held by Nassau Broadcasting III L.L.C.
Group Owner: Nassau Broadcasting Partners L.P.; (acq 3-16-2004; grpsl).
Nat'l Reps: McGavren Guild
Format: Contemporary Hits/Top 40, Adult Contemp *Hrs. of News Programming:* News progmg 5 hrs wkly *Target Audience:* 25-54; baby boomers *Adv. Rates:* 32; 32; 32; na

Louis Mercatanti, President
Jim Cande, Operations Dir
Rob Fulmer, General Manager
Ron Piro, General Sales Mgr
Molly King, Promotions Manager
Dirk Nadon, Chief Engineer
Pat Kelly, Operations Director
Andy Mack, PromotionsDirector

New Jersey

Asbury Park

WADB(AM)

01-01-1926; 1310 khz AM; 2.5 kw-D, 1 kw-N, DA-2; N40 13 47 W74 05 27
2351 Sunset Blvd., Suite 170-218, Rocklin, CA 95765
(916) 251-1600, *Fax:* (916) 251-1650
www.air1.com
info@air1.com
License: Asbury Park, Monmouth County, NJ held by Millennium Shore License Holdco LLC.
Group Owner: Millennium Radio Group LLC; (acq 6-11-2002; grpsl)
Nat'l Network: Fox Sports
Population Served: 8,383 *Arbitron Metro Market:* Denison IA
Format: Alternative, Christian

Mike Novak, President

WJLK

11-20-1947; 94.3 mhz FM; 1.3 kw; 499 ft.; N40 13 45 W74 5 25
619 Alexander Road, 3rd Floor, Princeton, NJ 08540 US
(732) 897-8282, *Fax:* (732) 897-8283
License: Asbury Park, Monmouth County, NJ
Group Owner: Millennium Radio Group LLC
Arbitron Metro Market: New York *Format:* Adult Contemp

Lou Russo, Operations Dir
Tara Hessline, News Director
Debbie Mazzella, Music Director

*WYGG

88.1 mhz FM; 0.001 kw horiz, 0.92 kw vert; 112 ft.; N40 13 2 W74 0 38
1488 New York Avenue, Brooklyn, NY 11210 US
(908) 775-0821
www.radiobonnenouvelle.com
License: Asbury Park, Monmouth County, NJ held by Minority Business & Housing Development, Inc.
Arbitron Metro Market: Asbury Park, NJ *Format:* Religious

Ethel Huff, Chairman
Gene Huff, General Manager

Atlantic City

*WAJM

01-01-1997; 88.9 mhz FM; 0.15 kw vert; 102 ft.; N39 21 54 W74 28 31
Mailing Address: 1809 Pacific Avenue, Atlantic City, NJ 08401 US
Second Address: 1809 Pacific Ave., Atlantic City, NJ 8402
(609) 343-7300, *Fax:* (609) 343-7347
wajm@comcast.net
License: Atlantic City, Atlantic County, NJ held by Atlantic City Board of Education.
Arbitron Metro Market: Atlantic City, NJ *Format:* Variety/Diverse

Pamela Lewis, General Manager
Albert Horner, Station Manager

WAYV

04-01-1961; 95.1 mhz FM *Hrs Open:* 24; 50 kw; 331 ft.; N39 22 51 W74 27 3 *Rebroadcasts:* Simulcast with WAIV(FM) Cape May 100%
8025 Black Horse Pike, Suite 100, West Altantic City, NJ 08232 US
wrnf@moody.edu
License: Atlantic City, Atlantic County, NJ held by Equity Communications L.P.
Group Owner: Equity Communications LP; (acq 6-21-96; $3.1 million).
Nat'l Reps: Katz Radio
Arbitron Metro Market: Selma AL *Format:* Religious *Adv. Rates:* 200; 200; 200; 50

Rob Moore, General Manager

WENJ

01-01-1940; 1450 khz AM *Hrs Open:* 24; 1 kw-U, ND1; N39 22 42 W74 26 53
1750 Rockville Pike, Suite 20, Rockville, MD 20852 US
(609) 645-9797, *Fax:* (609) 272-9228
www.literock969.com
mike.ruble@mrgnj.com
License: Atlantic City, NJ held by Millennium Atlantic City License Holdco LLC.
Group Owner: Millennium Radio Group LLC; (acq 5-11-2001; grpsl).
Nat'l Network: CBS
Arbitron Metro Market: Atlantic City-Cape May, NJ *Format:* Talk *Hrs. of News Programming:* news progmg 24 hrs wkly *No. News Employees:* 1 *Target Audience:* 25 plus; the population of South Jersey

Dan Sullivan, General Manager
Mike Ruble, General Sales Mgr
Gary Guida, Programming Director
Jennifer Smith, Promotions Manager
Tom McNally, Chief Engineer
Zoe Burdine-Fly, Regional Market Manager
Mike Ruble, Market Manager
JoeMitchell, Local Sales Manager
Chris Coleman, Production Director

WFPG

09-01-1962; 96.9 mhz FM *Hrs Open:* 24; 50 kw; 361 ft.; N39 22 42 W74 26 53
1750 Rockville Pike, Suite 20, Rockville, MD 20852 US
(609) 645-9797, *Fax:* (609) 272-9228
www.literock969.com
mike.ruble@mrgnj.com
License: Atlantic City, Atlantic County, NJ
Group Owner: Millennium Radio Group LLC
Arbitron Metro Market: Atlantic City-Cape May, NJ *Format:* Adult Contemp, Light Rock *No. News Employees:* 1 *Target Audience:* 25-54.

Gary Guida, Programming Director
Jennifer Smith, Promotions Manager
Tom McNally, Chief Engineer
Zoe Burdine-Fly, Regional Market Manager
Mike Ruble, Market Manager
Joe Mitchell, Local Sales Manager
Chris Coleman, ProductionDirector

WMGM

06-14-1961; 103.7 mhz FM *Hrs Open:* 24; 50 kw; 348 ft.; N39 23 24 W74 30 45
1601 New Road, Linwood, NJ 08221 US
(609) 653-1400, *Fax:* (609) 601-0450
www.1037wmgm.com
wmgm1037@aol.com
License: Atlantic City, Atlantic County, NJ held by Atlantic Broadcasting of Linwood NJ Limited Liability Co.
Group Owner: Atlantic Broadcasting; (acq 10-15-2008; grpsl)
Nat'l Reps: McGavren Guild
Arbitron Metro Market: Atlantic City, NJ *Format:* Rock/AOR
Target Audience: 25-54; men

Brett DeNafo, CEO
Dick Irland, General Manager
Nick Giorno, Programming Director
Anne Pratt, News Director
Dan Merlo, Chief Engineer

WMID

05-30-1947; 1340 khz AM *Hrs Open:* 24; 0.89 kw-U, ND1; N39 22 35 W74 27 8
2922 Atlantic Avenue, #201, Atlantic City, NJ 08401 US
(609) 484-8444, *Fax:* (609) 646-6331
www.classicoldieswmid.com
rgarcia@equitycommunications.net
License: Atlantic City, NJ held by Equity Communications L.P.
Group Owner: Equity Communications LP; (acq 3-29-2002; grpsl).
Nat'l Reps: Katz Radio
Arbitron Metro Market: Atlantic City, NJ *Format:* Oldies *Target Audience:* 35-64; adults *Adv. Rates:* 50; 50; 50; 50

Gary Fisher, Operations Dir
Cindy Hesley, General Sales Mgr
Rob Garcia, Programming Director
Shannon Wray, Promotions Manager

*WNJN-FM

09-01-1996; 89.7 mhz FM; 0.025 kw horiz, 6 kw vert; 276 ft.; N39 27 40 W74 41 6
25 South Stockton Street, P.O. Box 777, Trenton, NJ 08625 US
(215) 351-1200, *Fax:* (215) 351-0398
www.whyy.org
talkback@whyy.org
License: Atlantic City, Atlantic County, NJ held by New Jersey Public Broadcasting Authority.
Nat'l Network: NPR; PRI
Arbitron Metro Market: Atlantic City, PA *Format:* News, News/Talk, 86 *Target Audience:* General.

William Marrazzo, CEO/COO
Kyra McGrath, Operations Dir
Pharoah Cranston, Station Manager
Chris Satullo, News Director

WPUR

06-01-1998; 107.3 mhz FM; 25 kw; 308 ft.; N39 22 42 W74 26 53
1750 Rockville Pike, Rockville, MD 20852 US
(609) 645-9797, *Fax:* (609) 272-9224
www.catcountry1073.com
License: Atlantic City, Atlantic County, NJ held by Millennium Atlantic City License Holdco LLC.
Group Owner: Millennium Radio Group LLC; (acq 5-11-01; grpsl).
Nat'l Reps: McGavren Guild
Arbitron Metro Market: Atlantic City-Cape May, NJ *Format:* Country *Target Audience:* 25-54.

Andy Santoro, General Manager
Mike Ruble, General Sales Mgr
Joe Kelly, Programming Director
Hank Weisbecher, News Director
Tom McNally, Chief Engineer

Avalon

WIBG-FM

03-29-1976; 94.3 mhz FM *Hrs Open:* 24; 3 kw; 300 ft; N39 07 48 W74 47 20
3208 Pacific Ave., Wildwood, NJ 8260
(609) 522-1987, *Fax:* (609) 522-3666
www.wilw.com
wilwradio@mac.com
License: Avalon, Cape May County, NJ held by Coastal Broadcasting Systems Inc.
Group Owner: Coastal Broadcasting Systems Inc.; (acq 3-5-98; $470,000)
Population Served: 43,114 *Arbitron Metro Market:* Atlantic City-Cape May, NJ *Format:* Oldies

Bob Maschio, General Manager
Rick Rock, Programming Director

Barnegat

*WBNJ

91.9 mhz FM; 0 kw horiz, 4.5 kw vert; 226 ft.; N39 45 54 W74 19 12
US
(609) 660-2028
www.wbnj.org
License: Barnegat, Ocean County, NJ held by WWN Educational Radio Corp.
Arbitron Metro Market: Barnegat, NJ *Format:* Oldies

William Clanton Jr., President

Beach Haven West

*WVBH

01-01-2003; 88.3 mhz FM; 0.001 kw horiz, 0.1 kw vert; 427 ft.; N39 42 56 W74 17 32 *Rebroadcasts:* Simulcast of WXHL (FM) Christiana 100%
12 Oak Glen Lane, Colts Neck, NJ 07722 US
(302) 731-0690, *Fax:* (302) 738-3090
www.thereachfm.com
listenercare@myreachradio.com
License: Beach Haven West, Ocean County, NJ held by Priority Radio Inc.
Group Owner: Priority Radio Inc.; (acq 11-14-2003; $400,000).
Arbitron Metro Market: Newark, DE *Format:* Adult Contemp

Dan Edwards, Operations Dir
Steve Hare, General Manager

Belvidere

WWYY

10-15-1992; 107.1 mhz FM; 1.2 kw; 719 ft.; N40 56 53 W75 9 38
11 Skyline Drive, Hawthorne, NJ 10532 US
(570) 421-2100, *Fax:* (570) 421-2040
www.107thebone.fm
info@lite935.com
License: Belvidere, Warren County, NJ held by Nassau Broadcasting Holdings Inc.
Group Owner: Nassau Broadcasting Partners L.P.; (acq 2-25-03; grpsl).
Nat'l Network: ABC
Arbitron Metro Market: Allentown-Bethlehem-Easton, PA

Maureen Barth, Operations Dir

Berlin

*WNJS-FM
08-21-1992; 88.1 mhz FM; 0.001 kw horiz, 0.08 kw vert; 942 ft.; N39 43 41 W74 50 39
Mailing Address: 25 South Stockton Street, P.O. Box 777, Trenton, NJ 08625 US
Second Address: 25 S. Stockton St., Trenton, NJ 8608
(215) 351-1200, *Fax:* (215) 351-0398
www.whyy.org
talkback@whyy.org
License: Berlin, Camden County, NJ held by New Jersey Public Broadcasting Authority
Nat'l Network: NPR; PRI
Arbitron Metro Market: Berlin, PA *Format:* News, News/Talk, 86 *Target Audience:* General.
William Marrazzo, CEO/COO
Kyra McGrath, Operations Dir
Anthony Fleury, General Sales Mgr
Chris Satullo, News Director

Blackwood

*WDBK
06-07-1979; 91.5 mhz FM; 0.1 kw; 82 ft.; N39 47 6 W75 2 19
P. O. Box 200, Blackwood, NJ 08012 US
(856) 227-7200, *Fax:* (856) 374-4969
www.camdencc.edu/studentlife/WDBK-Radio.cfm
JMyerson@camdencc.edu
License: Blackwood, Camden County, NJ held by Camden County College.
Arbitron Metro Market: Blackwood, New Jersey *Format:* Alternative
James Canonica, General Manager
Jamie Myerson, Station Manager

Blairstown

WHCY
10-21-1973; 106.3 mhz FM *Hrs Open:* 24; 0.43 kw; 860 ft.; N41 2 53 W74 58 21
619 Alexander Road, 3rd Floor, Princeton, NJ 08540 US
(973) 827-2525, *Fax:* (973) 827-2135
www.max1063.com
License: Blairstown, Warren County, NJ held by Aloha States Trust, LLC
Group Owner: Clear Channel Communications Inc.; (acq 2-13-2001).
Nat'l Reps: Katz Radio
Arbitron Metro Market: Wilkes Barre-Scranton, PA *Format:* Adult Contemp *Special Programming:* Public Affairs one hr wkly
Target Audience: 18-49; Women
Krystal Reilly, CFO
Ken O'Brien, Operations Dir
Dick Taylor, General Sales Mgr
Art Eddy, Programming Director

Bridgeton

*WNJB-FM
01-01-1998; 89.3 mhz FM *Hrs Open:* 5 AM-midnight; 0.001 kw horiz, 2.5 kw vert; 220 ft.; N39 27 35 W75 9 28
Cn777, Trenton, NJ 08625 US
(215) 351-1200, *Fax:* (215) 351-0398
www.whyy.org
talkback@whyy.org
License: Bridgeton, Cumberland County, NJ held by New Jersey Public Broadcasting Authority.
Nat'l Network: NPR; PRI
Arbitron Metro Market: Bridgeton, PA *Format:* News, News/Talk, 86 *Target Audience:* General.
William Marrazzo, CEO/COO
Kyra McGrath, Operations Dir
Pharoah Cranston, Station Manager
Steve Prido, General Sales Mgr
Chris Satullo, News Director
Bill Schorbus, Engineering Dir

WSNJ
08-01-1937; 1240 khz AM *Hrs Open:* 5:30 AM-midnight
P.O. Box 69, 1771 South Burlington Rd, Bridgeton, NJ 08302 US
(856) 451-2930, *Fax:* (856) 453-9440
wsnjam.com
information@wsnjam.com
License: Bridgeton, NJ held by Quinn Broadcasting Inc.
Format: Variety/Diverse *Special Programming:* Big band, MOR, news/talk, farm 10 hrs wkly *Hrs. of News Programming:* news progmg 10 hrs wkly *No. News Employees:* 1 *Target Audience:* 25 plus.
Toni Coogan, CFO
James Quinn, President
Greg Hennis, General Manager
Fred Sharkey, Programming Director
Richard Arsenault, Chief Engineer
John Casey, Music Director

Bridgewater

WWTR
12-23-1971; 1170 khz AM *Hrs Open:* 6am - 8pm
55 Horsehill Road, Cedar Knolls, NJ 07927 US
(732) 821-6009, *Fax:* (732) 821-6003
www.ebcmusic.com
info@ebcmusic.com
License: Bridgewater, NJ held by The Sentinel Publishing Co.
Group Owner: Greater Media Inc.; (acq 7-12-2001; grpsl)
Arbitron Metro Market: Monmouth Junction, NJ *Format:* Ethnic *Hrs. of News Programming:* new progmg one hr wkly *No. News Employees:* 5 *Target Audience:* Indian *Adv. Rates:* 30; 20; 30; 20
Arvind Agarwal, CEO/COO
Kulraaj Anand, Programming Director
Neal Newman, Chief Engineer
Alka Agrawal, COO

Brigantine

*WWFP
01-01-2006; 90.5 mhz FM; 0.077 kw vert; 307 ft.; N39 22 46 W74 25 45
US
(800) 357-4226, *Fax:* (208) 736-1958
www.csnradio.com
csn@csnradio.com
License: Brigantine, Atlantic County, NJ held by CSN International
Group Owner: CSN International
Arbitron Metro Market: Brigantine, NJ *Format:* Christian
Mike Kestler, President
Daniel Davidson, Operations Dir
Mike Stocklin, General Manager
Don Mills, Network Programming Director / Music Director
Kelly Carlson, Engineering Dir
Jerry Johnson, Engineering Dir
Ray Gorney, AssistantDirector of Engineering
Dustin Pamplona, Engineer
Nolan Mather, Graphics / Website Maintenance
Mike Stocklin, National Underwriting
Austin Morris, Accounting
Lois Mills, FCC Applications / Translator Site Manager

Burlington

WPEN-FM
01-19-1949; 97.5 mhz FM; 26 kw; Ant 682 ft; N40 04 57 W75 10 53
One Bala Plaza, Mail Stop 429, Bala Cynwyd, PA 08540
(610) 771-9750
www.nowismusic.com
License: Burlington, Burlington County, NJ held by Greater Philadelphia Radio Inc.
Group Owner: Greater Media Inc.; (acq 11-15-2006; exchange for WCRB(FM) Lowell, MA)
Population Served: 500,000 *Arbitron Metro Market:* Philadelphia
Peter Smyth, Chairman
John Fullam, General Manager
Jim Brown, Station Manager
Don Gosselin, Programming Director
Chrissy Sirianni, Promotions Manager
Margo Marano, Music Director

Camden

WWIQ
07-23-1968; 106.9 mhz FM; 38 kw; 600 ft; N39 54 33 W75 06 00
1341 N. Delaware Ave., Suite 400, Philadelphia, PA 94621
(215) 278-4200
www.iq1069.com
License: Camden, Camden County, NJ held by Merlin Media License LLC
Group Owner: Merlin Media LLC; (acq 3-6-2012; $22.5 million)
Arbitron Metro Market: Philadelphia
Al Gardner, Vice President of Programming

WEMG
09-01-1925; 1310 khz AM *Hrs Open:* 24; 1 kw-D, ND2; 0.25 kw-N, ND2; N39 57 28 W75 6 54
8121 Georgia Ave 10th Fl, Silver Spring, MD 20910 US
(215) 426-1900, *Fax:* (215) 426-1550
http://mega1310am.com
mtaub@davidsonmediagroup.com
License: Camden, NJ held by Davidson Media Station WEMG Licensee LLC.
Group Owner: Davidson Media Group LLC; (acq 1-31-2006; $8.75 million)
Nat'l Reps: Interep
Arbitron Metro Market: Philadelphia *Hrs. of News Programming:* news in am/pm drive *No. News Employees:* 1
Marc Taub, General Manager
Uriel Rendon, General Sales Mgr
Maria Pilar, Programming Director

WTMR
11-01-1948; 800 khz AM; 5 kw-D, DA2; 0.5 kw-N, DA2; N39 54 33 W75 6 0
3033 Riviera Drive, Suite 200, Naples, FL 33940 US
(856) 962-8000, *Fax:* (856) 962-8004
www.wtmrradio.com
radioman@voicenet.com
License: Camden, NJ held by KAAY License L.P.
Group Owner: Beasley Broadcast Group Inc.; (acq 9-4-98; $8 million).
Arbitron Metro Market: Camden, NJ *Format:* Talk, Religious
Louise Bessler, General Manager
Mike Smith, Programming Director

Canton

WJKS
01-15-1972; 101.7 mhz FM; 3 kw; 263 ft; N39 25 51 W75 20 13
First Federal Plaza Bldg., 704 King St., Suite 604, Wilmington, DE 19801
(302) 622-8895, *Fax:* (302) 622-8678
www.wjks1017.com
steven@wlks1017.com
License: Canton, Salem County, NJ held by QC Communication Inc.
Population Served: 700,000 *Arbitron Metro Market:* Wilmington, DE *Target Audience:* 18-44.
Mel Brittingham, Operations Dir
Steven Chanin, General Manager
Maria Sylvanus, General Sales Mgr
Jeff DePaulo, Chief Engineer

Cape May

WAIV
06-03-1967; 102.3 mhz FM; 3.2 kw; 292 ft.; N39 0 33 W74 52 13
Rebroadcasts: Simulcast with WAYV(FM) Atlantic City 100%
2922 Atlantic Avenue, #201, Atlantic City, NJ 08401 US
(609) 484-8444, *Fax:* (609) 646-6331
www.951wayv.com
gfequity@aol.com
License: Cape May, Cape May County, NJ held by Equity Communications L.P.
Group Owner: Equity Communications LP; (acq 3-29-2002; grpsl).
Nat'l Reps: Katz Radio
Arbitron Metro Market: Atlantic City-Cape May, NJ *Format:* Adult Contemp *Target Audience:* 18-49; adults *Adv. Rates:* 200; 200; 200; 50
Gary Fisher, Operations Dir
Keith Fader, General Sales Mgr
Rob Garcia, Programming Director

*WWCJ
09-01-1999; 89.1 mhz FM *Hrs Open:* 24; 8.2 kw horiz, 13.5 kw vert; 385 ft.; N39 7 27.6 W74 45 56.4 *Rebroadcasts:* Rebroadcasts WWFM(FM) Trenton 100%
Mailing Address: 1200 Old Trenton Road, Trenton, NJ 08690 US
Second Address: 1200 Old Trenton Road, West Windsor, NJ 8550
(609) 570-3189, *Fax:* (609) 570-3863
www.jazzon2.org
License: Cape May, Cape May County, NJ held by Mercer County Community College.
Nat'l Network: NPR
Arbitron Metro Market: Cape May, NJ *Format:* Classical
Peter Fretwell, General Manager

Cape May Court House

*WNJZ
08-01-1999; 90.3 mhz FM; 6 kw; 236 ft.; N39 6 18 W74 48 6
PO Box 777, Trenton, NJ 08625 US
(215) 351-1200, *Fax:* (215) 351-0398
www.whyy.org
talkback@whyy.org
License: Cape May Court House, Cape May County, NJ held by New Jersey Public Broadcasting Authority.
Nat'l Network: NPR; PRI
Arbitron Metro Market: Berlin, PA *Format:* News, News/Talk, 86

William Marrazzo, CEO/COO
Kyra McGrath, Operations Dir
Pharoah Cranston, Station Manager
Chris Satullo, News Director

WSNQ
09-05-1985; 105.5 mhz FM *Hrs Open:* 24; 3.3 kw; 295 ft.; N39 7 32 W74 49 26 *Rebroadcasts:* Simulcast with WZBZ(FM) Atlantic City 100%
2922 Atlantic Ave #201, Atlantic City, NJ 08401 US
(609) 484-8444, *Fax:* (609) 646-6331
993thebuzz.com
info@993thebuzz.com
License: Cape May Court House, Cape May County, NJ held by Equity Communications L.P.
Group Owner: Equity Communications LP; (acq 5-31-2002; grpsl)
Nat'l Reps: Katz Radio
Arbitron Metro Market: Atlantic City-C *Format:* Contemporary Hits/Top 40 *Target Audience:* 18-49; adults *Adv. Rates:* 200; 200; 200; 50
Gary Fisher, Operations Dir
Rob Garcia, Programming Director
Denise Carrington, News Director

***WJPG**
01-01-2004; 88.1 mhz FM; 0 kw horiz, 0.55 kw vert; 213 ft.; N39 7 32 W74 49 27
Joy Communications Inc, P O Box 490, Green Creek, NJ 20036 US
(877) 300-8105, *Fax:* (609) 861-3730
www.praise899.org
letters@praise899.org
License: Cape May Court House, Cape May County, NJ held by Maranatha Ministries.
Arbitron Metro Market: Cape May, NJ *Format:* Religious *Special Programming:* Gospel one hr wkly *Hrs. of News Programming:* News progmg 10 hrs wkly *Target Audience:* 25-54; women
Kenneth Manri, General Manager

Cherry Hill

***WKVP**
01-07-1985; 89.5 mhz FM *Hrs Open:* 24; 1.9 kw vert; 200 ft.; N39 54 43 W74 59 21 *Rebroadcasts:* Rebroadcasts KLVR(FM) Santa Rosa, CA 100%
P.O. Box 895, Cherry Hill, NJ 08003 US
(800) 525-5683, *Fax:* (916) 251-1650
www.klove.com
License: Cherry Hill, Camden County, NJ held by Educational Media Foundation.
Group Owner: EMF Broadcasting; (acq 1-10-2007; $2.45 million)
Nat'l Network: K-Love
Arbitron Metro Market: Philadelphia *Format:* Religious
Darrell Chambliss, Chairman
Alan Mason, COO
Mike Novak, President
Glenn Goodwin, Operations Dir

Delaware Township

***WDVR**
02-19-1990; 89.7 mhz FM *Hrs Open:* 24; 0.006 kw horiz, 3.8 kw vert; 725 ft.; N40 30 36 W74 57 34
P.O. Box 191, Sergeantsville, NJ 08557 US
(609) 397-1620, *Fax:* (609) 397-5991
www.wdvrfm.org
webmaster@wdvrfm.org
License: Delaware Township, Hunterdon County, NJ held by Penn-Jersey Educational Radio Corp.
Nat'l Network: ABC
Arbitron Metro Market: Delaware, NJ *Format:* Variety/Diverse *Special Programming:* Folk 6 hrs, relg 6 hrs, jazz 11 hrs, oldies 13 hrs, bluegrass 6 hrs, country classic, 12 hrs; Americana country 6 hrs wkly. *Hrs. of NewsProgramming:* News progmg 2 hrs wkly *Target Audience:* 30 plus.
Frank Napurano, President
Ginny Lee, Promotions Manager
Carla Van Dyk, Music Director

Dover

WDHA-FM
02-22-1961; 105.5 mhz FM *Hrs Open:* 24; 1 kw; 574 ft.; N40 51 19 W74 30 42
55 Horsehill Road, Cedar Knolls, NJ 07927 US
(973) 538-1250(973) 455-1055, *Fax:* (973) 538-3060
www.wdhafm.com
ckay@greatermedianj.com
License: Dover, Morris County, NJ held by The Sentinel Publishing Co.
Group Owner: Greater Media Inc.; (acq 7-6-01; grpsl).
Nat'l Reps: Katz Radio
Arbitron Metro Market: New Jersey *Format:* Classic Rock *Target Audience:* 18-49. *Adv. Rates:* 250; 250; 250; 75
Nancy McKinley, Station Manager
Matt DeVoti, General Sales Mgr
Curtis Kay, Music Director
Scott Kohlhepp, Music Director
Pete Forester, National Sales Manager

East Orange

***WFMU**
01-01-1958; 91.1 mhz FM *Hrs Open:* 24; 1.25 kw; 495 ft.; N40 47 19 W74 15 20
P.O. Box 2011, Jersey City, NJ 07303 US
(201) 521-1416, *Fax:* (201) 521-1286
www.wfmu.org
wfmu@wfmu.org
License: East Orange, Essex County, NJ held by Auricle Communications.
Arbitron Metro Market: New York *Format:* Variety/Diverse *Special Programming:* International 15 hrs wkly *Target Audience:* General.
Ken Freedman, General Manager
Ken Freedman, Station Manager
Ken Freedman, Programming Director
John Fogarazzo, Chief Engineer
Liz Berg, Assistant General Manager
Brian Turner, Music Director
Scott William, Public ServiceAnnouncement Dorector
Joe McGasko, Listener Service Director
Mike Adler, Technology Director
Jason Sigal, Free Music Achieve Managing Director

Eatontown

WHTG
11-01-1957; 1410 khz AM; 0.5 kw-D, ND1; 0.126 kw-N, ND1; N40 16 10 W74 4 19
1129 Hope Road, Asbury Park, NJ 07712 US
(732) 774-4755, *Fax:* (732) 774-4974
www.1410amradio.com
johnf@presscommradio.com
License: Eatontown, NJ held by Press Communications L.L.C.
Group Owner: Press Communications L.L.C.; (acq 11-4-2000; $15 million with co-located FM)
Nat'l Reps: Christal
Arbitron Metro Market: New York *Format:* Contemporary Hits/Top 40 *Special Programming:* Baseball 20 hrs, football 3 hrs, basketball 6 hrs *Target Audience:* 35 plus; general
Robert McAllan, CEO
John Dziuba, General Manager
Cindy Brennan, Station Manager
John Kaszuba, General Sales Mgr
Jack Aponte, Programming Director
Mathew Schwenker, Promotions Manager
Mike Heilman, Chief Engineer
Richard Morena,CFO

WKMK
10-11-1961; 106.3 mhz FM; 1.1 kw; Ant 528 ft; N40 16 41 W74 04 51
2355 W. Bangs Ave., Neptune, NJ 07712
(732) 774-4755, *Fax:* (732) 774-4974
www.grockradio.com
g1063@g1063.com
License: Eatontown, Monmouth County, NJ held by Press Communications L.L.C.
Group Owner: Press Communications L.L.C.
Arbitron Metro Market: New York *Target Audience:* 18-34. *Adv. Rates:* 100; 100; 100; 55
John Kaszuba, General Sales Mgr
Michael Gavin, Programming Director
Brian Phillips, Music Director

Egg Harbor City

WSJO
09-23-1971; 104.9 mhz FM; 10 kw; 509 ft.; N39 32 49 W74 38 19
8121 Georgia Avenue, 10th Floor, Silver Spring, MD 20910 US
(609) 645-9797, *Fax:* (609) 272-9224
www.sojo1049.com
jennifersmith@townsquaremedia.com
License: Egg Harbor City, Atlantic County, NJ held by Millennium Egg Harbor License Holdco LLC.
Group Owner: Millennium Radio Group LLC; (acq 11-23-2004; $14 million).
Nat'l Network: AP Radio
Arbitron Metro Market: Egg Harbor City, NJ *Format:* Adult Contemp *Special Programming:* Relg 4 hrs wkly *Target Audience:* 35 plus.
Andy Santoro, President
Joe Kelly, Programming Director
Jennifer Smith, Promotions Manager
Tom McNally, Chief Engineer

Egg Harbor Township

***WXGN**
01-01-2000; 90.5 mhz FM *Hrs Open:* 24; 0 kw horiz, 0.5 kw vert; 82 ft.; N39 16 46 W74 34 34
1102 New Road, Northfield, NJ 08225 US
(609) 938-0012, *Fax:* (609) 926-5185
www.wxgnradio.org
wxgn90.5fm@gmail.com
License: Egg Harbor Township, Atlantic County, NJ held by Joy Broadcasting Inc.
Arbitron Metro Market: Egg Harbor City, NJ *Format:* Christian *Target Audience:* Teens - Young Adults
Bill Link, Station Manager
Bob Green, License Holder

Elizabeth

WJDM
03-11-1970; 1530 khz AM; 0.67 kw-C, NDD; 1 kw-D, NDD; N40 41 25 W74 15 40
8400 N.W. 52nd St., Suite 101, Miami, FL 33166 US
(908) 352-3400, *Fax:* (908) 352-4268
www.puertadepaz.com
info@1530restauradion.com
License: Elizabeth, NJ held by Multicultural Radio Broadcasting Licensee LLC.
Group Owner: Multicultural Radio Broadcasting Inc.; (acq 2-4-2004; grpsl).
Arbitron Metro Market: New York
Richard Dirocco, General Manager
Didier Ugalde, Station Manager

Ewing

WIMG
01-01-1923; 1300 khz AM *Hrs Open:* 24; 3.2 kw-D, DA2; 1.3 kw-N, DA2; N40 17 16 W74 52 23
Mailing Address: 1842 South Broad Street, Trenton, NJ 08610 US
Second Address: 1842 S. Broad St., Trenton, NJ 8610
(609) 695-1300, *Fax:* (609) 278-1588
www.wimg1300.com
wimg1300@aol.com
License: Ewing, NJ held by Morris Broadcasting Co. of New Jersey Inc.
Nat'l Network: American Urban; NBC; Westwood One *Nat'l Reps:* Williams Radio Sales
Arbitron Metro Market: Trenton, NJ *Format:* Adult Contemp, Gospel *Hrs. of News Programming:* News progmg 6 hrs wkly *Target Audience:* 25-54.
Louise Morris, Chairman
Johnny Morris, CEO
Michael Morris, President
Felicia Brannon, Operations Dir
Pamela Pruitt, General Sales Mgr
Maggie Guzzardo, Executive Vice President

Flemington

***WCVH**
04-01-1974; 90.5 mhz FM *Hrs Open:* 25.?Â ?; 0.078 kw; 449 ft.; N40 33 25 W74 54 18
State Hwy. 31, Flemington, NJ 08822 US
(908) 782-9595, *Fax:* (908) 284-7109
www.wcvhfm.com
mail@wcvhfm.com
License: Flemington, Hunterdon County, NJ held by Hunterdon Central Board of Education.
Arbitron Metro Market: Flemington, NJ *Format:* Country *Target Audience:* 18-54. *Adv. Rates:* 5; 4; 5; 2
Chris Puorro, General Manager
Nick Biando, Promotions Manager
Bryan Leoni, News Director
John Anastasio, Chief Engineer
Ryan Gill, Music Director
Travis Rainey, Music Director

WNJE
01-05-1998; 1040 khz AM *Hrs Open:* 24*Rebroadcasts:* Rebroadcasts WEPN(AM) New York, NY 100%
449 Broadway, New York, NY 10013 US
(212) 613-3800, *Fax:* (212) 613-3861
www.1050espnradio.com
License: Flemington, NJ held by Nassau Broadcasting II L.L.C.
Group Owner: Nassau Broadcasting Partners L.P.; (acq 2-15-2002; grpsl)

Nat'l Network: ESPN Radio
Format: Sports
Tim McCarthy, General Manager

Florence

WIFI
01-01-1985; 1460 khz AM *Hrs Open:* 24; 5 kw-D, 500 w-N, DA-2; N40 04 53 W74 47 41
2025 Burlington-Columbus Rd., Burlington, NJ 08016
(609) 499-4800, *Fax:* (609) 499-4905
License: Florence, Burlington County, NJ held by Real Life Broadcasting.
Nat'l Network: USA
Population Served: 2,000,000 *Arbitron Metro Market:* Philadelphia
Ron Graban, General Manager

Franklin

WSUS
02-28-1965; 102.3 mhz FM; 0.59 kw; 715 ft.; N41 8 36 W74 32 21
600 Alexander Road; Bldg Tw0, Princeton, NJ 08540 US
(973) 827-2525, *Fax:* (973) 827-2135
www.wsus1023.com
info@wsus1023.com
License: Franklin, Sussex County, NJ held by CC Licenses LLC.
Group Owner: Clear Channel Communications Inc.; (acq 2-15-2001; grpsl).
Nat'l Reps: Katz Radio *Wire Services:* AP
Arbitron Metro Market: Sussex, NJ *Format:* Adult Contemp *Hrs. of News Programming:* news progmg 10 hrs wkly *Target Audience:* 18-54; Adults & Families
John Hogan, CEO
Ken O'Brien, Operations Dir
Dick Taylor, General Sales Mgr
Maria Lake, Programming Director
Art Eddy, Director of Online
Krystal Reilly, Market Controller

Freehold

***WFJS-FM**
89.3 mhz FM
Domestic Church Media, PO Box 7509, Trenton, NJ
(609)882-9357, *Fax:* (609)403-2908
www.domesticchurchmedia.org
info@domesticchurchmedia.org
License: Freehold, Monmouth County, NJ

Jim Manfredonia, President
Cheryl Manfredonia, General Manager

Freehold Township

***WRDR**
02-20-1997; 89.7 mhz FM *Hrs Open:* 24; 0.001 kw horiz, 1.6 kw vert; 328 ft.; N40 7 49 W74 7 19
299 Summerhill Rd, East Brunswick, NJ 08816 US
(732) 901-9953, *Fax:* (732) 901-0356
www.bridgefm.org
License: Freehold Township, Monmouth County, NJ held by Bridgelight LLC
Format: Christian *Special Programming:* Relg 6 hrs wkly *Target Audience:* 25-62.
Brian J. Rechton, General Manager
John Gates, Programming Director

Glassboro

***WGLS-FM**
01-01-1964; 89.7 mhz FM *Hrs Open:* 24; 0.75 kw; 489 ft.; N39 41 41 W75 17 55
201 Mullica Hill Road, Glassboro, NJ 08028 US
(856) 863-9457, *Fax:* (856) 256-4704
www.wgls.rowan.edu
wgls@rowan.edu
License: Glassboro, Gloucester County, NJ held by Rowan University.
Nat'l Network: ABC
Arbitron Metro Market: Philadelphia *Format:* Variety/Diverse
Special Programming: Black 10 hrs wkly *Hrs. of News Programming:* one *No. News Employees:* 1 *Target Audience:* 18-45; general
Mandy Rippert, Operations Dir
Frank J. Hogan, General Manager
Derek Jones, Station Manager
Frank Sippel, Chief Engineer

Hackensack

WNYM
01-01-1921; 970 khz AM
4880 Santa Rosa Rd #300, Camarillo, CA 93012 US
(201) 298-9700, *Fax:* (201) 298-5797
www.am970theanswer.com
contact@nycradio.com
License: Hackensack, NJ held by Salem Media of New York LLC.
Group Owner: Salem Communications Corp.; (acq 8-3-94)
Arbitron Metro Market: Hackensack, NJ *Format:* News, News/Talk, 86 *Target Audience:* 25-44.
Edward Atsinger, President
Joe Davis, Operations Dir
Sean O'Neill, General Manager
Steven Viemeyer, General Sales Mgr
Peter Thiele, Programming Director

Hackettstown

***WNTI**
12-05-1957; 91.9 mhz FM *Hrs Open:* 24; 5.5 kw horiz, 5.6 kw vert; 509 ft.; N40 51 7 W74 52 35
400 Jefferson Street, Hackettstown, NJ 07840 US
(908) 852-4545, *Fax:* (908) 852-8515
www.wnti.org
delrej@centenarycollege.edu
License: Hackettstown, Warren County, NJ held by Centenary College.
Nat'l Network: PRI
Arbitron Metro Market: Warren, NJ *Format:* Variety/Diverse
Special Programming: Big band 4 hrs, blues 11 hrs, heavy metal 6 hrs, r *Hrs. of News Programming:* News progmg 2 hrs wkly *Target Audience:* 15 plus.
John Del Re, Operations Dir
Paul Massen, General Manager

WRNJ
01-01-1996; 1510 khz AM
P.O. Box 1000, Hackettstown, NJ 07840 US
(908) 850-1000, *Fax:* (908) 852-8000
www.wrnj.com
info@oldies1510.com
License: Hackettstown, NJ held by WRNJ Radio Inc.
Nat'l Network: ABC *Wire Services:* AP
Format: News, News/Talk, 64, Talk *Special Programming:* Talk 10 hrs wkly *Hrs. of News Programming:* news progmg 10 hrs wkly *No. News Employees:* 3 *Target Audience:* 25-50 plus; upwardly mobile *Adv. Rates:* 55; 40; 50; 30
L.J. Tighe, President
Russ Long, Operations Dir
Norman Worth, General Manager
Dan Hollis, General Sales Mgr
Chuck Reiger, Programming Director
Pat Layton, News Director
Larry Tighe, Chief Engineer

Hammonton

WGYM
05-11-1961; 1580 khz AM; 1 kw-D, ND1; 0.006 kw-N, ND1; N39 37 33 W74 47 44 *Rebroadcasts:* Rebroadcasts WOND(AM) Atlantic City 100%
1601 New Road, Linwood, NJ 08221 US
(609) 601-1100, *Fax:* (609) 601-0450
License: Hammonton, NJ held by Access.1 New Jersey License Co. LLC.
Group Owner: Access.1 Communications Corp.; (acq 11-17-2003; grpsl).
Nat'l Network: Westwood One *Nat'l Reps:* McGavren Guild
Arbitron Metro Market: Atlantic City-C *TV Affiliate:* Talk *No. News Employees:* Adults 35+. *Target Audience:* Sydney Small

Hazlet

***WPDI**
05-24-1979; 104.7 mhz FM; 10 w; Ant 125 ft; N40 25 37 W74 11 40
49 Briscoe Terr., Hazlet, PA 07730
(732) 452-0777
www.dhoomfm.org
info@dhoomfm.com
License: Hazlet, Monmouth County, NJ held by WVRM Inc.
James Manfredonia, President

Hopatcong

***WDNJ**
01-01-2009; 88.1 mhz FM; 0.5 kw vert; 387 ft.; N40 56 25 W74 36 48
US
(888) 776-9365, *Fax:* (804) 353-8549
www.wdnjfm.com
License: Hopatcong, Sussex County, NJ held by Youngshine Media Inc.
Arbitron Metro Market: Hopatcong, NJ *Format:* Christian, Spanish
Sun Young Joo, General Manager

Jersey City

WSNR
12-01-1948; 620 khz AM; 3 kw-D, DA2; 7.6 kw-N, DA2; N40 47 53 W74 6 24
1935 Techny Rd, Suite18, Northbrook, IL 60062 US
(847) 509-1661, *Fax:* (646) 424-2232
www.sportingnews.com
License: Jersey City, NJ held by Rose City Radio Corp.
Group Owner: Rose City Radio Corp.; acq 3-23-01; grpsl).
Nat'l Network: CBS *Wire Services:* CBS
Arbitron Metro Market: New York *Format:* Sports *Target Audience:* General.
Clancy Woods, President
Colleen Mamzella, News Director

WWRU
12-08-1995; 1660 khz AM
8400 N.W. 52nd St., Suite 101, Miami, FL 33166 US
(212) 966-8700, *Fax:* (212) 966-9580
www.krbusa.com
License: Jersey City, NJ held by Multicultural Radio Broadcasting Licensee LLC.
Group Owner: Multicultural Radio Broadcasting Inc.; (acq 2-4-2004; grpsl).
Arbitron Metro Market: Jersey City, NJ *Format:* Korean
Gene Heinemeyer, General Manager

Lakehurst

***WLNJ**
91.7 mhz FM *Hrs Open:* 24; 3.5 kw; 49 m HAAT 160 ft/32 m AGL; N40 04 07 W74 28 09 *Rebroadcasts:* WYRS 90.7
Box 730, Manahawkin, NJ
(609) 978-1678, *Fax:* (609) 597-4146
www.wyrs.org
info@wyrs.org
License: Lakehurst, Ocean County, NJ held by WYRS Broadcasting.
Nat'l Network: IRN/USA News
Arbitron Metro Market: Monmouth/Ocgan
Bob Wick, General Manager

Lakewood Township

WOBM
11-20-1970; 1160 khz AM; 5 kw-D, DA2; 8.9 kw-N, DA2; N40 8 9 W74 13 48
P O Box 927, Toms River, NJ 08754 US
848-221-8000, *Fax:* (732) 269-9292
www.wobmam.com
Brad.Burascano@townsquaremedia.com
License: Lakewood Township, NJ held by Millennium Shore License Holdco LLC.
Group Owner: Millennium Radio Group LLC; (acq 5-14-02; grpsl).
Nat'l Network: AP Radio *Nat'l Reps:* Katz Radio
TV Affiliate: Oldies *Format:* Talk *Special Programming:* news progmg 14 hrs wkly *Hrs. of News Programming:* 5 *No. News Employees:* 45 plus; educated
General Sales Manager, Steve Ardolina
Program Director, Brad Burascano
Promotions Director, Promotions Manager

Lawrenceville

***WRRC**
09-23-1989; 107.7 mhz FM *Hrs Open:* 16; 0.02 kw; 36 ft.; N40 16 44 W74 44 15
2083 Lawrenceville Rd., Lawrenceville, NJ 08648 US
(609) 896-5369, *Fax:* (609) 219-4724
License: Lawrenceville, Mercer County, NJ held by Rider University Board of Trustees.
Format: Variety/Diverse *Special Programming:* Black 10 hrs, heavy metal 10 hrs wkly *Hrs. of News Programming:* news progmg 4 hrs wkly *No. News Employees:* 3 *Target Audience:* 16-21; high school & collegestudents
Charles Benfer, General Manager

Lincroft

***WBJB-FM**
01-13-1975; 90.5 mhz FM *Hrs Open:* 24; 0.9 kw; 371 ft.; N40 19 19 W74 7 57
765 Newman Springs Road, Lincroft, NJ 07738 US

(732) 224-2252, *Fax:* (732) 224-2494
www.wbjb.org
comments@wbjb.org
License: Lincroft, Monmouth County, NJ held by Board of Trustees of Brookdale Community College.
Nat'l Network: NPR
Arbitron Metro Market: Lincroft, NJ *Format:* News, Triple A
Special Programming: Haitian 3 hrs, pub affrs 5 hrs, bluegrass 3 hrs, Sp 4 hrs, blues 4 hrs wkly *Hrs. of News Programming:* News progmg 16 hrs wkly *TargetAudience:* ages 25-54.
Michelle McBride, Operations Dir
Tom Brennan, Station Manager
Jeff Raspe, Programming Director
George Marshall, Chief Engineer

Lindenwold

WTTM
05-01-1999; 1680 khz AM
600 Alexander Rd, Bldg 2, Princeton, NJ 08540 US
(267) 527-9886, *Fax:* (267) 527-1684
www.radiowttm1680.com
wttm1680@yahoo.com
License: Lindenwold, NJ held by Multicultural Radio Broadcasting Licensee LLC.
Group Owner: Multicultural Radio Broadcasting Inc.; (acq 5-24-2002; grpsl).
Arbitron Metro Market: Philadelphia, PA *Format:* Ethnic

Long Branch

WWZY
06-01-1960; 107.1 mhz FM; 5 kw; 361 ft.; N40 18 17 W73 59 8
11 Skyline Drive, Hawthorne, NY 10532 US
(732) 774-4755, *Fax:* (732) 774-7315
www.breezeradio.com
info@breezeradio.com
License: Long Branch, Monmouth County, NJ held by Press Communications LLC
Group Owner: Press Communications L.L.C.; acq 6-18-2003; $20 million).
Nat'l Reps: Eastman Radio *Wire Services:* AP
Arbitron Metro Market: Long Branch, NJ *Format:* Adult Contemp
Target Audience: Women; 25-54
Rich Morena, General Manager
John Furno, General Sales Mgr
Dan Turi, Programming Director
Diana Pellegrino, Promotions Manager
Mike Heilman, Chief Engineer

Mahwah

*WRPR
07-15-1980; 90.3 mhz FM *Hrs Open:* 18; 0.1 kw horiz; -66 ft.; N41 4 51 W74 10 34
505 Ramapo Valley Rd., Mahwah, NJ 07430 US
(201) 825-1234,(201) 825-7998, *Fax:* (201) 327-9036
phobos.ramapo.edu/wrpp
wrpr@ramapo.edu
License: Mahwah, Bergen County, NJ held by Ramapo College of New Jersey.
Format: Contemporary Hits/Top 40 *Special Programming:* Pub affrs 12 hrs wkly *Hrs. of News Programming:* news progmg 10 hrs wkly *No. News Employees:* 4 *Target Audience:* 18-24; college students
Evan Brown, General Manager
Andrew Bernstein, Programming Director
Sarah Tucci, Music Director
Delores Smith, Traffic Manager

Manahawkin

WCHR-FM
01-01-2002; 105.7 mhz FM; 13 kw; 459 ft.; N39 42 56 W74 17 31
P.O. Box 658, Union, NJ 07083 US
(848)221-8000, *Fax:* (732) 269-9292
www.1057thehawk.com
Wendy.Wesley@townsquaremedia.com
License: Manahawkin, Ocean County, NJ held by Millennium Shore License Holdco LLC.
Group Owner: Millennium Radio Group LLC; (acq 3-15-2004; $12 million).
Arbitron Metro Market: Atlantic City, NJ *Format:* Classic Rock
Phil LoCascio, Operations Dir
Bill Saurer, General Manager
Russ DelCore, General Sales Mgr
Steve Ardolina, Programming Director
Brad Burascano, Promotions Manager
Tom Monzeli, News Director
Jay Pierce, Engineering Dir
TomDunphy, Digital Managing Editor
Zoe Burdine-Fly, Regional Vice President
Andy Chase, Music Director/APD
James Thomas, Director of Digital Sales
Wendy Wesley, Director of Live Events & Non-Traditional Revenue
Mario Forcellati, ProductionDirector

WJRZ-FM
07-04-1976; 100.1 mhz FM *Hrs Open:* 24; 1.7 kw; 436 ft.; N39 47 54 W74 12 10
Mailing Address: PO Box 1000, Manahawkin, NJ 08050 US
Second Address: 610 Main Street, Belmar, NJ 7719
(609) 597-1100, *Fax:* (609) 597-4400
www.wjrz.com
License: Manahawkin, Ocean County, NJ held by Jersey Shore Broadcasting Corp.
Group Owner: Greater Media Inc.; (acq 7-19-02).
Nat'l Network: AP Radio *Nat'l Reps:* Katz Radio
Format: Contemporary Hits/Top 40, Adult Contemp *Hrs. of News Programming:* news progmg 4 hrs wkly *No. News Employees:* 1 *Target Audience:* 35-54.
Dan Finn, Operations Dir
Marge Guglielmo, General Sales Mgr
Doug Sjonvall, Promotions Manager
Sharon Zarnowski, News Director
Bill Clanton Sr., Chief Engineer
Mike Normand, Local Sales Manager
Jeff Rafter, Operations Manager

*WNJM
08-01-1999; 89.9 mhz FM; 0.001 kw horiz, 0.2 kw vert; 259 ft.; N39 41 57 W74 14 5
P.O. Box 777, Trenton, NJ 08625 US
(215) 351-1200, *Fax:* (215) 351-0398
www.whyy.org
talkback@whyy.org
License: Manahawkin, Ocean County, NJ held by New Jersey Public Broadcasting Authority.
Nat'l Network: NPR; PRI
Arbitron Metro Market: Bridgeton, PA *Format:* News, News/Talk, 86
William Marrazzo, CEO/COO
Kyra McGrath, Operations Dir
Pharoah Cranston, Station Manager
Chris Satullo, News Director

*WYRS
03-27-1995; 90.7 mhz FM *Hrs Open:* 24; 0.001 kw horiz, 15 kw vert; 262 ft.; N39 38 24 W74 17 32
P.O. Box 730, Manahawkin, NJ 08050 US
(609) 978-1678, *Fax:* (609) 597-4146
www.wyrs.org
info@wyrs.org
License: Manahawkin, Ocean County, NJ held by WYRS Broadcasting
Nat'l Network: USA
Arbitron Metro Market: Manahawkin, NJ *Format:* Children *Target Audience:* General.
Bob Wick, CEO

Margate City

WTTH
11-19-1991; 96.1 mhz FM *Hrs Open:* 24; 2.8 kw; 400 ft.; N39 21 2 W74 26 55 *Rebroadcasts:* Simulcast with WDTH(FM) Wildwood Crest 100%
2922 Atlantic Ave, S 201, Atlantic City, NJ 08401 US
(609) 484-8444, *Fax:* (609) 646-6331
www.961wtth.com
961wtth@gmail.com
License: Margate City, Atlantic County, NJ held by Equity Communications L.P.
Group Owner: Equity Communications LP; (acq 5-30-2003; grpsl).
Nat'l Reps: Katz Radio
Arbitron Metro Market: Atlantic City-C *Format:* Adult Contemp
Special Programming: Gospel 5 hrs, relg one hr wkly *Target Audience:* 18-49; adults *Adv. Rates:* 200; 200; 200; 50
Gary Fisher, Operations Dir
Rob Garcia, Programming Director
Shannon Wray, Promotions Manager
Cindy Hesley, Sales Director

Medford Lakes

*WVBV
01-01-2005; 90.5 mhz FM *Hrs Open:* 24; 0 kw horiz, 21 kw vert; 453 ft.; N39 33 20 W74 44 48
US
(856) 983-1662, *Fax:* (856) 983-1814
www.hopefm.net
info@hopefm.net
License: Medford Lakes, Burlington County, NJ held by Hope Christian Church of Marlton Inc.
Arbitron Metro Market: Medford Lakes, NJ *Format:* Christian, Talk
William Luebkemann Jr., President

Millville

WMVB
12-01-1953; 1440 khz AM *Hrs Open:* 24; 1 kw-D, DA2; 0.065 kw-N, DA2; N39 25 19 W75 1 14 *Rebroadcasts:* Simulcast with WSNJ(AM) Bridgeton
2073 Fairton Road, Millville, NJ 08332 US
(856) 327-8800, *Fax:* (856) 327-0408
www.wsmjam.com
information@wsnjam.com
License: Millville, NJ held by Quinn Broadcasting Inc
Arbitron Metro Market: Millville, NJ *Format:* Variety/Diverse
Special Programming: Sp 2 hrs, gospel 8 hrs, children 3 hrs wkly *No. News Employees:* 4 *Target Audience:* 25-54; general public
Adv. Rates: 23; 23; 23; 23
Jim Quinn, President
Carl Elwood, General Manager
Richard Hoch, General Sales Mgr

Morristown

*WJSV
02-22-1971; 90.5 mhz FM *Hrs Open:* 8 AM-10 PM (M-F); 0.125 kw; 16 ft.; N40 50 10 W74 29 16
50 Early Street Rm. 163, Morristown, NJ 07960 US
(973) 292-2168, *Fax:* (973) 539-5573
www.wjsv.org
norman.wallerstein@msdk12.net
License: Morristown, Morris County, NJ held by Morris School District Board of Education.
Format: Rock/AOR *Special Programming:* News/talk 3 hrs, sports 3 hrs wkly *Hrs. of News Programming:* news progmg 3 hrs wkly *No. News Employees:* 1 *Target Audience:* General.
Norman Wallerstein, General Manager
Dame Mallan, Station Manager
Michael O'Brien, Programming Director
Ryan Whitenack, Promotions Manager
Lee Tyler, Promotions Director

WMTR
12-12-1948; 1250 khz AM
55 Horsehill Road, Cedar Knolls, NJ 07927 US
(973) 538-1250, *Fax:* (973) 538-3060
www.wmtram.com
cedwards@greatermedianj.com
License: Morristown, NJ held by The Sentinel Publishing Co.
Group Owner: Greater Media Inc.; (acq 7-6-01; grpsl).
Arbitron Metro Market: Morristown, NJ *Format:* Oldies *Special Programming:* Community connection 5 hrs wkly *Target Audience:* 35 plus.
Dan Finn, President
Chris Edwards, Operations Dir
Nancy McKinley, General Manager
Matt DeVoti, General Sales Mgr
Chris Edwards, Programming Director
Scott Kohlhepp, Promotions Manager

Mount Holly

WWJZ
11-01-1992; 640 khz AM
50 Tensaw Drive, Browns Mills, NJ 08015 US
(215) 591-0100, *Fax:* (215) 591-4527
www.radiodisney.com
License: Mount Holly, NJ held by Radio Disney Group LLC.
Group Owner: ABC Inc.; (acq 12-30-99).
Arbitron Metro Market: Philadelphia, PA *Format:* Children *Target Audience:* 45 plus. *Adv. Rates:* 35; 25; 35; 20
Phil Guerini, Vice President and General Manager
Ray De La Garza, VP of Programming
Rita Ferro, Executive Vice President, Disney Media Sales and M
Kelly Edwards, Executive Director Music & Programming, Radio Disn
Ivan Heredia, VP,Marketing
Anne Sweeney, Co-Chair

Netcong

*WNJY
01-01-2008; 89.3 mhz FM; 0.001 kw horiz, 0.52 kw vert; 430 ft.; N40 53 14 W74 41 55 *Rebroadcasts:* Rebroadcasts WNJT-FM Trenton 100%
PO Box 777, Trenton, NJ 08625 US
(609) 777-5000, *Fax:* (609) 777-5217
www.njn.net

License: Netcong, Morris County, NJ held by New Jersey Public Broadcasting Authority.
Regional Network: NJN Public Radio
Arbitron Metro Market: Netcong, NJ *Format:* News, News/Talk, 86
Josh Weston, Chairman
Pharoah Cranston, Station Manager
Andre Butts, Programming Director

New Brunswick

WCTC

12-12-1946; 1450 khz AM *Hrs Open:* 24; 0.25 kw-U, ND1; 1 kw-U, ND1; N40 28 33 W74 29 34; N40 29 32 W74 25 11
Mailing Address: P. O. Box 1059, East Brunswick, NJ 08816 US
Second Address: 78 Veronica Ave., Somerset, NJ 8873
(732) 249-2600, *Fax:* (732) 545-9282
www.wctcam.com
License: New Brunswick, NJ held by The Sentinel Publishing Co.
Group Owner: Greater Media Inc.; (acq 5-1-57)
Arbitron Metro Market: New York *Format:* Oldies *Special Programming:* Rutgers Univ. & high school sports *Hrs. of News Programming:* news progmg 15 hrs wkly *No. News Employees:* 6 *Target Audience:* 35-54.*Adv. Rates:* 125; 90; 90; 30
Dan Finn, Operations Dir
Frank Calderaro, General Manager
John Ford, Station Manager
Jack Cahill, General Sales Mgr
Dave Kirby, Promotions Manager
Keith Smeal, Chief Engineer
Bruce Johnson, Operations Manager
Susan Young,Traffic Manager

WMGQ

01-01-1947; 98.3 mhz FM *Hrs Open:* 24; 1.2 kw; 518 ft.; N40 28 37 W74 29 33
Mailing Address: P. O. Box 1059, East Brunswick, NJ 08816 US
Second Address: 78 Veronica Ave., Somerset, NJ 8873
(732) 249-2600, *Fax:* (732) 249-9010
www.magic983.com
License: New Brunswick, Middlesex County, NJ
Group Owner: Greater Media Inc.
Arbitron Metro Market: New York, NY *Format:* Adult Contemp *Hrs. of News Programming:* News progmg 3 hrs wkly *Target Audience:* 25-54.
Dan Henrickson, Station Manager
Ed Silver, General Sales Mgr
Jeff Rafter, Programming Director
Dave Kirby, Promotions Manager
Chris McCoy, News Director
Keith Smeal, Engineering Dir

*WRSU-FM

04-01-1974; 88.7 mhz FM *Hrs Open:* 24; 1.35 kw; 125 ft.; N40 28 0 W74 26 15
126 College Avenue, New Brunswick, NJ 08901 US
(732) 932-7800, *Fax:* (732) 932-1768
www.wrsu.org
wrsu@wrsu.rutgers.edu
License: New Brunswick, Middlesex County, NJ held by Board of Governors Rutgers University.
Wire Services: AP
Format: Variety/Diverse *Hrs. of News Programming:* News progmg 6 hrs wkly *Target Audience:* 15-30; college students, div group of young adults
Tim Espar, Operations Dir
Alex Gulbin, General Manager
Rebecca Granet, Programming Director
Joe Leiding, Promotions Manager
Kevin Lanza, News Director

Newark

*WBGO

02-07-1948; 88.3 mhz FM *Hrs Open:* 24; 2.5 kw; 883 ft.; N40 45 22 W73 59 12
54 Park Place, Newark, NJ 07102 US
(973) 624-8880, *Fax:* (973) 824-8888
www.wbgo.org
jazz88@wbgo.org
License: Newark, Essex County, NJ held by Newark Public Radio Inc.
Nat'l Network: NPR *Wire Services:* AP
Arbitron Metro Market: New York *Format:* Jazz *Hrs. of News Programming:* news progmg 5 hrs wkly *No. News Employees:* 2 *Target Audience:* General.
Tim Porter, Chairman
David Tallacksen, Operations Dir
Cephas Bowles, General Manager
Amy Niles, General Sales Mgr
Thurston Briscoe, Programming Director
Brandy Wood, Promotions Manager
Doug Doyle, News Director
David Antoine,Chief Engineer
Stevan Smith, Traffic Manager
Brandy Wood, Marketing Manager
David Tallacksen, Vice President, Operations and Engineering

WQXR-FM

08-01-1992; 105.9 mhz FM; 2.4 kw; Ant 722 ft; N40 45 04 W73 58 25
485 Madison Ave., New York, NY 75219
(212) 310-6000, *Fax:* (212) 888-3694
www.univision.com
License: Newark, Essex County, NJ held by WADO-AM License Corp. (WADO).
Group Owner: Univision Radio; (acq 9-22-2003; grpsl)
Population Served: 18,000,000 *Arbitron Metro Market:* New York
Joe Pagan, General Manager

WFME

01-01-1959; 94.7 mhz FM *Hrs Open:* 24; 23.5 kw; 679 ft.; N40 47 17 W74 15 19
4135 Northgate Blvd., Suite 1, Sacramento, CA 95834 US
(973) 736-3600, *Fax:* (973) 736-4832
www.wfme.net
wfme@wfme.net
License: Newark, Essex County, NJ held by Family Stations Inc.
Group Owner: Family Stations Inc.; acq 3-10-66).
Nat'l Network: Family Radio
Arbitron Metro Market: New York *Format:* Christian, Religious *Target Audience:* General.
Harold Camping, President
Jason Frentses, Operations Dir
Charles Menut, Station Manager

WHTZ

06-01-1961; 100.3 mhz FM; 6 kw; 1362 ft.; N40 44 54 W73 59 10
333 Meadowlands Parkway, Secaucus, NJ 07094 US
(212) 239-2300, *Fax:* (212) 239-2308
www.z100.com
z100radio@aol.com
License: Newark, Essex County, NJ held by AMFM Radio Licenses L.L.C.
Group Owner: Clear Channel Communications Inc.; (acq 8-30-00; grpsl)
Nat'l Reps: Christal
Arbitron Metro Market: New York *Format:* Contemporary Hits/Top 40
Rob Williams, President
Tom Poleman, Operations Dir
Bob McCuin, General Sales Mgr
Josh Hadden, Engineering Dir

WNSW

01-01-1947; 1430 khz AM *Hrs Open:* 24
499 Broadway, New York, NY 10013 US
(212) 966-1059, *Fax:* (212) 966-9580
geneh@mrbi.net
License: Newark, NJ held by Multicultural Radio Broadcasting Licensee LLC.
Group Owner: Multicultural Radio Broadcasting Inc.; (acq 1-30-98; grpsl)
Nat'l Reps: Katz Radio
Arbitron Metro Market: New York, NY *Format:* Christian
Gene Heinemeyer, General Manager
Harold Chou, Chief Engineer

Newton

WTOC

12-15-1953; 1360 khz AM *Hrs Open:* 24
619 Alexander Road, 3rd Floor, Princeton, NJ 08540 US
(973) 881-8700, *Fax:* (973) 881-8324
www.trueoldies1360.com
License: Newton, NJ held by Aloha Station Trust, LLC
Group Owner: Clear Channel Communications Inc.; (acq 1-31-2001; grpsl)
Nat'l Network: ABC Music Radio *Nat'l Reps:* Katz Radio *Wire Services:* AP
Arbitron Metro Market: Sussex, NJ *Format:* Oldies *Special Programming:* Relg half hr, pub affrs one hr wkly *Hrs. of News Programming:* news progmg 5 hrs wkly *Target Audience:* 35 plus; mature adults with highincomes
Krystal Reilly, CFO
Ken O'Brien, Operations Dir
Art Eddy, Programming Director
Dick Taylor, Promotions Manager

WNNJ

10-15-1961; 103.7 mhz FM *Hrs Open:* 24; 2.3 kw; 892 ft.; N41 11 12 W74 46 4
619 Alexander Road, 3rd Floor, Princeton, NJ 08540 US
(973) 827-2525, *Fax:* (973) 827-2135
www.wnnj.com
rob@wnnj.com
License: Newton, Sussex County, NJ held by CC Licenses LLC
Group Owner: Clear Channel Communications Inc.
Arbitron Metro Market: Sussex, NJ *Target Audience:* 18-54; adults and families
John Hogan, CEO
Ken O'Brien, Operations Dir
Dick Taylor, General Sales Mgr
Rob Moorhead, Programming Director
Art Eddy, Director of Online
Krystal Reilly, Market Controller

North Cape May

WJSE

01-01-1993; 106.3 mhz FM; 6 kw; 80 m; N38 57 32 W74 55 23
3208 Pacific Ave., Wildwood, NJ 08210
(609) 522-3666,(609) 522-1987
www.1067coastcountry.com
info@1067coastcountry.com
License: North Cape May, Cape May County, NJ held by Coastal Broadcasting Systems Inc.
Group Owner: Coastal Broadcasting Systems Inc.; (acq 11-1-2004; $700,000)
Nat'l Network: USA; Moody
Arbitron Metro Market: Atlantic City-Cape May, NJ *Special Programming:* Class 3 hrs wkly
Bob Maschio, Operations Dir
Mark Hunter, Programming Director

Oakland

WVNJ

12-13-1993; 1160 khz AM *Hrs Open:* 24; 20 kw-D, DA2; 2.5 kw-N, DA2; N41 3 23 W74 14 58
1086 Teaneck Road, Ste 4f, Teaneck, NJ 07666 US
(201) 837-0400, *Fax:* (201) 837-9664
www.wvnj.com
advertising@wvnj.com
License: Oakland, NJ held by Universal Broadcasting of New York Inc.
Group Owner: Universal Broadcasting of New York Inc.; acq 3-24-94; $12,050,000. with WTHE(AM) Mineola, NY;
Nat'l Reps: Universal Broadcasting Inc *Regional Reps:* Universal Broadcasting Inc
Arbitron Metro Market: Oakland, NJ *Format:* News, Talk *Special Programming:* Health related *Hrs. of News Programming:* news progmg 8 hrs wkly *No. News Employees:* 1 *Target Audience:* 35-64; upscale *Adv.Rates:* 100; 100; 100; 40
Miriam Warshaw, President
Howard Warshaw, Operations Dir
Abe Warshaw, General Manager
Dave Margalotti, Program & Production Director
Pete Bucky, Program & Production Director
Howard Warshaw, Vice President

Ocean Acres

WBBO(FM)

01-01-1992; 98.5 mhz FM *Hrs Open:* 24; 6 kw; Ant 328 ft; N39 45 06 W74 15 39
2355 W. Bangs Ave., Neptune, NJ 7753
(732) 774-4755, *Fax:* (732) 774-7315
www.k985.com
License: Ocean Acres, Ocean County, NJ held by Press Communications LLC.
Group Owner: Press Communications L.L.C.; (acq 8-9-2004; $17 million)
Nat'l Reps: Eastman Radio
Population Served: 400,000*Target Audience:* 25-55; women
Richard Morena, General Manager
John Furno, General Sales Mgr
Diana Pellegrino, Promotions Manager

Ocean City

WWAC

08-01-1991; 102.7 mhz FM *Hrs Open:* 24; 3.3 kw; Ant 295 ft; N39 12 18 W74 39 33
1601 New Rd., Linwood, NJ 08244
(609) 653-1400, *Fax:* (609) 601-0450
www.theace1027.com
License: Ocean City, Cape May County, NJ held by Atlantic Broadcasting of Linwood NJ Limited Liability Co.
Group Owner: Atlantic Broadcasting; (acq 10-15-2008; grpsl)
Population Served: 325,000 *Arbitron Metro Market:* Atlantic City-Cape May, NJ
Brett DeNafo, CEO
Dick Irland, General Manager

***WRTQ**
09-27-1994; 91.3 mhz FM *Hrs Open:* 24; 1.36 kw horiz, 13.5 kw vert; 394 ft.; N39 19 14 W74 46 18 *Rebroadcasts:* Rebroadcasts WRTI(FM) Philadelphia 100%
C/O Wrti, Annenberg Hall, Philadelphia, PA 19122 US
(215) 204-8405, *Fax:* (215) 204-7027
www.wrti.org
comments@wrti.org
License: Ocean City, Cape May County, NJ held by Temple University of the Commonwealth System of Higher Education.
Nat'l Network: NPR; AP Radio
Format: Jazz *Hrs. of News Programming:* news progmg 15 hrs wkly *No. News Employees:* 1 *Target Audience:* 30-65.
Dave Conant, General Manager
William Johnson, Station Manager
Jack Moore, Programming Director
Lorna Dixon, News Director
Jeff DePolo, Chief Engineer

Ocean City/Somers Po

WIBG
10-01-1992; 1020 khz AM *Hrs Open:* Sunrise-sunset
3328 Simpson Avenue, Ocean City, NJ 08226 US
(609) 398-1020, *Fax:* (609) 398-3736
www.wibg.com
wibg@wibg.com
License: Ocean City/Somers Po, NJ held by Enrico S. Brancadora.
Arbitron Metro Market: Atlantic City-Cape May, NJ *Format:* Christian, News, 86 *Hrs. of News Programming:* news progmg 7 hrs wkly *No. News Employees:* 1 *Target Audience:* 25-45; young urban-suburban professional*Adv. Rates:* 30; 30; 30; 30
Rick Brancadora, CEO
Josh Hennig, Operations Dir
Harry Hurley, Programming Director
David Angel, News Director

Parsippany-Troy Hill

WXMC
01-13-1973; 1310 khz AM *Hrs Open:* 24; 1 kw-D, DA1; 0.088 kw-N, DA1; N40 51 51 W74 21 6
20 Waterside Plaza, #26, New York, NY 10010 US
(973) 575-5561, *Fax:* (973) 575-5637
hoyestudia@hotmail.com
License: Parsippany-Troy Hill, NJ held by James Chladek
Arbitron Metro Market: Parsippany, NJ *Format:* Religious *Hrs. of News Programming:* news progmg 4 hrs wkly *No. News Employees:* 1 *Target Audience:* 25 plus; young upper middle class business professionals
James Chladek, CEO
Otto Gust, Operations Dir
Edwin Blas, Station Manager

Paterson

WPAT
05-03-1941; 930 khz AM; 5 kw-D, DA2; 5 kw-N, DA2; N40 50 59 W74 10 59
449 Broadway, 2nd Floor, New York, NY 10013 US
(212) 966-1059, *Fax:* (212) 966-9580
License: Paterson, NJ held by Multicultural Radio Broadcasting Licensee LLC.
Group Owner: Multicultural Radio Broadcasting Inc.; (acq 7-22-98).
Arbitron Metro Market: New York *Format:* Sports
Gene Heinemeyer, General Manager
Harold Chou, Chief Engineer

WPAT-FM
03-29-1957; 93.1 mhz FM; 5.4 kw; 1421 ft.; N40 42 43 W74 0 49
3191 Coral Way, Suite 805, Miami, FL 33145 US
(212) 541-9200, *Fax:* (212) 246-9239
License: Paterson, Passaic County, NJ held by WPAT Licensing Inc.
Group Owner: Spanish Broadcasting System Inc.; (acq 1996; $83.5 million)
Arbitron Metro Market: New York *Format:* Adult Contemp
Raul Alarcon Sr., Chairman
Raul Alarcon Jr., CEO
Jose Garcia, CFO

Pemberton

***WBZC**
01-24-1995; 88.9 mhz FM *Hrs Open:* 24; 0.47 kw horiz, 10 kw vert; 220 ft.; N39 50 34 W74 32 40
County Route 530, Pemberton, NJ 08068 US
(609) 894-9311 EXT. 1189, *Fax:* (609) 894-9440
www.z889.org
bholcumb@bcc.edu
License: Pemberton, Burlington County, NJ held by Burlington County College.
Arbitron Metro Market: Pemberton, NJ *Format:* Adult Contemp
Special Programming: Folk 4 hrs, jazz 4 hrs, bluegrass 4 hrs, reggae 4 hrs, *Hrs. of News Programming:* News progmg 4 hrs wkly *Target Audience:* 18-35.
Brett Holcomb, Operations Dir
Brett T. Holcomb, Station Manager
Neil Shore, Music Director
Jason ""Jaybird"" Varga, Production Director

Pennsauken

WPHI-FM
11-01-1982; 107.9 mhz FM *Hrs Open:* 24; 0.78 kw; 906 ft.; N39 57 9 W75 10 5
P O Box 69, 1771 South Burlington Rd, Bridgeton, NJ 08302 US
(610) 276-1100, *Fax:* (610) 276-1139
www.1003thebeaatphilly.com
1003@thebeatphilly.com
License: Pennsauken, Delaware County, NJ held by Radio One Licenses LLC.
Group Owner: Radio One Inc.; (acq 11-8-2001; grpsl).
Arbitron Metro Market: Philadelphia *Format:* Blues *No. News Employees:* 1 *Target Audience:* 18-44; savvy suburban educated professional
Helen Little, Operations Dir
Chester Schofield, General Manager

Petersburg

WTKU-FM
04-01-1983; 98.3 mhz FM *Hrs Open:* 24; 6 kw; 328 ft.; N39 12 18 W74 39 33
1601 New Road, Linwood, NJ 08221 US
(609) 653-1400, *Fax:* (609) 601-0450
www.kool983.com
jcroce@longportmedia.com
License: Petersburg, Cape May County, NJ held by Atlantic Broadcasting of Linwood NJ Limited Liability Co.
Group Owner: Atlantic Broadcasting; (acq 10-15-2008; grpsl)
Nat'l Reps: McGavren Guild
Arbitron Metro Market: Atlantic City, NJ *Format:* Oldies *Hrs. of News Programming:* News progmg 5 hrs wkly *Target Audience:* 25-64.
Brett DeNafo, CEO
Dick Irland, General Manager
Joe Croce, General Sales Mgr
Paul Kelly, Programming Director
Scott Reilly, Promotions Manager
Anne Pratt, News Director
Dan Merlo, Chief Engineer

Piscataway

***WVPH**
05-01-1976; 90.3 mhz FM; 0.1 kw; 254 ft.; N40 31 21 W74 25 52.5
C/O Lisa Ferguson, 100 Behemer Road, Piscataway, NJ 08854 US
(732) 981-0153, *Fax:* (732) 981-1985
www.thecore.fm
news@thecore.fm
License: Piscataway, Middlesex County, NJ held by Board of Education Piscataway High School.
Arbitron Metro Market: Middlesex, NJ *Format:* News, Talk *No. News Employees:* 1
Katherine O'Keefe, Operations Dir
Mary Kate Riecks, General Manager
David Rips, Programming Director
Nathan Seto, Promotions Manager
Kinako Abe, Business Director
Gina Rizze, Public Affairs Director
Kelly Terez, ProductionDirector
Stephen Yanick, IT Director
Audrey Krum, Development Director

Pleasantville

WBSS(AM)
01-01-1955; 1490 khz AM *Hrs Open:* 24 hrs; 400 w-U; N39 23 24 W74 30 45
1601 New Rd., Linwood, NJ 8221
(609) 653-1400, *Fax:* (609) 601-0450
www.kool983.com
License: Pleasantville, Atlantic County, NJ held by Atlantic Broadcasting of Linwood NJ Limited Liability Co.
Group Owner: Atlantic Broadcasting; (acq 10-15-2008; grpsl)
Nat'l Network: La Gran D *Nat'l Reps:* McGavren Guild
Population Served: 27,000 *Arbitron Metro Market:* Atlantic City-Cape May, NJ
Brett DeNafo, CEO
Dick Irland, General Manager

WOND
07-01-1950; 1400 khz AM; 1 kw-U, ND1; N39 23 24 W74 30 45
Rebroadcasts: Rebroadcasts WGYM(AM) Hammonton 100%
1601 New Road, Linwood, NJ 08221 US
(609) 653-1400, *Fax:* (609) 601-0450
www.wond1400am.com
License: Pleasantville, NJ held by Atlantic Broadcasting of Linwood NJ Limited Liability Co.
Group Owner: Atlantic Broadcasting; (acq 10-15-2008; grpsl)
Nat'l Network: Westwood One *Nat'l Reps:* McGavren Guild
Arbitron Metro Market: Atlantic City-C *TV Affiliate:* Talk *No. News Employees:* Adults 35 +.
CEO, CEO/COO

WBSS
03-30-1992; 1490 khz AM *Hrs Open:* 24; Ant 1,440 ft*Rebroadcasts:* Simulcast with WBUS(FM) Boalsburg 100%
1601 New Road, Linwood, NJ 08221 US
(814) 643-9620,(814) 643-1063, *Fax:* (814) 643-9625
www.thebus.net
License: Pleasantville, NJ held by Megahertz Licenses LLC.
Group Owner: Forever Broadcasting; (acq 3-13-2002; $620,000)
Nat'l Reps: Dome
Format: Classic Rock *No. News Employees:* 1 *Adv. Rates:* 16; 14; 16; 12
Kristen Cantrell, General Manager

WZBZ
01-01-1974; 99.3 mhz FM *Hrs Open:* 24; 3 kw; 328 ft.; N39 22 35 W74 27 8 *Rebroadcasts:* Simulcast with WGBZ(FM) Cape May Court House 100%
2922 Atlantic Avenue, #201, Atlantic City, NJ 08401 US
(609) 484-8444, *Fax:* (609) 646-6331
993thebuzz.com
993kissfm@gmail.com
License: Pleasantville, Atlantic County, NJ held by Equity Communications L.P.
Group Owner: Equity Communications LP; acq 5-31-2002; grpsl).
Nat'l Reps: Katz Radio
Arbitron Metro Market: Atlantic City-C *Format:* Urban Contemporary *Target Audience:* 18-49; adults *Adv. Rates:* 200; 200; 200; 50
Gary Fisher, Operations Dir
Cindy Hesley, General Sales Mgr
Rob Garcia, Programming Director
Shannon Wray, Promotions Manager

Point Pleasant

WRAT
10-04-1968; 95.9 mhz FM *Hrs Open:* 24; 4 kw; 240 ft.; N40 10 15 W74 1 42
Mailing Address: 55 Horsehill Road, Cedar Knolls, NJ 07927 US
Second Address: 610 Main St., Belmar, NJ 7719
(732) 681-3800, *Fax:* (732) 681-5995
www.wrat.com
License: Point Pleasant, Ocean County, NJ held by The Sentinel Publishing Co.
Group Owner: Greater Media Inc.; (acq 7-6-01; grpsl).
Nat'l Reps: Katz Radio
Target Audience: 21-44; men 25-54
Dan Finn, Operations Dir
Marge Guglielmo, General Sales Mgr
William Clanton Sr., Chief Engineer
Mike Normand, Local Sales Manager
Carl Craft, Operations Manager

Pomona

***WLFR**
10-16-1984; 91.7 mhz FM *Hrs Open:* 6 AM-2 AM; 0.82 kw; 148 ft.; N39 28 34.3 W74 32 20.3
Jim Leeds Road, Pomona, NJ 08240 US
(609) 652-4781, *Fax:* (609) 652-4958
www.wlfr.fm
License: Pomona, Atlantic County, NJ held by Stockton State College
Format: Alternative *Special Programming:* Folk 3 hrs, class 4 hrs, jazz 10 hrs wkly *Hrs. of News Programming:* News progmg one hr wkly *Target Audience:* General.
Christine Farina, General Manager

Pompton Lakes

WGHT
10-03-1964; 1500 khz AM *Hrs Open:* Sunrise-sunset; 1 kw-D, DAD; N40 58 51 W74 17 6
1878 Lincoln Ave., PO Box 316, Pompton Lakes, NJ 07442 US

(973) 839-1500, *Fax:* (973) 839-2400
www.ghtradio.com
livestudio@ghtradio.com
License: Pompton Lakes, NJ held by Mariana Broadcasting Inc.
Nat'l Network: AP Radio
Arbitron Metro Market: New York *Format:* Oldies, Talk *Special Programming:* Relg 2 hrs, polka one hr, loc sports 3 hrs wkly *Hrs. of News Programming:* news progmg 10 hrs wkly *No. News Employees:* 3 *TargetAudience:* 25-54; general
John Silliman, President
Tom Niven, Operations Dir
John Silliman, General Manager
Mary Hamilton, General Sales Mgr
Jimmy Howes, Programming Director
Deborah Valentine, News Director
Tom Niven, Chief Engineer
Greta Latona,Assistant Program Director
Jon Fass, Sports Director
Carmela Minervini, Office Manager
Mary Hamilton, Sales Director

Port Republic

*WEHA(FM)
01-01-2003; 88.7 mhz FM; 760 w vert; Ant 131 ft; N39 35 34 W74 26 15
300 Philadelphia Ave., Little Egg Harbor, NJ 8087
(609) 965-9100, *Fax:* (609) 965-9190
wgxm@verison.net
License: Port Republic, Atlantic County, NJ held by WXXY Broadcasting Inc.
Arbitron Metro Market: Little Egg Harbor, NJ *Format:* Gospel
George Krementz, General Manager

Princeton

WHWH
09-07-1963; 1350 khz AM *Hrs Open:* 24; 5 kw-D, DA2; 5 kw-N, DA2; N40 22 0 W74 44 38
619 Alexander Road, 3rd Floor, Princeton, NJ 08540 US
(212) 431-4300, *Fax:* (212) 966-9580
www.mrbi.net
info@mrbi.net
License: Princeton, NJ held by Multicultural Radio Broadcasting Licensee LLC.
Group Owner: Multicultural Radio Broadcasting Inc.; (acq 5-24-2002; grpsl)
Arbitron Metro Market: Trenton, NJ *TV Affiliate:* *KHIZ-TV
Arthur Liu, President

WPRB
10-01-1955; 103.3 mhz FM *Hrs Open:* 24; 14 kw; 728 ft.; N40 16 58 W74 41 11
P. O. Box 108, Princeton, NJ 08540 US
(609) 258-3655, *Fax:* (609) 258-1806
www.wprb.com
manager@wprb.com
License: Princeton, Mercer County, NJ held by Princeton Broadcasting Service Inc.
Arbitron Metro Market: Trenton, NJ *Format:* Jazz *Special Programming:* Asian Indian 6 hrs wkly *Target Audience:* 13-60. *Adv. Rates:* 22; 22; 22; 22
Spencer Salazar, General Manager

Princeton Junction

*WWPH
11-01-1975; 107.9 mhz FM; 0.017 kw horiz; 36 ft.; N40 18 20 W74 37 16
346 Clarksville Road, P.O. Box 248, Princeton Junction, NJ 08550 US
(609) 716-5050, *Fax:* (609) 716-5092
www.wwph1079.com
wwph107.9fmlogin@ww-p.org
License: Princeton Junction, Mercer County, NJ held by West Windsor Plainsboro Regional Board of Education.
Arbitron Metro Market: Princeton Junction, NJ *TV Affiliate:* WWPH-TV *Format:* Variety/Diverse *Target Audience:* 14-30; West Windsor & Plainsboro residents interested in their community
Glenn Allison, General Manager

Salem

WFAI
09-01-1966; 1510 khz AM *Hrs Open:* 6 AM-6 PM; 2.5 kw-D, DAD; N39 34 58 W75 27 39
704 King Street, Suite 604, Wilmington, DE 19801 US
(302) 622-8895, *Fax:* (302) 622-8678
www.faith1510.com
tonyq@faith1510.com
License: Salem, NJ held by QC Communication Inc.
Arbitron Metro Market: Wilmington, DE *Format:* Gospel *Special Programming:* Farm 8 hrs wkly *Hrs. of News Programming:* news progmg 3 hrs wkly *No. News Employees:* 2 *Target Audience:* 18 plus.
Tony Quartarone, General Manager
Manuel Mena, Programming Director

South Orange

*WSOU
04-14-1948; 89.5 mhz FM *Hrs Open:* 24; 2.4 kw; 312 ft.; N40 44 28 W74 14 42
400 South Orange Avenue, South Orange, NJ 07079 US
(973) 313-6110, *Fax:* (973) 761-7593
www.wsou.net
wsou@shu.edu
License: South Orange, Essex County, NJ held by Seton Hall University.
Wire Services: AP
Arbitron Metro Market: New York *Format:* Rock/AOR *Special Programming:* Pol 2 hrs, Ethnic 10 hrs, pub affrs 5 hrs, relg 5 hrs wkly *Hrs. of News Programming:* News progmg 7 hrs wkly *Target Audience:* 18-34.
Mark Maben, General Manager
Alexander Castiglione, Programming Director
Jen Wilcox, Promotions Manager
Eric Bishop, News Director
Frank Scafidi, Chief Engineer
Danielle Maffei, Music Director
Brian Wisowaty, Sports Director

Stirling

WKMB
02-01-1972; 1070 khz AM *Hrs Open:* Sunrise-sunset; 0.25 kw-D, NDD; N40 40 35 W74 28 36
1390 Valley Road, Stirling, NJ 07980 US
(908) 822-1515, *Fax:* (908) 822-1927
www.harvestradio.net
mprayer@harvestradio.com
License: Stirling, NJ held by World Harvest Communications Inc.
Arbitron Metro Market: New York *Format:* Christian, Talk
Gary Kirkwood Sr., CEO
Robert Hunt, Operations Dir
Melissa Prayer, General Manager

Sussex

*WNJP
01-01-1998; 88.5 mhz FM; 0.45 kw; 636 ft.; N41 8 37 W74 32 18
Cn777, Trenton, NJ 08625 US
(646) 829-4400, *Fax:* (609) 777-5217
www.njpublicradio.org
listenerservicesNJPR@nypublicradio.org
License: Sussex, Sussex County, NJ held by New Jersey Public Broadcasting Authority.
Nat'l Network: NPR; PRI
Arbitron Metro Market: Sussex, NJ *Format:* News, News/Talk, 86 *Target Audience:* General.
Pharoah Cranston, Operations Dir

Teaneck

*WFDU
08-30-1971; 89.1 mhz FM *Hrs Open:* 1:15 AM-3:45 PM (M-F); 24 (S, Su); 550 w; 550 ft; N40 57 39 W73 55 23
1000 River Rd., Teaneck, NJ 07666
(201) 692-2806, *Fax:* (201) 692-2807
www.wfdu.fm
barrys@fdu.edu
License: Teaneck, Bergen County, NJ held by Fairleigh Dickinson University.
Wire Services: AP
Population Served: 18,000,000 *Arbitron Metro Market:* New York *Special Programming:* Sp 3 hrs hrs wkly *Hrs. of News Programming:* News progmg 2 hrs wkly *Target Audience:* General.
Barry Sheffield, Operations Dir
Carl Kraus, General Manager
Barry Sheffield, Programming Director

Toms River

WOBM-FM
03-01-1968; 92.7 mhz FM; 1.4 kw; 486 ft.; N39 52 31 W74 9 57.3
P. O. Box 927, Toms River, NJ 08754 US
848-221-8000, *Fax:* (732) 269-9292
www.wobmam.com
Brad.Burascano@townsquaremedia.com
License: Toms River, Ocean County, NJ held by Millennium Shore Holdco LLC.
Group Owner: Millennium Radio Group LLC; (acq 5-14-02; grpsl).
TV Affiliate: Adult contemp
General Sales Manager, Steve Ardolina
Program Director, Brad Burascano
Promotions Director, Promotions Manager

*WNJO
01-01-2008; 90.3 mhz FM; 0.001 kw horiz, 4 kw vert; 121 ft.; N39 54 52 W74 4 58 *Rebroadcasts:* Rebroadcasts WNJT-FM Trenton 100%
US
(609) 777-5000, *Fax:* (609) 777-5217
www.njpublicradio.org
License: Toms River, Ocean County, NJ held by New Jersey Public Broadcasting Authority.
Nat'l Network: NPR *Regional Network:* NJN Public Radio
Arbitron Metro Market: Toms River, NJ *Format:* Jazz
Pharoah Cranston, Station Manager

Toms River Township

*WWNJ
12-01-1991; 91.1 mhz FM *Hrs Open:* 24; 0.05 kw horiz, 50 kw vert; 151 ft.; N39 58 7 W74 4 19 *Rebroadcasts:* Rebroadcasts WWFM(FM) Trenton 100%
Mailing Address: 1200 Old Trenton Road, Trenton, NJ 08690 US
Second Address: 1200 Old Trenton Road, West Windsor, NJ 8550
(609) 587-8989, *Fax:* (609) 570-3863
www.wwfm.org
info@wwfm.org
License: Toms River Township, Ocean County, NJ held by Mercer County Community College Board of Trustees.
Nat'l Network: NPR
Arbitron Metro Market: Toms River, NJ *Format:* Classical *Target Audience:* General.
Peter Fretwell, General Manager
Alice Weiss, Programming Director
David Osenberg, Development Producer
Diane Guvenis, Development Director
Glenn Smith, Music Director
Marcia Galambos, Membership Coordinator

Trenton

WFJS
01-20-1947; 1260 khz AM
1350 Campus Parkway, Suite 106, Wall, NJ 07753 US
(609)882-9357, *Fax:* (609)403-2908
www.wfjs.org
info@domesticchurchmedia.org
License: Trenton, NJ held by Domestic Church Media Foundation
Nat'l Network: EWTN Radio
Arbitron Metro Market: Trenton, NJ *Format:* Christian
James Manfredonia, President

WCHR
04-11-1941; 920 khz AM *Hrs Open:* 24
224 Maugers Mill Road, Pottstown, PA 19464 US
(609)454-4185, *Fax:* (215) 321-5583
www.wchram.net
jwhite@nassaubroadcasting.com
License: Trenton, NJ held by Nassau Broadcasting II L.L.C.
Group Owner: Nassau Broadcasting Partners L.P.; (acq 4-25-2002; with co-located FM)
Arbitron Metro Market: Trenton, NJ *Format:* Religious *Target Audience:* General; relg adults *Adv. Rates:* 40; 40; 40; 20
Curt Simpson, Operations Dir
John White, General Manager
John White, Station Manager
Chuck Zulker, General Sales Mgr
Dwain Decker, Programming Director

WKXW
08-27-1962; 101.5 mhz FM; 15.5 kw; 902 ft.; N40 16 58 W74 41 11
Mailing Address: 1350 Campus Parkway, Suite 106, Wall, NJ 07753 US
Second Address: 109 Walters Ave., Trenton, NJ 8638
(609) 771-8181, *Fax:* (609) 406-7956
www.nj1015.com
info@wkxw.com
License: Trenton, Mercer County, NJ
Group Owner: Millennium Radio Group LLC
Nat'l Reps: Christal
Arbitron Metro Market: Trenton, NJ *Format:* Talk *Hrs. of News Programming:* news progmg 75 hrs wkly *No. News Employees:* 15 *Target Audience:* General; New Jersey residents
Eric Johnson, Programming Director
Laurie Roth, News Director

WPST
08-07-1965; 94.5 mhz FM; 50 kw horiz, 48 kw vert; 492 ft.; N40 11 22 W74 50 47
224 Maugers Mill Road, Pottstown, PA 19464 US
(609) 419-0300, *Fax:* (609) 419-0143
www.wpst.com
dmckay@wpst.com
License: Trenton, Mercer County, NJ held by Nassau Broadcasting II L.L.C.
Group Owner: Nassau Broadcasting Partners L.P.; (acq 4-25-2002; with co-located AM)
Arbitron Metro Market: Trenton, NJ *Format:* Contemporary Hits/Top 40
Jim Spector, Programming Director
Angela Hartman, News Director
Randy Ellis, Music Director

***WNJT-FM**
05-20-1991; 88.1 mhz FM; 0.11 kw vert; 689 ft.; N40 16 58 W74 41 11
25 South Stockton Street, P.O. Box 777, Trenton, NJ 08625 US
(646) 829-4400, *Fax:* (609) 777-5217
www.njpublicradio.org
listenerservicesNJPR@nypublicradio.org
License: Trenton, Mercer County, NJ held by New Jersey Public Broadcasting Authority.
Nat'l Network: NPR; PRI
Arbitron Metro Market: Trenton, NJ *Format:* News, News/Talk, 86 *Target Audience:* General.
Pharoah Cranston, Station Manager
Andre Butts, Programming Director

***WTSR**
09-01-1966; 91.3 mhz FM *Hrs Open:* 24; 1.5 kw; 36 ft.; N40 16 17 W74 46 55
Kendall Hall Cn 4700, Ewing, NJ 08628 US
(609) 771-3200, *Fax:* (609) 637-5113
www.wtsr.org
wtsr@wtsr.org
License: Trenton, Mercer County, NJ held by The College of New Jersey Radio System.
Arbitron Metro Market: Trenton, NJ *Format:* Alternative *Special Programming:* Gospel 6 hrs, pub affrs 8 hrs, folk 4 hrs, jazz 4 *Hrs. of News Programming:* News progmg 15 hrs wkly *Target Audience:* 13-40; peoplewho listen to div mus formats
Pat Hall, Operations Dir
Kevin Potucek, General Manager
Alli Wentling, Station Manager
Alec Plasker, Promotions Manager
Melissa Radzimski, News Director
Matt Jannetti, Music Director
Kyle Greco, Production Director
Kyle Smith,PR Director
James Goetschius, Sports Director
Victoria Calafut, Web Director
Taylor Velardi, Automation Director

***WWFM**
09-06-1982; 89.1 mhz FM *Hrs Open:* 24; 1.15 kw; 292 ft.; N40 15 30 W74 38 59
Mailing Address: 1200 Old Trenton Rd., Trenton, NJ 08690 US
Second Address: 1200 Old Trenton Rd., West Windsor, NJ 8550
(609) 587-8989, *Fax:* (609) 570-3863
www.wwfm.org
info@wwfm.org
License: Trenton, Mercer County, NJ held by Mercer County Community College
Nat'l Network: NPR; PRI
Arbitron Metro Market: Trenton, NJ *Format:* Classical *Hrs. of News Programming:* 3.5 hrs wkly
Alice Weiss, Operations Dir
Peter Fretwell, General Manager
Heidi Jamieson, General Sales Mgr
Alice Weiss, Programming Director
David Osenberg, Development Producer
Diane Guvenis, Development Director
Glenn Smith, MusicDirector
Marcia Galambos, Membership Coordinator
Rachel Katz, Production Manager

Tuckerton

WBHX
01-01-1999; 99.7 mhz FM; 5.6 kw; 108 ft.; N39 33 41 W74 14 27
1018 Hillcrest Drive, Neshanic Station, NJ 08853 US
(732) 774-4755, *Fax:* (732) 774-7315
www.breezeradio.com
DanT@presscommradio.com
License: Tuckerton, Ocean County, NJ held by Press Communications L.L.C.
Group Owner: Press Communications L.L.C.; acq 9-18-02; $1.15 million).
Arbitron Metro Market: Neptune, N.J. *Format:* Adult Contemp
Rich Morena, General Manager
John Furno, General Sales Mgr
Dan Turi, Programming Director
Diana Pellegrino, Promotions Manager

Union Township

***WKNJ-FM**
01-01-1980; 90.3 mhz FM *Hrs Open:* 24/7; 0.009 kw; 16 ft.; N40 40 35 W74 14 2
PO Box Morris Avenue, Union, NJ 07083 US
(908) 737-0440, *Fax:* (908) 737-0445
www.wknjfm.com
wknj@kean.edu
License: Union Township, Union County, NJ held by Kean University.
Format: Rock/AOR *Special Programming:* Rock block, sports, classic times, Irish *Target Audience:* University students/administration; music lovers
Scott McHugh, General Manager
Cathleen Londino, Station Manager

Upper Montclair

***WMSC**
12-09-1974; 90.3 mhz FM *Hrs Open:* 7 AM-1 AM; 0.001 kw; 673 ft.; N40 51 53 W74 12 3
College Hall Room 235, Upper Montclair, NJ 07043 US
(973) 655-4257, *Fax:* (973) 655-7433
www.wmscradio.com
License: Upper Montclair, Essex County, NJ held by Montclair State University.
Arbitron Metro Market: Montclair, NJ *Format:* Variety/Diverse *Special Programming:* Black 4 hrs, gospel 2 hrs, jazz 2 hrs, Sp 2 hrs, s *Hrs. of News Programming:* News progmg 5 hrs wkly *Target Audience:* Under 35.
Andrew Ward, Operations Dir
Walter Soto, General Manager
Dan Maxwell, Programming Director
Dave Giumara, Promotions Manager
Lisa Hresko, Music Director

Villas

WCZT
02-01-1992; 98.7 mhz FM *Hrs Open:* 24; 6 kw; 328 ft.; N38 59 45 W74 50 19
403 Route 47 South, Cape May Court House, NJ 08210 US
(609) 522-1987, *Fax:* (609) 522-3666
www.987thecoast.com
coastalproduction@gmail.com
License: Villas, Cape May County, NJ held by Coastal Broadcasting Systems Inc.
Group Owner: Coastal Broadcasting Systems Inc.; (acq 5-21-2001; $1.4 million for stock)
Arbitron Metro Market: Villas, NJ *Format:* Adult Contemp
Bob Maschio, President /General Manager
Ed Rosenfeld, General Sales Mgr
Scott Wahl, Vice President/ News Director
Ray Bradley, Chief Engineer

Vineland

WMIZ
08-19-1959; 1270 khz AM; 0.36 kw-D, DA1; 0.21 kw-N, DA1; N39 29 53 W75 4 31
Mailing Address: P. O. Box 689, Vineland, NJ 08360 US
Second Address: 632 Maurice River Parkway, Vineland, NJ 8360
(856) 692-8888, *Fax:* (856) 696-2568
www.wmizradio.com
License: Vineland, NJ held by Clear Communications Inc.
Arbitron Metro Market: Vineland, NJ *Format:* Spanish *Target Audience:* Hispanic.
Carl Hemple, Sr, CEO
W. Withers, Jr, President
Dana Withers, General Manager
Scott Smolis, General Sales Mgr
Nicholas Lemay, News Director

WNJC
07-29-1946; 1360 khz AM *Hrs Open:* 6 AM-midnight
2 Wissa Powey Trail, Shamong, NJ 08088 US
(856) 227-1360, *Fax:* (856) 232-9093
www.wnjc1360.com
missradiochick@hotmail.com
License: Vineland, NJ held by Forsyth Broadcasting LLC
Arbitron Metro Market: Sewell, NJ *Format:* Gospel, Talk *Special Programming:* Relg 6 hrs wkly *Hrs. of News Programming:* news progmg 20 hrs wkly *No. News Employees:* 3 *Target Audience:* 30 plus; 52% women,upper income
John Forsythe, President
Al Jones, General Manager

WVLT
10-01-1968; 92.1 mhz FM; 6 kw; 328 ft.; N39 29 53 W75 4 31
P.O. Box 689, Vineland, NJ 08360 US
(856) 692-8888, *Fax:* (856) 696-2568
www.wvlt.com
psa@wvlt.com
License: Vineland, Cumberland County, NJ held by Clear Communications Inc.
Nat'l Network: ABC; Jones Radio Networks
Arbitron Metro Market: Vineland, NJ *Format:* Oldies *Target Audience:* 25-54; baby boomers *Adv. Rates:* 30; 27; 30; 22
Carl Hemple Sr., CEO/General Manager
Cheryl Kinderman, General Manager
Carson Raleton, Station Manager
Shaun Harvey, Programming Director
Heather Dooley, News Director
Chuck Niday, Chief Engineer

Wayne

***WPSC-FM**
11-01-1988; 88.7 mhz FM *Hrs Open:* 9 am-3 am M-F; 6 am-3 am S-S; 0.2 kw; 259 ft.; N40 59 46 W74 16 51
300 Pompton Road, Wayne, NJ 07470 US
(973) 720-3319, *Fax:* (973) 720-2454
wpsc887fm@wpunj.edu
License: Wayne, Passaic County, NJ held by William Paterson University of New Jersey.
Format: Alternative *Special Programming:* Punk 3 hrs, hip hop 18 hrs, metal 18 hrs, classic rock 12 hrs, jazz 12 hrs wkly *Target Audience:* 18-35; independent thinking
Ron Stotyn, General Manager

West Long Branch

***WMCX**
05-02-1974; 88.9 mhz FM *Hrs Open:* 24; 1 kw; 118 ft; N40 16 44 W74 00 26
Monmouth Univ., 400 Cedar Ave., West Long Branch, NJ 07764
(732) 571-3482, *Fax:* (732) 263-5145
www.wmcx.com
wmcxradio@monmouth.edu
License: West Long Branch, Monmouth County, NJ held by Monmouth University.
Nat'l Network: AP Radio
Population Served: 200,000*Special Programming:* Sports 11 hrs, jazz 3 hrs, changes w/semester *Hrs. of News Programming:* News progmg 2.5 hrs wkly *Target Audience:* 18-25; college students, recent grads, young adults
Kahlil Thomas, General Manager

Wildwood

WCMC
11-25-1951; 1230 khz AM *Hrs Open:* 24; 1 kw-U, ND1; N39 0 9 W74 48 46
Mailing Address: 8025 Black Horse Pike, Suite 100, W. Atlantic City, NJ 08232 US
Second Address: 3010 New Jersey Ave., Wildwood, NJ 8260
(919) 890-6299, *Fax:* (919) 890-6146
www.espntriangle.com
contact@999thefan.com
License: Wildwood, NJ held by Equity Communications L.P.
Group Owner: Equity Communications LP; (acq 11-4-97; $7.1 million with co-located FM).
Nat'l Network: ABC *Nat'l Reps:* Katz Radio
Arbitron Metro Market: Atlantic City-Cape May, NJ *Format:* Adult Contemp *Target Audience:* Adults 35-64. *Adv. Rates:* 50; 50; 50; 50
Gary Fisher, President
Jim MacMillan, Programming Director

WZXL
12-17-1959; 100.7 mhz FM *Hrs Open:* 24; 38 kw; 331 ft.; N39 7 28 W74 45 56
8025 Black Horse Pike, Suite 100, W. Atlantic City, NJ 08232 US
(609) 484-8444, *Fax:* (609) 646-6331
www.wzxl.com
STEVE@WZXL.COM
License: Wildwood, Cape May County, NJ
Group Owner: Equity Communications LP
Nat'l Reps: Katz Radio
Arbitron Metro Market: West Atlantic City, NJ *Format:* Classic Rock *Target Audience:* Adults 18-49. *Adv. Rates:* 200; 200; 200; 50

Steve Raymond, Programming Director
Shannon Wray, Promotions Manager
Cindy Hesley, Director of Sales

Wildwood Crest

WEZW
08-15-1993; 93.1 mhz FM *Hrs Open:* 24; 4.1 kw; 223 ft.; N38 59 34 W74 48 48 *Rebroadcasts:* Simulcast with WTTH(FM) Margate City 100%
2922 Atlantic Ave., Suite 201, Atlantic City, NJ 08401 US
(318)843-6929, *Fax:* (609) 646-6331
www.wezw1066fm.com/
bosstalker@bellsouth.net
License: Wildwood Crest, Cape May County, NJ held by Equity Communications L.P.
Group Owner: Equity Communications LP; (acq 5-30-2003; grpsl).
Nat'l Reps: Katz Radio
Arbitron Metro Market: Gibsland,La *Format:* Adult Contemp *Target Audience:* 18-49; adults *Adv. Rates:* 200; 200; 200; 50
Gary Fisher, Operations Dir
Rob Garcia, Programming Director
Denise Carrington, News Director

Woodbine

*WJPH
02-16-1999; 89.9 mhz FM *Hrs Open:* 24; 1 kw; 105 ft.; N39 16 51 W74 51 11
418 Washington Ave, PO Box 603, Woodbine, NJ 08270 US
(609) 861-3700
www.praise899.org
letters@praise899.org
License: Woodbine, Cape May County, NJ held by Maranatha Ministries/Joy Communications Inc.
Format: Religious *Special Programming:* Gospel one hr wkly *Hrs. of News Programming:* News progmg 10 hrs wkly *Target Audience:* 25-54; women
Kenneth Manri, President

Zarephath

WAWZ
08-22-1954; 99.1 mhz FM *Hrs Open:* 24; 50,000 watts; Ant 656 ft; N40 36 41 W74 34 12
Box 9058, Zarephath, NJ 08890
(732) 469-0991, *Fax:* (732) 469-2115
www.star991fm.com
info@star991fm.com
License: Zarephath, Somerset County, NJ held by Pillar of Fire Inc.
Group Owner: Pillar of Fire Inc.
Arbitron Metro Market: New York *Target Audience:* 25-54. *Adv. Rates:* 160; 160; 160; 75
Nancy Walter, Operations Dir
Rea Crawford, General Manager
Scott Taylor, Station Manager
Lorraine Shaw, General Sales Mgr
Therese Romano, Programming Director
Ron Habegger, Engineering Dir

New Mexico

Alamo

*KYGR
88.1 mhz FM; 400 w; Ant -195 ft; N34 25 01 W107 30 04
Box 907, Magdalena, NM
(505) 854-2632, *Fax:* (505) 854-2545
License: Alamo, Magdalena County, NM held by Alamo Navajo School Board Inc.

Sarah Apache, General Manager

Alamo Community

*KABR
107.5 mhz FM; 10000 w; -41 m; N34 25 01 W107 30 04
PO Box 907, Magdalena, NM
(575)854-2543, *Fax:* (575)854-2545
www.ansbi.org
License: Alamo Community, Socorro County, NM
Group Owner: Alamo Navajo School Board Inc.

Steve Guerro, President
Stanley Herrera, Vice President

Alamogordo

KINN
06-10-1957; 1270 khz AM *Hrs Open:* 24; 1 kw-D, ND2; 0.08 kw-N, ND2; N32 53 13 W105 57 4
440 Northlake Center, Suite 206, Dallas, TX 75238 US
(505) 434-1414, *Fax:* (505) 434-2213
License: Alamogordo, NM held by Burt Broadcasting Inc.
Group Owner: Burt Broadcasting Inc.; (acq 4-1-2001; with co-located FM)
Format: News, News/Talk, 86 *Hrs. of News Programming:* News progmg 22 hrs wkly *Target Audience:* 24-50; military & civil service personnel employed in high-tech jobs
William Burt, President
Lori Swinford, General Sales Mgr
James White, Programming Director
Ken Bass, Engineering Dir
Donnie Burt, Traffic Manager

KRSY
01-01-1954; 1230 khz AM *Hrs Open:* 24; 1 kw; 150 ft; N33 10 45 W105 53 53
Mailing Address: Box 2710, Alamogordo, NM 88201
Second Address: 119 N. Canyon Rd., Alamogordo, NM 88310
(575) 437-1505, *Fax:* (575) 437-5566
www.snmradio.com
Lhenke@snmradio.com
License: Alamogordo, Otero County, NM held by WP Broadcasting LLC.
Group Owner: Westburg Media Capital LP; (acq 5-19-2006; grpsl).
Nat'l Network: ESPN Radio
Dave Westberg, Chairman
John Weller, CEO/COO
Les Henke, General Manager
Kelly Lynch, Programming Director
Ken Bass, Chief Engineer

KNMZ
01-01-1997; 103.7 mhz FM *Hrs Open:* 24; 6 kw; 1,338 ft; N33 10 45 W105 53 53
Mailing Address: Box 2710, Alamogordo, NM 88201
Second Address: 119 N. Canyon Rd., Alamogordo, NM 88310
(575) 437-1505, *Fax:* (575) 437-5566
www.snmradio.com
Lhenke@snmradio.com
License: Alamogordo, Otero County, NM held by WP Broadcasting LLC.
Group Owner: Westburg Media Capital LP; (acq 5-19-2006; grpsl).
Nat'l Network: ESPN
Dave Westberg, Chairman
John Weller, CEO/COO
Les Henke, General Manager
Kelly Lynch, Programming Director
Ken Bass, Chief Engineer

*KUPR
10-14-2000; 91.7 mhz FM *Hrs Open:* 24; 1.4 kw; 1680 ft.; N32 49 47 W105 53 10
1505 Crescent Dr, Alamogordo, NM 88310 US
(505) 277-4806, *Fax:* (505) 434-6060(505) 437-9917
www.kunm.org
membership@kunm.org
License: Alamogordo, Otero County, NM held by Southern New Mexico Radio Foundation.
Arbitron Metro Market: Alamogordo, NM *Format:* Country, Gospel *Hrs. of News Programming:* News progmg 4 hrs wkly *Target Audience:* 25-60; adults
Bob Flotte, President
Scott MacNicholl, Operations Dir
Tristan Clum, Programming Director
Steve Young, News Director
Mike Stark, Chief Engineer
Roman Garcia, Production Director
Roberta Rael, Youth Radio Project Manager
OakleyMerideth, Music Assistant
Nicole Candelaria, Production Assistant
Melissa Rios, Management Assistant
Matthew Finch, Music Director

KYEE
07-21-1980; 94.3 mhz FM *Hrs Open:* 24; 3 kw; -384 ft.; N32 56 42 W105 56 47
P.O. Box 1848, Alamogordo, NM 88310 US
(505) 434-1414, *Fax:* (505) 434-2213
www.totacc.com/94Key
94key@totacc.com
License: Alamogordo, Otero County, NM held by Burt Broadcasting Inc.
Group Owner: Burt Broadcasting Inc.; acq 11-88; $230,000; *Arbitron Metro Market:* Alamogordo, NM *Format:* Contemporary Hits/Top 40 *Target Audience:* 18-44; young adults
William Burt, President
Donnie Burt, Operations Dir
Lori Swinford, General Sales Mgr

KZZX
01-01-1979; 105.3 mhz FM *Hrs Open:* 24; 0.91 kw; 1614 ft.; N32 49 48 W105 53 12
P O Box 618, 501 South Florida, Alamogordo, NM 88311 US
(505) 434-1414, *Fax:* (505) 434-2213
www.country1053.net/
Burt Broadcasting@bbiradio.net
License: Alamogordo, Otero County, NM held by Burt Broadcasting Inc.
Group Owner: Burt Broadcasting Inc.
Arbitron Metro Market: Alamogordo, NM *Format:* Country *Hrs. of News Programming:* News progmg 22 hrs wkly *Target Audience:* 20-55.
Steve Herling, Operations Dir
Teddie Gibbon, Station Manager
George Kessler, General Sales Mgr
Maynard Cohen, Programming Director
Roger Nelson, Promotions Manager
Jolene Longwill, News Director
Tim Anderson, Chief Engineer
Catherine Bruntlett, Research Director

KQEL
01-01-2006; 107.9 mhz FM *Hrs Open:* 24; 3 kw; -594 ft.; N32 53 13 W105 57 4
505 Turtle Creek Drive, Brentwood, TN 37027 US
(505) 434-1414, *Fax:* (505) 434-2213
www.1079coolfm.net
Broadcasting@bbiradio.net
License: Alamogordo, Otero County, NM held by Burt Broadcasting Inc.
Group Owner: Burt Broadcasting Inc.; (acq 10-29-2003; $93,000 for CP).
Arbitron Metro Market: Alamogordo, NM *Format:* Oldies
William Burt, General Manager
Lori Swinford, General Sales Mgr

*KYCM
01-01-2006; 89.9 mhz FM; 0.8 kw; 1631 ft.; N32 49 47 W105 53 13 *Rebroadcasts:* Rebroadcasts KYCC(FM) Stockton, CA 100%
9019 West Lane, Stockton, CA 95210 US
(209) 477-3690, *Fax:* (209) 477-2762
www.kycc.org
kycc@kycc.org
License: Alamogordo, Otero County, NM held by Your Christian Companion Network Inc.
Arbitron Metro Market: Alamogordo, NM *Format:* Adult Contemp, Gospel, 74
Shirley Garner, General Manager
Scott Mearns, Office Manager
John Ramos, Office Manager
Gary Harding, Production Manager

Albuquerque

KABQ
01-01-1947; 1350 khz AM *Hrs Open:* 8am - 5:30pm; 5 kw-D, DAN; 0.5 kw-N, DAN; N35 6 2 W106 40 34
5867 Locksley Place, Los Angeles, CA 90068 US
(505) 338-7400, *Fax:* (505) 830-6543
www.abqtalk.com
License: Albuquerque, NM held by Clear Channel Broadcasting Licenses.
Group Owner: Clear Channel Communications Inc.; (acq 3-01-00; grpsl)
Nat'l Reps: Lotus Entravision Reps LLC
Arbitron Metro Market: Albuquerque, NM *Format:* Alternative, Talk *Target Audience:* General.
Chuck Hammond, General Manager
Bill May, Programming Director
Chris Williams, Chief Engineer

*KANW
10-01-1950; 89.1 mhz FM *Hrs Open:* 24; 17 kw; 4154 ft.; N35 12 44 W106 26 57
2020 Coal Ave Se, Albuquerque, NM 87106 US
(505) 242-7163
www.kanw.com
larry@kanw.com
License: Albuquerque, Bernalillo County, NM held by Board of Education of the City of Albuquerque.
Nat'l Network: NPR; PRI
Arbitron Metro Market: Albuquerque, NM *Hrs. of News Programming:* News progmg 20 hrs wkly
Michael Brasher, General Manager

KDAZ
01-01-1969; 730 khz AM *Hrs Open:* 24; 1 kw-D, DA2; 0.076 kw-N, DA2; N35 0 31 W106 42 52
Mailing Address: P.O. Box 4338, Albuquerque, NM 87196 US
Second Address: 5010 4th St. N.W., Albuquerque, NM 87107
(505) 345-1991, *Fax:* (505) 345-5669
www.kdaz.org
birga@kdaz.org
License: Albuquerque, NM held by Pan American Broadcasting Inc.
Nat'l Network: USA
Arbitron Metro Market: Albuquerque, NM *Format:* Variety/Diverse *Target Audience:* 25-54. *Adv. Rates:* 16.50;16.50;16.50;16.50
Blackie Gonzalez, CEO
Annette Garcia, Operations Dir
Jim Sandell, Programming Director
Vickie Archiveque, CFO

KDEF
09-01-1953; 1150 khz AM; 5 kw-D, DAN; 0.5 kw-N, DAN; N35 12 6 W106 35 54
2900 Louisiana N.E., Suite 250, Albuquerque, NM 87110 US
(505) 265-0991, *Fax:* (505) 265-1081
info@kdefam.com
License: Albuquerque, NM held by RAMH Corp.
Nat'l Network: CNN Radio
Arbitron Metro Market: Albuquerque, NM *Format:* News, Sports, 2 *Target Audience:* General.
Henry Tafoya, General Manager

KIVA
05-14-1956; 1600 khz AM *Hrs Open:* 24; 10 kw-D, 128 w-N; N35 10 14 W106 37 51
307 Los Ranchos Rd. N.W., Albuquerque, NM 84101
(505) 899-5029, *Fax:* (505) 899-6865
www.realoldies1600.com
realoldies1600@realoldies1600
License: Albuquerque, Bernalillo County, NM held by Vanguard Media LLC
Nat'l Network: CNN Radio *Nat'l Reps:* Christal
Population Served: 600,000 *Arbitron Metro Market:* Albuquerque, NM *Target Audience:* 30-50.
Don Davis, CEO
Craig Collins, Operations Dir
Crystal Felice, Promotions Manager
Doris Budris, Promotions Director

*KFLQ
02-20-1983; 91.5 mhz FM *Hrs Open:* 24; 20 kw; 4042 ft.; N35 12 51 W106 27 2
7355 No. Orcale Rd #200, Tucson, AZ 85704 US
(505) 296-9100, *Fax:* (505) 296-6262
www.myflr.org
kflqonair@flc.org
License: Albuquerque, Bernalillo County, NM held by Family Life Broadcasting System.
Group Owner: Family Life Communications Inc.; (acq 1982).
Nat'l Network: Moody; USA
Arbitron Metro Market: Albuquerque, NM *Format:* Religious
Special Programming: Children's stories 10 hrs wkly. *No. News Employees:* 2 *Target Audience:* Christian families
Randy Carlson, President
Dan Rosecrans, Station Manager
Adam Nash, Programming Director

KBZU
11-01-1954; 96.3 mhz FM *Hrs Open:* 24; 17.5 kw; 4134 ft.; N35 12 44 W106 26 58
City Center West, 7201 W. Lake Mead Blvd, Las Vegas, NV 89128 US
(505) 767-6700, *Fax:* (505) 767-6767
License: Albuquerque, Bernalillo County, NM held by The Last Bastion Station Trust LLC, as Trustee
Nat'l Network: ESPN Deportes *Nat'l Reps:* McGavren Guild
Arbitron Metro Market: Albuquerque, NM *Format:* Sports
Eddie Haskell, Operations Dir
Jeff Berry, General Sales Mgr
Bill Harris, Engineering Dir
Art Ortega, Public Affairs Director

KNML
03-28-1928; 610 khz AM *Hrs Open:* 24
900 Oakmont Lane, Ste 210, Westmont, IL 60559 US
(505) 767-6700, *Fax:* (505) 767-6767
www.610thesportsanimal.com
610.knml@citcomm.com
License: Albuquerque, NM
Group Owner: Cumulus Media Inc.; (acq 3-23-00; swap with KSVA(AM) Albuquerque).
Arbitron Metro Market: Albuquerque, NM *Format:* Sports *Target Audience:* 25-54.
Pat Frisch, Operations Dir
Milt McConnell, General Manager
Ian Martin, Programming Director

KKIM
04-15-1972; 1000 khz AM; 10 kw-D, ND1; 0.038 kw-N, ND1; N35 10 14 W106 37 51
Mailing Address: P.O. Box 2700, Bakersfield, CA 93303 US
Second Address: 4125 Carlisle Blvd. N.E., Albuquerque, NM 87107-4806
(505) 878-0980, *Fax:* (505) 878-0098
www.mykkim.com
License: Albuquerque, NM held by AGM-Nevada L.L.C.
Group Owner: American General Media; (acq 12-22-97; grpsl)
Arbitron Metro Market: Albuquerque, NM *Format:* Christian, Talk
Special Programming: Black 2 hrs wkly *Target Audience:* 25-54.
Dewey Moede, Station Manager

KKOB
04-05-1922; 770 khz AM *Hrs Open:* 24; 50 kw-D, DAN; 50 kw-N, DAN; ND1; 0.23 kw; N35 12 9 W106 36 41; N35 4056 W105 5821
City Center West, 7201 W. Lake Mead Blvd, Las Vegas, NV 89128 US
(505) 767-6700, *Fax:* (505) 767-6767
www.770kkob.com
kkobam@citcomm.com
License: Albuquerque, NM
Group Owner: Cumulus Media Inc.; (acq 3-15-94; $7.8 million with co-located FM;
Nat'l Reps: McGavren Guild
Arbitron Metro Market: Albuquerque, NM *Format:* News, News/Talk, 86
Pat Frisch, Operations Dir
Milt McConnell, General Manager
Jeff M Berry, General Sales Mgr
Pat Frish, Programming Director
Alex Cuellar, News Director
Bill Harris, Chief Engineer
Art Ortega, Public Affairs Director
Joey Root,Webmaster

KKOB-FM
08-01-1967; 93.3 mhz FM *Hrs Open:* 24; 20 kw; 4150 ft.; N35 12 42 W106 26 59
City Center West, 7201 W. Lake Mead Blvd., Las Vegas, NV 89128 US
(505) 767-6700, *Fax:* (505) 767-6767
www.kobfm.com
License: Albuquerque, Bernalillo County, NM
Group Owner: Cumulus Media Inc.
Arbitron Metro Market: Albuquerque, NM *Format:* Adult Contemp
Kris Abrans, Operations Dir
Milt McConnell, General Manager
Tim Gannon, General Sales Mgr
Kris Abrams, Programming Director
Mark Anderson, Promotions Manager
Linda Land, News Director
Carlos Duran, Disc Jockey
Randy Savage,Disc Jockey
Carlos Duran, Disc Jockey
Greg Fite

*KLYT
09-11-1976; 88.3 mhz FM *Hrs Open:* 24; 4.1 kw; 4245 ft.; N35 12 49 W106 27 1
3107 Eubank Ne, Ste #2, Albuquerque, NM 87111 US
(505) 344-9146, *Fax:* (505) 344-9193
www.m88.org
License: Albuquerque, Bernalillo County, NM held by Calvary Chapel of Albuquerque, Inc.
Arbitron Metro Market: Albuquerque, NM *Format:* Christian
Chip Lusko, General Manager
Lynn Gilstrap, Station Manager
Darren Arnold, General Sales Mgr

KPEK
12-01-1974; 100.3 mhz FM *Hrs Open:* 8am - 5:30pm; 22.5 kw; 4111 ft.; N35 12 51 W106 27 2
900 Oakmont Lane, Ste 210, Westmont, IL 60559 US
(505) 830-6400, *Fax:* (505) 830-6543
www.1003thepeak.com
info@1003thepeak.com
License: Albuquerque, Bernalillo County, NM held by Citicasters Licenses L.P.
Group Owner: Clear Channel Communications Inc.; (acq 9-28-99; grpsl).
Arbitron Metro Market: Albuquerque, NM *Format:* Adult Contemp *Target Audience:* 25-54; adults, high income professional and technical
Bill May, Operations Dir
Chuck Hammond, General Manager

KKRG
10-01-1994; 101.3 mhz FM *Hrs Open:* 24; 3.7 kw; 420 ft.; N35 4 4 W106 46 47
57 West South Temple, Suite 700, Salt Lake City, UT 84101 US
(505) 262-1142, *Fax:* (505) 254-7106
www.lakalle1013.com
License: Albuquerque, Bernalillo County, NM held by Univision Radio License Corp.
Group Owner: Univision Radio; (acq 9-22-2003; grpsl).
Arbitron Metro Market: Albuquerque, NM *Format:* Ethnic *Target Audience:* 35-54.
Pat Delaney, President
John France, Operations Dir
Sue Thomsen, General Manager

KRST
09-15-1965; 92.3 mhz FM *Hrs Open:* 24; 22 kw; 4160 ft.; N35 12 55 W106 27 2
City Center West, 7201 W. Lake Mead Blvd, Las Vegas, NV 89128 US
(505) 767-6700, *Fax:* (505) 767-6767
www.923krst.com
License: Albuquerque, Bernalillo County, NM
Group Owner: Cumulus Media Inc.; (acq 9-30-96; grpsl).
Arbitron Metro Market: Albuquerque, NM *Format:* Country *Adv. Rates:* 150; 140; 140; 100
Eddie Haskell, Operations Dir
Milt McConnell, General Manager
Jeff Berry, General Sales Mgr
Richard Piombino, Promotions Manager
Bill Harris, Engineering Dir
Paul Bailey, Music Director
Art Ortega, Public Affairs Director
LindaRosenberg, Sales Manager

KRZY
06-01-1956; 1450 khz AM *Hrs Open:* 24; 1 kw-U, ND1; N35 7 56 W106 37 18
2905 South King Road, San Jose, CA 95122 US
(505) 342-4141, *Fax:* (505) 344-8714
www.entravision.com
mwilder@entravision.com
License: Albuquerque, NM held by Entravision Holdings LLC.
Group Owner: Entravision Communications Corp.; (acq 3-14-2000; grpsl).
Arbitron Metro Market: Albuquerque, NM *Format:* Tejano
Jeff Liberman, President
Margarita Wilder, General Manager
Juan Vavala, Promotions Manager

KSVA
03-28-1998; 920 khz AM *Hrs Open:* 24; 1 kw-D, ND1; 0.13 kw-N, ND1; N35 7 56 W106 37 18
City Center West, 7201 W. Lake Mead Blvd, Las Vegas, NV 89128 US
(800) 775-4673, *Fax:* (505) 890-0808
www.lifetalk.net
tim@lifetalk.net
License: Albuquerque, NM held by Lifetalk Radio Inc.
Nat'l Network: USA
Arbitron Metro Market: Corrales, NM *Format:* Christian, Religious
Special Programming: Sp 4 hrs wkly *Hrs. of News Programming:* News progmg 2 hrs wkly *Target Audience:* 35 plus; Christians
Jep Choate, Chairman
Phil Folett, CEO
Robert Hardy, Operations Dir
Ricardo Baratta, Station Manager
Clare Gallimore, General Sales Mgr
Jeremy Woodruff, Programming Director
Elvin Vence, Chief Engineer

KDRF
04-20-1988; 103.3 mhz FM *Hrs Open:* 24; 20 kw; 4242 ft.; N35 12 50 W106 27 1
City Center West, 7201 W. Lake Mead Blvd, Las Vegas, NC 89128 US
(505) 767-6700, *Fax:* (505) 767-6767
www.ed.fm
License: Albuquerque, Bernalillo County, NM
Group Owner: Cumulus Media Inc.; (acq 1996; $5 million).
Nat'l Reps: Christal
Arbitron Metro Market: Albuquerque, NM *Format:* Contemporary Hits/Top 40 *Target Audience:* 18-49.
Linda Rosenberg, General Sales Mgr

KBQI
04-27-1979; 107.9 mhz FM *Hrs Open:* 24; 22.5 kw; 4131 ft.; N35 12 43 W106 26 57
900 Oakmont Lane, Suite 210, Westmont, IL 60559 US

(505) 875-1079, *Fax:* (505) 830-6543
www.bigi1079.com
info@bigi1079.com
License: Albuquerque, Bernalillo County, NM held by Citicasters Licenses L.P.
Group Owner: Clear Channel Communications Inc.; (acq 9-28-99; grpsl).
Arbitron Metro Market: Albuquerque, NM *Format:* Country *Target Audience:* 18-49.
Bill May, Operations Dir
Chuck Hammond, General Manager

*KUNM

10-17-1966; 89.9 mhz FM *Hrs Open:* 24; 18.5 kw; 4108 ft.; N35 12 44 W106 26 57
Kunm Onate Hall, Albuquerque, NM 87131 US
(505) 277-4806, *Fax:* (505) 277-8004
www.kunm.org
kunm@kunm.org
License: Albuquerque, Bernalillo County, NM held by Regents of the University of New Mexico.
Nat'l Network: NPR; PRI
Arbitron Metro Market: Albuquerque, NM *Format:* News, News/Talk, 86, Variety/Diverse *Special Programming:* Class 12 hrs, Sp 9 hrs, Indian 9 hrs wkly *Hrs. of News Programming:* news progmg 50 hrs wkly *No. NewsEmployees:* 3 *Target Audience:* 25-54; those who enjoy NPR and diverse community-produced programs *Adv. Rates:* 45; 30; 45; 30
Scott MacNicholl, Operations Dir
Richard Towne, General Manager
Mary Bokuniewicz, General Sales Mgr
Tristan Clum, Programming Director
Steve Young, News Director
Mike Stark, Chief Engineer
Roman Garcia, Production Director
Roberta Rael, Youth Radio Project Manager
Oakley Merideth, Music Assistant
Nicole Candelaria, Production Assistant
Melissa Rios, Management Assistant
Matthew Finch, Music Director

KXKS

12-16-1969; 1190 khz AM *Hrs Open:* 24; 10 kw-D, ND2; 0.024 kw-N, ND2; N35 3 4 W106 38 34
803 N. Rexford Drive, Beverly Hills, CA 90210 US
(864) 585-1885, *Fax:* (864) 597-0687
www.wilkinsradio.com
info@wilkinsradio.com
License: Albuquerque, NM held by Wild West Radio Corp.
Group Owner: Wilkins Communications Network Inc.; (acq 12-16-2004; $775,000).
Arbitron Metro Market: Spartanburg, SC *Format:* Christian, Talk *Target Audience:* 35 plus.
Bob Wilkins, CEO
LuAnn Wilkins, President
Doug Cekander, Station Manager
Greg Garrett, Programming Director
Mitchell Mathis, President/COO

KZRR

06-25-1961; 94.1 mhz FM *Hrs Open:* 24; 19.5 kw; 4131 ft.; N35 12 44 W106 26 58
900 Oakmont Lane, #210, Westmont, IL 60559 US
(505) 830-6400, *Fax:* (505) 830-6543
www.94rock.com
kzrr@94rock.com,PhilMahoney@clearchannel.com
License: Albuquerque, Bernalillo County, NM held by Clear Channel Broadcasting Licenses Inc.
Group Owner: Clear Channel Communications Inc.; (acq 9-28-99; grpsl)
Nat'l Network: Westwood One
Arbitron Metro Market: Albuquerque, NM *Format:* Rock/AOR
Chuck Hammond, General Manager

Angel Fire

KKTC

01-15-1990; 99.9 mhz FM *Hrs Open:* 24; 1.75 kw; 2119 ft.; N36 33 30 W105 11 38
Mailing Address: P.O. Box 2158, Ketchum, ID 83340 US
Second Address: 125A Camino de la Merced, Taos, NM 87571-5119
(505) 758-4491, *Fax:* (505) 758-4452
www.kktctruecountry.com
License: Angel Fire, Colfax County, NM held by DMC Broadcasting Inc.
Group Owner: DMC Broadcasting Inc.; (acq 3-19-2003; $645,000 with KXMT(FM) Taos).
Nat'l Network: ABC
Format: Country *Special Programming:* Jazz 4 hrs, relg 8 hrs wkly *Hrs. of News Programming:* news progmg 7 hrs wkly *No. News Employees:* 1 *Target Audience:* 25-54; adults middle-upper-income residents & tourists*Adv. Rates:* 15; 15; 15; 10
Darren Cordova, CEO
Jeff Singer, Operations Dir
Jojo Valdez, General Sales Mgr
Jennifer Trujillo, News Director
Andrew Alanz, Web Administrator

Armijo

KNKT

12-17-1991; 107.1 mhz FM *Hrs Open:* 24; 17.5 kw; 705 ft.; N35 3 15 W106 51 31
4001 Osuna Road, Albuquerque, NM 87109 US
(505) 344-9146, *Fax:* (505) 344-9193
www.calvaryabq.org
License: Armijo, Bernalillo County, NM held by Calvary Chapel of Albuquerque Inc.
Arbitron Metro Market: Albuquerque, NM *Format:* Religious *Hrs. of News Programming:* News progmg 4 hrs wkly *Target Audience:* 25-54.
Chip Lusko, General Manager
Lynn Gilstrap, Station Manager
Darren Arnold, General Sales Mgr

Arroyo Seco

*KRRT

04-03-2008; 90.9 mhz FM; 5.1 kw horiz; -610 ft.; N36 23 52 W105 32 36 *Rebroadcasts:* Rebroadcasts KUNM(FM) Albuquerque 100%
Room 326 Onate Hall, University of New Mexico, Albuquerque, NM 87131 US
(505) 277-4806
www.kunm.org
kunm@kunm.org
License: Arroyo Seco, Taos County, NM held by Regents of the University of New Mexico.
Arbitron Metro Market: Albuquerque, NM *Format:* News, News/Talk, 86, Variety/Diverse
Richard Towne, General Manager
Tristan Clum, Programming Director
Mike Stark, Chief Engineer
Alaina George, Production Assistant
Jeff Maness, Engineering Assistant
Jonathan Longcore, Network Administrator
Roman Garcia, ProductionDirector
Scott MacNicholl, Operations Manager
Tristan Clum, Program Director

Artesia

KSVP

11-14-1946; 990 khz AM *Hrs Open:* 24; 1 kw-D, ND1; 0.25 kw-N, ND1; N32 49 29 W104 23 59
317 West Quay, Artesia, NM 88210 US
(505) 746-2751, *Fax:* (505) 748-3748
www.ksvpradio.com
info@ksvpradio.com
License: Artesia, NM held by Pecos Valley Broadcasting Co.
Group Owner: Pecos Valley Broadcasting Co.; (acq 1993; $150,000 with co-located FM;
Nat'l Network: CBS
Arbitron Metro Market: Artesia, NM *Format:* Talk *Hrs. of News Programming:* news progmg 18 hrs wkly *No. News Employees:* 1 *Target Audience:* General. *Adv. Rates:* 11.45; 11.45; 11.45; 11.45
Gene Dow, General Manager
Thomas Beard, General Sales Mgr
Mike Jaxon, News Director
Mike Montgomery, Chief Engineer

KTZA

05-09-1969; 92.9 mhz FM *Hrs Open:* 24; 100 kw; 1089 ft.; N32 47 38 W104 12 29
317 West Quay Avenue, Artesia, NM 88210 US
(575) 628-8402, *Fax:* (575) 941-3000
www.kz93.com
gene.dow@pvbcradio.com
License: Artesia, Eddy County, NM
Group Owner: Pecos Valley Broadcasting Co.
Nat'l Network: ABC
Arbitron Metro Market: Artesia, NM *Format:* Country *Hrs. of News Programming:* News progmg 3 hrs wkly *Target Audience:* 25-54.
Gene Dow, Operations Dir
Gene Dow, Vice President & General Manager
Thomas Beard, Sales Manager
Mike Jaxson, News Director
Mike Montgomery, Chief Engineer
Tana Steinback, Traffic Director
Marlee Smith, Traffic Assistant
MikeWinters, Operations Manager
Miguel Bernal, Production Assistant
Lana Faber, Public Affairs Director
Lauren Romero, Account Executive

Aztec

KCQL

09-04-1959; 1340 khz AM *Hrs Open:* 24; 1 kw-U, ND1; N36 49 17 W107 59 58
600 Congress Ave., Suite 1400, Austin, TX 78701 US
(505) 325-1716, *Fax:* (505) 325-6797
www.foxsports1340.com
License: Aztec, NM held by Capstar TX L.P.
Group Owner: Clear Channel Communications Inc.; (acq 8-30-2000; grpsl).
Nat'l Network: Fox Sports *Wire Services:* UPI
Arbitron Metro Market: Farmington, NM *Format:* Sports *Special Programming:* Sp 6 hrs wkly *Hrs. of News Programming:* News progmg 14 hrs wkly *Target Audience:* 18-54.
Steve Bortstein, Programming Director

KWYK-FM

01-02-1978; 94.9 mhz FM *Hrs Open:* 24; 100 kw; 433 ft.; N36 41 54 W108 13 18
1515 West Main Street, Farmington, NM 87401 US
(505) 325-1996, *Fax:* (505) 327-2019
www.kwykradio.com
productionroom@basinbroadcasting.com
License: Aztec, San Juan County, NM held by Basin Broadcasting Co.
Arbitron Metro Market: Farmington, NM *Format:* Adult Contemp *Hrs. of News Programming:* News progmg 15 hrs wkly *Target Audience:* 25-54; mainstream population *Adv. Rates:* 19; 17; 19; 16
Kerwin Gober, General Manager
Dana Childs, Programming Director
Jim Burk, Chief Engineer

Bayard

KNFT

07-04-1968; 950 khz AM
Mailing Address: P.O. Box 720, Alamogordo, NM 88310 US
Second Address: 5 Racetrack Rd., Silver City, NM 88061
(505) 388-1958, *Fax:* (505) 388-5000
events@silvercityradio.com
License: Bayard, NM held by SkyWest Licenses New Mexico LLC.
Group Owner: SkyWest Media L.L.C.; (acq 6-1-2006; grpsl).
Format: Sports, Talk
Matthew Runnell, General Manager
Anna Gallegos, News Director
Rita Niccum, Chief Engineer

KNFT-FM

06-15-1981; 102.9 mhz FM; 5.1 kw; 1578 ft.; N32 51 49 W108 14 27
Mailing Address: P.O. Box 720, Alamogordo, NM 88310 US
Second Address: 5 Racetrack Rd., Bayard, NM 88061
(505) 388-1958, *Fax:* (505) 388-5000
www.gilanet.com
events@silvercityradio.com
License: Bayard, Grant County, NM
Group Owner: SkyWest Media L.L.C.
Format: Country
Tim Brown, CEO
David Bach, Operations Dir
Colleen Barill, General Manager
Dave Rogers, CFO

Belen

KARS

10-07-1961; 860 khz AM *Hrs Open:* 24; 1.3 kw-D, ND1; 0.186 kw-N, ND1; N34 41 43 W106 46 13
P.O. Box 2700, Bakersfield, CA 93303 US
(505) 864-3024, *Fax:* (505) 864-2719
www.americangeneralmedia.com
rbrandon@americangeneralmedia.com
License: Belen, NM held by AGM-Nevada L.L.C.
Group Owner: American General Media; (acq 12-22-97; grpsl)
Nat'l Reps: Lotus Entravision Reps LLC
Arbitron Metro Market: Belen, NM *Format:* Country *Special Programming:* Relg *Hrs. of News Programming:* news progmg 30 hrs wkly *No. News Employees:* 1 *Target Audience:* 25 plus.
Rogers Brandon, General Manager
Dewey Moede, Station Manager
Ron Travis, Programming Director
Bob Picknell, Chief Engineer
Russ Ortego, Disc Jockey

KLVO
01-01-1982; 97.7 mhz FM *Hrs Open:* 24; 100 kw; Ant 859 ft; N34 47 55 W106 48 59
4125 Carlisle NE, Albuquerque, NM 93303
(505) 878-0980, *Fax:* (505) 878-0098
www.americangeneralmedia.com
License: Belen, Valencia County, NM held by AGM-Nevada L.L.C.
Group Owner: American General Media
Population Served: 600,000 *Arbitron Metro Market:* Albuquerque, NM
Russ Ortego, Programming Director

Bloomfield

KKFG
01-01-1988; 104.5 mhz FM; 100 kw; 1086 ft.; N36 38 33 W107 46 54
600 Congress Ave., Suite 1400, Austin, TX 78701 US
(505) 325-1716, *Fax:* (505) 325-6797
www.kool1045.com
License: Bloomfield, San Juan County, NM held by Capstar TX L.P.
Group Owner: Clear Channel Communications Inc.; (acq 8-30-2000; grpsl).
Arbitron Metro Market: Santa Fe, NM *Format:* Oldies
Dave Shaefer, Operations Dir
Hope Romero, General Manager
Sherry Curry, Programming Director

Bosque Farms

KABQ-FM
07-01-1987; 104.7 mhz FM; 100 kw; 843 ft.; N34 46 12 W106 51 42
803 N Rexford Drive, Beverly Hills, CA 90210 US
(505) 830-6400, *Fax:* (505) 830-6543
www.classiccountry1047.com
info@abtalk.com
License: Bosque Farms, Valencia County, NM held by Aloha Station Trust LLC, as Trustee
Arbitron Metro Market: Albuquerque, NM *Format:* Country *No. News Employees:* 1 *Target Audience:* 25-54.
Bill May, Operations Dir
Chuck Hammond, General Manager

***KQLV(FM)**
11-16-2001; 105.5 mhz FM *Hrs Open:* 24; 22 kw; Ant 745 ft; N34 47 55 W106 48 59
PO Box 2098, Omaha, NE 68103
(800) 525-5683, *Fax:* (916) 251-1650
www.klove.com
klove@klove.com
License: Bosque Farms, Valencia County, NM held by Educational Media Foundation.
Group Owner: EMF Broadcasting
Nat'l Network: K-Love
Format: Christian *No. News Employees:* 3 *Target Audience:* 25-44; Judeo-Christian, female
Mike Novak, President
Jim Marable, Operations Dir
Eric Allen, General Sales Mgr
David Pierce, Programming Director
Ed Lenane, News Director
Sam Wallington, Engineering Dir
Marya Morgan, News Reporter
Richard Hunt, NewsReporter

***KQRI**
01-01-2004; 105.5 mhz FM; 97.58 kw; 745 ft.; N34 47 55 W106 48 59 *Rebroadcasts:* Rebroadcasts KLRD(FM) Yucaipa, CA 100%
1425 North Market Blvd., Suite 9, Sacramento, CA 95834 US
(888) 937-2471, *Fax:* (916) 251-1650
www.air1.com
info@air1.com
License: Bosque Farms, Valencia County, NM held by Educational Media Foundation.
Group Owner: EMF Broadcasting
Nat'l Network: Air 1
Arbitron Metro Market: Bosque Farms, NM *Format:* Christian
Darrell Chambliss, Chairman
Alan Mason, COO
Mike Novak, President and CEO
Ed Lenane, News Director
Sam Wallington, Engineering Dir
Dan Antonelli, Chief Business Development Officer
Eric Moser, Chief Financial Officer
BrianBurger, Vice President of Human Resources
D. Kevin Blair, Secretary and General Counsel
Larry Moody, Director
Mitch Barnhart, Director

Cannon Afb

***KKCJ**
01-01-2006; 90.7 mhz FM; 25 kw; 194 ft.; N34 26 58 W103 37 3 *Rebroadcasts:* Rebroadcasts KSGR(FM) Portland, TX 100% US
(361) 814-7775, *Fax:* (361) 814-7779
www.coreradionetwork.org
jim.shepherd@csnradio.com
License: Cannon Afb, Curry County, NM held by CSN International
Group Owner: CSN International
Nat'l Network: CSN
Arbitron Metro Market: Canon, NM *Format:* Christian
Jim Shepherd, Station Manager

Carlsbad

KAMQ
06-10-1938; 1240 khz AM; 1 kw-D, ND1; 1 kw-N, ND1; N32 23 43 W104 14 48
Mailing Address: P. O. Box 1538, Carlsbad, NM 88220 US
Second Address: 1609 Radio Blvd., Carlsbad, NM 88220
(575) 887-7563, *Fax:* (575) 887-7000
www.carlsbadradio.com
don@carlsbadradio.com
License: Carlsbad, NM held by KAMQ Inc.
Arbitron Metro Market: Carlsbad, NM *Format:* Adult Contemp, Christian
Don Hughes, General Manager
Reginald James, Programming Director
Frank Nymeyer, Chief Engineer

KATK
05-17-1950; 740 khz AM; 1 kw-D, ND1; 0.5 kw-N, ND1; N32 27 2 W104 12 47
714 N. Canyon, Carlsbad, NM 88220 US
(575) 887-7563, *Fax:* (575) 887-7000
www.carlsbadradio.com
don@carlsbadradio.com
License: Carlsbad, NM held by Stubbs Broadcasting Co. Inc.
Arbitron Metro Market: Carlsbad, NM *Format:* Adult Contemp *Special Programming:* Gospel 2 hrs wkly *Hrs. of News Programming:* News progmg 70 hrs wkly *Target Audience:* 50 plus; bilingual Hispanics *Adv. Rates:* 8; 8; 8
Don Hughes, General Manager
Don Hughes, General Sales Mgr
Reginald James, Programming Director
Frank Nymeyer, Chief Engineer

KATK-FM
09-15-1966; 92.1 mhz FM; 6 kw; 190 ft.; N32 27 2 W104 12 47
714 N. Canyon, Carlsbad, MN 88220 US
(575) 887-7563, *Fax:* (575) 887-7000
www.carlsbadradio.com
don@carlsbadradio.com
License: Carlsbad, Eddy County, NM held by Stubbs Broadcasting Co. Inc.
Arbitron Metro Market: Carlsbad, NM *Format:* Country *Hrs. of News Programming:* News progmg 70 hrs wkly *Target Audience:* 18-54.
Tom Hoyt, Operations Dir
Don Hughes, General Sales Mgr
Kari Lynn, Programming Director

KPZE-FM
01-01-2000; 106.1 mhz FM *Hrs Open:* 24; 39 kw; 558 ft.; N32 34 22 W104 5 32
1908 E. Alameda, Roswell, NM 88201 US
(505) 746-2751, *Fax:* (505) 748-3748
www.pecosvalletbroadcasting.com
gene.dow@pvbcradio.com
License: Carlsbad, Eddy County, NM held by Pecos Valley Broadcasting Co.
Group Owner: Pecos Valley Broadcasting Co.; (acq 2005; $475,000).
Arbitron Metro Market: Artesia, NM *Format:* Tejano *Hrs. of News Programming:* news progmg one hr wkly *No. News Employees:* 1 *Adv. Rates:* 12; 12; 12; 10
Gene Dow, General Manager

KCCC
07-01-1966; 930 khz AM *Hrs Open:* 24; 1 kw-D, ND1; 0.06 kw-N, ND1; N32 24 20 W104 11 21
930 N. Canal, Carlsbad, NM 88220 US
(505) 887-5521, *Fax:* (505) 885-5481
kccc@carlsbadnm.com
License: Carlsbad, NM held by Compass Enterprises Inc.
Arbitron Metro Market: Carlsbad, NM *Format:* Oldies
Nick Jenkins, President
Michelle McCutcheon, Operations Dir
Phil Tozier, News Director
Frank Nymeyer, Chief Engineer

KCDY
07-01-1989; 104.1 mhz FM; 100 kw; 676 ft.; N32 34 22 W104 5 32
Mailing Address: P. O. Box 1538, Carlsbad, NM 88220 US
Second Address: 1609 Radio Blvd., Carlsbad, NM
(505) 887-7563, *Fax:* (505) 887-7000
License: Carlsbad, Eddy County, NM held by KAMQ Inc.
Format: Adult Contemp
Steve Sparks, Programming Director

Chama

KZRM
10-08-1999; 96.1 mhz FM *Hrs Open:* 24; 25 kw; 302 ft.; N36 53 56 W106 36 6
1217 Valencia N.E., Albuquerque, NM 87110 US
(505) 756-1617, *Fax:* (505) 756-1317
www.kzrmradio.com
info@kzrm.com
License: Chama, Rio Arriba County, NM held by Lance Broadcasting LLC
Arbitron Metro Market: Chama, NM *Format:* Classic Rock
Scott Flury, General Manager

Church Rock

KYVA-FM
08-07-1997; 103.7 mhz FM *Hrs Open:* 24; 100 kw; 1378 ft.; N35 36 22 W108 41 26
405 S. 2nd St., Gallup, NM 87301 US
(505) 863-6851, *Fax:* (505) 863-2429
www.gallupradio.com
sammyc@gallupradio.com
License: Church Rock, Cibola County, NM held by Millennium Media Inc.
Nat'l Network: ABC
Arbitron Metro Market: Church Rock, NM *Format:* Oldies *Special Programming:* American Indian 10 hrs, Sp 4 hrs wkly. *Hrs. of News Programming:* news progmg 12 hrs wkly *No. News Employees:* 1 *Target Audience:* 25+. 0
George Malti, CEO
Sammy Chioda, General Manager
Thomas Devlin, General Sales Mgr
John McBreen, News Director
Keith Desautels, Chief Engineer

Clayton

KLMX
11-10-1949; 1450 khz AM; 1 kw-U, ND1; N36 26 39 W103 11 24
P.O. Box 547, Clayton, NM 88415 US
(505) 374-2555, *Fax:* (505) 374-2557
License: Clayton, NM held by Johnson County Broadcasters Inc.
Arbitron Metro Market: Santa Fe NM *Format:* Country *Special Programming:* Sp 2 hrs wkly
Avis Tucker, President
Jim McCollum, Operations Dir
Janet Dillon, General Manager
Paula Maestas-Ballew, Programming Director
Henry Walker, Chief Engineer

***KUHC**
90.5 mhz FM; 1 kw horiz; Ant 256 ft; N36 26 39 W103 11 24
116 Hillcrest Dr., Seminole, OK
(405) 380-3516
bpba.us
info@bpba.us
License: Clayton, Union County, NM held by Better Public Broadcasting Association.
Dennis Burton, General Manager

Cloudcroft

***KHII**
01-01-2004; 88.9 mhz FM *Hrs Open:* 24; 0.1 kw; 1188 ft.; N32 59 48 W105 42 38 *Rebroadcasts:* Rebroadcasts KUPR(FM) Alamogordo 80%
1505 Crescent Drive, Alamogordo, NM 88310 US
(505) 437-0917, *Fax:* (505) 434-6060
khii889@yahoo.com
License: Cloudcroft, Otero County, NM held by Southern New Mexico Radio Foundation.
Format: Gospel
Bob Flotte, President
DeVere Johnson, Programming Director

KNMB
96.7 mhz FM; 25 kw; 2881 ft.; N33 24 14 W105 46 56
Post Office Drawer 2010, Ruidoso Downs, NM 88356 US
(505) 258-9922, *Fax:* (505) 258-2363
www.mymix967.com
mix@mtdradio.com
License: Cloudcroft, Otero County, NM held by MTD Inc.
Group Owner: MTD Inc.
Arbitron Metro Market: Ruidoso Downs, NM *Format:* Country
Tim Keithley, General Manager

Clovis

***KAQF**
03-01-1998; 91.1 mhz FM; 1.35 kw; 174 ft.; N34 24 5 W103 12 12
Po Drawer 2440, Tupelo, MS 38803 US
(662) 844-8888, *Fax:* (662) 842-6791
www.afr.net
comments@afr.net
License: Clovis, Curry County, NM held by American Family Association.
Group Owner: American Family Radio
Arbitron Metro Market: Tupelo, MO *Format:* Christian, Religious
Marvin Sanders, General Manager

KCLV
02-01-1953; 1240 khz AM *Hrs Open:* 24; 1 kw-U, ND1; N34 22 40 W103 12 17
Mailing Address: P.O. Box 1907, Clovis, NM 88102 US
Second Address: 2112 Thornton St., Clovis, NM 88101
(505) 763-4401, *Fax:* (505) 769-2564
www.kclvsports.com
kclv@allsups.com
License: Clovis, NM held by Zia Broadcasting Co.
Group Owner: Zia Broadcasting Co.; (Acq 7-1-71)
Nat'l Network: ESPN Radio
Arbitron Metro Market: Clovis, NM *Format:* Sports *Adv. Rates:* 6.50; 6.50; 6.50; 6.50
Lonnie Allsup, President
Rick Keefer, Genral Manager and General Sales Manager
Lorraine Weingates, News Director
Gary Jackson, Chief Engineer

KCLV-FM
01-08-1970; 99.1 mhz FM *Hrs Open:* 24; 74 kw; 230 ft.; N34 23 18 W103 11 7
Mailing Address: P.O. Box 1907, Clovis, NM 88101 US
Second Address: 2112 Thornton St., Clovis, NM 88101
(505) 763-4401, *Fax:* (505) 769-2564
www.kclvsports.com
kclv@allsups.com
License: Clovis, Curry County, NM held by Zia Broadcasting Co.
Group Owner: Zia Broadcasting Co.; (acq 11-12-81)
Nat'l Network: ABC
Arbitron Metro Market: Clovis, NM *Format:* Country *Target Audience:* 30 plus. *Adv. Rates:* 8.50; 8.50; 8.50; 8.50
Lonnie Allsup, President
Rick Keefer, Genral Manager and General Sales Manager
Lorraine Weingates, News Director
Gary Jackson, Chief Engineer

KICA
01-01-1933; 980 khz AM *Hrs Open:* 24
1000 Sycamore Street, Clovis, NM 88101 US
(505) 762-6200, *Fax:* (505) 762-8800
www.kkyckica@plateautel.net
info@kkyckica@plateautel.net
License: Clovis, NM held by Tallgrass Broadcasting LLC.
Group Owner: Tallgrass Broadcasting LLC; (acq 4-2-2007; grpsl)
Nat'l Network: USA
Format: Talk *Special Programming:* Farm 5 hrs, high school sports 4 hrs wkly *Target Audience:* 30 plus.
Dana Taylor, Operations Dir

KKYC
01-01-1993; 102.3 mhz FM *Hrs Open:* 24; 25 kw horiz; 177 ft.; N34 24 31 W103 11 15
1000 Sycamore Street, Clovis, NM 88101 US
(505) 762-6200, *Fax:* (505) 762-8800
www.1023myfm.com
clovis@tallgrassnation.com
License: Clovis, Curry County, NM held by Tallgrass Broadcasting LLC.
Group Owner: Tallgrass Broadcasting LLC; (acq 4-2-2007; grpsl)
Arbitron Metro Market: Sante Fe, NM *Format:* Contemporary Hits/Top 40 *Hrs. of News Programming:* news progmg 2 hrs wkly *No. News Employees:* 1 *Target Audience:* 25-54.
Anne Bradshaw, Promotions Manager

KSMX-FM
11-01-1982; 107.5 mhz FM; 100 kw; 541 ft.; N34 11 34 W103 16 44
Mailing Address: 2508 N. Prince, Suite 312, Clovis, NM 88101 US
Second Address: 42437 U.S. 70, Portales, NM 88130
(505) 763-4649, *Fax:* (505) 359-0724
www.bettermix.com
bettermix@bettermix.com
License: Clovis, Curry County, NM held by Rooney Moon Broadcasting Inc.
Group Owner: Rooney Moon Broadcasting Inc.; (acq 7-15-2002; grpsl)
Arbitron Metro Market: Clovis, NM *Format:* Adult Contemp
Steve Rooney, President
Duffy Moon, Operations Dir
Len Vohs, General Sales Mgr
Kevin Robbins, News Director
Jeff Burmeister, Chief Engineer
Lisa Schmidt, Traffic Manager

KTQM-FM
03-01-1963; 99.9 mhz FM *Hrs Open:* 24; 100 kw; 299 ft.; N34 21 48 W103 13 5
Mailing Address: P.O. Box 869, 710 Curry Rd K, Clovis, NM 88101 US
Second Address: 710 Curry Rd. K, Clovis, NM 88101
(505) 762-4411, *Fax:* (505) 769-0197
www.ktqm.com
ktqm@plateautel.net
License: Clovis, Curry County, NM held by Curry County Broadcasting, Inc.
Nat'l Network: ABC
Arbitron Metro Market: Clovis, NM *Format:* Adult Contemp *Hrs. of News Programming:* News progmg 3 hrs wkly *Target Audience:* 25-54; young affluent *Adv. Rates:* 17; na; 16; 10
Hewel Jones, President
Grant McGee, Operations Dir
Bob Coker, General Sales Mgr
Marty Berry, News Director

KWKA
01-01-1971; 680 khz AM *Hrs Open:* 24; 0.5 kw-U, DA1; N34 21 48 W103 13 5
Mailing Address: P.O. Box 869, 710 Curry Rd., Clovis, NM 88101 US
Second Address: 710 Curry Rd. K, Clovis, NM 88101
(505) 762-4411, *Fax:* (505) 769-0197
ktqm@plateautel.net
License: Clovis, NM held by Curry County Broadcasting Inc.
Nat'l Network: CNN Radio *Regional Reps:* Rgnl Reps.
Arbitron Metro Market: Clovis, NM *Format:* News, News/Talk, 86 *Special Programming:* Sean Hannity Talk Show *Hrs. of News Programming:* News progmg 3 hrs wkly *Target Audience:* 35 - 64; *Adv. Rates:* 11:25;8; 9:35; 6.50
Hewel Jones, President
Grant McGee, Operations Dir
Bob Coker, General Manager
Marty Berry, News Director

KRMQ-FM
01-01-2003; 101.5 mhz FM; 100 kw; 453 ft.; N34 15 8 W103 14 21
Box 4937, Casper, WY 82604 US
(505) 359-1759, *Fax:* (505) 359-0724
q1015.com
info@q1015.com
License: Clovis, Curry County, NM held by Rooney Moon Broadcasting Inc.
Group Owner: Rooney Moon Broadcasting Inc.; (acq 1-13-2006; $595,000)
Arbitron Metro Market: Clovis, NM *Format:* Oldies
Steve Rooney, President

***KELU**
01-01-2006; 90.3 mhz FM; 14 kw; 397 ft.; N34 26 21 W103 12 22
Rebroadcasts: Rebroadcasts KLVR(FM) Middletown, CA 100% US
(800) 525-5683, *Fax:* (916) 251-1650
www.klove.com
klove@klove.com
License: Clovis, Curry County, NM held by Educational Media Foundation.
Group Owner: EMF Broadcasting; (acq 9-22-2005; $40,000 for CP)
Nat'l Network: K-Love
Arbitron Metro Market: Clovis, NM *Format:* Christian *No. News Employees:* 13
Darrell Chambliss, Chairman
Mike Novak, President and CEO
David Pierce, Programming Director
Ed Lenane, News Director
Sam Wallington, Engineering Dir
Dan Antonelli, Chief Business Development Officer
Eric Moser, Chief FinancialOfficer
Brian Burger, Vice President of Human Resources
D. Kevin Blair, Secretary and General Counsel
Tim Luttrell, News Reporter

***KCOI**
88.1 mhz FM; 1.1 kw; 174 ft.; N34 24 5 W103 12 12 US
(662) 844-5036, *Fax:* (662) 842-6791
www.afr.net
contact@afa.net
License: Clovis, Curry County, NM held by Salt & Light Communications Inc.
Arbitron Metro Market: Clovis, NM *Format:* Christian
Donald E. Wildmon, Founder
Larry Durham, President
Buster Wilson, General Manager
Jennifer Hagman, Programming Director

Corrales

KKNS
07-15-1985; 1310 khz AM *Hrs Open:* 24; 5 kw-D, DAN; 0.5 kw-N, DAN; N35 12 0 W106 35 59 *Rebroadcasts:* 95.9FM Simulcast
57 West South Temple, Suite 700, Salt Lake City, UT 84101 US
(505) 255-5015, *Fax:* (505) 262-4792
www.elcaminocomm.com
vcamino@elcaminocomm.com
License: Corrales, NM held by El Camino Communications LLC
Arbitron Metro Market: Albuquerque, NM *Format:* Tejano *Target Audience:* H-18-49
Victor Camino, President

KLQT
04-27-1996; 95.1 mhz FM *Hrs Open:* 24; 3 kw; Ant -531 ft; N35 14 42 W106 36 18
5411 Jefferson St. N.E., Suite 100, Albuquerque, NM 60559
(505) 830-6400, *Fax:* (505) 830-6543
www.951abq.com
License: Corrales, Sandoval County, NM held by Clear Channel Broadcasting Licenses Inc.
Group Owner: Clear Channel Communications Inc.; (acq 9-28-99)
Chuck Hammond, General Manager

Deming

KDEM
04-15-1977; 94.3 mhz FM; 3 kw; 194 ft.; N32 15 5 W107 45 28
PO Box 470, Deming, NM 88031 US
(575) 546-9011, *Fax:* (575) 546-9342
www.demingradio.com
radio@demingradio.com
License: Deming, Luna County, NM
Nat'l Network: Westwood One *Wire Services:* AP
Arbitron Metro Market: Deming, NM *Format:* Adult Contemp *Hrs. of News Programming:* news progmg 5 hrs wkly *No. News Employees:* 1 *Target Audience:* 18-54. *Adv. Rates:* Same as AM
Candie Sweetser, General Manager

KOTS
03-10-1954; 1230 khz AM *Hrs Open:* 24; 1 kw-U, ND1; N32 15 5 W107 45 28
P.O. Box 470, Deming, NM 88031 US
(575) 546-9011, *Fax:* (575) 546-9342
www.demingradio.com
radio@demingradio.com
License: Deming, NM held by Luna County Broadcasting Co.
Nat'l Network: Westwood One *Wire Services:* AP
Format: Country *Special Programming:* Farm 5 hrs, Sp 8 hrs wkly *Hrs. of News Programming:* news progmg 13 hrs wkly *No. News Employees:* 1 *Target Audience:* General. *Adv. Rates:* 10; 10; 10; 10
Candie Sweetser, General Manager

***KZPI**
03-25-1996; 91.7 mhz FM *Hrs Open:* 24; 0.6 kw; 62 ft.; N32 15 31 W107 46 45
307 East Jackson Ave., McAllen, TX 78501 US
(956) 686-6382, *Fax:* (956) 686-2999
www.kcpiradio.com
info@kzpiradio.com.
License: Deming, Luna County, NM held by Paulino Bernal Evangelism.
Arbitron Metro Market: Baton Rouge, LA *Format:* Christian, Religious *Target Audience:* General.
Paulino Bernal, President

Des Moines

*KENU
10-04-2012; 88.5 mhz FM; 0.24 kw; 2011 ft.; N36 42 20 W103 52 36 *Rebroadcasts:* KENW-FM
Mailing Address: US
Second Address: Eastern New Mexico University, 1500 South Avenue K, Portales, NM 88130-9989
(575) 562-2112, *Fax:* (575) 562-2590
www.kenw.org
kenwfm@enmu.edu
License: Des Moines, Union County, NM held by Eastern New Mexico University.
Nat'l Network: NPR; BSN; APM; PRX
Arbitron Metro Market: Des Moines, NM
Dr. Steven G. Gamble, President
Duane Ryan, General Manager
Dr. James Lee, News Director
Jeff Burmeister, Engineering Dir
Carla Chacon, Development Director
Don Criss, Production/Community Services Director, TV
Duane W. Ryan,Director of Broadcasting
Karen Leonhardt', Accountant
Mickey Morgan, Audio Engineer

Dexter

KALN
01-01-2009; 96.1 mhz FM; 50 kw; 453 ft.; N33 23 57 W104 22 30 US
(575) 623-3914
License: Dexter, Chaves County, NM held by Hispanic Target Media Inc.
Group Owner: Hispanic Target Media Inc.
Arbitron Metro Market: Dexter, NM *Format:* Tejano
Francisco San Millan, President

Dulce

*KCIE
12-03-1990; 90.5 mhz FM *Hrs Open:* 24; 0.1 kw horiz, 0.093 kw vert; 1535 ft.; N36 59 0 W106 58 12
Aie Bldg/Narrow Gauge Rd, P.O. Box 603, Dulce, NM 87528 US
(575) 759-3681, *Fax:* (575) 759-9140
www.nv1.org/kcie.html
kcie@zianet.com
License: Dulce, Rio Arriba County, NM held by Jicarilla Apache Tribe.
Arbitron Metro Market: Dulce, NM *Format:* Variety/Diverse *Hrs. of News Programming:* news progmg 2 hrs wkly *No. News Employees:* 1 *Target Audience:* General.
Lisa Vigil-Gomez, General Manager
Lisa Vigil-Gomez, Station Manager
Romaine Wood, Programming Director
Annette Martinez, News Director
William Vicente, Engineering Tech
Jim Burt, Chief Engineer
Darnell Muniz, Music Director
Jordan Vigil, Computer Tech
Donna Shorty, Secretary
Carlos Davis, Production Assistant
Rita King, Custodian

Encino

*KXNM
88.7 mhz FM; kw
US
(505) 246-4780, *Fax:* (505) 384-3110
www.tcponm.com
License: Encino, Torrance County, NM held by Torrance County.
Arbitron Metro Market: Encino, NM
Joy Ansley, General Manager
Valerie Arevalo, Executive Director
Patty Ruiz, Administrative Assistant

Espanola

KDCE
01-01-1963; 950 khz AM; 4.2 kw-D, ND1; 0.08 kw-N, ND1; N36 0 8 W106 3 59
403 West Pueblo Dr., Espanola, NM 87533 US
(505) 753-2201, *Fax:* (505) 753-8685
www.kdce.net
kdce@zianet.com
License: Espanola, NM held by Richard L. Garcia Broadcasting Inc.
Arbitron Metro Market: Espanola, NM
Richard Garcia, President
Casey Gallegos, General Manager
Ray Casias, Programming Director
Ester Marquez, News Director
Ken Bass, Chief Engineer

KYBR
07-06-1981; 92.9 mhz FM; 15.5 kw; 417 ft.; N36 5 52 W106 7 18
403 West Pueblo Road, Espanola, NM 87532 US
(505) 753-2201, *Fax:* (505) 753-8685
www.radiooso.com
kdce@zianet.com
License: Espanola, Rio Arriba County, NM held by Rio Chama Broadcasting Co.
Arbitron Metro Market: Espanola, NM
Efrem Galindo, Programming Director

*KRAR
04-01-2008; 91.9 mhz FM; 5.9 kw; 530 ft.; N36 9 8 W106 2 21
Rebroadcasts: Rebroadcasts KUNM(FM) Albuquerque 100%
403 West Pueblo Drive, Espanola, NM 87532 US
(505) 277-4806
www.kunm.org
kunm@kunm.org
License: Espanola, Rio Arriba County, NM held by Regents of the University of New Mexico
Arbitron Metro Market: Espanola, NM *Format:* Public Affairs, Variety/Diverse
Richard Towne, General Manager
Tristan Clum, Programming Director
Mike Stark, Chief Engineer
Alaina George, Production Assistant
Jeff Maness, Engineering Assistant
Jonathan Longcore, Network Administrator
Roman Garcia, ProductionDirector
Scott MacNicholl, Operations Manager
Tristan Clum, Program Director

Eunice

KEJL
01-01-1996; 100.9 mhz FM *Hrs Open:* 24; 50 kw; 364 ft.; N32 28 5 W103 9 27
Mailing Address: 511 S. 93rd Street, Omaha, NE 68114 US
Second Address: 1423 W. Bender, Hobbs, NM 88241
(505) 393-6000, *Fax:* (505) 397-6088
www.hobbsradio.com/eagle/
larryphilpot@basinbreadband.com
License: Eunice, Lea County, NM held by FiveStar Enterprises L.C.
Nat'l Network: Jones Radio Networks
Arbitron Metro Market: Eunice, NM *Format:* Classic Rock *No. News Employees:* 1 *Target Audience:* 18-49. *Adv. Rates:* 12; 12; 12; 12
Larry Philpot, General Manager
Al Lobeck, General Sales Mgr

Farmington

KDAG
09-01-1969; 96.9 mhz FM *Hrs Open:* 24; 100 kw; 994 ft.; N36 48 52 W107 53 32
600 Congress Ave., Suite 1400, Austin, TX 78701 US
(505) 325-1716, *Fax:* (505) 325-6797
www.bigdog969.com
License: Farmington, San Juan County, NM held by Capstar TX L.P.
Group Owner: Clear Channel Communications Inc.; (acq 8-30-2000; grpsl).
Arbitron Metro Market: Farmington, NM *Format:* Classic Rock *Target Audience:* 18-49.
Dave Schaefer, Operations Dir
Bill Kruger, General Manager
Jenny Burgan, General Sales Mgr
Randy Burton, Promotions Manager
Jeff Ahrens, Chief Engineer

KENN
11-01-1951; 1390 khz AM; 5 kw-D, DAN; 1.3 kw-N, DAN; N36 42 27 W108 8 50
427 Bedford Road, Pleasantville, NY 10570 US
(505) 325-3541, *Fax:* (505) 327-5796
www.kennradio.com
License: Farmington, NM held by Winton Road Broadcasting Co. LLC
Group Owner: Winton Road Broadcasting Co. LLC; (acq 5-3-2001; grpsl)
Arbitron Metro Market: Farmington, NM *Format:* News, News/Talk, 84, Talk *Target Audience:* 25-54; upper middle class
Bill Kruger, General Manager
Randy Klock, General Sales Mgr

KNDN
08-01-1957; 960 khz AM *Hrs Open:* 6 AM-10 PM; 5 kw-D, ND1; 0.163 kw-N, ND1; N36 43 48 W108 13 47
1515 West Main, Farmington, NM 87401 US
(505) 325-1996, *Fax:* (505) 327-2019
productionroom@basinbroadcasting.com
License: Farmington, NM held by Basin Broadcasting Co.
Format: Native American *Target Audience:* General; Navajo Indian reservation; all Navajo language
Kerwin Gober, General Manager
George Werito, Programming Director
Jim Burt, Chief Engineer

*KNMI
03-18-1980; 88.9 mhz FM *Hrs Open:* 24; 27 kw vert; 663 ft.; N36 40 16 W108 13 54
Mailing Address: PO Box 1230, Farmington, NM 87499 US
Second Address: 2103 W. Main St., Farmington, NM 87401
(505) 327-4357, *Fax:* (505) 325-9035
www.verticalradio.org
email@verticalradio.org
License: Farmington, San Juan County, NM held by Navajo Missions Inc.
Nat'l Network: USA
Format: Christian, Talk *Hrs. of News Programming:* News progmg 9 hrs wkly *Target Audience:* 24-40; general
Darren Nez, General Manager

*KPCL
12-14-1988; 95.7 mhz FM *Hrs Open:* 24; 80 kw; 1040 ft.; N36 48 53 W107 53 31
Mailing Address: Box 232, Farmington, NM 87499 US
Second Address: 1105 W. Apache, Farmington, NM 87401
(505) 327-7202, *Fax:* (505) 327-2163
www.kpcl.org
kpcl@kpcl.org
License: Farmington, San Juan County, NM held by Voice Ministries of Farmington Inc.
Nat'l Network: Salem Radio Network
Format: Christian *Special Programming:* Class one hr, Navajo 7 hrs wkly *Hrs. of News Programming:* news progmg 3 hrs wkly *No. News Employees:* 1 *Target Audience:* General; relg audience
Fareed Ayoub, President

KRWN
01-01-1974; 92.9 mhz FM *Hrs Open:* 24; 62 kw; 394 ft.; N36 41 45 W108 13 23
427 Bedford Road, Pleasantville, NY 10570 US
(505) 327-4449, *Fax:* (505) 327-5796
www.krwn.com
License: Farmington, San Juan County, NM held by Winton Road Broadcasting Co. LLC.
Group Owner: Winton Road Broadcasting Co. LLC
Arbitron Metro Market: Farmington, NM *Format:* Classic Rock *Target Audience:* 18-49.
Dan Buchta, General Manager
Randy Klock, General Sales Mgr

*KSJE
11-01-1990; 90.9 mhz FM *Hrs Open:* 24; 15 kw; 390 ft.; N36 41 52 W108 13 14
4601 College Boulevard, Farmington, NM 87401 US
(505) 566-3517, *Fax:* (505) 566-3385
www.ksje.com
michlins@sanjuancollege.edu
License: Farmington, San Juan County, NM held by San Juan College.
Nat'l Network: PRI
Arbitron Metro Market: Framington, NM *Format:* Classical, Jazz, 60 *Special Programming:* Jazz 15 hrs, folk 15 hrs wkly *Hrs. of News Programming:* news progmg 15 hrs wkly *No. News Employees:* 1 *Target Audience:* 25-65.
Carol Spenser, President
Scott Michlin, General Manager
Constance Gotsch, Programming Director
Jim Burt, Chief Engineer

KTRA-FM
02-19-1987; 102.1 mhz FM *Hrs Open:* 24; 100 kw; 994 ft.; N36 48 52 W107 53 32
600 Congress Ave., Suite 1400, Austin, TX 78701 US
(505) 325-1716, *Fax:* (505) 325-6797
www.102ktra.com
License: Farmington, San Juan County, NM held by Clear Channel Radio Licenses Inc.
Group Owner: Clear Channel Communications Inc.; (acq 8-30-2000; grpsl)
Nat'l Network: ABC
Arbitron Metro Market: Farmington, NM *Format:* Country *Target Audience:* 25-54.
Dave Schaefer, Programming Director

***KUUT**
01-01-2008; 89.7 mhz FM; 1.35 kw vert; 663 ft.; N36 40 16 W108 13 54 *Rebroadcasts:* Rebroadcasts KUTE(FM) Ignacio, CO 100%
P.O. Box 737, Ignacio, CO 81137 US
(970) 563-0255, *Fax:* (970) 563-0399
www.ksut.org
info@ksut.org
License: Farmington, San Juan County, NM held by KUTE Inc.
Group Owner: KUTE Inc.
Arbitron Metro Market: Hobbs, NM *Format:* Triple A
Eddie Box Jr., President
Beth Warren, General Manager

Flora Vista

***KUSW**
01-01-2008; 88.1 mhz FM; 4.1 kw vert; 663 ft.; N36 40 16 W108 13 54 *Rebroadcasts:* Rebroadcasts KUTE(FM) Ignacio, CO 100%
US
(970) 563-0255, *Fax:* (970) 563-0399
www.ksut.org
info@ksut.org
License: Flora Vista, San Juan County, NM held by KUTE Inc.
Group Owner: KUTE Inc.; (acq 6-7-2006)
Arbitron Metro Market: Flora Vista, NM *Format:* News, Native American
Eddie Box Jr., President
Beth Warren, General Manager
Ken Brott, Programming Director
Bruce Campbell, Development Director
Denny Rahilly, Programmer
Jim Belcher, Programmer/PSA Director
Rob Rawls, Administrative Director
SheilaNanaeto, Tribal Radio Director

Fruitland

***KTGW**
91.7 mhz FM *Hrs Open:* 24; 12.5 kw; 394 ft.; N36 41 46 W108 13 13
Mailing Address: P.O. Box 232, Farmington, NM 87499 US
Second Address: 1103 W. Apache St., Farmington, NM 87401
(505) 327-7202, *Fax:* (505) 327-2163
www.kpcl.org
kpcl@kpcl.org
License: Fruitland, San Juan County, NM held by Native American Christian Voice Inc.
Arbitron Metro Market: Farmington, NM *Format:* Christian, Talk
Fareed Ayoub, President
Annette Ayoub, Executive Vice President

Gallup

KFMQ
01-01-1996; 106.1 mhz FM; 100 kw; 187 ft.; N35 29 39 W108 44 32
427 Bedford Road, Pleasantville, NY 10570 US
(505) 722-4442, *Fax:* (505) 722-7745
maryannarmijo@clearchannel.com
License: Gallup, McKinley County, NM held by Clear Channel Broadcasting Licenses Inc.
Group Owner: Clear Channel Communications Inc.; (acq 4-17-97)
Arbitron Metro Market: Gallup, NM
Ted Foster, Operations Dir
Mary Ann Armijo, General Manager
Blas Saucedo, Programming Director

KGAK
02-09-1945; 1330 khz AM *Hrs Open:* 5am-10pm; 5 kw-D, DAN; 1 kw-N, DAN; N35 32 34 W108 44 11
1515 West Main, Farmington, NM 84701 US
(505) 863-4444, *Fax:* (505) 722-7381
kgak@cia-g.com
License: Gallup, NM held by KRJG Inc.
Nat'l Network: CBS
Arbitron Metro Market: Gallup, NM *Format:* Native American *Target Audience:* 30-55.
Jim Gober, CEO
Leaudro Jodie, Programming Director
Jim Burt, Chief Engineer

***KGLP**
09-01-1992; 91.7 mhz FM *Hrs Open:* 24; 0.88 kw; 1147 ft.; N35 36 13 W108 40 45 *Rebroadcasts:* Rebroadcasts KSUT(FM) Ignacio, CO 50%
Board of Directors, 200 College Road, Gallup, NM 87301 US
(505) 863-7626, *Fax:* (505) 863-7532
www.kglp.org
kglpradio@kglp.org
License: Gallup, McKinley County, NM held by Gallup Public Radio.
Nat'l Network: NPR
Format: News, Variety/Diverse *Special Programming:* 3 hrs jazz, 2 hrs latin *Hrs. of News Programming:* News progmg 40 hrs wkly
Target Audience: General; adult professional, academic, business community
David Pracy, Operations Dir
Rachel Kaub, Station Manager
Tom Funk, Music Director

KGLX
03-01-1989; 99.1 mhz FM *Hrs Open:* 24; 51 kw; 1250 ft.; N35 36 18 W108 41 11
427 Bedford Road, Pleasantville, NY 10570 US
(505) 863-9391, *Fax:* (505) 863-9393
www.991kglx.com
maryannarmijo@clearchannel.com
License: Gallup, McKinley County, NM held by Clear Channel Broadcasting Licenses Inc.
Group Owner: Clear Channel Communications Inc.; (acq 8-18-00; grpsl).
Format: Country *Special Programming:* American Indian 3 hrs wkly *Hrs. of News Programming:* news progmg 14 hrs wkly *No. News Employees:* 2 *Target Audience:* 25-54.
Ted Foster, Operations Dir
Mary Armijo, General Manager
Sylvester Paquin, General Sales Mgr
Pat Jarvison, News Director

KYAT
10-06-1974; 94.5 mhz FM *Hrs Open:* 24; 100 kw; 1,388 ft; N35 28 03 W108 14 25
Box 420, Gallup, NM 87305
(505) 863-5567, *Fax:* (505) 863-2429
www.gallupradio.com
License: Gallup, McKinley County, NM
Population Served: 180,000*No. News Employees:* 1 *Target Audience:* 25-44; young families with buying power
Phil Lizotte, President
Jimmy Cole, General Sales Mgr
Hans Nelson, Programming Director
Tony Evans, Chief Engineer

KYVA
07-15-1959; 1230 khz AM *Hrs Open:* 24
P.O. Box 420, Gallup, NM 87305 US
(505) 863-6851, *Fax:* (505) 863-2429
www.gallupradio.com
License: Gallup, NM held by Millennium Media Inc.
Nat'l Network: ABC
Arbitron Metro Market: Gallup, NM *Format:* Country *Hrs. of News Programming:* news progmg 12 hrs wkly *No. News Employees:* 1 *Target Audience:* 35-54; mature, with buying power
Sammy Chioda, President
Sammy Chioda, General Manager
Tom Devlin, General Sales Mgr
Brian Smith, Promotions Manager
John McBreen, News Director
Keith Desautels, Engineering Dir
Keith DeSautels, Chief Engineer

KXXI
08-15-1975; 93.7 mhz FM *Hrs Open:* 24; 100 kw; 1378 ft.; N35 36 22 W108 41 26
Mailing Address: P.O. Box 420, Gallup, NM 87305 US
Second Address: 300 W. Aztec, Suite 200, Gallup, NM 87301
(505) 863-6851, *Fax:* (505) 863-2429
www.gallupradio.com
sammyc@gallupradio.com
License: Gallup, McKinley County, NM held by Millennium Media Inc.
Nat'l Network: ABC
Arbitron Metro Market: Gullap, NM *Format:* Classic Rock *Target Audience:* 25-44.
George Malti, CEO
Sammy Chioda, President
Thomas Devlin, General Sales Mgr
John McBreen, News Director
Keith Desautles, Engineering Dir
Keith Desautels, Chief Engineer
Tom Devlin, Sales Manager
Deni Gonzales, Marketing

***KGGA**
01-01-2008; 88.1 mhz FM; 1 kw; 16 ft.; N35 32 27 W108 44 36 *Rebroadcasts:* Rebroadcasts KLRD(FM) Yucaipa, CA 100%
188 South Bellevue, Suite 222, Memphis, TN 38104 US
(800) 877-5600, *Fax:* (916) 251-1650
www.air1.com
info@air1.com
License: Gallup, McKinley County, NM held by Educational Media Foundation.
Group Owner: EMF Broadcasting; (acq 7-23-2007; grpsl)
Nat'l Network: Air 1
Arbitron Metro Market: Sioux Falls, SD *Format:* Alternative, Christian
Mike Novak, President

***KLLU**
01-01-2008; 88.9 mhz FM; 0.65 kw; 1165 ft.; N35 36 15 W108 41 10 *Rebroadcasts:* Rebroadcasts KLVR(FM) Middletown, CA 100%
1425 North Market Blvd, Suite 9, Sacramento, CA 95834 US
(800) 877-5600, *Fax:* (916) 251-1650
www.klove.com
License: Gallup, McKinley County, NM held by Educational Media Foundation.
Group Owner: EMF Broadcasting
Nat'l Network: K-Love
Arbitron Metro Market: El Paso, TX *Format:* Christian
Mike Novak, President

Grants

KDSK
06-01-1997; 92.7 mhz FM *Hrs Open:* 24; 26 kw; 171 ft.; N35 7 9 W107 54 8
P.O. Box 11102, Albuquerque, NM 87192 US
(505) 285-5598, *Fax:* (505) 285-5575
License: Grants, Cibola County, NM held by KD Radio Inc.
Group Owner: KD Radio Inc.; (acq 11-16-00; with KMIN(AM) Grants).
Arbitron Metro Market: Albuquerque, NM *Format:* Oldies *Target Audience:* 30-50; earning boom
Derek Underhill, President
Debbie Anderson, General Sales Mgr
Tom Anderson, Promotions Manager

KMIN
09-01-1956; 980 khz AM *Hrs Open:* 24; 1 kw-D, 250 kw-N; N35 09 05 W107 52 31
733 Roosevelt, Grants, NM 84103
(505) 285-5598, *Fax:* (505) 285-5575
www.kmin980.com
info@kmin980.com
License: Grants, Cibola County, NM held by KD Radio Inc.
Group Owner: KD Radio Inc.; (acq 1-2-01; $145,000 with KDSK(FM) Grants).
Population Served: 25,000 *Arbitron Metro Market:* Albuquerque, NM *Target Audience:* 25-54; active, working adults
Derek Underhill, President
Debbie Anderson, General Sales Mgr
Tom Anderson, Promotions Manager

***KDRI**
01-01-2006; 90.3 mhz FM; 1 kw; Ant 2,713 ft; N35 15 08 W107 35 45 *Rebroadcasts:* Rebroadcasts KLVR(FM) Santa Rosa, CA 100%
2351 Sunset Blvd., Suite 170-218, Rocklin, CA 95834
(916) 251-1600, *Fax:* (916) 251-1650
www.air1.com
License: Grants, Cibola County, NM held by Educational Media Foundation.
Group Owner: EMF Broadcasting
Nat'l Network: Air 1
Mike Novak, President

***KIDS**
88.1 mhz FM; 100 w; Ant 162 ft; N35 07 09 W107 54 02
2020 Coal Ave. S.E., Albuquerque, NM 87106
(505) 242-7163
www.kanw.com
brasher@aps.edu
License: Grants, Cibola County, NM held by Board of Education of the City of Albuquerque, NM.
Population Served: 30,000
Michael Brasher, General Manager

Hatch

KVLC
04-01-1994; 101.1 mhz FM *Hrs Open:* 24; 100 kw; 1033 ft.; N32 41 35 W107 4 6
6808 Academy Parkway E., Ne, #B2, Albuquerque, NM 87109 US
(505) 527-1111, *Fax:* (505) 527-1100
www.101gold.com
contact@101gold.com
License: Hatch, Dona Ana County, NM held by Bravo Mic Communications LLC.
Group Owner: Bravo Mic Communications LLC; (acq 1-7-2005; $1.3 million)

Arbitron Metro Market: Albuquerque, NM *TV Affiliate:* KVLC-TV *Format:* Oldies *Special Programming:* Bi-lingual Sp/English 6 hrs wkly *Hrs. of News Programming:* news progmg 3 hrs wkly *No. News Employees:* 1 *Target Audience:* 25-54.
Allen Moore, Operations Dir
Michael Smith, General Manager
K.C. Counts, Programming Director

Hobbs

KHOB
08-07-1954; 1390 khz AM *Hrs Open:* 24; 5 kw-D, DAN; 0.5 kw-N, DAN; N32 44 21 W103 10 48
1000 East Sanger, Hobbs, NM 88240 US
(505) 392-9292, *Fax:* (505) 392-7579
khobam@aol.com
License: Hobbs, NM held by American Asset Management Inc. *TV Affiliate:* ESPN *Format:* Sports *Hrs. of News Programming:* news progmg 48 hrs wkly *No. News Employees:* 2 *Target Audience:* Males 18-45
Harmon Hann, General Manager
Pat Hann, Programming Director

KIXN
02-01-1996; 102.9 mhz FM *Hrs Open:* 24; 100 kw; 387 ft.; N32 47 12 W103 7 3
202 West 19th Street, El Dorado, AR 71730 US
(505) 397-4969, *Fax:* (505) 393-4310
www.1radiosquare.com
paul@1radiosquare.com
License: Hobbs, Lea County, NM held by Noalmark Broadcasting Corp.
Group Owner: Noalmark Broadcasting Corp.; acq 1995; $53,000 for CP).
Format: Country *Hrs. of News Programming:* news progmg 5 hrs wkly *No. News Employees:* 1 *Target Audience:* Adults 18-49. *Adv. Rates:* 16; 14; 16; 12.
William Nolan, CEO
Paul Starr, Operations Dir
Harry Harlan, General Sales Mgr
Dawn Morgan, News Director
Ken Bass, Engineering Dir
Edwin Alderson, Executive Vice President
Cathy Cox, Traffic Manager

KLMA
11-01-1993; 96.5 mhz FM *Hrs Open:* 24; 100 kw; 377 ft.; N32 28 5 W103 9 27
108 S. Willow, P.O. Box 457, Hobbs, NM 88240 US
(575) 391-9650, *Fax:* (575) 397-9373
www.klmaradio.com
License: Hobbs, Lea County, NM held by Ojeda Broadcasting Inc.
Arbitron Metro Market: El Paso, TX *Format:* Spanish *Target Audience:* Hispanic. *Adv. Rates:* 12; 12; 12; 12
Hermilo Ojeda, CEO
Pearl Ojeda, President
Letiicia Ojeda, Promotions Manager

KPER
08-01-1965; 95.7 mhz FM *Hrs Open:* 24; 25 kw; 328 ft.; N32 43 27 W103 9 4
Mailing Address: 202 West 19th St., El Dorado, AR 71730 US
Second Address: 1423 W. Bender St., Hobbs, NM 88240
(505) 393-1551, *Fax:* (505) 397-6088
www.hobbsradio.com
License: Hobbs, Lea County, NM held by Noalmark Broadcasting Corp.
Group Owner: Noalmark Broadcasting Corp.; acq 1-99)
Format: Country *No. News Employees:* 1 *Target Audience:* 25-54.
Al Lobeck, General Manager
Tyler Robinson, News Director
Ken Fine, Chief Engineer

***KOBH**
91.7 mhz FM; 0.25 kw; 157 ft.; N32 42 48 W103 5 28
88 Casey Jones Blvd, Jackson, TN 38305 US
(662) 844-5036, *Fax:* (662) 842-7798
www.afr.net
contact@afa.net
License: Hobbs, Lea County, NM held by American Family Association.
Group Owner: American Family Radio; (acq 8-27-2007)
Nat'l Network: American Family Radio
Arbitron Metro Market: Hobbs, NM *Format:* Christian
Donald E. Wildmon, Founder
Buster Wilson, General Manager
Jennifer Hagman, Programming Director

Humble City

KYKK
07-17-1971; 1110 khz AM *Hrs Open:* 6 AM-sunset; 2.5 kw-C, NDD; 5 kw-D, NDD; N32 48 59 W103 13 56
Mailing Address: 202 West 19th Street, El Dorado, AR 71730 US
Second Address: 1423 W. Bender Blvd., Hobbs, NM 88240
(505) 393-1551, *Fax:* (505) 397-6088
www.hobbsradio.com
License: Humble City, NM held by Noalmark Broadcasting Corp.
Group Owner: Noalmark Broadcasting Corp.; acq 8-8-77).
Nat'l Network: Premiere Radio Networks; Sporting News Radio Network; ABC Information & Entertainment
Arbitron Metro Market: Hobbs, NM *Format:* News, News/Talk, 84, Talk *Hrs. of News Programming:* news progmg 10 hrs wkly *No. News Employees:* 1 *Target Audience:* 25-54; men & women
William Nolan, President
Al Lobeck, General Manager
Tyler Robinson, News Director
Ken Fine, Chief Engineer

Hurley

***KOOT**
88.1 mhz FM; 2 kw vert; 167 ft.; N32 49 29 W108 14 54 US
(505) 534-0130
www.catsilver.org
catstv@comcast.net
License: Hurley, Grant County, NM held by Community Access Television of Silver.
Arbitron Metro Market: Hurley, NM *Format:* Variety/Diverse
Trent Petty, President
James Bumpous, General Manager
Betty Vega, Vice President
Charles Marquez, Treasurer
Brad Logan, Secretary
Lori Ford, Executive Director

Isleta

KOAZ
08-01-1983; 1510 khz AM; 5 kw-D, 25 w-N, 4.2 kw-CH; N34 25 01 W107 30 04
Box 907, Magdalena, NM 87825
(505) 854-2632,(505) 854-2641, Ext 1600-01, *Fax:* (505) 854-2545
www.alamo.bia.edu
info@kabram.com
License: Isleta, Bernalillo County, NM held by Martha Whitman dba Isleta Radio Co.
Special Programming: American Indian 10 hrs wkly *Target Audience:* General; Native Americans, loc ranchers, tourists, teachers & health professionals *Adv. Rates:* 55; 55; 55; na
Ann Kerr, President
Sarah Apache, General Manager

Jal

KPZA-FM
11-01-1998; 103.7 mhz FM *Hrs Open:* 24; 100 kw; 371 ft.; N32 25 53 W103 9 8
619 North Turner, Hobbs, NM 88240 US
(505) 397-4969, *Fax:* (505) 393-4310
www.1radiosquare.com
mail@1radiosquare.com
License: Jal, Lea County, NM held by Noalmark Broadcasting Corp.
Group Owner: Noalmark Broadcasting Corp.; (acq 5-29-98; $10,000 for CP).
Format: News, Sports *Hrs. of News Programming:* news progmg 5 hrs wkly *No. News Employees:* 1 *Target Audience:* Hispanic. *Adv. Rates:* 14; 12; 14; 10.
William Nolan, CEO
Edwin Alderson, Operations Dir
Paul Starr, General Manager
Tony Guerrero, Station Manager
Harry Harlan, General Sales Mgr
Tony Guerrero, Programming Director
Cathy Cox, News Director

Kirtland

KAZX
01-01-1999; 102.9 mhz FM; 100 kw; 994 ft.; N36 48 52 W107 53 32
4204 Sedona Court, Farmington, NM 87402 US
(505) 325-1716, *Fax:* (505) 325-6797
www.star1029.com
License: Kirtland, Bernalillo County, NM held by Capstar TX L.P.
Group Owner: Clear Channel Communications Inc.; (acq 12-19-00; $1.26 million).
Arbitron Metro Market: Farmington, NM *Format:* Contemporary Hits/Top 40
Bill Kruger, General Manager

La Luz

KRSY-FM
01-17-1987; 92.7 mhz FM *Hrs Open:* 24; 6 kw; -217 ft.; N32 58 13 W105 59 21
1805 East Bland, Roswell, NM 88201 US
(505) 437-1505, *Fax:* (505) 437-5566
www.snmradio.com
License: La Luz, Otero County, NM held by WP Broadcasting LLC.
Group Owner: Westburg Media Capital LP
Nat'l Network: ABC
Format: Country *Special Programming:* NASCAR *Hrs. of News Programming:* news progmg 2 hrs wkly *No. News Employees:* 2 *Target Audience:* 18-34; active adults, young adults
Les Henke, General Manager

Las Cruces

***KMBN**
01-01-2000; 89.7 mhz FM; 0.5 kw; 171 ft.; N32 16 41 W106 54 39
820 North Lasalle Blvd, Chicago, IL 60610 US
(505) 521-8053
www.mbn.org/kmbn
kmbn@moody.edu
License: Las Cruces, Dona Ana County, NM held by Moody Bible Institute of Chicago.
Group Owner: The Moody Bible Institute of Chicago
Format: Christian

KSNM
12-15-1955; 570 khz AM *Hrs Open:* 24; 5 kw-D, ND1; 0.155 kw-N, ND1; N32 18 33 W106 49 24
Mailing Address: PO Box 968, Las Cruces, NM 88004 US
Second Address: 1355 E. California Ave., Las Cruces, NM 88001
(575) 525-9298, *Fax:* (575) 525-9419
www.ksnm570.am
radiolc@kgrt.com
License: Las Cruces, NM held by Sunrise Broadcasting Inc.
Group Owner: Sunrise Broadcasting Corp.
Nat'l Network: CNN Radio
Arbitron Metro Market: Las Cruces, NM *Format:* News, Sports, 86 *Hrs. of News Programming:* news progmg 15 hrs wkly *No. News Employees:* 2 *Target Audience:* 25 plus; adults
Allen Lumeyer, Operations Dir
Tamara Blaeser, General Sales Mgr
Ernesto Garcia, Operations Manager

KGRT-FM
09-08-1966; 103.9 mhz FM *Hrs Open:* 24; 6 kw; 151 ft.; N32 18 33 W106 49 24
Mailing Address: PO Box 968, Las Cruces, NM 88004 US
Second Address: 1355 E. California Ave., Las Cruces, NM 88001
(575) 525-9298, *Fax:* (575) 525-9419
www.kgrt.com
radiolc@kgrt.com
License: Las Cruces, Dona Ana County, NM held by Sunrise Broadcasting Inc.
Group Owner: Sunrise Broadcasting Corp.; (acq 12-30-88; with co-located AM;
Nat'l Network: CNN Radio
Arbitron Metro Market: Las Cruces, NM *Format:* Country *No. News Employees:* 2 *Target Audience:* 25-54; adults
Allen Lumeyer, Operations Dir
Veronica Vaillancourt-Test, General Sales Mgr
Sheila Kirsch, Music Director
Tamara Blaeser, National Sales Manager
Ernesto Garcia, Operations Manager

KOBE
04-01-1947; 1450 khz AM *Hrs Open:* 24; 1 kw-U, ND1; N32 18 7 W106 48 8
Mailing Address: P.O. Drawer 1838, Las Cruces, NM 88004 US
Second Address: 1832 W. Amador, Las Cruces, NM 88005
(505) 526-2496, *Fax:* (505) 523-3918
kobeam1450.com
kmvr-kobe@totacc.com
License: Las Cruces, NM held by Bravo Mic Communications II LLC.
Group Owner: Bravo Mic Communications LLC; (acq 1-24-2007; $1.9 million with KMVR(FM) Mesilla Park)
Nat'l Network: CBS
Format: News, News/Talk, 84, Talk *Hrs. of News Programming:* news progmg 25 hrs wkly *No. News Employees:* 1 *Target Audience:* 25 plus.

Amanda Riordan, Operations Dir
Larry Edwards, General Manager
Keith Lamonica, Chief Engineer

KXPZ
05-01-1994; 99.5 mhz FM *Hrs Open:* 24; 100 kw; 1024 ft.; N32 41 35 W107 4 6
6900 Commerce Street, El Paso, TX 79915 US
(505) 527-1111, *Fax:* (505) 527-1100
www.rocket995.com
rocket@bravomic.com
License: Las Cruces, Dona Ana County, NM held by Bravo Mic Communications LLC.
Group Owner: Bravo Mic Communications LLC; (acq 4-18-2006; $1.4 million)
Arbitron Metro Market: Las Cruses and southern NM *Format:* Rock/AOR
Michael Smith, General Manager
Edmundo Resendez, General Sales Mgr
K.C. Counts, Programming Director
Glen Leffler, Chief Engineer

***KRUC**
03-01-1998; 88.9 mhz FM *Hrs Open:* 24; 0.5 kw; 197 ft.; N32 16 41 W106 54 39
Box 3333, McAllen, TX 78502 US
(915) 544-9192
www.wrn-rcm.org
License: Las Cruces, Dona Ana County, NM held by World Radio Network Inc.
Group Owner: World Radio Network Inc.
Arbitron Metro Market: El Paso, TX *Format:* Religious
Neil Torquiano, Station Manager

***KRUX**
09-20-1989; 91.5 mhz FM *Hrs Open:* 7 AM-2 AM; 1 kw; -194 ft.; N32 17 3 W106 45 0
Box 3z, Hadley 210, Las Cruces, NM 88003 US
(505) 646-4640, *Fax:* (505) 646-5219
www.kruxradio.com
krux_music@hotmail.com
License: Las Cruces, Dona Ana County, NM held by Board of Regents New Mexico State University.
Arbitron Metro Market: Las Cruces, NM *Format:* Variety/Diverse *Hrs. of News Programming:* news progmg 2 hrs wkly *No. News Employees:* 1 *Target Audience:* General.
Jonathan Goke, General Manager
Adrian Perez, Programming Director
Mathias Ortiz, Promotions Manager
Bianca Villani, News Director
Jesus Ramos, Chief Engineer
Leandra Gamboa, Business Manager

***KRWG**
10-03-1964; 90.7 mhz FM *Hrs Open:* 24; 100 kw; 351 ft.; N32 15 24 W106 58 34
Mailing Address: P. O. Box 3000, Las Cruces, NM 88003 US
Second Address: 2915 McFie Cir., Rm. 120, Las Cruces, NM 88003
(575) 646-2222, *Fax:* (575) 646-1974
krwg.org
krwgfm@nmsu.edu
License: Las Cruces, Dona Ana County, NM held by Regents of New Mexico State University.
Nat'l Network: NPR; PRI *Wire Services:* AP
Arbitron Metro Market: Las Cruces, NM *TV Affiliate:* *KRWG-TV affil *Format:* Jazz, News *Special Programming:* Sp 10 hrs, bluegrass/folk 8 hrs wkly *Hrs. of News Programming:* news progmg 39 hrs wkly *No. NewsEmployees:* 4 *Target Audience:* 18-60.
Carrie Hamblen, Operations Dir
Edmundo Resendez, Station Manager
L. Ford Ballard, General Sales Mgr
Fred Martino, Programming Director
Sloan Patton, News Director
Glen Cerny, Director, University Broadcasting

KHQT
12-12-1974; 103.1 mhz FM *Hrs Open:* 24; 1 kw; 551 ft.; N32 24 18 W106 45 41
Mailing Address: P.O. Box 880, Las Cruces, NM 88004 US
Second Address: 1355 E. California Ave., Las Cruces, NM 88001
(575) 525-9298, *Fax:* (575) 525-9419
www.hot103.fm
radiolc@kgrt.com
License: Las Cruces, Dona Ana County, NM held by Richardson Commercial Corp.
Arbitron Metro Market: Las Cruces, NM *TV Affiliate:* KHQT-TV aff. *Format:* Contemporary Hits/Top 40 *No. News Employees:* 2 *Target Audience:* 18-34; adult
Allen Lumeyer, Operations Dir
Tamara Blaeser, General Sales Mgr
Damien Willis, Music Director
Ernesto Garcia, Operations Manager
Veronica Vaillancourt-Test, Sales Manager

Las Vegas

KBAC
11-10-1989; 98.1 mhz FM *Hrs Open:* 24; 100 kw; 1037 ft.; N35 22 20 W105 22 2
427 Bedford Road, Pleasantville, NY 10570 US
(505) 471-1067, *Fax:* (505) 473-2667
www.santefe.com/kbac
info@kbacfm.com
License: Las Vegas, San Miguel County, NM held by Hutton Broadcasting LLC.
Group Owner: Hutton Broadcasting LLC; (acq 10-16-2007; $650,000)
Arbitron Metro Market: Santa Fe, NM
Edward Hutton, President
Scott Hutton, General Manager
Brad Brown, Eric Davis
Ted Levin, Chief Engineer

***KEDP**
09-01-1968; 91.1 mhz FM; 1.32 kw horiz; -199 ft.; N35 35 39 W105 13 15
Mass Communication Depar, Las Vegas, NM 87701 US
(505) 454-3238
www.nmhu.edu
martinezda@nmhu.edu
License: Las Vegas, San Miguel County, NM held by Board of Regents, New Mexico Highlands University.
Arbitron Metro Market: Las Vegas, NM *Format:* Oldies
Donna Martinez, General Manager
David Chavez, Programming Director
Doyle Hanschulz, Engineering Dir
Miriam Langer, Department Head
Mary Basler, Administrative Associate
Doyle Hauschulz, Instructor

KFUN
12-25-1941; 1230 khz AM *Hrs Open:* 24; 1 kw-U, ND1; N35 35 48 W105 12 21
Box 700, Radio Heights, Las Vegas, NM 87701 US
(505) 425-6766, *Fax:* (505) 425-6767
www.kfunonline.com
jpbaca1946@yahoo.com
License: Las Vegas, NM held by Meadows Media LLC.
Arbitron Metro Market: Las Vegas, NV *Format:* Country *Special Programming:* Spanish 20 hrs wkly, Oldies 7 hrs wkly *Target Audience:* General. *Adv. Rates:* 7.50; 7.50; 7.50; 7.50
Joseph Baca Jr., General Manager
Loretta Baca, News Director

KLVF
06-19-1973; 100.7 mhz FM *Hrs Open:* 24; 10 kw; -75 ft.; N35 35 48 W105 12 21 *Rebroadcasts:* (CP: COL Pecos. 3.7 kw horiz, ant 686 ft. TL: N35 39 06 W105 33 15)
P.O. Box 700, Radio Heights, Las Vegas, NM 87701 US
(505) 425-6766, *Fax:* (505) 425-6767
jpbaca1946@yahoo.com
License: Las Vegas, San Miguel County, NM held by Meadows Media LLC.
Format: Adult Contemp *Target Audience:* 17-40. *Adv. Rates:* 7.50; 7.50; 7.50; 7.50
Georgia Carrera, Operations Dir
Bill Shadorf, General Sales Mgr
Jose Santos, Programming Director

KNMX
10-01-1980; 540 khz AM *Hrs Open:* Sunrise-sunset; 5 kw-D, DA1; 0.02 kw-N, DA1; N35 34 25 W105 10 17
300 S. Grand Ave., Los Vegas, NM 87701 US
(505) 425-3555, *Fax:* (505) 425-3557
mattmartinez@knmx.com
License: Las Vegas, NM held by Sangre de Cristo Broadcasting Co.
Format: News, News/Talk, 86 *Hrs. of News Programming:* news progmg 15 hrs wkly *No. News Employees:* 1 *Target Audience:* 25-55; Hispanic, Anglo
Matt Martinez, President
John Chichester, Chief Engineer

KMDZ
01-01-2000; 96.7 mhz FM *Hrs Open:* 24; 4.4 kw; 381 ft.; N35 36 16 W105 15 35
300 S. Grand, Las Vegas, NM 87701 US
(505) 425-5669, *Fax:* (505) 425-3557
mattmartinez@knmx.com
License: Las Vegas, San Miguel County, NM held by Sangre de Cristo Broadcasting Co.
Arbitron Metro Market: Las Vegas, NM *Format:* Classic Rock
Matt Martinez, General Manager

***KRRE**
01-01-2008; 91.9 mhz FM; 0.1 kw; -38 ft.; N35 37 59 W105 14 10
Rebroadcasts: Rebroadcasts KUNM(FM) Albquerque 100% US
(505) 277-4806
www.kunm.org
kunm@kunm.org
License: Las Vegas, San Miguel County, NM held by Regents of the University of New Mexico.
Nat'l Network: NPR
Arbitron Metro Market: Las Vegas, NM *Format:* Public Affairs, Variety/Diverse
Richard Towne, General Manager
Tristan Clum, Programming Director
Mike Stark, Chief Engineer
Alaina George, Production Assistant
Jeff Maness, Engineering Assistant
Jonathan Longcore, Network Administrator
Roman Garcia, ProductionDirector
Scott MacNicholl, Operations Manager
Tristan Clum, Program Director

KBQL
92.7 mhz FM; 23 kw; 341 ft.; N35 34 23 W105 10 16 US
(505) 425-5669, *Fax:* (505) 425-3557
License: Las Vegas, San Miguel County, NM held by Matias C. Martinez.
Arbitron Metro Market: Las Vegas, NM
Matias Martinez, General Manager

Lordsburg

KPSA-FM
07-04-1986; 97.9 mhz FM *Hrs Open:* 24; 0.25 kw; -135 ft.; N32 20 57 W108 42 18
P.O Box 720, Alamogordo, NM 88310 US
(505) 538-3396, *Fax:* (505) 388-5000
www.977theplanet.com (coming soon)
events@silvercityradio.com
License: Lordsburg, Hidalgo County, NM held by SkyWest Licenses New Mexico LLC.
Group Owner: SkyWest Media L.L.C.; (acq 6-1-2006; grpsl).
Format: Classic Rock
Sabrina Pack, General Manager
Ted Tucker, Programming Director

Los Alamos

KABG
06-01-1956; 98.5 mhz FM; 100 kw; 1906 ft.; N35 46 49 W106 31 37
P.O. Box 2700, Bakersfield, CA 93303 US
(505) 878-0980, *Fax:* (505) 878-0098
www.big985.com
License: Los Alamos, Los Alamos County, NM held by AGM-Nevada L.L.C.
Group Owner: American General Media
Arbitron Metro Market: Albuquerque, NM *Format:* Oldies *Target Audience:* 25-54; affluent, upscale male professionals
Scott Hutton, General Manager
Scott Sherwood, Programming Director

KDLW
03-19-1987; 106.7 mhz FM *Hrs Open:* 24; 15.5 kw; Ant 1,948 ft; N35 47 15 W106 31 35
4125 Carlisle N.E., Albuqerque, NM 62864
(505) 878-0980, *Fax:* (505) 878-0098
www.radiolobo.net
License: Los Alamos, Los Alamos County, NM held by A.G.M.-Nevada L.L.C.
Group Owner: American General Media; (acq 8-9-2000; grpsl)
Population Served: 103,000 *Arbitron Metro Market:* Santa Fe, NM *Hrs. of News Programming:* News progmg 7 hrs wkly *Target Audience:* 25-54; mainstream audience with all socio-economic cells represented
Scott Hutton, General Manager

KQBA
03-01-1998; 107.5 mhz FM *Hrs Open:* 12a-12a; 100 kw; 797 ft.; N36 5 21 W106 1 41
3501 Broadway, P.O. Box 1508, Mount Vernon, IL 62864 US
(505) 471-1067, *Fax:* (505) 473-2667
1075outlawcountry.com
info@huttonbroadcasting.com
License: Los Alamos, Los Alamos County, NM held by Hutton Broadcasting LLC.
Group Owner: Hutton Broadcasting LLC; (acq 12-4-2000; $1 million)
Nat'l Network: Jones Radio Networks

Arbitron Metro Market: Santa Fe, NM *Format:* Country *Target Audience:* 18-49; male
Edward Hutton, President
Scott Hutton, General Manager
Chris Destler, Programming Director
Eric Davis, Promotions Manager
Ted Levin, Chief Engineer

KRSN
12-09-1946; 1490 khz AM *Hrs Open:* 24; 1 kw-U, ND1; N35 53 46 W106 17 21
1218 17th Street, Los Alamos, NM 87544 US
(505) 663-1490, *Fax:* (505) 663-0011
www.krsnam1490.com
info@krsnam1490.com
License: Los Alamos, NM held by Gillian Sutton
Nat'l Network: CBS; Westwood One
Arbitron Metro Market: Santa Fe, NM *Format:* News, Sports *Special Programming:* hs sports, interviews on hot topics *Hrs. of News Programming:* news progmg 20 hrs wkly *No. News Employees:* 1 *Target Audience:* 35 plus; well educated, affluent *Adv. Rates:* 16;16;16;
Gillian Sutton, CEO
David Sutton, Operations Dir

Los Lunas

KIOT
07-06-1981; 102.5 mhz FM *Hrs Open:* 24; 21 kw; 4075 ft.; N35 12 47 W106 26 59
57 West South Temple, Suite 700, Salt Lake City, UT 84101 US
(505) 262-1142, *Fax:* (505) 254-7106
License: Los Lunas, Valencia County, NM held by The Univision Albuquerque Trust, Bob Woodward, Trustee
Arbitron Metro Market: Albuquerque, NM *Format:* Classic Rock *Special Programming:* Gospel 4 hrs wkly *No. News Employees:* 1 *Target Audience:* 25-49; hip adults who like diversity & have disposable income
Chuck Morgan, General Manager

KAGM
01-01-1995; 106.3 mhz FM *Hrs Open:* 24; 98.1 kw; 856 ft.; N34 47 55 W106 48 59
P.O. Box 2700, Bakersfield, CA 93303 US
(505) 878-0980, *Fax:* (505) 878-0098
www.power106abq.com
srufail@americangeneralmedia.com
License: Los Lunas, Valencia County, NM held by AGM-Nevada L.L.C.
Group Owner: American General Media; (acq 12-22-97; grpsl).
Arbitron Metro Market: Los Lunas, NM *Format:* Country *Special Programming:* Club mix 18 hrs wkly *Target Audience:* 18-49.
Rogers Brandon, President
Scott Hutton, Promotions Manager
Matt Rader, Promotions Director

Los Ranchos

KTBL
12-16-1987; 1050 khz AM; 1 kw-D, DA1; 1 kw-N, DA1; N34 58 46 W106 44 13
City Center West, 7201 W. Lake Mead Blvd, Las Vegas, NV 89128 US
(505) 767-6700, *Fax:* (505) 767-6767
www.1050kbull.com
License: Los Ranchos, NM
Group Owner: Cumulus Media Inc.; (acq 6-28-96; $5.725 million with KBZU(FM) Albuquerque).
Arbitron Metro Market: Albuquerque, NM *Format:* News, News/Talk, 86 *Target Audience:* 25-54.
Pat Frisch, Operations Dir
Milt McConnell, General Manager
Blake Mendenhall, General Sales Mgr
Glenn Herbert, Promotions Manager
Lynda Ortega, News Director
Bill Harris, Chief Engineer
Art Ortega, Public Affairs Director

Los Ranchos De Albuquerque

KALY
01-01-1982; 1240 khz AM *Hrs Open:* 24
P.O. Box 6492, 2505 6th St., NW, Albuquerque, NM 87197 US
(505) 244-1100, *Fax:* (505) 244-0612
www.radiodisney.com
License: Los Ranchos De Albuquerque, NM
Group Owner: KD Radio Inc.; (acq 2-21-03; $650,000).
Arbitron Metro Market: Albuquerque, NM *Format:* Children *Target Audience:* 25-49.
Lynn Southard, General Manager

Lovington

KLEA
12-25-1952; 630 khz AM *Hrs Open:* 24; 0.5 kw-D, ND1; 0.069 kw-N, ND1; N32 56 30 W103 19 12
P.O. Box 877, Lovington, NM 88260 US
(505) 396-2244, *Fax:* (505) 396-3355
www.107oldies.com
klea@valornet.com
License: Lovington, NM held by Lea County Broadcasting Co.
Arbitron Metro Market: El Paso, TX *Format:* Sports, Contemporary Hits/Top 40 *Special Programming:* Relg 3 hrs wkly *Hrs. of News Programming:* news progmg 12 hrs wlky *No. News Employees:* 1 *Target Audience:* 25-54.
Susan Coe, General Manager
Keith Kelly, Programming Director
Rita Niccum, Chief Engineer
Annette Giese, Traffic Manager

KLEA-FM
10-01-1965; 101.7 mhz FM *Hrs Open:* 24; 25 kw; 289 ft.; N32 56 30 W103 19 12
P. O. Box 877, Lovington, NM 88260 US
(505) 396-2244, *Fax:* (505) 396-3355
www.107oldies.com
klea@valornet.com
License: Lovington, Lea County, NM
Arbitron Metro Market: El Paso, TX *Format:* Oldies *Hrs. of News Programming:* news progmg 10 hrs wkly *No. News Employees:* 1
Susan Coe, President

Maljamar

***KMTH**
02-14-1985; 98.7 mhz FM *Hrs Open:* 24; 100 kw; 709 ft.; N32 54 55 W103 46 31 *Rebroadcasts:* Rebroadcasts KENW-FM Portales 100%
Eastern N.M University, 52 Broadcast Street, Portales, NM 88130 US
(505) 562-2112, *Fax:* (505) 562-2590
kenw.org
License: Maljamar, Lea County, NM held by Eastern New Mexico University.
Nat'l Network: NPR; PRI *Wire Services:* AP
Format: News *Hrs. of News Programming:* news progmg 41 hrs wkly *No. News Employees:* 1 *Target Audience:* General.
Steven Gamble, President
Ronnie Birdsong, Operations Dir
Duane Ryan, General Manager
Carla Howard, General Sales Mgr
Virginia McReynolds, Promotions Manager
James Lee, News Director
Jeff Burmeister, Engineering Dir
Bob Scott,Engineering Manager
Shannon Hearn

KWMW
01-17-1990; 105.1 mhz FM; 100 kw; 925 ft.; N32 52 50 W103 41 1
P.O. Drawer 2010, Ruidoso Downs, NM 88346 US
(505) 396-0499, *Fax:* (505) 396-8349
kruikwmw@trailnet.com
License: Maljamar, Lea County, NM held by M.T.D. Inc.
Group Owner: MTD Inc.
Arbitron Metro Market: Ruidoso Downs, NM *Format:* Country
Tim Keithley, General Manager
Will Rooney, Station Manager

Mentmore

***KPKJ**
88.5 mhz FM; 1.45 kw; 489 ft.; N35 33 36 W109 6 30
3000 W. Macarthur Blvd, Santa Ana, CA 92704 US
(208) 734-6633, *Fax:* (208) 736-1958
www.csnradio.com
License: Mentmore, McKinley County, NM held by CSN International.
Group Owner: CSN International
Arbitron Metro Market: North Platte, NE
Mike Kestler, President

Mesilla Park

KMVR
06-01-1974; 104.9 mhz FM *Hrs Open:* 24; 3 kw; -33 ft.; N32 18 7 W106 48 8
P.O. Drawer 1838, Las Cruces, NM 88004 US
(575) 527-1111, *Fax:* (575) 527-1100
www.kmvrfm.com
kmvr-kobe@totacc.com
License: Mesilla Park, Dona Ana County, NM held by Bravo Mic Communications II LLC.
Group Owner: Bravo Mic Communications LLC; (acq 1-24-2007; $1.9 million with KOBE(AM) Las Cruces)
Format: Adult Contemp *Target Audience:* 18-54.
Larry Edwards, General Manager

Mesquite

***KELP-FM**
02-01-2004; 89.3 mhz FM *Hrs Open:* 24; 3 kw; 184 ft.; N32 5 5 W106 44 1
120 Colina Alta Dr., El Paso, TX 79912 US
(915) 779-0016, *Fax:* (915) 779-6641
www.kelpradio.com
tina@kelpradio.com
License: Mesquite, Dona Ana County, NM held by Sky High Broadcasting Inc.
Nat'l Network: Salem Radio Network
Arbitron Metro Market: El Paso, TX *Format:* Christian *Target Audience:* 25-55 plus.
Tina Casano, Operations Dir
Arniold McClatchey, Owner, General Manager
Jay Gilliland, Programming Director
Jay Gilliland, Minister, Director of Operations
Tina Casano, Office Manager
Eydie Copeland, Reception, ProductionAssistant
Clark Peters, Minister, Morning Producer
Jeff Popoff, Prison Minister, Saturday Producer
Steve Strub, Sunday Producer

Milan

KRKE
09-01-1989; 1100 khz AM *Hrs Open:* 24; 250 w-D, 20 w-N; N35 05 51 W107 52 19
809 Wellesly N.E., Albuqueque, NM 98901
(505) 899-5029, *Fax:* (505) 899-6865
joy@joyam.com
License: Milan, Cibola County, NM held by Cibola Radio Co.
Population Served: 22,000*Target Audience:* 25-54; upscale men *Adv. Rates:* 7; 7; 7; 3
Don Davis, President

KQNM
02-22-1971; 1100 khz AM *Hrs Open:* 24
P.O. Box 1675, 211 W. Sabte Fe Ave, Grants, NM 87020 US
(505) 899-5029
www.nmtruth.com
joyam@joyam
License: Milan, NM held by Vanguard Media L.L.C.
Arbitron Metro Market: Albuquerque, NM *Format:* Adult Contemp *Hrs. of News Programming:* News progmg 5 hrs wkly *Target Audience:* 35-64; mature upscale adults *Adv. Rates:* 20; 20; 20; 5
Don Davis, CEO
Craig Collins, Operations Dir
Josie Bunch, Station Manager
Crystal Felice, Promotions Manager

***KXXQ**
06-01-1991; 100.7 mhz FM *Hrs Open:* 24; 100 kw; 1362 ft.; N35 28 7 W108 14 24
809 Wellesley N.E., Albuquerque, NM 87106 US
(916) 535-0500, *Fax:* (916) 535-0504
www.ihradio.org
info@ihradio.org
License: Milan, Cibola County, NM held by IHR Educational Broadcasting.
Group Owner: IHR Educational Broadcasting; (acq 5-31-2005; $450,000).
Format: Christian
Douglas Sherman, President

***KVLK**
01-01-2007; 89.5 mhz FM *Hrs Open:* 24; 0.11 kw; 2625 ft.; N35 15 12 W107 35 50 *Rebroadcasts:* Rebroadcasts KLVR(FM) Santa Rosa, CA 100%
US
(800) 525-5683, *Fax:* (916) 251-1650
www.klove.com
klove@klove.com
License: Milan, Socorro County, NM held by Educational Media Foundation.
Group Owner: EMF Broadcasting
Nat'l Network: K-Love
Arbitron Metro Market: Socorro, NM *Format:* Christian *No. News Employees:* 13
Darrell Chambliss, Chairman
Mike Novak, President and CEO
Jim Marable, Operations Dir
David Pierce, Programming Director

Ed Lenane, News Director
Sam Wallington, Engineering Dir
Dan Antonelli, Chief Business DevelopmentOfficer
Eric Moser, Chief Financial Officer
Brian Burger, Vice President of Human Resources
D. Kevin Blair, Secretary and General Counsel
Tim Luttrell, News Reporter

Pecos

KLBU
08-01-2001; 102.9 mhz FM; 3.7 kw horiz, 0 kw vert; N35 39 6 W105 33 15
551 Cordova Road #142, Santa Fe, NM 87501 US
(505) 471-1067, *Fax:* (505) 984-0880
www.blu1029.com
info@klbu.com
License: Pecos, San Miguel County, NM held by Hutton Broadcasting LLC.
Group Owner: Hutton Broadcasting LLC; (acq 10-16-2007; $450,000)
Arbitron Metro Market: Santa Fe, NM *Format:* Adult Contemp
Edward Hutton, President
Scott Hutton, General Manager
Ira Gordon, Programming Director
Eric Davis, Promotions Manager
Ted Levin, Chief Engineer

KVSF-FM
01-01-2004; 101.5 mhz FM; 25 kw horiz; -92 ft.; N35 34 57 W105 46 34
1809 Lightsey Rd., Austin, TX 78704 US
(505) 438-7007, *Fax:* (505) 438-7007
www.santafe.com/project
License: Pecos, San Miguel County, NM held by Hutton Broadcasting LLC.
Group Owner: Hutton Broadcasting LLC; (acq 10-16-2007; $700,000)
Arbitron Metro Market: Santa Fe, NM *Format:* Variety/Diverse
James Bumpous, General Manager

Portales

***KENW-FM**
10-01-1968; 89.5 mhz FM *Hrs Open:* 24; 100 kw; Ant 590 ft; N34 15 08.11 W103 14 20.63
Mailing Address: Eastern New Mexico Univ., 52 Broadcast Center, Portales, NM 88130
Second Address: Eastern New Mexico Univ., 1500 S. Ave. K, Portales, NM 88130
(575) 562-2112, *Fax:* (575) 562-2590
www.kenw.org
kenwfm@enmu.edu
License: Portales, Roosevelt County, NM held by Eastern New Mexico University.
Nat'l Network: NPR; BSN
Population Served: 350,000*TV Affiliate:* *KENW-TV affil *Hrs. of News Programming:* news progmg 41 hrs wkly *No. News Employees:* 1 *Target Audience:* General.
Steven Gamble, President
Ronnie Birdsong, Vice President
Duane Ryan, General Manager
Duane Ryan, Station Manager
Duane Ryan, Programming Director
James Lee, News Director
Jeff Burmeister, Engineering Dir
Mickey Morgan, AudioEngineer
Shannon Hearn, Operations Director

KSEL
02-01-1950; 1450 khz AM *Hrs Open:* 24
P.O. Box 886, Portales, MN 88130 US
(505) 359-4649, *Fax:* (505) 359-0724
License: Portales, NM held by Rooney Moon Broadcasting Inc.
Group Owner: Rooney Moon Broadcasting Inc.; (acq 7-15-2002; grpsl)
Nat'l Network: CNN Radio
Arbitron Metro Market: Portales, NM *Format:* News, News/Talk, 86 *Hrs. of News Programming:* News progmg 168 hrs wkly *Target Audience:* 35+.
Steve Rooney, President
Duffy Moon, Operations Dir
Lisa Schmidt, News Director
Jeff Burmeister, Chief Engineer

KSEL-FM
03-01-1980; 105.9 mhz FM; 100 kw; 463 ft.; N34 15 8 W103 14 21
P.O. Box 886, Portales, MN 88130 US
(505) 359-4649, *Fax:* (505) 359-0724
License: Portales, Roosevelt County, NM held by Rooney Moon Broadcasting Inc.
Group Owner: Rooney Moon Broadcasting Inc.
Nat'l Network: CNN Radio
Arbitron Metro Market: Portales, NM *Format:* Country *Special Programming:* Farm 4 hrs wkly *Target Audience:* 18-54.
Lisa Schmidt, News Director

***KPCV**
02-01-2005; 91.7 mhz FM *Hrs Open:* 24; 9 kw; 315 ft.; N34 8 6 W103 36 58 *Rebroadcasts:* Rebroadcasts KPCC(FM) Pasadena 100%
US
(626) 583-5100, *Fax:* (626) 583-5101
www.scpr.org
mail@kpcc.org
License: Portales, Riverside County, NM held by American Public Media Group
Nat'l Network: NPR; PRI
Arbitron Metro Market: Portales, NM *Format:* Talk *Target Audience:* General.
Bill Davis, President and CEO
Mark Crowley, Vice President and General Manager
Craig Curtis, Programming Director
Lance Harper, Chief Engineer
Russ Stanton, Vice President, Content
Melanie Sill, Executive Editor
Gregory PierreCox, Vice President, Development
Julie Allen, Vice President, Underwriting Sales
Alex Schaffert, Director, Digital Media
Melanie Sauer, Manager, Finance & Accounting

Questa

KLNN
01-01-2006; 103.7 mhz FM; 51 kw horiz; -211 ft.; N36 39 23 W105 37 57
US
(505) 758-5826, *Fax:* (505) 758-8430
www.luna1037.com
ktaoo@newmex.com
License: Questa, Taos County, NM held by West Waves Inc.
Arbitron Metro Market: Questa, NM *Format:* Adult Contemp
David Rahn, President
Dave Noll, General Manager

Ramah

***KTDB**
04-24-1972; 89.7 mhz FM *Hrs Open:* 5 AM-11 PM; 15 kw; 289 ft.; N34 57 59 W108 25 31
P. O. Box 40, Pine Hill, NM 87357 US
(505) 775-3215, *Fax:* (505) 775-3551
www.ktdbfm.com
info@ktkb.com
License: Ramah, McKinley County, NM held by Ramah Navajo School Board Inc.
Nat'l Network: NPR
Arbitron Metro Market: Pine Hill, NM *Format:* Country *Special Programming:* Navajo *Target Audience:* General; Native American
Barbara Maria, General Manager
Irene Beaver, Programming Director
Earl Ericcho, News Director
Bernard Bustos, Chief Engineer

Ranchos De Taos

***KCEY**
89.5 mhz FM; 9000 w; 2877 ft; N36 14 54 W105 39 19
Cultural Energy, 125 A La Posta, Taos, NM
(575)758-9791
www.culturalenergy.org
energy@culturalenergy.org
License: Ranchos De Taos, Taos County, NM
Group Owner: Cultural Energy
Robin Collier, Production, Outreach & Member Station Devlopment
Ernie Atencio, Earth Beat
Roberta Salazar, Farming
Lisa Fox, Native Momentum

Raton

KBKZ
12-20-2001; 96.5 mhz FM; 5.4 kw; 968 ft.; N36 59 33 W104 28 24
705 South Fifth Street, Raton, NM 87740 US
(719) 846-3355, *Fax:* (719) 846-4711
www.kcrtradio.com
kcrt@comcast.net
License: Raton, Colfax County, NM held by Phillips Broadcasting Co. Inc.
Group Owner: Phillips Broadcasting Inc.
Arbitron Metro Market: Trinidad, CO *Format:* Country
Lory Phillips, General Manager

KRTN
01-01-1948; 1490 khz AM *Hrs Open:* 24
P.O. Box 638, 1128 State St., Raton, NM 87740 US
(505) 445-3652, *Fax:* (505) 445-2911
krtn@bacavalley.com
License: Raton, NM held by Enchanted Air Inc.
Arbitron Metro Market: Raton, NM *Format:* Adult Contemp *Target Audience:* General.
Bill Donati, Station Manager
Adrean Slocum, News Director
Jim Veltri, Chief Engineer

KRTN-FM
04-01-1982; 93.9 mhz FM *Hrs Open:* 24; 26 kw; 1447 ft.; N36 40 59 W104 24 50
P.O Box 638, Raton, NM 87740 US
(505) 445-3652, *Fax:* (505) 445-2911
License: Raton, Colfax County, NM
Arbitron Metro Market: Raton, NM *Format:* Oldies
Robbie Ley, Programming Director
Mike Higgins, Disc Jockey
Billy Donoti, Disc Jockey

Red River

***KCEI**
01-01-2002; 90.1 mhz FM; 3.2 kw vert; Ant 718 ft; N36 41 25 W105 33 43
Box 788, Questa, NM 87558
(505) 586-1919, *Fax:* (505) 586-2332
www.krdr.com
krdr@newmex.com
License: Red River, Taos County, NM held by Red River Radio Inc.

Mike Nolen, General Manager
Lynn Nolen, Station Manager

Rincon

KSIL
01-01-2002; 105.5 mhz FM *Hrs Open:* 24; 11 kw; 1063 ft.; N32 50 40 W108 14 19
13915 Lakeview Dr, Austin, TX 78732 US
(505) 534-1055, *Fax:* (505) 534-1400
www.ksilradio.com
info@ksilradio.com
License: Rincon, Grant County, NM held by James S. Bumpous dba Yellow Dog Radio.
Arbitron Metro Market: Rincon, NM *Format:* Variety/Diverse *Hrs. of News Programming:* News progmg 5 hrs wkly *Target Audience:* 25-54.
Steve Bumpous, General Manager

Rio Rancho

KQTM
11-02-1984; 101.7 mhz FM; 3 kw; 98 ft.; N35 11 35 W106 28 15
57 West South Temple, Suite 700, Salt Lake City, UT 84101 US
(505) 239-4771, *Fax:* (505) 254-7106
www.1017theteam.com
joe@1017theteam.com
License: Rio Rancho, Sandoval County, NM held by Team Broadcasting Inc.
Nat'l Network: Fox Sports *Nat'l Reps:* Christal
Arbitron Metro Market: Albuquerque, NM *Format:* Sports
Joe O'Neill, President
Chuck Morgan, General Manager

Roswell

KBCQ-FM
10-15-1977; 97.1 mhz FM *Hrs Open:* 24; 100 kw; 361 ft.; N33 24 5 W104 22 45
P.O. Box 670, Roswell, NM 88202 US
(505) 622-6450, *Fax:* (505) 622-9041
www.q971fm.com
License: Roswell, Chaves County, NM held by Roswell Radio Inc.
Group Owner: Roswell Radio Inc./Quay Broadcasters Inc.; (acq 11-2000; grpsl)
Arbitron Metro Market: Roswell, NM *Format:* Contemporary Hits/Top 40 *No. News Employees:* 1 *Target Audience:* 18-49.
Adv. Rates: 25; 20; 22; 20
John Dunn, CEO
Jeff Chase, General Manager
Gary Babcock, Engineering Dir

KBIM
05-01-1953; 910 khz AM *Hrs Open:* 24; 5 kw-D, DAN; 0.5 kw-N, DAN; N33 26 26 W104 31 35
Mailing Address: P.O. Box 2308, Roswell, NM 88201 US
Second Address: 1301 N. Main, Roswell, NM 88201
(505) 623-9100, *Fax:* (505) 623-4775
www.kbim910.com
kevin@kbimradio.com
License: Roswell, NM held by Noalmark Broadcasting Corp.
Group Owner: Noalmark Broadcasting Corp.; (acq 11-30-2007; $1.5 million with co-located FM)
Nat'l Network: ABC
Arbitron Metro Market: Roswell, NM *Format:* News, News/Talk, 86 *Hrs. of News Programming:* News progmg 16 hrs wkly *Target Audience:* 25-54; upscale male & active working female *Adv. Rates:* 16; 15; 14; 12
William Nolan Jr., President
Don Niccum, Operations Dir
Kevin Bonner, General Manager
Darryl Burkfield, General Sales Mgr
Tom A. Ruiz, News Director

KBIM-FM
06-01-1959; 94.9 mhz FM *Hrs Open:* 24; 100 kw; 1880 ft.; N33 3 20 W103 49 12
P.O.Box 2308, Roswell, NM 88201 US
(505) 623-9100, *Fax:* (505) 623-4775
www.kbim949.com
kevin@kbimradio.com
License: Roswell, Chaves County, NM held by Noalmark Broadcasting Corp.
Group Owner: Noalmark Broadcasting Corp.
Arbitron Metro Market: Roswell, NM *Format:* Adult Contemp *Hrs. of News Programming:* News progmg 16 hrs wkly *Target Audience:* 25-54. *Adv. Rates:* Same as AM
Kevin Bonner, General Manager
Darryl Burkfield, General Sales Mgr
Tom A. Ruiz, News Director
John King, General Sales Manager

KCKN
12-20-1965; 1020 khz AM *Hrs Open:* 24
P.O. Box 670, Rosewell, NM 88202 US
(505) 622-0658, *Fax:* (505) 622-0852
kckn1020.com
kckn@swwmail.net
License: Roswell, NM held by JCE Licenses L.L.C.
Group Owner: James Crystal Inc.; (acq 2000; $2.5 million).
Nat'l Network: AP Network News; Jones Radio Networks
Arbitron Metro Market: Kansas City, KS *Format:* Country, Religious *Special Programming:* local news 6 X daily *Hrs. of News Programming:* news progmg 5 hrs wkly *No. News Employees:* 2 *Target Audience:* 25-54; adult professionals
Jim Hilliard, President
Don Niccum, Operations Dir
Jerry Kiefer, General Manager
Bob Souza, General Sales Mgr
Don Nicuum, News Director
Bob Williams, Regional Sales Manager
Kathi Silvas, Traffic Manager

KCRX
03-15-1927; 1430 khz AM *Hrs Open:* 24; 5 kw-D, DAN; 1 kw-N, DAN; N33 26 11 W104 36 18
Mailing Address: P.O. Box 2052, Roswell, NM 88201 US
Second Address: 200 W. 1st St., Roswell, NM 88203-2052
(505) 622-1432, *Fax:* (505) 622-1432
kcrx.tripod.com
kcrx@digicominc.net
License: Roswell, NM held by Rosendo Casarez Jr.
Nat'l Network: CBS; Westwood One
Arbitron Metro Market: Roswell, NM *Format:* Oldies *No. News Employees:* 1 *Target Audience:* 35 plus. *Adv. Rates:* 5; 5; 5; 2.50
Rosendo Casarez Jr., President

KEND
05-30-1990; 106.5 mhz FM *Hrs Open:* 24; 65 kw; 135 ft.; N33 23 5 W104 43 22
P.O. Box 388, Roswell, NM 88201 US
(505) 625-2098, *Fax:* (505) 622-3877
www.themix1065.com
License: Roswell, Chaves County, NM held by Pecos Valley Broadcasting Co.
Group Owner: Pecos Valley Broadcasting Co.; (acq 4-1-2007; $500,000)
Arbitron Metro Market: Roswell, NM *Format:* Rock/AOR *Hrs. of News Programming:* News progmg 6 hrs wkly *Target Audience:* 18-34; upscale adults
Mike Winters, General Manager
K.C. Coggins, General Sales Mgr
Sean McKellips, News Director

KMOU
08-01-1992; 104.7 mhz FM *Hrs Open:* 24; 100 kw; 328 ft.; N33 24 49 W104 22 49
Mailing Address: 5206 West 2nd Street, Roswell, NM 88201 US
Second Address: 5206 W. 2nd St., Roswell, NM 88203
(505) 625-6450, *Fax:* (505) 622-9041
www.,roswellradio.org
License: Roswell, Chaves County, NM held by Roswell Radio Inc.
Group Owner: Roswell Radio Inc./Quay Broadcasters Inc.; (acq 11-22-2000; $750,000).
Format: Country *Hrs. of News Programming:* news progmg 12 hrs wkly *No. News Employees:* 2 *Adv. Rates:* 25; 20; 22; 20
John Dunn, CEO
Jeff Chace, Station Manager
Caiti Chace, General Sales Mgr

KRDD
01-01-1963; 1320 khz AM; 1 kw-D, ND2; 0.188 kw-N, ND2; N33 24 14 W104 28 12
P.O. Box 3, Santa Cruz, NM 87576 US
(505) 623-8111
krddam@yahoo.com
License: Roswell, NM held by Media Mining Group LLC
Carlos Espinoza, President
Monica Cardeas, General Sales Mgr
Ramiro Vasquez, Programming Director

KBCQ
05-01-1947; 1230 khz AM *Hrs Open:* 24
Mailing Address: 323 South Main, Roswell, NM 88210 US
Second Address: 5206 W. 2nd St., Roswell, NM 88201
, *Fax:* (505) 622-9041
www.roswellradio.org
penny@roswellradio.org
License: Roswell, NM held by Roswell Radio Inc.
Group Owner: Roswell Radio Inc./Quay Broadcasters Inc.; (acq 2-28-2003)
Nat'l Network: CNN Radio
Arbitron Metro Market: Roswell, NM *Format:* Oldies *Special Programming:* Talk 15 hrs wkly *Target Audience:* 35-75. *Adv. Rates:* 98; 115; 115; 98
John Dunn, President
Jeff Chace, Station Manager
Caiti Chace, General Sales Mgr

KSFX
03-15-1991; 100.5 mhz FM *Hrs Open:* 24; 100 kw; 121 ft.; N33 23 37 W104 36 16
Mailing Address: 5206 W. 2nd Street, Roswell, New Mexico, NY 88201 US
Second Address: 5206 W. 2nd St., Roswell, NM 88201
(505) 622-6450, *Fax:* (505) 622-9041
www.1005ksfx.com/
License: Roswell, Chaves County, NM held by Roswell Radio Inc.
Group Owner: Roswell Radio Inc./Quay Broadcasters Inc.; (acq 11-2000; grpsl)
Arbitron Metro Market: Rosewell, NM *Format:* Contemporary Hits/Top 40, Adult Contemp *Hrs. of News Programming:* news progmg 12 hrs wkly *No. News Employees:* 2 *Target Audience:* 25-49; mainstream upscale *Adv.Rates:* 25; 20; 22; 20
John Dunn, CEO
Gary Babock, President
Jeff Chace, Station Manager
Caiti Chace, General Sales Mgr
Tony Clayton, Promotions Manager
Gary Babcock, Engineering Dir

***KWFL**
12-21-1989; 99.3 mhz FM *Hrs Open:* 24; 16.5 kw; 436 ft.; N33 21 47 W104 38 11
P.O. Box 2684, Roswell, NM 88201 US
(800) 776-1050, *Fax:* (505) 296-6262
www.flc.org/flr/kwfl
kflqonair@flc.org
License: Roswell, Chaves County, NM held by Family Life Broadcasting System.
Group Owner: Family Life Communications Inc.; (acq 5-24-2004; $1)
Nat'l Network: Moody
Arbitron Metro Market: Albuquerque, NM *Format:* Religious *Target Audience:* Christian community.
Randy Carlson, President
Dan Rosecrans, General Manager

***KRLU**
01-01-2004; 90.1 mhz FM *Hrs Open:* 24; 2.4 kw vert; 394 ft.; N33 21 47 W104 38 11 *Rebroadcasts:* Rebroadcasts KLVR(FM) Middletown, CA 100%
US
(800) 525-5683, *Fax:* (916) 251-1650
www.klove.com
klove@klove.com
License: Roswell, Chaves County, NM held by Educational Media Foundation.
Group Owner: EMF Broadcasting
Nat'l Network: K-Love
Arbitron Metro Market: Roswell, NM *Format:* Christian *No. News Employees:* 13 *Target Audience:* 25-44; Judeo Christian, female
Darrell Chambliss, Chairman
Mike Novak, President and CEO
David Pierce, Programming Director
Ed Lenane, News Director
Sam Wallington, Engineering Dir
Dan Antonelli, Chief Business Development Officer
Eric Moser, Chief FinancialOfficer
Brian Burger, Vice President of Human Resources
D. Kevin Blair, Secretary and General Counsel
Tim Luttrell, News Reporter

***KQAI**
01-01-2007; 89.1 mhz FM; 2 kw vert; 207 ft.; N33 23 36 W104 37 27 *Rebroadcasts:* Rebroadcasts KLRD(FM) Yucaipa, CA 100%
US
(888) 937-2471, *Fax:* (916) 251-1650
www.air1.com
info@air1.com
License: Roswell, Chaves County, NM held by Educational Media Foundation.
Group Owner: EMF Broadcasting; (acq 9-22-2005; $40,000 for CP)
Nat'l Network: Air 1
Arbitron Metro Market: Roswell, NM *Format:* Alternative, Christian
Darrell Chambliss, Chairman
Alan Mason, COO
Mike Novak, President and CEO
Jim Marable, Operations Dir
Ed Lenane, News Director
Sam Wallington, Engineering Dir
Eric Moser, Chief Financial Officer
Brian Burger, Vice President ofHuman Resources
D. Kevin Blair, Secretary and General Counsel
Larry Moody, Director
Mitch Barnhart, Director

***KGCN**
91.7 mhz FM; 3.5 kw vert; 394 ft.; N33 21 47 W104 38 11
188 South Bellevue, Suite 222, Memphis, TN 38104 US
(916) 251-1600, *Fax:* (916) 251-1650
www.nuevavida.com
info@nuevavida.com
License: Roswell, Chaves County, NM held by Educational Media Foundation.
Group Owner: EMF Broadcasting; (acq 7-23-2007; grpsl)
Arbitron Metro Market: Roswell, NM *Format:* Christian, Spanish
Mike Novak, President

Ruidoso

KBUY
11-01-1959; 1360 khz AM *Hrs Open:* 24
Mailing Address: P.O. Box 39, Ruidoso, NM 88345 US
Second Address: 1096 Mechen Dr., Suite 230, Ruidoso, NM 88345
(505) 258-2222, *Fax:* (505) 258-2224
www.kwes.net
kwesradio@kwes.net
License: Ruidoso, NM held by Walton Stations New Mexico Inc.
Group Owner: Walton Stns; (acq 10-22-82; $475,000 with co-located FM;
Nat'l Network: Fox News Radio
Arbitron Metro Market: Ruidoso, NM *Format:* Oldies *Special Programming:* Sp 4 hrs wkly *Hrs. of News Programming:* news progmg 14 hrs wkly *No. News Employees:* 1 *Target Audience:* 38 plus; 25-54 females*Adv. Rates:* 10; 10; 10; 10
Steve Hall, Programming Director
Gary Herron, News Director
Steve Swayze, Chief Engineer

KWES-FM
01-01-1982; 93.5 mhz FM *Hrs Open:* 24; 25 kw; 187 ft.; N33 23 12 W105 40 14
P.O. Box 39, Ruidoso, NM 88355 US

(505) 258-2222, *Fax:* (505) 258-2224
www.kwes.net
shall@kwes.net
License: Ruidoso, Lincoln County, NM held by Walton Stations New Mexico Inc.
Group Owner: Walton Stns
Nat'l Network: Jones Radio Networks
Arbitron Metro Market: Ruidoso, NM *Format:* Country *Hrs. of News Programming:* news progmg 17 hrs wkly *No. News Employees:* 1 *Target Audience:* 18-54. *Adv. Rates:* Same as AM
Steve Swayze, General Manager
Juanita, General Sales Mgr
Steve Swayze, Programming Director
Kelly Capece, Promotions Manager
Gary Herron, News Director

KIDX
01-01-2000; 101.5 mhz FM; 0.92 kw; 2851 ft.; N33 24 14 W105 46 56
P.O. Drawer 2010, Ruidoso, NM 88346 US
(505) 258-9922, *Fax:* (505) 258-2363
www.kidxradio.com
kidx@mtdradio.com
License: Ruidoso, Lincoln County, NM held by MTD Inc.
Group Owner: MTD Inc.
Arbitron Metro Market: Ruidoso, NM *Format:* Classic Rock
Tim Keithley, General Manager

*KYCT
91.3 mhz FM; 0.235 kw; 2894 ft.; N33 24 15.2 W105 46 54.7
9019 West Lane, Stockton, CA 95210 US
(209) 477-3690, *Fax:* (209) 477-2762
www.kycc.org
kycc@kycc.org
License: Ruidoso, Lincoln County, NM held by Your Christian Companion Network Inc.
Arbitron Metro Market: Ruidoso, NM *Format:* Adult Contemp, Gospel, 74
Shirley Garner, General Manager
Scott Mearns, Office Manager
John Ramos, Office Manager
Gary Harding, Production Manager

KWES
01-01-2008; 1450 khz AM
US
(575) 258-2222, *Fax:* (575) 258-2224
www.kwes.net
shall@kwes.net
License: Ruidoso, NM held by Walton Stations New Mexico Inc.
Group Owner: Walton Stns
Nat'l Network: Fox Sports
Arbitron Metro Market: Ruidoso, NM *Format:* Sports
John Walton, President
Steve Swayze, General Manager
Juanita Jones, General Sales Mgr

Ruidoso Downs

KRUI
04-01-1984; 1490 khz AM *Hrs Open:* 24; 1 kw-U, ND1; N33 19 17 W105 35 24
105 Sierra Lane, Ruidoso Downs, NM 88346 US
(505) 258-9922, *Fax:* (505) 258-2363
www.1490krui.com
production@mtbradio.com
License: Ruidoso Downs, NM held by MTD Inc.
Group Owner: MTD Inc.; acq 12-88; $20,000;
Nat'l Network: Westwood One
Arbitron Metro Market: Ruidoso, NM *Format:* News, Sports, 86 *Hrs. of News Programming:* News progmg 14 hrs wkly *Adv. Rates:* 20; 10; 10; 5
Tim Keithley, General Manager

Santa Clara

KNUW
01-01-1996; 95.1 mhz FM *Hrs Open:* 24; 7.7 kw; 1549 ft.; N32 51 47 W108 14 28
106 South Bullard Street, Silver City, NM 88061 US
(505) 534-8700, *Fax:* (505) 534-8702
knuw@zianet.com
License: Santa Clara, Grant County, NM held by Duran-Hill, Inc.
Target Audience: General; Hispanic
George Mesa, President
Cecilia Soza, General Sales Mgr
Ken Bass, Engineering Dir

Santa Fe

KJFA
09-28-1985; 105.1 mhz FM; 100 kw; 1896 ft.; N35 46 49 W106 31 34
57 West South Temple, Suite 700, Salt Lake City, UT 84101 US
(505) 262-1142, *Fax:* (505) 254-7106
www.kjfa.univision.com/?origRef=http%3A%2F%2Ftunein.com%2Fradio%2FLa-Jefa-1051-s33580
License: Santa Fe, Santa Fe County, NM held by Univision Radio License Corp.
Group Owner: Univision Radio; (acq 9-22-2003; grpsl)
Arbitron Metro Market: Albuquerque, NM *Format:* Tejano *Target Audience:* 35-54.
Chuck Morgan, General Manager

KKOB Exp S
01-01-1986; 770 khz AM; 230 w-U; N35 40 56 W105 58 21
Rebroadcasts: Rebroadcasts KKOB(AM) Albuquerque 100%
500 4th St. N.W., Suite 500, Albuquerque, NM 87102
(505) 767-6700, *Fax:* (505) 767-6767
www.770kkob.com
License: Santa Fe, Santa Fe County, NM held by Citadel Broadcasting Co.
Nat'l Reps: McGavren Guild
Format: Adult Contemp
Pat Frisch, Operations Dir
Milt McConnell, Station Manager
Dennis Logsdon, General Sales Mgr
Pat Frish, Programming Director
Glen Hebert, Promotions Manager
Mike Langner, Chief Engineer
Art Ortega, Public Affairs Director

KKSS
03-01-1969; 97.3 mhz FM *Hrs Open:* 24; 94 kw; 1877 ft.; N35 46 50 W106 31 35
57 West South Temple, Suite 700, Salt Lake City, UT 84101 US
(505) 262-1142, *Fax:* (505) 254-7106
License: Santa Fe, Santa Fe County, NM held by Univision Radio License Corp.
Group Owner: Univision Radio; (acq 9-22-2003; grpsl).
Nat'l Reps: D & R Radio
Arbitron Metro Market: Albuquerque, NM *Format:* Contemporary Hits/Top 40 *Target Audience:* 18-34; Hispanic females
Chuck Morgan, General Manager

KTEG
11-24-1983; 104.1 mhz FM *Hrs Open:* 24; 100 kw; 1877 ft.; N35 46 50 W106 31 35
900 Oakmont Lane, #210, Westmont, IL 60559 US
(505) 830-6400, *Fax:* (505) 830-6599
www.1041theedge.com
info@ktegfm.com
License: Santa Fe, Santa Fe County, NM held by Citicasters Licenses Inc.
Group Owner: Clear Channel Communications Inc.; (acq 1-27-2009)
Arbitron Metro Market: Albuquerque, NM *Format:* Alternative
Bill May, Operations Dir
Chuck Hammond, General Manager

KHFM
08-15-1965; 95.5 mhz FM *Hrs Open:* 24; 17.5 kw; 1791 ft.; N35 46 49 W106 31 37
P.O. Box 2700, Bakersfield, CA 93303 US
(505) 878-0980, *Fax:* (505) 889-0617
www.classicalkhfm.com
lgold@americangeneralmedia.com,kallen@americangeneralmedia.com
License: Santa Fe, Santa Fe County, NM held by AGM-Nevada L.L.C.
Group Owner: American General Media
Arbitron Metro Market: Albuquerque, NM *Format:* Talk *Target Audience:* 18-49.
Bob Bishop, Programming Director

KRZY-FM
11-02-1983; 105.9 mhz FM *Hrs Open:* 24; 100 kw; 1919 ft.; N35 46 49 W106 31 34
2905 South King Road, San Jose, CA 95122 US
(505) 342-4141, *Fax:* (505) 344-8714
www.jose1059.com
mwilder@entravision.com
License: Santa Fe, Santa Fe County, NM held by Entravision Holdings LLC.
Group Owner: Entravision Communications Corp.; (acq 3-14-2000; grpsl).
Arbitron Metro Market: Albuquerque, NM *Target Audience:* 18-34.
Margarita Wilder, General Manager

KSWV
06-01-1966; 810 khz AM
P.O. Box 1088, Santa Fe, NM 87504 US
(505) 989-7441, *Fax:* (505) 989-7607
kswvanthonygonzales@yahoo.com
License: Santa Fe, NM held by La Voz Broadcasting Co.
Arbitron Metro Market: Santa Fe, NM *Format:* Spanish *Target Audience:* 25-54.
Celine Gonzales, President
George Gonzales, General Manager
George Gonzales, General Sales Mgr
Anthony Gonzales, Programming Director
John Chidester, Chief Engineer

KVSF
02-20-1947; 1400 khz AM; 1 kw-U, ND1; N35 40 56 W105 58 21
PO Box 1508, 3501 Broadway, Mount Vernon, IL 62864 US
(505) 471-1067, *Fax:* (505) 473-2667
www.espnsantafe.com
scott@huttonbroadcasting.com
License: Santa Fe, NM held by Hutton Broadcasting LLC.
Group Owner: Hutton Broadcasting LLC; (acq 6-5-2006; $350,000) .
Nat'l Network: ESPN Radio
Arbitron Metro Market: Santa Fe, NM *Format:* Sports
Edward Hutton, President
Scott Hutton, General Manager
Ira Gordon, Programming Director
Eric Davis, Promotions Manager
Ted Levin, Chief Engineer

KTRC
01-01-1935; 1260 khz AM *Hrs Open:* 12a-12a; 5 kw-D, ND1; 1 kw-N, ND1; N35 40 56 W105 58 21
3501 Broadway, PO Box 1508, Mount Vernon, IL 62864 US
(505) 471-1067, *Fax:* (505) 473-2667
www.santafe.com/espn
talk@talk1260.com
License: Santa Fe, NM held by Hutton Broadcasting L.L.C.
Group Owner: Hutton Broadcasting LLC; acq 11-2008
Nat'l Network: Air America; CNN Radio
Arbitron Metro Market: Santa Fe, NM *Format:* Alternative, News, 86 *Target Audience:* 35-64; involved affluent adults
Edward Hutton, President
Scott Hutton, General Manager
Ira Gordon, Programming Director
Eric Davis, Promotions Manager
Ted Levin, Chief Engineer

KKIM-FM
01-01-2000; 94.7 mhz FM; 100 kw; 797 ft.; N36 5 21 W106 1 41
P.O. Box 1508, 3501 Broadway, Mount Vernon, IL 62864 US
(505) 878-0980, *Fax:* (505) 878-0098
www.mykkim.com/
dewey@mykkim.com
License: Santa Fe, Santa Fe County, NM held by AGM Nevada LLC.
Group Owner: American General Media; (acq 1996; $96,250)
Arbitron Metro Market: Santa Fe, NM *Format:* Christian, News, 62, Talk
Dewey Moede, Station Manager
Dewey Moede, General Sales Mgr

Santa Rosa

KSSR-FM
01-01-2001; 95.9 mhz FM; 1.5 kw; Ant 118 ft; N34 56 47 W104 39 10 *Rebroadcasts:* Rebroadcasts KSSR(AM) Santa Rosa 100%
Mailing Address: HC 69 Box 78, Santa Rosa, NM 87110
Second Address: 2818 Historic Rt. 66, Santa Rosa, NM 88435
(505) 472-5777,(505) 472-3752, *Fax:* (505) 472-5777
License: Santa Rosa, Guadalupe County, NM held by Cibola Radio Co.

Gabriel Esquibel, General Manager

*KNLK
01-01-2004; 91.9 mhz FM; 0.1 kw; -26 ft.; N34 57 20 W104 40 53
2020 Coal Ave., S.E., Albuquerque, NM 87106 US
(505) 242-7163
www.kanw.com
larry.smith@aps.edu
License: Santa Rosa, Guadalupe County, NM held by Board of Education of the City of Albuquerque, NM.
Arbitron Metro Market: Santa Rosa, NM
Michael Brasher, General Manager

Shiprock

*KFDC
90.5 mhz FM; kw

US
(505) 368-1028
License: Shiprock, San Juan County, NM held by Dine Agriculture Inc.
Arbitron Metro Market: Shiprock, NM
Gilbert Yazzie, General Manager

Silver City

KSCQ
11-28-1989; 92.9 mhz FM *Hrs Open:* 24; 11.5 kw; 1024 ft.; N32 50 40 W108 14 18
Mailing Address: 1872 Highway 180 East, Silver City, NM 88061 US
Second Address: 1560 N. Corbin St., Silver City, NM 88061
(505) 388-4116, *Fax:* (505) 388-1759
theq929.com
events@silvercityradio.com
License: Silver City, Grant County, NM held by Skywest Media LLC
Group Owner: SkyWest Media L.L.C.; (acq 10-31-2005; $330,000).
Arbitron Metro Market: Silver City, NM *Format:* Adult Contemp *Hrs. of News Programming:* News progmg 3 hrs wkly *Target Audience:* 25-55; baby boomers, generation X *Adv. Rates:* 10; 10; 10; 10
Sabrina Pack, General Manager
Ted Tucker, Programming Director

Socorro

KMXQ
01-22-1995; 92.9 mhz FM *Hrs Open:* 24; 0.137 kw; -177 ft.; N34 2 43 W106 54 21
Mailing Address: P.O. Box 30570, Albuquerque, NM 87190 US
Second Address: 834 Hwy. 60 W., Socorro, NM 87801
(505) 835-1286, *Fax:* (505) 835-2015
kmxq@sdc.org,vvigil@sdc.org
License: Socorro, Socorro County, NM held by Lakeshore Media L.L.C.
Format: Country *Special Programming:* Farm 2 hrs, talk one hr wkly *Hrs. of News Programming:* 167 hrs wkly *No. News Employees:* 4 *Target Audience:* 12 plus. *Adv. Rates:* 14; 14; 14; 14
Virgil Vigil, General Manager
George Funkhoustol, News Director
Deb Hoyland, News Commentator
John Gonzales

*KXFR
01-01-2008; 91.9 mhz FM; 25 kw; 243 ft.; N34 23 44 W107 0 42
Rebroadcasts: Rebroadcasts KUFR(FM) Salt Lake City, UT 100%
4135 Northgate Blvd, Suite 1, Sacramento, CA 95834 US
(800) 543-1495, *Fax:* (801) 359-8112
www.familyradio.com
familyradio@familyradio.org
License: Socorro, Socorro County, NM held by Family Stations Inc.
Group Owner: Family Stations Inc.
Nat'l Network: Family Radio
Arbitron Metro Market: Socorro, NM *Format:* Christian
Harold Egbert, President
Jennifer Grant, Operations Dir
Harold Egbert, General Manager
Dan Elyea, Station Manager
Pattie Wagner, General Sales Mgr
Eel Dearborn, Chief Engineer

*KBOM
02-15-2008; 88.7 mhz FM; 0.1 kw; 1877 ft.; N34 4 17 W106 57 44 *Rebroadcasts:* Rebroadcasts KUNM(FM) Albuquerque 100%
Room 326 Onate Hall, University of Nm, Aluquerque, NM 87131 US
(505) 277-4806
www.kunm.org
kunm@kunm.org
License: Socorro, Socorro County, NM held by Regents of the University of New Mexico.
Arbitron Metro Market: Socorro, NM *Format:* Public Affairs, Variety/Diverse
Richard Towne, General Manager
Tristan Clum, Programming Director
Mike Stark, Chief Engineer
Alaina George, Production Assistant
Jeff Maness, Engineering Assistant
Jonathan Longcore, Network Administrator
Roman Garcia, ProductionDirector
Scott MacNicholl, Operations Manager
Tristan Clum, Program Director

KYRN
01-01-2009; 102.1 mhz FM; 0.25 kw; -476 ft.; N34 4 35 W106 54 29
US
(920) 271-1000, *Fax:* (920) 271-1010
www.sovcity.com
info@sovcity.com
License: Socorro, Socorro County, NM held by Sovereign City Radio Services LLC.
Arbitron Metro Market: Socorro, NM
Scott Krusinski, Operations Dir

Taos

KXMT
12-01-2000; 99.1 mhz FM; 60 kw; 2136 ft.; N36 51 32 W106 0 28
Mailing Address: P.O. Box 2158, Ketchum, ID 83340 US
Second Address: 125A Camino de la Merced, Taos, NM 87571-5119
(575) 758-4491, *Fax:* (505) 758-4452
www.kxmt.com
darren@kxmt.com; cordova@kxmt.com; brenda@kxmt.com; jojo@kxmt.com; gerryk@kxmt.com; karen@kxmt.com;
License: Taos, Taos County, NM held by DMC Broadcasting Inc.
Group Owner: DMC Broadcasting Inc.; (acq 3-19-2003; $645,000 with KKTC(FM) Angel Fire).
Format: Tejano *Target Audience:* Locals, Spanish speakers
Darren Cordova, President
Jeff Singer, Operations Dir
Jojo Valdez, General Sales Mgr
Jennifer Trujillo, News Director
Darren Lee Cordova, Vice President
Brenda Cordova, VP Human Resources
Andrew Alaniz, Web Administrator

KTAO
01-01-1978; 101.9 mhz FM *Hrs Open:* 6 AM-2 AM; 1.2 kw; 2795 ft.; N36 14 48 W105 39 15
P.O. Box 1844, Taos, NM 87571 US
(575) 758-5826, *Fax:* (505) 758-8430
www.ktao.com
ktaoo@newmex.com
License: Taos, Taos County, NM held by Taos Communications Corp.
Arbitron Metro Market: Taos, NM *Format:* Triple A *Special Programming:* Jazz 3 hrs, Roots & Wires, 5 hrs; maccasin wire, 3 hrs; world on tour, 2 hrs; celtic 4 hrs; Sonido del sol, 3 hrs. *Hrs. of News Programming:* newsprogmg 7 hrs wkly *No. News Employees:* 2 *Target Audience:* 25-49; educated, responsive, upwardly mobile *Adv. Rates:* 18; 18; 18; 5
Brad Hockmeyer, CEO
Dave Noll, Operations Dir
Paddy Mac, Music Director

KKIT
01-01-2005; 95.9 mhz FM *Hrs Open:* 24; 4 kw; -630 ft.; N36 23 22 W105 35 9
Mailing Address: US
Second Address: 125A Camino de la Merced, Taos, NM 87571-5119
(505) 758-4491, *Fax:* (505) 758-4452
www.radiotaos.com
production@kxmt.com
License: Taos, Taos County, NM held by DMC Broadcasting Inc.
Group Owner: DMC Broadcasting Inc.
Nat'l Network: ABC
Format: Adult Contemp
Jeff Singer, Operations Dir
Pattee Brown, General Sales Mgr
Jennifer Trujillo, News Director

KVOT
01-01-2005; 1340 khz AM *Hrs Open:* 25.?Â ?
Mailing Address: US
Second Address: 125A Camino de la Merced, Taos, NM 87571-5119
(505) 758-4491, *Fax:* (505) 758-4452
License: Taos, NM held by DMC Broadcasting Inc.
Group Owner: DMC Broadcasting Inc.; (acq 12-20-2005)
Nat'l Network: ABC
Arbitron Metro Market: Tucson, AZ *Format:* Talk
Jeff Singer, Operations Dir
Pattee Brown, General Sales Mgr
Jennifer Trujillo, News Director

Tatum

KTUM
01-01-2003; 107.1 mhz FM; 100 kw; 919 ft.; N32 52 50 W103 41 1
P O Drawer 2010, Ruidoso Downs, NM 88346 US
(505) 396-0499, *Fax:* (505) 396-8349
www.1071thenerve.com
thenerve@mtdradio.com
License: Tatum, Lea County, NM held by MTD Inc.
Group Owner: MTD Inc.
Arbitron Metro Market: Ruidoso, NM *Format:* Classic Rock
Tim Keithley, General Manager
Will Rooney, Station Manager

Thoreau

KXTC
10-21-1991; 99.9 mhz FM *Hrs Open:* 24; 100 kw; 1211 ft.; N35 36 13 W108 40 45
427 Bedford Road, Suite 300, Pleasantville, NY 10570 US
(505) 863-9391, *Fax:* (505) 863-9393
www.999xtc.com
maryannarmijo@clearchannel.com
License: Thoreau, McKinley County, NM held by Clear Channel Broadcasting Licenses Inc.
Group Owner: Clear Channel Communications Inc.; (acq 9-7-2000)
Arbitron Metro Market: Gallup, NM *Format:* Contemporary Hits/Top 40 *Special Programming:* American Indian one hr, Sp 8 hrs wkly *Hrs. of News Programming:* news progmg 2 hrs wkly *No. News Employees:* 2 *TargetAudience:* 18-44; Women *Adv. Rates:* 14; 14; 14; 8
MaryAnn Armijo, General Manager

Truth or Consequence

*KRJY
01-01-1938; 91.1 mhz FM *Hrs Open:* 24; kw
Mailing Address: US
Second Address: Box 1228, Sacramento, CA 95812
(916) 553-3000, *Fax:* (916) 553-3013
License: Truth or Consequence, Sacramento County, NM held by Diamond Broadcasting
Nat'l Network: CBS Radio
Arbitron Metro Market: Sacramento, CA *Format:* Gospel *Target Audience:* 18 plus.
Frank Redfield, Operations Dir
Paula Nelson, General Manager
Misty Pryce, General Sales Mgr
Kydd Mossie, Programming Director
Tony Williams, Promotions Manager

Truth or Consequences

KCHS
09-01-1944; 1400 khz AM *Hrs Open:* 6am-11pm 7days a wk; 1 kw-U; N33 08 26 W107 13 55
Mailing Address: Box 351, Truth or Consequences, NM 87901
Second Address: 1747 E Third Ave., Truth or Consequences, NM 87901
(575) 894-2400, *Fax:* (575) 894-3998
www.gpkmedia.com
kchs@gpkmedia.com
License: Truth or Consequences, Sierra County, NM held by Myrna Baird-Kohs dba GPK Media LLC
Nat'l Network: AP Radio
Population Served: 13,000*No. News Employees:* 4 *Target Audience:* General; area residents & visitors at lake
Patrick Kohs, President
Patrick Kohs, Operations Dir
Patrick Kohs, General Manager
Patrick Kohs, Station Manager
Frances Luna, General Sales Mgr
Patrick Kohs, Programming Director
Frances Luna, Promotions Manager
Patrick Kohs,News Director

KKVS
11-01-1984; 98.7 mhz FM *Hrs Open:* 24; 49 kw; Ant 2,644 ft; N32 58 15 W107 13 26
Mailing Address: P.O. Box 968, Las Cruces, NM 88004
Second Address: 1355 E. California Ave., Las Cruces, NM 88001
(575) 525-9298, *Fax:* (575) 525-9419
www.vista.fm
radiolc@kgrt.com
License: Truth or Consequences, Sierra County, NM held by Richardson Commercial Corp.
Nat'l Network: La Gran D
Population Served: 174,100 *Arbitron Metro Market:* Las Cruces, NM *No. News Employees:* 1 *Target Audience:* 25-54; Hispanic
Allen Lumeyer, Operations Dir
Veronica Vaillancourt-Test, General Sales Mgr
Ernesto Garcia, Programming Director
Tamara Blaeser, National Sales Manager

Tse Bonito

KHAC
03-21-1967; 880 khz AM; 10 kw-D, ND1; 0.43 kw-N, ND1; N35 38 41 W109 1 13
P.O. Box 9090, Window Rock, AZ 86515 US
(505) 371-5587, *Fax:* (505) 371-5588
www.westernindian.org
khac@westernindian.org
License: Tse Bonito, NM held by Western Indian Ministries.
Format: Christian *Special Programming:* children's 8 hrs wkly *No. News Employees:* 1 *Target Audience:* American Indian
Larry Harper, General Manager
Greg Lewis, Station Manager
Bruce Kinde, Engineering Dir
Scott Hill, Chief Engineer

Tucumcari

KQAY-FM
01-19-1968; 92.7 mhz FM; 3 kw; 412 ft.; N35 8 23 W103 44 35
P.O. Box 668, Tucumcari, NM 88401 US
(505) 461-0522, *Fax:* (505) 461-0092
www.tucumari.was
ktmnkqay@yahoo.com
License: Tucumcari, Quay County, NM
Group Owner: Roswell Radio Inc./Quay Broadcasters Inc.
Format: Country
Mike Martin, General Manager

KTNM
01-01-1941; 1400 khz AM; 1 kw-U, ND1; N35 10 15 W103 42 25
P.O. Box 668, Tucumcari, NM 88202 US
(505) 461-0522(505) 461-1400, *Fax:* (505) 461-0092
www.tucumcari.ws
ktnmkqay@yahoo.com
License: Tucumcari, NM held by Quay Broadcasters Inc.
Group Owner: Roswell Radio Inc./Quay Broadcasters Inc.; (acq 1-10-2003; with co-located FM)
Nat'l Network: ABC
Arbitron Metro Market: Tucumcari, NM *Format:* Country *Special Programming:* Sp 18 hrs wkly *Target Audience:* General.
Diane Paris, General Manager
Greg Carnefix, Programming Director

*KVLP
01-01-2009; 91.7 mhz FM; 0.57 kw; 312 ft.; N35 8 23 W103 44 35 *Rebroadcasts:* Rebroadcasts KLVR(FM) Middletown, CA 100%
P. O. Box 1458, Washington, DC 20013 US
(916) 251-1600, *Fax:* (916) 251-1650
www.klove.com
klove@klove.com
License: Tucumcari, Quay County, NM held by Educational Media Foundation.
Group Owner: EMF Broadcasting; (acq 3-23-2007; grpsl)
Nat'l Network: K-Love
Arbitron Metro Market: Tucumcari, NM *Format:* Christian
Darrell Chambliss, Chairman
Alan Mason, CEO/COO
Mike Novak, CEO
David Pierce, Chief Creative Officer
Dan Antonelli, Chief Business Development Officer
Eric Moser, Chief Financial Officer
Brian Burger, Vice President of HumanResources
D. Kevin Blair, Secretary and General Counsel

*KENM
09-03-2011; 88.9 mhz FM; 3 kw; 869 ft.; N35 8 3 W103 41 53 *Rebroadcasts:* KENW-FM
US
(575) 562-2112, *Fax:* (575) 562-2590
www.kenw.org
kenwfm@enmu.edu
License: Tucumcari, Quay County, NM held by Eastern New Mexico University.
Nat'l Network: NPR; BSN; APM; PRX
Arbitron Metro Market: Tucumcari, NM *No. News Employees:* 2
Orlando Ortega, Operations Dir
Duane Ryan, General Manager
Jenifer Baca, Programming Director
Rena Garrett, Promotions Manager
James Lee, News Director
Jeff Burmeister, Engineering Dir
Martin Quintero, Chief Engineer
CarlaChacon, Development Director, FM
Don Criss, Production/Community Services Director

Tularosa

*KNMA
05-05-2008; 88.1 mhz FM; 7 kw vert; 1900 ft.; N32 49 49 W105 53 25 *Rebroadcasts:* Rebroadcasts KAWZ(FM) Twin Falls, ID 100%
US
(505) 533-6100, *Fax:* (503) 533-6103
www.csnradio.com
License: Tularosa, Otero County, NM held by Calvary Chapel of Twin Falls Inc.
Group Owner: CSN International
Nat'l Network: CSN
Format: Christian
Mike Kestler, President
Don Mills, Station Manager

White Rock

KSFR
01-01-1991; 101.1 mhz FM *Hrs Open:* 24; 2.5 kw; Ant 1,863 ft; N35 53 09 W106 23 16
6401 S. Richards Ave., Santa Fe, NM 87505
(505) 428-1527, *Fax:* (505) 424-8938
www.ksfr.org
info@ksfr.org
License: White Rock, Los Alamos County, NM held by Santa Fe Community College
Population Served: 147,000 *Arbitron Metro Market:* Santa Fe, NM *Special Programming:* American Indian 4 hrs, Sp 4 hrs wkly *Hrs. of News Programming:* news progmg 14 hrs wkly *No. News Employees:* 1 *TargetAudience:* General.
Sean Conlon, Operations Dir
Linda Highill, General Manager
William Dupuy, News Director

Zuni

*KSHI
04-06-1978; 90.9 mhz FM *Hrs Open:* 8am - 5pm; 0.1 kw; -249 ft.; N35 5 18 W108 47 22
P.O. Box 339, Zuni, NM 87327 US
(505) 782-4811, *Fax:* (505) 782-2232
zuniradio@gmail.com
License: Zuni, McKinley County, NM held by Zuni Communications Authority.
Special Programming: Indian 20 hrs wkly *Target Audience:* 18-34; primarily Indian
Duane Chimoni, General Manager

New York

Acra

*WGXC
90.7 mhz FM; 0.125 kw horiz, 3.3 kw vert; 312 ft.; N42 19 43 W73 58 15
US
(518) 622-2598
www.wgxc.org
info@wgxc.org
License: Acra, Greene County, NY held by free103point9
Arbitron Metro Market: Acra, NY *Format:* Reggae
Melissa Dubbin, President
Galen Joseph-Hunter, General Sales Mgr
Tom Roe, Programming Director

Albany

*WAMC
01-01-1934; 1400 khz AM *Rebroadcasts:* wamc(FM) 97%
Mailing Address: 12 Dennis Terrace, Schenectady, NY 12303 US
Second Address: 318 Central Ave., Albany, NY 12206
(662) 844-8888, *Fax:* (662) 842-6791
www.afr.net
License: Albany, NY held by WAMC.
Group Owner: WAMC/Northeast Public Radio; (acq 4-24-03; $500,000).
Nat'l Network: NPR; PRI *Wire Services:* AP
Arbitron Metro Market: Tyler-Longview TX *Format:* Christian
Marvin Sanders, General Manager

*WAMC-FM
10-01-1958; 90.3 mhz FM *Hrs Open:* 24; 10 kw; 1969 ft.; N42 38 14 W73 10 7
318 Central Avenue, Albany, NY 12206 US
(518) 465-5233(800) 323-9262, *Fax:* (518) 432-6974
www.wamc.org
mail@wamc.org
License: Albany, Albany County, NY held by WAMC.
Group Owner: WAMC/Northeast Public Radio; (acq 7-1-82)
Nat'l Network: NPR; PRI *Wire Services:* AP
Arbitron Metro Market: Albany NY *Format:* News, Talk *Special Programming:* Jazz 18 hrs, folk 7 hrs *Hrs. of News Programming:* news progmg 48 hrs wkly *No. News Employees:* 11 *Target Audience:* General.
Alan Chartock, CEO
Selma Kaplan, Operations Dir
David Galletly, Vice President

*WCDB
03-01-1978; 90.9 mhz FM *Hrs Open:* 24; 0.1 kw; 210 ft.; N42 41 16 W73 49 19
1400 Washington Avenue, Albany, NY 12222 US
(518) 442-5234(518) 442-5262, *Fax:* (518) 442-4366
www.wcdb.albany.edu
info@wcdb.com
License: Albany, Albany County, NY held by State University of New York.
Arbitron Metro Market: Albany, NY *Format:* Rock/AOR, Variety/Diverse *Special Programming:* Gospel 3 hrs, Sp 3 hrs, dance 3 hrs, jazz 10 hrs, metal 10 hrs wkly *Hrs. of News Programming:* News progmg 15 hrs wkly*Target Audience:* 15-55; students & surrounding community
Michael Di Pietro, General Manager

WDDY
06-14-1924; 1460 khz AM *Hrs Open:* 24; 5 kw-D, DAN; 5 kw-N, DAN; N42 37 21 W73 48 9
600 Congress Ave., Suite 1400, Austin, TX 78701 US
(518) 464-1311, *Fax:* (518) 464-4185
www.radiodisney.com
License: Albany, NY held by Radio Disney Group LLC.
Group Owner: ABC Inc.; (acq 2-12-02; $2 million).
Nat'l Network: ABC *Nat'l Reps:* Katz Radio
Arbitron Metro Market: Albany-Schenectady-Troy, NY *Format:* Children *No. News Employees:* 1 *Target Audience:* 25-54; general
Rob Thomson, General Manager
Sarah Wiseman, Promotions Manager

WGNA-FM
12-01-1973; 107.7 mhz FM; 12.5 kw; 984 ft.; N42 38 13 W73 59 51
600 Congress Ave., Suite 1400, Austin, TX 78701 US
(518) 881-1515, *Fax:* (518) 881-1516
www.wgna.com
wgna1077@aol.com
License: Albany, Albany County, NY
Group Owner: Townsquare Media; (acq 8-24-2001; grpsl).
Arbitron Metro Market: Albany-Schenectady-Troy, NY *Format:* Country
Robert Ausfeld, General Manager
John Hirsch, Station Manager

WGY-FM
09-01-1966; 103.1 mhz FM; 6 kw; 328 ft; N42 39 46 W73 40 37
1203 Troy-Schenectady Rd., Latham, NY 17106
(518) 452-4800, *Fax:* (518) 452-4855
www.wgy.com
feedback@channel1031.com
License: Albany, Albany County, NY held by CC Licenses LLC.
Group Owner: Clear Channel Communications Inc.; (acq 8-5-98; grpsl)
Nat'l Reps: Clear Channel
Population Served: 114,873 *Arbitron Metro Market:* Albany-Schenectady-Troy, NY *Target Audience:* 21-54; upscale arrivers *Adv. Rates:* 50; 45; 45; 35
Kristen Delaney, Operations Dir
John Cooper, Station Manager
Lisa Biello, Operations Director

WKLI-FM
01-01-1972; 100.9 mhz FM *Hrs Open:* 24; 6 kw; 299 ft.; N42 43 54 W73 52 56
320 West College Ave., Pleasant Gap, PA 16823 US
(518) 786-6600, *Fax:* (518) 786-6610
www.albanymagic.com
info@albanymagic.com
License: Albany, Albany County, NY held by 6 Johnson Road Licenses Inc.
Group Owner: Pamal Broadcasting Ltd.; (acq 10-9-2001).
Nat'l Network: CBS Radio
Arbitron Metro Market: Albany-Schenectady-Troy, NY *Format:* Adult Contemp *Target Audience:* 25-54; upscale women *Adv. Rates:* 150; 140; 140; 50
Kevin Callahan, Operations Dir
Dan Austin, General Manager
Suzette Anthony, General Sales Mgr
Jay Scott, Programming Director
Jillian Shuhart, Promotions Manager
Mike Carey, News Director

WPYX
09-16-1980; 106.5 mhz FM *Hrs Open:* 24; 15.5 kw; 902 ft.; N42 38 9 W74 0 5
600 Congress Ave., Suite 1400, Austin, TX 78701 US
(518) 452-4800, *Fax:* (518) 452-4855
www.pyx106.com
feedback@pyx106.com
License: Albany, Albany County, NY held by Capstar TX L.P.
Group Owner: Clear Channel Communications Inc.; (acq 8-30-00; grpsl).
Arbitron Metro Market: Albany-Schenectady-Troy, NY *Format:* Classic Rock *Target Audience:* 25-54.
Kristen Delaney, Operations Dir
John Cooper, Station Manager
Nicholas Lombardi, General Sales Mgr
John Cooper, Programming Director
Jill Manti, Promotions Manager

WROW
09-30-1947; 590 khz AM *Hrs Open:* 24; 5 kw-D, DA2; 1 kw-N, DA2; N42 34 25 W73 47 12
6 Johnson Road, Latham, NY 12110 US
(518) 786-6600, *Fax:* (518) 786-6610
www.wrow.com
info@wrow.com
License: Albany, NY held by 6 Johnson Road Licenses Inc.
Group Owner: Pamal Broadcasting Ltd.; (acq 10-19-2001; grpsl).
Nat'l Network: CBS *Nat'l Reps:* McGavren Guild *Wire Services:* AP
Arbitron Metro Market: Albany-Schenectady-Troy, NY *Format:* News, News/Talk, 86 *Special Programming:* Gospel 3 hrs wkly *Hrs. of News Programming:* news progmg 8 hrs wkly *No. News Employees:* 3 *Target Audience:* 35 plus; affluent, educated, white collar, upwardly mobile, homeowners
Jim Morrell, President
Kevin Callahan, Operations Dir
Dan Austin, General Manager
Suzette Anthony, General Sales Mgr
Paul Vandenburg, Programming Director
Mike Carey, News Director

WYJB
10-01-1966; 95.5 mhz FM; 12 kw; 1024 ft.; N42 38 11 W74 0 0
6 Johnson Road, Latham, NY 12110 US
(518) 786-6600, *Fax:* (518) 786-6610
www.b95.com
info@b95.com
License: Albany, Albany County, NY
Group Owner: Pamal Broadcasting Ltd.
Nat'l Reps: McGavren Guild
Arbitron Metro Market: Albany, NY *Format:* Adult Contemp *No. News Employees:* 3 *Target Audience:* 25-54. *Adv. Rates:* 275; 275; 250; 75
Kevin Callahan, Operations Dir
Chuck Taylor, Programming Director
Chad O'Hara, Promotions Manager
Darrin Kibbey, Marketing

Albion

***WJCA**
12-27-2001; 102.1 mhz FM; 3.7 kw; 423 ft.; N43 11 19 W78 8 53
Mailing Address: 3000 W. Macarthur Blvd., 3rd Floor, Santa Ana, CA 92704 US
Second Address: 8917 World Ministry Ave., Baton Rouge, LA 70810
(225) 768-8300, *Fax:* (225) 768-3729
www.jsm.org
kawikfish@yahoo.com
License: Albion, Orleans County, NY held by Family Worship Center Church Inc.
Group Owner: Family Worship Center Church Inc.; (acq 1-30-2006; $950,000).
Arbitron Metro Market: Baton Rouge, LA *Format:* Christian
David Whitelaw, COO
Jimmy Swaggart, President
John Santiago, Programming Director

Alfred

***WALF**
01-01-1971; 89.7 mhz FM; 0.2 kw; -20 ft.; N42 15 17 W77 47 13
C/O Dr. Joseph Gow, Saxon Drive, Alfred, NY 14802 US
(607) 871-2287
www.walf.fm
info@walf.org
License: Alfred, Allegany County, NY held by Alfred University.
Nat'l Network: NPR
Arbitron Metro Market: Alfred, NY *Format:* Variety/Diverse
Ben Duffy, General Manager

***WETD**
03-19-1973; 90.7 mhz FM *Hrs Open:* 24; 3.2 kw; 299 ft.; N42 15 37 W77 47 51
State University Plaza, Albany, NY 12246 US
(607) 587-2907
www.wetd.fm
wetd@alfredstate.edu
License: Alfred, Allegany County, NY held by State University of New York.
Arbitron Metro Market: Alfred, NY *Format:* Rock/AOR *Target Audience:* 18-22; college students
Mark Amman, Operations Dir
Chris Schwarz, General Manager
Kyle Mason, Chief Engineer
Andy Jones, Treasurer
Kyle Mason, Chief Webmaster
Brandon Cross, Production
Michael Coviello ?, Music
Colton Conrad, Music
Greg Boyd, PublicRelations

WZKZ
02-28-1999; 101.9 mhz FM *Hrs Open:* 24; 1 kw; 801 ft.; N42 11 25 W77 49 17
1705 Lake Road, Elmira, NY 14901 US
(585) 593-9553, *Fax:* (585) 593-9554
www.wzkzradio.com
wzkz@wzkzradio.com
License: Alfred, Allegany County, NY held by Pembrook Pines Inc.
Group Owner: Pembrook Pines Media Group
Nat'l Network: Jones Radio Networks *Nat'l Reps:* Interep *Wire Services:* AP
Arbitron Metro Market: Alfred, NY *Format:* Country *Hrs. of News Programming:* news progmg 10 hrs wkly *No. News Employees:* 2 *Target Audience:* 18-54. *Adv. Rates:* 10; 10; 10; 10
Robert Pfuntner, CEO
Bob Weigand, Operations Dir
Rod Biehler, General Manager
Jim Davison, Programming Director

WZKZ(FM)
101.9 mhz FM; 1000 watts; 845 meters; 42 11 25N 77 49 17W
Mailing Address: 1705 Lake Road, Elmira, NY 14901 USA
Second Address: 3012 Eastside Avenue, Wellsville, NY 14895
(585) 593-9553, *Fax:* (585) 593-9554
wwww.kz102fm.com
License: Alfred, Allegany County, NY held by Pembrook Pines Inc
Group Owner: Pembrook Pines Inc
Target Audience: Adults 25-54
Robert J Pfuntner, President

Altamont

WZMR
06-26-1968; 104.9 mhz FM *Hrs Open:* 24; 0.53 kw; 932 ft.; N42 38 11 W74 0 2
6 Johnson Road, Latham, NY 12110 US
(518) 786-6600, *Fax:* (518) 786-6610
albanyedge.com
jreilly@albanybroadcasting.com?subject=Programming%20Questions%20from%20Website
License: Altamont, Albany County, NY held by 6 Johnson Road Licenses Inc.
Group Owner: Pamal Broadcasting Ltd.; (acq 10-19-2001; grpsl).
Arbitron Metro Market: Altamont, NY *Format:* Rock/AOR *Target Audience:* 18-44; men *Adv. Rates:* 50; 50; 50; 25
Kevin Callahan, Operations Dir
Dan Austin, General Manager
Suzette Anthony, General Sales Mgr
Jon Reilly, Programming Director
Mike Carey, News Director

Amherst

WUFO
01-01-1948; 1080 khz AM *Hrs Open:* Sunrise-sunset; 1 kw-D, NDD; N42 56 46 W78 49 43
960 Penn Ave, Ste 200, Pittsburgh, PA 15219 US
(716) 834-1080, *Fax:* (716) 837-1438
www.wufoam.com
wufo1080am@aol.com
License: Amherst, NY held by McL/McM New York LLC.
Group Owner: Sheridan Broadcasting Corp.; (acq 3-1-72)
Nat'l Network: American Urban
Arbitron Metro Market: Buffalo, NY *Format:* Gospel *Special Programming:* Talk 8 hrs wkly *Hrs. of News Programming:* News progmg 5 hrs wkly *Target Audience:* 25-54; Black adults, relg foundation, strong workethics
Ron Davenport, President
Alan Lincoln, General Manager
Sheila L. Brown, Station Manager
Lee Pettigrew, Program/Music Director
Porsha Coaxum, Program/Music Director
Hasan Sanders, Music & Production Director
Lee Ann Carr, AccountExecutive
Fatima Croom, Account Executive

Amsterdam

***WEXT**
08-01-1975; 97.7 mhz FM; 1.6 kw; 623 ft.; N42 59 5 W74 10 49
P.O. Box 219, Clifton Park, NY 12065 US
(518) 880-3400, *Fax:* (518) 880-3409
www.exit977.org
info@wmht.org
License: Amsterdam, Montgomery County, NY held by WMHT Educational Telecommunications
Arbitron Metro Market: Troy, NY *Format:* Classical
Deborah Onslow, President

WVTL
08-16-1961; 1570 khz AM *Hrs Open:* 24; 1 kw-D, ND1; 0.204 kw-N, ND1; N42 54 38 W74 13 4
P. O. Box 4490, Utica, NY 13504 US
(518) 843-9284, *Fax:* (518) 843-5225
www.wvtlfm.com
info@wvtl.com
License: Amsterdam, NY held by Roser Communications Network Inc.
Group Owner: Roser Communications Network Inc.; (acq 10-21-94; $400,000 with WBUG-FM Fort Plain;
Arbitron Metro Market: Amsterdam, NY *Format:* News, Sports, 86 *Hrs. of News Programming:* news progmg 10 hrs wkly *No. News Employees:* 2 *Target Audience:* 25 -54
Ken Roser Jr., General Manager
Roxanne Roser, Station Manager
Grant Roser, General Sales Mgr

WCSS
04-08-1948; 1490 khz AM *Hrs Open:* 24; 1 kw-U; N42 57 40 W74 10 35
Box 1250 Riverfront Ctr., Amsterdam, NY 12010
(518) 843-2500, *Fax:* (518) 684-6044
www.wcss1490.com
wcss@cranesville.com
License: Amsterdam, Montgomery County, NY held by Cranesville Block Co.
Nat'l Network: ABC/Classic Hits
Population Served: 800,000 *Arbitron Metro Market:* Albany-Schenectady-Troy, NY *Special Programming:* Local progmg & talk 20 hrs wkly *Hrs. of News Programming:* news progmg 20 hrs wkly *No. News Employees:* 1*Target Audience:* 25 plus; adults interested in loc, community info & mus *Adv. Rates:* 15; 10; 12; 8
Joseph Isabel, Operations Dir

Arcade

***WCOF**
01-01-2005; 89.5 mhz FM; 1 kw; 593 ft.; N42 27 41 W78 18 26
Rebroadcasts: Rebroadcasts WCIK(FM) Bath 100%
US
(607) 776-4151, *Fax:* (607) 776-6929
www.fln.org
mail@fln.org
License: Arcade, Wyoming County, NY held by Family Life Ministries Inc.
Group Owner: Family Life Network
Nat'l Network: Salem Radio Network *Wire Services:* Metro Weather Service Inc.
Arbitron Metro Market: Bath, NY *Format:* Christian *Hrs. of News Programming:* news progmg 14 hrs wkly *No. News Employees:* 3 *Target Audience:* 30-54; general
Dick Snavely, CFO
Rick Snavely, President, CEO
Sammy Carrillo, Programming Director
Gary Farnham, Engineering Dir
Jim Travis, Chief Engineer
Jeff Harmon, Chief Operating Officer (COO)
Katie Bernier, Youth Coordinator
LydiaBest, Ticket Agent
Dave Best, Business Manager
Trudi Cook, Radio Receptionist
Debbie Fero, Events Coordinator

Argyle

***WNGN**
08-01-1994; 91.9 mhz FM *Hrs Open:* 24; 2 kw; 571 ft.; N43 13 33 W73 26 34

Box 36 King Road, Buskirk, NY 12028 US
(518) 686-0975, *Fax:* (518) 686-0975
www.wngn.org
wngn@wngn.net
License: Argyle, Washington County, NY held by Northeast Gospel Broadcasting Inc.
Nat'l Network: Moody
Arbitron Metro Market: Buskirk, NY *Format:* Christian, Religious *Hrs. of News Programming:* News progmg one hr wkly *Target Audience:* 35-54; general
Brian Larson, President

Arlington

WRRB
12-01-1989; 96.9 mhz FM *Hrs Open:* 24; 0.31 kw; 1007 ft.; N41 43 9 W73 59 47 *Rebroadcasts:* Rebroadcasts WDST(FM) Woodstock 100%
Mailing Address: P.O. Box 416, Poughkeepsie, NY 12602 US
Second Address: 2 Pendell Rd., Poughkeepsie, NY 12602
(845) 471- 1500, *Fax:* (845) 454-1204
www.wrrv.com
boris@wrrv.com
License: Arlington, Dutchess County, NY held by Cumulus Licensing Corp.
Group Owner: Cumulus Media Inc.; (acq 1-23-02; grpsl).
Arbitron Metro Market: Arlington, NY *Format:* Alternative *Hrs. of News Programming:* News progmg 5 hrs wkly *Target Audience:* 25-54; upscale professionals
Charles Benfer, General Manager
Andrew Boris, Programming Director
Jeremiah Johnsen, Promotions Manager

Attica

***WCOU**
12-14-1992; 88.3 mhz FM; 11 kw; 535 ft.; N42 49 36 W78 12 25
Rebroadcasts: Rebroadcasts WCIK(FM) Bath 100%
Mailing Address: P.O. Box 506, Bath, NY 14810 US
Second Address: 7634 Campbell Creek Rd., Bath, NY 14810
(607) 776-4151, *Fax:* (607) 776-6929
www.fln.org
mail@fln.org
License: Attica, Wyoming County, NY held by Family Life Ministries Inc.
Group Owner: Family Life Network
Nat'l Network: Salem Radio Network *Wire Services:* Metro Weather Service Inc.
Arbitron Metro Market: Bath,NY *Format:* Christian *Hrs. of News Programming:* news progmg 14 hrs wkly *No. News Employees:* 3 *Target Audience:* 30-54; general
Dick Snavely, CFO
Rick Snavely, President
Sammy Carrillo, Programming Director
Sammy Carrillo, Promotions Manager
Jim Travis, Chief Engineer

Au Sable

WZXP
97.9 mhz FM; 18 kw; Ant 830 ft; N44 46 30 W73 36 48
1717 Dixie Hwy., Suite 650, Fort Wright, KY
(859) 331-9100
License: Au Sable, Clinton County, NY held by Radioactive LLC.
Group Owner: Radioactive LLC
Arbitron Metro Market: Burlington-Plattsburgh, VT-NY
Benjamin Homel, President

Auburn

WAUB
12-24-1959; 1590 khz AM
Box 160, Experimental Rd, Auburn, NY 13021 US
(315) 258-0937, *Fax:* (315) 258-9248
www.fingerlakes1.com
tbaker@flradiogroup.com
License: Auburn, NY held by Auburn Broadcasting Inc.
Group Owner: Finger Lakes Radio Group; (acq 7-2-97; $70,000 plus additonal consideration)
Nat'l Network: CBS
Arbitron Metro Market: Fargo-Moorhead, ND-MN *Format:* Talk *Target Audience:* General.
Bill Askew, General Sales Mgr
Mike Smith, Programming Director
Ted Baker, News Director

***WDWN**
10-31-1972; 89.1 mhz FM; 3 kw; 102 ft; N42 56 40 W76 32 33
197 Franklin St., Auburn, NY 13021
(315) 255-1743, *Fax:* (315) 255-2690
www.wdwn.fm
License: Auburn, Cayuga County, NY held by Cayuga County Community College.
Population Served: 250,000 *Arbitron Metro Market:* Syracuse, NY *Target Audience:* 18-25; high school & college students, young adults
Steven Keeler, General Manager
Jeff Szczesniak, Programming Director
Douglas Brill, Chief Engineer

WWLF
01-26-1927; 1340 khz AM; 1 kw-U, ND1; N42 57 5 W76 35 5
401 W. Kirkpatrick Street, Syracuse, NY 13204 US
(315) 472-0222, *Fax:* (315) 478-7745
www.radiodisney.com
info@radiodisney.com
License: Auburn, NY held by WOLF Radio Inc.
Group Owner: WOLF Radio Inc.; acq 6-26-98; $103,000).
Nat'l Network: Radio Disney
Format: Children
Sam Furco, General Manager
Becky Mullen, Promotions Manager

Avon

WYSL
01-23-1987; 1040 khz AM *Hrs Open:* 24
Mailing Address: 5620 South Lima Road, Avon, NY 14414 US
Second Address: 5620 S. Lima Rd., Avon, NY 14414
(585) 346-3000, *Fax:* (585) 346-0450
www.wysl1040.com
info@wysl1040.com
License: Avon, NY held by Radio Livingston Ltd.
Nat'l Network: ABC; Westwood One
Arbitron Metro Market: Avon, NY *Format:* News, Sports *Special Programming:* Relg 4 hrs wkly *Hrs. of News Programming:* news progmg 160 hrs wkly *No. News Employees:* 3 *Target Audience:* 35 plus; general
Robert Savage, CEO
Bob D'Angelo, Operations Dir
J.C. Delass, Station Manager
James Stevenson, CFO

Babylon

WBAB
08-27-1958; 102.3 mhz FM *Hrs Open:* 24; 6 kw; 269 ft.; N40 47 58 W73 20 8
3773 Howard Hughes Pkwy, Las Vegas, NV 89109 US
(506) 455-0923, *Fax:* (506) 455-3602
www.fredfm.ca
License: Babylon, Suffolk County, NY held by Cox Radio Inc.
Group Owner: Cox Radio Inc.; (acq 5-22-98; grpsl)
Nat'l Reps: Christal
Arbitron Metro Market: Fredericton NB *Format:* Oldies
Brad Muir, Operations Dir
Hilary Montbourquette, General Manager

Baldwinsville

***WBXL**
01-29-1975; 90.5 mhz FM *Hrs Open:* 7 AM-11 PM; 0.175 kw; 207 ft.; N43 9 47 W76 18 47
E. Oneida Street Complex, Baldwinsville, NY 13027 US
(315) 638-6010
License: Baldwinsville, Onondaga County, NY held by Baldwinsville Central School District.
Arbitron Metro Market: Baldwinsville, NY *Format:* Contemporary Hits/Top 40 *Target Audience:* Family of school district students
Peter Hunn, General Manager

WSEN
02-25-1959; 1050 khz AM *Hrs Open:* 24; 2.5 kw-D, DA2; 0.019 kw-N, DA2; N43 10 46 W76 20 19 *Rebroadcasts:* Rebroadcasts WSEN-FM Baldwinsville
Mailing Address: 166 West Putnam Avenue, Greenwich, CT 06830 US
Second Address: 8456 Smoky Hollow Rd., Baldwinsville, NY 13027
(315) 635-3971, *Fax:* (315) 635-3490
www.wsenfm.com
d.wagner@lmgiradio.com
License: Baldwinsville, NY held by Buckley Broadcasting of New York LLC.
Group Owner: Buckley Broadcasting Corp.; (acq 8-20-80; $700,000 with co-located FM;
Nat'l Network: CBS *Nat'l Reps:* McGavren Guild
Arbitron Metro Market: Baldwinsville, NY *Format:* Oldies *Target Audience:* 35 plus; well-educated professionals with disposable income
Richard Buckley, President
Judith Kelly, Operations Dir
Don Wagner, General Manager
Jody Frawley, General Sales Mgr
Jim Tate, Programming Director
Kristine Gladle, Promotions Manager
Al Jenner, Chief Engineer
Dan Elliott,Account Executive
Paul Davie, Account Executive

WSEN-FM
11-10-1967; 92.1 mhz FM *Hrs Open:* 24; 25 kw; 299 ft.; N43 10 46 W76 20 19
Mailing Address: 166 West Putnam Avenue, Greenwich, CT 06830 US
Second Address: 8456 Smoky Hollow Rd., Baldwinsville, NY 13027
(315) 635-3971, *Fax:* (315) 635-3490
www.wsenfm.com
webmaster@wsenfm.com
License: Baldwinsville, Onondaga County, NY
Nat'l Reps: McGavren Guild
Arbitron Metro Market: Syracuse, NY *Format:* Contemporary Hits/Top 40, Adult Contemp *Target Audience:* 35-64; well-educated professionals with disposable income
Don Wagner, General Manager

Ballston Spa

WKKF
05-27-1968; 102.3 mhz FM *Hrs Open:* 24; 4.1 kw; 387 ft.; N42 52 44 W73 51 47
200 Concord Plaza, Suite 600, San Antonio, TX 78216 US
(518) 452-4800, *Fax:* (518) 452-4885
www.1023kissfm.com
License: Ballston Spa, Saratoga County, NY held by CC Licenses LLC.
Group Owner: Clear Channel Communications Inc.; (acq 3-6-97)
Nat'l Reps: Clear Channel
Arbitron Metro Market: Ballstone Spa, NY *Format:* Contemporary Hits/Top 40 *Target Audience:* 18-34; upscale, hip women
Rob Dawes, Operations Dir
Kristen Delaney, VP/General Manager
John Cooper, Station Manager
Randy McMartin, Programming Director
Jill Manti, Marketing Director
Josh Farrell, Internet Content Director
Jim Stagnitti, Director ofSales

Batavia

WBTA
02-06-1941; 1490 khz AM *Hrs Open:* 24
438 East Main Street, Batavia, NY 14020 US
(585) 344-1490, *Fax:* (585) 344-1441
www.wbta1490.com
debbie@wbta1490.com
License: Batavia, NY held by HPL Communications Inc.
Nat'l Reps: Rgnl Reps
Arbitron Metro Market: Batavia, NY *Format:* News, News/Talk, 86 *Special Programming:* Sports 9 hrs wkly *Hrs. of News Programming:* news progmg 10 hrs wkly *No. News Employees:* 2 *Target Audience:* PrimaryDemographic: Adults 25-54;Secondary Demographic: 35-64 *Adv. Rates:* 14; 14; 14; 8
Daniel Fischer, President
Lorne Way, General Sales Mgr

***WGCC-FM**
11-13-1985; 90.7 mhz FM *Hrs Open:* 6 AM-1 AM; 0.88 kw; 164 ft.; N43 1 3 W78 8 18
1 College Road, Batavia, NY 14020 US
(585) 343-0055, *Fax:* (585) 345-6806
cmplatt@genesee.edu
License: Batavia, Genesee County, NY held by Genesee Community College Board of Trustees.
Format: Rock/AOR *Hrs. of News Programming:* news progmg 5 hrs wkly *No. News Employees:* 1 *Target Audience:* 13-30; high school & college youth
Chuck Platt, President
Melody Nardone, Station Manager
Andrew Scutt, Programming Director
Ashley Mouting, Music Director
Jeremy Canute, Station Manager

Bath

WABH
11-02-1962; 1380 khz AM *Hrs Open:* 19
1705 Lake Rd, Elmira, NY 14902 US
(607) 776-4151, *Fax:* (607) 776-6929
www.fln.org
License: Bath, NY held by Pembrook Pines Mass Media Inc.
Group Owner: Pembrook Pines Media Group; (acq 4-13-90; with co-located FM;
Nat'l Network: CBS

Arbitron Metro Market: Texarkana TX-AR *Format:* Christian
Rick Snavely, General Manager

WVIN-FM
10-10-1971; 98.3 mhz FM *Hrs Open:* 19; 4.5 kw; 367 ft.; N42 19 6 W77 21 27
1705 Lake Road, Elmira, NY 14902 US
(607) 776-3326, *Fax:* (607) 776-6161
wvinbath.com
wvinsales@stny.rr.com
License: Bath, Steuben County, NY
Arbitron Metro Market: Bath, NY *Format:* Adult Contemp *Special Programming:* Jazz 2 hrs wkly
Chip Miller, President
Paul Pesce, Station Manager

Bay Shore

WBZO
02-01-1993; 103.1 mhz FM *Hrs Open:* 24; 3 kw; 141 meters; N40 45 04 W73 12 52
234 Airport Plaza Blvd., Suite 5, Farmingdale, NY 11747
(631) 770-4200, *Fax:* (631) 770-0101
www.b103.com
webmaster@b103.com
License: Bay Shore, Suffolk County, NY held by Connoisseur Media of Long Island LLC
Group Owner: JVC Broadcasting; (acq 7-3-12; $12.45 million)
Nat'l Reps: D & R Radio
Population Served: 8,219 *Arbitron Metro Market:* Farmingdale, NY *Hrs. of News Programming:* news progmg 25 hrs wkly *No. News Employees:* 1 *Target Audience:* General.
Dave Widmer, General Manager
Bill Wise, Programming Director
Frank Brinka, News Director
Michael Glaser, Chief Engineer

Beacon

WBNR
12-17-1959; 1260 khz AM *Hrs Open:* 24; 1 kw-D, DA2; 0.4 kw-N, DA2; N41 29 32 W73 58 43 *Rebroadcasts:* Simulcast with WLNA(AM) Peekskill 100%
Mailing Address: 475 South Avenue, Beacon, NY 12508 US
Second Address: 715 Rt. 52, Beacon, NY 12508
(845) 838-6000, *Fax:* (845) 838-2109
www.hvradionet.com/
bowens@pamal.com
License: Beacon, NY held by 6 Johnson Road Licenses Inc.
Group Owner: Pamal Broadcasting Ltd.; (acq 10-19-2001; grpsl).
Nat'l Network: ABC
Arbitron Metro Market: Beacon, NY *Format:* Classic Rock *Special Programming:* Relg 5 hrs wkly *Hrs. of News Programming:* news progmg 2 hrs wkly *No. News Employees:* 2 *Target Audience:* 35 plus. *Adv.Rates:* 35; 25; 15; 10
James Morrell, CEO
Fred Bennett, President
Bruce Owens, Programming Director
Michael Molda, Webmaster

Big Flats

WENI-FM
04-01-1989; 97.7 mhz FM *Hrs Open:* 24; 0.61 kw; 722 ft.; N42 8 31 W77 4 40
P.O.Box 1047, 2309 Davis Road, Corning, NY 14830 US
(607) 937-8181, *Fax:* (607) 962-1138
cnj@route81radio.com
License: Big Flats, Chemung County, NY held by WS2K Radio LLC.
Group Owner: WS2K Radio LLC dba WS Media; (acq 7-14-2008; grpsl)
Nat'l Network: ABC *Nat'l Reps:* Roslin
Arbitron Metro Market: Elmira-Corning, NY *Format:* Oldies *Target Audience:* 25-54.
Paul Lyle, General Manager
Jamie Evans, General Sales Mgr
Dave Shoen, News Director

Binghamton

WAAL
03-01-1954; 99.1 mhz FM *Hrs Open:* 24; 8.7 kw; 955 ft.; N42 3 31 W75 57 6
Mailing Address: 405 Park Avenue, Suite 702, New York, NY 10022 US
Second Address: 59 Court St., Binghamton, NY 13901
(662) 844-8888, *Fax:* (662) 842-6791
www.afr.net
License: Binghamton, Broome County, NY held by Citadel Broadcasting Co.
Arbitron Metro Market: El Dorado AR *Format:* Christian
Marvin Sanders, General Manager

*WHRW
03-01-1966; 90.5 mhz FM *Hrs Open:* 24; 1.45 kw horiz, 0 kw vert; N42 5 24 W75 58 5
Mailing Address: P.O. Box 2000, Binghamton, NY 13902 US
Second Address: 4400 Vestal Pkwy, P.O. Box 2000, Binghamton, NY 13902-6000
(607) 777-2139, *Fax:* (607) 777-6501
www.whrwfm.org
gm@whrwfm.org
License: Binghamton, Broome County, NY held by State University of New York.
Wire Services: UPI
Arbitron Metro Market: Binghamton, NY *Format:* Variety/Diverse *Special Programming:* It 3 hrs, Jazz 9 hrs, Pol 3 hrs, Relg 6 hrs, Sp 9 *Hrs. of News Programming:* News progmg 5 hrs wkly *Target Audience:* General.
Mike Saltzman, General Manager
Brian Napolitano, Chief Engineer

WHWK
09-01-1956; 98.1 mhz FM; 6.7 kw; 1296 ft.; N42 3 40 W75 56 45
140 S. Ash Ave., Tempe, AZ 85281 US
(607) 772-8400, *Fax:* (607) 772-9806
www.981thehawk.com
License: Binghamton, Broome County, NY
Group Owner: Cumulus Media Inc.
Arbitron Metro Market: Binghamton, NY *Format:* Country *Target Audience:* 25-54.
Ed Walker, Programming Director

WINR
01-01-1946; 680 khz AM *Hrs Open:* 24
3646 George F. Highway, Endwell, NY 13760 US
(607) 584-5800, *Fax:* (607) 584-5900
www.680winr.com
JeffreySohinki@clearchannel.com
License: Binghamton, NY held by AMFM Radio Licenses LLC.
Group Owner: Clear Channel Communications Inc.; (acq 2-13-2001; $1 million).
Nat'l Network: CBS
Arbitron Metro Market: Binghamton, NY *Format:* Adult Contemp, News, 62, Talk *Hrs. of News Programming:* news progmg 10 hrs wkly *No. News Employees:* 1 *Target Audience:* 35 plus.
Doug Mosher, Operations Dir
Tom Barney, General Manager

WYOS
06-01-1947; 1360 khz AM *Hrs Open:* 24
Mailing Address: 405 Park Avenue, Suite 702, New York, NY 10022 US
Second Address: Box 414, Binghamton, NY 13902
(607) 772-8850, *Fax:* (607) 772-9806
www.wnbf.com
rodger.neel@cumulus.com
License: Binghamton, NY
Group Owner: Cumulus Media Inc.; (acq 6-9-99; grpsl)
Nat'l Network: ESPN Radio *Nat'l Reps:* McGavren Guild
Arbitron Metro Market: Binghamton, NY *Format:* Sports
Roger Neel, Programming Director
Rick Elliker, Chief Engineer
Marybeth Walsh, Market Manager
Eric Donaldson, Sales Manager
Alex Palmieri, Sales Manager

WNBF
01-01-1928; 1290 khz AM
140 S. Ash Ave., Tempe, AZ 85281 US
(607) 772-8400, *Fax:* (607) 772-9806
www.wnbf.com
License: Binghamton, NY
Group Owner: Cumulus Media Inc.; (acq 6-9-99; grpsl).
Arbitron Metro Market: Binghamton, NY *Format:* News, News/Talk, 86 *Target Audience:* 35-64.
Roger Neal, Programming Director
Bernie Fionte, News Director
Larry Hodge, Chief Engineer

*WSKG-FM
10-22-1975; 89.3 mhz FM *Hrs Open:* 24; 11.5 kw; 1040 ft.; N42 3 40 W75 56 46
PO Box 3000, Binghamton, NY 13902 US
(607) 729-0100, *Fax:* (607) 729-7328,
www.wskg.com
wskg_mail@wskg.pbs.org
License: Binghamton, Broome County, NY held by WSKG Public Telecommunications Council.
Nat'l Network: NPR; PRI
Arbitron Metro Market: Binghamton, NY *TV Affiliate:* *WSKG-TV affil. *Format:* News *Special Programming:* Jazz, folk 5 hrs wkly *Hrs. of News Programming:* news progmg 33 hrs wkly *No. News Employees:* 1 *Target Audience:* General.
Ken Campbell, Operations Dir
Ken Campbell, Programming Director
Stacy Mosteller, News Director
Mike Pufky, Engineering Dir
William Snyder, Music Director
Linda Cohen, Underwriting Director

*WSQX-FM
01-17-1995; 91.5 mhz FM *Hrs Open:* 24; 3.5 kw; 381 ft.; N42 7 54 W75 55 56
PO Box 3000, Binghamton, NY 13902 US
(607) 729-0100, *Fax:* (607) 729-7328
www.wskg.com
wskg_mail@wskg.pbs.org
License: Binghamton, Broome County, NY held by WSKG Public Telecommunications Council.
Nat'l Network: NPR; PRI
Arbitron Metro Market: Binghamton, NY *TV Affiliate:* *WSKG-TV affil *Format:* Jazz, News *Special Programming:* Talk 10 hrs wkly *Target Audience:* General.
Brian Sickora, President
Nancy Christensen, Operations Dir
Ken Campbell, Programming Director
Stacy Mosteller, News Director
Linda Cohen, Underwriting Director

Black River

WBLH
08-11-2008; 92.5 mhz FM; 6 kw; Ant 328 ft; N44 03 17.8 W75 57 15.3
223 J.B. Wise Pl., Suite 10, Watertown, NY
(315) 786-0925, *Fax:* (315) 786-0920
License: Black River, Jefferson County, NY held by Radioactive LLC.
Group Owner: Radioactive LLC
Arbitron Metro Market: Watertown, NY *No. News Employees:* 5-11 *Adv. Rates:* 10-12 dollars primetime
Michael Stapleford, CEO/COO
Benjamin Homel, President
Johnny Keagan, Operations Dir
Tim Sweeney, General Manager
Tim Sweeney, Station Manager
Tim Sweeney, General Sales Mgr
Robert Shackley, Programming Director

Blue Mountain Lake

*WXLH
11-01-1992; 91.3 mhz FM *Hrs Open:* 24; 0.078 kw; 1729 ft.; N43 52 18 W74 24 2 *Rebroadcasts:* Rebroadcasts WSLU(FM) Canton 100%
N. Country Public Radio, Canton, NY 13617 US
(315) 229-5356, *Fax:* (315) 229-5373
www.ncpr.org
info@ncpr.org
License: Blue Mountain Lake, Hamilton County, NY held by St. Lawrence University.
Arbitron Metro Market: Blue Mountain Lake, NY *Format:* Talk *Special Programming:* Gospel, jazz, class, folk, pub affrs *Hrs. of News Programming:* news progmg 35 hrs wkly *No. News Employees:* 4 *Target Audience:* General.
Shelly Pike, Operations Dir
Ellen Rocco, Station Manager
Jacqueline Sauter, Programming Director
Martha Foley, News Director
Joel Hurd, Production Manager
June Peoples, Membership Director
Naomi Weller, Office Manager
DaleHobson, Web Manager
Sandy Demarest, Development Director

Boonville

WBRV
06-22-1955; 900 khz AM *Hrs Open:* 24; 1 kw-D, ND1; 0.052 kw-N, ND1; N43 30 47 W75 21 46 *Rebroadcasts:* Rebroadcasts WLLG(FM) Lowville 50%
3399 Moose River Road, Boonville, NY 13309 US
(315) 376-7500, *Fax:* (315) 376-8549
www.themoose.net
sales@themoose.net
License: Boonville, NY held by Flack Broadcasting Group L.L.C.
Nat'l Network: USA
Arbitron Metro Market: Lowville, NY *Format:* Country *Hrs. of News Programming:* News progmg 18 hrs wkly *Target Audience:* General.
William Flack, President
Sara Flack, Operations Dir

Brian Best, News Director
Dana Cowles, Disc Jockey

WBRV-FM
01-31-1989; 101.3 mhz FM *Hrs Open:* 24; 4.7 kw; 374 ft.; N43 26 52 W75 20 50 *Rebroadcasts:* Rebroadcasts WLLG (FM) Lowville 50%
3399 Moose River Road, Boonville, NY 13309 US
(315) 376-7500, *Fax:* (315) 376-8549
www.themoose.net
sales@themoose.net
License: Boonville, Oneida County, NY
Arbitron Metro Market: Lowville, NY *Special Programming:* Farm 3 hrs, relg 3 hrs wkly *Hrs. of News Programming:* News progmg 10 hrs wkly *Target Audience:* General.
Jon Zucker, General Manager
Marianna Faircloth, Station Manager
Mark Stackowski, General Sales Mgr
Chris Novello, Programming Director
Olivia Hoffman, Promotions Manager
Kaitlyn Laabs, News Director

***WXLB**
01-01-2009; 91.7 mhz FM; 0.1 kw; 351 ft.; N43 26 53 W75 20 48 *Rebroadcasts:* Rebroadcasts WSLU(FM) Canton 100% US
(315) 229-5356, *Fax:* (315) 229-5373
www.northcountrypublicradio.org
radio@ncpr.org
License: Boonville, Oneida County, NY held by The St. Lawrence University.
Nat'l Network: NPR; PRI
Arbitron Metro Market: Boonville, NY *Format:* Talk
Shelly Pike, Operations Dir
Ellen Rocco, General Manager
Jackie Sauter, Programming Director
Martha Foley, News Director
Bob Sauter, Chief Engineer
Naomi Weller, Office Manager
Joel Hurd, Production Manager

Brentwood

***WXBA**
06-21-1975; 88.1 mhz FM *Hrs Open:* 24; 0.18 kw; 95 ft.; N40 46 19 W73 15 19
Third Avenue, Brentwood, NY 11717 US
(631) 434-2581, *Fax:* (631) 273-6572
wxba@88x.net
License: Brentwood, Suffolk County, NY held by Brentwood Public School District.
Arbitron Metro Market: Brentwood, NY *Format:* Christian *Special Programming:* Black 5 hrs wkly *Hrs. of News Programming:* news progmg 3 hrs wkly *No. News Employees:* 2 *Target Audience:* 18-54; general
Les Black, General Manager
Jaimie Ottone, Station Manager
Charles Vollmer, Programming Director
Paul Bryant, News Director
Frank Lapple, Chief Engineer
Pete Mandzych, Sports Commentator

Brewster

WPUT
07-03-1958; 1510 khz AM; 1 kw-D, NDD; N41 24 34 W73 37 29
600 14th St., N.W., Suite 800, Washington, DC 20005 US
(203) 775-1212, *Fax:* (203) 775-6452
License: Brewster, NY held by Cumulus Licensing Corp.
Group Owner: Cumulus Media Inc.
Nat'l Network: ESPN Radio
Arbitron Metro Market: New York *Format:* Sports
Matt Carey, Programming Director

Briarcliff Manor

WXPK
04-08-1960; 107.1 mhz FM *Hrs Open:* 24; 1.9 kw; 591 ft.; N41 4 49 W73 48 26
11 Skyline Drive, Hawthorne, NY 10532 US
(845) 838-6000, *Fax:* (848) 838-2109
www.1071thepeak.com
info@1071thepeak.com
License: Briarcliff Manor, Westchester County, NY held by 6 Johnson Road Licenses Inc.
Group Owner: Pamal Broadcasting Ltd.; (acq 11-5-2004; $18.4 million).
Arbitron Metro Market: New York *Format:* Triple A *No. News Employees:* 1 *Target Audience:* 18-44; upscale, young, suburban
Darren DiPrima, Station Manager

Bridgehampton

WBAZ
01-01-1996; 102.5 mhz FM *Hrs Open:* 24; 4.8 kw; 348 ft.; N40 53 58 W72 23 6
Mailing Address: P.O. Box 1200, Southold, NY 11971 US
Second Address: 249 Montauk Hwy., Amagansett, NY 11930
(631) 267-7800, *Fax:* (631) 267-1018
www.wbaz.com
info@wbaz.com
License: Bridgehampton, Suffolk County, NY held by AAA Licensing LLC.
Group Owner: Long Island Radio Broadcasting LLC; (acq 8-22-2000; $2.75 million with WBEA(FM) Southold).
Arbitron Metro Market: Watermill, NY *Format:* Adult Contemp *Special Programming:* News, sports *Target Audience:* 25-44; adults with active lifestyles
Don Maguire, President
Hedy Krebs-DeMaio, General Manager
Steve Harper, Programming Director

Bridgeport

WTKW
11-09-1992; 99.5 mhz FM *Hrs Open:* 24; 5.7 kw; 338 ft.; N43 9 24 W75 57 25
7636 Murray Drive, Cicero, NY 13039 US
(315) 472-9111, *Fax:* (315) 472-1888
www.tk99.net
asktk@tk99.net
License: Bridgeport, Madison County, NY held by Galaxy Syracuse Licensee LLC.
Group Owner: Galaxy Communications L.P.; (acq 4-6-2000; grpsl)
Arbitron Metro Market: Syracuse, NY *Format:* Classic Rock *Hrs. of News Programming:* news progmg 3 hrs wkly *No. News Employees:* 1 *Target Audience:* 25-54 plus; stable, peak-earning adults
Mike Lucarelli, CFO
Ed Levine, President
Ed Levine, General Manager
Lisa Morrow, General Sales Mgr
Mimi Grizwold, Programming Director

Brighton

WZNE
11-01-1996; 94.1 mhz FM *Hrs Open:* 24; 1.8 kw; 407 ft.; N43 8 7 W77 35 7
600 New Hampshire Ave., N.W., Suite 1200, Washington, DC 20037 US
(585) 399-5700, *Fax:* (585) 399-5750
www.thezone941.com
scott.hixson@smgny.com
License: Brighton, Monroe County, NY held by Stephens Media Group-Rochester LLC.
Group Owner: Stephens Family L.P.; (acq 7-14-2008; grpsl)
Nat'l Network: CNN Radio *Nat'l Reps:* Christal
Arbitron Metro Market: Moca, PR *Format:* Alternative *Target Audience:* Men 18-34; affluent fans of alternative rock music
Michael Ninnie, General Manager
Nik Rivers, Programming Director
Scott Hixson, Promotions Manager
Ray Noone, Sales Director

Brockport

WASB
02-15-1970; 1590 khz AM *Hrs Open:* 24; 1 kw-D, DA2; 1 kw-N, DA2; N43 11 44 W77 57 5
7280 Sandy Shore Drive, Hamlin, NY 14464 US
(585) 637-7040
www.sonshinenetwork.com
info@sonshinenetwork.com
License: Brockport, NY held by David L. Wolfe
Arbitron Metro Market: Brockport, NY *Format:* Christian *Target Audience:* All ages; rural audience, western Rochester & suburbs
Daniel Wolfe, General Manager
Gail Reed, Programming Director

***WBSU**
01-14-1981; 89.1 mhz FM *Hrs Open:* 24; 7.33 kw; 160 ft; N43 12 45 W77 57 17
135 Seymour Union, Brockport, NY 14420
(585) 395-2580, *Fax:* (585) 395-5334
www.891thepoint.com
wkozires@brockport.edu
License: Brockport, Monroe County, NY held by State University of New York.
Nat'l Network: AP Radio *Wire Services:* AP
Population Served: 500,000 *Arbitron Metro Market:* Rochester, NY *Special Programming:* Pub affrs 6 hrs wkly *Hrs. of News Programming:* News progmg 3 hrs wkly *Target Audience:* 17-34; college & young professional
Dr. John Halstead, President
Warren Kozireski, General Manager
Dean King, Chief Engineer

***WKDL-FM**
01-01-1999; 104.9 mhz FM; 6 kw; 328 ft.; N43 9 51 W77 47 2
P.O. Box 155, Canadaigua, NY 14424 US
(916) 251-1600, *Fax:* (916) 251-1650
www.klove.com
License: Brockport, Monroe County, NY held by Brockport Licenses LLC.
Group Owner: EMF Broadcasting; (acq 1-27-2006; $4 million)
Nat'l Network: K-Love
Format: Christian
Mike Novak, President
Glenn Goodwin, Operations Dir

Bronxville

WFAS-FM
09-01-1947; 103.9 mhz FM; 0.6 kw; 667 ft.; N41 1 32 W73 49 39
601 University Avenue, Suite 211, Sacramnto, CA 95825 US
(914) 693-2400, *Fax:* (914) 693-0000
www.wfasfm.com
Marty.Sheehan@cumulus.com
License: Bronxville, Westchester County, NY
Group Owner: Cumulus Media Inc.
Arbitron Metro Market: Bronxville, NY *Format:* Adult Contemp *Hrs. of News Programming:* News progmg one hr wkly *Target Audience:* 25-54.
Joan Franzino, Operations Dir
Marty Sheehan, Advertising & Sales Department
Bob Barnum, Program Director and News Department
Jennifer D'Ambrosio, Program Director and News Department
Pam Puso, News Director
Jennifer D'Ambrosio, WebMaster
Valencia Cichorek, Traffic Manager

Brooklyn

***WKRB**
05-28-1978; 90.3 mhz FM *Hrs Open:* 24; 0.01 kw; 134 ft.; N40 34 36 W73 56 4
2001 Oriental Boulevard, Brooklyn, NY 11235 US
(718) 368-5817, *Fax:* (718) 368-4776
www.wkrb.org
gm@wkrb.org
License: Brooklyn, Kings County, NY held by Kingsborough Community College.
Arbitron Metro Market: New York *Format:* Variety/Diverse *Target Audience:* General; young adults
Regina Peruggi, President
Rob Herklotz, General Manager

Brookville

***WCWP**
04-01-1965; 88.1 mhz FM *Hrs Open:* 24; 0.1 kw; 190 ft.; N40 49 0 W73 35 49 *Rebroadcasts:* Rebroadcasts WLIU(FM) Southampton 85%
700 Northern Blvd, University Center, Brookville, NY 11548 US
(516) 299-2683(516) 299-2626, *Fax:* (516) 299-2767
www.wcwp.org
wcwp@cwpost.liu.edu
License: Brookville, Nassau County, NY held by Long Island University.
Nat'l Network: NPR
Arbitron Metro Market: Nassau County, NY *Format:* Jazz, News *Hrs. of News Programming:* news progmg 15 hrs wkly *No. News Employees:* 1 *Target Audience:* General
Dan Cox, General Manager
Nick Sekela, Programming Director

Buffalo

WBEN
09-08-1930; 930 khz AM *Hrs Open:* 24; 5 kw-D, DAN; 5 kw-N, DAN; N42 58 42 W78 57 27
10706 Beaver Dam Road, Cockeysville, MD 21030 US
(716) 803-0930, *Fax:* (716) 832-3080
www.wben.com
newsroom@wben.com
License: Buffalo, NY held by Entercom Buffalo License L.L.C.
Group Owner: Entercom Communications Corp.; (acq 1999)
Nat'l Network: CBS *Nat'l Reps:* D & R Radio
Arbitron Metro Market: Buffalo, NY *Format:* News, News/Talk, 84, Talk *Special Programming:* Buffalo Bills football *Hrs. of*

News Programming: news progmg 20 hrs wkly *No. News Employees:* 10 *Target Audience:* 35-64; general
Im Wenger, Operations Dir
L. Greene, General Manager
Tim Holly, Sales Director
Tim Wenger, Programming Director
Cheryl Klocke, Promotions Manager
John Zach, News Director
Dennis Kavanaugh, Engineering Dir
Mike Krupa, NationalSales Manager
Kevin Sylvester, Sports Commentator
Susan Rose, Morning Anchor
Dave Debo, Anchor/Reporter/wben.com Editor

***WBFO**
01-07-1959; 88.7 mhz FM *Hrs Open:* 24; 50 kw; 384 ft.; N43 0 12 W78 45 56
State University Plaza, Albany, NY 12246 US
(716) 845-7040, *Fax:* (716)-845-7036
www.wbfo.org
mail@wbfo.org
License: Buffalo, Erie County, NY held by State University of New York.
Nat'l Network: NPR
Arbitron Metro Market: Buffalo, NY *Format:* Jazz *Special Programming:* Blues 8 hrs, bluegrass 3 hrs, class one hr, Pol 3 hrs wkly *Hrs. of News Programming:* news progmg 50 hrs wkly *No. News Employees:* 2*Target Audience:* General; educated professionals
Carole Smith Petro, Operations Dir
Joan Wilson, General Sales Mgr
Mark Scott, News Director
Mark Wozniak, Operations Manager

***WBNY**
01-01-1982; 91.3 mhz FM *Hrs Open:* 24; 0.1 kw; 112 ft.; N42 55 59 W78 52 59
1300 Elmwood Avenue, Buffalo, NY 14222 US
(716) 878-5104(716) 878-3080, *Fax:* (716) 878-6600
www.buffalostate.edu/wbny/
wbnygeneralmanager@gmail.com
License: Buffalo, Erie County, NY held by State University of New York.
Arbitron Metro Market: Buffalo, NY *Format:* Alternative *Special Programming:* Black 12 hrs, jazz 3 hrs, reggae 3 hrs, heavy metal 3 hrs, folk 3 hrs wkly *Hrs. of News Programming:* News progmg 6 hrs wkly *TargetAudience:* 18-25; college student
Nick Stutzman, General Manager
Megan Jones, Programming Director
Trever Dugan, Promotions Manager
Amanda Matthews, News Director
Sam Mines, Sports Director
Amber Llano Nigro, Music Director
Brian Mcdermott, Treasurer
MeganJones, Webmaster

WDCX-FM
02-01-1963; 99.5 mhz FM *Hrs Open:* 24; 110 kw; 640 ft.; N42 38 7 W78 46 5
P.O. Box 3003, Blue Bell, PA 19422 US
(716) 883-3010, *Fax:* (716) 883-3606
www.wdcxfm.com
info@wdcxfm.com
License: Buffalo, Erie County, NY held by Kimtron Inc.
Group Owner: Crawford Broadcasting Co.
Arbitron Metro Market: Buffalo-Niagara Falls, NY *Format:* Christian, Talk, 74 *Target Audience:* General.
Donald Crawford, President
Nevin Larson, General Manager

WEDG
01-01-1947; 103.3 mhz FM; 49 kw; 348 ft.; N42 55 34 W78 50 28
350 Park Ave, 20th Floor, New York, NY 10022 US
(716) 881-4555, *Fax:* (716) 888-9773
www.wedg.com
License: Buffalo, Erie County, NY
Group Owner: Cumulus Media Inc.; (acq 2-23-00; grpsl).
Nat'l Reps: Eastman Radio
Arbitron Metro Market: Buffalo, NY *Target Audience:* 18-44
Chet Osadchey, General Manager
Ross DiFranco, General Sales Mgr
Jim Kurdrdziel, Programming Director
Tom Ragan, News Director

***WFBF**
01-01-1989; 89.9 mhz FM; 16 kw; 295 ft.; N42 41 19 W78 45 15
Mailing Address: 4135 Northgate Blvd., Suite 1, Sacramento, CA 95834 US
Second Address: 290 Hegenberger Rd., Oakland, CA 94621
(800) 543-1495, *Fax:* (916) 641-8238
www.familyradio.com
info@familyradio.com
License: Buffalo, Erie County, NY held by Family Stations Inc.
Group Owner: Family Stations Inc.
Arbitron Metro Market: Buffalo-Niagara Falls, NY *Format:* Christian, Religious
Harold Camping, President

WGR
05-22-1922; 550 khz AM *Hrs Open:* 24
10706 Beaver Dam Road, Cockeysville, MD 21030 US
(716) 843-0600, *Fax:* (716) 843-0250
www.wgr550.com
info@wgr550.com
License: Buffalo, NY held by Entercom Buffalo License LLC.
Group Owner: Entercom Communications Corp.; (acq 12-13-99; grpsl).
Nat'l Network: ESPN Radio
Arbitron Metro Market: Buffalo-Niagara Falls, NY *Format:* Sports *Target Audience:* 25-54; men
Greg Ried, Operations Dir
Jill Kowalski, General Sales Mgr
Andy Roth, Programming Director
Tim Wenger, Operations Manager

WGRF
09-14-1959; 96.9 mhz FM; 24 kw; 712 ft.; N42 57 13 W78 52 36
350 Park Ave, 20th Floor, New York, NY 10022 US
(716) 881-4555, *Fax:* (716) 882-8329
www.97rock.com
License: Buffalo, Erie County, NY
Group Owner: Cumulus Media Inc.; (acq 2-23-00; grpsl).
Arbitron Metro Market: Buffalo-Niagara Falls, NY *Format:* Classic Rock *Target Audience:* 25-49; classic rock listeners
John Hager, Operations Dir
Chet Osadchey, General Manager
Ryan McCrohan, Promotions Manager
Chris Klein, News Director
Al Marranca, Chief Engineer

WHTT-FM
10-03-1954; 104.1 mhz FM *Hrs Open:* 24; 50 kw; 387 ft.; N42 49 50 W78 48 1
350 Park Ave, 20th Floor, New York, NY 10022 US
(716) 881-4555, *Fax:* (716) 884-2931
www.whtt.com
info@whtt.com
License: Buffalo, Erie County, NY
Group Owner: Cumulus Media Inc.; (acq 2-23-2000; grpsl).
Nat'l Network: ABC *Nat'l Reps:* Eastman Radio
Arbitron Metro Market: Buffalo-Niagara Falls, NY *Format:* Adult Contemp *Target Audience:* 35-64; women and adults
Steve Bearance, General Manager
Rose Porter, General Sales Mgr
Joe Siragusa, Programming Director
Mike Battaglia, Promotions Manager
Chet Osadchey, General Sales Manager

WJYE
11-11-1966; 96.1 mhz FM *Hrs Open:* 24; 47 kw; 505 ft.; N42 53 10 W78 52 25
600 New Hampshire Ave NW, Suite 1200, Washington, DC 20037 US
(716) 856-3550, *Fax:* (716) 852-0537
www.961joyfm.com
joe.russo@townsquaremedia.com
License: Buffalo, Erie County, NY
Group Owner: Townsquare Media; (acq 12-15-2006; grpsl)
Nat'l Reps: Christal
Arbitron Metro Market: Buffalo-Niagara Falls, NY *Format:* Adult Contemp *Special Programming:* Pub affrs 2 hrs wkly *Hrs. of News Programming:* news progmg 23 hrs wkly *No. News Employees:* 1 *Target Audience:* 25-54.
Jeff Silver, Operations Dir
Andrea DeFazio, General Sales Mgr
Joe Russo, Programming Director
Katie Benson, Promotions Manager
Bob Hill, News Director

WBUF
01-01-1947; 92.9 mhz FM; 76 kw; 640 ft.; N42 57 13 W78 52 36
600 New Hampshire Ave NW, Suite 1200, Washington, DC 20037 US
(716) 852-9292, *Fax:* (716) 852-9290
www.wbuf.com
joe.russo@townsquaremedia.com
License: Buffalo, Erie County, NY
Group Owner: Townsquare Media; (acq 12-15-2006; grpsl)
Nat'l Network: CBS Radio; CNN Radio *Nat'l Reps:* Christal
Arbitron Metro Market: Buffalo-Niagara Falls, NY *Format:* Talk *Target Audience:* 18-34; men
Jeff Silver, Operations Dir
Dan Walding, General Sales Mgr
Joe Russo, Programming Director
Jean Tod, Promotions Manager
Bob Hill, News Director

WTSS
11-11-1946; 102.5 mhz FM *Hrs Open:* 24; 110 kw; 1,340 ft; N42 39 33 W78 37 33
500 Corporate Pkwy., Suite 200, Amherst, NY 21030
(716) 843-0600, *Fax:* (716) 832-2872
www.star1025.com
License: Buffalo, Erie County, NY
Nat'l Reps: Katz
Arbitron Metro Market: Buffalo-Niagara Falls, NY *Target Audience:* 18-49.
Sue O'Neil, Operations Dir

WBBF
09-01-1947; 1120 khz AM; 1 kw-D, NDD; N42 49 50 W78 48 1
350 Park Ave, 20th Floor, New York, NY 10022 US
(716) 783-7522, *Fax:* (716) 783-7524
License: Buffalo, NY
Group Owner: Cumulus Media Inc.
Arbitron Metro Market: Buffalo, NY *Format:* Spanish
Natalie Hutchen, Operations Dir
Michael Brummer, General Manager
John Young, Operations Manager

***WNED**
10-14-1924; 970 khz AM *Hrs Open:* 24; 5 kw-U, DA1; N42 44 41 W78 53 13
Mailing Address: P.O. Box 1263, Buffalo, NY 14240 US
Second Address: 140 Lower Terr., Buffalo, NY 14202
(716) 845-7000, *Fax:* (716) 845-7043
www.wned.org
info@wned.org
License: Buffalo, NY held by Western New York Public Broadcasting Assoc.
Nat'l Network: PRI; NPR
Arbitron Metro Market: Buffalo, NY *Format:* News, News/Talk, 86 *Special Programming:* Pub affrs *No. News Employees:* 8 *Target Audience:* 35 plus.
Donald Boswell, President
Richard Daly, Station Manager
Cynthia Dwyer, General Sales Mgr
Al Wallack, Programming Director
Gwen Mysiak, Promotions Manager
Sam Anson, News Director
Jon Herrington, Engineering Dir
Monica Wilson,Local News Editor
Jim Dimino, Sales VP

WNED-FM
06-06-1960; 94.5 mhz FM; 105 kw; 709 ft.; N42 38 13 W78 46 5
P.O. Box 1263, Buffalo, NY 14240 US
(716) 845-7000, *Fax:* (716) 845-7043
www.wned.org
info@wned.org
License: Buffalo, Erie County, NY held by Western New York Public Broadcasting Assoc.
Nat'l Network: PRI
Arbitron Metro Market: Buffalo, NY *TV Affiliate:* *WNED-TV affil *Format:* Talk
Peter Goldsmith, Programming Director

WWKB
01-01-1925; 1520 khz AM *Hrs Open:* 24; 50 kw-U, DA1; N42 46 10 W78 50 34
10706 Beaver Dam Road, Cockeysville, MD 21030 US
(716) 843-0600, *Fax:* (716) 832-3323
www.kb1520.com
License: Buffalo, NY held by Entercom Buffalo License LLC.
Group Owner: Entercom Communications Corp.; (acq 12-13-99; grpsl)
Nat'l Reps: D & R Radio
Arbitron Metro Market: Buffalo, NY *Format:* Alternative, Talk *Hrs. of News Programming:* news progmg 20 hrs wkly *No. News Employees:* 4 *Target Audience:* 25-54.
Tim Wenger, Operations Dir
Gregory Ried, General Manager
Tim Wenger, Programming Director
Krystyna Jackson, Promotions Manager
Kevin Carr, Assistant Program Director
Tim Holly, Sales Director
Tell Vickers, Web Developer

WWWS
01-01-1934; 1400 khz AM
10706 Beaver Dam Road, Cockeysville, MD 21030 US
(716) 843-0600, *Fax:* (716) 843-3323
www.am1400solidgoldsoul.com
License: Buffalo, NY held by Entercom Buffalo License LLC.
Group Owner: Entercom Communications Corp.; (acq 12-13-99; grpsl)

Nat'l Reps: Katz Radio
Arbitron Metro Market: Buffalo, NY *Format:* Urban Contemporary *Target Audience:* 35-54.
Larry Robb, General Manager
Sue O'Neil, Programming Director
Lindsay Truesdell, Promotions Manager
Tom Karvelis, Chief Engineer
TellVickers, Web Developer
Matt Giansante, Internet Sales

WYRK
11-14-1962; 106.5 mhz FM; 50 kw; 466 ft.; N42 53 10 W78 52 25
600 New Hampshire Ave NW, Suite 1200, Washington, DC 20037 US
(716) 852-7444, *Fax:* (716) 852-5683
www.wyrk.com
info@wyrk.com
License: Buffalo, Erie County, NY
Group Owner: Townsquare Media; (acq 12-15-2006; grpsl)
Nat'l Reps: Katz Radio *Wire Services:* UPI
Arbitron Metro Market: Buffalo-Niagara *Format:* Country *Target Audience:* 25-54; adults
Jeff Silver, Operations Dir
Mark Plimpton, General Sales Mgr
Wendy Lynn, Programming Director
Dean Sarago, Promotions Manager
Bob Hill, News Director

Calcium

WOTT
01-01-2009; 94.1 mhz FM; 21.5 kw; 354 ft.; N43 58 0 W75 48 11 US
(315) 786-9552, *Fax:* (315) 782-0312
www.94rockwott.com
lancer.rockradio@gmail.com
License: Calcium, Jefferson County, NY held by Community Broadcasters LLC.
Group Owner: Community Broadcasters LLC; (acq 1-8-2009; $200,000 for CP)
Arbitron Metro Market: Calcium, NY
James Leven, President
Jim Leven, General Manager
Lance Hale, Programming Director

Calverton-Roanoke

WPTY
01-01-1998; 105.3 mhz FM *Hrs Open:* 24; 1 kw; Ant 492 ft; N40 51 18 W72 46 12
3075 Vets Memorial Hwy. #201, Ronkonkoma, NY 11530
(631) 648-2500, *Fax:* (516) 222-1391
info@wlir.com
License: Calverton-Roanoke, Suffolk County, NY held by Jarad Broadcasting Co. of Calverton Inc.
Group Owner: JVC Broadcasting; (acq 10-2-98).
Nat'l Reps: Christal
Arbitron Metro Market: New York
Beverly Fortune, General Manager

Canajoharie

***WCAN**
10-01-1988; 93.3 mhz FM *Hrs Open:* 24; 6 kw; 269 ft.; N42 53 46 W74 35 45 *Rebroadcasts:* Rebroadcast WAMC-FM Albany 100%
318 Central Avenue, Albany, NY 12206 US
(518) 465-5233(800) 323-9262, *Fax:* (518) 432-6974
www.wamc.org
mail@wamc.org
License: Canajoharie, Montgomery County, NY held by WAMC.
Group Owner: WAMC/Northeast Public Radio
Nat'l Network: PRI; NPR *Wire Services:* AP
Arbitron Metro Market: Albany, NY *Format:* News, Talk *Special Programming:* Jazz 17 hrs, folk 7 hrs wkly *Hrs. of News Programming:* News progmg 48 hrs wkly *Target Audience:* General.
Alan Chartock, CEO
Alan Chartock, President
Selma Kaplan, Operations Dir
David Galletly, Vice President

Canandaigua

WCGR
04-05-1961; 1550 khz AM *Hrs Open:* 6 AM-6 PM; 0.25 kw-D, NDD; N42 52 52 W77 15 2
P.O. Box 155, Canandaigua, NY 14424 US
(315) 781-7000, *Fax:* (315) 781-7700
www.k1017.com/Home.html
License: Canandaigua, NY held by The Fingerlakes Radio Group Inc.
Group Owner: Finger Lakes Radio Group; (acq 12-93; with co-located FM;
Arbitron Metro Market: Geneva, NY *Format:* News, News/Talk, 86 *Hrs. of News Programming:* news progmg 10 hrs wkly *No. News Employees:* 1 *Target Audience:* General.
George Kimble, President
Alan Bishop, General Manager
Paula Triplett, General Sales Mgr
Mike Smith, Programming Director
Ted Baker, News Director

***WCIY**
12-14-1992; 88.9 mhz FM; 0.68 kw; 1063 ft.; N42 44 44 W77 25 34 *Rebroadcasts:* Rebroadcasts WCIK(FM) Bath 100%
Mailing Address: P.O. Box 506, Bath, NY 14810 US
Second Address: 7634 Campbell Creek Rd., Bath, NY
(607) 776-4151, *Fax:* (607) 776-6929
www.fln.org
mail@fln.org
License: Canandaigua, Ontario County, NY held by Family Life Ministries Inc.
Group Owner: Family Life Network
Nat'l Network: Salem Radio Network *Wire Services:* Metro Weather Service Inc.
Arbitron Metro Market: Bath, NY *Format:* Christian *Hrs. of News Programming:* news progmg 14 hrs wkly *No. News Employees:* 3 *Target Audience:* 30-54.
Dick Snavely, CFO
Rick Snavely, President
Cecil Van Houten, Radio Operations Manager
Sammy Carrillo, Programming Director
Sammy Carrillo, Promotions Manager
Jim Travis, Chief Engineer

WVOR
07-16-1974; 102.3 mhz FM *Hrs Open:* 24; 3.4 kw; 282 ft.; N42 51 47 W77 19 22
50 East Rivercenter Bvld., Suite 1200, Covington, KY 41011 US
(585) 393-1240, *Fax:* (585) 454-5081
www.radiosunny.com
DaveLeFrois@clearchannel.com
License: Canandaigua, Ontario County, NY held by Citicasters Licenses L.P.
Group Owner: Clear Channel Communications Inc.; (acq 5-4-99; grpsl).
Arbitron Metro Market: Rochester, NY *Format:* Adult Contemp *Hrs. of News Programming:* News progmg 3 hrs wkly *Target Audience:* 25-54.
Dave LeFrois, Operations Dir
Karen Carey, General Manager
Bonnie Dolan, General Sales Mgr
Matt Basile, Webmaster

WRSB
04-05-1997; 1310 khz AM; 1 kw-D, DA2; 1 kw-N, DA2; N42 53 20 W77 19 9 *Rebroadcasts:* Rebroadcasts WASB(AM) Brockport 100%
7280 Sandy Shore Dr., Hamlin, NY 14464 US
(585) 637-7040
License: Canandaigua, NY held by David Wolfe
Nat'l Network: ABC
Arbitron Metro Market: Rochester, NY *Format:* Christian *Target Audience:* Everyone; all ages
Dr. David Wolfe, General Manager
Gail Reed, Programming Director

Canton

WRCD
01-01-1997; 101.5 mhz FM *Hrs Open:* 24; 50 kw; 453 ft.; N44 35 56 W74 46 24
515 Skylake Court, Incline Village, NV 89451 US
(315) 769-3333, *Fax:* (315) 769-3299
www.1015thefox.com
studio@1015thefox.com
License: Canton, St. Lawrence County, NY held by Stephens Media Group-Massena LLC.
Group Owner: Stephens Family L.P.
Hrs. of News Programming: news progmg 7 hrs wkly *No. News Employees:* 2 *Target Audience:* 30-50; country fans
Michael Boldt, General Manager
Drew Scott, Programming Director
Bob Larue, News Director
Bob Sauder, Chief Engineer

***WSLU**
12-01-1964; 89.5 mhz FM *Hrs Open:* 24; 40 kw; 299 ft.; N44 32 1 W75 5 50
North Country Public Rad, Canton, NY 13617 US
(315) 229-5356, *Fax:* (315) 229-5373
www.ncpr.org
radio@ncpr.org
License: Canton, St. Lawrence County, NY held by St. Lawrence University.
Nat'l Network: NPR; PRI
Format: Variety/Diverse *Special Programming:* Gospel, jazz, class, folk, pub affrs, Black *Hrs. of News Programming:* news progmg 35 hrs wkly *No. News Employees:* 2 *Target Audience:* General.
Ellen Rocco, General Manager
Ellen Rocco, Station Manager
Jacqueline Sauter, Programming Director
Martha Foley, News Director
Robert Sauter, Chief Engineer
Sandra Demarest, Underwriting Director

WNCQ-FM
07-01-1984; 102.9 mhz FM *Hrs Open:* 24; 23.5 kw; Ant 338 ft; N44 32 10 W75 05 46
1 Bridge Plaza, Suite 204, Ogdensburg, NY 89451
(315) 393-1220, *Fax:* (315) 393-3974
www.q1029.com
john@q1029.com
License: Canton, St. Lawrence County, NY held by Stephens Media Group-Ogdensburg LLC.
Group Owner: Stephens Family L.P.
Population Served: 100,000*Target Audience:* 25-54; adults *Adv. Rates:* 26; 22; 26; 22
John Winter, General Manager

***WREM**
88.7 mhz FM; 2.6 kw; Ant 233 ft; N44 32 01 W75 05 50
North Country Public Radio, St. Lawrence University, Canton, NY
(315) 229-5356, *Fax:* (315) 229-5373
www.northcountrypublicradio.org
License: Canton, St. Lawrence County, NY held by The St. Lawrence University.
Ellen Rocco, Station Manager

Cape Vincent

WLYK
04-21-1997; 102.7 mhz FM *Hrs Open:* 24; 6 kw; 328 ft.; N44 6 58 W76 20 21
199 Wealtha Avenue, Watertown, NY 13601 US
(414) 935-3000, *Fax:* (414) 935-3015
www.vcyamerica.org
kvfl@vcyamerica.org
License: Cape Vincent, Jefferson County, NY held by Border International Broadcasting Inc.
Group Owner: Clancy-Mance Communications; (acq 10-15-98; $50,000)
Nat'l Reps: Roslin
Arbitron Metro Market: Colorado Springs CO *Format:* Christian, Religious
Vic Eliason, Operations Dir
Jim Schneider, Programming Director

***WMHI**
10-01-1990; 94.7 mhz FM *Hrs Open:* 24; 6 kw; 284 ft; N44 02 42 W76 15 37 *Rebroadcasts:* Rebroadcasts WMHR(FM) Syracuse 98%
4044 Makyes Rd., Syracuse, NY 13215
(315) 469-5051
www.marshillnetwork.org
mhn@marshillnetwork.org
License: Cape Vincent, Jefferson County, NY held by Mars Hill Broadcasting Co. Inc. dba Mars Hill Network.
Group Owner: Mars Hill Network
Nat'l Network: Moody; Salem Radio Network *Wire Services:* AP
Arbitron Metro Market: Watertown, NY *Hrs. of News Programming:* News progmg 6 hrs wkly *Target Audience:* General; Christian families
Clayton Roberts, President
Mark Hard, Operations Dir
Wayne Taylor, General Manager
Chris Tetta, Programming Director
Craig Case, Promotions Manager
Valerie Smith, News Director
Rich McVicar, Traffic Manager
Mike Dwinell,Engineering

***WSLZ**
88.1 mhz FM; 2 kw; 302 ft.; N44 6 58 W76 20 21 US
(315) 229-5356, *Fax:* (315) 229-5373
www.ncpr.org
radio@ncpr.org
License: Cape Vincent, Jefferson County, NY held by The St. Lawrence University.
Arbitron Metro Market: Cape Vincent, NY *No. News Employees:* 4
Shelly Pike, Operations Dir
Ellen Rocco, General Manager

Ellen Rocco, Station Manager
Jackie Sauter, Programming Director
Martha Foley, News Director
Bob Sauter, Chief Engineer
Sandy Demarest, Development Director
Joel Hurd,Production Manager
June Peoples, Membership Director
Naomi Weller, Office Manager

Carthage

WTOJ
11-01-1984; 103.1 mhz FM *Hrs Open:* 24; 1.8 kw; 594 ft.; N43 57 15 W75 43 45
199 Wealtha Ave., Watertown, NY 13601 US
(315) 782-1240, *Fax:* (315) 782-0312
www.magic103.com
jim_leven@commbroadcasters.com
License: Carthage, Jefferson County, NY held by Community Broadcasters LLC.
Group Owner: Community Broadcasters LLC; (acq 2-8-2007; grpsl)
Nat'l Reps: Roslin
Arbitron Metro Market: Watertown, NY *Format:* Adult Contemp *Target Audience:* 25-54.
Todd Dalesandro, Operations Dir
James Leven, General Manager
Joseph Brosk, Station Manager
Ken Martin, Programming Director

Catskill

WCKL
02-06-1970; 560 khz AM *Hrs Open:* 24; 1 kw-D, DA2; 0.043 kw-N, DA2; N42 12 3 W73 50 9
5620 Route 9g, Hudson, NY 12534 US
(518) 828-3940, *Fax:* (518) 828-1080
www.familybroadcasting.net
License: Catskill, NY held by Black United Fund of New York Inc.
Arbitron Metro Market: Mid-Hudson Region *Format:* Talk
Kermit Eady, President

WCTW
09-01-1990; 98.5 mhz FM *Hrs Open:* 24; 4.7 kw; 374 ft.; N42 12 3 W73 50 9
5620 Route 9g, Hudson, NY 12534 US
(518) 828-5006, *Fax:* (518) 828-1080
www.985thecat.com
billwilliams@clearchannel.com
License: Catskill, Greene County, NY held by CC Licenses LLC.
Group Owner: Clear Channel Communications Inc.; (acq 1-17-2002; grpsl)
Nat'l Network: Fox News Radio *Nat'l Reps:* Katz Radio *Wire Services:* AP
Arbitron Metro Market: Hudson, NY *Format:* Adult Contemp *Hrs. of News Programming:* news progmg 7 hrs wkly *No. News Employees:* 1 *Target Audience:* 25-44; female
Reggie Osterhoudt, Operations Dir
Frank Curcio, General Manager
Rob VanDerbeck, General Sales Mgr
Bill Williams, Programming Director
Brian Powers, Promotions Manager
Cameron Hendrix, News Director

Cazenovia

***WITC**
04-01-1978; 88.9 mhz FM *Hrs Open:* Noon-midnight; 0.13 kw; 33 ft.; N42 55 53 W75 51 15
Seminary Street, Cazenovia, NY 13035 US
(315) 655-7154
License: Cazenovia, Madison County, NY held by Cazenovia College.
Format: Alternative *Special Programming:* News/talk 3 hrs, div 10 hrs wkly *Hrs. of News Programming:* News progmg 3 hrs wkly *Target Audience:* 15-35; college & young area residents
Roger Benn, General Manager

Center Moriches

WJVC
03-03-1997; 96.1 mhz FM *Hrs Open:* 24; 2.65 kw; Ant 499 ft; N40 51 08 W72 45 55
3241 Rt. 112, Bldg. #7, Medford, NY 11901
(631) 451-1039, *Fax:* (631) 451-0891
www.wrcn.com
info@wrcn.com
License: Center Moriches, Suffolk County, NY held by IW Limited Liability Co.
Group Owner: JVC Broadcasting; acq 1-13-2004; $3.75 million).

Dave Widmer, General Manager
Sal Abetamarco, General Sales Mgr
Charlie Lombardo, Programming Director
Megan Moir, Promotions Manager
Jen Moran, News Director
Bob Anderson, Chief Engineer

Champlain

WCHP
08-20-1985; 760 khz AM *Hrs Open:* Sunrise-sunset
1601 Belvedere Road, 204 E., West Palm Beach, FL 33406 US
(518) 298-2800, *Fax:* (518) 298-2604
www.wchp.com
wchp@primelink1.net
License: Champlain, NY held by Champlain Radio Inc.
Arbitron Metro Market: Detroit, MI *Format:* Talk, Religious
Special Programming: Fr, Sp *Target Audience:* 25 plus.
Tonya Billiter, Operations Dir
Teri Billiter, General Manager
Brandi Lloyd, Programming Director

Chateaugay

WYUL
04-15-1997; 94.7 mhz FM *Hrs Open:* 24; 50 kw horiz, 49 kw vert; 449 ft.; N44 46 56 W74 13 9
955 S. Virginia, Reno, NV 89502 US
(518) 483-1100, *Fax:* (518) 483-1382
License: Chateaugay, Franklin County, NY held by Cartier Communications Inc.
Group Owner: Martz Communications Group
Arbitron Metro Market: Chateaugay, NY *Format:* Contemporary Hits/Top 40
Timothy Martz, CEO
Michael Boldt, General Manager
Kim Scott, General Sales Mgr
Drew Scott, Programming Director
Neil Drew, News Director

Cheektowaga

WECK
08-01-1956; 1230 khz AM; 1 kw-D, ND1; 1 kw-N, ND1; N42 55 27 W78 46 41
600 New Hampshire Ave NW, Suite 1200, Washington, DC 20037 US
(716) 783-9120, *Fax:* (716) 783-9121
www.breezebuffalo.com/
License: Cheektowaga, NY held by Culver Communications II Inc.
Nat'l Network: Westwood One *Nat'l Reps:* Christal
Arbitron Metro Market: Buffalo, NY *Format:* Talk *Special Programming:* Pol 2 hrs wkly *Target Audience:* 35-64.
Richard Greene, President

Chenango Bridge

WWYL
07-01-1996; 104.1 mhz FM; 0.93 kw; 833 ft.; N42 3 29 W75 57 15
140 S. Ash Ave., Tempe, AZ 85281 US
(607) 772-8400, *Fax:* (607) 772-9806
www.wild104fm.com
License: Chenango Bridge, Broome County, NY
Group Owner: Cumulus Media Inc.; (acq 6-9-99; grpsl).
Arbitron Metro Market: Binghamton, NY *Format:* Contemporary Hits/Top 40
Mary Beth Walsh, General Manager
Eric Donaldson, General Sales Mgr
Matt Johnson, Programming Director
Andrew Smith, Promotions Manager

Cherry Valley

WJIV
01-01-1949; 101.9 mhz FM *Hrs Open:* 24; 11.5 kw; 1024 ft.; N42 47 36 W74 41 41
Mailing Address: 3 Computer Dr. West, Suite 126, Albany, NY 12205 US
Second Address: 1668 Country Hwy. 50, Cherry Valley, NY 13320
(607) 264-3062, *Fax:* (607) 264-8277
www.wjivradio.com
wjiv@hughes.net
License: Cherry Valley, Otsego County, NY held by Christian Broadcasting System Ltd.
Group Owner: Christian Broadcasting System Ltd.; acq 6-5-00; $1.3 million).
Wire Services: UPI
Format: Talk, Religious *Target Audience:* 25-54.

John Yinger, President
Rob Baltodano, General Manager
Alfin Maynor, Station Manager
Steve Crapser, Programming Director
Kim Pratt, Business Manager

Clayton

***WRVH**
08-16-1989; 89.3 mhz FM *Hrs Open:* 24; 7.9 kw; 86 ft.; N44 15 3 W76 1 50.6
US
(570) 323-8200, *Fax:* (570) 327-9138
License: Clayton, Lycoming County, NY held by South Williamsport SabreCom Inc.
Group Owner: Backyard Broadcasting LLC; (acq 12-1-2002; grpsl)
Nat'l Network: ABC *Nat'l Reps:* Christal
Arbitron Metro Market: Williamsport, P *Format:* Adult Contemp *Hrs. of News Programming:* news progmg one hr wkly *No. News Employees:* 1 *Target Audience:* 25-54. *Adv. Rates:* 15; 15; 15; 15
Robin Smith, CFO
Barry Drake, President
Dan Farr, General Manager

Clifton Park

WDCD-FM
11-01-1985; 96.7 mhz FM *Hrs Open:* 24; 4.7 kw; 328 ft; N42 52 44 W73 51 47
4243 Albany St., Albany, NY 19422
(518) 862-1540, *Fax:* (518) 862-1545
www.crawfordbroadcasting.com
info@crawfordbroadcasting.com
License: Clifton Park, Saratoga County, NY held by Kimtron Inc.
Group Owner: Crawford Broadcasting Co.; (acq 1996; $820,000).
Population Served: 850,000 *Arbitron Metro Market:* Albany-Schenectady-Troy, NY *Target Audience:* 30-64; financially capable
Donald Crawford, Jr., President
Peter Kaye, Programming Director
David Groth, Chief Engineer
Donald Crawford, President

Clinton

***WHCL-FM**
02-18-1963; 88.7 mhz FM *Hrs Open:* 24; 0.27 kw; 95 ft.; N43 3 4 W75 24 24
% Office of Student Act., 198 College Hill Rd, Clinton, NY 13323 US
(315) 859-4200
www.whcl.org
mngrwhcl@hamilton.edu
License: Clinton, Oneida County, NY held by The Trustees of Hamilton College.
Format: Rock/AOR, Variety/Diverse *Special Programming:* Class 9 hrs, jazz 9 hrs, relg 2 hrs wkly *Target Audience:* General.
Alex Price, Programming Director

Clyde

***WCOV-FM**
12-05-1995; 93.7 mhz FM; 3.8 kw; 328 ft.; N42 59 38 W76 51 59
Rebroadcasts: Rebroadcasts WCIK(FM) Bath 100%
Mailing Address: 5990 Experimental Road, Auburn, NY 13021 US
Second Address: 7634 Campbell Creek Rd., Bath, NY 14810
(607) 776-4151, *Fax:* (607) 776-6929
www.fln.org
mail@fln.org
License: Clyde, Wayne County, NY held by Family Life Ministries Inc.
Group Owner: Family Life Network; (acq 10-3-00).
Nat'l Network: Salem Radio Network *Wire Services:* Metro Weather Service Inc.
Format: Christian *Hrs. of News Programming:* news progmg 14 hrs wkly *No. News Employees:* 3 *Target Audience:* 30-54.
Dick Snavely, CFO
Rick Snavely, President
John Owens, Programming Director
Jim Travis, Chief Engineer

Cobleskill

WQBJ
09-01-1986; 103.5 mhz FM; 50 kw; 492 ft.; N42 58 21 W74 29 30
Rebroadcasts: Rebroadcasts WQBK-FM Rensselaer 100%
200 Concord Plaza, Suite 600, San Antonio, TX 78216 US

(518) 881-1515, *Fax:* (518) 881-1516
www.wqbk.com
License: Cobleskill, Schoharie County, NY
Group Owner: Townsquare Media; (acq 8-7-2000; grpsl)
Arbitron Metro Market: Albany-Schenectady-Troy, NY *Format:* Rock/AOR *Target Audience:* 18-49; general
Robert Ausfeld, General Manager
Bob O'Neal, Chief Engineer

WSDE
07-01-1981; 1190 khz AM *Hrs Open:* 6 AM-sunset
1525 Aviation Blvd., Ste-213, Redondo Beach, CA 90278 US
(518) 234-3400, *Fax:* (518) 234-4567
www.1190wsde.com
License: Cobleskill, NY held by Viva Communications Group LLC
Nat'l Network: CNN Radio
Arbitron Metro Market: Cobleskill, NY *Format:* Classic Rock *Target Audience:* General.
Ed Sherlock, President/General Manager
Bob Taylor, Operations/Traffic
Alla Horak, Office Manager

Cold Brook

***WMHU(FM)**
91.1 mhz FM; 560 watts; 143.2 meters; 43 12 01N 74 53 17W
4044 Makyes Road, Syracuse, NY 13215 USA
(800) 677-1881, *Fax:* (716) 488-1471
www.marshallhillnetwork.org
License: Cold Brook, Herkimer County, NY
Group Owner: Mars Hill Network
Wayne Taylor, General Manager
Mark Hard, Programming Director
Mike Dwinell, Engineering Dir

Conklin

WKGB-FM
02-11-1989; 92.5 mhz FM *Hrs Open:* 24; 1.45 kw; 676 ft.; N42 6 48 W75 51 9
Suite 200, 776 Conklin Rd., Binghamton, NY 13903 US
(607) 584-5800, *Fax:* (607) 584-5900
www.925kgb.com
info@925kgb.com
License: Conklin, Broome County, NY held by CC Licenses LLC.
Group Owner: Clear Channel Communications Inc.; (acq 4-14-2000; grpsl)
Nat'l Reps: D & R Radio
Arbitron Metro Market: Binghamton, NY *Format:* Classic Rock, Rock/AOR *Special Programming:* Jazz 2 hrs, farm one hr wkly *Hrs. of News Programming:* News progmg one hr wkly *Target Audience:* 25-49; baby boomerswho grew up with rock and roll of the 60s & 70s
Jim Free, Operations Dir
Tom Burney, General Manager
Michele Page, General Sales Mgr
Tom Barney, Promotions Manager

Copenhagen

WBDR
01-01-1994; 106.7 mhz FM *Hrs Open:* 24; 1.8 kw; 1191 ft.; N43 52 47 W75 43 11
199 Wealtha Ave, Watertown, NY 13601 US
(315) 782-1240, *Fax:* (315) 782-0312
www.wbdr.com
blade@theborder.com
License: Copenhagen, Lewis County, NY held by Community Broadcasters LLC.
Group Owner: Community Broadcasters LLC; (acq 2-8-2007; grpsl)
Nat'l Reps: Roslin
Arbitron Metro Market: Watertown, NY *Format:* Contemporary Hits/Top 40
James Leven, President
Todd Dalesandro, Operations Dir
David Mance, General Manager
Dick Whelan, General Sales Mgr

Corinth

WFFG-FM
06-26-1967; 107.1 mhz FM *Hrs Open:* 24; 2.85 kw; 482 ft.; N43 14 40 W73 46 18
89 Everts Avenue, Queensbury, NY 12804 US
(518) 793-7733, *Fax:* (518) 793-0838
www.froggy107.com
mthompson@adirondackbroadcasting.com
License: Corinth, Saratoga County, NY held by 6 Johnson Road Licenses Inc.
Group Owner: Pamal Broadcasting Ltd.; (acq 4-1-2004; grpsl).
Format: Country *Hrs. of News Programming:* news progmg 2 hrs wkly *No. News Employees:* 1 *Target Audience:* 18-54. *Adv. Rates:* 30; 28; 30; 15.
Walt Adams, Operations Dir
Mike Thompson, General Manager

Corning

WCBA
11-01-1948; 1350 khz AM *Hrs Open:* 24; 1 kw-D, ND1; 0.037 kw-N, ND1; N42 6 59 W77 2 24
P.O. Box 1047, Corning, NY 14830 US
(607) 962-4646, *Fax:* (607) 962-1138
cnj@route81radio.com
License: Corning, NY held by WS2K Radio LLC.
Group Owner: WS2K Radio LLC dba WS Media; (acq 7-14-2008; grpsl)
Nat'l Network: Westwood One *Nat'l Reps:* Roslin
Arbitron Metro Market: Corning, NY *Format:* Sports *Target Audience:* 50 plus.
Jamie Evans, Station Manager

WGMM
02-01-1989; 98.7 mhz FM *Hrs Open:* 24; 1.2 kw; 722 ft.; N42 8 31 W77 4 40 *Rebroadcasts:* Rebroadcasts WENY-FM Elmira 100%
P.O. Box 1047, Corning, NY 14830 US
(607) 937-8181, *Fax:* (607) 962-1138
www.987gemfm.com/
wenyfrankIyspeaking@gmail.com
License: Corning, Steuben County, NY held by WS2K Radio LLC.
Group Owner: WS2K Radio LLC dba WS Media; (acq 7-14-2008; grpsl)
Nat'l Network: ABC *Nat'l Reps:* McGavren Guild
Arbitron Metro Market: Corning, NY *Format:* Adult Contemp
Frank Acomb, Operations Dir
Jamie Evans, General Manager
Scott Benjamin, Sales Manager
Betty Coccho, Business Manager

WENI
11-01-1949; 1450 khz AM; 1 kw-D, ND1; 0.93 kw-N, ND1; N42 6 59 W77 2 24 *Rebroadcasts:* Rebroadcasts WENY(AM) Elmira 100%.
PO Box 1047, Corning, NY 14830 US
(607) 962-4646, *Fax:* (607) 962-1138
cnj@route81radio.com
License: Corning, NY held by WS2K Radio LLC.
Group Owner: WS2K Radio LLC dba WS Media; (acq 7-14-2008; grpsl)
Nat'l Network: USA *Nat'l Reps:* McGavren Guild
Arbitron Metro Market: Corning, NY *Format:* News, News/Talk, 86 *Target Audience:* 25-64.
Paul Lyle, General Manager

WNKI
05-01-1947; 106.1 mhz FM; 40 kw; 531 ft.; N42 9 43 W77 2 15
1685 Four Mile Drive, Williamsport, PA 17701 US
(607) 732-4400, *Fax:* (607) 732-7774
www.wink106.com
smitty.oloughlin@bybradio.com
License: Corning, Steuben County, NY held by Chemung County Radio Inc.
Group Owner: Backyard Broadcasting LLC; (acq 12-1-02; grpsl).
Nat'l Reps: Christal
Arbitron Metro Market: Elmira, NY *Format:* Adult Contemp *Hrs. of News Programming:* news progmg one hr wkly *No. News Employees:* 1 *Target Audience:* 25-54; women
Scott Free, Operations Dir
Smitty O'Loughlin, General Manager
Brian Povancher, General Sales Mgr
Scott Free, Programming Director

***WSQE**
01-01-1995; 91.1 mhz FM *Hrs Open:* 24; 3.6 kw; 653 ft.; N42 6 20 W76 52 17 *Rebroadcasts:* Rebroadcasts WSKG-FM Binghamton 100%
P.O. Box 3000, Binghamton, NY 13902 US
(607) 729-0100
www.wskg.com
info@wskg.org
License: Corning, Steuben County, NY held by WSKG Public Telecommunications Council.
Nat'l Network: NPR; PRI; AP Radio
Arbitron Metro Market: Elmira-Corning, NY *Format:* News *Special Programming:* Jazz, folk 5 hrs wkly *Hrs. of News Programming:* news progmg 33 hrs wkly *No. News Employees:* 1 *Target Audience:* General.
Brian Sickora, President
Nancy Christensen, Operations Dir
Ken Campbell, Programming Director
Stacy Mosteller, News Director
Linda Cohen, Underwriting Director

Cornwall

WWLE
11-22-1969; 1170 khz AM; 0.8 kw-D, DAD; N41 26 24 W74 4 25
1153 Route 44-55, Clintondale, NY 12515 US
(845) 569-7010, *Fax:* (845) 562-1348
License: Cornwall, NY held by 1170 Broadcast Radio Inc.
Nat'l Network: USA
Arbitron Metro Market: Newburgh-Middletown, NY *Format:* News, News/Talk, 86 *Special Programming:* Farm one hr wkly
Charles Stewart, General Manager

Cortland

WIII
11-15-1947; 99.9 mhz FM *Hrs Open:* 24; 26 kw; 682 ft.; N42 33 23 W76 9 19
1064 James Street, Syracuse, NY 13203 US
(607) 257-6400, *Fax:* (607) 257-6497
www.i100rocks.com
i100@wiii.com
License: Cortland, Cortland County, NY held by Saga Communications of New England LLC.
Group Owner: Saga Communications Inc.; (acq 9-1-2007; $4 million with co-located AM)
Nat'l Reps: Katz Radio
Arbitron Metro Market: Ithaca, NY *Format:* Classic Rock *Hrs. of News Programming:* news progmg one hr wkly *No. News Employees:* 1 *Target Audience:* 25-54; men
Chris Allinger, Operations Dir
Susan Johnston, General Manager

WYBY
11-15-1947; 920 khz AM *Hrs Open:* 24
1064 James Street, Syracuse, NY 13203 US
(704) 523-5555
www.bbnradio.org
bbn@bbnradio.org
License: Cortland, NY held by Bible Broadcasting Network Inc.
Group Owner: Bible Broadcasting Network; (acq 9-1-2007; donation)
Arbitron Metro Market: Ithaca, NY *Format:* Religious
Lowell Davey, President

***WSUC-FM**
11-17-1976; 90.5 mhz FM *Hrs Open:* 24; 0.21 kw; -59 ft.; N42 35 48 W76 11 23
Graham Ave Brockway Hall, Cortland, NY 13045 US
(607) 753-2936, *Fax:* (607) 753-2807
info@wsuc.com
License: Cortland, Cortland County, NY held by State University of New York.
Nat'l Network: AP Radio
Format: Variety/Diverse *Target Audience:* 12-50.
Peter Johams, General Manager

Dannemora

***WKVJ**
01-01-2005; 89.7 mhz FM *Hrs Open:* 24; 4.4 kw; 1096 ft.; N44 34 24 W73 40 31
Mailing Address: 1601 Belvedere Road, 204 E, West Palm Beach, FL 33406 US
Second Address: Box 888, Studio, Champlain, NY 12919
(800) 525-5683, *Fax:* (916) 251-1650
www.klove.com
klove@klove.com
License: Dannemora, Clinton County, NY held by American Educational Broadcasting Inc.
Arbitron Metro Market: Dannemora, NY *Format:* Christian
Darrell Chambliss, Chairman
Mike Novak, President and CEO
Fred Hodges, General Manager
Eric Allen, General Sales Mgr
David Pierce, Chief Creative Officer and Programming Director
Ed Lenane, News Director
Sam Wallington,Engineering Dir
Marya Morgan, News Reporter
Richard Hunt, News Reporter
Alan Mason, Chief Operating Officer
Dan Antonelli, Chief Business Development Officer
Eric Moser, Chief Financial Officer
Brian Burger, Vice President of HumanResources

WNMR
01-01-2008; 107.1 mhz FM; 1 kw; 276 ft.; N44 43 15.8 W73 44 10.5 *Rebroadcasts:* Simulcast with WCLX(FM) Westport 100% US

(804) 759-4000
www.fixationradio.com
License: Dannemora, Clinton County, NY held by Radioactive LLC.
Group Owner: Radioactive LLC
Arbitron Metro Market: Dannemora, NY *Format:* Classic Rock
Benjamin Homel, President

Dansville

WDNY
10-20-1978; 1400 khz AM *Hrs Open:* 19; 0.88 kw-D, ND1; 1 kw-N, ND1; N42 32 19 W77 40 57
129 Main Street, Dansville, NY 14437 US
(585) 335-9369, *Fax:* (585) 335-9677
www.wdnyradio.com
wdny@frontiernet.net
License: Dansville, NY held by Miller Media Inc.
Nat'l Network: Jones Radio Networks; Westwood One
Arbitron Metro Market: Rochester, NY *Format:* Contemporary Hits/Top 40 *Hrs. of News Programming:* news progmg 8 hrs wkly *No. News Employees:* 1 *Adv. Rates:* 21; 12; 12; 12.
Mark Miller, Programming Director

WDNY-FM
03-01-1990; 93.9 mhz FM *Hrs Open:* 24; 0.57 kw; 741 ft.; N42 30 45 W77 38 7
129 Main St., Dansville, NY 14437 US
(585) 335-9369, *Fax:* (585) 335-9677
www.wdnyradio.com
wdny@frontiernet.net
License: Dansville, Livingston County, NY held by Miller Media Inc.
Nat'l Network: Jones Radio Networks; Westwood One
Arbitron Metro Market: Rochester, NY *Format:* Adult Contemp *Special Programming:* Relg one hr, big band 3 hrs, sports 4 hrs wkly *Hrs. of News Programming:* news progmg 8 hrs wkly *No. News Employees:* 1 *TargetAudience:* 25-54. *Adv. Rates:* 21; 14; 14; 12
Dorothy Hotchkiss, General Manager

DeRuyter

WOLF-FM
01-01-1948; 105.1 mhz FM; 42 kw; Ant 541 ft; N42 46 58 W75 50 28
500 Plum St., Suite 100, Syracuse, NY 13204
(315) 472-9797, *Fax:* (315) 472-2323
www.y94fm.com
License: DeRuyter, Madison County, NY held by CC Licenses LLC.
Group Owner: Clear Channel Communications Inc.; (acq 3-12-2001; $5 million).
Population Served: 145,151 *Arbitron Metro Market:* Syracuse, NY *Format:* Adult Contemp *Target Audience:* 18-40; general
Rich Lauber, Operations Dir
Joel Delmonico, General Manager
Rick Yacobush, General Sales Mgr
Kathy Rowe, Programming Director
Joel Delmonico, Market Manager

WOLF-FM
105.1 mhz FM; 33000 w; 607 ft; N42 46 58 W75 50 28
401 W. Kirkpatrick Street, Syracuse, NY 13204
(315)472-0222, *Fax:* (315)478-7745
www.1051thewolf.com
License: DeRuyter, Madison County, NY
Group Owner: Foxfur Communications LLC
Keli Williams, Director of Sales

Delhi

WDHI
03-16-1992; 100.3 mhz FM *Hrs Open:* 16; 1.6 kw; 643 ft.; N42 22 43 W74 50 22
92 Main Street, Delhi, NY 13753 US
(607) 432-1030, *Fax:* (607) 432-6909
www.wdhifm.com
George.Wells@townsquaremedia.com
License: Delhi, Delaware County, NY held by Double O Central New York Corp.
Group Owner: Double O Radio L.L.C.; (acq 10-22-2004; grpsl)
Nat'l Network: USA
Arbitron Metro Market: Delhi, NY *Format:* Contemporary Hits/Top 40
George Wells, General Manager
Charlene Sugihara, Director of Sales

WTBD-FM
01-01-2008; 97.5 mhz FM; 6 kw; 328 ft.; N42 14 9 W74 57 12 US
(607) 432-1030, *Fax:* (607) 432-6909
www.wtbdfm.com
info@centralnewyorkradio.com
License: Delhi, Delaware County, NY held by Double O Central New York Corp.
Group Owner: Double O Radio L.L.C.
Arbitron Metro Market: Delhi, NY
Charlene Sugihara, Director of Sales
George Wells, Brand Manager

Depew

WBLK
12-01-1964; 93.7 mhz FM; 47 kw; 505 ft.; N42 53 10 W78 52 25
701 Northpoint Parkway, Suite 500, West Palm Beach, FL 33407 US
(716) 852-9393, *Fax:* (716) 852-9390
www.wblk.com
chris.reynolds@townsquaremedia.com
License: Depew, Erie County, NY
Group Owner: Townsquare Media; (acq 12-15-2006; grpsl)
Nat'l Network: CBS Radio *Nat'l Reps:* Katz Radio
Arbitron Metro Market: Buffalo, NY *Format:* Urban Contemporary *Target Audience:* General.
Jeff Silver, Operations Dir
Rose Vecchiarelli, General Sales Mgr
Chris Reynolds, Programming Director

Deposit

WIYN
01-16-1991; 94.7 mhz FM *Hrs Open:* 16; 0.77 kw; 643 ft.; N42 1 44 W75 28 25
P.O. Box 58, Walton, NY 13856 US
(607) 432-1030, *Fax:* (607) 432-6909
info@centralnewyorkradio.com
License: Deposit, Broome County, NY held by Double O Central New York Corp.
Group Owner: Double O Radio L.L.C.; (acq 10-22-2004; grpsl)
Arbitron Metro Market: Binghamton, NY *Format:* Oldies *Target Audience:* 28-55.
George Wells, General Manager

Dundee

WFLR
10-01-1956; 1570 khz AM *Hrs Open:* 24; 5 kw-D, ND1; 0.442 kw-N, ND1; N42 32 40 W76 59 35
260 Washington St., Watertown, NY 13601 US
(607) 243-7158, *Fax:* (607) 243-7662
www.fingerlakesdailynews.com
License: Dundee, NY held by Finger Lakes Radio Group Inc.
Group Owner: Finger Lakes Radio Group; (acq 3-5-2004; $600,000 with co-located FM)
Nat'l Network: Motor Racing Net
Format: Country, News, 62, Talk *Special Programming:* Relg 5 hrs wkly *Hrs. of News Programming:* news progmg 40 hrs wkly *No. News Employees:* 1 *Target Audience:* 25-55.
Dick Evans, General Manager
Mark Feiock, Promotions Manager

Dunkirk

WDOE
12-24-1949; 1410 khz AM
PO Box 1199, Jamestown, NY 14048 US
(716) 366-1410(716) 366-8580, *Fax:* (716) 366-1416
www.wdoe1410.com
community@wdoe1410.com
License: Dunkirk, NY held by Chadwick Bay Broadcasting Corp.
Nat'l Network: ABC
Arbitron Metro Market: Dunkirk, NY *Format:* News, News/Talk, 64, Talk *Special Programming:* Pol 6 hrs, Sp 2 hrs wkly *Hrs. of News Programming:* News progmg 12 hrs wkly *Target Audience:* 45-65.
John Bulmer, President
Mark James, Operations Dir
Patti Pritchard, General Manager
Dave Rowley, News Director

E. Syracuse

WSIV
12-06-1955; 1540 khz AM *Hrs Open:* 24; 1 kw-D, ND2; N43 5 40 W76 2 0
4853 Manor Hill Drive, Syracuse, NY 13215 US
(315) 656-2231, *Fax:* (315) 656-2259
www.wsiv1540.com
info@wsiv1540.com
License: E. Syracuse, NY held by CRAM Communications L.L.C.
Group Owner: Cram Communications LLC; (acq 1-6-97; $900,000 with WVOA(FM) DeRuyter)
Arbitron Metro Market: Syracuse, NY *Format:* Religious *Special Programming:* Black 20 hrs, Gospel music *Adv. Rates:* 6; 6; 6; 4
Sam Furco, CEO
Allen Elson, Operations Dir
James Wall, General Manager
Suzanne Anderson, Station Manager
Keith Copes, General Sales Mgr

East Hampton

WEHN
03-01-1993; 96.9 mhz FM *Hrs Open:* 24; 4.3 kw; 384 ft.; N40 59 37 W72 10 19 *Rebroadcasts:* Simulcast with WEHM(FM) Southampton 100%
Mailing Address: P.O. Box 7162, Amagansett, NY 11930 US
Second Address: 249 Montauk Hwy., Amagansett, NY 11930
(631) 267-7800, *Fax:* (631) 267-1018
www.wehm.com
License: East Hampton, Suffolk County, NY held by AAA Licensing LLC.
Group Owner: Long Island Radio Broadcasting LLC; (acq 5-31-2000; grpsl).
Nat'l Network: CNN Radio
Arbitron Metro Market: Water Mill, NY *Format:* Alternative *Target Audience:* 24-54; upscale Hamptons residents and NYC second homeowners
Don Maguire, President
Steve Harper, Operations Dir
Hedy Krebs-DeMaio, General Manager

Ellenville

WJIP
12-01-1964; 1370 khz AM; 5 kw-D; N41 44 19 W74 23 48
Mailing Address: 20 Tucker Dr., Poughkeepsie, NY 12603
Second Address: 30 Scotts Corners, Montgomery, NY 12549
(845) 471-2300, *Fax:* (845) 471-2683
www.1370welg.com
License: Ellenville, Ulster County, NY held by CC Licenses LLC.
Group Owner: Clear Channel Communications Inc.; (acq 7-14-2000; grpsl)
Nat'l Network: Fox News Radio; ABC News/Talk; Premiere Radio Networks; Talk Radio Network *Nat'l Reps:* Katz Radio *Wire Services:* AP
Population Served: 50,000*Hrs. of News Programming:* 12 hours *No. News Employees:* 1 *Target Audience:* 30-64.
Reggie Osterhoudt, Operations Dir
Frank Curcio, General Manager
Peter Clark, General Sales Mgr
Reg Osterhoudt, Programming Director
Brian Powers, Promotions Manager
Cameron Hendrix, News Director

WRWB-FM
08-01-1970; 99.3 mhz FM *Hrs Open:* 24; 115 w; Ant 1,630 ft; N41 41 06 W74 21 23 *Rebroadcasts:* Simulcast with WRWD-FM Highland
Mailing Address: 20 Tucker Dr., Poughkeepsie, NY 12603
Second Address: 30 Scotts Cornerns, Montgomery, NY 12549
(845) 471-2300, *Fax:* (845) 471-2683
www.wrwdfm.com
License: Ellenville, Ulster County, NY
Group Owner: Clear Channel Communications Inc.
Nat'l Network: Fox News Radio *Nat'l Reps:* Katz Radio
Population Served: 400,000 *Arbitron Metro Market:* Newburgh-Middletown, NY (Mid-Hudson Valley) *Hrs. of News Programming:* 7 hours *No. News Employees:* 1
Reggie Osterhoudt, Operations Dir
Frank Curcio, General Manager
Pete Clark, General Sales Mgr
Paty Quyn, Programming Director
Brian Powers, Promotions Manager

Elma

WLOF
11-09-1977; 101.7 mhz FM; 2.8 kw; 486 ft.; N42 46 58 W78 27 28
438 East Main Street, Batavia, NY 14020 US
(716) 839-6117, *Fax:* (716) 839-0400
www.wlof.net
info@thestationofthecross.com
License: Elma, Wyoming County, NY held by Holy Family Communications Inc.
Group Owner: Holy Family Communications; acq 12-20-99; $655,000).
Arbitron Metro Market: Elma, NY *Format:* Religious *Target Audience:* 25-54; blue collar, housewives
Jim Wright, President/General Manager
Bill Havas, Technical Operations Manager
Gina Zanicky, Programming Director
Zach Krajacic, Vice President of Development, Marketing, and

RADIO - U.S.

PR
Rick Paolini, Business Manager
Sarah Buttino,Executive Assistant
Debbie Daigler, Administrative Assistant

Elmira

*WCIH

07-31-1989; 90.3 mhz FM *Hrs Open:* 24; 4 kw; 527 ft.; N41 53 39 W76 51 32 *Rebroadcasts:* Rebroadcasts WCIK(FM) Bath 100%
Mailing Address: P.O. Box 506, Bath, NY 14810 US
Second Address: 7634 Campbell Creek Rd., Bath, NY 14810
(607) 776-4151, *Fax:* (607) 776-6929
www.fln.org
mail@fln.org
License: Elmira, Chemung County, NY held by Family Life Ministries Inc.
Group Owner: Family Life Network
Nat'l Network: Salem Radio Network *Wire Services:* Metro Weather Service Inc.
Arbitron Metro Market: Elmira-Corning, NY *Format:* Christian *Hrs. of News Programming:* news progmg 14 hrs wkly *No. News Employees:* 3 *Target Audience:* 30-54; general Christian public
Dick Snavely, CFO
Rick Snavely, President
Cecil Van Houten, Radio Operations Manager
Sammy Carrillo, Programming Director
Sammy Carrillo, Promotions Manager
Jim Travis, Chief Engineer

*WECW

01-19-1959; 107.7 mhz FM; 0.009 kw; -338 ft.; N42 5 48 W76 49 0
One Park Place, Elmira, NY 14901 US
(607) 735-1800
wecw@elmira.edu
License: Elmira, Chemung County, NY held by Elmira College.
Arbitron Metro Market: Elmira, NY *Format:* Classic Rock, Contemporary Hits/Top 40 *Target Audience:* 18-30.
Lauren Sanclementi, General Manager
Paul Riley, Programming Director

WELM

04-01-1947; 1410 khz AM *Hrs Open:* 24; 5 kw-D, DAN; 1 kw-N, DAN; N42 7 11 W76 48 37
1705 Lake Street, Elmira, NY 14901 US
(607) 733-5626(607) 732-1400, *Fax:* (607) 733-5627
www.welm1410.com/
rayross@yahoo.com
License: Elmira, NY held by Pembrook Pines Elmira Ltd.
Group Owner: Pembrook Pines Media Group; (acq 10-1-77).
Nat'l Network: CBS; ESPN Radio
Arbitron Metro Market: Elmira, NY *Format:* Sports *Special Programming:* Relg one hr wkly *Hrs. of News Programming:* news progmg 10 hrs wkly *No. News Employees:* 1 *Target Audience:* 25-54.
Robert Pfuntner, CEO
Nancy Nicastro, Operations Dir
Bob Michaels, Programming Director

WENY

01-01-1939; 1230 khz AM *Hrs Open:* 24*Rebroadcasts:* Rebroadcasts WCLI(AM) Corning 100%
P.O. Box 208, Elmira, NY 14902 US
(607) 962-4646, *Fax:* (607) 962-1138
cnj@route81radio.com
License: Elmira, NY held by WS2K Radio LLC.
Group Owner: WS2K Radio LLC dba WS Media; (acq 7-14-2008; grpsl)
Nat'l Reps: McGavren Guild
Arbitron Metro Market: Elmira, NY *Format:* News, News/Talk, 86 *Target Audience:* 30 plus.
Paul Lyle, General Manager

WENY-FM

08-15-1965; 92.7 mhz FM *Hrs Open:* 24; 1.2 kw; 715 ft.; N42 1 55 W76 47 2 *Rebroadcasts:* Rebroadcasts WCBA-FM Corning 100%
P. O. Box 208, Elmira, NY 14902 US
(607) 962-4646, *Fax:* (607) 962-1138
cnj@route81radio.com
License: Elmira, Chemung County, NY held by WS2K Radio LLC.
Group Owner: WS2K Radio LLC dba WS Media; (acq 7-14-2008; grpsl)
Nat'l Network: ABC
Arbitron Metro Market: Elmira, NY *Format:* Adult Contemp
Jennifer Cox-Hensley, President

WLVY

08-01-1966; 94.3 mhz FM; 1.15 kw; 745 ft.; N42 7 51 W76 47 26
1705 Lake Road, Elmira, NY 14901 US
(607) 733-5626, *Fax:* (607) 733-5627
www.94rockfm.com
airstaff@wlvy94rock.com
License: Elmira, Chemung County, NY
Group Owner: Pembrook Pines Media Group
Nat'l Network: Westwood One *Regional Reps:* Pembrook Pines
Arbitron Metro Market: Elmira, NY *Format:* Adult Contemp, Contemporary Hits/Top 40 *Hrs. of News Programming:* news progmg 5 hrs wkly *No. News Employees:* 1 *Target Audience:* 18-36; young vibrant adults
Dave Crum, General Sales Mgr
Mike Strobel, Programming Director
Donna Bogart, News Director

Elmira Hts-Horsehds

WEHH

07-04-1956; 1600 khz AM *Hrs Open:* 24
660 Hawleyton Road, Binghamton, NY 13903 US
(607) 733-5626, *Fax:* (607) 733-5627
wehhelmira.com
rayross@yahoo.com
License: Elmira Hts-Horsehds, NY held by Pembrook Pines Elmira Ltd.
Group Owner: Pembrook Pines Media Group; (acq 5-19-99).
Nat'l Network: CBS Radio
Arbitron Metro Market: Elmira Heights, NY *Format:* Adult Contemp *Hrs. of News Programming:* News progmg 2 hrs wkly *Target Audience:* 45 plus; upscale adults
Robert Pfuntner, CEO

Endicott

WENE

09-01-1947; 1430 khz AM *Hrs Open:* 24; 5 kw-D, DAN; 5 kw-N, DAN; N42 4 56 W76 1 53
3301 Country Club Road, Suite 2218, Endwell, NY 13760 US
(607) 584-5800, *Fax:* (607) 584-5900
www.1430theteam.com
jonscaptura@clearchannel.com
License: Endicott, NY held by CC Licenses LLC.
Group Owner: Clear Channel Communications Inc.; (acq 4-14-2000; grpsl)
Nat'l Network: Westwood One *Nat'l Reps:* McGavren Guild
Arbitron Metro Market: Endicott, NY *Format:* Sports, Talk *Hrs. of News Programming:* news progmg 28 hrs wkly *No. News Employees:* 2 *Target Audience:* 35 plus. *Adv. Rates:* 20; 15; 15; 5
Tom Barney, General Manager
Tom Barney, General Sales Mgr
Jon Scaptura, Programming Director

WMRV-FM

01-01-1969; 105.7 mhz FM *Hrs Open:* 24; 35 kw; 571 ft.; N42 8 17 W75 59 59
3301 Country Club Road, Suite 2218, Endwell, NY 13790 US
(607) 584-5800, *Fax:* (607) 584-5900
www.star1057fm.com
Theboss@binghamtonstar.com
License: Endicott, Broome County, NY
Group Owner: Clear Channel Communications Inc.
Arbitron Metro Market: Binghamton, NY *Format:* Contemporary Hits/Top 40 *Target Audience:* 18-34. *Adv. Rates:* 35; 25; 25; 10
Marilee Morrow, General Manager

Endwell

WBBI

01-01-1998; 107.5 mhz FM; 2.2 kw; 545 ft.; N42 8 17 W75 59 59
3301 Country Club Rd., Suite 2218, Endwell, NY 13760 US
(306) 862-2468, *Fax:* (306) 862-2660
www.lighthousefm.ca
info@lighthousefm.ca
License: Endwell, Broome County, NY held by CC Licenses LLC.
Group Owner: Clear Channel Communications Inc.; (acq 4-14-2000; grpsl)
Format: Christian *No. News Employees:* 1 *Target Audience:* 20-55.
Rod Petersen, Programming Director
Angela Petersen, News Director
Andrew Hildebrandt, Music Director
Andrew Clark, Programming Director

Essex

WCPV

10-01-1994; 101.3 mhz FM; 1 kw; 797 ft.; N44 24 12 W73 26 2
600 Congress Ave., Suite 1400, Austin, TX 78701 US
(802) 654-0093, *Fax:* (802) 655-0478
www.1013espn.com
Chris@1013ESPN.com
License: Essex, Essex County, NY held by Vox AM/FM LLC.
Group Owner: Vox AM/FM LLC; (acq 7-25-2008; grpsl)
Arbitron Metro Market: Burlington-Plattsburgh, VT-NY *Format:* Classic Rock
Steve Cormier, Operations Dir
Karen Marshall, General Manager
John Hill, General Sales Mgr

Fairport

WFKL

01-01-1993; 93.3 mhz FM *Hrs Open:* 24; 4.4 kw; 384 ft.; N43 10 37 W77 28 39
401 City Avenue, Suite 409, Bala Cynwyd, PA 19004 US
(585) 423-2900, *Fax:* (585) 325-5139
www.wfkl-fm.fimc.net
License: Fairport, Monroe County, NY held by Stephens Media Group-Rochester LLC.
Group Owner: Stephens Family L.P.; (acq 7-14-2008; grpsl)
Nat'l Reps: Katz Radio
Arbitron Metro Market: Rochester, NY *Format:* Oldies *No. News Employees:* 1 *Target Audience:* 25-54; upscale
Michael Doyle, General Manager
Mike Rockwell, General Sales Mgr
Christine Neenan, Promotions Manager
Steve Hausmann, News Director
Joe Fleming, Chief Engineer
Mike Johnson, Regional Sales Manager

Fenner

*WXXE

12-21-1998; 90.5 mhz FM; 0.049 kw; 413 ft.; N42 58 12 W75 47 7
P.O. Box 6365, Syracuse, NY 13217 US
(315) 863-6013
www.wxxe.org
info@wxxe.org
License: Fenner, Madison County, NY held by Syracuse Community Radio Inc.
Arbitron Metro Market: Syracuse, NY *Format:* Variety/Diverse
Dana Bonn, President
Danny Danhauser, General Manager

Fort Plain

WBUG-FM

03-01-1990; 101.1 mhz FM *Hrs Open:* 24; 1.25 kw; 719 ft.; N42 52 44 W74 47 7
P.O. Box 4490, Utica, NY 13504 US
(315) 734-9245, *Fax:* (315) 624-9245
www.bugcountry.com
License: Fort Plain, Montgomery County, NY held by Roser Communications Network Inc.
Group Owner: Roser Communications Network Inc.; (acq 10-21-94; $400,000 with WVTL(AM) Amsterdam;
Nat'l Network: ABC
Arbitron Metro Market: Utica, NY *Format:* Country *Hrs. of News Programming:* news progmg 10 hrs wkly *No. News Employees:* 2 *Target Audience:* 25 plus. *Adv. Rates:* 20; 15; 15; 15
Dave Silvers, Operations Dir
Ken Roser, General Manager
Grant Roser, General Sales Mgr

Frankfort

WKLL

02-12-1990; 94.9 mhz FM; 34 kw; 568 ft.; N43 8 40 W75 10 32
7536 Murray Drive, Cicero, NY 13039 US
(315) 797-1330, *Fax:* (315) 738-1073
www.krock.com
info@krock.com
License: Frankfort, Herkimer County, NY held by Galaxy Communications L.P.
Group Owner: Galaxy Communications L.P.; (acq 4-6-2000; grpsl).
Nat'l Network: ABC *Nat'l Reps:* D & R Radio
Arbitron Metro Market: Utica-Rome, NY *Format:* Rock/AOR
Paul Sznal, Operations Dir
Beth Coughlin, General Manager
Mimi Griswald, Programming Director

Fredonia

WBKX

04-01-1989; 96.5 mhz FM *Hrs Open:* 24; 1.4 kw; 686 ft.; N42 22 2 W79 23 12
PO Box 1199, Jamestown, NY 14701 US
(716) 366-8580(716) 366-1410, *Fax:* (716) 366-1416
www.wbkxcountry.com
License: Fredonia, Chautauqua County, NY held by Chadwick Bay Broadcasting Corp.

Nat'l Network: ABC
Arbitron Metro Market: New York,Jamestown, NY *Format:* Country *Hrs. of News Programming:* News progmg 12 hrs wkly *No. News Employees:* 1 *Target Audience:* 25-54.
Alan Bishop, President
Patti Pritchard, General Manager
Mike McAdam, Programming Director
Dave Rowley, News Director
Dan Palmer, Sports Director

***WCVF-FM**
07-06-1978; 88.9 mhz FM *Hrs Open:* 24; 0.13 kw; -115 ft.; N42 27 8 W79 20 14
Svny Fredonia, 115 McEwen Hall, Fredonia, NY 14063 US
(716) 673-3420, *Fax:* (716) 673-3427
www.fredoniaradio.com
wcvf@fredoniaradio.com
License: Fredonia, Chautauqua County, NY held by State University of New York.
Nat'l Network: NPR *Wire Services:* UPI
Arbitron Metro Market: Fredonia, NY *Format:* Variety/Diverse *Special Programming:* Reggae 4 hrs, folk 4 hrs, world 4 hrs, spanish 4 hrs, new age 4 hrs, polka 3 hours weekly *Hrs. of News Programming:* News progmg 28 hrswkly *Target Audience:* All ages of campus & community of Fredonia
Bill Miller, Operations Dir
Lisa Tait, General Sales Mgr
Peter Solomon, Operations Manager

Freeport

WGBB
08-01-1924; 1240 khz AM; 1 kw-D, ND1; 1 kw-N, ND1; N40 38 44 W73 34 39
45 John Street, #907, New York, NY 10038 US
(516) 623-1240, *Fax:* (516) 623-1240
www.am1240wgbb.com
support@am1240wgbb.com
License: Freeport, NY held by WGBB-AM Inc.
Group Owner: Cox Radio Inc.; (acq 5-22-98; grpsl)
Arbitron Metro Market: New York *Format:* Variety/Diverse *Special Programming:* Relg 6 hrs, Sp 2 hrs wkly *Target Audience:* 25-65.
Josephine Chain, President
Jeff Lo, Operations Dir
Josephine Chain, General Manager
Jeff Lo, Station Manager
Tom Ross, Programming Director
Neil Newman, Chief Engineer
Curry Kid, Assistant Program Director
Robert Kowal, SportsDirector
Robert Kowal, Account Executive
Trevor Vassell, Sound Engineer
Adam Kern, Sound Engineer

Friendship

***WCID**
01-01-1989; 89.1 mhz FM *Hrs Open:* 24; 7 kw; 492 ft.; N42 7 7 W78 10 43 *Rebroadcasts:* Rebroadcasts WCIK(FM) Bath 100%
P.O. Box 506, Bath, NY 14810 US
(607) 776-4151, *Fax:* (607) 776-6929
www.fln.org
mail@fln.org
License: Friendship, Allegany County, NY held by Family Life Ministries Inc.
Group Owner: Family Life Network
Nat'l Network: Salem Radio Network *Wire Services:* Metro Weather Service Inc.
Arbitron Metro Market: Bath, NY *Format:* Christian *Hrs. of News Programming:* news progmg 14 hrs wkly *No. News Employees:* 3 *Target Audience:* 30-54; general
Dick Snavely, CFO
Rick Snavely, President
Sammy Carrillo, Programming Director
Sammy Carrillo, Promotions Manager
Jim Travis, Chief Engineer
Cecil Van Houten, Radio Operations Manager

Fulton

WBBS
08-01-1961; 104.7 mhz FM; 50 kw; 492 ft.; N43 12 50 W76 23 47
200 Concord Plaza, Suite 600, San Antonio, TX 78216 US
(662) 844-8888, *Fax:* (662) 842-6791
www.afr.net
License: Fulton, Oswego County, NY held by Citicasters Licenses L.P.
Group Owner: Clear Channel Communications Inc.; (acq 5-4-99; grpsl).
Format: Christian
Marvin Sanders, General Manager

WOSW
08-19-1949; 1300 khz AM *Hrs Open:* 24; 1 kw-D; N43 17 41 W76 26 35
401 W. Kirkpatrick St., Syracuse, NY 13069
(315) 472-0222, *Fax:* (315) 478-7745
License: Fulton, Oswego County, NY held by Cram Communications LLC.
Group Owner: Cram Communications LLC; (acq 11-14-2007)
Nat'l Network: ABC
Population Served: 300,000 *Arbitron Metro Market:* Syracuse, NY *Special Programming:* It 2 hrs, Pol 5 hrs wkly *Target Audience:* 35 plus; hometown listeners, county coverage *Adv. Rates:* 15; 15; 12; 8
Don Derosa, General Manager

Garden City

***WHPC**
10-12-1972; 90.3 mhz FM *Hrs Open:* 24; 0.5 kw; 213 ft.; N40 43 47 W73 35 33
One Education Drive, Garden City, NY 11530 US
(516) 572-7439, *Fax:* (516) 572-7831
www.sunynassau.edu
WHPC@ncc.edu
License: Garden City, Nassau County, NY held by Nassau Community College Board of Trustees.
Format: Adult Contemp, Variety/Diverse *Hrs. of News Programming:* news progmg 5 hrs wkly *No. News Employees:* 2 *Target Audience:* 20-65; general
Sean Fanelli, CEO
Jack Ostling, President
Jim Green, Operations Dir

WQBU-FM
01-01-1988; 92.7 mhz FM; 2 kw; 522 ft.; N40 45 26 W73 42 52
1103 Stewart Avenue, Garden City, NY 11530 US
(212) 310-6000, *Fax:* (212) 310-6095
www.univision.com
info@univision.com
License: Garden City, Nassau County, NY held by Univision Radio License Corp.
Group Owner: Univision Radio; (acq 1-12-2004; $60 million)
Arbitron Metro Market: New York
Joe Pagan, Operations Dir

Geneseo

***WGSU**
02-18-1963; 89.3 mhz FM *Hrs Open:* 24; 1.8 kw horiz; 10 ft.; N42 47 51 W77 49 13
State University College, Geneseo, NY 14454 US
(585) 245-5486, *Fax:* (585) 245-5240
www.geneseo.edu/~wgsu/
pruszyns@geneseo.edu
License: Geneseo, Livingston County, NY held by State University of New York.
Format: Alternative, News *Hrs. of News Programming:* News progmg 7 hrs wkly *Target Audience:* 12-55; college, immediate community
Chris Pruszynski, General Manager

Geneva

***WEOS**
03-30-1971; 89.7 mhz FM *Hrs Open:* 24; 4 kw; 312 ft.; N42 48 32 W77 5 12
Mailing Address: 300 Pulteney Street, Geneva, NY 14456 US
Second Address: 113 Hamilton St., Geneva, NY 14456
(315) 781-3456(315) 781-3897, *Fax:* (315) 781-3916
www.weos.org
underwriting@wxxi.org
License: Geneva, Ontario County, NY held by The Colleges of the Seneca.
Nat'l Network: NPR; PRI *Wire Services:* AP
Arbitron Metro Market: Geneva, NY *Format:* Jazz, News, 62, Talk *Special Programming:* AAA 12 hrs, world 10 hrs, metal 6 hrs, gospel 3 hrs, reggae 3 hrs wkly *Hrs. of News Programming:* news progmg 40 hrs wkly *No.News Employees:* 1 *Target Audience:* 18-plus. *Adv. Rates:* 13; 1113; 13; 7.50
Greg Cotterill, General Manager
Michael Black, Radio Program Manager
Sara Henegan, News Director
Mike Monteiro, Music Director
Anessa Amer, Music Director
Alison Jones, Underwriting

WFLK
01-01-1974; 101.7 mhz FM *Hrs Open:* 24; 5.4 kw; 125 ft.; N42 51 34 W77 0 29
481 Hamilton Street, Geneva, NY 14456 US
(315) 781-7000, *Fax:* (315) 781-7077
www.k1017.com
k1017@rochester.rr.com
License: Geneva, Ontario County, NY held by MB Communications Inc.
Group Owner: M.B. Communications; (acq 1993)
Arbitron Metro Market: Rochester, NY *Format:* Country *Hrs. of News Programming:* news progmg 10 hrs wkly *No. News Employees:* 2 *Target Audience:* 25-49. *Adv. Rates:* 12; 12; 12; 12
Russ Kimble, President
John Thomas, Operations Dir
Lori Rose, General Sales Mgr
Matt Ripley, Promotions Manager
Deb Hunt, General Sales Manager

WGVA
01-01-1947; 1240 khz AM *Hrs Open:* 24; 1 kw-U, ND1; N42 51 37 W77 0 59
3568 Lenox Road, Geneva, NY 14456 US
(315) 781-1240, *Fax:* (315) 781-7700
www.fingerlakesdailynews.com
info@fingerlakesdailynews.com
License: Geneva, NY held by Geneva Broadcasting Inc.
Arbitron Metro Market: Rochester, NY *Format:* News, News/Talk, 86 *Hrs. of News Programming:* news progmg 10 hrs wkly *No. News Employees:* 1 *Target Audience:* General. *Adv. Rates:* 15; 12; 15; 10
George Kimble, President
Alan Bishop, Operations Dir
Paula Triplett, General Sales Mgr
Mike Smith, Programming Director
Ted Baker, News Director

Glens Falls

***WGFR**
01-01-1977; 92.7 mhz FM; 0.013 kw horiz; 49 ft.; N43 18 44 W73 38 58
Bay Road, Queensbury, NY 12804 US
(518) 743-2311, *Fax:* (518) 745-1433
www.wgfr.org
ankenyk@sunyacc.edu
License: Glens Falls, Warren County, NY held by Board of Trustees of Adirondack Community College.
Format: Triple A *Target Audience:* 18 plus; adults
Kevin Ankeny, General Manager
Steve Tefft, Station Manager

***WLJH**
01-01-2001; 90.7 mhz FM; 0.04 kw vert; 1325 ft.; N43 25 12 W73 45 37 *Rebroadcasts:* Rebroadcasts WFGB(FM) Kingston 100%
P O Box 777, Lake Katrine, NY 12449 US
(845) 336-6199, *Fax:* (845) 336-7205
www.soundoflife.org
License: Glens Falls, Warren County, NY held by Sound of Life Inc.
Format: Christian
Bob Conti, Operations Dir
Tom Zahradnik, General Manager
Joe Hunter, Programming Director

WMML
05-28-1959; 1230 khz AM *Hrs Open:* 24; 1 kw-U, ND1; N43 19 43 W73 38 58
89 Everts Avenue, Queensbury, NY 12804 US
(518) 793-7733, *Fax:* (518) 793-0838
License: Glens Falls, NY held by 6 Johnson Road Licenses Inc.
Group Owner: Pamal Broadcasting Ltd.; (acq 4-1-2004; grpsl).
Nat'l Network: ESPN Radio
Arbitron Metro Market: Glenn Falls, NY *Format:* Sports *Special Programming:* Relg 3 hrs wkly *Hrs. of News Programming:* news progmg 6 hrs wkly *No. News Employees:* 1 *Target Audience:* 18-54 plus. *Adv.Rates:* 10; 10; 10; 2.
Clay Ashworth, General Manager

WWSC
12-18-1946; 1450 khz AM *Hrs Open:* 24
128 Glen St., Glens Falls, NY 12801 US
(518) 761-9890, *Fax:* (518) 761-9893
www.radiowins.com
License: Glens Falls, NY held by Regional Radio Group LLC.
Group Owner: Regional Radio Group LLC; (acq 9-10-2008; grpsl)
Nat'l Network: ABC; Wall Street; Westwood One
Arbitron Metro Market: Glens Falls, NY *Format:* News, News/Talk, 84, Talk *Hrs. of News Programming:* news progmg 166 hrs wkly *No. News Employees:* 15 *Target Audience:* 12 plus; people who want full news radio &talk
Steve Babson, Operations Dir
Clay Ashworth, General Manager
Dan Miner, Station Manager
Pete Cloutier, Promotions Manager

Jim Scott, News Director
Ken Leccese, Sports Director
Mike Dubray, Traffic Director

Gloversville

WENT
07-01-1944; 1340 khz AM *Hrs Open:* 5:30 AM-midnight; 1 kw-U; N43 01 30 W74 21 10
Box 831, 138 Harrison St. Ext., Gloversville, NY 12078
(518) 725-7175, *Fax:* (518) 725-7177
www.am1340went.com
went@capital.net
License: Gloversville, Fulton County, NY held by Whitney Radio Broadcasting Inc.
Nat'l Network: CNN Radio; ESPN Radio *Wire Services:* AP
Population Served: 102,000*Special Programming:* Talk one hr wkly *Hrs. of News Programming:* news progmg 14 hrs wkly *No. News Employees:* 2 *Target Audience:* 30 plus.
Jack Scott, President
Jon Clark, Operations Dir
Tim Murphy, Promotions Manager
Tom Roehl, News Director
Lloyd Simon, Chief Engineer

WFNY
03-01-2003; 1440 khz AM
US
(518) 725-1108, *Fax:* (518) 773-3349
am1440wfny@gmail.com
License: Gloversville, NY held by Michael A. Sleezer.
Arbitron Metro Market: Gloversville, NY
Michael A. Sleezer, Owner and General Manager

Gouverneur

WLFK
12-05-1967; 95.3 mhz FM *Hrs Open:* 24; 6 kw; Ant 328 ft; N44 20 22 W75 24 00
2315 Knox St., Ogdensburg, NY 13669
(315) 393-1100, *Fax:* (315) 393-6673
www.coololdies.us
License: Gouverneur, St. Lawrence County, NY held by Community Broadcasters LLC.
Group Owner: Community Broadcasters LLC; (acq 2-8-2007; grpsl)
Population Served: 120,000*Hrs. of News Programming:* news progmg 7 hrs wkly *No. News Employees:* 3 *Target Audience:* 35-54.
James Leven, President
Tobi Newcombe, General Sales Mgr
Ken Ruhland, Chief Engineer

***WSLG**
90.5 mhz FM; 2 kw; 207 ft.; N44 15 32 W75 34 40
US
(315) 229-5356, *Fax:* (315) 229-5373
www.ncpr.org
radio@ncpr.org
License: Gouverneur, St. Lawrence County, NY held by The St. Lawrence University.
Arbitron Metro Market: Gouverneur, NY *Format:* Public Affairs
Shelly Pike, Operations Dir
Ellen Rocco, Station Manager
Jackie Sauter, Programming Director
Martha Foley, News Director
Bob Sauter, Chief Engineer
Naomi Weller, Office Manager
Joel Hurd, Production Manager

Grand Gorge

***WGKR**
11-01-1997; 105.3 mhz FM; 0.06 kw; 1358 ft.; N42 23 55 W74 35 23 *Rebroadcasts:* Rebroadcasts WFGB(FM) Kingston 100%.
Mailing Address: Post Office Box 777, Lake Katrine, NY 12449 US
Second Address: 199 Tuytenbridge Rd., Lake Katrine, NY 12449
(845) 336-6199, *Fax:* (845) 336-7205
www.soundoflife.org
email@soundoflife.org
License: Grand Gorge, Delaware County, NY held by Sound of Life Inc.
Format: Christian
Jay Cookingham, Chairman
Tom Michaels Zahradnik, CEO
Bob Conti, Operations Dir
Tom Zahradnik, General Manager
Joe Hunter, Programming Director
Paul Grimsland, Production Director
Connie Van Kleeck, Assistant Program Director
Donna Quiles, Office Administrator

Greece

***WGMC**
11-11-1973; 90.1 mhz FM *Hrs Open:* 24; 15 kw; 138 ft.; N43 14 40 W77 41 36
Mailing Address: P.O. Box 300, North Greece, NY 14515 US
Second Address: 1139 Maiden Ln., Rochester, NY 14615
(585) 966-2660, *Fax:* (585) 581-8185
www.jazz901.org
jazzinfo@jazz901.org
License: Greece, Monroe County, NY held by Greece Central School District.
Arbitron Metro Market: Rochester, NY *Format:* Jazz *Special Programming:* Pol 2 hrs, Sp 10 hrs, Lithuanian one hr, Turkish o *Target Audience:* 25-50; upscale, educated, mus lovers
Jack Mindy, Operations Dir
Rob Linton, Station Manager
Derrick Lucas, Music Director
Laurylann Romneo, Development Director
Joelle VanBuren, Production Director
Jack Mindy, Community Calendar Coordinator

Hamilton

***WRCU-FM**
03-22-1970; 90.1 mhz FM; 1.9 kw; 154 ft.; N42 48 38 W75 31 58
Student Activites Office, Hamilton, NY 13346 US
(315) 228-7901, *Fax:* (315) 228-7028
www.wrcu.colgate.edu
License: Hamilton, Madison County, NY held by Colgate University.
Format: Jazz, Variety/Diverse *Special Programming:* Jazz 12 hrs, class 4 hrs, Black 10 hrs wkly
Lydia Gulick, General Manager
Tracy Hoole, Programming Director
Paul Osmolskis, News Director

Hampton Bays

WLIR-FM
11-20-1980; 107.1 mhz FM; 4.1 kw; 397 ft.; N40 53 7 W72 41 33.6 *Rebroadcasts:* Rebroadcasts WEPN(AM) New York 100%
11 Skyline Drive, Hawthorne, NY 10532 US
(516) 495-8504, *Fax:* (516) 222-1391
wlir.fm
info@wlir.com
License: Hampton Bays, Suffolk County, NY held by Jarad Broadcasting Co. of Hampton Bays LLC
Group Owner: The Morey Organization Inc.; (acq 2-27-2004; $2 million)
Nat'l Network: ESPN Radio *Nat'l Reps:* Roslin
Arbitron Metro Market: New York *Format:* Sports
John Caracciolo, General Manager
Harlan Friedman, Programming Director

Hempstead

WHLI
07-22-1947; 1100 khz AM *Hrs Open:* Sunrise-sunset; 10 kw-D, DAD; N40 41 6 W73 36 36
1055 Franklin Ave #306, Garden City, NY 11530 US
(631) 770-4200, *Fax:* (631) 770-0101
www.whli.com
info@whli.com
License: Hempstead, NY held by Long Island Broadcasting Inc.
Group Owner: JVC Broadcasting; (acq 12-15-84; $5 million with co-located FM;
Nat'l Reps: Katz Radio
Arbitron Metro Market: New York *Format:* Adult Contemp *Special Programming:* Black one hr wkly *Hrs. of News Programming:* news progmg 2 hrs wkly *No. News Employees:* 1 *Target Audience:* 35-64; adults
Dave Widmer, President
Mike Banks, General Sales Mgr
Paul Richards, Programming Director
Cheryl Kampanis, Promotions Manager
Frank Brinka, News Director
Joe Satta, Disc Jockey
Antoinette Rodriguez, Traffic Manager

WKJY
07-22-1947; 98.3 mhz FM *Hrs Open:* 24; 3 kw; 328 ft.; N40 41 8 W73 36 37
1055 Franklin Ave #306, Garden City, NY 11530 US
(631) 770-4200, *Fax:* (631) 770-0090
www.whli.com
info@whli.com
License: Hempstead, Nassau County, NY held by Long Island Broadcasting Inc.
Group Owner: JVC Broadcasting
Nat'l Reps: Katz Radio
Arbitron Metro Market: New York *Format:* Adult Contemp *Special Programming:* Black one hr wkly *No. News Employees:* 1 *Target Audience:* 25-54.
Bill George, Programming Director
Alissa Marty, Promotions Manager
Antoinette Rodriguez, News Director
Mike Glaser, Engineering Dir
Jim Douglas, Disc Jockey
Bill Edwards, Disc Jockey
Jodi Vale, Disc Jockey
Kim Berk, DiscJockey

***WRHU**
06-09-1959; 88.7 mhz FM *Hrs Open:* 24; 0.47 kw; 180 ft.; N40 43 3 W73 36 12
111 Hofstra University, Hempstead, NY 11549 US
(516) 463-5667, *Fax:* (516) 463-5668
www.wrhu.org
mail@wrhu.org
License: Hempstead, Nassau County, NY held by Hofstra University.
Wire Services: AP
Format: Variety/Diverse *Hrs. of News Programming:* News progmg 11 hrs wkly *Target Audience:* General.
Kathleen Reddington, Station Manager

Henderson

WEFX
01-01-1991; 100.7 mhz FM; 6 kw; 328 ft.; N43 49 13 W76 5 29
199 Wealtha Ave., Watertown, NY 13601 US
(203) 845-3030, *Fax:* (203) 845-3097
www.realrock1007.com
License: Henderson, Jefferson County, NY held by Community Broadcasters LLC.
Group Owner: Community Broadcasters LLC; (acq 2-8-2007; grpsl)
Nat'l Reps: Roslin
Arbitron Metro Market: Watertown, NY *Format:* Rock/AOR
James Leven, President
Todd Dalesandro, Operations Dir
Glenn Curry, General Manager
Vickie Fenn, General Sales Mgr
Johnny Keegan, Programming Director

Henrietta

***WITR**
03-07-1975; 89.7 mhz FM *Hrs Open:* 24; 0.91 kw; 125 ft.; N43 5 8 W77 40 5
32 Lomb Memorial Drive, Rochester, NY 14623 US
(585) 475-2000, *Fax:* (585) 475-4988
www.witr.rit.edu
www.witr.rit.edu
License: Henrietta, Monroe County, NY held by Rochester Institute of Technology.
Format: Contemporary Hits/Top 40 *Special Programming:* Reggae 5 hrs, jazz 8 hrs, contemp Christian rock 1 *Target Audience:* General.
Arun Blatchley, General Manager
Dan Mansen, Programming Director
Michelle Comeau, Promotions Manager
Louis Moskowitz, News Director
Phil Betley, Chief Engineer
AJ Colosimo, Development Director
Eli Clampett, Business Director
Joe Makowski, Music Director
Ryan Aquilino, Webmaster
Vlad Ionescu, Staff Engineer
Jake Walsh, Event Manager

Herkimer

WNRS
10-01-1956; 1420 khz AM *Hrs Open:* 24; 1 kw-D, ND2; 0.064 kw-N, ND2; N43 3 40 W75 1 44
P.O. Box 927, Ilion, NY 13357 US
(315) 797-9270, *Fax:* (315) 733-5438
wxur@hotmail.com
License: Herkimer, NY held by Arjuna Broadcasting Corp.
Nat'l Network: ESPN Radio *Nat'l Reps:* Roslin
Arbitron Metro Market: Herkimer, NY *Format:* Sports *No. News Employees:* 1 *Target Audience:* 18 plus; men *Adv. Rates:* 30; 25; 25; 20
Mindy Barstein, President
Tim Barstein, General Sales Mgr
Tom Davenport, Programming Director
Anthony Falvo, Chief Engineer

***WVHC**
10-01-1993; 91.5 mhz FM *Hrs Open:* 24; 0.35 kw vert; -115 ft.; N43 1 58 W75 0 31

100 Reservoir Road, Herkimer, NY 13350 US
(315) 866-0300, *Fax:* (315) 866-7253
www.herkimer.edu
License: Herkimer, Herkimer County, NY held by Herkimer County Community College.
Arbitron Metro Market: Herkimer, NY *Format:* Jazz *Hrs. of News Programming:* News progmg 5 hrs wkly *Target Audience:* General; residents of southern Herkimer county & college community
Wade Lamb, General Manager

WXUR
04-28-1979; 92.7 mhz FM *Hrs Open:* 24; 6.4 kw; 659 ft.; N43 8 38 W75 10 40
381 Otsego Street, Ilion, NY 13357 US
(315) 866-9700, *Fax:* (315) 733-5438
www.927thedrive.net
License: Herkimer, Herkimer County, NY held by Arjuna Broadcasting Corp.
Nat'l Network: Westwood One
Arbitron Metro Market: Utica-Rome, NY *Format:* Contemporary Hits/Top 40, Adult Contemp *No. News Employees:* 1 *Adv. Rates:* 35; 30; 30; 25
Tim Barstein, General Sales Mgr
Chris Miller, Programming Director
Jenna Davenport, Promotions Manager
Max Davenport, News Director
Tony Falvo, Engineering Dir
Robert Huyck, Sports Commentator

Highland

WRWD-FM
10-03-1989; 107.3 mhz FM; 0.33 kw; 968 ft.; N41 41 58 W74 0 11
42 Holt Road, Hyde Park, NY 12536 US
(845) 471-2300, *Fax:* (845) 471-2683
www.wrwdfm.com
License: Highland, Ulster County, NY held by AMFM Radio Licenses LLC.
Group Owner: Clear Channel Communications Inc.; (acq 12-10-97; $7.5 million with WBWZ(FM) New Paltz).
Nat'l Network: Jones Radio Networks *Nat'l Reps:* Katz Radio
Arbitron Metro Market: Poughkeepsie, N *Format:* Country *Special Programming:* Farm one hr wkly *Target Audience:* 18 plus. *Adv. Rates:* 80; 65; 75; 35
Chris Marino, Operations Dir
Frank Curcio, General Manager
Rob VanDerbeck, General Sales Mgr
Chris Marino, Programming Director
Jeff Helion, Promotions Manager
Cameron Hendrix, News Director
Jeanette Relyea, National SalesManager
Brian Powers, NTR Director

Homer

WXHC
01-01-1991; 101.5 mhz FM *Hrs Open:* 24; 1.3 kw; 495 ft.; N42 41 12 W76 11 54
P.O. Box 386, 12 South Main Street, Homer, NY 13077 US
(607) 749-9942, *Fax:* (607) 749-2374
www.wxhc.com
johneves@wxhc.com
License: Homer, Cortland County, NY held by John Eves.
Nat'l Reps: Roslin
Arbitron Metro Market: Homer, NY *Format:* Oldies *Hrs. of News Programming:* news progmg 10 hrs wkly *No. News Employees:* 1 *Target Audience:* 25-54.
John Eves, General Manager
Bruce Eves, General Sales Mgr
Bobby Comstock Jr., Programming Director
Eric Mulvihill, News Director
Mike Eves, Traffic / Office Manager
Sonny King, Vice President, Operations

Honeoye Falls

WQBW
01-01-1948; 95.1 mhz FM *Hrs Open:* 24; 50 kw; Ant 479 ft; N43 02 01 W77 25 18
1700 HSBC Plaza, 100 Chestnut Street, Rochester, NY 41011
(585) 454-4884, *Fax:* (585) 454-5081
www.fox951.com
License: Honeoye Falls, Monroe County, NY held by Citicasters Licenses Inc. (NEW).
Group Owner: Clear Channel Communications Inc.; (acq 1999; grpsl).
Population Served: 120,000 *Arbitron Metro Market:* Rochester, NY *Target Audience:* 25-54.
Dave LeFrois, Operations Dir
Karen Carey, General Manager

Hoosick Falls

WHAZ-FM
07-04-1991; 97.5 mhz FM; 0.42 kw; 1184 ft.; N42 51 49 W73 13 59
27 Chastellux Ave, Newport, RI 02840 US
(518) 237-1330, *Fax:* (518) 235-4468
www.whaz.com
events@aliveradionetwork.com
License: Hoosick Falls, Rensselaer County, NY held by Capital Media Corp.
Group Owner: Capital Media Corp.; (acq 7-19-2005; $1.1 million)
Arbitron Metro Market: Albany-Schenect *Format:* Christian, Oldies
Paul Lotters, General Manager
Rex Gregory, Programming Director
Bill Rosenfeld, Chief Engineer

Hornell

WCKR
06-01-1981; 92.1 mhz FM *Hrs Open:* 24; 2.55 kw; 509 ft.; N42 20 38 W77 37 36
5942 Ashbaugh Hill Rd, Hornell, NY 14843 US
(607) 324-1480, *Fax:* (607) 324-5415
www.wckr.com
kpd@wlea.net
License: Hornell, Steuben County, NY held by PMJ Communications Inc.
Nat'l Network: USA *Wire Services:* AP
Arbitron Metro Market: Elmira-Corning, NY *Format:* Country *Hrs. of News Programming:* news progmg 11 hrs wkly *No. News Employees:* 2 *Target Audience:* 21 plus.
Kevin P. Doran, President
Glenn Lee, Operations Dir
Tom Booth, General Sales Mgr
Brian O'Neil, News Director
Ralph Van Derlinden, Chief Engineer

WKPQ
01-01-1946; 105.3 mhz FM *Hrs Open:* 24; 43 kw; 531 ft.; N42 17 32 W77 40 27
P.O. Box 726, Hornell, NY 14843 US
(607) 324-1596, *Fax:* (877) 575-1320
www.wkpq.hornellradio.com
sales@hornellradio.com
License: Hornell, Steuben County, NY held by Bilbat Radio Inc.
Arbitron Metro Market: Elmira-Corning, NY *Format:* Adult Contemp *Target Audience:* 18-54; females
Kevin White, General Manager

WLEA
09-01-1951; 1480 khz AM *Hrs Open:* 24; 2.5 kw-D, ND1; 0.019 kw-N, ND1; N42 17 15 W77 38 47
5942 Ashbaugh Hill Road, Hornell, NY 14843 US
(607) 324-1480, *Fax:* (607) 324-5415
www.wlea.net
kpd@wlwa.net
License: Hornell, NY held by PMJ Communications Inc.
Wire Services: AP
Arbitron Metro Market: Elmira-Corning, NY *Format:* News, News/Talk, 86 *Hrs. of News Programming:* news progmg 16 hrs wkly *No. News Employees:* 2 *Target Audience:* 35 plus.
Tom Booth, General Manager
Brian O'Neil, News Director

*WSQA
01-01-2000; 88.7 mhz FM; 4.5 kw; 495 ft.; N42 16 2 W77 37 55
PO Box 3000, Binghamton, NY 13902 US
(607) 729-0100, *Fax:* (607) 729-7328
www.wskg.com
wskg_mail@wskg.pbs.org
License: Hornell, Steuben County, NY held by WSKG Public Telecommunications Council.
Format: Jazz, News
Brian Sickora, President
Nancy Christensen, Operations Dir
Ken Campbell, Programming Director
Stacy Mosteller, News Director
Linda Cohen, Underwriting Director

Horseheads

WLNL
05-07-1967; 1000 khz AM *Hrs Open:* Sunrise-sunset; 2.5 kw-C, NDD; 5 kw-D, NDD; N42 9 14 W76 50 47
3134 Lake Road, Horseheads, NY 14845 US
(607) 737-9208, *Fax:* (607) 737-9210
www.wlnlradio.com
inbox@wlnlradio.com
License: Horseheads, NY held by Trinity Media Ltd.
Nat'l Network: USA; Salem Radio Network
Arbitron Metro Market: Elmira-Corning, NY *Format:* Religious *Special Programming:* Country/bluegrass one hr wkly *Target Audience:* 25-54; Christian families, women/mothers who work at home
Mike Cuomo, Operations Dir
Heather Clark, General Manager
John Earley, General Sales Mgr
Heather Clark, News Director

WPGI
07-04-1970; 100.9 mhz FM; 3.8 kw; 246 ft.; N42 12 0 W76 51 30
1685 Four Mile Drive, Williamsport, PA 17701 US
(607) 732-4400, *Fax:* (607) 732-7774
License: Horseheads, Chemung County, NY held by Chemung County Radio Inc.
Group Owner: Backyard Broadcasting LLC
Arbitron Metro Market: Elmira-Corning, NY *Format:* Country *Target Audience:* General.
John Rohm, Operations Dir
Fred Traynor, General Sales Mgr
Jay Bohannon, Programming Director

WWLZ
04-01-1966; 820 khz AM; 4.1 kw-D, DAN; 0.85 kw-N, DAN; N42 9 14 W76 50 47
1685 Four Mile Drive, Williamsport, PA 17701 US
(607) 732-4400, *Fax:* (607) 732-7774
www.wwlzam820.com
License: Horseheads, NY held by Chemung County Radio Inc.
Group Owner: Backyard Broadcasting LLC; (acq 12-1-2002; grpsl).
Arbitron Metro Market: Horseheads, NY *Format:* News, News/Talk, 86 *Target Audience:* 25-54; baby boomers
Scott Free, Operations Dir
Smitty O' Loughlin, General Manager
Jim Poteat, Promotions Manager
Ally Payne, Webmaster

Houghton

*WXXY(FM)
01-18-1979; 90.3 mhz FM *Hrs Open:* 24; 6 kw; 216 ft; N42 22 39 W78 10 45 *Rebroadcasts:* Rebroadcasts WMHR(FM) Syracuse 70%
Box 30021, Rochester, NY 14603
(585) 325-7500, *Fax:* (585) 258-0339
www.wxxi.org
newsroom@wxxi.org
License: Houghton, Allegany County, NY held by WXXI Public Broadcasting Council.
Population Served: 150,000*Special Programming:* Class 5 hrs wkly *Target Audience:* 18-36; college
Norm Silverstein, CEO
Sue Rogers, Operations Dir

*WXXY
08-02-1957; 90.3 mhz FM *Hrs Open:* 24; 6 kw; 217 ft.; N42 22 39 W78 10 45
280 State Street, Rochester, NY 14614 US
(302) 731-1777
License: Houghton, Kent County, NY held by WXXY Broadcasting Inc.
Format: Black, Gospel
George Krementz, General Manager

Hudson

WHUC
01-01-1947; 1230 khz AM *Hrs Open:* 24; 1 kw-U, ND1; N42 15 13 W73 45 45
Mailing Address: 5620 Route 9g, Hudson, NY 12534 US
Second Address: 5620 Rt. 96, Hudson, NY 12534
(518) 828-5006, *Fax:* (518) 828-1080
www.1230whuc.com
jeffreyhelion@clearchannel.com
License: Hudson, NY held by CC Licenses LLC.
Group Owner: Clear Channel Communications Inc.; (acq 1-17-2002; grpsl)
Nat'l Network: Jones Radio Networks *Nat'l Reps:* Katz Radio
Format: Adult Contemp *Hrs. of News Programming:* news progmg 4 hrs wkly *No. News Employees:* 1 *Target Audience:* 35 plus; loc people in Columbia & Greene counties
Steven Giuttari, Operations Dir
Frank Curcio, General Manager
Rob VanDerbeck, General Sales Mgr
Bill Williams, Programming Director
Jeffrey Helion, Promotions Manager
Cameron Hendrix, News Director
Deirdre Burns, Webmaster
Chuck Benfer, Market Manager

***WHVP**
05-01-1998; 91.1 mhz FM; 0.22 kw vert; 1043 ft.; N42 18 28 W73 29 35 *Rebroadcasts:* Rebroadcasts WFGB(FM) Kingston 100%
P.O. Box 777, Lake Katrine, NY 12449 US
(845) 336-6199, *Fax:* (845) 336-7205
www.soundoflife.org
email@soundoflife.org
License: Hudson, Columbia County, NY held by Sound of Life Inc.
Format: Christian
Bob Conti, Operations Dir
Tom Zahradink, General Manager
Joe Hunter, Programming Director

WZCR
01-20-1969; 93.5 mhz FM *Hrs Open:* 24; 5.8 kw; -16 ft.; N42 15 13 W73 45 45
Mailing Address: 5620 Route 9g, Hudson, NY 12534 US
Second Address: 5620 Rt. 96, Hudson, NY 12534
(518) 828-5006, *Fax:* (518) 828-1080
www.oldies93-5.com
DeirdreBurns@clearchannel.com
License: Hudson, Columbia County, NY held by CC Licenses LLC.
Group Owner: Clear Channel Communications Inc.
Nat'l Network: Westwood One *Nat'l Reps:* Katz Radio
Arbitron Metro Market: Hudson, NY *Format:* Oldies *Hrs. of News Programming:* News progmg 3 hrs wkly *Target Audience:* General; adults 35-54
Steven Giuttari, Operations Dir
Dan Baughman, General Manager
Rob VanDerbeck, General Sales Mgr
Bill Williams, Programming Director
Deirdre Burns, Webmaster

Hudson Falls

WNYQ
09-19-1983; 101.7 mhz FM *Hrs Open:* 24; 4.6 kw; 180 ft.; N43 22 40 W73 39 56
89 Everts Avenue, Queensbury, NY 12804 US
(518) 793-7733, *Fax:* (518) 793-0838
www.classichitswnyq.com/
jdonovan@adirondackbroadcasting.com
License: Hudson Falls, Washington County, NY held by 6 Johnson Road Licenses Inc.
Group Owner: Pamal Broadcasting Ltd.; (acq 4-1-2004; grpsl).
Arbitron Metro Market: Hudson Falls, NY *Format:* Adult Contemp *No. News Employees:* 1 *Target Audience:* 35-64.
Clay Ashworth, General Manager

Huntington

WNYH
09-01-1951; 740 khz AM *Hrs Open:* 24; 25 kw-D, DA2; 0.043 kw-N, DA2; N40 51 4 W73 26 16
Mailing Address: 900 Walt Whitman Road, Melville, NY 11747 US
Second Address: 131 Jericho Tpke., Suite 306, Jericho, NY 11753
(718) 335-3333
www.radiocanticonuevo.com
License: Huntington, NY held by Win Radio Broadcasting Corp.
Arbitron Metro Market: New York *Format:* Alternative
Richard Yoon, President

Hyde Park

WCZX
08-18-1970; 97.7 mhz FM *Hrs Open:* 24; 0.3 kw; 1030 ft.; N41 43 11 W73 59 45
P.O. Box 416, Poughkeepsie, NY 12602 US
(845) 471-1500, *Fax:* (845) 454-1204
www.mix97fm.com
chuck.bortnick@cumulus.com
License: Hyde Park, Dutchess County, NY held by Cumulus Licensing Corp.
Group Owner: Cumulus Media Inc.; (acq 1-23-02; grpsl).
Nat'l Reps: Katz Radio
Arbitron Metro Market: Hudson Valley, NY *Format:* Adult Contemp *Hrs. of News Programming:* news progmg 10 hrs wkly *No. News Employees:* 1 *Target Audience:* 25-54.
John Dickie, CEO
Lew Dickie, President
Charles Benfer, General Manager
Frankenberry, Programming Director
Jeremiah Johnsen, Promotions Manager

WHVW
07-04-1963; 950 khz AM *Hrs Open:* 24; 0.5 kw-D, ND1; 0.057 kw-N, ND1; N41 44 46 W73 54 46
316 Main Mall, Poughkeepsie, NY 12601 US
(845) 471-9500, *Fax:* (845) 452-8696
www.whvw.org
whvw@whvw.net
License: Hyde Park, NY held by Joseph-Paul Ferraro.
Arbitron Metro Market: Poughkeepsie, NY *Format:* Oldies *Special Programming:* Ger one hr, It one hr, Irish one hr wkly *Target Audience:* 25-54. *Adv. Rates:* 30; 20
J.P. Ferraro, President

Irondequoit

WKGS
03-01-1992; 106.7 mhz FM *Hrs Open:* 24; 4.6 kw horiz, 4.51 kw vert; 374 ft.; N43 8 5 W77 35 7
50 East Rivercenter Blvd., Suite 1200, Covington, KY 41011 US
(585) 454-4884, *Fax:* (585) 454-5081
www.1067kissfm.com
License: Irondequoit, Monroe County, NY held by Citicasters Licenses L.P.
Group Owner: Clear Channel Communications Inc.; (acq 1999; grpsl).
Arbitron Metro Market: Rochester, NY *Format:* Contemporary Hits/Top 40 *Target Audience:* 18-34.
Karen Carey, General Manager
Joe Bonacci, Programming Director

Islip

WLIE
01-01-1960; 540 khz AM *Hrs Open:* 24
425 Smith Street, Farmingdale, NY 11735 US
(631) 580-0540, *Fax:* (631) 471-5401
www.wlie540am.com
Info@wlie.com
License: Islip, NY held by Stuart Henry
Nat'l Network: USA; Jones Radio Networks
Arbitron Metro Market: Islip, NY *Format:* Ethnic *Special Programming:* Relg 3 hrs wkly *Hrs. of News Programming:* News progmg 10 hrs wkly *Target Audience:* 45 plus. *Adv. Rates:* 55; 55; 55; 40
Stuart Henry, President

Ithaca

WHCU
01-23-1923; 870 khz AM *Hrs Open:* 24
1751 Hanshaw Road, Ithaca, NY 14850 US
(607) 257-6400, *Fax:* (607) 257-6497
www.whcu870.com
info@whcu870.com
License: Ithaca, NY held by Saga Communications of New England LLC.
Group Owner: Saga Communications Inc.; (acq 5-31-2005; grpsl)
Nat'l Network: CBS; Westwood One; AP Radio *Nat'l Reps:* Christal
Arbitron Metro Market: Ithaca, NY *Format:* News, News/Talk, 84, Talk *Hrs. of News Programming:* news progmg 40 hrs wkly *No. News Employees:* 3 *Target Audience:* 25-64.
Edward Christian, President
Chris Allinger, Operations Dir
Susan Johnston, General Manager
Geoff Dunn, Programming Director
Connie Fairfax-Ozmun, Promotions Manager

***WICB**
01-14-1947; 91.7 mhz FM *Hrs Open:* 24; 4.1 kw; 135 ft.; N42 25 7 W76 29 39
326 Park Hall, Ithaca, NY 14850 US
(607) 274-1040
www.wicb.org
wicb@ithaca.edu
License: Ithaca, Tompkins County, NY held by Ithaca College.
Nat'l Network: ABC
Arbitron Metro Market: Ithaca, NY *Format:* Rock/AOR, Urban Contemporary *Special Programming:* Jazz 13 hrs, folk 2 hrs, blues 2 hrs, reggae 2 hrs *Hrs. of News Programming:* News progmg 6 hrs wkly *Target Audience:* 18-34; young audience with taste for innovative mus
Christopher Wheatley, General Manager

WQNY
01-01-1948; 103.7 mhz FM *Hrs Open:* 24; 16.5 kw; 863 ft.; N42 23 10 W76 40 9
1751 Hanshaw Rd, Ithaca, NY 14850 US
(607) 257-6400, *Fax:* (607) 257-6497
License: Ithaca, Tompkins County, NY held by Saga Communications of New England LLC
Group Owner: Saga Communications Inc.
Arbitron Metro Market: Ithaca, NY *Format:* Country *No. News Employees:* 3 *Target Audience:* 25-54.
Chris Allinger, Programming Director

***WSQG-FM**
01-01-1988; 90.9 mhz FM *Hrs Open:* 24; 5 kw; 325 ft.; N42 34 55 W76 33 22 *Rebroadcasts:* Rebroadcasts WSKG-FM Binghamton 100%
P.O. Box 3000, Binghamton, NY 13902 US
(607) 729-0100, *Fax:* (607) 729-7328
www.wskg.com
wskg_mail@wskg.pbs.org
License: Ithaca, Tompkins County, NY held by WSKG Public Telecommunications Council.
Nat'l Network: NPR; PRI
Arbitron Metro Market: Ithaca, NY *Format:* News *Special Programming:* Jazz 7 hrs, folk/bluegrass 5 hrs wkly *Hrs. of News Programming:* news progmg 33 hrs wkly *No. News Employees:* 1 *Target Audience:* General.
Brian Sickora, President
Nancy Christensen, Operations Dir
Ken Campbell, Programming Director
Stacy Mosteller, News Director
Linda Cohen, Underwriting Director

WNYY
04-01-1956; 1470 khz AM *Hrs Open:* 24; 5 kw-D, DAN; 1 kw-N, DAN; N42 23 32 W76 28 29
1751 Hanshaw Road, Ithaca, NY 14850 US
(607) 257-6400, *Fax:* (607) 257-6497
www.1470wnyy.com
cosadchey@cyradiogroup.com
License: Ithaca, NY held by Saga Communications of New England LLC.
Group Owner: Saga Communications Inc.; (acq 5-31-2005; grpsl)
Nat'l Network: Westwood One *Nat'l Reps:* Christal
Arbitron Metro Market: Ithaca, NY *Format:* Alternative, Talk *No. News Employees:* 3 *Target Audience:* 35-54.
Edward Christian, President
Chris Allinger, Operations Dir
Chet Osadchey, General Manager
Geoff Dunn, Programming Director
Connie Fairfax-Ozmun, Promotions Manager
Geoff Dunn, News Director
Brian Kerkan, Chief Engineer
ChrisAllinger, Operations Manager
Andrew Longcore, Webmaster

WVBR-FM
06-07-1958; 93.5 mhz FM *Hrs Open:* 24; 3 kw; 249 ft.; N42 25 42 W76 26 57
227 Linden Avenue, Ithaca, NY 14850 US
(607) 273-4000, *Fax:* (607) 273-4069
www.wvbr.com
concert@wvbr.com
License: Ithaca, Tompkins County, NY held by Cornell Radio Guild Inc.
Nat'l Network: Westwood One *Nat'l Reps:* Eastman Radio; Katz Radio
Arbitron Metro Market: Ithaca, NY *Format:* Rock/AOR *Special Programming:* Oldies 5 hrs, heavy metal 6 hrs, folk 8 hrs,blues *Hrs. of News Programming:* News progmg 10 hrs wkly *Target Audience:* 18-49; highlyeducated listeners
Drew Endick, General Manager
Nischay Rege, Programming Director
Michael Mallon, News Director
Jeff Gotlieb, Sports Director
Jay Sage, Marketing Director
Kevin Boyle, IT Director
Jeff Haber, Music Director

WYXL
09-01-1947; 97.3 mhz FM; 26 kw; 879 ft.; N42 27 54 W76 22 23
1751 Hanshaw Rd, Ithaca, NY 14850 US
(607) 257-6400, *Fax:* (607) 257-6497
License: Ithaca, Tompkins County, NY held by Saga Communications of New England LLC.
Group Owner: Saga Communications Inc.
Arbitron Metro Market: Ithaca, NY *Format:* Adult Contemp *Target Audience:* 25-54.
Chris Allinger, Programming Director

***WITH**
90.1 mhz FM; 1 kw; 286 ft.; N42 34 55 W76 33 22
300 Pulteney Street, Geneva, NY 14456 US
(315) 781-3456, *Fax:* (315) 781-3916
www.weos.org
weos@hws.edu
License: Ithaca, Tompkins County, NY held by The Colleges of the Seneca.
Arbitron Metro Market: Ithaca, NY
Greg Cotterill, General Manager
Michael Black, Programming Director

Jamestown

*WCOT
12-14-1992; 90.9 mhz FM; 12 kw; 653 ft.; N42 0 6 W79 3 19
Rebroadcasts: Rebroadcasts WCIK(FM) Bath 100%
P.O. Box 506, Bath, NY 14810 US
(607) 776-4151, *Fax:* (607) 776-6929
www.fln.org
mail@fln.org
License: Jamestown, Chautauqua County, NY held by Family Life Ministries Inc.
Group Owner: Family Life Network
Nat'l Network: Salem Radio Network *Wire Services:* Metro Weather Service Inc.
Arbitron Metro Market: Bath,NY *Format:* Christian *Hrs. of News Programming:* news progmg 14 hrs wkly *No. News Employees:* 3 *Target Audience:* 30-54.
Dick Snavely, CFO
Rick Snavely, President
Sammy Carrillo, Programming Director
Sammy Carrillo, Promotions Manager
Jim Travis, Chief Engineer

WHUG
02-01-1965; 101.9 mhz FM; 6 kw; 328 ft.; N42 7 53 W79 13 13
P.O. Box 1199, Jamestown, NY 14702 US
(716) 664-2313, *Fax:* (716) 488-1471
www.whug.com
A ahill@radiojamestown.com
License: Jamestown, Chautauqua County, NY
Group Owner: Media One Group
Format: Country *Hrs. of News Programming:* news progmg 2 hrs wkly *No. News Employees:* 2
Jason Finkleburg, General Manager
Steven Petrone, Programming Director

WJTN
12-01-1924; 1240 khz AM *Hrs Open:* 24
Mailing Address: 2 Orchard Road, W.E., Jamestown, NY 14701 US
Second Address: 2 Orchard Rd. W.E., Jamestown, NY 14701
(716) 487-1151, *Fax:* (716) 664-9326
www.wjtn.com
wjtn@wjtn.com
License: Jamestown, NY held by Media One Group LLC
Group Owner: Media One Group; (acq 8-30-2002; $5.05 million with co-located FM)
Nat'l Network: Westwood One *Nat'l Reps:* Rgnl Reps *Wire Services:* AP
Format: News, Sports, 86 *Special Programming:* It one hr, Sp one hr, Swedish one hr, farm one hr *Hrs. of News Programming:* news progmg 16 hrs wkly *No. News Employees:* 3 *Target Audience:* 35 plus; adultsseeking full service progmg *Adv. Rates:* 26; 26; 26; 26
Nick Keefe, Operations Dir
Merrill Rosen, General Manager
Larry Sazacki, General Sales Mgr
Kathy Roselle, News Director
Wayne Goff, Chief Engineer
Dennis Webster, Farm Director
Terry Frank, Local News Editor
Jason Sample, NewsReporter

WKSN
01-26-1948; 1340 khz AM
P. O. Box 1199, Jamestown, NY 14701 US
(716) 664-2313, *Fax:* (716) 488-1471
www.wksn.com
A ahill@radiojamestown.com
License: Jamestown, NY held by Media One Group II LLC.
Group Owner: Media One Group; (acq 5-31-2005; grpsl)
Format: Oldies *Special Programming:* Relg 2 hrs, Swedish one hr wkly *Hrs. of News Programming:* news progmg 3 hrs wkly *No. News Employees:* 2
Daniel Fischer, Operations Dir
Guy Ditonto, General Sales Mgr
Tom Marshall, Programming Director
Joel Keefer, News Director
Burton Waterman, Chief Engineer
Roseanne De Frisco, Traffic Manager

*WNJA
01-01-1991; 89.7 mhz FM *Hrs Open:* 24; 6 kw; 755 ft.; N42 2 48 W79 5 26
Mailing Address: P.O. Box 1263, Buffalo, NY 14240 US
Second Address: 140 Lower Terr., Buffalo, NY 14202-1263
(716) 845-7000, *Fax:* (716) 845-7043
www.wned.org
info@wnja.org
License: Jamestown, Chautauqua County, NY held by Western New York Public Broadcasting Association.
Arbitron Metro Market: Buffalo, NY *Format:* Talk *Target Audience:* 35 plus.
Donald Boswell, CEO
Richard Daly, Operations Dir
Ron Santora, Station Manager
Sylvia Bennett, General Sales Mgr
Gabe DiMaio, Programming Director
Jim Ranney, News Director
Michael Sutton, CFO

*WUBJ
07-11-1994; 88.1 mhz FM *Hrs Open:* 24; 2.7 kw; 499 ft.; N42 10 47 W79 20 29 *Rebroadcasts:* Rebroadcasts WBFO(FM) Buffalo 100%
3435 Main Street, Buffalo, NY 14214 US
(716) 845-7000, *Fax:* (716) 845-7036
www.wbfo.org
mail@wbfo.org
License: Jamestown, Chautauqua County, NY held by State University of New York.
Nat'l Network: NPR
Arbitron Metro Market: Jamestown, NY *Format:* Jazz, News
Special Programming: Blues 8 hrs, bluegrass music 3 hrs, Pol 3 hrs wkly *Hrs. of News Programming:* news progmg 50 hrs wkly *No. News Employees:* 2*Target Audience:* General; educated professional
Carole Smith Petro, Operations Dir
Carole Petro, General Manager
Joan Wilson, General Sales Mgr
Mark Scott, News Director
Mark Wozniak, Operations Manager

WWSE
10-01-1947; 93.3 mhz FM *Hrs Open:* 24; 26.5 kw; 643 ft.; N42 5 6 W79 17 22
Mailing Address: 2 Orchard Road, N.E., Jamestown, NY 14701 US
Second Address: 2 Orchard Rd. W.E., Jamestown, NY 14701
(716) 664-9393, *Fax:* (716) 664-9326
www.se933.com
wwsefm@wwsefm.com
License: Jamestown, Chautauqua County, NY held by Media One Group LLC.
Group Owner: Media One Group
Arbitron Metro Market: Jamestown, NY *Format:* Adult Contemp *Hrs. of News Programming:* news progmg 7 hrs wkly *No. News Employees:* 3 *Target Audience:* 12554; female *Adv. Rates:* 32; 32; 32; 32
Cheryl Akin, General Sales Mgr
Nick Keefe, Programming Director
Sammie Green, News Director
Brian Papalia, Assistant Music Director
Andrew Hill, Disc Jockey
Bill Dossion, Disc Jockey
Lee John, Disc Jockey
Matthew Hanley, NewsReporter

Jeffersonville

*WJFF
02-12-1990; 90.5 mhz FM *Hrs Open:* 24; 3.7 kw; 630 ft.; N41 48 58 W74 47 15
Rte 52 , Box 797, Jeffersonville, NY 12748 US
(845) 482-4141, *Fax:* (845) 482-WJFF
www.wjffradio.org
wjff@wjffradio.org
License: Jeffersonville, Sullivan County, NY held by Radio Catskill.
Nat'l Network: NPR; PRI
Format: News, News/Talk, 86 *Hrs. of News Programming:* News progmg 75 hrs wkly *Target Audience:* 16-60; general
Bill Duncan, President
Christine Aherne, Station Manager

WPDA
01-01-1993; 106.1 mhz FM; 1.6 kw; 627 ft.; N41 48 57 W74 45 42 *Rebroadcasts:* Rebroadcasts WPDH(FM) Poughkeepsie 100%
10 Circular Road, Poughkeepsie, NY 12601 US
(845) 471-1500, *Fax:* (845) 454-1204
www.wpdh.com
License: Jeffersonville, Sullivan County, NY held by Cumulus Licensing Corp.
Group Owner: Cumulus Media Inc.; (acq 1-23-02; grpsl).
Nat'l Reps: Katz Radio
Format: Rock/AOR
Charles Benfer, General Manager

WDNB
11-15-1999; 102.1 mhz FM *Hrs Open:* 24; 6 kw; 253 ft.; N41 44 30 W74 51 23
1151 Route 44-55, Clintondate, NY 12515 US
(570) 292-7535, *Fax:* (570) 292-7529
www.thunder102.com
pciliberto@boldgoldmedia.com
License: Jeffersonville, Sullivan County, NY held by Bold Gold Media Group L.P.
Group Owner: Bold Gold Media Group LP; (acq 5-23-2005; grpsl).
Arbitron Metro Market: Liberty, NY *Format:* Country *Hrs. of News Programming:* news progmg 5 hrs wkly *No. News Employees:* 1 *Target Audience:* 25 plus; male & female general high school education plus *Adv.Rates:* 20; 15; 18; 12
Vince Benedetto, CEO
Paul Ciliberto, NY Market Manager and General Manager
Paul Ciliberto, General Sales Mgr
George Schmitt, Programming Director
ReginaHensley, Promotions Manager
Theresa Opeka, News Director
Mike Sakell,Community Events and News Contact

Johnson City

WLTB
09-03-1972; 101.7 mhz FM; 0.58 kw; 1024 ft.; N42 3 22 W75 56 39
Mailing Address: 1 Delaware Ave, Ste 2, Endicott, NY 13760 US
Second Address: 1808 Vestal Pkwy. E., Vestal, NY 13851
(607) 748-9131, *Fax:* (607) 748-0061
www.magic1017fm.com
info@magic1017fm.com
License: Johnson City, Broome County, NY held by GM Broadcasting Inc.
Nat'l Network: CNN Radio *Nat'l Reps:* Christal
Arbitron Metro Market: Binghamton, NY *Format:* Adult Contemp
Target Audience: 25 - 54; emphasis on females
Thomas Mollen, President
Steve Gilinsky, General Manager

Johnstown

WIZR
01-01-1964; 930 khz AM *Hrs Open:* 24; 1 kw-D, ND1; 0.028 kw-N, ND1; N42 59 54 W74 21 31
6 Johnson Road, Latham, NY 12110 US
(518) 762-4631, *Fax:* (518) 762-0105
www.930wizr.com
License: Johnstown, NY held by 6 Johnson Road Licenses Inc.
Group Owner: Pamal Broadcasting Ltd.; (acq 10-19-2001; grpsl).
Arbitron Metro Market: Albany-Schenectady-Troy, NY *Format:* Adult Contemp *Special Programming:* It one hr, Pol one hr, Sp one hr wkly *Hrs. of News Programming:* news progmg 6 hrs wkly *No. News Employees:* 1*Target Audience:* 25-54. *Adv. Rates:* 10; 10; 10; 10
Joey Caruso, General Manager

Kingston

*WAMK
03-01-1988; 90.9 mhz FM *Hrs Open:* 24; 0.94 kw; 1486 ft.; N42 4 35 W74 6 26 *Rebroadcasts:* Rebroadcasts WAMC-FM Albany 100%
318 Central Avenue, Albany, NY 12206 US
(518) 465-5233(800) 323-9262, *Fax:* (518) 432-6974
www.wamc.org
mail@wamc.org
License: Kingston, Ulster County, NY held by WAMC.
Group Owner: WAMC/Northeast Public Radio
Nat'l Network: PRI; NPR *Wire Services:* AP
Arbitron Metro Market: Poughkeepsie NY *Format:* News, News/Talk, 86 *Special Programming:* Jazz 13 hrs, folk 7 hrs *Hrs. of News Programming:* News progmg 77 hrs wkly *Target Audience:* General.
Alan Chartock, CEO
David Galletly, Operations Dir
Selma Kaplan, Vice President

WKXP
12-13-1965; 94.3 mhz FM *Hrs Open:* 24; 2.25 kw; 545 ft.; N41 53 44 W73 59 32
Mailing Address: 427 Bedford Road, Suite 300, Pleasantville, NY 10570 US
Second Address: 2 Pendell Rd., Poughkeepsie, NY 12602
(845) 471-1500, *Fax:* (845) 454-1204
www.hudsonvalleycountry.com/
kathy.butsko@cumulus.com
License: Kingston, Ulster County, NY held by Cumulus Licensing Corp.
Group Owner: Cumulus Media Inc.; (acq 2-11-2004; $3.5 million).
Arbitron Metro Market: Poughkeepsie, NY *Format:* Country
Target Audience: 18-49; women *Adv. Rates:* 35; 25; 30; na
Charles Benfer, General Manager
Beth Christy, Programming Director

Jeremiah Johnsen, Promotions Manager
Kathy Butsko, Business Manager

***WFGB**
01-01-1985; 89.7 mhz FM *Hrs Open:* 24; 3.1 kw; 1486 ft.; N42 4 35 W74 6 26
P.O. Box 777, Lake Katrine, NY 12449 US
(800) 724-8518, *Fax:* (845) 336-7205
www.soundoflife.org
email@soundoflife.org
License: Kingston, Ulster County, NY held by Sound of Life Inc.
Arbitron Metro Market: Kingston, NY *Format:* Christian *Hrs. of News Programming:* News progmg 3 hrs wkly *Target Audience:* General.
Jay Cookingham, Chairman
Tom Michaels Zahradnik, CEO
Bob Conti, Operations Dir
Tom Zahradnik, General Manager
Joe Hunter, Programming Director
Donna Quiles, Office Administrator / Director of Partner Relatio
Connie Van Kleeck,Assistant Program Director
Derek Duncan, Business Partnership Representative
Paul Grimsland, Production Director
Tim Millard, Secretary

***WFRH**
09-01-1993; 91.7 mhz FM *Hrs Open:* 24; 1.2 kw vert; 325 ft.; N41 59 14 W74 1 13
4135 Northgate Blvd., Suite 1, Sacramento, CA 95834 US
(315) 331-7482, *Fax:* (410) 268-0931
www.familyradio.com
info@familyradio.com
License: Kingston, Ulster County, NY held by Family Stations Inc.
Group Owner: Family Stations Inc.
Format: Religious
Harold Camping, President
Dan Elmendorf, Station Manager

WGHQ
03-04-1956; 920 khz AM *Hrs Open:* 24; 5 kw-D, DA1; 0.078 kw-N, DA1; N41 53 9 W73 58 15
427 Bedford Road, Suite 300, Pleasantville, NY 10570 US
(845) 838-6000, *Fax:* (845) 838-6088
License: Kingston, NY held by 6 Johnson Road Licenses Inc.
Group Owner: Pamal Broadcasting Ltd.; (acq 4-1-2007; grpsl)
Format: News, News/Talk, 86 *Special Programming:* Relg 3 hrs wkly *No. News Employees:* 1 *Target Audience:* 30 plus.
Jason Finkelberg, General Manager

WKNY
08-01-1939; 1490 khz AM *Hrs Open:* 24; 1 kw-U, ND1; N41 56 11 W74 0 30
Mailing Address: P.O. Box 416, Poughkeepsie, NY 12602 US
Second Address: Box 1398, Kingston, NY 12402
(845) 331-1490, *Fax:* (845) 331-9569
www.1490wkny.com
wknynews@pendellrd.com
License: Kingston, NY held by Cumulus Licensing Corp.
Group Owner: Cumulus Media Inc.; (acq 1-23-02; grpsl).
Nat'l Network: CBS *Nat'l Reps:* Katz Radio *Wire Services:* AP
Format: Adult Contemp *Special Programming:* Ger one hr, Pol one hr, Irish one hr wkly *Hrs. of News Programming:* news progmg 26 hrs wkly *No. News Employees:* 2 *Target Audience:* 25-54; 60% female *Adv. Rates:* 28; 22; 24; 20
Chuck Benfer, General Manager
Dominic Fusco, General Sales Mgr
Warren Lawrence, Programming Director
Linda Rosner, News Director

Lake George

WCKM-FM
04-21-1994; 98.5 mhz FM *Hrs Open:* 24; 0.37 kw; 1289 ft.; N43 25 12 W73 45 37
128 Glen Street, Glens Falls, NY 12801 US
(518) 761-9890, *Fax:* (518) 761-9893
www.radiowins.com
wckm@regionalradiogroup.com
License: Lake George, Warren County, NY held by Regional Radio Group LLC.
Group Owner: Regional Radio Group LLC; (acq 9-10-2008; grpsl)
Nat'l Network: ABC
Arbitron Metro Market: Albany-Schenectady-Troy, NY *Format:* Oldies *Special Programming:* Interviews *Hrs. of News Programming:* news progmg 7 hrs wkly *No. News Employees:* 15 *Target Audience:* 25-54; upscalebaby boomers *Adv. Rates:* 37; 25; 30; 15
Steve Babson, Operations Dir
Clay Ashworth, General Manager
Dan Miner, Station Manager
Pete Cloutier, Promotions Manager
Robin Truax, News Director
Ken Leccese, Sports Director

Lake Luzerne

WBAR-FM
06-30-1992; 94.7 mhz FM *Hrs Open:* 24; 1.25 kw; 722 ft.; N43 18 16.7 W73 45 6.6 *Rebroadcasts:* Rebroadcasts WHAZ(AM) Troy 100%
30 Park Ave, Cohoes, NY 12047 US
(985) 839-3782, *Fax:* (985) 839-3783
License: Lake Luzerne, Warren County, NY held by Capital Media Corp.
Group Owner: Capital Media Corp.; acq 10-1-92;
Arbitron Metro Market: Tylertown MS *Format:* Gospel
C. Wayne Dowdy, President
William Giles, General Manager

Lake Placid

WIRD
11-21-1961; 920 khz AM *Hrs Open:* 24; 5 kw-D, ND1; 0.087 kw-N, ND1; N44 15 36 W74 1 22
P.O. Box 831, 17 Wilmington Rd, Lake Placid, NY 12946 US
(518) 891-1544, *Fax:* (518) 891-1545
brandy@mtnradio.com
License: Lake Placid, NY held by Radio Lake Placid Inc.
Group Owner: Mountain Communications; (acq 1-10-2005)
Nat'l Network: ESPN Radio
Format: Sports *Hrs. of News Programming:* news progmg 20 hrs wkly *No. News Employees:* 2 *Target Audience:* 25-54; working blue collar/college educated
Virgle Strictland, General Manager

WLPW
10-01-1979; 105.5 mhz FM *Hrs Open:* 24; 3 kw; -236 ft.; N44 15 36 W74 1 22
P.O. Box 831, 17 Wilmington Rd, Lake Placid, NY 12946 US
(518) 891-1544, *Fax:* (518) 891-1545
www.theclassicrock105.com
brandy@mtnradio.com
License: Lake Placid, Essex County, NY held by Radio Lake Placid Inc.
Group Owner: Mountain Communications
Format: Classic Rock
Clarence Barinowski, General Manager

Lake Ronkonkoma

***WSHR**
01-01-1966; 91.9 mhz FM *Hrs Open:* 24; 6 kw; 177 ft.; N40 50 10 W73 5 59
212 Smith Road, Lake Ronkonkoma, NY 11779 US
(631) 471-1472, *Fax:* (631) 471-1491
License: Lake Ronkonkoma, Suffolk County, NY held by Board of Education Sachem Central School District at Holbrook.
Format: Variety/Diverse *Target Audience:* General.
Mark Laura, General Manager
Isaic Ramaswamy, Station Manager

Lake Success

WKTU
01-01-1940; 103.5 mhz FM *Hrs Open:* 24; 6 kw; 1362 ft.; N40 44 54 W73 59 10
433 E. Las Colinas Blvd, #1130, Irving, TX 75039 US
(201) 420-3700, *Fax:* (201) 420-3737
www.ktu.com
1035ktu@clearchannel.com
License: Lake Success, Nassau County, NY held by AMFM Radio Licenses LLC.
Group Owner: Clear Channel Communications Inc.; (acq 8-30-2000; grpsl)
Nat'l Reps: D & R Radio
Arbitron Metro Market: New York *Format:* Contemporary Hits/Top 40 *No. News Employees:* 1 *Target Audience:* 18-54.
Rob Williams, General Manager

Lakewood

WKZA
03-01-2001; 106.9 mhz FM; 5.1 kw; 738 ft.; N41 57 31 W79 16 11
1914 Maple Leaf Drive, Windermere, FL 34786 US
(716) 487-1106, *Fax:* (716) 488-2169
www.1069kissfm.com
sherriewkza@hotmail.com
License: Lakewood, Chautauqua County, NY held by Cross Country Communications LLC.
Arbitron Metro Market: Jamestown, NY *Format:* Contemporary Hits/Top 40 *Target Audience:* 25-54.
John Newman, General Manager
Sherrie Brookmire, Sales Manager
Steve Rockford, Programming Director
Megan Arnone, Media Consultant
Jamie Trusler, Media Consultant
Jerod Zahn, Media Consultant
Bill Dorrion, Media Consultant

***WYRR**
88.9 mhz FM; 0.42 kw horiz, 0.336 kw vert; 335 ft.; N42 10 33 W79 19 2
US
(225)768-3224
www.jsm.org
onair@jsm.org
License: Lakewood, Chautauqua County, NY held by Muncy Hills Broadcasting Inc.
Arbitron Metro Market: Baton Rouge, LA *Format:* Religious
Van Michael, President

Lancaster

WXRL
01-01-1964; 1300 khz AM *Hrs Open:* 24
5426 William Street, Post Office Box 170, Lancaster, NY 14086 US
(716) 681-1313, *Fax:* (716) 681-7172
www.wxrl.com
wxrl@aol.com
License: Lancaster, NY held by Dome Broadcasting Inc.
Nat'l Network: CNN Radio
Arbitron Metro Market: Buffalo, NY *Format:* Country *Special Programming:* German one hr, Polish 19 hrs wkly *Target Audience:* 35 plus; Mature men & women 35 and older *Adv. Rates:* 40; 40; 45; 30
Louis Schriver, President
Lynn Carol Supparits, Operations Dir
Lori Arumygam, General Sales Mgr
Linda Sukennik, Promotions Manager
Joan Schriver, Executive Vice President

Liberty

***WGWR**
11-01-1997; 88.1 mhz FM *Hrs Open:* 24; 0.06 kw; 561 ft.; N41 48 55 W74 45 48 *Rebroadcasts:* Rebroadcasts WFGB(FM) Kingston 100%
P O Box 777, Lake Katrine, NY 12449 US
(845) 336-6199, *Fax:* (845) 336-7205
www.soundoflife.org
wmial@soundoflife.org
License: Liberty, Sullivan County, NY held by Sound of Life Inc.
Format: Christian
Bob Conti, Operations Dir
Tom Zahradnik, General Manager
Joe Hunter, Programming Director

WVOS
01-01-1947; 1240 khz AM *Hrs Open:* 5 AM-11 PM; 1 kw-U, ND1; N41 46 54 W74 43 49
P. O. Box 150, Liberty, NY 12754 US
(845) 794-9898, *Fax:* (845) 794-0125
www.wvosfm.com
mail@wVOSFM.com
License: Liberty, NY held by Watermark Communications LLC
Arbitron Metro Market: Liberty, NY *Format:* Country
Helena Manzione, General Manager

WVOS-FM
12-01-1964; 95.9 mhz FM *Hrs Open:* 24; 6 kw; 328 ft.; N41 45 9 W74 43 1
P. O. Box 150, Liberty, NY 12754 US
(845) 794-9898, *Fax:* (845) 794-0125
www.wvosfm.com
mail@wVOSFM.com
License: Liberty, Sullivan County, NY
Arbitron Metro Market: Liberty, NY *Format:* Oldies *Target Audience:* 25-54.
Karen Carey, Operations Dir
David LeFrois, Programming Director

Little Falls

WIXT
06-10-1952; 1230 khz AM *Hrs Open:* 24; 1 kw-U, ND1; N43 2 33 W74 51 31
P.O. Box 4490, Utica, NY 13504 US
(315) 797-0803, *Fax:* (315) 797-7813
www.starsradionetwork.com
info@galaxycommunication.com
License: Little Falls, NY held by Galaxy Utica Licensee LLC.

Group Owner: Galaxy Communications L.P.; (acq 10-24-2007; grpsl)
Arbitron Metro Market: Utica-Rome, NY *Format:* Sports *Special Programming:* Farm one hr, relg one hr wkly *Hrs. of News Programming:* news progmg 16 hrs wkly *No. News Employees:* 1 *Target Audience:* 25-54.
Brian Delaney, General Manager

WSKU
01-03-1991; 105.5 mhz FM *Hrs Open:* 24; 2.25 kw; 528 ft.; N42 59 27 W74 55 6
P.O. Box 4490, Utica, NY 13502 US
(315) 734-9245, *Fax:* (315) 624-9245
www.cnykiss.com
License: Little Falls, Herkimer County, NY held by Roser Communications Network Inc.
Group Owner: Roser Communications Network Inc.; (acq 10-24-2007; grpsl)
Nat'l Reps: Roslin
Arbitron Metro Market: Utica-Rome, NY *Format:* Contemporary Hits/Top 40 *Hrs. of News Programming:* news progmg one hr wkly *No. News Employees:* 1 *Target Audience:* 25-54.
Stephen Lawrence, Operations Dir
Brian Delaney, General Manager

Lockport

WLVL
05-08-1947; 1340 khz AM
Mailing Address: P.O. Box 477, 320 Michigan Street, Lockport, NY 14095 US
Second Address: 320 Michigan St., Lockport, NY 14094
(716) 433-5944, *Fax:* (716) 433-6588
www.wlvl.com
wlvl@wlvl.com
License: Lockport, NY held by Culver Communications Inc.
Nat'l Network: Westwood One
Arbitron Metro Market: Lockport, NY *Format:* News, News/Talk, 84, Talk *Special Programming:* Farm one hr, It 2 hrs, Pol one hr, relg 3 hrs wkly *Target Audience:* 25-64; adult Lockport area citizens
Richard Greene, President
Doug Young, News Director

Loudonville

*WVCR-FM
04-26-1963; 88.3 mhz FM *Hrs Open:* 24; 2.8 kw; 840 ft.; N42 38 13 W74 0 5
515 Loudon Road/Route 9, Loudonville, NY 12211 US
(518) 782-6750, *Fax:* (518) 782-6498
www.wvcr.com
dkibbey@siena.edu
License: Loudonville, Albany County, NY held by Siena College.
Arbitron Metro Market: Loudonville, NY *Format:* Variety/Diverse *Special Programming:* Pol 3 hrs, Sp 3 hrs, gospel 3 hrs, Irish 3 hrs *Target Audience:* 12-34; female *Adv. Rates:* 20; 20; 20; 20
Joseph Doty, Operations Dir
Darrin Kibbey, General Manager
Dean Charette, Programming Director
Stacy Rogers, Marketing Director
Sean Robbins, Web Director
John.F.Kelly, Director

Lowville

WLLG
04-01-1987; 99.3 mhz FM *Hrs Open:* 24; 1 kw; 561 ft.; N43 45 12 W75 33 50
3399 Joose River Road, Boonville, NY 13309 US
(315) 376-7500, *Fax:* (315) 376-8549
www.themoose.net
sales@themoose.net
License: Lowville, Lewis County, NY held by The Flack Broadcasting Group L.L.C.
Nat'l Network: USA
Format: Country, News *Special Programming:* Farm 3 hrs, relg 2 hrs wkly *Hrs. of News Programming:* news progmg 18 hrs wkly *No. News Employees:* 1 *Target Audience:* General.
William Flack, President
Brian Best, News Director
Ken Ruhlend, Chief Engineer

Malone

WICY
11-04-1946; 1500 khz AM *Hrs Open:* 18; 1 kw-U, ND1; N44 50 46 W74 16 7
1120 Mar West Street, Suite A, Tiburon, CA 44022 US
(518) 483-1100, *Fax:* (518) 483-1382
www.oldiesradioonline.com
License: Malone, NY held by Cartier Communications Inc.
Group Owner: Martz Communications Group; (acq 6-30-97; $761,000 with co-located FM)
Nat'l Reps: Rgnl Reps
Format: Oldies *Special Programming:* Farm one hr wkly *Hrs. of News Programming:* news progmg 15 hrs wkly *No. News Employees:* 2 *Target Audience:* 25-54.
Michael Boldt, General Manager

*WSLO
02-01-1989; 90.9 mhz FM *Hrs Open:* 24; 0.2 kw; 348 ft.; N44 49 46 W74 22 31 *Rebroadcasts:* Rebroadcasts WSLU(FM) Canton 100%
N. Country Public Radio, Canton, NY 13617 US
(315) 229-5356, *Fax:* (315) 229-5373
www.ncpr.org
radio@ncpr.org
License: Malone, Franklin County, NY held by St. Lawrence University.
Format: Variety/Diverse *Hrs. of News Programming:* news progmg 35 hrs wkly *No. News Employees:* 2 *Target Audience:* General.
Shelly Pike, Operations Dir
Ellen Rocco, General Manager
Ellen Rocco, Station Manager
Jackie Sautler, Programming Director
Martha Foley, News Director
Robert Sauter, Chief Engineer
Sandra Demarest, Underwriting Director

WVNV
05-01-1993; 96.5 mhz FM *Hrs Open:* 20; 16 kw horiz, 15.5 kw vert; 400 ft.; N44 46 56 W74 13 9
515 Skylake Court, Incline Village, NV 89451 US
(518) 483-1100, *Fax:* (518) 483-1382
www.country965.com
bhill@davidsonmediagroup.com
License: Malone, Franklin County, NY held by Cartier Communications Inc.
Group Owner: Martz Communications Group
Arbitron Metro Market: Malone, NY *Format:* Country *Hrs. of News Programming:* news progmg 2 hrs wkly *No. News Employees:* 2 *Target Audience:* 18-54.
Michael Boldt, General Manager
Kim Kiser, General Sales Mgr
Drew Scott, Programming Director

*WMHQ
12-03-2003; 90.1 mhz FM *Hrs Open:* 24; 2.7 kw; 354 ft.; N44 49 41 W74 22 43 *Rebroadcasts:* Rebroadcasts WMHR(FM) Syracuse 99%
4044 Makyes Rd, Syracuse, NY 13215 US
(315) 469-5051, *Fax:* (315) 469-4066
www.marshillnetwork.org
mhn@marshillnetwork.org
License: Malone, Franklin County, NY held by Mars Hill Broadcasting Co. Inc.
Group Owner: Mars Hill Network
Nat'l Network: Moody; Salem Radio Network *Wire Services:* AP
Arbitron Metro Market: Burlington, VT *Format:* Christian *Hrs. of News Programming:* News progmg 6 hrs wkly *Target Audience:* General; Christian families
Clayton Roberts, President
Wayne Taylor, General Manager
Mark Hard, Programming Director
Jeremy Miller, News Director
Mike Dwindell, Chief Engineer
Valerie Smith, Traffic Manager
Wayne Taylor, Network General Manager
LindaRockefeller, Business Manager
Yolanda Thompson, Administrative Assistant
Craig Case, Public Relations and Network Development Director
Phil Pilalas, IT Support/Webmaster/Afternoon host

Malta

WQSH
10-01-1996; 105.7 mhz FM; 7.1 kw; Ant 613 ft; N42 47 09 W73 37 43
1241 Kings Rd., Schenectady, NY 12804
(518) 881-1515, *Fax:* (518) 881-1516
www.buzz1057.com
comments@buzz1057.com
License: Malta, Saratoga County, NY
Group Owner: Townsquare Media; (acq 1-4-2007; $4.9 million)
Population Served: 275,000 *Arbitron Metro Market:* Albany-Schenectady-Troy, NY *Target Audience:* 18-54; general *Adv. Rates:* 30; 28; 30; 15
Robert Ausfeld, General Manager

Manlius

WAQX-FM
08-23-1978; 95.7 mhz FM *Hrs Open:* 24; 25 kw; 300 ft; N43 00 25 W76 05 38
1064 James St., Syracuse, NY 13203
(315) 472-0200, *Fax:* (315) 472-1146
www.95x.com
hunter.scott@cumulus.com
License: Manlius, Onondaga County, NY
Group Owner: Cumulus Media Inc.; (acq 4-26-01; grpsl).
Nat'l Network: ABC *Nat'l Reps:* D & R Radio
Arbitron Metro Market: Syracuse, NY *Special Programming:* Pub service one hr wkly *Hrs. of News Programming:* News progmg 3 hrs wkly *Target Audience:* 19-49; male
Tom Mitchell, Operations Dir
Dan Austin, General Manager
Hunter Scott, Programming Director
Dave Edwards, Chief Engineer
Angela Moonan, Sales Director

Manorville

WEHM
07-21-2003; 92.9 mhz FM; 6 kw; Ant 276 ft; N40 52 10 W72 34 37
Mailing Address: Box 7162, Amagansett, NY 11971
Second Address: 249 Montauk Hwy., Amagansett, NY 11930
(631) 267-7800, *Fax:* (631) 267-1018
www.wehm.com
info@wehm.com
License: Manorville, Suffolk County, NY held by AAA Licensing LLC.
Group Owner: Long Island Radio Broadcasting LLC; (acq 4-30-2003).

Don Maguire, President
Steve Harper, Operations Dir
Hedy Krebs-DeMaio, General Manager

Massena

WMSA
10-12-1945; 1340 khz AM *Hrs Open:* 5:30 AM-10:15 PM
515 Skylake Court, Incline Village, NV 89451 US
(315) 769-3333, *Fax:* (315) 769-3299
www.1340wmsa.com
info@1340wmsa.com
License: Massena, NY held by Stephens Media Group-Massena LLC.
Group Owner: Stephens Family L.P.
Arbitron Metro Market: Massena, NY *Format:* Adult Contemp *Hrs. of News Programming:* news progmg 16 hrs wkly *No. News Employees:* 1 *Target Audience:* 18 plus.
Michael Boldt, General Manager
Bob LaRue, News Director
Bob Sauder, Chief Engineer

WYBG
08-18-1958; 1050 khz AM *Hrs Open:* 6 AM-7 PM; 1 kw-D, 500 w-N; N44 53 42 W74 56 05
Box 298, 24 Andrews St., Massena, NY 13662
(315) 764-0554, *Fax:* (315) 764-0118
www.wybg1050.com
wybgradio@nnymail.com
License: Massena, St. Lawrence County, NY held by Wade Communications Inc.
Nat'l Network: USA *Nat'l Reps:* Commercial Media Sales
Population Served: 295,000*Special Programming:* American Indian, children, farm, folk *Hrs. of News Programming:* news progmg 14 hrs wkly *No. News Employees:* 2 *Target Audience:* 25-65; baby boomers & seniors*Adv. Rates:* 15; 15; 15; 15
Curran Wade, President
Dorothy Wade, Operations Dir

Mechanicville

WTMM-FM
01-04-1993; 104.5 mhz FM *Hrs Open:* 24; 5 kw; 351 ft.; N42 52 44 W73 51 47
600 Congress Avenue, Suite 1400, Austin, TX 78701 US
(805) 240-2070
License: Mechanicville, Rensselaer County, NY
Group Owner: Townsquare Media; (acq 8-24-2001; grpsl)
Nat'l Network: ESPN Radio
Arbitron Metro Market: Duluth-Superior MN-WI
Neal Robinson, President

WABY
10-19-1981; 1160 khz AM *Hrs Open:* 24; 5 kw-D, ND1; 0.57 kw-N, ND1; N42 55 12 W73 42 8
645 Church Street, Suite 400, Norfolk, VA 23510 US

(518) 899-3000, *Fax:* (518) 889-3057
www.saratogamoon.com
wabymoon@aol.com
License: Mechanicville, NY held by The Anastos Media Group Inc.
Group Owner: Anastos Media Group Inc.; (acq 12-7-00; $280,000).
Nat'l Network: ABC
Arbitron Metro Market: Albany, NY *Format:* Big Band *Hrs. of News Programming:* news progmg 50 hrs wkly *No. News Employees:* 1 *Target Audience:* 40 plus; adults, male & female *Adv. Rates:* 35; 30; 30; 10
Scott Collins, President
John Meaney, Operations Dir
John Measey, Station Manager
Fran Dingman, General Sales Mgr
Amanda Albright, Promotions Manager

Medford

WNYG
01-01-1958; 1440 khz AM *Hrs Open:* 24; 1 kw-D, 38 w-N; N40 42 32 W73 21 53
404 Rt. 109, West Babylon, NY 11704
(631) 321-9640, *Fax:* (631) 422-5992
www.wnygspiritofny.com
spiritny@optimum.net
License: Medford, Suffolk County, NY held by Multicultural Radio Broadcasting Licensee LLC.
Group Owner: Multicultural Radio Broadcasting Inc.; (acq 6-14-00; $850,000).
Population Served: 2,500,000 *Arbitron Metro Market:* New York *Hrs. of News Programming:* news progmg 3 hrs wkly *No. News Employees:* 1 *Target Audience:* 25-64. *Adv. Rates:* 600; 300; 600; 240
Phyllis Rose, General Manager
Doug Edwards, Programming Director

Medina

*WFWO
89.7 mhz FM; 0.4 kw; 131 ft.; N43 14 33 W78 18 27 US
(207) 865-3448, *Fax:* (207) 865-1763
www.positive.fm
info@positive.fm
License: Medina, Orleans County, NY held by The Positive Radio Network.
Arbitron Metro Market: Freeport, ME *Format:* Gospel
Mie Stoddard, Chairman
Suzanne Happs, General Manager
Kenny Robinson, Programming Director
Mark Marston, Office Manager
Erica Cook, Business Development Representative
Holly Norburg, Administrative Assistant / VolunteerCoordinator

Mexico

WVOA-FM
01-01-1997; 103.9 mhz FM; 3 kw; 292 ft; N43 28 36 W76 16 44
Renard Communications Corp., 401 W. Kirkpatrick St., Syracuse, NY 13215
(315) 472-0222, *Fax:* (315) 478-7745
WVOARadio.com
programming@WVOARadio.com
License: Mexico, Oswego County, NY held by Renard Communications Corp.
Special Programming: Ger 2 hrs, It 2 hrs, Pol 4 hrs , Sp 15 hrs wkly
Sam Furco, General Manager

Middletown

WALL
08-06-1942; 1340 khz AM *Hrs Open:* 24
Mailing Address: P.O. Box 416, Poughkeepsie, NY 12602 US
Second Address: 2 Pendel Rd., Poughkeepsie, NY 12602
(845) 471-1500, *Fax:* (845)-454-1204
www.wallhasitall.com
MarkWest@WallHasItAll.com
License: Middletown, NY held by Cumulus Licensing Corp.
Group Owner: Cumulus Media Inc.; (acq 1-23-02; grpsl).
Arbitron Metro Market: Middletown, NY *Format:* Children *Hrs. of News Programming:* news progmg 30 hrs wkly *No. News Employees:* 2 *Target Audience:* 35-64; educated, upscale families
Beth Christie, Operations Dir
Victor Goodman, General Sales Mgr
Nick Robbins, Programming Director
Bryan Jones, News Director

*WOSR
02-03-1992; 91.7 mhz FM *Hrs Open:* 24; 1.8 kw; 630 ft.; N41 36 4 W74 33 17 *Rebroadcasts:* Rebroadcasts WAMC-FM Albany 100%
Mailing Address: 318 Central Avenue, Albany, NY 12206 US
Second Address: 318 Central Ave., Middletown, NY 12206-6600
(518) 465-5233,(800) 323-9262, *Fax:* (518) 432-6974
www.wamc.org
mail@wamc.org
License: Middletown, Orange County, NY held by WAMC.
Group Owner: WAMC/Northeast Public Radio
Nat'l Network: NPR; PRI *Wire Services:* AP
Arbitron Metro Market: Newburgh-Middletown, NY (Mid-Hudson Valley) *Format:* News, Talk *Special Programming:* Folk 7 hrs, jazz 13 hrs wkly *Hrs. of News Programming:* News progmg 77 hrs wkly *Target Audience:* General.
Alan Chartock, CEO
Selma Kaplan, Operations Dir
David Galletly, Vice President

WRRV
11-11-1966; 92.7 mhz FM *Hrs Open:* 24; 6 kw; 269 ft.; N41 27 25 W74 26 24
Mailing Address: P.O. Box 416, Poughkeepsie, NY 12602 US
Second Address: 2 Pendel Rd., Middletown, NY 12602
(845) 471-1500, *Fax:* (845) 454-1204
www.cumulus.com
License: Middletown, Orange County, NY
Arbitron Metro Market: Newburgh-Middletown, NY (Mid-Hudson Valley) *Format:* Alternative *Special Programming:* New mus 2 hrs wkly *Hrs. of News Programming:* news progmg 3 hrs wkly *No. News Employees:* 1 *TargetAudience:* 18-44; younger, mobile, upscale families
Mike Harris, President
Bill Palmeri, General Manager
Greg O'Brien, Programming Director
Andrew Boris, Music Director

Milford

WYNY(AM)
1400 khz AM; 1 kw-U, DA-D; N41 28 26 W74 27 01
2927 US Route 6, Slate Hill, NY 10973
(845) 355-4001, *Fax:* (845) 355-4002
License: Milford, PA held by Digital Radio Broadcasting Inc.
Group Owner: Digital Radio Broadcasting Inc.
Arbitron Metro Market: Newburgh-Middletown, NY (Mid-Hudson Valley)
Bud Williamson, President

*WUOW
88.5 mhz FM; 0.1 kw vert; 732 ft.; N42 35 44 W74 51 53 US

www.external.oneonta.edu/WUOW
License: Milford, Otsego County, NY
Group Owner: State University of New York College at Oneonta
Gary Wickham, General Manager

Mineola

WTHE
01-01-1964; 1520 khz AM; 0.347 kw-C, NDD; 1 kw-D, NDD; N40 44 45 W73 37 29
1086 Teaneck Road, Teaneck, NJ 07666 US
(516) 742-1520, *Fax:* (516) 742-2878
www.wthe1520am.com
nygospelradio@aol.com
License: Mineola, NY held by Universal Broadcasting of New York Inc.
Group Owner: Universal Broadcasting of New York Inc.; acq 7-10-69; $235,000).
Arbitron Metro Market: Mineola, NY *Format:* Black, Gospel, 74 *Hrs. of News Programming:* news progmg 10 hrs wkly *No. News Employees:* 1 *Target Audience:* General. *Adv. Rates:* 30;30;30;30
Howard Warshaw, CEO
Miriam Warshaw, President
Abe Warshaw, Operations Dir
Darren Greggs, Programming Director
Darren Greggs, Vice President, Operations
Howard Warshaw Sr., Vice President

Minetto

WKRH
10-01-1996; 106.5 mhz FM; 5 kw; 328 ft.; N43 25 4 W76 27 54
7536 Murray Drive, Cicero, NY 13039 US
(315) 472-9111, *Fax:* (315) 472-1888
www.krock.com
generalinfo@krock.com
License: Minetto, Oswego County, NY held by Galaxy Syracuse Licensee LLC.
Group Owner: Galaxy Communications L.P.; (acq 8-31-2000).
Arbitron Metro Market: Syracuse, NY *Format:* Alternative *Hrs. of News Programming:* news progmg 2 hrs wkly *No. News Employees:* 1 *Target Audience:* 18-49; men
Michael Lucarelli, CFO
Ed Levine, President
Lisa Morrow, Operations Dir
Mimi Griswold, Programming Director
Scott Petibone, Programming Director

Monroe

*WLJP
05-01-1991; 89.3 mhz FM; 0.2 kw; 1040 ft.; N41 22 38 W74 7 55
Rebroadcasts: Rebroadcasts WFGB(FM) Kingston 100%
PO Box 777, Lake Katrine, NY 12449 US
(845) 336-6199, *Fax:* (845) 336-7205
www.soundoflife.org
email@soundoflife.org
License: Monroe, Orange County, NY held by Sound of Life Inc.
Format: Christian *Target Audience:* General.
Bob Conti, Operations Dir
Tom Zahradnik, General Manager
Joe Hunter, Programming Director

Montauk

WELJ
02-19-1993; 104.7 mhz FM *Hrs Open:* 24; 6 kw; Ant 328 ft; N41 01 57 W71 58 31
7 Governor Winthrop Blvd., New London, NY 11930
(866) 441-9653, *Fax:* (860) 444-7970
www.wxlm.fm
info@wxlm.fm
License: Montauk, Suffolk County, NY
Group Owner: Cumulus Media Inc.; (acq 4-3-2003)
Arbitron Metro Market: New York *Hrs. of News Programming:* news progmg 5 hrs wkly *No. News Employees:* 2 *Target Audience:* 21-54; adults who grew up in the 60s & 70s
Steve Ardolina, Operations Dir
Julie Johnson, Programming Director
Kevin O'Connor, Operations Director

*WEER
01-01-2004; 88.7 mhz FM; 8 w horiz, 2.7 kw vert; Ant 226 ft; N41 01 53 W71 58 32 *Rebroadcasts:* Rebroadcasts WPKN(FM) Bridgeport, CT 100%
244 University Ave., Bridgeport, CT 06604
(203) 331-9756
www.wpkn.org
wpkn@wpkn.org
License: Montauk, Suffolk County, NY held by WPKN Inc.
Harry Minot, General Manager

Monticello

*WJUX
11-01-1994; 99.7 mhz FM *Hrs Open:* 24; 6 kw; 299 ft.; N41 45 9 W74 43 1
11 Old Tappan Road, Old Tappan, NJ 07675 US
(732) 901-9953, *Fax:* (732) 901-0356
www.bridgefm.org
info@bridgefm.org
License: Monticello, Sullivan County, NY held by Bridgelight LLC
Format: Religious *Target Audience:* 35-54.
Brian Rechten, General Manager
Patti Gates, General Sales Mgr

WSUL
04-16-1977; 98.3 mhz FM *Hrs Open:* 24; 2.2 kw; 535 ft.; N41 39 38 W74 41 14
198 Bridgeville Rd., PO Box 983, Monticello, NY 12701 US
(845) 794-9898,(845) 794-0242, *Fax:* (845) 794-0125
www.wsul.com
office@wsul.com
License: Monticello, Sullivan County, NY held by Watermark Communications LLC
Format: Adult Contemp *No. News Employees:* 2 *Target Audience:* 25-54. *Adv. Rates:* 42; 36; 42; 26
Joni Shaughnessy, Operations Dir
Helena Manzione, General Manager
Yannika Sonic, Promotions Manager
Bill James, News Director

Montour Falls

WNGZ
06-01-1973; 104.9 mhz FM *Hrs Open:* 24; 1 kw; 479 ft.; N42 15 5 W76 52 53
1685 Four Mile Drive, Williamsport, PA 17701 US

(607) 732-4400, *Fax:* (607) 732-7774
www.wngz.com
smitty.oloughlin@bybradio.com
License: Montour Falls, Schuyler County, NY held by Chemung County Radio Inc.
Group Owner: Backyard Broadcasting LLC; (acq 12-1-02; grpsl).
Arbitron Metro Market: Elmira, NY *Format:* Classic Rock *No. News Employees:* 1 *Target Audience:* 20-49; baby boomers, young adults
Scott Free, Operations Dir
Smitty O'Loughlin, General Manager
Brian Povancher, General Sales Mgr
Vinnie Pagano, Programming Director

Morristown

WYSX
11-01-1998; 96.7 mhz FM *Hrs Open:* 24; 17 kw; 354 ft.; N44 34 43 W75 30 51
515 Skylake Court, Incline Village, NV 89451 US
(315) 393-1220, *Fax:* (315) 393-3974
www.yesfm.com
john@q1029.com
License: Morristown, St. Lawrence County, NY held by Stephens Media Group-Ogdensburg LLC.
Group Owner: Stephens Family L.P.
Arbitron Metro Market: Morristown, NY *Format:* Contemporary Hits/Top 40 *Target Audience:* 18-34. *Adv. Rates:* 25; 25; 25; 25
John Winter, General Manager
Dave Merz, Programming Director

Mount Hope

*WMFU(FM)
09-01-1994; 90.1 mhz FM *Hrs Open:* 24; 1.1 kw; Ant 600 ft; N41 25 36 W74 34 54
Mailing Address: Box 2011, Jersey City, NJ 07303-2011
Second Address: 4th Floor, 43 Montgomery St., Jersey City, NJ 7302
(201) 521-1416, *Fax:* (201) 521-1286
www.wfmu.org
info@wxhd.com
License: Mount Hope, Orange County, NY held by Auricle Communications.
Population Served: 7,018 *Arbitron Metro Market:* Mount Hope, NY *Format:* Variety/Diverse *Target Audience:* General.
Ken Freedman, Station Manager & Program Director
Brian Turner, Programming Director
John Fogarazzo, Chief Engineer
Mike Adler, Technology Director
Brian Turner, Music Director
Liz Berg, Assistant General Manager

Mount Kisco

WRVP
10-27-1957; 1310 khz AM *Hrs Open:* 6 AM-6 PM
20 Winston Dr., Rheinbeck, NY 12572 US
(973) 881-8700, *Fax:* (973) 881-8324
www.radiovision.net
License: Mount Kisco, NY held by Radio Vision Cristiana Management Corp.
Arbitron Metro Market: Paterson, NJ *Format:* Christian *No. News Employees:* 3 *Target Audience:* General. *Adv. Rates:* 40; 30; 40; na
Milton Donato, Station Manager

WDVY
01-15-1964; 106.3 mhz FM; 1.4 kw; Ant 440 ft; N41 11 56 W73 41 37 *Rebroadcasts:* Rebroadcasts WPDH(FM) Poughkeepsie 100%
Mailing Address: 365 Secor Rd., Hartsdale, NY 95825
Second Address: 2 Pendell Rd., Poughkeepsie, NY 12602
(914) 693-2400, *Fax:* (914) 693-4489
www.wfafm.com
License: Mount Kisco, Westchester County, NY held by Cumulus Licensing Corp.
Group Owner: Cumulus Media Inc.; (acq 1-23-2002; grpsl)
Population Served: 150,000*Adv. Rates:* 190; 190; 190; 190
Rob Calarco, General Manager

*WWES
88.9 mhz FM; 0.2 kw vert; 115 ft.; N41 14 20 W73 42 48 US
(518) 465-5233, *Fax:* (518) 432-6974
www.wamc.org
License: Mount Kisco, Westchester County, NY held by WAMC.
Group Owner: WAMC/Northeast Public Radio
Arbitron Metro Market: Mount Kisco, NY
Alan Chartock, CEO
Katie Britton, News Director
Joe Donahue, Vice President, News and Programming

Napeague

*WEGB
90.7 mhz FM; 4.6 kw; 262 ft.; N41 1 56 W71 58 30 US
(631) 725-4155, *Fax:* (631) 725-4155
cbchamptons.com
office@cbchamptons.com
License: Napeague, Suffolk County, NY held by Community Bible Church.
Arbitron Metro Market: Napeague, NY
Doug Kinney, President

New City

WRKL
07-04-1964; 910 khz AM *Hrs Open:* 24
4320 Dundee Road, Northbrook, IL 60062 US
(845) 354-2000, *Fax:* (845) 354-4796
www.polskieradio.com
wrkl@polskieradio.com
License: New City, NY held by Polnet Communications Ltd.
Group Owner: Polnet Communications Ltd.; acq 3-19-99).
Arbitron Metro Market: New York *Format:* Polish *Hrs. of News Programming:* news progmg 50 hrs wkly *No. News Employees:* 1 *Target Audience:* 18-54; Polish language audience *Adv. Rates:* 60; 60; 60; 30
Kent Gustafson, CEO
Walter Kotaba, President
Grzegorz Sliwecki, Operations Dir

New Paltz

WBWZ
11-19-1992; 93.3 mhz FM *Hrs Open:* 24; 0.33 kw; 968 ft.; N41 41 58 W74 0 11
42 Holt Road, Hyde Park, NY 12536 US
(845) 471-2300, *Fax:* (845) 471-2683
www.rock933.com
JeffreyHelion@clearchannel.com
License: New Paltz, Ulster County, NY held by AMFM Radio Licenses LLC.
Group Owner: Clear Channel Communications Inc.; (acq 12-22-2000; with WRWD-FM Highland).
Nat'l Network: Fox News Radio *Nat'l Reps:* Katz Radio *Wire Services:* AP
Arbitron Metro Market: Poughkeepsie, NY *Format:* Adult Contemp *Hrs. of News Programming:* news progmg 7 hrs wkly *No. News Employees:* 1 *Target Audience:* 25-54; baby boomers
Reggie Osterhoudt, Operations Dir
Frank Curcio, General Manager
Rob VanDerbeck, Sales Manager
Reg Osterhoudt, Programming Director
Jeffrey Helion, Promotions Manager
Cameron Hendrix, News Director
Deirdre Burns, Digital ContentDirector

New Rochelle

WVIP
01-01-1953; 93.5 mhz FM *Hrs Open:* 24; 1.75 kw; 433 ft.; N40 52 48 W73 52 40
1 Broadcast Forum, New Rochelle, NY 10801 US
(914) 636-1460, *Fax:* (914) 636-2900
don@wvox.com
License: New Rochelle, Westchester County, NY held by Hudson-Westchester Radio, Inc.
Nat'l Network: Fox News Radio; Music of Your Life
Arbitron Metro Market: New York *Format:* Variety/Diverse *Hrs. of News Programming:* 12 *No. News Employees:* 2 *Target Audience:* 18 plus; adults
Cindy Gallagher, Chairman
William O'Shaughnessy, President
David O'Shaughnessy, Operations Dir
Don Stevens, Programming Director

WVOX
01-01-1950; 1460 khz AM *Hrs Open:* 24; 0.5 kw-D, ND1; 0.122 kw-N, ND1; N40 55 42 W73 46 30
One Broadcast Forum, New Rochelle, NY 10801 US
(914) 636-1460, *Fax:* (914) 636-2900
www.wvox.com
don@wvox.com
License: New Rochelle, NY held by Hudson-Westchester Radio Inc.
Nat'l Network: Fox News Radio; Music of Your Life
Arbitron Metro Market: Westchester, NY *Format:* Variety/Diverse *Hrs. of News Programming:* 6 hours daily *No. News Employees:* 4 *Target Audience:* 24 plus; community minded *Adv. Rates:* 110; 90; 72; na
Cindy Hall Gallagher, Vice Chairman
William O'Shaughnessy, President
David O'Shaughnessy, Operations Dir
Judy Fremont, Station Manager
Bob Marrone, News Director
Maggie Hernandez, Office & Marketing Manager
Kevin Elliott,Director Of Informational Services

New York

WABC
10-07-1921; 770 khz AM
77 West 66th Street, 16th Fl, New York, NY 10023 US
(276) 632-2152, *Fax:* (276) 632-4500
www.martinsvillemedia.com
93.5@waxm.com
License: New York, NY
Group Owner: Cumulus Media Inc.; (acq 6-12-2007; grpsl)
Nat'l Reps: Interep
Arbitron Metro Market: Lafayette LA *Format:* Talk
Bill Wyatt, President

WADO
03-12-1934; 1280 khz AM *Hrs Open:* 24
100 Crescent Court, Suite 1777, Dallas, TX 75201 US
(334) 887-3401, *Fax:* (334) 826-9599
info@thetiger.fm
License: New York, NY held by Wado-Am License Corp.
Group Owner: Univision Radio; (acq 9-22-2003; grpsl).
Nat'l Reps: Katz Radio
Arbitron Metro Market: Dubuque IA *Format:* Big Band, Jazz, 84 *Hrs. of News Programming:* news progmg 7 hrs wkly *No. News Employees:* 1 *Target Audience:* 25 plus.
Chris Bailey, General Manager

WAXQ
12-01-1956; 104.3 mhz FM; 6 kw; 1362 ft.; N40 44 54 W73 59 10
1180 Ave of the Americas, 5th Floor, New York, NY 10036 US
(800) 729-9829, *Fax:* (414) 935-3015
www.vcyamerica.org
License: New York, New York County, NY held by AMFM Radio Licenses LLC.
Group Owner: Clear Channel Communications Inc.; (acq 8-30-2000; grpsl).
Arbitron Metro Market: Wittenberg WI *Format:* Christian, Religious
Vic Eliason, Operations Dir
Jim Schneider, Programming Director
Andy Eliason, Chief Engineer

WBAI
01-01-1960; 99.5 mhz FM *Hrs Open:* 24; 4.3 kw; 1362 ft.; N40 44 54 W73 59 10
505 8th Avenue, 19th Floor, New York, NY 10018 US
(800) 877-5600, *Fax:* (916) 251-1650
www.air1.com
info@air1.com
License: New York, New York County, NY held by Pacifica Foundation.
Group Owner: Pacifica Foundation Inc.; (acq 1-9-60)
Arbitron Metro Market: Scottsbluff NE *Format:* Alternative, Christian
Mike Novak, President

WBBR
02-13-1991; 1130 khz AM; 50 kw-D, DAN; 50 kw-N, DAN; N40 48 39 W74 2 24
499 Park Ave. 15th Floor, New York, NY 10022 US
(800) 877-5600, *Fax:* (916) 251-1650
www.klove.com
License: New York, NY held by Bloomberg Communications Inc.
Format: Christian
Mike Novak, President

WBLS
09-15-1965; 107.5 mhz FM *Hrs Open:* 24; 4.2 kw; 1362 ft.; N40 44 54 W73 59 10
3 Park Avenue, 40th Floor, New York, NY 10016 US
(212) 447-1000, *Fax:* (212) 447-5193
www.wbls.com
Deon@wbls.com
License: New York, New York County, NY held by Urban Radio I L.L.C.
Group Owner: Inner City Broadcasting
Nat'l Network: ABC
Arbitron Metro Market: New York *Format:* Black *Target Audience:* 25-54; upscale, urban
Charles Warfield, CEO/COO
Charles Warfield, President
Kernie Anderson, General Manager
Deon Levingston, General Sales Mgr
Skip Dillard, Programming Director
Koren Vaughan, Promotions Manager
Lucella Duncan, News Director

BillStallman, Engineering Dir
Jeff Fox, Disc Jockey
Charles Mitchell, Disc Jockey
J.C. Jordan, Disc Jockey
Raymond Anthony, Disc Jockey
Larry Hardesty, Sports Commentator

WCBS
01-01-1924; 880 khz AM *Hrs Open:* 24; 50 kw-U, ND1; N40 51 35 W73 47 9
600 New Hampshire Avenue, NW, Suite 1200, Washington, DC 20037 US
(212) 975-4321, *Fax:* (212) 975-4674
www.newyork.cbslocal.com/station/wcbs-880/
tscheld@wcbs880.com
License: New York, NY held by CBS Radio East Inc.
Group Owner: CBS Radio; (acq 11-13-98; grpsl)
Nat'l Network: CBS
Arbitron Metro Market: New York, NY *Format:* News *Target Audience:* 25-54.
Chad Brown, Operations Dir
Matt Timothy, General Sales Mgr
Cry Quimby, Programming Director
Manny Severin, Promotions Manager
Tim Scheld, News Director
Mark Olkowski, Chief Engineer
Mary Butler, National Sales Manager

WCBS-FM
01-01-1941; 101.1 mhz FM; 6.7 kw; 1339 ft.; N40 44 54 W73 59 10
600 New Hampshire Avenue, NW, Suite 1200, Washington, DC 20037 US
800) 367-1101, *Fax:* (212) 846-5188
www.wcbsfm.cbslocal.com/
License: New York, New York County, NY
Group Owner: CBS Radio
Arbitron Metro Market: New York, NY *Format:* Oldies
Chad Brown, Operations Dir
Ezio Torres, General Sales Mgr
Joe McCoy, Programming Director

WEPN
08-28-1922; 1050 khz AM *Hrs Open:* 24; 50 kw-U; N40 48 26 W74 04 11
2 Penn Plaza, 17th Fl., New York, NY 10001
(212) 613-3800, *Fax:* (212) 613-3861
www.espndeportes.espn.go.com
License: New York, New York County, NY held by New York AM Radio LLC.
Group Owner: ABC Inc.; (acq 4-28-2003; $78 million)
Nat'l Network: ESPN Deportes
Population Served: 15,340,000 *Arbitron Metro Market:* New York *No. News Employees:* 2 *Target Audience:* Men 25-54.
Tim McCarthy, President
Mike Thompson, Programming Director

WFAN
01-01-1930; 660 khz AM *Hrs Open:* 24; 50 kw-U, ND1; N40 51 35 W73 47 9
600 New Hampshire Ave, Suite 1200, Washington, DC 20037 US
(212) 314-9200, *Fax:* (718) 361-1059
www.wfan.com
espitz@wfan.com
License: New York, NY held by CBS Radio East Inc.
Group Owner: CBS Radio; (acq 2-25-92; $70 million;
Nat'l Network: CBS *Nat'l Reps:* CBS Radio *Wire Services:* SportsTicker; Sports Wire
Arbitron Metro Market: New York, NY *Format:* Sports, Talk *No. News Employees:* 34 *Target Audience:* 25-54; sports fans
Chuck Ortick, General Manager
Tony Hammel, General Sales Mgr
Eric Spitz, Programming Director

***WFUV**
07-01-1947; 90.7 mhz FM *Hrs Open:* 24; 46 kw; 509 ft.; N40 52 48 W73 52 40
Keating Hall, Bronx, NY 10458 US
(718) 817-4550, *Fax:* (718) 365-9815
www.wfuv.org
thefolks@wfuv.org
License: New York, Bronx County, NY held by Fordham University, Executive Committee, Board of Trustees.
Nat'l Network: NPR; PRI *Wire Services:* AP
Arbitron Metro Market: New York *Format:* News, Sports, 90, Variety/Diverse *Special Programming:* Irish 10 hrs wkly *Hrs. of News Programming:* news progmg 8 hrs wkly *No. News Employees:* 2 *Target Audience:* 25 plus; intelligent & sophisticated mus listeners
Joseph McShane, President
John Hollwitz, Operations Dir
Ralph Jennings, General Manager

Chuck Singleton, Programming Director
John Platt, Promotions Manager
Julianne Welby, News Director
Rita Houston, Music Director
GeorgeEvans, Operations Director
Janeen Shalteman, Promotions Director
George Bodarky, Public Affairs Director
Russ Borris, Assistant Music Director and Dics Jockey
Claudia DeVivo, Disc Jockey

***WHCR-FM**
02-01-1985; 90.3 mhz FM *Hrs Open:* 24; 0.008 kw; 266 ft.; N40 49 9 W73 56 59
138th St. & Covenant Ave, New York City, NY 10031 US
(212) 650-7481, *Fax:* (212) 650-7480
www.whcr.org
info@whcr.org
License: New York, New York County, NY held by City College of New York.
Arbitron Metro Market: New York *Format:* Black, Jazz *Hrs. of News Programming:* News progmg 70 hrs wkly *Target Audience:* Community of Harlem.
Angela Harden, General Manager

WINS
01-01-1924; 1010 khz AM *Hrs Open:* 24
600 New Hampshire Avenue, NW, Suite 1200, Washington, DC 20037 US
(212) 315-7000, *Fax:* (212) 315-7015
www.1010wins.com
info@1010wins.com
License: New York, NY held by CBS Radio East Inc.
Group Owner: CBS Radio
Nat'l Network: ABC; CNN Radio *Nat'l Reps:* CBS Radio *Wire Services:* AP
Arbitron Metro Market: New York *TV Affiliate:* WCBS-TV affil.
Format: News *Hrs. of News Programming:* news progmg 168 hrs wkly *No. News Employees:* 50 *Target Audience:* General.
Joel Hollander, CEO
Greg Janoff, General Manager
Mike Felicetti, General Sales Mgr
Mark Mason, Programming Director
Ben Mevorach, News Director
Mark Olkowski, Engineering Dir

***WKCR-FM**
10-01-1941; 89.9 mhz FM *Hrs Open:* 24; 1.35 kw; 932 ft.; N40 45 22 W73 59 12
535 West 116th Street, 313 Low Library, New York, NY 10027 US
(212) 854-9920, *Fax:* (212) 854-9296
www.wkcr.org
bored@wkcr.org
License: New York, New York County, NY held by Trustees of Columbia University.
Arbitron Metro Market: New York *Format:* Jazz, Variety/Diverse *Special Programming:* Country 6 hrs, news/sports 6 hrs, international 8 *Hrs. of News Programming:* News progmg 3 hrs wkly *Target Audience:* General.
Jordan Paul, Station Manager
Shira Burton, Promotions Manager

WKDM
01-01-1927; 1380 khz AM; 5 kw-U, DA1; N40 49 13 W74 4 9
449 Broadway 2nd Floor, New York, NY 10013 US
(212) 966-1059, *Fax:* (212) 966-9580
www.mrbi.net/wkdm.htm
info@mrbi.net/wkdm.htm
License: New York, NY held by Multicultural Radio Broadcasting Licensee LLC.
Group Owner: Multicultural Radio Broadcasting Inc.; (acq 6-30-2003; $37 million)
Arbitron Metro Market: New York *Format:* Chinese
Arthur Liu, President
Gene Heinemeyer, General Manager

WLIB
01-01-1942; 1190 khz AM *Hrs Open:* 24; 10 kw-D, DA2; 30 kw-N, DA2; N40 47 48 W74 6 6
Koteen & Naftalin, Llp, 1150 Connecticut Ave, NW, Washington, DC 20036 US
(212) 447-1000, *Fax:* (212) 447-5193
www.wlib.com
info@wlib.com
License: New York, NY held by Urban Radio I L.L.C.
Group Owner: Inner City Broadcasting; (acq 7-72).
Nat'l Reps: McGavren Guild
Arbitron Metro Market: New York *Format:* Black, Gospel
Pierre Sutton, Chairman
Deon Levingston, Operations Dir
Leon Van Gelder, General Sales Mgr

Gwen Kingsberry, Promotions Manager
Vinny Brown, Operations Manager

WLTW
01-26-1961; 106.7 mhz FM; 6 kw; 1362 ft.; N40 44 54 W73 59 10
1515 Broadway, 40th Floo, New York, NY 10036 US
(212) 377-7900, *Fax:* (212) 603-4602
www.1067litefm.com
info@wltw.com
License: New York, New York County, NY held by AMFM Radio Licenses LLC.
Group Owner: Clear Channel Communications Inc.; (acq 8-30-2000; grpsl).
Nat'l Network: AP Radio *Nat'l Reps:* Katz Radio
Arbitron Metro Market: New York, NY *Format:* Adult Contemp
Andrew Rosen, General Manager
Steve Chessare, General Sales Mgr
Jim Ryan, Programming Director
Bridget Sullivan, Promotions Manager

WMCA
01-01-1925; 570 khz AM *Hrs Open:* 24; 5 kw-U, DA1; N40 45 10 W74 6 15
4880 Santa Rosa Rd, #300, Camarillo, CA 93012 US
(201) 298-5700, *Fax:* (201) 298-5757
www.wmca.com
contact@nycradio.com
License: New York, NY held by Salem Media of New York LLC.
Group Owner: Salem Communications Corp.; (acq 9-15-89; $13 million;
Arbitron Metro Market: New York, NY *Format:* Christian, Talk
Special Programming: Jewish 9 hrs wkly *Hrs. of News Programming:* News progmg 5 hrs wkly *Target Audience:* General.
Edward Atsinger III, President
Joe Davis, Operations Dir
Sean O'Neill, General Manager
Steve Viehmeyer, General Sales Mgr
Peter Thiele, Programming Director
Peter Thiele, Operations Manager

WWFS
08-01-1958; 102.7 mhz FM *Hrs Open:* 24; 6 kw; 1362 ft.; N40 44 54 W73 59 10
600 New Hampshire Avenue, NW, Suite 1200, Washington, DC 20037 US
(212) 242-6190, *Fax:* (212) 489-1263
www.fresh1027.com
License: New York, New York County, NY held by CBS Radio East Inc.
Group Owner: CBS Radio; (acq 12-89; grpsl;
Nat'l Network: Westwood One
Arbitron Metro Market: New York, NY *Format:* Classic Rock
Target Audience: 24-44; women
Maire Mason, General Manager
Mark Olkowski, Chief Engineer

***WNYC**
07-08-1924; 820 khz AM
1 Centre Street, 26th Floor, New York, NY 10007 US
(646) 829-4400, *Fax:* (212) 669-8986
www.wnyc.org
listenerservices@wnyc.org.
License: New York, NY held by WNYC Radio Broadcasting Foundation
Nat'l Network: PRI; NPR
Arbitron Metro Market: New York *TV Affiliate:* Public radio
Format: Big Band *No. News Employees:* General.
President and CEO, CEO/COO
General Manager, General Manager
CFO, Ellen Reynolds
Development Director

WNYC-FM
09-21-1943; 93.9 mhz FM; 5.2 kw; 1362 ft.; N40 44 54 W73 59 10
1 Centre Street, 26th Floor, New York, NY 10007 US
(646) 829-4400, *Fax:* (212) 669-8986
www.wnyc.com
listenerservices@wnyc.org.
License: New York, New York County, NY held by WNYC Radio Broadcasting Foundation
Arbitron Metro Market: New York *TV Affiliate:* Public radio
Format: Jazz *Special Programming:* News progmg 35 hrs wkly
President and CEO, CEO/COO
General Manager, General Manager
Operations Manager

***WNYE**
11-01-1938; 91.5 mhz FM *Hrs Open:* WNYE-TV affil; 2 kw; 922 ft.; N40 45 22 W73 59 12
112 Tillary Street, Brooklyn, NY 11201 US

(718) 250-5800, *Fax:* (718) 855-8863
http://www.nyc.gov/html/media/html/radio/radio.shtml
License: New York, Kings County, NY held by New York City Dept. of Info Technology & Telecommunications.
Nat'l Network: NPR; PRI
Arbitron Metro Market: New York *TV Affiliate:* Public radio *No. News Employees:* General.

***WNYU-FM**
05-03-1973; 89.1 mhz FM; 8.3 kw; 256 ft.; N40 51 26 W73 54 48
70 Washiingtion Square S., New York, NY 10003 US
(212) 998-1660, *Fax:* (212) 998-1652
www.wnyu.org
License: New York, New York County, NY held by New York University.
Nat'l Network: ABC
Arbitron Metro Market: New York *TV Affiliate:* College *Format:* Black, Reggae *Special Programming:* News progmg 4 hrs wkly
General Manager, General Manager
Program Director, Momo Araki
Engineering Director, Engineering Dir
Business Director

WOR
02-22-1922; 710 khz AM *Hrs Open:* 24; 50 kw-U, DA-1; N40 47 50 W74 05 24
Mailing Address: 111 Broadway, New York, NY 06830
Second Address: 166 West Putnam Ave., Greenwich, CT 6830
(212) 642-4500, *Fax:* (212) 642-4486
www.wor710.com
License: New York, New York County, NY held by Buckley Broadcasting/WOR LLC.
Group Owner: Buckley Broadcasting Corp.; (acq 12-89; $25.1 million;
Nat'l Network: NBC Radio News *Nat'l Reps:* Eastman Radio
Population Served: 18,000,000 *Arbitron Metro Market:* New York *Special Programming:* Relg 4 hrs wkly *Hrs. of News Programming:* news progmg 4 hrs wkly *No. News Employees:* 5 *Target Audience:* 35-64.
Joseph Bilotta, CEO/COO
Joseph Bilotta, President
Thomas R. Ray III, Vice President/Corporate Director of Engineering
Jerry Crowley, General Manager
Jennifer Buckley, General Sales Mgr
Scott Lakefield, Programming Director
Gregory Bilotta, Local Sales Manager
Joseph Bartlett, News Director
Thomas R. Ray III, Vice President/Corporate Director of Engineering
Thomas R. Ray III, Vice President/Corporate Director of Engineering

WPLJ
01-18-1960; 95.5 mhz FM *Hrs Open:* 24; 6.7 kw; 1339 ft.; N40 44 54 W73 59 10
77 West 66th Street, 16th Floor, New York, NY 10023 US
(212) 613-8900, *Fax:* (212) 613-8956,(212) 613-8950
www.plj.com
writeus@Plj.com
License: New York, New York County, NY
Group Owner: Cumulus Media Inc.
Nat'l Reps: Interep
Arbitron Metro Market: New York *Format:* Adult Contemp *Hrs. of News Programming:* News progmg 5 hrs wkly *Target Audience:* 18-54; females
Tom Cuddy, Operations Dir
Steven Borneman, Station Manager
Scott Shannon, Programming Director
Theresa Angela, Promotions Manager
Patty Steele, News Director
Kevin Plumb, Engineering Dir
Tony Mascaro, Music Director

WFAN-FM
01-01-1945; 101.9 mhz FM *Hrs Open:* 24; 6.2 kw; Ant 1,355 ft; N40 44 54 W73 59 10
345 Hudson Street, 10th Floor, New York, NY 91505
(212) 314-9200, *Fax:* (212) 929-8559
www.1019rxp.com
mail.1019@rxp.com
License: New York, New York County, NY held by Merlin Media License LLC
Group Owner: Merlin Media LLC; (acq 3-26-98; grpsl)
Nat'l Reps: Katz Radio
Population Served: 1,245,000 *Arbitron Metro Market:* New York *Hrs. of News Programming:* news progmg 5 hrs wkly *No. News Employees:* 1 *Target Audience:* 25-54 Sports Fans
Eric Spitz, Programming Director

WQEW
12-03-1936; 1560 khz AM
229 West 43rd St., New York, NY 10036 US
(212) 615-3250, *Fax:* (212) 615-3268
www.radiodisney.com
Jospeh.M.Weinholtz@radiodisney.com
License: New York, NY held by Radio Disney New York LLC.
Group Owner: ABC Inc.; (acq 5-24-2007; $40 million)
Wire Services: Reuters
Arbitron Metro Market: New York *Format:* Children *Target Audience:* 25-64; educated & affluent
Jospeph M. Weinholtz, Station Manager

WQHT
01-01-1940; 97.1 mhz FM *Hrs Open:* 24; 6.7 kw; Ant 1,338 ft; N40 44 54 W73 59 10
395 Hudson St., 7th Floor, New York, NY 91505
(212) 229-9797, *Fax:* (212) 929-8559
www.hot97.com
License: New York, New York County, NY held by Emmis License Corp. of New York.
Group Owner: Emmis Communications Corp.
Nat'l Reps: Katz Radio
Population Served: 2,000,000 *Arbitron Metro Market:* New York *Target Audience:* General.
Alexandra Cameron, General Manager
Biancarlo Negovetti, General Sales Mgr
Ebro Darden, Programming Director
Brian D'Aurelio, Promotions Manager
Alex Roman, Engineering Dir

WXNY-FM
11-08-1939; 96.3 mhz FM *Hrs Open:* 24; 6 kw; 1,361 ft; N40 44 54 W73 59 10
122 5th Ave., 3rd Fl., New York, NY 10011
(212) 633-7600,(212) 633-7650, *Fax:* (212) 633-7666
WQXR@WQXR.COM
License: New York, New York County, NY held by The New York Times Electronic Media Co.
Wire Services: Reuters
Arbitron Metro Market: New York
Tom Bartunek, President
Hester Furman, Programming Director

WEPN-FM
01-01-1941; 98.7 mhz FM *Hrs Open:* 24; 6 kw; 1, 361ft; N40 44 54 W73 59 10
395 Hudson St., 7th Floor, New York, NY 91505
(212) 242-9870, *Fax:* (212) 929-8559
www.987kissfm.com
987kissfm@987kissfm.com
License: New York, New York County, NY held by Emmis Radio License Corp. of New York.
Group Owner: Emmis Communications Corp.; (acq 10-26-94; $68 million;
Nat'l Reps: Katz Radio
Population Served: 2,500,000 *Arbitron Metro Market:* New York *No. News Employees:* 1 *Target Audience:* 25-54; African American
Alexandra Cameron, General Manager
Jill Strada, Programming Director
Brian D'Aurelio, Promotions Manager
Harry Clark, DOS

WSKQ-FM
01-01-1950; 97.9 mhz FM; 6 kw; 1362 ft.; N40 44 54 W73 59 10
3191 Coral Way, Suite 805, Miami, FL 33145 US
(212) 541-9200, *Fax:* (212) 541-9408
www.lamega.com
License: New York, New York County, NY held by WSKQ Licensing Inc.
Group Owner: Spanish Broadcasting System Inc.; (acq 2-1-89; $55 million)
Nat'l Reps: McGavren Guild
Arbitron Metro Market: New York *Target Audience:* 18-49; Hispanic
Raul Alarcon Sr., Chairman
Raul Alarcon Jr., CEO
Jose Garcia, CFO

WWPR-FM
12-14-1953; 105.1 mhz FM *Hrs Open:* 24; 6 kw; 1362 ft.; N40 44 54 W73 59 10
1120 Avenue of the Ameri, 18th Floor, New York, NY 10036 US
(212) 704-1051, *Fax:* (212) 398-3299
www.power1051fm.com
info@power105fm.com
License: New York, New York County, NY held by AMFM Radio Licenses LLC.
Group Owner: Clear Channel Communications Inc.; (acq 8-30-00; grpsl).
Arbitron Metro Market: New York, NY *Format:* Urban Contemporary *No. News Employees:* 1 *Target Audience:* 25-54.
Rob Williams, General Manager

WWRL
08-26-1926; 1600 khz AM
1333 New Hampshire Ave, Suite 1000, Washington, DC 20036 US
(212) 631-0800, *Fax:* (212) 239-7203
www.wwrl1600.com
adriane@wwrl1600.com
License: New York, NY held by Access. 1 New York License Co. LLC.
Group Owner: Access.1 Communications Corp.; (acq 9-28-89; $1.98 million;
Nat'l Network: Air America; ABC; Fox News Radio; Westwood One
Arbitron Metro Market: New York, NY *Format:* Alternative, Talk
Adriane Gaines, President/General Manager
Anthony Small, Sr. Vice President, Operations
Adriane Gaines, General Manager
Michael Hill, General Sales Mgr
Rennie Bishop, Programming Director
Jeffrey Haveson, ExecutiveProducer
John Campanario, Digital Media/Sr. Account Executive
Shevette Watson-Brunn, Office Manager

***WWRV**
05-01-1972; 1330 khz AM *Hrs Open:* 24
Mailing Address: 419 Broadway, Paterson, NJ 07501 US
Second Address: 419 Broadway, Paterson, NJ 7501
(973) 881-8700, *Fax:* (973) 881-8324
www.radiovision.net
dtlrado@radiovision.net
License: New York, NY held by Radio Vision Christiana Management Corp.
Arbitron Metro Market: New York, NY *Format:* Christian, Religious *No. News Employees:* 1 *Target Audience:* General.
Rev. Milton Donato, President
Jose Lastra, Operations Dir
Julio Carbrera, Station Manager

WXRK
01-01-1951; 92.3 mhz FM *Hrs Open:* 24; 6 kw; 1362 ft.; N40 44 54 W73 59 10
600 New Hampshire Ave., Suite 1200, Washington, DC 20037 US
(212) 314-9230, *Fax:* (212) 314-9282
www.923now.com
wxrk923@aol.com
License: New York, New York County, NY held by CBS Radio East Inc.
Group Owner: CBS Radio
Nat'l Network: ABC *Nat'l Reps:* CBS Radio
Arbitron Metro Market: New York, NY *Format:* Contemporary Hits/Top 40
Tom Chiusano, Operations Dir
Alan Leinwand, General Sales Mgr
Mike Peer, Programming Director
Richard Herby, Engineering Dir

WZRC
01-01-1925; 1480 khz AM; 5 kw-D, DA2; 5 kw-N, DA2; N40 50 42 W74 1 12
449 Broadway, New York, NY 10013 US
(212) 966-1059, *Fax:* (212) 966-9580
www.mrbi.net/wzrc.htm
jimg@mrbi.net
License: New York, NY held by Multicultural Radio Broadcasting Licensee LLC.
Group Owner: Multicultural Radio Broadcasting Inc.; (acq 1-30-98; grpsl).
Arbitron Metro Market: New York, NY *Format:* Chinese *Target Audience:* 12-34.
Sherman Ngan, General Manager
Betty Yeh, Advertising Sales Contact

Newark

WACK
10-19-1957; 1420 khz AM *Hrs Open:* 24; 5 kw-D, DA2; 0.5 kw-N, DA2; N43 1 8 W77 4 41
PO Box 1420, Newark, NY 14513 US
(956) 487-8015
License: Newark, NY held by Waynco Radio Inc.
Nat'l Network: CNN Radio; Motor Racing Net; Westwood One
Arbitron Metro Market: De Queen AR *Adv. Rates:* 25; 20; 25; 15
Eloy Vera, General Manager

Newburgh

WGNY
02-25-1933; 1220 khz AM *Hrs Open:* 24; 5 kw-D, DA; N41 29 57 W74 03 54

Mailing Address: Box 2307, Newburgh, NY 12550
Second Address: 661 Little Britain Rd., New Windsor, NY 12553
(845) 561-2131,(845) 561-2132, *Fax:* (845) 561-2138
www.wgny.net
License: Newburgh, Orange County, NY held by Sunrise Broadcasting Corp.
Group Owner: Sunrise Broadcasting Corp.; (acq 8-90; $10,000 with co-located FM;
Nat'l Reps: Katz Radio
Arbitron Metro Market: Newburgh-Middletown, NY (Mid-Hudson Valley) *Special Programming:* Relg 4 hrs, Sp one hr wkly *Target Audience:* General.
Joerg Klebe, President
Robert Maines, Operations Dir
Robert A. DeFelice, General Manager
Tom Duff, News Director
Lori Grecco, Public Affairs Director

WJGK(FM)
10-29-1966; 103.1 mhz FM; 6 kw; 275 ft; N41 28 22 W74 08 22
Mailing Address: Box 2307, Newburgh, NY 12550
Second Address: 661 Little Britain Rd., Newburgh, NY 12553
(845) 561-2131,(845) 561-2132, *Fax:* (845) 561-2138
www.wgnyfm.com
License: Newburgh, Orange County, NY
Group Owner: Sunrise Broadcasting Corp.
Arbitron Metro Market: Newburgh-Middletown, NY (Mid-Hudson Valley) *Adv. Rates:* 50; 50; 50; 35
Patricia Van Zandt, General Manager

Newport Village

WBGK
01-01-2001; 99.7 mhz FM; 1.4 kw; 676 ft.; N43 8 28 W75 1 49
3460 Torrance Blvd., Suite 303, Torrance, CA 90503 US
(315) 734-9245, *Fax:* (315) 624-9245
www.bugcountry.com
License: Newport Village, Herkimer County, NY held by Roser Communications Network Inc.
Group Owner: Roser Communications Network Inc.; (acq 5-29-2001; $575,000)
Nat'l Network: ABC
Arbitron Metro Market: Utica-Rome, NY *Format:* Country
Dave Silvers, Operations Dir
Ken Roser, General Manager
Roxanne Roser, Station Manager
Grant Roser, General Sales Mgr

Niagara Falls

WHLD
05-20-1940; 1270 khz AM *Hrs Open:* 19
2692 Staley Rd., Grand Island, NY 14072 US
(716) 881-4555, *Fax:* (716) 855-4681
www.swing1270.com
License: Niagara Falls, NY
Group Owner: Cumulus Media Inc.
Arbitron Metro Market: Buffalo-Niagara Falls, NY *Format:* Gospel
Brian Cashdollar, CFO
Ray Marks, Operations Dir
Dave Polito, General Sales Mgr

WJJL
12-21-1947; 1440 khz AM *Hrs Open:* 24; 1 kw-D, ND1; 0.055 kw-N, ND1; N43 4 43 W79 0 40
Mailing Address: 1224 Main Street, Niagara Falls, NY 14301 US
Second Address: portage&pine, Niagara Falls, NY 14304
(716) 674-9555, *Fax:* (716) 674-0400
www.wjjl.com
radio1440@verizon.net
License: Niagara Falls, NY held by M.J. Phillips Communications Inc.
Arbitron Metro Market: Buffalo-Niagara Falls, NY *Format:* Rock/AOR, Oldies *Special Programming:* Black 2 hrs, It 4 hrs, news/talk 5 hrs wkly, gospe *Hrs. of News Programming:* news progmg 3 hrs wkly *No. NewsEmployees:* 1 *Target Audience:* 25-54; baby boomers
Earl Morgan, Chairman
Mark Phillips, CEO
John Phillips, President
M.J. Phillips, Operations Dir
Dennis Westberg, CFO

WKSE
01-01-1946; 98.5 mhz FM *Hrs Open:* 24; 46 kw; 420 ft.; N43 0 18 W78 59 34
10706 Beaver Dam Road, Cockeysville, MD 21030 US
(716) 843-0600, *Fax:* (716) 843-0250
www.kiss985.com
Info@kiss985.com
License: Niagara Falls, Niagara County, NY held by Entercom Buffalo License LLC.
Group Owner: Entercom Communications Corp.; (acq 12-13-99; grpsl).
Nat'l Network: ABC *Nat'l Reps:* D & R Radio
Arbitron Metro Market: Buffalo-Niagara Falls, NY *Format:* Contemporary Hits/Top 40 *No. News Employees:* 3 *Target Audience:* 12-49.
Larry Robb, General Manager
Steve Fortunato, General Sales Mgr
Sue O'Neil, Programming Director

North Creek

***WXLG**
01-01-1995; 89.9 mhz FM *Hrs Open:* 24; 0.2 kw; 1995 ft.; N43 40 22 W74 2 58 *Rebroadcasts:* Rebroadcasts WSLU(FM) Canton 100%
N. Country Public Radio, Canton, NY 13617 US
(315) 229-5356, *Fax:* (315) 229-5373
www.ncpr.org
info@ncpr.org
License: North Creek, Warren County, NY held by St. Lawrence University.
Arbitron Metro Market: North Creek, NY *Format:* Talk *Hrs. of News Programming:* news progmg 35 hrs wkly *No. News Employees:* 4 *Target Audience:* General.
Shelly Pike, Operations Dir
Ellen Rocco, Station Manager
Jacqueline Sauter, Programming Director
Martha Foley, News Director
Joel Hurd, Production Manager
June Peoples, Membership Director
Naomi Weller, Office Manager
DaleHobson, Web Manager
Sandy Demarest, Development Director

North Salem

***WJZZ**
90.1 mhz FM; 0.44 kw; -43 ft.; N41 23 3 W73 34 35 US
(404) 765-9750, *Fax:* (404) 688-7686
www.majicatl.com
Jhavis@radio-one.com
License: North Salem, Westchester County, NY held by Foothills Public Radio Inc.
Arbitron Metro Market: North Salem, NY
Dennis Jackson, President

***WJZZ(FM)**
90.1 mhz FM; 4.3 kw; Ant 232 ft; N42 58 47 W76 32 40
16 Walker Avenue, Westfield, MA 30309
(413) 572-4864
www.vivaatlanta.com
License: North Salem, Cayuga County, NY held by Quaboag Hills Public Radio
Population Served: 432,427 *Arbitron Metro Market:* Atlanta, GA
Aaron Read, General Manager
Justin Schaflander, General Sales Mgr
Raffy Contigo, Programming Director
Liz Leos, Promotions Manager

North Syracuse

WKRL-FM
03-01-1972; 100.9 mhz FM; 6 kw; 164 ft.; N43 9 6 W76 7 58
7536 Murray Drive, Cicero, NY 13039 US
(315) 472-9111, *Fax:* (315) 472-1888
www.krock.com
sales@galaxycommuncations.com
License: North Syracuse, Onondaga County, NY
Group Owner: Galaxy Communications L.P.
Nat'l Network: ABC
Arbitron Metro Market: Syracuse, NY *Format:* Rock/AOR *Target Audience:* 18-34; upscale, educated
Kamala Dworski, General Manager

WTLA
08-01-1959; 1200 khz AM *Hrs Open:* 24; 1 kw-D, DAN; 1 kw-N, DAN; N43 9 6 W76 7 58
7536 Murray Drive, Cicero, NY 13039 US
(315) 472-9111, *Fax:* (315) 472-1888
www.espncny.com
askespn@espncny.com
License: North Syracuse, NY held by Galaxy Syracuse Licensee LLC.
Group Owner: Galaxy Communications L.P.; (acq 4-6-2000; grpsl)
Nat'l Network: Jones Radio Networks
Arbitron Metro Market: Syracuse, NY *Format:* Sports *Special Programming:* Ger 2 hrs, Pol 2 hrs, relg 2 hrs wkly *Hrs. of News Programming:* news progmg 2 hrs wkly *No. News Employees:* 1 *Target Audience:* 35-64; white collar executives
Ed Levine, President
Mimi Griswald, Programming Director
Tim Backer, Chief Engineer

Norwich

WBKT
06-01-1997; 95.3 mhz FM *Hrs Open:* 24; 0.47 kw; 841 ft.; N42 26 8 W75 30 47
36 Chestnut Street, Oneonta, NY 13820 US
(607) 432-1030, *Fax:* (607) 432-6909
www.wbktfm.com/
George.Wells@townsquaremedia.com
License: Norwich, Chenango County, NY held by Double O Central New York Corp.
Group Owner: Double O Radio L.L.C.; (acq 10-22-2004; grpsl)
Nat'l Network: ABC
Arbitron Metro Market: Oneonta, NY *Format:* Country *No. News Employees:* 2 *Target Audience:* 25-54; general
George Wells, General Manager
John Hayen, Director of Sales
George Wells, Programming Director
Bud Williamson, Chief Engineer

WCHN
01-01-1953; 970 khz AM *Hrs Open:* 24
36 Chestnut Street, Oneonta, NY 13820 US
(607) 334-2218, *Fax:* (607) 334-9867
License: Norwich, NY held by Double O Central New York Corp.
Group Owner: Double O Radio L.L.C.; (acq 10-22-2004; grpsl)
Nat'l Network: ABC
Format: Classic Rock *Hrs. of News Programming:* News progmg 20 hrs wkly *Target Audience:* 35-65; mature
George Wells, General Manager

WKXZ
01-01-1961; 93.9 mhz FM *Hrs Open:* 5 AM-1 AM; 26 kw; 676 ft.; N42 32 51 W75 27 9
36 Chestnut Street, Oneonta, NY 13820 US
(607) 334-2218, *Fax:* (607) 334-9867
www.wkxzfm.com
License: Norwich, Chenango County, NY
Group Owner: Double O Radio L.L.C.
Nat'l Network: ABC
Format: Adult Contemp *Hrs. of News Programming:* News progmg 10 hrs wkly *Target Audience:* 25-54; growing families
Shawn McIntire, General Manager
Dan Hawthorne, News Director

Norwood

WVLF
01-01-2001; 96.1 mhz FM; 25 kw; 328 ft.; N44 54 11 W74 53 2
6936 Henderson Rd., Jamesville, NY 13078 US
(315) 769-3333, *Fax:* (315) 769-3299
www.mymix961.com
License: Norwood, St. Lawrence County, NY held by Stephens Media Group-Massena LLC.
Group Owner: Stephens Family L.P.
Arbitron Metro Market: Odessa-Midland
Paulino Bernal Jr., President

Noyack

***WSUF**
09-15-1996; 89.9 mhz FM *Hrs Open:* 24; 1.9 kw horiz, 12 kw vert; 358 ft.; N41 6 35 W72 22 5 *Rebroadcasts:* Rebroadcasts WSHU(FM) Fairfield, CT 30%
5151 Park Avenue, Fairfield, CT 06432 US
(203) 365-6604, *Fax:* (203) 371-7991
www.wshu.org
lombardi@wshu.org
License: Noyack, Suffolk County, NY held by Sacred Heart University Inc.
Nat'l Network: NPR; PRI *Wire Services:* AP
Format: News, News/Talk, 86 *Special Programming:* Folk 5 hrs, new age 6 hrs wkly *Hrs. of News Programming:* news progmg 45 hrs wkly *No. News Employees:* 4 *Target Audience:* General.
Barbara Bashar, Operations Dir
George Lombardi, General Manager
Gillian Anderson, General Sales Mgr

Nyack

***WNYK**
05-05-1982; 88.7 mhz FM; 0.01 kw; 56 ft.; N41 4 59 W73 55 45
One South Blvd, Nyack, NY 10960 US
(845) 358-1710, *Fax:* (845) 358-1718
wnyk@nyack.edu
License: Nyack, Rockland County, NY held by Nyack College.

TV Affiliate: College *Format:* Black, Religious *No. News Employees:* 18-35; 60%/40% -F/M, well

Odessa

WFIZ
08-20-1968; 95.5 mhz FM *Hrs Open:* 24; 0.85 kw; 869 ft.; N42 23 13 W76 40 11
260 Washinton St., Watertown, NY 13601 US
(607) 330-4848, *Fax:* (607) 330-4851
www.z955.net
gabe@z955.net
License: Odessa, Schuyler County, NY held by Finger Lakes Radio Group Inc.
Group Owner: Finger Lakes Radio Group; (acq 3-5-2004; $600,000 with co-located AM)
Arbitron Metro Market: Ithaca, NY *Format:* Contemporary Hits/Top 40
Frank Lischak, General Manager
Gabe, Programming Director
Alan Bishop, Managing Partner
Ashley Stewart, Marketing Consultant
John Wiedemer, Marketing Consultant
Gina Lamannis, Senior Marketing Consultant
Paula Triplett, RegionalSales Manager

*WINO
89.9 mhz FM; 0.25 kw; 341 ft.; N42 18 7 W76 48 1 US
(202) 965-7880, *Fax:* (202) 965-1729
www.wino.com
License: Odessa, Schuyler County, NY held by Ithaca Community Radio Inc.
Arbitron Metro Market: Washington, DC
Diane Cohen, Chairman
John Crigler, General Manager

Ogdensburg

WQTK
07-01-1981; 92.7 mhz FM; 3 kw; 312 ft.; N44 42 21 W75 27 55
P.O. Box 239, Ogdensburg, NY 13669 US
(315) 393-1100, *Fax:* (315) 393-6673
License: Ogdensburg, St. Lawrence County, NY held by Community Broadcasters LLC.
Group Owner: Community Broadcasters LLC; (acq 2-8-2007; grpsl)
Nat'l Network: CNN Radio *Nat'l Reps:* Eastman Radio; Katz Radio *Wire Services:* AP
Format: Talk *Hrs. of News Programming:* News progmg 10 hrs wkly *Target Audience:* 25-49; community connected, active, mature, responsible & responsive
Bryan Mallette, General Manager

WSLB
01-01-1940; 1400 khz AM *Hrs Open:* 24; 1 kw-U, ND1; N44 42 21 W75 27 55
2315 Knox Street, Box 239, Ogdensburg, NY 13669 US
(315) 393-1100, *Fax:* (315) 393-6673
burgproduction@commbroadcasters.com
License: Ogdensburg, NY held by Community Broadcasters LLC.
Group Owner: Community Broadcasters LLC; (acq 2-8-2007; grpsl)
Nat'l Network: ESPN Radio *Nat'l Reps:* Eastman Radio; Katz Radio *Wire Services:* AP
Format: Sports
James Leven, President
John Astolfi, Operations Dir
Bryan Mallette, General Manager

WPAC
06-01-1998; 98.7 mhz FM *Hrs Open:* 24; 3 kw; Ant 92 ft; N44 43 41 W75 26 36
1 Bridge Plaza, Suite 204, Ogdensburg, NY 89451
(315) 393-1220, *Fax:* (315) 393-3974
pac987.com
john@q1029.com
License: Ogdensburg, St. Lawrence County, NY held by Stephens Media Group-Ogdensburg LLC.
Group Owner: Stephens Family L.P.
Population Served: 112,000*No. News Employees:* 1 *Adv. Rates:* 20; 20; 20; 20
John Winter, General Manager

Olean

WHDL
02-01-1929; 1450 khz AM *Hrs Open:* 24; 1 kw-U, ND1; N42 4 39 W78 28 32
1685 Four Mile Drive, Williamsport, PA 17701 US
(716) 372-0161, *Fax:* (716) 372-0164
www.whdlradio.com
wpig.production@bybradio.com
License: Olean, NY held by Arrow Communication of N.Y. Inc.
Group Owner: Backyard Broadcasting LLC; (acq 12-1-2002; grpsl).
Regional Reps: Rgnl Reps.
Format: Oldies *Hrs. of News Programming:* news progmg 6 hrs wkly *No. News Employees:* 2 *Target Audience:* 25-54.
John Morton, General Manager
Mark Thomson, Programming Director

WOEN
05-20-1957; 1360 khz AM *Hrs Open:* 24; 1 kw-D, ND1; 0.03 kw-N, ND1; N42 6 18 W78 23 25
PO Box 609, Russell, PA 16345 US
(716) 375-1015, *Fax:* (716) 375-7705
www.newstalkwoen.com
traffic@mix101.com
License: Olean, NY held by Pembrook Pines Inc.
Group Owner: Pembrook Pines Media Group; (acq 2-22-2005; $950,000 with co-located FM).
Nat'l Network: CBS; Westwood One *Nat'l Reps:* Dome
Arbitron Metro Market: Olean, NY *Format:* News, News/Talk, 86 *No. News Employees:* 1 *Target Audience:* 45-65.
Robert Pfuntner, President
John Sirianni, General Manager
Michael McAdam, Programming Director
Ralph Vanderlinden, Chief Engineer

WMXO
11-01-1978; 101.5 mhz FM; 4 kw; 404 ft.; N42 6 18 W78 23 25
P.O. Box 609, Russell, PA 16345 US
(716) 375-1015, *Fax:* (716) 375-7705
www.themixwmxo.com
traffic@mix101.com
License: Olean, Cattaraugus County, NY held by Pembroke Pines Inc.
Group Owner: Pembrook Pines Media Group
Nat'l Network: CBS; Westwood One
Arbitron Metro Market: Olean, NY *Format:* Adult Contemp *Target Audience:* 18-49. *Adv. Rates:* 13; 13; 13; 9
Ron Livengood, President
Gene Sisk, Operations Dir
Campbell Smith, Operations Director

*WOLN
03-01-1993; 91.3 mhz FM; 1 kw; 656 ft.; N42 2 8 W78 26 47
Rebroadcasts: Rebroadcasts WBFO(FM) Buffalo 100%
3435 Main Street, Buffalo, NY 14214 US
716-845-7000, *Fax:* 716-845-7036
www.wbfo.org
mail@wbfo.org
License: Olean, Cattaraugus County, NY held by State University of New York.
Nat'l Network: NPR
TV Affiliate: Public *Special Programming:* news progmg 50 hrs wkly *Hrs. of News Programming:* 2 *No. News Employees:* General; educated profess
Operations Manager

WPIG
02-01-1949; 95.7 mhz FM *Hrs Open:* 24; 43 kw; 741 ft.; N42 2 8 W78 26 47
1685 Four Mile Drive, Williamsport, PA 17701 US
(716) 372-0161, *Fax:* (716) 372-0164
www.wpig.com
wpig.production@bybradio.com
License: Olean, Cattaraugus County, NY held by Arrow Communications of N.Y. Inc.
Group Owner: Backyard Broadcasting LLC
Nat'l Network: ABC
Format: Country
Vernon Baker, Chairman
Edward Baker, President

Olivebridge

*WFSO
12-27-1996; 88.3 mhz FM *Hrs Open:* 27/7; 80 W Circular; Ant 195 ft; N41 54 30 W74 14 46
PO Box 1520, Olivebridge, NY 12572
(888) 724-4427
www.redeemerbroadcasting.org
dce@redeemerbroadcasting.org
License: Olivebridge, Ulster County, NY held by Redeemer Broadcasting Inc.
Population Served: 120,000 *Arbitron Metro Market:* Hudson Valley *Special Programming:* Classic Christian
Dan Elmendorf, President
Dan Elmendorf, Operations Dir
Dan Elmendorf, General Manager
Clarence Elmendorf, Station Manager
N/A, General Sales Mgr
Dan Elmendorf, Engineering Dir
Deb Elmendorf, Treasurer
John Vance, Secretary

Oneida

WMCR
09-26-1956; 1600 khz AM *Hrs Open:* 16; 1 kw-D, ND1; 0.02 kw-N, ND1; N43 5 4 W75 41 35
237 Genessee St., Oneida, NY 13421 US
(315) 635-3971, *Fax:* (315) 635-3490
www.cnytalkradio.com
info@wmcr.com
License: Oneida, NY held by Warren Broadcasting Co. Inc.
Arbitron Metro Market: Syracuse, NY *Format:* News, News/Talk, 86 *Target Audience:* General.
Joel Meltzer, General Manager

WMCR-FM
09-01-1972; 106.3 mhz FM; 1.25 kw; 719 ft.; N43 2 48 W75 39 58
237 Genesee Street, Oneida, NY 13421 US
(315) 363-6050, *Fax:* (315) 363-9149
www.wmcronline.com
info@wmcr.com
License: Oneida, Madison County, NY held by Warren Broadcasting Co. Inc.
Arbitron Metro Market: Syracuse, NY *Format:* Contemporary Hits/Top 40
Marvin Sanders, General Manager

Oneonta

WDOS
12-01-1947; 730 khz AM
P.O. Box 649, Oneonta, NY 13820 US
(607) 432-1030, *Fax:* (607) 432-6909
cnynews.com/
info@centralnewyorkradio.com
License: Oneonta, NY held by Double O Central New York Corp.
Group Owner: Double O Radio L.L.C.; (acq 11-4-2005; $3.8 million with co-located FM)
Arbitron Metro Market: Oneonta, NY *Format:* Country *Special Programming:* Big band 7 hrs, nostalgia 2 hrs, relg 7 hrs wkly
Target Audience: General; adult
George Wells, General Manager
Janet Laytham, Programming Director

*WONY
01-01-1975; 90.9 mhz FM; 0.18 kw horiz; -72 ft.; N42 28 2 W75 3 40
State University Plaza, Albany, NY 12246 US
(607) 436-2712, *Fax:* (607) 436-2713
License: Oneonta, Otsego County, NY held by State University of New York.
TV Affiliate: Educ, div *No. News Employees:* General.

*WRHO
01-01-1970; 89.7 mhz FM *Hrs Open:* 18; 0.27 kw; -13 ft.; N42 27 24 W75 4 28
Radio Station Wrho, Oneonta, NY 13820 US
(607) 431-4555,(607) 431-4556, *Fax:* (607) 431-4064
License: Oneonta, Otsego County, NY held by Hartwick College.
Nat'l Network: AP Radio
Format: Classic Rock, Rock/AOR *Special Programming:* Folk 5 hrs, jazz 4 hrs, Sp 2 hrs, world beat 2 hrs, children's 2 hrs wkly *Hrs. of News Programming:* News progmg 4 hrs wkly *Target Audience:* General; teenagers,college students & young adults
Brian Knox, General Manager

*WSQC-FM
01-01-1992; 91.7 mhz FM *Hrs Open:* 24; 0.57 kw horiz, 2.3 kw vert; 528 ft.; N42 25 27 W75 2 33 *Rebroadcasts:* Rebroadcasts WSKG-FM Binghamton 100%
P. O. Box 3000, Binghamton, NY 13902 US
(607) 729-0100, *Fax:* (607) 729-7328
www.wskg.com
wskg_mail@wskg.pbs.org
License: Oneonta, Otsego County, NY held by WSKG Public Telecommunications Council.
Nat'l Network: NPR; PRI
Format: News *Special Programming:* Jazz, folk 5 hrs wkly *Hrs. of News Programming:* news progmg 33 hrs wkly *No. News Employees:* 1 *Target Audience:* General.
Brian Sickora, President
Nancy Christensen, Operations Dir
Ken Campbell, Programming Director
Stacy Mosteller, News Director
Linda Cohen, Underwriting Director

WSRK
01-26-1970; 103.9 mhz FM *Hrs Open:* 5 AM-midnight; 1.4 kw; 591 ft.; N42 25 26 W75 2 33
P.O. Box 649, Oneonta, NY 13820 US
(607) 432-1030, *Fax:* (607) 432-6909
www.wsrk.com
info@centralnewyorkradio.com
License: Oneonta, Otsego County, NY
Group Owner: Double O Radio L.L.C.
Format: Adult Contemp *Special Programming:* Class 2 hrs wkly *Hrs. of News Programming:* News progmg 5 hrs wkly *Target Audience:* 25-54; adult males & females
Charlie Ferguson, General Manager

WZOZ
11-28-1972; 103.1 mhz FM *Hrs Open:* 24; 2 kw; 361 ft.; N42 25 28 W75 4 36
P.O. Box 552, Norwich, NY 13815 US
(607) 432-1030, *Fax:* (607) 432-6909
www.wzozfm.com
George.Wells@townsquaremedia.com
License: Oneonta, Otsego County, NY held by Double O Central New York Corp.
Group Owner: Double O Radio L.L.C.; (acq 10-22-2004; grpsl)
Arbitron Metro Market: Oneonta, NY *Format:* Oldies *Special Programming:* Jazz 2 hrs, blues 2 hrs, oldies 2 hrs wkly *Hrs. of News Programming:* news progmg 8 hrs wkly *No. News Employees:* 2 *Target Audience:* 25-54.
George Wells, General Manager
George Wells, Programming Director
Steven Dillon, Director of Sales

Ontario

WYNY(AM)
1450 khz AM; 1 kw-D, 2 kw-N, DA-2; N43 10 49 W77 18 15
135 White Bridge Rd., Middletown, NY 10940
(845) 355-4001, *Fax:* (845) 355-4002
bud@dre.cc
License: Ontario, Wayne County, NY held by Digital Radio Broadcasting Inc.
Group Owner: Digital Radio Broadcasting Inc.
Arbitron Metro Market: Rochester, NY
Bud Williamson, President

Ossining

***WDFH**
07-15-1995; 90.3 mhz FM *Hrs Open:* 24; 53 w; Ant 476 ft; N41 09 07 W73 47 10
21 Brookside Ln., Dobbs Ferry, NY 10522
(914) 674-0900
www.wdfh.org
info@wdfh.org
License: Ossining, Westchester County, NY held by Hudson Valley Community Radio Inc.
Population Served: 625,000*Special Programming:* Pub affrs 20 hrs wkly *Target Audience:* 18+
Marc Sophos, President

***WOSS**
02-22-1972; 91.1 mhz FM *Hrs Open:* 24; 0.015 kw horiz; 69 ft.; N41 9 36 W73 51 38
Mailing Address: 190 Croton Avenue, Ossining, NY 10562 US
Second Address: 29 S. Highland Ave., Ossining, NY 10562
(914) 762-5760 x370
License: Ossining, Westchester County, NY held by Board of Education Union Free School District 1.
Format: Contemporary Hits/Top 40 *No. News Employees:* 3 *Target Audience:* General.
Martin McDonald, Station Manager

Oswego

***WNYO**
01-01-1993; 88.9 mhz FM; 0.1 kw; 10 ft.; N43 27 7 W76 32 40
State University Plaza, Albany, NY 12246 US
(315) 312-2101, *Fax:* (315) 312-3542
http://www.wnyo.org/
wnyo@wnyo.org
License: Oswego, Oswego County, NY held by State University of New York.
TV Affiliate: Variety *Format:* News, News/Talk, 86 *No. News Employees:* 13-34.
General Manager, General Manager
PR Director, Jessica Salamone
Production Director

WWLF-FM
07-01-1990; 96.7 mhz FM *Hrs Open:* 24; 3 kw; Any 328 ft; N43 29 12 W76 23 10
401 W. Kirkpatrick St., Syracuse, NY 13024
(315) 472-0222, *Fax:* (315) 478-7745
movin100.com
programming@movin100.com
License: Oswego, Oswego County, NY held by WOLF Radio Inc.
Group Owner: WOLF Radio Inc.; (acq 8-4-97; $65,000)
Regional Reps: Rgnl Reps
Population Served: 140,000 *Arbitron Metro Market:* Syracuse, NY
Sam Furco, General Manager

***WRVO**
01-06-1969; 89.9 mhz FM *Hrs Open:* 24; 50 kw horiz, 49.01 kw vert; 440 ft.; N43 25 14 W76 32 39
Lanigan Hall, Oswego, NY 13126 US
(315) 312-3690, *Fax:* (315) 312-3174
www.wrvo.fm
feedback@wrvo.fm
License: Oswego, Oswego County, NY held by State University of New York.
Nat'l Network: NPR *Wire Services:* AP
Arbitron Metro Market: Syracuse, NY *Format:* Variety/Diverse *Hrs. of News Programming:* news progmg 140 hrs wkly *No. News Employees:* 4 *Target Audience:* 25-55. *Adv. Rates:* 60; 50; 60; 10
Pam Cantine, Operations Dir
John Krauss, General Manager
Thomas Herbert, General Sales Mgr
Fred Vigeant, Programming Director
Catherine Loper, News Director
Jeff Windsor, Chief Engineer

WSGO
01-01-1960; 1440 khz AM *Hrs Open:* 24; 1 kw-D, ND1; 0.045 kw-N, ND1; N43 24 56 W76 28 0 *Rebroadcasts:* Rebroadcasts WTLA(AM) North Syracuse 100%
7536 Murray Dr., Cicero, NY 13039 US
(315) 472-9111, *Fax:* (315) 472-1888
License: Oswego, NY held by Galaxy Syracuse Licensee LLC.
Group Owner: Galaxy Communications L.P.; (acq 4-6-2000; grpsl)
Nat'l Network: Jones Radio Networks
Arbitron Metro Market: Syracuse, NY *Format:* Sports *Special Programming:* Ger 2 hrs, Pol 2 hrs wkly *Hrs. of News Programming:* News progmg one hr wkly *Target Audience:* 40 plus; retired & mobile
Ed Levine, President
Mimi Griswold, Programming Director
Tim Backer, Chief Engineer

WTKV
03-15-1973; 105.5 mhz FM *Hrs Open:* 24; 4 kw; 397 ft.; N43 24 56 W76 27 54 *Rebroadcasts:* Rebroadcasts WTKW(FM) Bridgeport 100%
7536 Murray Dr., Cicero, NY 13039 US
(325) 472-9111, *Fax:* (315) 472-1888
www.classicrock.com
asktk@tk99.net
License: Oswego, Oswego County, NY
Group Owner: Galaxy Communications L.P.
Arbitron Metro Market: Syracuse, NY *Format:* Classic Rock *Special Programming:* Folk 3 hrs, blues one hr wkly *Hrs. of News Programming:* news progmg 2 hrs wkly *No. News Employees:* 1 *Target Audience:* 25-54.
Ed Levine, General Manager
Mimi Griswold, Programming Director

Owego

WEBO
07-27-1957; 1330 khz AM *Hrs Open:* 5 AM-10 PM
Executive Inn, Bldg 3 #2, 1 Delaware Ave., Endicott, NY 13760 US
(607) 687-9933, *Fax:* (607) 687-9033
www.newsradiowebo.com/
news@newsradiowebo.com
License: Owego, NY held by Tioga Media Inc.
Nat'l Network: USA *Nat'l Reps:* D & R Radio
Arbitron Metro Market: Owego, NY *Format:* News, Talk *Special Programming:* NASCAR racing 16 hrs, relg 6 hrs wkly *No. News Employees:* 2 *Target Audience:* 35 plus.
Dave Radigan, General Manager

Palmyra

***WZXV**
05-01-1993; 99.7 mhz FM *Hrs Open:* 24; 2.8 kw; 486 ft.; N43 2 0 W77 25 17
Mailing Address: P.O. Box 25099, Farmington, NY 14425 US
Second Address: 1777 Rt. 332, Farmington, NY 14425
(315) 597-9574;, *Fax:* (585) 398-3250
www.wzxv.org
wzxv@ccfingerlake.org
License: Palmyra, Wayne County, NY held by Calvary Chapel of the Finger Lakes Inc.
Arbitron Metro Market: Farmington, NY *Format:* Christian
Jeff Gallatin, General Manager

Patchogue

WALK
05-20-1952; 1370 khz AM *Hrs Open:* 24; 0.5 kw-D, ND1; 0.102 kw-N, ND1; N40 45 14 W72 59 14
66 Colonial Drive, Patchogue, NY 11772 US
(631) 475-5200, *Fax:* (631) 475-9016
www.1370walk.com
info@1370walk.com
License: Patchogue, NY held by AMFM Radio Licenses LLC.
Group Owner: Clear Channel Communications Inc.; (acq 8-30-00; grpsl)
Arbitron Metro Market: Long Island, NY *Format:* Oldies *Hrs. of News Programming:* News progmg 15 hrs wkly *Target Audience:* 50 plus.
Andy Rosen, Operations Dir
Jim Condron, General Sales Mgr
Rob Miller, Programming Director
Linda Healy, Promotions Manager
John Lorentz, Chief Engineer
Bill Terry, Promotions Director

WALK-FM
12-01-1952; 97.5 mhz FM; 39 kw; 554 ft.; N40 50 41 W73 2 1
66 Colonial Dr, Parchogue, NY 11772 US
(631) 475-5200, *Fax:* (631) 475-9016
walkradio.com
psa@walkradio.com
License: Patchogue, Suffolk County, NY
Arbitron Metro Market: Long Island, NY *Format:* Adult Contemp *Special Programming:* Hits of the 70s, love songs *Target Audience:* 25-54.
Cindi Clifford, Programming Director
Freddie Colom, Disc Jockey
K.T. Mills, Disc Jockey
Mark Daniels, Disc Jockey

WBLI
12-01-1958; 106.1 mhz FM *Hrs Open:* 24; 49 kw; 499 ft.; N40 50 32 W73 2 25
3773 Howard Hughes Pwy, Suite 300n, Las Vegas, NV 89109 US
(631) 669-9254, *Fax:* (631) 376-0569
www.wbli.com
requests@wbli.com
License: Patchogue, Suffolk County, NY held by Cox Radio Inc.
Group Owner: Cox Radio Inc.; (acq 5-22-98; grpsl)
Nat'l Network: AP Radio *Nat'l Reps:* Christal
Arbitron Metro Market: West Babylon, NY *Format:* Contemporary Hits/Top 40 *Hrs. of News Programming:* news progmg 5 hrs wkly *No. News Employees:* 1 *Target Audience:* 18-34; women
Austin Vali, Operations Dir
John Shea, General Manager
Jeremy Rice, Programming Director
Nancy Cambino, Operations Manager
Suzanne Riccio, Public Affairs Director

WLIM
12-01-1951; 1580 khz AM *Hrs Open:* 24
Mailing Address: Woodside Avenue, Patchogue, NY 11772 US
Second Address: 41 Pennsylvania Ave, Medford, NY 11763
(631) 475-1580, *Fax:* (631) 475-1523
www.radio-formula.us
radioformula@radio-formula.us
License: Patchogue, NY held by Polnet Communications Ltd.
Group Owner: Polnet Communications Ltd.; acq 6-1-01; $850,000 including five-year noncompete agreement).
Arbitron Metro Market: New York *Format:* Spanish *Special Programming:* Spanish language 24 hrs/day, 7 days/week *Hrs. of News Programming:* news progmg 20 hrs wkly *No. News Employees:* 1 *Target Audience:* 18-54; Spanish language audience *Adv. Rates:* 54; 54; 52; 50
Kent Gustafson, CEO
Walter Kotaba, President
Brad Behnke, Station Manager

Patterson

WDBY
01-17-1982; 105.5 mhz FM *Hrs Open:* 24; 0.9 kw; 610 ft.; N41 31 18 W73 38 6
600 14th St., N.W., Suite 800, Washington, DC 20005 US
(800) 877-5600, *Fax:* (916) 251-1650
www.air1.com
info@air1.com
License: Patterson, Putnam County, NY held by Cumulus Licensing Corp.

Group Owner: Cumulus Media Inc.; (acq 1-23-2002; grpsl).
Nat'l Network: Westwood One
Arbitron Metro Market: Nanty Glo PA *Format:* Alternative, Christian
Darrell Chambliss, Chairman
Mike Novak, President

Pattersonville

*WPGL
08-15-1994; 90.7 mhz FM *Hrs Open:* 24; 0.03 kw; 653 ft.; N42 51 0 W74 3 58 *Rebroadcasts:* Rebroadcasts WFGB(FM) Kingston 95%
Mailing Address: P.O. Box 777, Lake Katrine, NY 12449 US
Second Address: 199 Tuytenbridge Rd., Lake Katrine, NY 12449
(845) 336-6199, *Fax:* (845) 336-7205
www.soundoflife.org
email@soundoflife.org
License: Pattersonville, Schenectady County, NY held by Sound of Life Inc.
Format: Christian *Hrs. of News Programming:* News progmg 3 hrs wkly *Target Audience:* General.
Bob Conti, Operations Dir
Tom Zahradnik, General Manager
Joe Hunter, Programming Director

Peekskill

WHUD
10-24-1958; 100.7 mhz FM; 50 kw; 499 ft.; N41 20 18 W73 53 41
6 Johnson Road, Latham, NY 12110 US
(914) 838-6000, *Fax:* (914) 838-2109
www.whud.com
info@whud.com
License: Peekskill, Westchester County, NY held by 6 Johnson Road Licenses Inc.
Group Owner: Pamal Broadcasting Ltd.
Nat'l Network: ABC
Arbitron Metro Market: New York *Format:* Adult Contemp *Target Audience:* Upscale adults.
Jason Finkleburg, General Manager
Bruce Feniger, General Sales Mgr
Steven Petrone, Programming Director
Sam Favata, Promotions Manager

Penn Yan

WYLF
01-01-1988; 850 khz AM *Hrs Open:* 24; 1 kw-D, ND1; 0.045 kw-N, ND1; N42 39 41 W77 7 14
100 Main Street, Penn Yan, NY 14527 US
(315) 536-0850, *Fax:* (315) 536-3299
www.wylf.com
wylf@airxcess.net
License: Penn Yan, NY held by M.B. Communications.
Group Owner: M.B. Communications; (acq 10-88)
Arbitron Metro Market: Penn Yan, NY *Format:* Adult Contemp *No. News Employees:* 2 *Target Audience:* 35 plus.
Russ Kimble, President
Don Radigan, Operations Dir
Phil Mann, General Sales Mgr

Peru

*WXLU
01-01-1991; 88.1 mhz FM *Hrs Open:* 24; 1 kw; 1119 ft.; N44 34 25 W73 40 29 *Rebroadcasts:* Rebroadcasts WSLU(FM) Canton 100%
N Country Public Radio, Canton, NY 13617 US
(315) 229-5356
www.ncpr.org
radio@mcpr.org
License: Peru, Clinton County, NY held by St. Lawrence University.
Arbitron Metro Market: Burlington, NY *Format:* Talk *Hrs. of News Programming:* news progmg 35 hrs wkly *No. News Employees:* 4 *Target Audience:* General.
Shelly Pike, Operations Dir
Ellen Rocco, Station Manager
Jacqueline Sauter, Programming Director
Martha Foley, News Director
Joel Hurd, Production Manager
June Peoples, Membership Director
Naomi Weller, Office Manager
DaleHobson, Web Manager
Sandy Demarest, Development Director

Phoenix

WZUN
05-22-1995; 102.1 mhz FM *Hrs Open:* 24; 6 kw; 266 ft.; N43 6 4 W76 16 58
6813 Van Buren Road, Warners, NY 13164 US
(315) 472-9111, *Fax:* (315) 472-1888
www.thesunnyspot.com
License: Phoenix, Oswego County, NY held by Galaxy Syracuse Licensee LLC.
Group Owner: Galaxy Communications L.P.; (acq 12-15-2000; $3.75 million).
Arbitron Metro Market: Syracuse, NY *Format:* Adult Contemp *Target Audience:* 25-54; general
Mike Lucarelli, CFO
Ed Levine, President
Lisa Morrow, General Sales Mgr
Mimi Griswold, Programming Director
Ted Bradford, Programming Director

Plainview

*WPOB
09-01-1973; 88.5 mhz FM; 0.125 kw; 259 ft.; N40 47 48 W73 27 44
Jfk Bldg., 50 Kennedy Dr, Plainview, NY 11803 US
(516) 937-6373,(516) 937-6344, *Fax:* (516) 937-6384
License: Plainview, Nassau County, NY held by Plainview-Old Bethpage Central School District.
Format: Rock/AOR *Target Audience:* General.
Joel Genero, Operations Dir
Adam Weinstock, General Manager

Plattsburgh

WBTZ
02-03-1960; 99.9 mhz FM *Hrs Open:* 24; 100 kw; 984 ft.; N44 46 13.9 W73 36 48.49
3206 Route 9, Peru, NY 12972 US
(802) 860-2440, *Fax:* (802) 860-1818
www.99thebuzz.com
mailbag@99thebuzz.com
License: Plattsburgh, Clinton County, NY held by Hall Communications Inc.
Group Owner: Hall Communications Inc.; (acq 7-31-2006; $2.5 million)
Arbitron Metro Market: Winooski, VT *Format:* Alternative *Target Audience:* 18-44.
Dan Dubonnet, General Manager
Matt Grasso, Programming Director

*WCEL
01-14-1991; 91.9 mhz FM *Hrs Open:* 24; 0.38 kw; 853 ft.; N44 46 27 W73 36 48 *Rebroadcasts:* Rebroadcasts WAMC-FM Albany 100%
Mailing Address: 318 Central Ave., Albany, Ny, NY 12206 US
Second Address: 318 Central Ave., Albany, NY 12206
(518) 465-5233(800) 323-9262, *Fax:* (518) 432-6974
www.wamc.org
news@wamc.org
License: Plattsburgh, Clinton County, NY held by WAMC.
Group Owner: WAMC/Northeast Public Radio; (acq 1996; $160,000)
Nat'l Network: PRI; NPR *Wire Services:* AP
Format: News, Talk *Special Programming:* Folk 7 hrs, jazz 13 hrs wkly *Hrs. of News Programming:* News progmg 77 hrs wkly *Target Audience:* General.
Alan Chartock, CEO
Selma Kaplan, Operations Dir
Stacie Monz, General Manager
David Galletly, Vice President

WTWK
01-01-1998; 1070 khz AM; 5 kw-D, NDD; N44 36 14 W73 27 18
P.O. Box 8260, Essex, VT 05451 US
(802) 524-2133, *Fax:* (802) 527-1450
www.wtwk1070.com/
sales@champlainradio.com
License: Plattsburgh, NY held by Champlain Communications Corp.
Group Owner: Northeast Broadcasting Company Inc.; (acq 1-11-2002; $150,000)
Nat'l Network: Air America
Arbitron Metro Market: Plattsburgh, NY *Format:* Talk *Target Audience:* 25-54; women
Richard DeLancey Sr., General Manager
J.J. Prieve, Programming Director

WEAV
02-03-1935; 960 khz AM
3206 Route 9 Lake Shore, Peru, NY 12972 US
(802) 655-0093, *Fax:* (802) 654-9376
www.thezone960am.com/
jamiedennis@thezone960am.com
License: Plattsburgh, NY held by Vox AM/FM LLC.
Group Owner: Vox AM/FM LLC; (acq 7-25-2008; grpsl)
Arbitron Metro Market: Plattsburgh, NY *Format:* Sports, Talk
Target Audience: General.
Steve Cormier, Operations Dir
Karen Marshall, General Manager
Jamie Dennis, Programming Director

WIRY
01-30-1950; 1340 khz AM *Hrs Open:* 24 hours; 1 kw-D, 940 w-N; N44 40 12 W73 26 41
4712 State Route 9, Plattsburgh, NY 12901
(518) 563-1340, *Fax:* (518) 563-1343
www.wiry.com
wiry@wiry.com
License: Plattsburgh, Clinton County, NY held by Hometown Radio Inc.
Nat'l Network: NBC News Radio; Dial Global Radio Network *Nat'l Reps:* Roslin
Population Served: 25,000*Hrs. of News Programming:* news progmg 14 hrs wkly *No. News Employees:* 2 *Target Audience:* 18 plus.
William Santa, President
Bob Pooler, Vice President
Bob Pooler, General Manager
Alan Drake, News Director
Roy Edmonds, Chief Engineer

WKOL
08-22-1994; 105.1 mhz FM *Hrs Open:* 24; 23.5 kw; 338 ft.; N44 31 31 W73 31 7
Mailing Address: P.O. Box 4368, Lancaster, PA 17604 US
Second Address: 70 Joy Dr., South Burlington, VT 5403
(802) 658-1230, *Fax:* (802) 862-0786
www.wkol.com
kool105@hallradio.com
License: Plattsburgh, Clinton County, NY held by Hall Communications Inc.
Group Owner: Hall Communications Inc.; acq 6-13-95; $1.1 million)
Nat'l Reps: D & R Radio *Wire Services:* AP
Arbitron Metro Market: Burlington-Plattsburgh, VT-NY *Format:* Contemporary Hits/Top 40, Adult Contemp *Target Audience:* 25-54.
Bonnie Rowbotham, Chairman
Arthur Rowbotham, President
Dan Dubonnet, General Manager
Rod Hill, Programming Director
Bill Baldwin, Executive Vice President

*WQKE
04-01-1979; 93.9 mhz FM *Hrs Open:* 7 AM-2:30 PM; 0.009 kw; 26 ft.; N44 41 40 W73 28 0
101 Broad Street, Kehoe 202, Plattsburgh, NY 12901 US
(518) 564-2727, *Fax:* (518) 564-3994
License: Plattsburgh, Clinton County, NY held by State University of N.Y.
Format: Alternative *Special Programming:* Heavy metal 10 hrs, classic rock 12 hrs, Black 9 hrs, relg 3 hrs wkly *Target Audience:* 18-24.
Phil Czterwastek, Operations Dir
Andy Martinez, Programming Director

Plattsburgh West

WPLB
100.7 mhz FM; 2.3 kw; 221 meters; N43 47 14 W73 58 53
23 Town Common Road, Georgia, VT
(518) 894-9967
License: Plattsburgh West, Essex County, NY held by Westport Radio Partners
Group Owner: Radioactive LLC
Jose Ortiz Y Pino, President

Port Chester

WKLV-FM
10-18-1974; 96.7 mhz FM *Hrs Open:* 24; 3 kw; Ant 328 ft; N41 02 49 W73 31 36
444 Westport Ave., Norwalk, CT 78701
(203) 845-3030, *Fax:* (203) 845-3097
967thecoast.com
info@967thecoast.com
License: Port Chester, Fairfield County, NY held by Cox Radio Inc.
Group Owner: Cox Radio Inc.; (acq 8-25-2000; grpsl).
Nat'l Reps: Katz Radio
Population Served: 123,000 *Arbitron Metro Market:* New York
Target Audience: 25-54; upscale
Robin Faller, General Manager
Jim Stagnitti, General Sales Mgr
Eric McDonald, Programming Director
Steve Soyland, Promotions Manager
Steve Rugh, News Director

Clark Burgard, Chief Engineer
Helaine Greenbaum, National SalesManager
Kelli McLaughlin, Regional Sales Manager

Port Dickinson

WRRQ

01-01-2006; 106.7 mhz FM *Hrs Open:* 24; 1.2 kw; 725 ft.; N42 3 22 W75 56 39
US
(607) 772-1005, *Fax:* (607) 772-2945
myq107.com
License: Port Dickinson, Broome County, NY held by Equinox Broadcasting Corp.
Nat'l Reps: Katz Radio
Arbitron Metro Market: Port Dickinson, NY *Format:* Adult Contemp *Target Audience:* 18-45.
George Hawras, President

Port Henry

WVTK

09-05-1982; 92.1 mhz FM *Hrs Open:* 24; 18 kw; 10 ft.; N44 1 38 W73 28 54
20 Stanford Drive, Farmington, CT 06032 US
(802) 655-0093, *Fax:* (802) 655-0478
www.trueoldieschannel.com
info@trueoldieschannel.com
License: Port Henry, Essex County, NY held by Vox AM/FM LLC.
Group Owner: Vox AM/FM LLC; (acq 7-25-2008; grpsl)
Arbitron Metro Market: Burlington, VT *Format:* Oldies *Hrs. of News Programming:* News progmg one hr wkly *Target Audience:* 25-54.
Karen Marshall, General Manager

Port Jervis

WDLC

07-04-1953; 1490 khz AM *Hrs Open:* 24; 1 kw-U, ND1; N41 21 49 W74 40 41
P.O. Box 920, Port Jervis, NY 12771 US
(845) 856-5185, *Fax:* (845) 856-4757
www.country1077.com
info@foxcountry.us
License: Port Jervis, NY held by PJ Radio L.L.C.
Arbitron Metro Market: Sussex, NJ *Format:* Country
James Morley, General Manager

*WRPJ

10-01-1992; 88.9 mhz FM; 0.5 kw; 591 ft.; N41 25 36 W74 34 54
Rebroadcasts: Rebroadcasts WFGB(FM) Kingston 100%
Mailing Address: Post Office Box 777, Lake Katrine, NY 12449 US
Second Address: 199 Tuytenbridge Rd., Lake Katrine, NY 12449
(845) 336-6199,(800) 724-8518, *Fax:* (845) 336-7205
www.soundoflife.org
email@soundoflife.org
License: Port Jervis, Orange County, NY held by Sound of Life Inc.
Format: Christian *Target Audience:* General.
Bob Conti, Operations Dir
Tom Zahradnik, General Manager
Joe Hunter, Programming Director

Portville

WVTT

96.7 mhz FM; 460 w; 509 ft; N42 03 04 W78 25 11
9 South Main Street, Coudersport, PA 16915
www.colonial.cc/WVTT
License: Portville, Cattaraugus County, NY
Group Owner: Colonial Radio Group Inc.

Potsdam

*WAIH

09-10-1998; 90.3 mhz FM; 0.1 kw; -16 ft.; N44 39 43 W74 58 26
State University Plaza, Albany, NY 12246 US
(315) 267-2511, *Fax:* (315) 267-2798
www.waih.fm
generalmanager@waih.fm.
License: Potsdam, St. Lawrence County, NY held by State University of New York.
Arbitron Metro Market: Potsdam, NY *Format:* Talk
Dan Laskaris, General Manager

WPDM

04-30-1955; 1470 khz AM; 1 kw-D, ND1; 0.044 kw-N, ND1; N44 38 38 W75 3 32
P. O. Box 348, Potsdam, NY 13676 US
(315) 265-5510, *Fax:* (315) 265-4040
hits@99hits.com
License: Potsdam, NY held by St. Lawrence Radio Inc.
Format: Adult Contemp *Hrs. of News Programming:* news progmg 5 hrs wkly *No. News Employees:* 1 *Target Audience:* 25 plus; div audience *Adv. Rates:* 20; 13; 16; 13
Jane Kyle, President
William Solomon, Operations Dir
Derry Loucks, General Sales Mgr
Justin James, Programming Director
Scott Dosztan, News Director
Dan Simmons, Chief Engineer
Drew Bradley, Disc Jockey
Betty Bombarn, TrafficManager

WSNN

10-15-1968; 99.3 mhz FM *Hrs Open:* 6 AM-midnight; 3 kw; 154 ft.; N44 38 38 W75 3 32
P. O. Box 348, Potsdam, NY 13676 US
(315) 265-5510, *Fax:* (315) 265-4040
www.99hits.com
hits@99hits.com
License: Potsdam, St. Lawrence County, NY held by Zoe Communications Inc.
Format: Country *Hrs. of News Programming:* news progmg 5 hrs wkly *No. News Employees:* 1 *Target Audience:* 25-54. *Adv. Rates:* 19.80; 13; 15.65; 13
Derry Loucks, Station Manager
Justin Gonyea, Programming Director
Drew Bradley, Disc Jockey
Dave Williams, Disc Jockey
Justin James, Disc Jockey
Josh Henry, Disc Jockey
Andy Van Duyne, Disc Jockey

*WTSC-FM

11-03-1963; 91.1 mhz FM *Hrs Open:* 24 hrs a day; 0.7 kw horiz; 135 ft.; N44 39 45 W75 0 7
Clarkson University, Box 5546, Potsdam, NY 13699 US
(315) 268-7658
radio.clarkson.edu
radio@clarkson.edu
License: Potsdam, St. Lawrence County, NY held by Clarkson University.
Arbitron Metro Market: Potsdam, NY *Format:* Alternative
Jess Halfacre, General Manager
Devon Jedamski, Chief Engineer
Ben Morton-Black, Sports Director

Poughkeepsie

WEOK

10-01-1949; 1390 khz AM *Hrs Open:* 24; 5 kw-D, DA2; 0.106 kw-N, DA2; N41 43 14 W73 54 29
Mailing Address: P.O. Box 416, Poughkeepsie, NY 12602 US
Second Address: 2 Penvell Rd., Poughkeepsie, NY 12602-0416
(404) 949-0700, *Fax:* (404) 949-0740
www.cumulus.com
License: Poughkeepsie, NY held by Cumulus Licensing Corp.
Group Owner: Cumulus Media Inc.; (acq 1-23-2002).
Arbitron Metro Market: Poughkeepsie, NY *Special Programming:* Farm 2 hrs, Pol one hr, relg 2 hrs, talk 5 hrs, Sinatra 2 hrs wkly *No. News Employees:* 3 *Target Audience:* 35 plus.
Lewis W. Dickey, Jr., Chairman, President & CEO
Jonathan G. Pinch, COO
Charles Benfer, President
Nick Robbins, Operations Dir
Victor Goodman, General Sales Mgr
John W. Dickey, Executive Vice President & Co-Chief Operating Offi
Richard S. Denning, Senior Vice President, Secretary & General Counsel
Joseph P. Hannan, Senior Vice President, Treasurer & Chief Financial
Linda A. Hill, Vice President, Corporate Controller & Chief Accou

WKIP

06-01-1940; 1450 khz AM; 1 kw-D, DAD; 1 kw-N, DAD; N41 42 18 W73 53 16
12 Tucker Drive, Poughkeepsie, NY 12603 US
(845) 471-2300, *Fax:* (845) 471-2683
www.newstalkwkip.com
ChuckBenfer@clearchannel.com
License: Poughkeepsie, NY held by CC Licenses LLC.
Group Owner: Clear Channel Communications Inc.; (acq 7-12-2000; grpsl)
Nat'l Network: ABC News/Talk; Fox News Radio; Premiere Radio Networks; Talk Radio Network *Nat'l Reps:* Katz Radio *Wire Services:* AP
Arbitron Metro Market: Poughkeepsie, NY *Format:* News, News/Talk, 86 *Hrs. of News Programming:* news progmg 24 hrs wkly *No. News Employees:* 1 *Target Audience:* 35-64.
Chris Marino, Operations Dir
Chuck Benfer, General Manager
Pete Clark, General Sales Mgr
Chris Marino, Programming Director
Jeffery Helion, Promotions Manager
Cameron Hendrix, News Director
Deirdre Burns, Digital ContentDirector
Rob Vanderbeck, Sales

WPDH

12-01-1962; 101.5 mhz FM *Hrs Open:* 24; 4.4 kw; 1539 ft.; N41 43 9 W73 59 47
P.O. Box 416, Poughkeepsie, NY 12602 US
(845) 471-1500, *Fax:* (845) 454-1204
www.wpdh.com
License: Poughkeepsie, Dutchess County, NY
Arbitron Metro Market: Poughkeepsie, NY *Format:* Classic Rock
Special Programming: Blues deluxe, flashback 4 hrs wkly
Nick Robbins, Operations Dir
Greg O'Brien, Programming Director

*WRHV

09-05-1990; 88.7 mhz FM; 0.23 kw vert; 1289 ft.; N41 43 9 W73 59 47 *Rebroadcasts:* Rebroadcasts Wmht-FM Schenectady 60%
P.O. Box 17, 17 Fern Avenue, Schenectady, NY 12301 US
(518) 880-3400, *Fax:* (518) 880-3409
www.wmht.org
info@wmht.org
License: Poughkeepsie, Dutchess County, NY held by WMHT Educational Telecommunications.
Nat'l Network: PRI
Arbitron Metro Market: Poughkeepsie, NY *Format:* Talk *Special Programming:* Jazz 2 hrs, ethnic one hr wkly *Target Audience:* 35-54; class mus lovers
Deborah Onslow, President
Dave Nicosia, Chief Engineer

WRNQ

06-30-1989; 92.1 mhz FM *Hrs Open:* 24; 0.52 kw; 1030 ft.; N41 43 9 W73 59 47
12 Tucker Drive, Poughkeepsie, NY 12603 US
(845) 471-2300, *Fax:* (845) 471-2683
www.921litefm.com
License: Poughkeepsie, Dutchess County, NY held by CC Licenses LLC.
Group Owner: Clear Channel Communications Inc.
Nat'l Network: Fox News Radio *Nat'l Reps:* Katz Radio *Wire Services:* AP
Arbitron Metro Market: Poughkeepsie, NY *Format:* Adult Contemp *Hrs. of News Programming:* news progmg 7 hrs wkly *No. News Employees:* 1 *Target Audience:* 35-54; primary market is women
Reggie Oserhoudt, Operations Dir
Pete Clark, General Sales Mgr
Michelle Taylor, Programming Director
Frank Curcio, Promotions Manager
Jeanette Relyea, National Sales Manager
Brian Powers, Promotions Director

WSPK

12-07-1947; 104.7 mhz FM *Hrs Open:* 24; 7.4 kw; 1250 ft.; N41 29 19 W73 56 52
475 South Avenue, Beacon, NY 12508 US
(845) 838-8600,(845) 838-6000, *Fax:* (845) 838-2109
www.k104online.com
License: Poughkeepsie, Dutchess County, NY held by 6 Johnson Road Licenses Inc.
Group Owner: Pamal Broadcasting Ltd.; (acq 10-19-2001; grpsl).
Nat'l Network: Westwood One; ABC *Nat'l Reps:* Katz Radio
Arbitron Metro Market: Poughkeepsie, NY *Format:* Contemporary Hits/Top 40 *No. News Employees:* 1 *Target Audience:* 18-49.
James Morrell, CEO
Fred Bennett, Operations Dir
Jason Finkelberg, General Manager
Arthur Heller, General Sales Mgr
Paul Thurst, Chief Engineer

WPKF

01-01-1996; 96.1 mhz FM *Hrs Open:* 24; 4.4 kw; 184 ft.; N41 44 25 W73 54 17
12 Tucker Drive, Poughkeepsie, NY 12603 US
(845) 471-2300, *Fax:* (845) 471-2683
www.kissfmhv.com
DeirdreBurns@clearchannel.com
License: Poughkeepsie, Dutchess County, NY held by CC Licenses LLC.
Group Owner: Clear Channel Communications Inc.; (acq 7-14-2000; grpsl).
Nat'l Network: Fox News Radio *Nat'l Reps:* Clear Channel; Katz Radio *Wire Services:* AP
Arbitron Metro Market: Poughkeepsie, NY *Format:* Christian

Reggie Osterhoudt, Operations Dir
Frank Curcio, General Manager
Rob VanDerBeck, General Sales Mgr
Chris Marino, Programming Director
Jeffrey Helion, Promotions Manager
Cameron Hendrix, News Director
Deirdre Burns, Digital ContentDirector
Chris Marino, Interim Operations Manager
Chuck Benfer, Market Manager

***WVKR-FM**
01-01-1976; 91.3 mhz FM *Hrs Open:* 24; 3.7 kw horiz; 820 ft.; N41 38 25 W74 1 16
P.O. Box 166, Poughkeepsie, NY 12601 US
(845) 437-5475, *Fax:* (845) 437-7656
www.wvkr.org
License: Poughkeepsie, Dutchess County, NY held by Vassar College.
Arbitron Metro Market: Poughkeepsie, NY *Format:* Variety/Diverse *Hrs. of News Programming:* news progmg 5 hrs wkly *No. News Employees:* 4 *Target Audience:* General.
Nick De Leeuw, General Manager

Pulaski

***WGKV**
01-01-1987; 101.7 mhz FM; 5 kw; 358 ft.; N43 36 28 W75 58 23
5090 Us Rt #11, P.O. Box 640, Pulaski, NY 13142 US
(800) 525-5683
www.klove.com
klove@klove.com
License: Pulaski, Oswego County, NY held by Educational Media Foundation.
Group Owner: EMF Broadcasting; (acq 7-6-2007; grpsl)
Nat'l Network: K-Love
Format: Religious
Darrell Chambliss, Chairman
Alan Mason, COO
Mike Novak, President

Queensbury

WCQL
09-01-1967; 95.9 mhz FM *Hrs Open:* 24; 0.38 kw; 1273 ft.; N43 25 12 W73 45 37
128 Glen Street, Glens Falls, NY 12801 US
(518) 761-9890, *Fax:* (518) 761-9893
www.radiowins.com
cashworth@regionalradiogroup.com
License: Queensbury, Warren County, NY held by Regional Radio Group LLC.
Group Owner: Regional Radio Group LLC; (acq 9-10-2008; grpsl)
Nat'l Network: Jones Radio Networks
Arbitron Metro Market: Saratoga, NC *Hrs. of News Programming:* news progmg 3 hrs wkly *No. News Employees:* 15 *Target Audience:* 18-49. *Adv. Rates:* 32; 25; 28; 15
Steve Babson, Operations Dir
Clay Ashworth, General Manager
Dan Miner, Station Manager
Pete Cloutier, Promotions Manager
Jim Scott, News Director

Ramapo

WRCR
09-15-1977; 1700 khz AM *Hrs Open:* 24; 0.5 kw-D, DA2; 0.083 kw-N, DA2; N41 5 48 W74 0 18
20 Old Turnpike Road, Nanuet, NY 10954 US
(845) 624-1313, *Fax:* (845) 624-1639
www.wrcr.com
mail@wrcr.com
License: Ramapo, NY held by Alexander Broadcasting Inc.
Nat'l Network: USA
Arbitron Metro Market: New York *Format:* Adult Contemp, News *Hrs. of News Programming:* news progmg 18 hrs wkly *No. News Employees:* 2 *Target Audience:* 25-54; upscale
Alexander Medakovic, President
Alexander Madakovic, Programming Director

Rapids

***WLNF**
02-08-2012; 90.5 mhz FM; 250 w; Ant 74 ft; N43 05 12 W78 37 59
293 Niagara St., Lockport, NY
(716) 434-1733, *Fax:* (716) 434-2837
www.lctv.net
lctv@lctv.net
License: Rapids, Niagara County, NY held by Lockport Community Television.

Tom Riley, General Manager
Rich Zapp, Programming Director

Ravena

***WYKV**
01-01-1991; 94.5 mhz FM *Hrs Open:* 24; 3 kw; 328 ft.; N42 33 23 W73 52 5
12 Dennis Terrace, Schenectady, NY 12303 US
(817) 641-3495
License: Ravena, Albany County, NY held by Educational Media Foundation.
Group Owner: EMF Broadcasting; (acq 7-6-2007; grpsl)
Nat'l Network: K-Love
Arbitron Metro Market: Windom MN
Linda De Romanett, President

Remsen

WRCK
12-12-1966; 1480 khz AM *Hrs Open:* 24; 5 kw-D; N43 19 31 W75 10 29 *Rebroadcasts:* Rebroadcasts WRNY(AM) Rome 100%
239 Genesee St., Suite 500, Utica, NY 17110
(315) 797-0803, *Fax:* (315) 797-7813
www.starsradionetwork.com
License: Remsen, Oneida County, NY held by Roser Communications Network Inc.
Group Owner: Roser Communications Network Inc.; (acq 10-24-2007; grpsl)
Nat'l Network: Westwood One *Nat'l Reps:* Christal
Population Served: 175,000 *Arbitron Metro Market:* Utica-Rome, NY *Hrs. of News Programming:* News progmg 3 hrs wkly *Target Audience:* 35 plus; 60% female, 40% male
Brian Delaney, General Manager
Gene Conte, Programming Director
Joe Petro, Chief Engineer

***WOKR**
12-01-1982; 93.5 mhz FM *Hrs Open:* 24; 2.1 kw; 564 ft.; N43 16 51 W75 18 14
800 Corporate Circle, Suite 201, Harrisonburg, PA 17110 US
(916) 251-1600, (800) 464-5817, *Fax:* (916) 251-1650
www.godscountryradionetwork.com
info@happyjubilee.com
License: Remsen, Oneida County, NY held by Educational Media Foundation.
Group Owner: EMF Broadcasting; (acq 10-24-2007; $350,000)
Arbitron Metro Market: Utica-Rome, NY *Format:* Country, Gospel
Mike Novak, President

***WRUN**
12-16-2008; 90.3 mhz FM; 1.2 kw; Ant 669 ft; N43 20 47.8 W75 13 58.8 *Rebroadcasts:* Rebroadcasts WAMC-FM Albany 100%
P.O. Box 66600, Albany, NY 12206
(518) 465-5233, *Fax:* (518) 432-6974
www.wamc.org
mail@wamc.org
License: Remsen, Oneida County, NY held by WAMC.
Group Owner: WAMC/Northeast Public Radio
Population Served: 507 *Arbitron Metro Market:* Remsen, NY
Alan Chartock, COO
Katie Britton, Programming Director
Katie Britton, News Director
Joe Donahue, Vice President, News and Programming

Rensselaer

WQBK-FM
12-01-1972; 103.9 mhz FM *Hrs Open:* 24; 6 kw; 302 ft.; N42 35 6 W73 46 29
200 Concord Plaza, Suite 600, San Antonio, TX 78216 US
(518) 881-1515, *Fax:* (518) 881-1516
www.wqbk.com
License: Rensselaer, Rensselaer County, NY
Group Owner: Townsquare Media; (acq 2000; grpsl)
Arbitron Metro Market: Albany-Schenectady-Troy, NY
Bob Ausfeld, President
John Hirsch, Station Manager
Jim Clifford, General Sales Mgr
Shawn Murphy, Programming Director

WGDJ
12-03-1961; 1300 khz AM *Hrs Open:* 24
200 Concord Plaza, Suite 600, San Antonio, TX 78216 US
(518) 813-4975, *Fax:* (518) 813-9025
www.talk1300.com
Talk@talk1300.com
License: Rensselaer, NY held by Capital Broadcasting Inc.
Nat'l Network: ABC *Nat'l Reps:* Interep
Arbitron Metro Market: Albany, NY *Format:* Talk *Target Audience:* 35-64.

Paul Vandenburgh, President & General Manager
Jim Law, Sales Manager
Mike Carey, News Director
Angela Rosetti, Executive Producer/Traffic

Riverhead

WRCN-FM
08-14-1962; 103.9 mhz FM; 1.4 kw; 486 ft.; N40 51 8 W72 45 55
3241 Route 112, Bldg#112, Bldg #7, Medford, NY 11763 US
(631) 451-1039, *Fax:* (631) 451-0891,(631) 451-0896
www.wrcn.com
info@wrcn.com
License: Riverhead, Suffolk County, NY held by IW L.L.C.
Group Owner: JVC Broadcasting; (acq 10-1-97; grpsl).
Nat'l Reps: Katz Radio
Arbitron Metro Market: New York *Format:* Classic Rock *Target Audience:* 18-49.
Mike Kaneb, President
Dave Widmer, General Manager
Sal Abetamarco, General Sales Mgr
Charlie Lombardo, Programming Director
Megan Moir, Promotions Manager
Jen Moran, News Director
Bob Anderson, Chief Engineer

WFTU
08-08-1963; 1570 khz AM; 1 kw-D, DA2; 0.5 kw-N, DA2; N40 54 48 W72 39 16
3241 Route112 Bldg 7, Medford, NY 11763 US
(631) 424-7000,(631) 656-3192
www.wftu.net
License: Riverhead, NY held by Five Towns College
Arbitron Metro Market: New York *Format:* Talk
Rob Stern, General Manager

WRIV
06-01-1955; 1390 khz AM *Hrs Open:* 6 AM-midnight; 1 kw-D, ND1; 0.064 kw-N, ND1; N40 54 55 W72 39 28
Mailing Address: PO Box 1390, Riverhead, NY 11901 US
Second Address: 40 W. Main St., Riverhead, NY 11901
(631) 727-1390, *Fax:* (631) 369-WRIV (9748)
www.wrivonline.com
License: Riverhead, NY held by Crystal Coast Communications.
Arbitron Metro Market: New York *Format:* Adult Contemp *Special Programming:* Farm 8 hrs, Pol 4 hrs wkly *Hrs. of News Programming:* news progmg 14 hrs wkly *No. News Employees:* 1 *Target Audience:* 35-64.
Bruce Tria, General Manager

Rochester

WBZA
01-01-1939; 98.9 mhz FM *Hrs Open:* 24; 37 kw; 564 ft.; N43 10 14 W77 40 23
401 City Avenue, Suite 409, Bala Cynwyd, PA 19004 US
(306) 463-4411, *Fax:* (306) 882-3037
cjmmnews@goldenwestradio.com
License: Rochester, Monroe County, NY held by Entercom Rochester Inc.
Group Owner: Entercom Communications Corp.; (acq 4-23-98; grpsl)
Nat'l Network: Westwood One *Nat'l Reps:* Katz Radio
Arbitron Metro Market: Tri-Cities WA (Richland-Kennewick-Pasco) *Format:* Country
Keith Leask, General Manager

WBEE-FM
02-01-1961; 92.5 mhz FM *Hrs Open:* 24; 50 kw; 499 ft.; N43 10 37 W77 28 39
401 City Avenue, Suite 409, Bala Cynwyd, PA 19004 US
(305) 995-1717, *Fax:* (305) 995-2299
www.wlrn.org
info@wlrn.org
License: Rochester, Monroe County, NY held by Entercom Rochester License LLC
Group Owner: Entercom Communications Corp.; (acq 4-23-98; grpsl).
Nat'l Network: Westwood One
Arbitron Metro Market: Bakersfield CA *Format:* News, News/Talk, 86 *Special Programming:* Haitian 3 hrs wkly *Hrs. of News Programming:* news progmg 111 hrs wkly *No. News Employees:* 7 *Target Audience:* General; well educated, moderate to high income bracket
John LaBonia, General Manager
Ted Eldredge, Station Manager
Peter J. Moerz, Programming Director
Irina Lellemand, News Director

***WBER**
01-01-1974; 90.5 mhz FM *Hrs Open:* 24; 2.5 kw; 417 ft.; N43 2 0 W77 25 11

2596 Baird Road, Penfield, NY 14526 US
(585) 419-8190, *Fax:* (585)-383-6605
www.wber.monroe.edu
wber@monroe.edu
License: Rochester, Monroe County, NY held by Monroe B.O.C.E.S #1.
Arbitron Metro Market: Rochester, NY *Format:* Alternative *Target Audience:* 25-34; male & female
Joey Guisto, General Manager

WCMF-FM

06-09-1960; 96.5 mhz FM *Hrs Open:* 24; 48 kw; 466 ft.; N43 8 5.17 W77 35 6.6
600 New Hampshire Ave., N.W., Suite 1200, Washington, DC 20037 US
(585) 423-2900, *Fax:* (585) 325-5139
www.wcmf.com
smunn@entercom.com
License: Rochester, Monroe County, NY held by Entercom Rochester License LLC.
Group Owner: Entercom Communications Corp.; (acq 11-30-2007; grpsl)
Arbitron Metro Market: Rochester, NY *Format:* Classic Rock *Hrs. of News Programming:* news progmg 10 hrs wkly *No. News Employees:* 1
John Thomas, Operations Dir
Sue Munn, General Manager
Mike Johnson, Director of Sales
Chris Crowley, Programming Director

WDCX

02-01-1947; 990 khz AM *Hrs Open:* 24; 5 kw-D, DA2; 2.5 kw-N, DA2; N43 13 54 W77 52 0
P.O. Box 3003, Blue Bell, PA 19422 US
(716) 883-3010, *Fax:* (716) 883-3606
www.wdcxam.com
info@wdcxfm.com
License: Rochester, NY held by Kimtron Inc.
Group Owner: Crawford Broadcasting Co.; (acq 6-5-97; $650,000)
Arbitron Metro Market: Rochester, NY *Format:* Christian
Nev Larson, General Manager

WDKX

04-06-1974; 103.9 mhz FM *Hrs Open:* 24; 0.8 kw; 541 ft.; N43 9 17 W77 36 16
683 East Main Street, Rochester, NY 14605 US
(585) 262-2050, *Fax:* (585) 262-2626
www.wdkx.com
License: Rochester, Monroe County, NY held by Monroe County Broadcasting Co. Ltd.
Arbitron Metro Market: Rochester, NY *Format:* Urban Contemporary *Special Programming:* Jazz 4 hrs, gospel 7 hrs wkly *Hrs. of News Programming:* news progmg 6 hrs wkly *No. News Employees:* 2 *Target Audience:* General.
Andrew Langston, CEO
Camilla Maas, Operations Dir
Gloria Langston, Station Manager
Marietta Avery, CFO
Andre Langston, Operations Director

WROC

01-01-1947; 950 khz AM *Hrs Open:* 24; 1 kw-D, DA2; 1 kw-N, DA2; N43 6 25 W77 35 51
401 City Avenue, Suite 409, Bala Cynwyd, PA 19004 US
(585) 423-2900, *Fax:* (585) 325-5139
www.sportsradio950espn.com
smunn@entercom.com
License: Rochester, NY held by Entercom Rochester License LLC.
Group Owner: Entercom Communications Corp.
Nat'l Network: ESPN Radio
Arbitron Metro Market: Rochester, NY *Format:* Sports
Bob Barnett, Operations Dir
Sue Munn, VP/General Manager
Mike Johnson, Director of Sales
Chris Crowley, Programming Director
Steve Hausmann, News Director
Joe Fleming, Chief Engineer
Alana Katz, Traffic Manager

WHAM

07-11-1922; 1180 khz AM *Hrs Open:* 24; 50 kw-U, ND1; N43 4 55 W77 43 30
50 East Rivercenter Blvd, Suite 1200, Covington, KY 41011 US
(585) 454-4884, *Fax:* (585) 454-5081
www.wham1180.com
whamnews@wham1180.com
License: Rochester, NY held by Citicasters Licenses L.P.
Group Owner: Clear Channel Communications Inc.; (acq 3-7-97; grpsl).
Nat'l Network: CBS
Arbitron Metro Market: Rochester, NY *Format:* News, News/Talk, 86 *No. News Employees:* 6 *Target Audience:* Adults: 25-54.
Karen Carey, General Manager
Jeff Howlett, Station Manager
Randy Gorbman, Programming Director

WHTK

11-22-1947; 1280 khz AM *Hrs Open:* 24; 5 kw-D, DAN; 5 kw-N, DAN; N43 5 54 W77 35 1
50 E. Rivercenter Blvd., Ste 1200, Covington, KY 41001 US
(585) 454-4884, *Fax:* (585) 262-2334
www.whtk.com
info@whtk.com
License: Rochester, NY held by Citicasters Licenses L.P.
Group Owner: Clear Channel Communications Inc.; (acq 5-4-99; grpsl).
Nat'l Reps: McGavren Guild
Arbitron Metro Market: Rochester, NY *Format:* Talk *Target Audience:* 25-54; men
Jeff Howlett, General Manager
Scott Gordon, General Sales Mgr

*WIRQ

01-01-1960; 90.9 mhz FM *Hrs Open:* 1 PM-8 PM (M-F); Sept-June; 19 w; 35 meters; N43 12 59 W77 35 51
260 Cooper Rd., Rochester, NY 14617
(585) 336-3065, *Fax:* (589) 336-2929
www.wirqfm.org
License: Rochester, Monroe County, NY held by Board of Education West, Irondequoit Central School District.
Population Served: 600,000 *Arbitron Metro Market:* Rochester, NY *Special Programming:* Top-35 countdown 3 hrs, Progressive Pioneers 3 hrs *Hrs. of News Programming:* News progmg one hr wkly *Target Audience:* 13-45.
Hannah Jacobs, General Manager
Brendan Pistilli, Station Manager
Dave Desilet, Programming Director
Dalton Thomas, Music Director
Alfonzo Altland, Business Director
Jake Bigenwald, Webmaster
Garth Daunton, Engineer

WJZR

01-22-1993; 105.9 mhz FM *Hrs Open:* 24; 3 kw; 180 ft.; N43 9 35 W77 34 44
1237 East Main Street, Rochester, NY 14609 US
(585) 288-5020
License: Rochester, Monroe County, NY held by North Coast Radio Inc.
Nat'l Network: AP Radio
Arbitron Metro Market: Rochester, NY *Format:* Blues, Jazz
Special Programming: News review one hr wkly *Hrs. of News Programming:* News progmg 14 hrs wkly *Target Audience:* 25 plus.
Lee Rust, President
Barry Vee, General Sales Mgr

WPXY-FM

09-14-1959; 97.9 mhz FM; 50 kw; 466 ft.; N43 8 5.17 W77 35 6.6
600 New Hampshire Ave., N.W., Suite 1200, Washington, DC 20037 US
(585) 423-2900, *Fax:* (585) 325-5139
www.98pxy.com
License: Rochester, Monroe County, NY held by Entercom Rochester License LLC.
Group Owner: Entercom Communications Corp.; (acq 11-30-2007; grpsl)
Arbitron Metro Market: Rochester, NY *Format:* Contemporary Hits/Top 40
John Johnson, Operations Dir
Mike Danger, Programming Director

WRMM-FM

11-14-1966; 101.3 mhz FM; 27 kw; 640 ft.; N43 10 13 W77 40 23
600 New Hampshire Ave., N.W., Suite 1200, Washington, DC 20037 US
(585) 399-5700, *Fax:* (585) 399-5750
www.warm1013.com
info@warm1013.com
License: Rochester, Monroe County, NY held by Stephens Media Group-Rochester LLC.
Group Owner: Stephens Family L.P.; (acq 7-14-2008; grpsl)
Nat'l Reps: Christal
Arbitron Metro Market: Rochester, NY *Format:* Adult Contemp
Target Audience: 25-54; baby boomers
Michael Ninnie, General Manager
Terese Taylor, Programming Director
Ray Noone, Sales Director
Sarah Anken, Marketing Director

*WRUR-FM

03-06-1966; 88.5 mhz FM *Hrs Open:* 24; 15.1 kw; 378 ft.; N43 8 7 W77 35 3
Cpu 277356, River Statio, Rochester, NY 14627 US
(585) 275-9787, *Fax:* (585) 273-1357
www.wrur.org
License: Rochester, Monroe County, NY held by University of Rochester Broadcasting Corp.
Arbitron Metro Market: Rochester, NY *Format:* Variety/Diverse
Special Programming: Jazz, gospel 3 hrs, relg one hr, world 10 hrs, fol *Hrs. of News Programming:* News progmg 4 hrs wkly
Target Audience: General.
Paul Szymanski, Operations Dir
Mike Lindsay, General Manager
Ally Miller, Programming Director

WDVI

01-01-1962; 100.5 mhz FM *Hrs Open:* 24; 50 kw; 479 ft.; N43 2 1 W77 25 18
50 East Rivercenter Blvd, Suite 1200, Covington, KY 41011 US
(585) 454-4884, *Fax:* (585) 454-5081
www.mydrivefm.com
License: Rochester, Monroe County, NY
Group Owner: Clear Channel Communications Inc.
Arbitron Metro Market: Rochester, NY *Format:* Adult Contemp
Target Audience: 25-54.
Karen Carey, General Manager
Joe Bonacci, Programming Director
Becki Efing, Digital Advertising Sales Manager
Bonnie Dolan, Advertising Sales Manager
Matt Basile, Digital Content Director

WHIC

09-11-1925; 1460 khz AM *Hrs Open:* 24
Mailing Address: P.O. Box 2700, Bakersfield, CA 93303 US
Second Address: 2 Cambridge Pl., 1840 Winton Rd. S., Rochester, NY 14618
(585) 271-0530, *Fax:* (585) 271-0530
www.whicradio.com
info@thestationofthecross.com
License: Rochester, NY held by Holy Family Communications
Group Owner: Holy Family Communications; acq 7-1-2003; $300,000).
Arbitron Metro Market: Rochester, NY *Format:* Christian
James Wright, President
Jack Palvino, General Manager
Gina Zanicky, Programming Director
Zach Krajacic, Vice President of Development, Marketing, and PR
Rick Paolini, Business Manager
Bill Havas, Technical Operations Manager
Debbie Daigler, Administrative Assistant
Erica Ploucha, Fundraising and Account Information

*WXXI

01-01-1936; 1370 khz AM *Hrs Open:* 24; 5 kw-U, DA-N; N43 06 01 W77 34 23
280 State St., Rochester, NY 14601
(585) 325-7500, *Fax:* (585) 258-0339
www.wxxi.org
radio@wxxi.org
License: Rochester, Monroe County, NY held by WXXI Public Broadcasting Council.
Nat'l Network: NPR *Wire Services:* AP
Population Served: 941,600 *Arbitron Metro Market:* Rochester, NY
Noprm Silverstein, President
Susan Rogers, General Manager
Jeanne Fisher, Station Manager
Alison Jones, General Sales Mgr
Michael Black, Programming Director
Julie Phillip, News Director
Kent Hatfield, Engineering Dir
BudLowell, Reporter

*WXXI-FM

12-01-1974; 91.5 mhz FM *Hrs Open:* 24; 45 kw; 440 ft.; N43 8 7 W77 35 3
280 State St., Box 21, Rochester, NY 14601 US
(585) 258-0200
www.wxxi.org
radio@wxxi.org
License: Rochester, Monroe County, NY held by WXXI Public Broadcasting Council
Nat'l Network: PRI
Arbitron Metro Market: Rochester, NY *TV Affiliate:* *WXXI-TV affil. *Format:* Talk
Norm Silverstein, President
Julia Figueras, Programming Director
Richard Gladwell, Disc Jockey

Morderai Lipshutz, Disc Jockey
Simon Pontin, Disc Jockey

Rome

WODZ-FM
08-01-1968; 96.1 mhz FM; 7.4 kw; 604 ft.; N43 8 39 W75 10 45
One Forever Drive, Hollidaysburg, PA 16648 US
(315) 768-9500, *Fax:* (315) 736-0720
http://961wodz.com
License: Rome, Oneida County, NY
Group Owner: Townsquare Media; (acq 11-5-99; grpsl)
Arbitron Metro Market: Utica-Rome, NY *TV Affiliate:* Oldies
General Manager, General Manager
Director of Sales, General Sales Mgr

WRNY
10-12-1959; 1350 khz AM *Hrs Open:* 24; 0.5 kw-D, ND1; 0.057 kw-N, ND1; N43 12 18 W75 29 8
800 Corporate Circle, Suite 201, Harrisonburg, PA 17110 US
(315) 797-0803, *Fax:* (315) 797-7813
info@galaxycommunication.com
License: Rome, NY held by Galaxy Utica Licensee LLC.
Group Owner: Galaxy Communications L.P.; (acq 10-24-2007; grpsl)
Arbitron Metro Market: Utica-Rome, NY *Format:* Sports *Special Programming:* Black 3 hrs wkly *No. News Employees:* 1 *Target Audience:* 25 plus.
Brian Deleney, General Manager
Chuck Hebbard, General Sales Mgr
Gene Conte, Programming Director
Joe Petro, Chief Engineer

WUMX
05-01-1983; 102.5 mhz FM *Hrs Open:* 24; 27 kw; 650 ft.; N43 2 14 W75 26 40
P O Box 60547, Harrisburg, PA 17106 US
(315) 797-1330, *Fax:* (315) 738-1073
mix1025.com
askmix@mix1025.com
License: Rome, Oneida County, NY
Group Owner: Clear Channel Communications Inc.
Arbitron Metro Market: Utica-Rome, NY *Format:* Variety/Diverse *Special Programming:* Pub affrs one hr wkly *No. News Employees:* 1 *Target Audience:* 18-49.
Stew Schantz, Programming Director
Chris Spiwak, Promotions Manager
Ed O'Brien, News Director
Joe Petro, Chief Engineer

WKAL
09-01-1946; 1450 khz AM *Hrs Open:* 24; 1 kw-U; N43 12 18 W75 28 48
Box 7300, Charlotte, NC 28273
(704) 523-5555, *Fax:* (704) 522-1967
www.bbnradio.org
License: Rome, Oneida County, NY held by Bible Broadcasting Network Inc.
Group Owner: Bible Broadcasting Network; (acq 5-7-99; $50,000).
Population Served: 275,000 *Arbitron Metro Market:* Utica-Rome, NY
Jason Padgett, Station Manager

Rosendale

*WFNP
09-05-1990; 88.7 mhz FM *Hrs Open:* 7 PM-5 AM; 0.23 kw vert; 1289 ft.; N41 43 9 W73 59 47
State Unversity Plaza, Albany, NY 12246 US
(845) 257-3090, *Fax:* (845) 257-3099
www.wfnp.org
wfnp.sm@gmail.com
License: Rosendale, Ulster County, NY held by State University of New York, Albany.
Nat'l Network: ABC; AP Radio
Format: Talk *Special Programming:* Black 14 hrs, jazz 4 hrs, Sp 3 hrs, news/talk 5 hr *Hrs. of News Programming:* News progmg 3 hrs wkly *Target Audience:* General; demographic-specific programs
William Clark, Operations Dir

Rotterdam

WTRY-FM
12-15-1986; 98.3 mhz FM *Hrs Open:* 24; 6 kw; 318 ft.; N42 44 43 W74 4 10
600 Congress Ave., Suite 1400, Austin, TX 78701 US
(518) 452-4800, *Fax:* (518) 452-4813
www.wtry.com
johncooper@clearchannel.com
License: Rotterdam, Schenectady County, NY held by Capstar TX L.P.
Group Owner: Clear Channel Communications Inc.; (acq 8-30-00; grpsl).
Nat'l Reps: Clear Channel
Arbitron Metro Market: Albany, NY *Format:* Oldies *Hrs. of News Programming:* news progmg 20 hrs wkly *No. News Employees:* 1 *Target Audience:* 35-54.
Kristen Delaney, VP & General Manager
Vera Hope, General Sales Mgr
John Cooper, Operations Manager & Program Director
Jill Manti, Marketing Director
Mike Arce, Online Content Director

Rouses Point

*WKYJ
01-01-2005; 88.7 mhz FM; 0.42 kw vert; 13 ft.; N44 56 44 W73 25 41
1601 Belvedere Rd, 204e, West Palm Beach, FL 33406 US
(800) 525-5683, *Fax:* (916) 251-1650
www.klove.com
klove@klove.com
License: Rouses Point, Clinton County, NY held by American Educational Broadcasting Inc.
Arbitron Metro Market: Rouses Point, NY *Format:* Christian, Gospel *No. News Employees:* 13
Darrell Chambliss, Chairman
Carl Auel, CEO
Mike Novak, President and CEO
Fred Hodges, General Manager
David Pierce, Programming Director
Ed Lenane, News Director
Sam Wallington, Engineering Dir
Dan Antonelli, Chief BusinessDevelopment Officer
Eric Moser, Chief Financial Officer
Brian Burger, Vice President of Human Resources
D. Kevin Blair, Secretary and General Counsel
Tim Luttrell, News Reporter

Roxbury

*WIOX
91.3 mhz FM; 3.3 kw; -600 ft.; N42 16 13 W74 34 16 US
(607) 326-7641
www.wioxradio.org
License: Roxbury, Delaware County, NY held by Town of Roxbury.
Arbitron Metro Market: Roxbury, NY
Thomas Hynes, General Manager

Sag Harbor

WLNG
04-13-1969; 92.1 mhz FM; 5.3 kw; 350 ft; N40 58 19 W72 20 54
Mailing Address: Box 2000, Sag Harbor, NY 11963
Second Address: 23 Redwood Road, Sag Harbor, NY 11963
(631) 725-2300, *Fax:* (631) 725-5897
www.wlng.com
info@wlng.com
License: Sag Harbor, Suffolk County, NY held by Mainstreet Broadcasting Co.
Arbitron Metro Market: New York
Gary Sapiane, President
Gary Sapiane, Operations Dir
Rusty Potz, General Sales Mgr
David Kline, Promotions Manager
Brion Bannon, Engineering Dir
Gary Sapiane, Vice President

Salamanca

WGGO
06-18-1957; 1590 khz AM; 5 kw-D, ND2; 0.014 kw-N, ND2; N42 10 24 W78 41 7
Mailing Address: P.O. Box 62, Salamanca, NY 14779 US
Second Address: 4104 Killbuck Rd., Salamanca, NY 14779
(716) 945-1590, *Fax:* (716) 945-1515
wgrt983@direcway.com
License: Salamanca, NY held by Pembrook Pines Inc.
Group Owner: Pembrook Pines Media Group; (acq 6-9-2006; $1.25 million with co-located FM).
Nat'l Network: ESPN Radio
Format: Sports *Special Programming:* Country 5 hrs, Pol one hr wkly *Target Audience:* General.
Robert Pfuntner, President
Michael Washington, General Manager
Sue Washington, General Sales Mgr
Scott Douglas, News Director
Russ Ehman, Chief Engineer

WQRS
10-15-1988; 98.3 mhz FM; 3.2 kw; 443 ft.; N42 6 32 W78 36 28
Mailing Address: P.O. Box 62, Salamanca, NY 14779 US
Second Address: 4104 Killbuck Rd., Salamanca, NY 14779
(716) 945-1590, *Fax:* (716) 945-1515
wqrt983@direcway.net
License: Salamanca, Cattaraugus County, NY
Group Owner: Pembrook Pines Media Group
Format: Classic Rock
Mike Novak, President

Sandy Creek-Pulaski

WSCP
08-08-1974; 1070 khz AM; 2.5 kw-D, NDD; N43 36 19 W76 7 48
5090 Us Rt #11, P.O. Box 640, Pulaski, NY 13142 US
(315) 298-3185, *Fax:* (315) 298-6181
License: Sandy Creek-Pulaski, NY held by Galaxy Syracuse Licensee LLC.
Group Owner: Galaxy Communications L.P.; (acq 7-17-2001; $400,000 with WSCP-FM Pulaski).
Nat'l Network: Jones Radio Networks
Arbitron Metro Market: Syracuse, NY *Format:* Sports *Hrs. of News Programming:* news progmg one hr wkly *No. News Employees:* 1 *Target Audience:* 35 plus.
Mimi Griswold, Programming Director

Saranac

WYZY
07-12-1989; 106.3 mhz FM *Hrs Open:* 24; 1.47 kw; 2316 ft.; N44 41 43 W73 53 0
Box 211, Colony Ct. Ext., Saranac Lake, NY 12983 US
(518) 891-1544, *Fax:* (518) 891-1545
www.y1063i.com
brandy@mtnradio.com
License: Saranac, Franklin County, NY held by Saranac Lake Radio LLC
Group Owner: Mountain Communications
Format: Contemporary Hits/Top 40 *Hrs. of News Programming:* news progmg 10 hrs wkly *No. News Employees:* 2 *Target Audience:* 18-49; adults *Adv. Rates:* Same as AM
Crystal Tatro, Operations Dir
Ted Morgan, General Sales Mgr
Steve Borst, Programming Director

Saranac Lake

WNBZ
09-11-1927; 1240 khz AM *Hrs Open:* 24; 1 kw-U, ND1; N44 18 58 W74 7 8
Mailing Address: 6786 Standing Boy Rd., Columbus, GA 31904 US
Second Address: Colony Ct. Ext., Saranac Lake, NY 12983
(518) 891-1544, *Fax:* (518) 891-1545
www.wnbz.com
mail@wnbz.com
License: Saranac Lake, NY held by Saranac Lake Radio L.L.C.
Group Owner: Mountain Communications; (acq 6-1-98; $397,500 with co-located FM)
Arbitron Metro Market: Sarnak Lake, NY *Format:* News, News/Talk, 86 *Hrs. of News Programming:* news progmg 36 hrs wkly *No. News Employees:* 1 *Target Audience:* 35 plus; loc community *Adv. Rates:* 20; 20;20; 15
Ted Morgan, President
John Gagnon, Operations Dir
James Williams, General Sales Mgr
Chris Knight, News Director
Chris Brescia, Chief Engineer
Steve Borst, Disc Jockey
Crystal Tatro, Public Affairs Director

*WSLL
07-01-1989; 90.5 mhz FM; 0.6 kw; 351 ft.; N44 20 28 W74 7 43
Rebroadcasts: Rebroadcasts WSLU(FM) Canton 100%
N. Country Public Radio, Canton, NY 13617 US
(315) 229-5356, *Fax:* (315) 229-5373
www.ncpr.org
radio@ncpr.org
License: Saranac Lake, Franklin County, NY held by St. Lawrence University.
Format: Variety/Diverse *Target Audience:* General.
Ellen Rocco, Station Manager
Jackie Sauter, Programming Director
Martha Foley, News Director
Robert Sauter, Chief Engineer
Sandra Demarest, Underwriting Director

WSLP
01-01-2007; 93.3 mhz FM; 11 kw; -207 ft.; N44 15 36 W74 1 22 US

(518) 523-4900, *Fax:* (518) 523-4290
www.wslpfm.com
info@wslpfm.com
License: Saranac Lake, Franklin County, NY held by North Country Radio Inc.
Nat'l Network: CNN Radio
Arbitron Metro Market: Saranac Lake, NY *Format:* Adult Contemp *Target Audience:* 25-54.
Jon Lundin, General Manager
Jim Williams, General Sales Mgr

Saratoga Springs

*WSPN
09-09-1974; 91.1 mhz FM *Hrs Open:* 24; 0.25 kw horiz; 98 ft.; N43 5 55 W73 47 10
815 North Broadway, Saratoga Springs, NY 12866 US
(518) 580-5783
License: Saratoga Springs, Saratoga County, NY held by Skidmore College.
Nat'l Network: AP Radio
Format: Talk *Special Programming:* Folk 3 hrs, Pol 3 hrs, Sp 3 hrs, blues 9 hrs, world mus 3 hrs wkly *Hrs. of News Programming:* News progmg 5 hrs wkly *Target Audience:* All ages.
Alissa DeVogel, General Manager
Lily Gedney, Programming Director

*WSSK
01-01-2001; 89.7 mhz FM; 0.05 kw vert; 430 ft.; N43 11 35 W73 45 25
P.O. Box 777, Lake Katrine, NY 12449 US
(845) 336-6199, *Fax:* (845) 336-7205
www.soundoflife.org
info@soundoflife.org
License: Saratoga Springs, Saratoga County, NY held by Sound of Life Inc.
Format: Christian
Bob Conti, Operations Dir
Tom Zahradnik, General Manager
Joe Hunter, Programming Director

Saugerties

WBPM
01-01-1999; 92.9 mhz FM *Hrs Open:* 24; 6 kw; 289 ft.; N41 59 20 W74 1 8
12 Tucker Drive, Poughkeepsie, NY 12603 US
(845) 838-6000, *Fax:* (845) 838-6088
www.wbpmfm.com
License: Saugerties, Ulster County, NY held by 6 Johnson Road Licenses Inc.
Group Owner: Pamal Broadcasting Ltd.; (acq 4-1-2007; grpsl)
Arbitron Metro Market: Poughkeepsie, NY *Format:* Contemporary Hits/Top 40, Adult Contemp
Jason Finkelberg, General Manager

Schenectady

WGY
02-01-1922; 810 khz AM *Hrs Open:* 24; 50 kw-U, ND1; N42 47 37 W74 0 36
800 Corporate Circle, Suite 201, Harrisonburg, PA 17110 US
(518) 452-4800, *Fax:* (518) 452-4855
www.wgy.com
paulihander@clearchannel.com
License: Schenectady, NY held by CC License LLC.
Group Owner: Clear Channel Communications Inc.; (acq 8-5-98; grpsl)
Nat'l Network: Fox News Radio; Premiere Radio Networks *Nat'l Reps:* Clear Channel *Wire Services:* AP
Arbitron Metro Market: Albany-Schenectady-Troy, NY *Format:* News, News/Talk, 86 *Hrs. of News Programming:* news progmg 23 hrs wkly *No. News Employees:* 12 *Target Audience:* 25-54; college graduate, married,homeowner
Kristen Delaney, Operations Dir
John Cooper, Station Manager
Vera Hope, General Sales Mgr
Paul Ihander, Programming Director
Paul Ihander, News Director
Dave Abdoo, Chief Engineer
Joe Gallagher, Disc Jockey
Ed Martin, DiscJockey
Don Weeks, Disc Jockey
Greg Foster, Operations Director

*WMHT-FM
06-08-1972; 89.1 mhz FM; 11 kw; 928 ft.; N42 38 13 W74 0 6
17 Fern Avenue, P.O. Box 17, Schenectady, NY 12301 US
(518) 880-3400, *Fax:* (518) 880-3409
www.wmht.org
info@wmht.org
License: Schenectady, Schenectady County, NY held by WMHT Educational Telecommunications.
Arbitron Metro Market: Albany, NY *TV Affiliate:* WMHT-TV.
Format: Talk *Special Programming:* Jazz one hr wkly
Deborah Onslow, General Manager
Dave Nicosia, Chief Engineer

*WRUC
05-09-1975; 89.7 mhz FM; 0.1 kw; -89 ft.; N42 49 4 W73 55 45
College Ctr, Union Coll, Schenectady, NY 12308 US
(518) 388-6151, *Fax:* (518) 388-6790
http://wruc.union.edu/wruc/
License: Schenectady, Schenectady County, NY held by Trustees of Union College.
Nat'l Network: AP Radio
Arbitron Metro Market: Albany-Schenect *Format:* Rock/AOR
Special Programming: It one hr, Sp 3 hrs, jazz 15 hrs, sports 4 hrs wkl *Target Audience:* 18 plus; general
Zach Pearce, General Manager
Michelle Goldberg, Promotions Manager

WRVE
04-01-1940; 99.5 mhz FM *Hrs Open:* 24; 14.5 kw; 925 ft.; N42 38 13 W73 59 45
800 Corporate Circle, Suite 201, Harrisonburg, PA 17110 US
(518) 452-4800, *Fax:* (518) 452-4855
www.wrve.com
rivermorningcrew@yahoo.com
License: Schenectady, Schenectady County, NY
Group Owner: Clear Channel Communications Inc.
Nat'l Network: Premiere Radio Networks
Arbitron Metro Market: Albany-Schenect *Format:* Adult Contemp *Hrs. of News Programming:* news progmg 3 hrs wkly *No. News Employees:* 1 *Target Audience:* 25-54.
Randy McCarten, Programming Director

WPTR(AM)
04-15-1942; 1240 khz AM *Hrs Open:* 24; 1 kw-U; N42 48 37 W73 59 04
100 Saratoga Village Blvd., Ste. 21, Malta, NY 12020
(518) 899-3000, *Fax:* (518) 899-3057
www.trueoldies1240.com
fran@anastosmedia.com
License: Schenectady, Schenectady County, NY held by Empire Broadcasting Corp
Group Owner: Anastos Media Group Inc.; (acq 4-10-2000; $137,500).
Population Served: 97,660 *Arbitron Metro Market:* Albany, NY *No. News Employees:* 1 *Target Audience:* 45 plus.
Scott Collins, President
John Meaney, Station Manager
Amanda Albright, Promotions Manager
Fran Dingeman, Advertising Contact

Schoharie

WMYY
01-01-1990; 97.3 mhz FM *Hrs Open:* 24; 0.8 kw; 896 ft.; N42 37 51 W74 16 1 *Rebroadcasts:* Rebroadcasts WHAZ(AM) Troy 100%
30 Park Avenue, Cohoes, NY 12047 US
(518) 237-1330, *Fax:* (518) 235-4468
www.aliveradionetwork.com
events@aliveradionetwork.com
License: Schoharie, Schoharie County, NY held by Capital Media Corp.
Group Owner: Capital Media Corp.; acq 2-14-92;
Arbitron Metro Market: Albany, NY *Format:* Christian *Special Programming:* Gospel, relg *Target Audience:* 25-75; young to old
Paul Lotters, President
Steven Klob, Operations Dir
Rex Gregory, Programming Director

Schuyler Falls

*WOXR
01-01-2004; 90.9 mhz FM; 2.7 kw; 1073 ft.; N44 34 24 W73 40 31
P O Box 583, Essex Jct, VT 05453 US
(802) 655-9451, *Fax:* (802) 655-2799
www.vpr.net
vermontedition@vpr.net
License: Schuyler Falls, Clinton County, NY held by Vermont Public Radio
Regional Network: Vermont Public Radio
Arbitron Metro Market: Schuyler Falls, NY *Format:* Classical
Robin Turnau, President & CEO
Victoria St. John, Operations Dir
Mark Vogelzang, General Manager
Franny Bastian, Director Of Programming & Production
Rich Parker, Engineering Dir
Mike Seguin, Engineering Dir
Asa Sourdiffe, ITManager
Brian Tagliaferro, Manager Of Special Giving
Ty Robertson, Coordinator of Community Engagement
Will Pearson, Corporate Support Associate
Sam Sanders, Senior Production Engineer
Brian Jones, Corporate Support Specialist

Scotia

*WYAI
12-01-1981; 93.7 mhz FM; 1.25 kw; 705 ft.; N42 51 24 W74 4 3
89 Everts Avenue, Queensbury, NY 12804 US
(888) 937-2471, *Fax:* (916) 251-1650
www.air1.com
info@air1.com
License: Scotia, Schenectady County, NY held by Educational Media Foundation.
Group Owner: EMF Broadcasting; (acq 7-6-2007; grpsl)
Nat'l Network: Air 1
Arbitron Metro Market: Omaha, NE *Format:* Alternative, Christian *Target Audience:* 18-35; Judeo-Christian, female
Darrell Chambliss, Chairman
Mike Novak, President & CEO
Larry Moody, Director
Mitch Barnhart, Director
David R. Ferry, Director
Walter Golembeski, Director
David Pierce, Chief Creative Officer
Alan Mason, Chief OperatingOfficer

Seneca Falls

WSFW
10-01-1968; 1110 khz AM *Hrs Open:* Sunrise-sunset
P.O. Box 608, Seneca Falls, NY 13148 US
(315) 781-7000, *Fax:* (315) 781-7700
www.calvaryradionetwork.com
wnyr@flare.net
License: Seneca Falls, NY held by Auburn Broadcasting Inc.
Group Owner: Finger Lakes Radio Group; (acq 3-2-2001; with co-located FM)
Nat'l Reps: Rgnl Reps
Format: Religious *Special Programming:* Irish 2 hrs, It 2 hrs, jazz one hr, oldies 3 hrs, *Hrs. of News Programming:* news progmg 24 hrs wkly *No. News Employees:* 1 *Target Audience:* 25-54.
Allan Bishop, General Manager

WLLW
11-01-1968; 99.3 mhz FM *Hrs Open:* 24; 5 kw; 358 ft.; N42 59 38 W76 51 59
P.O. Box 608, Seneca Falls, NY 13148 US
(315) 781-7000, *Fax:* (315) 781-7700
License: Seneca Falls, Seneca County, NY
Format: Classic Rock *Adv. Rates:* 14; 12; 14; 10
Ken Paradise, Programming Director

Sidney

WCDO
01-01-1983; 1490 khz AM; 1 kw-U, ND1; N42 19 24 W75 22 57
75 Main Street, Sidney, NY 13838 US
(607) 563-3588, *Fax:* (607) 563-7805
www.wcdoonline.com
wcdo@wcdofm.com
License: Sidney, NY held by CDO Broadcasting Inc.
Group Owner: Clancy-Mance Communications; (acq 3-8-86; $180,000 with co-located FM;
Format: Adult Contemp *Target Audience:* 25-54.
Craig Harris, General Manager
Jim Tomeo, Programming Director

WCDO-FM
05-01-1982; 100.9 mhz FM; 1.9 kw; 577 ft.; N42 17 33 W75 22 3
75 Main Street, Sidney, NY 13838 US
(607) 563-3588, *Fax:* (607) 563-7805
www.wcdoonline.com
wcdo@wcdofm.com
License: Sidney, Delaware County, NY
Group Owner: Clancy-Mance Communications
Format: Adult Contemp, Oldies *Target Audience:* 25-54.
Craig Stevens, General Manager
Greg Davie, General Sales Mgr

Silver Creek

*WCOM-FM
89.3 mhz FM; 8 kw; 272 ft.; N42 34 41 W78 57 47
US
(787)622-9475, *Fax:* (787)622-9477
License: Silver Creek, Chautauqua County, NY
Group Owner: Family Life Ministries Inc.

Smithtown

*WFRS
10-17-1988; 88.9 mhz FM *Hrs Open:* 24; 1.5 kw horiz, 1.45 kw vert; 433 ft.; N40 48 27 W73 10 48
4135 Northgate Blvd. #1, Sacramento, CA 95834 US
(631) 234-4151, *Fax:* (631) 234-4628
www.familyradio.com
License: Smithtown, Suffolk County, NY held by Family Stations Inc.
Group Owner: Family Stations Inc.; acq 9-27-83)
Nat'l Network: Family Radio
Format: Christian *Hrs. of News Programming:* News progmg 5 hrs wkly *Target Audience:* General.
Bruce Clark, General Manager
Craig Hulsobus, Programming Director

WIGX
05-21-1957; 94.3 mhz FM *Hrs Open:* 24; 2.6 kw; Ant 315 ft; N40 48 08 W73 17 12
234 Airport Plaza Blvd., Suite 5, Farmingdale, NY 11747
(631) 770-4200, *Fax:* (631) 770-0101
www.island943.com
jon@my94x.com
License: Smithtown, Suffolk County, NY held by Connoisseur Media of Long Island LLC
Group Owner: JVC Broadcasting; (acq 10-1-97; grpsl)
Nat'l Network: AP Radio *Wire Services:* Standard Broadcast Wire
Population Served: 2,000,000 *Arbitron Metro Market:* New York, NY *Hrs. of News Programming:* news progmg 2 hrs wkly *No. News Employees:* 1 *Target Audience:* 25-54; men & women
Adv. Rates: 45; 50; 45; 40
Dave Widmer, General Manager

Sodus

WUUF
01-01-1991; 103.5 mhz FM *Hrs Open:* 24; 6 kw; 243 ft.; N43 16 5 W77 9 40
P.O. Box 1420, Newark, NY 14513 US
(315) 331-9667, *Fax:* (315) 331-7101
www.bigdogcountry1035.com
bigdogfm@rochester.rr.com
License: Sodus, Wayne County, NY held by Waynco Radio
Nat'l Network: Motor Racing Net; Westwood One
Arbitron Metro Market: Rochester, NY *Format:* Country *Hrs. of News Programming:* news progmg one hr wkly *No. News Employees:* 1 *Target Audience:* 25-54. *Adv. Rates:* 30; 25; 30; 20
John Tickner, President
Jim Hill, Operations Dir
Rus Jeffrey, News Director

South Bristol Township

WODX
01-22-1996; 107.3 mhz FM *Hrs Open:* 24; 650 w; Ant 994 ft; N42 44 47 W77 25 35
1700 HSBC Plaza, 100 Chestnut Street, Rochester, NY 41011
(585) 454-4884, *Fax:* (585) 454-5081
www.mycountryfm.com
License: South Bristol Township, Ontario County, NY held by Citicasters Licenses L.P.
Group Owner: Clear Channel Communications Inc.; (acq 1999; grpsl)
Target Audience: 25-54.
Dave LeFrois, Operations Dir
Karen Carey, General Manager

South Glen Falls

WENU
09-01-1988; 1410 khz AM *Hrs Open:* 24
89 Everts Avenue, Queensbury, NY 12804 US
(518) 793-7733, *Fax:* (518) 793-0838
www.pamal.com/pamal/wenu.html
License: South Glen Falls, NY held by 6 Johnson Road Licenses Inc.
Group Owner: Pamal Broadcasting Ltd.; (acq 4-1-2004; grpsl).
Nat'l Network: Westwood One
Arbitron Metro Market: Queensbury, NY *Format:* Contemporary Hits/Top 40 *No. News Employees:* 1 *Target Audience:* 35 plus.
Adv. Rates: 15; 15; 15; 5
James Morrell, President
Mike Morgan, Operations Dir

Southampton

WHFM
10-01-1971; 95.3 mhz FM; 5 kw; 354 ft.; N40 56 5 W72 23 15
3773 Howard Hughes Prwy, Suite 300n, Las Vegas, NV 89109 US
(631) 587-1023, *Fax:* (631) 283-9506
www.wbab.com
License: Southampton, Suffolk County, NY held by Cox Radio Inc.
Group Owner: Cox Radio Inc.; (acq 5-22-98; grpsl)
Nat'l Reps: Christal
Arbitron Metro Market: New York *Format:* Adult Contemp, Rock/AOR *Target Audience:* 25-49; upscale
Kim Guthrie, Operations Dir
John Shea, General Manager
Todd Dinetz, General Sales Mgr
Chris Lloyd, Programming Director
Lori DeFilliis, News Director
Ted Ronneburger, Chief Engineer
Donovan Welsh, General Sales Manager
VinnyDiMarco, National Sales Manager
John Olsen, Programming Director

*WPPB
03-03-1979; 88.3 mhz FM *Hrs Open:* 24; 5.9 kw horiz, 25 kw vert; 217 ft; N40 53 17 W72 26 43
Box 1410, Southhampton, NY 11548
(631) 591-7000, *Fax:* (631) 591-7080
www.peconicpublicbroadcasting.org
wally@peconicpublicbroadcasting.org
License: Southampton, Suffolk County, NY held by Peconic Public Broadcasting
Nat'l Network: PRI; NPR *Wire Services:* AP
Population Served: 115,000*Special Programming:* Pub affrs one hr wkly *Hrs. of News Programming:* news progmg 34 hrs wkly *No. News Employees:* 2 *Target Audience:* 34-55; upscale, educ, public radio listeners
Jamie Berger, Operations Dir
Dr. Wallace Smith, General Manager
Nancye Simpson, Programming Director
Robert Anderson, Chief Engineer
Bonnie Grice, Music Director

*WRLI-FM
07-01-1999; 91.3 mhz FM; 10 kw; 312 ft.; N40 56 5 W72 23 15
Rebroadcasts: Rebroadcasts WPKT(FM) Meriden 100%
240 New Britain Avenue, Hartford, CT 06106 US
(860) 278-5310, *Fax:* (860) 244-9624
www.wnpr.org
info@wnpr.org
License: Southampton, Suffolk County, NY held by Connecticut Public Television & Radio.
Nat'l Network: NPR; PRI
Format: News, News/Talk, 86
Jerry Franklin, CEO
Kim Grehn, Operations Dir

Southold

WBEA
07-03-1985; 101.7 mhz FM *Hrs Open:* 24; 6 kw; 283 ft.; N40 52 10 W72 34 37
P.O. Box 1200, Southold, NY 11971 US
(541) 298-4141
License: Southold, Suffolk County, NY held by AAA Licensing LLC.
Group Owner: Long Island Radio Broadcasting LLC; (acq 8-22-2000; $2.75 million with WBAZ(FM) Bridgehampton).
Nat'l Network: Westwood One
Arbitron Metro Market: Omaha-Council Bluffs NE-IA
Danny Manciu, President

Southport

WOKN
09-15-1993; 99.5 mhz FM; 1.25 kw; 725 ft.; N42 7 51 W76 47 26
1705 Lake Street, Elmira, NY 14901 US
(607) 733-5626, *Fax:* (607) 733-5627
http://995woknelmira.com/
License: Southport, Chemung County, NY held by Pembrook Pines Elmira Ltd.
Group Owner: Pembrook Pines Media Group
Nat'l Network: Jones Radio Networks
Arbitron Metro Market: Elmira-Corning, *TV Affiliate:* Country
Special Programming: news progmg 2 hrs wkly *Hrs. of News Programming:* 1 *No. News Employees:* 18-49; female *Adv. Rates:* 25; 25; 25; 20
CEO, CEO/COO

Spectacular

WYVS
96.5 mhz FM; 2.6 kw; 152 m; N43 31 26 W74 21 39
1250 Riverfront Center, Amsterdam, NY
(518)684-6007
tesiero@cranesville.com
License: Spectacular, Hamilton County, NY
Group Owner: Tesiero, Joseph C.
Joseph C. Tesiero, CEO/COO

Spencer

*WCII
10-01-1989; 88.5 mhz FM *Hrs Open:* 24; 17 kw; 591 ft.; N42 0 50 W76 15 53 *Rebroadcasts:* Rebroadcasts WCIK(FM) Bath 100%
P.O. Box 506, Bath, NY 14810 US
(607) 776-4151, *Fax:* (607) 776-6929
www.fln.org
mail@fln.org
License: Spencer, Tioga County, NY held by Family Life Ministries Inc.
Group Owner: Family Life Network
Nat'l Network: Salem Radio Network *Wire Services:* Metro Weather Service Inc.
Arbitron Metro Market: Bath, NY *Format:* Christian *Special Programming:* News 14 hrs wkly *Hrs. of News Programming:* news progmg 14 hrs wkly *No. News Employees:* 3 *Target Audience:* 30-54; general public
Dick Snavely, CFO
Rick Snavely, President
Cecil Van Houten, Radio Operations Manager
Sammy Carrillo, Programming Director
Sammy Carrillo, Promotions Manager
Jim Travis, Chief Engineer

Springville

WSPQ
04-20-1986; 1330 khz AM *Hrs Open:* 24; 1 kw-D, DA2; 1 kw-N, DA2; N42 29 53 W78 41 10
51 Franklin Street, Springville, NY 14141 US
(716) 592-9500, *Fax:* (716) 592-9522
fredhaier@verizon.net
License: Springville, NY held by Hawk Communications Ltd.
Nat'l Network: CNN Radio; ESPN Radio; Motor Racing Net
Arbitron Metro Market: Buffalo-Niagara Falls, NY *Format:* Adult Contemp, Country, 84, Variety/Diverse *Special Programming:* Farm 5 hrs, relg 2 hrs wkly *Hrs. of News Programming:* news progmg 10 hrs wkly *No. NewsEmployees:* 1 *Target Audience:* 25-54. *Adv. Rates:* 20; 18; 20; 15
Kevin Bower, General Manager

Staten Island

*WSIA
08-31-1981; 88.9 mhz FM *Hrs Open:* 24; 0.011 kw; 630 ft.; N40 35 51 W74 6 53
1c-106 2800 Victory Blvd, Staten Island, NY 10314 US
(718) 982-3050, *Fax:* (718) 982-3052
www.wsia.fm
mailbox@wsia.fm
License: Staten Island, Richmond County, NY held by College of Staten Island.
Arbitron Metro Market: New York *Format:* Triple A *Target Audience:* General.
Philip Masciantonio, General Manager
John Ladley, Chief Engineer

Stillwater

WJKE(FM)
10-03-1988; 101.3 mhz FM *Hrs Open:* 24; 2.9 kw; 470 ft; N43 00 42 W73 41 01
100 Saratoga Blvd., Ste. 21, Malta, NY 12020
(518) 899-3000,(518) 899-1013, *Fax:* (518) 899-3057
www.star1013.com
wabymoon@aol.com
License: Stillwater, Saratoga County, NY held by Empire Broadcasting Corp
Group Owner: Anastos Media Group Inc.; acq 9-4-98; $900,000).
Arbitron Metro Market: Albany-Schenectady-Troy, NY *Special Programming:* Saratoga Forum one hr *Hrs. of News Programming:* news progmg 6 hrs wkly *No. News Employees:* 1 *Target Audience:* 25-54; upscale
Scott Collins, President
J. Scott Collins, General Manager
John Meaney, Station Manager
Fran Dingman, General Sales Mgr
Amanda Albright, Promotions Manager

Stony Brook

*WUSB
06-27-1977; 90.1 mhz FM *Hrs Open:* 24; 3.6 kw; 531 ft.; N40 50 32 W73 2 23
State University Plaza, Albany, NY 12246 US

(631) 632-6501, *Fax:* (631) 632-7182
www.wusb.org
md@wusb.fm
License: Stony Brook, Suffolk County, NY held by State University of New York.
Wire Services: AP
Arbitron Metro Market: Stony Brook, NY *Format:* News, News/Talk, 86, Variety/Diverse *Special Programming:* Black 12 hrs, Pol one hr, Sp 3 hrs, Chinese one hr *Hrs. of News Programming:* News progmg 20 hrs wkly *TargetAudience:* 18-49; progsv & musically adventurous
Marko Srdanovic, Operations Dir
Norman Prusslin, General Manager

Sylvan Beach

WMVN
04-01-1999; 100.3 mhz FM; 6 kw; Ant 328 ft; N43 14 46 W75 46 25
401 W. Kirkpatrick St., Syracuse, NY 13476
(315) 472-0222, *Fax:* (315) 478-7745
www.wolf1051.com
sfurco@wolf1051.com
License: Sylvan Beach, Oswego County, NY held by WOLF Radio Inc.
Group Owner: WOLF Radio Inc.; (acq 2-28-2002; $350,000)
Population Served: 145,151 *Arbitron Metro Market:* Syracuse, NY
Sam Furco, General Manager
Sam Furco, Station Manager
John Hunt, General Sales Mgr
Skip Clark, Programming Director
Taylor Smith, Promotions Manager

Syosset

*WKWZ
07-24-1973; 88.5 mhz FM; 0.125 kw; 259 ft.; N40 47 48 W73 27 44
Pell Lane, Syosset, NY 11791 US
(516) 364-5745, *Fax:* (516) 364-5737
www.wkwz.org
BigDave5@aol.com
License: Syosset, Nassau County, NY held by Syosset Central School District.
Format: Variety/Diverse *Special Programming:* C&W 6 hrs, class 6 hrs, jazz 12 hrs wkly
David Favilla, General Manager
Chris Hoffman, Station Manager
Roy Dippel, Chief Engineer

Syracuse

*WAER
04-01-1947; 88.3 mhz FM *Hrs Open:* 24; 50 kw; 276 ft.; N43 2 1 W76 7 53
215 University Place, Syracuse, NY 13244 US
(315) 443-4021, *Fax:* (315) 443-2148
www.waer.org
waer@waer.org
License: Syracuse, Onondaga County, NY held by Syracuse University.
Nat'l Network: NPR
Arbitron Metro Market: Syracuse NY *Format:* Jazz, News, 84 *Special Programming:* Gospel 3 hrs, blues 3 hrs, world mus 4 hrs, new age 3 hrs wkly *Hrs. of News Programming:* news progmg 20 hrs wkly *No. News Employees:* 3 *Target Audience:* 25-49.
Joe Lee, General Manager
Ron Ockert, Programming Director
Eric Cohen, Music Director

*WCNY-FM
12-04-1971; 91.3 mhz FM *Hrs Open:* 5 AM-midnight; 18.5 kw; 741 ft.; N42 56 42 W76 1 28
Mailing Address: P.O. Box 2400, 506 Old Liverpool Rd, Syracuse, NY 13220 US
Second Address: 506 Old Liverpool Rd., Liverpool, NY 13088
(315) 453-2424, *Fax:* (315) 451-8824
www.wcny.org
wcny-fm@wcny.org
License: Syracuse, Onondaga County, NY held by Public Broadcasting Council of Central New York.
Nat'l Network: NPR
Arbitron Metro Market: Syracuse, NY *TV Affiliate:* *WCNY-TV affil *Format:* Classical *Special Programming:* Bluegrass 3 hrs, jazz 7 hrs wkly *Target Audience:* General.
Colleen Edwards, CFO
Don Dolloff, Programming Director
Peter Hirsch, Promotions Manager
John Duffy, Chief Engineer

WFBL
02-04-1922; 1390 khz AM; 5 kw-D, DA2; 5 kw-N, DA2; N43 9 10 W76 11 35
P.O. Box 3003, Blue Bell, PA 19422 US
(315) 635-3971, *Fax:* (315) 635-3490
www.wfbl.com
d.wagner@lmgiradio.com
License: Syracuse, NY held by Buckley Broadcasting of New York LLC.
Group Owner: Buckley Broadcasting Corp.; (acq 11-10-2003; $1.2 million)
Arbitron Metro Market: Syracuse, NY *Format:* Talk
Judith Kelly, Operations Dir
Don Wagner, General Manager
Kristine Gladle, Promotions Manager
Bryan Richards, Operations Manager

WHEN
04-14-1941; 620 khz AM *Hrs Open:* 24; 5 kw-D, DAN; 1 kw-N, DAN; N43 5 32 W76 11 22; N43 5 34 W76 11 17
200 Concord Plaza, Suite 600, San Antonio, TX 78216 US
(315) 472-9797, *Fax:* (315) 472-1904
www.sportsradio620.com
wsyrnews@clearchannel.com
License: Syracuse, NY held by CC Licenses LLC.
Group Owner: Clear Channel Communications Inc.; (acq 1999)
Arbitron Metro Market: Syracuse, NY *Format:* Sports *Special Programming:* Syracuse Chiefs, Buffalo Bills, Syracuse Crunch
Rich Lauber, Operations Dir
Joel Delmonico, General Manager
Rick Yacobush, General Sales Mgr
Jason Furst, Programming Director
Joel Delmonico, Market Manager
Rob Wegman, Executive Producer

*WJPZ-FM
01-30-1985; 89.1 mhz FM *Hrs Open:* 24; 0.1 kw; 121 ft.; N43 2 1 W76 7 53
P. O. Box 239, Syracuse, NY 13210 US
(315) 443-4689, *Fax:* (315) 443-4379
www.z89.com
info@wjr.net
License: Syracuse, Onondaga County, NY held by WJPZ Radio Inc.
Arbitron Metro Market: Syracuse, NY *Format:* Contemporary Hits/Top 40 *Special Programming:* Black 12 hrs, pub service 13 hrs wkly *Target Audience:* 12-34; women & teenagers
Scott Purdy, Operations Dir
Geoff Herbert, General Manager
Louise Vazquez, General Sales Mgr
David McKinley, Programming Director
Joan Kump, Promotions Manager

WXTL
04-08-1996; 105.9 mhz FM *Hrs Open:* 24; 4 kw; 200 ft; N43 05 23 W76 09 10
1064 James St., Syracuse, NY 13203
(315) 472-0200, *Fax:* (315) 478-5625
www.lite1059.com
License: Syracuse, Onondaga County, NY
Group Owner: Cumulus Media Inc.; (acq 2000; grpsl).
Nat'l Network: CBS Radio
Population Served: 536,300 *Arbitron Metro Market:* Syracuse, NY *Target Audience:* 25-54; general
Tom Mitchell, Operations Dir
Dan Austin, General Manager
Angela Moonan, Programming Director

*WMHR
03-09-1969; 102.9 mhz FM *Hrs Open:* 24; 20 kw; 784 ft.; N42 58 1 W76 12 0
4044 Makyes Road, Syracuse, NY 13215 US
(315) 469-5051
www.marshillnetwork.org
mhn@marshillnetwork.org
License: Syracuse, Onondaga County, NY held by Mars Hill Broadcasting Co. Inc. dba Mars Hill Network.
Group Owner: Mars Hill Network
Nat'l Network: Moody; Salem Radio Network *Wire Services:* AP
Arbitron Metro Market: Syracuse, NY *Format:* Christian *Special Programming:* Children 11 hrs wkly *Hrs. of News Programming:* News progmg 6 hrs wkly *Target Audience:* General; Christian families
Clayton Roberts, President
Wayne Taylor, General Manager
Chris Tetta, Programming Director
Jeremy Miller, News Director
Valerie Smith, Traffic Manager

WSKO
01-01-1946; 1260 khz AM *Hrs Open:* 24; 5 kw-U, DA-2; N43 09 10 W76 11 35
1064 James St., Syracuse, NY 13203
(315) 472-0200, *Fax:* (315) 478-5625
www.espnradio1260.com
License: Syracuse, Onondaga County, NY
Group Owner: Cumulus Media Inc.
Nat'l Network: ESPN Radio
Population Served: 536,300 *Arbitron Metro Market:* Syracuse, NY *Target Audience:* 25-54; men
Tom Mitchell, Operations Dir
Dan Austin, General Manager
Angela Moonan, Programming Director

WNTQ
01-01-1956; 93.1 mhz FM *Hrs Open:* 24; 97 kw; 659 ft.; N42 56 48 W76 1 28
1064 James Street, Syracuse, NY 13203 US
(315) 472-0200, *Fax:* (315) 478-5625
www.93q.com
License: Syracuse, Onondaga County, NY
Group Owner: Cumulus Media Inc.; (acq 4-26-01; grpsl).
Nat'l Reps: McGavren Guild
Arbitron Metro Market: Syracuse, NY *Format:* Contemporary Hits/Top 40 *Target Audience:* 25-54; women
Tom Mitchell, Operations Dir
Dan Austin, General Manager
Janice Cole, Programming Director
Dave Edwards, Chief Engineer
Angela Moonan, Sales Director
Elizabeth Marcy, Traffic Manager

WOLF
04-27-1940; 1490 khz AM; 1 kw-D, DAD; 1 kw-N, DAD; N43 3 30 W76 10 0
401 West Kirkpatrick St., Syracuse, NY 13204 US
(315) 472-0222, *Fax:* (315) 478-7745
www.radiodisney.com
wolfam/fm@aol.com
License: Syracuse, NY held by WOLF Radio Inc.
Group Owner: WOLF Radio Inc.; acq 10-5-82).
Nat'l Network: Radio Disney
Arbitron Metro Market: Syracuse, NY *TV Affiliate:* Children

*WRVD
06-01-1999; 90.3 mhz FM *Hrs Open:* 24; 0.28 kw; 43 ft.; N43 2 27 W76 8 22 *Rebroadcasts:* Rebroadcasts WRVO(FM) Oswego 100%
14 Lanigan Hall, Oswego, NY 13126 US
(315) 312-3690, *Fax:* (315) 312-3174
wrvo.fm
feedback@wrvo.fm
License: Syracuse, Onondaga County, NY held by State University of New York.
Nat'l Network: NPR
Arbitron Metro Market: Syracuse, NY *Format:* Variety/Diverse *Hrs. of News Programming:* news progmg 140 hrs wkly *No. News Employees:* 4 *Target Audience:* 35-54. *Adv. Rates:* 60, 50, 60, 40
Pam Cantine, Operations Dir
Michael S. Ameigh, General Manager
Matt Seuert, General Sales Mgr
Fred Vigeant, Programming Director
Jeff Windsor, Chief Engineer

WSYR
01-01-1922; 570 khz AM *Hrs Open:* 24; 5 kw-D, DA2; 5 kw-N, DA2; N42 59 13 W76 9 9
200 Concord Plaza, Suite 600, San Antonio, TX 78216 US
(315) 472-9797, *Fax:* (315) 472-1904
www.sybercuse.com
License: Syracuse, NY held by CC Licenses LLC.
Group Owner: Clear Channel Communications Inc.
Nat'l Network: PRI
Arbitron Metro Market: Syracuse, NY *Format:* News, News/Talk, 86 *Hrs. of News Programming:* News progmg 35 hrs wkly *Target Audience:* 25-54.
Joel Delmonico, General Manager

WWHT
09-01-1958; 107.9 mhz FM *Hrs Open:* 24; 50 kw; 499 ft.; N42 57 21 W76 6 36
200 Concord Plaza, Suite 600, San Antonio, TX 78216 US
(315) 472-9797, *Fax:* (315) 472-2323
www.hot1079.com
joeldelmonico@clearchannel.com
License: Syracuse, Onondaga County, NY held by CC Licenses LLC.
Group Owner: Clear Channel Communications Inc.

Arbitron Metro Market: Syracuse, NY *Format:* Contemporary Hits/Top 40
Rich Lauber, Operations Dir
Vincent Sparzak, General Manager
Rick Yacobush, General Sales Mgr
A.J., Programming Director
Joel Delmonico, Market Manager

WYYY
01-01-1946; 94.5 mhz FM; 100 kw; 650 ft.; N42 56 46 W76 7 7
200 Concord Plaza, Suite 600, San Antonio, TX 78216 US
(315) 472-9797, *Fax:* (315) 472-1904
www.sybercuse.com
License: Syracuse, Onondaga County, NY
Group Owner: Clear Channel Communications Inc.
Arbitron Metro Market: Syracuse, NY *Format:* Adult Contemp
Jim Storey, COO
J.P. Ferrell, General Sales Mgr
Karla Melvin, News Director

Ticonderoga

***WANC**
09-06-1982; 103.9 mhz FM *Hrs Open:* 24; 1.55 kw; 381 ft.; N43 49 55 W73 24 28 *Rebroadcasts:* Rebroadcasts WAMC-FM Albany 100%
318 Central Avenue, Albany, NY 12206 US
(518) 465-5233(800) 323-9262, *Fax:* (518) 432-6974
www.wamc.org
mail@wamc.org
License: Ticonderoga, Essex County, NY held by WAMC.
Group Owner: WAMC/Northeast Public Radio; (acq 8-90; $400,000;
Nat'l Network: NPR; PRI *Wire Services:* AP
Arbitron Metro Market: Ticonderoga, NY *Format:* News, Talk *Special Programming:* Folk 6 hrs, jazz 17 hrs wkly *Target Audience:* General.
Alan Chartock, CEO
Selma Kaplan, Operations Dir
David Galletly, Vice President

Troy

WFLY
08-01-1948; 92.3 mhz FM *Hrs Open:* 24; 17 kw; 850 ft.; N42 38 16 W73 59 55
6 Johnson Road, Latham, NY 12110 US
(518) 786-6600, *Fax:* (518) 786-6610
www.fly92.com
ally@fly92.com
License: Troy, Rensselaer County, NY held by 6 Johnson Road Licenses Inc.
Group Owner: Pamal Broadcasting Ltd.; (acq 10-19-2001; grpsl)
Nat'l Network: ABC *Nat'l Reps:* McGavren Guild
Arbitron Metro Market: Albany-Schenectady-Troy, NY *Format:* Contemporary Hits/Top 40 *Hrs. of News Programming:* news progmg 5 hrs wkly *No. News Employees:* 1 *Target Audience:* 18-49. *Adv. Rates:* 175; 150;175; 100
Kevin Callahan, Operations Dir
Dan Austin, General Manager
Suzette Anthony, General Sales Mgr
Terry O'Donnell, Programming Director
Justin Chabot, Promotions Manager
Mike Carey, News Director

WHAZ
08-01-1922; 1330 khz AM *Hrs Open:* 24; 1 kw-D, ND1; 0.049 kw-N, ND1; N42 46 35 W73 41 10
30 Park Ave, Cohoes, NY 12047 US
(518) 237-1330, *Fax:* (518) 235-4468
www.whaz.com
events@aliveradionetwork.com
License: Troy, NY held by Capital Media Corp.
Group Owner: Capital Media Corp.; (acq 9-24-87)
Arbitron Metro Market: Albany-Schenectady-Troy, NY *Format:* Christian *Special Programming:* Gospel, rel *Target Audience:* 25-75; young to old
Paul Lotters, President
Steven Klob, Operations Dir
Rex Gregory, Programming Director
Bill Rosenfeld, Chief Engineer

***WRPI**
11-01-1957; 91.5 mhz FM *Hrs Open:* 6 AM-2 AM; 10 kw; 371 ft.; N42 41 14 W73 42 22
110 8th Street, Troy, NY 12180 US
(518) 276-6248, *Fax:* (518) 276-2360
www.wrpi.org
License: Troy, Rensselaer County, NY held by Rensselaer Polytechnic Institute.
Arbitron Metro Market: Albany-Schenectady-Troy, NY *Format:* Variety/Diverse *Hrs. of News Programming:* News progmg 5 hrs wkly *Target Audience:* General; open minded, educated listeners
John Corbett, President
Colin Fredericks, General Manager

WOFX
04-15-1940; 980 khz AM; 5 kw-D, DAN; 5 kw-N, DAN; N42 46 56 W73 50 7
600 Congress Ave., Suite 1400, Austin, TX 78701 US
(518) 452-4800, *Fax:* (518) 452-4813
www.wofx.com
info@wofx.com
License: Troy, NY held by Capstar TX L.P.
Group Owner: Clear Channel Communications Inc.; (acq 8-30-00; grpsl).
Nat'l Reps: Clear Channel
Arbitron Metro Market: Albany, NY *Format:* Sports, Talk *Target Audience:* 18-49.
Kristen Delaney, VP & General Manager
Vera Hope, General Sales Mgr
John Cooper, Operations Manager & Program Director
Jill Manti, Marketing Director
Mike Arce, Online Content Director

Trumansburg

WPIE
01-15-1990; 1160 khz AM *Hrs Open:* 24; 5 kw-D, DA2; 0.31 kw-N, DA2; N42 32 42 W76 42 39
1705 Lake Street, Elmira, NY 14901 US
(607) 733-5626, *Fax:* (607) 733-5627
wpieradio.com
ppinesmedia1@stny.rr.com
License: Trumansburg, NY held by Pembrook Pines Ithaca Ltd.
Group Owner: Pembrook Pines Media Group; (acq 3-3-93; $150,000;
Nat'l Network: ESPN Radio
Arbitron Metro Market: Ithaca, NY *Format:* Sports *Hrs. of News Programming:* news progmg 18 hrs wkly *No. News Employees:* 1 *Target Audience:* 25-54; mature, upscale adults
Robert Pfuntner, President
Todd Mallison, Station Manager

Tupper Lake

WRGR
02-29-1980; 102.1 mhz FM *Hrs Open:* 24; 0.14 kw; 1447 ft.; N44 9 35 W74 28 34 *Rebroadcasts:* Rebroadcasts WLPW(FM) Lake Placid 100%
P.O. Box 831, Lake Placid, NY 12946 US
(518) 891-1544, *Fax:* (518) 891-1545
www.wnbz.com
sales@wnbz.com
License: Tupper Lake, Franklin County, NY held by Radio Lake Placid Inc.
Group Owner: Mountain Communications; (acq 2003; grpsl)
Nat'l Network: ABC *Wire Services:* UPI
Format: Adult Contemp, Classic Rock *Special Programming:* Relg one hr, big band 2 hrs wkly *Hrs. of News Programming:* news progmg 2 hrs wkly *No. News Employees:* 2 *Target Audience:* 25-54; men
Ted Morgan, President

***WXLS**
88.3 mhz FM; 0.11 kw; 1421 ft.; N44 9 34 W74 28 34
US
(315) 229-5356, *Fax:* (315) 229-5373
www.ncpr.org
radio@ncpr.org
License: Tupper Lake, Franklin County, NY held by The St. Lawrence University.
Arbitron Metro Market: Tupper Lake, NY *Format:* Public Affairs *No. News Employees:* 3
Shelly Pike, Operations Dir
Ellen Rocco, General Manager
Ellen Rocco, Station Manager
Jackie Sauter, Programming Director
Martha Foley, News Director
Bob Sauter, Chief Engineer
Bill Haenel, New Media Developer
Joel Hurd,Production Manager
Naomi Weller, Office Manager

Unadilla

***WCIJ**
88.9 mhz FM; 5 kw vert; 791 ft.; N42 23 27 W75 19 41
US
(607) 776-4151, *Fax:* (607) 776-6929
www.fln.org
mail@fln.org
License: Unadilla, Sullivan County, NY held by Family Life Ministries Inc.
Group Owner: Family Life Network
Arbitron Metro Market: Unadilla, NY *Format:* Christian
Dick Snavely, Founder, CFO
Rick Snavely, President, CEO
Rick Snavely, General Manager
Sammy Carrillo, Program Director / Promotions Director
Gary Farnham, Engineering Dir
Jeff Harmon, Chief Operating Officer
Katie Bernier, YouthCoordinator
Dave Best, Business Manager
Debbie Fero, Events Coordinator
Nick Finlayson, Head Chef
Tom Fuest, Public Relations / Underwriting Director

Utica

WFRG-FM
10-10-1948; 104.3 mhz FM; 100 kw; 456 ft.; N43 3 22.9 W75 25 2
One Forever Drive, Hollidaysburg, PA 16648 US
(315) 768-9500, *Fax:* (315) 736-3311
www.bigfrog104.com
info@bigfrog104.com
License: Utica, Oneida County, NY
Group Owner: Townsquare Media; (acq 11-5-99; grpsl)
Arbitron Metro Market: Utica-Rome, NY *Format:* Country *Target Audience:* 25-54.
Mary Jo Beach, General Manager
Tracy DeCarr, General Sales Mgr
Bill McAdams, Programming Director
Dave Andrews, News Director

WIBX
12-05-1925; 950 khz AM *Hrs Open:* 24; 5 kw-U, DA1; N43 6 12 W75 20 31
One Forever Drive, Hollidaysburg, PA 16648 US
(315) 768-9500, *Fax:* (315) 736-0720
www.wibx950.com
jeff.monaski@townsquaremedia.com
License: Utica, NY
Group Owner: Townsquare Media; (acq 2-11-2000; grpsl)
Nat'l Network: CBS
Arbitron Metro Market: Utica-Rome, NY *Format:* News, News/Talk, 84, Talk *Special Programming:* Pol 3 hrs, farm 14 hrs wkly *No. News Employees:* 5 *Target Audience:* 35-64; middle to upper income adults
Tom Jacobson, Operations Dir
Mary Jo Beach, General Manager
Tracy DeCarr, General Sales Mgr
Jeff Monaski, Programming Director

WLZW
01-01-1972; 98.7 mhz FM *Hrs Open:* 24; 25 kw; 659 ft.; N43 8 39 W75 10 45
One Forever Drive, Hollidaysburg, PA 16648 US
(315) 768-9500, *Fax:* (315) 736-0720
www.lite987.com
eric.meier@townsquaremedia.com
License: Utica, Oneida County, NY
Group Owner: Townsquare Media
Arbitron Metro Market: Utica-Rome, NY *Format:* Adult Contemp *No. News Employees:* 6 *Target Audience:* 25-54; middle to upper income & educ levels
Mary Jo Beach, General Manager
Tracy DeCarr, General Sales Mgr
Eric Meier, Programming Director

WOUR
06-01-1967; 96.9 mhz FM; 19.5 kw; 791 ft.; N43 8 46 W75 10 40
800 Corporate Circle, Suite 201, Harrisonburg, PA 17110 US
(315) 797-0803
www.wour.com,www.galaxycommunications.com
License: Utica, Oneida County, NY held by Galaxy Utica Licensee LLC.
Group Owner: Galaxy Communications L.P.; (acq 9-21-2007; grpsl)
Arbitron Metro Market: Utica-Rome, NY *Format:* Rock/AOR *Target Audience:* 25-49; adults
Brian Delaney, General Manager
Jerry Kraus, Promotions Manager

***WPNR-FM**
11-01-1977; 90.7 mhz FM; 0.43 kw; -141 ft.; N43 5 47 W75 16 19
1600 Burrstone Road, Deperno Hall Room 413, Utica, NY 13502 US
(315) 792-3066,(315) 792-3069, *Fax:* (315) 792-3292
License: Utica, Oneida County, NY held by Utica College.
Arbitron Metro Market: Utica-Rome, NY *Format:* Rock/AOR, Variety/Diverse *Special Programming:* Class 10 hrs, jazz 14 hrs, reggae 5 hrs wkly

Todd Hutton, President

***WKVU**
04-23-1962; 107.3 mhz FM; 50 kw; Ant 499 ft; N43 08 40 W75 10 32
2351 Sunset Blvd., Suite 170-218, Rocklin, CA 13039
(916) 251-1600, *Fax:* (916) 251-1650
www.air1.com
info@air1.com
License: Utica, Oneida County, NY held by Educational Media Foundation.
Group Owner: EMF Broadcasting; (acq 10-24-2007; $1,224,000)
Nat'l Network: Air 1
Population Served: 8,500 *Arbitron Metro Market:* Utica-Rome, NY
Mike Novak, President

WUTI
04-24-1948; 1150 khz AM; 5 kw-D, 1 kw-N, DA-2; N43 10 31 W75 21 03
318 Central Ave., Albany, NY 16648
(518) 465-5233, *Fax:* (518) 432-6974
www.wamc.org
mail@wamc.org
License: Utica, Oneida County, NY held by WAMC.
Group Owner: WAMC/Northeast Public Radio; (acq 7-6-2005; $275,000)
Nat'l Network: NPR; PRI *Wire Services:* AP
Population Served: 91,611 *Arbitron Metro Market:* Utica-Rome, NY
Alan Chartock, CEO
Selma Kaplan, Operations Dir
David Galletly, Vice President

***WRVN**
06-04-1986; 91.9 mhz FM; 1.9 kw; -62 ft.; N43 8 31 W75 13 36
Rebroadcasts: Rebroadcasts WRVO(FM) Oswego 100%
State University Plaza, Albany, NY 12246 US
(315) 312-3690, *Fax:* (315) 312-3174
www.wrvo.fm
feedback@wrvo.fm
License: Utica, Oneida County, NY held by State University of New York.
Nat'l Network: NPR; PRI *Wire Services:* AP
Arbitron Metro Market: Utica-Rome, NY *Format:* Variety/Diverse *Hrs. of News Programming:* news progmg 140 hrs wkly *No. News Employees:* 3 *Adv. Rates:* 60; 50; 60; 40
Pam Cantine, Operations Dir
John Krauss, General Manager
Thomas Herbert, General Sales Mgr
Fred Vigeant, Programming Director
Catherine Loper, News Director
Jeff Windsor, Chief Engineer

WTLB
01-01-1946; 1310 khz AM *Hrs Open:* 24; 5 kw-D, DA2; 0.5 kw-N, DA2; N43 3 24 W75 16 42
7536 Murray Drive, Cierco, NY 13039 US
(315) 797-1330, *Fax:* (315) 738-1073
wour.com
askwour@wour.com
License: Utica, NY held by Galaxy Communications L.P.
Group Owner: Galaxy Communications L.P.; (acq 4-6-2000; grpsl)
Arbitron Metro Market: Utica, NY *Format:* Adult Contemp *Hrs. of News Programming:* News progmg one hr wkly *Target Audience:* 55 plus.
Ed Levine, President
Jason Passante, General Manager
Dave Doughty, Chief Engineer

***WUNY**
10-30-1985; 89.5 mhz FM *Hrs Open:* 5 AM-midnight; 6.3 kw; 778 ft.; N43 8 38 W75 10 40
P.O. Box 2400, 506 Old Liverpool Rd, Syracuse, NY 13220 US
(315) 453-2424, *Fax:* (315) 451-8824
www.wcny.org
wcny—online@wcny.org
License: Utica, Oneida County, NY held by Public Broadcasting Council of Central New York.
Nat'l Network: NPR
Arbitron Metro Market: Utica, NY *Format:* Talk *Special Programming:* Bluegrass 3 hrs, jazz 7 hrs wkly *Target Audience:* General.
Colleen Edwards, CFO
Peter Hirsch, Promotions Manager

WUSP
01-29-1962; 1550 khz AM *Hrs Open:* 24; 1 kw-D; N43 06 48 W75 15 25 *Rebroadcasts:* Rebroadcasts WRNY(AM) Rome 100%
Mayro Bldg., 239 Genesee St., Utica, NY 17110
(315) 797-0803, *Fax:* (315) 797-7813
License: Utica, Oneida County, NY held by Roser Communications Network Inc.
Group Owner: Roser Communications Network Inc.; (acq 10-24-2007; grpsl)
Nat'l Network: Westwood One *Nat'l Reps:* Christal
Population Served: 91,611 *Arbitron Metro Market:* Utica-Rome, NY *Special Programming:* It 2 hrs, Pol 4 hrs wkly *Target Audience:* 35 plus; 60% female, 40% male
Brian Delaney, General Manager
Gene Conte, Programming Director
Jack Moran, News Director
Joe Petro, Chief Engineer

WUTQ-FM
07-11-1994; 100.7 mhz FM *Hrs Open:* 24; 1.2 w; 551 ft; N43 09 12 W75 09 32
1017 Higby Rd., New Hartford, NY 13413
(315) 793-1007, *Fax:* (315) 793-1044
www.klove.com
License: Utica, Oneida County, NY held by Roser Communications Network
Group Owner: EMF Broadcasting; (acq 6-7-01; $1.25 million).
Nat'l Network: K-Love
Arbitron Metro Market: Utica-Rome, NY *Target Audience:* 25-45.
Bob Cain, Operations Dir

Valhalla

***WARY**
10-03-1973; 88.1 mhz FM *Hrs Open:* 10 AM-10 PM (M-F); 0.042 kw horiz, 0.039 kw vert; 404 ft.; N41 4 13 W73 47 25
75 Grasslands Road, Valhalla, NY 10595 US
(914) 606-6752(914) 606-6753, *Fax:* (914) 606-6260
www.881wary.webs.com
radprime1@aol.com
License: Valhalla, Westchester County, NY held by Westchester Community College.
Arbitron Metro Market: New York *Format:* Rock/AOR *Special Programming:* Pub svc 10 hrs wkly *Target Audience:* 12-24.
Radames Ocasio, General Manager

Vestal

WMXW
06-02-1989; 103.3 mhz FM *Hrs Open:* 24; 0.52 kw; 1099 ft.; N42 3 40 W75 56 45
3301 Country Club Road, Suite 2218, Endwell, NY 13760 US
(607) 584-5800, *Fax:* (607) 584-5900
www.mix1033fm.com
TomBarney@clearchannel.com
License: Vestal, Broome County, NY held by CC Licenses LLC.
Group Owner: Clear Channel Communications Inc.; (acq 9-2000; grpsl)
Nat'l Reps: Katz Radio
Arbitron Metro Market: Binghamton, NY *Format:* Adult Contemp *No. News Employees:* 1 *Target Audience:* 25-54.
Jim Free, Operations Dir
Tom Barney, General Manager
Dave Lozzi, Programming Director

Voorheesville

WAJZ
05-24-1991; 96.3 mhz FM *Hrs Open:* 24; 0.47 kw; 961 ft.; N42 38 11 W74 0 2
6 Johnson Road, Latham, NY 12110 US
(518) 786-6624, *Fax:* (518) 786-6610
www.jamz963.com
pryan@albanybroadcasting.com
License: Voorheesville, Albany County, NY held by 6 Johnson Road Licenses Inc.
Group Owner: Pamal Broadcasting Ltd.; (acq 10-19-2001; grpsl).
Nat'l Reps: McGavren Guild
Arbitron Metro Market: Voorheesville, NY *Format:* Christian *Special Programming:* Relg one hr wkly *Hrs. of News Programming:* news progmg 3 hrs wkly *No. News Employees:* 2 *Target Audience:* 18-49. *Adv.Rates:* 100; 100; 125; 75
Dan Austin, General Manager
Suzette Anthony, General Sales Mgr
Rob Torres, Programming Director
J.D. Reoman, Promotions Manager
Mike Carey, News Director
Peter Baumann, General Sales Manager
Christa Gardner, PromotionsDirector

Walton

WDLA
05-30-1951; 1270 khz AM; 5 kw-D, ND1; 0.089 kw-N, ND1; N42 8 10 W75 4 48
Route 206, Atop Bear Mountain, Walton, NY 13856 US
(607) 432-1030, *Fax:* (607) 865-4189
www.cnynews.com
George.Wells@townsquaremedia.com
License: Walton, NY held by Double O Central New York Corp.
Group Owner: Double O Radio L.L.C.; (acq 10-22-2004; grpsl)
Arbitron Metro Market: Walton, NY *Format:* Oldies *Special Programming:* When Radio Was *Target Audience:* 28-55; general
Donald L. Perkins, Operations Dir
George Wells, General Manager
Steven Dillon, Director of Sales

WDLA-FM
11-16-1973; 92.1 mhz FM; 0.69 kw; 656 ft.; N42 8 10 W75 4 48
Route 6, Atop Bear Spring Mtn., Walton, NY 13856 US
(607) 432-1030
www.wdlafm.com/
George.Wells@townsquaremedia.com
License: Walton, Delaware County, NY
Group Owner: Double O Radio L.L.C.
Arbitron Metro Market: Walton, NY
Brian Cleary, Operations Dir
George Wells, General Manager
Steven Dillon, Director of Sales
Dixie Penner, Promotions Manager
Marie Merrill, News Director

Warrensburg

WKBE
01-01-1990; 100.3 mhz FM *Hrs Open:* 24; 1.45 kw; 1312 ft.; N43 25 12 W73 45 39
320 West College Ave., Pleasant Gap, PA 16823 US
(518) 786-6600, *Fax:* (518) 786-6610
License: Warrensburg, Warren County, NY held by 6 Johnson Road Licenses Inc.
Group Owner: Pamal Broadcasting Ltd.; (acq 10-9-2001).
Format: Contemporary Hits/Top 40 *Hrs. of News Programming:* news progmg 10 hrs wkly *No. News Employees:* 1 *Target Audience:* 18-34; women
Bill Hunt, General Manager

Warsaw

WCJW
05-16-1973; 1140 khz AM *Hrs Open:* Sunrise-sunset
3258 Merchant Rd., Warsaw, NY 14569 US
(585) 786-8131, *Fax:* (585) 786-2241
www.wcjw.com
wcjw@wcjw.com
License: Warsaw, NY held by Lloyd Lane Inc.
Nat'l Network: USA *Regional Reps:* Regional Reps
Arbitron Metro Market: Warsaw, NY *Format:* Agriculture, Country, 60, Sports *Special Programming:* Farm 11 hrs wkly *Hrs. of News Programming:* news progmg 20 hrs wkly *No. News Employees:* 1 *Target Audience:* 25-54; adults *Adv. Rates:* 16; 16; 16; na
Lloyd Lane, President
Lee Richey, Programming Director
Jenny Snow, News Director

Warwick

WTBQ
07-24-1969; 1110 khz AM *Hrs Open:* Sunrise-sunset
46 Old Middletown Road, Rockaway, NJ 07866 US
(845) 651-1110, *Fax:* (845) 651-1025
www.wtbq.com
am1110@magiccarpet.com
License: Warwick, NY held by FST Broadcasting Corp.
Nat'l Network: ABC; Jones Radio Networks
Arbitron Metro Market: Florida, NY *Format:* Oldies, Talk *Special Programming:* Folk one hr, Irish 2 hrs wkly *Hrs. of News Programming:* news progmg 10 hrs wkly *No. News Employees:* 2 *Target Audience:* 24-55; affluent Orange County-New York City commuters *Adv. Rates:* 20; 20; 20; 20
Frank Truatt, President
Rob McLean, General Sales Mgr
Logan Moscovitz, Programming Director
Rich Ball, Programming Director

Waterloo

WNYR-FM
04-19-1989; 98.5 mhz FM; 3.2 kw; 446 ft.; N42 48 22 W76 50 47
3568 Lenox Road, Geneva, NY 14456 US
(315) 781-7000, *Fax:* (315) 781-7700
License: Waterloo, Seneca County, NY held by Lake Country Broadcasting.
Arbitron Metro Market: Rochester, NY *TV Affiliate:* Adult Contemp *Special Programming:* news progmg 5 hrs wkly *Hrs. of News Programming:* 1 *No. News Employees:* 25-54. *Adv. Rates:* 18; 15; 18; 12

Operations Manager

Watertown

WATN
02-03-1941; 1240 khz AM *Hrs Open:* 24; 1 kw-U, ND1; N43 58 49 W75 56 12
199 Wealtha Ave., Watertown, NY 13601 US
(315) 782-1240, *Fax:* (315) 782-0312
www.gisco.net/watn/
watn1240@gisco.net
License: Watertown, NY held by Community Broadcasters LLC.
Group Owner: Community Broadcasters LLC; (acq 2-8-2007; grpsl)
Nat'l Reps: Roslin
Arbitron Metro Market: Watertown, NY *Format:* Talk
James Leven, President
Todd Dalesandro, Operations Dir
David Mance, General Manager

WCIZ-FM
08-25-1986; 93.3 mhz FM *Hrs Open:* 24; 6 kw; 328 ft.; N43 57 23 W75 50 45
One Forever Drive, Hollidaysbrg, PA 16648 US
(315) 788-0790, *Fax:* (315) 788-4379
www.z93.fm
lisa.kerber@smgny.com
License: Watertown, Jefferson County, NY held by Stephens Media Group-Watertown LLC.
Group Owner: Stephens Family L.P.
Arbitron Metro Market: Watertown, NY *Format:* Oldies *Hrs. of News Programming:* news progmg 2 hrs wkly *No. News Employees:* 3 *Target Audience:* 35-54.
Dick Snavely, CFO
Rick Snavely, President
John Owens, Programming Director
Jim Travis, Chief Engineer

WFRY-FM
11-22-1968; 97.5 mhz FM; 97 kw; 476 ft.; N43 57 23 W75 50 45
134 Mullin Street, Watertown, NY 13601 US
(315) 788-0790, *Fax:* (315) 788-4379
www.froggy97.com
eliva.gaines@smgny.com
License: Watertown, Jefferson County, NY held by Stephens Media Group-Watertown LLC.
Group Owner: Stephens Family L.P.
Arbitron Metro Market: Watertown, NY *Format:* Country
Matt Raisman, Programming Director
Web Foote, Disc Jockey
Annie Croakly, Disc Jockey
James Pond, Disc Jockey

*WJNY
07-24-1986; 90.9 mhz FM *Hrs Open:* 5 AM-midnight; 7.1 kw; 449 ft.; N43 51 44 W75 43 40 *Rebroadcasts:* Rebroadcasts WCNY-FM Syracuse
Mailing Address: 506 Old Liverpool Rd, PO Box 2400, Syracuse, NY 13220 US
Second Address: 506 Old Liverpool Pl., Syracuse, NY 13220
(315) 453-2424, *Fax:* (315) 451-8824
www.wcny.org
wcny-online@wcny.org
License: Watertown, Jefferson County, NY held by Public Broadcasting Council of Central New York Inc.
Nat'l Network: NPR
Arbitron Metro Market: Watertown, NY *Format:* Talk *Special Programming:* Bluegrass 3 hrs, jazz 5 hrs wkly
Coleen Edwards, CFO
Peter Hirsch, Promotions Manager

*WRVJ
07-01-1989; 91.7 mhz FM *Hrs Open:* 24; 1.6 kw; 443 ft.; N43 51 44 W75 43 40 *Rebroadcasts:* Rebroadcasts WRVO(FM) Oswego 100%
Lanigan Hall, Oswego, NY 13126 US
(315) 312-3690, *Fax:* (315) 312-3174
www.wrvo.com
feedback@wrvo.fm
License: Watertown, Jefferson County, NY held by State University of New York.
Nat'l Network: NPR; PRI *Wire Services:* AP
Arbitron Metro Market: Watertown, NY *Format:* Variety/Diverse *Hrs. of News Programming:* news progmg 140 hrs wkly *No. News Employees:* 4 *Target Audience:* 25-55. *Adv. Rates:* 60; 50; 60; 40
Lee Mitchell, Operations Dir
Michael S. Ameigh, General Manager
Matt Seubert, General Sales Mgr
Fred Vigeant, Programming Director
Chris Ulanowski, News Director
Jeff Windsor, Chief Engineer

*WSLJ
01-01-1992; 88.9 mhz FM *Hrs Open:* 24; 0.2 kw; 453 ft.; N43 57 23 W75 50 28 *Rebroadcasts:* Rebroadcasts WSLU(FM) Canton 100%
North Country Public Rad, Canton, NY 13617 US
(315) 229-5356, *Fax:* (315) 229-5373
www.ncpr.org
radio@ncpr.org
License: Watertown, Jefferson County, NY held by St. Lawrence University.
Arbitron Metro Market: Watertown, NY *Format:* Variety/Diverse *Hrs. of News Programming:* news progmg 35 hrs wkly *No. News Employees:* 2 *Target Audience:* General.
Shelly Pike, Operations Dir
Ellen Rocco, General Manager
Ellen Rocco, Station Manager
Jacqueline Sauter, Programming Director
Martha Foley, News Director
Robert Sauter, Chief Engineer
Sandra Demarest, Underwriting Director

WTNY
04-29-1941; 790 khz AM *Hrs Open:* 24; 1 kw-D, DAN; 1 kw-N, DAN; N43 56 44 W75 56 54
One Forever Drive, Hollidaysburg, PA 16648 US
(315) 788-0790, *Fax:* (315) 788-4379
www.production@790wtny.com
eliva.gaines@smgny.com
License: Watertown, NY held by Stephens Media Group-Watertown LLC.
Group Owner: Stephens Family L.P.
Nat'l Network: CBS
Arbitron Metro Market: Watertown, NY *Format:* News *Special Programming:* Farm 3 hrs wkly *Hrs. of News Programming:* news progmg 20 hrs wkly *No. News Employees:* 3 *Target Audience:* 25 plus.
Don Wagner, General Manager
Lance Thomas, Programming Director

WNER
11-02-1959; 1410 khz AM
One Forever Drive, Hollidaysburg, PA 16648 US
(315) 788-0790, *Fax:* (315) 788-4379
www.wner1410.com
eliva.gaines@smgny.com
License: Watertown, NY held by Stephens Media Group-Watertown LLC.
Group Owner: Stephens Family L.P.
Nat'l Network: ESPN Radio
Arbitron Metro Market: Watertown, NY *Format:* Sports *Target Audience:* 35-64.
Don Wagner, CFO
Lance Thomas, Programming Director

*WKWV
06-26-2000; 90.1 mhz FM *Hrs Open:* 24; 0.4 kw; 679 ft.; N43 57 15 W75 43 45 *Rebroadcasts:* Rebroadcasts KLVR(FM) Santa Rosa, CA 100%
Network Inc, 17102 Cty Rt 53 Pob 563, Dexter, NY 13634 US
(800) 525-5683, *Fax:* (916) 251-1650
www.klove.com
klove@klove.com
License: Watertown, Jefferson County, NY held by Educational Media Foundation.
Group Owner: EMF Broadcasting; (acq 1-13-2006; $300,000)
Nat'l Network: K-Love
Arbitron Metro Market: Omaha, NE *Format:* Christian *No. News Employees:* 13
Darrell Chambliss, Chairman
MIke Novak, President & CEO
David Pierce, Programming Director
Ed Lenane, News Director
Sam Wallington, Engineering Dir
Marya Morgan, News Reporter
Richard Hunt, News Reporter
Laura Daniels, NewsReporter
Tim Luttrell, News Reporter
Kenny Noble Cortes, News Reporter
Darren Vinson, News Reporter

Watervliet

WUAM
03-23-1964; 900 khz AM *Hrs Open:* 24
8 Broadcast Plaza, Armonk, NY 10504 US
(518) 899-3000, *Fax:* (518) 899-3057
www.alnews9.com
wabymoon@aol.com
License: Watervliet, NY held by Anastos Media Group Inc.
Group Owner: Anastos Media Group Inc.; (acq 9-99; $100,000)
Arbitron Metro Market: Albany-Schenectady-Troy, NY *Format:* News *Target Audience:* 25 plus.
Fran Dingman, General Manager
John Meaney, Station Manager
Fran Dingham, Promotions Manager

Watkins Glen

WRCE
06-22-1968; 1490 khz AM
Mailing Address: 1685 Four Mile Drive, Williamsport, PA 17701 US
Second Address: 1685 Four Mile Dr., Williamsport, PA 17701
(607) 732-4400, *Fax:* (607) 732-7774
License: Watkins Glen, NY held by Chemung County Radio Inc.
Group Owner: Backyard Broadcasting LLC; (acq 12-1-2002; grpsl)
Nat'l Reps: D & R Radio
Format: Country *Target Audience:* 20-49; baby boomers
Scott Free, Operations Dir
Margaret Tollner, General Manager
Brian Povancher, General Sales Mgr

*WRFI
91.9 mhz FM; 0.42 kw; -374 ft.; N42 23 20 W76 53 27 US
(607) 319-5445, *Fax:* (202) 965-1729
www.ithacaradio.org
License: Watkins Glen, Schuyler County, NY held by Ithaca Community Radio Inc.
Arbitron Metro Market: Watkins Glen, NY
Diane Cohen, Chairman
John Crigler, General Manager

Waverly

WAVR
10-01-1974; 102.3 mhz FM; 4.1 kw; 400 ft.; N42 3 48 W76 31 28
Rebroadcasts: Rebroadcasts WATS(AM) Sayre 100%
204 Desmond Street, Sayre, PA 18840 US
(307) 326-8642, *Fax:* (307) 326-8340
www.bigfoot99.com
bigfoot@bigfoot99.com
License: Waverly, Tioga County, NY held by Wats Broadcasting Inc.
Arbitron Metro Market: Saratoga WY *Format:* Country *No. News Employees:* 3 *Adv. Rates:* 21; 16; 20; 12
Jim O'Reilly, General Manager

Webster

WLGZ-FM
02-15-1993; 102.7 mhz FM *Hrs Open:* 24; 6 kw; 328 ft.; N43 10 14 W77 40 23
P.O. Box 3003, Blue Bell, PA 19422 US
(585) 264-1027, *Fax:* (585) 264-1165
legends1027.com
info@legends1027.com
License: Webster, Monroe County, NY held by Kimtron Inc.
Group Owner: Crawford Broadcasting Co.; (acq 11-25-92; $950,000;
Arbitron Metro Market: Rochester, NY *Format:* Oldies
Don Crawford Jr., General Manager
Mark Shuttleworth, Programming Director
Brian Cunningham, Chief Engineer

*WFRW
10-01-1988; 88.1 mhz FM *Hrs Open:* 24; 11 kw horiz, 8.5 kw vert; 338 ft.; N43 4 18 W77 5 35
4135 Northgate Blvd., Suite 1, Sacramento, CA 95834 US
(315) 331-7482, *Fax:* (410) 268-0931
www.familyradio.com
info@familyradio.com
License: Webster, Monroe County, NY held by Family Stations Inc.
Group Owner: Family Stations Inc.
Format: Religious *Special Programming:* Class 2 hrs wkly *Hrs. of News Programming:* News progmg 4 hrs wkly *Target Audience:* General.
Harold Camping, President

*WMHN
02-29-1988; 89.3 mhz FM *Hrs Open:* 24; 1 kw; 75 ft; N43 13 45 W77 26 52 *Rebroadcasts:* Rebroadcasts WMHR(FM) Syracuse 99%
4044 Makyes Rd., Syracuse, NY 13215
(315) 469-5051
www.marshillnetwork.org
mhn@marshillnetwork.org
License: Webster, Monroe County, NY held by Mars Hill Broadcasting Co. Inc.
Group Owner: Mars Hill Network

RADIO - U.S.

Nat'l Network: Moody; Salem Radio Network *Wire Services:* AP *Population Served:* 1,000,000*Special Programming:* Children 11 hrs wkly *Hrs. of News Programming:* News progmg 13 hrs wkly *Target Audience:* Christian families
Clayton Roberts, President
Mark Hard, Operations Dir
Wayne Taylor, General Manager
Kevin Kloss, Programming Director
Kevin Kloss, Traffic Manager
Mike Dwinell, Engineering

Wellsville

WJQZ
02-03-1986; 103.5 mhz FM; 1.75 kw; 620 ft.; N42 3 24 W78 0 34
2 Green Acres Court, Ellenville, NY 12428 US
(585) 593-6070, *Fax:* (585) 593-6212
oldiesz103.topcities.com
wjqzradio@yahoo.com
License: Wellsville, Allegany County, NY held by DBM Communications Inc.
Format: Oldies *Target Audience:* 25-54.
Robert Mangels, Programming Director

WLSV
10-31-1955; 790 khz AM; 1 kw-D, ND1; 0.041 kw-N, ND1; N42 4 37 W77 55 47
2 Green Acres Court, Ellenville, NY 12428 US
(585) 593-6070, *Fax:* (585) 593-6212
www.wlsv1.topcities.com
wlsv790am@yahoo.com
License: Wellsville, NY held by DBM Communications Inc.
Format: Country *Target Audience:* General.
Richard Mangels, President
Bob Mangels, News Director

WQRW
02-14-2007; 93.5 mhz FM; 1.1 kw; 768 ft.; N42 11 25 W77 49 17 US
(585) 593-9553, *Fax:* (585) 593-9554
www.q935fm.com
warw@93radioyahoo.com
License: Wellsville, Allegany County, NY held by Pembrook Pines Mass Media N.A. Corp.
Group Owner: Pembrook Pines Media Group
Arbitron Metro Market: Wellsville, NY *Format:* Contemporary Hits/Top 40
Robert Pfuntner, President
Jeff Wilson, Operations Dir
Rod Biehler, General Manager
Bob Lee, General Sales Mgr

Westhampton

WBON
11-18-1993; 98.5 mhz FM *Hrs Open:* 24; 0.95 kw; 525 ft.; N40 51 18 W72 46 11
1103 Stewart Ave, Garden City, NY 11530 US
(865) 693-1020, *Fax:* (865) 693-3791
www.lafiestali.com
johnc@moreyorg.com
License: Westhampton, Suffolk County, NY held by Jarad Broadcasting Co. of Westhampton Inc.
Group Owner: The Morey Organization Inc.
Nat'l Reps: Christal
Arbitron Metro Market: Westhampton, NY
John Caracciolo, President

Westport

WCLX
01-01-1995; 102.9 mhz FM *Hrs Open:* 24; 6 kw; Ant 312 ft; N44 13 15 W73 24 41
Mailing Address: Westport Broadcasting, 19 Boas Lane, Wilton, CT 06897
Second Address: 560 Lake St., Bridport, VT 05734-9593
(203) 762-9425, *Fax:* (802) 758-5000
www.wclxfm.com
wwdj@optonline.net
License: Westport, Essex County, NY held by Westport Broadcasting.
Population Served: 150,000 *Arbitron Metro Market:* Burlington-Plat *Target Audience:* 25-54.
Dennis Jackson, CEO
Chip Morgan, General Manager
Kathy Morgan, Programming Director
Chip Morgan, Chief Engineer

Wethersfield Twnshp

WLKK
01-01-1948; 107.7 mhz FM *Hrs Open:* 24; 19.5 kw; 801 ft.; N42 37 23 W78 17 16
5500 Main Street, Williamsville, NY 14221 US
(716) 843-0600, *Fax:* (716) 832-3323
www.wben.com
License: Wethersfield Twnshp, Wyoming County, NY held by Entercom Buffalo License LLC.
Group Owner: Entercom Communications Corp.; (acq 5-5-2004; $9 million).
Nat'l Network: Westwood One
Arbitron Metro Market: Buffalo, NY *Format:* Classic Rock *Target Audience:* 25-54; adults
Tim Wegner, Operations Dir
Larry Robb, General Manager
Hank Dole, Programming Director
Jeff Surdej, Promotions Manager

White Plains

WFAS
08-11-1932; 1230 khz AM; 1 kw-U, ND1; N41 1 32 W73 49 39
601 University Avenue, Suite 211, Sacramnto, CA 95825 US
(914) 693-2400, *Fax:* (914) 693-0000
www.wfasam.com
Marty.Sheehan@cumulus.com
License: White Plains, NY held by Cumulus Licensing Corp.
Group Owner: Cumulus Media Inc.; (acq 1-23-2002; grpsl)
Nat'l Network: AP Radio *Nat'l Reps:* McGavren Guild
Arbitron Metro Market: White Plains, NY *Format:* Adult Contemp *Special Programming:* Sports progmg 8 hrs wkly *Hrs. of News Programming:* news progmg 5 hrs wkly *No. News Employees:* 2 *Target Audience:* General.
Dave Ashton, Operations Dir
Rod Colarco, General Manager
Marty Sheehan, Advertising & Sales Department
Bob Barnum, Program Director and News Department
Jennifer D'Ambrosio, Program Director and News Department
Val Cichorek, NewsDirector
Jennifer D'Ambrosio, Web Master

Whitehall

WNYV
07-14-1990; 94.1 mhz FM; 3 kw; 328 ft.; N43 28 37 W73 26 56
Mailing Address: PO Box 568, East Poultney, VT 05741 US
Second Address: Box 568, East Poultney, VT 5741
(802) 287-9031
License: Whitehall, Washington County, NY held by Pine Tree Broadcasting.
Nat'l Reps: Commercial Media Sales
TV Affiliate: Adult contemp *Format:* Big Band, Religious *Special Programming:* news progmg 3 hrs wkly *Hrs. of News Programming:* 1 *No. News Employees:* 25-55; active community o

Whitesboro

WSKS
01-01-1994; 97.9 mhz FM; 1.5 kw; 669 ft; N43 02 14 W75 26 40
Rebroadcasts: Rebroadcasts WOWB(FM) Little Falls 100%
185 Genesee St., Suite 1606, Utica, NY 13502
(315) 734-9245, *Fax:* (315) 624-9245
www.cnykiss.com
License: Whitesboro, Oneida County, NY held by Roser Communications Network Inc.
Group Owner: Roser Communications Network Inc.; (acq 10-24-2007; grpsl)
Arbitron Metro Market: Utica-Rome, NY
Ken Roser, President
Dave Silvers, Operations Dir
Ken Roser, General Manager
Granty Roser, General Sales Mgr
Shaun Andrews, Programming Director
Sean Morelle, Promotions Manager
Ken Ruhland, Chief Engineer

Willsboro

WXZO
01-01-1997; 96.7 mhz FM *Hrs Open:* 24; 1 kw; 797 ft.; N44 24 12 W73 26 2
600 Congress Ave., Suite 1400, Austin, TX 78701 US
(802) 655-0093, *Fax:* (802) 655-0478
www.theplanet967.com
Slater@theplanet967.com
License: Willsboro, Essex County, NY held by Vox AM/FM LLC.
Group Owner: Vox AM/FM LLC; (acq 7-25-2008; grpsl)
Arbitron Metro Market: Willsboro, NY *Format:* Talk
Tom Barney, General Manager
Jamie Dennis, Public Service Announcement Director

Windham

WRIP
08-05-1999; 97.9 mhz FM *Hrs Open:* 24; 580 w; Ant 1,056 ft; N42 17 06 W74 15 52
134 South St., PO Box 979, Windham, NY 06897
(518) 734-4747, *Fax:* (518) 734-9147
www.wripfm.com
wrip@mhcable.com
License: Windham, Greene County, NY held by Rip Radio LLC.
Nat'l Network: AP Network News *Regional Reps:* Local Focus - NYC
Population Served: 125,000 *Arbitron Metro Market:* Albany-Schenectady-Troy, NY *Special Programming:* AAA 5 hours, Classic Hits 4 hrs, Jazz 2 hrs, Christian contemp 2 hrs wkly *Hrs. of News Programming:* Approx 6 hrswkly (Net) *Target Audience:* 25 plus; mass appeal *Adv. Rates:* 25; 18; 18; 15
Dennis Jackson, CEO
Guy Garraghan, General Manager
Jay Fink, Station Manager

Windsor

*WIFF
01-01-1995; 90.1 mhz FM *Hrs Open:* 24; 0.1 kw; 686 ft.; N42 3 10 W75 42 7
1 Harry L Drive, Johnson City, NY 13790 US
(607) 732-2484, *Fax:* (607) 732-8704
www.csnradio.com
csnny@q969online.com
License: Windsor, Broome County, NY held by CSN International
Group Owner: CSN International; acq 5-30-2003; $67,000).
Arbitron Metro Market: Binghamton, NY *Format:* Adult Contemp, Christian *Hrs. of News Programming:* news progmg 8 hrs wkly *No. News Employees:* 2 *Target Audience:* General.
Lorenzo Galletti, General Manager
Gina Galletti, Programming Director

Woodstock

WDST
04-29-1980; 100.1 mhz FM *Hrs Open:* 24; 3 kw; 315 ft.; N41 59 24 W74 1 7
Mailing Address: 118 Tinker Street, P.O Box 367, Woodstock, NY 12498 US
Second Address: 293 Tinker St., Woodstock, NY 12498
(845) 679-7266(845) 679-7600, *Fax:* (845) 679-5395
www.radiowoodstock.com
live@radiowoodstock.com
License: Woodstock, Ulster County, NY held by CHET-5 Broadcasting L.P.
Nat'l Network: CBS Radio *Nat'l Reps:* Katz Radio
Arbitron Metro Market: Woodstock, NY *Format:* Alternative *Hrs. of News Programming:* news progmg 5 hrs wkly *No. News Employees:* 1 *Target Audience:* 24-55; upscale professionals
Gary Chetkof, Chairman
Gary Chetkof, GM
Mike Tuttle, Operations Dir
Stan Beinstein, General Sales Mgr
Jimmy Buff, Programming Director
Drew Frankel, Promotions Manager
Ike Phillips, National Sales Manager

Wurtsboro

WZAD
09-01-1990; 97.3 mhz FM *Hrs Open:* 24; 0.62 kw; 719 ft.; N41 36 4 W74 33 17
P.O. Box 416, Pendall Road, Poughkeepsie, NY 12602 US
(845) 471-1500, *Fax:* (845) 454-1204
License: Wurtsboro, Sullivan County, NY held by Cumulus Licensing Corp.
Group Owner: Cumulus Media Inc.; (acq 1-23-2002; grpsl).
Arbitron Metro Market: Newburgh-Middle *Format:* Country *Hrs. of News Programming:* news progmg 5 hrs wkly *No. News Employees:* 1 *Target Audience:* 25-54; upscale, educated
Lew Dickie, President
Charles Benfer, General Manager

Youngstown

WTOR
05-06-1998; 770 khz AM
21700 Northwestern Hwy., Twr 14, Ste 1190, Southfield, MI 48075 US
(248) 557-3500, *Fax:* (248) 557-2950
www.birach.com
sima@birach.com
License: Youngstown, NY held by Birach Broadcasting Corp.

Group Owner: Birach Broadcasting Corp.; acq 1996; $409,000 less land cost for CP)
Arbitron Metro Market: Southfield, MI *Format:* Religious *Target Audience:* Ethnic, Serbian, Lithuanian, Sp, Pol, Macedonian
Sima Birach, CEO

North Carolina

Ahoskie

***WBKU**
01-01-2002; 91.7 mhz FM; 87 kw; 430 ft.; N36 5 45 W77 12 30
P O Drawer 2440, Tupelo, MS 38803 US
(662) 844-8888, *Fax:* (662) 842-6791
www.afa.net/Radio/
License: Ahoskie, Hertford County, NC held by American Family Association.
Group Owner: American Family Radio
Arbitron Metro Market: Ahoskie, NC *Format:* Christian
Marvin Sanders, General Manager

WRCS
04-25-1948; 970 khz AM *Hrs Open:* 24; 1 kw-D, ND2; 0.08 kw-N, ND2; N36 16 46 W77 1 59
Route 1, Box B, Ahoskie, NC 27910 US
(252) 332-3101, *Fax:* (252) 332-3103
wrcs@gate811.net
License: Ahoskie, NC held by WRCS-AM 970 Inc.
Format: Gospel *Target Audience:* 12-70. *Adv. Rates:* 10; 10; 10; 10
J. Watford, General Manager

Albemarle

WSPC
07-01-1947; 1010 khz AM *Hrs Open:* 24; 1 kw-D, ND2; 0.064 kw-N, ND2; N35 22 40 W80 11 38
Mailing Address: P.O. Box 550, Albemarle, NC 28002 US
Second Address: 1234 Magnolia St., Albemarle, NC 28001
(704) 983-1580, *Fax:* (704) 983-1436
1010wspc.com
wspc@ctc.net
License: Albemarle, NC held by Stanly Communications Inc.
Format: News, News/Talk, 86 *No. News Employees:* 1 *Target Audience:* General. *Adv. Rates:* 18,18,18,10
Matt Smith, General Manager

WZKY
07-09-1956; 1580 khz AM *Hrs Open:* 24; 1 kw-D, ND1; 0.012 kw-N, ND1; N35 21 38 W80 10 39
Post Office Box 550, Albemarle, NC 28001 US
(704) 983-1580, *Fax:* (704) 983-1436
www.1010wspc.com
mattsmith@1010wspc.com
License: Albemarle, NC held by Stanly Communications Inc.
Regional Network: N.C. News Net.
Arbitron Metro Market: Albemarle, NC *Format:* News, Oldies, 84 *Target Audience:* 30 plus.
Matt Smith, President
Sherri Smith, Operations Dir
Leon Warren, News Director/Morning Show Host
Matt Smith, Manager/Owner
Jodi Johnson, Account Specalist

Asheboro

WKRR
11-01-1948; 92.3 mhz FM *Hrs Open:* 24; 100 kw; 1289 ft.; N35 49 59 W79 50 2
192 East Lewis Street, Greensboro, NC 27406 US
(336) 274-8042, *Fax:* (336) 274-1629
www.rock92.com
jgoodman@dbcradio.com
License: Asheboro, Randolph County, NC held by Dick Broadcasting Co. Inc. of Tennessee
Arbitron Metro Market: Greensboro-Winston Salem-High Point, NC *Format:* Classic Rock *Target Audience:* 18-49. *Adv. Rates:* 175; 125; 125; 30
James Kerr, Operations Dir
Bruce Wheeler, General Manager

WKXR
05-24-1947; 1260 khz AM *Hrs Open:* 24; 5 kw-D, DA2; 0.5 kw-N, DA2; N35 43 26 W79 48 21
1119 Eastview Drive, Asheboro, NC 27203 US
(336) 625-2187
www.wkxr.com
wkxr@atomic.net
License: Asheboro, NC held by Randolph Broadcasting Inc.
Nat'l Network: AP Network News; Jones Radio Networks
Regional Network: N.C. News Net.
Arbitron Metro Market: Greensboro-Winston Salem-High Point, NC *Format:* Country *Special Programming:* Farm one hr, gospel 10 hrs wkly *Hrs. of News Programming:* News progmg 8 hrs wkly *Target Audience:* 18 plus.
Edward Swicegood II, President
Ted Swicegood, Operations Dir
Larry Reid, Promotions Manager

***WTJY**
06-30-1999; 89.5 mhz FM *Hrs Open:* 24; 9.7 kw horiz, 7.8 kw vert; 535 ft.; N35 36 55 W79 53 28 *Rebroadcasts:* Rebroadcasts WXRI(FM) Winston-Salem Joy FM Network
P.O. Box 889, Blacksburg, VA 24063 US
(336) 788-1155, *Fax:* (336) 788-7199
www.joyfm.org
office@joyfm.org
License: Asheboro, Randolph County, NC held by Positive Alternative Radio Inc.
Group Owner: Positive Alternative Radio Inc.
Nat'l Network: Salem Radio Network
Arbitron Metro Market: Asheboro, NC *Format:* Gospel
Daniel Britt, Operations Dir
Sam Stutts, General Sales Mgr
Adam McCain, Promotions Manager
Candi Chandler, Director & Co-Host
Wanda Taylor, BusinessSupportRepresentative
Shelley Hicks, Office Manager
Stephanie Craddock Cook,Promotions & Office Assistant
Dona Martin, Events Calendar Coordinator & Office Assistant

WZOO
05-03-1971; 710 khz AM; 1 kw-D, DAD; N35 45 50 W79 50 4
P. O. Box 460, Asheboro, NC 27204 US
(336) 672-0944
www.wzooradio.com
License: Asheboro, NC held by Faith Enterprises Inc.
Format: Gospel
Huey Turner, General Manager

Asheville

***WCQS**
01-01-1975; 88.1 mhz FM *Hrs Open:* 24; 1.6 kw; 1168 ft.; N35 35 23 W82 40 26
73 Broadway, Asheville, NC 28801 US
(828) 210-4800, *Fax:* (828) 210-4801
www.wcqs.org
info@wcqs.org
License: Asheville, Buncombe County, NC held by Western N.C. Public Radio Inc.
Nat'l Network: NPR; PRI
Arbitron Metro Market: Asheville, NC *Format:* Jazz, News *Special Programming:* Folk 9 hrs wkly *Hrs. of News Programming:* news progmg 35 hrs wkly *No. News Employees:* 1 *Target Audience:* 25 plus. *Adv.Rates:* 36; 24; 36; 18
Lee Wilcher, Operations Dir
Ed Subkis, General Manager
Steve Busey, General Sales Mgr
Barbara Sayer, Programming Director
David Hurand, News Director
Tom Spaight, Chief Engineer
Michelle Keenan, Customer Support
Myra Fuller,Customer Support
Richard Kowal, Music Director

WISE
01-01-1939; 1310 khz AM *Hrs Open:* 24; 5 kw-D, DAN; 1 kw-N, DAN; N35 37 9 W82 34 21
P.O. Box 607, 401 Sawmill Road, Burnsville, NC 28714 US
(828) 253-1310, *Fax:* (828) 253-5619
www.wise-radio.com
wise-radio@hotmail.com
License: Asheville, NC held by Saga Communications of North Carolina, LLC
Nat'l Network: ESPN Radio
Arbitron Metro Market: Asheville, NC *Format:* Sports *Hrs. of News Programming:* news progmg 15 hrs wkly *No. News Employees:* 1 *Target Audience:* 35 plus; mature upscale audience *Adv. Rates:* 36; 25; 30; 21
Randy Cable, General Manager

***WLFA**
01-01-1975; 91.3 mhz FM; 440 w; 3,340 ft; N35 36 02 W82 39 07
2420 Wade Hampton Blvd., Greenville, SC 28802
(800) 849-8930,(828) 254-9532, *Fax:* (864) 292-8428
www.hisradio.com
comments@hisradio.com
License: Asheville, Buncombe County, NC held by Asheville Educational Association Inc.
Arbitron Metro Market: Asheville, NC
Ken Brantley, General Manager

WSKY
04-11-1947; 1230 khz AM *Hrs Open:* 20; 1 kw-U, ND1; N35 35 43 W82 33 57
P.O. Box 444, Spartanburg, SC 29304 US
(828) 251-2000, *Fax:* (828) 251-2135
www.wilkinsradio.com
wsky@wilkinsradio.com
License: Asheville, NC held by Wilkins Communications Network Inc.
Group Owner: Wilkins Communications Network Inc.; (acq 1996).
Nat'l Network: CBS; Salem Radio Network
Arbitron Metro Market: Asheville, NC *Format:* Oldies, Talk *Target Audience:* 35 plus. *Adv. Rates:* 30; 30; 30; 30
Mitchell Mathis, Pres/COO
Greg Garrett, Operations Dir
Ruthie Spears, General Manager
Tyger Elton, Chief Engineer
LuAnn Wilkins, Executive Vice President
Steve Stigall, Operations Director

WWNC
02-22-1927; 570 khz AM *Hrs Open:* 24
600 Congress Avenue, Suite 1400, Austin, TX 78701 US
(828) 257-2700, *Fax:* (828) 255-7850
www.wwnc.com
info@wwnc.com
License: Asheville, NC held by Capstar TX L.P.
Group Owner: Clear Channel Communications Inc.; (acq 8-30-2000; grpsl)
Nat'l Network: Motor Racing Net *Nat'l Reps:* McGavren Guild
Arbitron Metro Market: Asheville, NC *Format:* News, News/Talk, 86 *Special Programming:* Farm one hr, gospel 3 hrs, relg 3 hrs wkly *Hrs. of News Programming:* news progmg 30 hrs wkly *No. News Employees:* 3*Target Audience:* 25-54.
Mike Afflerbach, General Manager
John Rawson, General Sales Mgr
Brian Hall, Programming Director
Gene Austin, Sales Manager
Skip Wilson, Digital Sales Manager
Jessica Lee, Digital Content Director

Atlantic

WTKF
05-01-1992; 107.1 mhz FM; 46 kw; 625 ft.; N34 53 1 W76 30 22.3
Mailing Address: P.O. Box 70, Newport, NC 28570 US
Second Address: 5447 Hwy. 70, Morehead City, NC 28557
(252) 247-6343, *Fax:* (252) 247-7343
www.wtkf107.com
news@thetalkstation.com
License: Atlantic, Carteret County, NC held by Atlantic Ridge Telecasters Inc.
Nat'l Network: Westwood One; Motor Racing Net; USA *Regional Network:* N.C. News Net.
Arbitron Metro Market: Morehead City, NC *Format:* News, News/Talk, 84, Talk *Target Audience:* 25 plus; educated, informed
Lockwood Phillips, CEO
Shane Willis, Operations Dir
Ben Ball, Station Manager

Atlantic Beach

***WBJD**
01-01-1999; 91.5 mhz FM *Hrs Open:* 24; 85 kw; 384 ft.; N34 45 34 W76 51 16
800 College Court, New Bern, NC 28562 US
(252) 222-9832, *Fax:* (252) 638-3538
www.publicradioeast.org
jmcguire@publicradioeast.org
License: Atlantic Beach, Carteret County, NC held by Craven Community College.
Arbitron Metro Market: New Bern, NC *Format:* News
Kelly Batchelor, Operations Dir
Charles Wethington, General Manager
Chris Wethington, Station Manager
Jill McGuire, Programming Director
George Olsen, News Director
J. Howard Jones, Chief Engineer
Kathleen Beal, ExecutiveDirector
Jill McGuire, Assistant General Manager

Aurora

WSTK
104.5 mhz FM; 4.2 kw; 393 ft.; N35 18 9 W76 34 0
P.O. Box 1087, Angier, NC 27501 US
(704) 878-9004
License: Aurora, Beaufort County, NC held by Media East LLC.
Group Owner: Conner Media Corp.; (acq 1-15-2003)

Ronald Benfield, President

***WZGO**
08-01-2006; 91.1 mhz FM *Hrs Open:* 24; 40 kw; 351 ft.; N35 18 9 W76 34 0 *Rebroadcasts:* Rebroadcasts WAGO(FM) Snow Hill
107 Fairway Road, Jacksonville, NC 28546 US
(252) 747-8887, *Fax:* (252) 747-7888
www.gomixradio.org
wago@gomixradio.org
License: Aurora, Beaufort County, NC held by Pathway Christian Academy Inc.
Nat'l Network: Moody; Salem Radio Network
Arbitron Metro Market: Aurora, NC *Format:* Christian *Hrs. of News Programming:* news progmg 14 hrs wkly *No. News Employees:* 1 *Target Audience:* General.
T.D. Worthington, President
Keith Aycock, Programming Director
Ashley Lovett, Promotions Manager
Joe Patton, Chief Engineer
Tiffany Johnson, Music Director

Banner Elk

WZJS
08-05-1989; 100.7 mhz FM *Hrs Open:* 24; 0.15 kw; 1946 ft.; N36 11 3 W81 52 48
One Radio Lane, Cleveland, OH 44114 US
(828) 264-2411, *Fax:* (828) 264-2412
www.1007macfm.com
info@1007macfm.com
License: Banner Elk, Avery County, NC held by High Country Adventures LLC.
Group Owner: Curtis Media Group; (acq 3-3-2009; grpsl)
Nat'l Network: Motor Racing Net
Arbitron Metro Market: Banner Elk, NC *Format:* Classic Rock *Target Audience:* 18-44. *Adv. Rates:* 15; 15; 15; 7.50
Andy Glass, Operations Dir

Bath

***WZPE**
01-01-2005; 90.1 mhz FM *Hrs Open:* 24; 4.5 kw; 128 ft.; N35 28 32 W76 48 44
PO Box 868, Wake Forest, NC 27588 US
(919) 556-5178, *Fax:* (919) 556-9273
www.wcpe.org
music@TheClassicalStation.org
License: Bath, Beaufort County, NC held by Educational Information Corp.
Arbitron Metro Market: Bath, NC *Format:* Classical
Deborah Proctor, General Manager & Chief Engineer
Rae Weaver, General Sales Mgr
Dick Storck, Programming Director
John Graham, Engineering Dir
Will Woltz, Music Director
John Graham, Engineering Services
Peter Blume, BusinessDevelopment Director
Rae Weaver, Development Director
Rae Weaver, Development Director
Jane O'Connor, Volunteer Director

Bayboro

WNBB
01-01-2001; 97.9 mhz FM *Hrs Open:* 24; 50 kw; 433 ft.; N35 0 2 W76 49 58
702 Hartness Road, Statesville, NC 28677 US
(800)608-9798, *Fax:* (252) 638-8597
www.bear979.com
sue@bearpad.com
License: Bayboro, Pamlico County, NC held by Coastal Carolina Radio LLC
Nat'l Network: Fox News Radio *Nat'l Reps:* Rgnl Reps
Arbitron Metro Market: New Bern, NC *Format:* Country *Target Audience:* 35-64; adults *Adv. Rates:* 27; 27; 27; 5
Dann Miller, General Manager

Beaufort

***WXBE**
01-01-2005; 88.3 mhz FM; 1 kw; 180 ft.; N34 43 26 W76 43 18
P.O. Drawer 2440, Tupelo, MS 38803 US
(662) 844-8888, *Fax:* (662) 842-6791
www.afr.net
faq@afr.net
License: Beaufort, Carteret County, NC held by American Family Association.
Group Owner: American Family Radio
Arbitron Metro Market: Beaufort, NC *Format:* Christian
Marvin Sanders, General Manager

Beech Mountain

WECR-FM
01-01-1996; 102.3 mhz FM *Hrs Open:* 24; 0.15 kw; 1957 ft.; N36 11 3 W81 52 48
317 Old Turnpike Road, NW, Banner Elk, NC 28604 US
(828) 733-0188, *Fax:* (828) 733-0189
www.wecr1023.com
close_calendar@wecr1130am.com
License: Beech Mountain, Watauga County, NC held by High Country Adventures LLC.
Group Owner: Curtis Media Group; (acq 3-3-2009; grpsl)
Nat'l Network: CBS Radio
Arbitron Metro Market: Beech Mountain, NC *Format:* Adult Contemp *Hrs. of News Programming:* news progmg 2 hrs wkly *No. News Employees:* 2 *Target Audience:* 25-54. *Adv. Rates:* 14; 14; 14; 14
Gary Rozynek, President
Dan Lea, Operations Dir
George Roberts, General Manager
Rick Roberts, Station Manager
Lynn Bieritz, General Sales Mgr
Bill Holden, Chief Engineer
Dan Gainey, Regional Sales Manager

Belhaven

WQZL
10-15-1980; 101.1 mhz FM *Hrs Open:* 24; 50 kw; 463 ft.; N35 28 30 W76 51 51 *Rebroadcasts:* Rebroadcasts WQSL(FM) Jacksonville 100%
1705 West NW Hwy, Suite 275, Grapevine, TX 76051 US
(252) 639-7900, *Fax:* (252) 639-7976
www.carolinatouch.com
info@wqzl.com
License: Belhaven, Beaufort County, NC held by NM Licensing LLC.
Group Owner: NextMedia Group Inc.; (acq 11-26-2001; grpsl)
Nat'l Reps: Eastman Radio
Arbitron Metro Market: Belhaven, NC *Format:* Blues *Hrs. of News Programming:* News progmg 3 hrs wkly *Target Audience:* 25-54
Larry Weiss, General Manager

Belmont

WCGC
12-11-1954; 1270 khz AM *Hrs Open:* 24
P.O. Box 18614, Charlotte, NC 28210 US
(704) 596-1240, *Fax:* (704) 825-2127
www.heavenradio.org
wcgc1270am@yahoo.com
License: Belmont, NC held by WHVN Inc.
Group Owner: GHB Radio Group; (acq 4-17-98; $250,000)
Nat'l Network: Westwood One
Arbitron Metro Market: Charlotte, NC *Format:* Talk, Religious *Hrs. of News Programming:* news progmg 8 hrs wkly *No. News Employees:* 2 *Target Audience:* General.
Tom Gentry, President

Benson

WPYB
09-01-1961; 1130 khz AM
Mailing Address: State Road 1705, Benson, NC 27504 US
Second Address: 2234 Hodges Chapel Road, Benson, NC 27504
(919) 894-1130, *Fax:* (919) 894-1530
wpyb@dockpoint.net
License: Benson, NC held by Benson-Dunn Broadcasting Inc.
Arbitron Metro Market: Raleigh-Durham, NC *Format:* Country, Gospel *Target Audience:* General.
Jasper Tart, President
Mable Sue Tart, Executive Vice President

Bethel

WNBR-FM
12-05-1988; 98.9 mhz FM *Hrs Open:* 24; 11.2 kw; Ant 489 ft; N35 47 29 W77 22 54
233 Middle Street, Suite 107B, New Bern, NC 27983
(252) 638-8500, *Fax:* (252) 638-8597
www.bear989.com
mail@bear989.com
License: Bethel, Pitt County, NC held by Coastal Carolina Radio LLC
Nat'l Network: Fox News Radio *Nat'l Reps:* Rgnl Reps
Population Served: 697 *Arbitron Metro Market:* Greenville-New Bern-Jacksonville, NC *Target Audience:* 35-64; Adults *Adv. Rates:* 27; 27; 27; 5
Dann Miller, General Manager

Biltmore Forest

WOXL-FM
01-01-2002; 96.5 mhz FM; 2.1 kw; 1112 ft.; N35 36 4 W82 39 7
89 North Liberty Street, Asheville, NC 28801 US
(828) 259-9695, *Fax:* (828) 253-5619
www.theriverasheville.com
gbrown@avlradio.com
License: Biltmore Forest, Buncombe County, NC held by Saga Communications of North Carolina LLC.
Group Owner: Saga Communications Inc.; (acq 1-31-2008; $8 million)
Arbitron Metro Market: Asheville, NC *Format:* Light Rock
Bob Bolak, General Manager
Garry Brown, General Sales Mgr
Josh Strickland, Programming Director
Bill McClement, News Director

Black Mountain

WFGW
05-27-1962; 1010 khz AM *Hrs Open:* 24; 19 kw-C, DA3; 50 kw-D, DA3; DA3; 0.5 kw-; N35 36 19 W82 21 0
P.O. Box 159, Black Mountain, NC 28711 US
(828) 669-8477, *Fax:* (828) 298-0017
www.wfgw.org
thankyou@brb.org
License: Black Mountain, NC held by Blue Ridge Broadcasting Corp.
Nat'l Network: Salem Radio Network
Arbitron Metro Market: Black Mountain, NC *Format:* Christian, Talk *Special Programming:* Black one hr wkly *Hrs. of News Programming:* News progmg 3 hrs wkly *Target Audience:* 35 plus.
Billy Graham, Chairman
Dr. David Bruce, President
Jim Kirkland, General Manager
Wayne Roper, General Sales Mgr
Tom Greene, Programming Director
Keith Pittman, News Director
Paul Zettle, Engineering Dir

WMIT
06-01-1942; 106.9 mhz FM *Hrs Open:* 24; 36 kw; 3091 ft.; N35 44 6 W82 17 10
P.O. Box 159, 1330 U.S. Highway 70, Black Mountain, NC 28711 US
(828) 669-8477, *Fax:* (828) 298-0117
www.1069thelight.org
License: Black Mountain, Buncombe County, NC
Nat'l Network: Fox News Radio
Arbitron Metro Market: Asheville, NC *Format:* Christian *Target Audience:* 35-54; women
Matt Stockman, Programming Director

WZGM
02-26-1966; 1350 khz AM *Hrs Open:* 24
109 Charlotte Street, Black Mountain, NC 28711 US
(828) 505-8439
1350wzgm.com
agnes@mattandagnes.com;matt@mattandagnes.com
License: Black Mountain, NC held by HRN Broadcasting Inc.
Group Owner: HRN Broadcasting Inc.; (acq 4-28-2005; $850,000)
Arbitron Metro Market: Asheville, NC *Format:* Gospel *Target Audience:* General.
D. Mark Boyd III, President
Lanny Ford, General Manager

Bladenboro

***WRDK**
90.7 mhz FM; 0.16 kw; 190 ft.; N34 32 59 W78 48 30 US
(803) 581-9030, *Fax:* (803) 581-9932
License: Bladenboro, Bladen County, NC held by Richburg Educational Broadcasters Inc.
Arbitron Metro Market: Bladenboro, NC
Jeff Sigmon, General Manager

Blowing Rock

WXIT
01-01-1983; 1200 khz AM
P.O. Box 2533, Blowing Rock, NC 28605 US
(828) 265-1023, *Fax:* (828) 264-8902
www.gobIueridge.net
robinwohlbruck@gmail.com
License: Blowing Rock, NC held by High Country Adventures LLC.
Group Owner: Curtis Media Group; (acq 3-3-2009; grpsl)
Nat'l Network: CBS

Arbitron Metro Market: Blowing Rock, NC *Format:* News, News/Talk, 86 *Special Programming:* Relg 8 hrs, big band 4 hrs wkly *No. News Employees:* 1 *Target Audience:* 25-60; professionals *Adv. Rates:* 14;14;14;14
Donna Hoffman, Operations Dir
Jonathan Hoffman, General Manager
Phillip Greene, Station Manager
Steve, News Director
Andy Zlass, Operations Manager
Tom Lanier, Account Executive
Jennifer Smith, Account Executive
RobinWohlbruck, Market Manager

Boiling Spring Lakes

WKXB

12-13-1964; 99.9 mhz FM *Hrs Open:* 24; 35 kw; 584 ft.; N34 3 2 W77 57 20
201 N Front St, Ste 705, Wilmington, NC 28401 US
(910) 791-3088, *Fax:* (910) 791-0112
www.jammin999sm.com
stanleyb@nextmediagroup.com
License: Boiling Spring Lakes, Pender County, NC held by Sunrise Broadcasting LLC.
Group Owner: Capitol Broadcasting Co. Inc.; (acq 11-18-2008; grpsl)
Nat'l Reps: McGavren Guild
Arbitron Metro Market: Wilmington, NC *Format:* Contemporary Hits/Top 40 *Hrs. of News Programming:* news progmg 3 hrs wkly *No. News Employees:* 1 *Target Audience:* 25-54.
Barry Brown, Operations Dir
Barbara Raybourne, General Manager
Gayle Brown, General Sales Mgr
Stanley B., Programming Director
Missy Andrus, Promotions Manager
Doug Carlisle, News Director

Boiling Springs

*WGWG

01-22-1974; 88.3 mhz FM *Hrs Open:* 24; 50 kw; 302 ft.; N35 13 52 W81 42 57
P.O. Box 997, 106 Emily Lane, Boiling Springs, NC 28017 US
(704) 406-3525, *Fax:* (704) 434-4338
www.wgwg.org
info@wgwg.org
License: Boiling Springs, Cleveland County, NC held by Gardner-Webb University.
Format: Triple A *Special Programming:* Gospel 15 hrs wkly *Hrs. of News Programming:* News progmg one hr wkly *Target Audience:* General. *Adv. Rates:* 10; 10; 10; 10
Frank Campbell, President
Matt Webber, General Manager
Dan McClellan, Station Manager

Bolivia

WLTT

09-20-1986; 106.3 mhz FM *Hrs Open:* 24; 6 kw; 305 ft.; N34 2 50 W78 16 12
3084 Frontage Road, Shallotte, NC 28459 US
(800) 770-8190, *Fax:* (910) 772-6310
www.thebigtalker1063fm.com
aimee.b@hometownwilmington.com
License: Bolivia, Brunswick County, NC held by Sea-Comm Inc.
Group Owner: Sea-Comm Inc.; (acq 12-30-2003; with WBNE(FM) Shallotte)
Nat'l Network: ABC; Jones Radio Networks
Arbitron Metro Market: Wilmington, NC *Format:* News, News/Talk, 86 *Special Programming:* Beach mus 6 hrs wkly *Target Audience:* 25 plus; mature professionals
Paul Knight, General Manager
Max Deutsch, Station Manager

Boone

*WASU-FM

05-18-1972; 90.5 mhz FM; 0.14 kw; 1251 ft.; N36 13 59 W81 41 55
Director of B/Cg Speech, Wey Hall, Boone, NC 28608 US
(828) 262-3170, *Fax:* (828) 262-6521
www.wasuradio.com
License: Boone, Watauga County, NC held by Appalachian State University.
Arbitron Metro Market: Boone, NC. *Format:* Alternative *Special Programming:* Urban contemp 6 hrs, blues 2 hrs, Christian rock 3 hrs, country 8 hrs wkly *Hrs. of News Programming:* News progmg 2 hrs wkly *TargetAudience:* 18-30; college students & area residents
Richard Davis, General Manager

WATA

09-01-1950; 1450 khz AM *Hrs Open:* 5 AM-midnight (M-S); 6 AM-midnight; 1 kw-U, ND1; N36 12 59 W81 42 6
One Radio Lane, Cleveland, OH 44114 US
(828) 264-2411, *Fax:* (828) 264-2412
www.wataradio.com
tom@wecr1023.com
License: Boone, NC held by High Country Adventures LLC.
Group Owner: Curtis Media Group; (acq 3-3-2009; grpsl)
Nat'l Network: ABC
Arbitron Metro Market: Boone, NC. *Format:* News *Special Programming:* Gospel 5 hrs, Paul Harvey 2.5 hrs.,Watauga High sports wkly *Hrs. of News Programming:* news progmg 4 hrs wkly *No. News Employees:* 1 *TargetAudience:* 25-54. *Adv. Rates:* 15; 15; 15; 15
Andy Glass, Operations Dir
Jonathan Hoffman, General Manager
Tom Lanier, General Sales Mgr

Brevard

WSQL

07-06-1950; 1240 khz AM; 1 kw-U, ND1; N35 13 23 W82 42 20
Mailing Address: 1319 Wilson Rd., Pisgah Forest, NC 28768 US
Second Address: 1319 Wilson Rd., Pisgah Forest, NC 28768
(828) 877-5252, *Fax:* (828) 877-5253
info@wqsl.com
License: Brevard, NC held by A & L Broadcasting Inc.
Nat'l Network: CBS
Format: Adult Contemp, Talk *Special Programming:* Jazz 10 hrs, gospel 8 hrs, relg 4 hrs wkly *Target Audience:* General.
Allen Reese, General Manager
Leah Reese, Programming Director

Bryson City

WBHN

10-01-1967; 1590 khz AM; 0.5 kw-D, ND1; 0.037 kw-N, ND1; N35 25 41 W83 26 18
P.O. Box 1309, Bryson City, NC 28713 US
(708) 488-2682, *Fax:* (708) 488-3594
www.1590wbhn.com
wbhn@verizon.net
License: Bryson City, NC held by Starcast South Inc.
Format: Contemporary Hits/Top 40, Adult Contemp
Jack Mullen Jr., President
Jason Nations, General Manager
J.B. Jacobs, Chief Engineer

Buies Creek

*WCCE

10-07-1974; 90.1 mhz FM *Hrs Open:* 24; 0 kw horiz, 15 kw vert; 302 ft.; N35 12 39 W78 50 1
PO Box 1030, Buies Creek, NC 27506 US
(919)256-9787, *Fax:* (919)256-9559
www.hisradiowrtp.com
Management@hisradiowrtp.com
License: Buies Creek, Harnett County, NC held by Campbell University.
Arbitron Metro Market: Raleigh, NC *Format:* Jazz, Smooth Jazz, 74 *Special Programming:* Bluegrass 3 hrs, big band 4 hrs wkly *Hrs. of News Programming:* News progmg 10 hrs wkly *Target Audience:* General.
Carolyn Bowden, Operations Dir
Travis Autry, General Manager

Bunn

WFXK

09-01-1952; 104.3 mhz FM *Hrs Open:* 24; 100 kw; 987 ft; N35 48 40 W77 44 33 *Rebroadcasts:* 100% Simulcast with WFXC. WFXC, Durham, NC, 100%
8001-101 Creedmoor Rd., Raleigh, NC 78216
(919) 848-9736, *Fax:* (919) 848-4724
www.foxyhits.com
mmarinaro@radio-one.com
License: Bunn, Franklin County, NC held by Radio One Licenses LLC.
Group Owner: Radio One Inc.; (acq 11-8-01; grpsl).
Population Served: 870,000 *Arbitron Metro Market:* Raleigh-Durham, NC *Special Programming:* Gospel 3 hrs, jazz 4 hrs wkly *Hrs. of News Programming:* news progmg 3 hrs wkly *No. News Employees:* 1 *TargetAudience:* 25-54.
Cy Young, Operations Dir
Gary Weiss, General Manager
Kim Gattis, General Sales Mgr
Bruce Farmer, Promotions Manager
Jim Davis, Chief Engineer
Jodi Berri, Music Director
Jodi Luke, National Sales Manager

Burgaw

WVBS

06-21-1963; 1470 khz AM *Hrs Open:* Sunrise-sunset; 0.88 kw-D, ND1; 0.093 kw-N, ND1; N34 31 22 W77 54 17
520 Roberts Road, Newport, NC 28570 US
(910) 259-5718
www.fbnradio.com
License: Burgaw, NC held by Grace Christian School.
Arbitron Metro Market: Wilmington, NC *Format:* Christian
Carl Gibbs, General Manager
Dick Jones, Station Manager

Burlington

WZTK

12-01-1946; 101.1 mhz FM *Hrs Open:* 24; 100 kw; 1176 ft.; N35 56 15 W79 26 30
Mailing Address: 3012 Highwoods Blvd, Suite 201, Raleigh, NC 27604 US
Second Address: 1109 Tower Dr., Burlington, NC 27215
(336) 584-0126, *Fax:* (336) 854-1039
www.fmtalk1011.com
info@fmtalk1011.com
License: Burlington, Alamance County, NC held by Carolina Radio Group Inc.
Group Owner: Curtis Media Group
Arbitron Metro Market: Greensboro-Winston Salem-High Point, NC *Format:* Talk *Special Programming:* Bluegrass 3 hrs wkly *Target Audience:* 25-54.
Bryon Tucker, Programming Director

Burlington-Graham

WBAG

01-01-1946; 1150 khz AM *Hrs Open:* 24; 1 kw-D, 48 w-N; N36 06 48 W79 27 00
Mailing Address: Box 2450, Burlington, NC 27253
Second Address: 1745 Burch Bridge Rd., Burlington-Graham, NC 27217
(336) 226-1150, *Fax:* (336) 226-1180
www.wbag1150.com
License: Burlington-Graham, Alamance County, NC held by Gray Broadcasting LLC
Regional Network: N.C. News Net.
Population Served: 108,000 *Arbitron Metro Market:* Greensboro-Winston Salem-High Point, NC *Special Programming:* Relg 5 hrs wkly *Hrs. of News Programming:* news progmg 25 hrs wkly *No. News Employees:* 2 *TargetAudience:* 25-54; general
Harry Myers, Operations Dir
Joe Gray, General Manager
Gailes Stuckey, General Sales Mgr
Harry Myers, News Director
Tim Walker, Chief Engineer

WPCM

09-01-1941; 920 khz AM; 5 kw-D, ND1; 0.055 kw-N, ND1; N36 5 50 W79 29 3
Mailing Address: 3012 Highwoods Blvd, Ste 201, Raleigh, NC 27609 US
Second Address: 1109 Tower Dr., Burlington, NC 27215
(336) 584-0126, *Fax:* (336) 584-6333
www.920wpcm.com
License: Burlington-Graham, NC held by Carolina Radio Group Inc.
Group Owner: Curtis Media Group; (acq 3-1-90).
Arbitron Metro Market: Greensboro-Winston Salem-High Point, NC *Format:* Oldies *Target Audience:* 25 plus; upscale *Adv. Rates:* 10; 10; 10; 10
Bill Whitley, General Manager

Burnsville

WKYK

05-28-1967; 940 khz AM *Hrs Open:* 24; 4.6 kw-D, DAN; 0.25 kw-N, DAN; N35 55 32 W82 16 20
Mailing Address: P. O. Box 744, Burnsville, NC 28714 US
Second Address: 749 Sawmill Road, Burnsville, NC 28714
(828) 682-3510, *Fax:* (828) 682-6227
www.wkyk.com
940@wkyk.com
License: Burnsville, NC held by Mark Media Inc.
Group Owner: Mark Media Group; (acq 4-10-69)
Nat'l Network: ABC *Regional Network:* N.C. News Net.
Format: Country *Special Programming:* Gospel 12 hrs wkly *Hrs. of News Programming:* news progmg 10 hrs wkly *No. News Employees:* 1 *Target Audience:* 18-55. *Adv. Rates:* 20; 17; 20; 12
J. Ardell Sink, CEO
Michael Sink, Operations Dir
Steve Murphy, News Director

Remelle Sink, Executive Vice President
Holly Hall, Operations Manager
Mary Marsh, Promotions Director

Buxton

***WBUX**
01-01-1999; 90.5 mhz FM; 5.9 kw; 154 ft.; N35 16 1 W75 32 38 *Rebroadcasts:* Rebroadcasts WCPE(FM) Wake Forest 99.9%
Box 0915, Chapel Hill, NC 27599 US
(919) 445-9150, *Fax:* (919) 966-5955
www.wunc.org
wunc@wunc.org
License: Buxton, Dare County, NC held by Board of Trustees/University of North Carolina at Chapel Hill.
Nat'l Network: NPR; PRI; CBC Radio One
Arbitron Metro Market: Buxton, NC *Format:* Classical *Special Programming:* Folk 20 hrs wkly *Hrs. of News Programming:* news progmg 124 hrs wkly *No. News Employees:* 7
Bob Levin, COO
Connie Walker, General Manager
David Brower, Programming Director
Nandini Sen, Director of Technologies & Engineering
Regina Yeager, Director of Development
Susan Anderson, Accounting Coordinator
JacquelineEdwards, Business Assistant
Nathan Olawsky, Business Services Coordinator
Jennifer Bowling, Corporate Support Associate
Nancy Brookshire, Corporate Support Manager

WHDX
01-01-2008; 99.9 mhz FM; 0.11 kw; 56 ft.; N35 15 43 W75 31 23 US
(703) 527-1434
www.whdzx.com
radiobuxton@yahoo.com
License: Buxton, Dare County, NC held by David Wilson
David Wilson, General Manager

WHDZ
01-01-2008; 101.5 mhz FM; 0.11 kw; 66 ft.; N35 15 43 W75 31 23
US
(703) 527-1434
www.whdzx.com
radiobuxton@yahoo.com
License: Buxton, Dare County, NC held by David Wilson
David Wilson, General Manager

Calabash

WYNA
06-01-1964; 104.9 mhz FM; 15 kw; 338 ft.; N33 49 19 W78 46 18
P.O. Box 186, Narbeth, PA 19072 US
(843) 903-9962, *Fax:* (843) 903-1797
www.1049bobfm.com
License: Calabash, Brunswick County, NC held by Qantum of Myrtle Beach License Co. LLC.
Group Owner: Qantum Communications Corp.; (acq 4-23-2008; $4 million)
Arbitron Metro Market: Calabash, NC *Format:* Adult Contemp *Target Audience:* 25-54; adults
Frank Osborn, President
Will Isaacs, General Manager

Camp Lejeune

WSME
09-08-1980; 1120 khz AM
P.O. Box 401, 12731 Chapel Chase Dr, Clarkesville, MD 21029 US
(910) 355-9763, *Fax:* (910) 355-9763
www.ctc-media.com/WSME.html
amoseley@suddenlink.net
License: Camp Lejeune, NC held by CTC Media Group Inc.
Group Owner: CTC Media Group Inc.
Arbitron Metro Market: New Bern, NC *Format:* Country
Edwin Afflerbach, Operations Dir
Ashley Moseley, General Manager

Canton

WPTL
08-03-1963; 920 khz AM *Hrs Open:* 6 AM-6:30 PM; 0.5 kw-D, ND2; 0.038 kw-N, ND2; N35 31 15 W82 48 24
P.O. Box 909, Canton, NC 28716 US
(828) 648-3576,(828) 648-3577, *Fax:* (828) 648-3577
www.wptlradio.net
admin@wptlradio.net
License: Canton, NC held by Skycountry Broadcasting Inc.
Nat'l Network: AP Radio; Jones Radio Networks
Arbitron Metro Market: Asheville, NC *Format:* Religious, Country *Hrs. of News Programming:* News progmg 8 hrs wkly *Target Audience:* 25 plus; adult family *Adv. Rates:* 10 10 10 na
William Reck, President
Linda Reck, Operations Dir

WYSE
07-12-1954; 970 khz AM; 5 kw-D, ND1; 0.03 kw-N, ND1; N35 31 58 W82 51 58
117 Radio Hill Road, Maggie Valley, NC 28716 US
(828) 259-9695, *Fax:* (828) 253-5619
www.1310bigwise.com
gbrown@avlradio.com.
License: Canton, NC held by Saga Communications of North Carolina LLC.
Group Owner: Saga Communications Inc.; (acq 3-11-2003).
Nat'l Network: ESPN Radio
Arbitron Metro Market: Asheville, NC *Format:* Sports
Ed Christian, President
Bob Bolak, General Manager
Ken Carson, Programming Director
Nikki Mitchell, Promotions Manager
Bill McClement, News Director

Carolina Beach

WMYT
10-01-1996; 106.7 mhz FM *Hrs Open:* 24; 5.6 kw; Ant 341 ft; N34 03 02 W77 57 20 *Rebroadcasts:* Simulcast with WPPG(FM) Fair Bluff.
122 Cinema Dr., Wilmington, NC 29429
(910) 772-6300
www.carolinapenguin.com
info@carolinapenguin.com
License: Carolina Beach, New Hanover County, NC held by Ocean Broadcasting II LLC
Paul Knight, General Manager
Beau Gunn, Programming Director

WSFM
07-01-1989; 1180 khz AM; 10 kw-D, DA; N34 09 03 W78 04 48
Box 957, Wilmington, NC 28403
(910) 763-2452, *Fax:* (910) 763-6578
www.life905.com
life@life905.com
License: Carolina Beach, New Hanover County, NC held by Carolina Christian Radio Inc.
Group Owner: Carolina Christian Radio; (acq 3-2-2001; $100,000 with WDVV(FM) Wilmington)
Arbitron Metro Market: Wilmington, NC *Target Audience:* General Sp
Jim Stephens, General Manager
Roger Brace, Engineering Dir

Carrboro

WQOK
10-01-1960; 97.5 mhz FM *Hrs Open:* 24; 50 kw; 479 ft.; N35 58 39 W78 48 58
200 Concord Plaza, Suite 600, San Antonio, TX 78216 US
(919) 848-9736, *Fax:* (919) 848-4724
www.k975.com
mmarinaro@radio-one.com
License: Carrboro, South Boston City County, NC held by Radio One Licenses LLC.
Group Owner: Radio One Inc.; (acq 11-8-01; grpsl).
Nat'l Network: ABC *Nat'l Reps:* Christal
Arbitron Metro Market: Raleigh-Durham, NC *Format:* Urban Contemporary *Special Programming:* Gospel 9 hrs wkly *Hrs. of News Programming:* news progmg 20 hrs wkly *No. News Employees:* 1 *Target Audience:* 25-54; upwardly mobile with discretionary income
Cy Young, Operations Dir
Gary Weiss, General Manager
Saundra Lemaster, General Sales Mgr
Jodi Luke, National Sales Manager

Cary

WKSL
01-01-1946; 93.9 mhz FM; 100 kw; 1486 ft.; N35 42 50 W78 49 4
600 Congress Ave.,S1400, Austin, TX 78701 US
(919) 877-0939, *Fax:* (919) 876-2929
License: Cary, Wake County, NC held by Capstar TX L.P.
Group Owner: Clear Channel Communications Inc.; (acq 8-30-2000; grpsl)
Arbitron Metro Market: Raleigh-Durham, NC *Format:* Adult Contemp *Target Audience:* 25-49; men
Dick Harlow, General Manager
Chris Shebel, Programming Director
Fred Pace, Chief Engineer

Chadbourn

WVOE
04-23-1962; 1590 khz AM; 1 kw-D, NDD; N34 21 5 W78 50 38
1528 Old 74 Highway West, Chadbourn, NC 28431 US
(910) 654-5621, *Fax:* (910) 654-4385
License: Chadbourn, NC held by Ebony Enterprises Inc.
Arbitron Metro Market: Chadbourn, NC *Format:* Gospel *Target Audience:* General; white & blue collar workers, housewives, students, sr citizens
Willie Walls, President
Willie Walls, General Manager

Chapel Hill

WCHL
01-25-1953; 1360 khz AM *Hrs Open:* 24; 5 kw-D, DAN; 1 kw-N, DAN; N35 56 18 W79 1 36
3012 Highwoods Blvd., Suite 201, Raleigh, NC 27604 US
(919) 933-4165, *Fax:* (919) 968-3748
www.chapelboro.com
cdixon@wchl.com
License: Chapel Hill, NC held by Vilcom Interactive Media LLC
Nat'l Network: ABC; CBS Radio; Jones Radio Networks *Regional Network:* N.C. News Net. *Wire Services:* AP
Arbitron Metro Market: Raleigh-Durham, NC *Format:* News, News/Talk, 86 *Hrs. of News Programming:* news progmg 25 hrs wkly *No. News Employees:* 3 *Target Audience:* 25-54; educated adults with high median incomes
Christy Jones Taylor, General Manager
Christy Dixon, Station Manager
Ron Stutts, Programming Director

WLLQ
12-01-1973; 1530 khz AM *Hrs Open:* Sunrise-sunset; 10 kw-D, DAD; N35 58 7 W79 0 10
P.O. Box 15400, Durham, NC 27704 US
(202) 638-1959, *Fax:* (202) 638-6127
estuardovaldemar@hotmail.com
License: Chapel Hill, NC held by Estuardo Valdemar Rodriguez and Leonor Rodriguez.
Group Owner: Radio La Grande; (acq 2-2-2005; grpsl)
Arbitron Metro Market: Raleigh-Durham, *Target Audience:* Spanish young adult.
Estuardo Rodriguez, General Manager

***WUNC**
11-03-1952; 91.5 mhz FM *Hrs Open:* 24; 100 kw; 1362 ft.; N35 51 59 W79 10 0
Cb#6230, Swain Hall, Unc-Ch, Chapel Hill, NC 27599 US
(919) 445-9150, *Fax:* (919) 966-5955
www.wunc.org
wunc@wunc.org
License: Chapel Hill, Orange County, NC held by University of North Carolina at Chapel Hill.
Nat'l Network: NPR; PRI; CBC Radio One
Arbitron Metro Market: Chapel Hill, NC *Format:* News *Special Programming:* Folk 20 hrs wkly *Hrs. of News Programming:* news progmg 124 hrs wkly *No. News Employees:* 7 *Target Audience:* 25-54; highlyeducated, pro-active in the community, concerned about local issues
Kevin Wolf, Operations Dir
Connie Walker, General Manager
David Brower, Programming Director
Regina Yeager, Director of Development
Jacqueline Edwards, Business Assistant
Robin Copley, Audio Manager
Laura Shaffer, DevelopmentAssistant

***WXYC**
03-18-1977; 89.3 mhz FM *Hrs Open:* 24; 400 w; 280 ft; N35 54 15 W79 02 50
CB 5210, Carolina Union, Chapel Hill, NC 27599
(919) 962-8989
www.wxyc.org
info@wxyc.org
License: Chapel Hill, Orange County, NC held by Student Educational Broadcasting Inc.
Population Served: 25,000 *Arbitron Metro Market:* Raleigh-Durham, NC *Hrs. of News Programming:* News progmg 3 hrs wkly *Target Audience:* General.
Karina Soni, Station Manager
JJ Lang, Programming Director
Wilson Sayre, Programming Director
Ari Hines, Promotions Manager
Howard Hoyt, Chief Engineer

Charlotte

WBCN
05-01-1968; 1660 khz AM; 771 ft

600 New Hampshire Ave., Suite 1200, Washington, DC 20037 US
(208) 734-6633, *Fax:* (208) 736-1958
www.csnradio.com
License: Charlotte, NC held by Hemisphere Broadcasting Corp.
Group Owner: CBS Radio; (acq 11-13-98; grpsl)
Nat'l Network: CBS
Arbitron Metro Market: Artesia NM
Mike Kestler, President
Mike Stockland, General Manager
Don Mills, Programming Director

WBCN(AM)
12-01-2003; 1660 khz AM; 10 kw-D, 1 kw-N; N35 14 57 W80 51 41
1520 South Blvd., Suite 300, Charlotte, NC 28203
(704)319-9369, *Fax:* (704)319-3934
www.charlotte.cbslocal.com/
bschoening@cbs.com
License: Charlotte, Mecklenburg County, NC held by Infinity Radio Holdings Inc.
Group Owner: CBS Radio
Nat'l Network: Sporting News Radio Network *Nat'l Reps:* D & R Radio; Katz Radio
Population Served: 751,087 *Arbitron Metro Market:* Charlotte,NC
Format: Sports
D.J. Stout, Operations Dir
Bill Schoening, General Manager
Dustin Shearon, General Sales Mgr
DJ Stout, Programming Director
Bill Schoening, Market Manager
Shannon Scarborough, Director of Digital Content
Amanda Knepp, MarketingDirector

WBT
04-10-1922; 1110 khz AM *Hrs Open:* 24; 50 kw-D, DAN; 50 kw-N, DAN; N35 7 56 W80 53 23
One Julian Price Place, Charlotte, NC 28208 US
(704) 374-3500, *Fax:* (704) 374-3889
www.wbt.com
tsavery@wbt.com
License: Charlotte, NC held by Greater Media of Charlotte Inc.
Group Owner: Greater Media Inc.; (acq 1-31-2008; grpsl)
Nat'l Network: CBS
Arbitron Metro Market: Charlotte, NC *Format:* News, News/Talk, 86 *Hrs. of News Programming:* news progmg 20 hrs wkly *No. News Employees:* 5 *Target Audience:* 35-54; men
Rick Jackson, Operations Dir
Terry Mace, General Sales Mgr
Carl East, Programming Director
Matt Dubois, Promotions Manager
Marshall Adams, News Director
Jerry Dowd, Chief Engineer
Lisa Gergely, General Manager
Zach Simpson,Webmaster
Matt DuBois, Marketing Director
Jessica ""Reeves"" RoBards, Marketing Administrator

*WFAE
06-29-1981; 90.7 mhz FM *Hrs Open:* 24; 100 kw; 1086 ft.; N35 17 14 W80 41 45
8801 Jm Keynes Dr, Suite 91, Charlotte, NC 28262 US
(704) 549-9323, *Fax:* (704) 547-8851
www.wfae.org
wfae@wfae.org
License: Charlotte, Mecklenburg County, NC held by University Radio Foundation Inc.
Nat'l Network: NPR; PRI
Arbitron Metro Market: Charlotte, NC *Format:* News, News/Talk, 86 *Hrs. of News Programming:* news progmg 42 hrs wkly *No. News Employees:* 4 *Target Audience:* 35-49; professionals
Jennie Buckner, Chairman
Roger Sarow, President and General Manager
Tena Simmons, Operations Dir
Barbara Vermeire, General Sales Mgr
Paul Stribling, Programming Director
Renee Rallos, Promotions Manager
Mark Rumsey, NewsDirector
Jobie Sprinkle, Engineering Dir
Renee Ballos, Public Affairs Director
Catherine Little, Sales Director
Nash E. Long, III, Vice-Chair
Cyrus Johnson, Jr., Secretary
Michelle Maidt, Treasurer

WFNZ
01-01-1941; 610 khz AM
C/O Cbs Radio, 600 New, Hampshire Ave, S1200, Washington, DC 20037 US
(704) 319-9369, *Fax:* (704) 319-3934
www.charlotte.cbslocal.com/station/the-fan-610-am
License: Charlotte, NC held by CBS Radio Holdings Inc.
Group Owner: CBS Radio; (acq 11-13-98; grpsl).
Arbitron Metro Market: Charlotte-Gastonia-Rock Hill, NC-SC-Rock Hill, NC- *Format:* Sports *Target Audience:* 18 plus; male, sports oriented
D.J. Stout, Operations Dir
Bill Schoening, General Manager
Scott Vandivier, General Sales Mgr
DJ Stout, Programming Director
Chele Fassig, Promotions Manager
Eric Lakey, Chief Engineer
Bill Schoening, Market Manager
AmandaKnepp, Marketing Director
Shannon Scarborough, Director of Digital Content
Art Greene, Local Sales Manager
Dustin Shearon, National Sales Manager
Don Williams, Digital Sales Manager

WGFY
01-18-1955; 1480 khz AM *Hrs Open:* 24
866 2nd Ave., 2nd Fl, New York, NY 10017 US
(704) 377-2223, *Fax:* (704) 373-2245
www.radiodisney.com
info@radiodisney.com
License: Charlotte, NC held by Radio Disney Group LLC.
Group Owner: ABC Inc.; (acq 8-22-00; grpsl).
Arbitron Metro Market: Charlotte-Gastonia-Rock Hill, NC-SC
Format: Children *Hrs. of News Programming:* news progmg 25 hrs wkly *No. News Employees:* 6 *Target Audience:* Under 12; kids, mothers, families
Carolyn Renfro, Promotions Manager

WGSP
08-23-1958; 1310 khz AM
645 Church St, Suite 400, Norfolk, VA 23510 US
(704) 442-7277, *Fax:* (704) 442-9518
License: Charlotte, NC held by Norsan Consulting and Management Inc.
Group Owner: Norsan Consulting and Management Inc.; (acq 12-13-2004; $2 million).
Arbitron Metro Market: Charlotte-Gastonia-Rock Hill, NC-SC
Format: Spanish
Norberto Sanchez, President
Javier Placencia, Programming Director

WHVN
01-01-1958; 1240 khz AM; 1 kw-D, ND2; 1 kw-N, ND2; N35 12 0 W80 48 39
P.O. Box 18614, Charlotte, NC 28218 US
(704) 596-1240, *Fax:* (704) 596-6939
www.heavenradio.org
whvn@bellsouth.net
License: Charlotte, NC held by WHVN Inc.
Group Owner: GHB Radio Group; (acq 7-11-83)
Arbitron Metro Market: Charlotte-Gastonia-Rock Hill, NC-SC
Format: Religious *Target Audience:* 35 plus; Christian
George Buck, President
Brant Hart, Operations Dir
Tom Gentry, General Manager
Buddy Boone, Programming Director
Gary Hattaway, Chief Engineer

WLNK
08-15-1962; 107.9 mhz FM *Hrs Open:* 24; 100 kw; 1693 ft.; N35 21 51 W81 11 13
One Julian Price Place, Charlotte, NC 28208 US
(704) 374-3500, *Fax:* (704) 338-3062
www.1079thelink.com
License: Charlotte, Mecklenburg County, NC held by Greater Media of Charlotte Inc.
Group Owner: Greater Media Inc.; (acq 1-31-2008; grpsl)
Arbitron Metro Market: Charlotte-Gastonia-Rock Hill, NC-SC
Format: Adult Contemp
Nancy Haynes, General Sales Mgr
Tony Sciotto, Programming Director
Jennifer Staron, Promotions Manager
Nancy Albright, News Director
Derek James, Music Director
Jim Barroll, News Reporter
Pete Kaliner, Reporter

WNKS
07-21-1962; 95.1 mhz FM; 100 kw; 1542 ft.; N35 21 44 W81 9 19
600 New Hampshire Avenue, N.W., Suite 1200, Washington, DC 20037 US
(704) 331-9510, *Fax:* (704) 344-8656
www.kiss951.com
License: Charlotte, Mecklenburg County, NC
Group Owner: CBS Radio
Arbitron Metro Market: Charlotte, NC *Format:* Contemporary Hits/Top 40
John Renolds, Operations Dir
Keith Cornwell, General Manager
Rob Whitehead, General Sales Mgr
Natalie Kirby, Promotions Manager
Chad Fitzsimmons, Promotions Manager

WOGR
05-07-1964; 1540 khz AM
Mailing Address: P.O. Box 16408, Charlotte, NC 28297 US
Second Address: 1501 N. Carrier Dr., Charlotte, NC 28216
(704) 393-1540, *Fax:* (704) 393-1527
wordnet.org
info@wordnet.org
License: Charlotte, NC held by Victory Christian Center Inc.
Nat'l Network: Salem Radio Network
Arbitron Metro Market: Charlotte-Gasto *TV Affiliate:* Relg *No. News Employees:* General.
Operations Manager, Operations Dir
Programming Manager, Programming Director

WSOC-FM
01-01-1947; 103.7 mhz FM; 100 kw; 1348 ft.; N35 15 6 W80 41 12
Cbs Corp., Suite 1200, 600 New Hampshire Ave,NW, Washington, DC 20037 US
(704) 522-1103, *Fax:* (704) 523-2104
www.wsocfm.com
License: Charlotte, Mecklenburg County, NC held by Infinity Radio Holdings Inc.
Group Owner: CBS Radio; (acq 11-13-98; grpsl).
Arbitron Metro Market: Charlotte-Gastonia-Rock Hill, NC-SC
Format: Country *Target Audience:* 25-54.
Bill Schoening, Operations Dir
Billy Grooms, General Sales Mgr
Rick McCracken, Programming Director
Chele Fassig, Promotions Manager
Shirley Biers, News Director
Eric Lakey, Chief Engineer
Dustin Shearon, National SalesManager
D.J. Stout, Operations Manager
Frank Laseter, Public Affairs Director

WKQC
01-01-1972; 104.7 mhz FM *Hrs Open:* 24; 96 kw; 1211 ft.; N35 15 6 W80 41 12
600 New Hampshire Avenue, N.W., Suite 1200, Washington, DC 20037 US
(704) 372-1104, *Fax:* (704) 523-1047
www.star1047.com
License: Charlotte, Mecklenburg County, NC held by Infinity Radio Holdings Inc.
Group Owner: CBS Radio; (acq 11-13-98; grpsl).
Arbitron Metro Market: Charlotte-Gastonia-Rock Hill, NC-SC
Format: Oldies *No. News Employees:* 2 *Target Audience:* 25-54.
Keith Cornwell, General Manager
John Reynolds, Promotions Manager

*WYFQ
10-14-1933; 930 khz AM *Hrs Open:* 24; 5 kw-D, DAN; 1 kw-N, DAN; N35 16 0 W80 54 5
8030 Arrowridge Boulevar, Charlotte, NC 28273 US
(704) 523-5555, *Fax:* (704) 291-7807
www.bbnradio.org
bbn@bbnradio.org
License: Charlotte, NC held by Bible Broadcasting Network Inc.
Group Owner: Bible Broadcasting Network; acq 2-6-92; $475,000;
Arbitron Metro Market: Charlotte, NC *Format:* Christian *Hrs. of News Programming:* News progmg 3 hrs wkly *Target Audience:* General.
Dan Austin, Station Manager
John Woolery, Programming Director
Ron Muffley, Engineering Dir

Cherryville

WCSL
06-28-1967; 1590 khz AM *Hrs Open:* 24
P. O. Box 370, Cherryville, NC 28021 US
(704) 732-8011, *Fax:* (704) 732-9567
www.hrnb.com
info@hrnb.com
License: Cherryville, NC held by HRN Broadcasting Inc.
Group Owner: HRN Broadcasting Inc.; (acq 4-14-2004; $500,000 with WLON(AM) Lincolnton)
Nat'l Network: Westwood One *Regional Network:* N.C. News Net.
Arbitron Metro Market: Charlotte, NC *Format:* Christian *Special Programming:* Loc sports 3 hrs wkly *Target Audience:* General.
Mark Boyd, President
Lanny Ford, General Manager

Calvin Hastings, General Sales Mgr
Milton Baker, Programming Director
Larry Seagle, News Director
Josh Pierce, Chief Engineer
Wendy Stout, Music Director

China Grove

WRNA

11-17-1980; 1140 khz AM *Hrs Open:* 6 AM-2 hrs past sunset; 0.25 kw-C, DAD; 1 kw-D, DAD; N35 34 20 W80 35 21
P. O. Box 8146, Kannapolis, NC 28083 US
(704) 857-1101, *Fax:* (704) 857-0680
www.fordbroadcasting.com
info@fordbroadcasting.com
License: China Grove, NC held by South Rowan Broadcasting Co.
Nat'l Network: USA
Arbitron Metro Market: Charlotte-Gastonia-Rock Hill, NC-SC
Format: Gospel *Target Audience:* General.
Carl Ford, President
Angela Ford, Operations Dir
Taylor Ford, Executive Vice President

Claremont

WCXN

09-05-1985; 1170 khz AM; 1 kw-C, NDD; 7.7 kw-D, NDD; N35 43 34 W81 8 52
400 Alleghany Street, Blacksburg, VA 24063 US
(248) 557-3500, *Fax:* (248) 557-2950
www.birach.com/wcxn.htm
sima@BIRACH.Com
License: Claremont, NC held by Birach Broadcasting Corp.
Group Owner: Birach Broadcasting Corp.; (acq 8-1-2007; $800,000 with KXLQ(AM) Indianola, IA)
Nat'l Network: USA
Arbitron Metro Market: Claremont, NC *Target Audience:* General.
Abel Orozco, General Manager

Clayton

WHPY

01-01-1974; 1590 khz AM *Hrs Open:* Sunrise-sunset; 5 kw-D, ND1; 0.025 kw-N, ND1; N35 38 49 W78 30 21
P.O. Box 535, Clayton, NC 27520 US
(919) 553-6774, *Fax:* (919) 359-0016
www.whpyradio.com
WHPY@radio.com
License: Clayton, NC held by Fellowship Baptist Church Inc. dba Fellowship Christian Academy.
Arbitron Metro Market: Raleigh-Durham, NC *Format:* Christian
Charles Ennis, President
Keith Holland, General Manager

Clemmons

WMKS

05-03-1947; 105.7 mhz FM *Hrs Open:* 24; 30 kw; 1549 ft.; N36 22 36.4 W80 22 8.6
600 Congress Avenue, Suite 1400, Austin, TX 78701 US
(336) 822-2000, *Fax:* (336) 887-0104
www.1057kissfm.com
jojo@1057now.com
License: Clemmons, Forsyth County, NC held by Clear Channel Broadcasting Licenses Inc.
Group Owner: Clear Channel Communications Inc.; (acq 9-12-2006;. $15.65 million)
Arbitron Metro Market: Greensboro-Winston Salem-High Point, NC *Format:* Adult Contemp
Tim Satterfield, Operations Dir
Morgan Bohannon, General Manager
Pierre Proupe, General Sales Mgr
Brian Anthony, Programming Director
Alan Chapman, Director of Marketing and Promotions
Dennis Elliot, Digital Content Director

Clinton

WCLN

09-27-1975; 1170 khz AM *Hrs Open:* Sunrise-sunset; 1 kw-C, NDD; 5 kw-D, NDD; N35 1 21 W78 20 58
P.O. Box 28, Clinton, NC 28328 US
(910) 592-8949, *Fax:* (910) 592-3732
www.oldies1170.com
grandpas@oldies1170.com
License: Clinton, NC held by CLINTON SAMPSON RADIO CO INC
Nat'l Network: ABC *Regional Network:* N.C. News Net.
Arbitron Metro Market: Clinton, NC *Format:* Oldies *Special Programming:* Community, gospel 8 hrs wkly *Hrs. of News Programming:* news progmg 4.5 hrs. wkly *No. News Employees:* 7 *Target Audience:* 35 PLUS*Adv. Rates:* 10.35; 10.35; 10.35.; 10.35
Pat ""Grandpa"" Dixon, GM
Delma Patrick Dixon, General Manager
DONNA BASS, General Sales Mgr
Nolan Wiggins, Programming Director
Don Smith, News Director
NICOLE NELSON, PSA Director
JOYCE DIXON, Sales Director
Debbie BAKER,Traffic Manager

WCLN-FM

06-11-1967; 107.3 mhz FM *Hrs Open:* 24; 9.2 kw; 535 ft.; N35 7 37 W78 35 19
P O Box 217, Sterling, VA 20167 US
(910) 864-5028, *Fax:* (910) 864-6270
www.christian107.com
wcln@christian107.com
License: Clinton, Sampson County, NC held by Christian Listening Network Inc.
Group Owner: Christian Listening Network Inc.; (acq 7-94).
Arbitron Metro Market: Fayetteville, NC *Format:* Christian, Religious
George Wilson, President
Dan DeBruler, General Manager
Steve Turley, Programming Director
Cindy Long, Promotions Manager
Van Clough, Chief Engineer

WRRZ

04-05-1947; 880 khz AM; 1 kw-D, NDD; N34 58 40 W78 18 15
P.O. Box 1800, Raleigh, NC 27602 US
(910) 592-2165, *Fax:* (910) 592-8556
wrrzradio@webtv.net
License: Clinton, NC held by Sanchez Broadcasting Corp.
Regional Network: N.C. News Net.
Special Programming: Black 5 hrs, relg 6 hrs, Sp 5 hrs wkly
Target Audience: 25 plus. *Adv. Rates:* 8.75; 8.25; 8.75; 8.25
Victor Sanchez, President
Martha Sanchez, General Manager

Columbia

WERX-FM

03-14-1983; 102.5 mhz FM *Hrs Open:* 24; 64 kw; 689 ft.; N35 55 5 W76 20 48
Mailing Address: P.O. Box 1017, Edenton, NC 27932 US
Second Address: 2422 S. Wrightsville Ave., Nags Head, NC 27959
(252) 441-1024, *Fax:* (252) 441-2109
www.1025theshark.com
jennifer@ecri.net
License: Columbia, Tyrrell County, NC held by East Carolina Radio of Elizabeth City Inc.
Group Owner: East Carolina Radio Group
Arbitron Metro Market: Columbia, NC *Format:* Oldies *Special Programming:* Flashback, in concert, off the record, BBC classic tracks *Target Audience:* 18-49; moderate to high income, mobile professionals & families withchildren
Rick Loesch, President
Tom Charity, Operations Dir
R. Loesch, General Manager
Rick Loesch, General Sales Mgr

WRSF

06-13-1983; 105.7 mhz FM *Hrs Open:* 24; 100 kw; 614 ft.; N35 53 18 W76 13 50
Mailing Address: P.O. Box 1800, Raleigh, NC 27602 US
Second Address: 2422 S. Wrightsville Ave., Nags Head, NC 27959
(252) 449-8331, *Fax:* (252) 449-8354
www.ecri.net
License: Columbia, Tyrrell County, NC held by East Carolina Radio of Elizabeth City Inc.
Group Owner: East Carolina Radio Group; (acq 1996).
Format: Country *Hrs. of News Programming:* news progmg 5 hrs wkly *No. News Employees:* 1 *Target Audience:* 18-54; young & mid-range adults
Tom Charity, Operations Dir
John Maloney, General Sales Mgr
Ray Hall, Programming Director
Jerry Barco, News Director

Concord

WPEG

06-15-1962; 97.9 mhz FM; 94 kw; 1611 ft.; N35 21 44 W81 9 19
600 New Hampshire Avenue, N.W., Suite 1200, Washington, DC 20037 US
(704) 342-2644, *Fax:* (704) 227-8979
www.power98fm.com
License: Concord, Cabarrus County, NC held by Infinity Radio Holdings Inc.
Group Owner: CBS Radio; (acq 11-13-98; grpsl).
Nat'l Network: Westwood One *Nat'l Reps:* Katz Radio
Arbitron Metro Market: Charlotte-Gastonia-Rock Hill, NC-SC
Format: Urban Contemporary *Special Programming:* Gospel 6 hrs, mix show 8 hrs wkly *Hrs. of News Programming:* news progmg 20 hrs wkly *No. News Employees:* 1 *Target Audience:* 12 plus; Black
Terri Avery, Operations Dir
Bill Schoening, General Manager
Montressa Barber, General Sales Mgr
Lindsay Slocum, Programming Director

Cramerton

WZGV

08-21-1946; 730 khz AM *Hrs Open:* 24; 1 kw-D, 168 w-N; N35 17 27 W81 34 05
1511 W. Dixon Blvd., Shelby, NC 28021
(704) 482-4510,(704) 487-6313, *Fax:* (704) 482-4680
www.theboss.us
thebossradio@bellsouth.net
License: Cramerton, Gaston County, NC held by HRN Broadcasting Inc.
Group Owner: HRN Broadcasting Inc.; (acq 10-6-2006; $1.5 million with WGNC(AM) Gastonia)
Nat'l Network: ABC *Regional Network:* N.C. News Net. *Regional Reps:* T-N.
Population Served: 500,000 *Arbitron Metro Market:* Charlotte-Gastonia-Rock Hill, NC-SC *No. News Employees:* 2
Target Audience: General.
D. Mark Boyd III, President
Calvin Hastings, General Manager

Creedmore

WDRU

09-01-1989; 1030 khz AM *Hrs Open:* Daytime; 50 kw-D, DA; N36 10 43 W78 45 30 *Rebroadcasts:* Simulcast with WTRU(AM) Kernersville
4405 Providence Lane, Ste D, Winston-Salem, NC 24063
(336) 759-0363, *Fax:* (336) 759-0366
www.wtru.com
info@wtru.com
License: Creedmore, Granville County, NC held by Truth Broadcasting Corp.
Group Owner: Truth Broadcasting Corp.; (acq 5-2-2005; swap for WWBG(AM) Greensboro and WTOB(AM) Winston-Salem).
Nat'l Network: Salem Radio Network
Arbitron Metro Market: Raleigh-Durham, NC *Target Audience:* 25-54; middle-class families *Adv. Rates:* 356; 35; 35; 30
Bryan Brown, COO
Stuart Epperson Jr., President
Ed Park, Programming Director
Mandel Owens, Chief Engineer
Doug Marshall, Sales Manager

Cullowhee

*WWCU

01-15-1977; 90.5 mhz FM *Hrs Open:* 24; 0.24 kw horiz, 0.23 kw vert; 948 ft.; N35 26 23 W83 7 11
Sta Dept Western Car. Un, Cullowhee, NC 28723 US
(828) 227-7454, *Fax:* (828) 227-7099
www.wwcufm.com
info@wwcufm.com
License: Cullowhee, Jackson County, NC held by Western Carolina University.
Nat'l Network: ABC *Wire Services:* Reuters
Arbitron Metro Market: Cullowhee, NC *Format:* Sports *Target Audience:* 25-54; univ students & faculty, general public
Aaron D'Innocenzi, Operations Dir
Kyle McCurry, General Manager

Dallas

WCRU

01-01-1963; 960 khz AM *Hrs Open:* 6 AM-midnight
Mailing Address: P.O. Box 477, Dallas, NC 28034 US
Second Address: 407 Robinson Clemmer Rd., Dallas, NC 28034
(704) 922-3411(704) 922-5960, *Fax:* (704) 922-6998
www.wzrh.com
monty@wzrh.com
License: Dallas, NC held by Truth Broadcasting Corp.
Group Owner: Truth Broadcasting Corp.; (acq 6-30-2004; $775,000)
Arbitron Metro Market: Charlotte, NC *Format:* Talk *Hrs. of News Programming:* News progmg 10 hrs wkly *Target Audience:* Male 25-59; college educ, income 50K *Adv. Rates:* 180; 180; 180; 180
Stuart Epperson, President
Monty Monaghan, Station Manager

***WSGE**
10-27-1980; 91.7 mhz FM *Hrs Open:* 24; 7.5 kw; 853 ft.; N35 24 26 W81 7 48
201 Highway 321 South, Dallas, NC 28034 US
(704) 922-4286, *Fax:* (704) 922-2347
www.wsge.org
hall.cathis@gaston.edu
License: Dallas, Gaston County, NC held by Gaston College Board of Trustees.
Format: Triple A *Hrs. of News Programming:* News progmg 5 hrs wkly *Target Audience:* General.
Pat Skinner, President
Cathis Hall, Station Manager
David Baez, News Director

Davidson

***WDAV**
09-01-1973; 89.9 mhz FM *Hrs Open:* 24; 100 kw; 807 ft.; N35 26 54 W80 50 23
Mailing Address: P.O. Box 1540, Ridge Rd., Davidson, NC 20836 US
Second Address: 423 N. Main St., Davidson, NC 28036
(877) 333-8990, *Fax:* (704) 894-2997
www.wdav.org
wdav@davidson.edu
License: Davidson, Mecklenburg County, NC held by Trustees of Davidson College.
Nat'l Network: PRI; NPR
Arbitron Metro Market: Charlotte, NC *Format:* Talk *Hrs. of News Programming:* News progmg 2 hrs wkly *Target Audience:* General.
Joe Brant, Operations Dir
Scott Nolan, General Manager
Frank Dominguez, Programming Director
Larry Schropp, Chief Engineer
Kim Cline, Assistant General Manager
Ted Weiner, Music Director
Joe Brant, On-Air Host
Jennifer Foster,On-Air Host
Mike McKay, On-Air Host
Ted Weiner, Music Director

Dillsboro

***WNQS**
11-30-2012; 89.7 mhz FM; 18.5 w; 932 ft; N35 26 23 W83 07 11
179 Cross Creek Drive, Toccoa, GA
License: Dillsboro, Jackson County, NC
Group Owner: Toccoa Foundation Inc.

Dobson

WYZD
10-10-1978; 1560 khz AM
P.O. Box 797, Dobson, NC 27017 US
(336) 356-1560
License: Dobson, NC held by Gospel Broadcasting Inc.
Regional Network: N.C. News Net.
Arbitron Metro Market: Dobson, NC *Format:* Gospel
Ricky Cothren, General Manager

Dunn

WCKB
12-07-1946; 780 khz AM *Hrs Open:* Sunrise-sunset
Mailing Address: P. O. Box 789, Dunn, NC 28335 US
Second Address: 17336 US Hwy 421 S., Dunn, NC 28334
(910) 892-3133, *Fax:* (910) 892-3135
www.wckb780.com
wckb@wckb780.com
License: Dunn, NC held by N.C. Central Broadcasters Inc.
Regional Network: N.C. News Net.
Arbitron Metro Market: Dunn, NC *Format:* Gospel, Religious
Special Programming: Good Morning, Charlie,Southern Gospel Concert Update,Hymnal Harmony *Hrs. of News Programming:* News progmg 6 hrs wkly *Target Audience:* 25 plus; Christian, family-oriented with regional interests *Adv. Rates:* 11; 11; 11; 11; na
Charles Fowler, President
Ronald Tart, General Manager
Lottie Squires, Programming Director
Neal Wood, Assistant Music Director

WRCQ
05-17-1971; 103.5 mhz FM *Hrs Open:* 24; 48 kw; 502 ft.; N35 3 9 W78 38 54
Post Office Box 35297, Fayetteville, NC 28303 US
(910) 864-5222, *Fax:* (910) 864-3065
www.rock103rocks.com
License: Dunn, Harnett County, NC held by Cumulus Licensing Corp.
Group Owner: Cumulus Media Inc.; (acq 3-12-01; grpsl).
Nat'l Network: ABC
Arbitron Metro Market: Fayetteville, NC *Format:* Rock/AOR *Hrs. of News Programming:* news progmg one hr wkly *No. News Employees:* 1 *Target Audience:* 18-49.
Alan Buffaloe, General Manager
Al Fields, Programming Director

Durham

WDCG
02-28-1948; 105.1 mhz FM; 73 kw; 1112 ft.; N35 42 50 W78 49 4
600 Congress, Austin, TX 78701 US
(919) 871-1051, *Fax:* (919) 876-2929
www.g105.com
zacdavis@clearchannel.com
License: Durham, Durham County, NC held by Capstar TX L.P.
Group Owner: Clear Channel Communications Inc.; (acq 8-30-00; grpsl).
Nat'l Network: ABC
Arbitron Metro Market: Raleigh-Durham, NC *Format:* Contemporary Hits/Top 40 *Target Audience:* 18-49.
Jon Robbins, Operations Dir
Ken Spitzer, General Manager
Tammy O'Dell, General Sales Mgr
Zac Davis, Programming Director
Larry Jessup, Promotions Manager
Tracy Leonard, News Director
Fred Pace, Chief Engineer
Myron Bethea,General Sales Manager
Dan McLeod, Public Affairs Director

WDNC
04-09-1934; 620 khz AM *Hrs Open:* 24
407 Blackwell Street, Durham, NC 27701 US
(919) 890-6290, *Fax:* (919) 890-6146
www.espntriangle.com
contact@999thefan.com
License: Durham, NC held by WCHL-WDNC Inc.
Group Owner: Curtis Media Group; (acq 12-30-86)
Nat'l Network: Sporting News Radio Network *Nat'l Reps:* McGavren Guild *Wire Services:* AP
Arbitron Metro Market: Raleigh-Durham, NC *Format:* Sports *Adv. Rates:* 30; 26; 30; 18
Brian Maloney, General Manager
Adam Gold, Programming Director
Mike Stangl, Promotions Manager

WDUR
01-01-1947; 1490 khz AM *Hrs Open:* 24; 1 kw-U, ND1; N35 58 3 W78 53 18
200 Concord Plaza, Suite 600, San Antonio, TX 78216 US
(770) 825-0095, *Fax:* (770) 246-0054
www.prietobroadcasting.com
License: Durham, NC held by Prieto Broadcasting Inc.
Group Owner: Prieto Broadcasting Inc.; (acq 10-15-2007; $900,000)
Nat'l Network: ESPN Radio
Arbitron Metro Market: Durham, NC *Format:* Sports
Filiberto Prieto, President

WFXC
05-15-1971; 107.1 mhz FM *Hrs Open:* 24; 8 kw; 479 ft.; N35 58 39 W78 48 58
200 Concord Plaza, Suite 600, San Antonio, TX 78216 US
(919) 848-9736, *Fax:* (919) 863-4859
www.foxyhits.com
License: Durham, Durham County, NC held by Radio One Licenses LLC.
Group Owner: Radio One Inc.; (acq 11-8-2001; grpsl).
Wire Services: UPI
Arbitron Metro Market: Raleigh-Durham, NC *Format:* Urban Contemporary *Special Programming:* Gospel 4 hrs wkly *Hrs. of News Programming:* news progmg 5 hrs wkly *No. News Employees:* 1 *Target Audience:* 25-54; African American
Cy Young, Operations Dir
Gary Weiss, General Manager

***WNCU**
08-01-1995; 90.7 mhz FM *Hrs Open:* 24; 50 kw; 433 ft.; N36 3 33 W78 57 14
Post Office Box 19363, Durham, NC 27707 US
(919) 530-7445, *Fax:* (919) 530-5031
www.wncu.org
lsykes@nccu.edu
License: Durham, Durham County, NC held by North Carolina Central University.
Nat'l Network: NPR; PRI
Arbitron Metro Market: Durham, NC *Format:* Jazz, News, 62, Talk *Hrs. of News Programming:* news progmg 33 hrs wkly *No. News Employees:* 1 *Target Audience:* 25-54; middle class/middle age
Chris Whitfield, Operations Dir
Lackisha Freeman, General Manager
Uchenna Johnson, General Sales Mgr
Kimberley Pierce, News Director
James Davis, Chief Engineer
B.H. Hudson, Music Director

WRJD
10-14-1954; 1410 khz AM *Hrs Open:* 24
645 Church St, Suite 400, Norfolk, VA 23510 US
(919) 220-3226, *Fax:* (919) 220-0006
www.1410wrjd.com
License: Durham, NC held by Davidson Media Station WSRC Licensee LLC.
Group Owner: Davidson Media Group LLC; (acq 3-20-2006; $1.2 million).
Arbitron Metro Market: Raleigh-Durham, NC *Format:* Gospel, Talk *No. News Employees:* 5 *Target Audience:* 25-54.
Linda Greenwood, General Manager

WTIK
01-01-1945; 1310 khz AM *Hrs Open:* 24; 5 kw-D, DA2; 1 kw-N, DA2; N36 1 30 W78 54 8
P.O. Box 889, Blacksburg, VA 24063 US
(704) 987-3585
www.lameganc.com
info@wtik.com
License: Durham, NC held by Davidson Media Carolinas Stations LLC.
Group Owner: Davidson Media Group LLC; (acq 5-10-2004; grpsl).
Arbitron Metro Market: Durham, NC *Format:* Spanish
Peter Davidson, President

***WXDU**
11-01-1983; 88.7 mhz FM *Hrs Open:* 24; 2.15 kw; 253 ft.; N36 2 8 W79 4 48
P.O. Box 90834, Durham, NC 27708 US
(919) 684-2957, *Fax:* (919) 684-3260
www.wxdu.org
wxdu@duke.edu
License: Durham, Durham County, NC held by Duke University.
Arbitron Metro Market: Durham, NC *Format:* Variety/Diverse
Special Programming: Jazz 18 hrs, urban sound & hip hop 12 hrs wkly *Target Audience:* General.
Addie, General Manager
Kelly, Programming Director
Candace, Promotions Manager
Jim Davis, Chief Engineer
Ross, Local Music Director
Georg, World Music Director

East Fayetteville

***WWFJ**
88.1 mhz FM; 0.13 kw; 117 ft.; N35 0 4.4 W78 48 33.2 US
(910) 693-7729
License: East Fayetteville, Cumberland County, NC held by Highland Baptist Church.
Arbitron Metro Market: East Fayetteville, NC *Format:* Christian
Bill Vaughn, President

Eden

WCLW
08-16-1970; 1130 khz AM; 1 kw-D; N36 31 21 W79 45 55
116 S. Franklin St., Reidsville, NC 27320
(336) 634-1774, *Fax:* (336) 342-6497
www.carolinabaptistcollege.com/radio.html
License: Eden, Rockingham County, NC held by Dr. Jerry L. Carter dba Reidsville Baptist Church.
Target Audience: all
Dean Lundy, General Manager

WLOE
12-20-1946; 1490 khz AM *Hrs Open:* 5 AM-10 PM; 1 kw-U, ND1; N36 30 21 W79 46 18 *Rebroadcasts:* Rebroadcasts WMYN Mayodan NC 100%.
P. O. Box 311, Madison, NC 27025 US
(336) 427-9696, *Fax:* (336) 548-4636
www.wloewmyn.com
info@wloewmyn.com
License: Eden, NC held by Mayo Broadcasting Corp.
Nat'l Network: Salem Radio Network; USA
Format: Talk, Religious *Hrs. of News Programming:* news progmg 30 hrs wkly *No. News Employees:* 1 *Target Audience:* 25 plus; general *Adv. Rates:* 25; 25; 25; 25
Richard Hall, President
Mike Moore, General Manager
Annette Moore, Station Manager

WPTI
03-20-1949; 94.5 mhz FM; 100 kw; Ant 981 ft; N36 20 48 W79 54 30
2-B Pai park, Greensboro, NC 78216
(336) 822-2000, *Fax:* (336) 887-0104
License: Eden, Rockingham County, NC held by Clear Channel Broadcasting Licenses Inc.
Group Owner: Clear Channel Communications Inc.; (acq 1996; grpsl).
Nat'l Reps: Clear Channel
Population Served: 15,871 *Arbitron Metro Market:* Greensboro-Winston Salem-High Point, NC
Morgan Bohannon, General Manager
Pierre Proupe, General Sales Mgr
Carlos Pivano, Programming Director

Edenton

WBXB
06-18-1976; 100.1 mhz FM *Hrs Open:* 24; 50 kw; 302 ft.; N36 7 11 W76 35 29
Mailing Address: C/O Putbrese Hunsaker, P. O. Box 217, Sterling, VA 20167 US
Second Address: 1900 Paradise Rd., Edenton, NC 27932
(252) 482-8680, *Fax:* (252) 482-4260
robbmal@aol.com
License: Edenton, Chowan County, NC held by Willis Family Broadcasting Inc.
Group Owner: Willis Broadcasting Corp.; acq 3-4-92; grpsl;
Nat'l Network: American Urban
Arbitron Metro Market: Sterling, VA *Format:* Gospel *Hrs. of News Programming:* News progmg 8 hrs wkly *Target Audience:* General. *Adv. Rates:* 15; 12; 15; 12
Bishop L.E. Willis Sr., President
Toina Willis, General Manager

WZBO
11-01-1955; 1260 khz AM; 1 kw-D, ND2; 0.034 kw-N, ND2; N36 5 0 W76 36 0
P.O. Box 1800, Raleigh, NC 27602 US
(252) 482-2104, *Fax:* (252) 482-5591
www.ecri.net
swalker@ecri.net
License: Edenton, NC held by East Carolina Radio of Elizabeth City Inc.
Group Owner: East Carolina Radio Group; (acq 3-12-90; $400,000 with co-located FM;
Arbitron Metro Market: Edenton, NC *Format:* Tejano
Rick Loesch, President
Tom Charity, Operations Dir
Sam Walker, Programming Director

Elizabeth City

WCNC
09-01-1939; 1240 khz AM *Hrs Open:* 24; 1 kw-U, ND1; N36 18 38 W76 13 56
Mailing Address: Post Office Box 950, Edenton, NC 27932 US
Second Address: 911 Parsonage St. Ext., Elizabeth City, NC 27909
(252) 335-4379, *Fax:* (252) 441-2109
www.ecri.net
psa@ecri.net
License: Elizabeth City, NC held by East Carolina Radio of Elizabeth City Inc.
Group Owner: East Carolina Radio Group; (acq 10-29-98; $230,000)
Arbitron Metro Market: Elizabeth City-Nags Head, NC *Format:* Tejano
Rick Loesch, President
Cuervo Curtis, Operations Dir
Tom Charity, General Sales Mgr
Sam Walker, Programming Director

WGAI
11-02-1947; 560 khz AM *Hrs Open:* 24
P.O. Box 1040, Kill Devil Hills, NC 27948 US
(252) 480-4655, *Fax:* (252) 441-8063
www.newsradio560.com
info@wgai.com
License: Elizabeth City, NC held by Max Radio of the Carolinas Licenses LLC.
Group Owner: MAX Media L.L.C.; (acq 11-12-2002; grpsl).
Nat'l Network: CNN Radio *Regional Network:* Agrinet
Format: News, News/Talk, 84, Talk *Special Programming:* Relg 4 hrs, farm 7 hrs, Black 4 hrs, relg 4 hrs wk *Hrs. of News Programming:* news progmg 30 hrs wkly *No. News Employees:* 3 *Target Audience:* General.
Tim Boze, Operations Dir
Mike Smith, General Manager

WKJX
08-21-1984; 96.7 mhz FM *Hrs Open:* 24; 50 kw; 407 ft.; N36 12 10 W75 52 23
Mailing Address: Post Office Box 950, Eddenton, NC 27932 US
Second Address: 911 Parsonage St. Ext., Elizabeth City, NC 27909
(252) 338-0196, *Fax:* (252) 338-5275
www.ecri.net
swalker@ecri.net
License: Elizabeth City, Pasquotank County, NC held by East Carolina Radio of Elizabeth City Inc.
Group Owner: East Carolina Radio Group; (acq 5-21-98; $475,000).
Nat'l Network: NBC Radio; Westwood One *Regional Network:* N.C. News Net.
Format: Adult Contemp *Hrs. of News Programming:* news progmg one hr wkly *No. News Employees:* 1 *Target Audience:* 18-55. *Adv. Rates:* 15; 15; 15; 12
Rick Loesch, President
Cuervo Curtis, Operations Dir
Tom Charity, General Sales Mgr
Sam Walker, Programming Director

***WRVS-FM**
03-18-1986; 89.9 mhz FM *Hrs Open:* 24; 41 kw; 230 ft.; N36 16 55 W76 12 44
1704 Weedsville Road, Campus Box 790, Elizabeth City, NC 27909 US
(252) 335-3400, *Fax:* (252) 335-3745
www.ecsu.edu/wrvs/
mybrown@mail.ecsu.edu
License: Elizabeth City, Pasquotank County, NC held by Elizabeth City State University.
Nat'l Network: NPR; PRI
Format: Variety/Diverse *Special Programming:* Jazz 6 hrs, Black 20 hrs, gospel 20 *Hrs. of News Programming:* news progmg 5 hrs wkly *No. News Employees:* 1 *Target Audience:* 18-24; young adult, college
Willie Gilchnist, CEO
Melba Smith, General Manager
Ben Shaner, Chief Engineer

***WVRL**
02-01-2003; 88.3 mhz FM; 50 kw; Ant 446 ft; N36 18 40 W76 17 34
905 Halstead Blvd., Suite 29, Elizabeth City, NC 92704
(252) 334-1883, *Fax:* (252) 333-1459
www.wgpsradio.com
wgpsradio@earthlink.net
License: Elizabeth City, Pasquotank County, NC held by CSN International
Group Owner: CSN International

Jeff Ozanne, General Manager
Darla Ozanne, Programming Director
Maria Van DeWalker, Music Director

Elizabethtown

WBLA
08-03-1956; 1440 khz AM *Hrs Open:* 24
Mailing Address: 1602 Greenwood Street, Elizabethtown, NC 28337 US
Second Address: Box 28, Clinton, NC 28329
(910)488-7729, *Fax:* (910) 872-0100
www.wgqr1057.com
wgqr1057@carolina.net
License: Elizabethtown, NC held by Sound Business of Elizabethtown Inc.
Regional Network: N.C. News Net.
Format: Oldies *Special Programming:* Black gospel/relg 8 hrs wkly *Hrs. of News Programming:* News progmg 5 hrs wkly *Target Audience:* 25-54.
Lee Hauser, President
Bruce Dickerson, Operations Dir
Patrick Dixon, General Manager
Al Radlein, Programming Director
Buddy Wommack, Chief Engineer
Paul Reese, Disc Jockey
Bill Monroe, Disc Jockey
Don Arnsan, Disc Jockey

Elkin

WIFM-FM
01-01-1949; 100.9 mhz FM *Hrs Open:* 24; 600 w; 709 ft; N36 11 33 W80 50 59
Mailing Address: Box 1038, Elkin, NC 20120
Second Address: 813 N. Bridge St., Elkin, NC 28621
(336) 835-2511, *Fax:* (336) 835-5248
www.wifmradio.com
wifm@wifmradio.com
License: Elkin, Surry County, NC held by Yadkin Valley Broadcasting Corp.
Nat'l Network: ABC
No. News Employees: 1 *Target Audience:* 25-45. *Adv. Rates:* 24; 22.25; 24; 19.50
Gary York, President
Ronda Johnson, General Manager
Danny Hall, Programming Director
Stoney Owen, Engineering Dir
Joel Harper, Sports Director

Elm City

WRSV
01-01-1949; 92.1 mhz FM *Hrs Open:* 24; 2.35 kw; 531 ft.; N35 48 40 W77 44 33
Mailing Address: P.O. Box 2666, Rocky Mount, NC 27802 US
Second Address: 115 N. Church St., Rocky Mount, NC 27802
(252) 937-7400, *Fax:* (252)443-5977
www.soul92jams.com
soul92_2000@yahoo.com
License: Elm City, Nash County, NC
Nat'l Network: Premiere Radio Networks
Arbitron Metro Market: Rocky Mount-Wil *Format:* Urban Contemporary *Hrs. of News Programming:* news progmg 3 hrs wkly *No. News Employees:* 25 *Target Audience:* General; African American consumers of all age groups*Adv. Rates:* Call for rates
Sonya Johnson, Operations Dir
Charles Johnson, II, General Manager
Chuck Johnson, Music Director

Elon College

***WSOE**
11-01-1978; 89.3 mhz FM; 0.5 kw; 121 ft.; N36 6 25 W79 30 22
100 Campus Drive, 6000 Campus Box, Elon College, NC 27244 US
(336) 278-7210, *Fax:* (336) 278-7298
www.elon.edu/wsoe
wsoe@elon.edu
License: Elon College, Alamance County, NC held by Elon University.
Format: Alternative
Nikki Wasikowski, General Manager
Ryan Sweeney, Programming Director

Enfield

WVRA
07-14-2007; 107.3 mhz FM *Hrs Open:* 24; 4.1 kw; Ant 279 ft; N36 09 59 W77 46 46
301 S. Church St., Suite 270, Rocky Mount, NC
(252) 446-9262, *Fax:* (252) 446-9261
www.thepromise1073.com
bwilliams@newlitemedia.com
License: Enfield, Halifax County, NC held by Julie Epperson.
Nat'l Network: American Urban
Arbitron Metro Market: Rocky Mount-Wilson, NC
Bronson Williams, Programming Director

Erwin

***WUAW**
05-11-1990; 88.3 mhz FM *Hrs Open:* 24; 3 kw; 207 ft.; N35 20 15 W78 39 49
215 Maynard Lake Road, Erwin, NC 28339 US
(910) 897-8070, *Fax:* (910) 897-3148
www.wuaw.homestead.com
wuaw883fm@gaggle.net
License: Erwin, Harnett County, NC held by Central Carolina Community College.
Arbitron Metro Market: Fayetteville, NC *Format:* Variety/Diverse
Matt Garrett, President
Ron McLamb, General Manager
Dr. Jim Davis, Chief Engineer

Fair Bluff

WQTM
07-01-1988; 1480 khz AM *Hrs Open:* 24; 1 kw-D, 48 w-N; N34 19 23 W79 00 07
Mailing Address: Box 424, Cerrogordo, NC 28439
Second Address: 12045 Andrew Jackson Hwy., Fair Bluff, NC 28439
(910) 649-1480, *Fax:* (910) 649-7266
wsrc1480@emdarqmail.com
License: Fair Bluff, Columbus County, NC held by Rama Radio of North Carolina Inc.

Population Served: 250,000
Anthony Lee, Station Manager

WODR
01-01-2003; 105.3 mhz FM; 11 kw; 492 ft.; N34 17 1 W78 48 9
P O Box 10300, Florence, SC 29501 US
(910) 642-2013, *Fax:* (866) 927-2180
www.coolbeach1053.com
mailto:request@coolbeach1053.com
License: Fair Bluff, Columbus County, NC held by The Padner Group LLC
Arbitron Metro Market: Whiteville, NC *Format:* Oldies
William Polk, General Manager

Fairmont

WFMO
07-13-1953; 860 khz AM; 1 kw-D, ND1; 0.012 kw-N, ND1; N34 31 3 W79 6 19
P.O. Box 665, Fairmont, NC 28340 US
(910) 486-9438, *Fax:* (910) 484-4040
License: Fairmont, NC held by Pro Media Inc.
Regional Network: N.C. News Net.
Arbitron Metro Market: Fayetteville, NC *Format:* Black, Gospel, 74 *Special Programming:* Farm 5 hrs wkly *Target Audience:* 25-54.
James Clark, President

WSTS
08-01-1975; 100.9 mhz FM; 50 kw; 489 ft.; N34 16 17 W78 56 24
P.O. Box 665, Fairmont, NC 28340 US
(910) 628-6781, *Fax:* (910) 628-6648
wstf@carolina.net
License: Fairmont, Robeson County, NC held by Davidson Media Station WSTS Licensee LLC.
Group Owner: Davidson Media Group LLC; (acq 10-31-2005)
Regional Network: N.C. News Net.
Arbitron Metro Market: Fayetteville, NC *Format:* Gospel
James Clark, General Manager
Shanna Todd, Programming Director

Fairview

WPEK
07-04-1997; 880 khz AM
1470 Ben Sawyer Blvd, Ste 16, Mount Pleasant, SC 29464 US
(828) 257-2700, *Fax:* (828) 255-7850
www.880therevolution.com
brianhall@clearchannel
License: Fairview, NC held by Clear Channel Broadcasting Licenses Inc.
Group Owner: Clear Channel Communications Inc.; (acq 3-21-01; grpsl).
Nat'l Network: CBS
Arbitron Metro Market: Asheville, NC *Format:* Talk *Target Audience:* 25-64; generally upscale adults
Ken Salyer, General Manager
Gene Austin, General Sales Mgr
Brian Hall, Programming Director
Skip Wilson, Digital Sales Manager

Farmville

WGHB
12-12-1959; 1250 khz AM *Hrs Open:* 24; 5 kw-D, DA2; 2.5 kw-N, DA2; N35 36 17 W77 34 29
Box 229, Hwy 121 N., Farmville, NC 27828 US
(252) 317-1250, *Fax:* (252) 317-1255
www.pirateradio1250.com
info@pirateradio1250.com
License: Farmville, NC held by Pirate Media Group LLC
Nat'l Network: USA
Arbitron Metro Market: Greenville-New Bern-Jacksonville, NC *Format:* Sports, Talk *Hrs. of News Programming:* News progmg 8 hrs wkly *Target Audience:* 25-54.
Troy Dreyfus, General Manager
Wesley Hines, Programming Director

WRHD
03-24-1974; 94.3 mhz FM *Hrs Open:* 24; 3.9 kw; Ant 407 ft; N35 36 25 W77 28 05
211 Commerce St., Suite C, Greenville, NC 27834
(252) 355-1037, *Fax:* (252) 355-2234
www.talkfm943.com
License: Farmville, Pitt County, NC held by Inner Banks Media LLC.
Group Owner: Inner Banks Media LLC; (acq 3-12-2007; grpsl)
Regional Network: N.C. News Net.
Population Served: 100,000 *Arbitron Metro Market:* Greenville-New Bern-Jacksonville, NC *Hrs. of News Programming:* News progmg 3 hrs wkly *Target Audience:* 25-54.

Henry Hinton, General Manager

Fayetteville

WAZZ
01-01-1947; 1490 khz AM *Hrs Open:* 24
3012 Highwood Blvd. #201, Raleigh, NC 27604 US
(901) 726-8970, *Fax:* (901) 375-0041
mail@flinn.com
License: Fayetteville, NC held by WFLB License L.P.
Group Owner: Beasley Broadcast Group Inc.; (acq 1996; $228,635).
Nat'l Reps: D & R Radio
Arbitron Metro Market: Charleston WV
George Flinn Jr., President

WFAY
01-01-1947; 1230 khz AM *Hrs Open:* 24*Rebroadcasts:* Simulcast with WCIE(AM) Spring Lake 100%
346 Wagoner Drive, Fayetteville, NC 28303 US
(910) 867-4129, *Fax:* (704) 537-9735
www.espnfay.com
wfayespnradio@gmail.com
License: Fayetteville, NC held by Norsan Consulting and Management Inc.
Group Owner: Norsan Consulting and Management Inc.; (acq 5-25-2006; $850,000)
Nat'l Network: ESPN Radio
Arbitron Metro Market: Fayetteville, NC *Format:* Sports
Norberto Sanchez, CEO
Paul Lawing, General Manager

WFNC
01-01-1940; 640 khz AM *Hrs Open:* 24; 10 kw-D, ND1; 1 kw-N, ND1; N35 4 46 W78 55 58
P.O. Box 35297, Fayettevillle, NC 28303 US
(910) 864-5222, *Fax:* (910) 864-3065
www.wfnc640am.com
jimcooke@cumulus.com
License: Fayetteville, NC held by Cumulus Licensing Corp.
Group Owner: Cumulus Media Inc.; (acq 3-12-2001; grpsl)
Nat'l Network: CBS *Wire Services:* AP
Arbitron Metro Market: Fayetteville, NC *Format:* News, News/Talk, 86 *Hrs. of News Programming:* news progmg 20 hrs wkly *No. News Employees:* 4 *Target Audience:* 35 plus.
Alan Buffaloe, General Manager
Jim Cooke, Programming Director
Patrick Jackson, Promotions Manager
Gail Galbreath, Engineering Dir
Stephen Roberts, Market Manager and Director of Sales
Greg Sher, Regional Market Manager

***WFSS**
12-07-1977; 91.9 mhz FM *Hrs Open:* 24; 100 kw; 351 ft.; N35 4 22 W78 53 27
1200 Murchison Road, Fayetteville, NC 28301 US
(910) 672-2650, *Fax:* (910) 672-1964
wfss.org
wfss@uncfsu.edu
License: Fayetteville, Cumberland County, NC held by Fayetteville State University Board of Trustees.
Nat'l Network: NPR; PRI *Wire Services:* AP
Arbitron Metro Market: Fayetteville, NC *Format:* Jazz, News
Special Programming: Gospel 2 hrs, African rhythms 2 hrs, class 5 hrs, *Hrs. of News Programming:* news progmg 38 hrs wkly *No. News Employees:* 1*Target Audience:* 18 plus; general
Joe Ross, General Manager
Yvonne Jackson, General Sales Mgr
Janet Wright, Programming Director
Kathy Klaus, News Director
Ron Martin, Chief Engineer
Jimmy Miller, Music Director
Arvetra Jones Jr., Religion Ed
Dorothy Director,Development Director
Jimmy Miller, Music Director
Karen Andrews, Administrative Support Associate

WIDU
01-20-1958; 1600 khz AM *Hrs Open:* 24; 5 kw-D, DA2; 0.147 kw-N, DA2; N35 5 54 W78 53 12
Mailing Address: P. O. Box 2247, Fayetteville, NC 28302 US
Second Address: 1338 Bragg Blvd., Fayetteville, NC 28301
(910) 483-6111, *Fax:* (910) 483-6601
www.rejoicewidu.com
widu1600@aol.com
License: Fayetteville, NC held by Charles W. Cookman
Arbitron Metro Market: Fayetteville, NC *Format:* Black, Gospel, 60, News/Talk, Talk
Wes Cookman, President
Sandra Lofton, General Manager
Val Holiday, Programming Director

WQSM
01-01-1947; 98.1 mhz FM; 100 kw; 830 ft.; N35 4 46 W78 55 58
P. O. Box 35297., Fayetteville, NC 28303 US
(910) 864-5222, *Fax:* (910) 864-6208
www.cumulus.com
jeffdavis@cumulus.com
License: Fayetteville, Cumberland County, NC
Arbitron Metro Market: Fayetteville, NC *Format:* Contemporary Hits/Top 40 *Target Audience:* General.
Paul Michels, General Sales Mgr
Chris Chaos, Programming Director
Robin Duff, News Director
Rick O'Shea, Disc Jockey
Rick Jensen, Disc Jockey

***WYBH**
01-01-2008; 91.1 mhz FM; 0.255 kw; 640 ft.; N35 3 35 W78 59 24 *Rebroadcasts:* Rebroadcasts WYFQ(AM) Charlotte 100%
8030 Arrowridge Blvd., Charlotte, NC 28273 US
(704) 523-5555
www.bbnradio.org
License: Fayetteville, Cumberland County, NC held by Bible Broadcasting Network Inc.
Group Owner: Bible Broadcasting Network
Nat'l Network: Bible Bcstg Net
Arbitron Metro Market: Fayetteville, NC *Format:* Christian
Lowell Davey, President

Fletcher

WQNQ
02-05-1991; 104.3 mhz FM *Hrs Open:* 24; 0.47 kw; 1145 ft.; N35 31 39 W82 29 49
1470 Ben Sawyer Blvd., Suite 16, Mount Pleasant, SC 29464 US
(828) 257-2700, *Fax:* (828) 255-7850
www.star1043.com
info@star1043.com
License: Fletcher, Henderson County, NC held by Clear Channel Broadcasting Licenses Inc.
Group Owner: Clear Channel Communications Inc.; (acq 3-21-2001; grpsl).
Arbitron Metro Market: Asheville, NC *Special Programming:* Relg 2 hrs, news/talk 5 hrs wkly *Hrs. of News Programming:* news progmg 10 hrs wkly *No. News Employees:* 2 *Target Audience:* 25-54. *Adv. Rates:* 40; 30; 40; 15
Ken Salyer, General Manager
Caroline Earley, General Sales Mgr
Josh Michael, Programming Director

Forest City

WTPT
09-10-1947; 93.3 mhz FM; 93 kw; 2031 ft.; N35 16 19 W82 14 0
1250 Connecticut Avenue, NW, Suite 800, Washington, DC 20036 US
(864) 271-9200, *Fax:* (864) 242-1567
www.newrock933.com
info@newrock933.com
License: Forest City, Rutherford County, NC held by Entercom Greenville License LLC.
Group Owner: Entercom Communications Corp.; (acq 10-7-2005; grpsl).
Arbitron Metro Market: Greenville, SC *Format:* Rock/AOR *No. News Employees:* 1
David Field, President
Sharon Day, General Manager
Randy Cables, General Sales Mgr
Mark Hendrix, Programming Director
Paige Pirtle, News Director

WWOL
09-10-1947; 780 khz AM *Hrs Open:* Sunrise-sunset; 10 kw-D, NDD; N35 21 2 W81 54 4
1381 West Main Street, Forest City, NC 28043 US
(828) 245-0078, *Fax:* (828) 245-8528
www.wwol780.com
wwol@wwol780.com
License: Forest City, NC held by Holly Springs Baptist Church.
Nat'l Network: USA
Arbitron Metro Market: Forest City, NC *Format:* Gospel, Religious
Special Programming: Our community forum, NC family policy issues *No. News Employees:* 3 *Target Audience:* General.
Wade Huntley, President
Ray Davis, Operations Dir
Terri Frashier, General Sales Mgr
Jean Bruce, News Director

WAGY
10-15-1958; 1320 khz AM; 1 kw-D, DAN; 0.5 kw-N, DAN; N35 21 19 W81 52 52
P. O. Box 280, Forest City, NC 28043 US

RADIO - U.S.

(828) 245-9887, *Fax:* (828) 245-9880
License: Forest City, NC held by WAGY Inc.
Arbitron Metro Market: Forest City, NC *Format:* Country
Malcolm Watson, General Manager

Fort Dodge

*KWOP(FM)

88.7 mhz FM; 200 watts; 37.8 meters; N42 33 18.1 W94 07 46.6
6704 NC Highway 8 South, Germantown, NC 27019 USA
(336) 591-9076
License: Fort Dodge, IA held by Church Planters of America
William Danny Hawkins, President

Franklin

*WFQS

03-31-1989; 91.3 mhz FM *Hrs Open:* 24; 0.265 kw horiz, 0.255 kw vert; 2303 ft.; N35 10 24 W83 34 52 *Rebroadcasts:* Rebroadcasts WCQS(FM) Asheville 100%
73 Broadway, Asheville, NC 28801 US
(828) 253-6875, *Fax:* (828) 253-6700
www.wcqs.org
info@wcqs.org
License: Franklin, Macon County, NC held by Western N.C. Public Radio Inc.
Nat'l Network: NPR; PRI
Format: Jazz, News *Special Programming:* Folk 9 hrs wkly *Hrs. of News Programming:* news progmg 35 hrs wkly *No. News Employees:* 1 *Target Audience:* 25 plus.
Lee Wilcher, Operations Dir
Edward Subkis, General Manager
Steve Busey, General Sales Mgr
Barbara Sayer, Programming Director
David Hurand, News Director
Tom Spaight, Chief Engineer
Richard Kowal, Music Director
Vicky Gerald,Taffic Manager
Trent Henley, Public Service Announcements Producer
Michelle Keenan, Membership Director
Dick Kowal, Director of Music Programming

WFSC

05-05-1957; 1050 khz AM *Hrs Open:* 24/7
Mailing Address: P. O. Box 470, Franklin, NC 28734 US
Second Address: 180 Radio Hill Rd., Franklin, NC 28734
(828) 524-4418, *Fax:* (828) 524-2788
www.1050wfsc.com
gibson@gacaradio.com
License: Franklin, NC held by Sutton Radiocasting Corp.
Group Owner: Georgia-Carolina Radiocasting Companies; (acq 12-14-2001; grpsl).
Nat'l Network: CBS; ABC *Regional Network:* N.C. News Net.
Format: News, Oldies *Hrs. of News Programming:* Local news progmg 12 hrs wkly *No. News Employees:* 1 *Target Audience:* 35 plus.
Douglas M. Sutton Jr., President
M Terry Carter, Operations Dir
Sean Gibson, General Manager
Keith Giles, News Director
Marty Lee, Chief Engineer
Benita Snyder, Office Manager
George Young, Operation Manager

WPFJ

05-24-1979; 1480 khz AM *Hrs Open:* 24
106 Palmer Street, Franklin, NC 28734 US
(828) 369-5033, *Fax:* (828) 369-3197
www.wpfj.com
thedove@wpfj.com
License: Franklin, NC held by Drake Enterprises Ltd.
Nat'l Network: Salem Radio Network
Format: Religious *Hrs. of News Programming:* News progmg 12 hrs wkly *Target Audience:* 25-54.
Johnny Lee, General Sales Mgr
Brenda Wooten, Promotions Manager
Rick Cruse, Chief Engineer

WNCC-FM

09-01-1965; 96.7 mhz FM *Hrs Open:* 24; 6 kw horiz; -331 ft.; N35 12 40 W83 22 7
Mailing Address: P. O. Box 470, Franklin, NC 28734 US
Second Address: 180 Radio Hill Rd., Franklin, NC 28744
(828) 524-4418,(828) 524-5395, *Fax:* (828) 524-2788
www.967wncc.com
gibson@gacaradio.com
License: Franklin, Macon County, NC held by Sutton Radiocasting Corporation
Group Owner: Georgia-Carolina Radiocasting Companies
Nat'l Network: ABC
Format: Country *Special Programming:* NASCAR, Local Sports *Hrs. of News Programming:* news progmg 6 hrs wkly *No. News Employees:* 1 *Target Audience:* 25 plus.
Douglas M. Sutton, Jr., President
George Young, Operations Dir
Keith Giles, Programming Director
Marty Lee, Chief Engineer
Benita Snyder, Office Manager
Sean Gibson, Vice President
M. Terry Carter, Vice President

Franklinton

*WRTP

07-04-1994; 88.5 mhz FM *Hrs Open:* 24; 24 kw; 479 ft.; N36 17 44 W78 6 21
230-B Roanoke Ave., Roanoke Rapids, NC 27870 US
(919) 256-9787, *Fax:* (919) 256-9559
www.hisradiowrtp.com
Management@hisradiowrtp.com
License: Franklinton, Halifax County, NC held by Radio Training Network Inc.
Nat'l Network: Salem Radio Network *Nat'l Reps:* Salem
Arbitron Metro Market: Raleigh, NC *Format:* Christian *Hrs. of News Programming:* News progmg 14 hrs wkly *Target Audience:* 25-54; Christian
James Campbell, President
Mark Parker, General Manager
Randy Jordan, General Sales Mgr
Charlyne Laudrille, Underwriting Representative
Donna C, Public Service Director
Johanna, Director Of Support

Fuquay-Varina

WNNL

12-01-1980; 103.9 mhz FM *Hrs Open:* 24; 7.9 kw; 577 ft.; N35 35 47 W78 45 18
200 Concord Plaza, Suite 600, San Antonio, TX 78216 US
(919) 863-4430, *Fax:* (919) 863-4859
www.thelightnc.com
mmarinaro@radio-one.com
License: Fuquay-Varina, Wake County, NC held by Radio One Licenses LLC.
Group Owner: Radio One Inc.; (acq 11-8-01; grpsl).
Nat'l Network: ABC *Nat'l Reps:* Christal
Arbitron Metro Market: Raleigh, NC *Format:* Gospel, Religious *Hrs. of News Programming:* News progmg 20 hrs wkly *Target Audience:* 25-54; educated, upper income, professionals
Cy Young, Operations Dir
Gary Weiss, General Manager
Kim Gattis, General Sales Mgr
Jerry Smith, Programming Director
Steven Walker, General Sales Manager
Jodi Luke, National Sales Manager

Garner

WRTG

08-11-1969; 1000 khz AM *Hrs Open:* Daytime Only; 1 kw-D, NDD; N35 43 50 W78 36 12 *Rebroadcasts:* Rebroadcasts WRTP(AM) Chapel Hill 100%
P.O. Box 15400, Durham, NC 27704 US
(919) 477-7222, *Fax:* (919) 477-4424
estuardovaldemar@hotmail.com
License: Garner, NC held by Estuardo Valdemar Rodriguez and Leonor Rodriguez.
Group Owner: Radio La Grande; (acq 2-2-2005; grpsl)
Nat'l Network: USA
Arbitron Metro Market: Raleigh-Durham,
Leonor Rodriguez, President
Estuardo Rodriguez, General Manager

Garysburg

*WZRU

12-08-1972; 90.1 mhz FM *Hrs Open:* 24; 11 kw; 505 ft.; N36 14 39 W77 34 40
P.O. Box 2061, Bristol, TN 37621 US
(252) 308-0885, *Fax:* (252) 537-3333
www.wzru.org
License: Garysburg, Halifax County, NC held by Roanoke Valley Communications Inc.
Nat'l Network: NPR
Format: Adult Contemp *Special Programming:* Gospel 6 hrs, jazz 6 hrs, folk 5 hrs, oldies 4 hrs *Hrs. of News Programming:* news progmg 30 hrs wkly *No. News Employees:* 2 *Target Audience:* 35 plus; communityoriented, above-average education
Allen Garrett, General Manager

Gaston

WTRG

11-28-1988; 97.9 mhz FM *Hrs Open:* 24; 1.35 kw; 489 ft.; N36 27 38 W77 33 52
P.O. Box 910, Roanoke Rapids, NC 27870 US
(252) 538-9790, *Fax:* (252) 538-0378
www.thegreat98fm.com
al@bestradioaround.com
License: Gaston, Northampton County, NC held by First Media Radio LLC.
Group Owner: First Media Radio LLC; (acq 7-22-2003; grpsl)
Regional Network: N.C. News Net.; Va. News Net.
Format: Oldies *Hrs. of News Programming:* News progmg 2 hrs wkly *Target Audience:* 21-54.
CJ Riddick, Operations Dir
Al Haskins, General Manager
Marsha Collier, Business Manager

Gastonia

WBAV-FM

09-01-1947; 101.9 mhz FM; 99 kw; 988 ft.; N35 13 57 W81 16 35
C/O Cbs Radio. 600 New, Hampshire Ave., Ste 1200, Washington, DC 20037 US
(760) 947-4300, *Fax:* (760) 245-6268
www.ondasdevida.com
comentarios@ondadevida.com
License: Gastonia, Gaston County, NC held by Infinity Radio Holdings Inc.
Group Owner: CBS Radio; (acq 11-13-98; grpsl).
Nat'l Reps: Christal
Arbitron Metro Market: Barstow CA
Hector Manzo, CEO

WGNC

03-01-1939; 1450 khz AM *Hrs Open:* 24; 1 kw-U, ND1; N35 16 32 W81 12 4
P.O. Box 370, Cherryville, NC 28021 US
(704) 868-8222, *Fax:* (704) 482-4680
www.theboss.us
netoldies@aol.com
License: Gastonia, NC held by HRN Broadcasting Inc.
Group Owner: HRN Broadcasting Inc.; (acq 10-6-2006; $1.5 million with WOHS(AM) Shelby)
Nat'l Network: ABC; CBS Radio; Westwood One *Regional Network:* N.C. News Net.
Arbitron Metro Market: Charlotte-Gastonia-Rock Hill, NC-SC
Format: Oldies, Sports *Hrs. of News Programming:* news progmg 5 hrs wkly *No. News Employees:* 1 *Target Audience:* 18-49. *Adv. Rates:* 14.20;14.20; 14.20; 14.20
D. Mark Boyd III, President
Terresa Hastings, Operations Dir
Calvin Hastings, General Manager
Harold Watson, General Sales Mgr
Mike Slade, Programming Director
Lori Deitz, Promotions Manager
Anna McGinnis, News Director
AndyFoster, Music Director

Gatesville

WQDK

09-02-1968; 99.3 mhz FM *Hrs Open:* 24; 3.7 kw; 420 ft.; N36 16 29 W76 43 17
P.O. Box 1040, Kill Devil Hills, NC 27948 US
(252) 332-7993, *Fax:* (252) 332-6887
License: Gatesville, Hertford County, NC held by Max Radio of the Carolinas Licenses LLC.
Group Owner: MAX Media L.L.C.; (acq 11-12-2002; grpsl).
Regional Network: Agrinet
Format: Country *Special Programming:* Farm 7 hrs wkly
Don Upchurch, General Manager

Goldsboro

WFMC

11-11-1951; 730 khz AM *Hrs Open:* 24; 1 kw-D, 98 w-N; N35 22 25 W78 00 41
2581 U.S. Hwy. 70 W., Goldsboro, NC 27604
(919) 736-1150, *Fax:* (919) 736-3876
www.730wfmc.com
bjohnston@curtismedia.com
License: Goldsboro, Wayne County, NC held by New Age Communications Inc.
Group Owner: Curtis Media Group; (acq 6-95; $300,000)
Population Served: 120,000 *Arbitron Metro Market:* Raleigh-Durham, NC *Hrs. of News Programming:* news progmg 10 hrs wkly *No. News Employees:* 1 *Target Audience:* 25+.
Donald Curtis, President
Bill Johnston, General Manager

Averill Williams, Programming Director
Robyn Wade, News Director

WGBR
01-01-1939; 1150 khz AM *Hrs Open:* 24
3012 Highwoods Blvd., Raleigh, NC 27609 US
(919) 736-1150, *Fax:* (919) 736-3876
www.wgbr.com
License: Goldsboro, NC held by New Age Communications L.P.
Group Owner: Curtis Media Group; (acq 2-15-89; $2.2 million with co-located FM;
Nat'l Network: CNN Radio *Regional Network:* N.C. News Net. *Wire Services:* AP
Format: News, News/Talk, 86 *Hrs. of News Programming:* news progmg 11 hrs wkly *No. News Employees:* 1 *Target Audience:* 25 plus.
Donald Curtis, President
Kari DelaCruz, Operations Dir
Bill Johnston, General Manager
Wayne Alley, Programming Director
Robyn Wade, News Director

WYMY
01-01-1946; 96.9 mhz FM *Hrs Open:* 24; 100 kw; 984 ft.; N35 23 52 W78 8 7
3012 Highwoods Blvd, Raleigh, NC 27609 US
(919) 790-9392, *Fax:* (919) 736-3876
www.laley969.com
License: Goldsboro, Wayne County, NC
Group Owner: Curtis Media Group
Regional Network: N.C. News Net. *Wire Services:* AP
Arbitron Metro Market: Raleigh-Durham, NC *Format:* Tejano, Spanish *Hrs. of News Programming:* News progmg 2 hrs wkly *Target Audience:* 25-54.
Jon Bloom, General Manager

WSSG
10-22-1955; 1300 khz AM; 1 kw-D, ND1; 0.049 kw-N, ND1; N35 24 8 W78 1 20
P. O. Box 1141, Goldsboro, NC 27530 US
(919) 734-1300
License: Goldsboro, NC held by Robert Swinson
Arbitron Metro Market: Goldsboro, NC *Format:* Christian
Reginald Swinson, General Manager

Graham

WSML
12-02-1967; 1200 khz AM *Hrs Open:* 24*Rebroadcasts:* Rebroadcasts WSJS-AM 600, Winston-Salem NC 90%
200 Concord Plaza, Suite 600, San Antonio, TX 78216 US
(336) 227-4254, *Fax:* (336) 227-4254
License: Graham, NC held by Crescent Media Group LLC.
Group Owner: Curtis Media Group; (acq 2-14-2007; grpsl)
Arbitron Metro Market: Greensboro-Winston Salem-High Point, NC *Format:* News, News/Talk, 86 *Special Programming:* Black 18 hrs wkly *Adv. Rates:* 15; 15; 15; 12
Tom Hamilton, General Manager
Larry Ingold, Programming Director
George Newman, Chief Engineer

Granite Falls

WYCV
02-22-1963; 900 khz AM *Hrs Open:* 5 AM-11 PM (M-S); 6 AM-9 PM (Su)
P. O. Box 486, Granite Falls, NC 28630 US
(828) 396-3361, *Fax:* (828) 396-9193
www.gospel9.com
wycvradio@charter.net
License: Granite Falls, NC held by Freedom Broadcasting Corp.
Nat'l Network: USA; AP Radio
Arbitron Metro Market: Granite Falls, NC *Format:* Gospel, Religious *Special Programming:* Gospel *Hrs. of News Programming:* news progmg 2 hrs wkly *No. News Employees:* 1 *Target Audience:* 3-100.
Marvin Sizemore, President
Buddy Sizemore, General Manager
Clyde Smith, General Sales Mgr
Teresa Sizemore, News Director
Ted Fuller, Engineering Dir

Greensboro

WCOG
05-22-1948; 1320 khz AM *Hrs Open:* 24; 5 kw-D, DA2; 5 kw-N, DA2; N36 9 1 W79 54 48
600 Congress Ave.,S1400, Austin, TX 78701 US
(336) 777-3900, *Fax:* (336) 777-3915
www.triadsports.com
comments@triadsports.com
License: Greensboro, NC held by Radio Disney Group LLC.
Group Owner: ABC Inc.; (acq 5-6-2005; $1.675 million)
Arbitron Metro Market: Winston Salem, NC *Format:* Children *Target Audience:* General.
Gerry Franzer., Station Manager
Chris Nowak, Promotions Manager

WEAL
10-05-1962; 1510 khz AM *Hrs Open:* Sunrise-sunset
10706 Beaver Dam Road, Cockeysville, MD 21030 US
(336) 605-5200, *Fax:* (336) 605-0138
www.1510weal.com/
License: Greensboro, NC held by Entercom Greensboro License LLC
Group Owner: Entercom Communications Corp.
Nat'l Reps: McGavren Guild
Arbitron Metro Market: Greensboro, NC *Format:* Gospel *Target Audience:* 25-54; North Carolina A&T State Univ
Shilynne Cole, Programming Director

WKEW
02-16-1942; 1400 khz AM *Hrs Open:* 24 hrs 7 days; 1 kw-U, ND1; N36 4 0 W79 47 49
256 Four Seasons, Town Centre, Greensboro, NC 27407 US
(336) 759-0363, *Fax:* (336) 759-0366
www.1340thelight.com
info@1340thelight.com
License: Greensboro, NC held by Truth Broadcasting Corp.
Group Owner: Truth Broadcasting Corp.; acq 8-9-00; $800,000)
Arbitron Metro Market: Greensboro-Winston Salem-High Point, NC *Format:* Gospel, Religious *Target Audience:* 35 plus; African-American *Adv. Rates:* 206; 206; 20; 20
Stuart Epperson, President

WSMW
01-09-1958; 98.7 mhz FM *Hrs Open:* 24; 100 kw; 1230 ft.; N35 56 42 W79 51 45
One Television Place, Charlotte, NC 28232 US
(336) 605 5200, *Fax:* (336) 387-7206
www.987simon.com
mcassady@intercom.com
License: Greensboro, Guilford County, NC held by Entercom Greensboro License LLC.
Group Owner: Entercom Communications Corp.
Arbitron Metro Market: Greensboro-Winston Salem-High Point, NC *Format:* Adult Contemp *Target Audience:* 18-49.
Sean Sellers, Programming Director

***WNAA**
01-01-1979; 90.1 mhz FM *Hrs Open:* 24; 10 kw; 433 ft.; N36 4 58 W79 46 8
1601 East Market Street, Greensboro, NC 27411 US
(336) 334-7936, *Fax:* (336) 334-7960
www.wnaa-online.ncat.edu
wnaamail@gmail.com
License: Greensboro, Guilford County, NC held by North Carolina Agricultural & Technical State University.
Arbitron Metro Market: Greensboro, NC *Format:* Gospel, Jazz *Special Programming:* Blues 4 hrs, Reggae 5 hrs, Gospel Hip Hop 3 hrs *Hrs. of News Programming:* News prog 5 hrs wkly *Target Audience:* 35-45; general
D. Cherie Lofton, Operations Dir
Tony Welborne, General Manager
Cherie Lofton, Programming Director
Larry Allen, Chief Engineer

WPET
01-01-1954; 950 khz AM
One Television Place, Charlotte, NC 28205 US
(336) 605-5200, *Fax:* (336) 387-7206
www.wpetam950.com
mcassady@intercom.com
License: Greensboro, NC held by Entercom Greensboro License LLC.
Group Owner: Entercom Communications Corp.; (acq 1-28-2002; $20.5 million with co-located FM).
Arbitron Metro Market: Greensboro-Winston Salem-High Point, NC *Format:* Gospel *Target Audience:* 25-54.
Brent Miller, General Manager
Dave Compton, Programming Director

***WQFS**
01-01-1970; 90.9 mhz FM *Hrs Open:* 24; 1.9 kw; 200 ft.; N36 5 39 W79 53 21
5800 W. Friendly Avenue, Greensboro, NC 27410 US
(336) 316-2352,(336) 316-2444, *Fax:* (336) 316-2949
www.guilford.edu
wqts@guilford.edu
License: Greensboro, Guilford County, NC held by Guilford College Board of Trustees.
Arbitron Metro Market: Greensboro-Winston Salem-High Point, NC *Format:* Variety/Diverse *Hrs. of News Programming:* news progmg 4 hrs wkly *No. News Employees:* 1 *Target Audience:* 15-50.
Elizabeth Bass, General Manager

WQMG
07-08-1962; 97.1 mhz FM *Hrs Open:* 24; 100 kw; 1073 ft.; N35 56 42 W79 51 45
10706 Beaver Dam Road, Cockeysville, MD 21030 US
(336) 605-5200, *Fax:* (336) 605-0138
www.wqmg.com
info@wqmg.com
License: Greensboro, Guilford County, NC held by Entercom Greensboro License LLC
Group Owner: Entercom Communications Corp.; (acq 12-13-99; grpsl).
Nat'l Network: ABC *Nat'l Reps:* McGavren Guild
Arbitron Metro Market: Greensboro-Winston Salem-High Point, NC *Format:* Black, Blues *No. News Employees:* 1 *Target Audience:* 18-49; Black
Brant Millar, General Manager
Lisa Powell, General Sales Mgr
Joyce Staley, Promotions Manager
Brian McCall, News Director
Larry Allen, Chief Engineer

***WUAG**
07-20-1964; 103.1 mhz FM *Hrs Open:* 24; 18.1 w; 230 ft; N36 03 51 W79 48 37
402 Tate Street,Brown Building Room 210, UNCG, Greensboro, NC 27412
(336) 334-5450
www.wuag.net
wuag@uncg.edu
License: Greensboro, Guilford County, NC held by University of North Carolina at Greensboro Board of Trustees.
Population Served: 273,425 *Arbitron Metro Market:* Greensboro, NC *Special Programming:* Hip hop 6 hrs, world music 2 hrs, bluegrass 2 hrs, *Hrs. of News Programming:* news progmg 2 hrs wkly *No. News Employees:* 4*Target Audience:* 12-40; high school & college students *Adv. Rates:* 10; 10; 10; 10
Olivia Corteaux, General Manager
Spencer Auten, Programming Director
Magena Morris, Promotions Manager
Carla Guzman, News Director
Randall Quillian, Music Director
Kelly Fahey, Production Director
Terrence Gantt, SportsDirector

WWBG
01-01-1998; 1470 khz AM
3780 Will Scarlet Road, Winston-Salem, NC 27104 US
(336) 714-7516, *Fax:* (336) 714-0435
www.quepasamedia.com
quepasa@quepasamedia.com
License: Greensboro, NC held by Davidson Media Station WWBG Licensee LLC.
Group Owner: Davidson Media Group LLC; (acq 3-25-2005; swap with WTOB(AM) Winston-Salem for WDRU(AM) Wake Forest).
Nat'l Reps: Salem
Arbitron Metro Market: Greensboro, NC *Format:* Tejano
Jose Isasi, President & CEO
Roger Martinez, General Manager
Hernando Santos Ramirez, Executive Editor
German Navy, Commercial Director
Roberto Aisenberg, Commercial Manager

Greenville

WNCT
01-01-1940; 1070 khz AM *Hrs Open:* 24
3033 Riveria Dr, Ste 200, Naples, FL 33940 US
(252) 757-0011, *Fax:* (252) 757-0286
www.1070wnct.com
Brad@1079wnct.com
License: Greenville, NC held by WNCT License L.P.
Group Owner: Beasley Broadcast Group Inc.; (acq 1996)
Arbitron Metro Market: Greenville, NC *Format:* Blues *Target Audience:* General.
Brad Hood, General Manager
Lisa McHugh, General Sales Mgr

WNCT-FM
12-22-1963; 107.9 mhz FM *Hrs Open:* 24; 100 kw; 1699 ft.; N35 21 55 W77 23 38
3033 Riviera Dr, Ste 200, Naples, FL 33940 US
(252) 757-0011, *Fax:* (252) 757-0286
www.1079wnct.com
carlyle@1079wnct.com
License: Greenville, Pitt County, NC held by WNCT License LP
Group Owner: Beasley Broadcast Group Inc.

Arbitron Metro Market: Greenville, NC *TV Affiliate:* WNCT-TV affil. *Format:* Oldies
Brad Hood, General Manager
Lisa McHugh, General Sales Mgr
Wayne Carlyle, Programming Director
Richard Banks, Chief Engineer

***WZMB**
02-02-1982; 91.3 mhz FM *Hrs Open:* 8am - 5pm; 0.28 kw; 135 ft.; N35 36 1 W77 21 53
Mendenhall Student Ctr., Greenville, NC 27858 US
(252) 328-4751, *Fax:* (252) 328-4773
www.ecu.edu/cs-studentaffairs/wzmb
wzmb@ecu.edu
License: Greenville, Pitt County, NC held by East Carolina University Media Board.
Nat'l Network: ABC
Arbitron Metro Market: Greenville, NC *Format:* Alternative, Variety/Diverse *Hrs. of News Programming:* News progmg 12 hrs wkly *Target Audience:* 18-24; univ students
Michael Crenshaw, General Manager
Rashaad Toney, Music Manager
Jared Roach, Production Manager

Grifton

WXNR
09-11-1989; 99.5 mhz FM *Hrs Open:* 24; 16.5 kw; 843 ft.; N35 12 7 W77 11 15
3033 Riviera Drive, Suite 200, Naples, FL 33940 US
(252) 633-1500, *Fax:* (252) 633-6546
www.995thex.com
License: Grifton, Pitt County, NC held by WXNR License L.P.
Group Owner: Beasley Broadcast Group Inc.
Nat'l Reps: D & R Radio
Arbitron Metro Market: Greenville, WA *Format:* Rock/AOR *Target Audience:* 18-34.
Bruce Simel, General Manager
Wilbur Vitols, Director of Sales
Cindy Miller, Programming Director
Richard Banks, Chief Engineer
Wilbur Vitols, General Sales Manager

Hamlet

WJSG
08-25-1991; 104.3 mhz FM; 6 kw; 489 ft.; N34 48 39 W79 43 38
180 Airport Rd, Rockingham, NC 28379 US
(910) 895-3787, *Fax:* (910) 895-8811
www.g104fm.com
g104fm@104fm.com
License: Hamlet, Richmond County, NC held by Jackson Broadcasting Co.
Format: Christian, Country
Sherrell Jackson, General Manager
Jerry Stout, News Director

WKDX
06-30-1957; 1250 khz AM; 1 kw-D, ND1; 0.08 kw-N, ND1; N34 53 6 W79 40 50
208 South Rutherford St., Wadesboro, NC 28170 US
(910) 582-1997, *Fax:* (910) 582-1920
www.wkdx.net
wkdx@carolina55.com
License: Hamlet, NC held by The McLaurin Group
Format: Gospel
Howard McLaurin Jr., President

Harkers Island

WLGP
08-01-1996; 100.3 mhz FM *Hrs Open:* 24; 100 kw; 486 ft.; N34 48 17 W76 54 23
3213 Huxley Drive, Augusta, GA 30909 US
(706) 309-9610, *Fax:* (706) 309-9669
www.gnnradio.org
ctbarinowski@gnnradio.org
License: Harkers Island, Carteret County, NC held by Barinowski Investment Co.
Group Owner: Good News Network
Format: Christian
Clarence Barinowski, General Manager

Harrisburg

WPZS
01-01-1995; 92.7 mhz FM; 6 kw; Ant 328 ft; N35 16 20 W80 45 54
140 Est Market Street, York, PA 31901
(704) 358-0211, *Fax:* (704) 358-3752
www.my927charlotte.com
License: Harrisburg, Cabarrus County, NC held by Radio One of North Carolina LLC.
Group Owner: Radio One Inc.; (acq 6-7-2000)
Nat'l Reps: McGavren Guild
Population Served: 751,087 *Arbitron Metro Market:* Charlotte-Gastonia-Rock Hill, NC-SC *Target Audience:* Adults 25-54.
Debbie Kwei, General Manager
Michael Taylor, General Sales Mgr
Latoya Whitt, Promotions Manager
Gaynell Nichols, News Director
Phil Woods, Chief Engineer

Hatteras

WCMS-FM
05-01-1999; 94.5 mhz FM *Hrs Open:* 24; 100 kw; 981 ft.; N35 29 10 W75 59 58
P.O. Box 1040, Kill Devil Hills, NC 27948 US
(252) 480-4655, *Fax:* (252) 441-8063
www.wcms.com
bob@maxradionc.com
License: Hatteras, Dare County, NC held by Max Radio of the Carolinas Licenses LLC.
Group Owner: MAX Media L.L.C.; (acq 11-12-2002; grpsl)
Nat'l Network: Jones Radio Networks
Arbitron Metro Market: Hatteras, NC *Format:* Country *No. News Employees:* 2 *Adv. Rates:* 35; 35; 35; 35
Mike Smith, Operations Dir
Bob Davis, Station Manager
Mark Stevens, Programming Director
Tim Boze, Business Manager

WYND-FM
03-01-1995; 97.1 mhz FM *Hrs Open:* 24; 59 kw; 558 ft.; N35 27 48 W76 2 7
2422 Wrightsville Avenue, Nags Head, NC 27959 US
(252) 475-1888, *Fax:* (252) 475-1881
www.wilburandorville.com
hunt@capsanmedia.com
License: Hatteras, Dare County, NC held by CapSan Media LLC.
Group Owner: CapSan Media LLC; (acq 6-30-2006; grpsl)
Nat'l Network: Westwood One
Arbitron Metro Market: Hatteras, NC *Format:* Country
William Whitlow, President
Hunt Thomas, Operations Dir

Havelock

WANG
06-16-1962; 1330 khz AM *Hrs Open:* Sunrise-sunset; 1 kw-D; N34 55 24 W76 56 37 *Rebroadcasts:* Rebroadcasts WSSM-FM Morehead City 100%
1361 Colony Dr., New Bern, NC 75050
(252) 639-7900, *Fax:* (252) 639-7979
License: Havelock, Craven County, NC held by NM Licensing LLC.
Group Owner: NextMedia Group Inc.; (acq 11-26-2001; grpsl)
Nat'l Reps: Eastman Radio
Population Served: 5,283 *Arbitron Metro Market:* Greenville-New Bern-Jacksonville, NC *Target Audience:* 25-54
Larry Weiss, General Manager

***WLVG**
11-12-1971; 105.1 mhz FM; 18.5 kw; Ant 384 ft; N34 45 07 W76 52 57 *Rebroadcasts:* Rebroadcasts KLVR(FM) Middletown, CA 100%
5700 W. Oaks Blvd, Rocklin, CA 76051
(916) 251-1600, *Fax:* (916) 251-1650
www.klove.com
License: Havelock, Craven County, NC held by Educational Media Foundation
Group Owner: NextMedia Group Inc.; (acq 5-27-2010)
Population Served: 17,035 *Arbitron Metro Market:* Greenville-New Bern-Jacksonville, NC
Mike Novak, President
Larry Weiss, Operations Dir

Henderson

WHNC
06-20-1945; 890 khz AM *Hrs Open:* Sunrise-sunset*Rebroadcasts:* Rebroadcasts WCBQ(AM) Oxford 100%
Mailing Address: P.O. Box 336, Oxford, NC 27565 US
Second Address: 1 Alvin Augustus Jones Way, Oxford, NC 27565
(919) 693-3540, *Fax:* (919) 693-9054
www.dralvinjones.com
alvin@dralvinjones.com
License: Henderson, NC held by The Paradise Network Of North Carolina (TPN)
Nat'l Reps: Keystone (unwired net) *Regional Reps:* T-N.
Format: Gospel, Talk *Hrs. of News Programming:* news progmg 7 hrs wkly *No. News Employees:* 1 *Target Audience:* 18 plus.
Alvin Jones, CEO

WIZS
05-01-1955; 1450 khz AM *Hrs Open:* 24; 1 kw-U, ND1; N36 19 31 W78 24 36
Box 192, Henderson, NC 27536 US
(252) 492-3001, *Fax:* (252) 492-3002
www.wizs.com
wizs@vance.net
License: Henderson, NC held by Rose Farm and Rentals Inc.
Regional Network: N.C. News Net.
Format: Country, Oldies, 86 *Special Programming:* TownTalk, Tradio, Sports Mayhem *Hrs. of News Programming:* news proraming 6 hrs wkly *No. News Employees:* 2 *Target Audience:* 25 plus; fans of Country, Oldiesand Beach music *Adv. Rates:* 22.50; 22.50; 22.50; 22.50
George Rush, General Manager
Don Simmons, Programming Director
John Rose III, Chief Engineer
Dan Simmons, Programming Director

***WYFL**
01-01-1948; 92.5 mhz FM; 100 kw; 1020 ft.; N36 13 23 W78 12 7
8030 Arrowridge Blvd., Charlotte, NC 28273 US
704) 523-5555, *Fax:* (704) 522-1967
www.bbnradio.org
bbn@bbnradio.org
License: Henderson, Vance County, NC held by Bible Broadcasting Network Inc.
Group Owner: Bible Broadcasting Network; acq 10-3-81; $335,000;
Arbitron Metro Market: Henderson, NC *Format:* Religious *Target Audience:* General.
Bryant Nelson, General Manager

Hendersonville

WHKP
10-24-1946; 1450 khz AM *Hrs Open:* 25.?Â ?
P.O. Box 2470, Hendersonville, NC 28793 US
(828) 693-9061, *Fax:* (828) 696-9329
www.whkp.com
1450@whkp.com
License: Hendersonville, NC held by Radio Hendersonville Inc.
Nat'l Network: ABC Information & Entertainment
Format: Variety/Diverse *Special Programming:* Var 18 hrs wkly *Hrs. of News Programming:* 10 hrs news progmg wkly *No. News Employees:* 10 *Target Audience:* 25 plus; middle to upper income *Adv. Rates:* 22;22; 22; 11
Art Cooley, President
Art Cooley, General Manager
Richard Rhodes, General Sales Mgr
Larry Freeman, Programming Director
Larry Freeman, News Director
Dave Lyons, Chief Engineer
Chuck Hill, Disc Jockey
Tippy Creswell, DiscJockey
Marge Duncan, Women's Int Ed
Paul Adams, Advertising Consultant
Richard Rhodes, V.P., Advertising anf Sports Director
Marge Duncan, Traffic Director

WMYI
04-15-1958; 102.5 mhz FM *Hrs Open:* 24; kw
600 Congress Ave., Suite 1400, Austin, TX 78701 US
(864) 235-1025, *Fax:* (864) 242-2536
www.wmyi.com
marnemason@clearchannel.com
License: Hendersonville, Henderson County, NC held by Clear Channel Radio Licenses, Inc.
Group Owner: Clear Channel Communications Inc.; (acq 8-30-00; grpsl).
Arbitron Metro Market: Greenville, SC *Format:* Adult Contemp *No. News Employees:* 1
Bill McMartin, General Manager
Chris Leavitt, General Sales Mgr
Megan Culbreth, Promotions Manager

WTZQ
12-25-1964; 1600 khz AM *Hrs Open:* 24; 1 kw-D, ND1; 0.012 kw-N, ND1; N35 18 53 W82 25 58
Mailing Address: P.O. Box 607, Burnsville, NC 28714 US
Second Address: 418 Duncun Rd., Hendersonville, NC 28793
(828) 692-1600, *Fax:* (828) 697-1416
www.wtzq.com
1600@wtzq.com
License: Hendersonville, NC held by Houston Broadcasting Inc.
Group Owner: Mark Media Group; (acq 5-3-2008)
Nat'l Network: ABC *Regional Network:* N.C. News Net.

Arbitron Metro Market: Hendersonville, NC *Format:* Classic Rock *Special Programming:* Gospel 4 hrs wkly *Hrs. of News Programming:* news progmg 8 hrs wkly *No. News Employees:* 1 *Target Audience:* 35 plus;mature upscale audiences *Adv. Rates:* 36; 20; 24; 10

J. Ardell Sink, President
Michael A. Sink, Operations Dir
Mark Warwick, General Manager
George Henry, Programming Director
Michael Sink, Chief Engineer
Kathy Gallagher, Traffic Manager
Remelle K. Sink, Vice President, Admin
Paige Posey, Traffic Coordinator
Tom Brown, Engineer

Hertford

WFMZ

12-01-1997; 104.9 mhz FM *Hrs Open:* 24; 50 kw; 492 ft.; N36 5 59 W76 28 31
300 East Rock Road, Allentown, PA 18103 US
(252) 475-1888, *Fax:* (252) 475-1881
www.classichits1049.com
classichits@maxradio.com
License: Hertford, Perquimans County, NC held by CapSan Media LLC.
Group Owner: CapSan Media LLC; (acq 6-30-2006; grpsl).
Nat'l Network: USA
Format: Contemporary Hits/Top 40, Adult Contemp *Target Audience:* 25-54.

William Whitlow, President
Hunt Thomas, Operations Dir
William Whitlow, General Manager

*WHGO

06-01-1976; 91.3 mhz FM *Hrs Open:* 24; kw
US
(228) 388-2001, *Fax:* (228) 896-9736
www.bob1059.com
License: Hertford, Jackson County, NC held by Monterey Licenses LLC.
Group Owner: Triad Broadcasting Co. L.L.C.; (acq 7-14-99; grpsl)
Nat'l Network: ABC *Nat'l Reps:* Katz Radio
Arbitron Metro Market: Biloxi-Gulfport, MS *Format:* Contemporary Hits/Top 40, Adult Contemp *Target Audience:* 25-54; male/female

Kenny West, Operations Dir
David Manning, General Manager
Ricky Mitchell, Director of Sales
Wayne Watkins, Programming Director
Mindy Patton, Promotions Manager
Buddy Birch, General Manager
Michelle Shortridge, HR Director

Hickory

*WFHE

08-31-1995; 90.3 mhz FM *Hrs Open:* 24; 4 kw; 417 ft.; N35 50 59 W81 26 40 *Rebroadcasts:* Rebroadcasts WFAE(FM) Charlotte 100%
1 University Pl, # 91, Charlotte, NC 28262 US
(704) 549-9323, *Fax:* (704) 547-8851
www.wfae.org
wfae@wfae.org
License: Hickory, Catawba County, NC held by University Radio Foundation Inc.
Arbitron Metro Market: Hickory, NC *Format:* News/Talk, Variety/Diverse

Jennie Buckner, Chairman
Debra Peterson, CFO
Roger Sarow, President and General Manager
Tena Simmons, Operations Dir
Barbara Vermeire, General Sales Mgr
Paul Stribling, Programming Director
Renee Rallos, Promotions Manager
MarkRumsey, News Director
Catherine Little, Development Director
Nash E. Long, III, Vice-Chair
Cyrus Johnson, Jr., Secretary
Michelle Maidt, Treasurer

WHKY

06-10-1940; 1290 khz AM *Hrs Open:* 24
P.O. Box 1059, Hickory, NC 28603 US
(828) 322-1290, *Fax:* (828) 322-8256
www.whky.com
whky@whky.com
License: Hickory, NC held by Long Communications LLC
Nat'l Network: ABC; ESPN Radio *Regional Network:* N.C. News Net. *Nat'l Reps:* Rgnl Reps *Regional Reps:* Rgnl Reps
TV Affiliate: WHKY-TV affil. *Format:* News, News/Talk, 86 *Hrs. of News Programming:* news progmg 50 hrs wkly *No. News Employees:* 4 *Target Audience:* 35-54.

Thomas Long, General Manager
Jeff Long, Station Manager
Patty Guthrie, General Sales Mgr
Heather Isenhour, News Director

WAIZ

12-05-1948; 630 khz AM *Hrs Open:* 24 hrs; 1 kw-D, ND1; 0.057 kw-N, ND1; N35 43 22 W81 16 41
Mailing Address: P.O. Box 940, Newton, NC 28658 US
Second Address: Box 430, Newton, NC 28658
(828) 322-9472, *Fax:* (828) 464-9662
www.mytotalradio.com
totalradio@aol.com
License: Hickory, NC held by Newton-Conover Communications Inc.
Nat'l Network: ABC
Format: Oldies *Target Audience:* 25 plus. *Adv. Rates:* 30; 15; 15; 10.75

Dave Lingafelt, President
Jim Turner, General Sales Mgr
Karol Lowery, News Director

WLKO

01-20-1959; 102.9 mhz FM; 31 kw; 1,545 ft; N35 24 26 W81 07 47
801 Wood Ridge Center Dr., Charlotte, NC 78701
(704) 714-9444, *Fax:* (704) 332-8805
www.lite1029.com
License: Hickory, Catawba County, NC held by Capstar TX L.P.
Group Owner: Clear Channel Communications Inc.; (acq 8-30-00; grpsl).
Population Served: 150,000 *Arbitron Metro Market:* Charlotte,NC *Target Audience:* 25-54.

Nick Allen, Operations Dir
Morgan Johannon, General Manager
Kim Kyle, General Sales Mgr
Jeff Kent, Programming Director
Amanda Knepp, Promotions Manager
Linda Silver, News Director
Ben Birnitzer, Chief Engineer
Alan Lane, Chiefof Engineering
Anthony Testa, Promotions Director
Tom Hunt, Sales Director

*WPIR

12-03-1985; 88.1 mhz FM *Hrs Open:* 24; 26.5 kw horiz, 21 kw vert; 253 ft.; N35 43 34 W81 8 52 *Rebroadcasts:* Rebroadcasts WXRI(FM) East Bend 60%
Mailing Address: Post Office Box 889, Blacksburg, VA 24063 US
Second Address: 3289 WCXN Radio Rd., Claremont, NC 28610
(828) 459-2772, *Fax:* (828) 459-9805
office@joyfm.org
License: Hickory, Catawba County, NC held by Positive Alternative Radio Inc.
Group Owner: Positive Alternative Radio Inc.
Format: Gospel

Brian Sanders, General Manager

WXRC

12-07-1962; 95.7 mhz FM *Hrs Open:* 24; 100 kw; 1,276 ft; N35 42 32 W81 31 32
PO Box 430, Newton, NC 28658
(828) 464-4041, *Fax:* (828) 464-9662
957theride.com
totalradio@aol.com
License: Hickory, Catawba County, NC held by Pacific Broadcasting Group Inc.
Nat'l Reps: McGavren Guild
Arbitron Metro Market: Charlotte-Gasto *Target Audience:* 25-54.

Dave Lingafelt, President
Karol Lowery, News Director
Larry Schropp, Chief Engineer

*WRYN

89.1 mhz FM; 0.85 kw; 295 ft.; N35 41 23 W81 25 16
P O Drawer 2440, Tupelo, MS 38803 US
(662) 844-5036, *Fax:* (662) 842-7798
www.afr.net
contact@afa.net
License: Hickory, Catawba County, NC held by American Family Association.
Group Owner: American Family Radio
Arbitron Metro Market: Hickory, NC *Format:* Christian

Donald E. Wildmon, Founder
Buster Wilson, General Manager
Jennifer Hagman, Programming Director

High Point

WGOS

07-01-1947; 1070 khz AM *Hrs Open:* Sunrise-sunset; 1 kw-D, NDD; N35 54 58 W80 1 0
6223 Old Menden Hall Rd., High Point, NC 27263 US
(336) 434-5024, *Fax:* (336) 434-6018
www.wgos.net
wgosradio@triad.rr.com
License: High Point, NC held by Iglesia Nueva Vida of High Point Inc.
Nat'l Network: USA
Arbitron Metro Market: Greensboro-Winston Salem-High Point, NC *Format:* Talk *Special Programming:* Loc college sports 10 hrs wkly *Hrs. of News Programming:* News progmg 2 hrs wkly *Target Audience:* General.*Adv. Rates:* 25; 20; 25; na

Javier Fernandez, President
Lynn Ritchy, General Manager
Max Parrish, Station Manager
Simon Ritchy, Programming Director

*WHPE-FM

11-01-1947; 95.5 mhz FM *Hrs Open:* 24; 100 kw; 522 ft.; N35 55 10 W80 1 47
8030 Arrowridge Blvd., Charlotte, NC 28273 US
(336) 889-9473, *Fax:* (336) 889-9773
www.bbnradio.org
whpe@bbnradio.org
License: High Point, Guilford County, NC held by Bible Broadcasting Network.
Nat'l Network: USA
Arbitron Metro Market: Greensboro-Winston Salem-High Point, NC *Format:* Religious

Lowell Davey, President
Dan Austin, General Manager

WVBZ

06-01-1953; 100.3 mhz FM *Hrs Open:* 24; 100 kw; 1037 ft.; N35 58 9 W79 49 29
650 Madison Ave, New York, NY 10022 US
(336) 822-2000, *Fax:* (336) 887-0104
www.buzzardrocks.com
alanchapman@clearchannel.com
License: High Point, Guilford County, NC held by Capstar TX L.P.
Group Owner: Clear Channel Communications Inc.; (acq 8-30-00; grpsl).
Arbitron Metro Market: Greensboro-Winston Salem-High Point, NC *Target Audience:* 25-54.

Morgan Bohannon, General Manager
Brian Grube, General Sales Mgr
Tim Fattafield, Programming Director
Travis Moore, Disc Jockey

WMAG

01-01-1946; 99.5 mhz FM *Hrs Open:* 24; 100 kw; 1496 ft.; N35 52 13 W79 50 25
600 Congress Ave.,S1400, Austin, TX 78701 US
(336) 822-2000, *Fax:* (336) 887-0104
www.955wmag.com
jeffcushman@clearchannel.com
License: High Point, Guilford County, NC held by Capstar TX L.P.
Group Owner: Clear Channel Communications Inc.; (acq 8-30-00; grpsl).
Arbitron Metro Market: Greensboro, NC *Format:* Adult Contemp *Target Audience:* 25-54.

Cheryl Salamone, Operations Dir
Morgan Bohannon, General Manager
Rob Garner, General Sales Mgr
Jeff Cushman, Programming Director
James Newton, Promotions Manager
Pam Furr, News Director
Bill Flynn, Disc Jockey
Scott Keith,Operations Manager

WMFR

10-15-1935; 1230 khz AM *Hrs Open:* 5:30 AM-1 AM; 1 kw-U, ND1; N35 57 20 W80 0 22
600 Congress Ave.,S1400, Austin, TX 78701 US
(336) 777-3900, *Fax:* (336) 885-3915
www.triadsports.com/
comments@triadsports.com
License: High Point, NC held by Crescent Media Group LLC.
Group Owner: Curtis Media Group; (acq 2-14-2007; grpsl)
Arbitron Metro Market: Greensboro, NC *Format:* Sports

Tom Hamilton, Operations Dir
Marty Holbrook, Promotions Manager
Bob Costner, News Director
George Newman, Chief Engineer

WYSR
06-01-1953; 1590 khz AM
327 North Main Street, High Point, NC 27260 US
(336) 883-8852, *Fax:* (336) 882-1594
wysr@northstate.net
License: High Point, NC held by Latino Broadcasting LLC
Arbitron Metro Market: Greensboro-Wins *TV Affiliate:* Talk, sports *No. News Employees:* General.

Highlands

WHLC
07-01-1993; 104.5 mhz FM *Hrs Open:* 24; 0.46 kw; 1158 ft.; N35 3 40 W83 11 5
Mailing Address: P.O. Box 1889, Highlands, NC 28741 US
Second Address: 2420 Hwy. 64 E., Highlands, NC 28741
(828) 526-1045, *Fax:* (828) 526-4900
www.whlc.com
info@whlc.com
License: Highlands, Macon County, NC held by Charisma Radio Corp.
Arbitron Metro Market: Greenville-Spartanburg, SC *Format:* Easy Listening *Target Audience:* 35 plus.
Charles Cooper, President
Will Amari, Operations Dir

Hillsborough

WPLW
12-05-1989; 102.5 mhz FM *Hrs Open:* 24; 1.5 kw; 203.8 m; N36 07 12 W78 22 48
Box 463, Louisburg, NC 27549
(919) 496-3105, *Fax:* (919) 496-5864
License: Hillsborough, Orange County, NC held by New Century Media Group LLC
Group Owner: Curtis Media Group
Arbitron Metro Market: Raleigh-Durham, NC *Special Programming:* News, birthday celebration, country exchange, sports *Hrs. of News Programming:* News progmg 6 hrs wkly
Jackie Ayscue, News Director

Holly Springs

WCMC-FM
02-01-1993; 99.9 mhz FM *Hrs Open:* 24; 26.5 kw; 676 ft.; N35 40 35 W78 32 8
Mailing Address: P.O. Box 305, Chase City, VA 23924 US
Second Address: Box 10100, Raleigh, NC 27603
(919) 890-6299, *Fax:* (919) 890-6199
www.wralsportsfan.com
info@wralsportsfan.com
License: Holly Springs, Granville County, NC held by Capitol Broadcasting Co. Inc.
Group Owner: Capitol Broadcasting Co. Inc.; (acq 4-22-2005; $7.25 million)
Nat'l Reps: Katz Radio *Wire Services:* AP
Arbitron Metro Market: Raleigh-Durham, NC *Format:* Sports, Talk
Dan McGrath, CFO
Jim Goodmon, President
Ardie Gregory, Operations Dir
Karen Cates, General Sales Mgr
Dave Shore, Programming Director
Brandon Alexander, Promotions Manager
Mark Tarak, National Sales Manager
Joe Formicola,Operations Manager

Hope Mills

WCCG
07-01-1997; 104.5 mhz FM; 6 kw; 276 ft.; N34 56 34 W78 51 41
115 Gillespie Street, Fayetteville, NC 28301 US
(910) 484-4932, *Fax:* (910) 485-5192
www.wccg1045fm.com/
ccg1045@aol.com
License: Hope Mills, Cumberland County, NC held by James E. Carson.
Arbitron Metro Market: Fayetteville, NC *Format:* Oldies, Blues
James Carson, General Manager

Indian Trail

WQNC
02-01-1958; 100.9 mhz FM *Hrs Open:* 24; 5.2 kw; 107 meters; N35 22 40 W80 11 38
Box 2307, Newburgh, NY 17401
(845) 561-2131, *Fax:* (845) 561-2138
License: Indian Trail, Stanly County, NC held by Radio One of North Carolina LLC.
Group Owner: Radio One Inc.; (acq 11-12-2004; $11.5 million).
Population Served: 4,646 *Arbitron Metro Market:* Windom MN
Joerg Klebe, President

Jacksonville

WJCV
10-10-1968; 1290 khz AM *Hrs Open:* 24; 5 kw-D, 47 w-N; N34 45 58 W77 23 28
Box 1216, Jacksonville, NC 28541
(910) 347-6141, *Fax:* (910) 347-1290
www.wjcv.com
License: Jacksonville, Onslow County, NC held by Down East Broadcasting Co. Inc.
Nat'l Network: USA *Nat'l Reps:* Salem
Population Served: 250,000 *Arbitron Metro Market:* Greenville-New *Target Audience:* 25-54; general *Adv. Rates:* 12; 10; 12; 5
Michael Bland, President
Melvin Bland, Operations Dir
Michael Bland, Station Manager
Michael Bland, Promotions Manager
Joe North, Disc Jockey
Charlie Joyner, Disc Jockey
Tim Bland

WJNC
10-16-1945; 1240 khz AM; 1 kw-U, ND1; N34 44 56 W77 24 51
PO Box 81, Jacksonville, NC 28541 US
(910) 455-7222, *Fax:* (252) 247-7343
License: Jacksonville, NC held by Heritage Broadcasting LLC.
Group Owner: Conner Media Corp.; (acq 8-10-2001; $358,500)
Nat'l Network: Westwood One
Arbitron Metro Market: Greenville-New Bern-Jacksonville, NC
Format: News, News/Talk, 84, Talk *Target Audience:* 18-45 plus.
Ben Ball, General Manager
Dave Gremoske, Chief Engineer

WRMR(FM)
04-28-1965; 98.7 mhz FM *Hrs Open:* 24; 100 kw; Ant 1,015 ft; N34 29 38 W77 29 18
25 N. Kerr Ave., Wilmington, NC 28405
(910) 791-3088, *Fax:* (910) 791-0112
www.lagrand987.com
License: Jacksonville, Onslow County, NC held by Sunrise Broadcasting LLC.
Group Owner: Capitol Broadcasting Co. Inc.; (acq 11-18-2008; grpsl)
Population Served: 1,000,000 *Arbitron Metro Market:* Greenville-New Bern-Jacksonville, NC
Jeff Sanchez, Operations Dir

WQSL
11-01-1993; 92.3 mhz FM *Hrs Open:* 24; 22.5 kw; 725 ft.; N34 31 10 W77 26 52
111 East Kilbourn Ave., Suite 2700, Milwaukee, WI 53202 US
(252) 639-7900, *Fax:* (252) 639-7979
www.carolinatouch.com
info@carolinatouch.com
License: Jacksonville, Onslow County, NC held by NM Licensing LLC.
Group Owner: NextMedia Group Inc.; (acq 11-26-2001; grpsl)
Nat'l Reps: Eastman Radio
Arbitron Metro Market: Greenville-New Bern-Jacksonville, NC
Format: Adult Contemp
Larry Weiss, Operations Dir

WSRP
06-21-1954; 910 khz AM *Hrs Open:* 24
702 Hartness Road, Statesville, NC 28677 US
(910) 455-2202, *Fax:* (910) 355-2203
License: Jacksonville, NC held by Estuardo Valdemar Rodriguez & Leonor Rodriguez.
Group Owner: Radio La Grande; (acq 6-30-2006; $475,000)
Arbitron Metro Market: Greenville-New Bern-Jacksonville, NC
Henry Gonzalez, Station Manager

WXQR-FM
03-14-1966; 105.5 mhz FM *Hrs Open:* 24; 19 kw; 794 ft.; N34 31 10 W77 26 52
111 East Kilbourn Ave., Suite 2700, Milwaukee, WI 53202 US
(252) 639-7900, *Fax:* (252) 639-7979
www.carolinaspurerock.com
info@carolinaspurerock.com
License: Jacksonville, Onslow County, NC held by NM Licensing LLC.
Group Owner: NextMedia Group Inc.; (acq 11-26-2001; grpsl)
Nat'l Reps: Eastman Radio
Arbitron Metro Market: Greenville-New Bern, NC *Format:* Rock/AOR
Larry Weiss, VP/GM
Wes Styles, Programming Director
Laura Nichols, Promotions Manager
Dave Wood, Interactive Specialist

***WJKA**
01-01-2008; 90.1 mhz FM; 17 kw vert; 281 ft.; N34 38 52 W77 37 28 *Rebroadcasts:* Rebroadcasts WAFR(FM) Tupelo, MS 100%
P O Drawer 2440, Tupelo, MS 38803 US
(662) 844-8888, *Fax:* (662) 842-6791
www.afr.net
License: Jacksonville, Onslow County, NC held by American Family Association.
Group Owner: American Family Radio
Nat'l Network: American Family Radio
Arbitron Metro Market: Eagle Pass, TX *Format:* Christian
Marvin Sanders, General Manager

WAVQ
01-01-2008; 1400 khz AM
US
(252) 633-1490, *Fax:* (888) 878-5251
www.rfenc.com
info@rfenc.com
License: Jacksonville, NC held by Conner Media Corp.
Group Owner: Conner Media Corp.
Arbitron Metro Market: Jacksonville, NC *Format:* Sports, Talk
Ronald Benfield, President

Jefferson

WMMY
10-01-1999; 106.1 mhz FM; 10.5 kw; 509 ft.; N36 19 53 W81 35 17
872 Allen Road, Murfreesboro, TN 37129 US
(828) 264-2411, *Fax:* (828) 264-2412
www.highway106.com
sindy@wecr1023.com
License: Jefferson, Ashe County, NC held by High Country Adventures LLC.
Group Owner: Curtis Media Group; (acq 3-3-2009; grpsl)
Arbitron Metro Market: Jefferson, NC *Format:* Country *Special Programming:* Southern Fried Friday Night; Mountainhome Music Live Bluegrass Saturday Nights *Target Audience:* 18-49; adults
Robert Zurowesti, Operations Dir
Jeff Stevens, Operations Manager

Kannapolis

WRFX
10-01-1964; 99.7 mhz FM; 84 kw; 1056 ft.; N35 17 14 W80 41 45
650 Madison Ave, New York, NY 10022 US
(704) 714-9444, *Fax:* (704) 371-3238
www.wrfx.com
License: Kannapolis, Cabarrus County, NC held by Capstar TX L.P.
Group Owner: Clear Channel Communications Inc.; (acq 8-30-2000; grpsl)
Arbitron Metro Market: Charlotte-Gastonia-Rock Hill, NC-SC
Format: Classic Rock, Rock/AOR *Special Programming:* Talk 3 hrs wkly *Target Audience:* 25-54; male
Nick Allen, Operations Dir
Morgan Bohannon, General Manager
Kim Kyle, General Sales Mgr
Jeff Kent, Programming Director
Amanda Knepp, Promotions Manager
Linda Silver, News Director
Ben Brinitzer, Chief Engineer

WRKB
12-11-1960; 1460 khz AM *Hrs Open:* 24*Rebroadcasts:* Rebroadcasts WRNA(AM) China Grove 90%
P.O. Box 8146, Kannapolis, NC 28083 US
(704) 857-1101, *Fax:* (704) 857-0680
www.fordbroadcasting.com
info@fordbroadcasting.com
License: Kannapolis, NC held by Ford Broadcasting Inc.
Nat'l Network: USA
Arbitron Metro Market: Charlotte-Gastonia-Rock Hill, NC-SC
Format: Gospel
Carl Ford, President
Angela Ford, Operations Dir
Taylor Ford, Executive Vice President

Kernersville

WTRU
08-16-1970; 830 khz AM *Hrs Open:* 24; 50 kw-D, DA2; 10 kw-N, DA2; N36 11 58 W80 12 25
888 - 7th Avenue, New York, NY 10106 US
(336) 759-0363, *Fax:* (336) 759-0366
www.wtru.com
info@wtru.com
License: Kernersville, NC held by Truth Broadcasting Corp.
Group Owner: Truth Broadcasting Corp.; (acq 7-20-2000; $3.5 million with WGTK(AM) Louisville, KY)

Nat'l Network: Salem Radio Network
Arbitron Metro Market: Greensboro, NC *Format:* Christian, News *Hrs. of News Programming:* News progmg 24 hrs wkly *Target Audience:* General. *Adv. Rates:* 306; 306; 30; 20
Stuart Epperson, President
Beth Ann McBride, Programming Director
Joey Roberson, Assistant Program Director
Melanie Martin, Traffic Manager
Andrew Fox, Production Director
Paul Scott, Market Manager

Kill Devil Hills

WCXL
01-01-1993; 104.1 mhz FM *Hrs Open:* 24; 100 kw; 971 ft.; N36 8 8 W75 49 28
P.O. Box 1040, Kill Devil Hills, NC 27948 US
(252) 480-4655, *Fax:* (252) 441-4827
www.beach104.com
info@beach104.com
License: Kill Devil Hills, Dare County, NC held by Max Radio of the Carolinas Licenses LLC.
Group Owner: MAX Media L.L.C.; (acq 11-12-2002; grpsl).
Arbitron Metro Market: Hampton Roads, Outer Banks *Format:* Adult Contemp *Special Programming:* Farm 2 hrs wkly *No. News Employees:* 2 *Target Audience:* 18-54. *Adv. Rates:* 75; 45; 75; 35.
Tim Boze, General Manager
Bob Davis, General Sales Mgr
Mike Smith, General Manager

King

WKTE
12-04-1963; 1090 khz AM; 1 kw-D, NDD; N36 17 48 W80 22 18
Route 2, Box 88d, King, NC 27021 US
(336) 983-3111, *Fax:* (336) 368-1090
www.wktelogo.com
info@wktelogo.com
License: King, NC held by Booth-Newsom Broadcasting Inc.
Regional Network: Southern Farm
Arbitron Metro Market: Greensboro-Winston Salem-High Point, NC *Format:* Country, Gospel *Special Programming:* Farm 2 hrs wkly
P.W. Booth, President
Rodney Booth, General Manager
Elizabeth Club, General Sales Mgr
Mike Bertaux, Programming Director
Dan Sykes, Chief Engineer
Ron Wishon, Disc Jockey

Kings Mountain

WDYT
03-12-1953; 1220 khz AM *Hrs Open:* 5 AM-midnight
P.O. Box 1220, Kings Mountain, NC 28086 US
(704) 295-7901, *Fax:* (704) 295-7919
License: Kings Mountain, NC held by CRN Communications LLC
Arbitron Metro Market: Charlotte-Gastonia-Rock Hill, NC-SC
Deanna Greco, General Manager

Kinston

WELS
09-01-1950; 1010 khz AM *Hrs Open:* 8 AM-5 PM; 1 kw-D, ND1; 0.078 kw-N, ND1; N35 17 3 W77 39 53
Mailing Address: 645 Church Street, Suite 400, Norfolk, VA 23510 US
Second Address: 313 N. Queen St., Kinston, NC 28501
(252) 523-5151, *Fax:* (252) 523-9357
welsradio@juno.com
License: Kinston, NC held by Willis Broadcasting.
Regional Network: N.C. News Net. *Nat'l Reps:* Clayton-Davis
Arbitron Metro Market: Kinston, NC *Format:* Gospel *Target Audience:* 25-54; middle income
Anthony Gonzales, General Manager

WELS-FM
11-21-1990; 102.9 mhz FM *Hrs Open:* 24; 3 kw; 295 ft.; N35 17 3 W77 39 53
Mailing Address: 645 Church Street, Suite 400, Norfolk, VA 23510 US
Second Address: 313 N. Queen St., Kinston, NC 28501
(252) 523-5151, *Fax:* (252) 523-9357
welsradio@juno.com
License: Kinston, Lenoir County, NC
Nat'l Network: ABC
Arbitron Metro Market: Kinston, NC *Special Programming:* East Carolina Univ. sports, Kinston Indians baseball *Target Audience:* General; middle to upper income, married, working, college grads
Anthony Gonzales, Programming Director

*WKNS
03-26-1977; 90.3 mhz FM; 35 kw horiz, 34 kw vert; 322 ft.; N35 25 1 W77 48 57 *Rebroadcasts:* Rebroadcasting WTEB(FM) New Bern 100%
800 College Ct, New Bern, NC 28562 US
(252) 638-3434, *Fax:* (252) 638-3538
www.publicradioeast.org
License: Kinston, Lenoir County, NC held by Craven Community College.
Format: Public Affairs, News *Special Programming:* Jazz 6 hrs wkly
Kelly Batchlor, Operations Dir
Charles Wethington, Station Manager
Kathleen Beal, General Sales Mgr
Jill McGuire, Programming Director
George Olsen, News Director
J. Howard Jones, Chief Engineer

WLNR
05-01-1954; 1230 khz AM *Hrs Open:* 24; 1 kw-U, ND1; N35 15 31 W77 36 33
1223 West New Bern Rd, Kinston, NC 28504 US
(202) 638-1959, *Fax:* (202) 638-6127
www.wlrn.org
estuardovaldemar@hotmail.com
License: Kinston, NC held by Estuardo Valdemar Rodriguez & Leonor Rodriguez.
Group Owner: Radio La Grande; (acq 1-2004; $315,000)
Arbitron Metro Market: Greenville-New Bern-Jacksonville, NC
Estuardo Rodriguez, General Manager

WRNS
02-28-1937; 960 khz AM *Hrs Open:* 24; 5 kw-D, DAN; 1 kw-N, DAN; N35 16 57 W77 39 9
1705 W. Northwest Hwy, Ste 275, Grapevine, TX 76051 US
(252) 639-7900, *Fax:* (252) 639-7979
www.wrns.com
mail@wrns.com
License: Kinston, NC held by NM Licensing LLC
Group Owner: NextMedia Group Inc.
Arbitron Metro Market: Greenville-New Bern-Jacksonville, NC
Format: Country *Target Audience:* 25-64.
Wayne Carlyle, Programming Director

WRNS-FM
10-12-1968; 95.1 mhz FM *Hrs Open:* 24; 100 kw; 1506 ft.; N35 6 15 W77 20 12
Route 2 Box 182, Banks Scholl Road, Kinston, NC 28501 US
(252) 639-7900, *Fax:* (252) 639-7979
www.wrns.com
mail@wrns.com
License: Kinston, Lenoir County, NC held by NM Licensing LLC
Group Owner: NextMedia Group Inc.; (acq 11-26-01; grpsl).
Nat'l Reps: Eastman Radio
Arbitron Metro Market: Greenville-New Bern-Jacksonville, NC
Format: Country *Special Programming:* NASCAR racing 6 hrs wkly *No. News Employees:* 1 *Target Audience:* 25-54. *Adv. Rates:* 1440; 1440; 1440; 600
Larry Weiss, Operations Dir

Knightdale

WRDU
03-01-1961; 106.1 mhz FM *Hrs Open:* 24; 27.5 kw; 1604 ft.; N35 40 28 W78 31 40
600 Congress Ave.,S1400, Austin, TX 78701 US
(919) 876-1061, *Fax:* (919) 876-2929
www.1061rdu.com
info@1061rdu.com
License: Knightdale, Wilson County, NC held by Clear Channel Communications
Group Owner: Clear Channel Communications Inc.; (acq 8-30-2000; grpsl).
Arbitron Metro Market: Raleigh-Durham, NC *Format:* Country *Hrs. of News Programming:* news progmg 3 hrs wkly *No. News Employees:* 1
Ken Spitzer, General Manager

La Grange

WZUP
01-01-1993; 104.7 mhz FM; 25 kw; 249 ft.; N35 15 31 W77 36 33
1223 West New Bern Road, Kinston, NC 28504 US
(252) 753-3202, *Fax:* (910) 355-2203
License: La Grange, Lenoir County, NC held by Conner Media Corp.
Group Owner: Conner Media Corp.
Arbitron Metro Market: Farmville, NC *Format:* Spanish
Rodney Rainey, General Manager

Laurinburg

WEWO
09-01-1947; 1460 khz AM *Hrs Open:* 24; 5 kw-D, DA2; 5 kw-N, DA2; N34 47 0 W79 30 40
1338 Bragg Blvd., Fayetteville, NC 28301 US
(910) 280-5209, *Fax:* (910) 276-9787
www.widuradio.com
wewo1460@aol.com
License: Laurinburg, NC held by Service Media Inc.
Arbitron Metro Market: Laurinburg, NC *Format:* Gospel *Target Audience:* 25-54.
Westley Johnson, General Manager

WFLB
05-01-1951; 96.5 mhz FM *Hrs Open:* 24; 100 kw; 1043 ft.; N34 46 49 W79 2 45
C/O Beasley Brdcstng Grp, 3033 Riviera Dr, Ste 200, Naples, FL 33940 US
(910) 486-4114, *Fax:* (910) 323-5635
Stoney@965bobfm.com
License: Laurinburg, Scotland County, NC held by Beasley FM Acquisition Corp.
Group Owner: Beasley Broadcast Group Inc.; (acq 7-31-96; $4.2 million with co-owned AM).
Nat'l Reps: D & R Radio
Arbitron Metro Market: Fayetteville, NC *Format:* Adult Contemp
Special Programming: University of North Carolina football & basketball *Target Audience:* 25-54; affluent men & women in their peak earning years *Adv.Rates:* 65; 85; 65; 30
George Beasley, President
Mac Edwards, Operations Dir
Angela Godwin, General Sales Mgr
Dave Stone, Programming Director
Clara Glover, News Director
Van Clough, Chief Engineer
Bryan Kusilka, National Sales Manager
DannyHighsmith, Regional Vice President

WLNC
01-02-1962; 1300 khz AM *Hrs Open:* sunrise-sunset; 0.5 kw-D, ND2; 0.074 kw-N, ND2; N34 47 0 W79 26 22
Mailing Address: P. O. Box 1748, Laurinburg, NC 28352 US
Second Address: 1300 Lila Dr., Laurinburg, NC 28352
(910) 276-1300
www.wlncradio.com
wlncradio@carolina.net
License: Laurinburg, NC held by Fox Broadcasting Inc.
Format: Adult Contemp *Special Programming:* Gospel 4 hrs wkly
Target Audience: General.
Fred Fox, General Manager

Leland

WAAV
12-20-1957; 980 khz AM *Hrs Open:* 24; 5 kw-D, DAN; 5 kw-N, DAN; N34 14 54 W78 0 6
111 East Kilbourn Ave., Suite 2700, Milwaukee, WI 53202 US
(620) 665-5758, *Fax:* (620) 665-6655
production@adastra.kscoxmail.com
License: Leland, NC held by Cumulus Licensing Corp.
Group Owner: Cumulus Media Inc.; (acq 7-2-97; $1.6 million with co-located FM)
Nat'l Reps: McGavren Guild *Wire Services:* AP
Arbitron Metro Market: Dallas-Fort Worth *Format:* Oldies *Hrs. of News Programming:* news progmg 2 hrs wkly *No. News Employees:* 1
Aaron West, Operations Dir
Cliff C Shank, General Manager
Michael Hill, General Sales Mgr
Lucky Kidd, News Director
Susie Deines, Office Manager

WKXS-FM
12-10-1994; 94.5 mhz FM *Hrs Open:* 24; 3.8 kw; 416 ft.; N34 12 35 W77 56 53
111 East Kilbourn Ave, Suite 2700, Milwaukee, WI 53202 US
(505) 242-7163
www.kanw.com
brasher@aps.edu
License: Leland, Brunswick County, NC
Arbitron Metro Market: San Francisco
Michael Brasher, General Manager

Lenoir

WJRI
03-15-1947; 1340 khz AM *Hrs Open:* 24; 1 kw-U, ND1; N35 53 39 W81 33 30
Mailing Address: Post Office Box 1350, Lenoir, NC 28645 US
Second Address: Box 1678, Lenoir, NC 28645

(828) 754-5361, *Fax:* (828) 757-3300
www.foothillsradio.com
info@foothillsradio.com
License: Lenoir, NC held by Foothills Radio Group LLC
Group Owner: Foothills Radio Group LLC; acq 11-28-01).
Regional Network: N.C. News Net.
Format: News, News/Talk, 86 *Hrs. of News Programming:* news progmg 14 hrs wkly *No. News Employees:* 1 *Target Audience:* 20-45.
Al Bunch, President
Davy Crockett, Operations Dir
Steve Zushin, News Director
Stoney Owen, Chief Engineer
Shannon Hefner, Traffic Manager

WKGX
02-13-1969; 1080 khz AM *Hrs Open:* 12; 2.5 kw-C, NDD; 5 kw-D, NDD; N35 54 38 W81 33 35
P.O. Box 1080, Lenoir, NC 28645 US
(828) 758-1033, *Fax:* (828) 757-3300
www.foothillsradio.com
wxgx@twave.net
License: Lenoir, NC held by Foothills Radio Group LLC
Group Owner: Foothills Radio Group LLC; acq 11-28-01).
Format: Country *Special Programming:* Trading post show 16 hrs wkly *Hrs. of News Programming:* news progmg 6 hrs wkly *No. News Employees:* 1 *Target Audience:* 24-55; older, mature wise spenders
Patty Guthrie, General Manager

WKVS
09-27-1993; 103.3 mhz FM; 0.91 kw; 843 ft.; N35 58 30 W81 33 7
Post Office Box 1678, Lenoir, NC 28645 US
(828) 758-1033, *Fax:* (828) 757-3300
www.foothillsradio.com
pam@kicksradio.com
License: Lenoir, Caldwell County, NC held by Foothills Radio Group LLC.
Group Owner: Foothills Radio Group LLC; (acq 11-28-2001)
Format: Country *Target Audience:* 18-54.
Al Bunch, President
Rocky Brooks, Operations Dir
Davy Crockett, Programming Director
Steve Zushin, News Director
Stonie Owen, Engineering Dir
Bill Nolin, Disc Jockey

Lewisville

WSGH
01-01-1986; 1040 khz AM *Hrs Open:* 24; 9.1 kw-D, DA2; 0.182 kw-N, DA2; N36 8 6 W80 30 14
Box 889, Blacksburg, VA 24060 US
(336) 768-0050, *Fax:* (336) 768-0032
www.radiolamovidita.com
License: Lewisville, NC held by Davidson Media Carolinas Stations LLC.
Group Owner: Davidson Media Group LLC; (acq 5-10-2004; grpsl).
Nat'l Network: USA
Arbitron Metro Market: Greensboro-Wins *Target Audience:* 17-28.
Marco Antonio Saucedo, President
Lucy Saucedo, Operations Dir
Samuel Saucedo, General Manager

Lexington

WLXN
09-22-1946; 1440 khz AM *Hrs Open:* 24
200 Radio Drive, Lexington, NC 27292 US
(336) 242-1440, *Fax:* (336) 248-2800
www.wlxn.com
License: Lexington, NC held by Davidson County Broadcasting Co. Inc.
Regional Network: N.C. News Net.
Arbitron Metro Market: Greensboro, NC *Format:* News, News/Talk, 84, Talk *Hrs. of News Programming:* news progmg 30 hrs wkly *No. News Employees:* 1 *Target Audience:* 35 plus; those interested in news & sports
Greeley Hilton Jr., President
Tom Collins, Operations Dir
Harold Bowen, Programming Director
Willie Edwards, Promotions Manager
Bob Mahoney, News Director
Hal McGee, Engineering Dir

WWLV(FM)
08-24-1949; 94.1 mhz FM *Hrs Open:* 24; 100 kw; 1,014 ft; N35 55 02 W80 17 37
200 Radio Dr., Lexington, NC 27292
(336) 248-2716, *Fax:* (336) 248-2800
www.majic941.com
info@hitz94.com
License: Lexington, Davidson County, NC held by Davidson County Broadcasting Co. Inc.
Regional Reps: T-N.
Population Served: 273,425 *Arbitron Metro Market:* Greensboro, NC *Format:* Adult Contemp *Hrs. of News Programming:* news progmg one hr wkly *No. News Employees:* 1 *Target Audience:* General; 25-49
Greeley Hilton Jr., President
Bob Campbell, Programming Director
Hal McGee, Chief Engineer

Lillington

***WLLN**
02-12-1979; 1370 khz AM *Hrs Open:* Day time; 5 kw-D, DA2; 0.049 kw-N, DA2; N35 23 16 W78 48 22
Mailing Address: P.O. Box 1166, Dunn, NC 28335 US
Second Address: 910 E. McNeil St., Lillington, NC 27546
(910) 893-2811, *Fax:* (910) 893-2811
License: Lillington, NC held by Estuardo Valdemar Rodriguez
Format: Spanish *Target Audience:* General.
Estuardo Rodriguez, Chairman
Leonor Rodriguez, President
Helen Hernandez, Station Manager
Orlando Henao, Programming Director

Lincolnton

WLON
08-28-1953; 1050 khz AM *Hrs Open:* 24; 1 kw-D, ND1; 0.231 kw-N, ND1; N35 29 28 W81 16 3 *Rebroadcasts:* Rebroadcasts WCSL(AM) Cherryville 80%
P.O. Box 730, Cherryville, NC 28021 US
(704) 735-8071, *Fax:* (704) 732-9567
www.hrnb.com
info@hrnb.com
License: Lincolnton, NC held by HRN Broadcasting Inc.
Group Owner: HRN Broadcasting Inc.; (acq 4-14-2004; $500,000 with WCSL(AM) Cherryville).
Nat'l Network: Westwood One *Regional Network:* N.C. News Net.
Arbitron Metro Market: Charlotte-Gastonia-Rock Hill, NC-SC *Format:* Oldies, Sports *Special Programming:* Gospel 5 hrs wkly *Target Audience:* 25 plus.
Mark Boyd, President
Milton Baker, Operations Dir
Lanny Ford, General Manager

Lockwoods Folly Town

***WGHW**
01-01-2006; 88.1 mhz FM; 10 kw vert; 311 ft.; N34 3 48 W78 5 32
520 Roberts Rd, New Port, NC 28570 US
(910) 253-6593
www.kjbbfm.com
info@kjbbfm.com
License: Lockwoods Folly Town, Brunswick County, NC held by Church Planters of America
Arbitron Metro Market: Modesto, CA *Format:* Christian
Danny Hawkins, President

Louisburg

WYRN
09-12-1958; 1480 khz AM *Hrs Open:* 24; 0.5 kw-D, ND1; 0.035 kw-N, ND1; N36 6 46 W78 16 50
P. O. Box 463, Louisburg, NC 27549 US
(919) 496-3105, *Fax:* (919) 496-5864
License: Louisburg, NC held by New Century Media Group LLC.
Group Owner: Curtis Media Group; (acq 6-1-2003; $2.8 million with co-located FM)
Regional Network: N.C. News Net.
Arbitron Metro Market: Raleigh-Durham, *Format:* Talk *Special Programming:* Black *Hrs. of News Programming:* news progmg 20 hrs wkly *No. News Employees:* 1 *Target Audience:* Adults 25-54. *Adv. Rates:* 25; 23; 25; 15
William McClatchey Jr., President
Randy Jordan, General Manager
Jackie Ayscue, News Director

Lumberton

WAGR
11-27-1954; 1340 khz AM *Hrs Open:* 24; 1 kw-U, ND1; N34 35 58 W79 0 33
Mailing Address: 145 Rowan Street A-3, Fayetteville, NC 28301 US
Second Address: 145 Rowen Street A-3, Fayetteville, NC 28301
(910)486-9438, *Fax:* (910) 739-1349
wcookman@aol,com
License: Lumberton, NC held by WAGR Broadcasting Inc.
Regional Reps: Williams
Arbitron Metro Market: Fayetteville, NC *Format:* Gospel *Hrs. of News Programming:* News progmg 4 hrs wkly *Target Audience:* 25-54. *Adv. Rates:* 19; 17; 19; 14
Charles Cookman, President
Val Holiday, Operations Dir
Sandra Lofton, General Manager

WFVL
07-19-1964; 102.3 mhz FM *Hrs Open:* 24; 6 kw; 85.1 meters; N34 35 58 W79 00 33
2700 West Paks Blvd, Rocklin, CA 28303
(916) 251-1600, *Fax:* (916) 251-1650
www.oldiesradionc.com
License: Lumberton, Robeson County, NC held by Educational Media Foundation
Group Owner: Cumulus Media Inc.; (acq 8-10-2012)
Population Served: 103,000 *Arbitron Metro Market:* Fayetteville, NC
Mike Novak, President
Alan Buffaloe, General Manager

WKML
12-01-1960; 95.7 mhz FM *Hrs Open:* 24; 100 kw; 1043 ft.; N34 46 49 W79 2 45
Mailing Address: C/O Beasley Broadcastng Group, 3033 Riviera Dr, Ste 200, Naples, FL 33940 US
Second Address: 508 Person St., Fayetteville, NC 28301
(910) 483-9565, *Fax:* (910) 483-6008
www.wkml.com
info@wkml.com
License: Lumberton, Robeson County, NC held by Beasley Broadcasting of Eastern North Carolina Inc.
Group Owner: Beasley Broadcast Group Inc.; (acq 1981).
Nat'l Reps: D & R Radio
Arbitron Metro Market: Fayetteville, NC *Format:* Country *Hrs. of News Programming:* news progmg 5 hrs wkly *No. News Employees:* 1 *Target Audience:* 25-54.
George Beasley, President
Mac Edwards, Operations Dir
J. Daniel Highsmith, General Manager
Angela Godwin, General Sales Mgr
Paul Johnson, Programming Director
Van Clough, Chief Engineer
Larry K. Smith, Disc Jockey
Don Chase,Disc Jockey
Bryan Kusilka, National Sales Manager

***WLPS-FM**
89.5 mhz FM; 2 kw vert; 440 ft.; N34 42 2 W79 6 32
3463 Oak Grove Church Rd, Lumberton, NC 28358 US
(910) 521-3101
License: Lumberton, Robeson County, NC held by Billy Ray Locklear Evangelistic Association.
Arbitron Metro Market: Lumberton,NC *Format:* Gospel
Billy Ray Locklear, Chairman

Manteo

WOBX-FM
01-01-2001; 98.1 mhz FM *Hrs Open:* 24; 40 kw; 233 ft.; N35 51 52 W75 39 1
Mailing Address: 2401 S. Croatan Highway, Nags Head, NC 27959 US
Second Address: 2422 S. Wrightsville Ave., Nags Head, NC 27959
(252) 441-1024, *Fax:* (252) 449-8354
www.wobx.net
wobx@ecri.net
License: Manteo, Dare County, NC held by East Carolina Radio of Elizabeth City Inc.
Arbitron Metro Market: Nags Head, NC *Format:* News, Talk
Rick Loesch, President
Cliff Curtis, Operations Dir
R. Loesch, General Manager
Rick Loesch, General Sales Mgr

WVOD
03-28-1986; 99.1 mhz FM *Hrs Open:* 24; 50 kw; 492 ft.; N35 50 44 W75 38 50
P.O. Box 789, Nags Head, NC 27959 US
(252) 475-1888, *Fax:* (252) 475-1881
www.991thesound.com
matt@maxradionc.com
License: Manteo, Dare County, NC held by CapSan Media LLC.
Group Owner: CapSan Media LLC; (acq 6-30-2006; grpsl)
Arbitron Metro Market: Manteo, NC *Format:* Triple A *Special Programming:* Class 6 hrs, blues 2 hrs, reggae 2 hrs wkly *No. News Employees:* 1 *Target Audience:* 25-49.

Hunt Thomas, Operations Dir
William Whitlow, General Manager
Matt Cooper, Programming Director
Sharon Pro, News Director
Andy Booth, Chief Engineer
Tad Abbey, Music Director

*WURI
01-01-1999; 90.9 mhz FM *Hrs Open:* 24; 3.9 kw; 187 ft.; N35 54 28 W75 40 26 *Rebroadcasts:* Rebroadcasts WCPE(FM) Wake Forest 99.9%
Campus Box 0915, Chapel Hill, NC 27599 US
(919) 445-9150, *Fax:* (919) 966-5955
www.wunc.org
wunc@wunc.org
License: Manteo, Dare County, NC held by Board of Trustees/University of North Carolina at Chapel Hill.
Nat'l Network: CBC Radio One; NPR; PRI
Arbitron Metro Market: Chapel Hill, NC *Format:* Classical *Special Programming:* Folk 20 hrs wkly.
Bob Levin, COO
Kevin Wolf, Operations Dir
Connie Walker, General Manager
David Brower, Programming Director
Nandini Sen, Director of Technologies & Engineering
Regina Yeager, Director of Development
Susan Anderson, AccountingCoordinator
Jacqueline Edwards, Business Assistant
Nathan Olawsky, Business Services Coordinator
Jennifer Bowling, Corporate Support Associate

*WUND-FM
01-01-2004; 88.9 mhz FM *Hrs Open:* 24; 50 kw horiz, 47 kw vert; 1371 ft.; N35 54 0 W76 20 45 *Rebroadcasts:* Rebroadcasts WUNC(FM) Chapel Hill 99.9%
Campus Boc 0915, Chapel Hill, NC 27599 US
(919) 445-9150, *Fax:* (919) 966-5955
www.wunc.org
wunc@wunc.org
License: Manteo, Dare County, NC held by Board of Trustees of the University of North Carolina at Chapel Hill.
Nat'l Network: NPR; PRI
Arbitron Metro Market: Elizabeth City, NC *Format:* News *Special Programming:* Folk 20 hrs wkly *Hrs. of News Programming:* news progmg 124 hrs wkly *No. News Employees:* 7
Bob Levin, COO
Connie Walker, General Manager
David Brower, Programming Director
Nandini Sen, Director of Technologies & Engineering
Regina Yeager, Director of Development
Susan Anderson, Accounting Coordinator
JacquelineEdwards, Business Assistant
Nathan Olawsky, Business Services Coordinator
Jennifer Bowling, Corporate Support Associate
Nancy Brookshire, Corporate Support Manager

Marion

WBRM
05-09-1949; 1250 khz AM *Hrs Open:* 24
137 Garden St., Marion, NC 28752 US
(704) 652-9500
wbrm@charterinternet.com
License: Marion, NC held by WBRM Inc.
Arbitron Metro Market: Marion, NC *Format:* Country *Special Programming:* Gospel 5 hrs, relg 7 hrs wkly *Hrs. of News Programming:* news progmg 9 hrs wkly *No. News Employees:* 1 *Target Audience:* 25-55; youngadult to mature *Adv. Rates:* 12.50; 12,50; 12.50; na
Annette Bryant, CEO
Kevin Estes, Operations Dir

Mars Hill

*WYQS
01-01-1974; 90.5 mhz FM *Hrs Open:* 24; 0.25 kw; 1276 ft.; N35 53 12 W82 33 23
P. O. Box 94-T, Mars Hill, NC 28754 US
(828) 210-4800, *Fax:* (828) 210-4801
www.wcqs.org
info@wcqs.org
License: Mars Hill, Madison County, NC held by Western North Carolina Public Radio Inc.
Nat'l Network: NPR
Arbitron Metro Market: Asheville, NC *Format:* News, News/Talk, 86 *Hrs. of News Programming:* news progmg 7 hrs wkly *No. News Employees:* 3 *Target Audience:* 14-30; college students & college community
Lee Wilcher, Operations Dir
Ed Subkis, General Manager
Steve Busey, General Sales Mgr
Barbara Sayer, Programming Director
David Hurand, News Director
Tom Spaight, Chief Engineer
Lee Wilcher, Operations Manager
Vicky Gerald,Traffic Manager
Jody Evans, Executive Director
Jessica Frantz, Membership Associate

Marshall

WHBK
09-20-1956; 1460 khz AM *Hrs Open:* 24; 5 kw-D, ND1; 0.139 kw-N, ND1; N35 48 4 W82 40 48
351 Skyway Drive, Marshall, NC 28753 US
(828) 649-3914, *Fax:* (828) 649-2869
www.1460whbk.com
1460whbk@gmail.com
License: Marshall, NC held by Southern Broadcasting Inc.
Arbitron Metro Market: Asheville, NC *Format:* Gospel *Special Programming:* Farm 3 hrs wkly
Bruce Philips, President
Ricky Seay, General Manager
Ricky West, Programming Director
Ricky West, Disc Jockey

Mayodan

WMYN
07-15-1957; 1420 khz AM *Hrs Open:* 5 AM-10 PM*Rebroadcasts:* Rebroadcasts WLOE(AM) Eden 100%
Post Office Box 311, Madison, NC 27025 US
(336) 427-9696, *Fax:* (336) 548-4636
www.wloewmyn.com
info@rockinghamcountyradio.com
License: Mayodan, NC held by Mayo Broadcasting Corp.
Nat'l Network: Salem Radio Network; USA
Arbitron Metro Market: Mayodan, NC *Format:* Talk, Religious *Hrs. of News Programming:* news progmg 30 hrs wkly *No. News Employees:* 1 *Target Audience:* 25 plus; general *Adv. Rates:* 25; 25; 25; 25
Richard Hall, President
Mike Moore, General Manager
Annette Moore, Station Manager

Mebane

WGSB
12-07-1973; 1060 khz AM *Hrs Open:* Sunrise-sunset; 0.5 kw-C, DAD; 1 kw-D, DAD; N36 3 28 W79 16 36 *Rebroadcasts:* Rebroadcasts WRTP(AM) Chapel Hill 100%
3013 Guess Rd, Durham, NC 27705 US
(202) 638-1959, *Fax:* (202) 638-6127
www.hisradiowrtp.com
estuardovaldemar@hotmail.com
License: Mebane, NC held by Estuardo Valdemar Rodriguez and Leonor Rodriguez.
Group Owner: Radio La Grande; (acq 2-2-2005; grpsl)
Arbitron Metro Market: Raleigh-Durham, NC
Estuardo Valdemar Rodriguez, General Manager

Mint Hill

WNOW
08-01-1987; 1030 khz AM *Hrs Open:* Sunrise-sunset
Pob 889, Blacksburg, VA 24060 US
(704) 831-2478, *Fax:* (704) 949-2606
www.wnow-am.com
License: Mint Hill, NC held by Davidson Media Carolinas Stations LLC.
Group Owner: Davidson Media Group LLC; (acq 5-10-2004; grpsl)
Arbitron Metro Market: Charlotte, NC
Peter Davidson, President
Russ Douglass Jones, General Manager
Aura Gavilan, Promotions Manager
Maria Zarate, News Director
Winston Hawkins, Chief Engineer

Mocksville

WDSL
10-01-1964; 1520 khz AM; 1 kw-C, NDD; 5 kw-D, NDD; N35 52 50 W80 32 26
Mailing Address: 603 Jennings Road, Statesville, NC 28677 US
Second Address: 125 W. Deport St., Mocksville, NC 27028
(336) 751-9375
www.wdsl1520.com/
wdsl1520am@yahoo.com
License: Mocksville, NC held by Davie Broadcasting Inc.
Arbitron Metro Market: Mocksville, NC *Format:* Country, Gospel *Target Audience:* 25-80; general
Craig Dalla Riva, General Manager
Sherry Miller, General Sales Mgr

Monroe

WDEX
12-01-1983; 1430 khz AM *Hrs Open:* 24; 2.5 kw-D, DA2; 2.5 kw-N, DA2; N34 59 4 W80 36 14
Mailing Address: P.O. Box 8146, Kannapolis, NC 22028 US
Second Address: Weddington Rd., Monroe, NC 28110
(704) 289-9444, *Fax:* (704) 857-0680
wdex1430am@yahoo.com
License: Monroe, NC held by New Life Community Temple of Faith Inc.
Arbitron Metro Market: Charlotte, NC *Format:* Gospel *Target Audience:* 25-55.
Ella Hood, CEO
Sharon Talford, General Manager

WIXE
05-03-1968; 1190 khz AM *Hrs Open:* 24
Mailing Address: P. O. Box 1007, 1700 Buena Vista Rd, Monroe, NC 28112 US
Second Address: 1700 Buena Vista Dr., Monroe, NC 28112
(704) 289-2525, *Fax:* (704) 289-1416
www.wixe.com
wixeradio@carolina.rr.com
License: Monroe, NC held by Monroe Broadcasting Co.
Regional Network: N.C. News Net.
Arbitron Metro Market: Charlotte-Gastonia-Rock Hill, NC-SC *Format:* Gospel, Talk, 30 *Special Programming:* Beach & oldies 5 hrs wkly *Hrs. of News Programming:* News progmg 8 hrs wkly *Target Audience:* 18-55.*Adv. Rates:* 21.25; 21.25; 21.25; na
Archie Morgan, President

WXNC
07-01-1947; 1060 khz AM
506 South Church Street, Monre, NC 28110 US
(704) 442-7277, *Fax:* (704) 442-9518
info@latremendaradio.com
License: Monroe, NC held by Norsan Consulting and Management Inc.
Group Owner: Norsan Consulting and Management Inc.; (acq 8-3-2005; $1.15 million).
Nat'l Network: CNN Radio
Arbitron Metro Market: Charlotte-Gastonia-Rock Hill, NC-SC *Hrs. of News Programming:* news progmg 5 hrs wkly *No. News Employees:* 1
Kris Phillips, CFO
Norberto Sanchez, President
Cheri Moore, News Director

Mooresville

WHIP
01-01-1950; 1350 khz AM *Hrs Open:* 6 AM-6:30 PM; 1 kw-D, 670 w-N; N35 36 04 W80 48 51
Box 600, 2432 Statesville Hwy., Mooresville, NC 82115
(704) 664-9447, *Fax:* (704) 664-5551
License: Mooresville, Iredell County, NC held by Mooresville Media Inc.
Nat'l Network: USA
Population Served: 225,000*Special Programming:* Black 6 hrs, relg 6 hrs wkly *Hrs. of News Programming:* News progmg 13 hrs wkly *Target Audience:* 25-45. *Adv. Rates:* 10; 10; 10
Glenn Hamrick, President
Martha Hamrick, Operations Dir
Norman Tindal, General Sales Mgr
Harrill Hamrick, Chief Engineer
Vivian Brandon, Disc Jockey
Kevin Burchett, Sports Commentator
Gary Trexler, Sports Commentator

Morehead City

*WOTJ
12-12-1988; 90.7 mhz FM *Hrs Open:* 24; 24 kw; 466 ft.; N34 46 41 W76 52 42
520 Roberts Road, Newport, NC 28570 US
(252) 223-4600/223-6088, *Fax:* (252) 223-2201
www.fbnradio.com
fbn@fbnradio.com
License: Morehead City, Carteret County, NC held by Grace Christian School.
Nat'l Network: USA
Format: Religious *Hrs. of News Programming:* News progmg 8 hrs wkly *Target Audience:* General; family
Michael Ebron, General Manager

WRHT
12-20-1972; 96.3 mhz FM *Hrs Open:* 24; 100 kw; 492 ft.; N34 45 7 W76 52 57 *Rebroadcasts:* Rebroadcasts WCBZ(FM) Williamston 100%
P.O. Box 1019, Morehead City, NC 28557 US
(252) 672-5900, *Fax:* (252) 637-6872
thehotfm@thehotfm.com
License: Morehead City, Carteret County, NC held by Inner Banks Media LLC.
Group Owner: Inner Banks Media LLC; (acq 3-12-2007; grpsl)
Arbitron Metro Market: Greenville-New Bern-Jacksonville, NC *Format:* Contemporary Hits/Top 40 *Hrs. of News Programming:* news progmg 7 hrs wkly *No. News Employees:* 1 *Target Audience:* 18-49; young active adults& military personnel
Bill Bailey, General Manager

Morganton

WCIS
03-01-1988; 760 khz AM *Hrs Open:* Day station
Mailing Address: 2824 N.C. Route 126, Morganton, NC 28655 US
Second Address: 1399 Bost Rd., Morganton, NC 28655
(828) 584-3076, *Fax:* (828) 433-1498
www.am760thecross.webs.com
powerhouse76@aol.com
License: Morganton, NC held by W.F.M. Inc.
Nat'l Network: USA
Arbitron Metro Market: Morganton, NC *Format:* Gospel
John Whisnant Sr., President
Jeff Whisnant, Operations Dir
John Whisnant Jr., Program Director
Bob Clark, News Director

WMNC
09-23-1947; 1430 khz AM *Hrs Open:* 24; 2.7 kw-D, ND1; 0.046 kw-N, ND1; N35 45 9 W81 43 19
Mailing Address: P.O. Box 969, Morganton, NC 28680 US
Second Address: 1103 N. Green St., Morganton, NC 28655
(828) 437-0521, *Fax:* (828) 433-8855
www.bigdawg92fm.com
wmnc@bellsouth.net
License: Morganton, NC held by Cooper Broadcasting Co.
Nat'l Network: CNN Radio
Arbitron Metro Market: Morganton, NC *Format:* Country
Joe Cooper, Station Manager
Cindy Byas, Programming Director
C.J. Stancil, News Director

WMNC-FM
08-03-1963; 92.1 mhz FM *Hrs Open:* 24; 25 kw; 328 ft.; N35 45 9 W81 43 19
Mailing Address: P.O. Box 969, Morganton, NC 28680 US
Second Address: 1103 N. Green Street, Morganton, NC 28655
(828) 437-0521, *Fax:* (828) 433-8855
www.bigdawg92fm.com
wmnc@bellsouth.net
License: Morganton, Burke County, NC held by Cooper Broadcasting Co.
Arbitron Metro Market: Charlotte, NC *Format:* Country

Mount Airy

WPAQ
02-01-1948; 740 khz AM *Hrs Open:* 6 AM-6:15 PM winter, loc sunset sum; 1 kw-C, ND1; 10 kw-D, ND1; ND1; 0.007 kw; N36 32 4 W80 35 48
P.O. Box 907, Mount Airy, NC 27030 US
(336) 786-6111, *Fax:* (336) 789-7792
wpaq740am@earthlink.net
License: Mount Airy, NC held by WPAQ Radio Inc.
Group Owner: Blue Ridge Radio Inc.
Format: Big Band *Special Programming:* Farm one hr, community affrs one hr, old time string mus 15 hrs wkly *Hrs. of News Programming:* news progmg 13 hrs wkly *No. News Employees:* 1 *Target Audience:* 25-64.*Adv. Rates:* 8.50; 8.50; 8.50; 8.50
Kelly Epperson, General Manager
Kathy Edmonds, General Sales Mgr
Susan Carroll, Promotions Manager
Bernie Phillips, News Director
John Mullins, Chief Engineer

WSYD
10-04-1951; 1300 khz AM *Hrs Open:* 24; 5 kw-D, DAN; 1 kw-N, DAN; N36 30 12 W80 35 35
Box 1678, Mt Airy, NC 27030 US
(336) 786-2147, *Fax:* (336) 789-9858
License: Mount Airy, NC held by Granite City Broadcasters Inc.
Group Owner: Blue Ridge Radio Inc.; (acq 1996)
Format: Gospel *Hrs. of News Programming:* news progmg 8 hrs wkly *No. News Employees:* 1 *Target Audience:* General.
Kelly Epperson, President
Deborah Cochran, Programming Director
Bernie Phillips, News Director
John Mullins, Chief Engineer

Mount Olive

WDJS
12-27-1961; 1430 khz AM
Mailing Address: P.O. Box 429, Mount Olive, NC 28365 US
Second Address: 990 N. Center St., Ext., Mount Olive, NC 28365
(919) 658-9751, *Fax:* (919) 658-4894
License: Mount Olive, NC held by The Mount Olive Broadcasting Co.
Arbitron Metro Market: Fayetteville, NC *Format:* Christian, Religious *Special Programming:* Black 5 hrs, gospel 5 hrs, Sp 5 hrs wkly
Ann Mayo, CEO
Nancy West, Programming Director

Moyock

WCDG(FM)
10-17-1974; 92.1 mhz FM; 18 kw; Ant 384 ft; N36 41 39 W76 02 57
1003 Norfolk Sq., Norfolk, VA 23502-4948
(757) 466-0009, *Fax:* (757) 466-7043
www.cool921.com
License: Moyock, Currituck County, NC held by CC Licenses LLC.
Group Owner: Clear Channel Communications Inc.
Population Served: 1,700,000 *Arbitron Metro Market:* Norfolk-Virginia Beach-Newport News, VA *Format:* Urban Contemporary *Target Audience:* 18-34; males 18-49
Lowery Mays, CEO
Travis Dylan, Operations Dir
Reggie Jordan, General Manager
Terry Ratliff, General Sales Mgr
Toni Jones, Promotions Manager
Michael Bov-e, Chief Engineer
Bill Davis, National Sales Manager

Murfreesboro

WDLZ
10-11-1970; 98.3 mhz FM; 3 kw; 328 ft.; N36 26 24 W77 8 10
P.O. Box 4005, Rocky Mount, NC 27803 US
(252) 398-4111, *Fax:* (252) 398-3581
License: Murfreesboro, Hertford County, NC
Group Owner: First Media Radio LLC
Arbitron Metro Market: Elizabeth City-Nags Head, NC *Format:* Adult Contemp
Steve Crumbely, Operations Dir
Gary Pizzati, General Manager

WWDR
03-20-1965; 1080 khz AM
Mailing Address: P.O. Box 4005, Rocky Mount, NC 27803 US
Second Address: 1714 W. Main St., Murfreesboro, NC 27855
(252) 398-4111, *Fax:* (252) 398-3581
License: Murfreesboro, NC held by First Media Radio LLC.
Group Owner: First Media Radio LLC; (acq 1-7-2003; grpsl)
Nat'l Network: Moody *Regional Network:* N.C. News Net.
Arbitron Metro Market: Murfreesboro, NC *Format:* Christian, Gospel *Special Programming:* Farm 10 hrs wkly
Earl Tellega, General Manager
Neil Haskins, General Sales Mgr
Bob Wood, Programming Director
Frank White, Chief Engineer

Murphy

WCNG
10-23-1990; 102.7 mhz FM *Hrs Open:* 5 AM-midnight; 3 kw; 236 ft.; N35 4 0 W83 59 58
P. O. Box 280, Murphy, NC 28906 US
704) 837-9264(704) 837-5509
info@wcng.com
License: Murphy, Cherokee County, NC
Arbitron Metro Market: Murphy,NC *Format:* Classic Rock
Dennis Gene, General Manager

WCVP
10-12-1958; 600 khz AM *Hrs Open:* 5 AM-10 PM; 1 kw-D, ND1; 0.02 kw-N, ND1; N35 4 0 W83 59 58
P. O. Box 280, Murphy, NC 28906 US
(828) 837-2151(828) 837-2152
info@wcvp.com
License: Murphy, NC held by Cherokee Broadcasting Co.
Arbitron Metro Market: Knoxville, TN *Format:* Adult Contemp, Gospel, 60 *Special Programming:* Farm 3 hrs, class 20 hrs, C&W 12 hrs wkly *Target Audience:* All ages.
Allan Blakemore, President
Jane Blakemore, General Manager
Dennis Blakemore, General Sales Mgr
Skip Ballard, Music Director

WKRK
08-08-1958; 1320 khz AM *Hrs Open:* 24; 5 kw-D, ND1; 0.062 kw-N, ND1; N35 6 42 W84 0 31
631 Andrews Road, Murphy, NC 28906 US
(828) 837-1320, *Fax:* (828) 837-8610
www.1320am.com
License: Murphy, NC held by Radford Communications Inc.
Nat'l Network: Jones Radio Networks *Nat'l Reps:* Rgnl Reps
Regional Reps: Commercial Media Sales *Wire Services:* AP
Arbitron Metro Market: Chattanooga, TN *Format:* Country *Special Programming:* Pub affrs 3 hrs wkly *Hrs. of News Programming:* AP Radio News, 2 minutes an hour *Target Audience:* 35-64 *Adv. Rates:* 17; 15;17; 8
Tim Radford, President
Ab Radford, Operations Dir
Larry Nelson, Programming Director
Emma Ramsey, Promotions Manager
Bill Yonce, Disc Jockey
Marty Montell, Disc Jockey
John St. John, Disc Jockey

Nags Head

WZPR
04-04-1990; 92.3 mhz FM *Hrs Open:* 24; 10 kw; 384 ft.; N35 50 49 W75 37 20
637 Harbor Road, Wanchese, NC 27981 US
(252) 475-1888, *Fax:* (252) 475-1881
www.classichits1049.com
classichits@maxradionc.com
License: Nags Head, Dare County, NC held by CapSan Media LLC.
Group Owner: CapSan Media LLC; (acq 6-30-2006; grpsl)
Nat'l Network: ESPN Radio
Arbitron Metro Market: Wanchese, NC *Format:* Contemporary Hits/Top 40
William Whitlow, President
Hunt Thomas, Operations Dir

Nashville

WZAX
02-01-1997; 99.3 mhz FM *Hrs Open:* 24; 6 kw; 328 ft.; N35 57 1 W77 57 26
P O Box 910, Roanoke Rapids, NC 27870 US
(252) 442-8092, *Fax:* (252) 977-6664
www.jammin993.com
License: Nashville, Nash County, NC held by First Media Radio LLC
Group Owner: First Media Radio LLC; (acq 7-22-2003; grpsl)
Nat'l Reps: Interep
Arbitron Metro Market: Rocky Mount-Wil *Format:* Oldies
Alex Kolobielski, President
Mike Binkley, Promotions Manager

New Bern

***WAAE**
01-01-1997; 91.9 mhz FM *Hrs Open:* 24 hours; 1.35 kw; 164 ft.; N35 8 14 W77 0 22 *Rebroadcasts:* Rebroadcasts WAFR(FM) Tupelo 100%
P O Drawer 2440, Tupelo, MS 38803 US
(662) 844-8888, *Fax:* (662) 840-3187
www.afr.net
www.afr.net
License: New Bern, Craven County, NC held by American Family Association.
Group Owner: American Family Radio
Nat'l Network: American Family Radio
Arbitron Metro Market: New Bern, NC *Format:* Talk
Marvin Sanders, General Manager
Joey Moody, Chief Engineer

WIKS
08-01-1977; 101.9 mhz FM *Hrs Open:* 24; 100 kw; 981 ft.; N35 12 7 W77 11 15
3033 Riviera Dr., Suite 200, Naples, FL 33940 US
(252) 633-1500, *Fax:* (252) 633-6546
www.1019online.com
License: New Bern, Craven County, NC held by Beasley FM Acquisition Corp.
Group Owner: Beasley Broadcast Group Inc.
Nat'l Reps: D & R Radio

Arbitron Metro Market: Greenville-New Bern-Jacksonville, NC *Format:* Adult Contemp *Special Programming:* Gospel 4 hrs, jazz 2 hrs wkly
Bruce Beasley, President
Bruce Simel, Operations Dir
J Dot, Promotions Manager

WNOS
04-23-1942; 1450 khz AM *Hrs Open:* 24; 1 kw-U, ND1; N35 6 3 W77 4 33
1331 South Glenburnie, New Bern, NC 28562 US
(252) 633-1490, *Fax:* (888) 878-5251
www.rfenc.com
info@rfenc.com
License: New Bern, NC held by CTC Media Group Inc.
Group Owner: CTC Media Group Inc.; acq 7-1-00; $65,000).
Nat'l Network: Fox Sports; Westwood One *Regional Network:* N.C. News Net.
Arbitron Metro Market: Greenville, NC *Format:* Sports, Talk
Target Audience: 12+, Male 12-45
Lee Afflerbach, President
Mike Afflerbach, General Manager

WSFL-FM
07-20-1968; 106.5 mhz FM *Hrs Open:* 24; 100 kw; 915 ft.; N35 2 27 W77 21 11
1602 Highway 70 East, New Bern, NC 28560 US
(252) 633-1500, *Fax:* (252) 633-6546
www.wsfl.com
cindymiller@wsfl.com
License: New Bern, Craven County, NC held by W & B Media Inc.
Group Owner: Beasley Broadcast Group Inc.; (acq 7-10-91; $500,000 with co-located AM;
Nat'l Reps: D & R Radio
Arbitron Metro Market: Greenville-New *Format:* Rock/AOR
Target Audience: 18-54.
Bruce Simel, General Manager
Wilbur Vitols, General Sales Mgr
Cindy Miller, Programming Director
Wendy Gatlin, Promotions Manager
Richard Banks, Engineering Dir

***WTEB**
06-04-1984; 89.3 mhz FM *Hrs Open:* 24; 99 kw; 482 ft.; N35 6 32 W77 6 10
800 College Court, New Bern, NC 28562 US
(800) 222-9832, *Fax:* (252) 638-3538
www.publicradioeast.org
hsegar@publicradioeast.org
License: New Bern, Craven County, NC held by Board of Trustees, Craven Community College.
Nat'l Network: NPR; PRI
Arbitron Metro Market: Greenville-New Bern, NC *Format:* News *Special Programming:* Jazz 4 hrs wkly *Hrs. of News Programming:* News progmg 44 hrs wkly *Target Audience:* 35 plus; highly educated professionals
Kelly Batchelor, Operations Dir
Charles Wethington, General Manager
Kathleen Beal, General Sales Mgr
Jill McGuire, Programming Director
George Olsen, News Director
J. Howard Jones, Chief Engineer
Michael.R.Foster, BusinessAccount Executive

WWNB
07-05-1953; 1490 khz AM *Hrs Open:* 24; 1 kw-U, ND1; N35 7 59 W77 3 56
P.O. Box 401, Clarksville, MD 21029 US
(252) 633-1490, *Fax:* (888) 878-5251
www.rfenc.com
info@rfenc.com
License: New Bern, NC held by CTC Media Group Inc.
Group Owner: CTC Media Group Inc.; acq 11-15-90; $75,000).
Nat'l Network: ESPN Radio; Westwood One
Arbitron Metro Market: Greenville, NC *Format:* Sports *Target Audience:* Men 12-54; general
Mike Afflerbach, General Manager
Chris Butler, General Sales Mgr

***WZNB**
01-01-2006; 88.5 mhz FM; 0.3 kw; 121 ft.; N35 6 32 W77 6 10
800 College Court, New Bern, NC 28562 US
(800) 222-9832, *Fax:* (252) 638-3538
www.publicradioeast.org
kbatchelor@publicradioeast.org?subject=Contact%20from%20PRE%20Website
License: New Bern, Craven County, NC held by Craven Community College.
Arbitron Metro Market: Greenville, NC *Format:* Public Affairs, News
Kelly Batchelor, Operations Dir
Charles Wethington, Station Manager
Kathleen Beal, General Sales Mgr
Jill McGuire, Programming Director
George Olsen, News Director
J. Howard Jones, Chief Engineer
Kelly Batchelor, BroadcastSupervisor
Jared Brumbaugh, Announcer / Reporter and Producer

New Hope

WAUG
07-20-1987; 750 khz AM; 0.5 kw-D, NDD; N35 47 28 W78 37 10
1315 Oakwood Avenue, Raleigh, NC 97610 US
(919) 516-4750
waug@st-aug.edu
License: New Hope, NC held by Saint Augustine's College.
Nat'l Network: American Urban
Format: Gospel, News, 62, Talk, Religious *Target Audience:* 18 plus; Black adults
Diane Suber, President
Frank Butler, Operations Dir
Alan Riggs, Station Manager
John Hardee, Chief Engineer

Newland

WECR
08-14-1978; 1130 khz AM; 1 kw-D, NDD; N36 4 39 W81 54 59
317 Old Turnpike Road, NW, Banner Elk, NC 28604 US
(828) 733-0188, *Fax:* (828) 733-0189
www.wecr1130am.com/
wecr@bellsouth.net
License: Newland, NC held by High Country Adventures LLC.
Group Owner: Curtis Media Group; (acq 3-3-2009; grpsl)
Arbitron Metro Market: Newland, NC *Format:* Country *Special Programming:* Gospel 10 hrs, relg 5 hrs, bluegrass 2 hrs wkly
Target Audience: 25-54; middle class, blue collar *Adv. Rates:* 11.40; 11.40; 11.40; na
Jonathan Hoffman, General Manager

Newport

WMGV
09-04-1983; 103.3 mhz FM *Hrs Open:* 24; 100 kw; 981 ft.; N35 7 55 W76 52 32
3033 Riviera Drive, Suite 200, Naples, FL 33940 US
(252) 633-1500, *Fax:* (252) 633-0718
www.v1033.com
info@wmgv.com
License: Newport, Carteret County, NC held by WMGV License L.P.
Group Owner: Beasley Broadcast Group Inc.; (acq 2-3-2000; grpsl)
Nat'l Reps: D & R Radio
Arbitron Metro Market: Greenville, NC *Format:* Classic Rock
Target Audience: 18-54.
Bruce Simel, General Manager
Wilbur Vitols, General Sales Mgr
Colleen Jackson, Programming Director

Newton

WNNC
06-18-1948; 1230 khz AM *Hrs Open:* 24; 1 kw-U, ND1; N35 40 20 W81 14 12
P.O. Box 940, Newton, NC 28658 US
(828) 464-4041, *Fax:* (828) 464-9662
www.mytotalradio.com
totalradio@aol.com
License: Newton, NC held by Newton-Conover Communications Inc.
Arbitron Metro Market: Newton, NC *Format:* Adult Contemp *Special Programming:* Black 2 hrs, jazz 3 hrs wkly *No. News Employees:* 1 *Target Audience:* 25-49. *Adv. Rates:* 30; 15; 15; 12
Dave Lingafelt, President
Jim Turner, General Sales Mgr
Karol Lowery, News Director

Newton Grove

***WYBJ**
01-01-2007; 90.7 mhz FM; 3 kw; 354 ft.; N35 13 54 W78 22 11
2630 Mirror Lake Drive, Fayetteville, NC 28303 US
(252) 223-4600, *Fax:* (252) 223-2201
www.fbnradio.com
License: Newton Grove, Sampson County, NC held by Grace Missionary Baptist Church Inc.
Arbitron Metro Market: Newton Grove, NC
Michael Ebron, General Manager

Norlina

***WVRH**
01-01-2001; 94.3 mhz FM *Hrs Open:* 24; 6 kw; Ant 328 ft; N36 29 46 W78 11 14 *Rebroadcasts:* Rebroadcasts WAJC(FM) Zebulon 100%
5 W. Hargett St., Raleigh, NC 92704
(919) 899-6778, *Fax:* (919) 899-6779
License: Norlina, Warren County, NC held by CSN International
Group Owner: CSN International; acq 12-18-98).

Jim Walker, General Manager

***WZRN**
90.5 mhz FM; 2.3 kw; Ant 298 ft; N36 29 38 W78 11 23
232 Roanoke Ave., Roanoke Rapids, NC
(252) 308-0885, *Fax:* (252) 537-3333
www.gomixradio.org
License: Norlina, Warren County, NC held by Roanoke Valley Communications Inc.
Nat'l Network: WZRU
Target Audience: 23 and older
Dr. T.D. Worthington, President
Allen Garrett, General Manager
Glenda Browder, General Sales Mgr
Rusty Draper, Chief Engineer

North Wilkesboro

WKBC
06-01-1947; 800 khz AM *Hrs Open:* 24; 1 kw-D, ND1; 0.308 kw-N, ND1; N36 11 16 W81 8 30
Box 938, 400 C Street, North Wilkesboro, NC 28659 US
(336) 667-2221, *Fax:* (336) 667-3677
wkbctraffic@charter.net
License: North Wilkesboro, NC held by Wilkes Broadcasting Co. Inc.
Nat'l Network: CBS Radio *Wire Services:* AP
Format: Country *No. News Employees:* 1 *Adv. Rates:* 22; 14; 18; 12
Robert Brown, President
Ed Racey, News Director

WKBC-FM
07-01-1962; 97.3 mhz FM *Hrs Open:* 24; 100 kw horiz, 92 kw vert; 1322 ft.; N36 4 34 W81 7 43
P.O. Box 938, North Wilkesboro, NC 28659 US
(336) 667-2221, *Fax:* (336) 667-3677
License: North Wilkesboro, Wilkes County, NC held by Wilkes Broadcasting Co. Inc.
Format: Contemporary Hits/Top 40 *Adv. Rates:* 48; 40; 44; 30
Robert Brown, General Manager
Bob Brown, Programming Director
Ed Racey, Chief Engineer

Oak Island

WUIN
07-01-2000; 98.3 mhz FM *Hrs Open:* 24; 18.5 kw; 380 ft; N33 57 40 W78 01 37
25 N. Kerr Ave., Suite C, Wilmington, NC 28677
(910) 791-3088, *Fax:* (910) 791-0112
www.surf983.com
mud@surf983.com
License: Oak Island, Brunswick County, NC held by Sunrise Broadcasting LLC.
Group Owner: Capitol Broadcasting Co. Inc.; (acq 11-18-2008; grpsl)
Barbara Raybourne, General Manager
Mike Kennedy, Programming Director
Missy Andrus, Promotions Manager
Walt Howard, Engineering Dir

Ocean Isle Beach

WLQB
01-01-1999; 93.5 mhz FM; 6 kw; 328 ft.; N33 55 37 W78 23 48
Rebroadcasts: Simulcast with WGTR(FM) Bucksport, SC 100%
Two Bala Plaza, Suite 801, Bala-Cynwyd, PA 19004 US
(843) 293-0107, *Fax:* (843) 293-1717
License: Ocean Isle Beach, Brunswick County, NC held by Qantum of Myrtle Beach License Co. LLC.
Group Owner: Qantum Communications Corp.; (acq 7-2-2003; grpsl).
Arbitron Metro Market: Ocean Isle Beach, NC *Format:* Country
Serap Jackson, Operations Dir
Michael Meeks, General Manager

Ocracoke

***WOVV**
90.1 mhz FM; 0.65 kw; 62 ft.; N35 6 43 W75 58 38.2

RADIO - U.S.

US
(252) 921-0365
www.wovv.org
License: Ocracoke, Hyde County, NC held by Ocracoke Foundation.
Arbitron Metro Market: Ocracoke, NC *Format:* Variety/Diverse
Robin Payne, President

Old Fort

WKSF

08-01-1947; 99.9 mhz FM *Hrs Open:* 24; 48 kw; 2621 ft.; N35 25 32 W82 45 25
600 Congress Avenue, Suite 1400, Austin, TX 78701 US
(828) 257-2700, *Fax:* (828) 255-7850
www.99kisscountry.com
info@99kisscountry.com
License: Old Fort, Buncombe County, NC held by Capstar TX L.P.
Arbitron Metro Market: Asheville, NC *Format:* Country *Hrs. of News Programming:* News progmg 3 hrs wkly *Target Audience:* 25-44.
Larry Robb, General Manager
Steve Fortunato, General Sales Mgr
Sue O'Neil, Programming Director

Oriental

WNBU(FM)

03-18-1993; 94.1 mhz FM *Hrs Open:* 24; 11 kw; Ant 485 ft; N35 00 02 W76 49 58
1308 Glenburnie Rd., New Bern, NC 28562
(252) 355-1037, *Fax:* (252) 355-2234
www.wnbufm.com
dmckay@ibxmedia.com
License: Oriental, Pamlico County, NC held by Inner Banks Media LLC.
Group Owner: Inner Banks Media LLC; (acq 3-12-2007; grpsl)
Population Served: 250,000 *Arbitron Metro Market:* Grenville, NC *Format:* Talk *Target Audience:* 25 plus; adults with disposable incomes
Henry Hinton, General Manager
Hank Hinton, General Sales Mgr

Oxford

WCBQ

06-09-1949; 1340 khz AM *Hrs Open:* 18; 1 kw-U, ND1; N36 18 27 W78 34 37 *Rebroadcasts:* Rebroadcasts WHNC(AM) Henderson 100%
Mailing Address: P. O. Box 336, Oxford, NC 27565 US
Second Address: 1 Alvin Augustus Jones Way, Oxford, NC 27565
(919) 693-3540(919) 693-1340, *Fax:* (919) 693-9054
dralvin.com
alvin@dralvinjones.com
License: Oxford, NC held by The Paradise Network Of North Carolina (TPN)
Format: Gospel, Talk *Special Programming:* Farm, professional & college sports, news/talk *Hrs. of News Programming:* News progmg 10 hrs wkly *Target Audience:* General.
Dr. Alvin Jones, CEO

Pilot Mountain

*WGIW

01-01-2008; 89.7 mhz FM; 0.43 kw vert; 373 ft.; N36 25 23.6 W80 37 52.6
US
(605) 868-0525
License: Pilot Mountain, Surry County, NC held by Church Planters of America.
Arbitron Metro Market: Pilot Mountain, NC *Format:* Gospel
Danny Hawkins, President

Pine Knoll Shores

WBNK

01-01-2009; 92.7 mhz FM *Hrs Open:* 24 7; 11.5 kw; 748 ft.; N34 53 0.4 W76 30 21.3
Mailing Address: US
Second Address: 1305 S Glenburnie Road, New Bern, NC
(252) 636-3333
www.bigfishfm.com
traffic@bigfishfm.com
License: Pine Knoll Shores, Carteret County, NC held by Tower Investment Trust Inc.
Group Owner: Tower Investment Trust Inc.
Arbitron Metro Market: Pine Knoll Shores, NC *Format:* Christian *Target Audience:* w 25 -54 w 18 - 34
William Brothers, President

Pinehurst

*WBFY

09-01-2003; 90.3 mhz FM; 3.5 kw vert; 328 ft.; N35 9 13 W79 34 16
P O Drawer 2440, Tupelo, MS 38803 US
(662) 844-8888, *Fax:* (662) 840-3187
www.afr.net
faq@afr.net
License: Pinehurst, Moore County, NC held by American Family Association.
Group Owner: American Family Radio
Nat'l Network: American Family Radio
Arbitron Metro Market: Pinehurst, NC *Format:* Christian *Hrs. of News Programming:* 24 hours
Marvin Sanders, General Manager
Joey Moody, Chief Engineer

WIOZ

03-25-1980; 550 khz AM *Hrs Open:* 24; 1 kw-D, DA2; 0.26 kw-N, DA2; N35 9 4 W79 28 40
P. O. Box 1677, Southern Pines, NC 28387 US
(910) 692-2107, *Fax:* (910) 692-6849
www.wioz.com
License: Pinehurst, NC held by Muirfield Broadcasting Inc.
Group Owner: Muirfield Broadcasting Inc.; acq 12-28-83)
Format: Adult Contemp *Hrs. of News Programming:* news progmg 5 hrs wkly *No. News Employees:* 1 *Target Audience:* General.
Walker Morris, President
Rich Rushforth, Operations Dir
Tiffany Hewitt, General Manager

Pinetops

WPWZ

12-02-1996; 95.5 mhz FM *Hrs Open:* 24; 12.5 kw; 459 ft.; N35 56 45 W77 39 37
3012 Highwoods Blvd., Suite 201, Raleigh, NC 27604 US
(252) 442-8092, *Fax:* (252) 977-6664
www.powerhits95.com
License: Pinetops, Edgecombe County, NC held by First Media Radio LLC.
Group Owner: First Media Radio LLC; (acq 12-3-2003; grpsl)
Nat'l Reps: Interep
Arbitron Metro Market: Rocky Mount-Wilson, NC *Format:* Urban Contemporary *No. News Employees:* 1 *Target Audience:* 24-54.
Alex Kolobielski, President
David Perkins, Operations Dir
Mike Binkley, General Manager
Mike Binkley, Promotions Manager
Angie Webb, Office Manager
Laura Boyles, Administrative Assistant
Kat Leonard, Internet ProductionDirector
Rick Braswell, Public Service Announcements
Paul Andre, Disc Jockey

Pineville

WGIV

03-08-1948; 1370 khz AM *Rebroadcasts:* Rebroadcasts WRNA(AM) China Grove 90%
P.O. Box 861, Rock Hill, SC 29731 US
(803) 329-2760, *Fax:* (803) 329-3317
www.wgivcharlotte.com
fneely@rejoiceradio.com
License: Pineville, NC held by Wisdom LLC.
Group Owner: Wisdom LLC; (acq 2-2-2009; grpsl)
Nat'l Network: USA
Arbitron Metro Market: Charlotte-Gastonia-Rock Hill, NC-SC
Format: Blues *Target Audience:* 30 plus Black
Emma Neely, Operations Dir
Frank Neely, General Manager
Frankie Hemphill, Station Manager

Pisgah Forest

WGCR

09-16-1985; 720 khz AM
1950 Old Hendersonville, Highway, Pisgah Forest, NC 28768 US
(828) 884-9427, *Fax:* (828) 883-9427
www.wgcr.net
License: Pisgah Forest, NC held by Anchor Baptist Broadcasting Association.
Nat'l Network: USA *Regional Network:* N.C. News Net.
Format: News, Religious *Special Programming:* Gospel *Target Audience:* General.
Randy Barton, President
Shanna Barton, Promotions Manager
Shamma Barton, News Director
Lamar Owen, Chief Engineer

Plymouth

WPNC-FM

12-01-1979; 95.9 mhz FM *Hrs Open:* 24; 2.6 kw; 331 ft.; N35 50 48 W76 45 22
P.O. Box 686, Plymouth, NC 27962 US
(252) 793-9995, *Fax:* (252) 793-4673
magic959production@yahoo.com
License: Plymouth, Washington County, NC held by Durlyn Broadcasting Inc.
Nat'l Network: CBS Radio *Regional Network:* N.C. News Net.
Format: Adult Contemp *Target Audience:* 25-54. *Adv. Rates:* 10; 10; 10; 10.
Bill Benjamin, CEO
Marie Cox, Operations Dir
Alex Rains, Operations Manager

Raeford

WMFA

04-25-1963; 1400 khz AM *Hrs Open:* 6 AM-10 PM; 1 kw-U, ND1; N34 58 43 W79 12 32
1085 E. Central Ave., Raeford, SC 28376 US
(910) 875-6225, *Fax:* (910) 875-3220
wmfa1400@yahoo.com
License: Raeford, NC held by W & V Broadcasting Enterprises Inc.
Arbitron Metro Market: Raeford, NC *Format:* Gospel *Special Programming:* Sp 6 hrs wkly *Target Audience:* General. Black
William Hollingsworth, CEO
Jeremy Hollingsworth, General Manager
Vera Hollingsworth, CFO

*WRAE

01-01-2006; 88.7 mhz FM; 6 kw; 472 ft.; N34 54 57 W79 7 28
Rebroadcasts: Rebroadcasts WAFR(FM) Tupelo, MS 100%
P O Box 2440, Tupelo, MS 38803 US
(662) 844-8888, *Fax:* (662) 842-6791
www.afr.net
faq@afr.net
License: Raeford, Hoke County, NC held by American Family Association.
Group Owner: American Family Radio
Arbitron Metro Market: Raeford, NC *Format:* Christian
Marvin Sanders, General Manager

Raleigh

WBBB

01-01-1947; 96.1 mhz FM *Hrs Open:* 24; 98 kw; 984 ft.; N35 41 7 W78 43 14
3012 Highwoods Blvd.#201, Raleigh, NC 27604 US
(413) 597-3265, *Fax:* (413) 597-2259
wcfm.williams.edu
wcfmbd@wso.williams.edu
License: Raleigh, Wake County, NC held by Carolina Media Group Inc.
Group Owner: Curtis Media Group; (acq 1996; $16 million)
Nat'l Reps: McGavren Guild
Arbitron Metro Market: Twin Falls ID
Adam Ain, General Manager

WCLY

08-15-1962; 1550 khz AM
3012 Highwoods Blvd., Suite 201, Raleigh, NC 27604 US
(919) 890-6299, *Fax:* (919) 890-6146
www.espntriangle.com
contact@999thefan.com
License: Raleigh, NC held by Triangle Broadcast Associates LLC.
Group Owner: Curtis Media Group; (acq 4-5-99)
Arbitron Metro Market: Raleigh-Durham, NC *Format:* Christian, Gospel, 74 *Target Audience:* 25-65; primarily Black
Rick Heilmann, General Manager

*WCPE

07-17-1978; 89.7 mhz FM *Hrs Open:* 24; 96.7 kw; 1178 ft.; N35 56 25 W78 28 45
P.O. Box 828, Wake Forest, NC 27588 US
(919) 556-5178, *Fax:* (919) 556-9273
theclassicalstation.org
webmaster@TheClassicalStation.org
License: Raleigh, Wake County, NC held by Educational Information Corp.
Arbitron Metro Market: Raleigh-Durham, NC *Format:* Classical *Special Programming:* Sacred music, Opera *Target Audience:* 35 plus; class mus listeners
Deborah Proctor, CEO
Rae Weaver, General Sales Mgr
Dick Storck, Programming Director
Deborah Proctor, Chief Engineer
Will Woltz, Music Director

***WKNC-FM**
10-09-1966; 88.1 mhz FM *Hrs Open:* 24/7/365; 25 kw; 259 ft; N35 47 15 W78 40 14
343 Witherspoon Student Ctr., Campus Box 8607, Raleigh, NC 27695
(919) 515-2401, *Fax:* (919) 515-5333
www.wknc.org
gm@wknc.org
License: Raleigh, Wake County, NC held by North Carolina State University.
Population Served: 1,000,000 *Arbitron Metro Market:* Raleigh-Durham, NC *Special Programming:* South Asian, A capella, Americana, Punk *Hrs. of News Programming:* 4 hrs wkly *Target Audience:* 18-59; adults & highschool & college students of all demographics *Adv. Rates:* 40; 30; 40; 30
Michael D'Argenio, Operations Dir
Michaek Jones, General Manager
Bri Aab, Programming Director
Zach Dorsett, Promotions Manager
Anastassia Tretikova, Music Director
Christophe Bequet, Music Director
Cameren Dolecheck, MusicDirector
Billy Cunningham, Music Director

WPJL
03-01-1939; 1240 khz AM *Hrs Open:* 5:30 AM-midnight; 1 kw-U, ND1; N35 46 25 W78 37 9
P. O. Box 27946, 515 Bart Street, Raleigh, NC 27611 US
(919) 834-6401
License: Raleigh, NC held by WPJL Inc.
Nat'l Network: USA
Arbitron Metro Market: Raleigh-Durham, NC *Format:* Christian *Special Programming:* Black gospel *Hrs. of News Programming:* News progmg 10 hrs wkly *Target Audience:* 25-54; Evangelical Christian community ofgreater Raleigh area *Adv. Rates:* 30; 25; 30; 20
William Suttles, President
LaRue Porter, Operations Dir
Jon Hardee, Chief Engineer

WPTF
09-22-1924; 680 khz AM *Hrs Open:* 24; 50 kw-N, DAN; N35 47 38 W78 45 41
3012 Highwoods Blvd #201, Raleigh, NC 27604 US
(919) 790-9392, *Fax:* (919) 790-8369
www.wptf.com
License: Raleigh, NC held by First State Communications.
Group Owner: Curtis Media Group
Nat'l Network: CBS *Regional Network:* Southern Farm *Nat'l Reps:* McGavren Guild
Arbitron Metro Market: Raleigh-Durham, NC *Format:* News, News/Talk, 86 *Special Programming:* Farm 10 hrs wkly *Hrs. of News Programming:* News progmg 20 hrs wkly *Target Audience:* 35-64.
David Stuckey, General Manager

WQDR-FM
08-01-1949; 94.7 mhz FM *Hrs Open:* 24; 96 kw; 1,679 ft; N35 40 35 W78 32 09
3012 Highwoods Blvd., Suite 200, Raleigh, NC 27604
(919) 876-6464, *Fax:* (919) 790-8893
www.wqdr.net
info@curtismedia.com
License: Raleigh, Wake County, NC held by Carolina Media Group Inc.
Group Owner: Curtis Media Group
Regional Network: Southern Farm
Population Served: 1,000,000 *Arbitron Metro Market:* Raleigh-Durham, NC *Special Programming:* NASCAR racing, bluegrass *Hrs. of News Programming:* news progmg 2 hrs wkly *No. News Employees:* 1 *Target Audience:* 25-54.
Trip Savery, General Manager

WRAL
01-01-1947; 101.5 mhz FM *Hrs Open:* 24; 96 kw; 1821 ft.; N35 40 35 W78 32 8
Mailing Address: P. O. Box 12800, Raleigh, NC 27605 US
Second Address: 711 Hillsborough St., Raleigh, NC 27603
(919) 890-6101, *Fax:* (919) 890-6146
www.wralfm.com
mixonline@wralfm.com
License: Raleigh, Wake County, NC held by Capitol Broadcasting Co. Inc.
Group Owner: Capitol Broadcasting Co. Inc.; acq 1946)
Regional Network: N.C. News Net. *Nat'l Reps:* Katz Radio *Wire Services:* AP
Arbitron Metro Market: Raleigh-Durham, NC *TV Affiliate:* WRAL-TV affil. *Format:* Adult Contemp *Special Programming:* Public Affairs Block - 6:30-8:00am Sundays *Hrs. of News Programming:* 7 hrs wkly news progmg*Target Audience:* 25-54.
Dan McGrath, CFO
Jim Goodmon, President
Ardie Gregory, Operations Dir
Robert Wallace, General Sales Mgr
Paige Ellis Longest, Promotions Manager
Keith Harrison, Engineering Dir
Mark Turak, National Sales Manager
Barry Fox,Operations Director
Kirk Kirkland, Regional Sales Manager

WPTK(AM)
01-01-1947; 850 khz AM *Hrs Open:* 24; 10 kw-D, 5 kw-N, DA-N; N35 48 04 W78 48 51
4601 Six Forks Rd., Suite 520, Raliegh, NC 27609-5287
(919) 875-9100, *Fax:* (919) 510-6990
www.850thebuzz.com
brianm@850thebuzz.com
License: Raleigh, Wake County, NC held by McClatchey Broadcasting Co. LLC
Nat'l Network: Westwood One; Fox Sports *Nat'l Reps:* McGavren Guild *Wire Services:* AP
Population Served: 1,490,000 *Arbitron Metro Market:* Raleigh-Durham, NC *Hrs. of News Programming:* News progmg 5 hrs wkly *Target Audience:* 25-54.
Brian Maloney, General Manager
Adam Gold, Programming Director
Mike Stangl, Promotions Manager
Ted Sawyer, News Director

WFNL
12-01-1981; 570 khz AM *Hrs Open:* 24; 500 w-D, 54 w-N; N35 45 37 W78 39 27
3012 Highwoods Blvd., Raleigh, NC 27604
(919) 855-9383, *Fax:* (919) 790-6654
www.570wdox.com
License: Raleigh, Wake County, NC held by Triangle Broadcast Associates LLC.
Group Owner: Curtis Media Group; (acq 6-1-99).
Nat'l Network: ABC *Nat'l Reps:* McGavren Guild
Population Served: 600,000 *Arbitron Metro Market:* Raleigh-Durham, NC *Adv. Rates:* 18; 15; 24; 15
Rick Heilmann, General Manager
Peter Richon, Programming Director

***WSHA**
11-18-1968; 88.9 mhz FM *Hrs Open:* 24; 50 kw; 456 ft.; N35 45 5 W78 36 1
118 East South Street, Raleigh, NC 27602 US
(919) 546-8430, *Fax:* (919) 546-8315
www.wshafm.org
wsha@shawu.edu
License: Raleigh, Wake County, NC held by Shaw University.
Nat'l Network: NPR
Arbitron Metro Market: Raleigh-Durham, *Format:* Jazz *Special Programming:* Sp 3 hrs, African 3 hrs, Caribbean 3 hrs, blues 8 *Hrs. of News Programming:* News progmg 13.5 hrs wkly *Target Audience:* 25-55; highincome, well educated
Dr. Emeka Emekauwa, General Manager
Sharon Berry-Vivian, Programming Director
Jim Davis, Chief Engineer
Rashad Mulhaimin, Assistant General Manager
Michael Rochelle, Senior Underwriting

WKIX-FM
01-01-2000; 102.9 mhz FM; 1.7 kw; Ant 620 ft; N35 47 38 W78 45 41
3012 Highwoods Blvd., Suite 201, Raleigh, NC 27604
(919) 790-6961, *Fax:* (919) 790-8369
www.y1029.com
bcampbell@curtismedia.com
License: Raleigh, Wake County, NC held by WWND LLC.
Group Owner: Curtis Media Group; (acq 10-2-98; $495,000 for stock)
Nat'l Reps: McGavren Guild
Population Served: 1,100,000 *Arbitron Metro Market:* Raleigh-Durham, NC
Mike Hartel, General Manager
Bill Campbell, Programming Director
Shalon Lenfestry, Promotions Manager
Ali Diatta, News Director
Allen Sherrill, Chief Engineer

Red Springs

WTEL
06-15-1970; 1160 khz AM *Hrs Open:* 17; 5 kw-D, ND1; 0.25 kw-N, ND1; N34 50 19 W79 10 36
3033 Riviera Drive, #200, Naples, FL 33940 US
(910) 843-5946, *Fax:* (910) 843-8694
info@wtel.com
License: Red Springs, NC held by WDAS License L.P.
Group Owner: Beasley Broadcast Group Inc.; (acq 6-12-97; $1.2 million with WUKS(FM) Saint Pauls).
Regional Network: Southern Farm
Arbitron Metro Market: Red Springs, NC *Format:* Black, Gospel *Special Programming:* Farm 5 hrs wkly *No. News Employees:* 2 *Target Audience:* 24-54.
Danny Highsmith, General Manager
Towanna Locklear, General Sales Mgr
Garrette Davis, Programming Director
Deanna Hodges, Promotions Manager
Gilbert Baez, News Director
Van Clough, Chief Engineer
Montana Locklear, Disc Jockey
George McPhaul, Local News Editor

Reidsville

WJMH
09-06-1948; 102.1 mhz FM *Hrs Open:* 24; 99 kw; 1204 ft.; N36 16 33 W79 56 26
10706 Beaver Dam Road, Cockeysville, MD 21030 US
(336) 605-5200, *Fax:* (336) 605-5219
www.102jamz.com
info@102jamz.com
License: Reidsville, Rockingham County, NC held by Entercom Greensboro License LLC.
Group Owner: Entercom Communications Corp.; (acq 12-13-99; grpsl)
Nat'l Reps: McGavren Guild
Arbitron Metro Market: Greensboro-Winston Salem-High Point, NC *Format:* Adult Contemp *Target Audience:* 16-35; 65% Black, 35% white
Brent Millar, General Manager
Erin Casey, General Sales Mgr
Brian Douglas, Programming Director
Valerie Dickens, News Director
Larry Allen, Chief Engineer

WREV
01-01-1948; 1220 khz AM; 1 kw-D, NDD; N36 23 19 W79 38 51
Rebroadcasts: Rebroadcasts WRTP(AM) Chapel Hill 100%
1720 E. Garry Ave., Suite #228, Santa Ana, CA 92705 US
(202) 638-1959, *Fax:* (202) 638-6127
estuardovaldemar@hotmail.com
License: Reidsville, NC held by Estuardo Valdemar Rodriguez and Leonor Rodriguez.
Group Owner: Radio La Grande; (acq 8-5-2004; $125,000).
Format: Tejano
Estuardo Valdemar Rodriguez, General Manager

Rennert

WGQR
12-01-1989; 105.7 mhz FM *Hrs Open:* 24; 7.7 kw; 583 ft.; N34 44 5 W78 47 25
Mailing Address: 1602 Greenwood Street, Elizabethtown, NC 28337 US
Second Address: Box 28, Elizabethtown, NC 28329
(910) 488-7729
www.wgqr1057.com
License: Rennert, Bladen County, NC
Arbitron Metro Market: Fayetteville, NC *Format:* Gospel *Hrs. of News Programming:* News progmg 6 hrs wkly
Paul Brian, Programming Director
Al Radlein, News Director
Dan Arnsan, Disc Jockey
Buddy Edwards, Disc Jockey
K.C Evers, Disc Jockey

Roanoke Rapids

WCBT
11-01-1940; 1230 khz AM *Hrs Open:* 24; 1 kw-U, ND1; N36 26 45 W77 39 51
P.O. Box 910, Roanoke Rapids, NC 27870 US
(919) 537-4184, *Fax:* (919) 535-2686
haskinsal@yahoo.com
License: Roanoke Rapids, NC held by First Media Radio LLC.
Group Owner: First Media Radio LLC; (acq 7-22-2003; grpsl)
Nat'l Network: ABC; ESPN Radio *Regional Network:* N.C. News Net.
Format: Sports
John Green, Operations Dir
Al Haskin, General Manager
Allen Garrett, Programming Director
Frank White, Chief Engineer

WPTM
01-01-1973; 102.3 mhz FM *Hrs Open:* 24; 6 kw; 317 ft.; N36 30 13 W77 44 20
Mailing Address: P.O. Box 910, Roanoke Rapids, NC 27870 US
Second Address: 3 E. 4th St., Weldon, NC 27890

(252) 536-3115, *Fax:* (252) 538-0378
www.wptm1023.com
amyhmoran@yahoo.com
License: Roanoke Rapids, Halifax County, NC held by First Media Radio LLC.
Group Owner: First Media Radio LLC; (acq 7-22-2003; grpsl)
Regional Network: Southern Farm *Wire Services:* UPI
Format: Country *Special Programming:* Farm15 hrs, relg 3 hrs wkly *Hrs. of News Programming:* news progmg 14 hrs wkly *No. News Employees:* 3 *Target Audience:* 25-54; females with spendable income, decision-makers
Al Haskins, General Manager

***WVRP**
01-01-2001; 91.1 mhz FM; 2 kw; Ant 69 ft; N36 28 08 W77 39 02
Rebroadcasts: Rebroadcasts WGPS(FM) Elizabeth City 100%
Winchester Stn., 905 Halstead Blvd., Elizabeth City, NC 27870
(252) 334-1883, *Fax:* (252) 333-1459
wpgt@csnradio.com
License: Roanoke Rapids, Halifax County, NC held by CSN International
Group Owner: CSN International; (acq 5-5-2000; $20,000 for CP).
Hrs. of News Programming: News progmg one hr wkly
Jeff Ozanne, General Manager
Darla Ozanne, Programming Director
Maria VanDeWalker, Music Director

Robbins

WLHC
06-02-2003; 103.1 mhz FM *Hrs Open:* 24; 6 kw; 328 ft.; N35 26 33 W79 26 37
Mailing Address: P O Box 1087, Angier, NC 27501 US
Second Address: Box 1963, Pinehurst, NC 28370
(919) 775-1031, *Fax:* (919) 775-1397
www.life1031.com
whlc@life1031.com
License: Robbins, Moore County, NC held by Woolstone Corporation
Nat'l Network: ABC *Regional Network:* N.C. News Net.
Arbitron Metro Market: Robbins, NC *Format:* Adult Contemp
Special Programming: Jazz 2 hrs, Christian 5 hrs, bluegrass 5 hrs wkly *No. News Employees:* 1 *Adv. Rates:* 30; 26; 29; 20
Alan Button, President
Steve Koranda, Station Manager
Mary Button, Marketing/Sales Staff
Patrick Neal, Marketing/Sales Staff
Charlie Peterson, Marketing/Sales Staff
Pete Saunders, Marketing/Sales Staff

Robbinsville

WCVP-FM
01-01-1987; 95.9 mhz FM *Hrs Open:* 5:30 AM-10 PM (M-F); 6 AM-10 PM (S); 0.12 kw; 2008 ft.; N35 15 28 W83 47 44
P.O. Box 280, Murphy, NC 28906 US
(828) 479-8080(828) 479-2296, *Fax:* (828) 479-2296
info@wcvp.com
License: Robbinsville, Graham County, NC held by Cherokee Broadcasting Co.
Arbitron Metro Market: Knoxville, TN *Format:* Country *Target Audience:* General.
Dennis Blakemore, President
Penny Wade, Operations Dir

Rockingham

WAYN
09-01-1946; 900 khz AM *Hrs Open:* 6 AM-10 PM; 1 kw-D, ND1; 0.297 kw-N, ND1; N34 55 30 W79 44 35
Mailing Address: P.O. Box 519, Rockingham, NC 28379 US
Second Address: 1223 Rockingham Rd., Rockingham, NC 28380
(406) 721-6800, *Fax:* (406) 329-1850
www.jackfmmissoula.com
rharsell@simmonsmedia.com
License: Rockingham, NC held by WAYN Inc.
Regional Network: N.C. News Net.
Arbitron Metro Market: Missoula MT *Format:* Adult Contemp
Target Audience: 25-54; adults
Rod Harsell, General Manager

WLWL
10-27-1969; 770 khz AM; 5 kw-D, NDD; N34 55 30 W79 47 11
Mailing Address: P.O. Box 1536, Rockingham, NC 28379 US
Second Address: 275 River Rd., Rockingham, NC 28379
(910) 997-2526, *Fax:* (910) 997-2527
bigwaveradio@gmail.com
License: Rockingham, NC held by Sandhills Broadcasting Co. Inc.
Regional Network: N.C. News Net.
Arbitron Metro Market: Rockingham, NC *Format:* Oldies *Target Audience:* 25-60.
Keith Davis, Operations Dir
Beth Ballard, General Manager

***WRSH**
05-01-1973; 91.1 mhz FM; 0.34 kw; 161 ft.; N34 56 59 W79 42 52
Mailing Address: P.O. Box 1259, Hamlet, NC 28345 US
Second Address: Richmond Sr. High School, 838 N. US Hwy. 1, Rockingham, NC 28379
(910) 997-9812, *Fax:* (910) 997-9816
License: Rockingham, Richmond County, NC held by Richmond County Board of Education.
Kim Newton, General Manager

Rocky Mount

WEED
09-10-1933; 1390 khz AM *Hrs Open:* 24
Mailing Address: P.O. Box 2666, Rocky Mounty, NC 27802 US
Second Address: 115 N. Church St., Rocky Mount, NC 27802
(252) 443-5976, *Fax:* (252) 443-5977
License: Rocky Mount, NC held by Northstar Broadcasting Corp.
Nat'l Network: Premiere Radio Networks
Arbitron Metro Market: Rocky Mount, NC *Format:* Religious *Hrs. of News Programming:* news progmg 14 hrs wkly *No. News Employees:* 10 *Target Audience:* Males; 18+
Sonya Johnson, Operations Dir
Charles Johnson II, General Manager
Charles Johnson, II, Programming Director
Ethan Arrington, Music Director

WRMT
12-15-1958; 1490 khz AM *Hrs Open:* 24; 1 kw-U, ND1; N35 55 57 W77 49 49
12714 East Nc 97, Rocky Mount, NC 27803 US
(252) 442-8092, *Fax:* (252) 977-6664
License: Rocky Mount, NC held by First Media Radio LLC
Group Owner: First Media Radio LLC; (acq 1-7-2003; grpsl)
Regional Network: N.C. News Net. *Nat'l Reps:* Interep
Arbitron Metro Market: Rocky Mount-Wilson, NC *Format:* Sports
Target Audience: 30 plus.
Alex Kolobielski, President
Mike Binkley, Promotions Manager

***WRQM**
04-01-1996; 90.9 mhz FM *Hrs Open:* 24; 7.5 kw; 627 ft.; N35 48 40 W77 44 33 *Rebroadcasts:* Rebroadcasts WUNC(FM) Chapel Hill 99.9%
434 Falls Road, Rocky Mount, NC 27803 US
(919) 966-5454, *Fax:* (919) 966-5955
www.wunc.org
wunc@unc.edu
License: Rocky Mount, Edgecombe County, NC held by The Board of Trustees of the University of NC at Chapel Hill
Nat'l Network: NPR; PRI; CBC Radio One
Format: News *Hrs. of News Programming:* news progmg 124 hrs wkly *No. News Employees:* 7 *Target Audience:* 35 plus; educated, successful, community active
Kevin Wolf, Operations Dir
Joan Rose, General Manager

WDWG
12-18-1989; 98.5 mhz FM; 16 kw; 410 ft.; N35 54 43 W77 50 6
12714 East Nc 97, Rocky Mount, NC 27803 US
(252) 442-8092, *Fax:* (252) 977-6664
www.bigdawg985.com
License: Rocky Mount, Nash County, NC
Group Owner: First Media Radio LLC
Nat'l Reps: Interep
Arbitron Metro Market: Rocky Mount-Wil *Format:* Country *Target Audience:* 18 plus.
Alex Kolobielski, President
David Perkins, Operations Dir
Mike Binkley, General Sales Mgr
Mike Binkley, Promotions Manager

Rose Hill

WEGG
01-01-1971; 710 khz AM *Hrs Open:* Sunrise-sunset
Mailing Address: 1223 West New Bern Rd, Kinston, NC 28504 US
Second Address: 3228 U.S. Hwy. 117, Rose Hill, NC 28458
(252) 341-8327, *Fax:* (252) 497-2486
info@wegg.com
License: Rose Hill, NC held by Conner Media Corp.
Group Owner: Conner Media Corp.
Regional Network: Southern Farm *Nat'l Reps:* Keystone (unwired net)
Arbitron Metro Market: Rose Hill, NC *Format:* Black, Gospel, 74
Special Programming: Farm 9 hrs, bluegrass gospel 10 hrs wkly
Suzanne Wilson, General Manager
Don Brown, Chief Engineer
C.D. Melvin, Religion Ed

Roxboro

WKRX
01-01-1958; 96.7 mhz FM *Hrs Open:* 5:30 AM-11 PM; 3 kw; 299 ft.; N36 22 4 W78 59 58
P. O. Box 1176, Roxboro, NC 27573 US
(336) 599-0266, *Fax:* (336) 599-9411
www.radioroxboro.com
radio@aol.com
License: Roxboro, Person County, NC held by Roxboro Broadcasting Co.
Nat'l Network: ABC *Regional Network:* N.C. News Net.
Hrs. of News Programming: news progmg 7 hrs wkly *No. News Employees:* 1 *Target Audience:* 18-49. *Adv. Rates:* Same as AM
David Bradsher, Promotions Manager
David Ramsey, Disc Jockey
Bill Lester, Disc Jockey
Don Carroll, Disc Jockey

WRXO
01-01-1949; 1430 khz AM *Hrs Open:* 6 AM-sunset; 1 kw-D, NDD; N36 22 4 W78 59 58 *Rebroadcasts:* Simulcast with WKRX(FM) Roxboro
P. O. Box 1176, Roxboro, NC 27573 US
(336) 599-0266, *Fax:* (336) 599-9411
www.radioroxboro.com
radiod@aol.com
License: Roxboro, NC held by Roxboro Broadcasting Co.
Nat'l Network: ABC *Regional Network:* N.C. News Net.
Arbitron Metro Market: Raleigh-Durham, *Format:* Country *Special Programming:* Black 4 hrs, farm 5 hrs, Southern gospel 5 hrs wkl
Hrs. of News Programming: news progmg 7 hrs wkly *No. News Employees:* 1 *TargetAudience:* 18-49. *Adv. Rates:* 9.40; 9.40; 9.40; 9.40
David Bradsher, President
Wayne Tuck, News Director
Conrad Kimbrough, Chief Engineer
Don Carroll, Disc Jockey
Bill Lester, Disc Jockey
David Ramsey, Disc Jockey

Rutherfordton

WCAB
10-19-1966; 590 khz AM *Hrs Open:* 24
P. O. Box 511, Rutherfordton, NC 28139 US
(828) 287-3356, *Fax:* (828) 287-7182
www.wcab59.com
wcabam59@bellsouth.net
License: Rutherfordton, NC held by Isothermal Broadcasting Corp.
Regional Network: N.C. News Net.
Arbitron Metro Market: Rutherfordton, NC *Format:* Country, News, 62, Sports, Talk *Hrs. of News Programming:* News progmg 25 hrs wkly *Target Audience:* 25 plus; adult consumers
Adv. Rates: 12.70; 11.70; 12.70;11.70
James Bishop, President
Van Austin, Programming Director
Lou Gilliam, News Director

Salisbury

WEND
03-16-1946; 106.5 mhz FM *Hrs Open:* 24; 84 kw; 1047 ft.; N35 35 32 W80 37 44
10828 Lockland Road, Potomac, MD 20854 US
(704) 376-1065, *Fax:* (704) 334-9525
www.1065.com
jackdaniel@1065.com
License: Salisbury, Rowan County, NC held by Capstar TX L.P.
Group Owner: Clear Channel Communications Inc.; (acq 3-12-01).
Nat'l Reps: McGavren Guild
Arbitron Metro Market: Salisbury, NC *Format:* Alternative *Target Audience:* 18-34.
Liz Luke, Operations Dir
Della Pizzati, General Sales Mgr
Jack Daniel, Programming Director
Shelia Taylor, Promotions Manager
Rob Caskey, Chief Engineer
Kristen Pettus, Disc Jockey
Chris Rozak, Disc Jockey
Jack Anthony, DiscJockey

***WOGR-FM**
11-01-1996; 93.3 mhz FM; 0.01 kw; 180 ft.; N35 40 3 W80 28 13
Rebroadcasts: Rebroadcasts WOGR(AM) Charlotte 100%
Box 16408, Charlotte, NC 28297 US
(704) 393-1540, *Fax:* (704) 393-1527
www.wordnet.org
info@wordnet.org
License: Salisbury, Rowan County, NC held by Victory Christian Center Inc.
TV Affiliate: Relg
Operations Manager, Operations Dir
Programming Manager, Programming Director

WSAT
06-01-1947; 1280 khz AM *Hrs Open:* 24; 1 kw-D, DAN; 1 kw-N, DAN; N35 40 30 W80 30 30
1525 Jake Alex. Blvd. W, Salisbury, NC 28144 US
(704) 633-0621, *Fax:* (704) 636-2955
www.1280wsat.com
buddy@WSAT1280.com
License: Salisbury, NC held by Cap Communications Inc.
Nat'l Network: Motor Racing Net
Arbitron Metro Market: Charlotte-Gasto *Format:* Oldies *Target Audience:* 25-64; people that can afford high ticket items
Charles Poole, President
Bubby Poole, Programming Director
Ted Fuller, Chief Engineer
Eddie Fuller, Disc Jockey
Buddy Poole, Disc Jockey
Lance Anderson, Disc Jockey

WSTP
01-01-1939; 1490 khz AM *Hrs Open:* 24; 1 kw-U, ND1; N35 41 18 W80 29 44
Mailing Address: 200 Radio Drive, Lexington, NC 27292 US
Second Address: 1105 Statesville Blvd., Salisbury, NC 28144
(704) 636-3811, *Fax:* (704) 637-1490
www.1490wstp.com
newsradio1490@yahoo.com
License: Salisbury, NC held by Rowan Media INC.
Nat'l Network: Fox News Radio; Talk Radio Network; Jones Radio Networks *Regional Network:* N.C. News Net. *Regional Reps:* Capital Radio
Arbitron Metro Market: Charlotte-Gastonia-Rock Hill, NC-SC *Format:* News, News/Talk, 86 *Hrs. of News Programming:* News progmg 24 hrs daily *Target Audience:* 25-59. *Adv. Rates:* 22; 15; 22; 12
Timothy Coates, President
Mike Mangan, Operations Dir
Nicole Brown, Programming Director
Mark Brown, News Director
Hal McGee, Chief Engineer

Sanford

***WDCC**
01-01-1971; 90.5 mhz FM *Hrs Open:* 24; 2 kw; 236 ft.; N35 28 22.7 W79 8 32
1105 Kelly Drive, Sanford, NC 27330 US
(919) 718-7257, *Fax:* (919) 718-7429
www.wdccfm.com
wdcc@cccc.edu
License: Sanford, Lee County, NC held by Central Carolina Community College.
Arbitron Metro Market: Sanford, NC *Format:* Alternative, Contemporary Hits/Top 40
Bill Freeman, General Manager

WFJA
01-01-1950; 105.5 mhz FM *Hrs Open:* 24; 2.3 kw; 486 ft.; N35 26 34 W79 18 41
P. O. Drawer R, Sanford, NC 27330 US
(919) 775-3525, *Fax:* (919) 775-4503
www.classichitsandoldies.com
info@wfja.com
License: Sanford, Lee County, NC held by WWGP Broadcasting Corp.
Format: Oldies *No. News Employees:* 1 *Target Audience:* 25-54. *Adv. Rates:* 19; 18; 19; 17
Richard Feindel, President & General Manager
Jessica Tarleton, Operations Dir
Cindy Johnson, General Sales Mgr
Tommy Franks, Programming Director
Margaret Murchison, News Director
Maria Danza, Disc Jockey
Steve Gunn, DiscJockey
Kevan Browning, Disc Jockey
Larry King, Disc Jockey
Johnny Miller, Disc Jockey

WWGP
01-01-1946; 1050 khz AM *Hrs Open:* 6 AM-1 AM
P.O. Drawer 3457, Sanford, NC 27330 US
(919) 775-3525, *Fax:* (919) 775-4503
www.wwgp1050.com
production@wfjaradio.com
License: Sanford, NC held by Richard K. Feindel.
Arbitron Metro Market: Sanford, NC *Format:* Country *Special Programming:* Farm 7 hrs wkly *Hrs. of News Programming:* news progmg 7 hrs wklyone *No. News Employees:* 1 *Target Audience:* 18-54. *Adv. Rates:* 18; 17; 18; 16
Richard Feindel, President
Jessica Tarleton, Operations Dir
Cindy Johnson, General Sales Mgr
Audrey R. Mason, Programming Director
Margaret Murchison, News Director
Jim Vest, Chief Engineer

WXKL
10-02-1952; 1290 khz AM *Hrs Open:* 6 AM-8 PM; 1 kw-D, ND1; 0.04 kw-N, ND1; N35 27 1 W79 9 30
P. O. Box 25488, Raleigh, NC 27611 US
(919) 774-1290, *Fax:* (919) 774-1118
License: Sanford, NC held by Thomas Broadcasting Inc.
Nat'l Network: NBC
Arbitron Metro Market: Sanford, NC *Format:* Christian, Gospel *Hrs. of News Programming:* News progmg 6 hrs wkly *Target Audience:* 25 plus; general
James Thomas, President
Amos Marks, Programming Director
Tommy Mack, Disc Jockey
Marilyn Cross, Disc Jockey
Danny Davis, Disc Jockey

Scotland Neck

WYAL
04-03-1960; 1280 khz AM; 5 kw-D, NDD; N36 8 9 W77 26 9
Highway 125, Weldon Road, Scotland Neck, NC 27874 US
(252) 826-3866
License: Scotland Neck, NC held by Sky City Communications Inc.
Regional Network: N.C. News Net.
Arbitron Metro Market: Scotland Neck, NC *Format:* Gospel, Religious *Special Programming:* Farm 2 hrs wkly
Richard Petway, President

Scotts Hill

***WZDG**
03-23-2007; 88.5 mhz FM; 8.9 kw vert; 545 ft.; N34 30 7 W78 4 58
Mailing Address: P O Box 957, Wilmington, NC 28401 US
Second Address: 201 North Front Street, Suite 805, Wilmington, NC 28401
(910) 202-0946, *Fax:* (910) 763-6578
www.edgeonover.com
matt@edgeonover.com
License: Scotts Hill, Pender County, NC held by Carolina Christian Radio Inc.
Group Owner: Carolina Christian Radio
Arbitron Metro Market: Wilmington, NC *Format:* Alternative, Christian
Jim Stephens, General Manager
Matt Wall, Programming Director

Selma

WTSB
08-04-1964; 1090 khz AM *Hrs Open:* Sunrise-sunset
Post Office Box 1, Selma, NC 27567 US
(919) 934-6789, *Fax:* (919)934-6824
www.wtsbradio.com
info@wtsbradio.com
License: Selma, NC held by Lamm Media Group LLC
Arbitron Metro Market: Smithfield, NC *Format:* Country
Mickey Lamm, General Manager

Semora

***WKVK**
03-01-1996; 106.7 mhz FM; 50 kw; 492 ft.; N36 25 7 W79 11 49
107 Northmont Blvd, Danville, VA 24541 US
(916) 251-1600, (843) 267-0036, *Fax:* (916) 251-1650, (843) 399-9031
www.klove.com
License: Semora, Caswell County, NC held by Educational Media Foundation.
Group Owner: EMF Broadcasting
Nat'l Network: K-Love
Format: Christian
Mike Novak, President
Len Bagwell, Operations Dir

Shallotte

WVCB
06-11-1964; 1410 khz AM; 0.5 kw-D, ND1; 0.168 kw-N, ND1; N33 58 20 W78 23 2
Mailing Address: Hwy. 17, Main St., Shallotte, NC 28459 US
Second Address: 4640 Main St., Shallotte, NC 28459
(910) 754-4512, *Fax:* (910) 754-3461
wvcb@atmc.net
License: Shallotte, NC held by John G. Worrell.
Regional Network: N.C. News Net.
Arbitron Metro Market: Shallotte, NC *Format:* Gospel, Religious *Target Audience:* General.
Rhonda Worrell, Station Manager

Sharpsburg

WLQC
103.1 mhz FM; 6 kw; Ant 295 ft; N35 57 01 W77 57 26
2619 Western Ave., Raleigh, NC
(919) 821-8933, *Fax:* (919) 890-6095
License: Sharpsburg, Nash County, NC held by Capitol Broadcasting Co. Inc.
Group Owner: Capitol Broadcasting Co. Inc.; (acq 10-1-2008; $825,000 for CP)
Arbitron Metro Market: Rocky Mount-Wilson, NC
James Goodmon, President

Shelby

WOHS
07-09-1958; 1390 khz AM *Hrs Open:* 24; 1 kw-D, 500 w-N, DA-N; N35 19 28 W81 32 00
Mailing Address: 1366 Startown Rd, Lincolnton, NC 29340
Second Address: Box 2266, Shelby, NC 28151-2266
(704) 482-1390, *Fax:* (704) 481-9007
www.us1390.com
info@hrnb.com
License: Shelby, Cleveland County, NC held by HRN Broadcasting Inc.
Group Owner: HRN Broadcasting Inc.; (acq 2006; $350,000).
Nat'l Network: ABC
Population Served: 250,000*Target Audience:* 25-54; middle and older
D. Mark Boyd III, President
Joe Martin, Station Manager
Andy Johnson, General Sales Mgr

WHQC
01-01-1948; 96.1 mhz FM *Hrs Open:* 24; 100 kw; 1,738 ft; N35 21 44 W81 09 19
801 Woodbridge Center Dr., Charlotte, NC 20854
(704) 338-9600, *Fax:* (704) 334-9525
www.magic96.com
License: Shelby, Cleveland County, NC held by Clear Channel Broadcasting Licenses Inc.
Group Owner: Clear Channel Communications Inc.; (acq 10-18-2000).
Nat'l Reps: McGavren Guild
Population Served: 2,000,000 *Arbitron Metro Market:* Charlotte-Gastonia-Rock Hill, NC-SC *Hrs. of News Programming:* news progmg 4 hrs wkly *No. News Employees:* 1 *Target Audience:* 25-54.
Morgan Bohannon, General Manager
Graves Upchurch, General Sales Mgr
Nick Allen, Programming Director
Linda Silver, News Director
Ben Brinitzer, Chief Engineer
Bobby Lane, Disc Jockey
Ron Harper, Disc Jockey
Harriet Coffey, DiscJockey
Brenda Grubb, Traffic Manager

Siler City

WNCA
08-19-1952; 1570 khz AM *Hrs Open:* 6am - midnight
P. O. Box 429, Siler City, NC 27344 US
(919) 742-2135, *Fax:* (919) 663-2843
License: Siler City, NC held by Chatham Broadcasting Co. Inc. of Siler City.
Regional Network: N.C. News Net.
Arbitron Metro Market: Siler City, NC *Format:* Christian, News, 62, Talk *Special Programming:* Gospel 5 hrs, relg 12 hrs, loc sports 6 hrs & Span *Hrs. of News Programming:* news progmg 15+ hrs wkly *No. NewsEmployees:* 2 *Target Audience:* 25-55; rural, agri-oriented, blue-collar, growing spanish community *Adv. Rates:* 12; 10; 10; 8

Barry Hayes, President
Renee Kennedy, Station Manager
Dacia Hayes, General Sales Mgr
Jose Alvarado, Spanish Director
Debbie Applewhite, Traffic Manager

Smithfield

WWPL

02-02-1972; 102.3 mhz FM *Hrs Open:* 24; 2.6 kw; Ant 561 ft; N35 23 54 W78 00 38 *Rebroadcasts:* Simulcast with WWMY(FM) Raleigh 100%
3012 Highwoods Blvd., Suite 201, Raleigh, NC 27604
(919) 790-9392, *Fax:* (919) 790-8369
www.y1029.com
bcampbell@curtismedia.com
License: Smithfield, Johnston County, NC held by New Age Communications Inc.
Group Owner: Curtis Media Group; (acq 7-1-96; $550,000)
Population Served: 120,000*No. News Employees:* 4
Don Curtis, President
Mike Hartel, General Manager

WMPM

01-01-1950; 1270 khz AM; 5 kw-D, ND2; 0.145 kw-N, ND2; N35 31 33 W78 20 1
P. O. Box 240, Smithfield, NC 27577 US
(919) 934-2434, *Fax:* (919) 989-6388
www.1270wmpm.com
lynda@1270wmpm.com
License: Smithfield, NC held by Family Media Group LLC
Nat'l Network: CBS
Arbitron Metro Market: Raleigh, NC *Format:* Christian *Special Programming:* Farm 2 hrs, relg 8 hrs, news/talk 12 hrs wkly
Target Audience: 30 plus; general
Ellis Barbour Jr., President
Lynda Lamm Carroll, General Manager

Snow Hill

*WAGO

07-01-1998; 88.7 mhz FM *Hrs Open:* 24; 17 kw; 292 ft.; N35 26 49 W77 39 20
P. O. Box 1895, Goldsboro, NC 27533 US
(252) 747-8887, *Fax:* (252) 747-7888
www.gomixradio.org
wago@gomixradio.org
License: Snow Hill, Greene County, NC held by Pathway Christian Academy Inc.
Nat'l Network: Moody; Salem Radio Network
Arbitron Metro Market: Greenville NC *Format:* Christian *Hrs. of News Programming:* news progmg 14 hrs wkly *No. News Employees:* 1 *Target Audience:* General.
T.D. Worthington, President
Keith Aycock, Programming Director
Ashley Worthington, Promotions Manager
Joe Patton, Chief Engineer
Tim Sutton, Music Director

South Gastonia

*WGAS

08-14-1959; 1420 khz AM *Rebroadcasts:* Rebroadcasts WOGR(AM) Charlotte
P.O. 16408, Charlotte, NC 28297 US
(704) 393-1540, *Fax:* (704) 393-1527
www.wordnet.org
info@wordnet.org
License: South Gastonia, NC held by Victory Christian Center Inc.
Arbitron Metro Market: Charlotte-Gastonia-Rock Hill, NC-SC *TV Affiliate:* WGTB- TV *Format:* Gospel *Target Audience:* General.
Robyn Gool, President
Terry Hammond, General Manager

Southern Pines

WEEB

11-15-1947; 990 khz AM *Hrs Open:* 24; 5 kw-C, ND1; 10 kw-D, ND1; ND1; 0.026 kw; N35 11 37 W79 24 42
Box 1855, Midland Rd., Southern Pines, NC 28388 US
(910) 692-7440, *Fax:* (888) 390-5186
www.weeb990.com
steve@weeb990.com
License: Southern Pines, NC held by Pinehurst Broadcasting Corp.
Nat'l Network: ABC; Fox News Radio; Salem Radio Network
Regional Network: N.C. News Net.
Arbitron Metro Market: Southern Pines, NC *Format:* News, News/Talk, 86 *Special Programming:* High school & college sports, gospel 6 hrs wkly *Hrs. of News Programming:* news progmg 26 hrs wkly *No. News Employees:* 3 *Target Audience:* 25 plus; business professionals, CEOs, retirees *Adv. Rates:* $12,00 per spot
Steve Adams, CFO
Charles Bennett, General Sales Mgr
Steve Leader, Programming Director
Al Mangum, News Director
Rich McCarthy, Operations Manager
Rose Sharp, Religion Ed

WIOZ-FM

01-01-1995; 102.5 mhz FM; 3.4 kw; 436 ft.; N35 9 4 W79 28 40
P.O. Box 1677, Southern Pines, NC 28388 US
(910) 692-2107, *Fax:* (910) 692-6849
www.star1025fm.com
License: Southern Pines, Moore County, NC held by Meridian Communications L.L.C.
Group Owner: Muirfield Broadcasting Inc.; (acq 6-17-97; $316,500)
Format: Adult Contemp
Walker Morris, President
Rich Rushforth, Operations Dir
Tiffany Hewitt, General Manager

WMGU

08-14-1973; 106.9 mhz FM *Hrs Open:* 24; 50 kw; 469 ft.; N34 59 53 W79 15 47
P.O. Box 1677, Southern Pines, NC 28387 US
(910) 864-5222, *Fax:* (910) 864-3065
www.magic1069.com
License: Southern Pines, Moore County, NC held by Cumulus Licensing Corp.
Group Owner: Cumulus Media Inc.; (acq 3-12-2001; $6.15 million)
Arbitron Metro Market: Fayetteville, NC *Format:* Urban Contemporary *Hrs. of News Programming:* news progmg 18 hrs wkly *No. News Employees:* 2 *Target Audience:* 35 plus.
Alan Buffaloe, General Manager
Jim Cook, Programming Director

Southern Shores

WFMI

01-01-2003; 100.9 mhz FM; 39 kw; 486 ft.; N36 12 10 W75 52 23
P.O. Box 539, McLean, VA 22101 US
(757) 774-7148, *Fax:* (757) 490-2524
www.rejoice1009.com
rejoice@rejoice100point9.com
License: Southern Shores, Dare County, NC held by Communications Systems Inc.
Arbitron Metro Market: Virginia Beach, VA *Format:* Gospel, Talk
Mike Chandler, General Manager
Karol Scott, Station Manager

Southport

WAZO

04-15-1978; 107.5 mhz FM *Hrs Open:* 24; 75 kw; 449 ft.; N34 3 2 W77 57 20
224 West Canebrake Blvd., Hattiesburg, MS 39402 US
(910) 791-3088, *Fax:* (910) 791-0112
www.z1075.com
mark@z1075.com
License: Southport, Brunswick County, NC held by Sunrise Broadcasting LLC.
Group Owner: Capitol Broadcasting Co. Inc.; (acq 11-18-2008; grpsl)
Nat'l Reps: McGavren Guild
Arbitron Metro Market: Wilmington, NC *Format:* Contemporary Hits/Top 40 *Hrs. of News Programming:* news progmg one hr wkly *No. News Employees:* 1 *Target Audience:* 18-49; young, upwardly mobile professionals
Barry Brown, Operations Dir
Bea Raybourne, General Manager
Gayle Brown, General Sales Mgr
Mark Jacobs, Programming Director
Doug Carlisle, News Director
Walt Howard, Chief Engineer

Sparta

WCOK

04-01-1967; 1060 khz AM
P. O. Box 637, Sparta, NC 28675 US
(336) 372-5700, *Fax:* (336) 372-5863
www.wyzdradio.org
wcoksparta@yahoo.com
License: Sparta, NC held by Mountain Empire Broadcasting Inc.
Arbitron Metro Market: Piedmont Triad, NC *Format:* Religious, Country *Target Audience:* General.
Bro. Ricky Cothren, President
Jos Reynoso, General Manager
Bro. Jake Easter, Programming Director
Johnathan Johnson, Disc Jockey
Michael Sexton, Disc Jockey

Spindale

WGMA

10-01-1982; 1520 khz AM *Hrs Open:* Sunrise-sunset; 500 w-D; N35 21 00 W81 56 18
Box 805, 301 W. Main St., Spindale, NC 28160
(828) 287-5151, *Fax:* 1-828-287-0081
WGMA1520AM@BellSouth.Net
License: Spindale, Rutherford County, NC held by Blue Mountain Broadcasting LLC
Population Served: 35,000*Hrs. of News Programming:* news progmg 20 hrs wkly *No. News Employees:* 1 *Target Audience:* 30-50; adults *Adv. Rates:* 3.90; 3.90; 3.90; 3.90
Barbara Martin, President
Andy Foster, Operations Dir
Kaye Cantrell, General Manager
Neil Murray, Programming Director
Jerrell Bedford, Engineering Dir

*WNCW

10-13-1989; 88.7 mhz FM *Hrs Open:* 24; 17 kw horiz, 9.6 kw vert; 3028 ft.; N35 44 6 W82 17 11
Post Office Box 804, Spindale, NC 28160 US
(828) 287-8000, *Fax:* (828) 287-8012
www.wncw.org
info@wncw.org
License: Spindale, Rutherford County, NC held by Isothermal Community College.
Nat'l Network: PRI; NPR
Arbitron Metro Market: Spindale, NC *Format:* News, Triple A *Special Programming:* Blues 4 hrs, jazz 5 hrs, folk 12 hrs, drama 3 hrs, *Hrs. of News Programming:* news progmg 31 hrs wkly *No. News Employees:* 1*Target Audience:* 35-49; anyone interested in diverse info & culture
Dave Kester, Operations Dir
David Gordon, General Manager
Kate Barkschat, General Sales Mgr
Elle Ellis, Programming Director
Ele Ellis, News Director
Dennis Jones, Chief Engineer
Martin Anderson, Music Director

Spring Lake

WFBX

05-22-1963; 1450 khz AM *Hrs Open:* 24*Rebroadcasts:* Simulcast with WFAY(AM) Fayetteville 100%
777 Carpenters Way, Lakeland, FL 33809 US
(910) 867-4129, *Fax:* (910) 223-1451
www.espnfay.com/
wfayespnradio@gmail.com
License: Spring Lake, NC held by WCIE-AM Inc.
Nat'l Network: ESPN Radio
Arbitron Metro Market: Fayetteville, NC *Format:* Sports
JoAnn Germers Hausen, Operations Dir
Kevin Fennessy, General Manager

*WZRI

01-01-2005; 89.3 mhz FM *Hrs Open:* 24; 2 kw vert; 179 ft.; N35 10 14 W78 57 44
2630 Mirror Lake Drive, Fayetteville, NC 28303 US
(888) 937-2471, *Fax:* (916) 251-1650
www.air1.com
info@air1.com
License: Spring Lake, Cumberland County, NC held by Educational Media Foundation.
Group Owner: EMF Broadcasting; (acq 11-12-2002).
Nat'l Network: Air 1
Arbitron Metro Market: Spring Lake, NC *Format:* Alternative, Christian *No. News Employees:* 3 *Target Audience:* 18-35; Judeo-Christian, female
Darrell Chambliss, Chairman
Alan Mason, COO
Mike Novak, President and CEO
Len Bagwell, Operations Dir
Paul Goldsmith, Programming Director
Ed Lenane, News Director
Sam Wallington, Engineering Dir
Richard Hunt, News Reporter
Marya Morgan, News Reporter
Dan Antonelli, Chief Business Development Officer
Eric Moser, Chief Financial Officer
Brian Burger, Vice President of Human Resources
D. Kevin Blair, Secretary and General Counsel

Spruce Pine

WTOE
12-24-1955; 1470 khz AM *Hrs Open:* 24; 5 kw-D, ND1; 0.103 kw-N, ND1; N35 54 24 W82 6 21
Mailing Address: P.O. Box 607, 401 Sawmill Road, Burnsville, NC 28714 US
Second Address: 749 Sawmill Road, Burnsville, NC 28714
(828) 765-7441, *Fax:* (828) 682-6227
www.wtoe.com
1470@wtoe.com
License: Spruce Pine, NC held by Mountain Valley Media Inc.
Group Owner: Mark Media Group; (acq 9-27-91)
Nat'l Network: ABC *Regional Network:* N.C. News Net.
Arbitron Metro Market: Burnsville, NC *Format:* Oldies *Special Programming:* Relg 8 hrs wkly *Hrs. of News Programming:* news progmg 10 hrs wkly *No. News Employees:* 1 *Target Audience:* 25 plus. *Adv.Rates:* 18; 16; 18; 10
Remelle Sink, CEO
Michael Sink, President and General Manager
Laura Phillips, Programming Director
Remelle Sink, Chief Financial and Administrative Officer
Bruce Ikard, Community Affairs Director
Mary Marsh, Promotions Director
Dennis Renfro, Gospel Music Director
Mary Allen Marsh, Senior Account Representative

St. Pauls

WUKS
10-16-1994; 107.7 mhz FM; 5.2 kw; 656 ft.; N34 52 17 W79 8 49
3033 Riviera Drive, #200, Naples, FL 33940 US
(910) 486-4114, *Fax:* (910) 486-2124
www.kiss1077.com
info@kiss1077.com
License: St. Pauls, Robeson County, NC held by WDAS License L.P.
Group Owner: Beasley Broadcast Group Inc.; (acq 6-12-97; $1.2 million with WTEL(AM) Red Springs).
Nat'l Network: ABC *Nat'l Reps:* D & R Radio
Arbitron Metro Market: Fayetteville, NC *Format:* Adult Contemp *Target Audience:* 25-54.
George Beasley, Chairman
Caroline Beasley, CFO
Bruce Beasley, President
Tila Comstock, General Sales Mgr
Jeff Anderson, Programming Director
Mac Edwards, Promotions Manager
Brian Beasley, Executive Vice President
Bryan Kusilka,National Sales Manager
Taylor Morgan, Promotions Director

Statesville

WAME
10-07-1957; 550 khz AM *Hrs Open:* 24
PO Box 18614, Charlotte, NC 28218 US
(704) 872-0550, *Fax:* (704) 872-5547
www.wame550.com
john@wame550.com
License: Statesville, NC held by Statesville Family Radio Corp.
Group Owner: GHB Radio Group; (acq 4-22-86; $210,000;
Arbitron Metro Market: Charlotte-Gastonia-Rock Hill, NC-SC
Format: Country *Target Audience:* Adults 25- 54, Adults 35+
John Cornett, Operations Dir
Susan Childress, General Manager
Susie Miller, Station Manager
Gary Hattaway, Engineering Dir
Tammy Stephens, Traffic Manager
Leon Ijames, Sports
Jeff Davis, Announcer
Billy Blevins, DiscJockey
Kathy Cobbs, Marketing Consultant
Robin Adams, Marketing Consultant

WKKT
03-16-1961; 96.9 mhz FM *Hrs Open:* 24; 100 kw; 1549 ft.; N35 31 57 W80 47 47
200 E. Basse Road, Austin, TX 78701 US
(704) 714-9444, *Fax:* (704) 332-8805
www.wkktfm.com
info@wkktfm.com
License: Statesville, Iredell County, NC held by Capstar TX L.P.
Group Owner: Clear Channel Communications Inc.; (acq 8-30-00; grpsl).
Arbitron Metro Market: Charlotte-Gastonia-Rock Hill, NC-SC
Format: Country *Target Audience:* 25-54; middle to upper income adults
Bruce Logan, Operations Dir
Morgan Bohannon, General Manager
Robin Colfax, General Sales Mgr
John Roberts, Programming Director
Valerie Gladden, Promotions Manager
Linda Silver, News Director
Ben Brinitzer, Chief Engineer

WSIC
05-03-1947; 1400 khz AM *Hrs Open:* 24; 1 kw-D, ND2; 1 kw-N, ND2; N35 48 9 W80 53 30
600 Congress Avenue, Suite 1400, Austin, TX 78701 US
(704) 872-6345, *Fax:* (704) 873-6921
www.wsicweb.com
License: Statesville, NC held by Iredell Broadcasting Inc.
Nat'l Reps: Rgnl Reps *Regional Reps:* T-N.
Format: News, Sports *Hrs. of News Programming:* news progmg 21 hrs wkly *No. News Employees:* 1 *Target Audience:* 35 plus; upscale
Billy Blevins, Operations Dir
Mark Sanger, General Manager

Swansboro

*WKGV
09-12-1993; 104.1 mhz FM *Hrs Open:* 24; 5.4 kw; 345 ft.; N34 43 26 W77 14 57 *Rebroadcasts:* Rebroadcasts KLVR(FM) Middletown, CA 100%
4309 West Ocean Avenue, Emerald Isle, NC 28554 US
(800) 525-5683, *Fax:* (916) 251-1650
www.klove.com
klove@klove.com
License: Swansboro, Onslow County, NC held by Educational Media Foundation.
Group Owner: EMF Broadcasting; (acq 11-29-2007)
Nat'l Network: K-Love
Arbitron Metro Market: Omaha, NE *Format:* Christian *No. News Employees:* 13
Darrell Chambliss, Chairman
MIke Novak, President & CEO
Laura Daniels, News Reporter
Tim Luttrell, News Reporter
Kenny Noble Cortes, News Reporter
Darren Vinson, News Reporter

Sylva

WRGC
11-08-1957; 540 khz AM *Hrs Open:* 24; 5 kw-D, 140 w-N; N35 23 35 W83 11 38
Box 1044, 1846 Skyland Dr., Sylva, NC 28779
(828) 586-2221, *Fax:* (828) 586-6834
www.wrgc.com
jduke@gacaradio.com
License: Sylva, Jackson County, NC held by Georgia-Carolina Radiocasting Co. LLC.
Group Owner: Georgia-Carolina Radiocasting Companies; (acq 1-17-2002; $450,000).
Nat'l Network: ABC *Regional Network:* N.C. News Net.
Population Served: 86,663*Special Programming:* NASCAR, Local Sports *Hrs. of News Programming:* news progmg 14 hrs wkly *No. News Employees:* 1 *Target Audience:* General.
Douglas M. Sutton Jr., President
Terry Carter, Operations Dir
Jeremy, General Manager
Marty Lee, Chief Engineer
Tammie Pressley, Office Manager
Eric Moore, Operations Manager
Jeremy Duke, Vice President

Tabor City

WTAB
07-01-1954; 1370 khz AM *Hrs Open:* 6 AM-midnight; 5 kw-D, ND1; 0.109 kw-N, ND1; N34 9 0 W78 51 40
Mailing Address: Avon and 701 Bypass, Tabor City, NC 28463 US
Second Address: 210 Avon St., Tabor City, NC 28463
(910) 653-2131, *Fax:* (910) 653-5146
www.wtabradio.com
wtab@wtabradio.com
License: Tabor City, NC held by WTAB Inc.
Regional Network: N.C. News Net.
Arbitron Metro Market: Myrtle Beach, SC *Format:* Country, Gospel *Special Programming:* Swap shop, 12hrs wkly *Hrs. of News Programming:* News progmg 7 hrs wkly *Target Audience:* General. *Adv. Rates:* 12
Jack Miller, President
Bobby Pait, Programming Director
Bob Gause, Engineering Dir
Bonnie Miller, Executive Vice President

Tarboro

WCPS
01-01-1947; 760 khz AM *Hrs Open:* Sunrise-sunset; 1 kw-D; N35 55 40 W77 34 15
Mailing Address: Box 1202, Tarboro, NC 27604
Second Address: 1406 St Andrew St., Tarboro, NC 27886
(252) 824-7878, *Fax:* (252) 824-7818
ww.wcpsam760.com
jjwcpsam@embarqmail.com
License: Tarboro, Edgecombe County, NC held by Johnson Broadcast Ventures Ltd.
Regional Network: N.C. News Net.
Population Served: 13,000 *Arbitron Metro Market:* Rocky Mount-Wilson, NC *Target Audience:* General. *Adv. Rates:* 20 ROS
Jimmy Johnson, President
Stephanie Randolph, Station Manager

Taylorsville

WACB
05-02-1964; 860 khz AM *Hrs Open:* 24; 1 kw-D; N35 55 57 W81 10 19
133 E. Main Ave., Taylorsville, NC 28681
(828) 632-4621, *Fax:* (828) 632-9081
License: Taylorsville, Alexander County, NC held by Apple City Broadcasting Co. Inc.
Regional Network: N.C. News Net.
Population Served: 500,000*Special Programming:* Gospel 12 hrs wkly *Hrs. of News Programming:* news progmg 4 hrs wkly *No. News Employees:* 2 *Target Audience:* General.
Roger Brown, CEO
Norris Keever, President
Mary Brown, Operations Dir
Joyce Brown, General Sales Mgr
Lonnie Carrigan, Programming Director
Lisa McLain, Promotions Manager
Pete Ray, Assistant Music Director

WTLK
06-17-1962; 1570 khz AM
239 E. Main St., Taylorsville, NC 28681 US
(828) 632-4621, *Fax:* (828) 632-9081
License: Taylorsville, NC held by Apple City Broadcasting Co. Inc.
Regional Network: N.C. News Net.
Arbitron Metro Market: Taylorsville, NC *Format:* Gospel
Roger Brown, CEO
Norris Keever, President
Joyce Brown, General Sales Mgr
Lisa McLain, Promotions Manager
Jeff Watts, Chief Engineer
Mary Alice Brown, Executive Vice President

Thomasville

WBLO
09-01-1947; 790 khz AM *Hrs Open:* 24 hrs
Mailing Address: 645 Church Street, Suite 400, Norfolk, VA 23510 US
Second Address: 1607 Country Club Dr., High Point, NC 27262
(336) 887-0983, *Fax:* (336) 887-3055
License: Thomasville, NC held by GHB Radio Inc.
Group Owner: GHB Radio Group; (acq 4-3-2001; $350,000).
Nat'l Network: Fox Sports
Arbitron Metro Market: Charlotte, NC *Format:* Sports, Talk *Target Audience:* Men 25-54
Edgar Saucedo, General Manager
Sergio Garcia, Programming Director
Don West, Regional Sales
Koji Kryzwosz, Local Sales

Topsail Beach

WNTB
11-27-2000; 93.7 mhz FM *Hrs Open:* 24; 6 kw; 328 ft.; N34 18 4 W77 48 7
P.O. Box 3071, Bald Head Island, NC 28461 US
(910) 332-6390, *Fax:* (910) 772-6310
www.thebigtalkerfm.com
aimee.b@hometownwilmington.com
License: Topsail Beach, New Hanover County, NC held by Sea-Comm Inc.
Group Owner: Sea-Comm Inc.; (acq 6-30-2000; $1.2 million for CP)
Arbitron Metro Market: Wilmington, NC *Format:* Classic Rock
Paul Knight, General Manager
Max Deutsch, General Sales Mgr
Zach McHugh, Programming Director
Jonathan Knight, News Director

Troy

WJRM
12-08-1961; 1390 khz AM *Hrs Open:* 5 AM-9 PM
Box 550, Albenare, NC 28002 US
(910) 576-1390, *Fax:* (910) 576-1393
www.wjrm.com
jeffrey@wjrm.com
License: Troy, NC held by Family Worship Ministries Inc.
Format: Christian, Gospel *No. News Employees:* 1
Harold Pope, President
Jeffrey Pope, Operations Dir

Tryon

WJFJ
10-01-1954; 1160 khz AM *Hrs Open:* 24; 10 kw-D, DAN; 0.5 kw-N, DAN; N35 14 7 W82 14 27
1950 Old Hendersonville, Hwy, Pisgah Forest, NC 28768 US
(828) 894-5858, *Fax:* (828) 894-2957
www.wjfjradio.com
wjfjradio@wjfjradio.com
License: Tryon, NC held by Columbus Broadcast Corp. Inc.
Nat'l Network: USA
Format: Christian *Hrs. of News Programming:* news progmg 25 hrs wkly *No. News Employees:* 1 *Target Audience:* 25 plus; middle-to-upper income *Adv. Rates:* 9.50; 9.50; 9.50; 9.50
John Owens, General Manager

Valdese

WSVM
10-06-1961; 1490 khz AM *Hrs Open:* 24; 1 kw-U, ND1; N35 44 3 W81 34 4
P. O. Box 99, Valdese, NC 28690 US
(828) 874-0000, *Fax:* (828) 874-2123
www.1490wsvm.com
manager@1490wsvm.com
License: Valdese, NC held by GHB of Waxhaw Inc.
Group Owner: GHB Radio Group; (acq 10-28-2002; $450,000 with WEGO(AM) Concord).
Format: Talk *No. News Employees:* 4 *Target Audience:* 25+
Jerry Clegg, General Manager

Wadesboro

WADE
07-23-1947; 1340 khz AM *Hrs Open:* 24; 1 kw-U, ND1; N34 57 9 W80 3 0
P.O. Box 416, Waxhaw, NC 28173 US
License: Wadesboro, NC held by Inspirational Deliverance Center Inc.

*WYFQ-FM
01-01-1994; 93.5 mhz FM *Hrs Open:* 24; 8.7 kw; 554 ft.; N35 2 57 W80 18 38
8030 Arrowridge Blvd., Charlotte, NC 28273 US
(704) 523-5555, *Fax:* (704) 522-1967
www.bbnradio.org
bbn@bbnradio.org
License: Wadesboro, Anson County, NC held by Bible Broadcasting Network Inc.
Group Owner: Bible Broadcasting Network; acq 1996; $2,425,000)
Arbitron Metro Market: Wadesboro, NC *Format:* Religious *Target Audience:* 18-55.
Lowell Davey, CEO
Richard Johnson, Operations Dir
Hank Crull, Station Manager

Wake Forest

WRVA-FM
11-01-1947; 100.7 mhz FM; 100 kw; 1969 ft.; N35 49 53 W78 8 50
600 Congress Ave.,S1400, Austin, TX 78701 US
(919) 878-1500, *Fax:* (919) 876-8578
www.1007theriver.com
info@1007theriver.com
License: Wake Forest, Edgecombe County, NC held by Capstar TX L.P.
Group Owner: Clear Channel Communications Inc.; (acq 8-30-2000; grpsl).
Nat'l Network: ABC
Arbitron Metro Market: Raleigh, NC *Format:* Classic Rock *Target Audience:* 25-54; upscale adults
Jon Robbins, Operations Dir
Ken Spitzer, General Manager
Tammy O'Dell, General Sales Mgr
Jessica Hayes, Promotions Manager
Tracy Leonard, News Director
Fred Pace, Chief Engineer
Myron Bethea, General Sales Manager

Wallace

WZKB
07-20-1972; 94.3 mhz FM; 6 kw; 328 ft.; N34 45 30 W77 59 52
P.O. Box 520, Wallace, NC 28466 US
910-864-5028, *Fax:* 910-864-6270
www.wgqr.com
dan@wgqe1057.com
License: Wallace, Duplin County, NC held by Christian Listening Network Inc.
Group Owner: Christian Listening Network Inc.; (acq 12-15-2003; $425,000).
Nat'l Network: Salem Radio Network *Nat'l Reps:* Salem
Arbitron Metro Market: Wallace, NC *Format:* Gospel *Hrs. of News Programming:* News progmg 11 hrs wkly *Target Audience:* 35-54; women *Adv. Rates:* 15; 15; 15; 15
George Wilson, President
Dan DeBruler, General Manager
Steve Turley, Programming Director

Walnut Creek

WEQR
09-15-1976; 97.7 mhz FM *Hrs Open:* 24; 2.65 kw; 501 ft.; N35 17 28 W77 49 25
P.O. Box 1019, Morehead City, NC 28557 US
(919) 736-1150, *Fax:* (919) 736-3876
www.q977fm.com
bjohnston@curtismedia.com
License: Walnut Creek, Wayne County, NC held by New Age Communications Inc.
Group Owner: Curtis Media Group; (acq 8-30-2004; $875,000)
Wire Services: AP
Arbitron Metro Market: Walnut Creek, NC *Format:* Adult Contemp
Hrs. of News Programming: 3 hrs/week *No. News Employees:* 1
Donald Curtis, President
Bill Johnston, General Manager
Jeff Farrow, Programming Director
Robyn Wade, News Director

Wanchese

WOBX
05-29-1970; 1530 khz AM; 1 kw-D, DAD; N35 51 52 W75 39 1
Mailing Address: 1331 Paradise Road, Edenton, NC 17932 US
Second Address: 3855 Mill Landing Rd., Hwy. 345, Wanchese, NC 27981
(252) 473-5402, *Fax:* (252) 473-5838
License: Wanchese, NC held by East Carolina Radio Inc.
Group Owner: East Carolina Radio Group; (acq 8-82; $110,000;
TV Affiliate: Relg *No. News Employees:* Christian.

WOBR-FM
06-01-1973; 95.3 mhz FM; 25 kw; 295 ft.; N35 51 52 W75 39 1
1331 Paradise Rd, Edemtpm, NC 27932 US
(252) 441-1024, *Fax:* (252) 441-2109
jsweet@ecri.net
License: Wanchese, Dare County, NC held by East Carolina Radio Inc.
Group Owner: East Carolina Radio Group
Nat'l Network: ABC
TV Affiliate: Rock *Hrs. of News Programming:* 1 *No. News Employees:* 25-54; upscale, affluent

Warrenton

WARR
01-01-1970; 1520 khz AM *Hrs Open:* sun up-sun down; 1 kw-C, NDD; 5 kw-D, NDD; N36 24 18 W78 8 9
PO Box 611, Warrenton, NC 27589 US
(252) 257-5557/257-9277
www.warr-1520am.com
License: Warrenton, NC held by Quad Divisions Inc. dba Darensburg Broadcasting
Regional Network: N.C. News Net.
Arbitron Metro Market: Warrenton, NC *Format:* Black, Gospel
Hrs. of News Programming: News progmg 5 hrs wkly *Target Audience:* 25-56.
Logan Darensburg, President
Ann Alston, Station Manager

Washington

WLGT
12-01-1988; 98.3 mhz FM *Hrs Open:* 24; 1.35 kw; 489 ft.; N35 29 14 W77 2 42
P.O. Box 874, Greenville, NC 27834 US
(252) 446-9262, *Fax:* (252) 446-9261
www.wlgtfm.com
contact@wlgtfm.com
License: Washington, Beaufort County, NC held by Media East LLC
Arbitron Metro Market: Greenville-New Bern-Jacksonville, NC
Format: Gospel *Target Audience:* 25-54; upscale, affluent audience
Wesley Hines, General Manager

WDLX
03-03-1942; 930 khz AM
Mailing Address: 1705 W. Northwest Hwy, Ste 275, Grapevine, TX 76051 US
Second Address: 525 S. Evans St., Greenville, NC 27858
(252) 317-1250, *Fax:* (252) 317-1255
www.pirateradio930.com
troy@pirateradio1250.com
License: Washington, NC held by Pirate Media Group LLC
Regional Network: N.C. News Net.
Arbitron Metro Market: Greenville-New Bern-Jacksonville, NC
Format: Talk *Target Audience:* 35 plus.
Troy Dreyfus, General Manager
Troy Dreyfus, Owner
Jonathan Ellerbe, Owner

WERO
01-20-1961; 93.3 mhz FM *Hrs Open:* 24; 100 kw; 1781 ft.; N35 21 55 W77 23 38
PO Bx 1707, Washington, NC 27889 US
(252) 639-7900, *Fax:* (252) 639-7979
www.bob933.com
hollywood@bob933.com
License: Washington, Beaufort County, NC held by NM Licensing LLC.
Group Owner: NextMedia Group Inc.; (acq 11-26-2001; grpsl)
Nat'l Reps: Eastman Radio
Arbitron Metro Market: Washington, NC *Format:* Contemporary Hits/Top 40 *Hrs. of News Programming:* news progmg 12 hrs wkly *No. News Employees:* 1 *Target Audience:* 18-49
Larry Weiss, General Manager
Chris ""Hollywood"" Mann, Programming Director
Laura Nichols, Promotions Manager
Gina Gray, Assistant Program Director
Crystal Legends, Music Director

Waxhaw

WOLS
03-01-1995; 106.1 mhz FM *Hrs Open:* 24; 21 kw; 617 ft.; N34 53 1 W80 47 37
1776 Briarcliff Road, Ne, Atlanta, GA 30306 US
(704) 405-3172, *Fax:* (704) 405-3174
www.larazalaraza.com
jmiguel@norsanmultimedia.com
License: Waxhaw, Union County, NC held by GHB of Waxhaw Inc.
Group Owner: GHB Radio Group; (acq 6-95; $325,000)
Arbitron Metro Market: Charlotte, NC
George Buck Jr., President
Julian Miguel, Operations Dir
Edgar Saucedo, General Manager
Ronnie Coates, General Sales Mgr
Sergio Garcia, Programming Director

Waynesville

WMXF
08-01-1947; 1400 khz AM *Hrs Open:* 24; 1 kw-U, ND1; N35 30 14 W82 58 25
2014 North Irby Street, Florence, SC 29506 US
(828) 257-2700, *Fax:* (828) 281-3299
www.wwnc.com
brian@wwnc.com
License: Waynesville, NC held by Clear Channel Broadcasting Licenses Inc.
Group Owner: Clear Channel Communications Inc.; (acq 3-21-2001; grpsl)
Nat'l Reps: Keystone (unwired net)
Format: Adult Contemp *Special Programming:* Relg 3 hrs wkly *No. News Employees:* 1 *Target Audience:* General. *Adv. Rates:* 12; 12; 12; 10
Jeff Schwartz, Operations Dir
James Pastor, General Manager
John Craveno, General Sales Mgr
Justin Craig, Programming Director
John Hurni, Chief Engineer
Jon Paul Rexing, Regional Sales Manager

WQNS
10-01-1979; 104.9 mhz FM *Hrs Open:* 24; 0.245 kw; 1581 ft.; N35 34 7 W82 54 27

2014 North Irby Street, Florence, SC 29506 US
(828) 257-2700, *Fax:* (828) 281-3299
www.rock104rocks.com
License: Waynesville, Buncombe County, NC held by Clear Channel Broadcasting Licenses Inc.
Group Owner: Clear Channel Communications Inc.
Arbitron Metro Market: Asheville, NC *Format:* Classic Rock
Target Audience: General. *Adv. Rates:* 14; 14; 14; 12
Chris Bailey, General Manager

Weaverville

WTMT

10-01-1989; 105.9 mhz FM *Hrs Open:* 24; 9.5 kw; 1112 ft.; N35 36 4 W82 39 7
3223 West Wolf Valley Rd, Clinton, TN 37716 US
(828) 259-9695, *Fax:* (828) 253-5619
1059themountain.com
gbrown@avlradio.com
License: Weaverville, Buncombe County, NC held by Saga Communications of North Carolina LLC.
Group Owner: Saga Communications Inc.; (acq 8-7-2006; $650,000)
Arbitron Metro Market: Asheville, NC
Edward Christian, President
Randy Cable, Operations Dir
Bob Bolak, General Manager
Garry Brown, General Sales Mgr
Ken Carson, Programming Director
Nikki Mitchell, Promotions Manager
Bill McClement, News Director

Weldon

WSMY

01-01-1957; 1400 khz AM *Hrs Open:* 24; 1 kw-U, ND1; N36 24 43 W77 37 6
P.O. Box 910, Roanoke Rapids, NC 27870 US
(252) 536-0209, *Fax:* (252) 538-0378
www.wsmy1400.com
info@wsmy1400.com
License: Weldon, NC held by First Media Radio LLC.
Group Owner: First Media Radio LLC; (acq 7-22-2003; grpsl)
Format: Religious *Target Audience:* 18 plus; affluent adults
Allen Garrett, Operations Dir
Al Haskins, General Manager
John Green, Station Manager

Wendell-Zebulon

WETC

06-16-1959; 540 khz AM *Hrs Open:* 24
P.O. Box 103, Knightdale, NC 27545 US
(919) 772-9540, *Fax:* (770) 246-0054
www.vision540.com
vision540am@gmail.com
License: Wendell-Zebulon, NC held by Prieto Broadcasting Inc.
Group Owner: Prieto Broadcasting Inc.; (acq 6-1-2004; $1.8 million)
Arbitron Metro Market: Wendell, NC
Everado Morales, Station Manager

West Jefferson

WKSK

05-27-1959; 580 khz AM *Hrs Open:* 24 hours a day; 5 kw-D, 34 w-N; N36 24 39 W81 29 46
Box 729, West Jefferson, NC 28694
(336) 246-6001
www.580wksk.com
wksk@skybest.com
License: West Jefferson, Ashe County, NC held by Caddell Broadcasting, Inc.
Nat'l Network: AP Radio *Wire Services:* AP
Population Served: 80,000*Special Programming:* Farm 3 hrs, gospel 5 hrs, Sp one hr wkly *Hrs. of News Programming:* news progmg 16 hrs wkly *No. News Employees:* 1 *Target Audience:* General. *Adv. Rates:* 15; 15; 15; 12
Jan Caddell, President
Graham Caddell, Operations Dir
Nathan Roland, Programming Director
Mike Powers, News Director
Stoney Owen, Chief Engineer

Whiteville

WENC

07-14-1946; 1220 khz AM *Hrs Open:* 6 AM-10 PM; 5 kw-D, ND1; 0.152 kw-N, ND1; N34 18 30 W78 43 0
211 N. 2nd Street, Wilmington, NC 28401 US
(910) 642-2133, *Fax:* (910) 642-5981
License: Whiteville, NC held by DHA Communications.
Regional Network: N.C. News Net.
Format: Blues, Gospel *Special Programming:* Farm 5 hrs, relg 4 hrs, talk 5 hrs wkly *Hrs. of News Programming:* news progmg 10 hrs wkly *No. News Employees:* 1 *Target Audience:* 25-54; women *Adv. Rates:* 12;12; 12; 12;
Jesse Lee Godwin, General Manager
Bob Gause, Engineering Dir

WTXY

01-01-1976; 1540 khz AM *Hrs Open:* Sunrise-sunset; 1 kw-D, NDD; N34 19 23 W78 42 47
P.O. Box 1038, Whiteville, NC 28472 US
(910) 207-0019
www.wtxy1540.com
kendall@wtxy1540.com;dozier@wtxy1540.com
License: Whiteville, NC held by Stanley Broadcasting System Inc.
Nat'l Network: Westwood One; Motor Racing Net *Regional Network:* Tenn. Agri-Net
Arbitron Metro Market: Whiteville, NC *Format:* News, News/Talk, 86 *Special Programming:* Farm 2 hrs, relg 10 hrs wkly *Hrs. of News Programming:* news progmg 84 hrs wkly *No. News Employees:* 2 *Target Audience:* General. *Adv. Rates:* 15; 13.50; 15; 8.50
Thomas Stanley Jr., President
Robby Kendall, Owner & Operations
Jason Dozier, Owner & Operations
Franklin Davis, Advertising Sales Contact
Suzanne King, Advertising Sales Contact

WZFX

02-21-1962; 99.1 mhz FM; 100 kw; 981 ft.; N34 44 5 W78 47 25
Mailing Address: 3033 Riviera Drive, Suite 200, Naples, FL 33940 US
Second Address: 508 Person St, Fayetteville, NC 28301
(910) 486-4991, *Fax:* (910) 486-6720
www.fox99.com
License: Whiteville, Columbus County, NC held by WDAS License L.P.
Group Owner: Beasley Broadcast Group Inc.; (acq 5-8-97; $11.5 million)
Nat'l Reps: Katz Radio
Arbitron Metro Market: Fayetteville, N *Format:* Urban Contemporary *Target Audience:* 18-49.
George Beasley, CEO
Daniel Highsmith, Operations Dir
Mac Edwards, General Manager
Tila Comstock, General Sales Mgr
Mike Nicholson, Programming Director
Van Clough, Chief Engineer

Wilkesboro

*WSIF

04-06-1977; 90.9 mhz FM *Hrs Open:* 24; 1 kw; -171 ft.; N36 8 12 W81 11 2
Mailing Address: P.O. Box 120, Wilkesboro, NC 28697 US
Second Address: 1328 S. Collegiate Dr., Wilkesboro, NC 28697
(336) 838-6179, *Fax:* (336) 838-6277
www.wncw.org
al.delachica@wilkescc.edu
License: Wilkesboro, Wilkes County, NC held by Wilkes Community College.
Format: Triple A
Dave Kester, Operations Dir
Dave Kester, Programming Director

WWWC

01-26-1970; 1240 khz AM; 1 kw-U; N36 09 00 W81 09 42
Mailing Address: Box 580, Wilkesboro, NC 28697
Second Address: 413 Wilkesboro Blvd., Wilkesboro, NC 28697
(336) 838-1241/838-9992, *Fax:* (336) 838-9040
www.12403wc.com
onair@12403wc.com
License: Wilkesboro, Wilkes County, NC held by Foothills Media Inc.
Nat'l Network: USA *Regional Network:* N.C. News Net.
Population Served: 60,000*Target Audience:* General.
John Wishon, President
Petrice Edwards, General Sales Mgr
Angela Henley, News Director
Stoney Owen, Chief Engineer

Williamston

WTIB

08-01-1962; 103.7 mhz FM *Hrs Open:* 24; 100 kw; Ant 981 ft; N35 53 47 W76 58 58 *Rebroadcasts:* Rebroadcasts WRHT(FM) Morehead City 100%
408 W. Arlington Blvd., Suite 101-C, Greenville, NC 28557
(252) 355-1037, *Fax:* (252) 355-2234
www.thehotfmonline.com
License: Williamston, Martin County, NC held by Inner Banks Media LLC.
Group Owner: Inner Banks Media LLC; (acq 3-12-2007; grpsl)
Population Served: 300,000 *Arbitron Metro Market:* Greenville-New Bern-Jacksonville, NC *Target Audience:* 18-49; young adults
Mike Biddle, Operations Dir
Henry Hinton, General Manager
Paul Kingman, General Sales Mgr
Mike Middle, Programming Director
Donna Spivey, News Director
Eddie Harrell, Chief Engineer
Christine Cashwell, Business Manager

WIAM

03-01-1951; 900 khz AM *Hrs Open:* 24; 1 kw-D, ND1; 0.258 kw-N, ND1; N35 51 27 W77 2 34
P.O. Box 590, Williamston, NC 27892 US
(252) 792-4161, *Fax:* (252) 809-0039
www.opendoorradio.com
bryant@opendoorradio.com
License: Williamston, NC held by Lifeline Ministries Inc.
Regional Network: N.C. News Net.
Format: Gospel, Religious *Target Audience:* General.
Johnny Bryant, President

Wilmington

WLSG

12-24-1946; 1340 khz AM *Hrs Open:* 24
Mailing Address: 25 North Kerr Avenue, Suite C, Wilmington, NC 28405 US
Second Address: Box 957, Wilmington, NC 28402
(910) 763-2452, *Fax:* (910) 763-6578
www.homecominggospel.com
jim@life905.com
License: Wilmington, NC held by Carolina Christian Radio Inc.
Group Owner: Carolina Christian Radio; (acq 6-30-2000; $75,000)
Nat'l Network: Salem Radio Network
Arbitron Metro Market: Wilmington, NC *Format:* Gospel, Religious *Target Audience:* 30 plus.
Jim Stephens, General Manager
Roger Brace, Engineering Dir

*WDVV

01-01-1999; 89.7 mhz FM; 13.5 kw vert; 348 ft.; N34 10 52 W78 2 33
Mailing Address: 2002 Hawthorne Place, Wilmington, NC 28403 US
Second Address: 201 North Front Street, Suite 805, Wilmington, NC 28401
(910) 763-2452, *Fax:* (910) 763-6578
www.thedoveonline.org
thedove@thedoveonline.org
License: Wilmington, New Hanover County, NC held by Carolina Christian Radio Inc.
Group Owner: Carolina Christian Radio; (acq 2-16-2001; $100,000 with WMYT(AM) Carolina Beach)
Nat'l Network: USA
Arbitron Metro Market: Wilmington, NC *Format:* Christian
Roger Brace, Operations Dir
Jim Stephens, General Manager

WGNI

03-01-1970; 102.7 mhz FM *Hrs Open:* 24; 100 kw; 981 ft.; N34 3 6 W78 4 57
1009 Drayton Road, Fayetteville, NC 28403 US
(910) 763-9977, *Fax:* (910) 762-0456
www.cumulus.com
info@cumulus.com
License: Wilmington, New Hanover County, NC held by Cumulus Licensing LLC.
Group Owner: Cumulus Media Inc.
Nat'l Reps: McGavren Guild *Wire Services:* AP
Arbitron Metro Market: Wilmington, NC *Format:* Adult Contemp
No. News Employees: 2
Perry Stone, Operations Dir
Jim Principi, General Manager
Jennifer McLean, General Sales Mgr
Mike Farrow, Programming Director
David Carroll, Promotions Manager
Tim Nelson, Chief Engineer

*WHQR

04-24-1984; 91.3 mhz FM *Hrs Open:* 24; 100 kw; 1142 ft.; N34 7 53 W78 11 17
254 North Front Street, Wilmington, NC 28401 US
(910) 343-1640, *Fax:* (910) 251-8693
www.whqr.org
whqr@whqr.org

License: Wilmington, New Hanover County, NC held by Friends of Public Radio Inc.
Nat'l Network: NPR; PRI *Regional Reps:* Megan Gorham *Wire Services:* AP
Arbitron Metro Market: Wilmington, NC *Format:* News *Hrs. of News Programming:* news progmg 63 hrs wkly *No. News Employees:* 3 *Target Audience:* 35 plus.
George Scheibner, Operations Dir
John Milligan, General Manager
Bob Klorkmon, Programming Director
Ann Berry, Promotions Manager
Catherine Welch, News Director

WMFD
04-15-1935; 630 khz AM *Hrs Open:* 24
25 North Kerr Avenue, Suite C, Wilmington, NC 28405 US
(910) 791-3088
www.am630.net
bschimmel@cbc-sunrise.com
License: Wilmington, NC held by Sunrise Broadcasting LLC.
Group Owner: Capitol Broadcasting Co. Inc.; (acq 11-18-2008; grpsl)
Nat'l Network: CBS
Arbitron Metro Market: Wilmington, NC *Format:* Sports *Hrs. of News Programming:* news progmg 3 hrs wkly *No. News Employees:* 1 *Target Audience:* 30 plus; upscale audience
Carolyn Stewart, Chairman
David Stewart, President
Carol Casey, Programming Director

WMNX
02-24-1970; 97.3 mhz FM *Hrs Open:* 24; 100 kw; 884 ft.; N34 3 6 W78 4 57
1890 Dawson Street, Wilmington, NC 28403 US
(910) 763-9977, *Fax:* (910) 762-0456
www.coast973.com
info@coast973.com
License: Wilmington, New Hanover County, NC held by Cumulus Licensing Corp.
Group Owner: Cumulus Media Inc.; (acq 3-12-2001; grpsl)
Nat'l Reps: McGavren Guild *Wire Services:* AP
Arbitron Metro Market: Wilmington, NC *Format:* Urban Contemporary *No. News Employees:* 1 *Target Audience:* 18-49; general
Perry Stone, Operations Dir
Jim Principi, General Manager

WILT
02-01-1994; 104.5 mhz FM; 3.1 kw; 449 ft.; N34 10 0 W77 56 40
25 North Kerr Ave., Suite C, Wilmington, NC 28405 US
(910) 791-3088, *Fax:* (910) 791-0112
www.1045sunnyfm.com
License: Wilmington, New Hanover County, NC held by Sunrise Broadcasting LLC.
Group Owner: Capitol Broadcasting Co. Inc.; (acq 11-18-2008; grpsl)
Arbitron Metro Market: Wilmington, NC *Format:* Adult Contemp *Target Audience:* 25-54.
Dave Patella, General Manager
Jennifer McLean-Bloech, General Sales Mgr
Brian White, Programming Director

WWIL
08-25-1963; 1490 khz AM *Hrs Open:* 24; 1 kw-U, ND1; N34 13 52 W77 57 18
Mailing Address: P.O. Box 957, Wilmington, NC 28402 US
Second Address: 201 North Front Street, Suite 805, Wilmington, NC 28401
(910) 763-2452, *Fax:* (910) 763-6578
www.gospeljoy1490.com
life@life905.com
License: Wilmington, NC held by Carolina Christian Radio Inc.
Group Owner: Carolina Christian Radio; (acq 10-28-92; $35,000;
Nat'l Network: USA
Arbitron Metro Market: Wilmington, NC *Format:* Black, Gospel *Target Audience:* 25-49.
Jim Stephens, General Manager
Pastor James Utley, Station Manager

*WWIL-FM
12-01-1995; 90.5 mhz FM *Hrs Open:* 24; 1 kw horiz, 20 kw vert; 328 ft.; N34 10 52 W78 2 33
Mailing Address: P.O. Box 957, Wilmington, NC 28402 US
Second Address: 201 North Front Street, Suite 805, Wilmington, NC 28401
(910) 763-2452, *Fax:* (910) 763-6578
www.life905.com
Church@Life905.com
License: Wilmington, New Hanover County, NC
Group Owner: Carolina Christian Radio; (Acq 6-95;
Nat'l Network: USA
Arbitron Metro Market: Wilmington, NC *Format:* Adult Contemp, Christian *Target Audience:* 25-54.
Jim Stephens, General Manager

WWQQ-FM
03-31-1969; 101.3 mhz FM *Hrs Open:* 24; 40 kw; 545 ft.; N34 3 2 W77 57 20
111 East Kilbourn Ave., Suite 2700, Milwaukee, WI 53202 US
(910) 763-9977, *Fax:* (910) 762-0456
www.wwqq101.com
Joyce.Thomas@cumulus.com
License: Wilmington, New Hanover County, NC held by Cumulus Licensing Corp.
Group Owner: Cumulus Media Inc.; (acq 7-3-97;
Nat'l Reps: McGavren Guild *Wire Services:* AP
Arbitron Metro Market: Wilmington, NC *Format:* Country *No. News Employees:* 1 *Target Audience:* 25-54. *Adv. Rates:* 60; 50; 55; 40
Perry Stone, Operations Dir
Jim Principi, General Manager
Robin Batson, General Sales Mgr
Brian Sims, Programming Director
Kerry Hinshaw, Promotions Manager
Tim Nelson, Chief Engineer
Joyce Thomas, Assistant Business Manager

Wilson

WVOT
06-01-1948; 1420 khz AM *Hrs Open:* 24; 1 kw-D, DAN; 0.5 kw-N, DAN; N35 44 8 W77 53 2
2108 Beekman Place N.W., Wilson, NC 27896 US
(252) 243-5157(252) 243-1420, *Fax:* (252) 291-5000
www.wvot1420am.com
License: Wilson, NC held by Kingdom Expansion Corp.
Arbitron Metro Market: Wilson, NC *Format:* Christian, Sports *Hrs. of News Programming:* News progmg 25 hrs wkly *Target Audience:* 25-55. *Adv. Rates:* 20; 15; 20; 15
Pastor MK Smith, CEO/COO
M.K. Smith, President
Noel Johnson, Operations Dir
Joyce Farmer, Station Manager
Geri Kidd Brown, Programming Director

WLLY
01-01-1961; 1350 khz AM *Hrs Open:* Daylight; 1 kw-D, ND1; 0.079 kw-N, ND1; N35 43 24 W77 55 16
7354 Lindley Mill Road, Graham, NC 27253 US
(252) 237-5171, *Fax:* (252) 237-5172
info@wlly.com
License: Wilson, NC held by Estuardo Valdemar Rodriguez and Leonor Rodriguez, joint tenants.
Group Owner: Radio La Grande; (acq 10-11-2002; $255,000)
Nat'l Network: USA *Regional Network:* N.C. News Net.
Format: Gospel *Target Audience:* General.
Vivien Ogburn, Station Manager

Windsor

WBTE
01-01-1969; 990 khz AM; 1 kw-D, ND2; 0.025 kw-N, ND2; N35 58 0 W76 56 54
645 Church Street, Suite 400, Norfolk, VA 23510 US
(252) 582-8680, *Fax:* (252)482-4260
wbte@earthlink.net
License: Windsor, NC held by Dr. Tine Hicks & Associate
Arbitron Metro Market: Norfolk, VA *Format:* Gospel
Arbutis Walston, General Manager

Winfall

*WGTI
01-01-1980; 97.7 mhz FM *Hrs Open:* 24; 31 kw; 157 m; N36 04 06 W76 58 35
Box 590, Williamston, NC 23510
(252) 792-4161, *Fax:* (252) 809-0039
www.opendoorradio.com
bryant@opendoorradio.com
License: Winfall, Perquimans County, NC held by Lifeline Ministries Inc.
Johnny Bryant, President

Wingate

*WRCM
06-14-1993; 91.9 mhz FM *Hrs Open:* 24; 30 kw; 495 ft.; N35 3 34 W80 40 14
Mailing Address: P. O. Box 3122, Columbia, SC 29230 US
Second Address: 1092 Radio Drive, Indian Trail, NC 28079
(704) 821-9293,(704) 570-9200, *Fax:* (704) 821-9285
www.wrcm.org
newlife91.9@wrcm.org
License: Wingate, Union County, NC held by Columbia Bible College Broadcasting Co.
Nat'l Network: Salem Radio Network *Wire Services:* UPI
Format: Adult Contemp, Christian *Target Audience:* 25-44; female
Joyce Younts, Operations Dir
Joe Paulo, General Manager
Dwayne Harrison, Programming Director
Elizabeth Poplin, Promotions Manager
Dave Morrison, Chief Engineer
Steve McCranie, Special Events Coordinator

Winston-Salem

WEGO(AM)
10-28-1950; 980 khz AM; 1.3 kw-D, 49 w-N; N36 06 40 W80 14 36
Mailing Address: Box 5663, High Point, NC 27262
Second Address: 1607 Country Club Dr., High Point, NC 27262
(336) 887-0983, *Fax:* (336) 887-3055
schildress@ghbradio.com
License: Winston-Salem, Forsyth County, NC held by GHB Radio Inc.
Group Owner: GHB Radio Group; (acq 3-6-2006; $235,000)
Nat'l Network: ESPN Radio
Population Served: 150,000 *Arbitron Metro Market:* Greensboro-Winston Salem-High Point, NC *Target Audience:* Men 25-54
George Buck Jr., President
Wes Jones, Operations Dir
Susan Childress, General Manager
Gary Hattaway, Engineering Dir

WBFJ
10-01-1960; 1550 khz AM *Hrs Open:* Sunrise-sunset; 1 kw-D, NDD; N36 6 33 W80 14 44
1249 Trade Street, Winston Salem, NC 27101 US
(336) 721-1560, *Fax:* (336) 777-1032
www.wbfj.fm
live@wbfjfm.com
License: Winston-Salem, NC held by Word of Life Broadcasting Inc.
Nat'l Network: USA
Arbitron Metro Market: Winston Salem, NC *Format:* Christian, Talk *Target Audience:* 29-54; general *Adv. Rates:* 15; 15; 15; na
Philip Watson, President
Wally Decker, General Manager
John Hill, Programming Director
Larry Schropp, Chief Engineer
Bonnie Hilton, Volunteer Coordinator
Cindy Davis, Donor Services
Jeff Foster, Production/Web/On-Air

*WBFJ-FM
09-01-1994; 89.3 mhz FM *Hrs Open:* 24; 2.5 kw; 423 ft.; N36 5 56 W80 15 0
1249 Trade Street, Winston-Salem, NC 27101 US
(336) 721-1560(336) 777-1893, *Fax:* (336) 777-1032
www.wbfj.fm
live@wbfjfm.com
License: Winston-Salem, Forsyth County, NC held by Triad Family Network Inc.
Nat'l Network: USA
Arbitron Metro Market: Winston Salem, NC *Format:* Christian *Target Audience:* 25-49.
Wally Decker, General Manager
Kurt Myers, Promotions Manager
Verne Hill, News Director
Larry Shropp, Chief Engineer
Bonnie Hilton, Volunteer Coordinator
Cindy Davis, Donor Services
Jeff Foster, Production/Web/On-Air

*WFDD
03-13-1961; 88.5 mhz FM *Hrs Open:* 24; 60 kw; 935 ft.; N35 55 2 W80 17 37
Mailing Address: P. O. Box 7405, Winston-Salem, NC 27109 US
Second Address: 56 Wake Forest Rd., Winston-Salem, NC 27109
(336) 758-8850, *Fax:* (336) 758-5193
www.wfdd.org
wfdd@wfu.edu
License: Winston-Salem, Forsyth County, NC held by Trustees of Wake Forest University.
Nat'l Network: PRI; NPR *Regional Reps:* Public Radio Adv. Alliance
Arbitron Metro Market: Winston-Salem, NC *Format:* News *Special Programming:* Jazz 16 hrs wkly *Hrs. of News Programming:* news progmg 29 hrs wkly *No. News Employees:* 3 *Target Audience:* General;educated/public radio

Marian Wilson Reich, Operations / Production / Webmaster
Tom Dollenmayer, General Manager
Denise Franklin, News Director
ShaDonna Crosby, Listener Services and Volunteer Coordinator
Molly Davis, Marketing & Community Outreach
Audrey Fannin, Multimedia Producer
Eddie Garcia, Operations Technician
Karen Davis Kantziper, Account Manager
Greg Keener, Membership Operations Coordinator

WKZL
01-01-1972; 107.5 mhz FM; 100 kw; 994 ft.; N36 16 33 W79 56 27
192 E. Lewis St, PO Box 36070, Greensboro, NC 27406 US
(336) 274-8042, *Fax:* (336) 274-1629
www.1075kzl.com
bwheeler@dbcradio.com
License: Winston-Salem, Forsyth County, NC held by Dick Broadcasting Co. Inc. of Tennessee
Arbitron Metro Market: Greensboro-Winston Salem-High Point, NC *Format:* Contemporary Hits/Top 40 *Target Audience:* 25-49; women *Adv. Rates:* 175; 125; 125; 30
Allen Dick, CEO
Bruce Wheeler, Operations Dir
Bruce Wheeler, General Manager
Jennifer Hart, General Sales Mgr
Jason Goodman, Programming Director
Lauren McCombs, Promotions Manager
Josie Paza, Music Director
James Kerr,Operations Manager
Jared Pike, Disc Jockey
Katie O'Brien, Disc Jockey

WPAW
04-01-1947; 93.1 mhz FM *Hrs Open:* 24; 99 kw; 1099 ft.; N36 16 33 W79 56 26
10706 Beaver Dam Road, Cockeysville, MD 21030 US
(336) 605-5200, *Fax:* (336) 605-5221
www.931wolfcountry.com
info@wpaw.com
License: Winston-Salem, Forsyth County, NC held by Entercom Greensboro License LLC.
Group Owner: Entercom Communications Corp.; (acq 12-13-99; grpsl)
Nat'l Network: CBS *Nat'l Reps:* McGavren Guild
Arbitron Metro Market: Greensboro,NC *Format:* Country *Target Audience:* General
Brent Millar, General Manager
Lisa Powell, General Sales Mgr
Randy Bliss, Programming Director
Jill Dyson, Promotions Manager
Valerie Dickens, News Director
Larry Allen, Chief Engineer
Greg Carpenter, General Sales Manager

WPIP
06-01-1995; 880 khz AM *Hrs Open:* Sunrise-sunset
4135 Thomasville Road, Winston Salem, NC 27107 US
(336) 785-0527, *Fax:* (336) 785-0529
www.wpipbereanradio.org
wpip880am@triad.rr.com
License: Winston-Salem, NC held by Berean Baptist Church.
Nat'l Network: USA
Arbitron Metro Market: Greensboro-Winston Salem-High Point, NC *Format:* Christian
Jeff Baity, Operations Dir
Ron Baity, General Manager

WPOL
03-25-1937; 1340 khz AM *Hrs Open:* 24; 1 kw-U, ND1; N36 4 26 W80 15 19
645 Church Street, Suite 400, Norfolk, VA 23510 US
(336) 759-0363, *Fax:* (336) 759-0366
www.1340thelight.com
info@1340thelight.com
License: Winston-Salem, NC held by Truth Broadcasting Corp.
Group Owner: Truth Broadcasting Corp.; (acq 5-10-2000)
Arbitron Metro Market: Greensboro-Winston Salem-High Point, NC *Format:* Gospel, Religious *Hrs. of News Programming:* News progmg one hr wkly *Target Audience:* Relg *Adv. Rates:* 206; 20; 20; 20
Stuart Epperson Jr., President

WSJS
04-17-1930; 600 khz AM; 5 kw-D, DA2; 5 kw-N, DA2; N36 7 0 W80 21 26
200 Concord Plz., Ste 600, San Antonio, TX 78216 US
(336) 777-3900, *Fax:* (336) 777-3915
www.wsjs.com
License: Winston-Salem, NC held by Crescent Media Group LLC.
Group Owner: Curtis Media Group; (acq 2-14-2007; grpsl)
Nat'l Network: Wall Street *Nat'l Reps:* Clear Channel
Arbitron Metro Market: Greensboro-Wins *Format:* News *Target Audience:* 25-64.
Tom Hamilton, General Manager
Beth Ann McBride, Programming Director
Marty Holbrook, Promotions Manager
Bob Costner, News Director
George Newman, Chief Engineer

WSMX
10-01-1964; 1500 khz AM *Hrs Open:* Sunrise-sunset
P.O. Box 16056, Winston-Salem, NC 27115 US
(336) 391-1497, *Fax:* (336) 724-6368
wsmxradio@aol.com
License: Winston-Salem, NC held by Gospel Media Inc.
Arbitron Metro Market: Greensboro-Winston Salem-High Point, NC *Format:* Gospel *Hrs. of News Programming:* News progmg 12 hrs wkly *Target Audience:* 30-50 plus; blue collar, minorities, church members *Adv. Rates:* 10.00 per min
Joe Watson, President

***WSNC**
01-01-1982; 90.5 mhz FM *Hrs Open:* 24; 10 kw; 194 ft.; N36 5 24 W80 13 20
P.O. Box 13095, Winston-Salem, NC 27110 US
(336) 750-2321, *Fax:* (336) 750-2329
www.wssu.edu
WSNCFM@wssu.edu
License: Winston-Salem, Forsyth County, NC held by Winston-Salem State University.
Nat'l Network: NPR; PRI
Arbitron Metro Market: Greensboro-Winston Salem-High Point, NC *Format:* Jazz, News *Target Audience:* 30-70; African-Americans *Adv. Rates:* 10; 35; 35; 20
Ben Donnelly, Operations Dir
Elvin Jenkins, General Manager
Monica Melton, Programming Director
Baxter Griffin, Chief Engineer

WTOB
04-22-1947; 1380 khz AM *Hrs Open:* 18; 5 kw-D, DA2; 2.5 kw-N, DA2; N36 8 53 W80 19 11
3789 Will Scarlet Road, Winston-Salem, NC 27104 US
(336) 714-7516, *Fax:* (336) 714-0435
www.quepasamedia.com
quepasa@quepasamedia.com
License: Winston-Salem, NC held by Davidson Media Station WTOB Licensee LLC.
Group Owner: Davidson Media Group LLC; (acq 3-25-2005; swap with WWBG(AM) Greensboro for WDRU(AM) Wake Forest).
Regional Network: N.C. News Net.
Arbitron Metro Market: Greensboro, NC *Target Audience:* 35 plus; affluent audience
Jose Isasi, President & CEO
Roger Martinez, General Manager
Executive Editor, German Navy
Commercial Director, Roberto Aisenberg
Commercial Manager

WTQR
12-01-1947; 104.1 mhz FM *Hrs Open:* 24; 99 kw; 1732 ft.; N36 22 36.4 W80 22 8.6
200 Concord Plz., Ste 600, San Antonio, TX 78216 US
(336) 822-2000, *Fax:* (336) 887-0104
www.wtqr.com
brucelogan@clearchannel.com
License: Winston-Salem, Forsyth County, NC held by Clear Channel Radio Licenses Inc.
Group Owner: Clear Channel Communications Inc.; (acq 1996; grpsl).
Arbitron Metro Market: Greensboro, NC *Format:* Country *Special Programming:* NASCAR, bluegrass 2 hrs wkly *Target Audience:* 25-54.
Morgan Bohannon, General Manager
Bobby Tatum, General Sales Mgr
Bruce Logan, Programming Director
Jason Newton, Promotions Manager
Dennis Elliott, Digital Content Director
Alan Chapman, Internship Director

***WXRI**
05-17-1997; 91.3 mhz FM *Hrs Open:* 24; 50 kw; 217 ft.; N36 8 6 W80 30 14
P.O. Box 889, Blacksburg, VA 24063 US
(336) 788-1155, *Fax:* (336) 788-7199
www.joyfm.org
office@joyfm.org
License: Winston-Salem, Forsyth County, NC held by Positive Alternative Radio Inc.
Group Owner: Positive Alternative Radio Inc.; (acq 5-21-92)
Nat'l Network: Salem Radio Network
Arbitron Metro Market: Greensboro, NC *Format:* Gospel *Target Audience:* Female; middle-aged
Vernon Baker, President
Edward Baker, Operations Dir
Daniel Britt, Network Operations Manager
Brian Sanders, Vice President

Winterville

WECU
02-07-2006; 1570 khz AM *Hrs Open:* 24
US
(252) 931-9328, *Fax:* (252) 931-9328
www.wecu1570.com
Info@Wecu1570.com
License: Winterville, NC held by CTC Media Group.
Group Owner: CTC Media Group Inc.
Arbitron Metro Market: Winterville, NC *Format:* Gospel
Edwin Afflerbach, President
Michael Afflerbach, Station Manager

Wrightsville Beach

WBNE
10-31-1977; 103.7 mhz FM *Hrs Open:* 24; 35 kw; 510 ft.; N34 3 2 W77 57 20
3021 Bethel Road, Suite 208, Columbus, OH 43220 US
(910) 772-6300, *Fax:* (910) 772-6310
www.937thebone.com
newsroom@seacomm.com
License: Wrightsville Beach, Brunswick County, NC held by Sea-Comm Inc.
Group Owner: Sea-Comm Inc.; (acq 12-30-2003; with WLTT(FM) Shallotte)
Nat'l Network: Jones Radio Networks
Arbitron Metro Market: Wilmington, NC *Format:* Classic Rock *Hrs. of News Programming:* news progmg 7 hrs wkly *No. News Employees:* 1 *Target Audience:* 25-54; upscale female
Paul Knight, General Manager
Amy Besterfeldt, General Sales Mgr
Beau Gunn, Programming Director
Jonathan Knight, Promotions Manager

Yadkin

***WWQY**
90.3 mhz FM; 1.6 kw; 105 ft.; N35 48 13 W80 17 42
US
License: Yadkin, Yadkin County, NC
Group Owner: The Power Foundation

Yanceyville

WYNC
11-09-1979; 1540 khz AM *Hrs Open:* sun up-sun down; 1 kw-C, NDD; 2.5 kw-D, NDD; N36 24 52 W79 20 6
Mailing Address: P.O. Box 670, Yanceyville, NC 27379 US
Second Address: 545 Firetower Rd., Yanceyville, NC 27379
(336) 694-7343, *Fax:* (336) 694-7514
wync@earthlink.net
License: Yanceyville, NC held by Semora Broadcasting Inc.
Nat'l Network: Westwood One
Arbitron Metro Market: Yanceyville, NC *Format:* Gospel *Special Programming:* Gospel 16 hrs wkly *Target Audience:* General; rural Caswell county & Danville, VA
George Thaxton, Station Manager
Leroy Connally, Chief Engineer

Zebulon

***WVRD**
05-01-1990; 90.5 mhz FM *Hrs Open:* 24; 1.2 kw; Ant 210 ft; N35 49 19 W78 18 36
5 W. Hargett St., Raleigh, NC 27601
(919) 899-6778, *Fax:* (919) 899-6779
www.88wajc.com
jill@88wajc.com
License: Zebulon, Wake County, NC held by CSN International.
Group Owner: CSN International; (acq 6-23-2000; $150,000)
Population Served: 416,468 *Arbitron Metro Market:* Raleigh, NC
Jim Walker, General Manager

North Dakota

Arthur

KVMI
04-01-1994; 103.9 mhz FM; 25 kw; 328 ft.; N47 7 20 W97 19 29
PO Box 954, West Fargo, SD 58078 US
(701) 866-0799, *Fax:* (218) 287-8274
License: Arthur, Cass County, ND held by Vision Media Inc.

Nat'l Network: Westwood One
Arbitron Metro Market: Fargo-Moorhead, ND-MN *Format:* Country
Mike McCain, General Manager

Belcourt

*KEYA
10-01-1975; 88.5 mhz FM *Hrs Open:* 19; 19 kw; 361 ft.; N48 50 37 W99 45 2
P.O. Box 190, Belcourt, ND 58316 US
(701) 477-5686(701) 477-5687, *Fax:* (701) 477-3252
keya.utma.com/885
keya@utma.com
License: Belcourt, Rolette County, ND held by KEYA Inc.
Nat'l Network: NPR *Wire Services:* AP
Arbitron Metro Market: Belcourt, ND *Format:* Oldies, Rock/AOR, 30 *Special Programming:* American Indian 6 hrs, relg 10 hrs, old-time fiddle mus 4 hrs, Chippewa 3 hrs wkly *Hrs. of News Programming:* news progmg 7 hrswkly *Target Audience:* General; members of the Turtle Mountain Band of Chippewa Indians
Kimberly Thomas, General Manager
Jarle Kvale, Programming Director
Janice Keplin, Chief Engineer
Jarle Kvale, Programming Director

*KSIH
90.1 mhz FM; kw
US
(540) 459-7646, *Fax:* (540) 459-7656
www.radiomaria.us
License: Belcourt, Rolette County, ND held by Friends of Radio Maria Inc.
Arbitron Metro Market: Belcourt, ND
Florinda Iannace, President
John Trent, General Manager

Belfield

KXDI
93.9 mhz FM; 100 kw; 253.6 m; N46 43 31 W102 55 0.4
910 E. Broadway, Williston, ND
(701)572-4478, *Fax:* (701)572-1419
License: Belfield, Stark County, ND held by Williston Community Broadcasting Corp.
Stephen A. Marks, President

Beulah

KDKT
10-05-1978; 1410 khz AM *Hrs Open:* 24; 1 kw-D, 180 w-N; N47 17 15 W101 45 46
Mailing Address: 547 S. 7th Street, Bismarck, ND 58523
Second Address: 547 S. 7th St., Suite 166, Bismarck, ND 58504
(701) 873-2215, *Fax:* (701) 873-2363
www.foxsports1410.com
info@dsnradio.com
License: Beulah, Mercer County, ND held by Digital Syndicate Network LLC
Nat'l Network: Fox Sports *Regional Network:* American Ag
Population Served: 83,000 *Arbitron Metro Market:* Bismarck, ND *Hrs. of News Programming:* news progmg 14 hrs wkly *No. News Employees:* 35 *Target Audience:* 22-54; general
Guy Giuliano, President
Derek Stacklie, Station Manager

Bismarck

KACL
04-22-1997; 98.7 mhz FM *Hrs Open:* 24; 100 kw; 837 ft.; N46 35 24 W100 47 46
330 East Kilbourn Avenue, Suite 250, Milwaukee, WI 53202 US
(701) 250-6602, *Fax:* (701) 250-6632
www.cool987fm.com
License: Bismarck, Burleigh County, ND held by Cumulus Licensing Corp.
Group Owner: Cumulus Media Inc.; (acq 5-11-98; grpsl)
Arbitron Metro Market: Bismarck, ND *Format:* Oldies
Syd Stewart, General Manager
Bob Beck, Programming Director
Elliott Davidson, Chief Engineer

KBMR
08-15-1958; 1130 khz AM *Hrs Open:* 24
P.O. Box 1233, 3500 E. Rosser Ave., Bismarck, ND 58502 US
(701) 255-1234, *Fax:* (701) 222-1131
www.kbmr.com
kbmr@clearchannel.com
License: Bismarck, ND held by CC Licenses LLC.
Group Owner: Clear Channel Communications Inc.; (acq 2-13-2004;. grpsl).
Nat'l Reps: McGavren Guild
Arbitron Metro Market: Bismarck, ND *Format:* Country *Special Programming:* Farm 6 hrs wkly *Target Audience:* 25 plus.
Bob Denver, General Manager
Neil Cary, General Sales Mgr
Charlie Williams, Programming Director
Jeff Alexander, News Director
Elliott Davidson, Chief Engineer
Clarissa Lynn, Disc Jockey

KBYZ
06-01-1985; 96.5 mhz FM; 100 kw; 963 ft.; N46 35 24 W100 47 46
330 East Kilbourn Avenue, Suite 250, Milwaukee, WI 53202 US
(701) 663-9600, *Fax:* (701) 663-8790
www.965thefox.com
kbyz@cumulus.com
License: Bismarck, Burleigh County, ND
Group Owner: Cumulus Media Inc.
Arbitron Metro Market: Bismarck, ND *Format:* Classic Rock *No. News Employees:* 1 *Target Audience:* 25-54. *Adv. Rates:* 25; 25; 25; 25
Dee Daniels, Programming Director
Syd Stewart, Promotions Manager

*KCND
09-01-1981; 90.5 mhz FM *Hrs Open:* 24; 50 kw; 1217 ft.; N46 35 23 W100 48 2
P.O. Box 3240, Fargo, ND 58108 US
(701) 241-6900, *Fax:* (701) 239-7650
www.prairiepublic.org
info@prairiepublic.org
License: Bismarck, Burleigh County, ND held by Prairie Public Broadcasting Inc.
Nat'l Network: PRI; NPR
Arbitron Metro Market: Bismarck, ND *TV Affiliate:* *KBME-TV affil. *Format:* Jazz, News *Special Programming:* American Indian 2 hrs, folk 6 hrs, blues 2 hrs wkly *Hrs. of News Programming:* news progmg 40 hrs wkly*No. News Employees:* 2 *Target Audience:* General.
John Harris, President & CEO
Duane Lee, Operations Dir
Bill Thomas, General Sales Mgr
David Thompson, News Director
Jack Anderson, Engineering Dir
Beth Bradley, Business Development Representative
Ann Clark, Director ofDevelopment
Bob Dambach, Director of Television
Troy Davis, Membership Manager
Russell Ford-Dunker, Business Development Manager
John Gast, Director of Finance

KFYR
01-01-1925; 550 khz AM; 5 kw-D, DAN; 5 kw-N, DAN; N46 51 12 W100 32 37
Mailing Address: 50 East Rivercenter Boulevard, #1200, Covington, KY 41011 US
Second Address: 3500 E. Rosser Ave., Bismarck, ND 58501
(701) 255-1234, *Fax:* (701) 222-1131
www.kfyr.com
kfyr@clearchannel.com
License: Bismarck, ND held by Citicasters Licenses L.P.
Group Owner: Clear Channel Communications Inc.; (acq 5-4-99; grpsl)
Arbitron Metro Market: Bismarck, ND *Format:* News, News/Talk, 86 *Special Programming:* Oldies 6 hrs wkly
Bob Denver, General Manager
Neil Cary, General Sales Mgr

KKCT
01-01-1994; 97.5 mhz FM; 100 kw; 837 ft.; N46 35 24 W100 47 46
330 East Kilbourn Ave., Suite 250, Milwaukee, WI 53202 US
(701) 250-6602, *Fax:* (701) 250-6632
www.hot975fm.com
License: Bismarck, Burleigh County, ND held by Cumulus Licensing Corp.
Group Owner: Cumulus Media Inc.; (acq 5-11-98; grpsl)
Arbitron Metro Market: Bismarck, ND *Format:* Contemporary Hits/Top 40
Connie Schroeder, Operations Dir
Syd Stewart, General Manager
Bill Schmid, Station Manager
Mia Amini, Programming Director
Elliott Davidson, Chief Engineer

KQDY
09-13-1968; 94.5 mhz FM *Hrs Open:* 24; 100 kw; 1119 ft.; N46 56 31 W100 41 38
P. O. Box 1233, Bismarck, ND 58502 US
(701) 255-1234, *Fax:* (701) 222-1131
www.kqdy.com
info@kqdy.com
License: Bismarck, Burleigh County, ND held by CC Licenses LLC.
Group Owner: Clear Channel Communications Inc.; (acq 2-13-2004; grpsl).
Arbitron Metro Market: Bismarck-Mandan *Format:* Country *Hrs. of News Programming:* News progmg 4 hrs wkly *Target Audience:* 18-49.
Jim Lowe, General Manager
Neil Cary, General Sales Mgr

KSSS
08-01-1994; 101.5 mhz FM *Hrs Open:* 24; 100 kw; 988 ft.; N46 56 31 W100 41 37
Mailing Address: PO Box 1233, Bismarck, ND 58501 US
Second Address: Box 2156, Bismarck, ND 58502
(701) 255-1234, *Fax:* (701) 222-1131
www.1015.fm
info@1015.fm
License: Bismarck, Burleigh County, ND held by CC Licenses LLC.
Group Owner: Clear Channel Communications Inc.; (acq 2-13-2004; grpsl).
Arbitron Metro Market: Bismarck, ND *Format:* Classic Rock
Bob Denver, General Manager
Terry Flack, General Sales Mgr
Rick Anthony, Programming Director
Jeff Alexander, News Director
Cindy Lindsay, Traffic Manager

KXMR
03-20-1999; 710 khz AM *Hrs Open:* 24
Mailing Address: P.O. Box 1233, 3500 East Rosser Avenue, Bismarck, ND 58501 US
Second Address: Box 2156, Bismarck, ND 58502
(701) 255-1234, *Fax:* (701) 222-1131
www.espn710am.com
jjimlowe@clearchannel.com
License: Bismarck, ND held by CC Licenses LLC.
Group Owner: Clear Channel Communications Inc.; (acq 12-10-2003).
Arbitron Metro Market: Bismarck, ND *Format:* Sports
Jim Lowe, General Manager
Neil Cary, General Sales Mgr
Rick Anthony, Programming Director
Rick Anthony, Public Service Announcements

KYYY
08-15-1966; 92.9 mhz FM; 100 kw; 988 ft.; N46 56 31 W100 41 37
Mailing Address: 50 East Rivercenter Boulevard, #1200, Covington, KY 41011 US
Second Address: 3500 E. Rosser Ave., Bismarck, ND 58501
(701) 255-1234, *Fax:* (701) 222-1131
www.y93.com
y93@y93.fm
License: Bismarck, Burleigh County, ND held by Citicasters Licenses L.P.
Group Owner: Clear Channel Communications Inc.
Arbitron Metro Market: Bismarck, ND *Format:* Adult Contemp
Jim Lowe, General Manager
Neil Cary, General Sales Mgr
Todd Mitchell, Programming Director

*KBFR
10-01-2003; 91.7 mhz FM *Hrs Open:* 24; 0.78 kw; 348 ft.; N46 49 38 W100 46 28
Mailing Address: 4135 Northgate Blvd., Suite 1, Sacramento, CA 95834 US
Second Address: 290 Hegenberger Rd., Oakland, CA 94621
(800) 543-1495, *Fax:* (916) 641-8238
www.familyradio.com
info@familyradio.com
License: Bismarck, Burleigh County, ND held by Family Stations Inc.
Group Owner: Family Stations Inc.
Arbitron Metro Market: Bismarck, ND *Format:* Christian, Religious
Harold Camping, President
Don Horton, Operations Dir

*KBMK
01-01-2006; 88.3 mhz FM; 8.5 kw vert; 381 ft.; N46 49 38 W100 46 28 *Rebroadcasts:* Rebroadcasts KLVR(FM) Santa Rosa, CA 100%.
188 South Bellevue, Suite 222, Memphis, TN 38104 US
(800) 525-5683, *Fax:* (916) 251-1650
www.klove.com
klove@klove.com

License: Bismarck, Burleigh County, ND held by Educational Media Foundation
Group Owner: EMF Broadcasting
Nat'l Network: K-Love
Arbitron Metro Market: Bismarck, ND *Format:* Christian *No. News Employees:* 13
Darrell Chambliss, Chairman
Mike Novak, President and CEO
John Clements, General Sales Mgr
David Pierce, Chief Creative Officer and Programming Director
Ed Lenane, News Director
Sam Wallington, Engineering Dir
Marya Morgan, NewsReporter
Richard Hunt, News Reporter
Alan Mason, Chief Operating Officer
Dan Antonelli, Chief Business Development Officer
Eric Moser, Chief Financial Officer
Brian Burger, Vice President of Human Resources

***KNRI**
01-01-2006; 89.7 mhz FM *Hrs Open:* 24; 1.3 kw; 361 ft.; N46 49 38 W100 46 28
1425 N Market Blvd., Suite 9, Sacramento, CA 95834 US
(888) 937-2471, *Fax:* (916) 251-1650
www.air1.com
info@air1.com
License: Bismarck, Burleigh County, ND held by Educational Media Foundation.
Group Owner: EMF Broadcasting
Nat'l Network: Air 1
Arbitron Metro Market: Bismarck, ND *Format:* Alternative, Christian *No. News Employees:* 3 *Target Audience:* 18-35; Judeo Christian female
Darrell Chambliss, Chairman
Alan Mason, COO
Mike Novak, President and CEO
John Clements, Operations Dir
David Pierce, Programming Director
Ed Lenane, News Director
Sam Wallington, Engineering Dir
Richard Hunt, News Reporter
Marya Morgan, News Reporter
Dan Antonelli, Chief Business Development Officer
Eric Moser, Chief Financial Officer
Brian Burger, Vice President of Human Resources
D. Kevin Blair, Secretary and General Counsel

Bismarck-Mandan

KLXX
01-01-1925; 1270 khz AM *Hrs Open:* 24; 1 kw-D, ND1; 0.25 kw-N, ND1; N46 48 37 W100 50 10
330 East Kilbourn Avenue, Suite 250, Milwaukee, WI 53202 US
(701) 663-6411, *Fax:* (701) 663-8790
supertalk1270.com
syd.stewart@cumulus.com
License: Bismarck-Mandan, ND held by Cumulus Licensing Corp.
Group Owner: Cumulus Media Inc.; (acq 5-11-98; grpsl)
Nat'l Network: CNN Radio *Nat'l Reps:* Katz Radio
Arbitron Metro Market: Bismarck, ND *Format:* News, News/Talk, 84, Talk *Special Programming:* Sports 6 hrs wkly *Hrs. of News Programming:* news progmg 90 hrs wkly *No. News Employees:* 1 *Target Audience:* 35plus. *Adv. Rates:* 15; 15; 15; 15
Syd Stewart, General Manager
Dean Mastel, Programming Director
Elliot Davidson, Chief Engineer

Bottineau

KBTO
11-09-1980; 101.9 mhz FM *Hrs Open:* 24; 94 kw; 489 ft.; N48 51 10 W100 20 1
P.O. Box 105, Rugby, ND 58368 US
(701) 228-5151, *Fax:* (701) 228-2483
sunnyradio@hotmail.com
License: Bottineau, Bottineau County, ND held by Programmers Broadcasting Inc.
Group Owner: Programmers Broadcasting Inc.; (acq 1-2-2002; $595,000).
Nat'l Network: ABC *Regional Network:* American Ag
Arbitron Metro Market: Bottineau, ND *Format:* Country *Hrs. of News Programming:* News progmg 15 hrs wkly *Adv. Rates:* 11.88; 9.90; 9.90; 9.90
John Kircher, President
Jean Kircher, Operations Dir
Jean Schemmp, Station Manager
J. Davis, General Sales Mgr
Jeff Bliss, Chief Engineer

Bowman

KPOK
08-09-1980; 1340 khz AM *Hrs Open:* 24; 1 kw-U, ND1; N46 10 48 W103 22 12
PO Box 829, Bowman, ND 58623 US
(701) 523-3883, *Fax:* (701) 523-3885
www.kpokradio.com
kpok@ndsupernet.com
License: Bowman, ND held by Tri-State Communications Inc.
Nat'l Network: Westwood One
Format: Country *Special Programming:* Farm 2 hrs wkly *Hrs. of News Programming:* news progmg 14 hrs wkly *No. News Employees:* 1 *Target Audience:* 25-54.
Larry Kemnitz, President
Richard Peterson, Operations Dir
Brian Fischer, General Manager

Burlington

KWGO
01-01-2005; 102.9 mhz FM *Hrs Open:* 24; 98 kw; 512 ft.; N48 3 4 W101 20 23
US
(701) 852-7449, *Fax:* (701) 837-6925
pbiminot@srt.com
License: Burlington, Ward County, ND held by Programmers Broadcasting Inc.
Group Owner: Programmers Broadcasting Inc.
Arbitron Metro Market: Burlington, ND *Format:* Adult Contemp *Hrs. of News Programming:* News progmg 5 hrs wkly *Target Audience:* 18-49.
John Kircher, President
Jean Kircher, Operations Dir
Jean Schemmp, Station Manager
J. Davis, General Sales Mgr
Jeff Bliss, Chief Engineer

Cannon Ball

KXRV
107.5 mhz FM; 100 kw; 778 ft.; N46 34 19 W100 47 42
US
(701) 751-4757, *Fax:* (701) 751-4312
www.mojo1075.com
mojo@mojo1075.com
License: Cannon Ball, Sioux County, ND held by World Radio Link Inc.
Group Owner: World Radio Link Inc.
Arbitron Metro Market: Bismarck, ND *Format:* Contemporary Hits/Top 40, Adult Contemp
Bob Denver, Owner/General Manager

Carrington

KDAK
10-16-1961; 1600 khz AM *Hrs Open:* 24; 0.5 kw-D, ND1; 0.09 kw-N, ND1; N47 25 43 W99 5 3
Mailing Address: 232 Third Street, Ne, Valley City, ND 58072 US
Second Address: Box1170, Jamestown, ND 58402
(701) 652-3151, *Fax:* (701) 652-2916
kdakam@daktel.com
License: Carrington, ND held by Two Rivers Broadcasting Inc.
Group Owner: Robert Ingstad Broadcast Properties; (acq 7-1-94)
Nat'l Network: ABC *Regional Network:* N.D. News Net.
Format: Country, News *Target Audience:* 30 plus.
Janice Ingstad, President
Dave Reed, Station Manager

KXGT
01-01-1997; 98.3 mhz FM; 100 kw; 866 ft.; N47 5 38 W99 2 11
Mailing Address: 232 Third Street, Ne, Valley City, ND 58072 US
Second Address: 2625 8th Avenue SW, Jamestown, ND 58401
(701) 252-1400, *Fax:* (701) 252-1402
www.750thegame.com
License: Carrington, Foster County, ND held by Two Rivers Broadcasting Inc.
Group Owner: Robert Ingstad Broadcast Properties
Arbitron Metro Market: Portland, OR *Format:* Adult Contemp
Dave Reed, General Manager
Bill Ashenden, Director of Sales
Scott Mahalick, Programming Director

Cavalier

KAOC
09-29-1998; 105.1 mhz FM *Hrs Open:* 24; 100 kw; 764 ft.; N48 38 38 W97 58 46
232 3rd Street, Ne, Valley City, ND 58072 US
(701) 256-1080, *Fax:* (701) 256-1081
www.maverick105fm.com
kndkicksbs@utma.com
License: Cavalier, Pembina County, ND held by Simmons Broadcasting Inc.
Group Owner: Simmons Broadcasting Inc.; (acq 9-7-2004; $1).
Arbitron Metro Market: Langdon, ND *Format:* Country
Jen Taylor, Operations Dir
Bob Simmons, General Manager

Devils Lake

KDLR
01-25-1925; 1240 khz AM; 1 kw-U, ND1; N48 6 42 W98 50 43
400 12th Ave., Devils Lake, ND 58301 US
(701) 662-7563, *Fax:* (701) 662-7564
lrradioworks.com
kdlrkdvl@stellarnet.com
License: Devils Lake, ND held by Double Z Broadcasting Inc.
Group Owner: Lake Region Radio Works; (acq 1-1-2003; $820,000 with KDVL(FM) Devils Lake)
Arbitron Metro Market: Devils Lake, ND *Format:* Country, News *Special Programming:* Minnesota Twins baseball, Vikings football *Target Audience:* 25 plus; general
Curt Teigen, President
Roger Mertens, General Sales Mgr
Eric Arndt, News Director

KDVL
01-01-1967; 102.5 mhz FM *Hrs Open:* 24; 100 kw; 469 ft.; N47 59 16 W98 55 59
Mailing Address: 400 12th Ave., Devils Lake, ND 58301 US
Second Address: 400 12 Ave., Devils Lake, ND 58301
(701) 662-7563, *Fax:* (701) 662-7564
lrradioworks.com
kdlrkdvl@stellarnet.com
License: Devils Lake, Ramsey County, ND held by Double Z Broadcasting Inc.
Group Owner: Lake Region Radio Works; (acq 1-1-2003; $820,000 with KDLR(AM) Devils Lake).
Arbitron Metro Market: Devil's Lake, ND *Format:* Oldies *No. News Employees:* 1 *Target Audience:* 18-54.
Curt Teigen, President
Roger Mertens, General Sales Mgr
Bob Gunderson, Programming Director
Eric Arndt, News Director
Kara Danelle, Disc Jockey
Mark Beighley, Sports Commentator
Paul Clementich, Traffic Manager

KQZZ
08-01-1996; 96.7 mhz FM *Hrs Open:* 24; 38 kw; 561 ft.; N47 58 49 W99 3 11
232 Third Street, Ne, Valley City, ND 58072 US
(701) 662-7563, *Fax:* (701) 662-7564
kdlrkdul@stellarnet.com
License: Devils Lake, Ramsey County, ND held by Two Rivers Broadcasting Inc.
Group Owner: Robert Ingstad Broadcast Properties; (acq 3-11-99; $250,000)
Format: Adult Contemp
Curt Teigen, General Manager

KZZY
03-01-1984; 103.5 mhz FM *Hrs Open:* 24; 100 kw; 453 ft.; N47 58 49 W99 3 11
C/O Fisher Wayland: Ddo, 2001 Penn Ave NW Ste 400, Washington, DC 20006 US
(701) 662-7563, *Fax:* (701) 662-7564
www.lrradioworks.com/kzzy
kzzyfm@stellarnet.com
License: Devils Lake, Ramsey County, ND held by Double Z Broadcasting Inc.
Group Owner: Lake Region Radio Works; (acq 4-11-90).
Arbitron Metro Market: Devils Lake, ND *Format:* Country *No. News Employees:* 1
Curt Teigen, General Manager
Roger Mertens, General Sales Mgr
Rob Hendricks, Programming Director
Kaye Schwab, News Director

***KDVI**
01-01-2007; 89.9 mhz FM; 0.25 kw; 171 ft.; N48 8 5 W98 46 20
Rebroadcasts: Rebroadcasts WAFR(FM) Tupelo, MS 100%
P.O. Box 1458, Washington, DC 20013 US
(662) 844-5036, *Fax:* (662) 842-6791
www.afr.net
contact@afa.net
License: Devils Lake, Ramsey County, ND held by American Family Association.
Group Owner: American Family Radio; (acq 6-9-2006)
Nat'l Network: American Family Radio
Arbitron Metro Market: Devils Lake, ND *Format:* Christian

RADIO - U.S.

Donald E. Wildmon, Founder
Buster Wilson, General Manager
Jennifer Hagman, Programming Director

***KPPD**
91.7 mhz FM; 24 kw; 703 ft.; N48 3 47.8 W99 20 8.7
US
(701) 241-6900, *Fax:* (701) 239-7650
www.prairiepublic.org
info@prairiepublic.org
License: Devils Lake, Ramsey County, ND held by Prairie Public Broadcasting Inc.
Arbitron Metro Market: Devils Lake, ND *Format:* Jazz, Triple A
John Harris, President & CEO
John Harris, General Manager
Dave Thompson, News Director
Jack Anderson, Engineering Dir
Ann Clark, Director of Development
Bob Dambach, Director of Television
Troy Davis, Membership Manager
RussellFord-Dunker, Business Development Manager
John Gast, Director of Finance
Barbara Gravel, Production Manager

Dickinson

KCAD
11-20-1996; 99.1 mhz FM *Hrs Open:* 24; 100 kw; 400 ft.; N46 56 9 W102 43 55
427 Bedford Road, Pleasantville, NY 10570 US
(701) 227-1876, *Fax:* (701) 483-1959
www.roughridercountry.net
clearaudio@clearchannel.com
License: Dickinson, Stark County, ND held by CC Licenses LLC
Group Owner: Clear Channel Communications Inc.; (acq 9-1-2000; grpsl).
Nat'l Network: AP Radio; Jones Radio Networks
Arbitron Metro Market: Dickinson, ND *Format:* Country *Target Audience:* 16-50; general
Jim Lowe, General Manager
Bill Palenuk, Programming Director

KDIX
01-01-1947; 1230 khz AM *Hrs Open:* 24
119 Second Avenue, West, Dickinson, ND 58601 US
(701) 225-5133(800) 934-1230, *Fax:* (701) 225-4136
www.kdix.net
kdix@kdix.net
License: Dickinson, ND held by Starrdak Inc.
Nat'l Network: CBS
Arbitron Metro Market: Dickinson, ND *Format:* Adult Contemp, Oldies *Special Programming:* College sports *Hrs. of News Programming:* news progmg 6 hrs wkly *No. News Employees:* 8 *Target Audience:* 35-60.*Adv. Rates:* 10.85; 10.85; 10.85; 8.85
Lee Leiss, Chairman
Rod Kleinjan, Operations Dir

***KDPR**
10-12-1987; 89.9 mhz FM *Hrs Open:* 24; 12.5 kw; 492 ft.; N46 43 34 W102 54 56 *Rebroadcasts:* Rebroadcast KCND(FM) Bismark 100%
P.O. Box 3240, Fargo, ND 58108 US
(701) 241-6900, *Fax:* (701) 239-7650
www.prairiepublic.org
program@prairiepublic.org
License: Dickinson, Stark County, ND held by Prairie Public Broadcasting Inc.
Nat'l Network: PRI; NPR
Arbitron Metro Market: Bismarck, ND *Format:* Jazz, News *Special Programming:* American Indian 2 hrs, folk 6 hrs wkly *Hrs. of News Programming:* news progmg 40 hrs wkly *No. News Employees:* 2 *Target Audience:* General.
John Harris, CEO/COO
John Harris, President
John Peterson, Operations Dir
Bill Thomas, General Manager
Steve Wennblom, Programming Director
Dave Thompson, News Director
Stephanie Chimeziri, Special Events Coordinator

KLTC
07-04-1978; 1460 khz AM *Hrs Open:* 24; 5 kw-D, DAN; 5 kw-N, DAN; N46 50 54 W102 49 49
427 Bedford Road, Pleasantville, NY 10570 US
(701) 227-1876, *Fax:* (701) 483-1959
www.1460kltc.com
clearaudio@clearchannel.com
License: Dickinson, ND held by CC Licenses LLC
Group Owner: Clear Channel Communications Inc.
Nat'l Reps: Hyett/Ramsland
Arbitron Metro Market: Dickinson, ND *Format:* Country *Target Audience:* General.

Dana Demerjiah, Operations Dir
Pat McClean, General Manager
Cristina Valarezo, General Sales Mgr
Jose Santos, Programming Director
Gloria Salvador, News Director
Manny Garcia, Chief Engineer

KZRX
08-15-1983; 92.1 mhz FM *Hrs Open:* 5 AM-midnight; 17 kw; 400 ft.; N46 56 9 W102 43 55
427 Bedford Road, Suite 300, Pleasantville, NY 10570 US
(701) 227-1876, *Fax:* (701) 483-1959
www.kzrx921.com/
clearaudio@clearchannel.com
License: Dickinson, Stark County, ND held by CC Licenses LLC.
Group Owner: Clear Channel Communications Inc.; (acq 9-1-2000; grpsl).
Nat'l Reps: Hyett/Ramsland
Arbitron Metro Market: Dickinson, ND *No. News Employees:* 1 *Target Audience:* 18-45.
Jim Lowe, General Manager
Don Reisenauer, General Sales Mgr
Chad Barta, Programming Director
Kim Kramer, News Director
Brian Funk, Chief Engineer

Fargo

***KDSU**
01-17-1966; 91.9 mhz FM *Hrs Open:* 24; 100 kw; 991 ft.; N47 0 48 W97 11 37
PO Box 5347, Fargo, ND 58105 US
(701) 241-6900, *Fax:* (701) 231-8899
www.prairiepublic.org
info@kdsufm.com
License: Fargo, Cass County, ND held by North Dakota State University.
Nat'l Network: NPR; PRI *Wire Services:* AP
Arbitron Metro Market: Fargo-Moorhead, ND-MN *Format:* Variety/Diverse *Hrs. of News Programming:* news progmg 45 hrs wkly *No. News Employees:* 3 *Target Audience:* 24 plus; general
John Harris, CEO/COO
John Harris, President
John Peterson, Operations Dir
Bill Thomas, General Manager
Nancy Wood, General Sales Mgr
Steve Wennblom, Programming Director

***KFBN**
12-08-1997; 88.7 mhz FM; 30 kw horiz, 100 kw vert; 869 ft.; N47 0 48 W97 11 37
2500 18th Street South, Fargo, ND 58103 US
(701) 232-5500, *Fax:* (701) 241-4260
www.kfbn.org
info@kfbfm.com
License: Fargo, Cass County, ND held by Fargo Baptist Church.
Arbitron Metro Market: Fargo-Moorhead, ND-MN *Format:* News
T.C. Scheving, President
Michael Jordahl, Operations Dir
T.C. Scheving, General Manager
Tim Schaefer, Station Manager

KFGO
03-14-1948; 790 khz AM; 5 kw-D, DAN; 5 kw-N, DAN; N46 43 5 W96 48 5
Mailing Address: 1020 25th Street South, Fargo, ND 58103 US
Second Address: P.O. 10097, Fargo, ND 58106
(701) 237-5346, *Fax:* (701) 237-0980
www.kfgo.com
studio@kfgo.com
License: Fargo, ND held by Radio Fargo-Moorhead Inc.
Group Owner: Radio Fargo-Moorhead Inc.; (acq 1-19-2007; grpsl)
Nat'l Network: CBS Radio *Regional Network:* MNN *Nat'l Reps:* Eastman Radio *Wire Services:* AP
Arbitron Metro Market: Fargo-Moorhead, ND-MN *Format:* News, News/Talk, 86 *No. News Employees:* 4 *Target Audience:* 25+
Nancy Odney, COO
Joel Heitkamp, Operations Dir
Jack Sunday, Programming Director

KRWK
02-23-1984; 101.9 mhz FM; 96 kw; 1001 ft.; N47 0 36 W97 11 41
Mailing Address: 1020 25th Street South, Fargo, ND 58103 US
Second Address: 1020 25th St. S., Fargo, ND 58103
(701) 237-5346, *Fax:* (701) 237-0980
www.rock102online.com
studio@rock102online.com
License: Fargo, Cass County, ND held by Radio Fargo-Moorhead Inc.
Group Owner: Radio Fargo-Moorhead Inc.

Nat'l Reps: Eastman Radio
Arbitron Metro Market: Fargo-Moorhead, ND-MN *Format:* Classic Rock *Target Audience:* Men 25 - 54
Nancy Odney, COO
John Austin, Operations Dir
Bret Amundson, Programming Director

***KFNW-FM**
03-12-1965; 97.9 mhz FM *Hrs Open:* 24; 100 kw; 1001 ft.; N47 0 36 W97 11 41
3003 Snelling Ave.North, Roseville, MN 55113 US
(701) 282-5910, *Fax:* (701) 282-5781
www.kfnw.org
knfw@knfw.org
License: Fargo, Cass County, ND held by Northwestern College.
Group Owner: Northwestern College & Radio
Arbitron Metro Market: Fargo-Moorhead, ND-MN *Format:* Christian *Target Audience:* 25-54.
Desiree Smith, General Manager

KPFX
01-04-1993; 107.9 mhz FM *Hrs Open:* 24; 100 kw; 659 ft.; N46 32 46 W96 37 39
Mailing Address: P.O. Box 9439, Fargo, ND 58103 US
Second Address: 2720 Seventh Ave. S., Fargo, ND 58103
(701) 237-4500, *Fax:* (701) 235-9082
www.1079thefox.com/
studio@1079thefox.com
License: Fargo, Cass County, ND held by Monterey Licenses LLC.
Group Owner: Triad Broadcasting Co. L.L.C.; (acq 8-18-99; grpsl).
Nat'l Reps: Christal
Arbitron Metro Market: Fargo-Moorhead, ND-MN *Format:* Classic Rock *No. News Employees:* 4 *Target Audience:* 25-54; skews male
Micheal Kapel, Operations Dir
Micheal Brooks, General Manager
David Howland, General Sales Mgr
Moose Johnson, Programming Director
Dave Jacobs, Mornings Host

WDAY
05-22-1922; 970 khz AM *Hrs Open:* 24
301 Eight St. S. Po 2466, Fargo, ND 58103 US
(701) 237-6500, *Fax:* (701) 241-5253
www.wday.com
wday@wday.com
License: Fargo, ND held by Forum Communications Co. Inc.
Group Owner: Forum Communications Co.
Nat'l Network: ABC *Regional Network:* American Ag *Nat'l Reps:* Christal *Wire Services:* NWS (National Weather Service)
Arbitron Metro Market: Fargo-Moorhead, ND-MN *Format:* News, News/Talk, 84, Talk *Hrs. of News Programming:* news progmg 35 hrs wkly *No. News Employees:* 3 *Target Audience:* 35-64.
William Marcil Sr., CEO
Mark Prather, General Manager
Carol Anhorn, General Sales Mgr
Ben Ziegler, Programming Director
Steven Wagner, News Director
Dave Johnson, Chief Engineer

WDAY-FM
01-01-1965; 93.7 mhz FM *Hrs Open:* 24; 100 kw; 1007 ft.; N47 0 36 W97 11 41
Mailing Address: 2501 13th Avenue, Sw, Fargo, ND 58103 US
Second Address: P.O. Box 10097, Fargo, ND 58106
(701) 237-4487, *Fax:* (701) 235-0980
www.y94.com
studio@y94.com
License: Fargo, Cass County, ND held by Radio Fargo-Moorhead Inc.
Group Owner: Radio Fargo-Moorhead Inc.; (acq 1-19-2007; grpsl)
Nat'l Reps: Eastman Radio
Arbitron Metro Market: Fargo-Moorhead, ND-MN *Format:* Contemporary Hits/Top 40 *Target Audience:* Adults 18 - 44
Nancy Odeny, COO
JT, Programming Director

KVOX
01-01-2007; 740 khz AM
Mailing Address: US
Second Address: P.O. Box 10097, Fargo, ND 58106
(701) 237-5346, *Fax:* (701) 237-0980
www.740thefan.com
studio@740thefan.com
License: Fargo, ND held by Radio Fargo-Moorhead Inc.
Group Owner: Radio Fargo-Moorhead Inc.; (acq 7-31-2007)
Nat'l Network: Fox Sports *Nat'l Reps:* Eastman Radio
Arbitron Metro Market: Fargo, ND *Format:* Sports *Target Audience:* Men 25-54

Nancy Odney, COO
Tank McNamara, Programming Director

Flasher

KKBO
01-01-2008; 105.9 mhz FM; 100 kw; 912 ft.; N46 35 23 W100 47 39
US
(701) 751-8000
www.1059bobfm.com
License: Flasher, Morton County, ND held by Connoisseur Media of Bismarck LLC.
Group Owner: Connoisseur Media LLC
Arbitron Metro Market: Flasher, ND *Format:* Adult Contemp
Michael Driscoll, General Manager

Fort Totten

*KABU
03-15-1999; 90.7 mhz FM; 28 kw; 397 ft.; N47 59 31 W98 56 53
Mailing Address: P.O. Box 7, Fort Totten, ND 58335 US
Second Address: KABU Radio Station, 7889 Hwy. 57, St. Michael, ND 58370-9000
(701) 766-1995, *Fax:* (701) 766-4774
kabu@stellarnet.com
License: Fort Totten, Benson County, ND held by Dakota Circle Tipi Inc.
Arbitron Metro Market: Fort Totten, ND *Format:* Public Affairs, Variety/Diverse *Special Programming:* American Indian 19 hrs, children 12 hrs, gospel 7 *Target Audience:* General; community on Spirit Lake Nation &surrounding areas to reach all age groups
Adv. Rates: 55; 55; 55; na
John Chaske, General Manager

Four Bears

*KMHA
03-01-1984; 91.3 mhz FM *Hrs Open:* 24; 97 kw; 449 ft.; N47 44 23 W102 43 24
Hcr 3, P.O.Box 1, New Town, ND 58763 US
(701) 627-3333, *Fax:* (701) 627-3376
kmha_fm@restel.net
License: Four Bears, McKenzie County, ND held by Fort Berthold Communications Enterprise.
Format: Variety/Diverse *Special Programming:* American Indian-Mandan/Hidatsa/Arikara 4 hrs, coun *No. News Employees:* 1 *Target Audience:* Ranchers, farmers, Native Americans.
Clarence Sun, Operations Dir
Rose Crow Flies High, General Manager

Georgetown

KLJA(FM)
107.7 mhz FM; 10,500 watts; 154.8 meters; N46 26 43 W97 39 07
57 West South Temple, Suite 700, Salt Lake City, UT 78759
(310) 348-3600
www.lajefa1077.univision.com
License: Georgetown, TX held by Jose J. Garcia Jr.
Population Served: 820,611 *Arbitron Metro Market:* Austin, TX
Dan Wilson, General Manager
Andrew E. Olivera, General Sales Mgr
Claudia Talamantez, Programming Director
Karem Hocking, National Sales Manager

Grafton

KXPO
07-12-1958; 1340 khz AM *Hrs Open:* 6 AM-midnight; 1 kw-U, ND1; N48 23 53 W97 26 56
856 West 12th Street, Grafton, ND 58237 US
(701) 352-0431, *Fax:* (701) 352-0436
www.walshcountydailynews.com
kxpoaj@polarcomm.com
License: Grafton, ND held by KGPC Co.
Nat'l Network: ABC *Regional Network:* American Ag; N.D. News Net. *Wire Services:* AP
Arbitron Metro Market: Grafton, ND *Format:* Country *Special Programming:* Farm 18 hrs, gospel 5 hrs, relg 4 hrs wkly *Hrs. of News Programming:* news progmg 15 hrs wkly *No. News Employees:* 2 *Target Audience:* 30-70.
Del Nygard, President
Andrea Johnston, General Manager
Todd Ingstad, General Sales Mgr
Scott Karnik, News Director
Don Brintmall, Chief Engineer
Sean Ford, Sports Director
Brain James, Marketing Consultant/ CRMC
NanciGale-Wilson, Adminsitrative Assistant/ RMP

KAUJ
09-17-1984; 100.9 mhz FM *Hrs Open:* 24; 3 kw; 125 ft.; N48 23 53 W97 26 56
856 West 12th Street, Grafton, ND 58237 US
(701) 352-0431, *Fax:* (701) 352-0436
kxpoaj@polarcomm.com
License: Grafton, Walsh County, ND
Format: Oldies *Hrs. of News Programming:* news progmg 2 hrs wkly *No. News Employees:* 1 *Target Audience:* 18-60.
Nick Amico, News Director

Grand Forks

*KFJM
03-06-1995; 90.7 mhz FM *Hrs Open:* 24; 4 kw; 112 ft.; N47 54 17 W97 6 53
P.O. Box 8117, Grand Forks, ND 58202 US
(701) 777-2577, *Fax:* (701) 777-4263
http://www.prairiepublic.org/radio/roots-rock-and-jazz/
License: Grand Forks, Grand Forks County, ND held by University of North Dakota.
Nat'l Network: NPR; PRI
Arbitron Metro Market: Grand Forks, ND *Format:* Jazz, Triple A
Special Programming: Blues 3 hrs wkly, car talk 1 hr wkly, *Hrs. of News Programming:* news progmg 15 hrs wkly *No. News Employees:* 3 *TargetAudience:* 25-44; well-educated
Bill Thomas, Operations Dir
Michael Olson, General Manager
Dave Thompson, News Director

KJKJ
08-01-1985; 107.5 mhz FM *Hrs Open:* 24; 100 kw; 456 ft.; N47 57 52 W97 1 46
Mailing Address: 4701 East Lake Harriet Pkwy, Minneapolis, MN 55409 US
Second Address: 505 University Ave., Grand Forks, ND 58203
(701) 746-1417, *Fax:* (701) 746-1410
www.kjkj.com
patmclean@clearchannel.com
License: Grand Forks, Grand Forks County, ND held by Citicasters Licenses L.P.
Group Owner: Clear Channel Communications Inc.; (acq 10-26-99; grpsl).
Arbitron Metro Market: Grand Forks, ND-MN *Format:* Rock/AOR *Hrs. of News Programming:* News progmg 5 hrs wkly *Target Audience:* 18-49.
Jeff Hoberg, General Manager
Pat McLean, Station Manager
Laura Hammack, General Sales Mgr

KKXL
01-01-1941; 1440 khz AM *Hrs Open:* 24; 0.6 kw-D, ND1; 0.3 kw-N, ND1; N47 57 52 W97 1 46
Mailing Address: PO Box 1248, Minnetonka, MN 55345 US
Second Address: 505 University Ave., Grand Forks, ND 58203
(701) 746-1417, *Fax:* (701) 746-1410
www.1440kkxl.com
patmclean@clearchannel.com
License: Grand Forks, ND held by Citicasters Licenses L.P.
Group Owner: Clear Channel Communications Inc.; (acq 10-26-99; grpsl).
Nat'l Network: Jones Radio Networks
Arbitron Metro Market: Grand Forks, ND *Format:* News, Adult Contemp *Hrs. of News Programming:* news progmg 10 hrs wkly *No. News Employees:* 1 *Target Audience:* 25-54; farm community
Pat McLean, General Manager

KKXL-FM
03-01-1975; 92.9 mhz FM; 100 kw; 358 ft.; N47 57 52 W97 1 46
Mailing Address: 4701 East Lake Harriet Parkway, Minneapolis, MN 55409 US
Second Address: 505 University Ave., Grand Forks, ND 58203
(701) 746-1417, *Fax:* (701) 746-1410
www.xl93.com
patmclean@clearchannel.com
License: Grand Forks, Grand Forks County, ND
Arbitron Metro Market: Grand Forks, ND *Format:* Contemporary Hits/Top 40 *Target Audience:* 18-34.
Joe Schwartz, President

KNOX
09-07-1947; 1310 khz AM *Hrs Open:* 24; 5 kw-D, DAN; 5 kw-N, DAN; N47 50 39 W97 1 30
Mailing Address: PO Box 1458, St. Cloud, MN 56301 US
Second Address: Old Belmont Rd. S., Grand Forks, ND 58208
(701) 775-4611, *Fax:* (701) 772-0540
www.leightonbroadcasting.com
License: Grand Forks, ND held by Leighton Enterprises Inc.
Group Owner: Leighton Enterprises Inc.; acq 10-23-96; $1.1 million with co-located FM)
Nat'l Network: ABC *Regional Network:* MNN *Wire Services:* AP
Arbitron Metro Market: Grand Forks, ND *Format:* News, News/Talk, 86 *Hrs. of News Programming:* news progmg 80 hrs wkly *No. News Employees:* 3 *Target Audience:* 35 plus.
Jarrod Thomas, Operations Dir
Jack Hansen, General Manager
Lynn Hodgson, General Sales Mgr
Doug Barrett, News Director

KZGF
02-04-1967; 94.7 mhz FM *Hrs Open:* 24; 100 kw; Ant 325 ft; N48 00 20 W97 04 18
1185 9th St. N.E., Thompson, ND 56301
(701) 775-4611, *Fax:* (701) 772-0540
www.power947rocks.com
License: Grand Forks, Grand Forks County, ND held by Leighton Enterprises Inc.
Group Owner: Leighton Enterprises Inc.
Nat'l Network: ABC
Population Served: 43,765 *Arbitron Metro Market:* Grand Forks, ND-MN *Target Audience:* 18-45.
William Kling, President
Erik Nycklemoe, Operations Dir

*KWTL
10-22-1923; 1370 khz AM *Hrs Open:* 24
P.O. Box 8117, Grand Forks, ND 58202 US
(701) 795-0122
www.youram1370.com
License: Grand Forks, ND held by Real Presence Radio
Arbitron Metro Market: Grand Forks, ND *Format:* Christian
Steve Loegering, President

*KUND-FM
05-30-1976; 89.3 mhz FM; 50 kw; 292 ft.; N48 11 39.8 W97 11 28.4
Box 8117, Grand Forks, ND 58202 US
(701) 241-6900, *Fax:* (701) 239-7650
www.prairiepublic.org
info@prairiepublic.org
License: Grand Forks, Grand Forks County, ND held by University of North Dakota.
Arbitron Metro Market: Grand Forks, ND *Format:* Talk *Special Programming:* New age 5 hrs wkly
John Harris, President & CEO
John Peterson, Operations Dir
Gary Olson, Station Manager
Steve Wennblom, Program Manager
Dave Thompson, News Director
Jack Anderson, Engineering Dir
Beth Bradley, Business DevelopmentRepresentative
Ann Clark, Director of Development
Troy Davis, Membership Manager
John Gast, Director of Finance
Barbara Gravel, Production Manager
Kirstin Lindbery, Executive Assistant

Harvey

KHND
07-21-1981; 1470 khz AM; 1 kw-D, ND1; 0.161 kw-N, ND1; N47 45 23 W99 55 6
Mailing Address: 718 Lincoln Avenue, Harvey, ND 59341 US
Second Address: 718 Lincoln Ave., Harvey, ND 58341
(701) 324-4848, *Fax:* (701) 324-2043
www.khnd1470.com
studio@khnd1470.com
License: Harvey, ND held by Three Way Broadcasting Inc.
Nat'l Network: ABC
Format: Adult Contemp *Special Programming:* weather, news, talk, classic rock programs, polka *Hrs. of News Programming:* 15 hrs News Programing wkly *Target Audience:* 12 -85.
Sheila Jensen, President
Rick Jensen, Operations Dir
Sheila Jensen, General Sales Mgr
Seth David, Sports Director

Harwood

*KKLQ
01-01-2001; 100.7 mhz FM; 40 kw; 328 ft.; N47 8 43 W96 58 18
2001 Pennsylvania Ave,NW, Suite 400, Washington, DC 20006 US
(800) 525-5683, *Fax:* (916) 251-1650
www.klove.com
License: Harwood, Cass County, ND held by Educational Media Foundation.
Group Owner: EMF Broadcasting; (acq 1-8-2004; $750,000).
Nat'l Network: K-Love
Arbitron Metro Market: Fargo-Moorhead *Format:* Christian
Mike Novak, President
John Clements, General Sales Mgr

David Pierce, Programming Director
Ed Lenane, News Director
Sam Wallington, Engineering Dir
Richard Hunt, News Reporter
Marya Morgan, News Reporter

Hazelton

KUSB
01-01-2006; 103.3 mhz FM; 100 kw; 965 ft.; N46 35 23.8 W100 47 46.2
US
(701) 250-6602, *Fax:* (701) 250-6632
License: Hazelton, Emmons County, ND held by Cumulus Licensing LLC.
Group Owner: Cumulus Media Inc.
Arbitron Metro Market: Hazelton, ND *Format:* Country
Syd Stewart, General Manager
Mike Rose, Programming Director
Elliott Davidson, Chief Engineer

Hettinger

KNDC
03-01-1954; 1490 khz AM *Hrs Open:* 12:ooam -11:59pm; 1 kw-U, ND1; N46 1 11 W102 41 33
509 Jade Court, Lemmon, SD 57638 US
(701) 567-2421, *Fax:* (701) 567-4636
www.kndc.com
kndc1490@ndsupernet.com
License: Hettinger, ND held by Schweitzer Media Inc.
Nat'l Network: ABC News/Talk *Regional Network:* N.D. News Net.; S.D. News Net.
Format: Country *Special Programming:* Farm *Hrs. of News Programming:* News progmg 24 hrs wkly *Target Audience:* 24-52; rural residents
Mike Schweitzer, President
Nolan Dix, General Manager

KNDH
102.3 mhz FM; 51 kw; 59 meters; N46 09 12.97 W102 46 24.4
1282 Smallwood Dr., Suite 372, Waldorf, MD
(815) 346-2657, *Fax:* (301) 645-1426
contact@midnationmedia.com
License: Hettinger, Adams County, ND held by Midnation Media LLC
Group Owner: Alma Corp.
Dennis Wallace, General Manager

Hope

KMJO
01-01-2002; 104.7 mhz FM *Hrs Open:* 24; 100 kw; 702 ft.; N47 3 15 W97 24 44
Mailing Address: 7901 Stoneridge Drive, Cheyenne, WY 82009 US
Second Address: P.O. Box 10097, Fargo, ND 58106
(701) 297-6656, *Fax:* (701) 237-0980
www.1047popsterfm.com
nancyodney@radiofargomoorhead.com
License: Hope, Steele County, ND held by Radio Fargo-Moorhead Inc.
Group Owner: Radio Fargo-Moorhead Inc.; (acq 1-19-2007; grpsl)
Nat'l Reps: Eastman Radio
Arbitron Metro Market: Fargo, ND *Format:* Contemporary Hits/Top 40, Adult Contemp *Target Audience:* Adults 25-64
Nancy Odney, COO
Nancy Odney, General Manager
Mike Waters, Programming Director
Carlos Quintero, Director of Interactive Marketing

Jamestown

*KPRJ
01-01-1993; 91.5 mhz FM *Hrs Open:* 24; 18.5 kw; 354 ft.; N46 46 36 W98 31 20 *Rebroadcasts:* Rebroadcasts KCND(FM) Bismarck 100%
P.O. Box 3240, Fargo, ND 58108 US
(701) 241-6900, *Fax:* (701) 239-7650
www.prairiepublic.org
info@prairiepublic.org
License: Jamestown, Stutsman County, ND held by Prairie Public Broadcasting Inc.
Nat'l Network: NPR; PRI
Format: Jazz, News *Special Programming:* American Indian 2 hrs, folk 6 hrs wkly *No. News Employees:* 3 *Target Audience:* General.
John Harris, CEO
Duane Lee, Operations Dir
Bill Thomas, General Sales Mgr
David Thompson, News Director

KQDJ
08-12-1954; 1400 khz AM *Hrs Open:* 24; 1 kw-U, ND1; N46 53 37 W98 41 20
Mailing Address: 232 Third St, Ne, Valley City, ND 58072 US
Second Address: 2625 8th Ave. S.W., Jamestown, ND 58401
(701) 252-1400, *Fax:* (701) 252-1402
www.newsdakota.com
bigdog@daktel.com
License: Jamestown, ND held by Two Rivers Broadcasting Inc.
Group Owner: Robert Ingstad Broadcast Properties; (acq 1994; $600,000)
Nat'l Network: Fox Sports
Format: Contemporary Hits/Top 40
Dave Reed, General Manager

KSJB
01-01-1937; 600 khz AM *Hrs Open:* 24; 5 kw-U, DA1; N46 49 3 W98 42 34
Mailing Address: 4700 South Lewis Blvd, Sioux City, IA 51106 US
Second Address: 2400 8th Ave. S. W., Jamestown, ND 58402-1840
(701) 252-3570, *Fax:* (701) 252-1277
www.ksjbam.com
info@ksjbam.com
License: Jamestown, ND held by Chesterman Communications Inc.
Arbitron Metro Market: Jamestown, ND *Format:* Country *Special Programming:* Farm 12 hrs wkly *Hrs. of News Programming:* news progmg 13 hrs wkly *No. News Employees:* 1 *Target Audience:* 25 plus.
Patrick Pfieffer, General Manager
Patrick Pfeiffer, General Sales Mgr

KSJZ
01-01-1968; 93.3 mhz FM *Hrs Open:* 6 AM-midnight; 100 kw; 449 ft.; N46 49 6.6 W98 42 38.7
Mailing Address: 4700 South Lewis Blvd., Sioux City, IA 51106 US
Second Address: 2400 8th Ave. S. W., Jamestown, ND 58402
(701) 252-3570, *Fax:* (701) 252-1277
www.ksjbam.com
info@ksjbam.com
License: Jamestown, Stutsman County, ND
Arbitron Metro Market: Jamestown, ND *Format:* Adult Contemp *Target Audience:* 28-52; 60% male, 40% female
Marvin Sanders, General Manager
Bonnie Weatherly, Office Manager

KYNU
08-25-1984; 95.5 mhz FM *Hrs Open:* 24; 100 kw; 646 ft.; N46 56 21 W98 18 30
Mailing Address: 232 Third Street, Ne, Valley City, ND 58072 US
Second Address: 2625 8th Ave. S.W., Jamestown, ND 58402
(701) 252-1400, *Fax:* (701) 252-1402
License: Jamestown, Stutsman County, ND held by Two Rivers Broadcasting Inc.
Group Owner: Robert Ingstad Broadcast Properties
Nat'l Network: ABC
Format: Country *Target Audience:* 18-65.
Dave Reed, General Manager

*KLUU
01-01-2008; 89.1 mhz FM; 1.7 kw vert; 285 ft.; N46 50 5 W98 41 31 *Rebroadcasts:* Rebroadcasts KLVR(FM) Middletown, CA 100%
1425 North Market Blvd, Suite 9, Sacramento, CA 95834 US
(800) 877-5600, *Fax:* (916) 251-1650
www.klove.com
License: Jamestown, Stutsman County, ND held by Educational Media Foundation.
Group Owner: EMF Broadcasting
Nat'l Network: K-Love
Arbitron Metro Market: Tulsa, OK *Format:* Christian
Mike Novak, President

*KJTW
89.9 mhz FM; 0.4 kw; 154 ft.; N46 53 30 W98 42 46
88 Casey Jones Blvd, Jackson, TN 38305 US
(662) 844-5036, *Fax:* (662) 842-7798
www.afr.net
contact@afa.net
License: Jamestown, Stutsman County, ND held by American Family Association.
Group Owner: American Family Radio; (acq 8-27-2007)
Nat'l Network: American Family Radio
Arbitron Metro Market: Jamestown, ND *Format:* Christian
Donald E. Wildmon, Founder
Buster Wilson, General Manager
Jennifer Hagman, Programming Director

Kindred

KFNL
06-06-1986; 92.7 mhz FM *Hrs Open:* 24; 25 kw; 328 ft.; N46 39 37 W96 43 1
1020 25th Street South, Fargo, ND 58108 US
(651) 631-5000, *Fax:* (612) 631-5086
License: Kindred, Cass County, ND held by Northwestern College.
Group Owner: Northwestern College & Radio; (acq 1-19-2007; donation)
Arbitron Metro Market: Fargo-Moorhead, ND-MN *Format:* Rock/AOR
Robert Ingstad, President

Langdon

KNDK
06-27-1967; 1080 khz AM *Hrs Open:* 16
Route 5 Box 9, Langdon, ND 58249 US
(701) 256-1080, *Fax:* (701) 256-1081
www.kndkradio.com
kndk1080@utma.com
License: Langdon, ND held by KNDK Inc.
Group Owner: Simmons Broadcasting Inc.; (acq 12-1-87).
Nat'l Network: CBS
Format: Country, News, 62, Talk *Special Programming:* Farm 12 hrs, relg 4 hrs wkly *Hrs. of News Programming:* news progmg 42 hrs wkly *No. News Employees:* 3 *Target Audience:* 25 plus.
Bob Simmons, President
Brain Matthews, Operations Dir
Courtney Bodnar, Traffic Manager
Diane Simmons, CFO

KNDK-FM
01-15-1992; 95.7 mhz FM *Hrs Open:* 24; 6 kw; 328 ft.; N48 45 18 W98 21 38
Route 5, P.O. Box 9, Langdon, ND 58249 US
(701) 256-1080, *Fax:* (701) 256-1081
www.kndkradio.com
kndk1080@utma.com
License: Langdon, Cavalier County, ND
Group Owner: Simmons Broadcasting Inc.; (Acq 11-20-91; $90,000;
Format: Adult Contemp
Bob Simmons, President
Brain Matthews, Operations Dir
Courtney Bodnar, Traffic Manager
Diane Simmons, CFO

Lisbon

KQLX
11-01-1984; 890 khz AM
PO Box 1008, Lisbon, ND 58054 US
(701) 356-1156, *Fax:* (701) 356-1155
www.agnews890.com
studio@agnews890.com
License: Lisbon, ND held by Loomis Broadcasting Inc.
Regional Network: Agrinet
Arbitron Metro Market: Fargo-Moorhead *Format:* Agriculture, News, 62, Talk *Special Programming:* Farm 18 hrs, Gospel 6 hrs wkly *Hrs. of News Programming:* news progmg 5 hrs wkly *No. News Employees:* 1 *TargetAudience:* 18-65; farmers *Adv. Rates:* 22; 22; 17; 12
Terry Loomis, President
Rita Loomis, Operations Dir
Lisa A. Hook, General Manager
Jeff Ogden, Programming Director
Emily West, Promotions Manager

KQLX-FM
10-24-1986; 106.1 mhz FM; 100 kw; 715 ft.; N46 44 39 W97 25 38
PO Box 1008, Lisbon, ND 58054 US
(701) 356-1156, *Fax:* (701) 356-1155
www.thunder1061.com
thunderstudio@thunder1061.com
License: Lisbon, Ransom County, ND held by Sheyenne Valley Broadcasting Inc.
Nat'l Network: CNN Radio
Arbitron Metro Market: Fargo-Moorhead *Format:* Country *Hrs. of News Programming:* news progmg 5 hrs wkly *No. News Employees:* 1 *Target Audience:* 18-54; general *Adv. Rates:* 18; 18; 14; 10
Richard Jenkins, President
Broadway Boe, Operations Dir
Keith Whipple, General Sales Mgr
Broadway Boe, Programming Director
Ed Lenane, News Director
Sam Wallington, Engineering Dir
Eric Allen, National Sales Manager

KarenJohnson, News Reporter
Marya Morgan, News Reporter
Richard Hunt, News Reporter

Mandan

KNDR
06-19-1977; 104.7 mhz FM *Hrs Open:* 24; 100 kw; 853 ft.; N46 35 11 W100 48 20
Mailing Address: PO Box 516, Mandan, ND 58554 US
Second Address: ND
(701) 663-2345, *Fax:* (701) 663-2347
www.kndr.fm
kndr@midconetwork.com
License: Mandan, Morton County, ND held by Central Dakota Enterprise Inc.
Wire Services: AP
Arbitron Metro Market: Bismarck, ND *Format:* Adult Contemp, Christian *Target Audience:* 25-54; women and famlies (with children)
Paul Grosz, Chairman
Brad Bales, General Manager
LaRue Goetz, Vice Chairman

Mayville

KMSR
10-20-1967; 1520 khz AM *Hrs Open:* Sunrise-sunset; 2.5 kw-D; N47 29 45 W97 21 03
Box 216, Mayville, ND 58257
(701) 786-2335, *Fax:* (701) 786-2268
www.kmavradio.com
sports@kmavradio.com
License: Mayville, Traill County, ND held by KMSR Inc.
Nat'l Network: ESPN Radio *Regional Network:* N.D. News Net.
Population Served: 150,000*Target Audience:* 25-55. *Adv. Rates:* 14; 14; 14; 10
Marylou Keating, President
Dan Keating, General Manager
Mary Keating, General Sales Mgr
Greg Keating, Promotions Manager
Dan Keating, News Director
Rich Haraldson, Executive Vice President

KMAV-FM
01-10-1977; 105.5 mhz FM *Hrs Open:* 24; 25 kw; Ant 328 ft; N47 29 45 W97 21 03
Box 216, Mayville, ND 58257
(701) 786-2335, *Fax:* (701) 786-2268
kmav.com
License: Mayville, Traill County, ND held by KMSR Inc.
Nat'l Network: CBS; ESPN; Premiere; Dial Global *Regional Network:* Red River Farm Network; Dakota News Network; American DC Network
Population Served: 150,000*Target Audience:* 18-54 *Adv. Rates:* $7.00 30s; $11.00 60s
Marylou Keating, President
Dan Keating, General Manager

Minot

KCJB
09-01-1950; 910 khz AM
Mailing Address: P. O. Box 1686, Minot, ND 58701 US
Second Address: PO Box 10
701-852-4646, *Fax:* (701) 852-1390
www.kcjb910.com/main.html
RickStensby@ClearChannel.com
License: Minot, ND held by CC Licenses LLC.
Group Owner: Clear Channel Communications Inc.; (acq 1-12-2000; grpsl).
Nat'l Network: Fox News Radio
Arbitron Metro Market: Bismarck, ND *Format:* Country *Special Programming:* Loc sports, various loc talk segments, farm 4 hrs wkly *Target Audience:* 25 plus.
Allison Bostow, Operations Dir
Rick Stensby, General Manager
Allison Bostow, Operations Manager
Mike Budeau, Accounts Receivable
Dave Lehner, Mornings/Web Administrator

KHRT
11-17-1957; 1320 khz AM *Hrs Open:* 24; 2.5 kw-D, ND1; 0.31 kw-N, ND1; N48 11 48 W101 14 0
Mailing Address: P.O. Box 1210, Minot, ND 58702 US
Second Address: 3600 County Rd. 195 S., Minot, ND 58702
(701) 852-3789, *Fax:* (701) 852-8498
www.khrt.com
khrt@srt.com
*License:*Minot, ND held by Faith Broadcasting Inc.
Format: Gospel, News, 62, Talk, Religious *Special Programming:* Family 10 hrs wkly *Hrs. of News Programming:* news progmg 10 hrs wkly *No. News Employees:* 1 *Target Audience:* 25-54; large families, loyal,upper-income professionals
Richard Leavitt, President
Roy Leavitt, General Manager
John Kennedy, News Director
John McCann, Chief Engineer
Johas Nelson, Music Director
Marcia Leavitt, Traffic Manager

KIZZ
09-07-1968; 93.7 mhz FM *Hrs Open:* 24; 100 kw; 554 ft.; N48 3 11 W101 26 4
Mailing Address: 427 Bedford Road, Pleasantville, NY 10570 US
Second Address: 101 S. Main St., Minot, ND 58702
(701) 852-2494, *Fax:* (701) 852-1390
minotprod@clearchannel.com
License: Minot, Ward County, ND held by CC Licenses LLC.
Group Owner: Clear Channel Communications Inc.; (acq 9-1-2000; grpsl).
Format: Adult Contemp *Hrs. of News Programming:* news progmg 3 hrs wkly *No. News Employees:* 1 *Target Audience:* 25-54.
Allison Bostow, Operations Dir
Rick Stensby, General Manager
Don May, News Director
Brian Funk, Chief Engineer
Cat Collins, Disc Jockey
Tim Webster, Disc Jockey
Bill Allen, Disc Jockey
Rhonda Jensen, Traffic Manager

***KMPR**
11-23-1983; 88.9 mhz FM *Hrs Open:* 24; 50 kw; 928 ft.; N48 3 3 W101 23 24 *Rebroadcasts:* Rebroadcasts KCND(FM) Bismarck 100%
P.O. Box 3240, Fargo, ND 58108 US
(701) 224-1700, *Fax:* (701) 224-0555
www.prairiepublic.org
info@prairiepublic.org
License: Minot, Ward County, ND held by Prairie Public Broadcasting Inc.
Nat'l Network: PRI; NPR
TV Affiliate: *KSRE(TV) affil. *Format:* Jazz, News *Special Programming:* American Indian 2 hrs, folk 6 hrs wkly *Hrs. of News Programming:* news progmg 40 hrs wkly *No. News Employees:* 2 *Target Audience:* General.
John Harris, CEO
Duane Lee, Operations Dir
Bill Thomas, General Sales Mgr
David Thompson, News Director

KMXA-FM
04-01-1984; 99.9 mhz FM *Hrs Open:* 24; 100 kw; 466 ft.; N48 10 57 W101 31 57
3425 South Broadway, Minot, ND 58701 US
(701) 852-2494, *Fax:* (701) 852-1390
www.mix999fm.com
minotprod@clearchannel.com
License: Minot, Ward County, ND held by CC Licenses LLC.
Group Owner: Clear Channel Communications Inc.; (acq 1-12-2000; grpsl).
Format: Adult Contemp *Hrs. of News Programming:* News progmg 4 hrs wkly *Target Audience:* 25-54; adult upper middle class with teens at home
Allison Bostow, Operations Dir
Rick Stensby, General Manager

KRRZ
10-28-1929; 1390 khz AM; 5 kw-D, ND1; 1 kw-N, ND1; N48 12 45 W101 14 30
427 Bedford Road, Pleasantville, NY 10570 US
(701) 852-4646, *Fax:* (701) 852-1390
www.oldies1390.com
RickStensby@clearchannel.com
License: Minot, ND held by CC Licenses LLC.
Group Owner: Clear Channel Communications Inc.; (acq 9-1-2000; grpsl).
Regional Network: N.D. News Net. *Nat'l Reps:* Roslin
Format: Adult Contemp *Special Programming:* Sports *Target Audience:* 25-54.
Allison Bostow, Operations Dir
Rick Stensby, General Manager

KYYX
11-15-1966; 97.1 mhz FM *Hrs Open:* 24; 95 kw; 984 ft.; N48 3 2 W101 20 29
P. O. Box 1686, Minot, ND 58702 US
(701) 852-4646, *Fax:* (701) 852-1390
www.97kicksfm.com/
License: Minot, Ward County, ND held by CC Licenses LLC.
Group Owner: Clear Channel Communications Inc.
Arbitron Metro Market: Minot, ND *Hrs. of News Programming:* news progmg 6 hrs wkly *No. News Employees:* 1 *Target Audience:* 18-49; young families
Allison Bostow, Operations Dir
Rick Stensby, General Manager

KZPR
07-08-1985; 105.3 mhz FM *Hrs Open:* 24; 100 kw; 554 ft.; N48 3 11 W101 26 4
427 Bedford Road, Pleasantville, NY 10570 US
(701) 852-4646, *Fax:* (701) 852-1390
www.1053thefox.com/
License: Minot, Ward County, ND
Group Owner: Clear Channel Communications Inc.
Arbitron Metro Market: Minot, ND *Format:* Classic Rock *Special Programming:* Farm 4 hrs wkly *Hrs. of News Programming:* News progmg 4 hrs wkly
Allison Bostow, Operations Dir
Allison Bostow, General Sales Mgr
Rick Stensby, Programming Director
Rick Anthony, Disc Jockey

KHRT-FM
01-01-1992; 106.9 mhz FM; 50 kw; 344 ft.; N48 9 48 W101 17 55
Mailing Address: P.O. Box 1210, Minot, ND 58702 US
Second Address: 3600 County Rd. 195 S., Minot, ND 58702
(701) 852-3789, *Fax:* (701) 852-8498
www.khrt.com
khrt@srt.com
License: Minot, Ward County, ND held by Faith Broadcasting Inc.
Arbitron Metro Market: Minot, ND *Format:* Christian
Johas Nelson, Programming Director

New England

KLTQ
01-01-2008; 95.7 mhz FM; 700 w; Ant 610 ft; N46 27 48 W102 58 46
5331 Mt. Alifan Dr., San Diego, CA
(858) 277-4991, *Fax:* (858) 277-1365
License: New England, Hettinger County, ND held by Horizon Christian Fellowship.
Group Owner: Horizon Christian Fellowship; (acq 2-9-2006; grpsl)

Mike MacIntosh, President

Oakes

KDDR
07-31-1959; 1220 khz AM; 1 kw-D, ND1; 0.327 kw-N, ND1; N46 7 23 W98 5 21 *Rebroadcasts:* Rebroadcast KOVC(AM) Valley City
232 Third Street Ne, Valley City, ND 58072 US
(701) 845-1490, *Fax:* (701) 845-1245
kddr@drtel.net
License: Oakes, ND held by Sioux Valley Broadcasting Co.
Group Owner: Robert Ingstad Broadcast Properties; (acq 2-1-93; $85,000;
Regional Network: N.D. News Net.
Format: Country, News *Target Audience:* 28-59; farm/agriculture
Tim Ost, General Manager
Terry James, Programming Director

Rugby

KZZJ
08-21-1961; 1450 khz AM *Hrs Open:* 24; 1 kw-U, ND1; N48 21 14 W99 59 31
Highway 2, East, Rugby, ND 58368 US
(701) 776-5254, *Fax:* (701) 776-6154
www.kzzj.com
kzzj@kzzj.com
License: Rugby, ND held by Rugby Broadcasters Inc.
Arbitron Metro Market: Rugby, ND *Format:* Country *No. News Employees:* 1 *Target Audience:* 25-65. *Adv. Rates:* 8; 7; 6; 5
Jay Schmalz, Operations Dir
Lila D. Harstad, General Manager
Cheryl Holm, General Sales Mgr
Bruce Allen, News Director
Dee Dee Bishoff, Traffic Manager

South Heart

KDXN
11-01-2008; 105.7 mhz FM; 100 kw; 545 ft.; N46 56 53 W102 59 25
US
(701) 483-8344, *Fax:* (701) 483-8345
www.themix1057.com
License: South Heart, Stark County, ND held by Western Edge Media LLC

Arbitron Metro Market: South Heart, ND *Format:* Country
Bill Palanuk, President
Blake Messer, Operations Dir

Tioga

KTGO
02-27-1966; 1090 khz AM; 1 kw-D, NDD; N48 23 30 W102 56 12
Mailing Address: Box 457, Tioga, ND 58852 US
Second Address: 301 S.E. 2nd St., Tioga, ND 58852
(701) 664-3322(701) 664-3432, *Fax:* (701) 664-3322
ktgo@wccray.com
License: Tioga, ND held by Tioga Broadcasting Corp.
Nat'l Network: CBS
Arbitron Metro Market: Tioga, ND *Format:* Country *Special Programming:* Gospel 11 hrs wkly *Target Audience:* 18-55.
David Guttormson, General Manager
Dustin Moore, Programming Director
Scott Hennen, News Director
Jim Offerdahl, Engineering Dir
Cristi Trulson-Management

KZTW
104.1 mhz FM; 100 kw; 116 m; N48 20 40 W103 12 27
3325 Conservancy Lane, Middleton, WI
(608) 831-8708
License: Tioga, Williams County, ND held by L. Topaz Enterprises Inc.
Dale A. Ganske, President

Valley City

KOVC
10-19-1936; 1490 khz AM *Hrs Open:* 19; 1 kw-U, ND1; N46 54 48 W98 1 2
232 Third Street, Ne, Valley City, ND 58072 US
(701) 845-1490, *Fax:* (701) 845-1245
License: Valley City, ND held by Sioux Valley Broadcasting Co.
Group Owner: Robert Ingstad Broadcast Properties
Format: Country, News, 84 *Hrs. of News Programming:* News progmg 7 hrs wkly *Target Audience:* 25 plus.
Dave Reed, Operations Dir
Tim Ost, General Manager
Kerry Johnson, General Sales Mgr
Ron Lee, Promotions Manager
Ryan Cunningham, News Director
Don Brintnall, Chief Engineer
Rod Reel, Edit Director
Terri Suhr, Traffic Manager

KQDJ-FM
08-01-1983; 101.1 mhz FM *Hrs Open:* 19; 100 kw; 646 ft.; N46 56 21 W98 18 30
232 3rd Street, Ne, Valley City, ND 58072 US
(701) 845-1490, *Fax:* (701) 845-1245
www.newsdakota.com
License: Valley City, Barnes County, ND
Arbitron Metro Market: Jamestown-Valley City *Format:* Contemporary Hits/Top 40 *Target Audience:* 25-54.
Dave Reed, Programming Director

Velva

KTZU
01-01-2005; 94.9 mhz FM *Hrs Open:* 24; 98 kw; 512 ft.; N48 3 4 W101 20 23
US
(701) 852-7449, *Fax:* (701) 837-6925
pbiminot@srt.com
License: Velva, McHenry County, ND held by Programmers Broadcasting Inc.
Group Owner: Programmers Broadcasting Inc.
Arbitron Metro Market: Velva, ND *Format:* Classic Rock *Hrs. of News Programming:* News progmg 5 hrs wkly *Target Audience:* 25-54.
John Kircher, President
Jean Kircher, Operations Dir
Jean Schempp, Station Manager
J. Davis, General Sales Mgr
Jeff Bliss, Chief Engineer

Wahpeton

KEGK
05-21-1989; 106.9 mhz FM *Hrs Open:* 24; 41 kw; 538 ft.; N46 32 46 W96 37 39
Mailing Address: 605 Dakota Avenue, Wahpeton, ND 58074 US
Second Address: 605 Dakota Ave., Wahpeton, ND 58075
(701) 642-1156, *Fax:* (701) 642-1155
www.youreagle1069.com
studio@youreagle1069.com
License: Wahpeton, Richland County, ND held by Guderian Broadcasting Inc.
Nat'l Reps: Midwest Radio *Regional Reps:* Quest Marketing.
Format: Oldies *Hrs. of News Programming:* news progmg 5 hrs wkly *No. News Employees:* 1 *Target Audience:* 25-54.
Broadway Boe, Operations Dir
Lisa Hook, General Manager
Michael Brooks, General Sales Mgr
Breck Von Bank, Programming Director

Walhalla

KYTZ
09-01-1998; 106.7 mhz FM *Hrs Open:* 24; 16 kw; 837 ft.; N48 38 38 W97 58 46
P. O. Box 907, Valley City, ND 58072 US
(701) 256-1080, *Fax:* (701) 256-1081
www.thevalleysbiggesthits.com
bmatthews@utma.com
License: Walhalla, Pembina County, ND held by Simmons Broadcasting Inc.
Group Owner: Simmons Broadcasting Inc.; (acq 9-7-2004).
Arbitron Metro Market: Langdon, ND *Format:* Adult Contemp
Bob Simmons, CEO
Brian Matthews, Operations Dir
Bob Simmons, General Manager

West Fargo

*KFNW
10-28-1955; 1200 khz AM *Hrs Open:* 24
3003 N. Snelling Ave, Roseville, MN 55113 US
(701) 282-5910, *Fax:* (701) 282-5781
www.kfnw.org
kfnw@kfnw.org
License: West Fargo, ND held by Northwestern College.
Group Owner: Northwestern College & Radio
Arbitron Metro Market: Fargo-Moorhead, ND-MN *Format:* Religious *Hrs. of News Programming:* news progmg 6 hrs wkly *No. News Employees:* 1 *Target Audience:* 25-54.
Gary Herr, Station Manager
Phil Kvamme, Programming Director
Gary Ellingson, Chief Engineer

KQWB
09-01-2000; 1660 khz AM
2001 Penn. Ave., NW, Ste 400 Dms, Washington, DC 20006 US
(701) 237-4500, *Fax:* (701) 235-9082
www.123fargo.com
info@123fargo.com
License: West Fargo, ND held by Monterey Licenses LLC.
Group Owner: Triad Broadcasting Co. L.L.C.; (acq 8-18-99; grpsl)
Nat'l Network: Westwood One *Nat'l Reps:* Christal
Arbitron Metro Market: Fargo-Moorhead *Format:* Oldies *Target Audience:* 35 plus.
Tom Douglas, CFO
David Benjamin, President
Anne Phibian, Operations Dir
Nancy Odney, General Manager
John Austin, Programming Director

Williston

KDSR
02-28-1985; 101.1 mhz FM *Hrs Open:* 18; 98 kw; 801 ft.; N48 3 30 W104 0 0
723 15th Street West, Williston, ND 58801 US
(701) 572-4478, *Fax:* (701) 572-1419
kdsr@dia.net
License: Williston, Williams County, ND held by Williston Community Broadcasting Corp. dba KDSR(FM)
Nat'l Network: CNN Radio
Hrs. of News Programming: News progmg 7 hrs wkly
Stephen Marks, President
Ben Buckles, Operations Dir
P. Sturlausson, General Manager

KEYZ
01-01-1948; 660 khz AM *Hrs Open:* 24; 5 kw-D, DA2; 5 kw-N, DA2; N48 14 20 W103 39 1
Mailing Address: P.O. Box 3309, Great Falls, MT 59403 US
Second Address: 410 E. 6th, Williston, ND 58801
(701) 572-5371, *Fax:* (701) 572-7511
www.keyzradio.com
License: Williston, ND held by CCR-Williston IV LLC.
Group Owner: Cherry Creek Radio LLC; (acq 12-19-2003; grpsl)
Nat'l Network: ABC *Regional Network:* American Ag
Arbitron Metro Market: Williston, ND *Format:* Country, News, 62, Talk *Special Programming:* Relg 5 hrs wkly *No. News Employees:* 1 *Target Audience:* 25-54. *Adv. Rates:* 15; 15; 15; 8.25
Penny Lalim, Operations Dir
Joel Swanson, General Manager
Lyla Semenko, Station Manager
Scott Haugen, Programming Director
Earl Gross, News Director

*KPPR
11-20-1986; 89.5 mhz FM *Hrs Open:* 24; 10.5 kw; 492 ft.; N48 8 30 W103 53 34 *Rebroadcasts:* Rebroadcasts KCND(FM) Bismarck 100%
207 N 5th St/PO Box 3240, Fargo, ND 58108 US
(701) 241-6900, *Fax:* (701) 239-7650
www.prairiepublic.org
info@prairiepublic.org
License: Williston, Williams County, ND held by Prairie Public Broadcasting.
Nat'l Network: PRI; NPR
TV Affiliate: KWSE(TV) affil *Format:* Triple A *Special Programming:* American Indian 2 hrs, folk 6 hrs wkly *Hrs. of News Programming:* news progmg 40 hrs wkly *No. News Employees:* 2 *Target Audience:* General.
John Harris, CEO
John Harris, President
Bill Thomas, General Sales Mgr
Dave Thompson, News Director
Jack Anderson, Engineering Dir

KYYZ
12-01-1979; 96.1 mhz FM *Hrs Open:* 24; 100 kw; 869 ft.; N48 2 52 W103 59 1
Mailing Address: P.O. Box 3309, Great Falls, MT 59403 US
Second Address: 410 E. 6th, Williston, ND 58801
(701) 572-5371, *Fax:* (701) 572-7511
www.kyyzradio.com
License: Williston, Williams County, ND held by CCR-Williston IV LLC.
Group Owner: Cherry Creek Radio LLC
Nat'l Network: Fox News Radio
Arbitron Metro Market: Williston, ND *Format:* Country *No. News Employees:* 1 *Target Audience:* 25-54.
Joel Swanson, General Manager
Lyla Semenko, General Sales Mgr
Scott Haug, Programming Director
Penny Lalim, News Director

*KNDW
91.7 mhz FM; 0.25 kw; 118 ft.; N48 10 45 W103 33 54
US
(662) 844-5036, *Fax:* (662) 842-7798
www.afr.net
contact@afa.net
License: Williston, Williams County, ND held by Salt & Light Communications Inc.
Arbitron Metro Market: Williston, ND *Format:* Christian
Donald E. Wildmon, Founder
Larry Durham, President
Buster Wilson, General Manager
Jennifer Hagman, Programming Director

*KJND-FM
12-05-2011; 90.7 mhz FM *Hrs Open:* 24; 2 kw; 574 ft.; N48 8 30 W103 53 34
US
(406) 265-5845, *Fax:* (406) 265-8860
www.ynopradio.org
ynop@ynop.org
License: Williston, Williams County, ND held by Hi-Line Radio Fellowship Inc.
Arbitron Metro Market: Havre, MT *Adv. Rates:* Non-comm
Roger Lonnquist, General Manager
Brenda Boyum, KXEI Station Manager
Clark Berg, KALS Sales Manager
David Brown, YNOP Program Director
Nicholas Tobiason, Music/IT Director
Ron Huckeby, Chief Engineer
Crystal MacInnes, ProductionAssistant
Elizabeth McClenahan, Office Manager at KXEI/Webmaster
Joe McGee, KALS Account Executive
Carlene Prince, YNOP Associate Network Manager
Dan Shepherd, KALS Account Executive

Wimbledon

KRVX
01-01-2005; 103.1 mhz FM; 99 kw; 472 ft.; N46 56 21 W98 18 30
Mailing Address: US
Second Address: 2625 8th Ave. S.W., Jamestown, ND 58402
(701) 252-1400, *Fax:* (701) 252-1402
bigdog@daktel.com
License: Wimbledon, Barnes County, ND held by James River Broadcasting Inc.
Group Owner: Robert Ingstad Broadcast Properties

Nat'l Network: NBC Radio
Arbitron Metro Market: Lubbock, TX *Target Audience:* 18-54.
Dave Reed, General Manager
Lynn Lambrecht, General Sales Mgr

Ohio

Ada

***WONB**
10-18-1991; 94.9 mhz FM; 3 kw; 328 ft.; N40 45 58 W83 50 14
525 South Main Street, Ada, OH 45810 US
(419) 772-1194, *Fax:* (419) 772-2794
www.wonbradio.net
wonb@onu.edu
License: Ada, Hardin County, OH held by Ohio Northern University.
Nat'l Network: CNN Radio *Wire Services:* CNN
Arbitron Metro Market: Lima, OH *TV Affiliate:* var/div *Special Programming:* News progmg 8 hrs wkly *No. News Employees:* 18-49; general
General Manager, Nichole Tebbe
Station Manager, Station Manager
News Director, News Director

Akron

WAKR
10-16-1940; 1590 khz AM *Hrs Open:* 24; 5 kw-D, DAN; 5 kw-N, DAN; N41 1 14 W81 30 20
1795 West Market Street, Akron, OH 44333 US
(330) 869-9800, *Fax:* (330) 864-6799
www.wakr.net,www.akronnewsnow.com
ccollins@rcrg.net
License: Akron, OH held by Rubber City Radio Group Inc.
Group Owner: Rubber City Radio Group Inc.; acq 10-6-93; $9.3 million with co-located FM;
Nat'l Network: ABC *Nat'l Reps:* Christal *Wire Services:* AP
Arbitron Metro Market: Akron, OH *Format:* News, Oldies, 84 *Hrs. of News Programming:* news progmg 40 hrs wkly *No. News Employees:* 10 *Target Audience:* 35 plus.
Thomas Mandel, CEO
Chuck Collins, Operations Dir
Dominic Rizzo, General Sales Mgr
Joyce Lagios, Promotions Manager
Ed Esposito, News Director
Henry Zelman, CFO
Al Hruska, Chief of Operations
Chuck Collins, OperationsDirector
Mark Biviano, Senior Vice President

***WAPS**
10-04-1955; 91.3 mhz FM *Hrs Open:* 24; 800 w; Ant 151 ft; N41 03 18 W81 31 35
65 Steiner Ave., Akron, OH 44301
(330) 761-3099, *Fax:* (330) 761-3240
www.913thesummit.com
tommybruno@913thesummit.com
License: Akron, Summit County, OH held by Board of Education, Akron City School District.
Population Served: 300,000 *Arbitron Metro Market:* Akron, OH *Special Programming:* Ger 2 hrs, It 2 hrs, Hungarian one hr, Slovenian 2 hrs, Latin 2 hrs wkly *Target Audience:* 25-54; college educated adults
Andrew James, Operations Dir
Tommy Bruno, General Manager
Garrett Hart, Director of Creative Content
Jim Chenot, General Sales Mgr
Bill Gruber, Programming Director
Liz Mozzocco, Music Director
Jim Morgan, Chief Engineer

WHLO
10-01-1944; 640 khz AM *Hrs Open:* 24; 5 kw-D, DA2; 0.5 kw-N, DA2; N41 4 47 W81 38 45
4880 Santa Rosa Road, Suite 300, Camarillo, CA 93012 US
(330) 836-4700, *Fax:* (330) 492-1350
www.640whlo.com
info@newstalk.com
License: Akron, OH held by CC Licenses LLC.
Group Owner: Clear Channel Communications Inc.; (acq 12-31-2001; $4.5 million).
Arbitron Metro Market: Akron, OH *Format:* News, News/Talk, 86
Don Lankford, General Manager

WAKS
01-01-1950; 96.5 mhz FM; 31 kw; 620 ft.; N41 16 50 W81 37 22
1867 W. Market Street, Akron, OH 44313 US
(216) 520-2600, *Fax:* (216) 981-8167
www.waks.com
License: Akron, Summit County, OH held by Aloha Station Trust LLC
Arbitron Metro Market: Akron, OH *Format:* Contemporary Hits/Top 40
Mike Kenney, General Manager
Kris Foley, General Sales Mgr
Bo Matthews, Programming Director
Jeff Zukauckas, Promotions Manager

WONE-FM
10-01-1947; 97.5 mhz FM; 12 kw; 889 ft.; N41 3 53 W81 34 59
1795 West Market Street, Akron, OH 44333 US
(330) 869-9800, *Fax:* (330) 864-6799,
www.wone.net
License: Akron, Summit County, OH
Group Owner: Rubber City Radio Group Inc.
Arbitron Metro Market: Akron, OH *TV Affiliate:* Rock *No. News Employees:* 18-49.
Disc Jockey, Sandra Miller
Disc Jockey, Dana Durban
News Reporter

WARF
01-01-1926; 1350 khz AM; 5 kw-U, DA1; N41 10 5 W81 30 45
1867 W. Market Street, Akron, OH 44313 US
(330) 492-4700, *Fax:* (330) 492-1350
www.sportsradio1350.com
info@sportsradio1350.com
License: Akron, OH held by Capstar TX L.P.
Group Owner: Clear Channel Communications Inc.; (acq 2000; grpsl)
Nat'l Network: Sporting News Radio Network
Arbitron Metro Market: Akron, OH *Format:* Sports, Talk
Dan Lankford, Operations Dir
Mark Boarman, General Manager
Keith Kenendy, Operations/Production Manager

***WZIP**
12-10-1962; 88.1 mhz FM *Hrs Open:* 24; 7.5 kw; 820 ft.; N41 4 58 W81 38 2
1004 Guzzetta, Akron, OH 44325 US
(330) 972-7105, *Fax:* (330) 972-5521
www.wzip.fm
wzip@uakron.edu
License: Akron, Summit County, OH held by University of Akron.
Nat'l Network: AP Network News *Wire Services:* AP
Arbitron Metro Market: Akron, OH *Format:* Rock/AOR, Contemporary Hits/Top 40 *Special Programming:* Polka 4 hrs, pub affrs 11 hrs, sports talk 3 hrs w *Target Audience:* 18-34.
Thomas Beck, General Manager
Blake Thompson, Chief Engineer

Alliance

WDPN
09-02-1953; 1310 khz AM *Hrs Open:* 24; 1 kw-D, DA2; 0.48 kw-N, DA2; N40 55 34 W81 7 41
Mailing Address: 393 Smyth Ave Ne, Po2356, Alliance, OH 44601 US
Second Address: 392 Smyth Ave., Alliance, OH 44601
(330) 821-1111, *Fax:* (330) 821-0379
www.1310wdpn.com/
info@wdpn.com
License: Alliance, OH held by D.A. Peterson Inc.
Arbitron Metro Market: Alliance, OH *Format:* Urban Contemporary *Special Programming:* Relg 4 hrs wkly *Hrs. of News Programming:* news progmg 21 hrs wkly *No. News Employees:* 2 *Target Audience:* 35-64.
Doug Lane, Programming Director
Rex Coombs, News Director

***WRMU-FM**
10-17-1970; 91.1 mhz FM *Hrs Open:* 24/7; 2.8 kw horiz; 190 ft.; N40 54 16 W81 6 45
1972 Clark Avenue, Alliance, OH 44601 US
(330) 823-2414,(330) 823-3777, *Fax:* (330) 829-4913
www.muc.edu/wrmu
wrmu@muc.edu
License: Alliance, Stark County, OH held by Mount Union College.
Wire Services: AP
Arbitron Metro Market: Canton, OH *Format:* Jazz, Oldies, 76, Smooth Jazz *Special Programming:* Gospel 2 hrs, news/talk 5 hrs wkly *Hrs. of News Programming:* news progmg 8 hrs wkly *No. News Employees:* 1
Richard Giese, President
Mark Bergmann, General Manager
William Weisinger, Chief Engineer

WDJQ
04-01-1947; 92.5 mhz FM *Hrs Open:* 24; 50 kw horiz, 49.7 kw vert; 499 ft.; N40 47 25 W81 6 26
Mailing Address: 393 Smyth Ave, Ne, PO Box 2356, Alliance, OH 44601 US
Second Address: 392 Smyth Ave., Alliance, OH 44601
(330) 450-9250, *Fax:* (330) 821-0379
www.q92radio.com
radiosales@alliancelink.com
License: Alliance, Stark County, OH held by D.A. Peterson Inc.
Arbitron Metro Market: Alliance, OH *Format:* Adult Contemp *Hrs. of News Programming:* news progmg 4 hrs wkly *No. News Employees:* 2 *Target Audience:* 25-54.
Don Peterson, General Manager
Mark O'Brian, General Sales Mgr
John Stewart, Programming Director
Clint M, News Director
Steve Hundt, Chief Engineer
Mark O'Brien, General Sales Manager
Dee Zink, Traffic Manager

Anna

***WHJM**
06-01-2006; 88.7 mhz FM; 1 kw vert; 318 ft.; N40 28 1.8 W84 11 24.2
352 West 44th Street, New York, NY 10036 US
(888) 333-6279, *Fax:* (318) 449-9954
www.radiomaria.us
info.usa@radiomaria.org
License: Anna, Shelby County, OH held by Friends of Radio Maria Inc.
Group Owner: Radio Maria Inc.
Arbitron Metro Market: Anna, OH *Format:* Christian
Father Duane Stenzel, Operations Dir

Archbold

***WBCY**
12-01-1992; 89.5 mhz FM *Hrs Open:* 24; 20 kw; 315 ft.; N41 28 59 W84 16 58
1025 W. Rudisill Blvd., Fort Wayne, IN 46807 US
(541) 963-4121, *Fax:* (541) 963-3117
License: Archbold, Fulton County, OH held by Taylor University Broadcasting Inc.
Wire Services: UPI
Arbitron Metro Market: Portales NM *Format:* Oldies *Target Audience:* 25-54.
Mark Bolland, President
Linda Ashlock, General Manager

WMTR-FM
03-01-1968; 96.1 mhz FM *Hrs Open:* 24; 3.8 kw; Ant 400 ft; N41 33 29 W84 11 08
303 1/2 N. Defiance St., Archbold, OH 43502
(419) 445-9050, *Fax:* (419) 445-3531
www.961wmtr.com
wmtr@rtecexpress.net
License: Archbold, Fulton County, OH held by Nobco Inc.
Nat'l Network: Westwood One *Nat'l Reps:* Rgnl Reps
Population Served: 125,000 *Arbitron Metro Market:* Toledo, OH *Hrs. of News Programming:* news progmg 8 hrs wkly *No. News Employees:* 1 *Target Audience:* 25-54.
Max Smith Sr., President
Max Smith Jr., General Manager
Mark Knapp, Programming Director
Larry Christy, News Director

Ashland

WNCO
01-01-1949; 1340 khz AM *Hrs Open:* 24; 1 kw-U, ND1; N40 50 25 W82 21 26
2435 Mansfield Road, Ashland, OH 44805 US
(419) 529-2211, *Fax:* (419) 529-2516
www.wncoam.com
ronaldcolman@clearchannel.com
License: Ashland, OH held by Capstar TX L.P.
Group Owner: Clear Channel Communications Inc.; (acq 2-12-01; grpsl).
Nat'l Reps: Rgnl Reps
Arbitron Metro Market: Mansfield, OH *Format:* Adult Contemp *Special Programming:* Farm 3 hrs wkly *Hrs. of News Programming:* news progmg 20 hrs wkly *No. News Employees:* 2 *Target Audience:* 35 plus.
Diana Coon, General Manager

WNCO-FM
05-01-1947; 101.3 mhz FM *Hrs Open:* 24; 50 kw; 499 ft.; N40 50 25 W82 21 26
P. O. Box 311, Ashland, OH 44805 US
(419) 529-2211, *Fax:* (419) 529-2516
www.wncoafm.com
ronaldcolman@clearchannel.com
License: Ashland, Ashland County, OH held by Capstar TX LP

Group Owner: Clear Channel Communications Inc.
Arbitron Metro Market: Ashland, OH *Format:* Country *Hrs. of News Programming:* news progmg 14 hrs wkly *No. News Employees:* 3 *Target Audience:* 25 plus.
Dean Stampfli, Operations Dir
Martin Larsen, General Sales Mgr
Lori Johnson, News Director
Gene Davis, Local News Editor
Darla Stampfli, Promotions Manager
Steve Crabtree, Sports Commentator

*WRDL
08-24-1967; 88.9 mhz FM *Hrs Open:* 6 AM-1 AM; 3 kw; 171 ft.; N40 51 41 W82 19 11
401 College Avenue, Ashland, OH 44805 US
(419) 289-5678,(419) 289-5311, *Fax:* (419) 289-5329
License: Ashland, Ashland County, OH held by Ashland University.
Format: Rock/AOR *Special Programming:* Christian contemp 7 hrs, jazz 5 hrs, oldies 4 hrs wkly *Hrs. of News Programming:* News progmg 7 hrs wkly *Target Audience:* 18-35; general
Dr. G. William Benz, President
Tom Griffiths, General Manager

Ashtabula

WFUN
11-01-1937; 970 khz AM *Hrs Open:* 24; 5 kw-D, DA2; 1 kw-N, DA2; N41 48 52 W80 46 45
P. O. Box 738, Ashtabula, OH 44004 US
(440) 993-2126, *Fax:* (440) 992-2658
www.wfunam97.com
info@wfunam97.com
License: Ashtabula, OH held by Sweet Home Ashtabula LLC.
Group Owner: Sweet Home Ashtabula LLC; (acq 9-17-2007; grpsl)
Nat'l Network: ESPN Radio
Format: Sports *Target Audience:* General.
Dana Schulte, Operations Dir
Dennis Brockman, Operations Director

WREO-FM
01-01-1949; 97.1 mhz FM; 50 kw; 499 ft.; N41 48 58 W80 46 52
P. O. Box 738, Ashtabula, OH 44004 US
(440) 993-2126, *Fax:* (440) 992-2658
www.star97.com
star97@star97.com
License: Ashtabula, Ashtabula County, OH
Group Owner: Sweet Home Ashtabula LLC
Format: Adult Contemp *Target Audience:* 25-54; professionals
Dennis O'Brien, Programming Director

WYBL
01-01-2005; 98.3 mhz FM; 5.3 kw; 344 ft.; N41 50 23 W80 44 36
P O Box 738, Ashtabula, OH 44004 US
(440) 993-2126, *Fax:* (440) 992-2658
www.983thebull.com
rogermccoy@983thebull.com
License: Ashtabula, Ashtabula County, OH held by Sweet Home Ashtabula LLC.
Group Owner: Sweet Home Ashtabula LLC; (acq 9-17-2007; grpsl)
Arbitron Metro Market: Ashtabula, OH *Format:* News
Dana Schulte, General Manager
Kim Frustere, Sales Manager
Roger McCoy, Programming Director
Roger McCoy, Internet Content Manager

Ashville

WODC
07-01-1961; 93.3 mhz FM *Hrs Open:* 24; 50 kw; 335 ft; N39 19 52 W82 59 49
2323 W. Fifth Ave., Suite 200, Columbus, OH 45202
(614) 486-6101, *Fax:* (614) 487-2537
www.933wlzt.com
info@933wlzt.com
License: Ashville, Ross County, OH held by CC Licenses LLC.
Group Owner: Clear Channel Communications Inc.; (acq 4-11-2003).
Nat'l Network: ABC
Population Served: 100,000 *Arbitron Metro Market:* Columbus, OH *No. News Employees:* 3 *Target Audience:* 24-54. *Adv. Rates:* 35; 35; 35; 35
Tom Thon, General Manager
Dave Daugherty, General Sales Mgr
Michael McCoy, Programming Director

Athens

WATH
10-25-1950; 970 khz AM *Hrs Open:* 24; 1 kw-D, ND1; 0.026 kw-N, ND1; N39 20 40 W82 6 21
Mailing Address: 300 N. Columbus Rd., Athens, OH 45701 US
Second Address: 300 Columbus Rd., Athens, OH 45701
(740) 593-6651(740) 593-7982 (News), *Fax:* (740) 594-3488
www.970wath.com
palmerd@wxtq.com
License: Athens, OH held by WATH Inc.
Nat'l Network: CBS Radio *Regional Network:* Ohio News Network *Nat'l Reps:* Rgnl Reps *Regional Reps:* Rgnl Reps. *Wire Services:* AP
Arbitron Metro Market: Athens,OH *Format:* Adult Contemp, News, 62, Sports, Talk *Special Programming:* Big band 15 hrs wkly *Hrs. of News Programming:* 25 hrs wkly *No. News Employees:* 3 *Target Audience:* 40+
David Palmer, President
Bob Stilson, Operations Dir
Thom Williams, General Manager
Thom Williams, Station Manager
Marianne Williams, General Sales Mgr
Bob Beyette, Programming Director
Zahid Mumtaz, Chief Engineer
SallieSauber, Production Director
Robin Barnes, Public Service Director
Caleb Troop, Sports Director
Angie Marks, Traffic Director

WJKW
09-01-1998; 95.9 mhz FM *Hrs Open:* 24; 5.5 kw; 341 ft.; N39 14 10 W82 4 16
P.O. Box 247, Castalia, OH 44824 US
(740) 592-9879, *Fax:* (740) 592-9952
www.wjkw.net
wjkw@cfbroadcast.net
License: Athens, Athens County, OH held by Christian Faith Broadcast Inc.
Group Owner: Christian Faith Broadcasting Inc.
Format: Adult Contemp, Christian *Target Audience:* 25-44.
Rusty Yost, General Manager
Kevin Ingle, Station Manager

*WOUB
09-14-1957; 1340 khz AM *Hrs Open:* 24; 0.5 kw-D, ND2; 1 kw-N, ND2; N39 19 45 W82 5 29
9 South College Street, Athens, OH 45701 US
(740) 593-4554, *Fax:* (740) 593-0240
www.woub.org
woub@woub.org
License: Athens, OH held by Ohio University.
Nat'l Network: NPR; PRI
Format: News, News/Talk, 86 *Special Programming:* Black 8 hrs wkly *No. News Employees:* 3
David Wiseman, Operations Dir
Carolyn Lewis, General Manager
Tim Myers, Programming Director
Doug Partusch, Promotions Manager
Tim Sharp, News Director
Ted Ross, Engineering Director
Steve Skidmore, Operations Director
ScottMartin, Operations Manager
Bryan Gibson, Programming Director

*WOUB-FM
12-13-1949; 91.3 mhz FM *Hrs Open:* 24; 50 kw; 492 ft.; N39 18 52 W82 8 59
9 South College Street, Athens, OH 45701 US
(740) 593-4554, *Fax:* (740) 593-0240
www.woub.org
woub@woub.org
License: Athens, Athens County, OH held by Ohio University
Wire Services: UPI
TV Affiliate: *WOUB-TV affil. *Format:* Adult Contemp *No. News Employees:* 3
Rusty Smith, Programming Director
Mark Hellenberg, Assistant Music Director
Jan Sole, Assistant Music Director

WXTQ
09-16-1964; 105.5 mhz FM *Hrs Open:* 24; 6 kw; 312 ft.; N39 21 18 W82 5 32
Mailing Address: 300 North Columbus Road, Athens, OH 45701 US
Second Address: 300 Columbus Rd., Athens, OH 45701
(740) 593-6651, *Fax:* (740) 594-3488
www.wxtq.com
palmerd@wxtq.com
License: Athens, Athens County, OH held by WATH Inc.
Nat'l Network: Superadio *Regional Network:* Ohio News Network
Nat'l Reps: Rgnl Reps *Regional Reps:* Rgnl Reps *Wire Services:* AP
Arbitron Metro Market: Athens, OH *Format:* Adult Contemp
Special Programming: Ohio University Sports *Hrs. of News Programming:* news progmg 5 hrs wkly *No. News Employees:* 2
Target Audience: 18-34.
Dave Palmer, President
Robin Barnes, Operations Dir
Thom Williams, Station and General Sales Manager
Thom Williams, Station Manager
Bob Beyette, Programming Director
Bob Beyette, News Director
Zahid Mumtaz, Chief Engineer
Sallie Sauber, Production Director
Marianne Williams, National Sales Manager
Caleb Troop, Sports Director
Angie Marks, Traffic Director
Scott Dailey, Account Executive
Maryjane Burch, Account Executive

Bainbridge

*WKHR
05-06-1977; 91.5 mhz FM; 0.75 kw; 463 ft.; N41 27 49 W81 17 38
17419 Snyder Road, Chagrin Falls, OH 44023 US
(440) 543-9646, *Fax:* (440) 543-9012
www.wkhr.org
info@wkhr.com
License: Bainbridge, Ross County, OH held by Kenston Local School District.
Arbitron Metro Market: Cleveland, OH *Format:* Big Band *Target Audience:* 55 plus; well established, mature
Chris Kofron, General Manager

Baltimore

WWCD
07-08-1924; 1240 khz AM *Hrs Open:* 24; 1 kw-U; 130 meters; N39 46 14.8 w82 44 25.3
503. South Front Street, Suite 101, Columbus, OH 43701
(614) 221-9923, *Fax:* (614) 227-0021
www.whizamfmtv.com
License: Baltimore, Muskingum County, OH held by Southeastern Ohio Broadcasting System Inc.
Nat'l Reps: Roslin; Rgnl Reps
Population Served: 33,045*Special Programming:* Farm progmg 2 hrs wkly *Hrs. of News Programming:* news progmg 30 hrs wkly *No. News Employees:* 10 *Target Audience:* 25-54; general
N.J. Littick, Chairman
Henry Littick, President
Van Vannelli, Operations Dir
Jay Benson, General Sales Mgr
George Hiotis, News Director
Ken Cash, Chief Engineer
Brian Wagner, Operations Director

Barnesville

WBNV
07-01-1991; 93.5 mhz FM *Hrs Open:* 24; 2.5 kw; 489 ft.; N39 54 10 W81 12 37
Mailing Address: 63021 Ridgewood Drive, Cambridge, OH 43725 US
Second Address: Box 293, 175 E. Main St., Barnesville, OH 43713-0293
(740) 432-5605, *Fax:* (740) 432-1991
www.yourradioplace.com
webmaster@yourradioplace.com
License: Barnesville, Belmont County, OH held by W. Grant Hafley.
Nat'l Network: USA *Nat'l Reps:* Rgnl Reps
Arbitron Metro Market: Cambridge, Oh *Format:* Adult Contemp
Hrs. of News Programming: News progmg 15 hrs wkly *Target Audience:* 25-54.
Grant Hafley, CEO/COO
Grant Hafley, President
Dave Wilson, Operations Dir
Joel Losego, General Manager

Batavia

*WOBO
07-30-1981; 88.7 mhz FM; 15.5 kw horiz, 12.5 kw vert; 466 ft.; N39 3 43 W84 5 50
P. O. Box 338, Owensville, OH 45160 US
(513) 724-3939
www.wobofm.com
df1littman@cs.com
License: Batavia, Clermont County, OH held by Educational Community Radio Inc.

Arbitron Metro Market: Cincinnati, OH *TV Affiliate:* Var/div
Format: Ethnic *No. News Employees:* 35 plus.

Beach City

***WOFN**
09-27-2000; 88.7 mhz FM; 3.5 kw horiz, 22.5 kw vert; 344 ft.; N40 35 41 W81 34 39
Mailing Address: P.O. Box 1924, Tulsa, OK 74101 US
Second Address: 4916 Spruce Hill Dr., Suite 400, Canton, OH 44617
(330) 244-9151, *Fax:* 330-244-9153
www.oasisnetwork.org
mail@oasisnetwork.org
License: Beach City, Stark County, OH held by Creative Educational Media Corp. Inc.
Arbitron Metro Market: Canton, OH *TV Affiliate:* Relg *No. News Employees:* General.

Beavercreek

WXEG
06-18-1972; 103.9 mhz FM *Hrs Open:* 24; 2.9 kw; 479 ft.; N39 43 19 W84 12 33
50 East Rivercenter Boulevard, Suite 1200, Covington, KY 41011 US
(937) 224-1137, *Fax:* (937) 224-3667
www.wxeg.com
info@ccedayton.com
License: Beavercreek, Greene County, OH held by Citicasters Licenses L.P.
Group Owner: Clear Channel Communications Inc.; (acq 1999; grpsl).
Arbitron Metro Market: Dayton, OH *Format:* Alternative *No. News Employees:* 1 *Target Audience:* 18-34.
Tony Tilford, Operations Manager/Programming Director
Dave Litteral, General Sales Mgr
Steve Dent, Promotions Manager
Paul Jellison, Chief Engineer

Bellaire

WOMP
12-02-1947; 1290 khz AM; 1 kw-D, ND1; 0.033 kw-N, ND1; N40 2 9 W80 46 16
200 Gateway Towers, Pittsburgh, PA 15222 US
(740) 676-5661, *Fax:* (740) 676-2742
kool105@hotmail.com
License: Bellaire, OH held by Keymarket Licenses LLC.
Group Owner: Keymarket Communications LLC; (acq 1-15-93; $575,000 with co-located FM;
Nat'l Network: ESPN Radio *Nat'l Reps:* Rgnl Reps
Arbitron Metro Market: Wheeling, WV *TV Affiliate:* Sports *Format:* Ethnic *Special Programming:* news progmg 20 hrs wkly *Hrs. of News Programming:* 2

WYJK-FM
01-01-1947; 100.5 mhz FM *Hrs Open:* 24; 48 kw; Ant 518 ft; N40 02 09 W80 46 16
Box 448, Rt. 214, Bellaire, OH 43952
(740) 676-5661, *Fax:* (740) 671-4487
www.wompfm.com
License: Bellaire, Belmont County, OH held by Keymarket Licenses LLC.
Group Owner: Keymarket Communications LLC
Wire Services: AP
Arbitron Metro Market: Wheeling, WV *No. News Employees:* 1 *Target Audience:* 18-44; educated adults
Michael Kestler, President

Bellefontaine

WBLL
01-01-1951; 1390 khz AM *Hrs Open:* 24; 0.5 kw-D, ND1; 0.081 kw-N, ND1; N40 22 5 W83 44 2
1501 Road 235, Bellefontaine, OH 43311 US
(937) 592-1045, *Fax:* (937) 592-3299
www.peakofohio.com
lhoyles@wpko.com
License: Bellefontaine, OH held by V-Teck Communications Inc.
Nat'l Network: ABC; ESPN Radio *Regional Network:* ABN Radio
Nat'l Reps: Rgnl Reps *Wire Services:* AP
Arbitron Metro Market: Bellefontaine, OH *Format:* News, News/Talk, 84, Talk *Special Programming:* Relg 6 hrs wkly *Hrs. of News Programming:* news progmg 126 hrs wkly *No. News Employees:* 2 *Target Audience:* General.
Lou Vito, President
Chad Wilkinson, Operations Dir
Sheryl Godwin, General Sales Mgr
Ken Keller, Promotions Manager
Bill Tipple, News Director
Bill Bowin, Chief Engineer
Amie Huffman, Advertising Director

WPKO-FM
07-15-1969; 98.3 mhz FM *Hrs Open:* 24; 1.75 kw; 430 ft.; N40 22 5 W83 44 2
1501 Road 235, Bellefontaine, OH 43311 US
(937) 592-1045, *Fax:* (973) 592-3299
www.wpko.com
cwilkinson@wpko.com
License: Bellefontaine, Logan County, OH
Format: Adult Contemp *No. News Employees:* 2 *Target Audience:* 12 plus.
Chad Wilkinson, Programming Director
Pam Allen, Promotions Manager
Bill Bowin, Engineering Dir
Louie Vito, Assistant Music Director
Matt Hull, Disc Jockey
Mark Brake, Disc Jockey
Ken Keller, Disc Jockey

Bellevue

WOHF
04-04-1973; 92.1 mhz FM *Hrs Open:* 24; 6 kw; 328 ft.; N41 14 19 W82 50 16
107 1/2 East Main Street, Bellevue, OH 44811 US
(419) 332-8218, *Fax:* (419) 333-8226
www.wohf.basohio.com
jonkerns@basbroadcasting.com
License: Bellevue, Huron County, OH held by BAS Broadcasting Inc.
Group Owner: BAS Broadcasting Inc.; (acq 10-1-2003; $550,000)
Nat'l Network: ABC *Regional Network:* ABN Radio *Regional Reps:* Rgnl Reps
Arbitron Metro Market: Fremont, OH *Format:* Contemporary Hits/Top 40 *Hrs. of News Programming:* news progmg 5 hrs wkly *No. News Employees:* 1 *Adv. Rates:* 20; 20; 20; 15
Tom Klein, CEO
Jim Lorenzen, President
Jon Kerns, Programming Director

Belpre

***WCVV**
01-01-1986; 89.5 mhz FM *Hrs Open:* 24; 4.4 kw; 384 ft.; N39 19 27 W81 37 33
P.O. Box 405, Belpre, OH 45714 US
(740) 423-5895, *Fax:* (740) 423-9951
www.wcvv.thecalvarycommunitychurch.com
License: Belpre, Washington County, OH held by Belpre Educ. Broadcasting Foundation.
Arbitron Metro Market: Parkersburg-Marietta, WV-OH *Format:* Christian, News *Target Audience:* General.
Clay Sloan, General Manager
Ralph Matheny, Chief Engineer

***WLKP**
05-01-1991; 91.9 mhz FM; 5.2 kw; 325 ft.; N39 20 46 W81 29 55
PO Box 568, 2411 1/2 Washington Blv, Belpre, OH 45714 US
(800) 525-5683, *Fax:* (916) 251-1650
www.klove.com
License: Belpre, Washington County, OH held by Educational Media Foundation.
Group Owner: EMF Broadcasting; (acq 3-31-2005; $700,000 with WLKV(FM) Ripley, WV).
Nat'l Network: K-Love
Arbitron Metro Market: Rocklin, CA *Format:* Christian
Mike Novak, President
David Pierce, Programming Director
Ed Lenane, News Director
Sam Wallington, Engineering Dir
Marya Morgan, News Reporter
Richard Hunt, News Reporter

WNUS
09-12-1981; 107.1 mhz FM *Hrs Open:* 24; 4.7 kw; 351 ft.; N39 18 36 W81 35 49
Mailing Address: 6006 Grand Central Ave., Vienna, WV 26105 US
Second Address: 6006 Grand Central Ave., Vienna, WV 26105
(304) 295-9441, *Fax:* (304) 295-4389
www.107nus.com
roadcrew@wnus.com
License: Belpre, Washington County, OH held by CC Licenses LLC.
Group Owner: Clear Channel Communications Inc.; (acq 4-17-2001; grpsl).
Nat'l Reps: Clear Channel
Arbitron Metro Market: Parkersburg, WV *Format:* Country *Hrs. of News Programming:* news progmg 2 hrs wkly *No. News Employees:* 2 *Target Audience:* 18 plus. *Adv. Rates:* 37.50; 35; 20; 16
Chuck Poet, General Manager

Berea

***WBWC**
03-02-1958; 88.3 mhz FM *Hrs Open:* 19; 4 kw; 256 ft.; N41 25 5 W81 54 3
275 Eastland Road, Berea, OH 44017 US
(440) 826-2145, *Fax:* (440) 826-3426
www.wbwc.com
comments@wbwc.com
License: Berea, Cuyahoga County, OH held by Baldwin-Wallace College.
Nat'l Network: AP Radio
Arbitron Metro Market: BEREA, OH *Format:* Rock/AOR *Target Audience:* 12-25; alternative mus listeners
Allen Thompson, Operations Dir
Alex Hooper, General Sales Mgr
Amy Popik, Programming Director
Anthony Hrestak, Promotions Manager
Danielle Schwinn, News Director
Eddy Janson, Sports Director

Bowling Green

***WBGU**
11-01-1951; 88.1 mhz FM *Hrs Open:* 24; 0.45 kw; 177 ft.; N41 22 33 W83 38 34
West Hall, Bowling Green, OH 43403 US
(419) 372-8657, *Fax:* (419) 372-0202
www.wbgufm.com
smerril@bgsu.edu
License: Bowling Green, Wood County, OH held by Bowling Green State University.
Arbitron Metro Market: Bowling Green,OH *TV Affiliate:* *WBGU-TV affil. *Format:* Black, Jazz, 94 *Special Programming:* Country 4 hrs, class 3 hrs, folk 4 hrs, Sp 4 hrs wkly *Hrs. of News Programming:* News progmg 7hrs wkly *Target Audience:* General.
Ron Tolbert, Operations Dir
Rebecca Priebe, General Manager
Paige Dunham, Programming Director
Neil Carrier, Promotions Manager
Jim Davis, Chief Engineer
Chris Cedar, Music Director
Josh Clay, Production Director

WJYM
12-01-1964; 730 khz AM *Hrs Open:* 6 AM-midnight; 1 kw-D, DA2; 0.359 kw-N, DA2; N41 31 57 W83 33 55
8761 Freemont Pike, Perrysburg, OH 43551 US
(225) 768-3202, *Fax:* (225) 768-3729
www.jsm.org
kawikfish@yahoo.com
License: Bowling Green, OH held by Family Worship Center Church Inc.
Group Owner: Family Worship Center Church Inc.; acq 12-15-99).
Nat'l Network: USA
Arbitron Metro Market: Toledo, OH *Format:* Religious *Hrs. of News Programming:* News progmg 3 hrs wkly *Target Audience:* 25-49.
David Whitelaw, COO

WRQN
06-01-1964; 93.5 mhz FM; 7 kw; 397 ft.; N41 27 28 W83 39 33
111 East Kilbourn Ave., Suite 2700, Milwaukee, WI 53202 US
(419) 725-5700, *Fax:* (419) 385-2902
www.935wrqn.com
info@935wrqn.com
License: Bowling Green, Wood County, OH held by Cumulus Licensing Corp.
Group Owner: Cumulus Media Inc.; (acq 9-11-97; grpsl)
Arbitron Metro Market: Toledo, OH *Format:* Oldies *Special Programming:* Pub service one hr wkly *Target Audience:* 25-54.
Skip Schmidt, General Manager
Ron Finn, Programming Director

***WNOC**
89.7 mhz FM; 5.3 kw; 288 ft.; N41 25 39 W83 36 30 US
(419) 754-1009
www.annunciationradio.com
License: Bowling Green, Wood County, OH held by Ministry to Catholic Charismatic Renewal.
Arbitron Metro Market: Bowling Green, OH *Format:* Religious
Roy Handy, General Manager

Brunswick

***WKJA**
91.9 mhz FM; 25 kw; 318 ft.; N40 54 56 W81 55 56
US
(714) 825-9663, *Fax:* (714) 825-9660
www.krtmradio.com
License: Brunswick, Medina County, OH held by CSN International.
Group Owner: CSN International
Arbitron Metro Market: Brunswick, OH
Jeffrey Smith, President

Bryan

WBNO-FM
06-30-1966; 100.9 mhz FM *Hrs Open:* 24; 6 kw; 299 ft.; N41 28 44 W84 34 50
P.O. Box 603, Bryan, OH 43506 US
(419) 636-3175, *Fax:* (419) 636-4570
www.wbno-wqct.com/WBNO
wbno@wbno-wqct.com
License: Bryan, Williams County, OH held by Impact Radio LLC
Group Owner: Impact Radio LLC; (acq 8-1-2002; grpsl).
Nat'l Network: ABC *Regional Reps:* Rgnl Reps *Wire Services:* AP
Arbitron Metro Market: Toledo, OH *Format:* Contemporary Hits/Top 40, Adult Contemp *Hrs. of News Programming:* news progmg 27 hrs wkly *No. News Employees:* 1 *Target Audience:* 25-54; loc oriented *Adv. Rates:* 10; 9; 9; na
Dennis Rumsey, President
Andy Brigle, Programming Director
Sports Director

***WGBE**
01-01-1996; 90.9 mhz FM *Hrs Open:* 24; 0.85 kw; 394 ft.; N41 28 47 W84 35 50 *Rebroadcasts:* Rebroadcasts WGTE-FM Toledo 100%
136 N Huron Street, Toledo, OH 43697 US
(419) 380-4600, *Fax:* (419) 380-4710
www.wgte.org
info@wgte.com
License: Bryan, Williams County, OH held by The Public Broadcasting Foundation of Northwest Ohio.
Nat'l Network: NPR; PRI
TV Affiliate: WGTE-TV *Format:* News *Special Programming:* Jazz 16 hrs wkly *Hrs. of News Programming:* News progmg 23 hrs wkly *Target Audience:* General.
George Jones, Chairman
Marlon Kiser, CEO
Chris Pfeiffer, Operations Dir
Ross Pfeiffer, General Sales Mgr

WQCT
12-01-1962; 1520 khz AM *Hrs Open:* 24
P.O. Box 603, Bryan, OH 43506 US
(419) 636-3175, *Fax:* 419) 636-4570
License: Bryan, OH held by Impact Radio LLC
Group Owner: Impact Radio LLC; .
Regional Reps: Rgnl Reps
Arbitron Metro Market: Toledo, OH *Format:* Oldies *Hrs. of News Programming:* news progmg 3 hrs wkly *No. News Employees:* 1 *Target Audience:* 35-65; general
Dennis Rumsey, President

Buchtel

WAIS
12-03-1984; 770 khz AM *Hrs Open:* Sunrise-sunset; 1 kw-D, NDD; N39 25 56 W82 12 2
15751 Us Route 33, Nelsonville, OH 45764 US
(740) 753-4094, *Fax:* (740) 753-4965
wseo33@sbcglobal.net
License: Buchtel, OH held by Nelsonville TV Cable Inc.
Nat'l Network: ABC
Arbitron Metro Market: Buchtel, OH *Format:* News, News/Talk, 86 *Special Programming:* Farm 5 hrs, gospel 3 hrs wkly *Hrs. of News Programming:* news progmg 21 hrs wkly *No. News Employees:* 3 *Target Audience:* 35 plus.
Eugene Edwards, President
Sharon Elliott, Station Manager

Bucyrus

WBCO
12-22-1962; 1540 khz AM
403 East Rensselaer St., P.O. Box 1140, Bucyrus, OH 44820 US
(530) 257-6100, *Fax:* (530) 257-6107
dennis@jackfm963.com
License: Bucyrus, OH held by Franklin Communications Inc.
Group Owner: Saga Communications Inc.; (acq 12-1-2003; $2.2 million with co-located FM).
Nat'l Network: CBS *Nat'l Reps:* Rgnl Reps
Arbitron Metro Market: Yakima WA *Format:* Adult Contemp
Gary Katz, President
Dennis Carlson, General Manager

WQEL
09-05-1964; 92.7 mhz FM *Hrs Open:* 24; 3 kw; 305 ft.; N40 45 49 W82 56 0
403 East Rensselaer St, Post Office Box 1140, Bucyrus, OH 44820 US
(419) 562-2222, *Fax:* (419) 562-0520
License: Bucyrus, Crawford County, OH
Group Owner: Saga Communications Inc.
Nat'l Network: CBS *Nat'l Reps:* Rgnl Reps
Format: Classic Rock, Sports *Hrs. of News Programming:* news progmg 10 hrs wkly *No. News Employees:* 2 *Target Audience:* 25-54.
Will Beard, Programming Director
Jim Hahn, Disc Jockey

Byesville

WILE-FM
10-29-1994; 97.7 mhz FM *Hrs Open:* 24; 1.8 kw; 413 ft.; N40 2 24 W81 38 50
Mailing Address: 114 North Sixth Street, Coshocton, OH 43812 US
Second Address: 4988 Skyline Dr., Cambridge, OH 43725
(740) 432-5605, *Fax:* (740) 432-1991
www.yourradioplace.com
License: Byesville, Guernsey County, OH held by AVC Communications Inc.
Group Owner: AVC Communications Inc.; acq 7-13-00).
Format: Adult Contemp
W. Grant Hafley, CEO
Dave Wilson, Operations Dir
Joel Losego, General Manager

Cadiz

WCDK
08-28-1985; 106.3 mhz FM *Hrs Open:* 24; 2.7 kw; 495 ft.; N40 15 14 W80 50 35
51 West Long Beach Avenue, Du Bois, PA 15801 US
(304) 723-1444, *Fax:* (304) 723-1688
www.106.3theriver.com
dharrison@1063theriver.com
License: Cadiz, Harrison County, OH held by Priority Communications Ohio LLC.
Group Owner: Priority Communications; (acq 12-98; $475,000 with WEIR(AM) Weirton, WV)
Nat'l Network: Jones Radio Networks *Nat'l Reps:* Dome
Arbitron Metro Market: Weirton, WV *Format:* Contemporary Hits/Top 40, Adult Contemp *Special Programming:* OSU football, Cleveland Browns football, high school football *Hrs. of News Programming:* news progmg 5 hrs wklyNo. *News Employees:* 1 *Target Audience:* 25-54; general
Jay Philippone, President
Jude Sheets, Operations Dir
Judy Vavrek, Station Manager
Cindy Taylor, Programming Director

Caldwell

WWKC
07-01-1989; 104.9 mhz FM *Hrs Open:* 24; 3 kw; 328 ft.; N39 48 47 W81 36 38
Mailing Address: 63021 Ridgewood Drive, Cambridge, OH 43725 US
Second Address: Box 19, Caldwell, OH 43724
(740) 432-5605, *Fax:* (740) 432-1991
www.yourradioplace.com
info@yourradioplace.com
License: Caldwell, Noble County, OH held by W. Grant Hafley.
Nat'l Reps: Rgnl Reps
Arbitron Metro Market: Caldwell, OH *Format:* Country *Target Audience:* 25-54.
Grant Hafley, President & CEO
David Wilson, Operations Dir
Joel Losego, General Manager
Dave Wilson, Operations Manager

Caledonia

WYNT
10-01-1986; 95.9 mhz FM *Hrs Open:* 19; 4.6 kw; 374 ft.; N40 40 55 W83 0 27
P.O. Box 316, Upper Sandusky, OH 43351 US
(740) 383-1131, *Fax:* (740) 387-3697
www.majic959.com
License: Caledonia, Wyandot County, OH held by CC Licenses LLC.
Group Owner: Clear Channel Communications Inc.; (acq 4-2-2002; $825,000).
Arbitron Metro Market: Caledonia, OH *Format:* Adult Contemp *Special Programming:* Farm 3 hrs wkly *Target Audience:* 27 plus; general
Diana Coon, General Manager
Steve Scott, Programming Director
James Howell, News Director

Cambridge

WCMJ
10-01-1964; 96.7 mhz FM; 2.3 kw; 367 ft.; N40 2 24 W81 38 50
Mailing Address: P.O. Box 338, Cambridge, OH 43725 US
Second Address: 4988 Skyline Dr., Cambridge, OH 43725
(740) 432-5605, *Fax:* (740) 432-1991
www.yourradioplace.com
webmaster@yourradioplace.com
License: Cambridge, Guernsey County, OH held by AVC Communications Inc.
Group Owner: AVC Communications Inc.; (acq 5-5-83)
Regional Reps: Rgnl Reps
Arbitron Metro Market: Cambridge, Oh *Format:* Adult Contemp *Hrs. of News Programming:* 2 *Target Audience:* 18-49.
Grant Hafley, CEO
Dave Wilson, Operations Dir
Joel Losego, General Manager

WILE
04-09-1948; 1270 khz AM; 1 kw-D, ND2; 0.035 kw-N, ND2; N40 2 24 W81 38 50
4988 Skyline Drive, PO Box 338, Cambridge, OH 43725 US
(419) 946-0016
www.yourradioplace.com
License: Cambridge, OH held by St. Gabriel Radio Inc.
Nat'l Network: ESPN Radio
Format: Sports *Target Audience:* 25-54.
Christopher Gabrelcik, President

***WOUC-FM**
05-11-1987; 89.1 mhz FM *Hrs Open:* 24; 5 kw; 499 ft.; N40 5 32 W81 17 19 *Rebroadcasts:* Rebroadcasts WOUB-FM Athens 100%
9 South College Street, Athens, OH 45701 US
(740) 593-4554, *Fax:* (740) 593-0240
www.woub.org
woub@woub.org
License: Cambridge, Guernsey County, OH held by Ohio University.
Nat'l Network: PRI; NPR
TV Affiliate: *WOUC-TV affil *Format:* News, News/Talk, 86 *No. News Employees:* 3
David Wiseman, Operations Dir
Carolyn Lewis, General Manager
Steve Skidmore, Operations Director
Scott Martin, Operations Manager

***WYFY**
88.1 mhz FM; 1.5 kw; 144 ft.; N40 1 37 W81 33 9
US
(800) 888-7077
www.bnbradio.org
bbn@bbnmedia.org
License: Cambridge, OH
Format: Religious, Talk

Campbell

WGFT
10-16-1955; 1330 khz AM
401 North Blair Ave., Youngstown, OH 44505 US
(330) 744-5115, *Fax:* (330) 744-4020
www.1330wgft.com
Savannah@ytownradio.com
License: Campbell, OH held by Bernard of Ohio LLC.
Group Owner: Bernard Radio LLC; (acq 1-22-2007; grpsl)
Nat'l Network: CNN Radio
Arbitron Metro Market: Campbell, OH *Format:* Talk *Target Audience:* General; family
Skip Bednarczyk, General Manager
Tiffany Allen, Promotions Manager

Canton

WHBC
03-09-1925; 1480 khz AM; 15 kw-D, DA2; 5 kw-N, DA2; N40 53 51 W81 19 10; N40 43 15 W81 26 28
P.O. Box 9917, Canton, OH 44711 US
(330) 456-7166, *Fax:* (330) 456-7199
www.whbc.com
pcook@whbc.com
License: Canton, OH held by NM Licensing LLC.

Group Owner: NextMedia Group Inc.; (acq 9-30-2000; with WHBC-FM Canton)
Nat'l Reps: Christal
Arbitron Metro Market: Canton, OH *Format:* Oldies *Special Programming:* Farm one hr wkly *Target Audience:* 25 plus.
Richard Bossler, General Manager

WHBC-FM
02-02-1948; 94.1 mhz FM; 45 kw; 515 ft.; N40 53 53 W81 19 7
P.O. Box 9917, Canton, OH 44711 US
(330) 456-7166, *Fax:* (330) 456-7199
www.mix941.com
pcook@whbc.com
License: Canton, Stark County, OH held by NM Licensing LLC.
Group Owner: NextMedia Group Inc.; (acq 9-30-2000; with WHBC(AM) Canton)
Arbitron Metro Market: Canton, OH *Format:* Adult Contemp *Target Audience:* 25-54.
Terry Simmons, Programming Director

WINW
04-14-1966; 1520 khz AM *Hrs Open:* Sunrise-sunset; 1 kw-D, DAD; N40 50 41 W81 21 2
P.O. Box 616, Cuyahoga Falls, OH 44222 US
(330) 453-1520, *Fax:* (330) 454-3030
License: Canton, OH held by Pinebrook Corp.
Nat'l Reps: Rgnl Reps
Arbitron Metro Market: Canton, OH *Format:* Gospel *Target Audience:* 35-54; professionals
Patrick Barb, President
Curtis Perry, General Manager

WILB
08-11-1946; 1060 khz AM
4601 Hills and Dale Rdnw, Canton, OH 44718 US
(330) 966-2903, *Fax:* (330) 966-3177
www.livingbreadradio.com
License: Canton, OH held by Living Bread Radio Inc.
Arbitron Metro Market: Canton, OH *Format:* Talk, Christian
Barbara Gaskell, President
Dan Clark, Operations Dir
Kate Sell, Station Manager

WRQK-FM
03-01-1961; 106.9 mhz FM *Hrs Open:* 24; 27.5 kw; 338 ft.; N40 49 22 W81 25 40
13o Main Street, Suite 202, Westport, CT 06880 US
(330) 492-4700, *Fax:* (330) 492-1350
www.wrqk.com
wrqk@wrqk.com
License: Canton, Stark County, OH held by Capstar TX L.P.
Group Owner: Clear Channel Communications Inc.; (acq 3-15-00; grpsl).
Arbitron Metro Market: Canton, OH *Format:* Rock/AOR *Hrs. of News Programming:* News progmg one hr wkly *Target Audience:* 18-49; emphasis on men
Don Lankford, General Manager

Carrollton

***WJDD**
90.9 mhz FM; 0.27 kw horiz, 0 kw vert; 318 ft.; N40 34 15 W81 10 48
US
(330) 875-7181
www.dennyhazen.com
License: Carrollton, Carroll County, OH held by Denny and Marge Hazen Ministries Inc.
Arbitron Metro Market: Carrollton, OH
Denny Hazen, President

Castalia

WGGN
01-01-1975; 97.7 mhz FM *Hrs Open:* 24; 0.64 kw; 725 ft.; N41 23 48 W82 47 31
Mailing Address: 3809 Maple Avenue, Castalia, OH 44824 US
Second Address: P. O. Box 247, Castalia, OH 44824
(419) 684-5311, *Fax:* (419) 684-5378
www.fm977.net
fm977@cfbroadcast.net
License: Castalia, Erie County, OH held by Christian Faith Broadcasting Inc.
Group Owner: Christian Faith Broadcasting Inc.
Nat'l Network: USA
Format: Adult Contemp, Christian *Target Audience:* 25-49; general
Shelby Gillam, President
Rusty Yost, General Manager
Jeff Ferback, General Sales Mgr
Dave Yost, Programming Director

Cedarville

***WKDC-FM**
12-01-1962; 90.3 mhz FM *Hrs Open:* 24; 30 kw; 354 ft; N39 45 46 W83 53 05
Box 601, Cedarville, OH 45314-0601
(937) 766-7815, *Fax:* (937) 766-7927
www.thepath.fm
info@thepath.fm
License: Cedarville, Greene County, OH held by The Cedarville University.
Nat'l Network: AP Radio; CNN Radio; Moody
Population Served: 400,000*Special Programming:* Black 2 hrs wkly *Hrs. of News Programming:* news progmg 16 hrs wkly *No. News Employees:* 1 *Target Audience:* 35-54.
William Brown, President
Martin Clark, Operations Dir
Paul Gathany, General Manager
Keith Hamer, Operations Manager

Celina

WCSM
09-11-1963; 1350 khz AM *Hrs Open:* 24; 0.5 kw-D, DA2; 0.011 kw-N, DA2; N40 32 17 W84 35 20
P. O. Box 492, Celina, OH 45822 US
(419) 586-5133, *Fax:* (419) 586-3814
www.wcsmradio.com
wcsm@bright.net
License: Celina, OH held by Hayco Broadcasting Inc.
Regional Network: Agrinet
Arbitron Metro Market: Lima, OH *Hrs. of News Programming:* news progmg 20 hrs wkly *No. News Employees:* 1 *Target Audience:* 18-49. *Adv. Rates:* 12.75; 12.75; 12.75; 12.75
John Coe, President
Sue Heiser, General Sales Mgr
Jim Hyatt, Programming Director
Kevin Sandler, News Director

WCSM-FM
01-01-1968; 96.7 mhz FM *Hrs Open:* 24; 2.2 kw; 384 ft.; N40 33 10 W84 31 2
P. O. Box 492, Celina, OH 45822 US
(419) 586-5133, *Fax:* (419) 586-3814
www.wcsmradio.com
wcsm@bright.net
License: Celina, Mercer County, OH
Nat'l Network: ABC; Jones Radio Networks *Regional Network:* Agrinet
Arbitron Metro Market: Lima, OH *Format:* Sports *Adv. Rates:* Same as AM
Jeff Hall, Station Manager

WKKI
12-18-1960; 94.3 mhz FM *Hrs Open:* 24; 2.2 kw; 448 ft; N40 33 08 W84 30 46
126 W. Fayette St., Celina, OH 45822
(419) 586-7715, *Fax:* (419) 586-1074
www.wkki.net
k94@bright.net
License: Celina, Mercer County, OH held by The Sonshine Communications Corp.
Rgnl Reps
Population Served: 250,000 *Arbitron Metro Market:* Lima, OH *Special Programming:* Contemp Christian 2 hrs wkly *Target Audience:* 25-54.
Paul Schmitmeyer, President
Dan Dietz, Operations Dir

Centerville

***WCWT-FM**
09-20-1971; 107.3 mhz FM; 0.023 kw; 190 ft.; N39 37 38 W84 8 54
111 Virginia Avenue, Centerville, OH 45459 US
(937) 439-3558(937) 439-3557, *Fax:* (937) 439-3574
www.wcwtfm.com
wcwt@centerville.k12.oh.us
License: Centerville, Montgomery County, OH held by Centerville City Board of Education.
Arbitron Metro Market: Centerville, Oh *Format:* Classic Rock *Target Audience:* General.
Bob Romond, General Manager

Chillicothe

WBEX
09-01-1947; 1490 khz AM *Hrs Open:* 24; 1 kw-U, ND1; N39 19 52 W82 59 49
Mailing Address: 50 East River Center Blvd., Covington, KY 41011 US
Second Address: 45 W.Main St., Chillicothe, OH 45601
(740) 773-3000, *Fax:* (740) 774-4494
www.wbex.com
newsroom@wkkj.com
License: Chillicothe, OH held by Citicasters Licenses L.P.
Group Owner: Clear Channel Communications Inc.; (acq 1999; grpsl).
Nat'l Network: CBS; Westwood One *Nat'l Reps:* Katz Radio
Arbitron Metro Market: Chillicothe, OH *Format:* News, News/Talk, 86 *Hrs. of News Programming:* news progmg 10 hrs wkly *No. News Employees:* 3 *Target Audience:* 30-50.
Dan Latham, Operations Dir
JoshuaKoch, Sales Departments
Dan Ramey, Programming Director
Dan Latham, Market Manager
MikeSmith, News/Sports Director
KobyDoughty, Online Content Director

WCHI
10-01-1951; 1350 khz AM *Hrs Open:* 24
45 W. Main Street, Chillicothe, OH 45601 US
(740) 775-1350(740) 773-3000, *Fax:* (740) 774-4494
www.927wchi.com
newsroom@wkkj.com
License: Chillicothe, OH held by CC Licenses LLC.
Group Owner: Clear Channel Communications Inc.; (acq 10-19-99; $4 million with co-located FM).
Nat'l Network: ABC *Nat'l Reps:* Katz Radio
Arbitron Metro Market: Chillicothe, Oh *Format:* Oldies *No. News Employees:* 2 *Target Audience:* 25-65. *Adv. Rates:* 10; 10; 10; 10
Bob Neal, Operations Dir
Dan Latham, General Manager
Tracy Taylor, General Sales Mgr

WKKJ
12-22-1978; 94.3 mhz FM *Hrs Open:* 24; 19 kw; 353 ft.; N39 19 52 W82 59 49
P.O.Box 98, 45 W.Main St, Chillicothe, OH 45601 US
(740) 773-3000, *Fax:* (740) 774-4494
www.wkkj.com
newsroom@wkkj.com
License: Chillicothe, Ross County, OH
Group Owner: Clear Channel Communications Inc.
Nat'l Network: ABC
Arbitron Metro Market: Chillicothe, OH *Format:* Country *Hrs. of News Programming:* news progmg 14 hrs wkly *No. News Employees:* 3 *Adv. Rates:* 60; 50; 50; 50
Dan Latham, Operations Dir
Mike Smith, News Director

***WOHC**
05-01-1992; 90.1 mhz FM; 2 kw vert; 394 ft.; N39 20 45 W83 11 15 *Rebroadcasts:* Rebroadcasts WCDR(FM) Cedarville 100%
Box 601, 251 N. Main St, Cedarville, OH 45314 US
937-766-5595, *Fax:* 937-766-7927
thepath.fm
info@thepath.fm
License: Chillicothe, Ross County, OH held by The Cedarville University.
Nat'l Network: AP Radio; CNN Radio; Moody
TV Affiliate: Relg *Format:* Black *Special Programming:* news progmg 16 hrs wkly *Hrs. of News Programming:* 1 *No. News Employees:* 35-54; information-orient
Assistant Manager

***WOUH-FM**
10-01-1992; 91.9 mhz FM *Hrs Open:* 24; 0.75 kw; 650 ft.; N39 19 46 W82 48 8 *Rebroadcasts:* Rebroadcasts WOUB-FM Athens 100%
9 S. College Street, Athens, OH 45701 US
(740) 593-4554, *Fax:* (740) 593-0240
www.woub.org
woub@woub.org
License: Chillicothe, Ross County, OH held by Ohio University.
Format: News, News/Talk, 86 *No. News Employees:* 3
David Wiseman, Operations Dir
Carolyn Lewis, General Manager
Tim Myers, Programming Director
Kelly Martin, Promotions Manager
Tim Sharp, News Director
Ted Ross, Engineering Dir
Steve Skidmore, Operations Director
Scott Martin,Operations Manager
Rusty Smith, Programming Director

WQLX
07-15-1956; 1590 khz AM; 500 w-D; N39 09 58 W83 36 25
Mailing Address: Box 9, Hillsboro, OH 45133
Second Address: 5675 St., Rt. 247, Hillsboro, OH 45133
(937) 393-1590, *Fax:* (937) 393-1611
www.wsrwam.com
wsrw@clearchannel.com

License: Chillicothe, Highland County, OH held by CC Licenses LLC.
Group Owner: Clear Channel Communications Inc.; (acq 10-26-99; $2.5 million with WSRW-FM Hillsboro)
Nat'l Network: Jones Radio Networks *Nat'l Reps:* Katz Radio
Population Served: 75,000*Hrs. of News Programming:* News progmg 3 hrs wkly *Target Audience:* 35-54; general *Adv. Rates:* 10; 10; 10; 10
Dan Latham, Operations Dir
John Barney, General Sales Mgr
Damon Scott, Programming Director
Paul Levo, Chief Engineer
Kim Scaggs, Operations Manager

***WZCP**
01-15-1988; 89.3 mhz FM *Hrs Open:* 24; 2.5 kw vert; 351 ft.; N39 20 45 W83 11 15
3800 Victory Parkway, Cincinnati, OH 45207 US
614-289-5704
www.chillicothe.riverradio.com
promise@riverradio.com
License: Chillicothe, Ross County, OH held by Christian Voice of Central Ohio Inc.
Group Owner: Christian Voice of Central Ohio Inc.; (acq 5-15-2007; grpsl)
Arbitron Metro Market: Chillicothe, OH *Format:* Christian
Scott Thomson, CFO
Dan Baughman, President/CEO
Dan Baughman, General Manager
Craig Bennington, National Sales Manager
Scott Saunders, Programming Director
Matt Levin, Chief Engineer
Bill Montogomery, Chief Sales Officer
JonDennings, Traffic Coordinator
Eric Faulds, Music Director
Andy Meyer, Director of Brand Development
Todd Stach, Chief Creative Officer
Matt Waddell, Marketing Consultant

Cincinnati

WAKW
11-21-1961; 93.3 mhz FM *Hrs Open:* 24; 50 kw horiz, 49 kw vert; 492 ft.; N39 12 19 W84 33 23
6275 Collegevue Place, Cincinnati, OH 45224 US
(513) 542-9259, *Fax:* (513) 542-9333
www.mystar933.com
info@wakw.com
License: Cincinnati, Hamilton County, OH held by Pillar of Fire Inc.
Group Owner: Pillar of Fire Inc.
Nat'l Network: Moody
Arbitron Metro Market: Cincinnati, OH *Format:* Christian *No. News Employees:* 1 *Target Audience:* General; families *Adv. Rates:* 90; 75; 75; 56
Gerald Croucher, General Manager

WSAI
06-07-1923; 1360 khz AM *Hrs Open:* 24; 5 kw-D, DAN; 5 kw-N, DAN; N39 14 51 W84 31 52
50 E. Rivercenter Blvd., Suite 1200, Covington, KY 41011 US
(513) 686-8300, *Fax:* (513) 665-9700
www.foxsports1360.com
chuckfredrick@clearchannel.com
License: Cincinnati, OH held by Clear Channel Communication Inc.
Group Owner: Clear Channel Communications Inc.; (acq 4-29-99; grpsl)
Nat'l Network: ESPN Radio
Arbitron Metro Market: Cincinnati, OH *Format:* Sports
Chuck Fredrick, President
Darryl Parks, Operations Dir
Mike Kenney, General Manager
Mike Jamison, General Sales Mgr
Scott Reinhart, Programming Director
Matt Overla, Promotions Manager
Ted Ryan, Engineering Dir
Dave Abbott,Chief Engineer
Vince Marotta, Promotions Director

WEBN
08-27-1967; 102.7 mhz FM; 16 kw; 866 ft.; N39 6 59 W84 30 7
50 East Rivercenter Blvd, Suite 1200, Covington, KY 41011 US
(513) 686-8300, *Fax:* (513) 749-3299
www.webn.com
License: Cincinnati, Hamilton County, OH held by Jacor Broadcasting Corp.
Group Owner: Clear Channel Communications Inc.; (Acq 2-86; $8 million;
Arbitron Metro Market: Cincinnati, OH *Format:* Rock/AOR
Chuck Fredrick, President
Jeff Sigmon, General Manager
Paul Frodge, General Sales Mgr
Chris Williams, Programming Director
Matt Overla, Promotions Manager

***WGUC**
09-21-1960; 90.9 mhz FM *Hrs Open:* 24; 18.5 kw; 686 ft.; N39 7 29.9 W84 29 56.2
1223 Central Parkway, Cincinnati, OH 45214 US
(513) 241-8282, *Fax:* (513) 241-8456
www.wguc.org
info@wguc.org
License: Cincinnati, Hamilton County, OH held by Cincinnati Public Radio, Inc.
Nat'l Network: PRI
Arbitron Metro Market: Cincinnati, OH *Format:* Talk *Target Audience:* 35 plus; well-educated
Richard Eiswerth, CEO
Sherri Mancini, General Sales Mgr
Robin Gehl, Programming Director
Chris Phelps, Promotions Manager
Don Danko, Engineering Dir
Barry Weinstein, CFO
David Schackmann, Corporate Sales Manager
Gordon Bayliss,Sales VP

WKRC
01-01-1922; 550 khz AM; 5 kw-D, DA2; 1 kw-N, DA2; N39 0 29 W84 26 39
50 East Rivercenter Blvd, Suite 1200, Covington, KY 41011 US
(513) 686-8300
www.55krc.com
info@55krc.com
License: Cincinnati, OH held by Jacor Broadcasting Corp.
Group Owner: Clear Channel Communications Inc.; (acq 5-4-99; grpsl).
Nat'l Network: Westwood One; CBS
Arbitron Metro Market: Cincinnati, OH *Format:* News, News/Talk, 86 *Target Audience:* 35-64; adult, affluent, conservative
Chuck Fredrick, President
Mike Kenney, Operations Dir
Karrie Sudbrack, General Manager
Bill Mountel, General Sales Mgr
Scott Reinhart, Programming Director
Dave Abbott, Chief Engineer
Justin Tabas, Integrated MarketingDirector
Kelley Snider, Community Engagement Coordinator

WKRQ
01-01-1947; 101.9 mhz FM; 16 kw; 866 ft.; N39 6 59 W84 30 7
600 New Hampshire Ave NW, Suite 1200, Washington, DC 20037 US
(513) 699-5102, *Fax:* (513) 699-5000
www.wkrq.com
jeff@wkrg.com
License: Cincinnati, Hamilton County, OH held by Bonneville Holding Co.
Group Owner: Bonneville International Corporation; (acq 3-14-2008; grpsl)
Nat'l Reps: Katz Radio
Arbitron Metro Market: Cincinnati, OH *Format:* Adult Contemp
Jim Bryant, Operations Dir
Bryson Lair, General Sales Mgr
Patti Marshall, Programming Director
Brian Douglas, Music Director

WLW
03-22-1922; 700 khz AM; 50 kw-U, ND1; N39 21 11 W84 19 30
50 East Rivercenter Blvd, Suite 1200, Covington, KY 41011 US
(513) 686-8300, *Fax:* (513) 665-9700
www.700wlw.com
info@700wlw.com
License: Cincinnati, OH held by Jacor Broadcasting Corp.
Group Owner: Clear Channel Communications Inc.; (acq 4-99; grpsl).
Arbitron Metro Market: Cincinnati, OH *Format:* News, News/Talk, 86
Chuck Fredrick, President
Tom Alexander, General Manager
Tom Horan, General Sales Mgr
Scott Reinhart, Programming Director
Dave Abbot, Chief Engineer

WOFX-FM
08-19-1964; 92.5 mhz FM; 16 kw; 866 ft.; N39 6 59 W84 30 7
Suite 1200, 50 East Rivercenter Blvd, Covington, KY 41011 US
(513) 241-9898, *Fax:* (513) 241-6689
www.foxcincinnati.com
License: Cincinnati, Hamilton County, OH held by Cumulus Licensing LLC.
Group Owner: Cumulus Media Inc.; (acq 4-10-2009; grpsl)
Arbitron Metro Market: Cincinnati, OH *TV Affiliate:* Classic rock *No. News Employees:* 25-54.
Sales Manager, Chris Geisen
Program Director, Vincent Moses
Promotions, Promotions Manager

WRRM
10-01-1959; 98.5 mhz FM; 17.5 kw; 807 ft.; N39 7 19 W84 32 52
140 East Market Street, York, PA 17401 US
(513) 241-9898, *Fax:* (513) 241-6689
www.warm98.com
License: Cincinnati, Hamilton County, OH held by WRRM Lico Inc.
Group Owner: Cumulus Media Partners LLC; (acq 1-72)
Arbitron Metro Market: Cincinnati, OH *Format:* Adult Contemp
TJ Holland, Operations Dir

WCKY
09-16-1929; 1530 khz AM; 50 kw-D, DAN; 50 kw-N, DAN; N39 4 7 W84 36 20; N39 3 55 W84 36 27
50 E. Rivercenter Blvd, Suite 1200, Covington, KY 41011 US
(513) 686-8300, *Fax:* (513) 333-4269
www.wcky.com
License: Cincinnati, OH held by Clear Channel Communications
Group Owner: Clear Channel Communications Inc.
Nat'l Network: ESPN Radio; Fox Sports; Westwood One
Arbitron Metro Market: Cincinnati, OH *Format:* Sports *Target Audience:* 35 plus; special focus on ages 35-64
Darryl Parks, Operations Dir

WCVX
01-01-1947; 1050 khz AM *Hrs Open:* 24; 1 kw-D, ND1; 0.279 kw-N, ND1; N39 4 50 W84 31 18
4880 Santa Rosa Rd, Suite 300, Camarillo, CA 93012 US
(513) 579-1050, *Fax:* (513) 533-2528
christiantalk1050.com
carl.behanan@cbslradio.com
License: Cincinnati, OH held by Christian Broadcasting System Ltd.
Group Owner: Christian Broadcasting System Ltd.; (acq 2-10-2006; swap of WCVX(AM) and WDJO(AM) Florence, KY plus $6.75 million cash for WLQV(AM) Detroit, MI)
Nat'l Network: Salem Radio Network
Arbitron Metro Market: Cincinnati, OH *Format:* Talk, Religious
Special Programming: Gospel 15 hrs, Sp 3 hrs wkly *Hrs. of News Programming:* News progmg 10 hrs wkly *Target Audience:* 24-54; family oriented youngadults
Jon Yinger, President
Errol Dengler, Operations Dir
Gaither Stephens, General Manager
Carl Behanan, Programming Director

WDBZ
01-01-1927; 1230 khz AM *Hrs Open:* 24
625 Eden Park Drive, Suite 1050, Cincinnati, OH 45202 US
(513) 679-6000, *Fax:* (513) 948-1985
www.1230thebuzz.com
jtolliver@radio-one.com
License: Cincinnati, OH held by Blue Chip Broadcasting Licenses Ltd.
Group Owner: Radio One Inc.; (acq 7-20-2007; $2.69 million)
Nat'l Reps: Christal
Arbitron Metro Market: Cincinnati, OH *Format:* Gospel *No. News Employees:* 1 *Target Audience:* 25-54.
Barry.A.Mayo, President
Lincoln Ware, Operations Dir
Lisa Thal, General Manager
Josh Guttman, General Sales Mgr
Jeri Tolliver, Program Director/Marketing
Sharon McCormick, Sales

WUBE-FM
07-20-1949; 105.1 mhz FM; 14.5 kw; 915 ft.; N39 7 30 W84 29 56
625 Eden Park Drive, Suite 1050, Cincinnati, OH 45202 US
(513) 699-5105, *Fax:* (513-) 699-5000
www.b105.com
License: Cincinnati, Hamilton County, OH held by Bonneville Holding Co.
Group Owner: Bonneville International Corporation; (acq 3-14-2008; grpsl)
Arbitron Metro Market: Cincinnati, OH *Format:* Country
Jim Bryant, Operations Dir
Christine Mello, General Sales Mgr
Travis Moon, Programming Director
Duke Hamilton, Music Director

WNNF
01-01-1955; 94.1 mhz FM *Hrs Open:* 24; 16 kw; 866 ft.; N39 6 59 W84 30 7
50 East Rivercenter Blvd, Suite 1200, Covington, KY 41011 US

(513) 241-9898, *Fax:* (513) 241-6689
www.radio941.com
info@radio941.net
License: Cincinnati, Hamilton County, OH held by Cumulus Licensing LLC.
Group Owner: Cumulus Media Inc.; (acq 4-10-2009; grpsl)
Arbitron Metro Market: Cincinnati, OH *Format:* Adult Contemp *No. News Employees:* 1 *Target Audience:* 25-54.
Karrie Sudbrack, General Manager
Bobby Dayer, Programming Director

***WVXU**
10-01-1971; 91.7 mhz FM; 26 kw; 682 ft.; N39 7 31 W84 29 57
3800 Victoria Parkway, Cincinnati, OH 45207 US
(513) 352-9170, *Fax:* (513) 241-8456
www.wvxu.org
wvxu@wvxu.org
License: Cincinnati, Hamilton County, OH held by Cincinnati Public Radio, Inc.
Nat'l Network: PRI; NPR
Arbitron Metro Market: Cincinnati, OH *Format:* News *Hrs. of News Programming:* 107 hrs wkly *No. News Employees:* 6 *Target Audience:* 35 yrs plus; well educated
Mr.William Fee, Chairman
Barry Weinstein, CFO
Richard Eiswerth, General Manager
Sherri Mancini, General Sales Mgr
Robin Gehl, Programming Director
Chris Phelps, Promotions Manager
Maryanne Zeleznik, News Director
Don Danko,Engineering Dir
David Schackmann, Corporate Sales Manager

Circleville

WNKK
10-01-1965; 107.1 mhz FM; 3 kw; 328 ft.; N39 39 52 W82 51 4
600 New Hampshire Ave., NW, Suite 1200, Washington, DC 20037 US
(956) 686-6382, *Fax:* (956) 686-2999
License: Circleville, Pickaway County, OH held by Wilks License Co.-Columbus LLC.
Group Owner: Wilks Broadcast Group LLC; (acq 1-10-2007; grpsl)
Nat'l Reps: Christal
Paulino Bernal Jr., President

Cleveland

WWGK
01-01-1947; 1540 khz AM; 1 kw-D, NDD; N41 30 10 W81 37 57
8000 Euclid Avenue, Cleveland, OH 44103 US
(805) 240-2070
License: Cleveland, OH held by Good Karma Broadcasting L.L.C.
Group Owner: Good Karma Broadcasting L.L.C.; (acq 10-27-2006; $2.5 million)
Nat'l Network: ESPN Radio; Fox Sports; Premiere Radio Networks
Arbitron Metro Market: Altus OK
Neal Robinson, President

WFHM-FM
04-01-1960; 95.5 mhz FM *Hrs Open:* 24; 31 kw; 620 ft.; N41 26 32 W81 29 28
26501 Renaissance Pkwy, Cleveland, OH 44128 US
(216) 901-0921, *Fax:* (216) 901-1104
www.955thefish.com
office@whkradio.com
License: Cleveland, Cuyahoga County, OH held by Salem Media Group LLC.
Group Owner: Salem Communications Corp.; (acq 12-22-2000; grpsl)
Nat'l Reps: Salem
Arbitron Metro Market: Cleveland, OH *Format:* Adult Contemp, Christian *Hrs. of News Programming:* News progmg one hr wkly *Target Audience:* 25-54; female
Edward Atsinger, President
Joe Sweeney, Operations Dir
Mark Jaycox, General Manager
Tim Vaughan, General Sales Mgr
Len Howser, Programming Director

***WCPN**
09-08-1984; 90.3 mhz FM *Hrs Open:* 24; 47 kw; 509 ft.; N41 22 18 W81 42 48
Suite 300, 3100 Chester Avenue, Cleveland, OH 44114 US
(216) 916-6100, *Fax:* (216) 916-6101
www.wcpn.org
License: Cleveland, Cuyahoga County, OH held by Ideastream
Nat'l Network: PRI; NPR
Arbitron Metro Market: Cleveland, OH *Format:* Jazz, News, 86 *Special Programming:* Ger one hr, Hungarian one hr, Lithuanian one hr, Pol one hr, Slovak one hr wkly *Hrs. of News Programming:* news progmg 50 hrs wkly*No. News Employees:* 16 *Target Audience:* General.
Jerry Wareham, CEO
Keith Turner, Operations Dir
Maureen Paschke, General Sales Mgr

***WCRF-FM**
11-23-1958; 103.3 mhz FM *Hrs Open:* 24; 25.5 kw; 659 ft.; N41 17 48 W81 39 27
820 North La Salle St., Chicago, IL 60610 US
(440) 526-1111, *Fax:* (440) 526-1319
www.moodyradiocleveland.fm
wcrf@moody.edu
License: Cleveland, Cuyahoga County, OH held by Moody Bible Institute of Chicago.
Group Owner: The Moody Bible Institute of Chicago
Nat'l Network: Moody; Salem Radio Network *Wire Services:* AP
Arbitron Metro Market: Cleveland, OH *Format:* Religious *Target Audience:* 25-55.
Dr. Michael Easley, President
Richard Lee, Station Manager
Phil Villareal, Programming Director
Doug Hainer, Chief Engineer

***WCSB**
05-10-1976; 89.3 mhz FM *Hrs Open:* 24; 0.63 kw; 203 ft.; N41 30 12 W81 40 30
1983 East 24th St., Cleveland, OH 44115 US
(216) 687-3515
www.wcsb.org
gm@wcsb.org
License: Cleveland, Cuyahoga County, OH held by Cleveland State University.
Arbitron Metro Market: Cleveland, OH *Format:* Alternative *Hrs. of News Programming:* News progmg 7 hrs wkly *Target Audience:* General.
Sara Corrigan, General Manager
Brian Detrow, General Sales Mgr
Jae Kristoff, Programming Director
Mark Manolio, Chief Engineer

WDOK
04-30-1950; 102.1 mhz FM; 12 kw; 1004 ft.; N41 22 58 W81 42 7
1 Radio Lane, Cleveland, OH 44114 US
(216) 696-0123, *Fax:* (216) 363-7104
new102.cbslocal.com/
info@new102.com
License: Cleveland, Cuyahoga County, OH held by Infinity Radio Inc.
Group Owner: CBS Radio; (acq 2000; grpsl).
Arbitron Metro Market: Cleveland, OH *Format:* Classic Rock *Target Audience:* 25-54; general
Chris Maduri, General Manager
Dave Popovich, Programming Director

WENZ
07-14-1959; 107.9 mhz FM *Hrs Open:* 24; 16 kw horiz, 15 kw vert; 892 ft.; N41 27 54 W81 17 13
5900 Princess Garden Parkway, 8th Floor, Lanham, MD 20706 US
(216) 579-1111, *Fax:* (216) 771-4164
www.zhiphopcleveland.com/
cforgy@radio-one.com
License: Cleveland, Cuyahoga County, OH held by Radio One Licenses LLC.
Group Owner: Radio One Inc.; (acq 11-8-01; grpsl).
Nat'l Reps: Christal
Arbitron Metro Market: Cleveland, OH *Format:* Rock/AOR *No. News Employees:* 1 *Target Audience:* 18-34.
Chris Forgy, Operations Dir
paul guy, General Sales Mgr
Colby Colb, Programming Director
Rohnesha Horne, Promotions Manager
gary zocolo, Engineering Dir
Kim Johnson, Operations Manager

WJMO
07-06-1949; 1300 khz AM *Hrs Open:* 24; 5 kw-U, DA1; N41 20 28 W81 44 30
5900 Princess Garden Parkway, 8th Floor, Lanham, MD 20706 US
(216) 579-1111, *Fax:* (216) 621 2176
www.praisecleveland.com
elogan@radio-one.com
License: Cleveland, OH held by Radio One Licenses LLC.
Group Owner: Radio One Inc.; (acq 11-8-2001; grpsl)
Nat'l Reps: Christal
Arbitron Metro Market: Cleveland, OH *Format:* Gospel *Hrs. of News Programming:* news progmg 4 hrs wkly *No. News Employees:* 2 *Target Audience:* 25-54; Black adults
Colby Colb, Operations Dir
Elisabeth Logan, General Sales Mgr
Haig Meguerditchian, National Sales Manager

WGAR-FM
07-01-1948; 99.5 mhz FM *Hrs Open:* 24; 50 kw; 499 ft.; N41 22 18 W81 43 4
50 East Rivercenter Boulevard, Suite 1200, Covington, KY 41011 US
(216) 520-2600, *Fax:* (216) 524-2600
www.wgar.com
feedback@wgar.com
License: Cleveland, Cuyahoga County, OH held by Citicasters Licenses L.P.
Group Owner: Clear Channel Communications Inc.; (acq 5-4-99; grpsl).
Nat'l Network: AP Radio *Nat'l Reps:* Christal
Arbitron Metro Market: Cleveland, OH *Format:* Country *No. News Employees:* 2 *Target Audience:* 25-54.
Mike Kenney, General Manager
Rodger Moorman, General Sales Mgr
Brian Jennings, Programming Director
Chuck Collier, Music Director
Cindy Hunter, Local Sales Manager
Kristen Heiss, Sales Assistant

WHK
07-28-1921; 1420 khz AM; 5 kw-D, DAN; 5 kw-N, DAN; N41 21 30 W81 40 3
4880 Santa Rosa Rd, Ste 300, Camarillo, CA 93012 US
(216) 901-0921, *Fax:* (216) 901-5517
www.whkradio.com
office@whkradio.com
License: Cleveland, OH held by Caron Broadcasting Inc.
Group Owner: Salem Communications Corp.; (acq 9-1-2004; $10 million).
Nat'l Network: Salem Radio Network *Wire Services:* AP
Arbitron Metro Market: Cleveland, OH *Format:* Talk *Target Audience:* 25-54; male & female
Len Howser, Programming Director

WHKW
12-01-1930; 1220 khz AM; 50 kw-U, DA1; N41 18 26 W81 41 21
600 Congress Ave., Suite 1400, Austin, TX 78701 US
(216) 901-0921, *Fax:* (216) 901-5517
www.whkwradio.com
info@whkwradio.com
License: Cleveland, OH held by Caron Broadcasting Inc.
Group Owner: Salem Communications Corp.; (acq 8-24-2000; grpsl).
Arbitron Metro Market: Cleveland, OH *Format:* Christian, Talk
Errol Dengler, General Manager

WMJI
12-06-1948; 105.7 mhz FM *Hrs Open:* 24; 16 kw; 1129 ft.; N41 23 2 W81 41 44
50 East Rivercenter Boulevard, Suite 1200, Covington, KY 41011 US
(216) 520-2600, *Fax:* (216) 524-3200
www.wmji.com
feedback@wmji.com
License: Cleveland, Cuyahoga County, OH held by Citicasters Licenses L.P.
Group Owner: Clear Channel Communications Inc.; (acq 5-4-99; grpsl).
Nat'l Network: AP Radio *Nat'l Reps:* Christal *Wire Services:* UPI
Arbitron Metro Market: Cleveland, OH *Format:* Contemporary Hits/Top 40 *Hrs. of News Programming:* news progmg 5 hrs wkly *No. News Employees:* 4 *Target Audience:* 25-54.
Kevin Metheny, Operations Dir
Mike Kenney, General Manager
Roger Moorman, General Sales Mgr

WMMS
11-11-1948; 100.7 mhz FM; 34 kw; 600 ft.; N41 21 30 W81 40 3
50 East Rivercenter Boulevard, Suite 1200, Covington, KY 41011 US
(216) 520-2600, *Fax:* (216) 901-8166
www.wmms.com
feedback@wmms.com
License: Cleveland, Cuyahoga County, OH held by Citicasters Licenses L.P.
Group Owner: Clear Channel Communications Inc.; (acq 1999; grpsl).
Arbitron Metro Market: Cleveland, OH *Target Audience:* 18-34.
Bo Matthews, Operations Dir
Mike Kenney, General Manager
Kris Foley, General Sales Mgr

WHLK
05-04-1960; 106.5 mhz FM *Hrs Open:* 24; 11.3 kw; 1,036 ft; N41 22 45 W81 43 12
6200 Oak Tree Blvd., 4th Fl., Independence, OH 41011
(216) 520-2600, *Fax:* (216) 520-3008
www.wmvx.com
License: Cleveland, Cuyahoga County, OH
Group Owner: Clear Channel Communications Inc.
Population Served: 2,200,000 *Arbitron Metro Market:* Cleveland, OH *Adv. Rates:* 240; 240; 240; 75
Mike Kenney, Station Manager
Dawn Lesiak, News Director
Dave Snyder, Sports Commentator

WNCX
10-23-1948; 98.5 mhz FM *Hrs Open:* 24; 16 kw; 961 ft.; N41 20 28 W81 44 24
600 New Hampshire Avenue, N.W., Suite 1200, Washington, DC 20037 US
(216) 861-0100, *Fax:* (216) 696-0385
www.wncx.com
info@wncx.com
License: Cleveland, Cuyahoga County, OH held by Infinity Radio License Inc.
Group Owner: CBS Radio
Nat'l Network: ABC; Westwood One
Arbitron Metro Market: Cleveland, OH *Format:* Light Rock *Target Audience:* 25-54; adults *Adv. Rates:* 300; 250; 250; 75
Tom Herschel, Operations Dir
Linda Rodriguez, General Sales Mgr
Bill Louis, Programming Director
Marshall Goudy, Promotions Manager
George Cohn, National Sales Manager

WQAL
01-01-1948; 104.1 mhz FM *Hrs Open:* 24; 12 kw; 961 ft.; N41 20 28 W81 44 24
1621 Euclid Avenue, Cleveland, OH 44115 US
(216) 696-0123, *Fax:* (216) 348-0107
www.q104.com
License: Cleveland, Cuyahoga County, OH held by Infinity Radio Inc.
Group Owner: CBS Radio; (acq 12-14-00; grpsl).
Arbitron Metro Market: Cleveland, OH *Format:* Adult Contemp
No. News Employees: 1 *Target Audience:* 25-49; women
Chris Maduri, General Manager

WKNR
01-01-1926; 850 khz AM *Hrs Open:* 24; 50 kw-D, DA2; 4.7 kw-N, DA2; N41 19 0 W81 43 51
1 Radio Lane, Cleveland, OH 44114 US
(440) 838-8585, *Fax:* (440) 838-1546
www.espncleveland.com
License: Cleveland, OH held by Good Karma Broadcasting LLC.
Group Owner: Good Karma Broadcasting L.L.C.; (acq 2-7-2007; $7 million)
Nat'l Network: ESPN Radio
Arbitron Metro Market: Cleveland, OH *Format:* Sports *Target Audience:* 25-54; male sports fans
Craig Karmazin, CEO
Sam Pines, Station Manager
Jason Gibbs, Promotions Manager

***WRUW-FM**
02-26-1967; 91.1 mhz FM *Hrs Open:* 24; 15 kw; 292 ft.; N41 31 14 W81 35 3
2040 Adelbert Road, Cleveland, OH 44106 US
(216) 368-2207,
www.wruw.org
gm@wruw.org
License: Cleveland, Cuyahoga County, OH held by Case Western Reserve University.
Arbitron Metro Market: Cleveland, OH *Format:* Variety/Diverse
Target Audience: General; Cleveland & CWRU community
Tessa Greene, Operations Dir
Katy Witkowski, General Manager
Peter McCall, Station Manager
Natalie Agresta, Programming Director
Roger Ganley, Promotions Manager

WTAM
01-01-1923; 1100 khz AM *Hrs Open:* 24; 50 kw-U, ND1; N41 16 50 W81 37 22
50 East Rivercenter Boulevard, Suite 1200, Covington, KY 41011 US
(216) 520-2600, *Fax:* (216) 901-8152 (progmg)
www.wtam.com
info@wtam.com
License: Cleveland, OH held by Clear Channel Broadcasting Inc.
Group Owner: Clear Channel Communications Inc.; (acq 5-4-99; grpsl)
Arbitron Metro Market: Cleveland, OH *Format:* News, News/Talk, 84, Talk *Hrs. of News Programming:* news progmg 25 hrs wkly
No. News Employees: 14 *Target Audience:* 25-54. *Adv. Rates:* 250; 250; 375; 150
Jim Meltzer, Operations Dir
Gary Mincer, General Sales Mgr
Ray Davis, Programming Director
Jeff Zukauckas, Promotions Manager
R.C. Bauer, News Director
Dave Ianni, General Sales Manager
Gaye Ramstrom, National Sales Manager
Kevin Metheny, Operations Manager
Cheryl Zivich, Public Affairs Director

WWMK
04-03-1950; 1260 khz AM *Hrs Open:* 24; 10 kw-D, DA2; 5 kw-N, DA2; N41 17 10 W81 38 34
77 W. 66th St., 16th Fl, Attn: Sam Antar, New York, NY 10023 US
(440) 746-1010, *Fax:* (440) 746-1720
www.radiodisney.com
License: Cleveland, OH held by Radio Disney Group LLC.
Group Owner: ABC Inc.; (acq 8-26-98; $3.9 million).
Nat'l Network: USA
Arbitron Metro Market: Cleveland, OH *Format:* Children *Target Audience:* 3-12, women 21-44; children & families *Adv. Rates:* 80; 80; 80; 45
Michelle Kulball, Station Manager
Jeniffer Hansen, General Sales Mgr

WZAK
05-26-1963; 93.1 mhz FM *Hrs Open:* 24; 27.5 kw; 620 ft.; N41 16 50 W81 37 22
2510 Saint Claire, Cleveland, OH 44114 US
(216) 579-1111, *Fax:* (216) 621 2176
www.931wzak.com
cforgy@radio-one.com
License: Cleveland, Cuyahoga County, OH held by Radio One Licenses LLC.
Group Owner: Radio One Inc.; (acq 11-8-01; grpsl).
Nat'l Reps: Christal
Arbitron Metro Market: Cleveland, OH *Format:* Adult Contemp
No. News Employees: 1 *Target Audience:* 25-54 Black adults
Kim Johnson, Operations Dir
Chris Forgy, General Manager
haig megurditchian, General Sales Mgr

Cleveland Heights

WERE
01-01-1947; 1490 khz AM *Hrs Open:* 24; 1 kw-D, ND2; 1 kw-N, ND2; N41 30 48 W81 36 5
2510 Saint Claire, Cleveland, OH 44114 US
(216) 579-1111, *Fax:* (216) 621 2176
www.newstalk1490.com
cforgy@radio-one.com
License: Cleveland Heights, OH held by Radio One Licenses LLC.
Group Owner: Radio One Inc.; (acq 8-7-2000; grpsl)
Nat'l Reps: Christal
Arbitron Metro Market: Cleveland, OH *Format:* News, News/Talk, 86 *Hrs. of News Programming:* news progmg 30 hrs wkly *No. News Employees:* 4
Cathy Hughes, CEO
Chris Forgy, Operations Dir
haig meguerditchian, General Sales Mgr
kimberly Hill, Programming Director

WKRK-FM
11-23-1960; 92.3 mhz FM *Hrs Open:* 24; 40 kw horiz, 36 kw vert; 548 ft.; N41 26 32 W81 29 28
2510 Saint Claire, Cleveland, OH 44114 US
(216) 861-0100, *Fax:* (216) 696-3710
www.krockcleveland.com
License: Cleveland Heights, Cuyahoga County, OH held by CBS Radio Stations Inc.
Group Owner: CBS Radio; (acq 12-14-2000; grpsl)
Nat'l Network: ABC
Arbitron Metro Market: Cleveland, OH *Format:* Alternative *Target Audience:* 18-34; mass appeal, young adults
Tom Herschel, Operations Dir
Jeff Miller, General Sales Mgr
Marshall Goudy, Promotions Manager
George Cohn, National Sales Manager

Clyde

WMJK
07-16-1981; 100.9 mhz FM *Hrs Open:* 24; 3 kw; 299 ft.; N41 14 57 W82 54 47
50 East Rivercenter Blvd., Suite 1200, Covington, KY 41011 US
(419) 625-1010, *Fax:* (419) 625-1348
www.coast1009.com
randyhugg@basbroadcasting.com
License: Clyde, Sandusky County, OH held by BAS Broadcasting Inc.
Group Owner: BAS Broadcasting Inc.; (acq 6-30-2008; grpsl)
Nat'l Network: ABC *Nat'l Reps:* Katz Radio *Regional Reps:* Rgnl Reps.
Arbitron Metro Market: Sandusky/Port Clinton, Ohio *Format:* Country *Hrs. of News Programming:* news progmg 4 hrs wkly
No. News Employees: 2 *Target Audience:* 18-34 and 25-54
Adv. Rates: 20; 20; 20; 14
Randy Hugg, Operations Dir
Lisa Rich, General Manager
Adam Klein, Director of Sales
Steve Shoffner, News Director
Gary Homza, Chief Engineer

***WHVT**
12-01-1986; 90.5 mhz FM; 2.7 kw; 154 ft.; N41 17 45 W82 58 26
P.O. Box 273 144 Lemmon, Cldye, OH 43410 US
(419) 547-8254, *Fax:* (419) 547-7195
www.whvtfm.com
radio@whvtfm.com
License: Clyde, Sandusky County, OH held by Clyde Educ. Broadcasting Foundation.
Format: Religious
James Lewis, President
Pastor Lewis, Station Manager
Pastor Mott, Disc Jockey

Coal Grove

WBVB
02-01-1990; 97.1 mhz FM; 3 kw; 472 ft; N38 25 27 W82 32 04
Mailing Address: Box 2288, Huntington, WV 78701
Second Address: 134 4th Ave., Coal Grove, OH 25701
(304) 525-7788, *Fax:* (304) 525-6281,(304) 525-7861 (Sales)
www.B97fm.com
info@B97fm.com
License: Coal Grove, Lawrence County, OH held by Capstar TX L.P.
Group Owner: Clear Channel Communications Inc.; (acq 8-30-00; grpsl)
Arbitron Metro Market: Huntington-Ashland, WV-KY *Special Programming:* Winston Cup racing *Target Audience:* 18-34.
Judy Jennings, General Manager
Judy Jennings, Station Manager
Newman Adkins, General Sales Mgr
Mark Wood, Programming Director
Megan Kelley, Promotions Manager
Scott Hensley, Chief Engineer

Columbus

WBNS
01-01-1922; 1460 khz AM *Hrs Open:* 24; 5 kw-D, DAN; 1 kw-N, DAN; N39 57 6 W82 54 23
175 South Third Street, Columbus, OH 43215 US
(614) 460-3850, *Fax:* (614) 460-3757
www.espncolumbus.com/
License: Columbus, OH held by RadiOhio Incorporated
Group Owner: Dispatch Broadcast Group; (acq 1933).
Nat'l Network: ESPN Radio *Regional Network:* Ohio News Network *Nat'l Reps:* Christal *Wire Services:* AP
Arbitron Metro Market: Columbus, OH *Format:* Sports *Target Audience:* Men 25-54.
Dave VanStone, General Manager
Chris Crawford, General Sales Mgr
Jimmy Powers, Programming Director
Todd Reigle, Promotions Manager
Steve Clawson, Chief Engineer
Jay Taylor, Programmign Director
Mike Kearney, General SalesManager

WBNS-FM
06-01-1959; 97.1 mhz FM *Hrs Open:* 24; 20.5 kw; Ant 781 ft; N39 58 16 W83 01 40
605 S. Front St., 3rd Fl., Columbus, OH 43215
(614) 460-3850, *Fax:* (614) 460-3757
www.971thefan.com
License: Columbus, Franklin County, OH held by RadiOhio Incorporated
Group Owner: Dispatch Broadcast Group
Regional Network: Ohio News Network *Nat'l Reps:* Christal *Wire Services:* AP
Population Served: 1,773,120 *Arbitron Metro Market:* Columbus, OH *Target Audience:* Adults 25-54.
Dave Van Stone, General Manager
Mike Kearney, General Sales Mgr
Jay Taylor, Programming Director

Todd Reigle, Promotions Manager
Greg Armstrong, Chief Engineer
Chris Crawford, Sales Director
Todd Markiewicz, Sales Director
JoeHardin, Local Sales Mgr
Lisa Shackman, Regional Sales Mgr

WRKZ
04-26-1962; 99.7 mhz FM *Hrs Open:* 24; 20 kw; 784 ft.; N39 58 16 W83 1 40
1458 Dublin Road, Marble Cliff, OH 43215 US
(614) 821-9970, *Fax:* (614) 481-8070
www.wbzx.com
mail@wbzx.com
License: Columbus, Franklin County, OH held by North American Broadcasting Co. Inc.
Group Owner: North American Broadcasting Co. Inc.
Nat'l Reps: D & R Radio *Wire Services:* AP
Arbitron Metro Market: Columbus, OH *No. News Employees:* 5 *Target Audience:* 18-49.
Norma Mnich, Chairman
Matthew Mnich, CEO
Mark Jividen, Operations Dir
Jim Pontius, General Sales Mgr
Hal Fish, Programming Director
Greg Moebius, Promotions Manager
Eric Feucht, General Sales Manager
Ronni Hunter, MusicDirector

***WCBE**
09-26-1956; 90.5 mhz FM *Hrs Open:* 24; 11 kw; 531 ft.; N39 57 48 W83 0 17
270 E. State Street, Columbus, OH 43215 US
(614) 365-5555, *Fax:* (614) 365-5060
www.wcbe.org
wcbe@wcbe.org
License: Columbus, Franklin County, OH held by Board of Education, City School District of Columbus, Ohio.
Nat'l Network: NPR; PRI *Wire Services:* AP
Arbitron Metro Market: Columbus, OH *Format:* News *Special Programming:* Jazz 4 hrs, blues 3 hrs, Celtic 4 hrs wkly *Hrs. of News Programming:* news progmg 37 hrs wkly *No. News Employees:* 3 *Target Audience:* 35-54.
Dan Mushalko, General Manager
Wendy Craver, General Sales Mgr
Maggie Brennan, Programming Director
Jim Letizia, News Director

WCKX
02-01-1996; 107.5 mhz FM *Hrs Open:* 24; 1.9 kw; 413 ft.; N39 57 46 W82 59 46
1821 Summit Road, Suite 400, Cincinnati, OH 45237 US
(614) 487-1444, *Fax:* (614) 487-5862
mycolumbuspower.com/
info@wckx.com
License: Columbus, Franklin County, OH held by Blue Chip Broadcasting Licenses Ltd.
Group Owner: Radio One Inc.; (acq 4-30-01; grpsl).
Nat'l Network: ABC *Nat'l Reps:* D & R Radio
Arbitron Metro Market: Columbus, OH *Format:* Urban Contemporary *Hrs. of News Programming:* News progmg one hr wkly
Eddie Harrell Jr., General Manager
JD Kunes, Programming Director

WCOL-FM
01-01-1947; 92.3 mhz FM *Hrs Open:* 24; 22 kw; 755 ft.; N39 58 16 W83 1 40
50 East Rivercenter Boulevard, Suite 1200, Covington, KY 41011 US
(614) 486-6101, *Fax:* (614) 487-2559
www.wcol.com
daveman@clearchannel.com
License: Columbus, Franklin County, OH held by Citicasters Licenses L.P.
Group Owner: Clear Channel Communications Inc.; (acq 5-4-99; grpsl)
Arbitron Metro Market: Columbus, OH *Format:* Country *No. News Employees:* 1 *Target Audience:* 18-49.
Tom Thon, General Manager
Daveman, Webmaster

WYTS
01-01-1922; 1230 khz AM; 1 kw-U, ND1; N39 56 31 W83 1 20
50 East Rivercenter Boulevard, Suite 1200, Covington, KY 41011 US
(614) 486-6101, *Fax:* (614) 487-2559
talk1230wyts.com
jeffrehl@clearchannel.com
License: Columbus, OH held by Citicasters Licenses Inc.
Group Owner: Clear Channel Communications Inc.
Nat'l Network: Fox Sports
Arbitron Metro Market: Columbus, OH *Format:* Sports *Target Audience:* 35 plus; general
Jeff Rehl, General Sales Mgr
Steve Konrad, Programming Director
Sis Campbell, News Director
Daveman, Online Content Director

WLVQ
04-01-1959; 96.3 mhz FM *Hrs Open:* 24; 18 kw; 751 ft.; N39 58 16 W83 1 40
600 New Hampshire Ave., NW, Suite 1200, Washington, DC 20037 US
(614) 227-9696, *Fax:* (614) 461-1059
www.qfm96.com
License: Columbus, Franklin County, OH held by Wilks License Co.-Columbus LLC.
Group Owner: Wilks Broadcast Group LLC; (acq 1-10-2007; grpsl)
Nat'l Reps: Christal
Arbitron Metro Market: Columbus, OH *Format:* Classic Rock *Hrs. of News Programming:* news progmg 2 hrs wkly *No. News Employees:* 1 *Target Audience:* 25-54.
Scott Russell, General Sales Mgr
Ross Wagner, Programming Director
Megan Slater, Program Director
Mike Dorsey, Promotions Director

WMNI
04-26-1958; 920 khz AM *Hrs Open:* 24; 1 kw-D, DA2; 0.5 kw-N, DA2; N39 53 32 W83 2 51
1458 Dublin Road, Marble Cliff, OH 43215 US
(614) 481-7800, *Fax:* (614) 481-8070
www.wmni.com
mail997@wrkz.com
License: Columbus, OH held by North American Broadcasting Inc.
Group Owner: North American Broadcasting Co. Inc.
Nat'l Network: AP Network News *Wire Services:* AP
Arbitron Metro Market: Columbus, OH *Format:* News *Special Programming:* Relg 4 hrs wkly *Hrs. of News Programming:* news progmg 20 hrs wkly *No. News Employees:* 5 *Target Audience:* 35 plus.
Neil Orlikoff, General Manager

WNCI
07-01-1961; 97.9 mhz FM *Hrs Open:* 24; 175 kw horiz, 105 kw vert; 561 ft.; N39 58 10 W83 0 10
50 East Rivercenter Boulevard, Suite 1200, Covington, KY 41011 US
(614) 486-6101, *Fax:* (614) 487-2559
www.wnci.com
TonyTravatto@clearchannel.com
License: Columbus, Franklin County, OH held by Citicasters Licenses L.P.
Group Owner: Clear Channel Communications Inc.; (acq 1999; grpsl).
Arbitron Metro Market: Columbus, OH *Format:* Adult Contemp *Hrs. of News Programming:* news progmg 4 hrs wkly *No. News Employees:* 1 *Target Audience:* 18-49.
Tom Thon, General Manager
Rob O'Boyle, General Sales Mgr
Tony Travatto, Programming Director

***WVSG**
04-24-1922; 820 khz AM *Hrs Open:* 24; 5 kw-D, 790 w-N (L-WBAP Ft. Worth, Tex.); N40 01 44 W82 03 22
2400 Olentangy River Rd., Columbus, OH 43210
(614) 292-9678, *Fax:* (614) 292-0513
www.wosu.org
License: Columbus, Franklin County, OH held by Ohio State University.
Nat'l Network: NPR; PRI *Wire Services:* AP
Population Served: 1,200,000 *Arbitron Metro Market:* Columbus, OH *Special Programming:* Black one hr, bluegrass 12 hrs wkly *Hrs. of News Programming:* news progmg 114 hrs wkly *No. News Employees:* 9 *TargetAudience:* 35 plus; general
Thomas Rieland, General Manager
Tim Eby, Station Manager

***WOSU-FM**
12-13-1949; 89.7 mhz FM *Hrs Open:* 24; 40 kw; 552 ft.; N40 1 2 W83 1 11
950 Stimmel Road, Columbus, OH 43223 US
(614) 292-9678, *Fax:* (614) 292-0513
www.wosu.org
License: Columbus, Franklin County, OH held by Ohio State University
Nat'l Network: PRI *Wire Services:* AP
Arbitron Metro Market: Columbus, OH *TV Affiliate:* *WOSU-TV affil. *Format:* Contemporary Hits/Top 40 *Target Audience:* 25 plus.
Martin McDonald, Station Manager

WSNY
08-12-1982; 94.7 mhz FM; 22 kw; 755 ft.; N39 58 16 W83 1 40
4401 Carriage Hill Lane, Columbus, OH 43220 US
(614) 451-2191, *Fax:* (614) 451-1831
www.sunny95.com
info@sunny95.com
License: Columbus, Franklin County, OH held by Franklin Communications Inc.
Group Owner: Saga Communications Inc.; (acq 9-86).
Nat'l Reps: Christal; Katz Radio *Wire Services:* AP
Arbitron Metro Market: Columbus, OH *Format:* Adult Contemp *Hrs. of News Programming:* news progmg 3 hrs wkly *No. News Employees:* 1 *Target Audience:* 25-64; women, upscale families
Alan Goodman, President
Katie Cyr, General Sales Mgr
Michelle Hurley, Promotions Manager
Jill McCarron, National Sales Manager

WTVN
01-01-1924; 610 khz AM *Hrs Open:* 24
50 East Rivercenter Blvd, Suite 1200, Covington, KY 41011 US
(614) 486-6101, *Fax:* (614) 487-2559
www.610wtvn.com
info@610wtvn.com
License: Columbus, OH held by Citicasters Licenses L.P.
Group Owner: Clear Channel Communications Inc.; (acq 1999; grpsl).
Arbitron Metro Market: Columbus, OH *Format:* News, News/Talk, 86 *Target Audience:* 25-54; leaning male
Tom Thon, Operations Dir
Jeff Rehl, General Sales Mgr
Mike Elliott, Programming Director
Bruce Kamp, News Director
Joe Bradley, Producer
Daveman, Online Content Director
Matt McCoy, Sports Director

***WUFM**
03-22-1996; 88.7 mhz FM *Hrs Open:* 24; 5 kw; 774 ft.; N39 56 16 W83 1 16
Mailing Address: P.O. Box 8470, Westerville, OH 43086 US
Second Address: 116 County Line Rd., Westerville, OH 43082
(614) 839-7100, *Fax:* (614) 839-1329
www.radiou.com
radiou@radiou.com
License: Columbus, Franklin County, OH held by Spirit Communications Inc.
Arbitron Metro Market: Westerville, OH *Format:* Contemporary Hits/Top 40 *Target Audience:* 12-24; Male
John Shumate Sr., President
Kathy Shumate, Operations Dir
Michael Buckingham, General Manager
Nikki Cantu, Programming Director
Cole Drake, Promotions Manager

WVKO
11-21-1951; 1580 khz AM *Hrs Open:* 24
4401 Carriage Hill Lane, Columbus, OH 43220 US
(614) 538-1580
www.stgabrielradio.com
info@stgabrielradio.com
License: Columbus, OH held by Bernard Ohio LLC.
Group Owner: Bernard Radio LLC; (acq 1-22-2007; grpsl)
Nat'l Network: EWTN Radio
Arbitron Metro Market: Columbus, OH *Format:* Christian
Marc Hawk, President
Kevin Riecke, General Manager
Lori Crock, Promotions Manager
Bill Messerly, Executive Director
Dave Orsborn, Production Manager
Christina Klein, Vice President
Jim Stefaniak, Secretary

***WHKC**
09-01-2007; 91.5 mhz FM; 15 kw; Ant 689 ft; N39 56 14 W83 01 16
1630 Strathshire Hall Pl., Powell, OH 43065
(740) 548-5919, *Fax:* (740) 548-5911
License: Columbus, Franklin County, OH held by Christian Broadcasting Services Inc.
Arbitron Metro Market: Columbus, OH
Penny Neilsen, CEO
Nate Adams, Operations Dir
John Malone, General Manager
Nate Adams, General Sales Mgr
Don Roden, Chief Engineer

Columbus Grove

WBKS
01-01-2003; 93.9 mhz FM; 14 kw; Ant 436 ft; N40 57 21 W84 07 59
667 W. Market St., Lima, OH 43545
(419) 223-2060, *Fax:* (419) 229-3888
www.wild939.com
russryder@clearchannel.com
License: Columbus Grove, Putnam County, OH held by CC Licenses LLC.
Group Owner: Clear Channel Communications Inc.; (acq 8-10-2000).
Hrs. of News Programming: News progmg one hr wkly
Russ Ryder, Operations Dir
Mark Gierhart, Chief Engineer

Columbus-Worthington

WRFD
09-27-1947; 880 khz AM *Hrs Open:* Sunrise-sunset; 6.1 kw-C, NDD; 23 kw-D, NDD; N39 56 31 W83 1 20
4880 Santa Rosa Rd, #300, Camarillo, CA 93012 US
(614) 885-0880, *Fax:* (614) 885-6322
www.wrfd.com
mail@wrfd.com
License: Columbus-Worthington, OH held by Salem Media of Ohio
Group Owner: Salem Communications Corp.
Nat'l Network: Salem Radio Network *Nat'l Reps:* Christal; Salem
Arbitron Metro Market: Columbus, OH *Format:* Talk, Religious
Hrs. of News Programming: News progmg one hr wkly *Target Audience:* 30-60; conservatives, Christians, farmers
David Ruleman, Operations Dir
Tom Heyl, General Manager
Greg Sauold, Engineering Dir
Ryan Moran, Operations Manager

Conneaut

WGOJ
105.5 mhz FM *Hrs Open:* 24; 6 kw horiz, 5.8 kw vert; 295 ft.; N41 51 42 W80 31 1
Mailing Address: 236 State Street, PO Box 725, Conneaut, OH 44030 US
Second Address: 235 Miill St., Conneaut, OH 44030
(440) 599-1055, *Fax:* (440) 593-4761
www.wgoj-christian-radio.com
wgoj@suite224.net
License: Conneaut, Ashtabula County, OH held by Bible Brodcasting Inc.
Format: Christian *Target Audience:* General.
Dr. Roger Hogle, General Manager

WWOW
10-25-1959; 1360 khz AM *Hrs Open:* 24
239 Broad Street, Conneaut, OH 44030 US
(440) 593-2233, *Fax:* (440) 593-6885
www.1360wwow.com
mlandon@1360wwow.com
License: Conneaut, OH held by Cause Plus Marketing LLC
Arbitron Metro Market: Conneaut, OH *Format:* News, News/Talk, 86
John Marra, President
Marty Landon, Operations Dir
Gary Gersin, Programming Director
Pat Williams, News Director

Cortland

WKTX
04-01-1985; 830 khz AM; 1 kw-D; N41 24 56 W80 43 49
11906 Madison Ave., Lakewood, OH 44140
(216) 221-0330, *Fax:* (216) 221-3638
License: Cortland, Trumbull County, OH held by Miklos Kossanyi, Maria Kossanyi
Nat'l Network: USA
Arbitron Metro Market: Youngstown-Warren, OH *Special Programming:* Slovenian 2 hrs, Greek 2 hrs, Pol one hr, German 5 hrs wkly *Target Audience:* 35 plus; homeowners
Attila Kossanyl, President
Jim Georgiades, General Manager
Jack Cory, Programming Director
Tom Derrit, Promotions Manager
Andrew Huston, News Director
Jim Gorgiades, Engineering Dir

Coshocton

***WOSE**
01-01-1996; 91.1 mhz FM; 6 kw; 322 ft.; N40 20 30 W81 57 56
Rebroadcasts: Rebroadcasts WOSU-FM Columbus 100%
2400 Olentangy River Rd, Columbus, OH 43210 US
(614) 292-9678, *Fax:* (614) 292-7625
www.wosu.org
wosu@osu.edu
License: Coshocton, Coshocton County, OH held by The Ohio State University.
Nat'l Network: PRI; NPR *Wire Services:* AP
Format: Talk
Kevin Petrilla, Operations Dir
Thomas Rieland, General Manager
Tim Eby, Station Manager

WTNS
11-09-1947; 1560 khz AM; 1 kw-D; N40 16 30 W81 49 37
114 N. 6th St., Coshocton, OH 43812
(740) 622-1560, *Fax:* (740) 622-7940
License: Coshocton, Coshocton County, OH held by Coshocton Broadcasting Co.
Group Owner: Coshocton Broadcasting Co.; acq 9-86; $560,653;
Population Served: 13,747
Bruce Wallace, President
Tom Thompson, General Sales Mgr
Mike Bechtol, Programming Director
Ken Smailes, News Director
John Hartmeyer, Chief Engineer

WTNS-FM
04-25-1968; 99.3 mhz FM; 1.2 kw; 440 ft.; N40 16 30 W81 49 37
114 North 6th Street, Coshocton, OH 43812 US
(740) 622-1560, *Fax:* (740) 622-7940
www.mywtnsradio.com
License: Coshocton, Coshocton County, OH
Arbitron Metro Market: Coshocton, OH *Format:* Adult Contemp
Flo Murdock, Programming Director
Brad Haynes, Disc Jockey
Tom Thompson, Disc Jockey
Jim Parr, Disc Jockey

Crestline

***WYKL**
12-10-1990; 98.7 mhz FM *Hrs Open:* 24; 1.8 kw; 400 ft.; N40 46 13 W82 45 23
538 Broad St. P.O. Box 4006, Elyria, OH 44036 US
(916) 251-1600, *Fax:* (916) 251-1650
www.klove.com
klove@klove.com
License: Crestline, Crawford County, OH held by Educational Media Foundation.
Group Owner: EMF Broadcasting; (acq 12-18-03; $900,000).
Nat'l Network: K-Love
Arbitron Metro Market: Crestline, OH *Format:* Christian *Target Audience:* 25-44; Judeo Christian female
Mike Novak, President
Eric Allen, General Sales Mgr
David Pierce, Programming Director
Ed Lenane, News Director
Sam Wallington, Engineering Dir
Richard Hunt, News Reporter
Marya Morgan, News Reporter

Cridersville

WVLO
99.3 mhz FM; 6 kw; 74 meters; n40 45 19 w84 05 20
2700 West Oaks Blvd, Rocklin, CA
(916) 251-1600, *Fax:* (916) 251-1650
www.emfbroadcasting.com
info@emfbroadcasting.com
License: Cridersville, OH held by Educational Media Foundation
Mike Novak, President/CEO

Crooksville

WYBZ
10-26-1990; 107.3 mhz FM *Hrs Open:* 24; 3 kw; 328 ft; N39 47 23 W82 05 39
2895 Maysville Pike, Zanesville, OH 43707
(740) 453-6004, *Fax:* (740) 453-5865
www.wybz.com
jenny@wybz.com
License: Crooksville, Perry County, OH held by Y Bridge Broadcasting Inc.
Nat'l Network: NBC
Hrs. of News Programming: news progmg 9 hrs wkly *No. News Employees:* 1 *Target Audience:* 35-64.
Rick Sabine, President
Jenny McCloy, Operations Dir
Jenny McCloy, Station Manager
Monica Martinelli, General Sales Mgr
Ron Strong, Programming Director
Mark Hiner, Chief Engineer

Cuyahoga Falls

***WCUE**
01-01-1950; 1150 khz AM *Hrs Open:* 24
Mailing Address: 4135 Northgate Blvd., Sacramento, CA 95834 US
Second Address: 4075 Bellaire Ln., Peninsula, OH 44264
(800)-543-1495
www.familyradio.com
familyradio@familyradio.org
License: Cuyahoga Falls, OH held by Family Stations Inc.
Group Owner: Family Stations Inc.; acq 10-22-86)
Arbitron Metro Market: Akron, OH *Format:* Religious *Special Programming:* Class 2 hrs wkly *Hrs. of News Programming:* News progmg 4 hrs wkly *Target Audience:* 25 plus; Christians
Harold Camping, President

Dayton

WDAO
03-01-1955; 1210 khz AM; 1 kw-D, NDD; N39 43 36 W84 12 23
4309 West Mlk, Jr Way, Dayton, OH 45417 US
(937) 222-9326, *Fax:* (937) 461-6100
www.wdaoradio.com
wdao1210@aol.com
License: Dayton, OH held by Johnson Communications Inc.
Nat'l Reps: Christal
Arbitron Metro Market: Dayton, OH *Format:* Blues
Jim Johnson, GM
Sophia Carr, General Sales Mgr
Jim Johnston, Programming Director

***WDPR**
04-09-1977; 88.1 mhz FM *Hrs Open:* 24; 0.6 kw; 781 ft.; N39 43 16 W84 15 0
126 N. Main St., Dayton, OH 45402 US
(937) 496-3850, *Fax:* (937) 496-3852
www.dpr.org
dpr@dpr.org
License: Dayton, Montgomery County, OH held by Dayton Public Radio Inc.
Nat'l Network: USA
Arbitron Metro Market: Dayton, OH *Format:* Talk *Target Audience:* 24-50.
Larry Coressel, Operations Dir
Georganne Woessner, General Manager
Shaun Yu, Programming Director

***WDPS**
01-01-1976; 89.5 mhz FM *Hrs Open:* 9:15 AM-4:30 PM; 6 kw horiz, 5.8 kw vert; 210 ft.; N39 45 28 W84 11 36
348 West First Street, Dayton, OH 45402 US
(937) 542-7182, *Fax:* (937) 542-6714
www.dps.k12.oh.us/departments/PIO/wdps-fm.html
License: Dayton, Montgomery County, OH held by Dayton Public Schools.
Arbitron Metro Market: Dayton, OH *Format:* Jazz, Triple A
P.R. Frank, Operations Dir
Ken Kreitzer, General Manager
Christopher Hartley, Programming Director
Tom Nornhold, Chief Engineer
Jennifer Bryant, Assistant Music Director

WHIO
02-09-1935; 1290 khz AM *Rebroadcasts:* Simulcast with WHIO-FM Piqua 100%
Mailing Address: 3773 Howard Hughes Pwy, Suite 300n, Las Vegas, NV 89109 US
Second Address: 1414 Wilmington Ave., Dayton, OH 45420
(937) 259-2111, *Fax:* (937) 259-2168
1290whio.com
info@1290whio.com
License: Dayton, OH held by Cox Radio Inc.
Group Owner: Cox Radio Inc.
Nat'l Reps: D & R Radio
Arbitron Metro Market: Dayton, OH *TV Affiliate:* WHIO-TV affil.
Format: News, News/Talk, 86 *Special Programming:* Relg 2 hrs wkly *Hrs. of News Programming:* news progmg 30 hrs wkly *No. News Employees:* 4 *Target Audience:* 35-54.
Donna Hall, Operations Dir
Lisa Allan, General Sales Mgr
Larry Hansgen, Programming Director
Vicky Forrest, Promotions Manager
Jim Barrett, News Director
Marc Herbst, National Sales Manager
Tracey Slife, Promotions Manager
Kathy Eagle-Norris, Regional Sales Manager

WHKO
01-01-1946; 99.1 mhz FM; 50 kw; 1066 ft.; N39 44 2 W84 14 53

Mailing Address: 3773 Howard Hughes Pwy, Suite 300n, Las Vegas, NV 89109 US
Second Address: 1414 Wilmington Ave., Dayton, OH 45420
(937) 259-2111, *Fax:* (937) 259-2168
1290whio.com
info@1290whio.com
License: Dayton, Montgomery County, OH held by Cox Radio Inc.
Group Owner: Cox Radio Inc.
Nat'l Reps: Christal
Arbitron Metro Market: Dayton, OH *TV Affiliate:* WHIO-TV affil.
Format: Country
Nick Roberts, Operations Dir

WING
05-24-1921; 1410 khz AM; 5 kw-D, DAN; 5 kw-N, DAN; N39 40 56 W84 9 33
200 Concord Plaza, Suite 600, San Antonio, TX 78216 US
(937) 294-5858, *Fax:* (937) 297-5233
www.wingam.com
info@wingam.com
License: Dayton, OH held by MLB-Dayton IV LLC.
Group Owner: Main Line Broadcasting LLC; (acq 9-12-2007; grpsl)
Nat'l Network: CBS; Westwood One *Nat'l Reps:* Katz Radio
Arbitron Metro Market: Dayton, OH *Format:* Sports *Target Audience:* 25-54; well educated
Andrea Scott, General Manager

WMMX
09-01-1964; 107.7 mhz FM *Hrs Open:* 24; 28 kw; 656 ft.; N39 43 19 W84 12 33
50 East Rivercenter Boulevard, Suite 1200, Covington, KY 41011 US
(937) 224-1137, *Fax:* (937) 224-3667
www.wmmx.com
info@ccedayton.com
License: Dayton, Montgomery County, OH held by Citicasters Licenses L.P.
Group Owner: Clear Channel Communications Inc.; (acq 1999; grpsl).
Arbitron Metro Market: Dayton, OH *Format:* Adult Contemp *Target Audience:* 25-54.
Robert Zurowesti, Operations Dir
Jeff Stevens, Operations Manager

WONE
03-20-1949; 980 khz AM; 5 kw-D, DAN; 5 kw-N, DAN; N39 40 3 W84 10 1
50 East Rivercenter Boulevard, Suite 1200, Covington, KY 41011 US
(937) 224-1137, *Fax:* (937) 224-5015
www.wone.com
info@ccedayton.com
License: Dayton, OH held by Citicasters Licenses L.P.
Group Owner: Clear Channel Communications Inc.; (acq 5-4-99; grpsl).
Arbitron Metro Market: Dayton, OH *TV Affiliate:* Sports *Special Programming:* news progmg 18 hrs wkly *Hrs. of News Programming:* 3 *No. News Employees:* 35-64.
Operations Manager, Operations Dir
General Sales Manager, Tony Tilford
Programming Director, Aaron Klauber
Promotions Director, Promotions Manager
Operations Manager

***WQRP**
01-01-1976; 89.5 mhz FM; 6 kw; 210 ft.; N39 45 28 W84 11 36
P.O. Box 482, 915 E. Central Ave., West Carrollton, OH 45449 US
(916) 251-1600, *Fax:* (916) 251-1650
www.klove.com
License: Dayton, Montgomery County, OH held by Educational Media Foundation.
Group Owner: EMF Broadcasting; (acq 7-9-2008; $350,000)
Nat'l Network: K-Love
Arbitron Metro Market: Dayton, OH *Format:* Christian
Mike Novak, President

WTUE
01-01-1959; 104.7 mhz FM *Hrs Open:* 24; 28 kw; 656 ft.; N39 43 19 W84 12 33
200 Concord Plaza, Suite 600, San Antonio, TX 41011 US
(937) 224-1137, *Fax:* (937) 224-5015
www.wtue.com
wtue@wtue.com
License: Dayton, Montgomery County, OH held by Citicasters Licenses L.P.
Group Owner: Clear Channel Communications Inc.
Arbitron Metro Market: Dayton, OH *Format:* Rock/AOR *Hrs. of News Programming:* news progmg 2 hrs wkly *No. News Employees:* 1 *Target Audience:* 18-49.
Tony Tilford, Operations Dir
Dave Litteral, General Sales Mgr
Tony Tilford, Programming Director
Aaron Klauber, Promotions Manager
Paul Jellison, Chief Engineer
Karen Hohman, Continuity Director
Brittany Tankersley, WebsiteDirector

***WUDR**
01-01-2003; 98.1 mhz FM; 0.013 kw; 90 ft.; N39 47 14 W84 14 23
300 College Park Drive, Dayton, OH 45469 US
(937) 229-1000
flyer-radio.udayton.edu
info@udayton.edu
License: Dayton, Montgomery County, OH held by University of Dayton.
Arbitron Metro Market: Dayton, OH *Format:* Variety/Diverse
Roy Flynn, Operations Dir
Casey Drottar, General Manager
Laura Steffey, General Manager

De Graff

***WDEQ-FM**
09-01-1967; 91.7 mhz FM; 0.1 kw; 10 ft.; N40 18 54 W83 55 23
200 West Moore Street, Degraff, OH 43318 US
(937) 585-5981, *Fax:* (937) 585-4599
www.riverside.k12.oh.us
License: De Graff, Logan County, OH held by Riverside Local Board of Education.
Arbitron Metro Market: De Graff, Ohio
Gene Kirby, General Manager
Steve Webb, Station Manager

Defiance

WDFM
06-25-1985; 98.1 mhz FM *Hrs Open:* 24; 50 kw; 499 ft.; N41 17 28 W84 32 17
50 E. Rivercenter Blvd., # 1200, Covington, KY 41011 US
(419) 782-9336, *Fax:* (419) 784-0306
www.mix981fm.com
ricksmall@clearchannel.com
License: Defiance, Defiance County, OH held by Citicasters Licenses L.P.
Group Owner: Clear Channel Communications Inc.; (acq 5-4-99; grpsl).
Nat'l Network: CNN Radio *Nat'l Reps:* Katz Radio
Arbitron Metro Market: Defiance, Oh *Format:* Adult Contemp *Special Programming:* Relg 3 hrs wkly *Hrs. of News Programming:* news progmg 7 hrs wkly *No. News Employees:* 1 *Target Audience:* 25-54. *Adv.Rates:* 35; 20; 30; 12
Rick Small, Operations Dir
Bob McLimans, General Manager
Rick Small, Programming Director

***WGDE**
03-14-1999; 91.9 mhz FM *Hrs Open:* 24; 6 kw; 305 ft.; N41 17 41 W84 23 24 *Rebroadcasts:* Rebroadcasts WGTE-FM Toledo 100%
136 N. Huron St., Toledo, OH 43692 US
(419) 380-4600, *Fax:* (419) 380-4710
www.wgte.org
info@wgte.com
License: Defiance, Defiance County, OH held by Public Broadcast Foundation of NW Ohio.
Format: News *Special Programming:* Jazz 16 hrs, new age 4 hrs wkly *Hrs. of News Programming:* News progmg 23 hrs wkly *Target Audience:* General.
George Jones, Chairman
Marlon Kiser, CEO

WONW
01-01-1949; 1280 khz AM *Hrs Open:* 24; 1 kw-D, 500 w-N, DA-N; N41 16 44 W84 23 50
Mailing Address: 2110 Radio Dr., Defiance, OH 43545
Second Address: 709 N. Perry St., Napoleon, OH 43545
(419) 782-8126, *Fax:* (419) 784-4154
www.wonw1280.com
bobmclimans@clearchannel.com
License: Defiance, Defiance County, OH held by CC Licenses LLC.
Group Owner: Clear Channel Communications Inc.; (acq 11-5-99; grpsl)
Nat'l Network: ABC Radio *Nat'l Reps:* Katz Radio *Wire Services:* AP
Special Programming: Rush Limbaugh *No. News Employees:* 1 *Target Audience:* General. *Adv. Rates:* 25; 15; 20; 8
Bob McLimans, General Manager
John Schuette, General Sales Mgr
Rick Small, Programming Director
Rick Small, Operations Manager

WZOM
08-25-1989; 105.7 mhz FM *Hrs Open:* 24; 6 kw; 328 ft.; N41 13 23 W84 22 36
Mailing Address: 709 North Perry Street, Napoleon, OH 43545 US
Second Address: 709 N. Perry St., Napoleon, OH 43512
(419) 782-8126, *Fax:* (419) 784-4154
www.1057thebull.com
bethplummer@clearchannel.com
License: Defiance, Defiance County, OH held by CC Licenses LLC.
Group Owner: Clear Channel Communications Inc.; (acq 1-1-2000; grpsl)
Nat'l Reps: Katz Radio *Regional Reps:* Rgnl Reps.
Arbitron Metro Market: Defiance, OH *Format:* Country *Special Programming:* Relg 6 hrs wkly *Hrs. of News Programming:* news progmg 4 hrs wkly *No. News Employees:* 1 *Target Audience:* 25-54. *Adv. Rates:* 30; 20; 25; 10
Robert McLimans, Operations Dir
Bill Murphy, Programming Director
Rick Small, Operations Director
Josh Busch
John Schuette
Judy Damman, Business Manager

Delaware

WDLR
01-18-1961; 1550 khz AM *Hrs Open:* 24; 0.5 kw-D, DA2; 0.029 kw-N, DA2; N40 17 56 W83 2 46
5031 Latrobe Drive, Windemere, FL 34786 US
(740) 368-9357, *Fax:* (740) 369-9463
www.lakalle1550am.com
anuelrojas@laquebuenaohio.com
License: Delaware, OH held by The Fifteen Fifty Corp.
Arbitron Metro Market: Columbus, OH
Luis Orozco, General Manager

***WJJE**
01-01-2005; 89.1 mhz FM; 6 kw vert; 328 ft.; N40 24 2 W82 46 43
1984 Old Peachtree Rd, Lawrenceville, GA 30043 US
(662) 844-8888, *Fax:* (662) 842-6791
www.afa.net
randall@afa.net
License: Delaware, Delaware County, OH held by American Family Association.
Group Owner: American Family Radio; (acq 12-15-2003; $10 for CP).
Arbitron Metro Market: Delaware, OH *Format:* Religious
Marvin Sanders, General Manager

Delhi Hills

WNLT
09-01-1991; 104.3 mhz FM; 2 kw; 175 meters; N39 15 02 W84 50 10
8686 Michael Ln., Fairfield, OH 45014
(513) 829-7700
www.klove.com
License: Delhi Hills, Hamilton County, OH held by Vernon R. Baldwin Inc.
Group Owner: Vernon R Baldwin Inc.
Nat'l Network: K-Love
Population Served: 2,000,000 *Arbitron Metro Market:* Cincinnati, OH
Vernon Baldwin, President
Marci Baldwin, Operations Dir

Delphos

***WBIE**
01-01-2001; 91.5 mhz FM; 5.5 kw; 322 ft.; N40 56 48 W84 15 24
P O Drawer 2440, Tupelo, MS 38801 US
(662) 844-8888, *Fax:* (662) 842-6791
www.afa.net
info@afa.net
License: Delphos, Allen County, OH held by American Family Association.
Group Owner: American Family Radio
Arbitron Metro Market: Delphos, OH *Format:* Gospel
Marvin Sanders, General Manager

WDOH
12-16-1972; 107.1 mhz FM; 3.3 kw; 299 ft.; N40 49 55 W84 21 11
P.O. Box 100, Delphos, OH 45833 US

(419) 331-1600, *Fax:* (419) 228-5085
www.wdoh.com
philaustin@maverick-media.ws
License: Delphos, Allen County, OH held by Maverick Media of Lima License LLC.
Group Owner: Maverick Media LLC; (acq 11-15-2004; $1.15 million).
Nat'l Network: CBS
Arbitron Metro Market: Delphos, OH *Format:* Classic Rock
Special Programming: Farm 8 hrs wkly *Hrs. of News Programming:* news progmg 7 hrs wkly *No. News Employees:* 1
Target Audience: 25 plus. *Adv.Rates:* 10; 8; 10; 8
Gary Rozynek, President
Deb Klaus, Operations Dir
David Roach, General Manager
Tiffany Kayser, Director of Sales
Phil Austin, Programming Director
Bob Ulm, News Director

Delta

WLQR-FM

09-01-1994; 106.5 mhz FM; 3 kw; 328 ft; N41 35 13 W83 54 11
3225 Arlington Ave., Toledo, OH 43614
(419) 725-5700, *Fax:* (419) 725-5805
www.1065thezone.com
matt.spaulding@cumulus.com
License: Delta, Fulton County, OH held by Cumulus Licensing Corp.
Group Owner: Cumulus Media Inc.; (acq 11-18-99; $4,925,000).
Population Served: 286,038 *Arbitron Metro Market:* Toledo, OH *Format:* Alternative *Target Audience:* 18-34; male
Matt Spaulding, General Manager
Skip Schmidt, General Sales Mgr
Dan McClintock, Programming Director
Keith Bosworth, Chief Engineer

Dover-New Philadelphia

WJER

02-10-1950; 1450 khz AM *Hrs Open:* 24; 1 kw-U; N40 30 46 W81 27 24
646 Boulevard, Dover, OH 44622
(330) 343-7755, *Fax:* (330) 364-4538
www.wjer.com
wjer@wjer.com
License: Dover-New Philadelphia, Tuscarawas County, OH held by WJER Radio LLC
Nat'l Network: A.P. *Nat'l Reps:* Rgnl Reps
Population Served: 86,000*No. News Employees:* 3 *Target Audience:* Adult
Gary Petricola, President
Bob Scanlon, General Manager
Dan Pitzo, General Sales Mgr
Jennifer Clark, News Director
Bruce Whitsel, Chief Engineer

Dublin

WCGX

04-01-1953; 106.7 mhz FM; 7.3 kw; Ant 590 ft; N40 09 33 W82 55 23
2323 W. 5th Ave., Suite 200, Columbus, OH 41011
(614) 486-6101, *Fax:* (614) 487-3575
www.radio1067.com
tomthon@clearchannel.com
License: Dublin, Franklin County, OH held by Citicasters Licenses L.P.
Group Owner: Clear Channel Communications Inc.; (acq 1999; grpsl).
Arbitron Metro Market: Columbus, OH
Tom Thon, General Manager

East Liverpool

WOHI

12-01-1949; 1490 khz AM; 1 kw-U, ND1; N40 37 47 W80 36 9
Post Office Box 2338, East Liverpool, OH 43920 US
(724) 378-1271, *Fax:* (724) 378-4653
http://www.picklefm.com
License: East Liverpool, OH held by Keymarket Licenses LLC.
Group Owner: Keymarket Communications LLC; (acq 2000; grpsl).
Nat'l Network: Jones Radio Networks *Nat'l Reps:* Rgnl Reps
TV Affiliate: Adult Contemp *No. News Employees:* General.

Eaton

WEDI

01-01-1979; 1130 khz AM; 0.25 kw-D, DAD; N39 44 55 W84 35 2 *Rebroadcasts:* Rebroadcasts WBZI(AM) Xenia 80%
320 Woodside Drive, West Alexandria, OH 45381 US
(937) 372-3531, *Fax:* (937) 372-3508
www.myclassiccountry.com
myclassiccountry@myclassiccountry.com
License: Eaton, OH held by Town and Country Broadcasting Inc.
Group Owner: Town and Country Broadcasting Inc.; (acq 1-4-2005; $175,000).
Nat'l Network: Fox News Radio *Regional Network:* Agrinet *Nat'l Reps:* Rgnl Reps *Wire Services:* AP
Arbitron Metro Market: Dayton, OH *Format:* Country *Special Programming:* Gospel 5 hrs., Farm 2 hrs. wkly *Hrs. of News Programming:* news progmg 3 hrs wkly *No. News Employees:* 2
Target Audience: 35-64;adults *Adv. Rates:* 18; 18; 18; na
Joe Mullins, President
Roy Hatfield, Programming Director
Darrin Johnston, News Director
Bucks Braun, Morning Host
Megan Brugger, Traffic Manager

WGTZ

11-28-1960; 92.9 mhz FM *Hrs Open:* 24; 40 kw; 551 ft.; N39 50 10 W84 24 16
200 Concord Plaza, Suite 600, San Antonio, TX 78216 US
(937) 294-5858, *Fax:* (937) 297-5233
www.fly929.com
info@fly929.com
License: Eaton, Preble County, OH held by MLB-Dayton IV LLC.
Group Owner: Main Line Broadcasting LLC; (acq 9-12-2007; grpsl)
Nat'l Reps: Katz Radio
Arbitron Metro Market: Dayton, OH *Format:* Adult Contemp
Target Audience: 18-49; contemp middle America
Andrea Scott, General Manager

Edgewood

WZOO-FM

01-23-1989; 102.5 mhz FM *Hrs Open:* 24; 5.8 kw; 328 ft.; N41 49 44 W80 49 28
P.O. Box 102, Ashtabula, OH 44004 US
(440) 993-2126, *Fax:* (440) 992-2658
www.magicoldies1025.com/main.php
KathyDavis@magicoldies1025.com,
JeremyJames@magicoldies1025.com
License: Edgewood, Ashtabula County, OH held by Sweet Home Ashtabula LLC.
Group Owner: Sweet Home Ashtabula LLC; (acq 9-17-2007; grpsl)
Arbitron Metro Market: Ashtabula, OH *Format:* Oldies *No. News Employees:* 3 *Target Audience:* General.
Dana Schulte, Operations Dir
Dana Schulte, General Manager
Dennis O'Brien, Operations Manager
Roger McCoy, Internet Content Manager

Elyria

WEOL

10-01-1948; 930 khz AM *Hrs Open:* 24
P.O. Box 4006, Elyria, OH 44036 US
(440) 322-3761, *Fax:* (440) 284-3189
www.weol.northcoastnow.com
lgronek@elbc.net
License: Elyria, OH held by Elyria-Lorain Broadcasting Co.
Group Owner: Elyria-Lorain Broadcasting Co.
Nat'l Network: ABC *Nat'l Reps:* McGavren Guild *Regional Reps:* Rgnl Reps. *Wire Services:* AP
Arbitron Metro Market: Elyria, OH *Format:* News, News/Talk, 84, Talk *Special Programming:* Sp 2 hrs wkly; H.S. Sports *No. News Employees:* 4 *Target Audience:* 35 plus.
Bruce Van Dyke, Operations Dir
Lonnie Gronek, General Manager
Tim Alcorn, Sales Manager
Bruce VanDyke, Programming Director
Suzy Peters, Promotions Manager
Craig Adams, News Director

WNWV

10-01-1948; 107.3 mhz FM; 20 kw; 781 ft.; N41 16 10 W82 0 16
538 Broad Street, Elyria, OH 44036 US
216-828-1073
www.wnwv.com
info@wnwv.com
License: Elyria, Lorain County, OH
Group Owner: Elyria-Lorain Broadcasting Co.
Nat'l Reps: McGavren Guild *Regional Reps:* Regional Reps *Wire Services:* AP
Arbitron Metro Market: Cleveland, OH *TV Affiliate:* Jazz *Special Programming:* News progmg 4 hrs wkly *No. News Employees:* 25 plus; upscale
Sr. V.P. Exec. Director of Operations, Lonnie Gronek
Program Director/Music Director, Tiffany Broz
Promotions Director, Promotions Manager

Englewood

WLQT

02-20-1962; 94.5 mhz FM *Hrs Open:* 24; 3.6 kw; 427 ft.; N39 49 3 W84 14 53
50 East Rivercenter Boulevard, Suite 1200, Covington, KY 41011 US
(937) 224-1137, *Fax:* (937) 224-3667
www.wlqt.com
info@ccedayton.com
License: Englewood, Montgomery County, OH held by Citicasters Licenses L.P.
Group Owner: Clear Channel Communications Inc.; (acq 1999; grpsl).
Arbitron Metro Market: Dayton, OH *Format:* Adult Contemp
Target Audience: 35-64; persons 35-64
Robert Zurowesti, Operations Dir
Karrie Sudbrack, General Manager
Jeff Stevens, Operations Manager

Enon

WCLI-FM

08-01-1965; 101.5 mhz FM *Hrs Open:* 24; 6 kw; 328 ft; N39 53 02 W84 04 17
2963 Derr Rd., Springfield, OH 44256
(937) 399-5300,(937) 294-5858, *Fax:* (937) 399-3661
www.click1015.com
email@kisscountry.com
License: Enon, Champaign County, OH held by MLB-Dayton IV LLC.
Group Owner: Main Line Broadcasting LLC; (acq 9-12-2007; grpsl)
Population Served: 250,000 *Arbitron Metro Market:* Dayton, OH
Target Audience: 25-54; above-average income, blue-collar *Adv. Rates:* 30; 26; 26; 22
Jim Beard, General Manager
Kert Radel, Station Manager
Lee Riley, Programming Director
Andy Lawrence, Promotions Manager
Chris Daniels, News Director
Gene Simmons, Chief Engineer
Mickie Cooper, Traffic Manager

Fairborn

WGNZ

09-01-1968; 1110 khz AM
8010 North Main, Dayton, OH 45405 US
(937) 454-9000, *Fax:* (937) 454-1980
www.wgnz.com
wgnz@wgnz.com
License: Fairborn, OH held by L & D Broadcasters Inc.
Nat'l Network: Salem Radio Network
Arbitron Metro Market: Dayton, OH *Format:* Gospel, Religious
Target Audience: General; listeners who like family radio
Tim Livingston, President

*WWSU

04-04-1977; 106.9 mhz FM *Hrs Open:* 24; 0.02 kw; 210 ft.; N39 46 57.2 W84 3 42
Office of General Counse, 120g Allyn Hall -, Dayton, OH 45435 US
(937) 775-5554, *Fax:* (937) 775-5553
www.listen.to/wwsu
wwsugeneralmanager@yahoo.com
License: Fairborn, Montgomery County, OH held by Wright State University.
Arbitron Metro Market: Dayton, OH *Format:* Variety/Diverse
Special Programming: Black 12 hrs, relg 11 hrs, gospel 3 hrs, jazz 3 hr *Target Audience:* 15-26; college & high school students
H.R. Downey, General Manager
Meryn Conine, Programming Director
Jason Johnston, Chief Engineer
Kate McGaffin, Music Director
Jason McKever, Production/Training Director
Max Livada, Marketing Director
Ali Hamdan, SportsDirector

Fairfield

WCNW

02-14-1964; 1560 khz AM; 1 kw-C, DA2; 5 kw-D, DA2; N39 20 20 W84 31 30
8686 Michael Lane, Fairfield, OH 45014 US
(513) 829-7700, *Fax:* (513) 829-1560
info@wcnw.com
License: Fairfield, OH held by Vernon R. Baldwin Inc.

Group Owner: Vernon R Baldwin Inc.; acq 6-11-84; $700,000; *Arbitron Metro Market:* Cincinnati, OH *Format:* Gospel
Vernon Baldwin, President
Mark Mitchell, Station Manager

Findlay

WFIN
12-15-1941; 1330 khz AM *Hrs Open:* 24
Mailing Address: 551 Lake Cascade Parkway, Findlay, OH 45839 US
Second Address: 551 Lake Cascades Pkwy., Findlay, OH 45840
(419) 422-4545, *Fax:* (419) 422-6736
www.wfin.com
wfin@wfin.com
License: Findlay, OH held by Blanchard River Broadcasting Co.
Group Owner: The Findlay Publishing Co.; (acq 1949).
Nat'l Network: ABC *Regional Network:* ABN Radio *Regional Reps:* Rgnl Reps.
Arbitron Metro Market: Findlay, OH *Format:* News, News/Talk, 86
Special Programming: Farm 7 hrs, sports 12 hrs wkly *No. News Employees:* 2 *Target Audience:* 45 plus.
David Glass, President
Kurt Heminger, Operations Dir
Mike Holman, General Manager
Bill Rice, Programming Director
Doug Jenkins, News Director
Dennis Rund, Chief Engineer
Vaun Wickerham, Ag Services Director
Roger Kranz,Production Director
Chris Miller, Sports Director

WKXA-FM
01-01-1948; 100.5 mhz FM *Hrs Open:* 24; 20 kw; 440 ft.; N40 55 0 W83 35 45
Mailing Address: 551 Lake Cascade Parkway, Findlay, OH 45840 US
Second Address: 551 Lake Cascades Pkwy., Findlay, OH 45840
(415) 422-4545, *Fax:* (419) 422-6736
www.wkxa.com
wkxa@wkxa.com
License: Findlay, Hancock County, OH held by Blanchard River Broadcasting Co.
Group Owner: The Findlay Publishing Co.
Regional Reps: Regional Reps
Format: Contemporary Hits/Top 40, Adult Contemp *No. News Employees:* 2 *Target Audience:* 25-54.
Dave Glass, President
Kurt Heminger, Operations Dir
Sandy Kozlevcar, General Manager
Meg Stevens, Programming Director
Chris Miller, News Director
Dennis Rund, Chief Engineer
Vaun Wickerham, Ag Services Director
ShirleyNebergall, Business Manager
Roger Kranz, Production Director

*WTKC
07-01-2006; 89.7 mhz FM; 0.2 kw; 85 ft.; N41 3 11 W83 39 13
P. O. Box 1212, Findley, OH 45840 US
(419) 423-3285
www.wtkc897.com
wtkc89.7@sbcglobal.net
License: Findlay, Hancock County, OH held by Church of the Living God Ministries.
Arbitron Metro Market: Findlay, OH *Format:* Christian, Talk
Juan Salinas, General Manager
Richard Lugo, Programming Director

Fort Shawnee

WZRX-FM
01-01-1991; 107.5 mhz FM *Hrs Open:* 24; 1.35 kw; 495 ft.; N40 39 50 W84 5 7
50 East Rivercenter Boulevard, Suite 1200, Covington, KY 41011 US
(419) 223-2060, *Fax:* (419) 229-3888
www.wzrxfm.com
brittanytankersley@clearchannel.com
License: Fort Shawnee, Allen County, OH held by Jacor Broadcasting Corp.
Group Owner: Clear Channel Communications Inc.; (acq 5-4-99; grpsl).
Nat'l Reps: Clear Channel
Arbitron Metro Market: Lima, OH *Format:* Oldies, Rock/AOR *Hrs. of News Programming:* News progmg one hr wkly *Target Audience:* 18-49; male dominated *Adv. Rates:* 28; 22; 25; 11
Eric Michaels, Operations Dir
Jordan Treadway, Sales Manager
Renee Scott, Programming Director
Brittany Tankersley, Webmaster

Fostoria

WBVI
01-01-1946; 96.7 mhz FM *Hrs Open:* 24; 3 kw; 289 ft.; N41 6 0 W83 28 32
Mailing Address: US
Second Address: Box 1624, Findlay, OH 45839
(419) 422-9284, *Fax:* (419) 425-8019
www.wbvi.com
Josh@wbvi.com
License: Fostoria, Seneca County, OH held by TCB Holdings Inc.
Nat'l Network: Westwood One *Regional Reps:* OAB
Arbitron Metro Market: Findlay, OH *Format:* Adult Contemp *No. News Employees:* 1 *Target Audience:* 18-50. *Adv. Rates:* 18; 18; 18; 18
Shannon Miller, General Sales Mgr
Brian Cooper, Rhc Affiliate Manager

WFOB
12-09-1952; 1430 khz AM *Hrs Open:* 25.?Â ?; 1 kw-D, DA2; 1 kw-N, DA2; N41 6 6 W83 23 59
Mailing Address: P.O. Box 1157, 101 N. Main Street, Fostoria, OH 44830 US
Second Address: Box 1624, Findlay, OH 45840
(419) 435-1430, *Fax:* (419) 435-6611
www.wfob.com
production@wfob.com
License: Fostoria, OH held by TCB Holdings Inc. c/o Roppe Corp.
Nat'l Network: CBS *Nat'l Reps:* Rgnl Reps
Format: Sports *Special Programming:* Sp 3 hrs wkly *Target Audience:* General.
Donald P. Miller, Chairman
Burley Stapley, Operations Dir
Ahannon Miller, General Manager
Shannon Miller, General Sales Mgr
Josh Hohman, Programming Director
Karen Waltermeyer, Administrative Assistant
Deanna White, Traffic andBilling
Mike Fry, Account Executive
Todd Groves, Account Executive

Fredericktown

WMAN-FM
09-14-1987; 98.3 mhz FM *Hrs Open:* 24; 1.8 kw; Ant 423 ft; N40 34 27 W82 30 27 *Rebroadcasts:* Rebroadcasts WFXN-FM Galion 100%
1197 US Hwy. Rt. 42, Ashland, OH 44805
(419) 289-2605, *Fax:* (419) 289-0304
jeffschendel@clearchannel.com
License: Fredericktown, Knox County, OH held by Capstar TX L.P.
Group Owner: Clear Channel Communications Inc.; (acq 2-12-2001; grpsl).
Nat'l Network: Fox News Radio
Special Programming: Underground Garage, House of Hair
Target Audience: 25-54; Male
Eric Hansen, Operations Dir
Diana Coon, General Manager
Joe Rinehart, Station Manager
Margie Tasseff, General Sales Mgr

Fremont

WFRO-FM
12-15-1946; 99.1 mhz FM *Hrs Open:* 24; 11.5 kw; 364 ft.; N41 21 58 W83 5 20
905 West State Street, Fremont, OH 43420 US
(419) 332-8218, *Fax:* (419) 333-8226
www.wfroradio.com
jonkerns@basbroadcasting.com
License: Fremont, Sandusky County, OH held by BAS Broadcasting Inc.
Group Owner: BAS Broadcasting Inc.; (acq 9-11-2002; $1.3 million)
Nat'l Network: ABC *Regional Network:* Agrinet *Regional Reps:* Rgnl Reps
Format: Adult Contemp *Hrs. of News Programming:* news progmg 5 hrs wkly *No. News Employees:* 2 *Target Audience:* 25-54; adults *Adv. Rates:* 20; 20; 20; 15
Tom Klein, CEO
Jim Lorenzen, President
Dave Campbell, Operations Dir
Jon Kerns, Programming Director
Tom Fullen, News Director
Adam Klien, Sales Representative
Russ Rutherford, Production Manager

Gahanna

WCVO
10-13-1972; 104.9 mhz FM *Hrs Open:* 24; 6 kw; 313 ft.; N40 4 4 W82 51 38
Mailing Address: P.O. Box 7, New Albany, OH 43054 US
Second Address: 4400 Reynoldsburg-New Albany Road, New Albany, OH 43054
(614) 289-5700, *Fax:* (614) 289-5796
www.1049theriver.com
theriver@1049theriver.com
License: Gahanna, Franklin County, OH held by Christian Voice of Central Ohio Inc.
Group Owner: Christian Voice of Central Ohio Inc.
Arbitron Metro Market: Columbus, Oh *Format:* Adult Contemp, Christian *Hrs. of News Programming:* 1.5 *Target Audience:* 25-54; Christian, politically aware, female, middle aged professionals
Dan Baughman, President
Todd Stack, Programming Director
Mike Russell, Music Director

Galion

WFXN-FM
11-08-1974; 102.3 mhz FM *Hrs Open:* 24; 3.5 kw; 430 ft.; N40 45 26 W82 47 23
2435 Mansfield Road, Box 311, Ashland, OH 44805 US
(800) 529-1013, *Fax:* (419) 289-0304
www.foxclassicrock.com
jeffschendel@clearchannel.com
License: Galion, Crawford County, OH held by Capstar TX L.P.
Group Owner: Clear Channel Communications Inc.; (acq 2-12-2001; grpsl).
Nat'l Network: Fox News Radio
Format: Classic Rock *Special Programming:* Underground Garage 2hrs, House of Hair 2hrs *Target Audience:* 25-54; Male
Eric Hanson, Operations Dir
Diana Coon, General Manager
Margie Tasseff, General Sales Mgr
Jeff Schendel, Programming Director

Gallipolis

WJEH
06-19-1950; 990 khz AM *Hrs Open:* 24
Mailing Address: 117 Portsmouth Road, Gallipolis, OH 45631 US
Second Address: 117 Portsmouth Rd., Gallipolis, OH 45631
(740) 446-3543, *Fax:* (740) 446-3001
davediddle@sunny931.com
License: Gallipolis, OH held by Sunny Broadcasting LLC
Nat'l Reps: Rgnl Reps
Format: Contemporary Hits/Top 40 *Hrs. of News Programming:* news progmg 10 hrs wkly *No. News Employees:* 1 *Target Audience:* 35 plus.
Dave Diddle, Station Manager
Tina Merry, Programming Director
Bob Triplett, Chief Engineer

WXBW
12-15-1961; 101.5 mhz FM *Hrs Open:* 24; 50 kw; 492 ft.; N38 48 19 W82 13 36
Mailing Address: 117 Portsmouth Road, Gallipolis, OH 45631 US
Second Address: 919 Fifth Ave., Suite 210, Huntington, WV 25701
(304) 523-8401, *Fax:* (304) 523-8045
www.bigbuck1015.com
License: Gallipolis, Gallia County, OH held by Connoisseur Media of WV-OH LLC.
Group Owner: Connoisseur Media LLC; (acq 6-21-2006; $3.1 million)
Nat'l Network: Westwood One *Nat'l Reps:* McGavren Guild
Arbitron Metro Market: Huntington-Ashl *Format:* Adult Contemp
Target Audience: 24-49.
Newman Adkins, General Manager

Gambier

*WKCO
01-01-1975; 91.9 mhz FM *Hrs Open:* 19; 0.265 kw horiz; 190 ft.; N40 22 25 W82 23 45
P.O. Box 312, Gambier, OH 43022 US
(740) 427-5412
www.wkco.kenyon.edu
wkco@kenyon.edu
License: Gambier, Knox County, OH held by Kenyon College.
Format: Variety/Diverse *Hrs. of News Programming:* News progmg 8 hrs wkly *Target Audience:* 18-25; college population
Elizabeth DeBruin, General Manager
Ellen Pierson, Co-General Manager
Prenton Lange, Co-General Manager
Eugene Rutigliano, Co-General Manager

Geneva

WKKY
11-02-1987; 104.7 mhz FM *Hrs Open:* 24; 6 kw; 328 ft; N41 47 30 W81 05 31
95 W. Main St., Geneva, OH 44041
(440) 466-9559, *Fax:* (440) 466-3138
www.wkky.com
wkky@wkky.com
License: Geneva, Ashtabula County, OH held by Music Express Broadcasting Corp. of Northeast Ohio
Nat'l Network: ABC
Population Served: 128,000*Special Programming:* Pub affrs 2 hrs wkly *Hrs. of News Programming:* News progmg 6 hrs wkly
Target Audience: 25-54.
Warren Jones, President
Gary Hayes, General Manager
Clarence Bucaro, General Sales Mgr
Garth Cornell, Programming Director
Jim Pogras, Chief Engineer

Georgetown

WRAC
12-15-1981; 103.1 mhz FM *Hrs Open:* 24; 6 kw; 328 ft.; N38 52 14 W83 45 55
411 West Walnut, West Union, OH 45693 US
(937) 544-9722, *Fax:* (937) 544-5523
c103country@yahoo.com
License: Georgetown, Adams County, OH held by DreamCatcher Communications Inc.
Group Owner: DreamCatcher Communications Inc.; acq 9-21-81; $4,820;
Nat'l Reps: Rgnl Reps
Format: Country, Gospel *Special Programming:* Farm 10 hrs wkly *Target Audience:* General.
Donald Bowles, President
Venita Bowles, Operations Dir
Ted Foster, Station Manager
Brad Rolfe, Music Director

Gibsonburg

WIMX
01-24-1989; 95.7 mhz FM *Hrs Open:* 24; 3.5 kw; 433 ft.; N41 28 19 W83 25 5
3750 University Avenue, Suite 610, Riverside, CA 92501 US
(419) 868-7914, *Fax:* (419) 868-8765
www.mix957.net
brandibrown@urbanradio.fm
License: Gibsonburg, Sandusky County, OH held by Urban Radio Licenses LLC.
Group Owner: Urban Radio Licenses LLC; (acq 5-13-2005; $2 million)
Nat'l Reps: Interep *Regional Reps:* Regional Reps
Arbitron Metro Market: Toledo, OH *Format:* Adult Contemp
Special Programming: 0 *Target Audience:* 20-40.
Barbara Hubley, Operations Dir
Jillian Wiggs, General Sales Mgr
Brandi Brown, Programming Director
Curtis Downey, Promotions Manager
John Guzan, Market Director of Sales

Granville

***WDUB**
02-07-1962; 91.1 mhz FM *Hrs Open:* 24; 0.1 kw; 171 ft.; N40 4 16 W82 31 24
PO Box F, Granville, OH 43023 US
(740) 587-6382(740) 587-0810, *Fax:* (740) 587-8364
www.911wdub.com/
wdub@denison.edu
License: Granville, Licking County, OH held by Denison University.
Nat'l Network: USA *Wire Services:* UPI
Arbitron Metro Market: Granville, OH. *Format:* Classic Rock
Special Programming: Black 9 hrs, reggae 2 hrs, Sp 2 hrs, Swedish 2 hrs wkly *No. News Employees:* 3 *Target Audience:* General; college students,faculty & loc residents
Jessie Kanelos, Station Manager
Patrick Hunt, Station Manager

Greenfield

WVNU
05-01-1994; 97.5 mhz FM *Hrs Open:* 24; 2.3 kw; 538 ft.; N39 24 26.6 W83 21 14
321 Jefferson Street, Greenfield, OH 45123 US
(937) 981-5050, *Fax:* (937) 981-2107
wvnu.com
License: Greenfield, Highland/Fayette County, OH held by Southern Ohio Broadcasting Inc.
Nat'l Network: Jones Radio Networks; CNN Radio *Regional Network:* ABN Radio
Arbitron Metro Market: Cincinnati, OH *Format:* Adult Contemp
Target Audience: 24-54.
Patrick Hays, President
Nelson Eads, Programming Director
Elaine Hays, Promotions Manager
Christian Wheel, Chief Engineer

Greenville

WDSJ
10-26-1990; 106.5 mhz FM *Hrs Open:* 24; 50 kw; 479 ft.; N40 8 49 W84 36 36
50 East Rivercenter Boulevard, #1200, Covington, KY 41011 US
(937) 224-1137, *Fax:* (937) 224-5015
www.big1065.com
TonyTilford@clearchannel.com
License: Greenville, Darke County, OH held by Aloha Station Trust LLC, as Trustee
Nat'l Network: Jones Radio Networks
Arbitron Metro Market: Dayton, OH *Format:* Country *Target Audience:* 25-54.
Tony Tilford, Operations Dir
Tony Tilford, Programming Director
Aaron Klauber, Promotions Manager

***WDPG**
02-01-1994; 89.9 mhz FM *Hrs Open:* 24; 50 kw; 403 ft; N40 08 49 W84 36 36 *Rebroadcasts:* Rebroadcasts WDPR(FM) West Carrollton 100%
126 N. Main St., Dayton, OH 45402
(937) 496-3850, *Fax:* (937) 496-3852
www.dpr.org
dpr@dpr.org
License: Greenville, Darke County, OH held by Dayton Public Radio Inc.
Larry Coressel, Operations Dir
Shaun Yu, General Manager
Nick Wilson, General Sales Mgr
Shaun Yu, Programming Director
Stephanie Llacuna, Promotions Manager
Jim Stitt, Chief Engineer

Grove City

WOSA
08-21-1990; 101.1 mhz FM *Hrs Open:* 24; 6 kw; 328 ft; N39 48 50 W83 03 19
2400 Olentangy River Road, Columbus, OH 43215
(614) 292-9678, *Fax:* (614) 292-0513
www.beta.wosu.org/clasiical101
License: Grove City, Franklin County, OH held by The Ohio State University
Arbitron Metro Market: Columbus, OH *Target Audience:* 21-40; well educated, upscale professionals with discretionary income
Adv. Rates: 95; 95; 95; 45
Tom Rieland, General Manager

***WWGV**
01-01-2008; 88.1 mhz FM; 5.4 kw vert; 272 ft.; N39 43 16 W83 8 36 *Rebroadcasts:* Rebroadcasts WAFR(FM) Tupelo, MS 100%
Po Drawer 2440, Tupelo, MS 38803 US
(662) 844-5036, *Fax:* (662) 842-7798
www.afr.net
contact@afa.net
License: Grove City, Franklin County, OH held by American Family Association.
Group Owner: American Family Radio
Nat'l Network: American Family Radio
Arbitron Metro Market: Grove City, OH *Format:* Christian
Donald E. Wildmon, Founder
Buster Wilson, General Manager
Jennifer Hagman, Programming Director

Hamilton

WGRR
04-15-1961; 103.5 mhz FM *Hrs Open:* 24; 11 kw; 1037 ft.; N39 12 1 W84 31 22
600 New Hampshire Avenue, N.W., Suite 1200, Washington, DC 20037 US
(513) 241-9898, *Fax:* (513) 241-6689
www.wgrr.com
info@cumulus.com
License: Hamilton, Butler County, OH held by WVAE LICO Inc.
Group Owner: Cumulus Media Partners LLC; (acq 11-29-2007; exchange for WSWD(FM) Fairfield)
Arbitron Metro Market: Cincinnati, OH *Format:* Classic Rock
Joe Wickman, General Sales Mgr
Keith Mitchell, Promotions Manager

***WHSS**
05-12-1975; 89.5 mhz FM *Hrs Open:* Midnight-noon; 190 w; 282 ft; N39 25 51 W84 37 40
5440 Moeller Avenue, Cincinnati, OH 45012
(513) 731-7740, *Fax:* (513) 731-6465
www.sacredheartradio.com
info@sacredheartradio.com
License: Hamilton, Butler County, OH held by Hamilton City Schools Board of Education.
Population Served: 432,000*Target Audience:* 12 plus; general
Bill Leavitt, Station Manager

WMOH
08-15-1944; 1450 khz AM *Hrs Open:* 24
2081 Fairgrove Avenue, Hamilton, OH 45011 US
(513) 863-1111, *Fax:* (513) 863-6856
www.wmoh.com
christheiss@wmoh.com
License: Hamilton, OH held by Vernon R. Baldwin Inc.
Group Owner: Vernon R Baldwin Inc.; acq 1-7-03; $950,000).
Nat'l Network: ESPN Radio *Nat'l Reps:* Rgnl Reps
Arbitron Metro Market: Cincinnati, OH *Format:* News, News/Talk, 84, Talk *Hrs. of News Programming:* news progmg 25 hrs wkly
No. News Employees: 5 *Target Audience:* 35-64; adults above medium income *Adv.Rates:* 22; 18; 20; 12
Chris Theiss, General Manager
Chris Theiss, Station Manager
Brian Kauffmann, General Sales Mgr
Bill Douglas, Programming Director
Steve Vaughn, News Director
Jay Crawford, Engineering Dir
Jake Neal, Account Manager
AnnelieseLess, Business Manager
Gail Moore, Traffic Manager

Harrison

***WORI**
07-01-1998; 90.1 mhz FM *Hrs Open:* 24; 15 kw; Ant 335 ft; N39 13 34 W84 42 59
2351 Sunset Blvd., Suite 170-218, Rocklin, CA 98901
(916) 251-1600, *Fax:* (916) 251-1650
www.air1.com
info@air1.com
License: Harrison, Hamilton County, OH held by Educational Media Foundation.
Group Owner: EMF Broadcasting; (acq 10-2-2003; grpsl)
Nat'l Network: Air 1
Arbitron Metro Market: Cincinnati, OH *Target Audience:* 18-35; Judeo Christian, female
Mike Novak, President
David Pierce, Programming Director
Ed Lenane, News Director
Sam Wallington, Engineering Dir
Marya Morgan, News Reporter
Richard Hunt, News Reporter

Heath

WHTH
10-16-1970; 790 khz AM *Hrs Open:* 24; 1 kw-D, DA-1; N40 03 05 W82 28 08
Box 1057, 1000 N. 40th St., Newark, OH 43055
(740) 522-8171, *Fax:* (740) 522-8174
www.wnko.com
sales@wnko.com
License: Heath, Licking County, OH held by Runnymede Corp.
Nat'l Network: CNN Radio *Wire Services:* AP
Population Served: 140,000 *Arbitron Metro Market:* Columbus, OH *Target Audience:* 35-54. *Adv. Rates:* 15; 12; 15; 10
Charles Franks, President
John Franks, Operations Dir
J. Thomas Swank, General Manager

Hicksville

WFGA
01-01-2002; 106.7 mhz FM; 2.8 kw; 492 ft.; N41 25 24 W84 51 36
12 Glenmoor Place, Hilton Head, SC 29926 US
(260) 471-5100, *Fax:* (260) 920-3604
ilovefroggy.com
feedback@thefanfortwayne.com
License: Hicksville, Defiance County, OH held by Fallen Timber Communications, LLC
Arbitron Metro Market: Fort Wayne, IN *Format:* Variety/Diverse
Leann Didier, General Manager

Hilliard

WBWR
02-06-1991; 105.7 mhz FM *Hrs Open:* 24; 2.4 kw; 522 ft.; N39 58 10 W83 0 10
1301 Dublin Rd., Colombus, OH 43215 US
(614) 486-6101, *Fax:* (614) 487-3575
www.thebrew1057.com
tomthom@clearchannel.com
License: Hilliard, Franklin County, OH held by Citicasters Licenses L.P.
Group Owner: Clear Channel Communications Inc.; (acq 1999; grpsl).
Nat'l Network: ABC
Arbitron Metro Market: Columbus, OH *Format:* Classic Rock *No. News Employees:* 1 *Target Audience:* 18-34.
Tom Thon, General Manager
Rob O'Boyle, General Sales Mgr
John Crenshaw, Programming Director

Holland

***WPOS-FM**
09-01-1966; 102.3 mhz FM *Hrs Open:* 24; 6 kw; 312 ft.; N41 37 32 W83 42 41
Mailing Address: PO Box 457, Holland, OH 43528 US
Second Address: 7112 Angola Rd., Holland, OH 43528
(419) 865-5551, *Fax:* (419) 865-0112
www.wposfm.com
radio@wposfm.com
License: Holland, Lucas County, OH held by Maumee Valley Broadcasting Association.
Format: Christian *Special Programming:* Gospel 20 hrs wkly *Hrs. of News Programming:* News progmg 10 hrs wkly
Al Gaige, General Manager

Hubbard

WRBP
08-16-1993; 101.9 mhz FM; 3 kw; 328 ft.; N41 5 29 W80 30 5
600 Superior Ave. East, Suite 800, Cleveland, OH 44114 US
(330) 744-5115, *Fax:* (330) 744-4020
www.jamz1019.com
skip@ytownradio.com
License: Hubbard, Trumbull County, OH held by Bernard of Ohio LLC.
Group Owner: Bernard Radio LLC; (acq 1-22-2007; grpsl)
Nat'l Network: NBC Radio
Arbitron Metro Market: Youngstown-Warren, OH *Format:* Urban Contemporary, Blues *Special Programming:* Black, news/talk, jazz 12 hrs, relg 6 hrs, Sp 2 hrs wkly *Target Audience:* 25-54; general
Dawn Hartzell, Operations Dir
Skip Benarczyk, General Manager
Lucky Penny, Programming Director
Tiffany Allen, Promotions Manager
Savannah Thomas, Account Manager
Charles Rhodes, Senior Account Manager
Angie Magazine, BUSINESSMANAGER/TRAFFIC
Dan Gonder, PRODUCTION DIRECTOR

Huron

WKFM
04-01-1996; 96.1 mhz FM *Hrs Open:* 24; 3.4 kw; 436 ft.; N41 18 5 W82 29 16
P.O. Box 4006, Elyria, OH 44036 US
(419) 609-5961, *Fax:* (419) 609-2679
www.wkfm.com
k96@wkfm.com
License: Huron, Erie County, OH held by Elyria-Lorain Broadcasting Co.
Group Owner: Elyria-Lorain Broadcasting Co.; acq 7-1-96; $450,000)
Nat'l Network: Westwood One *Regional Network:* ABN Radio
Nat'l Reps: McGavren Guild
Arbitron Metro Market: Cleveland, OH *Format:* Country *Hrs. of News Programming:* news progmg one hr wkly *No. News Employees:* 1 *Target Audience:* General.
Gary Kneisley, President
Lonnie Gronek, General Manager
Bill Forthofer, Station Manager

Ironton

WLRX
07-01-1973; 107.1 mhz FM *Hrs Open:* 18; 3.1 kw; Ant 449 ft; N38 31 23 W82 39 11
Box 2288, Huntington, WV 78701
(304) 525-7788, *Fax:* (304) 525-3299
www.1071kiss.com
kiss107fm@clearchannel.com
License: Ironton, Lawrence County, OH held by Aloha Station Trust LLC
Arbitron Metro Market: Huntington-Ashland, WV-KY *Special Programming:* Relg 2 hrs wkly *Hrs. of News Programming:* News progmg 3 hrs wkly *Target Audience:* 35 plus; affluent, middle-aged
Judy Cornett, General Manager
Matt Tweel, General Sales Mgr
Jim Davis, Programming Director
Bill Cornwell, News Director
Scott Hensley, Chief Engineer
Gary Miller, Music Director

WIRO
09-01-1951; 1230 khz AM *Hrs Open:* 24; 1 kw-U, ND1; N38 32 22 W82 40 17
600 Congress Avenue, Suite 1400, Austin, TX 78701 US
(304) 525-7788, *Fax:* (304) 525-6281
www.800wvhu.com
paulswann@clearchannel.com
License: Ironton, OH held by Aloha Station Trust LLC
Nat'l Reps: Keystone (unwired net); Rgnl Reps
Arbitron Metro Market: Huntington-Ashland, WV-KY *Format:* News, News/Talk, 86 *Special Programming:* Relg 7 hrs wkly *Hrs. of News Programming:* News progmg 5 hrs wkly *Target Audience:* 21-49.
Judy Jennings, General Manager
Matt Tweet, General Sales Mgr
Paul Swann, Programming Director

***WOUL-FM**
10-12-1987; 89.1 mhz FM *Hrs Open:* 24; 50 kw; 400 ft.; N38 31 23 W82 39 20 *Rebroadcasts:* Rebroadcasts WOUB-FM Athens 100%
9 South College Street, Athens, OH 45701 US
(740) 593-4554, *Fax:* (740) 593-0240
www.woub.org
woub@woub.org
License: Ironton, Lawrence County, OH held by Ohio University.
Nat'l Network: PRI; NPR
Format: News, News/Talk, 86 *No. News Employees:* 3
David Wiseman, Operations Dir
Carolyn Lewis, General Manager
Steve Skidmore, Operations Director
Scott Martin, Operations Manager

Jackson

WCJO
01-01-1971; 97.7 mhz FM *Hrs Open:* 24; 3 kw; 299 ft.; N39 1 45 W82 35 51
Mailing Address: 235 Water Street, Jackson, OH 45640 US
Second Address: 295 E. Main St., Jackson, OH 45640
(740) 286-3023, *Fax:* (740) 286-6679
jmossbarger@jcbiradio.com
License: Jackson, Jackson County, OH held by Jackson County Broadcasting Inc.
Group Owner: Jackson County Broadcasting Inc.; (acq 6-15-99; grpsl).
Nat'l Network: Westwood One
Arbitron Metro Market: Jackson, Oh *Format:* Country *Hrs. of News Programming:* news progmg 8 hrs wkly *No. News Employees:* 1 *Target Audience:* General; current-country music lovers *Adv. Rates:* 17; 14; 17;9
Jerry Mossbarger, General Manager
Ron Speakman, General Sales Mgr
John Pelletier, Programming Director

Jefferson

***WCVJ**
01-01-1978; 90.9 mhz FM; 1.85 kw; 643 ft.; N41 37 50 W80 45 36
4422 Lenox New Lyme Road, Jefferson, OH 44047 US
(888) 937-2471, *Fax:* (916) 251-1650
www.air1.com
info@air1.com
License: Jefferson, Ashtabula County, OH held by Educational Media Foundation.
Group Owner: EMF Broadcasting; (acq 10-14-2005; $650,000)
Nat'l Network: Air 1
Arbitron Metro Market: Jefferson, Oh *Format:* Alternative, Christian
Alan Mason, COO
Mike Novak, President
David Pierce, Programming Director
Ed Lenane, News Director
Sam Wallington, Engineering Dir
Marya Morgan, News Reporter
Richard Hunt, News Reporter

Johnstown

WVKO-FM
06-16-1975; 103.1 mhz FM; 1.6 kw; 443 ft.; N40 13 44 W82 39 35.8
600 Superior Ave, East, Suite 800, Cleveland, OH 44114 US
(614) 821-0002,(614) 469-1930, *Fax:* (614) 821-0002,(614) 224-6208
wvko1580am@gmail.com
License: Johnstown, Licking County, OH held by Bernard Ohio LLC.
Group Owner: Bernard Radio LLC; (acq 1-22-2007; grpsl)
Nat'l Reps: D & R Radio
Arbitron Metro Market: Columbus, OH *Format:* Tejano *Special Programming:* Jazz 10 hrs, relg 13 hrs, reggae 5 hrs wkly *Target Audience:* 18-54; upscale, professional; homeowners with disposable incomes *Adv. Rates:* 34; 25; 34; 22
Tom Morris, Operations Dir
Hector Villarreal, General Manager

Kent

WJMP
03-01-1964; 1520 khz AM; 1 kw-D, DAD; N41 9 37 W81 18 16
Mailing Address: Box 2170, Akron, OH 44309 US
Second Address: 2449 S.R. 59, Kent, OH 44240
(330) 673-2323, *Fax:* (330) 673-0301
License: Kent, OH held by Media-Com Inc.
Arbitron Metro Market: Akron, OH *Format:* Sports *Target Audience:* 18 plus.
Richard Klaus, President
William Klaus, Station Manager
Robert Klaus, General Sales Mgr
Jim Midock, News Director
Bob Sassman, Chief Engineer
Mary Stein, Traffic Manager

***WKSU-FM**
01-01-1950; 89.7 mhz FM *Hrs Open:* 24; 14.5 kw; Ant 909 ft; N41 04 58 W81 38 02
Mailing Address: Box 5190, Kent, OH 44242
Second Address: 1613 E. Summit St., Kent, OH 44242-0001
(330) 672-3114, *Fax:* (330) 672-4107
www.wksu.org
letters@wksu.org
License: Kent, Portage County, OH held by Kent State University.
Nat'l Network: PRI; NPR; AP Radio
Population Served: 2,650,000 *Arbitron Metro Market:* Akron, OH *Special Programming:* Folk 12 hrs wkly *Hrs. of News Programming:* news progmg 35 hrs wkly *No. News Employees:* 5 *Target Audience:* 35-65;college grad, professional & upper income
Allen Bartholet, General Manager
M L Schutlze, News Director
Ronald Bartlebaugh, Engineering Dir
Kerry Kurchak, Assistant General Manager

WNIR
02-19-1962; 100.1 mhz FM; 4.2 kw; 394 ft.; N41 6 28 W81 21 19
Mailing Address: P. O. Box 2170, Akron, OH 44309 US
Second Address: 2449 S.R. 59, Kent, OH 44240
(330) 673-2323, *Fax:* (330) 673-0301
www.wnir.com
bobklaus@wnir.com
License: Kent, Portage County, OH held by Media-Com Inc.
Wire Services: AP
Arbitron Metro Market: Akron, OH *Format:* Talk *Target Audience:* General.
Bill Klaus, CEO/COO
Bob Klaus, President
Phil Ferguson, News Director
Dan Mammone, Chief Engineer

Kenton

WKTN
06-20-1963; 95.3 mhz FM *Hrs Open:* 5 AM-midnight; 3.5 kw; 276 ft.; N40 38 41 W83 33 59
C/O Susan Marshall, 1050 Connecticut Avenue, Washington, DC 20036 US
(419) 675-2355, *Fax:* (419) 673-1096
www.wktn.com
wktn@dbscorp.net
License: Kenton, Hardin County, OH held by Radio General Ltd.
Format: Adult Contemp *Special Programming:* Farm 2 hrs wkly *Hrs. of News Programming:* news progmg 10 hrs wkly *No. News Employees:* 1 *Target Audience:* 25-54.
Keith Gensheimer, President

Kettering

*WKET
05-05-1975; 98.3 mhz FM; 0.013 kw horiz; 249 ft.; N39 41 46 W84 9 43
3750 Far Hills Avenue, Kettering, OH 45429 US
(937) 296-7669, *Fax:* (937) 297-7435
ettering.k12.oh.us
info@wket.com
License: Kettering, Montgomery County, OH held by Kettering City School District.
Arbitron Metro Market: Dayton, OH *Format:* Classic Rock, Rock/AOR *Target Audience:* 13-18; high school students
Karl Bremer, General Manager

Lancaster

*WFCO
08-01-1988; 90.9 mhz FM *Hrs Open:* 24; 0 kw horiz, 1.2 kw vert; 256 ft.; N39 40 49 W82 35 51
2150 Joy Lane, Lancaster, OH 43130 US
(740) 689-0909, *Fax:* (740) 654-8581
wfcofm.com
wfco@wfcofm.com
License: Lancaster, Fairfield County, OH held by Lancaster Educational Broadcasting Foundation.
Nat'l Network: Salem Radio Network
Arbitron Metro Market: Lancaster, OH *Format:* Christian, News, 62, Talk *Special Programming:* Live coverage of sports & community events *Hrs. of News Programming:* news progmg one hr wkly *No. News Employees:* 1*Target Audience:* 30 plus; Christian audience & those interested in community events
John Hablitzel, Operations Dir
Steve Rauch, General Manager
Steve Rauch, Station Manager
Jim George, Sales and Marketing Manager
Josh Messerly, News and Production Director
Dallas Lambert, Sports Director
Amy Fratturo, OfficeManager
Andy Smeltzer, Sports Assistant

WHOK-FM
12-01-1958; 95.5 mhz FM *Hrs Open:* 24; 21 kw; 761 ft.; N39 40 32 W82 40 34
600 New Hampshire Ave., NW, Suite 1200, Washington, DC 20037 US
(614) 227-9696, *Fax:* (614) 461-1059
www.k95.fm
License: Lancaster, Fairfield County, OH held by Wilks License Co.-Columbus LLC.
Group Owner: Wilks Broadcast Group LLC; (acq 1-10-2007; grpsl)
Nat'l Reps: Christal
Arbitron Metro Market: Columbus, OH *Format:* Country *Hrs. of News Programming:* news progmg 2 hrs wkly *No. News Employees:* 1 *Target Audience:* 25-54.
Scott Russell, General Sales Mgr
Ross Wagner, Programming Director
George Wolf, Programming Director
Mike Dorsey, Promotions Director

WLOH
10-01-1948; 1320 khz AM *Hrs Open:* 24
PO Box 116, Lancaster, OH 43130 US
(740) 653-4373, *Fax:* (740) 653-0702
www.wloh.net
community@wloh.net
License: Lancaster, OH held by Frontier Broadcasting LLC No. 3
Nat'l Reps: D & R Radio
Arbitron Metro Market: Columbus, OH *Format:* Talk *Special Programming:* Farm one hr wkly *Hrs. of News Programming:* news progmg 24 hrs wkly *No. News Employees:* 2 *Target Audience:* General; Fairfield,Franklin & surrounding county residents
Bart Johnson, CEO
Mark Bohach, General Manager
Michael O'Riley, General Sales Mgr

Lebanon

WFTK
05-26-1958; 96.5 mhz FM *Hrs Open:* 24; 19.5 kw; 810 ft.; N39 21 11 W84 19 30
625 Eden Park Drive, Suite 1050, Cincinnati, OH 45202 US
(513) 241-9898, *Fax:* (513) 241-6689
www.purerock96.com
License: Lebanon, Warren County, OH held by WVAE Lico Inc.
Group Owner: Cumulus Media Partners LLC; (acq 5-5-2006; grpsl)
Nat'l Reps: Christal
Arbitron Metro Market: Lebanon, OH
Gary Lewis, General Manager
Jeff Davis, Promotions Manager

Lexington

*WFOT
02-01-2007; 89.5 mhz FM; 0.36 kw vert; 304 ft.; N40 43 36 W82 36 59
240 Rudy Road, Mansfield, OH 44903 US
(614) 442-1270, *Fax:* (714) 845-0411
www.stgabrielradio.com
info@stgabrielradio.com
License: Lexington, Richland County, OH held by St. Gabriel Radio Inc.
Nat'l Network: EWTN Radio
Arbitron Metro Market: Lexington, OH *Format:* Christian
Christopher Gabrelcik, President
Michael Barone, Station Manager
Bill Messerly, Executive Director
Dave Orsborn, Production Manager

Lima

WEGE
11-25-1970; 104.9 mhz FM *Hrs Open:* 24; 3 kw; 220 ft.; N40 43 21 W84 5 4
One Forever Dirve, Hollidaysburg, PA 16648 US
(419) 331-1600, *Fax:* (419) 222-3755
www.1049theeagle.com/
WEGE@Maverick-Media.ws
License: Lima, Allen County, OH held by Maverick Media of Lima License LLC.
Group Owner: Maverick Media LLC; (acq 12-4-2003; grpsl)
Nat'l Network: ABC *Nat'l Reps:* Christal
Arbitron Metro Market: Allen County, OH *Format:* Classic Rock *Target Audience:* 25-54; affluent, community involved
Dave Roach, General Manager
Matt Childers, General Sales Mgr
Bill Rice, Programming Director
Brandy Rader, News Director

*WGLE
12-02-1981; 90.7 mhz FM *Hrs Open:* 24; 50 kw horiz, 46 kw vert; 420 ft.; N40 39 15 W84 6 36 *Rebroadcasts:* Rebroadcasts WGTE-FM Toledo 100%
136 N. Huron St. Box 30, Toledo, OH 43697 US
(419) 380-4600, *Fax:* (419) 380-4710
www.wgte.org
info@wgte.com
License: Lima, Allen County, OH held by The Public Broadcasting Foundation of Northwest Ohio.
Nat'l Network: PRI; NPR
Arbitron Metro Market: Lima, OH *TV Affiliate:* *WGTE-TV affil.
Format: News, Public Affairs *Special Programming:* Jazz 16 hrs, new age/eclectic 4 hrs wkly *Hrs. of News Programming:* News progmg 23 hrs wkly*Target Audience:* General.
George Jones, Chairman
Marlon Kiser, CEO
Chris Pfeiffer, Operations Dir
Ross Pfeiffer, General Sales Mgr

WIMA
12-05-1948; 1150 khz AM *Hrs Open:* 24; 1 kw-D, DAN; 1 kw-N, DAN; N40 40 47 W84 6 34
50 East Rivercenter Boulevard, Suite 1200, Covington, KY 41011 US
(419) 223-2060, *Fax:* (419) 229-3888
www.1150wima.com
comments@1150wima.com
License: Lima, OH held by Jacor Broadcasting Corp.
Group Owner: Clear Channel Communications Inc.; (acq 5-4-99; grpsl)
Nat'l Network: Fox News Radio; Fox Sports *Nat'l Reps:* Clear Channel *Wire Services:* AP
Arbitron Metro Market: Lima, OH *Format:* News, News/Talk, 84, Talk *Special Programming:* Farm 5 hrs wkly *Hrs. of News Programming:* news progmg 20 hrs wkly *No. News Employees:* 1 *Target Audience:* 35 plus.*Adv. Rates:* 35; 32; 28; 12
Art Versnick, Operations Dir
David Cook, Station Manager
Jack Wheelbarger, General Sales Mgr
Dave Woodward, Programming Director
Doug Jenkins, News Director
Mark Gierhart, Chief Engineer
Phil Austin, Operations Manager

WIMT
12-01-1948; 102.1 mhz FM *Hrs Open:* 24; 11 kw; 1060 ft.; N40 38 3 W84 12 29
50 East Rivercenter Boulevard, Suite 1200, Covington, KY 41011 US
(419) 223-2060, *Fax:* (419) 229-3888
www.t102.com
comments@t102.com
License: Lima, Allen County, OH held by Jacor Broadcasting Corp.
Group Owner: Clear Channel Communications Inc.; (acq 5-4-99)
Wire Services: AP
Arbitron Metro Market: Lima, OH *Format:* Country *Hrs. of News Programming:* news progmg one hrs wkly *No. News Employees:* 1 *Target Audience:* 25-54. *Adv. Rates:* 55; 45; 50; 15
Brian Steel, Programming Director

WCIT(AM)
08-22-1963; 940 khz AM *Hrs Open:* 24; 250 w-D, DA-2; N40 43 21 W84 05 04
1301 N. Cable Rd., Lima, OH 45805
(419) 331-1600, *Fax:* (419) 222-5085
www.940jamz.com
info@940jamz.com
License: Lima, Allen County, OH held by Maverick Media of Lima License LLC.
Group Owner: Maverick Media LLC; (acq 12-4-2003; grpsl)
Nat'l Reps: Christal; Rgnl Reps
Population Served: 220,000 *Arbitron Metro Market:* Lima, OH *Format:* Urban Contemporary *Special Programming:* Jazz 2 hrs, relg 11 hrs wkly *Hrs. of News Programming:* news progmg 20 hrs wkly *No. News Employees:* 2 *Target Audience:* 35-54; affluent, community involved
Gary Rozynek, President
Bill McAdams, Operations Dir
Dave Roach, General Manager
Mark Mackey, Station Manager

*WTGN
09-27-1966; 97.7 mhz FM; 6 kw; 299 ft.; N40 45 23 W84 8 0
1600 Elida Road, Lima, OH 45805 US
(419) 227-2525, *Fax:* (419) 222-5438
www.wtgn.org
wtgn@wcoil.com
License: Lima, Allen County, OH held by Associated Christian Broadcasters Inc.
Arbitron Metro Market: Lima, OH *Format:* Christian
Wesley Lytle, President
Scott Young, General Manager
Dave Morris, Engineering Dir
Sue Gatchel, Secretary
Judi Skonieczny, Administrative Assistant

WWSR
07-01-1964; 93.1 mhz FM *Hrs Open:* 24; 3 kw; 318 ft.; N40 45 47 W84 10 59
Mailing Address: One Forever Drive, Hollidaysburg, PA 16648 US
Second Address: 1301 N. Cable Rd., Lima, OH 45805
(419) 331-1600, *Fax:* (419) 228-5085
www.931thefan.com
sportstalkwithkoza@wcoil.com
License: Lima, Auglaize County, OH held by Maverick Media of Lima License LLC.
Group Owner: Maverick Media LLC; (acq 12-4-2003; grpsl).
Nat'l Reps: Christal *Regional Reps:* Rgnl Reps.
Arbitron Metro Market: Lima, OH *Format:* Contemporary Hits/Top 40 *Hrs. of News Programming:* news progmg 6 hrs wkly *No. News Employees:* 1 *Target Audience:* 18-49; young, affluent women *Adv. Rates:* 30; 25;27; 18
Gary Rozynek, President
Dave Roach, General Manager
Matt Childers, General Sales Mgr
Ryan Wrecker, Programming Director
Cami Marlowe, Promotions Manager
Bob Ulm, News/Information Director
Matt Childers, Market Manager
PhilAustin, Operations Manager
Rick Burgei, Sports/Community Director
Deb Klaus, Business Manager
Tiffany Kayser, Director of Sales

*WYSM
01-01-2001; 89.3 mhz FM; 3 kw; Ant 220 ft; N40 39 15 W84 06 36
5105 Glendale Ave., Suite C, Toledo, OH 43537
(419) 389-0893, *Fax:* (419) 381-0731
www.yeshome.com
yesfm@yeshome.com
License: Lima, Allen County, OH held by Side by Side Inc.
Arbitron Metro Market: Lima, OH
J. Todd Hostetler, General Manager
Jeff Howe, Programming Director

Logan

WLGN

12-01-1967; 1510 khz AM *Hrs Open:* Sunrise-sunset
Mailing Address: P. O. Box 429, Logan, OH 43138 US
Second Address: One Radio Ln., Logan, OH 43138
(740) 385-2151, *Fax:* (740) 385-4022
wlgn@magicohio.com
License: Logan, OH held by WLGN LLC.
Group Owner: Baker Family Stations; (acq 1-4-2005; $675,000 with co-located FM)
Nat'l Network: ABC *Nat'l Reps:* Rgnl Reps
Format: Oldies *Target Audience:* 18-54.
Scott Blazer, General Manager
Vicki Lutz, General Sales Mgr

WKNA

12-10-1965; 98.3 mhz FM *Hrs Open:* 24; 6 kw; 220 ft.; N39 31 43 W82 23 6
P. O. Box 429, Logan, OH 43138 US
(740) 385-2151, *Fax:* (740) 385-4022
License: Logan, Hocking County, OH held by WLGN LLC.
Group Owner: Baker Family Stations
Format: Country *Hrs. of News Programming:* news progmg 25 hrs wkly *No. News Employees:* 1
Scott Blazer, General Manager
Vicki Lutz, News Director

London

WXMG

01-01-1965; 106.3 mhz FM *Hrs Open:* 24; 6 kw; 328 ft; N39 53 05 W83 25 23
350 E. 1st Ave., Suite 100, Columbus, OH 45237
(614) 487-1444, *Fax:* (614) 487-5862
www.joy106.com
info@wjod.com
License: London, Franklin County, OH held by Blue Chip Broadcasting Licenses Ltd.
Group Owner: Radio One Inc.; (acq 4-30-01; grpsl).
Nat'l Network: ABC *Nat'l Reps:* D & R Radio
Population Served: 1,603,000 *Arbitron Metro Market:* Columbus, OH *Special Programming:* Gospel 10 hrs wkly *No. News Employees:* 3 *Target Audience:* 18-34.
Jeff Wilson, General Manager

Lorain

WDLW

12-01-1969; 1380 khz AM *Hrs Open:* 24; 0.5 kw-D, ND1; 0.057 kw-N, ND1; N41 25 48 W82 9 7
Mailing Address: 8686 Michael Lane, Fairfield, OH 45014 US
Second Address: 45624 State Rt. 20, Oberlin, OH 44047
(440) 774-1320, *Fax:* (440) 774-1336
www.woblwdlw.com
dwilber@woblwdlw.com
License: Lorain, OH held by WDLW Radio Inc.
Wire Services: AP
Arbitron Metro Market: Cleveland, OH *Format:* Oldies *Hrs. of News Programming:* news progmg 10 hrs wkly *No. News Employees:* 3 *Target Audience:* 35-64. *Adv. Rates:* 22.50; 21.50; 22.50; 19.50
Doug Wilber, Station Manager
Lorie Wilber, Operations Dir
Peggy Brown, General Sales Mgr
Brian Engle, Programming Director

*WNZN

01-01-1992; 89.1 mhz FM; 2.2 kw; 374 ft.; N41 18 34 W82 26 31
P.O. Box 330184, Ponce, PR 0733 US
(419) 588-3700
tony10491@adelphia.net
License: Lorain, Lorain County, OH held by Spanish Cultural Network.
Arbitron Metro Market: Cleveland, OH *TV Affiliate:* Sp

WCLV

04-01-1961; 104.9 mhz FM *Hrs Open:* 24; 6 kw; 328 ft.; N41 28 32 W81 59 24
50 E. Rivercenter Blvd., #1200, Covington, KY 41011 US
(216) 464-0900, *Fax:* (216) 464-2206
www.wclv.com
wclv@wclv.com
License: Lorain, Lorain County, OH held by Radio Seaway Inc.
Nat'l Reps: D & R Radio; Interep *Wire Services:* AP
Arbitron Metro Market: Lorain, OH *Format:* Classical *Special Programming:* Jazz 5 hrs, financial news one hr wkly *Hrs. of News Programming:* News progmg 5 hrs wkly *Target Audience:* 35-64; high-income, collegegraduates & professionals *Adv. Rates:* 80; 80; 80; 80
Rich Marschner, CFO
Robert Conrad, President
John Simna, Operations Dir
Jenny Northern, Senior Vice President, General and Sales Manager,
Jenny Northern, Senior Vice President, General and Sales Manager,
Bill O'Connell, VicePresident; Program Manager; Afternoon Drive H
Randy Davis, Chief Engineer
Richard Marschner, Executive Vice President and Chief Financial Offic
John Simna, Music and Operations Manager
Jim Mehrling, First Program Host, Producer
AnnieBartlett, Vice President, Business Manager
Ken Kreutzer, Traffic Manager
Charlie Schnell, Senior Account Executive

Loudonville

WXXF

03-01-1990; 107.7 mhz FM *Hrs Open:* 24; 6 kw; 328 ft.; N40 36 58 W82 5 34 *Rebroadcasts:* Rebroadcasts WFXN-FM Galion 100%
Suite 2, 115 S. Water St., Loudonville, OH 44842 US
(419) 529-2211, *Fax:* (419) 529-2516
www.wfxnthefox.com/main.html
TOMMYBARNES@CLEARCHANNEL.COM
License: Loudonville, Ashland County, OH held by Capstar TX L.P.
Group Owner: Clear Channel Communications Inc.; (acq 2-12-2001; grpsl).
Nat'l Network: Fox News Radio
Arbitron Metro Market: Mansfield, OH *Format:* Classic Rock
Special Programming: Underground Garage, House of Hair
Target Audience: 25-54; Male
Eric Hansen, Operations Dir
Diana Coon, General Manager
Joe Rinehart, Station Manager
Margie Tasseff, General Sales Mgr
Jeff Schendel, Programming Director

Luckey

WPFX-FM

07-30-1990; 107.7 mhz FM; 5.2 kw; 350 ft; N41 07 04 W83 32 38
720 Water Street, 4th Floor, Toledo, OH 41011
(419) 255-0107, *Fax:* (419) 241-1077
www.1077wolf.com
License: Luckey, Wood County, OH held by Toledo Radio LLC
Group Owner: BAS Broadcasting Inc.; (acq 6-30-2008; grpsl)
Arbitron Metro Market: Toledo, OH
Daniel Dudley, President

Manchester

WAGX

10-26-1992; 101.3 mhz FM *Hrs Open:* 24; 3 kw; 299 ft; N38-36-03, W83-40-22
Mailing Address: PO Box 492, Manchester, OH 41001
Second Address: 9503 Mason Lewis Road, Maysville, KY 41056
(606) 564-8474, *Fax:* (606) 564-8383
License: Manchester, Adams County, OH held by Jewell Schaeffer Broadcasting Inc.
Population Served: 125,000 *Arbitron Metro Market:* Cincinnati, OH *Hrs. of News Programming:* local, 7 hrs per week *Target Audience:* 25-54; upscale adults *Adv. Rates:* upon request
James Wagner, President

Mansfield

WMAN

12-04-1939; 1400 khz AM *Hrs Open:* 24; 0.92 kw-U, ND1; 0.958 kw-U, ND1; N40 46 13 W82 32 36; N40 46 0 W82 32 48
1400 Radio Lane, Mansfield, OH 44901 US
(419) 529-2211, *Fax:* (419) 529-2516
www.wmanfm.com
rustycates@clearchannel.com
License: Mansfield, OH held by Capstar TX L.P.
Group Owner: Clear Channel Communications Inc.; (acq 8-7-00; grpsl).
Nat'l Network: CBS; Westwood One
Arbitron Metro Market: Mansfield, OH *Format:* News, News/Talk, 86 *Hrs. of News Programming:* news progmg 30 hrs wkly *No. News Employees:* 3 *Target Audience:* 35 plus; upscale, active mgmt/exec
Shawn Katzbeck, General Sales Mgr
Jim Medley, Programming Director
Lisa Bougie, News Director
Chuck Gennaro, Chief Engineer

*WOSV

06-27-1989; 91.7 mhz FM *Hrs Open:* 24; 0.75 kw; 449 ft.; N40 42 33 W82 29 11 *Rebroadcasts:* Rebroadcasts WOSU-FM Columbus 100%
2400 Olentangy River Rd, Columbus, OH 43210 US
(614) 292-9678, *Fax:* (614) 292-7625
www.wosu.org
wosu@osu.edu
License: Mansfield, Richland County, OH held by The Ohio State University.
Nat'l Network: PRI; NPR *Wire Services:* AP
Format: Classical *Hrs. of News Programming:* News progmg 28 hrs wkly *Target Audience:* 35 plus.
Kevin Petrilla, Operations Dir
Thomas Rieland, General Manager
Tim Eby, Station Manager

*WVMC-FM

03-01-1979; 90.7 mhz FM *Hrs Open:* 24; 170 w; 100 ft; N40 43 19 W82 31 52
500 Logan Rd., Mansfield, OH 44907
(419) 756-5651 ext 225, *Fax:* (419) 756-7470
www.wvmcfm.com
License: Mansfield, Richland County, OH held by Mansfield Christian School.
Population Served: 35,000*Target Audience:* 18-34; middle income adults, mostly female
Scott Sullind, General Manager

WVNO-FM

08-11-1962; 106.1 mhz FM; 40 kw; 545 ft.; N40 45 50 W82 37 4
2900 Park Avenue West, Mansfield, OH 44906 US
(419) 529-5900, *Fax:* (419) 529-2319
www.wvno.com
info@wvno.com
License: Mansfield, Richland County, OH held by Johnny Appleseed Broadcasting Co.
Regional Reps: Rgnl Reps
Arbitron Metro Market: Mansfield, OH *Format:* Adult Contemp *Hrs. of News Programming:* news progmg 10 hrs wkly *No. News Employees:* 5 *Target Audience:* 25-54; female
Gunther Meisse, President
Tony Mitchell, Operations Dir

WYHT

10-18-1962; 105.3 mhz FM; 50 kw; 371 ft.; N40 46 9 W82 32 23
1400 Radio Lane, Mansfield, OH 44901 US
(419) 529-2211, *Fax:* (419) 529-2516
www.wyht.com
License: Mansfield, Richland County, OH held by Capstar TX L.P.
Arbitron Metro Market: Mansfield, OH *Format:* Adult Contemp
Mike Fredrick, General Manager
Christine Mello, General Sales Mgr
Travis Moon, Programming Director

Marietta

*WCMO

10-01-1960; 98.5 mhz FM; 0.004 kw; 105 ft.; N39 25 7 W81 26 32
215 Fifth Street, Marietta, OH 45750 US
(740) 376-3345, *Fax:* (740) 376-4807
www.marietta.edu
sinclaij@marietta.edu
License: Marietta, Washington County, OH held by Marietta College.
Arbitron Metro Market: Marietta, Oh *Format:* Rock/AOR
Marilee Morrow, General Manager
Jennifer Sinclair, Station Manager

WMOA

09-08-1946; 1490 khz AM *Hrs Open:* 24
925 Lancaster Street, Marietta, OH 45750 US 45750
(740) 373-1490, *Fax:* (740) 373-1717
www.wmoa1490.com
jwharff@wmoa1490.com
License: Marietta, OH held by JAWCO Inc.
Nat'l Network: ABC Information & Entertainment *Regional Network:* Ohio News Network
Arbitron Metro Market: Parkersburg, OH *Format:* Adult Contemp, News, 84 *Special Programming:* Farm one hr, relg one hr, sports 15 hrs wkly *Hrs. of News Programming:* news progmg 5 hrs wkly *No. News Employees:* 1*Target Audience:* 35 plus; mature, middle-class to affluent
John Wharff, President
Jamey Styer, Operations Dir
John Wharff III, General Manager
Stephanie Wiles, Station Manager
Andy Rex, Programming Director
Kyle Wenzel, Music Director

***WMRT**
11-13-1975; 88.3 mhz FM; 9.2 kw; 203 ft.; N39 25 7 W81 26 32
211 Fifth Street, Marietta, OH 45750 US
(740) 376-4800, *Fax:* (740) 376-4807
www.wmrtfm.com
License: Marietta, Washington County, OH held by Marietta College.
Arbitron Metro Market: Parkersburg, OH *Format:* Jazz, News, 62, Talk
Marilee Morrow, General Manager
David St Peter, Station Manager

WRVB
12-01-1964; 102.1 mhz FM *Hrs Open:* 24; 11 kw; 492 ft.; N39 19 27 W81 37 33
6006 Grand Central Ave., Vienna, WV 26105 US
(304) 295-6070, *Fax:* (304) 295-4389
www.102theriver.com
info@102theriver.com
License: Marietta, Washington County, OH held by CC Licenses LLC.
Group Owner: Clear Channel Communications Inc.; (acq 4-17-2001; grpsl).
Arbitron Metro Market: Parkersburg-Mar *Format:* Contemporary Hits/Top 40 *Target Audience:* 25-54; general *Adv. Rates:* 14; 12; 14; 12
Chuck Poet, General Manager

WLTP
05-08-1996; 910 khz AM *Hrs Open:* 24
3711 Whipple Ave., NW., Canton, OH 44718 US
(304) 295-6070, *Fax:* (304) 295-4389
www.newstalk910wltp.com
info@wltp.com
License: Marietta, OH held by CC Licenses LLC.
Group Owner: Clear Channel Communications Inc.; (acq 9-4-2002).
Nat'l Network: CBS; Westwood One; AP Radio
Arbitron Metro Market: Marietta, OH *Format:* Talk *Hrs. of News Programming:* news progmg 8 hrs wkly *No. News Employees:* 1 *Target Audience:* 18-54; males
Chuck Poet, General Manager

Marion

WMRN-FM
02-27-1975; 94.3 mhz FM *Hrs Open:* 24; 3 kw; 299 ft.; N40 36 27 W83 14 14
50 East Rivercenter Boulevard, Suite 1200, Covington, KY 41011 US
(740) 383-1131, *Fax:* (740) 387-3697
www.buckeyecountry943.com
License: Marion, Marion County, OH held by Citicasters Licenses L.P.
Group Owner: Clear Channel Communications Inc.; (acq 1999; grpsl)
Nat'l Reps: Rgnl Reps
Arbitron Metro Market: Upper Sandusky- Marion- Bucyrus, Oh *Format:* Country *Target Audience:* 25-54.
Scott Shawver, Operations Dir
Diana Coon, General Manager
Mike Mitchell, General Sales Mgr

WMRN
12-23-1940; 1490 khz AM
50 East Rivercenter Boulevard, Suite 1200, Covington, KY 41011 US
(740) 383-1131, *Fax:* (740) 387-3697
www.wmrn.com
License: Marion, OH held by Citicasters Licenses L.P.
Group Owner: Clear Channel Communications Inc.; (acq 1999; grpsl)
Arbitron Metro Market: Marion, OH *Format:* News, News/Talk, 64, Talk *Special Programming:* Farm 5 hrs wkly *Target Audience:* 35-65
Diane Glassmeyer, General Manager

***WOSB**
04-14-1998; 91.1 mhz FM; 2.5 kw horiz, 6.8 kw vert; 285 ft.; N40 41 4 W83 15 24 *Rebroadcasts:* Rebroadcasts WOSU-FM Columbus
2400 Olentagy River Rd, Columbus, OH 43210 US
(614) 292-9678, *Fax:* (614) 292-7625
www.wosu.org
info@wosu.org
License: Marion, Marion County, OH held by The Ohio State University.
Nat'l Network: NPR *Wire Services:* AP
TV Affiliate: var

***WXMF**
91.9 mhz FM; 6 kw; 305 ft.; N40 36 51 W83 12 56
PO Box 158, Upper Sandusky, OH 43351 US
(419) 294-2900
License: Marion, Marion County, OH held by Kayser Broadcast Ministries Inc.
Arbitron Metro Market: Marion, OH *Format:* Christian, Religious
Daniel Kayser, President

Marysville

WQTT
12-01-1983; 1270 khz AM *Hrs Open:* 24; 500 w-U, DA-2; N40 14 46 W83 19 50
1585 Bethel Rd, Suite 101-LL, Columbus, OH 43081
(614) 442-1270, *Fax:* (714) 845-0411
www.stgabrielradio.com
info@stgabrielradio.com
License: Marysville, Union County, OH held by St. Gabriel Radio Inc
Nat'l Network: EWTN Radio
Population Served: 40,000 *Arbitron Metro Market:* Columbus, OH
Chris Gabrelcik, President
Michael Barone, Station Manager
Bill Cusack, General Sales Mgr
Farris Wilhite, Engineering Dir

Mason

WOXY
12-24-1959; 97.7 mhz FM *Hrs Open:* 24; 3.5 kw; 436 ft.; N39 20 56.8 W84 12 8.2
5120 College Corner Pike, Oxford, OH 45056 US
(513) 523-4114, *Fax:* (513) 523-1412
License: Mason, Butler County, OH held by First Broadcasting Capital Partners LLC.
Group Owner: First Broadcasting Operating Inc.; (acq 3-17-2004; $5.64 million).
Wire Services: AP
Arbitron Metro Market: Cincinnati, OH *Format:* Alternative *Target Audience:* 18-34. *Adv. Rates:* 50; 50; 50; 50
Heather Frye, General Manager

Massillon

WTIG
08-01-1957; 990 khz AM *Hrs Open:* 24; 0.25 kw-D, DA2; 0.112 kw-N, DA2; N40 49 56 W81 33 40
Mailing Address: P.O. Box 573, Massillon, OH 44648 US
Second Address: 3580 Karen Ave. N.W., Massillon, OH 44647
(330) 837-9900, *Fax:* (330) 837-9844
www.espn990.com
espn990@gmail.com
License: Massillon, OH held by WTIG Inc.
Arbitron Metro Market: Massillon, OH *Format:* Sports *Special Programming:* Loc church svcs 6 hrs wkly *Target Audience:* 25-54; male
Ray Jeske, President
Donovan Resh, Operations Dir

Maumee

***WYSZ**
11-14-1992; 89.3 mhz FM *Hrs Open:* 24; 2.45 kw horiz, 1.85 kw vert; 305 ft.; N41 38 55 W83 42 22
9035 Salisbury Road, Mouclova, OH 43542 US
(419) 389-0893, *Fax:* (419) 381-0731
License: Maumee, Lucas County, OH held by Side By Side Inc.
Arbitron Metro Market: Toledo, OH *Format:* Christian *Target Audience:* 15-25.
J. Todd Hostetler, General Manager
Janet Yonke, General Sales Mgr
Jeff Howe, Programming Director

McArthur

WYRO
01-01-1994; 98.7 mhz FM *Hrs Open:* 24; 5.4 kw; 344 ft.; N39 9 18 W82 35 49
Mailing Address: P.O. Box 606, Jackson, OH 45640 US
Second Address: 295 E. Main St., Jackson, OH 45640
(740) 286-3023, *Fax:* (740) 286-6679
jmossbarger@jcbradio.com
License: McArthur, Vinton County, OH held by Davis Broadcasting Media Inc.
Nat'l Network: Westwood One *Regional Reps:* Rgnl Reps.
Format: Classic Rock *No. News Employees:* 1 *Target Audience:* 18-65. *Adv. Rates:* 18; 14; 18; 10
Jerry Mossbarger, General Manager
Ron Speakman, General Sales Mgr
John Pelletier, Programming Director

McConnelsville

WJAW-FM
10-01-1992; 100.9 mhz FM *Hrs Open:* 24; 0.93 kw; 577 ft.; N39 33 24 W81 51 6
Mailing Address: 925 Lancaster Street, Marietta, OH 45750 US
Second Address: PO Box 547, McConnelsville, OH 43756
(740) 373-1490, *Fax:* (740) 373-1717
www.espnwjaw.com
kwenzel@wmoa1490.com
License: McConnelsville, Morgan County, OH held by JAWCO Inc.
Nat'l Network: ESPN Radio *Regional Network:* Ohio News Network
Arbitron Metro Market: Columbus, OH *Format:* Sports *No. News Employees:* 1 *Target Audience:* 18-34; male
Jamey Styer, Operations Dir
John Wharff III, General Manager
Stephanie Wiles, Station Manager
Andy Rex, Programming Director

Medina

WQMX
01-01-1960; 94.9 mhz FM *Hrs Open:* 24; 16 kw; 879 ft.; N41 4 58 W81 38 0
1795 West Market Street, Akron, OH 44313 US
(330) 869-9800, *Fax:* (330) 864-6799
wqmx.com
thom@wakr.net
License: Medina, Medina County, OH held by Rubber City Radio Group Inc.
Group Owner: Rubber City Radio Group Inc.; (acq 1988)
Nat'l Network: ABC *Nat'l Reps:* Christal *Wire Services:* AP
Arbitron Metro Market: Akron, OH *Format:* Country *Hrs. of News Programming:* news progmg 10 hrs wkly *No. News Employees:* 10 *Target Audience:* 25-54; adults
Thomas Mandel, CEO
Nick Anthony, Operations Dir
Paul Christopherson, General Sales Mgr
Sue Wilson, Programming Director
Joyce Lagios, Promotions Manager
Ed Esposito, News Director
Al Hruska, COO
Ken Steel, Music Director
MarkBiviano, Senior Vice President

Miamisburg

WFCJ
01-07-1961; 93.7 mhz FM *Hrs Open:* 24; 50 kw; 492 ft.; N39 39 35 W84 18 53
Mailing Address: P.O. Box 93.7, Dayton, OH 45449 US
Second Address: 7333 Manning Rd., Miamisburg, OH 45342
(937) 866-2471, *Fax:* (937) 866-2062
www.wfcj.com
inspiration@wfcj.com
License: Miamisburg, Montgomery County, OH held by Miami Valley Christian Broadcasting Association Inc.
Nat'l Network: USA; Salem Radio Network *Nat'l Reps:* Salem
Wire Services: AP
Arbitron Metro Market: Miamisburg, OH *Format:* Christian, Religious *Special Programming:* Black 3 hrs, children 2 hrs wkly *Hrs. of News Programming:* News progmg 10 hrs wkly *Target Audience:* 35-64; EvangelicalChristians *Adv. Rates:* 25; 21; 25; 21
Bud Schindler, President
Clair Miller, Operations Dir
Bill Nance, Programming Director
John Graham, Chief Engineer
Diane Akers, Office Manager

Miamitown

***WMWX**
08-05-2006; 88.9 mhz FM *Hrs Open:* 24; 4.6 kw; 374 ft.; N39 19 18 W84 57 33
5114 Princeton Glendale, Hamilton, OH 45011 US
(513) 436-0089
classxradio.com
classx@classxradio.com
License: Miamitown, Hamilton County, OH held by Spryex Communications Inc.
Arbitron Metro Market: Miamitown, OH *Format:* Classic Rock *Target Audience:* 30-58.
Bill Spry, Founder, General Manager and Programming Director
Alex O'Bryan, Station Manager
Melodi C. Moon, Creative Content Coordinator

Middleport

WYVK

08-27-1973; 92.1 mhz FM *Hrs Open:* 19; 4.7 kw; 364 ft.; N39 3 30 W82 2 31
P.O. Box 889, Blacksburg, VA 24063 US
(740) 992-6485, *Fax:* (740) 992-6486
www.wyvk.com
office@wyvk.com
License: Middleport, Meigs County, OH held by Positive Radio Group Inc. of Ohio
Arbitron Metro Market: Middleport, OH *Format:* Contemporary Hits/Top 40 *Hrs. of News Programming:* News progmg 3 hrs wkly *Target Audience:* 25-54.
Brenda Merritt, General Manager
Kevin Nott, Programming Director

Middleport-Pomeroy

WMPO

08-28-1959; 1390 khz AM
P.O. Box 889, Blacksburg, VA 24063 US
(740) 992-6485, *Fax:* (740) 992-6486
www.espnblacksburg.com
office@wyvk.com
License: Middleport-Pomeroy, OH held by Positive Radio Group Inc. of Ohio.
Group Owner: Baker Family Stations; (acq 1999; $492,000 with WYVK(FM) Middleport)
Nat'l Network: ESPN Radio *Nat'l Reps:* Rgnl Reps
Arbitron Metro Market: Middleport, OH *Format:* Sports *Special Programming:* Relg 6 hrs, farm one hr, gospel 18 hrs wkly
Target Audience: 35 plus.
Brenda Merritt, Station Manager
Mick Childs, News Director

Middletown

WPFB

09-01-1947; 910 khz AM *Hrs Open:* 24
4505 Central Avenue, Middletown, OH 45044 US
(513) 422-3625, *Fax:* (513) 424-9732
www.wpfb.com
info@wpfb.com
License: Middletown, OH held by Radio Stations WPAY/WPFB Inc.
Group Owner: Radio Stations WPAY/WPFB Inc.
Nat'l Reps: Roslin
Arbitron Metro Market: Dayton, OH *Format:* Country *Special Programming:* Radio Movie of the Week 2 hrs wkly *Hrs. of News Programming:* news progmg 26 hrs wkly *No. News Employees:* 2
Douglas Braden, President

WNKN

07-01-1959; 105.9 mhz FM *Hrs Open:* 24; 34 kw; 590 ft; N39 30 57 W84 21 05
4505 Central Ave., Middletown, OH 45044
(513) 422-3625, *Fax:* (513) 424-9732
www.therebel1059.com
info@wpfb.com
License: Middletown, Butler County, OH held by Radio Stations WPAY/WPFB Inc.
Group Owner: Radio Stations WPAY/WPFB Inc.
Population Served: 48,767 *Arbitron Metro Market:* Dayton, OH *Target Audience:* 25-54.
John Sheftic, General Manager

Milford

WKFS

08-01-1969; 107.1 mhz FM; 2.8 kw; 866 ft.; N39 6 59 W84 30 7
50 E. Rivercenter Blvd., Suite 1200, Covington, KY 41011 US
(513) 686-8300
www.kisscincinnati.com
info@kisscincinnati.com
License: Milford, Clermont County, OH held by Jacor Broadcasting Corp.
Group Owner: Clear Channel Communications Inc.; (acq 5-4-99; grpsl)
Arbitron Metro Market: Cincinnati, OH *Format:* Contemporary Hits/Top 40
Chuck Fredrick, Operations Dir
Mike Kenney, General Manager
Mark Anderson, Promotions Manager

Millersburg

WKLM

01-01-1988; 95.3 mhz FM *Hrs Open:* 5:30 AM-midnight; 3 kw; 328 ft.; N40 29 9 W81 50 45
114 North Sixth Street, Coshocton, OH 43812 US
(330) 674-1953, *Fax:* (330) 674-9556
www.wlkm.com
wklmradio@earthlink.net
License: Millersburg, Holmes County, OH held by Coshocton Broadcasting Co.
Group Owner: Coshocton Broadcasting Co.; acq 7-10-90; $490,000;
Nat'l Network: ABC
Format: Adult Contemp *Special Programming:* Loc sports *Hrs. of News Programming:* news progmg 12 hrs wkly *No. News Employees:* 1 *Target Audience:* General.
Bruce Wallace, President
Tom Thompson, General Sales Mgr
Matt Croy, Programming Director

*WVML

06-01-2004; 90.5 mhz FM *Hrs Open:* 24; 4.8 kw; 367 ft.; N40 36 8 W81 44 32 *Rebroadcasts:* Rebroadcasts WCRF(FM) Cleveland 100%
820 N. Lasalle Blvd, Chicago, IL 60610 US
(440) 526-1111, *Fax:* (440) 526-1319
wcrfradio.org
wcrf@moody.edu
License: Millersburg, Holmes County, OH held by The Moody Bible Institute of Chicago
Group Owner: The Moody Bible Institute of Chicago
Wire Services: AP
Arbitron Metro Market: Cleveland, OH *Format:* Religious *Target Audience:* 25-55; Adults
Dr. Michael Easley, President
Dick Lee, Station Manager
Phil Villareal, Programming Director
Doug Hainer, Chief Engineer

Mount Gilead

WVXG

03-01-1994; 95.1 mhz FM; 6 kw; 328 ft.; N40 35 15 W82 48 20
3800 Victory Parkway, Cincinnati, OH 45207 US
(161) 4935-1038
www.951rocks.com
mschnell@icsohio.com
License: Mount Gilead, Morrow County, OH held by ICS Holdings Sub 1 Inc.
Arbitron Metro Market: Mount Gilead, OH *Format:* Classic Rock
Mike Schnell, General Sales Mgr

Mount Vernon

WMVO

11-26-1953; 1300 khz AM; 0.41 kw-D, DA2; 0.051 kw-N, DA2; N40 24 17 W82 26 23
2435 Mansfield Road, Ashland, OH 44805 US
(740) 397-1000, *Fax:* (740) 392-9300
www.wmvo.com
Tdouglas@basbroadcasting.com
License: Mount Vernon, OH held by BAS Broadcasting Inc.
Group Owner: BAS Broadcasting Inc.; (acq 10-1-2005; $2 million with WQIO(FM) Mount Vernon)
Nat'l Network: ABC *Nat'l Reps:* Rgnl Reps *Wire Services:* AP
Arbitron Metro Market: Mt. Vernon, OH *Format:* News, News/Talk, 86 *Special Programming:* Relg 7 hrs wkly
Tommy Douglas, Operations Dir
Doug Berg, General Manager
Diana Coon, Promotions Manager

*WNZR

05-01-1986; 90.9 mhz FM *Hrs Open:* 24; 1300 w; 300 ft; N40 22 14 W82 28 05
800 Martinsburg Rd., Mount Vernon, OH 43050
(740) 392-9090, *Fax:* (740) 392-9155
www.wnzr.fm
wnzr@mvnu.edu
License: Mount Vernon, Knox County, OH held by Mt. Vernon Nazarene University.
Nat'l Network: AP Radio *Wire Services:* AP
Population Served: 61,275*Hrs. of News Programming:* News progmg 5 hrs wkly *Target Audience:* 25-54; Christian adults
Joe Rinehart, Operations Dir
Marcy Rinehart, Station Manager

WQIO

05-26-1951; 93.7 mhz FM *Hrs Open:* 24; 37 kw; 564 ft.; N40 24 18 W82 26 20
2435 Mansfield Road, Ashland, OH 44805 US
(740) 397-1000, *Fax:* (740) 392-9300
www.wqiofm.com
info@ohioradio.com
License: Mount Vernon, Knox County, OH held by BAS Broadcasting Inc.
Group Owner: BAS Broadcasting Inc.; (acq 10-1-2005; $2 million with WMVO(AM) Mount Vernon)
Arbitron Metro Market: Columbus, OH *Format:* Adult Contemp
Special Programming: Hit mus 4 hrs, gospel 2 hrs wkly *No. News Employees:* 1 *Target Audience:* 35-54.
G.S. Walker, Operations Dir
Rick Humphrey, General Manager
J. Morgan Dowdy, Partner

Munroe Falls

WKDD

11-19-1961; 98.1 mhz FM *Hrs Open:* 24; 50 kw; 453 ft.; N41 12 0 W81 31 23
4880 Santa Rosa Road, Suite 300, Camarillo, CA 93012 US
(330) 492-4700, *Fax:* (330) 492-1350
www.wkdd.com
info@wkdd.com
License: Munroe Falls, Stark County, OH held by Citicasters Licenses L.P.
Group Owner: Clear Channel Communications Inc.; (acq 12-22-2000; grpsl).
Arbitron Metro Market: Canton, OH *Format:* Adult Contemp
Tom Lopez, Operations Dir
Dan Lankford, General Manager
Vince Ing, General Sales Mgr
Keith Kennedy, Programming Director
Tom Duresky, News Director
John Hovenec, Chief Engineer
Ellen Force, Traffic Manager

Napoleon

WNDH

06-01-1972; 103.1 mhz FM *Hrs Open:* 24; 3.3 kw; 300 ft; N41 18 00 W84 09 22
709 N. Perry St., Napoleon, OH 43545
(419) 592-8060, *Fax:* (419) 592-1085
www.wndh1031.com
wndh@clearchannel.com
License: Napoleon, Henry County, OH held by CC Licenses LLC.
Group Owner: Clear Channel Communications Inc.; (acq 1-1-2000; grpsl)
Nat'l Network: CBS *Regional Reps:* Rgnl Reps *Wire Services:* AP
No. News Employees: 1 *Target Audience:* General. *Adv. Rates:* 30; 25; 28; 12
Bob McLimans, General Manager
John Schuette, General Sales Mgr
Adam Gubernath, Programming Director
Rick Small, Operations Manager

Nelsonville

WSEO

09-01-1990; 107.7 mhz FM *Hrs Open:* 24; 3 kw; 328 ft.; N39 27 38 W82 13 9
15751 U.S. Rt 33 South, Nelsonville, OH 45764 US
(740) 753-4094, *Fax:* (740) 753-4965
wseo33@sbcglobal.net
License: Nelsonville, Athens County, OH held by Nelsonville TV Cable Inc.
Format: Country *Special Programming:* Farm *Hrs. of News Programming:* news progmg 15 hrs wkly *No. News Employees:* 3 *Target Audience:* 25-49.
Eugene Edwards, President
Nick Brooks, Programming Director

New Albany

WNKO

12-08-1972; 101.7 mhz FM *Hrs Open:* 24; 22 kw; 351 ft.; N40 8 38 W82 38 20
P. O. Box 1057, Newark, OH 43055 US
(740) 522-8171, *Fax:* (740) 522-8174
www.wnko.com
studio@wnko.com
License: New Albany, Licking County, OH held by Runnymede Corp.
Nat'l Network: CNN Radio *Wire Services:* AP
Arbitron Metro Market: Columbus, OH *Format:* Contemporary Hits/Top 40 *No. News Employees:* 2 *Target Audience:* 25-54.
Adv. Rates: 25; 20; 23; 18
Charles Franks, President
John Franks, Operations Dir
Tom Swank, General Manager
Ben Krooze, Programming Director
Dave Doney, News Director

New Boston

WIOI

09-02-1959; 1010 khz AM; 1 kw-D, ND1; 0.022 kw-N, ND1; N38 43 48 W82 57 10

16044 State Route 348, Lucasville, OH 45648 US
(606) 932-4796, *Fax:* (606) 932-4796
www.wioiradio.com
chip@wioiradio.com
License: New Boston, OH held by Maillet Media Inc.
Format: Adult Contemp
Chip Maillet, General Manager

WNKE
06-15-1948; 104.1 mhz FM; 100 kw; Ant 1,486 ft; N38 41 00 W83 00 46
1009 Gallia St., Portsmouth, OH 45044
(740) 353-5176, *Fax:* (740) 353-1715
www.104wpay.com
License: New Boston, Scioto County, OH held by Radio Stations WPAY/WPFB Inc.
Group Owner: Radio Stations WPAY/WPFB Inc.
Nat'l Network: CBS
Population Served: 88,500
Brent Millar, General Manager
Lisa Powell, General Sales Mgr
Randy Bliss, Programming Director
Valerie Dickens, News Director
Larry Allen, Chief Engineer
Greg Carpenter, General Sales Manager

New Concord

***WMCO**
01-28-1961; 90.7 mhz FM *Hrs Open:* 6 AM-midnight; 1.3 kw; 85 ft.; N39 59 46 W81 43 18
163 Stormont St, Muskingum College, New Concord, OH 43762 US
(740) 826-8189
www.muskingum.edu/~wmco
wmco@muskingum.edu
License: New Concord, Muskingum County, OH held by Muskingum College.
Arbitron Metro Market: New Concord, OH *Format:* Variety/Diverse *Special Programming:* Class 4 hrs, jazz 10 hrs, relg 2 hrs wkly *Hrs. of News Programming:* News progmg 10 hrs wkly *Target Audience:* General,students
Jeffrey Harman, General Manager
Lisa Marshall, Station Manager
Matthew Hott, Programming Director

New Lexington

WWJM
05-01-1978; 106.3 mhz FM *Hrs Open:* 24; 1.7 kw; 627 ft.; N39 46 37 W82 9 54
Mailing Address: 210 South Jackson St., New Lexington, OH 43764 US
Second Address: 247 Market St., Zanesville, OH 43701
(740) 342-1988, *Fax:* (740) 342-1036
wwjm.com
wwjm@aol.com
License: New Lexington, Perry County, OH held by Perry County Broadcasting Co.
Nat'l Network: Westwood One
Arbitron Metro Market: New Lexington, OH *Format:* Adult Contemp *Hrs. of News Programming:* news progmg 2 hrs wkly *No. News Employees:* 1 *Target Audience:* 18-54; young to middle-aged *Adv. Rates:* 16,16,16,16
Charles Edwards, Chairman
Chuck T. Edwards, General Manager
Cheyenne Campbell, General Sales Mgr
Bill O'Reed, Operations Manager

New Philadelphia

***WKRJ**
07-12-1994; 91.5 mhz FM; 2 kw; 240 ft.; N40 33 50 W81 31 5
Rebroadcasts: Rebroadcasts WKSU-FM Kent 100%
Mailing Address: 1613 East Summit Street, Kent, OH 44242 US
Second Address: 1613 E. Summit St, Kent, OH 44242-0001
(330) 672-3114, *Fax:* (330) 672-4107
www.wksu.org
letters@wksu.org
License: New Philadelphia, Tuscarawas County, OH held by Kent State University.
Nat'l Network: NPR; PRI
Format: News *Hrs. of News Programming:* news progmg 35 hrs wkly *No. News Employees:* 5 *Target Audience:* 35-65; college grad, professional & upper income
Allen Bartholet, General Manager
David Roden, Programming Director
Robert Burford, Promotions Manager
M.L. Schultze, News Director
Ronald Bartlebaugh, Engineering Dir

WNPQ
02-02-1969; 95.9 mhz FM *Hrs Open:* 24; 3 kw; 400 ft; N40 35 51 W81 29 32
3969 Convenience Cir. N.W., Suite 205, Canton, OH 44683
(330) 492-9590, *Fax:* (330) 492-3702
www.thelight959.com
License: New Philadelphia, Tuscarawas County, OH held by Tuscarawas Broadcasting Co.
Nat'l Network: SRN Radio
Population Served: 300,000 *Arbitron Metro Market:* Canton, OH
Special Programming: Black 4 hrs, southern gospel 4 hrs wkly
Target Audience: 18-49; family oriented *Adv. Rates:* 15; 13; 15; 10.
James Natoli Jr., President
Tom Bishop, General Manager
Tom Bishop, General Manager
Jan Markowitz, Programming Director
Jan Markowitz, Promotions Manager

Newark

WCLT
01-04-1949; 1430 khz AM *Hrs Open:* 24; 0.5 kw-D, ND1; 0.048 kw-N, ND1; N40 2 2 W82 24 8
Mailing Address: PO Box 5150, Newark, OH 43058 US
Second Address: 674 Jacksontown Rd. S.E., Heath, OH 43056
(740) 345-4004, *Fax:* (740) 345-5775
www.wclt.com
wclt@wclt.com
License: Newark, OH held by WCLT Radio Inc.
Nat'l Network: AP Radio; Fox News Radio *Wire Services:* AP
Arbitron Metro Market: Columbus, OH *Format:* News, News/Talk, 86 *Hrs. of News Programming:* news progmg 12 hrs wkly *No. News Employees:* 2 *Target Audience:* General.
Robert Pricer, CEO
Douglas Pricer, President

WCLT-FM
08-07-1947; 100.3 mhz FM *Hrs Open:* 24; 50 kw; 390 ft; N40 02 02 W82 24 08
Mailing Address: Box 5150, Newark, OH 43055
Second Address: 674 Jacksontown Rd. S.E., Newark, OH 43056
(740) 345-4004, *Fax:* (740) 345-5775
www.wclt.com
wclt@wclt.com
License: Newark, Licking County, OH
Nat'l Network: ABC *Wire Services:* AP
Arbitron Metro Market: Columbus, OH *Target Audience:* 25-54.
Douglas Pricer, President
Bony Kale, Operations Dir
Buth Arney, Station Manager
Tom Bunyard, General Sales Mgr
Wally Schneider, Programming Director
Bill Clifford, News Director
Jim Fergusen, Chief Engineer
Dave Johnson,Traffic Manager

***WZNP**
01-01-2008; 89.3 mhz FM; 4.5 kw vert; 325 ft.; N39 58 45 W82 12 7
2620 South River Road, Zanesville, OH 43701 US
(614) 289-5700, *Fax:* (614) 289-5796
www.newark.riverradio.com
License: Newark, Licking County, OH held by Riverside Ministries.
Arbitron Metro Market: Newark, OH *Format:* Christian
Dan Baughman, CEO
Dan Baughman, General Manager
Craig Bennington, General Sales Mgr
Matt Levin, Chief Engineer
Scott Thompson, Chief Financial Officer
Todd Stach, Chief Creative Officer
Bill Montgomery, Chief Sales Officer

Niles

WBBG
05-15-1988; 106.1 mhz FM; 3 kw; 328 ft.; N41 15 52 W80 45 35
50 East Rivercenter Blv, Covington, KY 41011 US
(330) 965-0057, *Fax:* (330) 729-9991
www.oldies1061radio.com
jeffkelly@clearchannel.com
License: Niles, Trumbull County, OH held by Citicasters Licenses L.P.
Group Owner: Clear Channel Communications Inc.; (acq 5-4-99; grpsl).
Arbitron Metro Market: Youngstown, OH *Format:* Oldies *Target Audience:* 18-49.
Dan Rivers, Operations Dir
Bill Kelly, General Manager
Jeff Kelly, Programming Director
John Nagy, News Director
John Clark, Chief Engineer

WYCL
11-10-1976; 1540 khz AM *Hrs Open:* 24; 0.5 kw-D, DAD; Ant 1,407 ft; N41 7 56 W80 45 40
50 East Rivercenter Blvd, Covington, KY 41011 US
(850) 473-0400, *Fax:* (850) 473-0907
www.my107.com
License: Niles, OH held by Clear Channel Broadcasting Licenses Inc.
Group Owner: Clear Channel Communications Inc.; (acq 9-30-2003; $2.2 million).
Nat'l Reps: McGavren Guild
Arbitron Metro Market: Pensacola, FL *Format:* Classic Rock *Hrs. of News Programming:* news progmg 15 hrs wkly *No. News Employees:* 2 *Target Audience:* 25-54.
Steve Powers, Operations Dir
Jeanie Hufford, General Manager
Eddie Hill, General Sales Mgr

North Baltimore

***WLFC**
11-01-1973; 88.3 mhz FM *Hrs Open:* 24 hours; 4.6 kw; 328 ft.; N41 7 4 W83 32 38
1000 North Main St., Findlay, OH 45840 US
(419) 434-4747, *Fax:* (419) 434-4305
www.myspace.com/wlfc88_3
wlfc@findlay.edu
License: North Baltimore, Hancock County, OH held by University of Findlay
Wire Services: AP
Arbitron Metro Market: Toledo, OH *Format:* Rock/AOR *Special Programming:* AOR/metal, Saturday; Christian/jazz Sunday *Hrs. of News Programming:* News progmg hourly *Target Audience:* 18-40. *Adv. Rates:* underwriting only
Chris Underation, Operations Dir
Jesse Wilder, General Manager

North Canton

WHOF
08-29-1968; 101.7 mhz FM *Hrs Open:* 24; 6 kw; 266 ft.; N40 49 22 W81 25 41
646 Boulevard, Dover, OH 44622 US
(330) 492-4700
www.my1017.com
License: North Canton, Stark County, OH held by CC Licenses LLC.
Group Owner: Clear Channel Communications Inc.; (acq 1-30-2004; $4.3 million with WJER(AM) Dover-New Philadelphia)
Arbitron Metro Market: Canton, OH *Format:* Adult Contemp
Special Programming: Farm 2 hrs wkly
Scott Meier, General Manager
Scott Stein, Programming Director

North Kingsville

WFXJ-FM
04-08-2002; 107.5 mhz FM; 3.6 kw; 427 ft.; N41 53 4 W80 38 28
1204 Pennsylvania Avenue, Ashtabula, OH 44004 US
(440) 998-1075, *Fax:* (440) 992-2658
www.thefox1075.com
hunter@thefox1075.com
License: North Kingsville, Ashtabula County, OH held by Sweet Home Ashtabula LLC.
Group Owner: Sweet Home Ashtabula LLC; (acq 9-17-2007; grpsl)
Arbitron Metro Market: Ashtabula, OH *Format:* Classic Rock
Target Audience: 18-54; males
Dana Schulte, Operations Dir
Michelle Baird, General Sales Mgr
Hunter, Programming Director
Dennis O'Brien, Operations Director
Paula Taylor, Advertising Manager

North Ridgeville

WJTB
09-16-1984; 1040 khz AM; 2.5 kw-C, NDD; 5 kw-D, NDD; N41 22 37 W82 0 27
612 Wayne St, Elyria, OH 44035 US
(440) 327-1844, *Fax:* (440) 322-8942
wjtb.njit.edu
wjtb1040am@aol.com
License: North Ridgeville, OH held by Taylor Broadcasting Co.
Arbitron Metro Market: Cleveland, OH *Format:* Gospel
James Taylor, President
Henry Dunn, Operations Dir

Norwalk

WLKR-FM

09-17-1962; 95.3 mhz FM *Hrs Open:* 24; 3.3 kw; 299 ft.; N41 16 49 W82 39 27
P. O. Box 547, Norwalk, OH 44857 US
(419) 609-5961, *Fax:* (419) 609-2679
wlkrradio.com
wlkr@wlkrradio.com
License: Norwalk, Huron County, OH held by Elyria-Lorain Broadcasting Co.
Group Owner: Elyria-Lorain Broadcasting Co.
Nat'l Reps: McGavren Guild
Arbitron Metro Market: Cleveland, OH *Format:* Adult Contemp *No. News Employees:* 1 *Target Audience:* General; residents of Huron & Erie counties *Adv. Rates:* 21; 21; 21; 21
Carol Walters, Operations Dir
Bill Forthofer, Station Manager
Scott Truxel, News Director
Mike Jeffries, Program & Production Manager

WLKR

03-18-1968; 1510 khz AM *Hrs Open:* Sunrise-sunset; 0.5 kw-D, DAD; N41 16 45 W82 39 23
202 Old State Road South, Norwalk, OH 44857 US
(419) 609-5961, *Fax:* (419) 609-2679
www.wlkrradio.com
wikr@acc.com; wlkr@accnorwalk.com
License: Norwalk, OH held by Elyria-Lorain Broadcasting Co.
Group Owner: Elyria-Lorain Broadcasting Co.; acq 4-9-02; with co-located FM).
Nat'l Network: Westwood One; ESPN Radio
Arbitron Metro Market: Milan, OH *Format:* Oldies *Hrs. of News Programming:* news progmg 2 hrs wkly *No. News Employees:* 1 *Target Audience:* 40 plus. *Adv. Rates:* 12; 12; 12; 12
Tim Kelly, Station Manager
B, General Sales Mgr
Bill Forthofer, Programming Director
Scott Truxell, News Director
Ken Wilde, Chief Engineer
Shelly Luipold, Regional Sales Manager
Mike Jeffries, Traffic Manager
Carol Walters,Office Manager
Mike Adelman, Account Executive
Maria Smith, Account Executive
Steve Krick, Account Executive

*WNRK

01-01-2004; 90.7 mhz FM *Hrs Open:* 24; 4 kw; Ant 407 ft; N41 10 50 W82 23 21 *Rebroadcasts:* Rebroadcasts WKSU-FM Kent 100%
Mailing Address: c/o WKSU-FM, Box 5190, Kent, OH 44242
Second Address: 1613 E. Summit St., Kent, OH 44242-0001
(330) 672-3114, *Fax:* (330) 672-4107
www.wksu.org
letters@wksu.org
License: Norwalk, Huron County, OH held by Kent State University.
Nat'l Network: AP Radio; NPR; PRI
Allen Bartholet, General Manager
M L Schultze, News Director
Ronald Bartlebaugh, Engineering Dir
Kerry Kurchak, Assistant General Manager

Norwood

WMOJ-FM

02-27-1948; 100.3 mhz FM *Hrs Open:* 24; 3.1 kw; 463 ft.; N39 7 19 W84 32 52
2301 West Main Street, Richmond, IN 47374 US
(513) 679-6000, *Fax:* (513) 679-6014
www.mojocincy.com
info@wmoj.com
License: Norwood, Fayette County, OH held by Blue Chip Broadcasting Licenses Ltd.
Group Owner: Radio One Inc.; (acq 9-21-2006; $18 million)
Format: Adult Contemp
Lisa Thal, General Manager

Oak Harbor

WJZE

08-01-1993; 97.3 mhz FM *Hrs Open:* 24; 4.3 kw; 387 ft.; N41 28 19 W83 25 5
1600 Woodville Rd, Ste 2, Millbury, OH 43447 US
(419) 868-7914, *Fax:* (419) 868-8765
www.hot973.net
brandibrown@urbanradio.net
License: Oak Harbor, Ottawa County, OH held by Urban Radio Licenses LLC.
Group Owner: Urban Radio Licenses LLC; (acq 6-30-2005; $2.6 million)
Nat'l Reps: Interep *Regional Reps:* Regional Reps
Arbitron Metro Market: Toledo, OH *Format:* Contemporary Hits/Top 40 *No. News Employees:* 1 *Target Audience:* Adults 18-34 *Adv. Rates:* 25; 25; 25; 15
Jillian Wiggs, General Sales Mgr
Brandi Brown, Programming Director
Curtis Downey, Promotions Manager
John Guzan, Market Director of Sales

Oberlin

*WOBC-FM

11-01-1951; 91.5 mhz FM; 1 kw; 135 ft.; N41 17 38 W82 13 20
Wilder Hall, Room 319, 135 West Lorain Street, Oberlin, OH 44074 US
(440) 775-8107, *Fax:* (440) 775-6678
www.wobc.org
License: Oberlin, Lorain County, OH held by Oberlin College Student Network Inc.
TV Affiliate: College *Format:* Jazz *Special Programming:* News progmg 5 hrs wkly *No. News Employees:* General.
Operations Manager, Will Floyd
General Manager, General Manager
Program Director, Programming Director

WOBL

12-24-1971; 1320 khz AM; 1 kw-D, DA2; 1 kw-N, DA2; N41 16 5 W82 12 40
P.O. Box 277, Oberlin, OH 44074 US
(440) 774-1320, *Fax:* (440) 774-1336
woblwdlw@earthlink.net
License: Oberlin, OH held by WOBL Inc.
Wire Services: AP
Arbitron Metro Market: Cleveland, OH *TV Affiliate:* Country *Special Programming:* news progmg 14 hrs wkly *Hrs. of News Programming:* 3 *No. News Employees:* 35-55. *Adv. Rates:* 22.50; 20.50; 22.50; 16.50
Program Director, Programming Director
News Director, News Director

Ontario

WRGM

07-17-1987; 1440 khz AM *Hrs Open:* 24; 1 kw-D, DA2; 0.028 kw-N, DA2; N40 46 5 W82 37 4
2900 Park Ave West, Mansfield, OH 44906 US
(419) 529-5900, *Fax:* (419) 529-2319
www.wrgm.com
info@wrgm.com
License: Ontario, OH held by GSM Media Corp.
Nat'l Network: ESPN Radio *Nat'l Reps:* Rgnl Reps
Format: Sports *Special Programming:* High school football & basketball, NASCAR races *Hrs. of News Programming:* 10 hrs news progmg wkly *No. News Employees:* 5 *Target Audience:* 25 plus.
Gunther Meisse, President
Tony Mitchell, Operations Dir

Ottawa

WBUK

02-04-1977; 106.3 mhz FM *Hrs Open:* 24; 1.4 kw; 489 ft.; N40 57 21 W83 54 42
50 East Rivercenter Boulevard, Suite 1200, Covington, KY 41011 US
(419) 223-2060, *Fax:* (419) 229-3888
www.wbuk.com
info@wbuk.com
License: Ottawa, Putnam County, OH held by The Blanchard River Broadcasting Co.
Group Owner: The Findlay Publishing Co.; (acq 12-3-2008; $500,000)
Format: Classic Rock *Special Programming:* Farm 5 hrs, sports 2 hrs, MOR 4 hrs wkly *Hrs. of News Programming:* news progmg 3 hrs wkly *No. News Employees:* 1 *Target Audience:* 18-49; affluent, upscale adults
Kim Field, General Manager

Oxford

*WMUB

01-01-1950; 88.5 mhz FM *Hrs Open:* 24; 24.5 kw; 505 ft.; N39 33 26 W84 47 35
Williams Hall, Oxford, OH 45056 US
(513) 352-9170, *Fax:* (513) 241-8456
www.wmub.org
WMUB@WMUB.org
License: Oxford, Butler County, OH held by President & Trustees of Miami University.
Nat'l Network: NPR; PRI *Regional Network:* Ohio Educ. Telecommunications *Wire Services:* AP
Arbitron Metro Market: Dayton, OH *Format:* Jazz, News, 62, Talk *Target Audience:* General.
Richard Eiswerth, General Manager
Maryanne Zeleznik, News Director

Painesville

WABQ

04-25-1956; 1460 khz AM *Hrs Open:* 24; 1 kw-D, DA2; 0.5 kw-N, DA2; N41 44 20 W81 14 9
713 Forbes Street, Painesville, OH 44077 US
(440) 951-1460, *Fax:* (216) 231-9803(440) 357-7701
www.talk1460.com/
joecleveland@talk1460.com
License: Painesville, OH held by Radio Advantage One LLC
Arbitron Metro Market: Cleveland, OH *Format:* Gospel
Dale Edwards, President
Danelle Caldwell, Operations Dir
Almira Byrd, Executive Vice President

Parma

WCCD

01-09-1973; 1000 khz AM; 0.5 kw-D, DAD; N41 19 11 W81 46 7
4880 Santa Rosa Road, Suite 300, Camarillo, CA 93012 US
(216) 320-0000, *Fax:* (216) 321-9878
www.radio1000.org
Latreradio1000@yahoo.com
License: Parma, OH held by New Spirit Revival Center Ministries, Inc.
Arbitron Metro Market: Cleveland, OH *Format:* Christian, Gospel, 86 *Special Programming:* Black 3 hrs, Greek 2 hrs, Ukrainian one hr wkly *Target Audience:* 52.2% Female, 47.8% Male MEDIAN HOUSEHOLD INCOME:$35,236-$46,879 *Adv. Rates:* 30; 30; 30; 20
Latre Mattis, General Manager

Paulding

WKSD

08-14-1989; 99.7 mhz FM *Hrs Open:* 24; 3 kw; 328 ft.; N41 3 32 W84 35 30
PO Box 487, Van Wert, OH 45891 US
(419) 238-1220, *Fax:* (419) 238-2578
www.vwindependent.com
wert@bright.net
License: Paulding, Paulding County, OH held by First Family Broadcasting Inc.
Nat'l Network: ESPN Radio *Nat'l Reps:* Rgnl Reps
Format: Oldies, Sports *Adv. Rates:* 20; 10; 12; 8
Chris Roberts, President
Mona Kennedy, General Sales Mgr

Pemberville

WCKY-FM

07-11-1963; 103.7 mhz FM; 50 kw; 430 ft.; N41 8 20 W83 14 45
P.O. Box 338, Tiffin, OH 44883 US
(419) 240-1037, *Fax:* (419) 422-2954
www.1037wcky.com
johnyd@1037wcky.com
License: Pemberville, Seneca County, OH held by Citicasters Licenses L.P.
Group Owner: Clear Channel Communications Inc.
Arbitron Metro Market: Toledo, Oh *Format:* Country
Kim Field, General Manager

Pickerington

WNND

10-07-1989; 103.5 mhz FM *Hrs Open:* 24; 4 kw; 435 ft; N39 51 52 W82 38 19
4401 Carriage Hill Ln., Columbus, OH 43017
(614) 451-2191, *Fax:* (614) 451-1831
www.wjza.com
info@wjza.com
License: Pickerington, Fairfield County, OH held by Franklin Communications Inc.
Group Owner: Saga Communications Inc.; (acq 10-1-2003; $13 million)
Nat'l Reps: Christal *Wire Services:* AP
Population Served: 1,500,000 *Arbitron Metro Market:* Columbus, OH *Special Programming:* Various 15 hrs wkly *Hrs. of News Programming:* News progmg 2 hrs wkly *Target Audience:* 25-54.
Alan Goodman, President
Katie Cyr, General Sales Mgr
Bill Harman, Programming Director
Michelle Hurley, Promotions Manager

Piketon

WXZQ
12-01-1997; 100.1 mhz FM *Hrs Open:* 24; 6 kw; 328 ft.; N39 5 53 W82 57 20
P. O. Box 894, Piketon, OH 45661 US
(740) 947-0059, *Fax:* (740) 947-4600
wxiz@roadrunner.com
License: Piketon, Pike County, OH held by Piketon Communications.
Arbitron Metro Market: Piketon, OH *Format:* Contemporary Hits/Top 40 *Target Audience:* 18-49.
Gerald Davis, General Manager
Brad Lambert, General Sales Mgr

Piqua

WPTW
11-01-1947; 1570 khz AM *Hrs Open:* 24; 0.25 kw-U, ND1; N40 8 25 W84 16 7
623 Park Meadow Road, Suite J, Westerville, OH 43081 US
(937) 773-3513, *Fax:* (937) 773-4345
www.1570wptw.com
wptwnews@1570wptw.com
License: Piqua, OH held by Miami Valley Radio LLC
Nat'l Network: CBS *Regional Network:* ABN Radio
Arbitron Metro Market: Dayton, OH *Format:* Oldies *Special Programming:* Farm 2 hrs, sports 30 hrs wkly *Hrs. of News Programming:* news progmg 8 hrs wkly *No. News Employees:* 1 *Target Audience:* 35 plus.*Adv. Rates:* 14; 11; 14; 6.25
Dave Johnson, Operations Dir
David Roederer, General Manager
Bruce Welker, General Sales Mgr
Marty Selby, Programming Director
Lehra Mayfield, Promotions Manager
Jim Herrin, News Director

Pleasant City

WBIK
01-01-2002; 92.1 mhz FM *Hrs Open:* 24; 6 kw; 169 ft.; N40 1 37 W81 33 9
4988 Skyline Drive, Cambridge, OH 43725 US
(740) 432-5605, *Fax:* (740) 432-1991
yourradioplace.com/wbik/
webmaster@yourradioplace.com
License: Pleasant City, Guernsey County, OH held by David L. Wilson
Regional Reps: Rgnl Reps
Arbitron Metro Market: Cambridge, Oh *Format:* Classic Rock
Grant Hafley, CEO/COO
Grant Hafley, President
Joel Losego, General Manager
Dave Wilson, Operations Manager

Pleasant Hill

WHIO-FM
11-30-1960; 95.7 mhz FM *Hrs Open:* 24; 50 kw; Ant 476 ft; N40 13 02 W84 17 35 *Rebroadcasts:* Simulcast with WHIO(AM) Dayton 100%
1414 Wilmington Ave., Dayton, OH 89109
(937) 259-2111, *Fax:* (937) 259-2168
1290whio.com
info@1290whio.com
License: Pleasant Hill, Miami County, OH held by Cox Radio Inc.
Group Owner: Cox Media Group; (acq 1998; grpsl)
Population Served: 1,463,000 *Arbitron Metro Market:* Dayton, OH *Target Audience:* 35-54.
Nick Roberts, Operations Dir
Donna Hall, General Manager
Todd Pitt, General Sales Mgr

Port Clinton

WXKR
10-04-1961; 94.5 mhz FM *Hrs Open:* 24; 30 kw; 617 ft.; N41 30 3 W83 16 16
111 East Kilbourn Ave., Suite 2700, Milwaukee, WI 53202 US
(419) 725-5700, *Fax:* (419) 385-2902
www.wxkr.com
info@wxkr.com
License: Port Clinton, Ottawa County, OH held by Cumulus Licensing Corp.
Group Owner: Cumulus Media Inc.; (acq 12-18-97; $5 million cash)
Nat'l Network: ABC
Arbitron Metro Market: Toledo, OH *Format:* Classic Rock *Special Programming:* Sp one hr wkly *Hrs. of News Programming:* news progmg one hr wkly *No. News Employees:* 1 *Target Audience:* 25-49.
Matt Spaulding, General Manager
Dan McClintock, Programming Director
Ryan Young, Promotions Manager
London Mitchell, News Director
Kevin Hawley, Engineering Dir
Keith Bosworth, Chief Engineer
Debbie Calevro, Traffic Manager

Portsmouth

WNXT
08-30-1951; 1260 khz AM; 5 kw-D, DA2; 1 kw-N, DA2; N38 48 38 W82 59 21
PO Box 685, Greenup, KY 41144 US
(740) 353-1161, *Fax:* (740) 353-8080
www.wnxtradio.com
wnxtradio@yahoo.com
License: Portsmouth, OH held by Hometown Broadcasting of Portsmouth Inc.
Nat'l Network: ABC; ESPN Radio *Nat'l Reps:* Rgnl Reps
TV Affiliate: ESPN sports radio/talk *Special Programming:* news progmg 35 hrs wkly *Hrs. of News Programming:* 1 *No. News Employees:* Adult males; 25-54

WNXT-FM
09-15-1965; 99.3 mhz FM; 2.55 kw; 512 ft.; N38 43 22 W82 59 56
PO Box 685, Greenup, KY 41144 US
(740) 353-1161, *Fax:* (740) 353-3191
www.wnxtradio.com
wnxtradio@yahoo.com
License: Portsmouth, Scioto County, OH
TV Affiliate: Variety *Special Programming:* news progmg one hr wkly *Hrs. of News Programming:* 1 *No. News Employees:* 25-54.

***WUKV**
02-18-1992; 88.3 mhz FM *Hrs Open:* 24; 1 kw; 643 ft.; N38 43 20 W83 00 05 *Rebroadcasts:* Rebroadcasts WCDR-FM Cedarville 100%
Box 601, 251 N. Main St., Cedarville, OH 45314
(937) 766-7815, *Fax:* (937) 766-7927
www.thepath.fm
License: Portsmouth, Scioto County, OH held by The Cedarville University.
Population Served: 100,000*Special Programming:* Black 2 hrs wkly *Hrs. of News Programming:* news progmg 16 hrs wkly *No. News Employees:* 1 *Target Audience:* 35-54; church oriented audience
William Brown, President
Keith Hamer, Operations Dir
Marvin Sparks, General Manager
Chad Bresson, News Director
John Tocknell, Chief Engineer
Eric Johnson, Assistant Manager

***WOSP**
05-25-1993; 91.5 mhz FM *Hrs Open:* 24; 0.11 kw; 1207 ft.; N38 45 42 W83 3 41 *Rebroadcasts:* Rebroadcasts WOSU-FM Columbus 100%
2400 Olentangy River Rd., Columbus, OH 43210 US
(614) 292-9678, *Fax:* (614) 292-7625
www.wosu.org
wosu@osu.edu
License: Portsmouth, Scioto County, OH held by The Ohio State University.
Nat'l Network: PRI; NPR; AP Radio *Wire Services:* AP
TV Affiliate: *WPBO-TV affil. *Format:* Classical *Target Audience:* 35 plus.
Kevin Petrilla, Operations Dir
Thomas Rieland, General Manager
Tim Eby, Station Manager

WZZZ
01-01-2003; 107.5 mhz FM *Hrs Open:* 24; 2.6 kw; 495 ft.; N38 43 22 W82 59 56
Mailing Address: 2350 One Ppg Place, Pittsburgh, PA 15222 US
Second Address: 602 Chillicothe St., Portsmouth, OH 45662
(740) 353-1979, *Fax:* (740) 353-8080
www.wzzz.com
classicrock1075thebreeze@yahoo.com
License: Portsmouth, Scioto County, OH held by Hometown Broadcasting of Portsmouth 2 Inc.
Regional Reps: Rgnl Reps
Arbitron Metro Market: Portsmouth, OH *Format:* Classic Rock *Hrs. of News Programming:* news progmg .25 hrs wkly *No. News Employees:* 1 *Target Audience:* 35-54; working class & professional adults
Steve Hayes, Operations Dir
Rick Mayne, General Manager
Bill Murphy, Programming Director
Sam McKibbin, News Director
Tyrone Henry, Chief Engineer

Proctorville

***WHKU**
01-25-1986; 91.9 mhz FM *Hrs Open:* 24; 3 kw; 299 ft.; N38 27 14 W82 25 5
P.O. Box 7575, Huntington, WV 25704 US
(916) 251-1600, *Fax:* (916) 251-1650
www.klove.com
License: Proctorville, Lawrence County, OH held by Educational Media Foundation.
Group Owner: EMF Broadcasting; (acq 2-29-2008; $900,000 with WCKU(FM) Clarksburg, WV)
Nat'l Network: K-Love
Arbitron Metro Market: Proctorville, CA *Format:* Christian *Target Audience:* General.
Michael Novak, President

Racine

WNTO
07-15-1996; 93.1 mhz FM; 4.1 kw; 397 ft.; N38 56 56 W82 3 2
Mailing Address: P.O. Box 667, Ravenswood, WV 26164 US
Second Address: 117 Portsmouth Rd., Gallipolis, OH 45631
(740) 446-3543, *Fax:* (740) 446-3001
davediddle@sunny931.com
License: Racine, Meigs County, OH held by Sunny Boradcasting LLC
Arbitron Metro Market: Racine, OH *Format:* Adult Contemp
Special Programming: American Indian one hr, Black one hr, farm one hr, *Target Audience:* 18-50; general
Dave Diddle, Station Manager
Tina Merry, Programming Director

Reading

***WMKV**
01-01-1995; 89.3 mhz FM *Hrs Open:* 24; 0.41 kw; 236 ft.; N39 13 23 W84 25 56
11100 Springfield Pike, Springdale, OH 45246 US
(513) 782-2427, *Fax:* (513) 782-2720
www.wmkvfm.org
gzahn@lifesphere.org
License: Reading, Hamilton County, OH held by Lifesphere.
Arbitron Metro Market: Cincinnati, OH *Format:* Big Band *Target Audience:* 40 plus.
George Zahn, Station Manager

Republic

***WYOR**
09-01-1999; 88.5 mhz FM; 0.1 kw; 105 ft.; N41 6 32 W83 0 11 US
(540) 582-9700
www.bluegrassfm.org
License: Republic, Laurens County, OH held by Peregon Broadcasting LLC
Arbitron Metro Market: Saint George UT *Format:* Blues
Peter Stover, President

Richwood

WNNP
11-30-1995; 104.3 mhz FM *Hrs Open:* 24; 3.4 kw; Ant 436 ft; N40 21 52 W83 15 34
4401 Carriage Hill Ln., Columbus, OH 43017
(614) 451-2191, *Fax:* (614) 451-1831
www.bighits1043.com
info@wjza.com
License: Richwood, Union County, OH held by Franklin Communications Inc.
Group Owner: Saga Communications Inc.; (acq 10-1-2003; $13 million with WJZA(FM) Lancaster).
Nat'l Reps: Christal *Wire Services:* AP
Population Served: 1,500,000 *Arbitron Metro Market:* Columbus, OH *Special Programming:* Various 15 hrs wkly *Hrs. of News Programming:* News progmg 2 hrs wkly *Target Audience:* 25-54.
Alan Goodman, General Manager
Katie Cyr, General Sales Mgr
Bill Harman, Programming Director
Michelle Hurley, Promotions Manager

Ripley

WAOL
01-01-1993; 99.5 mhz FM; 13 kw; 459 ft.; N38 38 55 W84 0 42
35 Island Dr.,#16, Eastpoint, FL 32328 US

(937) 378-6151, *Fax:* (937) 377-2200
www.radiomaxfm.com
info@waol.com
License: Ripley, Brown County, OH held by First Broadcasting Capital Partners LLC.
Group Owner: First Broadcasting Operating Inc.; (acq 3-17-2004; $4.06 million with WAXZ(FM) Georgetown)
Arbitron Metro Market: Cincinnati, OH *Format:* Adult Contemp
Heather Frye, General Manager
Brian Elliott, Programming Director

Rossford

WNWT
11-28-1966; 1520 khz AM
1520 South Reynolds Road, Maumee, OH 43537 US
(916) 251-1600, *Fax:* (916) 251-1650
www.klove.com
License: Rossford, OH held by Educational Media Foundation.
Group Owner: EMF Broadcasting; (acq 4-21-2009; $2,825,000 with WNKL(FM) Wauseon)
Nat'l Network: K-Love
Arbitron Metro Market: Toledo, OH *Format:* Christian
Alan Mason, COO
Mike Novak, CEO

Rushville

*WLRY
12-01-1998; 88.9 mhz FM *Hrs Open:* 24; 1.1 kw vert; 299 ft.; N39 46 41 W82 25 26
P.O. Box 220, Rushville, OH 43150 US
(740) 536-0885, *Fax:* (740) 536-1885
www.wlry.org
wlry@wlry.org
License: Rushville, Fairfield County, OH held by Arcangel Broadcasting Foundation.
Nat'l Network: USA
Format: Christian *Special Programming:* Issues talk 16 hrs wkly *Hrs. of News Programming:* News progmg 40 hrs wkly *Target Audience:* 15-55; youth & adult mentors
Richard Finke, General Manager

Salem

WQXK
11-25-1958; 105.1 mhz FM; 88 kw; 446 ft.; N40 53 8 W80 49 55
351 South Warren Street, Syracus, NY 13202 US
(330) 783-1000, *Fax:* (330) 783-0060
www.k105country.com
License: Salem, Columbiana County, OH
Arbitron Metro Market: Youngstown-Warren, OH *Format:* Country *Target Audience:* 25-54.
Brian Schimmel, General Manager

WSOM
06-02-1965; 600 khz AM
351 South Warren Street, Suite 600, Syracuse, NY 13202 US
(330) 783-1000, *Fax:* (330) 783-2287
www.600wsom.com
License: Salem, OH held by Cumulus Licensing Corp.
Group Owner: Cumulus Media Inc.; (acq 3-15-00; grpsl).
Arbitron Metro Market: Youngstown-Warren, OH *Format:* Oldies *Special Programming:* Farm 2 hrs wkly *Target Audience:* 35 plus.
Lou Dickey, CEO
Brian Schimmel, General Manager
Wes Boyd, Chief Engineer

Sandusky

WLEC
12-07-1947; 1450 khz AM *Hrs Open:* 24; 1 kw-U, ND1; N41 26 28 W82 41 14
50 East Rivercenter Blvd., Suite 1200, Covington, KY 41011 US
(419) 625-1010, *Fax:* (419) 625-1348
www.wlec.com
License: Sandusky, OH held by BAS Broadcasting Inc.
Group Owner: BAS Broadcasting Inc.; (acq 6-30-2008; grpsl)
Regional Reps: Rgnl Reps.
Format: Sports *Hrs. of News Programming:* News progmg 2 hrs wkly
Tom Booth, General Manager
Brian O'Neil, News Director

WCPZ
08-15-1959; 102.7 mhz FM; 50 kw; 135 ft.; N41 26 28 W82 41 14
50 East Rivercenter Blvd., Suite 1200, Covington, KY 41011 US
(419) 625-1010, *Fax:* (419) 625-1348
www.mix1027.com
randyhugg@basbroadcasting.com
License: Sandusky, Erie County, OH held by BAS Broadcasting Inc.
Group Owner: BAS Broadcasting Inc.; (acq 6-30-2008; grpsl)
Arbitron Metro Market: Cleveland, OH *Format:* Adult Contemp *Hrs. of News Programming:* News progmg 2 hrs wkly *Target Audience:* 18-54.
Paul Mize, General Manager
Randy Hugg, Programming Director
Tammy Harrison, News Director

*WVMS
12-01-1993; 89.5 mhz FM *Hrs Open:* 24; 2.1 kw horiz, 5.4 kw vert; 69 ft.; N41 26 29 W82 48 20 *Rebroadcasts:* Rebroadcasts WCRF(FM) Cleveland 100%
820 N. Lasalle Drive, Chicago, IL 60610 US
(440) 526-1111, *Fax:* (440) 526-1319
www.wcrfradio.org
wcrf@moody.edu
License: Sandusky, Erie County, OH held by The Moody Bible Institute of Chicago.
Group Owner: The Moody Bible Institute of Chicago
Wire Services: AP
Arbitron Metro Market: Sandusky, OH *Format:* Christian, Religious *Target Audience:* 25-55; Adults
Michael Easley, President
Paul Carter, Operations Dir
Richard Lee, Station Manager
Gary Bittner, Programming Director
Doug Hainer, Chief Engineer
Alice Andrews, Office Administrator
Jonathan Dentler, Production Assistant
DickLee, Manager

Shadyside

WVKF
09-01-1990; 95.7 mhz FM *Hrs Open:* 24; 6.8 kw horiz, 6.67 kw vert; 627 ft.; N40 3 41 W80 45 9
C/O Gene McCoy, P.O. Box 30, Arlington, VA 22210 US
(304) 232-1170, *Fax:* (304) 234-0067
www.kisswheeling.com/
chuckpoet@clearchannel.com
License: Shadyside, Belmont County, OH held by Capstar TX L.P.
Group Owner: Clear Channel Communications Inc.; (acq 2-26-2004; $930,000).
Nat'l Reps: Christal
Arbitron Metro Market: Wheeling, WV *Format:* Contemporary Hits/Top 40
Scott Miller, General Manager
Jon Dickerson, General Sales Mgr
Keith Mac, Programming Director

Shelby

*WAUI
11-01-1998; 88.3 mhz FM; 0.9 kw vert; 138 ft.; N40 53 14 W82 38 51
P.O. Drawer 2440, Tupelo, MS 38803 US
(662) 844-8888, *Fax:* (662) 842-6791
www.afr.net
License: Shelby, Richland County, OH held by American Family Association.
Group Owner: American Family Radio
Format: Christian, Religious
Marvin Sanders, General Manager

WSWR
12-01-1981; 100.1 mhz FM; 3 kw; 299 ft.; N40 56 42 W82 39 42
50 E. Rivercenter Blvd., Suite 180, Covington, KY 41011 US
(419) 529-2211, *Fax:* (419) 529-2516
www.cruisin100.com
License: Shelby, Richland County, OH held by Capstar TX L.P.
Group Owner: Clear Channel Communications Inc.; (acq 8-24-2000; grpsl).
Format: Oldies
Diana Coon, General Manager

Sidney

WMVR-FM
11-28-1963; 105.5 mhz FM *Hrs Open:* 24; 6 kw; 154 ft.; N40 18 4 W84 12 21
2929 Russell Road, Sidney, OH 45365 US
(937) 492-1270, *Fax:* (937) 498-2277
www.hits1055.com
loretta@hits1055.com
License: Sidney, Shelby County, OH held by Dean Miller Broadcasting Corp.
Regional Network: ABN Radio; Ohio News Network *Nat'l Reps:* Rgnl Reps; ABN Radio & TV
Arbitron Metro Market: Sidney, OH *Format:* Adult Contemp *No. News Employees:* 6 *Target Audience:* 18-54; women
Julie Burns, Operations Dir
Loretta Kinney, General Manager
Scott Foxx, Programming Director
Becca Woolley, Promotions Manager
Joe Laber, Music Director

South Vienna

*WOAR
01-01-2006; 88.3 mhz FM; 1 kw vert; 278 ft.; N39 55 54 W83 36 36
P. O. Box 1458, Washington, DC 20013 US
(800) 877-5600, *Fax:* (916) 251-1650
www.air1.com
info@air1.com
License: South Vienna, Clark County, OH held by Educational Media Foundation.
Group Owner: EMF Broadcasting; (acq 3-23-2007; grpsl)
Nat'l Network: Air 1
Arbitron Metro Market: South Vienna, OH *Format:* Alternative, Christian
Darrell Chambliss, Chairman
Mike Novak, President
Alan Mason, Operations Dir

South Webster

*WEKV
01-01-1996; 94.9 mhz FM *Hrs Open:* 24; 2.2 kw; 459 ft.; N38 42 30 W82 40 15
P.O. Box 35, Jackson, OH 45640 US
(916) 251-1600, *Fax:* (916) 251-1650
www.klove.com
License: South Webster, Scioto County, OH held by Educational Media Foundation.
Group Owner: EMF Broadcasting; (acq 12-30-2005; $450,000).
Nat'l Network: K-Love
Arbitron Metro Market: South Webster, OH *Format:* Christian
Mike Novak, President

South Zanesville

*WHIZ(FM)
01-05-1983; 92.7 mhz FM *Hrs Open:* 24; 16 kw; Ant 407 ft; N39 42 52 W82 04 10
Mailing Address: 2477 E. Pike, South Zanesville, OH 43701-4626
Second Address: Box 3208, Zanesville, OH 43701
(740) 455-3181, *Fax:* (740) 455-6195
www.whiznews.com/fm/
License: South Zanesville, Muskingum County, OH held by Southeastern Ohio Broadcasting Systems Inc.
Nat'l Network: USA
Population Served: 250,000*Hrs. of News Programming:* News progmg 10 hrs wkly *Target Audience:* General; young children 5-10 to senior citizens
Henry Littick II, President
Tate Luck, Operations Dir
Dan Baughman, General Manager
Michael James, Programming Director
Mike Russell, Music Director

WHIZ-FM
12-16-1961; 92.7 mhz FM *Hrs Open:* 24; 16 kw; 407 ft.; N39 42 52 W82 4 10
4400 Reynoldsburg-, New Albany Rd, New Albany, OH 43054 US
(740) 452-5431, *Fax:* (740) 452-6553
www.whizamfmtv.com
License: South Zanesville, Muskingum County, OH held by Southeastern Ohio Broadcasting System Inc.
TV Affiliate: WHIZ-TV affil. *Format:* Adult Contemp *Special Programming:* Relg one hr, sports 3 hrs wkly *Hrs. of News Programming:* News progmg 12 hrs wkly *Target Audience:* 25 plus; general
Brian Wagner, General Sales Mgr
Jeff Ball, Programming Director
George Hiotis, News Director
Jared Stewart, Disc Jockey
Andy Jones, Sports Commentator

Spencerville

*WBCJ
09-01-1997; 88.1 mhz FM; 3.1 kw; 469 ft.; N40 42 41 W84 23 1
1025 W. Rudisill Blvd., Fort Wayne, IN 46807 US
(580) 658-9292
kfxi@cableone.net
License: Spencerville, Allen County, OH held by Taylor University Broadcasting Inc.
Arbitron Metro Market: Tulsa OK *Format:* Classic Rock

Ken Austin, General Manager
Sherry Lynn, General Sales Mgr
Jennifer James, Programming Director
James Wilson, Engineering Dir
Steve Michaels, Music Director

Springfield

WULM
01-01-1947; 1600 khz AM *Hrs Open:* 24; 1 kw-D, ND1; 0.034 kw-N, ND1; N39 57 11 W83 52 7
1529 Miracle Mile Road, Springfield, OH 45503 US
(888)408-0201, *Fax:* (318)449-9954
www.radiomaria.us/
info.usa@radiomaria.org
License: Springfield, OH held by Radio Maria Inc.
Group Owner: Radio Maria Inc.; (acq 5-30-2008; $225,000)
Arbitron Metro Market: Alexandria, LA *Format:* Christian
Robert Pitsch, General Manager
Marco Simmons, Station Manager

*WEEC
12-15-1961; 100.7 mhz FM *Hrs Open:* 24; 50 kw; 469 ft.; N39 57 42 W83 52 5
2265 Troy Road, Springfield, OH 45504 US
(937) 399-7837, *Fax:* (937) 399-7802
www.weec.org
info@weec.org
License: Springfield, Clark County, OH held by World Evangelistic Enterprise Corp.
Nat'l Network: USA; Moody; AP Radio *Wire Services:* AP
Arbitron Metro Market: Springfield, OH *Format:* Christian, Talk
Special Programming: Black one hr, farm one hr wkly *Hrs. of News Programming:* news progmg 16 hrs wkly *No. News Employees:* 1 *Target Audience:* 40 plus; general
Tracy Figley, CEO
Duane Helman, President
Newell Moore, Operations Dir
Chris Grindrod, Programming Director

WIZE
11-01-1940; 1340 khz AM *Hrs Open:* 24; 1 kw-D, ND2; 1 kw-N, ND2; N39 56 33 W83 47 15 *Rebroadcasts:* Simulcasts WONE(AM) Dayton 100%
50 East Rivercenter Blvd, Suite 1200, Covington, KY 41011 US
(937) 224-1137, *Fax:* (937) 224-3667
www.wone.com
info@ccedayton.com
License: Springfield, OH held by Citicasters Licenses L.P.
Group Owner: Clear Channel Communications Inc.; (acq 5-4-99; grpsl).
Regional Reps: Rgnl Reps.
Arbitron Metro Market: Dayton, OH *Format:* Sports *Hrs. of News Programming:* news progmg 14 hrs wkly *No. News Employees:* 1 *Target Audience:* 25 plus; upper income, businesses, offices
Adv. Rates: 20; 18;20; 12
Robert Zurowesti, Operations Dir
Tony Tilford, Programming Director
Jeff Bennett, Chief Engineer

*WUSO
02-20-1966; 89.1 mhz FM *Hrs Open:* 24; 0.1 kw vert; 85 ft.; N39 56 9 W83 48 41
C/O Wittenberg Universit, Box 720, P.O. Box 6100, Springfield, OH 45501 US
(937) 327-7026, *Fax:* (937) 327-6340
wuso.org
wusoprogrock@yahoo.com
License: Springfield, Clark County, OH held by Wittenberg University.
Arbitron Metro Market: Springfield, OH *Format:* Alternative, Rock/AOR *Special Programming:* Jazz 6 hrs, class 3 hrs, blues 3 hrs, urban contem *No. News Employees:* 1 *Target Audience:* General; liberal artsstudents & residents of Springfield, OH
Shelly Gregory, General Manager
Andrew Bowen, Programming Director
Amber Reyes, Promotions Manager
Nishant Makhija, News Director
Sven Isaacson, Engineering Dir
Caity Valley, Head Music Director
Adam Markins, Treasurer
NateDorow, Secretary

St. Marys

WMLX
01-01-1998; 103.3 mhz FM *Hrs Open:* 24; 1.95 kw; 558 ft.; N40 38 3 W84 12 29
50 East Rivercenter Boulevard, Suite 1200, Covington, KY 41011 US
(419) 223-2060, *Fax:* (419) 229-3888
www.mix1033.com
comments@wmlx.com
License: St. Marys, Auglaize County, OH held by Clear Channel Radio Licenses, Inc.
Group Owner: Clear Channel Communications Inc.; (acq 5-4-99; grpsl)
Arbitron Metro Market: St. Marys, OH *Format:* Adult Contemp
Hrs. of News Programming: News progmg 2 hrs wkly *Target Audience:* 18-49; women *Adv. Rates:* 30; 25; 28; 13
Renee Scott, Operations Dir
Matt Nesler, General Sales Mgr
Mark Gierhart, Engineering Dir
Jolene Molaski, National Sales Manager
Matt Bell, Regional Sales Manager

Steubenville

*WBJV
01-01-2002; 88.9 mhz FM; 0.125 kw; 256 ft.; N40 21 56 W80 43 36
P.O. Drawer 2440, Tupelo, MS 38803 US
(662) 844-8888, *Fax:* (662) 842-6791
www.afa.net/Radio/
License: Steubenville, Jefferson County, OH held by American Family Association.
Group Owner: American Family Radio
Arbitron Metro Market: Steubenville, OH *Format:* Christian
Marvin Sanders, General Manager

WDIG
09-25-1973; 950 khz AM *Hrs Open:* 24; 1 kw-D, DA2; 0.035 kw-N, DA2; N40 26 49 W80 34 6
500 North 5th Street, Steubenville, OH 43952 US
(740) 264-1760, *Fax:* (740) 264-5035
www.wdigradio.com
License: Steubenville, OH held by World Witness For Christ Ministries Inc.
Nat'l Network: ABC
Arbitron Metro Market: Wheeling, WV *Format:* Oldies *Special Programming:* Gospel *Target Audience:* 25-54; general
Roy Dawkins, CEO
Del King, General Manager

WSTV
11-04-1940; 1340 khz AM *Hrs Open:* 24; 1 kw-U, ND1; N40 20 30 W80 37 8
Mailing Address: 200 Gateway Towers, Pittsburgh, PA 15222 US
Second Address: 320 Market St., Steubenville, OH 43952
(740) 283-4747, *Fax:* (740) 283-3655
www.wstv.com
wstv@wstv.com
License: Steubenville, OH held by Keymarket Licences LLC.
Group Owner: Keymarket Communications LLC; (acq 3-20-2000; grpsl).
Nat'l Network: ESPN Radio *Nat'l Reps:* Rgnl Reps
Format: Sports *Special Programming:* Po 2 hrs, Czech 2 hrs wkly *Hrs. of News Programming:* news progmg 5 hrs wkly *No. News Employees:* 2
Gerald Getz, President
Joyce Nicholson, Operations Dir
Jim Seemiller, General Manager
Frank Bell, Programming Director
Marjie De Fede, News Director
Greg Harper, Chief Engineer

Streetsboro

*WSTB
09-01-1973; 88.9 mhz FM *Hrs Open:* 7 AM-midnight; 0.68 kw; 373 ft.; N41 9 4 W81 20 13
1900 Annalane Drive, Streetsboro, OH 44241 US
(330) 626-4906, *Fax:* (330) 626-4906
www.rock889.com
mail@rock889.com
License: Streetsboro, Portage County, OH held by Streetsboro City Schools.
Format: Rock/AOR *Hrs. of News Programming:* news progmg 4 hrs wkly *No. News Employees:* 1 *Target Audience:* 16-34.
Billy Germani, Operations Dir
Robert Long, General Manager

Struthers

*WKTL
09-06-1965; 90.7 mhz FM; 13.5 kw; 23 ft.; N41 3 6 W80 35 56
111 Euclid Avenue, Struthers, OH 44471 US
(330) 755-8578, *Fax:* (330) 755-4525
www.913thesummit.com
License: Struthers, Mahoning County, OH held by Struthers Board of Education.
Format: Adult Contemp, Classic Rock
Tom Krestal, General Manager

Swanton

WJUC
02-27-1997; 107.3 mhz FM *Hrs Open:* 24; 3 kw; 328 ft.; N41 38 30 W83 54 3
Mailing Address: P.O. Box 351450, Toledo, OH 43635 US
Second Address: 5902 Southwyck Blvd., Toledo, OH 43614
(419) 861-9582, *Fax:* (419) 861-2866
www.thejuice1073.com
wcharleswelch@aol.com
License: Swanton, Fulton County, OH held by Welch Communications Inc.
Regional Reps: Interep *Wire Services:* AP
Arbitron Metro Market: Toledo, OH *Format:* Adult Contemp, Blues *Special Programming:* Blues, gospel *Target Audience:* 18-54; African Americans 70%, others 30% *Adv. Rates:* 65; 65; 75; 60
W. Charles Welch, CEO

Sylvania

WWWM-FM
11-29-1968; 105.5 mhz FM *Hrs Open:* 24; 4.3 kw; 389 ft.; N41 38 49 W83 36 18
Mailing Address: 111 East Kilbourn Ave., Suite 2700, Milwaukee, WI 53202 US
Second Address: 2965 Pickle Rd., Oregon, OH 43616
(419) 725-5700, *Fax:* (419) 385-2902
www.star105toledo.com
info@star105toledo.com
License: Sylvania, Lucas County, OH held by Cumulus Licensing Corp.
Group Owner: Cumulus Media Inc.; (acq 9-11-97; $10 million with WLQR(AM) Toledo)
Nat'l Reps: D & R Radio
Arbitron Metro Market: Toledo, OH *Format:* Adult Contemp
Target Audience: 25-54.
MattSpaulding, General Manager
Ron Finn, Programming Director
Ryan Young, Promotions Manager
London Mitchell, News Director
Keith Bosworth, Chief Engineer
Debbie Calevro, Traffic Manager

Thompson

*WKSV
06-01-1997; 89.1 mhz FM *Hrs Open:* 24; 50 kw; Ant 472 ft; N41 41 34 W81 02 51 *Rebroadcasts:* Rebroadcasts WKSU-FM Kent 100%
Mailing Address: c/o WKSU-FM, Box 5190, Kent, OH 44242
Second Address: 1613 E.Summit St, Kent, OH 44242-0001
(330) 672-3114, *Fax:* (330) 672-4107
www.wksu.org
letters@wksu.org
License: Thompson, Geauga County, OH held by Kent State University.
Nat'l Network: NPR; PRI; AP Radio
Population Served: 191,723 *Arbitron Metro Market:* Cleveland, OH *Hrs. of News Programming:* news progmg 35 hrs wkly *No. News Employees:* 5 *Target Audience:* 35-65; college grad, professional & upper income
Allen Bartholet, General Manager
M L Schultze, News Director
Ronald Bartlebaugh, Engineering Dir
Kerry Kurchak, Assistant General Manager

Tiffin

WTTF
12-19-1959; 1600 khz AM *Hrs Open:* 6 AM-10 PM; 500 w-D, 20 w-N, DA-1; N41 07 32 W83 13 45
1624 Tiffin Ave., Findlay, OH 44883
(419) 427-1077, *Fax:* (419) 422-2954
www.wttf.com
License: Tiffin, Seneca County, OH held by Tiffen Broadcasting LLC
Group Owner: BAS Broadcasting Inc.; (acq 10-15-2008)
Population Served: 65,000*Hrs. of News Programming:* news progmg 18 hrs wkly *No. News Employees:* 2 *Target Audience:* General.
Jim Lorenzen, General Manager

Toledo

WCWA
04-10-1938; 1230 khz AM; 1 kw-U, ND1; N41 38 13 W83 33 52
50 East Rivercenter Blvd, Suite 1200, Covington, KY 41011 US

(419) 244-8321, *Fax:* (419) 244-7631
www.1230foxsports.com
tomriggs@clearchannel.com
License: Toledo, OH held by Jacor Broadcasting Corp.
Group Owner: Clear Channel Communications Inc.; (acq 1999; grpsl)
Nat'l Reps: Clear Channel
Arbitron Metro Market: Toledo, OH *Format:* News, News/Talk, 86 *Special Programming:* Ger one hr, Pol one hr, relg 3 hrs, sports 15 hrs wkly *Target Audience:* 25-54; male *Adv. Rates:* 20; 125; 25; 10
John Hogan, CEO
Andy Stuart, Operations Dir
Kellie Holeman, General Sales Mgr
Tom Riggs, Programming Director
Jack Jolly, General Sales Manager

***WGTE-FM**

05-02-1976; 91.3 mhz FM *Hrs Open:* 24; 13.5 kw; 948 ft.; N41 39 27 W83 25 55
136 N Huron St PO Box 30, Toledo, OH 43692 US
(419) 380-4600, *Fax:* (419) 380-4710
www.wgte.org
info@wgte.com
License: Toledo, Lucas County, OH held by The Public Broadcasting Foundation of Northwest Ohio.
Nat'l Network: NPR; PRI
Arbitron Metro Market: Toledo, OH *TV Affiliate:* *WGTE-TV affil. *Format:* News, Public Affairs *Special Programming:* Jazz 16 hrs, new age 4 hrs wkly *Hrs. of News Programming:* News progmg 23 hrs wkly *TargetAudience:* General.
George Jones, Chairman
Marlon Kiser, CEO
Chris Pfeiffer, Operations Dir
Ross Pfieffer, General Sales Mgr

WIOT

10-01-1949; 104.7 mhz FM *Hrs Open:* 24; 50 kw; 541 ft.; N41 40 23 W83 25 31
50 East Rivercenter, Suite 1200, Covington, KY 41011 US
(419) 244-8321, *Fax:* (419) 244-7631
www.wiot.com
wiot@wiot.com
License: Toledo, Lucas County, OH
Group Owner: Clear Channel Communications Inc.; (Acq 1997).
Arbitron Metro Market: Toledo, OH *Format:* Rock/AOR *Special Programming:* Progsv rock 2 hrs, metal 2 hrs wkly
Nathan Reed, Operations Dir
Kellie Holeman, General Sales Mgr
Don Grosselin, Programming Director
Beth Plummer, Webmaster
Grizzly Brown, Disc Jockey

WKKO

12-07-1956; 99.9 mhz FM *Hrs Open:* 24; 50 kw; 500 ft.; N41 40 5 W83 27 11
111 East Kilbourn Ave., Suite 2700, Milwaukee, WI 53202 US
(419) 725-5700, *Fax:* (419) 385-2902
www.k100country.com
info@k100country.com
License: Toledo, Lucas County, OH
Nat'l Network: ABC
Arbitron Metro Market: Toledo, OH
Gary Outlaw, Programming Director

WLQR

10-01-1954; 1470 khz AM; 1 kw-D, DA2; 1 kw-N, DA2; N41 37 54 W83 28 38
111 East Kilbourn Ave., Suite 2700, Milwaukee, WI 53202 US
(419) 725-5700, *Fax:* (419) 385-2902
www.1470theticket.com
info@1470theticket.com
License: Toledo, OH held by Cumulus Licensing Corp.
Group Owner: Cumulus Media Inc.; (acq 9-11-97; $10 million with WWWM-FM Sylvania)
Arbitron Metro Market: Toledo, OH *Format:* Sports *Target Audience:* 25-54.
Skip Schmidt, General Manager

***WOTL**

03-24-1988; 90.3 mhz FM; 0.7 kw; 377 ft.; N41 38 48 W83 36 22
Mailing Address: 4135 Northgate Blvd, Suite 1, Sacramento, CA 95834 US
Second Address: 716 N. Westwood Ave., Toledo, OH 43607
(815) 725-1331
www.familyradio.com
License: Toledo, Lucas County, OH held by Family Stations Inc.
Group Owner: Family Stations Inc.
Arbitron Metro Market: Toledo, OH *Format:* Religious *Target Audience:* General.
Harold Camping, President
John Rorvik, General Manager

WRVF

08-11-1946; 101.5 mhz FM; 33 kw; 538 ft.; N41 40 23 W83 25 31
50 East Rivercenter Blvd, Suite 1200, Covington, KY 41011 US
(419) 244-8321, *Fax:* (419) 244-7631
www.wrvf.com
License: Toledo, Lucas County, OH
Group Owner: Clear Channel Communications Inc.
Nat'l Reps: Clear Channel
Arbitron Metro Market: Toledo, OH *Format:* Adult Contemp *Special Programming:* Jazz 6 hrs wkly *Target Audience:* 25-54; mostly female *Adv. Rates:* 175; 250; 225; 50
Nathan Reed, Operations Dir
Maureen DeTange, General Sales Mgr
Don Gosselin, Programming Director

WSPD

04-15-1921; 1370 khz AM; 5 kw-D, DAN; 5 kw-N, DAN; N41 36 3 W83 32 11
50 East Rivercenter Blvd, Suite 1200, Covington, KY 41011 US
(419) 244-8321, *Fax:* (419) 244-7631
www.wspd.com
License: Toledo, OH held by Citicasters Licenses L.P.
Group Owner: Clear Channel Communications Inc.; (acq 5-4-99; grpsl).
Regional Reps: Rgnl Reps.
Arbitron Metro Market: Toledo, OH *Format:* News, News/Talk, 86 *Special Programming:* Relg 5 hrs, farm 3 hrs wkly *Target Audience:* 25-54; mostly males
Andy Stuart, Operations Dir
Kellie Holeman, General Sales Mgr
Al Law, Programming Director
A.T. Simen, Promotions Manager
Jack Jolly, General Sales Manager

WWYC

06-16-1946; 1560 khz AM; 5 kw-D, DA; N41 36 59 W83 37 22
3225 Arlington Ave., Toledo, OH 53202
(419) 725-5700, *Fax:* (419) 385-2902
www.am1560wtod.com
info@am1560wtod.com
License: Toledo, Lucas County, OH held by Cumulus Licensing Corp.
Group Owner: Cumulus Media Inc.; (acq 9-11-97; grpsl)
Population Served: 383,318 *Arbitron Metro Market:* Toledo, OH *Special Programming:* Pol 4 hrs wkly *Hrs. of News Programming:* news progmg 3 hrs wkly *No. News Employees:* 1 *Target Audience:* 25-54; adults
Kathy Stinehour, General Manager
Gary Shores, Programming Director
London Mitchell, News Director
Kevin Hawley, Chief Engineer

WVKS

10-14-1957; 92.5 mhz FM *Hrs Open:* 24; 50 kw; 479 ft.; N41 31 55 W83 35 37
50 East Rivercenter Blvd, Suite 1200, Covington, KY 41011 US
(419) 244-8321, *Fax:* (419) 244-7631
www.925kissfm.com
License: Toledo, Lucas County, OH held by Citicasters Licenses L.P.
Group Owner: Clear Channel Communications Inc.; (acq 5-15-99; grpsl).
Nat'l Reps: Clear Channel *Wire Services:* AP
Arbitron Metro Market: Toledo, OH *Format:* Contemporary Hits/Top 40 *Hrs. of News Programming:* news progmg one hr wkly *No. News Employees:* 1 *Target Audience:* 18-49; educated, employed adults, mostly females*Adv. Rates:* 125; 110; 125; 75
Andrew Stuart, Operations Dir
Kellie Holeman, General Sales Mgr
Amy Simon, Promotions Manager
Nathan Reed, Operations Manager
Beth Plummett, Website Issue

***WXTS-FM**

02-01-1975; 88.3 mhz FM *Hrs Open:* 24; 0.105 kw; 125 ft.; N41 40 7 W83 33 15
2400 Collingwood Blvd., Toledo, OH 43620 US
(419) 244-6875, *Fax:* (419) 249-8248
License: Toledo, Lucas County, OH held by Toledo Board of Education.
Arbitron Metro Market: Toledo, OH *Format:* Jazz *Special Programming:* Blues 5 hrs wkly *Target Audience:* 28-55.
John Kuschell, General Manager

***WXUT**

11-04-1990; 88.3 mhz FM *Hrs Open:* 8 PM-2 AM (M-W); 8 PM-4 AM (Th, F);; 0.1 kw horiz; 190 ft.; N41 39 26 W83 36 57
2801 W. Bancroft Street, Student Union 2515, Toledo, OH 43606 US
(419) 530-4172, *Fax:* (419) 530-2210
www.wxut.com
wxut@wxut.com
License: Toledo, Lucas County, OH held by University of Toledo.
Arbitron Metro Market: Toledo, OH *Format:* Alternative *Special Programming:* Black 8 hrs, heavy metal 4 hrs, rhythm and blues 2 *Hrs. of News Programming:* News progmg 4 hrs wkly *Target Audience:* General.
Terrance Teagarden, General Manager
Tyler Mattson, Station Manager
Sarah Avery, Programming Director
Breon Mitchell, Promotions Manager
David Sherline, Chief Engineer
Sean Weirich, Production Director
Derrick Lawson, SportsDirector
Claire Dale, Music Director

Troy

***WOKL**

01-01-1991; 96.9 mhz FM *Hrs Open:* 24; 6 kw; 312 ft.; N39 56 49 W84 11 29 *Rebroadcasts:* Rebroadcasts KLVR(FM) Santa Rosa 100%
211 South Main Street, Suite 1200, Dayton, OH 45402 US
(916) 251-1600, *Fax:* (916) 251-1650
www.klove.com
klove@klove.com
License: Troy, Miami County, OH held by Educational Media Foundation.
Group Owner: EMF Broadcasting; (acq 7-17-03; $1.2 million).
Nat'l Network: K-Love
Arbitron Metro Market: Dayton, OH *Format:* Christian *No. News Employees:* 3 *Target Audience:* 25-44; Judeo Christian, female
Mike Novak, President
David Pierce, Programming Director
Ed Lenane, News Director
Sam Wallington, Engineering Dir
Richard Hunt, News Reporter
Marya Morgan, News Reporter

Uhrichsville

WBTC

12-13-1963; 1540 khz AM
2305 North Water Street, Uhrichsville, OH 44683 US
(740) 922-2700, *Fax:* (740) 922-2702
www.wbtclive.com/
wbtc@tusco.net
License: Uhrichsville, OH held by Tuscarawas Broadcasting Co.
Nat'l Network: CBS *Nat'l Reps:* Rgnl Reps
Arbitron Metro Market: Uhrichsville, OH *Format:* News, News/Talk, 84, Talk *Special Programming:* Relg 2 hrs wkly *Target Audience:* 30-55.
James Natoli Jr., President
Kevin Baker, Sales Director
J.R. Richards, Programming Director
Adam Mackey, News & Sports
Kathy Chaney, Secretary

WTUZ

05-01-1990; 99.9 mhz FM *Hrs Open:* 24; 5.3 kw; 348 ft.; N40 26 19 W81 26 1
2695 Possum Hollow Rd Se, New Philadelphia, OH 44663 US
(330) 339-2222, *Fax:* (330) 339-5930
www.wtuz.com
info@wtuz.com
License: Uhrichsville, Tuscarawas County, OH held by WTUZ Radio Inc.
Nat'l Network: Fox News Radio *Wire Services:* AP
Arbitron Metro Market: New Philadelphia, OH *Format:* Country *Special Programming:* Farm 2 hr, relg 4 hr wkly *Hrs. of News Programming:* news progmg 7 hrs wkly *No. News Employees:* 2 *Target Audience:* 25-45;adults *Adv. Rates:* 50;50;50;30
Edward Schumacher, President
Melanie Osborn, General Sales Mgr
Brad Shupe, Programming Director
Pat Smith, Promotions Manager
Jennifer Lourenco, News Director
John Demuth, Chief Engineer

Union City

WTGR

12-31-1994; 97.5 mhz FM *Hrs Open:* 24; 6 kw; 325 ft.; N40 11 32 W84 47 58
P.O. Box 889, Blacksburg, VA 24063 US
(937) 548-5085, *Fax:* (937) 548-5089
www.wtgr.com
info@wtgr.com
License: Union City, Darke County, OH held by Positive Radio Group Inc. of Ohio.
Group Owner: Baker Family Stations

Nat'l Network: CNN Radio *Regional Network:* Ohio News Network *Nat'l Reps:* ABN Radio & TV
Arbitron Metro Market: Union City, OH *Format:* Country *Hrs. of News Programming:* news progmg one hr wkly *No. News Employees:* 1 *Target Audience:* 25-54; 25-49 female
Vernon Baker, CEO
Edward Baker, Operations Dir
Scott Ward, Station Manager
Kevin Nott, General Sales Mgr
Alex Mikos, News Director
Jeff Peters, Engineering Dir

University Heights

***WJCU**
05-13-1969; 88.7 mhz FM *Hrs Open:* 24; 2.5 kw; 341 ft.; N41 29 24 W81 31 54
20700 North Park Blvd, University Heights, OH 44118 US
(216) 397-4437, *Fax:* (216) 397-4439
www.wjcu.org
wjcu@jcu.edu
License: University Heights, Cuyahoga County, OH held by John Carroll University.
Arbitron Metro Market: Cleveland, OH *Format:* Variety/Diverse *Special Programming:* It 2 hrs, Chinese one hr, Pol 2 hrs, Lithuanian 2 *Hrs. of News Programming:* News progmg one hr wkly *Target Audience:* General.
Mark Krieger, General Manager
Joe Madigan, Station Manager

Upper Arlington

WJKR
05-25-1989; 98.9 mhz FM *Hrs Open:* 24; 3 kw; 328 ft; N39 58 16 W83 01 40
350 E 1st Ave., Suite 100, Columbus, OH 45237
(614) 487-1444, *Fax:* (614) 487-5862
www.magic989.com
info@wxmg.com
License: Upper Arlington, Franklin County, OH held by Blue Chip Broadcasting Licenses Ltd.
Group Owner: Radio One Inc.; (acq 4-30-01; grpsl).
Nat'l Reps: Christal
Arbitron Metro Market: Columbus, OH *No. News Employees:* 1 *Target Audience:* 25-54; upscale, educated, active & responsive
Jeff Wilson, General Manager

Upper Sandusky

***WXML**
12-26-1992; 90.1 mhz FM *Hrs Open:* 24; 15 circular; Ant 500 ft; N40 54 53 W83 07 32
Box 158, 1800 E. Wyandot Ave., Upper Sandusky, OH 43351
(419) 294-2900, *Fax:* (419) 294-1786
www.newvision.fm
wtactus@newvision.fm
License: Upper Sandusky, Wyandot County, OH held by Kayser Broadcast Ministries Inc.
Nat'l Network: SRN News
Population Served: 695,051*Hrs. of News Programming:* News progmg 8 hrs wkly *Target Audience:* General.
Daniel Kayser, CEO
Daniel Kayser, President
Daniel Kayser, General Manager
Jon Bowlus, Programming Director
Susan Kayser, Secretary/Director
Joe Emert, Treasurer
Dick Johnson, Vice President
Joe Perri, Director
Doug Doran,Director
Jenny Emert, Director

Urbana

WDHT
08-01-1958; 102.9 mhz FM *Hrs Open:* 24; 50 kw; 492 ft; N39 57 11 W83 52 07
717 E. David Rd., Dayton, OH 78216
(937) 294-5858, *Fax:* (937) 297-5233
www.hot1029.com
info@hot1029.com
License: Urbana, Clark County, OH held by MLB-Dayton IV LLC.
Group Owner: Main Line Broadcasting LLC; (acq 9-12-2007; grpsl)
Nat'l Reps: Katz Radio *Wire Services:* UPI
Population Served: 81,926 *Arbitron Metro Market:* Dayton, OH *Target Audience:* General.
Andrea Scott, General Manager

Van Wert

WERT
11-27-1958; 1220 khz AM *Hrs Open:* 24; 0.25 kw-D, ND2; 0.029 kw-N, ND2; N40 52 19 W84 33 15
PO Box 487, Van Wert, OH 45891 US
(419) 238-2092, *Fax:* (419) 238-2578
www.vwindependent.com
editor@thevwindependent.com
License: Van Wert, OH held by First Family Broadcasting Inc.
Nat'l Network: ABC *Nat'l Reps:* Rgnl Reps
Arbitron Metro Market: Van Wert, OH *Format:* Adult Contemp *Special Programming:* Gospel 3 hrs, Sp one hr wkly *Hrs. of News Programming:* news progmg 30 hrs wkly *No. News Employees:* 2 *Target Audience:* 35plus; spendable income
Chris Roberts, President

Wapakoneta

WFGF
01-01-1985; 92.1 mhz FM *Hrs Open:* 24; 3 kw; 328 ft.; N40 39 20 W84 6 54
Mailing Address: One Forever Drive, Hollidaysburg, PA 16648 US
Second Address: Box 1487, Lima, OH 45802
(419) 331-1600, *Fax:* (419) 228-5085
www.921thefrog.com
johntaylor@maverick-media.ws
License: Wapakoneta, Allen County, OH held by Maverick Media of Lima License LLC.
Group Owner: Maverick Media LLC; (acq 12-4-2003; grpsl).
Arbitron Metro Market: Wapakoneta, OH *Format:* Country
Special Programming: Nascar Nextel Races *Target Audience:* 25-54; young, affluent *Adv. Rates:* 17; 14; 15; 10
Gary Rozynek, President
Dave Roach, General Manager
Bill McAdams, Station Manager
Tiffany Kayser, Sales Manager
JP Taylor, Programming Director
Dave Woodward, Promotions Manager
Brandy Rader, News Director
Deb Klaus, BusinessManager

Warren

WHTX
04-07-1971; 1570 khz AM *Hrs Open:* 24; 500 w-D, 116 w-N, DA-1; N41 12 22 W80 50 29
Box 1798, Warren, OH 44483
(330) 394-7700, *Fax:* (330) 394-7701
www.wanr1570.com
License: Warren, Trumbull County, OH held by Beacon Broadcasting Inc.
Group Owner: Beacon Broadcasting Inc.; (acq 9-14-2005; grpsl)
Nat'l Network: Westwood One
Population Served: 41,358 *Arbitron Metro Market:* Warren, OH *Hrs. of News Programming:* news progmg 20 hrs wkly *No. News Employees:* 1 *Target Audience:* 25-49; adult men
Harold Glunt, CFO
Rich Esbenshade, General Manager

WHKZ
11-11-1941; 1440 khz AM; 5 kw-D, DA2; 5 kw-N, DA2; N41 9 52 W80 50 47 *Rebroadcasts:* Rebroadcasts WHKW(AM) Cleveland 100%
124 North Park Avenue, Warren, OH 44481 US
(216) 901-0921, *Fax:* (216) 901-5517
office@whkradio.com
License: Warren, OH held by Pentecostal Temple Development Corp.
Nat'l Reps: Salem
Arbitron Metro Market: Youngstown-Warren, OH *Format:* Christian, Talk
Errol Dengler, General Manager

Washington Court Hou

WCHO-FM
12-01-1968; 105.5 mhz FM; 6 kw; 328 ft.; N39 24 1 W83 26 48
50 East Rivercenter Blvd, Suite 1200, Covington, KY 41011 US
(304) 342-8131, *Fax:* (740) 335-6869
www.wcho.com
news@buckeyecountry105.com
License: Washington Court Hou, Fayette County, OH
Nat'l Network: ABC
Arbitron Metro Market: Washington Court House, OH *Format:* Country
Kevin Friedman, General Manager

Washington Ct House

WCHO
02-01-1952; 1250 khz AM; 0.5 kw-D, ND1; 0.042 kw-N, ND1; N39 32 59 W83 27 10
50 East Rivercenter Blvd, Suite 1200, Covington, KY 41011 US
(740) 335-0941, *Fax:* (740) 335-6869
www.wchoam.com
news@buckeyecountry105.com
License: Washington Ct House, OH held by Citicasters Licenses L.P.
Group Owner: Clear Channel Communications Inc.; (acq 5-4-99; grpsl).
Nat'l Network: ABC *Nat'l Reps:* Katz Radio
Arbitron Metro Market: Washington Court House, OH *Format:* Adult Contemp *Special Programming:* Farm 5 hrs wkly *Hrs. of News Programming:* News progmg 18 hrs wkly *Adv. Rates:* 10; 10; 10; 10
Dan Latham, Operations Dir
Tracy Taylor, General Sales Mgr
Carl Staffan, News Director
Todd Jellison, Engineering Dir
John Barney, General Sales Manager
Kim Skaggs, Vice President, Operations

Wauseon

***WYSA**
01-01-1996; 88.5 mhz FM *Hrs Open:* 24; 10 kw; 292 ft.; N41 33 29 W84 11 8
PO Box 8930, Maumee, OH 43537 US
(419) 389-0893, *Fax:* (419) 381-0731
www.yeshome.com
License: Wauseon, Fulton County, OH held by Side by Side Inc.
Arbitron Metro Market: Wauseon, OH *Format:* Christian *Target Audience:* 15-25.
Jim Oedy, President
J. Todd Hostetler, General Manager
Jeff Howe, Programming Director

***WNKL**
01-01-2003; 96.9 mhz FM; 5 kw; 358 ft.; N41 36 3 W83 54 27
2965 Pickle Road, Wauseon, OH 43616 US
(800) 525-5683, *Fax:* (916) 251-1650
www.klove.com
klove@klove.com
License: Wauseon, Fulton County, OH held by Educational Media Foundation.
Group Owner: EMF Broadcasting; (acq 4-21-2009; $2,825,000 with WNWT(FM) Rossford)
Nat'l Network: K-Love
Arbitron Metro Market: Omaha, NE *Format:* Christian *No. News Employees:* 13
Darrell Chambliss, Chairman
MIke Novak, President & CEO
Laura Daniels, News Reporter
Tim Luttrell, News Reporter
Kenny Noble Cortes, News Reporter
Darren Vinson, News Reporter

Waverly

WXIC
01-01-1954; 660 khz AM *Hrs Open:* Sunrise-sunset; 1 kw-D, NDD; N39 7 50 W83 0 46
P.O. Bx 227, Waverly, OH 45690 US
(740) 947-2166, *Fax:* (740) 947-4600
License: Waverly, OH held by Crystal Communications Corp.
Nat'l Reps: Keystone (unwired net)
Arbitron Metro Market: Waverly, OH *Format:* Gospel *Target Audience:* Gospel music lovers *Adv. Rates:* 11; 9; 11; 9
Gerald Davis, President
Rick Schweinburg, Operations Dir
Brad Lambert, General Sales Mgr
Rick Schweinburgh, Programming Director
Rick Schweinsburg, Promotions Manager

WXIZ
03-01-1971; 100.9 mhz FM *Hrs Open:* 24; 0.92 kw; 499 ft.; N39 13 17 W82 59 33
P.O. Box 227, Waverly, OH 45690 US
(740) 947-2166
www.wxiz.com
License: Waverly, Pike County, OH held by Crystal Communications Corp.
Arbitron Metro Market: Waverly,OH *Format:* Country *Hrs. of News Programming:* news progmg 10 hrs wkly *No. News Employees:* 1 *Target Audience:* 25-50.
Gerald Davis, Station Manager
Brad Lambert, General Sales Mgr
Tim Hughes, Programming Director
Roy Belt, News Director

***WWVY**
88.5 mhz FM; kw
P O Box 100, Lovejoy, GA 30250 US
(662) 844-5036, *Fax:* (662) 842-6791
www.afr.net
contact@afa.net
License: Waverly, Pike County, OH held by American Family Association.
Group Owner: American Family Radio; (acq 3-4-2008; $10 for CP)
Arbitron Metro Market: Tupelo, MS *Format:* Christian
Donald E. Wildmon, Founder
Buster Wilson, General Manager
Jennifer Hagman, Programming Director

Waynesville

***WYNS**
01-01-2009; 89.3 mhz FM; 0.1 kw; 49 ft.; N39 29 14 W84 4 29 US
(724) 516-6252
www.hybridfm.net
hybridfm@hotmail.com
License: Waynesville, Warren County, OH held by 24-7 Broadcasting Inc.
Arbitron Metro Market: Waynesville, OH *Format:* Variety/Diverse
Deborah Ives, Operations Dir

Wellston

WKOV-FM
07-17-1971; 96.7 mhz FM *Hrs Open:* 24; 16 kw; 129 meters; N39 01 45 W82 35 51
Box 667 295 E. Main, Jackson, OH 45640
(740) 286-3023, *Fax:* (740) 286-6679
License: Wellston, Jackson County, OH held by Jackson County Broadcasting Inc.
Group Owner: Jackson County Broadcasting Inc.
Nat'l Network: Dial Global
Population Served: 585,000*Hrs. of News Programming:* news progmg 21 hrs wkly *No. News Employees:* 1 *Target Audience:* 20-55. *Adv. Rates:* 19; 16; 19; 13
Jerry Mossbarger, General Manager
Ron Speakman, General Sales Mgr
John Pelletier, Programming Director

WYPC
01-01-1953; 1330 khz AM *Hrs Open:* 24; 500 w-D, 50 w-N; N39 06 22 W82 34 44
Box 667, 295 E. Main, Jackson, OH 45640
(740) 286-3023, *Fax:* (740) 286-6679
jmossbarger@jcbiradio.com
License: Wellston, Jackson County, OH held by Jackson County Broadcasting Inc.
Group Owner: Jackson County Broadcasting Inc.; acq 9-14-70)
Nat'l Network: Westwood One
Population Served: 42,000*Hrs. of News Programming:* news progmg 8 hrs wkly *No. News Employees:* 1 *Target Audience:* 50 plus. *Adv. Rates:* 9; 7; 9; 6
Jerry Mossbarger, General Manager
Ron Speakman, General Sales Mgr
John Pelletier, Programming Director

West Carrollton

WROU-FM
11-25-1991; 92.1 mhz FM *Hrs Open:* 24; 0.89 kw; 597 ft.; N39 43 15 W84 15 39
211 South Main Ste. 400, Dayton, OH 45402 US
(937) 294-5858, *Fax:* (937) 297-5233
www.921wrou.com
info@921wrou.com
License: West Carrollton, Montgomery County, OH held by MLB-Dayton IV LLC.
Group Owner: Main Line Broadcasting LLC; (acq 9-12-2007; grpsl)
Nat'l Network: ABC *Nat'l Reps:* Katz Radio
Arbitron Metro Market: Dayton, OH *Format:* Urban Contemporary *Target Audience:* 25-54.
Andrea Scott, General Manager

West Chester

***WLHS**
09-03-1976; 89.9 mhz FM *Hrs Open:* 9 AM-5 PM; 0.1 kw horiz; 341 ft.; N39 19 10 W84 22 4
5050 Tylersville Road, West Chester, OH 45069 US
(616) 987-2549, *Fax:* (616) 987-2547
www.wlhsradio.org
License: West Chester, Butler County, OH held by Lakota School District.
Wire Services: UPI
Format: Rock/AOR *Target Audience:* General; div, open minded crowd
R.C. Anderson, Operations Dir
Mark Hattersley, Station Manager
Corey Wyatt, General Sales Mgr
Matt Townsley, Programming Director
Brandon Enright, Assistant Music Director
Danny Hall, Music Director

West Union

***WZWP**
01-01-1990; 89.5 mhz FM *Hrs Open:* 24; 3.2 kw; 381 ft.; N38 51 26 W83 36 38 *Rebroadcasts:* Simulcasts WZCP(FM) Chillicothe 100%
3800 Victory Parkway, Cincinnati, OH 45207 US
(309) 674-9292, *Fax:* (309) 676-5000
www.powerpeoria.com
amanda.king@cumulus.com
License: West Union, Adams County, OH held by Christian Voice of Central Ohio Inc.
Group Owner: Christian Voice of Central Ohio Inc.; (acq 5-15-2007; grpsl)
Arbitron Metro Market: Peoria, IL *Format:* Contemporary Hits/Top 40
Brad Creek, Director of Sales
Amanda King, Programming Director

Westerville

WMNI-FM
01-01-1998; 103.9 mhz FM *Hrs Open:* 24; 6 kw; Ant 328 ft; N40 09 33 W82 55 21
1458 Dublin Rd., Columbus, OH 43215
(614) 481-7800, *Fax:* (614) 481-8070
www.tedfm.com
mail997@wrkz.com
License: Westerville, Franklin County, OH held by North American Broadcasting Co. Inc.
Group Owner: North American Broadcasting Co. Inc.; (acq 1999; $5 million)
Nat'l Network: Fox Sports *Nat'l Reps:* D & R Radio *Wire Services:* AP
Population Served: 1,200,000 *Arbitron Metro Market:* Columbus, OH
Norma Mnich, Chairman
Matthew Mnich, CEO
Mark Jividen, Operations Dir

***WOBN**
10-08-1958; 97.5 mhz FM; 29 w horiz; Ant 66 ft; N40 07 28 W82 56 06
Otterbein College, 33 College view Rd., Westerville, OH 43081
(614) 823-2975, *Fax:* (614) 823-3367
ocwobn.otterbein.edu
License: Westerville, Franklin County, OH held by Otterbein College.
Population Served: 12,530*Special Programming:* College Alternative University *Hrs. of News Programming:* News progmg one hr wkly *Target Audience:* General; Westerville & Otterbein College community
Janice Windborne, Faculty Advisor

WVMX
06-21-1991; 107.9 mhz FM *Hrs Open:* 24; 3 kw; 469 ft.; N40 14 41.5 W82 55 49.1
200 Gateway Towers, Pittsburgh, PA 15222 US
(614) 451-2191, *Fax:* (614) 451-1831
www.themix1079.com
info@b1079.com
License: Westerville, Delaware County, OH held by Franklin Communications Inc.
Group Owner: Saga Communications Inc.; (acq 3-27-2003; $9 million)
Nat'l Reps: Christal *Wire Services:* AP
Arbitron Metro Market: Columbus, OH *Format:* Adult Contemp *Hrs. of News Programming:* news progmg 10 hrs wkly *No. News Employees:* 1 *Target Audience:* 25-44.
Alan Goodman, President
Bill Shannon, Programming Director
Michelle Hurley, Promotions Manager

Whitehouse

***WTPG**
88.9 mhz FM; 11 kw; 266 ft.; N41 25 39 W83 36 30 US
(714) 545-7868, *Fax:* (208) 736-1958
www.csnradio.com
License: Whitehouse, Wood County, OH held by CSN International.
Group Owner: CSN International
Arbitron Metro Market: Whitehouse, Ohio
Mike Kestler, President
Don Mills, Network Programming Director / Music Director
Kelly Carlson, Engineering Dir
Ray Gorney, Assistant Director of Engineering
Jerry Johnson, Engineer / Outage Coordinator
Dustin Pamplona,Engineer
O.J. Edwards, Engineer
Jeremy Estabrooks, Engineer
Mickel Pruden, Engineer

Wilberforce

***WCSU-FM**
12-15-1962; 88.9 mhz FM; 1 kw; 174 ft.; N39 42 57 W83 52 27
1400 Brush Row Rd, Cosby Center, Wilberforce, OH 45384 US
(937) 376-9278, *Fax:* (937) 376-6015
www.wcsufm.org
wcsufm@gmail.com
License: Wilberforce, Greene County, OH held by Central State University.
Arbitron Metro Market: Wilberforce,OH *Format:* Jazz *Target Audience:* 12-49; African-Americans
J.C. Logan, General Manager
Tony Chappel, Programming Director

Willard

WLRD
01-01-2000; 96.9 mhz FM; 6 kw; 328 ft.; N40 57 36 W82 37 16
3809 Maple Avenue, Castalia, OH 44824 US
(419) 684-5311, *Fax:* (419) 684-5378
www.wlrd.net
fm977@cfbroadcast.net
License: Willard, Huron County, OH held by Christian Faith Broadcast Inc.
Group Owner: Christian Faith Broadcasting Inc.
Format: Gospel *Target Audience:* 25-54.
Rusty Yost, General Manager

Willoughby

WELW
01-25-1965; 1330 khz AM *Hrs Open:* 24; 0.5 kw-D, DA2; 0.042 kw-N, DA2; N41 38 57 W81 25 25
P.O. Box 1330, Willoughby, OH 44094 US
(440) 946-1330, *Fax:* (440) 953-0320
www.welw.com
email@welw.com
License: Willoughby, OH held by Spirit Broadcasting Corp.
Nat'l Network: USA; Westwood One; Radio America; Talk Radio Network
Arbitron Metro Market: Cleveland, OH *Format:* Sports, Talk
Special Programming: Ger one hr; Croation 3 hrs, It one hr; Pol one hr; Spanish contemporary 1 hr; Polka 15 hrs wkly *Target Audience:* 35 plus; communityadults
Tony Petkovsek, President
Ray Somich, General Manager
Ron Somich, Station Manager
Van Lane, General Sales Mgr
Kathy Gee, News Director

Wilmington

WKFI
01-01-1963; 1090 khz AM; 1 kw-D, DAD; N39 26 12 W83 51 21
Rebroadcasts: Rebroadcasts WBZI(AM) Xenia 80%
P.O. Box 1, Wilmington, OH 45177 US
(937) 372-3531, *Fax:* (937) 372-3508
www.myclassiccountry.com
myclassiccountry@myclassiccountry.com
License: Wilmington, OH held by Town and Country Broadcasting Inc.
Group Owner: Town and Country Broadcasting Inc.; (acq 12-16-2004; $300,000).
Nat'l Network: Fox News Radio *Regional Network:* Agrinet *Nat'l Reps:* Rgnl Reps *Wire Services:* AP
Format: Country *Special Programming:* Big band 5 hrs wkly *Hrs. of News Programming:* news progmg 3 hrs wkly *No. News Employees:* 1 *Target Audience:* General. *Adv. Rates:* 18; 18; 18; 0
Joe Mullins, General Manager
Roy Hatfield, Programming Director
Megan Brugger, News Director
Bucks Braun, Morning Host
Darrin Johnston, News Commentator

WKLN
01-01-1974; 102.3 mhz FM; 3 kw; 299 ft.; N39 21 54 W83 46 8
200 R Gordon Drive, Wilmington, OH 45177 US

(513) 829-7700
www.klove.com
info@wkln.com
License: Wilmington, Clinton County, OH held by Vernon R. Baldwin Inc.
Group Owner: Vernon R Baldwin Inc.; (acq 4-22-2003; $1.2 million with co-located AM).
Nat'l Network: K-Love
Format: Christian
Vernon Baldwin, President

Wooster

*WCWS-FM
04-01-1968; 90.9 mhz FM *Hrs Open:* 24; 1.05 kw; 223 ft.; N40 49 41 W81 52 14
P.O. Box 3177, Wooster, OH 44691 US
(330) 263-2240, *Fax:* (330) 263-2690
www.woo91.sites.wooster.edu
wcws@wooster.edu
License: Wooster, Wayne County, OH held by The College of Wooster.
Arbitron Metro Market: Wooster, Oh *Format:* Variety/Diverse *Special Programming:* Edu 8 hrs wkly *Hrs. of News Programming:* News progmg 10 hrs wkly *Target Audience:* General; college students & people of thesurrounding area
David Mallinson, General Manager
Jeremy Ludemann, Programming Director
Kenneth Perry, Promotions Manager
Cerissa Dellavecchia, News Director
Nick Sekela, Music Director

*WKRW
03-29-1993; 89.3 mhz FM *Hrs Open:* 24; 2.1 kw; 318 ft; N40 46 28 W81 55 05 *Rebroadcasts:* Rebroadcasts WKSU-FM Kent 99%
Mailing Address: Box 5190, Kent, OH 44242
Second Address: 1613 E. Summit St, Kent, OH 44242-0001
(330) 672-3114, *Fax:* (330) 672-4107
www.wksu.org
letters@wksu.org
License: Wooster, Wayne County, OH held by Kent State University.
Nat'l Network: NPR; PRI
Population Served: 91,826*Special Programming:* Folk 12 hrs wkly *Hrs. of News Programming:* news progmg 35 hrs wkly *No. News Employees:* 5 *Target Audience:* 35-65; college grad, professional & upper income
Allen Bartholet, General Manager
M L Schultze, News Director
Ronald Bartlebaugh, Engineering Dir
Kerry Kurchak, Assistant General Manager

WKVX
01-01-1947; 960 khz AM *Hrs Open:* 24; 1 kw-D, ND1; 0.032 kw-N, ND1; N40 47 31 W81 54 17
Mailing Address: 186 South Hillcrest Drive, Wooster, OH 44691 US
Second Address: 186 S. Hillcrest Dr., Wooster, OH 44691
(330) 264-5122, *Fax:* (330) 264-3571
www.wkvx.com
wkvx@aol.com
License: Wooster, OH held by WWST Corp. L.L.C.
Group Owner: Wooster Republican Printing Co.
Nat'l Network: Westwood One; CNN Radio *Regional Reps:* Rgnl Reps *Wire Services:* AP
Format: Oldies
Ken Nemeth, General Manager
Ron Hamilton, Programming Director

WQKT
01-01-1947; 104.5 mhz FM *Hrs Open:* 24; 52 kw; 331 ft.; N40 47 31 W81 54 17
Mailing Address: 186 South Hillcrest Drive, Wooster, OH 44691 US
Second Address: 186 S. Hillcrest Dr., Wooster, OH 44691
(330) 264-5122, *Fax:* (330) 264-3571
www.wqkt.com
wqkt@aol.com
License: Wooster, Wayne County, OH held by WWST Corp. L.L.C.
Group Owner: Wooster Republican Printing Co.
Nat'l Network: Westwood One; CNN Radio *Regional Reps:* Rgnl Reps *Wire Services:* AP
Format: Country, Sports *No. News Employees:* 3 *Target Audience:* 35-54.
Ken Nemeth, General Manager
Craig Walton, General Sales Mgr
Ron Hamilton, Programming Director
Mike Breckenridge, News Director

Xenia

WBZI
11-11-1963; 1500 khz AM *Hrs Open:* Sunrise-sunset; 0.5 kw-D, NDD; N39 42 48 W83 54 48
486 W. Second St., Xenia, OH 45385 US
(866) 372-3531, *Fax:* (937) 372-3508
www.myclassiccountry.com
myclassiccountry@myclassiccountry.com
License: Xenia, OH held by Town & Country Broadcasting Inc.
Group Owner: Town and Country Broadcasting Inc.; (acq 10-4-95; $140,000).
Nat'l Network: Fox News Radio *Regional Network:* Agrinet *Nat'l Reps:* Rgnl Reps *Wire Services:* AP
Arbitron Metro Market: Xenia, OH *Format:* Country *Special Programming:* Gospel 5 hrs, farm 2 hrs wkly *Hrs. of News Programming:* news progmg 3 hrs wkly *No. News Employees:* 1 *Target Audience:* 35-64; upperincome, married, homeowners *Adv. Rates:* 26; 26; 26
Joe Mullins, General Manager
Roy Hatfield, Programming Director
Darrin Johnston, News Director
Bucks Braun, Morning Host
Megan Brugger, Traffic Manager

WZLR
03-03-1967; 95.3 mhz FM *Hrs Open:* 24; 6 kw; 322 ft.; N39 37 52 W83 53 39
3773 Howard Hughes Pwy, Suite 300n, Las Vegas, NV 89109 US
(937) 259-2111, *Fax:* (937) 259-2168
953theeagle.com
nick.roberts@cmgohio.com, jennifer.perkins@cmgohio.com
License: Xenia, Greene County, OH held by Cox Radio Inc.
Group Owner: Cox Radio Inc.; (acq 1998; grpsl)
Nat'l Reps: Christal
Arbitron Metro Market: Xenia, OH *Format:* Contemporary Hits/Top 40, Adult Contemp *Target Audience:* 25-54.
Donna Hall, Operations Dir
Kathy Eagle-Norris, General Sales Mgr
Nick Roberts, Programming Director
Jennifer Perkins, Promotions Manager

Yellow Springs

*WYSO
02-08-1958; 91.3 mhz FM *Hrs Open:* 24; 50 kw horiz, 45.85 kw vert; 400 ft.; N39 45 46 W83 52 59
795 Livermore Street, Yellow Springs, OH 45387 US
(937) 767-6420, *Fax:* (937) 769-1382
www.wyso.org
wyso@wyso.org
License: Yellow Springs, Greene County, OH held by Antioch University.
Nat'l Network: PRI; NPR *Regional Network:* Ohio Educ. Telecommunications
Arbitron Metro Market: Yellow Springs, OH *Format:* News, Triple A *Special Programming:* Folk 2 hrs, jazz 12 hrs, blues 4 hrs, new age 4 hr *Hrs. of News Programming:* news progmg 77 hrs wkly *No. News Employees:* 2*Target Audience:* 25-54; college educated, professional, mid-upper income *Adv. Rates:* 45; 30; 35; 20
Tom Faecke, CFO
Paul Maassen, General Manager
Jacki Mayer, General Sales Mgr

Youngstown

WNCD
06-01-1959; 93.3 mhz FM; 50 kw; 279 ft.; N41 4 50 W80 38 54
7621 Little Ave., Charlotte, NC 28226 US
(306) 236-6494, *Fax:* (306) 236-6141
License: Youngstown, Mahoning County, OH held by Citicasters Licenses LP
Group Owner: Clear Channel Communications Inc.
Arbitron Metro Market: Eugene-Springfield OR
Jim Hamm, General Manager

WBBW
02-20-1949; 1240 khz AM; 1 kw-U, ND1; N41 4 50 W80 38 54
4040 Simon Road, Youngstown, OH 44512 US
(864) 476-7184, *Fax:* (864) 476-0474
License: Youngstown, OH held by Cumulus Licensing Corp.
Group Owner: Cumulus Media Inc.; (acq 3-15-00; grpsl).
Nat'l Network: Westwood One
Arbitron Metro Market: Elko NV *Format:* Religious
T.C. Lewis, General Manager

WASN
05-09-1976; 1500 khz AM *Hrs Open:* Sunrise-sunset; 0.25 kw-C, DAD; 0.5 kw-D, DAD; N41 6 26 W80 34 57
34 Federal Plaza West, Suite 1200, Wick Bldg, Youngstown, OH 44503 US
(330) 744-5115, *Fax:* (330) 744-4020
www.1500wasn.com
Derrick@ytownradio.com
License: Youngstown, OH held by Bernard of Ohio LLC.
Group Owner: Bernard Radio LLC; (acq 1-22-2007; grpsl)
Nat'l Network: CNN Radio
Arbitron Metro Market: Youngstown-Warren, OH *Format:* News, Talk *Hrs. of News Programming:* News progmg 4 hrs wkly *Target Audience:* General; families
Skip Bednarczyk, General Manager
Derrick McKinney, Sales Associate
Savannah Thomas, Sales Associate
Jammin Janay, Sales Associate
Skip Bednarczyk, Sales Associate

WHOT-FM
11-01-1959; 101.1 mhz FM; 24 kw; Ant 711 ft; N41 03 28 W80 38 24
4040 Simon Rd., Youngstown, OH 44512
(330) 783-1000, *Fax:* (330) 783-0060
www.hot101.com
License: Youngstown, Mahoning County, OH held by Cumulus Media
Arbitron Metro Market: Youngstown-Warren, OH *Target Audience:* 18-54.
Lewis Dirkey, President
Rick Parrish, General Manager
Brad Marshall, General Sales Mgr
Joe Dobbins, Programming Director
Leah Brenner, Promotions Manager
Kelly Stevens, News Director
Rick Foley, Engineering Dir
Wes Boyd, ChiefEngineer

WKBN
01-01-1926; 570 khz AM *Hrs Open:* 24
Mailing Address: 200 Concord Plaza, Suite 600, San Antonio, TX 78216 US
Second Address: 7461 South Ave., Boardman, OH 44512
(330) 965-0057, *Fax:* (330) 965-8277
www.570wkbn.com
danrivers@clearchannel.com
License: Youngstown, OH held by Citicasters Licenses L.P.
Group Owner: Clear Channel Communications Inc.; (acq 1-22-99; $11 million with co-located FM).
Nat'l Network: ABC; CBS
Arbitron Metro Market: Youngstown-Warren, OH *Format:* News, News/Talk, 84, Talk *Special Programming:* Polka 2 hrs, Croation 2 hrs wkly
Bill Kelly, Operations Dir
Dan Rivers, Programming Director
Jim Michaels, News Director

WMXY
08-26-1947; 98.9 mhz FM; 5.9 kw; 1371 ft.; N41 3 24 W80 38 44
200 Concord Plaza, Suite 600, San Antonio, TX 78216 US
(330) 729-2576, *Fax:* (330) 729-9991
www.mix989.com
stevegranato@clearchannel.com
License: Youngstown, Mahoning County, OH held by Citicasters Licenses L.P.
Group Owner: Clear Channel Communications Inc.
Arbitron Metro Market: Youngstown-Warren, OH *Format:* Adult Contemp
Steve Granato, Programming Director

WNIO
09-07-1939; 1390 khz AM *Hrs Open:* 24
7621 Little Ave., Ste 505, Charlotte, NC 28226 US
(330) 729-2565, *Fax:* (330) 729-9991
www.wnio.com
info@wnio.com
License: Youngstown, OH held by Citicasters Licenses L.P.
Group Owner: Clear Channel Communications Inc.; (acq 1-15-2004; grpsl).
Arbitron Metro Market: Youngstown-Warr *Format:* Oldies *Special Programming:* It 3 hrs wkly *Hrs. of News Programming:* news progmg 3 hrs wkly *No. News Employees:* 2 *Target Audience:* General.
Bill Kelly, General Manager
Karl Brandt, General Sales Mgr
Mark French, Programming Director
Dan Rivers, Advertising Director

*WYSU
09-01-1969; 88.5 mhz FM *Hrs Open:* 24; 50 kw; 376 ft.; N41 3 23.2 W80 38 43.7
410 Wick Avenue, Youngstown, OH 44555 US

(330) 941-3363, *Fax:* (330) 941-1501
www.wysu.org
info@wysu.org
License: Youngstown, Mahoning County, OH held by Youngstown State University.
Nat'l Network: PRI; NPR
Arbitron Metro Market: Youngstown-Warr *Format:* News *Special Programming:* Folk 3 hrs wkly *Hrs. of News Programming:* News progmg 48 hrs wkly *Target Audience:* General. *Adv. Rates:* 18; 13.75; 18; 8.25
David Luscher, Operations Dir
Gary Sexton, General Manager
Ron Krauss, Chief Engineer

***WYTN**
05-01-1991; 91.7 mhz FM *Hrs Open:* 24; 0.9 kw; 594 ft.; N41 3 28 W80 38 42
Mailing Address: 4135 Northgate Blvd, Suite 1, Sacramento, CA 95834 US
Second Address: 3930 Sunset Blvd., Youngstown, OH 60435
(815) 725-1331
www.familyradio.com
License: Youngstown, Mahoning County, OH held by Family Stations Inc.
Group Owner: Family Stations Inc.
Arbitron Metro Market: Youngstown-Warr *Format:* Religious *Special Programming:* Class 2 hrs wkly *Target Audience:* 25 plus; Christians
Harold Camping, President
John Rorvik, General Manager

Zanesville

***WJIC**
01-01-2000; 91.7 mhz FM *Hrs Open:* 24; 6 kw; 318 ft.; N39 58 2 W82 12 49
Dba Riverside Ministries, 2620 South River Road, Zanesville, OH 43701 US
(414) 935-3000, *Fax:* (414) 935-3015
www.wcyamerica.org
wjic@vcyamerica.org
License: Zanesville, Muskingum County, OH held by VCY/America Inc.
Group Owner: VCY America Inc.
Nat'l Network: USA
Format: Christian, Religious
Vic Eliason, General Manager
Jim Schneider, Programming Director
Andy Eliason, Chief Engineer

***WOUZ-FM**
11-01-1993; 90.1 mhz FM *Hrs Open:* 24; 3 kw vert; 279 ft.; N39 48 50 W81 57 21 *Rebroadcasts:* Rebroadcasts WOUB-FM Athens 100%
9 South College Street, Athens, OH 45701 US
(740) 593-4554, *Fax:* (740) 593-0240
www.woub.org
woub@woub.org
License: Zanesville, Muskingum County, OH held by Ohio University.
Format: News, News/Talk, 86 *No. News Employees:* 3
Carolyn Lewis, General Manager

Oklahoma

Ada

KADA
09-01-1934; 1230 khz AM; 1 kw-U, ND1; N34 47 6 W96 40 44
Mailing Address: PO Box 609, Ada, OK 74820 US
Second Address: 1019 N. Broadway, Ada, OK 74820
(580) 332-1212, *Fax:* (580) 332-0128
www.kadaradio.net
kada@cable1.net
License: Ada, OK held by The Chickasaw Nation.
Group Owner: The Chickasaw Nation
Regional Network: Okla. News Net.
Arbitron Metro Market: Ada, OK *Format:* Sports *Special Programming:* Gospel 5 hrs wkly *Target Audience:* 25-54.
Roger Harris, General Manager

KADA-FM
01-01-1979; 99.3 mhz FM; 5.5 kw; 276 ft.; N34 42 31 W96 44 24
PO Box 609, Ada, OK 74820 US
(580) 332-1212, *Fax:* (580) 332-0128
www.kadaradio.net
kada@cable1.net
License: Ada, Pontotoc County, OK held by The Chickasaw Nation
Group Owner: The Chickasaw Nation; (acq 7-88)
Arbitron Metro Market: Ada, OK *Format:* Country *Adv. Rates:* 15; 15; 15; 15
Roger Harris, Promotions Manager

***KCNP**
01-01-1999; 89.5 mhz FM *Hrs Open:* 24; 5.8 kw; 581 ft.; N34 41 1 W96 45 44
Route 5, Box 119, Ada, OK 74820 US
(580) 436-2603, *Fax:* (580)272-5267
www.kcnpradio.org/index.htm
License: Ada, Pontotoc County, OK held by The Chickasaw Nation.
Group Owner: The Chickasaw Nation; (acq 9-24-2008; $470,000)
Arbitron Metro Market: Ada, OK
Brian Brashier, General Manager

***KAJT**
01-01-2006; 88.7 mhz FM *Hrs Open:* 24; 31 kw; 240 ft.; N34 46 32 W96 35 15
Mailing Address: P O Drawer 2440, Tupelo, MS 38803 US
Second Address: 8919 World Ministry Ave., Baton Rouge, LA 70810
(225) 768-3288, *Fax:* (225) 768-3729
www.jsm.org
onair@jsm.org
License: Ada, Pontotoc County, OK held by Family Worship Center Church Inc.
Group Owner: Family Worship Center Church Inc.; (acq 10-7-2005; $500,000 with CP for KSSO(FM) Norman)
Arbitron Metro Market: Ada, OK *Format:* Gospel
David Whitelaw, COO
Van Michael, President
John Santiago, Programming Director

***KAKO**
01-01-2006; 91.3 mhz FM; 100 kw vert; 442 ft.; N35 13 36 W96 55 42
P O Drawer 2440, Tupelo, MS 38803 US
(662) 844-8888, *Fax:* (662) 842-6791
www.afa.net
License: Ada, Pontotoc County, OK held by American Family Association.
Group Owner: American Family Radio
Nat'l Network: American Family Radio
Arbitron Metro Market: Ada, OK *Format:* Christian
Marvin Sanders, General Manager

Altus

KEYB
12-25-1988; 107.9 mhz FM *Hrs Open:* 24; 50 kw; 492 ft.; N34 46 15 W99 32 20
Mailing Address: P.O. Box 1077, Altus, OK 73522 US
Second Address: 808 N. Main St., Altus, OK 73521
(580) 482-1555, *Fax:* (580) 482-8353
www.keyb.net
keyb@keyb.net
License: Altus, Jackson County, OK held by Altus FM Inc.
Group Owner: Altus FM Inc.; (acq 2-5-91;
Nat'l Network: Westwood One; AP Network News
Arbitron Metro Market: Altus, OK *Format:* Country *Special Programming:* Farm 2 hrs wkly *Hrs. of News Programming:* news progmg 3 hrs wkly *No. News Employees:* 1 *Target Audience:* 25-54.
Gayle Ledbetter, CEO
Sam Schroeder, Programming Director
Tracie Tobitt, News Director
Richard Bustos, Engineering Dir

***KKVO**
01-01-1985; 90.9 mhz FM *Hrs Open:* 24; 4 kw; 820 ft.; N34 58 39 W99 24 35
P.O. Box 837, Altus, OK 73522 US
(916) 251-1600, *Fax:* (916) 251-1650
www.klove.com
License: Altus, Jackson County, OK held by Educational Media Foundation.
Group Owner: EMF Broadcasting; (acq 6-6-2005; $150,000)
Nat'l Network: K-Love
Arbitron Metro Market: Sacramento, CA *Format:* Christian
Darrell Chambliss, Chairman
Mike Novak, CEO
Mike Novak, President
Alan Mason, Operations Dir
Eric Moser, General Sales Mgr
David Pierce, Programming Director
Ed Lenane, News Director
Sam Wallington, Engineering Dir
ScottSmith, Music Director
Marya Morgan, News Reporter
Scott Smith, News Reporter
Richard Hunt, Regional Manager
Evan Falat, Traffic Manager

KWHW-FM
04-01-1974; 93.5 mhz FM; 45 kw; Ant 528 ft; N34 37 35 W99 20 10
Mailing Address: Box 577, Altus, OK 73522
Second Address: 212 W. Cypress, Altus, OK 73522
(580) 482-1450, *Fax:* (580) 482-3420
mward@kwhw.com
License: Altus, Jackson County, OK
Population Served: 50,000
Lisa Korry Cheek, General Manager

KWHW
04-02-1947; 1450 khz AM
Mailing Address: P. O. Box 577, Altus, OK 73522 US
Second Address: 212 W. Cypress, Altus, OK 73522
(580) 482-1450, *Fax:* (580) 482-3420
www.kwhw.com
mward@kwhw.com
License: Altus, OK held by Monarch Broadcasting Inc.
Group Owner: Monarch Broadcasting Inc.; (acq 12-31-2003; grpsl)
Regional Network: Okla. News Net.
Arbitron Metro Market: Altus, OK *Format:* Agriculture, News, 62, Talk, Country *Special Programming:* Sp 16 hrs wkly
Jimmy Young, General Manager

***KOCU**
07-01-2002; 90.1 mhz FM; 5 kw; 85 ft.; N34 40 14 W99 20 13
Rebroadcasts: Rebroadcasts KCCU(FM) Lawton 100%
2800 West Gore, Lawton, OK 73505 US
(580) 581-2472, *Fax:* (580) 581-5571
www.kccu.org
kccu@cameron.edu
License: Altus, Jackson County, OK held by Cameron University.
Nat'l Network: NPR; PRI
Arbitron Metro Market: Lawton, OK *Format:* Classical, News
Ted Riley, General Manager, Director of Broadcasting
Doug Cole, Station Manager & Operations Director
Clinton Wieden, News Director
Cynthia Sosa, Production Director
Zach McGrew, Development Director

***KTHL**
89.3 mhz FM; 1.5 kw; 253 ft.; N34 38 21 W99 21 19
US
(580) 767-1400, *Fax:* (580) 765-1700
www.thehousefm.com
mail@thehousefm.com
License: Altus, Jackson County, OK held by The Love Station Inc.
Arbitron Metro Market: Altus, OK
Doyle Brewer, CEO/COO
Tony Weir, Music Director
Janelle Keith, Music Director
Darcey Christianson, Chief Engineer
Shaun Michaels, Production Director
Andy Youso, Assistant Program Director
Donna Hollifield, Office Manager

Alva

KALV
10-18-1956; 1430 khz AM *Hrs Open:* 24; 0.5 kw-D, DA2; 0.5 kw-N, DA2; N36 49 6 W98 38 38
Rt 1, Box 53, Alva, OK 73117 US
(405) 327-1430, *Fax:* (405) 327-1433
kalvradio@yahoo.com
License: Alva, OK held by MM&K of Alva Inc.
Arbitron Metro Market: Alva, OK *Format:* Oldies *Hrs. of News Programming:* news progmg 8 hrs wkly *No. News Employees:* 1 *Target Audience:* 45-70; loc residents
Randy Mitchel, President

KPAK
97.5 mhz FM; 50 kw; 492 ft.; N37 1 27 W98 41 22
188 South Bellevue#222, Memphis, TN 38104 US
(888) 251-8427, *Fax:* (620) 825-4324
www.kpak.net
License: Alva, Woods County, OK held by George S. Flinn Jr.
Arbitron Metro Market: Kiowa, KS *Format:* Alternative
George Flinn Jr., President

Anadarko

KVSP
09-01-1981; 103.5 mhz FM *Hrs Open:* 24; 100 kw; 1969 ft.; N35 15 4 W98 36 53
115 West Broadway, PO Box 1360, Anadarko, OK 73005 US

(405) 427-5877, *Fax:* (405) 424-8811
www.kvsp.com ??
rmperry@kvsp.com
License: Anadarko, Oklahoma County, OK held by Perry Broadcasting of Southwest Oklahoma Inc.
Group Owner: Perry Publishing & Broadcasting Co.; (acq 11-22-2002; grpsl).
Nat'l Network: ABC
Arbitron Metro Market: OK City area, rural areas west of OK
Format: Urban Contemporary *Target Audience:* 18 plus.
Russell Perry, Operations Dir
Kevin Perry, General Manager

Antlers

KDOE
01-01-2006; 102.3 mhz FM; 3.3 kw; 276 ft.; N34 13 35 W95 37 20
US
(580) 326-5541, *Fax:* (580) 326-5236
www.kdoe1023.com
License: Antlers, Pushmataha County, OK held by Will Payne.
Arbitron Metro Market: Antlers, OK *Format:* Variety/Diverse
Will Payne, General Manager

Apache

KACO
01-01-1989; 98.5 mhz FM *Hrs Open:* 24; 18.5 kw; 305 ft.; N34 56 30 W98 22 33
5946 Club Oaks Drive, Dallas, TX 75248 US
(405) 247-6682, *Fax:* (405) 247-1051
www.superstarcountry985.com
joyc@kjmz.com
License: Apache, Caddo County, OK held by Perry Publishing & Broadcasting
Group Owner: Perry Publishing & Broadcasting Co.; (acq 1-5-98; $475,000).
Nat'l Network: ABC
Arbitron Metro Market: Anadarko, OK *Format:* Country *Target Audience:* 25-54.
Kevin Perry, Operations Dir
Joy Chapman, General Manager
Terry Monday, Programming Director
Mark Edwards, News Director
Russell Perry, Operations Manager

Ardmore

*KLCU
06-19-1998; 90.3 mhz FM; 25 kw; 213 ft.; N34 12 10 W97 9 12
Rebroadcasts: Rebroadcasts KCCU(FM) Lawton 98%
2800 W Gore Blvd., Lawton, OK 73505 US
(580) 581-2425, *Fax:* (580) 581-5571
www.kccu.org
kccu@cameron.edu
License: Ardmore, Carter County, OK held by Cameron University.
Nat'l Network: NPR; PRI
Arbitron Metro Market: Lawton, OK *Format:* Classical
Ted Riley, General Manager
Terry Anderson, General Sales Mgr
Michael Leal, Programming Director

KVSO
09-01-1935; 1240 khz AM *Hrs Open:* 24; 1 kw-U, ND1; N34 10 54 W97 8 48
P.O. Box 429, Ardmore, OK 73402 US
(580) 226-0421, *Fax:* (580) 226-0464
www.kvso.com
webmaster@kvso.com
License: Ardmore, OK held by LKCM Radio Group L.P.
Group Owner: LKCM Radio Group L.P.
Nat'l Reps: Christal
Arbitron Metro Market: Ardmore, OK *Format:* Christian *Hrs. of News Programming:* news progmg 4 hrs wkly *No. News Employees:* 1 *Target Audience:* 25 plus.
Michael Baer, General Manager

*KQPD
01-01-2003; 91.1 mhz FM; 0.25 kw; 167 ft.; N34 11 1 W97 7 23
P.O. Drawer 2440, Tupelo, MS 38803 US
(662) 844-8888, *Fax:* (662) 842-6791
www.afa.net
faq@afr.net
License: Ardmore, Carter County, OK held by American Family Association.
Group Owner: American Family Radio
Arbitron Metro Market: Tupelo, MS *Format:* Christian
Marvin Sanders, General Manager

Atoka

KHKC-FM
06-15-1984; 102.1 mhz FM; 0.75 kw; 449 ft.; N34 25 8 W96 11 24
Mailing Address: 4410 10th Street, Lubbock, TX 79476 US
Second Address: Hwy. 75 N., Atoka, OK 74525
(580) 226-9797, *Fax:* (580) 889-9308
www.khkc1021.com
khkc103@yahoo.com
License: Atoka, Atoka County, OK held by Keystone Broadcasting Corp.
Format: Country *Target Audience:* Adults *Adv. Rates:* 5; 5; 5; na
Ricky Chase, General Manager

Bartlesville

KWON
04-01-1942; 1400 khz AM *Hrs Open:* 24; 1 kw-U, ND1; N36 45 53 W95 57 35
Mailing Address: 1200 S.E. Frank Phillips, Bartlesville, OR 74005 US
Second Address: 1200 S.E. Frank Phillips Blvd., Bartlesville, OK 74003
(918) 336-1001, *Fax:* (918) 336-6939
www.bartlesvilleradio.com
radio@bartlesvilleradio.com
License: Bartlesville, OK held by KCD Enterprises Inc.
Group Owner: KCD Enterprises Inc.; acq 2-1-97; $625,000 with co-located FM)
Nat'l Network: CBS *Regional Network:* Okla. News Net. *Regional Reps:* Rgnl Reps *Wire Services:* AP
Arbitron Metro Market: Bartlesville, OK *Format:* News, News/Talk, 86 *Special Programming:* Relg 5 hrs wkly *Hrs. of News Programming:* news progmg 25 hrs wkly *No. News Employees:* 2 *Target Audience:* 25-54;general *Adv. Rates:* 22; 22; 20; 22
Kevin Potter, President and General Manager
Charlie Taraboletti, Operations Dir
Tami Brinkman, General Sales Mgr
Dorea Potter, Promotions Manager
Sharon Frahm, Production
Joy West, Office Manager and Traffic and Biling
MikeSauter, Announcer and Website News
David Crawford, Sports Director
Phil Weaver, Music and Fun
Adam Hooper, Sports and News

KYFM
11-06-1961; 100.1 mhz FM *Hrs Open:* 24; 25 kw; Ant 695 ft; N36 37 42 W96 11 26
Mailing Address: Box 1100, Bartlesville, OK 74005
Second Address: 1200 S.E. Frank Phillips Blvd., Bartlesville, OK 74003
(918) 336-1001, *Fax:* (918) 336_6939
www.bartlesvilleradio.com
License: Bartlesville, Washington County, OK held by KCD Enterprises Inc.
Group Owner: KCD Enterprises Inc.
Nat'l Network: ABC *Regional Network:* Agri-Net *Regional Reps:* Rgnl Reps *Wire Services:* AP
Population Served: 720,000*Special Programming:* Gospel 4 hrs wkly *Hrs. of News Programming:* News progmg 15 hrs wkly *Target Audience:* 25-49. *Adv. Rates:* 22; 22; 22; 22
Kevin Potter, CEO
Charlie Taraboletti, Operations Dir
Kevin Potter, GM/President
Tami Brinkman, General Sales Mgr
David Crawford, Programming Director
Dorsa Potter, Promotions Manager
Mike Sauter, News Director
Sharon Frahm,Traffic Manager

*KWRI
01-01-2004; 89.1 mhz FM *Hrs Open:* 24; 100 kw vert; 627 ft.; N36 42 13 W95 30 57
1425 N. Market Blvd., Suite 9, Sacramento, CA 95834 US
(888) 937-2471, *Fax:* (916) 251-1650
www.air1.com
info@air1.com
License: Bartlesville, Washington County, OK held by Educational Media Foundation.
Group Owner: EMF Broadcasting
Nat'l Network: Air 1
Arbitron Metro Market: Tulsa, OK *Format:* Alternative, Christian *No. News Employees:* 3 *Target Audience:* 18-35; Judeo-Christian, female
Darrell Chambliss, Chairman
Alan Mason, COO
Mike Novak, President and CEO
David Pierce, Programming Director
Ed Lenane, News Director
Sam Wallington, Engineering Dir
Marya Morgan, News Reporter
Richard Hunt, News Reporter
Larry Moody, Director
Mitch Barnhart, Director
David R. Ferry, Director
Walter Golembeski, Director

Beaver

*KLXO
91.9 mhz FM; 0.1 kw horiz; -72 ft.; N36 49 3 W100 31 36
US
(405) 380-3516
www.bpba.us
info@bpba.us
License: Beaver, Beaver County, OK held by Better Public Broadcasting Association.
Arbitron Metro Market: Beaver, OK
Dennis Burton, General Manager

Bennington

KZRC
11-01-1979; 96.1 mhz FM *Hrs Open:* 5 AM-1 AM; 6 kw; 328 ft.; N33 53 51 W96 8 18
5946 Club Oaks Dr., Dallas, TX 75248 US
(979) 323-7771, *Fax:* (708) 671-1202
info@kfyzfm.com
License: Bennington, Bryan County, OK held by North Texas Radio Group L.P.
Arbitron Metro Market: Dallas, TX
Richard Witkovski, General Manager

Bethany

KKWD
10-29-1965; 104.9 mhz FM *Hrs Open:* 24; 6 kw; 328 ft.; N35 29 53 W97 37 10
518 17th Street, Suite 980, Denver, CO 80202 US
(405) 848-0100, *Fax:* (405) 843-5288
www.wild1049hd.com
info@wild1049hd.com
License: Bethany, Oklahoma County, OK held by The Last Bastion Station Trust LLC, as Trustee
Arbitron Metro Market: Oklahoma City, OK *Format:* Adult Contemp *Target Audience:* 35-49 & 25-34; young, professional
Larry Bastida, General Manager
Joe Jeldy, Station Manager
Chris Baker, Station Manager

Bixby

KJMM
11-01-1994; 105.3 mhz FM *Hrs Open:* 24; 10 kw; 879 ft.; N35 51 41 W95 46 3
1528 NE23rd Street, Oklahoma City, OK 73111 US
(918) 494-9886, *Fax:* (918) 494-9683
www.perry_pub_broadcasting.com
License: Bixby, Tulsa County, OK held by KJMM Inc.
Group Owner: Perry Publishing & Broadcasting Co.; (acq 1-95).
Nat'l Network: ABC; American Urban; Westwood One
Arbitron Metro Market: Tulsa, OK *Format:* Urban Contemporary *Hrs. of News Programming:* news progmg 10 hrs wkly *No. News Employees:* 1 *Target Audience:* 18-35; General
Russell Perry, CEO
Martha Vaughn, General Manager

Blackwell

KOKB
10-01-1952; 1580 khz AM *Hrs Open:* 6 AM-9 PM; 1 kw-D, ND1; 0.049 kw-N, ND1; N36 48 35 W97 15 50 *Rebroadcasts:* Rebroadcasts KOKP(AM) Perry 80%
Mailing Address: P.O. Box 2509, Ponca City, OK 74602 US
Second Address: 122 N. Third St., Ponca City, OK 74602
(580) 765-2485, *Fax:* (580) 767-1103
www.eteamradio.com
kokb@eteamradio.com
License: Blackwell, OK held by Team Radio LLC
Group Owner: Team Radio LLC; acq 10-18-96; $90,000).
Format: Sports, Talk *Hrs. of News Programming:* News progmg 30 hrs wkly *Target Audience:* 35-75; adult, upper-middle income
Bill Coleman, President

Blanchard

KKNG-FM
08-18-1977; 97.3 mhz FM *Hrs Open:* 24; 1 kw; Ant 800 ft; N35 10 38 W97 36 10

5101 S. Shields Blvd., Oklahoma City, OK 73005
(405) 616-5500, *Fax:* (405) 616-5505
www.jackokc.com
License: Blanchard, McClain County, OK held by Nick Radio LLC.
Group Owner: Tyler Media Broadcasting Corp.; (acq 1-31-2006; $1 million).
Nat'l Reps: D & R Radio
Population Served: 100,000 *Arbitron Metro Market:* Oklahoma City, OK
Skip Stow, CEO
Becca Sharp, Station Manager

Boise City

*KJHL
01-01-2009; 90.9 mhz FM; 10 kw; 351 ft.; N36 44 5 W102 29 53 US
(620) 873-2991, *Fax:* (620) 873-2755
www.kjil.com
kjil@kjil.com
License: Boise City, Cimarron County, OK held by Great Plains Christian Radio Inc.
Arbitron Metro Market: Boise City, OK *Format:* Christian, Religious *No. News Employees:* 1
Robert Hughes, CEO
Michael Luskey, CEO
Glenn Hascall, Station Manager
Bill Lurwick, Music Director
Delvin Kinser, News Director

Bristow

KREK
11-14-1978; 104.9 mhz FM *Hrs Open:* 24; 5 kw; 351 ft.; N35 47 11 W96 27 35
P.O. Box 1280, Bristow, OK 74010 US
(918) 367-5501, *Fax:* (918) 367-5502
krekfm@yahoo.com
License: Bristow, Creek County, OK held by Big Chief Broadcasting Co. of Bristow Inc.
Arbitron Metro Market: Tulsa, OK *Format:* Country *Target Audience:* 0-100.
Clifford Smith, President

Broken Arrow

*KNYD
08-19-1986; 90.5 mhz FM *Hrs Open:* 24; 80 kw; 1483 ft.; N35 53 0 W95 46 13
Mailing Address: 11717 S 129th East Ave., Broken Arrow, OK 74011 US
Second Address: 11717 S. 129th East Ave., Broken Arrow, OK 74011
(918) 455-5693, *Fax:* (918) 455-0411
www.oasisnetwork.org
mail@oasisnetwork.org
License: Broken Arrow, Tulsa County, OK held by Creative Educational Media Inc.
Arbitron Metro Market: Tulsa, OK *Format:* Religious *Target Audience:* General.
David Ingles, President

KTBT
12-23-1970; 92.1 mhz FM *Hrs Open:* 24; 27 kw; 656 ft.; N36 6 38 W96 1 57
200 Concord Plaza, Suite 600, San Antonio, TX 78216 US
(918) 388-5100, *Fax:* (918)388-5400
www.921thebeat.com
License: Broken Arrow, Tulsa County, OK held by Clear Channel Broadcasting Licenses Inc.
Group Owner: Clear Channel Communications Inc.
Nat'l Reps: Clear Channel
Arbitron Metro Market: Tulsa, OK *Format:* Contemporary Hits/Top 40 *Target Audience:* 18-34; women
Don Cristi, Operations Dir
Michael Oppenheimer, General Manager

Broken Bow

KKBI
01-01-1983; 106.1 mhz FM *Hrs Open:* 24; 17 kw; 817 ft.; N34 14 45 W94 46 58
103 Hastings Court, Idabel, OK 74745 US
(580) 584-3388, *Fax:* (580) 584-3341
www.kkbifm.com
kkbi@pine-net.com
License: Broken Bow, McCurtain County, OK held by J.D.C. Radio Inc.
Nat'l Network: Jones Radio Networks *Wire Services:* CNN
Arbitron Metro Market: Texarkana, TX *Format:* Country *Special Programming:* Farm 5 hrs, gospel 4 hrs wkly *Hrs. of News Programming:* news progmg 5 hrs wkly *No. News Employees:* 1
Target Audience: 24-55.*Adv. Rates:* 14; 14; 14; 12
David Smulyan, General Manager
Jay Lindley, Programming Director

*KBWW
88.3 mhz FM; 3.4 kw; 689 ft.; N34 12 31 W94 46 58 US
(580) 420-6687
License: Broken Bow, McCurtain County, OK held by Golden Baptist Church.
Arbitron Metro Market: Golden, OK
Ron Carroll, General Manager

Byng

KYKC
09-17-1992; 100.1 mhz FM *Hrs Open:* 24; 50 kw; 492 ft; N34 43 43 W96 42 45
Mailing Address: Box 609, Ada, OK 74820
Second Address: 1019 N. Broadway, Ada, OK 74820
(580) 436-1616, *Fax:* (580) 436-1617
www.kykc.net
kykc@cableone.net
License: Byng, Pontotoc County, OK held by The Chickasaw Nation.
Group Owner: The Chickasaw Nation; (acq 1-14-2005; $900,000).
Target Audience: 12 plus; across the board *Adv. Rates:* 12; 10; 12; 6
Roger Harris, General Manager
Pete Roper, General Sales Mgr
Mike Manos, Programming Director

Cache

KJMZ
10-23-1970; 97.9 mhz FM *Hrs Open:* 24; 6 kw; 318 ft.; N34 35 30.5 W98 32 54.5
1528 N.E. 23rd, Oklahoma City, OK 73111 US
(580) 355-1050, *Fax:* (580) 355-1056
www.kjmz.com
spots@kjmz.com
License: Cache, Comanche County, OK held by Perry Broadcasting of Lawton Inc.
Group Owner: Perry Publishing & Broadcasting Co.
Arbitron Metro Market: Lawton, OK *Format:* Oldies
Tony Foster, Programming Director

*KARU
01-01-2005; 88.9 mhz FM *Hrs Open:* 24; 0.44 kw vert; 259 ft.; N34 38 10 W98 41 32 US
(888) 937-2471, *Fax:* (916) 251-1650
www.air1.com
info@air1.com
License: Cache, Comanche County, OK held by Educational Media Foundation.
Group Owner: EMF Broadcasting
Nat'l Network: Air 1
Arbitron Metro Market: Cache, OK *Format:* Alternative, Christian *No. News Employees:* 3 *Target Audience:* 18-35; Judeo-Christian, female
Darrell Chambliss, Chairman
Alan Mason, COO
Mike Novak, President and CEO
Evan Falat, Operations Dir
Eric Allen, General Sales Mgr
Ed Lenane, News Director
Sam Wallington, Engineering Dir
Paul Goldsmith, Music Director
LarryMoody, Director
Mitch Barnhart, Director
David R. Ferry, Director
Walter Golembeski, Director
David Pierce, Chief Creative Officer

Carnegie

*KJCC
01-01-2005; 89.5 mhz FM; 0.35 kw vert; 194 ft.; N35 6 59 W98 28 26
Mailing Address: US
Second Address: 300 Towakkonie Rd., Fort Cobb, OK 73038
(800) 357-4226, *Fax:* (208) 736-1958
www.csnradio.com
csn@csnradio.com
License: Carnegie, Caddo County, OK held by CSN International
Group Owner: CSN International
Arbitron Metro Market: Carnegie, OK *Format:* Christian
Mike Kestler, President
Daniel Davidson, Operations Dir
Leanna Farmer, Station Manager
Don Mills, Network Programming Director / Music Director
Kelly Carlson, Engineering Dir
Jerry Johnson, Engineering Dir
Ray Gorney, AssistantDirector of Engineering
Dustin Pamplona, Engineer
Nolan Mather, Graphics / Website Maintenance
Mike Stocklin, National Underwriting
Austin Morris, Accounting
Lois Mills, FCC Applications / Translator Site Manager

Catoosa

KEOR
01-29-1968; 1120 khz AM *Hrs Open:* Sunrise-sunset
P. O. Box 68, Atoka, OK 74525 US
(580) 889-3392, *Fax:* (580) 889-9308
info@dioceseoftula.org
License: Catoosa, OK held by Catholic Diocese of Tulsa
Arbitron Metro Market: Tulsa, OK *Target Audience:* General.
Edward Slattery, CEO

KZLI
07-03-1950; 1570 khz AM *Hrs Open:* Daytime
P.O. Box 1270, Tulsa, OK 74101 US
(918) 496-7700, *Fax:* (918) 746-7615
License: Catoosa, OK held by Reunion Broadcasting L.L.C.
Regional Network: Okla. News Net.
Arbitron Metro Market: Tulsa, OK *Format:* Adult Contemp *Hrs. of News Programming:* news progmg 10 hrs wkly *No. News Employees:* 1 *Target Audience:* 35 plus. *Adv. Rates:* 30; 30; 30;
Stan Tacker, General Manager
Terri Tacker, General Sales Mgr

Chelsea

KTFR
03-01-2001; 100.7 mhz FM *Hrs Open:* 24; 6 kw; 328 ft.; N36 30 12 W95 26 29 *Rebroadcasts:* Rebroadcasts KXOJ-FM Sapulpa
P.O. Box 1250, Sapulpa, OK 74067 US
(918) 492-2660, *Fax:* (918) 492-8840
www.kxoj.com
kxoj@kxoj.com
License: Chelsea, Rogers County, OK held by Michael P. Stephens.
Group Owner: Adonai Radio Group; (acq 2-17-95;
Arbitron Metro Market: Tulsa, OK *Format:* Christian
Mike Stephens, President
David Stephens, General Manager
Bob Thornton, Programming Director

Chickasha

KWCO-FM
11-04-1966; 105.5 mhz FM *Hrs Open:* 24; 3.3 kw; 443 ft; N35 00 38 W97 55 54
627 West Chickasha Ave., Oklahoma City, OK 73129
(405) 224-9105, *Fax:* (405) 224-2890
www.ktuz.com
License: Chickasha, Grady County, OK held by Molmon Communications Inc.
Nat'l Network: Jones Radio Networks
Population Served: 100,000 *Arbitron Metro Market:* Oklahoma City, *Hrs. of News Programming:* News progmg 10 hrs wkly
Target Audience: 18-54; Spanish persons *Adv. Rates:* 18; 15; 14.50; 10
Matthew Mollman, General Manager
Bruce McGreen, Programming Director
George Plummer, News Director
Patrick Roberts, Chief Engineer

*KFXU
01-01-2008; 90.5 mhz FM; 10 kw; 322 ft.; N34 54 33 W97 57 29
1101 81 Highway North, Marlow, OK 73055 US
(580) 658-9292
kfxi@cableone.net
License: Chickasha, Grady County, OK held by Sister Sherry Lynn Foundation Inc.
Arbitron Metro Market: Tulsa, OK *Format:* Classic Rock
Ken Austin, General Manager
Sherry Lynn, General Sales Mgr
Jennifer James, Programming Director
James Wilson, Engineering Dir
Steve Michaels, Music Director

Claremore

*KRSC-FM
08-04-1980; 91.3 mhz FM *Hrs Open:* 7 AM-11 PM; 2.2 kw; 364 ft.; N36 19 6 W95 38 18

1701 W.Will Rogers Blvd., Claremore, OK 74017 US
(918) 343-7777(918) 343-7669, *Fax:* (918) 343-7952
www.rsu.edu
sdoyle@rsu.edu
License: Claremore, Rogers County, OK held by Board of Regents of the University of Oklahoma.
Regional Network: Okla. News Net.
Arbitron Metro Market: Claremore, OK *TV Affiliate:* *KRSC-TV affil. *Format:* Alternative *Special Programming:* Folk 5 hrs, jazz 5 hrs, progsv 12 hrs, country 5 hrs wkly *Target Audience:* General; college &community, young & older adults
Steve Doyle, Operations Dir
Cathy Coomer, General Manager

KRVT
01-17-1958; 1270 khz AM *Hrs Open:* 24
P.O. Box 1270, Tulsa, OK 74101 US
(918) 496-7700, *Fax:* (918) 746-7615
www.krvt.com
krvt@krvt.com
License: Claremore, OK held by Reunion Broadcasting L.L.C.
Nat'l Network: CBS Radio
Arbitron Metro Market: Tulsa, OK *Format:* Oldies *Special Programming:* St. Louis Cardinal Baseball *Hrs. of News Programming:* News progmg 4 hrs wkly *Target Audience:* 35 plus; upscale adults *Adv. Rates:* 30; 30; 30; 20
D. Stanley Tacker, President

Cleveland

***KJOG**
91.1 mhz FM; 25 kw vert; 276 ft.; N36 18 47 W96 46 20 US
(864) 297-0216, *Fax:* (864) 297-0344
networkofglory.com
info@networkofglory.org
License: Cleveland, Pawnee County, OK held by Network of Glory Inc.
Arbitron Metro Market: Cleveland, OK
Lola Richey, President

Clinton

KCLI
04-15-1949; 1320 khz AM
5105 South Shields Blvd, Oklahoma City, OK 73129 US
(580) 323-0617, *Fax:* (580) 323-0717
www.newstalkkcli.com
sales@wrightradio.com
License: Clinton, OK held by Wright Broadcasting Systems Inc.
Group Owner: Wright Broadcasting Systems; (acq 9-13-2000; $25,000).
Regional Network: Okla. News Net.
Arbitron Metro Market: Oklahoma city, OK *Format:* News, Talk *Target Audience:* General.
Harold Wright, President and CEO
Todd Brunner, Operations Dir
Harold Wright, General Manager
Heston Wright, Station and Sales Manager
Ray Bagby, Technical Director
Dianna Scott, Office Manager
Amanda Benton, Area SalesManager
Brianna Reherman, Area Sales Manager
John Liddle, Sports Director/Account Executive
Kelli Haan, Account Executive, Websites and Graphics

KWEY-FM
04-09-1978; 95.5 mhz FM *Hrs Open:* 24; 18.5 kw; 828 ft.; N35 26 43 W98 59 19
P.O. Box 587, Weatherford, OK 73096 US
(580) 772-5939, *Fax:* (580) 772-1590
www.kwey.com
sales@wrightradio.com
License: Clinton, Custer County, OK held by Wright Broadcasting Systems Inc.
Group Owner: Wright Broadcasting Systems; (acq 1996; $300,000)
Nat'l Network: ABC *Wire Services:* AP
Format: Country *Hrs. of News Programming:* News progmg 8 hrs wkly *Target Audience:* 18-54; upwardly mobile adults
Harold Wright, CEO
Todd Brunner, Operations Dir
Heston Wright, General Manager
Heston Wright, General Sales Mgr
Vanessa Valli, Programming Director
Mike Smith, News Director
Ray Bagby, Engineering Dir

***KYCU**
09-01-2002; 89.1 mhz FM; 40 kw; 633 ft.; N35 26 40 W98 59 22
Rebroadcasts: Rebroadcasts KCCU(FM) Lawton 100%
US
(888) 454-7800, *Fax:* (580) 581-5571
www.kccu.org
kccu@cameron.edu
License: Clinton, Custer County, OK held by Cameron University.
Nat'l Network: NPR; PRI
Arbitron Metro Market: Lawton, OK *Format:* Classical, News
Ted Riley, General Manager, Director of Broadcasting
Doug Cole, Station Manager
Clinton Wieden, News Director
Cynthia Sosa, Production Director
Zach McGrew, Development Director

Coalgate

KXFC
12-07-2001; 105.5 mhz FM *Hrs Open:* 24; 20 kw; 364 ft.; N34 41 43 W96 23 17
P. O. Box 1016, Broken Bow, OK 74728 US
(580) 332-1212, *Fax:* (580) 332-0128
www.kxfcradio.com
score@cableone.net
License: Coalgate, Coal County, OK held by The Chickasaw Nation.
Group Owner: The Chickasaw Nation; (acq 10-1-2008; $1.5 million with KTLS-FM Holdenville)
Nat'l Network: AP Radio; Jones Radio Networks
Arbitron Metro Market: Coalgate, OK *Format:* Contemporary Hits/Top 40 *Target Audience:* 25+. *Adv. Rates:* 20; 20; 20
Howard Stone, Operations Dir
Rick Woodward, General Manager
Craig Stone, Programming Director
Renae Woodward, News Director

Collinsville

KIZS
06-25-1996; 101.5 mhz FM; 6.2 kw; 656 ft.; N36 20 2 W95 47 8
200 Concord Plaza, Suite 600, San Antonio, TX 78216 US
(918) 388-5100, *Fax:* (918) 388-5400
www.tulsa.lapreciosa.com
License: Collinsville, Tulsa County, OK held by Clear Channel Broadcasting Licenses Inc.
Group Owner: Clear Channel Communications Inc.; (acq 10-6-97; $1.9 million).
Arbitron Metro Market: Tulsa, OK *Target Audience:* 25-54; general
Don Cristi, Operations Dir
Michael Oppenheimer, Station Manager

Comanche

KDDQ
04-01-1982; 105.3 mhz FM *Hrs Open:* 24; 6 kw; 299 ft.; N34 26 12 W97 54 47
Hc-69, Box 11, Kingston, OK 73439 US
(580) 255-1350, *Fax:* (580) 470-9993
www.perrybroadcasting.net/KDDQ/index.html
kken@cableone.net
License: Comanche, Stephens County, OK held by Perry Broadcasting of Southwest Oklahoma Inc.
Group Owner: Perry Publishing & Broadcasting Co.; (acq 1-9-2003; grpsl).
Nat'l Network: ABC
Arbitron Metro Market: Duncan, OK *Format:* Classic Rock
Special Programming: Gospel 2 hrs wkly *Hrs. of News Programming:* news progmg 4 hrs wkly *No. News Employees:* 1
Target Audience: 25-54; females withmid-level income
Joy Chapman, General Manager
Dale Weakley, Chief Engineer

Cordell

KCLI-FM
09-01-1988; 99.3 mhz FM *Hrs Open:* 24; 10.5 kw; 505 ft; N35 26 49 W98 59 17
700 Frisco Ave., Clinton, OK 73401
(580) 772-5939, *Fax:* (580) 323-0717
kcdl.com
sales@wrightradio.com
License: Cordell, Washita County, OK held by Wright Broadcasting Systems Inc.
Group Owner: Wright Broadcasting Systems; (acq 8-30-99; $350,000)
Nat'l Network: ABC; CNN Radio *Regional Network:* Agrinet
Target Audience: General. *Adv. Rates:* 15; 10; 15; 7.50
Harold Wright, CEO
Todd Brunner, Operations Dir
Rob Grogan, Programming Director

Coweta

***KDIM**
02-01-2005; 88.1 mhz FM *Hrs Open:* 24; 0.05 kw horiz, 100 kw vert; 551 ft.; N35 42 24 W96 5 39
Mailing Address: P.O. Box 1924, Tulsa, OK 74101 US
Second Address: 11717 S. 129th E. Ave., Broken Arrow, OK 74011
(918) 455-5693, *Fax:* (918) 455-0411
www.oasisnetwork.org
mail@oasisnetwork.org
License: Coweta, Wagoner County, OK held by Creative Educational Media Corp. Inc.
Arbitron Metro Market: Coweta, OK *Format:* Religious *Target Audience:* General.
David Ingles, President

Cushing

KUSH
01-01-1953; 1600 khz AM; 1 kw-D, ND1; 0.07 kw-N, ND1; N35 59 11.3 W96 42 37
P.O. Box 791, Cushing, OK 74023 US
(918) 225-0922, *Fax:* (918) 225-0925
www.1600kush.com
kush@yahoo.com
License: Cushing, OK held by Cimarron Valley Broadcasters Inc.
Arbitron Metro Market: Cushing, OK *Format:* News, News/Talk, 84, Talk
Evert Rossiter, Chairman
Sean Kelly, General Manager
Joe Manning, Jr, Vice Chairman
Brent Thompson, Executive Director

Davis

KKAJ-FM
06-24-1974; 95.7 mhz FM *Hrs Open:* 24; 100 kw; 449 ft.; N34 5 53 W97 10 54
P.O. Box 429, 1205 Northglen, Ardmore, OK 73402 US
(580) 226-0421, *Fax:* (580) 226-0464
www.kkaj.com
michael@sokradio.com
License: Davis, Carter County, OK held by LKCM Radio Group L.P.
Group Owner: LKCM Radio Group L.P.; (acq 2-26-2007; grpsl)
Format: Country *Hrs. of News Programming:* news progmg 25 hrs wkly *No. News Employees:* 1 *Target Audience:* 18-54. *Adv. Rates:* 36; 34; 36; 32
Dave Hilton, Operations Dir
Michael Baer, General Manager

Del City

KEBC
11-01-1946; 1560 khz AM *Hrs Open:* 24; 1 kw-D, 250 w-N, DA-2; N35 26 26 W97 29 24 (D), N35 26 27 W97 29 24 (N)
5101 S. Shields, Oklahoma City, OK 73023
(405) 616-5500, *Fax:* (405) 616-5551
www.radio.disney.go.com
License: Del City, Oklahoma County, OK held by Oklahoma Land Co. L.L.C.
Group Owner: Tyler Media Broadcasting Corp.; (acq 12-15-2003; $250,000).
Nat'l Network: Radio Disney
Population Served: 45,000 *Arbitron Metro Market:* Oklahoma City, OK *Special Programming:* Loc sports *Hrs. of News Programming:* news progmg 8 hrs wkly *No. News Employees:* 1 *Target Audience:* 18 plus.*Adv. Rates:* 20; 20; 20; 5.
Skip Stow, General Manager

Dickson

KTRX
06-01-2001; 92.7 mhz FM *Hrs Open:* 24; 5.5 kw; 341 ft.; N34 6 56 W97 0 6
P O Box 429, Ardmore, OK 73407 US
(580) 226-0421, *Fax:* (580) 226-0464
www.texomarocks.com
andle@sokradio.com
License: Dickson, Carter County, OK held by LKCM Radio Group L.P.
Group Owner: LKCM Radio Group L.P.; (acq 2-26-2007; grpsl)
Nat'l Network: Jones Radio Networks *Nat'l Reps:* Christal
Arbitron Metro Market: Ardmore, OK *Format:* Classic Rock *Hrs. of News Programming:* news progmg 25 hrs wkly *No. News Employees:* 1 *Target Audience:* 25-54; men
Gerry Schlegel, Operations Dir
Michael Baer, General Manager
Dave Hilton, Operations Manager

Duncan

KPNS
10-31-1947; 1350 khz AM *Hrs Open:* 6 AM-midnight; 0.18 kw-D, ND1; 0.07 kw-N, ND1; N34 30 43 W97 58 5
115 W. Broadway, Anadarko, OK 73005 US
(580) 255-1350, *Fax:* (580) 470-9993
www.perrybroadcasting.net/KPNS
License: Duncan, OK held by Perry Broadcasting of Southwest Oklahoma Inc.
Group Owner: Perry Publishing & Broadcasting Co.; (acq 11-22-02; grpsl).
Arbitron Metro Market: Lawton, OK *Format:* Sports, Talk *Hrs. of News Programming:* news progmg 20 hrs wkly *No. News Employees:* 1 *Target Audience:* General.
Peggy Richardson, Operations Dir
Jay Chapman, General Manager
Joy Chatman, General Sales Mgr
Terry Monday, Programming Director
Mark Edwards, News Director

KKEN
12-31-1975; 97.1 mhz FM; 6 kw; 328 ft.; N34 30 43 W97 58 4
115 W. Broadway, Anadarko, OK 73005 US
(580) 255-1350, *Fax:* (580) 470-9993
www.kickincountry971.com
License: Duncan, Stephens County, OK
Arbitron Metro Market: Lawton, OK *Format:* Country *Target Audience:* 25-54. *Adv. Rates:* 15; 9; 12; 8
Joy Chapman, General Manager
Pam Peck, General Sales Mgr
Terry Monday, Programming Director
Mark Edwards, News Director

Durant

***KAYC**
01-01-2000; 91.1 mhz FM; 0.403 kw; 210 ft.; N34 1 17 W96 28 18
P O Drawer 2440, Tupelo, MS 38803 US
(662) 844-8888, *Fax:* (662) 842-6791
www.afr.net
comments@afr.net
License: Durant, Bryan County, OK held by American Family Association.
Group Owner: American Family Radio
Arbitron Metro Market: Tupelo, MS *Format:* Christian, Religious
Marvin Sanders, General Manager

KLBC
11-01-1958; 106.3 mhz FM *Hrs Open:* 24; 16.5 kw; 404 ft.; N34 2 12 W96 25 37
401 West Evergreen, Durant, OK 74701 US
(580) 924-3100, *Fax:* (580) 920-1426
www.klbcfm.com
scott@klbcfm.com
License: Durant, Bryan County, OK held by Texoma Broadcasting Inc.
Group Owner: Texoma Broadcasting Inc.
Nat'l Network: ABC
Arbitron Metro Market: Lawton, OK *Format:* Country *Hrs. of News Programming:* news progmg 20 hrs wkly *No. News Employees:* 1 *Target Audience:* General. *Adv. Rates:* 18; 18; 18; 9
Todd Tidwell, General Manager
Bob McKinzie, Promotions Manager

KSEO
05-01-1947; 750 khz AM *Hrs Open:* 6 AM-7 PM
401 West Evergreen, Durant, OK 74701 US
(580) 924-3100, *Fax:* (580) 920-1426
www.klbcfm.com
margie@klbcfm.com
License: Durant, OK held by Texoma Broadcasting Inc.
Group Owner: Texoma Broadcasting Inc.; (acq 5-28-99; with co-located FM)
Arbitron Metro Market: Durant, OK *Format:* Christian *Hrs. of News Programming:* news progmg 3 hrs wkly *No. News Employees:* 1 *Target Audience:* Adults; 18-54 *Adv. Rates:* 10; 10; 10; na
Todd Tidwell, President
Bob McKenzie, Operations Dir
Bob McKinzie, Programming Director
Scott Corbin, News Director
Jim Reagan, Public Affairs Director

***KSSU**
02-01-1972; 91.9 mhz FM *Hrs Open:* 24; 1.5 kw; 341 ft; N34 00 45 W96 19 45
1405 N. 4th St., PMB 4226, Durant, OK 74701
(580) 745-7483, *Fax:* (580) 745-7475
License: Durant, Bryan County, OK held by Southeastern Oklahoma State University.
Population Served: 35,000*Target Audience:* 18-25; college, high school students & area residents
Prof. Dell McLain, Chairman

Edmond

***KCSC**
04-01-1966; 90.1 mhz FM *Hrs Open:* 24; 100 kw; 840 ft.; N35 34 24 W97 29 8
100 N. University Drive, Edmond, OK 73034 US
(405) 974-3333, *Fax:* (405) 974-3844
www.kcscfm.com
kcscfm@uco.edu
License: Edmond, Oklahoma County, OK held by University of Central Oklahoma.
Nat'l Network: PRI
Arbitron Metro Market: Edmond, OK *Format:* Talk *Hrs. of News Programming:* One *Target Audience:* 35 plus; educated, affluent
Zachary Dumas, Operations Dir
Brad Ferguson, General Manager
Susan Clark, General Sales Mgr
Hal Smith, Chief Engineer

***KOKF**
09-01-1977; 90.9 mhz FM *Hrs Open:* 24; 100 kw; 436 ft.; N35 33 59 W97 28 28
P.O. Box 22000, Oklahoma City, OK 73132 US
(916) 251-1600, *Fax:* (916) 251-1650
www.air1.com
info@air1.com
License: Edmond, Oklahoma County, OK held by Educational Media Foundation.
Group Owner: EMF Broadcasting; (acq 5-25-2006; $4 million).
Nat'l Network: Air 1
Arbitron Metro Market: Oklahoma City, OK *Format:* Alternative, Christian
Mike Novak, Operations Dir
David Pierce, Programming Director
Ed Lenane, News Director
Sam Wallington, Engineering Dir
Marya Morgan, News Reporter
Richard Hunt, News Reporter
Evan Falat, Regional Manager

El Reno

KZUE
09-09-1962; 1460 khz AM *Hrs Open:* Daytime only; 0.5 kw-D, NDD; N35 30 30 W97 54 0
2715 S. Radio Road, El Reno, OK 73036 US
(405) 262-1460, *Fax:* (405) 262-1886
www.latremendaok.com
kzue@aol.com
License: El Reno, OK held by La Tremenda Inc.
Nat'l Reps: Keystone (unwired net)
Arbitron Metro Market: El Reno, OK.
Nancy Galvan, General Manager

Elk City

KADS
10-01-1932; 1240 khz AM *Hrs Open:* 24; 1 kw-U, ND1; N35 22 51 W99 24 25
P.O. Box 1270, Tulsa, OK 74101 US
(580) 225-9696, *Fax:* (580) 225-9699
kecofm.com
info@kads.com
License: Elk City, OK held by Paragon Communications Inc.
Group Owner: Paragon Communications Inc.; acq 6-15-01; $15,000).
Nat'l Network: ESPN Radio *Wire Services:* AP
Arbitron Metro Market: Elk City, OK *Format:* Sports *No. News Employees:* 1 *Adv. Rates:* 12; 9; 12; 6
Blake Brewer, General Manager

KECO
07-20-1982; 96.5 mhz FM *Hrs Open:* 24; 100 kw; 689 ft.; N35 24 22 W99 29 54
Mailing Address: P.O. Box 945, 220 S. Pioneer, Elk City, OK 73648 US
Second Address: 220 S. Pioneer Rd., Elk City, OK 73644
(580) 225-9696, *Fax:* (580) 225-9699
www.kecofm.com
info@keco.com
License: Elk City, Beckham County, OK held by Paragon Communications Inc.
Group Owner: Paragon Communications Inc.; acq 4-22-98; $100,000 for 72% with KXOO(FM) Elk City).
Arbitron Metro Market: Elk City, OK *Format:* Country *Hrs. of News Programming:* news progmg 2.5 hrs wkly *No. News Employees:* 1 *Target Audience:* General. *Adv. Rates:* 23; 16; 23; 10
Blake Brewer, President
Connie Legrand, Operations Dir
Blake Brewer, Owner Operator
Connie Swearingen, Traffic Director
Shawn Wilson, Sales Executive

KTIJ
07-15-2000; 106.9 mhz FM; 100 kw; 981 ft.; N34 58 39 W99 24 35
PO Box 349, Dover, NH 03825 US
(580) 726-5656, *Fax:* (580) 726-2222
thezone@itlnet.net
License: Elk City, Beckham County, OK held by Fuchs Radio LLC.
Group Owner: Fuchs Radio L.L.C.
Format: Contemporary Hits/Top 40
Shelly Fox, Operations Dir
Chad Fox, General Manager

KXOO
04-01-1995; 94.3 mhz FM *Hrs Open:* 24; 12 kw; 469 ft.; N35 24 22 W99 29 54
P.O. Box 945, Elk City, OK 73648 US
(580) 225-5966, *Fax:* (580) 225-9699
www.kxoofm.com
kxoo@cableone.net
License: Elk City, Beckham County, OK held by Paragon Communications Inc.
Group Owner: Paragon Communications Inc.; acq 4-22-98; $100,000 for 72% with KECO(FM) Elk City).
Arbitron Metro Market: Elk City, OK *Format:* Adult Contemp, Christian *Hrs. of News Programming:* news progmg 2 hrs wkly *No. News Employees:* 1 *Adv. Rates:* 12; 9; 12; 6
Blake Brewer, President
Nathan Brewer, News Director
Gabe Ednay, Chief Engineer
Kim Brooks, Account Exc
Connie LeGrand, Traffic Director/ Office Manager
Shawn Wilson, Sports Director
Gabe Edney, Web Designer

Enid

KFXY
01-01-2004; 1640 khz AM *Hrs Open:* 24
Mailing Address: 316 E. Willow, Enid, OK 73701 US
Second Address: 316 E. Willow, Enid, OK 73701
(580) 237-1390, *Fax:* (580) 242-1390
www.knid.com
hchamplin@knid.com
License: Enid, OK held by Chisholm Trail Broadcasting Co.
Arbitron Metro Market: Enid, OK *Format:* Sports *Target Audience:* 18-54
Ricky Roggow, Operations Dir
Hiram Champlin, General Manager
Sandy Daniels, General Sales Mgr
Chad McKee, Programming Director
Suzi Lakin, Promotions Manager

***KKRD**
10-01-1986; 91.1 mhz FM *Hrs Open:* 24; 0.41 kw; 312 ft.; N36 23 48 W97 52 38
901 South Cleveland Road, Enid, OK 73703 US
(916) 251-1600, *Fax:* (916) 251-1650
www.air1.com
info@air1.com
License: Enid, Garfield County, OK held by Educational Media Foundation.
Group Owner: EMF Broadcasting; (acq 10-15-2004; $102,500)
Nat'l Network: Air 1
Arbitron Metro Market: Rocklin, CA *Format:* Alternative, Christian
Mike Novak, President
Evan Falat, General Sales Mgr
David Pierce, Programming Director
Ed Lenane, News Director
Sam Wallington, Engineering Dir
Marya Morgan, News Reporter
Richard Hunt, News Reporter
Tracy Butler, TrafficManager

KCRC
01-01-1926; 1390 khz AM *Hrs Open:* 24; 1 kw-U, DA1; N36 25 11 W97 52 28
Mailing Address: 316 East Willow, Enid, OK 73701 US
Second Address: 316 E. Willow, Enid, OK 73701
(580) 237-1390, *Fax:* (580) 242-1390
www.knid.com
ctbradio@yahoo.com
License: Enid, OK held by Chisholm Trail Holding Co. Inc.

RADIO - U.S.

Nat'l Network: Jones Radio Networks; ESPN Radio *Regional Network:* Okla. News Net.
Format: News *Hrs. of News Programming:* news progmg 2 hrs wkly *No. News Employees:* 1 *Target Audience:* General.
Hiram Champlin, President
Ricky Roggow, Operations Dir
Sandy Daniels, General Sales Mgr
Chad McKee, Programming Director
Suzi Lakin, Promotions Manager
Rob Houston, News Director
G.B. Bonham, Chief Engineer

KGWA
01-01-1950; 960 khz AM *Hrs Open:* 24; 1 kw-U, DA1; N36 26 13 W97 55 16
Mailing Address: 300 North Van Buren, P.O.Box 3128, Enid, OK 73703 US
Second Address: 1710 W. Willow Rd., Suite 300, Enid, OK 73703
(580) 234-4230, *Fax:* (580) 234-2971
www.kgwanews.com
radio@kofm.com
License: Enid, OK held by Williams Broadcasting LLC.
Nat'l Network: Fox News Radio *Regional Network:* Okla. News Net.
Format: News, News/Talk, 86 *Special Programming:* Farm 3 hrs wkly, finance 20 hrs wkly, lifestyle 4 hrs wkly *Hrs. of News Programming:* news progmg 60 hours wkly *No. News Employees:* 4 *Target Audience:* P25-54*Adv. Rates:* 35,35,35,20
Daniel J. Smith, General Manager
Cheryl Myatt, General Sales Mgr
J. Curtis Huckleberry, Programming Director

KQOB
05-01-1967; 96.9 mhz FM; 98 kw; 1480 ft.; N35 58 50 W97 41 42
Mailing Address: 316 East Willow, Enid, OK 73702 US
Second Address: 316 E. Willow, Enid, OK 73701
(580) 237-1390, *Fax:* (580) 242-1390
License: Enid, Garfield County, OK held by Champlin Broadcasting Inc.
Regional Network: Okla. News Net.
Format: Variety/Diverse *Target Audience:* 18-54.
Michael Presnell, President

KOFM
03-01-1982; 103.1 mhz FM *Hrs Open:* 24; 25 kw; 299 ft.; N36 26 13 W97 55 16
Mailing Address: 300 North Van Buren, P.O.Box 3128, Enid, OK 73703 US
Second Address: 1710 W. Willow Rd., Suite 300, Enid, OK 73703
(580) 234-6371, *Fax:* (580) 234-2971
www.kofm.com
radio@kofm.com
License: Enid, Garfield County, OK held by Williams Broadcasting LLC.
Nat'l Network: Fox News Radio
Format: Country *Hrs. of News Programming:* 1 hour weekly *No. News Employees:* 3 *Target Audience:* P25-54 *Adv. Rates:* 35,35,35,20
Daniel J. Smith, General Manager
Cheryl Myatt, General Sales Mgr
Alan Clepper, Programming Director

Eufaula

KTNT
06-15-1967; 102.5 mhz FM *Hrs Open:* 24; 10.5 kw; 505 ft.; N35 6 9 W95 36 53
Route 6, Box 374, Eufaula, OK 74432 US
(918) 689-3663, *Fax:* (918) 689-5451
www.kfoxradio.com
mrogers@k955.com
License: Eufaula, McIntosh County, OK held by K95.5 Inc.
Group Owner: K95.5 Inc.; acq 9-24-98; $400,000)
Nat'l Network: Fox News Radio *Regional Network:* Okla. News Net.
Arbitron Metro Market: Eufaula, Ok *Format:* Country *Special Programming:* Gospel 3 hrs wkly
William Payne, President
Mike Rogers, General Manager
Rodney Haltom, Promotions Manager
Lisa Cotten, News Director
Lisa Cotton-Traffic Director

Fairview

***KHEV**
01-01-2009; 90.3 mhz FM; 0.49 kw; 607 ft.; N36 13 25 W98 36 7 US
(620) 873-2991, *Fax:* (620) 873-2755
www.khym.org
khym@khym.com
License: Fairview, Major County, OK held by Great Plains Christian Radio Inc.
Arbitron Metro Market: Fairview, OK *Format:* Religious
Don Hughes, General Manager

Frederick

***KSYE**
07-01-1992; 91.5 mhz FM *Hrs Open:* 24; 100 kw; 509 ft.; N34 21 52 W98 50 4
P.O. Box 619000, Dallas, TX 75261 US
(866) 355-5793(580) 335-5500, *Fax:* (580) 335-5900
www.ksye.org
info@ksye.org
License: Frederick, Tillman County, OK held by Criswell College.
Group Owner: Criswell Communications
Nat'l Network: ABC
Arbitron Metro Market: Oklahoma City, OK *Format:* Religious
Target Audience: General.
Dr. Royce Laycock, Chairman
Dr. Jerry Johnson, President
Mike Tyrone, General Manager
Keith Mayo, Station Manager
Sharon Geiger, Programming Director

KTAT
01-01-1948; 1570 khz AM; 0.25 kw-D, ND2; 0.006 kw-N, ND2; N34 23 30 W99 1 51
Mailing Address: P.O. Box 1088, Frederick, OK 73542 US
Second Address: 207 W. Grand Ave., Frederick, OK 73542
(580) 335-3874, *Fax:* (580) 335-7659
License: Frederick, OK held by Morey Broadcasting LLC
Arbitron Metro Market: Frederick, OK *Format:* Easy Listening
Brent Morey, General Manager

KYBE
08-15-1982; 95.9 mhz FM; 6 kw; 249 ft.; N34 23 30 W99 1 51
P.O. Box 1088, Frederick, OK 73542 US
(580) 335-5923, *Fax:* (580) 335-7659
www.coyotenews.com
kybe959@pldi.net
License: Frederick, Tillman County, OK held by Fort Worth Media Group G.P. LLC.
Group Owner: LKCM Radio Group L.P.; (acq 9-9-2005; $325,000)
Arbitron Metro Market: Frederick, OK *Format:* Country
Scott Maguire, Operations Dir
Don Jacobs, General Manager
Dan Rahman, Programming Director

Glenpool

KTSO
05-24-1976; 94.1 mhz FM *Hrs Open:* 24; 100 kw; 691 ft.; N36 7 52 W96 4 13
149 Penn Avenue, Scranton, PA 18503 US
(918) 665-3131, *Fax:* (918) 663-6622
www.941THESOUND.com
production@shamrocktuosa.com
License: Glenpool, Tulsa County, OK held by Shamrock Communications Inc.
Group Owner: Shamrock Communications Inc.; acq 1996; $1.8 million)
Nat'l Reps: McGavren Guild
Arbitron Metro Market: Tulsa, OK *Format:* Contemporary Hits/Top 40, Adult Contemp *Hrs. of News Programming:* news progmg 35 hrs wkly *No. News Employees:* 1 *Target Audience:* 35-54. *Adv. Rates:* 65; 60; 60;40
William Lynett, CEO
Chuck Browning, General Manager
Tom Holiday, General Sales Mgr
Paul Kaiegler, Programming Director

Goltry

***KGVV**
90.5 mhz FM; 35 kw; Ant 397 ft; N36 40 47 W98 10 43
Box 697, Waukomis, OK
(580) 758-3045
License: Goltry, Alfalfa County, OK held by Waukomis Baptist Church Inc.
Danny Marney, President

Goodwell

***KPSU**
09-01-1977; 91.7 mhz FM *Hrs Open:* 10 AM to midnight; 0.38 kw; 121 ft.; N36 35 41 W101 38 10
P.O. Box 430, Goodwell, OK 73939 US
(580) 349-2611, *Fax:* (580) 349-2302
www.opsu.edu
opsu@opsu.edu
License: Goodwell, Texas County, OK held by Oklahoma Panhandle State University.
Target Audience: College age.
Dr. David Bryant, President
Russell Guthrie, General Manager

Grandfield

***KWKL**
09-19-2003; 89.9 mhz FM *Hrs Open:* 24; 45 kw vert; 499 ft.; N34 16 19 W98 25 30
US
(800) 525-5683, *Fax:* (916) 251-1650
www.klove.com
klove@klove.com
License: Grandfield, Tillman County, OK held by Educational Media Foundation.
Group Owner: EMF Broadcasting
Nat'l Network: K-Love
Arbitron Metro Market: Grandfield, OK *Format:* Christian *No. News Employees:* 3 *Target Audience:* 25-44; Judeo Christian, female
Darrell Chambliss, Chairman
Mike Novak, President and CEO
David Pierce, Programming Director
Ed Lenane, News Director
Sam Wallington, Engineering Dir
Marya Morgan, News Reporter
Richard Hunt, News Reporter
Laura Daniels, NewsReporter
Tim Luttrell, News Reporter
Kenny Noble Cortes, News Reporter
Darren Vinson, News Reporter

Granite

KZBS
01-01-2008; 104.3 mhz FM; 1.7 kw; 909 ft.; N34 58 39 W99 24 35
US
(580) 332-0902, *Fax:* (580) 332-0922
www.thegospelstation.com
email@thegospelstation.com
License: Granite, Greer County, OK held by Bcvision.
Arbitron Metro Market: Granite, OK *Format:* Gospel
Randall Christy, President
Rick Cody, Vice President
Sharla Frederick, Treasurer and CFO

***KHEB**
91.9 mhz FM; 0.1 kw; 774 ft.; N34 58 39 W99 24 35
US
(580) 332-0902
www.thegospelstation.com
email@thegospelstation.com
License: Granite, Greer County, OK held by South Central Oklahoma Christian Broadcasting Inc.
Arbitron Metro Market: Granite, OK
Randall Christy, President
Rick Cody, General Manager
Rick Cody, Vice President
Sharla Frederick, Treasurer / CFO

Grove

KGVE
12-12-1980; 99.3 mhz FM *Hrs Open:* 24; 14.5 kw; 430 ft.; N36 41 3 W94 53 11
P.O. Box 451749, Grove, OK 74345 US
(918) 786-2211, *Fax:* (918) 786-2284
info@kgvefm.com
License: Grove, Delaware County, OK held by Caleb Corp.
Nat'l Network: ABC *Regional Network:* Okla. News Net.
Format: Country *No. News Employees:* 1 *Target Audience:* General.
Larry Hestand, President
Janell Hestand, Operations Dir

***KWXC**
01-01-2008; 88.9 mhz FM; 6 kw vert; 240 ft.; N36 35 42 W94 38 5
Route 4 Box 481-4, Grove, OK 74344 US
(918) 854-3523
License: Grove, Delaware County, OK held by Grove Broadcasting Inc.
Format: Talk *Target Audience:* 30-45.
Darral Martin, President
Travis Martin, Programming Director
Margaret Van Dyke, Promotions Manager

Guthrie

KMFS
11-16-1955; 1490 khz AM *Hrs Open:* 24; 1 kw-U, ND1; N35 52 56 W97 23 34
Mailing Address: 1515 East Tropicana, Suite 240, Las Vegas, NV 89119 US
Second Address: 8919 World Ministry Ave., Baton Rouge, LA 70810
(225) 768-3688/8300, *Fax:* (225) 768-3729
www.jsm.org
kawikfish@yahoo.com
License: Guthrie, OK held by Family Worship Center Church Inc.
Group Owner: Family Worship Center Church Inc.; acq 9-27-2002; $150,000).
Nat'l Network: ABC; AP Radio
Arbitron Metro Market: Oklahoma City, OK *Format:* Religious
David Whitelaw, COO
Jimmy Swaggart, President
John Santiago, Programming Director

Guymon

KGYN
12-12-1948; 1210 khz AM *Hrs Open:* 24; 10 kw-D, DAN; 10 kw-N, DAN; N36 40 34 W101 22 58
P. O. Box 130, Guymon, OK 73942 US
(580) 338-1210, *Fax:* (580) 338-8255
www.kgynradio.com
kgyn@kgynradio.com
License: Guymon, OK held by Steckline Communications
Nat'l Network: Jones Radio Networks; AP Network News
Format: Country *Special Programming:* Relg 8 hrs, Sp 8 hrs wkly *Hrs. of News Programming:* news progmg 12 hrs wkly *No. News Employees:* 1 *Target Audience:* 25-65; broad based listenership
Todd Thrasher, General Manager
Debbie Browning, Programming Director
Bobby Gee, News Director
Chane Deming, Engineering Dir
Richard Ryther, Chief Engineer
Lisa Bryce, Traffic Manager

KKBS
12-25-1983; 92.7 mhz FM *Hrs Open:* 24; 11.5 kw; 486 ft.; N36 40 13 W101 28 48
P.O. Box 1756, Guymon, OK 73942 US
(580) 338-5493, *Fax:* (580) 338-0717
www.kkbs.com
kkbs@kkbs.com
License: Guymon, Texas County, OK held by MLS Communications Inc.
Arbitron Metro Market: Lawton, OK *Format:* Rock/AOR *Special Programming:* Financial markets 5 hrs wkly *Hrs. of News Programming:* news progmg 17 hrs wkly *No. News Employees:* 2 *Target Audience:* 25-54+;working people, 2 income families, farmers
Ramey Cozart, Operations Dir
Marsha Strong, General Manager
Amy Ford, General Sales Mgr
Ramey Cozart, Programming Director
Frank Riviera, Music Director
JJ Micheals, Webmaster

*KBIJ
01-01-2008; 99.5 mhz FM; 100 kw; 269 ft.; N36 50 42 W101 12 15
US
(800) 687-9112, *Fax:* (806) 353-1542
radiobygrace.com
info@krbgfm.com
License: Guymon, Texas County, OK held by Grace Community Church of Amarillo
Arbitron Metro Market: Guymon, OK *Format:* Christian
William Gehm, President

*KNGM
88.9 mhz FM; 25 kw; Ant 321 ft; N36 40 27 W101 28 09
Box 14, Abilene, KS
(877) 813-5366, *Fax:* (785) 263-3876
www.kjil.com
kjil@kjil.com
License: Guymon, Texas County, OK held by Great Plains Christian Radio Inc.
Population Served: 24,971 *Arbitron Metro Market:* Emporia, KS *No. News Employees:* 1
Michael Luskey, CEO
Linda Emig, Music Director
Mark Hinca, Station Manager
Delvin Kinser, News Director
Steve Larson, Chief Engineer

Jennifer Pooler, Production Director
Deb Hustus, Director of Underwriting / Development
JerryMann, Business Manager

Hammon

*KTHF
89.9 mhz FM; 26.5 kw; 295 ft.; N35 37 16 W99 22 32
US
(580) 767-1400, *Fax:* (580) 765-1700
www.thehousefm.com
mail@thehousefm.com
License: Hammon, Roger Mills County, OK held by The Love Station Inc.
Arbitron Metro Market: Hammon, OK
Doyle Brewer, CEO/COO
Tony Weir, Music Director
Janelle Keith, Music Director
Darcey Christianson, Chief Engineer
Shaun Michaels, Production Director
Andy Youso, Assistant Program Director
Donna Hollifield, Office Manager

Healdton

KICM
10-01-1978; 97.7 mhz FM; 50 kw; 492 ft.; N34 20 57 W97 27 24
5946 Club Oaks Drive, Dallas, TX 75248 US
(580) 226-9797, *Fax:* (580) 226-5113
www.kicm.com
mike@kicm.com
License: Healdton, Carter County, OK held by Keystone Broadcasting Corp.
Format: Country *Special Programming:* Relg 6 hrs wkly *Target Audience:* 21-49.
Bill Countrymen, General Manager

*KAZC
89.3 mhz FM; 0.3 kw; 56 ft.; N34 13 9 W97 28 27
US
(580) 332-0902, *Fax:* (580) 332-0922
www.thegospelstation.com/dyn/index.php
email@thegospelstation.com
License: Healdton, Carter County, OK held by First Free Will Baptist Church of Healdton.
Arbitron Metro Market: Healdton, OK
Sharla Frederick, Treasurer / CFO
Randall Christy, Founder and President
David Lomineck, General Manager
Rick Cody, Vice President/ Program Director

Heavener

KPRV-FM
10-01-1989; 92.5 mhz FM *Hrs Open:* 24; 1.55 kw; 640 ft.; N34 53 54 W94 34 30
P.O. Box 368, Poteau, OK 74953 US
(918) 647-3221, *Fax:* (918) 647-5092
www.kprvradio.com
kprv@windstream.net
License: Heavener, Le Flore County, OK held by LeRoy Billy.
Nat'l Network: ABC *Regional Network:* Okla. News Net.
Arbitron Metro Market: Fort Smith, AR *Format:* Country, Gospel *Special Programming:* Gospel 24 hrs Sun only *Hrs. of News Programming:* News progmg 24 hrs wkly *Target Audience:* 24-54.
LeRoy Billy, President
LeRoy Billy, Operations Dir
David Billy, Programming Director
Allen Riley, Chief Engineer

Henryetta

KXBL
12-20-1966; 99.5 mhz FM *Hrs Open:* 24; 100 kw; 981 ft.; N35 50 2 W96 7 28
3355 S. Valley View Boulevard, Las Vegas, NV 89102 US
(918) 743-7814, *Fax:* (918) 743-7613
bigcountry995.com
psutterfield@journalbroadcastgroup.com
License: Henryetta, Okmulgee County, OK held by Journal Broadcast Corp.
Group Owner: Journal Communications Inc.; (acq 6-11-99; grpsl).
Arbitron Metro Market: Tulsa, OK *Format:* Country *Target Audience:* 18-34.
Ron Kurtis, CFO
Carl Gardner, President
Randy Bush, Operations Dir
Randy Bush, General Manager
Brian Gann, News Director
Ray Klotz, Engineering Dir

Ric Hampton, Operations Manager
April Sailsbury, General Manager

*KVAZ
12-26-1985; 91.5 mhz FM *Hrs Open:* 24; 7.8 kw vert; 564 ft.; N35 32 53 W95 58 14
R#1 Box 65 A, Weleetka, OK 74880 US
(580) 332-0902, *Fax:* (580) 332-0922
www.thegospelstation.com
email@thegospelstation.com
License: Henryetta, Okmulgee County, OK held by South Central Oklahoma Broadcasting Inc.
Arbitron Metro Market: Henryetta, OK *Format:* Gospel
Sharla Frederick, CFO
Randall Christy, Founder and President
Rick Cody, General Manager
Rick Cody, Vice President/ Program Director

Hobart

KQTZ
05-28-1979; 105.9 mhz FM *Hrs Open:* 24; 100 kw; 1020 ft.; N34 52 15 W99 17 36
Mailing Address: P.O. Box 577, Altus, OK 73522 US
Second Address: 212 W. Cypress, Altus, OK 73521
(580) 482-1450, *Fax:* (580) 482-3420
www.kwhw.com
mward@kwhw.com
License: Hobart, Kiowa County, OK held by Monarch Broadcasting Inc.
Group Owner: Monarch Broadcasting Inc.; (acq 12-31-2003; grpsl)
Arbitron Metro Market: Lawton, OK *Format:* Adult Contemp
Target Audience: General; contemp adults during the day, rockers at night
Matthew Ward, President
Michael Barnes, Operations Dir

KTJS
06-21-1947; 1420 khz AM *Hrs Open:* 24; 1 kw-D, ND1; 0.36 kw-N, ND1; N35 2 57 W99 5 48
1515 N. Broadway, Hobart, OK 73651 US
(580) 726-5656, *Fax:* (580) 726-2222
www.ktjs.com
thezone@itlnet.net
License: Hobart, OK held by Fuchs Radio LLC.
Group Owner: Fuchs Radio L.L.C.; (acq 11-24-98; $182,000)
Arbitron Metro Market: Hobart, OK *Format:* Country, News, 62, Talk *Special Programming:* Relg 12 hrs wkly *Hrs. of News Programming:* News progmg 19 hrs wkly *Target Audience:* 30 plus; agri-related businessmen*Adv. Rates:* 10; 10; 8; 4
Chad Fox, President

Holdenville

KTLS-FM
11-30-1991; 106.5 mhz FM *Hrs Open:* 24; 25 kw; 328 ft.; N34 54 50 W96 31 20
5105 S Shields Boulevard, Oklahoma City, OK 73129 US
(580) 332-2211, *Fax:* (580) 436-1629
www.ktlsradio.com
ktls@ktlsradio.com
License: Holdenville, Hughes County, OK held by The Chickasaw Nation.
Group Owner: The Chickasaw Nation; (acq 10-1-2008; $1.5 million with KXFC(FM) Coalgate)
Nat'l Network: Jones Radio Networks
Arbitron Metro Market: Ada, OK *Format:* Classic Rock *No. News Employees:* 1 *Target Audience:* 25-54. *Adv. Rates:* 26; 26; 26; 26
Roger Harris, General Manager
Craig Stone, Programming Director
Renae Woodward, News Director

Hollis

KKRE
01-01-2005; 92.5 mhz FM; 6 kw; 328 ft.; N34 36 34 W99 50 57
Mailing Address: US
Second Address: 808 N. Main St., Altus, OK 73521
(580) 482-1555, *Fax:* (580) 482-8353
www.keyb.net
gayle@keyb.net
License: Hollis, Harmon County, OK held by Altus FM Inc.
Group Owner: Altus FM Inc.
Arbitron Metro Market: Hollis, OK *Format:* Country
Scott Wilmes, Operations Dir
Gayle Ledbetter, General Manager

KJOK
102.7 mhz FM; 50 kw; 95 meters; n34 36 34 w99 50 57
PO Box 1077, Altus, OK

(580) 482-1555, *Fax:* (580) 482-8353
License: Hollis, OK held by Altus FM Inc
Group Owner: Altus FM Inc.

Paul Wilmes, President

Hugo

KIHN
10-01-1948; 1340 khz AM *Hrs Open:* 16; 1 kw-U, ND1; N34 0 15 W95 29 20
P.O. Box 430, E.E. of Hugo, OK 74743 US
(580) 326-6411, *Fax:* (580) 326-7921
kihn@1starnet.com
License: Hugo, OK held by Little Dixie Broadcasting Co.
Format: News *Special Programming:* Gospel music 5 hrs, children one hr, farm one hr w *Hrs. of News Programming:* news progmg 20 hrs wkly *No. News Employees:* 1 *Target Audience:* General. *Adv. Rates:* 8.50;8.50; 8.50; 6
Leeta Henson, President

KITX
06-01-1983; 95.5 mhz FM; 50 kw; 492 ft.; N33 54 56 W95 28 4
3405 East Louisville, Broken Arrow, OK 74014 US
(580) 326-2555, *Fax:* (580) 326-2623
www.k955.com
K955@K955.com
License: Hugo, Choctaw County, OK held by K95.5 Inc.
Group Owner: K95.5 Inc.; (acq 10-95; $400,000)
Arbitron Metro Market: Hugo, OK *Format:* Country *Target Audience:* General.
Will Payne, General Manager
Will Payne, Programming Director

Idabel

KBEL-FM
10-01-1973; 96.7 mhz FM *Hrs Open:* 24; 25 kw; 299 ft.; N33 52 54 W94 49 10
Mailing Address: Box 67, Gordonville, TX 76245 US
Second Address: 813 Lincoln Rd., Idabel, OK 74745
(580) 286-6642, *Fax:* (580) 286-6643
www.kbelradio.com
kbel967@yahoo.com
License: Idabel, McCurtain County, OK held by Box Broadcasting Corp.
Nat'l Network: Salem Radio Network *Regional Network:* Agrinet
Arbitron Metro Market: Idabel, OK *Format:* Country *Hrs. of News Programming:* news progmg 6 hrs wkly *No. News Employees:* 1 *Target Audience:* 18 plus; country audience *Adv. Rates:* 14; 12; 14; 10
Paul W. Box, CEO

KQIB
08-01-1999; 102.9 mhz FM *Hrs Open:* 24; 6 kw; 318 ft.; N33 59 57 W94 47 29
103 Hastings Court, Idabel, OK 74745 US
(580) 584-3388, *Fax:* (580) 584-3341
www.theq102.com (Under Construction)
kkbi@pine-net.com
License: Idabel, McCurtain County, OK held by JDC Radio Inc.
Nat'l Network: ABC
Arbitron Metro Market: Paris, TX *Format:* Adult Contemp *Hrs. of News Programming:* news progmg 5 hrs wkly *No. News Employees:* 1 *Target Audience:* 25-44. *Adv. Rates:* 9; 9; 9; 8
David Smulyan, General Manager
Shellye Copeland, Programming Director

*KXRT
01-01-2003; 90.9 mhz FM; 0.5 kw; 210 ft.; N33 53 33 W94 49 26
P. O. Box 1458, Washington, DC 20013 US
(662) 844-8888, *Fax:* (662) 842-6791
www.afa.net
faq@afr.net
License: Idabel, McCurtain County, OK held by American Family Association.
Group Owner: American Family Radio; (acq 1-31-2001).
Arbitron Metro Market: Tupelo, MS *Format:* Christian
Marvin Sanders, General Manager

Ketchum

*KOSN
05-26-1989; 107.5 mhz FM *Hrs Open:* 24; 100 kw; 981 ft.; N36 46 13 W95 27 7 *Rebroadcasts:* Simulcast with KOSU-FM Stillwater 100%
1 West Third Street, P O Box 451750, Grove, OK 74345 US
(405) 744-6352, *Fax:* (405) 744-9970
www.kosu.org
info@kosu.org
License: Ketchum, Craig County, OK held by PRC Tulsa I-LLC
Nat'l Network: NPR
Arbitron Metro Market: Tulsa, OK *Format:* News, News/Talk, 86 *Special Programming:* Classical 30 hrs wkly *Hrs. of News Programming:* news progmg 130 hrs wkly *No. News Employees:* 2 *Target Audience:* General.
Rachel Hubbard, General Manager
Don Crider, General Sales Mgr
Dan Schroeder, Engineering Dir
Kelly Burley, Director
Joanna Self, Administrative Assistant

Kingfisher

KINB
01-01-2000; 105.3 mhz FM; 0.93 kw; 833 ft.; N35 43 38 W97 52 30
8225 NW 29, Bethany, OK 73008 US
(405) 848-0100, *Fax:* (405) 843-5288
www.laindomable.com
info@laindomable.com
License: Kingfisher, Kingfisher County, OK held by The Last Bastion Station Trust LLC, as Trustee
Arbitron Metro Market: Oklahoma City, OK *Target Audience:* 35-49 & 25-34; Yooung professionals
Luis Medina, Operations Dir
Joe Jelddy, Station Manager

Lahoma

KXLS
11-01-1995; 95.7 mhz FM; 14 kw; 449 ft.; N36 32 13 W98 0 39
Mailing Address: 205 W Maple, Suite 900, Enid, OK 73701 US
Second Address: 316 E. Willow Rd., Enid, OK 73701
(580) 237-1390, *Fax:* (580) 242-1390
hchamplin@knid.com
License: Lahoma, Garfield County, OK held by Chisholm Trail Broadcasting Co.
Nat'l Network: ABC
Format: Adult Contemp *Hrs. of News Programming:* news progmg 2 hrs wkly *No. News Employees:* 1 *Target Audience:* 30-60; female
Ricky Roggow, Operations Dir
Hiram Champlin, General Manager
Sandy Daniels, General Sales Mgr
Suzi Lakin, Promotions Manager
Rob Houston, News Director
G.B. Bonham, Chief Engineer

Langston

*KALU
03-03-1975; 89.3 mhz FM *Hrs Open:* 24; 0.15 kw; 200 ft.; N35 56 36 W97 15 32
P.O. Box 837, Langston, OK 73050 US
(405) 466-2924, *Fax:* (405) 466-2921
www.langston.edu
bishop@yahoo.com
License: Langston, Logan County, OK held by Langston University.
Arbitron Metro Market: Langston, OK *Format:* Jazz, Religious
Bishop Kendrick, General Manager

Lawton

KBZQ
05-01-1992; 99.5 mhz FM *Hrs Open:* 24; 25kw; 330 ft; N34 35 31 W98 32 55
Mailing Address: 2331 SW Lee Blvd, Lawton, OK 73506
Second Address: 1006 N.W. 47th St., Suite B, Lawton, OK 73505
(580) 357-9950, *Fax:* (580) 357-9995
www.hitsandfavorites.com
kbzq@sbcglobal.net
License: Lawton, Comanche County, OK held by William R. Fritsch Jr.
Nat'l Network: ABC
Population Served: 113,000 *Arbitron Metro Market:* Lawton, OK *Special Programming:* Jazz 2 hrs, Hits of the 80s5 hrs, Sp 4 hrs wkly *Hrs. of News Programming:* news progmg one hr wkly *No. News Employees:* 3*Target Audience:* 25-54; baby boomers, upscale white collar workers *Adv. Rates:* 10; 15; 10; 5
Chuck Pettigrew, Operations Dir
Rick Fritsch, General Manager
Lino Roldan, Spanish Director

*KCCU
07-13-1989; 89.3 mhz FM *Hrs Open:* 24; 0.05 kw horiz, 2 kw vert; 463 ft.; N34 37 26 W98 16 15
2800 West Gore Blvd, Lawton, OK 73505 US
(888) 454-7800
www.kccu.org
kccu@cameron.edu
License: Lawton, Comanche County, OK held by Cameron University.
Nat'l Network: NPR; PRI
Arbitron Metro Market: Lawton, OK *Format:* Classical, News *Special Programming:* Jazz *Hrs. of News Programming:* news progmg 40 hrs wkly *No. News Employees:* 5 *Target Audience:* General.
Ted Riley, General Manager

KKRX
05-27-1956; 1050 khz AM *Hrs Open:* 24; 0.25 kw-D, DA2; 0.006 kw-N, DA2; N34 35 27 W98 21 10
1528 N.E. 23rd, Oklahoma City, OK 73111 US
(580) 355-1050, *Fax:* (580) 355-1056
www.kjmz.com
spots@kjmz.com
License: Lawton, OK held by Perry Broadcasting of Lawton Inc.
Group Owner: Perry Publishing & Broadcasting Co.; (acq 1-31-97; $486,000 with co-located FM).
Nat'l Reps: D & R Radio
Arbitron Metro Market: Lawton, OK *Format:* Oldies *Special Programming:* Ger one hr wkly
Joy Chapman, General Manager
Mark Edwards, News Director
Dale Weakley, Chief Engineer

KLAW
01-01-1965; 101.3 mhz FM *Hrs Open:* 24; 100 kw; 584 ft.; N34 32 59 W98 32 21
600 Congress Avenue, Suite 1400, Austin, TX 78701 US
(580) 581-3600, *Fax:* (580) 357-2880
www.klaw.com
klaw@gapbroadcasting.com
License: Lawton, Comanche County, OK held by GAP Broadcasting Lawton License LLC.
Group Owner: GAP Broadcasting LLC; (acq 8-3-2007; grpsl)
Nat'l Reps: Katz Radio
Arbitron Metro Market: Lawton, OK *Format:* Country *Hrs. of News Programming:* news progmg 4 hrs wkly *No. News Employees:* 1 *Target Audience:* 25-54; adults *Adv. Rates:* 38; 38; 38; 17
Michelle Anders, Operations Dir
Kim Dodds, General Manager
JoAnne Taylor, General Sales Mgr
David Crawford, Programming Director

KMGZ
11-01-1982; 95.3 mhz FM *Hrs Open:* 24; 14 kw; 312 ft.; N34 34 36 W98 28 30
P.O. Box 7953, Lawton, OK 73506 US
(580) 536-9530, *Fax:* (580) 536-3299
www.kmgz.com
gm@kmgz.com
License: Lawton, Comanche County, OK held by Broadco of Texas Inc.
Arbitron Metro Market: Lawton, OK *Format:* Adult Contemp *Hrs. of News Programming:* News progmg one hr wkly *Target Audience:* 18-49.
Chuck Morgan, President
Albert Young, Programming Director

*KVRS
12-01-1989; 90.3 mhz FM *Hrs Open:* 24; 9.8 kw vert; 262 ft.; N34 31 51 W98 33 10
11 Winding Creek Road, Lawton, OK 73505 US
(580) 536-8886, *Fax:* (580) 536-8891
www.afr.net
kvvs@kvvsfm.com
License: Lawton, Comanche County, OK held by American Family Association.
Group Owner: American Family Radio; (acq 4-29-2004; $10).
Nat'l Network: American Family Radio
Arbitron Metro Market: Lake Charles, LA *Format:* Christian, Religious *Hrs. of News Programming:* News progmg 14 hrs wkly *Target Audience:* General.
Dan Meir, Station Manager

KVRW
03-13-1992; 107.3 mhz FM *Hrs Open:* 24; 26 kw; 584 ft.; N34 32 59 W98 32 21
6210 NW Oak, Lawton, OK 73505 US
(580) 581-3600, *Fax:* (580) 357-2880
www.my1073fm.com
psa@my1073fm.com
License: Lawton, Comanche County, OK held by GAP Broadcasting Lawton License LLC.
Group Owner: GAP Broadcasting LLC; (acq 10-1-2007; grpsl)
Nat'l Reps: Katz Radio
Arbitron Metro Market: Lawton, OK *Format:* Adult Contemp *Hrs. of News Programming:* News progmg 2 hrs wkly *Target Audience:* 25-54.

Michelle Anders, Operations Dir
Kim Dodds, General Manager
Joanne Taylor, General Sales Mgr
Steve Kelly, Programming Director
Sasha Spielman, Digital Managing Editor

KXCA
05-01-1941; 1380 khz AM *Hrs Open:* 24; 1 kw-D, DA2; 1 kw-N, DA2; N34 35 24 W98 21 44
115 W. Broadway, Anadarko, OK 73005 US
(580) 355-1064, *Fax:* (580) 355-1056
www.perrybroadcasting.net/kxca/
spots@kjmz.com
License: Lawton, OK held by Perry Broadcasting of Southwest Oklahoma Inc.
Group Owner: Perry Publishing & Broadcasting Co.; (acq 11-22-2002; grpsl).
Nat'l Reps: Roslin
Arbitron Metro Market: Lawton, OK *Format:* Sports, Talk *Target Audience:* 35 plus.
Joy Chapman, General Manager
James Stanley, Programming Director

KZCD
06-08-1987; 94.1 mhz FM *Hrs Open:* 24; 35 kw; 584 ft.; N34 32 59 W98 32 21
600 Congress Avenue, Suite 1400, Austin, TX 78701 US
(580) 581-3600, *Fax:* (580) 357-2880
www.z94.com
z94@gapbroadcasting.com
License: Lawton, Comanche County, OK held by GAP Broadcasting Lawton License LLC.
Group Owner: GAP Broadcasting LLC; (acq 8-3-2007; grpsl)
Nat'l Reps: Katz Radio
Arbitron Metro Market: Lawton, OK *Hrs. of News Programming:* news progmg 2 hrs wkly *No. News Employees:* 1 *Target Audience:* 18-49; males *Adv. Rates:* 17; 17; 17; 10
Michelle Anders, Operations Dir
Kim Dodds, General Manager
JoAnne Taylor, General Sales Mgr
Don "Critter" Brown, Programming Director

***KJRF**
01-01-2001; 91.1 mhz FM *Hrs Open:* 24; 100 kw; 413 ft.; N34 41 22 W98 7 34
2405 Sw Lee Blvd., Lawton, OK 73505 US
(580) 357-4498, *Fax:* (580) 357-1818
www.thechristian-center.org
covenant@lawtonchristiancenter.org
License: Lawton, Comanche County, OK held by The Christian Center Inc.
Arbitron Metro Market: Lawton, OK *Format:* Christian
Paul Craig, President
Alan Hampton, Operations Dir
Randy Muirhead, Station Manager
Allan Hampton, Engineering Dir

Lindsay

KBLP
10-01-1988; 105.1 mhz FM *Hrs Open:* 24; 2 kw; 564 ft.; N34 54 1 W97 33 56
204 South Main Street, Lindsay, OK 73052 US
(405) 756-4438, *Fax:* (405) 756-2040
www.kblpradio.net
jason@kblpradio.net
License: Lindsay, Garvin County, OK held by South Central Oklahoma Broadcasting & Advertising Corp.
Regional Network: Okla. News Net.
Arbitron Metro Market: Lindsay, OK *Format:* Country *Hrs. of News Programming:* news progmg 10.5 hrs wkly *No. News Employees:* 2 *Target Audience:* 21-65; working consumers
Charlie Jones, President

Locust Grove

KEMX
02-14-1991; 94.5 mhz FM *Hrs Open:* 24; 2.3 kw; 367 ft.; N36 15 5 W95 13 21 *Rebroadcasts:* Rebroadcasts KXOJ-FM Sapulpa 100%
P.O. Box 1250, Sapulpa, OK 74067 US
(918) 492-2660, *Fax:* (918) 492-8840
www.kxoj.com
kxoj@kxoj.com
License: Locust Grove, Mayes County, OK held by KXOJ Inc.
Group Owner: Adonai Radio Group; (acq 4-29-92; grpsl)
Arbitron Metro Market: Tulsa, OK *Format:* Christian *Target Audience:* 18-35; young married or single Christians
Mike Stephens, President
David Stephens, General Manager
Bob Thornton, Programming Director

Lone Grove

KYNZ
05-25-1988; 107.1 mhz FM *Hrs Open:* 24; 24.5 kw; 335 ft.; N34 17 52 W97 9 12
P.O Box 1609, Ardmore, OK 73402 US
(580) 226-0421, *Fax:* (580) 226-0464
www.kynz.com
sarah@sokradio.com
License: Lone Grove, Carter County, OK held by LKCM Radio Group L.P.
Group Owner: LKCM Radio Group L.P.; (acq 2-26-2007;. grpsl)
Nat'l Reps: Christal
Arbitron Metro Market: Lone Grove, OK. *Format:* Oldies *Hrs. of News Programming:* news progmg 25 hrs wkly *No. News Employees:* 1 *Target Audience:* 18-54.
Gerry Schlegel, Operations Dir
Michael Baer, General Manager
Terry Bell, Programming Director
Dave Hilton, Operations Director

Madill

KMAD
05-20-1962; 1550 khz AM *Hrs Open:* Sunrise-sunset; 0.25 kw-D, ND2; 0.09 kw-N, ND2; N34 6 24 W96 46 30
1913 West Elm Street, Durant, OK 74701 US
(580) 795-2345, *Fax:* (580) 795-5623
www.kmad1550.com
kmad1550@yahoo.com
License: Madill, OK held by Robert S. Sullins
Nat'l Network: Jones Radio Networks *Regional Network:* Okla. News Net.
Format: Country *Special Programming:* Farm 2 hrs wkly *Hrs. of News Programming:* News progmg 12 hrs wkly *Target Audience:* General. *Adv. Rates:* 5.25; 5; 5; 4.60
jason Smith, General Manager

Mangum

KHIM
01-01-1998; 97.7 mhz FM; 0.54 kw; 1079 ft.; N34 58 39 W99 24 35
Mailing Address: P.O. Box 837, Altus, OK 73522 US
Second Address: 1515 N. Broadway, Hobart, OK 73651
(580) 726-5656, *Fax:* (580) 726-2222
thezone@itlnet.net
License: Mangum, Greer County, OK held by Fuchs Radio L.L.C.
Group Owner: Fuchs Radio L.L.C.; (acq 4-4-2006; $250,000 with KJCM(FM) Snyder)
Format: Rock/AOR
Chad Fox, General Manager

Marlow

KFXI
08-01-1987; 92.1 mhz FM *Hrs Open:* 24; 100 kw; 545 ft.; N34 40 50 W98 1 2
1101 Highway 81 North, Marlow, OK 73055 US
(580) 658-9292, *Fax:* (580) 658-2561
www.kfxi.com
kfxi@cableone.net
License: Marlow, Stephens County, OK held by DFWU Inc.
Arbitron Metro Market: Marlow, OK *Format:* Country *Special Programming:* Gospel 8 hrs wkly *Target Audience:* 25-55.
Amy Helton, Operations Dir
K.D. Austin, General Manager
Sherry Lynn, General Sales Mgr
Jennifer James, Programming Director

***KFXH**
88.7 mhz FM; 2.15 kw; 364 ft.; N34 40 3 W97 56 49.1
US
(580) 658-9292, *Fax:* (580) 658-2561
License: Marlow, Stephens County, OK held by The Sister Sherry Lynn Foundation.
Arbitron Metro Market: Marlow, OK
Sherry Austin, President

McAlester

***KBCW-FM**
01-01-1999; 91.9 mhz FM *Hrs Open:* 24; 0.7 kw; 446 ft.; N34 59 13 W95 42 10 *Rebroadcasts:* Rebroadcasts KCSC(FM) Edmond 100%
100 N. University Drive, Edmond, OK 73003 US
(405) 974-3333, *Fax:* (405) 974-3844
www.kcscfm.com
kcscfm@uco.edu
License: McAlester, Pittsburg County, OK held by The University of Central Oklahoma.
Nat'l Network: PRI
Arbitron Metro Market: Edmond, OK *Format:* Talk *Hrs. of News Programming:* One *Target Audience:* 35 plus; educ, affluent
Barbara Hendrickson, Operations Dir
Bradford Ferguson, General Manager

KNED
03-14-1950; 1150 khz AM *Hrs Open:* 24; 1 kw-D, DAN; 0.5 kw-N, DAN; N34 56 12 W95 43 59
Mailing Address: P. O. Box 1068, McAlester, OK 74501 US
Second Address: 1801 E. Electric Ave., McAlester, OK 74501
(918) 423-1460, *Fax:* (918) 423-7119
mcalesterradio.com
kmcokned@mcalesterradio.com
License: McAlester, OK held by Southeastern Oklahoma Radio LLC.
Group Owner: Southeastern Oklahoma Radio LLC; (acq 1-18-2005; $222,223).
Wire Services: AP
Format: Country *Hrs. of News Programming:* News progmg 10 hrs wkly *Target Audience:* 45 plus.
Lee Anderson, General Manager
Sheila Turnbow, General Sales Mgr
Megan Waters, Programming Director
John Yates, News Director

KTMC
03-03-1946; 1400 khz AM *Hrs Open:* 24
Mailing Address: 209 E. Wyandotte, Suite 200, McAlester, OK 74501 US
Second Address: 1801 E. Electric Ave., McAlester, OK 74502
(918) 426-1050, *Fax:* (918) 423-7119
mcalesterradio.com
kmconed@mclesteradio.com
License: McAlester, OK held by Southeastern Oklahoma Radio LLC.
Group Owner: Southeastern Oklahoma Radio LLC; (acq 1-18-2005; $444,445 with co-located FM)
Nat'l Network: ABC
Arbitron Metro Market: McAlester, OK *Format:* Classic Rock
Special Programming: Gospel 5 hrs wkly *Hrs. of News Programming:* News progmg 2 hrs wkly *Target Audience:* 50 plus; older, middle-aged, mature & retiredadults
Lee Anderson, General Manager
Bob Turnbow, General Sales Mgr
John Yates, News Director
Tom Dolph-Production Manager

KTMC-FM
06-24-1987; 105.1 mhz FM *Hrs Open:* 24; 1.6 kw; 505 ft.; N34 59 13 W95 42 10
Mailing Address: P.O. Box 1068, McAlester, OK 74502 US
Second Address: 1801 E. Electric Ave., McAlester, OK 74502
(918) 426-1050, *Fax:* (918) 423-7119
www.mcalesterradio.com
License: McAlester, Pittsburg County, OK
Group Owner: Southeastern Oklahoma Radio LLC
Arbitron Metro Market: McAlester, OK *Format:* Classic Rock
Target Audience: 34-50.
Lee Anderson, General Manager
Bob Turnbow, General Sales Mgr
Tom Dolph-Production Manager

Miami

KGLC
12-01-1975; 100.9 mhz FM; 6 kw; 276 ft.; N36 53 24 W94 47 8
P.O. Box 1555, Miami, OK 74355 US
(918) 786-2211, *Fax:* (918) 542-1819
www.okradiostation.com
larry@okradiostation.com
License: Miami, Ottawa County, OK held by Northeast Oklahoma Broadcast Network Inc.
Group Owner: Northeast Oklahoma Broadcast Network Inc.; (acq 4-3-2006; $800,000 with KVIS(AM) Miami)
Nat'l Network: USA
Format: Contemporary Hits/Top 40 *Target Audience:* 25-44.
Adv. Rates: 8; 8; 8; 8
Christy Benton, General Manager
Larry Hestand, Station Manager
Meg Davis, General Sales Mgr
Whitney Thomas, Programming Director
Nicole Arnzen, Promotions Manager
Mike Cossey, Chief Engineer

KVIS
02-01-1948; 910 khz AM *Hrs Open:* 24; 1 kw-U, DA1; N36 53 27 W94 47 0
P.O. Box 1555, Miami, OK 74355 US
(918) 542-1818, *Fax:* (918) 542-1819
www.okradiostation.com/kvis.html
info@kvis.com

License: Miami, OK held by Northeast Oklahoma Broadcast Network Inc.
Group Owner: Northeast Oklahoma Broadcast Network Inc.; (acq 4-3-2006; $800,000 with KGLC(FM) Miami)
Arbitron Metro Market: Miami, OK *Format:* Gospel *Hrs. of News Programming:* news progmg 9 hrs wkly *No. News Employees:* 1 *Target Audience:* Christian/family. *Adv. Rates:* 8; 8; 8; 8
Robert Suman, General Manager
Larry Hestand, Station Manager
Shanda Daugherty, Promotions Manager
Kimberley Barnes, News Director
Rusty Wynn, Chief Engineer

Midwest City

KGHM
01-01-1922; 1340 khz AM *Hrs Open:* 24; 1 kw-U; N35 29 58 W97 30 33
50 Penn Pl., Suite 1000, Oklahoma City, OK 78216
(405) 840-5271, *Fax:* (405) 840-5808
www.1340thegame.com
derricknance@clearchannel.com
License: Midwest City, Oklahoma County, OK held by Clear Channel Broadcasting Licenses Inc.
Nat'l Network: Fox Sports *Nat'l Reps:* Katz
Population Served: 800,400 *Arbitron Metro Market:* Oklahoma City, OK
Bill Hurley, General Manager
Derrick Nance, General Sales Mgr
Tom Travis, Programming Director

KTLV
04-01-1973; 1220 khz AM *Hrs Open:* 6 am-7 pm; 0.25 kw-D, DA2; 0.005 kw-N, DA2; N35 23 50 W97 27 4
1325 S.W. 107th Pl., Oklahoma City, OK 73170 US
(405) 672-1220(405) 672-3886, *Fax:* (405) 672-5858
www.ktlv1220.com
ktlv1220@aol.com
License: Midwest City, OK held by First Choice Broadcasting Inc.
Arbitron Metro Market: Oklahoma City, OK *Format:* Christian, Gospel *Target Audience:* 24 plus.
Howard Williams, President
Dale Williams, General Manager

Moore

*KMSI
03-26-1991; 88.1 mhz FM *Hrs Open:* 24; 50 kw vert; 581 ft.; N35 12 7 W97 35 18
Mailing Address: 11717 S. 129 East Ave, Broken Arrow, OK 74011 US
Second Address: 120 S.W. 4th St., Moore, OK 73160
(405) 794-5674, *Fax:* (405) 794-5112
www.oasisnetwork.org
mail@oasisnetwork.org
License: Moore, Cleveland County, OK held by Creative Educational Media Corp. Inc.
Arbitron Metro Market: Oklahoma City, OK *Format:* Religious *Target Audience:* General.
David Ingles, President
Cherri Willis, General Manager
David Warren, Programming Director
Hal Smith, Chief Engineer

KWPN(AM)
09-26-1922; 640 khz AM; 5,000 w-Day, 1,000 w- Night; 35Â° 17' 21"" N, 97Â° 30' 08"" W
4045 N.W. 64th St., Suite 600, Oklahoma, OK 73116
(405) 848-0100, *Fax:* (405) 848-5288
www.thesportsanimal.com
dax.davis@citcomm.com
License: Moore, Cleveland County, OK
Group Owner: Cumulus Media Inc.; (acq 10-28-99; grpsl).
Population Served: 591,967 *Arbitron Metro Market:* Oklahoma City, OK *Format:* Sports, Talk
Chris Baker, Operations Dir
Larry Bastida, General Manager
Dax Davis, Programming Director
Jay Davis, Contact Person
Tricia York, Contact Person

Muldrow

KXMX
05-18-1959; 105.1 mhz FM *Hrs Open:* 24; kw
US
(818) 956-5552, *Fax:* (818) 551-1110
info@kkla.com,kxmx@kxmx.com
License: Muldrow, Orange County, OK held by Chase Radio Properties L.L.C.
Group Owner: Salem Communications Corp.; (acq 8-24-00; grpsl).
Arbitron Metro Market: Glendale, CA *Format:* Arabic, Korean, 86 *Special Programming:* Gospel, relg, Pol, Sp, Vietnamese 2 hrs wkly *Target Audience:* Specialized ethnic groups. *Adv. Rates:* 125; 100; 100; 75
Terry Fahy, General Manager
Dawn McKahan, General Sales Mgr
Bob Hastings, Programming Director
Mark Pollock, Chief Engineer

Muskogee

KBIX
05-01-1936; 1490 khz AM *Hrs Open:* 24
215 N. State Street, Suite 910, Muskogee, OK 74401 US
(918) 682-9700, *Fax:* (918) 682-6775
www.sportsanimaltulsa.com
info@kbixam.com
License: Muskogee, OK held by KMMY Inc.
Group Owner: Adonai Radio Group; (acq 12-11-2002; $1 million with KCXR(FM) Taft).
Arbitron Metro Market: Wagoner, OK *Format:* Sports
David Stephens, General Manager

KHTT
02-01-1972; 106.9 mhz FM *Hrs Open:* 24; 94 kw; 1010 ft.; N35 51 43 W95 46 1
Broadcast Plaza, Crane Ave., Pittsburgh, PA 15220 US
(918) 492-2020, *Fax:* (918) 496-2681
www.khits.com
License: Muskogee, Muskogee County, OK held by Renda Broadcasting Corp.
Group Owner: Renda Broadcasting Corp.; (acq 4-15-93; $1.6 million;
Arbitron Metro Market: Tulsa, OK *Format:* Contemporary Hits/Top 40 *Target Audience:* 18-34; young adults *Adv. Rates:* 110; 110; 110; 50
Tony Renda, President
Brian Gann, Operations Dir
Phillip Sutterfield, General Sales Mgr
Bill Sexauer, Promotions Manager
David Thompson, Interactive Manager
Jet Black, Program Director

KYAL-FM
01-19-1984; 97.1 mhz FM *Hrs Open:* 24; 100 kw; 1969 ft.; N35 24 48 W95 21 55
P.O. Box 1250, Sapulpa, OK 74067 US
(918) 492-2660, *Fax:* (918) 492-8840
www.thesportsanimal.com
kxoj@kxoj.com
License: Muskogee, Muskogee County, OK held by KMMY Inc.
Group Owner: Adonai Radio Group; (acq 9-15-93; $500,000;
Arbitron Metro Market: Tulsa, OK *Format:* Sports *Special Programming:* Farm 5 hrs wkly *Target Audience:* 21-49; middle, upper-middle class *Adv. Rates:* 28; 26; 26; 22
David Stephens, General Manager

Mustang

KZLS
02-01-1981; 99.7 mhz FM *Hrs Open:* 24; 47 kw; 509 ft.; N35 35 30 W97 51 58
Mailing Address: 316 East Willow, Enid, OK 73701 US
Second Address: 316 E. Willow Rd., Enid, OK 73701
(580) 237-1390, *Fax:* (580) 242-1390
License: Mustang, Canadian County, OK held by Chisholm Trail Holding Co. Inc.
Nat'l Network: ABC *Regional Network:* Mid-America Ag
Arbitron Metro Market: Oklahoma City, OK *Format:* Country *Hrs. of News Programming:* news progmg 2 hrs wkly *No. News Employees:* 1 *Target Audience:* 25-49.
Hiram Champlin, President
Ricky Roggow, Operations Dir
Sandy Daniels, General Manager
Suzi Lakin, Promotions Manager
G.B. Bonham, Chief Engineer

Newcastle

KJKE
04-15-1971; 93.3 mhz FM; 100 kw; 797 ft; N35 11 28 W97 35 49
5101 S. Shields Blvd., Oklahoma City, OK 73129
(405) 616-5500, *Fax:* (405) 616-5505
www.kkng.com
info@kkng.com
License: Newcastle, McClain County, OK held by Tyler Broadcasting Corp.
Group Owner: Tyler Media Broadcasting Corp.; (acq 10-95; $441,000).
Nat'l Network: AP Radio *Nat'l Reps:* D & R Radio
Population Served: 19,300*Special Programming:* Sunday Morning Gospel 7a-11a *Target Audience:* 25-54. *Adv. Rates:* 14; 10; 12; 6
Skip Stow, CEO
Kevin Young, Operations Dir
Harold Patterson, General Sales Mgr
Randy Mullinax, Chief Engineer

Norman

*KGOU
09-25-1970; 106.3 mhz FM *Hrs Open:* 24; kw
780 Van Vleet Oval, Norman, OK 73019 US
(405) 325-3388, *Fax:* (405) 325-7129
www.kgou.org
manager@kgou.org
License: Norman, Cleveland County, OK held by University of Oklahoma.
Nat'l Network: NPR
Arbitron Metro Market: Oklahoma City, OK *Format:* News, News/Talk, 86 *Special Programming:* Blues 8 hrs, jazz 15 hrs, automotive 2 hrs wkly *Hrs. of News Programming:* news progmg 82 hrs wkly *No. News Employees:* 1 *Target Audience:* 25-54; general
Brian Hardzinski, Operations Dir
Karen Holp, General Manager
Jolly Brown, General Sales Mgr
Jim Johnson, Programming Director
Kurt Gwartney, News Director
Patrick Roberts, Chief Engineer
Susan Shannon, Office Manager
KathyHawkins, Business Manager

KREF
11-01-1949; 1400 khz AM *Hrs Open:* 24; 1 kw-U, ND1; N35 13 4 W97 24 37
2020 Alameda Street, Norman, OK 73072 US
(405) 321-1400, *Fax:* (405) 321-6820
www.kref.com
production@kref.com
License: Norman, OK held by Fox Broadcasting, Co.
Regional Network: Okla. News Net.
Arbitron Metro Market: Oklahoma City, OK *Format:* Sports *No. News Employees:* 1 *Target Audience:* 25-54; middle, upper class adults
John Fox, President
Mike Holt, General Manager
T.J. Perry, Programming Director

*KSSO
01-01-2007; 89.3 mhz FM; 5.6 kw; 173 ft.; N35 13 22 W97 26 21
Mailing Address: 1101 North 81 Highway, Marlow, OK 73055 US
Second Address: 8919 World Ministry Ave., Baton Rouge, LA 70810
(225) 768-3688, *Fax:* (225) 768-3729
www.jsm.org
kawikfish@yahoo.com
License: Norman, Cleveland County, OK held by Family Worship Center Church Inc.
Group Owner: Family Worship Center Church Inc.; (acq 10-7-2005; $500,000 for CP with KQUJ(FM) Ada)
David Whitelaw, COO
Jimmy Swaggart, President
John Santiago, Programming Director

North Enid

KNID
01-01-2008; 107.1 mhz FM *Hrs Open:* 24; 14 kw; 449 ft.; N36 32 13 W98 0 39
US
(580) 237-1390, *Fax:* (580) 242-1390
www.todaysbestcountryonline.com
License: North Enid, Garfield County, OK held by Champlin Broadcasting Inc.
Arbitron Metro Market: North Enid, OK *Format:* Country *Target Audience:* 18-54; men and women
Hiram Champlin, President

Nowata

KRIG-FM
01-01-1965; 104.9 mhz FM *Hrs Open:* 24/7; 8.3 kw; 564 ft.; N36 43 37 W95 46 18
Mailing Address: 1200 Se Frank Phillips Sq., P O Box 1100, Bartlesville, OK 74005 US
Second Address: 1200 S.E. Frank Phillips Blvd., Bartlesville, OK 74003
(918) 336-1001, *Fax:* (918) 336-6939
www.bartlesvilleradio.com
radio@bartlesvilleradio.com

License: Nowata, Nowata County, OK held by KCD Enterprises Inc.
Group Owner: KCD Enterprises Inc.; acq 6-26-98; $775,000)
Nat'l Network: ABC *Regional Network:* Okla. News Net.; Agri-Net
Nat'l Reps: Rgnl Reps *Regional Reps:* Rgnl Reps *Wire Services:* AP
Format: Country *Special Programming:* Gospel 4 hrs wkly *Hrs. of News Programming:* News progmg 20 hrs wkly *No. News Employees:* 2 *Target Audience:* 35-65; mature buyers *Adv. Rates:* 22; 22; 20; 22
Kevin Potter, President
Charlie Taraboletti, Operations Dir
Kevin Potter, General Manager
Tami Brinkman, General Sales Mgr
Dorea Potter, Promotions Manager
Charlie Taraboletti, News Director
Charlie Taraboletti, Chief Engineer

Okarche

KTUZ-FM
09-01-1968; 106.7 mhz FM *Hrs Open:* 24; 13 kw; 958 ft.; N35 36 49 W97 52 19
5105 South Shields Blvd, Oklahoma City, OK 73129 US
(405) 616-5500, *Fax:* (405) 616-0328
www.ktuz.com
gabriel.o@tylermedia.com
License: Okarche, Kingfisher County, OK held by Tyler Broadcasting Corp.
Group Owner: Tyler Media Broadcasting Corp.; (acq 1-27-98; $100,000 with co-located AM).
Nat'l Reps: Univision Radio National Sales
Arbitron Metro Market: Oklahoma City, OK *Hrs. of News Programming:* News progmg 16 hrs wkly *Target Audience:* 18-65. *Adv. Rates:* 30; 30; 30; 15
Ty Tyler, General Manager

Okemah

*KYLK
11-01-2002; 103.7 mhz FM *Hrs Open:* 24; 100 kw; Ant 607 ft; N34 59 13 W95 42 10
3738 W. Charleston Street, Broken Arrow, OK 74502
918-805-0099, *Fax:* 918-517-3317
www.smoothjazzoklahoma.co
Rick@rcparrish.com
License: Okemah, Okfuskee County, OK held by KESC Enterprises LLC
Arbitron Metro Market: Tulsa, OK *Target Audience:* 25-54.
Rick Parrish, Operations Dir

Oklahoma City

KATT-FM
10-17-1960; 100.5 mhz FM; 28.87 kw; 1542 ft.; N35 33 37 W97 29 7
518 17th Street, #980, Denver, CO 80202 US
(405) 848-0100, *Fax:* (405) 843-5288
www.katt.com
infor@katt.com
License: Oklahoma City, Oklahoma County, OK
Group Owner: Cumulus Media Inc.; (acq 10-28-99; grpsl).
Arbitron Metro Market: OK City, OK *Format:* Rock/AOR *Target Audience:* 18-34; Men
Larry Bastida, General Manager
Tricia York, General Sales Mgr
Chris Baker, Programming Director

KTLR
01-01-1946; 890 khz AM *Hrs Open:* 24; 1 kw-D, NDD; N35 33 59 W97 28 28
5105 S. Shields Blvd., Oklahoma City, OK 73129 US
(405) 616-5500, *Fax:* (405) 616-5505
www.ktlr.com
License: Oklahoma City, OK held by Tyler Broadcasting Corp.
Group Owner: Tyler Media Broadcasting Corp.; (acq 1999; $40,000).
Nat'l Reps: D & R Radio
Arbitron Metro Market: OK City, OK *Format:* Talk *Special Programming:* Sp 3 hrs wkly *Target Audience:* 10-80.
Skip Stow, CEO
Mike Miller, Station Manager

KJYO
04-09-1961; 102.7 mhz FM *Hrs Open:* 24; 94.1 kw; 1220 ft.; N35 35 52 W97 29 22
200 Concord Plaza, Suite 600, San Antonio, TX 78216 US
(405) 840-5271, *Fax:* (405) 858-5333
www.kj103fm.com
License: Oklahoma City, Oklahoma County, OK held by Clear Channel Broadcasting Licenses, Inc.
Arbitron Metro Market: Oklahoma City, OK *Format:* Contemporary Hits/Top 40
Mike McCoy, Programming Director

KMGL
11-25-1965; 104.1 mhz FM *Hrs Open:* 24; 92 kw; 1549 ft.; N35 33 36 W97 29 7
Mailing Address: Broadcast Plaza, Crane Ave., Pittsburgh, PA 15220 US
Second Address: 400 E. Britton Rd., Oklahoma City, OK 73114
(405) 478-5104, *Fax:* (405) 478-0448
www.magic104.com
sobrien@rendabroadcasting.com
License: Oklahoma City, Oklahoma County, OK held by Renda Broadcasting.
Group Owner: Renda Broadcasting Corp.; acq 4-88)
Arbitron Metro Market: Oklahoma City, OK *Format:* Adult Contemp *Target Audience:* 25-54; women
Don Pollnow, General Manager
Bob Delancey, General Sales Mgr
Steve O'Brien, Programming Director
Dennis Orcutt, Chief Engineer

KOKC
12-24-1922; 1520 khz AM *Hrs Open:* 24; 50 kw-D, DAN; 50 kw-N, DAN; N35 20 0 W97 30 16
Mailing Address: 1459 Crane Avenue, Pittsburgh, PA 15220 US
Second Address: 400 E. Britton Rd., Oklahoma City, OK 73113
(405) 478-5104, *Fax:* (405) 478-0448
www.1520kokc.com
jperkey@rendabroadcasting.com
License: Oklahoma City, OK held by Renda Broadcasting Corp. of Nevada.
Group Owner: Renda Broadcasting Corp.; (acq 6-30-98; grpsl).
Nat'l Network: ABC *Nat'l Reps:* ABC Radio Sales
Arbitron Metro Market: Oklahoma City, OK *Format:* News, News/Talk, 84, Talk *Target Audience:* 25-54.
Don Pallnow, General Manager
J. Perkey, Programming Director

KOMA
01-01-1964; 92.5 mhz FM *Hrs Open:* 24; 94 kw; 1549 ft.; N35 33 36 W97 29 7
1459 Crane Avenue, Pittsburgh, PA 15220 US
(405) 478-5104, *Fax:* (405) 475-7021
www.komaradio.com
License: Oklahoma City, Oklahoma County, OK held by Renda Broadcasting Corp. of Nevada.
Group Owner: Renda Broadcasting Corp.; (acq 6-30-98; grpsl).
Arbitron Metro Market: Oklahoma City, OK *Format:* Contemporary Hits/Top 40, Adult Contemp *Target Audience:* 25-54.
Don Pollnow, General Manager
Sibyl Overstreet, General Sales Mgr
Kent Jones, Programming Director
Lisa Sykes, Promotions Manager
Stephen Bennett, News Director

KQCV
01-01-1948; 800 khz AM *Hrs Open:* 24
10550 Barkley, Ste 108, Overland Park, KS 66212 US
(913) 642-7770, *Fax:* (913) 642-1319
www.bottradionetwork.com
comments@bottradionetwork.com
License: Oklahoma City, OK held by Bott Broadcasting Co.
Group Owner: Bott Radio Network; (acq 1-76)
Arbitron Metro Market: OK City, OK *Format:* Christian, News *Target Audience:* 25-54; family oriented
Richard Bott, Sr., Chairman
Richard Bott, II, President
Eben Fowler, Operations Dir
Paul Sublett, General Manager
Pat Rulon, General Sales Mgr
Candy Green, Programming Director
Jerry McCall, Operations Director

KBRU
06-06-1967; 94.7 mhz FM *Hrs Open:* 24; 98 kw; 1,387 ft; N35 32 58 W97 29 50
Box 1000, Oklahoma City, OK 78216
(405) 840-5271, *Fax:* (405) 842-1315
www.947thebuzz.com
info@947thebuzz.com
License: Oklahoma City, Oklahoma County, OK held by Clear Channel Broadcasting Licenses, Inc.
Group Owner: Clear Channel Communications Inc.; (acq 1-94; $7.5 million).
Population Served: 850,000 *Arbitron Metro Market:* Oklahoma City, OK *No. News Employees:* 1 *Target Audience:* 25-54.
Jrod, Programming Director

KRXO
08-07-1987; 107.7 mhz FM *Hrs Open:* 24; 92 kw; 1542 ft.; N35 33 37 W97 29 6
Mailing Address: 1459 Crane Avenue, Pittsburgh, PA 15220 US
Second Address: 400 E. Britton Rd., Oklahoma City, OK 73113
(405) 478-5104, *Fax:* (405) 478-0448
www.krxo.com
bwiley@krxo.com
License: Oklahoma City, Oklahoma County, OK held by Renda Broadcasting Corp of Nevada.
Group Owner: Renda Broadcasting Corp.
Arbitron Metro Market: Oklahoma City, OK *Format:* Classic Rock
Jim Williston, General Manager
Buddy Wiley, Programming Director
Cara Rice, Promotions Manager
Steve Bennett, News Director

KTOK
01-29-1927; 1000 khz AM *Hrs Open:* 24; 5 kw-D, DA2; 5 kw-N, DA2; N35 21 29 W97 27 48
Mailing Address: 3305 W. Mountain Rd, #60, Las Vegas, NV 89102 US
Second Address: 1900 Northwest Expressway, Ste 1000, Oklahoma City, OK 73118
(405) 840-5271, *Fax:* (405) 858-5333
www.ktok.com
License: Oklahoma City, OK held by Clear Channel Broadcasting Licences, Inc.
Group Owner: Clear Channel Communications Inc.; acq 8-5-92)
Regional Network: Okla. News Net. *Nat'l Reps:* Clear Channel
Arbitron Metro Market: Oklahoma City, OK *Format:* News, News/Talk, 86
Derric Nance, General Sales Mgr
Lee Matthews, Programming Director
Bill Hurley-Market Manager

KTST
03-16-1962; 101.9 mhz FM *Hrs Open:* 24; 94.4 kw; 1220 ft.; N35 35 52 W97 29 22
Suite 600, 200 Concord Plaza, San Antonio, TX 78216 US
(405) 841-0200, *Fax:* (405) 848-1106
www.thetwister.com
mikemccoy@clearchannel.com
License: Oklahoma City, Oklahoma County, OK held by Clear Channel Broadcasting Licenses, Inc.
Group Owner: Clear Channel Communications Inc.; acq 1996; grpsl)
Arbitron Metro Market: Oklahoma City, OK *Format:* Country *No. News Employees:* 1 *Target Audience:* 18-49.
Tom Travis, Operations Dir
Bill Hurley, General Manager
Tom Travis, Programming Director
Bill Hurley, Radio VP/Market Manager
Derrick Nance, Sales Contact

KRMP
1140 khz AM; 1 kw-D, NDD; N35 23 14 W97 29 56
1528 N.E. 23rd Street, Oklahoma City, OK 73111 US
(405) 427-5877, *Fax:* (405) 424-6708
okcheartandsoul.com
info@krmp.com
License: Oklahoma City, OK held by Perry Broadcasting Co. Inc.
Group Owner: Perry Publishing & Broadcasting Co.; (acq 3-3-93; $375,000;
Arbitron Metro Market: Oklahoma City, OK *Format:* Urban Contemporary
Russell Perry, CEO
Terry Monday, Operations Dir
Kevin Perry, General Sales Mgr

KXXY-FM
10-01-1964; 96.1 mhz FM *Hrs Open:* 24; 94.9 kw; 1220 ft.; N35 35 52 W97 29 22
200 Concord Plaza, Ste 600, San Antonio, TX 78216 US
(405) 840-5271, *Fax:* (405) 842-1315
www.kxy.com
License: Oklahoma City, Oklahoma County, OK held by Clear Channel Broadcasting Licenses Inc.
Group Owner: Clear Channel Communications Inc.; (acq 1996; grpsl).
Arbitron Metro Market: Oklahoma City, OK *Format:* Country
Bill Reed, Programming Director

KYIS
06-01-1969; 98.9 mhz FM *Hrs Open:* 24; 100 kw; 1542 ft.; N35 33 37 W97 29 7
518 17th Street, Ste 980, Denver, CO 80202 US
(405) 848-0100, *Fax:* (405) 843-5288
www.kiss989.com
info@klis.com
License: Oklahoma City, Oklahoma County, OK

Group Owner: Cumulus Media Inc.; (acq 10-28-99; grpsl).
Nat'l Network: AP Radio
Arbitron Metro Market: Oklahoma City, OK *Format:* Adult Contemp *No. News Employees:* 1 *Target Audience:* 25-54; female
Larry Bastida, General Manager
Tricia York, General Sales Mgr
Chris Baker, Programming Director
Don Sweeney, Promotions Manager

*KYLV
11-03-1980; 88.9 mhz FM *Hrs Open:* 24; 5.9 kw; 1522 ft.; N35 33 37 W97 29 6 *Rebroadcasts:* Rebroadcasts KLVR(FM) Middletown, CA 100%
2501 E. Memorial Rd., Oklahoma City, OK 73136 US
(800) 525-5683, *Fax:* (916) 251-1650
www.klove.com
info@klove.com
License: Oklahoma City, Oklahoma County, OK held by Educational Media Foundation.
Group Owner: EMF Broadcasting; (acq 11-9-98; $1.2 million)
Nat'l Network: K-Love
Arbitron Metro Market: Oklahoma City, OK *Format:* Christian
Special Programming: Black 3 hrs, relg 2 hrs, gospel 4 hrs, pub affrs 4 hrs wkly *No. News Employees:* 3 *Target Audience:* 25-44; Judeo-Christian female
Darrell Chambliss, Chairman
Mike Novak, CEO/COO
Mike Novak, President
Evan Falat, Operations Dir
David Pierce, Programming Director
Ed Lenane, News Director
Sam Wallington, Engineering Dir
David Pierce, Chief CreativeOfficer
Alan Mason, Chief Operating Officer
Dan Antonelli, Chief Business Development Officer
Eric Moser, Chief Financial Officer
Mitch Barnhart, Director
Larry Moody, Director

WKY
01-01-1920; 930 khz AM *Hrs Open:* 24; 5 kw-D, DAN; 5 kw-N, DAN; N35 33 43 W97 30 27
P.O.Box 25125, Oklahoma City, OK 73125 US
(405) 848-0100, *Fax:* (405) 843-5288
www.jox930.com
info@jox930.com
License: Oklahoma City, OK
Group Owner: Cumulus Media Inc.; (acq 1-31-2003; $7.7 million)
Arbitron Metro Market: OK City, OK *Format:* Sports *Target Audience:* 25-54; Men
Chris Baker, Operations Dir
Larry Bastida, General Manager
Dan Davis, Programming Director

Okmulgee

KOKL
10-01-1937; 1240 khz AM *Hrs Open:* 24; 1 kw-U, ND1; N35 36 31 W95 58 19
Box 756, Okmulgee, OK 74447 US
(918) 756-3646, *Fax:* (918) 756-1800
www.kokl.net
koklradio@aol.com
License: Okmulgee, OK held by Regency Radio Inc.
Nat'l Network: ABC
Arbitron Metro Market: Tulsa, OK *Format:* Country, News, 62, Sports, Talk *Special Programming:* Tulsa Univ. sports 10 hrs *Hrs. of News Programming:* news progmg 16 hrs wkly *No. News Employees:* 1 *TargetAudience:* 25 plus; mid to upper income *Adv. Rates:* 18.95; 15.95; 18.95; 11.25
James Brewer, President
Paul Brown, General Manager

Owasso

KTGX
10-01-1981; 106.1 mhz FM *Hrs Open:* 24; 100 kw; Ant 1,315 ft; N36 31 36 W95 39 12
2625 South Memorial, Tulsa, OK 78216
(918) 388-5100, *Fax:* (918) 388-5400
www.kooltulsa.com
License: Owasso, Tulsa County, OK held by Clear Channel Broadcasting Licenses Inc.
Group Owner: Clear Channel Communications Inc.; (acq 1997; grpsl)
Arbitron Metro Market: Tulsa, OK *Target Audience:* Adults 35-54.
Don Cristi, Operations Dir
Michael Oppenheimer, General Manager

Pawhuska

KOSG
01-01-1997; 103.9 mhz FM; 6 kw; 328 ft.; N36 44 56 W96 17 51
609 Kihekah, Pawhuska, OK 74056 US
(580) 332-0902, *Fax:* (580) 332-0922
www.thegospelstation.com
info@kosgfm.com
License: Pawhuska, Osage County, OK held by Tallgrass Broadcasting LLC
Group Owner: Tallgrass Broadcasting LLC; (acq 10-25-2006; $294,000)
Arbitron Metro Market: Ada, OK *Format:* Gospel
Joe Walker, President

KPGM
10-19-1963; 1500 khz AM *Hrs Open:* 6 AM-6 PM; 0.5 kw-D, NDD; N36 45 42 W96 11 58
Mailing Address: 4415 East 25th Street, Tulsa, OK 74114 US
Second Address: 129 W. Main, Pawhuska, OK 74056
(918) 287-1145, *Fax:* (918) 287-1473
www.bartlesvilleradio.com/kpgm
kpgm@bartlesvilleradio.com
License: Pawhuska, OK held by Potter Radio LLC.
Group Owner: KCD Enterprises Inc.; (acq 7-1-2005; $100,000).
Nat'l Network: Salem Radio Network
Arbitron Metro Market: Tulsa, OK *Format:* Christian, News, 86 *Hrs. of News Programming:* news progmg 20 hrs wkly *No. News Employees:* 1 *Adv. Rates:* 12; 12; 12; 12
Kevin Potter, President
Charlie Taraboletti, Programming Director

Perry

KOKP
07-06-1986; 1020 khz AM *Hrs Open:* 24; 0.4 kw-D, DA2; 0.25 kw-N, DA2; N36 15 35 W97 13 1
3130 South Utica, Tulsa, OK 74105 US
(580) 765-2485, *Fax:* (580) 767-1103
www.eteamradio.com
bill@eteamradio.com
License: Perry, OK held by Team Radio L.L.C.
Group Owner: Team Radio LLC; (acq 7-14-98; $308,000 with co-located FM).
Format: Sports *Target Audience:* 24 plus; agriculture-related country
Bill Coleman, President
Chris Johnson, Programming Director

KOSB
11-24-1988; 105.1 mhz FM *Hrs Open:* 24; 6 kw; 328 ft.; N36 14 15 W97 21 59
3130 South Utica, Tulsa, OK 74105 US
(580) 765-2485, *Fax:* (580) 767-1103
www.eteamradio.com
bill@eteamradio.com
License: Perry, Noble County, OK held by Team Radio, LLC
Group Owner: Team Radio LLC
Nat'l Network: Westwood One
Format: Sports *No. News Employees:* 1 *Target Audience:* 25-55.
Chris Johnson, Programming Director

Piedmont

*KZTH
04-01-2008; 88.5 mhz FM; 50 kw; 597 ft.; N35 31 17 W98 9 33
Rebroadcasts: Rebroadcasts KJTH(FM) Ponca City 100%
P.O. Box 14, Ponca City, OK 74602 US
(580) 767-1400, *Fax:* (580) 765-1700
www.thehousefm.com
mail@thehousefm.com
License: Piedmont, Canadian County, OK held by The Love Station Inc.
Arbitron Metro Market: Piedmont, OK *Format:* Christian
Doyle Brewer, CEO and Founder
Tony Weir, Music Director
Janelle Keith, Music Director
Darcey Christianson, Chief Engineer
Shaun Michaels, Production Director
Andy Youso, Assistant Program Director
Donna Hollifield, OfficeManager
Jennifer Vaughan, Promotions Assistant

Pocola

*KKRI
06-11-2002; 88.1 mhz FM *Hrs Open:* 24; 0.001 kw horiz, 17 kw vert; 374 ft.; N35 13 30 W94 18 4
1425 North Market Blvd, Suite 9, Sacramento, CA 95834 US
(888) 937-2471, *Fax:* (916) 251-1650
www.air1.com
info@air1.com
License: Pocola, Le Flore County, OK held by Educational Media Foundation.
Group Owner: EMF Broadcasting
Nat'l Network: Air 1
Arbitron Metro Market: Fort Smith, AR *Format:* Alternative, Christian *No. News Employees:* 3 *Target Audience:* 18-35; Judeo-Christian, female
Darrell Chambliss, Chairman
Alan Mason, COO
Mike Novak, President and CEO
Evan Falat, Operations Dir
David Pierce, Programming Director
Tracy Butler, News Director
Sam Wallington, Engineering Dir
Marya Morgan, News Reporter
Richard Hunt, News Reporter
Larry Moody, Director
Mitch Barnhart, Director
David R. Ferry, Director
Walter Golembeski, Director

Ponca City

KIXR
06-01-1984; 104.7 mhz FM *Hrs Open:* 24; 25 kw; 292 ft.; N36 47 21 W97 2 53
Mailing Address: Post Office Box 2631, Ponca City, OK 74602 US
Second Address: 3924 Santa Fe Rd., Ponca City, OK 74602
(580) 765-5491, *Fax:* (580) 762-8329
www.kixr.com
kixr@kixr.com
License: Ponca City, Kay County, OK held by Mur-Thom Broadcasting Inc.
Nat'l Network: Westwood One
Format: Talk *Special Programming:* Native American 3 hrs wkly *Hrs. of News Programming:* news progmg 4 hrs wkly *No. News Employees:* 5 *Target Audience:* 24-55; core audience of females between the ages of 24-45*Adv. Rates:* 13; 12; 13; 11
Carol Murphy, President
Gordon Thompson, General Manager
Dave Foster, Chief Engineer

KLOR-FM
12-01-1965; 99.3 mhz FM *Hrs Open:* 24; 3 kw; 289 ft.; N36 46 59 W97 4 15
3130 S. Utica Ave., Tulsa, OK 74105 US
(580) 762-9930, *Fax:* (580) 767-1103
www.eteamradio.com
billc@eteamradio.com
License: Ponca City, Kay County, OK held by Team Radio L.L.C.
Group Owner: Team Radio LLC; acq 3-18-99).
Regional Network: Okla. News Net.
Arbitron Metro Market: Tulsa, OK *Format:* Classic Rock, Oldies *Hrs. of News Programming:* news progmg 75 hrs wkly *No. News Employees:* 1 *Target Audience:* 18-55.
Bill Coleman, President
Darrel Dye, General Sales Mgr
Sean Anderson, Programming Director

*KLVV
12-01-1992; 88.7 mhz FM *Hrs Open:* 24; 11.5 kw; 479 ft.; N36 41 25 W97 10 20
Mailing Address: P O Box 14, Ponca City, OK 74602 US
Second Address: 6600 W. Hwy. 60, Ponca City, OK 74601
(580) 767-1400, *Fax:* (580) 765-1700
www.klvv.com; www.mychristianfm.com,www.mypraisefm.com
mail@mypraisefm.com
License: Ponca City, Kay County, OK held by The Love Station Inc.
Format: Christian, Religious *Target Audience:* 25-45; young Christian adults
Doyle Brewer, CEO
Tony Weir, Programming Director
Janelle Keith, Promotions Manager
Darcy Christianson, Chief Engineer

KPNC
06-05-1979; 100.7 mhz FM *Hrs Open:* 24; 25 kw; 253 ft.; N36 46 59 W97 4 15
Mailing Address: PO Box 2509, Ponca City, OK 74602 US
Second Address: 122 N. 3rd St., Ponca City, OK 74601
(580) 765-2485, *Fax:* (580) 767-1103
www.eteamradio.com
billc@eteamradio.com
License: Ponca City, Kay County, OK held by Team Radio L.L.C.
Group Owner: Team Radio LLC; (acq 7-20-90)

Format: Country *Special Programming:* Farm 5 hrs wkly *Hrs. of News Programming:* News progmg 20 hrs wkly *Target Audience:* 25-54; working middle class
Bill Coleman, Chairman
Darrel Dye, General Sales Mgr
Ryan Diamond, Programming Director

WBBZ
01-01-1927; 1230 khz AM *Hrs Open:* 24; 1 kw-U, ND1; N36 41 46 W97 3 7
Box 191, Ponca City, OK 74602 US
(800) 877-5600, *Fax:* (916) 251-1650
www.air1.com
info@air1.com
License: Ponca City, OK held by Ponca City Publishing Co.
Nat'l Network: AP Radio
Arbitron Metro Market: Sioux Falls SD *Format:* Alternative, Christian
Mike Novak, President

***KJTH**
01-01-2004; 89.7 mhz FM *Hrs Open:* 24; 100 kw; 1007 ft.; N36 35 42 W97 34 38
Mailing Address: P.O. Box 14, Ponca City, OK 74602 US
Second Address: 6600 W. Hwy. 60, Ponca City, OK 74601
(580) 767-1400, *Fax:* (580) 765-1700
www.thehousefm.com
mail@thehousefm.com
License: Ponca City, Kay County, OK held by The Love Station Inc.
Arbitron Metro Market: Ponca City, OK *Format:* Christian *Target Audience:* 25-45; young Christian adults
Doyle Brewer, CEO and Founder
Tony Weir, Program/Music Director
Janelle Keith, Program/Music Director
Darcey Christianson, Chief Engineer
Shaun Michaels, Production Director
Janelle Keith, Promotions Director
Andy Youso,Assistant Program Director
Donna Hollifield, Office Manager
Jennifer Vaughan, Promotions Assistant
Stacey Husted, Office Assistant

Poteau

***KARG**
06-01-1998; 91.7 mhz FM; 2.5 kw; 1867 ft.; N35 4 17 W94 40 47
P O Drawer 2440, Tupelo, MS 38803 US
(662) 844-8888, *Fax:* (662) 842-6791
www.afr.net
License: Poteau, Le Flore County, OK held by American Family Association.
Group Owner: American Family Radio
Arbitron Metro Market: Tupelo, MO *Format:* Christian, Religious
Marvin Sanders, General Manager

KOMS
10-18-1969; 107.3 mhz FM *Hrs Open:* 24; 100 kw; 1893 ft.; N34 57 47.3 W94 22 30.7
111 East Kilbourn Avenue, Suite 2700, Milwaukee, WI 53202 US
(479) 474-3422, *Fax:* (479) 474-2649
www.bigcountry1073.com
cindywilson@cumulus.com
License: Poteau, Le Flore County, OK held by Cumulus Licensing Corp.
Group Owner: Cumulus Media Inc.; (acq 5-17-99; $950,000)
Nat'l Network: CNN Radio *Wire Services:* AP
Arbitron Metro Market: Fort Smith, AR *Format:* Country *Hrs. of News Programming:* News progmg 60 hrs wkly *Target Audience:* 25-54.
Michael Hauser, Programming Director
Smitty O'Loughlin, Promotions Manager
Don Jones, Engineering Dir
J.P. Morgan, Disc Jockey

KPRV
11-25-1953; 1280 khz AM *Hrs Open:* 24
PO Box 368, Poteau, OK 74953 US
(918) 647-3221, *Fax:* (918) 647-5092
www.kprvradio.com
kprv@windstream.net
License: Poteau, OK held by LeRoy Billy.
Nat'l Network: ABC *Regional Network:* Okla. News Net.
Arbitron Metro Market: Fort Smith, AR *Format:* Country, Gospel *Hrs. of News Programming:* News progmg 24 hrs wkly *Target Audience:* 24-54.
LeRoy Billy, President
Joann Billy, General Manager
LeRoy Billy, General Sales Mgr

KZBB
01-01-1967; 97.9 mhz FM *Hrs Open:* 24; 100 kw; 2001 ft.; N35 4 19 W94 40 46
600 Congress Ave., Suite 1400, Austin, TX 78701 US
(479) 782-8888, *Fax:* (479) 782-0366
www.kzbb.com
mikeburgess@clearchannel.com
License: Poteau, Le Flore County, OK held by Capstar TX L.P.
Group Owner: Clear Channel Communications Inc.; (acq 8-30-00; grpsl)
Arbitron Metro Market: Poteau, OK *Format:* Contemporary Hits/Top 40 *Special Programming:* Black 2 hrs, jazz 2 hrs, relg one hr wkly *Hrs. of News Programming:* News progmg one hr wkly *Target Audience:* 18-49;upscale
Ralph Cherry, Operations Dir
Paul Swint, General Manager
Mike Burgess, General Sales Mgr
Maverick, Programming Director
Allan Riley, Chief Engineer

Pryor

KMYZ-FM
07-03-1969; 104.5 mhz FM *Hrs Open:* 24; 70 kw; 1129 ft.; N36 1 10 W95 39 24
149 Penn Ave., Scranton, PA 18501 US
(918) 665-3131, *Fax:* (918) 663-6622
www.edgetulsa.com
production@shamrocktuosa.com
License: Pryor, Mayes County, OK held by Shamrock Communications Inc.
Group Owner: Shamrock Communications Inc.; acq 4-14-84)
Arbitron Metro Market: Tulsa, OK *Format:* Alternative
William Lynett, CEO
Chuck Browning, General Manager

Rattan

***KDBQ**
89.7 mhz FM; kw
US
(940) 668-7971
License: Rattan, Pushmataha County, OK held by 1 A Chord Inc.
Arbitron Metro Market: Santa Cruz, CA
Mary Fay Jackson, General Manager

Roland

KREU
12-29-1995; 92.3 mhz FM; 0.74 kw horiz, 0.73 kw vert; 932 ft.; N35 31 22 W94 23 32
2201 1/2 N. 58th Street, Fort Smith, AR 72904 US
(479) 785-2527, *Fax:* (501) 782-9127
License: Roland, Sequoyah County, OK held by Star 92 Co.
Arbitron Metro Market: Fort Smith, AR *Format:* Spanish
Fred Baker Jr., Operations Dir
Gary Keifer, General Manager
Carol Patterson, General Sales Mgr
Martin Miranda, Programming Director
Dale Davenport, Chief Engineer

Sallisaw

KKBD
05-18-1972; 95.9 mhz FM *Hrs Open:* 24; 30 kw; 623 ft.; N35 24 26 W94 41 25
600 Congress Avenue, Suite 1400, Austin, TX 78701 US
(479) 782-8888
www.bigdog959.com
info@bigdog959.com
License: Sallisaw, Sequoyah County, OK held by Clear Channel Radio Licenses, Inc.
Group Owner: Clear Channel Communications Inc.; (acq 8-30-00; grpsl).
Arbitron Metro Market: Fort Smith, AR *Format:* Classic Rock *Target Audience:* 25-49; adults
Paul Swint, General Manager
Phil Robken, General Sales Mgr

Sand Springs

KRMG-FM
06-01-1989; 102.3 mhz FM *Hrs Open:* 24; 50 kw; 492 ft.; N36 12 39 W96 6 3 *Rebroadcasts:* Simulcast with KRMG(AM) Tulsa 100%
8107 East Admiral Place, Tulsa, OK 74115 US
(918) 493-7400, *Fax:* (918) 493-2376
www.krmg.com
info@krmg.com
License: Sand Springs, Tulsa County, OK held by Cox Radio Inc.
Group Owner: Cox Radio Inc.; (acq 3-16-99; $3.5 million)
Arbitron Metro Market: Tulsa, OK *Format:* News, News/Talk, 86 *Target Audience:* 25-44.
Dan Lawrie, General Manager
Levi May, Programming Director
Randy Heller, Promotions Manager
Joe Kelley, News Director
Wayne Smith, Chief Engineer

KJMU
07-22-1961; 1340 khz AM *Hrs Open:* 24
8107 East Admiral Place, Tulsa, OK 74115 US
(248) 557-3500, *Fax:* (248) 557-2950
www.laquemandaentulsa.com
djpercy@perezmediagroup.com
License: Sand Springs, OK held by Birach Broadcasting Corp.
Group Owner: Birach Broadcasting Corp.; (acq 1-31-2008; $1.5 million with KTUV(AM) Little Rock, AR)
Arbitron Metro Market: Southfield, MI *Format:* Urban Contemporary
Sima Birach, General Manager

Sapulpa

KYAL
06-15-1962; 1550 khz AM *Hrs Open:* 24; 2.5 kw-D, DA2; 0.04 kw-N, DA2; N36 1 8 W96 5 55
P. O. Box 1250, Sapulpa, OK 74067 US
(918) 492-2660, *Fax:* (918) 492-8840
www.sportsanimaltulsa.com
studio@sportsanimaltulsa.com
License: Sapulpa, OK held by KXOJ Inc.
Group Owner: Adonai Radio Group; (acq 5-2-73)
Arbitron Metro Market: Tulsa, OK *Format:* Sports *Target Audience:* 35 plus.
David Stephens, General Manager

KXOJ-FM
02-22-1977; 100.9 mhz FM *Hrs Open:* 24; 5 kw; 361 ft.; N36 3 38 W96 6 3
P. O. Box 1250, Sapulpa, OK 74067 US
(918) 492-2660, *Fax:* (918) 492-8840
www.kxoj.com
kxoj@kxoj.com
License: Sapulpa, Creek County, OK held by KXOJ, Inc.
Group Owner: Adonai Radio Group
Arbitron Metro Market: Tulsa, OK *Format:* Christian
Mike Stephens, CEO
David Stephens, General Manager

Sayre

***KESG**
88.7 mhz FM; 0.225 kw horiz; 85 ft.; N35 21 47 W99 42 59
US
(580) 928-2345, *Fax:* (580) 928-3271
License: Sayre, Beckham County, OK held by Trinity Fellowship Ministries Inc.
Arbitron Metro Market: Sayre, OK
Andy Taylor, President

Seminole

KIRC
01-01-1986; 105.9 mhz FM *Hrs Open:* 24; 4.4 kw; 384 ft.; N35 18 28 W96 45 18
2 E. Main Street, Shawnee, OK 74801 US
(405) 878-1803,(405) 382-0105, *Fax:* (405) 878-0162
kirc1059@aol.com
License: Seminole, Seminole County, OK held by One Ten Broadcast Group Inc.
Group Owner: One Ten Broadcast Group Inc.; (acq 4-16-2008)
Arbitron Metro Market: Oklahoma City, OK *Format:* Country *Special Programming:* Area tribes one hr wkly *Hrs. of News Programming:* news progmg 2 hrs wkly *No. News Employees:* 9 *Target Audience:* 12-55;general *Adv. Rates:* 22; 20; 22; 18
Linda Jones, President
Dennis Burton, General Manager
David Beerley, General Sales Mgr
Nichole Johnson, News Director
Jim Stanford, Chief Engineer

***KXTH**
10-01-2003; 89.1 mhz FM *Hrs Open:* 24; 2.6 kw; 377 ft.; N35 12 53 W96 44 26
Mailing Address: P O Drawer 2440, Tupelo, MS 38803 US
Second Address: 6600 W. Hwy. 60, Ponca City, OK 74601
(580) 767-1400, *Fax:* (580) 765-1700
www.thehousefm.com
mail@thehousefm.com
License: Seminole, Seminole County, OK held by The Love Station Inc.

Arbitron Metro Market: Ponca City, OK *Format:* Adult Contemp, Christian *Target Audience:* 25-45; young Christian adults
Doyle Brewer, CEO and Founder
Tony Weir, Program/Music Director
Janelle Keith, Program/Music Director
Darcey Christianson, Chief Engineer
Shaun Michaels, Production Director
Andy Youso, Assistant Program Director
DonnaHollifield, Office Manager
Jennifer Vaughan, Promotions Assistant
Stacey Husted, Office Assistant

Shawnee

KGFF
12-10-1930; 1450 khz AM *Hrs Open:* 24; 1 kw-U; N35 21 39 W96 53 41
Mailing Address: Box 9, Shawnee, OK 74801
Second Address: 1570 S. Gordon Cooper Drive, Shawnee, OK 74801
(405) 273-4390, *Fax:* (405) 273-4530
www.kgff.com
mike@kgff.com
License: Shawnee, Pottawatomie County, OK held by Citizen Band Potawatomi Indian Tribe of Oklahoma I
Nat'l Network: Dial Global; St. Louis Cardinals (sports) *Regional Network:* Okla. News Net.; Learfield Sports
Population Served: 45,000 *Arbitron Metro Market:* Oklahoma City, *Special Programming:* school, University of Oklahoma, Oklahoma Baptist U *Hrs. of News Programming:* news progmg 20 hrs wkly *No. News Employees:* 1*Target Audience:* General
Michael Askins, General Manager
Michael Askins, Station Manager
Carrie Kieffer, General Sales Mgr
Michael Askins, Programming Director
Carrie Kieffer, Promotions Manager
Michael Askins, News Director
Michael Askins, EngineeringDir

KQCV-FM
04-13-1998; 95.1 mhz FM; 100 kw; 1,004 ft; N35 15 47 W96 22 43
1919 N. Broadway, Oklahoma City, OK 64052
(405) 521-0800, *Fax:* (405) 521-1391
www.bottradionetwork.com
License: Shawnee, Pottawatomie County, OK held by Community Broadcasting Inc.
Group Owner: Bott Radio Network
Arbitron Metro Market: Oklahoma City,
Jerry McCall, Operations Dir
Paul Sublett, General Manager
Joseph Palmer, General Sales Mgr
Paul Sublett, Chief Engineer

Snyder

KJCM
01-01-2000; 100.3 mhz FM; 18 kw; 384 ft.; N34 38 42 W99 5 3
Mailing Address: Post Office Box 837, Altus, OK 73522 US
Second Address: 1515 N. Broadway, Hobart, OK 73651
(580) 726-5656, *Fax:* (580) 726-2222
thezone@itlnet.net
License: Snyder, Kiowa County, OK held by Fuchs Radio L.L.C.
Group Owner: Fuchs Radio L.L.C.; (acq 4-4-2006; $250,000 with KHIM(FM) Mangum)
Format: Adult Contemp
Chad Fox, General Manager
Lance Perritt, Programming Director

Soper

KMMY
01-01-2008; 96.5 mhz FM *Hrs Open:* 24; 3.4 kw; 443 ft.; N33 59 25 W95 46 48
US
(580) 326-5541, *Fax:* (580) 326-5236
www.myrock965.com
License: Soper, Choctaw County, OK held by Will Payne.
Arbitron Metro Market: Soper, OK *Format:* Rock/AOR
Will Payne, General Manager

Spencer

*KROU
01-28-1993; 105.7 mhz FM *Hrs Open:* 24 hrs; 1.6 kw; 638 ft.; N35 34 6.8 W97 29 19.9 *Rebroadcasts:* Rebroadcasts KGOU(FM) Norman 100%
Mailing Address: 780 Van Vleet Oval, Norman, OK 73019 US
Second Address: The University of Oklahoma, Spencer, OK
(405) 325-3388, *Fax:* (405) 325-7129
www.kgou.org
manager@kgou.org
License: Spencer, Oklahoma County, OK held by University of Oklahoma.
Nat'l Network: NPR
Arbitron Metro Market: OK City, OK *Format:* Blues, Jazz *Special Programming:* Blues 8 hrs *Hrs. of News Programming:* news progmg 82 hrs wkly *No. News Employees:* 1 *Target Audience:* 25-54; general
Brian Hardzinski, Operations Dir
Karen Holp, General Manager
Jim Johnson, Programming Director
Kurt Gwartney, News Director
Patrick Roberts, Chief Engineer

Sperry

KMUS
01-01-2004; 1380 khz AM *Hrs Open:* 24
P.O. Box 52311, 320 S. Boston, Suite 920, Tulsa, OK 74152 US
(918) 250-8484, *Fax:* (918) 250-6464
www.radiodisney.com/tulsa
info@kmusam.com
License: Sperry, OK held by Radio Disney Group LLC.
Arbitron Metro Market: Tulsa, OK *Format:* Children *Adv. Rates:* 14; 14; 14; 14
Barbara Jacaby, General Manager
Mark Gould, General Sales Mgr
Amanda Lucie, Promotions Manager

Stigler

*KTKL
01-01-2003; 88.5 mhz FM *Hrs Open:* 24; 0.001 kw horiz, 22 kw vert; 643 ft.; N35 8 30 W95 21 20
US
(800) 525-5683, *Fax:* (916) 251-1650
www.klove.com
klove@klove.com
License: Stigler, Haskell County, OK held by Educational Media Foundation.
Group Owner: EMF Broadcasting
Nat'l Network: K-Love
Arbitron Metro Market: Stigler, OK *Format:* Christian *No. News Employees:* 3 *Target Audience:* 25-44; Judeo Christian, female
Darrell Chambliss, Chairman
Mike Novak, President and CEO
Evan Falat, Operations Dir
David Pierce, Programming Director
Ed Lenane, News Director
Sam Wallington, Engineering Dir
Marya Morgan, News Reporter
Richard Hunt, NewsReporter
Laura Daniels, News Reporter
Tim Luttrell, News Reporter
Kenny Noble Cortes, News Reporter
Darren Vinson, News Reporter

Stillwater

KGFY
02-06-1967; 105.5 mhz FM *Hrs Open:* 24; 4.2 kw; 393 ft.; N36 10 47 W97 0 38
Box 4584, Springfield, MO 65808 US
(405) 372-7800, *Fax:* (405) 372-6969
www.stillwaterradio.net
ken@stillwaterradio.net
License: Stillwater, Payne County, OK held by Stillwater Broadcasting LLC.
Group Owner: Mahaffey Enterprises Inc.; (acq 9-28-2001).
Format: Country *Special Programming:* Sports News 10 hrs wkly *Hrs. of News Programming:* news progmg 5 hrs wkly *No. News Employees:* 1 *Target Audience:* 18-54; young, college community & upscale educated people*Adv. Rates:* 30; 20; 30; 10
Ken Fearnow, General Manager
Diane Keenom, Station Manager
Jay McRae, Programming Director
Bill Van Ness, News Director
Carder Price, Creative Service Director
Rex Holt, Sports Director

*KOSU
12-29-1955; 91.7 mhz FM *Hrs Open:* 24; 100 kw; 1010 ft.; N35 46 50 W97 31 29
Rm 302 Paul Miller Bldg., Stillwater, OK 74078 US
(405) 744-6352, *Fax:* (405) 744-9970
www.kosu.org
info@kosu.org
License: Stillwater, Payne County, OK held by Oklahoma State University.
Nat'l Network: NPR
Format: News *Special Programming:* American Indian one hr wkly *Hrs. of News Programming:* news progmg 48 hrs wkly *No. News Employees:* 2 *Target Audience:* General.
Craig Beeby, General Manager
Don Crider, General Sales Mgr
Rachel Hubbard, News Director
Dan Schroeder, Engineering Dir

KSPI
06-01-1947; 780 khz AM *Hrs Open:* 6 AM-6 PM; 0.25 kw-D, NDD; N36 4 56 W97 3 13
Mailing Address: 211 West 9th Street, Stillwater, OK 74074 US
Second Address: 408 E. Thomas Rd., Stillwater, OK 74076
(405) 372-7800, *Fax:* (405) 372-6969
www.stillwaterradio.net
stillwaterradio@coxinet.net
License: Stillwater, OK held by Stillwater Broadcasting LLC.
Group Owner: Mahaffey Enterprises Inc.; (acq 7-21-97; $650,000 with co-located FM)
Nat'l Network: ESPN Radio
Arbitron Metro Market: Stillwater, OK *Format:* News, News/Talk, 84, Talk *Special Programming:* News, sports, features *Hrs. of News Programming:* news progmg 12 hrs wkly *No. News Employees:* 1 *Target Audience:* 30 plus. *Adv. Rates:* 25; 25; 25; 20
John Mahaffey, President
Ken Fearnow, General Manager
Ken Fearnow, General Sales Mgr
Jay McRae, Programming Director
Bill Van Ness, News Director

KSPI-FM
11-01-1947; 93.7 mhz FM *Hrs Open:* 24; 16 kw; 886 ft.; N36 6 30 W97 11 47
Mailing Address: P.O. Box 2288, Stillwater, OK 74076 US
Second Address: 408 E. Thomas Rd., Stillwater, OK 74076
(405) 372-7800, *Fax:* (405) 372-6969
www.stillwaterradio.net
stillwaterradio@coxinet.net
License: Stillwater, Payne County, OK held by Stillwater Broadcasting LLC
Group Owner: Mahaffey Enterprises Inc.
Arbitron Metro Market: Stillwater, OK *Format:* Adult Contemp *Hrs. of News Programming:* news progmg 11 hrs wkly *No. News Employees:* 2 *Target Audience:* 18 plus. *Adv. Rates:* 30; 25; 30; 10
Ken Fearnow, General Manager
Ken Fearnow, General Sales Mgr
Jay McRae, Programming Director
Bill Vanness, News Director

KVRO
04-12-1997; 101.1 mhz FM *Hrs Open:* 24; 6 kw; 328 ft.; N36 13 6 W97 9 43
Mailing Address: 217 1/2 S. Washington, Stillwater, OK 74074 US
Second Address: 408 E. Thomas, Stillwater, OK 74075
(405) 372-7800, *Fax:* (405) 372-6969
www.stillwaterradio.net
ken@stillwaterradio.net
License: Stillwater, Payne County, OK held by Stillwater Broadcasting LLC.
Group Owner: Mahaffey Enterprises Inc.; (acq 9-28-2001)
Arbitron Metro Market: Stillwater, OK *Format:* Oldies *Hrs. of News Programming:* 24 hrs news progmg wkly *No. News Employees:* 2 *Target Audience:* 25-54.
Bill Van Ness, News/ Operations
Ken Fearnow, General Manager/ Sales Manager
Jay McRae, Programming Director
Bill Van Ness, News Director
Diane Keenom, Traffic/ Office Manager
Carder Price, Creative Services Director
JackiePadgett, Sr. Account Executive
Rex Holdt, Sports Director/ Account Executive

Stuart

*KLRB
01-01-2003; 89.9 mhz FM *Hrs Open:* 24; 31 kw vert; 308 ft.; N34 54 57 W96 8 10
Rt 6 Box 158, McAlester, OK 74501 US
(918) 697-4019, *Fax:* (580) 892-3941
whitehouseradio@hotmail.com
License: Stuart, Hughes County, OK held by Lighthouse of Prayer Inc.
Arbitron Metro Market: Tulsa, OK *Format:* Christian, Country, 44
Walter Kuhlman, President
Stephen Burke, General Manager

Sulphur

*KFXT
01-01-2000; 90.7 mhz FM *Hrs Open:* 24; 7 kw; 299 ft.; N34 32 57 W96 58 34
1101 North 81 Highway, Marlow, OK 73055 US
(580) 658-9292, *Fax:* (580) 658-2561
License: Sulphur, Murray County, OK held by Sister Sherry Lynn Foundation Inc.
Arbitron Metro Market: Marlow, OK *Format:* Gospel *Target Audience:* 18-54
Ken Austin, General Manager
Sherry Lynn, General Sales Mgr
Jennifer James, Programming Director
James Wilson, Engineering Dir

KIXO
11-11-1979; 106.1 mhz FM *Hrs Open:* 24; 2.65 kw; 499 ft.; N34 39 3 W96 59 24
1101 North 81 Highway, Marlow, OK 73055 US
(580) 658-9292
License: Sulphur, Murray County, OK held by DFWU Inc.
Format: Country *Target Audience:* 25-52.
Ken Austin, General Manager
Sherry Lynn, General Sales Mgr
Jennifer James, Programming Director
Amy Helton, News Director

Taft

KCXR
03-20-1990; 100.3 mhz FM *Hrs Open:* 24; 3.9 kw; 410 ft.; N35 48 42 W95 34 12
215 N. State Street #910, PO Box 2418, Muskogee, OK 74401 US
(918) 492-2660, *Fax:* (918) 492-8840
www.thekross.fm
kxoj@kxoj.com
License: Taft, Muskogee County, OK held by KXOJ Inc.
Group Owner: Adonai Radio Group; (acq 12-11-2002; $1 million with KBIX(AM) Mukogee).
Arbitron Metro Market: Tulsa, OK *Format:* Christian *Target Audience:* Christian 18-49
Michael Stephens, President
David Stevens, General Manager

Tahlequah

KEOK
08-20-1966; 102.1 mhz FM; 6 kw; 285 ft.; N35 53 42.67 W94 57 12.16
P.O. Box 1793, Springdale, AR 72765 US
(918) 456-2511, *Fax:* (918) 456-3231
www.lakescountry1021.com
info@lakescountry1021.com
License: Tahlequah, Cherokee County, OK held by Payne 5 Communications LLC
Arbitron Metro Market: Tahlequah, OK *Format:* Country *Target Audience:* 25-60.
Shane Sellers, Operations Dir
Ralph Lynch, General Manager
Cindy Sellers, Programming Director

KTLQ
08-01-1957; 1350 khz AM *Hrs Open:* 24; 1 kw-D, ND1; 0.061 kw-N, ND1; N35 53 43 W94 57 12
P.O. Box 1793, Springdale, AR 72765 US
(918) 456-2511, *Fax:* (918) 456-3231
www.ktlq1350.com
Ralph@ktlq1350.com
License: Tahlequah, OK held by Payne 5 Communications LLC
Nat'l Network: Westwood One
Arbitron Metro Market: Tahlequah, OK *Format:* Country, Sports *Hrs. of News Programming:* news progmg 6 hrs wkly *No. News Employees:* 1 *Target Audience:* 25-54.
Shane Sellers, Operations Dir
Ralph Lynch, General Manager

Tishomingo

*KTGS
09-29-1998; 88.3 mhz FM; 5.5 kw; 922 ft.; N34 21 34 W96 33 34
Route 5, Box 119, Ada, OK 74820 US
(580) 332-0902, *Fax:* (580) 332-0922
www.thegospelstation.com
email@thegospelstation.com
License: Tishomingo, Johnston County, OK held by South Central Oklahoma Christian Broadcasting Inc.
Arbitron Metro Market: Ada, OK *Format:* Gospel
Randall Christy, President
Rick Cody, General Manager

KBBC
99.7 mhz FM; 15.5 kw; 128 meters; N34 11 36 W96 32 11
1418 North 1st Avenue, Durant, OK
(580) 924-3100
License: Tishomingo, OK held by Texoma Broadcasting Inc
Group Owner: Texoma Broadcasting Inc.

Gerald Todd Tidwell, President

Tonkawa

*KAYE-FM
06-01-1976; 90.7 mhz FM *Hrs Open:* 7 AM-midnight (M-F); 1.2 kw; 66 ft.; N36 40 42 W97 17 50
1220 E. Grand, PO Box 310, Tonkawa, OK 74653 US
(580) 628-6446, *Fax:* (580) 628-6209
www.north-ok.edu
kaye@north-ok.edu
License: Tonkawa, Kay County, OK held by Northern Oklahoma College.
Arbitron Metro Market: Tonkawa, OK *Format:* Contemporary Hits/Top 40 *Hrs. of News Programming:* News progmg 6 hrs wkly *Target Audience:* 13-25.
Dr. Joe Kinzer, President

Tulsa

KAKC
07-15-1938; 1300 khz AM *Hrs Open:* 24; 5 kw-D, DA2; 1 kw-N, DA2; N35 59 40 W95 51 27
200 Concord Plaza, Suite 600, San Antonio, TX 78216 US
(918) 664-2810, *Fax:* (918) 388-5400
www.buzztulsa.com
License: Tulsa, OK held by Clear Channel Broadcasting Licenses Inc.
Group Owner: Clear Channel Communications Inc.; (acq 8-5-92)
Nat'l Network: ESPN Radio; Fox Sports *Nat'l Reps:* Clear Channel
Arbitron Metro Market: Tulsa, OK *Format:* Sports *Target Audience:* 25-54; men
M. Oppenheimer, General Manager
Garry Weaver, Promotions Manager

KBEZ
03-01-1964; 92.9 mhz FM *Hrs Open:* 24; 100 kw; 1319 ft.; N36 11 26 W96 5 50
Broadcast Plaza, Crane Ave., Pittsburgh, PA 15220 US
(918) 492-2020, *Fax:* (918) 496-1937
www.929bobfm.com
bgann@jrn.com
License: Tulsa, Tulsa County, OK held by Renda Broadcasting Corp.
Group Owner: Renda Broadcasting Corp.; acq 6-8-90; grpsl;
Arbitron Metro Market: Tulsa, OK *Format:* Adult Contemp *Target Audience:* 25-54.
Brian Gann, Operations Dir
Jon Phillips, General Manager
Jet Black, Programming Director
Samantha Matthews, Promotions Manager
Richard Harley, Chief Engineer

KCFO
01-01-1946; 970 khz AM *Hrs Open:* 24; 2.5 kw-D, DA2; 1 kw-N, DA2; N36 11 46 W96 2 22
3737 S. 37 W. Avenue, Tulsa, OK 74107 US
(918) 622-0970, *Fax:* (918) 622-0985
www.kcfo.com
info@kcfo.com
License: Tulsa, OK held by Friendship Broadcasting L.P.
Nat'l Network: USA
Arbitron Metro Market: Tulsa, OK *Format:* Sports, Talk, 74 *Hrs. of News Programming:* News progmg 3 hrs wkly *Target Audience:* 25-54; Men & women
Ray Clatworthy, President
Kenneth Staley, General Manager

KGTO
01-01-1998; 1050 khz AM
3773 Howard Hughes Prwy, Suite 300n, Las Vegas, NV 89109 US
(918) 494-9886, *Fax:* (918) 494-9683
www.kgto.com
License: Tulsa, OK held by KJMM Inc.
Group Owner: Perry Publishing & Broadcasting Co.; (acq 3-30-01; $455,000).
Nat'l Network: Westwood One
Arbitron Metro Market: Tulsa, OK *Format:* Adult Contemp *Target Audience:* 35-54.
Martha Vaughan, General Manager

KJSR
11-01-1966; 103.3 mhz FM *Hrs Open:* 24; 100 kw; 1296 ft.; N36 1 10 W95 39 24
3773 Howard Hughes Prwy, Suite 300n, Las Vegas, NV 89109 US
(918) 493-3434, *Fax:* (918) 493-2397
www.star103fm.com
info@kjsrfm.com
License: Tulsa, Tulsa County, OK held by Cox Radio Inc.
Group Owner: Cox Radio Inc.; (acq 3-28-97; grpsl)
Arbitron Metro Market: Tulsa, OK *Format:* Classic Rock *Special Programming:* Pub affrs 2 hrs wkly *No. News Employees:* 1 *Target Audience:* 25-44.
Wavy Davy Michaels, Operations Dir
Lisa Hizer, General Manager
Rick Collier, General Sales Mgr
Dena Fletcher, Programming Director
Kim Dallow, Promotions Manager
Jack Conway, Web Master

KMOD-FM
10-10-1959; 97.5 mhz FM; 100 kw; 1486 ft.; N36 11 46 W96 5 53
200 Concord Plaza, Suite 600, San Antonio, TX 78216 US
(918) 388-5100, *Fax:* (918) 388-5400
www.kmod.com
License: Tulsa, Tulsa County, OK held by Clear Channel Broadcasting Licenses Inc.
Group Owner: Clear Channel Communications Inc.
Arbitron Metro Market: Tulsa, OK *Format:* Rock/AOR *Target Audience:* 25-49; men
Keith Sanderson, Station Manager
Daniel Boyd, Programming Director
Delvin Kinser, News Director

KTBZ
01-22-1934; 1430 khz AM
200 Concord Plaza, Suite 600, San Antonio, TX 78216 US
(918) 664-2810, *Fax:* (918) 388-5400
www.buzztulsa.com
License: Tulsa, OK held by Clear Channel Broadcasting Licenses Inc.
Group Owner: Clear Channel Communications Inc.; (acq 1997; grpsl)
Arbitron Metro Market: Tulsa, OK *Format:* Sports *Target Audience:* 25-49; men
Michael Oppenheimer, General Manager
Serene Rogers, General Sales Mgr
Chris Plank, Programming Director
Dave Hays, Promotions Manager
Brett Gilbert, Engineering Dir
Dave Hays, Webmaster

KRAV-FM
11-21-1962; 96.5 mhz FM; 100 kw; 1486 ft.; N36 11 46 W96 5 53
3773 Howard Hughes Prwy, Suite 300n, Las Vegas, NV 89109 US
(918) 491-9696, *Fax:* (918) 493-5385
www.mix96tulsa.com
License: Tulsa, Tulsa County, OK held by Cox Radio Inc.
Group Owner: Cox Radio Inc.; (acq 11-21-96; $5.5 million with co-located AM)
Arbitron Metro Market: Tulsa, OK *Format:* Adult Contemp *Target Audience:* 25-54; 30% men, 70% women
Robert Neil, President
Steve Hunter, Operations Dir
Dan Lawrie, General Manager
Lisa Hizer, General Sales Mgr
Dena Fletcher, Programming Director
Kim Dallow, Promotions Manager
Marc Morgan, Executive Vice President

KRMG
12-31-1949; 740 khz AM *Hrs Open:* 24; 50 kw-D, DA2; 25 kw-N, DA2; N36 4 50 W96 17 9
1400 Lake Hearn Drive, N.E., Atlanta, GA 30319 US
(918) 493-7400, *Fax:* (918) 493-2376
www.krmg.com
info@krmg.com
License: Tulsa, OK held by Cox Radio Inc.
Group Owner: Cox Radio Inc.; (acq 3-28-97; grpsl)
Arbitron Metro Market: Tulsa, OK *Format:* News, News/Talk, 86 *No. News Employees:* 7 *Target Audience:* 25-54; those interested in news, info & issue oriented talk
Dan Laurie, General Manager
Rick Collier, General Sales Mgr
Drew Anderssen, Programming Director
Randy Heller, Promotions Manager
Joe Kelley, News Director

KFAQ
01-23-1925; 1170 khz AM *Hrs Open:* 24

3355 S. Valley View Boulevard, Las Vegas, NV 89102 US
(918) 743-7814, *Fax:* (918) 743-6461
www.1170kfaq.com
bgann@journalbroadcastgroup.com
License: Tulsa, OK held by Journal Broadcast Corp.
Group Owner: Journal Communications Inc.; (acq 6-11-99; grpsl)
Nat'l Network: Fox News Radio *Nat'l Reps:* Clear Channel
Arbitron Metro Market: Tulsa, OK *Format:* Talk *Special Programming:* Farm 5 hrs, gospel 2 hrs wkly *Hrs. of News Programming:* news progmg 24 hrs wkly *No. News Employees:* 3 *Target Audience:* 35 plus.
Ron Kurtis, CFO
Carl Gardner, President
Brian gann, Operations Dir
Randy Bush, General Manager
April Sailsbury, Promotions Manager
Ray Klotz, Engineering Dir
Phillip Sutterfield, Advertising
Pat Campbell, Host
Elvis Polo,Host
Eddie Huff, Host

KVOO-FM
11-16-1973; 98.5 mhz FM *Hrs Open:* 24; 99 kw; 1227 ft.; N36 11 26 W96 5 50
3355 S. Valley View Boulevard, Las Vegas, NV 89102 US
(918) 743-7814, *Fax:* (918) 743-7613
www.kvoo.com
ljensen@journalbroadcastgroup.com
License: Tulsa, Tulsa County, OK held by Journal Broadcast Corp.
Group Owner: Journal Communications Inc.
Arbitron Metro Market: Tulsa, OK *Format:* Country *Target Audience:* 25-54.
Ron Kurtis, CFO
Carl Gardner, President
Brian Gann, Operations Dir
Randy Bush, General Manager
Crash Poteet, Programming Director
April Sailsbury, Promotions Manager
Ray Klotz, Engineering Dir
Phillip Sutterfield, AdvertisingSales Manager

KWEN
01-01-1961; 95.5 mhz FM *Hrs Open:* 24; 100 kw; 1486 ft.; N36 11 46 W96 5 53
3773 Howard Hughes Prwy, Suite 300n, Las Vegas, NV 89109 US
(918) 493-9500, *Fax:* (918) 493-2889
www.k955fm.com
info@kwen.com
License: Tulsa, Tulsa County, OK held by Cox Radio, Inc
Group Owner: Cox Radio Inc.
Wire Services: NWS (National Weather Service)
Arbitron Metro Market: Tulsa, OK *Format:* Country *No. News Employees:* 1 *Target Audience:* 25-54; country life group
Jim Dyer, General Sales Mgr
Karla Cantrell, Program Director
Kim Dallow, Program Director
Rick Collier, National Sales Manager
Pogie Freeman, Internet Sales Manager
Jack Conway, Web Master
Matt Bradley, Afternoon Personality/Asst. Program Director

*KWGS
10-19-1947; 89.5 mhz FM *Hrs Open:* 24; 50 kw; 1066 ft.; N36 1 15 W95 40 32
600 S. College, Tulsa, OK 74104 US
(918) 631-2577, *Fax:* (918) 631-3695
www.kwgs.org
public@publicradiotulsa.org
License: Tulsa, Tulsa County, OK held by The University of Tulsa.
Nat'l Network: NPR; PRI *Regional Reps:* Wayne Blackmon
Arbitron Metro Market: Tulsa, OK *Format:* News *Hrs. of News Programming:* News progmg 84 hrs wkly *No. News Employees:* 1 *Target Audience:* General. *Adv. Rates:* 30; 20; 30; 20
Steve Clem, Operations Director and Documentary Host
Rich Fisher, General Manager and host of Stodio Tulsa
P. Casey Morgan, General Sales Mgr
Frank Christel, Programming Director
John Durkee, News Director & Morning EditionAnchor
Brad Newman, Chief Engineer
Frank Christel, Director of Broadcast Services
Marshall Stewatr, Reporter and All Things Considered Anchor
P.Casey Morgan, Development Director
Scott Gregory, Production Director and host of All This isJazz

*KWTU
10-15-2004; 88.7 mhz FM *Hrs Open:* 24; 5 kw; 1066 ft.; N36 1 15 W95 40 32
Mailing Address: 600 S. College, Tulsa, OK 20036 US
Second Address: OK
(918) 631-2577, *Fax:* (918) 631-3695
www.publicradiotulsa.org
public@publicradiotulsa.org
License: Tulsa, Tulsa County, OK held by The University of Tulsa.
Regional Reps: Wayne Blackmon
Arbitron Metro Market: Tulsa, OK *Format:* Classical *Target Audience:* 50+.
Steve Clem, Operations Dir
Rich Fisher, General Manager
Frank Christel, Programming Director
John Durkee, News Director
Brad Newman, Chief Engineer
Frank Christel, Director of Broadcast Services
P. Casey Morgan, DevelopmentDirector
Scott Gregory, Production Director

Vinita

KGND
12-07-1954; 1470 khz AM *Hrs Open:* 24; 0.5 kw-D, ND1; 0.088 kw-N, ND1; N36 38 34 W95 7 35
Mailing Address: 402 North Wilson, P. O. Box 961, Vinita, OK 74301 US
Second Address: 402 N. Wilson St., Vinita, OK 74301
(918) 256-2255, *Fax:* (918) 256-2633
don@kitofm.com
License: Vinita, OK held by KXOJ Inc.
Group Owner: Stephens Family L.P.; 7-Sep
Nat'l Network: Fox Sports
Arbitron Metro Market: Tulsa, OK *Format:* Sports *Special Programming:* Oklahoma State University Sports *No. News Employees:* 4 *Target Audience:* 30-50.

KITO-FM
04-09-1981; 96.1 mhz FM *Hrs Open:* 24; 50 kw; 492 ft.; N36 34 56 W95 1 35
Mailing Address: 402 N.Wilson, P.O. Box 961, Vinita, OK 74301 US
Second Address: 402 N. Wilson St., Vinita, OK 74301
(918) 256-2255, *Fax:* (918) 256-2633
don@kitofm.com
License: Vinita, Craig County, OK held by KXOJ Inc.
Group Owner: Stephens Family L.P.; (acq 8-1-2007; $1.8 million with co-located AM)
Nat'l Network: Jones Radio Networks *Regional Network:* Okla. News Net.
Arbitron Metro Market: Tulsa, OK *Format:* Country *Special Programming:* Oklahoma University Sports *Hrs. of News Programming:* News progmg 28 hrs wkly *No. News Employees:* 4 *Target Audience:* General;traditional country music fans

Wagoner

KXTD
03-01-1966; 1530 khz AM *Hrs Open:* Daytime; 5 kw-D, DAD; N35 58 30 W95 29 30
2715 S. Radio Rd., El Reno, OK 73036 US
(918) 254-7556, *Fax:* (918) 252-0036
www.quebuenatulsa.com
kxtbr@tulsacoxmail.com
License: Wagoner, OK held by Gaytan-Galvan Limited Liability Co.
Nat'l Reps: Rgnl Reps
Arbitron Metro Market: Tulsa, OK *Format:* Tejano *Special Programming:* LiverPulga *Hrs. of News Programming:* Top of the hour *Target Audience:* 18-49 A *Adv. Rates:* 18;20;20;10
Maria DeLeon, CEO

Warner

KTFX-FM
03-01-1995; 101.7 mhz FM *Hrs Open:* 24; 25 kw; 276 ft.; N35 34 39 W95 12 36
8107 East Admiral Place, Tulsa, OK 74115 US
(918) 683-1017, *Fax:* (918) 686-6159
www.okiecountry1017.com
ktfx@k955.com
License: Warner, Muskogee County, OK held by K95.5 Inc.
Group Owner: K95.5 Inc.
Arbitron Metro Market: Muskogee, OK *Format:* Country *Hrs. of News Programming:* news progmg 2 hrs wkly *No. News Employees:* 1 *Target Audience:* 25-54; Adults
William H. Payne, CEO
Cliff Casteel, Operations Dir
Aleese Fielder, General Manager
Travis Reeves, General Sales Mgr
Cliff Casteel, Programming Director
Mick Reed, News Director

Watonga

KIMY
12-12-1987; 93.9 mhz FM *Hrs Open:* 24; 4.2 kw; 394 ft.; N35 50 27 W98 19 9
502 Santa Fe, Anthony, KS 67003 US
(580) 332-0902
www.thegospelstation.com
email@thegospelstation.com
License: Watonga, Blaine County, OK held by South Central Oklahoma Broadcasting Inc.
Format: Gospel *Target Audience:* 25-54; general *Adv. Rates:* 12; 11; 12; 11
Randall Christy, President
Rick Cody, General Manager

Weatherford

*KAYM
01-01-2000; 90.5 mhz FM; 2.7 kw; 282 ft.; N35 29 47 W98 44 10
Po Drawer 2440, Tupelo, MS 38803 US
(662) 844-8888, *Fax:* (662) 842-6791
www.afr.net
comments@afr.net
License: Weatherford, Custer County, OK held by American Family Association.
Group Owner: American Family Radio
Arbitron Metro Market: Tupelo, MS *Format:* Christian, Religious
Marvin Sanders, General Manager

KWEY
06-01-1970; 1590 khz AM; 1 kw-D, DA2; 0.032 kw-N, DA2; N35 33 33 W98 43 11
P.O. Box 587, Weatherford, OK 73096 US
(580) 772-5939, *Fax:* (580) 772-1590
www.kwey.com
info@kwey.com
License: Weatherford, OK held by Wright Broadcasting Systems Inc.
Group Owner: Wright Broadcasting Systems; (acq 7-17-91; $407,435 with co-located FM;
Nat'l Network: ABC *Regional Network:* Agrinet; Okla. News Net.
Arbitron Metro Market: Weatherford, OK *Format:* Country *Hrs. of News Programming:* news progmg 14 hrs wkly *No. News Employees:* 1 *Target Audience:* 25 plus; full service station *Adv. Rates:* 25; 16; 20; 15.
G. Harold Wright, CEO
Todd Brunner, Operations Dir
Heston Wright, General Manager
Vanessa Valli, Programming Director
Mike Smith, News Director
Ray Bagby', Technical Director
Amanda Benton, Area Sales Manager
Brianna Arherman,Area Sales Manager
John Liddle, Sports Director/ Account Executive
Kelli Haan, Account Executive, Websites and Graphics

Wewoka

KWSH
07-01-1951; 1260 khz AM; 1 kw-D, DAN; 1 kw-N, DAN; N35 10 10 W96 32 30
2 E. Main Street, Shawnee, OK 74801 US
(405) 382-1260(405)-257-5441, *Fax:* (405) 257-2011(405) 382-0128
onetenbroadcast@onetenbroadcast.com
License: Wewoka, OK held by One Ten Broadcast Group Inc.
Group Owner: One Ten Broadcast Group Inc.; (acq 4-16-2008)
Regional Network: Okla. News Net.
Format: Country *Special Programming:* American Indian one hr wkly *Target Audience:* 21-61.
Linda Jones, President
Garry Walker, Operations Dir
Dennis Burton, Station Manager
Jim Stanford, Chief Engineer

KSLE
10-01-1997; 104.7 mhz FM *Hrs Open:* 24; 1.7 kw; 505 ft.; N35 5 31 W96 32 29
2 E. Main Street, Shawnee, OK 74801 US
(405) 382-0186, *Fax:* (405) 382-0128
onetenbroadcast@onetenbroadcast.org
License: Wewoka, Seminole County, OK held by One Ten Broadcast Group Inc.
Group Owner: One Ten Broadcast Group Inc.; (acq 4-16-2008)
Format: Oldies
Linda Jones, Promotions Manager

Wilburton

KMCO
11-01-1965; 101.3 mhz FM *Hrs Open:* 24; 100 kw; 617 ft.; N34 59 13 W95 42 10
Mailing Address: P.O. Box 1068, McAlester, OK 74502 US
Second Address: 1801 E. Electric Ave., McAlester, OK 74502
(918) 426-1050, *Fax:* (918) 423-7119
www.mcalesterradio.com
info@mcalesterradio.com
License: Wilburton, Latimer County, OK
Group Owner: Southeastern Oklahoma Radio LLC; (Acq 1-18-2005; $766,666).
Format: Country *Hrs. of News Programming:* News progmg 5 hrs wkly *Target Audience:* 18-45.
Lee Anderson, General Manager
Sheila Turnbow, General Sales Mgr

Woodward

*KJOV
01-01-1998; 90.7 mhz FM; 25 kw; 397 ft.; N36 24 8 W99 25 47
Mailing Address: 922 Webster, P.O Box 1888, Woodward, OK 73802 US
Second Address: 922 Webster, Woodward, OK 73802
(620) 873-2991, *Fax:* (620) 873-2755
License: Woodward, Woodward County, OK held by Christian Community Radio.
Format: Christian
Micheal Luskey, CEO
Bill Lurwick, Programming Director
Delvin Kinser, News Director
Steve Larson, Chief Engineer
Polly Hughes, Traffic Manager

KZCU
01-01-2001; 95.9 mhz FM; 6 kw; 328 ft.; N36 24 40 W99 21 5
Third Coast Jt Venture, 3050 Post Oak Blvd #1700, Houston, TX 77056 US
(580) 581-2425, *Fax:* (580) 581-5571
www.kccu.org
kccu@cameron.edu
License: Woodward, Woodward County, OK held by Cameron University
Ted Riley, General Manager

KMZE
10-15-1989; 92.1 mhz FM *Hrs Open:* 24; 2.15 kw; 1099 ft.; N36 16 6 W99 26 56
2728 Williams Avenue #4d, Woodward, OK 73801 US
(580) 256-3692, *Fax:* (580) 256-3825
License: Woodward, Woodward County, OK held by FM 92 Broadcasters Inc.
Nat'l Network: Jones Radio Networks
Arbitron Metro Market: Oklahoma City, OK *Format:* Adult Contemp *No. News Employees:* 1 *Target Audience:* 25-54.
Mike Mitchel, CEO

KSIW
09-01-1947; 1450 khz AM *Hrs Open:* 24; 1 kw-U, ND1; N36 25 42 W99 24 10
Mailing Address: 1515 N. Broadway, Hobart, OK 73651 US
Second Address: 1922 22nd St., Woodward, OK 73801
(580) 256-0935, *Fax:* (580) 254-9102
www.woodwardradio.com
License: Woodward, OK held by Classic Communications Inc.
Group Owner: Classic Communications Inc.; (acq 6-20-2005).
Nat'l Network: ESPN Radio
Arbitron Metro Market: Woodward, OK *Format:* Sports, Talk *Target Audience:* Male 18-49.
Sherre House, President
Bret Brewer, Programming Director
Sam Piel, Programming Director

KWDQ
01-09-1990; 102.3 mhz FM; 100 kw; 868 ft.; N36 22 31 W99 28 31
P.O. Box 1600, Woodward, OK 73802 US
(580) 254-9102, *Fax:* (580) 254-9103
www.woodwardradio.com
cciradio@sbcglobal.net
License: Woodward, Woodward County, OK held by Classic Communications Inc.
Group Owner: Classic Communications Inc.; (acq 3-20-92)
Regional Network: Okla. News Net.
Arbitron Metro Market: Woodward, OK *Format:* Rock/AOR *Target Audience:* 18-49.
Sherre House, President
Bret Brewer, Programming Director

KWFX
11-01-1974; 100.1 mhz FM *Hrs Open:* 24; 100 kw; 868 ft.; N36 22 31 W99 28 31
Mailing Address: P O Box 1600, Woodward, OK 73802 US
Second Address: 1922 22nd St., Woodward, OK 73801
(580) 256-0935, *Fax:* (580) 254-9103
www.woodwardradio.com
License: Woodward, Woodward County, OK held by Classic Communications Inc.
Group Owner: Classic Communications Inc.; (acq 4-30-96)
Regional Network: Okla. News Net.
Arbitron Metro Market: Woodward, OK *Format:* Country *Target Audience:* 25-65; affluent, males & females
Sherre House, President
Bret Brewer, Operations Dir
LaDonna Herber, General Sales Mgr
Mikel Frederickson, Account Executive
Kendra Wyatt, Account Executive

KWOX
12-16-1983; 101.1 mhz FM *Hrs Open:* 24; 100 kw; 1,204 ft; N36 16 06 W99 26 56
101 Centre, 2728 Williams Ave., Woodward, OK 73801
(580) 256-4101, *Fax:* (580) 256-3825
k101@k101online.com
License: Woodward, Woodward County, OK held by Omni Communications Corp.
Nat'l Network: Westwood One; ABC *Regional Network:* Radio Oklahoma Net *Regional Reps:* Regional Reps
Population Served: 150,000 *Arbitron Metro Market:* Oklahoma City, OK *TV Affiliate:* KOMI-TV affil. *Special Programming:* Morning Show *No. News Employees:* 2 *Target Audience:* General.
J. Douglas Williams, President/GM
Shawn Miller, COO
Kevin Grice, General Manager
J Douglas Williams, General Sales Mgr
Patrick Ley, Programming Director
Cynthia Spencer, Promotions Manager
Pete Mundo, News Director
Kevin Grice,Engineering Dir
Shirley Webb, CFO
Matt Storm, Morning Show Host

Ontario

New Liskeard

CJTT-FM
06-26-1998; 104.5 mhz FM; 10 kw
Mailing Address: PO Box 1058, New Liskeard, ON P0J 1P0 Canada
Second Address: 55 Whitewood Ave., New Liskeard, ON P0J 1P0
(705) 647-7334, *Fax:* (705) 647-8660
www.cjttfm.com
cjtt@cjttfm.com
License: New Liskeard, ON held by Connelly Communications Corp.
Nat'l Reps: Canadian Broadcast Sales
Population Served: 20,000*No. News Employees:* 1
Gail Moore, General Manager

Petersburgh

CJWV-FM
06-07-2011; 96.7 mhz FM; 6 kw; 233 meters
360 George Street N, Unit 1, Petersburgh, ON K9H 7E7 Canada
(707) 876-7773
www.magic967.fm
License: Petersburgh, ON held by Pineridge Broadcasting Inc
Don Conway, President

Oregon

Albany

KHPE
01-12-1969; 107.9 mhz FM *Hrs Open:* 24; 100 kw; 1161 ft.; N44 38 46 W123 16 11
P. O. Box 278, 34545 Hwy 20, Albany, OR 97321 US
(541) 926-2233, *Fax:* (541) 926-3925
www.hope1079.com
paul@hope1079.com
License: Albany, Linn County, OR held by Extra Mile Media Inc.
Format: Christian *Special Programming:* Talk 30 hrs wkly *Target Audience:* 25-54; female
Bill Zipp, President
Jeff McMahon, Operations Dir
Randy Davison, General Manager
Vicki Webber, News Director
John Kenneke, Chief Engineer

KTHH
01-01-1959; 990 khz AM *Hrs Open:* 24; 0.25 kw-D, ND1; 0.009 kw-N, ND1; N44 35 43 W123 7 34
50 East Rivercenter Blvd, Suite 1200, Covington, KY 41011 US
(541) 926-8628, *Fax:* (541) 928-1261
www.comedy990.com
License: Albany, OR held by Bicoastal Willamette Valley LLC.
Group Owner: Bicoastal Media L.L.C.; (acq 7-2-2007; grpsl)
Nat'l Reps: Tacher
Format: Comedy *Hrs. of News Programming:* news progmg 10 hrs wkly *No. News Employees:* 1 *Target Audience:* 25-54.
Robert Dove, General Manager
Jason Henson, General Sales Mgr
Angie Foster, Programming Director
Kimberly Littler, Promotions Manager
Scott Schuler, Advertising Director

KRKT-FM
06-01-1978; 99.9 mhz FM; 100 kw; 1070 ft.; N44 38 46 W123 16 11
50 East Rivercenter Blvd, Suite 1200, Covington, KY 41011 US
(541) 926-8628, *Fax:* (541) 928-1261
www.krkt.com
License: Albany, Linn County, OR
Group Owner: Bicoastal Media L.L.C.
Format: Country
Jason Henson, General Sales Mgr
Scott Schuler, Programming Director
Kimberly Littler, Promotions Manager

KWIL
01-14-1941; 790 khz AM *Hrs Open:* 24; 1 kw-D, DA2; 1 kw-N, DA2; N44 37 54 W123 0 57
P. O. Box 278, 34545 Hwy 20, Albany, OR 97321 US
(541) 926-2233, *Fax:* (541) 926-3925
www.kwil790.com
pauldelury@kwil790.com
License: Albany, OR held by Extra Mile Media Inc.
Arbitron Metro Market: Albany, OR *Format:* Christian
Tim Murphy, General Manager
Jodie Bates, General Sales Mgr
Neal Larson, News Director
Rhett Downing, Chief Engineer

Aloha

KNRQ-FM
12-26-1958; 97.9 mhz FM; 10 kw; 470 meters; N44 0 8 W123 6 50
City Center West, 7201 W. Lake Mead Blvd, Las Vegas, NV 89128 US
(541) 284-8500, *Fax:* (541) 284-8500
www.nrq.com
info@nrq.com
License: Aloha, Lane County, OR
Arbitron Metro Market: Eugene, OR *Format:* Alternative
Chris Crowley, Programming Director

Altamont

KRAT(FM)
01-01-1991; 97.7 mhz FM; 22 kw; Ant 1,712 ft; N42 10 06 W122 09 06
Box 235, Klamath Falls, OR 97601
(541) 884-8167, *Fax:* (541) 884-8226
License: Altamont, Klamath County, OR held by George J. Wade.
Format: Oldies *Adv. Rates:* 4; 4; 4; 4
Richard Towne, General Manager

Ashland

KCMX-FM
07-20-1978; 101.9 mhz FM *Hrs Open:* 24; 42 kw; 1470 ft.; N42 17 55 W122 44 53
City Center West, 7201 W. Lake Mead Blvd, Las Vegas, NV 89128 US
(541) 779-1550, *Fax:* (541) 776-2360
www.lite102.com
news@kcmxam.com
License: Ashland, Jackson County, OR held by Mapleton License of Medford LLC.
Group Owner: Mapleton Communications LLC
Nat'l Network: ABC
Arbitron Metro Market: Ashland, OR *Format:* Adult Contemp *No. News Employees:* 1 *Target Audience:* 25-54.
Joe Mussio, General Manager
Leslie Haze, Programming Director
Kelly Kline, Disc Jockey

Jean Backus, Sales
Kendall Hess, Sales
Joe Mussio, Market Manager

KIFS
11-25-1996; 107.5 mhz FM; 5.8 kw; 1375 ft.; N42 17 54 W122 44 53
50 E. Rivercenter Blvd., #1200, Covington, KY 41011 US
(541) 858-5423, *Fax:* (541) 857-0326
www.107kiss.com
info@107kiss.com
License: Ashland, Jackson County, OR held by Bicoastal Rogue Valley LLC.
Group Owner: Bicoastal Media L.L.C.; (acq 7-2-2007; grpsl)
Nat'l Reps: Tacher
Arbitron Metro Market: Medford, OR *Format:* Contemporary Hits/Top 40 *Target Audience:* 18-49.
Bill Nielsen, General Manager

***KSMF**
11-07-1987; 89.1 mhz FM *Hrs Open:* 5 AM-2 AM; 2.3 kw; 1352 ft.; N42 17 54 W122 44 59
P. O. Box 3175, Eugene, OR 97403 US
(541) 552-6301, *Fax:* 9541) 552-8565
www.ijpr.org
jprinfo@sou.edu
License: Ashland, Jackson County, OR held by The State of Oregon, acting by and through the State Board of Higher Education.
Nat'l Network: NPR; PRI *Wire Services:* AP
Arbitron Metro Market: Ashland, OR *Format:* Jazz, News, 90 *Special Programming:* Blues 6 hrs, folk 3 hrs, pub affrs 7 hrs wkly *Hrs. of News Programming:* news progmg 45 hrs wkly *No. News Employees:* 1 *TargetAudience:* General.
Ronald Kramer, CEO
Bryon Lambert, Operations Dir
Jessica Robinson, Engineering Dir
Mitchell Christian, CFO

***KSOR**
04-01-1969; 90.1 mhz FM *Hrs Open:* 5 AM-2 AM; 38 kw; 2657 ft.; N42 41 30 W123 13 44
P.O. Box 3175, Eugene, OR 97403 US
(541) 552-6301, *Fax:* (541) 552-8565
www.ijpr.org
info@ijpr.org
License: Ashland, Jackson County, OR held by The State of Oregon, acting by and through the State Board of Higher Education.
Nat'l Network: PRI; NPR *Wire Services:* AP
Arbitron Metro Market: Medford-Ashland, OR *Format:* News *Special Programming:* Pub affrs 7 hrs wkly *Hrs. of News Programming:* news progmg 35 hrs wkly *No. News Employees:* 1 *Target Audience:* General.
Ronald Kramer, CEO

***KSRG**
01-01-1995; 88.3 mhz FM *Hrs Open:* 5 AM- 2 AM; 0.23 kw; 1345 ft.; N42 17 52 W122 44 58
P.O. Box 3175, Eugene, OR 97403 US
(541) 552-6301, *Fax:* (541) 552-8565
www.ijpr.org
info@ijpr.org
License: Ashland, Jackson County, OR held by The State of Oregon, acting by and through the State Board of Higher Education, for the benefit of Southern Oregon State University.
Nat'l Network: NPR; PRI *Wire Services:* AP
Arbitron Metro Market: Ashland, OR *Format:* Classical, Variety/Diverse *Hrs. of News Programming:* news progmg 35 hrs wkly *No. News Employees:* 1 *Target Audience:* General.
Ronald Kramer, CEO
Ransom,Darin, Engineering Dir

Astoria

KAST
01-01-1922; 1370 khz AM *Hrs Open:* 5 AM-midnight
1006 West Marine Drive, Astoria, OR 97103 US
(503) 861-6620, *Fax:* (503) 325-5570
www.kast1370.com
kris.edwards@nnbproduction.com
License: Astoria, OR held by New Northwest Broadcasters LLC.
Group Owner: New Northwest Broadcasters LLC; (acq 10-26-99; grpsl)
Arbitron Metro Market: Warrenton, OR *Format:* News, News/Talk, 84, Talk *Hrs. of News Programming:* News progmg 50 hrs wkly *Target Audience:* 35 plus.
Paul Mitchell, General Manager

***KMUN**
02-02-1982; 91.9 mhz FM *Hrs Open:* 5 AM-1 AM; 7.2 kw; 1089 ft.; N46 15 46 W123 53 9
Mailing Address: P.O. Box 269, 1445 Exchange St., Astoria, OR 97103 US
Second Address: 1445 Exchange St., Astoria, OR 97103
(503) 325-0010, *Fax:* (503) 325-3956
www.kmun.org
kmun@kmun.org
License: Astoria, Clatsop County, OR held by Tillicum Foundation.
Nat'l Network: NPR
Format: Easy Listening *Special Programming:* Folk 18 hrs, children's 6 hrs, Sp 3 hrs, American *Hrs. of News Programming:* news progmg 12 hrs wkly *No. News Employees:* 1 *Target Audience:* General.
Ray Merritt, President
David Hammock, General Manager
Stephanie Stern, General Sales Mgr

***KGIO**
01-01-2006; 90.5 mhz FM; 0 kw horiz, 0.048 kw vert; 469 ft.; N46 10 56 W123 48 9 *Rebroadcasts:* Rebroadcasts KRUC(FM) Las Cruces, NM 100%.
Box 3333, McAllen, TX 78502 US
(956) 787-9788, *Fax:* (956) 787-9783
www.worldradionetwork.org
info@kvmv.com
License: Astoria, Clatsop County, OR held by Carlos Arana Ministries
Arbitron Metro Market: Astoria, OR *Format:* Spanish, Religious
Glenn Lafitte, CEO
Dr. William Haney, General Manager
Kitty Stinson, Chief Operations Officer
James Gamblin, Director of Broadcast Operations
Jamie Sepulveda, Director of Finance and Administration
Dwight Lind, Western RegionalCoordinator
David Soper, Vice Chairman
Glenn Lafitte, Secretary

***KLOY**
01-01-2006; 88.7 mhz FM; 0.25 kw; 1053 ft.; N46 15 46 W123 53 9 *Rebroadcasts:* Rebroadcasts KLVR(FM) Santa Rosa, CA 100%
P.O. Box 269, Astoria, OR 97103 US
(800) 525-5683, *Fax:* (916) 251-1650
www.klove.com
klove@klove.com
License: Astoria, Clatsop County, OR held by Educational Media Foundation.
Group Owner: EMF Broadcasting; (acq 2-2-2004).
Nat'l Network: K-Love
Arbitron Metro Market: Astoria, OR *Format:* Christian *No. News Employees:* 13
Darrell Chambliss, Chairman
Mike Novak, President and CEO
Eric Allen, General Sales Mgr
David Pierce, Programming Director
Ed Lenane, News Director
Sam Wallington, Engineering Dir
Scott Smith, Music Director
Marya Morgan, NewsReporter
Richard Hunt, News Reporter
Mike Lee, Regional Manager
Tracy Butler, Traffic Manager

Athena

KHSS
11-05-1986; 100.7 mhz FM *Hrs Open:* 24; 6.3 kw; 1322 ft.; N45 59 23 W118 10 31
1230 Colonial Drive, College Place, WA 99324 US
(509) 525-7878, *Fax:* (509) 522-2046
www.khssradui.com
comments@khssradio.com
License: Athena, Walla Walla County, OR held by Two Hearts Communications L.L.C.
Nat'l Reps: Katz Radio
Format: Talk, Christian *Special Programming:* Relg 3 hrs wkly *Target Audience:* 18-34.
Rodney Fazzari, General Manager
Todd Brandenburg, Chief Engineer

Baker

KBKR
01-01-1939; 1490 khz AM *Hrs Open:* 24; 1 kw-U, ND1; N44 47 18 W117 48 35 *Rebroadcasts:* Rebroadcasts KLBM(AM) La Grande 100%
38194 NE85th Avenue, La Center, WA 98629 US
(541) 963-4121, *Fax:* (541) 963-3117
supertalk@eoni.com
License: Baker, OR held by Pacific Empire Radio Corp.
Group Owner: Pacific Empire Radio Corp.; acq 7-19-2004; grpsl).
Nat'l Network: Westwood One *Nat'l Reps:* McGavren Guild
Arbitron Metro Market: La Grande, OR *Format:* News, News/Talk, 86 *Special Programming:* Farm 2 hrs wkly *Hrs. of News Programming:* news progmg 25 hrs wkly *No. News Employees:* 1 *Target Audience:* 25-54.*Adv. Rates:* 22; 20; 22; 16
Mark Bolland, President
Steve Ryner, Station Manager
Bobby Hollowwa, Programming Director

KKBC-FM
02-01-1981; 95.3 mhz FM *Hrs Open:* 24; 6 kw; -200 ft.; N44 47 18 W117 48 35
38104 NE85th Ave., La Center, WA 98629 US
(541) 523-4431, *Fax:* (541) 963-3117
theboomer@eoni.com
License: Baker, Baker County, OR held by Pacific Empire Radio Corp.
Group Owner: Pacific Empire Radio Corp.
Nat'l Reps: McGavren Guild
Format: Oldies *Hrs. of News Programming:* news progmg 6 hrs wkly *No. News Employees:* 1 *Target Audience:* 25-54. *Adv. Rates:* 24; 24; 24; 18
Steve Darnell, General Manager
Otis Warren, General Sales Mgr
Kathy King, News Director
Bob Turner, Chief Engineer

***KANL**
01-01-2005; 90.7 mhz FM; 0.25 kw; 653 ft.; N44 45 58 W117 52 54
P.O. Drawer 2440, Tupelo, MS 38803 US
(662) 844-8888, *Fax:* (662) 842-6791
www.afr.net
faq@afr.net
License: Baker, Baker County, OR held by American Family Association.
Group Owner: American Family Radio
Arbitron Metro Market: Baker, OR *Format:* Christian
Marvin Sanders, General Manager

***KDJC**
01-01-2005; 88.1 mhz FM; 0.775 kw vert; 1810 ft.; N45 7 26 W117 46 48
US
(800) 357-4226, *Fax:* (208) 736-1958
www.csnradio.com
csn@csnradio.com
License: Baker, Baker County, OR held by CSN International.
Group Owner: CSN International
Arbitron Metro Market: Baker City-La Grande, OR *Format:* Religious
Mike Kestler, President
Daniel Davidson, Operations Dir
Wade Twilegar, General Manager
Don Mills, Network Programming Director / Music Director
Kelly Carlson, Engineering Dir
Jerry Johnson, Engineering Dir
Ray Gorney, AssistantDirector of Engineering
Dustin Pamplona, Engineer
Nolan Mather, Graphics / Website Maintenance
Mike Stocklin, National Underwriting
Austin Morris, Accounting
Lois Mills, FCC Applications / Translator Site Manager

***KANC**
89.9 mhz FM; kw
US
(662) 844-5036, *Fax:* (662) 842-7798
www.afr.net
contact@afa.net
License: Baker, Baker County, OR held by Abundant Life Broadcasting.
Arbitron Metro Market: Tupelo, MS *Format:* Christian
Donald E. Wildmon, Founder
Tamara Durham, Operations Dir
Buster Wilson, General Manager
Jennifer Hagman, Programming Director

Baker City

KCMB
06-26-1988; 104.7 mhz FM; 100 kw; 1,747 ft; N45 07 26 W117 46 48
1009-C Adams Ave., La Grande, OR 97814
(541) 963-3405, *Fax:* (541) 963-5090
www.1047kcmb.com
License: Baker City, Baker County, OR held by KCMB, LLC
Group Owner: Elkhorn Media Group
Nat'l Network: ABC *Nat'l Reps:* Tacher
Target Audience: 25-54.

Randy McKone, President
Tori Gandy, General Sales Mgr
Colleen Kaseberg, Programming Director
Lionel Shuntloff, Engineering Dir

***KESY**
01-01-2005; 91.9 mhz FM; 0.32 kw; 1132 ft.; N44 44 22 W117 44 42
US
(314) 921-9330
X93@knsx.com
License: Baker City, Crawford County, OR held by East Central Broadcasting LLC
Arbitron Metro Market: Baker City, OR *Format:* Country
Ruth Choate, General Manager
Randy Wachter, Chief Engineer

***KOBK**
01-01-2007; 88.9 mhz FM *Hrs Open:* 24; 0.6 kw; 1834 ft.; N44 35 57 W117 46 58 *Rebroadcasts:* Rebroadcasts KOPB-FM Portland 100%
7140 Sw Macadam Ave., Portland, OR 97219 US
(503) 244-9900, *Fax:* (503) 293-4877
www.opb.org
License: Baker City, Baker County, OR held by Oregon Public Broadcasting.
Nat'l Network: NPR *Regional Network:* Ore. Pub. Bcstg Radio Net.
Arbitron Metro Market: Baker City, OR *Format:* News, News/Talk, 86
Steve Bass, CEO
Jeff Douglas, Operations Dir

Bandon

KBDN
10-01-1996; 96.5 mhz FM; 1.5 kw; 1296 ft.; N42 57 27 W124 16 13
P. O. Box 250, Coquille, OR 97423 US
(541) 267-2121, *Fax:* (541) 267-5229
www.kbdn.com
License: Bandon, Coos County, OR held by Bicoastal Media Licenses III LLC.
Group Owner: Bicoastal Media L.L.C.; (acq 10-16-2003; grpsl)
Nat'l Reps: Tacher
Arbitron Metro Market: Bandon, OR *Format:* Country *Target Audience:* 25-54.
Ken Dennis, CEO
Mike Wilson, President
Mike O'Brien, Operations Dir
Joe de Groot, Regional Vice President

Banks

KXJM
06-01-1990; 107.5 mhz FM *Hrs Open:* 24; 68 kw; 1646 ft.; N45 30 58.4 W122 43 58.8
600 New Hampshire Avenue, N.W., Suite 1200, Washington, DC 20037 US
(503) 323-6400, *Fax:* (503) 323-6664
www.wild1075portland.com
License: Banks, Washington County, OR held by Citicasters Licenses Inc.
Group Owner: Clear Channel Communications Inc.; (acq 4-1-2009; grpsl)
Nat'l Network: Westwood One
Arbitron Metro Market: Portland, OR *Format:* Oldies *Target Audience:* 25-49; adult
Robert Dove, General Manager

Bay City

KTIL-FM
10-01-1998; 95.9 mhz FM *Hrs Open:* 24; 0.45 kw; 1181 ft.; N45 27 59 W123 55 11
US
(503) 842-4422, *Fax:* (503) 842-2755
www.ktil-kmbd.com
comments@ktil-kmbol.com
License: Bay City, Tillamook County, OR held by Oregon Eagle Inc.
Arbitron Metro Market: Tillamook, OR *Format:* Adult Contemp *Target Audience:* General.
Van Moe, President

KIXT(FM)
01-01-2005; 95.9 mhz FM; 450 w; Ant 1,181 ft; N45 27 59 W123 55 11
1600 Gray Lynn Dr., Walla Walla, WA 99362
(509) 527-1000, *Fax:* (509) 529-5534
www.kix106online.com
License: Bay City, Tillamook County, OR held by Alexandra Communications Inc.
Group Owner: Alexandra Communications Inc.; (acq 8-2-2005; $150,000 for CP)
Population Served: 13,767 *Arbitron Metro Market:* Hewitt, TX
Tom Hodgins, President

Beaverton

KKCW
02-01-1984; 103.3 mhz FM *Hrs Open:* 24; 95 kw; 1542 ft.; N45 31 21 W122 44 45
50 East Rivercenter Blvd, Suite 1200, Covington, KY 41011 US
(503) 323-6400, *Fax:* (503) 241-1033
www.k103.com
info@kkcwfm.com
License: Beaverton, Washington County, OR held by Citicasters Licenses L.P.
Group Owner: Clear Channel Communications Inc.; (acq 5-4-99; grpsl).
Nat'l Reps: D & R Radio
Arbitron Metro Market: Portland, OR *Format:* Adult Contemp *No. News Employees:* 3 *Target Audience:* 25-54.
Tony Coles, Operations Dir
Robert Dove, General Manager

Bend

KBND
01-01-1938; 1110 khz AM *Hrs Open:* 24; 10 kw-D, DAN; 5 kw-N, DAN; N44 6 25 W121 14 39
Mailing Address: P.O. Box 5037, Eugene, OR 97708 US
Second Address: 711 N.E. Butler Market Rd., Bend, OR 97701
(541) 382-5263, *Fax:* (541) 388-0456
www.kbnd.com
news@kbnd.com
License: Bend, OR held by Combined Communications.
Group Owner: Combined Communications; acq 4-27-90)
Nat'l Network: Fox News Radio *Nat'l Reps:* McGavren Guild
Format: News, Sports, 86 *No. News Employees:* 2 *Target Audience:* 35-64; upscale, professionals
Mike Chaney, General Manager
Dave Junis, Programming Director

KMGX
07-04-1973; 100.7 mhz FM; 50 kw horiz, 20 kw vert; 518 ft.; N44 4 40 W121 19 49
P.O. Box 751, Bend, OR 97709 US
(541) 388-3300, *Fax:* (541) 388-3303
www.kgmx.com
mike@kgmx.com
License: Bend, Deschutes County, OR held by GCC Bend LLC.
Group Owner: GCC Bend LLC
Nat'l Reps: Katz Radio
Arbitron Metro Market: Bend, OR *Format:* Adult Contemp *Target Audience:* 25 plus; middle to upper income consumers
Ed Lambert, Operations Dir
Jim Gross, General Manager
Mick Green, Programming Director
Mike Groff, Disc Jockey

KNLR
12-31-1984; 97.5 mhz FM *Hrs Open:* 24; 97 kw horiz, 42 kw vert; 535 ft.; N44 4 38 W121 19 49
P.O. Box 7408, Bend, OR 97708 US
(541) 389-8873, *Fax:* (541) 389-5291
www.knlr.com
info@knlr.com
License: Bend, Deschutes County, OR held by Cowan Broadcasting LLC.
Nat'l Network: USA *Wire Services:* AP
Arbitron Metro Market: Bend, OR *Format:* Adult Contemp, Christian
Terry Cowan, General Manager

***KOAB-FM**
01-01-1994; 91.3 mhz FM; 75 kw; 653 ft.; N44 4 41 W121 19 57
7140 S.W. Macadam Ave., Portlamd, OR 97219 US
(503) 293-1905, *Fax:* (503) 293-1919
www.opb.org
info@opb.org
License: Bend, Deschutes County, OR held by Oregon Public Broadcasting.
Nat'l Network: NPR
TV Affiliate: *KOAB-TV affil. *Format:* News *Hrs. of News Programming:* news progmg 146 hrs wkly *No. News Employees:* 5
Jack Galmiche, COO

KQAK
09-05-1986; 105.7 mhz FM *Hrs Open:* 24; 40 kw; 591 ft.; N44 4 40 W121 19 49
854 NE4th Street, Bend, OR 97701 US
(541) 383-3825, *Fax:* (541) 383-3403
www.kqakfm.com
License: Bend, Deschutes County, OR held by Horizon Broadcasting Group L.L.C.
Group Owner: Horizon Broadcasting Group, LLC; acq 2000; $3.45 million).
Nat'l Reps: Christal
Arbitron Metro Market: Bend, OR *Format:* Contemporary Hits/Top 40 *Special Programming:* Inside Central Oregon (Public Affairs) *No. News Employees:* 1 *Target Audience:* 25-54.
Keith Shipman, General Manager
Dave Clemens, Programming Director
Bill Baker, News Director
Regan Brick, Business Manager
John Edwards, General Sales Manager

KTWS
12-21-1990; 98.3 mhz FM *Hrs Open:* 24; 5.2 kw; 732 ft.; N44 4 39 W121 19 57
Mailing Address: 4222 Commerce Street, Eugene, OR 97402 US
Second Address: 711 N.E. Butler Market Rd., Bend, OR 97701
(541) 382-5263, *Fax:* (541) 388-0456
www.thetwins.com
thetwins@thetwins.com
License: Bend, Deschutes County, OR held by Combined Communications, Inc.
Group Owner: Combined Communications; acq 9-1-96)
Nat'l Reps: McGavren Guild
Arbitron Metro Market: Bend, OR *Format:* Classic Rock *Target Audience:* 25-54. *Adv. Rates:* 36; 32; 34; 24
Chuck Chackel, President and General Manager
Mike Cheney, General Manager
Christine Limburg, Director of Corporate Sales
Ron Alvarez, Programming Director

KICE
02-04-1960; 940 khz AM *Hrs Open:* 24
PO Box 5068, 1500 NEButler Market Rd, Bend, OR 97701 US
(541) 388-3300, *Fax:* (541) 388-3303
www.espn940.com
mflanagan@bendradiogroup.com
License: Bend, OR held by GCC Bend LLC.
Group Owner: GCC Bend LLC; (acq 1999)
Nat'l Network: ESPN Radio *Nat'l Reps:* Katz Radio
Arbitron Metro Market: Bend, OR *Format:* Sports, Talk *Hrs. of News Programming:* news progmg 2 hrs wkly *No. News Employees:* 1 *Target Audience:* 35 plus.
Ed Lambert, Operations Dir
Jim Gross, General Manager
Mick Green, Programming Director
Mike Flanagan, Programming Director

KMTK
01-01-2000; 99.7 mhz FM *Hrs Open:* 24; 26 kw; 682 ft.; N44 4 39 W121 19 57
59 Constantine Place, Eugene, OR 97405 US
(541) 382-5263, *Fax:* (541) 388-0456
www.mountain997.com
steveries@combinedcommunications.com
License: Bend, Deschutes County, OR held by Combined Communications Inc.
Group Owner: Combined Communications
Arbitron Metro Market: StreetBend, OR *Format:* Country
Chuck Chackel, CEO
Mike Cheney, General Manager
Steve Leon, Programming Director

***KVLB**
01-01-2003; 90.5 mhz FM *Hrs Open:* 24; 1.4 kw vert; 633 ft.; N44 4 40 W121 19 48
P O Drawer 2440, Tupelo, MS 38803 US
(800) 525-5683, *Fax:* (916) 251-1650
www.klove.com
klove@klove.com
License: Bend, Deschutes County, OR held by Educational Media Foundation.
Group Owner: EMF Broadcasting; (acq 3-11-03; grpsl).
Nat'l Network: K-Love
Arbitron Metro Market: Bend, OR *Format:* Christian *No. News Employees:* 3 *Target Audience:* 25-44; Judeo Christian, female
Darrell Chambliss, Chairman
Mike Novak, President and CEO
Marya Morgan, News Reporter
Mike Lee, General Sales Mgr
David Pierce, Programming Director
Ed Lenane, News Director
Sam Wallington, Engineering Dir
Richard Hunt, NewsReporter
Laura Daniels, News Reporter
Tim Luttrell, News Reporter

Kenny Noble Cortes, News Reporter
Darren Vinson, News Reporter

***KLBR**
88.1 mhz FM; 5 kw; Ant 850 ft; N44 02 49 W121 31 50
Rebroadcasts: Rebroadcasts KLCC(FM) Eugene 100%
136 W. 8th Ave., Eugene, OR 97405
(541) 463-6000, *Fax:* (541) 463-6046
www.klcc.org
klcc@klcc.org
License: Bend, Deschutes County, OR held by Lane Community College.
Steve Barton, General Manager
Cheryl Crumbley, General Sales Mgr
Don Hein, Programming Director

KRXF
01-01-2006; 92.9 mhz FM; 86 kw; 994 ft.; N44 2 49 W121 31 50
P. O. Box 5068, 1500 NEButler Market Rd, Bend, OR 97708 US
(541)388-3300, *Fax:* (541) 388-3303
www.929online.com
mflanagan@bendradiogroup.com
License: Bend, Deschutes County, OR held by Fields Pond Group.
Nat'l Reps: Katz Radio
Arbitron Metro Market: Bend, OR *Format:* Rock/AOR
Charles Wilkinson, CEO
Nancy Reino, General Sales Mgr
Mike Flanagan, Programming Director
Bart Platt, Promotions Manager

KBNW
08-25-2008; 1340 khz AM *Hrs Open:* 24*Rebroadcasts:* Simulcast with KWLZ-FM Warm Springs 100%
US
(541) 383-3825, *Fax:* (541) 383-3403
www.newsradiocentraloregon.com
License: Bend, OR held by Summit Broadcasting Group LLC
Nat'l Network: ABC Information & Entertainment; Premiere Radio Networks; Westwood One; Jones Radio Networks; Talk Radio Network *Nat'l Reps:* Christal *Wire Services:* AP
Arbitron Metro Market: Bend, OR *Format:* News, News/Talk, 86 *Hrs. of News Programming:* 17.5 weekly (local) *No. News Employees:* 3 *Target Audience:* Adults 25-54
Regan Brick, Operations Dir
Keith Shipman, General Manager
John Edwards, General Sales Mgr
Brian Canady, Programming Director
Bill Baker, News Director
Annette Weston, Program Director

Bonanza

***KYSF**
01-01-1999; 102.9 mhz FM; 460 w; Ant 2,106 ft; N42 05 48 W121 37 57
5700 W. Oaks Blvd., Rocklin, CA 98006
(916) 251-1600, *Fax:* (916) 251-1650
www.klove.com
License: Bonanza, Klamath County, OR held by Educational Media Founation
Group Owner: New Northwest Broadcasters LLC; (acq 1-4-2012).
Mike Novak, President/CEO
Rob Siems, General Manager

Brightwood

***KZME**
91.1 mhz FM; 0.125 kw; 1430 ft.; N45 19 44 W121 42 35
US
(503) 618-1071, *Fax:* (503) 667-7710
www.kzme.fm
PD@kzme.fm
License: Brightwood, Clackamas County, OR held by MetroEast Community Media.
Arbitron Metro Market: Portland, OR *Format:* Contemporary Hits/Top 40, Public Affairs
Rob Brading, CEO
Dennise M. Kowalczyk, Director of Organizational Advancement
Taaj Middleton, Director of Volunteer Services

Brookings

KURY
05-02-1958; 910 khz AM *Hrs Open:* 24; 1 kw-D, ND1; 0.037 kw-N, ND1; N42 2 34 W124 14 37
P.O. Box 1029, 605 Railroad St., Brookings, OR 97415 US
(541) 469-2111, *Fax:* (541) 469-6397
www.kuryradio.com
kury@kuryradio.com
License: Brookings, OR held by Eureka Broadcasting Co. Inc.
Group Owner: Eureka Broadcasting Co.; (acq 4-19-2005; $775,000 with co-located FM).
Nat'l Network: Jones Radio Networks *Nat'l Reps:* Tacher
Arbitron Metro Market: Brookings, OR *Format:* Oldies *No. News Employees:* 4 *Target Audience:* General. *Adv. Rates:* contact for rate card
Hugo Papstein, President
Brian Papstein, General Manager
Debby Phillips, General Sales Mgr
Kevin Bane, Programming Director
Tina Williams, News Director

KURY-FM
05-01-1977; 95.3 mhz FM *Hrs Open:* 24; 8.7 kw; 1165 ft.; N42 7 23 W124 17 56
P.O. Box 1029, 605 Railroad St, Brookings, OR 97415 US
(541) 469-2111, *Fax:* (541) 469-6397
www.kuryradio.com
debby@kuryradio.com
License: Brookings, Curry County, OR
Group Owner: Eureka Broadcasting Co.; 5/5/2005
Nat'l Reps: Tacher *Wire Services:* AP
Arbitron Metro Market: Brookings, OR *Format:* Oldies *Hrs. of News Programming:* news progmg 11 hrs wkly *No. News Employees:* 4 *Adv. Rates:* Contact for rate card
Brian Papstein, Station Manager
Debby Phillips, General Sales Mgr
Kevin Bane, Programming Director
Tina Williams, News Director
Steve Braun, Disc Jockey
Robert Brown, Disc Jockey
Josh Voight, Disc Jockey

***KMWR**
10-31-2002; 90.7 mhz FM *Hrs Open:* 24; 100 w; Ant 1,233 ft; N42 07 23 W124 17 56 *Rebroadcasts:* Rebroadcasts KVIP-FM Redding, CA 100%
1139 Hartnell Ave., Redding, CA 96049
(530) 222-4455, *Fax:* (530) 222-4484
www.kvip.org
info@kvip.org
License: Brookings, Curry County, OR held by Pacific Cascade Communications Corp.
Group Owner: Pacific Cascade Communications Corp.
Population Served: 15,000*No. News Employees:* 2
David Morrow, Operations Dir
Steve Hafen, General Manager
Ted Hering, Programming Director
Paul Brown, Chief Engineer

Brownsville

KEHK
04-01-1991; 102.3 mhz FM *Hrs Open:* 24; 100 kw horiz, 43 kw vert; 919 ft.; N44 0 8 W123 6 50
City Center West, 7201 W. Lake Mead Blvd, Las Vegas, NV 89128 US
(541) 284-8500, *Fax:* (541) 485-0969
www.starfm1023.com
License: Brownsville, Linn County, OR held by Cumulus Licensing Corp.
Group Owner: Cumulus Media Inc.; (acq 8-24-00; grpsl)
Nat'l Network: Jones Radio Networks *Nat'l Reps:* McGavren Guild
Arbitron Metro Market: Eugene-Springfield, OR *Format:* Adult Contemp *Hrs. of News Programming:* news progmg 2 hrs wkly *No. News Employees:* 1 *Target Audience:* 25-54.
Bill Bradley, President
BJ O'Brien, General Manager
Maverick, Programming Director

Burns

KORC(FM)
09-01-1997; 92.7 mhz FM *Hrs Open:* 24; 750 w; 905 ft; N43 34 22 W119 07 50
69470 S. Egan Rd., PO Box 877, Burns, OR 97720
(541) 573-2055, *Fax:* (541) 573-5223
kzzr_amkqhc_fm@centurytel.net
License: Burns, Harney County, OR
Nat'l Network: Jones Radio Networks *Nat'l Reps:* Tacher
Population Served: 10,000*Format:* Adult Contemp *Adv. Rates:* Same as AM
Trever Carson, Operations Dir
Toni Carson, General Manager
Kristina Spurlock, Programming Director

***KOBN**
90.1 mhz FM; 0.6 kw; 899 ft.; N43 34 23 W119 7 49
US
(503) 293-1905, *Fax:* (503) 293-1919
www.opb.org
opb.org/contactus
License: Burns, Harney County, OR held by Oregon Public Broadcasting.
Arbitron Metro Market: Burns, OR
Steven M. Bass, CEO
Dan Metziga, Senior Vice President, Development and Marketing
Lynne Clendenin, Vice President, Programming
David Davis, Vice President, TV Production
Morgan Holm, Vice President, News and Public Affairs
SteveAmen, Executive Producer

Canyon City

KJDY-FM
12-13-1996; 94.5 mhz FM *Hrs Open:* 24; 39 kw; 1365 ft.; N44 17 50 W119 2 9
P.O. Box 399, John Day, OR 97845 US
(541) 575-1185, *Fax:* (541) 575-2313
kjdy@centurytel.net
License: Canyon City, Grant County, OR held by Blue Mountain Broadcasting Co. Inc.
Nat'l Network: ABC
Format: Country *Target Audience:* 25-54.
Phil Gray, General Manager

Canyonville

***KMKR**
10-22-1990; 92.1 mhz FM; 6 kw; -686 ft.; N42 55 42 W123 17 5
1574 Coburg Rd, Suite 237, Eugene, OR 97401 US
(541) 782-2231, *Fax:* (541) 782-4692
www.geocites.com/kave921
kave921@hotmail.com
License: Canyonville, Lane County, OR held by School District #76.
Arbitron Metro Market: Canyonville, OR *Format:* Contemporary Hits/Top 40 *Target Audience:* General.
Debbie Gillespie, General Manager
Aaron Stone, Programming Director
Abbie Pierce, Promotions Manager

Cave Junction

KCNA
04-30-1985; 102.7 mhz FM *Hrs Open:* 24; 100 kw; 1975 ft.; N42 15 30 W123 39 38
1257 No. Riverside, Ave, Suite 10, Medford, OR 97501 US
(541) 772-0322, *Fax:* (541) 772-4233
1027TheDrive.com
jim@opusradio.com
License: Cave Junction, Josephine County, OR held by Opus Broadcasting Systems Inc.
Group Owner: Opus Broadcasting Systems Inc.; acq 12-94).
Nat'l Reps: Tacher
Arbitron Metro Market: Cave Junction, OR *Format:* Contemporary Hits/Top 40, Adult Contemp
Henry Flock, President
Dean Flock, General Manager

Central Point

KFJL
02-14-2012; 1400 khz AM; 1 kw-U; N42 21 00 W122 54 27
672 Mason Way, Medford, OR
(541) 245-2727, *Fax:* (541) 773-9554
License: Central Point, Jackson County, OR held by Fjarli Broadcasting, a General Partnership.
Arbitron Metro Market: Medford-Ashland
Jo Ann Fjarli, President
Bruce Fjarli, General Manager

Chemult

***KSKX**
89.5 mhz FM; 0.1 kw; 1896 ft.; N43 18 20 W121 42 58
US
(541) 552-6301, *Fax:* (541) 552-8565
www.ijpr.org
License: Chemult, Klamath County, OR held by The State of Oregon Acting By and Through the Oregon State Board of Higher Education for Southern Oregon University.
Arbitron Metro Market: Colorado Springs, CO
Ron Kramer, General Manager

Coburg

KSHL
12-01-1992; 97.7 mhz FM *Hrs Open:* 24; 7 kw; 850 ft.; N44 45 24 W124 2 53

PO Box 1180, Newport, OR 97365 US
(541) 265-6477, *Fax:* (541) 265-6478
www.kshl.com
info@kshl.com
License: Coburg, Lincoln County, OR held by Stephanie Linn.
Regional Reps: McGavren Guild
Arbitron Metro Market: Newport, OR *Format:* Country *Hrs. of News Programming:* News progmg 2 hrs wkly *Target Audience:* 25-55; general
Stephanie Linn, President
Dick Linn, General Manager

Coos Bay

KDCQ
05-24-1995; 92.9 mhz FM *Hrs Open:* 24; 4.5 kw; 524 ft.; N43 21 15 W124 14 34
P.O. Box 478, Coos Bay, OR 97420 US
(541) 269-0929, *Fax:* (541) 267-9376
www.kdcq.com
oldies@kdcq.com
License: Coos Bay, Coos County, OR held by Bay Cities Building Co. Inc.
Nat'l Network: ABC *Nat'l Reps:* Tacher *Wire Services:* AP
Arbitron Metro Market: Coos Bay, OR *Format:* Contemporary Hits/Top 40, Adult Contemp *Hrs. of News Programming:* News progmg 5 hrs wkly *No. News Employees:* 1 *Target Audience:* 35-54; baby boomers
Bruce Latta, President
Mike Chavez, Operations Dir
Stephanie Kilmer, General Manager
Cindi Miller, General Sales Mgr
Evan O, Public Service Director
Julie Cummings, Accounts Executive

KHSN
03-15-1928; 1230 khz AM *Hrs Open:* 24
340 Central, Coos Bay, OR 97420 US
(541) 267-2121, *Fax:* (541) 267-5229
www.khsn1230.com
License: Coos Bay, OR held by W7 Broadcasting LLC
Regional Reps: Allied Radio Partners.
TV Affiliate: ESPN *Format:* Talk *Hrs. of News Programming:* News progmg 14 hrs wkly *Target Audience:* 35- plus. *Adv. Rates:* 13; 11; 13; 7
Mike O'Brien, Operations Dir
Lee Taft, General Manager

KMHS
12-07-1956; 1420 khz AM
1330 Teakwood, Coos Bay, OR 97420 US
(541) 267-1451, *Fax:* (541) 269-0161
www.marshfield.coos-bay.k12.or.us/kmhs/index.htm
stevew@coosbay.k12.or.us
License: Coos Bay, OR held by Coos Bay School District No. 9
Format: Country
Steve Walker, General Manager

*KSBA
11-04-1988; 88.5 mhz FM *Hrs Open:* 5 AM-2 AM; 2.2 kw; 531 ft.; N43 23 26 W124 7 46
PO Box 3175, Eugene, OR 97403 US
(541) 552-6301, *Fax:* (541) 552-8565
www.ijpr.org
jprinfo@sou.edu
License: Coos Bay, Coos County, OR held by The State of Oregon, acting by and through the State Board of Higher Education.
Nat'l Network: NPR; PRI *Wire Services:* AP
Arbitron Metro Market: Ashland, OR *Format:* Jazz, News, 90
Special Programming: Blues 6 hrs, folk 3 hrs, pub affrs 7 hrs wkly *Hrs. of News Programming:* news progmg 45 hrs wkly *No. News Employees:* 1 *TargetAudience:* General.
Ronald Kramer, CEO
Darin Ransom, Engineering Dir
Betsy Byers, Administrative Assistant
Paul Westhelle, Executive Director

KYSJ
11-01-1979; 105.9 mhz FM; 15 kw; 902 ft.; N43 27 49 W124 5 44
580 Kingwood Avenue, Coos Bay, OR 97420 US
(800) 447-7664, *Fax:* (541) 267-0114
www.lighthouseradio.com
kysj@lighthouseradio.com
License: Coos Bay, Coos County, OR held by Lighthouse Radio Group.
Wire Services: AP
Arbitron Metro Market: Coos Bay, OR *Format:* Jazz, Smooth Jazz
Rick Stevens, General Manager
David DeAndrea, Programming Director

KYTT-FM
11-01-1978; 98.7 mhz FM *Hrs Open:* 24; 12.55 kw; 961 ft.; N43 27 49 W124 5 44
580 Kingwood Avenue, Coos Bay, OR 97420 US
(800) 447-7664, *Fax:* (541) 267-0114
www.lighthouseradio.com
License: Coos Bay, Coos County, OR held by Lighthouse Radio Group.
Nat'l Network: Salem Radio Network *Wire Services:* AP
Arbitron Metro Market: Coos Bay, OR *Format:* Christian *Hrs. of News Programming:* News progmg 8 hrs wkly
Dave DeAndrea, Operations Dir
Rick Stevens, General Manager
Steve Ramberg, General Sales Mgr
David DeAndrea, Programming Director

*KJCH
04-01-2005; 90.9 mhz FM *Hrs Open:* 24; 3.5 kw; 1463 ft.; N42 57 32 W124 16 23
Mailing Address: 3000 W Macarthur Blvd., Santa Ana, CA 92704 US
Second Address: CSN International, 4002 N 3300 E, Twin Falls, ID 83301
(800) 357-4226, *Fax:* (208) 736-1958
www.csnradio.com
csn@csnradio.com
License: Coos Bay, Coos County, OR held by CSN International
Group Owner: CSN International
Arbitron Metro Market: Coos Bay, OR *Format:* Religious
Mike Kestler, President
Daniel Davidson, Operations Dir
Joshua Tanner, General Manager
Don Mills, Network Programming Director / Music Director
Kelly Carlson, Engineering Dir
Jerry Johnson, Engineering Dir
Ray Gorney, AssistantDirector of Engineering
Dustin Pamplona, Engineer
Nolan Mather, Graphics / Website Maintenance
Mike Stocklin, National Underwriting
Austin Morris, Accounting
Lois Mills, FCC Applications / Translator Site Manager

*KMHS-FM
01-01-2008; 91.3 mhz FM; 10 kw horiz; -33 ft.; N43 22 7 W124 12 11
1330 Teakwood, Coos Bay, OR 97420 US
(541) 267-3104
www.kmhsradio.cbd9.net
License: Coos Bay, Coos County, OR held by Coos Bay School District No. 9.
Arbitron Metro Market: Coos Bay, OR *Format:* Contemporary Hits/Top 40
Steve Walker, General Manager

Coquille

KSHR-FM
11-01-1981; 97.3 mhz FM; 25 kw horiz, 5.9 kw vert; 856 ft.; N43 14 51 W124 6 46
Mailing Address: P.O. Box 250, Coquille, OR 97423 US
Second Address: 1270 W. 13th, Coquille, OR 97423
(541) 396-2121, *Fax:* (541) 267-5229
www.kshr.com
License: Coquille, Coos County, OR held by Bicoastal Media Licenses III LLC.
Group Owner: Bicoastal Media L.L.C.
Arbitron Metro Market: Coos Bay, OR *Format:* Country
Bill Buchanan, CEO
Barbara Moss, Operations Dir
Eric Latz, Programming Director
Tiffany York, News Director
James Stephenson, Chief Engineer

KWRO
02-01-1949; 630 khz AM; 5 kw-D, ND2; 0.046 kw-N, ND2; N43 10 17 W124 11 54
Mailing Address: Box 250, Coquille, OR 97423 US
Second Address: 1270 W. 13th, Coquille, OR 97423
(541) 396-2121, *Fax:* (541) 267-5229
www.kwro.com
connie@crbradio.com
License: Coquille, OR held by Bicoastal Media Licenses III LLC.
Group Owner: Bicoastal Media L.L.C.; (acq 10-16-2003; grpsl)
Nat'l Reps: McGavren Guild
Arbitron Metro Market: Coos Bay, OR *Format:* News, News/Talk, 86
Connie Williamson, General Manager

Corvallis

*KBVR
10-26-1965; 88.7 mhz FM *Hrs Open:* 24; 0.34 kw; -82 ft.; N44 33 50 W123 16 30
Mu East 218, Corvallis, OR 97331 US
(541) 737-2008, *Fax:* (541) 737-4545
www.oregonstate.edu/dept/kbvr/fmradio
info@kbvrfm.com
License: Corvallis, Benton County, OR held by State Board of Higher Education.
Arbitron Metro Market: Corvallis, OR *Format:* Alternative, Jazz
Special Programming: Class 4 hrs, Sp 4 hrs, folk 4 hrs wkly
Target Audience: 15-45; general
Ian Rose, Station Manager

KEJO
08-01-1955; 1240 khz AM; 1 kw-U; N44 35 44 W123 14 54
2840 Marion St. S.E., Albany, OR 78216
(541) 926-8628, *Fax:* (541) 928-1261
www.kejoam.com
License: Corvallis, Benton County, OR held by Bicoastal Willamette Valley LLC.
Group Owner: Bicoastal Media L.L.C.; (acq 7-2-2007; grpsl)
Population Served: 76,600*Target Audience:* ages 25-54 men
Larry Roger, General Manager
Jason Henson, General Sales Mgr
Jon Warren, Programming Director
Kimberly Littler, Promotions Manager
Robin O'Kelly, Chief Engineer

KFLY
10-01-1966; 101.5 mhz FM; 27.5 kw; 2320 ft.; N44 17 28 W123 32 18
200 Concord Plaza, Suite 600, San Antonio, TX 78216 US
(541) 284-3600
www.kflyfm.com
info@kflyfm.com
License: Corvallis, Benton County, OR held by Bicoastal Willamette Valley LLC.
Group Owner: Bicoastal Media L.L.C.
Arbitron Metro Market: Corvallis, OR *Format:* Rock/AOR *Special Programming:* Comedy 20 hrs wkly *Target Audience:* 25-49; general
Larry Rogers, Promotions Manager

KLOO
08-23-1947; 1340 khz AM *Hrs Open:* 24
50 East Rivercenter Boulevard, Suite 1200, Covington, KY 41011 US
(541) 926-8628, *Fax:* (541) 928-1261
www.news1340.com
License: Corvallis, OR held by Bicoastal Willamette Valley LLC.
Group Owner: Bicoastal Media L.L.C.; (acq 7-2-2007; grpsl)
Arbitron Metro Market: Eugene, OR *Format:* News, News/Talk, 84, Talk *Hrs. of News Programming:* news progmg 83 hrs wkly
No. News Employees: 1 *Target Audience:* 35-54.
Robert Dove, General Manager
Larry Rogers, General Sales Mgr
Rick Rogers, News Director
Robin O'Kelley, Chief Engineer

KLOO-FM
01-01-1973; 106.3 mhz FM *Hrs Open:* 24; 100 kw; 1138 ft.; N44 38 47 W123 16 10
50 East Rivercenter Boulevard, Suite 1200, Covington, KY 41011 US
(541) 926-8628, *Fax:* (541) 928-1261
www.kloo.com
License: Corvallis, Benton County, OR
Group Owner: Bicoastal Media L.L.C.
Arbitron Metro Market: Eugene, OR *Format:* Classic Rock *Hrs. of News Programming:* News progmg 15 hrs wkly *Target Audience:* 18-54.
Richard Jenkins, President
Mike Novak, Operations Dir
Keith Whipple, General Sales Mgr
David Pierce, Programming Director
Sam Wallington, Engineering Dir
Marya Morgan, News Reporter
Richard Hunt, Marya Morgan
Karen Johnson,News Reporter
Ed Lenane, Operations Director

*KOAC
12-07-1922; 550 khz AM *Hrs Open:* 5 AM-midnight; 5 kw-D, DA2; 5 kw-N, DA2; N44 38 12 W123 11 33
7140 S.W. Macadam Avenue, Portland, OR 97219 US
(503) 293-1905,(541) 737-5332, *Fax:* (503) 293-1919
info@opb.org
License: Corvallis, OR held by Oregon Public Broadcasting.
Nat'l Network: PRI; NPR

TV Affiliate: *KOAC-TV affil *Format:* News, News/Talk, 86 *Special Programming:* Jazz 12 hrs wkly *Hrs. of News Programming:* news progmg 40 hrs wkly *No. News Employees:* 5 *Target Audience:* 25-54; collegeeducated with an interest in news & mus
Lynne Clendenin, Operations Dir
Roger Dominigues, Chief Engineer

Cottage Grove

KMME(FM)
03-21-1994; 100.5 mhz FM *Hrs Open:* 24; 6 kw; Ant 115 ft; N43 44 41 W123 05 29
4222 Commerce St., Suite E, Box 10, Eugene, OR 97402
(541) 683-3392, *Fax:* (541) 338-7067
License: Cottage Grove, Lane County, OR held by Diamond Peak Investments LLC
Nat'l Reps: Tacher
Arbitron Metro Market: Eugene-Springfield, OR *Format:* Contemporary Hits/Top 40 *Hrs. of News Programming:* News progmg 6 hrs wkly *Target Audience:* 25-49. *Adv. Rates:* 12; 12; 12; na
Steve Master, General Manager

KNND
08-01-1953; 1400 khz AM *Hrs Open:* 24
321 Main Street, Cottage Grove, OR 97424 US
(541) 942-2468, *Fax:* (541) 942-5797
paul@knnd.com
License: Cottage Grove, OR held by Schwartzberg Communications Inc.
Nat'l Network: AP Radio
Arbitron Metro Market: Eugene, OR *Format:* Country, News, 62, Talk *Special Programming:* Relg 3 hrs wkly *Hrs. of News Programming:* news progmg 40 hrs wkly *No. News Employees:* 1 *Target Audience:* General.*Adv. Rates:* 14; 12; 12; 10
Paul Schwartzberg, President

Creswell

KUJZ
09-01-1983; 95.3 mhz FM; 0.63 kw; 1207 ft.; N44 0 4 W123 6 45
One Office Park Circle, Suite 300, Birmingham, AL 35223 US
(541) 484-8500, *Fax:* (541) 485-0969
www.1320thescore.com
License: Creswell, Lane County, OR held by Cumulus Licensing Corp.
Group Owner: Cumulus Media Inc.; (acq 2-29-00;; grpsl).
Nat'l Network: ESPN Radio *Nat'l Reps:* Christal
Arbitron Metro Market: Eugene, OR *Format:* Sports *Target Audience:* 18-34.
B.J. O'Brien, General Manager

Dallas

KWIP
04-15-1955; 880 khz AM; 5 kw-D, ND1; 1 kw-N, ND1; N44 55 45 W123 17 22
Box 469, Dallas, OR 97338 US
(503) 623-0245, *Fax:* (503) 623-6733
www.kwip.com
info@kwip.com
License: Dallas, OR held by Jupiter Communications Corp.
Arbitron Metro Market: Dallas, OR *Special Programming:* Talk 5 hrs wkly *Target Audience:* 18-54; families & blue collar workers
Diana Burns, General Manager

Depoe Bay

KPPT-FM
12-01-1980; 100.7 mhz FM; 17.5 kw; 837 ft.; N44 45 23 W124 3 1
Mailing Address: P.O. Box 456, 304 S. Coast Highway, Newport, OR 97365 US
Second Address: 145 N. Coast Hwy., Newport, OR 97365
(541) 265-5000, *Fax:* (541) 265-9576
www.bossfmradio.net
info@bossradio.net
License: Depoe Bay, Lincoln County, OR held by Agpal Broadcasting Inc.
Arbitron Metro Market: Central OR Coast *Format:* Talk
Cheryl Harle, Operations Dir

Eagle Point

KZZE
03-01-1995; 106.3 mhz FM; 1 kw; 1575 ft.; N42 21 12 W122 47 8
50 Rivercenter Blvd., #1200, Covington, KY 41011 US
(541) 857-4170, *Fax:* (541) 858-5416
www.kzze.com
donhurley@bicoastalmedia.com
License: Eagle Point, Jackson County, OR held by Bicoastal Rogue Valley LLC.
Group Owner: Bicoastal Media L.L.C.; (acq 7-2-2007; grpsl)
Nat'l Reps: Tacher
Arbitron Metro Market: Eagle Point, OR *Format:* Rock/AOR *Hrs. of News Programming:* news progmg one hr wkly *No. News Employees:* 1 *Target Audience:* 18-49; rock listeners
Bill Nielsen, General Manager
Boss Hogg, Programming Director

Elgin

KRJT
01-01-2005; 105.9 mhz FM *Hrs Open:* 24; 0.115 kw; 1916 ft.; N45 26 26 W117 53 31
Mailing Address: US
Second Address: 2510 E. Cove Ave., La Grande, OR 97850
(541) 963-4121, *Fax:* (541) 963-3117
License: Elgin, Union County, OR held by Pacific Empire Radio Corp.
Group Owner: Pacific Empire Radio Corp.
Nat'l Reps: Interep; McGavren Guild
Arbitron Metro Market: Portales, NM *Format:* Oldies *Target Audience:* 25-54. *Adv. Rates:* 24; 24; 24; 24
Mark Bolland, President
Linda Ashlock, General Manager

Enterprise

KWVR
06-01-1960; 1340 khz AM *Hrs Open:* 24; 1 kw-U, ND1; N45 26 14 W117 17 30
220 West Main Street, Enterprise, OR 97828 US
(541) 426-4577, *Fax:* (541) 426-4578
kwvrradio.net
kwvrradio@gmail.com
License: Enterprise, OR held by Wallowa Valley Radio LLC
Nat'l Network: ABC
Arbitron Metro Market: Enterprise, OR *Format:* News, News/Talk, 86 *Special Programming:* Farm 4 hrs wkly *Hrs. of News Programming:* news progmg 11 hrs wkly *No. News Employees:* 2 *Target Audience:* General.
Lee Perkins, President
Alyssa Werst, Operations Dir
David Frasch, General Manager
Patrick Channing, II, General Sales Mgr
Alyssa Werst, News Director

KWVR-FM
01-01-1986; 92.1 mhz FM *Hrs Open:* 24; 6 kw; -689 ft.; N45 19 19 W117 13 18
220 West Main Street, Enterprise, OR 97828 US
(541) 426-4577, *Fax:* (541) 426-4578
kwvrradio.net
kwvrradio@gmail.com
License: Enterprise, Wallowa County, OR held by Wallowa Valley Radio LLC
Nat'l Network: ABC; Jones Radio Networks
Arbitron Metro Market: Enterprise, OR *Format:* Country
Alyssa Werst, Operations Dir
David Frasch, General Manager

*KETP
88.7 mhz FM; 0.1 kw; 1755 ft.; N45 23 58 W117 23 16 US
(503) 293-1905, *Fax:* (503) 293-1919
www.opb.org
opb.org/contactus
License: Enterprise, Wallowa County, OR held by Oregon Public Broadcasting.
Arbitron Metro Market: Enterprise, OR
Steven M. Bass, CEO
Dan Metziga, Senior Vice President, Development and Marketing
Lynne Clendenin, Vice President, Programming
David Davis, Vice President, TV Production
Morgan Holm, Vice President, News and Public Affairs
SteveAmen, Executive Producer

Eugene

KOPB
09-19-1947; 1600 khz AM
3545 Highway 20, PO Box 278, Albany, OR 97321 US
(503) 293-9900, *Fax:* (503) 293-1919
www.opb.org
License: Eugene, OR held by Oregon Public Broadcasting
Nat'l Network: NPR *Regional Network:* Ore. Pub. Bcstg Radio Net.
Arbitron Metro Market: Eugene-Springfield, OR *Format:* News, News/Talk, 86
Steven Bass, President
Cheryl Ikemiya, Director
Julie Arnzen, Associate Director
Jordan Anderson, Associate Director

KKNX
01-01-1992; 840 khz AM *Hrs Open:* 24; 1 kw-D, ND2; 0.17 kw-N, ND2; N44 4 54 W123 6 34
945 Garfield Street, Eugene, OR 97402 US
(541) 342-1012, *Fax:* (541) 342-6201
www.radio84.com
john@radio84.com
License: Eugene, OR held by John S. Mielke, Susan J. Mielke.
Nat'l Network: AP Radio *Regional Reps:* Tacher & Co. *Wire Services:* AP
Arbitron Metro Market: Eugene, OR *Format:* Oldies *Special Programming:* Black 3 hrs wkly *Hrs. of News Programming:* news progmg 7 hrs wkly *No. News Employees:* 1 *Target Audience:* 25-64; general *Adv.Rates:* 18; 16; 18; 10
John Mielke, President

KLZS
09-07-1954; 1450 khz AM *Hrs Open:* 24; 1 kw-U, ND1; N44 4 54 W123 6 34
925 County Club Road, Eugene, OR 97401 US
(541) 343-4100, *Fax:* (541) 343-0448
www.radio84.com
info@alzx660am.com
License: Eugene, OR held by Churchill Communications LLC
Group Owner: Churchill Communications LLC; (acq 11-3-2004; $87,500).
Nat'l Network: CNN Radio
Arbitron Metro Market: Eugene, OR *Format:* Oldies *Hrs. of News Programming:* news progmg 30 hrs wky *No. News Employees:* 2 *Target Audience:* 25-54.
Mike Triem, General Manager

*KLCC
02-17-1967; 89.7 mhz FM *Hrs Open:* 24; 81 kw horiz, 54 kw vert; Ant 1,161 ft; N44 00 05 W123 06 48
136 W. 8th Ave., Eugene, OR 97405
(541) 463-6000, *Fax:* (541) 463-6046
www.klcc.org
klcc@klcc.org
License: Eugene, Lane County, OR held by Lane Community College.
Nat'l Network: NPR
Population Served: 750,000 *Arbitron Metro Market:* Eugene-Springfield, OR *Special Programming:* Sp 5 hrs, folk 12 hrs, Black 3 hrs, blues 4 hrs, world 3 hrs, electronic 6 hrs wkly *Hrs. of News Programming:* news progmg60 hrs wkly *No. News Employees:* 1 *Target Audience:* 25-54.
Steve Barton, General Manager
Cheryl Crumbley, General Sales Mgr
Don Hein, Programming Director
Tripp Sommer, News Director

KMGE
10-10-1965; 94.5 mhz FM; 49 kw horiz, 21 kw vert; 1299 ft.; N44 0 4 W123 6 45
Koteen & Naftalin, L.L.P, 1150 Conn. Ave., N.W., Washington, DC 20036 US
(541) 484-9400, *Fax:* (541) 344-9424
www.kmge.com
License: Eugene, Lane County, OR held by McKenzie River Broadcasting Co. Inc.
Group Owner: McKenzie River Broadcasting Company, Inc.; (acq 3-87; $950,000;
Arbitron Metro Market: Eugene, OR *Format:* Adult Contemp *Target Audience:* 18-49.
John Tilson, President
Jeff Baird, Programming Director

KSCR
06-12-1962; 1320 khz AM; 1 kw-D, ND1; 0.048 kw-N, ND1; N44 5 25 W123 6 43
One Office Park Circle, Suite 300, Birmingham, AL 35223 US
(541) 485-5846, *Fax:* (541) 485-0969
License: Eugene, OR held by Cumulus Licensing Corp.
Group Owner: Cumulus Media Inc.; (acq 2-29-00; grpsl).
Nat'l Network: ESPN Radio *Nat'l Reps:* Christal
Arbitron Metro Market: Eugene, OR *Format:* Sports *Target Audience:* 18-44; general
Steve Ries, General Manager

KODZ
11-01-1968; 99.1 mhz FM; 100 kw; 1631 ft.; N44 6 57 W122 59 57
Mailing Address: 4700 S.W. Macadam Ave., Portland, OR 97201 US
Second Address: OR
(541) 485-1120, *Fax:* (541) 484-5769

License: Eugene, Lane County, OR
Group Owner: Bicoastal Media L.L.C.
Arbitron Metro Market: Eugene-Springfield, OR *Format:* Adult Contemp *Target Audience:* 25-54; working women
Larry Rogers, Promotions Manager

KPNW
07-22-1968; 1120 khz AM *Hrs Open:* 24; 50 kw-U, DA1; N43 57 24 W123 2 10
Mailing Address: 4700 S.W. Macadam Ave., Portland, OR 97201 US
Second Address: OR 97440
(541) 485-1120, *Fax:* (541) 484-5769
www.kpnw.com
1120kpnw@gmail.com
License: Eugene, OR held by Bicoastal Willamette Valley LLC.
Group Owner: Bicoastal Media L.L.C.; (acq 7-2-2007; grpsl)
Arbitron Metro Market: Eugene-Springfield, OR *Format:* News, News/Talk, 86 *Special Programming:* Portland Trail Blazers *No. News Employees:* 2 *Target Audience:* 35 plus; upper income, conservative
Robert Dove, Promotions Manager

*KRVM
11-09-1949; 1280 khz AM *Hrs Open:* 24; 5 kw-D, 1.5 kw-N, DA-N; N44 06 03 W123 03 06
P.M.B. 237, 1574 Cobug Rd., Eugene, OR 97402
(541) 790-6680, *Fax:* (541) 790-6688
www.krvm.org
info@krvm.org
License: Eugene, Lane County, OR held by Lane County School District 4J.
Nat'l Network: NPR *Nat'l Reps:* McGavren Guild
Arbitron Metro Market: Eugene-Springfield, OR
Randy Larson, Operations Dir
Randy Larson, General Manager

*KRVM-FM
12-08-1947; 91.9 mhz FM *Hrs Open:* 24; 1.1 kw; Ant 745 ft; N44 00 08 W123 06 50
P.M.B. 237, 1574 Cobug Rd., Eugene, OR 97402
(541) 790-6680, *Fax:* (541) 790-6688
www.krvm.org
info@krvm.org
License: Eugene, Lane County, OR held by Lane County School District No. 4J.
Nat'l Network: NPR
Population Served: 200,000 *Arbitron Metro Market:* Eugene-Springfield, OR *Special Programming:* Black 2 hrs, country one hr, folk 3 hrs, Native American 2 hrs wkly *Target Audience:* General.
Marti Ashcraft, Operations Dir
Jana Smith, General Manager
Gordon Ames, General Sales Mgr
Glenn Taylor, Programming Director
Diane Philips, News Director
Monica Smith, Sales

KUGN
07-04-1946; 590 khz AM *Hrs Open:* 24; 5 kw-D, DAN; 5 kw-N, DAN; N44 6 3 W123 3 6
City Center West, 7201 W. Lake Mead Blvd., Las Vegas, NV 89128 US
(541) 284-8500, *Fax:* (541) 485-0969
www.kugn.com
kugnpsa@gmail.com
License: Eugene, OR held by Cumulus Licensing Corp.
Group Owner: Cumulus Media Inc.; (acq 6-15-00; grpsl).
Nat'l Network: CBS *Wire Services:* NWS (National Weather Service)
Arbitron Metro Market: Eugene, OR *Format:* News, News/Talk, 86 *Hrs. of News Programming:* news progmg 28 hrs wkly *No. News Employees:* 6 *Target Audience:* 30-65; general
Bill Bradley, General Manager
Troy Murphy, General Sales Mgr
Jerry Allen, Programming Director
Wendy Wintrode, Promotions Manager
Rick Little, News Director
Cory Schruth, Chief Engineer

*KWAX
04-04-1951; 91.1 mhz FM *Hrs Open:* 24; 21.5 kw horiz, 12.5 kw vert; 1214 ft.; N44 0 4 W123 6 45
139 Susan Campbell Hall, University of Oregon, Eugene, OR 97403 US
(541) 345-0800, *Fax:* (541) 343-2123
www.kwax.com
inquiry@kwax.com
License: Eugene, Lane County, OR held by State Board of Higher Education.
Arbitron Metro Market: Eugene-Springfield, OR *Format:* Talk *Hrs. of News Programming:* News progmg 7 hrs wkly *Target Audience:* 35 plus.
Paul Bjornstad, General Manager

*KWVA
05-27-1993; 88.1 mhz FM *Hrs Open:* 24; 1 kw; 177 ft.; N44 4 55 W123 6 34
Mailing Address: Erb Memorial Union Ste.4, Univ. of Oregon, Eugene, OR 97403 US
Second Address: Univ. of Oregon, EMU, Suite M-112, Eugene, OR 97403
(541) 346-4091, *Fax:* (541) 346-0648
gladstone.uoregon.edu/~kwva
kwva@gladstone.uoregon.edu
License: Eugene, Lane County, OR held by Associated Students of University of Oregon.
Arbitron Metro Market: Eugene-Springfield, OR *Format:* Variety/Diverse *Special Programming:* Asian 4 hrs, Black 4 hrs, jazz 6 hrs, country 3 hrs, Japanese 2 hrs, Sp 6 hrs wkly *Hrs. of News Programming:* News progmg 12hrs wkly *Target Audience:* 3-30; college, alternative, underrepresented, varying educ levels & music lover
Charlotte Nisser, General Manager
Steven Murschel, Programming Director
Michael Zarkesh, Promotions Manager
Sarah Mollner, News Director
Hiring, Assistant General Manager
Lyzi Diamond, Music Department
Brandon O Rourke, SportsDepartmeent
Lex Chase, Marketing Department

KZEL-FM
04-22-1962; 96.1 mhz FM; 100 kw horiz, 43 kw vert; 1093 ft.; N44 0 5 W123 6 48
One Office Park Circle, Suite 300, Birmingham, AL 35223 US
(541) 284-8500, *Fax:* (541) 485-4070
www.96kzel.com/main
kteige@cumuluseugene.com
License: Eugene, Lane County, OR held by Cumulus Licensing Corp.
Group Owner: Cumulus Media Inc.; (acq 2-29-00; grpsl)
Nat'l Network: Westwood One *Nat'l Reps:* Christal
Arbitron Metro Market: Eugene, OR *Format:* Classic Rock *Target Audience:* 18-44.
Russ Davidson, Operations Dir
Steve Ries, General Manager

Florence

KCFM(AM)
05-05-1985; 1250 khz AM *Hrs Open:* 24; 1 kw-D, 68 w-N; N44 00 38 W124 05 37
Mailing Address: Box 20000, Florence, OR 97439
Second Address: Radio Center Bldg., 4480 Hwy. 101 N., Florence, OR 97439
(541) 997-9136, *Fax:* (541) 997-9165
www.kcst.com
radiowaves@kcst.com
License: Florence, Lane County, OR held by Coast Broadcasting Co. Inc.
Population Served: 370,000 *Arbitron Metro Market:* Florence, OR *Format:* Contemporary Hits/Top 40 *Target Audience:* 55+. *Adv. Rates:* 13; 13; 13; 13
John Thompson, General Manager

KCST-FM
10-01-1992; 106.9 mhz FM *Hrs Open:* 24; 2.3 kw; 509 ft.; N43 57 19 W124 4 26
Mailing Address: P.O. Box 20000, Florence, OR 97439 US
Second Address: 4480 Hwy 101 N., Radio Centre Bldg., Florence, OR 97439
(541) 997-9136, *Fax:* (541) 997-9165
www.kcst.com
radiowaves@kcst.com
License: Florence, Lane County, OR held by Coast Broadcasting Co. Inc.
Nat'l Network: ABC *Regional Reps:* Tacher Company *Wire Services:* AP
Arbitron Metro Market: Florence, OR *Format:* Adult Contemp, Country, 64 *Target Audience:* 35+. *Adv. Rates:* 15; 15; 15; 15
Greg Jacquay, General Manager

KDUK-FM
11-21-1983; 104.7 mhz FM *Hrs Open:* 24; 66 kw; 2320 ft.; N44 17 28 W123 32 18
Mailing Address: 4700 S.W. Macadam Avenue, Portland, OR 97201 US
Second Address: 1345 Olive St., Eugene, OR 977401
(541) 485-1120, *Fax:* (541) 484-5769
www.kduk.com
info@kduk.com
License: Florence, Lane County, OR held by Bicoastal Willamette Valley LLC.
Group Owner: Bicoastal Media L.L.C.; (acq 7-2-2007; grpsl)
Arbitron Metro Market: Eugene-Springfield, OR *Format:* Contemporary Hits/Top 40
Larry Rogers, Promotions Manager

*KLFO
08-16-1999; 88.1 mhz FM *Hrs Open:* 24; 250 w; Ant 548 ft; N43 57 26 W124 04 26 *Rebroadcasts:* Rebroadcasts KLCC(FM) Eugene 100%
136 W. 8th Ave., 4000 E. 30th Ave., Eugene, OR 97405
(541) 463-6000, *Fax:* (541) 463-6046
www.klcc.org
klcc@klcc.org
License: Florence, Lane County, OR held by Lane Community College.
Steve Barton, General Manager
Cheryl Crumbley, General Sales Mgr
Don Hein, Programming Director
Chris Heck, Chief Engineer

*KWVZ
01-01-2001; 91.5 mhz FM; 0.15 kw; 548 ft.; N43 57 26 W124 4 26 *Rebroadcasts:* Rebroadcasts KWAX(FM) Eugene 100%
139 Susan Campbell Hall, University of Oregon, Eugene, OR 97403 US
(541) 345-0800
info@kwax.com
License: Florence, Lane County, OR held by Oregon State Board of Higher Education.
Format: Classical
Marvin Sanders, General Manager

Garibaldi

KDEP
01-01-2001; 105.5 mhz FM; 0.32 kw; 1181 ft.; N45 27 59 W123 55 11
Mailing Address: 415 Cliff Street, P O Box 516, Depoe Bay, OR 97341 US
Second Address: 1550 N. Main, Tillamook, OR 97141
(503) 842-3888, *Fax:* (503) 842-5640
www.coast105.com
tommy@coast105.com
License: Garibaldi, Tillamook County, OR held by Alexandra Communications Inc.
Group Owner: Alexandra Communications Inc.; (acq 9-21-2005; $250,000).
Format: Classic Rock
Chris Gilbreth, General Manager

Gladstone

KRYP
05-10-1981; 93.1 mhz FM; 1.55 kw; 1270 ft.; N45 29 20 W122 41 40
1006 W Marine Drive, Astoria, OR 97103 US
(503) 786-0600, *Fax:* (503) 786-1551
www.931elrey.com
License: Gladstone, Clackamas County, OR held by Salem Media of Oregon Inc.
Group Owner: Salem Communications Corp.; (acq 1-19-2005)
Arbitron Metro Market: Portland, OR
Dennis Hayes, General Manager

Gleneden Beach

*KOGL
01-01-2008; 89.3 mhz FM; 0.21 kw; 73 ft.; N44 53 8 W124 0 51 *Rebroadcasts:* Rebroadcasts KOPB-FM Portland 100%
7140 Sw Macadam Ave, Portland, OR 97219 US
(503) 293-1905, *Fax:* (503) 293-1919
www.opb.org
opb.org/contactus
License: Gleneden Beach, Lincoln County, OR held by Oregon Public Broadcasting.
Regional Network: Ore. Pub. Bcstg Radio Net.
Arbitron Metro Market: Portland, OR *Format:* News
Steven M. Bass, CEO and General Manager
Dan Metziga, Senior Vice President, Development and Marketing
Lynne Clendenin, Vice President, Programming
David Davis, Vice President, TV Production
Morgan Holm, Vice President, News andPublic Affairs
Steve Amen, Executive Producer

*KQOC
06-01-2008; 88.1 mhz FM; 8.8 kw; 928 ft.; N44 45 23 W124 2 52 *Rebroadcasts:* Rebroadcasts KQAC(FM) Portland 100%
515 N E 15 Th Ave, Portland, OR 97232 US

(503) 943-5828, *Fax:* (503) 802-9456
www.allclassical.org
License: Gleneden Beach, Lincoln County, OR held by KBPS Public Radio Foundation.
Arbitron Metro Market: Portland, OR *Format:* Classical
Jack Allen, CEO
Kelly Palin, CFO
Andrea Rennie, Executive Assistant
Jenn Woodward, HR & Office Coordinator
John Burk, Vice President of Programming

Gold Beach

KGBR
12-01-1984; 92.7 mhz FM *Hrs Open:* 24; 265 w; 2700 ft; N42 23 50 W124 21 50
Box 787, Gold Beach, OR 97444
(541) 247-7211,(541) 247-7418, *Fax:* (541) 247-4155
www.kgbr.com
info@kgbr.com
License: Gold Beach, Curry County, OR held by St. Marie Communications Inc.
Nat'l Reps: Tacher
Population Served: 20,000*Hrs. of News Programming:* news progmg 4 hrs wkly *No. News Employees:* 2 *Target Audience:* 25-54. *Adv. Rates:* 18; 18; 18; 18
Dale St Marie, Chairman
Dale St Marie, President
Diana St Marie, Operations Dir
Dale St Marie, General Manager
Diana St Marie, Station Manager
Lucie Labonte, General Sales Mgr
Bill Bailey, Programming Director
Diana St Marie,Promotions Manager
Bill Bailey, News Director
Dale St Marie, Engineering Dir

Gold Hill

KRWQ
08-11-1980; 100.3 mhz FM *Hrs Open:* 24; 30 kw; 1004 ft.; N42 27 11 W123 3 22
50 E. Rivercenter Blvd., #1200, Covington, KY 41011 US
(541) 772-4170, *Fax:* (541) 858-5416
www.krwq.com
License: Gold Hill, Jackson County, OR held by Bicoastal Rogue Valley LLC.
Group Owner: Bicoastal Media L.L.C.; (acq 7-2-2007; grpsl)
Nat'l Reps: Tacher
Arbitron Metro Market: Medford-Ashland, OR *Format:* Country
No. News Employees: 1 *Target Audience:* 18-54.
Bill Nielsen, General Manager
Larry Neal, Programming Director

Government Camp

KZZR
09-28-1957; 94.3 mhz FM *Hrs Open:* 24; 3.4 kw; 1683 ft.; N45 20 1 W121 42 45
190 Queen Anne Avenue North, Suite 100, Seattle, WA 98109 US
(541) 573-2055, *Fax:* (541) 573-5223
www.lazeta943.com
License: Government Camp, Harney County, OR held by B&H Radio Inc.
Group Owner: Bustos Media LLC; (acq 10-1-2007; $209,700 with co-located FM)
Nat'l Network: ABC; Jones Radio Networks *Nat'l Reps:* Tacher
Wire Services: AP
Format: Country, News, 86 *Special Programming:* Farm 6 hrs wkly *Hrs. of News Programming:* News progmg 30 hrs wkly
Target Audience: 18-55. *Adv. Rates:* 26; 26; 26; 26
Trever Carson, Operations Dir
Toni Carson, General Manager
Kristina Spurlock, Programming Director

Grants Pass

*KAGI
12-16-1939; 930 khz AM *Hrs Open:* 24 hrs; 5 kw-D, ND1; 0.123 kw-N, ND1; N42 26 16 W123 21 27
P. O. Box 3175, Eugene, OR 97403 US
(541) 552-6301, *Fax:* (541) 552-8565
www.ijpr.org
jprinfo@sou.edu
License: Grants Pass, OR held by The State of Oregon, acting by and through the State Board of Higher Education, for the benefit of Southern Oregon University.
Nat'l Network: PRI; NPR
Arbitron Metro Market: Ashland, OR *Format:* News *Special Programming:* Sp 6 hrs wkly
Ronald Kramer, CEO
Bryon Lambert, Operations Dir
Paul Westhelle, General Sales Mgr
Eric Teel, Programming Director
Darin Ransom, Engineering Dir
Mitchell Christian, CFO
Eric Alan, Music Director

KAJO
08-15-1957; 1270 khz AM *Hrs Open:* 24
Box 230, Grants Pass, OR 97526 US
(541) 476-6608, *Fax:* (541) 476-4018
www.kajo.com
kajo@kajo.com
License: Grants Pass, OR held by Grants Pass Broadcasting Corp.
Nat'l Network: AP Radio *Nat'l Reps:* Tacher *Regional Reps:* Tacher *Wire Services:* AP
Arbitron Metro Market: Grants Pass, OR *Format:* News, News/Talk, 86, Adult Contemp *Special Programming:* Gospel one hr, relg 8 hrs wkly *Hrs. of News Programming:* news progmg 22 hrs wkly *No. News Employees:* 2*Target Audience:* 35 plus.
Carl Wilson, CEO
Brian Diatte, General Sales Mgr
Jeanette Stark, Programming Director
Jill Hamm, Promotions Manager
Chuck Benson, News Director
Joe Torsistano, Chief Engineer
Carl Wilson, CFO

*KAPK
04-01-1998; 91.1 mhz FM; 0.5 kw; 72 ft.; N42 27 51 W123 18 19
P.O. Drawer 2440, Tupelo, MS 38803 US
(662) 844-8888, *Fax:* (662) 842-6791
www.afr.net
comments@afr.net
License: Grants Pass, Josephine County, OR held by American Family Association.
Group Owner: American Family Radio
Arbitron Metro Market: Tupelo, MO *Format:* Christian, Religious
Marvin Sanders, General Manager

KROG
10-02-1981; 96.9 mhz FM *Hrs Open:* 24; 25 kw; 2228 ft.; N42 22 56 W123 16 29
1257 N. Riverside, #10, Medford, OR 97501 US
(541) 772-0322, *Fax:* (541) 772-4233
www.969therogue.com
License: Grants Pass, Josephine County, OR held by Opus Broadcasting Systems Inc.
Group Owner: Opus Broadcasting Systems Inc.; acq 3-6-91; $63,634 with KRTA(AM) Medford;
Nat'l Reps: Tacher
Arbitron Metro Market: Medford, OR, Ashland *Format:* Rock/AOR
No. News Employees: 1 *Target Audience:* 25-54; affluent middle America
Dean Flock, General Manager
Brian Fraser, General Sales Mgr

KCMD
10-18-1925; 99.3 mhz FM *Hrs Open:* 24; 0.25 kw; 1535 ft.; N42 29 22 W123 18 16
US
(541) 476-2137, *Fax:* (503) 497-2314
www.kcmd993.com
info@kufo.com
License: Grants Pass, Multnomah County, OR held by CBS Radio Stations Inc.
Group Owner: CBS Radio; (acq 11-13-98; grpsl)
Arbitron Metro Market: Grants Pass, OR *Format:* Country *Target Audience:* 35 plus.
Dave McDonald, General Manager
Mark Whaler, General Sales Mgr

Gresham

*KMHD
01-01-1984; 89.1 mhz FM *Hrs Open:* 24; 7.9 kw; 1434 ft.; N45 30 58 W122 43 59
26000 S. E. Stark Street, Gresham, OR 97030 US
(503) 661-8900, *Fax:* (503) 491-6999
www.kmhd.org
station-manager@knhd.fm
License: Gresham, Multnomah County, OR held by Mt. Hood Community College.
Nat'l Network: NPR
Arbitron Metro Market: Portland, OR *Format:* Blues, Jazz *Special Programming:* Blues 15 hrs, news 5 hrs wkly *Hrs. of News Programming:* News progmg 5 hrs wkly *Target Audience:* 35-65; music lovers
Dan Gurin, Operations Dir
Doug Sweet, General Manager
Calvin Walker, General Sales Mgr
Greg Gomez, Programming Director

KSZN(AM)
09-28-1956; 1230 khz AM *Hrs Open:* 24; 1 kw-U; N45 29 35 W122 24 40
5110 S.E. Stark St., Portland, WA 97215
(503) 234-5550, *Fax:* (503) 234-5583
www.bustosmedia.com
rtatum@bustosmedia.com
License: Gresham, Multnomah County, OR held by Bustos Media of Oregon License LLC.
Group Owner: Bustos Media LLC; (acq 7-15-2003; $1.13 million)
Population Served: 300,000 *Arbitron Metro Market:* Portland, OR
Special Programming: News 3 hrs, relg one hr wkly *Hrs. of News Programming:* News progmg 3 hrs wkly *Target Audience:* 12-54; lower to upper middleincome *Adv. Rates:* 35; 35; 35
Amador Bustos, President
Rick Tatum, General Manager
Tom Oberg, General Sales Mgr
Henry Cuallo, Promotions Manager
James Boyd, Chief Engineer
Chitra Gade, Office Manager

KRYN(AM)
1230 khz AM; 920 watts; non-directional; 45 29 03N 122 24 40W
Mailing Address: 24 South A Street, Suite C, Washougal, WA 98671 USA
Second Address: Bustos Media Holdings, 5110 SE Stark Street, Portland, OR 87215
(503) 234-5550
License: Gresham, Multnomah County, OR
Group Owner: Bustos Media Holdings LLC

Harbeck-Fruitdale

KLDR
05-03-1991; 98.3 mhz FM *Hrs Open:* 24; 1.85 kw; 2093 ft.; N42 22 56 W123 16 29
P.O. Box 230, Grants Pass, OR 97526 US
(541) 474-7292, *Fax:* (541) 474-7300
www.kldr.com
kldr@kldr.com
License: Harbeck-Fruitdale, Josephine County, OR held by Grants Pass Broadcasting Corp.
Nat'l Network: AP Network News *Nat'l Reps:* Tacher
Arbitron Metro Market: Medford, OR *Format:* Adult Contemp *Hrs. of News Programming:* news progmg 10 hrs wkly *No. News Employees:* 3 *Target Audience:* 25-54; Middle Age demo-actually a wide range in listeners*Adv. Rates:* 25; 15; 15; 10
Matt Wilson, CEO
Brian Diatte, General Sales Mgr
Marty Sether, Programming Director
Carl Wilson, CFO

Harrisburg

*KXPC-FM
04-08-1974; 103.7 mhz FM *Hrs Open:* 24; 90 kw; 2047 ft.; N44 34 49 W122 30 7
4915 Auburn Ave, Ste 100, Bethesda, MD 20814 US
(541) 928-1926, *Fax:* (541) 791-1054
www.kxpc.com
kxpc@kxpc.com
License: Harrisburg, Linn County, OR held by Portland Broadcasting L.L.C.
Nat'l Reps: McGavren Guild
Arbitron Metro Market: Portland, OR *Format:* Country *Hrs. of News Programming:* News progmg 2 hrs wkly *Target Audience:* 18-54. *Adv. Rates:* 24; 24; 24; 20
Rich Coleman, General Manager

Hermiston

KOHU
02-06-1956; 1360 khz AM *Hrs Open:* 24; 4.3 kw-D, DAN; 0.5 kw-N, DAN; N45 51 57 W119 18 45
P.O. Box 886, Baker City, OR 97814 US
(541) 567-6500, *Fax:* (541) 567-6068
kqfm@eotnet.net
License: Hermiston, OR held by Westend Radio L.L.C.
Nat'l Network: ABC *Nat'l Reps:* Farmakis *Regional Reps:* Target.
Format: Country *Special Programming:* Sp 6 hrs wkly *Hrs. of News Programming:* news progmg 10 hrs wkly *No. News Employees:* 1 *Target Audience:* General; two county loc audience *Adv. Rates:* 20; 16; 20; 14
Ron Hughes, President
Jeff Walker, Operations Dir
Angela Pursel, General Manager
Adam Russell, News Director
Richard Wilson, Engineering Dir

KQFM
09-18-1978; 100.1 mhz FM *Hrs Open:* 24; 5.3 kw; 308 ft.; N45 51 57 W119 18 42
PO Box 886, Baker City, OR 97814 US
(541) 567-6500, *Fax:* (541) 567-6068
kqfm@eotnet.net
License: Hermiston, Umatilla County, OR
Nat'l Network: ABC
Format: Adult Contemp *Hrs. of News Programming:* news progmg 5 hrs wkly *No. News Employees:* 1 *Target Audience:* 25-54.
Angela Pursel, General Sales Mgr
Jeff Walker, Programming Director
Ron Hughes, Promotions Manager
Pam Rebman, News Director

Hillsboro

KUIK
01-01-1954; 1360 khz AM *Hrs Open:* 24; 5 kw-D, DAN; 5 kw-N, DAN; N45 29 13 W122 54 31
Mailing Address: P. O. Box 566, Hillsboro, OR 97123 US
Second Address: 3355 N.E. Cornell Rd., Hillsboro, OR 97124
(503) 640-1360, *Fax:* (503) 640-6108
www.kuik.com
amradio@kuik.com
License: Hillsboro, OR held by Dolphin Communications Inc.
Regional Network: Agrinet *Wire Services:* AP
Arbitron Metro Market: Hillsboro, OR *Format:* News, News/Talk, 84, Talk *Special Programming:* Relg 2 hrs, Sp 21 hrs wkly *Hrs. of News Programming:* news progmg 24 hrs wkly *No. News Employees:* 1 *TargetAudience:* 25-54; Seekers of locally produced unique programming *Adv. Rates:* 44; 38; 44; 32
Don McCoun, President
Donna McCoun, Operations Dir
Paul Warren, Operations Manager

Hines

***KQDL**
01-01-2008; 89.1 mhz FM; 0.3 kw; 875 ft.; N43 34 23 W119 7 50
Rebroadcasts: Rebroadcasts KBPS-FM Portland 100% US
(503) 943-5828, *Fax:* (503) 802-9456
www.allclassical.org
License: Hines, Wasco County, OR held by KBPS Public Radio Foundation.
Arbitron Metro Market: Hines, OR *Format:* Classical
John Schumann, CEO/COO
Jack Allen, President
Robert Ridgley, Vice President
Kelly Palin, CFO
Andrea Rennie, Executive Assistant
Jenn Woodward, HR & Office Coordinator
Deborah Rochford, Director of Member Services
John Burk,Vice President of Programming

Hood River

KCGB-FM
12-04-1978; 105.5 mhz FM; 1 kw; 787 ft.; N45 39 45 W121 28 14
Mailing Address: 1190 22nd St,PO Box 360, Hood River, OR 97031 US
Second Address: 1190 22nd St., Hood River, OR 97031
(541) 386-1511, *Fax:* (541) 386-7155
License: Hood River, Hood River County, OR held by Bicoastal Media Licenses IV LLC.
Group Owner: Bicoastal Media L.L.C.; (acq 12-1-2007; grpsl)
Nat'l Network: ABC
Format: Adult Contemp *Target Audience:* 18-49. *Adv. Rates:* 19; 17; 19; 12
Jeff Skye, Programming Director
Gwen Troutner, News Director
Mark Bailey, Local News Editor

KIHR
10-17-1950; 1340 khz AM *Hrs Open:* 24
Mailing Address: P.O. Box 360, Hood River, OR 97031 US
Second Address: 1190 22nd St., Hood River, OR 97031
(541) 386-1511, *Fax:* (541) 386-7155
www.kihrk105.com
info@kihrk105.com
License: Hood River, OR held by Bicoastal Media Licenses IV LLC.
Group Owner: Bicoastal Media L.L.C.; (acq 12-1-2007; grpsl)
Arbitron Metro Market: Hood River, OR *Format:* Country *Hrs. of News Programming:* news progmg 12 hrs wkly *No. News Employees:* 3 *Target Audience:* 25-54. *Adv. Rates:* 19; 17; 19; 12
Kenneth Dennis, CEO
Gary Grossman, Station Manager
Rick Cavagnaro, General Sales Mgr
Jeff Skye, Programming Director
Mark Bailey, News Director
Jim Keightley, Engineering Dir
Ismael Pinedo, Spanish Director
Gwen Troutner,Traffic Manager

***KHRV**
90.1 mhz FM; 0.065 kw; 745 ft.; N45 39 45 W121 28 14
515 N E 15th Ave, Portland, OR 97323 US
(503) 293-1905, *Fax:* (503) 293-1919
www.opb.org
License: Hood River, Hood River County, OR held by Oregon Public Broadcasting.
Regional Network: Ore. Pub. Bcstg Radio Net.
Arbitron Metro Market: Hood River, OR
Steve Bass, General Manager

John Day

KJDY
12-13-1963; 1400 khz AM *Hrs Open:* 24; 1 kw-U, ND1; N44 25 17 W118 57 9 *Rebroadcasts:* Rebroadcasts KJDY-FM Canyon City 100%
P.O. Box 399, John Day, OR 97845 US
(541) 575-1400, *Fax:* (541) 575-2313
kjdy@centurytel.net
License: John Day, OR held by Blue Mountain Broadcasting Co.
Nat'l Network: ABC *Regional Reps:* Tacher
Format: Country *No. News Employees:* 1
Phil Gray, General Manager
Patricia Webb, General Sales Mgr
Kelly Workman, Programming Director
J. Kelly Carlson, Chief Engineer

***KOJD**
89.7 mhz FM; 0.9 kw; -128 ft.; N44 26 3 W118 57 28 US
(503) 293-1905, *Fax:* (503) 293-1919
www.opb.org
License: John Day, Grant County, OR held by Oregon Public Broadcasting.
Regional Network: Ore. Pub. Bcstg Radio Net.
Arbitron Metro Market: John Day, OR
Elizabeth Schwartz, Chairman
Steve Bass, CEO
Mary Gardner, Programming Director
Keith Mobley, Vice Chairman
Dan Metziga, Senior VP, Development
Lynne Clendenin, VP, Programming
Dave Davis, VP, TV Production
Don McKay, VP,Engineering
Debbie Rotich, VP, HR and Administration

Jordan Valley

***KGCL**
01-01-2005; 90.9 mhz FM *Hrs Open:* 24; 21.5 kw vert; 2161 ft.; N43 0 26 W116 42 23
1425 N. Market Blvd., #9, Sacramento, CA 95834 US
(800) 260-5676
www.nuevavida.com
info@nuevavida.com
License: Jordan Valley, Malheur County, OR held by Educational Media Foundation.
Group Owner: EMF Broadcasting
Arbitron Metro Market: Jordan Valley, OR *Format:* Christian *No. News Employees:* 3 *Target Audience:* 18-35; Judeo-Christian, female
Mike Novak, President

Junction City

KXOR
01-01-1998; 660 khz AM *Hrs Open:* 24; 10 kw-D, ND1; 0.075 kw-N, ND1; N44 12 36 W123 10 56
10209 Southeast Division, Portland, OR 97266 US
(541) 343-4100, *Fax:* (541) 343-0448
www.lax660.com
info@alax660am.com
License: Junction City, OR held by Churchill Communications LLC.
Group Owner: Churchill Communications LLC; (acq 1-14-2005; $550,000).
Nat'l Reps: Univision Radio National Sales *Regional Reps:* Julie Schneidar & Paul Danitz *Wire Services:* AP
Arbitron Metro Market: Junction City, OR. *Hrs. of News Programming:* 6am-6pm on the hour *No. News Employees:* 1 *Target Audience:* 25-54; 18-49.
Paul Danitz, General Manager
Phil Polter, General Sales Mgr

***KPIJ**
01-01-2008; 88.5 mhz FM; 0.55 kw; 2314 ft.; N44 16 44 W123 35 38 *Rebroadcasts:* Rebroadcasts KAWZ(FM) Twin Falls, ID 100%
Mailing Address: 3000 West Macarthur Blvd, Santa Ana, CA 92704 US
Second Address: 4002 N. 3300 E., Twin Falls, ID 83301
, *Fax:* (208) 734-6633
www.csnradio.com
License: Junction City, Lane County, OR held by CSN International.
Group Owner: CSN International
Nat'l Network: CSN
Arbitron Metro Market: Junction City, OR *Format:* Christian
Mike Stocklin, General Manager

Keizer

KYKN
01-01-1951; 1430 khz AM *Hrs Open:* 24; 5 kw-U; N44 55 36 W122 57 19
Mailing Address: Box 1430, Salem, OR 97308
Second Address: 4205 Cherry Ave. N.E., Keizer, OR 97303
(503) 390-3014, *Fax:* (503) 390-3728
www.kykn.com
mfrith@kykn.com
License: Keizer, Marion County, OR held by Willamette Broadcasting Co. Inc.
Nat'l Network: Premiere Radio Networks; Talk Radio Network; Westwood One; Salem Radio Network *Nat'l Reps:* McGavren Guild *Regional Reps:* McGavren Guild
Population Served: 500,000 *Arbitron Metro Market:* Portland, OR *Special Programming:* LOCAL TALK/TRAFFIC/ WEATHER/ NEWS...RUSH LIMBAUGH, SEAN HANNITY, LAURA INGRAHAM, BILL POST, GLENN BECK *Hrs. of News Programming:* news progmg 20 hrs wkly *No. News Employees:* 2 *Target Audience:* 25-64; $50-90K income, homeowners, white collar *Adv. Rates:* 20-40
Michael Frith, General Manager

Klamath Falls

KAGO
07-19-1923; 1150 khz AM
5455 Highland Drive, Bellevue, WA 98006 US
(541) 882-8833, *Fax:* (541) 882-8836
www.mybasin.com
License: Klamath Falls, OR
Group Owner: Basin Mediactive LLC; acq 3-16-99; $1.6 million with co-located FM).
Nat'l Network: CBS
Arbitron Metro Market: Klamath Falls, OR *Format:* News, News/Talk, 86 *Special Programming:* Farm 3 hrs, Sp 5 hrs wkly *Target Audience:* 35-65; upscale, professional
Brian Mobley, Operations Dir
Rob Siems, General Manager

KAGO-FM
10-15-1973; 99.5 mhz FM; 60 kw; 367 ft.; N42 12 56 W121 47 51
5455 Highland Drive, Bellevue, WA 98006 US
(541) 882-8833, *Fax:* (541) 882-8836
www.mybasin.com
License: Klamath Falls, Klamath County, OR held by New Northwest Broadcasters LLC
Group Owner: New Northwest Broadcasters LLC
Nat'l Network: CBS
Arbitron Metro Market: Klamath Falls, OR *Format:* Classic Rock
Rob Siems, General Manager

KFLS
01-01-1946; 1450 khz AM *Hrs Open:* 24; 1 kw-U, ND1; N42 12 19 W121 46 4
1338 Oregon Avenue, Klamath Falls, OR 97601 US
(541) 882-4656, *Fax:* (541) 884-2845
www.klamathradio.com
bob@klamathradio.com
License: Klamath Falls, OR held by Wynne Enterprises LLC.
Group Owner: Wynne Enterprises LLC; (acq 1-1-71)
Nat'l Network: ABC *Regional Reps:* Tacher.
Arbitron Metro Market: Klamath Falls, OR *Format:* News, News/Talk, 84, Talk *Target Audience:* 35 plus.
Robert Wynne, CEO

KKRB
04-01-1983; 106.9 mhz FM; 100 kw; Ant 1,200 ft; N42 13 26 W121 49 02
Mailing Address: Box 1450, Klamath Falls, OR 97601
Second Address: 1338 Oregon Ave., Klamath Falls, OR 97601
(541) 882-4656, *Fax:* (541) 884-2845
bob@klamathradio.com

License: Klamath Falls, Klamath County, OR held by Wynne Enterprises LLC.
Group Owner: Wynne Enterprises LLC
Robert Wynne 2, General Manager
Robbie Rush, General Sales Mgr
Randy Adams, Programming Director

KLAD
09-01-1955; 960 khz AM
Mailing Address: 5455 Highland Drive, Bellevue, WA 98006 US
Second Address: 4509 S. 6th St., Suite 201, Klamath Falls, OR 97601
(541) 882-8833, *Fax:* (541) 882-8836
License: Klamath Falls, OR
Group Owner: Basin Mediactive LLC; (acq 10-20-98; grpsl)
Arbitron Metro Market: Medford, OR *Format:* Sports *Target Audience:* 25-54; mature with spendable income *Adv. Rates:* 40; 40; 40; 40
Rob Siems, General Manager
Aaron Bentson, Programming Director
James Boyd, Chief Engineer

KLAD-FM
07-19-1974; 92.5 mhz FM; 63 kw; 2142 ft.; N42 5 50 W121 37 59
Mailing Address: 5455 Highland Drive, Bellevue, WA 98006 US
Second Address: 4509 S. 6th St., Suite 201, Klamath Falls, OR 97601
(541) 882-8833, *Fax:* (541) 882-8836
License: Klamath Falls, Klamath County, OR
Group Owner: Basin Mediactive LLC
Nat'l Network: ABC *Regional Reps:* Allied Radio Partners.
Arbitron Metro Market: Medford, OR *Format:* Country
Rob Siems, General Manager

***KSKF**
11-10-1989; 90.9 mhz FM *Hrs Open:* 5 AM-2 AM; 6.5 kw horiz, 2 kw vert; 2254 ft.; N42 5 50 W121 37 59
P.O. Box 3175, Eugene, OR 97403 US
(541) 552-6301, *Fax:* (541) 552-8565
ww.ijpr.org
info@ijpr.org
License: Klamath Falls, Klamath County, OR held by The State of Oregon, acting by and through the State Board of Higher Education.
Nat'l Network: NPR; PRI
Arbitron Metro Market: Ashland, OR *Format:* Jazz, News, 90 *Special Programming:* Blues 6 hrs, folk 3 hrs, pub affrs 7 hrs wkly *Hrs. of News Programming:* news progmg 45 hrs wkly *No. News Employees:* 1 *TargetAudience:* General.
Ronald Kramer, CEO
Bryon Lambert, Operations Dir
Paul Westhelle, General Sales Mgr
Jessica Robinson, News Director
Betsy Byers, Administrative Assistant

***KTEC**
12-19-1950; 89.5 mhz FM *Hrs Open:* 9 AM-midnight; 0.21 kw; 184 ft.; N42 12 59 W121 47 57
Oregon Institute of Tech, Klamath Falls, OR 97601 US
(541) 885-1840(541) 885-1841, *Fax:* (541) 885-1857
www.oit.edu/-ktec
ktec@oit.edu
License: Klamath Falls, Klamath County, OR held by Oregon State Board of Higher Education.
Arbitron Metro Market: Klamath Falls, OR *Format:* Variety/Diverse *Special Programming:* American Indian one hr, Black 3 hrs, folk 3 hrs, Sp 3 hrs, world mus 6 hrs, electronic 9 hrs wkly *Hrs. of News Programming:* newsprogmg 5 hrs wkly *No. News Employees:* 1 *Target Audience:* 15 plus; eclectic, free thinking, progsv individuals
Christipher G.Mapels, President
Carola Roufs, General Manager
Jake Byron, Programming Director
Len Simpson, Music Director

KFEG
01-01-2002; 104.7 mhz FM *Hrs Open:* 24; 51 kw; 645 ft.; N42 13 24 W121 49 2
P.O. Box 218, Cheney, WA 99004 US
(541) 882-4656, *Fax:* (541) 884-2845
www.klamathradio.com
bob@klamathradio.com
License: Klamath Falls, Klamath County, OR held by Cove Road Publishing LLC
Arbitron Metro Market: Klamath Falls, OR *Format:* Classic Rock *Target Audience:* 25-54.
Bill Ifft, President
Robert Wynne, General Manager
Robbie Rush, Sales Manager
Randy Adams, Programming Director
Carol Fritch, Traffic Manager

***KLMF**
01-01-2002; 88.5 mhz FM; 0.095 kw; 2162 ft.; N42 5 50 W121 37 59
Or St College, P O Box 3175, Eugene, OR 97403 US
(541) 552-6301
www.ijpr.org
jprinfo@sou.edu
License: Klamath Falls, Klamath County, OR held by The State of Oregon, acting by and through the State Board of Higher Education, for the benefit of Southern Oregon University.
Nat'l Network: NPR; PRI *Wire Services:* AP
Arbitron Metro Market: Klamath Falls, OR *Format:* News *Hrs. of News Programming:* News progmg 35 hrs wkly *No. News Employees:* 1
Ronald Kramer, CEO
Bryon Lambert, Operations Dir
Paul Westhelle, General Sales Mgr
Eric Teel, Director of FM Network Programming / Music Directo
Darin Ransom, Engineering Dir
Mitchell Christian, CFO
Betsy Byers, AdministrativeAssistant
Mitchell Christian, Director of Finance & Administration
Jill Hernandez, Accountant Technician
Valerie Ing-Miller, Northern CA Program Coordinator
Abby Kraft, Development Associate / Editor Jefferson Monthly

***KKLJ**
03-14-2003; 88.9 mhz FM *Hrs Open:* 24; 0.11 kw; 2185 ft.; N42 4 5 W121 58 13 *Rebroadcasts:* Rebroadcasts KLVR(FM) Middletown, CA 100%
1425 N. Market Blvd, Suite 9, Sacramento, CA 95834 US
(800) 525-5683, *Fax:* (916) 251-1650
www.klove.com
klove@klove.com
License: Klamath Falls, Klamath County, OR held by Educational Media Foundation.
Group Owner: EMF Broadcasting
Nat'l Network: K-Love
Arbitron Metro Market: Klamath Falls, OR *Format:* Christian *No. News Employees:* 13 *Target Audience:* 25-44; Judeo Christian, female
Darrell Chambliss, Chairman
Mike Novak, President and CEO
Eric Allen, General Sales Mgr
David Pierce, Chief Creative Officer and Programming Director
Ed Lenane, News Director
Sam Wallington, Engineering Dir
Tracy Butler, TrafficManager
Alan Mason, Chief Operating Officer
Dan Antonelli, Chief Business Development Officer
Eric Moser, Chief Financial Officer
Brian Burger, Vice President of Human Resources
D. Kevin Blair, Secretary and General Counsel

La Grande

***KEOL**
10-01-1973; 91.7 mhz FM *Hrs Open:* 24; 0.31 kw horiz; -748 ft.; N45 19 16 W118 5 26
1410 ""L"" Avenue, La Grande, OR 97850 US
(541) 962-3698
www.eou.edu/keol
91.7keol@gmail.com
License: La Grande, Union County, OR held by Oregon State Board of Higher Education.
Arbitron Metro Market: Le Grande, OR *Format:* Contemporary Hits/Top 40, Variety/Diverse *Special Programming:* Black 12 hrs, class 4 hrs, jazz 6 hrs, reggae 7 hrs wkly *Target Audience:* 14-25; college students & locyouth
Dave McDermot, Station Manager

KLBM
01-01-1938; 1450 khz AM *Hrs Open:* 24; 1 kw-U, ND1; N45 19 45 W118 4 0 *Rebroadcasts:* Rebroadcasts KBKR(AM) Baker City 100%
Mailing Address: 38104 NE85th Avenue, La Center, WA 98629 US
Second Address: 2510 E. Cove Ave., La Grande, OR 97850
(541) 963-4121, *Fax:* (541) 963-3117
supertalk@eoni.com
License: La Grande, OR held by Pacific Empire Radio Corp.
Group Owner: Pacific Empire Radio Corp.; acq 7-19-2004; grpsl).
Nat'l Network: Westwood One; ABC *Regional Reps:* McGavren Guild
Arbitron Metro Market: Richland, WA *Format:* News, News/Talk, 86 *Special Programming:* Farm 2 hrs wkly *Hrs. of News Programming:* news progmg 25 hrs wkly *No. News Employees:* 1 *Target Audience:* 25-54.*Adv. Rates:* 22; 20; 22; 16
Mark Bolland, President
Steve Ryner, General Manager
Bobby Hollowwa, Programming Director

KUBQ
08-15-1977; 98.7 mhz FM *Hrs Open:* 24; 2.25 kw; 1942 ft.; N45 26 26 W117 53 31
Mailing Address: 38104 NE85th Avenue, La Center, WA 98629 US
Second Address: 2510 E. Cove Ave., La Grande, OR 97850
(541) 963-4121, *Fax:* (541) 963-3117
www.987kubq.com
q98@eoni.com
License: La Grande, Union County, OR
Group Owner: Pacific Empire Radio Corp.
Nat'l Reps: McGavren Guild
Arbitron Metro Market: La Grande, OR *Format:* Classic Rock *Hrs. of News Programming:* news progmg 6 hrs wkly *No. News Employees:* 1 *Target Audience:* 25-54. *Adv. Rates:* 24; 24; 24; 18
Hugo Morales, CEO
Maria Erana, Operations Dir
Maria Esana, Programming Director

KWRL
09-27-1988; 99.9 mhz FM *Hrs Open:* 24; 25 kw; 1657 ft.; N45 7 21 W117 46 44
2021 Court Avenue, Baker City, OR 97814 US
(541) 963-7911, *Fax:* (541) 963-5090
www.999kwrl.com
999@eoni.com
License: La Grande, Union County, OR held by KSRV Inc.
Group Owner: Capps Broadcast Group; (acq 12-14-98; $800,000).
Nat'l Network: ABC; Jones Radio Networks *Nat'l Reps:* Tacher *Regional Reps:* Tacher.
Arbitron Metro Market: La Grande, OR *Format:* Adult Contemp *Target Audience:* 18-49; general
Dave Capps, President
Randy McKone, General Manager

***KTVR-FM**
01-01-2004; 90.3 mhz FM; 0.4 kw; 2520 ft.; N45 18 33 W117 43 54
7140 Sw Macadam Ave., Portland, OR 97219 US
(800) 241-8123, *Fax:* (503) 293-1919
www.opb.org
info@opb.org
License: La Grande, Union County, OR held by Oregon Public Broadcasting.
Arbitron Metro Market: Portland, OR *Format:* News *Hrs. of News Programming:* news progmg 146 hrs wkly *No. News Employees:* 5
Elizabeth Schwartz, Chairman
Jack Galmiche, COO
Steven M. Bass, President and CEO
Dan Metziga, Senior VP, Development
Lynne Clendenin, VP, Programming
Dave Davis, VP, TV Production
Mary Gardner, Director, TV Programming
MorganHolm, VP, News and Public Affairs
Don McKay, VP, Engineering

La Pine

***KKLP**
01-01-2005; 90.1 mhz FM *Hrs Open:* 24; 2.5 kw vert; 177 ft.; N43 34 50 W121 34 13 *Rebroadcasts:* Rebroadcasts KLVR(FM) Santa Rosa, CA 100%
1425 N Market Blvd., Suite 9, Sacramento, CA 95834 US
(800) 525-5683, *Fax:* (916) 251-1650
www.klove.com
klove@klove.com
License: La Pine, Deschutes County, OR held by Educational Media Foundation.
Group Owner: EMF Broadcasting
Nat'l Network: K-Love
Arbitron Metro Market: La Pine, OR *Format:* Christian *No. News Employees:* 3 *Target Audience:* 25-44; Judeo Christian, female
Darrell Chambliss, Chairman
Mike Novak, President and CEO
Mike Lee, General Sales Mgr
David Pierce, Programming Director
Ed Lenane, News Director
Sam Wallington, Engineering Dir
Marya Morgan, News Reporter
Richard Hunt, NewsReporter
Laura Daniels, News Reporter
Tim Luttrell, News Reporter
Kenny Noble Cortes, News Reporter
Darren Vinson, News Reporter

Lake Oswego

KDZR
01-01-1996; 1640 khz AM
PO Box 3003, Blue Bell, PA 19422 US
(503) 228-4322, *Fax:* (503) 228-4325
www.radiodisney.com
info@kdzra.com
License: Lake Oswego, OR held by Radio Disney Group LLC.
Group Owner: ABC Inc.; (acq 2-03; $3.8 million with KKSL(AM) Lake Oswego).
Nat'l Network: Radio Disney
Arbitron Metro Market: Portland, OR *Format:* Children
Jean-Paul Colaco, President
Pamela Herrold, Station Manager

KLTH
08-01-1977; 106.7 mhz FM *Hrs Open:* 24; 96 kw; 1647 ft.; N45 30 58 W122 43 59
600 New Hampshire Ave., N.W., Suite 1200, Washington, DC 20037 US
(503) 323-6400, *Fax:* (503) 323-6664
www.khits1067.com
info@klthfm.com
License: Lake Oswego, Clackamas County, OR held by Citicasters Licenses Inc.
Group Owner: Clear Channel Communications Inc.; (acq 4-1-2009; grpsl)
Arbitron Metro Market: Portland, OR *Format:* Oldies *No. News Employees:* 1 *Target Audience:* 35-54; 55% women, 45% men
Robert Dove, General Manager

Lakeview

KLCR
01-01-2003; 95.3 mhz FM *Hrs Open:* 24; 0.78 kw; 1378 ft.; N42 12 40 W120 19 35
Post Office Box 509, Ruidoso Downs, NM 88346 US
(541) 947-3325
warrenstation@gooseke.like.com
License: Lakeview, Lake County, OR held by Woodrow Michael Warren.
Group Owner: Woodrow Michael Warren Stns
Arbitron Metro Market: Medford, OR *Format:* Classic Rock
Mike Warren, General Manager

KQIK
12-05-1956; 1230 khz AM *Hrs Open:* 24; 1 kw-U, ND1; N42 12 30 W120 21 39
P.O. Box 189, Lakeview, OR 97630 US
(541) 947-3351, *Fax:* (541) 947-3375
kqik@tnet.biz
License: Lakeview, OR held by Crystal Clear Broadcasting Co. Inc.
Nat'l Network: ABC *Wire Services:* AP
Format: Country *Special Programming:* Relg 2 hrs wkly *Hrs. of News Programming:* news progmg 2 hrs wkly *No. News Employees:* 1 *Target Audience:* General. *Adv. Rates:* 8; 7; 7; 7
Tommie Dodd, General Manager

KORV-FM
01-01-1987; 93.5 mhz FM *Hrs Open:* 24; 1 kw; Ant 951 ft; N42 12 18 W120 19 39
629 Center St., PO Box 189, Lakeview, OR 97630
(541) 947-3351, *Fax:* (541) 947-3375
kqik@tnet.biz
License: Lakeview, Lake County, OR
Nat'l Network: ABC *Wire Services:* AP
Population Served: 30,000*Format:* Contemporary Hits/Top 40
Target Audience: General. *Adv. Rates:* Same as AM
Walt Lawton, Programming Director

*KOAP
01-01-2000; 88.7 mhz FM; 0.17 kw; -591 ft.; N42 10 42 W120 21 19
7140 Sw Macadam Ave, Portland, OR 97219 US
(503) 244-9900, *Fax:* (503) 293-4877
www.opb.org
cikemiya@opb.org
License: Lakeview, Lake County, OR held by Oregon Public Broadcasting.
Nat'l Network: NPR *Regional Network:* Ore. Pub. Bcstg Radio Net.
Arbitron Metro Market: Portland, OR *Format:* News
Steve Bass, CEO
Jeff Douglas, Operations Dir
Cheryl Ikemiya, Director, Leadership Giving
Julie Arnzen, Associate Director, Leadership Giving
Jordan Anderson, Associate Director, Foundation Relations

KORV
93.5 mhz FM; 1 kw; 951 ft.; N42 12 18 W120 19 39
P.O. Box 189, Lakeview, OR 97630 US
(541) 482-3999
www.mcaso.org
mcaso@mcaso.org
License: Lakeview, Jackson County, OR held by Multicultural Association of Southern Oregon.
Arbitron Metro Market: Lakeview, OR *Format:* Adult Contemp
Jim Bauermeister, President

Lebanon

KGAL
08-05-1995; 1580 khz AM *Hrs Open:* 24; 1 kw-U, DA1; N44 34 25 W122 55 5
36991 Kgal Drive, Lebanon, OR 97355 US
(541) 451-5425, *Fax:* (541) 451-5429
www.kgal.com
charlie@kgal.com
License: Lebanon, OR held by EADS Broadcasting Corp.
Nat'l Network: CBS; Westwood One; Salem Radio Network; Sporting News Radio Network *Nat'l Reps:* McGavren Guild *Wire Services:* AP
Arbitron Metro Market: Portland, OR *Format:* News, Sports, 86
Special Programming: Local interview show 5 hrs wkly *Hrs. of News Programming:* news progmg 22 hrs wkly *No. News Employees:* 5 *Target Audience:* 25-54; active listeners
Florence Eads, CFO
Richard ""Charlie"" Eads, President
Susie Dowding, Operations Dir
Ted Jenne, Programming Director
Weldon Greig, News Director
Jim Willhight, Operations Manager

KSHO
01-01-1950; 920 khz AM *Hrs Open:* 24; 1 kw-U, DA1; N44 34 30 W122 55 15
36991 Kgal Drive, Lebanon, OR 97355 US
(541) 451-5425, *Fax:* (541) 451-5429
www.ksho.net
kgal@kgal.com
License: Lebanon, OR held by Eads Broadcasting Corp.
Nat'l Network: Jones Radio Networks; AP Radio *Nat'l Reps:* McGavren Guild *Wire Services:* AP
Arbitron Metro Market: Lebanon, OR *Format:* Adult Contemp *Hrs. of News Programming:* news progmg 7 hrs wkly *No. News Employees:* 5 *Target Audience:* 35 plus; mature adults with money & leisure
Florence Eads, CFO
Richard ""Charlie"" Eads, President
Susie Dowding, Operations Dir
Charlie Eads, General Manager
Ted Jenne, Programming Director
Ted 'Bill Diamond""Jenne, Promotions Manager
Weldon Greig, News Director
harlie,Engineering Dir
Weldon Greig, News Director
Jim Willhight, Operations Manager

*KGRI
01-01-2005; 88.1 mhz FM *Hrs Open:* 24; 0.001 kw horiz, 0.17 kw vert; 2474 ft.; N44 28 59 W122 34 55 *Rebroadcasts:* Rebroadcasts KLRD(FM) Yucaipa, CA 100%
1425 N. Market Blvd., Sacramento, CA 95834 US
(888) 937-2471, *Fax:* (916) 251-1650
www.air1.com
info@air1.com
License: Lebanon, Linn County, OR held by Educational Media Foundation.
Group Owner: EMF Broadcasting
Nat'l Network: Air 1
Arbitron Metro Market: Lebanon, OR *Format:* Alternative, Christian *No. News Employees:* 3 *Target Audience:* 18-35; Judeo-Christian, female
Darrell Chambliss, Chairman
Alan Mason, COO
Mike Novak, President and CEO
Eric Allen, General Sales Mgr
David Pierce, Programming Director
Ed Lenane, News Director
Sam Wallington, Engineering Dir
Paul Goldsmith, MusicDirector
Richard Hunt, News Reporter
Marya Morgan, News Reporter
Dan Antonelli, Chief Business Development Officer
Eric Moser, Chief Financial Officer
Brian Burger, Vice President of Human Resources

Lincoln City

KBCH
05-27-1955; 1400 khz AM; 1 kw-U; N44 59 27 W123 58 45
Box 1430, Newport, OR 97367
(541) 265-2266, *Fax:* (541) 265-6397
kbcham.com
info@kbcham.com
License: Lincoln City, Lincoln County, OR held by Pacific West Broadcasting Inc.
Group Owner: Pacific West Broadcasting Inc.
Regional Reps: Tacher
Population Served: 12,000*Hrs. of News Programming:* news progmg 4 hrs wkly *No. News Employees:* 2
David Miller, President
Larry Blair, Sales Manager

KCRF-FM
11-01-1981; 96.7 mhz FM *Hrs Open:* 24; 19.5 kw; Ant 872 ft; N44 45 22 W124 02 57
Box 1430, Newport, OR 97367
(541) 265-2266, *Fax:* (541) 265-6397
kcrffm.com
info@kcrffm.com
License: Lincoln City, Lincoln County, OR held by Pacific West Broadcasting Inc.
Group Owner: Pacific West Broadcasting Inc.; acq 11-15-00; grpsl).
Regional Reps: Tacher
Population Served: 68,000*Hrs. of News Programming:* news progmg 2 hrs wkly *No. News Employees:* 2
David Miller, President
Larry Blair, Sales Manager

McMinnville

KLYC
06-18-1949; 1260 khz AM *Hrs Open:* 24; 1 kw-U, DA-N; N45 13 19 W123 10 21
Mailing Address: Box 1099, McMinnville, OR 97128
Second Address: 1975 N.E. Colvin Ct., McMinnville, OR 97128
(503) 472-1260, *Fax:* (503) 472-3243
klyc@viclink.com
License: McMinnville, Yamhill County, OR held by Bohnsack Strategies Inc.
Nat'l Network: NBC News
Population Served: 90,000 *Arbitron Metro Market:* Portland, OR *No. News Employees:* 1 *Target Audience:* 25-54.
Laurel Bohnsack, President

*KSLC
01-17-1972; 90.3 mhz FM *Hrs Open:* 6 AM-noon; 0.75 kw; 335 ft.; N45 9 28 W123 17 22
900 S. Baker, Mc Minnville, OR 97128 US
(503) 883-2550
www.kslcfm.com
License: McMinnville, Yamhill County, OR held by Linfield College.
Arbitron Metro Market: McMinnville, OR *Format:* Alternative
Special Programming: Black 2 hrs, heavy metal 7 hrs wkly, relg 2 hrs wkly *Hrs. of News Programming:* News progmg 3 hrs wkly
Target Audience: 12-25;young people looking for new mus
Nancy Cornwell, General Manager

Medford

KBOY-FM
02-01-1958; 95.7 mhz FM *Hrs Open:* 24; 60 kw; 981 ft.; N42 27 11 W123 3 21
City Center West, 7201 W. Lake Mead Blvd, Las Vegas, NV 89128 US
(541) 779-1550, *Fax:* (541) 776-2360
www.957kboy.com
cbaker@radiomedford.com
License: Medford, Jackson County, OR held by Mapleton License of Medford LLC.
Group Owner: Mapleton Communications LLC; (acq 10-26-2001; grpsl)
Arbitron Metro Market: Medford-Ashland, OR *Format:* Classic Rock *Hrs. of News Programming:* One
Ron Hren, Operations Dir
Jamy Gilinsky, General Sales Mgr
Casey Baker, Programming Director
Joe Mussio, Promotions Manager
Maria Chaney, News Director
Robert Probert, Engineering Dir

*KDOV
08-01-1995; 91.7 mhz FM *Hrs Open:* 24; 26 kw; -364 ft.; N42 17 44 W122 48 15
7355 North Oracle, Suite 200, Tucson, AZ 85740 US
(541) 776-5368, *Fax:* (541) 776-0618
www.kdov.net
kdov@kdov.net
License: Medford, Jackson County, OR held by UCB USA Inc.
Nat'l Network: Salem Radio Network *Wire Services:* AP

Arbitron Metro Market: Medford-Ashland, OR *Format:* News, News/Talk, 86, Religious *Hrs. of News Programming:* news progmg 5 hrs wkly *No. News Employees:* 1 *Target Audience:* 25-54; women
Perry Atkinson, President
Dallas Rhoden, Operations Dir
Pat Daly, Operations Manager

KLDZ
08-19-1991; 103.5 mhz FM *Hrs Open:* 24; 100 kw; 479 ft.; N42 17 13 W123 0 15
50 E. Rivercenter Blvd., Suite 1200, Covington, KY 41011 US
(541) 774-1324, *Fax:* (541) 857-0326
www.kool103.net
info@kool103.net
License: Medford, Jackson County, OR held by Bicoastal Rogue Valley LLC.
Group Owner: Bicoastal Media L.L.C.; (acq 7-2-2007; grpsl)
Nat'l Reps: Tacher
Arbitron Metro Market: Medford, OR *Format:* Contemporary Hits/Top 40 *Target Audience:* 25 plus.
Bill Nielsen, General Manager

***KEZX**
05-31-1954; 730 khz AM *Hrs Open:* 24; 1 kw-D, ND1; 0.074 kw-N, ND1; N42 18 36 W122 48 41
1425 N. Market Blvd, Suite 9, Sacramento, CA 95834 US
(541) 772-0322, *Fax:* (541) 772-4233
sportsradio730.com
License: Medford, OR held by Opus Broadcasting Systems Inc.
Group Owner: Opus Broadcasting Systems Inc.; (acq 12-17-2003; $70,000)
Nat'l Network: Fox Sports *Nat'l Reps:* Tacher
Arbitron Metro Market: Medford, OR *Format:* Sports *No. News Employees:* 3
Dean Flock, General Manager
Brian Fraser, General Sales Mgr

KMED
01-01-1922; 1440 khz AM *Hrs Open:* 24; 5 kw-D, ND2; 1 kw-N, ND2; N42 18 36 W122 48 41
50 East Rivercenter Blvd., 31200, Covington, KY 41011 US
(541) 773-1440, *Fax:* (541) 857-0326
www.kmed.com
news@kmed.com
License: Medford, OR held by Bicoastal Rogue Valley LLC.
Group Owner: Bicoastal Media L.L.C.; (acq 7-2-2007; grpsl)
Nat'l Network: Westwood One; CBS
Arbitron Metro Market: Medford, OR *Format:* News, News/Talk, 86 *Hrs. of News Programming:* news progmg 14 hrs wkly *No. News Employees:* 1 *Target Audience:* 35 plus.
Bill Nielsen, General Manager
Bill Meyer, Station Manager

KRTA
10-01-1947; 610 khz AM *Hrs Open:* 24; 2.5 kw-D, DA2; 5 kw-N, DA2; N42 23 15 W122 46 11
1257 N. Riverside Ave., #10, Medford, OR 97501 US
(541) 772-0322, *Fax:* (541) 772-4233
brian@opusradio.com
License: Medford, OR held by Opus Broadcasting Systems Inc.
Group Owner: Opus Broadcasting Systems Inc.; acq 7-9-91; $63,634 with KROG(FM) Grants Pass;
Nat'l Network: La Gran D *Nat'l Reps:* Tacher
Arbitron Metro Market: Medford-Ashland, OR *Format:* Tejano *Hrs. of News Programming:* News progmg 9 hrs wkly *Target Audience:* 12 plus; Hispanic
Dean Flock, General Manager
Brian Fraser, General Sales Mgr
Oscar Bonilla, Programming Director

KTMT-FM
10-15-1970; 93.7 mhz FM *Hrs Open:* 24; 27 kw; 3215 ft.; N42 4 52 W122 43 9
City Center West, 7201 W. Lake Mead Blvd, Las Vegas, NV 89128 US
(541) 779-1550, *Fax:* (541) 776-2360
www.937mike.com
info@937mike.com
License: Medford, Jackson County, OR held by Mapleton License of Medford LLC.
Group Owner: Mapleton Communications LLC
Arbitron Metro Market: Medford-Ashland, OR *Format:* Adult Contemp *Hrs. of News Programming:* news progmg 3 hrs wkly *No. News Employees:* 1 *Target Audience:* 18-49.
Casey Baker, Promotions Manager
Ron Scott, Disc Jockey
Leslie Haze, Disc Jockey
Richard Tempelton, Promotions Director

Merrill

KKKJ
01-01-2008; 105.5 mhz FM; 18 kw; 686 ft.; N42 13 24 W121 49 2
P.O. Box 218, Cheney, WA 99004 US
(541) 882-4656, *Fax:* (541) 884-2845
www.klamathradio.com
webmaster@klamathradio.com
License: Merrill, Klamath County, OR held by Klamath Basin Broadcasting.
Arbitron Metro Market: Merrill, OR *Format:* Adult Contemp *Target Audience:* 18-49.
Robert Wynne, General Manager
Randy Adams, Programming Director
Paul Hanson, News Director
Robbie Rush, Director of Sales
Carol Fritch, Traffic Director

Milton-Freewater

***KLRF**
01-01-1999; 88.5 mhz FM *Hrs Open:* 24; 5 kw; Ant 1,302 ft; N45 47 16 W118 10 31
PO Box 500, Sun Valley, CA 98901
(509) 524-0885, *Fax:* (509) 524-0884; (423) 884-2802
www.lifetalk.net
office@lifetalk.net
License: Milton-Freewater, Umatilla County, OR held by Lifetalk Radio Inc
Nat'l Network: Lifetalk Radio Network
Warren Judd, President
Ted Duncan, General Manager

KZTB
09-10-1992; 97.9 mhz FM *Hrs Open:* 24; 100 kw; 899 ft.; N45 47 41 W118 10 6
City Center West, 7201 W. Lake Mead Blvd., Las Vegas, NV 89128 US
(509) 543-3334, *Fax:* (509) 452-0541
zorro@radiozorro.com
License: Milton-Freewater, Umatilla County, OR
Group Owner: Adelante Media Group LLC; (acq 2-22-2006; $900,000 plus swap for KUJJ(FM) Weston).
Arbitron Metro Market: Tri-Cities, WA (Richland-Kennewick-Pasco)
Bob Berry, General Manager

Milwaukie

KOOR
02-01-1988; 1010 khz AM; 1.1 kw-C, NDD; 4.5 kw-D, NDD; N45 29 3 W122 24 40
6035 S.E. Milwaukie Ave, Portland, OR 97202 US
(503) 234-5550, *Fax:* (503) 234-5583
www.bustosmedia.com
rtatum@bustosmedia.com
License: Milwaukie, OR held by Bustos Media of Oregon License LLC.
Group Owner: Bustos Media LLC; (acq 11-19-2003; $1 million)
Arbitron Metro Market: Portland, OR *Format:* Adult Contemp *Adv. Rates:* 25; 20; 25; 15
Chitra Gade, Operations Dir
Ricky Tatum, General Manager
Tom Oberg, General Sales Mgr
Henry Cualio, Programming Director
James Boyd, Chief Engineer

Molalla

KRSK
07-03-1970; 105.1 mhz FM; 21 kw; 1542 ft.; N45 31 21 W122 44 45
401 City Avenue, Suite 409, Bala Cynwyd, PA 19004 US
(503) 223-1441, *Fax:* (503) 223-6909
www.1051thebuzz.com
info@1051thebuzz.com
License: Molalla, Clackamas County, OR held by Entercom Portland License L.L.C.
Group Owner: Entercom Communications Corp.; (acq 4-23-98; grpsl).
Arbitron Metro Market: Portland, OR *Format:* Adult Contemp
David Field, President
Erin Hubert, General Manager
Brian Lee, General Sales Mgr
Jeff McHugh, Programming Director
Liz Kay, Promotions Manager
Sheryl Steward, Music Director

Monmouth

KSND
03-23-1995; 95.1 mhz FM *Hrs Open:* 24; 1 kw; 1565 ft.; N44 53 19 W123 36 26
PO Box 484, Newport, OR 97365 US
(503) 763-9951, *Fax:* (503) 763-2676
www.ksnd.com
ernie@ksnd.com
License: Monmouth, Polk County, OR held by Radio Beam LLC
Wire Services: AP
Arbitron Metro Market: Salem, OR *Format:* Adult Contemp *Hrs. of News Programming:* news progmg 5 hrs wkly *No. News Employees:* 1 *Target Audience:* 25-54. *Adv. Rates:* 30; 22; 30; 20
Ernie Hopseker, President
Frank Rippey, Operations Dir
Scott Forrest, Programming Director
Lyndi Miles, News Director

Mount Angel

KQRR(AM)
1130 AM; 25,000 watts; 490 watts; 45 04 35N 122 48 27W
5110 SE Stark Street, Portland, OR 97215 USA
(503) 234-5550
License: Mount Angel, Marion County, OR
Group Owner: Bustos Media Holdings LLC

Myrtle Point

***KOOZ**
08-01-1996; 94.1 mhz FM *Hrs Open:* 5 AM-2 AM; 1 kw; 1457 ft.; N42 57 32 W124 16 23
Post Office Box 1760, Roseburg, OR 97470 US
(541) 552-6301(541) 552-8565
www.ijpr.org
info@ijpr.org
License: Myrtle Point, Coos County, OR held by JPR Foundation Inc.
Nat'l Network: NPR; PRI *Wire Services:* AP
Arbitron Metro Market: Ashland, OR *Format:* News *Hrs. of News Programming:* news progmg 35 hrs wkly *No. News Employees:* 1
Ronald Kramer, CEO
Bryon Lambert, Operations Dir
Paul Westhelle, General Sales Mgr
Ransom,Darin, Engineering Dir
Mitchell Christian, CFO

Newport

KNCU
06-01-2000; 92.7 mhz FM; 3.8 kw; 840 ft; N44 45 22 W124 02 57
Box 1430, Newport, OR 97365
(541) 265-2266, *Fax:* (541) 265-6397
www.u92fm.com
info@u92fm.com
License: Newport, Lincoln County, OR held by Pacific West Broadcasting Inc.
Group Owner: Pacific West Broadcasting Inc.; acq 10-27-00; grpsl).
Regional Reps: Tacher.
Population Served: 44,000*Hrs. of News Programming:* news progmg 2 hrs wkly *No. News Employees:* 1 *Target Audience:* 24-54; adults
David Miller, President
Larry Blair, Sales Manager

***KLCO**
09-11-1990; 90.5 mhz FM *Hrs Open:* 24; 3.2 kw; 256 ft; N44 45 22 W124 02 57 *Rebroadcasts:* Rebroadcasts KLCC(FM) Eugene 100%
136 W. 8th Ave., Eugene, OR 97405
(541) 463-6000, *Fax:* (541) 463-6046
www.klcc.org
klcc@klcc.org
License: Newport, Lincoln County, OR held by Lane Community College.
Nat'l Network: NPR
Population Served: 50,000*Format:* Jazz, News, 94 *Special Programming:* Sp 5 hrs, Black 3 hrs, folk 12 hrs, blues 4 hrs, world 3 hrs, electronic 6 hrs wkly *Hrs. of News Programming:* news progmg 60 hrs wkly *No. NewsEmployees:* 1 *Target Audience:* 25-54.
Steve Barton, General Manager
Cheryl Crumbley, General Sales Mgr
Don Hein, Programming Director
Gayle Chisholm, Promotions Manager
Tripp Sommer, News Director

KNPT
06-28-1948; 1310 khz AM *Hrs Open:* 24; 5 kw-D, 1 kw-N, DA-N; N44 37 40 W123 59 15
Box 1430, 906 S.W. Alder St., Newport, OR 97365
(541) 265-2266, *Fax:* (541) 265-6397
knptam.com
info@knptam.com
License: Newport, Lincoln County, OR held by Yaquina Bay Communications Inc.
Regional Reps: Tacher.
Population Served: 18,000*Special Programming:* 1 hour religious programming *Hrs. of News Programming:* news progmg 21 hrs wkly *No. News Employees:* 2 *Target Audience:* 34 plus. *Adv. Rates:* 18.40; 13.60;18.40; 6.40
David Miller, President
Larry Blair, General Sales Mgr
Johnny Randolph, Programming Director

KYTE
10-25-1976; 102.7 mhz FM *Hrs Open:* 24; 66 kw; Ant 881 ft; N44 45 22 W124 02 57
Box 1430, 906 S.W. Alder St., Newport, OR 97365
(541) 265-2266, *Fax:* (541) 265-6397
www.kytefm.com
info@kytefm.com
License: Newport, Lincoln County, OR held by Yaquina Bay Communications Inc.
Regional Reps: Tacher.
Population Served: 120,000*Hrs. of News Programming:* news progmg 4 hrs wkly *No. News Employees:* 2 *Target Audience:* 24-49.
David Miller, President
Johnny Randolph, Program Director/Announcer
Howard Wright, Announcer
Heather Hollingsworth, Announcer
Howard Wright, Music Director
Larry Blair, Music Director

***KYOR**
01-01-2006; 88.9 mhz FM; 0.035 kw; 899 ft.; N44 45 23 W124 2 59 *Rebroadcasts:* Rebroadcasts KUFR(FM) Salt Lake City, UT 100%
4136 Northgate Blvd., Suite 1, Sacramento, CA 95834 US
(801) 359-3147, *Fax:* (801) 359-8112
www.familyradio.com
info@familyradio.com
License: Newport, Lincoln County, OR held by Family Stations Inc.
Group Owner: Family Stations Inc.
Arbitron Metro Market: Newport, OR *Format:* Christian, Religious
Harold Camping, General Manager

North Bend

KOOS
10-01-1990; 107.3 mhz FM *Hrs Open:* 24; 51 kw; 692 ft.; N43 12 18 W124 18 7
Mailing Address: 340 Central, Coos Bay, OR 97420 US
Second Address: 320 Central Ave., Suite 519, Coos Bay, OR 97420
(541) 267-2121, *Fax:* (541) 267-5229
www.power1073.com
License: North Bend, Coos County, OR held by Bicoastal Media Licenses III LLC.
Group Owner: Bicoastal Media L.L.C.; (acq 10-16-2003; grpsl)
Nat'l Network: Jones Radio Networks *Regional Reps:* Tacher
Arbitron Metro Market: Coos Bay, OR *Format:* Contemporary Hits/Top 40 *Hrs. of News Programming:* News progmg 14 hrs wkly *Target Audience:* 18-44. *Adv. Rates:* 18; 14; 18; 7
Ken Dennis, CEO
Mike O'Brien, Operations Dir
Mike Wilson, President/CEO
Joe de Groot, Regional Vice President

KBBR
12-01-1950; 1340 khz AM *Hrs Open:* 24
Mailing Address: 340 Central Avenue, Coos Bay, OR 97420 US
Second Address: 320 Central Ave., Suite 519, Coos Bay, OR 97420
(541) 267-2121, *Fax:* (541) 267-5229
www.1340kbbr.com
License: North Bend, OR held by Bicoastal Media Licenses III LLC.
Group Owner: Bicoastal Media L.L.C.
Nat'l Network: CBS Radio; Jones Radio Networks; Westwood One *Nat'l Reps:* Katz Radio; Tacher
Arbitron Metro Market: North Bend, OR *Format:* News, News/Talk, 86 *Hrs. of News Programming:* News progmg 40 hrs wkly *Target Audience:* 25-54. *Adv. Rates:* 13; 11; 13; 7
Ken Dennis, CEO
Mike Wilson, President
Joe de Groot, Operations Dir

KTEE
12-10-1979; 94.9 mhz FM; 89 kw; 627 ft.; N43 12 18 W124 18 7
340 Central, Coos Bay, OR 97420 US
(541) 267-2121, *Fax:* (541) 267-5229
www.southcoastradio.com
License: North Bend, Coos County, OR held by Bicoastal Media Licenses III LLC.
Group Owner: Bicoastal Media L.L.C.; (acq 10-16-2003; grpsl)
Nat'l Reps: Tacher
Format: Triple A, Christian *Hrs. of News Programming:* News progmg 8 hrs wkly *Target Audience:* 25-54. *Adv. Rates:* 14; 12; 14; 10
Kenneth Dennis, CEO
Mike Wilson, President
Joe de Groot, Operations Dir

North Powder

***KEFS**
01-01-2006; 89.5 mhz FM; 0.165 kw; 1787 ft.; N45 7 26 W117 46 48
US
(541) 963-5884
www.effectradio.com
License: North Powder, Union County, OR held by CSN International.
Group Owner: CSN International
Format: Christian
Mike Kestler, President
Wade Twilegar, General Manager

Nyssa

***KARO**
01-01-1997; 98.7 mhz FM *Hrs Open:* 24; 82 kw; 1001 ft.; N43 24 9 W116 54 9 *Rebroadcasts:* Rebroadcasts KLRD(FM) Yucaipa, CA 100%
402 Carilion Tower West, 13601 Preston Road, Dallas, TX 75240 US
(916) 251-1600, *Fax:* (916) 251-1650
www.air1.com
info@air1.com
License: Nyssa, Malheur County, OR held by Educational Media Foundation
Group Owner: EMF Broadcasting; (acq 2-25-03; $1 million).
Nat'l Network: Air 1
Arbitron Metro Market: Boise, ID *Format:* Alternative, Christian
Target Audience: 18-54
Mike Novak, President

Oakridge

***KAVE**
01-01-2006; 88.5 mhz FM *Hrs Open:* 24; 400 w; Ant -1,286 ft; N43 44 27 W122 26 50
Lane County School District 4J, 200 N. Monroe St., Eugene, OR
(541) 790-6680, *Fax:* (541) 790-6688
www.krvm.org
randy@krvm.org
License: Oakridge, Lane County, OR held by Lane County School District 4J.
Target Audience: 18-35.
Randhy Larson, Operations Dir
Randy Larson, Station Manager
Ken Martin, Programming Director

Ontario

KSRV
11-23-1946; 1380 khz AM *Hrs Open:* 24
P.O. Box 693, Milwaukee, WI 53201 US
(541) 889-8651, *Fax:* (541) 889-8733
www.1380thebull.com
dale@impactradiogroup.com
License: Ontario, OR held by FM Idaho Co. LLC
Group Owner: FM Idaho Co. LLC dba Impact Radio Group; (acq 9-9-2004; $2.5 million with co-located FM)
Nat'l Network: ABC *Wire Services:* AP
Arbitron Metro Market: Ontario, OR *Format:* Country, News
Special Programming: Farm 15 hrs wkly *Hrs. of News Programming:* news progmg 15 hrs wkly *No. News Employees:* 1 *Target Audience:* 25-54 plus.
Dale Jeffries, Operations Dir
Mark Broz, General Sales Mgr
Don Jarrett, Programming Director
Gary Knox, News Director

KSRV-FM
07-04-1977; 96.1 mhz FM *Hrs Open:* 24; 47 kw; 2674 ft.; N43 45 18 W116 5 51
P.O. Box 693, Milwaukee, WI 53201 US
(208) 465-9966, *Fax:* (208) 465-2922
www.961bobfm.com
mikey@impactradiogroup.com
License: Ontario, Malheur County, OR
Group Owner: FM Idaho Co. LLC dba Impact Radio Group
Arbitron Metro Market: Nampa, ID *Format:* Adult Contemp *Hrs. of News Programming:* News progmg 40 hrs wkly
Mikey Fuentes, Operations Dir
Darrell Calton, General Manager
Mark Broz, General Sales Mgr

Oregon City

KGDD
07-04-1947; 1520 khz AM *Hrs Open:* 24; 50 kw-D, DA2; 15 kw-N, DA2; N45 24 44 W122 34 37
401 City Ave., Suite 409, Bala Cynwyd, PA 19004 US
(503) 234-5550, *Fax:* (503) 234-5583
www.lagrand1520.com
License: Oregon City, OR held by Bustos Media of Oregon License LLC.
Group Owner: Bustos Media LLC; (acq 11-17-2003; $2.8 million).
Nat'l Reps: D & R Radio
Arbitron Metro Market: Portland, OR *No. News Employees:* 1 *Adv. Rates:* 70; 70; 70; 50
Amador Bustos, President
Ricky Tatum, General Manager
Tom Oberg, General Sales Mgr
Henry Cualio, Promotions Manager
Chitra Gade, News Director
James Boyd, Chief Engineer

Pendleton

***KRBM**
04-18-1970; 90.9 mhz FM; 24.5 kw horiz, 10.5 kw vert; 591 ft.; N45 35 21 W118 59 53
7140 S.W. Macadam Avenue, Portland, OR 97219 US
(503) 293-1905, *Fax:* (503) 293-1919
www.opb.org
opb.org/contactus
License: Pendleton, Umatilla County, OR held by Oregon Public Broadcasting.
Nat'l Network: PRI; NPR *Regional Network:* Ore. Pub. Bcstg Radio Net.
Format: News, News/Talk, 86 *Hrs. of News Programming:* news progmg 146 hrs wkly *No. News Employees:* 5 *Target Audience:* Teens to adults.
Jack Galmiche, COO

KTIX
01-01-1941; 1240 khz AM *Hrs Open:* 24
1000 S W 6th St, P.O. Box 640, Pendleton, OR 97801 US
(541) 278-2500, *Fax:* (541) 276-1480
www.1240ktix.com
License: Pendleton, OR held by KSRV Inc.
Group Owner: Capps Broadcast Group; (acq 5-14-98; $1.2 million with co-located FM).
Nat'l Network: ESPN Radio *Nat'l Reps:* Tacher
Arbitron Metro Market: Pendleton, OR *Format:* Sports *No. News Employees:* 1 *Target Audience:* 25-54; upscale adults *Adv. Rates:* 23; 19; 21; 17
Randy McKone, President
J.J. Ford, Operations Dir
John Thomas, Programming Director

KUMA
08-25-1955; 1290 khz AM *Hrs Open:* 24; 5 kw-D, DAN; 5 kw-N, DAN; N45 40 25 W118 44 48
P.O. Box 886, Baker City, OR 97814 US
(541) 276-1511, *Fax:* (541) 276-1480
www.1290kuma.com
jthompson@cappsbroadcastgroup.com
License: Pendleton, OR held by Round-Up Radio Inc.
Group Owner: Capps Broadcast Group; (acq 7-1-93; $340,000 with co-located FM;
Regional Reps: Tacher.
Arbitron Metro Market: Pendleton, OR *Format:* News, Talk
Special Programming: Farm 10 hrs wkly *Hrs. of News Programming:* news progmg 20 hrs wkly *No. News Employees:* 1 *Target Audience:* 25 plus; adults
Dave Capps, President
Randy McKone, Operations Dir
Julie Thompson, Sales Manager
Butch Thurman, News and Sports Director
J.J. Ford, Operations Manager
Stacie Cummings, Traffic Director

KWHT
05-01-1984; 103.5 mhz FM *Hrs Open:* 24; 100 kw; 719 ft.; N45 48 2 W118 22 36
P.O. Box 640, Pendleton, OR 97801 US
(800) 225-5948, *Fax:* (541) 276-6842
www.1035kwheat.com
stayseejc@yahoo.com
License: Pendleton, Umatilla County, OR
Group Owner: Capps Broadcast Group
Nat'l Network: ABC
Arbitron Metro Market: Pendleton, OR *Format:* Country *Hrs. of News Programming:* News progmg 2 hrs wkly *Target Audience:* 25-54; adults
Randy McKone, General Manager
Julie Thompson, General Sales Mgr
Emily Jaceks, News Director
J.J. Ford, Engineering Dir
Connie Shurtleff, Engineer
Joe Oertel, Sports Director

Phoenix

KAKT
01-01-1991; 105.1 mhz FM *Hrs Open:* 24; 52 kw; 545 ft.; N42 25 41 W123 0 4
City Center West, 7201 W. Lake Mead Blvd, Las Vegas, NV 89128 US
(541) 779-1550, *Fax:* (541) 776-2360
www.thewolf1051.com
bbishop@radiomedford.com
License: Phoenix, Jackson County, OR held by Mapleton License of Medford LLC.
Group Owner: Mapleton Communications LLC; (acq 10-26-2001; grpsl)
Arbitron Metro Market: Medford, OR *Format:* Country *No. News Employees:* 1 *Target Audience:* 25-49; female
Ron Hren, Operations Dir
Joe Mussio, General Manager
Jamy Gilinsky, General Sales Mgr
Joe Mussio, Promotions Manager
Maria Chaney, News Director
Robert Probert, Engineering Dir
Casey Baker, Operations Manager

***KAPL**
01-02-1977; 1300 khz AM; 20 kw-D, DAN; 5 kw-N, DAN; N42 17 44 W122 48 15
P.O. Box 1090, Jacksonville, OR 97530 US
(541) 899-5275, *Fax:* (541) 899-8068
www.kaplradio.com
kaplradio@gmail.com
License: Phoenix, OR held by Applegate Media Inc.
Arbitron Metro Market: Jacksonville, OR *Format:* Christian, News, 62, Talk *Target Audience:* 25-54.
Chris Thompson, General Manager

KCMX
04-07-1962; 880 khz AM *Hrs Open:* 24; 1 kw-U, ND1; N42 18 36 W122 48 41
City Center West, 7201 W. Lake Mead Blvd, Las Vegas, NV 89128 US
(541) 779-1550, *Fax:* (541) 776-2360
www.kcmxam.com
news@kcmxam.com
License: Phoenix, OR held by Mapleton License of Medford LLC.
Group Owner: Mapleton Communications LLC; (acq 10-26-2001; grpsl)
Regional Reps: Art Moore.
Arbitron Metro Market: Medford, OR *Format:* News, Talk *No. News Employees:* 1 *Target Audience:* 18 plus.
Ron Hren, Operations Dir
Jamy Gilinsky, General Sales Mgr
Rosemary Harrington, Programming Director
Devin Harpole, Promotions Manager
Robert Probert, Engineering Dir
Garth Harrington, Disc Jockey
Joe Mussio, Marketing Manager

Pilot Rock

KUMA-FM
10-01-1978; 92.1 mhz FM; 6.9 kw; 633 ft.; N45 35 21 W118 59 54
US
(541) 276-1511, *Fax:* (541) 276-1480
www.921kuma.com
jthompson@cappsbroadcastgroup.com
License: Pilot Rock, Umatilla County, OR
Group Owner: Capps Broadcast Group
Nat'l Network: ABC
Arbitron Metro Market: Pilot Rock, OR *Format:* Adult Contemp *Target Audience:* 18 plus. *Adv. Rates:* 26; 20; 24; 15
Julie Thompson, Sales Manager
J.J. Ford, Programming Director
Butch Thurman, News and Sports Director
Stacie Cummings, Traffic Director

Pine Grove

***KPFR**
06-22-2005; 89.5 mhz FM *Hrs Open:* 24; 7 kw vert; 1673 ft.; N45 19 58 W121 42 48
Mailing Address: 1425 N Market Blvd, Suite 9, Sacramento, CA 95834 US
Second Address: 290 Hegenberger Rd., Oakland, CA 94621
(800) 543-1495, *Fax:* (916) 641-8238
www.familyradio.com
info@familyradio.com
License: Pine Grove, Hood River County, OR held by Family Stations Inc.
Group Owner: Family Stations Inc.; (acq 9-9-2002).
Arbitron Metro Market: Portland, OR *Format:* Christian, Religious
Harold Camping, President

Portland

KBNP
01-01-1949; 1410 khz AM *Hrs Open:* 24; 5 kw-D, ND1; 0.009 kw-N, ND1; N45 28 24 W122 39 36
278 S.W. Arthur Street, Portland, OR 97201 US
(503) 223-6769, *Fax:* (503) 223-4305
www.kbnp.com
kbnp@kbnp.com
License: Portland, OR held by 2nd Amendment Foundation.
Arbitron Metro Market: Portland, OR *Format:* News *Special Programming:* People w/disabilities, computer shows, home improv *Hrs. of News Programming:* news progmg 163 hrs wkly *No. News Employees:* 2 *TargetAudience:* General; corporations & individuals concerned with how-to's of making & keeping money *Adv. Rates:* 75; 65; 75; 35
Keith Lyons, General Manager

***KBOO**
06-01-1968; 90.7 mhz FM *Hrs Open:* 24; 25.5 kw; 1266 ft.; N45 29 20 W122 41 40
20 S.E. 8th Ave, Portland, OR 97214 US
(503) 231-8032, *Fax:* (503) 231-7145
kboo.fm
program@kboo.org
License: Portland, Multnomah County, OR held by KBOO Foundation.
Arbitron Metro Market: Portland, OR *Format:* Variety/Diverse *Special Programming:* Sp 10 hrs, Indian one hr, ethnic 4 hrs, African/r *Hrs. of News Programming:* news progmg 5 hrs wkly *No. News Employees:* 2*Target Audience:* General.
Arthur Davis, General Manager
Justin Miller, General Sales Mgr
Chris Merrick, Programming Director
John Mackey, Chief Engineer
Denise Kowalczyk, General Manager

***KBPS**
03-23-1923; 1450 khz AM *Hrs Open:* 18; 1 kw-D, ND2; 1 kw-N, ND2; N45 31 38 W122 39 3
515 N.E. 15th Avenue, Portland, OR 97232 US
(503) 916-5830, *Fax:* (503) 916-2642
www.allclassical.org
music.info@allclassical.org
License: Portland, OR held by School District No. 1 Multnomah County, OR.
Arbitron Metro Market: Portland, OR *Format:* Children *Special Programming:* Sp one hr wkly *Hrs. of News Programming:* News progmg one hr wkly
Sally Lewis, General Sales Mgr

***KQAC**
08-01-1983; 89.9 mhz FM *Hrs Open:* 24; 5.9 kw; 1444 ft.; N45 30 58 W122 43 59
515 N.E. 15th Avenue, Portland, OR 97232 US
(503) 943-5828, *Fax:* (503) 802-9456
www.allclassical.org
License: Portland, Multnomah County, OR held by KBPS Public Radio Foundation
Nat'l Network: PRI
Arbitron Metro Market: Portland, OR *Format:* Classical *Hrs. of News Programming:* News progmg 5 hrs wkly
Sally Lewis, General Sales Mgr
Larry Holtz, Chief Engineer

***KBVM**
12-08-1989; 88.3 mhz FM *Hrs Open:* 24; 3.5 kw; 1434 ft.; N45 30 58 W122 43 59
Mailing Address: P. O. Box 5888, 5000 N. Willamette Blvd., Portland, OR 97212 US
Second Address: 5000 N. Willamette, No. 44, Portland, OR 97203
(503) 285-5200, *Fax:* (503) 285-3322
www.kbvm.com
info@kbvm.fm
License: Portland, Multnomah County, OR held by Catholic Broadcasting NW Inc.
Arbitron Metro Market: Portland, OR *Format:* Religious *Special Programming:* Sp 14 hrs wkly *Target Audience:* General; anyone desiring Christian mus, inspiration, Catholic prayer & evangelism
Steven Moffitt, CEO
Tony Galati, General Sales Mgr
Mark Andreas, Programming Director
Dina Hale, Programming Director

KPOJ
03-25-1922; 620 khz AM *Hrs Open:* 24
20 Concord Plaza, Ste 600, San Antonio, TX 78216 US
(503) 323-6400, *Fax:* (503) 323-6664
www.620kpoj.com
deaveosporne@clearchannel.com
License: Portland, OR held by Citicasters Licenses L.P.
Group Owner: Clear Channel Communications Inc.; (acq 1999; grpsl).
Nat'l Network: ABC
Arbitron Metro Market: Portland, OR *Format:* News, News/Talk, 86 *Target Audience:* 25-54.
Mike Dirkx, Operations Dir
Robert Dove, General Manager

KEX
12-24-1926; 1190 khz AM *Hrs Open:* 24
200 Concord Plaza, Ste 600, San Antonio, TX 78216 US
(503) 225-1190, *Fax:* (503) 227-5873
www.1190kex.com
info@kexam.com
License: Portland, OR held by Citicasters Licenses L.P.
Group Owner: Clear Channel Communications Inc.
Arbitron Metro Market: Portland, OR *Format:* News, Talk *Special Programming:* Portland Trailblazers basketball *Hrs. of News Programming:* News progmg 25 hrs wkly *Target Audience:* 25-54; general
Ron Saito, President
Mike Dirkx, Operations Dir
dave Milner, General Sales Mgr
Scott Thompson, Promotions Manager
Brad Ford, News Director
Shane Ruark, Chief Engineer
Mike Lulich, National Sales Manager
Teri Rodrigues,Promotions Manager

KGON
12-01-1967; 92.3 mhz FM *Hrs Open:* 24; 97 kw; 1266 ft.; N45 29 20 W122 41 40
401 City Ave., Suite 409, Bala Cynwyd, PA 19004 US
(503) 223-1441, *Fax:* (503) 223-6909
www.kgon.com
jhutchison@entercom.com
License: Portland, Multnomah County, OR held by Entercom Portland License LLC.
Group Owner: Entercom Communications Corp.; (acq 8-1-95; grpsl)
Nat'l Reps: D & R Radio
Arbitron Metro Market: Portland, OR *Format:* Classic Rock *Hrs. of News Programming:* news progmg one hr wkly *No. News Employees:* 3
David Field, President
Jack Hutchinson, Operations Dir
Erin Hubert, General Manager
Dick Loughney, General Sales Mgr
Clark Ryan, Programming Director
Keevin Wagner, Promotions Manager
Bonnie Knox, Music Director

KINK
12-24-1968; 101.9 mhz FM *Hrs Open:* 24; 99 kw; 1646 ft.; N45 30 58.4 W122 43 58.8
600 New Hampshire Avenue, N.W., Suite 1200, Washington, DC 20037 US
(503) 517-6000, *Fax:* (503) 517-6100
www.kink.fm
lwarren@kink.fm
License: Portland, Multnomah County, OR held by Infinity Radio Inc.
Group Owner: CBS Radio; (acq 11-13-98; grpsl).
Nat'l Network: AP Radio

Arbitron Metro Market: Portland, OR *Format:* Triple A *Hrs. of News Programming:* news progmg 3 hrs wkly *No. News Employees:* 2 *Target Audience:* 25-54; primary, secondary
Leana Warren, Operations Dir
Stan Mak, General Manager
Maureen Pulicella, General Sales Mgr
Dennis Constantine, Programming Director
Candace Gonzales, Promotions Manager
Sheila Hamilton, News Director

KKPZ
11-12-1923; 1330 khz AM *Hrs Open:* 5 am-12 am (M-F); 6 am-12 am (S, Su; 5 kw-U, DA1; N45 27 13 W122 32 45
P.O. Box 3003, Blue Bell, PA 19422 US
(503) 242-1950, *Fax:* (503) 242-0155
www.kkpz.com
info@kkpz.com
License: Portland, OR held by KPHP Radio Inc.
Group Owner: Crawford Broadcasting Co.; (acq 1995; $2 million)
Arbitron Metro Market: Portland, OR *Format:* Christian, Talk
Special Programming: Hispanic Christian talk, Hispanic Christian music *Target Audience:* 34-54.
Donald Crawford Sr., President
Sunny Hudson, General Manager
James Autry, Station Manager
John White, Chief Engineer

KKRZ
05-01-1946; 100.3 mhz FM; 95 kw; 1542 ft.; N45 31 21 W122 44 45
50 East Rivercenter Blvd, Suite 1200, Covington, KY 41011 US
(503) 226-0100, *Fax:* (503) 295-9281
www.2100portland.com
info@kkrzfm.com
License: Portland, Multnomah County, OR held by Citicasters Licenses L.P.
Group Owner: Clear Channel Communications Inc.
Arbitron Metro Market: Portland, OR *Format:* Contemporary Hits/Top 40 *Target Audience:* 18-49.
Michael Hayes, Programming Director
Jen Dalton, Promotions Manager
Shane Raurk, News Director

KYCH-FM
04-01-1980; 97.1 mhz FM; 97 kw; 1266 ft.; N45 29 20 W122 41 40
401 City Avenue, Suite 409, Bala Cynwyd, PA 10004 US
(503) 223-1441, *Fax:* (503) 223-6909
www.charliefm.com
cryan@entercom.com
License: Portland, Multnomah County, OR held by Entercom Portland License L.L.C.
Group Owner: Entercom Communications Corp.; (acq 4-23-98; grpsl)
Nat'l Reps: Christal
Arbitron Metro Market: Portland, OR *Format:* Adult Contemp
Target Audience: 25-54.
David Field, President
Maureen Pulicella, General Sales Mgr
Dan Persigehl, Programming Director
Shel Bailey, Promotions Manager
Gary Hilliard, Chief Engineer
Jack Hutchinson, Executive Vice President

***KOPB-FM**
01-01-1962; 91.5 mhz FM; 70 kw; 1542 ft.; N45 31 21 W122 44 45
7140 S.W. Macadam Ave., Portland, OR 97219 US
(503) 293-1905, *Fax:* (503) 293-1919
www.opb.org
opbnews@opb.org
License: Portland, Multnomah County, OR held by Oregon Public Broadcasting.
Nat'l Network: NPR; PRI
Arbitron Metro Market: Portland, OR *TV Affiliate:* *KOPB-TV affil. *Format:* News *Hrs. of News Programming:* news progmg 146 hrs wkly *No. News Employees:* 5 *Target Audience:* 34-54.
Jack Galmiche, COO
Virginia Breen, Operations Dir

KFXX
01-17-1925; 1080 khz AM
100 4th Avenue North, Seattle, WA 98109 US
(503) 223-1441, *Fax:* (503) 223-6909
www.1080thefan.com
comments@koth.com
License: Portland, OR held by Entercom Portland License LLC.
Group Owner: Entercom Communications Corp.; (acq 12-18-2003; $44 million with co-located FM)
Arbitron Metro Market: Portland, OR *Format:* Sports *Target Audience:* 25-54.
Ron Carter, CFO

KPDQ
07-30-1947; 800 khz AM *Hrs Open:* 24
4880 Santa Rosa Rd, #300, Camarillo, CA 93012 US
(503) 786-0600, *Fax:* (503) 786-1551
www.kpdq.am
License: Portland, OR held by Salem Media of Oregon Inc.
Group Owner: Salem Communications Corp.
Arbitron Metro Market: Portland, OR *Format:* Christian, Talk
Target Audience: 18-54; listeners of talk
Dennis Hayes, General Manager
Justin Mansfield, Programming Director
Jordan Smith, Promotions Manager

KPDQ-FM
01-01-1961; 93.9 mhz FM *Hrs Open:* 24; 50 kw; 1270 ft.; N45 29 20 W122 41 40
4880 Santa Rosa Rd, #300, Camarillo, CA 93012 US
(503) 786-0600, *Fax:* (503) 786-1551
www.kpdq.com
License: Portland, Multnomah County, OR held by Salem Media of Oregon Inc.
Group Owner: Salem Communications Corp.; (acq 8-86; grpsl)
Arbitron Metro Market: Portland, OR *Format:* Christian, Talk
Target Audience: 25-54; listeners of Christian talk progmg
Dennis Hayes, General Manager
Mark Durkin, General Sales Mgr
Justin Mansfield, Programming Director
Jordan Smith, Promotions Manager
Georgene Rice, News Director
Don Perkins, Chief Engineer

***KRRC**
05-01-1958; 97.9 mhz FM; 0.0082 kw; 13 ft.; N45 28 51 W122 37 50
3203 Se Woodstock Blvd., Portland, OR 97202 US
(773) 332-6534, *Fax:* (503) 777-7769
www.krrcfm.com
jpape@reed.edu
License: Portland, Multnomah County, OR held by The Reed Institute.
Arbitron Metro Market: Southest Portland *Special Programming:* Black 10 hrs, class 4 hrs, country 2 hrs, Fr 2 hrs *Target Audience:* 17-21; Reed College student body
Kristin Holmberg, Operations Dir
Nicholas Wright, General Manager

KUFO-FM
05-01-1977; 101.1 mhz FM *Hrs Open:* 24; 100 kw; 1,640 ft; N45 30 58 W122 43 59
20040 S.W. 1st Ave., Portland, OR 97201
(503) 223-0300, *Fax:* (503) 497-2314
www.kufo.com
info@kufo.com
License: Portland, Multnomah County, OR held by Infinity Radio Inc.
Group Owner: CBS Radio
Population Served: 250,000 *Arbitron Metro Market:* Portland, OR *Format:* Rock/AOR
William Marcus, General Manager

KUPL
01-01-1948; 98.7 mhz FM *Hrs Open:* 24; 24 kw; 1647 ft.; N45 30 58.4 W122 43 58.7
Suite 1200, 600 New Hampshire NW, Washington, DC 20037 US
(503) 733-5000, *Fax:* (503) 517-6401
www.kupl.com
scott.mahalick@alphabroadcasting.com
License: Portland, Multnomah County, OR held by Radio Systems of Miami Inc.
Group Owner: CBS Radio; (acq 11-13-98; grpsl)
Nat'l Network: AP Radio
Arbitron Metro Market: Portland, OR *Format:* Country *No. News Employees:* 1 *Target Audience:* 25-54.
Mel Karmazin, Chairman
Dan Mason, President
Lee Rogers, Operations Dir
Mark Walen, General Manager
Amy Leimbach, General Sales Mgr
Scott Mahalick, Programming Director
Danny Dwyer, Promotions Manager
Lola Montgomery, MusicDirector
Carl Simpson, Street Team Captain
Rick Vodicka, Webmaster
Al McCutchan, Account Executive
Jim Garbett, Account Executive
Jeana Adkinson, Account Executive

KWJJ-FM
01-01-1968; 99.5 mhz FM; 50 kw; 1266 ft.; N45 29 20 W122 41 40
100 Fourth Avenue North, Seattle, WA 98109 US
(503) 223-1441, *Fax:* (503) 223-6909
www.thewolfonline.com
info@thewolfonline.com
License: Portland, Multnomah County, OR held by Entercom Portland License LLC.
Group Owner: Entercom Communications Corp.
Arbitron Metro Market: Portland, OR *Format:* Country *Target Audience:* 25-54.
William Glynn Jr., President

KXTG
06-18-1965; 750 khz AM *Hrs Open:* 24; Ant 990 ft
One Center Court, S 200, Suite 200, Portland, OR 97227 US
(503) 243-7595, *Fax:* (503) 417-7662
www.955thegame.com
License: Portland, OR held by Rose City Radio Corp.
Group Owner: Rose City Radio Corp.
Nat'l Network: Fox Sports
Arbitron Metro Market: Portland, OR *Format:* Sports
Tim McNamara, General Sales Mgr
James Derby, Programming Director

KXTG(AM)
01-01-1926; 750 khz AM; 50 kw-D, 20 kw-N, DA-2; N45 24 05 W122 26 47
0234 S.W. Bancroft, Portland, OR 97231
(503) 243-7595, *Fax:* (503) 417-7662
www.kxl.com
License: Portland, Multnomah County, OR held by Rose City Radio Corp.
Group Owner: Rose City Radio Corp.; (acq 11-30-98; $55 million with co-located FM)
Nat'l Network: CBS *Nat'l Reps:* McGavren Guild
Population Served: 593,820 *Arbitron Metro Market:* Portland, OR *Format:* News, News/Talk, 86 *Target Audience:* 25-54.
Rose City Radio, CFO
James Derby, Operations Dir
Tim McNamara, General Manager
Bill Ashenden, General Sales Mgr

KXET(AM)
1150 khz AM; 5000 watts; non-directional; 45 38 34N 122 36 50W
15240 SE 82nd Drive, Clackamas, OR 97015 USA
(503) 234-5550, *Fax:* (503) 234-5583
License: Portland, Multnomah County, OR
Group Owner: Bustos Media Holdings LLC

Prineville

KLTW-FM
04-08-1981; 95.7 mhz FM *Hrs Open:* 24; 100 kw; 182 meters; N44 04 40 W121 19 49 *Rebroadcasts:* Translators: 104.5 mhz Bend, OR and 104.5 mhz Madras, OR
854 NE 4th Street, Bend, OR 97754
(541) 383-3825
www.lite951.com
License: Prineville, Crook County, OR held by Horizon Broadcasting Group LLC.
Group Owner: Horizon Broadcasting Group, LLC; (acq 2000)
Nat'l Reps: Christal
Population Served: 200,000 *Arbitron Metro Market:* Bend, OR
Special Programming: Inside Central Oregon (Public Affairs) *No. News Employees:* 3 *Target Audience:* 25-54.
Keith Shipman, General Manager
Brian Canady, General Sales Mgr
Jeffrey Nelson, Programming Director
Bill Baker, News Director
Regan Brick, Business Manager
John Edwards, General Sales Manager

KRCO
02-01-1950; 690 khz AM *Hrs Open:* 24*Rebroadcasts:* Translator: 96.9 mhz Prineville, OR
P.O. Box K, Prineville, OR 97754 US
(541) 447-6770, *Fax:* (541) 383-3403
www.krcoam.com
License: Prineville, OR held by Horizon Broadcasting Group L.L.C
Group Owner: Horizon Broadcasting Group, LLC; (acq 3-2-2000; grpsl)
Nat'l Network: ABC *Nat'l Reps:* Christal
Arbitron Metro Market: Bend, OR *Format:* Country *No. News Employees:* 3 *Target Audience:* 35-64.
Keith Shipman, General Manager
Brian Canady, General Sales Mgr
Jack Friday, Programming Director
Bill Baker, News Director
Regan Brick, Business Manager
John Edwards, General Sales Manager

KNLX
01-01-2008; 104.9 mhz FM; 0.86 kw; 2215 ft.; N44 26 13 W120 57 11
Mailing Address: US
Second Address: 30 S.E. Bridgeford Blvd., Bend, OR 97702
(541) 389-8873, *Fax:* (541) 389-5291
www.knlr.com
info@knlr.com
License: Prineville, Crook County, OR held by Cowan Broadcasting LLC
Arbitron Metro Market: Prineville, OR *Format:* Christian
Terry Cowan, General Manager

Rainier

KPPK
11-01-2005; 98.3 mhz FM; 1.6 kw; 640 ft.; N46 10 59 W122 57 29
US
(360) 425-1500, *Fax:* (360) 423-1554
grodman@biocoastalmedia.com
License: Rainier, Columbia County, OR held by Bicoastal Media Licenses IV LLC.
Group Owner: Bicoastal Media L.L.C.
Arbitron Metro Market: Rainier, OR *Format:* Adult Contemp
Kevin Mostyn, Operations Dir

Redmond

KLRR
06-17-1985; 101.7 mhz FM; 23 kw; 732 ft.; N44 4 39 W121 19 57
P.O. Box 5037, Bend, OR 97708 US
(541) 382-5263, *Fax:* (541) 388-0456
www.clear1017.fm
clear@clear1017.fm
License: Redmond, Deschutes County, OR held by Combined Communications.
Group Owner: Combined Communications
Format: Adult Contemp, Triple A *Special Programming:* Jazz 5 hrs wkly *Target Audience:* 25-54; upscale, professional women & men
Chuck Chackel, CEO
Mike Cheney, General Manager
Doug Donolo, Programming Director

KSJJ
02-04-1981; 102.9 mhz FM *Hrs Open:* 24; 100 kw; 886 ft.; N44 2 49 W121 31 50
Mailing Address: PO Box 5068, 1500 NEButler Market Rd, Bend, OR 97701 US
Second Address: 1500 N.E. Butler Market Rd., Bend, OR 97702
(541) 388-3300, *Fax:* (541)389-7885
www.ksjj.com
info@ksjj.com
License: Redmond, Deschutes County, OR held by GCC Bend LLC.
Group Owner: GCC Bend LLC; (acq 1999; grpsl).
Arbitron Metro Market: Bend, OR *Format:* Country *Hrs. of News Programming:* news progmg 8 hrs wkly *No. News Employees:* 1 *Target Audience:* 25-54.
Dana Horner, General Sales Mgr

***KWRX**
01-01-2002; 88.5 mhz FM; 0.95 kw; 2198 ft.; N44 26 14 W120 57 12
139 Susan Campell Hall, Un of Oregon, Eugene, OR 97403 US
(541) 345-0800
www.kwax.com
inquiry@kwax.com
License: Redmond, Deschutes County, OR held by State Board of Higher Education for the University of Oregon.
Arbitron Metro Market: Eugene, OR *Format:* Classical
Paul Bjornstad, General Manager

KRDM
06-01-2004; 1240 khz AM *Hrs Open:* 24
Mailing Address: US
Second Address: 416 S.W. Black Bute Blvd., Redmond, OR 97756
(541) 548-7621, *Fax:* (541) 504-8145
www.radiolabronca.com
sales@radiolabronca.net
License: Redmond, OR held by Red Mountain Broadcasting LLC
Arbitron Metro Market: Redmond, OR *Format:* Tejano *Adv. Rates:* 18; 14; 18; 8
Juan Zendejas, President
Selene Zendejas, News Director

***KKJA**
07-18-2008; 89.9 mhz FM; 0.75 kw; 2218 ft.; N44 26 17 W120 57 14 *Rebroadcasts:* Rebroadcasts KAWZ(FM) Twin Falls, ID 100%
3000 Macarthur Blvd., Santa Ana, CA 92704 US
(208) 734-6633, *Fax:* (208) 736-1958
www.csnradio.com
License: Redmond, Deschutes County, OR held by CSN International.
Group Owner: CSN International
Nat'l Network: CSN
Arbitron Metro Market: San Antonio, TX *Format:* Christian
Mike Kestler, President
Mike Stocklin, General Manager

Reedsport

***KLFR**
01-01-1999; 89.1 mhz FM *Hrs Open:* 24; 1 kw; 400 ft; N43 43 21 W124 05 40
136 W. 8th Ave., Eugene, OR 38803
(541) 463-6000, *Fax:* (541) 463-6046
www.klcc.org
klcc@klcc.org
License: Reedsport, Douglas County, OR held by Lane Community College
Steve Barton, General Manager
Cheryl Crumbley, General Sales Mgr
Don Heim, Programming Director
Gayle Chisholm, Promotions Manager

KDUN
06-02-1961; 1030 khz AM *Hrs Open:* 24
1159 Fair Oaks Avenue, Arroyo Grande, CA 93420 US
(541) 271-1030, *Fax:* (541) 271-2598
www.kdun.com
traffic.kdun@gmail.com
License: Reedsport, OR held by Bill Schweitzer dba WKS Broadcasting Inc.
Nat'l Network: CBS Radio *Regional Reps:* McGavren-Guild
Arbitron Metro Market: Eugene, OR *Format:* News, Talk *Target Audience:* 25 plus. *Adv. Rates:* 30; 25; 20; 10
Joe Zelinski, Operations Dir
Bill Schweitzer, General Manager
Michael Nadeau, Business Manager

KJMX
01-01-1993; 99.5 mhz FM *Hrs Open:* 24; 11 kw; 400 ft.; N43 40 40 W124 6 36
1270 West 13th Street, Coquille, OR 97423 US
(541) 267-2121, *Fax:* (541) 267-5229
www.kjmxfm.com
License: Reedsport, Douglas County, OR held by Bicoastal Media Licenses III LLC.
Group Owner: Bicoastal Media L.L.C.; (acq 10-16-2003; grpsl)
Format: Classic Rock *Hrs. of News Programming:* news progmg 2 hrs wkly *No. News Employees:* 1
Mike O'Brien, Operations Dir
John Pundt, General Manager

***KSYD**
03-01-1990; 92.1 mhz FM *Hrs Open:* 24; 0.3 kw; 358 ft.; N43 39 26 W124 11 10 *Rebroadcasts:* KRVM FM 92.1
200 North Monroe, Eugene, OR 97402 US
(541) 790-6686, *Fax:* (541) 790-5786
www.krvm.org
info@krvm.org
License: Reedsport, Douglas County, OR held by School District 4J Lane County.
Arbitron Metro Market: Eugene, OR *Format:* Triple A *Target Audience:* 12-40.
Carl Sundberg, General Manager
Randy Larson, Station Manager
Bobbie Cirel, General Sales Mgr
Ken Martin, Programming Director
Randy Larson, Chief Engineer

Rockaway Beach

***KLON**
01-01-2005; 90.3 mhz FM *Hrs Open:* 24; 1.8 kw vert; 342 ft.; N45 36 18 W123 55 30 *Rebroadcasts:* Rebroadcasts KLVR(FM) Santa Rosa, CA 100%
1425 N Market Blvd., Suite 9, Sacramento, CA 95834 US
(800) 525-5683, *Fax:* (916) 251-1650
www.klove.com
klove@klove.com
License: Rockaway Beach, Tillamook County, OR held by Educational Media Foundation.
Group Owner: EMF Broadcasting
Nat'l Network: K-Love
Arbitron Metro Market: Rockaway Beach, OR *Format:* Christian *No. News Employees:* 13 *Target Audience:* 25-44; Judeo Christian, female
Darrell Chambliss, Chairman
Mike Novak, President and CEO
Mike Lee, General Sales Mgr
David Pierce, Programming Director
Ed Lenane, News Director
Sam Wallington, Engineering Dir
Marya Morgan, News Reporter
Richard Hunt, NewsReporter
Dan Antonelli, Chief Business Development Officer
Eric Moser, Chief Financial Officer
Brian Burger, Vice President of Human Resources
D. Kevin Blair, Secretary and General Counsel

Rocky River

KLMI(FM)
01-01-2006; 106.0 mhz FM; 6.9 kw; Ant 633 ft; N45 35 21 W118 59 54
45 Campbell Rd., Walla Walla, WA 99362
(509) 545-8836, *Fax:* (509) 529-5534
www.laestaciondelafamilia.org
laestaciondelafamilia@gmail.com
License: Rocky River, WY held by Greeley Broadcasting Corp
Population Served: 3,291 *Arbitron Metro Market:* Burbank, WA
Format: Oldies
Aaron Bruton, General Manager

Rogue River

KRRM
10-01-1994; 94.7 mhz FM *Hrs Open:* 24; 130 w; 2,043 ft; N42 26 44 W123 12 56
225 Rogue River Hwy., Grants Pass, OR 97527
(541) 479-6497, *Fax:* (541) 479-5726
www.krrm.com
krrm@krrm.com
License: Rogue River, Jackson County, OR held by Shirley M. Bell.
Population Served: 99,100 *Arbitron Metro Market:* Medford-Ashland, OR *Target Audience:* 35 plus.
Herb Bell, General Manager
Shirley Bell, General Sales Mgr

Roseburg

KQEN
09-19-1950; 1240 khz AM *Hrs Open:* 24; 1 kw-U, ND1; N43 11 35 W123 21 39
P.O. Box 5180, Roseburg, OR 97470 US
(541) 673-4464, *Fax:* (541) 673-7598
www.541radio.com
License: Roseburg, OR held by Brooke Communications Inc.
Group Owner: Brooke Communications Inc.; acq 5-1-86; $173,000)
Nat'l Network: ESPN Radio *Nat'l Reps:* Tacher
Format: News, Sports, 86 *Special Programming:* Sports *Hrs. of News Programming:* news progmg 4 hrs wkly *No. News Employees:* 2 *Target Audience:* 35 plus; general *Adv. Rates:* 17; 17; 17; 17
Patrick Markham, President
Mike Carter, Operations Dir
Brian Prawitz, News Director

KSKR
08-01-1935; 1490 khz AM *Hrs Open:* 24
P. O. Box 910, Roseburg, OR 97470 US
(541) 440-0101, *Fax:* (541) 673-7598
www.541radio.com
License: Roseburg, OR held by Brooke Communications Inc.
Group Owner: Brooke Communications Inc.; (acq 1-14-2005)
Nat'l Network: ESPN Radio *Nat'l Reps:* Tacher
Format: Sports *No. News Employees:* 2 *Target Audience:* 25 plus.
Patrick Markham, President
Mike Carter, General Manager
Pam Houck, General Sales Mgr

KRSB-FM
10-01-1970; 103.1 mhz FM *Hrs Open:* 24; 2.75 kw; 308 ft.; N43 12 24 W123 21 47
P.O. Box 5180, Roseburg, OR 97470 US
(541) 672-6641, *Fax:* (541) 673-7598
www.541radio.com
country@bciradio.com
License: Roseburg, Douglas County, OR held by Brooke Communications Inc.
Group Owner: Brooke Communications Inc.; acq 4-30-89)
Nat'l Network: ABC *Nat'l Reps:* Tacher
Arbitron Metro Market: Roseburg, OR *Format:* Country *Hrs. of News Programming:* news progmg 15 hrs wkly *No. News Employees:* 2 *Target Audience:* 25-54. *Adv. Rates:* 19; 19; 19; 19

Patrick Markham, President
Mike Carter, Operations Dir

***KSRS**
12-01-1990; 91.5 mhz FM *Hrs Open:* 5 AM-2 AM; 2 kw; 305 ft.; N43 12 22 W123 21 48
P.O. Box 3175, Eugene, OR 97403 US
(541) 552-6301, *Fax:* (541) 552-8565
www.ijpr.org
info@ijpr.org
License: Roseburg, Douglas County, OR held by The State of Oregon, Acting By and Through the State Board of Higher Education, for the benefit of Southern Oregon University.
Nat'l Network: NPR; PRI *Wire Services:* AP
Arbitron Metro Market: Ashland, OR *Format:* News *Hrs. of News Programming:* news progmg 35 hrs wkly *No. News Employees:* 1 *Target Audience:* General.
Ronald Kramer, CEO
Bryon Lambert, Operations Dir
Paul Westhelle, General Sales Mgr
Ransom,Darin, Engineering Dir

***KTBR**
11-01-1955; 950 khz AM *Hrs Open:* 24 hrs
P.O. Box 1760, Roseburg, OR 97470 US
(541) 552-6301
www.ijpr.org
info@ijpr.org
License: Roseburg, OR held by JPR Foundation Inc.
Nat'l Network: NPR; PRI
Arbitron Metro Market: Ashland, OR *Format:* News *No. News Employees:* 1 *Target Audience:* General.
Ronald Kramer, CEO
Bryon Lambert, Operations Dir
Paul Westhelle, General Sales Mgr
Ransom,Darin, Engineering Dir
Mitchell Christian, CFO

***KMPQ**
11-24-2004; 88.1 mhz FM; 950 w; Ant 351 ft; N43 12 22 W123 21 50
136 W. 8th Ave., Eugene, OR 97405
(541) 463-6000, *Fax:* (541) 463-6046
www.klcc.org
klcc@klcc.org
License: Roseburg, Douglas County, OR held by Lane Community College.
Nat'l Network: NPR
Steve Barton, General Manager
Cheryl Crumbley, General Sales Mgr
Don Hein, Programming Director

Salem

KBZY
05-01-1957; 1490 khz AM *Hrs Open:* 24; 1 kw-U, ND1; N44 57 3 W123 2 43
P. O. Box 14900, Salem, OR 97309 US
(503) 362-1490, *Fax:* (503) 362-6545
www.kbzy.com
kbzy@com.net
License: Salem, OR held by Capital Broadcasting Inc.
Regional Reps: Tacher
Arbitron Metro Market: Salem, OR *Format:* Oldies *Target Audience:* 25-54. *Adv. Rates:* 22; 16; 18; 16
Roy Dittman, President
Roy Dittman, General Manager
Terry Sol, Programming Director

KPJC
12-12-1961; 1220 khz AM *Hrs Open:* 24
4303 Market St., N.E., Salem, OR 97301 US
(503) 316-1220, *Fax:* (503) 364-1022
www.thejctown.com
info@thejcmediagroup.com
License: Salem, OR held by KCCS LLC
Nat'l Network: USA *Nat'l Reps:* Broadcast Reps Canada
Arbitron Metro Market: Salem, OR *Format:* Christian *Hrs. of News Programming:* News progmg 14 hrs wkly *Target Audience:* 25-54; family
Phil Swearingin, Operations Dir
Christina Evans, General Manager

***KWBX**
04-01-2002; 90.3 mhz FM *Hrs Open:* 24; 0.135 kw vert; 46 ft.; N44 52 57 W122 57 34
5000 Deer Park Drive Se, Salem, OR 97301 US
(503) 589-8197, *Fax:* (503) 585-4316
www.corban.edu/radio
kwbx@corban.edu
License: Salem, Marion County, OR held by Corban College
Nat'l Network: Air 1
Arbitron Metro Market: Portland, OR *Format:* Christian *Hrs. of News Programming:* news progmg one hr wkly *No. News Employees:* 1 *Target Audience:* 25-44; young adults
Josh Bartlett, COO
Reno Hoff, President
Steve Hunt, General Manager
Josh Bartlett, Station Manager
Steve Hunt, Vice President for Marketing

***KAJC**
01-01-2006; 90.1 mhz FM *Hrs Open:* 24; 0.56 kw; 128 ft.; N44 45 33 W123 13 34
3000 W. Macarthur Blvd., Santa Ana, CA 92704 US
(503) 837-1000, *Fax:* (503) 838-2476
www.kajcfm.org
kajc@kajcfm.org
License: Salem, Marion County, OR held by CSN International
Group Owner: CSN International
Arbitron Metro Market: Salem, OR *Format:* Religious
Matt Martin, General Manager
George King, Programming Director

Sandy

***KLVP**
01-01-1997; 88.7 mhz FM *Hrs Open:* 24; 3.7 kw; 1742 ft.; N45 20 1 W121 42 45 *Rebroadcasts:* Rebroadcasts KLVR(FM) Middletown, CA 100%
1425 N Market Blvd, Suite 9, Sacramento, CA 95834 US
(707) 528-9236, *Fax:* (707) 528-9246
www.klove.com
klove@klove.com
License: Sandy, Clackamas County, OR held by Educational Media Foundation.
Group Owner: EMF Broadcasting
Nat'l Network: K-Love
Arbitron Metro Market: Portland, OR *Format:* Christian *No. News Employees:* 3 *Target Audience:* 25-44; Judeo-Christian, female
Darell Chambliss, Chairman
Mike Novak, President

Scappoose

KFIS
05-01-1986; 104.1 mhz FM; 6.9 kw; 1266 ft.; N45 29 20 W122 41 40
190 Queen Anne Avenue North, Suite 100, Seattle, WA 98109 US
(503) 786-0600, *Fax:* (503) 786-1551
www.1041thefish.com
License: Scappoose, Columbia County, OR held by Caron Broadcasting Inc.
Group Owner: Salem Communications Corp.; (acq 9-20-2001; $35.8 million).
Format: Christian *Target Audience:* 25-54; women
Dennis Hayes, General Manager
Segar Kannan, General Sales Mgr
Chris Kelly, Programming Director
Laura Ahumada, Promotions Manager
Beckii Schiffer, Webmaster

Seaside

KCYS
11-26-1996; 96.5 mhz FM *Hrs Open:* 24; 6 kw; 328 ft; N45 57 11 W123 56 14
Mailing Address: Box 1258, Astoria, OR 97103
Second Address: 1324 N. Holladay Dr., Seaside, OR 97138
(503) 717-9643, *Fax:* (503) 717-9578
info@kcysfm.com
License: Seaside, Clatsop County, OR held by Dave's Broadcasting Corp
Regional Reps: Tacher.
Population Served: 40,000*Target Audience:* 35-44; working moms with kids, some college *Adv. Rates:* 12; 12; 12; na
Dave Heick, General Manager

KSWB
07-12-1968; 840 khz AM; 1 kw-D, ND1; 0.5 kw-N, ND1; N45 58 55 W123 55 2
P.O. Box 566, Hillsboro, OR 97138 US
(503) 738-8668, *Fax:* (503) 738-8778
License: Seaside, OR held by Cannon Beach Radio
Arbitron Metro Market: Seaside, OR *Format:* Oldies
John Chapman, General Manager

KCRX-FM
01-01-1998; 102.3 mhz FM; 25 kw; 328 ft.; N45 57 8 W123 56 14
P.O. Bpx 566, Hillsboro, OR 97138 US
(503) 325-2911, *Fax:* (503) 325-5570
www.kcrx1023.com
kcrx@nnbradio.com
License: Seaside, Clatsop County, OR
Group Owner: Ohana Media Group LLC; acq 8-24-99; grpsl).
Arbitron Metro Market: Astoria, OR *Format:* Classic Rock
Tom Freel, Operations Dir
Paul Mitchell, General Manager
Bob Castle, Programming Director

Selma

***KJKL**
01-01-2003; 88.7 mhz FM; 30 kw vert; 1916 ft.; N42 15 29 W123 39 32
1425 N Market Blvd, Suite 9, Sacrmento, CA 95834 US
(800) 525-5683, *Fax:* (916) 251-1650
www.klove.com
klove@klove.com
License: Selma, Josephine County, OR held by Educational Media Foundation.
Group Owner: EMF Broadcasting
Nat'l Network: K-Love
Arbitron Metro Market: Medford, OR *Format:* Christian *No. News Employees:* 3 *Target Audience:* 25-44; Judeo Christian, female
Darrell Chambliss, Chairman
Mike Novak, President and CEO
Mike Lee, Operations Dir
David Pierce, Programming Director
Ed Lenane, News Director
Sam Wallington, Engineering Dir
Marya Morgan, News Reporter
Richard Hunt, NewsReporter
Laura Daniels, News Reporter
Tim Luttrell, News Reporter
Kenny Noble Cortes, News Reporter
Darren Vinson, News Reporter

Shaniko

***KHJJ**
90.9 mhz FM; kw
US
(541) 815-1480
License: Shaniko, Wasco County, OR held by Educational Broadcast Service.
Arbitron Metro Market: Shaniko, OR
Dena Crane, President

Sisters

KWPK-FM
06-01-2001; 104.1 mhz FM *Hrs Open:* 24; 34 kw; 591 ft.; N44 4 40 W121 19 49
190 Queen Anne Ave., North, Suite 100, Seattle, WA 98109 US
(541) 383-3825, *Fax:* (541) 383-3403
www.thepeak1041.com
License: Sisters, Deschutes County, OR held by Horizon Broadcasting Group LLC.
Group Owner: Horizon Broadcasting Group, LLC; (acq 3-31-2005; $475,000).
Nat'l Reps: Christal
Arbitron Metro Market: Bend, OR *Format:* Adult Contemp *Special Programming:* Inside Central Oregon (Public Affairs) *No. News Employees:* 3 *Target Audience:* 18-49.
Keith Shipman, General Manager
Brian Canady, General Sales Mgr
Dave Clemens, Programming Director
Bill Baker, News Director
Regan Brick, Business Manager
John Edwards, General Sales Manager

***KVRA**
01-01-2006; 89.3 mhz FM; 1.4 kw vert; 633 ft.; N44 4 40 W121 19 48 *Rebroadcasts:* Rebroadcasts KLRD(FM) Yucaipa, CA 100%
1425 N Market Blvd, Suite 9, Sacramento, CA 95834 US
(888) 937-2471, *Fax:* (916) 251-1650
www.air1.com
info@air1.com
License: Sisters, Deschutes County, OR held by Educational Media Foundation.
Group Owner: EMF Broadcasting
Nat'l Network: Air 1
Arbitron Metro Market: Sisters, OR *Format:* Alternative, Christian
Darrell Chambliss, Chairman
Alan Mason, CEO/COO
Mike Novak, CEO
Mike Lee, Operations Dir
Ed Lenane, News Director
Sam Wallington, Engineering Dir
Marya Morgan, News Reporter
Richard Hunt, News Reporter
David Pierce, ChiefCreative Officer
Dan Antonelli, Chief Business Development Officer

Eric Moser, Chief Financial Officer
Brian Burger, Vice President of Human Resources

Springfield

***KQFE**
03-07-1989; 88.9 mhz FM *Hrs Open:* 24; 1.25 kw; 951 ft.; N44 0 11 W123 6 48
Mailing Address: 4135 Northgate Blvd., Suite 1, Sacramento, CA 95834 US
Second Address: 290 Hegenberger Rd., Oakland, CA 94621
(916) 641-8191, *Fax:* (916) 641-8238
www.familyradio.com
info@familyradio.com
License: Springfield, Lane County, OR held by Family Stations Inc.
Group Owner: Family Stations Inc.
Nat'l Network: Family Radio
Arbitron Metro Market: Eugene-Springfi *Format:* Christian *Target Audience:* 30 plus; older relg
Jim Abrahamson, Operations Dir
Harold Camping, General Manager

Springfield-Eugene

KKNU
12-18-1958; 93.3 mhz FM *Hrs Open:* 24; 100 kw horiz, 43 kw vert; 1296 ft.; N44 0 4 W123 6 45
925 Country Club Road, Eugene, OR 97401 US
(541) 484-9400, *Fax:* (541) 344-9424
www.kknu.com
License: Springfield-Eugene, Lane County, OR held by McKenzie River Broadcasting Co. Inc.
Group Owner: McKenzie River Broadcasting Company, Inc.; (acq 11-17-92; $1.01 million with KEED(AM) Eugene;
Nat'l Reps: D & R Radio
Arbitron Metro Market: Eugene, OR *Format:* Country *Target Audience:* 25-49; country life group
John Tilson, President
Dave Wiles, General Sales Mgr
Jim Davis, Programming Director

KORE
09-01-1927; 1050 khz AM *Hrs Open:* 24; 5 kw-D, ND1; 0.149 kw-N, ND1; N44 4 7 W123 1 45
2080 Laura Street, Springfield, OR 97477 US
(541) 747-5673
kore@kore1050am.com
License: Springfield-Eugene, OR held by Support Christian Broadcasting Inc.
Nat'l Network: USA
Arbitron Metro Market: Eugene-Springfield, OR *Format:* Christian *Target Audience:* 18 plus.
Larry Knight, General Manager

St. Helens

KOHI
03-02-1960; 1600 khz AM *Hrs Open:* 24; 1 kw-D, ND1; 0.012 kw-N, ND1; N45 51 15 W122 49 11 *Rebroadcasts:* Talkstar Radio Network
P.O. Box 398, St. Helens, OR 97051 US
(503) 397-1600, *Fax:* (503) 397-1601
www.am1600kohi.com
kohiradio@gmail.com
License: St. Helens, OR held by Mountain Broadcasting LLC
Nat'l Reps: Keystone (unwired net)
Format: News, Sports, 86 *Special Programming:* Sports Talk, Religion *Hrs. of News Programming:* news progmg 12 hrs wkly *No. News Employees:* 1 *Target Audience:* Adults 25-65. *Adv. Rates:* 25; 25; 25; 25
Marty Rowe, President
Alex Rowe, Programming Director

Stanfield

KLKY
01-01-2005; 96.1 mhz FM; 8.5 kw; 1178 ft.; N45 29 12 W119 25 52
US
(509) 527-1000, *Fax:* (509) 529-5534
www.urockfm.com
License: Stanfield, Umatilla County, OR held by Alexandra Communications Inc.
Group Owner: Alexandra Communications Inc.
Arbitron Metro Market: Stanfield, OR *Format:* Contemporary Hits/Top 40
Tom Hodgins, General Manager

Stayton

KCKX
06-01-1987; 1460 khz AM *Hrs Open:* 24; 1 kw-D, ND1; 0.015 kw-N, ND1; N44 48 10 W122 44 3
17579 S.W. Deemar Way, Lake Oswego, OR 97035 US
(503) 981-9400, *Fax:* (503) 981-3561
www.cowboycountryradio.net
request@cowboycountryradio.net
License: Stayton, OR held by Sanlee Broadcasting Corp.
Nat'l Network: ABC *Regional Reps:* Allied Radio Partners.
Arbitron Metro Market: Portland, OR *Format:* Country *Special Programming:* Portland Trailblazers basketball, Forest Dragons arena football, high school sports, farm 15 hrs wkly *Hrs. of News Programming:* News progmg 3hrs wkly *Target Audience:* 25 plus; stable, mature adults with above average income *Adv. Rates:* 24; 23; 24; 15
Donald Coss, President
Chris McCartney, General Manager
Andy McGarrett, General Sales Mgr
Dorecia Luse, Corporate Administrator

Sunriver

KXIX
12-01-1974; 94.1 mhz FM; 18.5 kw; 814 ft.; N44 2 49 W121 31 50
US
(541) 388-3300, *Fax:* (541) 388-3303
www.power94.fm
mflanagan@bendradiogroup.com
License: Sunriver, Deschutes County, OR held by GCC Bend LLC.
Group Owner: GCC Bend LLC; (acq 2000)
Nat'l Reps: Katz Radio
Format: Contemporary Hits/Top 40 *Target Audience:* 18-49.
Ed Lambert, Operations Dir
Jim Gross, General Manager
Mick Green, Programming Director
R. L. Garrigus, News Director
Mike Flanagan, Programming Director
Pam Hudspeth, Traffic Manager

Sutherlin

KSKR-FM
01-01-1999; 101.1 mhz FM *Hrs Open:* 24; 3.6 kw; 860 ft.; N43 22 19 W123 21 15
PO Box 5455, Portland, OR 97228 US
(541) 672-6641, *Fax:* (541) 673-7598
www.541radio.com
sales@bciradio.com
License: Sutherlin, Douglas County, OR held by Brooke Communications Inc.
Group Owner: Brooke Communications Inc.; (acq 12-16-2002)
Nat'l Network: ESPN Radio *Regional Reps:* Tacher
Arbitron Metro Market: Roseburg, OR *Format:* Sports
Pat Markham, President
Mike Carter, Operations Dir
Pam Houck, General Sales Mgr

Sweet Home

KFIR
08-07-1968; 720 khz AM
P.O. Box 720, Sweet Home, OR 97386 US
(541) 367-5115
www.kfir720am.com
info@kfir720am.com
License: Sweet Home, OR held by Radio Fiesta Network LLC
Regional Reps: Allied Broadcast Partners.
Arbitron Metro Market: Sweet Home, OR *Format:* Talk *Special Programming:* Law 3 hrs wkly, country store 7 hrs wkly, Sunday Lutheran 1 hr wkly *Hrs. of News Programming:* news progmg 100 hrs wkly *Target Audience:* 25-54 plus.
Michael Astalis, General Manager

***KLVU**
09-20-1989; 107.1 mhz FM *Hrs Open:* 24; 9.3 kw; 2431 ft.; N44 28 59 W122 34 55
1425 N. Market Boulevard, Suite 9, Sacramento, CA 95834 US
(707) 528-9236, *Fax:* (707) 528-9236
www.klove.com
klove@klove.com
License: Sweet Home, Linn County, OR held by Educational Media Foundation.
Group Owner: EMF Broadcasting; (acq 3-12-97; $4 million).
Nat'l Network: K-Love
Format: Christian *No. News Employees:* 3 *Target Audience:* 25-44; Judeo-Christian female
Darell Chambliss, Chairman
Mike Novak, President
Mike Lee, Operations Dir
David Pierce, Programming Director
Ed Lenane, News Director
Sam Wallington, Engineering Dir
Marya Morgan, News Reporter
Richard Hunt, Marya Morgan

Talent

***KSJK**
10-01-1960; 1230 khz AM *Hrs Open:* 24 hrs; 1 kw-U, ND1; N42 13 37 W122 44 33
P.O. Box 3175, Eugene, OR 97403 US
(541) 552-6301, *Fax:* (541) 552-8565
www.ijpr.org
info@ijpr.org
License: Talent, OR held by The State of Oregon, acting by and through the State Board of Higher Education. for the benefit of Southern Oregon University.
Nat'l Network: PRI; NPR
Arbitron Metro Market: Ashland, OR *Format:* News *Special Programming:* Talk 6 hrs wkly *Target Audience:* General.
Ronald Kramer, CEO
Bryon Lambert, Operations Dir
Paul Westhelle, General Sales Mgr
Ransom,Darin, Engineering Dir
Mitchell Christian, CFO

The Dalles

KACI
06-01-1955; 1300 khz AM *Hrs Open:* 24; 1 kw-D, ND2; 0.013 kw-N, ND2; N45 34 54 W121 7 53
1190 22nd Street, Hood River, OR 97031 US
(541) 296-2211, *Fax:* (541) 296-2213
www.newsradiokaci.com
gary@bicoastalmedia.com
License: The Dalles, OR held by Bicoastal Media Licenses IV LLC.
Group Owner: Bicoastal Media L.L.C.; (acq 12-1-2007; grpsl)
Nat'l Network: Jones Radio Networks
Arbitron Metro Market: The Dalles, OR *Format:* News, News/Talk, 86 *Special Programming:* Relg one hr, home improvement 3 hrs, financial tal *Hrs. of News Programming:* news progmg 14 hrs wkly *No. News Employees:* 1 *Target Audience:* 25-54.
Michael Wilson, President
Greg LeBlanc, Operations Dir
Gary Grossman, General Manager
Rick Cavagnaro, General Sales Mgr
Mark Bailey, Programming Director
Greg LaBlanc, News Director
Paulette LaRoque, Traffic Manager

KACI-FM
02-01-1985; 97.7 mhz FM *Hrs Open:* 24; 5.1 kw; 889 ft.; N45 38 58 W121 16 25
1190 22nd Street, Hood River, OR 97031 US
(541) 296-2211, *Fax:* (541) 296-2213
www.935kaci.com
gary@bicoastalmedia.com
License: The Dalles, Wasco County, OR held by Bicoastal Media Licenses IV LLC.
Group Owner: Bicoastal Media L.L.C.; (acq 12-1-2007; grpsl)
Arbitron Metro Market: The Dalles, OR *Format:* Oldies *Adv. Rates:* Same as AM
Greg LeBlanc, Operations Dir
Rick Cavagnaro, General Sales Mgr
Mark Bailey, Programming Director
Paulette LaRoque, News Director
Greg LeBlanc, Local News Editor

KODL
10-12-1940; 1440 khz AM; 5 kw-D, DAN; 1 kw-N, DAN; N45 35 31 W121 11 57
Mailing Address: 1709 Cherry Heights Road, The Dalles, OR 97058 US
Second Address: 404 E. 2nd St., The Dalles, OR 97058
(541) 296-2101, *Fax:* (541) 296-3766
www.kodl.com
web-master@kodl.net
License: The Dalles, OR held by Larson-Wynn Inc.
Format: Adult Contemp *Special Programming:* Farm 4 hrs, Sp 2 hrs wkly
Al Wynn, President
Marcia Wynn, Operations Dir

KMSW
10-01-2002; 92.7 mhz FM; 3.4 kw; 889 ft.; N45 38 58 W121 16 25
P. O. Box 360, Hood River, OR 97031 US

(541) 296-2211, *Fax:* (541) 296-2213
www.gorgeradio.com
gary@bicoastalmedia.com
License: The Dalles, Wasco County, OR held by Bicoastal Media Licenses IV LLC.
Group Owner: Bicoastal Media L.L.C.; (acq 12-1-2007; grpsl)
Regional Reps: Tacher
Arbitron Metro Market: The Dalles, OR *Format:* Classic Rock *Target Audience:* 25-54.
Michael Wilson, President
Gary Grossman, General Manager
Rick Cavagnaro, General Sales Mgr
Mark Bailey, Programming Director
Gary Grossman, Market Manager
Jeff Skye, Hood River Operations Director
Greg LeBlanc, The DallesOperations Director
Mary Brenneman, Account Executive
Tammy Dirks, Account Executive
Holly Humphrey-Gove, Account Executive

***KQHR**
01-01-2002; 88.1 mhz FM *Hrs Open:* 24; 4 kw; 1115 ft.; N45 43 19 W121 26 14 *Rebroadcasts:* Rebroadcasts KBPS-FM Portland 100%
US
(503) 943-5828, *Fax:* (503) 802-9456
www.allclassical.org
musicinfo@allclassical.org
License: The Dalles, Hood River County, OR held by KBPS Public Radio Foundation.
Arbitron Metro Market: Portland, OR *Format:* Classical *Hrs. of News Programming:* News progmg 5 hrs wkly
John Schumann, Chairman
Jack Allen, President & CEO
Suzanne White, General Manager
Kelly Palin, CFO
Andrea Rennie, Executive Assistant
Jenn Woodward, HR & Office Coordinator
Deborah Rochford, Director of Member Services
Katherine Lefever, Assistant Director of Member Services
Arianna Avena, Membership Associate

***KOTD**
01-01-2008; 89.7 mhz FM; 0.012 kw; 1932 ft.; N45 42 43 W121 6 58 *Rebroadcasts:* Rebroadcasts KOPB-FM Portland 100%
US
(503) 293-1905, *Fax:* (503) 293-1919
www.opb.org/radio/
License: The Dalles, Wasco County, OR held by Oregon Public Broadcasting.
Nat'l Network: NPR *Regional Network:* Ore. Pub. Bcstg Radio Net.
Arbitron Metro Market: The Dalles, OR
Raoul van Hall, Operations Dir
Steve Bass, General Manager
Lynne Clendenin, Vice President
Beth Hyams, News Director
Steven Kray, Chief Engineer
Morgan Holm, Vice President of News and Public Affairs
Eve Epstein, ManagingEditor

Tigard

***KXPD**
06-28-1993; 1040 khz AM *Hrs Open:* 24
1425 N Market Blvd #9, Sacramento, CA 95834 US
(541) 344-5500, *Fax:* (541) 485-2550
info@kxpd.com
License: Tigard, OR held by Churchill Communications LLC.
Group Owner: Churchill Communications LLC; (acq 7-31-2006; $1.8 million).
Arbitron Metro Market: Portland, OR
Suzanne Arlie, General Manager

Tillamook

KMBD(AM)
08-01-1947; 1590 khz AM; 5 kw-D, 1 kw-N, DA-N; N45 27 24 W123 52 36
Mailing Address: Box 40, Tillamook, OR 97141
Second Address: 170 W. 3rd St., Tillamook, OR 97141
(503) 842-4422, *Fax:* (503) 842-2755
www.ktil-kmbd.com
comments@ktil-kmbd.com
License: Tillamook, Tillamook County, OR held by Oregon Eagle Inc.
Population Served: 4,500*Format:* News, News/Talk, 84, Talk
Van Moe, President

***KTMK**
01-01-2005; 91.1 mhz FM; 0.14 kw; 1168 ft.; N45 27 59 W123 55 11
1445 Exchange, P O B 269, Astoria, OR 97103 US
(800) 241-8123, *Fax:* (503) 293-1919
www.opb.org
hr@opb.org
License: Tillamook, Tillamook County, OR held by Oregon Public Broadcasting
Arbitron Metro Market: Tillamook, OR *Format:* News, News/Talk, 86
Steve Bass, General Manager

***KAIK**
01-01-2006; 88.5 mhz FM; 0.06 kw vert; 1276 ft.; N45 27 59 W123 55 11 *Rebroadcasts:* Rebroadcasts KLRD(FM) Yucaipa, CA 100%
US
(888) 937-2471, *Fax:* (916) 251-1650
www.air1.com
info@air1.com
License: Tillamook, Tillamook County, OR held by Educational Media Foundation.
Group Owner: EMF Broadcasting
Nat'l Network: Air 1
Arbitron Metro Market: Tillamook, OR *Format:* Alternative, Christian *No. News Employees:* 3 *Target Audience:* 18-35; Judeo Christian female
Darrell Chambliss, Chairman
Alan Mason, COO
Mike Novak, President and CEO
Mike Lee, Operations Dir
David Pierce, Programming Director
Ed Lenane, News Director
Sam Wallington, Engineering Dir
Marya Morgan, News Reporter
Richard Hunt, News Reporter
Eric Moser, Chief Financial Officer
Brian Burger, Vice President of Human Resources
D. Kevin Blair, Secretary and General Counsel
Larry Moody, Director

***KTCB**
08-25-2004; 89.5 mhz FM *Hrs Open:* 24; 0.38 kw; 1152 ft.; N45 27 59 W123 55 11
7140 Sw Macadam Avenue, Portland, OR 97219 US
(503) 325-0010, *Fax:* (503) 325-3956
www.kmun.org
info@coastradio.org
License: Tillamook, Tillamook County, OR held by Tillicum Foundation
Nat'l Network: NPR *Wire Services:* AP
Arbitron Metro Market: Cheriton, VA *Format:* Public Affairs, Variety/Diverse *Hrs. of News Programming:* News progmg 35 hrs wkly
Joe Patenaude, Operations Dir
Joanne Rideout, General Manager
Arlene Layton, General Sales Mgr
Elizabeth Grant, Programming Director
Kathleen Morgain, News Director
Terry Wilson, Chief Engineer
David Paul, Front Desk
TomHartland, Membership Services
Elizabeth Menetrey, Music Tracking

Toledo

KCUP
09-26-1960; 1230 khz AM; 1 kw-U, ND1; N44 37 47 W123 56 35
P.O. Box 456, Newport, OR 97365 US
(541) 265-5000, *Fax:* (541) 265-9576
www.kcup.net
bobk@kcup.net
License: Toledo, OR held by Agpal Broadcasting Inc.
Nat'l Reps: McGavren Guild
Format: News, Talk *Target Audience:* 25-54. *Adv. Rates:* 16; 14; 16; 12
Cheryl Harle, General Manager
Ed Kowas, General Sales Mgr

Tri City

KKMX
06-01-1993; 104.3 mhz FM *Hrs Open:* 24; 5.6 kw; 1385 ft.; N43 0 13 W123 21 26
P.O. Box 5180, Roseburg, OR 97470 US
(541) 672-6641, *Fax:* (541) 673-7598
www.541radio.com
License: Tri City, Douglas County, OR held by Brooke Communications Inc.
Group Owner: Brooke Communications Inc.; acq 11-21-96)
Nat'l Reps: Tacher
Arbitron Metro Market: Medford, OR *Format:* Adult Contemp *Hrs. of News Programming:* news progmg 2 hrs wkly *No. News Employees:* 2 *Target Audience:* 25-54; general
Pat Markham, President
Mike Carter, Operations Dir

Troutdale

KPAM
01-01-1997; 860 khz AM *Hrs Open:* 24
10209 S.E. Division St, Portland, OR 97266 US
(503) 223-4321, *Fax:* (503) 294-0074
www.kpam.com
email@kpam.com
License: Troutdale, OR held by Pamplin Broadcasting-Oregon Inc.
Group Owner: Pamplin Broadcasting; (acq 12-29-97; $652,500 for 87% of stock)
Nat'l Network: ABC *Nat'l Reps:* Tacher *Regional Reps:* The Tacher Co.; Inc. *Wire Services:* AP
Arbitron Metro Market: Portland, OR *Format:* News, News/Talk, 86 *Special Programming:* Wall St. Journal *Hrs. of News Programming:* news progmg 35.4 hrs wkly *No. News Employees:* 11 *Target Audience:* 35-54;adults.
Mark Ail, Operations Dir
Paul Clithero, General Manager
Margaret Evans, General Sales Mgr
Paul Duckworth, Programming Director
Misty Osko, Promotions Manager
Bill Gallagher, News Director
Dave Bischoff, Chief Engineer
JeanneWinters, National Sales Manager
Robert Eisinger, Political Ed
Paul Blaviding, Traffic Manager

Turner

***KMUZ**
88.5 mhz FM; 0.032 kw; 794 ft.; N44 47 0 W122 59 44
US
(503) 990-6101
www.kmuz.org
info@kmuz.org
License: Turner, Marion County, OR held by Salem Folklore Community.
Arbitron Metro Market: Turner, OR
Tim Crosby, President
Karen Holman, General Manager

Umatilla

KLWJ(AM)
06-01-1980; 1090 khz AM *Hrs Open:* 6 AM-sunset; 2.5 kw-D; N45 52 46 W119 20 37
80898 Powerline Rd., Umatilla, OR 97882
(541) 567-2102, *Fax:* (541) 567-2103
klwjradio@hotmail.com
License: Umatilla, Umatilla County, OR held by Umatilla Broadcasting Inc.
Nat'l Network: USA
Population Served: 250,000*Format:* Christian, News, 62, Talk, Religious *Special Programming:* Farm one hr, Sp one hr wkly *No. News Employees:* 1 *Target Audience:* General. *Adv. Rates:* 8; 8; 8; 8
Darrell Marlow, President
John Marlow, Operations Dir

Veneta

KEUG
01-01-1998; 105.5 mhz FM *Hrs Open:* 24; 2.8 kw; 994 ft.; N44 0 11 W123 6 48
P. O. Box 3088, Portland, OR 97228 US
(541) 484-9400, *Fax:* (541) 344-9424
bob1055.com
License: Veneta, Lane County, OR held by McKenzie River Broadcasting Co. Inc.
Group Owner: McKenzie River Broadcasting Company, Inc.; (acq 1-28-2004; $1.02 million).
Nat'l Reps: D & R Radio
Arbitron Metro Market: Eugene-Springfield, OR *Format:* Adult Contemp *Target Audience:* 25-54; adults
John Tilson, President
Dave Wiles, General Sales Mgr
Jeff Baird, Programming Director

Warm Springs

***KWSO**
09-22-1986; 91.9 mhz FM *Hrs Open:* 18; 4.3 kw; 1096 ft.; N44 50 24 W121 13 56

Mailing Address: PO Box C, Warm Springs, OR 97761 US
Second Address: 97761 Kahneeta Hamlet Rd., Warm Springs, OR 97761
(541) 553-1968, *Fax:* (541) 553-3348
www.kwso.org
smatters@wstribes.org
License: Warm Springs, Jefferson County, OR held by Confederated Tribes of Warm Springs.
Arbitron Metro Market: Warm Springs, OR *Format:* Adult Contemp, Native American *Target Audience:* General.
Sue Matters, General Manager

Warrenton

*KCPB-FM

04-17-2006; 90.9 mhz FM; 0.24 kw; 1119 ft.; N46 15 46 W123 53 9
121st and Park, Tacoma, WA 98447 US
(503) 325-0010, *Fax:* (503) 325-3956
www.kmun.org
kmun@kmun.org
License: Warrenton, Clatsop County, OR held by Tillicum Foundation
Nat'l Network: NPR
Arbitron Metro Market: Spokane, WA
Ray Merritt, President

Welches

*KZRI

05-10-2001; 90.3 mhz FM *Hrs Open:* 24; 0.235 kw; 1742 ft.; N45 20 1 W121 42 45
1425 N Market Blvd., Suite 9, Sacramento, CA 95834 US
(888) 937-2471, *Fax:* (916) 251-1650
www.air1.com
info@air1.com
License: Welches, Clackamas County, OR held by Educational Media Foundation.
Group Owner: EMF Broadcasting
Nat'l Network: Air 1
Arbitron Metro Market: Omaha, NE *Format:* Alternative, Christian *No. News Employees:* 3 *Target Audience:* 18-35; Judeo-Christian, female
Darrell Chambliss, Chairman
Mike Novak, President & CEO
Mike Lee, Operations Dir
David Pierce, Programming Director
Ed Lenane, News Director
Sam Wallington, Engineering Dir
Marya Morgan, News Reporter
Richard Hunt, NewsReporter
Tracy Butler, Traffic Manager
Walter Golembeski, Director
David Pierce, Chief Creative Officer
Alan Mason, Chief Operating Officer

West Linn

KWLZ-FM

01-18-1986; 96.3 mhz FM *Hrs Open:* 24; 100 kw; 1089 ft.; N44 50 24 W121 13 56 *Rebroadcasts:* Simulcast with KBNW(AM) Bend 100%
P.O. Box K, Prineville, OR 97754 US
(541) 383-3825, *Fax:* (541) 383-3403
www.newsradiocentraloregon.com
License: West Linn, Jefferson County, OR held by Horizon Broadcasting Group L.L.C.
Group Owner: Horizon Broadcasting Group, LLC; (acq 3-2-2000; grpsl)
Nat'l Network: ABC Information & Entertainment; Premiere Radio Networks; Westwood One; Jones Radio Networks; Talk Radio Network *Nat'l Reps:* Christal
Arbitron Metro Market: Bend, OR *Format:* News, News/Talk, 86 *Special Programming:* Inside Central Oregon (public affairs) *Hrs. of News Programming:* 17.5 weekly (local) *No. News Employees:* 3 *Target Audience:* 25-64.
Keith Shipman, General Manager
John Edwards, General Sales Mgr
Annette Weston, Programming Director
Bill Baker, News Director
Regan Brick, Business Manager
Brian Canady, Sales Director

Weston

KZIU-FM

01-01-1997; 101.9 mhz FM *Hrs Open:* 24; 13.5 kw; Ant 958 ft; N45 47 41 W118 10 06
45 Campbell Rd., Walla Walla, WA 99362
(509) 527-1000, *Fax:* (509) 529-5534
License: Weston, Umatilla County, OR held by Alexandra Communications Inc.
Group Owner: Alexandra Communications Inc.; (acq 4-10-2006; swap for KMMG(FM) Milton-Freewater)
Format: Jazz, Smooth Jazz
Tom Hodgins, General Manager

Winchester

*KLOV

08-01-1997; 89.3 mhz FM *Hrs Open:* 24; 3.5 kw; 696 ft.; N43 14 8 W123 19 18
1425 N Market Blvd, Suite 9, Sacramento, CA 95834 US
(916) 251-1600, *Fax:* (916) 251-1650
www.klove.com
klove@klove.com
License: Winchester, Douglas County, OR held by Educational Media Foundation.
Group Owner: EMF Broadcasting
Nat'l Network: K-Love
Format: Christian *No. News Employees:* 3 *Target Audience:* 25-44; Judeo-Christian, female
Mike Novak, President
Mike Lee, Operations Dir
David Pierce, Programming Director
Ed Lenane, News Director
Sam Wallington, Engineering Dir
Marya Morgan, News Reporter
Richard Hunt, Marya Morgan
Tracy Butler, Traffic Manager

Winston

KGRV

02-12-1984; 700 khz AM *Hrs Open:* 24
Mailing Address: 1139 Hartnell Ave., PO Box 492727, Redding, CA 96049 US
Second Address: 196 S.E. Main St., Winston, OR 97496
(541) 679-8185, *Fax:* (541) 679-6456
www.kgrv700.net
info@kgru700.net
License: Winston, OR held by Pacific Cascade Communications Corp.
Group Owner: Pacific Cascade Communications Corp.; (acq 4-15-85)
Nat'l Network: Moody
Format: Christian, Religious *Special Programming:* Southern gospel 3 hrs wkly, Family 20 hrs wkly *Hrs. of News Programming:* News progmg 10 hrs wkly *Target Audience:* Christian Adults *Adv. Rates:* 8.50; 8.50;8.50; 8.50
David Morrow, President
Phil Morrow, General Manager

Woodburn

KWBY

07-10-1964; 940 khz AM *Hrs Open:* 24; 0.25 kw-D, ND1; 0.2 kw-N, ND1; N45 10 37 W122 50 58
P. O. Box 158, Woodburn, OR 97071 US
(503) 981-9400, *Fax:* (503) 981-3561
www.lapantera940.com
sam@lapantera940.com
License: Woodburn, OR held by Donald D. Coss
Nat'l Network: CNN Radio *Nat'l Reps:* Lotus Entravision Reps LLC
Arbitron Metro Market: Woodburn, OR *Format:* Tejano *Special Programming:* Relg 5 hrs, gospel 3 hrs wkly *Hrs. of News Programming:* news progmg 35 hrs wkly *No. News Employees:* 1 *Target Audience:* 18-49;younger-larger-than-gen mkt average Hispanic families *Adv. Rates:* 35; 30; 35; 25
Donald Coss, President
Dorecia Luse, General Manager
Gilberto Galvan, Programming Director
Natasha Holstein, Promotions Manager

Pennsylvania

Allentown

WAEB

01-01-1949; 790 khz AM; 3.6 kw-D, DA2; 1.5 kw-N, DA2; N40 39 37 W75 30 50
600 Congress Ave., Suite 1400, Austin, TX 78701 US
(920) 388-9286, *Fax:* (920) 743-9183
info@waun.com
License: Allentown, PA held by Capstar TX L.P.
Group Owner: Clear Channel Communications Inc.; (acq 8-30-00; grpsl).
Nat'l Network: CBS
Arbitron Metro Market: Durango CO *Format:* Jazz, Smooth Jazz *Special Programming:* Czech one hr, farm 10 hrs, relg 3 hrs wkly *Hrs. of News Programming:* news progmg 15 hrs wkly *No. News Employees:* 1 *TargetAudience:* 25-54.
Dave Magnum, President
Rick Jensen, Operations Dir
Frank Devillers, General Manager
Debbie Doyle, News Director

WAEB-FM

06-30-1961; 104.1 mhz FM; 50 kw; 499 ft.; N40 43 13 W75 35 44
600 Congress Ave., Suite 1400, Austin, TX 78701 US
(662) 844-8888(662) 844-8893 (call-in), *Fax:* (662) 842-6791
www.afr.net
comments@afr.net
License: Allentown, Lehigh County, PA
Arbitron Metro Market: Phoenix AZ *Format:* Christian
Marvin Sanders, General Manager

*WDIY

01-08-1995; 88.1 mhz FM *Hrs Open:* 24hrs/day; 0.1 kw vert; 843 ft.; N40 33 54 W75 26 26 *Rebroadcasts:* 93.7 & 93.9MHz translators
301 Broadway, Bethlehem, PA 18015 US
(610) 694-8100, *Fax:* (610) 954-9474
www.wdiy.org
info@wdiy.org
License: Allentown, Lehigh County, PA held by Lehigh Valley Community Broadcasters Association Inc.
Nat'l Network: NPR
Arbitron Metro Market: Lehigh Valley, PA *Format:* News, Variety/Diverse *Special Programming:* AAA 49hrs, Classical 17 hrs, Folk 13 hrs, Jazz 14 hrs, Ethnic 3hrs (Asian-Indian 1 hr, Arabic 1 hr, Jewish 1 hr), Local publicaffairs 3hrs weekly. *Hrs. of News Programming:* News progmg 41 hrs wkly *Target Audience:* General.
Anne Bedics, President
Mike Kraynak, Operations Dir
Bill Dautremont-Smith, Programming Director
Geoff Chambers, Secretary
James Mattern, Treasurer
Geoff Gutgold, Vice President

WHOL

09-12-1948; 1600 khz AM *Hrs Open:* 24; 0.5 kw-D, DA2; 0.056 kw-N, DA2; N40 35 33 W75 28 42
P.O. Box 153, Cheltenham, PA 19012 US
(610) 434-4801, *Fax:* (484) 223-0088
www.whol1600.com
info@whol1600.com
License: Allentown, PA held by Matthew P. Braccili
Nat'l Network: USA; Radio Unica *Nat'l Reps:* Salem
Arbitron Metro Market: Allentown-Bethlehem, PA *Format:* Contemporary Hits/Top 40, Spanish *Target Audience:* 18-65. *Adv. Rates:* 23; 21; 23; 30
Matthew Braccili, President
Jeffrey Maddox, Operations Dir
Matthew Braccili, Station Manager
Delia Torres, General Sales Mgr
Tony Rodriguez, Programming Director
Jeffrey Maddox, Traffic Manager
Alfa Lopez, Public ServiceDirector

*WJCS

02-29-1996; 89.3 mhz FM *Hrs Open:* 24; 0.0001 kw horiz, 0.12 kw vert; 915 ft.; N40 33 52 W75 26 25
Mailing Address: PO Box 8900, Allentown, PA 18103 US
Second Address: 300 E. Rock Rd., Suite 205, Allentown, PA 18103
(610) 791-7262, *Fax:* (610) 797-6922
www.wjcs.org
wjcs@wjcs.org
License: Allentown, Lehigh County, PA held by Beacon Broadcasting Corp.
Nat'l Network: Moody
Arbitron Metro Market: Allentown-Bethlehem, PA *Format:* Christian, News, 62, Talk, Religious *Target Audience:* General.
Frank Ginther, Station Manager

WSAN

05-24-1923; 1470 khz AM; 5 kw-D, DAN; 5 kw-N, DAN; N40 38 10 W75 29 6
600 Congress Ave., Suite 1400, Austin, TX 78701 US
(610) 434-1742, *Fax:* (610) 434-6288
www.1470wyhm.com
License: Allentown, PA held by Capstar TX L.P.
Group Owner: Clear Channel Communications Inc.; (acq 8-30-2000; grpsl)
Nat'l Reps: D & R Radio
Arbitron Metro Market: Allentown-Bethlehem, PA *Format:* Sports
Alison Ruppe, General Sales Mgr
Craig Stevens, Programming Director

WLEV

07-01-1947; 100.7 mhz FM; 11 kw; 1073 ft.; N40 33 54 W75 26 26

City Center West, 7201 W. Lake Mead Blvd, Las Vegas, NV 89128 US
(610) 266-7600, *Fax:* (610) 231-0400
www.wlevradio.com
License: Allentown, Lehigh County, PA
Group Owner: Cumulus Media Inc.; (acq 9-5-97; $23 million).
Nat'l Reps: Christal; Katz Radio
Arbitron Metro Market: Allentown-Bethlehem, PA *Format:* Adult Contemp
Shelly Easton, Operations Dir
John Fraunfelter, General Manager
Elizabeth Pembleton, General Sales Mgr

***WMUH**
02-06-1966; 91.7 mhz FM *Hrs Open:* 24; 0.44 kw; -3 ft.; N40 35 52 W75 30 38
2400 Chew Street, Allentown, PA 18104 US
(484) 664-3239, *Fax:* (484) 664-3539
www.muhlenberg.edu/wmuh
wmuh@muhlenberg.edu
License: Allentown, Lehigh County, PA held by Muhlenberg College.
Nat'l Network: NPR
Arbitron Metro Market: Allentown, PA *Format:* Variety/Diverse
Special Programming: Sp 4 hrs, Arabic 2 hrs, Ger 2 hrs, It 2 hrs, Pol *Target Audience:* General.
Joe Swanson, General Manager
Mike Calcagno, Station Manager
Rich Gensiak, Programming Director

WTKZ
09-01-1948; 1320 khz AM; 0.75 kw-D, DAN; 0.195 kw-N, DAN; N40 35 33 W75 28 42 *Rebroadcasts:* WEEX-AM Simulcast
961 Marcon Blvd., Ste 400, Allentown, PA 18105 US
(610) 258-6155, *Fax:* (610) 253-3384
www.espnlv.com
tomf@espnlv.com
License: Allentown, PA held by Nassau Broadcasting II L.L.C.
Group Owner: Nassau Broadcasting Partners L.P.; (acq 2-14-2005; $500,000).
Nat'l Network: ESPN Radio *Nat'l Reps:* Katz Radio *Regional Reps:* Glenn Jones
Arbitron Metro Market: Allentown, PA *Format:* Sports *Target Audience:* 18-49; Men
Pat Lincoln, General Manager
Tom Fallon, Programming Director
Sarah Weidner, Sales Coordinator

Altoona

WFBG
10-30-1924; 1290 khz AM *Hrs Open:* 24; 5 kw-D, DAN; 1 kw-N, DAN; N40 27 20 W78 23 50
One Forever Drive, Hollidaysburg, PA 16648 US
(814) 941-9800(814) 944-1290, *Fax:* (814) 943-2754(814) 941-7198
www.wfbg.com
dick@wfbg.com
License: Altoona, PA held by Forever of PA L.L.C.
Group Owner: Forever Broadcasting; (acq 12-24-90; $2.1 million with co-located FM;
Nat'l Reps: Christal
Arbitron Metro Market: Altoona, PA *Format:* Adult Contemp *Hrs. of News Programming:* news progmg 2 hrs wkly *No. News Employees:* 2 *Target Audience:* 25-54.
Dave Davies, General Manager

WFGY
10-17-1960; 98.1 mhz FM *Hrs Open:* 24; 30 kw; 942 ft.; N40 34 1 W78 26 32
One Forever Drive, Holliaysburg, PA 16648 US
(814) 941-9800(814) 944-1290, *Fax:* (814) 943-2754(814) 941-7198
www.froggyradio.com
info@foreverradio.com
License: Altoona, Blair County, PA
Nat'l Network: CBS
Arbitron Metro Market: Altoona, PA *Format:* Country *No. News Employees:* 1 *Target Audience:* 25-64.
Jay Crockett, Programming Director

WWOT
07-01-1976; 100.1 mhz FM; 3 kw; 955 ft.; N40 34 11 W78 26 25
2727 West Albert Drive, Altoona, PA 16602 US
(814) 941-9800, *Fax:* (814) 943-2754
www.hot100radio.com
info@foreverradio.com
License: Altoona, Blair County, PA
Group Owner: Forever Broadcasting
Arbitron Metro Market: Altoona, PA *Format:* Contemporary Hits/Top 40
Jonathan Reed, Programming Director
Mark Haze, News Director

WRTA
06-12-1946; 1240 khz AM *Hrs Open:* 19; 1 kw-U, ND1; N40 30 26 W78 25 15
P. O. Box 272, Altoona, PA 16603 US
(814) 943-6112, *Fax:* (814) 944-9782
www.wrta.com
contactus@wrta.com
License: Altoona, PA held by Handsome Brothers Inc.
Nat'l Network: Westwood One *Regional Reps:* Marv Roslin
Arbitron Metro Market: Altoona, PA *Format:* News, News/Talk, 86
Special Programming: Sports play-by-play/loc college & high schools *Hrs. of News Programming:* news progmg 15 hrs wkly *No. News Employees:* 2*Target Audience:* 25 plus; middle/upper income, college educated, professional *Adv. Rates:* 32; 30; 28; 14
David Barger, President
David Wolf, General Manager
Ken Maguda, Station Manager
Dave Weaver, News Director
Bob Taylor, Chief Engineer

WVAM
07-01-1948; 1430 khz AM; 5 kw-D, DAN; 1 kw-N, DAN; N40 29 42 W78 24 6
2727 West Albert Drive, Altoona, PA 16602 US
(814) 941-9800, *Fax:* (814) 943-2754
www.wvamam.com
info@foreverradio.com
License: Altoona, PA held by Forever Broadcasting LLC.
Group Owner: Forever Broadcasting; (acq 12-12-2003; $2.1 million with co-located FM).
Nat'l Network: ESPN Radio
Arbitron Metro Market: Altoona, PA *Format:* Sports *Special Programming:* Pol one hr wkly *Target Audience:* 25 plus; white collar professionals
Dave Davies, General Manager
Charlie Weston, Programming Director
Troy Barnhart, Chief Engineer

Ambridge

WMBA
05-01-1957; 1460 khz AM *Hrs Open:* 24; 0.5 kw-D, DA2; 0.5 kw-N, DA2; N40 35 8 W80 12 11
1000 Kennedy Drive, Ambridge, PA 15003 US
(724) 846-4100, *Fax:* (724) 843-7771
www.wbvp-wmba.com
1230@wbvp-wmba.com
License: Ambridge, PA held by Iorio Broadcasting Inc.
Group Owner: Iorio Broadcasting Inc.; (acq 5-23-2000; $325,000)
Nat'l Network: Talk Radio Network *Wire Services:* AP
Arbitron Metro Market: Pittsburgh, PA *Format:* Sports, Talk
Special Programming: Polka review 2 hrs, oldies 3 hrs, Polish 2 hrs wkl *Hrs. of News Programming:* news progmg 10 hrs wkly *No. News Employees:* 1*Target Audience:* 35+.
Frank Iorio, President
Mark Peterson, General Manager
John Nuzzo, Programming Director
Pat Septak, News Director
Bob Barrickman, Sports Commentator

Annville-Cleona

WWSM
08-04-1968; 1510 khz AM; 5 kw-D, DAD; N40 17 44 W76 27 46
Rt. 78, Exit 7, Strasstown, PA 19559 US
(717) 272-1510, *Fax:* (717) 832-0209
www.wwsm.us
wwsm2@evenlink.com
License: Annville-Cleona, PA held by Patrick H. Sickafus.
Nat'l Network: Westwood One; USA
Arbitron Metro Market: Lebanon, PA *Format:* Country *Special Programming:* Polka 2 hrs, bluegrass 3 hrs, gospel music 3 hrs w *No. News Employees:* 2 *Target Audience:* 34 plus. *Adv. Rates:* 20; 15; 15; na
Patrick Sickafus, President
Gary Gruver, General Manager
Carolyn Gruver, Production Assistant
Susan Sheetz, Account Executive

Apollo

WAVL
12-13-1947; 910 khz AM; 5 kw-D, DAD; 0.069 kw-N, DA2; N40 35 1 W79 31 34
P. O. Box 277, Apollo, PA 15613 US
(671) 478-0104, *Fax:* (671) 647-7840
www.kijifm104.com
License: Apollo, PA held by Evangel Heights Assembly of God
Nat'l Network: USA
Arbitron Metro Market: Tumon GU *Format:* Oldies *Adv. Rates:* 10; 10; 10; 10
Yasunori Kawauchi, President
Kevin Yamazaki, Operations Dir

Avis

WQBR
08-11-1989; 99.9 mhz FM *Hrs Open:* 24; 570 w; Ant 1,053 ft; N41 13 45 W77 22 02
Mailing Address: Box 999, McElhattan, PA 17701
Second Address: 330 McElhattan Dr., McElhattan, PA 17748
(570) 769-2327, *Fax:* (570) 769-7746
www.bear999.com
bear@kcnet.org
License: Avis, Clinton County, PA held by Maximum Impact Communications Inc.
Nat'l Network: Jones Radio Networks *Nat'l Reps:* Dome
Population Served: 300,000 *Arbitron Metro Market:* Williamsport, PA *Hrs. of News Programming:* news progmg 2 hrs wkly *No. News Employees:* 1 *Target Audience:* 25-54. *Adv. Rates:* 12; 12; 12; 12
Karyn O'Brien Stratton, President
Dave Stratton, General Sales Mgr
Michael Ferriola, Engineering Dir
Patti Knepp, Traffic Manager

Avoca

WILK-FM
04-02-1976; 103.1 mhz FM *Hrs Open:* 24; 6 kw; 72 ft.; N41 18 20 W75 45 38 *Rebroadcasts:* Simulcast with WILK(AM) Wilkes-Barre 100%
10706 Beaver Dam Road, Cockeysville, MD 21030 US
(570) 883-9850, *Fax:* (570) 883-9851
www.wilknetwork.com
jimr@102themountain.com
License: Avoca, Luzerne County, PA held by Entercom Wilkes-Barre Scranton LLC.
Group Owner: Entercom Communications Corp.; (acq 12-13-99; grpsl)
Arbitron Metro Market: Avoca, PA *TV Affiliate:* WILK-TV *Format:* News, News/Talk, 86 *Target Audience:* 18-54; general
Jim Rising, Operations Dir
Andy Zapotek, General Sales Mgr
Larry Serafin, Local Sales Manager
Tony Bartocci, Director of Strategic Sales &Marketing

Barnesboro

WNCC
10-15-1950; 950 khz AM *Hrs Open:* 24; 0.5 kw-D, ND2; 0.029 kw-N, ND2; N40 40 47 W78 44 26
P.O. Box 371, Kittanning, PA 16201 US
(814) 472-4060, *Fax:* (814) 948-0950
whpa@verizon.net
License: Barnesboro, PA held by Vernal Enterprises Inc.
Group Owner: Vernal Enterprises Inc.; (acq 3-19-97; $20,000 with WRDD(AM) Ebensburg).
Arbitron Metro Market: Northern Cambria, PA *Format:* Adult Contemp, Oldies *Hrs. of News Programming:* news progmg 6 hrs wkly *No. News Employees:* 1 *Target Audience:* 35 plus; females & males in the 35 plus agerange
Larry Schrengost, General Manager

Beaver Falls

WAOB-FM
01-01-1960; 106.7 mhz FM *Hrs Open:* 24; 37 kw; Ant 554 ft; N40 37 11 W80 05 36
21 Yost Blvd., Suite 505, Pittsburgh, PA 15221
(412) 829-1000, *Fax:* (412) 391-3559
www.wamo100.com
info@wamo100.com
License: Beaver Falls, Beaver County, PA held by McL/McM Pennsylvania LLC.
Group Owner: Sheridan Broadcasting Corp.
Nat'l Network: American Urban *Nat'l Reps:* McGavren Guild
Population Served: 307,484 *Arbitron Metro Market:* Pittsburgh, PA *Format:* Urban Contemporary *Hrs. of News Programming:* News progmg 2 hrs wkly
Ronald Davenport Jr., President
Kathy Gersna, Operations Dir
Michael Douglass, General Manager
Mickey Baker, General Sales Mgr
Ron Atkins, Programming Director
Tammy Sadler, Promotions Manager
Tene Croom, News Director
BobSharkey, Chief Engineer
Laura Varner-Norman, Regional Sales Manager
Jon Plesser, Regional Sales Manager

WBVP
05-25-1948; 1230 khz AM *Hrs Open:* 24; 1 kw-U, ND1; N40 44 16 W80 17 47
1316 7th Avenue, Beaver Falls, PA 15010 US
(724) 846-4100(412) 761-6600, *Fax:* (724) 843-7771
www.wbvp-wmba.com
1230@wbvp-wmba.com
License: Beaver Falls, PA held by Iorio Broadcasting Inc.
Group Owner: Iorio Broadcasting Inc.; (acq 1996)
Nat'l Network: Talk Radio Network *Wire Services:* AP
Arbitron Metro Market: Beaver Falls, Pa *Format:* News, Sports, 86 *Special Programming:* Polka music 2 hrs, relg 2 hrs, gospel 2 hsr wkly *No. News Employees:* 2 *Target Audience:* 35 plus.
Frank Iorio, President
John Nuzzo, Operations Dir
Mark Peterson, Station Manager
Diane Powers, Business Manager

Beaver Springs

WLZS
02-21-1993; 106.1 mhz FM *Hrs Open:* 24; 0.175 kw; 1312 ft.; N40 42 4 W77 12 50
Mailing Address: Old Rt 22 East, Mexico, PA 17056 US
Second Address: Box 146, Beaver Springs, PA 17812
(717) 436-5504, *Fax:* (717) 436-8155
www.wheels1061.com
wheels@wheels1061.com
License: Beaver Springs, Snyder County, PA held by Starview Media Inc.
Regional Network: Radio Pa.
Arbitron Metro Market: Beaver Springs, PA *Format:* Oldies *Hrs. of News Programming:* news progmg 2 hrs wkly *No. News Employees:* 1 *Target Audience:* 25-54.
Curt Dreibelbis, General Manager
Shane Nelson, Programming Director

Bedford

WAYC-FM
12-22-1966; 100.9 mhz FM *Hrs Open:* 24; 0.19 kw; 1280 ft.; N40 0 46 W78 33 12
Mailing Address: P. O. Box 1, Bedford, PA 15522 US
Second Address: 134 E. Pitt St., 2nd Fl., Bedford, PA 15522
(573) 701-9590, *Fax:* (573) 701-9696
License: Bedford, Bedford County, PA held by Cessna Communications Inc.
Group Owner: Cessna Communications Inc.; acq 3-22-93; $350,000 with WBFD(AM) Bedford;
Nat'l Network: Fox News Radio *Regional Network:* Radio Pa. *Regional Reps:* Commercial Media Sales.
Arbitron Metro Market: Arcadia MO *Format:* Contemporary Hits/Top 40 *Adv. Rates:* 16; 16; 16; 16
Chip Miller, President
Joel Jordan, Operations Dir

WHJB
08-05-1974; 1600 khz AM *Hrs Open:* 24; 2.7 kw-D, 18 w-N; N40 02 35 W78 30 13
Mailing Address: Box 1, Bedford, PA 19810
Second Address: 134 E. Pitt St., 2nd Fl., Bedford, PA 15522
(814) 623-1000, *Fax:* (814) 623-1020
johncesscomm@embarqmail.com
License: Bedford, Bedford County, PA held by Cessna Communications Inc.
Group Owner: Cessna Communications Inc.; (acq 2-29-2008; $15,000)
Nat'l Network: Fox News Radio *Regional Reps:* CommercialMedia Sales
Population Served: 35,000*No. News Employees:* 1 *Target Audience:* 35 plus. *Adv. Rates:* 16; 16; 16; 16
Jay Cessna, President
John Cessna, Operations Dir
Keith Bagley, News Director

WBFD
07-02-1955; 1310 khz AM; 2.5 kw-D, ND1; 0.085 kw-N, ND1; N40 2 37 W78 30 11
Mailing Address: P. O. Box One, Bedford, PA 15522 US
Second Address: 2nd Fl., 134 E. Pitt St., Bedford, PA 15522
(814) 623-1000, *Fax:* (814) 623-9692
www.oldiesradioonline.com
webmaster@greatestmojo.com
License: Bedford, PA held by Cessna Communications Inc.
Group Owner: Cessna Communications Inc.; acq 3-22-93; $350,000 with WAYC(FM) Bedford;
Nat'l Network: Salem Radio Network; Talk Radio Network; Premiere Radio Networks *Regional Network:* Radio Pa. *Regional Reps:* Commercial Media Sales.
TV Affiliate: News/talk *Format:* Sports *Hrs. of News Programming:* 1 *No. News Employees:* 30 plus; general *Adv. Rates:* 16; 16; 16; 16
Operations Manager

WBVE
08-15-1988; 107.5 mhz FM *Hrs Open:* 24; 0.37 kw; 1309 ft.; N40 0 46 W78 33 12
Mailing Address: P. O. Box 1, Bedford, PA 15522 US
Second Address: 2nd Fl., 134 E. Pitt St., Bedford, PA 15522
(814) 623-1000, *Fax:* (814) 623-9692
cesscomm@embarqmail.com
License: Bedford, Bedford County, PA held by Cessna Communications Inc.
Group Owner: Cessna Communications Inc.
Nat'l Network: Fox News Radio *Regional Reps:* Commerical Media Sales
Arbitron Metro Market: Bedford, PA *Format:* Classic Rock *Special Programming:* Motor Racing Network *No. News Employees:* 1 *Target Audience:* 25-54. *Adv. Rates:* 16; 16; 16; 16
Jay Cessna, President
John Cessna, Operations Dir
Chris Collins, Operations Manager

*WUFR
01-01-2008; 91.1 mhz FM; 2.5 kw vert; 1220 ft.; N40 17 40 W78 34 25 *Rebroadcasts:* Rebroadcasts WFSI(FM) Annapolis, MD 100%
4135 Northgate Blvd., Suite 1, Sacramento, CA 95834 US
(410) 268-6200, *Fax:* (410) 268-0931
www.familyradio.com
License: Bedford, Bedford County, PA held by Family Stations Inc.
Group Owner: Family Stations Inc.
Nat'l Network: Family Radio
Arbitron Metro Market: Tahlequah, OK *Format:* Religious
Harold Camping, President
W.A. Sadlier, Station Manager

Beech Creek

*WRWV
89.3 mhz FM; kw
US
(814) 867-3836, *Fax:* (814) 867-1922
www.revfm.net
info@revfm.net
License: Beech Creek, Elk County, PA held by Invisible Allies Ministries.
Arbitron Metro Market: Saint Marys, PA
Michael Schomer, General Manager

Bellefonte

WBLF
08-01-1958; 970 khz AM; 1 kw-D, NDD; 0.07 kw-N, ND1; N40 54 12 W77 46 6
City Center West, 7201 W. Lake Mead Blvd, Las Vegas, NV 89128 US
(814) 272-1320, *Fax:* (814) 272-3291
www.wblf.247exhibits.com
jerryfisher3@yahoo.com
License: Bellefonte, PA held by Magnum Broadcasting Inc.
Group Owner: Magnum Broadcasting Inc.; (acq 8-31-2005; $150,000) .
Nat'l Network: Fox News Radio; Fox Sports *Regional Network:* Agrinet *Nat'l Reps:* Interep
Arbitron Metro Market: State College, PA *Format:* News, News/Talk, 86 *Target Audience:* Adults 25+.
Michael Stapleford, President
Diana Stapleford, General Manager
Michael Brennen, General Sales Mgr

WZWW
09-15-1986; 95.3 mhz FM *Hrs Open:* 24; 790 w; Ant 636 ft; N40 53 35 W77 51 48
863 Benner Pike, Suite 200, State College, PA 16801
(814) 231-0953, *Fax:* (814) 231-0950
www.3wz.com
nancy@3wz.com
License: Bellefonte, Centre County, PA held by First Media Radio LLC.
Group Owner: First Media Radio LLC; (acq 11-2-2000)
Nat'l Network: CBS Radio *Regional Reps:* Commercial Media Sales.
Population Served: 124,000 *Arbitron Metro Market:* State College, *Special Programming:* Sports 3 hrs wkly *Hrs. of News Programming:* news progmg 7 hrs wkly *No. News Employees:* 2 *Target Audience:* 25-54;upscale families
Alex Kolobielski, President
Steve Williams, Operations Dir
Mike McGough, General Manager
Dave Kurten, Programming Director

Bellwood

WALY
03-28-1970; 103.9 mhz FM *Hrs Open:* 18; 0.38 kw; 919 ft.; N40 34 1 W78 26 32
One Forever Drive, Hollidaysburg, PA 16648 US
(814) 941-9800, *Fax:* (814) 943-2754
www.waly1039.com
kcoday@waly1039.com
License: Bellwood, Blair County, PA held by Forever Broadcasting LLC.
Group Owner: Forever Broadcasting; (acq 7-16-97; grpsl).
Nat'l Network: AP Radio *Nat'l Reps:* Katz Radio *Regional Reps:* Dome.
Arbitron Metro Market: Altoona, PA *Format:* Oldies *Target Audience:* 35-64; earlier boomers, socially & financially active
Carol Logan, President
Dave Davies, General Manager
Bobbi Castelluci, General Sales Mgr

Benton

WGGI
10-04-1985; 95.9 mhz FM; 4.2 kw; 384 ft.; N41 9 32 W76 24 6
10706 Beaver Dam Road, Cockeysville, MD 21030 US
(570) 883-1111, *Fax:* (570) 883-9851
www.froggy101.com
feedback@froggy101.com
License: Benton, Columbia County, PA held by Entercom Scranton Wilkes-Barre License LLC.
Group Owner: Entercom Communications Corp.; (acq 12-13-99; grpsl).
Arbitron Metro Market: Wilkes Barre-Scranton, PA *Format:* Country *Target Audience:* 25-54.
John Burkavage, Operations Dir
Jim Rising, Operations Manager

Berwick

WHLM-FM
02-14-1992; 103.5 mhz FM; 4.1 kw; 387 ft.; N41 5 11 W76 16 41
Rr1, Box 360, Sugarloaf, PA 18249 US
(570) 784-1200, *Fax:* (570) 784-6060
www.wkab.net
whlmam@aol.com
License: Berwick, Columbia County, PA held by Columbia FM Inc.
Arbitron Metro Market: Wilkes Barre-Scranton, PA *Format:* Contemporary Hits/Top 40, Adult Contemp *Target Audience:* 25-54; females at work, 18-39 men on weekends *Adv. Rates:* 18; 18; 18; 15
Joseph Reilly, General Manager

WBWX(AM)
08-01-1957; 1280 khz AM; 1 kw-D, 175 w-N; N41 04 36 W76 15 32
114 N. Market St., Berwick, PA 18603
(570) 752-8012, *Fax:* (570) 752-1131
way750am@aol.com
License: Berwick, Columbia County, PA held by Bold Gold Media Group L.P.
Group Owner: Bold Gold Media Group LP; (acq 1-11-2007; $10,000 plus assumption of debt)
Population Served: 50,000 *Arbitron Metro Market:* Wilkes Barre-Scranton, PA *Format:* Oldies
JoAnn Germers Hausen, Operations Dir
Kevin Fennessy, General Manager

Bethlehem

WGPA
02-14-1946; 1100 khz AM *Hrs Open:* Sunrise-sunset; 0.25 kw-D, NDD; N40 37 27 W75 21 19
528 North New Street, Bethlehem, PA 18018 US
(610) 866-8074, *Fax:* (610) 866-9381
www.regiononline.com/joetimmer
joetimmer@jollyjoetimmer.com
License: Bethlehem, PA held by Joseph Timmer dba Timmer Broadcasting Co.
Nat'l Network: USA
Arbitron Metro Market: Allentown-Bethlehem, PA *Format:* News, News/Talk, 86 *Special Programming:* Ger 2 hrs, polka 12 hrs, Sp 4 hrs wkly *Hrs. of News Programming:* news progmg 2 hrs wkly *No. News Employees:* 1*Target Audience:* General. *Adv. Rates:* 50; 20; 20; 20
Joe Timmer, President
Mark Staller, Operations Dir

***WLVR-FM**
05-03-1973; 91.3 mhz FM *Hrs Open:* 7 AM-4 AM; 0.013 kw; 558 ft.; N40 36 4 W75 21 34
University Center, 29 Trembley Drive, Bethlehem, PA 18015 US
(610) 758-4187, *Fax:* (610) 758-4186
www.wlvr.org
inwlvr@lehigh.edu
License: Bethlehem, Northampton County, PA held by Lehigh University.
Arbitron Metro Market: Bethlehem, PA *Format:* Variety/Diverse *Special Programming:* Black 12 hrs, class 8 hrs, reggae 6 hrs, jazz 12 h *Hrs. of News Programming:* News progmg 10 hrs wkly *Target Audience:* General.
Aimee Van House, General Manager
Geordie Connell, Station Manager
Adam Ponzek, Programming Director

WZZO
02-14-1946; 95.1 mhz FM; 30 kw; 630 ft.; N40 37 13 W75 17 37
600 Congress Ave., Suite 1400, Austin, TX 78701 US
(610) 434-1742, *Fax:* (610) 434-9511
www.wzzo.com
studio@wzzo.com
License: Bethlehem, Northampton County, PA held by Capstar TX L.P.
Group Owner: Clear Channel Communications Inc.; (acq 8-30-00; grpsl).
Nat'l Reps: Katz Radio
Arbitron Metro Market: Whitehall, PA *Format:* Rock/AOR
Pat Gremling, Sales Manager
Craig Stevens, Programming Director
Rich Lewis, Promotions Manager

Blairsville

WLCY
04-15-1985; 106.3 mhz FM *Hrs Open:* 24; 2.4 kw; 364 ft.; N40 31 10 W79 13 26
400 Unity Street, Suite 200, Latrobe, PA 15650 US
(724) 479-9093, *Fax:* (724) 349-6842
www.country1063fm.com
License: Blairsville, Indiana County, PA held by The St. Pier Group LLC.
Group Owner: Renda Broadcasting Corp.; (acq 8-1-2004; $900,000).
Nat'l Network: Jones Radio Networks *Regional Reps:* Dome.
Format: Country *Hrs. of News Programming:* news progmg 2 hrs wkly *No. News Employees:* 2 *Target Audience:* 25-54. *Adv. Rates:* 20; 20; 20; 20
Mark Bertig, General Manager

Bloomsburg

***WBUQ**
09-16-1986; 91.1 mhz FM *Hrs Open:* 16; 0.6 kw; -72 ft.; N41 0 29 W76 26 51
400 East Second Street, Bloomsburg, PA 17815 US
(570) 389-4686, *Fax:* (570) 389-2718
www.orgs.bloomu.edu/wbuq/
rsantico@bloomu.edu
License: Bloomsburg, Columbia County, PA held by Bloomsburg University of Pennsylvania.
Arbitron Metro Market: Bloomsburg, Pa *Format:* Alternative, Rock/AOR *Special Programming:* Talk 10 hrs, urban 10 hrs, metal 15 hrs, indie 10 hrs wkly *Hrs. of News Programming:* news progmg 2 hrs wkly *No. NewsEmployees:* 1 *Target Audience:* General; college & area high school students *Adv. Rates:* 8; 7; 8; 7
Richard Antico, General Manager
Kelly Barnett, Programming Director
Ed Kaul, News Director
Kelly Barnett, Marketing Director

WHLM
09-26-1947; 930 khz AM *Hrs Open:* 24
3185 Lackawanna Avenue, Bloomsburg, PA 17815 US
(570) 784-1200, *Fax:* (570) 784-6060
www.whlmam.com
hopperWHLM@aol.com
License: Bloomsburg, PA held by Columbia Broadcasting Co.
Nat'l Network: CBS Radio *Regional Network:* Radio Pa.
Arbitron Metro Market: St.Bloomsburg,PA *Format:* News, Oldies *Special Programming:* Farm one hr, relg 2 hrs wkly *Hrs. of News Programming:* news progmg 15 hrs wkly *No. News Employees:* 1 *Target Audience:* 25-54. *Adv. Rates:* 15; 10; 15; 8
Joseph Reilly, President
Larry Hopper, General Sales Mgr

WFYY
09-01-1956; 106.5 mhz FM; 10.5 kw; 1027 ft.; N40 56 18 W76 25 38
Mailing Address: 480 West Fifth Street, Bloomsburg, PA 17815 US
Second Address: 246 W. Main St., Bloomsburg, PA 17815
(570) 374-5711, *Fax:* (570) 784-1004
License: Bloomsburg, Columbia County, PA held by MMP License LLC.
Group Owner: MAX Media L.L.C.; (acq 10-17-03; grpsl).
Nat'l Network: Westwood One *Regional Reps:* Dome.
Arbitron Metro Market: Wilkes Barre-Scranton, PA *Format:* Adult Contemp *Target Audience:* 18-49.
John Trinder, President
Scott Richards, Operations Dir
Greg Adair, General Sales Mgr
Ted Koppen, Chief Engineer
Dawn Marie, Operations Director

Boalsburg

WBUS
04-13-1998; 93.7 mhz FM; 0.33 kw; 1362 ft.; N40 45 8 W77 45 16
2029 Cato Avenue, Suite 101, State College, PA 16801 US
(814) 237-9800, *Fax:* (814) 237-2477
www.thebus.net
foreverpsa@ gmail.com
License: Boalsburg, Centre County, PA held by Forever Broadcasting LLC.
Group Owner: Forever Broadcasting; (acq 5-1-2005; $2.65 million with WRSC(AM) State College)
Arbitron Metro Market: State College, PA *Format:* Classic Rock *Target Audience:* 25-54.
Scott Cohagan, General Manager
Wendy Lynch, Sales Manager
Tony Riccardi, Programming Director
Bob Taylor, Chief Engineer

Boyertown

WBYN-FM
10-31-1960; 107.5 mhz FM *Hrs Open:* 24; 30 kw; 610 ft.; N40 24 15 W75 39 9
P. O. Box 3022, Lancaster, PA 17604 US
(610) 369-7777, *Fax:* (610) 369-7780
www.wbynfm.com
info@wbynfm.com
License: Boyertown, Berks County, PA held by WDAC Radio Co.
Nat'l Reps: Katz Radio
Arbitron Metro Market: Boyertown, PA *Format:* Contemporary Hits/Top 40, Adult Contemp *Target Audience:* 25-54; families
Richard Crawford, President
John White, General Manager

Braddock

WLFP
06-01-1947; 1550 khz AM *Hrs Open:* 5 AM-midnight
7138 Kelly Street, Pittsburgh, PA 15208 US
(412) 942-0076
www.theedge1550.com
License: Braddock, PA held by WURP East Inc.
Group Owner: BusinessTalkRadio.Net Inc.; (acq 8-29-2007; $225,000)
Nat'l Network: American Urban
Arbitron Metro Market: Pittsburgh, PA *Format:* Talk *Hrs. of News Programming:* news progmg 6 hrs wkly *No. News Employees:* 1 *Target Audience:* 25-54.
Michael Metter, President
Chris Squire, General Manager
Shelia Corley, Station Manager
Coddy Anderson, General Sales Mgr

WRRK
06-01-1959; 96.9 mhz FM *Hrs Open:* 24; 45 kw; 531 ft.; N40 24 42 W79 55 53
7 Parkway Center, Suite 780, Pittsburgh, PA 15220 US
(412) 316-3342, *Fax:* (412) 316-3388
www.wrrk.com
info@wrrk.com
License: Braddock, Allegheny County, PA held by WPNT Associates.
Nat'l Network: ABC
Arbitron Metro Market: Pittsburgh, PA *Format:* Adult Contemp
Greg Frischling, General Manager
Chris Kohan, General Sales Mgr
John Robertson, Programming Director
Vicki Wolfe, Promotions Manager
Amy Crago, News Director
Paul Carroll, Chief Engineer
Ed Lang, Traffic Manager

WLFP(AM)
1550 khz AM; 500 w-D, 900 w-N, DA-2; N42 01 47 W80 07 06
4039 Sunset Blvd., Steubenville, OH 43952
(412) 936-1500
License: Braddock, Erie County, PA held by Wurp East Inc
Population Served: 53,515 *Arbitron Metro Market:* Kearsarge, PA
Randy Dietterich, General Manager

Bradford

WBRR
12-01-1987; 100.1 mhz FM *Hrs Open:* 24; 1.65 kw; 525 ft; N41 58 12 W78 42 03
Box 545, 1490 St. Francis Dr., Bradford, PA 16701
(814) 368-4141, *Fax:* (814) 368-3180
www.wbrrfm.com
dfredeen@wesb.com
License: Bradford, McKean County, PA held by Radio Station WESB Inc.
Arbitron Metro Market: Olean, NY *Target Audience:* 25-54. *Adv. Rates:* Same as AM
Donald J Fredeen, President

WESB
04-01-1947; 1490 khz AM *Hrs Open:* 24; 1 kw-U; N41 27 54 W78 37 01
Box 545, 1490 St. Francis Dr., Bradford, PA 16701
(814) 368-4141, *Fax:* (814) 368-3180
www.wesb.com
1490@wesb.com
License: Bradford, McKean County, PA held by Radio Station WESB Inc.
Nat'l Network: CNN Radio *Regional Network:* Radio Pa. *Nat'l Reps:* Dome
Population Served: 25,000 *Arbitron Metro Market:* Olean, NY
No. News Employees: 1 *Target Audience:* 25-54. *Adv. Rates:* 15; 15; 15; 15
Donald Fredeen, President
Frank Williams, Operations Dir
Peggy Austin, General Sales Mgr
Scott Douglas, Promotions Manager
Anne Holliday, News Director

***WTWT**
90.5 mhz FM; 2.5 kw; 568 ft.; N42 3 18 W78 27 28
Mailing Address: US
Second Address: Rt. 62 North, Russell, PA 16345
(814) 757-8744, *Fax:* (814) 757-8745
www.wtwtfm.org
jstowe@wtwtfm.org
License: Bradford, McKean County, PA held by Calvary Chapel of Russell.
Arbitron Metro Market: Bradford, PA *Format:* Christian
Jeffrey York, General Manager

Bristol

***WLBS**
04-01-1998; 91.7 mhz FM *Hrs Open:* 24; 0.1 kw vert; 69 ft.; N40 9 33 W74 51 24 *Rebroadcasts:* Rebroadcasts WRDV(FM) Warminster 100%
P. O. Box 2012, Warminster, PA 18974 US
(215) 674-8002, *Fax:* (215) 674-4586
www.wrdv.org
info@wrdv.org
License: Bristol, Bucks County, PA held by Bux-Mont Educational Radio Association.
Wire Services: AP
Format: Variety/Diverse
Charles Loughary, Chairman
Todd Allen, General Manager

Brookville

WKQL
01-17-2000; 103.3 mhz FM *Hrs Open:* 24; 10.5 kw; 495 ft.; N41 4 4 W79 4 59
Mailing Address: Broadcast Plaza, Crane Avenue, Pittsburgh, PA 15220 US
Second Address: Renda Radio Inc., Broadcast Plaza, Pittsburgh, PA 15767
(814) 938-6000, *Fax:* (814) 938-4237
www.kool1033fm.com/
rpolippo@rendabroadcasting.com
License: Brookville, Jefferson County, PA held by Renda Radio Inc.
Group Owner: Renda Broadcasting Corp.
Nat'l Network: ABC
Arbitron Metro Market: Punxsutawney, PA *Format:* Oldies *Hrs. of News Programming:* news progmg 2 hrs wkly *No. News*

Employees: 1 *Target Audience:* 35-54; adults *Adv. Rates:* 24; 20; 24; 16
Diana Albright, General Manager
Chuck Stevens, Station Manager
Renee Polippo, Business Manager

WMKX
08-22-1981; 105.5 mhz FM *Hrs Open:* 24; 16 kw; 413 ft.; N41 7 21 W79 3 51
51 Pickering Street, Brookville, PA 15825 US
(814) 849-8100, *Fax:* (814) 849-4585
www.megarock.fm
megarock@alltel.net
License: Brookville, Jefferson County, PA held by Strattan Broadcasting Inc.
Arbitron Metro Market: Brookville, PA *Format:* Light Rock *Special Programming:* Jazz 3 hrs, rock classics 6 hrs, oldies 8 hrs wkly *Hrs. of News Programming:* news progmg 5 hrs wkly *No. News Employees:* 1 *Target Audience:* 25-54; general
Jim Farley, President
Diana Farley, General Sales Mgr
Kevin Heinrich, Programming Director
Chris Condon, Promotions Manager

Burgettstown

WOGH
05-01-1947; 103.5 mhz FM *Hrs Open:* 24; 19.5 kw; Ant 810 ft; N40 20 33 W80 37 14
Mailing Address: 320 Market Street, Steubenville, PA 15222
Second Address: 320 Market Street, Steubenville, OH 43952
(740) 283-4747, *Fax:* (740) 283-3655
www.froggyland.com
License: Burgettstown, Washington County, PA held by Key market license
Nat'l Reps: Katz *Regional Reps:* Regional Reps
Target Audience: 25-54
Lynn Deppen, President
Paul Rothfuss, Operations Dir
Paul Rothfuss, General Manager
Scott Feist, Programming Director
Stu Schroeder, Promotions Manager
Greg Harper, Engineering Dir
Greg Harper, Chief Engineer

Burnham

WVNW
08-01-1994; 96.7 mhz FM *Hrs Open:* 24; 0.45 kw; 850 ft.; N40 35 10 W77 41 40
114 N. Logan Blvd., Burnham, PA 17009 US
(717) 248-7827
www.star967.com
wvnw@star967.com
License: Burnham, Mifflin County, PA held by WVNW Inc.
Nat'l Network: ABC; Fox News Radio *Regional Network:* Radio Pa.
Arbitron Metro Market: Burnham, PA *Format:* Country *Target Audience:* 25-54.
Jed Donahue, Operations Dir
Jed Donahue, General Manager
Tom Sheeder, Programming Director
Erik Lane, News Director
Dave Busman, Sports Commentator

Butler

WBUT
03-14-1949; 1050 khz AM *Hrs Open:* 24; 0.5 kw-D, ND2; 0.062 kw-N, ND2; N40 53 51 W79 53 22
1768 N. Main Street, PO Box 1645, Butler, PA 16001 US
(724) 287-5778, *Fax:* (724) 283-3005
www.wbut.com
frontdesk@bcnetwork.com
License: Butler, PA held by Butler County Radio Network Inc.
Group Owner: Butler County Radio Network Inc.; (acq 5-19-98; grpsl).
Nat'l Network: CNN Radio
Arbitron Metro Market: Butler, PA *Format:* Country *No. News Employees:* 2 *Target Audience:* General.
Victoria Hinterberger, General Manager
Bob Cupp, Programming Director
Bill Davis, News Director
Wes Briggs, Sports Director

WISR
09-26-1941; 680 khz AM *Hrs Open:* 24; 0.25 kw-D, ND1; 0.05 kw-N, ND1; N40 52 39 W79 54 9
1768 N. Main Street Ext., P.O. Box 1645, Butler, PA 16001 US
(724) 283-1500, *Fax:* (724) 283-3005
www.wisr680.com, www.insidebutlercounty.com
frontdesk@bcnetwork.com
License: Butler, PA held by Butler County Radio Network Inc.
Group Owner: Butler County Radio Network Inc.; acq 5-19-98; grpsl)
Nat'l Network: CBS *Regional Network:* Radio Pa.
Arbitron Metro Market: Pittsburgh, PA *Format:* News, News/Talk, 84, Talk *Special Programming:* Relg 6 hrs wlky *Hrs. of News Programming:* news progmg 28 hrs wkly *No. News Employees:* 2 *Target Audience:* 45plus.
Vicki Hinterberger, General Manager
Dave Malarkey, Programming Director
Wes Briggs, News Director
Scott Briggs, Engineering Dir

WLER-FM
03-14-1949; 97.7 mhz FM *Hrs Open:* 24; 4.6 kw; 374 ft.; N40 53 51 W79 53 22
1768 N. Main Street, PO Box 1645, Butler, PA 16001 US
(724) 287-5778, *Fax:* (724) 283-3005
frontdesk@bcrnetwork.com
License: Butler, Butler County, PA
Group Owner: Butler County Radio Network Inc.
Nat'l Network: Westwood One; CNN Radio
Arbitron Metro Market: Pittsburgh, PA *Format:* Contemporary Hits/Top 40 *No. News Employees:* 2
Victoria Hinterberger, Station Manager
Jay Kline, Programming Director
Bill Davis, News Director

California

*WCAL
09-01-1973; 91.9 mhz FM *Hrs Open:* 24; 3 kw; 161 ft.; N40 2 57 W79 54 1
428 Hickory Street, California, PA 15419 US
(724) 938-3000, *Fax:* (724) 938-5959
wcal.calu.edu
wheeler@cup.edu
License: California, Washington County, PA held by The Student Association Inc.
Nat'l Network: Westwood One
Arbitron Metro Market: California, PA *Format:* Rock/AOR *Special Programming:* Contemp Christian 6 hrs, urban contemp 12 hrs, rap *Hrs. of News Programming:* News progmg 5 hrs wkly *Target Audience:* 18-25; studentsat California Univ
J.R. Willer, General Manager

Cambridge Springs

WXMJ
07-14-1997; 104.5 mhz FM *Hrs Open:* 24; 2.55 kw; 512 ft.; N41 42 10 W80 9 54
908 Diamond Square, Meadville, PA 16335 US
(814) 432-2188, *Fax:* (814) 437-9372
www.mymajicspace.com
radio@zoominternet.com
License: Cambridge Springs, Crawford County, PA held by Forever Broadcasting LLC.
Group Owner: Forever Broadcasting; (acq 7-21-2000; grpsl)
Arbitron Metro Market: Cambridge Springs, PA *Format:* Adult Contemp *Target Audience:* 25-54.
Carol Logan, President
Todd Adkins, Operations Dir
Terry Deitz, General Manager
Joe Elan, General Sales Mgr

Canonsburg

WWCS
11-28-1957; 540 khz AM *Hrs Open:* 24; 5 kw-D, DA2; 0.5 kw-N, DA2; N40 17 22 W80 11 7
21700 Northwestern Hwy., Twr 14, Ste 1190, Southfield, MI 48075 US
(724) 745-5400, *Fax:* (724) 745-8790
www.radiodisney.com
License: Canonsburg, PA held by Birach Broadcasting Corp.
Group Owner: Birach Broadcasting Corp.; (acq 5-28-92; $475,000;
Arbitron Metro Market: Pittsburgh, PA *Format:* Children *Target Audience:* Educated adults, ethnic groups, open minded.
Phil Guerini, Vice President and General Manager
Ray De La Garza, VP of Programming
Rita Ferro, Executive Vice President, Disney Media Sales and M
Kelly Edwards, Executive Director Music & Programming, Radio Disn
Ivan Heredia, VP,Marketing
Anne Sweeney, Co-Chair

Canton

WHGL-FM
08-30-1978; 100.3 mhz FM *Hrs Open:* 24; 3.9 kw; 846 ft.; N41 44 32 W76 50 8
Mailing Address: 170 Redington Avenue, Troy, PA 16947 US
Second Address: 170 Redington Ave, Troy, PA 16947
(570) 297-0100, *Fax:* (570) 297-3193
www.wiggle100.com
whgl100@ptd.net
License: Canton, Bradford County, PA held by Cantroair Communications Inc.
Nat'l Network: ABC
Format: Country *No. News Employees:* 1 *Target Audience:* 25-54.
Mike Powers, President
Bob Gisler, Operations Dir
Shane Wilber, Programming Director
David Rockwell, Promotions Manager

Carbondale

WTRW(FM)
01-01-1965; 94.3 mhz FM *Hrs Open:* 24; 1.1 kw; Ant 770 ft; N41 32 37 W75 27 44
957 Broadcast Ctr., Avoca, PA 18641
(570) 414-1943, *Fax:* (570) 414-1944
www.lite943fm.com
License: Carbondale, Lackawanna County, PA held by WS2K Radio LLC.
Group Owner: WS2K Radio LLC dba WS Media; (acq 7-14-2008; grpsl)
Population Served: 821,623 *Arbitron Metro Market:* Lehigh Valley, PA *Format:* Adult Contemp
Ira Rosenblatt, Station Manager

WCDL
01-01-1950; 1440 khz AM; 5 kw-D, ND2; 0.037 kw-N, ND2; N41 33 28 W75 29 11
City Center West, 7201 W. Lake Mead Blvd, Las Vegas, NV 89128 US
(570) 282-8700, *Fax:* (570) 282-1435
License: Carbondale, PA held by WS2K Radio LLC.
Group Owner: WS2K Radio LLC dba WS Media; (acq 7-14-2008; grpsl)
Arbitron Metro Market: Wilkes Barre-Scranton, PA
Chuck Sebastian, Operations Dir
John Speeney, General Manager

WTRW
01-01-2008; 94.3 mhz FM; 0.97 kw; 817 ft.; N41 32 37 W75 27 44
City Center West, 7201 W. Lake Mead Blvd, Las Vegas, NV 89128 US
(570) 344-1221, *Fax:* (570) 344-0996
www.talker943.com
bspinelli@boldgoldmedia.com
License: Carbondale, Manitowoc County, PA held by Midwest Communications Inc.
Group Owner: Midwest Communications Inc.; (acq 8-20-2008; $1.73 million)
Arbitron Metro Market: Carbondale, PA
Duke Wright, President

Carlisle

*WDCV-FM
01-01-1972; 88.3 mhz FM *Hrs Open:* 7 AM-2 AM; 0.45 kw horiz; -43 ft.; N40 12 9 W77 11 46
P.O. Box 1773, Carlisle, PA 17013 US
(717) 245-1444, *Fax:* (717) 245-1899
www.blogs.dickinson.edu/wdcvfm
wdcvfm@gmail.com
License: Carlisle, Cumberland County, PA held by Board of Trustees Dickinson College.
Arbitron Metro Market: Carlisle, PA *Format:* Variety/Diverse *Special Programming:* Jazz 6 hrs, Ger one hr, Sp one hr, funk/rap 15 hrs, Russian one hr, politics one hr, blues 6 hrs wkly *Hrs. of News Programming:* newsprogmg 5 hrs wkly *No. News Employees:* 5
Nick Stamos, General Manager
Ben, Programming Director

WHYL
01-01-1948; 960 khz AM *Hrs Open:* 24; 5 kw-D, DA2; 0.022 kw-N, DA2; N40 11 34 W77 10 28
140 South Ash Avenue, Tempe, AZ 85281 US
(717) 249-1717, *Fax:* (717) 258-4638
www.whylradio.com
kevin@whylradio.com
License: Carlisle, PA held by WS2K Radio LLC.

Group Owner: WS2K Radio LLC dba WS Media; (acq 7-14-2008; grpsl)
Nat'l Reps: McGavren Guild
Arbitron Metro Market: Harrisburg-Lebanon-Carlisle, PA *Format:* News, News/Talk, 86 *Special Programming:* Polka 2 hrs *No. News Employees:* 1 *Target Audience:* 45 plus; older, mature adults
Kevin Kremer, Operations Dir
Bruce Collier, General Manager
Karen Peiffer, News Director

WCAT-FM
01-01-1959; 102.3 mhz FM *Hrs Open:* 24; 3 kw horiz, 2.75 kw vert; 328 ft.; N40 17 23 W77 8 10
Mailing Address: 140 South Ash Avenue, Tempe, AZ 85281 US
Second Address: 1703 Walnut Bottom Rd., Carlisle, PA 17013
(610) 266-7600, *Fax:* (717) 258-4638
www.red1023.com
rick.sten@cumulus.com
License: Carlisle, Cumberland County, PA
Group Owner: Cumulus Media Inc.; (acq 1999; $4.5 million with WHYL(AM) Carlisle).
Nat'l Network: CNN Radio
Arbitron Metro Market: Harrisburg-Lebanon-Carlisle, PA *Format:* Country *Target Audience:* 25-54.
John Fraunfelter, Operations Dir
Cindy Miller, General Manager
Will Robinson, Programming Director
Jay Hunter, Promotions Manager

WIOO
07-08-1965; 1000 khz AM *Hrs Open:* Sunrise-sunset/AM, 24/7/FM; 1 kw-D, NDD; Non-Directional; N40 9 30 W77 11 49
180 York Rd, Carlisle, PA 17013 US
(717) 243-1200, *Fax:* (717) 243-1277
www.wioo.com
wioo@pa.net
License: Carlisle, PA held by Harold Swidler.
Nat'l Network: Motor Racing Net; ABC Information & Entertainment; Westwood One *Regional Network:* Radio Pa.
Arbitron Metro Market: Harrisburg-Lebanon-Carlisle, PA *Format:* Country *Special Programming:* Relg 5 hrs wkly *Hrs. of News Programming:* news progmg 5 hrs wkly *No. News Employees:* 1 *Target Audience:* 21plus. *Adv. Rates:* 20; 20; 20; 15
Harold Swidler, President
Florence Fisher, General Manager
Sandy Loy, General Sales Mgr
Ray Thomas, Programming Director
Randy Freed, Senior Account Executive
Rebecca Greeger, Traffic Manager

Carnegie

WZUM
07-01-1962; 1590 khz AM *Hrs Open:* 6 AM-sunset; directional
P.O. Box 27, Monroeville, PA 15146 US
(724) 863-7804, *Fax:* (724) 864-9028
License: Carnegie, PA held by Starboard Media Foundation Inc.
Group Owner: Relevant Radio; (acq 9-23-2005; $435,000)
Arbitron Metro Market: Monroeville *Format:* News *Special Programming:* Ethnic 2 hrs wkly *Target Audience:* General.
Mike Horvath, General Manager

Cashtown

***WFKJ**
12-07-1988; 890 khz AM *Hrs Open:* 7 AM-6 PM; 0.89 kw-D, NDD; N39 52 59 W77 20 43
Mailing Address: P. O. Box 115, Cashtown, PA 17310 US
Second Address: 3425 Chambersburg Rd., Biglerville, PA 17307
(717) 337-1635, *Fax:* (717) 334-8914
www.wordbroadcast.org/WFKJ
WFKJ@wordbroadcast.org
License: Cashtown, PA held by Jesus is Lord Ministries International.
Nat'l Network: Moody
Arbitron Metro Market: York, PA *TV Affiliate:* livestream TV
Format: Religious *Special Programming:* Country 4 hrs, children 12 hrs wkly *Target Audience:* General.
Rev. Michael Yeager, President
Fred Bream, Promotions Manager
Larry Angle, Chief Engineer

Central City

WCCL
10-19-1972; 101.7 mhz FM *Hrs Open:* 24; 0.72 kw; 643 ft.; N40 6 42 W78 51 33
1348 Connel Drive, P.O. Box 1330, Somerset, PA 15501 US
(814) 534-8975, *Fax:* (814) 534-8979
www.cool101online.com
info@cool101online.com
License: Central City, Somerset County, PA held by 2510 Licenses LLC.
Group Owner: 2510 Licenses LLC; (acq 2-16-2005; grpsl).
Format: Oldies *Special Programming:* Relg 4 hrs wkly *No. News Employees:* 4 *Target Audience:* 25-54.
Nick Ferrara, General Manager

Centre Hall

WMAJ-FM
05-24-1989; 99.5 mhz FM *Hrs Open:* 24; 0.85 kw; 1368 ft.; N40 45 9 W77 45 16
112 West Shirley St., Mt. Union, PA 17066 US
(814) 237-9800, *Fax:* (814) 237-2477
www.majic99.com
majic99fm@gmail.com
License: Centre Hall, Centre County, PA held by Megahertz Licenses LLC.
Group Owner: Forever Broadcasting; (acq 4-29-2002; $875,000 with WHUN(AM) Huntingdon)
Arbitron Metro Market: State College, PA *Format:* Variety/Diverse
Chuck Hertzog, General Manager
Wendy Lynch, Sales Manager
Alexandra Rabb, Programming Director
Bob Taylor, Chief Engineer

Chambersburg

WCHA
08-11-1946; 800 khz AM; 1 kw-D, ND1; 0.196 kw-N, ND1; N39 55 41 W77 41 44
25 Penncraft Avenue, Chambersburg, PA 17201 US
(717) 264-7121, *Fax:* (717) 263-9649
mix95@mix95.com
License: Chambersburg, PA held by MLB-Hagerstown-Chambersburg IV LLC.
Group Owner: Main Line Broadcasting LLC; (acq 7-20-2005; grpsl).
Nat'l Network: ABC
Arbitron Metro Market: Hagerstown-Chambersburg-Waynesboro, MD-PA *Format:* News, News/Talk, 86 *Special Programming:* Relg 8 hrs, gospel 2 hrs wkly *No. News Employees:* 1 *Target Audience:* 25-54.
Rick Alexander, Operations Dir
Rich Bateman, General Manager
Craig Stevens, General Sales Mgr
Tammy Heckman, Promotions Manager

WIKZ
04-15-1948; 95.1 mhz FM; 50 kw; 449 ft.; N39 55 41 W77 41 44
25 Penncraft Avenue, Chambersburg, PA 17201 US
(717) 263-0813, *Fax:* (717) 263-9649
www.mix95.com
info@wikz.com
License: Chambersburg, Franklin County, PA
Group Owner: Main Line Broadcasting LLC
Arbitron Metro Market: Hagerstown-Chambersburg-Waynesboro, MD-PA *Format:* Adult Contemp *No. News Employees:* 1 *Target Audience:* 25-44.
Rick Alexander, Operations Dir
Lisa Harding, Promotions Manager
Barbara Turkenton, News Director
Jeff Baker, Engineering Dir
J.P. McCartney, Assistant Music Director
J.P. McCartneyu, Disc Jockey
Artie Shultz, Disc Jockey
LisaKline, Local News Editor

***WZXQ**
01-01-2005; 88.3 mhz FM; 110 w vert; Ant 1,155 ft; N39 57 40 W77 28 32 *Rebroadcasts:* Rebroadcasts WBYO(FM) Sellersville 100%
Box 186, Sellersville, PA 18960
(215) 721-2141, *Fax:* (215) 721-9811
www.wordfm.org
wordfm@wordfm.org
License: Chambersburg, Franklin County, PA held by Four Rivers Community Broadcasting Corp.
Arbitron Metro Market: Hagerstown-Chambersburg-Waynesboro, MD-PA
Charles Loughery, President
Meg Sabulsky, Operations Dir
David Baker, General Manager
Meg Sabulsky, Programming Director
William Dunn, Promotions Manager
Charles Loughery, Engineering Dir

Chester

***WDNR**
04-22-1977; 89.5 mhz FM *Hrs Open:* 9; 0.008 kw; 85 ft.; N39 51 42 W75 21 20
Box 1000 Widender Univ, Chester, PA 19013 US
(610) 499-4439(610) 499-4000, *Fax:* (610) 499-4531
www.wdnrfm.org
wdnr895@gmail.com
License: Chester, Delaware County, PA held by Widener University.
Arbitron Metro Market: Philadelphia, PA *Format:* Variety/Diverse *Special Programming:* Jazz 2 hrs, blues 2 hrs, oldies 2 hrs, children 2 hrs wkly *Target Audience:* 16-30; high school & college age population
Sean Sheenan, Operations Dir
Daniel Armenti, General Manager
Drena Gwin, Programming Director
Jaclyn Gutterman, Promotions Manager
John Blazek, Chief Engineer

WPWA
10-01-1947; 1590 khz AM *Hrs Open:* 24
8910 University Center Lane, #130, San Diego, CA 92122 US
(610) 358-1400, *Fax:* (610) 358-1845
www.wpwa.net
poder1590@wpwa.net
License: Chester, PA held by Mount Ocean Media L.L.C.
Group Owner: Mountain Broadcasting Corp.; (acq 8-20-2001; $675,000).
Arbitron Metro Market: Philadelphia *Format:* Christian, Gospel, 74 *Hrs. of News Programming:* News progmg 20 hrs wkly *Target Audience:* 25-64; affluent, mature adults
Steve Skalish, General Manager

WVCH
04-04-1948; 740 khz AM *Hrs Open:* 6 AM-6 PM; 1 kw-D, ND1; 0.006 kw-N, ND1; N39 52 38 W75 24 24
Mailing Address: Box 102, Springhouse, PA 19477 US
Second Address: 308 Dutton Mill Rd., Brookhaven, PA 19015
(610) 279-9000, *Fax:* (610) 279-9002
www.wvch.com
charcos@juno.com
License: Chester, PA held by WVCH Communications Inc.
Nat'l Network: Moody; USA
Arbitron Metro Market: Philadelphia, PA *Format:* Christian, Religious *Target Audience:* General.
Charlotte Cosden, Advertising Contact

Clarendon

WKNB
08-31-1995; 104.3 mhz FM *Hrs Open:* 24; 4.7 kw; 371 ft.; N41 48 50 W79 10 4
Mailing Address: 310 Second Ave, Warren, PA 16365 US
Second Address: 310 Second Ave, Warren, PA 16365
(814) 723-1310, *Fax:* (814) 723-3356
www.kibcoradio.com
info@kibcoradio.com
License: Clarendon, Warren County, PA held by Radio Partners LLC.
Group Owner: Radio Partners LLC; (acq 9-30-2005; grpsl)
Nat'l Network: AP Radio *Regional Reps:* Commercial Media Sales *Wire Services:* AP
Format: Country *No. News Employees:* 1 *Target Audience:* 18-45.
Frank Iorio, General Manager
David Whipple, General Sales Mgr
Mark Silvis, Programming Director
Dale Bliss, Promotions Manager
Dana Simmons, News Director

Clarion

WCCR
06-28-1985; 92.7 mhz FM *Hrs Open:* 24; 3 kw; 279 ft.; N41 14 41 W79 15 42
Mailing Address: 725 Wood St P.O. Box 688, Clarion, PA 16214 US
Second Address: 1168 Greenville Pike, Clarion, PA 16214
(814) 226-4500, *Fax:* (814) 226-5898
www.bonnie16224.tripod.com/c93.htm
clarionradio@comcast.net
License: Clarion, Clarion County, PA
Group Owner: Clarion County Broadcasting Corp.
Regional Reps: Dome & Associates
Arbitron Metro Market: Clarion, PA *Format:* Adult Contemp *Hrs. of News Programming:* news progmg 8 hrs wkly *No. News Employees:* 1 *Target Audience:* 25-54. *Adv. Rates:* 13; 13; 13; 13

***WCUC-FM**
04-01-1977; 91.7 mhz FM *Hrs Open:* 25.?Â ?; 3.2 kw; 318 ft.; N41 12 35 W79 22 39
Becker Hall, Clarion, PA 16214 US

(814) 393-2330(814) 393-2514, *Fax:* (814) 393-2065
www.wcuc.org
bexley@clarion.edu
License: Clarion, Clarion County, PA held by Clarion University of Pennsylvania.
Wire Services: AP
Arbitron Metro Market: Clarion, PA *Format:* Contemporary Hits/Top 40 *Special Programming:* Urban 6 hrs, country 6 hrs, jazz 3 hrs, community 12 hrs wkly
Bruce Exley, Operations Dir
Bill Adams, General Manager

WWCH
06-12-1960; 1300 khz AM *Hrs Open:* 24
Mailing Address: P.O. Box 688, 1300 Greenville Ave Ext., Clarion, PA 16214 US
Second Address: 1168 Greenville Pike, Clarion, PA 16214
(814) 226-4500, *Fax:* (814) 226-5898
www.clarioncountydailynews.com
clarionradio@comcast.net
License: Clarion, PA held by Clarion County Broadcasting Corp.
Group Owner: Clarion County Broadcasting Corp.
Nat'l Network: CBS Radio *Regional Network:* Radio Pa. *Nat'l Reps:* Dome
Arbitron Metro Market: Clarion, PA *Format:* Country, News, 62, Talk *Special Programming:* Pub affrs, relg 8 hrs wkly *Hrs. of News Programming:* news progmg 8 hrs wkly *No. News Employees:* 1 *Target Audience:* 25-54. *Adv. Rates:* 12.50; 12.50; 12.50; 10
William Hearst, President

Clearfield

WCPA
01-01-1947; 900 khz AM; 2.5 kw-D, DA2; 0.5 kw-N, DA2; N41 2 32 W78 26 54
110 Healy Avenue, Clearfield, PA 16830 US
(814) 371-6100, *Fax:* (814) 371-6100
License: Clearfield, PA held by First Media Radio LLC.
Group Owner: First Media Radio LLC; (acq 1-23-2007; $750,000 with co-located FM)
Nat'l Reps: Dome
Arbitron Metro Market: Clearfield- DuBois,PA *Format:* Oldies
Target Audience: 35 plus.
Francis Rosana, General Manager

WQYX
07-12-1967; 93.1 mhz FM *Hrs Open:* 24; 1.7 kw; 942 ft.; N41 4 5 W78 31 7
110 Healy Avenue, Clearfield, PA 16830 US
(814) 371-6100, *Fax:* (814) 765-6333
License: Clearfield, Clearfield County, PA
Group Owner: First Media Radio LLC
Format: Adult Contemp *Target Audience:* 18-44.
Francis Rosana, General Manager

Coatesville

***WCOJ**
11-29-1949; 1420 khz AM *Hrs Open:* 24
3721 East Lincoln Highwy, Thorndale, PA 19372 US
(215) 345-1570, *Fax:* (215) 345-1946
www.holyspiritradio.org
1570am@holyspiritradio.org
License: Coatesville, PA held by Holy Spirit Radio Foundation Inc.
Nat'l Network: EWTN Radio
Arbitron Metro Market: Chester County, PA *Format:* Christian
Dale Meier, President

***WRTJ**
89.3 mhz FM; 0.001 kw horiz, 0.46 kw vert; 287 ft.; N40 1 26 W75 48 48
2020 N 13th Street, Annenberg Hall, Philadephia, PA 19122 US
(215) 204-8405, *Fax:* (215) 204-7027
www.wrti.org
License: Coatesville, Chester County, PA held by Temple University of The Commonwealth System of Higher Education.
Arbitron Metro Market: Coatesville, PA *Format:* Classical, Jazz
David Conant, General Manager

Columbia

WVZN
01-01-1957; 1580 khz AM *Hrs Open:* 24
244 North Queen Street, Lancaster, PA 17603 US
(717) 823-9300
License: Columbia, PA held by Esfuerzo de Union Cristiana
Arbitron Metro Market: Lancaster, PA
Wilson Cortez, General Manager

Cooperstown

WUUZ
01-01-2002; 107.7 mhz FM *Hrs Open:* 24; 4.5 kw; 377 ft.; N41 29 23 W79 44 7
P.O. Box 738, Ashtabula, OH 44004 US
(814) 724-1111, *Fax:* (814) 333-9628
www.mywuzz.com
radio@zoominternet.net
License: Cooperstown, Venango County, PA held by Forever Broadcasting LLC.
Group Owner: Forever Broadcasting; (acq 7-5-01; $342,000 for CP).
Arbitron Metro Market: Meadville, PA *Format:* Contemporary Hits/Top 40, Adult Contemp
Terry Deitz, General Manager

Corry

WHYP(AM)
04-02-1955; 1370 khz AM *Hrs Open:* 6 AM-11 PM (M-F); 7 AM-11 PM (S);; 1 kw-D, 500 w-N, DA-N; N41 56 10 W79 39 20
Mailing Address: Box 4, Corry, PA 16407
Second Address: 418 N. Center, Corry, PA 16407
(814) 664-8694, *Fax:* (814) 664-8695
License: Corry, Erie County, PA held by Corry Communications Corp.
Nat'l Network: Motor Racing Net; Westwood One; CBS
Population Served: 101,807 *Arbitron Metro Market:* Erie, PA
Format: Classic Rock, Oldies, 84 *Target Audience:* General.
Adv. Rates: 10.25; 10.25; 10.25; 10.25
William Hammond III, President

Coudersport

WFRM
05-01-1953; 600 khz AM; 1 kw-D, ND1; 0.046 kw-N, ND1; N41 45 11 W78 0 3
9 South Main Street, Coudersport, PA 16915 US
(814) 274-8600, *Fax:* (814) 274-0760
gmiller@wfrm.net; radio@wfrm.net,wfrm@usa.net
License: Coudersport, PA held by Farm & Home Broadcasting Co.
Group Owner: Allegheny Mountain Network Stations
Nat'l Network: ABC *Nat'l Reps:* Dome
Format: Country, News, 62, Talk *Special Programming:* Farm 2 hrs wkly *Target Audience:* General.
Gerri Miller, General Sales Mgr

Covington

WDKC
01-01-1994; 101.5 mhz FM; 1.9 kw; 594 ft.; N41 43 25 W77 2 46
Mailing Address: 83 Jacobs Road, Marlboro, MA 01752 US
Second Address: 8767 Rt. 414, Liberty, PA 16930
(570) 662-9000, *Fax:* (570) 324-1015
kc101@sosbbs.com
License: Covington, Tioga County, PA held by Mid-Atlantic Broadcasting Inc.
Arbitron Metro Market: Elmira, NY *Format:* Country *Hrs. of News Programming:* news progmg 3 hrs wkly *No. News Employees:* 1 *Target Audience:* 25-54; 70% female *Adv. Rates:* 12; 8; 9; 5
Thomas Gluszczak, Chairman
Kevin Thomas, CEO
Kevin Gluszczak, General Manager

Cresson

WBRX
11-01-1981; 94.7 mhz FM *Hrs Open:* 24; 0.97 kw; 794 ft.; N40 24 11 W78 31 35
4000 5th Ave., Altoona, PA 16602 US
(814) 943-6112, *Fax:* (814) 944-9782
www.mymix947.com
License: Cresson, Cambria County, PA held by Sounds Good Inc.
Nat'l Network: Westwood One
Arbitron Metro Market: Altoona, PA *Format:* Adult Contemp *Hrs. of News Programming:* news progmg 7 hrs wkly *No. News Employees:* 1 *Target Audience:* 18-54; males
David Barger, General Manager

Curwensville

WOKW
08-01-1989; 102.9 mhz FM; 0.35 kw; 945 ft.; N41 4 29 W78 31 58
Mailing Address: P.O. Box 73, Clearfield, PA 16830 US
Second Address: 712 River Rd., Clearfield, PA 16830
(814) 765-4955, *Fax:* (814) 765-7038
www.wokw.com
news@wokw.com,sales@wokw.com
License: Curwensville, Clearfield County, PA held by Raymark Broadcasting Co. Inc.
TV Affiliate: Adult contemp *Format:* Oldies *Special Programming:* news progmg 14 hrs wkly *Hrs. of News Programming:* 1 *No. News Employees:* 21-54.
Executive Vice President

Dallas

WSJR
05-29-1989; 93.7 mhz FM *Hrs Open:* 24; 1.45 kw; 679 ft.; N41 15 43 W75 58 4 *Rebroadcasts:* Rebroadcasts WCTP(FM) Carbondale 100%
City Center West, 7201 W. Lake Mead Blvd, Las Vegas, NV 89128 US
(570) 824-9000, *Fax:* (570) 820-0520
www.jr937.us
License: Dallas, Luzerne County, PA
Group Owner: Cumulus Media Inc.; (acq 2-4-98; grpsl).
Nat'l Network: CBS *Nat'l Reps:* Roslin
Arbitron Metro Market: Wilkes Barre-Scranton, PA *Format:* Country *Special Programming:* Community affrs one hr wkly *Hrs. of News Programming:* news progmg 3 hrs wkly *No. News Employees:* 1 *Target Audience:* 25-54. *Adv. Rates:* 55; 40; 40; 40
Mark Lindow, Programming Director
Bill Palmeri, Promotions Manager
Erin Evans, Promotions Director

***WCIG**
01-01-2005; 107.7 mhz FM; 2.35 kw; 531 ft.; N41 18 54 W75 53 19 *Rebroadcasts:* Rebroadcasts WCIK(FM) Bath, NY 100%
City Center West, 7201 W. Lake Mead Blvd., Las Vegas, NV 89128 US
(607) 776-4151, *Fax:* (607) 776-6929
www.fln.org
mail@fln.org
License: Dallas, Lackawanna County, PA held by Family Life Ministries Inc.
Group Owner: Family Life Network
Nat'l Network: Salem Radio Network *Wire Services:* Metro Weather Service Inc.
Arbitron Metro Market: Dallas, PA *Format:* Christian *Hrs. of News Programming:* news progmg 14 hrs wkly *No. News Employees:* 3 *Target Audience:* 30-54.
Dick Snavely, CFO and Founder
Rick Snavely, President and CEO
Rick Snavely, Operations Dir
Sammy Carrillo, Program Director/Promotions Director
Bob Price, News Director
Gary Farnham, Engineering Dir
Jim Travis, Chief Engineer
Rob Wood, Information Services Director
Darcie Schwarz, Publicity Manager
Alan Gustafson, Creative Services Director
Dave Best, Business Manager
Sandy Parker, Office Manager / Executive Secretary
Jackie Snavely, Office Assistant

Danville

***WPGM**
06-01-1963; 1570 khz AM; 2.5 kw-D, ND1; 0.221 kw-N, ND1; N40 59 10 W76 37 37
8 E. Mkt. Street, Danville, PA 17821 US
(570) 275-1570, *Fax:* (570) 275-4071
www.wpgm.info
info@wpgm.org
License: Danville, PA held by Montrose Broadcasting Corp.
Group Owner: Montrose Broadcasting Corp.; (acq 1-6-64).
Format: Religious *Target Audience:* General; families
George Vacca, General Sales Mgr

***WPGM-FM**
09-06-1968; 96.7 mhz FM; 0.57 kw; 764 ft.; N40 59 16 W76 32 51
Eight East Market Street, PO Box 236, Danville, PA 17821 US
(570) 275-1570, *Fax:* (570) 275-4071
www.wpgm.info
info@wpgm.org
License: Danville, Montour County, PA held by Montrose Broadcasting Corp.
Group Owner: Montrose Broadcasting Corp.
Bob Conti, Operations Dir
Tom Zahradnik, General Manager
Joe Hunter, Programming Director

Doylestown

WISP
01-01-1948; 1570 khz AM *Hrs Open:* 24

Mailing Address: 977 Baron Drive, Yardley, PA 19067 US
Second Address: 40 Rickerts Rd., Doyelstown, PA 18901
(215) 345-1570, *Fax:* (215) 345-1946
www.holyspiritradio.org
1570am@holyspiritradio.org
License: Doylestown, PA held by Holy Spirit Radio Foundation Inc.
Arbitron Metro Market: Philadelphia *Format:* Religious *Hrs. of News Programming:* News progmg 14 hrs wkly *Target Audience:* General.
Dale Meier, CEO

Du Bois

WCED
02-01-1941; 1420 khz AM *Hrs Open:* 24
P.O. Box 1087, Dubois, PA 15801 US
(814) 375-5260, *Fax:* (814) 375-5262
www.1420wced.com
License: Du Bois, PA held by WCED Radio LLC.
Group Owner: Priority Communications; acq 11-28-2003; $150,000).
Nat'l Network: ABC; ESPN Radio
Arbitron Metro Market: DuBois, PA *Format:* News, News/Talk, 86 *Hrs. of News Programming:* news progmg 20 hrs wkly *No. News Employees:* 1
Beth Walters, Operations Dir
Jay Philippone, General Manager
Lori Lewis, Station Manager
Lindsey Schoening, Programming Director
Lindsey Schoening, News Director
Al Lockwood, Engineering Dir
Polly Slie, Traffic Manager

***WCOH-FM**
11-12-1975; 107.3 mhz FM *Hrs Open:* 24; 50 kw; 499 ft.; N41 11 28 W78 41 27
28 W. Scribner Ave., Du Bois, PA 15801 US
(607) 776-4151, *Fax:* (607) 776-6929
www.fln.org
mail@fln.org
License: Du Bois, Clearfield County, PA held by Family Life Ministries Inc.
Nat'l Reps: Salem Wire Services: AP
Arbitron Metro Market: DuBois, PA *Format:* Christian, Religious *Special Programming:* Children 2 hrs wkly, Southern Gospel 5 hrs wkly, Christian rock 5 hrs wkly *Hrs. of News Programming:* News progmg 6 hrs wkly*Target Audience:* 25-54; women
Daniel Brownlee, President
Gerald Meloon, Operations Dir
Dan Kennard, General Manager
Sammy Carrillo, Promotions Director

WOWQ
01-01-1948; 102.1 mhz FM *Hrs Open:* 24; 28 kw; 663 ft.; N41 2 43 W78 42 11
P.O. Box 1087, Dubois, PA 15801 US
(814) 371-6100, *Fax:* (814) 371-7724
www.q102radio.fm
q102@adelphia.net
License: Du Bois, Clearfield County, PA held by First Media Radio LLC.
Group Owner: First Media Radio LLC; (acq 4-10-2002; $4.2 million with WCED(AM) DuBois)
Format: Country *Hrs. of News Programming:* news progmg 10 hrs wkly *No. News Employees:* 1 *Target Audience:* 18 plus.
Alex Kolobielski, CEO
F. Rosana, General Manager

Dushore

WNKZ
08-01-1998; 103.9 mhz FM *Hrs Open:* 24; 4.3 kw; 202 ft.; N41 26 6 W76 28 28
P.O. Box 45, Eagles Mere, PA 17731 US
(570) 928-7200, *Fax:* (570) 928-2100
www.cozyradio.com
contact_us@cozy.com
License: Dushore, Sullivan County, PA held by Geos Communications.
Group Owner: Geos Communications; (acq 8-1-2008)
Arbitron Metro Market: Williamsport, PA *Format:* Adult Contemp *Hrs. of News Programming:* News progmg 4 hrs wkly *Target Audience:* 25-54; adults *Adv. Rates:* 12; 10; 12; 8
Ben Smith, General Manager
Cindi McCarty, General Sales Mgr
Kevin Fitzgerald, Engineering Dir

***WYSP**
08-01-1971; 88.1 mhz FM; 0.1 kw; -74 ft.; N41 31 33 W76 24 35 US
(215) 625-9460, *Fax:* (215) 625-6560
www.94wysp.com
info@94wysp.com
License: Dushore, Philadelphia County, PA held by CBS Radio East Inc.
Group Owner: CBS Radio; (acq 11-1-81; grpsl;
Nat'l Network: Westwood One *Nat'l Reps:* CBS Radio
Arbitron Metro Market: Philadelphia
Peter Kleiner, General Manager
Gil Edwards, Programming Director

East Nottingham

***WZXE**
88.3 mhz FM; 1 w horiz, 540 w vert; Ant 453 ft; N39 44 00 W75 57 56
Box 186, Sellersville, PA
(215) 721-2141, *Fax:* (215) 721-9811
www.wordfm.org
License: East Nottingham, Chester County, PA held by Four Rivers Community Broadcasting Corp.
Charles Loughery, President
Meg Sabulsky, Operations Dir
David Baker, General Manager
Meg Sabulsky, Programming Director
William Dunn, Promotions Manager
Charles Loughery, Engineering Dir

East Stroudsburg

***WESS**
03-10-1971; 90.3 mhz FM; 1 kw; -121 ft.; N40 59 50 W75 10 22
Communications Center, East Stroudsburg, PA 18301 US
(570) 422-3133, *Fax:* (570) 422-3777
www.esu.edu/wess
wess@po-box.esu.edu
License: East Stroudsburg, Monroe County, PA held by East Stroudsburg University Board of Trustees/Student Activities Association.
Arbitron Metro Market: East Stroudsburg, PA *Format:* Alternative, Sports, 94 *Special Programming:* Class 4 hrs, educ 7 hrs, jazz 6 hrs, news/talk 6 hrs,oldies 8 hrs wkly
Jillian Kane, Station Manager
Jennifer Haney, Promotions Manager
Nicholas Frey, News Director

Easton

WCTO
01-01-1948; 96.1 mhz FM *Hrs Open:* 24; 50 kw; 499 ft.; N40 35 55 W75 25 12
City Center West, 7201 W. Lake Mead Blvd., Las Vegas, NV 89128 US
(610) 266-760, *Fax:* (610) 231-0400
www.catcountry96.fm
studio@catcountry96.com
License: Easton, Northampton County, PA
Group Owner: Cumulus Media Inc.
Nat'l Reps: Christal; Katz Radio
Arbitron Metro Market: Allentown-Bethlehem, PA *Format:* Country
Shelly Easton, Operations Dir
John Fraunfelter, General Manager
Elizabeth Penbleton, General Sales Mgr

WEEX
05-01-1956; 1230 khz AM; 0.84 kw-D, DAD; 1 kw-N, DAD; N40 42 30 W75 13 0
200 Concord Plaza, Suite 600, San Antonio, TX 78216 US
(610) 258-6155, *Fax:* (610) 258-6292
www.espnlv.com
tomf@espnlv.com
License: Easton, PA held by Nassau Broadcasting II LLC.
Group Owner: Nassau Broadcasting Partners L.P.; (acq 1-31-01; grpsl).
Nat'l Network: ESPN Radio *Nat'l Reps:* Katz Radio *Regional Reps:* Glenn Jones
Arbitron Metro Market: Easton, PA *Format:* Sports *Target Audience:* 18-49; men
Rick Musselman, General Manager
Pat Lincoln, General Sales Mgr
Tom Fallon, Programming Director

WEST
04-01-2006; 1400 khz AM *Hrs Open:* 24; 1 kw-U, ND1; N40 40 23 W75 12 30 *Rebroadcasts:* WHOL-AM 100% Simulcast
300 East Rock Rd, Allentown, PA 18103 US
(610) 434-4801, *Fax:* (484) 223-0088
www.hola1600.com
matthewb@whol1600.com
License: Easton, PA held by WHOL Radio Inc.
Arbitron Metro Market: Allentown, PA *Format:* Spanish *Hrs. of News Programming:* 5 hrs per week *No. News Employees:* 8 *Target Audience:* Hispanic - 25 - 54 *Adv. Rates:* $38 - $52 Gross
Matthew J. Braccili, Owner/President
Jeffrey Maddox, Operations/Traffic Manager
Matthew Braccili, General Manager
Delia Torres, General Sales Mgr
Tony Rodriguez, Programming Director
Jorge Antonely, News Director
Mick Rapper,Chief Engineer
J. Miguel, Music Director
Jason Lee, Internet Technology
Victor Martinez, Programming Consultant

***WJRH**
03-01-1953; 104.9 mhz FM *Hrs Open:* 15; 0.008 kw; 23 ft.; N40 41 53 W75 12 30
115 Farinon College Cent, Ofc. of Stud. Activities, Easton, PA 18042 US
(610) 330-5316, *Fax:* (610) 250-5318
www.wjrh.org
info@lafayette.com
License: Easton, Northampton County, PA held by Lafayette College.
Arbitron Metro Market: Allentown-Bethlehem, PA *Format:* Variety/Diverse *Special Programming:* Jazz 9 hrs, reggae 6 hrs, metal 6 hrs, Sp 6 hrs, c *Hrs. of News Programming:* news progmg 6 hrs wkly *No. News Employees:* 3 *Target Audience:* General; college students & community
Sergey Tosninski, General Manager
Brian Hertz, Programming Director
Fred Lott, Chief Engineer

WODE-FM
06-01-1950; 99.9 mhz FM; 50 kw; 449 ft.; N40 42 30 W75 13 0
200 Concord Plaza, Suite 600, San Antonio, TX 78216 US
(610) 258-6155, *Fax:* (610) 253-3384
License: Easton, Northampton County, PA held by Nassau Broadcasting II LLC.
Group Owner: Nassau Broadcasting Partners L.P.; (acq 1-31-2001; grpsl)
Nat'l Reps: Katz Radio *Regional Reps:* Glenn Jones
Arbitron Metro Market: Allentown-Bethl *TV Affiliate:* Classic hits

Ebensburg

WRKW
07-15-1962; 99.1 mhz FM; 50 kw; 499 ft.; N40 24 41 W78 46 29
City Center West, 7201 W. Lake Mead Blvd, Las Vegas, NV 89128 US
(814) 255-4186, *Fax:* (814) 255-6145
www.rocky99.com
info@hot92fm.net
License: Ebensburg, Cambria County, PA held by Forever Broadcasting LLC.
Group Owner: Forever Broadcasting; (acq 5-1-2005; $2.73 million with WJHT(FM) Johnstown).
Verla Price, General Manager
Tina Perry, General Sales Mgr
Mike Stevens, Programming Director
Rick Shepard, News Director
Jim Boxler, Chief Engineer

WRDD
05-25-1961; 1580 khz AM *Hrs Open:* Sunrise-sunset; 0.25 kw-C, ND1; 1 kw-D, ND1; ND1; 0.004; N40 29 33 W78 42 54
Mailing Address: P.O. Box 371, Kittanning, PA 16201 US
Second Address: 104 S. Center St., Ebensburg, PA 15931
, *Fax:* (814) 471-0282
whpa@verizon.net
License: Ebensburg, PA held by Vernal Enterprises Inc.
Group Owner: Vernal Enterprises Inc.; acq 3-19-97; $20,000 with WNCC(AM) Northern Cambria).
Nat'l Network: USA
Format: News, News/Talk, 86 *Hrs. of News Programming:* News progmg 4 hrs wkly *Target Audience:* General; church goers
Denny Pompa, President
Larry Schrecongost, General Manager

Edinboro

***WFSE**
04-03-1979; 88.9 mhz FM *Hrs Open:* 24; 3 kw; 299 ft.; N41 52 38 W80 10 39
Faculty Annex, 110 Edinboro University, Edinboro, PA 16444 US
(814) 732-2641, *Fax:* (814) 732-2270
www.wfse.synthasite.com
wfse@edinboro.edu
License: Edinboro, Erie County, PA held by Edinboro University.
Arbitron Metro Market: Erie, PA *Format:* Alternative *Special Programming:* Football & basketball, Black 15 hrs, relg 4 hrs, l

Hrs. of News Programming: News progmg 18 hrs wkly *Target Audience:* 18-25; collegestudents with community interest
Terrence Warburton, Chairman
Dr. Frank Pogue, CEO
Glenn Thompson, General Manager
Richard Smith, General Sales Mgr
Brian Hagberg, Programming Director
Andy Alm, News Director
Steve Caldwell, Music Director
Mike Frank,Production Director
Tad Wissel, Konstantinos Fekos
Public Relations Director

WXTA
10-15-1988; 97.9 mhz FM *Hrs Open:* 24; 10 kw; 505 ft.; N41 57 59 W80 6 40
50 E. River Center Boulevard, Suite 180, Covington, KY 14011 US
(814) 864-4835, *Fax:* (814) 868-1876
www.country98wxta.com
License: Edinboro, Erie County, PA
Group Owner: Cumulus Media Inc.; (acq 5-12-2004; grpsl).
Nat'l Reps: Katz Radio
Arbitron Metro Market: Erie, PA *Format:* Country *Target Audience:* Adults; 25-64 *Adv. Rates:* 55; 50; 52; 15
Farid Suleman, CEO
Jim Riley, General Manager
Stephanie Lancaster, General Sales Mgr
Fred Horton, Programming Director
Dave Benson, News Director

Elizabethtown

WPDC
05-01-1958; 1600 khz AM *Hrs Open:* 24
939 Radio Road, Elizabethtown, PA 17022 US
(717) 367-1600
teamespn@earthlink.net
License: Elizabethtown, PA held by JVJ Communications Inc.
Nat'l Network: ESPN Radio
Arbitron Metro Market: Lancaster, PA *Format:* Sports *Hrs. of News Programming:* News progmg 10 hrs wkly *Target Audience:* 25-54; men *Adv. Rates:* 25; 25; 25; 18
Vincent Grande, President
Bill Wilson, Operations Dir
Sam Conrad, Operations Director

Elizabethville

WYGL-FM
12-07-1989; 100.5 mhz FM *Hrs Open:* 24; 1.2 kw; 515 ft.; N40 37 24 W76 49 54
P.O. Box 90, Rt 204 State School Rd., Selinsgrove, PA 17870 US
(570) 374-8819, *Fax:* (570) 374-7444
www.b983.com
bigcountryrequest@hotmail.com
License: Elizabethville, Dauphin County, PA held by MMP License LLC.
Group Owner: MAX Media L.L.C.; (acq 10-17-03; grpsl).
Nat'l Network: USA
Arbitron Metro Market: Elizabethville, PA *Format:* Country *Hrs. of News Programming:* news progmg 8 hrs wkly *No. News Employees:* 1 *Target Audience:* 25-54.
John Trinder, President
Scott Richards, Operations Dir
Greg Adair, General Sales Mgr
Ted Koppen, Chief Engineer

Ellwood City

WKPL
07-04-1968; 92.1 mhz FM; 2.5 kw; 512 ft.; N40 46 9 W80 16 56
50 E. Rivercenter Blvd, #1200, Covington, KY 41011 US
(724) 378-1271, *Fax:* (412) 279-5500
www.picklefm.com
License: Ellwood City, Lawrence County, PA held by Keymarket Licenses LLC.
Group Owner: Keymarket Communications LLC; (acq 6-30-2004; grpsl).
Format: Oldies
Edward Czelada, President
Jennifer Czelada, General Manager
Dave Russell, Programming Director
Tim Miller, Promotions Manager
Katie McGavitt, Production
Joyce Haywood, Billing
Melissa Kasula, Production

Emporium

WLEM
03-02-1958; 1250 khz AM *Hrs Open:* 16; 2.5 kw-D, ND1; 0.03 kw-N, ND1; N41 30 22 W78 13 26
51 West Long Avenue, Dubois, PA 15801 US
(814) 486-3712, *Fax:* (814) 486-1772
www.theriver989.com
License: Emporium, PA held by Salter Communications Inc.
Nat'l Network: Westwood One *Nat'l Reps:* Commercial Media Sales
Format: Country *Hrs. of News Programming:* news progmg 3 hrs wkly *No. News Employees:* 1 *Target Audience:* 25-65.
John Salter, President
Gary Mitchell, Operations Dir
J. Philippone, General Manager

WQKY
05-20-1985; 98.9 mhz FM; 2 kw; 548 ft.; N41 29 32 W78 15 19
51 West Long Avenue, Dubois, PA 15801 US
(814) 486-3712, *Fax:* (814) 486-1772
License: Emporium, Cameron County, PA
Format: Adult Contemp
Roger Haddon, Jr, CEO
Tricia Cease, General Sales Mgr
Drew Kelly, Programming Director
Matt Farrand, News Director
Rob Senter, Music Director

Ephrata

WIOV-FM
11-09-1962; 105.1 mhz FM; 25 kw; 702 ft.; N40 10 30 W76 9 31
P.O. Box 3353, Evansville, IN 47732 US
(717) 738-1191, *Fax:* (717) 738-1661
www.wiov.com
dick.raymond@citcomm.com
License: Ephrata, Lancaster County, PA
Group Owner: Cumulus Media Inc.; (acq 5-12-2004; grpsl).
Nat'l Reps: McGavren Guild
Arbitron Metro Market: Lancaster, PA *Format:* Country
Mitch Carroll, General Sales Mgr
Dick Raymond, Programming Director
Carrie Rey, News Director

***WRTL**
01-01-2000; 90.7 mhz FM *Hrs Open:* 24; 0.001 kw horiz, 0.65 kw vert; 869 ft.; N40 19 22 W76 11 52 *Rebroadcasts:* Rebroadcasts WRTI(FM) Philadelphia 100%.
Annenberg Hall (011-00), Philadelphia, PA 19122 US
(414) 778-5780, *Fax:* (414) 778-5785
www.wrtl.org
admin@wrtl.org
License: Ephrata, Lancaster County, PA held by Temple University of The Commonwealth System of Higher Education.
Nat'l Network: NPR
Arbitron Metro Market: Ephrata, PA *Format:* Classical, Jazz
Dave Conant, General Manager

Erie

***WEFR**
03-01-1992; 88.1 mhz FM *Hrs Open:* 24; 0.63 kw; 430 ft.; N41 57 59 W80 6 40
Mailing Address: 4135 Northgate Blvd.,#1, Sacramento, CA 95834 US
Second Address: 290 Hegenberger Rd., Oakland, CA 94621
1-(800)-543-1495, *Fax:* (916) 641-8238
www.familyradio.com
familyradio@familyradio.org
License: Erie, Erie County, PA held by Family Stations Inc.
Group Owner: Family Stations Inc.
Arbitron Metro Market: Erie, PA *Format:* Christian, Religious *Target Audience:* General.
Harold Camping, President
John Rorvik, Operations Dir

***WERG**
12-01-1972; 90.5 mhz FM *Hrs Open:* 24; 2.75 kw; 374 ft.; N42 2 34 W80 3 57
University Square, Erie, PA 16541 US
(814) 459-9374, *Fax:* (814) 871-7652
www.wergfm.com
womer003@gannon.edu
License: Erie, Erie County, PA held by Gannon University
Arbitron Metro Market: Erie, PA *Format:* Alternative *Special Programming:* Sp 3 hrs, Polka 4 hrs wkly *Hrs. of News Programming:* News progmg 3 hrs wkly *Target Audience:* 18-plus
Chet LaPrice, Operations Dir
Alex Womer, General Manager
Rob Lopez, Programming Director
Connor Sondel, Promotions Manager
Allison Kessler, News Director
Cristianne Johnson, Music Director
Zack Borland, Sports Director
MorganMurphy, Production Director
Deb Carlson, Underwriting Coordinator
Vanessa Cherry, Webmaster
Morgan Murphy, Secretary

WXBB
09-01-1993; 94.7 mhz FM *Hrs Open:* 24; 1.7 kw; 614 ft.; N42 2 26 W80 4 5
4216 Sterrettania Road, Erie, PA 16506 US
(814) 461-1000, *Fax:* (814) 874-0011
www.947bobfm.com
License: Erie, Erie County, PA held by Connoisseur Media of Erie LLC.
Group Owner: Connoisseur Media LLC; (acq 3-30-2006; grpsl)
Arbitron Metro Market: Erie, PA *Format:* Adult Contemp
Rick Rambaldo, General Manager

WFNN
01-01-1947; 1330 khz AM
One Broadcast Park, Erie, PA 16428 US
(814) 461-1000, *Fax:* (814) 874-0011
www.sportsradio1330.com
License: Erie, PA held by Connoisseur Media of Erie LLC.
Group Owner: Connoisseur Media LLC; (acq 3-31-2006; grpsl)
Nat'l Network: Fox Sports *Nat'l Reps:* Katz Radio
Arbitron Metro Market: Erie, PA *Format:* Sports
David Bevins, General Manager

WQHZ
10-15-1951; 102.3 mhz FM *Hrs Open:* 24; 1.7 kw; 614 ft.; N42 2 25 W80 4 8
4216 Sterrettania Road, Erie, PA 16506 US
(814) 868-5355, *Fax:* (814) 868-1876
www.z1023online.com
License: Erie, Erie County, PA
Group Owner: Cumulus Media Inc.; (acq 5-12-2004; grpsl).
Nat'l Reps: Katz Radio
Arbitron Metro Market: Erie, PA *Format:* Classic Rock *No. News Employees:* 1 *Target Audience:* 25-54; Adults *Adv. Rates:* 50; 45; 45; 20
Farid Suleman, CEO
Jim Riley, General Manager
Stephanie Lancaster, General Sales Mgr
Adam Reese, Programming Director
Dave Benson, News Director

WJET
01-01-1951; 1400 khz AM *Hrs Open:* 24; 1 kw-U, ND1; N42 7 28 W80 3 54
One Broadcast Park, Erie, PA 16428 US
(814) 461-1000, *Fax:* (814) 874-0011
www.jetradio1400.com
jet1400@jet1400.com
License: Erie, PA held by Connoisseur Media of Erie LLC.
Group Owner: Connoisseur Media LLC; (acq 3-31-2006; grpsl).
Regional Network: Radio Pa.
Arbitron Metro Market: Erie, PA *Format:* News, News/Talk, 86 *No. News Employees:* 1 *Target Audience:* 35 plus; middle to upper middle income, business owners, upscale
Rick Rambaldo, General Manager

***WMCE**
02-02-1989; 88.5 mhz FM *Hrs Open:* 24; 750 w; Ant 499 ft; N42 05 25 W79 56 37
501 E. 38th St., Erie, PA 16546
(814) 824-2260,(814) 824-2261, *Fax:* (814) 824-2590
www.mercyhurst.edu
wshannon@mercyhurst.edu
License: Erie, Erie County, PA held by Mercyhurst College.
Nat'l Network: AP Radio
Population Served: 280,000 *Arbitron Metro Market:* Erie, PA
Special Programming: Pol 3 hrs, Ger 4 hrs, Sp 3 hrs, jazz 4 hrs wkly *Hrs. of News Programming:* News progmg 6 hrs wkly
Target Audience: General;Adults 45+ *Adv. Rates:* 5; 5; 5; 3
Greg Granger, President
William Shannon, General Manager

WPSE
04-21-1935; 1450 khz AM *Hrs Open:* 24; 1 kw-U, ND1; N42 8 11 W80 2 25
5091 Station Rd, Erie, PA 16563 US
(814) 898-6495,(814) 898-6491
License: Erie, PA held by Board of Trustees, Pennsylvania State University.
Nat'l Network: CBS; Westwood One
Arbitron Metro Market: Erie, PA *Format:* News, Sports *Target Audience:* General.
Ron Slomski, General Manager

***WQLN-FM**
01-07-1973; 91.3 mhz FM *Hrs Open:* 24; 35 kw; 499 ft.; N42 2 31 W80 3 57
8425 Peach St, Erie, PA 16509 US
(814) 864-3001, *Fax:* (814) 864-4077
www.wqln.org
dmiller@wqin.org
License: Erie, Erie County, PA held by Public Broadcasting of Northwest Pennsylvania Inc.
Nat'l Network: NPR; PRI
Arbitron Metro Market: Erie, PA *TV Affiliate:* *WQLN(TV) affil. *Format:* Classical, Jazz, 60 *Special Programming:* Sp one hr, pub affrs 5 hrs, new age 2 hrs, call-in show 3 hrs wkly *Hrs. of News Programming:* newsprogmg 24 hrs wkly *No. News Employees:* 1 *Target Audience:* General.
Dwight Miller, President
Cindy Spizarny, Operations Dir
Sue Allen, Programming Director
Kim Young, News Director

WRIE
01-01-1941; 1260 khz AM *Hrs Open:* 24; 5 kw-D, DA2; 5 kw-N, DA2; N42 3 18 W80 2 24
50 E. River Center Boulevard, Suite 180, Covington, KY 14011 US
(814) 868-5355, *Fax:* (814) 868-1876
License: Erie, PA
Group Owner: Cumulus Media Inc.; (acq 5-12-2004; grpsl)
Nat'l Network: ESPN Radio *Nat'l Reps:* Katz Radio
Arbitron Metro Market: Erie, PA *Format:* Sports, Talk *Adv. Rates:* 25; 20; 22; 10
Farid Suleman, CEO
Marcia Diehl, Operations Dir
Gary Spurgeon, General Manager
Donna Palowitz, General Sales Mgr
Ron Arlen, Programming Director
Tina Achhammer, Promotions Manager
Dave Benson, News Director
Rick Pogson, ChiefEngineer
Judy Ellis, COO

WRTS
05-01-1969; 103.7 mhz FM *Hrs Open:* 24; 50 kw; 499 ft.; N42 5 25 W79 56 37
One Broadcast Park, North East, PA 16428 US
(814) 461-1000, *Fax:* (814) 455-6000
www.star104.com
star104@star104.com
License: Erie, Erie County, PA held by Connoisseur Media of Erie LLC.
Group Owner: Connoisseur Media LLC; (acq 3-30-2006; grpsl).
Arbitron Metro Market: Erie, PA *Format:* Contemporary Hits/Top 40 *Special Programming:* PSA one hr wkly *Hrs. of News Programming:* news progmg one hr wkly *No. News Employees:* 1 *Target Audience:* 25-54.
Richard Rambaldo, General Manager

WXKC
01-01-1949; 99.9 mhz FM *Hrs Open:* 24; 50 kw; 492 ft.; N42 5 24 W79 57 12
50 E. River Center Boulevard, Suite 180, Covington, KY 14011 US
(814) 868-5355, *Fax:* (814) 868-1876
www.classy100.com
License: Erie, Erie County, PA
Arbitron Metro Market: Erie, PA *Format:* Adult Contemp *No. News Employees:* 1 *Target Audience:* Adults; 35-64 *Adv. Rates:* 45; 46; 45; 15
Heather Rose, News Director

Everett

WZSK
03-15-1963; 1040 khz AM *Hrs Open:* 0600 - 1815; 4 kw-C, NDD; 10 kw-D, NDD; Non-Directional; N40 0 26 W78 21 44
Mailing Address: P. O. Box 187, Everett, PA 15537 US
Second Address: 151 E 1st Ave, Everett, PA 15537-1351
(814) 652-2600, *Fax:* (814) 652-9347
wzsk@penn.com
License: Everett, PA held by New Millennium Communications Group Inc.
Nat'l Network: ABC Information & Entertainment; Jones Radio Networks; Premiere Radio Networks; Radio America *Regional Network:* Radio Pa. *Regional Reps:* Dome & Associates
Arbitron Metro Market: Johnstown, PA *Format:* News, News/Talk, 86 *Hrs. of News Programming:* news progmg 10 hrs wkly *No. News Employees:* 1 *Target Audience:* 25-54
Shane Imler, President
John Imler, General Manager

WSKE
03-15-1988; 104.3 mhz FM *Hrs Open:* 24; 0.82 kw; 886 ft.; N40 0 11 W78 23 58
Mailing Address: P.O. Box 187, Everett, PA 15537 US
Second Address: 151 E 1st Ave, Everett, PA 15537-1351
(814) 652-2600, *Fax:* (814) 652-9347
wske@penn.com
License: Everett, Bedford County, PA held by New Millennium Communications Group Inc.
Nat'l Network: ABC Information & Entertainment; Jones Radio Networks *Regional Network:* Radio Pa. *Regional Reps:* Dome & Associates
Format: Country *Special Programming:* Bluegrass, Classic Country, Southern Gospel *Hrs. of News Programming:* news progmg 7 hrs wkly *No. News Employees:* 1 *Target Audience:* 25-54.
Shane Imler, President
John Imler, General Manager

Fairview

WTWF
10-01-2001; 93.9 mhz FM; 6 kw; 299 ft.; N42 1 36 W80 7 18
1300 N. 17th St, 11th Fl, Rosslyn, VA 22209 US
(814) 461-1000, *Fax:* (814) 874-0011
www.939thewolf.com
us939@us939.com
License: Fairview, Erie County, PA held by Connoisseur Media of Erie LLC.
Group Owner: Connoisseur Media LLC; (acq 3-30-2006; grpsl).
Arbitron Metro Market: Erie, PA *Format:* Country
Richard Rambaldo, General Manager

Fallon Station

KZTI(FM)
105.3 mhz FM; 100 kw horiz; 600 meters; N39 54 46 W118 55 18
149 Penn Avenue, Scranton, PA 18503
(570) 349-9103, *Fax:* (570) 348-9109
License: Fallon Station, Churchill County, NV held by Shamrock Communications Inc
William R Lynett, President

Farmington Township

***WCOP**
106.1 mhz FM; 3.2 kw; 443 ft.; N41 26 31 W79 26 40 US
(607) 776-4151
www.fln.org
License: Farmington Township, Clarion County, PA held by World Radio Link Inc.
Group Owner: World Radio Link Inc.
Arbitron Metro Market: Farmington, PA *Format:* Christian
Rick Snavely, CEO
Sammy Carrillo, Promotions Director
Bob Price, News Director
Jim Travis, Engineering Dir
Jeremy Hill, Chief Engineer
Jeff Harmon, Chief Operating Officer
Kevin VanBuren, Production Director
Cecil Van Houten,Radio Operations Manager
Dick Snavely, Founder / CFO

Farrell

WLOA
10-03-1954; 1470 khz AM
7621 Little Avenue, Ste 506, Charlotte, NC 28266 US
(330) 394-7700, *Fax:* (330) 394-7701
License: Farrell, PA held by Beacon Broadcasting Inc.
Group Owner: Beacon Broadcasting Inc.; (acq 10-4-2005; $295,000)
Arbitron Metro Market: Youngstown-Warren, OH *Format:* Country
Estuardo Rodriguez, General Manager

Folsom

***WRSD**
01-05-1983; 94.9 mhz FM; 0.014 kw; 20 ft.; N39 53 12 W75 20 1
1001 Morton Ave., Folsom, PA 19033 US
(610) 534-1900, *Fax:* (610) 461-7083
License: Folsom, Delaware County, PA held by Ridley School District.
Format: Adult Contemp, Variety/Diverse
Kevin Hitchens, General Manager

Forest City

WQFM
10-31-1973; 100.1 mhz FM *Hrs Open:* 24; 0.75 kw; 935 ft.; N41 35 35 W75 25 56 *Rebroadcasts:* Simulcast with WQFN(FM) Forest City
149 Penn Avenue, Scranton, PA 18503 US
(570) 346-6555, *Fax:* (570) 346-6038
www.921qfm.com
tbass@shamrocknepa.com
License: Forest City, Luzerne County, PA held by The Scranton Times L.P.
Group Owner: Shamrock Communications Inc.; (acq 8-10-94).
Nat'l Reps: Roslin
Arbitron Metro Market: Wilkes Barre-Scranton, PA *Format:* Adult Contemp *Special Programming:* Pol 3 hrs wkly *Hrs. of News Programming:* news progmg 5 hrs wkly *No. News Employees:* 1 *Target Audience:* 25-54.
William Lynett, CEO
Jim Loftus, General Manager

WQFN(FM)
01-01-2000; 100.1 mhz FM; 750 w; Ant 935 ft; N41 35 35 W75 25 56 *Rebroadcasts:* Simulcast with WQFM(FM) Nanticoke
149 Penn Ave., 5th Floor, Scranton, PA 18503
(570) 771-8484, *Fax:* (570) 346-6038
www.nepasespnradio.com
tbass@shamrocknepa.com
License: Forest City, Susquehanna County, PA held by The Scranton Times L.P.
Group Owner: Shamrock Communications Inc.; (acq 3-23-2000).
Population Served: 75,995 *Arbitron Metro Market:* Scranton, PA *Format:* Adult Contemp *Target Audience:* 35-64; adults
William Lynett, CEO
Sean O'Mealy, General Manager
Dave Mehall, Sales Manager
Mark Hoover, Promotions Manager
Kevin Fitzgerald, Chief Engineer
Janice Dowdell, Business Manager
Mari Olshefski, Traffic & Continuity Director
DonnaRyan, Traffic
Jim Morris, National Sales Manager
Judy Haudenschield, Account Executive
Dan Kosloski, Account Executive

Franklin

***WAWN**
01-01-1998; 89.5 mhz FM; 2 kw; 315 ft.; N41 23 39 W79 46 20
P O Drawer 2440, Tupelo, MS 38803 US
(603) 668-6470
www.rocksthebighorns.com
License: Franklin, Venango County, PA held by American Family Association.
Group Owner: American Family Radio
Arbitron Metro Market: Cody WY
Steven Silberberg, President

WFRA
04-13-1958; 1450 khz AM *Hrs Open:* 6 AM-midnight; 0.99 kw-U, ND1; N41 23 30 W79 48 41
P.O. Box 908, Franklin, PA 16323 US
(814) 432-2188, *Fax:* (814) 437-9372
radio@zoominternet.com
License: Franklin, PA held by Forever Broadcasting LLC.
Group Owner: Forever Broadcasting; (acq 7-20-2000; grpsl)
Format: Adult Contemp, News, 84 *Hrs. of News Programming:* news progmg 12 hrs wkly *No. News Employees:* 1 *Target Audience:* 45 plus.
Carol Logan, President
Terry Deitz, General Manager
Tim Snyder, Programming Director
Lynn Deppen, Engineering Dir
Tim Shaw, Sports Commentator

WHMJ
03-05-1971; 99.3 mhz FM *Hrs Open:* 6 AM-midnight; 7.3 kw; 600 ft.; N41 26 16 W79 55 29
P. O. Box 908, Franklin, PA 16323 US
(814) 432-2188, *Fax:* (814) 437-9372
radio@zoominternet.com
License: Franklin, Venango County, PA
Group Owner: Forever Broadcasting
Format: Adult Contemp *Hrs. of News Programming:* News progmg 4 hrs wkly *Target Audience:* 18-44.
Tim Snyder, Promotions Manager
Tim Shaw, News Director

Freeland

WKRZ
01-01-1947; 98.5 mhz FM; 8.7 kw; 1171 ft.; N41 11 56 W75 49 6
Rebroadcasts: Rebroadcasts WKRZ(FM) Tobyhanna 100%
10706 Beaver Dam Road, Cockeysville, MD 21030 US
(570) 883-9850, *Fax:* (570) 883-9851
www.wkrz.com
info@wkrz.com
License: Freeland, Luzerne County, PA held by Entercom Scranton Wilkes-Barre License LLC.
Group Owner: Entercom Communications Corp.; (acq 12-13-99; grpsl).
Arbitron Metro Market: Wilkes Barre-Scranton, PA *Format:* Contemporary Hits/Top 40 *Target Audience:* 19-54; women
Jim Rising, Operations Dir
John Burkavage, General Manager
Ryan Flynn, General Sales Mgr
Tias Schuster, Programming Director
Lamar Smith, Chief Engineer
Elizabeth Masich, Music Director

Galeton

***WCOG-FM**
01-01-1996; 100.7 mhz FM; 7.7 kw; 492 ft.; N41 39 36 W77 38 2
Rebroadcasts: Rebroadcasts WCIK(FM) Bath, NY 100%
Mailing Address: P.O. Box 506, Bath, NY 14810 US
Second Address: 7634 Campbell Creek Rd., Bath, NY 14810
(607) 776-4151, *Fax:* (607) 776-6929
www.fln.org
mail@fln.org
License: Galeton, Potter County, PA held by Family Life Ministries Inc.
Group Owner: Family Life Network; (acq 10-1-96; $20,130).
Nat'l Network: Salem Radio Network *Wire Services:* Metro Weather Service Inc.
Arbitron Metro Market: Bath,NY *Format:* Christian *Hrs. of News Programming:* news progmg 14 hrs wkly *No. News Employees:* 3 *Target Audience:* 30-54; general
Rick Snavely, President
Sammy Carrillo, Programming Director
Sammy Carrillo, Promotions Manager
Jim Travis, Chief Engineer

Gettysburg

WGET
08-27-1950; 1320 khz AM *Hrs Open:* 24; 1 kw-D, DA2; 0.5 kw-N, DA2; N39 50 30 W77 13 25
P.O. Box 3179, 1560 Fairfield Road, Gettysburg, PA 17325 US
(717) 334-3101, *Fax:* (717) 334-5822
www.foxsports1320.com
License: Gettysburg, PA held by Times and News Publishing Co.
Nat'l Network: CBS *Regional Network:* Radio Pa. *Wire Services:* AP
Arbitron Metro Market: York, PA *Format:* Adult Contemp, News, 84 *Hrs. of News Programming:* news progmg 40 hrs wkly *No. News Employees:* 3 *Target Audience:* 35-64; mainstream mature adults
Philip Jones, CEO
Cindy Ford, President
Dave Jackson, Operations Dir
John Martin, General Sales Mgr
Kim Alexander, News Director
Daryl Hancock, Engineering Dir
Larry Rhoten, Special Events Coordinator
Shannon Weishaar, TrafficManager

WGTY
07-05-1962; 107.7 mhz FM *Hrs Open:* 24; 16 kw horiz, 15.5 kw vert; 850 ft.; N39 51 23 W76 56 57
PO Box 3179, 1560 Fairfield Road, Gettysburg, PA 17325 US
(717) 334-3101, *Fax:* (717) 334-5822
www.wgty.com
info@wgty.com
License: Gettysburg, Adams County, PA held by Times and News Publishing Co.
Wire Services: AP
Arbitron Metro Market: York, PA *Format:* Country *Hrs. of News Programming:* News progmg 2 hrs wkly *Target Audience:* 25-54.
Cindy Ford, General Manager
Scott Donato, Programming Director
Lisa Snedden, Promotions Manager
Lou Ann Milhimes, News Director
Daryl Hancock, Chief Engineer
Dan Douglas, Music Director

***WZBT**
10-23-1976; 91.1 mhz FM *Hrs Open:* 8 AM-2 AM; 0.35 kw; 116 ft.; N39 50 29 W77 13 26
Mailing Address: P.O. Box 435, Gettysburg College, Gettysburg, PA 17325 US
Second Address: 300 N. Washington St., Gettysburg, PA 17325
(717) 337-6000, *Fax:* (717) 337-6666
www.gettesburg.edu/~wzbt/
wzbtexec@gettysburg.edu
License: Gettysburg, Adams County, PA held by Gettysburg College.
Arbitron Metro Market: Gettysburg, PA *Format:* Alternative
Special Programming: Class 3 hrs, folk 6 hrs, jazz 4 hrs, Sp 4 hrs, gos *Target Audience:* General.
Ryan Gottschall, Station Manager
Laura Benincasa, Programming Director

Glen Mills

***WZZE**
05-20-1975; 97.3 mhz FM; 0.018 kw; 184 ft.; N39 55 15 W75 29 58
Mailing Address: PO Box 1, Concordville, PA 19331 US
Second Address: Glen Mills Schools, Glen Mills Rd., Glen Mills, PA 19342
(610) 459-8100
msmith@glenmillerschools.org
License: Glen Mills, Delaware County, PA held by Glen Mills Schools.
Nat'l Network: ABC
Arbitron Metro Market: Concordville, PA *Format:* Contemporary Hits/Top 40
C.D. Ferrainola, President
Mark Smith, Operations Dir

Grantham

***WVMM**
09-29-1989; 90.7 mhz FM *Hrs Open:* 24/7 beginning 8/27; 0.1 kw; 164 ft.; N40 9 34 W76 59 0
Messiah College, Grantham, PA 17027 US
(717) 691-6081, *Fax:* (717) 796-5241
www.messiah.edu/wvmm
wvmm@messiah.edu,earke@messiah.edu
License: Grantham, Cumberland County, PA held by Messiah College.
Nat'l Network: PRI
Arbitron Metro Market: Grantham, PA *Format:* Christian, Triple A
Special Programming: Praise and worship—7hrs, Gospel—5 hrs, Big Band- *Hrs. of News Programming:* 25 *Target Audience:* 13-25.
Edward Arke, General Manager
Sheryl Ezbiansky, Promotions Manager

Greencastle

WQCM
05-06-1967; 94.3 mhz FM *Hrs Open:* 24; 3.5 kw; 430 ft.; N39 47 29 W77 40 30
25 Penncraft Avenue, Chambersburg, PA 17201 US
(717) 263-0813, *Fax:* (717) 263-9649
www.wqcmfm.com
info@wqcm.com
License: Greencastle, Franklin County, PA held by MLB-Hagerstown-Chambersburg IV LLC.
Group Owner: Main Line Broadcasting LLC; (acq 7-20-2005; grpsl)
Arbitron Metro Market: Chambersburg, PA *Format:* Classic Rock
No. News Employees: 1 *Target Audience:* 25-44.
Rich Bateman, General Manager
Mike Holder, Programming Director
Tammy Heckman, Promotions Manager

Greenville

WLVX(FM)
07-01-1965; 107.1 mhz FM *Hrs Open:* 24; 3 kw; Ant 328 ft; N41 22 50 W80 24 48
Mailing Address: 44 McCracken Rd., Greenville, PA 16125
Second Address: 124 N. Park Avenue, Warren, OH 44481
(877) 373-7723, *Fax:* (724) 962-2105
www.thefreq107.com
wocr@adelphia.net
License: Greenville, Mercer County, PA held by Beacon Broadcasting Inc.
Group Owner: Beacon Broadcasting Inc.; (acq 9-14-2005; grpsl)
Population Served: 66,571 *Arbitron Metro Market:* Youngstown, OH *Format:* Christian *No. News Employees:* 1 *Target Audience:* 14-34. *Adv. Rates:* 15; 15; 15; 15
Harold Glunt, General Manager
Matt Rhodes, Programming Director
Dana Schroyer, Disc Jockey
Bob Woodley, Office Manager

WGRP
09-19-1959; 940 khz AM *Hrs Open:* 24
P.O. Box 189, 44 McCracken Rd, Greenville, PA 16125 US
(330) 394-7700, *Fax:* (330) 394-7701
www.classiccountry940.com
License: Greenville, PA held by Beacon Broadcasting Inc.
Group Owner: Beacon Broadcasting Inc.; (acq 9-14-2005; grpsl)
Format: Country
Harold Glunt, President
Rich Esbenshade, General Manager

***WXTC**
05-14-1930; 88.1 mhz FM *Hrs Open:* 24; kw
US
(814) 255-4186, *Fax:* (814) 255-6145
www.wsposports.com
License: Greenville, Charleston County, PA held by Apex Broadcasting Inc.
Group Owner: Apex Broadcasting Inc.; (acq 8-24-2007; $70,000)
Nat'l Reps: McGavren Guild
Arbitron Metro Market: Charleston, SC *Format:* Black, Gospel
No. News Employees: 1 *Target Audience:* 35-54; women
Chris Johnson, General Manager

Grove City

WWGY
09-10-1962; 95.1 mhz FM *Hrs Open:* 24; 19 kw horiz, 17 kw vert; 804 ft.; N41 15 8 W80 21 28
7621 Little Avenue, Ste 506, Charlotte, NC 28226 US
(724) 346-5070, *Fax:* (724) 346-5075
fforeverradio.com
webmaster@foreverradio.com
License: Grove City, Mercer County, PA held by Forever Broadcasting LLC.
Group Owner: Forever Broadcasting; (acq 2-23-2004; $2.28 million).
Arbitron Metro Market: Youngstown-Warren, OH *Format:* Country
Hrs. of News Programming: news progmg 2 hrs wkly *No. News Employees:* 1 *Target Audience:* 18-34.
Scott Cohagan, General Manager
John Thomas, Programming Director

***WSAJ-FM**
09-01-1968; 91.1 mhz FM *Hrs Open:* 24; 2.7 kw; 502 ft.; N41 14 48 W79 54 1
100 Campus Drive, Grove City, PA 16127 US
(724) 458-2077, *Fax:* (724) 458-2329
wsaj.com/
wsaj@gcc.edu
License: Grove City, Mercer County, PA held by Grove City College.
Format: Talk *No. News Employees:* 1 *Target Audience:* General; listeners who are generally unfamiliar with class mus & arts
Bryce Vagt, General Manager
Darren Morton, Station Manager
Lindsay Hegeman, Programming Director
Kristin Hilfiger, News Director

Hanover

WHVR
01-09-1949; 1280 khz AM; 5 kw-D, DA2; 0.5 kw-N, DA2; N39 49 11 W77 0 25
Mailing Address: P. O. Box 234, Hanover, PA 17331 US
Second Address: 275 Radio Rd., Hanover, PA
(717) 637-3831, *Fax:* (717) 637-9006
www.realcountry1280whvr.com
License: Hanover, PA held by Radio Hanover Inc.
Arbitron Metro Market: York, PA *Format:* Country
Joan McAnall, General Manager
Rick McCauslin, General Sales Mgr
Deanna Forney, News Director
Daryll Harcock, Chief Engineer

Harrisburg

WHP
01-01-1924; 580 khz AM *Hrs Open:* 24; 5 kw-D, DAN; 5 kw-N, DAN; N40 18 11 W76 57 7
800 Corporate Circle, Suite 201, Harrisonburg, PA 17110 US
(717) 540-8800, *Fax:* (717) 541-0094
www.whp580.com
rjharris@whp580.com
License: Harrisburg, PA held by Clear Channel Radio License Inc.
Group Owner: Clear Channel Communications Inc.; (acq 8-5-98; grpsl)
Nat'l Network: Westwood One

Arbitron Metro Market: Harrisburg-Lebanon-Carlisle, PA *Format:* News, News/Talk, 86 *No. News Employees:* 4 *Target Audience:* 35-64.
Ron Roy, General Sales Mgr

***WITF-FM**
04-01-1971; 89.5 mhz FM *Hrs Open:* 24; 5.9 kw; 1362 ft.; N40 20 44 W76 52 7
Mailing Address: P.O. Box 2954, Harrisburg, PA 17105 US
Second Address: 1982 Locust Ln., Harrisburg, PA 17109
(717) 236-6000, *Fax:* (717) 232-7612
www.witf.org
info@witf.org
License: Harrisburg, Dauphin County, PA held by WITF Inc.
Nat'l Network: NPR; PRI
Arbitron Metro Market: Harrisburg-Lebanon-Carlisle, PA *TV Affiliate:* *WITF-TV affil. *Format:* News, News/Talk, 86 *Hrs. of News Programming:* news progmg 43 hrs wkly *No. News Employees:* 3
Kathleen Pavelko, President
Mitzi Trostle, Station Manager

WKBO
01-01-1922; 1230 khz AM *Hrs Open:* 24; 0.48 kw-U, ND1; N40 16 52 W76 52 6
600 Corporate Circle, Suite 100, Harrisburg, PA 17110 US
(717) 540-8800, *Fax:* (717) 540-8814
www.oneheartministries.com
fortress1230am@oneheartministries.com
License: Harrisburg, PA held by Clear Channel Broadcasting Licenses Inc.
Group Owner: Clear Channel Communications Inc.; (acq 8-5-98; grpsl).
Nat'l Reps: Salem
Arbitron Metro Market: Harrisburg-Lebanon-Carlisle, PA *Format:* Christian *Special Programming:* Pop standards, Music of Your Life *Hrs. of News Programming:* news progmg 168 hrs wkly *No. News Employees:* 6*Target Audience:* 35-54; well educated, upscale professionals
Pete Hamel, General Manager

WNNK-FM
01-01-1962; 104.1 mhz FM *Hrs Open:* 24; 22.5 kw; 725 ft.; N40 18 59 W76 57 4
600 Congress Ave., Suite 1400, Austin, TX 78701 US
(717)238-1041, *Fax:* (717) 234-4842
www.wink104.com
john.odea@cumulus.com
License: Harrisburg, Dauphin County, PA
Arbitron Metro Market: Harrisburg, PA *Format:* Contemporary Hits/Top 40 *Hrs. of News Programming:* news progmg 15 hrs wkly *No. News Employees:* 2
John Hogan, CEO
John O'Dea, Operations Dir
Lois Burmester, General Sales Mgr
Ken O'Brien, Programming Director
Marisa Allen, Promotions Manager
Art Eddy, Director of Online
Rob Moorhead, Morning Show
Frank Curci, PromotionsDirector

WRBT
09-30-1962; 94.9 mhz FM *Hrs Open:* 24; 25 kw horiz, 24.5 kw vert; 699 ft.; N40 18 58 W76 57 1
P O Box 60547, Harrisburg, PA 17106 US
(717) 671-9949, *Fax:* (717) 540-8814
www.bobradio.com
info@bobradio.com
License: Harrisburg, Dauphin County, PA held by Clear Channel Radio License Inc.
Group Owner: Clear Channel Communications Inc.; (acq 8-5-98; grpsl)
Nat'l Reps: Christal
Arbitron Metro Market: Harrisburg-Lebanon-Carlisle, PA *TV Affiliate:* WHP-TV. *Format:* Country *No. News Employees:* 1 *Target Audience:* 25-54.
Ronald Roy, General Manager

WRVV
01-01-1946; 97.3 mhz FM *Hrs Open:* 24; 15 kw; 853 ft.; N40 20 43 W76 52 9
P O Box 60547, Harrisburg, PA 17106 US
(717) 540-8800, *Fax:* (717) 671-9973
www.wrvv.com
wrvv@river973.com
License: Harrisburg, Dauphin County, PA held by Clear Channel Radio License Inc.
Group Owner: Clear Channel Communications Inc.
Arbitron Metro Market: Harrisburg-Leba *Format:* Rock/AOR *Target Audience:* 25-54.
Jennifer Sexton, General Manager
David Cash, Programming Director

WHGB
05-28-1945; 1400 khz AM *Hrs Open:* 24; 1 kw-U, ND1; N40 14 58 W76 52 3
600 Congress Ave., Suite 1400, Austin, TX 78701 US
(717) 238-1041, *Fax:* (717) 234-4842
www.espnradio1400.com
License: Harrisburg, PA held by Cumulus Licensing Corp.
Group Owner: Cumulus Media Inc.; (acq 11-28-2000; grpsl)
Nat'l Network: ESPN Radio
Arbitron Metro Market: Harrisburg, PA *Format:* Sports *Target Audience:* 25-54; men
Ron Vioanviannell, Promotions Manager

WTKT
02-01-1948; 1460 khz AM *Hrs Open:* 24
800 Corporate Circle, Suite 201, Harrisonburg, PA 17110 US
(717) 540-8800, *Fax:* (717) 540-8814
www.1460theticket.com
1460theticket@1460theticket.com
License: Harrisburg, PA held by Clear Channel Radio License Inc.
Group Owner: Clear Channel Communications Inc.; (acq 8-5-98; grpsl).
Nat'l Reps: Clear Channel
Arbitron Metro Market: Harrisburg, PA *Format:* Oldies, Sports *Special Programming:* Gospel 2 hrs, pub service 2 hrs wkly *Hrs. of News Programming:* news progmg 30 hrs wkly *No. News Employees:* 4 *TargetAudience:* General.
Ken Austin, Programming Director

WHKF
07-01-1965; 99.3 mhz FM; 1.35 kw; 679 ft.; N40 11 30 W76 52 5
800 Corporate Circle, Suite 201, Harrisburg, PA 17110 US
(717) 540-8800, *Fax:* (717) 540-8814
www.993kissfm.com
info@wwklfm.com
License: Harrisburg, Dauphin County, PA
Arbitron Metro Market: Harrisburg, PA *Format:* Contemporary Hits/Top 40 *Target Audience:* 18-34.women
Doug Baker, General Sales Mgr
Kraig Nace, Promotions Manager
Peter MacArthur, News Director
Tom Presite, Chief Engineer
Ron Walker, Sales

***WZXM**
01-01-1995; 88.1 mhz FM *Hrs Open:* 24; 540 w; Ant 105 ft; N40 15 44 W76 53 11
Box 186, Sellersville, PA 19104
(215) 721-2141, *Fax:* (215) 721-9811
www.wordfm.org
wordfm@wordfm.org
License: Harrisburg, Dauphin County, PA held by Four Rivers Community Broadcasting Corp.
Population Served: 400,000 *Arbitron Metro Market:* Harrisburg-Leba
Charles Loughery, President
Meg Sabulsky, Operations Dir
David Baker, General Manager
Meg Sabulsky, Programming Director
William Dunn, Promotions Manager
Charles Loughery, Engineering Dir

Havertown

***WHHS**
12-06-1949; 99.9 mhz FM *Hrs Open:* 2 PM-10 PM (M-F); 0.0095 kw; 161 ft.; N39 58 59 W75 18 10
1801 Darby Road, Havertown, PA 19083 US
(610) 446-7111, *Fax:* (610) 853-5952
www.whhs.org
whhsnewsdirector@yahoo.com
License: Havertown, Delaware County, PA held by School District of Haverford Township.
Format: Variety/Diverse *Target Audience:* General.
Kevin Moran, General Manager

Hawley

WYCY
09-13-1993; 105.3 mhz FM *Hrs Open:* 24; 2.9 kw; 479 ft; N41 35 01 W75 10 30
575 Grove St., Honesdale, PA 18431
(570) 253-1616, *Fax:* (570) 253-6297
www.boldgoldmedia.com
vbenedetto@boldgoldmedia.com
License: Hawley, Wayne County, PA held by Bold Gold Media Group L.P.
Group Owner: Bold Gold Media Group LP; (acq 5-23-2005; grpsl).
Nat'l Network: ABC
Hrs. of News Programming: news progmg 5 hrs wkly *No. News Employees:* 1 *Target Audience:* 25-55.
Vincent Benedetto, CEO
Vince Benedetto, President
Michael G Stanton, General Manager
Michael G Stanton, Station Manager
Michael G Stanton, General Sales Mgr
George Schmitt, Programming Director
Regina Hensley, PromotionsManager
Mikki Uzupes, News Director
Craig Seelig, Chief Engineer
Jessica Baglieri, Traffic Manager

***WBYH**
12-01-2000; 89.1 mhz FM *Hrs Open:* 24; 200 w; 525 ft; N41 24 43 W75 09 51 *Rebroadcasts:* Rebroadcasts WYBO (FM) Sellersville 100%
Box 186, Sellersville, PA 18960
(215) 721-2141, *Fax:* (215) 721-9811
www.wordfm.com
wordfm@wordfm.org
License: Hawley, Wayne County, PA held by Four Rivers Communications Broadcasting Co.
Population Served: 50,000
Charles Loughery, President
Meg Sabulsky, Operations Dir
David Baker, General Manager
Meg Sabulsky, Programming Director
William Dunn, Promotions Manager
Charles Loughery, Engineering Dir

Hazleton

WAZL
12-19-1932; 1490 khz AM *Hrs Open:* 24; 1 kw-U, ND1; N40 56 24 W75 58 4
City Center West, 7201 W. Lake Mead Blvd, Las Vegas, NV 89128 US
(902) 493-7133
License: Hazleton, PA held by WS2K Radio LLC.
Group Owner: WS2K Radio LLC dba WS Media; (acq 7-14-2008; grpsl)
Nat'l Network: Fox News Radio *Wire Services:* Metro Weather Service Inc.
Arbitron Metro Market: Halifax NS *Format:* News, News/Talk, 86 *Adv. Rates:* 15; 10; 15; 10
Jim Hamm, General Manager

WBSX
01-01-1949; 97.9 mhz FM *Hrs Open:* 24; 6.3 kw; 1335 ft.; N41 10 56 W75 52 22
City Center West, 7201 W. Lake Mead Blvd, Las Vegas, NV 89128 US
(570) 824-9000, *Fax:* (570) 820-0520
www.979x.com
License: Hazleton, Luzerne County, PA
Group Owner: Cumulus Media Inc.; (acq 5-29-97; grpsl).
Nat'l Network: ABC; Moody
Arbitron Metro Market: Wilkes Barre, PA *Format:* Rock/AOR *Target Audience:* 18-34.
John Crawford, General Sales Mgr
Kenny Wall, Programming Director
Erin Evans, Promotions Manager
Phil Galasso, Chief Engineer
John Rizzuto, Market Manager
Jeanne Kerr, Local Sales Manager
Joe Rae, IT Director

Hershey

WMHX(FM)
04-30-1964; 106.7 mhz FM *Hrs Open:* 24; 14 kw; Ant 928 ft; N40 10 16 W76 35 50
515 S. 32nd St., Camp Hill, PA 17011
(717) 635-7000, *Fax:* (717) 635-7551
www.mix1067fm.com
License: Hershey, Dauphin County, PA
Group Owner: Cumulus Media Inc.; (acq 5-29-97; grpsl).
Population Served: 1,500,000 *Arbitron Metro Market:* Harrisburg-Lebanon-Carlisle, PA *Format:* Adult Contemp
Bob Adams, General Manager

Hollidaysburg

WRKY-FM
12-01-1978; 104.9 mhz FM; 0.73 kw; 906 ft.; N40 34 1 W78 26 32
One Forever Drive, Hollidaysburg, PA 16648 US
(814) 941-9800, *Fax:* (814) 943-2754
www.rocky1049.com
xman@rocky1049.com

RADIO - U.S.

License: Hollidaysburg, Blair County, PA held by Forever of PA L.L.C.
Group Owner: Forever Broadcasting; (acq 2-18-97; $2 million with WKMC(AM) Roaring Spring).
Nat'l Reps: Roslin
Arbitron Metro Market: Altoona, PA *Format:* Adult Contemp
Target Audience: 25-54; adults with significant income
Carol Logan, President
David Davies, General Manager

***WHHN**
01-01-2008; 88.1 mhz FM; 0.85 kw horiz, 0.67 kw vert; 1352 ft.; N40 29 19 W78 21 20
352 West 44th Street, New York, NY 10036 US
(888) 408-0201, *Fax:* (318) 449-9954
www.radiomaria.us
License: Hollidaysburg, Blair County, PA held by Friends of Radio Maria.
Arbitron Metro Market: Hollidaysburg, PA *Format:* Christian, Talk, 74
Shane Connor, Operations Dir
Chip Thomas, General Manager
Phil Hickerson, General Sales Mgr
Jim Smith, Chief Engineer

Homer City

WCCS
10-25-1983; 1160 khz AM *Hrs Open:* 24; 10 kw-D, DA2; 1 kw-N, DA2; N40 34 18 W79 10 12
P. O. Box 73, Clearfield, PA 16830 US
(724) 479-1160(724) 465-4700
www.1160wccs.com
mbertig@rendabroadcasting.com
License: Homer City, PA held by The St. Pier Group LLC.
Group Owner: Renda Broadcasting Corp.; (acq 10-4-2002; $650,000)
Nat'l Network: ABC *Regional Reps:* Dome & Associates *Wire Services:* AP
Arbitron Metro Market: Indiana,PA *Format:* Adult Contemp
Special Programming: Pol 3 hrs, oldies 9 hrs wkly *Hrs. of News Programming:* news progmg 14 hrs wkly *No. News Employees:* 2 *Target Audience:* 25-49.*Adv. Rates:* 15; 15; 15; 15
Tony Renda Sr., CEO
Alan Serena, Operations Dir
Mark Bertig, General Manager
Ron Nocco, News Director
Jack Benedict, Operations Director

Honesdale

WDNH-FM
10-12-1981; 95.3 mhz FM *Hrs Open:* 24; 1.65 kw; 456 ft.; N41 34 45 W75 10 42
575 Grove Street, Honesdale, PA 18431 US
(570) 253-1616, *Fax:* (570) 253-6297
www.boldgoldlakeregion.com
mstanton@boldgoldmedia.com
License: Honesdale, Wayne County, PA held by Bold Gold Media Group L.P.
Group Owner: Bold Gold Media Group LP
Nat'l Network: USA
Arbitron Metro Market: Honesdale, PA *Format:* Adult Contemp
Hrs. of News Programming: news progmg 6 hrs wkly *No. News Employees:* 1 *Target Audience:* 25-54.
Michael G. Stanton, General Manager
George Schmitt, Programming Director

WPSN
09-01-1972; 1590 khz AM; 2.5 kw-D, ND2; 0.015 kw-N, ND2; N41 33 13 W75 15 18
575 Grove Street, Honesdale, PA 18431 US
(570) 253-1616, *Fax:* (570) 253-6297
www.waynepikenews.com
mstanton@boldgoldmedia.com
License: Honesdale, PA held by Bold Gold Media Group L.P.
Group Owner: Bold Gold Media Group LP; (acq 5-23-2005; grpsl)
Nat'l Reps: Dome
Arbitron Metro Market: Honesdale, PA *Format:* Sports *Target Audience:* General.
Michael.G.Stanton, General Manager
George Schmitt, Programming Director
John Emerson, News Director
Mikki Uzupes, Web Editor

***WZZH**
01-01-2008; 90.9 mhz FM; 200 w; Ant 912 ft; N41 35 35 W75 25 56 *Rebroadcasts:* Rebroadcasts WBYO(FM) Sellersville 100%
Box 186, Sellersville, PA 18960
(215) 721-2141, *Fax:* (215) 721-9811
www.wordfm.org
wordfm@wordfm.org
License: Honesdale, Wayne County, PA held by Four Rivers Community Broadcasting Corp.
Charles Loughery, President
Meg Sabulsky, Operations Dir
David Baker, General Manager
Meg Sabulsky, Programming Director
William Dunn, Promotions Manager
Charles Loughery, Engineering Dir

Hughesville

WRKK
08-04-1985; 1200 khz AM *Hrs Open:* 24; 10 kw-D, DA2; 0.25 kw-N, DA2; N41 12 43 W76 44 55 *Rebroadcasts:* Rebroadcasts WRAK(AM) Williamsport 100%
Mailing Address: 800 Corporate Circle, Suite 201, Harrisonburg, PA 17110 US
Second Address: 1559 W. 4th St., Williamsport, PA 17701
(570) 327-1400, *Fax:* (570) 327-8156
www.wrak.com
wrak@wrak.com
License: Hughesville, PA held by Clear Channel Broadcasting License Inc.
Group Owner: Clear Channel Communications Inc.; (acq 8-5-98; grpsl)
Nat'l Network: ABC; Westwood One
Arbitron Metro Market: Williamsport, PA *Format:* News, News/Talk, 86 *No. News Employees:* 1 *Target Audience:* 35 plus.
Bryan Kell, General Manager
Duke Rice, Programming Director

Huntingdon

WLLI
07-05-1972; 1150 khz AM; 5 kw-D, ND1; 0.036 kw-N, ND1; N40 27 18 W77 58 50
112 West Shirley Street, Mt. Union, PA 17066 US
(731) 427-3316, *Fax:* (731) 427-9338
License: Huntingdon, PA held by Forever South Licenses LLC.
Group Owner: Forever Communications Inc.; (acq 7-31-2006; grpsl)
Format: Country
Verla Price, General Manager

WLLI(AM)
03-02-1947; 1150 khz AM *Hrs Open:* 24; 5 kw-D, 36 w-N; N40 27 18 W77 58 50 *Rebroadcasts:* Simulcast with WRSC(AM) State College
RR 3 Box 225A, Huntington, PA 16652-8804
(814) 542-8648, *Fax:* (814) 643-9625
License: Huntingdon, Huntingdon County, PA held by Megahertz Licenses LLC.
Group Owner: Forever Broadcasting; (acq 4-29-2002; $875,000 with WLTS(FM) Mount Union)
Regional Reps: Commercial Media Sales Inc.
Population Served: 56,000*Format:* News, News/Talk, 86 *Special Programming:* Relg 2 hrs wkly *Hrs. of News Programming:* news progmg 15 hrs wkly *No. News Employees:* 1 *Target Audience:* 25 plus; general*Adv. Rates:* 14; 14; 14; 13
Kristin Cantrell, General Manager

***WKVR-FM**
03-01-1978; 92.3 mhz FM *Hrs Open:* 22; 0.013 kw; -266 ft.; N40 30 0 W78 0 52
1700 Moore Street, Huntingdon, PA 16652 US
(814) 643-5031, *Fax:* (814) 643-4477
License: Huntingdon, Huntingdon County, PA held by Juniata College Board of Trustees.
Format: Classic Rock, Rock/AOR *Special Programming:* CHR 15 hrs, jazz 3 hrs, Black 10 hrs, contemp Chr *Hrs. of News Programming:* News progmg 8 hrs wkly *Target Audience:* 18-25; college students
Chad Herzog, General Manager
J. Andrew Scott, Promotions Manager

WLAK
09-12-1967; 103.5 mhz FM *Hrs Open:* 24; 0.16 kw; 1427 ft.; N40 29 51 W78 8 0 *Rebroadcasts:* Rebroadcasts WMRF-FM Lewistown 95.7%
Mailing Address: 12 1/2 East Market St, Lewiston, PA 17044 US
Second Address: 12 East Market St., 2nd Floor, Lewistown, PA 17044
(717) 248-6757, *Fax:* (717) 248-6759
www.merfradio.com
pete@merfradio.com
License: Huntingdon, Huntingdon County, PA held by First Media Radio LLC.
Group Owner: First Media Radio LLC; (acq 3-28-2001; grpsl)
Format: Adult Contemp *Target Audience:* 18-44.
Jeff Stevens, Operations Dir
Peter Herman, General Manager
Mary Lee Shaffer, News Director

Indiana

WDAD
11-04-1945; 1450 khz AM *Hrs Open:* 24; 1 kw-U, ND1; N40 38 17 W79 8 47
21 North Fifth St., Indiana, PA 15701 US
(724) 465-4700, *Fax:* (724) 349-6842
www.wdadradio.com
info@wdadradio.com
License: Indiana, PA held by The St. Pier Group.
Group Owner: Renda Broadcasting Corp.; (acq 2-13-2004; $3.25 million).
Nat'l Network: CBS *Nat'l Reps:* Dome
Arbitron Metro Market: Indiana/Johnstown, PA *Format:* Oldies
Special Programming: Relg 2 hrs wkly *No. News Employees:* 1
Target Audience: 35 plus. *Adv. Rates:* 24; 20; 20; 16
Tony Renda Sr., President
Jim DeCesare, Operations Dir
Mark Bertig, General Manager
Nick Ruffner, News Director

***WIUP-FM**
10-01-1969; 90.1 mhz FM *Hrs Open:* 7 AM-2 AM; 1.5 kw; 89 ft.; N40 36 32.3 W79 10 0.9
121 Stouffer Hall, Indiana, PA 15705 US
(724) 357-9487, *Fax:* (724) 357-5503
www.wiupfm.org
ygkg@iup.edu
License: Indiana, Indiana County, PA held by Indiana University of Pennsylvania.
TV Affiliate: *WIUP-TV affil. *Format:* Variety/Diverse *Special Programming:* Black 14 hrs, class 15 hrs, folk 4 hrs, gospel one *Hrs. of News Programming:* News progmg 11 hrs wkly *Target Audience:* General.
James Rogers, General Manager
Bridget Clark, Station Manager
Ben Cunningham, Programming Director
Quinn Denio, Promotions Manager
Emily Krause, Music Director
Steve Mozes, Assistant Music Director
George Ribbich, TrainingDirector
Matthew Albright, Production Director
John Rockenbach, Traffic Manager
Steve Mozes, Webmaster

WQMU
08-14-1968; 92.5 mhz FM *Hrs Open:* 24; 3 kw; 328 ft.; N40 38 17 W79 8 47
21 North Fifth St., Indiana, PA 15701 US
(724) 465-4700, *Fax:* (724) 349-6842
www.wqmuradio.com
info@wqmuradio.com
License: Indiana, Indiana County, PA
Group Owner: Renda Broadcasting Corp.
Regional Reps: Dome
Format: Adult Contemp *Target Audience:* 21-41. *Adv. Rates:* Same as AM
Jack Gillen, President
Kevin Brenahan, Operations Dir
R.J. Shingleton, General Sales Mgr
Corey Duices, Programming Director
Heather Shingleton, News Director

Irwin

WKHB
10-28-1934; 620 khz AM *Hrs Open:* 24
245 Brown Street, Greensburg, PA 15601 US
(412) 823-7000
www.khbradio.com
License: Irwin, PA held by Broadcast Communications Inc.
Group Owner: Broadcast Communications Inc.; (acq 10-9-96; $300,000)
Arbitron Metro Market: Pittsburgh, PA *Format:* Variety/Diverse
Target Audience: Adults.
Robert Stevens, President
Ashley Stevens, Operations Dir
Barry Banker, Station Manager
Clark Ingram, Operations Manager

Jackson Township

***WRTY**
08-23-1991; 91.1 mhz FM *Hrs Open:* 24; 3.5 kw; 866 ft.; N41 2 40 W75 22 45 *Rebroadcasts:* Rebroadcasts WRTI(FM) Philadelphia 100%
Annenberg Hall (011-00), Philadelphia, PA 19122 US

(215) 204-8405, *Fax:* (215) 204-7027
www.wrti.org
comments@wrti.org
License: Jackson Township, Monroe County, PA held by Temple University of The Commonwealth System of Higher Education.
Nat'l Network: NPR
Arbitron Metro Market: Wilkes Barre-Sc *Format:* Jazz *Hrs. of News Programming:* news progmg 15 hrs wkly *No. News Employees:* 1 *Target Audience:* 30-65.
Tobias Poole, Operations Dir
Dave Conant, General Manager
William Johnson, Station Manager
Jack Moore, Programming Director
Jeffery DePolo, Engineering Dir

Jeannette

WKFB
01-28-1974; 770 khz AM *Hrs Open:* Sunrise-sunset
Mailing Address: 245 Brown Street, Greensburg, PA 15601 US
Second Address: 1918 Lincoln Hwy., North Versailles, PA 15137
(505) 758-4491, *Fax:* (505) 758-4452
License: Jeannette, PA held by Broadcast Communications Inc.
Group Owner: Broadcast Communications Inc.; (acq 4-98)
Arbitron Metro Market: Tucson AZ *Format:* Talk
Jeff Singer, Operations Dir
Pattee Brown, General Sales Mgr
Jennifer Trujillo, News Director

Jenkintown

WPPZ-FM
11-01-1960; 103.9 mhz FM *Hrs Open:* 24; 0.27 kw; 1109 ft.; N40 2 29.6 W75 14 11.4
5900 Princess Grdn Pkwy, 7th Floor, Lanham, MD 20706 US
, *Fax:* (215) 884-9400
www.praise1039.com
License: Jenkintown, Montgomery County, PA held by Radio One Licenses LLC.
Group Owner: Radio One Inc.; (acq 11-8-2001; grpsl).
Arbitron Metro Market: Philadelphia *Format:* Religious *Target Audience:* 18-34.
Chester Schofield, General Manager
Daisy Davis, Programming Director

Jersey Shore

WJSA
07-10-1979; 1600 khz AM *Hrs Open:* 24; 1 kw-D, ND1; 0.02 kw-N, ND1; N41 13 32 W77 16 1
262 Allegheny Street, Jersey Shore, PA 17740 US
(570) 398-7200, *Fax:* (570) 398-7201
www.wjsaradio.com
mail@wjsaradio.com
License: Jersey Shore, PA held by Covenant Broadcasting Co.
Nat'l Network: Salem Radio Network; Moody *Nat'l Reps:* Salem
Arbitron Metro Market: Williamsport, PA *Format:* Religious
Special Programming: Sacred Classics one hr, southern gospel 4 hrs, Chr *Hrs. of News Programming:* news progmg 14 hrs wkly *No. News Employees:* 1*Target Audience:* General.
John Hogg Jr., General Manager
Ann L. Hogg, Programming Director
Liz Brady, News Director

WJSA-FM
11-01-1984; 96.3 mhz FM *Hrs Open:* 24; 2.65 kw; 1004 ft.; N41 13 45 W77 22 2
262 Allegheny St., Jersey Shore, PA 17740 US
(570) 398-7200, *Fax:* (570) 398-7201
www.wjsaradio.com
mail@wjsaradio.com
License: Jersey Shore, Lycoming County, PA held by Covenant Broadcasting Co.
Nat'l Network: Moody; Salem Radio Network *Nat'l Reps:* Salem
Arbitron Metro Market: Williamsport, PA *Format:* Religious
Special Programming: Sacred classics one hr, southern gospel 3 hrs, Chr *Hrs. of News Programming:* news progmg 14 hrs wkly *No. News Employees:* 1
John K. Hogg, General Manager
Liz Brady, News Director
Ann L. Hogg, Traffic Manager

Johnsonburg

WJNG
07-01-1998; 100.5 mhz FM *Hrs Open:* 24; 1.3 kw; 666 ft.; N41 23 11 W78 41 32 *Rebroadcasts:* Rebroadcasts WMKX(FM) Brookville 100%
51 Pickering Street, Brookville, PA 15825 US
(814) 965-2921, *Fax:* (814) 965-2921
www.megarock.fm
megarock@windstream.net
License: Johnsonburg, Elk County, PA held by Strattan Broadcasting Inc.
Format: Classic Rock
Kevin Heinrick, Operations Dir
James Farley, General Manager
Diana Farley, General Sales Mgr
Kevin Heinrich, Programming Director
Chris Condon, Promotions Manager
Kevin Heinrich, News Director
Cindy Pierucci, Office Manager,Traffic and Billing
Sharon Stewart, Music Director

Johnstown

WCRO
09-01-1947; 1230 khz AM *Hrs Open:* 24; 1 kw-U, ND1; N40 19 55 W78 54 46
Mailing Address: 1091 Broad St., Johnstown, PA 15906 US
Second Address: 1089 Broad St, Johnstown, PA 15906
(814) 533-5533, *Fax:* (814) 533-5534
License: Johnstown, PA held by Greater Johnstown School District.
Wire Services: AP
Arbitron Metro Market: Johnstown PA *Format:* Adult Contemp
Special Programming: University of Pittsburgh Football, basketball, NASCAR racing *Hrs. of News Programming:* News progmg 35 hrs wkly *Target Audience:* 45 - 64; Fastest growing and most financially secure demographically *Adv. Rates:* 30; 30; 30; 23
Ed Sherlock, President
Ed Scherlock, Station Manager

*WFRJ
06-06-1986; 88.9 mhz FM *Hrs Open:* 24; 5.5 kw vert; 1214 ft.; N40 22 17 W78 58 56
4135 Northgate Blvd.#1, Sacramento, CA 95821 US
(916) 641-8191, *Fax:* (916) 641-8238
www.familyradio.com
info@familyradio.com
License: Johnstown, Cambria County, PA held by Family Stations Inc.
Group Owner: Family Stations Inc.
Format: Christian *Hrs. of News Programming:* News progmg 6 hrs wkly *Target Audience:* General; every age group
Harold Camping, President
Gary Johnson, Operations Dir

WJHT
09-01-1974; 92.1 mhz FM *Hrs Open:* 24; 0.58 kw; 1043 ft.; N40 22 15 W78 59 2
City Center West, 7201 W. Lake Mead Blvd, Las Vegas, NV 89128 US
(814) 255-4186, *Fax:* (814) 255-6145
www.hot92and100.com
info@hot92and100.com
License: Johnstown, Cambria County, PA held by Forever Broadcasting LLC.
Group Owner: Forever Broadcasting; (acq 5-1-2005; $2.73 million with WRKW(FM) Ebensburg).
Format: Contemporary Hits/Top 40
Terry Deitz, General Manager
Tina Perry, General Sales Mgr
Mitch Edwards, Programming Director
Rick Shepard, News Director

WKGE
04-01-1925; 850 khz AM; 10 kw-U, DA1; N40 10 54 W78 53 20
Rebroadcasts: Simulcasts WWGE(AM) Loretto 100%
One Forever Drive, Hollidaysburg, PA 16648 US
(814) 255-4186, *Fax:* (814) 255-6145
License: Johnstown, PA held by Birach Broadcasting Corp.
Group Owner: Birach Broadcasting Corp.; (acq 4-10-2008; $230,000)
Nat'l Reps: McGavren Guild; Dome
Format: News, News/Talk, 84, Talk
Sima Birach, President
Verla Price, General Manager
Mike Stevens, Programming Director
Rick Shepard, News Director
Jim Boxler, Chief Engineer

WFGI-FM
08-01-1949; 95.5 mhz FM; 57 kw; 1060 ft.; N40 22 18 W78 58 57
One Forever Drive, Hollidaysburg, PA 16648 US
(814) 255-4186, *Fax:* (814) 255-6145
www.myfroggy95.com
License: Johnstown, Cambria County, PA held by Forever Broadcasting LLC
Group Owner: Forever Broadcasting
Format: Country *Target Audience:* 25-54.
Terry Deitz, General Manager
Tina Perry, General Sales Mgr
Lara Mosby, Programming Director
Rick Shepard, News Director

WKYE
08-14-1973; 96.5 mhz FM *Hrs Open:* 24; 50 kw; 489 ft.; N40 19 45 W78 53 54
800 Corporate Circle, Suite 201, Harrisonburg, PA 17110 US
(814) 255-4186, *Fax:* (814) 255-6145
www.96key.com
info@hot92fm.net
License: Johnstown, Cambria County, PA held by Forever Broadcasting LLC.
Group Owner: Forever Broadcasting; (acq 1-30-2004; $9.13 million with co-located AM).
Arbitron Metro Market: Johnstown, PA *Format:* Adult Contemp
Verla Price, General Manager
Jack Michaels, Programming Director
Jim Boxler, Chief Engineer
Brian Wolfe, Music Director

WNTJ
08-01-1946; 1490 khz AM *Hrs Open:* 24; 1 kw-U, ND1; N40 19 25 W78 53 49
800 Corporate Circle, Suite 201, Harrisonburg, PA 17110 US
(814) 255-4186, *Fax:* (814) 255-6145
www.ntjnetwork.com
tdeitz@96key.com
License: Johnstown, PA held by 2510 Licenses LLC.
Group Owner: 2510 Licenses LLC; (acq 5-1-2005; grpsl)
Arbitron Metro Market: Johnstown, PA *Format:* News, News/Talk, 86 *Target Audience:* 18-54.
Terry Deitz, General Manager
Tina Perry, General Sales Mgr
Mitch Edwards, Programming Director

*WQEJ
10-01-1998; 89.7 mhz FM *Hrs Open:* 24; 8.4 kw; 1184 ft.; N40 22 17 W78 58 56 *Rebroadcasts:* Rebroadcasts WQED-FM Pittsburgh 100%
4802 Fifth Ave, Pittsburgh, PA 15213 US
(412) 622-1436, *Fax:* (412) 622-7073
www.wqed.org
radio@wqed.org
License: Johnstown, Cambria County, PA held by WQED Multimedia.
Nat'l Network: AP Radio; NPR; PRI
Format: Classical *Target Audience:* 35-64; educated, influential, professional, community leaders, mid to high income
George Miles Jr., CEO
Darryl Ford-Williams, Operations Dir
Dorothy Frank, General Sales Mgr
Bryan Sejvar, Programming Director
Paul Byers, Chief Engineer
Deborah Acklin, Executive Vice President
Lilli Mosco, Director ofDevelopment
Rosemary Martinelli, Director of Marketing

Kane

*WPSX
01-01-1995; 90.1 mhz FM; 17 kw; 761 ft; N41 37 04 W78 48 14
Rebroadcasts: Rebroadcasts WPSU(FM) 100%
WPSU-FM, 120 Outreach Bldg/, University Park, PA 16802
(814) 865-1877, *Fax:* (814) 865-4043
wpsu.org
wpsu@psu.edu
License: Kane, McKean County, PA held by The Pennsylvania State University.
Nat'l Network: NPR; PRI *Wire Services:* AP
Special Programming: Folk 10 hrs, jazz 3 hrs, blues 2 hrs wkly *Hrs. of News Programming:* news progmg 35 hrs wkly *No. News Employees:* 1 *Target Audience:* Upscale educated adults
Craig Johnson, Operations Dir
Ted Krichels, General Manager
Greg Petersen, Station Manager
Tom Yourchak, General Sales Mgr
Emily Reddy, Programming Director
Leslie Dyer, News Director
Russ Rockwell, Chief Engineer

Kane/Bradford

WLMI(FM)
09-17-1984; 103.9 mhz FM *Hrs Open:* 24; 6 kw; Ant 733 ft HAAT; N41 37 03 W78 48 13 *Rebroadcasts:* WBYB (FM)
Mailing Address: 29 Fraley St., Kane, PA 16735
Second Address: One Blue Bird Square, Olean, NY 16740
(814) 837-9564, *Fax:* (814) 975-1098
www.wlmi.net
wlmi@colonial.cc
License: Kane/Bradford, McKean County, PA held by Colonial Radio Group Inc.

Population Served: 125,000 *Arbitron Metro Market:* Olean, NY *Format:* Country *Special Programming:* Polka one hr *Hrs. of News Programming:* news progmg 12 hrs wkly *No. News Employees:* 1 *Target Audience:* 18-49; female-skewing *Adv. Rates:* 21; 15; 18; 12
Jeffrey Andrulonis, President
JJ Michaels, Operations Dir
Quentin Shutters, Station Manager
Christy Andrulonis, General Sales Mgr

King of Prussia

WFYL
12-01-1976; 1180 khz AM
22942 Captain Kidd Lane, Cudjoe Key, FL 33042 US
(610) 539-5015, *Fax:* (610) 539-1799
www.1180wfyl.com
info@1180wfyl.com
License: King of Prussia, PA held by Langer Broadcasting Group L.L.C.
Group Owner: Langer Broadcasting Group L.L.C.
Arbitron Metro Market: Philadelphia, PA *Format:* Talk
Helen Lenza, General Manager

Kittanning

WTYM
01-01-1948; 1380 khz AM; 1 kw-D, ND1; 0.028 kw-N, ND1; N40 47 19 W79 32 5
P. O. Box 371, Kittanning, PA 16201 US
(724) 543-1380, *Fax:* (724) 543-5572
www.wtymradio.com
wtym@alltel.net
License: Kittanning, PA held by Vernal Enterprises Inc.
Group Owner: Vernal Enterprises Inc.; acq 7-22-92; $85,000;
Arbitron Metro Market: Kittanning, PA *Format:* Oldies, Sports *Special Programming:* Relg 4 hrs wkly *Target Audience:* 20-55.
Larry Schrecongost, President
Nancy Schrecongost, Operations Dir
John DeFeo, General Sales Mgr

Kulpmont

*WZRG(FM)
91.9 mhz FM; 600 w; Ant 535 ft; N40 49 01 W76 27 00
101 Armorey Blvd, Lewisburg, PA 18960
(570) 523-1190
www.wordfm.org
License: Kulpmont, Northumberland County, PA held by Salt and Light Media Ministries
Population Served: 2,926 *Arbitron Metro Market:* Kulpmont, PA
Charles Loughery, President

Laceyville

*WCOZ
90.5 mhz FM; 0.1 kw; 71 ft.; N41 40 27 W76 10 3
US
(607) 427-0452
License: Laceyville, Wyoming County, PA held by Telikoja Educational Broadcasting Inc.
Arbitron Metro Market: Laceyville, PA
Kevin Fitzgerald, President

Lancaster

WDAC
12-13-1959; 94.5 mhz FM; 19 kw; 810 ft.; N39 53 46 W76 14 22
Mailing Address: P.O. Box 3022, Lancaster, PA 17604 US
Second Address: for UPS, Fed-Ex only:, 683 Lancaster Pike, New Providence, PA 17560
(717) 284-4123, *Fax:* (717) 284-2300
www.wdac.com
postmaster@wdac.com
License: Lancaster, Lancaster County, PA held by WDAC Radio Co.
Nat'l Network: Moody; Salem Radio Network
Arbitron Metro Market: Lancaster, PA *Format:* Christian, Talk *Special Programming:* Farm 4 hrs wkly *Hrs. of News Programming:* news progmg 8 hrs wkly *No. News Employees:* 1 *Target Audience:* 25-49;Evangelical Christians, families
Doug Myer, COO
Richard Crawford, President
Mike Stike, Operations Dir
Joe Hartman, General Sales Mgr
John Eby, Programming Director

*WFNM
05-01-1973; 89.1 mhz FM *Hrs Open:* 20; 0.1 kw; 151 ft.; N40 2 43 W76 19 14
630 College Avenue, Lancaster, PA 17604 US
(717) 291-4098, *Fax:* (717) 358-4437
www.wfnm.freeflux.net
adam.gould@fandm.edu
License: Lancaster, Lancaster County, PA held by Franklin and Marshall College.
Arbitron Metro Market: Lancaster, PA *Format:* Variety/Diverse *Special Programming:* Black 6 hrs, sports talk 2 hrs, class 2 hrs, jazz *Hrs. of News Programming:* News progmg 4 hrs wkly *Target Audience:* 13-35.
Pat Collins, Operations Dir
Adam Gould, General Manager
Tim Gatz, General Sales Mgr
Brian Hughes, Assistant General Manager and Technical Support
Dan Lewis, Academic Advisor
Dan Kober, Music Director
Aamer Bajwa, MusicDirector
Lauren Shor, Advertising
Katie Davidson, Advertising

*WJTL
08-27-1984; 90.3 mhz FM; 4.7 kw; 198 ft; N40 04 13 W76 17 19
Box 1614, Lancaster, PA 17601
(717) 392-3690, *Fax:* (717) 390-2892
www.wjtl.com
contact@wjtl.com
License: Lancaster, Lancaster County, PA held by Creative Ministries Inc.
Nat'l Network: USA
Arbitron Metro Market: Lancaster, PA
Fred McNaughton, Station Manager
John Shirk, Programming Director
John Staffieri, Promotions Manager

WLAN
08-09-1946; 1390 khz AM *Hrs Open:* 24
200 Concord Plaza, Suite 600, San Antonio, TX 78216 US
(717) 295-9700, *Fax:* (717) 295-7329
www.1390wlan.com
webmaster@1390wlan.com
License: Lancaster, PA held by Clear Channel Radio Licenses Inc.
Group Owner: Clear Channel Communications Inc.; (acq 1996; $7 million with co-located FM)
Nat'l Network: ABC *Nat'l Reps:* Clear Channel *Wire Services:* AP
Arbitron Metro Market: Lancaster, PA *Format:* Adult Contemp *Hrs. of News Programming:* news progmg 9 hrs wkly *No. News Employees:* 3 *Target Audience:* 35-64.
Dick Taylor, General Manager

WLAN-FM
01-01-1948; 96.9 mhz FM *Hrs Open:* 24; 50 kw; 500 ft; N40 02 52 W76 27 25
1685 Crown Ave., Suite 100, Lancaster, PA 78216
(717) 295-9700, *Fax:* (717) 295-7329
www.fm97.com
webmaster@fm97.com
License: Lancaster, Lancaster County, PA
Group Owner: Clear Channel Communications Inc.
Wire Services: AP
Population Served: 420,000 *Arbitron Metro Market:* Lancaster, PA *Hrs. of News Programming:* news progmg 9 hrs wkly *No. News Employees:* 3 *Target Audience:* 18-49.
Jt Bosch, Operations Dir
Dan Lankford, Marketing Manager
Julia Armstrong, General Sales Mgr
Derrick Cole, Programming Director
Joe Bleacher, Promotions Manager
Troy Becker, Engineering Dir

*WLCH
09-14-1987; 91.3 mhz FM; 0.16 kw; 135 ft.; N40 4 13 W76 17 19
545 Pershing Avenue, Lancaster, PA 17602 US
(717) 295-7996, *Fax:* (717) 295-7759
www.sacapa.org
info@sacapa.org
License: Lancaster, Lancaster County, PA held by Spanish American Civic Association for Equality Inc.
Arbitron Metro Market: Lancaster, PA *Format:* Variety/Diverse *Target Audience:* General; Hispanics
Mayra Guevar, CEO
Enid Vazquez, General Manager
Carlos Groupera, Executive Vice President

WLPA
01-01-1922; 1490 khz AM *Hrs Open:* 24; 0.6 kw-U, ND1; N40 3 38 W76 18 59
Mailing Address: P.O. Box 4368, Lancaster, PA 17604 US
Second Address: 1996 Auction Rd., Manheim, PA 17545
(717) 653-0800, *Fax:* (717) 653-0122
www.wlpa.com
www.wlpa.com
License: Lancaster, PA held by Hall Communications Inc.
Group Owner: Hall Communications Inc.; (acq 2-13-77)
Nat'l Network: Fox Sports *Regional Network:* Radio Pa. *Nat'l Reps:* Katz Radio
Arbitron Metro Market: Lancaster, PA *Format:* Sports *Hrs. of News Programming:* News progmg 8 hrs wkly *Target Audience:* 25-54; men
Bonnie Rowbotham, Chairman
Arthur Rowbotham, President
Sue Sensenig, Programming Director
William Baldwin, Executive Vice President

WROZ
01-01-1944; 101.3 mhz FM *Hrs Open:* 24; 7.4 kw; 1243 ft.; N40 2 4 W76 37 8
PO Box 4368, Lancaster, PA 17604 US
(717) 653-0800, *Fax:* (717) 653-0122
www.roseradio.com
wroz@hallradio.com
License: Lancaster, Lancaster County, PA held by Hall Communications Inc.
Group Owner: Hall Communications Inc.
Nat'l Reps: Katz Radio *Wire Services:* AP
Arbitron Metro Market: Lancaster, PA *Format:* Adult Contemp *No. News Employees:* 1 *Target Audience:* 25-54; women
Bonnie Hall Rowbotham, Chairman
Art Rowbotham, President
Michael Anthony, Programming Director
Justin Broka, News Director
Patsy Sympson, Air Personality
Bill Baldwin, Executive Vice President
Dennis Mitchell, Morning ShowHost
Michelle Cruz, Morning Show Host

Lansdale

WNPV
10-17-1960; 1440 khz AM *Hrs Open:* 24; 2.5 kw-D, DA2; 0.5 kw-N, DA2; N40 14 18 W75 19 0
1210 Synder Road, Lansdale, PA 19446 US
(215) 855-8211, *Fax:* (215) 368-0180
www.wnpv1440.com
dberger@wnpv1440.com
License: Lansdale, PA held by WNPV Inc.
Nat'l Network: Fox News Radio *Regional Network:* Radio Pa.
Arbitron Metro Market: Philadelphia, PA *Format:* News, News/Talk, 84, Talk *Special Programming:* Big band 3 hrs, relg 5 hrs, sports 6 hrs wkly *Hrs. of News Programming:* news progmg 20 hrs wkly *No. News Employees:* 2 *Target Audience:* 30 plus. *Adv. Rates:* 15; 15; 15; 15
Phillip Hunt, President
Linda Moskal, General Sales Mgr
Darryl Berger, Programming Director
Randy Brock, News Director
David McCrork, Engineering Dir

Lansford

WLSH
12-24-1952; 1410 khz AM *Hrs Open:* 24; 5 kw-D, DAD; N40 50 40 W75 50 37
Mailing Address: Route 209, Lansford, PA 18232 US
Second Address: Box D, Lansford, PA 18232
(570) 645-3123, *Fax:* (570) 645-2159
www.wmgh.com
wmgh@ptdprolog.net
License: Lansford, PA held by J-Systems Franchising Corp.
Group Owner: J-Systems Franchising Corp.; acq 1-89; $300,000;
Nat'l Network: Westwood One; USA *Regional Network:* Radio Pa.
Arbitron Metro Market: Allentown-Bethlehem, PA *Format:* Adult Contemp *Special Programming:* Big Band 4 hrs, Oldies 18 hrs wkly *Target Audience:* 35-64; Mature adults
Harold Fulmer III, CEO
Harold Fulmer, III, President
Christopher Fulmer, Operations Dir
Bill Lakatas, General Manager

Laporte

*WPAL
09-01-1968; 91.7 mhz FM *Hrs Open:* 24; 0.27 kw; 161 ft.; N41 26 6 W76 28 28
US
(843) 529-9293, *Fax:* (843) 746-9299
wayx.wayfm.com
License: Laporte, Dorchester County, PA held by Charles W. Cherry, Receiver for Gresham Communications Inc.
Arbitron Metro Market: Charleston, SC *Format:* Christian
Bret Bremberg, General Manager

*WPAL(FM)
91.7 mhz FM; 190 w; Ant 161 ft; N41 26 06 W76 28 28
Box 20155, Scranton, PA 18502
(607) 427-0452
License: Laporte, Sullivan County, PA held by Telikoja Educational Broadcasting Inc.
Population Served: 2,932 *Arbitron Metro Market:* Towanda, PA
Kevin Fitzgerald, President

Latrobe

WCNS
08-11-1956; 1480 khz AM *Hrs Open:* 24; 0.5 kw-D, DAN; 1 kw-N, DAN; N40 16 12 W79 23 13
400 Unity Street, Suite 200, Latrobe, PA 15650 US
(724) 537-3338, *Fax:* (724) 539-9798
www.1480wcns.com
mailbox@wcnsradio.com
License: Latrobe, PA held by Longo Media Group.
Nat'l Network: Westwood One
Arbitron Metro Market: Latrobe, Pennsylvania / Pittsburgh, PA
Format: Variety/Diverse *Special Programming:* Relg 2 hrs wkly *Hrs. of News Programming:* news progmg 15 hrs wkly *No. News Employees:* 3 *TargetAudience:* 25 +; general
John Longo, President
Greg Zahornacky, Station Manager
Dow Carnahan, Programming Director

WQTW
01-01-1952; 1570 khz AM; 1 kw-D, NDD; N40 18 7 W79 21 56
Rebroadcasts: Rebroadcasts WLSW(FM) Scottdale
R. D. #7, Box 56, Greensburg, PA 15601 US
(724) 532-1778, *Fax:* (724) 532-1779
License: Latrobe, PA held by L. Stanley Wall.
Arbitron Metro Market: Pittsburgh, PA *Format:* Adult Contemp
L. Stanley Wall, President

Lebanon

WADV
07-04-1976; 940 khz AM *Hrs Open:* 19; 1 kw-D, ND1; 0.005 kw-N, ND1; N40 22 22 W76 21 53
152 S. Spruce Street, Birdsboro, PA 19508 US
(662) 844-8888, *Fax:* (662) 842-6791
www.afr.net
License: Lebanon, PA held by WADV Radio Inc.
Nat'l Network: Moody
Format: Gospel
Marvin Sanders, General Manager

WLBR
11-13-1946; 1270 khz AM *Hrs Open:* 5 AM-1 AM; 5 kw-D, DA2; 1 kw-N, DA2; N40 21 35 W76 27 30
PO Box 1270, Lebanon, PA 17042 US
(717) 272-7651, *Fax:* (717) 274-0161
License: Lebanon, PA held by Lebanon Broadcasting Co.
Regional Network: Radio Pa. *Nat'l Reps:* Roslin *Regional Reps:* Dome
Arbitron Metro Market: Harrisburg-Lebanon-Carlisle, PA *Format:* News, News/Talk, 86 *No. News Employees:* 2 *Target Audience:* 25-64.
Robert Etter, Operations Dir
Mickey Santora, General Sales Mgr
Gordon Weise, News Director
Glenn Waybright, Chief Engineer
Greg Lyons, Music Director
Laura Lebeau, News Reporter
Scott Bradley, Sports Commentator
Gayle Reich,Traffic Manager

WQIC
01-01-1948; 100.1 mhz FM *Hrs Open:* 5 AM-1 AM; 3 kw; 266 ft.; N40 21 37 W76 27 31
PO Box 1270, Lebanon, PA 17042 US
(717) 272-7651, *Fax:* (717) 274-0161
License: Lebanon, Lebanon County, PA
Arbitron Metro Market: Harrisburg-Lebanon-Carlisle, PA *Format:* Adult Contemp *Target Audience:* 25-54.
Steve Todd, Programming Director
Gayle Reich, News Director
John Tuscano, Disc Jockey
Phil Liles, Disc Jockey
Mike Ebersole, Music Director
Scott Bradley, Sports Commentator

Lehighton

WBYN
04-12-1962; 1160 khz AM *Hrs Open:* 24; 4 kw-D, DA2; 1 kw-N, DA2; N40 49 3 W75 41 31 *Rebroadcasts:* Rebroadcasts WBYN-FM Boyertown 100%
P. O. Box 115, Lehighton, PA 18235 US
(610) 258-6155, *Fax:* (610) 253-3384
License: Lehighton, PA held by Nassau Broadcasting II LLC
Group Owner: Nassau Broadcasting Partners L.P.; (acq 4-25-2003; $375,000).
Nat'l Reps: Katz Radio *Regional Reps:* Glenn Jones
Arbitron Metro Market: Allentown-Bethl *Format:* Christian
Rick Musselman, General Manager

Lehman Township

WABT(FM)
10-30-1970; 96.7 mhz FM *Hrs Open:* 24; 3 kw; Ant 300 ft; N41 22 24 W74 43 49
15 Neversink Dr., Port Jervis, NY 12771
(845) 856-5185
kevinhalpenny@foxcountry.us
License: Lehman Township, Pike County, PA
Arbitron Metro Market: Newburgh-Middletown, NY (Mid-Hudson Valley) *No. News Employees:* 2
Rick Davis, Programming Director
Judi Edwards, News Director
Rob Ryan, Disc Jockey
Ryan Drean, Disc Jockey
Victoria Curtain, Disc Jockey
Bob Oefinger, Disc Jockey

Levittown

WBCB
12-08-1957; 1490 khz AM *Hrs Open:* 24; 1 kw-U, ND1; N40 10 8 W74 50 8
200 Magnolia Drive, Levittown, PA 19054 US
(800) 877-5600, *Fax:* (916) 251-1650
www.klove.com
License: Levittown, PA held by Progressive Broadcasting Co.
Nat'l Network: USA
Arbitron Metro Market: El Paso TX *Format:* Christian
Mike Novak, President

Lewisburg

WCXR
10-18-1990; 103.7 mhz FM *Hrs Open:* 24; 0.95 kw; 801 ft.; N40 58 38 W77 7 0 *Rebroadcasts:* Rebroadcasts WZXR(FM) South Williamsport 100%
1685 Four Mile Drive, Williamsport, PA 17701 US
(570) 323-8200, *Fax:* (570) 327-9138
www.wzxr.com
dan.farr@bybradio.com
License: Lewisburg, Union County, PA held by South Williamsport SabreCom Inc.
Group Owner: Backyard Broadcasting LLC; (acq 12-1-02; grpsl).
Nat'l Network: ABC *Nat'l Reps:* Christal
Arbitron Metro Market: Sunbury-Selinsgrove-Lewisburg, PA
Format: Classic Rock *No. News Employees:* 3 *Target Audience:* 25-54. *Adv. Rates:* 30; 30; 30; 20
Robin Smith, CFO
Barry Drake, President
Dan Farr, General Manager
Ted Minier, Programming Director
John Finn, News Director

*WGRC
04-22-1988; 91.3 mhz FM *Hrs Open:* 24; 3 kw; 322 ft.; N40 56 40 W76 52 45
150 Buffalo Rd #202, Lewisburg, PA 17837 US
(570) 523-1190, *Fax:* (570) 523-1114
www.wgrc.com
email@wgrc.com
License: Lewisburg, Union County, PA held by Salt and Light Media Ministries Inc.
Nat'l Network: Salem Radio Network *Wire Services:* AP
Format: Adult Contemp, Christian *Hrs. of News Programming:* news progmg 16 hrs wkly *No. News Employees:* 3 *Target Audience:* 25-54; young to middle-aged adult
Larry Weidman, General Manager
Don Casteline, Programming Director
Linda Dantonio, News Director
Chris Miller, Engineering Dir
Lamar Smith, Chief Engineer
Jim Diehl, News Reporter
John Callahan, News Reporter

*WVBU-FM
10-01-1965; 90.5 mhz FM *Hrs Open:* 8 AM-2 AM; 0.225 kw; -33 ft.; N40 57 18 W76 52 55
Box C-3956, Lewisburg, PA 17837 US
(570) 577-2000, *Fax:* (570) 577-1174
www.orgs.bucknell.edu/wvbu
wvbu@bucknell.edu
License: Lewisburg, Union County, PA held by Bucknell University.
Arbitron Metro Market: Lewisburg, PA *Format:* Rock/AOR
Special Programming: Jazz 3 hrs, dance/club 6 hrs, prison request 2 hrs *Hrs. of News Programming:* News progmg 7 hrs wkly *Target Audience:* 18-23; collegestudents
Jordan Gremli, General Manager
Alex Alam, Station Manager
Mike Estrich, General Sales Mgr
Duke Wellington, Programming Director
Michael Ajjan, Promotions Manager
Todd Fogle, Chief Engineer
Charlie Geitz, Music Director
AaronVockley, Production Manager
Matt Szucs, Business Manager

Lewistown

WCHX
07-01-1987; 105.5 mhz FM *Hrs Open:* 24; 3 kw; 817 ft; N40 39 43 W77 34 28
Mailing Address: Box 911, Lewistown, PA 17009
Second Address: 114 N. Logan Blvd., Burnham, PA 17009
(717) 242-1493, *Fax:* (717) 242-3764
www.chx105.com
License: Lewistown, Mifflin County, PA held by Mifflin County Communications Inc.
Nat'l Network: Fox News Radio *Regional Network:* Radio Pa.
Population Served: 125,000*Hrs. of News Programming:* news progmg 10 hrs wkly *No. News Employees:* 1 *Target Audience:* 25-54; mature, affluent, middle & upper class adults
Michelle Long, General Manager
Scott Brattan, General Sales Mgr
Steve Buda, Programming Director

WIEZ
06-01-1941; 670 khz AM *Hrs Open:* Sunrise-sunset; 5.4 kw-D, NDD; N40 36 30 W77 34 45
Mailing Address: 12 1/2 East Market St., Lewistown, PA 17044 US
Second Address: 12 E. Market St. 2nd Floor, Lewistown, PA 17044
(717) 248-6757, *Fax:* (717) 248-6759
www.new.wiez.com
pete@merfradio.com
License: Lewistown, PA held by First Media Radio LLC.
Group Owner: First Media Radio LLC; (acq 3-28-2001; grpsl)
Nat'l Reps: Dome
Format: News *Hrs. of News Programming:* news progmg 12 hrs wkly *No. News Employees:* 2 *Target Audience:* 45 plus; adults who control the area's disposable income
Jeff Stevens, Operations Dir
Pete Herman, General Manager
Mary Lee Schaeffer, News Director

*WJRC
07-01-1996; 90.9 mhz FM *Hrs Open:* 24; 0.094 kw; 1293 ft.; N40 34 20 W77 30 51 *Rebroadcasts:* Rebroadcasts WGRC(FM) Lewisburg 100%
150 Buffalo Road, Suite 202, Lewisburg, PA 17837 US
(570) 523-1190, *Fax:* (570) 523-1114
www.wgrc.com
email@wgrc.com
License: Lewistown, Mifflin County, PA held by Salt and Light Media Ministries Inc.
Nat'l Network: Salem Radio Network *Wire Services:* AP
Format: Christian *Hrs. of News Programming:* news progmg 9 hrs wkly *No. News Employees:* 3 *Target Audience:* 25-54.
Don Casteline, Operations Dir
Larry Weidman, General Manager
Linda Dantonio, News Director
Chris Miller, Engineering Dir
Lamar Smith, Chief Engineer
Jim Diehl, News Reporter
John Callahan, News Reporter

WKVA
12-04-1949; 920 khz AM *Hrs Open:* 5 AM-midnight; 1 kw-D, DAN; 0.5 kw-N, DAN; N40 34 45 W77 34 18
Mailing Address: 114 North Logan Boulevard, Burnham, PA 17009 US
Second Address: 114 N. Logan Blvd., Burnham, PA 17009
(717) 242-1055, *Fax:* (717) 242-3764
www.oldies920.com
wkva@oldies920.com
License: Lewistown, PA held by Mifflin County Communications Inc.
Nat'l Network: ABC; CBS Radio *Regional Network:* Radio Pa.
Format: Oldies *Hrs. of News Programming:* news progmg 31 hrs wkly *No. News Employees:* 2 *Target Audience:* 25-54; blue collar mix of agricultural & industrial adults

Anna Hain, President
Jed Donahue, Operations Dir
Erik Lane, News Director

WMRF-FM
10-01-1964; 95.7 mhz FM *Hrs Open:* 24; 3.9 kw; 407 ft.; N40 36 30 W77 34 45
12 E. Market St, 2nd Fl, Lewistown, PA 17044 US
(717) 248-6757, *Fax:* (717) 248-6759
www.merfradio.com
pete@merfradio.com
License: Lewistown, Mifflin County, PA held by First Media Radio LLC.
Group Owner: First Media Radio LLC; (acq 5-14-2001; grpsl)
Arbitron Metro Market: Lewistown, PA *Format:* Adult Contemp
Hrs. of News Programming: news progmg 8 hrs wkly *No. News Employees:* 2 *Target Audience:* 18-44.
Jeff Stevens, Operations Dir
Peter Herman, General Manager
Mary Lee Sheaffer, News Director

Lincoln University

***WWLU**
08-01-1975; 88.7 mhz FM; 0.003 kw horiz; 141 ft.; N39 48 36 W75 55 35
U.S. Route 131, Lincoln University, PA 19352 US
(610) 932-8300, *Fax:* (610) 932-1095
www.lincoln.edu
asims@lincoln.edu
License: Lincoln University, Chester County, PA held by Lincoln University.
Format: Urban Contemporary
Whitney G. Walton, General Manager

Linesville

WMVL
05-04-1970; 101.7 mhz FM *Hrs Open:* 24; 1.4 kw; 554 ft.; N41 42 38 W80 16 29
Mailing Address: P. O. Box 307, Linesville, PA 16424 US
Second Address: 16271Conneaut Lake Rd., Ste 102, Meadville, PA 16335
(814) 333-9011, *Fax:* (814) 333-2562
cool1017online.com
wmvl@zoominternet.net
License: Linesville, Crawford County, PA held by Vilkie Communications Inc.
Nat'l Network: ABC *Regional Reps:* Regional Reps; CLE; OH
Arbitron Metro Market: Meadville, PA *Format:* Oldies *Hrs. of News Programming:* News progmg 8 hrs wkly *Target Audience:* 29 plus. *Adv. Rates:* 16; 15; 16; 9
Joseph Vilkie, President
Eugene Vilkie, Operations Dir
Jim Jewell, General Sales Mgr
Chuck Stopp, Programming Director
Dave Hanahan, Sales Manager
Jenna Wagner, Sales

Lock Haven

WBPZ
02-20-1947; 1230 khz AM *Hrs Open:* 24; 1 kw-U, ND1; N41 8 3 W77 28 9
Mailing Address: P. O. Box 420, Lock Haven, PA 17745 US
Second Address: 21 E. Main St., Lock Haven, PA 17745
(717)748-4038, *Fax:* (717)-748-0092
wbpz@kcnet.org
License: Lock Haven, PA held by Lipez Broadcasting Corp.
Nat'l Reps: Keystone (unwired net); Dome
Arbitron Metro Market: Lock Haven, PA *Format:* Oldies *Special Programming:* Loc sports *Hrs. of News Programming:* news progmg 10 hrs wkly *No. News Employees:* 1 *Target Audience:* General.
John Lipez, President
John Lupez, General Sales Mgr
Randy Dorey, Programming Director
Mark Sohmer, News Director
Dennis Sherman, Chief Engineer
Bill Daney, Music Director
Michelle Grove, Traffic Manager

WSQV(FM)
09-01-1965; 92.1 mhz FM *Hrs Open:* 24; 3 kw; 255 ft; N41 08 49 W77 29 16
Mailing Address: Box 420, Lock Haven, PA 17745
Second Address: 21 E. Main St., Lock Haven, PA 17745
(570) 748-4038, *Fax:* (570) 748-0092
wbpz@kcnet.org
License: Lock Haven, Clinton County, PA
Population Served: 70,000 *Arbitron Metro Market:* Williamsport, PA *Format:* Adult Contemp *Hrs. of News Programming:* news progmg 6 hrs wkly *No. News Employees:* 1 *Target Audience:* 21-48.
Michelle Grove, News Director

Loretto

WWGE
12-07-1963; 1400 khz AM *Hrs Open:* 24; 1 kw-U, ND1; N40 30 12 W78 38 10
Mailing Address: 3425 Chambersburg Road, Biglerville, PA 17307 US
Second Address: 104 S. Center St., Suite 401, Ebensburg, PA 15931
(814) 619-3284, *Fax:* (814) 255-3343
www.edge-radio.com/
License: Loretto, PA held by Pennsylvania Radiowerks LLC
Nat'l Network: Jones Radio Networks
Arbitron Metro Market: Loretto, PA *Format:* News, News/Talk, 84, Talk *Adv. Rates:* 4; 3; 2; 1
Rev. Michael Yeager, President
Jennifer Strelnik, General Manager

Manchester Township

WGLD
10-22-1950; 1440 khz AM
P.O. Box 102, Springhouse, PA 19477 US
(717) 764-1155, *Fax:* (717) 252-4708
espn1440.com
info@wsba910.com
License: Manchester Township, PA held by Susquehanna License Co. LLC.
Group Owner: Cumulus Media Partners LLC; (acq 5-11-2005; $280,000)
Nat'l Network: ESPN Radio
Arbitron Metro Market: York, PA *Format:* Sports *Target Audience:* General.
John Dickey, President
Brian Shaffer, Director of Sales
Todd Toerper, Promotions Manager
Bob Adams, VP/Market Manager

Mansfield

WNBQ
06-01-1999; 92.3 mhz FM *Hrs Open:* 24; 1.6 kw; 643 ft.; N41 53 53 W77 5 38 *Rebroadcasts:* Rebroadcasts WNBT-FM Wellsboro 100%
Mailing Address: 9 S. Main Street, Coudersport, PA 16915 US
Second Address: 12385 Rt. 6 Box 198-B, Wellsboro, PA 16901
(570) 724-1490, *Fax:* (570) 724-6971
www.wnbt.net
wnbt@ynt.net
License: Mansfield, Tioga County, PA held by Farm & Home Broadcasting Co.
Group Owner: Allegheny Mountain Network Stations
Nat'l Network: Westwood One *Regional Reps:* Dome & Assoc.
Arbitron Metro Market: Wellsboro, PA *Format:* Adult Contemp
Adv. Rates: 223.80; 186; 223.80; 141.60
Cary Simpson, President
Al Harer, General Manager

***WNTE**
09-15-1968; 89.5 mhz FM; 0.115 kw; -279 ft.; N41 48 23 W77 4 25
311 South Hall., Mansfield, PA 16933 US
(570) 662-4653, *Fax:* (570) 662-4654
www.wnte.com
slatera@mounties.mansfield.edu
License: Mansfield, Tioga County, PA held by Mansfield University
Arbitron Metro Market: Mansfield, PA *Format:* Contemporary Hits/Top 40, Rock/AOR *Special Programming:* Black 5 hrs, jazz 2 hrs wkly *Target Audience:* 17-25; college students/community
Randolph Bell, President
Wayne DeSylvia, Station Manager
Kenny Ertel, Programming Director

Markleysburg

***WLOG**
01-01-2002; 89.1 mhz FM; 0.1 kw vert; 328 ft.; N39 43 32 W79 28 53
Dinner Bell Road, Farmington, PA 15437 US
(208) 733-3551, *Fax:* (208) 734-0674
www.edgewaterbroadcasting.com
License: Markleysburg, Fayette County, PA held by Edgewater Broadcasting Inc.
Arbitron Metro Market: Twin Falls, ID *Format:* Christian
Ben Mccarron, Chief Operating Engineer
Clark Parrish, President
Robert L. Jackson, Head of Programming & Operations
Jim Long, General Manager
Steve Atkin, Promotions Manager
Diana Atkin, Vice President
Earl Williamson, Secretary/ Treasurer
John Devine, Director
Dennis Clounch, Director

Martinsburg

WWBJ
02-27-1968; 1110 khz AM; 1 kw-D, NDD; N40 18 14 W78 15 59
R.D. 2, Box 87, Martinsburg, PA 16662 US
(814) 793-2188, *Fax:* (814) 793-9727
www.wwjb.com
License: Martinsburg, PA held by Martinsburg Broadcasting Inc.
Arbitron Metro Market: Altoona, PA *Format:* News, Talk, 74
Special Programming: Farm one hr wkly *Target Audience:* General.
Larry Walters, President
Deborah Walters, Operations Dir
Bill Reed, News Director
Cheryl Walters, Women's Int Ed

WJSM-FM
04-19-1965; 92.7 mhz FM; 1.9 kw; 591 ft.; N40 20 50 W78 24 57
R.D.2, Box 87, Martinsburg, PA 16662 US
(814) 793-2188, *Fax:* (814) 793-9727
www.wjsm.com
License: Martinsburg, Blair County, PA held by Martinsburg Broadcasting Inc.
Nat'l Network: USA
Arbitron Metro Market: Altoona, PA *Format:* Gospel, News, 62, Talk, Religious
Larry Walters, President
Larry Walters, General Manager
Byrle Hap Ritchey, General Sales Mgr
Byrle Hap Ritchey, Programming Director
Bill Reed, News Director
Terry MacAlarney, Transmitter Engineer
Cheryl Walters, TrafficManager
Matthew Lightner, Audio Engineer
Priscilla Ritchey, Sales Bookkeepers
Kenneth Ferry, Founder
Margaret Ferry, Co-Founder

Masontown

***WRIJ**
11-01-1990; 106.9 mhz FM *Hrs Open:* 19; 0.98 kw; 810 ft.; N39 42 17 W79 46 30 *Rebroadcasts:* Rebroadcasts WAIJ(FM) Grantsville, MD 100%
34 Springs Rd, P O Box 540, Grantsville, MD 21536 US
(301) 895-3292, *Fax:* (301) 895-3293
www.hesalive.net
hesalive@hesalive.net
License: Masontown, Fayette County, PA held by He's Alive Inc.
Group Owner: He's Alive Inc.
Nat'l Network: USA
Format: Adult Contemp, Christian, 44, Religious *Target Audience:* 18-35.
Sharon Johnson, President

***WYFU**
01-01-2003; 88.5 mhz FM; 16 kw vert; 328 ft.; N39 47 15 W79 59 20
8030 Arrowridge Blvd., Charlotte, NC 28273 US
(704) 523-5555, *Fax:* (704) 522-1967
www.bbnradio.org
bbn@bbnradio.org
License: Masontown, Fayette County, PA held by Bible Broadcasting Network Inc.
Group Owner: Bible Broadcasting Network; (acq 2-12-99; $250,000).
Arbitron Metro Market: Masontown, PA *Format:* Christian
Richard Johnson, General Manager

McConnellsburg

WEEO-FM
01-01-1997; 103.7 mhz FM; 0.135 kw; 1555 ft.; N39 55 25 W77 57 20
Cary H. Simpson Dba, 37 South Main Street, Chambersburg, PA 17201 US
(814) 272-1320, *Fax:* (717) 709-0802
www.weeofm.com/
ameyer@1059qwikrock.com
License: McConnellsburg, Fulton County, PA held by Allegheny Mountain Network.
Group Owner: Allegheny Mountain Network Stations; (acq 10-95; $18,000)
Regional Reps: Dome

Arbitron Metro Market: McConnellsburg, PA *Format:* Rock/AOR *Adv. Rates:* 33; 30; 33; 26
John Simpson, CEO

***WWCF**
01-01-2005; 88.7 mhz FM; 0.009 kw; 1194 ft.; N39 54 58 W77 57 25
Rural Delivery-1, Box 211-F, McConnelsburg, PA 17233 US
(717) 485-5526
License: McConnellsburg, Fulton County, PA held by Morris Broadcasting & Communications Inc.
Arbitron Metro Market: McConnellsburg, PA *Format:* Children
Glenn Morris, President

McKeesport

WEDO
01-01-1947; 810 khz AM *Hrs Open:* Sunrise-sunset
414 5th Avenue, McKeesport, PA 15132 US
(412) 664-4431, *Fax:* (412) 664-1236
www.wedo810.com/
wedoradio@comcast.net
License: McKeesport, PA held by 810 Inc.
Arbitron Metro Market: Mckeesport, PA *Format:* Talk *Special Programming:* Slovenian one hr, Slovak one hr, Greek one hr, Croation one hr, It one hr wkly *Target Audience:* 35-65, 25-54, 65+.
Judith Baron, President
John James, Operations Dir
Bill Korch, Programming Director

WMNY
04-01-1947; 1360 khz AM *Hrs Open:* 24; 5 kw-D, DAN; 1 kw-N, DAN; N40 24 30 W79 55 40; N40 18 41 W79 50 59
1459 Crane Avenue, Pittsburgh, PA 15220 US
(412) 875-9500, *Fax:* (412) 875-9474
www.wmnyradio.com
License: McKeesport, PA held by Renda Broadcasting Corp. of Nevada.
Nat'l Network: ABC *Nat'l Reps:* McGavren Guild *Wire Services:* AP; Metro Weather Service Inc.
Arbitron Metro Market: Pittsburgh, PA *Format:* Talk *Special Programming:* Oldies 9 hrs, polka 2 hrs wkly *Hrs. of News Programming:* News progmg 15 hrs wkly *Target Audience:* 25-54. *Adv. Rates:* 55; 55; 55;30
Tony Renda Sr., CEO
Tony Renda Jr., General Manager

Meadville

***WARC**
02-03-1963; 90.3 mhz FM; 0.4 kw; 66 ft.; N41 38 57 W80 8 38
520 N Main St - Box C, Meadville, PA 16335 US
(814) 332-3376
www.sites.allegheny.edu/warc
warc@allegheny.edu
License: Meadville, Crawford County, PA held by Allegheny College.
Arbitron Metro Market: Meadville, PA. *Format:* Alternative *Special Programming:* Black 8 hrs, class 10 hrs, jazz 4 hrs wkly
Jennifer Knapp, General Manager

WMGW
01-01-1947; 1490 khz AM; 1 kw-U, ND1; N41 37 53 W80 10 37
P.O. Box 397, Meadville, PA 16335 US
(814) 724-1111, *Fax:* (814) 333-9628
www.myantsnetwork.com/
License: Meadville, PA held by Forever Broadcasting LLC.
Group Owner: Forever Broadcasting; (acq 7-20-00; grpsl).
Arbitron Metro Market: Meadville, PA *Format:* News, News/Talk, 84, Talk *Target Audience:* 25-54.
Terry Dietz, General Manager
Dave Galentine, Programming Director

WGYY
01-01-1947; 100.3 mhz FM; 20 kw; 587 ft.; N41 37 53 W80 10 37
Downtown Mall, PO Bx 397, Meadville, PA 16335 US
(814) 724-1111, *Fax:* (814) 333-9628
www.froggyfun.com
radioron6668@yahoo.com
License: Meadville, Crawford County, PA held by Forever Broadcasting LLC
Group Owner: Forever Broadcasting
Arbitron Metro Market: Meadville, PA *Format:* Country
Kim Vacanti, Sales Manager

***WVME**
01-01-2002; 91.9 mhz FM *Hrs Open:* 24; 4.4 kw; 308 ft.; N41 37 50 W80 10 38 *Rebroadcasts:* Rebroadcasts WCRF(FM) Cleveland, OH 100%
820 North Lasalle Blvd, Chicago, IL 60610 US
(440) 526-1111, *Fax:* (440) 526-1319
www.wcrfradio.org
wcrf@moody.edu
License: Meadville, Crawford County, PA held by The Moody Bible Institute of Chicago.
Group Owner: The Moody Bible Institute of Chicago
Wire Services: AP
Arbitron Metro Market: Cleveland, OH *Format:* Religious *Target Audience:* 25-55; Adults
Michael Easley, President
Richard Lee, Station Manager
Phil Villareal, Programming Director
Gary Bittner, News Director
Doug Hainer, Chief Engineer
Alice Andrews, Office Administrator; Volunteer Coordinator
Keel Arlia, FrontOffice Receptionist; Secretary
Paul Carter, Operations Coordinator; Afternoon Announcer
Jonathan Dentler, Production Assistant
Cindy Grove, Front Office Receptionist; Secretary
Dick Lee, Manager

Mechanicsburg

WWKL
09-22-1959; 93.5 mhz FM; 1.25 kw; 719 ft.; N40 10 38 W76 52 38 *Rebroadcasts:* Rebroadcasts WTPA(FM) Mechanicsburg 100%
600congress Avenue, Suite 1400, Austin, TX 78701 US
(717) 238-1041, *Fax:* (717) 234-7780
www.hot935fm.com
info@hot92.com
License: Mechanicsburg, Lebanon County, PA held by Cumulus Licensing Corp.
Group Owner: Cumulus Media Inc.; (acq 11-28-2000; grpsl)
Regional Network: Radio Pa.
Arbitron Metro Market: Harrisburg, PA *Format:* Contemporary Hits/Top 40 *Special Programming:* Relg 6 hrs, Sp 14 hrs, Hershey Bears hockey, Hersh *Target Audience:* 25-54.
John O'Dea, Operations Dir
Ron Giovanniello, General Manager
Karen Richards, General Sales Mgr
John O'Dea, Programming Director
Marisa Allen, Promotions Manager
Dave Supplee, Chief Engineer
Todd Matthews, General SalesManager
Amy Warner, Music Director

Media

WRNB
01-01-1946; 100.3 mhz FM *Hrs Open:* 5:30 AM-midnight; 17 kw; 863 ft.; N40 2 36 W75 14 33
1001 E. Baltimore Pike, Media, PA 19063 US
(610) 276-1100, *Fax:* (610) 279-1139
License: Media, Camden County, PA held by Radio One Licenses LLC.
Group Owner: Radio One Inc.; (acq 2-2-2004; $35 million).
Arbitron Metro Market: Philadelphia *Format:* Urban Contemporary
Chester Schofield, General Manager

Mercer

WLLF
01-01-1985; 96.7 mhz FM *Hrs Open:* 24; 1.4 kw; 486 ft.; N41 18 43 W80 16 39
Box 1120, Hermitage, PA 16148 US
(724) 346-4113, *Fax:* (724) 981-4545
www.967theriver.com
bob.greenburg@cumulus.com
License: Mercer, Mercer County, PA held by Cumulus Licensing Corp.
Group Owner: Cumulus Media Inc.; (acq 3-15-00; grpsl).
Nat'l Network: Jones Radio Networks
Arbitron Metro Market: Youngstown-Warren, OH *Format:* Adult Contemp
Brian Schimmel, General Manager
Bob Popa, Programming Director
Joe Bilo, News Director
Wes Boyd, Chief Engineer

Mercersburg

WNUZ
01-01-1945; 92.1 mhz FM *Hrs Open:* 5 AM-11 PM; 4 kw; 295 ft.; N39 48 34 W77 48 22
4850 Connecticut Ave, NW, Suite 103, Washington, DC 20008 US
(717) 597-9200, *Fax:* (717) 597-9210
www.now921.com
License: Mercersburg, Talladega County, PA held by Birmingham Christian Radio Inc.
Arbitron Metro Market: Franklin, PA *Format:* Contemporary Hits/Top 40 *Special Programming:* Talk 5 hrs, Gospel 7 hrs, bluegrass 6 hrs wkly *No. News Employees:* 1 *Target Audience:* 25-70; middle/upper middle, blue& white collar *Adv. Rates:* 65; 47; 47; 37
L.E. Willis Sr., President
Jonnie Luster, General Manager
Louis Amerson, Programming Director

Mexico

WJUN
09-08-1955; 1220 khz AM *Hrs Open:* 24
Mailing Address: Old Rt. 22 East, Mexico, PA 17056 US
Second Address: 7452 William Penn Highway, Mifflintown, PA 17059
(717) 436-2135, *Fax:* (717) 436-8155
www.wjun925.com
wjun@nmax.net
License: Mexico, PA held by Starview Media Inc.
Nat'l Network: ESPN Radio *Regional Network:* Radio Pa. *Format:* Sports *Special Programming:* Relg 2 hrs wkly *No. News Employees:* 1 *Target Audience:* 25-54. *Adv. Rates:* available on request
Douglas George, President
Curt Dreibelbis, General Manager
Laurie Hower, News Director
John Hess, Chief Engineer

WJUN-FM
07-04-1989; 92.5 mhz FM *Hrs Open:* 24; 0.44 kw; 1181 ft.; N40 34 58 W77 29 48
Mailing Address: Old Rt 22 East, Mexico, PA 17056 US
Second Address: 7452 William Penn Highway, Mifflintown, PA 17059
(717) 436-2135, *Fax:* (717) 436-8155
www.wjun925.com
wjun@wjun925.com
License: Mexico, Juniata County, PA held by Starview Media Inc.
Nat'l Network: Motor Racing Net *Regional Network:* Radio Pa. *Format:* Country *Hrs. of News Programming:* news progmg 5 hrs wkly *No. News Employees:* 1
Curt Dreibelbis, General Manager
Mel Thomas, Programming Director

Meyersdale

WQZS
01-01-1992; 93.3 mhz FM; 0.63 kw; 965 ft.; N39 47 49 W79 10 5
128 Hunsrick Road, Meyersdale, PA 15552 US
(814) 634-9111, *Fax:* (814) 634-0882
helenwahl27@hotmail.com
License: Meyersdale, Somerset County, PA held by Roger Wahl. *Format:* Oldies *Special Programming:* Gospel 5 hrs wkly *No. News Employees:* 1 *Target Audience:* 25-60; females 60%, males 40%
Helen Wahl, General Manager
Jessy Chabol, General Sales Mgr

Middletown

***WMSS**
09-07-1978; 91.1 mhz FM *Hrs Open:* 7 AM-9 PM; 0.45 kw; 73 ft.; N40 12 44 W76 44 47
55 W. Water Street, Middletown, PA 17057 US
(717) 948-9136
www.wmssfm.com
sales@wmssfm.com
License: Middletown, Dauphin County, PA held by Middletown Area School District.
Regional Network: Va. News Net.
Arbitron Metro Market: Harrisburg, PA *Format:* Adult Contemp *Special Programming:* Sports 5 hrs, relg 8 hrs wkly *Hrs. of News Programming:* News progmg one hr wkly *Target Audience:* General.
Maureen Denis, Operations Dir
John Wilsbach, General Manager
Steve Leedy, Operations Manager

***WXPH**
01-01-2006; 88.7 mhz FM; 0.075 kw horiz, 7 kw vert; 709 ft.; N40 2 7 W76 37 19 *Rebroadcasts:* Rebroadcasts WXPN(FM) Philadelphia 100%
P O Box 186, Sellersville, PA 18960 US
(215) 898-6677, *Fax:* (215) 898-0707
www.xpn.org
wxpndesk@xpn.org
License: Middletown, Dauphin County, PA held by The Trustees of the University of Pennsylvania
Arbitron Metro Market: Middletown, PA *Format:* Alternative
Roger LaMay, General Manager
Quyen Shanahan, General Sales Mgr

Mifflinburg

WWBE

01-01-1975; 98.3 mhz FM *Hrs Open:* 24; 1.4 kw; 482 ft.; N40 53 27 W76 59 54 *Rebroadcasts:* Rebroadcasts WUNS(FM) Lewisburg 100%
P.O. Box 90, Rt. 204, State School Bd, Selinsgrove, PA 17870 US
(570) 374-8819, *Fax:* (570) 374-7444
www.b983.com
tmorgan@ptd.net
License: Mifflinburg, Union County, PA held by MMP License LLC.
Group Owner: MAX Media L.L.C.; (acq 10-17-03; grpsl).
Nat'l Network: Westwood One; Jones Radio Networks *Nat'l Reps:* Dome
Arbitron Metro Market: Mifflinburg, PA *Format:* Country *Special Programming:* Gospel 2 hrs wkly *Hrs. of News Programming:* news progmg 2 hrs wkly *No. News Employees:* 1 *Target Audience:* 25-54.
Tom Morgan, Operations Dir
Carol Pierson, General Manager
Greg Adair, Station Manager
Dawn Marie, Programming Director
Kyle Blessing, News Director
Ted Koppen, Chief Engineer
Shelly Marx, Assistant Program Director

Mifflintown

*WQJU

10-15-1985; 107.1 mhz FM *Hrs Open:* 24; 0.37 kw; 1302 ft.; N40 34 20 W77 30 51 *Rebroadcasts:* Rebroadcasts WTLR(FM) State College 100%
2020 Cato Street, State College, PA 16801 US
(814) 237-9857
mail@cpci.org
License: Mifflintown, Juniata County, PA held by Central Pennsylvania Christian Institute.
Nat'l Network: Moody; USA *Wire Services:* AP
Format: Christian *Hrs. of News Programming:* news progmg 8 hrs wkly *No. News Employees:* 1 *Target Audience:* 30-55; adults, family oriented
Mark Van Ouse, General Manager

Milford

WYNY(AM)

1450 khz AM; 1 kw-U; N41 20 10 W74 47 45
135 White Bridge Rd., Middletown, NY 10940
(845) 355-4001, *Fax:* (845) 355-4002
License: Milford, Pike County, PA held by Digital Radio Broadcasting Inc.
Group Owner: Digital Radio Broadcasting Inc.
Population Served: 1,014 *Arbitron Metro Market:* Milford, PA
Bud Williamson, President

Mill Hall

WVRT

08-20-1979; 97.7 mhz FM *Hrs Open:* 24; 6 kw; 295 ft.; N41 13 14 W77 16 39
Mailing Address: 309 West Southern Avenue, South Williamsport, PA 17701 US
Second Address: 1559 W 4th Street, Williamsport, PA 17701
(570) 327-1400, *Fax:* (570) 327-8156
www.variety977.com
kcote@clearchannel.com
License: Mill Hall, Clinton County, PA held by Clear Channel Radio Licenses, Inc.
Group Owner: Clear Channel Communications Inc.; (acq 3-12-01; $1.5 million).
Nat'l Reps: Christal
Arbitron Metro Market: Williamsport, PA *Format:* Adult Contemp *Target Audience:* 18-49. *Adv. Rates:* 17; 17; 17; 12
Karen Cote, General Sales Mgr
Tom Scott, Programming Director
Mike Myer, Engineering Dir

Millersburg

WQLV

02-24-1992; 98.9 mhz FM *Hrs Open:* 24; 0.78 kw; 896 ft.; N40 30 18 W77 7 3
309 Peachtree Drive, Gratz, PA 17030 US
(717) 692-2193, *Fax:* (717) 692-2080
www.wqlvfm.com
bob@wqlvfm.com
License: Millersburg, Dauphin County, PA held by UPOD Radio, LLC
Nat'l Network: ABC
Arbitron Metro Market: Harrisburg-Lebanon-Carlisle, PA *Format:* Adult Contemp *Special Programming:* seasonal High school sports *Hrs. of News Programming:* newscast every hour *Target Audience:* 25 plus *Adv.Rates:* 41.70; 30.70; 35.55; 20.65
Robert Kerstetter, General Manager
Mark West, Programming Director
JD Cooper, Promotions Manager
Ric Cooper, General Manager/Owner

Millersville

*WIXQ

01-01-1978; 91.7 mhz FM *Hrs Open:* 7 AM-3 AM; 0.096 kw; 21 ft.; N40 0 3.1 W76 21 43.4
Student Memorial Center, Millersville, PA 17551 US
(717) 872-3518, *Fax:* (717) 872-3383
www.wixq.com
comments@wixq.com
License: Millersville, Lancaster County, PA held by Millersville University.
Format: Black, Variety/Diverse *Special Programming:* Jazz 2 hrs wkly *Hrs. of News Programming:* News progmg one hr wkly
Target Audience: 18-24; college students
Greg Park, Station Manager
Steve Entrekin, Programming Director
Paul Galvin, Promotions Manager

Milroy

*WRYV

88.7 mhz FM; 2.2 kw; 869 ft.; N40 35 10 W77 41 40 US
(814) 867-3836, *Fax:* (814) 867-1922
www.revfm.net
tim@revfm.net
License: Milroy, Mifflin County, PA held by Invisible Allies Ministries.
Arbitron Metro Market: Milroy, PA *Format:* Christian
Michael Schomer, General Manager

Milton

WMLP

10-27-1955; 1380 khz AM *Hrs Open:* 24; 1 kw-D, ND1; 0.018 kw-N, ND1; N40 59 52 W76 52 17
Mailing Address: P. O. Box 334, Milton, PA 17847 US
Second Address: 1227 County Line Rd., Selingsrove, PA 17870
(570) 286-5838, *Fax:* (570) 743-7837
www.1380wmlp.com
License: Milton, PA held by Sunbury Broadcasting Corp.
Group Owner: Sunbury Broadcasting Corp.; (acq 2006; $3 million with co-located FM).
Nat'l Network: CNN Radio; Premiere Radio Networks; Salem Radio Network; Fox Sports *Nat'l Reps:* Dome; Roslin *Wire Services:* Accu-Weather
Arbitron Metro Market: Sunbury, PA *Format:* Talk *Hrs. of News Programming:* news progmg 12 hrs wkly *No. News Employees:* 4 *Target Audience:* 25-54. *Adv. Rates:* 24.50; 24.50; 24.50; 14.25
Roger Haddon Jr., President
Kevin Herr, Operations Dir
Nicole Shelley, General Sales Mgr
Sara Bartlett, News Director
Harry Bingaman, Chief Engineer

WVLY-FM

10-01-1967; 100.9 mhz FM *Hrs Open:* 24; 1.3 kw; 715 ft.; N40 57 12 W76 45 5
Mailing Address: P.O. Box 334, Milton, PA 17847 US
Second Address: 1227 County Line Rd., Selingsrove, PA 17870
(570) 286-5838, *Fax:* (570) 743-7837
www.wkok.com
equest@wvly.com
License: Milton, Northumberland County, PA held by Sunbury Broadcasting Corp.
Group Owner: Sunbury Broadcasting Corp.
Nat'l Network: Premiere Radio Networks *Nat'l Reps:* Dome; Roslin *Wire Services:* Accu-Weather
Arbitron Metro Market: Sunbury, PA *Format:* Adult Contemp *Special Programming:* Smooth jazz 6 hrs wkly *Hrs. of News Programming:* news progmg 5 hrs wkly *No. News Employees:* 4 *Target Audience:* 25-54;adults *Adv. Rates:* 25.50; 24.50; 24.50; 12.25
Roger Haddon Jr., President/CEO
Kevine Herr, Operations Dir
Nicole Shelley, General Sales Mgr
Drew Kelly, Programming Director
Sara Bartlett, News Director
Harry Bingaman, Chief Engineer
Jayme Dunkelberger, Director of Sales &Finance
Tina Fry, Business Manager
Lynn Hall, Production Director

Monroeville

WPGR

09-27-1964; 1510 khz AM *Hrs Open:* 24
Mailing Address: 3270 Blazer Parkway, Suite 101, Lexington, KY 40509 US
Second Address: Sheridan Broadcasting Co., 960 Penn Ave., Pittsburgh, PA 15222
(412) 456-4064, *Fax:* (412) 391-3559
mdouglass@sbcol.com
License: Monroeville, PA held by McL/McM Pennsylvania LLC.
Group Owner: Sheridan Broadcasting Corp.; (acq 9-28-2001; $625,000)
Nat'l Reps: McGavren Guild
Arbitron Metro Market: Monroeville, PA *Format:* Christian *Special Programming:* Relg 6 hrs wkly *Target Audience:* 25-54; middle class & higher income households *Adv. Rates:* 12; 12; 12; 12
Ronald Davenport Jr., Chairman
Michael Douglass, General Manager

Montrose

*WPEL

05-30-1953; 800 khz AM *Hrs Open:* 6 AM-sunset
P.O. Box 248, 9 Ocust Street, Montrose, PA 18801 US
(570) 278-2811, *Fax:* (570) 278-1442
wpel.org
mail@wpel.org
License: Montrose, PA held by Montrose Broadcasting Corp.
Group Owner: Montrose Broadcasting Corp.
Nat'l Network: AP Network News *Regional Network:* Radio Pa.
Wire Services: AP
Format: Gospel *Special Programming:* None *Hrs. of News Programming:* News progmg 7 hrs wkly *Target Audience:* General; families
Larry Souder, President
Lloyd Sheldon, General Manager
LaVerne Sollick, Promotions Manager
Robert Brigham, Chief Engineer

WPEL-FM

06-05-1961; 96.5 mhz FM *Hrs Open:* 24; 57 kw; 459 ft.; N41 51 16 W75 51 50
P.O. Box 248, Montrose, PA 18801 US
(570) 278-2811, *Fax:* (570) 278-1442
wpel.org
mail@wpel.org
License: Montrose, Susquehanna County, PA held by Montrose Broadcasting Corp.
Group Owner: Montrose Broadcasting Corp.
Nat'l Network: Moody; AP Network News; Salem Radio Network
Regional Network: Radio Pa. *Wire Services:* AP
Arbitron Metro Market: Wilkes Barre-Scranton, PA *Format:* Religious *Hrs. of News Programming:* News progmg 12 hrs wkly
Target Audience: General.
Larry Souder, President
Lloyd Sheldon, General Manager
Robert Brigham, Chief Engineer

Moon Township

WOGI(FM)

04-15-1959; 104.3 mhz FM *Hrs Open:* 24; 50 kw; 330 ft; N40 37 48 W80 36 10
131 Pleasant Dr., Suite 5U, Aliquippa, OH 15001
(724) 378-1271, *Fax:* (724) 378-4653
www.froggyland.com
License: Moon Township, Columbiana County, PA held by Keymarket Licenses LLC.
Group Owner: Keymarket Communications LLC
Population Served: 500,000 *Arbitron Metro Market:* Pittsburgh, PA *Target Audience:* 25-54.
Ron Aughinbaugh, General Manager
Kalen Boyd, Programming Director

Mount Carmel

WVRZ

03-01-1993; 99.7 mhz FM *Hrs Open:* 24; 0.79 kw; 646 ft.; N40 49 9 W76 27 45
612 N. Shamokin Street, Shamokin, PA 17872 US
(570) 327-1400, *Fax:* (570) 327-8156
www.variety997.com
License: Mount Carmel, Northumberland County, PA held by Clear Channel Broadcasting Licenses Inc.
Group Owner: Clear Channel Communications Inc.; (acq 5-26-2005; $460,000)
Format: Contemporary Hits/Top 40 *Target Audience:* 25-65.
Jim Dabney, General Manager

Mount Cobb

***WFTE**
90.3 mhz FM; 3 kw; 38 ft.; N41 23 9 W75 24 10 US
(570) 504-5803
www.wfte.org
License: Mount Cobb, Lackawanna County, PA held by Center for Creative Cooperation Inc.
Arbitron Metro Market: Mount Cobb, PA *Format:* Talk
Don Noll, President
Tom Borthwick, Operations Dir
Robert Apter, Office Manager

Mount Pleasant

WKVE
04-21-1978; 103.1 mhz FM *Hrs Open:* 24; 4.4 kw; 801 ft.; N39 54 49.6 W79 37 57.4
R.D. #3, Gordon Hill, Waynesburg, PA 15370 US
(724) 627-5555, *Fax:* (724) 627-4021
radiowanb@gmail.com
License: Mount Pleasant, Westmoreland County, PA held by Broadcast Communications Inc.
Group Owner: Broadcast Communications Inc.; (acq 4-1-2002; with co-located AM)
Nat'l Reps: Dome
Arbitron Metro Market: Mount Pleasant, PA *Format:* Country *Target Audience:* 20 plus. *Adv. Rates:* 17; 17; 17; 17.
Judy Rastoka, General Manager
Doug Wilson, Programming Director
Marcia Mackey, News Director
Rick Williams, Chief Engineer

Mount Pocono

WPLY
04-08-1981; 960 khz AM *Hrs Open:* 24; 1 kw-D, DA2; 0.024 kw-N, DA2; N41 4 41 W75 23 33 *Rebroadcasts:* Simulcast with WVPO(AM) Stroudsburg 100%
619 Alexander Road, 3rd Floor, Princeton, NJ 08540 US
(570) 421-2100, *Fax:* (570) 421-2040
info@lite935.com
License: Mount Pocono, PA held by Nassau Broadcasting II LLC.
Group Owner: Nassau Broadcasting Partners L.P.; (acq 6-28-2000).
Format: News, Talk
Rick Musselman, Operations Dir

Mountain Top

WBHT
09-01-1992; 97.1 mhz FM *Hrs Open:* 24; 0.5 kw; 1102 ft.; N41 10 57 W75 52 19
140 South Ash Avenue, Tempe, AZ 85281 US
(570) 824-9000, *Fax:* (570) 820-0520
www.97bht.com
License: Mountain Top, Luzerne County, PA
Group Owner: Cumulus Media Inc.; (acq 10-23-98; grpsl).
Arbitron Metro Market: Wilkes Barre, PA *Format:* Contemporary Hits/Top 40 *Target Audience:* 18-34. *Adv. Rates:* 40; 30; 40; 25
Jeanne Kerr, General Sales Mgr
A.J., Programming Director
Erin Evans, Promotions Manager
Bill Palmeri, Market Manager
Jeanne Kerr, Local Sales Manager
Ralphie Aversa, Website Manager

Muncy

WBZD-FM
08-11-1983; 93.3 mhz FM *Hrs Open:* 24; 1.7 kw; 1220 ft.; N41 12 42 W76 57 16
1685 Four Mile Drive, Williamsport, PA 17701 US
(570) 323-8200, *Fax:* (570) 327-9138
www.wbzd.com
dan.farr@bybradio.com
License: Muncy, Lycoming County, PA held by South Williamsport SaberCom Inc.
Group Owner: Backyard Broadcasting LLC; (acq 12-1-02; grpsl).
Nat'l Reps: Christal
Arbitron Metro Market: Williamsport, PA *Format:* Oldies *Hrs. of News Programming:* news progmg 3 hrs wkly *No. News Employees:* 1 *Target Audience:* 18-54; adult oriented, mass appeal
Robin Smith, CFO
Barry Drake, President
Dan Farr, General Manager
Bob Pawlikowski, General Sales Mgr
Ted Minier, Programming Director
Brian Hill, Engineering Dir

Murrysville

***WRWJ**
07-01-1994; 88.1 mhz FM *Hrs Open:* 19; 0.001 kw horiz, 1 kw vert; 302 ft.; N40 31 12 W79 39 29 *Rebroadcasts:* Rebroadcasts WAIJ(FM) Grantsville, MD 100%
34 Springs Road, P.O. Box 540, Grantsville, MD 21536 US
(301) 895-3292, *Fax:* (301) 895-3293
www.hesalive.net
info@hesalive.net
License: Murrysville, Westmoreland County, PA held by He's Alive Inc.
Nat'l Network: USA
Arbitron Metro Market: Pittsburgh, PA *Format:* Religious *Target Audience:* 18-35.
Sharon Johnson, President

Nanticoke

WZMF(AM)
02-01-1947; 730 khz AM; 1 kw-D, 38 w-N; N41 13 10 W75 59 28
Box 701, Tunkhannock, PA 18657
(570) 836-4200, *Fax:* (570) 836-7035
www.gem104.com
License: Nanticoke, Luzerne County, PA held by WS2K Radio LLC.
Group Owner: WS2K Radio LLC dba WS Media; (acq 7-14-2008; grpsl)
Population Served: 16,632 *Arbitron Metro Market:* Wilkes Barre, PA *Format:* Light Rock *Target Audience:* 35 plus.
Ira Rosenblatt, Station Manager

***WSFX**
10-25-1987; 89.1 mhz FM; 0.1 kw; -381 ft.; N41 11 42 W75 59 28
1333 S Prospect St., Advanced Tech Center, Nanticoke, PA 18634 US
(570) 740-0634, *Fax:* (570) 740-0605
http://depts.luzerne.edu/wsfx/
rreino@luzerne.edu
License: Nanticoke, Luzerne County, PA held by Luzerne County Community College.
Format: Variety/Diverse *Target Audience:* 16-25; college age alternative mus audience
Thomas P. Leary, President
Ron Reino, General Manager

Nanty Glo

***WPAI**
01-01-2006; 90.7 mhz FM; 2.1 kw vert; 482 ft.; N40 30 20 W78 48 12
P.O. Box 1452, Washington, DC 20013 US
(800) 877-5600, *Fax:* (916) 251-1650
www.air1.com
info@air1.com
License: Nanty Glo, Cambria County, PA held by Educational Media Foundation.
Group Owner: EMF Broadcasting; (acq 3-23-2007; grpsl)
Nat'l Network: Air 1
Arbitron Metro Market: Nanty Glo, PA *Format:* Alternative, Christian
Darrell Chambliss, Chairman
Mike Novak, President

New Berlin

***WBGM**
09-01-1996; 88.1 mhz FM; 0.55 kw; 417 ft.; N40 53 27 W76 59 54 *Rebroadcasts:* Rebroadcasts WPGM-FM Danville 100%
Post Office Box 236, Eight East Market St., Danville, PA 17821 US
(570) 275-1570, *Fax:* (570) 275-4071
www.wpgmfm.org/
info@wbgm.org
License: New Berlin, Union County, PA held by Montrose Broadcasting Corp.
Group Owner: Montrose Broadcasting Corp.
Arbitron Metro Market: Danville,PA *Format:* Christian, Religious
George Vacca, General Manager
Deanna Force, Programming Director

New Castle

WKST
08-25-1968; 1200 khz AM *Hrs Open:* 5:30 AM-1 AM; 5 kw-D, DAN; 1 kw-N, DAN; N40 56 22 W80 23 38
50 E. Rivercenter Blvd., #1200, Covington, KY 41011 US
(724) 346-5070, *Fax:* (724) 654-3101
www.wkst.com
khlebovy@foreverradio.com
License: New Castle, PA held by Forever Broadcasting LLC.
Group Owner: Forever Broadcasting; (acq 6-30-2004; grpsl).
Regional Reps: Commercial Media Sales.
Arbitron Metro Market: New Castle,PA *Format:* Sports, Talk
Special Programming: Ger one hr, Pol one hr, Greek one hr wkly *Hrs. of News Programming:* news progmg 7 hrs wkly *No. News Employees:* 2 *TargetAudience:* 34 plus.
Scott Cohagan, General Manager
Ken Hlebovy, Programming Director
Wade Sutton, News Director

WJST
10-23-1938; 1280 khz AM
50 E. Rivercenter Blvd, #1200, Covington, KY 41011 US
(724) 346-5070, *Fax:* (724) 654-3101
License: New Castle, PA held by Forever Broadcasting LLC.
Group Owner: Forever Broadcasting; (acq 6-30-2004; grpsl).
Nat'l Network: ABC *Nat'l Reps:* Dome; Rgnl Reps
Format: Oldies *Special Programming:* Black one hr, class one hr wkly *Target Audience:* 30 plus.
Scott Cohagan, General Manager

***WVMN**
11-22-1995; 90.1 mhz FM *Hrs Open:* 24; 2 kw; 236 ft.; N41 0 47 W80 17 36 *Rebroadcasts:* Rebroadcasts WCRF(FM) Cleveland, OH 100%
820 N. Lasalle Drive, Chicago, IL 60610 US
(440) 526-1111, *Fax:* (440) 526-1319
www.wcrfradio.org
wcrf@moody.edu
License: New Castle, Lawrence County, PA held by Moody Bible Institute of Chicago.
Group Owner: The Moody Bible Institute of Chicago
Wire Services: AP
Arbitron Metro Market: Cleveland, OH *Format:* Religious *Target Audience:* 25-55.
Michael Easley, President
Paul Carter, Operations Dir
Richard Lee, Station Manager
Gary Bittner, Programming Director
Doug Hainer, Chief Engineer
Dick Lee, Manager
Jonathan Dentler, Production Assistant
Alice Andrews, OfficeAdministrator

New Kensington

WGBN
10-01-1940; 1150 khz AM *Hrs Open:* 24; 1 kw-D, 70 w-N, DA-1; N40 34 24 W79 46 58
560 7th St., New Kensington, PA 15206
(724) 337-3588, *Fax:* (724) 337-1318
License: New Kensington, Westmoreland County, PA held by Pentecostal Temple Development Corp.
Nat'l Network: USA *Nat'l Reps:* Dome
Population Served: 1,209,000 *Arbitron Metro Market:* Pittsburgh, PA *Special Programming:* Pol 3 hrs, It 2 hrs, Irish 2 hrs, relg 2 hrs wkly *Hrs. of News Programming:* news progmg 19 hrs wkly *No. News Employees:* 1 *Target Audience:* 30 plus; older, upscale
Lauren Mann, General Manager
Calvin Penny, Programming Director
Del King, Chief Engineer

WBZZ(FM)
08-17-1967; 100.7 mhz FM *Hrs Open:* 24; 17 kw; Ant 850 ft; N40 29 43 W80 00 18
651 Holiday Dr., Foster Plaza Five, Pittsburgh, PA 15220
(412) 920-9400, *Fax:* (412) 920-9444
www.1007.com
john.damico@cbsradio.com
License: New Kensington, Westmoreland County, PA held by Infinity Radio Holdings Inc.
Group Owner: CBS Radio; (acq 6-8-98; grpsl).
Population Served: 307,484 *Arbitron Metro Market:* Pittsburgh, PA *Format:* Adult Contemp *Target Audience:* 18-49.
Joel Hollander, President
Christine Fallon, General Sales Mgr
Mark Anderson, Programming Director
John D'Amico, Promotions Manager
Scott Herman, Executive Vice President
Keith Belden, National Sales Manager
Michael Young, Sr.Vice President/Market Manager
Michael Spacc, Director of Sales
Anthony Fontana, Local Sales Manager

New Wilmington

***WWNW**
01-31-1968; 88.9 mhz FM *Hrs Open:* 24; 4 kw vert; Ant 128 ft; N41 06 41 W80 20 21
Box 89, Westminster College, New Wilmington, PA 16172

(724) 946-7242, *Fax:* (724) 946-7070
titanradio.net
barnerdl@westminster.edu
License: New Wilmington, Lawrence County, PA held by Westminster College Board of Trustees.
Nat'l Network: NBC News Radio *Wire Services:* AP
Population Served: 60,000*Special Programming:* Relg 3 hrs wkly *Hrs. of News Programming:* News progmg 3 hrs wkly
Target Audience: 18-49; college students & staff
Richard Dorman, President
David L. Barner, General Manager
Andrew Borts, Chief Engineer

Norristown

WNAP
08-06-1946; 1110 khz AM
3246 Fairway Drive, Montgomery, AL 36116 US
(610) 272-7600, *Fax:* (610) 272-5793
www.wnap1110am.com
gospel@wnap1110am.com
License: Norristown, PA held by George H. Buck.
Group Owner: GHB Radio Group; (acq 12-15-87; $725,000;
Arbitron Metro Market: Philadelphia, PA *Format:* Black, Gospel
Target Audience: General.
Fred Blain, General Manager
Orey Ferrell, General Sales Mgr
Tonya Ginyard, Programming Director
Dave McCrork, Chief Engineer

North East

WYNE
11-24-1966; 1530 khz AM *Hrs Open:* Sunrise-set; 0.25 kw-C, NDD; 1 kw-D, NDD; N42 12 5 W79 51 43
418 N. Center Street, Corry, PA 16407 US
(814) 725-6100, *Fax:* (814) 725-6112
northeast.mercyhurst.edu
License: North East, PA held by Mercyhurst College
Arbitron Metro Market: North East, PA *Format:* Oldies *Target Audience:* 35-64; men & women
William Shannon, General Manager

WRKT
03-29-1970; 100.9 mhz FM *Hrs Open:* 24; 4.2 kw; 797 ft.; N42 11 51 W79 45 10
One Broadcast Park, Erie, PA 16428 US
(814) 461-1000, *Fax:* (814) 461-1500
rocket101@rocket101.com
License: North East, Erie County, PA held by Connoisseur Media of Erie LLC.
Group Owner: Connoisseur Media LLC; (acq 3-30-2006; grpsl).
Arbitron Metro Market: Erie, PA *Format:* Classic Rock *Special Programming:* Loc bands one hr wkly *Hrs. of News Programming:* news progmg one hr wkly *No. News Employees:* 1 *Target Audience:* 25-54.
Richard Rambaldo, General Manager
Michael Malpiedi, General Sales Mgr

Northern Cambria

*WPCL
09-30-1991; 97.3 mhz FM *Hrs Open:* 19; 1.75 kw horiz, 1.7 kw vert; 610 ft.; N40 30 27 W78 48 14 *Rebroadcasts:* Rebroadcasts WAIJ (FM) Grantsville, MD 100%
P.O. Box 540, Grantsville, MD 21536 US
(301) 895-3292, *Fax:* (301) 895-3293
www.hesalive.com
hesalive@hesalive.net
License: Northern Cambria, Cambria County, PA held by He's Alive Inc.
Group Owner: He's Alive Inc.; acq 3-18-97; $105,000)
Nat'l Network: USA *Nat'l Reps:* Commercial Media Sales
Format: Adult Contemp, Christian, 44, Religious *Target Audience:* 18-35.
Sharon Johnson, President

Northumberland

WEGH
08-22-1994; 107.3 mhz FM *Hrs Open:* 24; 0.9 kw; 843 ft.; N40 47 10 W76 41 49
Mailing Address: Post Office Box 1070, Sunbury, PA 17801 US
Second Address: 1227 County Line Rd., Selinsgrove, PA 17870
(570) 286-5838(570) 743-1841, *Fax:* (570) 743-7837
www.wkok.com/Eagle_107/107_HOME.htm
eagle107@eagle107.com
License: Northumberland, Northumberland County, PA held by Sunbury Broadcasting Corp.
Group Owner: Sunbury Broadcasting Corp.
Nat'l Reps: Roslin *Regional Reps:* Dome. *Wire Services:* Accu-Weather
Arbitron Metro Market: Northumberland, PA *Format:* Contemporary Hits/Top 40, Adult Contemp *Hrs. of News Programming:* news progmg one hr wkly *No. News Employees:* 4 *Target Audience:* 25-54.
Roger Haddon Jr., CEO
Roger S. Haddon, Jr., President
Kevin Herr, Operations Dir
Nicole Shelley, General Sales Mgr
Rob Senter, Programming Director

Oil City

WKQW
12-01-1986; 1120 khz AM; 1 kw-D, NDD; N41 23 45 W79 39 53
Mailing Address: P.O. Box 970, Montrose, PA 81401 US
Second Address: www.venangocountydailynews.com
(814) 676-8254, *Fax:* (814) 677-4272
www.kqw.com
traffic@wkqw.com
License: Oil City, PA held by Clarion County Broadcasting Corp.
Group Owner: Clarion County Broadcasting Corp.; (acq 4-8-2005; $540,000 with co-located FM)
Nat'l Network: CBS Radio *Nat'l Reps:* Dome
Format: Oldies *Hrs. of News Programming:* news progmg 4 hrs wkly *No. News Employees:* 1 *Target Audience:* 25-54.
Tim Shaw, Programming Director
Mark Heim, News Director
Bill Hearst, Disc Jockey
Mike Snyder, Disc Jockey
Sammy Gordon, Disc Jockey
Steve Truitt, Traffic Manager

WKQW-FM
09-01-1992; 96.3 mhz FM *Hrs Open:* 24; 6 kw; 328 ft.; N41 23 45 W79 39 53
222 Seneca Street, Oil City, PA 16301 US
(814) 676-8254, *Fax:* (814) 677-4272
www.venangocountydailynews.com
traffic@kqw.com
License: Oil City, Venango County, PA held by Clarion County Broadcasting Corp.
Group Owner: Clarion County Broadcasting Corp.
Nat'l Network: CBS Radio *Regional Reps:* Dome & Assoc.
Format: Adult Contemp *Hrs. of News Programming:* news progmg 4 hrs wkly *No. News Employees:* 1
William Hearst, President
Steve Truitt, Operations Dir
Sammy Gordon, General Sales Mgr
Mark Heim, Programming Director
Tim Shaw, Program Manager
Joe Lodanowsky, Sports Director

WGYI
05-01-1957; 98.5 mhz FM; 20 kw; 299 ft.; N41 25 4 W79 42 53
908 Diamond Square, Meadville, PA 16335 US
(814) 676-5744, *Fax:* (814) 437-9372
radio@zoominternet.com
License: Oil City, Venango County, PA held by Forever Broadcasting LLC.
Format: Country
Nicholas Galli, President
David Bronham, General Manager
Greg Bolyard, Programming Director
Larry Smith, Chief Engineer

Oliver

WOGG
06-11-1993; 94.9 mhz FM *Hrs Open:* 24; 1.65 kw; 1234 ft.; N39 52 11 W79 38 22
P.O. Box 270, Brownsville, PA 15417 US
(724) 938-2000, *Fax:* (724) 938-7824
www.froggyland.com
jtrunzo@zoominternet.net
License: Oliver, Fayette County, PA held by Keymarket Licenses LLC.
Group Owner: Keymarket Communications LLC; (acq 8-31-99; $2.875 million with WASP(AM) Brownsville).
Arbitron Metro Market: Pittsburgh, PA *Format:* Country *No. News Employees:* 1 *Target Audience:* 25-54.
Gerald Getz, President
Andrew Powaski, General Sales Mgr
Jeffrey Trunzo, Chief Engineer

Olyphant

WQOR
07-20-1987; 750 khz AM *Hrs Open:* Sunrise-sunset; 1.6 kw-D, NDD; N41 28 34 W75 29 41
321 Spruce Street; 3rdfl, Scranton, PA 18503 US
(802) 626-9800, *Fax:* (802) 626-8500
wjpk@gmail.com
License: Olyphant, PA held by Holy Family Communications
Group Owner: Holy Family Communications; acq 3-24-2003; $170,000).
Arbitron Metro Market: Palm Springs CA *Format:* Country
Bruce James, General Manager

WBHD
01-01-1991; 95.7 mhz FM *Hrs Open:* 24; 0.6 kw; 1010 ft.; N41 26 9 W75 43 45 *Rebroadcasts:* Simulcast with WBHT(FM) Mountaintop
7201 W. Lake Mead Blvd, Suite 400, Las Vegas, NV 89128 US
(570) 824-9000, *Fax:* (570) 820-0520
www.97bht.com
License: Olyphant, Lackawanna County, PA
Group Owner: Cumulus Media Inc.; (acq 1999; $950,000).
Arbitron Metro Market: Wilkes Barre, PA *Format:* Contemporary Hits/Top 40 *Special Programming:* Talk *Target Audience:* 18-49; men, sports fans
Jeanne Kerr, Local Sales Manager
Erin Evans, Promotions Manager
Ralphia Aversa, Website Manager
John Rizzuto, Market Manager

Palmyra

WTPA
11-01-1978; 92.1 mhz FM; 1.5 kw; 601 ft.; N40 23 28 W76 43 31
600congress Avenue, Suite 1400, Austin, TX 78701 US
(717) 901-0738, *Fax:* (717) 234-4842
www.935WTPA.com
dina.acri@cumulus.com
License: Palmyra, Cumberland County, PA held by Cumulus Licensing Corp.
Group Owner: Cumulus Media Inc.; (acq 2000; grpsl)
Arbitron Metro Market: Harrisburg, VA *Format:* Rock/AOR *Target Audience:* 18-49.
John O'Dea, Operations Dir
Ron Giovaniello, Station Manager
Karen Richards, General Sales Mgr
Chris James, Programming Director
Phil George, Promotions Manager
Dave Supplee, Chief Engineer
Dina Acri, EEO Officer

Patton

WBXQ
01-01-1991; 94.3 mhz FM; 2.1 kw; 548 ft.; N40 39 17 W78 40 34
4000 5th Avenue, Altoona, PA 16602 US
(814) 943-6112, *Fax:* (814) 944-9782
www.wbxq.com
ken@theradiocampus.com
License: Patton, Cambria County, PA held by Sherlock Broadcasting Inc.
Arbitron Metro Market: Altoona, PA *Format:* Country *Target Audience:* 35-65.
Ken Maguda, Operations Dir
David Barger, General Manager
Diane Boslet, Sales Manager
Doug Herendeen, Public Service Director

Pen Argyl

*WWPJ
01-01-2001; 89.5 mhz FM *Hrs Open:* 24; 0.003 kw horiz, 0.1 kw vert; 1093 ft.; N40 53 1 W75 15 43 *Rebroadcasts:* Rebroadcasts WWFM(FM) Trenton, NJ 100%
1200 Old Trenton Rd, Trenton, NJ 08690 US
(609) 587-8989, *Fax:* (609) 570-3863
www.wwfm.org
info@wwfm.org
License: Pen Argyl, Northampton County, PA held by Mercer County Community College.
Arbitron Metro Market: Trenton, NJ *Format:* Classical
Jeffery Sekerka, General Manager
Alice Weiss, Programming Director
David Osenberg, Development Producer
Diane Guvenis, Development Director
Glenn Smith, Music Director
Marcia Galambos, Membership Coordinator
Rachel Katz,Production Manager/Public Affairs Host
Winifred Howard, JazzOn2 Program Manager

Philadelphia

KYW
01-01-1921; 1060 khz AM *Hrs Open:* 24
C/O Cbs Corporation, 600 New Hampshire Avenue, N.W. #1200, Washington, DC 20037 US
(215) 238-1060, *Fax:* (215) 238-4657
www.philadelphia.cbslocal.com
newstips@kyw1060info.com

License: Philadelphia, PA held by CBS Radio East Inc.
Group Owner: CBS Radio
Nat'l Network: ABC; CBS; CNN Radio *Nat'l Reps:* CBS Radio
Wire Services: AP
Arbitron Metro Market: Philadelphia, PA *TV Affiliate:* KYW-TV affil. *Format:* News *Hrs. of News Programming:* news progmg 168 hrs wkly *No. News Employees:* 34 *Target Audience:* 25-54; adults

David Yadgaroff, Operations Dir
Michael Berkowitz, General Sales Mgr
Steve Butler, Programming Director
Kyle Ruffin, Promotions Manager
Dee Patel, News Director
Frank Sippel, Chief Engineer
Rob Kaloustian, Regional SalesManager
Rich Iovanisci, Regional Sales Manager

WBEB
05-13-1963; 101.1 mhz FM *Hrs Open:* 24; 14 kw; 942 ft.; N40 2 19 W75 14 14
10 N. Presidential Blvd., Bala Cynwyd, PA 19004 US
(541) 463-6000, *Fax:* (541) 463-6046
www.klcc.org
klcc@klcc.org
License: Philadelphia, Philadelphia County, PA held by WEAZ-FM Radio Inc.
Nat'l Reps: McGavren Guild
Arbitron Metro Market: Odessa-Midland TX

Steve Barton, General Manager

WDAS-FM
01-01-1959; 105.3 mhz FM; 16.5 kw; 873 ft.; N40 2 30 W75 14 24
433 E. Las Colinas Blvd, #1130, Irving, TX 75039 US
(610) 784-3333, *Fax:* (610) 784-2098
www.wdasfm.com
info@wdasfm.com
License: Philadelphia, Philadelphia County, PA
Group Owner: Clear Channel Communications Inc.
Arbitron Metro Market: Philadelphia, PA *Format:* Adult Contemp, Black *Target Audience:* 25-54.

Craig Dalla Riva, General Manager
Sherry Miller, General Sales Mgr
Gail Nichols, Programming Director
Thoma Lesieur, News Director
David Jones, Chief Engineer
Veronica Wingate, Traffic Manager

WURD
07-23-1958; 900 khz AM
8121 Georgia Ave 10th Fl, Silver Spring, MD 20910 US
(215) 425-7875, *Fax:* (215) 634-6003
www,900amwurd.com/
900amwurd@wurdradio.com
License: Philadelphia, PA held by Levas Communications LLC
Nat'l Network: CNN Radio *Nat'l Reps:* McGavren Guild
Arbitron Metro Market: Philadelphia, PA *Format:* Talk *Special Programming:* Gospel 9 hrs, lt 3 hrs wkly *Adv. Rates:* 100; 100; 100; 50

Sara Lomax Reese, GM
Steve Ballard, Operations Dir
Cody Anderson, General Manager
Kimberly Everett, Director, Sales and Marketing
Stephanie Renee, Programming Director
Kia Long, News Director

WFIL
01-01-1922; 560 khz AM *Hrs Open:* 24; 5 kw-U, DA-2; N40 05 42 W75 16 38
117 Ridge Pike, Lafayette Hill, PA 93012
(610) 828-8879, *Fax:* (610) 828-8879
www.wfil.com
wfil@wfil.com
License: Philadelphia, Philadelphia County, PA held by Pennsylvania Media Associates Inc.
Group Owner: Salem Communications Corp.; (acq 11-1-93; $4 million)
Nat'l Network: Salem Radio Network *Nat'l Reps:* Salem
Population Served: 11,792,380 *Arbitron Metro Market:* Philadelphia *Hrs. of News Programming:* News progmg 2 hrs wkly *Target Audience:* 35-64; parents & grandparents

Russ Whitnah, Operations Dir
Carol Healey, General Sales Mgr
Ann Krill, Promotions Manager
Rene Tetro, Chief Engineer
Mark Daniels, Marketing Manager
David Handler, New Business Sales Manager
Kevin Manna, Operations Director

WHAT
01-01-1925; 1340 khz AM; 1 kw-U, ND1; N40 0 6 W75 12 35
3 Park Ave., New York, NY 10016 US
(267) 285-5161, *Fax:* (267) 285-5185
www.martiniloungeradio.com
License: Philadelphia, PA held by Marconi Broadcasting Co. LLC
Arbitron Metro Market: Philadelphia *Format:* Classic Rock

Tom Kelly, President
David Direnzo, General Sales Mgr

***WHYY-FM**
01-01-1954; 90.9 mhz FM *Hrs Open:* 24; 13.5 kw; 920 ft; N40 02 30 W75 14 24
150 N. 6th St., Independence Mall West, Philadelphia, PA 19106
(215) 351-1200,(215) 351-9204, *Fax:* (215) 351-3352
www.whyy.org
talkback@whyy.org
License: Philadelphia, Philadelphia County, PA held by WHYY Inc.
Nat'l Network: NPR; PRI
Population Served: 3,987,600 *Arbitron Metro Market:* Philadelphia *Special Programming:* Opera 4 hrs, folk 4 hrs, jazz 4 hrs wkly *Hrs. of News Programming:* news progmg 35 hrs wkly *No. News Employees:* 7 *TargetAudience:* 35-49.

Gerard Sweeney, Chairman
William Marrazzo, President/CEO
Kyra McGrath, EVP/CCO
Christine Dempsey, Station Manager
Roseann Oleyn, General Sales Mgr
Chris Satullo, VP/News
William Weber, VP/Chief Technical Officer
Jeffrey Bundy,Member Relations Director

WIOQ
01-01-1941; 102.1 mhz FM *Hrs Open:* 24; 27 kw; 669 ft.; N40 2 37 W75 14 32
Two Bala Plaza, Suite 201, Bala Cynwyd, PA 19004 US
(610) 784-3333, *Fax:* (610) 784-2075
www.q102philly.com
License: Philadelphia, Philadelphia County, PA held by AMFM Radio Licenses LLC.
Group Owner: Clear Channel Communications Inc.; (acq 8-30-00; grpsl).
Arbitron Metro Market: Philadelphia *Format:* Contemporary Hits/Top 40 *Special Programming:* Pub affrs *Target Audience:* 18-34; females & teens

Rich Lewis, Operations Dir
Cassandra Banko, General Sales Mgr
Brian Bridgman, Programming Director
Lisa Acchione, Promotions Manager
Michael Guidotti, Chief Engineer
Chris Marino, Disc Jockey
Marian Newsome, Music Director
JeffJordan, Promotions Director
Wendy McClure, Public Affairs Director
Elvis Duran, Disc Jockey
Ryan Seacrest, Disc Jockey

WIP
03-16-1922; 610 khz AM
600 New Hampshire Ave, N.W., Suite 1200, Washington, DC 20037 US
(610) 949-7800, *Fax:* (610) 949-7880
www.610wip.com
info@610wip.com
License: Philadelphia, PA held by CBS Radio Inc. of Philadelphia.
Group Owner: CBS Radio; (acq 8-12-93;
Nat'l Network: Westwood One *Nat'l Reps:* CBS Radio
Arbitron Metro Market: Philadelphia *Format:* Sports

Cecil Forster Jr., Operations Dir
Tom Bigby, Programming Director

WISX
11-11-1959; 106.1 mhz FM; 22.5 kw; 741 ft.; N40 4 58 W75 10 54
433 E. Las Colinas Blvd, #1130, Irving, TX 75039 US
(610) 508-1200, *Fax:* (610) 784-0501
www.phillys1061.com
info@phillys1061.com
License: Philadelphia, Philadelphia County, PA held by AMFM Radio Licenses LLC.
Group Owner: Clear Channel Communications Inc.; (acq 8-30-2000; grpsl).
Nat'l Reps: Christal
Arbitron Metro Market: Philadelphia *Format:* Adult Contemp
Target Audience: 25-54.

Joe Tenerelli, General Manager
David Sabaini, Programming Director
Dan Watson, Chief Engineer

***WKDU**
01-01-1970; 91.7 mhz FM *Hrs Open:* 24; 0.8 kw; 154 ft.; N39 57 36 W75 11 27
3210 Chestnut Streets, Philadelphia, PA 19104 US
(215) 895-5920, *Fax:* (215) 895-1050
www.wkdu.org
License: Philadelphia, Philadelphia County, PA held by Drexel University.
Arbitron Metro Market: Philadelphia *Format:* Alternative *Special Programming:* International 12 hrs, rhythm & blues 3 hrs, gospel
Target Audience: General.

Ryan McIntyre, Operations Dir
Evan Caposerri, General Manager
Casey Ross, Programming Director
Jim Cavanaugh, Chief Engineer

WMGK
01-01-1942; 102.9 mhz FM *Hrs Open:* 24; 8.9 kw; Ant 1,148 ft; N40 02 21 W75 14 13
One Bala Plaza, Suite 339, Bala Cynwyd, PA 08816
(610) 667-8500, *Fax:* (610) 771-9692
www.wmgk.com
ckirchner@wmgk.com
License: Philadelphia, Philadelphia County, PA held by Greater Philadelphia Radio Inc.
Group Owner: Greater Media Inc
Population Served: 1,800,000 *Arbitron Metro Market:* Philadelphia

Peter Smyth, President
John Fullam, General Manager
Chris Kirchner, General Sales Mgr
Charley Lake, Programming Director
Dan Fein, Promotions Manager
Larry Paulausky, Engineering Dir

WMMR
04-20-1942; 93.3 mhz FM *Hrs Open:* 24; 16.5 kw; 866 ft.; N39 57 9 W75 10 5
P.O. Box 1059, 2 Kennedy Blvd., East Brunswick, NJ 08816 US
(610) 771-0933, *Fax:* (610) 771-9667
www.wmmr.com
License: Philadelphia, Philadelphia County, PA held by Greater Philadelphia Radio Inc.
Group Owner: Greater Media Inc.; (acq 7-23-97; grpsl)
Nat'l Network: Westwood One *Nat'l Reps:* McGavren Guild
Arbitron Metro Market: Philadelphia, PA *Format:* Rock/AOR *Hrs. of News Programming:* news progmg 5 hrs wkly *No. News Employees:* 1 *Target Audience:* 25-54; suburban rockers

Richard Feinblatt, Operations Dir
John Fullam, General Manager
Jim Antes, General Sales Mgr
Bill Weston, Programming Director
Scott Segelbeum, Promotions Manager
Queen Chandler, News Director
Larry Paulauski, Chief Engineer
KenZipeto, Music Director

WNWR
07-11-1947; 1540 khz AM
2131 Crimmins Lane, Falls Church, VA 22043 US
(610) 664-6780, *Fax:* (610) 664-8529
www.wnwr.com
License: Philadelphia, PA held by Global Radio L.L.C.
Nat'l Reps: Roslin
Arbitron Metro Market: Philadelphia *TV Affiliate:* Var/div, ethnic multicultural *No. News Employees:* 25-54.

WOGL
05-16-1944; 98.1 mhz FM; 9.6 kw; 1109 ft.; N40 2 29.6 W75 14 11.4
C/O Cbs Corporation, 600 New Hampshire Avenue, N.W. #1200, Washington, DC 20037 US
(610) 668-5900, *Fax:* (610) 668-5977
www.wogl.com
questions@wogl.com
License: Philadelphia, Philadelphia County, PA held by CBS Radio East Inc.
Group Owner: CBS Radio
Arbitron Metro Market: Philadelphia *TV Affiliate:* Hits of the 60s & 70s *Special Programming:* news progmg 1.25 hrs wkly *Hrs. of News Programming:* 1 *No. News Employees:* 25-54.

General Manager, General Manager
Sales Manager, Anne Gress
Program Director, Samantha Black
Promotions Director, Promotions Manager
Music Director, Diane Santilippo
National Sales Manager

***WPEB**
05-15-1981; 88.1 mhz FM; 0.001 kw vert; 69 ft.; N39 56 57 W75 13 9
Suite 7b, 3901 Market Street, Philadelphia, PA 19104 US
(215) 387-6155
www.radiovolta.org
info@radiovolta.org

RADIO - U.S.

License: Philadelphia, Philadelphia County, PA held by West Philadelphia Educational Broadcasting Foundation.
Arbitron Metro Market: Philadelphia *Format:* Variety/Diverse *Target Audience:* General.
Alex Snipes, General Manager
Tersa Haire, General Sales Mgr
Tony Gee, Programming Director

WPEN
04-01-1929; 950 khz AM *Hrs Open:* 24
2 Kennedy Blvd, P.O. Box 1059, East Brunswick, NJ 08816 US
(610) 667-8500, *Fax:* (610) 771-9692
sr950.com
bdeblois@950espn.com
License: Philadelphia, PA held by Greater Philadelphia Radio Inc.
Group Owner: Greater Media Inc.; (acq 1-6-75)
Nat'l Network: ESPN Radio
Arbitron Metro Market: Philadelphia *Format:* Sports
John Fullam, General Manager
Bob DeBlois, Station Manager
Paul Blake, General Sales Mgr
Matt Nahigian, Programming Director
Mike McMonagle, Promotions Manager
Ralph Nieves, General Sales Manager

WPHT
01-01-1922; 1210 khz AM; 50 kw-U, ND1; N39 58 46 W74 59 13
C/O Cbs Corporation, 600 New Hampshire Avenue, N.W. #1200, Washington, DC 20037 US
(610) 668-5800, *Fax:* (610) 667-5886
www.thebigtalker1210.com
talkradio1210@cbs.com
License: Philadelphia, PA held by CBS Radio East Inc.
Group Owner: CBS Radio; (acq 8-58).
Nat'l Network: CBS; Westwood One *Nat'l Reps:* CBS Radio
Arbitron Metro Market: Philadelphia *Format:* Talk *Hrs. of News Programming:* 2 *Target Audience:* 25-64; adults
David Yadgaroff, General Manager
Mike Baldini, Station Manager
Grace Blazer, Programming Director
Jennifer Miller, News Director
Dave Skalish, Chief Engineer

***WRTI**
07-09-1953; 90.1 mhz FM *Hrs Open:* 24; 7.7 kw; 1217 ft.; N40 2 29.6 W75 14 11.5
Annenberg Hall, Philadelphia, PA 19122 US
(215) 204-8405, *Fax:* (215) 204-7027
www.wrti.org
comments@wrti.org
License: Philadelphia, Philadelphia County, PA held by Temple University of The Commonwealth System of Higher Education.
Nat'l Network: NPR; PRI *Wire Services:* AP
Arbitron Metro Market: Philadelphia *Format:* Jazz *Hrs. of News Programming:* news progmg 15 hrs wkly *No. News Employees:* 1 *Target Audience:* 30-65.
David Conant, CEO
Tobias Poole, Operations Dir
David Conant, General Manager
William Johnson, Station Manager
Patricia Prevost, General Sales Mgr
Jack Moore, Programming Director
Porsche Blakey, Promotions Manager
WindsorJohnston, News Director
Jeffrey DePolo, Engineering Dir
Vic Scarpato, CFO
Rick Torpey, National Sales Manager

WUSL
01-01-1961; 98.9 mhz FM *Hrs Open:* 24; 27 kw; 669 ft.; N40 2 37 W75 14 32
440 Domino Lane, Philadelphia, PA 19128 US
(610) 784-3333, *Fax:* (610) 784-0507
www.power99.com
License: Philadelphia, Philadelphia County, PA held by Clear Channel Radio Licenses, Inc.
Group Owner: Clear Channel Communications Inc.; (acq 8-30-00; grpsl).
Arbitron Metro Market: Bala Cynwyd, PA *TV Affiliate:* webphilly@clearchannel.com *Format:* Urban Contemporary
Special Programming: Gospel 4 hrs wkly *Hrs. of News Programming:* news progmg 4 hrs wkly *No. NewsEmployees:* 2 *Target Audience:* 18-49.
John Rohm, President
Wes Franks, General Sales Mgr
Tim Herbster, Director of Online Programming
Joe McCullum, Director of Online Programming
Chuck Gustafon, Traffic Manager
Richard Lewis, VP of Sales

WWDB
01-01-1925; 860 khz AM *Hrs Open:* Daytime
%Joseph D. Sullivan, 1001 Penn Ave, NW #1300, Washington, DC 20004 US
(610) 822-1321, *Fax:* (610) 667-5978
www.wwdbam.com
License: Philadelphia, PA held by Beasley Broadcasting of Eastern Pennsylvania Inc.
Group Owner: Beasley Broadcast Group Inc.; (acq 9-9-86; $2.4 million;
Arbitron Metro Market: Philadelphia, PA *Format:* Talk *Target Audience:* 18-49.
Tim Halloran, Operations Dir
Bruce Gilbert, General Manager

WRDW-FM
01-01-1957; 96.5 mhz FM *Hrs Open:* 24; 9.6 kw; 1108 ft.; N40 2 30 W75 14 11
166 E. Levering Mill Rd, Bala Cynwd, PA 19004 US
(610) 667-9000, *Fax:* (610) 667-2972
www.wired965.com
nconner@bbgiphilly.com
License: Philadelphia, Philadelphia County, PA held by WDAS License L.P.
Group Owner: Beasley Broadcast Group Inc.; (acq 3-11-97)
Nat'l Network: Wall Street *Nat'l Reps:* D & R Radio
Arbitron Metro Market: Philadelphia, PA *Format:* Contemporary Hits/Top 40 *Target Audience:* 18 plus; general
Bruce Beasley, CEO
Natalie Conner, VP/General Manager/Market Manager
Matt Smith, General Sales Mgr
Dan Hunt, Programming Director
Bethany Kent, Promotions Manager
Don Melnyk, Chief Engineer
Laura Lombardi, Local Sales Manager
Rafe D'Amico, National Sales Manager
Grooves, Music Director
Mark Vizza, Events Manager

***WXPN**
04-01-1957; 88.5 mhz FM *Hrs Open:* 24; 5 kw; 919 ft.; N40 2 36 W75 14 33
3905 Spruce Street, Philadelphia, PA 19104 US
(215) 898-6677, *Fax:* (215) 898-0707
www.xpn.org
wxpndesk@xpn.org
License: Philadelphia, Philadelphia County, PA held by Trustees of the University of Pennsylvania.
Nat'l Network: PRI; NPR
Arbitron Metro Market: Philadelphia, PA *Format:* Alternative
Special Programming: Children 5 hrs, folk 5 hrs wkly *Hrs. of News Programming:* News progmg 3 hrs wkly *Target Audience:* 25-54; educated
Roger LaMay, General Manager
Quyen Shanahan, General Sales Mgr
Bruce Warren, Programming Director
Bob Bumbera, News Director
Jay Goldman, Engineering Dir
Tom Mara, General Sales Manager
Dan Reed, Music Director
Debby Seitz,Promotions Manager
Jay Ricci, Sales VP

WXTU
09-01-1958; 92.5 mhz FM *Hrs Open:* 24; 15 kw; 915 ft.; N40 2 19 W75 14 14
555 City Line Avenue, Suite 330, Bala Cynwyd, PA 19004 US
(610) 667-9000, *Fax:* (610) 667-1355
www.925xtu.com
comments@925xtu.com
License: Philadelphia, Philadelphia County, PA held by Beasley Broadcasting of Eastern Pennsylvania Inc.
Group Owner: Beasley Broadcast Group Inc.; (acq 7-83; $6 million;
Nat'l Reps: D & R Radio
Arbitron Metro Market: Philadelphia, PA *Format:* Country *Special Programming:* Sundays 6am-6:30am-Philadelphia Focus *Adv. Rates:* 400;400;400;200
Bruce Beasley, President
Natalie Conner, VP/GM
Laura Lombardi, Local Sales Manager
Shelly Easton, Programming Director
Carrie Miller, Promotions Manager
Don Melnyk, Chief Engineer
Andie Summers, Disc Jockey
Scott Evans, DiscJockey
Leigh Richards, Disc Jockey
Kris Stevens, Disc Jockey
Rafe D'Amico, National Sales Manager
Matt Smith, Director of Sales

WBEN-FM
03-01-1949; 95.7 mhz FM *Hrs Open:* 24; 8.9 kw; 1148 ft.; N40 2 21 W75 14 13
Two Kennedy Blvd, P.O. Box 1059, East Brunswick, NJ 08816 US
(610) 771-0933, *Fax:* (610) 771-9690
www.957benfm.com
gdefrancesco@greaterphila.com
License: Philadelphia, Philadelphia County, PA held by Greater Philadelphia Radio Group.
Group Owner: Greater Media Inc.; (acq 5-29-97; $41.8 million)
Arbitron Metro Market: Philadelphia, PA *Format:* Adult Contemp
Hrs. of News Programming: News progmg 3 hrs wkly *Target Audience:* 25-54; professional, upscale executives
Bill Schultz, Operations Dir
John Fullam, General Manager
Bill Burns, General Sales Mgr
Jules Riley, Programming Director

WRFF
02-01-1965; 104.5 mhz FM *Hrs Open:* 24; 11.5 kw; 1010 ft.; N40 2 30 W75 14 24
1 Bala Plaza, Suite 243, Bala Cynwyd, PA 19004 US
(610) 784-3333, *Fax:* (610) 784-2011
www.radio1045.com
License: Philadelphia, Philadelphia County, PA held by AMFM Radio Licenses LLC.
Group Owner: Clear Channel Communications Inc.; (acq 8-30-2000; grpsl)
Arbitron Metro Market: Philadelphia *No. News Employees:* 1
L. Mays, CEO
Manuel Rodriguez, Operations Dir
Ron Decastro, General Sales Mgr
Brian Check, Programming Director
Shelvia Williams, Promotions Manager
Jennifer Ryan, News Director
Becki West, General Sales Manager
Margo Marano,Music Director
Sandra Johnson, Traffic Manager

WNTP
01-01-1923; 990 khz AM *Hrs Open:* 24; 50 kw-D, 10 kw-N, DA-2; N40 05 43 W75 16 37
117 Ridge Pike, Lafayette Hill, PA 93012
(610) 940-0990, *Fax:* (610) 828-8879
www.wntp.com
wntp@wntp.com
License: Philadelphia, Philadelphia County, PA held by Pennsylvania Media Associates Inc.
Group Owner: Salem Communications Corp.; (acq 1994; $3.5 million grpsl).
Nat'l Network: Salem Radio Network
Population Served: 7,927,724 *Arbitron Metro Market:* Philadelphia *Special Programming:* Sports, Sp *Hrs. of News Programming:* 4 times per hr *Target Audience:* 35-64; Adults
Russ Whitnah, Operations Dir
Carol Healey, General Sales Mgr
Ann Krill, Promotions Manager
Rene Tetro, Chief Engineer
Mark Daniels, Marketing Manager
David Handler, New Business Sales Manager
Kevin Manna, Operations Manager

Philipsburg

WPHB
06-01-1956; 1260 khz AM *Hrs Open:* 24; 5 kw-D, ND1; 0.034 kw-N, ND1; N40 53 39 W78 11 51
38 Radio Park, Philipsburg, PA 16866 US
(814) 342-2300, *Fax:* (814) 342-WPHB/9742
www.wphbradio.com
wphb1260@gmail.com
License: Philipsburg, PA held by Magnum Broadcasting Inc.
Group Owner: Magnum Broadcasting Inc.; (acq 11-24-2004; $2,022,527 with co-located FM)
Nat'l Network: CNN Radio *Regional Network:* Radio Pa. *Regional Reps:* Dome & Assoc
Arbitron Metro Market: State College, PA *Format:* Country, News, 62, Sports, Talk *Special Programming:* Bluegrass 4 hrs, polka 6 hrs, Gospel 6 hrs, big band 5 hrs wkly *Target Audience:* Men & women; generally 25+*Adv. Rates:* 18; 15; 15; 13
Michael Stapleford, President
Cliff Mack, Operations Dir
Laura Shore Mack, General Manager
Marian Kovach, General Sales Mgr
C.J. Daniels, Programming Director
Jason Torrance, Promotions Manager
Mary Beth Thompson, NewsDirector
Joe Portelli, Chief Engineer
Tor Michaels, News Reporter
Sherry Flick, Public Affairs Director

WQCK(FM)
03-01-1989; 105.9 mhz FM *Hrs Open:* 24; 710 w; Ant 951 ft; N40 47 34 W78 10 29
315 S. Atherton Street, State College, PA 16803
(814) 272-1320, *Fax:* (814) 342-9742
1059qwikrock.com
License: Philipsburg, Centre County, PA held by Magnum Broadcasting Inc.
Group Owner: Magnum Broadcasting Inc.
Population Served: 42,499 *Arbitron Metro Market:* State College, PA *Format:* Alternative *Hrs. of News Programming:* News progmg 2.5 hrs wkly *Target Audience:* 18-49; men & women
Adv. Rates: 26.50; 21;24.50; 19
Drew Shannon, Radio Jockey
AJ, Local Producer

Phoenixville

WPHE
08-23-1978; 690 khz AM; 1 kw-D, DAD; N40 8 8 W75 33 37
Mailing Address: P.O. Box 46327, Philadelphia, PA 19160 US
Second Address: 321 W. Sedgley Ave., Philadelphia, PA 19140
(215) 291-7532, *Fax:* (215) 739-1337
www.radiosalvation.com
rs@radiosalvation.com
License: Phoenixville, PA held by Salvation Broadcasting Co.
Arbitron Metro Market: Philadelphia *Format:* Variety/Diverse, Religious *Special Programming:* Por 3 hrs wkly
Sarrial Salva, President
Isabel Salva, General Sales Mgr
Juan Izquierdo, Programming Director
Juan Pydeck, Chief Engineer

Pittsburgh

KDKA
11-02-1920; 1020 khz AM *Hrs Open:* 24; 50 kw-U, ND1; N40 33 33 W79 57 11
C/O Cbs Corporation, 600 New Hampshire Avenue, N.W. #1200, Washington, DC 20037 US
(412) 575-2320
KDKAradio.com
madams@kdka.com
License: Pittsburgh, PA held by Infinity Broadcasting East Inc.
Group Owner: CBS Radio
Nat'l Network: CBS; CNN Radio; AP Network News; Premiere Radio Networks; Westwood One *Nat'l Reps:* CBS Radio *Wire Services:* AP; Accu-Weather
Arbitron Metro Market: Pittsburgh, PA *Format:* News, News/Talk, 86 *Hrs. of News Programming:* news progmg 75 hrs wkly *No. News Employees:* 35 *Target Audience:* P25-54
Michael Young, Operations Dir
Michael Spacc, General Sales Mgr
Marshall Adams, Programming Director
Amy Mauk, Promotions Manager
Jeff Hathhorn, News Director
Vic Pasquarelli, Chief Engineer
Dan Wonders, Edit Manager

KQV
11-19-1919; 1410 khz AM *Hrs Open:* 24; 5 kw-D, DA2; 5 kw-N, DA2; N40 31 24 W80 0 40
Center City Tower, 650 Smithfield St S620, Pittsburgh, PA 15222 US
(412) 562-5900, *Fax:* (412) 562-5936
www.kqv.com
kqvnews@kqv.com
License: Pittsburgh, PA held by Calvary Inc.
Nat'l Network: Wall Street; AP Radio *Regional Network:* Radio Pa. *Wire Services:* AP
Arbitron Metro Market: Pittsburgh metro area *Format:* News *Special Programming:* NFL football (regular season, playoffs & Superbowl *Hrs. of News Programming:* news progmg 168 hrs wkly *No. News Employees:* 15*Target Audience:* 35 plus; affluent, info-oriented adults
Robert W. Dickey Sr., President
Cheryl Scott, Operations Dir
Judith Ross, General Sales Mgr
Frank Gottlieb, News Director
Steve Conti, Chief Engineer
Susan Selby, Traffic Director

WXXF(FM)
07-19-1948; 93.7 mhz FM; 41 kw; Ant 550 ft; N40 26 28 W80 01 32
651 Holiday Dr., Suite 310, Pittsburgh, PA 15220
(412) 920-9400, *Fax:* (412) 920-9444
www.b94.com
wbzw@cbfradio.com
License: Pittsburgh, Allegheny County, PA held by CBS Radio Holdings Inc.
Group Owner: CBS Radio; (acq 11-13-98; grpsl)
Population Served: 64,294 *Arbitron Metro Market:* Pittsburgh, PA *Format:* Contemporary Hits/Top 40
Jacques Tortoroli, CFO
Joel Hollander, President
Michael Young, Operations Dir
Norm Slemenda, General Sales Mgr
Brandon Davis, Promotions Manager
Shelley Duffy, News Director
Scott Herman, Executive Vice President
Keith Clark,Vice President, Operations

WDSY-FM
09-01-1962; 107.9 mhz FM; 17.5 kw; 827 ft.; N40 28 20 W79 59 41
600 N. Hampshire Ave, NW, Suite 1200, Washington, DC 20037 US
(412) 920-9400, *Fax:* (412) 920-9449
y108.cbslocal.com/
jeff.davidson@cbsradio.com
License: Pittsburgh, Allegheny County, PA held by Infinity Radio Holdings Inc.
Group Owner: CBS Radio; (acq 12-14-00; grpsl).
Nat'l Network: Westwood One *Nat'l Reps:* Katz Radio
Arbitron Metro Market: Pittsburgh, PA *Format:* Country *Target Audience:* 25-54; general *Adv. Rates:* 275; 225; 250; 100
Jacques Tortoroli, CFO
Joel Hollander, President
Don Oyleaar, Operations Dir
Don Oylear, General Manager
Christine Fallon-McKenna, General Sales Mgr
Mark Anderson, Programming Director
Jeff Davidson, Promotions Manager
ScottHerman, Executive Vice President
Keith Belden, National Sales Manager
Keith Clark, Vice President, Operations
Norm Slemanda, Regional Sales Manager

***WESA**
12-15-1949; 90.5 mhz FM *Hrs Open:* 24; 25 kw; 480 ft; N40 25 52 W80 00 26
600 Forbes Ave., 67 Bedford Square, Pittsburgh, PA 15282
(412) 396-6030, *Fax:* (412) 396-5061
www.wesa.fm
info@wesa.fm
License: Pittsburgh, Allegheny County, PA held by Duquesne University.
Nat'l Network: NPR; PRI; APM; PRX *Nat'l Reps:* Interep
Arbitron Metro Market: Pittsburgh, PA *Hrs. of News Programming:* news progmg 47 hrs wkly *No. News Employees:* 5 *Target Audience:* Educated, moderately affluent
Helen Wigger, Operations Dir
DeAnne Hamilton, General Manager
Dorothy Frank, General Sales Mgr
Tammy Terwelp, Programming Director
Suzanne Meyer, Promotions Manager
Mark Nootbaar, News Director
Russ Lyod, Engineering Dir

WDVE
05-10-1962; 102.5 mhz FM; 55 kw; 820 ft.; N40 29 38 W80 1 9
600 Congress Ave., Suite 1400, Austin, TX 78701 US
(412) 937-1441, *Fax:* (412) 937-0323
www.dve.com
davidedgar@clearchannel.com
License: Pittsburgh, Allegheny County, PA held by Capstar TX L.P.
Group Owner: Clear Channel Communications Inc.; (acq 8-00; grpsl).
Nat'l Reps: Christal
Arbitron Metro Market: Pittsburgh, PA *Format:* News, Talk *No. News Employees:* 1 *Target Audience:* 25-54.
Missy Gawaldo, General Sales Mgr

WJAS
10-19-1921; 1320 khz AM
Broadcast Plaza Ii, 3rd Floor, 900 Parish St, Pittsburgh, PA 15220 US
(412) 875-9500, *Fax:* (412) 875-9970
www.1320wjas.com
rantill@1320wjas.com
License: Pittsburgh, PA held by Renda Broadcasting Corp.
Group Owner: Renda Broadcasting Corp.; (acq 7-16-85; $700,000;
Arbitron Metro Market: Pittsburgh, PA *Format:* Adult Contemp, Big Band, 64 *Special Programming:* Big band jump, Frank Sinatra 2 hrs wkly *Target Audience:* 35 plus; older, upscale *Adv. Rates:* 90; 90; 90; 50
Anthony Renda, President
Lawrence Weiss, General Manager
David Pavlic, General Sales Mgr
Ron Antill, Programming Director
Chris Shovlin, Promotions Manager
Jason Horvath, Chief Engineer
Chris Shovlin, Director of Marketing
Maureen Brady, NTR Director

WPGB
02-04-1963; 104.7 mhz FM *Hrs Open:* 24; 13 kw; 827 ft.; N40 28 20 W79 59 41
600 Congress Ave., Suite 1400, Austin, TX 78701 US
(412) 937-1441, *Fax:* (412) 937-0323
www.wpgb.com
info@wpgb.com
License: Pittsburgh, Allegheny County, PA held by Capstar TX L.P.
Group Owner: Clear Channel Communications Inc.; (acq 8-30-00; grpsl).
Nat'l Network: Fox News Radio *Wire Services:* AP
Arbitron Metro Market: Pittsburgh, PA *Format:* News, Sports, 86 *Hrs. of News Programming:* news progmg 5 hrs wkly *Target Audience:* 25-54; white collar workers
John Rohm, Operations Dir
Fred Traynor, General Sales Mgr
Jay Bohannon, Programming Director

WDDZ
02-12-1950; 1250 khz AM *Hrs Open:* 24 hrs; 5 kw-D, DAN; 5 kw-N, DAN; N40 23 50 W79 57 43
77 West 66th Street, 16th Floor, New York, NY 10023 US
(401) 722-0839, *Fax:* (401) 722-1459
radio.disney.go.com
License: Pittsburgh, PA held by Radio Disney Group LLC.
Group Owner: ABC Inc.; (acq 5-29-2001; $2.05 million).
Nat'l Network: Radio Disney
Arbitron Metro Market: Providence-Warwick-Pawtucket, RI
Format: Children *Target Audience:* Children & Teens 3-14, Parents 25-54, esp. moms.
Michael Kellogg, General Manager
Jaccalen Grillo, Promotions Manager
Adria Paquin, Marketing Account Executive
Scott Henderson, Senior Account Manager

WLTJ
04-04-1942; 92.9 mhz FM *Hrs Open:* 24; 43 kw; 853 ft.; N40 29 43 W80 0 17
7 Parkway Center, #780, Pittsburgh, PA 15220 US
(412) 316-3342, *Fax:* (412) 316-3388
q929fm.com
info@wltj.com
License: Pittsburgh, Allegheny County, PA held by WPNT Inc.
Nat'l Reps: McGavren Guild
Arbitron Metro Market: Pittsburgh, PA *Format:* Adult Contemp
Target Audience: 25-54; affluent, professional, working public
Saul Frischling, President
Greg Frischling, General Manager
Chris Kohan, General Sales Mgr
Chuck Stevens, Programming Director
Vicki Wolfe, Promotions Manager
Amy Crago, News Director
Paul Carroll, Chief Engineer

WORD-FM
01-01-1948; 101.5 mhz FM; 43 kw; 528 ft.; N40 29 2 W79 59 34
4880 Santa Rosa Rd, #300, Camarillo, CA 93012 US
(412) 937-1500, *Fax:* (412) 937-1576
www.wordfm.com
word@wordfm.com
License: Pittsburgh, Allegheny County, PA held by Pennsylvania Media Associates Inc.
Group Owner: Salem Communications Corp.
Arbitron Metro Market: Pittsburgh, PA *TV Affiliate:* Relg *No. News Employees:* 25-49.
Sales Manager, Gary Dickson
Program Director, Programming Director

WWNL
01-01-1947; 1080 khz AM *Hrs Open:* Sunrise-sunset; 25 kw-C, DAD; 50 kw-D, DAD; N40 36 17 W79 57 37
3270 Blazer Pkwy, Suite 101, Lexington, KY 40509 US
(724) 443-4844, *Fax:* (724) 443-4847
www.wilkinsradio.com
wwnl@wilkinsradio.com
License: Pittsburgh, PA held by Steel City Radio Inc.
Group Owner: Wilkins Communications Network Inc.; (acq 6-14-2001).
Arbitron Metro Market: Pittsburgh, PA *Format:* Christian, Talk
Target Audience: 35 plus. *Adv. Rates:* 60; 60; 60; 60
Bob Wilkins, CEO
Greg Garrett, Operations Dir
Fred Brucker, Station Manager
Julie Ziegler, General Sales Mgr
Terri Wehofer, Promotions Manager

Art White, Engineering Dir
Mitchell Mathis, COO
LuAnn Wilkins, Executive VicePresident
Barry Bright, Senior Director of Client

WKST-FM
08-08-1960; 96.1 mhz FM; 44 kw; 522 ft.; N40 23 49 W79 57 43
600 Congress Ave., Suite 1400, Austin, TX 78701 US
(412) 937-1441, *Fax:* (412) 937-0323
www.kissfm961.com
info@kissfm961.com
License: Pittsburgh, Allegheny County, PA held by Capstar TX L.P.
Group Owner: Clear Channel Communications Inc.; (acq 8-30-00; grpsl).
Arbitron Metro Market: Pittsburgh, PA *Format:* Contemporary Hits/Top 40
Missy Gawaldo, General Sales Mgr

WPIT
01-01-1947; 730 khz AM; 5 kw-D, ND1; 0.024 kw-N, ND1; N40 29 2 W79 59 34
4880 Santa Rosa Rd #300, Camarillo, CA 93012 US
(412) 937-1500, *Fax:* (412) 937-1576
www.wpitam.com
wpit@wpitam.com
License: Pittsburgh, PA held by Pennsylvania Media Associates Inc.
Group Owner: Salem Communications Corp.; (Acq 12-2-92; $6.5 million;
Arbitron Metro Market: Pittsburgh, PA *Format:* Christian
Jeff Baity, Operations Dir
Ron Baity, General Manager

***WPTS-FM**
08-26-1984; 92.1 mhz FM *Hrs Open:* 24; 0.016 kw; 463 ft.; N40 26 39 W79 57 12
4200 Fifth Avenue, Pittsburgh, PA 15260 US
(412) 648-7990, *Fax:* (412) 648-7988
www.wpts.pitt.edu
wpts@freelist.org
License: Pittsburgh, Allegheny County, PA held by University of Pittsburgh.
Arbitron Metro Market: Pittsburgh, PA *Format:* Variety/Diverse *Hrs. of News Programming:* news progmg 10 hrs wkly *No. News Employees:* 3 *Target Audience:* General.
Gregory Weston, General Manager

***WQED-FM**
01-25-1973; 89.3 mhz FM *Hrs Open:* 24; 28 kw; 653 ft.; N40 26 46 W79 57 51
4802 Fifth Avenue, Pittsburgh, PA 15213 US
(412) 622-1300, *Fax:* (412) 622-1488
www.wqed.org
radio@wqed.org
License: Pittsburgh, Allegheny County, PA held by WQED Multimedia.
Nat'l Network: NPR; PRI
Arbitron Metro Market: Pittsburgh, PA *TV Affiliate:* *WQED(TV) affil. *Format:* Talk *Hrs. of News Programming:* News progmg 5 hrs wkly *Target Audience:* 35-64; educated, influential, professional, communityleaders, mid to high income
George Miles Jr., President
B.J. Leber, Operations Dir
Michelle Heck, General Manager
Lilli Mosco, General Sales Mgr
Karen Colbert, Promotions Manager
George Hazimanois, Advertising Director
Ted Sohier, Operations Manager
GigiSaladna, Promotions Manager
Rick Vaccarielli, Sales Director

***WRCT**
04-01-1974; 88.3 mhz FM *Hrs Open:* 24; 1.75 kw; 72 ft.; N40 26 39 W79 56 37
5020 Forbes Avenue, Pittsburgh, PA 15213 US
(412) 621-0728,(412) 621-9728, *Fax:* (412) 268-6549
www.wrct.org
info@wrct.org
License: Pittsburgh, PA held by Carnegie Mellon Student Government Corp.
Arbitron Metro Market: Pittsburgh, PA *Format:* Variety/Diverse *Special Programming:* Black 12 hrs, class 3 hrs, country 3 hrs, folk 3 hrs, experimental 12 hrs, jazz 18 hrs wkly *Hrs. of News Programming:* News progmg 10hrs wkly *Target Audience:* General.
Matt Siko, General Manager
Pauline Law, Programming Director

WSHH
03-08-1948; 99.7 mhz FM; 15.5 kw; 899 ft.; N40 27 48 W80 0 16
1459 Crane Avenue, Pittsburgh, PA 15220 US
(412) 875-4800, *Fax:* (412) 875-9474
www.wshh.com
License: Pittsburgh, Allegheny County, PA held by Renda Broadcasting Corp.
Group Owner: Renda Broadcasting Corp.; (acq 11-83; $2.7 million;
Arbitron Metro Market: Pittsburgh, PA *Format:* Adult Contemp *Special Programming:* Pub affrs one hr wkly *No. News Employees:* 1 *Target Audience:* 25-54; white collar, upscale office workers, professionals,managers *Adv. Rates:* 130; 130; 125; 50
Allan Freed, Operations Dir
Susan Kelly, General Sales Mgr
Ron Antill, Programming Director

WBGG
01-01-1932; 970 khz AM *Hrs Open:* 24; 5 kw-D, DA2; 5 kw-N, DA2; N40 30 30 W80 0 30
433 E. Las Colina Blvd, #1130, Irving, TX 75039 US
(412) 937-1441, *Fax:* (412) 937-0323
www.fox970.com
License: Pittsburgh, PA held by AMFM Radio Licenses L.L.C.
Group Owner: Clear Channel Communications Inc.; (acq 8-30-2000; grpsl)
Nat'l Network: Fox Sports
Arbitron Metro Market: Pittsburgh, PA *Format:* Sports
John Rohm, General Manager
Fred Traynor, General Sales Mgr

WWSW-FM
01-01-1940; 94.5 mhz FM; 50 kw; 810 ft.; N40 27 48 W80 0 18
433 E. Las Colina Blvd, #1130, Irving, TX 75039 US
(412) 937-1441, *Fax:* (412) 937-0323
www.3wsradio.com
License: Pittsburgh, Allegheny County, PA held by AMFM Radio Licenses L.L.C.
Group Owner: Clear Channel Communications Inc.
Arbitron Metro Market: Pittsburgh, PA *Format:* Contemporary Hits/Top 40, Adult Contemp
David Edgar, Operations Dir
John Rohm, General Manager

WXDX-FM
01-01-1960; 105.9 mhz FM; 15.5 kw; 892 ft.; N40 29 38 W80 1 9
600 Congress Ave., Suite 1400, Austin, TX 78701 US
(412) 937-1441, *Fax:* (412) 937-0323
www.wxdx.com
info@wxdx.com
License: Pittsburgh, Allegheny County, PA held by Capstar TX L.P.
Group Owner: Clear Channel Communications Inc.; (acq 8-30-00; grpsl).
Nat'l Reps: Christal
Arbitron Metro Market: Pittsburgh, PA *Format:* Alternative *Target Audience:* 18-34.
David Edgar, Operations Dir
Missy Gawaldo, General Sales Mgr

***WYEP-FM**
04-30-1974; 91.3 mhz FM *Hrs Open:* 24; 18 kw; 381 ft.; N40 24 42 W79 55 53
2313 E. Carson Street, Pittsburgh, PA 15203 US
(412) 381-9900, *Fax:* (412) 381-9126
www.wyep.org
info@wyep.org
License: Pittsburgh, Allegheny County, PA held by Pittsburgh Community Broadcasting Corp.
Nat'l Network: PRI; NPR
Arbitron Metro Market: Pittsburgh, PA *Format:* Triple A *Special Programming:* Folk 9 hrs, blues 7 hrs, bluegrass 4 hrs, soul 3 h *Target Audience:* 25-49; socially, politically & culturally aware & active; well-educated
Blaine Lucas, Chairman
Sean Sebastian, President
Lee Ferraro, General Manager
Tony Pirollo, General Sales Mgr
Rosemary Welsch, Programming Director
Suzanne Meyer, Marketing Director

***WRCT(FM)**
04-01-1974; 88.3 mhz FM *Hrs Open:* 24; 1.75 kw; 53 ft; N40 26 39 W79 56 37
One WRCT Plaza, 5000 Forbes Ave., Pittsburgh, PA 15213
(412) 621-0728,(412) 621-9728, *Fax:* (412) 268-6549
www.wrct.org
info@wrct.org
License: Pittsburgh, Allegheny County, PA held by Carnegie Mellon Student Government Corp.
Population Served: 1,500,000 *Arbitron Metro Market:* Pittsburgh, PA *Special Programming:* Black 12 hrs, class 3 hrs, country 3 hrs, folk 3 hrs, experimental 12 hrs, jazz 18 hrs wkly *Hrs. of News Programming:* Newsprogmg 10 hrs wkly *Target Audience:* General.
Matt Siko, General Manager
Pauline Law, Programming Director

Pittston

WITK
06-21-1953; 1550 khz AM; 10 kw-D, DA2; 0.5 kw-N, DA2; N41 20 45 W75 47 8
633 East Drinker Turnpik, Dunmore, Pa 18512, PA 18512 US
(570) 207-6515, *Fax:* (877) 711-8500
License: Pittston, PA held by Steel City Radio Inc.
Group Owner: Wilkins Communications Network Inc.; (acq 10-10-2007; $400,000)
Arbitron Metro Market: Wilkes Barre-Scranton, PA *Format:* Christian
James Wright, General Manager

WDMT
11-01-1983; 102.3 mhz FM; 5.8 kw; 72 ft.; N41 18 20 W75 45 38
10706 Beaver Dam Road, Cockeysville, MD 21030 US
(570) 883-1111, *Fax:* (570) 883-9851
www.102themountain.com
info@102themountain.com
License: Pittston, Luzerne County, PA held by Entercom Wilkes-Barre Scranton LLC.
Group Owner: Entercom Communications Corp.; (acq 12-13-99; grpsl).
Nat'l Network: Jones Radio Networks *Nat'l Reps:* D & R Radio
Arbitron Metro Market: Wilkes Barre-Sc *Format:* Triple A *Special Programming:* Philadelphia Eagles, Penn State football *Target Audience:* 35-64; female
John Burkavage, General Manager
Jim Rising, Station Manager
Andy Zapotek, General Sales Mgr
Jerry Padden, Programming Director
Michael Ignatz, Promotions Manager
Lamar Smith, Chief Engineer
Elizabeth Masich, Music Director

Plains

WYCK
01-01-1923; 1340 khz AM *Hrs Open:* 24; 0.81 kw-U, ND1; N41 15 1 W75 49 32 *Rebroadcasts:* Rebroadcasts WICK(AM) Scranton 98%
1049 N. Skol Road, Scranton, PA 18504 US
(570) 344-1221, *Fax:* (570) 344-0996
www.boldgoldradionepa.com
License: Plains, PA held by Bold Gold Media WBS L.P.
Group Owner: Bold Gold Media Group LP; (acq 3-13-2006; grpsl).
Nat'l Network: Fox Sports *Wire Services:* Metro Weather Service Inc.
Arbitron Metro Market: Scranton, PA *Format:* Sports *Special Programming:* Relg 3 hrs wkly, Polish 3 hrs wkly *Hrs. of News Programming:* 8 hrs progmg wkly *No. News Employees:* 1 *Target Audience:* Adults35-64; adults who love original hits of top 40 era
Bob Vanderheyden, General Manager
Brian Spinelli, General Sales Mgr

Pleasant Gap

WEMR
06-13-1986; 98.7 mhz FM *Hrs Open:* 18; 2.2 kw; 551 ft.; N40 55 58 W77 45 40
One Forever Drive, Hollidaysburg, PA 16648 US
(570) 928-7200, *Fax:* (570) 928-2100
License: Pleasant Gap, Wyoming County, PA held by GEOS Communications.
Group Owner: Geos Communications; (acq 1-30-2004; $515,000 with co-located FM)
Arbitron Metro Market: Wilkes Barre. PA *Format:* News, News/Talk, 86
Ben Smith, General Manager

Pocono Pines

WPZX
01-01-2000; 105.9 mhz FM; 6 kw; 328 ft.; N41 5 6 W75 38 9
Rebroadcasts: Simulcast with WEZX(FM) Scranton
8280 Greensboro Drive, 7th Floor, McLean, VA 22102 US
(570) 346-6555, *Fax:* (570) 346-6038
www.rock107.com
License: Pocono Pines, Monroe County, PA held by The Scranton Times L.P.
Group Owner: Shamrock Communications Inc.; (acq 9-8-00).
Arbitron Metro Market: Scranton, PA *Format:* Classic Rock
William Lynett, CEO
Sean O'Mealy, General Manager

Dave Mehall, Sales Manager
Scott Laudani, Operations Manger / Program Director
Mark Hoover, Operations Manger / Program Director
Ruth Miller, News Director
Kevin Fitzgerald, ChiefEngineer
Jim Loftus, COO
Jim Morris, National Sales Manager
Krista Saar, Traffic Manager
Mari Olshefski, Traffic & Continuity Director
Donna Ryan, Traffic
Judy Haudenschield, Account Executive

Port Allegany

WHKS
01-01-1990; 94.9 mhz FM *Hrs Open:* 24; 1.15 kw; 758 ft.; N41 48 36 W78 23 10
Mailing Address: 59 Lent Hollow Rd, Coudersport, PA 16915 US
Second Address: 59 Lent Hollow Rd., Coudersport, PA 16915
(814) 642-7004, *Fax:* (814) 642-9491
whksradio.com
whks@verizon.net
License: Port Allegany, McKean County, PA held by L-Com Inc.
Nat'l Network: Jones Radio Networks; AP Radio *Regional Network:* Radio Pa. *Nat'l Reps:* Dome *Regional Reps:* Commercial Media Sales.
Format: Adult Contemp *Special Programming:* Relg 2 hrs wkly *Hrs. of News Programming:* News progmg 2 hrs wkly *Target Audience:* 25-54; general
David Lent, President
Joe Taylor, General Sales Mgr

Port Matilda

***WKVB**
10-17-1994; 107.9 mhz FM *Hrs Open:* 24; 0.45 kw; 1175 ft.; N40 55 11 W77 58 28
140 South Ash Avenue, Tempe, AZ 85281 US
(814) 238-5085, *Fax:* (814) 238-8993
www.klove.com
License: Port Matilda, Centre County, PA held by 2510 Licenses LLC.
Group Owner: 2510 Licenses LLC; (acq 2-16-2005; grpsl).
Nat'l Network: K-Love
Arbitron Metro Market: Port Matilda, PA *Format:* Christian
Nick Ferrara, General Manager

Portage

***WLKJ**
11-15-1990; 105.7 mhz FM *Hrs Open:* 24; 3 kw; 322 ft.; N40 22 59 W78 39 31
One Forever Drive, Hollidaysburg, PA 16648 US
(800) 525-5683, *Fax:* (814) 534-8979
www.klove.com
info@klove.com
License: Portage, Cambria County, PA held by 2510 Licenses LLC.
Group Owner: 2510 Licenses LLC; (acq 5-1-2005; grpsl)
Nat'l Network: K-Love
Format: Christian *Target Audience:* 18-54; middle to upper income
Nick Ferrara, Operations Dir
Amanda Carroll, Disc Jockey
Troy West, Disc Jockey
Monika Kelly, Disc Jockey

Pottstown

***WPAZ**
10-01-1951; 89.1 mhz FM *Hrs Open:* 6 AM-7 PM; kw
US
(610) 326-4000,(610) 326-6832, *Fax:* (610) 326-7984
www.1370wpaz.com
License: Pottstown, Montgomery County, PA held by Faye Scott.
Group Owner: Great Scott Broadcasting
Arbitron Metro Market: Philadelphia *Format:* News, News/Talk, 86 *Special Programming:* Pol one hr, relg 12 hrs wkly *Hrs. of News Programming:* news progmg 8 hrs wkly *No. News Employees:* 2 *Target Audience:* 25 plus; most affluent people
Adv. Rates: 20; 18; 20; 10
Faye Scott, President
Mike LiCata, General Manager
Jay Warren, Programming Director
Paul Fanelli, News Director
Terry Dalton, Chief Engineer

Pottsville

WAVT-FM
11-20-1948; 101.9 mhz FM *Hrs Open:* 24; 29 kw; 561 ft.; N40 49 50 W76 12 32
P.O. Box 540, Pottsville, PA 17901 US
(507) 345-4646, *Fax:* (507) 345-3299
www.957theblaze.com
dsturgeon@mankato.threeeagles.com
License: Pottsville, Schuylkill County, PA held by Pottsville Broadcasting Co. Inc.
Format: Rock/AOR *No. News Employees:* 1
Larry LeBlanc, Operations Dir
Dave Sturgeon, General Manager
Jen Jones, General Sales Mgr
Jeff Spence, Programming Director
Mike Schoen, Promotions Manager
Randall Harder, News Director
Jill Mason, Business Manager
Al Clennon,Local Sales Manager

WPAM
01-01-1946; 1450 khz AM *Hrs Open:* 24; 1 kw-U, ND1; N40 41 27 W76 11 39
Mailing Address: 101 N. Centre Street, Pottsville, PA 17901 US
Second Address: PO Box 732, Pottsville, PA 17901-0732
(570) 622-1450, *Fax:* (570) 622-4690
www.phoenix1450.com
bob@phoenix1450.com
License: Pottsville, PA held by Curran Communications Inc.
Nat'l Network: Jones Radio Networks
Format: Classic Rock *Special Programming:* Gospel, Talk 6 hrs wkly *Target Audience:* 25-54; active, upwardly mobile adults
Adv. Rates: 10; 10; 10; 10
Robert Murray, General Manager

WPPA
05-09-1946; 1360 khz AM *Hrs Open:* 24; 5 kw-D, DA2; 0.5 kw-N, DA2; N40 41 56 W76 11 43
P.O. Box 540, Pottsville, PA 17901 US
(570) 622-1360, *Fax:* (570) 622-2822
www.wpparadio.com
info@wpparadio.com
License: Pottsville, PA held by Pottsville Broadcasting Co. Inc.
Nat'l Network: CBS
Format: Adult Contemp *Hrs. of News Programming:* news progmg 14 hrs wkly *No. News Employees:* 2 *Target Audience:* 25-54.
Argie Tidmore, President
Les Blankenhorn, Operations Dir
William Tidmore, General Sales Mgr
Al Kovy, Programming Director
Jay Levan, News Director
Deb Daugherty, Public Affairs Director

Punxsutawney

WECZ
03-18-1953; 1540 khz AM *Hrs Open:* 12; 1 kw-C, NDD; 5 kw-D, NDD; N40 57 36 W79 0 8
1459 Crane Avenue, Pittsburgh, PA 15220 US
(814) 938-6000, *Fax:* (814) 938-4237
www.weczam1540.com/
dpavlic@weczam1540.com
License: Punxsutawney, PA held by Renda Radio Inc.
Group Owner: Renda Broadcasting Corp.; acq 6-1-81; $512,000;
Nat'l Network: Westwood One
Arbitron Metro Market: Punxsutawney, PA *Format:* News, Talk *Special Programming:* Pol 3 hrs wkly *Hrs. of News Programming:* news progmg 10 hrs wkly *No. News Employees:* 2 *Target Audience:* 45 plus. *Adv.Rates:* 12; 8; 6; na
Anthony Renda, President
Doug Metherey, General Manager
David Pavlic, Station Manager
Jennifer Black, General Sales Mgr
Jim Costanzo, Programming Director
Marty Palmer, Engineering Dir

WPXZ-FM
12-12-1973; 104.1 mhz FM *Hrs Open:* 24; 3 kw; 295 ft.; N40 57 36 W79 0 8
P.O. Box 458, Route 36 North, Punxsutawney, PA 15767 US
(814) 938-6000, *Fax:* (814) 938-4237
rendaradio@comcast.net
License: Punxsutawney, Jefferson County, PA
Nat'l Network: ABC
Format: Adult Contemp *Target Audience:* 35-64. *Adv. Rates:* 20; 16; 20; 12
Larry McGuire, Programming Director

Radnor Township

***WYBF**
08-01-1991; 89.1 mhz FM *Hrs Open:* 7 AM-2 AM (M, W, F); noon-2 AM (Su); 0.7 kw vert; 223 ft.; N40 3 22 W75 22 30
Rebroadcasts: Rebroadcasts WXVU(FM) Villanova
610 King of Prussia Rd., Radnor, PA 19087 US
610-902-8453
www.wybf.com
License: Radnor Township, Chester County, PA held by Cabrini College.
Arbitron Metro Market: Philadelphia *Format:* News, News/Talk, 86, Variety/Diverse
Justin Sillner, Operations Dir
Alyssa Mentzer, Promotions Manager
Liz Scopelliti, News Director
Megan Sokolowski, Sports Director

Reading

WEEU
01-01-1931; 830 khz AM *Hrs Open:* 24
34 North Fourth Street, Reading, PA 19601 US
(610) 376-7335, *Fax:* (610) 376-7756
www.weeu.com
weeu@weeu.com
License: Reading, PA held by WEEU Broadcasting Co.
Nat'l Reps: McGavren Guild
Arbitron Metro Market: Reading, PA *Format:* News, News/Talk, 84, Talk *Special Programming:* Folk 3 hrs, Ger 2 hrs wkly *Hrs. of News Programming:* news progmg 6 hrs wkly *No. News Employees:* 2 *Target Audience:* 30 plus; mature
Dave Kline, Station Manager

WIOV
09-01-1946; 1240 khz AM; 1 kw-U, ND1; N40 19 28 W75 56 31
P.O. Box 3353, Evansville, IN 57732 US
(717) 738-1191, *Fax:* (717) 738-1661
www.espn1240.com
widv@ptd.net
License: Reading, PA
Group Owner: Cumulus Media Inc.; (acq 5-12-2004; grpsl).
Nat'l Network: ESPN Radio
Arbitron Metro Market: Reading, PA *Format:* Sports *Target Audience:* 35-54; Male *Adv. Rates:* 20; 17; 15; 8
Mitch Carroll, Operations Dir
CJ Taylor, Promotions Manager
Brenda Perkins, National Sales Manager
Jim Rudley, Operations Manager
Susie Summer, Promotions Manager
Crissy Wall, Regional Sales Manager

WRAW
09-01-1922; 1340 khz AM *Hrs Open:* 24; 1 kw-U, ND1; N40 19 27 W75 55 10
1265 Perkiomen Avenue, Reading, PA 19602 US
(610) 376-7173,(610) 376-6671, *Fax:* (610) 376-1270
www.1340praiseradio.com
License: Reading, PA held by Clear Channel Radio Licenses Inc.
Group Owner: Clear Channel Communications Inc.; (acq 1996; grpsl)
Arbitron Metro Market: Reading, PA *Format:* Christian
Brian Check, Operations Dir
John Rizzuto, General Manager
Al Burke, Programming Director
Nick Harris, Promotions Manager
Steve McKenzie, Chief Engineer

WRFY-FM
09-23-1962; 102.5 mhz FM; 10 kw; 807 ft.; N40 19 19 W75 53 35
200 Concord Plaza, Suite 600, San Antonio, TX 78216 US
(610) 376-7173, *Fax:* (610) 376-6671
www.y102.com
License: Reading, Berks County, PA
Group Owner: Clear Channel Communications Inc.
Arbitron Metro Market: Reading, PA *Format:* Contemporary Hits/Top 40 *Target Audience:* 18-49.
Al Burke, Programming Director

***WXAC**
01-01-1967; 91.3 mhz FM; 0.22 kw horiz; -23 ft.; N40 21 39 W75 54 37
P. O. Box 15234, 13th & Bern St., Reading, PA 19612 US
(610) 921-7545, *Fax:* (610) 921-7685
www.wxac.squarespace.com
music@albright.edu
License: Reading, Berks County, PA held by Albright College.
Arbitron Metro Market: Reading, PA *Format:* Jazz, Rock/AOR
Target Audience: General; Albright college community & Reading area
Mindy Cohen, Station Manager
Kyrstyn, Program Director & Webmaster
Cassandra, Program Director & Webmaster
Jennifer, Treasurer/News Director
Yuliza, Music Librarian/Office Manager
Sam, Music Director/Productions Director
Anthony, Assistant
Peter, Assistant

Red Lion

WSOX
10-01-1960; 96.1 mhz FM; 13.5 kw; 951 ft.; N39 54 16 W76 34 48
P. O. Box 102, Springhouse, PA 19477 US
(717) 764-1155, *Fax:* (717) 252-4708
www.oldies961.com
info@oldies961.com
License: Red Lion, York County, PA held by Susquehanna License Co. LLC.
Group Owner: Cumulus Media Partners LLC; (acq 8-1-2003; $23 million).
Arbitron Metro Market: York, PA *Format:* Oldies
Bobby D., Programming Director
Todd Toerper, Promotions Manager
Bob Poff, Chief Engineer

Renovo

WQKK(FM)
09-19-1996; 106.9 mhz FM; 800 w; Ant 876 ft; N41 14 15 W77 45 02
240 11th Street, Renovo, PA 17764
(570) 923-9106, *Fax:* (570) 923-9106
www.1069thesurge.com
morninghive@yahoo.com
License: Renovo, Clinton County, PA held by Magnum Broadcasting Inc.
Group Owner: Magnum Broadcasting Inc.; (acq 7-21-2004; $200,000).
Population Served: 1,235 *Arbitron Metro Market:* Renovo, PA *Format:* Classic Rock
Michael Stapleford, President
Diana Stapleford, General Manager
Glenn Brooks, Station Manager
Michael Brennen, General Sales Mgr

Reynoldsville

WDSN
02-14-1990; 106.5 mhz FM *Hrs Open:* 24; 6 kw; 328 ft.; N41 8 41 W78 52 41
51 West Long Avenue, Dubois, PA 15801 US
(814) 375-5260, *Fax:* (814) 375-5262
www.sunny106.fm
sunny106@penn.com
License: Reynoldsville, Jefferson County, PA held by Priority Communications.
Group Owner: Priority Communications; (acq 11-6-90; $275,000; *Nat'l Network:* Jones Radio Networks; Fox News Radio *Regional Reps:* Commerical Media Sales *Wire Services:* AP
Arbitron Metro Market: Reynoldsville, PA *Format:* Adult Contemp *Hrs. of News Programming:* news progmg 18 hrs wkly *No. News Employees:* 1 *Target Audience:* 25-54.
Jay Philippone, President
Beth Walters, Operations Dir
Jay Philippone, General Manager
Lori Lewis, Station Manager
Lindsey Schoening, Programming Director
Lindsay Schoening, News Director
Al Lockwood, Public Affairs Director
Polly Slie, Traffic Manager

Ridgebury

WZKN(FM)
01-01-1991; 96.9 mhz FM *Hrs Open:* 24; 3.6 kw; Ant 430 ft; N41 55 43 W76 46 58
111 N. Main St., Elmira, NY 14901
(607) 732-2484, *Fax:* (607) 732-8704
q969online.com
wreq@csnradio.com
License: Ridgebury, Bradford County, PA held by CSN International.
Group Owner: CSN International; (acq 6-14-2001; $300,000).
Arbitron Metro Market: Elmira-Corning, NY *Format:* Christian *Hrs. of News Programming:* News progmg 4 hrs wkly *Target Audience:* 25-44; women with families (small children), heads of households
Mike Kessler, President
Lorenzo Galletti, General Manager
Gina Galletti, Programming Director

Riverside

WVSL-FM
10-25-1990; 92.3 mhz FM *Hrs Open:* 24; 440 w; 833 ft; N40 57 30 W76 42 53 *Rebroadcasts:* Rebroadcasts WYGL(AM) Selinsgrove
Box 90, Rt. 204, State School Rd, Selinsgrove, PA 17870
(570) 374-8819, *Fax:* (570) 374-7444
bigcountryrequest@hotmail.com
License: Riverside, Northumberland County, PA held by MMP License LLC.
Group Owner: MAX Media L.L.C.; (acq 10-17-03; grpsl).
Nat'l Network: Jones Radio Networks; CNN Radio *Regional Reps:* Dome & Associates.
Population Served: 150,000*Format:* Country *Hrs. of News Programming:* news progmg 5 hrs wkly *No. News Employees:* 1 *Target Audience:* 25-54.
Dawn Marie, Operations Dir
Scott Richards, General Manager
Greg Adair, General Sales Mgr
Ted Koppen, Chief Engineer
Shelly Marx, Promotions Director

Roaring Spring

WKMC
05-01-1955; 1370 khz AM; 5 kw-D, DA2; 0.038 kw-N, DA2; N40 19 26 W78 23 40
1345 S. Main St., Roaring Spring, PA 16673 US
(814) 224-7501, *Fax:* (814) 224-7504
www.wkmcam.com
wkmc@cove.net
License: Roaring Spring, PA held by Handsome Brothers Inc.
Arbitron Metro Market: Altoona, PA *Format:* Adult Contemp
Target Audience: 45 plus; mature, loyal listeners
David Barger, President
Mike Martin, General Manager
Robert Lynn, Chief Engineer

Russell

WQFX-FM
11-11-1984; 103.1 mhz FM; 2.5 kw; 351 ft.; N41 57 48 W79 9 42
P.O. Box 609, Russell, PA 16345 US
(716) 664-2313, *Fax:* (716) 488-1471
A ahill@radiojamestown.com
License: Russell, Warren County, PA held by Media One Group II LLC.
Group Owner: Media One Group; (acq 5-31-2005; grpsl).
Nat'l Reps: Dome
Format: Classic Rock *Target Audience:* 25-54.
Merrill Rosen, General Manager
Jason Sample, Programming Director
Joel Keefer, News Director

Saegertown

WUZZ
01-19-1979; 94.3 mhz FM; 2.15 kw; 551 ft.; N41 37 53 W80 10 37
P.O. Box 397, Meadville, PA 16335 US
(814) 724-1111, *Fax:* (814) 333-9628
www.mywuzz.com
License: Saegertown, Crawford County, PA held by Forever Broadcasting LLC.
Group Owner: Forever Broadcasting; (acq 7-20-2000; grpsl)
Arbitron Metro Market: Cooperstown, PA *Format:* Light Rock
James R. Shields, General Manager

Salladasburg

WBYL
01-01-1989; 95.5 mhz FM; 3.9 kw; 240 ft.; N41 14 0 W77 12 10
Mailing Address: P.O. Box 6477, Harrisburg, PA 17701 US
Second Address: 1559 W 4th Street, Williamsport, PA 17701
(570) 327-1400, *Fax:* (570) 327-8156
www.bill95.com
bill@billcountry.com
License: Salladasburg, Lycoming County, PA held by Clear Channel Radio License Inc.
Group Owner: Clear Channel Communications Inc.; (acq 8-5-98; grpsl)
Arbitron Metro Market: Williamsport, PA *Format:* Country *Hrs. of News Programming:* news progmg 4 hrs wkly *No. News Employees:* 1 *Target Audience:* 35 plus.
Ken Sawyer, Operations Dir
James Dabney, General Manager
Joe Daniels, General Sales Mgr
Tom Scott, Programming Director
Gary Chrisman, Promotions Manager
Kathy Thomas, News Director
Mike Myer, Engineering Dir

Sayre

WATS
06-01-1950; 960 khz AM; 5 kw-D, ND1; 0.05 kw-N, ND1; N41 59 48 W76 30 3 *Rebroadcasts:* Rebroadcasts WAVR-FM Waverly, NY 100%
204 Desmond Street, Sayre, PA 18840 US
(570) 888-7745, *Fax:* (570) 888-9005
wats.wavr@cqservices.com
License: Sayre, PA held by WATS Broadcasting Inc.
Arbitron Metro Market: Sayre, PA. *Format:* Adult Contemp
Special Programming: Farm one hr wkly *Target Audience:* 25-54. *Adv. Rates:* 21; 16; 20; 12
Charles Carver Jr., President

Schnecksville

***WXLV**
09-23-1983; 90.3 mhz FM *Hrs Open:* 24; 0.42 kw; 230 ft.; N40 39 43 W75 36 41
4525 Education Park Dr, Schnecksville, PA 18078 US
(610) 799-4141, *Fax:* (610) 799-1571
www.wxlvradio.com
info@wxlvradio.com
License: Schnecksville, Lehigh County, PA held by Lehigh Carbon Community College.
Arbitron Metro Market: Schnecksville, PA *Format:* Triple A
Special Programming: Country, Bluegrass, Rock *Target Audience:* General. *Adv. Rates:* 25; 20; 15
Burr Beard, Programming Director
Chris Andrew, Contact Person

Scottdale

WLSW
12-21-1971; 103.9 mhz FM *Hrs Open:* 24; 0.32 kw; 781 ft.; N40 0 51 W79 31 1
R.D.#7, Box 56, Greensburg, PA 15601 US
(724) 628-2800, *Fax:* (724) 628-7380
www.musicpower104.com/
info@wlsw.com
License: Scottdale, Westmoreland County, PA held by Wall Broadcasting.
Nat'l Network: Westwood One
Arbitron Metro Market: Pittsburgh, PA *Format:* Adult Contemp, Oldies *Target Audience:* 25-54; general
L. Stanley Wall, President
Chris Molton, General Manager
Debbie Larson, Programming Director
Connie LaPorte, News Director
Jerry Braveman, Disc Jockey
Charlie Apple, Disc Jockey
Jeff Allen, Disc Jockey
Jamie Allen, DiscJockey

Scranton

WARM
01-01-1940; 590 khz AM *Hrs Open:* 24; 5 kw-D, DA2; 5 kw-N, DA2; N41 28 44 W75 52 51
City Center West, 7201 W. Lake Mead Blvd, Las Vegas, NV 89128 US
(570) 824-9000, *Fax:* (570) 820-0520
www.warm590.com/
phil.galasso@citcomm.com
License: Scranton, PA
Group Owner: Cumulus Media Inc.; (acq 7-1-97; grpsl).
Nat'l Network: ABC
Arbitron Metro Market: Scranton, PA *Format:* Oldies *Special Programming:* Sinatra, 2 hrs wkly *Hrs. of News Programming:* news progmg 1 hrs wkly *No. News Employees:* 1 *Target Audience:* 35 plus. *Adv.Rates:* 15; 15; 15; 15
Tom Jenkins, Operations Dir
Jeanne Kerr, General Sales Mgr
Phil Galasso, Programming Director
Bill Palmeri, Promotions Manager
Brian Hughes, News Director
Erin Evans, Promotions Manager
Lori Law, Traffic Manager

WEJL
11-29-1922; 630 khz AM *Rebroadcasts:* Rebroadcasts WBAX(AM) Wilkes Barre 100%
149 Penn. Avenue, Scranton, PA 18503 US
(570) 207-8599, *Fax:* (570) 346-6038
www.wejl-wbax.com
willobee@shamrocknepa.com
License: Scranton, PA held by The Scranton Times LP.
Group Owner: Shamrock Communications Inc.; (acq 1922).
Arbitron Metro Market: Scranton, PA *Format:* Sports
William Lynett, CEO
Tim Durkin, General Sales Mgr
Michael Neff, Programming Director
Mark Hoover, Promotions Manager
Ruth Miller, News Director
Kevin Fitzgerald, Chief Engineer
Jim Loftus, COO

Jenny Arndt, National SalesManager
Krista Saar, Traffic Manager

WEZX
11-01-1967; 106.9 mhz FM; 1.45 kw; 617 ft; N41 20 52 W75 39 03
149 Penn Ave., Scranton, PA 18503
(570) 346-6555, *Fax:* (570) 346-6038
info@wejl-wbax.com
License: Scranton, Lackawanna County, PA
Group Owner: Shamrock Communications Inc.; (Acq 1967).
Population Served: 103,564 *Arbitron Metro Market:* Wilkes Barre-Scranton, PA
Sean O'Mealy, General Manager
Scott Laudani, Station Manager
Dave Mehall, General Sales Mgr
Scott Laudani, Programming Director
Mark Hoover, Promotions Manager
Kevin Fritzgerald, Engineering Dir

WBZU
01-12-1925; 910 khz AM *Hrs Open:* 24*Rebroadcasts:* Rebroadcasts WILK(AM) Wilkes Barre 100%
2000 W. 41st St., Baltimore, MD 21211 US
(570) 883-9850, *Fax:* (570) 883-0832
www.wilknewsradio.com
info@wilknewsradio.com
License: Scranton, PA held by Entercom Scranton Wilkes-Barre License LLC.
Group Owner: Entercom Communications Corp.; (acq 12-16-99; grpsl).
Nat'l Reps: D & R Radio *Wire Services:* ABC; AP; Metro Weather Service Inc.
Arbitron Metro Market: Wilkes Barre-Scranton, PA *Format:* News, News/Talk, 86 *Special Programming:* Relg one hr wkly *Hrs. of News Programming:* news progmg 25 hrs wkly *No. News Employees:* 6 *Target Audience:* 25-54; affluent, educated
Jim Rising, Operations Dir
John Burkavage, General Manager
Andy Zapotell, General Sales Mgr
Nancy Kman, Programming Director
Liz Masich, Promotions Manager
Joe Thomas, News Director
Lamar Smith, Chief Engineer
Bob DeMono,National Sales Manager
Tom Ragan, News Reporter
Shannon Ball, Traffic Manager

WGGY
12-25-1948; 101.3 mhz FM; 7 kw; 1198 ft.; N41 25 38 W75 44 53
10706 Beaver Dam Road, Cockeysville, MD 21030 US
(570) 883-1111, *Fax:* (570) 883-1360
www.froggy101.com
License: Scranton, Lackawanna County, PA
Group Owner: Entercom Communications Corp.
Nat'l Network: CBS *Nat'l Reps:* Interep
Arbitron Metro Market: Wilkes Barre-Scranton, PA *Format:* Country
John Burkavage, Operations Dir
Andy Zapotek, General Sales Mgr
Mike Krinik, Programming Director
Elizabeth Masieh, Promotions Manager
Kelly Green, Music Director
Jaymie Gordon, Music Director
Bob De Mono, National SalesManager
Jim Rising, Operations Manager
Cheryl Willis, Promotions Manager

WICK
04-17-1954; 1400 khz AM *Hrs Open:* 24; 1 kw-U, ND1; N41 25 5 W75 39 43
1049 North Sekol Rd, Scranton, PA 18504 US
(570) 344-1221, *Fax:* (570) 344-0996
www.thegame-radio.com
bspinelli@boldgoldmedia.com
License: Scranton, PA held by Bold Gold Media WBS L.P.
Group Owner: Bold Gold Media Group LP; (acq 3-13-2006; grpsl)
Nat'l Network: Fox Sports
Arbitron Metro Market: Wilkes Barre-Scranton, PA *Format:* Sports *Special Programming:* Relg 3 hrs, Pol 3 hrs wkly *Hrs. of News Programming:* news progmg 8 hrs wkly *No. News Employees:* 2 *Target Audience:* 35-64; adults who love original hits of Top 40 Era
Bob Vanderheyden, General Manager
Brian Spinelli, General Sales Mgr

***WUSR**
02-27-1993; 99.5 mhz FM *Hrs Open:* 11 AM-2 AM; 0.3 kw; 1014 ft.; N41 26 9 W75 43 33
St. Thomas Hall, Scranton, PA 18510 US
(570) 941-7648, *Fax:* (570) 941-4628
www.scranton.edu/wusr
wusr@scranton.edu
License: Scranton, Lackawanna County, PA held by University of Scranton.
Wire Services: Metro Weather Service Inc.
Arbitron Metro Market: Scranton, PA *Format:* Alternative, Blues, 52, Rock/AOR *Special Programming:* Class 5 hrs, relg 4 hrs, loud rock 8 hrs, urban co *No. News Employees:* 1 *Target Audience:* General.
Ken Sandrowicz, General Manager
Gina Staller, Station Manager
John Niemiec, News Director
Katie Goodwin, Alternative Director
Matt Tarantino, Technology Director

***WVIA-FM**
04-23-1973; 89.9 mhz FM *Hrs Open:* 24; 7.4 kw; 1250 ft.; N41 10 55 W75 52 17
70 Old Boston Rd., Pittston, PA 18640 US
(570) 826-6144, *Fax:* (570) 655-1180
www.wvia.org
webadmin@wvia.org
License: Scranton, Lackawanna County, PA held by N.E. Pa. Educational TV Association.
Nat'l Network: NPR; PRI *Regional Network:* Pennsylvania Public Television Network
Arbitron Metro Market: Scranton, PA *TV Affiliate:* *WVIA-TV affil.
Format: Jazz, News *Hrs. of News Programming:* News progmg 31 hrs wkly *Target Audience:* General.
A. William Kelly, CEO
Chris Norton, VP
George Graham, Programming Director
Joseph Glynn, Engineering Dir
Joe Glynn, Engineering Dir
Tom Curra, Executive Vice President & Executive Producer
Andrea O'Neill, Director of Education

***WVMW-FM**
09-01-1974; 91.7 mhz FM *Hrs Open:* 14; 2 kw; -285 ft.; N41 25 57 W75 38 6
2300 Adams Avenue, Scranton, PA 18509 US
(570) 348-6202, *Fax:* (570) 961-4769
www.vmfm917.com
staff@vmfm917.org
License: Scranton, Lackawanna County, PA held by Marywood College.
Arbitron Metro Market: Scranton, PA *Format:* Alternative *Special Programming:* Black 2 hrs, class 7 hrs, jazz 10 hrs wkly *Hrs. of News Programming:* news progmg 7 hrs wkly *No. News Employees:* 2 *TargetAudience:* 15-25; young adults
Earnest Mengoni, Station Manager
George D. Graham, Chief Engineer

WWRR
11-26-1964; 104.9 mhz FM *Hrs Open:* 24; 0.27 kw; 1093 ft.; N41 26 6 W75 43 35
1049 North Sekol Road, Scranton, PA 18504 US
(570) 344-1221, *Fax:* (570) 344-0996
www.boldgoldradionepa.com
bspinelli@boldgoldmedia.com
License: Scranton, Lackawanna County, PA held by Bold Gold Media WBS L.P.
Group Owner: Bold Gold Media Group LP
Arbitron Metro Market: Wilkes Barre, PA *Format:* Contemporary Hits/Top 40, Adult Contemp *Hrs. of News Programming:* news progmg 8 hrs wkly *No. News Employees:* 1 *Target Audience:* 25-54; men & women
Brian Spinelli, Market Manager & General Manager
Brian Spinelli, General Sales Mgr

Selinsgrove

***WQSU**
09-01-1967; 88.9 mhz FM *Hrs Open:* 24; 12 kw; 620 ft.; N40 57 6 W76 45 3
514 University Ave, Selinsgrove, PA 17870 US
(570) 372-4030, *Fax:* (570) 372-2757
www.wqsu.com
augustin@susqu.edu
License: Selinsgrove, Snyder County, PA held by Susquehanna University.
Nat'l Network: AP Radio *Wire Services:* AP
Arbitron Metro Market: Sunbury-Selinsgrove-Lewisburg, PA
Format: Rock/AOR *Special Programming:* Classic country 6 hrs, sports 4 hrs, bluegrass 7 hrs wkly *Hrs. of News Programming:* News progmg 7 hrs wkly *TargetAudience:* 18-34.
Larry Augustine, General Manager
Patricia Wendt, News Director
Harry Bingaman, Chief Engineer

WVSL(AM)
01-16-1967; 1240 khz AM *Hrs Open:* 24; 1 kw-U; N40 48 59 W76 52 13
Box 90, Rt. 204 & State School Rd., Selinsgrove, PA 17870
(570) 374-1155, *Fax:* (570) 374-7444
www.bigcountrynow.com
bigcountryrequest@hotmail.com
License: Selinsgrove, Snyder County, PA held by MMP License LLC.
Group Owner: MAX Media L.L.C.; (acq 10-17-03; grpsl).
Nat'l Network: USA
Population Served: 150,000*Format:* Country *Hrs. of News Programming:* news progmg 8 hrs wkly *No. News Employees:* 1 *Target Audience:* 18 plus.
John Trinder, President
Scott Richards, Operations Dir
Greg Adair, General Sales Mgr
Lisa Richards, Programming Director
Shelly Marks, Promotions Manager
Nat O'Brien, News Director
Ted Koppen, Chief Engineer
Dawn Marie,Operations Director

Sellersville

***WBYO**
03-01-1991; 88.9 mhz FM *Hrs Open:* 24; 900 w; Ant 436 ft; N40 23 02 W75 21 02
Box 186, Sellersville, PA 18960
(215) 721-2141, *Fax:* (215) 721-9811
www.wordfm.org
wordfm@wordfm.org
License: Sellersville, Bucks County, PA held by Four Rivers Community Broadcasting Corp.
Population Served: 300,000*Special Programming:* Country gospel 2 hrs, gospel bluegrass 2 hrs wkly *Hrs. of News Programming:* news progmg 10 hrs wkly *No. News Employees:* 1 *Target Audience:* General.
Charles Loughery, President
Meg Sabulsky, Operations Dir
David Baker, General Manager
Meg Sabulsky, Programming Director
William Dunn, Promotions Manager
Charles Loughery, Engineering Dir

Shamokin

WBLJ-FM
01-01-1968; 95.3 mhz FM; 1.25 kw; 505 ft.; N40 45 36 W76 32 19 *Rebroadcasts:* Rebroadcasts WBYL(FM) Salladasburg 100%
810 North Rock Street, Shamokin, PA 17872 US
(570) 327-1400, *Fax:* (570) 327-8156
www.billcountry.com
bill@billcountry.com
License: Shamokin, Northumberland County, PA held by Clear Channel Broadcasting Licenses Inc.
Group Owner: Clear Channel Communications Inc.; (acq 10-4-01; $800,000 with co-located AM).
Format: Country
Jim Dabney, General Manager
Joe Daniels, General Sales Mgr
Tom Scott, Programming Director
Gary Chrisman, Promotions Manager
Kathy Thomas, News Director

Sharon

WPIC
10-25-1938; 790 khz AM *Hrs Open:* 24
134 Main Street, Westport, CT 06880 US
(724) 346-4113, *Fax:* (724) 981-4545
www.wpic790.com
License: Sharon, PA held by Cumulus Licensing Corp.
Group Owner: Cumulus Media Inc.; (acq 3-15-00; grpsl).
Nat'l Network: ABC; Jones Radio Networks; Talk Radio Network; Westwood One
Arbitron Metro Market: Youngstown-Warren, OH *Format:* News, News/Talk, 86 *Special Programming:* Pol 3 hrs, It 2 hrs, relg 2 hrs, infomercials 12 hrs wkly *No. News Employees:* 1 *Target Audience:* 35 plus.
Brian Schimmel, General Manager
Bob Popa, Programming Director
Wes Boyd, Chief Engineer

WYFM
10-25-1947; 102.9 mhz FM; 33 kw; 604 ft.; N41 3 26 W80 38 22
Suite 202, 136 Main Street, Westport, CT 06880 US
704) 523-5555, *Fax:* (704) 522-1967
www.bbnradio.org
bbn@bbnradio.org

License: Sharon, Mercer County, PA held by Cumulus Licensing Corp.
Nat'l Network: Westwood One
Arbitron Metro Market: Sharon, PA *Format:* Classic Rock, Adult Contemp *Target Audience:* 25-54.
Brian Schimmel, General Manager
Scott Kennedy, Programming Director
Dave Messersmith, Disc Jockey

Sharpsville

WAKZ
12-28-1976; 95.9 mhz FM; 6 kw; 328 ft.; N41 13 5 W80 33 43
7621 Little Avenue, Ste 306, Charlotte, NC 28226 US
(330) 965-0057, *Fax:* (330) 729-9991
www.959kiss.com
stevegranato@clearchannel.com
License: Sharpsville, Mercer County, PA held by Citicasters Licenses L.P.
Group Owner: Clear Channel Communications Inc.; (acq 1-15-2004; grpsl).
Arbitron Metro Market: Youngstown, OH *Format:* Contemporary Hits/Top 40
Bill Kelly, General Manager
Bob Hotchkiss, General Sales Mgr
Steve Granato, Programming Director
John Thomas, Webmaster
Abbey Dawes, Internet Sales Director

Shenandoah

***WCIM**
01-01-2008; 91.5 mhz FM; 1.2 kw; 719 ft.; N40 50 58 W76 6 55
Rebroadcasts: Rebroadcasts WCIK(FM) Bath, NY 100%
P O Drawer 2440, Tupelo, MS 38803 US
(607) 776-4151, *Fax:* (607) 776-6929
www.fln.org
License: Shenandoah, Schuylkill County, PA held by Family Life Ministries Inc.
Group Owner: Family Life Network; (acq 7-24-2007; $800,000 for CP)
Arbitron Metro Market: Texarkana, TX-AR *Format:* Christian
Rick Snavely, General Manager

Shippensburg

WEEO
12-05-1961; 1480 khz AM *Hrs Open:* 6 AM-10 PM; 0.46 kw-D, ND1; 0.009 kw-N, ND1; N40 4 30 W77 32 9
601 Fifth Street, Tyrone, PA 16686 US
(717) 697-4297, *Fax:* (717) 243-1277
wioo.com
License: Shippensburg, PA held by Shippensburg Broadcasting Inc.
Regional Network: Radio Pa.
Arbitron Metro Market: Harrisburg-Leba *Format:* Country *Target Audience:* 30 plus. *Adv. Rates:* 10; 10; 10; 10
Eric Swidler, President
Eric Swidler, Operations Dir
Sandy Loy, General Manager
Sandy Loy, Station Manager
Ray Thomas, Programming Director
Matthew Becker, Promotions Manager

***WSYC-FM**
02-01-1975; 88.7 mhz FM *Hrs Open:* 24; 0.13 kw; -154 ft.; N40 4 30 W77 31 15
Prince Street, Shippensburg, PA 17257 US
(717) 532-6006, *Fax:* (717) 477-4024
www.wsyc.org
License: Shippensburg, Cumberland County, PA held by Shippensburg University.
Nat'l Network: Westwood One
Format: Variety/Diverse *Special Programming:* Black 9 hrs, class 2 hrs, jazz 3 hrs, blues 2 hrs, wkly *Hrs. of News Programming:* news progmg 3 hrs wkly *No. News Employees:* 7 *Target Audience:* 16-25; college &area high school students
Travis Hunt, Operations Dir
Sage Ober, General Manager
Jospeh Borreu, General Sales Mgr
Jim Shaffer, Programming Director
Jeff Hollinshead, Chief Engineer
Michael Gardner, Broadcasting Director

Shiremanstown

WHYF(AM)
06-01-1987; 720 khz AM *Hrs Open:* 6 AM-sunset; 2 kw-D; N40 11 28 W76 57 09
8 W. Main St., Shiremanstown, PA 17011
(717) 525-8110, *Fax:* (717) 731-4002
www.720therock.com
contact@yourholyfamilyradio.com
License: Shiremanstown, Cumberland County, PA held by Hensley Broadcasting.
Population Served: 49,673 *Arbitron Metro Market:* Harrisburg, PA *Format:* Christian *Special Programming:* Gospel 2 hrs, polka 7 hrs, Indian one hr, blues 4 *Hrs. of News Programming:* News progmg 2 hrs wkly*Target Audience:* 25 plus; Christian
Joe Green, General Manager
Tom Sullivan, Programming Director

Slippery Rock

***WSRU**
09-20-1991; 88.1 mhz FM *Hrs Open:* 14; 0.1 kw; 79 ft.; N41 3 43 W80 2 35
211 University Union Bld, Slippery Rock, PA 16057 US
(724) 738-2655,(724) 738-2931, *Fax:* (724) 738-2754
organizations.sru.edu/WRSK/index.asp
rockradio@hotmail.com
License: Slippery Rock, Butler County, PA held by Slippery Rock University.
Nat'l Network: ABC
Format: Classic Rock, Variety/Diverse *Special Programming:* Relg one hr, campus info one hr, sports one hr wkly *Hrs. of News Programming:* news progmg 14 hrs wkly *No. News Employees:* 1 *Target Audience:* 18-24;on & off campus students
Sean Lohrer, General Manager
Paul Joseph, Programming Director
Jami LoAlbo, Promotions Manager
Jason Fialkovich, News Director
Werner Ullrich, Chief Engineer
Sara Faletti, Music Director
Matt Miller, Sports Commentator

Smethport

WXMT
01-01-1990; 106.3 mhz FM *Hrs Open:* 24; 1.03 kw; 788 ft.; N41 48 36 W78 23 10
211 W. Main St., Smethport, PA 16749 US
(814) 837-9564, *Fax:* (814) 975-1098
www.colonial.cc/rockwithoutthehardedge/
wxmt@colonial.cc
License: Smethport, McKean County, PA held by Colonial Radio Group Inc.
Format: Classic Rock *Target Audience:* Men.
Jeffrey Andrulonis, President

Somerset

WLKH
06-15-1966; 97.7 mhz FM *Hrs Open:* 24; 3.5 kw; 430 ft.; N40 1 32 W79 5 44
One Forever Drive, Hollidaysburg, PA 16648 US
(814) 534-8975, *Fax:* (814) 534-8979
www.klove.com
info@klove.com
License: Somerset, Somerset County, PA held by 2510 Licenses LLC.
Group Owner: 2510 Licenses LLC; (acq 5-1-2005; grpsl)
Nat'l Network: K-Love
Format: Religious
Darrell Chambliss, Chairman
Alan Mason, COO
Mike Novak, President
Nick Ferrara, Operations Dir

WNTW
01-15-1951; 990 khz AM *Hrs Open:* 24; 10 kw-D, DA2; 0.1 kw-N, DA2; N40 1 31 W79 5 42 *Rebroadcasts:* Rebroadcasts WLYE(AM) Johnstown 100%
One Forever Drive, Hollidaysburg, PA 16648 US
(814) 255-4186, *Fax:* (814) 255-6145
www.ntjnetwork.com
tdeitz@96key.com
License: Somerset, PA held by Forever Broadcasting LLC.
Group Owner: Forever Broadcasting; (acq 9-9-97; grpsl).
Arbitron Metro Market: Somerset, PA *Format:* News, News/Talk, 86 *Hrs. of News Programming:* news progmg 8 hrs wkly *No. News Employees:* 1 *Target Audience:* 35-55.
Carol Logan, President
Terry Deitz, General Manager
Tina Perry, Sales Manager
Mitch Edwards, Programming Director
Rick Sheppard, News Director
Jim Boxler, Chief Engineer
Tegan Hayes, Traffic Manager
Shirley Lambert, BusinessManager

South Waverly

WPHD
01-01-2003; 96.1 mhz FM *Hrs Open:* 24; 1.8 kw; 613 ft.; N42 1 54.7 W76 47 2.2
Mailing Address: 583 Long Creek Road, Apalachin, NY 13732 US
Second Address: 495 Court St., 2nd Fl., Binghamton, PA 13904
(607) 795-0795, *Fax:* (607) 795-1095
www.cool96.coolesthits.com
themetrocks@aol.com
License: South Waverly, Bradford County, PA held by Fitzgerald and Hawras Partnership
Nat'l Reps: Katz Radio
Arbitron Metro Market: Elmira-Corning, NY *Format:* Oldies *Target Audience:* 35-64; adults *Adv. Rates:* 15; 15; 15; 10
Kevin Fitzgerald, Operations Dir
George Hawras, General Manager
Bob Smith, Station Manager
April Emerson, General Sales Mgr
Dave Paltrowitz, Promotions Manager
Steve Shimer, Operations Manager
Mina Smallacombe, BusinessManager
Trisha Philip, Office Manager
Kyle Mills, Assistant Promotions Director
Josh Evans, Sales

South Williamsport

WZXR
06-01-1968; 99.3 mhz FM; 0.41 kw; 1237 ft.; N41 12 42 W76 57 16
1685 Four Mild Drive, Williamsport, PA 17701 US
(570) 323-8200, *Fax:* (570) 323-5075
www.wzxr.com
dan.farr@bybradio.com
License: South Williamsport, Lycoming County, PA held by South Williamsport SabreCom Inc.
Group Owner: Backyard Broadcasting LLC; (acq 12-1-02; grpsl).
Nat'l Network: ABC *Nat'l Reps:* Christal
Arbitron Metro Market: Williamsport, PA *Format:* Classic Rock, Rock/AOR *Hrs. of News Programming:* news progmg 7 hrs wkly *No. News Employees:* 3 *Target Audience:* 25-54. *Adv. Rates:* 30; 30; 30; 20
Robin Smith, CFO
Barry Drake, President
Dan Farr, General Manager
Bob Pawlikowski, General Sales Mgr
Ted Minier, Programming Director
John Finn, News Director
Tom Atkins, Chief Engineer
Kelly Bailey, Production Director
IanEmerson, Webmaster
Georgia Stover, Office Manager
Doug Dodge, Sales Manager
Bob Pawlikowski, Sales Manager
Justin Lutz, Sales Assistant/Graphic Artist/Web Coordinator

St. Marys

WKBI
07-23-1950; 1400 khz AM *Hrs Open:* 24; 1 kw-U, ND1; N41 24 56 W78 33 56
P. O. Box 466, St. Marys, PA 15857 US
(814) 834-2821, *Fax:* (814) 834-4319
www.wkbi.net
b94@wkbi.net
License: St. Marys, PA held by Elk-Cameron Broadcasting Co.
Group Owner: Allegheny Mountain Network Stations
Nat'l Network: Westwood One *Regional Network:* Allegheny Mtn. Net. *Nat'l Reps:* Dome
Format: Adult Contemp, Oldies, 84 *Hrs. of News Programming:* news progmg 10 hrs wkly *No. News Employees:* 1 *Target Audience:* 35-55.
Cary Simpson, President
Erik Lane, Operations Dir
Ted Simpson, General Manager
Chris O'Donnell, Programming Director
Nancy Bowser, Promotions Manager
Phil Leslie, News Director
Robert Lynn, Chief Engineer
Jason Lang, DiscJockey

WKBI-FM
08-01-1966; 93.9 mhz FM *Hrs Open:* 24; 2.35 kw; 801 ft.; N41 23 11 W78 41 32
P.O. Box 466, St. Marys, PA 15857 US
(814) 834-2821, *Fax:* (814) 834-4319
www.wkbi.net
License: St. Marys, Elk County, PA held by Elk-Cameron Broadcasting Co.

Group Owner: Allegheny Mountain Network Stations
Nat'l Network: Westwood One; Jones Radio Networks
Special Programming: Relg 2 hrs wkly *Target Audience:* General; young adults
Chris O'Donnell, Programming Director
Jason Lang, Disc Jockey
Nancy Kelly, Disc Jockey
Erik Lane, Disc Jockey
Val Joseph, Disc Jockey

WDDH
04-22-1986; 97.5 mhz FM *Hrs Open:* 24; 19.5 kw; 801 ft.; N41 37 4 W78 48 14
P.O. Box 623, Ridgway, PA 15853 US
(814) 772-9700, *Fax:* (814) 772-9750
www.houndcountry.com
denny@houndcountry.com
License: St. Marys, Elk County, PA held by Laurel Media Inc.
Nat'l Network: Jones Radio Networks *Nat'l Reps:* Rgnl Reps
Regional Reps: Dome & AssociatesCommercial Media S
Arbitron Metro Market: State College, PA *Format:* Country *Target Audience:* 25-54. *Adv. Rates:* 16; 14; 16; 13
Dennis Heindl, President
Becky Towne, Station Manager

State College

WBHV-FM
10-23-1991; 94.5 mhz FM; 1.9 kw; 587 ft.; N40 54 4 W77 50 20
One Forever Drive, Hollidaysburg, PA 16648 US
(814) 238-5085, *Fax:* (814) 238-7932
www.b945live.com
B945LIVE@gmail.com
License: State College, Centre County, PA held by 2510 Licenses LLC.
Group Owner: 2510 Licenses LLC; (acq 2-1-2006; $1.2 million)
Nat'l Reps: Christal
Arbitron Metro Market: State College, PA *Format:* Christian
Nick Ferrara, General Manager
PJ Mullen, Programming Director
Chris Bickel, Assistant Program Director

***WKPS**
01-01-1995; 90.7 mhz FM *Hrs Open:* 24; 0.1 kw; 85 ft.; N40 47 58 W77 52 11
202 Wagner Building, University Park, PA 16802 US
(814) 865-7983, *Fax:* (814) 865-2751
www.thelion.fm
lion-officers@psu.edu
License: State College, Centre County, PA held by Board of Trustees of Pennsylvania State University.
Arbitron Metro Market: State College, PA *Format:* Variety/Diverse
Special Programming: Jazz 11 hrs, Sp 8 hrs wkly *Hrs. of News Programming:* News progmg 4 hrs wkly *Target Audience:* University students.
Tom Shakely, Operations Dir
Brandon Peach, General Manager
Tristan Vaughan, Operations Director

WQWK(AM)
01-01-1945; 1450 khz AM *Hrs Open:* 24; 1 kw-U; N40 48 32 W77 50 28
2551 Park Center Blvd., State College, PA 16801
(814) 237-9800, *Fax:* (814) 237-2477
www.1450espnradio.com
forever103@comcast.net
License: State College, Centre County, PA held by Forever Broadcasting LLC.
Group Owner: Forever Broadcasting; (acq 3-10-98; $2.9 million with co-located FM).
Nat'l Network: ESPN Radio *Regional Network:* Radio Pa. *Nat'l Reps:* Christal *Wire Services:* The Sports Network
Population Served: 110,000 *Arbitron Metro Market:* State College, PA *Format:* Sports *Target Audience:* 30 plus; college educated, upscale
Chuck Hertzog, General Manager
Bob Taylor, Programming Director
Pat Boland, News Director

***WPSU**
12-06-1953; 91.5 mhz FM *Hrs Open:* 24; 1.7 kw; Ant 1,197 ft; N40 48 32 W77 50 28
174 Outreach Bldg, University Park, PA 16802
(814) 865-1877, *Fax:* (814) 865-4043
www.wpsu.org
wpsu@psu.edu
License: State College, Centre County, PA held by Pennsylvania State University.
Nat'l Network: PRI; NPR *Wire Services:* AP
Population Served: 100,000 *Arbitron Metro Market:* State College, PA *Special Programming:* Folk 10, jazz 3 hrs, blues 2 hrs wkly *Hrs. of News Programming:* news progmg 35 hrs wkly *No. News Employees:* 1 *TargetAudience:* General; upscale, educated adults
Craig Johnsoqn, Operations Dir
Ted Krichels, General Manager
Greg Petersen, Station Manager
Tom Yourchak, General Sales Mgr
Kristine Allen, Programming Director
Emily Ready, News Director
Russ Rockwell, Chief Engineer
BillHiergeist, Regional Sales Manager
Sam Komlenic, Regional Sales Manager

WRSC
05-29-1961; 1390 khz AM; 2 kw-D, DAN; 1 kw-N, DAN; N40 48 30 W77 56 32
City Center West, 7201 W. Lake Mead Blvd, Las Vegas, NV 89128 US
(814) 237-9800, *Fax:* (814) 237-2477
www.newsradio1390.com
programming@newsradio1390.com
License: State College, PA held by Forever Broadcasting LLC.
Group Owner: Forever Broadcasting; (acq 5-1-2005; $2.65 million with WBUS(FM) Boalsburg)
Arbitron Metro Market: State College, PA *Format:* News, News/Talk, 86
Chuck Hertzog, General Manager
Pat Boland, Programming Director
Bob Taylor, Chief Engineer

***WTLR**
01-01-1978; 89.9 mhz FM *Hrs Open:* 24; 25 kw; 584 ft.; N40 53 32 W77 51 49
2020 Cato Avenue, State College, PA 16801 US
(814) 237-9857
www.cpci.org
info@wtlr.org
License: State College, Centre County, PA held by Central Pennsylvania Christian Institute Inc.
Wire Services: AP
Arbitron Metro Market: State College, PA *Format:* Christian *Hrs. of News Programming:* news progmg 9 hrs wkly *No. News Employees:* 1 *Target Audience:* 30-55; Adults, family oriented
Mark Van Ouse, General Manager
Dean Christian, Station Manager
Tom Betz, Production Coordinator
Chryss Griffin, Business Manager

***WRXV**
06-18-2004; 89.1 mhz FM *Hrs Open:* 24; 0.001 kw horiz, 4.4 kw vert; 1099 ft.; N40 43 56 W78 19 33
1313 Valley View Road, Bellefonte, PA 16823 US
(814) 867-3836, *Fax:* (814) 867-1922
www.revfm.net
info@revfm.net
License: State College, Centre County, PA held by Invisible Allies Ministries.
Arbitron Metro Market: State College, PA *Format:* Christian
Michael Schomer, General Manager
Erik Lane, Station Manager
Jim Schomer, Chief Engineer

***WKDN(FM)**
01-01-2008; 88.3 mhz FM *Hrs Open:* 24; 10 w horiz, 1.8 kw vert; Ant 686 ft; N40 53 35 W77 51 48 *Rebroadcasts:* Rebroadcasts WFSI(FM) Annapolis, MD 100%
918 Chesapeake Ave., Annapolis, MD 21403
(410) 268-6200, *Fax:* (410) 268-0931
www.familyradio.org
info@familyradio.org
License: State College, Centre County, PA held by Family Stations Inc.
Group Owner: Family Stations Inc.
Nat'l Network: Family Radio
Population Served: 10,706 *Arbitron Metro Market:* Vermillion, SD
Format: Religious
Harold Camping, President
W.A. Sadlier, Station Manager

Stroudsburg

***WBYX**
10-01-1999; 88.7 mhz FM *Hrs Open:* 24; 1 w horiz, 4 kw vert; Ant 794 ft; N41 02 40 W75 22 45 *Rebroadcasts:* Rebroadcasts WBYO(FM) Sellersville 100%
Box 186, Sellersville, PA 18960
(215) 721-2141, *Fax:* (215) 721-9811
www.wordfm.org
wordfm@wordfm.org
License: Stroudsburg, Monroe County, PA held by Four Rivers Community Broadcasting Corp.
Nat'l Network: ABC
Special Programming: Bluegrass Gospel; *Target Audience:* 25-45.
Charles Loughery, President
Meg Sabulsky, Operations Dir
David Baker, General Manager
Meg Sabulsky, Programming Director
William Dunn, Promotions Manager
Charles Loughery, Engineering Dir

WSBG
10-01-1964; 93.5 mhz FM; 0.55 kw; 764 ft.; N40 56 56 W75 9 29
449 Broadway, New York, NY 10013 US
(570) 421-2100, *Fax:* (570) 421-2040
www.lite935.com
info@lite935.com
License: Stroudsburg, Monroe County, PA
Arbitron Metro Market: Wilkes Barre-Sc *Format:* Easy Listening
Special Programming: Modern rock 3 hrs wkly *Target Audience:* 20 plus.
David Meszaros, General Manager
Patrick Lincoln, General Sales Mgr
Rod Bauman, Programming Director

WVPO
01-01-1947; 840 khz AM; 0.25 kw-D, NDD; N40 58 26 W75 11 43
449 Broadway, New York, NY 10013 US
(570) 421-2100, *Fax:* (570) 421-2040
info@lite935.com
License: Stroudsburg, PA held by Nassau Broadcasting II L.L.C.
Group Owner: Nassau Broadcasting Partners L.P.; (acq 2-15-02; grpsl).
Arbitron Metro Market: Stroudsburg, PA *Format:* Talk *Target Audience:* 35 plus.
Peter Tonks, CFO
Rick Musselman, General Manager
Michele Stevens, Programming Director
Bob Matthews, News Director
Tony Gervasi, Engineering Dir
George Guilda, Engineering Manager
Rod Bauman, Programming Director

Summerdale

***WJAZ**
01-10-1991; 91.7 mhz FM *Hrs Open:* 24; 1 kw; 702 ft.; N40 18 20 W77 0 27 *Rebroadcasts:* Rebroadcasts WRTI(FM) Philadelphia 100%
Anneberg Hall (011-00), Philadelphia, PA 19122 US
(215) 204-8405, *Fax:* (215) 204-7027
www.wrti.org
comments@wrti.org
License: Summerdale, Cumberland County, PA held by Temple University of the Commonwealth System of Higher Education
Nat'l Network: NPR *Wire Services:* AP
Format: Classical, Jazz *Hrs. of News Programming:* news progmg 15 hrs wkly *No. News Employees:* 1 *Target Audience:* 30-65.
Dave Conant, CEO
Tobias Poole, Operations Dir
Rick Torpey, General Sales Mgr
Jack Moore, Programming Director
Patty Prevost, Promotions Manager
Windsor Johnson, News Director
Jeff DePolo, Chief Engineer
Vic Scarpato, CFO
Porsche Blakey, Promotions Director

Sunbury

WKOK
01-01-1933; 1070 khz AM *Hrs Open:* 24
Mailing Address: P.O. Box 1070, Sunbury, PA 17801 US
Second Address: 1227 County Line Rd., Selinsgrove, PA 17870
(570) 286-5838, *Fax:* (570) 743-1605
www.wkok.com
wkok@wkok.com
License: Sunbury, PA held by Sunbury Broadcasting Corp.
Group Owner: Sunbury Broadcasting Corp.; (acq 5-33).
Nat'l Network: CBS; CNN Radio; Fox Sports; Wall Street; Westwood One *Nat'l Reps:* Roslin *Regional Reps:* Dome. *Wire Services:* AP; Accu-Weather
Format: News, News/Talk, 84, Talk *Hrs. of News Programming:* news progmg 168 hrs wkly *No. News Employees:* 4 *Target Audience:* 35-64.
Roger Haddon Jr., CEO
Kevin Herr, Operations Dir
Nicole Shelley, General Sales Mgr
Mark Lawrence, Programming Director
Sara Bartlett, News Director

WQKX
09-15-1948; 94.1 mhz FM *Hrs Open:* 24; 16 kw; 879 ft.; N40 47 10 W76 41 49
Mailing Address: P.O. Box 1070, Sunbury, PA 17801 US
Second Address: 1227 County Line Rd., Selinsgrove, PA 17870
(570) 286-5838,(570) 743-1841, *Fax:* (570) 743-7837
www.wqkx.com
equest@wqkx.com
License: Sunbury, Northumberland County, PA
Group Owner: Sunbury Broadcasting Corp.
Nat'l Reps: Roslin *Regional Reps:* Dome *Wire Services:* Accu-Weather; AP
Format: Adult Contemp *Hrs. of News Programming:* news progmg 7 hrs wkly *No. News Employees:* 4 *Target Audience:* 25-54.
Roger Haddon, Jr, CEO
Nicole Shelley, General Sales Mgr
Drew Kelly, Programming Director
Sara Bartlett, News Director
Rob Senter, Music Director

Susquehanna

WCDW
03-01-1995; 100.5 mhz FM *Hrs Open:* 24; 1.6 kw; 643 ft.; N42 3 10 W75 42 7
1907 Darby Road, Havertown, PA 19083 US
(607) 772-1005, *Fax:* (607) 772-2945
www.cool100oldies.com
cool100oldies@aol.com
License: Susquehanna, Susquehanna County, PA held by Equinox Broadcasting Corp.
Nat'l Reps: Katz Radio
Arbitron Metro Market: Binghamton, NY *Format:* Oldies *Special Programming:* Polish 5 hrs wkly *Target Audience:* 35-64. *Adv. Rates:* 23; 30; 22; 15
George Hawras, President

Swarthmore

***WSRN-FM**
12-31-1939; 91.5 mhz FM; 0.11 kw; 141 ft.; N39 54 18 W75 21 16
500 College Avenue, Swarthmore, PA 19081 US
(610) 328-8336,(610) 328-8335,(610) 328-8000
www.wsrnfm.org
License: Swarthmore, Delaware County, PA held by Swarthmore College.
Format: Variety/Diverse
Roger Shaw, General Manager

Sweet Valley

***WRGN**
10-15-1984; 88.1 mhz FM *Hrs Open:* 24; 0.5 kw; 302 ft.; N41 17 54 W76 7 28
Rr #3, Hunlock Creek, PA 18621 US
(570) 477-3688, *Fax:* (570) 477-2310
www.wrgn.com
wrgn@epix.net
License: Sweet Valley, Luzerne County, PA held by Gospel Media Institute Inc.
Format: Religious
Burl Updyke, President
Shirley Updyke, Promotions Manager

Sykesville

WZDB
05-05-2009; 95.9 mhz FM; 1.5 kw; 643 ft.; N41 2 44.1 W78 42 11.8
US
(814) 371-6100, *Fax:* (410) 822-0576
www.959zdb.com
License: Sykesville, Jefferson County, PA held by First Media Radio LLC.
Group Owner: First Media Radio LLC
Arbitron Metro Market: Sykesville, PA
Alex Kolobielski, President

Tafton

***WLKA**
01-01-2002; 88.3 mhz FM; 1.1 kw; 823 ft.; N41 32 37 W75 27 44
The Classical Network, 1200 Old Trenton Road, Trenton, NJ 08690 US
(800) 525-5683, *Fax:* (916) 251-1650
www.klove.com
klove@klove.com
License: Tafton, Pike County, PA held by Educational Media Foundation.
Group Owner: EMF Broadcasting; (acq 11-17-2006; $675,000)
Nat'l Network: K-Love
Arbitron Metro Market: Omaha, NE *Format:* Christian *No. News Employees:* 13
Darrell Chambliss, Chairman
MIke Novak, President & CEO
Glenn Goodwin, Operations Dir
Laura Daniels, News Reporter
Tim Luttrell, News Reporter
Kenny Noble Cortes, News Reporter
Darren Vinson, News Reporter

Tamaqua

WMGH-FM
06-14-1965; 105.5 mhz FM *Hrs Open:* 24; 1.4 kw; 486 ft.; N40 47 14 W76 1 59
Mailing Address: 1444 Hamilton St #606, Allentown, PA 18102 US
Second Address: P.O. Box D, Lansford, PA 18232
(570) 668-2992, *Fax:* (570) 645-2159
www.wmgh.com
wmgh@ptdprolog.net
License: Tamaqua, Schuylkill County, PA held by J-Systems Franchising Corp.
Group Owner: J-Systems Franchising Corp.; acq 2-28-87; $300,000;
Nat'l Network: Westwood One; ABC; USA *Regional Network:* Radio Pa.
Arbitron Metro Market: Tamaqua, PA *Format:* Adult Contemp
Special Programming: Oldies 7 hrs, polka 3 hrs wkly *Target Audience:* 25-54; primary women, secondary adults *Adv. Rates:* 45; 40; 45; 15
Harold Fulmer III, President
Christopher Fulmer, Operations Dir
Bill Lakatas, General Manager
Mark Marek, News Director
Joe Manjack, Chief Engineer
Kim Noel, Disc Jockey
Nicky Vee, Disc Jockey
Cheryl Lee, Disc Jockey

Telford

***WBMR**
06-01-1967; 91.7 mhz FM; 0.125 kw horiz, 0.5 kw vert; 253 ft.; N40 18 48.1 W75 17 29.1
7401 Powder Valley Rd., Zionsville, PA 18092 US
(610) 797-4530, *Fax:* (610) 791-3000
info@wbmr.com,info@wbmr.com
License: Telford, Montgomery County, PA held by United Ministries.
Group Owner: United Ministries; (acq 8-30-2002).
Arbitron Metro Market: Zionsville, PA *Format:* Religious
Marvin Sanders, General Manager

Tioga

WMTT
05-23-1991; 94.7 mhz FM *Hrs Open:* 24; 12 kw; 482 ft.; N42 3 43 W77 21 38
Mailing Address: 53 Bridge Street, Suite 2, Corning, NY 14830 US
Second Address: 495 Court St., 2nd Fl, Binghamton, NY 13904
(607) 795-0795,(607) 772-1005, *Fax:* (607) 795-1095,(607) 772-2945
www.themetrocks.com
themetrocks@aol.com
License: Tioga, Tioga County, PA held by Europa Communications Inc.
Nat'l Reps: Katz Radio
Arbitron Metro Market: Elmira-Corning, NY *Format:* Classic Rock, Rock/AOR *Hrs. of News Programming:* News progmg 2 hrs wkly *Target Audience:* 25-49. *Adv. Rates:* 40; 55; 45; 35
Kevin Fitzgerald, Operations Dir
George Harris, General Manager
Robert Smith, Station Manager
Justin McGregor, Promotions Manager
Stephen Shimer, Operations Manager

Titusville

WTIV
11-27-1955; 1230 khz AM *Hrs Open:* 6 AM-midnight
P.O. Box 184, Titusville, PA 16354 US
(814) 432-2188, *Fax:* (814) 827-1679
www.myantsnetwork.com
License: Titusville, PA held by Forever Broadcasting LLC.
Group Owner: Forever Broadcasting; (acq 7-20-00; grpsl).
Regional Network: Radio Pa.
Arbitron Metro Market: Titusville, PA *Format:* News, News/Talk, 86 *Hrs. of News Programming:* News progmg 13 hrs wkly *Target Audience:* 22-54; mixed *Adv. Rates:* 18; 13; 18; 11
Thomas Sauber, General Manager
Kim Vacanti, Advertising Head

Tobyhanna

WKRF
01-15-1993; 107.9 mhz FM *Hrs Open:* 24; 0.84 kw; 876 ft.; N41 2 37 W75 22 38 *Rebroadcasts:* Rebroadcasts WKRZ(FM) Wilkes-Barre 100%
10706 Beaver Dam Road, Cockeysville, MD 21030 US
(570) 839-5858, *Fax:* (570) 883-9851
www.wkrf.com
info@wkrf.com
License: Tobyhanna, Monroe County, PA held by Entercom Wilkes-Barre Scranton LLC.
Group Owner: Entercom Communications Corp.; (acq 5-11-00).
Nat'l Network: Jones Radio Networks
Arbitron Metro Market: Wilkes Barre-Scranton, PA *Format:* Contemporary Hits/Top 40 *Hrs. of News Programming:* news progmg one hr wkly *No. News Employees:* 1 *Target Audience:* 25-54.
Jim Rising, Operations Dir
John Burkavage, General Manager
Andy Zapotek, General Sales Mgr
Jerry Padden, Programming Director
Michael Ignatz, Promotions Manager
Tracy Iannaprone, News Director
Lamar Smith, Chief Engineer
JoeThomas, Local News Editor
Elizabeth Masich, Music Director
Bob Demono, National Sales Manager

Towanda

WTTC
01-01-1959; 1550 khz AM; 0.5 kw-D, ND2; 0.004 kw-N, ND2; N41 45 55 W76 29 10
204 Desmond St., Sayre, PA 18840 US
(570) 888-7745, *Fax:* (570) 888-9005
License: Towanda, PA held by WATS Broadcasting Inc.
Nat'l Network: Motor Racing Net
Arbitron Metro Market: Sayre, PA *Format:* Oldies *Target Audience:* General. *Adv. Rates:* 16; 12; 13; 11
Charles Carver Jr., President
Meade Murtland, Station Manager

WTTC-FM
11-01-1959; 95.3 mhz FM *Hrs Open:* 6 AM-11 PM; 5.4 kw; 125 ft.; N41 45 55 W76 29 10
204 Desmond St., Sayre, PA 18840 US
(570) 265-9530
www.953thebridge.com
whgl100@gmail.com
License: Towanda, Bradford County, PA
Arbitron Metro Market: Towanda, PA *Format:* Contemporary Hits/Top 40, Adult Contemp
Joel Clawson, General Sales Mgr

Trout Run

***WCIT-FM**
01-01-2001; 90.1 mhz FM; 0.35 kw; 295 ft.; N41 27 26 W77 6 55
Rebroadcasts: Rebroadcasts WCIK(FM) Bath, NY 100%
Mailing Address: US
Second Address: 7634 Campbell Creek Rd., Bath, NY 14810
(607) 776-4151, *Fax:* (607) 776-6929
www.fln.org
mail@fln.org
License: Trout Run, Lycoming County, PA held by Family Life Ministries Inc.
Group Owner: Family Life Network
Nat'l Network: Salem Radio Network *Wire Services:* Metro Weather Service Inc.
Arbitron Metro Market: Bath, NY *Format:* Christian *Hrs. of News Programming:* news progmg 14 hrs wkly *No. News Employees:* 3 *Target Audience:* 30-54.
Dick Snavely, Founder, CFO
Rick Snavely, President, CEO
Sammy Carrillo, Programming Director
Roger Settje, Promotions Manager
Bob Price, News Director
Jim Travis, Chief Engineer
Dave Best, Business Manager
Trudi Cook, RadioReceptionist
Gary Farnham, IT Director
Debbie Fero, Events Coordinator
Jeff Harmon, Chief Operating Officer

Troy

WTZN
03-03-1982; 1310 khz AM

Mailing Address: 170 Redington Ave, Troy, PA 16947 US
Second Address: 170 Redington Ave., Troy, PA 16947
(570) 297-0100, *Fax:* (570) 297-3193
www.wtzn.com
whgl100@ptd.net
License: Troy, PA held by Cantroair Communications Inc.
Format: Sports *Target Audience:* 25-54.
Mike Powers, President
Bob Gisler, Operations Dir
Kevin Smith, Chief Engineer

Tyrone

WFGE
08-15-1961; 101.1 mhz FM *Hrs Open:* 24; 8.5 kw; 1171 ft.; N40 55 10 W77 58 28
Washington Ave.,& 1st St, Tyrone, PA 16686 US
(814) 237-9800, *Fax:* (814) 237-2477
www.froggy103.com
scott@forevercomm.com
License: Tyrone, Blair County, PA held by Forever Broadcasting LLC.
Group Owner: Forever Broadcasting; (acq 7-2-2008; $2.5 million)
Arbitron Metro Market: State College, PA *Format:* Country
Scott Swalls, General Manager
Monty Buehler, General Sales Mgr

WTRN
01-12-1955; 1340 khz AM *Hrs Open:* 24
Mailing Address: Box 247, Tyrone, PA 16686 US
Second Address: Washington Ave. & 1st St., Tyrone, PA 16686
(814) 684-3200, *Fax:* (814) 684-1220
www.wtrn.net
amnnet@aol.com
License: Tyrone, PA held by Allegheny Mountain Network.
Group Owner: Allegheny Mountain Network Stations
Nat'l Network: Jones Radio Networks *Regional Network:* Allegheny Mtn. Net. *Nat'l Reps:* Dome
Arbitron Metro Market: Tyrone, PA *Format:* Adult Contemp
Special Programming: Relg 4 hrs wkly *Hrs. of News Programming:* News progmg 16 hrs wkly *Target Audience:* General; total community targeted *Adv. Rates:* 7; 7; 7; 7
Cary Simpson, President
Peg Baney, General Sales Mgr
Rich Saupp, Programming Director
Jean Dixon, News Director
Robert Lynn, Chief Engineer

Union City

WCTL
04-23-1967; 106.3 mhz FM; 3.4 kw; 430 ft.; N42 0 3 W79 52 33
10912 Route 19 North, Waterford, PA 16441 US
(814) 796-6000, *Fax:* (814) 796-3200
www.wctl.org
wctl@wctl.org
License: Union City, Erie County, PA held by Inspiration Time Inc.
Nat'l Network: USA *Nat'l Reps:* Salem
Arbitron Metro Market: Erie, PA *Format:* Adult Contemp, Christian *Special Programming:* Children one hr wkly *Hrs. of News Programming:* news progmg 2.5 hrs wkly *No. News Employees:* 1 *Target Audience:* 25-54; Christian families *Adv. Rates:* 25; 20; 20; 20
Ed Mattson, President
Ronald Raymond, General Manager
Adam Frase, Programming Director

Uniontown

WMBS
07-15-1937; 590 khz AM *Hrs Open:* 24; 1 kw-D, DAN; 1 kw-N, DAN; N39 51 35 W79 44 44
82 W. Fayette Street, Uniontown, PA 15401 US
(724) 438-3900, *Fax:* (724) 438-2406
www.wmbs590.com
sales590@wmbs590.com
License: Uniontown, PA held by Fayette Broadcasting Corp.
Nat'l Network: CBS Radio; Westwood One *Nat'l Reps:* Commercial Media Sales *Regional Reps:* West Media Group
Wire Services: AP; Metro Weather Service Inc.
Arbitron Metro Market: Pittsburgh, PA *Format:* Adult Contemp
Special Programming: Talk shows, polka 3 hrs wkly, Pittsburgh Pirates, *Hrs. of News Programming:* news progmg 24 hrs wkly *No. News Employees:* 1*Target Audience:* 25 plus; General *Adv. Rates:* 12; 12; 12; 10
Bob Pritts, President
Doreen Minafee, Operations Dir
Brian Mroziak, General Manager
Sandy Tracy, General Sales Mgr
Jim Morgan, News Director
Larry Campbell, Chief Engineer
Michael Pasqua, General Sales Manager
Timothy Schwer,Public Affairs Director

WPKL
12-20-1968; 99.3 mhz FM *Hrs Open:* 24; 3 kw; 295 ft.; N39 53 9 W79 46 29
133 E. Crawford Ave., Connellsville, PA 15425 US
(724) 938-2000, *Fax:* (724) 938-7842
oldiesradioonline.com
rherring@keymarketradio.com
License: Uniontown, Fayette County, PA held by Keymarket Licenses LLC
Group Owner: Keymarket Communications LLC; (acq 1-17-2001; $475,000 with WYJK(AM) Connellsville)
Nat'l Reps: Dome
Arbitron Metro Market: Pittsburgh, PA *Format:* Oldies *Target Audience:* 25 plus. *Adv. Rates:* 25; 25; 25; 25
Gerald Getz, President
Andrew Powaski, General Manager

University Park

WOWY
04-01-1965; 97.1 mhz FM; 2 kw; 404 ft.; N40 48 27 W77 56 29
City Center West, 7201 W. Lake Mead Blvd, Las Vegas, NV 89128 US
(814) 238-5085, *Fax:* (814) 238-7932
www.wowyonline.com
License: University Park, Centre County, PA held by 2510 Licenses LLC.
Group Owner: 2510 Licenses LLC; (acq 2-16-2005; grpsl)
Arbitron Metro Market: State College, PA *Format:* Oldies
Nick Ferrara, General Manager

Villanova

***WXVU**
08-01-1991; 89.1 mhz FM; 0.1 kw vert; 279 ft.; N40 1 58 W75 20 15
800 Lancaster Avenue, 210 Dougherty Hall, Villanova, PA 19085 US
(610) 519-7200, *Fax:* (610) 519-7956
www1.villanova.edu
info@wxvufm.com
License: Villanova, Delaware County, PA held by Villanova University.
Arbitron Metro Market: Villanova, PA *Format:* Sports, Talk
Special Programming: Black 10 hrs, relg 2 hrs wkly *Target Audience:* 15-25; youngsters
Kaitlin Santana, Operations Dir
Jarred Cannon, General Manager
Matilda Swartz, Programming Director
Nick Monzo, Promotions Manager
Suzanne Lee, Music Director
Chris Haring, Sports Director
Joe Orkwiszewski, Production Director

Warminster

***WRDV**
09-06-1976; 89.3 mhz FM *Hrs Open:* 24; 0.1 kw horiz, 1 kw vert; 118 ft.; N40 12 19 W75 6 27
Mailing Address: P. O. Box 2012, Warminster, PA 18974 US
Second Address: 126 S. York Rd., Hatboro, PA 19040
(215) 674-8002, *Fax:* (215) 674-4586
wrdv.org
License: Warminster, Bucks County, PA held by Bux-Mont Educational Radio Associates.
Arbitron Metro Market: Philadelphia *Format:* Variety/Diverse
Special Programming: C&W 4 hrs, blues 3 hrs, folk 4 hrs, new age 3 hrs, jazz 3 hrs wkly *Hrs. of News Programming:* News progmg 2 hrs wkly *TargetAudience:* General.
Charles Loughery, President
Todd Allen, General Manager

Warren

WNAE
12-31-1946; 1310 khz AM *Hrs Open:* 24 hours; 5 kw-D, ND1; 0.094 kw-N, ND1; N41 48 50 W79 10 4
Mailing Address: 310 Second Avenue, Warren, PA 16365 US
Second Address: 310 2nd Ave., Warren, PA 16365
(814) 723-1310, *Fax:* (814) 723-3356
www.kibcoradio.com
info@kibcoradio.com
License: Warren, PA held by Radio Partners LLC.
Group Owner: Radio Partners LLC; (acq 9-30-2005; grpsl)
Nat'l Network: AP Network News *Wire Services:* AP
Arbitron Metro Market: Warren, PA *Format:* Talk *Hrs. of News Programming:* news progmg 11 hrs wkly *No. News Employees:* 1 *Target Audience:* General.
Frank Iorio, CEO
Karen White, General Manager
David Whipple, Station Manager
David Whipple, General Sales Mgr
Mark Silvis, Programming Director
Dale Bliss, Promotions Manager
Dana Simmons, Traffic Manager

WRRN
03-01-1948; 92.3 mhz FM *Hrs Open:* 24; 50 kw; 410 ft.; N41 48 50 W79 10 4
310 Second Avenue, Warren, PA 16365 US
(814) 723-1310, *Fax:* (814) 723-3356
www.kibcoradio.com
info@kibcoradio.com
License: Warren, Warren County, PA held by Radio Partners LLC
Group Owner: Radio Partners LLC
Format: Oldies
Frank Iorio, CEO
Dave Whipple, Station Manager

Warwick

***WZZD**
12-01-2000; 88.1 mhz FM *Hrs Open:* 24; 180 w vert; 587 ft; N40 07 45 W75 52 43 *Rebroadcasts:* Rebroadcasts WBYO(FM) Sellersville 90%
Box 186, Sellersville, PA 18960
(215) 721-2141, *Fax:* (215) 721-9811
www.wordfm.org
wordfm@wordfm.org
License: Warwick, Chester County, PA held by Four Rivers Community Broadcasting Corp.
Population Served: 75,000*Special Programming:* Bluegrass/gospel 3 hrs wkly
Charles Loughery, President
Meg Sabulsky, Operations Dir
David Baker, General Manager
Meg Sabulsky, Programming Director
William Dunn, Promotions Manager
Charles Loughery, Engineering Dir

Washington

WJPA
02-01-1941; 1450 khz AM *Hrs Open:* 24; 1 kw-U, ND1; N40 11 23 W80 14 2
98 South Main Street, Washington, PA 15301 US
(724) 222-2110, *Fax:* (724) 228-2299
www.wjpa.com
email@wjpa.com
License: Washington, PA held by Washington Broadcasting Co.
Regional Network: Radio Pa.
Arbitron Metro Market: Pittsburgh, PA *Format:* Oldies *Hrs. of News Programming:* news progmg 6 hrs wkly *No. News Employees:* 2
Michael Siegel, President
Bob Gregg, Operations Dir
Pete Povich, Programming Director
Dale Allen, Promotions Manager
Jim Jefferson, News Director
Margie Konstantinou, Music Director

WJPA-FM
09-26-1964; 95.3 mhz FM *Hrs Open:* 24; 2.15 kw; 390 ft.; N40 11 23 W80 14 2
98 South Main Street, Washington, PA 15301 US
(724) 222-2110, *Fax:* (724) 228-2299
www.wjpa.com
email@wjpa.com
License: Washington, Washington County, PA held by Washington Broadcasting Co.
Arbitron Metro Market: Pittsburgh, PA *Format:* Oldies
Austin Davis, Programming Director
Sherry Flick, News Director
Jill Gleeson, Disc Jockey
Kenny Marks, Disc Jockey
Laura Mack, Disc Jockey
Tor Michaels, News Reporter

WKZV
08-01-1968; 1110 khz AM *Hrs Open:* Daylight; 1 kw-D, DAD; N40 13 16 W80 14 34
80 East Chestnut Street, Washington, PA 15301 US
(724) 228-6678, *Fax:* (724) 228-6678
License: Washington, PA held by My-Key Broadcasting Inc.
Nat'l Reps: Dome
Arbitron Metro Market: Pittsburgh, PA *Format:* Country *Special Programming:* Pol 3 hrs, polka 2 hrs, Croatian one hr, gospel on *Target Audience:* 35 plus.

Helen Supinski, President
Michael Panjuscek, Operations Dir

***WNJR**
11-26-1972; 91.7 mhz FM *Hrs Open:* 24; 0.95 kw; 112 ft.; N40 10 13 W80 14 43
1 South Lincoln Street, Washington, PA 15301 US
(724) 503-1001
www.wnjr.org
wnjr@washjeff.edu
License: Washington, Washington County, PA held by Washington and Jefferson College.
Wire Services: AP
Arbitron Metro Market: Washington, PA *Format:* Variety/Diverse *Hrs. of News Programming:* News progmg 4 hrs wkly *Target Audience:* All ages; college students, staff, community, alumni *Adv. Rates:* 150; 150; 150;150
Liz, Station Manager
Anthony Fleury, General Sales Mgr
Khyati, Programming Director
Allyse, Promotions Manager
Dana, Sponsorship Director
Sara, Music Director
Jake, Production Director

Waynesboro

WBHB-FM
02-03-1959; 101.5 mhz FM; 50 kw horiz, 48 kw vert; 230 ft.; N39 49 44 W77 33 10
Mailing Address: 4850 Conn. Ave NW Ste103, Washington, DC 20008 US
Second Address: 10960 John Wayne Dr., Waynesboro, PA 17225
(406) 755-8700, *Fax:* (406) 755-8770
www.1051cool.com
info@1051cool.com
License: Waynesboro, Franklin County, PA held by HJV L.P.
Group Owner: VerStandig Broadcasting
Arbitron Metro Market: Whitefish MT *Format:* Oldies
Cassie Bee, General Manager

WCBG
08-19-1953; 1380 khz AM; 1 kw-D, ND2; 0.02 kw-N, ND2; N39 44 20 W77 36 10
Mailing Address: 4850 Ct Ave., N.W., #103, Washington, DC 20008 US
Second Address: 10960 John Wayne Dr., Greencastle, PA 17225
(717) 597-9200, *Fax:* (717) 597-9210
wcbg.wagner.edu
wcbg@wagner.edu
License: Waynesboro, PA held by HJV L.P.
Group Owner: VerStandig Broadcasting; (acq 1-6-97; $1,068,699 with co-located FM).
Arbitron Metro Market: Hagerstown-Chambersburg-Waynesboro, MD-PA *Format:* Country *Target Audience:* 25-54.
Marge Martin, General Manager
Don Brake, Programming Director

Waynesburg

WANB
09-27-1956; 1210 khz AM *Hrs Open:* Sunrise-sunset
R.D #3, Gordon Hill, Waynesburg, PA 15370 US
(724) 627-5555, *Fax:* (724) 627-4021
wanbradio@gmail.com
License: Waynesburg, PA held by Broadcast Communications Inc.
Group Owner: Broadcast Communications Inc.
Arbitron Metro Market: Waynesburg, PA
Marcia Mackay, News Director

***WCYJ-FM**
07-06-1979; 99.5 mhz FM *Hrs Open:* 24; 0.007 kw; -3 ft.; N39 53 59 W80 11 7
51 West College St., Waynesburg, PA 15370 US
(724) 852-3310(724) 852-3297, *Fax:* (724) 627-4757
www.waynesburg.edu
wcyj@waynesburg.edu,mperry@waynesburg.edu
License: Waynesburg, Greene County, PA held by Waynesburg College.
Arbitron Metro Market: Waynesburg, PA *Format:* Adult Contemp *Special Programming:* Oldies 3 hrs, country 3 hrs, Christian 3 hrs, R&B 3 hrs, classic rock 3 hrs wkly *No. News Employees:* 1 *Target Audience:* 18-25;college & high school students
Travis Gongaware, Operations Dir
Ariel Dugan, General Manager
Mark Perry, Station Manager

Wellsboro

WNBT
05-13-1955; 1490 khz AM *Hrs Open:* 24; 1 kw-U, ND1; N41 44 41 W77 17 35
Mailing Address: 33 East Avenue, Wellsboro, PA 16901 US
Second Address: 198-B RR 7, Wellsboro, PA 16901
(570) 724-1490, *Fax:* (570) 724-6971
www.wnbt.net
wnbt@ynt.net
License: Wellsboro, PA held by Farm & Home Broadcasting Co.
Group Owner: Allegheny Mountain Network Stations
Nat'l Network: Westwood One *Regional Network:* Radio Pa. *Nat'l Reps:* Dome
Arbitron Metro Market: Wellsboro, PA *Format:* Adult Contemp *Hrs. of News Programming:* news progmg 10 hrs wkly *No. News Employees:* 1 *Target Audience:* 45+. *Adv. Rates:* 12; 12; 12; 12
Cary Simpson, President

WNBT-FM
07-02-1969; 104.5 mhz FM *Hrs Open:* 24; 50 kw; 381 ft.; N41 44 17 W77 21 50
33 East Avenue, Wellsboro, PA 16901 US
(570) 724-1490, *Fax:* (570) 724-6971
www.wnbt.net
wnbt@ynt.net
License: Wellsboro, Tioga County, PA held by Farm & Home Broadcasting Co.
Group Owner: Allegheny Mountain Network Stations
Nat'l Network: Westwood One
Arbitron Metro Market: Wellsboro, PA *Format:* Adult Contemp *Hrs. of News Programming:* news progmg 2 hrs wkly *No. News Employees:* 1 *Target Audience:* 18-55.
Dann Miller, General Manager

West Chester

WCHE
10-04-1963; 1520 khz AM *Hrs Open:* Sunrise-sunset
119 West Market Street, West Chester, PA 19382 US
(610) 692-3131, *Fax:* (610) 692-3133
www.wche1520.com
wche@wche1520.com
License: West Chester, PA held by Chester County Radio Inc.
Nat'l Network: USA; Westwood One
Arbitron Metro Market: West Chester,PA *Format:* Alternative, Talk *Special Programming:* Relg 8 hrs, country 2 hrs wkly *Hrs. of News Programming:* news progmg 20 hrs wkly *No. News Employees:* 1 *Target Audience:* 24-64; upscale
David Shur, President
Bill Mason, General Manager

***WCUR**
01-01-1999; 91.7 mhz FM; 0.1 kw vert; 112 ft.; N39 57 2 W75 35 58
211 Sykes Union Building, West Chester, PA 19383 US
(610) 436-2478, *Fax:* (610) 436-2477
www.wcur.org
web@wcur.org
License: West Chester, Chester County, PA held by Student Services Inc.
Arbitron Metro Market: West Chester, PA *Format:* Variety/Diverse
Matt Toal, General Manager
Jacki Marinich, General Sales Mgr
Brynn Pezzuti, Programming Director

West Hazleton

WKZN
01-01-1982; 1300 khz AM *Hrs Open:* 24; 5 kw-D, DA2; 0.5 kw-N, DA2; N40 56 26 W76 0 7 *Rebroadcasts:* Rebroadcasts WILK(AM) Wilks-Barre 100%.
10706 Beaver Dam Road, Cockeysville, MD 21030 US
(570) 883-9850, *Fax:* (570) 883-0832
www.wilknewsradio.com
info@wilknewsradio.com
License: West Hazleton, PA held by Entercom Scranton Wilkes-Barre License LLC.
Group Owner: Entercom Communications Corp.; (acq 12-13-99; grpsl).
Nat'l Reps: D & R Radio *Wire Services:* ABC; AP
Arbitron Metro Market: Wilkes Barre-Scranton, PA *Format:* News, News/Talk, 86 *Special Programming:* Relg one hr wkly *Hrs. of News Programming:* news progmg 25 hrs wkly *No. News Employees:* 6 *Target Audience:* General; affluent, educated *Adv. Rates:* 35; 45; 35; 25
Jim Rising, Operations Dir
John Burkavage, General Manager
Andy Zapotek, General Sales Mgr
Nancy Kman, Programming Director
Casey Consagra, Promotions Manager
Joe Thomas, News Director
Lamar Smith, Chief Engineer
Bob DeMond,National Sales Manager
Tom Ragan, News Reporter
Shannon Ball, Traffic Manager

West Middlesex

WWIZ
10-01-1972; 103.9 mhz FM; 6 kw; 89.7 meters; N41 12 16 W80 21 49
Station Wwiz PO Box 1120, Hermitage, PA 16148 US
(330) 783-1000, *Fax:* (330) 783-0060
www.realrock104.com
License: West Middlesex, Mercer County, PA held by Cumulus Licensing Corp.
Group Owner: Cumulus Media Inc.; (acq 3-15-00; grpsl).
Arbitron Metro Market: Youngstown, OH *Format:* Rock/AOR *Target Audience:* 25-54.
Brian Schimmell, General Manager

Whitneyville

WLIH
03-15-1987; 107.1 mhz FM *Hrs Open:* 6 AM-Midnight; 3.3 kw; 299 ft.; N41 46 13 W77 12 8
Mailing Address: P. O. Box 97, Wellsboro, PA 16901 US
Second Address: 2352 Charleston Rd, Wellsboro, PA 16901
(570) 724-4272, *Fax:* (570) 724-2302
www.wlih.com
wlih107@quik.com
License: Whitneyville, Tioga County, PA held by Good Christian Radio Broadcasting Inc.
Nat'l Network: USA
Format: Christian, News, 74 *Hrs. of News Programming:* News progmg 28 hrs wkly *Target Audience:* General; serving the Christian community of the county *Adv. Rates:* 6; 5; 6; na
Robert Makin, President
Carol Makin, General Manager
George Buickus, Programming Director

Wilkes-Barre

WBAX
05-01-1922; 1240 khz AM *Hrs Open:* 24; 1 kw-U, ND1; N41 15 13 W75 54 25 *Rebroadcasts:* Simulcasts with WEJL (AM) Scranton.
149 Penn Avenue, Scranton, PA 18503 US
(208) 263-2179, *Fax:* (208) 265-5440
www.1067thepoint.com
carolynp@953kpnd.com
License: Wilkes-Barre, PA held by The Scranton Times L.P.
Group Owner: Shamrock Communications Inc.
Arbitron Metro Market: Kootenai ID *Format:* Classic Rock
Dylan Benefield, General Manager
Mike Brown, News Director
John Goes, Chief Engineer

***WCLH**
02-06-1972; 90.7 mhz FM *Hrs Open:* 24; 0.205 kw; 971 ft.; N41 11 11 W75 51 33
187 South Franklin St, Wilkes-Barre, PA 18766 US
(570) 408-5907, *Fax:* (570) 408-5908
www.wclh.org
wclhpd@gmail.com .
License: Wilkes-Barre, Luzerne County, PA held by Wilkes University.
Nat'l Network: AP Network News
Arbitron Metro Market: Wilkes Barre-Scranton, PA *Format:* Alternative *Special Programming:* Ger 3 hrs, Sp 3 hrs wkly *Hrs. of News Programming:* News progmg 7 hrs wkly *Target Audience:* 12-44.
Renee Loftus, General Manager
Corey M and Joe P, Programming Director

WILK
02-13-1947; 980 khz AM *Hrs Open:* 24; 5 kw-D, DAN; 1 kw-N, DAN; N41 13 42 W75 56 53
10706 Beaver Dam Road, Cockeysville, MD 21030 US
(570) 883-9800, *Fax:* (570) 883-9851
www.wilknetwork.com
feedback@thewilknetwork.com
License: Wilkes-Barre, PA held by Entercom Scranton Wilkes-Barre License LLC.
Group Owner: Entercom Communications Corp.; (acq 12-13-99; grpsl)
Arbitron Metro Market: Wilkes Barre-Scranton, PA *Format:* News, News/Talk, 86 *Special Programming:* Relg one hr wkly *Target Audience:* 15-54.
Joseph Fields, President
John Burkavage, General Manager

WMGS
01-01-1946; 92.9 mhz FM *Hrs Open:* 24; 5.3 kw; 1385 ft.; N41 10 56 W75 52 22
City Center West, # 400, 7201 W. Lake Mead Blvd, Las Vegas, NV 89128 US
(570) 824-9000, *Fax:* (570)655-9393
www.magic93fm.com
License: Wilkes-Barre, Luzerne County, PA
Group Owner: Cumulus Media Inc.; (acq 7-1-97; grpsl).
Arbitron Metro Market: Wilkes Barre, PA *Format:* Adult Contemp
Special Programming: Farm one hr, relg 3 hrs wkly *Hrs. of News Programming:* news progmg 2 hrs wkly *No. News Employees:* 1
Target Audience: 25-54; adult women
Stan Phillips, Programming Director
Bill Palmeri, Promotions Manager
Erin Evans, Promotions Director

***WRKC**
09-18-1968; 88.5 mhz FM *Hrs Open:* 7 AM-2 AM; 1.5 kw; -459 ft.; N41 14 56 W75 52 45
133 North River Street, Wilkes-Barre, PA 18702 US
(570) 208-5931, *Fax:* (570) 825-9049
www.kings.edu/~wrke/
wrkc@kings.edu
License: Wilkes-Barre, Luzerne County, PA held by King's College.
Arbitron Metro Market: Wilkes Barre-Scranton, PA *Format:* Rock/AOR *Target Audience:* General; people who need wide-ranging svcs
Sue Henry, General Manager
Pat Barton, Station Manager
Katie Moore, Programming Director
Bob Decker, Metal
Michael Wasenda, Music Director

Wilkinsburg

WAMO
08-01-1948; 660 khz AM *Hrs Open:* 24
One Forever Drive, Hollidaysburg, PA 16648 US
(412) 829-1000, *Fax:* (412) 391-3559
www.wamo100.com
info@wamo100.com
License: Wilkinsburg, PA held by McL/McM Pennsylvania LLC.
Group Owner: Sheridan Broadcasting Corp.; (acq 3-1-73)
Nat'l Network: American Urban *Nat'l Reps:* McGavren Guild
Arbitron Metro Market: Pittsburgh, PA *Format:* Black, Blues
Ronald Davenport Sr., Chairman
Ronald Davenport Jr., President
Kathy Gersha, Operations Dir
Michael Davenport, General Manager
Mickey Baker, General Sales Mgr
Ron Atkins, Programming Director
Laura Varner-Norman, PromotionsManager
George Cook, Programming Director
Tammy Sadler, Promotions Director
Jon Plesser, Regional Sales Manager

Williamsport

WILQ
07-31-1949; 105.1 mhz FM *Hrs Open:* 24; 9.2 kw; 1135 ft.; N41 11 43 W76 58 18
1685 Four Mile Drive, Williamsport, PA 17701 US
(570) 323-8200, *Fax:* (570) 327-9138
www.wilq.com
dan.farr@bybradio.com
License: Williamsport, Lycoming County, PA held by South Williamsport SabreCom Inc.
Group Owner: Backyard Broadcasting LLC; (acq 12-1-02; grpsl).
Nat'l Reps: Christal
Arbitron Metro Market: Williamsport, PA *Format:* Country *Hrs. of News Programming:* news progmg 7 hrs wkly *No. News Employees:* 4 *Target Audience:* 25 plus; adults in a 10 county area *Adv. Rates:* 45; 45;45; 25
Robin Smith, CFO
Barry Drake, President
Dan Farr, General Manager
Doug Dodge, General Sales Mgr
Ted Minier, Programming Director
John Finn, News Director

WKSB
04-01-1948; 102.7 mhz FM *Hrs Open:* 24; 53 kw; 1270 ft.; N41 11 21 W76 58 53
P O Box 60547, Harrisburg, PA 17106 US
(570) 327-1400, *Fax:* (570) 327-8156
www.wksb.com
wksb@wksb.com
License: Williamsport, Lycoming County, PA
Arbitron Metro Market: Williamsport, PA *Format:* Adult Contemp
No. News Employees: 1 *Target Audience:* 25-54.
Russell Davidson, Operations Dir
Tom Scott, Programming Director
Liz Stroup, News Director
Dan Milliken, Engineering Dir
Tom Turner, Assistant Music Director
Mark Lawrence, Public Affairs Director

WLYC
06-01-1951; 1050 khz AM *Hrs Open:* 24; 1 kw-D, ND1; 0.03 kw-N, ND1; N41 15 44 W77 1 59
P.O. Box 545, Williamsport, PA 17703 US
(570) 327-1300, *Fax:* (570) 327-5565
www.espnwilliamsport.com
wlyc1050@yahoo.com
License: Williamsport, PA held by Sentry Communications License LLC
Nat'l Network: ESPN Radio; Westwood One *Regional Network:* Radio Pa. *Regional Reps:* .
Arbitron Metro Market: Williamsport, PA *Format:* Sports *Hrs. of News Programming:* Sports news only *Target Audience:* 25-54; male *Adv. Rates:* 25; 15; 20; 7.50
Jeffrey Andruionis, Operations Dir
James McKowne, General Manager
Christy Andruionis, General Sales Mgr

***WPTC**
09-03-1980; 88.1 mhz FM *Hrs Open:* 24; 494 w; -101 ft; N41 14 11 W77 01 26
One College Ave., Williamsport, PA 17701
(570) 326-3761, *Fax:* (570) 320-2423
www.pct.edu/wptc
wptc@pct.edu
License: Williamsport, Lycoming County, PA held by Pennsylvania College of Technology.
Wire Services: AP
Population Served: 99,000 *Arbitron Metro Market:* Williamsport, P *Special Programming:* Jazz inspired with Judy Carmichael, The Jazz Scene *Hrs. of News Programming:* 1 hour weekly
Target Audience: 18-24; collegestudents *Adv. Rates:* Underwriting $150 per semester
Davie Gilmour, President
Brad Nason, General Manager
Skip Smith, Chief Engineer

WRAK
04-10-1930; 1400 khz AM *Hrs Open:* 24; 1 kw-U, ND1; N41 14 22 W77 2 27 *Rebroadcasts:* Rebroadcasts WRKK(AM) Hughesville 100%
800 Corporate Circle, Suite 201, Harrisonburg, PA 17110 US
(570) 327-1400, *Fax:* (570) 327-8156
www.wrak.com
wrak@wrak.com
License: Williamsport, PA held by Clear Channel Radio License Inc.
Group Owner: Clear Channel Communications Inc.; (acq 8-5-98; grpsl)
Nat'l Network: Westwood One
Arbitron Metro Market: Williamsport, PA *Format:* News, News/Talk, 84, Talk *Hrs. of News Programming:* news progmg 3 hrs wkly *No. News Employees:* 1 *Target Audience:* 35 plus.
James Dabney, General Manager
Ken Sawyer, Programming Director
Tom Scott, Promotions Manager

***WRLC**
04-05-1976; 91.7 mhz FM *Hrs Open:* 24; 0.74 kw horiz; -299 ft.; N41 14 42 W76 59 50
College Place, Williamsport, PA 17701 US
(570) 321-4060, *Fax:* (570) 321-4372
www.lycoming.edu/orgs/wrlc
wrlc@lycoming.edu
License: Williamsport, Lycoming County, PA held by Lycoming College.
Arbitron Metro Market: Williamsport, PA *Format:* Alternative, Oldies *Special Programming:* Class one hr, gospel 6 hrs, pub affrs 2 hrs, Christian rock 3 hrs, jazz 8 hrs, blues 3 hrs wkly *Hrs. of News Programming:* Newsprogmg 15 hrs wkly *Target Audience:* General; Lycoming College & its surrounding communities
Alan Jackson, Station Manager
Skip Smith, Chief Engineer

WWPA
05-22-1949; 1340 khz AM *Hrs Open:* 24; 1 kw-U, ND1; N41 13 45 W77 0 45
309 West Southern Avenue, South Williamsport, PA 17701 US
(570) 323-8200, *Fax:* (570) 327-9138
www.wwpa1340amtalkradiowilliamsportpa.com
License: Williamsport, PA held by South Williamsport SabreCom Inc.
Group Owner: Backyard Broadcasting LLC; (acq 12-1-02; grpsl).
Nat'l Network: CSN *Nat'l Reps:* Christal
Arbitron Metro Market: Williamsport, PA *Format:* News, News/Talk, 86 *Special Programming:* Sports *Hrs. of News Programming:* news progmg 168 hrs wkly *No. News Employees:* 1 *Target Audience:* 35 plus.*Adv. Rates:* 15; 15; 15; 8
Robin Smith, CFO
Barry Drake, President
Dan Farr, General Manager
John Finn, News Reporter

***WVYA**
01-01-2003; 89.7 mhz FM *Hrs Open:* 24; 3.3 kw; -16 ft.; N41 14 54 W77 1 52 *Rebroadcasts:* Rebroadcasts WVIA-FM Scranton
Old Boston Rd, Pittston, PA 18640 US
(570) 826-6144, *Fax:* (570) 655-1180
www.wvia.org
danmattern@wvia.org
License: Williamsport, Lycoming County, PA held by Northeastern Pennsylvania Educational TV Association.
Nat'l Network: NPR *Wire Services:* AP
Arbitron Metro Market: Pittston, PA *Format:* Jazz, News *Hrs. of News Programming:* news progmg 30 hrs wkly *No. News Employees:* 1 *Target Audience:* Upscale, mature audience.
Harmar Brereton, M.D., Chairman
A. William Kelly, President & CEO
Chris Norton, Operations Dir
Larry Vojtko, Programming Director
Tom Curr, Executive Vice President & Executive Producer
Lynn Volk, Senior Vice President ofFinance
Chris Norton, Vice President of Radio
Joe Glynn, Vice President of Engineering
Doug Cook, Vice President of Marketing & Special Events
George Thomas, Vice President of Membership

***WCRG**
02-20-2002; 90.7 mhz FM *Hrs Open:* 24; 3 kw; Ant -216 ft; N41 13 50 W77 08 59 *Rebroadcasts:* Rebroadcasts WGRC(FM) Lewisburg 100%
101 Armory Blvd., Lewisburg, PA 17837
(570) 523-1190, *Fax:* (570) 523-1114
www.wgrc.com
email@wgrc.com
License: Williamsport, Lycoming County, PA held by Salt & Light Media Ministries Inc.
Wire Services: AP
Population Served: 150,000 *Arbitron Metro Market:* Williamsport, PA *Hrs. of News Programming:* news progmg 12 hrs wkly *No. News Employees:* 3 *Target Audience:* 25-54.
Larry Weidman, General Manager
Don Casteline, Programming Director
Jim Diehl, News Director
Chris Miller, Chief Engineer
Jim Diehl, News Reporter
John Callahan, News Reporter

Wyomissing

***WYTL**
01-01-2005; 91.7 mhz FM; 10 w horiz, 320 w vert; Ant 840 ft; W40 19 22 W76 11 52 *Rebroadcasts:* Rebroadcasts WBYO (FM) Sellersville 100%
Box 186, Sellersville, PA 18960
(215) 721-2141, *Fax:* (215) 721-9811
www.wordfm.org
wordfm@wordfm.org
License: Wyomissing, Berks County, PA held by Four Rivers Community Broadcasting Corp.
Charles Loughery, President
Meg Sabulsky, Operations Dir
David Baker, General Manager
Meg Sabulsky, Programming Director
William Dunn, Promotions Manager
Charles Loughery, Engineering Dir

York

WARM-FM
09-01-1962; 103.3 mhz FM *Hrs Open:* 24; 6.4 kw; 1306 ft.; N40 1 38 W76 36 0
Mailing Address: 140 East Market Street, York, PA 17401 US
Second Address: 5989 Susquehanna Plaza Dr., York, PA 17406
(717) 764-1155, *Fax:* (717) 252-4708
www.wink103.com
bobby.d@cumulus.com
License: York, York County, PA
Group Owner: Cumulus Media Partners LLC
Arbitron Metro Market: York, PA *Format:* Adult Contemp
Tom Ranker, Operations Dir
Brian Shaffer, General Sales Mgr
Bobby D, Programming Director

Jay Long, Promotions Manager
Joel Murphy, News Director
John London, Disc Jockey
Dennis Wagner, Disc Jockey
Dennis John Cahill, DiscJockey
Gina Koch, Special Events Coordinator

WOYK
03-01-1932; 1350 khz AM *Hrs Open:* 24; 5 kw-D, DAN; 1 kw-N, DAN; N39 56 0 W76 49 6
Mailing Address: 1360 Copenhaffer Road, York, PA 17404 US
Second Address: 1051 Dairy Ln., Elizabethtown, PA 17022
(717) 840-0355, *Fax:* (717) 840-0355
sportsradioespn1350.com
woyk1350@att.net
License: York, PA held by WOYK Inc.
Nat'l Network: Sporting News Radio Network *Regional Network:* Radio Pa.
Arbitron Metro Market: York, PA *Format:* Sports *Target Audience:* 25-64; men *Adv. Rates:* 40; 40; 40; 32
Douglas George, President
SAM CONRAD, Operations Dir
Vincent Grande, General Manager

WYYC
01-01-1948; 1250 khz AM *Hrs Open:* 24; 1 kw-D, ND1; 0.033 kw-N, ND1; N39 59 56 W76 41 43
City Center West, 7201 W. Lake Mead Blvd, Las Vegas, NV 89128 US
(717) 757-9402
www.wilkinsradio.com
wyyc@wilkinsradio.com
License: York, PA held by Steel City Radio Inc.
Group Owner: Wilkins Communications Network Inc.; (acq 10-11-2005; $250,000)
Arbitron Metro Market: York, PA *Format:* Talk *Target Audience:* 35 plus.
Bob Wilkins, CEO
LuAnn Wilkins, President
Greg Garrett, Operations Dir
Bob Moore, Station Manager
Mitchell Mathis, President/COO

WQXA-FM
01-01-1948; 105.7 mhz FM; 25 kw; 705 ft.; N39 59 56 W76 41 43
City Center West, 7201 W. Lake Mead Blvd, Las Vegas, NV 89128 US
(717) 635-7700, *Fax:* (717) 635-7551
License: York, York County, PA
Group Owner: Cumulus Media Inc.; (acq 5-29-97; grpsl)
Arbitron Metro Market: York, PA *Format:* Rock/AOR *Target Audience:* 18-49.
Bob Adams, General Manager

WSBA
09-01-1942; 910 khz AM *Hrs Open:* 24
Mailing Address: 140 East Market Street, York, PA 17401 US
Second Address: 5989 Susquehanna Plaza Dr., York, PA 17406
(717) 764-1155, *Fax:* (717) 252-4708
www.wsba910.com
info@wsba910.com
License: York, PA held by WSBA Lico Inc.
Group Owner: Cumulus Media Partners LLC
Arbitron Metro Market: York, PA *Format:* News, News/Talk, 86 *Special Programming:* Black 3 hrs, farm 4 hrs wkly *No. News Employees:* 5
Tom Rawker, General Manager
Brian Shaffer, General Sales Mgr
Jim Horn, Programming Director
Bob Popa, Chief Engineer

***WVYC**
11-18-1976; 88.1 mhz FM *Hrs Open:* 18; 0.036 kw horiz; -70 ft.; N39 56 49 W76 43 47
339 Country Club Rd., York, PA 17405 US
(717) 815-1932
www.wvyc.org
tgibson@ycp.edu
License: York, York County, PA held by York College of Pennsylvania.
Arbitron Metro Market: York, PA *Format:* Variety/Diverse *Special Programming:* Class 8 hrs, jazz 8 hrs, Sp one hr wkly *Hrs. of News Programming:* news progmg 3 hrs wkly *No. News Employees:* 1 *Target Audience:* 14-24; new mus lovers
Dr.Brian Furio, Chairman
Michelle Gorecki, General Manager
Thomas.K.Gibson, Faculty Advisor

York-Hanover

WYCR
12-22-1962; 98.5 mhz FM; 10.5 kw; 928 ft.; N39 51 26 W76 56 54
Mailing Address: P. O. Box 234, Hanover, PA 17331 US
Second Address: 275 Radio Rd., Hanover, PA 17331
(717) 792-0098, *Fax:* (717) 637-9006
www.thepeak985.com
info@thepeak.com
License: York-Hanover, York County, PA held by Radio Hanover Inc.
Arbitron Metro Market: York, PA *Format:* Contemporary Hits/Top 40, Adult Contemp
Tom Jackson, Programming Director
Beth Mowren, News Director
Jim Cooke, Disc Jockey
Paul Scott, Disc Jockey
Lee Sheldon, Disc Jockey
Davy Crockett, Disc Jockey
Jeff Brown, Disc Jockey

Youngsville

***WYVL(FM)**
01-19-1999; 88.5 mhz FM *Hrs Open:* 24; 100 w; -335 ft; N41 51 01 W79 18 41
409 E. Main St., Youngsville, PA 16371
(814) 563-4903, *Fax:* (814) 563-4903
www.wtmv.com
wtmv@verizon.net
License: Youngsville, Warren County, PA held by Living Word of Faith Christian Outreach.
Nat'l Network: American Family Radio; Moody
Population Served: 1,714 *Arbitron Metro Market:* Youngsville, PA *Format:* Christian *Special Programming:* Children 10 hrs, class 2.5 hrs wkly *Hrs. of News Programming:* 12.?A? *No. News Employees:* 5*Target Audience:* 21 plus; Christians of all ages
Rev. William Baker, President
Rev. Patricia Baker, Operations Dir
Khlare Bracken, Music Critic
Kathy Joy, Public Affairs Director

Puerto Rico

Adjuntas

WOQI
01-01-1997; 1020 khz AM
Box 1507 Cuepo No. 80, Utuado, PR 0761 US
(787) 829-1453, *Fax:* (787) 840-7077
administracion@wpabradio.com
License: Adjuntas, PR held by WPAB Inc.
Arbitron Metro Market: Puerto Rico *Format:* Variety/Diverse *Hrs. of News Programming:* news progmg 3 hrs wkly *No. News Employees:* 1 *Target Audience:* General; General Public *Adv. Rates:* 10; 10; 10; 8
Alfonso Gimenez-Lucchetti, General Manager

Aguada

WFDT
01-01-1975; 105.5 mhz FM *Hrs Open:* 24; 3 kw; 997 ft.; N18 18 57 W67 10 54
P. O. Box 847, Mayaguez, PR 0681 US
(787) 474-0630, *Fax:* (787) 767-9343
www.fidelitypr.com
License: Aguada, PR held by Arso Radio Corp.
Group Owner: Uno Radio Group; (acq 4-19-01; $3.2 million).
Nat'l Reps: McGavren Guild
Arbitron Metro Market: Puerto Rico *Format:* Adult Contemp *Target Audience:* 25-49; middle class
Luis Soto, President
Raymond Totti, Executive Vice President

Aguadilla

WABA
11-15-1951; 850 khz AM
P. O. Box 188, Aguadilla, PR 0603 US
(641) 752-4122, *Fax:* (641) 752-5121
ktdvradio.com
info@ktdvradio.com
License: Aguadilla, PR held by Aquadilla Radio & TV Corp. Inc.
Format: Adult Contemp, Christian
Mark Osmundson, General Manager

WIVA-FM
04-16-1964; 100.3 mhz FM *Hrs Open:* 24; 22 kw; 2014 ft.; N18 9 7 W66 59 15
P.O. Box 487, Caguas, PR 0726 US
(787) 834-2320, *Fax:* (787) 831-7969
www.salsoul.com
www.@unoradio.com
License: Aguadilla, PR held by Arso Radio Corp.
Group Owner: Uno Radio Group; (acq 3-85).
Arbitron Metro Market: Puerto Rico *Hrs. of News Programming:* news progmg 5 hrs wkly *No. News Employees:* 1 *Target Audience:* 12 plus.
Jesus Soto, CEO
Luis Soto, President
Maida Bedaya, General Manager
Raymond Totti, General Sales Mgr
Anthony Soto, Programming Director

WWNA
01-01-1956; 1340 khz AM
Mailing Address: Box 5734, Puerta De Tierra, San Juan, PR 0906 US
Second Address: Rd. 111, Aquadilla, PR 605
(787) 252-1730, *Fax:* (787) 868-1340
www.radiouna1340.com
License: Aguadilla, PR held by Dominga Barreto Santiago
Arbitron Metro Market: Puerto Rico *Format:* Spanish *Special Programming:* Jazz 3 hrs wkly *Target Audience:* 20-55.
Aureo Matos, General Manager
Ron Cushing, Chief Engineer
Felix Gonzalez, Disc Jockey

WTPM
05-27-1971; 92.9 mhz FM *Hrs Open:* 18; 50 kw; 1207 ft.; N18 18 47 W67 11 6
Sector Cuba #1060, Mayaguez, PR 0680 US
(787) 831-9200, *Fax:* (787) 831-9292
www.wtpm.org
info@wtpm.org
License: Aguadilla, PR held by Corp. of the 7th Day Adventists of West Puerto Rico
Arbitron Metro Market: Mayaguez, PR *Format:* Adult Contemp *Special Programming:* English one hr, class 7 hrs wkly *Hrs. of News Programming:* News progmg 11 hrs wkly *Target Audience:* General; traditionalChristian groups
Pastor James White, General Manager

Arecibo

WCMN
06-24-1947; 1280 khz AM *Hrs Open:* 24; 5 kw-D, ND1; 1 kw-N, ND1; N18 28 52 W66 41 16
Mailing Address: P. O. Box 436, Arecibo, PR 0612 US
Second Address: 55 Gonzalo Marin St., Arecibo, PR 612
(787) 878-0070(787) 781-6303, *Fax:* (787) 880-1112
www.notiuno.com
unoarecivo.aruba@gmail.com
License: Arecibo, PR held by Caribbean Broadcasting Corp.
Group Owner: Uno Radio Group; (acq 4-7-2004; $5.75 million for stock with co-located FM).
Arbitron Metro Market: Puerto Rico, PR *Format:* News, News/Talk, 86 *Hrs. of News Programming:* news progmg 50 hrs wkly *No. News Employees:* 3 *Target Audience:* 30 plus.
Byron Mitchell, Operations Dir
Maria Mitchell, General Sales Mgr
Jacquelyn Rames, News Director
Juan Rivera, Chief Engineer

WCMN-FM
01-01-1967; 107.3 mhz FM *Hrs Open:* 24; 50 kw; 1027 ft.; N18 14 52 W66 48 43
P O Box 436, 55 Ganzalo Marin Street, Arecibo, PR 0613 US
(787) 878-1073
www.1073miemisora.com
comentarios@tocadeto.com
License: Arecibo, PR held by Caribbean Broadcasting Corp.
Group Owner: Uno Radio Group
Arbitron Metro Market: Puerto Rico, PR *Format:* Contemporary Hits/Top 40 *Target Audience:* 18-42; young adults
Rick Duerson, General Manager

WMIA
02-21-1957; 1070 khz AM *Hrs Open:* 19; 0.5 kw-D, ND1; 2.5 kw-N, ND1; N18 27 33 W66 45 20
Mailing Address: P. O. Box 1055, Arecibo, PR 0613 US
Second Address: 1168 Miramar Ave., Arecibo, PR 612
(787) 878-2727, *Fax:* 787-878-1275
www.wmia1070.com
epifanioro@gmail.com
License: Arecibo, PR held by Abacoa Radio Corp.
Arbitron Metro Market: Puerto Rico *Format:* Oldies *Target Audience:* 25 plus; the buying power in the area
Epifanio Rodriguez-Velez, General Manager

WNIK
01-01-1957; 1230 khz AM; 1 kw-U, ND1; N18 27 20 W66 44 24

PO Box 0556, Arecibo, PR 0612 US
(787) 880-2461, *Fax:* (787) 880-2461
www.unicaradio1230.com
mss64radio@gmail.com
License: Arecibo, PR held by Unik Broadcasting System Corp.
Arbitron Metro Market: Puerto Rico *Format:* Variety/Diverse
Target Audience: General.
Manuel Santiago, General Manager

WNIK-FM
07-17-1965; 106.5 mhz FM; 25 kw; 20 ft.; N18 27 20 W66 44 24
PO Box 0556, Arecibo, PR 0613 US
(787) 880-2613, *Fax:* (787) 879-1011
License: Arecibo, PR held by Kelly Broadcasting System Inc.
Arbitron Metro Market: Puerto Rico *Format:* Spanish, Christian
Raul Santiago, General Manager

Barceloneta-Manati

WBQN
03-01-1975; 1160 khz AM; 5 kw-D, DAD; 2.5 kw-N, DAD; N18 26 23 W66 33 7
P.O.Box 993, Manati, PR 0701 US
(787) 854-2450, *Fax:* (787) 854-3738
www.wbqn1160.com/
riveraolmo@hotmail.com
License: Barceloneta-Manati, PR held by Radio Borinquen Inc.
Arbitron Metro Market: Manati, PR *Format:* Contemporary Hits/Top 40, Spanish, 86 *Target Audience:* General.
Angel Rivera, President
Luis Rivera Jr., General Manager

Barranquitas

WOLA
03-01-1986; 1380 khz AM; 1 kw-U, ND1; N18 11 1 W66 18 24
Carr 719 Km1 Bo Helechal, Baranquitas, PR 0618 US
(787) 857-1380, *Fax:* (787) 857-1381
info@radioprocer.com
License: Barranquitas, PR held by Torrecillas Broadcasting Corp.
Arbitron Metro Market: Puerto Rico *TV Affiliate:* Sp *Format:* Jazz
No. News Employees: General.
CEO, CEO/COO

Bayamon

WODA
12-03-1959; 94.7 mhz FM *Hrs Open:* 24; 31 kw; 1837 ft.; N18 16 44 W65 51 12
Mailing Address: P.O. Box 949, Guaynbo, PR 0970 US
Second Address: Amelia Industrial Park, Calle Frances 42, Guaynabo, PR 968
(787) 622-9700, *Fax:* (787) 622-9481
www.lanueva94.com
rogie@sbspuertorico.com
License: Bayamon, PR held by WLDI Inc.
Group Owner: Spanish Broadcasting System Inc.; (acq 11-29-99; grpsl)
Arbitron Metro Market: Guayanbo,PR *Format:* Contemporary Hits/Top 40 *Target Audience:* 12-24; males & females, middle/upper socio-economic
Raul Alarcon, President
Ismael Nieves, General Manager
Marie Martinez, General Sales Mgr
Rogie Gallart, Programming Director
Luis Rivera, Promotions Manager
Demare Ramirez, News Director
Alejandro Luciano, Chief Engineer

WCMA(AM)
01-01-1966; 1600 khz AM *Hrs Open:* 18; 5 kw-U; N18 21 38 W66 09 30
Mailing Address: Box 9394, San Juan, PR 00908-0394
Second Address: 403 Del Parque, 15 th Fl., Santurce, PR 00912-3709
(787) 785-1600,(787) 729-1600, *Fax:* (787) 785-2094,(787) 723-8685
ttrelles@yahoo.com
License: Bayamon, Bayamon County, PR held by Marketing Promotion Network Inc.
Population Served: 2,000,000 *Arbitron Metro Market:* Puerto Rico
Tony Trelles, President
Martha Villanueva, Operations Dir

WRSJ
01-01-1947; 1560 khz AM; 5 kw-D, ND1; 0.75 kw-N, ND1; N18 24 5 W66 7 14
Box 3986 Valle Arriba Hgts Station, Carolina, PR 0984 US
(787) 274-1800, *Fax:* (787) 281-9758
License: Bayamon, PR held by International Broadcasting Corp.
Group Owner: International Broadcasting Corp.; (acq 7-6-2004; $1.45 million with WCHQ(AM) Quebradillas).
Arbitron Metro Market: Puerto Rico
Pedro Collazo, President
Margarita Nazario, General Manager

WXYX
02-01-1979; 100.7 mhz FM *Hrs Open:* 24; 50 kw; 1093 ft.; N18 16 58 W66 10 47
Mailing Address: Bambbo Drive K-8, Ub Torrimar, Guaynabo, PR 0657 US
Second Address: Rd 174, KM 5.0 Bo. Guaraguao, Bayamon, PR 00956-9535
(787) 785-9390, *Fax:* (787) 785-9377
www.lax.fm
info@lax.fm
License: Bayamon, PR held by RAAD Broadcasting Corp.
Arbitron Metro Market: Bayamon, PR *Format:* Contemporary Hits/Top 40 *Target Audience:* 12-34; young teens, adults
Roberto Davila, President
Eduardo Cora, General Sales Mgr
Herman Davila, Programming Director
Michelle Torres, Promotions Manager
Edwardo Carrasguillo, News Director
Juan Rivera, Chief Engineer

Cabo Rojo

WYAC
01-09-1970; 930 khz AM *Hrs Open:* 21; 2.5 kw-U, ND1; N18 6 5 W67 9 17
Mailing Address: Post Office Box 9023916, San Juan, PR 0902 US
Second Address: Radio Centre, Post & Bosgue Sts., Mayaguez, PR 684
(787) 620-9898
www.radiopr740.com
info@wyac.com
License: Cabo Rojo, PR held by Bestov Broadcasting Inc.
Arbitron Metro Market: Mayagueez, PR *Format:* News, News/Talk, 86 *Target Audience:* General; Mayaguez county residents
Luis Majia, President
Francisco Acosta, General Manager

WMIO
01-10-1988; 102.3 mhz FM *Hrs Open:* 6 AM-midnight; 3 kw; 781 ft.; N17 59 37 W67 10 27
Post Office Box 9023916, San Juan, PR 0902 US
(787) 798-7878, *Fax:* (787) 620-0720
www.1073miemisora.com
License: Cabo Rojo, PR held by Arso Radio Corp.
Group Owner: Uno Radio Group; (acq 3-26-2007; $3.25 million)
Arbitron Metro Market: Puerto Rico *Format:* Contemporary Hits/Top 40 *Target Audience:* 18-45; general
Alan Mejia, General Manager

Caguas

WNEL
07-21-1947; 1430 khz AM *Hrs Open:* 24; 5 kw-D, ND1; 5 kw-N, ND1; N18 14 53 W66 1 25
P. O. Box 487, Caguas, PR 0625 US
(787) 640-3393, *Fax:* (787) 743-0252
www.radiotempo.net
leon@unoradio.com,lionprc@yahoo.com
License: Caguas, PR held by Turabo Radio Corp.
Group Owner: Uno Radio Group; (acq 4-1-73).
Arbitron Metro Market: Puerto Rico *Format:* Oldies *Hrs. of News Programming:* 15 *Target Audience:* 24 plus.
Jesus Soto, CEO
Luis Soto, President
Elba Esmirria, Operations Dir
Luis Leon, General Manager
Jaime Soto, Programming Director
Tanya Ramos, Promotions Manager
Luis Gonzales, CFO

WVJP
11-24-1947; 1110 khz AM *Hrs Open:* 24; 2.5 kw-D, ND1; 0.5 kw-N, ND1; N18 13 25 W66 1 11
Mailing Address: P. O. Box 207, Caguas, PR 0726 US
Second Address: Tomas de Castro #2, Caguas, PR 626
(787) 743-5790, *Fax:* (787) 746-6996
dimension103.com
License: Caguas, PR held by Borinquen Broadcasting Co. Inc.
Arbitron Metro Market: Caguas, PR *Format:* Adult Contemp
Jancel Pereira, CEO
Bienvenido Rodriguez, General Manager
Norma Rodriquez-Trinidad, Programming Director
Jesus Gomez, Chief Engineer

WVJP-FM
10-01-1968; 103.3 mhz FM; 28 kw; 1906 ft.; N18 16 41 W65 51 9
Mailing Address: P.O. Box 207, Caguas, PR 0726 US
Second Address: Tomas de Castro #2, Caguas, PR 626
(787) 743-5790, *Fax:* (787) 746-6996
dimension103.com
License: Caguas, PR
Arbitron Metro Market: Caguas, PR *Format:* Classic Rock, Tejano
Ranny Parks, General Manager
Debra Toler, General Sales Mgr
Jeff Halsey, Programming Director

Camuy

WDIN
08-15-1968; 102.9 mhz FM; 50 kw; 1053 ft.; N18 17 27 W66 39 39
Box 780, Camuy, PR 0627 US
(787) 743-5790, *Fax:* (787) 746-6996
www.dimension.fm
License: Camuy, PR held by HQ 103 Inc.
Arbitron Metro Market: Puerto Rico *Format:* Urban Contemporary
Bienvenido Rodriguez, General Manager
Maggie Lopez, Programming Director

Canovanas

WGIT
01-01-2001; 1660 khz AM
2001 Penn. Ave., NW, Ste 400 Frm, Washington, DC 20006 US
(787) 776-1616, *Fax:* (787) 281-9758
License: Canovanas, PR held by International Broadcasting Corp.
Group Owner: International Broadcasting Corp.; acq 5-29-03; $1.3 million).
Format: Sports
Pedro Roman-Collazo, General Manager
Margarita Nazario, Station Manager

Carolina

WIDA
03-16-1964; 1400 khz AM; 1 kw-U, ND1; N18 23 49 W65 56 6
Mailing Address: P.O. Box 188, Carolina, PR 0928 US
Second Address: Ignacio Arzuaga 203-7, Carolina, PR 987
(787) 757-1414, *Fax:* (787) 769-4103
www.cadenaradiovida.com
radiovida@cadenaradiovida.com
License: Carolina, PR held by Radio Vida Inc.
Arbitron Metro Market: Puerto Rico
Yexica Rosario, President
Wanda Pagan, Operations Dir
Hilda Dumont, General Sales Mgr
Alberto Periera, Chief Engineer

***WIDA-FM**
08-01-1983; 90.5 mhz FM; 25 kw; 1900 ft.; N18 6 48 W66 3 7
Mailing Address: Calle Arzuaga Number 203, Apartado 188, Carolina, PR 0630 US
Second Address: Ignacio Arzuaga 203-7, Carolina, PR 987
(787) 757-1414, *Fax:* (787) 769-4103
www.cadenaradiovida.com
radiovida@cadenaradiovida.com
License: Carolina, PR held by Radio Vida Inc.
Arbitron Metro Market: Puerto Rico
Yexika Rosario, President
Wanda Pagan, Operations Dir
Alberto Pereira, Engineering Dir
Hilda Dumont, Tesorera Junta

WVOZ-FM
03-03-1967; 107.7 mhz FM; 12 kw; 2759 ft.; N18 18 36 W65 47 41
#1554 Bori Street, Antonsanti Development, Rio Pedras, PR 0928 US
(787) 274-1800, *Fax:* (787) 281-9758
www.mix107.fm
License: Carolina, PR held by International Broadcasting Corp.
Group Owner: International Broadcasting Corp.
Arbitron Metro Market: Puerto Rico *Format:* Adult Contemp
Pedro Roman-Collazo, President
Margarita Nazario, General Manager

Cayey

WLEY
12-03-1965; 1080 khz AM *Hrs Open:* 19; 0.25 kw-U, ND1; N18 6 55 W66 8 28 *Rebroadcasts:* WSKN 1320 Radio Isla
G.P.O. Box 7213, Ponce, PR 0731 US

(787) 292-1700, *Fax:* (787) 292-1717
www.laley1079.com
noticias@radioisla1320.com
License: Cayey, PR held by Media Power Group Inc.
Group Owner: Media Power Group Inc.; (acq 9-30-2003; grpsl).
Nat'l Network: CNN Radio
Arbitron Metro Market: Puerto Rico *Format:* News, Talk *Hrs. of News Programming:* 24 hrs wkly *No. News Employees:* 40 *Target Audience:* 35 plus.
Eduardo Rivero, President
Ismael Nieves, Operations Dir
Nora Plaza, General Sales Mgr
Luis Penchi, Programming Director
Fernando Vazquez, Promotions Manager
Orlando Morales, Operations Manager

Ceiba

WFAB
01-01-1993; 890 khz AM; 0.25 kw-U, ND1; N18 12 16 W65 42 40
Apartado 318, Rio Blanco, PR 0744 US
(787) 874-0890, *Fax:* (787) 874-0190
www.radiounidadcristiana.com
wfab@osnetpr.com
License: Ceiba, PR held by Daniel Rosario Diaz.
Arbitron Metro Market: Ceiba, PR *Format:* Religious
Daniel Diaz, President
Jose Garcia, Administrative Officer

Cidra

WNVM
03-01-1972; 97.7 mhz FM *Hrs Open:* 24; 3 kw; 1093 ft.; N18 16 49.27 W66 6 35.3
P.O. Box 364701, San Juan, PR 0936 US
(787) 745-9700(787) 745-9770, *Fax:* (787) 745-9777
www.nuevavidafm.net
nuevavida@nuevavidafm.net
License: Cidra, PR held by New Life Broadcasting Inc.
Arbitron Metro Market: Caguas, PR *Format:* Christian *Hrs. of News Programming:* news progmg one hr wkly *No. News Employees:* 1 *Target Audience:* 25-54; women
Juan Matos, President
Orlando Mercado, General Manager

Coamo

WCPR
01-01-1967; 1450 khz AM *Hrs Open:* 16; 1 kw-U, ND1; N18 5 29 W66 22 15
P. O. Box 316, Coamo, PR 0640 US
(787) 825-7061, *Fax:* (787) 825-1905
License: Coamo, PR held by Coamo Broadcasting Corp.
Arbitron Metro Market: Puerto Rico PR *Format:* Adult Contemp *Hrs. of News Programming:* News progmg 9 hrs wkly *Target Audience:* General.
Jose David Soler, President

Corozal

WORO
07-01-1968; 92.5 mhz FM; 50 kw; 1198 ft.; N18 15 9 W66 19 58
Mailing Address: P.O. Box 9021967, San Juan, PR 0902 US
Second Address: Box 9021967, San Juan, PR 902
(787) 751-1380, *Fax:* (787) 758-9967
License: Corozal, PR held by Catholic Apostolic & Roman Church San Juan Archdiocese.
Arbitron Metro Market: Puerto Rico *TV Affiliate:* Sp
Chief of Engineering

Culebra

***WJVP**
01-01-1998; 89.3 mhz FM; 50 kw vert; 571 ft.; N18 19 37 W65 18 21
Mailing Address: P.O. Box 40,000, Bayamon, PR 0958 US
Second Address: An 167 Calle Granada AM Alahambra, Bayamon, PR 956
(787) 288-4336, *Fax:* (787) 740-7104
www.clamorpr.org
License: Culebra, Culebra County, PR held by Clamor Broadcasting Network Inc.
Arbitron Metro Market: Puerto Rico *Format:* Religious
Jorde Raschke, General Manager

WNVE
12-01-1996; 102.1 mhz FM *Hrs Open:* 24; 6 kw; 584 ft.; N18 19 19 W65 17 59
P.O. Box 847, Mayaguez, PR 0681 US
(787) 860-1065, *Fax:* (787) 860-1055
License: Culebra, PR held by Western New Life Inc
Arbitron Metro Market: Culebra, PR *Format:* Christian *No. News Employees:* 4 *Target Audience:* 25-54. *Adv. Rates:* 20; 17; 20; 14
Aureo Matos, General Manager

Fajardo

WRXD
02-15-1969; 96.5 mhz FM *Hrs Open:* 24; 11.5 kw; 2795 ft.; N18 18 36 W65 47 41
Mailing Address: 3191 Coral Way, Suite 805, Miami, FL 33145 US
Second Address: Amelia Industrial Park, Calle Frances #42, Guaynabo, PR 968
(787) 622-9700, *Fax:* (787) 622-9478
www.spanishbroadcastingsystem.com
License: Fajardo, PR held by WCMA Licensing Inc.
Group Owner: Spanish Broadcasting System Inc.; (acq 8-4-98; $8.25 million)
Arbitron Metro Market: Fajardo, PR *Format:* News
Falex Bonnet, General Manager

WMDD
05-31-1947; 1480 khz AM *Hrs Open:* 24; 5 kw-U, ND1; N18 21 46 W65 38 24
Puerta-Tierra, 306 Ponce Delon Avenue, San Juan, PR 0906 US
(787) 863-0202, *Fax:* (787) 863-0166
License: Fajardo, PR held by Pan Caribbean Broadcasting de P.R. Inc.
Arbitron Metro Market: Puerto Rico *Format:* Talk *Target Audience:* 25-49.
Rita Friedman, President

Guayama

***WCRP**
01-01-1991; 88.1 mhz FM; 27 kw; 1890 ft.; N18 6 47 W66 3 8
P.O. Box 344, Guayama, PR 0655 US
(787) 653-0880, *Fax:* (787) 653-1988
www.revelacion.fm
License: Guayama, PR held by Ministerio Radial Cristo Viene Pronto Inc.
Arbitron Metro Market: Puerto Rico *Format:* Religious
Carmita Rodriguez, President

WIBS
03-01-1981; 1540 khz AM; 1 kw-D, NDD; N17 59 44 W66 4 39
Box 1540, Guayama, PR 0655 US
(787) 274-1800, *Fax:* (787) 281-9758
License: Guayama, PR held by International Broadcasting Corp.
Group Owner: International Broadcasting Corp.; acq 12-3-01; $300,000).
Arbitron Metro Market: Puerto Rico
Pedro Roman-Collazo, CEO
Margarita Nazario, General Manager

WMEG
11-01-1966; 106.9 mhz FM; 24.5 kw; 1949 ft.; N18 6 48 W66 3 7
Mailing Address: 3191 Coral Way, Suite 805, Miami, FL 33145 US
Second Address: Amelia Industrial Park, Calle Frances 42, Guaynabo, PR 968
(787) 622-9700, *Fax:* (787) 622-9478
www.lamega.fm
info@broadcastingsystem.com
License: Guayama, PR held by WMEG Licensing Inc.
Group Owner: Spanish Broadcasting System Inc.; (acq 3-15-99; $16 million with WZET(FM) Hormigueros).
Arbitron Metro Market: Puerto Rico *Format:* Christian
Falex Bonnet, General Manager
Edgardo Aubray, General Sales Mgr

WXRF
07-01-1948; 1590 khz AM; 1 kw-U, ND1; N17 57 40 W66 8 20
1554 Bori St. Antonsanti Dev., San Juan, PR 0928 US
(787) 274-1800, *Fax:* (787) 281-9758
License: Guayama, PR held by International Broadcasting Corp.
Group Owner: International Broadcasting Corp.; (acq 10-7-2004; $1,382,961 with WVEO(TV) Aguadilla).
Arbitron Metro Market: Guayama, PR *Format:* Spanish
Pedro Roman-Collazo, President
Margarita Nazario, General Manager

Guayanilla

WOIZ
10-01-1986; 1130 khz AM; 0.2 kw-D, ND1; 0.7 kw-N, ND1; N18 1 3 W66 46 22
Mailing Address: Box 3800, Guayanilla, PR 0656 US
Second Address: 383 Road klmo.4, Bo Magas Arriba, Guayanilla, PR 656
787-835-3130, *Fax:* (787) 835-3130
www.radioantillas.4t.com
radioantillas@yahoo.com
License: Guayanilla, PR held by Radio Antillas of Harriet Broadcasters.
Arbitron Metro Market: Puerto Rico *TV Affiliate:* Sp *No. News Employees:* 35 plus. *Adv. Rates:* 12; 12; 12; 12

Hatillo

WMSW
01-01-1980; 1120 khz AM; 2.6 kw-D, DAN; 5 kw-N, DAN; N18 28 15 W66 50 24
Box 1652, Arecibo, PR 0613 US
(787) 879-4094, *Fax:* (787) 880-0441
www.radioonce.com
mss64radio@gmail.com
License: Hatillo, PR held by Aurora Broadcasting Corp.
Arbitron Metro Market: Puerto Rico *Format:* News, News/Talk, 86
Manuel Santos, President
Hector Santos, Operations Dir
Lloyd Santos, General Sales Mgr
Ronald Cushing, Chief Engineer

Hormigueros

WZET
10-12-1980; 92.1 mhz FM; 2.95 kw; 1106 ft.; N18 19 6 W67 10 42
Mailing Address: 3191 Coral Way, Suite 805, Miami, FL 33145 US
Second Address: Amelia Industrial Park, Calle Frances 42, Guaynabo, PR 968
(787) 622-9700, *Fax:* (787) 622-9478
www.spanishbroadcastingsystem.com
info@spanishbroadcastingsystem.com
License: Hormigueros, PR held by WSMA Licensing Inc.
Group Owner: Spanish Broadcasting System Inc.; (acq 3-15-99; $16 million with WMEG(FM) Guayama).
Arbitron Metro Market: Hormigueros, PR
Falex Bonnet, General Manager

WRRH
01-01-1998; 106.1 mhz FM; 0.8 kw horiz, 0.71 kw vert; 1932 ft.; N18 8 33 W66 58 56
P. O. Box 174, Lajas, PR 0667 US
(787) 849-1061, *Fax:* (787) 849-6106
www.renacer1061.com
renacer1061@yahoo.com
License: Hormigueros, PR held by Renacer Broadcasters Corp.
Arbitron Metro Market: Puerto Rico *Format:* Christian
Larry Ramos, General Manager
Kehmuel Ramos, Programming Director

Humacao

WALO
02-11-1958; 1240 khz AM *Hrs Open:* 19; 1 kw-U, ND1; N18 8 49 W65 48 49
Call Box 1240, Humacao, PR 0792 US
(787) 725-8265, *Fax:* (787) 852-1280
www.waloradio.com
wlo@prtc.net
License: Humacao, PR held by Ochoa Broadcasting Corp.
Wire Services: CNN
Arbitron Metro Market: Humacao, PR *Format:* Adult Contemp, News, 62, Sports, Talk *Special Programming:* Relg 2 hrs wkly *Hrs. of News Programming:* news progmg 60 hrs wkly *No. News Employees:* 2 *TargetAudience:* 18-54; general *Adv. Rates:* 42; 42; 42; 45
Efrain Archilla-Roig, CEO
Maribel Ortiz-Del Valle, Operations Dir
Beatriz Archilla, General Manager
Ken Allen, General Sales Mgr

Isabela

WISA
10-19-1961; 1390 khz AM; 1 kw-U, ND1; N18 30 6 W67 2 1
P.O. Box 9023916, San Juan, PR 0902 US
(787) 872-0100, *Fax:* (787) 872-0802
www.wisa1390.com
License: Isabela, PR held by Isabela Broadcasting Inc.
Arbitron Metro Market: Puerto Rico *Format:* Adult Contemp
David Marda, General Manager
Edwin Nieves, Programming Director

WELX
01-01-1987; 101.5 mhz FM; 42 kw; Ant -26 ft; N18 26 36 W67 08 50
Box 9023916, San Juan, PR 0902

(787) 620-9898
www.sistema102.com
License: Isabela, PR held by Isabela Broadcasting Inc.
Arbitron Metro Market: Puerto Rico
Luis Mejia, CEO

Island of Vieques

WIVV

12-08-1956; 1370 khz AM *Hrs Open:* 24; 5 kw-D, ND1; 1 kw-N, ND1; N18 6 7 W65 28 21 *Rebroadcasts:* Rebroadcasting WBMJ(AM) San Juan 100%
P.O. Box 367000, San Juan, PR 0936 US
(787) 724-1190, *Fax:* (787) 722-5395
radio@vrockradio.org
License: Island of Vieques, PR held by Calvary Evangelistic Mission Inc.
Group Owner: Calvary Evangelistic Mission Inc.
Nat'l Network: Salem Radio Network
Arbitron Metro Market: Puerto Rico *Format:* Adult Contemp, Talk, 74 *Special Programming:* News 7 hrs wkly *Hrs. of News Programming:* News progmg 7 hrs wkly *Target Audience:* General; eastern Puerto Rico & theLeeward Islands
Janet Luttrell, CEO

Juana Diaz

WCGB

11-23-1967; 1060 khz AM *Hrs Open:* 5 AM-midnight
Mailing Address: P. O. Box 9405, Grand Rapids, MN 49509 US
Second Address: Carretera Hwy. 1, KM 112.0, Juana Diaz, PR 795
(787) 837-1060, *Fax:* (787) 260-1060
www.therockradio.org
wcgb@therockradio.org
License: Juana Diaz, PR held by Calvary Evangelistic Mission Inc.
Group Owner: Calvary Evangelistic Mission Inc.; (acq 12-3-2004; $500,000)
Arbitron Metro Market: Juana Diaz,PR *Format:* Variety/Diverse, Religious *Hrs. of News Programming:* News progmg 10 hrs wkly *Target Audience:* Adult. *Adv. Rates:* 264; 192; 264; 120
Lawrence Trumbower, General Manager

Juncos

WRRE

01-01-1971; 1460 khz AM *Hrs Open:* 24
P.O. Box 827, Carolina, PR 0986 US
(787) 561-1460,(888) 561-1460, *Fax:* (787) 716-0808
www.sonidosantidad.com
sonidosantidad@hotmail.com
License: Juncos, PR held by Hacienda San Eladio Inc.
Arbitron Metro Market: Puerto Rico *Format:* Religious *Target Audience:* All.
Miguel A. Medina, General Manager

Lajas

WBSG

01-01-1986; 1510 khz AM *Hrs Open:* 16; 1 kw-U, DA1; N18 2 11 W67 4 58
Las Torres Sur Ste 10e, Bayamon, PR 0619 US
License: Lajas, PR held by Perry Broadcasting Systems

WXLX

01-05-1994; 103.7 mhz FM *Hrs Open:* 24; 50 kw; 456 ft; N17 59 37 W67 11 09 *Rebroadcasts:* Rebroadcasts WXYX(FM) Bayamon 100%
HC 67, Bayamon, PR 0956
(787) 255-2325, *Fax:* (787) 785-9377
License: Lajas, PR held by Radio X Broadcasting Corp.
Group Owner: RAAD Broadcasting Corp; (acq 1-20-98; $3 million)
Population Served: 600,000 *Arbitron Metro Market:* Puerto Rico
Roberto Davila, President
Roberto Davila Rios, Operations Dir
Carlos Alvarez, General Sales Mgr
Herman Davila, Programming Director
Wendy Armando, Promotions Manager
Alfredo Gomez, Chief Engineer

Lares

WGDL

02-01-1983; 1200 khz AM *Hrs Open:* 12; 0.25 kw-D, NDD; N18 17 40 W66 53 50
P.O. Box 872, Lares, PR 0669 US
(787) 897-1200, *Fax:* (787) 897-7821
wgdl1200@yahoo.com
License: Lares, PR held by Lares Broadcasting Corp.

Arbitron Metro Market: Puerto Rico *Hrs. of News Programming:* news progmg 20 hrs wkly *No. News Employees:* 1 *Target Audience:* General.
Pedro Hernandez, President
Julia Bello, General Manager
Angel Perez, Programming Director

Levittown

*WLUZ

10-01-1986; 88.5 mhz FM; 100 w vert; Ant 69 ft; N18 26 55 W66 10 26
Box 371177, Cayey, PR 0958
(787) 798-8850, *Fax:* (787) 798-8851
www.plenitudfm.com
info@plenitudfm.com
License: Levittown, PR held by La Gigante Siembra Inc.
Arbitron Metro Market: Puerto Rico
Shay Garcya, Station Manager

Luquillo

WYAS

01-01-1976; 92.1 mhz FM *Hrs Open:* 24; 6.9 kw; Ant 915 ft; N18 19 54 W65 41 11
Box 29027, Rio Piedras, PR 0929
(787) 767-1005, *Fax:* (787) 758-1055
www.radiosol.org
wzol@radiosol.org
License: Luquillo, Luquillo County, PR held by Radio Sol 92, WZOL Inc.
Arbitron Metro Market: Puerto Rico
Pedro Canales, President
William Irizarry, General Manager
Maria Navarro, Programming Director
Raymond Hernandez, Chief Engineer

Manati

WMNT

12-01-1959; 1500 khz AM *Hrs Open:* 16; 1 kw-D, ND1; 0.25 kw-N, ND1; N18 26 6 W66 29 54
Mailing Address: Calle Delta #1305, Caparra Terrace, San Juan, PR 0920 US
Second Address: Delta St. #1305 Caparra Terr., San Juan, PR 920
(787) 854-2223, *Fax:* (787) 781-7647
www.radioatenas.com
info@radioatenas.com
License: Manati, PR held by Manati Radio Corp.
Arbitron Metro Market: Manati, PR *Format:* News, News/Talk, 84, Talk *Special Programming:* NBA, World Series in Sp *Hrs. of News Programming:* news progmg 25 hrs wkly *No. News Employees:* 2 *Target Audience:* 25 plus; men & women *Adv. Rates:* 20; 20; 20; 10
Jose Dominicci, CEO
Jose Ribas-Dominicci, President
Freddy Ribas, Operations Dir
Maria Rodriguez, Station Manager

WNRT

01-01-1973; 96.9 mhz FM *Hrs Open:* 24 hours; 50 kw; 1125 ft.; N18 15 34 W66 32 15
PO Box 13324, Santurce, PR 0908 US
(787) 999-0360, *Fax:* (787) 999-1560
www.triunfofm.net
License: Manati, PR held by La Voz Evangelica de Puerto Rico Inc.
Arbitron Metro Market: Puerto Rico *Format:* Christian
Luis Barajas, President
Moises Flores, Operations Dir
Mosses Flores, General Manager
Carlos Flecha, Programming Director
Jorge Figueroa, Engineering Dir
Virgen Perez, Sales VP

Maricao

WAEL-FM

07-01-1970; 96.1 mhz FM *Hrs Open:* 24; 24 kw; 2011 ft.; N18 9 7 W66 59 15
Mailing Address: P.O. Box 1370, Mayaguez, PR 0681 US
Second Address: 600 Ramirez Pabon St., Guanajibo Homes, Mayaguez, PR 681
(787) 832-4560/ 832-0600, *Fax:* (787) 792-3140
www.waelfm96.com
waeline@prte.net
License: Maricao, PR held by WAEL Inc.
Arbitron Metro Market: Puerto Rico *Format:* Spanish, Christian *Target Audience:* 12-24.
Maria del Pilar-Pirallo, President
Luis Pirallo, Operations Dir

Lydia Vargas, News Director
Ivan Feliu, Chief Engineer

Mayaguez

WYEL

01-01-1949; 600 khz AM *Hrs Open:* 4:30 AM-midnight; 5 kw-D, DA1; 5 kw-N, DA1; N18 10 39 W67 10 15
Mailing Address: P.O. Box 1370, Mayaguez, PR 0681 US
Second Address: 600 Ramirez Pabon , Guanajibo Homes, Mayaguez, PR 680
(662) 844-8888, *Fax:* (662) 842-6791
www.afr.net
comments@afr.net
License: Mayaguez, PR held by Univision Radio Puerto Rico Inc.
Group Owner: Univision Radio; (acq 11-17-2006; $2 million)
Arbitron Metro Market: Sacramento CA *Format:* Religious
Marvin Sanders, General Manager

WIOB

10-12-1947; 97.5 mhz FM; 50 kw; 991 ft.; N18 19 33 W67 10 13
Rebroadcasts: Rebroadcasts WIOA(FM) San Juan 80%
Mailing Address: P.O. Box 101, San Juan, PR 0970 US
Second Address: Amelia Industrial Park, Calle Frances 42, Guaynabo, PR 968
(787) 622-9700, *Fax:* (787) 622-9478
www.spanishbroadcastingsystem.com
info@spanishbroadcastingsystem.com
License: Mayaguez, PR held by Cadena Estereotempo Inc.
Group Owner: Spanish Broadcasting System Inc.; (acq 11-29-99; grpsl)
Arbitron Metro Market: Puerto Rico *Format:* Spanish *Target Audience:* 30-50; women *Adv. Rates:* 25; 20; 25; 18
Falex Bonnet, General Manager

WKJB

12-06-1946; 710 khz AM; 10 kw-D, ND1; 0.75 kw-N, ND1; N18 10 8 W67 9 3
P. O. Box 1293, Mayaguez, PR 0681 US
(787) 834-6666, *Fax:* (787) 831-6925
License: Mayaguez, PR held by WKJB-AM Inc.
Arbitron Metro Market: Puerto Rico *Format:* News, News/Talk, 86 *Special Programming:* Sp 1 hr wkly
Dennis Bechara, President
Ada Ramos, General Sales Mgr
Eric Graniela, Programming Director
Rafy Aviles, News Director
Pedro Velez Jr., Chief Engineer
Jose Bechara Jr., Executive Vice President
Johhny Flores, SportsCommentators

WORA

05-12-1947; 760 khz AM; 5 kw-U, DA1; N18 11 30 W67 9 28
Calle Eleanor Roosevelt, #117, Hato Rey, PR 0918 US
(787) 758-1300, *Fax:* (787) 751-2319
www.notiuno.com
noticias@notiuno.com
License: Mayaguez, PR held by Arso Radio Corp.
Group Owner: Uno Radio Group; (acq 5-10-01; grpsl).
Arbitron Metro Market: Puerto Rico *TV Affiliate:* News

WNOD

01-01-1960; 94.1 mhz FM *Hrs Open:* 24; 25 kw; 1959 ft.; N18 9 5 W66 59 20 *Rebroadcasts:* Rebroadcasts WCOM(FM) San Juan 80%
Post Office Box 1718, Mayaguez, PR 0681 US
(787) 265-9494, *Fax:* (787) 622-9481
www.lamega.fm
License: Mayaguez, PR held by WOYE Inc.
Group Owner: Spanish Broadcasting System Inc.; (acq 11-29-99; grpsl).
Arbitron Metro Market: Puerto Rico *Format:* Contemporary Hits/Top 40 *Hrs. of News Programming:* news progmg 10 hrs wkly *No. News Employees:* 1 *Target Audience:* 18-49; young adults *Adv. Rates:* 30; 25; 30;20
Raul Alarcon, Chairman
Ismael Nieves, General Manager
Marie Martinez, General Sales Mgr
Pedro Arroyo, Programming Director
Luis Rivera, Promotions Manager
Demare Ramirez, News Director
Alejandro Luciano, Chief Engineer

WPRA

10-16-1937; 990 khz AM *Hrs Open:* 18; 0.91 kw-U, ND1; N18 10 8 W67 9 3
P.O. Box 1293, Mayaguez, PR 0681 US
(787) 834-6666, *Fax:* (787) 831-6925
License: Mayaguez, PR held by WPRA Inc.
Nat'l Network: AP Radio

Arbitron Metro Market: Puerto Rico *Format:* Contemporary Hits/Top 40, Talk *Target Audience:* General. *Adv. Rates:* 16; 16; 16; 16
Dennis Bechara, President
Jose Bechara, Operations Dir

*WRUO
12-01-1998; 88.3 mhz FM; 2 kw; 1004 ft.; N18 19 31 W67 10 13
P O Box 21305 Upr, San Juan, PR 0931 US
(787) 763-4699, *Fax:* (787) 764-1290
www.wrtu.PR
lluna@wrtu.pr
License: Mayaguez, PR held by University of Puerto Rico.
Arbitron Metro Market: Puerto Rico
Ezequiel Rodrguez, Operations Dir
Yolanda Zabala, General Manager
Carlos Camuas, Programming Director

WTIL
11-01-1950; 1300 khz AM; 1 kw-U, ND1; N18 11 0 W67 10 4
Mailing Address: Calle Post Esquina Bosqu, Mayaguez, PR 0681 US
Second Address: Post & Bosque Sts., Mayaguez, PR 680
(787) 832-1300, *Fax:* (787) 265-1300
www.radioutil.net
radioutil@gmail.commatos1040@gmail.com
License: Mayaguez, PR held by International Broadcasting Corp.
Group Owner: International Broadcasting Corp.; acq 5-12-2004; $700,000).
Arbitron Metro Market: Mayaguez, PR *Format:* Adult Contemp, Oldies, 86 *Target Audience:* 35 plus.
Lynette Matos, Dept.Sales and Programming
Jason Matos, Dept.Accounting

WUKQ-FM
01-15-1963; 99.1 mhz FM; 25 kw; 1972 ft.; N18 9 5 W66 59 19
P.O. Box 364668, San Juan, PR 0936 US
(787) 758-5800, *Fax:* (787) 763-1854
kq105.univision.com
ncordova@univisionradio.com
License: Mayaguez, PR held by El Mundo Broadcasting Corp.
Group Owner: Univision Radio; (acq 8-1-2003; grpsl).
Arbitron Metro Market: San Juan, PR *Format:* Contemporary Hits/Top 40 *Special Programming:* Jazz 6 hrs wkly
Jaime Bauza, CEO
Reynaldo Quinones, General Sales Mgr
Carlos Gonzalez, Programming Director
Aracelis Cruz, Promotions Manager
Luis Garcia, Sales Manager

Moca

WZNA
12-01-1983; 1040 khz AM
P.O. Box 7, Moca, PR 0676 US
(787) 745-9770, *Fax:* (787) 745-9777
www.nuevavidafm.com
nuevavuda@nuevavidafm.com
License: Moca, PR held by Western New Life Inc.
Arbitron Metro Market: Moca, PR *Format:* Christian
Juan Carlos Barreto, President
Orlando Mercede, General Manager

Morovis

WEKO
12-01-1981; 1580 khz AM; 5 kw-D, DAD; 2.5 kw-N, DAD; N18 20 32 W66 25 8
1554 Bori St. Caribe Dev., San Juan, PR 0927 US
(787) 864-2460, *Fax:* (787) 281-9758
License: Morovis, PR held by International Broadcasting Corp.
Group Owner: International Broadcasting Corp.; acq 9-29-98; $315,000).
Arbitron Metro Market: Puerto Rico *Format:* News *Target Audience:* 30 plus.
Pedro Roman-Collazo, President
Margarita Nazario, General Manager

Naguabo

WYQE
12-01-1994; 92.9 mhz FM *Hrs Open:* 24; 3.9 kw; 751 ft.; N18 16 50 W65 40 13
Mailing Address: Box 9300, Naguabo, PR 0718 US
Second Address: Apt. 2-A, Naguabo, PR 718
(809) 847-9300, *Fax:* (809) 874-9290
www.yunque93.com
wyqe@yunque93.com
License: Naguabo, Humacao County, PR held by Fajardo Broadcasting Co. Inc.
Arbitron Metro Market: Puerto Rico *Format:* Spanish *Hrs. of News Programming:* news progmg 20 hrs wkly *No. News Employees:* 2 *Target Audience:* 18 plus; general *Adv. Rates:* 44; 44; 44; 44
Efrain Archilla-Diez, President
Raul Rivera, Operations Dir
Edwin Glass, General Sales Mgr
Vanessa Jimenez, National Sales Manager

Pastillo

*WJDZ
01-01-2006; 90.1 mhz FM; 0.9 kw; -181 ft.; N17 59 57 W66 27 29
P.O. Box 8072, Ponce, PR 0732 US

www.somosfamilia.net
License: Pastillo, Santa Isabel County, PR held by Siembra Fertil P.R. Inc.
Arbitron Metro Market: Pastillo, PR *Format:* Christian, Spanish
Susanne Meyers, General Manager
Bill Phipps, Programming Director

Patillas

WEXS
01-01-1991; 610 khz AM *Hrs Open:* 5:30 AM-10 PM; 0.25 kw-D, ND2; 1 kw-N, ND2; N18 0 36 W66 1 28
P.O. Box 640, Patillas, PR 0723 US
(787) 839-0610, *Fax:* (787) 839-0960
www.leonespatillas.com
License: Patillas, PR held by Community Broadcasting Inc.
Arbitron Metro Market: Patillas, PR *Format:* Adult Contemp, News *Special Programming:* Relg 2 hrs, sports 6 hrs wkly *Target Audience:* 18-55.
Enrique Garcia, General Manager

Penuelas

WPPC
05-25-1976; 1570 khz AM *Hrs Open:* 12; 1 kw-D, ND1; 0.126 kw-N, ND1; N18 3 47 W66 43 4
P. O. Box 9064, Ponce, PR 0732 US
(809) 836-1570,(809) 848-4670, *Fax:* (787) 848-4670
www.wppc1570am.org
radiofelicidad@yahoo.com
License: Penuelas, PR held by Radio Felicidad Inc.
Arbitron Metro Market: Puerto Rico *Format:* Adult Contemp, Religious *Target Audience:* General. *Adv. Rates:* 4; 4; 4; N/A
Julio Valazquez, President
Rafael Acosta, Chief Engineer

Ponce

WUKQ
05-01-1957; 1420 khz AM *Hrs Open:* 24; 1 kw-U, ND1; N17 59 23 W66 37 21 *Rebroadcasts:* Rebroadcasts WKAQ(AM) San Juan 99%
2250 Las Americas Avenue, Suite 529, Ponce, PR 0731 US
(787) 758-5800, *Fax:* (787) 763-1854
www.univision.com
License: Ponce, PR held by El Mundo Broadcasting Corp.
Group Owner: Univision Radio; (acq 8-1-2003; grpsl).
Arbitron Metro Market: Ponce, PR *Format:* News, News/Talk, 86 *Target Audience:* 25-55; young professionals, retirees, middle & upper income
Jaime Bauza, General Manager

*WPUC-FM
05-17-1984; 88.9 mhz FM *Hrs Open:* 4 AM-midnight; 11 kw; 2913 ft.; N18 10 27 W66 35 32
2250 Las Americas Avenue, Ste 529, Ponce, PR 0731 US
(787) 844-8809, *Fax:* (787) 651-2022
www.catolicaradiopr.com
info@catolicaradiopr.com
License: Ponce, Ponce County, PR held by Pontifical Catholic University of Puerto Rico Service Association Inc.
Arbitron Metro Market: Ponce, PR *Format:* Adult Contemp *Hrs. of News Programming:* news progmg 30 hrs wkly *No. News Employees:* 2 *Target Audience:* 25-39/40-45; professional young adults, retirees-middle & upperclass
Julio Ramirez, General Manager
Jose Leon, Station Manager
Ediel Montalvo, Programming Director
Rolando Mendez, Promotions Manager
King Moreira, Chief Engineer
Jose ""Jossie"" Tizol, Shift Control Supervisor
Orsini Texeira Betzy,Administrative Officer
Marisel Salazar, Production
Jose ""Pepn"" Fernndez, Reporter
Luis R. Varela, Reporter - Sports

WIOC
01-01-1970; 105.1 mhz FM *Hrs Open:* 24; 47 kw; -200 ft.; N17 59 27 W66 37 45 *Rebroadcasts:* Rebroadcasts WIOA(FM) San Juan 80%
Mailing Address: P.O. Box 1718, Mayaguez, PR 0681 US
Second Address: Amelia Industrial Park, Calle Frances 42, Guaynabo, PR 978
(787) 622-9700, *Fax:* (787) 622-9478
www.lamega.fm
info@lamega.fm
License: Ponce, PR held by Cadena Estereotempo Inc.
Group Owner: Spanish Broadcasting System Inc.; (acq 11-29-99; grpsl)
Arbitron Metro Market: Puerto Rico *Format:* Adult Contemp *Hrs. of News Programming:* news progmg one hr wkly *No. News Employees:* 1 *Target Audience:* 30-50; women *Adv. Rates:* 25; 20; 25; 18
Raul Alarcon, President
Ismael Nieves, General Manager
Marie Martinez, General Sales Mgr
Pedro Arroyo, Programming Director
Luis Rivera, Promotions Manager
Demare Ramirez, News Director
Alejandro Luciano, Chief Engineer

WISO
09-15-1953; 1260 khz AM *Hrs Open:* 16
155 San Antonio St., Floral Park, Hato Rey, PR 0917 US
(787) 763-1066, *Fax:* (787) 763-4195
www.waparadio.net
jblanco25@hotmail.com
License: Ponce, PR held by Wilfredo G. Blanco Pi.
Arbitron Metro Market: Puerto Rico *Format:* News, News/Talk, 86 *Hrs. of News Programming:* News progmg 26 hrs wkly *Target Audience:* Adults.
Wilfredo Blanco, President
Jorge Blanco, Operations Dir
Carmen Blanco, General Sales Mgr

WDEP
02-01-1973; 1490 khz AM *Hrs Open:* 24; 5 kw-D, ND2; 1 kw-N, ND2; N17 58 52 W66 36 51
Post Office Box 7213, Ponce, PR 0732 US
(787) 292-1700, *Fax:* (787) 292-1717
www.wdepradio.com
noticias@radioisla1320.com
License: Ponce, PR held by Media Power Group Inc.
Group Owner: Media Power Group Inc.; (acq 9-30-2003; grpsl).
Nat'l Network: CNN Radio
Arbitron Metro Market: Puerto Rico *Format:* News, News/Talk, 86 *Hrs. of News Programming:* News progmg 24 hrs wkly *Target Audience:* 35 plus.
Eduardo Rivero, President
Ismaez Nieves, Operations Dir
Nora Plaza, General Sales Mgr
Luis Penchi, Programming Director
Fernando Vazquez, Promotions Manager
Orlado Moraless, Operations Manager

WPAB
08-14-1940; 550 khz AM *Hrs Open:* 24
Mailing Address: P.O. Box 7243, Playa Ponce, PR 0732 US
Second Address: 1643 Ave. Eduardo Ruberte, Ponce, PR 716
(787) 840-5550, *Fax:* (787) 840-7077
License: Ponce, PR held by WPAB Inc.
Nat'l Network: CNN Radio *Regional Reps:* Sayda Ortiz *Wire Services:* AP
Arbitron Metro Market: Puerto Rico *Format:* News, News/Talk, 86 *Hrs. of News Programming:* news progmg 15 hrs wkly *No. News Employees:* 4 *Target Audience:* 25 plus; concerned adults *Adv. Rates:* 25; 25;20; 10
Alfonso Gimenez-Porrata, CEO
Alfonso Gimenez-Lucchetti, Operations Dir
Sayda Ortiz, General Sales Mgr
Maria Luisa Gimenez-Lucchetti, Vice President, Operations

WPRP
01-01-1936; 910 khz AM; 4.4 kw-D, ND2; 4.4 kw-N, ND2; N17 59 27 W66 37 48
Mailing Address: 117 Eleanor Roosevelt St, Hato Rey, PR 0918 US
Second Address: WLEO/WZAR Bldg., Sector Puerto Viejo, Paseo Sauri, Playa de Po, Ponce, PR 732
(787) 842-0048, *Fax:* (787) 840-0049
www.unoradio.com
jsantiago@unoradio.com
License: Ponce, PR held by Arso Radio Corp.
Group Owner: Uno Radio Group; (acq 5-8-01; grpsl).
Arbitron Metro Market: Puerto Rico *Format:* News, News/Talk, 86 *Target Audience:* 35 plus. *Adv. Rates:* 24; 18; 18; 10

Jose Santiago, General Manager
Carlos Conesa, General Sales Mgr
Ray Cruz, Programming Director
Glerys Rivera, Promotions Manager
Oscar Vega, Engineering Dir

WRIO
01-01-1986; 101.1 mhz FM *Hrs Open:* 24; 50 kw; -46 ft.; N18 1 40 W66 39 14
P.O. Box 487, Caguas, PR 0726 US
(787) 842-0048, *Fax:* (787) 840-0049
www.salsoul.com,www.unoradio.com
License: Ponce, PR held by Arso Radio Corp.
Group Owner: Uno Radio Group
Arbitron Metro Market: Puerto Rico *Format:* Spanish *Adv. Rates:* 40; 25; 25; 20
Jose Santiago, General Manager
Vicente Veldodere, General Sales Mgr
Donny Cruz, Programming Director
Marianna Colon, News Director
Alberto Pereira, Chief Engineer
Vicente Bergodere, General Sales Manager

WZAR
03-17-1966; 101.9 mhz FM *Hrs Open:* 24; 14 kw; 2589 ft.; N18 9 15 W66 33 15
Mailing Address: Box 7213, Ponce, PR 0732 US
Second Address: 46 Sector Purto Viejo, Playa De Ponce, Ponce, PR 732
(787) 842-0048, *Fax:* (787) 840-0049
License: Ponce, PR
Arbitron Metro Market: Puerto Rico *Format:* Adult Contemp
Special Programming: Talk show 15 hrs wkly *Hrs. of News Programming:* News progmg 12 hrs wkly *Target Audience:* 18-49; blue & white collar, adults,professionals
Jose Juan Santiago, Operations Dir
Pedro Gonzales, Programming Director
Carmen Reyes, News Director
Rafael Acosta, Engineering Dir

WZMT
05-01-1969; 93.3 mhz FM *Hrs Open:* 20; 14.5 kw; -226 ft.; N17 59 26 W66 37 43 *Rebroadcasts:* Rebroadcasts WZNT(FM) San Juan 100%
Mailing Address: P.O. Box 7243, Ponce, PR 0732 US
Second Address: Amelia Industrial Park, Calle Frances 42, Guaynabo, PR 968
(787) 622-9700, *Fax:* (787) 622-9478
www.lamega.fm
rogie@sbspuertorico.com
License: Ponce, PR held by Potorican American Broadcasting Inc.
Group Owner: Spanish Broadcasting System Inc.; (acq 2000; grpsl)
Arbitron Metro Market: Ponce, PR *Format:* Spanish *Hrs. of News Programming:* news progmg 6 hrs wkly *No. News Employees:* 1 *Target Audience:* 18-49; affluent young adults
Raul Alarcon, President
Ismael Nieves, General Manager
Maria Martinez, General Sales Mgr
Rogie Gallart, Programming Director
Luis Rivera, Promotions Manager
Demare Ramirez, News Director
Alejandro Luciano, Chief Engineer
JoeMackay, National Sales Manager
Edgardo Aubray, Sales
Omar Rodriguez, Internet Web Manager

WLEO
11-03-1956; 1170 khz AM *Hrs Open:* 24
Mailing Address: Box 7213, Ponce, PR 0732 US
Second Address: WLEO/WZAR, 46 Sector Purto Viejo, Playa De Ponce, Ponce, PR 732
(787) 474-0630, *Fax:* (787) 758-1410
www.unoradio.com
ventasurg@unoradio.com
License: Ponce, PR held by Uno Radio of Ponce Inc.
Group Owner: Uno Radio Group; (acq 2-18-00; grpsl).
Arbitron Metro Market: San Juan, PR *Format:* Oldies *Special Programming:* Sports *Hrs. of News Programming:* news progmg 50 hrs wkly *No. News Employees:* 2 *Target Audience:* 25 plus; mature, blue-collar &professionals
Jose Juan Santiago, Station Manager
Carlos Conesa, General Sales Mgr
Ray Cruz, Programming Director
Oscar Vega, Chief Engineer
Jose Perez, Disc Jockey
Adam Asencio, Disc Jockey
Nathanael Paradiso, Disc Jockey
Luis Torres, NewsReporter
Carmen Reyes, Traffic Manager

Quebradillas

WDNO
02-01-1998; 960 khz AM; 1 kw-D, 1.7 kw-N, DA-2; N18 26 38 W66 57 43 *Rebroadcasts:* Rebroadcasts WZNA(AM) Moca 100%
Box 4039, Carolina, PR 0676
(787) 750-4090, *Fax:* (787) 750-6440
License: Quebradillas, PR held by International Broadcasting Corp.
Group Owner: International Broadcasting Corp.; (acq 7-6-2004; $1.45 million with WRSJ(AM) Bayamon).
Arbitron Metro Market: Puerto Rico
Luis Rosado, President
Josue Salgado, Programming Director

WIDI
11-17-1974; 98.3 mhz FM *Hrs Open:* 24; 3 kw; 1001 ft.; N18 23 33 W66 59 46
Box 980, Quebradillas, PR 0742 US
(787) 895-2725,(787) 895-0000, *Fax:* (787) 895-4198
www.magic973.com
magic973@prtc.net
License: Quebradillas, PR held by Jose J. Arzuaga.
Arbitron Metro Market: Puerto Rico *Format:* Oldies *Hrs. of News Programming:* News progmg 2 hrs wkly *Target Audience:* General.
Jose Arzuaga, President
Idalia Arzuaga, Operations Dir
Joshua Arzuaga, General Manager
Idalia Arrieta, Vice President, Operations

***WZCA**
91.7 mhz FM; 720 watts; -8 meters; 18 29 N16 66 56 W37
PO Box 980, Querbradillas, PR 0678

www.sacrafm.com
License: Quebradillas, PR

Rio Grande

WOYE
01-01-2003; 97.3 mhz FM; 0.8 kw; 1906 ft.; N18 16 46 W65 51 12
Avenue Ponce De Leon 760, Miramar, PR 0907 US
(787) 895-0000, *Fax:* (787) 895-4198
www.magic973.com
magic973@prtc.net
License: Rio Grande, Rio Grande County, PR held by Jose J. Arzuaga
Arbitron Metro Market: Quebradillas, PR *Format:* Oldies
Idalia Arzuaga, Operations Dir
Tommy Carrasquillo, General Manager
Eva Cordero, General Sales Mgr
Joshua Arzuaga, Programming Director
Rafael Brito, News Director
Jose Arzuaga, Engineering Dir
Arlene Perez, AdvertisingDirector
Nitza Mercado, Public Affairs Director
Roberto Toledo, Sales Director

Rio Piedras

WFID
11-17-1958; 95.7 mhz FM; 50 kw; 942 ft.; N18 16 0 W66 5 5
Mailing Address: 24th St. & Munoz Rivera Ave., Caguas, PR 0726 US
Second Address: 1581 Ponce DeLeon St., Rio Piedras, PR 926
(787) 773-7474, *Fax:* (787) 758-1410
www.unoradiogroup.com
ventasurg@unoradio.com
License: Rio Piedras, PR held by Madifide Inc.
Group Owner: Uno Radio Group; (acq 3-26-98; $11,537,500).
Nat'l Reps: McGavren Guild
Arbitron Metro Market: Rio Piedras, PR *Format:* Adult Contemp, Easy Listening *Target Audience:* 25-49; middle & upper income
Luis Soto, President
Jaime Soto, Programming Director
Tanya Ramos, Promotions Manager
Raymond Totti, Executive Vice President

Sabana

WJIT
03-31-2000; 1250 khz AM *Hrs Open:* 16
Mailing Address: P.O. Box 316, Coamo, PR 0769 US
Second Address: Road #2 km 30.5, Vega Alta, PR 769
(787) 449-9304, *Fax:* (787) 825-1905
License: Sabana, PR held by WJIT Broadcasting Corp.
Arbitron Metro Market: Puerto Rico *Format:* Variety/Diverse
Olga Fernandez, President
Jose Soler, Programming Director
Carlos Ortiz, News Director

Sabana Grande

WYKO
01-01-1990; 880 khz AM; 1 kw-D, ND1; 0.5 kw-N, ND1; N18 4 21 W66 57 6
34 Doctor Felix Tio St., Sabana Grande, PR 0637 US
, *Fax:* (787) 873-5795
License: Sabana Grande, PR held by Juan Galiano Rivera
Arbitron Metro Market: Sabana Grande, PR
Juan Rivera, President

Salinas

WHOY
04-06-1967; 1210 khz AM; 5 kw-D, DA2; 5 kw-N, DA2; N17 58 38 W66 18 14
Road 712 Km. 1.6, Salinas, PR 0751 US
(787) 824-3420, *Fax:* (787) 824-8054
whoyam@coquinet.com
License: Salinas, PR held by Colon Radio Corp.
Arbitron Metro Market: Puerto Rico
Martin Colon, General Manager
Rafael Pagan, Chief Engineer

San German

WEGM
02-01-1969; 95.1 mhz FM *Hrs Open:* 24; 25 kw; 1969 ft.; N18 8 55 W66 58 54
Mailing Address: P.O. Box 1718, Mayaguez, PR 0681 US
Second Address: Amelia Industrial Park, Calle Frances 42, Guaynabo, PR 968
(787) 622-9700, *Fax:* (787) 622-9478
www.lamega.fm
rogie@sbspuertorico.com
License: San German, PR held by WRPC Inc.
Group Owner: Spanish Broadcasting System Inc.; (acq 11-29-99; grpsl)
Arbitron Metro Market: Puerto Rico PR *Format:* Contemporary Hits/Top 40 *Target Audience:* 18-49; men
Raul Alarcon, President
Ismael Nieves, General Manager
Marie Martinez, General Sales Mgr
Pedro Arroyo, Programming Director
Luis Rivera, Promotions Manager
Demare Ramirez, News Director
Alejandro Luciano, Chief Engineer
RoqueGallart, Programming Director

WSOL
01-01-1955; 1090 khz AM; 0.25 kw-D, ND1; 0.73 kw-N, ND1; N18 4 44 W67 1 18
Box 5000, Suite 442, San German, PR 0683 US
(787) 892-2216,(787) 892-2975, *Fax:* (787) 264-1090
w1090sol@yahoo.com
License: San German, PR held by San German Broadcasters Group.
Arbitron Metro Market: Puerto Rico *Format:* News *Special Programming:* Farm 2 hrs wkly *Target Audience:* Adults.
Alfredo Cardona, President
Lucy Rivera, Operations Dir
Luz Maria Rivera, General Manager
Gloria Silva, Station Manager

***WNNV**
11-14-1996; 91.7 mhz FM *Hrs Open:* 24; 5 kw vert; 364 ft.; N18 4 8 W67 2 54
P.O. Box 847, Mayaguez, PR 0681 US
(787) 883-7100, *Fax:* (787) 833-7940
License: San German, San German County, PR held by Siembra Fertil P.R. Inc.
Arbitron Metro Market: Puerto Rico *Format:* Christian *Target Audience:* 25-49.
Miguel Marquez, Programming Director

San Juan

WAPA
01-15-1947; 680 khz AM
134 Domenech Ave, Hato Ray, PR 0918 US
(787) 759-9122, *Fax:* (787) 759-9122
www.waparadio.net
jblanco25@hotmail.com
License: San Juan, PR held by Wifredo G. Blanco Pi
Arbitron Metro Market: San Juan, PR *Format:* News, News/Talk, 86
Jorge Blanco, Operations Dir
Wilfredo Blanco, General Manager

WBMJ
07-19-1968; 1190 khz AM *Hrs Open:* 24; 10 kw-D, DA2; 5 kw-N, DA2; N18 21 0 W66 6 50
P.O. Box 367000, San Juan, PR 0936 US
(787) 724-1190, *Fax:* (787) 722-5395(787) 723-9633
www.therockradio.org/
radio@therockradio.org
License: San Juan, PR held by Calvary Evangelistic Mission Inc.
Group Owner: Calvary Evangelistic Mission Inc.; (acq 11-85).
Nat'l Network: Moody; USA; Salem Radio Network
Arbitron Metro Market: San Juan, PR *Format:* Adult Contemp, Talk, 74 *Hrs. of News Programming:* News progmg 7 hrs wkly
Target Audience: General; relg community of central Puerto Rico
Janet Luttrell, CEO
Janet Luttrell, President
Madeline Burgos, Operations Dir
Lawrence Trumbower, Chief Engineer
Nita Luttrell, VP
Judith Prez, Music Director

WCAD
03-05-1968; 105.7 mhz FM; 50 kw; 1099 ft.; N18 16 54 W66 6 46
Mailing Address: P.O. Box 9024188, San Juan, PR 0902 US
Second Address: 1667 Fernandez Juncos Ave., San Turce, PR 910
(787) 728-7280, *Fax:* (787) 268-3313
www.alfarock.com
alfa@alfarock.com
License: San Juan, PR held by Broadcasting & Programming Systems of Puerto Rico Inc.
Arbitron Metro Market: San Juan, PR *Format:* Rock/AOR
Ada Cox, Operations Dir
Ralph Perez, General Manager
Pedro Davila, Programming Director
T. Morales, Engineering Dir
Felipe Diaz, Sales Director

WIAC
01-01-1947; 740 khz AM *Hrs Open:* 24; 10 kw-U, DA1; N18 21 24 W66 14 5
PO Box 9023916, San Juan, PR 0902 US
(787) 620-9898, *Fax:* (787) 620-0730
www.radiopr740.com
tcarrasquillo@radiopr740.com
License: San Juan, PR held by Bestov Broadcasting Inc.
Arbitron Metro Market: Puerto Rico *Format:* News *Target Audience:* General.
Luis Mejia, President
Valerie Majia, Operations Dir
Luis Penchi, News Director
Rey Moraira, Chief Engineer
Johnny Men, Traffic Manager

WTOK-FM
03-01-1961; 102.5 mhz FM; 50 kw; Ant 1,139 ft; N18 25 25 W66 08 20
Box 9023916, San Juan, PR 0902
(787) 620-9898, *Fax:* (787) 620-0730
www.sistema102.com
losorio@sistem102.net
License: San Juan, PR held by MSG Radio Inc.
Arbitron Metro Market: Puerto Rico
Danny Gonzalez, Operations Dir
Glenn Valares, General Sales Mgr
Valerie Mejia, Programming Director

WIOA
03-01-1961; 99.9 mhz FM; 31 kw; 1837 ft.; N18 16 44 W65 51 12
Mailing Address: P.O. Box 949, Guaynabo, PR 0970 US
Second Address: Amelia Industrial Park, Calle Frances 42, Guaynabo, PR 968
(787) 622-9700, *Fax:* (787) 622-9478
www.lamega.fm
info@lamega.fm
License: San Juan, PR held by Cadena Estereotempo Inc.
Group Owner: Spanish Broadcasting System Inc.; (acq 11-29-99; grpsl)
Arbitron Metro Market: Puerto Rico *Format:* Adult Contemp
Target Audience: 18-49; predominantly women
Raul Alarcon, President
Ismael Nieves, General Manager
Maria Elena Martinez, General Sales Mgr
Fernando de Hostas, Programming Director
Luis Rivera, Promotions Manager
Demare Ramirez, News Director
Alejandro Luciano, ChiefEngineer

***WIPR**
01-26-1948; 940 khz AM *Hrs Open:* 24
P. O. Box 190909, San Juan, PR 0919 US
(787) 766-0505, *Fax:* (787) 250-7694
www.prnet.pr
License: San Juan, PR held by Puerto Rico Corp. for Public Broadcasting.
Nat'l Network: NPR
Arbitron Metro Market: Puerto Rico *Format:* News *Hrs. of News Programming:* news progmg 7 hrs wkly *No. News Employees:* 7
Luis Agrait, Chairman
Linda Hernandez, President
Susan Marte, Operations Dir
Raul Carbonell, General Manager
Vilma Reyes, Station Manager
Ileana Rivera, General Sales Mgr
Yolanda Zavala, Executive Vice President
Luis Santiago,Sales Director

***WIPR-FM**
06-03-1960; 91.3 mhz FM *Hrs Open:* 24; 105 kw; 2707 ft.; N18 6 42 W66 3 5
P. O. Box 190909, San Juan, PR 0919 US
(787) 766-0505, *Fax:* (787) 250-7694
www.prnet.pr
License: San Juan, PR held by Puerto Rico Corp. for Public Broadcasting.
Arbitron Metro Market: Puerto Rico *Format:* Talk
Sinta Seiber, Operations Dir
Bill Wheelhouse, General Manager
Lisa Clemmons-Stott, General Sales Mgr
Rick Bradley, News Director
Greg Manfroi, Chief Engineer

WKAQ
12-03-1922; 580 khz AM *Hrs Open:* 24; 10 kw-U, DA1; N18 25 56 W66 8 9
Mailing Address: P.O. Box 364668, San Juan, PR 0936 US
Second Address: 383 F.D. Roosevelt Ave., Third Floor, Hato Rey, PR 918
(787) 758-5800, *Fax:* (787) 763-1854
wkaq580.univision.com
License: San Juan, PR held by El Mundo Broadcasting Corp.
Group Owner: Univision Radio; (acq 8-1-2003; grpsl).
Arbitron Metro Market: Puerto Rico *Format:* News, News/Talk, 86 *No. News Employees:* 22 *Target Audience:* General.
Jamie Bauza, General Manager
Javier Cosme, Programming Director
Aracelis Cruz, Promotions Manager
Nestor Perez, Chief Engineer

WKAQ-FM
10-08-1958; 104.7 mhz FM; 50 kw; 1220 ft.; N18 16 51 W66 6 38
Mailing Address: G.P.O.Box 364668, San Juan, PR 0936 US
Second Address: 383 F.D. Roosevelt Ave., San Juan, PR 918
(787)758-5800, *Fax:* (787) 756-5220
www.kq105fm.com
License: San Juan, PR
Arbitron Metro Market: Puerto Rico *Format:* Contemporary Hits/Top 40
Huberto Biaggi, President
Raul Muxo, General Sales Mgr
Carlos Gonzalez, Programming Director

WKVM
01-01-1951; 810 khz AM; 50 kw-U, DA1; N18 21 47 W66 8 13
Mailing Address: P.O. Box 9021967, San Juan, PR 0902 US
Second Address: c/o Arquidiocesis de San Juan, Apartado 1967, San Juan, PR 00901-1967
(787) 751-1018, *Fax:* (787) 758-9967
License: San Juan, PR held by Catholic, Apostolic & Roman Church, San Juan Archdiocese.
Arbitron Metro Market: Puerto Rico *Format:* Oldies, Religious
Roberto Gonzalez, President
Allan Corales, Station Manager
Elsa Fernandez, General Sales Mgr
Jose Antonio Cruz, Programming Director
Placido Padilla, News Director
Jose Gomez, Chief Engineer
Judith Rivera, Local News Editor
Efrain Rodriguez, Religion Ed
Enrigue Liboy, Sports Commentator

WOSO
11-21-1977; 1030 khz AM *Hrs Open:* 24; 10 kw-U, DA-1; N18 22 07 W66 15 17
Box 11487, San Juan, PR 0902
(787) 724-4242, *Fax:* (787) 723-9676
www.woso.com
License: San Juan, PR held by Sherman Broadcasting Corp.
Nat'l Network: Wall Street; CBS; ABC
Arbitron Metro Market: Puerto Rico *Hrs. of News Programming:* news progmg 6 hrs wkly *No. News Employees:* 2 *Target Audience:* 25-49. *Adv. Rates:* 48; 24; 38; 20
Sherman Wildman, President
Mariano Calderon, Operations Dir
Sergio Fernandez, General Manager
Sherman Wildmon, Programming Director
Gary Tuominen, News Director
Rodolfo Rivas, Chief Engineer
Danette Hudoba, Traffic Manager

WPRM-FM
04-01-1959; 98.5 mhz FM *Hrs Open:* 24; 25 kw; 1905 ft.; N18 6 47 W66 3 6
P. O. Box 487, Caguas, PR 0625 US
(787) 744-3131, *Fax:* (787) 743-0252
www.salsoul.com
License: San Juan, PR held by Arso Radio Corp.
Group Owner: Uno Radio Group; (acq 4-1-73).
Arbitron Metro Market: Puerto Rico *Format:* Black *Hrs. of News Programming:* news progmg 3 hrs wkly *No. News Employees:* 1
Target Audience: 18-49.
Jesus Soto, CEO
Luis Soto, President
Maida Bedaya, General Manager
Raymond Totti, General Sales Mgr
Anthony Soto, Programming Director
Luis Gonzalez, CFO

WQBS
11-01-1954; 870 khz AM
129 Ave De Diego, San Juan, PR 0927 US
(787) 758-8700, *Fax:* (787) 765-2965
angel@aercobroadcasting.com
License: San Juan, PR held by Aerco Broadcasting Corp.
Arbitron Metro Market: Puerto Rico *TV Affiliate:* WSJU-TV
Format: Variety/Diverse
Luz Alvarez, General Manager

WQII
01-01-1947; 1140 khz AM; 10 kw-U, DA1; N18 21 30 W66 8 5
Mailing Address: P.O. Box 193779, San Juan, PR 0919 US
Second Address: Box 906 6590, San Juan, PR 00906-6590
(787) 723-4848, *Fax:* (787) 723-4035
postmaster@1140qpr.com
License: San Juan, PR held by Communications Council Group Inc.
Arbitron Metro Market: Puerto Rico *Format:* Talk
Nieves Gonzalez Avreu, President
Jorge Marquina, General Manager
William Padilla, General Sales Mgr
Danny Gonzalez, Programming Director
Raymond Hernandez, Chief Engineer

***WRTU**
02-08-1980; 89.7 mhz FM *Hrs Open:* 24; 50 kw; 801 ft.; N18 16 0 W66 5 5
Mailing Address: P.O. Box 21305, San Juan, PR 0931 US
Second Address: Mariana Bracetti St., Ponce de Leon Ave., San Juan, PR 931
(787) 763-4699, *Fax:* (787) 764-1290
www.wrtu.pr
lluna@wrtu.pr
License: San Juan, PR held by University of Puerto Rico.
Arbitron Metro Market: Puerto Rico *No. News Employees:* 8
Target Audience: General.
Ezequiel Rodrguez, Operations Dir
Yolanda Zabala, General Manager

WUNO
01-11-1960; 630 khz AM *Hrs Open:* 24; 5 kw-U, DA1; N18 26 0 W66 7 29
Mailing Address: Calle Eleanor Roosevelt, #117, Hato Rey, PR 0918 US
Second Address: 1581 Ponce de Leon St., Rio Peidras, PR 926
(787) 758-1300, *Fax:* (787) 754-1395
www.notiuno.com
FMKOOL929@aol.com
License: San Juan, PR held by Madifide Inc.
Group Owner: Uno Radio Group; (acq 5-8-01; grpsl).
Nat'l Reps: McGavren Guild
Arbitron Metro Market: Puerto Rico *Format:* News, News/Talk, 86 *No. News Employees:* 22 *Target Audience:* 25 plus.
Jesus Soto, CEO
Luis Soto, President
Jaime Soto, Programming Director
Raymond Totti, Executive Vice President

WSKN
10-15-1949; 1320 khz AM *Hrs Open:* 24
Box 363222, San Juan, PR 0936 US
(787) 292-1700, *Fax:* (787) 292-1717
www.radioisla1320.com
noticias@radioisla1320.com
License: San Juan, PR held by Media Power Group Inc.

Group Owner: Media Power Group Inc.; (acq 9-30-2003; grpsl).
Nat'l Network: CNN Radio
Arbitron Metro Market: San Juan, PR *Format:* News, News/Talk, 86 *Hrs. of News Programming:* news progmg 24 hrs wkly *No. News Employees:* 40 *Target Audience:* 35 plus.
Eduardo Rivero, President
Ismael Nieves, Operations Dir
Nora Plaza, General Sales Mgr
Luis Penchi, Programming Director
Fernando Vazquez, Promotions Manager
Orlando Morales, Operations Manager

WVOZ
07-04-1949; 1520 khz AM *Hrs Open:* 16
1554 Bori Street, Caribe Development, Rio Piedras, PR 0928 US
(787) 764-1077, *Fax:* (787) 281-9758
www.mix107.fm
License: San Juan, PR held by Pedro Roman Collazo.
Arbitron Metro Market: Puerto Rico *Format:* Sports *Special Programming:* Puerto Rican & Latin hits 15 hrs wkly *Target Audience:* 35 plus; medium & low income individuals
Pedro Roman-Collazo, President
Margarita Nazario, General Manager

WZNT
01-01-1959; 93.7 mhz FM *Hrs Open:* 24; 28 kw; 1837 ft.; N18 16 44 W65 51 12
Mailing Address: PO Box 949, Guaynabo, PR 0970 US
Second Address: Amelia Industrial Park, Calle Frances 42, Guaynabo, PR 968
(787) 622-9700, *Fax:* (787) 622-9478
www.lamega.fm
rogie@sbspuertorico.com
License: San Juan, PR held by WZNT Inc.
Group Owner: Spanish Broadcasting System Inc.; (acq 2000; grpsl)
Arbitron Metro Market: Guaynabo, PR *Target Audience:* 18-49; male
Raul Alarcon, President
Ismael Nieves, General Manager
Marie Martinez, General Sales Mgr
Rogie Gallart, Programming Director
Luis Rivera, Promotions Manager
Demare Ramirez, News Director
Alejandro Luciano, Chief Engineer
PedroArroyo, Programming Director
Nestor Rodriguez, Programming Director
Omar Rodriguez, Internet Web Manager
Joe Mackay, National Sales Manager SBS
Edgardo Aubray, National Sales Manager SBS
Andrew Polsky

San Sebastian

WLRP
02-15-1965; 1460 khz AM *Hrs Open:* 19; 0.5 kw-U, ND1; N18 20 50 W66 59 56
PO Box 1670, San Sebastian, PR 0755 US
(787) 896-1460, *Fax:* (787) 896-8100
www.radioracies.net
radioraices@prtc.net
License: San Sebastian, PR held by Las Raices Pepinianas Inc.
Arbitron Metro Market: Puerto Rico *Format:* Adult Contemp *No. News Employees:* 1
Ramon Colon Pratts, President
Carlos M. Aquino, General Manager
Alfredo Perez, General Sales Mgr
Jose Chaparro, Programming Director
Ramon Pratts, Promotions Manager
Juan Felin, Chief Engineer

WRSS
04-01-1984; 1410 khz AM; 1 kw-U, DA1; N18 19 14 W66 58 45
Mailing Address: P.O. Box 1410, San Sebastian, PR 0685 US
Second Address: Segundo Ruez # 52 St., San Sebastian, PR 685
(787) 896-2121, *Fax:* (787) 896-5753
tunuevafamilia@hotmail.com
License: San Sebastian, PR held by Angel Vera-Maury
Arbitron Metro Market: Puerto Rico *Format:* Oldies, Talk *Hrs. of News Programming:* news progmg 30 hrs wkly *No. News Employees:* 6 *Target Audience:* 30 plus.
Angel Vera, President
Cesar Vera, General Manager
Arturo Soto, General Sales Mgr
Nestor Gonzalez, Programming Director

Utuado

WUPR
04-18-1964; 1530 khz AM *Hrs Open:* 17; 1 kw-D, ND1; 0.25 kw-N, ND1; N18 16 4 W66 42 35
P. O. Box 868, Utuado, PR 0641 US
(787) 894-2460, *Fax:* (787) 894-4955
www.coqui.net
info@coqui.net
License: Utuado, PR held by Central Broadcasting Corp.
Arbitron Metro Market: Utuado, PR *Format:* News, News/Talk, 86 *Hrs. of News Programming:* news progmg 11 hrs wkly *No. News Employees:* 2 *Target Audience:* 18-49; middle income adults
Jose Martinez, President
Manuel Martinez, News Director
Epifanio Rodriguez Velez, Chief Engineer
Manuel Andujar, Music Director

Vega Alta

WERR
02-01-1970; 104.1 mhz FM *Hrs Open:* 24; 50 kw; 988 ft.; N18 17 29 W66 39 39
Mailing Address: P.O. Box 29404, San Juan, PR 0929 US
Second Address: San Felipe # 205, Arecibo, PR 612
(787) 751-1310, *Fax:* (787) 751-6854
www.redentor104fm.com
hernanpantoja@gmail.com
License: Vega Alta, PR held by Radio Redentor Inc.
Arbitron Metro Market: Vega Alta, PR *Format:* Adult Contemp, Christian *Hrs. of News Programming:* news progmg one hr wkly *No. News Employees:* 4 *Target Audience:* General.
Luis Quiones, COO
Rev. Miguel Cintron, President
Omayra Martinez, Operations Dir
Jesus M. Velez Rivera, General Manager
Pantoja Hernn, Programming Director
Brenda Lis Gines, Promotions Manager
Elizabeth Bosques, NewsDirector
Ramon Rivera, Engineering Dir
Omayra Martinez, Administrative Manager
Nydia Guzman, Accounting

Vega Baja

WEGA
10-01-1971; 1350 khz AM; 2.5 kw-D, DA2; 2.5 kw-N, DA2; N18 28 38 W66 23 43
Box 1488, Vega Baja, PR 0693 US
(787) 855-1350, *Fax:* (787) 855-0916
info@wega.com
License: Vega Baja, PR held by A Radio Company Inc.
Arbitron Metro Market: Puerto Rico *Format:* Variety/Diverse
Gerardo Angulo, President
Carmelo Santiago, General Manager
Hector Santiago, General Sales Mgr
Lloyd Santiago, Promotions Manager
Ronald Cushing, Chief Engineer

Vieques

WZOL
11-04-1978; 98.9 mhz FM; 50 kw; Ant 751 ft; N18 19 39 W65 18 05
Box 1047, Fajardo, PR 0929
(787) 860-1065, *Fax:* (787) 860-1055
License: Vieques, PR held by La Mas Z Radio Inc.
Arbitron Metro Market: Puerto Rico
Gary King Sr., CEO
James Brown, Operations Dir

WVIS
06-10-1973; 106.1 mhz FM; 50 kw; 558 ft.; N18 19 37 W65 18 21
P.O. Box 6556, Loiza Station, San Juan, PR 0914 US
(787) 355-0090, *Fax:* (787) 355-0079
www.radiojoe106.com
License: Vieques, PR held by V.I. Stereo Communications Corporation (PR)
Arbitron Metro Market: Vieques, PR *Format:* Adult Contemp, Oldies, 72
Michael Bahr, President

Yabucoa

WXEW
01-01-1978; 840 khz AM *Hrs Open:* 19; 5 kw-D, DAN; 1 kw-N, DAN; N18 2 58 W65 52 7
Mailing Address: P.O. Box 100, Yabucoa, PR 0767 US
Second Address: Box 100, Yabucoa, PR 767
(787) 893-3065, *Fax:* (787) 850-4055
www.victoria840.com
victor@victoria840.com
License: Yabucoa, PR held by Radio Victoria Inc.
Arbitron Metro Market: Yabucoa, PR *Format:* Adult Contemp, Talk
Victoria Vargas, President
Victor Calderon, Operations Dir
Caly Burmudez, General Sales Mgr
Luis Calderon, Programming Director
Brenda Calderon, Promotions Manager
Angel Bena, News Director
Alberto Pereira, Chief Engineer
JoseCalderon, Promotions Manager

Yauco

WENA
11-11-1978; 1330 khz AM *Hrs Open:* 24
P.O. Box 1338, Yauco, PR 0698 US
(787) 267-1330(787) 856-1330, *Fax:* (787) 267-1340
www.labuena1330.com
wena@cogui.net
License: Yauco, PR held by Southern Broadcasting Corp.
Arbitron Metro Market: Yauco, PR *Format:* Adult Contemp, News, 62, Talk *Hrs. of News Programming:* news progmg 28 hrs wkly *No. News Employees:* 5 *Target Audience:* 25 plus; young adults & women *Adv. Rates:* 216; 216; 200; 168
Nephtali Rodriguez, President
Israel Rodriguez, Operations Dir
Ramon Ramos, General Sales Mgr
Guillermo Valls, Programming Director
Isaac Pagan, Engineering Dir
Juan Diaz, Advertising Manager
Ronald Cushing, EngineeringManager
Pedro Gregory, Sales Director

WKFE
11-03-1961; 1550 khz AM *Hrs Open:* 24; 0.25 kw-U, ND1; N18 1 24 W66 52 2 *Rebroadcasts:* Rebroadcasts WSKN(AM) San Juan 70%
Box 7213, Ponce, PR 0732 US
(787) 292-1700, *Fax:* (787) 292-1717
noticias@radioisla1320.com
License: Yauco, PR held by Media Power Group Inc.
Group Owner: Media Power Group Inc.; (acq 9-30-2003; grpsl).
Arbitron Metro Market: Puerto Rico *Format:* News, News/Talk, 86 *Hrs. of News Programming:* news progmg 40 hrs wkly *No. News Employees:* 2 *Target Audience:* P35-64 P35+.
Eduardo Rivero, President
Jose Pagan, General Manager
Nora Plaza, General Sales Mgr
Orlando Morales, Programming Director

Rhode Island

Block Island

WCRI-FM
06-13-1994; 95.9 mhz FM *Hrs Open:* 24; 6 kw; 249 ft.; N41 10 28 W71 34 20
750 South Street, Waltham, MA 02154 US
(401) 294-9274, *Fax:* (401) 294-4034
www.classical959.com
wcri@classical959.com.
License: Block Island, Washington County, RI held by Judson Group Inc.
Arbitron Metro Market: Rhode Island *Format:* Talk *Special Programming:* New age 4 hrs, folk 4 hrs, big band 4 hrs, relg 2 hrs wkly *Target Audience:* General.
Christopher Jones, President
Mark Halliday, General Manager
Michael Abranson, Station Manager

WJZS
10-03-1988; 99.3 mhz FM *Hrs Open:* 24; 6 kw; 256 ft.; N41 10 28 W71 34 20
85 Beach Street, Westerly, RI 02891 US
(401) 846-1540, *Fax:* (401) 846-1598
www.wadk.com
rmelfi@wadk.com
License: Block Island, Washington County, RI held by Astro Tele-Communications Corp.
Group Owner: Astro Tele-Communications Corp. Rhode Island; (acq 8-24-99).
Arbitron Metro Market: Newport, RI *Format:* Adult Contemp *Target Audience:* 30-50; total community
Bobb Angel, Operations Dir
Bob Melfi, General Manager
Lisa Lancaster, News Director
Maurice Polayes, Chief Engineer
Lisa Lancaster, Traffic Director, Office Manager
Larry Beavers, Engineer

Bristol

***WQRI**
04-01-1989; 88.3 mhz FM; 0.2 kw horiz, 0.8 kw vert; 79 ft.; N41 38 54 W71 15 34

One Old Ferry Road, Bristol, RI 02809 US
(401) 254-3283,(401) 254-3282,(401) 253-1040, *Fax:* (401) 254-3355
License: Bristol, Bristol County, RI held by Roger Williams University.
Format: Rock/AOR
Becky Riopel, General Manager

Coventry

***WCVY**
10-19-1978; 91.5 mhz FM *Hrs Open:* 2pm - 10pm; 0.2 kw; 36 ft.; N41 41 10 W71 35 37
40 Reservoir Road, Coventry, RI 02816 US
(401) 822-9499, *Fax:* (401) 822-9492
www.coventryschools.net/wcvy
91.5wcvy@gmail.com
License: Coventry, Kent County, RI held by Coventry Public Schools.
Arbitron Metro Market: Coventry, RI *Format:* Contemporary Hits/Top 40 *Special Programming:* Sports 2 hrs wkly *Target Audience:* 12-30.
Scott P., Station Manager
Ronald Guillemette, General Sales Mgr
James Murphy, Advisor

East Providence

WPMZ
04-15-1947; 1110 khz AM; 5 kw-D, DAD; N41 49 40 W71 22 9
1270 Mineral Spring Ave., North Providence, RI 02904 US
(401) 726-8413, *Fax:* (401) 726-8649
www.poder1110.com
wpmz@aol.com
License: East Providence, RI held by Videomundo Broadcasting Co. L.L.C.
Arbitron Metro Market: Providence-Warwick-Pawtucket, RI *Target Audience:* General.
Dilson Mendez, President
Tony Mendez, General Manager
Johanna Petrarca, General Sales Mgr
Zoilo Garcia, Programming Director

Greenville

WALE
01-01-1948; 990 khz AM *Hrs Open:* 6 AM-midnight; 50 kw-D, DA2; 5 kw-N, DA2; N41 57 18 W71 35 39
1185 North Main Street, Providence, RI 02904 US
(401) 521-0990, *Fax:* (401) 521-5077
License: Greenville, RI held by Cumbre Communications Corp., debtor in possession
Arbitron Metro Market: Providence, RI *Target Audience:* .
Manolo Pazos, General Manager

Hope Valley

WCRI(AM)
10-07-1985; 1180 khz AM; 1.8 kw-D; N41 31 36 W71 44 35
400 S. County Trail, Exeter, RI 2822
(401) 596-6795, *Fax:* (401) 596-6782
www.newsradio1180.com
mail@classical959.com
License: Hope Valley, Washington County, RI held by Judson Group Inc.
Nat'l Network: USA
Population Served: 750,000 *Arbitron Metro Market:* Providence-Warwick-Pawtucket, RI *Format:* News *Adv. Rates:* 29; 20; 25; na
Christopher Jones, President
Mark Halliday, General Manager
Mike Abramson, Station Manager

Kingston

***WRIU**
02-16-1964; 90.3 mhz FM *Hrs Open:* 24; 3.4 kw; 420 ft.; N41 29 52 W71 31 43
50 Lower College Rd, (Memorial Union Bldg.), Kingston, RI 02881 US
(401) 874-4949, *Fax:* (401) 874-4349
www.wriu.org
License: Kingston, Washington County, RI held by University of Rhode Island.
Format: Variety/Diverse *Special Programming:* Folk 15 hrs, gospel 5 hrs, heavy metal 6 hrs, blues 3 hrs, reggae 7 hrs, Sp 3 hrs wkly *Target Audience:* Diverse.
James Proctor, General Manager

Middletown

WKKB
10-06-1978; 100.3 mhz FM *Hrs Open:* 24; 1.55 kw; 656 ft.; N41 35 48 W71 11 24
Suite 400, 7201 W. Lake Mead Blvd, Las Vegas, NV 89128 US
(401) 331-1003, *Fax:* (401) 521-5077
latina 1003.com
marcklowan@supermaxfm.com
License: Middletown, Newport County, RI held by Davidson Media Rhode Island Stations LLC.
Group Owner: Davidson Media Group LLC; (acq 1-31-2005; $7.5 million with WAKX(FM) Narragansett Pier)
Arbitron Metro Market: Providence-Warwick-Pawtucket, RI
Format: Spanish *Hrs. of News Programming:* news progmg 7 hrs wkly *No. News Employees:* 1 *Target Audience:* 12+; Latino Americans 1st & 2nd generation
Craig Rapoza, General Manager
Cesar Salas, General Sales Mgr
Enrique Ortaga, Programming Director
Juan Gonzalez, Programming Director

Narragansett Pier

***WRNI-FM**
07-15-1990; 102.7 mhz FM *Hrs Open:* 19; 1.95 kw; 226 ft.; N41 25 27 W71 28 38
1110 Central Avenue, Pawtucket, RI 02861 US
(401) 351-2800, *Fax:* (401) 351-0246
www.ripr.org
info@ripr.org
License: Narragansett Pier, Washington County, RI held by Rhode Island Public Radio
Nat'l Network: NPR
Arbitron Metro Market: Rhode Island *Format:* News, News/Talk, 86
Eugene Mihaly, President
James Baumgartner, Operations Dir
Joe O'Connor, General Manager
Catherine Welch, News Director
Donna Bannon, manager of corporate underwriting

Newport

WADK
11-06-1948; 1540 khz AM *Hrs Open:* 6am-6pm; 1 kw-D, NDD; N41 30 13 W71 18 43
85 Beach Street, Westerly, RI 02891 US
(315) 258-0937, *Fax:* (315) 258-9248
www.fingerlakes1.com
tbaker@flradiogroup.com
License: Newport, RI held by Astro Tele-Communications Corp.
Group Owner: Astro Tele-Communications Corp. Rhode Island; (acq 8-24-99).
Nat'l Network: ABC; Talk Radio Network
Arbitron Metro Market: Fargo-Moorhead ND-MN *Format:* Talk *Target Audience:* General.
Bill Askew, General Sales Mgr
Mike Smith, Programming Director
Ted Baker, News Director

Portsmouth

***WJHD**
04-03-1972; 90.7 mhz FM; 0.36 kw horiz; 79 ft.; N41 36 6 W71 16 20
285 Cory's Lane, Portsmouth, RI 02871 US
(401) 683-2000, *Fax:* (401) 683-5888
License: Portsmouth, Newport County, RI held by The Order of St. Benedict.
Format: Variety/Diverse
Edmund Adams, General Manager

Providence

WBRU
02-21-1966; 95.5 mhz FM *Hrs Open:* 24; 18.5 kw; 456 ft.; N41 49 40 W71 22 9
88 Benevolent Street, Providence, RI 02906 US
(401) 272-9550, *Fax:* (401) 272-9278
www.wbru.com
promotions@wbru.com
License: Providence, Providence County, RI held by Brown Broadcasting Service Inc.
Arbitron Metro Market: Providence, RI *Format:* Alternative
Special Programming: Black 20 hrs, jazz 18 hrs wkly *Hrs. of News Programming:* News progmg 3 hrs wkly *Target Audience:* 18-34; highly educatedprofessionals
Jon Zucker, General Manager
Marianna Faircloth, Station Manager
Mark Stackowski, General Sales Mgr
Chris Novello, Programming Director
Arnie Ramirez, Promotions Manager
Kaitlyn Laabs, News Director

***WDOM**
03-15-1966; 91.3 mhz FM *Hrs Open:* 18; 0.125 kw; 131 ft.; N41 50 39 W71 26 14
River Ave., & Eaton St., Providence, RI 02918 US
(401) 865-2091, *Fax:* (401) 865-2822
www.wdom913.com
musicdirectors@wdom913.com
License: Providence, Providence County, RI held by Providence College.
Arbitron Metro Market: Providence, RI *Format:* Alternative
Special Programming: Urban contemp 16 hrs, metal 6 hrs, country 2 hrs, classic rock 3 hrs, sports 2 hrs wkly *Hrs. of News Programming:* News progmg one hrwkly *Target Audience:* General; college students & professionals
Brian Wall, Operations Dir
Scott Seseske, General Manager
Jaclyn Schede, Assistant Music Director
Dan Devine, Music Director
Carlin Corrigan, Promotions Director
Sott Seseske, Special Events Coordinator

***WELH**
09-01-1994; 88.1 mhz FM *Hrs Open:* 24; 4 kw; 135 ft.; N41 51 26.7 W71 19 5.6
216 Hope Street, Providence, RI 02906 US
(401) 351-2800, *Fax:* (401) 751-7674
www.ripr.org/
info@ripr.org
License: Providence, Providence County, RI held by The Wheeler School.
Arbitron Metro Market: Providence, RI *Format:* Jazz, Variety/Diverse *Target Audience:* General.
Joe O'Connor, General Manager
Catherine Welch, News Director

WHJJ
09-06-1922; 920 khz AM *Hrs Open:* 24; 5 kw-D, DAN; 5 kw-N, DAN; N41 46 53 W71 19 55
600 Congress Ave., Suite 1400, Austin, TX 78701 US
(401) 781-9979, *Fax:* (401) 781-9329
www.920whjj.com
License: Providence, RI held by Capstar TX L.P.
Group Owner: Clear Channel Communications Inc.; (acq 8-30-2000; grpsl)
Nat'l Network: CBS *Nat'l Reps:* Clear Channel
Arbitron Metro Market: Providence-Warwick-Pawtucket, RI
Format: News, News/Talk, 86 *Target Audience:* 35-64.
Jim Corwin, General Manager
Kevin Hickey, General Sales Mgr
Bill George, Programming Director

WHJY
03-14-1966; 94.1 mhz FM; 50 kw; 456 ft.; N41 49 40 W71 22 9
600 Congress Ave., Suite 1400, Austin, TX 78701 US
(401) 781-9979, *Fax:* (401) 781-9329
www.whjy.com
jocks@whjy.com
License: Providence, Providence County, RI held by Capstar TX L.P.
Group Owner: Clear Channel Communications Inc.
Arbitron Metro Market: Providence-Warwick-Pawtucket, RI
Format: Rock/AOR *Target Audience:* 18-34; adults
Scott Laudani, Programming Director

WPRO
10-16-1931; 630 khz AM; 5 kw-D, DAN; 5 kw-N, DAN; N41 46 28 W71 19 23 *Rebroadcasts:* Simulcast with WEAN-FM Wakefield-Peacedale 100%
City Center West, 7201 W. Lake Mead Blvd, Las Vegas, NV 89128 US
(401) 433-4200, *Fax:* (401) 433-5967
www.630wpro.com
License: Providence, RI
Group Owner: Cumulus Media Inc.; (acq 5-29-97; grpsl)
Nat'l Reps: McGavren Guild
Arbitron Metro Market: Providence-Warwick-Pawtucket, RI
Format: News, News/Talk, 84, Talk
Barbara Haynes, General Manager
Joe Lembo, General Sales Mgr

WPRO-FM
04-01-1949; 92.3 mhz FM; 39 kw; 551 ft.; N41 48 18 W71 28 24
City Center West, 7201 W. Lake Mead Blvd, Las Vegas, NV 89128 US
(401) 433-4200, *Fax:* (401) 433-5967
www.92wpro.com
License: Providence, Providence County, RI held by Citadel Broadcasting Co.

Arbitron Metro Market: Providence-Warwick-Pawtucket, RI
Format: Contemporary Hits/Top 40
Steve Maully, General Sales Mgr
Tony Brisco, Programming Director

WSTL
06-16-1946; 1220 khz AM *Hrs Open:* 24; 1 kw-D, ND1; 0.166 kw-N, ND1; N41 49 15 W71 23 7
20 Park Plaza, Suite 720, Boston, MA 02116 US
(508) 336-4233, *Fax:* (508) 336-5789
shineradio.us
patricia.varner@shineradio.us
License: Providence, RI held by New England Christian Media Inc.
Arbitron Metro Market: Providence-Warwick-Pawtucket, RI
Format: Christian
Patricia Varner, General Manager
Mike Laliberte, Programming Director

WRNI
04-01-1948; 1290 khz AM *Hrs Open:* 24
890 Commonwealth Avenue, Boston, MA 02215 US
(401) 351-2800, *Fax:* (401) 351-0246
www.wrni.org
info@wrni.org
License: Providence, RI held by WRNI Foundation
Nat'l Network: NPR; PRI *Nat'l Reps:* Rgnl Reps
Arbitron Metro Market: Providence-Warwick-Pawtucket, RI
Format: News, News/Talk, 86 *Hrs. of News Programming:* news progmg 80 hrs wkly *No. News Employees:* 8 *Target Audience:* 25-54; intelligent adultsinterested in news & politics
Joe O'Connor, General Manager
Steve Callahan, Chief Engineer

WPRV
06-02-1922; 790 khz AM; 5 kw-D, DAN; 5 kw-N, DAN; N41 50 3 W71 21 56
City Center West, 7201 W. Lake Mead Blvd, Las Vegas, NV 89128 US
(401) 433-4200, *Fax:* (401) 433-2932
www.790business.com
ron.stpierre@cumulus.com
License: Providence, RI
Group Owner: Cumulus Media Inc.; (acq 5-29-97; grpsl)
Nat'l Reps: McGavren Guild
Arbitron Metro Market: Providence-Warw *Format:* Oldies *Target Audience:* 25-64; upper class, affluent, college educated
Joe Lembo, General Sales Mgr
Ron St. Pierre, Programming Director
Ryan Casey, Promotions Manager

WWBB
06-07-1968; 101.5 mhz FM *Hrs Open:* 24; 13.5 kw; 951 ft.; N41 52 13 W71 17 47
3305 West Spring Mt Rd, Suite 60, Las Vegas, NV 89102 US
(401) 781-9979, *Fax:* (401) 781-9329
www.b101.com
feedback@b101.com
License: Providence, Providence County, RI held by Clear Channel Radio Licenses Inc.
Group Owner: Clear Channel Communications Inc.
Nat'l Network: AP Radio; Premiere Radio Networks *Nat'l Reps:* Clear Channel
Arbitron Metro Market: Providence, RI *Format:* Contemporary Hits/Top 40, Adult Contemp *Target Audience:* 35-54; indispensable & powerful adults
Jim Corwin, General Manager
Mark Cottey, General Sales Mgr
Michelle Maker, Promotions Manager
Steve Lariviere, Chief Engineer

WWLI
07-11-1948; 105.1 mhz FM; 50 kw; 499 ft.; N41 48 24 W71 28 13
City Center West, 7201 W. Lake Mead Blvd, Las Vegas, NV 89128 US
(401) 433-4200, *Fax:* (401) 433-5967
www.lite105.com
License: Providence, Providence County, RI
Group Owner: Cumulus Media Inc.
Arbitron Metro Market: Providence, RI *Format:* Light Rock *Target Audience:* 25-54; mid to upper income professionals, general appeal format
Barbara Haynes, General Manager
Holly Paras, General Sales Mgr
Tony Bristol, Programming Director
Amy Albanese, Promotions Manager
Patrick Austin, Website

Smithfield

***WJMF**
08-01-1974; 88.7 mhz FM *Hrs Open:* 7 AM-2 AM; 1.2 kw; 535 ft.; N41 48 12 W71 33 27
1150 Douglas Pike, Bx 6, Smithfield, RI 02917 US
(401) 232-6044, *Fax:* (401) 232-6748
www.wjmfradio.com
wjmf@bryant.edu
License: Smithfield, Providence County, RI held by Bryant College of Business Administration.
Format: Alternative *Special Programming:* Folk 4 hrs, gospel 2 hrs, relg 2 hrs wkly *Hrs. of News Programming:* news progmg 12 hrs wkly *No. News Employees:* 1 *Target Audience:* 16-30; from teenagers to youngexecutives
Ricky McLaughlin, General Manager
Tyler Pepe, Programming Director
Katie Colton, Office Manager
Josh Grolman, Business Director
Nick Russell, Technology Director
Dylan Smith, Music Director
Brianne Brinkmann, ProductionDirector
Jeanetter Ferraro, Marketing Director

Wakefield-Peacedale

WEAN-FM
06-01-1995; 99.7 mhz FM *Hrs Open:* 24; 2.3 kw; 535 ft.; N41 34 22 W71 37 55 *Rebroadcasts:* Simulcast with WPRO(AM) Providence 100%
City Center West, 7201 W. Lake Mead Blvd, Las Vegas, NV 89128 US
(401) 433-4200, *Fax:* (401) 437-3297
www.630wpro.com
License: Wakefield-Peacedale, Washington County, RI
Group Owner: Cumulus Media Inc.; (acq 8-6-97; $8.5 million with WKKB(FM) Middletown)
Arbitron Metro Market: Providence, RI *Format:* News, News/Talk, 86 *No. News Employees:* 6
Barbara Haynes, General Manager
Bill Haberman, News Director
Duffy Egan, Chief Engineer

Warwick

WARV
08-12-1959; 1590 khz AM *Hrs Open:* 24; 5 kw-D, DA2; 5 kw-N, DA2; N41 43 40 W71 27 46
19 Luther Ave., Warwick, RI 02886 US
(401) 737-0700, *Fax:* (401) 737-1604
www.warv.net
warv@aol.com
License: Warwick, RI held by Blount Communications Inc.
Group Owner: Blount Communications Group; (acq 7-7-78)
Nat'l Network: Salem Radio Network
Arbitron Metro Market: Providence, RI *Format:* Religious *Special Programming:* Black 2 hrs wkly *Target Audience:* 25-54; Adults
William Blount, President
David Young, Operations Dir
Deborah Blount, Executive Vice President
Kevin Linegan, Operations Manager

West Warwick

WLKW
08-12-1986; 1450 khz AM *Hrs Open:* 24
866 2nd Ave., 2nd Fl, New York, NY 10017 US
(401) 467-4366, *Fax:* (401) 941-2795
www.wlkwradio.com/
twall@hallradio.com
License: West Warwick, RI held by Hall Communications Inc.
Group Owner: Hall Communications Inc.; acq 6-4-01; $410,000).
Nat'l Network: ESPN Radio *Nat'l Reps:* Eastman Radio
Arbitron Metro Market: West Warwick, RI *Format:* Sports *Special Programming:* Pol 2 hrs wkly *No. News Employees:* 1 *Target Audience:* 35-64. *Adv. Rates:* 30; 20; 20; 10
Bonnie Rowbotham, CEO
Arthur Rowbotham, President
Tom Wall, General Manager

Westerly

***WKIV**
12-08-1997; 88.1 mhz FM; 0.001 kw horiz, 1.2 kw vert; 105 ft.; N41 26 13 W71 52 55 *Rebroadcasts:* Rebroadcasts KLVR(FM) Middletown, CA 100%
4 Canal Street, Westerly, RI 02891 US
(800) 877-5600, *Fax:* (916) 251-1650
www.klove.com
info@klove.com
License: Westerly, Washington County, RI held by Educational Media Foundation.
Group Owner: EMF Broadcasting; (acq 3-21-2008; $100,000)
Nat'l Network: K-Love
Arbitron Metro Market: Omaha, NE *Format:* Christian
Darrell Chambliss, Chairman
Mike Novak, CEO/COO
Mike Novak, President
David Pierce, Chief Creative Officer
Alan Mason, Chief Operating Officer
Dan Antonelli, Chief Business Development Officer
Eric Moser, Chief FinancialOfficer
Mitch Barnhart, Director
Larry Moody, Director

WBLQ(AM)
07-01-1949; 1230 khz AM; 1 kw-U; N41 21 57 W71 50 11
Rebroadcasts: Rebroadcasts WRNI(AM) Providence 100%
One Union Station, Providence, RI 2903
(401) 351-2800, *Fax:* (401) 351-0246
www.wrni.org
info@wrni.org
License: Westerly, Washington County, RI held by WRNI Foundation
Nat'l Network: NPR; PRI
Population Served: 178,053 *Arbitron Metro Market:* Providence, RI *Format:* News, Talk *Hrs. of News Programming:* News progmg 80 hrs wkly *No. News Employees:* 3 *Target Audience:* 25-54; intelligent adultsinterested in news & politics
Joe O'Connor, General Manager
Catherine Welch, News Director
Steve Callahan, Chief Engineer

Woonsocket

WNRI
11-28-1954; 1380 khz AM; 2.5 kw-D, ND1; 0.018 kw-N, ND1; N42 0 58 W71 29 30
Longmeadow Way, Box 403, Hamilton, MA 01936 US
(401) 769-6925, *Fax:* (401) 762-0442
www.wnri.com
rogerwnri@prodigy.net
License: Woonsocket, RI held by Bouchard Broadcasting Inc.
Nat'l Network: USA
Arbitron Metro Market: Providence. RI *Format:* News, News/Talk, 86 *Special Programming:* Fr 4 hrs, Pol 2 hrs, Por 2 hrs wkly *Target Audience:* 35 plus.
Roger Bouchard, General Manager
Jeff Gamache, Programming Director

WOON
11-11-1946; 1240 khz AM
Longmeadow Way, Box 403, Hamilton, MA 01936 US
(401) 762-1240, *Fax:* (401) 769-8232
www.onworldwide.com
email@onworldwide.com
License: Woonsocket, RI held by O-N Radio Inc.
Arbitron Metro Market: Providence-Warw *TV Affiliate:* easy lstng *Format:* Black, Gospel *No. News Employees:* 35 plus.

WWKX
07-01-1949; 106.3 mhz FM; 1.15 kw; 518 ft.; N41 59 43 W71 26 54
1110 Central Ave, Pawtucket, RI 02861 US
(401) 433-4200, *Fax:* (401) 433-5967
www.hot1063.com
hot1063@hot1063.com
License: Woonsocket, Providence County, RI
Group Owner: Cumulus Media Inc.; (acq 1-24-2005; $16.5 million with WAKX(FM) Narragansett Pier)
Nat'l Network: Westwood One *Regional Reps:* Christal.
Arbitron Metro Market: Providence, RI *Format:* Christian *Target Audience:* 18-49.
Barbara Haynes, General Manager
Duffy Egan, Chief Engineer
Nancy-Jean, Contact Person

South Carolina

Abbeville

WABV
03-01-1956; 1590 khz AM; 1 kw-D, ND1; 0.027 kw-N, ND1; N34 9 3 W82 23 34
Hood Road, Jasper, GA 30143 US
(360) 533-3000, *Fax:* (360) 532-1456
www.jodesha.com
License: Abbeville, SC held by Hellinger Broadcasting Inc.
Arbitron Metro Market: Waterloo-Cedar Falls IA
Gabrielle Jordan, Operations Dir
Bill Wolfenbarger, General Manager
Sally Miller, General Sales Mgr

WZLA-FM
01-01-1990; 92.9 mhz FM *Hrs Open:* 24; 6 kw; 243 ft.; N34 11 13 W82 19 28
Mailing Address: P.O. Box 548, Abbeville, SC 29620 US
Second Address: 112 N. Main St., Abbeville, SC 29620
(864) 366-5785, *Fax:* (864) 366-9391
z93oldies.com
z93@wctel.net
License: Abbeville, Abbeville County, SC held by Shelley Reid.
Nat'l Network: Motor Racing Net; Salem Radio Network
Arbitron Metro Market: Abbeville, SC *Format:* Oldies *Special Programming:* Gospel 8 hrs wkly *Target Audience:* 25-65.
Shelley Reid, President
Oscar Reid Jr., Station Manager
Oscar Reid, News Director
Wayne Stevenson, Sports Commentator

Aiken

WKXC-FM
08-01-1966; 99.5 mhz FM; 24 kw; 712 ft.; N33 38 44 W81 55 45
1776 Briarcliff Rd, Ne, Atlanta, GA 30306 US
(706) 396-7000, *Fax:* (706) 396-7092
www.kicks99.com
License: Aiken, Aiken County, SC held by WGAC License LLC.
Group Owner: Beasley Broadcast Group Inc.; (acq 4-2-2001; $12 million with WHHD(FM) Clearwater).
Arbitron Metro Market: Augusta, GA *Format:* Country
Kent Dunn, General Manager
Mark Haddon, General Sales Mgr
T. Gentry, Programming Director

***WLJK**
01-01-1990; 89.1 mhz FM *Hrs Open:* 24; 10 kw; 1,374 ft; N33 24 18 W81 50 15 *Rebroadcasts:* Rebroadcasta WRJA-FM Sumter 100%
1101 George Rogers Blvd., Columbia, SC 29211
(803) 737-3200, *Fax:* (803) 737-3552
www.scern.org
gasque@scetv.org
License: Aiken, Aiken County, SC held by South Carolina Educational TV Commission.
Nat'l Network: NPR; PRI; APM
Hrs. of News Programming: News progrmg 120 hrs wkly
Linda O'Bryon, President
John Gasque, Operations Dir
Shari Hutchinson, General Manager
Shari Hutchinson, Station Manager
Melanie Boyer, General Sales Mgr
John Gasque, Programming Director
John Crockett, Engineering Dir
SkpBeach, Chief Engineer
Melanie Boyer, Underwriting Manager

WKSP
09-17-1966; 96.3 mhz FM; 17.5 kw; 846 ft.; N33 41 6 W81 55 36
111 East Kilbourn Ave., Suite 2700, Milwaukee, WI 53202 US
(706) 396-6000, *Fax:* (706) 396-6010
www.kiss963.com
License: Aiken, Aiken County, SC held by Capstar TX L.P.
Group Owner: Clear Channel Communications Inc.; (acq 12-19-00; grpsl).
Arbitron Metro Market: Augusta, GA *Format:* Blues, Oldies
Travis Dylan, Operations Dir
Mark Bass, General Manager
Brett Pomykala, General Sales Mgr
Minnesota Fattz, Programming Director
Cher Best, Promotions Manager

Allendale

WDOG-FM
08-29-1983; 93.5 mhz FM; 6 kw; 299 ft.; N33 1 22 W81 19 58
P. O. Box 442, Allendale, SC 29810 US
(803) 584-3500, *Fax:* (240) 358-7473
www.bigdogradio.com
wdog935@aol.com
License: Allendale, Allendale County, SC
Arbitron Metro Market: Allendale, SC
Carl Gooding, General Sales Mgr
Lisa Gooding, News Director
Ron Lopez, Disc Jockey
Rick Gooding, Disc Jockey
Jim Lowe, Local News Editor

Anderson

WAIM
04-01-1935; 1230 khz AM; 1 kw-U, ND1; N34 31 52 W82 36 50
2203 Old Williamston Rd, Anderson, SC 29621 US
(864) 226-1511(864) 225-1230, *Fax:* (864) 226-1513
www.waim.us
info@waim.us
License: Anderson, SC held by Palmetto Broadcasting Corp
Arbitron Metro Market: Anderson, SC *Format:* News, News/Talk, 86 *Target Audience:* 25-64.
Rick Driver, General Manager
Craig More, Disc Jockey
Deb Kent, Disc Jockey
Dave Shannon, Disc Jockey
Terry Mitchell, Disc Jockey
Dave Chastain, Disc Jockey
Dan Cooley, Disc Jockey

WANS
06-01-1949; 1280 khz AM *Hrs Open:* 24; 5 kw-D, DAN; 1 kw-N, DAN; N34 32 17 W82 41 28
Watson Village, Anderson, SC 29624 US
(864) 224-9267, *Fax:* (864) 224-9744
License: Anderson, SC held by FM 103 Inc.
Arbitron Metro Market: Anderson, SC *Format:* Sports
Ray Morris, General Manager

WJMZ-FM
08-01-1963; 107.3 mhz FM *Hrs Open:* 24; 100 kw; 1010 ft.; N34 42 7 W82 36 19
1250 Connecticut Avenue, NW, Suite 800, Washington, DC 20036 US
(864) 235-1073, *Fax:* (864) 370-3403
www.1073jamz.com
steve.crumbley@coxinc.com
License: Anderson, Anderson County, SC held by Cox Radio Inc.
Group Owner: Cox Radio Inc.; (acq 2-1-2001; grpsl)
Arbitron Metro Market: Greenville-Spartanburg, SC *Format:* Urban Contemporary
Steve Crumbley, Operations Dir
Steve Sinicropi, VP and General Manager
Karolyn Mulvaney, Station Manager
Bob Grossmall, General Sales Mgr
Doug Davis, Programming Director
Laurie Madden, Promotions Manager
Ed Bailey, NewsDirector
Lemont Bryant, Chief Engineer
K.J. Bland, Assistant Music Director
Cathy Tabor, National Sales Manager
Amy DeVries, National Sales Manager
Sara Polk, Director of Customer Care

WROQ
01-01-1947; 101.1 mhz FM; 100 kw; 971 ft.; N34 38 51 W82 16 13
, Greenville, SC 0 US
(864) 271-9200, *Fax:* (864) 242-1567
www.wroq.com
info@wroq.com
License: Anderson, Anderson County, SC held by Entercom Greenville License LLC.
Group Owner: Entercom Communications Corp.; (acq 10-7-2005; grpsl).
Arbitron Metro Market: Greenville-Spartanburg, SC *Format:* Classic Rock *Target Audience:* 25-54; baby boomers
David Field, President
Sharon Day, General Manager
Mark Hendrix, Programming Director

Andrews

WGTN-FM
08-19-1985; 100.7 mhz FM *Hrs Open:* 24; 3.1 kw; 446 ft.; N33 24 3 W79 27 30
1416 High Market Street, Georgetown, SC 29440 US
(843) 903-9962, *Fax:* (843) 903-1797
www.wgtnradio.com
License: Andrews, Georgetown County, SC held by Coastline Communications of Carolina Inc.
Arbitron Metro Market: Myrtle Beach, SC *Format:* Adult Contemp *Target Audience:* 25-54; Adults
Will Isaacs, General Manager
Jerome Bresson, News Director

Atlantic Beach

WMIR
10-01-1997; 1200 khz AM *Hrs Open:* Sunrise-sunset
C/O Purbrese Hunsaker &, Post Office 217, Sterling, VA 20167 US
(843) 399-2653, *Fax:* (843) 399-2659
wradio@sc.rr.com
License: Atlantic Beach, SC held by Atlantic Beach Radio Inc.
Arbitron Metro Market: Atlantic Beach, SC *Format:* Religious *Target Audience:* 25-65; Urban Black gospel
Dr. Gardner Altman, President
Reggie Dyson, General Manager

WSEA
01-01-1998; 100.3 mhz FM; 12 kw; 476 ft.; N33 47 4 W78 52 44
330 East Kilbourn Ave, Suite 250, Milwaukee, WI 53202 US
(843) 651-7869, *Fax:* (843) 651-3197
www.hot100fm.com
info@hot100fm.com
License: Atlantic Beach, Horry County, SC held by Cumulus Licensing Corp.
Group Owner: Cumulus Media Inc.; (acq 7-16-98; $1.3 million).
Arbitron Metro Market: Myrtle Beach, S *Format:* Contemporary Hits/Top 40
Bill Hazen, General Manager

Bamberg-Denmark

WVCD
06-23-1957; 790 khz AM; 1 kw-D, ND1; 0.1 kw-N, ND1; N33 18 50 W81 4 43
P.O. Box 244, Bamberg, SC 29003 US
(803) 703-7002, *Fax:* (803) 703-7022
License: Bamberg-Denmark, SC held by Voorhees College
Regional Network: S.C. News Net.
Format: Religious *Special Programming:* Farm one hr wkly
Annette Gantt, General Manager

Barnwell

WDOG
01-01-1966; 1460 khz AM
P.O. Box 442, Allendale, SC 28910 US
(803) 584-3500, *Fax:* (240) 358-7473
www.bigdogradio.com
wdog935@aol.com
License: Barnwell, SC held by Good Radio Broadcasting Inc.
Regional Network: S.C. News Net.
Arbitron Metro Market: Allendale, SC *Format:* Black, Country
H. Carl Gooding, President
Rick Gooding, Promotions Manager
Lisa Gooding, News Director
Carl Gooding, Farm Director
Jim Lowe, Local News Editor

***WHBJ**
99.1 mhz FM; 25 kw; 99 meters; N33 24 55 W81 18 10
414 Tennessee Avenue, New Ellington, SC
(803) 652-2696
License: Barnwell, SC held by Barnwell Community Radio

Donald W Hadden, President

Batesburg

WBLR
05-10-1956; 1430 khz AM *Hrs Open:* 24
3213 Huxley Drive, Augusta, GA 30909 US
1(800)926-4669
www.gnnradio.org
ctbarinowski@comcast.net
License: Batesburg, SC held by Barinowski Investment Company
Arbitron Metro Market: Grovetown,GA *Target Audience:* General.
Clarence Barinowski, President

WZMJ
08-05-1965; 93.1 mhz FM; 2.1 kw; 561 ft.; N33 54 2 W81 24 25
Rebroadcasts: Simulcast with WOIC(AM) Columbia 100%
2929 East Commercial Blvd., Ste 410, Ft. Lauderdale, FL 33308 US
(803) 785-9596, *Fax:* (803) 695-8605
www.lakemurrayradio.com
lakemurrayradio@comporium.net
License: Batesburg, Lexington County, SC held by Urban Radio II L.L.C.
Group Owner: Inner City Broadcasting; (acq 5-30-2003; $11.1 million with WHXT(FM) Orangeburg).
Nat'l Network: ESPN Radio; Jones Radio Networks
Arbitron Metro Market: Batesburg, SC *Format:* Christian, News, 86
Michael Willis, President/CEO
Steve Patterson, General Manager
Renee Lowder, Sales Manager
Dave Stewart, Programming Director
Richard Peterson, Public Affairs, Outreach & Special Projects

Beaufort

***WAGP**
10-10-1987; 88.7 mhz FM *Hrs Open:* 24; 100 kw; 338 ft.; N32 21 27.1 W80 55 11.2

Mailing Address: P.O. Box 119, Beaufort, SC 29901 US
Second Address: 4 Grober Hill Rd., Suite C, Beaufort, SC 29901
(843) 525-1859, *Fax:* (843) 522-3691
www.wagp.net
info@wagp.net
License: Beaufort, Beaufort County, SC held by The Christian Broadcasting Corp. of Beaufort.
Nat'l Network: Moody
Arbitron Metro Market: Savannah, GA *Format:* Religious *Hrs. of News Programming:* News progmg 20 hrs wkly *Target Audience:* General; evangelical Christians
Carl Broggi, President
Richard Forschner, General Manager

***WJWJ-FM**
08-01-1980; 89.9 mhz FM *Hrs Open:* 24; 47 kw; Ant 1,096 ft; N32 42 42 W80 40 54 *Rebroadcasts:* Rebroadcasts WRJA(FM) Sumter 100%
1101 George Rogers Blvd., Columbia, SC 29211
(803) 737-3200, *Fax:* (803) 737-3552
www.etvradio.org
gasque@scetv.org
License: Beaufort, Beaufort County, SC held by South Carolina Educational TV Commission.
Nat'l Network: NPR; PRI; APM
Hrs. of News Programming: News progmg 120 hrs wkly *Target Audience:* General.
Linda O'Bryon, President
John Gasque, Operations Dir
Shari Hutchinson, General Manager
Shari Hutchinson, Station Manager
Melanie Boyer, General Sales Mgr
John Gasque, Programming Director
John Crockett, Engineering Dir
SkipBeach, Chief Engineer
Melanie Boyer, Underwriting Manager

WVGB
01-01-1959; 1490 khz AM; 0.5 kw-D, ND1; 1 kw-N, ND1; N32 26 8 W80 41 54
806 Monson Street, Beaufort, SC 29902 US
(843) 524-4700, *Fax:* (843) 524-1329
vgbradio@earthlink.net
License: Beaufort, SC held by Vivian Broadcasting Inc.
Nat'l Network: American Urban
Arbitron Metro Market: Beaufort, SC *Format:* Classic Rock *Special Programming:* Community progmg, sports *Target Audience:* 18-65; African American
William Galloway, President
Vivian Galloway, General Manager
Darryl Jamison, Station Manager
Derrick Moon, Programming Director

WYKZ
08-08-1962; 98.7 mhz FM *Hrs Open:* 24; 99 kw; 715 ft.; N32 19 43 W80 56 17
600 Congress Ave., Suite 1400, Austin, TX 78701 US
(912) 964-7794, *Fax:* (912) 964-9414
www.987theriver.com
info@987theriver.com
License: Beaufort, Beaufort County, SC held by Capstar TX L.P.
Group Owner: Star Radio Company
Arbitron Metro Market: Beaufort, SC *Format:* Adult Contemp *Special Programming:* Oldies 5 hrs wkly *Hrs. of News Programming:* news progmg 3 hrs wkly *No. News Employees:* 1 *Target Audience:* 25-54; female
Steve Richards, Operations Dir
Mark Robertson, Programming Director
Craig Scott, Promotions Manager
Marty Foglia, Chief Engineer
Sheryl Collison, Sales Director

Belton

***WEPC**
05-01-1994; 88.5 mhz FM *Hrs Open:* 24; 50 kw; 299 ft.; N34 23 43 W82 29 49 *Rebroadcasts:* Rebroadcasts WRAF-FM Toccoa Falls, GA 100%
Mailing Address: Falls Road, Toccoa Falls, GA 30598 US
Second Address: 292 Old Clarkesville Hwy., Belton, SC 30577
(800) 251-8326(706) 282-6030, *Fax:* (706) 282-6090
www.myfavoritestation.net
radio@myfavoritestation.net
License: Belton, Anderson County, SC held by Toccoa Falls College.
Arbitron Metro Market: Belton, SC *Format:* Adult Contemp, Christian
Marty Lee, Operations Dir
David Cornelius, General Manager
Bryan Race, Station Manager and Program Director
Mike Shelley, Assistant Manager
Kevin Klump, Program Coordinator
Mike Shelley, Music Director
Debbie Faubion, Children'sProgramming
Cathy Klump, Social Networking Coordinator
Peggy Leff, Donor Relations Coordinator

WROP
10-01-1956; 1390 khz AM
490 South Main St, Belton, SC 29627 US
(713) 479-5358
www.wevg1470.com
clarson@yahoosportsradio.com
License: Belton, SC held by Big Fish Broadcasting LLC
Arbitron Metro Market: Greenville-Spartanburg, SC *Format:* Sports, Talk *Target Audience:* General.
David Gow, CEO
Jeffrey Roper, General Manager
Craig Larson, Programming Director
Christopher Morales, Assistant Porgram Director
Josh Vexler, Affiliate Relations
Gina Messick, Digital Sales Manager

Belvedere

***WAFJ**
08-01-1994; 88.3 mhz FM *Hrs Open:* 24; 4.5 kw; 1388 ft.; N33 24 29 W81 50 36
5015 South Florida Ave, # 104, Lakeland, FL 33813 US
(803) 819-3125, *Fax:* (803) 819-3129
www.wafj.com
info@wafj.com
License: Belvedere, Aiken County, SC held by Radio Training Network Inc.
Nat'l Network: Fox News Radio
Arbitron Metro Market: Augusta, GA *Format:* Christian *No. News Employees:* 1 *Target Audience:* 25-54; women
Steve Swanson, General Manager
Steve Swanson, Program Director
Cleve Walker, News Director
David Perry, Production Director

Bennettsville

WBSC
06-01-1947; 1550 khz AM; 10 kw-D, DAN; 5 kw-N, DAN; N34 40 52 W79 42 4
501 Sewanee Street, Bennettsville, SC 29512 US
(803) 479-7121, *Fax:* (803) 479- 4474
www.wbsc1550.com
wbsc@aol.com
License: Bennettsville, SC held by D. Mitch Broadcasting Inc.
Nat'l Network: ABC *Nat'l Reps:* Dora-Clayton
Format: Gospel, Oldies *Special Programming:* Black 15 hrs wkly
Dwight Johnson, CEO
Richard Gehm, Chief of Operations

Bishopville

WAGS
02-24-1954; 1380 khz AM *Hrs Open:* 6:30 AM-6 PM; 1 kw-D; N34 12 35 W80 13 34
142 Wags Dr., Bishopville, SC 29010
(803) 484-5415
wagsradio@sc.rr.com
License: Bishopville, Lee County, SC held by Beaver Communications
Group Owner: James D. Jenkins; (acq 11-01-99; $27,500).
Population Served: 22,000*Special Programming:* Live remotes-parades, civic events, festivals 2 hrs, relg 7 hrs wkly *Hrs. of News Programming:* News progmg 6 hrs wkly *Target Audience:* 25-55 plus. *Adv. Rates:* 8; 8; 8; 8
James D. Jenkins, Owner/General Manager

Blackville

WIIZ
04-01-1996; 97.9 mhz FM; 50 kw; 433 ft.; N33 6 52 W81 23 13
P.O. Box 814, Barnwell, SC 29812 US
(803) 259-9797, *Fax:* (803) 541-9700
www.wiizfm.com
thewiz@wiiz979.com
License: Blackville, Barnwell County, SC held by NicWild Communications Inc.
Arbitron Metro Market: Augusta, GA *Format:* Urban Contemporary
Bobby Nichols, CEO
Bobby Nichols, General Manager
Russ Parr, Disc Jockey
James Carter, Disc Jockey

Bluffon

WTYB
10-01-1977; 103.9 mhz FM; 50 kw; Ant 344 ft; N32 03 33 W81 00 57
214 Television Cir., Savannah, GA 53202
(912) 961-9000, *Fax:* (912) 961-7070
www.magic1039fm.com
info@diane.hubelcumulus.com
License: Bluffon, Chatham County, GA held by Volt Radio LLC
Group Owner: Cumulus Media Inc.; (acq 3-26-98; grpsl).
Arbitron Metro Market: Savannah, GA
Diane Hubel, General Manager

Blythewood

WBAJ
01-01-1999; 890 khz AM
25510 Mandarin Court, Loma Linda, CA 92354 US
(304) 765-7373, *Fax:* (304) 765-7836
www.105kqv.com
info@105kqv.com
License: Blythewood, SC held by Family First
Arbitron Metro Market: Cowen WV *Format:* Classic Rock *Target Audience:* 18-49.
Al Sergi, President

Bowman

WSPX
10-01-1997; 94.5 mhz FM *Hrs Open:* 24; 3.5 kw; 434 ft.; N33 19 13 W80 43 52
Mailing Address: P.Ob Box 1546, Orangeburg, SC 29116 US
Second Address: 1236 Five Chop Rd., Orangeburg, SC 29115
(803) 539-9450, *Fax:* (803) 539-9458
email@wfmv.com
License: Bowman, Orangeburg County, SC held by Glory Communications Inc.
Group Owner: Glory Communications Inc.; acq 4-19-01; $400,000).
Format: Gospel
Alex Snipes, General Manager

Branchville

WGFG
12-13-1993; 105.3 mhz FM *Hrs Open:* 24; 12.5 kw; 463 ft.; N33 26 35 W80 48 16
PO Box 1546, Orangeburg, SC 29115 US
(803) 536-1710, *Fax:* (803) 531-1089
mail@miller.fm
License: Branchville, Orangeburg County, SC held by Miller Communications Inc.
Group Owner: Miller Communications Inc.; (acq 4-30-2003; $1.25 million with WQKI-FM Orangeburg).
Nat'l Network: ABC
Format: Oldies *Target Audience:* 25-64; baby boomers
Harold Miller Jr., President
Russ Fender, Operations Dir
Theresa Miller, General Manager

Briarcliff Acres

WRXZ
04-05-1975; 107.1 mhz FM *Hrs Open:* 18; 50 kw; 492 ft.; N33 56 14 W78 57 53
Two Bala Plaza, Suite 801, Bala-Cynwyd, PA 19004 US
(843) 293-0107, *Fax:* (843) 293-1717
www.thesound1071.com
info@thesound1071.com
License: Briarcliff Acres, Horry County, SC held by Qantum of Myrtle Beach License Co. LLC.
Group Owner: Qantum Communications Corp.; (acq 7-2-2003; grpsl)
Arbitron Metro Market: Myrtle Beach, SC
Jimmy Feuger, General Manager
Shawn Small, Programming Director

Bucksport

WGTR
06-01-1993; 107.9 mhz FM; 20 kw; 784 ft.; N33 35 45 W79 3 11
Two Bala Plaza, Suite 801, Bala-Cynwyd, PA 19004 US
(843) 293-0107, *Fax:* (843) 293-1717
www.gator1079.com
info@gator1079.com
License: Bucksport, Horry County, SC held by Qantum of Myrtle Beach License Co. LLC.
Group Owner: Qantum Communications Corp.; (acq 7-2-2003; grpsl).
Arbitron Metro Market: Myrtle Beach, SC *Format:* Country
Special Programming: Motor racing 8 hrs wkly

Jimmy Feuger, General Manager

Camden

WCAM
07-23-1948; 1590 khz AM *Hrs Open:* 6 AM-11 PM
Mailing Address: P.O. Box 753, Camden, SC 29020 US
Second Address: 5 The Commons Ward Rd., Lugoff, SC 29078
(803) 438-9002, *Fax:* (803) 408-2288
www.kol1027.com
wpubradio@bellsouth.net
License: Camden, SC held by Kershaw Radio Corp.
Regional Network: S.C. News Net.
Arbitron Metro Market: Camden, SC *Format:* Oldies *Target Audience:* 45 plus.
Chris Johnson, General Manager
Bill Rogers, Programming Director

WPUB-FM
12-01-1974; 102.7 mhz FM; 6 kw; 299 ft.; N34 13 31 W80 40 44
Mailing Address: P.O. Box 753, Camden, SC 29020 US
Second Address: 5 The Commons Ward Rd., Camden, SC 29020
(803) 438-9002, *Fax:* (803) 408-2288
www.kol1027.com
wpubradio@camden.net
License: Camden, Kershaw County, SC
Format: Oldies *Target Audience:* 25-55. *Adv. Rates:* 13; 13; 13; 13
Gregory Weston, General Manager

Cameron

WTQS
01-01-2008; 1490 khz AM
US
(803) 939-9530, *Fax:* (803) 939-9469
wsmvproduction@wsmv.com
License: Cameron, SC held by Glory Communications Inc.
Group Owner: Glory Communications Inc.; (acq 2-10-2006; $50,000 for CP)
Arbitron Metro Market: Cameron, SC
Alex Snipe, President

Cayce

WLTY
07-11-1974; 96.7 mhz FM; 9 kw; 433 ft.; N34 0 18 W81 0 44
600 Congress Avenue, Suite 1400, Austin, TX 78701 US
(803) 343-1100, *Fax:* (803) 256-5255
www.967stevefm.com
info@wlty.com
License: Cayce, Lexington County, SC held by Capstar TX L.P.
Group Owner: Clear Channel Communications Inc.; (acq 8-30-00; grpsl).
Nat'l Reps: Clear Channel
Arbitron Metro Market: Columbia, SC *Format:* Variety/Diverse *Hrs. of News Programming:* News progmg 6 hrs wkly *Target Audience:* 25-44; professionals & young adults
Bob Huntley, General Manager
Todd Shuster, General Sales Mgr
LJ Smith, Programming Director

WGCV
08-22-1958; 620 khz AM *Hrs Open:* 24
1303 State Street, Cayce, SC 29033 US
(803) 939-9530, *Fax:* (803) 799-1620
www.wgcv.net
acampbell@wfmv.com
License: Cayce, SC held by Glory Communications Inc.
Group Owner: Glory Communications Inc.; acq 10-8-99).
Nat'l Network: American Urban
Arbitron Metro Market: Columbia, SC *Format:* Gospel *No. News Employees:* 1 *Target Audience:* 34-65; Black adults
Alex Snipe, CEO
Rev. Isaac Heyward, Station Manager
Alexis Campbell, General Sales Mgr
Tony Jamison, Programming Director
Armita Thomas, Traffic
Yvonne Carrington, Accounting
Ullanda M. Harp, Assistant Program Director

*WYFV
10-10-1990; 88.5 mhz FM *Hrs Open:* 24; 50 kw; 171 ft.; N33 54 32 W81 5 57
8030 Arrowridge Blvd., Charlotte, NC 28273 US
(704) 523-5555, *Fax:* (704) 522-1967
www.bbnradio.org
bbn@bbnradio.org
License: Cayce, Lexington County, SC held by Bible Broadcasting Network Inc.
Group Owner: Bible Broadcasting Network; acq 6-26-90; *Arbitron Metro Market:* Columbia, SC *Format:* Religious *Hrs. of News Programming:* News progmg 10 hrs wkly *Target Audience:* General.
Lowell Davey, President

Charleston

*WALC
04-04-1990; 100.5 mhz FM *Hrs Open:* 24; 13.5 kw; 448 ft.; N32 49 0.4 W79 50 9.7
50 E. Rivercenter Blvd, Suite 1200, Covington, KY 14011 US
(843) 884-2534, *Fax:* (843) 884-6096
www.drive1005.com
License: Charleston, Charleston County, SC held by Radio Training Network Inc.
Nat'l Reps: Katz Radio
Arbitron Metro Market: Charleston, SC *Format:* Christian
Allen Henderson, General Manager
Terri Hegel, General Sales Mgr
Willie Bennett, Chief Engineer
Alene Grevey, VP/Market Manager

WEZL
10-03-1970; 103.5 mhz FM *Hrs Open:* 24; 100 kw; 659 ft.; N32 49 4 W79 50 9
50 East Rivercentr Blvd, Suite 1200, Covington, KY 41011 US
(843) 884-2534, *Fax:* (843) 884-6096
www.wezlfm.com
AleneGrevey@ClearChannel.com?subject=Inquiry%20from%20WEZL-FM%20Web%20Site
License: Charleston, Charleston County, SC held by Citicasters Licenses L.P.
Group Owner: Clear Channel Communications Inc.; (acq 5-4-99; grpsl).
Arbitron Metro Market: Charleston, SC *Format:* Country *Hrs. of News Programming:* news progmg 3 to 4 hrs wkly *No. News Employees:* 1
Paul Smith, General Manager
Michelle Kelly, General Sales Mgr
Scott Johnson, Programming Director
Jonny Knight, Promotions Manager
Brian Worboys, News Director
Willie Bennett, Engineering Dir
Willie Bennett, Chief Engineer
Alene Grevey, VP/Market Manager
Bill West, PD / Music Director
Lisa Cooper, Business Manager
Mary Catherine Walker, Digital Content Director

*WFCH
12-01-1986; 88.5 mhz FM; 29.5 kw; 305 ft.; N32 49 4 W79 50 8
4135 Northgate Blvd, Suite 1, Sacramento, CA 95834 US
(800) 543-1495, *Fax:* (510) 568-6190
www.familyradio.com
info@familyradio.org
License: Charleston, Charleston County, SC held by Family Stations Inc.
Group Owner: Family Stations Inc.
Nat'l Network: Family Radio
Arbitron Metro Market: Charleston, SC *Format:* Religious
Harold Camping, General Manager
Joe Papp, Chief Engineer

WQNT
01-01-1948; 1450 khz AM; 1 kw-U; N32 48 15 W79 57 43
60 Markfield Dr., Suite 4, Charleston, SC 29418
(843) 763-6631, *Fax:* (843) 766-1239
ted@kirkmanbroadcasting.com
License: Charleston, Charleston County, SC held by Kirkman Broadcasting Inc.
Group Owner: Kirkman Broadcasting Inc.; (acq 1995)
Nat'l Network: Fox Sports
Population Served: 460,000 *Arbitron Metro Market:* Charleston, SC *Special Programming:* Relg one hr wkly *Target Audience:* 25-54; Men *Adv. Rates:* 20; 20; 20; 10
Gil Kirkman, President
Ted Byrne, Operations Dir
Rick Howze, General Sales Mgr
Wally Momeier, Chief Engineer

WQSC
01-01-1946; 1340 khz AM *Hrs Open:* 24; 1 kw-U; N32 49 07 W79 57 43
60 Markfield Dr., Suite 4, Charleston, SC 29418
(843) 763-6631, *Fax:* (843) 766-1239
www.1340theboardwalk.net
ted@kirkmanbroadcasting.com
License: Charleston, Charleston County, SC held by Kirkman Broadcasting Inc.
Group Owner: Kirkman Broadcasting Inc.; acq 11-1-94).
Population Served: 66,945 *Arbitron Metro Market:* Charleston, SC *Target Audience:* 25-54; Adults *Adv. Rates:* 20; 20; 20; 20
Gil Kirkman, President
Ted Byrne, Operations Dir
Rick Howze, General Sales Mgr
John Dixon, News Director
Wally Momeier, Chief Engineer

WLTQ
01-01-1947; 730 khz AM *Hrs Open:* 24
50 E. Rivercenter Blvd., #1200, Covington, KY 41011 US
(828) 859-6982
catholicradioinsc.com
info@thedrive100.com
License: Charleston, SC held by Indigo Radio LLC
Arbitron Metro Market: Charleston, SC *Format:* Religious
Mark Jorgenson, General Manager

*WSCI
01-01-1973; 89.3 mhz FM *Hrs Open:* 24; 97 kw; 540 ft; N32 47 44 W79 50 27 *Rebroadcasts:* Rebroadcasts WLTR(FM) Columbia 95%
1101 George Rogers Blvd., Columbia, SC 29211
(803) 737-3200, *Fax:* (803) 737-3552
www.etvradio.org
gasque@scetv.org
License: Charleston, Charleston County, SC held by South Carolina Educational TV Commission.
Nat'l Network: NPR; PRI; APM
Population Served: 66,945 *Arbitron Metro Market:* Charleston, SC *Hrs. of News Programming:* News progmg 70 hrs wkly
Linda O'Bryon, President
John Gasque, Operations Dir
Shari Hutchinson, General Manager
Shari Hutchinson, Station Manager
Melanie Boyer, General Sales Mgr
John Gasque, Programming Director
John Crockett, Engineering Dir
SkipBeach, Chief Engineer

WSSX-FM
01-01-1945; 95.1 mhz FM *Hrs Open:* 24; 100 kw; 1001 ft.; N32 47 44 W79 50 27
140 S. Ash Ave., Tempe, AZ 85281 US
(843) 277-1200, *Fax:* (843) 277-1212
www.95fx.com
info@95fx.com
License: Charleston, Charleston County, SC
Group Owner: Cumulus Media Inc.; (acq 6-9-99; grpsl).
Nat'l Network: Westwood One
Arbitron Metro Market: Charleston, SC *Format:* Adult Contemp, Contemporary Hits/Top 40 *No. News Employees:* 1 *Target Audience:* 18-34.
Paul O'Mailey, General Manager

WIWF
04-01-1948; 96.9 mhz FM; 99 kw; 1768 ft.; N32 55 28 W79 41 58
140 S. Ash Ave., Tempe, AZ 85281 US
(843) 277-1200, *Fax:* (843) 277-1212
www.sunny969.com
info@sunny969.com
License: Charleston, Charleston County, SC
Group Owner: Cumulus Media Inc.
Nat'l Reps: McGavren Guild
Arbitron Metro Market: Charleston, SC *Format:* Country
Paul O'Malley, General Manager
Bocky Gilleath, General Sales Mgr
Brian Driver, Programming Director
J.T. Tucker, Chief Engineer

WTMA
01-01-1939; 1250 khz AM *Hrs Open:* 24; 5 kw-D, 1 kw-N, DA-N; N32 49 20 W79 58 45
4230 Faber Place Dr., Suite 100, N. Charleston, SC 85281
(843) 277-1200, *Fax:* (843) 227-1212
www.wtma.com
mike.edwards@cumulus.com
License: Charleston, Charleston County, SC
Group Owner: Cumulus Media Inc.; (acq 6-9-99; grpsl).
Nat'l Network: Westwood One; ABC *Wire Services:* AP
Population Served: 15,000 *Arbitron Metro Market:* Charleston, SC *Hrs. of News Programming:* news progmg 5 hrs wkly *No. News Employees:* 2 *Target Audience:* 25-54.
Mike Edwards, Operations Dir
Paul O'Malley, General Manager

WSPO
05-01-1967; 1390 khz AM; 5 kw-D, DAN; 5 kw-N, DAN; Ant 340 ft; N32 49 28 W80 0 10
140 S. Ash Ave., Tempe, AZ 85281 US
(843) 972-1100, *Fax:* (843) 972-1200
www.wspsports.com
License: Charleston, SC held by Apex Broadcasting Inc.

Group Owner: Apex Broadcasting Inc.; (acq 8-4-2008; $1.5 million)
Arbitron Metro Market: Charleston, SC *Format:* Sports, Talk
G. Dean Pearce, President

Cheraw

WCRE

07-01-1953; 1420 khz AM *Hrs Open:* 24; 1 kw-D, 97 w-N / 250 24 hrs.; N34 40 48 W79 53 58
Mailing Address: Box 160, Cheraw, SC 29520
Second Address: 541 Hwy. #1 S., Cheraw, SC 29520
(843) 537-7887, *Fax:* (843) 537-7307
www.wcreradio.com,www.myfm939.com
janepigg@gmail.com
License: Cheraw, Chesterfield County, SC held by Pee Dee Broadcasting LLC
Population Served: 63,000*Special Programming:* Black 5 hrs wkly *Hrs. of News Programming:* news progmg 12 hrs wkly *No. News Employees:* 1 *Target Audience:* 25 plus; Adults *Adv. Rates:* 20; 20; 20; 20
Jane Elizabeth Davis-Pigg, President

WJMX-FM

07-17-1979; 103.3 mhz FM; 50 kw; 492 ft.; N34 30 18 W79 54 18
Two Bala Plaza, Suite 801, Bala-Cynwyd, PA 19004 US
(843) 667-9569, *Fax:* (843) 673-7390
www.103xonline.com
denis103@gmail.com
License: Cheraw, Chesterfield County, SC held by Qantum of Florence License Co. LLC.
Group Owner: Qantum Communications Corp.; (acq 7-2-2003; grpsl).
Regional Network: S.C. News Net. *Nat'l Reps:* McGavren Guild
Arbitron Metro Market: Florence, SC *Format:* Contemporary Hits/Top 40 *Target Audience:* 18-34.
Randy Wilcox, Operations Dir
Craig Dalla Riva, General Manager
Craig Dallariva, General Sales Mgr
Denis Davis, Programming Director
Sherry Miller, Director of Sales
Rene Caplan, Public Service Announcement Director

Chester

WBT-FM

08-30-1969; 99.3 mhz FM *Hrs Open:* 24; 7.7 kw; 598 ft.; N34 47 30 W81 16 6 *Rebroadcasts:* Rebroadcasts WBT(AM) Charlotte 100%
One Julian Price Place, Charlotte, NC 28208 US
(704) 374-3500, *Fax:* (704) 338-3062
www.wbt.com
tsavery@wbt.com
License: Chester, Chester County, SC held by Greater Media of Charlotte Inc.
Group Owner: Greater Media Inc.; (acq 1-31-2008; grpsl)
Arbitron Metro Market: Charlotte, NC *Format:* News, News/Talk, 86 *Special Programming:* Gospel 6 hrs wkly *Hrs. of News Programming:* news progmg 6 hrs wkly *No. News Employees:* 7 *Target Audience:* 25-54;information, sports seekers
Rick Jackson, Operations Dir
Terry Mace, General Sales Mgr
Carl East, Programming Director
Tom Jackson, Operations Director
Zach Simpson, Webmaster
Matt DuBois, Marketing Director
Jessica ""Reeves"" RoBards, MarketingAdministrator

WGCD

07-19-1948; 1490 khz AM; 1 kw-U, ND1; N34 41 54 W81 12 6
P. O. Box 117, Chester, SC 29706 US
(803) 329-2760, *Fax:* (803) 329-3317
License: Chester, SC held by Wisdom LLC.
Group Owner: Wisdom LLC; (acq 2-2-2009; grpsl)
Format: Gospel
Frank Neeley, General Manager
Frankie Hemphill, Station Manager

Chesterfield

WVSZ

01-01-1993; 107.3 mhz FM; 4.5 kw; 328 ft.; N34 43 12 W80 5 45
P.O. Box 307, Rock Hill, SC 29731 US
(843) 324-1340, *Fax:* (803) 324-2860
www.wrhi.com
almiller@wrhi.com
License: Chesterfield, Chesterfield County, SC held by Our Three Sons Broadcasting L.L.P.
Group Owner: Our Three Sons Broadcasting L.L.P.; acq 2-28-97; $142,500)
Nat'l Network: ABC *Regional Network:* S.C. News Net.
Arbitron Metro Market: Chesterfield, SC *Format:* Country *No. News Employees:* 2
Steven Stone, Operations Dir
Allan Miller, General Manager
Sheila Caldwell, Programming Director
Mike Crowder, News Director
Andrew Kiel, News Staff
Noreen Brake-Ruff, Traffic Director
Allan Miller, Managing Partner
MarioWashington, Program Director
Jasmine Rutledge, Programming Staff

*WRFE

01-01-2007; 89.3 mhz FM; 1.5 kw; 197 ft.; N34 43 15 W80 5 18
P O Box 7337, Mayaguez, PR 0681 US
(336) 788-1155, *Fax:* (336) 788-7199
www.joyfm.org
office@joyfm.org
License: Chesterfield, Chesterfield County, SC held by Positive Alternative Radio Inc.
Group Owner: Positive Alternative Radio Inc.; (acq 1-16-2008; $500,000)
Arbitron Metro Market: Chesterfield, SC *Format:* Gospel
Edward Baker, President
Brian Sanders, General Manager

Clearwater

WHHD

04-01-1987; 98.3 mhz FM *Hrs Open:* 24; 11.5 kw; 486 ft.; N33 30 44 W82 4 48
1776 Briarcliff Road Ne, Atlanta, GA 30306 US
(706) 396-7000, *Fax:* (706) 396-7100
www.hd983.com
mail@whhd.com
License: Clearwater, Aiken County, SC held by WGAC License LLC.
Group Owner: Beasley Broadcast Group Inc.; (acq 4-2-2001; $12 million with WKXC-FM Aiken).
Arbitron Metro Market: Augusta, GA *Format:* Contemporary Hits/Top 40 *Special Programming:* Kidd Kraddick in the Morning *Target Audience:* 18-49 females *Adv. Rates:* Inquiries only
Kent Murphy, General Sales Mgr
Chuck Whitaker, Programming Director
Kent Dunn, Promotions Manager
Charlie McCoy, Chief Engineer
Bryan Axelson, Promotions Director

Clemson

WAHT

07-27-1969; 1560 khz AM *Hrs Open:* 6 AM-8 PM; 0.5 kw-C, NDD; 1 kw-D, NDD; N34 42 4 W82 49 30
202 Lawrence Rd., P.O. Box 1560, Clemson, SC 29631 US
(864) 654-1560, *Fax:* (864) 654-3300
www.wahtam.com
waht@wahtam.com
License: Clemson, SC held by Golden Corners Broadcasting Inc.
Regional Network: S.C. News Net. *Wire Services:* CBS
Arbitron Metro Market: Clemson, SC *Format:* Oldies *Hrs. of News Programming:* news progmg 35 hrs wkly *No. News Employees:* 1 *Target Audience:* 35-58; older yuppies
George Clement, President
Faye Clement, Operations Dir
Jeff Bright, Station Manager

WCCP-FM

04-08-1993; 104.9 mhz FM *Hrs Open:* 24; 4.6 kw; 371 ft.; N34 38 13 W82 42 30
P.O. Box 1560, Clemson, SC 29633 US
(864) 654-4004, *Fax:* (864) 654-3300
www.wccpfm.com
info@wccpfm.com
License: Clemson, Pickens County, SC
Nat'l Network: CBS; Sporting News Radio Network
Arbitron Metro Market: Clemson, SC *Format:* Sports *Target Audience:* 91% of the WCCP audience is between the ages of 18-54 & 96% of the WCCP audience is male *Adv. Rates:* 30; 25; 21; 18
George Clement, CEO
Barry Clement, Operations Dir
Aly Darby, Station Manager
Chris Downey, General Sales Mgr

*WSBF-FM

03-16-1961; 88.1 mhz FM; 3 kw; 200 ft.; N34 40 42 W82 49 15
104 Holtzendorff, Clemson, SC 29634 US
(864) 656-4010, *Fax:* (864) 656-4011
wsbf.clemson.edu/
gm@wsbf.net
License: Clemson, Pickens County, SC held by Clemson University Board of Trustees.
Nat'l Network: Westwood One
Format: Alternative *Target Audience:* 16-25.
Farid Suleman, CEO
Judy Ellis, President
Mark Ericson, Operations Dir
Marty Lessard, General Manager
Andrew Harris, General Sales Mgr
Jonathan Smith, Programming Director
Derek Riker, Promotions Manager
Marc Fisher, ChiefEngineer

Clinton

WPCC

09-11-1957; 1410 khz AM *Hrs Open:* 24; 1 kw-D, ND1; 0.1 kw-N, ND1; N34 26 42 W81 53 24
Mailing Address: Hwy 72, S. Greenwood Hwy, Clinton, SC 29325 US
Second Address: 1766 Hwy 72 West, West Clinton, SC 29325
(864) 833-1410, *Fax:* (864) 833-2467
www.sportsradio1410wpcc.com
wpcc@charter.net
License: Clinton, SC held by Laurens County Communications Inc.
Nat'l Network: ESPN Radio
Format: Sports *Special Programming:* Moring Show- The Doghouse, Local and Regional Sports *Hrs. of News Programming:* news progmg one hr wkly *No. News Employees:* 1 *Target Audience:* General.
A. Cruickshanks, President
Rhonda Cruickshanks, General Manager
Chris Burgin, Programming Director

Cokesbury

*WKRI

91.9 mhz FM; 20.5 kw; 354 ft.; N34 21 26 W82 9 14 US
(866) 468-9533
www.i919wkri.com
License: Cokesbury, Greenwood County, SC held by Spirit Broadcasting Group Inc.
Arbitron Metro Market: Cokesbury, SC
C. Curtis Sigmon, President
Scott Garrison, General Sales Mgr

Columbia

WARQ

02-06-1971; 93.5 mhz FM *Hrs Open:* 24; 2.8 kw; 443 ft.; N34 0 4 W81 2 5
Mailing Address: 200 Concord Plz., Ste 600, San Antonio, TX 78216 US
Second Address: 1900 Pineview Rd., Columbia, SC 29290
(803) 695-8600, *Fax:* (803) 695-8605
www.warq.com
info@warq.com
License: Columbia, Richland County, SC held by Urban Radio II L.L.C.
Group Owner: Inner City Broadcasting; (acq 8-7-2000; grpsl).
Nat'l Network: Westwood One *Wire Services:* Accu-Weather
Arbitron Metro Market: Columbia, SC *Hrs. of News Programming:* news progmg 5 hrs wkly *No. News Employees:* 1 *Target Audience:* 18-49.
Steve Patterson, General Manager
Bryan Hendry, General Sales Mgr
Dave Stewart, Programming Director
Jamie Muldrow, Promotions Manager

WCOS

01-01-1939; 1400 khz AM *Hrs Open:* 24; 1 kw-U, ND1; N34 0 18 W81 0 43
600 Congres Avenue, Suite 1400, Austin, TX 78701 US
(803) 343-1100, *Fax:* (803) 798-5255
www.975wcos.com
kelleyroyster@clearchannel.com
License: Columbia, SC held by Capstar TX L.P.
Group Owner: Clear Channel Communications Inc.; (acq 9-1-00; grpsl)
Nat'l Reps: Clear Channel
Arbitron Metro Market: Columbia, SC *Format:* Sports *Target Audience:* Men 25-54.
Gary Barboza, Operations Dir
Tim McFalls, General Manager
Todd Shuster, General Sales Mgr
Gary Frakes, Promotions Manager
Mary Pais, News Director
Gary Robinson, Engineering Dir
Bobby Martin, General Manager
ChristopherThompson, News Reporter

WCOS-FM
03-01-1951; 97.5 mhz FM *Hrs Open:* 24; 100 kw; 981 ft.; N34 8 23 W81 3 22
600 Congress Avenue, Suite 1400, Austin, TX 78701 US
(803) 343-1100, *Fax:* (803) 798-5255
www.975wcos.com
kelleyroyster@clearchannel.com
License: Columbia, Richland County, SC
Arbitron Metro Market: Columbia, SC *Format:* Country *No. News Employees:* 1 *Target Audience:* 25-54.
Todd Shuster, General Sales Mgr
Ron Brooks, Programming Director
Susan Brown, Promotions Manager
Gary Robinson, Chief Engineer
Glen Garrett, Music Director

WCEO
01-01-1994; 840 khz AM *Hrs Open:* Sunrise-sunset; 50 kw-D, DAD; N34 12 42 W80 50 5
1320 Hidden Brook Lane, Acworth, GA 30144 US
(803) 419-7366, *Fax:* (803) 419-7363
www.latremendaradio.com
License: Columbia, SC held by Norsan Broadcasting WCEO LLC.
Group Owner: Norsan Consulting and Management Inc.; (acq 10-1-2006; $1.6 million)
Arbitron Metro Market: Columbia, SC *Adv. Rates:* 40; 35; 40; na
Lino Cruz, Station Manager

WISW
06-30-1954; 1320 khz AM *Hrs Open:* 24; 5 kw-D, DAN; 2.5 kw-N, DAN; N34 0 16 W81 4 15
P.O. Box 8, Bloomington, IL 61702 US
(803) 796-7600, *Fax:* (803) 796-5502
www.wisradio.com
License: Columbia, SC
Group Owner: Cumulus Media Inc.
Nat'l Reps: Christal
Arbitron Metro Market: Columbia, SC *Format:* Talk *Special Programming:* Sports *Hrs. of News Programming:* news progmg 168 hrs wkly *No. News Employees:* 5 *Target Audience:* 35-64.
William McElveen, President
Tim Miller, Operations Dir
Bill MacAvine, General Sales Mgr
Al Conner, Programming Director
Ray Allen, News Director
Ed Noyes, Engineering Dir

***WLTR**
07-01-1976; 91.3 mhz FM *Hrs Open:* 24; 96 kw; 761 ft; N34 07 07 W80 56 12
1101 George Rogers Blvd., Columbia, SC 29211
(803) 737-3200, *Fax:* (803) 737-3552
www.etvradio.org
gasque@scetv.org
License: Columbia, Richland County, SC held by South Carolina Educ. TV Commission.
Nat'l Network: NPR; PRI; APM
Population Served: 450,000 *Arbitron Metro Market:* Columbia, SC
Linda O'Bryon, President
John Gasque, Operations Dir
Shari Hutchinson, General Manager
Shari Hutchinson, Station Manager
Melanie Boyer, General Sales Mgr
John Gasque, Programming Director
John Crockett, Engineering Dir
SkipBeach, Chief Engineer

***WMHK**
08-30-1976; 89.7 mhz FM; 100 kw; 1398 ft.; N34 5 49 W80 45 51
Post Office Box 3122, Columbia, SC 29230 US
(803) 754-5400, *Fax:* (803) 714-0849
www.wmhk.com
wmhk@wmhk.com
License: Columbia, Richland County, SC held by Columbia Bible College Broadcasting Co.
Arbitron Metro Market: Columbia, SC *Format:* Christian *Target Audience:* 25-44; women
John Owens, Operations Dir
Jeff Cruz, Programming Director
Joe Paulo, Broadcasting Director
David Morrison, Technical Director

WNOK
07-15-1959; 104.7 mhz FM *Hrs Open:* 24; 90 kw; 1033 ft.; N34 9 3 W80 54 36
600 Congress Avenue, Suite 1400, Austin, TX 78701 US
(803) 343-1100, *Fax:* (803) 779-7874
www.wnok.com
ljsmith@clearchannel.com
License: Columbia, Richland County, SC held by Capstar TX L.P.
Group Owner: Clear Channel Communications Inc.; (acq 8-30-00; grpsl).
Arbitron Metro Market: Columbia, SC *Format:* Contemporary Hits/Top 40 *Target Audience:* 18-34; landed gentry
Bob Hentley, General Manager
Todd Shuster, General Sales Mgr
LJ Smith, Programming Director

WOIC
01-01-1947; 1230 khz AM; 1 kw-U, DA-N; N33 59 34 W81 02 45
Box 9127, Columbia, SC 78216
(803) 776-1013, *Fax:* (803) 695-8605
www.espn1230am.com
License: Columbia, Richland County, SC held by Urban Radio II L.L.C.
Group Owner: Inner City Broadcasting; (acq 8-7-2000; grpsl).
Nat'l Network: USA *Nat'l Reps:* Eastman
Population Served: 461,000 *Arbitron Metro Market:* Columbia, SC *Hrs. of News Programming:* News progmg 3 hrs wkly *Target Audience:* 25-54; Male
Steve Patterson, General Manager
Mark Fitzmayer, General Sales Mgr
Chris Connors, Programming Director
Michelle Alston, Promotions Manager
Trent Muldrow, Chief Engineer

WLXC
04-15-1989; 103.1 mhz FM; 6 kw; 308 ft.; N34 3 5 W81 0 7
P.O. Box 5106, Columbia, SC 29250 US
(803) 796-7600, *Fax:* (803) 739-1042
License: Columbia, Richland County, SC
Group Owner: Cumulus Media Inc.
Arbitron Metro Market: Columbia, SC *TV Affiliate:* Urban contemp *Special Programming:* news progmg one hr wkly *Hrs. of News Programming:* 1 *No. News Employees:* 25-54; upward, mobile, hi

WQXL
06-15-1945; 1470 khz AM *Hrs Open:* 6 AM-8:30 PM
1303 Sunset Drive, Columbia, SC 29230 US
(803) 779-7911, *Fax:* (803) 252-2158
wqxl1470@aol.com
License: Columbia, SC held by Glory Communications Inc.
Group Owner: Glory Communications Inc.; (acq 5-11-2007; $200,000)
Nat'l Network: USA
Arbitron Metro Market: Columbia, SC *Format:* Religious *Target Audience:* 25-49.
Alex Snipe, President
Olin Jenkins, Operations Dir
Donna Moore, Station Manager

WXBT
08-05-1975; 560 khz AM *Hrs Open:* 24; 5 kw-D, DAN; 5 kw-N, DAN; 331 ft; N34 2 0 W81 8 32
600 Congress Avenue, Suite 1400, Austin, TX 78701 US
(803) 343-1100, *Fax:* 803-748-WCOS
www.560theteam.com
License: Columbia, SC held by Capstar TX L.P..
Group Owner: Clear Channel Communications Inc.; (acq 8-30-00; grpsl).
Nat'l Network: CBS
Arbitron Metro Market: Columbia, SC *Format:* Sports *Hrs. of News Programming:* news progmg 17 hrs wkly *No. News Employees:* 1 *Target Audience:* 35 plus; mature adults
Kelley Royster, General Manager
Todd Shuster, General Sales Mgr
LJ Smith, Programming Director

***WUSC-FM**
01-17-1977; 90.5 mhz FM *Hrs Open:* 24; 2.5 kw; 253 ft.; N34 0 2 W81 1 19
Student Media Russell H., Columbia, SC 29208 US
(803) 777-5468, *Fax:* (803) 777-6482
wusc.sc.edu
wuscsm@sc.edu
License: Columbia, Richland County, SC held by University of South Carolina.
Arbitron Metro Market: Columbia, SC *Format:* Variety/Diverse *Hrs. of News Programming:* news progmg 3 hrs wkly *No. News Employees:* 1 *Target Audience:* General; alternative generation
Will Belenger, Station Manager
Gabe Crawford, Programming Director
John George, Chief Engineer
Joshua Rainwater, Music Director
Rupert Hudson, Music Director
Freddie Poweres, Secretary

WXBT(AM)
07-10-1930; 560 khz AM *Hrs Open:* 24; 5 kw-U, DA-N; N34 02 00 W81 08 32
316 Greystone Blvd., Columbia, SC 29210-8007
(803) 343-1100, *Fax:* (803) 256-1968
www.wvoc.com
jayflanagan@clearchannel.com
License: Columbia, Richland County, SC held by Capstar TX L.P.
Group Owner: Clear Channel Communications Inc.; (acq 8-30-00; grpsl).
Nat'l Network: CNN Radio *Regional Network:* S.C. News Net.
Wire Services: Dow Jones Financial News Services
Population Served: 130,591 *Arbitron Metro Market:* Columbia, SC *Format:* News, News/Talk, 84, Talk *Hrs. of News Programming:* news progmg 40 hrs wkly *No. News Employees:* 2 *Target Audience:* 35-64.
Tim McFalls, General Manager
Todd Shuster, General Sales Mgr
LJ Smith, Programming Director
Jay Flanagan, Online Content Director
Kelley Royster, Business Manager

Conway

***WHMC-FM**
09-15-1985; 90.1 mhz FM *Hrs Open:* 24; 30 kw; 706 ft; N33 57 05 W79 06 31 *Rebroadcasts:* Rebroadcasts WRJA-FM Sumter 100%
1101 George Rogers Blvd., Columbia, SC 29211
(803) 737-3200, *Fax:* (803) 737-3552
www.etvradio.org
gasque@scetv.org
License: Conway, Horry County, SC held by South Carolina Educational Television Commission.
Nat'l Network: NPR; PRI; APM
Arbitron Metro Market: Myrtle Beach, S *Hrs. of News Programming:* New progrmg 120 hrs wkly
Linda O'Bryon, President
John Gassque, Operations Dir
Shari Hutchinson, General Manager
Shari Hutchinson, Station Manager
Melanie Boyer, General Sales Mgr
John Gasque, Programming Director
John Crockett, Engineering Dir
SkipBeach, Chief Engineer
Melanie Boyer, Underwriting Director

WHSC
10-01-1946; 1050 khz AM *Hrs Open:* 24; 5 kw-D, DA2; 0.473 kw-N, DA2; N33 50 56 W79 5 3
111 East Kilbourn Ave., Suite 2700, Milwaukee, WI 53202 US
(843) 661-5000, *Fax:* (843) 661-0888
www.897wshc.org
wshc@sheperd.edu
License: Conway, SC held by Cumulus Licensing Corp.
Group Owner: Cumulus Media Inc.; (acq 4-20-98; 700,000 with co-located FM)
Regional Network: S.C. News Net.
Arbitron Metro Market: Florence, SC *Format:* Contemporary Hits/Top 40 *Special Programming:* Farm 3 hrs, gospel 3 hrs, relg 6 hrs, big band 3 h *Hrs. of News Programming:* News progmg 12 hrs wkly *Target Audience:* 19-49; those with buying power
Matt Scurry, Operations Dir
Jerry Stevens, General Manager
Gale Gilbraith, Chief Engineer

WHSC(AM)
02-23-1977; 1050 khz AM *Hrs Open:* 24; 5 kw-D, 473 w-N, DA-2; N33 50 56 W79 05 03
11640 Hwy. 17 Bypass, Murrells Inlet, SC 29576
(843) 651-7869, *Fax:* (843) 397-3197
License: Conway, Horry County, SC held by Cumulus Licensing Corp.
Group Owner: Cumulus Media Inc.; (acq 12-29-97; grpsl)
Regional Network: S.C. News Net.
Population Served: 256,000 *Arbitron Metro Market:* Myrtle Beach, SC *Format:* Sports *No. News Employees:* 1 *Target Audience:* 50 plus; affluent retirees *Adv. Rates:* 10; 10; 10; 10
Ron Raybourne, General Manager
Dave Solomon, Programming Director
Robert Kesler, News Director
Buddy Womack, Chief Engineer

WJXY-FM
10-01-1990; 93.9 mhz FM *Hrs Open:* 24; 3.7 kw; Ant 420 ft; N33 50 07 W78 52 06
11640 Hwy. 17 Bypass, Murrells Inlet, SC 53202
(843) 651-7869, *Fax:* (843) 397-3197

License: Conway, Horry County, SC held by Cumulus Licensing Corp.
Group Owner: Cumulus Media Inc.
Nat'l Network: ABC
Arbitron Metro Market: Myrtle Beach, SC *Hrs. of News Programming:* News progmg 2 hrs wkly *Target Audience:* 18-34.
Lou Dickey, President
Lisa Van Horn, Operations Dir
Dave Solomon, General Sales Mgr

WPJS
08-01-1945; 1330 khz AM
1720 Highway 501 West, Conway, SC 29526 US
(843) 248-9040, *Fax:* (843) 248-6365
License: Conway, SC held by WPJS Broadcasters Inc.
Arbitron Metro Market: Myrtle Beach, SC *Format:* Black, Gospel *Target Audience:* 12 plus.
P.J. Parrish, General Manager

Coward

WPDT
05-01-1995; 105.1 mhz FM; 18 kw; 384 ft.; N33 54 54 W79 50 19
Box 12699, Coward, SC 29504 US
(843) 374-5255, *Fax:* (843) 374-5256
www.wfmv.com
wpdt@ftc-i.net
License: Coward, Florence County, SC held by Glory Communications Inc.
Group Owner: Glory Communications Inc.; acq 5-20-02).
Arbitron Metro Market: Florence, SC *Format:* Religious
Alex Snipes, General Manager
Tersa Haire, General Sales Mgr
Tony Gee, Programming Director

Darlington

WDAR-FM
12-01-1965; 105.5 mhz FM *Hrs Open:* 24hrs; 17 kw; 400 ft.; N34 18 58 W79 53 17
Mailing Address: Two Bala Plaza, Suite 801, Bala-Cynwyd, PA 19004 US
Second Address: 181 E. Evans St., Suite 311, Florence, SC 29506
(843) 667-4600, *Fax:* (843) 673-7390
www.sunny1055online.com
contact@sunny1055online.com
License: Darlington, Darlington County, SC held by Qantum of Florence License Co. LLC
Group Owner: Qantum Communications Corp.; (acq 7-2-2003; grpsl).
Arbitron Metro Market: Florence, SC *Format:* Adult Contemp, Easy Listening
Craig Dalla Riva, General Manager
Sherry Miller, General Sales Mgr
Gail Nichols, Programming Director
Thoma Lesieur, News Director
David Jones, Chief Engineer
Veronica Wingate, Traffic Manager

WWRK
01-01-1955; 1400 khz AM
Mailing Address: Two Bala Plaza, Suite 801, Bala-Cynwyd, PA 19004 US
Second Address: 181 E. Evans St., Suite 311, Florence, SC 29506
(843) 667-4600, *Fax:* (843) 673-7390
License: Darlington, SC held by Qantum of Florence License Co. LLC
Group Owner: Qantum Communications Corp.
Arbitron Metro Market: Florence, SC *Format:* Black, Gospel *Target Audience:* 25 plus.
Terri Burgess, News Director

Dillon

WDSC
05-22-1946; 800 khz AM *Hrs Open:* 24
Mailing Address: Two Bala Plaza, Suite 801, Bala-Cynwyd, PA 19004 US
Second Address: 181 E. Evans St., Florence, SC 29506
(843) 667-4600, *Fax:* (843) 673-7390
License: Dillon, SC held by Qantum of Florence License Co. LLC.
Group Owner: Qantum Communications Corp.; (acq 7-2-2003; grpsl)
Format: Gospel *Target Audience:* General.
Craig Dalla Riva, General Manager
Sherry Miller, General Sales Mgr

WEGX
02-16-1954; 92.9 mhz FM *Hrs Open:* 24; 100 kw; 1617 ft.; N34 22 4 W79 19 21
Mailing Address: Two Bala Plaza, Suite 801, Bala-Cynwyd, PA 19004 US
Second Address: 181 E. Evans St., Suite 311, Florence, SC 29506
(843) 667-4600, *Fax:* (843) 673-7390
www.eagle929online.com
radioman203@gmail.com
License: Dillon, Dillon County, SC held by Qantum of Florence License Co. LLC.
Group Owner: Qantum Communications Corp.; (acq 7-2-2003; grpsl)
Arbitron Metro Market: Dillon, SC *Format:* Country *Special Programming:* Jazz one hr wkly
Sherry Miller, General Sales Mgr
Randy Wilcox, Programming Director

***WDLL**
01-01-2007; 90.5 mhz FM; 25 kw vert; 276 ft.; N34 19 53 W79 33 37 *Rebroadcasts:* Rebroadcasts WAFR(FM) Tupelo, MS 100%
P O Drawer 2440, Tupelo, MS 38803 US
(662) 844-8888, *Fax:* (662) 842-6791
www.afr.net
License: Dillon, Dillon County, SC held by American Family Association.
Group Owner: American Family Radio
Arbitron Metro Market: Dillon, SC *Format:* Christian
Donald Wildmon, Chairman

Dorchester Terrace-Brentwood

WTMZ
11-17-1960; 910 khz AM *Hrs Open:* 24; 500 w-U, DA-N; N34 09 03 W82 23 34
60 Markfield Dr., Charleston, SC 85281
(843) 763-6631, *Fax:* (843) 766-1239
www.kirkmanbroadcasting.com
ted@kirkmanbroadcasting.com
License: Dorchester Terrace-Brentwood, Dorchester County, SC held by Kirkman Broadcasting Inc.
Group Owner: Kirkman Broadcasting Inc.; (acq 1-5-2005; $500,000).
Nat'l Network: ESPN Radio
Population Served: 122,689 *Arbitron Metro Market:* Charleston, SC
Ted Byrne, Operations Dir
Gil Kirkman, General Manager
Rick Howze, General Sales Mgr

Easley

WELP
03-04-1951; 1360 khz AM *Hrs Open:* 24; 5 kw-D, ND1; 0.036 kw-N, ND1; N34 50 23 W82 38 22
P.O. Box 444, Spartanburg, SC 29304 US
(864) 855-9300, *Fax:* (864) 855-8444
www.wilkinsradio.com
welp@wilkinsradio.com
License: Easley, SC held by Upstate Radio Inc.
Group Owner: Wilkins Communications Network Inc.; (acq 1999; $150,000).
Arbitron Metro Market: Easley, SC *Format:* Christian, Talk *Hrs. of News Programming:* news progmg 22 hrs wkly *No. News Employees:* 2 *Target Audience:* 35 plus. *Adv. Rates:* 30; 30; 30; 30
Bob Wilkins, President
Mitchell Mathis, Operations Dir
Greg Garrett, Station Manager
Ted McCall, Engineering Dir
LuAnn Wilkins, Executive Vice President

WOLI-FM
01-01-1964; 103.9 mhz FM; 6 kw; 328 ft.; N34 50 21 W82 31 37
940 West Port Plaza, Suite 210, St. Louis, MO 63416 US
864-271-9200, *Fax:* 864-241-4343
License: Easley, Pickens County, SC held by Davidson Media Station WOLI Licensee LLC.
Group Owner: Davidson Media Group LLC; (acq 10-6-2005; grpsl).
Arbitron Metro Market: Greenville-Spar *TV Affiliate:* Sp

Eastover

WNKT
01-05-1971; 107.5 mhz FM *Hrs Open:* 24; 40 kw; 548 ft.; N33 45 46 W80 49 23
140 S. Ash Ave., Tempe, AZ 85281 US
(803) 796-7600, *Fax:* (803) 796-9291
www.1075thegame.com
License: Eastover, Richland County, SC
Group Owner: Cumulus Media Inc.; (acq 6-9-99; grpsl)
Nat'l Reps: McGavren Guild
Arbitron Metro Market: Columbia, SC *Format:* Sports
William McElveen, General Manager

Elloree

WORG
05-01-1988; 100.3 mhz FM; 25 kw; 328 ft.; N33 21 42 W80 41 5
3402 Foxfire Lane, Orangeburg, SC 29118 US
(803) 516-8400, *Fax:* (803) 516-0704
www.worg.com
worg@worg.com
License: Elloree, Orangeburg County, SC held by Garris Communications Inc.
TV Affiliate: Adult contemp *Format:* News/Talk *Special Programming:* 6am, 7am, 8am *No. News Employees:* 25-54.
Adv. Rates: 22; 22; 22; 12

Enoree

***WUBK(FM)**
88.1 mhz FM; 175 w; Ant 253 ft; N34 38 06 W81 58 47
PO Box 15, Chester, SC 29710
(803) 581-9030
License: Enoree, Spartanburg County, SC held by Richburg Educational Broadcasters
Population Served: 665 *Arbitron Metro Market:* Enoree, SC
C. Curtis Sigmon, President

Florence

WJMX
07-13-1947; 970 khz AM *Hrs Open:* 24; 5 kw-D, 3 kw-N, DA-N; N34 13 47 W79 48 07
Mailing Address: Box 103000, Florence, SC 19004
Second Address: Florence Bus. & Tech. Ctr., 181 E. Evans St., Florence, SC 29506
(843) 667-4600,(843) 665-0970, *Fax:* (843) 673-7390
newstalk970online.com
License: Florence, Florence County, SC held by Qantum of Florence License Co. LLC.
Group Owner: Qantum Communications Corp.; (acq 7-2-2003; grpsl)
Nat'l Network: CBS; AP Radio *Regional Network:* S.C. News Net.
Nat'l Reps: McGavren Guild
Population Served: 300,000 *Arbitron Metro Market:* Florence, SC *Special Programming:* Big band 3 hrs wkly *Hrs. of News Programming:* news progmg 49 hrs wkly *No. News Employees:* 1 *Target Audience:* 25-54.
Tom Koser, General Manager
Craig Riva, Station Manager

***WLPG**
05-15-1993; 91.7 mhz FM *Hrs Open:* 24; 20 kw; 482 ft.; N34 4 10.1 W79 40 42.3
3213 Huxley Drive, Augusta, GA 30909 US
(706) 309-9610
www.gnnradio.org
ctbarinowski@comcast.net
License: Florence, Florence County, SC held by Augusta Radio Fellowship Institute Inc.
Arbitron Metro Market: Florence, SC *Format:* Christian *Hrs. of News Programming:* News progmg 12 hrs wkly
Clarence Barinowski, General Manager

WOLH
11-18-1937; 1230 khz AM; 1 kw-U, ND1; N34 13 48 W79 44 49
151 S. Dargan, Florence, SC 29501 US
(843) 665-1230, *Fax:* (843) 665-8786
jjones1990@sc.rr.com
License: Florence, SC held by Miller Communications Inc.
Group Owner: Miller Communications Inc.; (acq 4-29-2008; $275,000 with WHYM(AM) Lake City)
Nat'l Network: ABC *Regional Reps:* Jim D. Jones
Arbitron Metro Market: Florence, SC *TV Affiliate:* Talk *Format:* Gospel, Jazz, 86 *Special Programming:* news progmg 4 hrs wkly *Hrs. of News Programming:* 1 *No. News Employees:* 21-101; within a 30 mile*Adv. Rates:* 7; 7; 15; 7

WYNN
11-05-1958; 540 khz AM *Hrs Open:* 24; 0.25 kw-D, ND1; 0.166 kw-N, ND1; N34 13 5 W79 48 30
111 East Kilbourn Avenue, Suite 2700, Milwaukee, WI 53202 US
(843) 661-5000, *Fax:* (843) 661-0888
License: Florence, SC held by Cumulus Licensing Corp.
Group Owner: Cumulus Media Inc.; (acq 12-17-98; with co-located FM)
Nat'l Network: American Urban
Arbitron Metro Market: Florence, SC *Format:* Black, Blues, 44 *Special Programming:* Jazz *Hrs. of News Programming:* news

progmg 12 hrs wkly *No. News Employees:* 1 *Target Audience:* 35 plus; Black
Matt Scurry, Operations Dir
Jerry Stevens, General Manager
Ollie Williams, Programming Director
Daniel Tindal, Assistant Music Director

WYNN-FM
10-01-1964; 106.3 mhz FM *Hrs Open:* 24; 6 kw; 328 ft.; N34 13 5 W79 48 30
111 East Kilbourn Avenue, Suite 2700, Milwaukee, WI 53202 US
License: Florence, Florence County, SC held by Cumulus Licensing Corp.
Arbitron Metro Market: Florence, SC *Format:* Urban Contemporary *Hrs. of News Programming:* news progmg one hr wkly *No. News Employees:* 1 *Target Audience:* 12-34.
Gerald McSwain, Programming Director

Folly Beach

WYBB
07-04-1988; 98.1 mhz FM *Hrs Open:* 24; 50 kw; 479 ft.; N32 39 57 W80 3 11
59 Windermere Blvd., Charleston, SC 29407 US
(843) 769-4799, *Fax:* (843) 769-4797
www.my98rock.com
License: Folly Beach, Charleston County, SC held by L.M. Communications of South Carolina Inc.
Group Owner: L M Communications Inc.; (acq 5-17-88)
Nat'l Network: ABC
Arbitron Metro Market: Charleston, SC *Format:* Rock/AOR *Hrs. of News Programming:* News progmg 28 hrs wkly *Target Audience:* 25-49; men *Adv. Rates:* 75; 60; 70; 30

Forest Acres

WWNQ
01-01-2005; 94.3 mhz FM; 2.55 kw; 446 ft.; N34 0 4 W81 2 5
1801 K Street, NW, Suite 400k, Washington, DC 20006 US
(803) 753-6800, *Fax:* (803) 753-6806
www.flashback943.com
kirk@hometowncolumbia.com
License: Forest Acres, Richland County, SC held by Double O South Carolina Corp.
Group Owner: Double O Radio L.L.C.; (acq 9-10-2004; $4.73 million for CP)
Arbitron Metro Market: Columbia, SC *Format:* Contemporary Hits/Top 40, Adult Contemp *Target Audience:* 25-50.
Kirk Litton, President/Owner
Chuck McKay, General Manager
Marty Hall, Operations Mgr/Program Director
Karen Starnes, Business Manager

Forestbrook

WKZQ-FM
03-11-1985; 96.1 mhz FM *Hrs Open:* 24; 8.5 kw; 871 ft.; N33 35 27 W79 2 55
1964 Ashley River Road, Charleston, SC 29407 US
(662) 844-8888, *Fax:* (662) 842-6791
www.afa.net
License: Forestbrook, Horry County, SC held by NM Licensing LLC.
Group Owner: NextMedia Group Inc.; (acq 10-28-2008; swap for WAVF(FM) Hanahan)
Arbitron Metro Market: Ada OK *Format:* Christian
Marvin Sanders, General Manager

Fort Mill

***WFBK**
91.5 mhz FM; 0.14 kw horiz, 0.11 kw vert; 118 ft.; N35 0 17 W80 58 54
US
(803) 581-9030, *Fax:* (803) 581-9932
www.wfbk.org
License: Fort Mill, York County, SC held by Richburg Educational Broadcasters Inc.
Arbitron Metro Market: Fort Mill, SC *Format:* Triple A
Jeff Sigmon, General Manager

Fountain Inn

WFIS
10-01-1956; 1600 khz AM *Hrs Open:* 24; 1 kw-D, ND1; 0.025 kw-N, ND1; N34 42 28 W82 13 40
Mailing Address: 1318 N. Main 14, P.O. Box 156, Fountain Inn, SC 29644 US
Second Address: 1318 N. Main St., Fountain Inn, SC 29644
(864) 963-5991, *Fax:* (864) 963-5992
www.wfisradio.com
wfis16@aol.com
License: Fountain Inn, SC held by Golden Strip Broadcasting Inc.
Nat'l Network: Westwood One; Jones Radio Networks; ABC
Regional Network: S.C. News Net. *Nat'l Reps:* Rgnl Reps
Arbitron Metro Market: Fountain Inn, SC *Format:* Sports, Talk
Special Programming: Gospel 4, Black 4 hrs, Christian 3 hrs wkly *Hrs. of News Programming:* news progmg 3 hrs wkly *No. News Employees:* 1 *TargetAudience:* 25-49; working adults
Joseph LaStringer, General Manager

Gaffney

WNOW-FM
01-01-1959; 105.3 mhz FM *Hrs Open:* 24; 51 kw; 1296 ft.; N35 21 51 W81 11 13
Mailing Address: P. O. Box 1210, Gaffney, SC 29340 US
Second Address: 340 Providence Rd., Gaffney, SC 29341
(704) 665-9355, *Fax:* (864) 489-9069
www.wnow-fm.com/
feedback@wagifm.com
License: Gaffney, Cherokee County, SC held by Gaffney Broadcasting Inc.
Group Owner: Davidson Media Group LLC; (acq 10-18-2007; $22 million with co-located AM)
Nat'l Network: CNN Radio *Wire Services:* AP
Arbitron Metro Market: Charlotte, NC *Format:* Country, Gospel
Special Programming: Clemson Univ. sports, loc sports, talk 10 hrs wkly *No. News Employees:* 1 *Target Audience:* 18-54. *Adv. Rates:* 22; 15:55;15:55; 15:55
Ronald Owenby, General Manager
Dennis Fowler, Station Manager
Ernie Payne, Jr., General Sales Mgr
Jonathan Fitch, Programming Director
Fabian Fuentes, Sports Director
Claudella Moss, Traffic Manager

WZZQ(AM)
09-28-1962; 1500 khz AM; 1 kw-D, 500 w-N; N35 05 18 W81 38 40
Mailing Address: Box 1210, Gaffney, SC 29342
Second Address: 340 Providence Rd., Gaffney, SC 29341
(864) 489-9066, *Fax:* (864) 489-9069
www.weac.org/
feedback@wagifm.com
License: Gaffney, Cherokee County, SC held by Gaffney Broadcasting Inc.
Group Owner: Davidson Media Group LLC
Regional Network: S.C. News Net. *Wire Services:* AP
Population Served: 12,456 *Arbitron Metro Market:* Gaffney, SC *Format:* Country *Hrs. of News Programming:* news progmg 2 hrs wkly *No. News Employees:* 1 *Target Audience:* 18-54. *Adv. Rates:* 22; 15; 15;12
Laura Haemker, Station Manager
Amy Garelick, Promotions Manager

WFGN
01-01-1948; 1180 khz AM *Hrs Open:* 6 AM-8 PM; 2.5 kw-D, NDD; N35 2 59 W81 38 42
470 Leadmine Road, PO Box 1388, Gaffney, SC 29340 US
(864) 489-9430, *Fax:* (864) 489-9440
License: Gaffney, SC held by Hope Broadcasting Inc.
Arbitron Metro Market: Gaffney, SC *Format:* Religious
Eddie Leroy Bridges Jr., President
Charles Montgomery, Operations Dir
Ed Ridges, General Manager
Rev. Eula Miller, General Sales Mgr
Clarence Quarles, Programming Director
Lonnie Dawkins, Disc Jockey
Caroline Allen, DiscJockey
Marianetta Smith, Disc Jockey

***WYFG**
10-12-1982; 91.1 mhz FM *Hrs Open:* 24; 100 kw; 669 ft.; N35 6 57 W81 46 42
8030 Arrowridge Blvd., Charlotte, NC 28273 US
(704) 523-5555, *Fax:* (704) 522-1967
www.bbnradio.org
bbn@bbnradio.org
License: Gaffney, Cherokee County, SC held by Bible Broadcasting Network Inc.
Group Owner: Bible Broadcasting Network
Nat'l Network: USA
Arbitron Metro Market: Gaffney, SC *Format:* Christian, Religious *No. News Employees:* 1 *Target Audience:* General.
Lowell Davey, President
Stan Schenkel, General Manager

Garden City

WWXM
09-25-1971; 97.7 mhz FM *Hrs Open:* 24; 100 kw; 719 ft.; N33 35 45 W79 3 11
Two Bala Plaza, Suite 801, Bala-Cynwyd, PA 19004 US
(843) 293-0107, *Fax:* (843) 293-1717
www.mix977online.com
info@977online.com
License: Garden City, Horry County, SC held by Qantum of Myrtle Beach License Co. LLC.
Group Owner: Qantum Communications Corp.; (acq 7-2-2003; grpsl).
Arbitron Metro Market: Garden City, SC *Format:* Contemporary Hits/Top 40 *Hrs. of News Programming:* news progmg 2 hrs wkly *No. News Employees:* 1 *Target Audience:* 18-49.
Jimmy Feuger, General Manager
Deby Emanuel, General Sales Mgr
Ron Roberts, Programming Director

Georgetown

WGTN
07-01-1949; 1400 khz AM *Hrs Open:* 24
2538 Millwood Avenue, Columbia, SC 29202 US
(843) 546-1400, *Fax:* (843) 527-2337
www.wgtnradio.com
License: Georgetown, SC held by R.J. Stalvey
Nat'l Network: Fox News Radio
Arbitron Metro Market: Myrtle Beach, SC *Format:* News, News/Talk, 86 *Hrs. of News Programming:* news progmg 12 hrs wkly *No. News Employees:* 1 *Target Audience:* 25-54; upscale adult; bus, professional andtechnical
Rod Stalvey, General Manager

WLMC
03-01-1962; 1470 khz AM; 1 kw-D, ND2; 0.147 kw-N, ND2; N33 22 15 W79 16 39
P.O. Drawer 1530, Georgetown, SC 29442 US
(843) 546-8863, *Fax:* (843) 546-6281
www.wlmcradio.com
wlmcradio@aol.com
License: Georgetown, SC held by Cumberland A & A Corp.
Nat'l Network: ABC
Format: Christian, Gospel, 74 *Special Programming:* Talk 4 hrs wkly *Target Audience:* 25 plus; African-Americans
Reggie Dyson, CEO

WLFF
05-01-1973; 106.5 mhz FM *Hrs Open:* 24; 50 kw; 492 ft.; N33 26 20 W79 8 11
111 East Kilbourn Ave., Suite 2700, Milwaukee, WI 53202 US
(843) 651-7869, *Fax:* (843) 651-3197
www.sunny1065.net
License: Georgetown, Georgetown County, SC held by Cumulus Licensing Corp.
Group Owner: Cumulus Media Inc.; (acq 1-27-98)
Arbitron Metro Market: Myrtle Beach, SC *Format:* Oldies
Bill Hazen, General Manager

WXJY
09-01-1990; 93.7 mhz FM *Hrs Open:* 24; 6 kw; 315 ft.; N33 16 5 W79 17 49
330 East Kilbourn Avenue, Suite 250, Milwaukee, WI 53202 US
(404) 949-0700, *Fax:* (404) 949-0740
www.teammyrtlebeach.com
License: Georgetown, Georgetown County, SC held by Cumulus Licensing Corp.
Group Owner: Cumulus Media Inc.; (acq 12-29-97; grpsl)
Arbitron Metro Market: Myrtle Beach, SC *Format:* Sports *Hrs. of News Programming:* News progmg 4 hrs wkly *Target Audience:* 25-49; career-oriented, college-educated adults
Roderick Smith, Operations Dir
Lyne Ryan, General Manager
Kellly Broderick, Programming Director
David Lewis, Market Manager
Todd Cartner, Advertising

Goose Creek

WSCC-FM
05-19-1983; 94.3 mhz FM; 25 kw; 328 ft.; N32 49 4 W79 50 8
11521 Innfields Drive, Odessa, FL 33556 US
(843) 856-6100, *Fax:* (843) 884-1218
www.wscfm.com
bjkay@clearchannel.com
License: Goose Creek, Berkeley County, SC held by Clear Channel Broadcasting Licenses Inc.
Group Owner: Clear Channel Communications Inc.; (acq 7-29-2003).
Nat'l Network: Fox News Radio *Nat'l Reps:* McGavren Guild
Arbitron Metro Market: Charleston, SC *Format:* Talk *No. News Employees:* 3 *Target Audience:* 25-54.
Paul Smith, General Manager
Willie Bennett, Chief Engineer

Gray Court

WSSL-FM
11-01-1960; 100.5 mhz FM *Hrs Open:* 24; 100 kw; 1250 ft.; N34 34 18 W82 6 44
7 North Laurens Street, Greenville, SC 29601 US
(864) 242-1005, *Fax:* (864) 271-3830
www.wsslfm.com
License: Gray Court, Laurens County, SC held by Capstar TX L.P.
Group Owner: Clear Channel Communications Inc.
Regional Network: S.C. News Net.
Arbitron Metro Market: Greenville-Spartanburg, SC *Format:* Country
Bill McMartin, Operations Dir
Libby Spencer, General Sales Mgr
Kix Layton, Programming Director
Vicky Sexton, Promotions Manager
Jim Graham, Chief Engineer
Steve Geofferies, Operations Manager

Greenville

***WEPR**
09-03-1972; 90.1 mhz FM *Hrs Open:* 24; 85 kw; 1,184 ft; N34 56 26 W82 24 38 *Rebroadcasts:* Rebroadcasts WLTR(FM) Columbia 100%
1101 George Rogers Blvd., Columbia, SC 29211
(803) 737-3200, *Fax:* (803) 737-3552
www.etvradio.org
gasque@scetv.org
License: Greenville, Greenville County, SC held by South Carolina Educ. TV Commission.
Nat'l Network: NPR; PRI; APM
Arbitron Metro Market: Greenville-Spar *Hrs. of News Programming:* New progrmg 70 hrs wkly
Linda O'Bryon, President
John Gasque, Operations Dir
Shari Hutchinson, General Manager
Shari Hutchinson, Station Manager
Melanie Boyer, General Sales Mgr
John Gasque, Programming Director
John Crockett, Engineering Dir
SkipBeach, Chief Engineer
Melanie Boyer, Underwriting Manager

WLFJ
03-01-1947; 660 khz AM; 50 kw-D, 10 kw-CH; N34 53 10 W82 28 03
2420 Wade Hampton Blvd., Greenville, SC 20036
(864) 292-6040, *Fax:* (864) 292-8428
www.christiantalk660.com
comments@hisradio.com
License: Greenville, Greenville County, SC held by Clear Channel Broadcasting Licenses Inc.
Group Owner: Clear Channel Communications Inc.; (acq 1998; grpsl).
Nat'l Network: Fox News Radio
Population Served: 61,208 *Arbitron Metro Market:* Greenville-Spartanburg, SC *Target Audience:* 25-54.
Allen Henderson, General Manager
Gary Miller, Station Manager
Isaac Fineman, General Sales Mgr
Brian Sumner, Promotions Manager

WESC-FM
03-01-1948; 92.5 mhz FM *Hrs Open:* 24; 95 kw; 2001 ft.; N35 8 16 W82 36 31
Mailing Address: 1250 Connecticut Avenue, NW, Suite 800, Washington, DC 20036 US
Second Address: 7 N. Laurens St., Suite 700, Greenville, SC 29601
(864) 242-4660, *Fax:* (864) 271-3830
www.wescfm.com
ChrisLeavitt@clearchannel.com
License: Greenville, Greenville County, SC held by Clear Channel Broadcasting Licenses Inc.
Group Owner: Clear Channel Communications Inc.; (acq 1998; grpsl).
Arbitron Metro Market: Greenville, SC *Format:* Country
Bruce Logan, Operations Dir
Bill McMartin, VP/General Manager
Bob Hooper, General Sales Mgr
Scott Johnson, Programming Director
Sandra Dill, Promotions Manager
Roger Davis, News Director
Jim Graham, Chief Engineer
Jessy Howard,Disc Jockey
John Landrum, Music Director
Vicky Sexton, Promotions Manager
Goldia Williams, Traffic Manager
Carole Sloan, Business Manager
Megan Culbreth, Coordinator

WFBC-FM
03-01-1947; 93.7 mhz FM *Hrs Open:* 24; 100 kw; 1811 ft.; N35 6 43 W82 36 24
10706 Beaver Dam Road, Cockeysville, MD 21030 US
(864) 271-9200, *Fax:* (864) 242-1567
www.b937online.com
rcable@entercom.com?subject=Advertising%20with%20B93.7
License: Greenville, Greenville County, SC held by Entercom Greenville License LLC
Arbitron Metro Market: Greenville, SC *Format:* Adult Contemp
Special Programming: Alternative 2 hrs wkly *Hrs. of News Programming:* news progmg one hr wkly *No. News Employees:* 4 *Target Audience:* 35-64.
Tias Schuster, Programming Director
Keaira Bray, Promotions Manager
Heidi Aiken, News Director
Tracy West, WebMistress

WGVL
01-01-1950; 1440 khz AM *Hrs Open:* 24; 5 kw-D, DAN; 5 kw-N, DAN; N34 52 6 W82 28 4
7 North Laurens Street, Greenville, SC 29601 US
(864) 220-1115, *Fax:* (864) 220-1120
www.lainvasora1440.com
info@lainvasora1440.com
License: Greenville, SC held by Capstar TX L.P.
Group Owner: Clear Channel Communications Inc.; (acq 8-30-00; grpsl)
Arbitron Metro Market: Greenville-Spartanburg, SC *Format:* Spanish *Hrs. of News Programming:* news progmg 4 hrs wkly *No. News Employees:* 2 *Target Audience:* 25-54.
George Kimble, President
Alan Bishop, Operations Dir
Paula Triplett, General Sales Mgr
Mike Smith, Programming Director
Ted Baker, News Director

***WLFJ-FM**
05-01-1983; 89.3 mhz FM *Hrs Open:* 24; 41 kw; 1,100 ft; N34 56 26 W82 24 44
2420 Wade Hampton Blvd., Greenville, SC 33807
(864) 292-6040,(864) 292-5683, *Fax:* (864) 292-8428
www.hisradio.com
comments@hisradio.com
License: Greenville, Greenville County, SC held by Radio Training Network Inc.
Population Served: 850,000 *Arbitron Metro Market:* Greenville-Spartanburg, SC
Allen Henderson, General Manager
Brian Sumner, Programming Director
Ted McCall, Chief Engineer

WPJF
09-15-1949; 1260 khz AM; 5 kw-D, ND1; 0.015 kw-N, ND1; N34 54 30 W82 20 41
920 Wade Hampton Blvd., Greenville, SC 29609 US
(864) 241-5355, *Fax:* (864) 241-5353
License: Greenville, SC held by WMUU Inc.
Arbitron Metro Market: Greenville, SC *Format:* Religious *Target Audience:* 35 plus.
Ed Dos Santos, General Manager
Joe Norris, Chief Engineer

WMUU-FM
08-15-1960; 94.5 mhz FM *Hrs Open:* 24; 100 kw; 1490 ft.; N34 56 29 W82 24 41
920 Wade Hamilton Blvd., Greenville, SC 29614 US
(864) 242-6240, *Fax:* (864) 370-3829
www.wmuu.com
generalmanager@wmuu.com
License: Greenville, Greenville County, SC held by WMUU Inc.
Arbitron Metro Market: Greenville, SC *Format:* Easy Listening
Special Programming: Class 14 hrs, relg 20 hrs wkly *Target Audience:* 35 plus.
Paul Wright, General Manager
Brigette Barrett, Programming Director
Jeff Gainous, Promotions Manager
Joe Norris, Engineering Dir

WPCI
02-08-1954; 1490 khz AM; 1 kw-U, ND1; N34 51 7 W82 24 54
840 North Highway, 25 Bypass, Greenville, SC 29617 US
(864) 836-3551,(864) 834-3193, EXT. 35
License: Greenville, SC held by Hunter Broadcast Group.
Arbitron Metro Market: Greenville-Spartanburg, SC *Format:* Oldies
Randy Mathena, President

***WTBI-FM**
06-01-1991; 91.5 mhz FM *Hrs Open:* 24; 22.5 kw; 420 ft.; N34 49 51 W82 26 55
3931 White Horse Road, Greenville, SC 29611 US
(864) 295-2145, *Fax:* (864) 295-6313
www.wtbi.org
jwatts@tabernacleministries.org
License: Greenville, Greenville County, SC held by Tabernacle Baptist Bible College
Arbitron Metro Market: Greenville-Spartanburg, SC *Format:* Gospel, Religious *Target Audience:* General.
Dr. W. Melvin Aiken, CEO
Carolyn Headrick, Operations Dir
Charles R. Garrett Sr., Programming Director
James H. Simpson, Promotions Manager
John H. Watts, COO

WYRD
05-01-1933; 1330 khz AM *Hrs Open:* 24; 5 kw-D, DAN; 5 kw-N, DAN; N34 51 18 W82 25 24 *Rebroadcasts:* Rebroadcasts WORD(AM) Spartanburg
10706 Beaver Dam Road, Cockeysville, MD 21030 US
(864) 271-9200, *Fax:* (864) 242-1567
www.newsradioword.com
info@newsradioword.com
License: Greenville, SC held by Entercom Greenville License LLC.
Group Owner: Entercom Communications Corp.; (acq 12-13-99; grpsl).
Nat'l Network: ABC; Salem Radio Network
Arbitron Metro Market: Greenville-Spar *Format:* News, News/Talk, 86 *Target Audience:* 30-64.
Tom Durney, General Manager

Greenwood

WCRS
09-01-1941; 1450 khz AM *Hrs Open:* 24; 1 kw-U, ND1; N34 12 34 W82 9 5
P O Box 5, Union, SC 29379 US
(864) 229-7984, *Fax:* (864) 229-5896
www.wlmawcrsradio.com
License: Greenwood, SC held by Peregon Broadcasting LLC
Nat'l Network: CBS *Regional Network:* S.C. News Net.
Arbitron Metro Market: Greenville SC *Format:* News, News/Talk, 86, Adult Contemp *Hrs. of News Programming:* news progmg 20 hrs wkly *No. News Employees:* 2 *Target Audience:* 25 plus; middle & upper income adults*Adv. Rates:* 12; 10; 10; 8
Mike Hatfield, Operations Dir

WCZZ
06-20-1973; 1090 khz AM *Hrs Open:* Sunrise-sunset; 2.25 kw-C, NDD; 5 kw-D, NDD; N34 9 46 W82 11 41
510 Sparrow Road, Greenwood, SC 29646 US
(864) 223-4300, *Fax:* (864) 223-4096
sunny@sunny103-5.com
License: Greenwood, SC held by Broomfield Broadcasting LLC
Nat'l Network: Westwood One
Arbitron Metro Market: Greenwood, SC *Format:* Gospel *Hrs. of News Programming:* News progmg 12 hrs wkly *Target Audience:* 25-65. *Adv. Rates:* 12; 12; 12; 12
John Broomfield, President
Rick Prusator, General Sales Mgr
Dave Fezler, Programming Director
Kathleen Prusator, Promotions Manager
Tonya Branyon, News Director
Stephanie White, Promotions Director

WZSN
03-01-1989; 103.5 mhz FM *Hrs Open:* 24; 25 kw; 328 ft.; N34 9 46 W82 11 41
510 Sparrow Road, Greenwood, SC 29646 US
(864) 223-4300, *Fax:* (864) 223-4096
www.sunny103-5.com
sunny@sunny103-5.com
License: Greenwood, Greenwood County, SC
Nat'l Network: Westwood One
Arbitron Metro Market: Greenwood, SC *Format:* Adult Contemp *Hrs. of News Programming:* News progmg 3 hrs wkly *Target Audience:* 25-54. *Adv. Rates:* 30; 30; 30; 30
Stephanie White, Promotions Manager

Greer

WCKI
03-03-1955; 1300 khz AM *Hrs Open:* 6 AM-6 PM; 1 kw-D; N34 55 39 W82 15 42
Box 170022, Spartanburg, SC 29652
(864) 877-8458,(864) 877-8459, *Fax:* (864) 877-8500
mbrennan@mediatrixsc.org
License: Greer, Greenville County, SC held by Mediatrix SC Inc.

Population Served: 10,642 *Arbitron Metro Market:* Greenville-Spartanburg, SC *Hrs. of News Programming:* News progmg one hr wkly *Target Audience:* 25-54; working people who spend money
Gary Towery, President
Michael Brennan, Executive Vice President
Gary Powery, Station Manager
Michael Brennan, Programming Director
Kevin Raper, Chief Engineer

WOLT
01-01-1993; 103.3 mhz FM; 2.7 kw; 495 ft.; N34 59 54 W82 8 17
3100 Smoketree Court, Suite 500, Raleigh, NC 27604 US
(864) 751-0113, *Fax:* 864-751-0117
www.wolt-fm.com
License: Greer, Greenville County, SC held by Davidson Media Station WOLT Licensee LLC.
Group Owner: Davidson Media Group LLC; (acq 10-6-2005; grpsl).
Arbitron Metro Market: Greenville-Spar *TV Affiliate:* Top 40
General Manager, General Manager
National Sales Manager

WPJM
06-15-1949; 800 khz AM; 1 kw-D, ND1; 0.438 kw-N, ND1; N34 56 59 W82 14 43
305 North Tryon St., Greer, SC 29651 US
(864) 877-1112,(864) 877-1821, *Fax:* (864) 877-0342
License: Greer, SC held by Full Gospel WPJM 800 AM Radio Inc.
Regional Network: S.C. News Net.
Arbitron Metro Market: Greenville-Spartanburg, SC *Format:* Gospel *Target Audience:* General.
Bobby Cohen, President
J.B. Adams, Programming Director

Hampton

WHGS
09-01-1957; 1270 khz AM *Hrs Open:* 24
P. O. Box 666, Hampton, SC 29924 US
(803) 943-2831, *Fax:* (803) 943-5450
License: Hampton, SC held by Bocock Communications LLC
Nat'l Network: CNN Radio *Regional Network:* S.C. News Net.
Nat'l Reps: Salem *Regional Reps:* Interep
Format: News, Talk *No. News Employees:* 1
John Bocock, President

WBHC-FM
09-01-1970; 92.1 mhz FM *Hrs Open:* 24/7; 6 kw; Ant 328 ft; N32 50 38 W81 07 31
Box 607, Hampton, SC 29924
(803) 943-2831, *Fax:* (803) 943-5450
www.varietyhits921.com
License: Hampton, Hampton County, SC held by Bocock Communications LLC
Nat'l Network: NBC Radio *Regional Network:* S.C. News Net.
Regional Reps: Interep
Special Programming: Relg 11 hrs wkly *No. News Employees:* 1 *Target Audience:* Adults.
John Bocock, President
Kevin Coan, Operations Dir
Kevin Coan, News Director

Hanahan

WAVF
07-03-1969; 101.7 mhz FM *Hrs Open:* 24; 100 kw; 782 ft.; N32 49 4 W79 50 8
P. O. Box 2389, Myrtle Beach, SC 29578 US
(843) 972-1100, *Fax:* (843) 972-1200
wavf-fm.fimc.net
License: Hanahan, Berkeley County, SC held by Apex Broadcasting Inc.
Group Owner: Apex Broadcasting Inc.; (acq 10-28-2008; swap for WKZQ-FM Forestbrook)
Nat'l Reps: Christal
Arbitron Metro Market: Charleston, SC *Format:* Variety/Diverse
Dean Pearce, CEO
John Anthony, Operations Dir
Chris Johnson, General Manager

Hardeeville

WLVH
08-30-1992; 101.1 mhz FM *Hrs Open:* 24; 50 kw; 476 ft.; N32 5 48 W81 19 17
600 Congress Ave., Suite 1400, Austin, TX 78701 US
(912) 231-1011, *Fax:* (912) 964-9414
www.love1011.com
info@love1011.com
License: Hardeeville, Jasper County, SC held by Capstar TX L.P.
Group Owner: Clear Channel Communications Inc.; (acq 8-30-00; grpsl)
Nat'l Network: ABC
Arbitron Metro Market: Savannah, GA *Format:* Urban Contemporary *Hrs. of News Programming:* News progmg one hr wkly *Target Audience:* 25-54; affluent Black adults
Steve Richards, Operations Dir
Sheryl Collison, Programming Director
Craig Scott, Promotions Manager
Marty Foglia, Chief Engineer
Gary Young, Program Director

Hartsville

WBZF
11-19-1992; 98.5 mhz FM; 6 kw; 328 ft.; N34 27 54 W80 5 45
111 East Kilbourn Ave., Suite 2700, Milwaukee, WI 53202 US
(843) 661-5000, *Fax:* (843) 661-0888
www.glory985-com
christy.mitchell@cumulus.com
License: Hartsville, Darlington County, SC held by Cumulus Licensing Corp.
Group Owner: Cumulus Media Inc.
Arbitron Metro Market: Florence, SC *Format:* Black, Religious
Matt Scurry, Operations Dir
David Jaye, Programming Director
Christy Mitchell, Business/HR Manager

WJDJ
12-04-1972; 1490 khz AM *Hrs Open:* 6:30 AM-6PM; 1 kw-U, ND1; N34 21 47 W80 4 28 *Rebroadcasts:* WAGS—WAGS/WJDJ are simulcast. Program originates at WAGS.
430 W. Lincoln St., Hartsville, SC 29550 US
(803) 484-5415
www.wagsradio.com
wagsradio@sc.rr.com
License: Hartsville, SC held by Beaver Communications
Nat'l Network: USA
Arbitron Metro Market: Bishopville, SC *Format:* Country, Gospel *Special Programming:* live remotes 2 hrs wkly, religious 7 hrs wkly *Hrs. of News Programming:* 6 hrs wkly *Target Audience:* 28 & up; Adults 28 & up*Adv. Rates:* 8; 8; 8; 8
James Jenkins, President

Hemingway

***WLGI**
07-01-1984; 90.9 mhz FM *Hrs Open:* 15; 50 kw; 505 ft.; N33 43 9 W79 19 50
1272 William Hill, Hemingway, SC 29527 US
(843) 558-9544, *Fax:* (843) 558-5778
wlgi@ufbnb.org
License: Hemingway, Williamsburg County, SC held by Regional Baha'i Council of the Southern States.
Wire Services: Weather Wire
Format: Black, Gospel *Special Programming:* Jazz *Target Audience:* General.
Jenn Czelada, General Manager
Ed Czelada, Programming Director

Hilton Head Island

WFXH(AM)
02-14-1983; 1130 khz AM *Hrs Open:* 24; 1 kw-D, 500 w-N, DA-N; N32 12 01 W80 43 27
One Saint Augustine Pl., Hilton Head Island, SC 29928
(843) 785-9569, *Fax:* (843) 842-3369
License: Hilton Head Island, Beaufort County, SC held by Monterey Licenses LLC.
Group Owner: Triad Broadcasting Co. L.L.C.; (acq 7-18-00; grpsl)
Population Served: 50,000 *Arbitron Metro Market:* Savannah, GA *Format:* News, Sports *Hrs. of News Programming:* news progmg 5 hrs wkly *No. News Employees:* 1 *Target Audience:* 35 plus.
Robert Leonard, General Manager

WFXH-FM
07-14-1973; 106.1 mhz FM; 10.5 kw; 794 ft; N32 19 50 W80 56 19
401 Mall Blvd., Suite 101 D, Savannah, GA 29928
(912) 351-9830, *Fax:* (912) 352-4821
www.adventureradio.com
mhalverson@adventureradio.fm
License: Hilton Head Island, Beaufort County, SC
Nat'l Reps: Christal
Population Served: 100,000 *Arbitron Metro Market:* Savannah, GA *No. News Employees:* 2 *Target Audience:* 18-49; more male than female
Mark Halverson, General Manager
Gabe Reynolds, Programming Director

Holly Hill

WJBS
12-01-1972; 1440 khz AM; 1 kw-D, NDD; N33 20 23 W80 26 18
P.O. Box 1087, Holly Hilly, SC 29059 US
(803) 496-5352, *Fax:* (803) 496-2526
wjbsam@yahoo.com
License: Holly Hill, SC held by Eugene Schoebinger.
Format: Gospel *Special Programming:* Black 17 hrs, fishing/hunting 2 hrs, farm 2 hrs wk
Harry Govan, General Manager
Robert Small, Promotions Manager

Hollywood

WXST
07-15-1988; 99.7 mhz FM *Hrs Open:* 24; 70 kw; 781 ft.; N32 49 4 W79 50 8
3 Yonah Drive, Atlanta, GA 30309 US
(843) 972-1100, *Fax:* (843) 972-1200
www.star997.com
info@star997.com
License: Hollywood, Charleston County, SC held by Apex Broadcasting Inc.
Group Owner: Apex Broadcasting Inc.; acq 11-20-01).
Nat'l Network: Jones Radio Networks
Arbitron Metro Market: Charleston, SC *Format:* Urban Contemporary *Target Audience:* 25-54; urban professional *Adv. Rates:* 25; 25; 25; na
Dean Pearce, CEO
John Anthony, Operations Dir
Walt Rosen, General Sales Mgr
Carl Wine, Promotions Manager

Homeland Park

WRIX
09-01-1986; 1020 khz AM; 3 kw-C, NDD; 10 kw-D, NDD; N34 28 14 W82 38 3
Watson Village, Anderson, SC 29624 US
(864) 224-6733, *Fax:* (864) 224-0260
License: Homeland Park, SC held by AM 1020 Inc.
Regional Network: S.C. News Net.
Arbitron Metro Market: Greenville-Spartanburg, SC *Format:* Religious *Special Programming:* Black 7 hrs wkly
Karen Small, General Manager

Honea Path

WRIX-FM
06-10-1977; 103.1 mhz FM *Hrs Open:* 24; 6 kw; 328 ft.; N34 25 31 W82 32 26
Watson Village, Anderson, SC 29624 US
(864) 224-9749, *Fax:* (864) 224-0260
License: Honea Path, Anderson County, SC held by FM 103 Inc.
Nat'l Network: ABC *Regional Network:* S.C. News Net.
Arbitron Metro Market: Greenville-Spartanburg, SC *Format:* News, News/Talk, 86 *Special Programming:* Talk 20 hrs wkly
Karen Small, General Manager

Irmo

WWNU
05-23-1987; 92.1 mhz FM *Hrs Open:* 24; 15 kw; 427 ft.; N34 4 55 W81 7 36
P.O Drawer I, Johnston, SC 29832 US
(803) 753-6800, *Fax:* (803) 753-6806
www.new92.com
kirk@hometowncolumbia.com
License: Irmo, Lexington County, SC held by Double O South Carolina Corp.
Group Owner: Double O Radio L.L.C.; (acq 11-1-2004; $4.7 million)
Arbitron Metro Market: Columbia, SC *Format:* Country *Hrs. of News Programming:* News progmg 7 hrs wkly *Adv. Rates:* 24; 20; 24; 16
Kirk Litton, President
Tyler Ryan, Operations Dir
Chuck McKay, General Manager

Isle of Palms

WMXZ
11-01-1974; 95.9 mhz FM *Hrs Open:* 24; 50 kw; 352 ft.; N32 49 27 W80 0 10
Post Office Box 543, Bamberg, SC 29003 US
(850) 654-1000, *Fax:* (850) 654-6510
www.mix1031online.com
License: Isle of Palms, Walton County, SC held by Qantum of Fort Walton Beach License Co. LLC.
Group Owner: Qantum Communications Corp.; (acq 7-2-2003; grpsl).

Nat'l Reps: Katz Radio
Arbitron Metro Market: Fort Walton Beach, FL *Format:* Adult Contemp *Hrs. of News Programming:* news progmg 20 hrs wkly *No. News Employees:* 1 *Target Audience:* 25-54; general
Frank Osborne, President
Georgia Edmiston, General Manager
Allyson Buckner, General Sales Mgr

Johnsonville

WALD
08-01-1947; 1080 khz AM *Hrs Open:* sunup-sundown
P. O. Box 2166, Walterboro, SC 29488 US
(843) 538-4780, *Fax:* (843) 538-5392
rswaldradio@lowcountry.com
License: Johnsonville, SC held by Glory Communications, Inc.
Format: Gospel
Annette Gantt, Operations Dir
Jesse Bowers, General Manager
Ronda Simpson, Programming Director

Johnston

WKSX-FM
08-26-1985; 92.7 mhz FM; 1.8 kw; 577 ft.; N33 45 19 W81 50 44
Mailing Address: P.O. Drawer I, Johnston, SC 29832 US
Second Address: 102 Slide Hill Rd., Johnston, SC 29832
(803) 275-4444, *Fax:* (803) 275-3185
fdaviksx@bellsouth.net
License: Johnston, Edgefield County, SC held by Edgefield Saluda Radio Co. Inc.
Nat'l Network: CNN Radio *Regional Network:* S.C. News Net.
Nat'l Reps: Keystone (unwired net)
Arbitron Metro Market: Augusta, GA *Format:* Oldies *Target Audience:* men & women age 25-54 *Adv. Rates:* quoted upon request
Mike Casey, President
Frank Davis, Operations Dir
Tony Baughman, News Director
Fayne Anderson, Chief Engineer

Kershaw

WKSC
12-21-1961; 1300 khz AM *Hrs Open:* 24; 0.5 kw-D, ND2; 0.088 kw-N, ND2; N34 33 30 W80 33 34
502 West Church Street, Kershaw, SC 29067 US
(803) 475-8585, *Fax:* (805) 966-3530
www.wkscradio.com
wksc@wkscradio.com
License: Kershaw, SC held by Kershaw Broadcasting Corp.
Nat'l Network: ABC
Format: Oldies *Target Audience:* 35-64.
John Griffin, President
Johnny Knight, General Manager

Kiawah Island

WCOO
12-07-1969; 105.5 mhz FM *Hrs Open:* 24; 50 kw; 436 ft.; N32 39 57 W80 3 11
59 Windermere Blvd, Charleston, SC 29407 US
(843) 769-4799, *Fax:* (843) 769-4797
www.1055thebridge.com
License: Kiawah Island, Charleston County, SC held by L.M. Communications II of South Carolina Inc.
Group Owner: L M Communications Inc.; (acq 3-30-95;
Nat'l Network: ABC
Arbitron Metro Market: Charleston, SC *Format:* Oldies *Target Audience:* 25-54; general *Adv. Rates:* 50; 50; 45; 20
Lynn Martin, President
Mike Allen, Operations Dir
Charlie Cohn, General Manager

Kingstree

WDKD
07-01-1949; 1310 khz AM *Hrs Open:* 24
P. O. Box 1125, Kingstree, SC 29556 US
(803) 775-2321, *Fax:* (803) 773-4856
www.miller.fm
production@miller.fm
License: Kingstree, SC held by Miller Communications Inc.
Group Owner: Miller Communications Inc.; (acq 12-18-2001; $1,415,456 assumption of debt with co-located FM).
Nat'l Network: ABC *Regional Network:* S.C. News Net.
Arbitron Metro Market: Florence, SC *Format:* Adult Contemp *Target Audience:* 25-54. *Adv. Rates:* 20; 20; 20; 20
Harold Miller, CEO
Harold Miller, Jr., President
Theresa Miller, Operations Dir
Kevin Ireland, General Sales Mgr
Dave Baker, Programming GM
Sarah Skinner, News Director
Dave Baker, Vice President, Operations
John Mcleod, PublicAffairs Director

WRZE
01-01-1998; 94.1 mhz FM *Hrs Open:* 24; 6 kw; 328 ft.; N33 43 32 W79 58 19
Two Bala Plaza, Suite 801, Bala-Cynwyd, PA 19004 US
(843) 667-4600, *Fax:* (843) 673-7390
www.therose.net
mcv@qantuncapecod.com
License: Kingstree, Williamsburg County, SC held by Qantum of Florence License Co. LLC.
Group Owner: Qantum Communications Corp.; (acq 7-2-2003; grpsl)
Format: Gospel *Target Audience:* 25-54; urban & caucasian
Jonathan Brewster, General Manager
Craig Dalla Riva, Station Manager

WWKT-FM
05-28-1966; 99.3 mhz FM *Hrs Open:* 24; 11 kw; 492 ft.; N33 54 7 W79 59 52
P.O.Box 1125, Kingstree, SC 29556 US
(803) 775-2321, *Fax:* (803) 773-4856
www.miller.fm
production@miller.fm
License: Kingstree, Williamsburg County, SC
Group Owner: Miller Communications Inc.
Arbitron Metro Market: Kingstree, SC *Format:* Country *Hrs. of News Programming:* news progmg 14 hrs wkly *No. News Employees:* 1 *Adv. Rates:* Same as AM
Kevin Ireland, General Sales Mgr
Johnny Green, Programming Director
Vakenya Brunson, News Director
Gary Mills, Disc Jockey

Ladson

WJNI
06-15-1998; 106.3 mhz FM *Hrs Open:* 24; 6 kw; 328 ft.; N32 55 42 W80 6 13
5081 Rivers Ave., North Charleston, SC 29418 US
(843) 763-6631, *Fax:* (843) 763-5636
www.wjnifm.com
License: Ladson, Berkeley County, SC held by Thomas B. Daniels.
Group Owner: Jabar Communications Inc.
Nat'l Reps: Interep
Format: Religious *Target Audience:* 25 plus. *Adv. Rates:* 360; 360; 360; 360.
Michael Baynard, General Manager

*WKCL
01-11-1982; 91.5 mhz FM *Hrs Open:* 24; 100 kw; 305 ft.; N33 0 24 W80 5 17
P. O. Box 809, 528 College Park Road, Ladson, SC 29456 US
(843) 553-5420, *Fax:* (843) 553-0636
www.wkclradio.com
wkcl@msn.com
License: Ladson, Berkeley County, SC held by Chapel of the Holy Spirit and Holy Spirit Bible College.
Format: Adult Contemp, Gospel *Target Audience:* General; baby boomers
Carl Wiggins Sr., President

Lake City

WHYM
10-09-1953; 1260 khz AM *Hrs Open:* 6 AM-6 PM; 5 kw-D, ND1; 0.055 kw-N, ND1; N33 51 42 W79 44 15 *Rebroadcasts:* Simulcasts WOLS(AM) Florence 75%.
Mailing Address: 1776 Briarcliff Road, Ne, Suite A, Atlanta, GA 30306 US
Second Address: 925 E. Main St., Lake City, SC 29560
(843) 665-1230
License: Lake City, SC held by Miller Communications Inc.
Group Owner: Miller Communications Inc.; (acq 4-29-2008; $275,000 with WOLH(AM) Florence)
Nat'l Network: ABC *Regional Network:* S.C. News Net. *Regional Reps:* Jim D.Jones
Arbitron Metro Market: Florence, SC *Format:* Country *Special Programming:* Loc news *Hrs. of News Programming:* news progmg 5 hrs wkly *No. News Employees:* 1 *Target Audience:* 35 plus. *Adv. Rates:* 7;7; 15; 7
Jeff Lonis, General Manager

WWFN-FM
05-11-1977; 100.1 mhz FM; 3.3 kw; 433 ft.; N33 58 36 W79 48 32
2014 N. Irby Street, Florence, SC 29501 US
(843) 661-5000, *Fax:* (843) 661-0888
www.thefanfm.com
christy.mitchell@cumulus.com
License: Lake City, Florence County, SC held by Cumulus Licensing Corp.
Group Owner: Cumulus Media Inc.; (acq 3-12-2001; $850,000).
Arbitron Metro Market: Florence, SC *Format:* Sports *Target Audience:* 25-54.
Matt Scurry, Operations Dir
Jerry Stevens, General Manager
Christy Mitchell, Business/HRManager

Lamar

WSIM
10-01-1992; 93.7 mhz FM *Hrs Open:* 24; 2.8 kw; 485 ft.; N34 12 12 W79 51 52
P.O. Box 1269, Sumter, SC 29151 US
(803) 775-2321, *Fax:* (803) 773-4856
www.star937.net
production@miller.fm
License: Lamar, Darlington County, SC held by Miller Communications Inc.
Group Owner: Miller Communications Inc.; (acq 11-14-2000; grpsl)
Nat'l Network: ABC
Arbitron Metro Market: Florence, SC *Format:* Classic Rock *No. News Employees:* 1 *Target Audience:* 35-64; adults *Adv. Rates:* 35; 30; 35; 20
Harold Miller Jr., CEO
Theresa Miller, Operations Dir
Dave Baker, Vice President, Operations

Lancaster

WAGL
08-07-1962; 1560 khz AM; 50 kw-C, DAD; 50 kw-D, DAD; N34 49 53 W80 52 8
Mailing Address: 101 South Woodland Drive, Lancaster, SC 29720 US
Second Address: 101 S. Woodland Drive, Lancaster, SC 29720
(803) 283-8431, *Fax:* (803) 286-4702
www.waglradio.com
waglradio@conporium.net
License: Lancaster, SC held by Palmetto Broadcasting System Inc.
Arbitron Metro Market: Charlotte, NC *Format:* Gospel, Oldies *No. News Employees:* 6 *Adv. Rates:* 25; 25; 25; 25
B.L. Phillips Jr., President

WRHM
07-27-1964; 107.1 mhz FM; 2.4 kw; 524 ft.; N34 51 34 W80 47 59
Mailing Address: P.O. Box 307, Rock Hill, SC 29731 US
Second Address: 142 N. Confederate Ave., Rock Hill, SC 29730
(803) 286-1071, *Fax:* (803) 324-2860
fm107.com
almiller@wrhi.com
License: Lancaster, Lancaster County, SC held by Our Three Sons Broadcasting L.L.P.
Nat'l Network: ABC *Regional Network:* S.C. News Net.
Arbitron Metro Market: Charlotte-Gastonia-Rock Hill, NC-SC
Format: Country, News, 84 *Target Audience:* 25-54.
Steven Stone, Operations Dir
Allan Miller, General Manager
Mike Crowder, News Director

Latta

WCMG
09-18-1970; 94.3 mhz FM *Hrs Open:* 24; 10.5 kw; 502 ft.; N34 26 20 W79 29 44
330 East Kilbourn Ave, Suite 250, Milwaukee, WI 53202 US
(843) 661-5000, *Fax:* (843) 661-0888
www.943thedam.com
matt.scurry@cumulus.com
License: Latta, Dillon County, SC held by Cumulus Licensing Corp.
Group Owner: Cumulus Media Inc.; (acq 6-99; $525,000)
Nat'l Network: USA
Arbitron Metro Market: Florence, SC *Format:* Urban Contemporary *Hrs. of News Programming:* news progmg 8 hrs wkly *No. News Employees:* 1 *Target Audience:* 21-54; African-American
Matt Scurry, Operations Dir
Gerry Stevens, General Manager
Pam Mathis, Programming Director
Martha Clark, News Director
Gail Gilbreath, Chief Engineer
Christy Mitchell, Business/HR Manager

Laurens

WLBG

03-01-1947; 860 khz AM *Hrs Open:* 24; 1 kw-D, ND1; 0.012 kw-N, ND1; N34 30 13 W82 1 6
P.O. Box 1289, Laurens, SC 29360 US
(864) 984-3544, *Fax:* (864) 984-3545
www.wlbg.com
mail@wlbg.com
License: Laurens, SC held by Southeastern Broadcast Associates Inc.
Nat'l Network: Fox News Radio; Fox Sports
Format: Variety/Diverse *Hrs. of News Programming:* News progmg 4 hrs wkly *Target Audience:* 30 plus; Black
Emil Finley, President
Michael Johnson, General Sales Mgr

Lexington

WDEK(AM)

01-01-1983; 1170 khz AM *Hrs Open:* Sunrise-sunset; 10 kw-D; N33 58 17 W81 16 43
Box 537, Irmo, SC 29063
(803) 407-5223, *Fax:* (803) 407-6160
myritmo.com
info@myritmo.com
License: Lexington, Lexington County, SC held by Peregon Communications Inc.
Arbitron Metro Market: Columbia, SC
Sergio Perez, General Manager
Beth Well, General Sales Mgr

WOMG

08-31-1994; 98.5 mhz FM *Hrs Open:* 24; 6 kw; 325 ft.; N33 53 58.5 W81 13 29.6
Mailing Address: P.O. Box 5106, Columbia, SC 29250 US
Second Address: 1801 Charleston Hwy., Suite J, Cayce, SC 29033
(803) 796-7600, *Fax:* (803) 223-6079
www.womg.com
doug.william@citcomm.com
License: Lexington, Lexington County, SC
Group Owner: Cumulus Media Inc.; (acq 5-30-2000; grpsl)
Arbitron Metro Market: Columbia, SC *Format:* Contemporary Hits/Top 40 *Target Audience:* 25-54. *Adv. Rates:* 35; 30; 30; 18
William McElveen, General Manager

Loris

WLSC

08-01-1958; 1240 khz AM *Hrs Open:* 6 AM-midnight
P. O. Box 578, Loris, SC 29569 US
(843) 756-1183
www.tigerradio.com
infor@wlsc.com
License: Loris, SC held by JARC Broadcasting Inc.
Regional Network: S.C. News Net. *Nat'l Reps:* Keystone (unwired net)
Arbitron Metro Market: Myrtle Beach, SC *Format:* Variety/Diverse *Target Audience:* 21-54.
Jerry Jenrette, General Manager

WVCO

11-19-1993; 94.9 mhz FM *Hrs Open:* 24; 11 kw; 489 ft.; N33 59 39 W78 46 16
P. O. Box 1036, Myrtle Beach, SC 29578 US
(843) 445-9491, *Fax:* (843) 445-9490
www.949thesurf.com
Surf949@yahoo.com
License: Loris, Horry County, SC held by Carolina Beach Music Broadcasting Corp.
Arbitron Metro Market: Myrtle Beach, SC *Format:* Oldies *Hrs. of News Programming:* News progmg 2 hrs wkly *Target Audience:* 25-45.
Harvey Graham, CEO
Selene Graham, Operations Dir

Manning

WYMB

07-15-1957; 920 khz AM; 2.3 kw-D, DAN; 1 kw-N, DAN; N33 41 24 W80 16 23
330 East Kilbourn Ave., Suite 250, Milwaukee, WI 53202 US
(843) 661-5000, *Fax:* (843) 661-0888
License: Manning, SC held by Cumulus Licensing Corp.
Group Owner: Cumulus Media Inc.; (acq 3-24-99; with co-located FM).
Nat'l Network: AP Radio *Nat'l Reps:* Katz Radio
Arbitron Metro Market: Manning, SC *Format:* Contemporary Hits/Top 40 *Target Audience:* General.
Jerry Stevens, General Manager

Marion

WHLZ

08-01-1991; 100.5 mhz FM; 25 kw; 328 ft.; N34 23 26 W79 35 25
330 East Kilbourn Ave., Suite 250, Milwaukee, WI 53202 US
(843) 661-5000, *Fax:* (843) 661-0888
www.whlz1005.com
info@whlz1005.com
License: Marion, Marion County, SC held by Cumulus Licensing Corp.
Group Owner: Cumulus Media Inc.; (acq 3-24-99; $3.8 million with WMXT(FM) Pamplico).
Arbitron Metro Market: Florence, SC *Format:* Country
Matt Scurry, Operations Dir
Jerry Stevens, General Manager
Gail Gilbreath, Engineering Dir

McClellanville

WAZS(FM)

12-01-1994; 98.9 mhz FM *Hrs Open:* 24; 50 kw; Ant 492 ft; N33 11 20 W79 33 25
60 Markfield Drive, Charleston, SC 29407
(843) 763-6613, *Fax:* (843) 763-5636
License: McClellanville, Charleston County, SC held by 98.9 Inc.
Group Owner: Kirkman Broadcasting Inc.; (acq 1-5-2001)
Population Served: 44,783 *Arbitron Metro Market:* Summerville, SC *Target Audience:* 18-25; adults
Gill Kirkman, CEO

Moncks Corner

WJKB

12-01-1963; 950 khz AM *Hrs Open:* 24
P.O. Box 67, Moncks Corner, SC 29461 US
(843) 763-6631, *Fax:* (843) 766-1239
www.charlestonsportsradio.com/
License: Moncks Corner, SC held by Kirkman Broadcasting Inc.
Group Owner: Kirkman Broadcasting Inc.; (acq 11-29-2000; $150,000).
Nat'l Network: Jones Radio Networks; Motor Racing Net
Arbitron Metro Market: Charleston, SC *Format:* Country *Special Programming:* Nascar *Target Audience:* 25-54; male *Adv. Rates:* 20; 20; 40; 15
Gil Kirkman, President
Ted Byrne, Operations Dir
Rick Howze, General Sales Mgr
John Dixon, News Director
Wally Momeier, Chief Engineer

Mount Pleasant

WRFQ

06-01-1985; 104.5 mhz FM *Hrs Open:* 24; 100 kw; 659 ft.; N32 49 4 W79 50 9
50 E. Rivercenter Blvd, Suite 1200, Covington, KY 14011 US
(843) 884-2534, *Fax:* (843) 884-6096
q1045.com
kevin@qious.com
License: Mount Pleasant, Charleston County, SC held by Citicasters Licenses L.P.
Group Owner: Clear Channel Communications Inc.; (acq 5-4-99; grpsl).
Arbitron Metro Market: Charleston, SC *Format:* Classic Rock *Target Audience:* 25-54; adults, men
Paul Smith, Operations Dir
Tom Bustard, General Sales Mgr
Kevin Harbison, Programming Director
Scott Johnson, Operations Manager

WZJY

05-21-1982; 1480 khz AM *Hrs Open:* 24; 0.88 kw-D, ND1; 0.044 kw-N, ND1; N32 49 30 W79 49 53 *Rebroadcasts:* simulcast w/ WAZS-AM
1434 Meeting Street Road, P.O. Box 6196, Charleston, SC 29405 US
(843) 554-1063, *Fax:* (843) 554-1088
License: Mount Pleasant, SC held by Thomas B. Daniels
Group Owner: Jabar Communications Inc.; (acq 6-24-2007; $375,000)
Nat'l Reps: Interep
Arbitron Metro Market: Charleston, SC *Format:* Spanish *Hrs. of News Programming:* news progmg 24 hrs wkly *No. News Employees:* 5 *Target Audience:* 18-35 *Adv. Rates:* 240; 240; 240; 240.
Michael Baynard, General Manager

Mullins

WJAY

06-01-1949; 1280 khz AM *Hrs Open:* 18; 4.2 kw-D, ND1; 0.27 kw-N, ND1; N34 11 30 W79 18 55
PO Box 1020, Marion, SC 29571 US
(843) 423-1140, *Fax:* (843) 423-2829
www.wjay.com
License: Mullins, SC held by The Greater Highway Church of Christ.
Nat'l Network: ABC *Regional Network:* S.C. News Net.
Format: Gospel *Special Programming:* Farm 10 hrs wkly *Hrs. of News Programming:* News progmg 8 hrs wkly *Target Audience:* General.
Curtis Campbell, President

Murrells Inlet

*WMBJ

01-01-1997; 88.3 mhz FM *Hrs Open:* 24; 0 kw horiz, 1.8 kw vert; 331 ft.; N33 26 35 W79 8 21 *Rebroadcasts:* His Radio Network
Post Office Box 2061, Bristol, TN 37621 US
(864) 292-6040, *Fax:* (864) 292-8428
www.hisradio.com
comments@hisradio.com
License: Murrells Inlet, Georgetown County, SC held by Radio Training Network Inc.
Format: Christian
Allen Henderson, General Manager

WYEZ

04-07-1991; 94.5 mhz FM *Hrs Open:* 24; 12 kw; 476 ft.; N33 33 13 W79 13 14
Mailing Address: 1705 West Northwest Hwy, Suite 275, Grapevine, TX 76051 US
Second Address: 3926 Wesley St., Suite 301, Myrtle Beach, SC 29579
(843) 903-9962, *Fax:* (843) 903-1797
www.movin945.net
general@movin945.net
License: Murrells Inlet, Georgetown County, SC held by Fidelity Broadcasting Corp.
Arbitron Metro Market: Myrtle Beach, SC *Format:* Oldies *Hrs. of News Programming:* news progmg 40 hrs wkly *No. News Employees:* 1 *Target Audience:* Adults 25-54
Will Isaacs, General Manager
Bob Gauss, Engineering Dir

Myrtle Beach

WMYB

01-11-1965; 92.1 mhz FM *Hrs Open:* 24; 94 kw; 863 ft.; N33 35 27 W79 2 55
1116 Ocala Street, Myrtle Beach, SC 29577 US
(843) 448-1041, *Fax:* (843) 626-5988
www.star921.net
License: Myrtle Beach, Horry County, SC held by NM Licensing LLC.
Group Owner: NextMedia Group Inc.; (acq 11-26-01; grpsl).
Arbitron Metro Market: Myrtle Beach, SC *Format:* Adult Contemp *Target Audience:* Women: 25-54.
Carl Hirsch, Chairman
Steven Dinetz, CEO
Skip Weller, President
Barry Brown, General Manager
Art Greene, General Sales Mgr
Bill Catcher, Programming Director
Liza Van Horne, Promotions Manager
Ginny Batchelder, NewsDirector
Paul Matthews, Chief Engineer
Jeff Dinetz, COO

WRNN

04-24-1965; 1450 khz AM; 1 kw-U, ND1; N33 42 20 W78 53 23
PO Box 2389, Myrtle Beach, SC 29578 US
(843) 448-1041, *Fax:* (843) 626-5988
www.wrnn.net
License: Myrtle Beach, SC held by NM Licensing LLC.
Group Owner: NextMedia Group Inc.; (acq 11-26-2001; grpsl)
Arbitron Metro Market: Myrtle Beach, SC *Format:* Sports *Target Audience:* 25-60.
Carl Hirsch, Chairman
Steven Dinetz, CEO
Skip Weller, President
Barry Brown, General Manager
Dave Priest, Programming Director

WYAV

07-01-1964; 104.1 mhz FM; 100 kw; 981 ft.; N33 35 27 W79 2 55
1705 West Northwest Hwy, Suite 275, Grapevine, TX 76051 US
(843) 448-1041, *Fax:* (843) 626-5988
www.wave104.net
License: Myrtle Beach, Horry County, SC held by NM Licensing LLC.
Group Owner: NextMedia Group Inc.; (acq 11-26-01; grpsl).
Arbitron Metro Market: Myrtle Beach, SC *Format:* Classic Rock *Target Audience:* 18-49.

Carl Hirsch, Chairman
Steven Dinetz, CEO
Skip Weller, President
Barry Brown, General Manager
Art Greene, General Sales Mgr
Mark McKinney, Programming Director
Liza Van Horne, Promotions Manager
Paul Matthews, Chief Engineer
Jeff Dinetz, COO
Scott Mann, Music Director

***DWKEL**
01-01-2008; 1450 khz AM; Ant 764 ft
310 Sproul Street, McKees Rocks, PA 15136 US
(916) 251-1600, *Fax:* (916) 251-1650
www.klove.com
klove@klove.com
License: Myrtle Beach, SC held by Educational Media Foundation.
Group Owner: EMF Broadcasting
Nat'l Network: K-Love
Arbitron Metro Market: Omaha, NE *Format:* Christian
Darrell Chambliss, Chairman
Alan Mason, CEO/COO
Mike Novak, CEO
David Pierce, Chief Creative Officer
Dan Antonelli, Chief Business Development Officer
Eric Moser, Chief Financial Officer
Brian Burger, Vice President of HumanResources
D. Kevin Blair, Secretary and General Counsel

New Ellenton

WGUS-FM
12-01-1989; 102.7 mhz FM *Hrs Open:* 24; 4.3 kw; 387 ft.; N33 30 49 W81 38 3
P. O. Box 211045, Augusta, GA 30917 US
(706) 396-7000, *Fax:* (706) 396-7092
www.1027wgus.com
License: New Ellenton, Aiken County, SC held by WGAC License LLC.
Group Owner: Beasley Broadcast Group Inc.; (acq 12-22-94; $700,000;
Arbitron Metro Market: Augusta, GA *Format:* Gospel *Hrs. of News Programming:* News progmg 7 hrs wkly *Target Audience:* 35-64; affluent audience loyal fan base
T. Gentry, Operations Dir
Kent Dunn, General Manager
Zach Taylor, Programming Director

Newberry

WKDK
10-01-1946; 1240 khz AM *Hrs Open:* 24 hrs; 1 kw-U, ND1; N34 17 30 W81 37 15
P.O. Box 753, Newberry, SC 29108 US
(803) 276-2957, *Fax:* (803) 276-3337
www.wkdk.com
jcoggins@wkdk.com
License: Newberry, SC held by Newberry Broadcasting Co.
Nat'l Network: ABC *Regional Network:* S.C. News Net.
Format: Adult Contemp, Oldies *Target Audience:* General. *Adv. Rates:* 10; 8; 10; 8
James Coggins, Operations Dir
Brice Zimmerman, News Director
Heather Hawkins, Operations Manager

WKMG
05-22-1968; 1520 khz AM *Hrs Open:* Sunrise-sunset; 1 kw-D, NDD; N34 15 12 W81 35 44
115-A West Church St, Batesburg, SC 29006 US
(803) 405-0111, *Fax:* (803) 276-5677
License: Newberry, SC held by Cornell Blakely
Format: Spanish *Special Programming:* Relg 2 hrs, gospel 3 hrs, Sp 10 hrs wkly
Cornell Blakely, General Manager

North Augusta

WNRR
07-30-1958; 1380 khz AM *Hrs Open:* 24; 4 kw-D, 70 w-N; N33 29 17 W81 56 46
2743 Perimeter Pkwy., Bldg. 100, Suite 200, Augusta, GA 53202
(706) 396-6000, *Fax:* (706) 396-6010
License: North Augusta, Aiken County, SC held by Capstar TX L.P.
Group Owner: Clear Channel Communications Inc.; (acq 12-19-2000; grpsl)
Population Served: 72,000 *Arbitron Metro Market:* Augusta, GA *Hrs. of News Programming:* news progmg 7 hrs wkly *No. News Employees:* 1
Mark Bass, General Manager

WKZK
05-09-1962; 1600 khz AM *Hrs Open:* 6 AM-sunset
Mailing Address: P.O. Box 1454, Augusta, GA 30903 US
Second Address: 2 Milledge Rd., Augusta, GA 30904
(706) 738-0044, *Fax:* (706) 481-8442
wkzk.net
wkzk1600@bellsouth.net
License: North Augusta, SC held by Gospel Radio Inc.
Nat'l Network: American Urban *Nat'l Reps:* Dora-Clayton
Arbitron Metro Market: Augusta, GA *Format:* Black, Gospel, 74
Target Audience: Black adults.
Garfield Turner, General Manager

North Charleston

WXLY
07-17-1962; 102.5 mhz FM *Hrs Open:* 24; 100 kw; 659 ft.; N32 49 4 W79 50 9
50 East Rivercenter Blvd, Suite 1200, Covington, KY 41011 US
(843) 884-2534, *Fax:* (843) 884-1218
www.wxly.com
lisacooper@clearchannel.com
License: North Charleston, Charleston County, SC held by Citicasters Licenses L.P.
Group Owner: Clear Channel Communications Inc.; (acq 5-4-99; grpsl).
Arbitron Metro Market: Charleston, SC *Format:* Oldies *No. News Employees:* 2 *Target Audience:* 25-54.
Paul Smith, Operations Dir
Tom Bustard, General Sales Mgr
Brian Cleary, Programming Director
Jonny Knight, Promotions Manager
Willie Bennett, Chief Engineer
Alene Grevey, VP/Market Manager
Lisa Cooper, Business Manager
MaryCatherine Walker, Digital Content Director

***WYFH**
07-07-1984; 90.7 mhz FM; 50 kw; 492 ft.; N32 58 23 W80 13 54
8030 Arrowridge Blvd., Charlotte, NC 28273 US
(704) 523-5555, *Fax:* (704) 522-1967
www.bbnradio.org
bbn@bbnradio.org
License: North Charleston, Charleston County, SC held by Bible Broadcasting Network Inc.
Group Owner: Bible Broadcasting Network
Nat'l Network: Bible Bcstg Net
Arbitron Metro Market: Charleston, SC *Format:* Christian, Religious
Dave Phillps, President

North Myrtle Beach

WNMB
04-01-1983; 900 khz AM; 0.5 kw-D, DA2; 0.5 kw-N, DA2; N33 49 26 W78 45 59
429 Pine Avenue, N. Myrtle Beach, SC 29582 US
(843) 249-6662, *Fax:* (843) 249-7823
www.wnmb900.com
License: North Myrtle Beach, SC held by Norman Communications NMB Inc.
Arbitron Metro Market: Myrtle Beach, SC *Format:* Religious
Bill Norman, General Manager

***WKVC**
09-09-1997; 88.9 mhz FM *Hrs Open:* 24; 100 kw vert; 581 ft.; N34 5 41 W78 28 27
2630 Mirror Lake Dr, Fayettville, NC 28303 US
(843) 399-9649, *Fax:* (843) 399-9031
www.klove.com
kreeder@klove.com
License: North Myrtle Beach, Horry County, SC held by Educational Media Foundation.
Group Owner: EMF Broadcasting; (acq 5-11-00; $1.2 million).
Nat'l Network: K-Love
Arbitron Metro Market: Little River, SC *Format:* Religious *Target Audience:* 25-65; contemp Christian
Richard Jenkins, CEO
Kurt Reeder, General Manager

WEZV
08-15-1972; 105.9 mhz FM *Hrs Open:* 24; 17 kw; 361 ft.; N33 51 16 W78 43 0
Mailing Address: 429 Pine Avenue, N. Myrtle Beach, SC 29582 US
Second Address: 3926 Wesley St., Suite 301, Myrtle Beach, SC 29579
(843) 903-9962, *Fax:* (843) 903-1797
www.wezv.com
License: North Myrtle Beach, Horry County, SC held by Fidelity Broadcasting Corp.
Arbitron Metro Market: Myrtle Beach, SC *Format:* Easy Listening
Target Audience: 35 plus.
Matt Sedota, General Manager

Orangeburg

WHXT
09-01-1973; 103.9 mhz FM; 9.2 kw; 531 ft.; N33 40 13 W80 52 25
2929 E. Commercial Blvd., Suite 410, Ft. Lauderdale, FL 33308 US
(803) 695-8680, *Fax:* (803) 695-8605
www.hot1039fm.com
mhanisch@innercity.sc.com
License: Orangeburg, Orangeburg County, SC held by Urban Radio II L.L.C.
Group Owner: Inner City Broadcasting; (acq 5-30-2003; $11.1 million with WZMJ(FM) Batesburg).
Arbitron Metro Market: Columbia, SC *Format:* Urban Contemporary
Steve Patterson, General Manager

WQKI-FM
10-10-1987; 102.9 mhz FM *Hrs Open:* 24; 3.1 kw; 457 ft.; N33 26 35 W80 48 16
PO Box 1546, Orangeburg, SC 29116 US
(803) 536-1710, *Fax:* (803) 531-1089
miller.fm
mail@miller.fm
License: Orangeburg, Orangeburg County, SC held by Miller Communications Inc.
Group Owner: Miller Communications Inc.; acq 4-30-03; $1.25 million with WGFG(FM) Branchville).
Nat'l Network: ABC
Format: Classic Rock *Special Programming:* Relg 6 hrs wkly *Hrs. of News Programming:* news progmg 10 hrs wkly *No. News Employees:* 1 *Target Audience:* 25-54.
Harold Miller Jr., President
Russ Fender, Operations Dir
Theresa Miller, General Manager
Sonny Pagan, General Sales Mgr
Dave Baker, Programming Director
Dave Dalesky, Engineering Dir

WPJK
11-03-1958; 1580 khz AM *Hrs Open:* Sunrise-sunset; 1 kw-D, NDD; N33 28 43 W80 52 46
2358 Amsterdam Dr., Augusta, GA 30906 US
(803) 534-4848, *Fax:* (803) 534-0888
License: Orangeburg, SC held by Radio Orangeburg Partnership.
Nat'l Network: USA
Format: Gospel, Religious
Bose Gowdy, President
Rev. Pinckney Palmer Jr., Operations Dir

***WSSB-FM**
03-15-1985; 90.3 mhz FM *Hrs Open:* 24; 80 kw horiz, 72 kw vert; 217 ft.; N33 29 55 W80 50 30
P.O. Box 7656, Orangeburg, SC 29117 US
(803) 536-8196, *Fax:* (803) 533-3652
www.scsu.edu
info@wssb.com
License: Orangeburg, Orangeburg County, SC held by South Carolina State University.
Nat'l Network: American Urban; NPR
Format: Gospel, Jazz *Special Programming:* Jazz 10 hrs, reggae 4 hrs, blues 2 hrs, rap 4 hrs wkly *Hrs. of News Programming:* news progmg 7 hrs wkly *No. News Employees:* 1
Target Audience: 8-65.
Milton McKissick, General Manager
Marion White, Programming Director
Ken Durst, Chief Engineer

WTCB
07-06-1967; 106.7 mhz FM; 100 kw; 787 ft.; N33 46 52 W80 55 14
Mailing Address: P.O. Box 5106, Columbia, SC 29250 US
Second Address: 1801 Charleston Hwy., Suite J, Cayce, SC 29033
(803) 796-7600, *Fax:* (803) 926-1067
www.b106fm.com
wtcb@b106fm.com
License: Orangeburg, Orangeburg County, SC
Group Owner: Cumulus Media Inc.; (acq 5-30-00; grpsl).
Nat'l Reps: Christal
Arbitron Metro Market: Columbia, SC *Format:* Adult Contemp
Target Audience: 25-54; affluent, upscale young adults
William McElveen, President
Brent Johns, Operations Dir

Pageland

WGSP-FM
02-22-1975; 102.3 mhz FM; 2.55 kw; 512 ft.; N34 53 57 W80 25 46
P.O. Box 5, Pageland, SC 29728 US
(843) 672-7839,(704) 442-7222
www.latremendaradio.com
License: Pageland, Chesterfield County, SC held by Norsan Media Group of South Carolina LLC.
Group Owner: Norsan Consulting and Management Inc.; (acq 7-13-2006; $975,000)
Nat'l Network: Salem Radio Network
Format: Tejano
Norberto Sanchez, President

Pamplico

WMXT
11-01-1990; 102.1 mhz FM *Hrs Open:* 24; 50 kw horiz, 49.4 kw vert; 479 ft.; N33 58 36 W79 48 32
330 East Kilbourn Ave., Suite 250, Milwaukee, WI 53202 US
(843) 661-5000, *Fax:* (843) 661-0888
www.1021thefox.com
buzz.bowman@cumulus.com
License: Pamplico, Florence County, SC held by Cumulus Licensing Corp.
Group Owner: Cumulus Media Inc.; (acq 3-24-99; $3.8 million with WHLZ(FM) Marion).
Arbitron Metro Market: Florence, SC *Format:* Light Rock *Special Programming:* Beach music 5 hrs wkly *Hrs. of News Programming:* news progmg 3 hrs wkly *No. News Employees:* 2 *Target Audience:* 25-54.
Matt Scurry, Operations Dir
Jerry Stevens, General Manager
Buzz Bowman, Programming Director
Gail Gilbreath, Chief Engineer

Parris Island

WGZO
07-01-1985; 103.1 mhz FM *Hrs Open:* 24; 17.5 kw; 328 ft; N32 26 10 W80 55 23
401 Mall Blvd., Suite 101 D, Savannah, GA 29928
(912) 351-9830, *Fax:* (912) 352-4821
www.1031thedrive.com,www.adventureradio.com
mhalverson@adventureradio.fm
License: Parris Island, Beaufort County, SC held by Monterey Licenses
Nat'l Reps: Christal
Population Served: 500,000*No. News Employees:* 1 *Target Audience:* 25-54 *Adv. Rates:* 25; 25; 25
Mark Halverson, General Manager
Scott Keith, Programming Director

Pawleys Island

WDAI
10-02-1993; 98.5 mhz FM *Hrs Open:* 24; 6.1 kw; 666 ft.; N33 35 27 W79 2 55
111 East Kilbourn Ave., Suite 2700, Milwaukee, WI 53202 US
(843) 651-7869, *Fax:* (843) 651-3197
www.985kissfm.net
david.lewis@cumulus.com
License: Pawleys Island, Georgetown County, SC held by Cumulus Licensing Corp.
Group Owner: Cumulus Media Inc.; (acq 1-27-98)
Nat'l Network: Westwood One
Arbitron Metro Market: Myrtle Beach, SC *Format:* Urban Contemporary *Hrs. of News Programming:* news progmg 6 hrs wkly *No. News Employees:* 1 *Target Audience:* 25-54.
Bill Hazen, General Manager
David Lewis, Market Manager

Pickens

WTBI
01-21-1984; 1540 khz AM *Hrs Open:* Sunrise-sunset; 1 kw-C, NDD; 10 kw-D, NDD; N34 51 37 W82 43 25 *Rebroadcasts:* Rebroadcasts WTBI-FM Greenville
P. O. Box 837, Pickens, SC 29671 US
(864) 295-2145, *Fax:* (864) 295-6313
www.wtbi.org
jwatts@tabernacleministries.org
License: Pickens, SC held by Tabernacle Christian Schools
Nat'l Network: USA
Arbitron Metro Market: Greenville-Spartanburg, SC *Format:* Christian *Target Audience:* All ages.
Dr. W. Melvin Aiken, CEO
Mary Parker, Operations Dir
Charles R. Garrett Sr., Programming Director
James Simpson, Promotions Manager
Tommy Anderson, Announcer/Operator
Sam Quinn, Announcer/Operator
John H. Watts, COO

Pinopolis

WTUA
05-01-1990; 105.9 mhz FM; 6 kw; 328 ft.; N33 29 36 W79 53 21
Mailing Address: 4011 Burns Drive, St. Stephen, SC 29479 US
Second Address: 4013 Burns Dr., Saint Stephen, SC 29479
(803) 939-9010
www.wfmv.com
wtuaradio@direcway.com
License: Pinopolis, Berkeley County, SC held by Praise Communications Inc.
Group Owner: Glory Communications Inc.; (acq 1-27-2005).
Arbitron Metro Market: Charleston, SC *Format:* Gospel *Hrs. of News Programming:* news progmg 5 hrs wkly *No. News Employees:* 1 *Target Audience:* 20-65; African American *Adv. Rates:* 8; 8; 8; 6
Alex Snipe, CEO
Alexis Campbell, General Sales Mgr
Lula Greene, Programming Director
Tony Green, Music Director
Kevin Fedler, Local Sales Manager
Emma Butler, Traffic
Armita Thomas, Traffic

Port Royal

WXYY(FM)
02-01-1988; 107.9 mhz FM *Hrs Open:* 24; 24 kw; Ant 725 ft; N32 13 36 W80 50 53
One St. Augustine Pl., Hilton Head Island, SC 29928
(843) 785-9569, *Fax:* (843) 842-3369
wlow1079@adventureradio.fm
License: Port Royal, Beaufort County, SC held by Monterey Licenses LLC.
Group Owner: Triad Broadcasting Co. L.L.C.; (acq 7-18-2000; grpsl)
Nat'l Reps: Christal
Population Served: 500,000 *Arbitron Metro Market:* Savannah, GA *Format:* Urban Contemporary *Target Audience:* 45 plus; active, affluent, older
Robert Leonard, General Manager

Ravenel

WMGL
02-01-1986; 107.3 mhz FM *Hrs Open:* 24; 16.5 kw; 410 ft.; N32 54 18 W79 55 19
140 S. Ash Ave., Tempe, AZ 85281 US
(843) 277-1207, *Fax:* (843) 277-1212
www.magic1073.com
info@magic1017.com
License: Ravenel, Charleston County, SC held by The Last Bastion Station Trust LLC, as Trustee
Arbitron Metro Market: Charleston, SC *Format:* Adult Contemp *Hrs. of News Programming:* news progmg 6 hrs wkly *No. News Employees:* 2 *Target Audience:* 25-54; upscale adults
Chris Hoffman, Operations Dir
Paul O'Malley, General Manager
Jerold Jackson, Programming Director
Charles Pack, Promotions Manager

Richburg

***WRBK**
01-01-1998; 90.3 mhz FM *Hrs Open:* 24; 7.5 kw horiz, 7.3 kw vert; 538 ft.; N34 41 46 W81 1 23
P O Box 15, Chester, SC 29706 US
(803) 581-9030, *Fax:* (803) 581-9932
WRBK@Truvista.net
License: Richburg, Chester County, SC held by Richburg Educational Broadcasters Inc.
Format: Oldies *Target Audience:* 30-60; middle aged adults who like beach flavored oldies
Jeff Sigmon, President

Ridgeland

WLHH(FM)
07-15-1986; 104.9 mhz FM *Hrs Open:* 24; 16 kw; Ant 410 ft; N32 26 10 W80 55 23
210 Montaque Ave., Greenwood, SC 29649
(248) 455-7200, *Fax:* (248) 304-4970
www.detroit.cbslocal.com
shows@cbsdetroit.com
License: Ridgeland, Beaufort County, SC held by JB Broadcasting LLC
Population Served: 500,000 *Arbitron Metro Market:* Savannah, GA *Format:* Oldies *No. News Employees:* 2 *Target Audience:* 18-49; general *Adv. Rates:* 50; 50; 50; 50
Robert Leonard, General Manager

Ridgeville

WAYA-FM
10-01-1989; 100.9 mhz FM *Hrs Open:* 24; 13 kw; 299 ft.; N33 4 25.7 W80 11 54.2
1717 Wappoo Rd., Charleston, SC 29407 US
(541) 963-5884
www.csnradio.com
License: Ridgeville, Meigs County, SC held by East Tennessee Radio Group III L.P.
Group Owner: East Tennessee Radio Group III L.P.; (acq 5-30-2008; grpsl)
Nat'l Reps: D & R Radio
Format: Christian
Mike Kestler, President
Wade Tilegar, General Manager

Rock Hill

WAVO
05-18-1948; 1150 khz AM *Hrs Open:* 24
Mailing Address: P. O. Box 18614, Charlotte, NC 28210 US
Second Address: 400 Pineview Rd., Rock Hill, SC 29731
(509) 527-1000, *Fax:* (509) 529-5534
www.urockfm.com
License: Rock Hill, SC held by WHVN Inc.
Group Owner: GHB Radio Group; (acq 2-4-92; $115,000;
Arbitron Metro Market: Stanfield OR *Format:* Contemporary Hits/Top 40
Tom Hodgins, General Manager

***WNSC-FM**
01-03-1978; 88.9 mhz FM *Hrs Open:* 24; 100 kw; Ant 600 ft; N34 50 24 W81 01 07
1101 George Rogers Blvd., Columbia, SC 29211
(803) 737-3200, *Fax:* (803) 737-3552
www.etvradio.org
gasque@scetv.org
License: Rock Hill, York County, SC held by South Carolina Educational Television Commission.
Nat'l Network: NPR; PRI; APM
Arbitron Metro Market: Charlotte-Gasto
Linda O'Bryon, President
John Gasque, Operations Dir
Shari Hutchinson, General Manager
Shari Hutchinson, Station Manager
Melanie Boyer, General Sales Mgr
John Gasque, Programming Director
John Crockett, Engineering Dir
SkipBeach, Chief Engineer

WRHI
12-14-1944; 1340 khz AM *Hrs Open:* 24 hours; 1 kw-U, ND1; N34 58 59 W81 1 11
Mailing Address: P.O. Box 307, Rock Hill, SC 29731 US
Second Address: 142 N. Confederate Ave., Rock Hill, SC 29730
(803) 324-1340, *Fax:* (803) 324-2860
www.wrhi.com
newsroom@wrhi.com
License: Rock Hill, SC held by Our Three Sons Broadcasting L.L.P.
Group Owner: Our Three Sons Broadcasting L.L.P.; acq 10-1-84)
Nat'l Network: ABC *Regional Network:* S.C. News Net.
Arbitron Metro Market: Charlotte-Gastonia-Rock Hill, NC-SC *Format:* News, News/Talk, 84, Talk *Hrs. of News Programming:* news progmg 14 hrs wkly *No. News Employees:* 2 *Target Audience:* 30 plus.
Steven Stone, Operations Dir
Allan Miller, General Manager
Mike Crowder, News Director

Saint Matthews

WSCZ(FM)
01-01-1990; 93.9 mhz FM *Hrs Open:* 24; 1.75 kw; Ant 607 ft; N33 45 46 W80 49 23
200 Regional Pkwy., Bldg. C, Suite 200, Orangeburg, SC 29118
(803) 534-2777, *Fax:* (803) 531-1089
mail@miller.fm.com
License: Saint Matthews, Calhoun County, SC held by Miller Communications Inc.
Group Owner: Miller Communications Inc.; (acq 6-30-2003; $900,000 with co-located AM)
Population Served: 100,000 *Arbitron Metro Market:* Columbia, SC
Theresa Miller, General Manager

Saint Stephen

WEAF
12-10-1970; 1120 khz AM; 390 w-D; N34 15 32 W80 34 47
Box 1165, Camden, SC 70116
(803) 432-8717, *Fax:* (803) 939-9469
wsmvproduction@wsmv.com
License: Saint Stephen, Kershaw County, SC held by Glory Communications Inc.
Group Owner: Glory Communications Inc.; (acq 7-13-2006; $222,500)
Population Served: 6,902 *Arbitron Metro Market:* Camden, SC
Alex Snipe, General Manager

Sans Souci

WCSZ
05-26-1966; 1070 khz AM *Hrs Open:* 24; 50 kw-D, DA2; 1.5 kw-N, DA2; N34 55 5 W82 27 21
11511 Dyrham Lane, Glen Dale, MD 20769 US
(864) 294-1071, *Fax:* (864) 246-8695
License: Sans Souci, SC held by WHYZ Radio L.P.
Nat'l Network: Westwood One; American Urban
Arbitron Metro Market: Greenville-Spartanburg, SC *Format:* Gospel, Religious *Target Audience:* 25-54; $50,000 plus houshold income, college educated, 60% male, 40% female
Glenn Cherry, CEO
Jerry Young, General Manager

Scranton

WZTF
01-01-1991; 102.9 mhz FM; 2.9 kw; 466 ft.; N34 0 39 W79 45 24
Two Bala Plaza, Suite 801, Bala-Cynwyd, PA 19004 US
(843) 667-4600,(843) 667-0970, *Fax:* (843) 673-7390
License: Scranton, Florence County, SC held by Qantum of Florence License Co. LLC.
Group Owner: Qantum Communications Corp.; (acq 7-2-2003; grpsl).
Arbitron Metro Market: Florence, SC *Format:* Urban Contemporary *Adv. Rates:* 25; 25; 25; 15
Jonathan Brewster, General Manager

Seneca

WSNW
06-01-1949; 1150 khz AM *Hrs Open:* 24*Rebroadcasts:* W277BX FM Translator
Mailing Address: P.O. Box 1557, Seneca, SC 29679 US
Second Address: 103 Ram Cat Alley, Seneca, SC 29678
(864) 882-9769, *Fax:* (864) 886-0082
www.wsnwradio.com
allgood@gacaradio.com
License: Seneca, SC held by Tugart Properties LLC.
Group Owner: Georgia-Carolina Radiocasting Companies; (acq 9-28-2001)
Nat'l Network: CBS Radio *Regional Network:* S.C. News Net.
Wire Services: AP
Format: Adult Contemp, News, 64, Talk *Special Programming:* Local Sports *Hrs. of News Programming:* news progmg 12 hrs wkly *No. News Employees:* 1 *Target Audience:* Adults 35 plus.
Art Sutton, President
Tug Carter, Operations Dir
Chad Dorsette, Programming Director
Marty Lee, Chief Engineer
Ian Lundin, Operations Manager
Adam Wright, Vice President

Simpsonville

WYRD-FM
07-10-1989; 106.3 mhz FM *Hrs Open:* 24; 25 kw; 328 ft.; N34 50 33 W82 9 59
1776 Briarcliff Road, Ne, Suite A, Atlanta, GA 30306 US
(864) 271-9200
www.newsradioword.com
twest@entercom.com
License: Simpsonville, Greenville County, SC held by Entercom Greenville License LLC.
Group Owner: Entercom Communications Corp.; (acq 10-7-2005; grpsl)
Arbitron Metro Market: Simpsonville, SC *Format:* News, News/Talk, 86 *Target Audience:* 25-54; adults
David Field, President
Sharon Day, General Manager
Bob McLain, Programming Director
Keaira Bray, Promotions Manager

Socastee

WRNN-FM
01-01-1997; 99.5 mhz FM; 21.5 kw; 354 ft.; N33 43 16 W78 53 45
1571 Trade Street, Myrtle Beach, SC 29577 US
(843) 448-1041, *Fax:* (843) 626-5988
www.wrnn.net
License: Socastee, Horry County, SC held by NM Licensing LLC.
Group Owner: NextMedia Group Inc.; (acq 11-26-2001; grpsl)
Arbitron Metro Market: Myrtle Beach, SCC *Format:* Talk
Carl Hirsch, Chairman
Steven Dinetz, CEO
Skip Weller, President
Barry Brown, General Manager
Art Greene, General Sales Mgr
Dave Priest, Programming Director
Liza Van Horne, Promotions Manager
Ginny Batchelder, News Director
Paul Matthews, Chief Engineer
Jeff Dinetz, COO

Society Hill

***WEBK**
91.1 mhz FM; 0.43 kw; 127 ft.; N34 32 13 W79 54 29 US
(803) 581-9030, *Fax:* (803) 581-9932
License: Society Hill, Darlington County, SC held by Richburg Educational Broadcasters Inc.
Arbitron Metro Market: Society Hill, SC
Jeff Sigmon, General Manager

South Congaree

WFMV
01-01-1993; 95.3 mhz FM *Hrs Open:* 24; 6 kw; 328 ft.; N33 53 58 W81 13 29
Mailing Address: P.O. Box 2355, West Columbia, SC 29171 US
Second Address: 2440 Millwood Ave., Columbia, SC 29205
(803) 939-9530, *Fax:* (803) 939-9469
www.wfmv.com
email@wfmv.com
License: South Congaree, Lexington County, SC held by Glory Communications.
Group Owner: Glory Communications Inc.
Arbitron Metro Market: Columbia, SC *Format:* Religious *Target Audience:* Primary : adult 25-54; secondary: Women 25-54
Alex Snipe, General Manager
Alexis Campbell, General Sales Mgr
Nate Stoney, Programming Director
Tony Green, Music Director
Tony Jamison, Network Operations
Kevin Felder, Local Sales Manager
Emma Butler, Traffic
Armita Thomas,Traffic

Spartanburg

WASC
01-15-1968; 1530 khz AM; 0.25 kw-C, NDD; 1 kw-D, NDD; N34 56 58 W81 57 33
Mailing Address: PO Box 5686, Spartanburg, SC 29301 US
Second Address: 840 Wofford St., Spartanburg, SC 29304
(864) 585-1530, *Fax:* (864) 573-7790
License: Spartanburg, SC held by New South Broadcasting Corp.
Arbitron Metro Market: Spartanburg, SC *Format:* Black
Sam Floyd, President
K. Joseph Sessoms, Operations Dir
K. Sessmos, General Manager
Ed Waddell, General Sales Mgr

WSPG
09-01-1952; 1400 khz AM; 1 kw-U, ND1; N34 58 26 W81 55 37
Mailing Address: P.O. Box 5416, Spartanburg, SC 29304 US
Second Address: 340 Garner Rd., Spartanburg, SC 29303
(864) 573-1400, *Fax:* (864) 573-8699
www.espnspartanburg.com
info@espn1400am.com
License: Spartanburg, SC held by Fulmer Broadcasting Inc.
Regional Network: S.C. News Net. *Wire Services:* AP
Arbitron Metro Market: Greenville-Spartanburg, SC *Format:* News, News/Talk, 84, Talk *Target Audience:* Adult male 25-54.
Matthew Fulmer, President
J. Dwayne Corn, General Manager
Jan Scruggs, Programming Director

WOLI
09-01-1940; 910 khz AM; 3.6 kw-D, DA2; 0.89 kw-N, DA2; N35 1 10 W82 0 36 *Rebroadcasts:* Rebroadcasts WYRD(AM) Greenville 100%
10706 Beaver Dam Road, Cockeysville, MD 21030 US
(864) 751-0113, *Fax:* (864) 751-0117
License: Spartanburg, SC held by Davidson Media Station WSPA Licensee LLC.
Group Owner: Davidson Media Group LLC; (acq 10-6-2005; grpsl).
Nat'l Network: CBS; ABC
Arbitron Metro Market: Greenville-Spar *TV Affiliate:* Sports
Format: Sports *Special Programming:* news progmg 50 hrs wkly
Hrs. of News Programming: 4 *No. News Employees:* 35-64.
News Reporter, Amy Hierder
News Reporter, Katherine Lambert
Traffic Manager

WORD
02-17-1930; 950 khz AM *Hrs Open:* 24
10706 Beaver Dam Road, Cockeysville, MD 21030 US
(864) 271-9200, *Fax:* (864) 242-1567
www.newsradioword.com
License: Spartanburg, SC held by Entercom Greenville License L.L.C.
Group Owner: Entercom Communications Corp.; (acq 12-13-99; grpsl).
Nat'l Network: CBS; Motor Racing Net *Regional Network:* S.C. News Net.
Arbitron Metro Market: Greenville-Spartanburg, SC *Format:* News, News/Talk, 86 *Hrs. of News Programming:* news progmg 45 hrs wkly *No. News Employees:* 4 *Target Audience:* 35-64.
David Field, CEO
Jim Kirkland, Operations Dir
Tom Durney, General Manager
Steve Fisher, CFO

WSPA-FM
08-29-1946; 98.9 mhz FM *Hrs Open:* 24; 100 kw; 1903 ft.; N35 10 11 W82 17 28
10706 Beaver Dam Road, Cockeysville, MD 21030 US
(864) 271-9200, *Fax:* (864) 370-1473
www.magic989online.com
License: Spartanburg, Spartanburg County, SC held by Entercom Greenville License LLC.
Group Owner: Entercom Communications Corp.; (acq 12-13-99; grpsl)
Arbitron Metro Market: Greenville-Spartanburg, SC *Format:* Adult Contemp *Special Programming:* Relg 3 hrs, jazz 6 hrs, 70s oldies 10 hrs wkly *Hrs. of News Programming:* News progmg one hr wkly
Jerry Stevens, General Sales Mgr
Michael McKeel, Programming Director
Stephen Hester, News Director
Jeff Cross, Disc Jockey
Ted Love, Disc Jockey
Lee Alexander, Disc Jockey
John Gosnell, Disc Jockey
Rick Woodell, DiscJockey
David Patella, National Sales Manager

St. Andrews

WMFX
01-23-1985; 102.3 mhz FM *Hrs Open:* 24; 6 kw; 328 ft.; N34 5 55 W81 4 48
Mailing Address: 200 Concord Plaza, Suite 600, San Antonio, TX 78216 US
Second Address: 1900 Pineview Rd., Columbia, SC 29209
(803) 695-8600, *Fax:* (803) 695-8605
www.fox102.com
mhanisch@innercity.sc.com
License: St. Andrews, Richland County, SC held by Urban Radio II L.L.C.
Group Owner: Inner City Broadcasting; (acq 8-7-2000; grpsl)
Arbitron Metro Market: Columbia, SC *Format:* Classic Rock, Rock/AOR *Hrs. of News Programming:* news progmg one hr wkly *No. News Employees:* 1 *Target Audience:* 18-49.
Maggie Hanisch, General Manager
Bryan Hendry, General Sales Mgr
Dave Stewart, Programming Director
Susan Morningstar, Promotions Manager

St. George

WQIZ
08-23-1962; 810 khz AM
309 Stono Dr., Charleston, SC 29412 US
(904) 859-0980
License: St. George, SC held by Mediatrix SC Inc.
Arbitron Metro Market: Charleston, SC *Format:* Christian
Paul Danese, General Manager
Bert Artlip, Station Manager

St. Matthews

WPOG
08-15-1975; 710 khz AM *Hrs Open:* 6 AM-6 PM
P.O. Box 777, St. Matthews, SC 29135 US
(803) 536-4300
License: St. Matthews, SC held by Grace Baptist Church of Orangeburg
Arbitron Metro Market: Columbia, SC *Format:* Gospel
Gene Soult, General Manager

Summerton

WLJI
01-01-1997; 98.3 mhz FM *Hrs Open:* 24; 16 kw; 328 ft.; N33 42 58 W80 20 44 *Rebroadcasts:* Simulcast of WFMV(FM) South Congaree 100%
1801 Charleston Highway, Suite A, Cayce, SC 29033 US
(803) 774-5512, *Fax:* (803) 774-5534
www.wfmv.com
info@wfmv.com
License: Summerton, Clarendon County, SC held by Glory Communications Inc.
Group Owner: Glory Communications Inc.; acq 4-1-97).
Format: Religious *Target Audience:* Adults 25-54.
Tony Jamison, Operations Dir
Alex Snipe, General Manager
Tezra Haire, General Sales Mgr

Summerville

WAZS
06-07-1963; 980 khz AM *Hrs Open:* 24*Rebroadcasts:* simulcast w/ WZJY-AM
P. O. Box 859, Summerville, SC 29483 US
(662) 844-8888, *Fax:* (662) 842-6791
www.afr.net
License: Summerville, SC held by Thomas B. Daniels.
Group Owner: Jabar Communications Inc.; (acq 9-1-2000).
Nat'l Reps: Interep
Arbitron Metro Market: Mertzon TX *Format:* Christian *Adv. Rates:* 240; 240; 240; 240.
Marvin Sanders, General Manager

WWWZ
05-10-1974; 93.3 mhz FM; 50 kw; 492 ft.; N32 54 18 W79 55 19
140 S. Ash Ave., Tempe, AZ 85281 US
(843) 277-1200, *Fax:* (843) 277-1212
www.z93jamz.com
License: Summerville, Dorchester County, SC
Group Owner: Cumulus Media Inc.; (acq 6-9-99; grpsl)
Arbitron Metro Market: Charleston, SC *Format:* Urban Contemporary
Paul O'Malley, General Manager
Star Israel, General Sales Mgr
Terry Base, Programming Director
Judy Herold, News Director
Justin Tucker, Chief Engineer
Stephanie Gaines, Women's Int Ed

Sumter

WDXY
05-23-1960; 1240 khz AM *Hrs Open:* 24; 1 kw-U, ND1; N33 54 16 W80 19 25
Mailing Address: P. O. Box 1269, Sumter, SC 29151 US
Second Address: 51 Commerce St., Sumter, SC 29150
(803) 775-2321, *Fax:* (803) 773-4856
www.newsstalk1240.am
production@miller.fm
License: Sumter, SC held by Miller Communications Inc.
Group Owner: Miller Communications Inc.; acq 1-2-2001; grpsl)
Nat'l Reps: Rgnl Reps
Arbitron Metro Market: Sumter, SC *Format:* Talk *Hrs. of News Programming:* news progmg 6 hrs wkly *No. News Employees:* 1 *Target Audience:* 35 plus. *Adv. Rates:* 12; 12; 12; 10
Harold Miller, CEO
Theresa Miller, Operations Dir
Dave Baker, Vice President, Operations

WWBD
06-21-1995; 94.7 mhz FM *Hrs Open:* 24; 8.1 kw; 571 ft.; N34 2 56 W80 12 51
Mailing Address: P.O. Box 1711, Sumter, SC 29150 US
Second Address: 51 Commerce St., Sumter, SC 29150
(803) 773-1859, *Fax:* (803) 773-4856
www.miller.fm
Tmiller55@aol.com
License: Sumter, Sumter County, SC held by Miller Communications Inc.
Group Owner: Miller Communications Inc.; (acq 9-27-2001)
Nat'l Network: American Urban
Format: Contemporary Hits/Top 40, Adult Contemp *No. News Employees:* 1 *Target Audience:* Adults 25 to 49 & secondary females 25-54 *Adv. Rates:* 40; 35; 40; 20
Harold Miller, Jr., CEO
Theresa Miller, Operations Dir
Dave Baker, Vice President, Operations

WWHM
03-16-1940; 1290 khz AM *Hrs Open:* 16
100 West College Street, Sumter, SC 29150 US
(803) 775-2321, *Fax:* (803) 773-4856
www.miller.fm
production@miller.fm
License: Sumter, SC held by Miller Communications Inc.
Group Owner: Miller Communications Inc.; (acq 11-12-2007; $60,000)
David Baker, Operations Dir

***WRJA-FM**
08-25-1975; 88.1 mhz FM *Hrs Open:* 24; 98 kw; 1001 ft.; N33 52 52 W80 16 14
1101 George Rogers Blvd, PO Box 11000, Columbia, SC 29211 US
(803) 737-3420, *Fax:* (803) 737-3552
www.etvradio.org
gasque@scetv.org
License: Sumter, Sumter County, SC held by South Carolina Educational TV Commission.
Nat'l Network: NPR; PRI
Format: News *Hrs. of News Programming:* News progrmg 120 hrs wkly
Moss Bresnahan, President
Tom Holloway, General Sales Mgr
John Gasque, Programming Director
Connie Murray, News Director

WSSC
04-27-1953; 1340 khz AM *Hrs Open:* 6 AM-midnight
2295 Harper Street, Sumter, SC 29153 US
(803) 469-0288, *Fax:* (803) 469-0297
www.sumterbaptisttemple.org
License: Sumter, SC held by Sumpter Baptist Temple Inc.
Regional Network: S.C. News Net.
Format: Christian *Target Audience:* 25-54.
Eddie Richardson, President

WWDM
01-01-1961; 101.3 mhz FM *Hrs Open:* 24; 100 kw horiz, 82 kw vert; 1322 ft.; N34 3 4 W80 40 55
200 Concord Plz., Ste 600, San Antonio, TX 78216 US
(803) 695-8600, *Fax:* (803) 695-8605
www.thebigdm.com
mhanisch@innercity.sc.com
License: Sumter, Sumter County, SC held by Urban Radio II L.L.C.
Group Owner: Inner City Broadcasting; (acq 8-7-2000; grpsl).
Nat'l Network: ABC; Westwood One *Nat'l Reps:* D & R Radio
Arbitron Metro Market: Columbia, SC *Format:* Urban Contemporary *Hrs. of News Programming:* news progmg 6 hrs wkly *No. News Employees:* 1 *Target Audience:* 25-49.
Maggie Hanisch, General Manager
Mark Fitzmayer, General Sales Mgr
Chris Connors, Programming Director
Michelle Alston, Promotions Manager

Sun City-Hilton Head

WNFO
01-01-1964; 1430 khz AM *Hrs Open:* Sunrise-sunset; 0.213 kw-D, NDD; N32 21 24 W80 55 23
9-B Wanderer Ln, Hilton Head Island, SC 29928 US
(843) 785-5769, *Fax:* (843) 785-8139
License: Sun City-Hilton Head, SC held by Walter M. Czura
Arbitron Metro Market: Hilton Head Island, SC *Format:* Spanish
Special Programming: Spanish *Target Audience:* General; incoming visitors to South Carolina & Spanish speaking people
Walter Czura, President

Surfside Beach

WSYN
04-04-1977; 103.1 mhz FM *Hrs Open:* 24; 8 kw; 528 ft.; N33 47 4 W78 52 44 *Rebroadcasts:* Rebroadcasts WVCO(FM) Loris 100%
2505 North Highway 360, Suite 620, Grand Prairie, TX 75050 US
(843) 651-7869, *Fax:* (843) 651-3197
www.cumulus.com
info@sunny1065.net
License: Surfside Beach, Horry County, SC held by Cumulus Licensing Corp.
Group Owner: Cumulus Media Inc.; (acq 4-30-2001; swap of WSYN(FM) for WQSL(FM) & WXQR(FM) Jacksonville, NC)
Nat'l Network: Westwood One
Arbitron Metro Market: Myrtle Beach, SC *Format:* Country *Hrs. of News Programming:* news progmg 4 hrs wkly *No. News Employees:* 1 *Target Audience:* 25-54; adults & families of loc towns & tourists
John Sheftic, General Manager
David Lewis, Market Manager

Union

WBCU
08-27-1949; 1460 khz AM *Hrs Open:* 24; 1 kw-D, DAN; 1 kw-N, DAN; N34 43 10 W81 39 44
P.O.Box 5, Union, SC 29379 US
(406) 728-5000, *Fax:* (406) 721-3020
License: Union, SC held by Union-Carolina Broadcasting Co. Inc.
Nat'l Network: ABC *Regional Network:* S.C. News Net.
Arbitron Metro Market: San Antonio TX *Adv. Rates:* 134; 120; 126; 91
Chad Parrish, General Manager

Walhalla

WGOG
09-01-1991; 105.5 mhz FM *Hrs Open:* 24; 6 kw; 302 ft.; N34 51 33 W83 3 31
Mailing Address: P.O. Box 10, Walhalla, SC 29691 US
Second Address: 2058 Westminster Hwy., Walhalla, SC 29691
(864) 638-3616, *Fax:* (864) 638-6810
www.wgog.com
wgog@wgog.com
License: Walhalla, Oconee County, SC held by Appalachian Broadcasting Co. Inc.
Group Owner: Georgia-Carolina Radiocasting Companies; (acq 10-16-2001; with co-located AM).
Nat'l Network: ABC
Format: Country, News *Hrs. of News Programming:* news progmg 15 hrs wkly *No. News Employees:* 1 *Target Audience:* 25-54.
Douglas M. Sutton Jr., President
M. Terry Carter, Operations Dir
Gary Butts, General Manager
Dick Mangrum, News Director
Marty Lee, Chief Engineer
Wayne Morton, Operations Manager

Walterboro

WALI
12-13-1991; 93.7 mhz FM *Hrs Open:* 24; 6 kw; 328 ft.; N32 50 58 W80 33 31
215 N Stonebedge Dr, Columbia, SC 29210 US
(843) 549-1543, *Fax:* (843) 549-2711
WALLY937@LOWCONTRY.COM
License: Walterboro, Colleton County, SC held by Hess Communications L.L.C.
Nat'l Network: ABC Information & Entertainment *Regional Network:* S.C. News Net. *Regional Reps:* Rgnl Reps.
Arbitron Metro Market: Columbia, SC *Format:* Country, Sports
Special Programming: 3 HOURS WEEKLY *Hrs. of News Programming:* News progmg 3 hrs wkly *Target Audience:* General.
Karl Hess, President

Wedgefield

WIBZ
03-01-1985; 95.5 mhz FM *Hrs Open:* 24; 4.4 kw; 387 ft.; N33 56 56 W80 23 34
Mailing Address: P O Box 1269, Sumter, SC 29151 US
Second Address: 51 Commerce St., Sumter, SC 29150
(803) 773-1859, *Fax:* (803) 773-4856
production@miller.fm
License: Wedgefield, Sumter County, SC held by Miller Communicatins Inc.
Group Owner: Miller Communications Inc.; acq 11-14-00; grpsl).
Nat'l Network: ABC
Format: Gospel *No. News Employees:* 1 *Target Audience:* 18-49. *Adv. Rates:* 35; 30; 35; 20
Harold Miller, CEO
Theresa Miller, Operations Dir
Dave Baker, Vice President, Operations

Whitmire

***WNBK**
01-01-2009; 90.9 mhz FM *Hrs Open:* 24; 1.8 kw horiz, 1.61 kw vert; 335 ft.; N34 29 52 W81 32 55 *Rebroadcasts:* WRBK 90.3 FM
US

(803) 581-9030, *Fax:* (803) 581-9932
License: Whitmire, Newberry County, SC held by Richburg Educational Broadcasters Inc.
Arbitron Metro Market: Whitmire, SC *Format:* Oldies *Target Audience:* 35-75+
Jeff Sigmon, General Manager

Williamston

WHZT
06-06-1953; 98.1 mhz FM *Hrs Open:* 24; 100 kw; 1,004 ft; N34 41 14 W82 59 12
220 N. Main St., Suite 402, Greenville, SC 29601
(864) 232-9810, *Fax:* (864) 370-3403
www.hot981.com
License: Williamston, Oconee County, SC held by Cox Radio Inc.
Group Owner: Cox Radio Inc.; (acq 2-1-2001; grpsl)
Nat'l Network: Westwood One; CBS
Population Served: 800,000 *Arbitron Metro Market:* Greenville-Spartanburg, SC *Hrs. of News Programming:* news progmg 18 hrs wkly *No. News Employees:* 2 *Target Audience:* 25-54; affluent adults
Steve Sinicropi, Operations Dir
Rob Grossman, General Sales Mgr
Murph Dawg, Programming Director
Laurie Madden, Promotions Manager
Lemont Bryant, Chief Engineer
Cathy Tabor, National Sales Manager

Williston

WAAW
08-12-1994; 94.7 mhz FM *Hrs Open:* 24; 2.55 kw; 509 ft.; N33 30 31 W81 37 27
Mailing Address: 1217 W. Medical Park Road, Augusta, GA 30909 US
Second Address: 2166 Park Ave. E, Aiken, SC 29801
(808) 521-4711, *Fax:* (808) 538-3269
License: Williston, Barnwell County, SC held by Wisdom LLC.
Group Owner: Wisdom LLC; (acq 2-2-2009; grpsl)
Arbitron Metro Market: Phoenix AZ
Wagdy Guirguis, President

Woodruff

WQUL
03-14-1972; 1510 khz AM *Hrs Open:* 6 AM-10 PM; 0.25 kw-C, NDD; 1 kw-D, NDD; 433 ft; N34 45 22 W82 3 18
360 Sloan Road, Post Office Box 340, Woodruff, SC 29388 US
(618) 997-8123,(618) 932-8121, *Fax:* (618) 993-2319
License: Woodruff, SC held by Withers Broadcasting of Southern Illinois LLC.
Group Owner: Withers Broadcasting Co.; (acq 3-17-2008; grpsl)
Arbitron Metro Market: Marion-Carbondale (Southern Illinois)
Format: Classic Rock *Hrs. of News Programming:* News progmg 2 hrs wkly *Target Audience:* 25-54; adult
Matt Mellen, Programming Director

WQUL(AM)
07-07-1967; 1510 khz AM; 1 kw-D, 250 w-CH; N34 45 22 W82 03 18
Box 547, Woodruff, SC 29388
(864) 476-7184, *Fax:* (864) 476-0474
License: Woodruff, Spartanburg County, SC held by B&B Media Inc.
Population Served: 18,546 *Arbitron Metro Market:* Elko, NV
Format: Religious
T.C. Lewis, General Manager

York

WBZK
04-19-1956; 980 khz AM *Hrs Open:* 24; 3 kw-D, DA2; 0.167 kw-N, DA2; N34 54 11 W81 5 33 US
(336) 759-0363, *Fax:* (336) 759-0366
www.wtru.com
info@truthnetwork.com
License: York, SC held by 980 AM Inc.
Nat'l Network: ABC
Arbitron Metro Market: Winston-Salem, NC *Format:* Christian, Spanish *Special Programming:* Chinese 10 hrs, Greek 10 hrs wkly *Hrs. of News Programming:* News progmg 6 hrs wkly *Target Audience:* 22-54.
Michael Glinter, President
Robert Freeze, Operations Dir
Russ Jones, General Manager
Humberto Martinez, Programming Director
Winston Hawkins, Chief Engineer

South Dakota

Aberdeen

KBFO
02-20-1999; 106.7 mhz FM *Hrs Open:* 24; 100 kw; 446 ft.; N45 27 57 W98 20 8
Mailing Address: 427 Bedford Road, Suite 330, Pleasantville, NY 10570 US
Second Address: 13541 386th Ave., Aberdeen, SD 57401
(605) 229-3632, *Fax:* (605) 229-4849
www.hubcityradio.com
info@hubcityradio.com
License: Aberdeen, Brown County, SD held by Armada Media - Aberdeen Inc.
Group Owner: Armada Media Corp.; (acq 10-31-2006; grpsl)
Regional Reps: Jones Satellite Audio.
Arbitron Metro Market: Aberdeen, SD *Format:* Adult Contemp *Target Audience:* 18-35. *Adv. Rates:* 10; 10; 9; 7
Brian Lundquist, General Manager
Rob Feller, General Sales Mgr
Doc Sebastian, Programming Director
Bri Matthews, News Director

KGIM
09-01-1933; 1420 khz AM
232 Third St Ne, Valley City, ND 58072 US
(605) 229-3632, *Fax:* (605) 229-4849
www.hubcityradio.com
brianlundquist@hubcityradio.com
License: Aberdeen, SD held by Armada Media - Aberdeen Inc.
Group Owner: Armada Media Corp.; (acq 10-31-2006; grpsl)
TV Affiliate: ESPN *Format:* Sports *Target Audience:* 25 plus; general
Jim Coursolle, President
Brian Lundquist, General Manager

***KKAA**
09-12-1974; 1560 khz AM *Hrs Open:* 24
Mailing Address: 427 Bedford Road, Pleasantville, NY 10570 US
Second Address: 290 Hegenberger Rd., Oakland, CA 94621
(916) 641-8191, *Fax:* (916) 641-8238
www.familyradio.com
info@familyradio.com
License: Aberdeen, SD held by Family Stations Inc.
Group Owner: Family Stations Inc.; (acq 11-30-2004; $75,000 with KQKD(AM) Redfield).
Format: Christian, Religious
Harold Camping, President

***KLRJ**
09-01-1979; 94.9 mhz FM *Hrs Open:* 5 AM-1 AM; 100 kw; 446 ft.; N45 27 57 W98 20 8 *Rebroadcasts:* Rebroadcasts KLVR(FM) Santa Rosa, CA
427 Bedford Road, Suite 330, Pleasantville, NY 10570 US
(800) 525-5683, *Fax:* (916) 251-1650
www.klove.com
klove@klove.com
License: Aberdeen, Brown County, SD held by Educational Media Foundation.
Group Owner: EMF Broadcasting; (acq 11-30-2004; $200,000).
Nat'l Network: K-Love
Format: Christian
Darrell Chambliss, Chairman
Mike Novak, CEO/COO
Mike Novak, President
Alan Mason, Operations Dir
David Pierce, Programming Director
Richard Hunt, News Director
Sam Wallington, Engineering Dir
Marya Morgan, News Reporter

KSDN
04-16-1947; 930 khz AM; 5 kw-D, DA2; 1 kw-N, DA2; N45 25 29 W98 31 3
Mailing Address: 427 Bedford Road, Pleasantville, NY 10570 US
Second Address: 13541 386th Ave., Aberdeen, SD 57401
(605) 225-1560, *Fax:* (605) 229-4849
www.aberdeenradioranch.com
info@aberdeenradioranch.com
License: Aberdeen, SD held by Armada Media - Aberdeen Inc.
Group Owner: Armada Media Corp.; (acq 10-31-2006; grpsl)
Nat'l Network: ABC
Arbitron Metro Market: Aberdeen, SD *Format:* Talk *Special Programming:* Farm 15 hrs wkly *Hrs. of News Programming:* news progmg 15 hrs wkly *No. News Employees:* 1 *Target Audience:* 25-54. *Adv. Rates:* 10; 10; 10; 9
Ron Feller, General Sales Mgr
Doug Pitts, Programming Director

KSDN-FM
11-18-1979; 94.1 mhz FM; 100 kw; 440 ft.; N45 25 26 W98 31 1
427 Bedford Road, Pleasantville, NY 10570 US
(605) 225-1560, *Fax:* (605) 229-4849
www.aberdeenradioranch.com
License: Aberdeen, Brown County, SD
Group Owner: Armada Media Corp.
Arbitron Metro Market: Aberdeen, SD *Format:* Classic Rock
Peggy Gordon-Miller, President
Jay Buchholz, General Manager

***KEEA**
90.1 mhz FM; 1 kw; 98 ft.; N45 28 22 W98 30 16 US
(662) 844-5036, *Fax:* (662) 842-6791
www.afr.net
contact@afa.net
License: Aberdeen, Brown County, SD held by American Family Association.
Group Owner: American Family Radio; (acq 4-7-2008)
Nat'l Network: American Family Radio
Arbitron Metro Market: Aberdeen, SD *Format:* Christian
Donald E. Wildmon, Founder
Buster Wilson, General Manager
Jennifer Hagman, Programming Director

Belle Fourche

KBFS
07-22-1959; 1450 khz AM *Hrs Open:* 24; 1 kw-U, ND1; N44 40 2 W103 51 22 *Rebroadcasts:* Rebroadcasts KYDT(FM) Sundance, WY 99%
Mailing Address: Box 787, 707 Harding Street, Belle Fourche, SD 57717 US
Second Address: 707 Harding St.
(605) 892-2571, *Fax:* (605) 892-2573
www.kbfs.com
karl@kbfs.com
License: Belle Fourche, SD held by Ultimate Caps Inc.
Nat'l Network: Jones Radio Networks; ESPN Radio; Motor Racing Net; Radio America; Westwood One *Wire Services:* AP
Arbitron Metro Market: Belle Fourche, SD *Format:* Country, News, 84, Talk *Special Programming:* Farm 20 hrs, relg 2 hrs wkly *Hrs. of News Programming:* News progmg 20 hrs wkly
Target Audience: 25-54; farmers,ranchers, sports fans
Karl Grimmelmann, President
Karl Grimmelmann, General Manager

KZZI
09-22-1995; 95.9 mhz FM *Hrs Open:* 24; 100 kw; 1788 ft.; N44 19 35 W103 50 6
842 Short Track Road, Sturgis, SD 57785 US
(605) 642-85747, *Fax:* (605) 642-7849
www.myeaglecountry.com/
ted@dberadio.com
License: Belle Fourche, Butte County, SD held by Western South Dakota Broadcasting L.L.C.
Nat'l Reps: Katz Radio
Arbitron Metro Market: Rapid City, SD *Format:* Country *Target Audience:* 18-54. *Adv. Rates:* 21; 19; 20; 19
Ted Peiffer, General Manager
Lil Anderson, General Sales Mgr

KFMH
101.9 mhz FM; 100 kw horiz, 0 kw vert; 1490 ft.; N44 19 40 W103 50 6
20001 Pennsylvania Ave., Washington, DC 20006 US
(605) 721-9005, *Fax:* (605) 721-9007
www.oldiesradio1019.com
License: Belle Fourche, Butte County, SD held by Bad Lands Broadcasting Co. Inc.
Group Owner: Northeast Broadcasting Company Inc.; (acq 9-6-2005; $915,000)
Arbitron Metro Market: Rapid City, SD *Format:* Oldies
Steven Silberberg, President
Mark Norby, Account Exectutive

Box Elder

KXMZ
01-01-2008; 102.7 mhz FM; 50 kw; 449 ft.; N44 5 33 W103 14 53 US
(203) 227-1978, *Fax:* (203) 227-2373
www.hits1027.com
hits1027@hits1027.com
License: Box Elder, Pennington County, SD held by Connoisseur Media LLC.
Group Owner: Connoisseur Media LLC
Arbitron Metro Market: Box Elder, SD *Format:* Contemporary Hits/Top 40

RADIO - U.S.

Brandon

KDEZ
01-01-2007; 100.1 mhz FM; 2.15 kw; 558 ft.; N43 31 7 W96 32 5 US
(605) 361-0300, *Fax:* (605) 361-5410
www.easy1001.com
scott.maguire@results-radio.com
License: Brandon, Minnehaha County, SD held by Cumulus Licensing LLC.
Group Owner: Cumulus Media Inc.
Arbitron Metro Market: Brandon, SD *Format:* Easy Listening
Lew Dickey, President
Don Jacobs, General Manager
Barry Roberts, Programming Director
Scott Maguire, Brand Manager
Rick Fink, Director of Sales

Brookings

KBRK
07-28-1955; 1430 khz AM; 1 kw-D, ND1; 0.1 kw-N, ND1; N44 18 12 W96 46 1
2227 22nd Ave., South, Brookings, SD 57006 US
(605) 692-1430, *Fax:* (605) 692-6434
www.brookingsradio.com
brookingsradio@brookings.net
License: Brookings, SD held by Three Eagles Communications Co.
Group Owner: Three Eagles Communications
Format: Religious *Special Programming:* Farm 9 hrs wkly
Cami Powers, General Manager

KBRK-FM
08-10-1968; 93.7 mhz FM *Hrs Open:* 24; 100 kw; 571 ft.; N44 20 22 W97 9 16
2227 22nd Ave., South, Brookings, SD 57006 US
(605) 692-1430, *Fax:* (605) 692-4441
www.b937.com
License: Brookings, Brookings County, SD held by Three Eagles of Huron Inc.
Nat'l Network: Westwood One
Format: Adult Contemp *Target Audience:* 20-45.
Cami Powers, General Manager

*KESD
07-01-1967; 88.3 mhz FM; 50 kw; 623 ft.; N44 20 10 W97 13 41
Box 5000, Vermillion, SD 57069 US
(605) 688-4191, *Fax:* (605) 677-5010
www.sdpb.org
sdpr@sdpb.org
License: Brookings, Brookings County, SD held by South Dakota Board of Directors for Educational Telecommunications.
Nat'l Network: NPR; PRI
Arbitron Metro Market: Vermillion, SD *TV Affiliate:* *KESD-TV affil. *Format:* News *Target Audience:* 35-65; upscale, higher educated & arts-oriented
Julie Andersen, President
Terry Spencer, General Sales Mgr
Joe Tlustos, Programming Director

*KSDJ
01-01-1993; 90.7 mhz FM *Hrs Open:* 24; 1 kw; 125 ft.; N44 19 1 W96 47 2
Administration 318, Brookings, SD 57007 US
(605) 688-5559
www.907ksdj.com
newrock907ksdj@hotmail.com
License: Brookings, Brookings County, SD held by South Dakota State University.
Arbitron Metro Market: Brookings, SD *Format:* Alternative *Special Programming:* Black 8 hrs, jazz 2 hrs wkly *Hrs. of News Programming:* news progmg 5 hrs wkly *No. News Employees:* 1 *Target Audience:* 17-22;college students
Peggy Gordon-Miller, President
Jay Buchholz, General Manager

Canton

KYBB
01-01-1996; 102.7 mhz FM; 50 kw; 486 ft.; N43 28 48 W96 41 5
122 S.W. Fourth Street, Rochester, MN 55901 US
(605) 339-0300, *Fax:* (605) 339-2735
www.81027.com
License: Canton, Lincoln County, SD held by Cumulus Licensing LLC.
Group Owner: Cumulus Media Inc.; (acq 3-29-2004; grpsl)
Nat'l Reps: Christal
Arbitron Metro Market: Sioux Falls *Format:* Classic Rock *Target Audience:* 25-49; men
Scott Maguire, Operations Dir
Don Jacobs, General Manager
Rick Fink, Director Of Sales
Dan Rahman, Programming Director

Clear Lake

KDBX
01-01-1999; 107.1 mhz FM; 9.8 kw; 531 ft.; N44 36 44 W96 40 41
206 S. 9th, Milbank, SD 57252 US
(605) 692-9125, *Fax:* (605) 692-6434
www.brookingsradio.com
brookingsradio@brookings.net
License: Clear Lake, Deuel County, SD held by Three Eagles of Joliet Inc.
Group Owner: Three Eagles Communications; (acq 5-17-2005; $250,000)
Format: Classic Rock
Cami Powers, General Manager

Custer

KAWK
11-01-1996; 105.1 mhz FM; 7 kw; 1312 ft.; N43 44 41 W103 28 52
145 Mount Rushmore Road, P.O. Box 804, Custer, SD 57730 US
(605) 745-3637, *Fax:* (605) 745-3517
info@kawk.com
License: Custer, Custer County, SD held by Mt. Rushmore Broadcasting Inc.
Group Owner: Mt. Rushmore Broadcasting Inc.
Format: Oldies
Dwyan Calvert, Chairman
Al Ross, Station Manager

KFCR
05-01-1988; 1490 khz AM; 0.83 kw-U, ND1; N43 43 3 W103 35 0
Mailing Address: 145 Mt Rushmore Rd, P.O. Box 804, Custer, SD 57730 US
Second Address: 145 Mount Rushmore Rd., Custer, SD 57730
(605) 745-3637, *Fax:* (605) 745-3517
License: Custer, SD held by Mount Rushmore Broadcasting Inc.
Group Owner: Mt. Rushmore Broadcasting Inc.; (acq 5-6-92;
Arbitron Metro Market: Hot Springs, SD *Format:* Adult Contemp
Gary Baker, General Manager

Deadwood

KDSJ
07-02-1947; 980 khz AM *Hrs Open:* 6:00 a.m.-10:00 p.m. Daily; 5 kw-D, DAN; 1 kw-N, DAN; N44 22 57 W103 39 44
745 Main P.O. Box 567, Deadwood, SD 57350 US
(605) 578-1826, *Fax:* (605) 578-1827
www.kdsj980.com
oldies@kdsj980.com
License: Deadwood, SD held by Goldrush Broadcasting
Nat'l Network: ABC *Regional Network:* S.D. News Net.
Arbitron Metro Market: Deadwood, SD *Format:* News, Oldies, 84 *Target Audience:* 25-50
Al Decker, President
Cody Oliver, Programming Director

KSQY
09-04-1982; 95.1 mhz FM *Hrs Open:* 24; 100 kw; 1709 ft.; N44 19 49 W103 50 10
Mailing Address: 666 Main Street, Deadwood, SD 57732 US
Second Address: 306 E. St. Joe, Rapid City, SD 57709
(605) 343-0888, *Fax:* (605) 342-3075
www.951ksky.com
License: Deadwood, Lawrence County, SD held by Haugo Broadcasting Inc.
Group Owner: Haugo Broadcasting Inc.
Nat'l Reps: Midwest Radio *Regional Reps:* Midwest Radio.
Arbitron Metro Market: Rapid City, SD *Format:* Triple A *Hrs. of News Programming:* News progmg 2 hrs wkly *Target Audience:* 18-49; young, active adults within a 5 state region
Houston Haugo, CEO
Chris Haugo, Executive Vice President

Dell Rapids

KSQB-FM
10-02-1998; 95.7 mhz FM *Hrs Open:* 24; 25 kw; 328 ft.; N43 45 48 W96 48 27
2301 West 50th Street, Sioux Falls, SD 57105 US
(605) 331-5350, *Fax:* (605) 336-0415
www.q957.com
License: Dell Rapids, Minnehaha County, SD held by Backyard Broadcasting South Dakota Licensee LLC.
Group Owner: Backyard Broadcasting LLC; (acq 8-1-2006; grpsl).
Nat'l Reps: Rgnl Reps *Wire Services:* AP
Arbitron Metro Market: Sioux Falls, SD *Format:* Contemporary Hits/Top 40, Adult Contemp *Target Audience:* 20-40; young, active adults with spending ability *Adv. Rates:* 20; 18; 20; 18
Mark Nelson, Operations Dir

Ethan

KUQL
01-01-1999; 98.3 mhz FM; 100 kw; 896 ft.; N43 45 33 W98 24 44
Mailing Address: 501 South Ohlman Street, Mitchell, SD 57301 US
Second Address: 501 S. Ohlman, Mitchell, SD 57301
(605) 996-9667, *Fax:* (605) 996-0013
www.kool98.com
timsmith@kmit.com; mikekelly@kool98.com; cj@kool98.com
License: Ethan, Jerauld County, SD held by Saga Communications of South Dakota LLC.
Group Owner: Saga Communications Inc.; (acq 5-1-2001; $4.05 million with KMIT(FM) Mitchell)
Format: Oldies *Special Programming:* Theme weekends
Tim Smith, General Manager
Nikki Frederickson, General Sales Mgr
Chris Johnson, Programming Director
John Cyr, Chief Engineer
Mike Kelly, Production Director

Faith

*KPSD-FM
06-01-1989; 97.1 mhz FM; 100 kw; 1526 ft.; N45 3 14 W102 15 47 *Rebroadcasts:* Rebroadcasts KUSD(FM) Vermillion.
Mailing Address: Cherry & Dakota Streets, Box 5000, Vermillion, SD 57069 US
Second Address: 555 N. Dakota St., Faith, SD 57069
(605) 677-5861, *Fax:* (605) 677-5010
www.sdpb.org
fritz.miller@state.sd.us; admin@sdpb.org
License: Faith, Meade County, SD held by South Dakota Board of Directors for Educational Telecommunications.
Nat'l Network: NPR
Format: Jazz, News
Julie Andersen, President
Terry Spencer, General Sales Mgr
Owen DeJong, Programming Director
Carol Robertson, Promotions Manager
Joe Tlustos, Radio Director

Flandreau

KXQL
10-01-2000; 107.9 mhz FM *Hrs Open:* 24; 21 kw; 761 ft.; N43 57 56 W96 49 11
2301 West 50th Street, Sioux Falls, SD 57105 US
(605) 331-5350, *Fax:* (605) 336-0415
www.kool1079fm.com
License: Flandreau, Moody County, SD held by Backyard Broadcasting South Dakota Licensee LLC.
Group Owner: Backyard Broadcasting LLC; (acq 8-1-2006; grpsl).
Nat'l Network: Jones Radio Networks *Nat'l Reps:* Rgnl Reps
Arbitron Metro Market: Sioux Falls, SD *Format:* Oldies *Target Audience:* Adults: 35-65. *Adv. Rates:* 20; 18; 20; 18
Mark Nelson, Programming Director

Fort Pierre

KJBI
12-01-2007; 100.1 mhz FM *Hrs Open:* 24; 51 kw; 530 ft.; N44 18 30 W100 20 49
Mailing Address: US
Second Address: 214 W. Pleasant Dr., Pierre, SD 57501
(605) 224-8686, *Fax:* (605) 224-8984
www.drgnews.com
License: Fort Pierre, Stanley County, SD held by James River Broadcasting Inc.
Group Owner: Robert Ingstad Broadcast Properties; (acq 7-31-2007; $450,000 for CP)
Arbitron Metro Market: Fort Pierre, SD *Format:* Contemporary Hits/Top 40, Adult Contemp
Mark Swendsen, General Manager

Frankfort

*KTUT
89.5 mhz FM; kw
US
(940) 668-7971
License: Frankfort, Spink County, SD held by 1 A Chord Inc.
Arbitron Metro Market: Frankfort, SD
Dorothy Fay Jones, General Manager

Freeman

***KVCF**
01-01-2002; 90.5 mhz FM; 9 kw; 807 ft.; N43 29 22 W97 26 33
3434 W. Kilbourn Ave., Milwaukee, WI 53208 US
(414) 935-3000, *Fax:* (414) 935-3015
www.vcyamerica.org
vcy@vcyamerica.org
License: Freeman, Hutchinson County, SD held by VCY America Inc.
Group Owner: VCY America Inc.
Arbitron Metro Market: Freeman, SD *Format:* Christian, Religious
Vic Eliason, General Manager
Jim Schneider, Programming Director
Andy Eliason, Chief Engineer

Gregory

***KVCX**
05-08-1982; 101.5 mhz FM; 100 kw; 640 ft.; N43 7 41 W99 26 1
3434 West Kilbourn Ave, Milwaukee, WI 53208 US
(414) 935-3000, *Fax:* (414) 935-3015
www.vcyamerica.org
vcy@vcyamerica.org
License: Gregory, Gregory County, SD held by VCY/America Inc.
Group Owner: VCY America Inc.; acq 4-87)
Nat'l Network: USA; Moody
Arbitron Metro Market: Milwaukee, WI *TV Affiliate:* KVCX-TV
Dr. Randall Melchert, President
Vic Eliason, Operations Dir
Jim Schneider, Programming Director
Gordon Morris, News Director
Andrew Eliason, Chief Engineer
Tom Schlueter, Music Director

Hermosa

***KWRC**
01-01-2008; 90.9 mhz FM; 0.4 kw; 1269 ft.; N43 44 40 W103 28 52 *Rebroadcasts:* Rebroadcasts KAWZ(FM) Twin Falls, ID 100%
3000 W Macarthur Blvd., Santa Ana, CA 92704 US
(800) 357-4226, *Fax:* (208) 736-1958
www.csnradio.com
csn@csnradio.com
License: Hermosa, Custer County, SD held by Calvary Chapel of Twin Falls Inc.
Group Owner: CSN International
Arbitron Metro Market: Hermosa, SD *Format:* Christian
Mike Kestler, President
Daniel Davidson, Operations Dir
Don Mills, Network Programming Director / Music Director
Kelly Carlson, Engineering Dir
Jerry Johnson, Engineering Dir
Ray Gorney, Assistant Director of Engineering
DustinPamplona, Engineer
Nolan Mather, Graphics / Website Maintenance
Mike Stocklin, National Underwriting
Austin Morris, Accounting
Lois Mills, FCC Applications / Translator Site Manager

Hot Springs

KZMX
07-04-1958; 580 khz AM; 2.3 kw-D, ND1; 0.31 kw-N, ND1; N43 27 24 W103 28 34
Mailing Address: 437 Montgomery Street, Custer, SD 57730 US
Second Address: North Wind Cave Rd., Hot Springs, SD 57747
(605) 745-3637, *Fax:* (605) 745-3517
info@kzmx.com
themorningshow@email.com
License: Hot Springs, SD held by Mount Rushmore Broadcasting Inc.
Group Owner: Mt. Rushmore Broadcasting Inc.; (acq 5-20-93; $45,000 with co-located FM;
Arbitron Metro Market: Hot Springs, SD *Format:* Country *Special Programming:* Farm 6 hrs wkly
Gary Baker, General Manager

KZMX-FM
02-10-1981; 96.7 mhz FM; 1.4 kw horiz; 443 ft.; N43 26 34 W103 27 27
Mailing Address: Box 611, Hot Springs, SD 57747 US
Second Address: North Wind Cave Rd., Hot Springs, SD 57747
(605) 745-3637, *Fax:* (605) 745-3517
info@kzmx.com
License: Hot Springs, Fall River County, SD
Group Owner: Mt. Rushmore Broadcasting Inc.
Arbitron Metro Market: Hot Springs, SD *Format:* Country
Lisa Cheek, General Manager
Sam Scholl, Programming Director

Huron

KIJV
07-01-1947; 1340 khz AM *Hrs Open:* 24
1726 Dakota Avenue South, Huron, SD 57350 US
(605) 352-8621, *Fax:* (605) 352-8622
License: Huron, SD held by Dakota Communications Ltd.
Group Owner: Dakota Communications Ltd.; (acq 3-11-2004; $400,000 with co-located FM)
Arbitron Metro Market: Huron, SD *Format:* Oldies, Sports, 86 *No. News Employees:* 1 *Target Audience:* 35 plus. *Adv. Rates:* 15; 12; 15; 9.
Duane Butt, President
John Speeney, General Manager
Matt Price, Programming Director
Curt Coleman, News Director
Nick Rottum, Disc Jockey
Sheri Barth, Sports Commentator

KOKK
01-13-1976; 1210 khz AM
P.O. Box 364, Pierre, SD 57501 US
(605) 352-8621, *Fax:* (605) 352-0911
www.kokk.com
traffic@kokk.com
License: Huron, SD held by Dakota Communications Ltd.
Group Owner: Dakota Communications Ltd.
Format: Country
Linda Marcus, General Manager
Dick Schultz, Chief Engineer

KZKK
01-01-1993; 105.1 mhz FM *Hrs Open:* 5:30 AM-midnight; 6 kw; 154 ft.; N44 21 44 W98 9 9
Mailing Address: P.O. Box 364, Pierre, SD 57501 US
Second Address: 1835 Dakota Ave., Huron, SD 57350
(605) 352-1933, *Fax:* (605) 352-0911
www.kokk.com
lmarcus@kokk.com
License: Huron, Beadle County, SD
Group Owner: Dakota Communications Ltd.
Arbitron Metro Market: Huron, SD *Format:* Adult Contemp *No. News Employees:* 1
Rhonda Hart, Operations Dir
Linda Marcus, General Manager
JoAnn Oxsen, General Sales Mgr
Steve Levin, Programming Director
Zach Nelson, News Director

***KVCH**
88.7 mhz FM; 60 kw; 528 ft.; N44 11 39 W98 19 5
US
(414) 935-3000, *Fax:* (414) 935-3015
www.vcyamerica.org
vcy@vcyamerica.org
License: Huron, Beadle County, SD held by VCY America Inc.
Group Owner: VCY America Inc.
Arbitron Metro Market: Huron, SD
Jeff Fitzgerald, Operations Dir
Andrew Kalb, Programming Director

Ipswich

KABD
12-21-2007; 107.7 mhz FM; 51 kw; Ant 354 ft; N45 27 13 W98 48 10
426 N. Hwy. 281, Suite 4, Aberdeen, SD
(605) 725-5551, *Fax:* (605) 725-5553
www.1077kabd.com
License: Ipswich, Edmunds County, SD held by Dakota Broadcasting LLC
Population Served: 90,000*Hrs. of News Programming:* 6a-5p *No. News Employees:* 9
Neil Lipetzky, CEO/COO
Joel Swanson, General Manager
Devin Reints, General Sales Mgr
Mike Johnson, Programming Director
Marnah Lee, News Director
Steve Heaton, Chief Engineer

***KSJP(FM)**
88.9 mhz FM; 20 kw vert; Ant 34 ft; N45 26 56.2 W99 15 08.8
6300 S Old Village Place, Suite 203, Sioux Falls, SD 28422
(605) 275-4659
License: Ipswich, Edmunds County, SD held by Agnes DEI Communications Inc
Population Served: 951 *Arbitron Metro Market:* Ipswich, SD
Joshua Hawkins, President

Keystone

KRKI
01-01-2003; 99.5 mhz FM; 100 kw horiz, 0 kw vert; N43 51 24 W103 45 50
Mailing Address: 7901 Stoneridge Drive, Cheyenne, WY 82009 US
Second Address: 1711 W. Main St., Rapid City, WY 57702
(877) 996-6369, *Fax:* (605) 721-9007
www.995thefan.com
jameskelley@clearchannel.com
License: Keystone, Weston County, SD held by Michael Radio Group.
Group Owner: Michael Radio Group
Nat'l Network: ESPN Radio
Arbitron Metro Market: Newcastle, WY *Format:* Sports
Scott McCormick, Operations Dir
Lonnie Glasford, General Manager
James Kelly, Online Program Director / Webmaster
Craig Hawkesworth, VP of Interactive Sales
Dan Metter, SVP/Director of Talk Radio Sales

Lemmon

KBJM
04-01-1966; 1400 khz AM *Hrs Open:* 24; 1 kw-U, ND1; N45 55 5 W102 11 55
Mailing Address: 500 1st Avenue, East, Lemmon, SD 57638 US
Second Address: 500 First Ave. E., Lemmon, SD 57638
(605) 374-5747, *Fax:* (605) 374-5332
www.kbjm.com
kbjm@sdplains.com
License: Lemmon, SD held by Media Associates Inc.
Nat'l Reps: Keystone (unwired net)
Arbitron Metro Market: Lemmon, SD *Format:* Oldies, Country *Hrs. of News Programming:* News progmg 30 hrs wkly *Target Audience:* General.
Mike Schweitzer, President
James Schwab, Programming Director

Lennox

KSOO-FM
01-01-2008; 99.1 mhz FM; 25 kw; 328 ft.; N43 22 36 W96 48 19 US
(605) 361-0300, *Fax:* (605) 361-5410
www.ksoo.com
dave@ksoo.com
License: Lennox, Lincoln County, SD held by Cumulus Licensing LLC.
Group Owner: Cumulus Media Inc.
Arbitron Metro Market: Sioux Falls, SD *Format:* News, News/Talk, 84, Talk
Don Jacobs, General Manager
Dave Roberts, Brand Manager
Rick Fink, Director of Sales

Little Eagle

***KLND**
06-25-1997; 89.5 mhz FM *Hrs Open:* 6 AM-midnight; 100 kw; 679 ft.; N45 44 54 W100 48 30
Hc 61 Box 1, McLaughlin, SD 57642 US
(605) 823-4661, *Fax:* (605) 823-4660
www.klnd.org
info@klndfm.com
License: Little Eagle, Corson County, SD held by Seventh Generation Media Services Inc.
Nat'l Network: PRI
Arbitron Metro Market: Rapid City, SD *Format:* Variety/Diverse *Special Programming:* Gospel 3 hrs, children 4 hrs, Sp one hr, elders 2 *Hrs. of News Programming:* news progmg 5 hrs wkly *No. News Employees:* 1*Target Audience:* General; tribal people on the Standing Rock & Cheyenne River Nations
Jana Shields Gipp, Chairman
Beau Fontenalla, General Manager

Lowry

KMLO
01-01-1996; 100.7 mhz FM; 100 kw; 587 ft.; N45 16 26 W99 58 21 *Rebroadcasts:* Rebroadcasts KPLO-FM Reliance 100%
232 Third Street Ne, Valley City, ND 58072 US
(605) 224-8686, *Fax:* (605) 224-8984
drgprod1@amfmradio.biz
License: Lowry, Walworth County, SD held by James River Broadcasting Inc.
Group Owner: Robert Ingstad Broadcast Properties
Format: Country
Robert Inqstad, President
Mark Swendsen, General Manager

***KQSD-FM**
01-01-1994; 91.9 mhz FM; 100 kw; 725 ft.; N45 16 34 W99 59 3 3
Mailing Address: P.O. Box 5000, Vermillion, SD 57069 US
Second Address: 555 N. Dakota St., Lowry, SD 57069
(605) 677-5861, *Fax:* (605) 677-5010
www.sdpb.org
License: Lowry, Walworth County, SD held by South Dakota Board of Directors for Educational Telecommunications.
Arbitron Metro Market: Vermillion, SD *Format:* Classical, Jazz, 60
Owen DeJong, Programming Director

Madison

KJAM
12-03-1959; 1390 khz AM *Hrs Open:* 18; 0.5 kw-D, ND1; 0.062 kw-N, ND1; N44 0 37 W97 10 18
101 South Eqan, Madison, SD 57042 US
(605) 256-4515, *Fax:* (605) 256-6477
www.kjamradio.com
info@kjamradio.com
License: Madison, SD held by Three Eagles of Brookings Inc.
Group Owner: Three Eagles Communications; (acq 12-8-99; $1.2 million with co-located FM)
Format: News, News/Talk, 86 *Special Programming:* National agriculture talk program 11 hrs wkly *Hrs. of News Programming:* news progmg 12 hrs wkly *No. News Employees:* 13 *Target Audience:* 21 plus. *Adv.Rates:* 35; 32; 32; 28.
Gary Buchanan, President
Lorin Larsen, General Manager
Peg Nordling, Programming Director
Sue Bergheim, News Director
Bob Cook, Chief Engineer
Dave Borman, Farm Director
Jim Hockett, General Sales Manager
Joyce Wiesman, Women'sInt Ed

KJAM-FM
12-17-1967; 103.1 mhz FM *Hrs Open:* 24; 33 kw; 305 ft.; N43 59 8 W97 7 42
101 South Egan Ave, Madison, SD 57042 US
(605) 256-4515, *Fax:* (605) 256-6477
www.kjamradio.com
manager@kjamradio.com
License: Madison, Lake County, SD held by Three Eagles of Brookings Inc.
Group Owner: Three Eagles Communications
Format: Country, News *Hrs. of News Programming:* news progmg 20 hrs wkly *No. News Employees:* 2 *Target Audience:* 21 plus.
Dan Sudenga, General Sales Mgr
Nicole Nordbye, News Director
James Wyngaard, Sports Commentator

Martin

***KZSD-FM**
07-03-1991; 102.5 mhz FM; 100 kw; 755 ft.; N43 26 6 W101 33 14
Mailing Address: P O Box 5000, Cherry & Dakota Streets, Vermillion, SD 57069 US
Second Address: 555 N. Dakota St., Martin, SD 57069
(605) 677-6443, *Fax:* (605) 677-5010
www.sdpb.org
sdpr@sdpb.org
License: Martin, Bennett County, SD held by South Dakota Board of Directors for Educational Telecommunications.
Arbitron Metro Market: Martin, SD *Format:* Classical, Jazz, 60 *No. News Employees:* 10
Owen DeJong, Programming Director
Joe Tlustos, Radio Director

Mibank

KMSD
03-20-1975; 1510 khz AM
232 Third Street, Ne, Valley City, ND 58072 US
(605) 432-5516, *Fax:* (605) 432-4231
kmsd@tnics.com
License: Mibank, SD held by Armada Media-Watertown Inc.
Group Owner: Armada Media Corp.; (acq 8-3-2007; grpsl)
Regional Network: S.D. News Net. *Wire Services:* UPI
Format: News, News/Talk, 64, Talk *Special Programming:* Farm 6 hrs wkly *Target Audience:* General.
Jeff Kurtz, General Manager

Milbank

KKSD
02-04-1991; 104.3 mhz FM *Hrs Open:* 24; 97 kw; 981 ft.; N45 10 31 W96 59 15
600 N Kiwanis, Sioux Falls, SD 57104 US
(605) 886-8444, *Fax:* (605) 886-2121
www.ksdr.com
A mneudecker@kwat.threeeagles.com
License: Milbank, Grant County, SD held by Three Eagles of Joliet Inc.
Group Owner: Three Eagles Communications; (acq 7-1-2004; grpsl)
Arbitron Metro Market: Sioux City, IA *Format:* Oldies *Special Programming:* Sports 5 hrs wkly *Target Audience:* 25-54.
Nancy Linneman, General Manager

KXLG
11-01-1972; 99.1 mhz FM; 37 kw; 548 ft.; N45 1 10 W96 56 43
1726 Dakota Ave South, Huron, SD 57350 US
(605) 753-9910, *Fax:* (605) 352-8622
www.kxlgradio.com/
carol.zillgitt@kxlgradio.com
License: Milbank, Grant County, SD held by Dakota Communications Ltd.
Group Owner: Dakota Communications Ltd.
Arbitron Metro Market: Milbank, SD *Format:* Country *Target Audience:* 25-54.
Linda Marcus, General Manager

Mitchell

KMIT
03-10-1975; 105.9 mhz FM *Hrs Open:* 24; 100 kw; 653 ft.; N43 44 16 W98 14 39
Mailing Address: P.O. Box 520, Mitchell, SD 57301 US
Second Address: 501 S. Ohlman, Mitchell, SD
(605) 996-9667, *Fax:* (605) 996-0013
www.kmit.com
kmit@kmit.com
License: Mitchell, Davison County, SD held by Saga Communications of South Dakota LLC.
Group Owner: Saga Communications Inc.; (acq 5-1-2001; $4.05 million with KUQL(FM) Wessington Springs).
Format: Country *Special Programming:* Farm 18 hrs wkly *No. News Employees:* 2 *Target Audience:* 18-54.
Tim Smith, General Manager
Nikki Frederickson, General Sales Mgr
Joel VanDover, Programming Director
Lisa Youngstrom, Promotions Manager
John Cyr, Chief Engineer
Eric Roozen, Disc Jockey
Joel Van Dover

KORN
01-01-1947; 1490 khz AM *Hrs Open:* 24; 1 kw-U, ND1; N43 42 14 W97 59 57
Mailing Address: 600 N. Kiwanis, Sioux Falls, SD 57104 US
Second Address: 319 N. Main, Mitchell, SD 57301
(605) 996-1490, *Fax:* (605) 996-6680
kornstudio@kornq107.com
License: Mitchell, SD held by Sorenson Broadcasting Corp.
Group Owner: Sorenson Broadcasting Corp.; (acq 7-1-97; $1.2 million with co-located FM)
Nat'l Network: Westwood One; ABC *Wire Services:* AP
Format: News, News/Talk, 84, Talk *Special Programming:* Farm 10 hrs wkly *Hrs. of News Programming:* news progmg 15 hrs wkly *No. News Employees:* 1 *Target Audience:* 35 plus; mature adults *Adv. Rates:* 12;10; 10; 8
Mary Quass, President
John Koons, General Manager
Clayton Mick, Programming Director
J.P. Skelly, News Director

KQRN
08-17-1980; 107.3 mhz FM *Hrs Open:* 24; 100 kw; 361 ft.; N43 42 14 W97 59 57
Mailing Address: 600 N. Kiewanis, Sioux Falls, SD 57104 US
Second Address: 319 N. Main, Mitchell, SD 57301
(605) 996-1073, *Fax:* (605) 996-6680
q107radio.com
kornstudio@kornq107.com
License: Mitchell, Davison County, SD
Group Owner: Sorenson Broadcasting Corp.
Wire Services: AP
Arbitron Metro Market: Mitchell, SD *Format:* Adult Contemp *Hrs. of News Programming:* news progmg 4 hrs wkly *No. News Employees:* 1 *Target Audience:* 10-49; adult female *Adv. Rates:* 20; 15; 20; 12
Steve Morgan, Operations Dir
John Koons, General Manager
Steve Morgan, Programming Director
JP Skelly, News Director

Mobridge

KOLY
08-10-1956; 1300 khz AM *Hrs Open:* 24; 5 kw-D, 111 w-N; N45 32 07 W100 20 45
Box 400, 118 E. 3rd St., Mobridge, SD 57601
(605) 845-3654, *Fax:* (605) 845-5094
koly@westriv.com
License: Mobridge, Walworth County, SD held by James River Broadcasting Co.
Group Owner: Robert Ingstad Broadcast Properties; (acq 7-8-97; $890,742 with co-locat
Population Served: 50,000*Special Programming:* Farm, American Indian *Hrs. of News Programming:* news progmg 21 hrs wkly *No. News Employees:* 1 *Target Audience:* General.
Mark Swendsen, General Manager
Dawn Konold, General Sales Mgr
John Schreier, Programming Director
Mel Hanson, Promotions Manager
Aaron Kurth, News Director
Don Britnall, Chief Engineer
Andy Shumacher, Disc Jockey
Pat Morrison,Sports Commentator

KOLY-FM
10-01-1973; 99.5 mhz FM; 56 kw; 560 ft; N45 31 50 W100 20 30
Box 400, 118 E. 3rd St., Mobridge, SD 57601
(605) 845-3654, *Fax:* (605) 845-5094
koly@westriv.com
License: Mobridge, Walworth County, SD

Cindy Dafnis, Operations Dir
Dawn Konold, Station Manager
John Schreier, Programming Director
Mel Hanson, Promotions Manager
Aaron Kurth, News Director
Don Britnal, Chief Engineer
John Schreier, Production Manager

Newell

KXZT
107.9 mhz FM; 4.8 kw horiz, 0 kw vert; 1493 ft.; N44 19 40 W103 50 6
US
(859) 879-0818
License: Newell, Butte County, SD held by JER Licenses LLC.
Group Owner: JER Licenses LLC
Arbitron Metro Market: Newell, SD
Jon Robinson, General Manager

Pierpont

***KDSD-FM**
04-01-1984; 90.9 mhz FM; 70 kw; 1060 ft.; N45 29 55 W97 40 35
Rebroadcasts: Rebroadcasts KUSD(FM) Vermillion.
Mailing Address: P.O. Box 5000, Vermillion, SD 57069 US
Second Address: 555 N. Dakota St., Vermillion, SD 57069
(605) 677-5861, *Fax:* (605) 677-5010
www.sdpb.org
sdpr@sdpb.org
License: Pierpont, Day County, SD held by South Dakota Board of Directors for Educational Telecommunications.
Nat'l Network: PRI; NPR *Regional Network:* S.D. Pub
Arbitron Metro Market: Vermillion, SD *Format:* Jazz, News *No. News Employees:* 8
Terry Spencer, General Sales Mgr
Owen DeJong, Programming Director
Joe Tlustos, Radio Director

Pierre

KCCR
02-04-1959; 1240 khz AM *Hrs Open:* 5:30 AM-midnight; 1 kw-U, ND1; N44 21 2 W100 19 8
600 N. Kiwanis, Sioux Falls, SD 57104 US
(605) 224-1240, *Fax:* (605) 945-4270
todaykccr.com
steve@todayskccr.com
License: Pierre, SD held by Sorenson Broadcasting Corp.
Group Owner: Sorenson Broadcasting Corp.; (acq 3-1-72)
Nat'l Network: CBS
Arbitron Metro Market: Pierre, SD *Format:* News, News/Talk, 64, Talk *Hrs. of News Programming:* news progmg 24 hrs wkly *No. News Employees:* 2 *Target Audience:* 35 plus; well-educated, upper income, politicallyaware business people, retirees, housewives
Dean Sorenson, President
Steve White, General Manager
Tanya Martin, General Sales Mgr

D.T. Meyer, Programming Director
Tony Mangan, News Director

KGFX
01-01-1927; 1060 khz AM *Hrs Open:* 24; 10 kw-D, DA2; 1 kw-N, DA2; N44 17 12 W100 20 18
Mailing Address: 232 Third Street, Ne, Valley City, ND 58072 US
Second Address: 214 W. Pleasant Dr., Pierre, SD 57501
(605) 224-8686, *Fax:* (605) 224-8984
www.drgnews.com
joansimons@amfmradio.biz
License: Pierre, SD held by James River Broadcasting.
Group Owner: Robert Ingstad Broadcast Properties; (acq 11-15-68)
Nat'l Network: ABC Information & Entertainment *Regional Network:* S.D. News Net. *Wire Services:* AP
Format: Country *Hrs. of News Programming:* news progmg 20 hrs wkly *No. News Employees:* 1 *Target Audience:* 25-54.
Janice Ingstad, President
Mark Swendsen, General Manager
Dawn Marso, General Sales Mgr
Paul Rollie, Programming Director
Chuck Hanson, Promotions Manager
Jeri Thomas, News Director
Dorene Foster, Farm Director

KGFX-FM
01-04-1982; 92.7 mhz FM *Hrs Open:* 24; 50 kw; 488 ft.; N44 18 30 W100 20 49
Mailing Address: 232 3rd Street N.W., Valley City, ND 58072 US
Second Address: 214 W. Pleasant Dr., Pierre, SD 57501
(605) 224-8686, *Fax:* (605) 224-8984
www.drgnews.com
joansimons@amfmradio.biz
License: Pierre, Hughes County, SD held by Robert E. Ingstad Properties.
Group Owner: Robert Ingstad Broadcast Properties
Format: Adult Contemp *Target Audience:* 25-49.
Mark Swendsen, General Manager
Dawn Marso, General Sales Mgr
Chuck Hanson, Promotions Manager
Patrick Callahan, News Director

KLXS-FM
04-15-1981; 95.3 mhz FM; 49 kw; 495 ft.; N44 18 42 W100 21 10
600 North Kiwanis, Sioux Falls, SD 57104 US
(605) 224-7381
info@todaykccr.com
License: Pierre, Hughes County, SD held by Sorenson Broadcasting Corp.
Group Owner: Sorenson Broadcasting Corp.
Nat'l Network: Westwood One
Arbitron Metro Market: Rapid City, SD *Format:* Adult Contemp *Target Audience:* 18-34; 55% female, 45% male
Gary Terrell, General Manager
Neal Gladner, General Sales Mgr
Craig Dale, Programming Director
Melissa Walters, News Director

***KVFL**
01-01-2006; 89.1 mhz FM *Hrs Open:* 24; 0.4 kw vert; 371 ft.; N44 25 33 W100 21 28
3434 West Kilbourn Ave, Milwaukee, WI 53208 US
(414) 935-3000, *Fax:* (414) 935-3015
www.vcyamerica.org
kvfl@vcyamerica.org
License: Pierre, Hughes County, SD held by VCY America Inc.
Group Owner: VCY America Inc.
Arbitron Metro Market: Colorado Springs, CO *Format:* Christian, Religious
Vic Eliason, Operations Dir
Jim Schneider, Programming Director

Pine Ridge

***KVAR**
07-01-2008; 93.7 mhz FM; 12 kw; 479 ft.; N42 49 47 W102 39 8
Mailing Address: US
Second Address: 709 Coleman Ave., Athens, AL 35611
(256) 497-4502, *Fax:* NA
varietyrock@hotmail.com
License: Pine Ridge, Shannon County, SD held by Alleycat Communications.
Arbitron Metro Market: Mesquite, TX *Format:* Variety/Diverse, Rock/AOR *Target Audience:* 18-54.
Richard Dabney, General Manager

***KVKR**
88.3 mhz FM; 10 kw; 436 ft.; N42 49 47 W102 39 8
US
(256) 497-4502
License: Pine Ridge, Shannon County, SD held by Southern Cultural Foundation.
Arbitron Metro Market: Pine Ridge, SD
Richard Dabney, General Manager

Porcupine

***KILI**
01-01-1984; 90.1 mhz FM; 100 kw; 509 ft.; N43 10 48 W102 19 25
Mailing Address: P.O. Box 150, Porcupine, SD 57772 US
Second Address: 901 Lamont Ln., Porcupine, SD 57772
(605) 867-5002, *Fax:* (605) 867-5634
www.kiliradio.org
on.air.person@gmail.com
License: Porcupine, Shannon County, SD held by Lakota Communications Inc.
Arbitron Metro Market: Porcupine, SD *Format:* Native American
Melanie Janis, General Manager

Rapid City

***KBHE-FM**
01-01-1984; 89.3 mhz FM; 9.8 kw; 410 ft.; N44 3 9 W103 14 38
Box 5000, Vermillion, SD 57069 US
(605) 677-5861, *Fax:* (605) 677-5010
www.sdpb.org
fritz.miller@state.sd.us
License: Rapid City, Pennington County, SD held by South Dakota Board of Educational Telecommunications.
Nat'l Network: PRI; NPR *Regional Network:* S.D. Pub
Arbitron Metro Market: Vermillion, SD *Format:* Classical, Jazz, 60
Joe Tlustos, Programming Director

KFXS
04-11-1977; 100.3 mhz FM *Hrs Open:* 24; 100 kw; 463 ft.; N44 4 13 W103 15 1
Mailing Address: Post Office Box 1248, Minnetonka, MN 55345 US
Second Address: 660 Flormann St., Suite 100, Rapid City, SD 57709
(605) 348-1100, *Fax:* (605) 348-1100
www.foxradio.com
request@foxradio.com
License: Rapid City, Pennington County, SD held by New Rushmore Radio Inc.
Group Owner: Schurz Communications Inc.; (acq 10-23-2006; grpsl)
Nat'l Reps: Christal
Arbitron Metro Market: Rapid City, SD *Format:* Classic Rock *Hrs. of News Programming:* news progmg 3 hrs wkly *No. News Employees:* 1 *Target Audience:* 25-54.
Charlie O'Douglas, Operations Dir
Lia Green, General Manager
Jake Michaels, Programming Director
Kay Duda, News Director
Gary Peterson, Engineering Dir

KIMM
03-16-1962; 1150 khz AM
PO Box 8164, Rapid City, SD 57709 US
(605) 342-1150, *Fax:* (605) 343-1096
KIMMproduction@rushmore.com
License: Rapid City, SD held by Aasen Publishing Inc.
Nat'l Reps: Christal
Arbitron Metro Market: Rapid City, SD *Format:* Talk *Special Programming:* Colorado Rockies baseball, farm one hr wkly *Target Audience:* 35-64. *Adv. Rates:* 20; 20; 20; 10
Carson Aasen, President
Gary Peterson, Operations Dir
Ron Hansen, General Manager
Michael Goodroad, General Sales Mgr
Wayne Janke, Programming Director
Dan Rahman, Disc Jockey
Gail Hanson, Disc Jockey
Dan Rahman

KIQK
01-07-1992; 104.1 mhz FM *Hrs Open:* 24; 100 kw; 538 ft.; N44 1 19 W103 15 33
666 Main Street, Deadwood, SD 57732 US
(605) 343-0888, *Fax:* (605) 342-3075
License: Rapid City, Pennington County, SD
Arbitron Metro Market: Rapid City, SD *Format:* Country *Hrs. of News Programming:* news progmg 3 hrs wkly *No. News Employees:* 1 *Target Audience:* 25-54.
Christian Haugo, General Manager

KKLS
06-07-1959; 920 khz AM *Hrs Open:* 24; 5 kw-D, DA2; 0.111 kw-N, DA2; N44 3 43 W103 10 32
Post Office Box 1248, Minnetonka, MN 55345 US
(605) 343-6161, *Fax:* (605) 343-9012
www.newrushmoreradio.com/kkls/
License: Rapid City, SD held by New Rushmore Radio Inc.
Group Owner: Schurz Communications Inc.; (acq 10-23-2006; grpsl)
Nat'l Network: Westwood One *Nat'l Reps:* Christal *Wire Services:* AP
Arbitron Metro Market: Rapid City, SD *Format:* Oldies *Target Audience:* 35-64.
Charlie O'Douglas, Operations Dir
Lia Green, General Manager
Michael Goodroad, General Sales Mgr
Jay Davis, Programming Director
Kurt Summers, Program/Music Director

KKMK
01-01-1971; 93.9 mhz FM *Hrs Open:* 24; 100 kw; 686 ft.; N44 2 49 W103 14 45
P.O. Box 1248, Minneytonka, MN 55345 US
(609) 343-6161, *Fax:* (605) 343-9012
www.kkmk.com
kkmk@rapidnet.comm
License: Rapid City, Pennington County, SD
Group Owner: Schurz Communications Inc.
Nat'l Reps: Christal *Wire Services:* AP
Arbitron Metro Market: Rapid City, SD *Format:* Adult Contemp *Target Audience:* 25-54.
John Hiatt, Operations Dir
Clint Culp, Senior Vice President

KTPT
10-01-1968; 97.9 mhz FM *Hrs Open:* 24; 100 kw; 1900 ft.; N44 19 42 W103 50 3
P.O. Box 168, Rapid City, SD 57709 US
(605) 342-6822, *Fax:* (605) 342-0854
www.979thepoint.com
info@ktpt.com
License: Rapid City, Pennington County, SD held by Bethesda Christian Broadcasting Inc.
Group Owner: Bethesda Christian Broadcasting; (acq 6-25-96; $350,000)
Arbitron Metro Market: Rapid City, SD *Format:* Christian
Mitch Hildebrandt, President
Tom Schoenstadt, General Manager
John Derrek, General Sales Mgr
Jennifer Crawford, Programming Director

KOTA
11-01-1936; 1380 khz AM *Hrs Open:* 24
518 St. Joe Street, Rapid City, SD 57701 US
(605) 342-2000, *Fax:* (605) 721-5732
www.kotaradio.com
les@dberadio.com
License: Rapid City, SD held by Duhamel Broadcasting Enterprises.
Group Owner: Duhamel Broadcasting Enterprises; acq 5-54)
Nat'l Network: CBS *Nat'l Reps:* Katz Radio *Wire Services:* AP
Arbitron Metro Market: Rapid City, SD *TV Affiliate:* KOTA-TV affil
Format: News, News/Talk, 86 *Hrs. of News Programming:* news progmg 10 hrs wkly *No. News Employees:* 2 *Target Audience:* 35 plus. *Adv.Rates:* 25; 28; 21; 17
William Duhamel, President
Les Tuttle, Station Manager

KOUT
01-01-1993; 98.7 mhz FM *Hrs Open:* 24; 100 kw; 463 ft.; N44 4 13 W103 15 1
Mailing Address: P.O. Box 1248, Minnetonka, MN 55345 US
Second Address: 660 Flormann St., Suite 100, Rapid City, SD 57701
(605) 343-6161, *Fax:* (605) 343-9012
www.katcountry.com
prod@newrushmore.com
License: Rapid City, Pennington County, SD held by New Rushmore Radio Inc.
Group Owner: Schurz Communications Inc.; (acq 10-23-2006; grpsl)
Nat'l Reps: Christal
Arbitron Metro Market: Rapid City, SD *Format:* Country *Target Audience:* Adults 25-54.
Charlie O'Douglas, Operations Dir
Lia Green, General Manager
Mark Houston, Programming Director
Kay Duda, News Director
Gary Peterson, Engineering Dir

KTOQ
09-26-1953; 1340 khz AM *Hrs Open:* 24; 1 kw-U, ND1; N44 4 6 W103 10 11
666 Main Street, Deadwood, SD 57732 US
(605) 343-0888, *Fax:* (605) 342-3075
www.ktalkam1340.com

License: Rapid City, SD held by Haugo Braodcasting Inc.
Group Owner: Haugo Broadcasting Inc.; acq 11-20-98; $1.97 million with co-located FM)
Nat'l Reps: McGavren Guild
Arbitron Metro Market: Rapid City, SD *Format:* Talk *Special Programming:* Farm 2 hrs wkly *Hrs. of News Programming:* news progmg 3 hrs wkly *No. News Employees:* 2 *Target Audience:* 35 plus; upscale
Houston Haugo, CEO
Christian Haugo, Operations Dir
Georgia McGaa, General Sales Mgr
Brad Anderson, News Director
Tracy Krsnak, Chief Engineer
Rose Jeffert, Public Affairs Director
Phil Amundson, Traffic Manager

KZLK
01-01-2001; 106.3 mhz FM *Hrs Open:* 24; 92 kw; 696 ft.; N44 4 7 W103 15 2
1515 Forest Court, Rapid City, SD 57701 US
(605) 721-1063, *Fax:* (605) 721-5732
www.1063maxfm.com
she1063@dberadio.com
License: Rapid City, Pennington County, SD held by Steven E. Duffy.
Nat'l Reps: Katz Radio *Wire Services:* AP
Arbitron Metro Market: Rapid City, SD *Target Audience:* Adult 25-54. *Adv. Rates:* 25; 22; 23; 18
Les Tuttle, General Manager

KQRQ
10-01-2002; 92.3 mhz FM *Hrs Open:* 24; 86 kw; 581 ft.; N44 4 7 W103 15 2
C/O Radio Station Kroc, 122 S W Fourth Street, Rochester, MN 55901 US
(605) 342-2000, *Fax:* (605) 721-5732
www.q923radio.com
ted@dberadio.com
License: Rapid City, Pennington County, SD held by New Generation Broadcasting LLC.
Nat'l Reps: Katz Radio *Wire Services:* AP
Arbitron Metro Market: Rapid City, SD *Format:* Contemporary Hits/Top 40, Adult Contemp *Target Audience:* Adults 25-44. *Adv. Rates:* 24; 23; 24; 18
Ted Peiffer, General Manager
Lil Anderson, General Sales Mgr
Rick Allen, Programming Director

*KQFR
08-05-2005; 89.9 mhz FM *Hrs Open:* 24; 2.3 kw; 1844 ft.; N44 19 42 W103 50 3
Mailing Address: 4135 Northgate Blvd., Suite 1, Sacramento, CA 95834 US
Second Address: 290 Hegenberger Rd., Oakland, CA 94621
(800) 543-1495, *Fax:* (916) 641-8238
www.familyradio.com
info@familyradio.com
License: Rapid City, Pennington County, SD held by Family Stations Inc.
Group Owner: Family Stations Inc.
Arbitron Metro Market: Rapid City, SD *Format:* Christian, Religious
Harold Camping, President
Don Horton, Operations Dir

*KLMP
02-17-2005; 88.3 mhz FM; 63 kw; Ant 1,712 ft; N44 19 42 W103 50 03
1853 Fountain Plaza Dr., Rapid City, SD 80920
(605) 342-6822, *Fax:* (605) 342-0854
www.klmp.com
info@klmp.com
License: Rapid City, Pennington County, SD held by Bethesda Christian Broadcasting Inc.
Group Owner: Bethesda Christian Broadcasting
Nat'l Network: Fox News Radio
Arbitron Metro Market: Rapid City, SD *Target Audience:* 35 plus; general
Tom Schoenstedt, General Manager
John Derrek, General Sales Mgr
Dave Masters, Programming Director
Joe Standish, Chief Engineer

*KASD
01-01-2006; 90.3 mhz FM; 1 kw; 407 ft.; N44 4 13 W103 15 1
Rebroadcasts: Rebroadcasts WAFR(FM) Tupelo, MS 100%
P O Drawe 2440, Tupelo, MS 38803 US
(662) 844-8888, *Fax:* (662) 842-6791
www.afr.net
faq@afr.net
License: Rapid City, Pennington County, SD held by American Family Association.
Group Owner: American Family Radio
Nat'l Network: American Family Radio
Arbitron Metro Market: Rapid City, SD *Format:* Christian
Marvin Sanders, General Manager

Redfield

KGIM-FM
04-07-1991; 103.7 mhz FM *Hrs Open:* 5:30 AM-midnight; 100 kw; 554 ft.; N45 12 30 W98 40 20
P.O. Box 907, Valley City, ND 58072 US
(605) 229-3632, *Fax:* (605) 229-4849
www.hubcityradio.com
brianlundquist@hubcityradio.com
License: Redfield, Spink County, SD held by Armada Media - Aberdeen Inc.
Group Owner: Armada Media Corp.; (acq 10-31-2006; grpsl)
Format: Country *Special Programming:* Farm 12 hrs wkly, Religious 2 hrs wkly *Hrs. of News Programming:* 10 hrs wkly *No. News Employees:* 1 *Target Audience:* 25-49.
Jim Coursolle, President
Doc Sebastian, Operations Dir
Bri Matthews, News Director
Sports Director, Ben Root

KNBZ
01-01-1999; 97.7 mhz FM; 100 kw; 561 ft.; N45 12 30 W98 40 20
Mailing Address: PO Box 907, Valley City, ND 58072 US
Second Address: 13541 386th Ave., Aberdeen, SD 57401
(605) 229-3632, *Fax:* (605) 229-4849
www.hubcityradio.com
info@hubcityradio.com
License: Redfield, Spink County, SD held by Armada Media - Aberdeen Inc.
Group Owner: Armada Media Corp.; (acq 10-31-2006; grpsl)
Format: Adult Contemp
Brian Lundquist, General Manager
Doc Sebastian, Programming Director

*KQKD
12-01-1962; 1380 khz AM *Hrs Open:* 24
Mailing Address: P.O. Box 907, Valley City, ND 58072 US
Second Address: 290 Hegenberger Rd., Oakland, CA 94621
(916) 641-8191, *Fax:* (916) 641-8238
www.familyradio.com
info@familyradio.com
License: Redfield, SD held by Family Stations Inc.
Group Owner: Family Stations Inc.; (acq 11-30-2004; $75,000 with KKAA(AM) Aberdeen).
Format: Christian, Religious
Harold Camping, President

Reliance

KPLO-FM
01-01-1986; 94.5 mhz FM *Hrs Open:* 24; 95 kw; 988 ft.; N43 57 57 W99 36 11
232 Third St., Ne, Valley City, ND 58072 US
(605) 224-8686, *Fax:* (605) 224-8984
drgprod1@amfmradio.biz
License: Reliance, Lyman County, SD held by James River Broadcasting Co.
Group Owner: Robert Ingstad Broadcast Properties; (acq 8-21-98; $98,000)
Arbitron Metro Market: Pierre, SD *Format:* Country *Special Programming:* Farm 5 hrs wkly *Target Audience:* 25-54.
Mark Swendsen, General Manager

*KTSD-FM
01-01-1984; 91.1 mhz FM; 100 kw; 1480 ft.; N43 57 55 W99 35 56 *Rebroadcasts:* Rebroadcasts KUSD-FM, Vermillion,SD 89.7%.
Mailing Address: P.O. Box 5000, Vermillion, SD 57069 US
Second Address: 555 N. Dakota St., Vermillion, SD 57069
(605) 394-2551, *Fax:* (605) 677-5010
www.sdpb.org
fritz.miller@state.sd.us
License: Reliance, Lyman County, SD held by S.D. Board of Educational Telecommunications.
Nat'l Network: PRI; NPR
Arbitron Metro Market: Reliance, SD *Format:* Classical, Jazz, 60 *Special Programming:* Sioux one hr wkly
Owen DeJong, Programming Director
Joe Tlustos, Radio Director

Roscoe

KMOM
12-11-2007; 105.5 mhz FM *Hrs Open:* 24; 100 kw; 456 ft.; N45 27 13 W98 48 10
US
(605) 725-5551, *Fax:* (605) 725-5553
www.dakotabroadcasting.com
License: Roscoe, Edmunds County, SD held by Dakota Broadcasting LLC
Arbitron Metro Market: Roscoe, SD *Format:* Country *No. News Employees:* 9 *Target Audience:* 18-34, 25-54.
Mike Johnson, Operations Dir
Joel Swanson, General Manager
Devin Reints, General Sales Mgr
Ward Hilger, Programming Director
Marnah Lee, News Director
Kate Von Brook, Office Manager
Adam St. Paul, Sports Director
SueChristensen, Senior Marketing Consultant

Rosebud

*KOYA
88.1 mhz FM; 51 kw vert; 640 ft.; N43 13 1 W100 47 28
US
(605) 747-2381
License: Rosebud, Todd County, SD held by Rosebud Sioux Tribe.
Arbitron Metro Market: Rosebud, SD
Ronald Neiss, General Manager

Salem

KIKN-FM
11-04-1993; 100.5 mhz FM *Hrs Open:* 24; 100 kw; 940 ft.; N43 29 22 W97 26 33
122 Sw Fourth Street, Rochester, MN 55901 US
(605) 361-0300, *Fax:* (605) 361-5410
www.kikn.com
License: Salem, McCook County, SD held by Cumulus Licensing LLC.
Group Owner: Cumulus Media Inc.; (acq 4-1-2004; grpsl)
Nat'l Reps: Christal
Format: Country *No. News Employees:* 1 *Target Audience:* 18-49.
Don Jacobs, General Manager
J.D. Collins, Programming Director

Sioux Falls

*KAUR
10-09-1972; 89.1 mhz FM *Hrs Open:* 10 AM-3 AM; 0.68 kw; 184 ft.; N43 31 37 W96 44 18
Mailing Address: 2001 S. Summit Avenue, Sioux Falls, SD 57197 US
Second Address: 2001 S. Summit Ave., Sioux Falls, SD 57197
(605) 274-0770, *Fax:* (605) 336-5465
www.kaur.com
inf@kaur.com
License: Sioux Falls, Minnehaha County, SD held by Augustana College Association.
Nat'l Network: ABC
Format: Alternative, Jazz *Special Programming:* Folk 2 hrs, world mus 6 hrs, blues 12 hrs wkly *Target Audience:* General.

*KCFS
07-01-1985; 94.5 mhz FM; 2 kw; 197 ft.; N43 31 56 W96 44 20
1101 W. 22nd Street, Sioux Falls, SD 57105 US
(605) 331-6691, *Fax:* (605) 331-6615
www.usiouxfalls.edu/campus/radio/index.html
kcfs@thecoo.edu
License: Sioux Falls, Minnehaha County, SD held by University of Sioux Falls.
Format: Variety/Diverse *Special Programming:* Urban 6 hrs wkly
Jesse Logterman, General Manager
Chris Stafford, Station Manager
Jason Peiser, Programming Director

*KCSD
07-01-1985; 90.9 mhz FM *Hrs Open:* 24; 6 kw; 262 ft.; N43 34 28 W96 39 19
1101 W. 22nd Street, Sioux Falls, SD 57105 US
(605) 331-6690, *Fax:* (605) 331-6692
www.sdpb.org
sdpr@sdpb.org
License: Sioux Falls, Minnehaha County, SD held by University of Sioux Falls.
Nat'l Network: NPR *Regional Network:* S.D. Pub
Arbitron Metro Market: Sioux Falls, SD *Format:* Talk *Special Programming:* Folk 5 hrs, jazz 10 hrs wkly *Hrs. of News Programming:* news progmg 44 hrs wkly *No. News Employees:* 1 *Target Audience:* 25 plus;educated males & females
Janice Davis, Station Manager

KELO
01-01-1937; 1320 khz AM *Hrs Open:* 24; 5 kw-D, DAN; 5 kw-N, DAN; N43 29 17 W96 38 14

500 South Phillips Ave., Sioux Falls, SD 57102 US
(605) 331-5350, *Fax:* (605) 336-0415
kelo.com
License: Sioux Falls, SD held by Backyard Broadcasting South Dakota Licensee LLC
Group Owner: Backyard Broadcasting LLC
Nat'l Network: Fox News Radio *Nat'l Reps:* Katz Radio
Arbitron Metro Market: Sioux Falls, SD *Format:* News, News/Talk, 86 *No. News Employees:* 6 *Target Audience:* 25-54.
Kurt Boney, General Sales Mgr
Greg Belfrage, Programming Director
Jack Taylor, News Director

KELO-FM
07-11-1965; 92.5 mhz FM *Hrs Open:* 24; 100 kw; 1821 ft.; N43 31 7 W96 32 5
500 South Phillips, Sioux Falls, SD 57102 US
(605) 331-5350, *Fax:* (605) 336-0415
kelofm.com
License: Sioux Falls, Minnehaha County, SD held by Backyard Broadcasting South Dakota Licensee LLC
Group Owner: Backyard Broadcasting LLC; (acq 4-2005; grpsl).
Nat'l Reps: Katz Radio
Arbitron Metro Market: Sioux Falls, SD *Format:* Adult Contemp
Barry Drake, President
Craig Hodgson, General Manager
Kurt Boney, General Sales Mgr
Greg Belfrage, Programming Director
Jack Taylor, News Director

KKLS-FM
03-01-1975; 104.7 mhz FM; 100 kw; 981 ft.; N43 43 46 W97 5 14
122 S.W. Fourth Street, Rochester, MN 55901 US
(605) 361-0300, *Fax:* (605) 361-5410
License: Sioux Falls, Minnehaha County, SD
Group Owner: Cumulus Media Inc.
Arbitron Metro Market: Sioux City, IA *Format:* Contemporary Hits/Top 40 *Target Audience:* 18-49.
Lew Dickey, President
Don Jacobs, General Manager
Don Jacobs, Station Manager
Rick Fink, General Sales Mgr
Andy Erickson, Programming Director

KMXC
10-01-1973; 97.3 mhz FM; 100 kw; 840 ft.; N43 43 46 W97 5 10
122 S.W. Fourth Street, Rochester, MN 55901 US
(605) 339-1140, *Fax:* (605) 339-2735
www.mix97-3.com
License: Sioux Falls, Minnehaha County, SD
Group Owner: Cumulus Media Inc.
Format: Adult Contemp *Target Audience:* 25-44; females
Lew Dickey, President
Don Jacobs, Station Manager
Scott Maguire, Programming Director

*KNWC
03-01-1961; 1270 khz AM *Hrs Open:* 24
3003 Snelling Ave. North, St. Paul, MN 55113 US
(605) 339-1270, *Fax:* (605) 339-1271
www.knwc.org
knwc@knwc.org
License: Sioux Falls, SD held by Northwestern College.
Group Owner: Northwestern College & Radio; (acq 1961).
Format: News, Religious *Hrs. of News Programming:* news progmg 24 hrs wkly *No. News Employees:* 1 *Target Audience:* 35-54.
David Martin, Operations Dir
Jeff Rupp, General Manager

*KNWC-FM
03-28-1969; 96.5 mhz FM *Hrs Open:* 24; 100 kw; 1601 ft.; N43 31 7 W96 32 5
3003 Snelling Ave. North, Roseville, MN 55113 US
(605) 339-1270, *Fax:* (605) 339-1271
www.knwc.org
License: Sioux Falls, Minnehaha County, SD
Format: Christian *Hrs. of News Programming:* news progmg 24 hrs wkly *No. News Employees:* 1 *Target Audience:* 20-54.
Tim Unsinn, Promotions Manager

KRRO
05-06-1969; 103.7 mhz FM *Hrs Open:* 24; 38 kw; 394 ft.; N43 27 28 W96 40 14
500 South Phillips Ave, Sioux Falls, SD 57104 US
(605) 331-5350, *Fax:* (605) 336-0415
www.krro.com
License: Sioux Falls, Minnehaha County, SD held by Backyard Broadcasting South Dakota Licensee LLC
Group Owner: Backyard Broadcasting LLC; (acq 4-2005; grpsl).
Nat'l Reps: Katz Radio *Wire Services:* AP
Arbitron Metro Market: Sioux Falls, SD *Format:* Classic Rock
Target Audience: 25-49; young adults, family-rearing age with disposable income
Barry Drake, President
Craig Hodgson, General Manager

*KRSD
05-11-1985; 88.1 mhz FM *Hrs Open:* 24; 2 kw; 184 ft.; N43 31 37 W96 44 18
45 East Seventh St., Saint Paul, MN 55101 US
(605) 335-6666(800) 228-7123, *Fax:* (605) 335-1259
www.mpr.org
mail@mpr.org
License: Sioux Falls, Minnehaha County, SD held by Minnesota Public Radio.
Nat'l Network: NPR; PRI
Arbitron Metro Market: Sioux Falls, SD *Format:* News *No. News Employees:* 1 *Target Audience:* General.
William Kling, President
Michael Olsen, General Manager
Mike Edgerly, News Director
Vince Fuhs, Chief Engineer

KSQB(AM)
06-13-1970; 1520 khz AM; 500 w-D; N43 33 28 W96 47 46
3205 S Meadow Avenue, Sioux Falls, SD 57104
(605) 335-6896, *Fax:* (605) 330-0047
www.q957.com
License: Sioux Falls, Minnehaha County, SD held by Backyard Broadcasting South Dakota Licensee LLC.
Group Owner: Backyard Broadcasting LLC; (acq 8-1-2006; grpsl)
Nat'l Network: Jones Radio Networks *Nat'l Reps:* Rgnl Reps *Wire Services:* AP
Format: Oldies *Target Audience:* 35-65. *Adv. Rates:* 15; 13; 15; 13
Mark Nelson, Programming Director

KSOO
01-01-1926; 1140 khz AM
122 S.W. Fourth Street, Rochester, MN 55901 US
(605) 339-1140, *Fax:* (605) 339-2735
www.ksoo.com
License: Sioux Falls, SD held by Cumulus Licensing LLC.
Group Owner: Cumulus Media Inc.; (acq 3-29-2004; grpsl)
Nat'l Reps: Christal
Arbitron Metro Market: Sioux Falls, SD *Format:* News, News/Talk, 84, Talk *Target Audience:* 35-54.
Lew Dickey, President
Don Jacobs, Station Manager
Dave Roberts, Programming Director
Gene Hetland, News Director
Mike Langford, Chief Engineer

KTWB
05-05-1990; 101.9 mhz FM *Hrs Open:* 24; 34 kw; 581 ft.; N43 45 5 W96 53 22
500 South Phillips Avenue, Sioux Falls, SD 55431 US
(605) 331-5350, *Fax:* (605) 336-0415
www.ktwb.com
ktwb@ktwb.com
License: Sioux Falls, Minnehaha County, SD held by Backyard Broadcasting South Dakota Licensee LLC.
Group Owner: Backyard Broadcasting LLC; (acq 4-2005; grpsl).
Nat'l Reps: Katz Radio *Wire Services:* AP
Arbitron Metro Market: Sioux Falls, SD *Format:* Country *Hrs. of News Programming:* news progmg 10 hrs wkly *No. News Employees:* 1 *Target Audience:* 25-54; adult
Barry Drake, President
Craig Hodgson, General Manager

KWSN
05-06-1948; 1230 khz AM *Hrs Open:* 24
500 South Phillips Ave, Sioux Falls, SD 57104 US
(605) 271-5873, *Fax:* (605) 336-0415
www.kwsn.com
studio@kwsn.com
License: Sioux Falls, SD held by Backyard Broadcasting South Dakota
Group Owner: Backyard Broadcasting LLC; .
Nat'l Network: ESPN Radio *Nat'l Reps:* Katz Radio *Wire Services:* AP
Arbitron Metro Market: Sioux Falls, SD *Format:* Sports *Hrs. of News Programming:* news progmg 27 hrs wkly *No. News Employees:* 2 *Target Audience:* 25-54; adults with disposable income, business leaders
Rob Powers, Operations Dir
Mike Newhouse, General Sales Mgr
Curtis Anderson, Programming Director
Laura Schiltz, Promotions Manager
Monica Mattoon, News Director
Stan Culley, Chief Engineer
Magda Orduno, Bilingual Sales
ShirleyDicus, Business Manager
Rhonda Johnson, Promotions Manager

KXRB
02-01-1969; 1000 khz AM *Hrs Open:* 24
122 S.W. Fourth Street, Rochester, MN 55901 US
(605) 361-0300, *Fax:* (605) 361-5410
www.kxrb.com
don.jacobs@townsquaremedia.com
License: Sioux Falls, SD held by Cumulus Licensing LLC.
Group Owner: Cumulus Media Inc.; (acq 3-29-2004; grpsl)
Nat'l Network: CNN Radio *Nat'l Reps:* Christal *Wire Services:* UPI
Arbitron Metro Market: Sioux Falls, SD *Format:* Country *Hrs. of News Programming:* news progmg 5 hrs wkly *No. News Employees:* 1 *Target Audience:* 25-54.
Lew Dickey, President
Don Jacobs, General Manager
Randy McDaniel, Programming Director
Jerry Dohmen, News Director
Mike Langford, Chief Engineer
Rick Flink, Director of Sales
Randy McDaniel, Brand Manager

*KSFS
01-01-2006; 90.1 mhz FM; 18 kw; 112 ft.; N43 32 41 W96 45 45
P O Drawer 2440, Tupelo, MS 38803 US
(800) 877-5600, *Fax:* (916) 251-1650
www.klove.com
License: Sioux Falls, Minnehaha County, SD held by Educational Media Foundation.
Group Owner: EMF Broadcasting; (acq 1-30-2009; $650,000)
Nat'l Network: K-Love
Arbitron Metro Market: Odessa-Midland, TX *Format:* Christian
Mike Novak, President

Sisseton

KBWS-FM
12-28-1983; 102.9 mhz FM; 100 kw; 459 ft.; N45 36 52 W97 24 51
232 Third St., Ne, Valley City, ND 58072 US
(605) 698-3471, *Fax:* (605) 698-3330
www.bigstoneradio.com
kbwsstudio@venturecomm.net
License: Sisseton, Roberts County, SD held by Armada Media-Watertown Inc.
Group Owner: Armada Media Corp.; (acq 8-3-2007; grpsl)
Arbitron Metro Market: Milbank, SD *Format:* Country *Target Audience:* General.
Jim Coursolle, President
Terry Heitman, Operations Dir
Jeff Kurtz, General Manager
Randy Peterson, General Sales Mgr
John Seiber, Programming Director
Don Brittnal, Chief Engineer
Jamie Rothe, Traffic Manager

Spearfish

*KBHU-FM
10-18-1974; 89.1 mhz FM *Hrs Open:* 24; 0.1 kw horiz; -348 ft.; N44 29 48 W103 52 13 *Rebroadcasts:* KJKT-FM
1200 University Blvd, Unisersity Stn Box 9665, Spearfish, SD 57799 US
(605) 642-6265, *Fax:* (605) 642-6762
www.thebuzzfm.net
thebuzzfm@thebuzzfm.net
License: Spearfish, Lawrence County, SD held by Black Hills State University.
Arbitron Metro Market: Spearfish, SD *TV Affiliate:* KBHU-TV
Format: Alternative *Hrs. of News Programming:* News progmg 3 hrs wkly *Target Audience:* 12-35.
Kay Schallenkamp, President
Erin Doering, General Manager
Cheyenne Griffin, News Director

KDDX
07-19-1985; 101.1 mhz FM *Hrs Open:* 24; 100 kw; 1788 ft.; N44 19 35 W103 50 6
PO Box 1760, Rapid City, SD 57709 US
(605) 642-5747, *Fax:* (605) 642-7849
www.xrock.fm
License: Spearfish, Lawrence County, SD held by Duhamel Broadcasting Enterprises.
Group Owner: Duhamel Broadcasting Enterprises; acq 3-16-92; $525,000;
Arbitron Metro Market: Rapid City, SD *Format:* Rock/AOR *Hrs. of News Programming:* news progmg 3 hrs wkly *No. News Employees:* 1 *Target Audience:* 18-49. *Adv. Rates:* 25; 23; 25; 19

Ted Peiffer, General Manager
Lil Anderson, General Sales Mgr
Jim Kallas, Programming Director

KSLT
02-17-1984; 107.3 mhz FM *Hrs Open:* 24; 100 kw; 1,702 ft; N44 19 36 W103 50 12
1853 Fountain Plaza Dr., Rapid City, SD 57709
(605) 342-6822, *Fax:* (605) 342-0854
www.kslt.com
info@kslt.com
License: Spearfish, Lawrence County, SD held by Bethesda Christian Broadcasting Inc.
Group Owner: Bethesda Christian Broadcasting
Nat'l Network: Fox News Radio
Arbitron Metro Market: Rapid City, SD *Target Audience:* 25-49; affluent, educated, 60% female, 40% male
Mitch Hildebrandt, President
Tom Schoenstadt, General Manager
John Derrek, General Sales Mgr
Dave Masters, Programming Director
Joe Standish, Chief Engineer

***KJKT**
04-11-2009; 90.7 mhz FM; 0.7 kw; 1644 ft.; N44 19 42 W103 50 3 *Rebroadcasts:* Simulcasts KBHU(FM) Spearfish 100%
P .O. Box 1452, Washington, DC 20013 US
(605) 642-6265
www.thebuzzfm.net
kbhufm@gmail.com
License: Spearfish, Lawrence County, SD held by Black Hills State University
Arbitron Metro Market: Spearfish, SD
Amber Bestgen, Operations Dir
Sean Freese, General Manager
Dr. Scott H. Clarke, General Sales Mgr
Dorothy Marvin, Programming Director
Cal Crooks, Chief Engineer

Sturgis

KBHB
09-27-1962; 810 khz AM *Hrs Open:* Sunrise-sunset
PO Box 1248, Minnetonka, MN 55345 US
(605) 347-4455, *Fax:* (605) 347-5120
www.newrushmoreradio.com/kbhb
info@kbhbradio.com
License: Sturgis, SD held by New Rushmore Radio Inc.
Group Owner: Schurz Communications Inc.; (acq 10-23-2006; grpsl)
Nat'l Network: ABC *Regional Network:* Agrinet
Arbitron Metro Market: Sturgis, SD *Format:* Agriculture *Special Programming:* American Indian one hr, gospel 3 hrs wkly *Hrs. of News Programming:* news progmg 17 hrs wkly *No. News Employees:* 1 *TargetAudience:* 35 plus. *Adv. Rates:* 16; 16; 16; na
Toni Kinney, Operations Dir
Dean Kinney, General Manager
Gary Matthews, Programming Director
Gary Maki, News Director
Gary Peterson, Chief Engineer

KRCS
12-05-1972; 93.1 mhz FM; 97.8 kw; 1060 ft.; N44 19 58 W103 32 20
P.O. Box 1248, Minneapolis, MN 55345 US
(605) 343-6161, *Fax:* (605) 343-9012
www.newrushmoreradio.com
prod@newrushmore.com
License: Sturgis, Meade County, SD held by New Rushmore Radio Inc.
Group Owner: Schurz Communications Inc.
Arbitron Metro Market: Rapid City, SD *Format:* Contemporary Hits/Top 40
Charlie O'Douglas, Operations Dir
Lia Green, General Manager
Michael Goodroad, General Sales Mgr
Jay Davis, Programming Director
D. Knight, News Director
Gary Peterson, Chief Engineer

Tulare

***KAMF**
91.7 mhz FM; kw
US
(605) 868-0525
License: Tulare, Spink County, SD held by Church Planters of America.
Arbitron Metro Market: Tulare, SD
Danny Hawkins, President

Vermillion

***KAOR**
09-01-1986; 91.1 mhz FM *Hrs Open:* 18; 120 w; 107 ft; N42 47 01 W96 55 26
Contemporary Media & Journalism, 414 E. Clark, Vermillion, SD 57069
(605) 677-5477, *Fax:* (605) 677-4250
www.usd.edu/kaor
kaor@usd.edu
License: Vermillion, Clay County, SD held by The University of South Dakota.
Population Served: 35,000*Special Programming:* American Indian 2 hrs wkly *Hrs. of News Programming:* News progmg 2 hrs wkly *Target Audience:* 16-30; college age students & the Vermillion Community
Michelle Van Maanen, Chairman
Janet Davison, General Manager
Don Harris, Chief Engineer

KVTK
11-16-1967; 1570 khz AM *Hrs Open:* 24; 0.5 kw-D, ND1; 0.071 kw-N, ND1; N42 47 32 W97 0 3
Mailing Address: P.O. Box 282, Vermillion, SD 57069 US
Second Address: 210 W. 3rd St., Yankton, SD 57078
(605) 665-2600, *Fax:* (605) 665-8875
www.kvtk.com
License: Vermillion, SD held by Culhane Communications Inc.
Nat'l Network: ESPN Radio; Westwood One
Format: Sports *Hrs. of News Programming:* news progmg 20 hrs wkly *No. News Employees:* 1 *Target Audience:* 25-54; general *Adv. Rates:* 21.50; 19.50; 15.25; 12
Kevin Culhane, CEO
Randy Hammer, Operations Dir
Kevin Culhane, General Manager

***KUSD**
10-01-1967; 89.7 mhz FM; 32 kw; 663 ft.; N43 3 0 W96 47 12
Mailing Address: Cherry & Oak. St Box 5000, Vermillion, SD 57069 US
Second Address: 555 N. Dakota St., Vermillion, SD 57069
(800) 456-0766, *Fax:* (605) 677-5010
www.sdpb.org
sdpr@sdpb.org
License: Vermillion, Clay County, SD held by South Dakota Board of Directors/Educational Telecommunications.
Nat'l Network: NPR; PRI *Regional Network:* S.D. Pub
Arbitron Metro Market: Vermillion, SD *TV Affiliate:* *KUSD-TV affil. *Format:* Classical, Jazz, 60 *Special Programming:* Sioux one hr wkly
Julie Anderson, President
Terry Spencer, General Sales Mgr
Owen DeJong, Programming Director
Joe Tlustos, Radio Director
Fritz Miller, Director of Marketing

KVHT
11-16-1967; 106.3 mhz FM *Hrs Open:* 24; 50 kw; 390 ft.; N42 59 45 W96 49 25
Mailing Address: P.O.Box 282, 1407 E. Cherry Street, Vermillion, SD 57069 US
Second Address: 210 West Third Street, Yankton, SD 57078
(605) 665-2600, *Fax:* (605) 665-8875
www.kvht.com
classichits1063@kvht.com
License: Vermillion, Clay County, SD held by Culhane Communications Inc.
Nat'l Network: ABC *Wire Services:* AP
Format: Oldies *Hrs. of News Programming:* news progmg 42 hrs wkly *No. News Employees:* 1 *Target Audience:* 25-64. *Adv. Rates:* 19.50; 19.50; 19.50; 15.25
Randy Eichelburg, Operations Dir
Kevin Culhane, General Manager
Bryce Phillipy, Sales Manager
Joe Van Goor, News Director
Dina Anderson, Traffic Manager

Volga

KJJQ
05-06-1981; 910 khz AM *Hrs Open:* 24; 0.5 kw-D, DA2; 0.5 kw-N, DA2; N44 15 1 W96 57 22
600 N. Kiwanis Avenue, Sioux Falls, SD 57104 US
(605) 692-1430, *Fax:* (605) 692-6434
www.brookingsradio.com
brookingsradio@brookings.net
License: Volga, SD held by Three Eagles of Joliet Inc.
Group Owner: Three Eagles Communications; (acq 7-1-2004; grpsl)
Nat'l Network: ESPN Radio
Format: Sports, Talk *Target Audience:* 25-54; 60% male, 40% female
Cami Powers, General Manager

KKQQ
04-15-1984; 102.3 mhz FM; 25 kw; 243 ft.; N44 15 1 W96 57 22
600 N. Kiwanis, Sioux Falls, SD 57104 US
(605) 692-9125, *Fax:* (605) 692-6434
www.kcountry102.com
brookingsradio@brookings.net
License: Volga, Brookings County, SD held by Three Eagles of Joliet Inc.
Group Owner: Three Eagles Communications; (acq 7-1-2004; grpsl)
Arbitron Metro Market: Sioux City, IA *Format:* Country *Target Audience:* 18-54.
Cami Powers, General Manager
Keith King, PR/Marketing/Advertising

Wall

KXZS
107.5 mhz FM; 8.4 kw horiz; 246 ft.; N43 56 9 W102 8 29 US
(859) 879-0818
License: Wall, Pennington County, SD held by JER Licenses LLC.
Group Owner: JER Licenses LLC
Arbitron Metro Market: Wall, SD
Jon Robinson, General Manager

Watertown

KDLO-FM
03-01-1968; 96.9 mhz FM *Hrs Open:* 24; 100 kw; 1572 ft.; N44 57 57 W97 35 22
600 N. Kiwanis, Sioux Falls, SD 57104 US
(605) 886-8444, *Fax:* (605) 886-9306
www.kdlocountry.com
A mneudecker@kwat.threeeagles.com
License: Watertown, Codington County, SD held by Three Eagles of Joliet Inc.
Group Owner: Three Eagles Communications; (acq 7-1-2004; grpsl)
Nat'l Network: USA
Arbitron Metro Market: Watertown, SD *Format:* Country *No. News Employees:* 1 *Target Audience:* 25-54.
Bruce Erlandson, Operations Dir
Dean Johnson, General Manager

KIXX
09-29-1968; 96.1 mhz FM *Hrs Open:* 6 AM-1 AM; 97 kw; 978 ft.; N45 10 31 W96 59 15
Mailing Address: 600 N. Kiwanis, Sioux Falls, SD 57104 US
Second Address: 921 9th Ave S. E., Watertown, SD 57201
(605) 886-9696, *Fax:* (605) 886-9306
Amneudecker@kwat.threeeagles.com
License: Watertown, Codington County, SD held by Three Eagles of Joliet Inc.
Group Owner: Three Eagles Communications; (acq 7-1-2004; grpsl)
Format: Adult Contemp *Target Audience:* 25-54.
Curt Crawford, Programming Director

KSDR
04-16-1961; 1480 khz AM *Hrs Open:* 6 AM-midnight; 1 kw-D, ND2; 0.05 kw-N, ND2; N44 55 58 W97 6 19
P.O. Box 1480, Watertown, SD 57201 US
(605) 886-5747, *Fax:* (605) 886-2121
A mnuedecker@kwat.threeeagles.com
License: Watertown, SD held by Three Eagles of Brookings Inc.
Group Owner: Three Eagles Communications; (acq 6-19-00; $3.25 million with co-located FM).
Arbitron Metro Market: Watertown, SD *Format:* Talk *Hrs. of News Programming:* news progmg 15 hrs wkly *No. News Employees:* 3 *Target Audience:* 25-54.
Gary Buchanan, President
Dean Johnsson, General Manager

KSDR-FM
03-10-1992; 92.9 mhz FM *Hrs Open:* 24; 97 kw; 978 ft.; N45 10 31 W96 59 15
P.O. Box 1480, Watertown, SD 57201 US
(605) 886-5747, *Fax:* (605) 886-2121
A mneudecker@kwat.threeeagles.com
License: Watertown, Codington County, SD
Regional Network: Tribune Radio Networks
Arbitron Metro Market: Watertown, SD *Format:* Country *Special Programming:* Farm 8 hrs, sports 8 hrs wkly *Hrs. of News Programming:* news progmg 12 hrs wkly *No. News Employees:* 1 *Target Audience:* General;rgnl country stn with wide var of ages

Erving Bales, General Manager

KWAT
03-08-1940; 950 khz AM *Hrs Open:* 5 AM-midnight; 1 kw-D, DAN; 1 kw-N, DAN; N44 52 12 W97 6 49
Mailing Address: 600 N. Kiwanis Plaza, Sioux Falls, SD 57104 US
Second Address: 921 9th Ave S. E., Watertown, SD 57201
(605) 886-8444, *Fax:* (605) 886-9306
A mneudecker@kwat.threeeagles.com
License: Watertown, SD held by Three Eagles of Joliet Inc.
Group Owner: Three Eagles Communications; (acq 7-1-2004; grpsl)
Nat'l Network: CBS
Arbitron Metro Market: Watertown, SD *Format:* Adult Contemp, News *Target Audience:* 35 plus.
Gary Buchanan, President
Dean Johnson, Operations Dir
Mike Blakenship, Programming Director
David Law, News Director
Todd Enderson, Disc Jockey
Wayne Hunter, Disc Jockey
Jim Thoreson, Farm Director
Bruce Erlandson, OperationsManager

***KJBB(FM)**
08-01-2000; 89.1 mhz FM *Hrs Open:* 24; 200 w vert; Ant 20 ft; N44 53 57 W97 06 18
6704 Highway H. South, Germantown, NC 27019
(877) 676-5372, *Fax:* (866) 812-2269
www.kjbbfm.com
oldpaths1611@gmail.com
License: Watertown, Codington County, SD held by Church Planters of America
Population Served: 4,523 *Arbitron Metro Market:* Germantown, NC
Sheila Hawkins, Operations Dir
Danny Hawkins, General Manager

Wessington Springs

KJRV
01-01-2005; 93.3 mhz FM; 65 kw; 623 ft.; N44 11 39 W98 19 5
2001 Pennsylvania Avenue, Suite 400, Washington, DC 20006 US
(605) 352-1933, *Fax:* (605) 352-1934
www.bigjimrocks.com
mlyon@kokk.com
License: Wessington Springs, Jerauld County, SD held by Alpena Broadcasting Co.
Group Owner: Dakota Communications Ltd.
Format: Classic Rock
Linda Marcus, General Manager
Mike Lyon, General Sales Mgr

Winner

KWYR
09-27-1957; 1260 khz AM *Hrs Open:* 24; 5 kw-D, ND1; 0.146 kw-N, ND1; N43 22 57 W99 54 38
Mailing Address: Box 491, Winner, SD 57580 US
Second Address: Box 491, Winner, SD 57580
(605) 842-3333, *Fax:* (605) 842-3875
www.kwyr.com
937radio@gwtc.net
License: Winner, SD held by Midwest Radio Corp.
Wire Services: AP
Arbitron Metro Market: Winner, SD *Format:* Country *Hrs. of News Programming:* news progmg 14 hrs wkly *No. News Employees:* 1 *Target Audience:* 25-60. *Adv. Rates:* 12; 8; 8; 8
Scott Schramm, President
John Driscoll, Operations Dir
Scott Schramm, General Manager
John Driscoll, General Sales Mgr
Darnell Novotny, Office Manager and Accounting

KWYR-FM
11-25-1971; 93.7 mhz FM *Hrs Open:* 24; 100 kw; 561 ft.; N43 17 46 W99 52 2
Mailing Address: 346 Main Street, Winner, SD 57580 US
Second Address: Box 491, Winner, SD 57580
(605) 842-3693, *Fax:* (605) 842-3875
www.kwyr.com
License: Winner, Tripp County, SD held by Midwest Radio Corp.
Nat'l Network: Jones Radio Networks *Wire Services:* AP
Arbitron Metro Market: Winner, SD *Format:* Adult Contemp
Target Audience: 18-45.
Scott Schramm, General Manager
John Driscoll, General Sales Mgr
Darnell Novotny, Office Manager and Accounting

Yankton

WNAX-FM
08-09-1973; 104.1 mhz FM *Hrs Open:* 24; 97 kw; 981 ft.; N42 38 24 W97 3 21
73 Kercheval Avenue, Grosse Pointe Farms, MI 48236 US
(605) 665-7442, *Fax:* (605) 665-8788
www.wnax.com
bholst@wnax.com
License: Yankton, Yankton County, SD held by Saga Communications Inc.
Wire Services: NOAA Weather
Arbitron Metro Market: Sioux City, IA *Format:* Country *Hrs. of News Programming:* news progmg 3 hrs wkly *No. News Employees:* 1 *Target Audience:* 25-54.
Steve Crawford, Operations Dir
Bill Holst, General Manager
Erin Tycz, Promotions Manager
Jerry Oster, News Director
Michelle Rook, Farm Director
Steve Imming, Sports Director
Dee Davis, Community Relations
Fred Forman,News/Sports
Matt Andes, Production Director

KKYA
05-25-1982; 93.1 mhz FM *Hrs Open:* 24; 100 kw; 469 ft.; N42 43 49 W97 24 13
Mailing Address: 600 N. Kiwanis, Sioux Falls, SD 57104 US
Second Address: 202 W. 2nd St., Yankton, SD 57078
(605) 665-7892, *Fax:* (605) 665-7892
www.kk93.com
davelee@kk93.com
License: Yankton, Yankton County, SD
Group Owner: Sorenson Broadcasting Corp.
Regional Network: Waitt Farm Net.
Arbitron Metro Market: Sioux City, IA *Format:* Country *Hrs. of News Programming:* news progmg 1.5 hrs wkly *No. News Employees:* 2 *Adv. Rates:* 15; 15; 15; 10
Dave Lesher, Operations Dir
Curt Dykstra, General Manager
Cynthia Miller, General Sales Mgr
David Leonard, News Director
Tammy Hauger, Traffic Manager
Doyle Becker, Co-Owner
Carolyn Becker, Co-Owner

KYNT
03-15-1955; 1450 khz AM *Hrs Open:* 24; 1 kw-U, ND1; N42 53 30 W97 25 10
Mailing Address: 600 N. Kiwanis, Sioux Falls, SD 57104 US
Second Address: 202 W. 2ndn St., Yankton, SD 57078
(605) 665-7892, *Fax:* (605) 665-0818
www.kynt1450.com
kynt1450@kynt1450.com
License: Yankton, SD held by Sorenson Broadcasting Corp.
Group Owner: Sorenson Broadcasting Corp.; (acq 7-1-73)
Nat'l Network: ABC *Regional Network:* Waitt Farm Net.
Arbitron Metro Market: Yankton, SD *Format:* Adult Contemp
Special Programming: Farm 5 hrs, polka one hr, Pol one hr wkly *Hrs. of News Programming:* news progmg 25 hrs wkly *No. News Employees:* 2 *TargetAudience:* General. *Adv. Rates:* 12; 12; 12; 8
Dave Lesher, Operations Dir
Curt Dykstra, General Manager
Cynthia Miller, General Sales Mgr
Dave Leonard, News Director
Troy Cowman, Public Service Director
Brady Dovonvin, Sports Director
Tammy Hauger, Traffic Manager

WNAX
11-01-1922; 570 khz AM *Hrs Open:* 24; 5 kw-D, DAN; 5 kw-N, DAN; N42 54 47 W97 18 58
73 Kercheval Avenue, Grosse Pointe Farms, MI 48236 US
(605) 665-7442, *Fax:* (605) 665-8788
www.wnax.com
wnax@wnax.com
License: Yankton, SD held by Saga Communications Inc.
Nat'l Network: CBS *Regional Network:* MNN *Nat'l Reps:* Katz Radio *Wire Services:* NOAA Weather; Knight-Ridder/Tribune Information S
Arbitron Metro Market: Sioux City, IA *Format:* News, News/Talk, 86 *Special Programming:* Relg 16 hrs, sports 10 hrs, weather 15 hrs, farm n *Hrs. of News Programming:* news progmg 23 hrs wkly *No. News Employees:* 4 *Target Audience:* 35 plus; farmers & agri-businesses
Edward Christian, President
Steve Crawford, Operations Dir
Bill Holst, General Manager
Jim Reimler, Programming Director
Erin Tycz, Promotions Manager
Jerry Oster, News Director

Tennessee

Alamo

WCTA
10-01-1983; 810 khz AM; 0.25 kw-D, DAD; N35 47 59 W89 7 20
234 S. Johnson St., Alamo, TN 38001 US
(731) 696-2781
billy@wcta810.com
License: Alamo, TN held by Billy H. Williams
Arbitron Metro Market: Jackson TN *Format:* News, Talk *Special Programming:* Relg 9 hrs wkly *Target Audience:* 30 plus.
Billy Williams, President
Dave Hacker, Chief Engineer

WWGM
08-10-1989; 93.1 mhz FM *Hrs Open:* 24; 14 kw; 443 ft.; N35 43 28 W89 3 35
6742 Highway 412, South, Bells, TN 38006 US
(731) 616-4015, *Fax:* (731) 855-1600
www.gracebroadcasting.com
lennis931@aol.com
License: Alamo, Crockett County, TN held by Grace Broadcasting Services Inc.
Group Owner: Grace Broadcasting Services Inc.; (acq 8-18-97; $800,000).
Arbitron Metro Market: Jackson, TN *Format:* Christian, Gospel *Hrs. of News Programming:* news progmg 3 hrs wkly *No. News Employees:* 1 *Target Audience:* 24-54; upscale women *Adv. Rates:* 16; 16; 16; 8
Lacy Ennis, President & CEO
John Blankenship, Operations Dir
Rodney Minyard Sr., General Manager
Geraldine Minyard, Programming Director
Phillip Chambers, Sales Representative
Ivan Hodge, Sales Representative

Alcoa

WBCR
08-25-1957; 1470 khz AM; 0.956 kw-D, ND1; 0.082 kw-N, ND1; N35 45 8 W83 55 4
Mailing Address: P.O. Box 130, Alcoa, TN 37701 US
Second Address: 118 Defoe Cir., Alcoa, TN 37701
(702) 731-5588
License: Alcoa, TN held by Blount County Broadcasting Co.
Arbitron Metro Market: Farmington NM
Carl Auel, CEO
Fred Hodges, General Manager

Algood

WATX
10-05-1981; 1600 khz AM *Hrs Open:* 6 AM-9 PM
275 Willow Avenue, Cookeville, TN 38501 US
(931) 528-6064, *Fax:* (931)520-1590
www.classiccountry1600.com
jimstapleton@jwcbroadcasting.com
License: Algood, TN held by JWC Broadcasting
Group Owner: JWC Broadcasting; acq 8-3-01).
Nat'l Network: Salem Radio Network *Nat'l Reps:* Rgnl Reps
Arbitron Metro Market: Cookeville, TN *Format:* Christian *Special Programming:* Gospel *Hrs. of News Programming:* news progmg 34 hrs wkly *No. News Employees:* 2 *Target Audience:* General. *Adv. Rates:* 12;10;10;8
Jim Stapleton, General Manager

Arlington

WEGR
03-01-1967; 102.7 mhz FM *Hrs Open:* 24; 100 kw; 942 ft.; N35 16 33 W89 46 38
200 Concord Plaza, Suite 600, San Antonio, TX 78216 US
(901) 259-1300, *Fax:* (901) 259-6456
www.rock103.com
rock103@aol.com
License: Arlington, Shelby County, TN
Group Owner: Clear Channel Communications Inc.
Nat'l Reps: Clear Channel
Arbitron Metro Market: Memphis, TN *TV Affiliate:* WPTY-TV, WLMT(TV) affils *Format:* Classic Rock *Special Programming:* Rockline, flashback, blues show *Hrs. of News Programming:* news progmg 15 hrs wkly *No. NewsEmployees:* 1 *Target Audience:* 25-54; 25-34 core audience-70% male, 30% female
Tim Spencer, Operations Dir
Felicia Moore, Promotions Manager

RADIO - U.S.

Ashland City

WQSV

07-14-1982; 790 khz AM
Mailing Address: Box 619, Ashland City, TN 37015 US
Second Address: 208 1/2 N. Main St., Ashland City, TN 37015-1316
(615) 792-6789, *Fax:* (615) 792-7795
www.wqsvam790.com
wqsvradio@bellsouth.net
License: Ashland City, TN held by Sycamore Valley Broadcasting Inc.
Nat'l Network: ABC *Regional Network:* Tenn. Radio Net.
Arbitron Metro Market: Nashville, TN *Format:* Variety/Diverse *No. News Employees:* 4 *Target Audience:* General. *Adv. Rates:* 7; 7; 7; 7
Richard Albright, CEO

Athens

WJSQ

12-01-1979; 101.7 mhz FM *Hrs Open:* 24; 7.5 kw; 528 ft.; N35 31 19 W84 27 29
2110 Oxnard Road, Athens, TN 37303 US
(423) 745-1000, *Fax:* (423) 745-2000
www.1017wlar.com
1017wlar@bellsouth.net
License: Athens, McMinn County, TN
Format: Country
Nancy Hall, CEO
Tom Barclay, Operations Dir
Bob Houghton, General Manager
Rob Maynard, Programming Director
Nancy Zintak, Promotions Manager
Susanna Capelouto, News Director
Bonnie Bean, CFO

WLAR

05-15-1946; 1450 khz AM *Hrs Open:* 24; 1 kw-U, ND1; N35 26 44 W84 36 43
P. O. Box 986, Athens, TN 37303 US
(423) 745-1000, *Fax:* (423) 745-2000
www.1017wlar.com
1017wlar@bellsouth.net
License: Athens, TN held by James C. Sliger.
Format: Country *Special Programming:* Farm 2 hrs wkly
James Sigler, General Manager

WYXI

10-05-1966; 1390 khz AM *Hrs Open:* 6 AM-7 PM; 2.5 kw-D, ND2; 0.062 kw-N, ND2; N35 26 48 W84 34 19
P. O. Box 1390, Athens, TN 37371 US
(423) 746-1390, *Fax:* (423) 744-1390
wyxi.com
wyxi@bellsouth.net
License: Athens, TN held by Cornerstone Broadcasting Inc.
Nat'l Network: ABC *Regional Reps:* Rgnl Reps
Arbitron Metro Market: Athens, TN *Format:* Talk *Special Programming:* Black one hr, relg 8 hrs wkly *Hrs. of News Programming:* news progmg 10 hrs wkly *No. News Employees:* 1 *Target Audience:* 25-64; maturemiddle class *Adv. Rates:* 8.82; 8.82; 8.82; na
Mark Lefler, President
Bob Ketchersid, Operations Dir

Atwood

WTKB-FM

01-01-1992; 93.7 mhz FM *Hrs Open:* 24; 15 kw; 325 ft.; N35 57 25 W88 41 44
P.O. Box 565, Milan, TN 38358 US
(731) 633-2327, *Fax:* (731) 633-2427
www.gracebroadcasting.com
lennis931@aol.com
License: Atwood, Carroll County, TN held by Grace Broadcasting Services Inc.
Group Owner: Grace Broadcasting Services Inc.; (acq 1-7-2005; grpsl).
Arbitron Metro Market: Atwood, TN *Format:* Christian, Gospel
Lacy Ennis, President & CEO
John Blankenship, Operations Dir
Rodney Minyard Sr., General Manager
Geraldine Minyard, Programming Director
Phillip Chambers, Sales Representative
Ivan Hodge, Sales Representative

Bartlett

WMPS

08-19-1986; 1210 khz AM *Hrs Open:* 24; 10 kw-D, DA2; 0.25 kw-N, DA2; N35 15 40 W89 49 50
6080 Mt. Moriah, Memphis, TN 38115 US
(901) 375-9324, *Fax:* (901) 375-0041
www.wmpsthepoint.com
mail@flinn.com
License: Bartlett, TN held by Arlington Broadcasting Co. Inc.
Regional Network: Tenn. Radio Net.
Arbitron Metro Market: Memphis, TN *Format:* Contemporary Hits/Top 40 *Special Programming:* Relg progmg 7 hrs wkly
Target Audience: 25 plus.
Fred Flinn, President
Shea Flinn, General Manager

WMFS-FM

05-01-1994; 92.9 mhz FM *Hrs Open:* 24; 6 kw; 328 ft; N35 10 20 W89 56 40
1835 Moriah Woods Blvd., Bldg. 1, Memphis, TN 38134

www.93xmemphis.com
License: Bartlett, Shelby County, TN held by Entercom Memphis License LLC.
Group Owner: Entercom Communications Corp.; (acq 11-30-2007; grpsl)
Nat'l Reps: Interep *Wire Services:* Metro Weather Servic
Population Served: 1,000,000 *Arbitron Metro Market:* Memphis, TN *Hrs. of News Programming:* News progmg one hr wkly
Target Audience: 18-49; adults
Terry Wood, Operations Dir
Kory Myers, General Sales Mgr
Rob Cressman, Programming Director
Scott Speropoulas, National Sales Manager

*WKVF

11-01-1994; 94.9 mhz FM *Hrs Open:* 24; 1.6 kw; 948 ft.; N35 9 16 W89 49 20
5141 Fire Tower Road, Franklin, TN 37064 US
(916) 251-1600, *Fax:* (916) 251-1650
www.klove.com
klove@klove.com
License: Bartlett, Marshall County, TN held by Educational Media Foundation.
Group Owner: EMF Broadcasting; (acq 2-1-00; $1.4 million).
Nat'l Network: K-Love
Arbitron Metro Market: Bartlett, TN *Format:* Christian *No. News Employees:* 3 *Target Audience:* 25-44; Judeo Christian, female
Mike Novak, President
Chip Bailey, Operations Dir
Eric Allen, General Sales Mgr
David Pierce, Programming Director
Tracy Butler, News Director
Sam Wallington, Engineering Dir
Scott Smith, Music Director
Richard Hunt, NewsReporter
Marya Morgan, News Reporter

Baxter

WBXE

10-01-1995; 93.7 mhz FM *Hrs Open:* 24; 6.1 kw; 659 ft.; N36 11 3 W85 24 40
259 S. Willow Avenue, Cookeville, TN 38501 US
(931) 528-6064, *Fax:* (931) 520-1590
www.rock937online.com
hoseppy@stonecomradio.com
License: Baxter, Putnam County, TN held by JWC Broadcasting
Group Owner: JWC Broadcasting; acq 8-29-01).
Nat'l Network: Westwood One *Nat'l Reps:* Rgnl Reps
Arbitron Metro Market: Cookeville, TN *No. News Employees:* 1
Target Audience: 18-45; Men 25 plus *Adv. Rates:* 32; 30; 28; 24
Jim Stapleton, General Manager

Belle Meade

WLVU

01-01-2008; 97.1 mhz FM; 44.37 kw; 517 ft.; N36 17 50 W86 45 11 *Rebroadcasts:* Rebroadcasts KLVR(FM) Middletown, CA 100%
3149 Gynnwood Drive, Nahshville, TN 37207 US
(800) 877-5600, *Fax:* (916) 251-1650
www.klove.com
License: Belle Meade, Dauphin County, TN held by Educational Media Foundation.
Group Owner: EMF Broadcasting; (acq 7-23-2007; grpsl)
Nat'l Network: K-Love
Arbitron Metro Market: Torrington, WY *Format:* Christian
Mike Novak, President

Benton

WBIN

05-18-1977; 1540 khz AM *Hrs Open:* Sunrise-sunset
601 Hidden Forrest Drive, Chattanooga, TN 37421 US
(615) 469-5122
www.lifetalk.net/
office@lifetalk.net
License: Benton, TN held by John A. Sines and L. Jane Sines, JTWROS
Regional Network: ABN Radio
Arbitron Metro Market: Collegedale, TN *Format:* Religious *Target Audience:* All ages; Includes baby boomers and seniors
John Geli, Operations Dir
Chris Harding, General Manager
John Geli, Programming Director
Deloris Trujillo, HR Director
Paul Willis, IT Director
Seth Wade, Webmaster

WSAA

11-01-1996; 93.1 mhz FM; 3.5 kw; 437 ft.; N35 9 54 W84 51 13
601 Hidden Forrest Drive, Chattanooga, TN 37421 US
(423) 485-8987, *Fax:* (423) 485-8946
http://www.air1.com/
License: Benton, Polk County, TN held by LB Radio of Chattanooga, LLC
TV Affiliate: Relg *Format:* Sports, Talk *No. News Employees:* 25-54. *Target Audience:* Darrell Chambliss *Adv. Rates:* 35; 20; 25; 15
Chairman, Mike Novak

*WTSE

01-01-2005; 91.1 mhz FM; 8.5 kw vert; 466 ft.; N35 19 25 W84 17 54
321 Freeman Circle, Norcross, GA 30071 US
(208) 733-3551, *Fax:* (208) 734-0674
www.edgewaterbroadcasting.com
License: Benton, Polk County, TN held by Radio Assist Ministry Inc.
Arbitron Metro Market: Benton, TN
Ben Mccarron, COO
Clark Parrish, President
Robert L. Jackson, Head of Programming & Operations
Jim Long, General Manager
Clark Parrish, Engineering Dir
Steve Atkin, Executive Director
Diana Atkin, Vice President
EarlWilliamson, Secretary / Treasurer
John Devine, Director
Dennis Clounch, Director

Berry Hill

WVOL

12-01-1951; 1470 khz AM *Hrs Open:* 24; 5 kw-D, DA2; 1 kw-N, DA2; N36 12 1 W86 46 47
Suite 901, 50 Music Sq. W., Nashville, TN 37203 US
(615) 226-9510, *Fax:* (615) 226-0709
www.wvol1470.com
wvol1470@aol.com
License: Berry Hill, TN held by Heidelberg Broadcasting LLC.
Arbitron Metro Market: Nashville, TN *Format:* Blues, Oldies
Special Programming: Gospel 6 hrs wkly *Target Audience:* 25-54; relg
John Heidelberg, Chairman
Roderick Heidelberg, Operations Dir
Betty Fykes, News Director
Watt Harriston, Chief Engineer

Blountville

WXSM

09-20-1967; 640 khz AM *Hrs Open:* 24; 10 kw-D, DAN; 0.81 kw-N, DAN; N36 31 19 W82 25 25
640 Radio Way, Blountville, TN 37617 US
(423) 477-1000, *Fax:* (423) 477-4747
www.640wxsm.com
SportsMonster@640wxsm.com
License: Blountville, TN
Group Owner: Cumulus Media Inc.; (acq 5-30-2000; grpsl)
Nat'l Network: ESPN Radio *Nat'l Reps:* Dora-Clayton
Arbitron Metro Market: Johnson City-Kingsport-Bristol, TN-VA
Format: Sports
Don Raines, General Manager
Debbie Caso, General Sales Mgr
Bill Meade, Programming Director
Al LeFevre, Chief Engineer
Paul Overbay, General Sales Manager

Bluff City

WFHG-FM

12-10-1966; 92.9 mhz FM *Hrs Open:* 24; 7.6 kw; 1240 ft.; N36 16 10 W82 20 17

Mailing Address: P.O. Box 1067, Abingdon, VA 24212 US
Second Address: Bristol Broadcasting Co Inc, 901 E Valley Dr, Bristol, VA 24201
(858) 277-4991, *Fax:* (858) 277-1365
www.horizonradio.org
kwoods@horizonsd.org
License: Bluff City, Washington County, TN held by Bristol Broadcasting Co. Inc.
Group Owner: Bristol Broadcasting Co. Inc.; acq 11-30-99; with co-located AM).
Arbitron Metro Market: Excelsior Springs MO *Format:* Christian
Mike MacIntosh, President

Bolivar

WBOL
10-19-1962; 1560 khz AM; 0.25 kw-D, NDD; N35 15 30 W88 58 50
P.O. Box 191, Bolivar, TN 38008 US
(731) 658-3633(731) 658-3690, *Fax:* (731) 658-3408
www.wbolam1560.com
wojg@aeneas.net
License: Bolivar, TN held by Shaw's Broadcasting Co.
Format: Blues, Jazz, 64
Johnny Shaw, General Manager
Dewayne Dickerson, General Sales Mgr
Opal Shaw, Programming Director

WMOD
01-27-1975; 96.7 mhz FM *Hrs Open:* 24; 3 kw; 299 ft.; N35 15 0 W88 53 28
PO Box 438, Bolivar, TN 38008 US
(731) 658-4320, *Fax:* (731) 658-7328
http://www.wmodradio.com
darrell@wmodradio.com
License: Bolivar, Hardeman County, TN held by WMOD Inc.
Nat'l Network: ABC *Regional Network:* Tenn. Radio Net.
Regional Reps: Midsouth.
Arbitron Metro Market: Bolivar, TN *Format:* Country *Hrs. of News Programming:* News progmg 7 hrs wkly *Target Audience:* 25-55; males & females *Adv. Rates:* 10; 9; 10; 7
D. Richard Teubner, President
Gail Teubner, Operations Dir

WOJG
06-01-1992; 94.7 mhz FM; 6 kw; 328 ft.; N35 16 39 W88 55 41
P. O. Box 191, Bolivar, TN 38008 US
731-658-3690, *Fax:* (731) 658-3408
http://www.wojg.com/
wojg@aeneas.net
License: Bolivar, Hardeman County, TN held by Johnny W. Shaw & Opal J. Shaw.
TV Affiliate: Black
CEO, CEO/COO
Operations Manager, Tracy Shaw
General Manager, General Manager

Brentwood

WNSR
09-04-1985; 560 khz AM
4314 Cherry Court, ', Evansville, IN 47714 US
(615) 844-1039, *Fax:* (615) 777-2284
www.wnsr.com
info@wnsr.com
License: Brentwood, TN held by Southern Wabash Communications Middle Tennessee Inc.
Group Owner: Southern Wabash Communications Corp.; (acq 11-25-97; $245,000).
Arbitron Metro Market: Nashville, TN *Format:* Sports *Target Audience:* 18-54; men
Ted Johnson, General Manager

Bristol

WIGN
08-18-1962; 1550 khz AM *Hrs Open:* 24 hours; omnidirectional
Mailing Address: P.O. Box 68, Bristol, TN 37621 US
Second Address: 101 Lee Street, Suite A, Bristol, VA 24201
(225) 768-3224
www.jsm.org
License: Bristol, TN held by Sunshine Broadcasters Inc.
Nat'l Network: CBS Radio; ABC
Arbitron Metro Market: Tucson AZ *Format:* Christian *Adv. Rates:* 16.00; 25:00;
David Whitelaw, COO

*WHCB
08-10-1984; 91.5 mhz FM *Hrs Open:* 24; 1.5 kw; 2346 ft.; N36 26 3 W82 8 3
Mailing Address: P.O. Box 2061, Bristol, TN 37621 US
Second Address: 340 Edgemont Ave., Suite 100, Bristol, TN 37620
(423) 878-6279, *Fax:* (423) 878-6520
www.whcbradio.org
whcb@aecc.org
License: Bristol, Sullivan County, TN held by Appalachian Educational Communication Corp.
Nat'l Network: Moody; Salem Radio Network
Arbitron Metro Market: Johnson City-Kingsport-Bristol, TN-VA
Format: Christian, Talk *Special Programming:* Class one hr, Appalachian culture 2 hrs, farm one *Hrs. of News Programming:* news progmg 14 hrs wkly *No.News Employees:* 1 *Target Audience:* General.
Kenneth Hill, President
Mike Cox, Operations Dir

WOPI
06-15-1929; 1490 khz AM *Hrs Open:* 24; 1 kw-U; N36 35 45 W82 09 42 *Rebroadcasts:* WKPT(AM) 85%
Mailing Address: 222 Commerce St., Kingsport, TN 37662
Second Address: 288 Delaney St., Bristol, TN 37620
(423) 764-5131, *Fax:* (423) 246-6261,(423) 247-9836
www.wopi.com
davidw@wtfm.com
License: Bristol, Sullivan County, TN held by Holston Valley Broadcasting Corp.
Group Owner: Glenwood Communications Corp.; (acq 5-16-96; $140,000;
Nat'l Network: ABC *Nat'l Reps:* Eastman Radio *Wire Services:* AP
Population Served: 200,000 *Arbitron Metro Market:* Johnson City-Kingsport-Bristol, TN-VA *Special Programming:* Weekend Blugrass/Classic Country *No. News Employees:* 2 *Target Audience:* 35 plus.
George DeVault, President
David Widener, EVP/General Manager
Scott Onks, Programming Director
Emily Pridemore, Traffic/Office Manager
Bette Lawson, VP/Treasurer

Brownsville

WNWS
10-14-1963; 1520 khz AM; 0.25 kw-D, NDD; N35 36 30 W89 14 40
PO Box 198, Brownsville, TN 38012 US
(731) 772-3700, *Fax:* (731) 423-8304
License: Brownsville, TN held by The Wireless Group Inc.
Group Owner: The Wireless Group Inc.; acq 4-80; $320,000 with co-located FM;
Nat'l Network: ABC
TV Affiliate: Sp

WTBG
11-09-1965; 95.3 mhz FM *Hrs Open:* 24; 5 kw; 151 ft.; N35 36 30 W89 14 40 *Rebroadcasts:* Rebroadcasts WNWS-FM Jackson 30%
42 South Washington St, Brownsville, TN 38012 US
(901) 772-3700
www.brownsvilleradio.com
License: Brownsville, Haywood County, TN held by The Wireless Group Inc.
Format: Country, News, 62, Talk *No. News Employees:* 1 *Target Audience:* 25-54.
Carlton Veirs, General Manager

Bulls Gap

WBGQ
01-01-2001; 100.7 mhz FM *Hrs Open:* 24; 0.33 kw; 1260 ft.; N36 22 48 W83 10 47
3125 Cherokee Dr., Morristown, TN 37814 US
(423) 235-4640
www.wbgqfm.com/
radiomanone@hotmail.com
License: Bulls Gap, Hawkins County, TN held by Cherokee Broadcasting
Nat'l Network: CNN Radio
Arbitron Metro Market: Morristown, TN *Format:* Adult Contemp
Target Audience: 18-54; female 65% & male 35%
Clark Quillen, CEO
David Quillen, Operations Dir

Calhoun

WCLE-FM
08-01-1993; 104.1 mhz FM *Hrs Open:* 24; 2.3 kw; 522 ft.; N35 15 59 W84 50 23
Mailing Address: 1311 Hamerhill Road, Athens, TN 37303 US
Second Address: 1860 Executive Park, Suite E, Cleveland, TN 37312
(423) 472-6700, *Fax:* (423) 476-4686
www.mix104.info
steve@mymix1041.com
License: Calhoun, McMinn County, TN held by Hartline LLC
Arbitron Metro Market: Cleveland, TN *Format:* Adult Contemp
No. News Employees: 1 *Target Audience:* 25-54.
Steve Hartline, General Manager

Camden

WFWL
09-18-1956; 1220 khz AM *Hrs Open:* 24; 0.25 kw-D, ND1; 0.14 kw-N, ND1; N36 3 10 W88 5 15
117 Vicksburg Avenue, Camden, TN 38320 US
(731) 584-7570, *Fax:* (731) 584-7553
wfwlwrjb@bellsouth.net
License: Camden, TN held by Community Broadcasting Services Inc.
Regional Network: Tenn. Radio Net. *Nat'l Reps:* Keystone (unwired net) *Regional Reps:* Midsouth.
Format: Country *Special Programming:* Gospel 8 hrs wkly
Target Audience: 25-49; adult *Adv. Rates:* 6.95, 6:95, 6.95, 6:65
Stan Medlin, President
Ron Lane, General Manager
Jim Hart, Programming Director
Larry Nunnery, Engineering Dir
Bobby Melton, Disc Jockey
Reid Bell, Disc Jockey

WRJB
06-20-1976; 95.9 mhz FM *Hrs Open:* 24; 6 kw; 285 ft.; N36 3 26 W88 6 14
117 Vicksburg Avenue, Camden, TN 38320 US
(731) 584-7570,(731) 584-4444, *Fax:* (731) 584-7553
wfwlwrjb@bellsouth.net
License: Camden, Benton County, TN held by Community Broadcasting Services Inc.
Format: Adult Contemp *Hrs. of News Programming:* News progmg 4 hrs wkly *Target Audience:* 20-50.
Stan Medlin, CFO
Charles Ennis, President
Jim Hart, Programming Director
Vickie Dodson, News Director
Larry Nannery, Engineering Dir

Carthage

WRKM
06-20-1959; 1350 khz AM *Hrs Open:* 12; 1 kw-D, ND1; 0.09 kw-N, ND1; N36 14 42 W85 56 44
Mailing Address: Box 179, Carthage, TN 37030 US
Second Address: 104 Z Country Ln., Carthage, TN 37030
(615) 735-1350, *Fax:* (615) 735-0381
www.wucz-wrkm.com
am1350@smithcounty.com
License: Carthage, TN held by Wood Broadcasting Inc.
Nat'l Network: Sporting News Radio Network
Format: Sports *Hrs. of News Programming:* news progmg 2 hrs wkly *No. News Employees:* 1 *Target Audience:* 35 plus. *Adv. Rates:* 8; 6:50; 6:50; na
Dennis Banka, President
John Wood, General Manager
Tracy Banka, News Director
Carl Campbell, Chief Engineer

WUCZ
07-18-1975; 104.1 mhz FM *Hrs Open:* 24; 4.9 kw; 361 ft.; N36 18 43 W85 57 8
Mailing Address: Box 179, Carthage, TN 37030 US
Second Address: 104 Z Country Ln., Carthage, TN 37030
(615) 735-1350, *Fax:* (615) 735-0381
www.1041theranch.net
info@1041theranch.net
License: Carthage, Smith County, TN
Nat'l Network: Westwood One
Arbitron Metro Market: Carthage, TN *Format:* Country *Hrs. of News Programming:* news progmg 2 hrs wkly *No. News Employees:* 1 *Target Audience:* 18-35. *Adv. Rates:* 14.75; 14.75; 14.75; 14.75
John Wood, Station Manager
Tracy Banka, News Director
Dennis Banka, Radio Jockey
Jim West, Sports/Sales

Celina

WVFB
08-01-1994; 101.5 mhz FM *Hrs Open:* 6AM - 11PM; 6 kw; 328 ft.; N36 33 28 W85 36 15
352 Radio Station Road, Tompkinsville, KY 42167 US
(270) 487-6119, *Fax:* (270) 487-8462
License: Celina, Clay County, TN held by Whittimore Enterprises

Nat'l Network: USA *Nat'l Reps:* Rgnl Reps
Arbitron Metro Market: Celina, TN *Format:* Country *Hrs. of News Programming:* news progmg 2 hrs wkly *No. News Employees:* 2 *Target Audience:* Male 18-55. *Adv. Rates:* 35; 28; 32; 28
Rebecca Brown, General Manager

Centerville

WNKX-FM
05-01-1974; 96.7 mhz FM *Hrs Open:* 24; 6 kw; 299 ft.; N35 49 39 W87 34 2
150 Highway 50 East, Centerville, TN 37033 US
(931) 729-5191, *Fax:* (931) 729-5467
www.countrykix96.com
kix96fm@bellsouth.net
License: Centerville, Hickman County, TN held by Hickman County Broadcasting Co. Inc.
Regional Network: Tenn. Radio Net. *Nat'l Reps:* Dora-Clayton
Regional Reps: Midsouth
Arbitron Metro Market: Nashville, TN *Format:* Country *Hrs. of News Programming:* news progmg 30 hrs wkly *No. News Employees:* 3 *Target Audience:* 6-80. *Adv. Rates:* Same as AM
Mickey Bunn, Operations Dir
Steve Turner, Station Manager
Mickey Bunn, Programming Director
Demetria Smith, Disc Jockey
Brent Atkinson, Disc Jockey
Kay Atkinson, Disc Jockey

Chattanooga

WDEF
12-31-1940; 1370 khz AM *Hrs Open:* 24
Mailing Address: 3300 Broad Street, Chattanooga, TN 37408 US
Second Address: 2615 S. Broad St., Chattanooga, TN 37408
(423) 321-6200, *Fax:* (423) 321-6270
www.foxsportschattanooga.com
dhoward@wdefradio.com
License: Chattanooga, TN held by Bahakel Communications
Group Owner: Bahakel Communications
Nat'l Network: Fox Sports
Arbitron Metro Market: Chattanooga, TN *Format:* Sports *No. News Employees* 1 *Target Audience:* 25-64; males
Bernie Barker, General Manager
Danny Howard, Station Manager
Jeff Fontana, General Sales Mgr

WDEF-FM
09-15-1964; 92.3 mhz FM *Hrs Open:* 24; 97 kw; 1181 ft.; N35 8 6 W85 19 25
Mailing Address: Box 11008, Chattanooga, TN 37401 US
Second Address: 2615 Broad St., Chattanooga, TN 37408
(423) 321-6200, *Fax:* (423) 321-6270
www.sunny923.com
info@sunny923.com
License: Chattanooga, Hamilton County, TN held by Bahakel Communications
Group Owner: Bahakel Communications; acq 1996; grpsl)
Nat'l Network: CBS
Arbitron Metro Market: Chattanooga, TN *Format:* Adult Contemp *Hrs. of News Programming:* news progmg 5 hrs wkly *No. News Employees:* 1 *Target Audience:* 25-54; upscale adults *Adv. Rates:* 150; 100; 115; 85
Bernie Barker, General Manager
Danny Howard, Station Manager
Jeff Fontana, General Sales Mgr

WDOD-FM
02-01-1960; 96.5 mhz FM; 100 kw horiz, 88 kw vert; 1102 ft.; N35 9 41 W85 19 5
P.O. Box 4232, Chattanooga, TN 37405 US
(423) 321-6200, *Fax:* (423) 321-6270
www.965themountain.com
dhoward@wdefradio.com
License: Chattanooga, Hamilton County, TN
Arbitron Metro Market: Chattanooga, TN *Format:* Contemporary Hits/Top 40 *Target Audience:* 18-54; upscale, contemp adults
Bernie Barker, General Manager
Danny Howard, Station Manager
Jeff Fontana, General Sales Mgr

*WYBK(FM)
06-01-1968; 89.7 mhz FM *Hrs Open:* 24; 100 kw; 205 ft; N35 10 17 W85 18 58
1815 Union Ave., Chattanooga, TN 37404
(423) 493-4382(423) 493-4383, *Fax:* (423) 493-4526
www.wdyn.com
wdyn@wdyn.com
License: Chattanooga, Hamilton County, TN held by Tennessee Temple University.
Nat'l Network: USA
Population Served: 170,136 *Arbitron Metro Market:* Chattanooga, TN *Format:* Religious *Hrs. of News Programming:* News progmg 2 hrs wkly *No. News Employees:* 1 *Target Audience:* General; conservativeChristians
Tommy Sneed, General Manager

WGOW
01-01-1936; 1150 khz AM; 5 kw-D, DAN; 1 kw-N, DAN; N35 4 5 W85 20 4
Mailing Address: P. O. Box 11202, Chattanooga, TN 37401 US
Second Address: 821 Pineville Rd., Chattanooga, TN 37405
(423) 756-6141, *Fax:* (423) 266-3629
www.wgow.com
info@wgow.com
License: Chattanooga, TN
Group Owner: Cumulus Media Inc.; (acq 5-30-00; grpsl).
Nat'l Reps: Christal
Arbitron Metro Market: Chattanooga, TN *Format:* News, News/Talk, 86
Dan Brown, President
Bill Lockhart, Programming Director

WJOC
07-04-1948; 1490 khz AM; 1 kw-U, ND1; N35 3 7 W85 16 24
722 South Germantown Rd, Chattanooga, TN 37412 US
(706) 861-0800, *Fax:* (706) 861-2299
www.am1490.net
WJOC1490@aol.com
License: Chattanooga, TN held by Sara Margarett Fryar.
Nat'l Network: USA
Arbitron Metro Market: Chattanooga, TN *Format:* Christian, Gospel
Trey Searcy, General Manager

WLMR
01-01-1961; 1450 khz AM *Hrs Open:* 24; 1 kw-U, ND1; N35 2 54 W85 16 26
P. O. Box 444, Spartanburg, SC 29304 US
(423) 624-4200, *Fax:* (423) 624-4722
www.wilkinsradio.com
wlmr@wilkinsradio.com
License: Chattanooga, TN held by Grace Media Inc.
Group Owner: Wilkins Communications Network Inc.
Nat'l Network: USA
Arbitron Metro Market: Chattanooga, TN *Format:* Christian, Talk *Target Audience:* 35 plus. *Adv. Rates:* 30; 30; 30; 30
Bob Wilkins, President
Mitchell Mathis, Operations Dir
John M. Burks, Station Manager
Charlie Edwards, Engineering Dir
LuAnn Wilkins, Executive Vice President
Greg Garrett, Operations Manager

*WMBW
08-01-1969; 88.9 mhz FM *Hrs Open:* 24; 98 kw; 1509 ft.; N34 57 43 W85 22 40 *Rebroadcasts:* WMKW 89.3FM;
Mailing Address: 820 N. Lasalle Drive, Chicago, IL 60610 US
Second Address: 1920 E. 24th St. PL., Chattanooga, TN 37404
(423) 629-8900, *Fax:* (423) 629-0021
www.moodyradiosouth.fm
wmbw@moody.edu
License: Chattanooga, Hamilton County, TN held by Moody Bible Institute of Chicago.
Group Owner: The Moody Bible Institute of Chicago; acq 5-18-73)
Nat'l Network: Moody
Arbitron Metro Market: Chattanooga, TN *Format:* Religious
Special Programming: Black one hr wkly *Hrs. of News Programming:* News progmg 12 hrs wkly *Target Audience:* 25-54.
Dr. Paul Nyquist, President
Leighton LeBoeuf, General Manager
Jim Young, News Director
David Morais, Chief Engineer
Paul Martin, Music Director
Andy Napier, Promotions Director

WNOO
06-01-1951; 1260 khz AM *Hrs Open:* 24
Box 5156, 1108 Hendricks, Chattanooga, TN 37406 US
(423) 698-8617, *Fax:* (423) 698-8796
www.wnooradio.com
wnoo@epbinternet.com
License: Chattanooga, TN held by Clear Media LLC
Nat'l Network: American Urban
Arbitron Metro Market: Chattanooga, TN *Format:* Gospel, Talk
No. News Employees: 8 *Target Audience:* 25-54; mature Black adults & children *Adv. Rates:* 25; 15; 20; 10
Lee Clear, President

WSKZ
11-01-1960; 106.5 mhz FM; 100 kw; 1079 ft.; N35 9 42 W85 19 6
Mailing Address: P.O. Box 8, Bloomington, IL 61702 US
Second Address: 821 Pineville Rd., Chattanooga, TN 37405
(423) 756-6141, *Fax:* (423) 266-3629
www.wskz.com
License: Chattanooga, Hamilton County, TN
Arbitron Metro Market: Chattanooga, TN *Format:* Triple A

*WUTC
03-01-1980; 88.1 mhz FM *Hrs Open:* 24; 30 kw; 889 ft; N35 12 28 W85 16 46
615 McCallie Ave., Chattanooga, TN 37403
(423) 425-4756, *Fax:* (423) 425-2379
www.wutc.org
License: Chattanooga, Hamilton County, TN held by Board of Trustees of University of Tennessee.
Nat'l Network: NPR; PRI; AP Radio
Population Served: 460,000 *Arbitron Metro Market:* Chattanooga, TN *Target Audience:* General.
John McCormack, General Manager
Ken Dryden, General Sales Mgr
Mark Colbert, Programming Director

Church Hill

WMCH
05-08-1954; 1260 khz AM *Hrs Open:* 24 hours; 1 kw-D, ND2; 0.021 kw-N, ND2; N36 31 15 W82 44 54
PO Box 128, Church Hill, TN 37642 US
(423) 357-5601, *Fax:* (423) 343-5173
www.wmchradio.com
wmchradio@yahoo.com
License: Church Hill, TN held by Media Link, Incorporated
Nat'l Network: USA
Arbitron Metro Market: Johnson City, TN *Format:* Religious, Talk
No. News Employees: 5 *Target Audience:* 25-54; adult audience
Ron W Gordon, General Manager

Clarksville

*WAPX-FM
10-01-1984; 91.9 mhz FM *Hrs Open:* 24; 6 kw; 194 ft.; N36 32 13 W87 21 26
Box 4627, Clarksville, TN 37044 US
(931) 221-7378, *Fax:* (931) 221-7265
www.apsu.edu/comm_thea/student_activities/wapxfm.htm
License: Clarksville, Montgomery County, TN held by Austin Peay State University.
Arbitron Metro Market: Clarksville, TN *Format:* Variety/Diverse
Special Programming: Black 6 hrs, jazz 6 hrs wkly *Hrs. of News Programming:* News progmg 8 hrs wkly *Target Audience:* 18-34; college students &young professionals
Dr. David Michael von Palko, General Manager

WKFN
11-12-1954; 540 khz AM *Hrs Open:* 24
P.O. Box 2249, Clarksville, TN 37042 US
(865) 675-4105, *Fax:* (865) 675-4859
License: Clarksville, TN held by Saga Communications of Tuckessee L.L.C.
Group Owner: Saga Communications Inc.; (acq 2-1-2001; grpsl)
Arbitron Metro Market: Clarksville, TN *Format:* Sports, Talk *Hrs. of News Programming:* news progmg 36 hrs wkly *No. News Employees:* 2 *Target Audience:* 25-54.
Scott Chase, Operations Dir
Katie Gambill, General Manager

WJZM
10-19-1941; 1400 khz AM *Hrs Open:* 24; 1 kw-U, ND1; N36 30 57 W87 20 57
Mailing Address: PO Box 648, Clarksville, TN 37041 US
Second Address: 925 Martin St., Clarksville, TN 37040
(931) 645-6414, *Fax:* (931) 551-8432
www.wjzm.com
14jzm@wjzm.com
License: Clarksville, TN held by Cumberland Radio Partners Inc.
Format: News, News/Talk, 84, Talk *Special Programming:* Relg
Hrs. of News Programming: News progmg 8 hrs wkly *Target Audience:* 25-60; blue collar, working women, businessmen
John Bastin, Operations Dir
Hank Bonecutter, General Manager
Angie Brown, Programming Director
Ivan Davis, Chief Engineer
Ken Baxter, Disc Jockey
Sharon Fewless, Disc Jockey
Jimmy Baird, Disc Jockey
Jeff Lyon, Disc Jockey

*WAYQ
10-22-2003; 88.3 mhz FM *Hrs Open:* 24; 14 kw; 745 ft.; N36 17 36 W87 18 20
P O Box 887, Brentwood, TN 37024 US

(888) 339-2936, *Fax:* (615) 261-3967
www.waym.wayfm.com
supportservices@wayfm.com
License: Clarksville, Montgomery County, TN held by WAY-FM Media Group Inc.
Group Owner: WAY-FM Media Group Inc.
Arbitron Metro Market: Franklin, TN *Format:* Christian
Teresa White, General Sales Mgr
Jeff Brown, Programming Director
Bob Augsburg, Founder

Cleveland

WBAC
06-18-1945; 1340 khz AM *Hrs Open:* 24; 1 kw-U, ND1; N35 9 54 W84 51 13
409 Chestnut Street, Suite a 154, Chattanooga, TN 37402 US
(508) 548-9600, *Fax:* (508) 548-5517
www.capeandislands.org
cainan@wgbh.org
License: Cleveland, TN held by East Tennessee Radio Group III L.P.
Group Owner: East Tennessee Radio Group III L.P.; (acq 5-30-2008; grpsl)
Nat'l Network: ABC *Regional Network:* Tenn. Radio Net. *Nat'l Reps:* D & R Radio
Arbitron Metro Market: Brewster MA *Format:* News, News/Talk, 86 *Adv. Rates:* 16; 14; 14; 7
John Voci, Station Manager

WCLE
05-02-1957; 1570 khz AM; 5 kw-D, ND1; 0.084 kw-N, ND1; N35 10 55 W84 50 55
1311 Hamerhill Road, Athens, TN 37303 US
(423) 472-6700, *Fax:* (423) 476-4686
www.mix104.info
steve@mymix1041.com
License: Cleveland, TN held by Hartline LLC
Arbitron Metro Market: Cleveland, TN *Format:* News, News/Talk, 86 *Target Audience:* 25-54. *Adv. Rates:* 14; 12; 12; 8.50
Steve Hartline Jr., President
Steve Hartline, General Manager

WUSY
08-01-1961; 100.7 mhz FM *Hrs Open:* 24; 100 kw; 1191 ft.; N35 12 26 W85 17 10
111 East Kilborn Avenue, Suite 2700, Milwaukee, WI 53202 US
(423) 892-3333, *Fax:* (423) 899-7224
www.us101country.com
jcruze@clearchannel.com
License: Cleveland, Bradley County, TN held by Capstar TX L.P.
Group Owner: Clear Channel Communications Inc.; (acq 8-7-2000; grpsl)
Arbitron Metro Market: Chattanooga, TN *Format:* Country
Gator Harrison, Operations Dir
Sammy George, General Manager
Jared Stehney, General Sales Mgr
Jay Cruze, Programming Director
Ed Buice, News Director
Andre Johnson, Chief Engineer
Daniel Wyatt, Webite

Clifton

WLVS-FM
01-01-2002; 106.5 mhz FM; 3.8 kw; 416 ft.; N35 28 41 W88 6 36
Rebroadcasts: Rebroadcasts WXFL(FM) Florence 100%
C/O Fletcher, Heald Plc, 1300 N. 17th St, 11th Fl, Arlington, VA 22209 US
(256) 764-8121, *Fax:* (256) 764-8169
www.kix96country.com
License: Clifton, Wayne County, TN held by Gold Coast Broadcasting Co.
Arbitron Metro Market: Florence, AL *Format:* Country
Nick Martin, General Manager
Rocky Reich, General Sales Mgr
Fletch Brown, Programming Director
Greg Pace, Chief Engineer

Clinton

*WDVX
11-01-1997; 89.9 mhz FM; 0.2 kw vert; 1962 ft.; N36 11 53 W84 13 51
P O Box 27568, Knoxville, TN 37927 US
(865) 544-1029, *Fax:* (865) 494-3299
www.wdvx.com
studio@wdvx.com
License: Clinton, Anderson County, TN held by Cumberland Communities Communications Corp.
Arbitron Metro Market: Clinton, TN *Format:* Triple A
Tony Lawson, General Manager

*WYFC
07-04-1966; 95.3 mhz FM *Hrs Open:* 24; 1.45 kw; 669 ft.; N36 4 21 W84 1 18
8030 Arrowridge Blvd, Charlotte, NC 28273 US
(704) 523-5555, *Fax:* (704) 522-1967
www.bbnradio.com
bbn@bbnradio.org
License: Clinton, Anderson County, TN held by Bible Broadcasting Network Inc.
Group Owner: Bible Broadcasting Network; acq 8-18-89; $450,000;
Arbitron Metro Market: Clinton, TN *Format:* Christian
Lowell Davey, President
Hank Crull, General Manager
Grant Bishop, Station Manager

WYSH
11-01-1960; 1380 khz AM *Hrs Open:* 24; 1 kw-D, DAN; 0.08 kw-N, DAN; N36 6 48 W84 8 30
Mailing Address: Box 329, Clinton, TN 37716 US
Second Address: 111 Hillcrest Dr., Clinton, TN 37716
(865) 457-1380, *Fax:* (865) 457-4440
www.wyshradio.com
ron@merle.com
License: Clinton, TN held by Clinton Broadcasters Inc.
Nat'l Network: AP Radio *Regional Network:* Tenn. Radio Net.
Nat'l Reps: Keystone (unwired net)
Arbitron Metro Market: Knoxville, TN *Format:* Country *Special Programming:* Relg 15 hrs wkly *Hrs. of News Programming:* news progmg 15 hrs wkly *No. News Employees:* 1 *Target Audience:* 25-54; families, bluecollar to upper income *Adv. Rates:* 12; 10; 12; 8
Ronald Meredith Jr., President

Coalmont

WSGM
06-21-1994; 104.7 mhz FM *Hrs Open:* 6 AM-10 PM; 1 kw; 548 ft.; N35 16 44 W85 44 2
Hcr 77, Box 123, Coalmont, TN 37313 US
(931) 592-7777, *Fax:* (931) 592-7778
wsgmfm@hotmail.com,wamo@wamo.com
License: Coalmont, Grundy County, TN held by Cumberland Communication Corp.
Format: Religious *Hrs. of News Programming:* News progmg 30 hrs wkly *Target Audience:* General; interested in community affrs
Dr. Byron Harbolt, President
Sam Harbolt, Operations Dir
Rocky Ruehling, Programming Director
Tom Wiseman, Chief Engineer
Jim McKnight, Disc Jockey
Gina Brady, Disc Jockey
Rhonda Pickett, Disc Jockey
Geniveve Harbolt, VicePresident

Collegedale

*WSMC-FM
11-01-1961; 90.5 mhz FM; 100 kw; 1030 ft.; N35 15 20 W85 13 34
P. O. Box 870, Collegedale, TN 37315 US
(423) 236-2905, *Fax:* (423) 236-1905
www.wsmc.org
License: Collegedale, Hamilton County, TN held by Southern Adventist University.
Nat'l Network: PRI; NPR
Format: News *Target Audience:* 25-54.
Gordon Bietz, President
Myrna Ott, Operations Dir
David Brooks, General Manager

Collierville

WCRV
10-01-1966; 640 khz AM *Hrs Open:* 24; 50 kw-D, DAN; 0.48 kw-N, DAN; N34 59 35 W89 53 58
10550 Barkley, Ste 108, Overland Park, KS 66212 US
(913)642-7770, *Fax:* (913)642-1319
www.bottradionetwork.com
comments@bottradionetwork.com
License: Collierville, TN held by Bott Broadcasting.
Group Owner: Bott Radio Network
Nat'l Network: USA *Nat'l Reps:* Salem
Arbitron Metro Market: Memphis, TN *Format:* Christian *Target Audience:* 25-54; family oriented
Richard Bott, President
Richard Bott II, Operations Dir
Todd Payne, General Manager
Byron Tyler, Programming Director
Shirley Gossett, Operations Manager

Collinwood

WMSR-FM
07-01-1991; 94.9 mhz FM *Hrs Open:* 24; 7.7 kw; 594 ft.; N35 1 46 W87 47 7
122 West Tombigbee, Florence, AL 35630 US
(256) 383-2525, *Fax:* (256) 383-4450
www.star94fm.net
thechief@star94.net
License: Collinwood, Wayne County, TN held by Urban Radio Licenses LLC
Nat'l Network: Fox News Radio *Nat'l Reps:* Katz Radio
Arbitron Metro Market: Florence, AL *Format:* Contemporary Hits/Top 40 *Hrs. of News Programming:* News progmg 8 hrs wkly *Target Audience:* 18-49; primary women, secondary adults
Adv. Rates: 35; 30; 35; 30
Kevin Wagner, General Manager
Derrick Robbinson, General Sales Mgr
Jon Marte, Programming Director
Kevin Whoreton, Promotions Manager

Colonial Heights

WPWT
12-31-1984; 870 khz AM *Hrs Open:* Sunrise-sunset; 10 kw-D, NDD; N36 27 40 W82 27 12
Mailing Address: P.O. Box 2061, Bristol, TN 37621 US
Second Address: 340 Edgemont Ave., Suite 100, Bristol, TN 3720
(423) 878-6279, *Fax:* (423) 878-6520
www.powertalk870.com
wpwt@aecc.org
License: Colonial Heights, TN held by Information Communications Corp.
Group Owner: Information Communications Corp.; (acq 6-29-2001).
Nat'l Network: Fox News Radio; Salem Radio Network; Talk Radio Network; Premiere Radio Networks
Arbitron Metro Market: Johnson City-Kingsport-Bristol, TN-VA *Format:* Talk *Special Programming:* Health Education one hr wkly *Hrs. of News Programming:* news progmg 5 hrs wkly *No. News Employees:* 1 *TargetAudience:* Adults 25-54.
Kenneth Hill, General Manager
Rusty Cury, General Sales Mgr
Mathew Hill, Programming Director
Jerome Jackson III, Promotions Manager
Art Countiss, News Director

WRZK
04-04-1997; 95.9 mhz FM *Hrs Open:* 24; 7.4 kw; Ant 1,253 ft; N36 31 36 W82 35 13
222 Commerce St., Kingsport, TN 37663
(423) 246-9578, *Fax:* (423) 247-9836
www.wrzk.com
david@wrzk.com
License: Colonial Heights, Sullivan County, TN held by Holston Valley Broadcasting Corp.
Group Owner: Glenwood Communications Corp.; (acq 8-14-2008; $3.65 million)
Nat'l Network: ABC *Nat'l Reps:* Eastman
Population Served: 396,400 *Arbitron Metro Market:* Johnson City-Kingsport-Bristol, TN-VA *TV Affiliate:* WKPT-TV *No. News Employees:* 2 *Target Audience:* 18-44; Men
George Devault, President
David Widener, General Manager
Tim Loy, General Sales Mgr
Scott Onks, Programming Director
Duane Nelson, News Director

Columbia

WKOM
01-01-1967; 101.7 mhz FM *Hrs Open:* 24; 4.1 kw; 387 ft.; N35 37 5 W87 2 33
Mailing Address: 315 West 7th Street, Columbia, TN 38401 US
Second Address: 315 W. 7th St., Columbia, TN 38401
(931) 388-3636, *Fax:* (931) 381-1017
License: Columbia, Maury County, TN held by Middle Tennessee Broadcasting Co.
Nat'l Network: Motor Racing Net; ABC
Format: Classic Rock *Hrs. of News Programming:* news progmg 8 hrs wkly *No. News Employees:* 1 *Target Audience:* 30-50.
Robert McKay III, CEO

WKRM
11-25-1946; 1340 khz AM *Hrs Open:* 24; 1 kw-U, ND1; N35 36 38 W87 3 22
Mailing Address: P. O. Box 1377, Columbia, TN 38401 US
Second Address: 315 W. 7th St., Columbia, TN 38401
(931) 388-3636, *Fax:* (931) 381-1017
License: Columbia, TN held by Robert M. McKay III.
Nat'l Network: ABC; Motor Racing Net; Premiere Radio Networks

Format: Adult Contemp *Special Programming:* Relg 4 hrs wkly *Hrs. of News Programming:* news progmg 8 hrs wkly *No. News Employees:* 1 *Target Audience:* 25-54.
Robert McKay III, President

WMCP

11-12-1956; 1280 khz AM *Hrs Open:* 24; 5 kw-D, DA2; 0.5 kw-N, DA2; N35 37 8 W86 58 52
Mailing Address: 816 South Garden, Columbia, TN 38401 US
Second Address: 1st Farmer & Merchants Bank Bldg., 816 S. Garden, Suite 306, Columbia, TN 38401
(931) 388-3241, *Fax:* (931) 381-2510
wmcp@edge.net
License: Columbia, TN held by Maury County Boosters Corp.
Regional Network: Tenn. Radio Net.
Arbitron Metro Market: Columbia, TN *Format:* Country *Special Programming:* Farm 4 hrs weekly *Hrs. of News Programming:* news progmg 13 hrs wkly *No. News Employees:* 1 *Target Audience:* 18 plus. *Adv.Rates:* 9.45; 9.45; 9.45; 9.45.
Edna Williford, President
Mack Shaw, Operations Dir

WMRB

08-14-1982; 910 khz AM; 0.5 kw-D, ND1; 0.101 kw-N, ND1; N35 36 24 W87 1 30
609 West 7th Street, Columbia, TN 38401 US
(931) 381-7100, *Fax:* (931) 381-0088
www.910theduck.net
chuck@910theduck.net
License: Columbia, TN held by Ogilvie Family Ministries Inc.
Nat'l Reps: Dora-Clayton
Arbitron Metro Market: Columbia, TN *Format:* Sports *Target Audience:* General; Christian families
Chuck Killion, CEO/COO
Trent Ogilvie, General Manager
David Boggs, Station Manager

Cookeville

WGIC

03-26-1964; 98.5 mhz FM *Hrs Open:* 20; 50 kw; 492 ft.; N36 8 34 W85 28 2
200 Concord Plaza, Suite 600, San Antonio, TX 78216 US
(931) 526-7144, *Fax:* (931) 528-8400
www.magic985.com
email@magic985.com
License: Cookeville, Putnam County, TN held by Cookeville Communications LLC.
Group Owner: Great Plains Media Inc.; (acq 5-30-2008; grpsl)
Nat'l Network: ABC *Nat'l Reps:* Clear Channel
Arbitron Metro Market: Cookeville, TN *Format:* Adult Contemp *Hrs. of News Programming:* news progmg 8 hrs wkly *No. News Employees:* 1
Scott Straube, General Sales Mgr
Marty McFly, Programming Director
Helen Daniels, News Director
Jerri-Lynn Zimmer, Public Service Announcement Manager

WGSQ

03-08-1963; 94.7 mhz FM *Hrs Open:* 24; 100 kw; 1319 ft.; N36 10 26 W85 20 37
200 Concord Plaza, Suite 600, San Antonio, TX 78216 US
(931) 526-7144, *Fax:* (931) 528-8400
www.countrygiant.com
info@countrygiant.com
License: Cookeville, Putnam County, TN held by Cookeville Communications LLC.
Group Owner: Great Plains Media Inc.; (acq 5-30-2008; grpsl)
Arbitron Metro Market: Cookeville, TN *Format:* Country *Hrs. of News Programming:* news progmg 28 hrs wkly *No. News Employees:* 2
Norberto Sanchez, President

*WHRS

10-01-1996; 91.7 mhz FM; 0.5 kw; 384 ft.; N36 8 34 W85 28 2
Rebroadcasts: Rebroadcasts WPLN(FM) 90.3, Nashville; 100%
630 Mainstream Drive, Nashville, TN 37228 US
(615) 760-2903, *Fax:* (615) 760-2904
www.wpln.org
info@wpln.org
License: Cookeville, Putnam County, TN held by Nashville Public Radio.
Format: News *Special Programming:* Bluegrass one hr, song writers one hr wkly
William Ivey, Chairman
Robert Gordon, General Manager

WHUB

07-20-1940; 1400 khz AM *Hrs Open:* 24; 1 kw-U, ND1; N36 10 25 W85 30 40
200 Concord Plaza, Suite 600, San Antonio, TX 78216 US
(931) 526-7144, *Fax:* (931) 528-8400
www.1400thehub.com
License: Cookeville, TN held by Cookeville Communications LLC.
Group Owner: Great Plains Media Inc.; (acq 5-30-2008; grpsl)
Nat'l Network: CBS *Regional Network:* Tenn. Radio Net.
Arbitron Metro Market: Cookeville, TN *Format:* Country, Gospel *Special Programming:* Sports 10 hrs, gospel 11 hrs wkly *Hrs. of News Programming:* news progmg 18 hrs wkly *No. News Employees:* 1 *Target Audience:* General.
Marty McFly, Operations Dir
Dave Thomas, General Manager
Jim Stapleton, General Sales Mgr
Mike Dinger, Programming Director
Lehra Heidel, Promotions Manager
Jim Herrin, News Director
Lehar Heidel, Promotions Director
JenniferHenson, Traffic Manager

WPTN

07-10-1962; 780 khz AM; 1 kw-D, NDD; N36 9 30 W85 31 15
200 Concord Plaza, Suite 600, San Antonio, TX 78216 US
(931) 526-7144, *Fax:* (931) 528-8400
License: Cookeville, TN held by Cookeville Communications LLC.
Group Owner: Great Plains Media Inc.; (acq 5-30-2008; grpsl)
Nat'l Reps: Clear Channel
Arbitron Metro Market: Cookeville, TN *Format:* News, News/Talk, 86 *Target Audience:* General.
Dave Johnson, Operations Dir
David Roederer, General Manager
Bruce Welker, General Sales Mgr
Marty Selby, Programming Director
Lehra Mayfield, Promotions Manager
Jim Herrin, News Director

*WTTU

05-22-1972; 88.5 mhz FM *Hrs Open:* 25.?Â ?; 2 kw horiz; 164 ft.; N36 10 36 W85 30 20
P.O. Box 5113, North Dixie Avenue, Cookeville, TN 38505 US
(931) 372-3688, *Fax:* (931) 372-6225
www.tntech.edu/wttu
davewttu@gmail.com
License: Cookeville, Putnam County, TN held by Tennessee Technological University.
Arbitron Metro Market: Cookeville, TN *Format:* Alternative *Special Programming:* Jazz, Metal, American, Folk, Rap represented with *Hrs. of News Programming:* news progmg 5 hrs wkly *No. News Employees:* 1*Target Audience:* 14-25.
Will Housley, Programming Director
Chuck Acheson, News and Sports Director
Will Sheckler, Music Director
Bridgette Buchanan, Public Affairs Director

*WWOG

01-01-1994; 90.9 mhz FM *Hrs Open:* 24; 40 kw; 682 ft.; N36 11 5 W85 22 30 *Rebroadcasts:* Rebroadcasts WSGP(FM) Glasgow, KY and WTHL(FM) Somerset, KY 100%
Mailing Address: 93 Rainbow Terrace, Somerset, KY 42501 US
Second Address: 93 Rainbow Terr., Somerset, TN 42503
(606) 679-6300, *Fax:* (606) 679-1342
www.kingofkingsradio.net
dcradio@alltel.net
License: Cookeville, Putnam County, TN held by Somerset Educational Broadcasting Foundation.
Arbitron Metro Market: Somerset, KY *Format:* Gospel, Religious
David Carr, General Manager
Carolyn Jones, Programming Director
Marvin Whittaker, Chief Engineer

Copper Hill

WLSB

12-02-1958; 1400 khz AM *Hrs Open:* 6 AM-10 PM; 1 kw-U, ND1; N34 58 4 W84 19 39 *Rebroadcasts:* Simulcast with WYHG(AM) Young Harris, GA
PO Box 430, Copperhill, TN 37317 US
(423) 496-3311, *Fax:* (423) 496-2635
www.wolfcreekbroadcasting.com
info@wlsb.com
License: Copper Hill, TN held by Copper Basin Broadcasting Co., Inc.
Group Owner: Wolf Creek Broadcasting Inc.; (acq 9-26-2002)
Format: Country
Rebecca St. John, Station Manager

Covington

WKBL

08-16-1954; 1250 khz AM *Hrs Open:* 24; 800 w-D, 106 w-N; N35 35 10 W89 38 35
101 WKBL Dr., Covington, TN 38019
(901) 476-7129, *Fax:* (901) 476-7120
www.us51country.com
billy.thomas@us51country.com
License: Covington, Tipton County, TN held by Covington Broadcasting Inc., LMA in 2007 by 51 Ra
Nat'l Network: Dial Global *Regional Network:* Tenn. Radio Net.
Regional Reps: N/A
Population Served: 100,000 *Arbitron Metro Market:* Memphis, TN *Special Programming:* Black 4 hrs wkly *Hrs. of News Programming:* news progmg 14 hrs wkly *No. News Employees:* 1 *Target Audience:* 35 - 64.*Adv. Rates:* 15; 15; 15; 15
Gloria Thomas, Operations Dir
Bill Thomas, General Manager
David Lane, General Sales Mgr
Ron Grayson, Programming Director

WKBQ

08-31-1965; 93.5 mhz FM *Hrs Open:* 24; 6 kw; Ant 328 ft; N35 35 12 W89 38 21
101 WKBL Dr., Covington, TN 38019
(901) 476-7129, *Fax:* (901) 476-7120
www.us51country.com
david.lane@us51country.com
License: Covington, Tipton County, TN held by Covington Broadcasting Inc.
Nat'l Network: AP Radio; Jones Radio Networks *Regional Network:* Tenn. Radio Net. *Regional Reps:* N/A
Population Served: 170,000 *Arbitron Metro Market:* Memphis, TN *Special Programming:* University of Tennessee Football, University of M *Hrs. of News Programming:* news progmg 6.5 hrs wkly *No. News Employees:* 1*Target Audience:* 18 - 54; Adults *Adv. Rates:* 30 (MF6a-7p) Sat 10a-3p
Bill Thomas, General Manager
Rob Grayson, Programming Director
Gloria Thomas, Business Manager
David Lane, Partner/EVP

Cowan

WZYX

03-10-1957; 1440 khz AM *Hrs Open:* 24; 5 kw-D, ND1; 0.066 kw-N, ND1; N35 9 39 W86 1 51
540 West Cumberland St., PO Box 398, Cowan, TN 37318 US
(931) 967-7471, *Fax:* (931) 962-1440
www.wzyxradio.net
sam_fm@wzyxradio.net
License: Cowan, TN held by Tims Ford Broadcasting Co. Inc.
Nat'l Network: CNN Radio *Wire Services:* NOAA Weather
Arbitron Metro Market: Cowan, TN *Format:* Country, Oldies, 86 *Special Programming:* Talk, gospel 10 hrs, farm 2 hrs, relg 12 hrs wkly *Hrs. of News Programming:* news progmg 15 hrs wkly *No. News Employees:* 1*Target Audience:* 35-55; middle-of-the-road working people
Mary Lou Garner, CEO
Jeff Pennington, Operations Dir

Crossville

WAEW

01-01-1952; 1330 khz AM *Hrs Open:* 24; 1 kw-D, ND1; 0.035 kw-N, ND1; N35 57 1 W85 2 9
P.O. Box 1505, Glasgow, KY 42142 US
(931) 707-1102, *Fax:* (931) 707-1220
www.waewradio.com
License: Crossville, TN held by Peg Broadcasting Crossville LLC
Group Owner: Peg Broadcasting Crossville LLC; acq 10-1-2003; grpsl).
Nat'l Network: ABC
Arbitron Metro Market: Cookeville, TN *Format:* Talk *Hrs. of News Programming:* news progmg 13 hrs wkly *No. News Employees:* 2 *Target Audience:* 35-64; adult *Adv. Rates:* 12; 12; 10; 6
Gordon Stack, Operations Dir
Steve Sweeney, General Sales Mgr
Jeff Shaw, Promotions Manager
Christy Lewis, News Director
Houston McDavitt, Engineering Dir
Kendra Williams, Traffic Manager

WCSV

06-15-1968; 1490 khz AM *Hrs Open:* 24; 1 kw-U, ND1; N35 57 1 W85 2 9
P.O. Box 1505, Glasgow, KY 42142 US
(931) 707-1102, *Fax:* (931) 707-1220
www.1490wcsv.com
steve@pegbroadcasting.com
License: Crossville, TN held by Peg Broadcasting Crossville LLC
Group Owner: Peg Broadcasting Crossville LLC; acq 10-1-2003; grpsl).
Nat'l Network: ABC

Arbitron Metro Market: Crossville, TN *Format:* Sports *Hrs. of News Programming:* news progmg 13 hrs wkly *No. News Employees:* 2 *Target Audience:* 25-54; men
Gordon Stack, Operations Dir
Steve Sweeney, General Sales Mgr
Jeff Shaw, Promotions Manager
Christy Lewis, News Director
Houston McDavitt, Engineering Dir
Kendra Williams, Traffic Manager

***WMKW**
11-01-1996; 89.3 mhz FM *Hrs Open:* 24; 0.5 kw vert; 1394 ft.; N35 46 38 W84 58 34 *Rebroadcasts:* Rebroadcasts WMBW(FM) Chattanooga 100%
Mailing Address: 820 N. Lasalle Boulevard, Chicago, IL 60610 US
Second Address: Box 73026, Chattanooga, TN 37407
423-629-8900, *Fax:* (423) 629-0021
www.moody.edu
License: Crossville, Cumberland County, TN held by The Moody Bible Institute of Chicago.
Format: News, News/Talk, 86, Religious *Target Audience:* General.
Dr. Paul Nyquist, President
Leighton LeBoeuf, General Manager
Jim Young, News Director
David Morais, Chief Engineer
Paul Martin, Music Director
Andy Napier, Promotions Director

WOWF
06-15-1990; 102.5 mhz FM *Hrs Open:* 24; 9 kw; 542 ft.; N36 1 18 W84 58 18
961 Miller Ave, Crossville, TN 38555 US
(931) 707-1102, *Fax:* (931) 707-1220
www.1025wowcountry.com
License: Crossville, Cumberland County, TN held by Peg Broadcasting Crossville LLC
Group Owner: Peg Broadcasting Crossville LLC; acq 1-3-01; $2.5 million).
Nat'l Network: Jones Radio Networks; Fox News Radio *Regional Reps:* Rgnl Reps. *Wire Services:* AP
Format: Country *Hrs. of News Programming:* news progmg 10 hrs wkly *No. News Employees:* 2 *Target Audience:* 25 -54; adults *Adv. Rates:* 40; 36; 40; 24
Gordon Stack, Operations Dir
Steve Sweeney, General Sales Mgr
Christy Lewis, News Director
Houston McDavitt, Engineering Dir
Kendra Williams, Traffic Manager

WPBX
05-12-1967; 99.3 mhz FM *Hrs Open:* 24; 1.4 kw; 572 ft.; N36 1 18 W84 58 18
P.O. Box 1505, Glasgow, KY 42142 US
(931) 484-5115, *Fax:* (931) 707-1220
mix993.net
info@993.net
License: Crossville, Cumberland County, TN held by Peg Broadcasting Crossville LLC
Group Owner: Peg Broadcasting Crossville LLC; acq 10-1-2003: grpsl).
Nat'l Network: ABC *Nat'l Reps:* Clear Channel
Arbitron Metro Market: Knoxville, TN *Format:* Adult Contemp *Hrs. of News Programming:* news progmg 10 hrs wkly *No. News Employees:* 2 *Target Audience:* 25-54; women *Adv. Rates:* 18; 14; 18; 9
Gordon Stack, Operations Dir
Jeffrey Shaw, General Manager
Steve Sweeney, General Sales Mgr
Gordon Stack, Programming Director
Christy Lewis, News Director
Kendra Williams, Traffic Manager

Dayton

WDNT
12-06-1957; 1280 khz AM *Rebroadcasts:* Rebroadcasts WBAC(AM) Cleveland 100%
P.O. Box 970, Spring City, TN 37381 US
(423) 284-6411, *Fax:* (423) 472-5290
www.rheacountyradio.com
comments@rheacountyradio.com
License: Dayton, TN held by East Tennessee Radio Group III L.P.
Group Owner: East Tennessee Radio Group III L.P.; (acq 5-30-2008; grpsl)
Nat'l Network: ABC *Regional Network:* Tenn. Radio Net. *Nat'l Reps:* D & R Radio
Arbitron Metro Market: Rhea County, TN *Format:* Adult Contemp *Hrs. of News Programming:* news progmg 26 hrs wkly *No. News Employees:* 1 *Target Audience:* 45 plus. *Adv. Rates:* 16; 14; 14; 7
Mike Powers, Operations Dir
Charles Sells, General Manager
John Holland, General Sales Mgr
Corky Whitlock, Programming Director

Dibrell

***WRCC**
88.3 mhz FM; 0.085 kw; 344 ft.; N35 50 20 W85 47 2 US
(580) 332-0902, *Fax:* (580) 332-0922
www.thegospelstation.com
License: Dibrell, Warren County, TN held by Pearl Communications Group.
Arbitron Metro Market: Dibrell, TN
Randall Christy, President
Rick Cody, Vice President
Sharla Frederick, Treasurer / CFO

Dickson

WDKN
01-01-1955; 1260 khz AM *Hrs Open:* 6 AM-6:30 PM; 5 kw-D, ND2; 0.018 kw-N, ND2; N36 6 31 W87 22 14
106a E. College Street, Dickson, TN 37055 US
(615) 446-4000, (615) 446-0752, *Fax:* (615) 446-9681
www.wdkn.com
sales@1015theone.com
License: Dickson, TN held by Edmission & Eubank Communications Inc.
Arbitron Metro Market: Nashville, TN *Target Audience:* General.
Tommy Edmisson, President
Oscar Eubank, Operations Dir
Kenneth Forte, General Manager
Big Zak, Programming Director
Chris Norman, Operations/News

***WNRZ**
04-07-1997; 91.5 mhz FM *Hrs Open:* 24; 8 kw; 262 ft.; N36 0 36 W87 30 47 *Rebroadcasts:* Rebroadcasts WNAZ-FM Nashville 100%
333 Murfreesboro Road, Nashville, TN 37210 US
(913) 642-7770, *Fax:* (913) 642-1319
www.bottradionetwork.com
comments@bottradionetwork.com
License: Dickson, Dickson County, TN held by Trevecca Nazarene University Inc.
Arbitron Metro Market: Dickson, TS *Format:* Christian *Target Audience:* 14-28; Christians
Mark Myers, CFO
Dr. Dan Boone, President
Dave Queen, Operations Dir
David Deese, General Manager
Paul Eby, Station Manager

Donelson

WCRT
04-12-1971; 1160 khz AM *Hrs Open:* 24; 50 kw-D, DAN; 1 kw-N, DAN; N36 9 49 W86 42 56
1617 Lebanon Road, Nashville, TN 37210 US
(913) 642-7770, *Fax:* (913) 642-1319
www.bottradionetwork.com
comments@bottradionetwork.com
License: Donelson, TN held by Bott Communications Inc.
Group Owner: Bott Radio Network; (acq 1-11-2006; $5 million)
Arbitron Metro Market: Nashville, TN *Format:* Christian
Richard Bott, President
Richard Bott II, Operations Dir
Randy Uselton, General Manager

Dresden

WCDZ
04-10-1992; 95.1 mhz FM *Hrs Open:* 24; 21.5 kw; 276 ft.; N36 15 50 W88 40 3
P.O. Box 318, Martin, TN 38237 US
(731) 587-9526, *Fax:* (731) 587-5079
www.wcmt.com
oldies951@crunet.com,ptinkle@crunet.com
License: Dresden, Weakley County, TN held by Thunderbolt Broadcasting Co.
Group Owner: Thunderbolt Broadcasting Co.; (acq 1-28-94; $320,000;
Format: Oldies *Special Programming:* Atlanta Braves and Tennessee Vols *Hrs. of News Programming:* news progmg one hr wkly *No. News Employees:* 1 *Adv. Rates:* 40; 30; 40; 25
Paul Tinkle, President

Dunlap

WSDQ
11-01-1980; 1190 khz AM; 1 kw-C, NDD; 5 kw-D, NDD; N35 21 41 W85 22 33
712 Old York Hwy North, Ste B, Dunlap, TN 37327 US
(423) 949-5806, *Fax:* (423) 949-5143
wsdq1190@gmail.com
License: Dunlap, TN held by Rodgson Inc.
Regional Network: Tenn. Radio Net.
Arbitron Metro Market: Chattanooga, TN *Format:* Country *Special Programming:* Gospel 7 hrs wkly
Charles Rodgers, President
Howard Staten, Station Manager

Dyer

WTJJ
02-01-1995; 94.3 mhz FM *Hrs Open:* 24; 6 kw; 328 ft.; N36 6 12 W89 7 45
P.O. Box 112, Humboldt, TN 38343 US
(731) 427-3316, *Fax:* (731) 427-9338
www.wtjs.com/
License: Dyer, Gibson County, TN held by Forever South Licenses LLC.
Group Owner: Forever Communications Inc.; (acq 7-31-2006; grpsl)
Arbitron Metro Market: Dyer, TN *Format:* News, News/Talk, 86 *Target Audience:* 18-49
Verla Price, General Manager

Dyersburg

WASL
07-01-1968; 100.1 mhz FM *Hrs Open:* 24; 26 kw; 676 ft.; N36 6 0 W89 29 12
Mailing Address: P.O. Boxc 100, Dyersburg, TN 38025 US
Second Address: 2555 Huish Rd, Dyersburg, TN 38024
(731) 285-1450(731) 285-1339, *Fax:* (731) 287-0100
www.sl100rocks.com
roger@burksb.com
License: Dyersburg, Dyer County, TN
Group Owner: Dr. Pepper Pepsi-Cola Bottling Co. of Dyersburg
Nat'l Network: ABC *Nat'l Reps:* Rgnl Reps *Wire Services:* AP
Special Programming: John Boy and Billy, Tenn Titans *No. News Employees:* 1 *Target Audience:* 18-54.
Roger Vestal, Operations Dir
Natalie Burks, General Sales Mgr
Dan DeFilippo, Programming Director
Brian Thomas, News Director
Dave Hacker, Engineering Dir

***WZKV**
10-30-1992; 90.7 mhz FM *Hrs Open:* 24; 9.9 kw horiz, 100 kw vert; 561 ft.; N36 6 0 W89 29 12
P.O. Box 241880, Memphis, TN 38124 US
(916) 251-1600, *Fax:* (916) 251-1650
www.klove.com
License: Dyersburg, Dyer County, TN held by Educational Media Foundation.
Group Owner: EMF Broadcasting; (acq 3-29-2007; $825,000)
Nat'l Network: K-Love
Format: Christian
Mike Novak, President

WTRO
07-13-1946; 1450 khz AM *Hrs Open:* 24; 1 kw-U, ND1; N36 3 2 W89 22 7 *Rebroadcasts:* FM Translator 101.7
Mailing Address: P.O. Box 100, Dyersburg, TN 38024 US
Second Address: 2555 Huish Rd, Dyersburg, TN 38024
(731) 285-1450, *Fax:* (731) 287-0100
wtroradio.net
roger@burksb.com
License: Dyersburg, TN held by Dr. Pepper/Pepsi Cola Bottling Co. of Dyersburg Inc.
Group Owner: Dr. Pepper Pepsi-Cola Bottling Co. of Dyersburg; (acq 1991)
Nat'l Network: ABC *Wire Services:* AP
Arbitron Metro Market: Dyersburg, TN *Format:* Oldies *Special Programming:* St. Louis Cardinals, Tenn Vols *Hrs. of News Programming:* news prgmg 5 hrs/week *No. News Employees:* 1 *Target Audience:* 35 plus.
Roger Vestal, General Manager
Natalie Burks, Sales Director
Tom Hunt, Programming Director
Tom Hunt, Partyline Host

East Ridge

WOGT
11-09-1990; 107.9 mhz FM; 25 kw; 328 ft.; N35 7 33 W85 17 25
P O Box 8, Bloomington, IL 61702 US

(423) 756-6141, *Fax:* 423-266-3629
http://www.1079bigfm.com/
License: East Ridge, Hamilton County, TN
Group Owner: Cumulus Media Inc.; (acq 5-30-00; grpsl).
Arbitron Metro Market: Chattanooga, TN *TV Affiliate:* Classic Hits

Elizabethton

WTZR
05-17-1968; 99.3 mhz FM; 3.6 kw; 810 ft.; N36 24 7 W82 12 12
Mailing Address: 901 East Valley Drive, Bristol, VA 24201 US
Second Address: 901 E. Valley Dr., Bristol, VA 24201
(276) 669-8112, *Fax:* (276) 669-0541
www.zrock993.com
jay@zrock993.com
License: Elizabethton, Carter County, TN held by Bristol Broadcasting Co.
Group Owner: Bristol Broadcasting Co. Inc.; (acq 2-13-97; $3 million).
Nat'l Reps: Christal
Arbitron Metro Market: Johnson City-Kingsport-Bristol, TN-VA *Format:* Alternative *Target Audience:* 18-49.
W.L. Nininger, President
Bruce Clark, Station Manager
Winnie Quaintance, General Sales Mgr
Jay Patrix, Programming Director
Anna Honaker, News Director
Chuck Lawson, Chief Engineer

WBEJ
07-01-1946; 1240 khz AM *Hrs Open:* 24; 1 kw-U, ND1; N36 20 7 W82 13 3
626 1/2 E. Elk Avenue, Elizabethton, TN 37643 US
(209) 477-3690, *Fax:* (209) 477-2762
www.kycc.org
kycc@kycc.org
License: Elizabethton, TN held by CB Radio Inc.
Nat'l Network: Westwood One
Arbitron Metro Market: Kerville TX *Format:* Gospel, Religious *Target Audience:* 35-55. *Adv. Rates:* 17; 15; 17; 15
Shirley Garner, General Manager

***WUMC**
01-01-1999; 90.5 mhz FM; 0.5 kw; -285 ft.; N36 17 58 W82 17 28
P O Box 9, Milligan College, TN 37682 US
(423) 461-8464
www.milliganradio.com
License: Elizabethton, Carter County, TN held by Milligan College.
Arbitron Metro Market: Milligan College, TN *Format:* Contemporary Hits/Top 40, Christian
Carrie Swanay, General Manager

Englewood

WENR
04-21-1967; 1090 khz AM; 1 kw-D, NDD; N35 25 35 W84 30 57
136 County Road 611, Athens, TN 37303 US
(423) 337-5025, *Fax:* (423) 337-5026
wenrradio@yahoo.com
License: Englewood, TN held by Paul Wilson dba 1090 Radio, a Tennessee sole proprietorship
Arbitron Metro Market: Englewood, TN *Format:* Gospel
Carolyne Wilson, General Manager

Erwin

WEMB
05-17-1956; 1420 khz AM; 5 kw-D, ND1; 0.02 kw-N, ND1; N36 6 58 W82 26 49
P.O. Box 280, Erwin, TN 37650 US
(423) 743-6123(423) 743-6124, *Fax:* (423) 743-6122
www.wemb.com/
License: Erwin, TN held by WEMB Inc.
Regional Network: Tenn. Radio Net.
Arbitron Metro Market: Erwin, TN *Format:* Country, Gospel, 84
Special Programming: Bluegrass 2 hrs, gospel 10 hrs wkly
Jim Crawford, President
Charles Ray, Operations Dir
Kathy Thornberry, News Director
Fred Lance, Edit Director

Etowah

WCPH
01-01-1955; 1220 khz AM; 1 kw-D, ND1; 0.109 kw-N, ND1; N35 19 15 W84 30 34
P. O. Box 676, Etowah, TN 37331 US
(423) 263-5555, *Fax:* (423) 263-2555
wcphradio@yahoo.com
License: Etowah, TN held by Starr Mountain Broadcasting Co.
Arbitron Metro Market: Chattanooga, TN *Format:* Easy Listening, News, 62, Sports, Talk
Carolyne Wilson, General Manager

WLLJ
01-01-1977; 103.1 mhz FM *Hrs Open:* 24; 50 kw; 492 ft.; N35 27 24 W84 40 43 *Rebroadcasts:* Rebroadcasts WBDX(FM) Trenton, GA 100%
Mailing Address: 12820 Greenwood Forest Dr., #325, Houston, TX 77066 US
Second Address: Box 212, McDonald, TN 37353
(423) 892-1200, *Fax:* (423) 892-1633
www.j103.com
info@j103.com
License: Etowah, McMinn County, TN held by Friendship Broadcasting LLC.
Nat'l Network: Salem Radio Network
Arbitron Metro Market: Etowah, TN *Format:* Adult Contemp, Christian *Hrs. of News Programming:* news progmg 2 hrs wkly *No. News Employees:* 1 *Target Audience:* 18-49; female
Bob Lubell, CEO
Steve Green, Station Manager
Debbie Lubell, Promotions Manager
Freda Thornton, News Director
Dave Skinner, CFO
Kendall Payne, Local News Editor

Farragut

WMTY
11-10-1988; 670 khz AM; 2.5 kw-D, NDD; N35 53 12 W84 14 48
412 Executive Tower Drive, Suite 205, Knoxville, TN 37922 US
(865) 671-7419, *Fax:* (865) 675-4859
www.wmtradio.com
License: Farragut, TN held by Horne Radio L.L.C.
Group Owner: Horne Radio Group; (acq 1999; $275,000).
Nat'l Network: USA
Arbitron Metro Market: Knoxville, TN *Format:* Talk *Target Audience:* 25-54; upscale adults
Doug Horne, President

Fayetteville

WEKR
10-01-1948; 1240 khz AM *Hrs Open:* 4:30 AM-10 PM; 1 kw-U, ND1; N35 9 28 W86 35 25
Mailing Address: P.O. Box 656, Fayetteville, TN 37334 US
Second Address: 7 Boonshill Rd., Fayetteville, TN 37334
(931) 433-3545, *Fax:* (931) 438-0620
License: Fayetteville, TN held by Joseph D. Young, Wanda Young & Mary Elizabeth Miller.
Nat'l Network: CNN Radio *Regional Network:* Tenn. Radio Net.
Arbitron Metro Market: Fayetteville, TN *Format:* Country, Gospel, 84 *Special Programming:* Farm one hr wkly *Hrs. of News Programming:* news progmg 5 hrs wkly *No. News Employees:* 1 *Target Audience:* 25plus; general *Adv. Rates:* 14.12; 14.12; 14.12; na
Joseph Young, CEO
Jim Young, Station Manager
Jennifer Denise, Programming Director
Wayne Thomas, News Director
Charles Hicks, Disc Jockey
Jack Atchley, Sports Commentator

WYTM-FM
03-27-1970; 105.5 mhz FM *Hrs Open:* 5 AM-10 PM; 6 kw; 295 ft.; N35 7 39 W86 34 49
P. O. Box 717, Fayetteville, TN 37334 US
(931) 433-1531, *Fax:* (931) 433-4110
License: Fayetteville, Lincoln County, TN held by Time Broadcasters Inc.
Nat'l Network: ABC
Arbitron Metro Market: Fayetteville, TN *Format:* Country
Joseph Young, President
Debbie Kawiecki, Operations Dir

Franklin

WAKM
03-18-1953; 950 khz AM *Hrs Open:* 24
222 Mallory Station Road, Franklin, TN 37067 US
(615) 794-1950, *Fax:* (615) 794-1595
www.wakm950am.tripod.com
wakm950@comcast.net
License: Franklin, TN held by Franklin Radio Associates Inc.
Nat'l Network: CNN Radio *Regional Network:* Tenn. Radio Net.
Arbitron Metro Market: Nashville, TN *Format:* Country, News, 62, Talk *Special Programming:* Relg 6 hrs, NASCAR racing 6 hrs wkly *Hrs. of News Programming:* news progmg 14 hrs wkly *No. News Employees:* 2 *TargetAudience:* 24 plus; community interested adults *Adv. Rates:* 20; 18; 20; 18
Jim Hayes, President
Tom Lawrence, Operations Dir
Linda Jackson Carden, General Sales Mgr
Darrell Williams, Programming Director
Charles Dibrell, News Director

WRLT
11-16-1961; 100.1 mhz FM *Hrs Open:* 24; 0.2 kw; 1181 ft.; N36 2 6 W86 50 54
401 Church Street, 30th Floor, Nashville, TN 37219 US
(615) 242-5600, *Fax:* (615) 523-2153
www.WRLT.com
comments@WRLT.com
License: Franklin, Williamson County, TN held by Tuned In Broadcasting Inc.
Nat'l Network: Westwood One *Nat'l Reps:* Roslin
Arbitron Metro Market: Nashville, TN *Format:* Triple A *Special Programming:* Retro Rock 4 hrs, Local Music 3 hrs, Music Business Talk 2 hrs, Indie Rock 1 hr, Blues 1 hr weekly *Target Audience:* Adults 18+
Lester Turner Jr., CEO
Fred Buc, General Manager
David Hall, Programming Director
Jayson Chalfant, Promotions Manager
Tom Hansen, Chief Engineer

Friendsville

WNML-FM
01-05-1989; 99.1 mhz FM *Hrs Open:* 24; 6 kw; 328 ft.; N35 47 10 W84 17 24 *Rebroadcasts:* Simulcast with WNML (AM) & WNRX (FM) Knoxville
Mailing Address: 4711 Old Kingston Pike, Knoxville, TN 37919 US
Second Address: 4711 Old Kingston Pike, Knoxville, TN 37919
(865) 588-6511, *Fax:* (865) 558-4218
www.sportsanimal99.com
License: Friendsville, Knoxville County, TN
Group Owner: Cumulus Media Inc.; (acq 8-2-00; grpsl).
Nat'l Network: ABC; Westwood One *Nat'l Reps:* Katz Radio
Regional Reps: Rgnl Reps. *Wire Services:* AP
Arbitron Metro Market: Knoxville, TN *Format:* Sports, Talk *Target Audience:* 25-54.
Mike Hammond, Operations Dir
Ed Brantley, General Manager
Jack Lee, General Sales Mgr
Mickey Dearstone, Promotions Manager
Tim Berry, Chief Engineer

Gallatin

WGFX
12-01-1960; 104.5 mhz FM *Hrs Open:* 24; 58 kw; 1207 ft.; N36 16 5 W86 47 45
P.O. Box 101604, Nashville, TN 37224 US
(615) 244-9533, *Fax:* (615) 259-1271
www.1045thezone.com
ken.bailey@citcom.com
License: Gallatin, Sumner County, TN
Group Owner: Cumulus Media Inc.; (acq 4-26-01; grpsl).
Nat'l Reps: Katz Radio
Arbitron Metro Market: Nashville, TN *Format:* Sports, Talk *Target Audience:* 18-49.
Ken Bailey, General Manager

WHIN
08-02-1948; 1010 khz AM *Hrs Open:* 24; 5 kw-D, ND1; 0.047 kw-N, ND1; N36 26 0 W86 28 0
1625 Highway 109 North, P.O. Box 1685, Gallatin, TN 37066 US
(615) 451-0450, *Fax:* (615) 452-9446
whinam@comcast.net
License: Gallatin, TN held by WHIN Inc.
Arbitron Metro Market: Nashville, TN *Format:* Country *Special Programming:* Black 2 hrs, farm 5 hrs wkly *Hrs. of News Programming:* news progmg 14 hrs wkly *No. News Employees:* 1 *Target Audience:* 25-54;upper middle to lower middle income
Jack Williams, President

WMRO
02-19-1994; 1560 khz AM *Hrs Open:* Daytime
701 North Blythe Street, Gallatin, TN 37066 US
(615) 451-2131, *Fax:* (615) 206-4207
www.magic1560.com
wmroam@comcast.net
License: Gallatin, TN held by Classic Broadcasting Inc.
Nat'l Network: ABC Music Radio *Regional Reps:* .
Arbitron Metro Market: Gallatin, TN *Format:* Adult Contemp *Special Programming:* Relg 11 hrs. wkly *Hrs. of News Programming:* news progmg 4 hrs wkly *No. News Employees:* 2 *Target Audience:* 25-54; middle toupper class adults *Adv. Rates:* 7; 6; 7; 2

Scott Bailey, President
Scott Bailey, General Manager

***WVCP**
01-04-1979; 88.5 mhz FM *Hrs Open:* 24; 1 kw; 390 ft; N36 22 36.1 W86 28 20.9
1480 Nashville Pike, Ramer Bldg., Ste. 101, Gallatin, TN 37066
(615) 230-3618, *Fax:* (615) 230-4803
www.wvcp.net
wvcp@volstate.edu
License: Gallatin, Sumner County, TN held by Volunteer State Community College.
Wire Services: AP
Arbitron Metro Market: Nashville, TN *Special Programming:* Christian Rock 4 hrs wkly, Classic country 2 hrs w *Hrs. of News Programming:* News progmg 5 hrs wkly *Target Audience:* General.
Dr Jerry Faulkner, President
Holly Nimmo, Operations Dir
Howard Espravnik, General Manager

WYXE
11-01-1966; 1130 khz AM; 0.94 kw-C, NDD; 2.3 kw-D, NDD; N36 24 38 W86 27 16
506 Red River Road, Gallatin, TN 37066 US
(615) 227-1130
License: Gallatin, TN held by Jon Gary Enterprises Inc.
Arbitron Metro Market: Nashville, TN *Format:* Religious
Richard Deck Jr., General Manager

Gatlinburg

WSEV-FM
01-01-1983; 105.5 mhz FM *Hrs Open:* 24; 0.53 kw; 1056 ft.; N35 42 13 W83 33 57
415 Middle Creek Road, Sevierville, TN 37862 US
(865) 932-6002, *Fax:* (865) 932-0167
www.mixx1055.com
studio@easttennesseeradio.com
License: Gatlinburg, Sevier County, TN held by East Tennessee Radio Group L.P.
Group Owner: East Tennessee Radio Group L.P.; (acq 3-22-2000; $1.45 million with WSEV(AM) Sevierville).
Nat'l Network: Fox News Radio *Regional Network:* Tenn. Radio Net.
Arbitron Metro Market: Knoxville, TN *Format:* Adult Contemp *No. News Employees:* 1 *Target Audience:* 25-54; loc adults, tourists
Steve Hartford, Operations Dir
Bill Burkett, Station Manager

Germantown

WHBQ-FM
06-01-1994; 107.5 mhz FM *Hrs Open:* 24; 3.9 kw; 407 ft.; N35 10 30 W89 44 26
188 South Bellevue, Suite 222, Memphis, TN 38104 US
(901) 375-9324, *Fax:* (901) 375-0041
www.q1075.com
info@q1075.com
License: Germantown, Shelby County, TN held by Flinn Broadcasting Corp.
Arbitron Metro Market: Memphis, TN *Format:* Contemporary Hits/Top 40
Donald Biggs, General Manager

WKQK
04-15-1977; 94.1 mhz FM; 50 kw; 472 ft.; N34 59 22 W89 51 45
10706 Beaver Dam Road, Cockeysville, MD 21030 US
(901) 384-5900, *Fax:* (901) 767-6076
www.941kqk.com
BCarson@941kqk.com
License: Germantown, Shelby County, TN held by Entercom Memphis License LLC.
Group Owner: Entercom Communications Corp.; (acq 12-13-99; grpsl)
Arbitron Metro Market: Memphis, TN *TV Affiliate:* Classic hits *Special Programming:* news progmg 2 hrs wkly *Hrs. of News Programming:* 1 *No. News Employees:* 18-49; adults with discre

WOWW
10-01-1955; 1430 khz AM
6080 Mt Moriah Road, Memphis, TN 38115 US
(901) 375-9324, *Fax:* (901) 375-0041
www.radiodisney.com
info@radiodisney.com
License: Germantown, TN held by Flinn Broadcasting Corp.
Arbitron Metro Market: Memphis, TN *Format:* Children *Target Audience:* 25-54.
George Flinn, President
Lonnie Treadaway, General Manager

Goodlettsville

WQZQ
01-24-1980; 830 khz AM *Hrs Open:* 24
P.O. Box 150846, Nashville, TN 37215 US
(615) 399-1029, *Fax:* (615) 361-9873
www.wqzq.com
jhampton@cromwellradio.com
License: Goodlettsville, TN held by Winston Communications Inc.
Group Owner: The Cromwell Group Inc.; (acq 10-17-91)
Arbitron Metro Market: Nashville, TN *Format:* Black, Gospel, 86 *Target Audience:* 24-56; talk radio audience
Bayard Walters, President
David Wilson, Operations Dir
Tincy Crouse, General Manager

WQQK
10-16-1970; 92.1 mhz FM *Hrs Open:* 24; 3.1 kw; 461 ft.; N36 17 50 W86 45 11
Suite 901, 50 Music Sq. W., Nashville, TN 37203 US
(615) 321-1067, *Fax:* (615) 321-5771
www.cumulus.com
danielle.haese@cumulus.com
License: Goodlettsville, Sumner County, TN held by Cumulus Licensing LLC.
Group Owner: Cumulus Media Inc.; (acq 3-28-2002; grpsl).
Nat'l Network: ABC
Arbitron Metro Market: Nashville, TN *Format:* Urban Contemporary *Special Programming:* Gospel 6 hrs wkly *Target Audience:* 18-49; relg *Adv. Rates:* 170; 170; 180; 150
John Columbus, General Manager
Timothy Meagher, General Sales Mgr
Kenny Smoov, Programming Director
Troy Pennington, Chief Engineer

Graysville

***WAYB-FM**
01-01-1994; 95.7 mhz FM; 6 kw; 328 ft.; N35 24 39 W85 7 54
Mailing Address: 532 North Hillcrest Dr., Spring City, TN 37381 US
Second Address: 8919 World Ministry Ave, Baton Rouge, LA 70810
(307) 745-4888, *Fax:* (307) 742-4576
www.1061theriver.com
klmi@myhits106.com
License: Graysville, Rhea County, TN held by Family Worship Center Church Inc.
Group Owner: Family Worship Center Church Inc.; acq 5-20-02).
Arbitron Metro Market: Rock River WY *Format:* Contemporary Hits/Top 40
Andy Hoefer, General Manager
Eric Henderson, General Sales Mgr

Greeneville

WGRV
01-01-1946; 1340 khz AM *Hrs Open:* 24; 1 kw-U, ND1; N36 10 10 W82 50 52
Mailing Address: P.O. Box 278, Greeneville, TN 37743 US
Second Address: 1004 Arnold Rd., Greeneville, TN 37743
(423) 638-4147, *Fax:* (423) 638-1979
www.greeneville.com
wgrv@greeneville.com
License: Greeneville, TN held by Radio Greeneville Inc.
Group Owner: Radio Greeneville Inc.
Regional Network: Tenn. Radio Net.
Format: Country *No. News Employees:* 3
Ron Metcalfe, Operations Dir
Paul Metcalfe, General Manager
Leroy Moon, General Sales Mgr
Brian Stayton, Programming Director
Ron Metcalfe, Promotions Manager
Bobby Rader, News Director
Ray Elliot, Chief Engineer
Charlie Hicks,Disc Jockey
Ray Elliott, Disc Jockey
Maxine Humphreys, Local News Editor
Nancy Ensor, News Reporter
Nathan Humbard, Music Director
Betty FletcherTraffic Director

WAEZ
01-01-1956; 94.9 mhz FM *Hrs Open:* 24; 100 kw horiz, 87 kw vert; 1089 ft.; N36 4 34 W82 41 28
P. O. Box 278, Greeneville, TN 37743 US
(276) 669-8112, *Fax:* (276) 669-0541
www.electric949.com
info@electric949.com
License: Greeneville, Greene County, TN held by Bristol Broadcasting Co. Inc.
Group Owner: Bristol Broadcasting Co. Inc.; acq 6-22-00)
Nat'l Reps: Rgnl Reps
Arbitron Metro Market: Johnson City-Kingsport-Bristol, TN-VA *Format:* Contemporary Hits/Top 40 *Special Programming:* Univ. of Tennessee football & basketball *No. News Employees:* 2 *Target Audience:* 25-49.
Pete Nininger, President
Bill Hickey, Operations Dir

WSMG
12-01-1961; 1450 khz AM *Hrs Open:* 24
Mailing Address: P. O. Box 727, Greeneville, TN 37744 US
Second Address: 10004 Arnold Rd., Greeneville, TN 37743
(423) 638-3188, *Fax:* (423) 638-1979
wsmg@greeneville.com
License: Greeneville, TN held by Radio Greeneville Inc.
Group Owner: Radio Greeneville Inc.; acq 6-22-00; $1.8 million with WIKQ(FM) Tusculum)
Wire Services: AP
Format: Oldies *Target Audience:* General. *Adv. Rates:* 12; 12; 12; 8.
Ronnie Metcalfe, President
Ron Metcalfe, Operations Dir

Halls Crossroads

WMYL
08-15-1991; 96.7 mhz FM; 2.8 kw; 489 ft.; N36 4 21 W84 1 18
Mailing Address: P.O. Box 719, Harrogate, TN 37752 US
Second Address: 111 Hillcrest Dr., Clinton, TN 37716
(865) 896-9670, *Fax:* (865) 457-4440
www.merlefm.com
ron@merle.com
License: Halls Crossroads, Knox County, TN held by M & M Broadcasting
Nat'l Network: ABC; CNN Radio *Nat'l Reps:* Rgnl Reps
Arbitron Metro Market: Knoxville, TN *Format:* Country *Special Programming:* Farm 2 hrs, gospel 2 hrs, relg 2 hrs wkly *Target Audience:* 25-54; community-oriented adults
Ronald Meredith Jr., General Manager
Garry Walden, Sales
Jim Harris, News & Sports Director
Will Housley, Website
Kelly Harris, Traffic & Billing
Jimmy Farmer, Advertising

Harriman

WIJV
01-21-1981; 92.7 mhz FM; 2.65 kw; 502 ft.; N35 52 4 W84 25 56
P.O. Box 387, Rockwood, TN 37854 US
(931) 484-1057
www.victory927.com
License: Harriman, Roane County, TN held by Progressive Media Inc.
Arbitron Metro Market: Knoxville, TN *Format:* Christian
Kirk Tollett, General Manager
Scott Humphrey, News Director
Jennifer Tollett, Traffic Manager

Harrison

WMPZ
01-01-1995; 93.5 mhz FM *Hrs Open:* 24; 6 kw horiz, 5.88 kw vert; 315 ft.; N35 7 33 W85 17 25
409 Chestnut Street, Suite A-154, Chattanooga, TN 37402 US
(423) 265-9494, *Fax:* (423) 266-2335
www.groove93.com
info@power94.com
License: Harrison, Catoosa County, TN held by J.L. Brewer Broadcasting L.L.C.
Group Owner: Brewer Broadcasting Corp.; (acq 11-96).
Nat'l Network: ABC *Nat'l Reps:* D & R Radio
Arbitron Metro Market: Chattanooga, TN *Format:* Adult Contemp *Target Audience:* 25-54; adults
Jim Brewer II, President
Keith Landecker, Operations Manager

Harrogate

***WLMU**
08-05-1987; 91.3 mhz FM *Hrs Open:* 24; 0.19 kw; 285 ft.; N36 35 10 W83 39 54
Highway 25e, Harrogate, TN 37752 US
(423) 869-6331
www.913thegap.com
info@wlmu.com
License: Harrogate, Claiborne County, TN held by Lincoln Memorial University.
Format: Country *Target Audience:* 25-54.
Dr. Nancy Moody, President
Dustin McCoy, Operations Dir

Travis Moody, General Manager
Larry Carter, General Sales Mgr

WCXZ
11-10-1980; 740 khz AM *Hrs Open:* 24
Box 2025, Sigmon Communication Ctr, Harrogate, TN 37752 US
(423) 869-7400, *Fax:* (423) 869-6435
www.74wcxz.com
tom@74wcxz.com
License: Harrogate, TN held by Pine Hills of Tenn. Inc.
Wire Services: AP
Arbitron Metro Market: Knoxville, TN *Format:* Talk *Hrs. of News Programming:* news progmg 150 hrs wkly *No. News Employees:* 4 *Target Audience:* 34-65. *Adv. Rates:* 19; 17; 19; 13
Tom Amis, General Manager
Dustin McCoy, Programming Director

Hartsville

WTNK
09-01-1966; 1090 khz AM *Hrs Open:* 24; 1 kw-D, 2 w-N; N36 23 17 W86 09 55
165 Marlene St., Hartsville, TN 37090
(615) 374-2111, *Fax:* (615) 374-3544
wtnk@ainweb.net
License: Hartsville, Trousdale County, TN held by G & L Aircasters Inc.
Nat'l Reps: Keystone (unwired net)
Population Served: 500,000*Special Programming:* Gospel 4 hrs wkly *Hrs. of News Programming:* News progmg 5 hrs wkly *Target Audience:* 35 plus. *Adv. Rates:* 7; 7; 7; na
Lisa C. Frank, CEO/COO
Jerry Richmond, News Director

Henderson

***WFHU**
05-22-1967; 91.5 mhz FM *Hrs Open:* 24; 10.5 kw; 308 ft.; N35 27 40 W88 40 51
158 East Main Street, Henderson, TN 38340 US
(731) 989-6691(731) 989-6749
www.fhu.edu/radio
webmaster@fhu.edu
License: Henderson, Chester County, TN held by Freed-Hardeman University.
Arbitron Metro Market: Henderson, TN *Format:* Classic Rock, Classical, 52 *Special Programming:* Class 10 hrs, gospel 9 hrs, jazz 45 hrs wkly *Hrs. of News Programming:* news progmg 5 hrs wkly *No. News Employees:* 1 *Target Audience:* General; young adults to senior citizens
Milton Sewell, President
Ron Means, General Manager

WFKX
02-01-1984; 95.7 mhz FM *Hrs Open:* 24; 4.4 kw; 383 ft.; N35 29 52 W88 42 29
425 East Chester, Jackson, TN 38302 US
(901) 427-9616, *Fax:* (901) 427-9302
cthomas@wwyn.fm
License: Henderson, Chester County, TN held by Thomas Radio LLC
Group Owner: Black Crow Media Group LLC; (acq 11-9-2001; grpsl).
Nat'l Network: ABC
Arbitron Metro Market: Jackson, TN *Format:* Black *Special Programming:* Gospel 3 hrs wkly *Hrs. of News Programming:* news progmg 5 hrs wkly *Target Audience:* 18-54; the general Black population & contemp women*Adv. Rates:* 36; 34; 38; 24
Billy Thomas, President
Chip Thomas, General Manager
Jim Smith, Chief Engineer

WHHM-FM
11-19-1990; 107.7 mhz FM *Hrs Open:* 24; 50 kw horiz, 49.07 kw vert; 459 ft.; N35 27 23 W88 37 36
P.O. Box 203, 111 East Main, Henderson, TN 38340 US
(731) 427-9616, *Fax:* (731) 424-2473
www.star1077.fm
info@star1077.fm
License: Henderson, Chester County, TN held by Thomas Radio LLC
Group Owner: Black Crow Media Group LLC; (acq 11-9-2001; grpsl).
Regional Network: Tenn. Agri-Net *Wire Services:* AP
Arbitron Metro Market: Jackson, TN *Format:* Adult Contemp
Special Programming: Gospel 10 hrs wkly *Hrs. of News Programming:* news progmg 5 hrs wkly *No. News Employees:* 1 *Target Audience:* 25-54; adults*Adv. Rates:* 24; 26; 24; 17
Shane Connor, Operations Dir
Chip Thomas, General Manager
Phil Hickerson, General Sales Mgr
Jim Smith, Chief Engineer

Hendersonville

WWTN
06-20-1962; 99.7 mhz FM; 100 kw; 1296 ft.; N35 49 3 W86 31 24
One Gaylord Drive, Nashville, TN 37214 US
(615) 321-1067, *Fax:* (615) 321-5771
www.997wtn.com
License: Hendersonville, Coffee County, TN held by Cumulus Licensing Corp.
Group Owner: Cumulus Media Inc.; (acq 7-21-2003; $65 million with WSM-FM Nashville).
Nat'l Network: ABC; CBS Radio *Wire Services:* UPI
Arbitron Metro Market: Nashville, TN *Format:* News, News/Talk, 84, Talk *Target Audience:* 25-54; general
John Columbus, General Manager
Tim Meagher, General Sales Mgr
Brian Wilson, Programming Director
Cori Vallentine, Promotions Manager

Henry

WMUF
04-12-1999; 104.7 mhz FM *Hrs Open:* 24; 2.9 kw; 476 ft.; N36 8 19 W88 15 52 *Rebroadcasts:* Rebroadcasts WMUF(AM) Paris 100%
P O Box 1239, 110 India Road, Paris, TN 38242 US
(731) 644-9455, *Fax:* (731) 644-9421
www.wmufradio.com
wmuf@bellsouth.net
License: Henry, Henry County, TN held by Benton-Weatherford Broadcasting Inc. of Tennessee
Group Owner: Benton-Weatherford Broadcasting Inc. of Tennessee
Nat'l Network: ABC
Arbitron Metro Market: Paris, TN *Format:* Country *Target Audience:* 25-54.
Gary Benton, President
Janice Benton, Operations Dir

Hohenwald

***WAUO**
01-01-1998; 90.7 mhz FM; 0.5 kw; 233 ft.; N35 33 56 W87 33 27
P O Drawer 2440, Tupelo, MS 38803 US
(662) 844-8888(662) 844-8893 (call-in), *Fax:* (662) 842-6791
www.afr.net
comments@afr.net
License: Hohenwald, Lewis County, TN held by American Family Association.
Group Owner: American Family Radio
Arbitron Metro Market: Phoenix, AZ *Format:* Christian
Marvin Sanders, General Manager

WMLR
07-04-1970; 1230 khz AM *Hrs Open:* 24; 1 kw-U, ND1; N35 31 22 W87 32 40
174 Gay Road, Hohenwald, TN 38462 US
(931) 796-5966, *Fax:* (931) 796-7353
harold@wmlr1230am.com
License: Hohenwald, TN held by Cochran Communication Corp. of Lewis County.
Nat'l Network: ABC
Arbitron Metro Market: Hohenwald, TN *Format:* Country *Special Programming:* Gospel *Adv. Rates:* 6; 4; 6; 4
Harold Cochran, President
Benjamin Cochran, General Sales Mgr
Josiah Cochran, Programming Director
Celeste Cochran, News Director

Humboldt

WIRJ
01-20-1949; 740 khz AM; 0.25 kw-D, ND1; 0.016 kw-N, ND1; N35 48 52 W88 54 51
Mailing Address: P.O. Box 740, Humbolt, TN 38343 US
Second Address: 2606 East End Dr., Humboldt, TN 38343
(731) 784-5000, *Fax:* (731) 784-2533
BRANDY@CLICK1.NET
License: Humboldt, TN held by John F. Warmath.
Format: Oldies, Talk
John Warmath, General Manager

WDVW(FM)
01-19-1989; 105.3 mhz FM *Hrs Open:* 24; 3 kw; Ant 328 ft; N35 50 41 W88 54 08
122 Radio Rd., Jackson, TN 38301
(731) 427-3316, *Fax:* (731) 427-9338
www.wtjs.com/
License: Humboldt, Gibson County, TN held by Forever South Licenses LLC
Group Owner: Forever Communications Inc.
Arbitron Metro Market: Jackson, TN *Target Audience:* 18-49.
Dave Hacker, Engineering Dir

WZDQ
09-01-1964; 102.3 mhz FM *Hrs Open:* 24; 6 kw; 299 ft.; N35 45 45 W88 51 42
P. O. Box 2763, Jackson, TN 38302 US
(731) 427-9616, *Fax:* (731) 424-2473
www.wzdq.fm
info@wzdq.fm
License: Humboldt, Gibson County, TN held by Thomas Radio LLC.
Group Owner: Black Crow Media Group LLC; (acq 11-9-2001; grpsl).
Nat'l Network: CNN Radio
Arbitron Metro Market: Jackson, TN *Target Audience:* 25-49; middle to upper class *Adv. Rates:* 28; 26; 28; 20
Shane Connor, Operations Dir
Chip Thomas, General Manager
Marsha Hulsey, General Sales Mgr

Huntingdon

WWDX
10-21-1975; 1530 khz AM *Hrs Open:* 7 AM-5 PM; 0.25 kw-C, NDD; 1 kw-D, NDD; N36 0 4 W88 26 2
PO Box 490, McKenzie, TN 38201 US
(800) 708-3276, *Fax:* (731) 986-8557
www.thefarmradio.com
License: Huntingdon, TN held by Jim W. Freeland.
Group Owner: Freeland Broadcasting Stations; (acq 3-13-2007; $110,000)
Arbitron Metro Market: Huntingdon, TN *Format:* Country *No. News Employees:* 2 *Target Audience:* General.
Mark Johnson, General Manager
Sarah Dunning, General Sales Mgr
Jay Jackson, News Director

WEIO(FM)
11-01-1979; 100.9 mhz FM *Hrs Open:* 24; 6 kw; 300 ft; N35 57 05 W88 27 47
215 Baker Rd., Huntingdon, TN 38344
(731) 986-8557
thefarmradio.com
wvhr@aeneas.net
License: Huntingdon, Carroll County, TN held by Jim W. Freeland.
Group Owner: Freeland Broadcasting Stations; (acq 9-16-2005; $650,000)
Regional Network: Tenn. Radio Net.
Population Served: 3,976 *Arbitron Metro Market:* Huntingdon, TN *Format:* Country
Michael Ray, Operations Dir
Jerry Vandiver, General Manager
Dave Hacker, Chief Engineer

Jackson

***WAMP**
01-01-1995; 88.1 mhz FM; 0.75 kw; 135 ft.; N35 39 38 W88 51 30
Post Office Drawer 2440, Tupelo, MS 38803 US
(662) 844-8888(662) 844-8893, *Fax:* (662) 842-6791
www.afr.net
faq@afr.net
License: Jackson, Madison County, TN held by American Family Association.
Group Owner: American Family Radio
Arbitron Metro Market: Jackson, TN *Format:* Christian
Marvin Sanders, General Manager

WDXI
10-31-1948; 1310 khz AM *Hrs Open:* 24; 5 kw-D, DAN; 1 kw-N, DAN; N35 39 50 W88 49 20
Mailing Address: One Radio Park, Jackson, TN 38301 US
Second Address: 1 Radio Park Dr., Jackson, TN 38305-4124
(731) 427-9611(731) 424-1310, *Fax:* (731) 424-1321
www.wdxi.com/
wdxi1310@yahoo.com
License: Jackson, TN held by Gerald W. Hunt
Nat'l Reps: D & R Radio
Arbitron Metro Market: Jackson, TN *Format:* News *Special Programming:* Farm 12 hrs, gospel 16 hrs, sports 16 hrs wkly *Hrs. of News Programming:* news progmg 10 hrs wkly *No. News Employees:* 1 *Target Audience:* 25 plus.
Gerald Hunt, General Manager

***WIGH**
09-30-1995; 88.7 mhz FM *Hrs Open:* 24; 14 kw; 538 ft.; N35 43 19 W88 36 7
Mailing Address: 1970-D N Highland Ave, Jackson, TN 38305 US
Second Address: 107 Park Gate Dr., Tupelo, MS 38801

(662) 844-8888, *Fax:* (662) 842-6791
License: Jackson, Henderson County, TN held by American Family Association.
Group Owner: American Family Radio; (acq 5-22-03; $20,000).
Nat'l Network: American Family Radio
Format: Christian *Target Audience:* Visually & physically impaired.
Marvin Sanders, General Manager

WJAK
11-14-1954; 1460 khz AM *Hrs Open:* 24; 1 kw-D, ND1; 0.128 kw-N, ND1; N35 38 37 W88 46 24
P. O. Box 2763, Jackson, TN 38302 US
(731) 427-9616, *Fax:* (731) 427-9302
License: Jackson, TN held by Thomas Radio L.L.C.
Group Owner: Black Crow Media Group LLC; (acq 7-21-2004; $318,000).
Nat'l Network: Moody; USA *Nat'l Reps:* Rgnl Reps
Format: Gospel *Hrs. of News Programming:* News progmg 14 hrs wkly *Target Audience:* 18-54; primarily Black Christian middle-class families with low to moderate income
Chip Thomas, General Manager

***WKNP**
12-17-1990; 90.1 mhz FM *Hrs Open:* 24; 18 kw; 512 ft.; N35 38 49 W88 50 0 *Rebroadcasts:* Rebroadcasts WKNO-FM Memphis 100%
Mailing Address: P.O. Box 241880, Memphis, TN 38124 US
Second Address: TN
(901) 458-2521, *Fax:* (901) 325-6505
www.wknofm.org
License: Jackson, Madison County, TN held by Mid-South Public Communications Foundation.
Nat'l Network: NPR; PRI
TV Affiliate: *WKNO-TV affil *Format:* Classical, News *Hrs. of News Programming:* news progmg 51 hrs wkly *No. News Employees:* 2 *Target Audience:* 35 plus.
Michael LaBonia, President
Darel Snodgrass, Operations Dir
Dan Campbell, General Manager
Charles McLarty, General Sales Mgr

WMXX-FM
05-09-1979; 103.1 mhz FM; 42 kw; 538 ft.; N35 32 39 W88 47 18
Mailing Address: PO Box 3845, Jackson, TN 38303 US
Second Address: 1 Radio Park Dr., Jackson, TN 38303
(731) 424-1310, *Fax:* (731) 424-1321
www.kool103.com
License: Jackson, Madison County, TN
Arbitron Metro Market: Jackson, TN *Format:* Oldies *Target Audience:* 25-54.
Dave Lozzi, Programming Director

WNWS-FM
08-01-1993; 101.5 mhz FM; 2.2 kw; 381 ft.; N35 38 59 W88 46 11
351 North Royal Street, Jackson, TN 38301 US
(731) 423-8316, *Fax:* (731) 423-8304
www.wnws.com
bnipp@wnws.com
License: Jackson, Madison County, TN held by Radiocorp of Jackson Inc.
Group Owner: The Wireless Group Inc.; (acq 12-6-00; $925,000).
Nat'l Network: CBS
TV Affiliate: Talk *Special Programming:* news progmg 25 hrs wkly *Hrs. of News Programming:* 2 *No. News Employees:* 25 plus; upscale adults
General Manager, Greg Wood
Office Manager, Station Manager
News Director, News Director

WTJS
01-01-1931; 1390 khz AM *Hrs Open:* 24; 5 kw-D, 1 kw-N, DA-N; N35 38 50 W88 50 00
122 Radio Rd., Jackson, TN 78701
(731) 427-3316, *Fax:* (731) 427-4576
License: Jackson, Madison County, TN held by Forever South Licenses LLC.
Group Owner: Forever Communications Inc.; (acq 5-12-2006; grpsl).
Regional Network: Tenn. Radio Net.
Population Served: 290,120 *Arbitron Metro Market:* Jackson, TN *Hrs. of News Programming:* news progmg 30 hrs wkly *No. News Employees:* 3 *Target Audience:* 35 plus; general
Christine Hilliard, President
Tabatha Eubank, Operations Dir
Verta Price, EVP
Verla Price, General Sales Mgr
Anthony Blackburn, Programming Director
Anna Gilmore, Promotions Manager
Ron Haney, News Director

Dave Hacker, ChiefEngineer
Connie Cain, Traffic Manager

WOGY
01-01-1947; 104.1 mhz FM; 100 kw; 682 ft.; N35 38 49 W88 50 0
600 Congress Ave., Suite 1400, Austin, TX 78701 US
(731) 427-3316, *Fax:* (731) 427-4576
eagle104.net
info@eagle104.net
License: Jackson, Madison County, TN
Group Owner: Forever Communications Inc.
Arbitron Metro Market: Jackson, TN *Format:* Country *Target Audience:* 18-54.
Deb Smith, Promotions Manager
Rusty Mac, News Director

Jamestown

WCLC
10-28-1957; 1260 khz AM; 1 kw-D, NDD; N36 26 10 W84 55 42
P. O. Box 1509, Jamestown, TN 38556 US
(931) 879-8188, *Fax:* (931) 879-1733
www.newlife105.com
info@newlife105.com
License: Jamestown, TN held by Bible Believers Network Inc.
Arbitron Metro Market: Jamestown, TN *Format:* Religious *Special Programming:* Farm 2 hrs, bluegrass 3 hrs wkly
Ryan Smith, Operations Dir
Connie Cody, Station Manager
Jim Cody, General Sales Mgr
Cheryl Wright, Programming Director
Steve Boutelle, News Director
Connie Cody, Business Manager
Sheliah Hughes, Traffic Manager

WCLC-FM
01-01-1985; 105.1 mhz FM; 6 kw; 328 ft.; N36 18 45 W84 56 13
P. O. Box 1509, Jamestown, TN 38556 US
(931) 879-8188, *Fax:* (931) 879-1733
www.newlife105.com
info@newlife105.com
License: Jamestown, Fentress County, TN
Arbitron Metro Market: Jamestown, TN *Format:* Religious
Colleen Condron, Operations Dir
Bruce Haines, General Manager
Connie Cody, Station Manager
Karen Fraser, General Sales Mgr
Cheryl Wright, Programming Director
Steve Boutelle, News Director
Janice Furtner, Music Director
JackieDidier, Traffic Manager

WDEB
01-12-1968; 1500 khz AM *Hrs Open:* Sunrise-sunset; 0.5 kw-C, NDD; 1 kw-D, NDD; N36 25 31 W84 56 32
Mailing Address: PO Box 69- Hwy 52 West, Jamestown, TN 38556 US
Second Address: 403 Livingston Ave., Jamestown, TN 38556
(931) 879-8164(931) 879-9332, *Fax:* (931) 879-7437
wderadio.com
wdebaudio@twlakes.net
License: Jamestown, TN held by BAZ Broadcasting Inc.
Regional Network: Tenn. Radio Net.
Arbitron Metro Market: Cookeville, TN *Format:* Country, Religious *Special Programming:* Farm 3 hrs wkly *Hrs. of News Programming:* news progmg 10 hrs wkly *No. News Employees:* 7 *Target Audience:* 18-54;household members who spend money in the marketplace
N.A. Baz, President
Jean Baz, Operations Dir
Gary Crocket, Programming Director
Gunther Muhsemann, Chief Engineer
Turk Baz, Local News Editor
Kevin Baz, Music Director

WDEB-FM
10-10-1972; 103.9 mhz FM *Hrs Open:* 5 AM-10:15 PM; 3.4 kw; 443 ft.; N36 25 31 W84 56 32
Mailing Address: P.O. Box 69, Jamestown, TN 38556 US
Second Address: 403 Livingston Ave., Jamestown, TN 38556
(931) 879-8164(931) 879-9332, *Fax:* (931) 879-7437
wderaudio@twlakes.net
License: Jamestown, Fentress County, TN
Wire Services: NOAA Weather
Arbitron Metro Market: Cookeville, TN *Format:* Country, Gospel
Jean Baz, General Sales Mgr
Cindy Mitchell, Programming Director
John Mullinix, Disc Jockey
Kevin Baz, Disc Jockey
Turk Baz, Disc Jockey
N. Baz, Regional Sales Manager

Jefferson City

WNRX
02-01-1976; 99.3 mhz FM *Hrs Open:* 24; 0.94 kw; 653 ft.; N36 4 28 W83 34 56
P.O. Box 5188 Eks, Johnson City, TN 37603 US
(865) 588-3725, *Fax:* (865) 428-2601
www.sportsanimal99.com
Jesse.Plunkett@citcomm.com
License: Jefferson City, Jefferson County, TN
Group Owner: Cumulus Media Inc.; (acq 7-20-2004; $1.65 million).
Arbitron Metro Market: Jefferson City, TN *Format:* Sports, Talk *Hrs. of News Programming:* news progmg 17 hrs wkly *No. News Employees:* 1
Luis Barajas, President
Moises Flores, Operations Dir
Mosses Flores, General Manager
Carlos Flecha, Programming Director
Jorge Figueroa, Engineering Dir
Virgen Perez, Sales VP

WJFC
11-01-1961; 1480 khz AM *Hrs Open:* 6 AM-6 PM; 0.5 kw-D, ND2; 0.034 kw-N, ND2; N36 6 15 W83 29 10
4045 Weaver Pike, Bluff City, TN 37618 US
(865) 475-3825, *Fax:* (865) 475-3800
www.wjfcradio.com
djmike@radiowjfc.com
License: Jefferson City, TN held by Lakeway Broadcasting LLC
Format: Country *Special Programming:* Farm one hr, relg 4 hrs wkly *Hrs. of News Programming:* news progmg 10 hrs wkly *No. News Employees:* 1 *Target Audience:* 25 plus; Jefferson, Grainger & Hamblen counties*Adv. Rates:* 15; 15; 15; 15.
M. Edward Stiner Jr., President
Kenneth Hill, General Manager
Beau Tucker, Station Manager
Susan Stiner, Programming Director
Mike Conner, Disc Jockey
Wendi Stiner, Disc Jockey
John Brown, Disc Jockey

Jellico

WEKX
01-01-1993; 102.7 mhz FM *Hrs Open:* 24; 0.63 kw; 1007 ft.; N36 41 28 W84 12 31
Rt. 550 West, Hindman, KY 41822 US
(606) 549-1027, *Fax:* (606) 549-5565
wekx@bellsouth.net
License: Jellico, Campbell County, TN held by Whitley Broadcasting Co. Inc.
Regional Reps: Rgnl Reps.
Arbitron Metro Market: Jellico, TN *Format:* Classic Rock *Hrs. of News Programming:* News progmg 5 hrs wkly
David Estes, General Manager
Rick Campbell, Programming Director
Frank Folsom, Chief Engineer

WJJT
02-01-1972; 1540 khz AM *Hrs Open:* Sunup to Sundown
Rt 550 West, Hindman, KY 41822 US
(423) 494-1582, *Fax:* (423) 784-5991
www.wjjtradio.com
wjjtradio@gmail.com
License: Jellico, TN held by Southeast Broadcasting Corp.
Nat'l Network: Salem Radio Network
Format: Gospel *Hrs. of News Programming:* news progmg 4 hrs wkly *No. News Employees:* 3
James Kilgore, President
Glenda Kilgore, Executive Vice President

Johnson City

WETB
10-01-1947; 790 khz AM *Hrs Open:* 6 AM-11 PM; 5 kw-D, ND1; 0.072 kw-N, ND1; N36 19 43 W82 24 39
Mailing Address: PO Box 4127, 231 Brandonwood Drive, Johnson City, TN 37602 US
Second Address: 231 Brandonwood Dr., Johnson City, TN 37604
(423) 928-7131, *Fax:* (423) 928-8392
webb@mounet.com
License: Johnson City, TN held by Mountain Signals Inc.
Nat'l Network: USA
Arbitron Metro Market: Johnson City, TN *Format:* Gospel *Hrs. of News Programming:* news progmg 3 hrs wkly *No. News Employees:* 1 *Target Audience:* General. *Adv. Rates:* 216; 216; 216; 216
Paul Gobble Jr., President
Paul Gobble, General Manager
Bob Morrison, Station Manager
Loretta Gouge, General Sales Mgr

***WETS-FM**
02-26-1974; 89.5 mhz FM *Hrs Open:* 24; 66 kw; 2270 ft.; N36 26 2 W82 8 8
P. O. Box 70630, Johnson City, TN 37614 US
(423) 439-6440(423) 439-6441, *Fax:* (423) 439-6449
www.wets.org
winklerw@etsu.edu
License: Johnson City, Washington County, TN held by East Tennessee State University.
Nat'l Network: NPR; PRI
Arbitron Metro Market: Johnson City, TN *Format:* News, News/Talk, 86 *Special Programming:* Blues 12 hrs, Sp one hr wkly *Hrs. of News Programming:* News progmg 22 hrs wkly
Target Audience: General.
Paul Stanton, President
Tony Coker, Operations Dir
Wayne Winkler, Station Manager
Larry Mayer, Programming Director
Dave Edwards, Engineering Dir
Mitch Sandidge, Chief Engineer
Mike Strickland, Announcer/Producer
Jim Blalock,Classical Music Director
Bob Hoffman, Producer/Announcer
Susan Lachmann, Women's Int Ed

WJCW
12-13-1938; 910 khz AM *Hrs Open:* 24; 5 kw-D, DAN; 1 kw-N, DAN; N36 24 37 W82 27 13
P.O. Box 8, Bloomington, IL 61702 US
(423) 477-1000, *Fax:* (423) 477-4747
www.wjcw.com
TalkRadio@wjcw.com
License: Johnson City, TN
Group Owner: Cumulus Media Inc.; (acq 5-30-2000; grpsl)
Nat'l Network: CBS; ABC
Arbitron Metro Market: Johnson City-Kingsport-Bristol, TN-VA
Format: Talk *Special Programming:* Relg 4 hrs wkly *Target Audience:* 25 plus.
Don Raines, Operations Dir
Debbie Caso, General Sales Mgr
Brian Bishop, Programming Director
Bob Lawrence, Promotions Manager
Richard Lovette, News Director
Al LeFevere, Chief Engineer
Paul Overbay, General Sales Manager
BobGordon, Operations Director

WQUT
03-01-1948; 101.5 mhz FM *Hrs Open:* 24; 99 kw; 1499 ft.; N36 16 7 W82 20 21
P.O. Box 8668, Gray, TN 37615 US
(423) 477-1015, *Fax:* (423) 477-4747
www.wqvt.com
classiccrock@wqut.com
License: Johnson City, Washington County, TN
Group Owner: Cumulus Media Inc.
Arbitron Metro Market: Johnson City-Kingsport-Bristol, TN-VA
Format: Classic Rock *Hrs. of News Programming:* news progmg 3 hrs wkly *No. News Employees:* 2 *Target Audience:* 18-49.
Randy Ross, General Sales Mgr
John Patrick, Programming Director
Jeri George, Promotions Manager
Susan Rines, News Director
Marc Tragler, Disc Jockey
John Boy Billy, Disc Jockey

Jonesborough

WKTP
10-01-1958; 1590 khz AM *Hrs Open:* 24; 5 kw-U, DA-2; N36 19 54 W82 28 27 *Rebroadcasts:* Rebroadcasts WKPT(AM) Kingsport 95%
222 Commerce St., Kingsport, TN 37662
(423) 246-9578, *Fax:* (423) 247-9836
www.wkptam.com
davidw@wtfm.com
License: Jonesborough, Washington County, TN held by Holston Valley Broadcasting Corp.
Group Owner: Glenwood Communications Corp.; (acq 1-25-90; $90,000;
Nat'l Network: ABC *Nat'l Reps:* Eastman *Wire Services:* AP
Population Served: 200,000 *Arbitron Metro Market:* Johnson City-Kingsport-Bristol, TN-VA *TV Affiliate:* WKPT-TV *Hrs. of News Programming:* news progmg 24 hrs wkly *No. News Employees:* 2 *Target Audience:* 35plus.
George Devault, President
David Widener, General Manager
Charles Aesque, General Sales Mgr
Scott Onks, Programming Director
Duane Nelson, News Director
N. David Widener, Executive Vice President

Karns

WCYQ
01-08-1989; 93.1 mhz FM; 2.4 kw; 512 ft.; N35 57 46 W84 1 23
P.O. Box 693, 720 East Capitol Drive, Milwaukee, WI 53212 US
(865) 824-1021, *Fax:* (865) 693-8493
www.q93country.com
info@wmyu.com
License: Karns, Knox County, TN held by Journal Broadcast Corp.
Group Owner: Journal Communications Inc.; (acq 5-19-97)
Arbitron Metro Market: Knoxville, TN *Format:* Country
Andy Laird, Operations Dir
Chris Protzman, General Manager
Dan McKee, General Sales Mgr
Mike Hammond, Programming Director
Rich Bailey, Operations Manager

Kingsport

***WCQR-FM**
12-01-1996; 88.3 mhz FM; 1.2 kw; 2133 ft.; N36 25 53 W82 8 16
P. O. Box 889, Blacksburg, VA 24063 US
(423) 477-5676, *Fax:* (423) 477-7060
www.wcqr.org
office@wcqr.org
License: Kingsport, Sullivan County, TN held by Positive Alternative Radio Inc.
Group Owner: Positive Alternative Radio Inc.
Nat'l Network: Salem Radio Network
Arbitron Metro Market: Johnson City-Kingsport-Bristol, TN-VA
Format: Christian *Target Audience:* 25-54.
Mike Perry, General Manager

***WCSK**
11-05-1984; 90.3 mhz FM; 195 w; 23 ft; N36 31 37 W82 35 12
Kingsport City Schools, 400, Clinchfield St. Ste 200, Kingsport, TN 37664
(423) 378-2111, *Fax:* (423) 378-8473
http://kingsport.schoolfusion.us
jhall@k12k.com
License: Kingsport, Sullivan County, TN held by Kingsport Board of Education.
Population Served: 70,000 *Arbitron Metro Market:* Johnson City-Ki
Jeff Hall, Station Manager

WHGG
06-01-1967; 1090 khz AM *Hrs Open:* 12
Mailing Address: P.O. Box 2061, Bristol, TN 37621 US
Second Address: 340 Edgemont Ave., Suite 100, Bristol, TN 37620
(423) 878-6279, *Fax:* (423) 878-6520
www.mighty1090.com
mshepard@bcaradio.com
License: Kingsport, TN held by Information Communication Corp.
Group Owner: Information Communications Corp.; (acq 1-1-2006; $250,000 with WABN(AM) Abingdon, VA).
Arbitron Metro Market: Johnson City-Kingsport-Bristol, TN-VA
Format: Oldies *Hrs. of News Programming:* news progmg 10 hrs wkly *No. News Employees:* 1 *Target Audience:* 24-55.
Kenneth Hill, President
Mike Shepard, Operations Dir
Tex Meyer, General Manager
Matthew Hill, Station Manager
Jerry Donadio, General Sales Mgr
Mike Shepard, Programming Director
Patrick Osburn, VP Director of Sales
Jim Shean,Sales Manager
Michael Projansky, National Sales Manager
Dwayne Taylor, Director of Sales
Jack Cronin, Executive Producer

WGOC
10-01-1951; 1320 khz AM *Hrs Open:* 24; 5 kw-D, DAN; 0.5 kw-N, DAN; N36 33 12 W82 28 58
Mailing Address: P. O. Box 8, Bloomington, IL 61702 US
Second Address: 162 Freehill Rd., Kingsport, TN 37615
(423) 477-1000, *Fax:* (423) 477-4747
www.640wxsm.com
bill.meade@cumulus.com
License: Kingsport, TN
Group Owner: Cumulus Media Inc.; (acq 5-30-2000; grpsl)
Nat'l Network: ESPN Radio; CBS Radio *Nat'l Reps:* Katz Radio
Wire Services: AP
Arbitron Metro Market: Johnson City-Kingsport-Bristol, TN-VA
Format: Sports
Bob Gordon, Operations Dir
Don Raines, General Manager
Paul Overbay, General Sales Mgr
John Patrick, Programming Director
Bob Lawrence, Promotions Manager
Richard Lovette, News Director
Wayne Sizemore, Chief Engineer
DebbieCaso, Market Manager
Patti Johnson, Business Manager
J.B. Stone, Program Director
Bill Meade, Program Director
Carl Swann, Director of Special Creative Services
Susan Rhea, Traffic Director

WKOS
02-21-1970; 104.9 mhz FM; 2.75 kw; 492 ft.; N36 33 14 W82 27 0
Mailing Address: P.O. Box 8, Bloomington, IL 61702 US
Second Address: 162 Freehill Rd., Kingsport, TN 37615
(423) 477-1000, *Fax:* (423) 477-4747
www.wkos.com
oldies@preferred.com
License: Kingsport, Sullivan County, TN
Group Owner: Cumulus Media Inc.
Nat'l Network: Westwood One
Arbitron Metro Market: Johnson City-Kingsport-Bristol, TN-VA
Format: Oldies *Target Audience:* 25-54.
Bob Lawrence, Operations Dir
Debbie Caso, General Sales Mgr
Alan Austin, Programming Director
Susan Ritea, News Director
Dennis Kelly, Disc Jockey
Don Gibson, Disc Jockey
Greg Price, National Sales Manager

WKPT
07-14-1940; 1400 khz AM *Hrs Open:* 24; 1 kw-U; N36 32 37 W82 31 21
222 Commerce St., Kingsport, TN 37662
(423) 246-9578, *Fax:* (423) 247-9836
www.wkptam.com
davidw@wtfm.com
License: Kingsport, Sullivan County, TN held by Holston Valley Broadcasting Corp.
Group Owner: Glenwood Communications Corp.; (acq 6-1-66)
Nat'l Network: ABC *Regional Network:* U T Vol Network *Nat'l Reps:* Eastman *Wire Services:* AP
Population Served: 650,000 *Arbitron Metro Market:* Johnson City-Kingsport-Bristol, TN-VA *TV Affiliate:* WKPT-TV *No. News Employees:* 2 *Target Audience:* 35 plus.
George Devault, President
David Widener, General Manager
Charles Aesque, General Sales Mgr
Scott Onks, Programming Director
Duane Nelson, News Director
N. David Widener, Executive Vice President
Roger Epperson, News Reporter
Emily Pridemore, Traffic Manager
David Light, Women's Int Ed

WTFM
02-01-1948; 98.5 mhz FM *Hrs Open:* 24; 74 kw; Ant 2,241 ft; N36 25 54 W82 08 15
222 Commerce St., Kingsport, TN 37662
(423) 246-9578, *Fax:* (423) 247-9836
www.wtfm.com
davidw@wtfm.com
License: Kingsport, Sullivan County, TN held by Holsten Valley Broadcasting
Group Owner: Glenwood Communications Corp.; 06-01-1966
Nat'l Network: ABC *Nat'l Reps:* Eastman *Wire Services:* AP
Population Served: 1,000,000 *Arbitron Metro Market:* Johnson City-Kingsport-Bristol, TN-VA *TV Affiliate:* WKPT-TV affil *No. News Employees:* 2 *Target Audience:* 25-54 Women
George Devault, President
N. David Widener, EVP/General Manager
Tim Loy, General Sales Mgr
Mark Baker, Programming Director
Brittany Moore, Promotions Manager
Duane Nelson, News Director
Lyle Musser, Chief Engineer
TaylorMorgan, Disc Jockey
Elva Marie, Disc Jockey
Steve Mann, Disc Jockey
Emily Pridemore, Traffic Manager

Kingston

WBBX
07-01-1978; 1410 khz AM *Hrs Open:* 8 AM-6 PM; 0.5 kw-D, NDD; N35 52 49 W84 30 56
Mailing Address: 705 Greenwood, Box 389, Kingston, TN 37763 US
Second Address: 705 Greenwood St., Kingston, TN 37763

(208) 734-6633, *Fax:* (208) 736-1958
www.csnradio.com
License: Kingston, TN held by Pilgrim Pathway Inc.
Arbitron Metro Market: North Platte NE
Mike Kestler, President

***WKTS**
09-11-2006; 90.1 mhz FM *Hrs Open:* 24; 0.055 kw vert; 633 ft.; N35 45 57 W84 34 33
838 Ray Drive, Oliver Springs, TN 37840 US
(865) 717-3335
www.bridgeradiofm.org
thebridgefm@yahoo.com
License: Kingston, Roane County, TN held by Foothills Broadcasting, Inc.
Arbitron Metro Market: Kingston, TN *Format:* Christian *Special Programming:* 2 church services, 2hrs *Hrs. of News Programming:* news progmg 3 hrs wkly *No. News Employees:* 1
David Wells, General Manager
Darrin Wilcox, Station Manager

Kingston Springs

WFFI
01-15-1993; 93.7 mhz FM *Hrs Open:* 24; 1.15 kw; 755 ft.; N36 8 10 W86 59 4 *Rebroadcasts:* Simulcasts with WFFH(FM) Smyrna
C/O Fisher Wayland: Jsr, 2001 Penn. Ave., #400, Washington, DC 20006 US
(615) 367-2210, *Fax:* (615) 367-0758
www.94fmthefish.net
94fm@thefish.com
License: Kingston Springs, Cheatham County, TN held by Caron Broadcasting Inc.
Group Owner: Salem Communications Corp.; (acq 12-18-2002; $5.6 million with WFFH(FM) Smyrna).
Nat'l Network: Salem Radio Network *Nat'l Reps:* Salem
Arbitron Metro Market: Nashville, TN *Format:* Christian *Target Audience:* 25-54; adults
Michael Miller, General Manager
Kevin Anderson, General Sales Mgr
Vance Dillard, Programming Director
Dick Marsh, Promotions Manager
Kim Bindel, News Director
Carl Campbell, Chief Engineer
Ed Evenson, Traffic Manager

Knoxville

WNPZ
05-21-1961; 1580 khz AM; 1 kw-C, NDD; 5 kw-D, NDD; N35 54 42 W83 53 33
1515 Magnolia Avenue, Knoxville, TN 37917 US
(423)231-8257
www.praisenglory.com
rejoice1580@aol.com
License: Knoxville, TN held by Metropolitan Management Corp. of Tennessee
Arbitron Metro Market: Knoxville, TN
Randal Mangham, President
Rev. Maurice Gaines, Programming Director

WVLZ
06-01-1988; 1180 khz AM; 2.6 kw-C, NDD; 10 kw-D, NDD; N35 58 48 W83 49 9
802 S Central, Knoxville, TN 37902 US
(865) 546-4653, *Fax:* (865) 637-7133
License: Knoxville, TN held by Kirkland Wireless Broadcasters Inc.
Arbitron Metro Market: Knoxville, TN *Format:* Sports *Target Audience:* 30 plus; young, married with small children
John Hodge, Station Manager

WIFA
01-21-1941; 1240 khz AM *Hrs Open:* 24; 1 kw-U, ND1; N35 57 17 W83 57 4
Mailing Address: P.O. Box 3848, Evansvill, IN 47736 US
Second Address: 818 N. Cedar Bluff Rd., Knoxville, TN 37923
(865) 531-2005, *Fax:* (865) 531-2006
www.1240radio.com
License: Knoxville, TN held by Progressive Media Inc.
Arbitron Metro Market: Knoxville, TN *Format:* Adult Contemp, Christian
Barry Culberson, President
Brian Brooks, General Manager

WIMZ-FM
10-01-1949; 103.5 mhz FM; 79 kw; 1722 ft.; N36 8 6 W83 43 29
P.O.. Box 3848, Evansvill, IN 47736 US
(865) 525-6000, *Fax:* (865) 525-2000
www.wimz.com
rcchambers@sccradio.com
License: Knoxville, Knox County, TN held by South Central Communications Corp.
Group Owner: South Central Communications Corp.; (acq 2-23-93; $3.5 million with co-located AM;
Arbitron Metro Market: Knoxville, TN *Format:* Classic Rock
Terry Gillingham, Operations Dir
Randy Ross, General Sales Mgr
Randy Chambers, Programming Director
Jeff Cutshaw, News Director
Billy Kidd, Music Director
Neda Gayle, National Sales Manager
Nikki Roberts, Public AffairsDirector

WITA
09-01-1960; 1490 khz AM *Hrs Open:* 24 hrs; 1 kw-U, ND1; N35 58 11 W83 57 56
2730 Loumor Ave, Metairie, LA 70001 US
(865) 588-2974
www.wwcr.com
wita1490@aol.com
License: Knoxville, TN held by RR Broadcast Group Inc.
Arbitron Metro Market: Knoxville, TN *Format:* Christian, Talk *Special Programming:* Black 8 hrs wkly *Target Audience:* General.
Rex Palmer, President
Greg McMahon, Operations Dir
Gail Scott, General Manager

WIVK-FM
12-16-1965; 107.7 mhz FM *Hrs Open:* 24; 91 kw; 2077 ft.; N35 48 41 W83 40 10
4711 Old Kingston Pike, Knoxville, TN 37919 US
(865) 588-6511, *Fax:* (865) 588-3725
www.wivk.com
License: Knoxville, Knox County, TN
Group Owner: Cumulus Media Inc.
Arbitron Metro Market: Knoxville, TN *Format:* Country
John Crooks, Programming Director

WKVL
01-16-1989; 850 khz AM; 50 kw-D, DAD; N36 4 12 W83 58 19
Box 2526, Knoxville, TN 37901 US
(865) 675-4105, *Fax:* (865) 675-4859
www.wkvl.com
info@wkvl.com
License: Knoxville, TN held by Horne Radio L.L.C.
Group Owner: Horne Radio Group; (acq 10-15-99; grpsl).
Arbitron Metro Market: Knoxville, TN *Format:* Talk *Target Audience:* 25 plus; educated, informed adults
Brian Tatum, General Manager

WJXB-FM
04-10-1967; 97.5 mhz FM *Hrs Open:* 24; 96 kw; 1,296 ft; N36 00 36 W83 55 57
1100 Sharps Ridge Mem Park Dr., Knoxville, TN 47736
(865) 525-6000, *Fax:* (865) 656-3292
www.b975.com
jjarnigan@sccradio.com
License: Knoxville, Knox County, TN held by South Central Communications Corp.
Group Owner: South Central Communications Corp.
Wire Services: UPI
Population Served: 174,589 *Arbitron Metro Market:* Knoxville, TN *Target Audience:* 25-54.
Terry Gillingham, Operations Dir
Randy Ross, General Sales Mgr
Jeff Jarnigan, Programming Director
Deborah Maulden, Promotions Manager
David Henley, News Director
Kevin Duplantis, Chief Engineer

***WKCS**
12-01-1952; 91.1 mhz FM *Hrs Open:* 8 AM-3:30 PM; 0.31 kw horiz; 72 ft.; N35 59 36 W83 55 24
2509 Broadway, N. E., Knoxville, TN 37917 US
(865) 594-1259
www.wkcsradio.org
wkcsradio@hotmail.com
License: Knoxville, Knox County, TN held by Fulton High School.
Arbitron Metro Market: Knoxville, TN *Format:* Oldies *Hrs. of News Programming:* News progmg 3 hrs wkly *Target Audience:* 18 plus; University of Tennessee
Russell Mayes, General Manager

WKGN
09-28-1947; 1340 khz AM; 1 kw-U, ND1; N35 57 20 W83 58 14
P.O. Box 10005, Knoxville, TN 37939 US
(865) 546-7900, *Fax:* (865) 546-7965
info@wkgn.com
License: Knoxville, TN held by Norsan Consulting and Management Inc.
Group Owner: Norsan Consulting and Management Inc.; (acq 3-8-2006; $500,000).
Nat'l Network: Westwood One *Nat'l Reps:* Roslin
Arbitron Metro Market: Knoxville, TN *Format:* Gospel *Special Programming:* Relg 5 hrs, medicine/health one hr wkly *Target Audience:* 18-34; young, mobile adults
Norberto Sanchez, President
Robert Stewart, General Manager
Thomas Henderson, Programming Director
Ed Martin, Chief Engineer

WKXV
02-01-1953; 900 khz AM *Hrs Open:* 24 hours; 1 kw-D, ND1; 0.258 kw-N, ND1; N35 58 52 W83 59 15
5106 Middlebrook Pike, Knoxville, TN 37921 US
(865) 558-0900, *Fax:* (865) 588-5848
wkxv@bellsouth.net
License: Knoxville, TN held by Ratel Broadcasting Co. Inc.
Arbitron Metro Market: Knoxville, TN *Format:* Gospel, Religious *Target Audience:* 18+ *Adv. Rates:* 12;20
Ted Lowe Sr., President
Ted Lowe Jr., General Manager
Ted Lowe Jr, Programming Director
Rick Whisman, News Director
Frank Folsom, Chief Engineer
Eva Ruffin, Office Manager

WETR
07-05-1995; 760 khz AM *Hrs Open:* Day-time; 2.4 kw-D, NDD; N35 59 18 W83 50 35
304 Crane Cove, Longwood, FL 32750 US
(865) 525-0620, *Fax:* (865) 521-8923
www.talkradio760.com
info@talkradio760.com
License: Knoxville, TN held by Thomas H. Moffit Jr.
Nat'l Network: Salem Radio Network; Talk Radio Network
Arbitron Metro Market: Knoxville, TN *Format:* News, News/Talk, 86 *Target Audience:* 25-54; blue collar men & women
David Wells, General Manager
David Wells, Programming Director

WNML
03-23-1953; 990 khz AM *Hrs Open:* 24
Mailing Address: 4711 Old Kingston Pike, Knoxville, TN 37919 US
Second Address: 4711 Old Kingston Pike, Knoxville, TN 37919
(865) 588-6511, *Fax:* (865) 558-4218
www.sportsanimal99.com
License: Knoxville, TN
Group Owner: Cumulus Media Inc.; (acq 4-26-2001; grpsl).
Arbitron Metro Market: Knoxville, TN *Format:* News, News/Talk, 84, Talk *Hrs. of News Programming:* news progmg 28 hrs wkly *No. News Employees:* 8 *Target Audience:* 25-54.
Farid Suleman, CEO
Mike Hammond, Operations Dir
Ed Brantley, General Manager
Charles Sells, General Sales Mgr
John Crooks, Programming Director
Steve Queisser, Promotions Manager
Donna Heffner, CFO
Lisa Rotton, National SalesManager
Jack Gillette, Regional Sales Manager

WKHT
11-01-1991; 104.5 mhz FM; 2.3 kw; 528 ft.; N36 0 8 W83 56 41
720 E. Capitol Drive, Milwaukee, WI 53212 US
(865) 693-1020,(865) 824-1021, *Fax:* (865) 824-1880
www.1045thebone.com
dmckee@journalbroadcastinggroup.com
License: Knoxville, Knox County, TN held by Journal Broadcast Corp.
Group Owner: Journal Communications Inc.; (acq 3-4-98; $5.745 million with WQBB(AM) Powell).
Nat'l Reps: Roslin
Arbitron Metro Market: Knoxville, TN *Format:* Classic Rock *Special Programming:* Pub affrs 2 hrs wkly *Target Audience:* 35 plus; female
Rich Bailey, Operations Dir
Chris Protzman, General Manager
Dodie Manalac, General Sales Mgr
Russ Allen, Programming Director
Eddy Roy, News Director
Mark Lucas, Chief Engineer

WRJZ
02-12-1927; 620 khz AM *Hrs Open:* 24; 5 kw-D, DAN; 5 kw-N, DAN; N35 59 24 W83 50 15
1621 E. Magnolia Ave, Knoxville, TN 37917 US
(865) 525-0620, *Fax:* (865) 521-8910
www.wrjz.com
joy62@wrjz.com

License: Knoxville, TN held by Tennessee Media Associates.
Nat'l Network: Salem Radio Network *Nat'l Reps:* Salem
Arbitron Metro Market: Knoxville, TN *Format:* Christian, Talk *Hrs. of News Programming:* News progmg 5 hrs wkly *Target Audience:* 25-54; white collar men & woman
Thomas Moffit Jr., President
David Wells, General Manager

***WUOT**
10-01-1949; 91.9 mhz FM *Hrs Open:* 24; 64 kw; 1752 ft.; N35 59 44 W83 57 23
232 Communications Bldg., Knoxville, TN 37996 US
(865) 974-5375, *Fax:* (865) 974-3941
www.wuot.org
wuot@utk.edu
License: Knoxville, Knox County, TN held by University of Tennessee.
Nat'l Network: PRI; NPR *Wire Services:* AP
Arbitron Metro Market: Knoxville, TN *Format:* Classical, Jazz, 60 *Hrs. of News Programming:* news progmg 37 hrs wkly *No. News Employees:* 3 *Target Audience:* 35-54.
David Williamson, CFO
Greg Hill, Operations Dir
Regina Dean, General Manager
Dan Berry, Programming Director
Matt Powell, News Director
Mike Murvell, Chief Engineer

***WUTK-FM**
01-04-1982; 90.3 mhz FM *Hrs Open:* 24; 0.8 kw vert; 69 ft.; N35 57 9 W83 55 34
333 Communications Bldg., Knoxville, TN 37996 US
(865) 974-2228, *Fax:* (865) 974-2814
www.wutkradio.com
wutk@utk.edu
License: Knoxville, Knox County, TN held by University of Tennessee.
Arbitron Metro Market: Knoxville, TN *Format:* Rock/AOR *Target Audience:* 18-45; male/female
Benny Smith, General Manager
Holly Gary, News Department Assistant
Todd Roberts, Production Director
Dallas Abel, Sports Director
Jennell Klussman, Underwriting Director

La Follette

WQLA
09-01-1983; 960 khz AM *Hrs Open:* 24 HRS; 1 kw-D, ND2; 0.033 kw-N, ND2; N36 22 2 W84 8 50
Box 1530, Lafollette, TN 37766 US
(423) 566-1000, *Fax:* (423) 566-7070
wqla@bellsouth.net
License: La Follette, TN held by JENN MEDIA INC..
Nat'l Reps: Roslin
Format: Classic Rock *Special Programming:* LET IT RIP *Hrs. of News Programming:* TOP OF HOUR *No. News Employees:* 3 *Target Audience:* General.
Cliff Jennings, President
BARBARA NULF, General Manager

WLAF
05-17-1953; 1450 khz AM *Hrs Open:* 24; 1 kw-U, ND1; N36 22 52 W84 7 32
Mailing Address: P.O. Box 1409, Lafollette, TN 37766 US
Second Address: 210 N 5th St, La Follette, TN 37766
(423) 562-1450, *Fax:* (423) 562-5764
www.1450wlaf.com
wlaf@campbellcounty.com
License: La Follette, TN held by Stair Co. Inc.
Nat'l Network: USA *Regional Network:* Tenn. Radio Net.
Format: Gospel *Special Programming:* Bluegrass 7 hrs wkly *Hrs. of News Programming:* news progmg 7 hrs wkly *No. News Employees:* 1 *Target Audience:* 12+ or 25+. *Adv. Rates:* 10; 10; 10; 10
Jim Stair, President
Bill Waddell, Operations Dir

WTNQ
09-01-1982; 104.9 mhz FM *Hrs Open:* 24; 2.3 kw; 499 ft.; N36 21 8 W84 5 20
P.O. Box 1530, Lafollette, TN 37766 US
(423) 562-0550, *Fax:* (423) 562-0105
License: La Follette, Campbell County, TN
Format: Sports, Country *Target Audience:* 18 plus. *Adv. Rates:* 15; 15; 15; 15
Barbara Nuls, General Sales Mgr

La Vergne

WBUZ
05-01-1962; 102.9 mhz FM *Hrs Open:* 24; 100 kw; 955 ft.; N35 48 1 W86 37 17
P.O. Box 150846, Nashville, TN 37215 US
(615) 399-1029, *Fax:* (615) 361-9873
www.1029thebuzz.com
programming@1029thebuzz.com
License: La Vergne, Rutherford County, TN held by WYCQ Inc.
Group Owner: The Cromwell Group Inc.; (acq 11-28-89).
Arbitron Metro Market: Nashville, TN *Format:* Rock/AOR *Special Programming:* Farm one hr wkly *Target Audience:* 18-34; residents in middle TN
Bayard Walters, President
Tincy Crouse, General Manager
Bob Reich, Station Manager
Troy Hanson, Program Director/Operations Manager
Chad Fournier, Program Director/Operations Manager
Jim Patrick, News Director
David Wilson, ChiefEngineer
Andra Kramer, Traffic Manager
Jana Hampton, Sales Manager
Cindy Marino, Marketing Coordinator
Lacey House, Digital Strategies Manager

Lafayette

WEEN
11-03-1958; 1460 khz AM *Hrs Open:* Daytime; 0.86 kw-D, ND1; 0.119 kw-N, ND1; N36 32 6 W86 0 27
P.O. Box 160, Lafayette, TN 37083 US
(615) 666-2169, *Fax:* (615) 666-8056
www.wlct.com/
wlct@nctc.com,schermars@nctc.com
License: Lafayette, TN held by Lafayette Broadcasting Co. Inc.
Nat'l Network: Salem Radio Network *Regional Network:* Tenn. Radio Net.
Arbitron Metro Market: Lafayette, TN *Format:* Gospel *Special Programming:* Farm 5 hrs wkly *Target Audience:* General; 25-54 year olds *Adv. Rates:* 8.95; 8.95; 8.95; n/a
Ivan Davis, CEO
Randall Swaffer, General Manager
Randy Swaffer, Station Manager

WLCT
07-01-1995; 102.1 mhz FM *Hrs Open:* 5 AM-11 PM; 6 kw; 325 ft.; N36 32 6 W86 0 27
P.O. Box 160, Lafayette, TN 37083 US
(615) 666-2169, *Fax:* (615) 666-8056
www.wlct.com
wlct@nctc.com
License: Lafayette, Macon County, TN held by Lafayette Broadcasting Co. Inc.
Format: Country *Target Audience:* 20-60. *Adv. Rates:* 8.95; 8.95; 8.95; 8.95
Randy Swaffer, General Manager
Jamie Dallas, General Sales Mgr
Melinda White, News Director
Jamie DAllas, Promotions Director

Lakeland

WMQM
04-27-1955; 1600 khz AM *Hrs Open:* 24
Mailing Address: Rt. 4 Box 114 Baker Roa, Huntingdon, TN 38344 US
Second Address: Sale Office, 1300 WWCR Ave., Nashville, TN 37218
(901) 327-2500, *Fax:* (901) 327-2777
www.wwcr.com
info@wwcr.com
License: Lakeland, TN held by WMQM Inc.
Group Owner: F W Robbert Broadcasting Co. Inc.
Arbitron Metro Market: Memphis, TN *Format:* Religious *Target Audience:* General.
Fred Werstenberger, President
Adam Lock, Operations Dir
George McClintock, General Manager
David Brown, Station Manager

Lakesite

WALV-FM
07-01-1976; 105.1 mhz FM *Hrs Open:* 24; 6 kw
1305 Carter Street, Chattanooga, TN 37381
(423) 265-9494, *Fax:* (423) 266-2335
espnchattanooga.com
License: Lakesite, Hamilton County, TN held by J.L. Brewer Broadcasting of Cleveland, LLC
Group Owner: Brewer Broadcasting Corp.; 1-May
Nat'l Network: ESPN Radio *Nat'l Reps:* Katz Radio
Population Served: 450,000 *Arbitron Metro Market:* Chattanooga, TN *Target Audience:* A18+ *Adv. Rates:* 30; 25; 30; 20
Jim Brewer, Chairman
Jim Brewer II, President
Keith Landecker, Operations Dir
Jim Brewer, General Manager
Jim Brewer, Station Manager
Mike Baskin, General Sales Mgr
Wells Guthrie, Programming Director
Sam Lewis, ChiefEngineer

Lawrenceburg

***WAWI**
01-01-1999; 89.7 mhz FM; 6 kw; 148 ft.; N35 16 4 W87 19 25
P O Drawer 2440, Tupelo, MS 38803 US
(603) 668-6470
License: Lawrenceburg, Lawrence County, TN held by American Family Association.
Group Owner: American Family Radio
Arbitron Metro Market: Mills WY *Format:* Adult Contemp
Steven Silberberg, President

WDXE
07-21-1951; 1370 khz AM; 1 kw-D, ND1; 0.044 kw-N, ND1; N35 15 25 W87 18 24
Rt 2 Box 10c, Houston, MS 38851 US
(931) 762-4411, *Fax:* (931) 762-4789
www.wdxeradio.com/
wdxe@wdxe.com
License: Lawrenceburg, TN held by Lakewood Communications LLC
Regional Network: Tenn. Radio Net.
Arbitron Metro Market: Lawrenceburg, TN *Format:* Country
Jack Cheatwood, General Manager
Ron Fisher, General Sales Mgr
Phillip Kemper, Chief Engineer
Ronnie Allen, Disc Jockey
Sunny Cull, Disc Jockey
Paula Walker, Women's Int Ed

WDXE-FM
08-28-1964; 106.7 mhz FM; 6 kw; 292 ft.; N35 15 25 W87 18 24
C/O Robin H. Mathis, Rt. 2, Box 10c, Houston, MS 38851 US
(931) 762-4411, *Fax:* (931) 762-4789
www.wdxeradio.com/
wdxe@wdxe.com
License: Lawrenceburg, Lawrence County, TN
Arbitron Metro Market: Lawrenceburg, TN *Format:* Adult Contemp
Jack Cheatwood, General Manager

WLLX
05-01-1991; 97.5 mhz FM *Hrs Open:* 24; 42 kw; 528 ft.; N35 16 56 W87 6 18
Mailing Address: PO Box 156, Lawrenceburg, TN 38464 US
Second Address: 1212 N. Locust Ave., Lawrenceburg, TN 38464
wllxradio@lorettotel.net
License: Lawrenceburg, Lawrence County, TN held by Roger W. Wright dba Prospect Communications
Format: Country *No. News Employees:* 1 *Target Audience:* 25-54.
Roger Wright, Operations Dir
Dan Hollander, Programming Director
Janet Wright, Promotions Manager
Dawn Washburn, Disc Jockey
Carolyn Thompson, Disc Jockey
Eddie Landtroop, Disc Jockey

WWLX
06-21-1987; 590 khz AM *Hrs Open:* 24
Mailing Address: PO Box 156, Lawrenceburg, TN 38464 US
Second Address: 1212 N. Locust Ave., Lawrenceburg, TN 38464
(931) 762-6200, *Fax:* (931) 762-6200
www.wlxonline.com
ben@wlxonline.com
License: Lawrenceburg, TN held by Roger W. Wright dba Prospect Communications.
Arbitron Metro Market: Lawrenceburg, TN *Format:* Country
Special Programming: Oldies R&R 8 hrs, old country 8 hrs wkly
Hrs. of News Programming: news progmg 10 hrs wkly *No. News Employees:* 1 *TargetAudience:* General.
Roger Wright, President
Janet Wright, General Sales Mgr
Dan Hollander, Programming Director
Michele Tankersley, News Director
Carolyn Thompson, Disc Jockey
Eddie Landtroop, Disc Jockey

***WZXX**
01-01-2005; 88.5 mhz FM; 0.076 kw; 545 ft.; N35 12 12 W87 19 39
P O Box 887, Brentwood, TN 37024 US
(208) 733-3551, *Fax:* (208) 733-3548
www.edgewaterbroadcasting.com
License: Lawrenceburg, Lawrence County, TN held by Radio Assist Ministry Inc.
Arbitron Metro Market: Florence, AL *Format:* Christian
Ben Mccarron, Chief Operating Engineer
Clark Parrish, President & Technical Director
Robert L. Jackson, Head of Programming & Operations
Jim Long, General Manager
Steve Atkin, Promotions Manager
Diana Atkin, Vice President
EarlWilliamson, Secretary / Treasurer
John Devine, Director
Dennis Clounch, Director

Lebanon

WANT
10-01-1993; 98.9 mhz FM *Hrs Open:* 24; 5 kw; 318 ft.; N36 12 24 W86 16 2
P.O. Box 1025, Lebanon, TN 37088 US
(615) 449-3699, *Fax:* (615) 443-4235
www.wantfm.com
info@WANTFM.com
License: Lebanon, Wilson County, TN held by Bay-Pointe Broadcasting Co. Inc.
Arbitron Metro Market: Lebanon, TN, *Format:* Country *No. News Employees:* 1 *Target Audience:* General.
Susan James, President
Billy Goodman, Operations Dir
Albert Jarratt Sr., Chief Engineer
M.J. Lucas, Music Director

WKDA
10-05-1949; 900 khz AM *Hrs Open:* 24
P.O. Box 1025, Lebanon, TN 37088 US
(615) 889-1960, *Fax:* (615)902-9108
www.wantfm.com
License: Lebanon, TN held by Wilson County Broadcasting, Inc.
Arbitron Metro Market: Nashville, TN *Format:* Spanish *No. News Employees:* 1 *Target Audience:* General.
Susan James, President
Billy Goodman, News Director
Gary Brown, Chief Engineer

***WFMQ**
12-15-1966; 91.5 mhz FM *Hrs Open:* 24; 0.5 kw horiz; 82 ft.; N36 12 13 W86 18 1
P.O. Box 609, Lebanon, TN 37087 US
(615) 444-2562, *Fax:* (615) 444-2569
License: Lebanon, Wilson County, TN held by Cumberland University.
Format: Jazz *Special Programming:* Class 6 hrs wkly
Dr. Harvill Eaton, President
Jeremiah McElwain, Station Manager
Albert Jarratt Sr., Chief Engineer

WRVW
08-31-1962; 107.5 mhz FM *Hrs Open:* 24; 46 kw; 1342 ft.; N36 15 50 W86 47 39
600 Congress Avenue, Suite 1400, Austin, TX 78701 US
(615) 664-2400, *Fax:* (615) 664-2434
www.1075theriver.com
programming@1075theriver.com
License: Lebanon, Wilson County, TN held by Capstar TX L.P.
Group Owner: Clear Channel Communications Inc.; (acq 8-30-00; grpsl).
Arbitron Metro Market: Nashville, TN *Format:* Contemporary Hits/Top 40 *Hrs. of News Programming:* news progmg 4 hrs wkly *No. News Employees:* 1 *Target Audience:* 18-49.
Keith Kaufman, Operations Dir
Gene McKay, General Manager
Darren Smith, General Sales Mgr
Rich Davis, Programming Director
Tom Schurr, Promotions Manager
Temple Hancock, Promotions Manager

WCOR
12-07-2005; 1490 khz AM *Hrs Open:* 24
US
(615) 444-9899, *Fax:* (615) 443-4235
www.wantfm.com
info@WANTFM.com
License: Lebanon, TN held by Finbar Broadcasting Company Inc.
Nat'l Network: ABC
Arbitron Metro Market: Lebanon, TN *Format:* News, News/Talk, 84, Talk
William Barry, President
Harry Stephenson, General Sales Mgr
Billy Goodman, News Director
Gary M. Brown, Chief Engineer
Jo Smith, Account Executive
Elaine Spence, Account Executive
Susie James, Account Executive

***WRSN**
88.1 mhz FM; 0.185 kw; 303 ft.; N36 17 36.3 W86 15 27
US
(615) 598-7677
www.heisrisenradio.com
listenerservice@heisrisenradio.com
License: Lebanon, Wilson County, TN held by St. John Vianney Roman Catholic School.
Nat'l Network: EWTN Radio
Arbitron Metro Market: Lebanon, TN *Format:* Christian
John Sappenfield, General Manager

Lenoir City

WBLC
06-15-1965; 1360 khz AM *Hrs Open:* 24; 1 kw-D, ND1; 0.024 kw-N, ND1; N35 47 32 W84 17 45
Mailing Address: 412 Executive Tower Drive, Suite 205, Knoxville, TN 37922 US
Second Address: 4787 Browder Hollow Rd., Lenoir City, TN 37771
(618)627-4651, *Fax:* (618)627-2726
www.3abn.org/
wblc3abn@bellsouth.net
License: Lenoir City, TN held by Three Angels Broadcasting Network Inc.
Arbitron Metro Market: West Frankfort,IL *Format:* Christian, Religious *Target Audience:* 35 plus. *Adv. Rates:* 6; 6; 6; 4
Jim Morris, General Manager

WLIL
05-30-1950; 730 khz AM *Hrs Open:* 24; 1 kw-D, ND1; 0.214 kw-N, ND1; N35 46 12 W84 16 47
PO Box 340, Lenoir City, TN 37771 US
(865) 986-7536, *Fax:* (865) 986-1716
www.wlilcountry.com
wlilcountry@aol.com
License: Lenoir City, TN held by B.P. Broadcasters L.L.C.
Nat'l Network: CNN Radio *Nat'l Reps:* Keystone (unwired net)
Regional Reps: Rgnl Reps.
Arbitron Metro Market: Knoxville, TN *Format:* Country *Special Programming:* Black one hr, farm one hr, gospel 18 hrs, American *Hrs. of News Programming:* news progmg 20 hrs wkly *No. News Employees:* 1 *TargetAudience:* General; adults *Adv. Rates:* 50; 50; 50; 40
Dale Anthony, General Manager

WKZX-FM
09-19-1967; 93.5 mhz FM; 2 kw; 577 ft.; N35 42 38 W84 10 46
P. O. Box 340, Lenoir City, TN 37771 US
(865) 455-2267, *Fax:* (865) 986-9850
www.laliderwkzx.com
wkzx@aol.com
License: Lenoir City, Loudon County, TN held by B.P. Broadcasters L.L.C.
Arbitron Metro Market: Knoxville, TN *Hrs. of News Programming:* news progmg 20 hrs wkly *No. News Employees:* 1 *Target Audience:* General; Adults
Dale Anthony, General Manager

Lewisburg

WAXO
09-01-1980; 1220 khz AM; 1 kw-D, ND2; 0.144 kw-N, ND2; N35 25 42 W86 46 22
217 W. Commerce St., Lewisburg, TN 37091 US
(225) 768-3102, *Fax:* (225) 768-3729
www.jsm.org
kawikfish@yahoo.com
License: Lewisburg, TN held by Marshall County Radio Corp.
Nat'l Network: AP Network News
Arbitron Metro Market: Grand Island NE *Format:* Christian, Religious *Adv. Rates:* Call for Rates (Radio and TV P
David Whitelaw, COO

WJJM
05-15-1947; 1490 khz AM; 1 kw-U; N35 27 03 W86 46 57
Mailing Address: Box 2025, Lewisburg, TN 37091
Second Address: 344 E. Church St., Lewisburg, TN 37091
(931) 359-4511, *Fax:* (931) 270-9556
www.wjjm.com
wjjm@wjjm.com
License: Lewisburg, Marshall County, TN held by WJJM Inc.
Regional Network: Tenn. Radio Net.; Fox Network News *Nat'l Reps:* Keystone (unwired net)
Population Served: 7,207*Hrs. of News Programming:* news progmg one hr wkly *No. News Employees:* 1 *Target Audience:* 25-65; manufacturing, business, family programming *Adv. Rates:* 5.50; 5.50; 5.50; 5.50
Michelle Haislip, President
Jeff Haislip, Operations Dir
Michelle Haislip, General Manager
Michelle Haislip, Station Manager
Jeff Haislip, Programming Director
Jeff Haislip, News Director
Don Roden, Chief Engineer
DougHazelwood, Music Director

WJJM-FM
02-20-1969; 94.3 mhz FM *Hrs Open:* 17; 6 kw; 115 ft.; N35 27 3 W86 46 57
Mailing Address: P. O. Box 2025, Lewisburg, TN 37091 US
Second Address: 344 E. Church St., Lewisburg, TN 37091
(931) 359-4511, *Fax:* (931) 270-9556
www.wjjm.com
wjjm@wjjm.com
License: Lewisburg, Marshall County, TN held by WJJM Inc.
Format: Country
Doug Cheek, General Sales Mgr
Doug Hazelwood, Programming Director
Tommy Allen, Disc Jockey
Jennifer St. John, Disc Jockey
Linda Dugan, Disc Jockey
Chris Bates, Disc Jockey

Lexington

WDXL
07-01-1954; 1490 khz AM *Hrs Open:* 24; 1 kw-U, ND1; N35 38 5 W88 23 34
Mailing Address: P. O. Box 170, Lexington, TN 38351 US
Second Address: 584 Smith Ave., Lexington, TN 38351
(731) 968-3500(731) 968-9990, *Fax:* (731) 968-0380
wzlt@netease.net
License: Lexington, TN held by Lexington Broadcast Service Inc.
Nat'l Network: Jones Radio Networks
Arbitron Metro Market: Lexington, TN *Format:* Gospel *Special Programming:* Black 4 hrs, gospel 10 hrs wkly *Hrs. of News Programming:* news progmg 10 hrs wkly *No. News Employees:* 1 *Target Audience:* 30plus.
Dan Hughes, General Manager
Terry Rhodes, Programming Director

WZLT
09-01-1964; 99.3 mhz FM *Hrs Open:* 24; 5 kw; 151 ft.; N35 38 5 W88 23 34
Mailing Address: P. O. Box 170, 584 Smith Street, Lexington, TN 38351 US
Second Address: 584 Smith Ave., Lexington, TN 38351
(731) 968-9990, *Fax:* (731) 968-0380
www.wzlt993.com
wzlt993@yahoo.com
License: Lexington, Henderson County, TN held by Lexington Broadcast Service Inc.
Arbitron Metro Market: Lexington, TN *Format:* Adult Contemp
Target Audience: General.
Todd Buttrey, Programming Director

Livingston

WLIV
11-26-1956; 920 khz AM *Hrs Open:* 24; 1 kw-D, ND1; 0.038 kw-N, ND1; N36 22 28 W85 18 20
1130 West Main Street, Livingston, TN 38570 US
(931) 823-1226, *Fax:* (931) 823-6005
www.wilv.com
License: Livingston, TN held by Sunny Broadcasting G.P.
Nat'l Network: CNN Radio *Regional Network:* Tenn. Radio Net.
Nat'l Reps: Keystone (unwired net)
Format: News, Sports *Special Programming:* Farm 2 hrs, relg 15 hrs, gospel 18 hrs wkly *Hrs. of News Programming:* news progmg 7 hrs wkly *No. News Employees:* 2 *Target Audience:* General. *Adv. Rates:* 9; 9;9; 9.
Millard Oakley, President
Craig Cantrell, Operations Dir
Joel Upton, General Manager
Carolyn Peterman, Station Manager
Shirley Burnette, News Director
Austin Stinnett, Chief Engineer
Mark Young, Public Service Director
RogerEaley, Sports Director

WLQK
12-01-1966; 95.9 mhz FM; 27 kw; 669 ft.; N36 11 3 W85 24 40
259 S. Willow, Cookeville, TN 38501 US

RADIO - U.S.

(931) 526-6064, *Fax:* (931) 520-1590
www.literock959.com
jimstapleton@jwcbroadcasting.com,sstevens@1069kicksfm.com
License: Livingston, Overton County, TN held by JWC Broadcasting
Group Owner: JWC Broadcasting; acq 12-18-98).
Nat'l Reps: Rgnl Reps
Arbitron Metro Market: Cookeville, TN *Format:* Classic Rock
Target Audience: General. *Adv. Rates:* 30; 28; 30; 24
Scott Stevens, Operations Dir
Jim Stapleton, General Manager

Lobelville

WHPY-FM
10-01-1974; 94.5 mhz FM *Hrs Open:* 24; 22 kw; Ant 715 ft; N35 45 56 W87 49 50
25 Stonebrook Place, Suite G 322, Jackson, TN 38305
(731) 663-2327, *Fax:* (731) 663-2427
www.gracebroadcasting.com
gminyard@gracebroadcasting.com
License: Lobelville, Dickson County, TN held by Grace Broadcasting Services Inc.
Group Owner: Grace Broadcasting Services Inc.; (acq 11-28-2003; $487,000).
Population Served: 590,807 *Arbitron Metro Market:* Nashville, TN *Format:* Christian *Hrs. of News Programming:* news progmg 14 hrs wkly *No. News Employees:* 1 *Target Audience:* 18-54; mid to upper incomeadults with purchasing power *Adv. Rates:* 132; 132; 132; 132
Lacy Ennis, President/ CEO
John Blankenship, Operations Man./ Production
Rodney Minyard Sr., General Manager
Geraldine Minyard, Secretary/ Programming
Phillip Chambers, Sales Representative
Brad McCoy, Sales Representative
TomMapes, Sales Representative
Tony Reeves, Sales Representative
Ivan Hodge, Sales Representative
Ronnie Ragan, Sales Representative

WNKX
11-16-1955; 1570 khz AM *Hrs Open:* 24
US
(731) 663-2327, *Fax:* (731) 663-2427
www.gracebroadcasting.com
info@gracebroadcasting.com
License: Lobelville, TN held by Grace Broadcasting Services Inc.
Group Owner: Grace Broadcasting Services Inc.; (acq 11-1-2008; $75,000)
Arbitron Metro Market: Nashville, TN
Lacy Ennis, CEO/COO
Charles Ennis, President
John Blackenship, Operations Dir
Rodney Minyard, General Manager
Geraldine Minyard, Programming Director

Lookout Mountain

WFLI
02-20-1961; 1070 khz AM *Hrs Open:* 24; 50 kw-D, DA2; 2.5 kw-N, DA2; N35 2 42 W85 21 44
621 O'Grady Dr., Chattanooga, TN 37409 US
(423) 821-3555, *Fax:* (423) 821-3557
flipaul@aol.com,benns@mindspring.com
License: Lookout Mountain, TN held by WFLI Inc.
Nat'l Network: USA
Arbitron Metro Market: Chattanooga, TN *Format:* Gospel, Religious *Special Programming:* College football *Target Audience:* 18-54. *Adv. Rates:* 18; 18; 18; 10
Ying Hua Benns, President
Paul White, Station Manager

Loretto

WKSR-FM
01-12-1970; 98.3 mhz FM; 18 kw; 377 ft.; N35 9 0 W87 17 45
Mailing Address: P.O. Box 738, Pulaski, TN 38478 US
Second Address: 104 S. Second St., Pulaski, TN 38478
(931) 363-2505, *Fax:* (931) 424-3157
www.wksr.com
wksr@igiles.net
License: Loretto, Lawrence County, TN held by Pulaski Broadcasting Inc.
Nat'l Network: ABC
Format: Country *No. News Employees:* 2 *Adv. Rates:* 18; 14; 16; 12
Ronnie Rose, General Manager
Ed Carter, Programming Director

Loudon

WFIV-FM
05-20-1991; 105.3 mhz FM *Hrs Open:* 24; 6 kw; 328 ft.; N35 48 40 W84 16 2
412 Executive Tower Drive, Suite 205, Knoxville, TN 37922 US
(865) 392-9585, *Fax:* (865) 738-0177
www.wkvl.com
info@wkvl.com
License: Loudon, Loudon County, TN held by Horne Radio L.L.C.
Group Owner: Horne Radio Group; (acq 8-29-2001; grpsl).
Nat'l Network: CBS
Arbitron Metro Market: Loudon, TN *Format:* Triple A *Hrs. of News Programming:* News progmg 3 hrs wkly *Target Audience:* 25-50; baby boomers *Adv. Rates:* 40; 40; 40; 20
Douglas Horne, President
Jim Christensen, General Manager
Shawn Nunally, General Sales Mgr
Todd Ethridge, Programming Director
Martha Lee, News Director
Brian Tatum, Chief Engineer

WLOD
01-01-1983; 1140 khz AM *Hrs Open:* Sunrise-sunset; 1 kw-D, NDD; N35 43 35 W84 20 49
412 Executive Tower Drive, Suite 205, Knoxville, TN 37922 US
(865) 675-4105, *Fax:* (865) 675-4859
License: Loudon, TN held by Horne Radio LLC.
Group Owner: Horne Radio Group; (acq 8-29-01; grpsl).
Nat'l Network: ABC
Arbitron Metro Market: Knoxville, TN *Format:* News, News/Talk, 86 *No. News Employees:* 1 *Target Audience:* 35 plus. *Adv. Rates:* 8; 8; 8; 6
Bill Tatum, General Manager

Lynchburg

***WGBQ**
91.9 mhz FM; 0.9 kw; 351 ft.; N35 16 32 W86 21 37
US
(864) 297-0216, *Fax:* (864) 297-0344
networkofglory.com
info@networkofglory.org
License: Lynchburg, Moore County, TN held by Network of Glory Inc.
Arbitron Metro Market: Lynchburg, TN *Format:* Christian, Gospel
Lola Richey, President

Madison

WPLN
09-14-1958; 1430 khz AM *Hrs Open:* 24
1617 Lebanon Road, Nashville, TN 37210 US
(615) 760-2903, *Fax:* (615) 760-2904
www.wpln.org
info@wpln.org
License: Madison, TN held by Nashville Public Radio
Arbitron Metro Market: Nashville, TN *Format:* News, News/Talk, 86 *Target Audience:* General.
Rob Gordon, President

Madisonville

WRKQ
07-12-1967; 1250 khz AM *Hrs Open:* 6 AM-6 PM; 0.5 kw-D, ND2; 0.084 kw-N, ND2; N35 30 29 W84 22 45
P. O. Box 489, Madisonville, TN 37354 US
(423) 442-1446, *Fax:* (423) 420-1020
www.wrkq.net
License: Madisonville, TN held by Beverly Broadcasting Co. LLC
Nat'l Network: CBS Radio
Format: News, News/Talk, 86 *No. News Employees:* 1 *Target Audience:* General.
Mike Beverly, President

WYGO
11-15-1992; 99.5 mhz FM *Hrs Open:* 24; 2.7 kw; 489 ft.; N35 31 19 W84 27 29
Mailing Address: Post Office Box 641, Sweetwater, TN 37874 US
Second Address: 2110 Oxnard Rd., Athens, TN 37303
(423) 337-0995, *Fax:* (423) 337-0880
www.todaysbesthits.com
License: Madisonville, Monroe County, TN held by Major Broadcasting Corp.
Arbitron Metro Market: Madisonville, TN *Format:* Oldies, Adult Contemp *Target Audience:* 18-54.
Randy Sliger, General Manager

Manchester

WFTZ
11-16-1992; 101.5 mhz FM *Hrs Open:* 24; 3 kw; 328 ft.; N35 23 51 W86 8 39
Mailing Address: Post Office Box 1015, Manchester, TN 37355 US
Second Address: 1025 Hillsboro Blvd., Manchester, TN 37355
(931) 728-3458, *Fax:* (931) 723-1099
www.fantasyradio.com
kahuna@fantasyradio.com
License: Manchester, Coffee County, TN held by Phase Two Communications Inc.
Nat'l Network: ABC *Wire Services:* AP
Arbitron Metro Market: Nashville, TN *Format:* Adult Contemp *Hrs. of News Programming:* news progmg 4 hrs wkly *No. News Employees:* 1 *Target Audience:* 25-45; white collar, educated
Roger Dotson, CEO
Amber V. Dotson, Operations Dir
Rodger H. Dotson, General Manager
Marsha Dotson, General Sales Mgr
Amber Dotson, Promotions Manager
Wayne Hudgens, News Director
Josh Kuhn, Local Sales Manager
Chris, OperationsAssistant
Mike Ray, Disc Jockey
Scott Shasteen, Disc Jockey

WMSR
04-07-1957; 1320 khz AM *Hrs Open:* 24; 5 kw-D, ND1; 0.079 kw-N, ND1; N35 28 3 W86 5 42
P.O. Box 759, McMinnville, TN 37110 US
(931) 728-3526, *Fax:* (931) 728-3527
www.thunder1320.com
wmsr@thunder1320.com
License: Manchester, TN held by Coffee County Broadcasting Inc.
Wire Services: AP
Arbitron Metro Market: Manchester, TN *Format:* Oldies, Sports, 86 *Special Programming:* High school sports, farm *Hrs. of News Programming:* news progmg 21 hrs wkly *No. News Employees:* 1 *Target Audience:* General.
Scott Vaughn, General Manager

Martin

WCMT
06-08-1957; 1410 khz AM *Hrs Open:* 24; 0.7 kw-D, ND1; 0.058 kw-N, ND1; N36 21 45 W88 50 57
P. O. Box 318, Martin, TN 38237 US
(731) 587-9526, *Fax:* (731) 587-5079
www.wcmt.com
cprince@crunet.com
License: Martin, TN held by Thunderbolt Broadcasting Co.
Group Owner: Thunderbolt Broadcasting Co.; (acq 3-1-80;
Nat'l Network: Westwood One; AP Radio
Arbitron Metro Market: Jackson, TN *Format:* News, News/Talk, 64, Talk *Hrs. of News Programming:* News progmg 10 hrs wkly *Target Audience:* 25-54; baby boomers *Adv. Rates:* 40; 25; 40; 15
Paul Tinkle, President

WCMT-FM
09-26-1967; 101.3 mhz FM *Hrs Open:* 24; 22 kw; 308 ft.; N36 29 0 W88 57 10
P. O. Box 318, Martin, TN 38237 US
(731) 587-9526, *Fax:* (731) 587-5079
www.wcmt.com
cprince@crunet.com
License: Martin, Obion County, TN
Group Owner: Thunderbolt Broadcasting Co.
Arbitron Metro Market: Jackson, TN *Format:* Adult Contemp *Hrs. of News Programming:* News progmg 25 hrs wkly *Adv. Rates:* 40; 35; 40; 15
Paul Tinkle, President

***WUTM**
09-01-1971; 90.3 mhz FM *Hrs Open:* 6 AM-midnight; 0.175 kw; 282 ft.; N36 20 23 W88 51 35
305 Gooch Hall, Martin, TN 38238 US
(731) 881-7095, *Fax:* (731) 881-7550
www.utm.edu/organizations/wutm
wutm@utm.edu
License: Martin, Weakley County, TN held by University of Tennessee.
Regional Network: Tenn. Radio Net.
Arbitron Metro Market: Martin, TN *Format:* Contemporary Hits/Top 40 *Target Audience:* General; Univ
Richard Robinson, Operations Dir
Harold Cochran, Chief Engineer

Maryville

WGAP
08-13-1947; 1400 khz AM *Hrs Open:* 24; 1 kw-U, ND1; N35 45 41 W83 58 57
620 Campbell Station Road, #2, Knoxville, IN 37922 US
(865) 983-4310, *Fax:* (865) 983-4314
www.wyshradio.com
License: Maryville, TN held by Horne Radio LLC.
Group Owner: Horne Radio Group; (acq 8-29-01; grpsl).
Nat'l Network: Motor Racing Net *Nat'l Reps:* Rgnl Reps
Arbitron Metro Market: Knoxville, TN *Format:* Country *Hrs. of News Programming:* news progmg 18 hrs wkly *No. News Employees:* 1 *Target Audience:* 25 plus; general *Adv. Rates:* 24; 20; 24; 14
Brian Tatum, General Manager

WKCE
01-01-1989; 1120 khz AM
802 S. Central Ave., Knoxville, TN 37902 US
(865) 546-4653, *Fax:* (865) 637-7133
License: Maryville, TN held by Kirkland Wireless Broadcasters Inc.
Nat'l Network: ESPN Deportes
Arbitron Metro Market: Knoxville, TN *Format:* Sports
Rob Robinson, Operations Dir

WQJK
02-02-1990; 95.7 mhz FM *Hrs Open:* 24; 6 kw; 322 ft.; N35 49 53 W84 1 25
P.O. Box 3848, Evansville, IN 47720 US
(865) 525-6000, *Fax:* (865) 656-4386
www.jackfmknoxville.com
rchambers@sccradio.com
License: Maryville, Blount County, TN held by South Central Communications Corp.
Group Owner: South Central Communications Corp.
Arbitron Metro Market: Knoxville, TN *Target Audience:* 35-59; adults
J.P. Engelbrecht, CEO
Craig Jacobus, President
Terry Gillingham, Operations Dir
Randy Chambers, Programming Director
Judy Dyke, News Director
Randy Ross, Sales Director

Maynardville

***WYLV(FM)**
01-01-2001; 88.3 mhz FM; 2.85 kw horiz; Ant 1,489 ft; N36 00 13 W83 56 34
1621 E. Magnolia Ave., Knoxville, TN 37917
(865) 521-8910, *Fax:* (865) 521-8923
life883.org
info@ez88.org
License: Maynardville, Union County, TN held by Foothills Broadcasting Inc.
Population Served: 2,423 *Arbitron Metro Market:* Maynardville, TN *Format:* Christian
David Wells, General Manager
Mike Blakemore, Programming Director
Marisa Lykins, Promotions Manager

***WYLV**
02-14-1993; 88.3 mhz FM *Hrs Open:* 24; 2.85 kw horiz; N36 0 13 W83 56 34
304 Crane Cove, Longwood, FL 32750 US
(865) 521-8910, *Fax:* (865) 521-8923
www.love89.org
info@love89.org
License: Maynardville, Blount County, TN held by Foothills Broadcasting Inc.
Arbitron Metro Market: Maynardville, TN *Format:* Christian
David Wells, General Manager
Jonathan Unthank, Programming Director
Marisa Lykins, Promotions Manager

McKenzie

WHDM
01-29-1954; 1440 khz AM; 500 w-D, 91 w-N; FM 1,000 kw; N36 07 20 W88 31 31
110 India Rd., Paris, TN 62959
(731) 352-1410, *Fax:* (731) 644-9970
License: McKenzie, Carroll County, TN held by WHDM Broadcasting Inc.
Group Owner: Benton-Weatherford Broadcasting Inc. of Tennessee; (acq 1-4-2002; $69,000).
Nat'l Network: ABC
Population Served: 5,651*Hrs. of News Programming:* news progmg 4 hrs wkly *No. News Employees:* 1 *Adv. Rates:* 7;30;9.
Gary Benton, President
Janice Benton, Operations Dir

WWYN
02-11-1963; 106.9 mhz FM *Hrs Open:* 24; 100 kw; 886 ft.; N35 54 5 W88 46 51
68 Federal Drive, Jackson, TN 38305 US
(731) 427-9616, *Fax:* (731) 424-2773
www.wwyn1069.jacksonnewsnow.com
cthomas@wwyn.fm
License: McKenzie, Carroll County, TN held by Rainbow Media Inc.
Group Owner: Black Crow Media Group LLC; (acq 11-9-2001).
Arbitron Metro Market: McKenzie, TN *Format:* Country *Hrs. of News Programming:* news progmg 4 hrs wkly *No. News Employees:* 1 *Target Audience:* 25-54; adults *Adv. Rates:* 28; 26; 27; 20
Chip Thomas, General Manager
Shane Conner, Programming Director
Ellen Bennet, News Director
Jim Smith, Chief Engineer

***WAJJ**
01-01-2002; 89.3 mhz FM *Hrs Open:* 24; 1 kw; 328 ft.; N36 6 55 W88 30 38
P. O. Box 281, Hardin, KY 42048 US
(731) 352-6034
www.wajjradio.org
comments@wajjradio.org
License: McKenzie, Carroll County, TN held by Temple Broadcasting Co.
Arbitron Metro Market: McKenzie, TN *Format:* Christian
Gary Hall, General Manager
Bro. Steve Vincent, Programming Director
Bro. Gary L. Hall, Pastor / Director
Ruth Back, Secretary

McKinnon

WTPR-FM
01-01-1992; 101.7 mhz FM *Hrs Open:* 24; 1.8 kw; 607 ft.; N36 24 39 W87 58 6 *Rebroadcasts:* Rebroadcasts WTPR(AM) Paris 100%
P.O. Box 648, Clarksville, TN 37040 US
(731) 642-7100, *Fax:* (731) 642-9367
www.wenkwtpr.com
thailey@wenkwtpr.com
License: McKinnon, Houston County, TN held by WENK of Union City Inc.
Group Owner: WENK of Union City Inc.; (acq 1996; $200,000)
Regional Reps: Rgnl Reps.
Arbitron Metro Market: Paris, TN *Format:* Oldies *Hrs. of News Programming:* news progmg 12 hrs wkly *No. News Employees:* 1 *Target Audience:* 35-54.
Terry L. Hailey, President and General Manager
Terry Hailey, Programming Director
Jim Adcock, Promotions Manager
Lorrie Matlock, Sales Representative

McMinnville

WAKI
01-01-1947; 1230 khz AM *Hrs Open:* 5 AM-midnight
PO Box 31, McMinnville, TN 37110 US
(931) 473-9253, *Fax:* (931) 473-4149
www.1230waki.com
jeffbarnes@clearchannel.com
License: McMinnville, TN held by Peg Broadcasting Crossville LLC.
Group Owner: Peg Broadcasting Crossville LLC; (acq 6-30-2008; grpsl)
Arbitron Metro Market: McMinnville, TN *Format:* News, News/Talk, 86 *Special Programming:* Farm 2 hrs wkly *Hrs. of News Programming:* news progmg 24 hrs wkly *No. News Employees:* 1 *Target Audience:* 25-54;general
David Roederer, General Manager

WBMC
05-01-1955; 960 khz AM *Hrs Open:* 5 AM-8 PM
P. O. Box 759, 230 West Colville St, McMinnville, TN 37110 US
(931) 473-9253, *Fax:* (931) 473-4149
www.960wbmc.com/
License: McMinnville, TN held by Peg Broadcasting Crossville LLC.
Group Owner: Peg Broadcasting Crossville LLC; (acq 6-30-2008; grpsl)
Nat'l Network: ABC
Arbitron Metro Market: McMinnville, TN *Format:* Contemporary Hits/Top 40, Country, 44 *Special Programming:* Farm 5 hrs wkly *Hrs. of News Programming:* news progmg 10 hrs wkly *No. News Employees:* 1 *TargetAudience:* General.
Bryan Kell, Station Manager
Jeff Barnes, Programming Director
Jay Walker, News Director
Homer Wilson Jr., Chief Engineer
Kathy Klasek, Traffic Manager

***WCPI**
02-01-1997; 91.3 mhz FM *Hrs Open:* 24; 1.6 kw; 157 ft.; N35 39 41 W85 45 6
110 South Court Street, McMinnville, TN 37110 US
(931) 506-9274, *Fax:* (931) 507-1005
www.wcpi913fm.webs.com
wcpi@blomand.net
License: McMinnville, Warren County, TN held by Warren County Education Foundation.
Wire Services: AP
Arbitron Metro Market: Cookeville, TN *Target Audience:* 6 plus.
Dr. Norman Rone, President
Gloria Grissom, Station Manager
Mary Cantrell, Promotions Manager
Richard Myers, Chief Engineer

Memphis

KOTC
07-19-1947; 830 khz AM *Hrs Open:* Sunrise-sunset; 10 kw-D; N36 13 29 W90 04 31
Mailing Address: Box 271, Kennett, MO 63967
Second Address: 700 N. Bypass, Kennett, MO 63857
(573) 686-3700, *Fax:* (573) 686-6116
www.foxradionetwork.com
kotc@sheltonbbs.com
License: Memphis, Shelby County, TN held by Eagle Bluff Enterprises
Population Served: 20,000*No. News Employees:* 1 *Target Audience:* 28-55. *Adv. Rates:* 10; 10; 10; na
Steven Fuchs, President
Charles Isabell, News Director
P.J. Johnson, Chief Engineer

KWAM
01-01-1946; 990 khz AM
200 Concord Plaza, Suite 600, San Antonio, TX 78216 US
(901) 259-1300, *Fax:* (901) 259-6449
www.kwam990.com/
License: Memphis, TN held by Concord Media Group Inc.
Arbitron Metro Market: Memphis, TN *Format:* News, Talk *Target Audience:* 25 plus; general
Tim Davies, General Manager
Jeffrey Jones, General Sales Mgr
Leonard Blakely, Programming Director

WBBP
04-11-1964; 1480 khz AM *Hrs Open:* 24; 5 kw-D, ND2; 0.041 kw-N, ND2; N35 3 18 W90 5 15
250 East Raines Rd, Memphis, TN 38109 US
(800) 877-5600, *Fax:* (916) 251-1650
www.air1.com
info@air1.com
License: Memphis, TN held by Bountiful Blessings Inc.
Format: Alternative, Christian *Adv. Rates:* 40; 30; 40; 30
Mike Novak, President
Mike Lee, Operations Dir
David Pierce, Programming Director
Ed Lenane, News Director
Sam Wallington, Engineering Dir
Marya Morgan, News Reporter
Richard Hunt, News Reporter

WDIA
06-07-1947; 1070 khz AM *Hrs Open:* 24; 50 kw-D, DA2; 5 kw-N, DA2; N35 16 5 W90 1 3
200 Concord Plaza, Suite 600, San Antonio, TX 78216 US
(901) 259-1300, *Fax:* (901) 259-6451
www.mywdia.com
info@am1070wdia.com
License: Memphis, TN held by CC Licenses LLC.
Group Owner: Clear Channel Communications Inc.; (acq 1996; grpsl)
Nat'l Network: ABC *Nat'l Reps:* Clear Channel
Arbitron Metro Market: Memphis, TN *Format:* Black *Special Programming:* Gospel *Target Audience:* 25-54; Black adults
Tim Davies, General Manager
Ralph Salierno, General Sales Mgr
Bobby O'Jay, Programming Director
Franklin Gilbert Jr., Promotions Manager
Alonzo Pendleton, Chief Engineer

***WEVL**
05-01-1976; 89.9 mhz FM *Hrs Open:* 20; 4.8 kw; 381 ft.; N35 8 37 W89 48 22

Mailing Address: P.O. Box 40952, Memphis, TN 38174 US
Second Address: 518 S. Main St., Memphis, TN 38103
(901) 528-0560(901) 528-0561
www.wevl.org
stnmgr@wevl.org
License: Memphis, Shelby County, TN held by Southern Communication Volunteers Inc.
Arbitron Metro Market: Memphis, TN *Format:* Blues *Special Programming:* Jazz 15 hrs, C&W 15 hrs, Fr one hr, Irish 4 hrs, Indian subcontinent one hr wkly *Hrs. of News Programming:* News progmg 2 hrs wkly *TargetAudience:* General.
Dan Phillips, President
Judy Dorsey, Station Manager
Brian Craig, Programming Director

WGKX

01-10-1968; 105.9 mhz FM *Hrs Open:* 24; 100 kw; 993 ft.; N35 9 16 W89 49 20
965 Ridgelake Blvd., Suite 102, Memphis, TN 38120 US
(901) 682-1106, *Fax:* (901) 767-9531
www.kix106.com
License: Memphis, Shelby County, TN
Group Owner: Cumulus Media Inc.; (acq 3-23-2004; grpsl).
Nat'l Reps: Katz Radio
Arbitron Metro Market: Memphis, TN *Format:* Country *Target Audience:* 25-54. *Adv. Rates:* 300; 250; 250; 100
Sheri Sawyer, General Manager
Dan Barron, General Sales Mgr
Tim Jones, Programming Director
Paula Davis, Promotions Manager
Gennora Reed, General Sales Manager

WHBQ

03-18-1925; 560 khz AM *Hrs Open:* 24; 5 kw-D, DA2; 1 kw-N, DA2; N35 15 12 W90 2 51
188 South Bellevue #222, Memhips, TN 38104 US
(901) 375-9324, *Fax:* (901) 375-4117
www.sports56whbq.com
License: Memphis, TN held by Flinn Broadcasting Corp.
Nat'l Network: CBS
Arbitron Metro Market: Memphis, TN *Format:* Sports *Hrs. of News Programming:* News progmg 2 hrs wkly *Target Audience:* 18-54.
George Flinn, President
Chris Coates, General Manager
Eli Savoie, Programming Director

WHRK

01-01-1961; 97.1 mhz FM *Hrs Open:* 24; 100 kw; 531 ft.; N35 13 23 W90 2 33
200 Concord Plaza, Suite 600, San Antonio, TX 78216 US
(901) 259-1300, *Fax:* (901) 259-6451
www.k97fm.com
info@k97fm.com
License: Memphis, Shelby County, TN
Group Owner: Clear Channel Communications Inc.
Arbitron Metro Market: Memphis, TN *Format:* Urban Contemporary *Target Audience:* 18-49.
Devin Steel, Programming Director

*WKNO-FM

03-01-1972; 91.1 mhz FM *Hrs Open:* 24; 100 kw; 574 ft.; N35 9 14 W89 49 19
Mailing Address: P.O. Box 241880, Memphis, TN 38124 US
Second Address: TN
(901) 458-2521, *Fax:* (901) 325-6505
www.wknofm.org
License: Memphis, Shelby County, TN held by Mid-South Public Communications Foundation.
Nat'l Network: NPR; PRI
Arbitron Metro Market: Memphis, TN *TV Affiliate:* *WKNO-TV affil *Format:* Classical, News *Hrs. of News Programming:* 51 hrs news progmg wkly *No. News Employees:* 2 *Target Audience:* 35 plus.
Michael LaBonia, President
Darel Snodgrass, Operations Dir
Dan Campbell, General Manager
Charles McCarty, General Sales Mgr

WLOK

03-01-1956; 1340 khz AM *Hrs Open:* 24; 1 kw-U; N35 07 01 W90 00 59
363 S. 2nd St., Memphis, TN 38103
(901) 527-9565, *Fax:* (901) 528-0335
www.wlok.com
License: Memphis, Shelby County, TN held by Gilliam Communications Inc.
Nat'l Reps: Local Focus
Population Served: 1,000,000 *Arbitron Metro Market:* Memphis, TN *No. News Employees:* 1 *Target Audience:* 25-54.
H. Gilliam Jr., General Manager
Walter Hunter, General Sales Mgr
Pamela Bridges, Programming Director
Delsa Fleming, Music Director
Falesha Stafford, Public Affairs Director

WMC

01-21-1923; 790 khz AM *Hrs Open:* 24
Rsa Tower, 20th Floor, 201 Monroe Street, Montgomery, AL 36104 US
(901) 384-5900, *Fax:* (901) 767-6076
www.sports790am.com
info@wmc79.com
License: Memphis, TN held by Entercom Memphis License Inc.
Group Owner: Entercom Communications Corp.; (acq 11-30-2007; grpsl)
Nat'l Reps: CBS Radio *Wire Services:* Metro Weather Service Inc.
Arbitron Metro Market: Memphis, TN *Format:* Sports *No. News Employees:* 1
Terry Wood, Operations Dir

WMC-FM

05-22-1947; 99.7 mhz FM *Hrs Open:* 24; 290 kw horiz, 96 kw vert; 909 ft.; N35 10 9 W89 53 10
Rsa Tower, 20th Floor, 201 Monroe Street, Montgomery, AL 36104 US
(901) 384-5900, *Fax:* (901) 767-6076
www.fm100memphis.com
License: Memphis, Shelby County, TN held by Entercom Memphis License Inc
Group Owner: Entercom Communications Corp.
Arbitron Metro Market: Memphis, TN *Format:* Adult Contemp *Target Audience:* 25-54; adults
William Shannon, General Manager

*WQOX

04-08-1974; 88.5 mhz FM *Hrs Open:* 24; 30 kw; 430 ft.; N35 9 17 W89 49 20
3333 Covington Pike, Memphis, TN 38128 US
(901) 320-3460, *Fax:* (901) 454-7673
www.wqoxmes/admin/avery/mes.com
License: Memphis, Shelby County, TN held by Board of Education Memphis City Schools.
Arbitron Metro Market: Memphis, TN *Format:* Adult Contemp *No. News Employees:* 1 *Target Audience:* 12-54; Students, teachers, parents & admin staff
Derek Wagner, General Manager
Paul Gubala, Programming Director
Derick McMillan, Chief Engineer
Chris Malone, Assistant Music Director
Sherman Austin, Public Affairs Director

WREC

09-01-1922; 600 khz AM *Hrs Open:* 24
200 Concord Plaza, Suite 600, San Antonio, TX 78216 US
(901) 259-1300, *Fax:* (901) 259-6451
www.wrecradio.com
info@recradio.com
License: Memphis, TN held by CC Licenses LLC.
Group Owner: Clear Channel Communications Inc.; (acq 1996; grpsl).
Nat'l Network: Westwood One; ABC *Regional Network:* Tenn. Radio Net. *Nat'l Reps:* Clear Channel *Wire Services:* NWS (National Weather Service)
Arbitron Metro Market: Memphis, TN *Format:* News, News/Talk, 84, Talk *Special Programming:* Farm 3 hrs, relg 4 hrs wkly *Hrs. of News Programming:* news progmg 5 hrs wkly *No. News Employees:* 2 *Target Audience:* 35 plus; upscale, professional, males 70%
Timothy Davies, General Manager
Ralph Salierno, General Sales Mgr
Steve Versnick, Programming Director
Frank Gilbert, Promotions Manager
Alonzo Pendleton, Chief Engineer

WRVR

09-15-1968; 104.5 mhz FM; 100 kw; 751 ft.; N35 9 16 W89 49 20
10706 Beaver Dam Road, Cockeysville, MD 21030 US
(901) 384-5900, *Fax:* (901) 767-6076
www.wrvr.com
river104@wrvr.com
License: Memphis, Shelby County, TN
Group Owner: Entercom Communications Corp.
Arbitron Metro Market: Memphis, TN *Format:* Adult Contemp *Hrs. of News Programming:* news progmg 2 hrs wkly *No. News Employees:* 1
Dan Barron, Operations Dir
Rondi Atkinson, General Sales Mgr
Jerry Dean, Programming Director
Mike Schwartz, Chief Engineer
Rachel Dewitt, General Sales Manager

WGSF

02-01-1984; 1030 khz AM *Hrs Open:* 24; 10 kw-C, DAN; 50 kw-D, DAN; DAN; 1 kw-N; N35 10 59 W89 56 17
C/O Putbrese Hunsaker, PO Box 217, Sterling, VA 20167 US
(901) 375-9324, *Fax:* (901) 375-4117
License: Memphis, TN held by Arlington Broadcasting Co. Inc.
Nat'l Network: Westwood One; CBS
Arbitron Metro Market: Memphis, TN *Adv. Rates:* 40; 40; 60; 30
Daniel Ybarra, General Manager

*WUMR

08-01-1979; 91.7 mhz FM *Hrs Open:* 6 AM-midnight; 25 kw horiz, 24 kw vert; 394 ft.; N35 9 17 W89 51 28
Dept of Communications, 3745 Central Ave, Memphis, TN 38152 US
(901) 678-3176, *Fax:* (901) 678-4331
www.memphis.edu/wumr/
rmcdowll@memphis.edu
License: Memphis, Shelby County, TN held by The University of Memphis.
Arbitron Metro Market: Memphis, TN *Format:* Jazz, Sports *Hrs. of News Programming:* news progmg 2 hrs wkly *No. News Employees:* 1 *Target Audience:* 18-49; upscale, college-educated *Adv. Rates:* 50; 50; 50;50
Robert McDowell, General Manager

*WYPL

04-17-1991; 89.3 mhz FM *Hrs Open:* 24; 100 kw; 1253 ft.; N35 28 3 W90 11 27
1850 Peabody Avenue, Memphis, TN 38104 US
(901) 415-2752, *Fax:* (901) 323-7902
www.memphislibrary.org
info@memphislibrary.org
License: Memphis, Shelby County, TN held by Memphis Public Library & Information Center.
Arbitron Metro Market: Memphis, TN *Format:* News *Special Programming:* Sp one hr wkly *Hrs. of News Programming:* News progmg 110 hrs wkly *Target Audience:* General.
Tommy Warren, General Manager

Middleton

WYDL

01-01-2001; 100.3 mhz FM; 25 kw; 328 ft.; N35 0 13 W88 39 39
188 South Bellevue, Suite 222, Memphis, TN 38104 US
(410) 268-6200, *Fax:* (410) 268-0931
www.familyradio.com
License: Middleton, Hardeman County, TN held by Flinn Broadcasting Corp.
Arbitron Metro Market: Tahlequah OK *Format:* Religious
Harold Camping, President
W.A. Sadlier, Station Manager

Milan

WYNU

12-12-1964; 92.3 mhz FM *Hrs Open:* 24; 100 kw; 991 ft.; N35 54 6 W88 46 55
600 Congress Ave., Suite 1400, Austin, TX 78701 US
(731) 427-3316, *Fax:* (731) 427-4576
www.rock923.net
steveburke@clearchannel.com
License: Milan, Gibson County, TN held by Forever South Licenses LLC.
Group Owner: Forever Communications Inc.; (acq 5-12-2006; grpsl).
Arbitron Metro Market: Jackson, TN *Format:* Classic Rock *Hrs. of News Programming:* news progmg 5 hrs wkly *No. News Employees:* 1 *Target Audience:* 18-54; middle/upper income adults with disposable income &buying power *Adv. Rates:* 50; 48; 52; 38
Dave Hacker, Operations Dir
Roger Vestal, General Manager
Gina Langley, General Sales Mgr
Steve Burke, Programming Director

Millersville

WNFN

01-01-1998; 106.7 mhz FM; 2.95 kw; 966 ft.; N36 15 50 W86 47 39
Suite 901, 50 Music Square West, Nashville, TN 37203 US
(615) 321-1067, *Fax:* (615) 321-5771
www.i106hits.com
kenny.smoov@cumulus.com
License: Millersville, Sumner County, TN held by Cumulus Licensing Corp.
Group Owner: Cumulus Media Inc.; (acq 2-12-2002; grpsl).
Arbitron Metro Market: Nashville, TN *Format:* Sports
John Columbus, General Manager
Rhonda Rollins, General Sales Mgr
Derick Corbett, Programming Director

Cori Vallentine, Promotions Manager
Dan Goodman, Chief Engineer

Millington

WLRM
06-22-1962; 1380 khz AM; 2.5 kw-D, DA2; 1 kw-N, DA2; N35 18 56 W89 55 23
2124 E. Holmes Road, Memphis, IN 38116 US
(901) 872-8861, *Fax:* (901) 872-8863
www.1380wlrm.com/
License: Millington, TN held by CPT & T Radio Station Inc.
Arbitron Metro Market: Memphis, TN *TV Affiliate:* Relg
Station Manager, Station Manager
Program Director, Programming Director

WXMX
04-12-1960; 98.1 mhz FM; 100 kw; 869 ft.; N35 9 16 W89 49 20
C/O Barnstable Bcst, Inc, Two Newton Exec. Park, Newton, MA 02162 US
(901) 682-1106, *Fax:* (901) 767-9531
www.981themax.com
License: Millington, Shelby County, TN
Group Owner: Cumulus Media Inc.; (acq 3-23-2004; grpsl).
Arbitron Metro Market: Memphis, TN *Format:* Oldies *Target Audience:* 25-54; adults, upwardly mobile with above average income
Sherri Sawyer, General Manager
Dan Baron, General Sales Mgr
Michael Webb, Programming Director
Paula Davis, Promotions Manager
Gennora Reed, General Sales Manager

Minor Hill

WEUZ
09-02-1983; 92.1 mhz FM; 2.6 kw; 479 ft.; N35 7 18 W87 11 17
Rebroadcasts: Simulcast with WEUP-FM Moulton, AL; 100%
Post Office Box 920, Huntsville, AL 35804 US
(256) 837-9387, *Fax:* (256) 837-9404
www.103weup.com
hundley@103weup.com
License: Minor Hill, Giles County, TN held by Broadcast One Inc.
Arbitron Metro Market: Minor Hill, TN *Format:* Blues
Hundley Batts, President
Steve Murry, Station Manager
Yvonne Craighead, News Director
John Hain, Chief Engineer

Monterey

WKXD-FM
03-03-1986; 106.9 mhz FM *Hrs Open:* 24; 23 kw; 735 ft.; N36 7 13 W85 14 44
259 South Willow Avenue, Cookville, TN 38501 US
(931) 528-6064, *Fax:* (931) 520-1590
www.1069kicksfm.com
jstapleton@jwcbroadcasting.com
License: Monterey, Putnam County, TN held by JWC Broadcasting
Group Owner: JWC Broadcasting; acq 8-3-01).
Nat'l Network: ABC *Nat'l Reps:* Rgnl Reps
Arbitron Metro Market: Cookeville, TN *Hrs. of News Programming:* news progmg one hr wkly *No. News Employees:* 1 *Target Audience:* 18-49; young, adult & affluent audiences
Adv. Rates: 28; 24; 26; 20
Jim Stapleton, General Manager

WLIV-FM
01-08-1997; 104.7 mhz FM *Hrs Open:* 24; 1.25 kw; 712 ft.; N36 15 42 W85 16 35
P.O. Box 520, 1024 West Main Street, Livingston, TN 38570 US
(931) 823-1226, *Fax:* (931) 823-6005
License: Monterey, Putnam County, TN held by Sunny Broadcasting G.P.
Nat'l Network: Westwood One; Fox News Radio *Wire Services:* AP
Format: Country, Sports *Hrs. of News Programming:* news progmg 4 hrs wkly *No. News Employees:* 1 *Target Audience:* General. *Adv. Rates:* 9; 9; 9; 9
Millard Oakley, President
Craig Cantrell, Operations Dir
Joel Upton, General Manager
Carolyn Peterman, Station Manager
Mark Young, General Sales Mgr
Shirley Burnette, News Director
Austin Stinnett, Chief Engineer
Roger Ealey,News & Sports Director

Morrison

WOWC
08-02-1964; 105.3 mhz FM *Hrs Open:* 24; 6 kw; 243 ft.; N35 37 27 W85 53 37
P.O. Box 1505, Glasgow, KY 42142 US
(931) 836-1055,(931) 836-2824, *Fax:* (931) 836-2320
rockdog1055.com
License: Morrison, Warren County, TN held by Peg Broadcasting Crossville LLC.
Group Owner: Peg Broadcasting Crossville LLC; (acq 6-30-2008; grpsl)
Format: Classic Rock *No. News Employees:* 1 *Target Audience:* 18-34.
Don Howard, Operations Dir

Morristown

WCRK
10-01-1947; 1150 khz AM *Hrs Open:* 24; 5 kw-D, DAN; 0.5 kw-N, DAN; N36 14 11 W83 18 33
308 College Street, Pulaski, TN 38478 US
(423) 586-9101, *Fax:* (423) 587-2866
www.wcrk.com
ed@wcrk.com
License: Morristown, TN held by Radio Acquisition Corp.
Nat'l Network: ABC *Nat'l Reps:* Rgnl Reps
Arbitron Metro Market: Morristown, TN *Format:* Contemporary Hits/Top 40 *Hrs. of News Programming:* news progmg 45 hrs wkly *No. News Employees:* 1 *Target Audience:* 25-54; slighty more female, average income$50,000 yearly
S. Herschel Lake, President
Geraldine Lake, Operations Dir
Edwin Arnold, General Manager
Matt Keaton, Programming Director
Mike Rypel, News Director
Dan Trombley, Engineering Dir
Stephanie Christian, Office/Traffic Manager

WMTN
10-19-1957; 1300 khz AM; 5 kw-D, ND1; 0.096 kw-N, ND1; N36 12 15 W83 19 57
Post Office Box 70, 510 West Economy Rd, Morristown, TN 37815 US
(423) 586-9101, *Fax:* (423) 587-2866
www.wmtnradio.com
ed@wcrk.com
License: Morristown, TN held by Radio Acquisition Corp.
Nat'l Network: USA *Regional Network:* Tenn. Radio Net.
Arbitron Metro Market: Morristown, TN *Format:* Country
Ed Arnold, General Manager
Mike Rypel, News Director
Stephanie Christian, Office/Traffic Manager

*WMXK
05-31-1964; 94.1 mhz FM; 1 kw; 810 ft.; N36 13 42 W83 19 56
P.O. Box 70, 510 West Economy Rd, Morristown, TN 37815 US
(916) 251-1600, *Fax:* (916) 251-1650
www.klove.com
License: Morristown, Hamblen County, TN held by Educational Media Foundation.
Group Owner: EMF Broadcasting; (acq 6-17-2008; $640,000)
Nat'l Network: K-Love
Arbitron Metro Market: Rocklin, CA *Format:* Christian
Mike Novak, President

Mount Pleasant

WXRQ
12-15-1981; 1460 khz AM *Hrs Open:* 6 AM-8 PM; 1 kw-D, ND1; 0.169 kw-N, ND1; N35 31 21 W87 11 34
P.O. Box 31, 209 Bond Street, Mt. Pleasant, TN 38474 US
(931) 379-3119, *Fax:* (931) 379-3129
www.1460wxrq.com
wxrq@yahoo.com
License: Mount Pleasant, TN held by New Life Broadcasting Inc.
Nat'l Network: USA
Arbitron Metro Market: Mount Pleasant, TN *Format:* Gospel
Special Programming: Black 4 hrs wkly *Hrs. of News Programming:* news progmg 7 hrs wkly *No. News Employees:* 1 *Target Audience:* General. *Adv.Rates:* 5.50; 5.50; 5.50; na.
Donald Paul, President
Monty Gilliam, General Sales Mgr
Tim Wright, News Director

Mountain City

WMCT
12-08-1967; 1390 khz AM *Hrs Open:* 6 AM-6 PM; 1 kw-D, ND2; 0.058 kw-N, ND2; N36 29 23 W81 47 12
1211 N. Church St, Mountain City, TN 37683 US
(423) 727-6701, *Fax:* (423) 727-9454
www.wmctradio.net
jim@wmct-1390.com
License: Mountain City, TN held by Johnson County Broadcasting Co.
Nat'l Network: ABC *Regional Network:* Tenn. Radio Net. *Nat'l Reps:* Rgnl Reps *Regional Reps:* Linley Grande
Arbitron Metro Market: Mountain City, TN *Format:* Country *No. News Employees:* 1 *Target Audience:* 25-50. *Adv. Rates:* 10; 10; 10; 10
Janice Russell, President

Munford

WKIM
01-01-1948; 98.9 mhz FM; 100 kw horiz, 98.1 kw vert; 614 ft.; N35 9 16 W89 49 20
720 Gordon Terrace, Suite 8b, Chicago, IL 60610 US
(901) 683-0989, *Fax:* (901) 767-9531
www.989kimfm.com
License: Munford, Tipton County, TN
Group Owner: Cumulus Media Inc.; (acq 3-23-2004; grpsl).
Nat'l Reps: Katz Radio
Arbitron Metro Market: Memphis, TN *Format:* Adult Contemp
Sherri Sawyer, General Manager
Dan Barron, General Sales Mgr
Marvin Nugent, Programming Director
Marvin Emilien, Promotions Manager
Krista Freeman-Advertising & Sales

Murfreesboro

*WFCM-FM
09-01-1997; 91.7 mhz FM *Hrs Open:* 24; 2.5 kw horiz, 2.48 kw vert; 758 ft.; N35 48 1 W86 37 17
820 N. Lasalle Drive, Chicago, IL 60610 US
(423) 629-8900, *Fax:* (423) 629-0021
www.wfcm.org
wfcm@moody.edu
License: Murfreesboro, Rutherford County, TN held by The Moody Bible Institute of Chicago.
Nat'l Network: Moody
Arbitron Metro Market: Murfreesboro, TN *Format:* Religious *Target Audience:* 25-54.
Dr. Paul Nyquist, President
Leighton LeBoeuf, General Manager
Andy Napier, Programming Director
David Morais, Chief Engineer
Dawn Rae, Music Director, Webmaster
Juanell Rice, Office Administrator

WGNS
12-31-1946; 1450 khz AM *Hrs Open:* 24; 1 kw-U, ND1; AM, TV and 2 FM translato; N35 50 26 W86 23 27 *Rebroadcasts:* 100% on FM 100.5; FM 101.9...FM translators rebroadcasting WGNS (AM)
306 South Church Street, Murfreesboro, TN 37130 US
(615) 893-5373, *Fax:* (615) 867-6397
www.wgnsradio.com
news@WGNSradio.com
License: Murfreesboro, TN held by The Rutherford Group Inc.
Nat'l Network: ABC; Premiere Radio Networks; Radio America *Regional Network:* Tenn. Radio Net.
Arbitron Metro Market: Nashville, TN *TV Affiliate:* WETV-class A (ch. 11) *Format:* News, News/Talk, 84, Talk *Special Programming:* Black 8 hrs, farm 3 hrs, relg 6 hrs wkly *Hrs. of News Programming:* News progmg80 hrs wkly *No. News Employees:* 4 *Target Audience:* 25 plus; active adults, movers & shakers in economic & educ groupings
Bart Walker, President
Lee Ann Walker, Operations Dir
Scott Walker, General Sales Mgr
Jeff Jordan, Programming Director
Zach Troutman, Promotions Manager
Gary Brown, Chief Engineer
Kristin Walker, Community Relations
BobbieHayes, Director, Religious Programming
Bryan Barrett, Operations Director
Melissa McCullough, Traffic Director

WMGC
11-01-1953; 810 khz AM; 5 kw-D, NDD; 0.006 kw-N, ND1; N35 50 14 W86 25 0 *Rebroadcasts:* Rebroadcasts WNSR(AM) Brentwood 55%
Post Office Box 90972, Nashville, TN 37209 US
(615) 251-1222, *Fax:* (615) 777-2284
www.lasabrosita810am.net/
License: Murfreesboro, TN held by Radio 810 Nashville Ltd.
Group Owner: Southern Wabash Communications Corp.; (acq 7-10-01).
Nat'l Network: ABC

RADIO - U.S.

Arbitron Metro Market: Nashville, TN *Special Programming:* Relg 4 hrs wkly *Target Audience:* 18-54; adults
Ted Johnson, General Manager

*WMOT

04-09-1969; 89.5 mhz FM *Hrs Open:* 24; 100 kw; 676 ft.; N36 5 7 W86 26 22
P.O. Box 3, Murfreesboro, TN 37132 US
(615) 898-2800, *Fax:* (615) 898-2774
www.wmot.org
wmot@mtsu.edu
License: Murfreesboro, Rutherford County, TN held by Middle Tennessee State University.
Nat'l Network: NPR; AP Radio
Arbitron Metro Market: Nashville, TN *Format:* Jazz *Hrs. of News Programming:* news progmg 10 hrs wkly *No. News Employees:* 2 *Target Audience:* 24 plus; general
John Egly, Operations Dir
John High, General Manager
Keith Palmer, General Sales Mgr
Greg Lee Hunt, Programming Director
Mike Osborne, News Director
Gary Brown, Chief Engineer

*WMTS-FM

01-01-1996; 88.3 mhz FM *Hrs Open:* 24; 0.68 kw; 138 ft.; N35 50 56 W86 21 11
P.O. Box 3, Murfreesboro, TN 37132 US
(615) 898-2636, *Fax:* (615) 898-5682
www.wmts.org
manager@wmts.org
License: Murfreesboro, Rutherford County, TN held by Middle Tennessee State University.
Arbitron Metro Market: Murfreesboro, TN *Format:* Variety/Diverse *Special Programming:* Polka 2 hrs, electronic 10 hrs, jazz 4 hrs, funk 2 *Target Audience:* 18-26; College age, diverse
Max Smith Sr., President
Ali Dorris, General Manager
Jonathan Stockdell, Programming Director
Sarah Raulerson, Promotions Manager
Larry Christy, News Director
Jacob Whisenaut, Music Director
Kelsey Griffith, Business Director
Andrew Croney, Technical Director
Andrew Kelly, Production Director
Logan Propst, Drive Time Producer

WCJK

08-10-1963; 96.3 mhz FM *Hrs Open:* 24; 39 kw; 1417 ft.; N36 15 50 W86 47 39
Mailing Address: PO Box 3848, Evansville, IN 47736 US
Second Address: 504 Rosedale Ave., Nashville, TN 37211
615-259-4567, *Fax:* 615-259-4594
www.963jackfm.com
License: Murfreesboro, Rutherford County, TN held by South Central Communications Corp.
Group Owner: South Central Communications Corp.; (acq 2-4-94; $6 million;
Nat'l Reps: Katz Radio *Wire Services:* NWS (National Weather Service)
Arbitron Metro Market: Nashville, TN *Format:* Adult Contemp *No. News Employees:* 1 *Target Audience:* A 25-54
Dennis Gwiazdon, Operations Dir
Craig Jones, Programming Director
Clinton Hooper, Chief Engineer
Pam Parks, Business Manager
Meredith Mazanek, Marketing Director
Marty Linck, Program Director
Gillian Baxter, Traffic Director

Nashville

WENO

05-23-1988; 760 khz AM *Hrs Open:* Sunrise-sunset; 1 kw-D, NDD; N36 8 28 W86 45 23
333 Murfreesboro Road, Nashville, TN 37210 US
(615) 742-6506, *Fax:* (615) 248-7786
www.760thegospel.com
info@760TheGospel.com
License: Nashville, TN held by WENO Inc.
Nat'l Network: AP Radio
Arbitron Metro Market: Nashville, TN *Format:* Christian, Religious *Hrs. of News Programming:* News progmg 6 hrs wkly *Target Audience:* 25-54.
Mark Myers, CFO
Dan Boone, President
David Deese, General Manager
Dave Queen, Station Manager
Jennifer Houchin, News Director
Dan Klimkowski, Chief Engineer

*WFSK-FM

04-14-1973; 88.1 mhz FM *Hrs Open:* 24; 0.7 kw horiz; 7 ft.; N36 10 0 W86 48 17
1000 17th Avenue North, Nashville, TN 37208 US
(615) 329-8500, *Fax:* (615) 329-9305
www.fisk.edu
webmaster@fisk.edu
License: Nashville, Davidson County, TN held by Fisk University.
Nat'l Network: PRI
Arbitron Metro Market: Nashville, TN *Format:* Jazz, Smooth Jazz, 86
Sharon Kay, General Manager
Xuam Lawson, Programming Director
Clinton Hooper, Chief Engineer

WJXA

04-03-1976; 92.9 mhz FM *Hrs Open:* 24; 97 kw; 1053 ft.; N36 7 14 W86 58 7
Mailing Address: P.O. Box 3848, Evansville, IN 47736 US
Second Address: 504 Rosedale Ave., Nashville, TN 37211
615-259-4567, *Fax:* (615) 259-4594
www.mix929.com
License: Nashville, Davidson County, TN held by South Central Communications Corp.
Group Owner: South Central Communications Corp.
Nat'l Reps: Katz Radio
Arbitron Metro Market: Nashville, TN *Format:* Adult Contemp *Target Audience:* A 25-54
Dennis Gwiazdon, Operations Dir
Craig Jones, Programming Director
Anna Marie Ritter, News Director
Clinton Hooper, Chief Engineer
Pam Parks, Business Manager
Meredith Mazanek, Marketing Director
Barbara Bridges, ProgramDirector
Gillian Baxter, Traffic Director

WAMB

12-21-2001; 1200 khz AM *Hrs Open:* 24
P. O. Box 399, Lebanon, TN 37088 US
(615) 889-1960, *Fax:* (615) 902-9108
www.wamb.net
wamb@bellsouth.net
License: Nashville, TN held by Great Southern Broadcasting Co. Inc.
Nat'l Network: CNN Radio
Arbitron Metro Market: Nashville, TN *Format:* Adult Contemp
William Barry, President
Will Baird, Operations Dir
Harry Stephenson, General Sales Mgr
Ronald Johnson, Programming Director
Beth Lane, News Director
Gary Brown, Chief Engineer

WKDF

01-01-1967; 103.3 mhz FM; 100 kw; 1234 ft.; N36 2 8 W86 50 56
506 2nd Ave, South, Nashville, TN 37210 US
(615) 244-9533, *Fax:* (615) 259-1271
www.103wkdf.com
ken.bailey@citcom.com
License: Nashville, Davidson County, TN
Group Owner: Cumulus Media Inc.; acq 4-26-01; grpsl).
Arbitron Metro Market: Nashville, TN *Format:* Country *Target Audience:* 18-34; general
Dave Kelly, General Manager
Cindy Francis, Promotions Manager
Jennifer Boucher, News Director
Cameron Adkins, Chief Engineer
Eddy Foxx, Music Director
Bud Ford, Programming Director

WLAC

11-24-1926; 1510 khz AM *Hrs Open:* 24
600 Congress Avenue, Suite 1400, Austin, TX 78701 US
(615) 664-2400, *Fax:* (615) 664-2457
www.1510wlac.com
info@1510wlac.com
License: Nashville, TN held by Capstar TX L.P.
Group Owner: Clear Channel Communications Inc.; (acq 8-30-00; grpsl)
Nat'l Network: Wall Street; ABC
Arbitron Metro Market: Nashville, TN *Format:* News, News/Talk, 86, Religious *Special Programming:* Black 20 hrs wkly *Hrs. of News Programming:* news progmg 18 hrs wly *No. News Employees:* 3 *Target Audience:* 35-64; professionals, business owners & managers
Dave Alpert, President
Keith Kaufman, Operations Dir
Darren Smith, General Sales Mgr
Bruce Collins, Programming Director
Mike Gideon, Chief Engineer
Temple Hancock, Promotions Director

WMDB

08-15-1983; 880 khz AM
3051 Stokers Lane, Nashville, TN 37218 US
(615) 742-6506 x 22, *Fax:* (615) 242-8223
www.760thegospel.com
License: Nashville, TN held by Davidson Media Station WMDB Licensee LLC.
Group Owner: Davidson Media Group LLC; (acq 9-1-2005; $1.6 million)
Arbitron Metro Market: Nashville, TN *Format:* Gospel *Target Audience:* 18 plus; Black relg
Armando Quintero, General Manager

WNAH

12-24-1949; 1360 khz AM *Hrs Open:* 24; 1 kw-D, ND1; 0.027 kw-N, ND1; N36 11 30 W86 46 26
44-Music Square East, Nashville, IN 37203 US
(615) 254-7611, *Fax:* (615) 467-8600
www.wnah.com
mail@wnah.com
License: Nashville, TN held by Hermitage Broadcasting Corp.
Arbitron Metro Market: Nashville, TN *Format:* Gospel *Hrs. of News Programming:* News progmg 5 hrs wkly *Target Audience:* 21-50.
Van Irwin Jr., President
Tony Cappuccilli, General Sales Mgr
Hoyt Carter Jr., Programming Director
Bill Grist, Promotions Manager
Bobby Lynn II, Music Director

*WECV-FM

05-23-1967; 89.1 mhz FM *Hrs Open:* 24; 1.4 kw; Ant 200 ft; N36 08 28 W86 45 23
2 Lakeview Place, Suite 101, Nashville, TN 37214
(615) 871-1160, *Fax:* (615) 871-9355
www.bottradionetwork.com
wcrt@bottradionetwork.com
License: Nashville, Davidson County, TN held by Trevecca Nazarene University Inc.
Population Served: 447,877 *Arbitron Metro Market:* Nashville, TN *Format:* Christian *Hrs. of News Programming:* News progmg 3 hrs wkly *Target Audience:* 18-30; college & young professionals
Lee Kelly, General Manager

WNQM

07-01-1948; 1300 khz AM *Hrs Open:* 24
1300 Wwcr Avenue, Nashville, TN 37218 US
(615) 255-1300, *Fax:* (615) 255-1311
www.wwcr.com
wnqm@wwcr.com
License: Nashville, TN held by WNQM Inc.
Group Owner: F W Robbert Broadcasting Co. Inc.; (acq 1-83; $700,000;
Nat'l Network: USA
Arbitron Metro Market: Nashville, TN *Format:* Religious *Special Programming:* Sp *Hrs. of News Programming:* News progmg 2 hrs wkly *Target Audience:* General.
Fred Westenberger, President
Brady Murray, Operations Dir
Eric Westenberger, General Manager

WNRQ

01-01-1953; 105.9 mhz FM *Hrs Open:* 24; 98 kw; 1234 ft.; N36 2 8 W86 50 56
600 Congress Avenue, Suite 1400, Austin, TX 78701 US
(615) 664-2400, *Fax:* (615) 742-1059
www.1059therock.com
info@1059.com
License: Nashville, Davidson County, TN
Arbitron Metro Market: Nashville, TN *Format:* Adult Contemp *Special Programming:* Christian 6 hrs wkly *Hrs. of News Programming:* news progmg 3 hrs wkly *No. News Employees:* 1 *Target Audience:* 25-54;upwardly mobile adults
Keith Kaufman, Operations Dir
David Alpert, General Manager
Temple Hancock, Promotions Manager

WNVL

01-01-1948; 1240 khz AM *Hrs Open:* 24; 1 kw-U, ND1; N36 9 23 W86 46 16
3270 Blazer Parkway, Suite 101, Lexington, KY 40509 US
(615) 242-1411, *Fax:* (615) 242-3823
www.activa1240.com
gerente@activa1240.com
License: Nashville, TN held by Davidson Media Station WNSG Licensee LLC.
Group Owner: Davidson Media Group LLC; (acq 8-1-2005; $2.7 million).

Arbitron Metro Market: Nashville, TN *Target Audience:* 25-54.
Peter Davidson, President
Orlaindo Rosa, Operations Dir
Armando Quintero, General Manager
Alberto Pena, Programming Director
Jay Shoemaker, Chief Engineer

***WPLN-FM**
12-17-1962; 90.3 mhz FM; 80 kw; 1132 ft.; N36 2 8 W86 50 56
630 Mainstream Drive, Nashville, TN 37228 US
(615) 760-2903, *Fax:* (615) 760-2904
www.wpln.org
info@wpln.org
License: Nashville, Davidson County, TN held by Nashville Public Radio.
Nat'l Network: NPR; PRI
Arbitron Metro Market: Nashville, TN *Format:* News *Target Audience:* General.
Nina Cardona, Operations Dir
Robert Gordon, General Manager
Laura Landress, General Sales Mgr
Henry Fennell, Programming Director
Anita Bugg, News Director
Tom Knox, Chief Engineer
Will Griffin, Music Director
Wendy Poston,Traffic Manager

***WCFL(FM)**
12-03-1971; 91.1 mhz FM *Hrs Open:* 24; 14.5 kw; 457 ft; N36 08 27 W86 51 56
Box 9100-B, Vanderbilt Univ., Nashville, TN 37235
(615) 322-3691, *Fax:* (615) 343-2582
www.wrvu.org
wrvugm@gmail.com
License: Nashville, Davidson County, TN held by Vanderbilt Student Communications.
Nat'l Network: ABC
Population Served: 447,877 *Arbitron Metro Market:* Nashville, TN *Format:* Variety/Diverse *Target Audience:* General; div, adventurous individuals
Robert Ackley, General Manager
Scott Cardone, Programming Director
Kate Koschewa, Promotions Manager

WSIX-FM
01-01-1948; 97.9 mhz FM *Hrs Open:* 24; 100 kw; 1145 ft.; N36 2 50 W86 49 48
600 Congress Avenue, Suite 1400, Austin, TX 78701 US
(615) 664-2400, *Fax:* (615) 664-2457
www.wsix.com
License: Nashville, Davidson County, TN held by Capstar TX L.P.
Group Owner: Clear Channel Communications Inc.; (acq 8-30-00; grpsl).
Arbitron Metro Market: Nashville, TN *Format:* Country *Hrs. of News Programming:* news progmg one hr wkly *No. News Employees:* 2 *Target Audience:* 25-54.
Melissa Kent, General Sales Mgr
Michael Bryan, Programming Director
Mollie Cochrane, Promotions Manager
Mike Gideon, Chief Engineer
Temple Hancock, Promotions Director

WSM
10-05-1925; 650 khz AM *Hrs Open:* 24; 50 kw-U, ND1; N35 59 50 W86 47 32
One Gaylord Drive, Nashville, TN 37214 US
(615) 889-6595, *Fax:* (615) 871-6384
www.wsmonline.com
License: Nashville, TN held by Grand Ole Opry LLC
Nat'l Network: ABC *Nat'l Reps:* Christal
Arbitron Metro Market: Nashville, TN *Format:* Country *Special Programming:* Farm 6 hrs, Grand Ole Opry 12 hrs wkly *Hrs. of News Programming:* news progmg 11 hrs wkly *No. News Employees:* 12 *Target Audience:* 35 plus; high school graduates, married homeowners, income $25,000 plus
Tom English, General Manager
Anthony Oldham, Programming Director
Nicole Judd, Promotions Manager
Jason Cooper, Chief Engineer
Joe Limardi, Operations Manager

WSM-FM
11-01-1962; 95.5 mhz FM; 100 kw; 1230 ft.; N36 8 27 W86 51 56
One Gaylord Drive, Nashville, TN 37214 US
(615) 321-1067, *Fax:* (615) 321-5808
www.955thewolf.com
License: Nashville, Davidson County, TN held by Cumulus Licensing LLC.
Group Owner: Cumulus Media Inc.; (acq 7-21-2003; $65 million with WWTN(FM) Manchester).
Arbitron Metro Market: Nashville, TN *Format:* Country *Target Audience:* 25-54.
Michael Dickey, General Manager

WYFN
01-07-1927; 980 khz AM; 5 kw-D, DAN; 5 kw-N, DAN; N36 12 25 W86 40 25
8030 Arrowridge Blvd, Charlotte, NC 28273 US
(704) 523-5555, *Fax:* (704) 522-1967
www.bbnradio.org
bbn@bbnradio.org
License: Nashville, TN held by Bible Broadcasting Network.
Group Owner: Bible Broadcasting Network; acq 1-31-91; $600,000;
Nat'l Reps: McGavren Guild
Arbitron Metro Market: Nashville, TN *Format:* Religious
Aaron Tuttle, Station Manager

New Johnsonville

***WAYW**
01-01-2001; 89.9 mhz FM *Hrs Open:* 24; 3.1 kw; 466 ft.; N35 56 17 W87 53 39
6910 NE2nd Terrace, Boca Raton, FL 33487 US
(719) 533-0300
www.main.wayfm.com
supportservices@wayfm.com
License: New Johnsonville, Humphreys County, TN held by WAY-FM Media Group Inc.
Group Owner: WAY-FM Media Group Inc.; acq 2-1-01).
Arbitron Metro Market: Colorado Springs, CO *Format:* Christian
Teresa White, General Sales Mgr
Jeff Brown, Programming Director

Newport

WLIK
04-09-1954; 1270 khz AM *Hrs Open:* 24; 5 kw-D, DAN; 0.5 kw-N, DAN; N35 57 49 W83 12 31
640 West Highway 25/70, Newport, TN 37821 US
(423) 623-3095, *Fax:* (423) 623-3096
wlik.net
wlik@planetc.com
License: Newport, TN held by WLIK Inc.
Nat'l Network: CNN Radio *Regional Network:* Tenn. Radio Net.
Regional Reps: Regional Reps
Format: Oldies *Special Programming:* Relg 18 hrs wkly *Hrs. of News Programming:* news progmg 7 hrs wkly *No. News Employees:* 1 *Target Audience:* General. *Adv. Rates:* 10; 10; 10; 6
Dwight Wilkerson, President
Angie Wilkerson, Operations Dir
Johnnie Swann, Chief of Operations

WLNQ-FM
02-01-1993; 92.9 mhz FM *Hrs Open:* 24; 3.1 kw; 459 ft; N35 57 27 W83 05 03 *Rebroadcasts:* Rebroadcasts WNPC(AM) Newport 100%
377 Graham St., Newport, TN 37821
(423) 623-8743, *Fax:* (423) 623-8744
www.thundercountry1047.com/
License: Newport, Cocke County, TN
Group Owner: Bristol Broadcasting Co. Inc.
Arbitron Metro Market: White Pine, TN
Jim Phillips, Programming Director

***WGSN**
01-01-2008; 90.7 mhz FM; 1 kw vert; Ant 2,296 ft; N35 54 20 W83 17 48
Box 1509, Jamestown, TN 38556
(931) 879-8188, *Fax:* (931) 879-1733
www.newlife105.com
License: Newport, Cocke County, TN held by Bible Believers Network Inc.

Fred Allred, President
Andy Lowe, General Manager
Stev Boutelle, News Director

Norris

WLYT(FM)
04-01-2001; 106.7 mhz FM *Hrs Open:* 24; 1.1 kw; Ant 751 ft; N36 07 12 W83 55 30 *Rebroadcasts:* Rebroadcasts WTXM(FM) Maryville 100%
6808 Hanna Lake S.E., Caledonia, MI 49316
(616) 698-1831
License: Norris, Anderson County, TN held by South Central Communications Corp.
Group Owner: South Central Communications Corp.; (acq 6-14-2001; $2.5 million).
Wire Services: AP
Population Served: 4,524 *Arbitron Metro Market:* Polson MT
Adv. Rates: 20; 20; 20; 10
P.R. Frank, Operations Dir
Ken Kreitzer, General Manager
Christopher Hartley, Programming Director
Tom Nornhold, Chief Engineer
Jennifer Bryant, Assistant Music Director

Oak Ridge

WNOX
04-20-1974; 100.3 mhz FM; 100 kw; 2001 ft.; N36 11 53 W84 13 51
Mailing Address: Post Office Boe 50006, Knoxville, TN 37950 US
Second Address: 4711 Old Kingston Pike, Knoxville, TN 37919
(865) 588-6511, *Fax:* (865) 588-3725
www.wnoxnewstalk.com
License: Oak Ridge, Anderson County, TN held by Oak Ridge FM Inc.
Nat'l Reps: Katz Radio *Wire Services:* AP
Arbitron Metro Market: Knoxville, TN *TV Affiliate:* News/talk
Operations Manager

Olive Hill

***WDNX**
01-10-1975; 89.1 mhz FM *Hrs Open:* 24; 52 kw; 591 ft.; N35 12 23 W88 3 32
Mailing Address: 3730 Lonesome Pine Road, Savannah, TN 38372 US
Second Address: WDNX Bldg., 3730 Lonesome Pine Rd., Savannah, TN 38372
(731) 925-3098, *Fax:* (731) 925-4238
www.harberthills.org
sheriwdnx@yahoo.com
License: Olive Hill, Hardin County, TN held by Rural Life Foundation.
Arbitron Metro Market: Savannah, TN *Format:* Christian, Religious *Special Programming:* Class 5 hrs, farm one hr wkly *Hrs. of News Programming:* news progmg 5 hrs wkly *No. News Employees:* 1 *Target Audience:* General; families
Charles Harris, Chairman
Steven Dickman, President
Steve Dickman, Chief Engineer
Sheri Durbin, General Sales Manager

Oliver Springs

WOKI
09-15-1989; 98.7 mhz FM *Hrs Open:* 24; 8 kw; 571 ft.; N36 6 48 W84 3 44
Mailing Address: 4711 Old Kingston Pike, P. O. Box 11167, Knoxville, TN 37939 US
Second Address: 4711 Old Kingston Pike, Knoxville, TN 37919
(865) 588-6511, *Fax:* (865) 656-7487
www.987earlfm.com
License: Oliver Springs, Anderson County, TN
Group Owner: Cumulus Media Inc.; (acq 4-26-2001; grpsl)
Nat'l Reps: Katz Radio *Regional Reps:* Rgnl Reps. *Wire Services:* AP
Arbitron Metro Market: Knoxville, TN *Format:* Oldies *Target Audience:* 18 plus.
Ed Brantley, Operations Dir
Tammy Browning, General Sales Mgr
Joe Stutler, Programming Director
Shanna Lingerfelt, Promotions Manager
Mike Hammond, Operations Manager

WJRV(FM)
106.1 mhz FM; 190 w; Ant 1,746 ft; N36 06 29 W84 20 08
217 Bayfront Dr., Bonita Springs, FL 34134
(239) 390-9987
License: Oliver Springs, Roane County, TN held by Momentum Broadcasting LLC.
Population Served: 253 *Arbitron Metro Market:* Louisville, KY
Norman Alpert, President

Oneida

WBNT-FM
06-10-1965; 105.5 mhz FM *Hrs Open:* 18; 3 kw horiz; 285 ft.; N36 30 3 W84 29 24
P.O. Box 4370, 1126 Buffalo Road, Oneida, TN 37841 US
(423) 569-8598, *Fax:* (423) 569-5572
www.hive105.com
wbnt@highland.net
License: Oneida, Scott County, TN held by Oneida Broadcasters Inc.
Nat'l Network: ABC
Arbitron Metro Market: Oneida, TN *Format:* Adult Contemp, Country *Target Audience:* 16-56; male/female working class-retirees

Paul C. Strunk, Operations Dir
Hillard Mattie, General Manager
Hillard Mattie, General Sales Mgr

WOCV
08-01-1959; 1310 khz AM; 1 kw-D, NDD; N36 30 3 W84 29 24
Rebroadcasts: Rebroadcasts WBNT-FM Oneida 100%
P.O. Box 4370, Oneida, TN 37841 US
(423) 569-8598, *Fax:* (423) 569-5572
www.hive105.com
wbnt@highland.net
License: Oneida, TN held by Oneida Broadcasters Inc.
Nat'l Network: ABC
TV Affiliate: Adult contemp *Special Programming:* news progmg 15 hrs wkly *Hrs. of News Programming:* 4 *No. News Employees:* 22-55; male & female *Adv. Rates:* 6.50; 6.50; 6.50; 6.50
General Manager, General Manager

Ooltewah

WPLZ
02-27-1980; 95.3 mhz FM *Hrs Open:* 24; 11 kw; Ant 499 ft; N34 57 23 W85 17 32
1305 Carter St., Chattanooga, TN 37402
(423) 265-9494, *Fax:* (423) 266-2335
www.catcountry953.com
Jim2@BrewerRadio.com
License: Ooltewah, Hamilton County, TN held by J.L. Brewer Broadcasting of Cleveland LLC.
Group Owner: Brewer Broadcasting Corp.; May-98
Nat'l Reps: Katz Radio *Regional Reps:* Eastman
Population Served: 500,000 *Arbitron Metro Market:* Chattanooga, TN *Target Audience:* A25-54 *Adv. Rates:* 30; 25; 30; 20
Jim Brewer, Chairman
Jim Brewer II, President
Keith Landecker, Operations Dir
Jim Brewer II, General Manager
Jim Brewer II, Station Manager
Mike Baskin, General Sales Mgr
Josh Weber, Programming Director
Sam Lewis, ChiefEngineer

Paris

WAKQ
09-01-1967; 105.5 mhz FM; 3.7 kw; 420 ft.; N36 16 45 W88 20 31 *Rebroadcasts:* Rebroadcasts WWKF(FM) Union City 100%
1729 Nailling Drive, Union City, TN 38261 US
(731) 642-7100, *Fax:* (731) 642-9367
kf99kg105.com
jadcock@wenkwtpr.com
License: Paris, Henry County, TN
Group Owner: WENK of Union City Inc.
Arbitron Metro Market: Clarksville TN *Format:* Contemporary Hits/Top 40 *Hrs. of News Programming:* news progmg one hr wkly *No. News Employees:* 1 *Target Audience:* adults 18-34 *Adv. Rates:* Same as AM
Terry Hailey, Programming Director

WLZK
11-01-1991; 94.1 mhz FM *Hrs Open:* 24; 10.5 kw; 328 ft.; N36 18 50 W88 17 33
P. O. Box 1239, Paris, TN 38242 US
(731) 644-9455, *Fax:* (731) 644-9421
wlzk@bellsouth.net
License: Paris, Henry County, TN held by Benton-Weatherford Broadcasting Inc. of Texas
Group Owner: Benton-Weatherford Broadcasting Inc. of Tennessee; (Acq 3-15-91;
Nat'l Network: Jones Radio Networks
Arbitron Metro Market: Paris, TN *Format:* Adult Contemp *Hrs. of News Programming:* news progmg 7 hrs wkly *No. News Employees:* 1 *Adv. Rates:* Same as AM
Olvie Sisk, President
Carolyn Jackson, General Manager
David Ever, Programming Director

WRQR(AM)
05-09-1980; 1000 khz AM; 5 kw-D, DA; N36 18 50 W88 17 33
110 India Rd., Paris, TN 38242
(731) 644-9455, *Fax:* (731) 644-9421
www.wmufradio.com
radionews@bellsouth.net
License: Paris, Henry County, TN held by Benton-Weatherford Broadcasting Inc.of Tennessee
Group Owner: Benton-Weatherford Broadcasting Inc. of Tennessee; acq 4-1-85).
Nat'l Network: ABC
Population Served: 50,000 *Arbitron Metro Market:* Paris, TN *Format:* Country *Special Programming:* Farm 2 hrs wkly *Hrs. of News Programming:* news progmg 3 hrs wkly *No. News Employees:* 1 *Target Audience:* 25-54; people with disposable income
Gary Benton, President
Tim Alsobrooks, News Director

WTPR
05-07-1947; 710 khz AM *Hrs Open:* Sunrise-sunset; 0.75 kw-D, NDD; N36 16 47 W88 20 32 *Rebroadcasts:* Reboadcasts WTPR-FM Paris 100%
1729 Nailing Drive, Union City, TN 38242 US
(731) 642-7100, *Fax:* (731) 642-9367
wenkwtpr.com
thailey@wenkwtpr.com
License: Paris, TN held by WENK of Uniion City Inc.
Group Owner: WENK of Union City Inc.; acq 10-28-89;
Nat'l Network: ABC *Regional Reps:* Rgnl Reps
Arbitron Metro Market: Paris, TN *Format:* Oldies *Hrs. of News Programming:* news progmg 12 hrs wkly *No. News Employees:* 1 *Target Audience:* 35-54. *Adv. Rates:* 11.75; 17.75; 17.75; 8.80
Terry L. Hailey, President and General Manager
Terry Hailey, Programming Director
Jim Adcock, Promotions Manager
Brad Hosford, Chief Engineer
Lorrie Matlock, Sales Representative

***WPRH**
90.9 mhz FM; 5.4 kw vert; 315 ft.; N36 15 29 W88 11 11
88 Casey Jones Blvd, Jackson, TN 38305 US
(662) 844-5036, *Fax:* (662) 842-6791
www.afr.net
contact@afa.net
License: Paris, Henry County, TN held by American Family Association.
Group Owner: American Family Radio; (acq 1-16-2007)
Nat'l Network: American Family Radio
Arbitron Metro Market: Paris, TN *Format:* Christian
Donald E. Wildmon, Founder
Buster Wilson, General Manager
Jennifer Hagman, Programming Director

Parker's Crossroads

WBFG
01-01-1999; 96.5 mhz FM; 6 kw; 328 ft.; N35 45 33 W88 23 15
Mailing Address: P.O. Box 279, Lexington, TN 38351 US
Second Address: 584 Smith Ave., Lexington, TN 38351
(731) 968-9990, *Fax:* (731) 968-0380
www.wbfg965.com
wbfg965@yahoo.com
License: Parker's Crossroads, Henderson County, TN held by Crossroads Broadcasting LLC.
Nat'l Network: ESPN Radio
Format: Sports
Lori Becker, Operations Dir
Dan Hughes, General Manager

Parsons

WKJQ-FM
06-04-1990; 97.3 mhz FM *Hrs Open:* 24; 6 kw; 256 ft.; N35 39 39 W88 7 5
PO Box 576, Iron Hill Road, Parsons, TN 38363 US
(731) 847-3011, *Fax:* (731) 847-4600
ralphclenney@yahoo.com
License: Parsons, Decatur County, TN held by Clenney Broadcasting Corp.
Format: Country *Target Audience:* 25-54. *Adv. Rates:* 10; 10; 10; na
Charles Dowdy, General Manager

Pegram

WPRT-FM
04-27-1964; 102.5 mhz FM *Hrs Open:* 24; 100 kw; 974 ft.; N36 17 36 W87 18 20
P. O. Box 150846, Nashville, TN 37215 US
(615) 399-1029, *Fax:* (615) 361-9873
www.v1025.com
programming@1025theparty.com
License: Pegram, Cheatham County, TN held by Montgomery Broadcasting.
Group Owner: The Cromwell Group Inc.; (acq 1990)
Nat'l Reps: McGavren Guild
Arbitron Metro Market: Nashville, TN *Format:* Adult Contemp *Target Audience:* 18-34; S. KY residents
Bayard Walters, President
Troy Hanson, Operations Dir
Tincy Crouse, General Manager
David Wilson, Chief Engineer

Pigeon Forge

WPFT
01-01-2007; 106.3 mhz FM; 0.5 kw; 1117 ft.; N35 42 13 W83 33 57
US
(423) 485-8987
License: Pigeon Forge, Sevier County, TN held by East Tennessee Radio Group L.P.
Group Owner: East Tennessee Radio Group L.P.
Arbitron Metro Market: Pigeon Forge, TN *Format:* Sports, Talk
Paul Fink, General Manager

Pikeville

WUAT
12-19-1972; 1110 khz AM; 0.25 kw-D, NDD; N35 36 18 W85 11 14
Mailing Address: P.O. Box 128, Pikeville, TN 37367 US
Second Address: 101 N. Main, Pikeville, TN 37367
(423) 447-2906, *Fax:* (423) 447-7309
www.wuatradio.com
wuat@wuatradio.com
License: Pikeville, TN held by Joyce V. Bownds.
Arbitron Metro Market: Pikeville, TN *Format:* Country, Gospel
Special Programming: Farm 5 hrs, relg 15 hrs wkly
Joyce Bownds, President

Portland

WQKR
07-15-1980; 1270 khz AM *Hrs Open:* 24
817 North Broadway, Portland, TN 37148 US
(615) 325-3250, *Fax:* (615) 325-0803
wqkr@comcast.net
License: Portland, TN held by Venture Broadcasting LLC
Nat'l Network: ABC *Regional Network:* Tenn. Radio Net.
Arbitron Metro Market: Nashville, TN *Format:* Oldies *No. News Employees:* 1 *Target Audience:* 25-54.
Lee Dorman, General Manager

Powell

WNFZ
02-01-1967; 94.3 mhz FM; 2.95 kw; 472 ft.; N35 57 58 W84 4 6
Mailing Address: Post Office Box 50006, Knoxville, TN 37950 US
Second Address: 1100 Sharps Ridge Rd., Knoxville, TN 37917
(865) 525-6000, *Fax:* (865) 525-2000
www.943thex.com
SCOX@SCCRADIO.COM
License: Powell, Anderson County, TN held by John A. Pirkle.
Arbitron Metro Market: Knoxville, TN *Format:* Alternative *Target Audience:* General.
John Pirkle, CEO
Johnathan Pirkle, President
Terry Gillingham, Operations Dir
Jeff Cutshaw, General Sales Mgr
Shane Cox, Programming Director

WKTI
08-15-1984; 1040 khz AM; 3 kw-C, NDD; 10 kw-D, NDD; N36 2 34 W84 2 51
Mailing Address: 3355 S. Valley View Blvd., Las Vegas, NV 09102 US
Second Address: Box 50158, Knoxville, TN 37950
(865) 824-1021, *Fax:* (865) 824-1880
www.studio1040.com
bpatrick@journalbroadcastgroup.com
License: Powell, TN held by Journal Broadcast Corp.
Group Owner: Journal Communications Inc.
Nat'l Network: AP Radio; Jones Radio Networks
Arbitron Metro Market: Knoxville, TN *Format:* Classic Rock
Dan McKee, General Sales Mgr
Bruce Patrick, Programming Director

Pulaski

WKSR
05-06-1947; 1420 khz AM
Mailing Address: 104 South Second Street, P.O.Box 738, Pulaski, TN 38478 US
Second Address: 104 S. Second St., Pulaski, TN 38478
(931) 363-2505, *Fax:* (931) 424-3157
www.wksr.com
wksr@igiles.net
License: Pulaski, TN held by Pulaski Broadcasting Inc.
Nat'l Network: ABC
Format: Oldies *Hrs. of News Programming:* one. *Target Audience:* 25-54.
Ronnie Rose, General Manager
Ed Carter, Programming Director

Red Bank

*WJBP

09-12-1980; 91.5 mhz FM *Hrs Open:* 24; 11 kw horiz, 10 kw vert; 328 ft.; N34 56 37 W85 18 1
4501 Amnicola Highway, Chattanooga, TN 37406 US
(800) 877-5600, *Fax:* (916) 251-1650
www.klove.com
License: Red Bank, Hamilton County, TN held by Family Life Broadcasting Inc.
Group Owner: Family Life Communications Inc.; (acq 12-10-2008; $1.5 million)
Arbitron Metro Market: Dripping Springs TX *Format:* Christian
Mike Novak, President
Eric Allen, General Sales Mgr
David Pierce, Programming Director
Ed Lenane, News Director
Sam Wallington, Engineering Dir
Scott Smith, Music Director
Marya Morgan, News Reporter
Richard Hunt, NewsReporter
Tracy Butler, Traffic Manager

WJTT

11-01-1972; 94.3 mhz FM *Hrs Open:* 24; 4.7 kw; 371 ft.; N35 7 33 W85 17 25
409 Chestnut St #A-154, Chattanooga, TN 37402 US
(423) 265-9494, *Fax:* (423) 266-2335
www.power94.com
info@power94.com
License: Red Bank, Hamilton County, TN held by Brewer Broadcasting of Chattanooga Inc.
Group Owner: Brewer Broadcasting Corp.; (acq 12-26-93; $1.68 million).
Nat'l Reps: D & R Radio
Arbitron Metro Market: Chattanooga, TN *Format:* Urban Contemporary *Special Programming:* Relg 4 hrs wkly *Target Audience:* 18-49.
Jim Brewer Sr., President
Jim Brewer II, Operations Dir
Jerry Ware, General Sales Mgr
Keith Landecker, Programming Director
Jay Holloway, Promotions Manager
Donna Harrison, News Director
Parks Hall, Chief Engineer
BradGuagriri, National Sales Manager

Ripley

*WAUV

01-01-2000; 89.7 mhz FM; 6.4 kw; 394 ft.; N35 46 31 W89 28 18
P.O. Drawer 2440, Tupelo, MS 38803 US
(662) 844-8888, *Fax:* (662) 842-6791
www.afr.net
comments@afr.net
License: Ripley, Lauderdale County, TN held by American Family Association.
Group Owner: American Family Radio
Arbitron Metro Market: Sacramento, CA *Format:* Religious
Marvin Sanders, General Manager

WTRB

12-11-1954; 1570 khz AM *Hrs Open:* 17; 1 kw-D, ND1; 0.053 kw-N, ND1; N35 43 46 W89 32 33
C.O Walton E. Williams, 420 20th St Suite 1600, Birmingham, AL 35203 US
(731) 635-1570, *Fax:* (731) 635-9722
www.1570wtrb.com
wtrb@newwavecomm.net
License: Ripley, TN held by West Tennessee Regional Broadcasting Inc.
Regional Network: Tenn. Radio Net. *Nat'l Reps:* Keystone (unwired net)
Arbitron Metro Market: Ripley, TN *Format:* Country *Special Programming:* Gospel 6 hrs wkly
Phillip Ennis, President
Palmer Johnson, General Manager
Mickey Hamlin, General Sales Mgr
Jerry Wilson, Programming Director
Randy Byrd, Sports Director
Mickey McLure, Disc Jockey
April Goodrich, Disc Jockey
Erin Little, DiscJockey

Rockwood

WYHM

05-12-1957; 580 khz AM; 1 kw-D, 49 w-N; N35 49 40 W84 39 19
319 W. Rockwood St., Rockwood, TN 37854
(865) 250-6717
License: Rockwood, Roane County, TN held by The Holler Inc.
Population Served: 607,315*Hrs. of News Programming:* news progrmg 3 hrs wkly *No. News Employees:* 3 *Target Audience:* 35 plus; adults *Adv. Rates:* 24; 18; 24; 12
Nick Barrett, General Manager

WIHG

07-09-1991; 105.7 mhz FM; 2.4 kw; 1014 ft.; N35 53 27 W84 52 1
P.O. Box 387, Rockwood, TN 37854 US
(931) 484-1057, *Fax:* (931) 707-0580
License: Rockwood, Roane County, TN held by Southern Media Group Inc.
Nat'l Network: CNN Radio *Regional Reps:* Rgnl Reps *Wire Services:* AP
Arbitron Metro Market: Knoxville, TN *TV Affiliate:* classic hits
Special Programming: News progmg 4 hrs wkly *No. News Employees:* 25-54. *Adv. Rates:* 42; 36; 42; 24

WIHG(FM)

105.7 mhz FM; 1.1 kw; Ant 760 ft; N36 29 26 W85 01 47
224 Charleston Ln., Unit 102, Crossville, TN 38555
(931) 248-4360
License: Rockwood, Pickett County, TN held by Crossville Radio LLC
Population Served: 65,187 *Arbitron Metro Market:* Jackson TN
Brandon Tollett, General Manager

Rogersville

WJDT

12-01-1990; 106.5 mhz FM *Hrs Open:* 24; 0.3 kw; 1378 ft.; N36 22 51 W83 10 47
Mailing Address: 2387 Warren Drive, Morristown, TN 37814 US
Second Address: N. Davy Crockett Pkwy., Morristown, TN 37814
(423) 235-4640
www.wjdtfm.com
wjdtfm@planetc.com
License: Rogersville, Hawkins County, TN held by C & S Broadcasting.
Nat'l Network: CNN Radio
Arbitron Metro Market: Johnson City-Kingsport-Bristol, TN-VA
Format: Country *Hrs. of News Programming:* News progmg 6 hrs wkly *Target Audience:* 18-59; female 65%, male 35%
Clark Quillen, President
David Quillen, Operations Dir

WRGS

08-20-1954; 1370 khz AM *Hrs Open:* 24; 1 kw-D, 40 w-N; N36 24 58 W82 59 04
211 Burem Rd., Rogersville, TN 37857
(423) 272-3900, *Fax:* (423) 272-0328
www.wrgsradio.com
stationmanager@wrgsradio.com
License: Rogersville, Hawkins County, TN held by WRGS Inc.
Nat'l Network: USA *Nat'l Reps:* Rgnl Reps
Population Served: 50,000 *Arbitron Metro Market:* Johnson City-Kingsport-Bristol, TN-VA *Target Audience:* General.
Debbie Beal, General Manager
Bill Durham, General Sales Mgr
Jay Phillips, Programming Director
Mike Reeves, News Director
Chuck Windham, Chief Engineer
Jeff Crigger, Gospel Manager

Savannah

*WAZD

01-01-2001; 88.1 mhz FM; 0.38 kw; 128 ft.; N35 12 58 W88 14 30
P O Drawer 2440, Tupelo, MS 38803 US
(601) 684-4116, *Fax:* (601) 684-4654
License: Savannah, Hardin County, TN held by American Family Association.
Group Owner: American Family Radio
Arbitron Metro Market: Centreville MS *Format:* Country
Charles Dowdy, General Manager

WKWX

93.5 mhz FM; 25 kw; 299 ft.; N35 17 8 W88 10 3
Mailing Address: P. O. Box 40, 1714 Wayne Road, Savannah, TN 38372 US
Second Address: 695 Wayne Rd., Savannah, TN 38372
(731) 925-9600, *Fax:* (731) 925-8828
www.wkwxfm.com
wkwx@bellsouth.net
License: Savannah, Hardin County, TN held by Melco Inc.
Nat'l Network: AP Radio *Regional Network:* Tenn. Radio Net.
Format: Country
Steve Carnal, President
Jane Haggard, General Manager
Jim Jerrolds, General Sales Mgr
Dennis Brown, Programming Director
Tom Treadway, Chief Engineer

WORM

06-29-1956; 1010 khz AM; 0.25 kw-D, ND1; 0.027 kw-N, ND1; N35 14 24 W88 14 29
P.O. Box 550, Savannah, TN 38372 US
(731) 925-4981, *Fax:* (731) 925-4981
thewormq105@yahoo.com
License: Savannah, TN held by Gerald W. Hunt.
Regional Network: Tenn. Radio Net.
TV Affiliate: Pure Gold
Music Director

WORM-FM

08-25-1966; 101.7 mhz FM; 3 kw horiz; 174 ft.; N35 14 24 W88 14 29
P. O. Box 550, Savannah, TN 38372 US
(731) 925-4981, *Fax:* (731) 925-4981
thewormq105@yahoo.com
License: Savannah, Hardin County, TN held by Gerald W. Hunt
TV Affiliate: Country

Selmer

WDTM

10-31-1967; 1150 khz AM; 1 kw-D, NDD; N35 11 27 W88 35 21
P.O. Box 388, Selmer, TN 38375 US
(731) 663-3931, *Fax:* (731) 663-9804
www.gracebroadcasting.com
License: Selmer, TN held by Grace Broadcasting Services Inc.
Group Owner: Grace Broadcasting Services Inc.; (acq 7-25-2005; $200,000 with co-located FM)
Arbitron Metro Market: Selmer, TN *Format:* Christian
Lacy Ennis, President

WSIB

01-01-1990; 93.9 mhz FM *Hrs Open:* 24; 6 kw; 328 ft.; N35 11 27 W88 35 21
P.O. Box 388, Selmer, TN 38375 US
(731) 663-2327, *Fax:* (731) 663-2427
www.gracebroadcasting.com
License: Selmer, McNairy County, TN
Group Owner: Grace Broadcasting Services Inc.
Format: Religious *Target Audience:* 20-45.
Lacy Ennis, President
John Blankenship, Operations Dir
Rodney Minyard Sr, General Manager
Geraldine Minyard, Programming Director
John Ladley, Chief Engineer

WXOQ

06-15-1986; 105.5 mhz FM *Hrs Open:* 24; 6 kw; 299 ft.; N35 13 11 W88 40 23
302 E. Poplar, Selmer, TN 38375 US
(731) 645-9880, *Fax:* (731) 925-4981
thewormQ105@yahoo.com
License: Selmer, McNairy County, TN held by Gerald W. Hunt.
Nat'l Network: Westwood One
Arbitron Metro Market: Selmer, TN *Format:* Country *No. News Employees:* 2 *Target Audience:* General.
Gerald Hunt, President
Dave Morgan, Programming Director
Randy Tucker, Music Director

*WXKV

01-01-2008; 90.5 mhz FM; 20 kw; 413 ft.; N35 10 44 W88 33 45
Rebroadcasts: Rebroadcasts KLVR(FM) Middletown, CA 100%
188 S. Bellevue, Suite 222, Memphis, TN 38104 US
(800) 877-5600, *Fax:* (916) 251-1650
www.klove.com
License: Selmer, McNairy County, TN held by Educational Media Foundation.
Group Owner: EMF Broadcasting; (acq 11-1-2006; grpsl)
Nat'l Network: K-Love
Arbitron Metro Market: Selmer, TN *Format:* Christian
Darrell Chambliss, Chairman
Mike Novak, President
Crystal Wojteczko, Operations Dir

Sevierville

WWST

02-03-1961; 102.1 mhz FM *Hrs Open:* 24; 15 kw; 1978 ft.; N35 48 41 W83 40 8
P.O. Box 693, Milwaukee, WI 53201 US
(865) 693-1020, *Fax:* (865) 656-8329
www.star1021fm.com
dmckee@journalbroadcastgroup.com
License: Sevierville, Sevier County, TN held by Journal Broadcast Corp.
Group Owner: Journal Communications Inc.; (acq 5-19-97)

Nat'l Network: ABC
Arbitron Metro Market: Knoxville, TN *Format:* Contemporary Hits/Top 40 *Hrs. of News Programming:* News progmg 4 hrs wkly *Target Audience:* 25-54. *Adv. Rates:* 115; 105; 95; 25
Rich Bailey, Operations Dir
Chris Protzman, General Manager
Dan McKee, General Sales Mgr
Rich Bailey, Programming Director
Rich Bailey, Promotions Manager
Brad Allen, Disc Jockey
Randy Chambers, Disc Jockey
Jerry Agar, DiscJockey
Scott Bohannon, Music Director
Dan McKee, Regional Sales Manager

WSEV
04-23-1955; 930 khz AM *Hrs Open:* 24; 5 kw-D, ND1; 0.148 kw-N, ND1; N35 52 42 W83 33 18
415 Middle Creek Rd, Sevierville, TN 37862 US
(865) 932-6002, *Fax:* (865) 429-2601
www.easttennesseeradio.com
studio@easttennesseeradio.com
License: Sevierville, TN held by Grand Crowne Resorts of Pigeon Forge LLC
Nat'l Network: CBS *Regional Network:* Tenn. Radio Net. *Nat'l Reps:* Rgnl Reps
Arbitron Metro Market: Knoxville, TN *Format:* Adult Contemp *Hrs. of News Programming:* news progmg 6 hrs wkly *No. News Employees:* 1 *Target Audience:* 25 plus.
Bill Burkett, Operations Dir

Sewanee

***WUTS**
05-01-1972; 91.3 mhz FM; 0.014 kw horiz; 656 ft.; N35 12 23 W85 55 4
735 University Ave, Sewanee, TN 37383 US
(931) 598-1206, *Fax:* (931) 598-1145
wutsfm.org
wuts@sewanee.edu
License: Sewanee, Franklin County, TN held by University of the South.
Arbitron Metro Market: Sewanee, TN *Format:* Variety/Diverse *Special Programming:* Black 2 hrs, class 4 hrs, country 2 hrs, jazz 4 hr *Target Audience:* General; college students
John Lee, General Manager
Austin Lacy, Programming Director
Greg Banworth, Chief Engineer

Seymour

WJBZ-FM
03-31-1991; 96.3 mhz FM *Hrs Open:* 24; 2.9 kw; 479 ft.; N35 56 17 W83 42 11
Box 2526, Knoxville, TN 37901 US
(865) 577-4885, *Fax:* (865) 579-4667
www.praise963.com
info@praise963.com
License: Seymour, Sevier County, TN held by Seymour Communications.
Arbitron Metro Market: Knoxville, TN *Format:* Gospel
Charlotte Mull, CEO
Doug Hutchison, President
Mike Clark, Operations Dir
Jamie Lewis, General Sales Mgr
Tim Guinn, Programming Director
Staci Beal, News Director
Tim Berry, Chief Engineer

Shelbyville

***WBIA**
01-01-1999; 88.3 mhz FM; 0.25 kw; 46 ft.; N35 28 54 W86 27 28
P O Drawer 2440, Tupelo, MS 38803 US
(662) 844-8888, *Fax:* (662) 842-6791
www.afa.net
License: Shelbyville, Bedford County, TN held by American Family Association.
Group Owner: American Family Radio
Arbitron Metro Market: Shelbyville, TN *Format:* Christian
Marvin Sanders, General Manager
John Riley, Programming Director
Joey Moody, Chief Engineer

WLIJ
12-02-1959; 1580 khz AM *Hrs Open:* 24; 5 kw-D, ND1; 0.012 kw-N, ND1; N35 27 19 W86 27 7
236 Woodland Drive, Shelbyville, TN 37160 US
(931) 684-1514, *Fax:* (931) 684-3956
License: Shelbyville, TN held by Jax Broadcasting, LLC
Format: Country, Gospel *Special Programming:* Black one hr, farm 3 hrs, relg 11 hrs wkly *Hrs. of News Programming:* news progmg 14 hrs wkly *No. News Employees:* 1 *Target Audience:* General.
Rusty Reed, President
Keith Cook, General Sales Mgr
Paul Hopkins, Chief Engineer
Wayne Hitchcock, Disc Jockey

WZNG
12-01-1946; 1400 khz AM *Hrs Open:* 24; 1 kw-U, ND1; N35 28 26 W86 26 45
Mailing Address: 3563 Highway 231 North, Shelbyville, TN 37160 US
Second Address: 236 Woodland Dr., Shelbyville, TN 37160
(931) 680-1214, *Fax:* (931) 684-3956
www.cflradio.net/1360_WZNG_AM.htm
License: Shelbyville, TN held by Jax Broadcasting, LLC
Arbitron Metro Market: Shelbyville, TN *Format:* Talk *Special Programming:* Relg 5 hrs wkly *Target Audience:* General; residents of the loc area
Rusty Reed, President

Signal Mountain

WLND
08-29-1994; 98.1 mhz FM *Hrs Open:* 24; 1 kw; 794 ft.; N35 5 16 W85 21 47
330 East Kilbourn Avenue, Suite 250, Milwaukee, WI 53202 US
(423) 892-3333, *Fax:* (423) 642-0097
www.thelegendonline.com
miller@981thelegend.com
License: Signal Mountain, Hamilton County, TN held by Capstar TX L.P.
Group Owner: Clear Channel Communications Inc.; (acq 8-15-2000; grpsl)
Arbitron Metro Market: Chattanooga, TN *Format:* Country *Hrs. of News Programming:* news progmg 4 hrs wkly *No. News Employees:* 1 *Target Audience:* 35-54.
Jay Cruze, Operations Dir
Sammy George, General Manager
Rhonda Rollins, General Sales Mgr

Smithville

WJLE
04-11-1964; 1480 khz AM *Hrs Open:* 16; 1 kw-D, ND1; 0.034 kw-N, ND1; N35 55 31 W85 49 14
2606 McMinnville Highway, Smithville, TN 37166 US
(615) 597-4265, *Fax:* (615) 597-6025
www.wjle.com
wjle@dtccom.net
License: Smithville, TN held by Center Hill Broadcasting Corp.
Format: Country *Special Programming:* Gospel 15 hrs wkly *Hrs. of News Programming:* news progmg 14 hrs wkly *No. News Employees:* 1 *Target Audience:* General.
W.E. Vanatta, President
Dwayne Page, General Sales Mgr
Homer Wilson Jr., Chief Engineer

WJLE-FM
01-01-1970; 101.7 mhz FM *Hrs Open:* 16; 4.4 kw; 194 ft.; N35 55 31 W85 49 14
2606 McMinnville Hwy, Smithville, TN 37166 US
(615) 597-4265, *Fax:* (615) 597-6025
www.wjle.com
wjle@dtccom.net
License: Smithville, De Kalb County, TN held by Center Hill Broadcasting Corp.
Format: Country
Til Levesque, General Manager
David Crumb, General Sales Mgr
K. J. Holiday, Programming Director
Charles Pugh, News Director
Thomas Christie, Chief Engineer
Brian Boettcher, General Sales Manager
Cheron Mans, Music Director

Smyrna

***WFCM**
01-01-1993; 710 khz AM *Hrs Open:* Sunrise-sunset; 0.25 kw-D, NDD; N35 58 31 W86 33 16
Mailing Address: 820 North Lasalle Blvd, Chicago, IL 60610 US
Second Address: 615 Potomac Pl., Smyrna, TN 37167
(423) 629-8900, *Fax:* (423) 629-0021
www.wfcm.org
wfcm@moody.edu
License: Smyrna, TN held by The Moody Bible Institute of Chicago.
Group Owner: The Moody Bible Institute of Chicago; acq 5-16-97; $162,500)
Nat'l Network: Moody
Arbitron Metro Market: Smyrna, TN *Format:* News, News/Talk, 86, Religious
Dr. Paul Nyquist, President
Leighton LeBoeuf, General Manager
Andy Napier, Programming Director
David Morais, Chief Engineer
Paul Martin, Music Director, Webmaster
Juanell Rice, Office Administrator

WFFH
10-07-1993; 94.1 mhz FM *Hrs Open:* 24; 3.2 kw; 453 ft.; N36 1 14 W86 38 18 *Rebroadcasts:* Simulcasts with WFFI(FM) Kingston Springs
401 Church Street, 30th Floor, Nashville, TN 37219 US
(615) 367-2210, *Fax:* (615) 367-0758
www.94fmthefish.net
License: Smyrna, Rutherford County, TN held by Caron Broadcasting Inc.
Group Owner: Salem Communications Corp.; (acq 12-18-02; $5.6 million with WFFI(FM) Kingston Springs).
Nat'l Network: Salem Radio Network *Nat'l Reps:* Salem
Arbitron Metro Market: Nashville, TN *Format:* Christian *Target Audience:* 25-54; adults
Michael Miller, General Manager
Kevin Anderson, General Sales Mgr
Vance Dillard, Programming Director
Dick Marsh, Promotions Manager
Kim Bindel, News Director
Carl Campbell, Chief Engineer
Ed Evenson, Traffic Manager
CarolynFelco, Traffic/Billing Manager

Soddy-Daisy

WGOW-FM
07-14-1977; 102.3 mhz FM; 6 kw; 285 ft.; N35 11 45 W85 13 45
Mailing Address: P.O. Box 8, Bloomington, IL 61702 US
Second Address: 821 Pineville Rd., Chattanooga, TN 37405
(423) 756-6141, *Fax:* (423) 266-3629
www.wgow.com
info@wgow.com
License: Soddy-Daisy, Hamilton County, TN
Group Owner: Cumulus Media Inc.; (acq 5-30-00; grpsl).
Arbitron Metro Market: Chattanooga, TN *Format:* News, News/Talk, 86 *Target Audience:* 18-54; baby boomers
Dan Brown, General Manager
Kennard Yamada, General Sales Mgr
Bill Lockhart, Programming Director
Kevin West, News Director
Dave Fisher, Chief Engineer

WSDT
02-27-1970; 1240 khz AM *Hrs Open:* 24; 1 kw-U, ND1; N35 16 16 W85 10 28
Mailing Address: 645 Church Street, Suite 400, Norfolk, VA 23510 US
Second Address: 4513 Hixson Pike, Suite 105, Hixson, TN 35373
(636) 586-8697, *Fax:* (636) 586-8697
www.svicommunications.com
svicomm@hughes.net
License: Soddy-Daisy, TN held by Serendipity Ventures II LLC
Nat'l Network: USA
Arbitron Metro Market: Chattanooga, TN *Format:* Oldies *Hrs. of News Programming:* TOH-Daytime
Steve Vogt, General Manager

South Pittsburg

WEPG
07-09-1954; 910 khz AM; 5 kw-D, 95 w-N; N35 00 57 W85 42 00
Mailing Address: Box 8, South Pittsburg, TN 37347
Second Address: 105 N. Ash Ave., South Pittsburg, TN 37380
(423) 837-8001, *Fax:* (423) 837-8002
wepg@att.net
License: South Pittsburg, Marion County, TN held by Stone/Collins Communications Inc.
Population Served: 80,000 *Arbitron Metro Market:* Chattanooga, TN *Special Programming:* Gospel 10 hrs wkly *Target Audience:* 18-50; females *Adv. Rates:* 7.25; 5.37; 6.25; 4.20
Charles Rodgers, Owner/Manager

WUUQ
11-05-1990; 97.3 mhz FM *Hrs Open:* 24; 16 kw; 856 ft.; N34 58 21 W85 37 58
Mailing Address: 111 East Kilbourn Avenue, Suite 2700, Milwaukee, WI 53202 US
Second Address: 307 N Market St, Chattanooga, TN 37414
(423) 643-2212, *Fax:* (423) 642-0096
www.wuuqradio.com
License: South Pittsburg, Marion County, TN held by 3 Daughters Media Inc.

Group Owner: 3 Daughters Media Inc.; (acq 6-22-2007; grpsl)
Arbitron Metro Market: Chattanooga, TN *Format:* Contemporary Hits/Top 40, Adult Contemp *Hrs. of News Programming:* news progmg 20 hrs wkly *No. News Employees:* 2 *Target Audience:* 18-54.
Joe Mule, General Manager
Dale Mitchell, Programming Director

Sparta

WSMT
04-26-1953; 1050 khz AM *Hrs Open:* 24
P.O. Box 1505, Glasgow, KY 42142 US
(931) 836-1055,(931) 836-2824, *Fax:* (931) 836-2320
License: Sparta, TN held by Peg Broadcasting Crossville LLC.
Group Owner: Peg Broadcasting Crossville LLC; (acq 7-1-2008; grpsl)
Format: Gospel *Special Programming:* Relg 10 hrs wkly *Hrs. of News Programming:* news progmg 10 hrs wkly *No. News Employees:* 1 *Target Audience:* General.
Duke Rice, Operations Dir
Bryan Kell, General Manager
Anthony Griffen, Engineering Dir

WTZX
11-26-1971; 860 khz AM *Hrs Open:* 24; 1 kw-D, ND1; 0.01 kw-N, ND1; N35 55 20 W85 26 50
P.O. Box 1505, Glasgow, KY 42142 US
(931) 836-1055, *Fax:* (931) 836-2320
License: Sparta, TN held by Peg Broadcasting Crossville LLC.
Group Owner: Peg Broadcasting Crossville LLC; (acq 7-1-2008)
Arbitron Metro Market: Cookeville, TN *Format:* Country *No. News Employees:* 1 *Target Audience:* General.
Duke Rice, Operations Dir
Bryan Kell, General Manager
Anthony Griffen, Engineering Dir

Spencer

WTRZ
08-01-1993; 107.3 mhz FM; 2 kw; 509 ft.; N35 39 55 W85 31 19
P.O. Box 31, McMinnville, TN 37110 US
(931) 473-9253, *Fax:* (931) 473-4149
www.kiss107radio.com
bryankell@clearchannel.com
License: Spencer, Van Buren County, TN held by Peg Broadcasting Crossville LLC.
Group Owner: Peg Broadcasting Crossville LLC; (acq 6-30-2008; grpsl)
Arbitron Metro Market: Spencer, TN *Format:* Contemporary Hits/Top 40
Bryan Kell, General Manager
Jeff Edwards, Programming Director
Homer Wilson, Chief Engineer

*WZYZ
01-01-2003; 90.1 mhz FM *Hrs Open:* 24; 0.03 kw; 591 ft.; N35 44 3 W85 27 33
P.O. Box 1452, Washington, DC 20013 US
(931) 946-7777
questions@wzyz.org,prayer@wzyz.org
License: Spencer, Van Buren County, TN held by Church Faith Trinity Assemblies
Format: Religious
Daniel Lawson, General Manager

Spring City

WRHA(AM)
07-12-1979; 970 khz AM *Hrs Open:* 6 AM-6 PM; 500 w-D; N35 39 59 W84 52 44 *Rebroadcasts:* Rebroadcasts WBAC(AM) Cleveland 100%
2640 Commerce Dr. N.E., Cleveland, TN 37311
(423) 242-7656, *Fax:* (423) 472-5290
www.wbacradio.com
License: Spring City, Rhea County, TN held by East Tennessee Radio Group III L.P.
Group Owner: East Tennessee Radio Group III L.P.; (acq 5-30-2008; grpsl)
Nat'l Network: ABC *Regional Network:* Tenn. Radio Net. *Nat'l Reps:* D & R Radio
Population Served: 41,723 *Arbitron Metro Market:* Cleveland, TN *Format:* News, News/Talk, 86 *Hrs. of News Programming:* news progmg 16 hrs wkly *No. News Employees:* 1 *Target Audience:* 35-64. *Adv. Rates:* 16; 14; 14; 7
Mike Powers, Operations Dir
Charles Sells, General Manager
John Holland, General Sales Mgr
Corky Whitlock, Programming Director

Spring Hill

*WAYM
01-01-1992; 88.7 mhz FM *Hrs Open:* 24; 5 kw; 1083 ft.; N36 2 49.7 W86 49 48.9
P.O. Box 887, Brentwood, TN 37024 US
(406) 721-6800, *Fax:* (406) 329-1850
www.u1045.com
tanthony@simmonsmedia.com
License: Spring Hill, Maury County, TN held by WAY-FM Media Group Inc.
Group Owner: WAY-FM Media Group Inc.; acq 3-13-91;
Arbitron Metro Market: Stevensville MT *Format:* Adult Contemp *No. News Employees:* 1 *Target Audience:* Adults 18-49.
Rod Harsell, General Manager

Springfield

WDBL
07-24-1950; 1590 khz AM *Hrs Open:* 19; 0.71 kw-D, ND1; 0.03 kw-N, ND1; N36 29 42 W86 54 22
101 Broadway, Nashville, TN 37201 US
(615) 384-5541, *Fax:* (615) 384-9325
www.wsgi1100.com
License: Springfield, TN held by Lightning Broadcasting LLC
Regional Network: Tenn. Radio Net.
Arbitron Metro Market: Springfield, TN *Format:* Christian *Special Programming:* Farm 10 hrs, gospel 10 hrs wkly *Hrs. of News Programming:* news progmg 16 hrs wkly *No. News Employees:* 1 *Target Audience:* 18plus.
Lee Logan, Operations Dir
Susan Quesenberry, General Manager
J.C. Morrow, Chief Engineer

WSGI
12-15-1982; 1100 khz AM *Hrs Open:* 6 AM-sunset; 1 kw-D, NDD; N36 31 0 W86 53 30
5628 S. Hillview Dr., Brentwood, TN 37027 US
(615) 384-9744, *Fax:* (615) 384-9746
wsgi1100@yahoo.com
License: Springfield, TN held by Lightning Broadcasting LLC
Regional Network: Tenn. Radio Net.
Arbitron Metro Market: Nashville, TN *Format:* Variety/Diverse *Special Programming:* Relg, farm 5 hrs, gospel 16 hrs wkly *Target Audience:* General. *Adv. Rates:* 7; 5.50; 4; na
Neil Petersen, President
Jo Petersen, Operations Dir
Billy Gray, General Sales Mgr

St. Joseph

WMXV
01-01-1991; 101.5 mhz FM; 2.85 kw; 484 ft.; N34 55 47 W87 31 44
PO Box 187, St. Joseph, TN 38481 US
(931) 845-4172, *Fax:* (931) 845-4172
www.wmxv1015.com
License: St. Joseph, Lawrence County, TN held by Urban Radio Licenses LLC.
Group Owner: Urban Radio Licenses LLC; (acq 5-13-2005; grpsl).
Arbitron Metro Market: Florence-Muscle Shoals, AL *Format:* Country, Gospel
Randy Paul, Operations Dir
Rick Brown, General Manager
Lance Knoll, General Sales Mgr
Lonnie Box, Programming Director
Tony Fowler, Promotions Manager
Sandi Summers, News Director
Craig Westbrook, Chief Engineer
Jane Hoslan,Advertising Manager

Static

WSBI
04-07-1986; 1210 khz AM *Hrs Open:* Sunrise-sunset
Route 4, Box 893, Albany, KY 42602 US
(606) 387-6625, *Fax:* (606) 387-8126
www.wsbiam.com
info@wsbiam.com
License: Static, TN held by Donnie S. Cox.
Nat'l Network: USA
Format: Country *Special Programming:* Gospel 10 hrs, bluegrass one hr wkly *Hrs. of News Programming:* news progmg 15 hrs wkly *No. News Employees:* 1 *Target Audience:* 25 plus.
Donnie Cox, General Manager
Robert Huddleston, Chief Engineer

Surgoinsville

WEYE
11-01-1990; 104.3 mhz FM *Hrs Open:* 24; 4.1 kw; 397 ft.; N36 32 5 W82 47 52
Mailing Address: Route 6, Box 1, Rogersville, TN 37857 US
Second Address: 439 Richmond St.., Church Hill, TN 37642
(800) 450-1043, *Fax:* (423) 357-3635
www.eagle1043fm.com
dsandz@yahoo.com
License: Surgoinsville, Hawkins County, TN held by ASRadio LLC
Nat'l Network: USA *Nat'l Reps:* Rgnl Reps
Arbitron Metro Market: Surgoinsville, TN *Format:* Country
David DeFranzo, Station Manager
Daryl Smith, Chief Engineer

Sweetwater

WDEH
01-01-1955; 800 khz AM *Hrs Open:* 24; 1 kw-D, ND1; 0.379 kw-N, ND1; N35 36 49 W84 27 33
Box 2526, Knoxville, TN 37901 US
(423) 337-5025, *Fax:* (423) 337-5026
wlodwdeh@yahoo.com
License: Sweetwater, TN held by Horne Radio L.L.C.
Group Owner: Horne Radio Group; (acq 1999; $425,000 with co-located FM).
Arbitron Metro Market: Sweetwater, TN *Format:* Gospel *Adv. Rates:* 12; 12; 12; 8
N.A. Baz, President
Jean Baz, Operations Dir
Gary Crocket, Programming Director
Gunther Muhsemann, Chief Engineer
Turk Baz, Local News Editor
Kevin Baz, Music Director

WMTY-FM
09-01-1967; 98.3 mhz FM *Hrs Open:* 24; 6 kw; Ant 135 ft; N35 36 49 W84 27 33
Box 330, Sweetwater, TN 37874
(423) 337-5025, *Fax:* (423) 337-5026
License: Sweetwater, Monroe County, TN
Population Served: 250,000
Tony Cox, President
Tony Cox, General Manager
Bob Wallace, Chief Engineer

Tazewell

WNTT
07-01-1960; 1250 khz AM *Hrs Open:* 6AM-sunset
Mailing Address: 115 Airport Rd, PO Box 95, Tazewell, TN 37879 US
Second Address: TN
(423) 626-4203, *Fax:* (423) 626-3040
www.wntt1250am.com
aileen@wntt1250am.com
License: Tazewell, TN held by WNTT Inc.
Group Owner: ABC Inc.; (acq 9-1-94; $90,000)
Nat'l Network: ABC
Arbitron Metro Market: Tazewell, TN *Format:* Country, News, 64 *Special Programming:* gospel,bluegrass *Hrs. of News Programming:* 12 hrs wkly *Target Audience:* 18-65; general.
Aileen Craft, CEO
Jennifer Duff, Operations Dir
Aileen Standifer-Craft, General Manager
Frank Folsom, Chief Engineer

Tiptonville

WTNV
07-01-2007; 97.3 mhz FM; 1.9 kw; 591 ft.; N36 16 11 W89 19 25 US
(731) 285-1339, *Fax:* (731) 287-0100
eagle973.net
roger@burksb.com
License: Tiptonville, Lake County, TN held by Dr. Pepper Pepsi-Cola Bottling Co. of Dyersburg.
Group Owner: Dr. Pepper Pepsi-Cola Bottling Co. of Dyersburg
Nat'l Network: Fox News Radio *Regional Network:* Tenn. Agri-Net; Tenn. Radio Net. *Nat'l Reps:* Rgnl Reps
Arbitron Metro Market: Tiptonville, TN *Format:* Country *Target Audience:* 18-54.
W.E. Burks, President
Brian Thomas, Operations Dir
Roger Vestal, General Manager
Natalie Burks, General Sales Mgr
Dan Defilippo, Programming Director
Tom Hunt, News Director
Dave Hacker, Engineering Dir

Trenton

WTNE
12-09-1966; 1500 khz AM *Hrs Open:* 24
P.O. Box 198, 42 S. Washington Avenue, Brownsville, TN 38012 US
(731) 663-2327, *Fax:* (731) 663-2427
www.gracebroadcasting.com
License: Trenton, TN held by Grace Broadcasting Services Inc.
Group Owner: Grace Broadcasting Services Inc.
Regional Reps: Midsouth.
Arbitron Metro Market: Jackson, TN *Format:* Adult Contemp
Special Programming: Sports *Target Audience:* General; Gibson county, news oriented people
Lacy Ennis, CEO/President
John Blankenship, Operations Dir
Rodney minyard Sr., General Manager
Geraldine Minyard, Programming Director
Phillip Chambers, Sales Rep
Glendell Fullerton, Sales Rep

Tullahoma

*WYLJ(FM)
01-01-1998; 88.5 mhz FM; 1.9 kw; 177 ft; N35 20 30 W86 11 05
Box 3206, American Family Radio, Tupelo, MS 38803
(662) 844-8888(662) 844-8893, *Fax:* (662) 842-6791
www.afr.net
comments@afr.net
License: Tullahoma, Coffee County, TN held by American Family Association.
Group Owner: American Family Radio
Population Served: 90,000 *Arbitron Metro Market:* Devil's Lake, ND *Format:* Religious
Marvin Sanders, General Manager

WHMT(AM)
08-01-1947; 740 khz AM *Hrs Open:* 24; 250 w-D, 67 w-N; N35 20 36 W86 12 00
WJIG AM 740, 2214 N. Jackson St., Tullahoma, TN 37388
(931) 455-7426, *Fax:* (931) 455-7438
wjig@charterinternet.com
License: Tullahoma, Coffee County, TN held by NRS Enterprises Inc.
Nat'l Network: Salem Radio Network *Regional Network:* Tenn. Radio Net.
Population Served: 18,000*Format:* Christian *Target Audience:* 35 plus. *Adv. Rates:* 12; 12; 12; 12
Roy Woods, President
Joyce Woods, General Manager
Heath Laws, Programming Director
Mark Tavernier, Disc Jockey

*WTML
01-01-2001; 91.5 mhz FM; 1.55 kw; 269 ft.; N35 23 53 W86 8 40
Rebroadcasts: Rebroadcasts WPLN-FM Nashville 100%
630 Mainstream Drive, Nashville, TN 37228 US
(615) 760-2903, *Fax:* (615) 760-2904
www.wpln.org
rgordon@wpln.org?subject=message%20from%20WPLN%20website
License: Tullahoma, Coffee County, TN held by Nashville Public Radio.
Arbitron Metro Market: Nashville, TN *Format:* Classical, News
Rob Gordon, President and General Manager
Scott Smith, Operations Dir
Laura Landress, General Sales Mgr
Henry Fennell, Programming Director
Anita Bugg, News Director
Tom Knox, Chief Engineer
Will Griffin, Music Director
WendyPoston, Traffic Manager
Donna Robinson, Director of Philanthropy
Molly Nicholas, Membership Director
Hilary Barnett, Development Coordinator
Laura Landress, Manager of Corporate Support

Tusculum

WIKQ
02-01-1996; 103.1 mhz FM *Hrs Open:* 24; 6 kw; -223 ft.; N36 7 40 W82 37 57
Mailing Address: 1204 Christie Court, Greeneville, TN 37743 US
Second Address: 1004 Arnold Rd., Greeneville, TN 37743
(423) 639-1831, *Fax:* (423) 638-1979
wsmg@greeneville.com
License: Tusculum, Greene County, TN held by Radio Greeneville Inc.
Group Owner: Radio Greeneville Inc.; (acq 6-22-2000; $1.8 million with WSMG(AM) Greeneville)
Format: Country *No. News Employees:* 1 *Target Audience:* 25-55; middle to upper middle income *Adv. Rates:* 14; 12; 12; 12
Ronnnie Metcalfe, President
Ron Metcalfe, Operations Dir
Ronnie Metcalfe, General Manager
Brian Stayton, Programming Director
Marty Ricker, News Director
Ray Elliott, Chief Engineer
Nathan Humbard, Music Director

*WZTH
91.1 mhz FM; 0 kw horiz, 17 kw vert; 285 ft.; N36 5 53 W82 56 37
US
(877) 746-7913
www.truthfm.net
info@truthfm.net
License: Tusculum, Greene County, TN held by Solid Foundation Broadcasting Corp.
Arbitron Metro Market: Greeneville, TN *Format:* Religious
James Smith, President

Union City

WENK
10-26-1946; 1240 khz AM *Hrs Open:* 24; 1 kw-U, ND1; N36 25 28 W89 2 17 *Rebroadcasts:* Rebroadcasts WTPR-FM McKinnon 100%
1729 Nailling Dr Pob 669, Union City, TN 38261 US
(731) 885-1240, *Fax:* (731) 885-3405
www.wenkwtpr.com/
thailey@wenkwtpr.com
License: Union City, TN held by WENK of Union City Inc.
Group Owner: WENK of Union City Inc.; (acq 1-74)
Nat'l Reps: Rgnl Reps
Arbitron Metro Market: Union City, TN *Format:* Oldies *Hrs. of News Programming:* news progmg 15 hrs wkly *No. News Employees:* 1 *Target Audience:* 35-54.
Terry Hailey, President
Richard Hall, General Sales Mgr
Brad Hosford, Chief Engineer

WQAK
03-01-1994; 105.7 mhz FM; 6 kw; 308 ft.; N36 31 7 W89 5 41
Mailing Address: P.O. Box 100, Union City, TN 38281 US
Second Address: 233 Westgate, Union City, TN 38281
(731) 885-0051, *Fax:* (731) 885-0250
www.wqakradio.com
ptinkle@crunet.com
License: Union City, Obion County, TN held by Thunderbolt Broadcasting Co.
Group Owner: Thunderbolt Broadcasting Co.; (acq 12-29-2005; $900,000 with WYVY(FM) Union City).
Format: Contemporary Hits/Top 40, Adult Contemp *No. News Employees:* 1 *Adv. Rates:* 40; 35; 40; 30.
Paul Tinkle, President

KYTN(FM)
09-20-1974; 104.9 mhz FM *Hrs Open:* 24; 6 kw; Ant 328 ft; N36 28 25 W88 56 41
Mailing Address: Box 5000, Union City, TN 38281
Second Address: 223 Westgate Dr., Union City, TN 38261
(731) 885-0051, *Fax:* (731) 885-0250
www.kytnradio.com
ptinkle@crunet.com
License: Union City, Obion County, TN held by Thunderbolt Broadcasting Co.
Group Owner: Thunderbolt Broadcasting Co.; (acq 12-29-2005; $900,000 with WQAK(FM) Union City)
Population Served: 301,843*Format:* Country *Hrs. of News Programming:* news progmg 25 hrs wkly *No. News Employees:* 1 *Target Audience:* 18 plus. *Adv. Rates:* 40; 35; 40; 30.
Paul Tinkle, President

*WTAI
01-01-2005; 88.9 mhz FM; 0.86 kw vert; 623 ft.; N36 24 48 W89 8 59
188 South Bellevue, Suite 222, Memphis, TN 38104 US
(888) 937-2471, *Fax:* (916) 251-1650
www.air1.com
info@air1.com
License: Union City, Obion County, TN held by Educational Media Foundation.
Group Owner: EMF Broadcasting; (acq 6-21-2005; $25,000 for CP)
Nat'l Network: Air 1
Arbitron Metro Market: Union City, TN *Format:* Alternative, Christian
Darrell Chambliss, Chairman
Alan Mason, COO
Mike Novak, President and CEO
Ed Lenane, News Director
Sam Wallington, Engineering Dir
Dan Antonelli, Chief Business Development Officer
Eric Moser, Chief Financial Officer
BrianBurger, Vice President of Human Resources
D. Kevin Blair, Secretary and General Counsel
Larry Moody, Director
Mitch Barnhart, Director

Wartburg

WECO
08-31-1970; 940 khz AM; 5 kw-D, ND2; 0.016 kw-N, ND2; N36 5 48 W84 35 31
Mailing Address: Box 100, Wartburg, TN 37887 US
Second Address: 305 N. Church St., Wartburg, TN 37887
(423) 346-3900, *Fax:* (423) 346-7686
www.wecoradio.com/
wecoradio@highland.net
License: Wartburg, TN held by Morgan County Broadcasting Co. Inc.
Regional Network: Tenn. Radio Net.
Arbitron Metro Market: Wartburg, TN *Format:* Gospel
Gary Stone, Operations Dir
Ed Knight, General Manager
Gary Stone, Programming Director
Aaron Harvey, News Director
Carl Stump, Chief Engineer

WECO-FM
08-01-1988; 101.3 mhz FM; 3.5 kw; 771 ft.; N36 11 25 W84 37 24
Mailing Address: P.O. Box 100, Wartburg, TN 37887 US
Second Address: 305 N. Church St., Wartburg, TN 37887
(423) 346-3900, *Fax:* (423) 346-7686
www.wecoradio.com/
wecoradio@highland.net
License: Wartburg, Morgan County, TN
Arbitron Metro Market: Wartburg, TN *Format:* Country *Target Audience:* 25-49.
Gary Rozynek, President
Gary Stone, Operations Dir
Ed Knight, General Manager
Rick Roberts, Station Manager
Lynn Bieritz, General Sales Mgr
Aaron Harvey, News Director
Bill Holden, Chief Engineer
Dan Gainey, Regional SalesManager

*WWQW(FM)
90.3 mhz FM; 550 w vert; Ant -47 ft; N36 05 48 W84 35 31
Box 604, Loudon, TN 37774
(865) 458-9563
www.wlntfm.com
License: Wartburg, Morgan County, TN held by Corporation for Radio Education Inc.
Population Served: 13,557 *Arbitron Metro Market:* Warsaw, IN
Richard Lynn, President

Waverly

WQMV
09-25-1963; 1060 khz AM *Hrs Open:* 24
201 Hall Lane, White Bluff, TN 37187 US
(931) 296-9768, *Fax:* (931) 296-9892
www.wqmv1060.com
wqmv@comcast.net
License: Waverly, TN held by C & L Broadcasting Corp.
Nat'l Network: ABC *Regional Network:* Tenn. Radio Net.
Format: Oldies *Target Audience:* Adults 35-65. *Adv. Rates:* 10.35; 10.35; 10.35; 10.35
Richard Albright, President

WVRY
09-26-1972; 105.1 mhz FM *Hrs Open:* 24; 50 kw; Ant 492 ft; N36 05 16 W87 51 19
2263 N. Highland Ave., 25 Stonebrook Pl., Suite #322, Jackson, TN 37228
(731) 855-9394, *Fax:* (731) 855-1600
www.gracebroadcasting.com
info@salemmusicnetwork.com
License: Waverly, Humphreys County, TN held by Reach Satellite Network Inc.
Group Owner: Salem Communications Corp.; (acq 3-31-2000; $3.1 million for stock with WBOZ(FM) Woodbury)
Nat'l Network: Salem Radio Network *Regional Network:* Tenn. Radio Net. *Nat'l Reps:* Salem
Population Served: 1,500,000 *Arbitron Metro Market:* Nashville, TN *Target Audience:* 25-54.
Jim Cumbee, CEO
Rodney Minyard, General Manager

Waynesboro

WWON
01-31-1970; 930 khz AM *Hrs Open:* 24; 0.47 kw-D, ND2; 0.091 kw-N, ND2; N35 18 30 W87 44 42
Mailing Address: P O Box 999, Waynesboro, Tn 38485, Ft. Worht, TX 76107 US
Second Address: 100 Public Sq. S., Waynesboro, TN 38485
(931) 722-3631, *Fax:* (931) 722-3632
www.bigoldies930.com
BIGOldies930@yahoo.com
License: Waynesboro, TN held by Small Potatoes Broadcasting Co. LLC
Arbitron Metro Market: Waynesboro, TN *Format:* Oldies *Hrs. of News Programming:* News progmg 13 hrs wkly *Target Audience:* 18-54; listeners interested in rgnl & natl issues
Chris Lash, General Manager

White Bluff

WQSE
07-18-1982; 1030 khz AM; 1 kw-D, DAN; 0.25 kw-N, DAN; N36 8 3 W87 12 58
201 Hall Place, White Bluff, TN 37187 US
(615) 797-9785, *Fax:* (615) 797-9788
dvanedjwqse@aol.com
License: White Bluff, TN held by Canaan Communications Inc.
Arbitron Metro Market: Nashville, TN *Format:* Gospel
Duane Jeffrey, President
Kerry Lampley, General Sales Mgr
Mary Jeffrey, Programming Director
Shery Swaw, News Director

White Pine

WLNQ
104.7 mhz FM; 2.8 kw; 492 ft.; N36 13 0 W83 11 38
377 Graham St., Newport, TN 37821 US
(423) 623-8743, *Fax:* (865) 458-0959
www.thundercountry1047.com
License: White Pine, Rhea County, TN held by Corporation for Radio Education Inc.
Arbitron Metro Market: White Pine, TN *Format:* Country
Richard Lynn, President

Winchester

WCDT
03-08-1948; 1340 khz AM *Hrs Open:* 24; 1 kw-U; N35 10 51 W86 05 34
1201 S. College St., Winchester, TN 37398
(931) 967-2201,(931) 967-2202, *Fax:* (931) 967-2201
www.wcdt1340.com
wcdt@bellsouth.net
License: Winchester, Franklin County, TN held by Franklin County Radio & Broadcasting Co. Inc.
Nat'l Network: ABC *Regional Network:* Tenn. Radio Net.
Population Served: 65,000*Special Programming:* Farm 15 hrs, Relg 6 hrs wkly *Hrs. of News Programming:* news progmg 15 hrs wkly *No. News Employees:* 1 *Target Audience:* General.
John Yarbrough, President
Jeanetta Shields, Operations Dir
Darryl Basham, General Manager
Karen Shetters, General Sales Mgr
Al Tipps, Programming Director
Jan Tavalin, News Director
Sharon Price, Sales

Woodbury

WBOZ
10-05-1994; 104.9 mhz FM *Hrs Open:* 24; 6 kw; 328 ft.; N35 49 33 W86 9 28
Mailing Address: 312 South Church St, Murfreesboro, TN 37130 US
Second Address: 402 BNA Dr., Suite 400, Nashville, TN 37217
(615) 890-3233, *Fax:* (615) 890-2990
www.solidgospel105.com
info@salemmusicnetwork.com
License: Woodbury, Cannon County, TN held by Reach Satellite Network Inc.
Group Owner: Salem Communications Corp.; (acq 4-1-00; $3.1 million for stock with WVRY(FM) Waverly).
Nat'l Network: Salem Radio Network *Nat'l Reps:* Salem
Arbitron Metro Market: Woodbury, TN *Format:* Christian, Country, 44 *Special Programming:* Sports 5 hrs wkly *Hrs. of News Programming:* News progmg 14 hrs wkly *Target Audience:* 35+; adults
Greg Anderson, President
Michael Miller, General Manager
Kevin Anderson, Station Manager
Vance Dillard, Programming Director
Dick Marsh, Promotions Manager
Carl Campbell, Chief Engineer

Texas

Abilene

*KACU
06-02-1986; 89.7 mhz FM *Hrs Open:* 24; 33 kw; 217 ft.; N32 28 34 W99 42 22
100 Don H, Morris Center, Abileen, TX 79699 US
(325) 674-2441, *Fax:* (325) 674-2417
www.kacu.org
bestj@acu.edu
License: Abilene, Taylor County, TX held by Abilene Christian University.
Nat'l Network: NPR
Arbitron Metro Market: Abilene, TX *Format:* Adult Contemp, News *Special Programming:* Jazz 3 hrs wkly *Hrs. of News Programming:* News progmg 42 hrs wkly *Target Audience:* 35 plus; middle-to-upper incomeprofessionals
Dave Smith, Operations Dir
John Best, General Manager
Kim Seidman, General Sales Mgr

*KAQD
01-01-1998; 91.3 mhz FM; 325 ft.; N32 29 58 W99 58 19
P.O. Drawer 2440, Tupelo, MS 38803 US
(662) 844-8888, *Fax:* (662) 842-6791
www.afr.net
comments@afr.net
License: Abilene, Taylor County, TX held by American Family Association.
Group Owner: American Family Radio
Arbitron Metro Market: Tupelo, MO *Format:* Christian, Religious
Marvin Sanders, General Manager

KYYW
10-01-1936; 1470 khz AM
3911 South First Street, Abilene, TX 79605 US
(325) 676-7711, *Fax:* (325) 676-3851
www.1470kyyw.com
karenhines@townsquaremedia.com
License: Abilene, TX held by GAP Broadcasting Abilene License LLC.
Group Owner: GAP Broadcasting LLC; (acq 8-3-2007; grpsl)
Nat'l Network: CBS
Arbitron Metro Market: Abilene, TX *Format:* Country
Karen Hines, General Manager
Robert Snyder, Programming Director
Gary Smith, Chief Engineer

KEAN-FM
07-01-1969; 105.1 mhz FM *Hrs Open:* 24; 100 kw; 886 ft.; N32 16 35 W99 35 38
1350 One Galleria Tower, Dallas, TX 75240 US
(325) 676-5326, *Fax:* (325) 676-3851
www.keanradio.com
kean@keanradio.com
License: Abilene, Taylor County, TX
Group Owner: GAP Broadcasting LLC
Nat'l Network: ABC
Arbitron Metro Market: Abilene, TX *Format:* Country
Karen Hines, General Manager
Karen Hines, General Sales Mgr
Rudy Fernandez, Programming Director

KEYJ-FM
04-30-1961; 107.9 mhz FM; 100 kw; 886 ft.; N32 16 35 W99 35 38
3911 South First St, Abilene, TX 79605 US
(325) 677-7225(325) 676-7711, *Fax:* (325) 676-3851
www.keyj.com
info@keyj.com
License: Abilene, Taylor County, TX held by GAP Broadcasting Abilene License LLC.
Group Owner: GAP Broadcasting LLC; (acq 8-3-2007; grpsl)
Arbitron Metro Market: Abilene, TX *Format:* Alternative *Target Audience:* 18-49; men
James Cameron, Operations Dir
Karen Hines, General Manager
Renee Gonzalez, General Sales Mgr
Frank Pain, Programming Director

KSLI
06-15-1957; 1280 khz AM *Hrs Open:* 24; 0.5 kw-D, ND1; 0.226 kw-N, ND1; N32 26 30 W99 43 8
Mailing Address: 1350 One Galleria Tower, Dallas, TX 75240 US
Second Address: 3911 S. First St., Abilene, TX 79605
(325) 676-7711, *Fax:* (325) 676-3851
www.1280ksli.com
rudyfernandez@townsquaremedia.com;
karenhines@townsquaremedia.com;
reneegonzalez@townsquaremedia.com
License: Abilene, TX held by GAP Broadcasting Abilene License LLC.
Group Owner: GAP Broadcasting LLC; (acq 8-3-2007; grpsl)
Nat'l Network: Jones Radio Networks
Arbitron Metro Market: Abilene, TX *Format:* Country *Hrs. of News Programming:* News progmg 4 hrs wkly *Target Audience:* 18-49; Hispanic *Adv. Rates:* 20; 20; 20; 20
Rudy Fernandez, Operations Dir
Karen Hines, General Manager
Renee Gonzalez, Station Manager

*KGNZ
03-07-1981; 88.1 mhz FM *Hrs Open:* 24; 91 kw; 827 ft.; N32 13 47 W99 37 42
Mailing Address: 1001 Cedar Crest, Abilene, TX 79601 US
Second Address: 1001 Cedar Crest St., Abilene, TX 79601
(325) 673-8801, *Fax:* (325) 672-7938
www.kgnz.com
gary@kgnz.com
License: Abilene, Taylor County, TX held by Christian Broadcasting Co.
Nat'l Network: USA
Arbitron Metro Market: Abilene, TX *Format:* Adult Contemp, Christian *Special Programming:* Black 2 hrs, gospel 2 hrs wkly
Larry Jack Hill, President
Doug Harris, Operations Dir
Gary Hill, General Manager
Randy Martinez, General Sales Mgr
Glenn Arnold, Engineering Dir
Holley Hill, Office Administrator
Crystal Rae, Special Events

KKHR
06-01-1988; 106.3 mhz FM *Hrs Open:* 24; 50 kw; Ant 184 ft; N32 28 34 W99 42 22
402 Cypress St., Suite 510, Abilene, TX 53202
(325) 672-5442, *Fax:* (325) 672-6128
radioabilene.com
License: Abilene, Taylor County, TX held by Canfin Enterprises Inc.
Group Owner: Canfin Enterprises Inc.; (acq 3-25-2005; $684,000).
Nat'l Reps: Lotus Entravision Reps LLC
Arbitron Metro Market: Abilene, TX *Hrs. of News Programming:* News progmg 3 hrs wkly *Target Audience:* 18-49.
Parker Cannon, General Manager
Ben Gonzalez, Programming Director
James Thompson, Chief Engineer

KZQQ
08-29-1962; 1560 khz AM *Hrs Open:* 24
3444 North First St., Suite 405, Abilene, TX 49603 US
(325) 672-5442, *Fax:* (325) 672-6128
www.radioabilene.com
License: Abilene, TX held by Canfin Enterprises Inc.
Group Owner: Canfin Enterprises Inc.
Nat'l Network: ESPN Radio *Regional Network:* Texas State Networks
Arbitron Metro Market: Abilene, TX *Format:* Sports, Talk *No. News Employees:* 1 *Target Audience:* 18 plus.
Parker Cannan, General Manager

KULL
09-01-1974; 100.7 mhz FM; 100 kw; 1,260 ft; N32 24 48 W100 06 25
3911 S. First St., Abilene, TX 79603
(325) 676-7111, *Fax:* (325) 676-3851
www.keyj.com
License: Abilene, Taylor County, TX held by GAP Broadcasting Abilene License LLC.
Group Owner: GAP Broadcasting LLC; (acq 8-3-2007; grpsl)
Population Served: 200,000 *Arbitron Metro Market:* Abilene, TX *Special Programming:* Oldies 2 hrs wkly *Target Audience:* 18-34; women
James Cameron, Operations Dir
Ted Warren, General Manager
Renee Gonzalez, General Sales Mgr

KMWX
04-01-1998; 92.5 mhz FM; 27.5 kw; Ant 663 ft; N32 16 35 W99 35 38
3911 S. 1st St., Abilene, TX 75240
(325) 677-7225, *Fax:* (325) 677-3851
info@kull.com
License: Abilene, Taylor County, TX held by GAP Broadcasting Abilene License LLC.
Group Owner: GAP Broadcasting LLC; (acq 8-3-2007; grpsl)

Nat'l Network: ABC
Population Served: 250,000 *Arbitron Metro Market:* Abilene, TX
Ted Wrenn, Operations Dir
James Cameron, Operations Manager

KWKC
06-19-1948; 1340 khz AM *Hrs Open:* 24; 1 kw-U, ND1; N32 25 14 W99 43 54
1740 North First Street, Abilene, TX 79603 US
(915) 673-1455, *Fax:* (915) 673-3485
www.radioabilene.com
parker@radioabilene.com
License: Abilene, TX held by Canfin Enterprises Inc.
Group Owner: Canfin Enterprises Inc.
Nat'l Network: CBS Radio *Regional Network:* Texas State Networks
Arbitron Metro Market: Abilene, TX *Format:* News, News/Talk, 86 *No. News Employees:* 2 *Target Audience:* 25 plus.
Parker Cannan, President

*KAGT
11-05-2002; 90.5 mhz FM *Hrs Open:* 24; 100 kw; 315 ft.; N32 30 37 W99 44 28
P.O. Box 16145, Abilene, TX 79698 US
(888) 937-2471, *Fax:* (916) 251-1650
www.air1.com
info@air1.com
License: Abilene, Taylor County, TX held by Educational Media Foundation.
Group Owner: EMF Broadcasting; (acq 12-31-2006; $450,000)
Nat'l Network: Air 1
Arbitron Metro Market: Abilene, TX *Format:* Alternative, Christian
Darrell Chambliss, Chairman
Alan Mason, COO
Mike Novak, President and CEO
Amy Yost, Operations Dir
Ed Lenane, News Director
Sam Wallington, Engineering Dir
Dan Antonelli, Chief Business Development Officer
Eric Moser, ChiefFinancial Officer
Brian Burger, Vice President of Human Resources
D. Kevin Blair, Secretary and General Counsel
Larry Moody, Director
Mitch Barnhart, Director

Alamo

KJAV
08-17-1980; 104.9 mhz FM; 6 kw; 324 ft.; N26 13 0 W98 5 23
PO Box 252, McAllen, TX 78502 US
(956) 992-8895, *Fax:* (956) 992-8897
www.bmpradio.com
info@bmpradio.com
License: Alamo, Hidalgo County, TX held by BMP RGV License Company L.P.
Group Owner: Border Media Partners LLC; (acq 1-26-2005; $7 million)
Arbitron Metro Market: McAllen-Brownsville-Harlingen, TX
Format: Adult Contemp
Thomas Castro, President
Jeff Koch, Operations Dir
Jose Munoz, General Manager

Alamo Heights

KDRY
11-08-1963; 1100 khz AM *Hrs Open:* 24
16414 San Pedro Avenue, Suite 460, San Antonio, TX 78232 US
(210) 545-1100, *Fax:* (210) 545-1139
www.kdry.com
License: Alamo Heights, TX held by KDRY Radio Inc.
Arbitron Metro Market: San Antonio, TX *Format:* Religious *Target Audience:* General.
Diane Rainey, General Manager

Alice

KNDA
01-01-1974; 102.9 mhz FM; 50 kw; 492 ft.; N27 42 26 W97 46 54
400 Spid, Suite 100, Corpus Christi, TX 78405 US
(361) 814-1030, *Fax:* (361) 814-1036
lilrichardbomb@aol.com
License: Alice, Jim Wells County, TX held by Encarnacion A. Guerra
Arbitron Metro Market: Corpus Christi, TX *Format:* Urban Contemporary, Blues
Jesse Rodriguez, General Manager

KOPY
01-01-1947; 1070 khz AM *Hrs Open:* 24; 1 kw-D, DAN; 1 kw-N, DAN; N27 46 39 W98 4 53
Mailing Address: 1501 N. Main Street, Cleburne, TX 76031 US
Second Address: 2722 N. Business Hwy. 281, Alice, TX 78332
(361) 664-1884, *Fax:* (361) 664-1886
License: Alice, TX held by Claro Communications Ltd.
Group Owner: Claro Communications Ltd.; (acq 8-31-2007; $300,000 with KOPY-FM Alice)
Format: Country *Hrs. of News Programming:* news progmg 2 hrs wkly *No. News Employees:* 12 *Target Audience:* 18-59. *Adv. Rates:* 13; 10; 13; 7
Bobby Pena, Station Manager
Jackie Hinojosa, General Sales Mgr

KOPY-FM
01-20-1976; 92.1 mhz FM *Hrs Open:* 24; 6 kw; 308 ft.; N27 46 39 W98 4 52
Mailing Address: Highway 281 North, P O Box 731, Alice, TX 78332 US
Second Address: 2722 N. Business Hwy. 281, Alice, TX 78332
(361) 664-1884, *Fax:* (361) 664-1886
License: Alice, Jim Wells County, TX held by Claro Communications Ltd.
Group Owner: Claro Communications Ltd.; (acq 8-31-2007; $300,000 with KOPY(AM) Alice)
Format: Tejano *Hrs. of News Programming:* News progmg 8 hrs wkly *Target Audience:* General. *Adv. Rates:* 13; 10; 13; 6
Bobby Pena, Programming Director

*KIFR
88.3 mhz FM; 23 kw vert; 292 ft.; N27 45 8 W98 7 55
Mailing Address: 4135 Northgate Blvd, Suite 1, Sacramento, CA 95834 US
Second Address: 290 Hegenberger Rd., Oakland, CA 94621
(800) 543-1495, *Fax:* (916) 641-8238
familyradio@familyradio.org
License: Alice, Jim Wells County, TX held by Family Stations Inc.
Group Owner: Family Stations Inc.
Arbitron Metro Market: Alice, TX
Harold Camping, President

Allen

KESN
12-01-1981; 103.3 mhz FM; 98 kw; 1988 ft.; N33 32 8 W96 49 54
P.O. Box 1292, Greenville, TX 75403 US
(817) 640-3778, *Fax:* (817) 695-3505
www.espn1033.com
License: Allen, Collin County, TX held by WBAP-KSCS Operating Ltd.
Group Owner: ABC Inc.; (acq 8-9-00; $18 million).
Arbitron Metro Market: Allen, TX *Format:* Sports *Target Audience:* 25-54; males and females
Peter Dits, General Manager
Tom Lee, Programming Director

Alpine

KALP
09-01-1986; 92.7 mhz FM *Hrs Open:* 6 AM-10 PM; 2.35 kw; 328 ft.; N30 19 9 W103 37 4
Mailing Address: P. O. Box 9650, Alpine, TX 79831 US
Second Address: 500 Hendryx Ave., Alpine, TX 79830
(432) 837-2144, *Fax:* (915) 837-3984
www.bigbenradio.com
ray@bigbenradio.com
License: Alpine, Brewster County, TX held by Rio Grande Broadcasting Co.
Arbitron Metro Market: Alpine, TX *Format:* Country
Gene Ray Hendryx, President
Gene Hendryx, General Manager

KVLF
02-27-1947; 1240 khz AM *Hrs Open:* 6 AM-10 PM; 1 kw-U, ND1; N30 22 25 W103 39 44
Mailing Address: 500 Hendryx Avenue, Alpine, TX 79830 US
Second Address: 500 Hendryx Ave., Alpine, TX 79831
(432) 837-2144, *Fax:* (432) 837-3984
www.bigbendradio.com
ray@bigbendradio.com
License: Alpine, TX held by Big Bend Broadcasters.
Nat'l Network: ABC
Arbitron Metro Market: Alpine, TX *Format:* Variety/Diverse
Special Programming: Sp 10 hrs wkly *Hrs. of News Programming:* News progmg 21 hrs wkly
Gene Ray Hendryx Jr., President
Ray Hendryx, General Manager
Jerry Sotello, General Sales Mgr

Alvin

*KACC
11-01-1993; 89.7 mhz FM *Hrs Open:* 24; 5.6 kw; 331 ft.; N29 24 1 W95 12 13
3110 Mustang Road, Alvin, TX 77511 US
(281) 756-3766, *Fax:* (281) 756-3885
www.kaccradio.com
License: Alvin, Brazoria County, TX held by Alvin Community College.
Wire Services: AP
Arbitron Metro Market: Alvin, TX *Format:* Rock/AOR *Hrs. of News Programming:* news progmg 3 hrs wkly *No. News Employees:* 1 *Target Audience:* General.
A. Rodney Allbright, President
Mark Moss, Operations Dir

KTEK
11-01-1981; 1110 khz AM *Hrs Open:* Sunrise-sunset; 2.5 kw-C, DAD; 2.5 kw-D, DAD; N29 22 51 W95 14 15
4880 Santa Rosa Road, Suite 300, Camarillo, CA 93012 US
(713) 979-2700
www.bizradio.com
License: Alvin, TX held by BusinessRadio Houston Licensee LLC
Nat'l Network: USA
Arbitron Metro Market: Houston, TX *Format:* Talk *Target Audience:* 25-54; upscale families, 60% women, 40% male
Daniel Frishberg, President

Amarillo

*KACV-FM
03-15-1976; 89.9 mhz FM *Hrs Open:* 6 AM-midnight; 100 kw; 1155 ft.; N35 20 33 W101 49 21
Mailing Address: P. O. Box 447, Amarillo, TX 79178 US
Second Address: 2408 S. Jackson, Amarillo, TX 79109
(806) 371-5000, *Fax:* (806) 345-5576
www.kacvfm.org
kacvfm90@actx.edu
License: Amarillo, Potter County, TX held by Amarillo Junior College District.
Nat'l Network: ABC
Arbitron Metro Market: Amarillo, TX *TV Affiliate:* *KACV-TV affil.
Format: Alternative *Special Programming:* Jazz 12 hrs, Texas 6 hrs wkly
Linda Pitner, General Manager
Brian Frank, Programming Director

*KJJP
12-06-1991; 105.7 mhz FM *Hrs Open:* 24; 43 kw; 525 ft.; N35 17 33 W101 50 48
1603 West 8th Avenue, Amarillo, TX 79101 US
(620) 275-7444, *Fax:* (620) 275-7496
www.hppr.org
License: Amarillo, Potter County, TX held by Kanza Society Inc.
Arbitron Metro Market: Garden City, KS *Format:* Christian *Target Audience:* General.
Richard Hicks, General Manager

KATP
03-11-1976; 101.9 mhz FM *Hrs Open:* 24; 100 kw; 935 ft.; N35 20 33 W101 49 21
5406 Winners Circle, Amarillo, TX 79110 US
(806) 355-9777, *Fax:* (806) 359-0136
www.blakefm.com
skipstow@townsquaremedia.com
License: Amarillo, Potter County, TX held by GAP Broadcasting Amarillo License LLC.
Group Owner: GAP Broadcasting LLC; (acq 10-1-2007; grpsl)
Arbitron Metro Market: Amarillo, TX *Format:* Country *Hrs. of News Programming:* News progmg 2 hrs wkly *Target Audience:* 18-49. *Adv. Rates:* 14; 12; 12; 10
Kevin Meyer, General Manager
Les Montgomery, General Sales Mgr
Debbie Davis, General Sales Manager

*KAVW
07-01-1998; 90.7 mhz FM; 1 kw; 213 ft.; N35 11 57 W101 48 43
P. O. Drawer 2440, Tupelo, MS 38803 US
(662) 844-8888, *Fax:* (662) 842-6791
www.afr.net
comments@afr.net
License: Amarillo, Potter County, TX held by American Family Association.
Group Owner: American Family Radio
Arbitron Metro Market: Tupelo, MS *Format:* Christian, Religious
Marvin Sanders, General Manager

KMXJ-FM
03-01-1946; 94.1 mhz FM *Hrs Open:* 24; 100 kw; 1083 ft.; N35 20 33 W101 49 21
600 Congress Avenue, Suite 1400, Austin, TX 78701 US

(806) 355-9777, *Fax:* (806) 355-5832
www.mix941kmxj.com
rickandrews@townsquaremedia.com
License: Amarillo, Potter County, TX held by GAP Broadcasting Amarillo License LLC.
Group Owner: GAP Broadcasting LLC; (acq 10-1-2007; grpsl)
Nat'l Network: ABC
Arbitron Metro Market: Amarillo, TX *Format:* Adult Contemp *Hrs. of News Programming:* news progmg 2 hrs wkly *No. News Employees:* 1 *Target Audience:* General.
Skip Stow, General Manager
Les Montgomery, General Sales Mgr
Rick Andrews, Programming Director
Lori Crofford, Promotions Manager
Jennifer Stephenson, News Director
Charlie Fuller, Chief Engineer
Debbie Davies, General SalesManager

KBZD
03-01-1994; 99.7 mhz FM; 21.5 kw; 351 ft.; N35 6 50 W101 49 16
3801 Skillern Blvd., Flower Mound, TX 75028 US
(806) 355-1044, *Fax:* (806) 457-0642
License: Amarillo, Potter County, TX held by Tejas Broadcasting Ltd. LLP
Group Owner: Tejas Broadcasting Ltd. LLP; (acq 11-15-2004; grpsl)
Arbitron Metro Market: Amarillo, TX *Format:* Tejano
Mac Douglas, General Manager
Brad Gonzalez, General Sales Mgr
Israel Salazar, Programming Director
Emelia Chacon, News Director
Charlie Singleton, Chief Engineer

KDJW
09-15-1955; 1360 khz AM
1759 Avondale, Amarillo, TX 79106 US
(806) 350-1360, *Fax:* (806) 350-1360
www.kdjw.com
stval@kdjw.org
License: Amarillo, TX held by Avondale Operating Inc.
Arbitron Metro Market: Amarillo, TX *Format:* Country *Target Audience:* 45 plus; adults with money
Ron Slover, President

KGNC
05-19-1922; 710 khz AM *Hrs Open:* 24; 10 kw-U, DA-2; N35 25 12 W101 33 20
Mailing Address: Box 710, Amarillo, TX 30903
Second Address: 3505 Olsen Blvd., Suite 117, Amarillo, TX 79109
(806) 355-9801, *Fax:* (806) 354-8779
www.kgncam.com
License: Amarillo, Potter County, TX held by Morris Communications Corp.
Group Owner: Morris Radio LLC; (acq 12-22-97; grpsl)
Nat'l Network: ABC *Regional Network:* Texas State Networks
Nat'l Reps: Katz Radio *Wire Services:* Reuters
Population Served: 400,000 *Arbitron Metro Market:* Amarillo, TX *Target Audience:* General; upscale adults & agricultural business listeners
Tim Butler, Operations Dir
Brice Edwards, General Manager
Brice Edwards, Station Manager
Brice Edwards, General Sales Mgr
Tim Butler, Programming Director
Russel Johnson, Promotions Manager
Mike Hill, News Director
CharlieFuller, Chief Engineer
Mike Roden, Sports Director
James Hunt, Director

KGNC-FM
12-24-1958; 97.9 mhz FM *Hrs Open:* 24; 100 kw; 1306 ft.; N35 18 53 W101 50 47
725 Broad Street, P.O. Box 936, Augusta, GA 30903 US
(806) 355-9801, *Fax:* (806) 354-8779
www.kgncfm.com
tim.butler@kgnc.com
License: Amarillo, Potter County, TX held by Morris Communications Corp.
Group Owner: Morris Radio LLC
Wire Services: Reuters
Arbitron Metro Market: Amarillo, TX *Format:* Country *Target Audience:* General; upscale adults & agricultural business listeners
Dan Gorman, Station Manager
Patrick Clark, Program Director

KIXZ
06-01-1947; 940 khz AM *Hrs Open:* 24
600 Congress Avenue, Suite 1400, Austin, TX 78701 US
(806) 355-9777, *Fax:* (806) 355-5832
www.newsradio940.com
kixz@clearchannel.com
License: Amarillo, TX held by GAP Broadcasting Amarillo License LLC.
Group Owner: GAP Broadcasting LLC; (acq 10-1-2007; grpsl)
Arbitron Metro Market: Amarillo, TX *Format:* News, News/Talk, 86 *Special Programming:* Talk 2 hrs, gospel 6 hrs wkly *Hrs. of News Programming:* news progmg 8 hrs wkly *No. News Employees:* 1 *Target Audience:* General.
Kevin Meyer, General Manager
Dusty Cagle, General Sales Mgr
David Emmons, Programming Director
Lori Crofford, Promotions Manager
Jennifer Stephenson, News Director
Charles Fuller, Chief Engineer

*KJRT
04-01-1994; 88.3 mhz FM; 20 kw horiz, 6 kw vert; 289 ft.; N35 11 57 W101 48 43 *Rebroadcasts:* Rebroadcasts KPDR(FM) Wheeler 100%
5754 Canyon Drive, Amarillo, TX 79114 US
(806) 359-8855, *Fax:* (806) 354-2039
www.kingdomkeys.org
kjrt@kingdomkeys.org
License: Amarillo, Potter County, TX held by Top o'Texas Educational Broadcasting Foundation.
Arbitron Metro Market: Amarillo, TX *Format:* Religious
Jeremy Pfeil, Operations Dir
Ricky Pfeil, General Manager
Ricky Pfeil, Station Manager
Diana Pfeil, General Sales Mgr

*KXLV
08-01-1989; 89.1 mhz FM *Hrs Open:* 24; 27.5 kw; 401 ft.; N35 15 41 W101 52 52
7355 North Oracle Rd., Tucson, AZ 85704 US
(916) 251-1600, *Fax:* (916) 251-1650
www.klove.com
klove@klove.com
License: Amarillo, Potter County, TX held by Educational Media Foundation.
Group Owner: EMF Broadcasting; (acq 11-4-99; $450,000).
Nat'l Network: K-Love
Arbitron Metro Market: Amarillo, TX *Format:* Christian *No. News Employees:* 3 *Target Audience:* 25-44; Judeo Christian, female
Mike Novak, President
Eric Allen, General Sales Mgr
David Pierce, Programming Director
Ed Lenane, News Director
Sam Wallington, Engineering Dir
Scott Smith, Music Director
Marya Morgan, Richard Hunt
News Reporter

KXSS-FM
03-01-1985; 96.9 mhz FM *Hrs Open:* 24; 100 kw; 614 ft.; N35 17 33 W101 50 48
600 Congress Avenue, Suite 1400, Austin, TX 78701 US
(806) 355-9777, *Fax:* (806) 355-5832
www.969kmml.com
kmml@kmml.com
License: Amarillo, Potter County, TX held by GAP Broadcasting Amarillo License LLC.
Group Owner: GAP Broadcasting LLC; (acq 10-1-2007; grpsl)
Nat'l Network: ABC
Arbitron Metro Market: Amarillo, TX *Format:* Contemporary Hits/Top 40 *Hrs. of News Programming:* news progmg 2 hrs wkly *No. News Employees:* 1 *Target Audience:* General.
Kevin Meyer, General Manager
Les Montgomery, General Sales Mgr
Lori Crofford, Promotions Manager
Jennifer Stephenson, News Director
Charlie Fuller, Chief Engineer
Debbie Davis, General Sales Manager

KPRF
10-01-1979; 98.7 mhz FM *Hrs Open:* 24; 100 kw; 469 ft.; N35 11 2 W101 58 11
600 Congress Avenue, Suite 1400, Austin, TX 78701 US
(806) 355-9777, *Fax:* (806) 355-5832
www.987jackfm.com
info@987jackfm.com
License: Amarillo, Potter County, TX held by GAP Broadcasting Amarillo License LLC.
Group Owner: GAP Broadcasting LLC; (acq 10-1-2007; grpsl)
Nat'l Network: ABC
Arbitron Metro Market: Amarillo, TX *Format:* Adult Contemp *Hrs. of News Programming:* news progmg 2 hrs wkly *No. News Employees:* 1 *Target Audience:* General.
Kevin Meyer, General Manager
Marshal Blevins, Programming Director
Jennifer Stephenson, News Director

KXGL
11-01-1997; 100.9 mhz FM *Hrs Open:* 24; 100 kw; 1306 ft.; N35 18 53 W101 50 47
1616 S. Kentucky, Bldg. C, Suite 215, Amarillo, TX 79102 US
(806) 351-2345, *Fax:* (806) 331-3170
www.1009theeagle.com
jameykarr@1009theeagle.com
License: Amarillo, Potter County, TX held by JMJ Broadcasting Co. Inc.
Nat'l Reps: Katz Radio *Wire Services:* AP
Arbitron Metro Market: Amarillo, TX *Format:* Talk *Hrs. of News Programming:* news progmg 5 hrs wkly *No. News Employees:* 1 *Target Audience:* 25-54.
Herbert McCord, President
Jamey Karr, Operations Dir
Bob Russell, General Manager
Brice Edwards, General Sales Mgr
Kelly James, News Director
Morgan Tanner, Production Manager

KPUR
08-01-1949; 1440 khz AM *Hrs Open:* 24; 5 kw-D, DAN; 1 kw-N, DAN; N35 7 20 W101 48 9
111 East Kilbourn Ave., Suite 2700, Milwaukee, WI 53202 US
(806) 342-5200, *Fax:* (806) 342-5202
www.cumulus.com
rickmatchett@cumulus.com
License: Amarillo, TX held by Cumulus Licensing Corp.
Group Owner: Cumulus Media Inc.; (acq 3-12-98; $820,000 with KPUR-FM Canyon)
Arbitron Metro Market: Amarillo, TX *Format:* Oldies *Target Audience:* 25-54. *Adv. Rates:* 14; 14; 14; 10
Lewis W Dickey, Jr., Chairman
Lewis W Dickey, Jr., CEO/COO
Lewis W Dickey, Jr., President
Jim Worthington, General Manager
Matt Darby, Programming Director
Craig Vaughn, Promotions Manager
J.P. Wolf, Chief Engineer

KQIZ-FM
11-01-1976; 93.1 mhz FM *Hrs Open:* 24; 100 kw; 699 ft.; N35 17 33 W101 50 48
111 East Kilbourn Ave., Suite 2700, Milwaukee, WI 53202 US
(806) 342-5200, *Fax:* (806) 342-5202
www.931thebeat.com
element@cumulus.com
License: Amarillo, Potter County, TX held by Cumulus Licensing Corp.
Group Owner: Cumulus Media Inc.; (acq 3-5-98; $3.057 million)
Arbitron Metro Market: Amarillo, TX *Format:* Contemporary Hits/Top 40 *Special Programming:* Relg 2 hrs wkly *Target Audience:* 18-44; young families
Jim Worthington, General Manager
Deana McGuire, Programming Director
Shea White, Promotions Manager
J.P. Wolf, Chief Engineer

*KRGN
10-06-1986; 102.9 mhz FM *Hrs Open:* 24; 100 kw; 292 ft.; N35 15 40 W101 52 52
Mailing Address: 7355 North Oracle Rd., Tucson, AZ 85704 US
Second Address: 910 S. Lamar, Amarillo, TX 79106
(806) 376-5746, *Fax:* (806) 376-4212
www.krgn.org
krgn@flc.org
License: Amarillo, Potter County, TX held by Family Life Broadcasting Inc.
Group Owner: Family Life Communications Inc.; (acq 6-24-98; grpsl)
Nat'l Network: USA
Arbitron Metro Market: Amarillo, TX *Format:* Religious *Hrs. of News Programming:* News progmg 4 hrs wkly *Target Audience:* 28 plus; mature Christian, mainstream evangelical
Steve Wright, Station Manager
Steve Johnson, News Director

KTNZ
01-01-1946; 1010 khz AM; 5 kw-D, DA2; 0.5 kw-N, DA2; N35 11 3 W101 41 28
3801 Skillern Blvd, Flower Mound, TX 75028 US
(806) 355-1044, *Fax:* (806) 457-0642
www.justplaincreativeproductions.com/
ctonzale@tegasb.com
License: Amarillo, TX held by Tejas Broadcasting Ltd. LLP
Group Owner: Tejas Broadcasting Ltd. LLP
Arbitron Metro Market: Amarillo, TX *Format:* Christian
Israel Salazar, Programming Director

*KXRI
11-01-1993; 91.9 mhz FM *Hrs Open:* 24; 4 kw; 459 ft.; N35 14 31 W101 48 43
8030 Arrowridge Blvd., Charlotte, NC 28273 US
(916) 251-1600, *Fax:* (916) 251-1650
www.air1.com
info@air1.com
License: Amarillo, Potter County, TX held by Educational Media Foundation.
Group Owner: EMF Broadcasting; (acq 5-1-2000; $750,000 with KKLU(FM) Lubbock).
Nat'l Network: Air 1
Arbitron Metro Market: Amarillo, TX *Format:* Alternative, Christian *No. News Employees:* 3 *Target Audience:* 18-35; Judeo Christian female
Mike Novak, President
Eric Allen, General Sales Mgr
David Pierce, Programming Director
Ed Lenane, News Director
Sam Wallington, Engineering Dir

KZIP
09-15-1955; 1310 khz AM *Hrs Open:* 6 AM-10 PM; 1 kw-D, ND2; 0.088 kw-N, ND2; N35 11 2 W101 58 11
1011 S. Jackson, Amarillo, TX 79101 US
(806) 355-1044, *Fax:* (806) 352-6525
cgonzzales@tejasbroadcasting.com
License: Amarillo, TX held by Del Norte Communications Inc.
Arbitron Metro Market: Amarillo, TX *Format:* Talk *Hrs. of News Programming:* news progmg one hr wkly *No. News Employees:* 1 *Target Audience:* General. *Adv. Rates:* 12; 12; 12; 12
Mac Douglas, General Manager

Andrews

KACT
01-12-1955; 1360 khz AM; 1 kw-D, ND1; 0.24 kw-N, ND1; N32 20 50 W102 33 23
Mailing Address: P.O. Box 1907, Clovis, NM 88101 US
Second Address: Box 524, Andrews, TX
(432) 523-2845, *Fax:* (432) 523-5671
www.kactradio.com
kact1055@windstream.net
License: Andrews, TX held by Zia Broadcasting Co.
Group Owner: Zia Broadcasting Co.; (acq 5-26-76)
Nat'l Network: CBS Radio; Radio America; Talk Radio Network; Westwood One
Arbitron Metro Market: Andrews, TX *Format:* News, Sports, 86 *Hrs. of News Programming:* CBS News hourly *No. News Employees:* 1 *Adv. Rates:* 5.25, 5.25, 5.25, 5.25
Lonnie Allsup, President
Gerald Reid, General Manager
Gerald Reid, Station Manager
Rick Keefer, General Sales Mgr

KACT-FM
01-01-1980; 105.5 mhz FM; 3 kw; 210 ft.; N32 20 50 W102 33 23
Mailing Address: P.O. Box 1907, Clovis, NM 88101 US
Second Address: Box 524, Andrews, TX
(432) 523-2845, *Fax:* (432) 523-5671
www.kactradio.com
kact1055@windstream.net
License: Andrews, Andrews County, TX held by Zia Broadcasting Co.
Group Owner: Zia Broadcasting Co.
Arbitron Metro Market: Andrews, TX *Format:* Country
Gerald Reid, General Manager
Geral Reid, Station Manager

Anson

KTLT
06-01-1988; 98.1 mhz FM *Hrs Open:* 24; 50 kw; 305 ft.; N32 39 49 W99 51 18
3301 South 14th, Suite10-A, Abilene, TX 79605 US
(940)763-1111, *Fax:* (940) 322-3166
http://www.the98x.com/
jimchristoferson@cumulus.com
License: Anson, Jones County, TX held by Cumulus Licensing Corp.
Group Owner: Cumulus Media Inc.; (acq 1999)
Arbitron Metro Market: Anson, TX *Format:* Alternative
Jim Christoferson, General Manager
John Scott, Programming Director
Chris Andrews, Chief Engineer

Aransas Pass

*KKWV
01-01-2008; 88.1 mhz FM; 28 kw vert; 367 ft.; N27 52 2 W97 13 7 *Rebroadcasts:* Rebroadcasts KLRD(FM) Yucaipa, CA 100%
188 South Bellevue, Suite 222, Memphis, TN 38104 US
(800) 877-5600, *Fax:* (916) 251-1650
www.air1.com
info@air1.com
License: Aransas Pass, San Patricio County, TX held by Educational Media Foundation.
Group Owner: EMF Broadcasting; (acq 7-23-2007; grpsl)
Nat'l Network: Air 1
Arbitron Metro Market: Belcourt, ND *Format:* Alternative, Christian
Mike Novak, President

Arlington

KLTY
04-01-1949; 94.9 mhz FM *Hrs Open:* 24; 99 kw; 1667 ft.; N32 35 19 W96 58 5
4880 Santa Rosa Road, Suite 300, Camarillo, CA 93012 US
(972) 870-9949, *Fax:* (214) 561-2156
www.klty.com
info@klty.com
License: Arlington, Tarrant County, TX held by Inspiration Media of Texas LLC.
Group Owner: Salem Communications Corp.; 2000
Nat'l Reps: Katz Radio
Arbitron Metro Market: Irving, TX *Format:* Adult Contemp *Hrs. of News Programming:* News progmg 2 hrs wkly *No. News Employees:* 1 *Target Audience:* 25-54; female dominant, family oriented, upscale, conservative*Adv. Rates:* 70; 50; 70; 40
John Peroyea, General Sales Mgr
Jerreshia Manuel, Promotions Manager
Kelly Trentham, Executive Assistant to General Manager & Regional
Teresa Chandler, Traffic Manager
John Hudson, Production Director
Bonnie Curry, CreativeServices Director
Jack Peddy, Graphic Designer/ Webmaster
Kevin Mote, Video Imaging Director

Athens

KLVQ
05-17-1948; 1410 khz AM; 1 kw-D, ND1; 0.139 kw-N, ND1; N32 9 22 W95 50 31
P. O. Box 489, Malakoff, TX 75148 US
(903) 489-1238, *Fax:* (903) 489-2671
www.kcklklvq.com
lakecountry@kcklfm.com
License: Athens, TX held by Lake Country Radio L.P.
Nat'l Network: Salem Radio Network *Wire Services:* NOAA Weather; UPI
Arbitron Metro Market: Tyler, TX *Hrs. of News Programming:* Southern gospel *No. News Employees:* Black one hr, relg 8 hrs *Target Audience:* news progmg 7 hrs wkly *Adv. Rates:* 16; 14;14;12
1, 35 plus.
Pat Isaacson, General Manager
Chris Quinn, Station Manager
Nancy Morrish, General Sales Mgr
Charrie Foster, Promotions Manager
Tim Howard, News Director
Wayne Blackwelder

Atlanta

KPYN
10-18-1950; 900 khz AM *Hrs Open:* 24; 1 kw-D, ND1; 0.033 kw-N, ND1; N33 4 58 W94 10 58
Mailing Address: PO Box 1166, Atlanta, TX 75551 US
Second Address: State Hwy. 43 S., Atlanta, TX 75551
(903) 796-2817, *Fax:* (903) 769-1000
www.kpyn.net
info@kpyn.net
License: Atlanta, TX held by Freed AM Corp.
Arbitron Metro Market: Atlanta, TX *Format:* Christian *Target Audience:*
Bob DelGiorno, CEO
Robert Delgiorno Jr., President
Randy Smith, Operations Dir
Don Peace, General Sales Mgr
Jeff Akin, Programming Director

*KNRB
12-22-1978; 100.1 mhz FM *Hrs Open:* 24; 50 kw; 492 ft.; N33 15 18 W94 5 16
Mailing Address: P.O. Drawer 1166, Atlanta, TX 75551 US
Second Address: 8919 World Ministry Ave., Baton Rouge, LA 70810
(225) 768-8300, *Fax:* (225) 768-3729
www.jsm.org
kawikfish@yahoo.com
License: Atlanta, Cass County, TX held by Family Worship Center Church Inc.
Group Owner: Family Worship Center Church Inc.; (acq 3-7-2002; grpsl)
Regional Reps: Riley.
Arbitron Metro Market: Texarkana, TX-AR *Format:* Christian *Hrs. of News Programming:* News progmg 15 hrs wkly *Target Audience:* General. *Adv. Rates:* 24; 18; 18; 18
David Whitelaw, COO
Jimmy Swaggart, President
John Santiago, Programming Director

Austin

KASE-FM
03-30-1969; 100.7 mhz FM *Hrs Open:* 24; 100 kw; 1191 ft.; N30 19 10 W97 48 6
600 Congress Avenue, Suite 1400, Austin, TX 78701 US
(512) 684-7300, *Fax:* (512) 684-7441
www.kase101.com
License: Austin, Travis County, TX held by Capstar TX L.P.
Group Owner: Clear Channel Communications Inc.; (acq 8-30-00; grpsl).
Arbitron Metro Market: Austin, TX *Format:* Country *Target Audience:* 18-44.
Mac Daniels, Operations Dir
Mike McDonald, General Sales Mgr
Joel Burke, Programming Director
Whitney Bond, Promotions Manager
Suzanne Munoz, News Director
Gil Garcia, Chief Engineer
Mitch Bordeno, Business Manager

*KAZI
08-29-1982; 88.7 mhz FM *Hrs Open:* 24; 1.6 kw; 351 ft.; N30 16 37 W97 49 34
4700 Loyola Ln #104, Austin, TX 78723 US
(512) 836-9544, *Fax:* (512) 836-9563
www.kazifm.org
steve@katzfm.org
License: Austin, Travis County, TX held by Austin Community Radio.
Arbitron Metro Market: Austin, TX *Format:* Gospel *Special Programming:* Reggae 6 hrs, blues 6 hrs, gospel 18 hrs, talk 10 *Hrs. of News Programming:* news progmg 12 hrs wkly *No. News Employees:* 1 *TargetAudience:* General; all ages, all ethnic groups
David Bursell, Chairman
Steven Savage, General Manager
Steve Savage, Station Manager
Marion Nickerson, Programming Director
Sharon Jones, Promotions Manager
James Davis, Chief Engineer
Avis Thomas, Music Director
Sharon Jaye,Music Director

KLGO
01-01-1922; 1490 khz AM *Hrs Open:* 24; 1 kw-U; N30 15 13 W97 42 25
912 S. Capital of Texas Hwy., Austin, TX 78216
(512) 416-1100, *Fax:* (512) 416-8205
License: Austin, Travis County, TX held by BMP Austin License Company L.P.
Group Owner: Border Media Partners LLC; (acq 2-10-2005; grpsl).
Population Served: 500,000 *Arbitron Metro Market:* Austin, TX *Target Audience:* 18 plus; men
Pedro Gasc, General Manager

KKMJ-FM
01-05-1968; 95.5 mhz FM *Hrs Open:* 24; 49 kw; 1306 ft.; N30 19 23 W97 47 58
600 New Hampshire Ave., N.W., Suite 1200, Washington, DC 20037 US
(512) 327-9595, *Fax:* (512) 329-6255
www.majic.com
jdhiatt@cbs.com
License: Austin, Travis County, TX held by Entercom Austin License LLC
Group Owner: Entercom Communications Corp.; (acq 11-30-2007; grpsl)
Nat'l Reps: Katz Radio
Arbitron Metro Market: Austin, TX *Format:* Adult Contemp *Target Audience:* 25-54.
John Hiatt, Operations Dir
Clint Culp, Senior Vice President

KLBJ
01-01-1939; 590 khz AM *Hrs Open:* 24; 5 kw-D, DAN; 1 kw-N, DAN; N30 14 16 W97 37 47
114 West Seventh St., Suite 300, Austin, TX 78701 US
(512) 832-4000, *Fax:* (512) 832-4081
www.590klbj.com
info@590klbj.com

License: Austin, TX held by LBJS Broadcasting Co. L.P.
Group Owner: Emmis Communications Corp.; (acq 4-25-03; grpsl).
Nat'l Network: ABC; Wall Street *Nat'l Reps:* McGavren Guild
Wire Services: NWS (National Weather Service)
Arbitron Metro Market: Austin, TX *Format:* News, News/Talk, 86
Hrs. of News Programming: news progmg 14 hrs wkly *No. News Employees:* 6
Brooke Gallagher, Operations Dir
Bruce Walden, General Manager
Mark Caesar, Programming Director
Julie Springer, Promotions Manager
Hal Kemp, News Director
Jim Henkel, Engineering Dir

KLBJ-FM

01-01-1960; 93.7 mhz FM; 97 kw; 1050 ft.; N30 18 36 W97 47 33
8309 North I-35, Suite 200, Austin, TX 78761 US
(512) 832-4000, *Fax:* (512) 832-4081
www.klbjfm.com
info@590klbj.com
License: Austin, Travis County, TX
Arbitron Metro Market: Austin, TX
Bob Sinclair, President
Scott Gillmore, Operations Dir
Jeff Carrol, Programming Director
Loris Lowe, News Director

*KMFA

01-01-1967; 89.5 mhz FM *Hrs Open:* 24; 40 kw; 1306 ft.; N30 19 23 W97 47 58
3001 N Lamar Blvd,S.100, Austin, TX 78705 US
(512) 476-5632, *Fax:* (512) 474-7463
www.kmfa.org
info@kmfa.org
License: Austin, Travis County, TX held by Capitol Broadcasting Association Inc.
Arbitron Metro Market: Austin, TX *Format:* Talk *Special Programming:* Educ 2 hrs wkly *Target Audience:* General.
Frank Bash, Chairman
Rich Upton, Operations Dir
Joan Kobayashi, General Manager

KPEZ

08-13-1976; 102.3 mhz FM *Hrs Open:* 24; 26 kw; 686 ft.; N30 13 24 W97 49 39
200 Concord Plaza, Suite 600, San Antonio, TX 78216 US
(512) 684-7300, *Fax:* (512) 684-7441
www.z1023.com
info@z1023.com
License: Austin, Travis County, TX held by CCB Texas Licenses L.P.
Group Owner: Clear Channel Communications Inc.; (acq 7-24-92).
Nat'l Reps: Clear Channel
Arbitron Metro Market: Austin, TX *Format:* Christian *Hrs. of News Programming:* news progmg 3 hrs wkly *No. News Employees:* 1
Target Audience: 25-54; young adults with families, above average income, education
Mac Daniels, Operations Dir
Ginger Nelson, General Sales Mgr
Tracy Walker, Programming Director
Pam McKay, Promotions Manager
Gil Garcia, Chief Engineer
Mitch Bordeno, Business Manager
Mel Jones, Sales Director

*KUT

11-10-1958; 90.5 mhz FM; 100 kw; 679 ft.; N30 18 51 W97 51 58
Communication Bldg B, Austin, TX 78712 US
(512) 471-1631, *Fax:* (512) 471-3700
www.kut.org
kut@kut.org
License: Austin, Travis County, TX held by University of Texas at Austin.
Nat'l Network: NPR; PRI
Arbitron Metro Market: Austin, TX *Format:* News *Special Programming:* Folk 4 hrs, blues 6 hrs wkly *Hrs. of News Programming:* news progmg 25 hrs wkly *No. News Employees:* 5 *Target Audience:* 25-54;educated; influential decision makers & arts community
Stewart Vanderwilt, General Manager
Sylvia Carson, General Sales Mgr
Jody Evans, Programming Director
Emily Donahue, News Director
Chris Collins, General Sales Manager

KVET

01-01-1946; 1300 khz AM *Hrs Open:* 24
600 Congress Avenue, Suite 1400, Austin, TX 78701 US
(512) 684-7300, *Fax:* (512) 684-7441
www.kvet.com

License: Austin, TX held by Capstar TX L.P.
Group Owner: Clear Channel Communications Inc.
Arbitron Metro Market: Austin, TX *Format:* Sports, Talk *Hrs. of News Programming:* news progmg 25 hrs wkly *No. News Employees:* 6 *Target Audience:* 25-64.
Mac Daniels, Operations Dir
Joel Burke, Programming Director
Whitney Bond, Promotions Manager
Gil Garcia, Chief Engineer
Lance Aldridge, Sales Manager
Brandon Blake, Webmaster
Kendra Jackson, Human Resources

KVET-FM

01-01-1950; 98.1 mhz FM *Hrs Open:* 24; 49.8 kw; 1302 ft.; N30 19 23 W97 47 58
600 Congress Avenue, Suite 1400, Austin, TX 78701 US
(512) 684-7300, *Fax:* (512) 684-7441
www.kvet.com
License: Austin, Travis County, TX held by Capstar TX L.P.
Group Owner: Clear Channel Communications Inc.; (acq 8-30-00; grpsl).
Nat'l Network: Westwood One
Arbitron Metro Market: Austin, TX *Format:* Country *No. News Employees:* 4 *Target Audience:* 35-64.
John Hogan, President
Charlie Ranilly, Operations Dir
Joel Burke, Programming Director
Whitney Bond, Promotions Manager
Gil Garcia, Chief Engineer
Lance Aldridge, Sales Manager
Brandon Blake, Webmaster
Kendra Jackson, HumanResources

*KVRX

11-01-1994; 91.7 mhz FM; 3 kw; 85 ft.; N30 16 0 W97 40 27
2500 Whitis Avenue, Austin, TX 78705 US
(512) 232-1559, *Fax:* (512) 232-5793
www.kvrx.org
cartergoss@austin.utexas.edu
License: Austin, Travis County, TX held by University of Texas at Austin.
Arbitron Metro Market: Austin, TX *Format:* Alternative *Special Programming:* Share frequency with KOOP-FM *Target Audience:* 18-34; general *Adv. Rates:* 25; 25; 25; 25
Michael Sedillo, Operations Dir
Katy A, Station Manager
Dan Knight, General Sales Mgr
Michael McAfee, Programming Director
Chelsey Blackmon, Music Director

Azle

KTCY

06-29-1967; 101.7 mhz FM *Hrs Open:* 24; 92 kw; 2034 ft.; N33 26 13 W97 29 5
1436 Auburn Boulevard, Sacramento, CA 95815 US
(214) 887-9107, *Fax:* (214) 841-4215
www.xoradio1017.com
License: Azle, Tarrant County, TX held by Liberman Broadcasting of Dallas License LLC.
Group Owner: Liberman Broadcasting Inc.; (acq 11-2-2006; grpsl)
Nat'l Reps: Lotus Entravision Reps LLC
Arbitron Metro Market: Azle, TX *Format:* Spanish *Target Audience:* 18-34; Hispanics
Rosa Cuellar, General Manager

Baird / Abilene

KABW

09-09-1999; 95.1 mhz FM *Hrs Open:* 24; 100 kw; Ant 872 ft; N32 17 06 W99 38 39
1740 N. First, Abilene, TX 75137
(325) 437-9596, *Fax:* (325) 673-1819
www.95q.fm
doudmediagroup@aol.com
License: Baird / Abilene, Callahan County, TX held by Doud Media Group LLC
Nat'l Network: Fox News Radio *Nat'l Reps:* Rgnl Reps
Population Served: 500,000 *Arbitron Metro Market:* Abilene, TX
Hrs. of News Programming: news prgmg 10 hrs wkly *No. News Employees:* 1 *Target Audience:* 18-49; women & teens
Ryan Doud, Operations Dir
Richard Doud, General Manager
Martin Mims, General Sales Mgr
Panama, Programming Director
James Thompson, Engineering Dir

Balch Springs

KSKY

09-30-1941; 660 khz AM *Hrs Open:* 24
433 E. Las Colinas Blvd, #1130, Irving, TX 75039 US
(214) 561-9660, *Fax:* (214) 561-9662
www.ksky.com
myopinion@ksky.com
License: Balch Springs, TX held by Bison Media Inc.
Group Owner: Salem Communications Corp.; (acq 4-24-2000; $7.5 million plus seller gets KMOM(FM) Fountain, CO).
Arbitron Metro Market: Irving, TX *Format:* News, Talk *Special Programming:* High school, college sports *Target Audience:* 35-59; middle income white female
David Darling, Operations Dir
John L Peroyea, General Manager
Mike Krejci, General Sales Mgr
David Sparkman, Promotions Manager
Andy Pickard, Chief Engineer
Bob Johnson, General Sales Manager

Ballinger

KKCN

04-01-2012; 103.1 mhz FM *Hrs Open:* 24; 100 kw; Ant 456 ft; N31 39 37 W100 05 23
1301 South Abe Street, San Angelo, TX 79762
(325) 655-7161, *Fax:* (325) 658-7377
www.103kkcn.com
License: Ballinger, Runnels County, TX
Group Owner: Double O Radio L.L.C.; (acq 3-15-2006; grpsl).
Population Served: 150,000 *Arbitron Metro Market:* San Angelo, TX
John Kerr, General Manager
Randy Phair, General Sales Mgr
Boomer Kingston, Programming Director
Garry Vaughn, Engineering Dir

KRUN

08-01-1947; 1400 khz AM *Hrs Open:* 24 hrs; 1 kw-U, ND1; N31 43 31 W99 57 42
6201 Andrews Highway, Odessa, TX 79762 US
(325) 365-5500, *Fax:* (325) 365-3407
www.krunam.com
krun1400@hotmail.com
License: Ballinger, TX held by Graham Brothers Communications L.L.C.
Nat'l Network: ABC *Regional Network:* Texas State Networks; Voice of Southwest Agriculture Radio
Arbitron Metro Market: Ballinger, TX *Format:* Country, Sports
Special Programming: Christian 4 hrs wkly *Hrs. of News Programming:* news progmg 2 hrs wkly *No. News Employees:* 1
Target Audience: 25-54.*Adv. Rates:* 15; 15; 15; 12.50
Glynne Collenbark, Operations Dir
Andy Allen, General Manager
Kody Mac, Programming Director
Toby Virden, News Director

Bandera

KEEP

07-11-1981; 103.1 mhz FM *Hrs Open:* 24; 3.5 kw; 430 ft.; N29 51 21 W99 5 26 *Rebroadcasts:* Rebroadcasts KFAN-FM Johnson City 100%
P.O. Box 311, Fredericksburg, TX 78624 US
(830) 997-2197, *Fax:* (830) 997-2198
www.texasrebelradio.com
txradio@ktc.com
License: Bandera, Bandera County, TX held by J. & J. Fritz Media Ltd.
Group Owner: J. & J. Fritz Media Ltd.; acq 7-99; $108,000).
Format: Triple A *No. News Employees:* 1 *Target Audience:* 25-49. *Adv. Rates:* 28; 28; 28; 28
Jayson Fritz, President
Jan Fritz, Operations Dir
Mac McClennahan, Programming Director
Rick Star, Music Director
Gloria Ottmers, Operations Manager
Ariana Fritz, Promotions Manager

Bastrop

*KHIB

01-01-1998; 88.5 mhz FM; 4 kw vert; 308 ft.; N30 12 57 W97 8 31
Suite 3, 8103 Brodie Lane, Austin, TX 78745 US
(713) 520-5200
www.khcb.org
License: Bastrop, Bastrop County, TX held by Houston Christian Broadcasters Inc.
Group Owner: Houston Christian Broadcasters Inc.; (acq 1-19-2005; $112,000).

RADIO - U.S.

Nat'l Network: Moody
Arbitron Metro Market: Huston, TX *Format:* Christian
Bruce Munsterman, General Manager
Bonnie BeMent, Assistant General Manager

Batesville

*KRZU
90.7 mhz FM; 100 kw; 149 meters; N28 47 54 W99 35 37
5005 East Belmont Avenue, Fresno, CA
(559) 455-5777, *Fax:* (559) 455-5778
www.radiobilingue.org
epaala@radiobilingue.org
License: Batesville, TX held by Radio Bilingue Inc
Hugh Morales, Executive Director
Ethel Meyer, Operations Dir
Walter Ramirez, News Director

Bay City

KMKS
07-27-1984; 102.5 mhz FM *Hrs Open:* 24; 100 kw; 466 ft.; N28 47 49 W96 9 20
Mailing Address: P.O.Box 789, Bay City, TX 77404 US
Second Address: 2309 5th St., Bay City, TX 77414
(979) 244-4242, *Fax:* (979) 245-0107
www.kmks.com
kmks@kmks.com
License: Bay City, Matagorda County, TX held by Sandlin Broadcasting Co. Inc.
Format: Country *Target Audience:* 24-54.
Margaret Sandlin, President
C.W. Simon, Operations Dir
Larry Sandlin, General Manager
Judith Gardiner, General Sales Mgr
Kay Sandlin, News Director
Ryan Stone, Promotions Manager

KNTE
09-25-1995; 101.7 mhz FM; 100 kw; 449 ft; N28 43 53 W96 05 26 *Rebroadcasts:* Simulcast KQQK Jefferson
3000 Bering Dr., Houston, TX 77414
(713) 315-3400, *Fax:* (713) 314-3506
License: Bay City, Matagorda County, TX held by Liberman Broadcasting of Houston License LLC.
Group Owner: Liberman Broadcasting Inc.; (acq 10-11-2002; $3.15 million with KNTE-FM El Campo)
Nat'l Network: ABC
Population Served: 670,000*Adv. Rates:* 22; 22; 22; 14
Leonard Liberman, CEO
Winter Horton, Operations Dir
Ezequiel Gonzalez, Programming Director
Meliza Posada, News Director
Mike Todd, Engineering Dir

*KZBJ
01-01-2005; 89.5 mhz FM; 35 kw; Ant 479 ft; N29 08 58 W95 59 14 *Rebroadcasts:* Rebroadcasts KSBJ(FM) Humble 100%
1722 Treble Dr., Humble, TX 33487
(281) 446-5725, *Fax:* (281) 540-2198
www.ksbj.org
webmaster@ksbj.org
License: Bay City, Matagorda County, TX held by KSBJ Educational Foundation
Population Served: 17,663 *Arbitron Metro Market:* Bay City, TX
Tim McDermott, President and General Manager
Tim McDermott, General Manager
Carlos Aguiar, Programming Director
Brittany Whatley, Promotions Manager
Don Chapman, Chief Engineer
Bill Hartman, Broadcast Engineer
Tim Dimas,Facilities Supervisor
Pam Kelly, Assistant Program Director
Rhonda Hall, Community Relations Director
Richard Silva, Special Events Manager
Stephanie Meeks, Director of Donor Relations

*KEDR
01-01-2007; 88.1 mhz FM; 3.6 kw; 1434 ft.; N28 48 3 W96 7 32 *Rebroadcasts:* Rebroadcasts WBFR(FM) Birmingham, AL 100%
4135 Northgate Blvd., Suite 1, Sacramento, CA 95834 US
(205) 942-3530, *Fax:* (510) 568-6190
www.familyradio.com
License: Bay City, Matagorda County, TX held by Family Stations Inc.
Group Owner: Family Stations Inc.
Arbitron Metro Market: Bay City, TX *Format:* Religious
Stanley Jackson, General Manager

Baytown

KWWJ
10-01-1947; 1360 khz AM *Hrs Open:* 24; 5 kw-D, DA2; 1 kw-N, DA2; N29 46 28 W95 0 55
Mailing Address: 4638 Decker Drive, Baytown, TX 77520 US
Second Address: 4638 Decker Dr., Baytown, TX 77522
(281) 837-8777, *Fax:* (281) 424-7588
www.kwwj.org
kwwj1360@yahoo.com
License: Baytown, TX held by Salt of the Earth Broadcasting Inc.
Nat'l Network: American Urban
Arbitron Metro Market: Baytown, TX *Format:* Gospel *No. News Employees:* 1 *Target Audience:* General.
Darrell Martin, CEO
Darrell Martin, President

Beaumont

KIKR
01-01-1938; 1450 khz AM; 1 kw-D, ND2; 1 kw-N, ND2; N30 3 52 W94 7 12
111 East Kilbourn Ave., Suite 2700, Milwaukee, WI 53202 US
(409) 833-9421, *Fax:* (409) 833-9296
www.lagrand1450.com
bshaw@cumulus.com; patrick.sanders@cumulus.com; ashlie.christie@cumulus.com
License: Beaumont, TX held by Cumulus Licensing Corp.
Group Owner: Cumulus Media Inc.; (acq 3-9-98; grpsl).
Nat'l Reps: McGavren Guild
Arbitron Metro Market: Beaumont-Port A *Format:* Sports *Target Audience:* 25-54.
B Shaw, Programming Director
Ashlie Christie, Promotions Manager
Greg Davis, Chief Engineer
Patrick Sanders, Assistant Program Director
Ashlie Christie, Program Director

KLVI
01-01-1924; 560 khz AM *Hrs Open:* 24
Mailing Address: 600 Congress Avenue, Suite 1400, Austin, TX 78701 US
Second Address: 2885 I-10 E., Beaumont, TX 77726
(409) 896-5555, *Fax:* (409) 896-5500
www.klvi.com
License: Beaumont, TX held by Clear Channel
Group Owner: Clear Channel Communications Inc.; (acq 8-30-00; grpsl).
Arbitron Metro Market: Golden Triangle *Format:* News, News/Talk, 86 *Hrs. of News Programming:* news progmg 5 hrs wkly *No. News Employees:* 4 *Target Audience:* 25-54; informed professionals *Adv. Rates:* 78;78; 78; 78
Lowry Mays, Chairman
John Hogan, CEO
Trey Poston, Operations Dir
Tim Thomas, General Manager
Susan Labure, General Sales Mgr
Jim Love, Programming Director
Mark Gusmon, Promotions Manager
Harold Mann, News Director
RandallMays, CFO
Rob Windham, Randall Mays
Trey Poston, Operations Director
Jim Love, Operations Manager
Mark Kopelman, Vice President

KQXY-FM
09-01-1966; 94.1 mhz FM *Hrs Open:* 24; 100 kw; 600 ft.; N30 6 56 W94 0 0
111 East Kilbourn Ave., Suite 2700, Milwaukee, WI 53202 US
(409) 833-9421, *Fax:* (409) 833-9296
www.kqxy.com
psanders@qt.rr.com
License: Beaumont, Jefferson County, TX held by Cumulus Licensing Corp.
Group Owner: Cumulus Media Inc.; (acq 3-9-98; grpsl)
Arbitron Metro Market: Beaumont-Port Arthur, TX *Format:* Contemporary Hits/Top 40 *Hrs. of News Programming:* news progmg 5 hrs wkly *No. News Employees:* 1 *Target Audience:* 18-49; skewed female
Rick Prusator, General Manager
Mike Simpson, General Sales Mgr
Greg Davis, Chief Engineer

KTCX
01-01-1996; 102.5 mhz FM; 50 kw; 492 ft.; N29 59 20 W94 14 42
111 East Kilbourn Ave., Suite 2700, Milwaukee, WI 53202 US
(409) 833-9421, *Fax:* (409) 833-9296
www.ktcx.com
info@ktcx.com
License: Beaumont, Jefferson County, TX held by Cumulus Licensing Corp.
Group Owner: Cumulus Media Inc.; (acq 3-26-98; $3.6 million)
Arbitron Metro Market: Beaumont-Port Arthur, TX *Format:* Urban Contemporary
Jim West, Operations Dir
Zanetta Kelley, General Manager
Ed Turner, Station Manager
Walter Brickhouse, General Sales Mgr
Douglas Harris, Programming Director
Mark Guzman, Promotions Manager
Greg Davis, Chief Engineer
AdrianScott, Assistant Music Director
Marco Camacho, Regional Sales Manager
Wes Matejka, Sales Director

*KTXB
01-23-1990; 89.7 mhz FM *Hrs Open:* 24; 9 kw vert; 568 ft.; N30 9 27 W93 48 6
4135 Northgate Blvd #1, Sacramento, CA 95834 US
(800) 543-1495, *Fax:* (916) 641-8238
www.familyradio.com
info@familyradio.com
License: Beaumont, Jefferson County, TX held by Family Stations Inc.
Group Owner: Family Stations Inc.
Arbitron Metro Market: Beaumont, TX *Format:* Christian
Harold Camping, President
Martha Tallent, Station Manager

*KVLU
01-01-1974; 91.3 mhz FM *Hrs Open:* 24; 40 kw; 449 ft.; N30 6 40 W94 3 10
PO Box 10064, Beaumont, TX 77710 US
(409) 880-8164
www.kvlu.org
License: Beaumont, Jefferson County, TX held by Lamar University.
Nat'l Network: NPR
Arbitron Metro Market: Beaumont-Port Arthur, TX *Format:* Jazz, News *Special Programming:* Sp 5 hrs wkly *Target Audience:* 35 plus.
Byron Balentine, Station Manager
Ken Wilson, Chief Engineer
Melanie Dishman, Station Manager-Advancement
Joe Elwell, Music Director
Stacey Dishman, Membership Coordinator/ Webmaster
Jason Miller, Production Director

KQQK
07-10-1967; 107.9 mhz FM *Hrs Open:* 24; 90 kw; 1955 ft.; N30 1 1 W94 32 47 *Rebroadcasts:* Simulcasts KXGJ(FM) Matagorda
1980 Post Oak Blvd., Suite 1500, Houston, TX 77056 US
(731) 315-3400, *Fax:* (713) 314-3506
www.xoradio.com
License: Beaumont, Jefferson County, TX held by Liberman Broadcasting of Houston License LLC.
Group Owner: Liberman Broadcasting Inc.; (acq 10-11-2002; $24 million)
Arbitron Metro Market: Huston, TX *Format:* Classic Rock, Tejano *Target Audience:* 18-49; bilingual Hispanics
Lenard Liberman, CEO
Winter Horton, Operations Dir
Brad Branson, General Sales Mgr
Ezequiel Gonzalez, Programming Director
Meliza Posada, News Director
Mike Todd, Engineering Dir

KYKR
02-01-1966; 95.1 mhz FM *Hrs Open:* 24; 100 kw; 430 ft.; N30 3 43 W93 58 50
Mailing Address: 600 Congress Avenue, Suite 1400, Austin, TX 78701 US
Second Address: 2885 Interstate 10 E., Beaumont, TX 77726
(409) 896-5555, *Fax:* (409) 896-5599
www.kykr.com
www.kicker951@clearchannel.com
License: Beaumont, Jefferson County, TX held by Capstar TX L.P.
Group Owner: Clear Channel Communications Inc.; (acq 8-30-2000; grpsl).
Nat'l Reps: Clear Channel *Wire Services:* AP
Arbitron Metro Market: Beaumont-Port Arthur, TX *Format:* Country *Hrs. of News Programming:* news progmg 2 hrs wkly *No. News Employees:* 3 *Target Audience:* 18-54. *Adv. Rates:* 63; 63; 63; 63
Lowry Mays, Chairman
John Hogan, CEO
Mark Mays, President
Mark Kopelman, Operations Dir
Vesta Brandt, General Manager

Elizabeth Blackstock, General Sales Mgr
Randall Mays, CFO
Rick Miles, National Sales Manager
JoeyArmstrong, Operations Director

KZZB
05-01-1947; 990 khz AM *Hrs Open:* 24; 1 kw-U, DA1; N30 8 57 W94 7 59
4638 Decker Drive, Baytown, TX 77520 US
(409) 833-0990, *Fax:* (409) 833-0995
www.kzzbradio.com
info@kzzb.com
License: Beaumont, TX held by Martin Broadcasting Inc.
Group Owner: Martin Broadcasting Inc.; (acq 7-28-92;
Nat'l Reps: Christal
Arbitron Metro Market: Beaumont, TX *Format:* Gospel *No. News Employees:* 1 *Target Audience:* 18-49.
Darrell Martin, President
Willie Mae McIver, Programming Director

***KLBT**
08-17-2006; 88.1 mhz FM; 0 kw horiz, 7 kw vert; 476 ft.; N29 54 52 W94 17 6
1601 Belvedere Rd, 204 E, W Palm Beach, FL 33406 US
(409) 833-0045
www.thekingsmusician.org
info@thekingsmusician.org
License: Beaumont, Jefferson County, TX held by The King's Musician Educational Foundation Inc
Arbitron Metro Market: Beaumont, TX *Format:* Christian
Leslie Jones, President

***KGHY**
88.5 mhz FM; 13.5 kw vert; 344 ft.; N30 16 23 W93 57 23
P O Box 34321, Houston, TX 77234 US
(888) 477-4273
www.thegospelhiway.org
License: Beaumont, Jefferson County, TX held by CCS Radio Inc.
Arbitron Metro Market: Beaumont, TX *Format:* Contemporary Hits/Top 40, Gospel
Otis Dyson, President

Beeville

KIBL
10-20-1949; 1490 khz AM *Hrs Open:* 5 AM-10 PM; 1 kw-U, ND1; N28 23 8 W97 43 42
P.O. Box 252, McAllen, TX 78502 US
(512) 358-1490, *Fax:* (956) 686-2999
License: Beeville, TX held by Paulino Bernal
Arbitron Metro Market: Beeville, TX *Format:* Christian
Eloy Bernal, General Manager
John Ross, Chief Engineer

KTKO
12-12-1976; 105.7 mhz FM *Hrs Open:* 24hours; 25 kw; 328 ft.; N28 28 16 W97 48 39
310 North Frio, Mathis, TX 78368 US
(361) 358-1490, *Fax:* (361) 358-7814
bebekicker106@yahoo.com
License: Beeville, Bee County, TX held by Texas Gulfwest Broadcasting Inc.
Wire Services: NOAA Weather
Arbitron Metro Market: Corpus Christi, TX *Format:* Country *Hrs. of News Programming:* news progmg 13 hrs wkly *No. News Employees:* 1 *Target Audience:* 18-64. *Adv. Rates:* 18: 16: 18: 16
Bebe Adamez, General Manager

***KVFM**
01-01-2000; 91.3 mhz FM; 1 kw vert; 302 ft.; N28 26 42 W97 45 50
P.O. Box 252, McAllen, TX 78505 US
(956) 781-5528, *Fax:* (956) 686-2999
License: Beeville, Bee County, TX held by Paulino Bernal Evangelism.
Arbitron Metro Market: McAllen, TX
Vic Eliason, Operations Dir
Jim Schneider, Programming Director

KRXB
12-02-1988; 107.1 mhz FM *Hrs Open:* 24; 1.5 kw; 337 ft.; N28 27 45 W97 46 50
Mailing Address: 8584 Katy Fwy., Ste 300, Houston, TX 77024 US
Second Address: TX
(361) 358-4941, *Fax:* (361) 358-0601
krxbfm@sbcglobal.net
License: Beeville, Bee County, TX held by Shaffer Communications Group Inc.
Nat'l Network: Jones Radio Networks
Arbitron Metro Market: Beeville, TX *Format:* Classic Rock *No. News Employees:* 4 *Target Audience:* 25 plus.
Joe Shaffer, President
Marlene Rivera, General Manager
Joy Burkhardt, News Director

Bellaire

KGOW
06-07-1961; 1560 khz AM *Hrs Open:* 6 AM-sunset
3633 Farm To Market, Road 437, Rogers, TX 76569 US
(713) 479-5300, *Fax:* (713) 479-5333
1560thegame.com
info@kgowam.com
License: Bellaire, TX held by Gow Communications L.L.C.
Arbitron Metro Market: Houston-Galvest *Format:* Sports
David Gow, President
Craig Larson, Programming Director
Michelle McDonald, Promotions Manager

Bells

KMKT
09-01-1997; 93.1 mhz FM; 6.8 kw; 627 ft.; N33 41 31 W96 26 36
The Katy Depot, 101 East Main Suite 255, Denison, TX 75020 US
(903) 465-6200, *Fax:* (903) 463-9816
www.931kmkt.com
jason@931kmkt.com
License: Bells, Grayson County, TX held by NM Licensing LLC.
Group Owner: NextMedia Group Inc.; (acq 11-26-01; grpsl).
Format: Country
Steven Dinetz, CEO
Jeff Dinetz, President
Jason Taylor, Operations Dir
David Smith, General Manager
David MacMullen, General Sales Mgr
Anne Oliver, Promotions Manager
Tiffany Reynolds, News Director
Vince Richardson, ChiefEngineer
Sean Stover, CFO

Bellville

KULF
08-08-1974; 1090 khz AM; 250 w-D; N29 56 50 W96 15 54
Rebroadcasts: Rebroadcasts KLTR(FM) Caldwell 100%
530 W. Main St., Brenham, TX 77001
(979) 836-9411, *Fax:* (979) 836-9435
lorihenderson01@hotmail.com
License: Bellville, Austin County, TX held by Roy E. Henderson

Roy Henderson, President

Belton

KQXB(FM)
04-25-1970; 106.3 mhz FM *Hrs Open:* 24; 11.5 kw; Ant 489 ft; N31 03 46 W97 31 54
608 Moody Ln., Temple, TX 76504
(254) 773-5252, *Fax:* (254) 773-0115
www.myb106.com
b106@cumulus.com
License: Belton, Bell County, TX held by Cumulus Licensing LLC.
Group Owner: Cumulus Media Inc.; (acq 2-2-2000; grpsl).
Population Served: 162,000 *Arbitron Metro Market:* Killeen-Temple, TX *Format:* Adult Contemp *No. News Employees:* 1 *Target Audience:* 25-54.
Bourdon Wooten, General Manager
CC Cruz, Programming Director

Benbrook

KZFO(FM)
01-01-1990; 107.1 mhz FM *Hrs Open:* 24; 74 kw; Ant 1,050 ft; N32 35 10 W97 49 52
7700 Carpenter Fwy., Dallas, TX 75247
(214) 525-0400, *Fax:* (214) 631-1196
univision.com
License: Benbrook, Tarrant County, TX held by KCYT-FM License Corp.
Group Owner: Univision Radio; (acq 9-22-2003; grpsl).
Population Served: 3,000,000 *Arbitron Metro Market:* Dallas-Fort Worth
Andy Lockridge, Operations Dir
Ivonne Flaherty, General Manager
Cipriano Robles, General Sales Mgr
Oscar Espinosa, Promotions Manager
Mirentxu Smith, News Director
Patrick Parks, Chief Engineer
Frank Carter, General Manager
Betsy Galleguillos, National Sales Manager
Myrna Vera, Research Director

Big Lake

***KPDB**
01-01-2001; 98.3 mhz FM; 50 kw; 430 ft.; N31 11 45 W101 25 40
P O Box 252, McAllen, TX 78502 US
(760) 947-4300
www.ondasdevida.com
radiodesafio@radiodesafio.org
License: Big Lake, Reagan County, TX held by Centro Cristiano de Fe Inc.
Arbitron Metro Market: Hesperia, CA *Format:* Christian, Religious
Larry Johnson, President
Elliott Klein, General Manager

Big Sandy

***KTAA**
11-06-1995; 90.7 mhz FM *Hrs Open:* 24; 5.8 kw vert; 515 ft.; N32 37 50 W94 53 44
P. O. Box 111, Big Sandy, TX 75755 US
(913) 642-7770, *Fax:* (913) 642-1319
www.bottradionetwork.com
comments@bottradionetwork.com
License: Big Sandy, Upshur County, TX held by Community Broadcasting Inc.
Group Owner: Bott Radio Network; (acq 9-6-2006; $450,000)
Nat'l Network: USA
Arbitron Metro Market: Overland Park, KS *Format:* Christian, Talk
Target Audience: 25-54; adults
Richard Bott II, President
Pat Rulon, General Sales Mgr
Candy Green, Programming Director
Rachel Moser, Promotions Manager
Jason Potocnik, News Director

Big Spring

***KBCX**
01-01-2001; 91.5 mhz FM; 1 kw; 305 ft.; N32 11 6 W101 27 56
Po Drawer 2440, Tupelo, MS 38803 US
(662) 844-8888, *Fax:* (662) 842-6791
www.afr.net
comments@afr.net
License: Big Spring, Howard County, TX held by American Family Association.
Group Owner: American Family Radio
Arbitron Metro Market: Tupelo, MS *Format:* Christian, Religious
Marvin Sanders, General Manager

KBST
12-23-1936; 1490 khz AM; 1 kw-U; N32 15 44 W101 27 37
Mailing Address: Box 1632, Big Spring, TX 78729
Second Address: 608 Johnson St., Big Spring, TX 79720
(432) 267-1490, *Fax:* (432) 267-1579
onair@kbst.com
License: Big Spring, Howard County, TX held by Rhattigan Broadcasting (Texas) LP
Group Owner: Rhattigan Broadcasting (Texas) LP; (acq 8-19-2004; grpsl)
Nat'l Network: Fox Sports *Regional Network:* Texas State Networks *Nat'l Reps:* Riley
Population Served: 28,735*Target Audience:* 25 plus.
Guy Gill, CEO
Charles Sagona, Operations Dir
Malinda Flenniken, General Manager
Bill Norris, News Director

KBST-FM
01-01-1961; 95.7 mhz FM; 33 kw; 459 ft.; N32 13 13 W101 26 25
Mailing Address: 13625 Pond Springs Rd, #105, Austin, TX 78729 US
Second Address: 608 Johnson St., Big Spring, TX 79720
(432) 267-6391, *Fax:* (432) 267-1579
www.kbst.com
kbst@kbst.com
License: Big Spring, Howard County, TX held by Rhattigan Broadcasting (Texas) LP.
Group Owner: Rhattigan Broadcasting (Texas) LP; (acq 8-19-2004; grpsl)
Format: Country, News, 62, Talk
Michael Rhattigan, General Manager

KBTS
08-14-1995; 94.3 mhz FM; 8.3 kw; 561 ft.; N32 13 13 W101 26 25
Mailing Address: 15 Stutz Court, Midland, TX 79705 US
Second Address: 608 Johnson St., Big Spring, TX 79720

(432) 267-6391, *Fax:* (432) 267-1579
www.943fuse.com
comments@kbst.com
License: Big Spring, Howard County, TX held by Rhattigan Broadcasting (Texas) LP
Group Owner: Rhattigan Broadcasting (Texas) LP; (acq 6-3-2004; grpsl).
Arbitron Metro Market: Big Spring, TX *Format:* Adult Contemp
Malinda Ellison Flenniken, General Manager
Tim Knox, Programming Director
Bill Norris, News Director

KBYG
01-01-1948; 1400 khz AM *Hrs Open:* 24; 1 kw-U, ND1; N32 13 22 W101 28 35
4410 10 Street, Lubbock, TX 79416 US
(432) 263-6351, *Fax:* (432) 263-8223
www.kbygradio.com
david@pappajhn.akbys.net
License: Big Spring, TX held by Ballard Drew.
Regional Network: Southwest Agri-Radio
Arbitron Metro Market: Big Spring, TX *Format:* Oldies, Talk *No. News Employees:* 1 *Target Audience:* 25-54; Anglo-Hispanic
Joe Murphy, Operations Dir
John Weeks, General Manager
Jennifer Patton, Station Manager
David Pappajohn, General Sales Mgr
Vents Allyn Solis, Programming Director
Mike Henry, News Director
David Pappajohn, General Manager

KBQX
730 khz AM
US
(432) 352-9110
License: Big Spring, TX held by Trade Media Corp.
Arbitron Metro Market: Big Spring, TX *Format:* Christian
Mark Nolte, Operations Dir

Bishop

KMZZ
06-15-1980; 106.9 mhz FM *Hrs Open:* 24; 25 kw; 246 ft.; N27 40 16 W97 44 17
P.O. Box 5206, Corpus Christi, TX 78465 US
(361) 289-0999, *Fax:* (361) 289-0810
davilabroadcasting@bizstx.rr.com
License: Bishop, Nueces County, TX held by Claro Communications Ltd.
Group Owner: Claro Communications Ltd.; (acq 11-4-2004; $550,000)
Arbitron Metro Market: Bishop, TX *Format:* Religious *No. News Employees:* 1 *Target Audience:* 18-49; people with buying power
Lionel Davila, General Manager
Mike Aradillias, General Sales Mgr
Jeremy Lopez, Programming Director
George Sanders, Chief Engineer

Bloomington

KLUB
12-01-1992; 106.9 mhz FM *Hrs Open:* 24; 18.5 kw; 381 ft.; N28 42 24 W96 50 6
Mailing Address: 600 Congress Avenue, Suite 1400, Austin, TX 78701 US
Second Address: Box 3325, Victoria, TX 77904
(361) 573-0777, *Fax:* (361) 578-0059
www.1069therock.com
kixs@gapbroadcasting.com
License: Bloomington, Victoria County, TX held by GAP Broadcasting Victoria License LLC.
Group Owner: GAP Broadcasting LLC; (acq 10-1-2007; grpsl)
Format: Classic Rock *Special Programming:* Blues *Hrs. of News Programming:* news progmg 4 hrs wkly *No. News Employees:* 1 *Target Audience:* 25-59; listeners in a growth & acquisition mode *Adv. Rates:* 15;13; 15; 13
Jeff Lyon, General Manager
Natalie Franz, General Sales Mgr
Adam West, Programming Director
James Love, News Director
Charles Smithey, Engineering Dir
Becky Snell, Traffic Manager

***KHVT**
01-01-2006; 91.5 mhz FM; 46 kw; 482 ft.; N29 0 4 W97 0 5
Rebroadcasts: Rebroadcasts KHCB-FM Houston 95%
2424 South Boulevard, Houston, TX 77098 US
(713) 520-5200
www.khcb.org
email@khcb.org
License: Bloomington, Victoria County, TX held by Houston Christian Broadcasters Inc.
Group Owner: Houston Christian Broadcasters Inc.
Arbitron Metro Market: Bloomington, TX *Format:* Christian
Special Programming: Sp Christian 6 hrs wkly
Bruce Munsterman, General Manager
Bonnie BeMent, Assistant General Manager

Boerne

KBRN
05-10-1982; 1500 khz AM; 0.25 kw-D, NDD; N29 48 44 W98 43 41
P.O. Box 252, McAllen, TX 78505 US
(361) 774-4354, *Fax:* (361) 241-7945
License: Boerne, TX held by Claro Communications Ltd.
Group Owner: Claro Communications Ltd.; (acq 6-25-2004; $200,000)

Gerry Benavides, General Manager

Bonham

KFYN
05-01-1948; 1420 khz AM *Hrs Open:* 5 AM-1 AM; 250 w-D, 148 w-N; N33 34 40 W96 09 55
Mailing Address: 811 E. Sam Rayburn Dr., Bonham, TX 75248
Second Address: Box 248, Bonham, TX 75418-4928
(903) 583-3151, *Fax:* (903) 583-2728
www.kfyn1420.com
kfyn@kfyn1420.com
License: Bonham, Fannin County, TX held by Vision Media Group Inc.
Nat'l Network: ABC *Regional Network:* Texas State Networks
Population Served: 238,000*Special Programming:* Farm 6 hrs, relg 6 hrs, oldies rock 6 hrs wkly *Adv. Rates:* 14; 12; 14; 12
C.L. Carter II, President
Jeff Davis, Operations Dir

Borger

***KASV**
01-01-1998; 88.7 mhz FM *Hrs Open:* 24; 10 kw horiz, 3 kw vert; 203 ft.; N35 40 42 W101 23 18 *Rebroadcasts:* Rebroadcasts KJRT(FM) Amarillo 100%
P.O. Box 469, Wheeler, TX 79096 US
(806) 359-8855, *Fax:* (806) 354-2039
www.kingdomkeysradio.org
License: Borger, Hutchinson County, TX held by Top O' Texas Ed. Broadcasting.
Arbitron Metro Market: Amarillo, TX *Format:* Religious
Jeremy Pfeil, Operations Dir
Ricky Pfeil, General Manager

KQFX
03-01-1975; 104.3 mhz FM; 100 kw; 574 ft.; N35 25 34 W101 36 47
2402 Broadmoor, Bldg D-2, Bryan, TX 77802 US
(806) 355-1044, *Fax:* (806) 457-0642
www.lamejorenvivo.com
License: Borger, Hutchinson County, TX held by Tejas Broadcasting Ltd. LLP.
Group Owner: Tejas Broadcasting Ltd. LLP; (acq 11-15-2004; grpsl).
Arbitron Metro Market: Amarillo area *Format:* Tejano
Matt Douglas, General Manager
Willie Palacios, General Sales Mgr
Jorge Saenz, Programming Director
Charlie Singleton, Chief Engineer

KQTY
01-10-1947; 1490 khz AM *Hrs Open:* 24; 1 kw-U; N35 41 05 W101 23 20
Box 165, 113 Union, Borger, TX 88101
(806) 273-7533,(806) 273-5889, *Fax:* (806) 273-3727
kqtyradio.com
kqtyradio@yahoo.com
License: Borger, Hutchinson County, TX held by Zia Broadcasting.
Group Owner: Zia Broadcasting Co.; (acq 12-1-79)
Population Served: 26,800*Target Audience:* 25-54; blue collar workers with traditional values & beliefs *Adv. Rates:* 12; 12; 12; 12
Lonnie Ausups, CEO
Rick Keefer, General Manager
George Grover, Station Manager

KQTY-FM
01-01-1999; 106.7 mhz FM *Hrs Open:* 24; 6 kw; Ant 259 ft; N35 41 05 W101 23 12
Mailing Address: Box 165, Borger, TX 88102
Second Address: 113 Union, Borger, TX 79007
(806) 273-5889, *Fax:* (806) 273-3727
www.kqtyradio.com
kqtyradio@yahoo.com
License: Borger, Hutchinson County, TX held by Zia Broadcasting Co.
Group Owner: Zia Broadcasting Co.
Nat'l Network: ABC
Population Served: 26,800*Special Programming:* Religious, 1hr; southern gospel, 3hrs; christian country, 5hrs; Texas country, 10hrs *Hrs. of News Programming:* News progmg 15 hrs wkly
Target Audience: 25-54; Bluecollar workers w/traditional values & beliefs *Adv. Rates:* 12; 12; 12; 12
Lonnie Allsups, CEO
Rick Keefer, General Manager
George Grover, Station Manager

Bovina

KKNM
01-01-2008; 96.5 mhz FM; 50 kw; 459 ft.; N34 41 17 W102 56 53
US
(817) 920-7599, *Fax:* (817) 920-9606
License: Bovina, Parmer County, TX held by Tejas Broadcasting Ltd. LLP.
Group Owner: Tejas Broadcasting Ltd. LLP
Arbitron Metro Market: Bovina, TX
Charles Brooks, President

***KOVA**
90.9 mhz FM; kw
US
(214) 525-7700, *Fax:* (214) 525-7750
License: Bovina, Parmer County, TX held by Ron Elmore Ministries Inc.
Arbitron Metro Market: Houston, TX
Ron Elmore, President

Bowie

KNTX
05-29-1959; 1410 khz AM *Hrs Open:* 24 hrs; 500 w-D, DA; N33 35 10 W97 48 23
Box 1080, State Hwy 59 & FM 1758, Bowie, TX 76230
(940) 872-2288, *Fax:* (940) 872-1228
kntxradio.com
chenderson@kntxradio.com
License: Bowie, Montague County, TX held by Henderson Broadcasting Co. L.P.
CBS Radio *Regional Network:* Texas State Networks
Population Served: 30,000 *Arbitron Metro Market:* Wichita Falls, *Special Programming:* Gospel 4 hrs wkly *Hrs. of News Programming:* news progmg 15 hrs wkly *No. News Employees:* 1 *Target Audience:* 25-54.*Adv. Rates:* 13; 10; 13; 7
Charley Henderson, President
Pamela Henderson, Station Manager
Ken Wood, Promotions
Doris McGuffey, News Director
Broadcast Works, Chief Engineer
Wendy Hill, Operations Director

Brady

KNEL
12-01-1935; 1490 khz AM; 1 kw-U, ND1; N31 7 48 W99 19 21
Mailing Address: 117 S. Blackburn, Brady, TX 76825 US
Second Address: 117 S. Blackburn St., Brady, TX 76825
(325) 597-2119, *Fax:* (325) 597-1925
www.knelradio.com
knel@airmail.net
License: Brady, TX held by Farris Broadcasting Inc.
Nat'l Network: ABC *Regional Network:* Texas State Networks
Format: Oldies *Target Audience:* General.
Lynn Farris, President
Stan Cooper, Chief Engineer

KNEL-FM
08-21-1979; 95.3 mhz FM; 6 kw; 299 ft.; N31 7 27 W99 21 34
Mailing Address: PO Box 630, Brady, TX 76825 US
Second Address: 117 S. Blackburn St., Brady, TX 76825
(325) 597-2119, *Fax:* (325) 597-1925
www.knelradio.com
License: Brady, McCulloch County, TX
Regional Network: Texas State Networks
Format: Country *Target Audience:* General.
Lynn Farris, General Manager

Breckenridge

KLXK
08-01-1982; 93.5 mhz FM; 12.5 kw; 459 ft.; N32 47 32 W98 56 24

Mailing Address: 114east Elm Street, Breckenridge, TX 76424 US
Second Address: 101 E. Walker St., Suite 201, Breckenridge, TX 76424
(254) 559-6543, *Fax:* 940-549-8628
www.todaysbestcountryonline.com
License: Breckenridge, Stephens County, TX
Group Owner: Graham Newspapers Inc.
Nat'l Network: ABC
Arbitron Metro Market: Abilene, TX *Format:* Country *Special Programming:* Agricultural programming 5 hrs wkly *Hrs. of News Programming:* news progmg 1.5 hrs wkly *No. News Employees:* 1 *Target Audience:* 25-54; general *Adv. Rates:* 15; 15; 15; 15
Roy Robinson, Operations Dir
Joe Graham, General Manager
Greg Tiller, Programming Director
Jim Jones, News Director

KROO

09-01-1947; 1430 khz AM *Hrs Open:* 24
Mailing Address: 114east Elm Street, Breckenridge, TX 76424 US
Second Address: 101 E. Walker St., Suite 201, Breckenridge, TX 76424
(254) 559-6543, *Fax:* (254) 559-6545
klxk@brazosnet.com
License: Breckenridge, TX held by Graham Newspapers Inc.
Group Owner: Graham Newspapers Inc.; (acq 4-12-2001; with co-located FM)
Nat'l Network: ABC
Arbitron Metro Market: Abilene, TX *Format:* Adult Contemp *Hrs. of News Programming:* news progmg 2.5 hrs wkly *No. News Employees:* 1 *Target Audience:* Adults 25-54; adults *Adv. Rates:* 15; 15; 15; 15
Roy Robinson, Operations Dir
Joe Graham, General Manager
Greg Tiller, Programming Director
Jim Jones, News Director

*KQXB

89.9 mhz FM; 17.9 kw; Ant 325 ft; N32 35 48 W98 44 26
Box 497933, Garland, TX
(469) 245-3604
License: Breckenridge, Stephens County, TX held by Gospel American Network.
William Wright, General Manager

Brenham

KTTX

09-15-1964; 106.1 mhz FM; 50 kw; 492 ft.; N30 21 48 W96 34 33
P. O. Box 1280, Brenham, TX 77833 US
(979) 836-3655, *Fax:* (979) 830-8141
www.ktex.com
mail@ktex.com
License: Brenham, Washington County, TX held by Tom S. Whitehead, Inc.
Nat'l Reps: Rgnl Reps
Arbitron Metro Market: Brenham, TX *Format:* Country *Hrs. of News Programming:* news progmg 1.5 hrs wkly *No. News Employees:* 1 *Target Audience:* 18-49. *Adv. Rates:* 20; 15; 18; 11
Tom D Whitehead, President/General Manager
Ken Murray, Operations Dir
Tom Whitehead, General Manager
Carolyn Warmke, Sales Manager
Ken Murray, Programming Director
Austen Hagood, Promotions Manager
Michele Daniels, NewsDirector
Kelly Outlaw, Promotions Director
Carolyn Warmke, Regional Sales Manager
Troy Arndt, Production Director
Ed Pothul, Sports Director
Michele Danielss, Traffic Director
Elizabeth Pomykal, Copy Writer

KLTR

08-01-1988; 94.1 mhz FM *Hrs Open:* 24; 6.4 kw; 328 ft.; N30 8 31 W96 25 0
306 East Main Street, Brenham, TX 77833 US
(979) 836-9411, *Fax:* (979) 836-9435
www.litefm941.com
kodiroberts@yahoo.com
License: Brenham, Washington County, TX held by Roy E. Henderson.
Group Owner: Fort Bend Broadcasting Co.; (acq 5-31-2001; $1.5 million)
Arbitron Metro Market: Brenham, TX *Format:* Adult Contemp *Special Programming:* Gospel 10 hrs wkly *Hrs. of News Programming:* news progmg 18 hrs wkly *No. News Employees:* 1 *Target Audience:* 18-49.
Roy Henderson, President
Ryan Henderson, General Sales Mgr
Amber Kyle, Programming Director
Lori Henderson, News Director

KWHI

04-15-1947; 1280 khz AM; 1 kw-D, ND1; 0.072 kw-N, ND1; N30 10 5 W96 25 20
Mailing Address: P. O. Box 1280, Brenham, TX 77833 US
Second Address: 223 E. Main St., Brenham, TX 77833
(979) 836-3655, *Fax:* (979) 830-8141
www.kwhi.com
mail@kwhi.com
License: Brenham, TX held by Tom S. Whitehead Inc.
Nat'l Network: ABC *Nat'l Reps:* Rgnl Reps
Arbitron Metro Market: Brenham, TX *Format:* Country, News, 62, Talk *Special Programming:* Polka 2 hrs, relg 3 hrs, farm 3 hrs wkly *Hrs. of News Programming:* news progmg 14 hrs wkly *No. News Employees:* 2*Target Audience:* 25-54. *Adv. Rates:* 24; 19; 22; 10
Tom D. Whitehead, President and General Manager
Ken Murray, Operations Dir
Carolyn Warmke, General Sales Mgr
Craig Mantey, Programming Director
Austen Hagood, Promotions Manager
Frank Wagner, News Director
Mark Whitehead, ChiefEngineer
Ed Pothul, Sports Director
Elizabeth Pomykal, Copywriter
Michele Daniels, Office Manager
Lynnett Ratchford, Account Executive
Lori Ligues, Accounting
LaVerne Krumrey, Account Executive

*KUBJ

01-01-2008; 89.7 mhz FM; 17.5 kw; 407 ft.; N30 3 17 W96 30 26
P.O. Drawer 2440, Tupelo, MS 38803 US
(281) 446-5725, *Fax:* (281 540-2198
www.ksbj.org
License: Brenham, Washington County, TX held by KSBJ Educational Foundation.
Arbitron Metro Market: Benton, AR *Format:* Christian
Tim McDermott, General Manager

Bridgeport

KBOC

08-02-1982; 98.3 mhz FM *Hrs Open:* 24; 93 kw; 2034 ft.; N33 26 13 W97 29 5
5946 Club Oaks Dr., Dallas, TX 75248 US
(817) 868-2900, *Fax:* (817) 868-2929
www.elnorteenlinea.com
License: Bridgeport, Wise County, TX held by Liberman Broadcasting of Dallas License LLC.
Group Owner: Liberman Broadcasting Inc.; (acq 11-2-2006; grpsl)
Arbitron Metro Market: Dallas-Fort Worth
Alex Sanchez, General Manager

Brookshire

KCHN

01-01-2001; 1050 khz AM
449 Broadway, New York, NY 10013 US
(713) 490-2538, *Fax:* (713) 984-1721
www.mrbi.net
terryl@mrbi.net
License: Brookshire, TX held by KCHN Licensee LLC.
Arbitron Metro Market: Greater Houston, TX *Format:* Ethnic
Terry Lowry, General Manager

Brownfield

KKUB

08-01-1949; 1300 khz AM
Mailing Address: 1277 Brownfield Radio, Inc., Brownfield, TX 79316 US
Second Address: 1722 Tahoka Rd., Brownfield, TX 79316
(806) 637-4531, *Fax:* (806) 637-4610
License: Brownfield, TX held by Dios Llega Al Hombre Ministries
Arbitron Metro Market: Lubbock, TX *Format:* Country *Target Audience:* 24 and up.
Adolph Hernandez, General Manager

KSTQ(FM)

11-12-1984; 104.3 mhz FM *Hrs Open:* 24; 50 kw; Ant 466 ft; N33 25 08 W102 08 58
9800 University Ave., Lubbock, TX 79423
(806) 745-3434, *Fax:* (806) 748-2470
idee@ramar.com
License: Brownfield, Terry County, TX held by Ramar Communications II Ltd.
Group Owner: Ramar Communications II Ltd.; (acq 3-26-99; $1.025 million)
Arbitron Metro Market: Lubbock, TX *Format:* Adult Contemp
Target Audience: 25-54.
Lew Dee, General Manager
Diana Dee, General Sales Mgr

*KPBB

01-01-1999; 88.5 mhz FM; 4.5 kw; 377 ft.; N33 9 18 W102 16 51
Mailing Address: P.O. Box 252, McAllen, TX 78505 US
Second Address: 4501 N. McCall Rd., McAllen, TX 78504
(956) 686-6382, *Fax:* (956) 686-2999
License: Brownfield, Terry County, TX held by Paulino Bernal Evangelism.
Format: Christian
Paulino Bernal, General Manager

Brownsville

*KBNR

04-10-1984; 88.3 mhz FM *Hrs Open:* 24; 5.5 kw; 289 ft.; N25 55 10 W97 31 44
Mailing Address: P.O. Box 3333, McAllen, TX 78502 US
Second Address: 901 Mexico Blvd., Brownsville, TX 78520
(956) 542-6933, *Fax:* (956) 542-0523
www.radiokbnr.org
kbnr@lwrn.org
License: Brownsville, Cameron County, TX held by World Radio Network Inc.
Group Owner: World Radio Network Inc.
Arbitron Metro Market: McAllen-Brownsville-Harlingen, TX *Format:* Religious *Hrs. of News Programming:* News progmg 3 hrs wkly *Target Audience:* 20-45; Hispanic, middle & upper income
Ted Haney, President
Abelardo Limon, Operations Dir
Moises Flores, Station Manager

KKPS

01-17-1978; 99.5 mhz FM *Hrs Open:* 24; 100 kw; 1037 ft.; N26 4 53 W97 49 44
1350 One Galleria Tower, 13355 Noel Road, Dallas, TX 75240 US
(956) 661-6000, *Fax:* (956) 661-6082
mquinn@entravision.com
License: Brownsville, Cameron County, TX held by Entravision Holdings L.L.C.
Group Owner: Entravision Communications Corp.; (acq 7-20-00; grpsl)
Arbitron Metro Market: McAllen, TX *Format:* Tejano *No. News Employees:* 1 *Target Audience:* 18-49; Hispanic females, young adults
Scott Savage, General Manager

KVNS

01-01-1999; 1700 khz AM *Hrs Open:* 24; 8.8 kw-D, ND1; 0.88 kw-N, ND1; N25 56 57 W97 33 15
1050 McIntosh, Brownsville, TX 78521 US
(956) 973-9202, *Fax:* (956) 973-9355
www.classic1700.com
License: Brownsville, TX held by Clear Channel Broadcasting Licenses Inc.
Group Owner: Clear Channel Communications Inc.; (acq 12-9-2003; grpsl).
Arbitron Metro Market: McAllen-Brownsville-Harlingen *Format:* Contemporary Hits/Top 40
Billy Santiago, Operations Dir
Tim Thomas, General Manager
Chris Aldrich, General Sales Mgr
Billy Santiago, Programming Director
Ken Meek, Chief Engineer

Brownwood

*KBUB

03-12-1987; 90.3 mhz FM; 5.5 kw; 289 ft.; N31 43 10 W99 0 57
P.O. Box 1522, 901 Cc Woodson Rd, Brownwood, TX 76804 US
(325) 641-2223, *Fax:* (325) 643-9772
License: Brownwood, Brown County, TX held by Living Word Church of Brownwood Inc.
Format: Christian
Angelia Schum, General Manager

KBWD

08-17-1941; 1380 khz AM; 1 kw-D, ND1; 0.5 kw-N, ND1; N31 42 36 W98 57 36
Mailing Address: P. O. Box 280, Brownwood, TX 76801 US
Second Address: 300 Carnegie St., Brownwood, TX 76801
(325) 646-3505, *Fax:* (325) 646-2220
www.koxe.com
upfront@koxe.com

License: Brownwood, TX held by Brown County Broadcasting Co.
Arbitron Metro Market: Brownwood, TX *Format:* Adult Contemp
Don Dillard, Operations Dir
Barbara McAnally, General Manager

***KHBW(FM)**
09-01-1998; 91.7 mhz FM *Hrs Open:* 24; 290 w; Ant 571 ft; N31 43 32 W99 00 48
300 Carnegie St., Brownwood, TX 77098
(713) 520-5200
www.khcb.org
License: Brownwood, Brown County, TX held by Houston Christian Broadcasters Inc.
Group Owner: Houston Christian Broadcasters Inc.; (acq 2-27-2009; $40,000)
Population Served: 25,000*Format:* Christian
Bruce Munsterman, General Manager

KOXE
05-17-1975; 101.3 mhz FM; 100 kw; 577 ft.; N31 43 45 W99 1 12
801 Carnegie Blvd, Brownwood, TX 76801 US
(325) 646-3505, *Fax:* (325) 646-2220
www.koxe.com
License: Brownwood, Brown County, TX held by Brown County Broadcasting Co.
Format: Country
Barbara McAnally, General Manager

***KPBE**
01-01-2000; 89.3 mhz FM; 6 kw; 328 ft.; N31 47 43 W98 49 7
Mailing Address: P.O. Box 252, McAllen, TX 78505 US
Second Address: 4501 N. McCall Rd., McAllen, TX 78504
(956) 686-6382, *Fax:* (956) 686-2999
License: Brownwood, Brown County, TX held by Paulino Bernal Evangelism.
Format: Christian
Paulino Bernal, President

KPSM
04-11-1981; 99.3 mhz FM; 100 kw; 446 ft.; N31 43 10 W99 0 57
Mailing Address: P.O. Box 1522, Brownwood, TX 76804 US
Second Address: 901 C.C. Woodson Rd., Brownwood, TX 76801
(325) 646-5993, *Fax:* (325) 643-9772
www.kpsm.net
kpsmfm@gmail.com
License: Brownwood, Brown County, TX held by Living Word Church of Brownwood Inc.
Nat'l Network: Salem Radio Network
Format: Christian *Special Programming:* Children 3 hrs, Christian hip hop 5 hrs, Southern
Jack Ruth, CEO
Angelia Schum, General Manager
Brigitte Rittenour, Station Manager
Erich Schnitz, Programming Director
Tom Zintgraff, Chief Engineer
Kevin Koontz, Promotions Manager

KQBZ
01-01-1953; 1240 khz AM *Hrs Open:* 24; 1 kw-U; N31 42 21 W98 59 45
600 Fisk Dr, Brownwood, TX 76801
(325) 646-3535, *Fax:* (325) 646-5347
wattsradio.net
ksta1000@web-access.net
License: Brownwood, Brown County, TX held by Tackett-Boazman Broadcasting LP
Group Owner: Tackett-Boazman Broadcasting LP
Regional Network: Texas State Networks *Nat'l Reps:* Roslin
Population Served: 35,000*Special Programming:* Christian Sp 36 hrs wkly *Hrs. of News Programming:* news progmg 8 hrs wkly
No. News Employees: 2 *Target Audience:* 18+; Spanish *Adv. Rates:* Same as AM
Chema Martinez, Programming Director
Helen Lehman, News Director

Bryan

KAGC
12-27-1977; 1510 khz AM; 0.5 kw-D, NDD; N30 39 6 W96 23 6
Mailing Address: P.O. Box 4066, Bryan, TX 77805 US
Second Address: 2700 Rudder Fwy. S., Suite 5000, College Station, TX 77845
(979) 695-9595, *Fax:* (979) 695-1933
kagcradio.com
christianfamilyradio@yahoo.com
License: Bryan, TX held by Divcon Associates Inc.
Group Owner: Bryan Broadcasting Corp.; (acq 3-87)
Nat'l Network: Salem Radio Network
Arbitron Metro Market: College Station, TX *Format:* Christian
Special Programming: Black 2 hrs, Czech music 2 hrs wkly *Hrs. of News Programming:* News progmg 6 hrs wkly *Target Audience:* 25-54; upscale, higherincome & conservative *Adv. Rates:* 12.50; 11; 12;50; na
Bill Hicks, President
Keith Kane, Operations Dir
Ben Downs, General Manager
Sam Jones, General Sales Mgr
Chris Dusterhoff, Chief Engineer
Michele McNew, Advertising Director

KNFX-FM
10-07-1991; 99.5 mhz FM *Hrs Open:* 24; 6 kw; 187 ft.; N30 39 9 W96 20 16
103 N. Main Street, Bryan, TX 77803 US
(979) 846-5597, *Fax:* (979) 268-9090
www.995thefox.com
kcwheeler@995thefox.com
License: Bryan, Brazos County, TX held by CCB Texas Licenses L.P.
Group Owner: Clear Channel Communications Inc.; (acq 7-20-01; $2.5 million).
Arbitron Metro Market: Bryan-College Station, TX *Format:* Light Rock *Target Audience:* General. *Adv. Rates:* 18; 18; 18; 18
Zack Owens, Operations Dir
Mike Gatons, General Sales Mgr
K.C. Wheeler, Programming Director

KKYS
07-28-1984; 104.7 mhz FM *Hrs Open:* 24; 50 kw; 285 ft.; N30 42 59 W96 22 20
2201 Cantu Court, Sarasota, FL 34232 US
(979) 846-5597, *Fax:* (979) 268-9090
www.mix1047.com
leslieguidry@clearchannel.com
License: Bryan, Brazos County, TX held by CCB Texas Licenses L.P.
Group Owner: Clear Channel Communications Inc.; (acq 10-10-00; grpsl).
Arbitron Metro Market: Bryan, TX *Format:* Adult Contemp *Hrs. of News Programming:* News progmg 15 hrs wkly *Target Audience:* 18-49; heavy office lstng *Adv. Rates:* 30; 40; 30; 25
Zack Owens, Operations Dir
Mike Gatons, General Manager
Evan Armstrong, Market Manager

KORA-FM
04-01-1966; 98.3 mhz FM; 0.9 kw; 528 ft.; N30 39 0.985 W96 20 57.34
Mailing Address: 2402 Broadmoor, Bldg, D-2, Suite 101, Bryan, TX 77802 US
Second Address: 1240 Villa Maria Rd, Bryan, TX 77802
(979) 776-1240, *Fax:* (979) 776-0123
License: Bryan, Brazos County, TX held by Brazos Valley Communications Ltd.
Group Owner: Brazos Valley Communications Ltd.
Nat'l Reps: Katz Radio
Arbitron Metro Market: Bryan-College Station, TX *Format:* Country *Special Programming:* ABC News *Target Audience:* P18-49, P25-54
Dan Ginzel, Operations Dir
Chris Kiske, General Manager
Nathan Peacock, General Sales Mgr
Roger Garrett, Programming Director
Lance Parr, Chief Engineer

KTAM
09-10-1947; 1240 khz AM
Mailing Address: 2402 Broadmoor, Bldg, D-2, Suite 101, Bryan, TX 77802 US
Second Address: 1240 Villa Maria Rd, Bryan, TX 77802
(979) 776-1240, *Fax:* (979) 776-0123
License: Bryan, TX held by Brazos Valley Communications Ltd.
Group Owner: Brazos Valley Communications Ltd.; (acq 8-31-2006; grpsl)
Nat'l Reps: Univision Radio National Sales
Arbitron Metro Market: Bryan-College Station, TX *Format:* Tejano
Special Programming: GLR News, ESPN Deportes *Target Audience:* 18-34, 18-49
Dan Ginzel, Operations Dir
Chris Kiske, General Manager
Nathan Peacock, General Sales Mgr
Carolyn Benavides, Programming Director
Lance Parr, Chief Engineer

Buda

KROX-FM
09-01-1984; 101.5 mhz FM *Hrs Open:* 24; 12.5 kw; 847 ft.; N30 19 20 W97 48 3
Norwood Tower, Suite 300 ,114 W. 7th St, Austin, TX 78701 US
(512) 832-4000, *Fax:* (512) 832-4071
www.101x.com
jwhite@krox.com
License: Buda, Hays County, TX held by LBJS Broadcasting Co. L.P.
Group Owner: Emmis Communications Corp.; (acq 4-25-03; grpsl).
Nat'l Reps: McGavren Guild
Arbitron Metro Market: Austin-Round Rock metro area *Format:* Alternative *Target Audience:* 18-34; young adults *Adv. Rates:* 140; 150; 160; 70
Bruce Walden, General Manager
James White, General Sales Mgr
Lynn Barstow, Programming Director
Andres Cantu, Promotions Manager
Todd Jeffries, News Director
Jim Henkle, Chief Engineer
Lisa Melton, Traffic Manager
Toby Ryan,Music Director

Buffalo

WTAW-FM
103.5 mhz FM; 6 kw; 96.1 meters; N31 21 42 W95 58 15
PO Box 3248, Bryan, TX
(979) 695-9595, *Fax:* (979) 695-1933
www.bryanbroadcasting.com
radio@bryanbroadcasting.com
License: Buffalo, TX held by Bryan Broadcasting Corp
William R Hicks, President
Ben Downs, Vice President
Sam Jones, General Sales Mgr
Louie Belina, Programming Director
Allison Meserole, Promotions Manager
Tom Turner, News Director

Burkburnett

KYYI
06-01-1989; 104.7 mhz FM *Hrs Open:* 24; 92 kw; 1017 ft.; N34 5 35 W98 52 44
111 East Kilbourn Avenue, Suite 2700, Milwaukee, WI 53202 US
(940) 691-2311, *Fax:* (940) 696-2255
www.bear104.com
bear104@bear104.com
License: Burkburnett, Wichita County, TX held by Cumulus Licensing Corp.
Group Owner: Cumulus Media Inc.; (acq 10-3-97; grpsl)
Arbitron Metro Market: Burkburnett, TX *Format:* Classic Rock
Keith Vaughn, Operations Dir
Lindy Parr, General Manager
John Tidwell, Sales Manager
Keith Vaughn, Programming Director
Dana Jameson, News Director
Jeff Chancey, Chief Engineer

Burleson

KCLE
07-22-1922; 1460 khz AM *Hrs Open:* 24
P.O. Box 1629, Cleburne, TX 76033 US
(817) 645-6643, *Fax:* (817) 645-6644
www.countrygoldradio.com
info@countrygoldradio.com
License: Burleson, TX held by M&M Broadcasters Ltd.
Arbitron Metro Market: Dallas, TX *Format:* Country
Gary Moss, General Manager

Burnet

KBEY
04-01-1993; 103.9 mhz FM; 1.8 kw; Ant 604 ft; N30 44 29 W98 19 05
5526 N. Hwy. 281, Marble Falls, TX 75244
(830) 693-5551, *Fax:* (830) 693-5107
www.radiohillcountry.com
realcountry@kbay.com
License: Burnet, Burnet County, TX held by Munbilla Broadcasting Properties Ltd.
Group Owner: Munbilla Broadcasting Properties Ltd.
Bill Woleben, Operations Dir
Cindi Ashford, General Manager

Bushland

***KTXP**
01-01-2004; 91.5 mhz FM *Hrs Open:* 24; 1 kw; 262 ft.; N35 8 51 W102 5 56 *Rebroadcasts:* Rebroadcasts KANZ(FM) Garden City 100%
210 North 7th Street, Garden City, KS 67846 US
(620) 275-7444, *Fax:* (620) 275-7496
www.hppr.org
hppr@hppr.org
License: Bushland, Potter County, TX held by Kanza Society Inc.
Nat'l Network: NPR; AP Radio; PRI

Arbitron Metro Market: Bushland, Texas *Format:* News, Variety/Diverse
Don Close, President
Richard Hicks, General Manager
Diana Gonzales, General Sales Mgr
Bob Kirby, Programming Director
Barb Blevins, Promotions Manager
Chuck Springer, Chief Engineer
Mary Palmer, Music Director
Rod Buchele, VicePresident
Quentin Hope, Treasurer
Gary Pitner, Secretary
Dean Yates, Texas Underwriting Representative

Byrne

*KLRW
01-01-2004; 88.5 mhz FM; 2.5 kw; 689 ft.; N31 25 16 W100 32 36
P. O. Box 1458, Washington, DC 20013 US
(800) 525-5683, *Fax:* (916) 251-1650
www.klove.com
klove@klove.com
License: Byrne, Tom Green County, TX held by Educational Media Foundation.
Group Owner: EMF Broadcasting; (acq 5-8-2003; $75,000 for CP).
Nat'l Network: K-Love
Arbitron Metro Market: San Angelo, TX *Format:* Christian *No. News Employees:* 13
Darrell Chambliss, Chairman
Mike Novak, President and CEO
Eric Allen, General Sales Mgr
David Pierce, Chief Creative Officer and Programming Director
Ed Lenane, News Director
Sam Wallington, Engineering Dir
Marya Morgan, NewsReporter
Richard Hunt, News Reporter
Alan Mason, Chief Operating Officer
Dan Antonelli, Chief Business Development Officer
Eric Moser, Chief Financial Officer
Brian Burger, Vice President of Human Resources

Caldwell

KAPN
01-01-2002; 107.3 mhz FM *Hrs Open:* 24; 6 kw; 328 ft.; N30 33 31 W96 34 50
P.O. Box 948, Houston, TX 77001 US
(979) 776-1240, *Fax:* (979) 776-0123
License: Caldwell, Burleson County, TX held by Brazos Valley Communications Ltd.
Group Owner: Brazos Valley Communications Ltd.; (acq 11-18-2008; $875,000)
Nat'l Reps: Katz Radio
Arbitron Metro Market: Bryan-College S *Format:* Adult Contemp *Special Programming:* Kidd Kraddick AM Show *Target Audience:* p18-34, p18-49
Dan Ginzel, Operations Dir
Chris Kiske, General Manager
Nathan Peacock, General Sales Mgr
Raquel Pena, Programming Director
Lance Parr, Chief Engineer

Callisburg

*KPFC
04-01-1998; 91.9 mhz FM *Hrs Open:* 24; 0.3 kw; 66 ft.; N33 40 11 W97 0 50
P O Box 918, Gainesville, TX 76241 US
(940) 665-2011, *Fax:* (940) 665-9467
www.kpfc.org
kpfc@gmail.com
License: Callisburg, Cooke County, TX held by Camp Sweeney.
Format: Contemporary Hits/Top 40
Dr. Ernie Fernandez, General Manager
Skip Rigsby, Programming Director

Cameron

KMIL
01-01-2002; 105.1 mhz FM; 15 kw; 328 ft.; N30 51 30 W97 1 47
P.O.Box 590209, Houston, TX 77259 US
(254) 697-6633, *Fax:* (254) 697-6330
www.kmil.com
kmil@kmil.com
License: Cameron, Milam County, TX held by Cameron Broadcasting Co.
Nat'l Network: CBS Radio
Format: Country *Special Programming:* Farm 5 hrs wkly *Hrs. of News Programming:* news progmg 5 hrs wkly
Rob Reed, Operations Dir
Clay Gish, General Manager
Bret Eberhart, Traffic Manager

KTAE
09-01-1955; 1330 khz AM; 0.5 kw-D, ND1; 0.097 kw-N, ND1; N30 50 48 W96 57 55
Mailing Address: P. O. Box 832, Cameron, TX 76520 US
Second Address: 901 E. First, Cameron, TX 76520
(254) 697-6633, *Fax:* (254) 697-6330
www.kmil.com
kmil@tlab.net
License: Cameron, TX held by Milam Broadcasting Co.
Nat'l Reps: Keystone (unwired net)
Format: Country *Special Programming:* Gospel 6 hrs, Czech 8 hrs wkly *Target Audience:* General.
Joe Smitherman, General Manager
Eric Haussecker, Programming Director
A.T. Sheffield, Disc Jockey
Nonito Martinez, A.T. Sheffield
Sarah Haussecker, Traffic Manager

Camp Wood

KAYG
01-01-2001; 99.1 mhz FM; 0.965 kw; 226 ft.; N29 42 53 W100 0 56
Mailing Address: P O Box 252, McAllen, TX 78505 US
Second Address: 4501 N. McCall Rd., McAllen, TX 78504
(956) 686-6382, *Fax:* (956) 686-2999
License: Camp Wood, Real County, TX held by La Radio Cristiana Network Inc.
Format: Christian
Paulino Bernal, President

Campbell

KRVA-FM
08-01-1969; 107.1 mhz FM; 3.6 kw; 423 ft.; N33 7 30 W95 44 32
1436 Auburn Boulevard, Sacramento, CA 95815 US
(817) 332-0959, *Fax:* (817) 348-8373
www.kfwr.com/#1
ContactUs@TheRanchRadio.com
License: Campbell, Hunt County, TX held by LKCM Radio Group L.P.
Group Owner: LKCM Radio Group L.P.; (acq 5-21-2004; $1 million with KRVF(FM) Kerens).
Arbitron Metro Market: Campbell, TX *Format:* Oldies *No. News Employees:* 2
Gerry Schlegel, President
Joel Gough, General Sales Mgr
Chuck Taylor, Programming Director
Molly Prince, Promotions Manager
Jane Wasson, News Director
Michael Margrave, Chief Engineer

Canton

KWJB
09-12-1963; 1510 khz AM *Hrs Open:* Sunrise-suset; 500 w-D; N32 41 02 W95 29 44
Box 868, Forney, TX 75103
(903) 567-5566, *Fax:* (903) 567-5567
info@krdh.com
License: Canton, Van Zandt County, TX held by RDH Land & Cattle Co. Inc.
Population Served: 50,000*Hrs. of News Programming:* News progmg 6 hrs wkly *Target Audience:* General. *Adv. Rates:* 15; 10; 10; na
Dee Cox, Operations Dir
Eric Jontra, General Manager

Canyon

KPUR-FM
01-12-1981; 107.1 mhz FM *Hrs Open:* 24; 6 kw; 315 ft.; N35 5 9 W101 54 48
111 East Kilbourn Ave., Suite 2700, Milwaukee, WI 53202 US
(806) 342-5200, *Fax:* (806) 342-5202
www.kpur107.com
rickmatchett@cumulus.com
License: Canyon, Randall County, TX held by Cumulus Licensing Corp.
Group Owner: Cumulus Media Inc.; (acq 5-98; $820,000 with KPUR(AM) Amarillo)
Arbitron Metro Market: Amarillo, TX *Format:* Country *Hrs. of News Programming:* news progmg 5 hrs wkly *No. News Employees:* 1 *Target Audience:* 35-55; boomers
Lewis W Dickey, Jr., Chairman
Lewis W Dickey, Jr., CEO/COO
Lewis W Dickey, Jr., President
Eric Stevens, Operations Dir
Jim Worthington, General Manager
Shannon Urton, General Sales Mgr
Shea White, Promotions Manager
J.P. Wolf,Chief Engineer

*KWTS
01-01-1971; 91.1 mhz FM *Hrs Open:* 24; 6 kw; 141 ft.; N34 59 22 W101 54 45
Wtamu Box 747, Canyon, TX 79016 US
(806) 651-2797, *Fax:* (806) 651-2818
www.wtamu.edu/kwts
kwtsgm@gmail.com
License: Canyon, Randall County, TX held by West Texas A & M University.
Arbitron Metro Market: Canyon, TX *Special Programming:* Class 4 hrs, jazz 3 hrs, Black 3 hrs, techo 5 hrs, acoustic 3 hrs, Britsh rock 3 hrs, Sp 3 hrs wkly *Hrs. of News Programming:* news progmg 3 hrs wkly *No. NewsEmployees:* 2 *Target Audience:* 16-25.
Dr. Leigh Browning, President
Tyler Sweeney, General Manager
Ricky Mariscal, Programming Director
Katie Perkins, News Director
Randy Ray, Engineering Dir
Dani Morton, Program Director
Alex Montoya, Marketing Director
WilsonLemieux, Music Director
Dani Morton, Production Director
Keltin Wiens, Sports Director

KZRK
05-08-1962; 1550 khz AM *Hrs Open:* 6 AM-6 PM; 1 kw-D, ND1; 0.219 kw-N, ND1; N34 58 54 W101 57 18
111 East Kilbourn Ave., Suite 2700, Milwaukee, WI 53202 US
(806) 342-5200, *Fax:* (806) 342-5202
rickmatchett@cumulus.com
License: Canyon, TX held by Cumulus Licensing Corp.
Group Owner: Cumulus Media Inc.
Arbitron Metro Market: Amarillo, TX *Format:* Sports, Talk *Adv. Rates:* 10; 10; 10; 8
Larry Boyd, General Manager
Chad Elliott, Programming Director
Jessica Leighman, Promotions Manager
Mel Williams, Chief Engineer

KZRK-FM
09-30-1985; 107.9 mhz FM *Hrs Open:* 24; 100 kw; 476 ft.; N35 13 36 W102 0 24
111 East Kilbourn Ave., Suite 2700, Milwaukee, WI 53202 US
(806) 342-5200, *Fax:* (806) 342-5202
amarillosrockstation.com/
chris.knight@cumulus.com,rick.matchett@cumulus.com
License: Canyon, Randall County, TX held by Cumulus Licensing Corp.
Group Owner: Cumulus Media Inc.; (acq 3-3-98; $1 million with co-located AM).
Nat'l Network: Westwood One *Nat'l Reps:* Roslin
Arbitron Metro Market: Amarillo, TX *Format:* Rock/AOR *Hrs. of News Programming:* news progmg 3 hrs wkly *No. News Employees:* 1 *Target Audience:* 18-34; general *Adv. Rates:* 35; 32; 35; 24
Eric Slayter, Operations Dir
Rick Matchett, General Manager
Stan Ross, General Sales Mgr
D'Lisa Pohnert, Promotions Manager
Matt Darby, News Director
J.P. Wolf, Chief Engineer
J. Curry, Assistant Music Director
Chris Collins,Music Director

Carrizo Springs

KBEN
08-09-1955; 1450 khz AM; 1 kw-U, ND1; N28 31 15 W99 51 30
Route 1, Box 168, Heritage Farms, Eagle Pass, TX 78852 US
(830) 876-3205
License: Carrizo Springs, TX held by Sylvia Mijares
Arbitron Metro Market: Carrizo Springs, TX *Format:* Religious *Target Audience:* English & Sp listeners.
Gordon Baehre, General Manager

*KCZO
01-01-1991; 92.1 mhz FM; 25 kw; 302 ft.; N28 33 24 W99 53 49
Mailing Address: 307 East Jackson, McAllen, TX 78501 US
Second Address: 4501 N. Mc Call Rd., McAllen, TX 78504
(956) 686-6382, *Fax:* (956) 686-2999
License: Carrizo Springs, Dimmit County, TX held by Paulino Bernal Evangelism.
Format: Christian
Eloy Bernal, General Manager

KAJP
01-01-2008; 93.5 mhz FM; 6 kw; 253 ft.; N28 30 32.3 W99 52 37 US
(202) 429-8970, *Fax:* (202) 293-7783
License: Carrizo Springs, Dimmit County, TX held by Hispanic Target Media Inc.
Group Owner: Hispanic Target Media Inc.
Arbitron Metro Market: Carrizo Springs, TX *Format:* Tejano
Francisco San Millan, President
Meredith Senter, General Manager

Carrollton

KJON
12-17-1970; 850 khz AM
115 West Broadway, P.O. Box 1360, Anadarko, OK 73005 US
(817) 923-3424, *Fax:* (817) 923-3451
info@kjonam.com
License: Carrollton, TX held by Chatham Hill Foundation Inc.
Arbitron Metro Market: Dallas, TX *Format:* Spanish, Christian
Bob Prouse, General Manager

Carthage

KGAS
10-01-1955; 1590 khz AM; 2.5 kw-D, ND1; 0.128 kw-N, ND1; N32 9 12 W94 18 52
226 South Shelby, Carthage, TX 75633 US
(903) 693-6668, *Fax:* (903) 693-7188
www.kgasradio.com
info@kgasradio.com
License: Carthage, TX held by Jerry T. Hanszen
Regional Network: Texas State Networks *Wire Services:* NOAA Weather
Arbitron Metro Market: Carthage, TX *Format:* Sports *Hrs. of News Programming:* News 20 hrs wkly *Target Audience:* General.
Jerry T. Hanszen, CEO/COO
Jerry Hanszen, General Manager
Melissa Ruffner, Station Manager

KGAS-FM
08-01-1992; 104.3 mhz FM; 6 kw; 328 ft.; N32 8 33 W94 25 39
226 South Shelby, Carthage, TX 75633 US
(903) 693-6668, *Fax:* (903) 693-7188
www.kgasradio.com
info@kgasradio.com
License: Carthage, Panola County, TX held by Jerry T. Hanszen.
Nat'l Network: ABC; Westwood One
Arbitron Metro Market: Carthage, TX *Format:* Country *Target Audience:* General.
Jerry T. Hanszen, CEO/COO
Jerry Hanszen, General Manager
Melissa Ruffner, Station Manager

KTUX
04-01-1985; 98.9 mhz FM *Hrs Open:* 24; 100 kw; 719 ft.; N32 23 19 W94 1 10
5005 W. Monkhouse, Shreveport, LA 71109 US
(318) 688-1130, *Fax:* (318) 688-9839
www.therockstation99x.com
PaulCannell@townsquaremedia.com
License: Carthage, Panola County, TX held by GAP Broadcasting Shreveport License LLC.
Group Owner: GAP Broadcasting LLC; (acq 8-3-2007; grpsl)
Arbitron Metro Market: Shreveport, LA *Format:* Rock/AOR *Target Audience:* 18-49; super-active adults
Lisa Janes, General Manager
Casey Ryan, Director of Sales
Paul Cannell, Brand Manager

Cedar Park

KGSR
08-01-1961; 93.3 mhz FM; 100 kw; Ant 1,948 ft; N30 43 34 W97 59 23
8309 N. I-35, Austin, TX 78761
(512) 832-4000, *Fax:* (512) 832-4081
www.kxmg.com
info@590klbj.com
License: Cedar Park, Williamson County, TX held by Emmis Austin Radio Broadcasting Co. L.P.
Group Owner: Emmis Communications Corp.; (acq 4-25-03; grpsl).
Population Served: 2,000,000 *Arbitron Metro Market:* Austin, TX *Special Programming:* Pub service 2 hrs, Sp one hr, Latino one hr wkly *Target Audience:* 18-34; women & men who like current music
Jeff Carrol, Operations Dir
Bruce Walden, General Manager
Brad Copland, General Sales Mgr
Bob Lewis, Programming Director
Todd Jeffries, News Director
Jim Henkel, Chief Engineer
Bradley Grein, Music Director
Lisa Melton,Traffic Manager

Center

KDET
02-22-1949; 930 khz AM; 1 kw-D, 36 w-N; N31 50 03 W94 12 53
Box 930, 307 San Augustine St., Center, TX 75935
(936) 598-3304, *Fax:* (936) 598-9537
License: Center, Shelby County, TX held by Center Broadcasting Co. Inc.
Group Owner: Center Broadcasting Co. Inc.; (acq 3-26-98; grpsl)
Regional Network: Texas State Networks *Nat'l Reps:* Riley
Population Served: 29,000
Lori Alvis, Station Manager
Lori Alvis, General Sales Mgr
Tracy Broadway, Programming Director
J J Lyons, News Director
Broadcast Works, Engineering Dir
Rob Rockett, Operations Manager

KQBB
07-05-1978; 100.5 mhz FM; 2.05 kw; Ant 567 ft; N31 43 34 W94 15 27
Mailing Address: Box 930, Center, TX 75766
Second Address: 307 San Augustine St., Center, TX 75935
(936) 598-3304, *Fax:* (936) 598-9537
License: Center, Shelby County, TX held by Center Broadcasting Co. Inc.
Group Owner: Center Broadcasting Co. Inc.
Target Audience: Shelby County
Barbara Harding, Operations Dir
Lori Alvis, General Manager
Rachel Shanz, News Director
Rob Rockett, Operations Manager

Centerville

***KUZN**
01-01-2001; 105.9 mhz FM *Hrs Open:* 24; 25 kw; 328 ft.; N31 16 56 W95 53 42
9279 Dutch Hill Road, West Valley, NY 14171 US
(509) 242-2400
www.hit961.com
michaellacrosse@clearchannel.com
License: Centerville, Leon County, TX held by Aleluya Christian Broadcasting Inc.
Group Owner: Aleluya Christian Broadcasting Inc.; (acq 2-26-2008)
Arbitron Metro Market: Spokane, WA *Format:* Religious
Ruben Villarreul, General Manager

Charlotte

KSAQ
102.3 mhz FM; 6 kw; 148 ft.; N28 45 47 W98 42 0 US
(772) 215-1634
License: Charlotte, Atascosa County, TX held by Gary S. Hess
Arbitron Metro Market: Charlotte, TX
Gary Hess, General Manager

Childress

KCTX
05-08-1947; 1510 khz AM *Hrs Open:* 6:30 AM-6 PM; 0.25 kw-D, NDD; N34 25 41 W100 13 47
Mailing Address: 1511 Ave. F, N. W., Childress, TX 79201 US
Second Address: 1111 16th St. N.W., Childress, TX 79201
(940) 937-6316, *Fax:* (940) 937-6551
www.kctxradi.com
kctxradio@gmail.com
License: Childress, TX held by James G. Boles
Format: Oldies
James Boles, General Manager
Chao Ware, General Sales Mgr
J. Scott, Programming Director
Mona Boles, News Director

KCTX-FM
07-01-1984; 96.1 mhz FM; 50 kw; 476 ft.; N34 26 20 W100 13 10
Mailing Address: 1511 Ave F. NW - Pob 5, Childress, TX 79201 US
Second Address: 1111 16th St. N.W., Childress, TX 79201
(940) 937-6316, *Fax:* (940) 937-6551
www.kctx.com
kctxradio@gmail.com
License: Childress, Childress County, TX held by James G. Boles
Nat'l Reps: Riley
Arbitron Metro Market: Childress, TX *Format:* Country *Special Programming:* Relg 5 hrs wkly *Target Audience:* General.
James Boles, General Manager
Chad Ware, General Sales Mgr
J. Scott, Programming Director

KCHT
104.1 mhz FM; 1 kw; 459 ft.; N34 26 30 W100 14 16 US
(571) 228-1258, *Fax:* (703) 299-6626
License: Childress, Childress County, TX held by Miriam Media Inc.
Group Owner: Miriam Media Inc.
Arbitron Metro Market: Childress, TX
Darryl Delawder, President

Clarendon

KEFH
09-01-2000; 99.3 mhz FM *Hrs Open:* 24; 44 kw; 522 ft.; N35 4 36 W100 53 33
P.O. Box 370, 207 South Sully Street, Clarendon, TX 79226 US
(806) 874-2296, *Fax:* (806) 874-4411
www.kool993.net
kefh@ka1993.net
License: Clarendon, Donley County, TX held by RoHo Broadcasting Co.
Arbitron Metro Market: Claredon, TX *Format:* Oldies
Ken Meinhart, General Manager
Carol Hinton, Station Manager
Patrick Robertson, General Sales Mgr
Carol Hinton, News Director
John Wolfe, Chief Engineer

Clarksville

KCAR
04-27-1956; 1350 khz AM *Hrs Open:* 24; 0.41 kw-D, ND1; 0.065 kw-N, ND1; N33 36 47 W95 1 3
P.O. Box 609, Clarksville, TX 75426 US
(903) 427-3861, *Fax:* (903) 427-5524
kool985@@neato.net
License: Clarksville, TX held by American Media Investments Inc.
Group Owner: American Media Investments Inc.; (acq 2-17-2009; grpsl)
Nat'l Network: Jones Radio Networks *Regional Network:* Texas State Networks
Arbitron Metro Market: Paris, TX *Format:* Country *Special Programming:* Gospel 6 hrs, sports 10 hrs, farm 2 hrs wkly *Hrs. of News Programming:* News progmg 10 hrs wkly *Target Audience:* General; rural,agricultural, middle-aged *Adv. Rates:* 25; 25; 25; 10
Tex Phillips, General Manager
Mike Monday, Programming Director
Dale Gorsuch, Chief Engineer

KGAP
12-11-1990; 98.5 mhz FM *Hrs Open:* 24; 50 kw; 308 ft.; N33 36 47 W95 1 3
P. O. Box 609, Clarksville, TX 75426 US
(903) 793-1109, *Fax:* (903) 794-4717
kool985@neato.net
License: Clarksville, Red River County, TX held by American Media Investments Inc.
Group Owner: American Media Investments Inc.; (acq 2-17-2009; grpsl)
Nat'l Network: ABC
Arbitron Metro Market: Clarksville, TX *Format:* Oldies *Hrs. of News Programming:* News progmg one hr wkly *Target Audience:* 25-64.

Claude

KARX
04-12-1992; 95.7 mhz FM *Hrs Open:* 24; 100 kw; 390 ft.; N35 6 16 W101 39 28
111 East Kilbourn Ave., Suite 2700, Milwaukee, WI 53202 US
(806) 342-5200, *Fax:* (806) 342-5202
www.957thekar.com
chris.matchett@cumulus.com
License: Claude, Armstrong County, TX held by Cumulus Licensing Corp.
Group Owner: Cumulus Media Inc.; (acq 2-2-98; $675,000).
Arbitron Metro Market: Amarillo, TX *Format:* Classic Rock *Hrs. of News Programming:* news progmg 10 hrs wkly *No. News Employees:* 1 *Target Audience:* 25-54; male *Adv. Rates:* 45; 50; 48; 34
Jim Worthington, General Manager
Stan Ross, General Sales Mgr
Eric Slayter, Programming Director
Shea White, Promotions Manager

Matt Darby, News Director
J.P. Wolf, Chief Engineer
Dale Miller, Music Director
Shannon Urton,Sales

Cleburne

KHFX
04-01-1947; 1140 khz AM *Hrs Open:* 24
Mailing Address: P.O. Box 1629, Cleburne, TX 76033 US
Second Address: 305 Milsap Hwy., Mineral Wells, TX 76067
(817) 645-1140, *Fax:* (817) 645-3944
info@kcleam.com
License: Cleburne, TX held by Siga Broadcasting Corp.
Group Owner: SIGA Broadcasting Corp.; (acq 9-24-2008; $1.4 million)
Arbitron Metro Market: Dallas-Fort Worth, TX *Format:* Country
Gabriel Arango, President

Cleveland

KTHT
01-17-1993; 97.1 mhz FM; 100 kw; 1847 ft.; N30 32 6 W95 1 4
50 East Rivercenter Blvd., Suite 1200, Covington, KY 41011 US
(713) 622-5533, *Fax:* (713) 993-9300
www.countrylegends971.com
License: Cleveland, Liberty County, TX held by Cox Radio Inc.
Group Owner: Cox Radio Inc.; (acq 8-15-2000; grpsl)
Arbitron Metro Market: Houston, TX *Format:* Country
Caroline Devine, General Manager
Judy Lakin, General Sales Mgr
John Chaing, Programming Director
Ed Wilson, Engineering Dir

Clifton

KWOW
01-01-1989; 104.1 mhz FM *Hrs Open:* 24; 21 kw; 470 ft.; N31 44 11 W97 19 27
919 N. Main, 91, Cleburne, TX 76033 US
(254) 772-6104, *Fax:* (254) 772-0642
www.laley104.com
License: Clifton, Bosque County, TX held by BMP Waco License Company L.P.
Group Owner: Border Media Partners LLC; (acq 11-9-2004; grpsl).
Nat'l Reps: Lotus Entravision Reps LLC
Arbitron Metro Market: Waco, TX *Format:* Spanish *Target Audience:* 18-54; adults *Adv. Rates:* 50 40; 50; 20
Bob Proud, Operations Dir
Jaime Martinez, Programming Director
Darrel Heckendorf, Chief Engineer
Cynthia Lopez, Operations Manager

Coahoma

KXCS(FM)
01-01-2006; 105.5 mhz FM; 5.1 kw; Ant 358 ft; N32 21 52 W101 19 35 *Rebroadcasts:* Rebroadcasts KSRD(FM) Saint Joseph, MO 100%
c/o KSRD(FM), 1212 Faraon St., Coahoma, TX 64501
(816) 233-5773, *Fax:* (816) 233-5777
www.ksrdradio.com
License: Coahoma, Howard County, TX held by Weeks Broadcasting Inc
Group Owner: Horizon Christian Fellowship; (acq 2-9-2006; grpsl)
Population Served: 820 *Arbitron Metro Market:* Coahoma, TX *Format:* Christian
Mike MacIntosh, President
Brian Jones, General Manager

Cockrell Hill

KRVA
09-29-1947; 1600 khz AM *Hrs Open:* 24
1436 Auburn Boulevard, Sacramento, CA 95815 US
License: Cockrell Hill, TX held by Mortenson Broadcasting Co. of Texas Inc.
Group Owner: Mortenson Broadcasting Co.; (acq 8-30-2004; $3.5 million)
Arbitron Metro Market: Dallas-Fort Worth *Format:* Ethnic
Rehan Siddiqi, General Manager
Naheed Raheel, Programming Director

Coleman

KSTA
11-01-1947; 1000 khz AM; 0.25 kw-D, NDD; N31 51 16 W99 25 36
One Texas Avenue, Brownwood, TX 76801 US
(325) 646-3535, *Fax:* (325) 646-5347
www.wendleebroadcasting.com/ksta-country-1000-the-voice-of-colemann-county/
ksta1000@web-access.net
License: Coleman, TX held by Tackett-Boazman Broadcasting LP.
Group Owner: Tackett-Boazman Broadcasting LP; (acq 4-11-2006; grpsl).
Nat'l Network: Jones Radio Networks *Regional Network:* Texas State Networks
Arbitron Metro Market: Brownwood, TX *Format:* Country *Special Programming:* Farm 14 hrs, Sp 5 hrs, gospel 7 hrs wkly *Target Audience:* General.
Jesse Jones, Operations Dir
Rex Tackett, General Manager
Joe Havnes, Station Manager
Mariann Tackett, General Sales Mgr
Stan Cooper, Chief Engineer

KXYL-FM
09-01-1965; 102.3 mhz FM *Hrs Open:* 24; 12 kw; 689 ft.; N31 44 54 W99 19 57
One Texas Avenue, Brownwood, TX 76801 US
(325) 646-3535, *Fax:* (325) 646-5347
www.wendleebroadcasting.com
ksta1000@web-access.net
License: Coleman, Brown County, TX held by Tackett-Boazman Broadcasting LP
Group Owner: Tackett-Boazman Broadcasting LP; (acq 4-11-2006; grpsl).
Nat'l Network: ABC
Arbitron Metro Market: Brownwood, TX *Format:* News, News/Talk, 86 *No. News Employees:* 3 *Target Audience:* 18+. *Adv. Rates:* 15; 12; 15; 10
Jesse Jones, Operations Manager/ Engineer
Rex Tackett, General Manager
Mariann Tackett, General Sales Mgr
Kyle Dennis, News Director
Stan Cooper, Chief Engineer
Cheryl Buse, Offive/ Traffic Manager
Mark Cope, Producer

College Station

***KAMU-FM**
03-30-1977; 90.9 mhz FM *Hrs Open:* 6 AM-midnight; 2.4 kw horiz, 32 kw vert; 341 ft.; N30 37 47 W96 20 33
Houston & Russell Street, College Station, TX 77843 US
(979) 845-5611, *Fax:* (979) 845-1643
kamu.publicbroadcasting.net
kamu@tamu.edu
License: College Station, Brazos County, TX held by Texas A&M University.
Nat'l Network: NPR; PRI
Arbitron Metro Market: College Station, TX *Format:* Jazz, News *Special Programming:* Folk 3 hrs, new age 5 hrs, international 5 hrs wkl *Hrs. of News Programming:* News progmg 35 hrs wkly *Target Audience:* General.
Rodney Zent, General Manager
Penny Zent, Station Manager
Elaine Hoyak, General Sales Mgr
Richard Howard, Programming Director
Yildiz McNew, News Director
Ken Nelson, Engineering Dir
Ed Hadden, Chief Engineer

WTAW
05-01-2000; 1620 khz AM
Mailing Address: PO Box 3248, Bryan, TX 77805 US
Second Address: 2700 Rudder Fwy., Suite 5000, College Station, TX 77845
(979) 695-9595, *Fax:* (979) 846-1933
www.wtaw.com
news@wtaw.com
License: College Station, TX held by Bryan Broadcasting Corp.
Group Owner: Bryan Broadcasting Corp.
Arbitron Metro Market: Bryan, TX *Format:* News, News/Talk, 86
Benjamin Downs, General Manager
Sam Jones, General Sales Mgr
Scott Delucia, Programming Director
Alisa Dusterhoff, News Director
Chris Dusterhoff, Chief Engineer

***KEOS**
03-25-1995; 89.1 mhz FM *Hrs Open:* 24; 100 w vert; 254 ft; N30 38 54 W96 23 23
Mailing Address: Box 78, College Station, TX 77841
Second Address: 202 E. Carson St., Bryan, TX 77801-1404
(979) 779-5367, *Fax:* (979) 779-7259
www.keos.org
keos@keos.org
License: College Station, Brazos County, TX held by Brazos Educational Radio.
Nat'l Network: PRI
Population Served: 130,000 *Arbitron Metro Market:* Bryan-College Station, TX *Special Programming:* Folk 10 hrs, gospel 3 hrs, jazz 3 hrs, Jewish & Israeli 2 hrs wkly *Hrs. of News Programming:* News progmg 25 hrs wkly*Target Audience:* General.
Jeff Cooper, Operations Dir
Steve Schlemmer, News Director
Lance Parr, Chief Engineer
John Roths, Music Director
George Weber, Public Affairs Director

KNDE
08-08-1964; 95.1 mhz FM; 38 kw; 561 ft.; N30 41 15 W96 25 32
2700 East Bypass, #5000, College Station, TX 77845 US
(979) 846-1150, *Fax:* (979) 846-1933
www.candy95.com
radio@wtaw.com
License: College Station, Brazos County, TX
Group Owner: Bryan Broadcasting Corp.
Arbitron Metro Market: College Station, TX *Format:* Contemporary Hits/Top 40
Sam Jones, General Sales Mgr
Tucker Young, Programming Director
Patrick Zeinert, Web Coordinator

KZNE
10-02-1922; 1150 khz AM *Hrs Open:* 24
2700 East Bypass, #5000, College Station, TX 77845 US
(979) 846-1150, *Fax:* (979) 846-1933
www.kzne.com
radio@wtaw.com
License: College Station, TX held by Bryan Broadcasting Corp.
Group Owner: Bryan Broadcasting Corp.; acq 8-7-97; with co-located FM).
Arbitron Metro Market: Bryan-College Station, TX *Format:* Sports *Special Programming:* Farm 10 hrs wkly *Hrs. of News Programming:* news progmg 58 hrs wkly *No. News Employees:* 3 *Target Audience:* 25-54.
William Hicks, President
Benjamin Downs, General Manager
Sam Jones, General Sales Mgr
Louie Belina, Programming Director
Chace Murphy, News Director

***KLGS**
01-01-2007; 89.9 mhz FM; 8.4 kw vert; 358 ft.; N30 28 35 W96 25 57 *Rebroadcasts:* Rebroadcasts WAFR(FM) Tupelo, MS 100%
P O Box 106, Roaring Springs, PA 16673 US
(662) 844-5036, *Fax:* (662) 842-6791
www.afr.net
contact@afa.net
License: College Station, Brazos County, TX held by American Family Association.
Group Owner: American Family Radio; (acq 1-3-2006; $10 for CP)
Arbitron Metro Market: College Station, TX *Format:* Christian
Donald E. Wildmon, Founder
Buster Wilson, General Manager
Jennifer Hagman, Programming Director

Colorado City

KAUM
03-29-1983; 107.1 mhz FM; 3 kw; 157 ft.; N32 23 15 W100 53 33
P. O. Box 990, Colorado City, TX 79512 US
(325) 728-5224, *Fax:* (325) 728-5224
License: Colorado City, Mitchell County, TX
Arbitron Metro Market: CO City, TX *Format:* Country
Jim Baum, General Manager

KVMC
06-16-1950; 1320 khz AM; 1 kw-D, NDD; N32 23 15 W100 53 33
PO Box 990, Colorado City, TX 79512 US
(325) 728-5530, *Fax:* (325) 728-5224
www.kvmckaum.blogspot.com
License: Colorado City, TX held by James G. Baum
Regional Network: Texas State Networks
Arbitron Metro Market: Colorado City, TX *Format:* Country
Jim Baum, General Manager
Gary Graham, Chief Engineer

Columbus

KULM-FM
09-03-1973; 98.3 mhz FM *Hrs Open:* 24; 6 kw; 253 ft.; N29 42 3 W96 34 24

RADIO - U.S.

Mailing Address: 2402 Broadmoor, Bldg D-2, Suite 101, Bryan, TX 77802 US
Second Address: 325 Radio Ln., Columbus, TX 78934
(979) 732-5766, *Fax:* (979) 732-6377
www.kulmradio.com
kulmradio@aol.com
License: Columbus, Colorado County, TX held by Roy E. Henderson.
Group Owner: Fort Bend Broadcasting Co.; (acq 5-16-2000; grpsl)
Nat'l Network: ABC *Regional Network:* Texas State Networks
Arbitron Metro Market: Columbus, TX *Format:* Country *Special Programming:* Polka 12 hrs wkly *Hrs. of News Programming:* News progmg 12 hrs wkly *Target Audience:* General. *Adv. Rates:* 12.50; 12.50; 12.50;12.50
Steve Smith, CFO
Roy Henderson, President
Carl Geisler, Station Manager
Judy Barrett, News Director
Ray Nelson, Chief Engineer

Comanche

KCOM
04-01-1962; 1550 khz AM *Hrs Open:* 24; 0.25 kw-D, ND1; 0.054 kw-N, ND1; N31 53 54 W98 35 14
105 North Sand St., Comanche, TX 76442 US
(325) 356-2558, *Fax:* (325) 356-3120
www.kcomam.com
kcom@comanchetx.com
License: Comanche, TX held by CCR-Stephenville III LLC.
Group Owner: Cherry Creek Radio LLC; (acq 8-2-2005; $164,000).
Regional Network: Texas State Networks
Arbitron Metro Market: Comanche, TX *Format:* Country, Gospel *Special Programming:* Gospel 5 hrs wkly *Target Audience:* 35-64; Men & Women *Adv. Rates:* 8; 8; 8; 8
Joseph Schwartz, President
Marcus Nettleton, General Manager
John Barnes, General Sales Mgr
Peggy Vineyard, Programming Director
Stan Cooper, Chief Engineer
Bill Cole, Disc Jockey

KYOX
03-01-1999; 94.3 mhz FM; 32 kw; 620 ft.; N31 54 51 W98 41 48
P.O. Box 289, Stephenville, TX 76401 US
(325) 356-3090, *Fax:* (325) 356-3120
www.kyoxfm.com
943theox@gmail.com
License: Comanche, Comanche County, TX held by CCR-Stephenville III LLC.
Group Owner: Cherry Creek Radio LLC; (acq 6-10-2004; grpsl).
Arbitron Metro Market: Comanche, TX *Format:* Country *Target Audience:* 35-64; men & women
Richard Niblett, General Manager
Pam Niblett, Programming Director
Justin McClure, Chief Engineer
Jerri Lynn Robinson, Music Director

Comfort

KGSX
02-26-1994; 95.1 mhz FM *Hrs Open:* 24; 100 kw; 659 ft.; N29 38 3 W98 47 57.8
1216-A Sidney Baker, Kervile, TX 78028 US
(210) 829-1075
www.lakalle951.univision.com
License: Comfort, Kendall County, TX held by Univision Radio License Corp.
Group Owner: Univision Radio; (acq 9-22-2003; grpsl)
Arbitron Metro Market: San Antonio, TX *Format:* Spanish *Hrs. of News Programming:* news progmg 4 hrs wkly *No. News Employees:* 1 *Target Audience:* 25-54; average, middle income with small town & rural lifestyle
Mac Tichenor, President
Rick Thomas, Operations Dir
Dan Wilson, General Manager
Barbara Carreon, General Sales Mgr
Ramon Loo, Programming Director
Robert De La Garza, Promotions Manager
Brett Huggins, Engineering Dir

Commerce

*KETR
04-07-1975; 88.9 mhz FM *Hrs Open:* 24; 100 kw; 381 ft.; N33 14 17 W95 55 27
2600 S. Neal, P.O. Box 4504, Commerce, TX 75429 US
(903) 886-5848, *Fax:* (903) 886-5850
ketr.org
ketr@ketr.org
License: Commerce, Hunt County, TX held by Board of Regents Texas A&M University-Commerce.
Nat'l Network: NPR
Arbitron Metro Market: Commerce, TX *Format:* Adult Contemp, Jazz, 60 *Special Programming:* Bluegrass 3 hrs wkly *Hrs. of News Programming:* news progmg 7 hrs wkly *No. News Employees:* 1 *Target Audience:* 21-66; general *Adv. Rates:* 11; 10; 11; 10
Jerrod Knight, General Manager
Beverly Nanos, General Sales Mgr
Kevin Jeffries, News Director
Robert Goodwin, Chief Engineer
Deborah Smith, Administrative Assistant
Brad Kellar, News Reporter
Deborah Smith, Traffic Manager

*KYJC
01-01-2005; 91.3 mhz FM; 0.35 kw horiz; 175 ft.; N33 15 37 W95 52 59
US
(800) 357-4226, *Fax:* (208) 736-1958
www.csnradio.com
csn@csnradio.com
License: Commerce, Hunt County, TX held by CSN International Inc.
Group Owner: CSN International; (acq 3-6-2003).
Arbitron Metro Market: Kasilof, AK *Format:* Christian, Gospel
Mike Kestler, President
Daniel Davidson, Operations Dir
Mike Stocklin, General Manager
Don Mills, Network Programming Director / Music Director
Kelly Carlson, Engineering Dir
Jerry Johnson, Engineering Dir
Ray Gorney, AssistantDirector of Engineering
Dustin Pamplona, Engineer
Nolan Mather, Graphics / Website Maintenance
Mike Stocklin, National Underwriting
Austin Morris, Accounting
Lois Mills, FCC Applications / Translator Site Manager

Conroe

*KAFR
10-01-1998; 88.3 mhz FM; 100 kw vert; 443 ft.; N30 27 52 W95 30 20
P O Drawer 2440, Tupelo, MS 38803 US
(662) 844-8888, *Fax:* (662) 842-6791
www.afr.net
comments@afr.net
License: Conroe, Montgomery County, TX held by American Family Association.
Group Owner: American Family Radio
Arbitron Metro Market: Tupelo, MS *Format:* Christian, Religious
Marvin Sanders, General Manager

KYOK
04-13-1981; 1140 khz AM; 5 kw-D, DAD; N30 20 40 W95 27 32
3124 Tidwell Street, Houston, TX 77093 US
(936) 441-1140, *Fax:* (936) 788-1140
www.kyokradio.com
info@kyokradio.com
License: Conroe, TX held by Martin Broadcasting Inc.
Group Owner: Martin Broadcasting Inc.; (acq 2-10-92; $175,000;
Arbitron Metro Market: Houston, TX *Format:* Gospel *Target Audience:* 24-55.
Darrell Martin, President
Nicholas Martin, Station Manager
Roland Booker, General Sales Mgr
Dave Biondi, Chief Engineer

KJOZ
04-16-1951; 880 khz AM; 10 kw-D, 1 kw-N, DA-2; N30 17 38 W95 25 55
Little Saigon Radio, 7080 Southwest Fwy., Houston, TX 78216
(713) 271-7888, *Fax:* (713) 271-9333
www.littlesaigonradio.com
License: Conroe, Montgomery County, TX held by Liberman Broadcasting of Houston License LLC.
Group Owner: Liberman Broadcasting Inc.; (acq 3-20-2001; grpsl)
Arbitron Metro Market: Houston-Galveston
Winter Horton, General Manager

KHPT
02-14-1965; 106.9 mhz FM; 91.6 kw; 1900 ft.; N30 13 53 W95 7 26
4880 Santa Rosa Road, Suite 300, Camarillo, CA 93012 US
(713) 963-1200, *Fax:* (713) 622-5457
www.1069thepoint.com
License: Conroe, Montgomery County, TX held by Cox Radio Inc.
Group Owner: Cox Radio Inc.; (acq 8-24-2000; grpsl)
Arbitron Metro Market: Houston, TX *Format:* Oldies
Mark Krieschen, Operations Dir
Beth Lavine, General Sales Mgr
Dain Craig, Programming Director
Shana Sonnier, Promotions Manager
Mike Murray, National Sales Manager

Converse

KTMR
07-28-1980; 1130 khz AM
Good News Brdct. of Tx, 2702 Pine Street, Laredo, TX 78046 US
(713) 868-5559, *Fax:* (713) 868-9631
www.bizradio.com
docarango@houston.rr.com
License: Converse, TX held by SIGA Broadcasting Corp.
Group Owner: SIGA Broadcasting Corp.; (acq 5-4-99; $333,750)
Arbitron Metro Market: San Antonio, TX *Format:* Talk
Gabriel Arango, General Manager

Copperas Cove

KSSM
11-21-1977; 103.1 mhz FM *Hrs Open:* 24; 8.6 kw; 558 ft.; N31 5 5 W97 57 7
Post Office Box 607, Copperas Cove, TX 76522 US
(254) 773-5252, *Fax:* (254) 773-0115
www.1031kissfm.com
bourdon.wooter@cumulus.com
License: Copperas Cove, Coryell County, TX held by Cumulus Licensing Corp.
Group Owner: Cumulus Media Inc.; (acq 2-2-00)
Nat'l Reps: Interep
Arbitron Metro Market: Killeen-Temple, TX *Format:* Adult Contemp *Special Programming:* Gospel *Hrs. of News Programming:* News progmg 3 hrs wkly *Target Audience:* 25-54.
Bourdon Wooten, General Manager
Mikie Cummings, General Sales Mgr
Mark Raymond, Programming Director
Jamie Garrett, Promotions Manager
Doug Bernhardt, Engineering Dir
Lisa Tanne, Promotions Director

Corpus Christi

*KBNJ
01-01-1985; 91.7 mhz FM *Hrs Open:* 24; 6.1 kw; 554 ft.; N27 45 23 W97 36 25
Box 3765, McAllen, TX 78502 US
(361) 855-0975, *Fax:* (361) 855-0977
www.kbnj.org
kbnj@lwrn.org
License: Corpus Christi, Nueces County, TX held by World Radio Network Inc.
Group Owner: World Radio Network Inc.; acq 6-5-84; $36,000;
Nat'l Network: Moody; USA
Arbitron Metro Market: Corpus Christi, TX *Format:* Religious *Hrs. of News Programming:* News progmg 7 hrs wkly *Target Audience:* General.
Joe Fahl, General Manager
Jimmy Stinson, Chief Engineer

KBSO
01-01-1992; 94.7 mhz FM; 25 kw; 285 ft.; N27 49 50 W97 32 34
107 Lost Creek, Portland, TX 78374 US
(361) 289-0999
davilabroadcasti@bizstx.rr.com
License: Corpus Christi, Nueces County, TX held by Reina Broadcasting Inc.
Arbitron Metro Market: Corpus Christi, TX *Format:* Tejano
Manuel Davila Jr., General Manager

KCCT
06-01-1954; 1150 khz AM *Hrs Open:* 24; 1 kw-D, DA2; 0.5 kw-N, DA2; N27 48 1 W97 28 44
P.O. Box 5278, Corpus Christi, TX 78465 US
(361) 289-0999, *Fax:* (361) 289-0810
davilabroadcasti@bizstx.rr.com
License: Corpus Christi, TX held by Radio KCCT Inc.
Arbitron Metro Market: Corpus Christi, TX *Format:* Talk
Manuel Davila Jr., President
George Sanders, Chief Engineer

KCTA
10-24-1959; 1030 khz AM *Hrs Open:* Sunrise-sunset
1602 S. Brownlee, Corpus Christi, TX 78403 US
(361) 882-7711, *Fax:* (361) 882-3038
www.kctaradio.com
kcta@usawide.net
License: Corpus Christi, TX held by Broadcasting Corp. of the Southwest.

Nat'l Network: USA
Arbitron Metro Market: Corpus Christi, TX *Format:* Religious
Special Programming: Sp 6 hrs wkly *Target Audience:* 35 plus.
Adv. Rates: 12; 12; 12; 12
Bill York, President
David Freymiller, Operations Dir
Russell Vaughan, Chief Engineer

*KEDT-FM
03-02-1982; 90.3 mhz FM *Hrs Open:* 24; 100 kw; 801 ft.; N27 39 12 W97 33 55
4455 S Padre Island #38, Corpus Christi, TX 78411 US
(361) 855-2213, *Fax:* (361) 855-3877
www.kedt.org
info@kedt.pbs.org
License: Corpus Christi, Nueces County, TX held by South Texas Public Broadcasting System Inc.
Nat'l Network: NPR
Arbitron Metro Market: Corpus Christi, TX *Format:* Jazz, News
Special Programming: Sp 4 hrs wkly *Hrs. of News Programming:* news progmg 37 hrs wkly *No. News Employees:* 1 *Target Audience:* General.
Don Dunlap, President
Don Dunlap, General Manager
Bob Scott, Programming Director
Shane Barker, News Director
Bob Scott, Engineering Dir
Myra Lombardo, Vice President

KEYS
03-01-1941; 1440 khz AM *Hrs Open:* 24; 1 kw-D, DAN; 1 kw-N, DAN; N27 47 2 W97 27 29
Mailing Address: P.O. Box 9757, Corpus Christi, TX 78469 US
Second Address: 2117 Leopard St., Corpus Christi, TX 78408
(361) 883-3516, *Fax:* (361) 882-9767
www.1440keys.com
johngifford1440@yahoo.com
License: Corpus Christi, TX held by Malkan AM Associates L.P.
Group Owner: Malkan Broadcast Associates; (acq 1965).
Nat'l Network: ABC Information & Entertainment *Regional Network:* Texas State Networks *Nat'l Reps:* Katz Radio *Wire Services:* Accu-Weather
Arbitron Metro Market: Corpus Christi, TX *Format:* News, News/Talk, 84, Talk *No. News Employees:* 2 *Target Audience:* 25+ *Adv. Rates:* $35
Glen Powers, President
Janice Raleigh, Programming Director
John Gifford, Program Director
Nick Russo, Promotions Director

*KKLM
03-11-1991; 88.7 mhz FM *Hrs Open:* 24; 8 kw; 866 ft.; N27 44 29 W97 36 9 *Rebroadcasts:* Rebroadcasts KLVR(FM) Middletown, CA 100%
P.O. Box 1177, Corpus Christi, TX 78403 US
(916) 251-1600 (860) 434-8400, *Fax:* (916) 251-1650
www.klove.com
info@klove.com
License: Corpus Christi, Nueces County, TX held by Educational Media Foundation.
Group Owner: EMF Broadcasting; (acq 6-5-2002; $500,000)
Nat'l Network: K-Love
Arbitron Metro Market: Corpus Christi, TX *Format:* Christian *Hrs. of News Programming:* News progmg 10 hrs wkly *Target Audience:* 35 plus.
Darrell Chambliss, Chairman
Mike Novak, CEO/COO
Mike Novak, President

KLTG
09-01-1967; 96.5 mhz FM; 97 kw; 955 ft.; N27 44 28 W97 36 8
13625 Ponds Spring Road, #105, Austin, TX 78729 US
(361) 883-1600, *Fax:* (361) 888-5685
www.thebeach965fm.com
License: Corpus Christi, Nueces County, TX held by Tejas Broadcasting Ltd. LLP.
Group Owner: Tejas Broadcasting Ltd. LLP; (acq 11-15-2004; grpsl).
Arbitron Metro Market: Corpus Christi, TX *Format:* Adult Contemp *Target Audience:* 25-54.
Gloria Apolinario, Programming Director

KMXR
01-01-1970; 93.9 mhz FM *Hrs Open:* 24; 100 kw; 932 ft.; N27 45 7 W97 38 17
600 Congress Ave., Suite 1400, Austin, TX 78701 US
(361) 289-0111, *Fax:* (361) 289-5035
www.939online.com
oldies939@aol.com
License: Corpus Christi, Nueces County, TX held by Capstar TX L.P.
Group Owner: Clear Channel Communications Inc.; (acq 8-30-00; grpsl).
Nat'l Network: AP Radio
Arbitron Metro Market: Corpus Christi, TX *Format:* Oldies *Hrs. of News Programming:* news progmg 5 hrs wkly *No. News Employees:* 1 *Target Audience:* 25-54.
Matt Martin, General Manager

KKTX
01-01-2002; 1360 khz AM *Hrs Open:* 24; 1 kw-U, ND1; N27 48 1 W97 27 41
600 Congress Ave., Suite 1400, Austin, TX 78701 US
(361) 289-0111, *Fax:* (361) 289-5024
www.1360online.com
scottjohnson@clearchannel.com
License: Corpus Christi, TX held by Capstar TX L.P.
Group Owner: Clear Channel Communications Inc.
Nat'l Network: ABC
Arbitron Metro Market: Corpus Christi, TX *Format:* News, News/Talk, 86 *Target Audience:* 2-18; children
Matt Martrin, General Manager
Chris Aldrich, General Sales Mgr
Frank Edwards, Programming Director
Russell Vaughn, Chief Engineer

KRYS-FM
12-05-1982; 99.1 mhz FM *Hrs Open:* 24; 100 kw; 932 ft.; N27 45 7 W97 38 17
600 Congress Ave., Suite 1400, Austin, TX 78701 US
(361) 289-0111, *Fax:* (361) 289-5024
www.krysfm.com
info@krysfm.com
License: Corpus Christi, Nueces County, TX held by Capstar TX L.P.
Group Owner: Clear Channel Communications Inc.; (acq 8-30-00; grpsl).
Nat'l Network: ABC
Arbitron Metro Market: Corpus Christi, TX *Format:* Country *No. News Employees:* 1 *Target Audience:* 25-54.
Matt Martin, General Manager
Chris Aldrich, General Sales Mgr
Frank Edwards, Programming Director
Frank Edwards, Promotions Manager
Pamela Anaya, News Director
Russell Vaughn, Chief Engineer
Lou Ramirez, Music Director

KSIX
09-01-1947; 1230 khz AM *Hrs Open:* 24
PO Box Tv-10, 301 Artesian, Corpus Christi, TX 78403 US
(361) 882-5749, *Fax:* (361) 884-1240
www.espn1230ksix.com
info@espn1230ksix.com
License: Corpus Christi, TX held by Withers Family Texas Holding LP
Nat'l Network: ESPN Radio
Arbitron Metro Market: Corpus Christi, TX *Format:* Sports
Jim Withers, General Manager
Scott Howe, General Sales Mgr
Bill Doerner, Programming Director
Valerie Smith, News Director

KUNO
05-01-1950; 1400 khz AM *Hrs Open:* 24; 1 kw-D, ND1; 1 kw-N, ND1; N27 45 36 W97 26 14
600 Congress Ave., Suite 1400, Austin, TX 78701 US
(361) 289-0111, *Fax:* (361) 289-5035
www.1400kuno.com
John.Richards@clearchannel.com
License: Corpus Christi, TX held by Capstar TX L.P.
Group Owner: Clear Channel Communications Inc.; (acq 8-30-00; grpsl)
Arbitron Metro Market: Corpus Christi, TX *Hrs. of News Programming:* News progmg 17 hrs wkly *Target Audience:* 25-64.
Matt Martin, General Manager
Dan Pena, Programming Director
Jeff ""Hitman"" DeWitt, Webmaster

KZFM
12-07-1964; 95.5 mhz FM *Hrs Open:* 24; 100 kw; 991 ft.; N27 39 33 W97 34 12
Mailing Address: P.O. Box 9757, Corpus Christi, TX 78469 US
Second Address: 2117 Leopard St., Corpus Christi, TX 78408
(361) 883-3516, *Fax:* (361) 882-9767
www.hotz95.com
thechief@star94.net
License: Corpus Christi, Nueces County, TX held by Malkan FM Associates L.P.
Group Owner: Malkan Broadcast Associates; (acq 1976).
Nat'l Reps: Katz Radio
Arbitron Metro Market: Corpus Christi, TX *Format:* Contemporary Hits/Top 40 *Target Audience:* 18-34 *Adv. Rates:* 68; 68; 68; 68
Glen Powers, President
Janice Raleigh, Programming Director
John Gifford, Chief Engineer
Arlene Cordell, Music Director
Ed Ocanas, Program Director
Gino Flores, Promotions Director

Corrigan

KYTM
99.3 mhz FM; kw
US
License: Corrigan, Polk County, TX held by Tammy L. Pearce.
Arbitron Metro Market: Corrigan, TX
Tammy Pearce, General Manager

Corsicana

KAND
05-17-1937; 1340 khz AM *Hrs Open:* 24; 1 kw-U, ND1; N32 6 53 W96 27 47
Mailing Address: 1201 Third Ave #3600, Seattle, WA 98101 US
Second Address: Box 2998, Corsicana, TX 75151
(903) 874-7421, *Fax:* (903) 874-0789
www.kandradio.com
mail@kandradio.com
License: Corsicana, TX held by Yates Communications LLC
Regional Network: Texas State Networks
Arbitron Metro Market: Corsicana, TX *Format:* Talk *Hrs. of News Programming:* news progmg 25 hrs wkly *No. News Employees:* 1 *Target Audience:* General.
Brad Rivers, Operations Dir
Mike Taylor, General Manager
Mary Sikes, General Sales Mgr
Bob Belcher, Programming Director
Dick Aldama, News Director
Jim Wiggins, Chief Engineer

Crane

KMMZ
01-01-1995; 101.3 mhz FM *Hrs Open:* 24; 100 kw; 486 ft.; N31 41 2 W102 19 13
Mailing Address: 620 N. Grant, Ste 1013, Odessa, TX 79761 US
Second Address: 12200 W. I-20 E., Crane, TX 79711
(432) 563-2266, *Fax:* (432) 563-2288
traffic@lacaliente101.com
License: Crane, Crane County, TX held by Don L. Cook.
Arbitron Metro Market: Odessa, TX *Format:* Contemporary Hits/Top 40 *Target Audience:* 25-54. *Adv. Rates:* 15; 15; 15; 9
Don Cook, General Manager

KXOI
12-01-1959; 810 khz AM *Hrs Open:* 6 AM-midnight; 1 kw-D, DA1; 0.5 kw-N, DA1; N31 28 39 W102 20 24
P.O. Box 2344, Odessa, TX 79760 US
(432) 333-5061, *Fax:* (432) 333-6067
License: Crane, TX held by Hispanic Outreach Ministries Inc.
Target Audience: General.
Rev. Pedro Emiliano, President
Eli Emiliano, General Manager
Don Cook, Chief Engineer

Creedmoor

KZNX
12-08-1962; 1530 khz AM *Hrs Open:* Sunrise-sunset
1707 N. Mays Street, Round Rock, TX 78664 US
(512) 416-1100, *Fax:* (512) 314-7442
www.espnaustin.com
controlroom@espnaustin.com
License: Creedmoor, TX held by Simmons-Austin, LS LLC.
Group Owner: Simmons Media Group; (acq 6-2-2004; $2 million).
Nat'l Network: ESPN Radio; Westwood One
Arbitron Metro Market: Austin-Round Rock metro area *Format:* Sports, Talk *Hrs. of News Programming:* News progmg 63 hrs wkly *Target Audience:* 25-54; 51% male, 49% female *Adv. Rates:* 55; 40; 60; na
Jeff Wolf, Operations Dir
John Hiatt, General Sales Mgr
Erin Hogan, Programming Director
Lauren Guerra, Promotions Manager
Flavia Chen, News Director
Ben Rippy, Engineering Dir
J. Cole McClellan, Chief Engineer
Bob Proud, Sr.VP/Marketing Manager
Evan Chancey, Production Manager

Crockett

KBHT
11-15-1982; 93.5 mhz FM *Hrs Open:* 24; 50 kw; 479 ft.; N31 20 3 W95 47 13
304 East Houston, Crockett, TX 75835 US
(936) 544-9350, *Fax:* (936) 544-9695
License: Crockett, Houston County, TX held by Weston Entertainment L.P.
Group Owner: Weston Entertainment L.P.; (acq 10-4-2005; $1.43 million)
Arbitron Metro Market: Crockett, TX *Format:* Country *Special Programming:* Gospel 6 hrs wkly *No. News Employees:* 7
Target Audience: 25-54.
Dennis Goodman, General Manager
Jeri Sulewski, General Sales Mgr

KIVY
11-11-1949; 1290 khz AM *Hrs Open:* 24; 2.5 kw-D, ND1; 0.175 kw-N, ND1; N31 18 20 W95 27 6
P. O. Box 1109, Crockett, TX 75835 US
(936) 544-2171,(936) 544-KIVY, *Fax:* (936) 544-4891
www.kivy.com
leon@kivy.com
License: Crockett, TX held by Leon Hunt
Nat'l Network: ABC *Regional Network:* Texas State Networks
Format: Oldies *Target Audience:* General. *Adv. Rates:* 18; 16; 16; 12
Leon Hunt, President
Chester Leediker, Chief Engineer

KIVY-FM
06-01-1970; 92.7 mhz FM *Hrs Open:* 24; 50 kw; 492 ft.; N31 18 20 W95 27 6
P. O. Box 1109, Crockett, TX 75835 US
(936) 544-2171,(936) 544-5489, *Fax:* (936) 544-4891
www.kivy.com
leon@kivy.com
License: Crockett, Houston County, TX held by Leon Hunt.
Nat'l Network: ABC *Regional Network:* Texas State Networks
Format: Country
Bryan King, General Manager

***KCKT**
02-01-2003; 88.5 mhz FM; 0.25 kw; 161 ft.; N31 19 37 W95 28 26
88 Casey Jones Blvd, Jackson, TN 38305 US
(662) 844-8888, *Fax:* (662) 842-6791
www.afr.net
faq@afr.net
License: Crockett, Houston County, TX held by American Family Association.
Group Owner: American Family Radio; (acq 1-17-01).
Arbitron Metro Market: Tupelo, MS *Format:* Christian
Marvin Sanders, General Manager

Crystal Beach

KSTB
01-01-1996; 101.5 mhz FM *Hrs Open:* 24; 6 kw; 184 ft.; N29 30 7 W94 31 15
8229 Maryland Avenue, St. Louis, MO 63105 US
(409) 833-9421, *Fax:* (409) 833-9296
www.kayd.com
License: Crystal Beach, Galveston County, TX held by Cumulus Licensing Corp.
Group Owner: Cumulus Media Inc.; (acq 5-20-02; $2.5 million).
Nat'l Reps: Roslin
Arbitron Metro Market: Beaumont, TX *Format:* Country *Hrs. of News Programming:* news progmg 12 hrs wkly *No. News Employees:* 2 *Target Audience:* 18-49.
Jim West, Operations Dir
Rick Prusater, General Manager
Liz Ferguson, News Director
Greg Davis, Chief Engineer

Crystal City

KHER
09-05-1985; 94.3 mhz FM; 3 kw; 135 ft.; N28 39 57 W99 48 58
Rt. 1 Box 168, Heritage Farms, Eagle Pass, TX 78852 US
(210) 374-2803
kherfm@yahoo.com
License: Crystal City, Zavala County, TX held by Sylvia Mijares.
Regional Network: Texas State Networks
Format: News, News/Talk, 86 *Special Programming:* Relg 2 hrs wkly *Target Audience:* 18-54; 90% Hispanic, 10% non-minority
Sylvia Mijares, President
Rudy Gomez, General Sales Mgr
Marie Martinez, News Director
Charlie Schmele, Chief Engineer
Becky Reyes, Traffic Manager

Cuero

***KTLZ**
01-01-2003; 89.9 mhz FM *Hrs Open:* 24; 5 kw; 243 ft.; N29 2 23 W97 19 24
2702 Pine St., Laredo, TX 78046 US
(208) 733-3551, *Fax:* (208) 734-0674
www.edgewaterbroadcasting.com
License: Cuero, DeWitt County, TX held by Radio Assist Ministry Inc.
Arbitron Metro Market: Cuero, TX *Format:* Christian, Spanish
Ben Mccarron, Chief Operating Engineer
Clark Parrish, President & Technical Director
Robert L. Jackson, Head of Programming & Operations
Jim Long, General Manager
Steve Atkin, Promotions Manager
Diana Atkin, Vice President
EarlWilliamson, Secretary / Treasurer
John Devine, Director
Dennis Clounch, Director

Cypress

KYND
12-01-1991; 1520 khz AM; 2.6 kw-C, DAD; 3 kw-D, DAD; N30 0 37 W95 41 40 *Rebroadcasts:* Rebroadcasts KJOJ(AM) Conroe 100%
740 Voss Road, Houston, TX 77024 US
(281) 373-1520, *Fax:* (713) 271-9333
www.littlesaigonradio.com
radio@littlesaigonradio.com
License: Cypress, TX held by Matthew Provenzano.
Arbitron Metro Market: Houston TX *Format:* Ethnic, Vietnamese
Target Audience: General.
Matt Provenzano, CEO

Daingerfield

KNGR
08-01-1966; 1560 khz AM *Hrs Open:* 24
Box 497931, Garland, TX 75049 US
(903) 645-4325, *Fax:* (903) 645-4357
www.kingcountry.org
License: Daingerfield, TX held by Network Communications Co.
Arbitron Metro Market: Tyler-Longview, TX *Format:* Country *Hrs. of News Programming:* News progmg 3 hrs wkly *Adv. Rates:* 10; 10; 10; 10
Bob Wilson, General Manager
Glory Wilson, Programming Director

Dalhart

KXIT
01-01-1948; 1240 khz AM *Hrs Open:* 24; 1 kw-U, ND1; N36 5 45 W102 30 38
P. O. Box 1350, Dalhart, TX 79022 US
(806) 249-4747
www.kxit.com
kxit@kxit.net
License: Dalhart, TX held by Dalhart Radio Inc.
Regional Network: Texas State Networks
Format: Country *Special Programming:* Farm 7 hrs wkly
George Chambers, President
Jusin Bliss, Programming Director

KXIT-FM
01-01-1962; 96.3 mhz FM *Hrs Open:* 24; 100 kw; Ant 472 ft; N35 53 46 W102 23 03
Box 1359, Hwy. 385 N., Dalhart, TX 79022
(806) 249-4747
License: Dalhart, Dallam County, TX held by Radio Dalhart
Population Served: 12,500
George Chambers, General Manager

***KTDA**
01-01-2009; 91.7 mhz FM; 0.83 kw; 128 ft.; N36 3 20 W102 30 34 *Rebroadcasts:* Rebroadcasts WAFR(FM) Tupelo, MS 100%
P.O. Box 1452, Washington, DC 20013 US
(662) 844-5036, *Fax:* (662) 842-6791
www.afr.net
contact@afa.net
License: Dalhart, Dallam County, TX held by American Family Association.
Group Owner: American Family Radio; (acq 6-9-2006)
Nat'l Network: American Family Radio
Arbitron Metro Market: Dalhart, TX *Format:* Christian
Donald E. Wildmon, Founder
Buster Wilson, General Manager
Jennifer Hagman, Programming Director

Dallas

KBFB
01-01-1965; 97.9 mhz FM; 99 kw; 1883 ft.; N32 35 2 W96 57 48
650 Madison Ave, New York, NY 10022 US
(972) 331-5400, *Fax:* (972) 331-5560
www.thebeatdfw.com
thebeatdfw@radio-one.com
License: Dallas, Dallas County, TX held by Radio One Licenses LLC.
Group Owner: Radio One Inc.; (acq 2000; grpsl)..
Nat'l Reps: CBS Radio
Arbitron Metro Market: Dallas, TX *Format:* Urban Contemporary
Target Audience: 25-50.
Alfred Liggine, President
John Candelaria, Operations Dir
George Laughlin, General Manager
Shawn Nunn, General Sales Mgr
Tony Fields, Programming Director
Joe Libios, Promotions Manager
Rowena Montgomery, News Director
DonStevenson, Chief Engineer

***KCBI**
05-19-1976; 90.9 mhz FM *Hrs Open:* 24; 98 kw; 1509 ft.; N32 35 22 W96 58 10
P.O.Box 619000, Dallas, TX 75261 US
(817) 792-3800, *Fax:* (817) 277-9929
www.kcbi.org
kcbi@kcbi.org
License: Dallas, Dallas County, TX held by Criswell College.
Group Owner: Criswell Communications
Nat'l Network: AP Radio
Arbitron Metro Market: Arlington, TX *Format:* Christian, Religious
Hrs. of News Programming: news progmg 4 hrs wkly *No. News Employees:* 4 *Target Audience:* 35-54; Christian families
Royce Laycock, Chairman
Ronald Harris, CEO
Doug Price, Operations Dir
Todd Chatman, Station Manager
James Nance, General Sales Mgr
Marc Anderson, Programming Director
Troy Kriechbaum, Promotions Manager
L.B. Lyon, NewsDirector
Doug Watson, Engineering Dir
Heidi Graham, Sales Director

KDMX
01-01-1965; 102.9 mhz FM *Hrs Open:* 24; 100 kw; 1591 ft.; N32 34 54 W96 58 32
50 East Rivercenter Boulevard, Suite 1200, Covington, KY 41011 US
(214) 866-8000, *Fax:* (214) 866-8201
www.mix1029.com
info@kdmxfm.com
License: Dallas, Dallas County, TX held by Citicasters Licenses L.P.
Group Owner: Clear Channel Communications Inc.; (acq 5-4-99; grpsl)
Arbitron Metro Market: Dallas-Fort Worth *Format:* Adult Contemp
Hrs. of News Programming: News progmg 3 hrs wkly *Target Audience:* 25-49; upper income females
Pat McMahon, Operations Dir
J.D. Freeman, General Manager
Jeff Mitchell, General Sales Mgr
Rick O'Bryan, Programming Director
Steve Lee, Promotions Manager
Louis Sutton, Engineering Dir

KBXD
01-01-1952; 1480 khz AM *Hrs Open:* 24; 5 kw-D, 1.9 kw-N, DA-2; N32 39 42 W96 39 20
2221 E. Lamar Blvd., Suite 300, Arlington, TX 75219
(817) 695-0878, *Fax:* (817) 695-3505
License: Dallas, Dallas County, TX held by JCE Licenses LLC.
Group Owner: James Crystal Inc.; (acq 2-3-2006; swap in exchange for WORL(AM) Altamonte Springs, FL)
Nat'l Network: ESPN Deportes
Arbitron Metro Market: Dallas-Fort Worth
Peter Dits, General Manager

***KERA**
07-11-1974; 90.1 mhz FM; 100 kw; 1273 ft.; N32 34 43 W96 57 12
3000 Harry Hines Blvd., Dallas, TX 75201 US
(214) 871-1390, *Fax:* (214) 740-9369
www.kera.org
kerafm@kera.org
License: Dallas, Dallas County, TX held by North Texas Public Broadcasting.
Nat'l Network: NPR; PRI *Wire Services:* AP

Arbitron Metro Market: Dallas-Fort Worth *Format:* News, News/Talk, 86 *Hrs. of News Programming:* news progmg 80 hrs wkly *No. News Employees:* 5 *Target Audience:* 35-54; general
Barger Tygart, Chairman
Kevin Martin, COO
Jeff Luchsinger, Station Manager
Patricia Lyons, General Sales Mgr

KGGR
06-08-1947; 1040 khz AM
3270 Blazer Pkwy, Suite 101, Lexington, KY 40509 US
(972) 572-5447, *Fax:* (214) 330-6133
www.kggram.com
info@kggram.com
License: Dallas, TX held by MBC of Texas-KGGR Inc.
Group Owner: Mortenson Broadcasting Co.; (acq 5-1-96; $1.15 million)
Nat'l Network: American Urban
Arbitron Metro Market: Dallas-Fort Worth *Format:* Black, Talk, 74 *Special Programming:* Scripture 5 hrs wkly *Target Audience:* 18 plus.
Ann Arnold, General Manager
Christie Wafer, General Sales Mgr

KKDA-FM
06-08-1947; 104.5 mhz FM *Hrs Open:* 24; 99 kw; 1667 ft.; N32 35 19 W96 58 5
Mailing Address: P.O. Box 30860, Grand Prairie, TX 75247 US
Second Address: 621 N.W. 6th St., Grand Prairie, TX 75050
(972) 263-9911, *Fax:* (972) 558-0010
www.k104fm.com
staff@k104fm.com
License: Dallas, Dallas County, TX held by Service Broadcasting Group LLC.
Group Owner: Service Broadcasting Group LLC; (acq 5-76)
Nat'l Reps: Christal
Arbitron Metro Market: Dallas, TX *Format:* Urban Contemporary
Hymen Childs, President
Chuck Smith, General Manager
Skip Cheatham, Programming Director
Gary Wachter, Chief Engineer

KLIF
06-26-1922; 570 khz AM *Hrs Open:* 24; 5 kw-D, DA2; 5 kw-N, DA2; N32 56 40 W96 59 25
140 East Market Street, York, PA 17401 US
(214) 526-2400, *Fax:* (214) 520-4343
www.klif.com
kilf@klif.com
License: Dallas, TX held by KLIF Lico Inc.
Group Owner: Cumulus Media Partners LLC; (acq 12-15-89)
Nat'l Network: Fox News Radio
Arbitron Metro Market: Dallas, TX *Format:* News, News/Talk, 86 *Hrs. of News Programming:* news progmg 15 hrs wkly *No. News Employees:* 1 *Target Audience:* 25-54; men
Lew Dickey, CEO
Jeff Catlin, Operations Dir
Tyler Cox, General Manager
Vanessa Thill, Promotions Manager
John Dickey, COO

KFXR
01-01-1947; 1190 khz AM *Hrs Open:* 24; 50 kw-D, DA2; 5 kw-N, DA2; N32 47 10 W96 57 0; N32 53 57 W96 24 47
600 New Hampshire Ave, N.W. , Suite 1200, Washington, DC 20037 US
(214) 866-8000, *Fax:* (214) 866-8091
www.dfw1190am.com
License: Dallas, TX held by Capstar TX L.P.
Group Owner: Clear Channel Communications Inc.; (acq 3-27-2001; $16 million)
Nat'l Network: CNN Radio
Arbitron Metro Market: Dallas, TX *Format:* News *Target Audience:* 25-54; general
Mick Anselmo, President
Todd Kalman, General Sales Mgr
Chad Abbott, Programming Director
Jess Meyer, Chief Engineer

KLUV
01-01-1961; 98.7 mhz FM *Hrs Open:* 24; 99 kw; 1663 ft.; N32 35 19 W96 58 5
600 New Hampshire Ave NW, Suite 1200, Washington, DC 20037 US
(214) 525-7098, *Fax:* (866) 717-2214
www.kluv.com
info@kluv.com
License: Dallas, Dallas County, TX held by CBS Radio Partner I Inc.
Group Owner: CBS Radio; (acq 9-17-94; $51 million)
Arbitron Metro Market: Dallas, TX *Format:* Oldies *No. News Employees:* 2 *Target Audience:* 35-54.
Mel Karmazin, President
Kevin Cassidy, General Manager
John Phillips, General Sales Mgr
Jay Cresswell, Programming Director
Liz Balon, Promotions Manager
Kathy Jones, News Director
Bill Taylor, Chief Engineer
Julie Davis,Traffic Manager
Tony Bishop, Digital Sales Manager
Mark Sanders, National Sales Manager

*KNON
08-03-1983; 89.3 mhz FM *Hrs Open:* 24; 55 kw; 850 ft.; N32 35 24 W96 58 21
Mailing Address: 4415 San Jacinto, Dallas, TX 75204 US
Second Address: 5353 Maples Ave., Dallas, TX 75235
(214) 828-9500, *Fax:* (214) 823-3051
www.knon.org
License: Dallas, Dallas County, TX held by Agape Broadcasting Foundation Inc.
Arbitron Metro Market: Dallas, TX *Format:* Variety/Diverse *Target Audience:* General.
Dave Chaos, Station Manager
Christian Lee, Programming Director
Pamela Parker, News Director

KJKK
12-25-1965; 100.3 mhz FM; 97 kw; 1884 ft.; N32 35 2 W96 57 48
600 New Hampshire Ave NW, Suite 1200, Washington, DC 20037 US
(214) 525-7000, *Fax:* (214) 905-5052
www.jackontheweb.cbslocal.com
jack@cbsradio.com
License: Dallas, Dallas County, TX held by CBS Radio Partner I Inc.
Group Owner: CBS Radio; (acq 11-13-98; grpsl)
Nat'l Network: ABC *Nat'l Reps:* CBS Radio
Arbitron Metro Market: Dallas-Fort Worth Metroplex *Format:* Adult Contemp *Target Audience:* 18-49.
Mel Karmazin, CEO
Lori Dodd, Operations Dir
Dave Siebert, General Manager
Kevin Cassidy, General Sales Mgr
Jeff McMurray, Programming Director
Marci Parrish, Promotions Manager
Connie Pena, News Director
Bob Henke, ChiefEngineer
Joel Gough, General Sales Manager
Bethany Parks, Music Director

KRLD
10-01-1926; 1080 khz AM *Hrs Open:* 24; 50 kw-D, DAN; 50 kw-N, DAN; N32 53 25 W96 38 44
600 New Hampshire Avenue, NW, Suite 1200, Washington, DC 20037 US
(214) 525-7000, *Fax:* (214) 525-7370
www.dfw.cbslocal.com
License: Dallas, TX held by CBS Radio Partner I Inc.
Group Owner: CBS Radio
Regional Network: Texas State Networks *Nat'l Reps:* CBS Radio
Arbitron Metro Market: Dallas-Fort Wor *Format:* News *Special Programming:* Texas Rangers baseball *Hrs. of News Programming:* news progmg 119 hrs wkly *No. News Employees:* 35 *Target Audience:* 25-54.
Brian Purdy, Operations Dir
Bob Waterman, General Sales Mgr
Gavin Spittle, Programming Director
Eric Disen, Chief Engineer
Tom Bigby, Operations Director

KTCK
01-01-1920; 1310 khz AM *Hrs Open:* 24
140 East Market Street, York, PA 17401 US
(214) 526-7400, *Fax:* (214) 525-2525
www.theticket.com
License: Dallas, TX held by KRBE Lico Inc.
Group Owner: Cumulus Media Partners LLC; (acq 1996; $14 million)
Arbitron Metro Market: Dallas-Fort Worth *Format:* Sports, Talk *Target Audience:* 25-54; men & sport enthusiasts
Dan Bennett, Operations Dir
Dan Bennett, General Manager
Alec Drake, General Sales Mgr
Jeff Catlin, Programming Director
Marie Hopkins, Promotions Manager
Kimberly Jolly, News Director
Rob Chickering, Engineering Dir
MarkFriedman, Assistant Programming Director
Ken Roberts, General Sales Manager
Jami Williams, National Sales Manager
Jamey Garner, Promotions Director

KRLD-FM
04-05-1968; 105.3 mhz FM *Hrs Open:* 24; 97 kw; 1884 ft.; N32 35 2 W96 57 48
600 New Hampshire Ave., Suite 1200, Washington, DC 20037 US
(214) 525-7000, *Fax:* (214) 905-5052
www.dfw.cbslocal.com/station/1053-the-fan/
info@live1053.com
License: Dallas, Dallas County, TX held by CBS Radio Partner I Inc.
Group Owner: CBS Radio; (acq 11-13-98; grpsl)
Nat'l Network: Fox Sports *Nat'l Reps:* CBS Radio
Arbitron Metro Market: Dallas, TX *Format:* Sports *Target Audience:* 18-49; general
Mel Karmazin, CEO
Brian Purdy, General Manager
Steve Sullivan, General Sales Mgr
Gavin Spittle, Programming Director
Jeff Burkett, Promotions Manager
Susan Wade, News Director
Bob Henke, Chief Engineer
Lynn Sornsen, NationalSales Manager

KZPS
04-01-1948; 92.5 mhz FM *Hrs Open:* 24; 99 kw; 1667 ft.; N32 35 19 W96 58 5
Suite 1200, 15851 Dallas Pkwy, Dallas, TX 75248 US
(214) 866-8000
www.lonestar925.com/
dondavis@clearchannel.com
License: Dallas, Dallas County, TX held by AMFM Texas Licenses L.P.
Group Owner: Clear Channel Communications Inc.; (acq 8-30-2000; grpsl)
Arbitron Metro Market: Dallas, TX *Format:* Classic Rock *No. News Employees:* 1 *Target Audience:* 25-44; upscale young adults
Pat McMahon, Operations Dir
J.D. Freeman, General Manager
Kelly Kibler, General Sales Mgr
Don Davis, Programming Director
Steve Lee, Promotions Manager
Anna DeHaro, News Director
Louis Sutton, Chief Engineer
Tracy Martin,General Sales Manager
Sylvia Sanchez, Traffic Manager

WRR
01-01-1948; 101.1 mhz FM *Hrs Open:* 24; 98 kw; 1667 ft.; N32 35 19 W96 58 5
Mailing Address: City Hall, 1500 Marilla, Street, Rm . 4/D/North, Dallas, TX 75201 US
Second Address: 1516 First Ave., Dallas, TX 75210
(214) 670-8888, *Fax:* (214) 670-8394
www.wrr101.com
License: Dallas, Dallas County, TX held by City of Dallas.
Nat'l Network: AP Network News *Nat'l Reps:* McGavren Guild
Arbitron Metro Market: Dallas-Fort Worth *Format:* Classical
Special Programming: Children 2 hrs wkly *No. News Employees:* 22 *Target Audience:* 25-54; all ages
Gregory Davis, Operations Dir

Decatur

*KDKR
01-01-1998; 91.3 mhz FM *Hrs Open:* 24; 40 kw horiz, 100 kw vert; 1785 ft.; N33 23 12 W97 33 57
P.O. Box 1924, Tulsa, OK 74101 US
(817) 831-9130
www.kdkr.org
kdkr@csnradio.com
License: Decatur, Wise County, TX held by CSN International
Group Owner: CSN International; acq 7-12-2000).
Arbitron Metro Market: Dallas-Fort Worth *Format:* Gospel, Religious
Kelly Rasulo, Operations Dir
Chris Rohloff, General Manager
Stephanie Rohloff, Programming Director

KRNB
08-15-1968; 105.7 mhz FM *Hrs Open:* 24; 100 kw; 492 ft; N32 11 11 W98 17 26
621 N.W. 6th St., Grand Prairie, TX 75053
(972) 263-9911, *Fax:* (972) 558-0010
www.krnb.com
License: Decatur, Wise County, TX held by Service Broadcasting Group LLC.
Group Owner: Service Broadcasting Group LLC; (acq 2-28-95;
Nat'l Network: ABC
Population Served: 75,000 *Arbitron Metro Market:* Dallas-Fort Wor

Hymen Childs, President
Chuck Smith, General Manager
Shay Moore, Programming Director
Gary Wachter, Chief Engineer

Deer Park

KAMA-FM

08-08-1968; 104.9 mhz FM; 8.7 kw; 984 ft.; N29 45 26 W95 20 19
3102 Oak Lawn Avenue, Suite 215, Dallas, TX 75219 US
(713) 965-2400, *Fax:* (713) 965-2401
info@univision.com
License: Deer Park, Fort Bend County, TX held by Tichenor License Corp.
Group Owner: Univision Radio; (acq 9-22-2003; grpsl)
Arbitron Metro Market: Houston-Galveston
Mark Masepohl, Operations Dir
Dave Burdette, General Sales Mgr
Arnulfo Ramirez, Programming Director
Nestor Enriquez, Promotions Manager
Kim Guerrero, National Sales Manager
Renzo Heredia, Public Affairs Director

Del Mar Hills

KVOZ

04-15-1952; 890 khz AM; 10 kw-D, DAN; 1 kw-N, DAN; N27 32 57 W99 22 21
P.O. Box 252, McAllen, TX 78502 US
(956) 781-5528(956) 686-6382, *Fax:* (956) 686-2999
www.laradiochristiana.com
License: Del Mar Hills, TX held by Consolidated Radio Inc.
Arbitron Metro Market: McAllen, TX *Format:* Gospel *Target Audience:* 18 plus.
Pete Guzman, Operations Dir
Paulino Bernal, General Manager
Eloy Bernal, Station Manager

Del Rio

KDLK-FM

08-15-1966; 94.1 mhz FM *Hrs Open:* 24; 18 kw; Ant 310 ft; N29 25 45 W100 54 17
Box 1489, Del Rio, TX 78840
(830) 775-9583, *Fax:* (830) 774-4009
www.kdlk.com
License: Del Rio, Val Verde County, TX
Nat'l Network: Westwood One
Target Audience: 18 plus.
Larry Mariner, President
Jay Gonzalez, Operations Dir
Travis Mariner, VP Sales
Jay Gonzalez, Programming Director

KTDR

03-31-1986; 96.3 mhz FM *Hrs Open:* 24; 100 kw; 505 ft.; N29 32 25 W101 7 21
P.O.Box 420848, Del Rio, TX 78842 US
(830) 775-6291(830) 775-6291(830) 774-6436, *Fax:* (830) 775-6545
www.themix96.com
production@themix96.com
License: Del Rio, Val Verde County, TX held by Grande Broadcasting of Del Rio Inc.
Arbitron Metro Market: Del Rio, TX *Format:* Adult Contemp *Special Programming:* Relg 3 hrs wkly *Hrs. of News Programming:* News progmg 1 hr wkly *Target Audience:* 25-54; male *Adv. Rates:* 35; 25; 30; 25
Frank Mendoza, President
Chris Russell, General Sales Mgr
Rodney Lyman, Programming Director
Margaritta Martinez, Research Director
Charlene Duncan, Traffic Manager

KLTO

01-01-1947; 1230 khz AM *Hrs Open:* 24; 860 w-U; N29 25 45 W100 54 17
Box 1489, Del Rio, TX 78840
(830) 775-9583, *Fax:* (830) 774-4009
www.ktjk.com
License: Del Rio, Val Verde County, TX held by Forum Broadcasting Inc.
Population Served: 50,000*Target Audience:* 25-54.
Larry Mariner, President
Rudy Briones, Operations Dir
Jay Gonzalez, Programming Director
Christina Rangel, News Director

KWMC

08-20-1967; 1490 khz AM *Hrs Open:* 24; 1 kw-U, ND1; N29 22 17 W100 51 55
903 E. Cortinas Street, Del Rio, TX 78840 US
(830) 775-3544, *Fax:* (830) 775-3546
www.kwmc1490.com/
kwmc1490@wcsonline.net
License: Del Rio, TX held by Minerva Garza Valdez.
Regional Network: Texas State Networks *Wire Services:* NOAA Weather
Arbitron Metro Market: Del Rio, TX *Format:* Oldies *Special Programming:* Relg 5 hrs wkly *No. News Employees:* 2
Alfredo Garza, President
Minerva Garza-Valdez, Operations Dir
Guillermo Garza, Station Manager
Javier Martinez, General Sales Mgr
Guillermo Garza, Engineer
Javier Martinez Jr, Manager
Angelina Rivera, Business Manager
ErnestMesta, Angelina Rivera
Angel Torres, Production Director

*KDLI

01-01-2007; 89.9 mhz FM; 1 kw; 171 ft.; N29 25 24 W100 54 21
Rebroadcasts: Rebroadcasts WAFR(FM) Tupelo, MS 100%
Po Drawer 2440, Tupelo, MS 38803 US
(662) 844-8888, *Fax:* (662) 842-6791
www.afr.net
License: Del Rio, Val Verde County, TX held by American Family Association.
Group Owner: American Family Radio
Arbitron Metro Market: Tupelo, MS *Format:* Christian
Marvin Sanders, General Manager

*KLIT

90.5 mhz FM; kw
P O Box 252, McAllen, TX 78505 US
(909) 248-9270, *Fax:* (916) 251-1650
License: Del Rio, Lea County, TX held by Broadcasting for the Challenged Inc.
Arbitron Metro Market: Fountain Valley, CA
George Flinn Jr., President

Del Valle

KIXL

08-08-1959; 970 khz AM *Hrs Open:* 24
11615 Angus Road, Suite 120 B, Austin, TX 78704 US
(512) 390-5495, *Fax:* (512) 241-0510
www.relevantradio.com
KIXL@relevantradio.com
License: Del Valle, TX held by Starboard Media Foundation Inc.
Group Owner: Relevant Radio; (acq 1-20-2006; $3.58 million)
Arbitron Metro Market: Austin, TX *Format:* Talk, Christian
Ted Wrenn, General Manager
Ruben Villarreal, Station Manager

Denison

*KYFB

01-19-2007; 91.5 mhz FM; 4.5 kw; 220 ft.; N33 42 10 W96 34 5
8030 Arrownridge Blvd, Charlotte, NC 28273 US
(704) 523-5555, *Fax:* (704) 522-1967
www.bbnradio.org
License: Denison, Grayson County, TX held by Bible Broadcasting Network Inc.
Group Owner: Bible Broadcasting Network
Arbitron Metro Market: Denison, TX *Format:* Christian
Lowell Davey, President

Denton

KDXX

09-01-1988; 99.1 mhz FM *Hrs Open:* 24; 100 kw; Ant 1,168 ft; N33 23 22 W97 33 53
7700 Carpenter Fwy., Dallas, TX 75219
(214) 525-0400,(214) 630-8531, *Fax:* (214) 689-3818,(214) 631-1196 (sales)
www.kick991.com,Netmio.com
info@kfzofm.com
License: Denton, Denton County, TX held by KHCK-FM License Corp.
Group Owner: Univision Radio; (acq 9-22-2003; grpsl).
Arbitron Metro Market: Dallas-Fort Worth *Hrs. of News Programming:* news progmg one hr wkly *No. News Employees:* 1 *Target Audience:* 25-54; affluent/educated adults
Andy Lockridge, Operations Dir
Frank Carter, General Manager
Howard Toole, General Sales Mgr
Frank Gonzales, Programming Director
Oscar Espinosa, Promotions Manager
Mirentxu Smith, News Director
Patrick Parks, Chief Engineer
Cipriano Robles, General Sales Manager
Betsy Galleguillos, National Sales Manager
Myrna Vera, Research Director

KHKS

01-01-1947; 106.1 mhz FM *Hrs Open:* 24; 99 kw; 1667 ft.; N32 35 19 W96 58 5
510 Lovett Blvd., Houston, TX 77006 US
(214) 866-8000, *Fax:* (214) 866-8588
www.1061kissfm.com
promotions@khksfm.com
License: Denton, Denton County, TX held by AMFM Texas Licenses L.P.
Group Owner: Clear Channel Communications Inc.; (acq 8-30-00; grpsl).
Arbitron Metro Market: Dallas-Fort Worth, TX *Format:* Contemporary Hits/Top 40 *No. News Employees:* 1 *Target Audience:* 18-49.
J.D. Freeman, General Manager
Jeff Mitchell, General Sales Mgr
Patrick Davis, Programming Director
Steve Lee, Promotions Manager
Sylvia Sanchez, News Director
Louis Sutton, Engineering Dir
Kelly Parker, National Sales Manager
Shawn McCalister, Regional Sales Manager

Devine

KRPT

11-17-1982; 92.5 mhz FM *Hrs Open:* 24; 50 kw; 492 ft.; N28 55 32 W99 2 53
200 Concord Plaza, Suite 600, San Antonio, TX 78216 US
(210) 736-9700, *Fax:* (210) 735-8811
www.sanantonioiswild.com/main.html
License: Devine, Medina County, TX held by CCB Texas Licenses L.P.
Group Owner: Clear Channel Communications Inc.; (acq 10-2-98; $1.5 million).
Arbitron Metro Market: San Antonio, TX *Format:* Country
Matt Martin, General Manager

Diboll

KAFX-FM

06-29-1960; 95.5 mhz FM *Hrs Open:* 24; 100 kw; 568 ft.; N31 24 28 W94 45 53
Mailing Address: 600 Congress Avenue, Suite 1400, Austin, TX 78701 US
Second Address: 1216 S. 1st St., Lufkin, TX 75901-4716
(936) 639-4455, *Fax:* (936) 639-5957
kfox95.com
johnnylathrop@gapbroadcasting.com
License: Diboll, Angelina County, TX held by GAP Broadcasting Lufkin License LLC.
Group Owner: GAP Broadcasting LLC; (acq 8-3-2007; grpsl)
Arbitron Metro Market: Lufkin, TX *Format:* Adult Contemp *Hrs. of News Programming:* news progmg 2 hrs wkly *No. News Employees:* 1 *Target Audience:* 25-44; female
Johnny Lathrop, General Manager
Tami Koonce, General Sales Mgr

KSML

06-02-1957; 1260 khz AM *Hrs Open:* 24
P.O. Box 1345, Lufkin, TX 75902 US
(409) 634-6661, *Fax:* (409) 632-5722
www.espn1260.net
info@ksml.com
License: Diboll, TX held by Stephen W. & Karla Yates.
Hrs. of News Programming: news progmg 14 hrs wkly *No. News Employees:* 1
Stephen Yates, President
Oscar Chavez, Programming Director
Steve Comer, Chief Engineer

Dilley

KVWG-FM

03-01-1984; 95.3 mhz FM; 0.1 kw; 121 ft.; N28 40 23 W99 10 8
8203vantage Dr., Suite 840, San Antonio, TX 78230 US
License: Dilley, Frio County, TX held by Pearsall Radio Works Ltd.
Arbitron Metro Market: Dilley, TX
Trace Taul, Operations Dir
Doug Downs, General Manager
Ron Allen, Programming Director

KLMO-FM

01-01-2001; 98.9 mhz FM; 92 kw; 722 ft.; N28 56 34 W99 16 47
115 West Avenue ""D"", Robstown, TX 78320 US
(210) 532-9858, *Fax:* (361) 289-7722
License: Dilley, Frio County, TX held by Dilley Broadcasters.
Arbitron Metro Market: Robstown, TX *Format:* Spanish

Jose Guzman, General Manager
Salvador Prieto, Programming Director

KKDL
93.7 mhz FM; 2.5 kw; 266 ft.; N28 38 53 W99 10 50
US
(956) 726-4738
License: Dilley, Frio County, TX held by La Nueva Cadena Radio Luz Inc.
Arbitron Metro Market: Dilley, TX
Israel Tellez, President

Dimmitt

KDHN
12-22-1963; 1470 khz AM; 0.5 kw-D, ND1; 0.149 kw-N, DA2; N34 35 11 W102 18 35
704 W. Cleveland St, Dimmitt, TX 79027 US
(806) 647-4161, *Fax:* (806) 647-4715
kdhn@1984yoohoo.com
License: Dimmitt, TX held by Collins Communications Co.
Format: Religious, Country *Special Programming:* Sp 17 hrs wkly *Hrs. of News Programming:* News progmg 8 hrs wkly *Target Audience:* General.
Wayne Collins, President

KNNK
06-13-1998; 100.5 mhz FM *Hrs Open:* 24; 43 kw; Ant 489 ft; N34 44 49 W102 29 37
Box 1635, 207 S. 25-Mile Ave., Hereford, TX 79045
(806) 363-1005, *Fax:* (806) 364-0226
www.knnk.net
knnk@wtrt.net
License: Dimmitt, Castro-Deaf Smith County, TX held by James D. Peeler.
Nat'l Network: Moody
Population Served: 253,002 *Arbitron Metro Market:* Amarillo, TX *Special Programming:* Soft instrumentals 35 hrs wkly *Target Audience:* General; mature adults
Terry Smothermon, Operations Dir
Alva Lee Peeler, General Manager

Doss

***KGLF**
88.1 mhz FM; 6 kw; 328 ft.; N30 22 22 W99 5 2
P.O. Box 26142, Austin, TX 78755 US
(800) 525-5683
www.klove.com
klove@klove.com
License: Doss, Gillespie County, TX held by Legacy Austin Broadcasting Foundation Inc.
Arbitron Metro Market: Omaha, NE *Format:* Christian *No. News Employees:* 13
Darrell Chambliss, Chairman
Mlke Novak, President and CEO
Pam Patrick-Thompson, Operations Dir
Eric Allen, General Manager
David Pierce, Programming Director
Ed Lenane, News Director
Sam Wallington, Engineering Dir
MaryaMorgan, News Reporter
Richard Hunt, News Reporter
Laura Daniels, News Reporter
Tim Luttrell, News Reporter
Kenny Noble Cortes, News Reporter
Darren Vinson, News Reporter

Dripping Springs

KTXX-FM
01-01-1984; 104.9 mhz FM *Hrs Open:* 24; 2.35 kw; Ant 531 ft; N30 11 54 W98 00 46
912 S. Capital of Texas Hwy., Suite 400, Austin, TX 75244
(512) 416-1100, *Fax:* (512) 416-8205
License: Dripping Springs, Hays County, TX held by BMP Austin License Company L.P.
Group Owner: Border Media Partners LLC; (acq 11-9-2004; grpsl)
Arbitron Metro Market: Austin, TX *Target Audience:* 25-54; upscale, retired, affluent
Jerry Del Core, General Manager

***KLLR**
01-01-2007; 91.9 mhz FM; 1.1 kw; 472 ft.; N30 11 53 W98 0 45
Rebroadcasts: Rebroadcasts KLVR(FM) Santa Rosa, CA 100%
8103 Brodie Lane, Suite #3, Austin, TX 78745 US
(800) 877-5600, *Fax:* (916) 251-1650
www.klove.com
License: Dripping Springs, Hays County, TX held by Educational Media Foundation.
Group Owner: EMF Broadcasting
Nat'l Network: K-Love
Arbitron Metro Market: Dripping Springs, TX *Format:* Christian
Mike Novak, President
Eric Allen, General Sales Mgr
David Pierce, Programming Director
Ed Lenane, News Director
Sam Wallington, Engineering Dir
Scott Smith, Music Director
Marya Morgan, News Reporter
Richard Hunt, NewsReporter
Tracy Butler, Traffic Manager

Dublin

KSTV-FM
08-15-1968; 93.1 mhz FM *Hrs Open:* 24; 7 kw; 584 ft.; N32 10 59 W98 17 12
3209 West Washington St, Stephensville, TX 76401 US
(254) 968-2141, *Fax:* (254) 968-6221
www.377net.com
kstv@htcomp.net
License: Dublin, Erath County, TX held by CCR-Stephenville III LLC.
Group Owner: Cherry Creek Radio LLC; (acq 6-24-2004; grpsl).
Arbitron Metro Market: Stephenville, TX *Format:* Country
Robert Elliot, General Manager
Robert Haschke, General Sales Mgr
Tony Hart, Programming Director
Nyki Wyatt, News Director
Justin McClure, Chief Engineer
Troy Stark, Traffic Manager

Dumas

KDDD
05-01-1948; 800 khz AM *Hrs Open:* 6 AM-sunset; 0.25 kw-D, ND2; 0.008 kw-N, ND2; N35 51 42 W101 55 50
Mailing Address: P. O. Box 555, Dumas, TX 79029 US
Second Address: 408 N. Dumas Ave., Dumas, TX 79029
(806) 935-4141, *Fax:* (806) 935-3836
kddd@amaonline.com
License: Dumas, TX held by PBI LLC
Format: Country *Target Audience:* General.
Candy Bray, News Director

KDDD-FM
06-29-1960; 95.3 mhz FM *Hrs Open:* 24; 6.6 kw; 259 ft.; N35 51 51 W101 55 44
Mailing Address: P. O. Box 555, Dumas, TX 79029 US
Second Address: 408 N. Dumas Ave., Dumas, TX 79029
(806) 935-4141, *Fax:* (806) 935-3836
License: Dumas, Moore County, TX held by PBI LLC
Nat'l Network: ABC
Format: Oldies *Special Programming:* Farm 5 hrs, gospel 5 hrs wkly *Hrs. of News Programming:* news progmg 13 hrs wkly *No. News Employees:* 1 *Target Audience:* 25-65; farmers, community, factory *Adv. Rates:* 20; 20; 20; 20
Steve Bayless, Operations Dir
Kandi Bray, General Manager
Ali Allison, News Director
Stephen White, Chief Engineer

Eagle Pass

***KEPI**
05-13-1995; 88.7 mhz FM *Hrs Open:* 24; 1 kw; 180 ft.; N28 39 26 W100 25 0
Box 3333, McAllen, TX 78502 US
(830) 757-0895, *Fax:* (830) 757-8950
www.887kepi.org/KEPI_88.7/Home.html
License: Eagle Pass, Maverick County, TX held by World Radio Network Inc.
Arbitron Metro Market: Eagle Pass, TX *Format:* Christian
James Gamblin, General Manager

KEPS
08-01-1957; 1270 khz AM
Mailing Address: 2402 Broadmoor, Bldg, D-2, Suite 101, Bryan, TX 77802 US
Second Address: 127 Kilowatt Dr., Eagle Pass, TX 78852
(830) 773-9247, *Fax:* (830) 773-9500
www.eaglepassradio.com
kinlkepsrg@bizzstx.rr.com
License: Eagle Pass, TX held by Rhattigan Broadcasting (Texas) LP
Group Owner: Rhattigan Broadcasting (Texas) LP; (acq 8-19-2004; grpsl)
Arbitron Metro Market: Eagle Pass, TX *Format:* Tejano *Target Audience:* 18-49; middle income, Texas-born Hispanics
Rosa De La Garza, General Manager
Rosa De La Garza, General Sales Mgr
Jose Perez, Programming Director
Mario Martinez, News Director
Gary Graham, Chief Engineer

***KEPX**
09-09-1994; 89.5 mhz FM *Hrs Open:* 24; 52 kw; 256 ft.; N28 39 26 W100 25 0
P.O. Box 3333, McAllen, TX 78502 US
(830) 757-0895, *Fax:* (830) 757-8950
www.kepx.net
License: Eagle Pass, Maverick County, TX held by World Radio Network Inc.
Arbitron Metro Market: Eagle Pass, TX *Format:* Christian *Hrs. of News Programming:* News progmg 3 hrs wkly *Target Audience:* Hispanic; Mexican
Arturo Lazano, General Manager

KINL
11-02-1971; 92.7 mhz FM; 20 kw; 184 ft.; N28 43 57 W100 29 34
Mailing Address: 2402 Broadmoor, Bldg, D-2, Suite 101, Bryan, TX 77802 US
Second Address: 127 Kilowatt Dr., Eagle Pass, TX 78852
(830) 773-9247, *Fax:* (830) 773-9500
kinlkepsrg@bizzstx.rr.com
License: Eagle Pass, Maverick County, TX held by Rhattigan Broadcasting (Texas) LP.
Group Owner: Rhattigan Broadcasting (Texas) LP
Format: Oldies
Cesar Galindo, Programming Director

Eastland

KATX
09-01-1986; 97.7 mhz FM *Hrs Open:* 24; 3 kw; 203 ft.; N32 23 47 W98 46 26
306 S. Seaman, Box 590, Eastland, TX 76448 US
(254) 629-2621, *Fax:* (254) 629-8520
www.hpnetwork.com/index_central.html
silverspursbroadcasting@gmail.com
License: Eastland, Eastland County, TX held by Partnership Broadcasting Inc.
Arbitron Metro Market: Abilene, TX *Format:* Classic Rock, Oldies *Hrs. of News Programming:* news progmg 8 hrs wkly *No. News Employees:* 3 *Target Audience:* 25-54; adults *Adv. Rates:* 7.00/14.00
Chuck Statler, President

***KQXE**
01-01-2008; 91.1 mhz FM; 14.5 kw; 436 ft.; N32 28 37.5 W98 48 34
206 Wiggs Lane, Weatherford, TX 76086 US
(817) 341-2337, *Fax:* (817) 596-9842
www.qxfm.com
License: Eastland, Eastland County, TX held by CSSI Non-Profit Educational Broadcasting Corp.
Arbitron Metro Market: Eastland, TX
John Peterson, General Manager

Edinburg

KBFM
02-01-1972; 104.1 mhz FM *Hrs Open:* 24; 100 kw; 1224 ft.; N26 6 2 W97 50 21
One Independence Plaza, 280 Hwy 35, Middletown, NJ 33408 US
(956) 973-9202, *Fax:* (956) 973-9355
www.wild104.net
kbfmm@aol.com
License: Edinburg, Hidalgo County, TX held by Capstar TX L.P.
Group Owner: Clear Channel Communications Inc.; (acq 8-15-00; grpsl).
Nat'l Reps: Christal
Arbitron Metro Market: Weslaco, TX *Format:* Contemporary Hits/Top 40 *Special Programming:* Community affrs *No. News Employees:* 1 *Target Audience:* 18-34; females *Adv. Rates:* 100; 75; 100; 50
Danny Fletcher, Operations Dir
Cyndi Torres, General Sales Mgr
Bobby Macias, Programming Director
Gloria Garcia, News Director
Ken Meek, Chief Engineer
Billy Santiago, Operations Manager

***KOIR**
02-05-1983; 88.5 mhz FM *Hrs Open:* 24; 3 kw; 285 ft.; N26 7 49 W98 10 51
4300 S. Business 281, Edinburg, TX 78539 US
(956) 380-8100,(956) 380-3435, *Fax:* (956) 380-8156
correo@radioesparanza.com
License: Edinburg, Hidalgo County, TX held by Rio Grande Bible Institute Inc.
Wire Services: UPI

Arbitron Metro Market: McAllen-Brownsville-Harlingen, TX
Format: Religious *Target Audience:* General.
Gerardo Lorenzo, General Manager
Jerry Jeske, Chief Engineer

KURV
10-01-1947; 710 khz AM *Hrs Open:* 24; 1 kw-D, DA2; 0.91 kw-N, DA2; N26 19 43 W98 9 35; N26 19 42 W98 9 36
2921 N. Closner, Edinburg, TX 78539 US
(956) 992-8895, *Fax:* (956) 992-8897
www.kurv.com
webmaster@kurv.com
License: Edinburg, TX held by BMP RGV License Co. L.P.
Group Owner: Border Media Partners LLC; (acq 2-6-2004; $7.5 million with KSOX(AM) Raymondville)
Nat'l Network: CBS *Regional Network:* Texas State Networks
Arbitron Metro Market: Edinburg, TX *Format:* News, News/Talk, 84, Talk *Hrs. of News Programming:* news progmg 30 hrs wkly *No. News Employees:* 2 *Target Audience:* 35-64.
Jose Munoz, General Manager

KVLY
01-01-1974; 107.9 mhz FM; 100 kw; 843 ft.; N26 5 18 W98 3 44
1350 One Galleria Tower, 13355 Noel Road, Dallas, TX 75240 US
(956) 661-6000, *Fax:* (956) 661-6081
www.mix1079.net
License: Edinburg, Hidalgo County, TX held by Entravision Holdings L.L.C.
Group Owner: Entravision Communications Corp.; (acq 7-20-00; grpsl)
Arbitron Metro Market: McAllen-Brownsville-Harlingen, TX
Format: Adult Contemp, Spanish *Target Audience:* 25-54.
Willie Rosales, General Manager
Alex Duran, Programming Director
Shirley Kennedy, News Director
Sonny Cavazos, Chief Engineer
Lilly Lopez, Music Director
Dora Borjas, Traffic Manager

Edna

KIOX-FM
09-20-1998; 96.1 mhz FM; 13 kw; 456 ft.; N29 6 5 W96 27 19
111 N. Main, Hallettsville, TX 77964 US
(974) 543-8282
www,kioxradio.com
License: Edna, Jackson County, TX held by Buckalew Media Inc.
Format: Country
Ryan Henderson, General Manager

El Campo

KXBJ
09-01-1968; 96.9 mhz FM *Hrs Open:* 24; 100 kw; 981 ft; N29 05 44 W96 27 25
3000 Bering Dr., Houston, TX 77404
(713) 315-3400, *Fax:* (713) 315-3565
www.xoradio.com
Houstoninfo@lbimedia.com
License: El Campo, Wharton County, TX held by Liberman Broadcasting of Houston License LLC.
Group Owner: Liberman Broadcasting Inc.; (acq 10-11-2002; $3.15 million with KXGJ(FM) Bay City)
Target Audience: 18-49; college, plant workers, business & agriculture
Cheryl Kirk, General Manager

KULP
01-01-1948; 1390 khz AM *Hrs Open:* 6 AM-10 PM; 0.5 kw-D, ND1; 0.18 kw-N, ND1; N29 12 34 W96 15 50
Mailing Address: P.O. Box 390, El Campo, TX 77437 US
Second Address: 515 E. Jackson St., El Campo, TX 77437
(979) 543-3303, *Fax:* (979) 543-1546
www.kulpradio.com
contact@kulpradio.com
License: El Campo, TX held by Wharton County Radio Inc.
Regional Network: Texas State Networks
Arbitron Metro Market: El Campo, TX *Format:* Country, News, 62, Sports, Talk *Special Programming:* Sp 14 hrs, Czech 5 hrs wkly *Hrs. of News Programming:* news progmg 5 hrs wkly *No. News Employees:* 2 *TargetAudience:* 25 plus. *Adv. Rates:* 276; 228; 228; 228
Bob Buckalew, President
Clint Robinson, Operations Dir
Stephen Zetsche, General Manager
Jerry Aulds, Station Manager
Bob Nason, News Director
Mike Wenglar, Engineering Dir
Kate Manrriquez, Traffic Manager

El Paso

KAMA
07-13-1972; 750 khz AM *Hrs Open:* 24
3102 Oak Lawn Ave., Suite 215, Dallas, TX 75219 US
(915) 544-9797, *Fax:* (915) 544-1247
www.univision.com
info@netmio.com
License: El Paso, TX held by Tichenor Media System Inc.
Group Owner: Univision Radio; (acq 9-22-2003; grpsl).
Arbitron Metro Market: El Paso, TX *Format:* Oldies *Hrs. of News Programming:* news progmg 8 hrs wkly *No. News Employees:* 1 *Target Audience:* 25-54; women
MacHenry Tichenor Jr., President
Cecilia Uebel, General Manager
Carlos Fourzan, General Sales Mgr
Pedro Skaggs, Programming Director
Fernando Rubio, News Director
Michael McCabe, Chief Engineer
Patricia Villasenor, TrafficManager

KYSE
11-29-1958; 94.7 mhz FM *Hrs Open:* 24; 97 kw horiz, 65 kw vert; 1191 ft.; N31 47 34 W106 28 47
4105 Rio Bravo, Ste 150, El Paso, TX 79902 US
(915) 581-1126, *Fax:* (915) 532-4970
www.superestrella947.com
info@superestrella947.com
License: El Paso, El Paso County, TX held by Entravision Holdings L.L.C.
Group Owner: Entravision Communications Corp.; (acq 10-19-99).
Nat'l Reps: Lotus Entravision Reps LLC
Arbitron Metro Market: El Paso, TX *Format:* Contemporary Hits/Top 40 *Target Audience:* 18-34.
Joe Garcia, Operations Dir
David Candelaria, General Manager
Phil Gabbard, General Sales Mgr
Susan Graham, News Director

KSVE
02-11-2004; 1650 khz AM
1400 16th St., NW, Ste 600, Washington, DC 20036 US
(915) 581-1126, *Fax:* (915) 532-4970
License: El Paso, TX held by Entravision Holdings LLC.
Group Owner: Entravision Communications Corp.
Arbitron Metro Market: El Paso, TX
Joe Garcia, Operations Dir
David Candelaria, General Manager
Phil Gabbard, General Sales Mgr
Leo Lugo, Promotions Manager
Susan Fleming, News Director
Jim Lotspeich, Chief Engineer

KQBU
06-01-1947; 920 khz AM; 1 kw-D, DAN; 0.36 kw-N, DAN; N31 44 9 W106 22 24
3102 Oak Lawn Ave., Suite 215, Dallas, TX 75219 US
(915) 544-9797, *Fax:* (915) 544-1247
License: El Paso, TX held by Tichenor License Corp.
Group Owner: Univision Radio; (acq 9-22-2003; grpsl)
Arbitron Metro Market: El Paso, TX *Format:* Talk
MacHenry Tichenor Jr., President
Jose Molina, Operations Dir
Cecilia Uebel, General Manager
Carlos Fourzan, General Sales Mgr
Leonel Arias, Promotions Manager
Patricia Villasenor, News Director
Michael McCabe, Chief Engineer

KBNA-FM
08-15-1969; 97.5 mhz FM; 100 kw horiz, 48 kw vert; 1089 ft.; N31 47 34 W106 28 47
3102 Oak Lawn Ave., Suite 215, Dallas, TX 75219 US
(915) 544-9797, *Fax:* (915) 544-1247
www.univision.com
info@netmio.com
License: El Paso, El Paso County, TX
Group Owner: Univision Radio
Arbitron Metro Market: El Paso, TX
Jose Molina, Operations Dir
Cecilia Uebel, General Manager
Carlos Fourzan, General Sales Mgr
Michael McCabe, Chief Engineer
Patricia Villasenor, Traffic Manager

KELP
04-10-1959; 1590 khz AM *Hrs Open:* 24; 5 kw-D, DA2; 0.8 kw-N, DA2; N31 44 38 W106 23 45
6900 Commerce, El Paso, TX 79915 US
(915) 779-0016, *Fax:* (915) 779-6641
www.kelpradio.com
tina@kelpradio.com
License: El Paso, TX held by McClatchey Broadcasting.
Nat'l Network: Salem Radio Network
Arbitron Metro Market: El Paso, TX *Format:* Christian, Talk
Special Programming: Spanish 12 hrs wklly *Target Audience:* 25-54; Christian community of El Paso, Las Cruces, Northern Mexico
Jay Gilliland, Operations Dir
Arnie McClatchey, General Manager
Jay Gilliland, Programming Director
Tina Casano, Office Manager

KXPL
09-16-1985; 1060 khz AM; 10 kw-D, NDD; N31 48 41 W106 31 53
2211 E. Missouri E-237, El Paso, TX 79903 US
(915) 587-8822, *Fax:* (915) 587-8602
newsroomlavoz@yahoo.com
License: El Paso, TX held by New Radio System Inc.
Arbitron Metro Market: El Paso, TX *Format:* News
Maria Lazo, General Manager
Jose Camacho, Programming Director
Paul Gregg, Chief Engineer

KTSM
01-01-1947; 690 khz AM *Hrs Open:* 24; 10 kw-D, DA2; 10 kw-N, DA2; N31 58 11 W106 21 15
200 Concord Plaza, Suite 600, San Antonio, TX 78216 US
(915) 351-5400, *Fax:* (915) 351-3102
www.ktsmradio.com
biltole@clearchannel.com
License: El Paso, TX held by CCB Texas Licenses L.P.
Group Owner: Clear Channel Communications Inc.; (acq 5-16-96; grpsl).
Nat'l Reps: Clear Channel
Arbitron Metro Market: El Paso, TX *Format:* News, News/Talk, 86 *Special Programming:* Relg 3 hrs, radio health journal one hr, El Paso p *Hrs. of News Programming:* News 100 hrs wkly *Target Audience:* 25-54; men
L. Lowry Mays, CEO
Bill Struck, Operations Dir
Karen Daniels-Pearson, General Sales Mgr
Tom Connelly, Programming Director
Christopher Lucy, Promotions Manager
Randall May, CFO
Frank Rodriquez, Promotions Director

KHEY-FM
08-01-1974; 96.3 mhz FM *Hrs Open:* 24; 88 kw; 1391 ft.; N31 47 47 W106 28 55
200 Concord Plaza, Suite 600, San Antonio, TX 78216 US
(915) 351-5400, *Fax:* (915) 351-3102
www.khey.com
info@khey.com
License: El Paso, El Paso County, TX
Nat'l Network: ABC
Arbitron Metro Market: El Paso, TX *Format:* Country *Target Audience:* 25-54.
Bill Tole, Operations Dir
Mike Ryan, General Manager
Michelle Haston, General Sales Mgr
Raul Rodriquez, Programming Director
Chris Lucy, Promotions Manager
Bobby Gutierrez, News Director
Enrique Lopez, Engineering Dir
Amy Page,Traffic Manager

KINT-FM
07-04-1975; 93.9 mhz FM; 96 kw; 1421 ft.; N31 47 46 W106 28 57
11900 Olympic Boulevard, Los Angeles, CA 90064 US
(915) 581-1126, *Fax:* (915) 585-4611
info@kint.com
License: El Paso, El Paso County, TX held by Entravision Communications Co. L.L.C.
Group Owner: Entravision Communications Corp.; (acq 6-4-97; grpsl)
Nat'l Reps: Lotus Entravision Reps LLC
Arbitron Metro Market: El Paso, TX *Format:* Adult Contemp *Hrs. of News Programming:* News progmg 4 hrs wkly *Target Audience:* 25-54.
Joe Garcia, Operations Dir
David Candelaria, General Manager
Phil Gabbard, General Sales Mgr
Leo Lugo, Promotions Manager
Ron Haney, Chief Engineer
Abel Rodriguez, Public Affairs Director

KLAQ
10-01-1978; 95.5 mhz FM; 88 kw; 1391 ft.; N31 47 47 W106 28 55
4150 Pinnacle, El Paso, TX 79902 US
(915) 544-9550, *Fax:* (915) 532-6342
www.klaq.com
info@klaq.com
License: El Paso, El Paso County, TX
Arbitron Metro Market: El Paso, TX *Format:* Rock/AOR *Target Audience:* 18-49; adults who grew up on FM rock and roll
Brad Dubow, General Manager
Mike Ramey, Programming Director
Ron Haney, Chief Engineer

KOFX
06-06-1978; 92.3 mhz FM *Hrs Open:* 24; 98 kw; 1860 ft.; N31 48 55 W106 29 20
4105 Rio Bravo, Ste 150, El Paso, TX 79902 US
(915) 581-1126, *Fax:* (915) 532-4970
www.923thefox.com
info@923thefox.com
License: El Paso, El Paso County, TX held by Entravision Holdings L.L.C.
Group Owner: Entravision Communications Corp.; (acq 10-19-99)
Arbitron Metro Market: El Paso, TX *Format:* Oldies *No. News Employees:* 2 *Target Audience:* 25-54; upscale
Joe Garcia, Operations Dir
David Candelaria, General Manager
Phil Gabbard, General Sales Mgr
Al Jones, Programming Director
Susan Graham, News Director
Jim Lotspeich, Chief Engineer

KPRR
12-05-1969; 102.1 mhz FM *Hrs Open:* 24; 100 kw horiz, 66 kw vert; 1191 ft.; N31 47 34 W106 28 47
200 Concord Plaza, Suite 600, San Antonio, TX 78216 US
(915) 351-5400, *Fax:* (915) 351-3102
www.kprr.com
info@kprr.com
License: El Paso, El Paso County, TX held by CCB Texas Licenses L.P.
Group Owner: Clear Channel Communications Inc.; (acq 5-16-96; grpsl).
Nat'l Reps: Clear Channel
Arbitron Metro Market: El Paso, TX *Format:* Contemporary Hits/Top 40 *Target Audience:* 18-34.
L. Lowry Mays, CEO
Bill Struck, Operations Dir
Mike Ryan, General Manager
Michelle Haston, General Sales Mgr
Patti Diaz, Programming Director
Christopher Lucy, Promotions Manager
Randall Mays, CFO
Frank Rodriguez, PromotionsDirector

KROD
06-01-1940; 600 khz AM *Hrs Open:* 24
4150 Pinnacle, El Paso, TX 79902 US
(915) 544-9550, *Fax:* (915) 532-6342
www.krod.com
info@krod.com
License: El Paso, TX
Group Owner: Townsquare Media; (acq 12-1-99; grpsl).
Regional Network: Texas State Networks *Nat'l Reps:* D & R Radio
Arbitron Metro Market: El Paso, TX *Format:* Sports *Hrs. of News Programming:* news progmg 3 hrs wkly *No. News Employees:* 1 *Target Audience:* 25-54; adult listeners who grew up on the roots of rock and roll
Brad Dubow, General Manager
JT Chapman, General Sales Mgr
Johnnie Walker, Programming Director
Ron Haney, Chief Engineer

KSII
12-30-1975; 93.1 mhz FM *Hrs Open:* 24; 98 kw; 1421 ft.; N31 47 46 W106 28 57
4150 Pinnacle, El Paso, TX 79902 US
(915) 544-9300, *Fax:* (915) 544-9536
www.ksiiinfo.com
info@ksii.com
License: El Paso, El Paso County, TX
Group Owner: Townsquare Media; (acq 12-1-99; grpsl).
Arbitron Metro Market: El Paso, TX *Format:* Adult Contemp *Hrs. of News Programming:* news progmg 2 hrs wkly *No. News Employees:* 1 *Target Audience:* 25-54; 60% male, 40% female
Brad Dubow, General Manager
Kelly Calvillo, General Sales Mgr
Chris Elliot, Programming Director
Diana Rivas, News Director
Robert King, Chief Engineer

KHRO
06-01-1958; 1150 khz AM *Hrs Open:* 24
11900 Olympic Boulevard, Los Angeles, CA 90064 US
(915) 581-1126, *Fax:* (915) 585-4611
www.khro1150.com
info@ksve.com
License: El Paso, TX held by Entravision Communications Co. L.L.C.
Group Owner: Entravision Communications Corp.
Nat'l Reps: Lotus Entravision Reps LLC
Arbitron Metro Market: El Paso, TX *Format:* Talk *Target Audience:* 18-54.
Claud Pettit, President

***KTEP**
09-14-1950; 88.5 mhz FM *Hrs Open:* 24; 94 kw; 732 ft.; N31 47 17 W106 28 46
500 W. University Ave, El Paso, TX 79968 US
(915) 747-5152(915) 880-5837, *Fax:* (915) 747-5641
www.ktep.org
ktep@utep.edu
License: El Paso, El Paso County, TX held by University of Texas at El Paso.
Nat'l Network: PRI; NPR
Arbitron Metro Market: El Paso, TX *Format:* Jazz, News *Special Programming:* Gospel 4 hrs, folk 3 hrs wkly *Hrs. of News Programming:* news progmg 39 wkly *No. News Employees:* 1 *Target Audience:* 35 plus;college educated, upper-income
Dennis Woo, Operations Dir
Patrick Piotrowaski, General Manager
Joe Torres, General Sales Mgr
Louie Saenz, News Director
Norbert Miles, Chief Engineer
Norma Martinez, Traffic Manager

KHEY
08-22-1929; 1380 khz AM *Hrs Open:* 24; 5 kw-D, ND1; 0.5 kw-N, ND1; N31 45 26 W106 22 33
200 Concord Plaza, Suite 600, San Antonio, TX 78216 US
(915) 351-5400, *Fax:* (915) 351-3102
www.khey1380.com
MIKERYAN3@clearchannel.com
License: El Paso, TX held by CCB Texas Licenses L.P.
Group Owner: Clear Channel Communications Inc.; (acq 5-29-98; $10.5 million with co-located FM)
Nat'l Reps: Clear Channel
Arbitron Metro Market: El Paso, TX *Format:* Sports *Target Audience:* General.
Mike Ryan, General Manager
Raul Rodriguez, Sales
Paul Whittler, Programming Director
Chris Lucy, Promotions Manager
Julie Bustillos, News Director
Enrique Lopez, Chief Engineer
Frank Rodriquez, Promotions Director
Bill Tole,Operations Manager
Raul Figueroa, Website Support
Chris Lucy, Marketing Director

KTSM-FM
06-11-1962; 99.9 mhz FM; 87 kw; 1821 ft.; N31 48 19 W106 28 57
200 Concord Plaza, Suite 600, San Antonio, TX 78216 US
(915) 351-5400, *Fax:* (915) 351-3102
www.sunny999fm.com
MIKERYAN3@clearchannel.com
License: El Paso, El Paso County, TX held by CCB Texas Licenses L.P.
Group Owner: Clear Channel Communications Inc.
Nat'l Network: CBS
Arbitron Metro Market: El Paso, TX *Format:* Adult Contemp
Melissa Kerr, Operations Dir
Mike Ryan, General Manager
Raul Rodriguez, Sales
Bill Tole, Programming Director
Chris Lucy, Promotions Manager
Krystal Watkins, News Director
Enrique Lopez, Engineering Dir
Sam Cassiano, MusicDirector
Bill Tole, Operations Manager
Raul Figueroa, Website Support
Chris Lucy, Marketing Director

***KVER**
01-01-1993; 91.1 mhz FM *Hrs Open:* 24; 0.51 kw; 1115 ft.; N31 47 34 W106 28 47
P. O. Box 3333, McAllen, TX 78502 US
(915) 544-9190
www.kver.org
kver@hcjb.org
License: El Paso, El Paso County, TX held by World Network Radio Inc.
Group Owner: World Radio Network Inc.
Arbitron Metro Market: El Paso, TX *Format:* Religious *Target Audience:* Hispanic
Marcos Barraza, Station Manager
Gracel Calleros, Programming Director

KVIV
12-03-1949; 1340 khz AM
4900 Montana Ave, El Paso, TX 79903 US
(915) 565-2999, *Fax:* (915) 880-5848
www.kviv1340.com
radiovictoria@mail.com
License: El Paso, TX held by El Paso y Juarez Companerismo-Cristiano
Arbitron Metro Market: El Paso, TX *Format:* Religious *Target Audience:* Mexican-American.
Alfonso Cabrera, President
Jesus Cruz, Programming Director

***KKLY**
05-01-1985; 89.5 mhz FM *Hrs Open:* 24; 3.5 kw; 1211 ft.; N31 47 42 W106 28 51
2023 Myrtle Avenue, El Paso, TX 79901 US
(916) 251-1600, *Fax:* (916) 251-1650
www.klove.com
klove@klove.com
License: El Paso, El Paso County, TX held by Educational Media Foundation.
Group Owner: EMF Broadcasting; (acq 11-18-2002; $1 million).
Nat'l Network: K-Love
Arbitron Metro Market: El Paso, TX *Format:* Christian *No. News Employees:* 3 *Target Audience:* 25-44.
Mike Novak, President
David Pierce, Programming Director
Ed Lenane, News Director
Sam Wallington, Engineering Dir
Marya Morgan, News Reporter
Richard Hunt, News Reporter

Eldorado

KLDE
01-01-2007; 104.9 mhz FM; 50 kw; 279 ft.; N30 51 55 W100 35 36
US
(325) 853-1049
www.klderadio.com
License: Eldorado, Schleicher County, TX held by Tenn-Vol Corp.
Arbitron Metro Market: Eldorado, TX *Format:* Oldies
Danny Ray Boyer, General Manager

Electra

KOLI
01-01-1998; 94.9 mhz FM; 50 kw; 492 ft.; N34 5 1 W98 59 29
Rt 6, Box 150, Hwy 303, Brunswick, GA 31520 US
(940) 691-2311, *Fax:* (940) 696-2255
www.culumus.com
info@cumulus.com
License: Electra, Wichita County, TX held by Cumulus Licensing Corp.
Group Owner: Cumulus Media Inc.; (acq 8-10-99; $238,400)
Arbitron Metro Market: Wichita Falls, TX *Format:* Country
Brent Warner, Operations Dir
Lindy Parr, General Manager
Andrea Lewis, General Sales Mgr
Jim Russell, News Director
Jeff Chan, Chief Engineer
Dana Jameson, Traffic Manager

Elgin

KVLR
08-14-1992; 92.5 mhz FM *Hrs Open:* 24; 1.6 kw; Ant 449 ft; N30 19 00 W97 20 22
912 South Capital of Texas Hwy, Suite 400, Austin, TX 78752
(512) 453-1491, *Fax:* (512) 453-6809
jdelcore@bmpradio.com
License: Elgin, Bastrop County, TX held by BMP Austin License Company L.P.
Group Owner: Border Media Partners LLC; (acq 2-10-2005; grpsl)
Nat'l Network: CNN Radio
Arbitron Metro Market: Austin, TX
Pedro Gasc, General Manager

Elkhart

***KATG**
01-01-2006; 88.1 mhz FM; 80 kw vert; Ant 544 ft; N32 02 41 W95 40 37
Box 2440, Tupelo, MS 38803
(662) 844-8888, *Fax:* (662) 842-6791
www.afr.net
License: Elkhart, Henderson County, TX held by American Family Association.
Group Owner: American Family Radio
Arbitron Metro Market: Tyler-Longview, TX
Marvin Sanders, General Manager

Fabens

KPAS
03-24-1979; 103.1 mhz FM *Hrs Open:* 18; 3 kw; 299 ft.; N31 35 42 W106 11 58
8564 North Loop Road, El Paso, TX 79907 US
(915) 851-3382, *Fax:* (915) 851-4360
www.kpasfmradio.com
License: Fabens, El Paso County, TX held by Algie A. Felder.
Nat'l Network: USA
Arbitron Metro Market: El Paso, TX *Format:* Religious *Hrs. of News Programming:* News progmg 6 hrs wkly *Adv. Rates:* 25.50; 25.50; 25.50
Algie Felder, General Manager

Fairfield

KNES
12-01-1983; 99.1 mhz FM *Hrs Open:* 24; 11.5 kw; 482 ft.; N31 40 55 W96 1 22
P.O. Box 347, Fairfield, TX 75840 US
(903) 389-5637, *Fax:* (903) 389-7172
www.texas99.com
texas99@texas99.com
License: Fairfield, Freestone County, TX held by J & J Communications Inc.
Nat'l Network: Jones Radio Networks *Regional Network:* Texas State Networks *Nat'l Reps:* Riley
Format: Country *Special Programming:* Farm 3 hrs, talk 15 hrs, Black 3 hrs, gospel 3 hrs *Hrs. of News Programming:* news progmg 6 hrs wkly *No. News Employees:* 1 *Target Audience:* General.
Joe Reid, General Manager
Buzz Russell, Programming Director

Falfurrias

KDFM
103.3 mhz FM; 3 kw; 328 ft.; N27 15 29 W98 7 8
P O Box 252, McAllen, TX 78505 US
(956) 686-6382(956) 686-2992, *Fax:* (956) 686-2999
www.kdfc.com
License: Falfurrias, Brooks County, TX held by La Radio Cristiana Network Inc.
Arbitron Metro Market: Falfurrias, TX
Bill Lueth, Operations Dir
Dwight Walker, General Manager
Joe Schembri, General Sales Mgr

KLDS
01-01-1953; 1260 khz AM *Hrs Open:* 6 AM-midnight; 0.5 kw-D, ND1; 0.33 kw-N, ND1; N27 14 11 W98 10 22
Mailing Address: 304 E Rice, Falfurrias, TX 78355 US
Second Address: 215 W. Adam St., Falfurrias, TX 78355
(361) 325-1212, *Fax:* (361) 325-5003
License: Falfurrias, TX held by The Evangelistic Worship Center
Arbitron Metro Market: Corpus Christi, TX *Format:* Christian *Target Audience:* General.
Timothy Trevino, General Manager
Steve Cantu, Chief Engineer

KPSO-FM
11-01-1983; 106.3 mhz FM *Hrs Open:* 6 AM-10 PM; 6 kw; 184 ft.; N27 14 11 W98 10 22
304 E Rice, Falfurrias, TX 78355 US
(361) 325-2112, *Fax:* (361) 325-2112
kpso@awesomenet.net
License: Falfurrias, Brooks County, TX held by Brooks Broadcasting Corp.
Regional Network: Texas State Networks
Arbitron Metro Market: Corpus Christi, TX *Format:* Tejano *Hrs. of News Programming:* News progmg 10 hrs wkly *Target Audience:* All groups. *Adv. Rates:* 11
Raymond Creely, General Manager
Steve Cantu, General Sales Mgr

Fannett

***KZFT**
10-31-2003; 90.5 mhz FM; 40 kw vert; 361 ft.; N29 53 33 W94 8 6
P.O. Drawer 2440, Tupelo, MS 38803 US
(662) 844-8888, *Fax:* (662) 842-6791
www.afa.net
randall@afa.net
License: Fannett, Jefferson County, TX held by American Family Association.
Group Owner: American Family Radio
Arbitron Metro Market: Fannett, TX *Format:* Christian
Marvin Sanders, General Manager

Farmersville

KFCD
11-01-1947; 990 khz AM *Hrs Open:* 24
P.O. Box 12345, Dallas, TX 75225 US
(972) 354-1990, *Fax:* (972) 354-0820
www.radioexitosfm.com
dagoberto@radioexitosfm.net
License: Farmersville, TX held by Bernard Dallas LLC
Group Owner: Bernard Radio LLC; (acq 1-31-2007; $9 million with KHSE(AM) Wylie)
Nat'l Network: CNN Radio
Arbitron Metro Market: Farmersville, TX *Format:* Talk *Target Audience:* 35 plus; men *Adv. Rates:* 100; 100; 100; 20.
Dagoberto Rodriguez, CEO/COO
Dave Marcum, Operations Dir
Jerry Overton, General Manager
Jesus Dominguez, Sales Manager
Leslie Cooke, News Director
Jose Sanchez ', Tech Support
Dave Schum, Chief Engineer

KXEZ
09-01-1998; 92.1 mhz FM; 1.95 kw; 584 ft.; N33 16 31 W96 22 2
P.O. Box 94094, Plano, TX 75094 US
(972) 633-0953, *Fax:* (972) 396-1643
www.kxez.com
info@kxez.com
License: Farmersville, Collin County, TX held by Metro Broadcasters-Texas Inc.
Nat'l Network: Jones Radio Networks
Arbitron Metro Market: Dallas, TX *Format:* Country
Ken Jones, CEO
Jack Bishop, Operations Dir
Joshua Jones, General Sales Mgr
Glenda Jones, CFO
Lou Rogers, Technical Support

Farwell

KICA-FM
09-15-1984; 98.3 mhz FM *Hrs Open:* 24; 51 kw; 174 ft.; N34 24 31 W103 11 15
1000 Sycamore Street, Clovis, NM 88101 US
(505) 762-6200, *Fax:* (505) 762-8800
License: Farwell, Parmer County, TX held by Tallgrass Broadcasting LLC.
Group Owner: Tallgrass Broadcasting LLC; (acq 4-2-2007; grpsl)
Format: Classic Rock *Hrs. of News Programming:* news progmg 3 hrs wkly *No. News Employees:* 1 *Target Audience:* 18-49.
Dana Taylor, Programming Director
Shannon Phillips, News Director

KIJN
04-17-1958; 1060 khz AM; 10 kw-D, DAD; N34 23 14 W103 1 51
3801 Skillern, Flower Mound, TX 75028 US
(806) 481-3318, *Fax:* (806) 481-3835
www.angelfire.com
inHIM@cheerful.com; w5urx@hotmail.com
License: Farwell, TX held by Metropolitan Radio Group Inc.
Group Owner: Metropolitan Radio Group Inc.; (acq 9-97; with co-located FM)
Format: Christian, Religious *Target Audience:* General. *Adv. Rates:* 15; 15; 15; na
Mike Rodriquez, General Manager
David Pollard, Programming Director

KIJN-FM
08-01-1985; 92.3 mhz FM *Hrs Open:* 24; 100 kw; 354 ft.; N34 32 26 W102 47 56
3801 Skillern, Flower Mound, TX 75028 US
(806) 481-3318, *Fax:* (806) 481-3835
www.angelfire.com
inHIM@cheerful.com; w5urx@hotmail.com
License: Farwell, Parmer County, TX held by Metropolitan Radio Group Inc.
Group Owner: Metropolitan Radio Group Inc.
Format: Christian, Religious *Adv. Rates:* 18; 18; 18; 15
Yasunori Kawauchi, President
Kevin Yamazaki, Operations Dir

KMUL
07-06-1956; 830 khz AM
1000 Sycamore Street, Clovis, NM 88101 US
(806) 272-4273, *Fax:* (806) 272-5067
info@kmulam.com
License: Farwell, TX held by Tallgrass Broadcasting LLC.
Group Owner: Tallgrass Broadcasting LLC; (acq 4-2-2007; grpsl)
Special Programming: Farm 3 hrs wkly
Noe Anzaldua, General Manager
Martha Alvarado, Programming Director
Rick Keefer, Chief Engineer

Ferris

KDFT
07-13-1988; 540 khz AM *Hrs Open:* 24
127 Mamanasco Road, Ridgefield, CT 06877 US
(972) 572-1540, *Fax:* (972) 572-1263
kdft540.com
kdft-kmny@mrbi.net
License: Ferris, TX held by Way Broadcasting Licensee LLC
Group Owner: Multicultural Radio Broadcasting Inc.; (acq 4-19-2000; grpsl).
Regional Reps: In Language Radio; San Francisco
Arbitron Metro Market: Dallas-Fort Worth *Format:* Christian *Target Audience:* 25-59; Sp
Ted Sauceman, CEO
Arthur Liu, President
Yary Uhing, Operations Dir
Ted Sauceman, General Manager
John Gabel, Regional Vice President

Floresville

KTFM
06-15-1977; 94.1 mhz FM *Hrs Open:* 24; 40 kw; 548 ft.; N29 11 3 W98 30 49
26 West 56th Street, New York, NY 10019 US
(210) 654-5100, *Fax:* (210) 340-1775
License: Floresville, Wilson County, TX held by BMP San Antonio License Co. L.P.
Group Owner: Border Media Partners LLC; (acq 4-28-2004; $24.4 million with KSAH(AM) Universal City)
Arbitron Metro Market: San Antonio, TX *Format:* Christian *Target Audience:* 18-49.
Lance Hawkins, General Manager
Bob Brown, General Sales Mgr

***KJMA**
01-01-1993; 89.7 mhz FM; 100 kw; 564 ft.; N28 57 40 W98 15 31
1905 Tenth Street, Floresville, TX 78114 US
(210) 821-5050, *Fax:* (210) 821-5052
www.grnonline.com
License: Floresville, Wilson County, TX held by La Promesa Foundation.
Group Owner: La Promesa Foundation; (acq 6-25-2007; $130,000)
Nat'l Network: EWTN Radio
Arbitron Metro Market: Floresville, TX *Format:* Christian
Leonard Oswald, President
Cissy Gonzalez, General Manager

Flower Mound

WBAP-FM
06-30-2008; 96.7 mhz FM *Hrs Open:* 24; 92 kw; Ant 2,034 ft; N33 26 13 W97 29 05
2221 E. Lamar Blvd., Suite 300, Arlington, TX 10023
(817) 695-3500, *Fax:* (817) 695-0860
www.platinum967.com
License: Flower Mound, Denton County, TX
Group Owner: Cumulus Media Inc.; (acq 6-12-2007; . grpsl)
Nat'l Network: ABC *Nat'l Reps:* McGavren Guild
Population Served: 132,000 *Arbitron Metro Market:* Dallas-Fort Worth *Target Audience:* 35-54 Adults
Lynn Sornsen, Programming Director
Neal Peden, Chief Engineer

Floydada

KFLP-FM
04-01-1985; 106.1 mhz FM *Hrs Open:* 24; 25 kw; 233 ft.; N33 58 7 W101 21 15
Rt. 2, Box 60, Floydada, TX 79235 US
(806) 983-5704
www.kflp.net
kflp @ kflp.net

License: Floydada, Floyd County, TX held by Anthony L. Ricketts.
Nat'l Reps: Interep
Arbitron Metro Market: Floydada, TX *Format:* Agriculture, News
Target Audience: Farmers
A.T. Moore, President
Dan Perkins, Operations Dir
Donna Cole, General Manager
Joe Miot, Programming Director

KFLP
01-01-1951; 900 khz AM
Rt. 2, Box 60, Floydada, TX 79235 US
(806) 983-5704
www.kflp.net
kflp@kflp.net
License: Floydada, TX held by Anthony L. Ricketts.
Nat'l Network: USA *Regional Network:* American Ag *Nat'l Reps:* Interep
Arbitron Metro Market: Floydada, TX *Format:* Country *Hrs. of News Programming:* news progmg 12 hrs wkly *No. News Employees:* 1 *Target Audience:* 18-64
Tony St. James, General Manager

Fort Stockton

KFST
05-08-1954; 860 khz AM *Hrs Open:* 24; 0.25 kw-D, ND1; 0.25 kw-N, ND1; N30 52 37 W102 53 30
Rt. 1, Box 165, Fort Stockton, TX 79735 US
(432) 336-2228, *Fax:* (432) 336-5834
www.kfstradio.com
kfst@sbcglobal.net
License: Fort Stockton, TX held by Fort Stockton Radio Co Inc.
Regional Network: Texas State Networks *Wire Services:* NOAA Weather
Arbitron Metro Market: Fort Stockton, TX *Format:* Adult Contemp, Religious *Special Programming:* School and seniors 1 hr wkly *Hrs. of News Programming:* news progmg 6 hrs wkly *No. News Employees:* 2 *TargetAudience:* General.
Ken Ripley, General Manager

KFST-FM
11-01-1974; 94.3 mhz FM; 3 kw; 236 ft.; N30 52 37 W102 53 30
Rt. 1, Box 165, Fort Stockton, TX 79735 US
(432) 336-2228, *Fax:* (432) 336-5834
www.kfstradio.com
kfst@sbcglobal.net
License: Fort Stockton, Pecos County, TX held by Fort Stockton Radio Co. Inc.
Wire Services: NOAA Weather
Arbitron Metro Market: Fort Stockton, TX *Format:* Country
Special Programming: School and seniors 1 hr wkly *Hrs. of News Programming:* news progmg 6 hrs wkly *Target Audience:* Families
Matthew Boan, Operations Dir
Don Priest, General Manager
Joe Moore, Station Manager
Frank Delgado, Programming Director
Matt Garcia, Music Director

Fort Worth

KEGL
04-01-1959; 97.1 mhz FM *Hrs Open:* 24; 97 kw; 1667 ft.; N32 35 19 W96 58 5
50 East Rivercenter Boulevard, Suite 1200, Covington, KY 41011 US
(214) 866-8000
www.kegl.com
License: Fort Worth, Tarrant County, TX held by Citicasters Licenses L.P.
Group Owner: Clear Channel Communications Inc.; (acq 5-4-99; grpsl)
Arbitron Metro Market: Dallas-Fort Worth
Pat McMahon, Operations Dir
J.D. Freeman, General Manager

KFLC
01-01-1922; 1270 khz AM *Hrs Open:* 24
3102 Oak Lawn Avenue, Suite 215, Dallas, TX 75219 US
(214) 525-0400, *Fax:* (214) 631-1196
www.univision.com
License: Fort Worth, TX held by KESS-AM License Corp.
Group Owner: Univision Radio; (acq 9-22-2003; grpsl)
Arbitron Metro Market: Dallas-Fort Worth *Format:* News, News/Talk, 84, Talk *Hrs. of News Programming:* news progmg 11 hrs wkly *No. News Employees:* 2 *Target Audience:* 25-54.
Andy Lockridge, Operations Dir
Frank Carter, General Manager
Cipriano Robles, General Sales Mgr
Herminio Ortuno, Programming Director
Oscar Espinosa, Promotions Manager
Mirentxu Smith, News Director
Patrick Parks, ChiefEngineer
Ivonne Flaherty, General Sales Manager
Karen Hocking, National Sales Manager
Myrna Vera, Research Director

KFJZ
02-15-1947; 870 khz AM
2214 East 4th Street, Fort Worth, TX 76102 US
(817) 429-1630, *Fax:* 817-338-1205
License: Fort Worth, TX held by SIGA Broadcasting Corp.
Group Owner: SIGA Broadcasting Corp.; (acq 1-10-2008; $1.8 million)
Arbitron Metro Market: Fort Worth, TX
Gabriel Arango, President

KHVN
12-06-1946; 970 khz AM *Hrs Open:* 24; 1 kw-D, ND1; 0.27 kw-N, ND1; N32 47 56 W97 17 43
600 New Hampshire Ave., N.W., Suite 1200, Washington, DC 20037 US
(214) 331-5486, *Fax:* (214) 331-1908
www.khvnam.com
khvncommunitycalendar@yahoo.com
License: Fort Worth, TX held by Mortenson Broadcasting Co. of Texas Inc.
Group Owner: Mortenson Broadcasting Co.; (acq 5-31-2002; $4.5 million with KNAX(AM) Fort Worth).
Nat'l Reps: Interep
Arbitron Metro Market: Dallas-Fort Worth *Format:* Gospel *Hrs. of News Programming:* news progmg 10 hrs wkly *No. News Employees:* 1 *Target Audience:* 25-54.
Jack Mortenson, CEO
Dion Mortenson, Operations Dir
Tonya King, General Manager
Karl Banks, General Sales Mgr
Robert Ashley, News Director
Carmina Barnett, Program/Music Director

KLNO
12-24-1964; 94.1 mhz FM *Hrs Open:* 24; 98 kw; 1591 ft.; N32 35 22 W96 58 10
12900 Preston Road, Suite 100, Dallas, TX 75230 US
(214) 525-0400, *Fax:* (214) 631-1196
aquebuena941.univision.com
info@klnofm.com
License: Fort Worth, Tarrant County, TX held by HBC License Corp.
Group Owner: Univision Radio; (acq 9-22-2003; grpsl).
Nat'l Network: ABC
Arbitron Metro Market: Dallas, TX *Format:* Tejano
Andy Lockridge, Operations Dir
Frank Carter, General Manager
Cipriane Robles, General Sales Mgr
Oscar Rios, Programming Director
Oscar Espinosa, Promotions Manager
Mirentxu Smith, News Director
Patrick Parks, Chief Engineer
Ivonne Flaherty, General Sales Manager
Karen Hecking, Ivonne Flaherty
Myrna Vera, Research Director

KMVK
02-08-1965; 107.5 mhz FM *Hrs Open:* 24; 16.5 kw; 1884 ft.; N32 35 2 W96 57 48
600 New Hampshire Ave., Suite 1200, Washington, DC 20037 US
(214) 526-9870, *Fax:* (214) 905-5052
www.mega1075.com
License: Fort Worth, Tarrant County, TX held by CBS Radio Partner I Inc.
Group Owner: CBS Radio; (acq 6-26-96; grpsl)
Arbitron Metro Market: Dallas-Fort Worth *Format:* Adult Contemp
Target Audience: 25-54.
Mel Karmazin, President
David Henry, General Manager
Rick Frisch, General Sales Mgr
Kurt Johnson, Programming Director
Liz Balon, Promotions Manager
Julie Davis, News Director
Vance Henley, Engineering Dir
Bill Taylor, ChiefEngineer
Mark Sanford, Music Director
Dave Dillon, National Sales Manager

KKGM
01-01-2002; 1630 khz AM *Hrs Open:* 24 hrs
600 N.Hampshire Ave., NW, Ste 1200, Washington, DC 20037 US
(214) 337-5700, *Fax:* (214) 337-5707
www.kkgmam.com
traffic@kkgmam.com
License: Fort Worth, TX held by Mortenson Broadcasting Co. of Texas Inc.
Group Owner: Mortenson Broadcasting Co.; (acq 5-31-2002; with KHVN(AM) Fort Worth).
Arbitron Metro Market: Dallas-Fort Worth *Format:* Gospel, Sports
Target Audience: 30-64. *Adv. Rates:* 50; 40; 50; 30
Paul Hughes, Operations Dir
Lon Sosh, General Manager
Jack Davis, Programming Director
Mike Price, Chief Engineer
Beverly Black, Office Manager
Nancy Burns, Public Service Director

KPLX
12-15-1962; 99.5 mhz FM *Hrs Open:* 24; 100 kw; 1677 ft.; N32 34 54 W96 58 32
140 East Market Street, York, PA 17401 US
(214) 520-4350, *Fax:* (214) 520-4343
www.995thewolf.com
info@kplzfm.com
License: Fort Worth, Tarrant County, TX held by KPLX Lico Inc.
Group Owner: Cumulus Media Partners LLC; (acq 1974)
Nat'l Network: AP Network News
Arbitron Metro Market: Dallas-Fort Worth *Format:* Country *Hrs. of News Programming:* news progmg 4 hrs wkly *No. News Employees:* 1 *Target Audience:* 25-54; loyal listeners throughout the day
Jim Quirk, General Sales Mgr
Dan Bennett, Promotions Manager
Rob Chickering, Chief Engineer

KSCS
03-08-1949; 96.3 mhz FM *Hrs Open:* 24; 99 kw; 1611 ft.; N32 35 15 W96 57 59
2221 East Lamar Blvd., Suite 400, Arlington, TX 76006 US
(817) 695-1820, *Fax:* (817) 695-0014
www.kscs.com
License: Fort Worth, Tarrant County, TX
Group Owner: Cumulus Media Inc.
Nat'l Reps: ABC Radio Sales
Arbitron Metro Market: Dallas-Fort Worth *Format:* Country
Greg Heitzman, General Sales Mgr
Robert Shiflet, Promotions Manager

*KTCU-FM
10-06-1964; 88.7 mhz FM *Hrs Open:* 6 AM-1 AM; 3 kw; 320 ft; N32 42 40 W97 22 00
Box 298020, Moudy Bldg., Fort Worth, TX 76129
(817) 257-7631,(817) 257-7634, *Fax:* (817) 257-7637
www.ktcu.net
ktcu@tcu.edu
License: Fort Worth, Tarrant County, TX held by Board of Trustees Texas Christian University.
Group Owner: TCU
Population Served: 1,000,000 *Arbitron Metro Market:* Dallas-Fort Worth *Special Programming:* some specialty shows
Russell Scott, General Manager
Janice McCall, Assistant Manager

WBAP
05-02-1922; 820 khz AM *Hrs Open:* 24; 50 kw-U, ND1; N32 36 38 W97 10 0
2221 East Lamar Blvd., Suite 400, Arlington, TX 76006 US
(702) 876-1460, *Fax:* (702) 876-6685
www.wearelv.com
info@espn1100.com
License: Fort Worth, TX
Group Owner: Cumulus Media Inc.; (acq 6-12-2007; grpsl)
Nat'l Reps: ABC Radio Sales
Arbitron Metro Market: Las Vegas NV *Format:* Sports
Tony Bonnici, General Manager
Jessee Leeds, General Sales Mgr
Mitch Moss, Programming Director
Andy Kaye, News Director

Fort Worth-Dallas

KDGE
04-10-1962; 102.1 mhz FM *Hrs Open:* 24; 100 kw; 1591 ft.; N32 34 54 W96 58 32
650 Madison Ave, New York, NY 10022 US
(214) 866-8000, *Fax:* (214) 866-8091
www.kdge.com
Josh@kdge.com
License: Fort Worth-Dallas, Tarrant County, TX held by Capstar TX L.P.
Group Owner: Clear Channel Communications Inc.; (acq 8-30-2000; grpsl).
Nat'l Reps: CBS Radio

Arbitron Metro Market: Fort Worth, TX *Format:* Alternative *Hrs. of News Programming:* news progmg 5 hrs wkly *No. News Employees:* 1 *Target Audience:* 20-44.
John Roberts, Operations Dir
J.D. Freeman, General Manager
Tracy Martin Taylor, Station Manager

Franklin

KJXJ
04-08-1985; 103.9 mhz FM *Hrs Open:* 24; 8.7 kw; 197.5 feet; 30-53-05.7 N 096-32-29.6 W
Mailing Address: Box 3069, Bryan, TX 77802
Second Address: 1240 E. Villa Maria Rd., Bryan, TX 77802
(979) 776-1240, *Fax:* (979) 776-0123
License: Franklin, Robertson County, TX held by Brazos Valley Communications Ltd.
Group Owner: Brazos Valley Communications Ltd.; (acq 8-31-2006; grpsl)
Nat'l Reps: Katz Radio
Population Served: 150,000 *Arbitron Metro Market:* Bryan-College Station, TX *Special Programming:* Letterman, SNL *Target Audience:* 18-49; 25-54.
Dan Ginzel, Operations Dir
Chris Kiske, General Manager
Nathan Peacock, General Sales Mgr
Lance Parr, Chief Engineer

Frankston

KOYE
06-15-1970; 96.7 mhz FM *Hrs Open:* 24; 50 kw; 492 ft.; N32 2 22 W95 24 39
101 South Fourth Street, P.O. Box 1067, Crockett, TX 75835 US
(903) 581-9966, *Fax:* (903) 534-5300
www.lainvasora.fm
request@koye.com
License: Frankston, Anderson County, TX held by Access.1 Texas License Company LLC.
Group Owner: Access.1 Communications Corp.; (acq 1-7-2005; grpsl)
Nat'l Reps: McGavren Guild
Arbitron Metro Market: Tyler, TX *Target Audience:* 18-49. *Adv. Rates:* 45; 45; 45; 45
Ginger Nimmons, General Manager
Dru Laborde, Programming Director
Robert Taylor, National Sales Manager

Fredericksburg

KNAF
11-01-1947; 910 khz AM; 1 kw-D, ND1; 0.174 kw-N, ND1; N30 17 12 W98 52 58
Mailing Address: 210 Woodcrest, Fredericksburg, TX 78624 US
Second Address: 210 Woodcrest, Fredericksburg, TX 78624
(830) 997-2197, *Fax:* (830) 997-2198
texasrebelradio@fbgn
License: Fredericksburg, TX held by J. & J. Fritz Media Ltd.
Group Owner: J. & J. Fritz Media Ltd.; (acq 1-23-91;
Format: Country, Talk *Special Programming:* Farm 5 hrs, Polka 4.5 hrs wkly *Adv. Rates:* 14; 14; 14; 14
Jayson Fritz, President
Jan Fritz, Operations Dir
Rick Star, Programming Director
Arziana Carruth, Promotions Manager
Holley Day, Music Director

KNAF-FM
01-01-2005; 105.7 mhz FM; 9.1 kw; 538 ft.; N30 21 49 W98 54 47
Mailing Address: P.O. Box 311, Fredericksburg, TX 78624 US
Second Address: 210 Woodcrest, Fredericksburg, TX 78624
(830) 997-2197, *Fax:* (830) 997-2198
www.knafam.com
txradio@ktc.com
License: Fredericksburg, Gillespie County, TX
Group Owner: J. & J. Fritz Media Ltd.
Arbitron Metro Market: Fredericksburg, TX *Format:* Country *Target Audience:* 18-54. *Adv. Rates:* 18; 18; 18; 18
Jayson Fritz, Engineering Dir

*KBLC
08-01-2008; 91.5 mhz FM; 3.1 kw; 394 ft.; N30 11 49 W98 38 19
2424 Blvd, Houston, TX 77098 US
(713) 520-5200
www.khcb.org
License: Fredericksburg, Gillespie County, TX held by Houston Christian Broadcasters Inc.
Group Owner: Houston Christian Broadcasters Inc.
Arbitron Metro Market: Fredericksburg, TX *Format:* Christian *Hrs. of News Programming:* News progmg 6 hrs wkly
Bruce Munsterman, General Manager
Bonnie BeMent, News Director

Freeport

KJOJ-FM
01-01-1987; 103.3 mhz FM; 100 kw; 994 ft.; N28 48 57 W95 36 3
200 Concord Plaza, Suite 600, San Antonio, TX 78216 US
(713) 315-3400, *Fax:* (713) 315-3565
www.laraza.fm
Houstoninfo@lbimedia.com
License: Freeport, Brazoria County, TX held by Liberman Broadcasting of Houston License LLC.
Group Owner: Liberman Broadcasting Inc.; (acq 3-20-2001; grpsl)
Arbitron Metro Market: Houston, TX *Target Audience:* 18-49.
Lenard Liberman, CEO
Winter Horton, Operations Dir
Gerardo Reyes, General Sales Mgr
Cheque Gonzalez, Programming Director
Meliza Posada, News Director

Freer

*KPBN
01-01-2004; 90.7 mhz FM; 0.7 kw; 312 ft.; N27 48 55 W98 41 45
P O Box 252, McAllen, TX 78505 US
(956) 686-6382, *Fax:* (956) 686-2999
License: Freer, Duval County, TX held by Paulino Bernal Evangelism.
Arbitron Metro Market: Freer, TX *Format:* Christian
Paulino Bernal Jr., President

Fremont

*KLBD(FM)
88.1 mhz FM; 100 w vert; Ant 220 ft; N27 17 20 W98 07 23
The Worship Center of Knoxville, PO Box 260715, Corpus Christi, TX 78480
(361) 299-1960
License: Fremont, Brooks County, TX held by The Worship Center of Knoxville
Population Served: 307,953 *Arbitron Metro Market:* Corpus Christi, TX
Nancy Doerner, General Manager

Friona

KGRW
11-01-1994; 94.7 mhz FM; 48 kw; 500 ft.; N34 41 17 W102 56 53
Rebroadcasts: Rebroadcasts KQFX(FM) Borger 100%
2402 Broadmoor, Bldg D-2, Suite 101, Bryan, TX 77802 US
(806) 355-1044, *Fax:* (806) 457-0642
www.gruvworks.com
gruvworks@aol.com
License: Friona, Parmer County, TX held by Tejas Broadcasting Ltd. LLP.
Group Owner: Tejas Broadcasting Ltd. LLP; (acq 11-15-2004; grpsl).
Format: Variety/Diverse *Target Audience:* 25-54; working class Texas born Hispanic audience
Matt Douglas, General Manager
Brad Gonzalez, General Sales Mgr
Daniel, Programming Director
Emilia Chacon, News Director
Charles Singleton, Chief Engineer

Frisco

KATH
10-01-1936; 910 khz AM
17719 Cedar Creek, Canyon Drive, Dallas, TX 75252 US
(214) 634-7780, *Fax:* (214) 634-7523
License: Frisco, TX held by Chatham Hill Foundation Inc.
Arbitron Metro Market: Dallas-Fort Worth *Format:* Sports *Target Audience:* Ages 18-44; Hispanic sports & music fans *Adv. Rates:* 60; 40; 80; 20
Gus Perez, General Manager
Fernando Gonzalez, General Sales Mgr
Arturo Canizalez, Programming Director
Adriana Balero, News Director

Gainesville

KSOC
01-01-1958; 94.5 mhz FM *Hrs Open:* 24; kw
15851 Dallas Parkway, Suite 1200, Dallas, TX 75248 US
(972) 331-5400, *Fax:* (972) 726-0940
www.oldschool945.com
Oldschool945@Radio-One.com
License: Gainesville, Cooke County, TX held by Radio One Licenses LLC.
Group Owner: Radio One Inc.; (acq 11-8-01; grpsl).
Arbitron Metro Market: Dallas-Fort Worth *Format:* Adult Contemp *Hrs. of News Programming:* news progmg one hr wkly *No. News Employees:* 1 *Target Audience:* 18-44; affluent generation X'ers
Gary Spurgeon, General Manager
John Candelaria, Programming Director
Don Stevenson, Chief Engineer
Barbara Wilson, Business Manager
Steve Walker, Assistant Engineer

KGAF
01-01-1947; 1580 khz AM; 0.25 kw-D, DAN; 0.25 kw-N, DAN; N33 37 42 W97 6 25
801 E. Ca. St.,PO Box996, Gainesville, TX 76240 US
(940) 665-5546, *Fax:* (940) 665-1580
www.memories1580.com
info@kgaf1580.com
License: Gainesville, TX held by First IV Media Inc.
Regional Network: Texas State Networks
Arbitron Metro Market: Gainesville, TX *Format:* Adult Contemp, News, 62, Oldies, Talk *Special Programming:* Farm 3 hrs, sports 3 hrs wkly, community 3 hrs wkly *No. News Employees:* 1 *Target Audience:* 25-54; m/f
Steve Eberhart, General Manager
Curt Spain, General Sales Mgr
Dee Blanton, Programming Director
Stephen Monahan, News Director
Frank Bonner, Chief Engineer
Chad Henderson, Disc Jockey
Erik Lesko, Disc Jockey
Clay Corbett,Sports Director

Galveston

KGBC
05-01-1947; 1540 khz AM *Hrs Open:* 24
No. 11, Pelican Island, Galveston, TX 77554 US
(409) 744-4567, *Fax:* (409) 740-0944
www.kgbc1540.com
sigabroadcasting@gmail.com
License: Galveston, TX held by SIGA Broadcasting Corp.
Group Owner: SIGA Broadcasting Corp.; acq 5-9-2002; $900,000).
Arbitron Metro Market: Galveston, TX *Format:* Chinese *Target Audience:* Chinese Adults
Gabriel Arango, President
Julian Arango, Station Manager
Bobby Coles, General Sales Mgr

KOVE-FM
07-01-2001; 106.5 mhz FM *Hrs Open:* 24; 98 kw; 1962 ft.; N29 18 0 W95 6 40
1980 Post Oak Blvd., Suite 1500, Houston, TX 77056 US
(713) 965-2400, *Fax:* (713) 965-2401
www.recuerdo1065.univision.com
info@univision.com
License: Galveston, Galveston County, TX held by HBC License Corp.
Group Owner: Univision Radio; (acq 9-22-2003; grpsl)
Arbitron Metro Market: Greater Houston *Format:* Spanish *Hrs. of News Programming:* news progmg 3 hrs wkly *No. News Employees:* 1 *Target Audience:* 18-49; assimilated Hispanics
Mark Masepohl, Operations Dir
Mark Masepohl, VP
Dave Burdette, Station Manager
Dave Burdett, General Sales Mgr
Eleazar Garcia, Programming Director
Nestor Enriquez, Promotions Manager
Marty Scruggs, Engineering Dir
Kim Mercier,National Sales Manager
Arnulfo Ramirez, Operations Director
Nestor Enriquez, Promotions Manager
Renzo Heredia, Public Affairs Director

Ganado

KHTZ
11-26-1997; 104.7 mhz FM *Hrs Open:* 24; 50 kw; 459 ft.; N28 55 37 W96 46 54
102 Jason Plaza, Victoria, TX 77901 US
(979) 836-9411, *Fax:* (361) 579-4105
www.lonestarfm.com
ego@lonestarfm.com
License: Ganado, Jackson County, TX held by Roy E. Henderson.
Group Owner: Fort Bend Broadcasting Co.; (acq 5-10-2001; $1.5 million)
Regional Network: Texas State Networks
Arbitron Metro Market: Ganado, TX *Format:* Country *Target Audience:* 25-64; skews males
Ryan Henderson, General Manager

Gardendale

KFZX

01-09-1984; 102.1 mhz FM *Hrs Open:* 24; 100 kw; 984 ft.; N31 57 55 W102 46 10
600 Congress Avenue, Suite 1400, Austin, TX 78701 US
(432) 563-9102, *Fax:* (432) 580-9102
www.classicrock102.net
License: Gardendale, Ector County, TX
Group Owner: ICA Radio Ltd.; (acq 10-1-2007; grpsl)
Nat'l Reps: Eastman Radio
Arbitron Metro Market: Odessa, TX *Format:* Classic Rock *Target Audience:* 25-54.
Mike Gatons, General Manager
Robert Hallmark, Programming Director
Rodney Norris, Chief Engineer

Garland

KAAM

01-01-1973; 770 khz AM *Hrs Open:* 24; 10 kw-D, 1 kw-N, DA-2; N33 01 58 W96 34 31
3201 Royalty Row, Irving, TX 75356
(972) 445-1700, *Fax:* (972) 438-6574
www.kaamradio.com
cbcstand@aol.com
License: Garland, Dallas County, TX held by DJRD Broadcasting
Group Owner: Crawford Broadcasting Co.; (acq 1979).
Population Served: 6,000,000 *Arbitron Metro Market:* Dallas-Fort Worth *Target Audience:* 35 plus; Christian
Don Crawford, President
Don Crawford Jr., General Manager

Gatesville

*KVLW

01-01-2005; 88.1 mhz FM; 16.5 kw vert; Ant 1,096 ft; N31 18 53 W97 19 36
Mailing Address: American Educational Broadcasting Inc., 3185 S. Highland Dr., Las Vegas, NV 33406
Second Address: 3411 Market Loop, Studio, Suite 108, Temple, TX 76502
(254) 791-5251, *Fax:* (254) 791-0200
License: Gatesville, McLennan County, TX held by American Educational Broadcasting Inc.
Nat'l Network: K-Love
Arbitron Metro Market: Waco, TX
Carl Auel, President
James Auel, General Manager

George West

KGWT

01-01-2008; 93.5 mhz FM; 22.5 kw; 344 ft.; N28 17 37 W98 13 16
US
(361) 449-1315
License: George West, Live Oak County, TX held by Hispanic Target Media Inc.
Group Owner: Hispanic Target Media Inc.
Arbitron Metro Market: George West, TX *Format:* Country
Francisco San Millan, President

Georgetown

KLJA(FM)

10-31-1991; 107.7 mhz FM *Hrs Open:* 24; 25 kw; Ant 508 ft; N30 42 17 W97 38 32
57 W. South Temple, Suite 107, Salt Lake City, UT 84101
(512) 419-1077, *Fax:* (512) 340-7169
www.netmio.com
info@kinvfm.com
License: Georgetown, Williamson County, TX held by Univision Radio License Corp.
Group Owner: Univision Radio; (acq 9-22-2003; grpsl)
Arbitron Metro Market: Austin, TX *Format:* Spanish, Christian *Target Audience:* 18-34; male *Adv. Rates:* 85; 85; 90; 20
Sandi Brown, General Manager

KHFI-FM

03-01-1972; 96.7 mhz FM *Hrs Open:* 24; 100 kw; 951 ft.; N30 19 20 W97 48 3
3305 W. Mountain Rd, #60, Las Vegas, NV 89102 US
(512) 684-7300, *Fax:* (512) 684-7441
www.967kissfm.com
info@967kissfm.com
License: Georgetown, Williamson County, TX held by CCB Texas Licenses L.P.
Group Owner: Clear Channel Communications Inc.; (acq 3-9-93; $3.5 million;
Nat'l Reps: Clear Channel
Arbitron Metro Market: Austin, TX *Format:* Rock/AOR *Hrs. of News Programming:* news progmg one hr wkly *No. News Employees:* 1 *Target Audience:* 18-49; adult women
Mac Daniels, Operations Dir
Melody Caldwell, General Sales Mgr
Tracy Walker, Programming Director
Pam McKay, Promotions Manager
Gil Garcia, Engineering Dir
Mitch Bordeno, Business Manager
Mel Jones, Sales Director

Giddings

*KANJ

10-28-1999; 91.1 mhz FM *Hrs Open:* 24; 0.45 kw; 335 ft.; N30 9 56 W96 52 15 *Rebroadcasts:* Rebroadcasts KHCB-FM Houston 95%
P. O. Box 933, Giddings, TX 78942 US
(713) 520-5200
www.khcb.org
email@khcb.org
License: Giddings, Lee County, TX held by Houston Christian Broadcasters Inc.
Group Owner: Houston Christian Broadcasters Inc.
Nat'l Network: Moody
Arbitron Metro Market: Houston, TX *Format:* Christian
Bruce Munsterman, General Manager
Bonnie BeMent, Assistant General Manager

Gilmer

KFRO-FM

07-24-1980; 95.3 mhz FM *Hrs Open:* 24; 5.9 kw; 666 ft.; N32 37 50 W94 53 44
13355 Noel Road, Dallas, TX 75240 US
(903) 586-2527, *Fax:* (903) 589-0677
License: Gilmer, Upshur County, TX held by Walller Media LLC.
Group Owner: Waller Broadcasting; (acq 6-15-98; $1.425 million with KFRO(AM) Longview).
Nat'l Reps: Roslin
Arbitron Metro Market: Gilmer, TX *Format:* Spanish *Target Audience:* 25-49.
Dudley Waller, General Manager

Gladewater

KEES

01-01-1947; 1430 khz AM; 5 kw-D, DAN; 1 kw-N, DAN; N32 31 46 W94 52 50
Mailing Address: 928 N.E. Loop 323, Tyler, TX 75708 US
Second Address: 1001 E Southeast Loop 323, Suite 455, Tyler, TX 75701-9600
(903) 593-2519, *Fax:* (903) 597-8378
www.ktbb.com
info@ktbb.com
License: Gladewater, TX held by Gleiser Communications LLC
Group Owner: Gleiser Communications LLC; acq 11-21-03; grpsl).
Nat'l Network: Westwood One *Nat'l Reps:* Riley
Arbitron Metro Market: Tyler-Longview, TX *Format:* Talk
Paul Gleiser, General Manager
Angie Mapes, News Director
Mike LaRoux, Chief Engineer

Glen Rose

KTFW-FM

01-01-1989; 92.1 mhz FM; 25 kw; 1417 ft.; N32 16 31 W98 1 22
P.O. Box 1629, Cleburne, TX 76033 US
(817) 332-0959, *Fax:* (817) 348-8373
www..countrylegends921.com
License: Glen Rose, Somervell County, TX held by LKCM Radio Group L.P.
Group Owner: LKCM Radio Group L.P.; (acq 1-13-2006; $10,142,816).
Regional Network: Texas State Networks
Arbitron Metro Market: Fort Worth, TX *Format:* Country *Target Audience:* 40 plus.
Gerry Schlegel, President
George Marti, Operations Dir
Mike Crow, Programming Director

Goldsmith

KTXO

94.7 mhz FM; 6 kw; 318 ft.; N31 52 2 W102 39 18
US
(512) 467-0643
License: Goldsmith, Ector County, TX held by Matinee Radio LLC.
Group Owner: Matinee Radio LLC
Arbitron Metro Market: Monterey-Salinas-Santa Cruz, CA
Robert Walker, President

Goliad

KHMC

01-01-1995; 95.9 mhz FM *Hrs Open:* 24; 25 kw; 322 ft.; N28 40 57 W97 18 50
115 West Avenue D, Robstown, TX 78380 US
(361) 575-9533, *Fax:* (361) 575-9502
www.majic95fm.com
majictejano@yahoo.com
License: Goliad, Goliad County, TX held by Cinco de Mayo Broadcasting.
Format: Tejano *Target Audience:* Spanish Adults
Homer Lopez, General Manager
Ralph Salezar, General Sales Mgr
Lilo Arguellez, Program Director

Gonzales

KCTI

12-17-1947; 1450 khz AM; 1 kw-U, ND1; N29 30 35 W97 24 51
707 St. Francis Street, Gonzales, TX 78629 US
(830) 672-3631, *Fax:* (830) 672-9603
www.kcti1450.com
kcti@kcti1450.com
License: Gonzales, TX held by Gonzales Communications, a Texas L.P.
Regional Network: Texas State Networks
Arbitron Metro Market: Gonzales, TX *Format:* Country *Target Audience:* General.
Steven Oakes, General Manager
Syble Kline, General Sales Mgr
Dian Bowman, Programming Director
Egon Barthels, Promotions Manager
L.D. Decker, News Director
Bill Woleben, Chief Engineer
Marina Mann, General Manager/Partner

*KMLR

03-01-1986; 106.3 mhz FM; 15 kw; 423 ft.; N29 41 17 W97 40 39
615 St. Paul, Gonzales, TX 78629 US
(916) 251-1600, *Fax:* (916) 251-1650
www.klove.com
License: Gonzales, Gonzales County, TX held by Educational Media Foundation.
Group Owner: EMF Broadcasting; (acq 3-31-2006; $6 million with KYLR(FM) Hutto).
Nat'l Network: K-Love
Arbitron Metro Market: Rocklin, CA *Format:* Christian
Mike Novak, President
Eric Allen, General Sales Mgr
David Pierce, Programming Director
Ed Lenane, News Director
Sam Wallington, Engineering Dir
Scott Smith, Music Director
Marya Morgan, News Reporter
Richard Hunt, NewsReporter
Tracy Butler, Traffic Manager

*KRNZ

01-01-2008; 88.1 mhz FM; 1.3 kw; Ant 384 ft; N29 29 09 W97 29 17 *Rebroadcasts:* Rebroadcasts KLRD(FM) Yucaipa, CA 100%
2351 Sunset Blvd., Suite 170-218, Rocklin, CA 78046
(916) 251-1600, *Fax:* (916) 251-1650
www.air1.com
info@air1.com
License: Gonzales, Gonzales County, TX held by Educational Media Foundation.
Group Owner: EMF Broadcasting; (acq 2-28-2006; $36,000 for CP)
Nat'l Network: Air 1
Mike Novak, President
David Pierce, Programming Director
Ed Lenane, News Director
Sam Wallington, Engineering Dir
Marya Morgan, News Reporter
Richard Hunt, News Reporter

Graham

KSWA

01-01-1948; 1330 khz AM *Hrs Open:* 24; 0.5 kw-D, NDD; 0.051 kw-N, ND1; N33 7 37 W98 35 35
620 Oak Street, Graham, TX 76046 US
(940) 549-1330, *Fax:* (940) 549-8628
gm@kwkq-kswa.com
License: Graham, TX held by Graham Newspapers Inc.
Group Owner: Graham Newspapers Inc.; (acq 1996)
Regional Network: Texas State Networks
Arbitron Metro Market: Graham, TX *Format:* Country *Special Programming:* Bluegrass 2 hrs, gospel 2 hrs, Texas mus 2 hrs

wkly *Hrs. of News Programming:* news progmg 10 hrs wkly *No. News Employees:* 1 *TargetAudience:* Adults 35 plus. *Adv. Rates:* 15; 15; 15; 15
Roy Robinson, Operations Dir
Joe Graham, General Manager
Cindy Lewis, General Sales Mgr
Greg Tiller, Programming Director
James Jones, News Director
Christy Garcia, Traffic Manager

KWKQ
08-01-1975; 94.7 mhz FM *Hrs Open:* 24; 10.5 kw; 486 ft.; N33 2 30 W98 46 44
620 Oak Street, Graham, TX 76450 US
(940) 549-1330, *Fax:* (940) 549-8628
License: Graham, Young County, TX
Group Owner: Graham Newspapers Inc.
Regional Network: Texas State Networks
Arbitron Metro Market: Graham, TX *Format:* Classic Rock
Special Programming: Alternative 6 hrs wkly *Hrs. of News Programming:* news progmg 5 hrs wkly *No. News Employees:* 1 *Target Audience:* Adults 25-54.*Adv. Rates:* 15; 15; 15; 15
Roy Robinson, Operations Dir
Joe Graham, General Manager
Jim Jones, News Director

Granbury

KPIR
03-13-1980; 1420 khz AM *Hrs Open:* 24; 0.5 kw-D, DA2; 0.5 kw-N, DA2; N32 27 43 W97 47 19
P. O. Box 1534, Granbury, TX 76048 US
(817) 736-0360, *Fax:* (817) 736-0344
www.kpir.com
License: Granbury, TX held by Pirate Broadcasters Inc.
Arbitron Metro Market: Dallas-Fort Worth *Format:* Country
Special Programming: Farm one hr wkly *Hrs. of News Programming:* news progmg 21 hrs wkly *No. News Employees:* 1 *Target Audience:* 25-55; general
Bob Haschke, General Manager
Shayne Hollinger, Programming Director
Sue Haschke, News Director
Justin McClure, Chief Engineer

Grand Prairie

KKDA
08-01-1957; 730 khz AM; 0.5 kw-D, DAN; 0.5 kw-N, DAN; N32 45 51 W96 59 26
P. O. Box 530860, Grand Prairie, TX 75053 US
(972) 263-9911, *Fax:* (972) 558-0010
www.k104fm.com
License: Grand Prairie, TX held by Service Broadcasting Group LLC.
Group Owner: Service Broadcasting Group LLC; (acq 12-22-76)
Arbitron Metro Market: Dallas, TX *Format:* Blues, Oldies
Hymen Childs, President
Chuck Smith, General Manager
Steve Watkins, General Sales Mgr
Willis Johnson, Programming Director
Gary Wachter, Chief Engineer

Greenville

KGVL
03-26-1946; 1400 khz AM; 1 kw-U; N33 10 02 W96 05 55
Mailing Address: Box 1015, Greenville, TX 75401
Second Address: 1517 Wolfe City Dr., Greenville, TX 75401
(903) 455-1400, *Fax:* (903) 455-5485
License: Greenville, Hunt County, TX held by Dynamic Broadcasting LLC
Group Owner: Hunt County Radio LLC; (acq 1-11-2005; $500,000).
Nat'l Network: Fox News Radio *Regional Network:* Texas State Networks
Population Served: 70,000*Special Programming:* farm 5 hrs, relg 6 hrs wkly *Hrs. of News Programming:* 14 *No. News Employees:* 2 *Target Audience:* 25 plus.
Mike Horne, General Manager
Jim Patrick, Programming Director
Jason Russell, Chief Engineer

KIKT
09-15-1978; 93.5 mhz FM *Hrs Open:* 24; 1.8 kw; Ant 328 ft; N33 11 00 W96 03 19
Mailing Address: 140 EAST MARKET STREET, York, PA 75403
Second Address: 1517 Wolfe City Dr., Greenville, TX 75401
(903) 455-1400, *Fax:* (903) 455-5485
hometownradiokikt@gmail.com
License: Greenville, Hunt County, TX held by KRBE Lico Inc.
Group Owner: Hunt County Radio LLC; (acq 9-2-99; with co-located AM).
Regional Network: Fox News Radio
Hrs. of News Programming: News progmg 15 hrs wkly *Target Audience:* General.
Mike Horne, General Manager

***KTXG**
01-01-2006; 90.5 mhz FM; 38 kw; 722 ft.; N33 19 0 W96 24 27
Rebroadcasts: Rebroadcasts WAFR(FM) Tupelo, MS 100%
P O Drawer 2440, Tupelo, MS 38803 US
(662) 844-8888, *Fax:* (662) 842-6791
www.afr.net
faq@afr.net
License: Greenville, Hunt County, TX held by American Family Association.
Group Owner: American Family Radio
Arbitron Metro Market: Greenville, TX *Format:* Christian
Marvin Sanders, General Manager

Gregory

KPUS
01-01-1999; 104.5 mhz FM *Hrs Open:* 24; 14 kw; 446 ft.; N27 52 2 W97 13 7
7755 Carondelet Ave., Clayton, MO 63105 US
(361) 814-3800, *Fax:* (361) 855-3770
classicrock1045.com
info@classicrook1045.com
License: Gregory, San Patricio County, TX held by Convergent Broadcasting Corpus Christi LP.
Group Owner: Convergent Broadcasting LP; (acq 1-12-2004; grpsl).
Arbitron Metro Market: Corpus Christi, TX *Format:* Classic Rock
Target Audience: Adults; 25-54
Scott Holt, Operations Dir
Mark White, General Manager
Dallas Garcia, General Sales Mgr
Amanda Moreno, News Director
Molly Cox, Music Director

Groves

KCOL-FM
09-17-1983; 92.5 mhz FM *Hrs Open:* 24; 31 kw; 430 ft.; N30 3 43 W93 58 50
P.O. Box 22257, Beaumont, TX 77720 US
(409) 896-5555, *Fax:* (409) 896-5566
www.cool925.com
info@cool1925.com
License: Groves, Jefferson County, TX held by Clear Channel Broadcasting Licenses Inc.
Group Owner: Clear Channel Communications Inc.; (acq 1-29-2004; $4.5 million).
Arbitron Metro Market: Beaumont-Port Arthur, TX *Format:* Oldies
Target Audience: 35 plus. *Adv. Rates:* 63; 63; 63; 63
John Hogan, CEO
Trey Poston, Operations Dir
Vesta Brandt, General Manager
Jim Love, Programming Director
Mark Guzman, Promotions Manager
Harold Mann, News Director
Randall Mays, CFO
Trey Poston, Operations Director
MarkKopelman, Vice President

Hallettsville

KTXM
10-29-1997; 99.9 mhz FM; 3.4 kw; 348 ft.; N29 27 45 W96 56 4
Rebroadcasts: Rebroadcasts KYKM(FM) Yoakum 100%
111 North Main Street, Hallettsville, TX 77964 US
(361) 798-4333, *Fax:* (361) 798-3798
www.texasthunderradio.com
texasthunderradio@yahoo.com
License: Hallettsville, Lavaca County, TX held by Kremling Enterprises Inc.
Arbitron Metro Market: Hallettsville, TX *Format:* Country
Laura Kremling, Station Manager
Travis Kremling, Programming Director

Haltom City

KLIF-FM
01-01-1995; 93.3 mhz FM; 50 kw; 276 ft; N32 54 44 W97 11 18
3500 Maple Ave., 13th Fl., Dallas, TX 17405
(214) 526-7400, *Fax:* (214) 525-2525
www.933thebone.com
License: Haltom City, Tarrant County, TX held by Texas Star Radio Inc.
Group Owner: Cumulus Media Partners LLC; (acq 1-28-97)
Arbitron Metro Market: Dallas-Fort Worth *Hrs. of News Programming:* News progmg 2 hrs wkly
Lew Dickey, CEO
Dan Bennett, Operations Dir
Carmen Lee, General Sales Mgr
Jerome Fischer, Programming Director
John Winchestor, Promotions Manager
Hue Beavers, Chief Engineer
John Dickey, Executive Vice President

Hamilton

KCLW
05-22-1948; 900 khz AM *Hrs Open:* 24; 0.25 kw-D, ND1; 0.01 kw-N, ND1; N31 43 8 W98 8 39
Mailing Address: P.O. Box 631, Hamilton, TX 76531 US
Second Address: 115 A N. Rice, Hamilton, TX 76531
(254) 221-4802, *Fax:* (254) 386-8804
www.kclw.com
tim@kclwradio.com
License: Hamilton, TX held by Lasting Value Broadcasting Group Inc.
Nat'l Network: CBS; Jones Radio Networks
Arbitron Metro Market: Killeen,TX *Format:* Country *Special Programming:* Relg 6 hrs, Sp 12 hrs wkly *Hrs. of News Programming:* news progmg 6 hrs wkly *No. News Employees:* 1 *Target Audience:* 18-65. *Adv.Rates:* 27; 22; 27; 10
Meredith Beal, President
Ronald Beal, Operations Dir
Sammie Casey, General Manager

Hamlin

KCDD
01-30-1987; 103.7 mhz FM; 98 kw; 984 ft.; N32 43 31 W100 4 19
111 East Kilbourn Ave., Suite 2700, Milwaukee, WI 53202 US
(325) 793-9700, *Fax:* (325) 692-1576
www.power103.com
ijim.christoferson@cumulus.com
License: Hamlin, Jones County, TX held by Cumulus Licensing Corp.
Group Owner: Cumulus Media Inc.; (acq 2-13-98; grpsl)
Arbitron Metro Market: Abilene, TX *Format:* Contemporary Hits/Top 40
Jim Christoferson, General Manager
Brad Elliott, Programming Director
Chris Andrews, Chief Engineer

Harker Heights

KUSJ
06-01-1987; 105.5 mhz FM; 33 kw; 600 ft.; N30 59 9 W97 37 51
608 Moody Lane, Temple, TX 76504 US
(254) 773-5252, *Fax:* (254) 773-0015
www.myus105.com
bourdon.wooten@townsquaremedia.com
License: Harker Heights, Bell County, TX held by Cumulus Licensing Corp.
Group Owner: Cumulus Media Inc.; (acq 2-2-00; grpsl).
Arbitron Metro Market: Harker Heights, TX *Format:* Country
Target Audience: 25-54.
Bourdon Wooten, Director of Sales
Jamie Garrett, Promotions Manager
Doug Bernhardt, Engineering Dir
Lisa Tanner, Promotions Director

Harlingen

KFRQ
01-01-1960; 94.5 mhz FM *Hrs Open:* 24; 100 kw; 1158 ft.; N26 8 55 W97 49 17
1350 One Galleria Tower, 13355 Noel Road, Dallas, TX 75240 US
(956) 661-6000, *Fax:* (956) 661-6082
www.kfrq.com
mquinn@entravision.com
License: Harlingen, Cameron County, TX held by Entravision Holdings LLC.
Group Owner: Entravision Communications Corp.; acq 1996; $6.1 million with KKPS(FM) Brownsville)
Arbitron Metro Market: Harlington TX *Format:* Rock/AOR *No. News Employees:* 1 *Target Audience:* 25-54.
Alex Duran, General Manager

KGBT
01-01-1941; 1530 khz AM *Hrs Open:* 24
3102 Oak Lawn Ave., Suite 215, Dallas, TX 75219 US
(956) 631-5499, *Fax:* (956) 631-0090
www.latremenda1530.com
info@netmio.com
License: Harlingen, TX held by Tichenor License Corp. (TLC).
Group Owner: Univision Radio; (acq 9-22-2003; grpsl)
Arbitron Metro Market: Harlington TX *No. News Employees:* 2 *Target Audience:* 18 plus.

Victoria Guerrero, President
Joe Morales, General Manager
Hugo Delacruz, Programming Director
Jorge Garza, Chief Engineer

KBTQ
07-01-1975; 96.1 mhz FM; 100 kw; Ant 449 ft; N26 10 34 W97 46 59
200 S. 10th, Suite 600, McAllen, TX 75219
(956) 631-5598, *Fax:* (956) 631-0090
www.netmio.com
info@netmio.com
License: Harlingen, Cameron County, TX held by Tichenor License Corp. (TLC).
Group Owner: Univision Radio
Population Served: 101,500 *Arbitron Metro Market:* McAllen-Brownsville-Harlingen, TX
Derek Underhill, President
Derrick Underhill, General Manager
Tom Anderson, Promotions Manager

***KMBH-FM**
04-30-1991; 88.9 mhz FM *Hrs Open:* 24; 3 kw; 299 ft.; N26 10 46 W97 30 6
Mailing Address: P.O. Box 2147, Harlingen, TX 78551 US
Second Address: 1701 Tennessee, Harlingen, TX 78551
(956) 421-4111, *Fax:* (956) 421-4150
www.kmbh.org
kmbhkhid@aol.com
License: Harlingen, Cameron County, TX held by RGV Educational Broadcasting Inc.
Nat'l Network: NPR
Arbitron Metro Market: McAllen, TX *TV Affiliate:* *KMBH(TV) affil
Format: Jazz, News *Special Programming:* Sp 3 hrs wkly *Hrs. of News Programming:* News progmg 34 hrs wkly *Target Audience:* General.
Fr. Pedro Briseno, CEO
Chris Maley, Programming Director

Hart

***KKFC**
89.3 mhz FM; 0.2 kw; 36 ft.; N34 23 23 W102 7 14
US
(940) 668-7971
www.kkfcradio.com
License: Hart, Castro County, TX held by 1 A Chord Inc.
Arbitron Metro Market: Gainesville, TX
Mary Fay Jackson, General Manager

Harts Bluff

***KPKP**
89.1 mhz FM; kw
US
(903) 466-6791
License: Harts Bluff, Red River County, TX held by Millennium Broadcasting Corp.
Arbitron Metro Market: Harts Bluff, TX
James Furlow Jr., President

Haskell

KVRP-FM
04-08-1981; 97.1 mhz FM *Hrs Open:* 24; 100 kw; 531 ft; N33 09 40 W99 48 57
Box 1118, 1406 N. First, Haskell, TX 79521
(940) 864-8505, *Fax:* (940) 864-8001
www.kvrp.com
gary@kvrp.com
License: Haskell, Haskell County, TX held by 1 Chronicles 14 L.P.
Group Owner: Weston Entertainment L.P.; (acq 8-4-2004; $700,000 with KVRP(A
Regional Network: Texas State Networks *Nat'l Reps:* Katz Radio
Population Served: 45,000 *Arbitron Metro Market:* Abilene, TX
Special Programming: Farm 5 hrs, relg 6 hrs wkly *Hrs. of News Programming:* News progmg 5 hrs wkly *Target Audience:* 25 plus.
Greg Weston, President
Gary Barrett, General Manager
Gary Barrett, General Sales Mgr
Dave Harrison, Programming Director
Dave Harrison, News Director
James Thompson, Chief Engineer
Tony St. James, Farm Director

Hearne

KVJM
05-15-1985; 103.1 mhz FM; 5 kw horiz, 4.9 kw vert; 361 ft.; N30 45 35 W96 28 0
219 North Main # 600, Bryan, TX 77803 US
(979) 779-3337, *Fax:* (979) 779-3444
www.mia1031.com
kvjmv103@aol.com
License: Hearne, Robertson County, TX held by Equal Access Media Inc.
Arbitron Metro Market: Bryan, TX *Target Audience:* 18-54.
Pluria Marshall Jr., General Manager
Edward Sanchez, Station Manager
Lester Pace, Programming Director
Ed Loftis, Chief Engineer
Plyria Marshall Jr., National Sales Manager

***KEDC**
88.5 mhz FM; 2.5 kw; 184 ft.; N30 46 12.6 W96 32 33
US
(979) 846-2825, *Fax:* (979) 846-0389
info@coalitionforlife.com
License: Hearne, Robertson County, TX held by Brazos Valley Coalition for Life.
Nat'l Network: EWTN Radio
Arbitron Metro Market: Hearne, TX *Format:* Christian
Shawn Carney, General Manager

Hebbronville

***KAZF**
11-01-2000; 91.9 mhz FM; 3 kw; 220 ft.; N27 19 0 W98 40 7
P O Box 252, McAllen, TX 78505 US
(956) 686-6382, *Fax:* (956) 686-2999
License: Hebbronville, Jim Hogg County, TX held by Paulino Bernal Evangelism.
Arbitron Metro Market: Hebbronville, TX *Format:* Christian
Gilbert Martinez, Station Manager

***KEKO**
01-01-2003; 101.7 mhz FM; 3 kw; 328 ft.; N27 18 46 W98 39 51
2702 Pine St, Laredo, TX 78043 US
(956) 726-4738, *Fax:* (928) 569-0456
www.lacadenaradioluz.com/keko.htm
info@israelsr.com
License: Hebbronville, Jim Hogg County, TX held by La Nueva Cadena Radio Luz Inc.
Format: Christian
Israel Tellez, President
Hiram Tellez, Programming Director

Helotes

KONO-FM
02-18-1971; 101.1 mhz FM *Hrs Open:* 24; 96 kw; 991 ft.; N29 31 25 W98 43 25
3773 Howard Hughes Pwy, Suite 300n, Las Vegas, NV 89109 US
(210) 615-5400, *Fax:* (210) 615-5300
www.kono101.com
License: Helotes, Bexar County, TX held by Cox Radio Inc.
Group Owner: Cox Radio Inc.; (acq 2-12-98; $23 million with KONO(AM) San Antonio)
Nat'l Reps: Katz Radio *Wire Services:* AP
Arbitron Metro Market: San Antonio, TX *Format:* Oldies *Hrs. of News Programming:* news progmg one hr wkly *No. News Employees:* 1 *Target Audience:* 25-54; total audience appeal
Bob Neil, CEO
Marty Choate, Operations Dir
Connie Tyra Kremer, General Sales Mgr
Roger Allen, Programming Director
Vera Flores, Promotions Manager
Chrissie Murnin, News Director
Paul Reynolds, Chief Engineer
Jeff Scott,National Sales Manager
Connye Rodriguez, Traffic Manager

Hemphill

KPBL
02-16-1978; 1240 khz AM
P. O. Box 1000, Hemphill, TX 75948 US
(409) 787-4796, *Fax:* (409) 787-2696
License: Hemphill, TX held by Phillip Burr Broadcasting Co.
Format: Country
Phillip Burr, President

KTHP
11-01-2000; 103.9 mhz FM *Hrs Open:* 24 hours; 4.5 kw; 377 ft.; N31 25 24 W93 50 30
595 San Antonio Ave, Many, LA 71449 US
(318) 256-5177, *Fax:* (318) 256-0950
www.bdcradio.com
kthp@sabinenet.com
License: Hemphill, Sabine County, TX held by Baldridge-Dumas Communications Inc.
Group Owner: Baldridge-Dumas Communications Inc.
Arbitron Metro Market: Shreveport, LA *Format:* Country
Michael Parker, Operations Dir
Rhonda Benson, VP/General Manager
Cindy Ezernack, Station Manager
Jenny Hodge, General Sales Mgr
Tedd Dumas, Owner
Ed Baldridge, Co-Owner

Hempstead

KTWL
01-01-1999; 105.3 mhz FM; 9.2 kw; 545 ft.; N30 18 19 W96 1 40
Rebroadcasts: Simulcasts KLTR(FM) Caldwell 100%
P.O. Box 948, Houston, TX 77001 US
(979) 836-0214, *Fax:* (979) 836-9435
www.texasmix.fm
lorihenderson01@hotmail.com
License: Hempstead, Waller County, TX held by Farmers Communications.
Arbitron Metro Market: Brenham, TX *Format:* Adult Contemp
Roy Henderson, CEO
Steve Britewell, Engineering Dir

Henderson

KWRD
03-01-1956; 1470 khz AM *Hrs Open:* 24; 5 kw-D, NDD; N32 10 55 W94 47 49
5946 Club Oaks Drive, Dallas, TX 75248 US
(903) 655-1800, *Fax:* (903) 655-1808
www.kwrdonline.com
info@kwrdonline.com
License: Henderson, TX held by Jerry Hanszen dba Hanszen Broadcasting Company
Nat'l Network: ESPN Radio *Regional Network:* Texas State Networks *Wire Services:* ABC
Arbitron Metro Market: Henderson, TX *Format:* Sports *No. News Employees:* 1 *Target Audience:* General.
David Jacobs, Operations Dir
David Chenault, General Manager
Julie Nichols, Sales Executive
Dennis Rivers, Sports Color Analyst
Jason Wade, Sports Director
Miles Toler, Sportscaster

Hereford

KJNZ
12-12-2000; 103.5 mhz FM; 50 kw; 279 ft.; N34 45 0 W102 22 54
C/O Fisher Wayland, 2001 Pennsylvania Ave NW, Washington, DC 20006 US
(806) 364-0277, *Fax:* (806) 363-6567
joelwithlaley@yahoo.com
License: Hereford, Deaf Smith County, TX held by Hereford Broadcasting LLC
Jose Aguillon, CEO
Joel Gallegos, General Manager

KPAN
08-01-1948; 860 khz AM *Hrs Open:* 24; 250 w-D, 231 w-N; N34 47 33 W102 25 45
Box 1757, 218 E. 5th St., Hereford, TX 79045
(806) 364-1860, *Fax:* (806) 364-5814
www.kpanradio.com
kpan@kpanradio.com
License: Hereford, Deaf Smith County, TX held by KPAN Broadcasters.
Nat'l Network: CBS *Regional Network:* Texas State Networks
Wire Services: AP
Population Served: 350,000*Special Programming:* Tejano 15 hrs, farm 12 hrs wkly *Hrs. of News Programming:* news progmg 20 hrs wkly *No. News Employees:* 1 *Target Audience:* General.
Chip Formby, General Manager
Brad Land, General Sales Mgr

KPAN-FM
09-01-1965; 106.3 mhz FM *Hrs Open:* 24; 30 kw; 259 ft; N34 47 33 W102 25 45 *Rebroadcasts:* Rebroadcasts KPAN(AM) Hereford.
Box 1757, 218 E. 5th St., Hereford, TX 79045
(806) 364-1860, *Fax:* (806) 364-5814
www.kpanradio.com
License: Hereford, Deaf Smith County, TX
Nat'l Network: CBS Radio *Regional Network:* Texas State Networks *Wire Services:* AP
Target Audience: General.
Chip Formby, General Manager

***KRLH**
01-01-2009; 90.9 mhz FM; 0.13 kw; 269 ft.; N34 51 2 W102 23 38 *Rebroadcasts:* Rebroadcasts KLVR(FM) Middletown, CA 100%
88 Casey Boulvard, Jackson, TN 38305 US
(916) 251-1600, *Fax:* (916) 251-1650
www.klove.com
klove@klove.com
License: Hereford, Deaf Smith County, TX held by Educational Media Foundation.
Group Owner: EMF Broadcasting; (acq 3-23-2007; grpsl)
Nat'l Network: K-Love
Arbitron Metro Market: Hereford, TX *Format:* Christian
Darrell Chambliss, Chairman
Alan Mason, CEO/COO
Mike Novak, CEO
David Pierce, Chief Creative Officer
Dan Antonelli, Chief Business Development Officer
Eric Moser, Chief Financial Officer
Brian Burger, Vice President of HumanResources
D. Kevin Blair, Secretary and General Counsel

Hico

KHHG
107.7 mhz FM
PO Box 1629, Cleburne, TX
(817) 645-6643
License: Hico, TX held by M&M Broadcasters LTD

Highland Park

KVCE
03-01-1960; 1160 khz AM *Hrs Open:* 24
7700 Carpenter Freeway, Dallas, TX 75247 US
(888) 839-2717
www.kvceradio.com
License: Highland Park, TX held by Dallas Broadcasting LLC
Arbitron Metro Market: Dallas-Fort Worth *Format:* Talk
Dan Patrick, General Manager

Highland Park-Dallas

KVIL
08-14-1961; 103.7 mhz FM *Hrs Open:* 24; 99 kw; 1663 ft.; N32 35 19 W96 58 5
600 New Hampshire Ave., N.W., Suite 1200, Washington, DC 20037 US
(214) 787-1037
www.kvil.com
feedback@kvil.com
License: Highland Park-Dallas, Dallas County, TX held by CBS Radio Partner I Inc.
Group Owner: CBS Radio; (acq 7-2-87)
Nat'l Network: CBS
Arbitron Metro Market: Dallas, TX *Format:* Light Rock
David Henry, General Manager

Highland Village

KWRD-FM
11-15-1988; 100.7 mhz FM *Hrs Open:* 18; 98 kw; 1988 ft.; N33 32 8 W96 49 54
P.O. Box 1080, Bowie, TX 76230 US
(972) 870-9949, *Fax:* (214) 561-9662
www.thewordfm.com
theword@thewordfm.com
License: Highland Village, Denton County, TX held by Inspiration Media of Texas LLC.
Group Owner: Salem Communications Corp.; (acq 1-17-2001; grpsl).
Arbitron Metro Market: Dallas-Fort Worth Metroplex/Sherman/Denison/Gaines *Format:* Christian, Talk
David Darling, Operations Dir
John L. Peoryea, General Manager
John L. Peroyea, General Sales Mgr
Ezio Torres, Programming Director
David Sparkman, Promotions Manager
Andy Pickard, Chief Engineer

Hillsboro

KBRQ
10-20-1959; 102.5 mhz FM *Hrs Open:* 24; 100 kw; 449 ft.; N31 49 23 W97 9 35
600 Congress Ave., Suite 1400, Austin, TX 78701 US
(254) 776-3900, *Fax:* (254) 761-6371
www.1025thebear.com
brenthenslee@clearchannel.com
License: Hillsboro, Hill County, TX held by Aloha Station Trust LLC, as Trustee
Arbitron Metro Market: Waco, TX *Format:* Classic Rock *Target Audience:* 25-49; men
Zack Owen, Operations Dir
Evan Armstrong, General Manager
Vernon Riggs, General Sales Mgr
Brent Henslee, Programming Director

KHBR
05-21-1948; 1560 khz AM *Hrs Open:* 12; 0.25 kw-D, NDD; N32 1 0 W97 6 32
Mailing Address: P. O. Box 569, Hillsboro, TX 76645 US
Second Address: 335 Country Club Rd., Hillsboro, TX 76645
(254) 582-3431, *Fax:* (254) 582-3800
www.khbrhillsboro.com
info@khbrhillsboro.com
License: Hillsboro, TX held by KHBR Radio Inc.
Regional Network: Texas State Networks *Wire Services:* NOAA Weather
Format: Country *Special Programming:* Czech 1.5 hrs, gospel 6 hrs wkly *Hrs. of News Programming:* News progmg 18 hrs wkly
Target Audience: General. *Adv. Rates:* 15;15; 15; na
Roger Galle, President
Rick Bailey, General Manager
Roger Creech, Programming Director

Holliday

KWFB
09-01-1982; 100.9 mhz FM *Hrs Open:* 24; 18.5 kw; 299 ft.; N33 49 42 W98 40 13
P. O. Box 29, Quanah, TX 79252 US
(940) 322-1009, *Fax:* (940) 767-3299
www.bobradio.fm
kixc@broadcast.net
License: Holliday, Hardeman County, TX held by KIXC-FM L.L.C.
Format: Variety/Diverse *Special Programming:* Farm 3 hrs, relg 2 hrs wkly *Hrs. of News Programming:* News progmg 10 hrs wkly *Target Audience:* General.
Glen Ingram, President
John White, Operations Dir
Michael Reeves, General Manager

***KGVB**
90.9 mhz FM; 7.5 kw; 351 ft.; N33 44 18 W98 54 28 US
(580) 332-0902, *Fax:* (580) 332-0922
www.thegospelstation.com
License: Holliday, Archer County, TX held by South Central Oklahoma Christian Broadcasting Inc.
Arbitron Metro Market: Holliday, TX
Randall Christy, President
Rick Cody, Vice President
Sharla Frederick, Treasurer / CFO

Hondo

KCWM
02-13-1970; 1460 khz AM *Hrs Open:* 6 AM-10 PM; 500 w-D, 226 w-N; N29 21 42 W99 07 42
Mailing Address: Box 447, Hondo, TX 78861
Second Address: 1605 Ave. K, Hondo, TX 78861
(830) 741-5296, *Fax:* (830) 426-3368
License: Hondo, Medina County, TX held by Hondo Communications Inc.
Regional Network: Texas State Networks *Nat'l Reps:* Keystone (unwired net)
Population Served: 35,000*Hrs. of News Programming:* news progmg 20 hrs wkly *No. News Employees:* 1 *Target Audience:* General.
Mike Carr, President
Mike Carr, General Sales Mgr
Tom Fusselmen, News Director
Paul McKay, Chief Engineer

KAHL-FM
01-01-1993; 105.9 mhz FM; 6 kw; Ant 328 ft; N29 18 48 W99 16 03
8023 Vantage Dr., Suite 840, San Antonio, TX 63017
(888) 522-7437, *Fax:* (210) 341-1777
License: Hondo, Medina County, TX held by Hondo RadioWorks Ltd.
John Barger, CEO

Hooks

KPWW
12-22-1985; 95.9 mhz FM *Hrs Open:* 24; 11.5 kw; 486 ft.; N33 27 25 W94 10 59
600 Congress Avenue, Suite 1400, Austin, TX 78701 US
(870) 772-3771, *Fax:* (870) 772-0364
www.power959.com
info@power959.com
License: Hooks, Bowie County, TX held by GAP Broadcasting Texarkana License LLC.
Group Owner: GAP Broadcasting LLC; (acq 8-3-2007; grpsl)
Nat'l Reps: McGavren Guild
Arbitron Metro Market: Texarkana *Format:* Contemporary Hits/Top 40 *No. News Employees:* 1 *Target Audience:* 18-49; contemp adults, upscale middle America
Ron Bird, General Manager
Phil Robken, General Sales Mgr
Wes Spicher, Programming Director
John Williams, News Director
Cindy Esterling, Traffic Manager

Hornsby

***KOOP**
11-01-1994; 91.7 mhz FM *Hrs Open:* 9 AM-7 PM (M-F); 9 AM-10 PM (S, Su); 3 kw; 85 ft.; N30 16 0 W97 40 27
Mailing Address: P. O. Box 49340, Austin, TX 78765 US
Second Address: 304 E. 5th St., Austin, TX 78768
(512) 472-1369,(512) 472-5667, *Fax:* (512) 472-6149
www.koop.org
info@koop.org
License: Hornsby, Travis County, TX held by Texas Educational Broadcasting Inc.
Format: Variety/Diverse *Special Programming:* American Indian one hr, Black 2 hrs, folk 7 hrs, Ger 5 hrs, Pol 5 hrs, Sp 10 hrs wkly *Hrs. of News Programming:* News progmg 14 hrs wkly
Amy Wright, Station Manager
Joanna Garfinkel, Programming Director
Lonny Stern, Promotions Manager

Houston

KBME
10-16-1944; 790 khz AM *Hrs Open:* 24; 5 kw-D, DA2; 5 kw-N, DA2; N29 54 54 W95 27 42
510 Lovett Blvd., Houston, TX 77006 US
(713) 212-8000, *Fax:* (713) 212-8790
www.790kbme.com
info@kbmeam.com
License: Houston, TX held by AMFM Texas Licenses L.P.
Group Owner: Clear Channel Communications Inc.; (acq 8-30-2000; grpsl).
Nat'l Network: ESPN Radio *Nat'l Reps:* Christal
Arbitron Metro Market: Houston-Galveston *Format:* Sports
Peggy Tuck, Operations Dir
Mark Copelman, General Manager
Pam McKay, General Sales Mgr
Ken Charles, Programming Director
Melissa Brezner, Promotions Manager
Bryan Erickson, News Director
David Armstrong, Chief Engineer
TimCollins, Programming Director
Dan Endom, Regional Sales Manager

KBXX
01-01-1958; 97.9 mhz FM; 95 kw; 1919 ft.; N29 34 34 W95 30 36
200 Concord Plaza, #600, San Antonio, TX 78216 US
(713) 623-2108, *Fax:* (713) 300-5751
www.theboxhouston.com
scorpio@kbxx.com
License: Houston, Harris County, TX held by Radio One Licenses LLC.
Group Owner: Radio One Inc.; (acq 2000).
Nat'l Reps: Clear Channel
Arbitron Metro Market: Houston, TX *Format:* Urban Contemporary *Target Audience:* 18-29; females
Ernest Jackson, President
Terri Thomas, Operations Dir
Doug Abernethy, General Manager
Bob McKay, General Sales Mgr
Terri Thomas, Programming Director
Jerry McCruse, Promotions Manager
David Ainslie, Engineering Dir
TomCallococci, Operations Manager

KCOH
01-01-1952; 1430 khz AM *Hrs Open:* 24
5011 Alameda, Houston, TX 77004 US
(713) 522-1001, *Fax:* (713) 521-0769
www.kcohradio.com
dsamuel@kcohradio.com
License: Houston, TX held by KCOH Inc.
Nat'l Network: Westwood One *Nat'l Reps:* Roslin
Arbitron Metro Market: Houston, TX *Format:* Black, Talk *Special Programming:* Sports *Hrs. of News Programming:* news progmg 15 hrs wkly *No. News Employees:* 2 *Target Audience:* 25-54; upbeat, knowledgeable,civic & politically minded adults
Mike Petrizzo, President
Travis Gardner, Operations Dir

Michael Harris, News Director
Don Samuel, Assistant Music Director

KNTH
01-17-1968; 1070 khz AM; 10 kw-D, DA2; 5 kw-N, DA2; N29 59 33 W95 28 23
4880 Santa Rosa Rd #300, Camarillo, CA 93012 US
(713) 260-3600, *Fax:* (713) 260-3628
www.1070knth.com
comment@knth.net
License: Houston, TX held by South Texas Broadcasting Inc.
Group Owner: Salem Communications Corp.; (acq 1-6-95; $2.5 million;
Nat'l Reps: Salem
Arbitron Metro Market: Houston-Galveston *Format:* News, News/Talk, 86
Paul Baker, Operations Dir
Chuck Jewell, General Manager
Dan Doster, General Sales Mgr
Kent McDonald, News Director
Sidney Jones, Chief Engineer
Ken Garza, Public Affairs Director

KEYH
11-01-1974; 850 khz AM; 10 kw-D, DA1; 0.185 kw-N, DA1; N29 39 19 W95 40 19
P.O. Box 311, Bellaire, TX 77402 US
(713) 315-3400, *Fax:* (713) 315-3506
www.estrellatv.com/radio
License: Houston, TX held by Liberman Broadcasting of Houston License LLC.
Group Owner: Liberman Broadcasting Inc.; (acq 4-22-2003; $5.70 million)
Arbitron Metro Market: Houston-Galveston *Target Audience:* 24-65; Hispanic, recent immigrants & primarily Sp speakers
Lenard Liberman, CEO
Winter Horton, General Manager
Gerardo Reyes, General Sales Mgr
Ezequiel Gonzalez, Programming Director
Meliza Posada, News Director
Mike Todd, Engineering Dir

*KHCB-FM
03-10-1962; 105.7 mhz FM *Hrs Open:* 24; 100 kw; 1614 ft.; N29 34 6 W95 29 57
2424 South Blvd., Houston, TX 77098 US
(713) 520-5200
www.khcb.org
email@khcb.org
License: Houston, Harris County, TX held by Houston Christian Broadcasters Inc.
Group Owner: Houston Christian Broadcasters Inc.
Nat'l Network: Moody
Arbitron Metro Market: Houston-Galveston *Format:* Christian
Special Programming: Sp 10 hrs, Chinese one hr wkly
Bruce Munsterman, General Manager
Bonnie BeMent, Programming Director
Dan Wales, Engineering Dir

KHMX
01-01-1961; 96.5 mhz FM; 97 kw; 1919 ft.; N29 34 34 W95 30 36
50 East Rivercenter Boulevard, Suite 1200, Covington, KY 41011 US
(713) 881-5100, *Fax:* (713) 881-5150
www.mix965houston.cbslocal.com
dsabetti@cbs.com
License: Houston, Harris County, TX held by CBS Radio Holdings Inc.
Group Owner: CBS Radio; (acq 4-1-2009; grpsl)
Arbitron Metro Market: Houston-Galveston *TV Affiliate:* CBS *Format:* Adult Contemp *Target Audience:* 25-40.
Brian Purdy, General Manager
Kate Harper, Programming Director
Bob Neumann, Program Director

KKHH
10-04-1959; 95.7 mhz FM *Hrs Open:* 24; 95 kw; 1919 ft.; N29 34 34 W95 30 36
600 New Hampshire Avenue, NW, Suite 1200, Washington, DC 20037 US
(713) 881-5100, *Fax:* (713) 881-5250
hothits957.cbslocal.com
License: Houston, Harris County, TX held by CBS Radio Partner I Inc.
Group Owner: CBS Radio; (acq 11-13-98; grpsl)
Nat'l Network: CBS *Nat'l Reps:* CBS Radio
Arbitron Metro Market: Houston-Galvest *Format:* Contemporary Hits/Top 40 *Target Audience:* 25-54.
Laura Morris, Operations Dir
Tony Belzer, General Sales Mgr
Mark Adams, Programming Director
Hunter Greene, Promotions Manager
Dan Woodard, Chief Engineer

KILT
01-01-1948; 610 khz AM *Hrs Open:* 8:30-5:00
600 New Hampshire Avenue, NW, Suite 1200, Washington, DC 20037 US
(713) 881-5100, *Fax:* (713) 881-5150
www.sportsradio610.com
houstonpsa@cbsradio.com
License: Houston, TX held by CBS Radio Partner I Inc.
Group Owner: CBS Radio; (acq 12-89)
Nat'l Reps: CBS Radio
Arbitron Metro Market: Houston-Galvest *Format:* Sports, Talk
Tim Gratzer, General Sales Mgr
Gavin Spittle, Programming Director
Maggie Wessel, Promotions Manager
Dan Woodard, Chief Engineer

KILT-FM
01-01-1961; 100.3 mhz FM *Hrs Open:* 24; 95 kw; 1919 ft.; N29 34 34 W95 30 36
600 New Hampshire Avenue, NW, Suite 1200, Washington, DC 20037 US
(713) 881-5100, *Fax:* (713) 881-5150
www.kilt.com
License: Houston, Harris County, TX held by CBS Radio Partner I Inc.
Group Owner: CBS Radio
Arbitron Metro Market: Houston-Galvest *Format:* Country
Tim Gratzer, General Sales Mgr

KKRW
01-01-1964; 93.7 mhz FM; 100 kw; 1719 ft.; N29 34 27 W95 29 37
650 Madison Ave, New York, NY 10022 US
(713) 212-8000, *Fax:* (713) 830-8099
www.kkrw.com
License: Houston, Harris County, TX held by Capstar TX L.P.
Group Owner: Clear Channel Communications Inc.; (acq 8-30-00; grpsl).
Arbitron Metro Market: Houston, TX *Format:* Classic Rock *Target Audience:* 25-54.
Vince Richards, Programming Director

KLAT
07-31-1961; 1010 khz AM; 5 kw-D, DA2; 3.6 kw-N, DA2; N29 53 47 W95 17 25; N29 51 44 W95 30 42
3102 Oak Lawn Ave., Suite 215, Dallas, TX 75219 US
(713) 407-1415, *Fax:* (713) 965-2401
www.univision.com
info@univision.com
License: Houston, TX held by Tichenor License Corp.
Group Owner: Univision Radio; (acq 9-22-2003; grpsl)
Arbitron Metro Market: Houston, TX *Format:* News, News/Talk, 86 *Target Audience:* 25-54; Hispanic
Mark Masepohl, Operations Dir
Dave Burdette, Station Manager
Kim McBride, General Sales Mgr
Rolando Becerra, Programming Director
Frances Jones, Promotions Manager
Renzo Heredia, News Director
Arnulfo Ramirez, OperationsManager
Pilar Torres, Arnulfo Ramirez
Manuel Cardona, Regional Sales Manager

KTBZ-FM
11-01-1964; 94.5 mhz FM; 97 kw; 1919 ft.; N29 34 34 W95 30 36
5353 W. Alabama, Houston, TX 77056 US
(713) 212-8000, *Fax:* (713) 212-8970
www.thebuzz.com
info@thebuzz.com
License: Houston, Harris County, TX held by AMFM Texas Licenses L.P.
Group Owner: Clear Channel Communications Inc.; (acq 8-30-00; grpsl).
Nat'l Reps: D & R Radio
Arbitron Metro Market: Houston, TX *Format:* Oldies *Special Programming:* Talk 2 hrs, relg one hr, pub affrs one hr wkly
Target Audience: 25-54; baby boomers
Ellen Cavanaugh, General Manager
Jim Trapp, Programming Director

KLOL
01-01-1947; 101.1 mhz FM; 96 kw; 1919 ft.; N29 34 34 W95 30 36
510 Lovett Blvd., Houston, TX 77006 US
(713) 881-5100, *Fax:* (713) 881-5150
www.mega101fm.com
info@klol.com
License: Houston, Harris County, TX held by CBS Radio Holdings Inc.
Group Owner: CBS Radio; (acq 4-1-2009; grpsl)
Nat'l Reps: CBS Radio
Arbitron Metro Market: Houston, TX *Target Audience:* 18-54.
Charlie Wilkinson, General Manager

KLTN
10-04-1960; 102.9 mhz FM *Hrs Open:* 24; 99.5 kw; 984 ft.; N29 45 26 W95 20 19
3102 Oak Lawn Avenue, Suite 215, Dallas, TX 75219 US
(713) 965-2400, *Fax:* (713) 965-2401
www.univision.com
info@univision.com
License: Houston, Harris County, TX held by Univision Radio Houston License Corp.
Group Owner: Univision Radio; (acq 9-22-2003; grpsl)
Arbitron Metro Market: Houston, TX *No. News Employees:* 1
Target Audience: 18-49; Hispanics
Mark Masepohl, Operations Dir
Dave Burdette, General Sales Mgr
Raul Brindis, Programming Director
Nestor Enriquez, Promotions Manager
Renzo Heredia, News Director
Marty Scruggs, Chief Engineer
Anna Munoz, National SalesManager
Arnulfo Ramirez, Kim Mercier

KMJQ
02-01-1964; 102.1 mhz FM *Hrs Open:* 24; 100 kw; 1719 ft.; N29 34 27 W95 29 37
Mailing Address: Suite 1508, 24 Greenway Plaza, Houston, TX 77046 US
Second Address: Box 22900, Houston, TX 77227-2900
(713) 623-2108, *Fax:* (713) 623-0106
www.kmjq.com
info@kmjqfm.com
License: Houston, Harris County, TX held by Radio One Licenses LLC.
Group Owner: Radio One Inc.; (acq 11-8-01; grpsl).
Nat'l Network: ABC *Nat'l Reps:* Clear Channel
Arbitron Metro Market: Houston, TX *Format:* Urban Contemporary *Special Programming:* Talk 3 hrs wkly *No. News Employees:* 2 *Target Audience:* 25-54; African-Americans
Carl Hamilton, Operations Dir
Mark McMillen, General Manager
Jerome Hutchinson, General Sales Mgr
Sam Choice, Programming Director
Bobrie Jefferson, Promotions Manager
Carmen Watkins, News Director
David Ainslie, EngineeringDir
Brenda Ford-Jones, National Sales Manager
Tom Callococci, Brenda Ford-Jones
Cindy Webster, Regional Sales Manager

KODA
11-09-1958; 99.1 mhz FM *Hrs Open:* 24; 96 kw; 1919 ft.; N29 34 34 W95 30 36
3050 Post Oak Blvd., 12th Floor, Houston, TX 77056 US
(713) 212-8000, *Fax:* (713) 830-8099
www.sunny99.com
License: Houston, Harris County, TX held by AMFM Texas License L.P.
Group Owner: Clear Channel Communications Inc.; (acq 8-30-00; grpsl).
Arbitron Metro Market: Houston-Galveston *Format:* Adult Contemp *Special Programming:* Jazz 4 hrs wkly *Hrs. of News Programming:* news progmg 22 hrs wkly *No. News Employees:* 1 *Target Audience:* 25-54.
Mark Kopelman, General Manager
Sandy Capell, General Sales Mgr
Vince Richards, Programming Director
Donna McCoy, Music Director

*KPFT
03-01-1970; 90.1 mhz FM *Hrs Open:* 24; 100 kw; 673 ft.; N29 53 15 W95 31 22
1929 Martin Luther King, Jr. Way, Berkeley, CA 94704 US
(713) 526-4000, *Fax:* (713) 526-5750
www.kpft.org
License: Houston, Harris County, TX held by Pacifica Foundation Inc.
Group Owner: Pacifica Foundation Inc.
Nat'l Network: PRI
Arbitron Metro Market: Houston-Galveston *Format:* News, Variety/Diverse *Special Programming:* Black 15 hrs *Target Audience:* General.
Dwande Bradley, General Manager
Donna Platt, General Sales Mgr
Otis Maclay, Programming Director
Ernesto Aguilar, News Director
Steve Brightwell, Engineering Dir

Phil Edwards, Music Director
Renee Feltz, News Director

KPRC
05-09-1925; 950 khz AM *Hrs Open:* 24
200 Concord Plaza, #600, San Antonio, TX 78216 US
(713) 212-8000, *Fax:* (713) 212-8950
www.950kprc.com
info@950kprc.com
License: Houston, TX held by CCB Texas Licenses L.P.
Group Owner: Clear Channel Communications Inc.; (acq 3-14-95;
Nat'l Network: CBS; Fox News Radio; Westwood One *Regional Network:* Texas State Networks *Nat'l Reps:* Clear Channel
Arbitron Metro Market: Greater Houston *Format:* News, News/Talk, 86 *Special Programming:* Gardening 7 hrs, home handyman 6 hrs, automotive 3 *Hrs. of News Programming:* news progmg 32 hrs wkly *No. News Employees:* 15 *Target Audience:* 25-54.
Michael Berry, Operations Dir
Mark Kopelman, General Manager
Paul Lambert, General Sales Mgr
Ken Charles, Programming Director
Brian Erickson, News Director
David Armstrong, Chief Engineer
Matt Thomas, Sports Commentator

KQUE
02-18-1948; 1230 khz AM *Hrs Open:* 24; 1 kw-U, ND1; 0.41 kw-U, ND1; N29 45 26 W95 20 18; N29 51 34 W95 33 32
Rebroadcasts: Simacasts KKRW (FM) Houston.
650 Madison Ave, New York, NY 10022 US
(713) 315-3400, *Fax:* (713) 315-3506
License: Houston, TX held by Liberman Broadcasting of Houston License LLC.
Group Owner: Liberman Broadcasting Inc.; (acq 3-20-2001; grpsl)
Arbitron Metro Market: Houston-Galveston *Format:* Tejano *Hrs. of News Programming:* News progmg 14 hrs wkly *Target Audience:* 35 plus; mature, upscale, high-income
Lenard Liberman, CEO
Winter Horton, Operations Dir
Gerardo Reyes, General Sales Mgr
Cheque Gonzalez, Programming Director
Meliza Posada, News Director
Ezequiel Gonzalez, Programming Director

KRBE
11-08-1959; 104.1 mhz FM; 92.18 kw; 1919 ft.; N29 34 34 W95 30 36
140 East Market Street, York, PA 17401 US
(713) 266-1000, *Fax:* (713) 954-2330
www.krbe.com
feedback@104krbe.com
License: Houston, Harris County, TX held by KRBE Lico Inc.
Group Owner: Cumulus Media Partners LLC; (acq 11-86; $25 million with co-located AM;
Arbitron Metro Market: Greater Houston *Format:* Contemporary Hits/Top 40 *Target Audience:* 18-34; general
Peter Brubaker, Chairman
David Kennedy, President
Nancy Vaeth, Operations Dir
Mark Shecterle, General Manager
Amy Dewbre, General Sales Mgr
Leslie Whittle, Programming Director
Lesley Brotamonte, Promotions Manager
Beth Lavine,National Sales Manager
Donna Baker, VP/Market Manager

KTRH
03-29-1930; 740 khz AM; 50 kw-D, DA2; 50 kw-N, DA2; N29 57 57 W94 56 32
510 Lovett Blvd, Houston, TX 77006 US
(713) 526-5874, *Fax:* (713) 212-8000
www.ktrh.com
info@ktrh.com
License: Houston, TX held by AMFM Texas Licenses L.P.
Group Owner: Clear Channel Communications Inc.; (acq 8-30-2000; grpsl).
Nat'l Network: ABC *Nat'l Reps:* Christal
Arbitron Metro Market: Houston-Galveston *Format:* News, Sports *Target Audience:* 25-54.
Mark Kopelman, General Manager
Betty Scott, Programming Director
Brian Mcdonald-Producer

***KTRU(FM)**
05-20-1971; 90.1 mhz FM *Hrs Open:* 24; 30 kw; 492 ft; N29 53 15 W95 31 22
Mailing Address: Rice University, 6100 S. Main, Houston, TX 77005
Second Address: P.O. Box 1892, Houston, TX 77251-1892
(713) 348-4098, *Fax:* n/a
www.ktru.org
ktru@ktru.org
License: Houston, Harris County, TX held by Rice University.
Population Served: 6,000,000 *Arbitron Metro Market:* Houston-Galveston *Special Programming:* Eclectic 104 hrs, jazz 9 hrs, world 2 hrs, Americana 1 hr, experimental 3 hrs, post-punk 1 hr, local 2 hrs, hip hop 3 hrs, reggae 2hrs, blues 2 hrs *Target Audience:* General.
Will Robedee, General Manager
Nick Ryder, Station Manager
Ross Cooper, Chief Engineer

***KTSU**
10-01-1973; 90.9 mhz FM *Hrs Open:* 24; 18.5 kw; 266 ft.; N29 43 25 W95 21 52
3100 Cleburne, Houston, TX 77004 US
(713) 313-7591, *Fax:* (713) 313-7479
www.ktsu.info
License: Houston, Harris County, TX held by Board of Regents Texas Southern University.
Arbitron Metro Market: Houston, TX *Format:* Jazz, Variety/Diverse *Special Programming:* Reggae 8 hrs wkly *Hrs. of News Programming:* news progmg 10 hrs wkly *No. News Employees:* 1 *Target Audience:* 25-54.
John Rudley, President
Charles Hudson, Operations Dir
George Thomas, General Manager
Larry Johson, General Sales Mgr
Charles Hudson, Operations Manager/Gospel Program Director
Maurice Hopethompson, News Director
Dave Biondi,Chief Engineer
Donna Franklin, Interim Assistant General Manager/Programming
Larry Johnson, Development Director
Deborah Chambers, Development Manager
Deborah Adams, Membership Coordinator
Sheldon T. Nunn, Music Director
Rick Lauderdale,Production Manager

***KUHF**
11-06-1950; 88.7 mhz FM *Hrs Open:* 24; 100 kw; 1719 ft.; N29 34 27 W95 29 37
4800 Calhoun Road, Houston, TX 77004 US
(713) 743-0887, *Fax:* (713) 743-0868
www.kuhf.org
communications@kuhf.org
License: Houston, Harris County, TX held by University of Houston.
Nat'l Network: NPR; PRI
Arbitron Metro Market: Houston, TX *Format:* News *Hrs. of News Programming:* news progmg 25 hrs wkly *No. News Employees:* 7 *Target Audience:* 25 plus.
Debra Fraser, Director of Operations & Stations Manager
Lisa Trapani Shumate, Executive Director & General Manager
Victor Kendall, General Sales Mgr
St. John Flynn, Programming Director
Jack Williams, News Director
Alex Schneider,Engineering Dir
Sidney Knight, Engineering Dir
Catherine Lu, Associate Producer
Ed Mayberry, News Reporter
Rod Rice, News Reporter
Jim Bell, News Reporter
Robert Stevenson, Producer, The Front Row
Troy Schulze, Production Assistant

KXYZ
08-08-1930; 1320 khz AM; 5 kw-D, DAN; 5 kw-N, DAN; N29 42 39 W95 10 30
8400 N.W. 52nd St., Suite 101, Miami, FL 33166 US
(713) 490-2538, *Fax:* (713) 984-1721
License: Houston, TX held by Multicultural Radio Broadcasting Licensee LLC.
Group Owner: Multicultural Radio Broadcasting Inc.; (acq 12-1-2003; grpsl).
Arbitron Metro Market: Huston, TX *Format:* Talk
Terry Lowry, General Manager

KMIC
01-01-1955; 1590 khz AM *Hrs Open:* 24
77 West 66th Street, 16th Floor, New York, NY 10023 US
(713) 552-1590, *Fax:* (713) 552-1588
www.disney.com,www.radiodisney.com
info@kmic.com
License: Houston, TX held by Radio Disney Group LLC.
Group Owner: ABC Inc.; (acq. 1999).
Nat'l Network: Radio Disney
Arbitron Metro Market: Houston, TX. *Format:* Children *Target Audience:* 6-14; 25-49; kids, parents *Adv. Rates:* 275.00; 275.00; 275.00; 50
Chris Martin, General Manager
Laura Pena, Promotions Manager
Johanna Anderson, News Director
A. Rigmaiden, Chief Engineer

Howe

KHYI
04-01-1949; 95.3 mhz FM *Hrs Open:* 24; 15 kw; 889 ft.; N33 28 12 W96 47 19
Mailing Address: 103-B West Main Street, Allen, TX 75013 US
Second Address: 12225 Greenville Ave. Ste.356, Suite 120, Dallas, TN 75074
(972) 633-0955, *Fax:* (972) 633-0957
www.khyi.com
josh@khyi.com; lhooks@khyi.com
License: Howe, Grayson County, TX held by Metro Broadcasters-Texas Inc.
Nat'l Network: Jones Radio Networks
Arbitron Metro Market: Dallas-Fort Worth *Format:* Country *Special Programming:* Gospel 4 hrs wkly, Agriculture 5 hrs wkly *Hrs. of News Programming:* news progmg 3 hrs wkly *No. News Employees:* 1 *TargetAudience:* 25-54; affluent, white collar, middle to upper income listeners
Ken Jones, CEO
Lisa Hooks, Operations Dir
Joshua Jones, General Manager
Glenda Jones, CFO

Hudson

KZXL
01-01-2002; 96.3 mhz FM; 13.5 kw; 491 ft.; N31 20 5 W94 40 10
Old Us Highway 35 North, Livingston, TX 77351 US
(877) 963-9696
www.963zxl.com
License: Hudson, Angelina County, TX held by The Turning Leaf LLC
Arbitron Metro Market: Lufkin-Nacogdoches, NY
Vance Barbee, General Manager

Humble

KGOL
07-18-1984; 1180 khz AM *Hrs Open:* 5 AM-midnight
1436 Auburn Boulevard, Sacramento, CA 95815 US
(713) 349-9880, *Fax:* (713) 349-0647
caguilar@entravision.com
License: Humble, TX held by Entravision Holdings LLC.
Group Owner: Entravision Communications Corp.; (acq 7-28-00; grpsl).
Arbitron Metro Market: Houston-Galvest, TX *Format:* Ethnic *Special Programming:* Hindi 15 hrs wkly *No. News Employees:* 1 *Target Audience:* General; Ethnic & Asian
Walter Ulloa, CEO
Jeff Liberman, President
David Padgett, Operations Dir
Carmen Aguilar, General Manager
Rick Hunt, Engineering Dir

***KSBJ**
07-06-1982; 89.3 mhz FM *Hrs Open:* 24; 100 kw; 837 ft.; N30 12 26 W95 5 28
Mailing Address: P.O. Box 187, Humble, TX 77347 US
Second Address: 1722 Treble Dr., Humble, TX 77338
(281) 446-5725, *Fax:* (281) 540-2198
www.ksbj.org
info@ksbj.org
License: Humble, Harris County, TX held by KSBJ Educational Foundation.
Arbitron Metro Market: Humble, TX *Format:* Christian *Hrs. of News Programming:* news progmg 4 hrs wkly *No. News Employees:* 31 *Target Audience:* 25-49; Christian adults
J.R. Hernandez, Operations Dir
Tim McDermott, General Manager
John Hull, Programming Director
Jason Ray, Promotions Manager
Amanda Carroll, News Director
George Schank, Chief Engineer
Jon Hull, Disc Jockey
Jim Beeler, MusicDirector
Tom Carter, Promotions Manager

Hunt

KRZS
99.9 mhz FM; 14.5 kw; 200 ft.; N30 5 8 W99 16 23
US

(830) 890-5229
www.roseradio999.com
License: Hunt, Kerr County, TX held by Munbilla Kerrville Ltd.
Group Owner: Munbilla Broadcasting Properties Ltd.
Arbitron Metro Market: Hunt, TX *Format:* Variety/Diverse
B. Shane Fox, General Manager

KYRT
97.9 mhz FM; 6 kw; Ant 279 ft; N30 44 48 W99 14 58
381 Casa Linda Plaza, Suite 347, Dallas, TX
(972) 241-2110, *Fax:* (830) 693-5107
License: Hunt, Mason County, TX held by Munbilla Broadcasting Properties Ltd.
Group Owner: Munbilla Broadcasting Properties Ltd.
B. Shane Fox, General Manager

Huntington

KSML-FM
03-01-1994; 101.9 mhz FM *Hrs Open:* 24; 15 kw; Ant 827 ft; N31 20 05 W94 40 10
Yates Broadcasting, 121 Cotton Sq., Lufkin, TX 77505
(936) 634-4584, *Fax:* (936) 632-5722
www.ksml.net
keith@yatesmedia.com
License: Huntington, Angelina County, TX held by Yates Broadcasting Corp.
Keith Sims, Operations Dir
Steven Yates, General Manager

Huntsville

***KHCH**
10-04-1982; 1410 khz AM *Hrs Open:* 24
2424 South Boulevard, Houston, TX 77098 US
(713) 520-5200
www.khcb.org
email@khcb.org
License: Huntsville, TX held by KHCB Inc.
Group Owner: Houston Christian Broadcasters Inc.; (acq 10-97; $145,000)
Format: Christian
Bruce Munsterman, General Manager
Dolly Martin, Programming Director
Miguel Jacinto, News Director

KHVL
11-03-1938; 1490 khz AM *Hrs Open:* 24; 1 kw-U, ND1; N30 41 48 W95 33 8
Mailing Address: P.O. Box 330, Huntsville, TX 77340 US
Second Address: 622 Interstate 45 S., Huntsville, TX 77340
(936) 295-2651, *Fax:* (936) 295-8201
www.khvl.com
steveeverett@ksam1017@.com
License: Huntsville, TX held by HEH Communications LLC
Nat'l Network: ABC
Arbitron Metro Market: Huntsville, TX *Format:* Oldies *Special Programming:* Black 5 hrs wkly *Hrs. of News Programming:* 5 local news casts per day *No. News Employees:* 1 *Target Audience:* 30 plus.
Brooke Addams, Operations Dir
Steve Everett, General Manager
Larry Crippen, News Director
Stacy Selman, Traffic Manager

KSAM-FM
08-01-1965; 101.7 mhz FM *Hrs Open:* 24; 3.7 kw; 420 ft.; N30 41 48 W95 33 8
Mailing Address: P.O. Box 330, Huntsville, TX 77342 US
Second Address: 622 Interstate 45 S., Huntsville, TX 77340
(936) 295-2651, *Fax:* (936) 295-8201
www.ksam1017.com
ksammail@yahoo.com
License: Huntsville, Walker County, TX held by HEH Communications LLC
Arbitron Metro Market: Huntsville, TX *Format:* Country *Hrs. of News Programming:* 6 local news casts per day *No. News Employees:* 1 *Target Audience:* 25-54; women
Brooke Addams, Operations Dir
Steve Everett, General Manager
Larry Crippen, News Director
Stacey Selman, Traffic Manager

***KSHU**
10-01-1973; 90.5 mhz FM *Hrs Open:* 24; 3 kw; 255 ft; N30 42 50 W95 32 58
Box 2207, 1804 Avenue J, Huntsville, TX 77341
(936) 294-3939,(936) 294-1342, *Fax:* (936) 294-1888
www.shsu.edu/~rtf_kshu
rtf_kshu@shsu.edu
License: Huntsville, Walker County, TX held by Sam Houston State University.
Population Served: 40,000*Special Programming:* Sp 4 hrs wkly *Hrs. of News Programming:* News progmg 25 hrs wkly *Target Audience:* General; rural
Le Ann Muns, Operations Dir
Steve Sandlin, Chief Engineer

Hurst

KMNY
04-01-1947; 1360 khz AM *Hrs Open:* 24
8400 N.W. 52nd St., Suite 101, Miami, FL 33166 US
(214) 631-1360, *Fax:* (972) 572-1260
www.rationalradio.org
License: Hurst, TX held by Multicultural Radio Broadcasting Licensee LLC.
Group Owner: Multicultural Radio Broadcasting Inc.; (acq 2-4-2004; grpsl)
Nat'l Network: Air America; USA
Arbitron Metro Market: Dallas, TX *Format:* Talk
Ted Sauceman, General Manager

Hutto

***KYLR**
02-01-1980; 92.1 mhz FM; 2.5 kw; 449 ft.; N30 32 4 W97 34 52
1707 N. Mays Street, Round Rock, TX 78664 US
(800) 525-5683, *Fax:* (916) 251-1650
www.klove.com
klove@klove.com
License: Hutto, Williamson County, TX held by Educational Media Foundation.
Group Owner: EMF Broadcasting; (acq 3-31-2006; $6 million with KMLR(FM) Gonzales).
Format: Christian
Mike Novak, President
David Pierce, Programming Director
Ed Lenane, News Director
Sam Wallington, Engineering Dir
Marya Morgan, News Reporter
Richard Hunt, News Reporter

Idalou

KRBL
09-18-1995; 105.7 mhz FM; 5.5 kw; 328 ft.; N33 39 47 W101 35 52
6257 Brisa Del Mar, El Paso, TX 79925 US
(806) 749-1057, *Fax:* (806) 749-1177
License: Idalou, Lubbock County, TX held by Triumph Communications Inc.
Arbitron Metro Market: Lubbock, TX *Format:* Religious *Target Audience:* 24-64.
Paul Beane, General Manager
Steve Ritchie, General Sales Mgr
Anthony Garza, Programming Director
Wanda Byers, Traffic Manager

Ingram

***KTXI**
11-01-1998; 90.1 mhz FM *Hrs Open:* 24; 50 kw; 453 ft.; N30 6 14 W99 4 36 *Rebroadcasts:* Rebroadcasts KPAC(FM) San Antonio 75% , KSTX(FM) San Antonio 25%
8401 Datapoint Drive, Suite 800, San Antonio, TX 78229 US
(210) 614-8977, *Fax:* (210) 614-8983
www.ktxi.fm
info@ktxi.fm
License: Ingram, Kerr County, TX held by Texas Public Radio.
Nat'l Network: NPR; PRI
Arbitron Metro Market: Ingram, TX *Format:* News *Target Audience:* 25 plus.
Dan Skinner, President and General Manager
Paul Flahive, Operations Dir
Laverne Dittx, General Sales Mgr
Paul Flahive, Program Contact
David Martin Davies, News Director
Wayne Coble, Engineering Dir
Randy Anderson, ClassicalMusic Director
Janet Grojean, Director of Corporate & Community Outreach
Cindy Alleman, Corporate Relations Associate
Nathan Cone, Director of Classical Programming
Stephen Custer, Corporate Membership Associate
Annette Ewer, TrafficDirector

KSYY
01-01-2007; 96.5 mhz FM; 8.4 kw; 430 ft.; N30 7 4 W99 11 40 US
(830) 896-4990
www.sunnyradio965.com
alyson@theranchfm92.com
License: Ingram, Kerr County, TX held by Radioactive LLC.
Group Owner: Radioactive LLC
Arbitron Metro Market: Ingram, TX *Format:* Adult Contemp
Benjamin Homel, President
Alyson Foster, General Sales Mgr
Ed Chandler, Programming Director
Mike Taylor, Assistant Program Director

Iowa Park

KXXN
06-01-2009; 96.3 mhz FM *Hrs Open:* 24 7; 6 kw; 256 ft.; N33 58 20 W98 45 35
Mailing Address: US
Second Address: 1305 S Glenburnie Road, New Bern, NC 28562
2526363333
bill@bigfishfm.com
License: Iowa Park, Wichita County, TX held by Tower Investment Trust Inc.
Group Owner: Tower Investment Trust Inc.
Arbitron Metro Market: Iowa Park, TX *Format:* Christian
William Brothers, President

Jacksboro

KFWR
03-01-1970; 95.9 mhz FM *Hrs Open:* 24; 80 kw; 1079 ft.; N32 39 50 W98 9 47
151 Fox Road, Weatherford, TX 76088 US
(817) 332-0959, *Fax:* (817) 348-8373
959theranch.com
ContactUs@TheRanchRadio.com
License: Jacksboro, Palo Pinto County, TX held by LKCM Radio Group L.P.
Group Owner: LKCM Radio Group L.P.; acq 9-30-02; $6 million).
Arbitron Metro Market: Mineral Wells, TX *Format:* Country *Target Audience:* 25-54; local, Texas country
Gerry Schlegel, President
Joel Gough, General Sales Mgr
Chuck Taylor, Programming Director
Molly Prince, Promotions Manager
Jane Wasson, News Director
Michael Margrave, Chief Engineer

Jacksonville

***KBJS**
05-16-1987; 90.3 mhz FM; 16 kw; 1286 ft.; N32 3 40 W95 18 50
P.O. Box 654, 416 Nacogdoches St, Jacksonville, TX 75766 US
(903) 586-5257, *Fax:* (903) 586-4986
www.kbjs.org
info@kbjs.org
License: Jacksonville, Cherokee County, TX held by East Texas Media Association Inc.
Nat'l Network: Moody
Arbitron Metro Market: Jacksonville, TX *Format:* Christian, Religious *Special Programming:* Black one hr, Sp one hr wkly
Bob Shivery, President
Randy Featherston, Station Manager
Eddie Baiseri, Programming Director

KEBE
01-12-1947; 1400 khz AM *Hrs Open:* 24; 1 kw-U, ND1; N31 58 11 W95 15 52
Mailing Address: P.O. Box 1648, Jacksonville, TX 75766 US
Second Address: Radio Ctr., 402 S. Ragsdale, Jacksonville, TX 75766
(903) 586-2527, *Fax:* (903) 586-1394
www.wallerbroadcasting.com,www.kooi.com
info@wallerbroadcasting.com
License: Jacksonville, TX held by Waller Broadcasting Inc.
Group Owner: Waller Broadcasting; (acq 11-58; $75,000).
Nat'l Reps: McGavren Guild
Arbitron Metro Market: Tyler-Longview, TX *Format:* Country *Special Programming:* Farm 9 hrs wkly *Hrs. of News Programming:* news progmg 6 hrs wkly *No. News Employees:* 2 *Target Audience:* 25-54. *Adv.Rates:* 10; 8; 6; 8
Dudley Waller, CEO
Alan Mather, Operations Dir
Tina Harper, CFO

KLJT
01-01-1993; 102.3 mhz FM *Hrs Open:* 24; 50 kw; 492 ft.; N31 52 18 W95 10 0
Mailing Address: P.O. Box 12, 402 S Ragsdale, Jacksonville, TX 75766 US
Second Address: 402 S. Ragsdale, Jacksonville, TX 75766
(903) 586-2527, *Fax:* (903) 589-0677
License: Jacksonville, Cherokee County, TX held by Waller Media LLC.
Group Owner: Waller Broadcasting; (acq 12-9-02).
Nat'l Network: ABC *Nat'l Reps:* McGavren Guild *Wire Services:* AP

Arbitron Metro Market: Tyler, TX *Format:* Adult Contemp *Hrs. of News Programming:* news progmg 6 hrs wkly *No. News Employees:* 1 *Adv. Rates:* 30; 24; 20; 16
Dudley Waller, CEO

KOOI
09-09-1967; 106.5 mhz FM *Hrs Open:* 24; 100 kw; 1480 ft.; N32 3 40 W95 18 50
Mailing Address: P.O. Box 1648, Jacksonville, TX 75766 US
Second Address: 210 S. Broadway, Tyler, TX 75702
(903) 581-9966, *Fax:* (903) 534-5300
www.kooi.com
kooi@etradiogroup.com
License: Jacksonville, Cherokee County, TX held by Access.1 Texas License Company LLC.
Group Owner: Access.1 Communications Corp.; (acq 1-7-2005; grpsl).
Nat'l Network: ABC *Regional Network:* Texas State Networks
Nat'l Reps: McGavren Guild
Arbitron Metro Market: Tyler-Longview, TX *Format:* Adult Contemp *Target Audience:* 25-54. *Adv. Rates:* 60; 60; 60; 60
Rick Guest, General Manager
Genni Causey, General Sales Mgr
Paul Orr, Programming Director
Shelley Miller, News Director
Tara Holley, Local Sales Manager
Robert Taylor, National Sales Manager

Jasper

KJAS
01-01-1996; 107.3 mhz FM *Hrs Open:* 24; 8 kw; 328 ft.; N30 58 31 W93 59 24
765 Hemphill St., Jasper, TX 75951 US
(409) 384-2626, *Fax:* (409) 383-1979
www.kjas.com
press@kjas.com
License: Jasper, Jasper County, TX held by DBA Rayburn Broadcasting Co.
Arbitron Metro Market: Beaumont-Port Arthur, TX *Format:* Adult Contemp *Special Programming:* Oldies 4 hrs wkly *Hrs. of News Programming:* news progmg 4 hrs wkly *No. News Employees:* 1 *Target Audience:* 24-54; females/buying group *Adv. Rates:* 14; 12; 9; 6.50
Jacque Hill, Operations Dir
Mike Lout, General Manager
Debra Foster, General Sales Mgr
Michael Love, Engineering Dir
Lowell Nunnally, Production Specialist
Steve Stewart, Public Affairs Director

KCOX
08-06-1948; 1350 khz AM *Hrs Open:* 24; 5 kw-D, ND1; 0.037 kw-N, ND1; N30 55 11 W93 58 13
Mailing Address: P.O. Box 2008, Jasper, TX 79951 US
Second Address: 1408 E. Gibson, Jasper, TX 75951
(409) 384-4500, *Fax:* (409) 384-4525
www.1027ktxj.com
request@1027KTXJ.com
License: Jasper, TX held by Cross Texas Media Inc.
Nat'l Network: Salem Radio Network
Arbitron Metro Market: Jasper, TX *Format:* Christian *Target Audience:* 18-35.
T.J. Bordelon, Operations Dir
Rick Tallent, General Manager
Dale Cucancic, General Sales Mgr
Barbara Bordelon, News Director
Carol Tallent, Business Manager

KTXJ-FM
11-01-1964; 102.7 mhz FM *Hrs Open:* 24; 46 kw; 513 ft.; N31 3 36 W93 57 42
Mailing Address: P.O. Box 2008, Jasper, TX 75951 US
Second Address: 1408 E. Gibosn, Jasper, TX 75951
(409) 384-4500, *Fax:* (409) 384-4525
www.1027ktxj.com
request@1027KTXK.com
License: Jasper, Jasper County, TX held by Cross Texas Media Inc.
Nat'l Network: Salem Radio Network
Arbitron Metro Market: Jasper, TX *Format:* Gospel *Target Audience:* Very broad receptive demographic
Dan Skinner, President
Laverne Dittx, General Sales Mgr
Nathan Cone, Programming Director
Dave Davies, News Director
Wayne Coble, Engineering Dir
Randy Anderson, Music Director
Janet Grojean, Sales

Jefferson

KJTX
10-01-1990; 104.5 mhz FM *Hrs Open:* 24; 4.4 kw; 384 ft.; N32 49 23 W94 28 32
707 Valentine Lane, Longview, TX 75604 US
(903) 759-1243, *Fax:* (903) 759-1243
www.kjtx1045fm.com
kj104fm@juno.com
License: Jefferson, Marion County, TX held by Wisdom Ministries Inc.
Format: Christian, Gospel *Hrs. of News Programming:* News progmg 2 hrs wkly *Target Audience:* 16 plus.
Leroy Richardson, President
Annie Thompson, Operations Dir
Brenda Richardson, General Sales Mgr
Sharon Herbert, News Director
Jocelyn Jordan, Music Director

***KHCJ**
01-01-2003; 91.9 mhz FM *Hrs Open:* 24; 3.2 kw; 459 ft.; N32 50 7 W94 28 53 *Rebroadcasts:* Rebroadcasts KHCB-FM Houston 95%
2424 S Boulevard, Houston, TX 77098 US
(713) 520-5200
www.khcb.org
email@khcb.org
License: Jefferson, Marion County, TX held by Houston Christian Broadcasters Inc.
Group Owner: Houston Christian Broadcasters Inc.
Nat'l Network: Moody
Arbitron Metro Market: Texarkana, TX *Format:* Christian
Bruce Munsterman, General Manager
Bonnie BeMent, Assistant General Manager

Johnson City

KFAN-FM
01-01-1991; 107.9 mhz FM *Hrs Open:* 24; 8.7 kw; 551 ft.; N30 11 49 W98 38 19
210 Woodcrest, Fredericksburg, TX 78624 US
(952) 417-3000, *Fax:* (612) 417-3001
www.kfan.com
info@k102.com
License: Johnson City, Blanco County, TX held by J. & J. Fritz Media Ltd.
Group Owner: J. & J. Fritz Media Ltd.
Arbitron Metro Market: Minneapolis-St. Paul, MN *Format:* Triple A *Special Programming:* Jazz 5 hrs wkly *No. News Employees:* 1 *Target Audience:* 25-49. *Adv. Rates:* 28; 28; 28; 28
Jayson Fritz, President
Jan Fritz, Operations Dir
Rick Star, Programming Director
Robbie Fish, News Director
Ariana Carruth, Promotions Manager
Kyle Province, Public Affairs Director

Jourdanton

KLEY-FM
01-01-2001; 95.7 mhz FM; 11 kw; 1037 ft.; N28 54 57.4 W98 39 39
1428 Wiltshire, San Antonio, TX 78209 US
(210) 654-5100, *Fax:* (210) 340-1775
License: Jourdanton, Atascosa County, TX held by BMP San Antonio License Co. L.P.
Group Owner: Border Media Partners LLC; (acq 12-23-2004; $7.5 million)
Format: Tejano
Lance Hawkins, General Manager
Bob Brown, General Sales Mgr

Junction

KMBL
01-01-1953; 1450 khz AM *Hrs Open:* 24; 1 kw-U, ND1; N30 29 34 W99 45 41
Mailing Address: 5550 Friendship Blvd, Chevy Chase, MD 20815 US
Second Address: 214 Pecan St., Junction, TX 76899
(830) 896-1230, *Fax:* (830) 792-4142
generalmanager@krvl.com
License: Junction, TX held by Foster Charitable Foundation Inc.
Group Owner: Revolution Broadcast Company of the West; (acq 5-31-2007)
Nat'l Network: Westwood One *Regional Network:* Texas State Networks
Format: Country *Special Programming:* Farm 6 hrs wkly *Hrs. of News Programming:* news progmg 6 hrs wkly *No. News Employees:* 1 *Target Audience:* General. *Adv. Rates:* 8; 7; 8; 4.20
David Greenwald, President
Harley Belew, Operations Dir
Monte Spearman, General Manager
Steve Alex, Station Manager
A.J. Hernandez, Programming Director
Monte Speaman, Advertising Director
Glen Taylor

KOOK
01-01-1997; 93.5 mhz FM *Hrs Open:* 24; 50 kw; 492 ft.; N30 29 31 W100 2 3
5550 Friendship Blvd., Suite 260, Chevy Chase, MD 20815 US
(830) 896-1230, *Fax:* (830) 792-4142
License: Junction, Kimble County, TX held by Foster Charitable Foundation Inc.
Group Owner: Revolution Broadcast Company of the West; (acq 5-31-2007)
Nat'l Network: ABC *Regional Network:* Texas State Networks
Format: Country *Special Programming:* Gospel 2 hrs wkly *Adv. Rates:* 7.90; 6.30; 7.90; 6.30
Donna Keese, Operations Dir
Monte Spearman, General Manager

Karnes City

KHHL
03-01-2005; 103.1 mhz FM; 34 kw; Ant 587 ft; N29 00 52 W97 40 02
4500 Eisenhauer Rd, San Antonio, TX 78701
(210) 654-5100, *Fax:* (210) 340-1775
License: Karnes City, Karnes County, TX held by Palm Broadcasting Co.

Lance Hawkins, General Manager
Bob Brown, General Sales Mgr

Keene

***KJRN**
06-13-1974; 88.3 mhz FM *Hrs Open:* 24; 23 kw; 180 ft; N32 24 19 W97 19 55
PO Box 567, Keene, TX 76059
(817) 202-6788, *Fax:* (817) 202-6790
www.kjrn.org
License: Keene, Johnson County, TX held by Southwestern Adventist University.
Population Served: 1,500,000 *Arbitron Metro Market:* Dallas-Fort Wor *Hrs. of News Programming:* News progmg 2 hrs wkly *Target Audience:* 25-54
Eric Anderson, President
Michael Agee, General Manager
Karen Knaubert, General Sales Mgr
Ron Macomber, Chief Engineer

Kempner

KHLE
12-15-1978; 106.9 mhz FM; 2.3 kw; 538 ft.; N31 6 1 W97 55 39
2402 Broadmoor, Bldg, D-2, Suite 101, Bryan, TX 77802 US
(254) 772-0330, *Fax:* (254) 833-8844
http://www.1660espn.com/
smoaky@1660espn.com
License: Kempner, Lampasas County, TX held by Munbilla Fort Hood Ltd.
Group Owner: Munbilla Broadcasting Properties Ltd.
Nat'l Network: ABC
TV Affiliate: ESPN *Format:* Sports *Hrs. of News Programming:* news progmg 3 hrs wkly *No. News Employees:* 2 *Target Audience:* 25-54. *Adv. Rates:* 20; 18; 18; 15.
Laura Uvalle, General Manager
Ben Shields, Programming Director
Bill Woleban, Chief Engineer
David Smoak, Program Director
Bill LeGrand, Marketing Director
Terry Taker, Sports Marketing Consultant

Kenedy

***KTNR**
09-01-1982; 92.1 mhz FM; 6 kw; 262 ft.; N28 45 35 W97 51 45
Post Office Box 1614, Laredo, TX 78044 US
(214) 879-0081, *Fax:* (214) 879-0083
License: Kenedy, Karnes County, TX held by Hispanic Christian Community Network Inc.
Arbitron Metro Market: Dallas, TX
Antonio Cesar Guel, President

Kenedy-Karnes City

KAML
11-01-1954; 990 khz AM *Hrs Open:* 24; 0.25 kw-D, ND1; 0.07 kw-N, ND1; N28 51 2 W97 52 48

Mailing Address: Rt. 1, Box 990, Kenedy, TX 78119 US
Second Address: Box 990, Karnes City, TX 78118
(830) 583-2990, *Fax:* (830) 583-3994
info@kamlam.com
License: Kenedy-Karnes City, TX held by SIGA Broadcasting Corp.
Group Owner: SIGA Broadcasting Corp.; acq 1-17-2002).
Nat'l Reps: Dome *Wire Services:* U.S. Weather Service
Arbitron Metro Market: Kenedy, TX *Format:* Country, News, 84 *Hrs. of News Programming:* news progmg 8 hrs wkly *No. News Employees:* 2 *Target Audience:* 24-54; male-female *Adv. Rates:* 12; 12; 12; 10
Gabriel Arango, President
Clyde Eckols, General Manager
Steve Eckols, Programming Director

Kerens

KRVF
05-23-1979; 106.9 mhz FM; 21.5 kw; 365 ft.; N32 6 12 W96 22 33
1436 Auburn Boulevard, Sacramento, CA 96815 US
(903) 874-8884, *Fax:* (903) 885-9107
www.1069theranch.com/
MikeCrow@TheRanchRadio.com
License: Kerens, Navarro County, TX held by LKCM Radio Group L.P.
Group Owner: LKCM Radio Group L.P.; (acq 5-21-2004; $1 million with KRVA-FM Campbell).
Arbitron Metro Market: Kerens, TX *Format:* Oldies
Bert Goldman, President
Chris McMurray, General Manager

Kermit

KERB
06-01-1950; 600 khz AM; 1 kw-D, DA2; 0.091 kw-N, DA2; N31 50 5 W103 8 10
P.O. Box 252, McAllen, TX 78502 US
(915) 586-3481, *Fax:* (915) 586-6757
License: Kermit, TX held by La Radio Cristiana Network Inc.
Regional Network: Texas State Networks *Nat'l Reps:* Keystone (unwired net)
Arbitron Metro Market: Odessa-Midland, TX *Format:* Christian
Eloy Bernal, General Manager
Gilbert Martinez, Programming Director

KERB-FM
01-01-1983; 106.3 mhz FM; 3 kw; 276 ft.; N31 50 5 W103 8 10
P.O. Box 252, McAllen, TX 78502 US
(956) 781-5528, *Fax:* (956) 686-2999
www.laradiocristiana.com
License: Kermit, Winkler County, TX held by La Radio Cristiana Network Inc.
Arbitron Metro Market: Odessa-Midland, TX
Barger Tygart, Chairman
Kevin Martin, COO
Jeff Luchsinger, Station Manager
Patricia Lyons, General Sales Mgr

Kerrville

*KKER
12-08-2000; 88.7 mhz FM *Hrs Open:* 24; 52 kw; 571 ft.; N30 3 30 W99 3 50
P O Drawer 2440, Tupelo, MS 38803 US
(713) 520-5200
www.khcb.org
email@khcb.org
License: Kerrville, Kerr County, TX held by Houston Christian Broadcasters Inc.
Group Owner: Houston Christian Broadcasters Inc.; acq 11-24-00; $3,500 for CP with CP of KHCP(FM) Paris).
Nat'l Network: Moody
Arbitron Metro Market: Houston, TX *Format:* Christian *Special Programming:* Sp 6 hrs, Chinese one hr wkly
Bruce Munsterman, General Manager
Bonnie BeMent, Assistant General Manager

KERV
11-05-1948; 1230 khz AM *Hrs Open:* 24; 0.99 kw-U, ND1; N30 4 14 W99 11 7
Suite 200, 1021 E. Main St., Kerrville, TX 78028 US
(830) 896-1230, *Fax:* (830) 792-4142
www.revfmradio.com
info@kerv.com
License: Kerrville, TX held by Foster Charitable Foundation Inc.
Group Owner: Revolution Broadcast Company of the West; (acq 5-31-2007)
Nat'l Network: ABC
Arbitron Metro Market: Kerville, TX *Format:* Jazz, Smooth Jazz, 86 *Hrs. of News Programming:* news progmg 3 hrs wkly *No. News Employees:* 1 *Target Audience:* 45 plus; educated professionals *Adv. Rates:* 14;12; 14; 12.
Dennis Anderson, President

KRNH
06-01-1994; 92.3 mhz FM *Hrs Open:* 24; 20 kw; 666 ft.; N30 3 42 W99 3 43
P.O. Drawer 2037, Canyon Lake, TX 78130 US
(830) 896-4990, *Fax:* (830) 896-4991
www.theranchfm92.com
daybreakshow@theranchfm92.com
License: Kerrville, Kerr County, TX held by Radio Ranch Ltd.
Format: Country *Target Audience:* 18-64.
JD Rose, Operations Dir
Mark Grubbs, General Manager
Kelli McLaughlin, General Sales Mgr

*KHKV
01-01-1998; 91.1 mhz FM *Hrs Open:* 24; 0.3 kw; 207 ft.; N30 2 37 W99 7 17 *Rebroadcasts:* Rebroadcasts KHCB(AM) Houston-Galveston 80%
2424 South Boulevard, Houston, TX 77098 US
(713) 520-5200
www.khcb.org
email@khcb.org
License: Kerrville, Kerr County, TX held by Houston Christian Broadcasters Inc.
Group Owner: Houston Christian Broadcasters Inc.
Arbitron Metro Market: San Antonio, TX *Format:* Christian
Bruce Munsterman, General Manager
Dolly Martin, Programming Director
Miguel Jacinto, News Director

KRVL
09-12-1975; 94.3 mhz FM *Hrs Open:* 24; 33 kw; 400 ft.; N30 15 8 W99 8 1
301 Junction Hwy, Suite 320, Kerrville, TX 78028 US
(830) 896-1230, *Fax:* (830) 792-4142
www.revfmradio.com
info@revfmradio.com
License: Kerrville, Kerr County, TX held by Foster Charitable Foundation Inc.
Group Owner: Revolution Broadcast Company of the West; (acq 5-31-2007)
Nat'l Network: ABC
Format: Triple A *Special Programming:* Gospel one hr, local church service one hr wkly *Target Audience:* 25-49. *Adv. Rates:* 25; 20; 25; 18.
Marti Ashcraft, Operations Dir
Jana Smith, General Manager
Gordon Ames, General Sales Mgr
Glenn Taylor, Programming Director
Diane Philips, News Director
Monica Smith, Sales

KKVR
09-01-2007; 106.1 mhz FM *Hrs Open:* 24; 6 kw; 328 ft.; N30 2 27 W99 10 19
US
(830) 896-4990, *Fax:* (830) 896-4991
www.theriver1061.com
alyson@ranchradiogroup.com
License: Kerrville, Kerr County, TX held by E-String Wireless Ltd.
Arbitron Metro Market: Kerrville, TX *Format:* Contemporary Hits/Top 40, Adult Contemp
Bret Huggins, General Manager
Alyson Foster, General Sales Mgr
Ed Chandler, Programming Director
Mike Taylor, Assistant Program Director

Kilgore

KKTX-FM
12-23-1976; 96.1 mhz FM; 50 kw; 492 ft.; N32 22 14 W94 56 20
600 Congress Avenue, Suite 1400, Austin, TX 78701 US
(903) 581-0606, *Fax:* (903) 581-2011
www.kktx.com
craigreininger@gapbroadcasting.com
License: Kilgore, Gregg County, TX held by GAP Broadcasting Tyler License LLC
Group Owner: GAP Broadcasting LLC; (acq 8-3-2007; grpsl)
Arbitron Metro Market: Tyler, TX *Format:* Classic Rock *Target Audience:* 25-54.
Craig Reininger, General Sales Mgr
Lisa Nix, Programming Director
Chris Jones, Regional Sales Manager

*KZLO
02-04-1991; 88.7 mhz FM *Hrs Open:* 19; 63 kw horiz, 79 kw vert; 551 ft.; N32 20 14 W95 2 41
904 Houston Street, Kilgore, TX 75662 US
(916) 251-1600, *Fax:* (916) 251-1650
www.klove.com
License: Kilgore, Gregg County, TX held by Educational Media Foundation.
Group Owner: EMF Broadcasting; (acq 2-15-2007; $2 million)
Nat'l Network: K-Love
Arbitron Metro Market: Tyler-Longview, TX *Format:* Christian
Mike Novak, CEO/COO
Mike Novak, President
Darrell Chambliss-Chairman

Killeen

KIIZ-FM
12-10-1990; 92.3 mhz FM *Hrs Open:* 24; 6 kw; 240 ft.; N31 6 29 W97 39 50
600 Congress Avenue, Suite 1400, Austin, TX 78701 US
(254) 699-5000, *Fax:* (254) 399-8134
www.kiiz.com
babysitter@clearchannel.com
License: Killeen, Bell County, TX held by Capstar TX L.P.
Group Owner: Clear Channel Communications Inc.; (acq 8-30-2000; grpsl)
Arbitron Metro Market: Killeen-Temple, TX *Format:* Urban Contemporary *Hrs. of News Programming:* News progmg 2 hrs wkly *Target Audience:* 18-49.
Tim Thomas, General Manager
Evan Armstrong, Station Manager
Chuck Redden, General Sales Mgr
Terry Steele, Promotions Manager
Julia Conner, News Director
Ron Davis, Engineering Dir
Brett Gilbert, Chief Engineer
Scott Shafer,Production Director

*KNCT-FM
11-23-1970; 91.3 mhz FM *Hrs Open:* 24; 50 kw; 1171 ft.; N30 59 12 W97 37 47
6200 W. Central Texas, Expressway, Killeen, TX 76542 US
(254) 526-1176, *Fax:* (254) 526-1850
www.knct.org
knctfm@knctfm.com
License: Killeen, Bell County, TX held by Central Texas College.
Nat'l Network: AP Network News
Arbitron Metro Market: Killeen-Temple, *TV Affiliate:* *KNCT(TV) affil *Format:* News *Special Programming:* Jazz 15 hrs wkly, big band 6 hrs wkly *Target Audience:* 45 plus.
Max Rudolph, General Manager
Dan Hull, Programming Director
Steve Sulzer, Chief Engineer

KRMY
07-04-1955; 1050 khz AM; 0.25 kw-D, ND2; 0.005 kw-N, ND2; N31 6 53 W97 42 0
Mailing Address: 4638 Decker Drive, Baytown, TX 77520 US
Second Address: 314 N. 2nd St., Killeen, TX 76514
(254) 628-7071, *Fax:* (254) 634-5263
License: Killeen, TX held by Martin Broadcasting Inc.
Group Owner: Martin Broadcasting Inc.; acq 11-89; grpsl;
Arbitron Metro Market: Killeen-Temple, *Format:* Gospel *Target Audience:* 18-44.
Darrell Martin, General Manager
Horatio Martinez, Programming Director

Kingsville

KFTX
05-02-1970; 97.5 mhz FM *Hrs Open:* 24; 97 kw; 955 ft.; N27 44 28 W97 36 8
1520 South Port Avenue, Corpus Christi, TX 78405 US
(361) 883-5987, *Fax:* (361) 883-3648
www.kftx.com
License: Kingsville, Kleberg County, TX held by Quality Broadcasting Corp.
Arbitron Metro Market: Corpus Christi, TX *Format:* Country *Special Programming:* Religious 10 hrs wkly *Hrs. of News Programming:* news progmg 2 hrs wkly *No. News Employees:* 1 *Target Audience:* 25-49;educated, affluent young adults
Cyndi Rowden, General Manager
Cyndi Rowden, General Sales Mgr
Chuck Abel, Programming Director
Wendy Hatley, News Director
Mark Earle, Chief Engineer
Austin Daniels, Music Director

KINE
11-01-1948; 1330 khz AM *Hrs Open:* 24; 1 kw-D, ND1; 0.28 kw-N, ND1; N27 36 36 W97 47 42
115 West Avenue D, Robstown, TX 78380 US
(361) 855-1330, *Fax:* (361) 289-7722
License: Kingsville, TX held by Cotton Broadcasting.

Arbitron Metro Market: Corpus Christi, TX *Format:* Religious *Target Audience:* 25-54.
Humberto Lopez, CEO
Carlos Lopez, General Manager
Minerva Lopez, General Sales Mgr
Homer Lopez, Programming Director
Manuel Lopez, Promotions Manager
Tommy Greg, Chief Engineer
Ernest Lopez, Sales VP

KKBA
11-01-1981; 92.7 mhz FM *Hrs Open:* 24; 12.5 kw; 869 ft.; N27 39 20 W97 33 55
Mailing Address: P. O. Box 9757, Corpus Christi, TX 78469 US
Second Address: 2117 Leopard St., CorpusChristi, TX 78408
(361) 883-3516, *Fax:* (361) 882-9767
www.927kkba.com
thechief@star94.net
License: Kingsville, Kleberg County, TX held by Malkan Broadcasting L.P.
Group Owner: Malkan Broadcast Associates; (acq 9-13-95;
Nat'l Reps: Katz Radio
Arbitron Metro Market: Corpus Christi, TX *Format:* Contemporary Hits/Top 40 *Special Programming:* John Tesh *Hrs. of News Programming:* 20 hrs wkly *No. News Employees:* 1 *Target Audience:* 25-54. *Adv.Rates:* 68; 68; 68; 68
Glen Powers, President
Janice Raleigh, Programming Director
John Gifford, Chief Engineer
Bart Allison, Program Director
Norma Morales, Promotions Director

*KTAI
02-23-1970; 91.1 mhz FM *Hrs Open:* Noon-12:30 AM (M-F); 4 PM-10 PM (Su; 0.1 kw horiz, 0 kw vert; N27 31 24 W97 52 42
Campus Box 178, Kingsville, TX 78363 US
(361) 593-3489
www.tamuk.edu/ktai
ktaifm@hotmail.com
License: Kingsville, Kleberg County, TX held by Texas A&M University-Kingsville.
Arbitron Metro Market: Kingsville, TX *Special Programming:* Black 8 hrs, gospel 6 hrs, mus from India 3 hrs, mus from Mexico 3 hrs wkly *Target Audience:* 16-25; high school & college ages
Rumaldo Juarez, President

Krum

KNOR
11-11-1984; 93.7 mhz FM *Hrs Open:* 24; 43 kw; 1969 ft.; N33 29 5 W97 24 44
5946 Club Oaks Drive, Dallas, TX 75248 US
(817) 868-2900, *Fax:* (817) 868-2116
www.laraza937.com
Dallasinfo@lbimedia.com; banditoraza@yahoo.com
License: Krum, Denton County, TX held by Liberman Broadcasting of Dallas License LLC.
Group Owner: Liberman Broadcasting Inc.; (acq 5-13-2004; $15.5 million)
Nat'l Reps: Roslin
Arbitron Metro Market: Dallas-Fort Worth *Hrs. of News Programming:* news 20 hrs wkly *Target Audience:* HISPANIC *Adv. Rates:* 15; 13; 15; 13
Rosa Cuellar-Khraish, General Manager

Kurten

KPWJ
107.7 mhz; 3500 w; 328 ft; N30 37 12 W96 15 13
2700 Rudder Freeway, Suite 5000, College Station, TX
(979)695-9595, *Fax:* (979)695-1933
radio@bryanbroadcasting.com
License: Kurten, Brazos County, TX held by Bryan Broadcasting License Corporation
William Hicks, President
Ben Downs, General Manager
Alisa Dusterhoff, Office Manager
Sam Jones, Sales Manager
Chris Dusterhoff, Chief Engineer

La Grange

KBUK
12-21-1970; 104.9 mhz FM; 1.75 kw; 527 ft.; N29 52 32 W96 52 39
PO Box 609, La Grange, TX 78945 US
(979) 968-3173, *Fax:* (979) 968-6196
www.kvlgkbuk.com
info@kvlgkbuk.com
License: La Grange, Fayette County, TX
Arbitron Metro Market: La Grange, TX
Roy Cerney, Station Manager
Mike Anders, Programming Director

KVLG
06-27-1959; 1570 khz AM; 0.25 kw-D, DA2; 0.011 kw-N, DA2; N29 52 58 W96 51 57
Mailing Address: 3901 Westheimer, #190, Houston, TX 77027 US
Second Address: FM 155 S., La Grange, TX 78945
(979) 968-3173, *Fax:* (409) 968 6196
www.kvlgkbuk.com
info@kvlgkbuk.com
License: La Grange, TX held by Fayette Broadcasting Corp.
Regional Network: Texas State Networks
Arbitron Metro Market: La Grange *Format:* Country *Special Programming:* Ger one hr, Black one hr, farm 4 hrs, Pol/Czech 12 hrs, relg 5 hrs wkly *Target Audience:* General.
Roy Cerney, General Manager
Mike Anders, Program Director/ Engineer
John Haworth, Co-Owner
Dan Mueller, Co-Owner/ Old Music Show Host/ Morning Newscaster
Sylvia Bookout, Copy Writer/ Webmaster/ Trading Post
Gary Dusek, SportsNewscaster

La Porte

KHJK
01-01-1992; 103.7 mhz FM; 94.86 kw; Ant 1,935 ft; N29 56 09 W94 30 38
2700 Post Oak Blvd., Suite 2300, Houston, TX 77301
(713) 300-3500, *Fax:* (713) 300-3585
www.houstonrock1037.com
License: La Porte, Harris County, TX held by A R Licensing LLC
Group Owner: Cumulus Media Partners LLC; (acq 5-3-2006; grpsl)
Arbitron Metro Market: Houston-Galveston
Patrick Fant, General Manager

Lake Jackson

KHTC(FM)
04-01-1963; 107.5 mhz FM *Hrs Open:* 24; 100 kw; Ant 2,000 ft; N29 17 16 W95 13 53
1990 Post Oak Blvd., Suite 2300, Houston, TX 77056
(713) 963-1200, *Fax:* (713) 622-5457
1075khits.com
License: Lake Jackson, Brazoria County, TX held by Cox Radio Inc.
Group Owner: Cox Radio Inc.; (acq 8-30-2000; grpsl)
Population Served: 47,743 *Arbitron Metro Market:* Houston-Galveston *Format:* Oldies *Hrs. of News Programming:* news progmg 5 hrs wkly *No. News Employees:* 2 *Target Audience:* 25-54; college grads from the60s, 70s & 80s
Johnny Chiang, Operations Dir
Jaymie Kosina, General Sales Mgr
Johnny Chiang, Programming Director
Candy Mendez, Promotions Manager
Paul Christy, Music Director
Mike Murray, National Sales Manager

*KYBJ
07-02-2012; 91.1 mhz FM; 5 kw; 459 ft; N29 02 37 W95 20 11
Rebroadcasts: Rebroadcasts KSBJ(FM) Humble 100%
1722 Treble, c/o KSBJ(FM), Humble, TX 77347
(281) 446-5725, *Fax:* (281) 540-2198
www.ngenradio.com
technology@ksbj.org
License: Lake Jackson, Brazoria County, TX held by KSJB Educational Foundation Inc.
Target Audience: 12-35
Tim McDermott, General Manager
Carlos Agular, Programming Director
Tamara Brubaker, Assistant General Manager
Mark Wanner, Sr. Dir. Planning & Technology Director
Nikki Sparks, Sr. Dir. Creative Services
Jon Hull, Sr. Dir.Outreach

Lamesa

*KBKN
91.3 mhz FM; 0.25 kw; 157 ft.; N32 45 34 W101 57 9
P O Drawer 2440, Tupelo, MS 38803 US
(432) 638-1150, *Fax:* (432) 682-5230
www.grnonline.com
robertd@grnonline.com
License: Lamesa, Dawson County, TX held by La Promesa Foundation.
Group Owner: La Promesa Foundation; (acq 5-4-2004; $108,000 including six translator stns).
Arbitron Metro Market: Lamesa, TX *Format:* Christian
Leonard Oswald, President

KPET
05-21-1947; 690 khz AM *Hrs Open:* 24; 0.25 kw-U, ND1; N32 42 27 W101 56 11
P. O. Box 1188, Lamesa, TX 79331 US
(806) 872-6511,(806) 872-6537, *Fax:* (806) 872-6514
kpet@pics.net
License: Lamesa, TX held by DCB License Sub LLC
Nat'l Network: ABC *Regional Network:* Texas State Networks
Format: Country *Hrs. of News Programming:* news progmg 2 hrs wkly *No. News Employees:* 1 *Target Audience:* 18-65. *Adv. Rates:* 10.50; 10.50; 10.50; 10.50
Don Sitton, General Manager
Elaine Githens, General Sales Mgr
Grover Clifft, News Director
Anthony Garza, Chief Engineer
DeeAnn Martin, Traffic Manager

KTXC
05-01-1988; 104.7 mhz FM *Hrs Open:* 24; 100 kw; 801 ft.; N32 23 47 W101 57 24
6999 East Highway 80, Odessa, TX 79762 US
(432) 567-9991, *Fax:* (432) 567-9999
www.newswest9.com
dmarino@kwes.com
License: Lamesa, Dawson County, TX held by Graham Brothers Comm. L.L.C.
Arbitron Metro Market: Lamesa, TX *Target Audience:* 25-54; college-educated, upper-income families
Richard Esparza, Station Manager
David Marino, News Director

*KRJA
88.9 mhz FM; 250 watts; 22 meters; N32 44 06.2 W101 57 35
1307 South Camp, Midland, TX
(432) 683-0972
License: Lamesa, TX held by Templo Piedra Angular

Lampasas

KCYL
01-01-1948; 1450 khz AM *Hrs Open:* 5 AM-11 PM; 0.8 kw-U, ND1; N31 2 57 W98 10 10
505 N. Key Ave., Lampasas, TX 76550 US
(512) 556-6193(512) 556-3671, *Fax:* (512) 556-2197
www.lampasasradio.com
info@lampasasraio.com
License: Lampasas, TX held by Ronald K. Witcher.
Regional Network: Texas State Networks
Arbitron Metro Market: Lampasas, TX *Format:* Country *Special Programming:* Farm 5 hrs, loc news & community service 14 hrs, sports 8 hrs, relg 10 hrs wkly *Hrs. of News Programming:* news progmg 15 hrs wkly *No. NewsEmployees:* 3 *Target Audience:* 30 plus; agriculture, farm & ranch
Ronnie Witcher, President
Joe Lombardi, Promotions Manager
Lela Cooper, News Director

Laredo

*KBNL
07-27-1985; 89.9 mhz FM *Hrs Open:* 24; 100 kw; 604 ft.; N27 39 27 W99 35 10
Mailing Address: P.O. Box 3333, McAllen, TX 78502 US
Second Address: 1620 E. Plum St., Laredo, TX 78043
(956) 724-9090, *Fax:* (956) 724-9919
www.kbnl.org
kbnl@lwrn.org
License: Laredo, Webb County, TX held by World Radio Network Inc.
Group Owner: World Radio Network Inc.; (acq 10-24-85)
Arbitron Metro Market: Laredo, TX *Format:* Spanish *Hrs. of News Programming:* News progmg 2 hrs wkly *Target Audience:* Male-Females 18-54.
Arturo Lozano, General Manager

*KHOY
11-01-1985; 88.1 mhz FM; 1.8 kw; 348 ft.; N27 31 14 W99 31 19
1901 Corpus Christi St., Laredo, TX 78044 US
(956) 722-4167, *Fax:* (956) 722-4464
www.khoy.org
khoy@khoy.org
License: Laredo, Webb County, TX held by Laredo Catholic Communications Inc.
Format: Religious, Spanish *Hrs. of News Programming:* news progmg 8 hrs wkly *Target Audience:* Christian Families
Bennett McBride, General Manager
Jose Angel Jimenez, Programming Director

KJBZ
12-29-1982; 92.7 mhz FM *Hrs Open:* 24; 3 kw; 289 ft.; N27 31 4 W99 31 20
902 East Calton Rd, Laredo, TX 78041 US

(956) 726-9393, *Fax:* (956) 724-9915
License: Laredo, Webb County, TX held by Encarnacion A. Guerra.
Arbitron Metro Market: Laredo, TX *Format:* Tejano *Target Audience:* General; all ages
Belinda Guerra, CEO
Jorge A. Arredondo, General Manager
Laura Lafaire, General Sales Mgr
Luis ""Bird"" Rodriguez, Programming Director
Arturo Trevino, Chief Engineer

KLAR
01-01-1956; 1300 khz AM *Hrs Open:* 24
Mailing Address: PO Box 2517, Laredo, TX 78044 US
Second Address: 3320 Anna Ave., Laredo, TX 78040-1070
(956) 723-1300, *Fax:* (956) 723-9539
info@klaramfeytoder.com
License: Laredo, TX held by Faith and Power Communications Inc.
Arbitron Metro Market: Laredo, TX *Format:* Christian *Hrs. of News Programming:* news progmg 18 hrs wkly *No. News Employees:* 2 *Target Audience:* 18-54; Hispanic & Anglo middle to upper-middle class
Hector Patino, President

KLNT
04-20-1990; 1490 khz AM *Hrs Open:* 24
505 Houston St/ Po 814, Laredo, TX 78040 US
(956) 725-1000, *Fax:* (956) 794-9155
info@klntam.com
License: Laredo, TX held by BMP 100.5 FM L.P.
Group Owner: Border Media Partners LLC; (acq 11-9-2004; grpsl).
Arbitron Metro Market: Laredo, TX
Thomas Castro, President
Ruben Villareal, Operations Dir
Raul Rodriguez, General Manager
Joe Flores, General Sales Mgr

KNEX
01-01-1992; 106.1 mhz FM; 6 kw; 177 ft.; N27 31 12 W99 31 19
P. O. Box 814, Laredo, TX 78042 US
(956) 725-1000, *Fax:* (956) 794-9155
www.hot1061.net
License: Laredo, Webb County, TX held by BMP 100.5 FM L.P.
Group Owner: Border Media Partners LLC; (acq 11-9-2004; grpsl).
Arbitron Metro Market: Laredo, TX *Format:* Contemporary Hits/Top 40, Spanish
Miguel Villarreal, General Manager

KQUR
02-02-1972; 94.9 mhz FM; 100 kw; 810 ft.; N27 31 14 W99 31 19
P. O. Box 1638, Laredo, TX 78044 US
(956) 725-1491, *Fax:* (956) 725-3424
License: Laredo, Webb County, TX held by Border Broadcasters Inc.
Nat'l Reps: Roslin
Arbitron Metro Market: Laredo, TX *Format:* Adult Contemp
Target Audience: 25-54; general
Miguel Villarreal, General Manager

KRRG
10-01-1982; 98.1 mhz FM; 96 kw; 699 ft.; N27 31 14 W99 31 19
Encarnacion A. Guerra, 902 E. Calton Rd, Laredo, TX 78041 US
(956) 724-9800, *Fax:* (956) 724-9915
www.bigbuck98.com
bigbuck@krrg.com
License: Laredo, Webb County, TX held by Guerra Enterprises
Nat'l Reps: D & R Radio
Arbitron Metro Market: Laredo, TX *Format:* Country
Belinda Guerra, CEO
Roberto Estrada, General Manager
David Gonzalez, Programming Director
Jeannette Alvarado, News Director
Arturo Trevino, Chief Engineer
Laura Lafaire, Local Sales Manager

Laughlin Afb

KDRX
106.9 mhz FM; 6 kw; 328 ft.; N29 24 21 W100 39 41
US
(772) 286-5586
License: Laughlin Afb, Edwards County, TX held by William H. Brothers.
Arbitron Metro Market: Del Rio, TX *Format:* Country
William Brothers, General Manager

League City

***KHCB**
01-01-1922; 1400 khz AM *Hrs Open:* 24; 1 kw-U DA; N29 25 35 W95 08 00
2424 South Blvd., Houston, TX 77098
(713) 520-7900, *Fax:* (713) 520-8104
www.radioamistad.net
License: League City, Galveston County, TX held by Houston Christian Broadcasters Inc.
Group Owner: Houston Christian Broadcasters Inc.; (acq 12-4-90; $150,000)
Population Served: 1,500,000 *Arbitron Metro Market:* Houston-Galveston *Special Programming:* Chinese 13 hrs, Vietnamese 4 hrs wkly *No. News Employees:* 1 *Target Audience:* General.
Bruce Munsterman, President
Dan Wales, Chief Engineer
Miguel Jacinto, Music Director
Dolly Martin, Programming Director

Leakey

KBLT
06-10-1997; 104.3 mhz FM; 1 kw; 594 ft.; N29 41 34 W99 48 56
Mailing Address: 8620 N. New Braunfels, San Antonio, TX 78217 US
Second Address: 935 East Main, Uvalde, TX 78801
(830) 278-3693, *Fax:* (830) 278-2329
www.kbnu.fm
kbradioranch@hotmail.com
License: Leakey, Real County, TX held by Radio Cactus Ltd.
Arbitron Metro Market: Leakey, TX *Format:* Christian *Target Audience:* General.
John Furr, President
Regenia Tumbarello, General Manager

KBDK
93.1 mhz FM; kw
US
(847) 674-0864
License: Leakey, Real County, TX held by KM Communications Inc.
Group Owner: KM Communications Inc.
Kevin Joel Bae, Operations Dir

Leander

KXBT
05-16-1976; 98.9 mhz FM *Hrs Open:* 24; 29 kw; Ant 515 ft; N30 23 26 W97 50 13
912 Capital of Texas Hwy, Suite 400, Austin, TX 18503
(512) 416-1100, *Fax:* (512) 416-8205
License: Leander, Williamson County, TX held by BMP Austin License Company L.P.
Group Owner: Border Media Partners LLC; (acq 11-9-2004; grpsl)
Nat'l Network: ABC; Westwood One *Nat'l Reps:* D & R Radio
Population Served: 926,300 *Arbitron Metro Market:* Austin, TX
Target Audience: 25-54; adults *Adv. Rates:* 38; 38; 38; 38
Ian Hernandez, Operations Dir
Paul Danitz, General Manager
Daniel Martinez, Programming Director

Levelland

KLVT
08-01-1949; 1230 khz AM; 1 kw-U, ND1; N33 35 54 W102 23 8
Mailing Address: 132 Liveoak, Hereford, TX 79045 US
Second Address: 611 N. West Ave., Levelland, TX 79336
(806) 894-3134, *Fax:* (806) 894-3135
www.hprnetwork.com/
office@hprnetwork.com
License: Levelland, TX held by Profit Programming of Northern Texas
Regional Network: Texas State Networks
Format: Country
Jody Rose, Operations Dir
Anthony Garza, Chief Engineer

KJDL-FM
11-08-1983; 105.3 mhz FM; 23.5 kw; 712 ft.; N33 25 24 W102 7 41
132 Liveoak, Hereford, TX 79045 US
(806) 744-6864, *Fax:* (806) 744-8018
1053jack.com
info@kjdlfm.com
License: Levelland, Hockley County, TX held by Walker FM Holdings LLC
Format: Country
Dennis Leverett, General Manager
Jess Walker, Station Manager

Lewisville

KESS-FM
04-10-1999; 107.9 mhz FM *Hrs Open:* 24; 100 kw; 981 ft.; N33 19 42 W97 3 56
3102 Oak Lawn Ave., Suite 215, Dallas, TX 75219 US
(214) 525-0400, *Fax:* (214) 631-1154
www.univisionradio.com
info@kessfm.com
License: Lewisville, Denton County, TX held by KECS-FM License Corp.
Group Owner: Univision Radio; (acq 9-22-2003; grpsl).
Arbitron Metro Market: Dallas, TX *Format:* Tejano
Andy Lockridge, Operations Dir
Frank Carter, General Manager
Cipriano Robles, General Sales Mgr
Herminio Ortuno, Programming Director
Oscar Espinosa, Promotions Manager
Karen Hocking, National Sales Manager

Liberty

KSHN
08-29-1991; 99.9 mhz FM *Hrs Open:* 24; 26 kw; 679 ft; N30 03 05 W94 31 37
2099 Sam Houston St., Liberty, TX 77575
(936) 336-5793, *Fax:* (936) 336-5250
www.kshn.com
bill@kshn.com
License: Liberty, Liberty County, TX held by Trinity River Valley Broadcasting Co.
Regional Network: Texas State Networks
Population Served: 700,000 *Arbitron Metro Market:* Houston-Galvest *Special Programming:* Black 4 hrs, bluegrass 2 hrs, relg 5 hrs wkly *Hrs. of News Programming:* news progmg 36 hrs wkly *No. News Employees:* 2*Target Audience:* 34 plus; Adults *Adv. Rates:* 15; 15; 15; 15
Bill Buchanan, CEO
Bill Buchanan, President
Jordan Day, Operations Dir
Bill Buchanan, General Manager
Eric Latz, News reporter
Tiffany York, Computer Director
James Stephenson, Chief Engineer
Barbara Moss, Traffic Manager
Brad Harrington, News, sales
J.R. Austin, Adv. Sales

Littlefield

KZZN
01-01-1947; 1490 khz AM; 1 kw-U, ND1; N33 56 17 W102 20 38
Box 510, Littlefield, TX 79339 US
(806) 385-4474(806) 385-1490, *Fax:* (806) 894-3135
www.hpnetwork.com
KZZN@HPRNetwork.com
License: Littlefield, TX held by Juan Alejandro Ibarra
Nat'l Network: USA *Regional Network:* Texas State Networks
Arbitron Metro Market: Littlefield, TX *Format:* Country, Gospel
Special Programming: Farm 7 hrs, relg 5 hrs wkly *Target Audience:* General; try to reach all ages
Paul Beane, General Manager
Emil Macha, General Sales Mgr
Mike Rader, Programming Director
Anthony Garza, Chief Engineer

Livingston

KETX
06-28-1957; 1440 khz AM *Hrs Open:* 6 AM-midnight; 5 kw-D, ND1; 0.091 kw-N, ND1; N30 44 23 W94 55 30
P. O. Box 1236, Livingston, TX 77351 US
(409) 327-8916, *Fax:* (409) 327-8477
License: Livingston, TX held by Peggy Sue Marsh, administrator
Format: Country
Curtis Walzel, President

KETX-FM
09-01-1970; 92.3 mhz FM; 32 kw; 607 ft.; N30 44 18 W94 55 26
P. O. Drawer 1236, Livingston, TX 77351 US
(936) 327-8916, *Fax:* (936) 327-8477
License: Livingston, Polk County, TX held by Peggy Sue Marsh, administrator
Format: Country *Target Audience:* General.
Curtis Walzel, President

Llano

KAJZ
01-01-2000; 96.3 mhz FM; 2.9 kw; 459 ft.; N30 41 12 W98 34 16
3939 Beltline Road, Suite 250, Dallas, TX 75244 US

(325) 247-4539
www.kajzradio.com
info@kajzradio.com
License: Llano, Llano County, TX held by Rawhide Radio LLC.
Group Owner: Univision Radio; (acq 9-22-2003; grpsl).
Arbitron Metro Market: Llano, TX *Format:* Adult Contemp
Dan Wilson, General Manager

KITY
01-01-2004; 102.9 mhz FM; 2 kw; 495 ft.; N30 40 37 W98 33 59
1809 Lightsey Road, Austin, TX 78704 US
(512) 444-9268
www.kityradio.com
kity@tstar.net
License: Llano, Llano County, TX held by Bryan A. King
Nat'l Network: CNN Radio; Westwood One
Arbitron Metro Market: Llano, TX *Format:* Oldies
Bryan King, General Manager

Lockhart

KFIT
02-01-1967; 1060 khz AM *Hrs Open:* 6 AM-8 PM; 2 kw-D, DAD; N30 19 13 W97 38 59
Mailing Address: 110 Wild Basin Road, Suite 375, Austin, TX 78746 US
Second Address: 110 Wild Basin Rd., Suite 375, Austin, TX 78746
(512) 328-8400, *Fax:* (512) 328-8437
www.gospel1060.com
kfitam@yahoo.com
License: Lockhart, TX held by KFIT Inc.
Nat'l Network: Westwood One
Arbitron Metro Market: Austin, TX *Format:* Gospel *No. News Employees:* 2 *Target Audience:* 18-65.
Darrell Marshi, CEO
Terri Lewis, General Manager

Lometa

KACQ
01-01-1996; 101.9 mhz FM; 6 kw; 328 ft.; N31 14 33 W98 19 19
Rt. 2, Box 32a, Lampasas, TX 76550 US
(512) 556-6193, *Fax:* (512) 556-2197
lampasasradio.com
License: Lometa, Lampasas County, TX held by Debra L. Witcher.
Arbitron Metro Market: Lampasas, TX *Format:* Country
Ronnie Witcher, General Manager
Norma Spinner, General Sales Mgr
Joe Lombardi, Programming Director
Lela Cooper, News Director

Longview

KFRO
02-06-1935; 1370 khz AM *Hrs Open:* 24; 1 kw-D, DAN; 1 kw-N, DAN; N32 30 7 W94 42 12
13355 Noel Road, 1350 One Galleria Tower, Dallas, TX 75240 US
(903) 663-9800, *Fax:* (903) 663-9458
gnimmons@etradiogroup.com
License: Longview, TX held by Access.1 Texas License Company LLC.
Group Owner: Access.1 Communications Corp.; (acq 1-7-2005; grpsl).
Nat'l Network: ABC; Westwood One
Arbitron Metro Market: Tyler, TX *Format:* Christian, Talk *Special Programming:* Black 3 hrs wkly *Hrs. of News Programming:* news progmg 30 hrs wkly *No. News Employees:* 1 *Target Audience:* 25-54; general
Sydney Small, CEO
Chesley Maddox-Dorsey, President
Richard Guest, General Manager
Robert Taylor, General Sales Mgr
Dru Laborde, Programming Director
Shelley Miller, News Director
Sans Hawkins, Engineering Dir
Debbie Tilley,CFO

KYKX
07-01-1974; 105.7 mhz FM *Hrs Open:* 24; 100 kw; 1155 ft.; N32 35 37 W94 49 10
1350 One Galleria Tower, Dallas, TX 75240 US
(903) 663-9800(903) 663-3700, *Fax:* (903) 663-1022
www.kykx.com
gnimmons@etradiogroup.com
License: Longview, Gregg County, TX held by Access.1 Texas License Company LLC.
Group Owner: Access.1 Communications Corp.; (acq 1-7-2005; grpsl).
Nat'l Reps: McGavren Guild
Arbitron Metro Market: Tyler-Longview, TX *Format:* Country *Hrs. of News Programming:* news progmg 6 hrs wkly *No. News Employees:* 1 *Target Audience:* General.
Ginger Nimmons, General Manager
Ginger Nimmons, General Sales Mgr
Dru LaBorde, Programming Director
Tom Metzger, News Director
Sans Hawkins, Chief Engineer
Shirley Bread, Traffic Manager
Harlen Lobley, Local Sales Manager

Lorena

***KYAR**
04-06-1976; 98.3 mhz FM *Hrs Open:* 24; 4.1 kw; 397 ft.; N31 24 45 W97 12 40
600 Congress Avenue, Suite 1400, Austin, TX 78701 US
(916) 251-1600, *Fax:* (916) 251-1650
www.air1.com
info@air1.com
License: Lorena, Coryell County, TX held by Educational Media Foundation.
Group Owner: EMF Broadcasting; (acq 3-21-2003; $100,000).
Nat'l Network: Air 1
Arbitron Metro Market: Rocklin, CA *Format:* Alternative, Christian *No. News Employees:* 3 *Target Audience:* 25-44; Judeo Christian, female
Mike Novak, President
Amy Yost, Operations Dir
David Pierce, Programming Director
Ed Lenane, News Director
Sam Wallington, Engineering Dir
Marya Morgan, News Reporter
Richard Hunt, News Reporter

Lorenzo

KKCL
01-01-1989; 98.1 mhz FM *Hrs Open:* 24; 36 kw; 574 ft.; N33 31 3 W101 51 24
600 Congress Avenue, Suite 1400, Austin, TX 78701 US
(806) 798-7078
www.98kool.com
INFO@KKCLF.COM
License: Lorenzo, Crosby County, TX held by GAP Broadcasting Lubbock License LLC.
Group Owner: GAP Broadcasting LLC; (acq 8-3-2007; grpsl)
Nat'l Network: ABC
Arbitron Metro Market: Lubbock, TX *Format:* Oldies *Special Programming:* Talk 17 hrs wkly *Hrs. of News Programming:* news progmg 14 hrs wkly *No. News Employees:* 8 *Target Audience:* 25-54; upscale 55% male,45% female *Adv. Rates:* 35; 45; 25; 10
Dale Harris, General Manager
Renee Gonzalez, General Sales Mgr
Ladon King, Programming Director

Los Ybanez

KBXJ
12-01-1990; 98.5 mhz FM *Hrs Open:* 24; 50 kw; 459 ft.; N32 43 22 W102 1 50
P.O Box 1143 (#15), Los Ybanez, TX 79331 US
(214) 341-3887
License: Los Ybanez, Dawson County, TX held by KYMI License Sub LLC
Arbitron Metro Market: Los Ybanez, TX
David Stewart, General Manager

Louise

***KABA**
12-25-1986; 90.3 mhz FM; kw
US
(907) 522-1018, *Fax:* (907) 522-1027
License: Louise, Anchorage County, TX held by Tati Broadcasting LLC
Arbitron Metro Market: Anchorage, AK *Format:* Talk
Mike Robbins, General Manager

Lovelady

KHMR
01-01-2009; 104.3 mhz FM; 10.5 kw; 500 ft.; N31 11 30 W95 29 32
US
(936) 636-2859
www.kmcommunications.com
License: Lovelady, Houston County, TX held by KM Communications Inc.
Group Owner: KM Communications Inc.
Arbitron Metro Market: Lovelady, TX *Format:* Contemporary Hits/Top 40, Adult Contemp
Kevin Bae, Operations Dir

Lubbock

***KAMY**
10-01-1990; 90.1 mhz FM *Hrs Open:* 24; 63 kw; 482 ft.; N33 30 8 W101 52 20
7355 North Oracle Rd., Tucson, AZ 85704 US
(806) 794-1766, *Fax:* (806) 798-3251
License: Lubbock, Lubbock County, TX held by Family Life Broadcasting Inc.
Group Owner: Family Life Communications Inc.; (acq 6-24-98; grpsl).
Arbitron Metro Market: Lubbock, TX *Format:* Christian *Target Audience:* 28 plus; 35-54 female; Christian community of Lubbock
Don Webster, General Manager
Dave Borowsky, Promotions Manager

KBZO
04-01-1953; 1460 khz AM *Hrs Open:* 24
1220 Broadcasting, Suite 500, Lubbock, TX 79401 US
(806) 763-6051, *Fax:* (806) 744-8363
www.1460jose.com
License: Lubbock, TX held by Entravision Holdings LLC.
Group Owner: Entravision Communications Corp.; (acq 10-7-99).
Nat'l Reps: Lotus Entravision Reps LLC
Arbitron Metro Market: Lubbock, TX *Format:* Tejano *Target Audience:* Hispanic.
Jose Sauceda, General Manager
Erick Segura, Promotions Manager

KQBR
07-15-1964; 99.5 mhz FM; 100 kw; 817 ft.; N33 31 5 W101 51 25
600 Congress Avenue, Suite 1400, Austin, TX 78701 US
(806) 798-7078, *Fax:* (806) 798-7052
www.kqbr.com
info@kqbr.com
License: Lubbock, Lubbock County, TX held by GAP Broadcasting Lubbock License LLC.
Group Owner: GAP Broadcasting LLC; (acq 8-3-2007; grpsl)
Arbitron Metro Market: Lubbock, TX *Format:* Country
Dale Harris, General Manager
Alyssa Rodriguez, Programming Director

KDAV
05-14-1947; 1590 khz AM
1714 Buddy Holly Avenue, Lubbock, TX 79401 US
(806) 744-5859(806) 770-5328
www.kdav.com
radio@door.net
License: Lubbock, TX held by Renaissance Broadcasting Inc.
Wire Services: ESSA Weather Service
Arbitron Metro Market: Lubbock, TX *Format:* Oldies *Hrs. of News Programming:* 5 hrs. news progmg wkly *No. News Employees:* 1 *Target Audience:* 50 plus.
Bill Clement, President
Bud Andrews, General Manager
Jan Reeves, General Sales Mgr

KEJS
01-01-1993; 106.5 mhz FM; 34 kw; 587 ft.; N33 30 8 W101 52 20
4319 57th Street, Lubbock, TX 79413 US
(806) 747-5951, *Fax:* (806) 747-3524
www.jalapenomix.com
ebarton@kejsfm.com
License: Lubbock, Lubbock County, TX held by Barton Broadcasting Co.
Arbitron Metro Market: Lubbock, TX *Format:* Tejano
Ernest Barton, General Manager
Gilbert Esparza, Programming Director
Debra Alcorte, News Director

KFMX-FM
08-01-1966; 94.5 mhz FM; 100 kw; 817 ft.; N33 31 5 W101 51 25
600 Congress Avenue, Suite 1400, Austin, TX 78701 US
(806) 798-7078, *Fax:* (806) 798-7052
www.kfmx.com
wesnessman@townsquaremedia.com;
daleharris@townsquaremedia.com;
jasonhenry@townsquaremedia.com
License: Lubbock, Lubbock County, TX held by Gap Broadcasting Lubbock License LLC.
Group Owner: GAP Broadcasting LLC
Arbitron Metro Market: Lubbock, TX *Format:* Rock/AOR *Target Audience:* 18-64
Dale Harris, General Manager
Jason Henry, General Sales Mgr
Wes Nessman, Programming Director

KFYO
09-06-1927; 790 khz AM *Hrs Open:* 24; 5 kw-D, DA2; 1 kw-N, DA2; N33 27 50 W101 55 30
600 Congress Avenue, Suite 1400, Austin, TX 78701 US
(801) 394-8833, *Fax:* (806) 798-7052
www.bbnradio.org
bbn@bbnmedia.org
License: Lubbock, TX held by GAP Broadcasting Lubbock License LLC.
Group Owner: GAP Broadcasting LLC; (acq 8-3-2007; grpsl)
Nat'l Network: CBS *Regional Network:* Texas State Networks
Arbitron Metro Market: Ogden, UT *Format:* News, News/Talk, 86 *Hrs. of News Programming:* news progmg 12 hrs wkly *No. News Employees:* 2 *Target Audience:* Christian Adults
Scott Parsons, General Manager
Robert Snyder, Programming Director
Roger Taylor, Chief Engineer

KKAM
01-01-1955; 1340 khz AM; 1 kw-U, ND1; N33 33 24 W101 51 46
600 Congress Avenue, Suite 1400, Austin, TX 78701 US
(806) 798-7078, *Fax:* (806) 798-7052
www.kfmx.com
info@kfmx.com
License: Lubbock, TX held by GAP Broadcasting Lubbock License LLC.
Group Owner: GAP Broadcasting LLC; (acq 8-3-2007; grpsl)
Nat'l Network: ABC; CBS
Arbitron Metro Market: Lubbock, TX *Format:* Rock/AOR
Wes Nessman, Operations Dir
Dale Harris, General Manager
Renee Gonzalez, General Sales Mgr
Mark Finkner, Programming Director

KJDL
11-15-1966; 1420 khz AM *Hrs Open:* 18
4410 10th Street, Lubbock, TX 79416 US
(806) 741-1420, *Fax:* (806) 744-8018
www.newsradio1420.com
dwalker@newsradio1420.com
License: Lubbock, TX held by Walker Broadcasting & Communications Ltd.
Regional Network: Texas State Networks
Arbitron Metro Market: Lubbock, TX *Format:* News, News/Talk, 86
David Walker, President
Helen Castro, Promotions Manager
Bill Enloe, Chief Engineer

KLLL-FM
03-01-1958; 96.3 mhz FM *Hrs Open:* 24; 100 kw; 817 ft.; N33 31 4 W101 51 23
1705 West Northwest Hwy, Suite 275, Grapevine, TX 76051 US
(806) 762-3000, *Fax:* (806) 770-5363
www.klll.com
License: Lubbock, Lubbock County, TX held by Wilks License Co. -Lubbock LLC.
Group Owner: Wilks Broadcast Group LLC; (acq 8-19-2005; grpsl).
Nat'l Network: ABC
Arbitron Metro Market: Lubbock, TX *Format:* Country *Target Audience:* 25-54.
Jeff Scott, Operations Dir
Jay Richardson, General Manager
Randy Smith, Promotions Manager
Kelli D'Angelo, News Director
Randy Hayes, Chief Engineer
Neely Yates, Music Director
Celeste Collins

***KTTZ-FM**
01-01-1973; 89.1 mhz FM *Hrs Open:* 24; 70 kw; Ant 567 ft; N33 34 55 W101 53 25
Mailing Address: 1901 University Ave., Suite 603-B, Lubbock, TX 79409
Second Address: Box 45891, Lubbock, TX 79409
(806) 742-3100, *Fax:* (806) 742-3716
www.kohm.org
kohm@ttu.edu
License: Lubbock, Lubbock County, TX held by Texas Tech University.
Nat'l Network: NPR; PRI
Population Served: 250,000 *Arbitron Metro Market:* Lubbock, TX *TV Affiliate:* *KTXT-TV affil.
Derrick Ginter, General Manager
Sherril Skibell, General Sales Mgr
Clinton Barrick, Programming Director

KONE
01-01-1975; 101.1 mhz FM *Hrs Open:* 24; 100 kw; 883 ft.; N33 26 31 W101 52 40
1705 West NW Highway, Suite 275, Grapevine, TX 76051 US
(806) 762-3000, *Fax:* (806) 762-8419
www.cr101.com
License: Lubbock, Lubbock County, TX held by Wilks License Co.-Lubbock LLC.
Group Owner: Wilks Broadcast Group LLC; (acq 8-19-2005; grpsl).
Nat'l Network: ABC
Arbitron Metro Market: Lubbock, TX *Format:* Adult Contemp, Classic Rock *Target Audience:* 25-54.
Jeff Scott, Operations Dir
Scott Harris, General Manager
Jay Richards, General Sales Mgr
Rick Gilbert, Promotions Manager
Stacey James, News Director
Randy Hayes, Chief Engineer
Kelly Greene, Music Director
Julia Aguilar,Traffic Manager

KRFE
09-19-1953; 580 khz AM *Hrs Open:* 24; 0.5 kw-D, DA2; 0.29 kw-N, DA2; N33 32 0 W101 49 14
6602 Martin L. King Blvd, Lubbock, TX 79404 US
(806) 745-1197, *Fax:* (806) 745-1088
www.am580lubbock.com
wade@wadewilkes.com
License: Lubbock, TX held by KRFE Radio Inc.
Nat'l Network: ABC
Arbitron Metro Market: Lubbock, TX *Format:* News, News/Talk, 86 *Special Programming:* News/talk 15 hrs wkly *Hrs. of News Programming:* news progmg 5 hrs wkly *No. News Employees:* 1 *Target Audience:* 40plus.
Wade Wilkes, OWN

***KTXT-FM**
04-01-1961; 88.1 mhz FM *Hrs Open:* 24; 35 kw; 423 ft.; N33 34 55 W101 53 25
P.O. Box 43082, Lubbock, TX 79409 US
(806) 742-3388, *Fax:* (806) 742-2434
www.ktxt.net
info@ktxtfm.com
License: Lubbock, Lubbock County, TX held by Texas Tech University.
Arbitron Metro Market: Lubbock, TX *Format:* Variety/Diverse
Nick Carissimi, Station Manager
Sheri Lewis, General Sales Mgr
Ali Rana, Programming Director

KJTV
11-01-1946; 950 khz AM *Hrs Open:* 24; 5 kw-D, DA2; 0.5 kw-N, DA2; N33 34 53 W101 49 38
Mailing Address: P.O. Box 3757, Lubbock, TX 79452 US
Second Address: 9800 University Ave., Lubbock, TX 79423
(806) 745-3434, *Fax:* (806) 748-2470
www.myfoxlubbock.com
License: Lubbock, TX held by Ramar Communications II Ltd.
Group Owner: Ramar Communications II Ltd.
Regional Network: Texas State Networks
Arbitron Metro Market: Lubbock, TX *Format:* News, News/Talk, 86 *Hrs. of News Programming:* news progmg 147 hrs wkly *No. News Employees:* 1 *Target Audience:* 25-54.
Brad Moran, General Manager
Sherry Saffle, General Sales Mgr
Jeff Klotzman, News Director
Paula Poole, Traffic Manager
Kay Boren, Assistant News Director

KXTQ-FM
11-01-1963; 93.7 mhz FM *Hrs Open:* 24; 100 kw; 743 ft.; N33 30 8 W101 52 20
Mailing Address: PO Box 3757, Lubbock, TX 79452 US
Second Address: 9800 University Ave., Lubbock, TX 79423
(806) 745-3434, *Fax:* (806) 748-1949
www.magic937fm.com
cfleming@ramarcom.com
License: Lubbock, Lubbock County, TX held by Ramar Communications II Ltd.
Group Owner: Ramar Communications II Ltd.; (acq 9-93; $362,500).
Nat'l Reps: Univision Radio National Sales
Arbitron Metro Market: Lubbock, TX *Format:* Tejano *Target Audience:* 18-49.
Brad Moran, President
Chris Fleming, General Manager
Connie Hayes, General Sales Mgr
Eddie Moreno, Programming Director
Susie Gonzales, News Director
Tee Thomas, Chief Engineer
Liz Marmalejo, Traffic Manager
Eddie Moreno,Program Director

***KKLU**
10-24-1993; 90.9 mhz FM *Hrs Open:* 24; 21 kw; 597 ft.; N33 31 33 W101 52 7
8030 Arrowridge Blvd., Charlotte, NC 28273 US
(916) 251-1600, *Fax:* (916) 251-1650
www.klove.com
License: Lubbock, Lubbock County, TX held by Educational Media Foundation.
Group Owner: EMF Broadcasting; (acq 5-1-2000; $750,000 with KXRI(FM) Amarillo).
Nat'l Network: K-Love
Arbitron Metro Market: Lubbock, TX *Format:* Christian *Target Audience:* All ages.
Richard Jenkins, President
Mike Novak, Programming Director

KZII-FM
03-10-1982; 102.5 mhz FM *Hrs Open:* 24; 100 kw; 817 ft.; N33 31 5 W101 51 25
600 Congress Avenue, Suite 1400, Austin, TX 78701 US
(806) 798-7078
www.1025kiss.com/
daleharris@townsquaremedia.com
License: Lubbock, Lubbock County, TX held by GAP Broadcasting Lubbock License LLC.
Group Owner: GAP Broadcasting LLC
Arbitron Metro Market: Lubbock, TX *Format:* Contemporary Hits/Top 40 *Target Audience:* 18-49.
Dale Harris, General Manager
Renee Gonzalez, Director of Sales

Lufkin

***KAVX**
12-25-1998; 91.9 mhz FM *Hrs Open:* 24; 23 kw; 728 ft.; N31 22 8 W94 38 45
Mailing Address: Route 17, Box 6395, Lufkin, TX 75904 US
Second Address: , Nacogdoches, TX
(936) 639-6400, *Fax:* (936) 639-5677
www.kavx.org
aloss@kavx.org
License: Lufkin, Angelina County, TX held by Lufkin Educational Broadcasting Foundation.
Nat'l Network: USA
Arbitron Metro Market: Lufkin, TX *Format:* Talk *Special Programming:* Praise & Worship - Weekends *Target Audience:* Persons 30 Plus *Adv. Rates:* 10, 20
Dwyan Calvert, President
Al Ross, General Manager
Michelle Ross, Programming Director
Tim Swanson, Production Director
Drew Wilson, Promotions Director

***KLDN**
05-02-1991; 88.9 mhz FM *Hrs Open:* 24; 50 kw; 650 ft.; N31 24 28 W94 45 53 *Rebroadcasts:* Rebroadcasts KDAQ(FM) Shreveport, LA 100%
One University Place, Shreveport, LA 71115 US
(318) 797-5150, *Fax:* (318) 797-5265
www.redriverradio.org
listenermail@redriverradio.org
License: Lufkin, Angelina County, TX held by Board of Supervisors of Louisiana State University.
Nat'l Network: NPR; PRI
Format: Classical, Jazz, 60 *Target Audience:* 25+.
Rick Shelton, Operations Dir
Kermit Poling, General Manager

KRBA
05-03-1938; 1340 khz AM *Hrs Open:* 24; 1 kw-U, ND1; N31 21 53 W94 43 8
Mailing Address: P.O. Box 1345, Lufkin, TX 75902 US
Second Address: 121 Cotton Sq., Lufkin, TX 75901
(936) 634-6661, *Fax:* (936) 632-5722
kybi@lcc.net
License: Lufkin, TX held by Stephen W. Yates.
Format: Country *Hrs. of News Programming:* news progmg 7 hrs wkly *No. News Employees:* 1 *Target Audience:* General.
Stephen Yates, General Manager
Kevin Sims, Programming Director
Jeremy Chance, News Director

***KSWP**
08-31-1985; 90.9 mhz FM *Hrs Open:* 24; 100 kw; 807 ft.; N31 22 8 W94 38 45
Mailing Address: Rt. 17, Box 6395, Lufkin, TX 75904 US
Second Address: , Nacogdoches, TX
(936) 639-6400, *Fax:* (936) 639-5677
www.kswp.org
aloss@kswp.org

License: Lufkin, Angelina County, TX held by Lufkin Educational Broadcasting Foundation.
Nat'l Network: USA
Arbitron Metro Market: Lufkin, TX *Format:* Christian *Special Programming:* Pub affrs talk show 2 hrs wkly *Target Audience:* Woman 25-54, Persons 25-54 *Adv. Rates:* 10, 20
Dwyan Calvert, President
Al Ross, General Manager
Michelle Ross, Programming Director
Tim Swanson, Production Director
Drew Wilson, Promotions Director

KYBI
05-01-1978; 100.1 mhz FM *Hrs Open:* 24; 20 kw; 787 ft.; N31 20 5 W94 40 10
Mailing Address: 3 Deerwood, Lufkin, TX 75901 US
Second Address: 121 Cotton Sq., Lufkin, TX 75902
(936) 634-4584, *Fax:* (936) 632-5722
www.kybiradio.com
traffic@yatesmedia.com
License: Lufkin, Angelina County, TX
Arbitron Metro Market: Lufkin, TX *Format:* Adult Contemp *Target Audience:* 25-54.
Stephen Yates, General Manager

KYKS
07-09-1976; 105.1 mhz FM *Hrs Open:* 24; 100 kw; 1066 ft.; N31 22 8 W94 38 45
Mailing Address: 600 Congress Avenue, Suite 1400, Austin, TX 78701 US
Second Address: 1216 S. First St., Lufkin, TX 75901
(936) 639-4455, *Fax:* (936) 632-5957
www.kicks105.com
info@kyks.com
License: Lufkin, Angelina County, TX held by GAP Broadcasting Lufkin License LLC.
Group Owner: GAP Broadcasting LLC; (acq 8-3-2007; grpsl)
Arbitron Metro Market: Lufkin, TX *Format:* Country *No. News Employees:* 1 *Target Audience:* 25-54.
Tami Jones, General Manager
Johnny Lathrop, General Sales Mgr
Danny Merrell, Promotions Manager
Brandy Abney, News Director
Sean Ericson, Music Director
Jeff Klein, Advertising Enquiry

KAGZ(FM)
01-01-2008; 93.9 mhz FM; 1.7 kw; Ant 610 ft; N31 21 55 W94 45 59
24018 Middle Fork, San Antonio, TX 78258
(830) 980-7111
License: Lufkin, Angelina County, TX held by E-String Wireless Ltd.
Population Served: 35,425 *Arbitron Metro Market:* Lufkin, TX
Bret Huggins, General Manager

Luling

KAMX
03-22-1987; 94.7 mhz FM *Hrs Open:* 24; 99 kw; 1306 ft.; N30 19 23 W97 47 58
600 New Hampshire Avenue, N.W., Suite 1200, Washington, DC 20037 US
(512) 327-9595, *Fax:* (512) 329-6255
mix947.com
akirshbom@entercom.com
License: Luling, Caldwell County, TX held by Entercom Austin License LLC.
Group Owner: Entercom Communications Corp.; (acq 11-30-2007; grpsl)
Nat'l Reps: Katz Radio
Arbitron Metro Market: Austin, TX *Format:* Adult Contemp
Special Programming: Pub affrs 2 hrs wkly *Target Audience:* 18-49; upscale adults
Clint Culp, Operations Dir
Alan Kirshbom, General Manager
John Hiatt, Senior Vice President

Lumberton

KSET
10-13-1959; 1300 khz AM *Hrs Open:* 24
103 Entrance Drive, Suite 1, Livingston, TX 77351 US
(409) 385-2883, *Fax:* (409) 386-1001
www.kset1300.com
kset@kset1300.com
License: Lumberton, TX held by Proctor-Williams Inc.
Regional Network: Texas State Networks
Arbitron Metro Market: Beaumont, TX *Format:* Sports *Target Audience:* General.
Dave Collier, CEO

KKHT-FM
12-01-1987; 100.7 mhz FM *Hrs Open:* 24; 100 kw; 1952 ft.; N30 3 5 W94 31 37
3102 Oak Lawn, Suite 215, Dallas, TX 75219 US
(713) 260-3600, *Fax:* (713) 260-3628
www.kkht.com
comments@kkht.com
License: Lumberton, Chambers County, TX held by Salem Media of Illinois LLC.
Group Owner: Salem Communications Corp.; (acq 1-7-2005; with WIND(AM) Chicago, IL and KNIT(AM) Dallas in exchange for WPPN(FM) Des Plaines, IL).
Nat'l Reps: Salem
Arbitron Metro Market: Houston, TX *Format:* Christian, Talk
Paul Baker, Operations Dir
Chuck Jewell, General Manager
Dan Doster, General Sales Mgr
Kent McDonald, News Director
Sidney Jones, Chief Engineer
Marsha Lambeth, Music Director
Ken Garza, Public Affairs Director

Lytle

*KZLV
01-20-1990; 91.3 mhz FM *Hrs Open:* 24; 50 kw; 492 ft.; N29 14 39 W98 44 27
1425 North Market Boulevard, Suite 9, Sacramento, CA 95839 US
(210) 824-9100, *Fax:* (210) 824-8870
www.klove.com
info@kzlv.com
License: Lytle, Atascosa County, TX held by Educational Media Foundation.
Group Owner: EMF Broadcasting; (acq 4-28-99).
Nat'l Network: K-Love
Format: Adult Contemp, Christian *Target Audience:* 25-49; professional adult & parents
Dick Jenkins, President
Ed Lenane, Operations Dir
Lloyd Parker, General Manager

Mabank

KTXV
01-01-2007; 890 khz AM; 20 kw-D, DA; N32 17 13 W95 58 39
10613 Bellaire Blvd., Suite 900, Houston, TX
(713) 917-0050, *Fax:* (713) 917-0213
www.radiosaigonhouston.com
License: Mabank, Kaufman County, TX held by Bustos Media Holdings L.L.C.
Group Owner: Bustos Media LLC; (acq 9-5-2007; $1 million)
Thuy Vu, General Manager

Madisonville

KAGG
12-05-1989; 96.1 mhz FM *Hrs Open:* 24; 40 kw; 538 ft.; N30 48 2 W96 7 0
13355 Noel Road, Dallas, TX 75240 US
(979) 846-5597, *Fax:* (979) 268-9090
www.aggie96.com
info@aggie96.com
License: Madisonville, Madison County, TX held by CCB Texas Licenses L.P.
Group Owner: Clear Channel Communications Inc.; (acq 10-10-00; grpsl).
Arbitron Metro Market: Bryan, TX *Format:* Country

KMVL
10-01-1989; 1220 khz AM *Hrs Open:* 24; 0.5 kw-D, ND1; 0.011 kw-N, ND1; N30 57 56 W95 53 52
102 West Main Street, Madisonville, TX 77864 US
(936) 348-9200, *Fax:* (936) 348-9201
www.kmvl.net
kmvlradio@ev1.net
License: Madisonville, TX held by Hunt Broadcasting.
Regional Network: Texas State Networks
Format: Adult Contemp *Hrs. of News Programming:* news progmg 15 hrs wkly *No. News Employees:* 1 *Target Audience:* General.
Leon Hunt, General Manager

KMVL-FM
04-01-1997; 100.5 mhz FM *Hrs Open:* 24; 25 kw; 449 ft; N31 00 42 W96 02 27
102 W. Main St., Madisonville, TX 77864
(936) 348-9200, *Fax:* (936) 348-9201
www.kmvl.net
License: Madisonville, Madison County, TX held by Leon Hunt
Nat'l Network: ABC
Target Audience: 25-49.
Leon Hunt, President
Leon Hunt, General Manager
Lance Parr, Chief Engineer

*KHML
01-01-2006; 91.5 mhz FM *Hrs Open:* 24; 95 kw; 341 ft.; N31 6 39.6 W95 57 8.6 *Rebroadcasts:* Rebroadcasts KHCB-FM Houston 95%
2424 South Boulevard, Houston, TX 77098 US
(713) 520-5200
www.khcb.org
email@khcb.org
License: Madisonville, Madison County, TX held by Houston Christian Broadcasters Inc.
Group Owner: Houston Christian Broadcasters Inc.
Nat'l Network: Moody
Arbitron Metro Market: Austin, TX *Format:* Christian *Special Programming:* Sp Christian 6 hrs wkly
Bruce Munsterman, General Manager
Bonnie BeMent, Assistant General Manager

KPWJ(FM)
101.3 mhz FM; 3.5 kw; 328 feet; N30 37 12 W96 15 13
PO Box 3248, Bryan, TX 77805
(979) 695-9595, *Fax:* (979) 695-1933
www.bryanbroadcasting.com
License: Madisonville, Madison County, TX held by Bryan Broadcasting License Corp
Group Owner: Bryan Broadcasting Corp.
Ben D Downs, Vice President

Malakoff

KCKL
08-08-1983; 95.9 mhz FM *Hrs Open:* 24; 6 kw; 295 ft.; N32 8 48 W95 58 25
P.O. Box 489, Malakoff, TX 75148 US
(903) 489-1238, *Fax:* (903) 489-2671
www.kcklfm.com
cquinn@kcklfm.com
License: Malakoff, Henderson County, TX held by Lake Country Radio L.P.
Nat'l Network: ABC
Arbitron Metro Market: Tyler-Longview, TX *Format:* Country
Special Programming: Relg 7 hrs wkly *Hrs. of News Programming:* news progmg 10 hrs wkly *No. News Employees:* 1 *Target Audience:* 25-54;country/city folk, weekenders & visitors to Cedar Creek Lake *Adv. Rates:* 22.50; 18.50; 22.50; 16.50
Pat Isaacson, Operations Dir
Chris Quinn, General Manager
Tim Howard, Program Director, Sports Director and News Directo
Rich Flowers, News Director
Wayne Blackwelder, Chief Engineer
Robin Smetak, Traffic Director
Nancy Morris,Business Manager
Tasha Crum, Promotions Coordinator
Tasha Crum, Public Service Announcements

Manor

KELG
04-22-1981; 1440 khz AM *Hrs Open:* 24; 0.8 kw-D, DA2; 0.5 kw-N, DA2; N30 19 36 W97 32 35
7524 North Lamar Blvd, Austin, TX 78752 US
(512) 453-1491, *Fax:* (512) 453-6809
License: Manor, TX held by Encino Broadcasting LLC.
Group Owner: Encino Broadcasting LLC; (acq 2-15-2008; grpsl)
Arbitron Metro Market: Austin, TX
Jerry Del Core, General Manager
Chayan Ortuno, Programming Director
Pam Walker, News Director
Ben Rippy, Chief Engineer

KTXW
1120 khz AM
US
License: Manor, TX held by JNE Investments Inc.
Group Owner: Bustos Media LLC
Arbitron Metro Market: Manor, TX

Marble Falls

*KBMD
01-01-2002; 88.5 mhz FM *Hrs Open:* 24; 6 kw vert; 89 ft.; N30 33 12 W98 15 30 *Rebroadcasts:* EWTN
P.O. Box 26142, Austin, TX 78755 US

(432) 638-1150, *Fax:* (432) 682-5230
www.grnonline.com
robertd@grnonline.com
License: Marble Falls, Burnet County, TX held by La Promesa Foundation.
Group Owner: La Promesa Foundation; (acq 2-24-2005; $130,000).
Arbitron Metro Market: Marble Falls, TX *Format:* Religious, Christian *No. News Employees:* 2 *Adv. Rates:* 10; 10; 10; 10
Leonard Oswald, President
Dick Bigelow, General Manager

Marfa

***KRTS**
01-01-2007; 93.5 mhz FM; 33 kw; 1463 ft.; N30 33 50.2 W104 9 44.8
Mailing Address: US
Second Address: 111 S. Highland Ave., Marfa, TX 79843
(432) 729-4578
www.marfapublicradio.org
info@marfapublicradio.org
License: Marfa, Presidio County, TX held by Matinee Radio LLC.
Group Owner: Matinee Radio LLC
Arbitron Metro Market: Marfa, TX *Format:* Triple A
Tom Michael, General Manager
Rachel Osier Lindley, Production Director
Anne Adkins, Office Manager & Volunteer Coordinator
Nicolas Miller, Operations & Traffic Manager

Marion

***KBIB**
09-21-1989; 1000 khz AM; 0.25 kw-D, DAD; N29 34 9 W98 9 47
Rt. 1, Box 95-C, Marion, TX 78124 US
(830) 914-2083
www.kbib.org
kbibam@juno.com
License: Marion, TX held by Hispanic Community College.
Arbitron Metro Market: San Antonio, TX *Format:* Religious *Target Audience:* General.
Pastor Ken Hutchinson, General Manager

Markham

KKHA
08-01-2000; 92.5 mhz FM *Hrs Open:* 24; 6 kw; 328 ft.; N28 52 26 W96 8 22
2104 Cedar Drive, La Marque, TX 77568 US
(979) 323-7771, *Fax:* (775) 719-2182
www.kkhafm.com
lee@happyradioonline.com
License: Markham, Matagorda County, TX held by Edwards Broadcasting Co.
Format: Contemporary Hits/Top 40, Adult Contemp *No. News Employees:* 1 *Target Audience:* 25-54; White equally mixed gender
Dick Witkovski, President
Ernie Cunnar, Operations Dir
Jill Moore, General Manager

Marlin

KRMX(FM)
04-02-1977; 92.9 mhz FM *Hrs Open:* 24; 3 kw; 500 ft; N31 19 31 W96 54 36
220 S. 2nd St., Apt. 282, Waco, TX 76701
(254) 772-0930, *Fax:* (254) 753-0499
star929fm.com
info@star929fm.com
License: Marlin, Falls County, TX held by Simmons Austin, LS LLC.
Group Owner: Simmons Media Group; (acq 6-4-2004; grpsl)
Nat'l Reps: Roslin
Population Served: 109,000 *Arbitron Metro Market:* Waco, TX *No. News Employees:* 1 *Target Audience:* 25-49. *Adv. Rates:* 40; 40; 40; NA
Rob Reed, Operations Dir
Daryl O'Neal, General Manager
Bill LeGrande, General Sales Mgr
Dustin Drew, Programming Director
Flavia Chen, News Director
Cole McClellan, Chief Engineer

KRMX
01-01-1958; 92.9 mhz FM *Hrs Open:* 24; 50 kw; 492 ft.; N31 24 45 W97 12 40 *Rebroadcasts:* KNKN Sunday mass 10:15 am
1018 N. Valley Mills Dr., Waco, TX 76710 US
(719) 545-2883, *Fax:* (719) 547-9301
knfoffice@qwestoffice.net
License: Marlin, Pueblo County, TX held by United States CP LLC.
Group Owner: United States CP LLC; (acq 3-10-2008; $1.75 million with KNKN(FM) Pueblo)
Arbitron Metro Market: Waco, TX *Format:* Country *Target Audience:* General; Hispanic families *Adv. Rates:* 26; 26; 26; 26
Lupe Brown, General Manager

Marshall

***KBWC**
03-01-1977; 91.1 mhz FM *Hrs Open:* 24; 0.135 kw; 112 ft.; N32 32 12 W94 22 29
711 Wiley Avenue, Marshall, TX 75670 US
(903) 927-3266, *Fax:* (903) 935-0153
www.wileyc.edu
info@kbwcfm.com
License: Marshall, Harrison County, TX held by Wiley College.
Nat'l Network: American Urban
Arbitron Metro Market: Marshall, TX *Format:* Adult Contemp *Target Audience:* 18-34.
Shanon Levingston, General Manager

KCUL
10-07-1957; 1410 khz AM *Hrs Open:* 5:30 AM-11 PM; 0.5 kw-D, DA2; 0.09 kw-N, DA2; N32 29 30 W94 21 52
Mailing Address: 3712 Cornell Drive, Shreveport, LA 71107 US
Second Address: 621 Chase Dr., Tyler, TX 75701
(903) 581-9966, *Fax:* (903) 534-5300
www.theranch.fm
License: Marshall, TX held by Access. 1 Texas License Co. LLC.
Group Owner: Access.1 Communications Corp.; (acq 5-9-2000; grpsl)
Nat'l Network: Fox News Radio *Regional Network:* Texas State Networks
Format: Country, News *Special Programming:* Farm 3 hrs wkly *Hrs. of News Programming:* news progmg 15 hrs wkly *No. News Employees:* 1 *Target Audience:* General.
Rick Quest, General Manager

KCUL-FM
01-01-1992; 92.3 mhz FM *Hrs Open:* 24; 5.8 kw; 328 ft.; N32 32 26 W94 24 3
Mailing Address: 3712 Cornell Drive, Shreveport, LA 71107 US
Second Address: 621 Chase Dr., Tyler, TX 75701
(903) 581-9966, *Fax:* (903) 534-5300
www.lainvasora.fm
License: Marshall, Harrison County, TX held by Access: 1 Texas License Co. LLC.
Group Owner: Access.1 Communications Corp.
Regional Network: Texas State Networks
Format: Tejano *Target Audience:* 25 plus.
Peter Tuluk, General Manager

KMHT
01-01-1947; 1450 khz AM; 0.65 kw-U, ND1; N32 33 50 W94 21 4
2323 Jefferson Avenue, Marshall, TX 75670 US
(903) 923-8000, *Fax:* (903) 935-2481
License: Marshall, TX held by Hanszen Broadcast Group Inc.
Format: Sports
Chris Paddie, General Manager

KMHT-FM
09-04-1977; 103.9 mhz FM; 1.85 kw; 423 ft.; N32 33 50 W94 21 4
2323 Jefferson Avenue, Marshall, TX 75670 US
(903) 923-8000, *Fax:* (903) 935-2481
www.kgasradio.com/
info@kmhtradio.com
License: Marshall, Harrison County, TX
Arbitron Metro Market: Marshall, TX *Format:* Country
Chris Paddie, General Manager

Mart

***KSUR**
01-01-2007; 88.9 mhz FM; 100 kw vert; 623 ft.; N31 23 2 W97 16 38 *Rebroadcasts:* Rebroadcasts WAFR(FM) Tupelo, MS 100%
P O Drawer 2440, Tupelo, MS 38803 US
(254) 772-1900
www.kbderadio.net
License: Mart, McLennan County, TX held by American Family Association.
Group Owner: American Family Radio
Arbitron Metro Market: Eagle Pass, TX *Format:* Christian
Marvin Sanders, General Manager

Mason

KOTY
01-01-2004; 95.7 mhz FM; 50 kw; 436 ft.; N30 33 53 W99 27 13
1809 Lightsey Rd., Austin, TX 78704 US
(512) 444-9268
www.kityradio.com
kity@tstar.net
License: Mason, Mason County, TX held by Bryan A. King
Arbitron Metro Market: Mason, TX *Format:* Oldies
Bryan King, General Manager

KHLB
01-01-2005; 102.5 mhz FM; 26 kw; 630 ft.; N30 42 3 W99 13 59
1818 N Street NW, Suite 700, Washington, DC 20036 US
(830) 693-5551, *Fax:* (830) 593-5107
License: Mason, Mason County, TX held by Munbilla Broadcasting Properties Ltd.
Group Owner: Munbilla Broadcasting Properties Ltd.
Arbitron Metro Market: Killeen, TX *Format:* Country
Cindi Ashford, General Manager
Ben Shields, Programming Director
Bill Woleban, Chief Engineer

Mc Allen

***KVMV**
03-01-1972; 96.9 mhz FM *Hrs Open:* 24; 100 kw; 1148 ft.; N26 4 53 W97 49 44
Mailing Address: P.O. Box 3333, McAllen, TX 78502 US
Second Address: 715 E. Thomas Dr., Pharr, TX 78502
(956) 787-9700, *Fax:* (956) 787-9783
www.kvmv.org
info@kvmv.com
License: Mc Allen, Hidalgo County, TX held by World Radio Network Inc.
Group Owner: World Radio Network Inc.; acq 8-27-84)
Nat'l Network: Moody
Arbitron Metro Market: Pharr, TX *Format:* Christian *Hrs. of News Programming:* News progmg 4 hrs wkly *Target Audience:* 30-65; general
James Gamblin, General Manager
Bob Malone, Music Director

McAllen

KGBT-FM
01-01-1964; 98.5 mhz FM; 100 kw; 997 ft.; N26 7 14 W97 49 18
3102 Oak Lawn Ave., Suite 215, Dallas, TX 75219 US
(956) 631-5499, *Fax:* (956) 631-0090
www.kgbt985.univision.com
info@netmio.com
License: McAllen, Hidalgo County, TX held by Tichenor License Corp.
Group Owner: Univision Radio; (acq 9-22-2003; grpsl).
Arbitron Metro Market: McAllen, TX *Format:* Tejano *Target Audience:* 18 plus
Mac Tichenor Jr., President
Joe Morales, General Manager
Angela Navarrete, General Sales Mgr
Hugo de la Cruze, Programming Director
Odie Chavez, News Director
Jorge Garza, Chief Engineer

***KHID**
07-16-1992; 88.1 mhz FM *Hrs Open:* 24; 2.1 kw; 253 ft.; N26 21 44 W98 19 26 *Rebroadcasts:* Rebroadcasts KMBH-FM Harlingen
Mailing Address: P.O. Box 2147, Harlingen, TX 78551 US
Second Address: 1701 E. Tennessee Ave., Harlingen, TX 78550
(956) 421-4111, *Fax:* (956) 421-4150
www.kmbh.org
publicradio@kmbh.org
License: McAllen, Hidalgo County, TX held by RGV Educational Broadcasting Inc.
Arbitron Metro Market: McAllen-Brownsv *Format:* Jazz, News *Hrs. of News Programming:* News progmg 34 hrs wkly *Target Audience:* General.
Pedro Briseno, General Manager
Chris Malley, News Director

KRIO
01-01-1947; 910 khz AM *Hrs Open:* 24
4300 S. Business 281, Edinburg, TX 78539 US
(956) 380-3435, *Fax:* (956) 380-8156
www.radioesperanza.com
correo@radioesperanza.com
License: McAllen, TX held by Rio Grande Bible Institute Inc.
Wire Services: UPI
Arbitron Metro Market: McAllen-Brownsville-Harlingen *Format:* Christian *Hrs. of News Programming:* News progmg 5 hrs wkly *Target Audience:* General.
Larry Windle, President
Gerardo Lorenzo, General Manager
Jerry Joske, Chief Engineer

RADIO - U.S.

McCamey

KPBM
95.3 mhz FM; 3 kw; 761 ft.; N31 12 41 W102 16 28
P O Box 252, McAllen, TX 78502 US
License: McCamey, Upton County, TX held by Paulino Bernal.
Paulino Bernal, General Manager

McCook

***KCAS**
01-01-2001; 91.5 mhz FM *Hrs Open:* 24; 2.5 kw; 358 ft.; N26 28 51 W98 23 45
Mailing Address: 4301 N Shary Rd., Mission, TX 78572 US
Second Address: PO Box 8106, Mission, TX 78572
(956) 424-9098, *Fax:* (956) 581-7786
www.kcasradio.org
kcas@kcasradio.org
License: McCook, Hidalgo County, TX held by Faith Baptist Church Inc.
Nat'l Network: USA
Arbitron Metro Market: Mission, TX *Format:* Religious *Hrs. of News Programming:* News progmg 20 hrs wkly *Target Audience:* 30-85; male & female
David Harris, President
Don Prentice, General Manager
Don Prentice, Station Manager
Jerry Jeske, Chief Engineer

McKinney

***KNTU**
11-01-1969; 88.1 mhz FM *Hrs Open:* 24; 100 kw; 443 ft.; N33 17 24 W97 8 10
Mailing Address: P.O. Box 13585, Denton, TX 76203 US
Second Address: 1179 Union Cir. #262, Denton, TX 76201
(940) 565-3688, *Fax:* (940) 565-2518
www.kntu.com
kntu@unt.edu
License: McKinney, Collin County, TX held by University of North Texas.
Nat'l Network: AP Radio *Wire Services:* AP
Arbitron Metro Market: Dallas, TX *Format:* Jazz *Special Programming:* Class 6 hrs, Sp 6 hrs, new mus 2 hrs, pub affrs 2 *Hrs. of News Programming:* News progmg 12.5 hrs wkly *No. News Employees:* 6 *TargetAudience:* 18 +.
Russ Campbell, General Manager
Mark Lambert, Programming Director

McQueeney

KZAR
07-01-1989; 97.7 mhz FM *Hrs Open:* 24; 100 kw; Ant 981 ft; N29 20 45 W97 38 44
1777 N.E. Loop 410, San Antonio, TX 77001
(210) 829-1075, *Fax:* (210) 824-9971
License: McQueeney, Guadalupe County, TX held by Rawhide Radio LLC.
Group Owner: Univision Radio; (acq 9-22-2003; grpsl)
Population Served: 1,206,495 *Arbitron Metro Market:* San Antonio, TX *Target Audience:* 12-17, 18-34.
Dan Wilson, Operations Dir
Rory Charitan, Programming Director
Bret Huggins, Program Director

Memphis

KLSR-FM
01-01-1982; 105.3 mhz FM *Hrs Open:* 24; 100 kw; 486 ft.; N34 51 52 W100 36 55
114 N. 17th, P.O. Box 400, Memphis, TX 79245 US
(806) 259-3511, *Fax:* (806) 259-2397
klsr105fm@arn.net
License: Memphis, Hall County, TX held by Davis Broadcast Company Inc.
Arbitron Metro Market: Amarillo, TX *Format:* Variety/Diverse, Country *Special Programming:* Sp 6 hrs, good time oldies 60s & 70s 10 hrs, relg
Donna Davis, President
Brandi Davis-Tatum, Operations Dir
Joe Davis, General Manager

Menard

KXXS
02-24-2012; 100.9 mhz FM; kw
US
(416) 416-1100, *Fax:* (512) 416-8205
License: Menard, Menard County, TX held by Katherine Pyeatt
Katherine Pyeatt, General Manager

KFON
05-18-2012; 106.3 mhz FM; kw
US
(416) 416-1100, *Fax:* (512) 416-8205
License: Menard, Menard County, TX held by Katherine Pyeatt
Katherine Pyeatt, General Manager

Mercedes

KTEX
01-01-1975; 100.3 mhz FM *Hrs Open:* 24; 100 kw; 1224 ft.; N26 6 1 W97 50 21
One Independence Plaza, 280 Hwy 35, Middletown, NJ 07701 US
(956) 973-2143, *Fax:* (956) 975-2101
www.ktex.net
ktexx@aol.com
License: Mercedes, Hidalgo County, TX held by Capstar TX L.P.
Group Owner: Clear Channel Communications Inc.; (acq 8-15-2000; grpsl)
Arbitron Metro Market: Weslaco, TX *Format:* Country *No. News Employees:* 1 *Target Audience:* 25-54; male & female *Adv. Rates:* 50; 40; 50; 30
Billy Santiago, Operations Dir
Danny Fletcher, General Manager
Chris Aldrich, General Sales Mgr
Jojo Cerda, Programming Director

Meridian

KOME-FM
95.3 mhz FM; 6 kw horiz; 226 ft.; N31 54 17 W97 40 49
US
(817) 332-0959
License: Meridian, Bosque County, TX held by LKCM Radio Group LP.
Group Owner: LKCM Radio Group L.P.
Arbitron Metro Market: Meridian, TX
Gerry Schlegel, President

Merkel

KHXS
11-04-1983; 102.7 mhz FM *Hrs Open:* 24; 99.2 kw; 745 ft.; N32 24 39 W100 6 26
330 East Kilbourn Avenue, Suite 250, Milwaukee, WI 53202 US
(325) 793-9700, *Fax:* (325) 692-1576
www.102thebear.com
jim.christoferson@cumulus.com; jb.cloud@cumulus.com; chris.andrews@cumulus.com
License: Merkel, Taylor County, TX held by Cumulus Licensing Corp.
Group Owner: Cumulus Media Inc.; (acq 6-15-98; $1.6 million)
Arbitron Metro Market: Abilene, TX *Format:* Classic Rock
John Scott, Operations Dir
Jim Christoferson, General Manager
Lori Barrett, News Director
Chris Andrews, Chief Engineer

KMXO
06-01-1963; 1500 khz AM; 0.25 kw-D, NDD; N32 28 17 W100 0 19
5234 North 3 Street, Abilene, TX 79603 US
(325) 928-3060, *Fax:* (325) 928-4683
www.kmxoradiofe.com
License: Merkel, TX held by Ray R. Silva.
Arbitron Metro Market: Merkel, TX *Format:* Christian
Zacarias Serrato, General Manager

Mertzon

***KMEO**
01-01-2006; 91.9 mhz FM; 6.5 kw vert; 522 ft.; N31 25 16 W100 32 36
P O Box 1452, Wasahington, DC 20013 US
(662) 844-8888, *Fax:* (662) 842-6791
www.afr.net
License: Mertzon, Irion County, TX held by American Family Association.
Group Owner: American Family Radio; (acq 8-9-2005)
Arbitron Metro Market: Mertzon, TX *Format:* Christian
Marvin Sanders, General Manager

Mesquite

***KEOM**
09-04-1984; 88.5 mhz FM *Hrs Open:* 24; 61 kw; 574 ft.; N32 45 46 W96 38 4
405 East Davis Street, Mesquite, TX 75149 US
(972) 888-7560
www.keom.fm
pbrooks@mesquiteisd.org
License: Mesquite, Dallas County, TX held by Mesquite Independent School District.
Regional Network: Texas State Networks
Arbitron Metro Market: Mesquite, TX *Format:* Variety/Diverse
Target Audience: General; citizens of Mesquite & surrounding area
Peggy Brooks, Station Manager

Mexia

KLRK
05-21-1956; 1590 khz AM *Hrs Open:* 24; 500 w-D, 128 w-N; N31 41 10 W96 27 18
Mailing Address: Box 1590, Mexia, TX 76667
Second Address: 1006-B Milam St., Mexia, TX 76667
(254) 562-5328, *Fax:* (254) 562-6729
radio@kycxfm.com
License: Mexia, Limestone County, TX held by Simmons Austin, LS LLC.
Group Owner: Simmons Media Group; (acq 8-19-2005; $390,000 with co-located FM)
Nat'l Network: ABC *Regional Network:* Texas State Networks
Population Served: 30,000*Special Programming:* Farm 12 hrs, Gospel 3 hrs wkly *Target Audience:* General; 20-59 *Adv. Rates:* 13; 10; 10; 9
Bill Ferris, Operations Dir
Susan Cholopisa, General Manager
Jan Phillips, News Director
Dave Campbell, Sports Commentator
Brandi Garza, Traffic Manager

KWBT
08-29-1983; 104.9 mhz FM; 2.85 kw; Ant 482 ft; N31 38 39 W96 36 51
Box 1590, Mexia, TX 76667
(254) 562-5328, *Fax:* (254) 562-6729
License: Mexia, Limestone County, TX
Group Owner: Simmons Media Group
Nat'l Network: CBS
Population Served: 30,000*Adv. Rates:* 13; 10; 10; 9.
Bill Ferris, Operations Dir
Susan Cholopisa, Station Manager
Brandi Garza, News Director
Dave Campbell, Sports Commentator

Midland

KZBT
01-01-1974; 93.3 mhz FM *Hrs Open:* 24; 100 kw; 440 ft.; N31 57 30 W102 3 59
111 East Kilbourn Avenue, Suite 2700, Milwaukee, WI 53202 US
(432) 563-9300, *Fax:* (915) 563-3823
www.b93.net
License: Midland, Midland County, TX held by Cumulus Licensing Corp.
Group Owner: Cumulus Media Inc.; (acq 12-17-98; grpsl)
Arbitron Metro Market: Odessa, TX *Format:* Contemporary Hits/Top 40 *Hrs. of News Programming:* news progmg 2 hrs wkly *No. News Employees:* 1 *Target Audience:* 18-44.
John Moesch, Operations Dir
George DeMarco, General Manager
Aleese Fielder, General Sales Mgr
Leo Caro, Programming Director
Rebecca Cruz, Promotions Manager
Robbie Green, Chief Engineer

KCHX
08-15-1988; 106.7 mhz FM *Hrs Open:* 24; 100 kw; 679 ft.; N31 54 53 W101 57 49
600 Congress Avenue, Suite 1400, Austin, TX 78701 US
(432) 563-9102, *Fax:* (432) 580-9102
www.mymix1067.com
info@mymix1067.com
License: Midland, Midland County, TX
Group Owner: ICA Radio Ltd.; (acq 10-1-2007; grpsl)
Arbitron Metro Market: Odessa-Midland, TX *Format:* Adult Contemp *Hrs. of News Programming:* News progmg 2 hrs wkly *Target Audience:* 25-54; general *Adv. Rates:* 60; 60; 50; 24
Gloria Apolinario, General Manager
Laura Florez, General Sales Mgr
Rob Norris, Engineering Dir

KCRS
12-20-1935; 550 khz AM *Hrs Open:* 24; 5 kw-D, DA2; 1 kw-N, DA2; N32 4 10 W102 1 46
1001 South Midkiff, Midland, TX 79701 US
(432) 563-9102, *Fax:* (432) 580-9102
www.newstalkkcrs.com
License: Midland, TX
Group Owner: ICA Radio Ltd.; (acq 8-3-2007; grpsl)
Regional Network: Texas State Networks

Arbitron Metro Market: Odessa-Midland, TX *Format:* News, News/Talk, 86 *Hrs. of News Programming:* news progmg 30 hrs wkly *No. News Employees:* 2 *Target Audience:* 25-54.
Steve Driscoll, Operations Dir
Gloria Apolinario, General Manager
Jesse Grimes, News Director
Rod Norris, Engineering Dir
Robert Hallmark, Operations Manager
Shelly Todd, Traffic Manager

KCRS-FM
05-25-1976; 103.3 mhz FM *Hrs Open:* 24; 95 kw; 919 ft.; N32 5 11 W102 17 10
1001 South Midkiff, Midland, TX 79701 US
(432) 563-9102, *Fax:* (432) 580-9102
www.1033kissfm.net
info@1033kissfm.net
License: Midland, Midland County, TX
Group Owner: ICA Radio Ltd.
Arbitron Metro Market: Odessa-Midland, TX *Format:* Adult Contemp
Jesse Grimes, Operations Dir
Ric Elliott, Programming Director
Shelly Todd, News Director
Robert Hallmark, Special Events Coordinator

KLPF
08-06-1950; 1150 khz AM *Hrs Open:* 24*Rebroadcasts:* EWTN
1903 S. Lames Sa Road, Midland, TX 79701 US
(432) 638-1150, *Fax:* (432) 682-5230
www.grnonline.com
robertd@grnonline.com
License: Midland, TX held by La Promesa Foundation.
Group Owner: La Promesa Foundation; (acq 2-11-2002; $85,000)
Arbitron Metro Market: Odessa-Midland, TX *Format:* Christian *No. News Employees:* 3 *Adv. Rates:* 10; 10; 10; 10
Robert Dominguez, General Manager
Toya Hall, Programming Director

KMND
11-27-1963; 1510 khz AM; 2.4 kw-D, NDD; N31 57 49 W102 4 53
111 East Kilbourn Avenue, Suite 2700, Milwaukee, WI 53202 US
(432) 563-5636, *Fax:* (432) 563-3823
www.kmnd.com
jmesher@aol.com
License: Midland, TX held by Cumulus Licensing Corp.
Group Owner: Cumulus Media Inc.; (acq 12-17-98; grpsl).
Nat'l Network: ESPN Radio
Arbitron Metro Market: Odessa, TX *Format:* Sports *Special Programming:* Jazz one hr wkly
George Demarco, General Manager
Mike Baer, General Sales Mgr
Robi Burns, Programming Director
Garry Vaughn, Chief Engineer

KNFM
11-02-1959; 92.3 mhz FM; 100 kw; 984 ft.; N32 5 51 W102 17 21
111 East Kilbourn Avenue, Suite 2700, Milwaukee, WI 53202 US
(432) 563-5636, *Fax:* (432) 563-3823
www.lonestar92.com
License: Midland, Midland County, TX
Arbitron Metro Market: Odessa, TX *Format:* Country
John Moesch, Operations Dir
Jeff Stone, General Manager
Aleese Fielder, General Sales Mgr
Spencer Bennett, Programming Director
Tonya Calloway, Promotions Manager
Robbie Green, Engineering Dir
Gwen McCown, Brand Manager

KQRX
10-20-1995; 95.1 mhz FM *Hrs Open:* 24; 10.5 kw; 505 ft.; N32 3 9 W102 17 39
P.O. Box 14895, Odessa, TX 79768 US
(432) 520-9912, *Fax:* (432) 520-0112
www.boblivesintexas.com
ooradio01@aol.com
License: Midland, Midland County, TX
Group Owner: Brazos Communications West LLC; (acq 2006; grpsl)
Nat'l Reps: Katz Radio
Arbitron Metro Market: Midland-Odessa *Format:* Adult Contemp
Kelly Peterson, Operations Dir
John Moesch, General Manager
Michael Todd, Programming Director

KWEL
04-01-1957; 1070 khz AM *Hrs Open:* 6 AM-9 PM; 2.5 kw-D, NDD; N31 57 44 W102 4 7
Mailing Address: 1110 E. Scharbauer Drive, Midland, TX 79705 US
Second Address: 310 W. Wall, Ste 104, Midland, TX 79701
(915) 685-1950, *Fax:* (915) 687-0586
www.kwel.com
craiganderson@kwel.com
License: Midland, TX held by Faustino Quiroz.
Nat'l Network: ABC
Arbitron Metro Market: Odessa, TX *Format:* News, Talk *Hrs. of News Programming:* News progmg 60 hrs wkly *Target Audience:* 35 plus; adults *Adv. Rates:* 20
Craig Anderson, CEO
Doris Anderson, News Director
Jason Moore, Engineering Dir
Garry Vaughn, Engineer

***KVDG**
09-01-2006; 90.9 mhz FM; 1.5 kw; 430 ft.; N31 54 32 W102 4 1
6910 NW 2nd Terrace, Boca Raton, FL 33487 US
(432) 682-1485, *Fax:* (432) 682-5230
robertd@grnonline.com
License: Midland, Midland County, TX held by La Promesa Foundation.
Group Owner: La Promesa Foundation; (acq 11-6-2007; $175,000)
Nat'l Network: EWTN Radio
Arbitron Metro Market: Midland, TX
Leonard Oswald, President

Mineola

KMOO-FM
09-01-1977; 99.9 mhz FM *Hrs Open:* 24; 6 kw; 295 ft.; N32 45 4 W95 33 18
Mailing Address: P. O. Box 628, Mineola, TX 75773 US
Second Address: Hwy. 69 N., Mineola, TX 75773
(903) 569-3823, *Fax:* (903) 569-6641
www.kmoo.com
jason@kmoo.com
License: Mineola, Wood County, TX held by Hightower Radio Inc.
Regional Network: Texas State Networks
Arbitron Metro Market: Tyler, TX *Format:* Country *Hrs. of News Programming:* news progmg 3 hrs wkly *No. News Employees:* 1 *Target Audience:* 25-64. *Adv. Rates:* 18;18;18;15
Jason Hightower, President
Amy Castleberry, Operations Dir
Marlene Keahey, Public Affairs Director

Mineral Wells

KVTT
12-01-1946; 1120 khz AM *Hrs Open:* 6 AM-sunset; 250 w-D; N32 47 12 W98 05 53
305 Millsap Hwy., Mineral Wells, TX 76067
(940) 325-1140, *Fax:* (940) 325-1164
www.bizradio.com
info@kjsaam.com
License: Mineral Wells, Palo Pinto County, TX held by M&M Broadcasters Ltd.
Population Served: 75,000 *Arbitron Metro Market:* Dallas-Fort Worth
Gary Moss, General Manager

Mirando City

KBDR
04-01-1993; 100.5 mhz FM *Hrs Open:* 24; 42 kw; 535 ft.; N27 21 17 W99 13 52
1919 Victoria Street, Laredo, TX 78040 US
(956) 725-1000, *Fax:* (956) 718-1000
www.laley1005.com
mrillstrsl@kbdrfm.com
License: Mirando City, Webb County, TX held by BMP 100.5 FM LP.
Group Owner: Border Media Partners LLC; (acq 5-30-2003; $8 million with KBUC(FM) Raymondville).
Arbitron Metro Market: Laredo, TX *Format:* Tejano *Target Audience:* 18-45; upper-income bracket
Tom Castro, CEO
Steve Stephenson, Operations Dir
Nestor Cobos, Station Manager
Joe Flores, General Sales Mgr
Rogelio Botello Rios, Programming Director
Robert Garcia, Promotions Manager
Joe Espinoza, Chief Engineer
Hugo DelPozzo, CFO
Issac Carrillo, Operations Manager

Mission

KIRT
02-23-1958; 1580 khz AM; 1 kw-D, ND1; 0.302 kw-N, ND1; N26 17 36 W98 19 50
608 S. 10th St., McAllen, TX 78501 US
(956) 519-9999, *Fax:* (956) 581-0546
www.radioimagen.net
kirtradio@aol.com
License: Mission, TX held by Bravo Broadcasting Co. Inc.
Regional Network: Texas State Networks
Arbitron Metro Market: McAllen-Brownsville-Harlingen, TX
Walter Gomez, General Manager
Rosie Pedraza, General Sales Mgr
Armando Pedraza, Programming Director
John Pankratz, Chief Engineer

KQXX-FM
01-01-1989; 105.5 mhz FM *Hrs Open:* 24; 3 kw; 285 ft.; N26 13 50 W98 20 18 *Rebroadcasts:* Rebroadcasts KTJN(FM) Brownsville 100%
1050 McIntosh, Brownsville, TX 78521 US
(956) 973-9202, *Fax:* (956) 544-0311
www.oldies1055.net
billysantiago@clearchannel.com
License: Mission, Hidalgo County, TX held by Clear Channel Broadcasting Licenses Inc.
Group Owner: Clear Channel Communications Inc.; (acq 12-9-2003; grpsl).
Arbitron Metro Market: McAllen-Brownsville-Harlingen, TX *Format:* Oldies *No. News Employees:* 3
Billy Santiago, Operations Dir
Danny Fletcher, General Manager
Cyndia Torres, General Sales Mgr
Gloria Garcia, News Director
Ken Meek, Chief Engineer

Missouri City

KBRZ
10-01-1952; 1460 khz AM
1914 North Hwy 523, Freeport, TX 77541 US
(713) 589-1336, *Fax:* (713) 589-1335
License: Missouri City, TX held by Aleluya Christian Broadcasting Inc.
Group Owner: Aleluya Christian Broadcasting Inc.; (acq 3-1-2001; $700,000)
Arbitron Metro Market: Houston-Galveston *Format:* Christian
Ruben Villarreal, General Manager

Monahans

KBAT
11-01-1983; 99.9 mhz FM *Hrs Open:* 24; 100 kw; 574 ft.; N31 45 40 W102 31 28
111 East Kilbourn Avenue, Suite 2700, Milwaukee, WI 53202 US
(432) 563-5499, *Fax:* (432) 563-5530
www.kbat.com
info@kbatfm.com
License: Monahans, Ward County, TX held by Cumulus Licensing Corp.
Group Owner: Cumulus Media Inc.; (acq 12-17-98; grpsl).
Arbitron Metro Market: Odessa, TX *Target Audience:* 25-54; general
John Moesch, Operations Dir
George DeMarco, General Manager
Aleese Fielder, General Sales Mgr
Kevin Chase, Programming Director
Brian Hill, Promotions Manager
Robbie Green, Chief Engineer

KCKM
03-12-1947; 1330 khz AM *Hrs Open:* 24
Box 270, Monahans, TX 79756 US
(432) 943-2588, *Fax:* (432) 943-7314
info@kckmam.com
License: Monahans, TX held by Sandhills Communication Inc.
Nat'l Network: CBS *Regional Network:* Texas State Networks
Nat'l Reps: Riley
Format: Oldies *Special Programming:* Gospel 3 hrs wkly *No. News Employees:* 1 *Target Audience:* 25-54; general
Rick Anderson, General Manager
David McCaffity, Programming Director
Allen Martin, News Director
Dexter Nichols, Sports Commentator

Mont Belvieu

KFNC
01-01-1948; 97.5 mhz FM *Hrs Open:* 24; 100 kw; Ant 1,955 ft; N29 41 52 W94 24 09
2700 Post Oak Blvd., Suite 2300, Houston, TX 53202

RADIO - U.S.

(713) 300-3500, *Fax:* (713) 300-3585
License: Mont Belvieu, Jefferson County, TX held by A R Licensing LLC
Group Owner: Cumulus Media Partners LLC; (acq 5-3-2006; grpsl)
Nat'l Network: ESPN Radio
Arbitron Metro Market: Houston-Galveston
Pat Fant, Promotions Manager

Morton

*KPGA

01-16-2009; 91.9 mhz FM; 100 kw; 522 ft.; N33 33 1 W102 13 7
Rebroadcasts: Rebroadcasts KLRD(FM) Yucaipa, CA 100%
P O Box 187, Humble, TX 77347 US
(888) 937-2471, *Fax:* (916) 251-1650
www.air1.com
info@air1.com
License: Morton, Cochran County, TX held by Educational Media Foundation.
Group Owner: EMF Broadcasting
Nat'l Network: Air 1
Arbitron Metro Market: Morton, TX *Format:* Alternative, Christian
Darrell Chambliss, Chairman
Alan Mason, CEO/COO
Mike Novak, CEO
David Pierce, Chief Creative Officer
Dan Antonelli, Chief Business Development Officer
Eric Moser, Chief Financial Officer
Brian Burger, Vice President of HumanResources
D. Kevin Blair, Secretary and General Counsel

Mount Pleasant

KIMP

10-08-1948; 960 khz AM; 1 kw-D, ND2; 0.075 kw-N, ND2; N33 9 54 W95 0 27
Mailing Address: PO Box 990, Mt. Pleasant, TX 75456 US
Second Address: 1798 U.S. Hw. 67 West, Mount Pleasant, TX 75455
(903) 572-8726, *Fax:* (903) 572-7232
easttexasradio.com
License: Mount Pleasant, TX held by East Texas Broadcasting Inc.
Group Owner: East Texas Broadcasting Inc.; (acq 11-21-91; $850,000 with co-located FM;
Hrs. of News Programming: news progmg 10 hrs wkly *No. News Employees:* 10 *Target Audience:* General. *Adv. Rates:* 17; 15; 17
John Mitchell, Chairman
Bud Kitchens, President
Bryan Frimesth, General Sales Mgr
Clint Cooper, News Director
Bill Hughes, Chief Engineer
Darrin Tripp, Operations Director

*KYZQ

88.3 mhz FM; 3 kw vert; Ant 149 ft; N33 10 10.4 W95 05 59.3
1039 CR 2920, Pittsburg, TX
(903) 466-6791
License: Mount Pleasant, Titus County, TX held by Millennium Broadcasting Corp.
James Furlow Jr., President

Mountain Home

KAXA

102.1 mhz FM; 6 kw; Ant 272 ft; N30 10 34 W99 23 02
Box 717, Pickerington, OH
(239) 877-4605
License: Mountain Home, Kerr County, TX held by In Phase Broadcasting Inc.
Peter Cea, President

Muenster

KZZA

12-23-1991; 106.7 mhz FM *Hrs Open:* 24; 75 kw; 2034 ft.; N33 26 13 W97 29 5
107 South Commerce St., Gainesville, TX 76240 US
, *Fax:* (817) 868-2900(817) 868-2929
casa1067.com
License: Muenster, Cooke County, TX held by Liberman Broadcasting of Dallas License LLC.
Group Owner: Liberman Broadcasting Inc.; (acq 11-2-2006; grpsl)
Nat'l Reps: Eastman Radio
Arbitron Metro Market: Dallas-Fort Worth *Format:* Ethnic *Target Audience:* 18-34.
Alex Sanchez, General Manager

*KTMU

88.7 mhz FM; 0.5 kw; 69 ft.; N33 43 32 W97 28 26 US
(940) 668-7971
License: Muenster, Cooke County, TX held by 1 A Chord Inc.
Arbitron Metro Market: Gainesville, TX
Mary Fay Jackson, President

Muleshoe

KMUL-FM

02-06-1966; 103.1 mhz FM; 6 kw; 75 ft.; N34 13 39 W102 44 10
1000 Sycamore Street, Clovis, NM 88101 US
(505) 762-6200, *Fax:* (505) 762-8800
License: Muleshoe, Bailey County, TX held by Tallgrass Broadcasting LLC.
Group Owner: Tallgrass Broadcasting LLC; (acq 4-2-2007; grpsl)
Format: Country
David Lippe, General Sales Mgr
Michael Jacinto, Programming Director

Nacogdoches

KJCS

05-01-1967; 103.3 mhz FM; 22.5 kw; 735 ft.; N31 25 59 W94 49 3
111 W. Pillar, Nacogdoches, TX 75961 US
(936) 559-8800, *Fax:* (936) 559-8801
info@kjcsfm.com
License: Nacogdoches, Nacogdoches County, TX held by Radio Licensing Inc.
Nat'l Network: ABC
Format: Country *Special Programming:* Gospel 3 hrs wkly
Bill Vance Jr., General Manager
Carolyn Gage, Station Manager
Della Huse, General Sales Mgr
Lou Bennett, Programming Director
Gwen Jordan, News Director

*KSAU

07-05-1975; 90.1 mhz FM *Hrs Open:* 10 AM-2 AM; 3.5 kw; 449 ft.; N31 37 45 W94 40 44
Mailing Address: P. O. Box 13048, Nacogdoches, TX 75962 US
Second Address: 1936 North St., Boynton Building, Nacogdoches, TX 75961
(936) 468-4000, *Fax:* (936) 468-1331
www.sfasu.edu/ksau
ksau@sfasu.edu
License: Nacogdoches, Nacogdoches County, TX held by Stephen F. Austin State University.
Nat'l Network: ABC *Wire Services:* AP
Arbitron Metro Market: Nacogdoches, TX *Format:* Jazz *Hrs. of News Programming:* News progmg 3 hrs wkly *Target Audience:* 18-54.
Sherry Williford, General Manager
John Chapman, Engineering Dir

KSFA

06-02-1947; 860 khz AM
600 Congress Avenue, Suite 1400, Austin, TX 78701 US
(936) 639-4455, *Fax:* (936) 639-4440
www.ksfa860.com
info@ksfa.com
License: Nacogdoches, TX held by GAP Broadcasting Lufkin License LLC.
Group Owner: GAP Broadcasting LLC; (acq 8-3-2007; grpsl)
Arbitron Metro Market: Lufkin, TX *Format:* News, News/Talk, 86
Special Programming: Houston Astros baseball, farm 7 hrs wkly
Target Audience: 25 plus; upscale, upper income level men
Tami Koonce, General Manager
Danny Merrell, Programming Director

KTBQ

07-15-1967; 107.7 mhz FM *Hrs Open:* 24; 13 kw; 400 ft.; N31 34 58 W94 39 59
600 Congress Avenue, Suite 1400, Austin, TX 78701 US
(936) 639-4455, *Fax:* (936) 639-4440
www.q1077.com
info@ktbq.com
License: Nacogdoches, Nacogdoches County, TX
Group Owner: GAP Broadcasting LLC
Arbitron Metro Market: Lufkin, TX *Format:* Classic Rock *No. News Employees:* 1 *Target Audience:* 18-49; upscale women
Tami Koonce, General Manager
Scott Parker, Station Manager

Natalia

*KYRQ

90.3 mhz FM; 3 kw; 135 ft.; N29 9 20 W98 53 6
P O Box 7337, Mayaguez, TX 0681 US
(210) 440-9894
www.oasisradio.tv
License: Natalia, Medina County, TX held by Community Public Radio Inc.
Arbitron Metro Market: Natalia, TX *Format:* Christian, Spanish
Penny Jackson, President

Navasota

*KWUP

03-01-1989; 92.5 mhz FM *Hrs Open:* 24; 3.3 kw; 446 ft.; N30 27 58 W96 2 57
304 East Houston, Crockett, TX 75835 US
(281) 446-5725, *Fax:* (281) 540-2198
info@thehippo.com
License: Navasota, Grimes County, TX held by KSBJ Educational Foundation
Arbitron Metro Market: Bryan-College S
Tim McDermott, General Manager

KWBC

09-21-1960; 1550 khz AM; 0.25 kw-D, ND2; 0.026 kw-N, ND2; N30 22 48 W96 6 1
304 East Houston, Crockett, TX 75835 US
(936) 825-9007, *Fax:* (936) 825-1019
navasotanews.com
news@navasotanews.com
License: Navasota, TX held by Bryan Broadcasting Corp.
Group Owner: Bryan Broadcasting Corp.; (acq 7-31-2007; $275,000)
Arbitron Metro Market: Navasota, TX *Format:* News, News/Talk, 86
Ben Downs, General Manager
Dave Hill, Station Manager
Michelle McNew, General Sales Mgr
Tom Turner, News Director
Chris Dusterhoff, Chief Engineer

Nederland

KBED

01-11-1969; 1510 khz AM *Hrs Open:* Sunrise-sunset; 5 kw-D, DAD; N30 3 40 W93 58 48
111 East Kilbourn Avenue, Suite 2700, Milwaukee, WI 53202 US
(409) 833-9421, *Fax:* (409) 833-9296
www.lagrand1450.com
info@cumulus.com
License: Nederland, TX held by Cumulus Licensing Corp.
Group Owner: Cumulus Media Inc.; (acq 3-9-98; grpsl).
Nat'l Network: ESPN Radio
Arbitron Metro Market: Beaumont-Port Arthur area *Format:* Tejano *Special Programming:* Relg 4 hrs wkly *Hrs. of News Programming:* news progmg 5 hrs wkly *No. News Employees:* 1 *Target Audience:* 18-49; males
Zanetta Kelley, General Manager
Wes Matejka, General Sales Mgr
Jim West, Programming Director
Mark Guzman, Promotions Manager
Richard Core, News Director
Greg Davis, Chief Engineer
Liz Ferguson, Traffic Manager

New Boston

KEWL-FM

07-01-1995; 95.1 mhz FM *Hrs Open:* 24; 25 kw; Ant 325 ft; N33 26 15 W94 25 11
1323 College Dr., Texarkana, TX 75503
(903) 793-1109, *Fax:* (903) 794-4717
www.kool951.com
License: New Boston, Bowie County, TX held by American Media Investments Inc.
Group Owner: American Media Investments Inc.; (acq 2-17-2009; grpsl)
Arbitron Metro Market: Texarkana, TX-A *Target Audience:* 35-64.
Mike Basso, General Manager

KLBW

11-16-1969; 1530 khz AM *Hrs Open:* 6 AM-6 PM; 2.5 kw-D, NDD; N33 28 56 W94 25 25
P.O. Box 848, New Boston, TX 75570 US
(903) 628-2561
info@knboam.com
License: New Boston, TX held by Chapel of Light
Arbitron Metro Market: Texarkana, TX *Format:* Adult Contemp, Christian *Target Audience:* General.
Carmen Johnson, General Manager

KZRB

11-16-1997; 103.5 mhz FM *Hrs Open:* 24; 50 kw; 492 ft.; N33 24 54 W94 38 10

3720 County Avenue, Texarkana, AR 75502 US
(903) 547-3223, *Fax:* (903) 547-3095
realcowboyassociation.com/kzrb.html
kzrb@NOSPAMtxk.com
License: New Boston, Bowie County, TX held by B & H Broadcasting System Inc.
Nat'l Network: American Urban *Nat'l Reps:* Christal
Arbitron Metro Market: New Boston, TX *Format:* Adult Contemp, Oldies *Hrs. of News Programming:* news progmg 9 hrs wkly *No. News Employees:* 1 *Target Audience:* 25-54; all age buyers
Ray Bursey Jr., CEO
Sandy Hunter, Operations Dir
Brigette Talbert, Programming Director
Gray Graham, Engineering Dir

KTTY
06-01-2009; 105.1 mhz FM; 4.3 kw; 387 ft.; N33 28 0 W94 27 48
Mailing Address: US
Second Address: 1305 S Glenburnie Road, New Bern, NC
2526363333
bill@bigfishfm.com
License: New Boston, Bowie County, TX held by Tower Investment Trust Inc.
Group Owner: Tower Investment Trust Inc.
Nat'l Reps: Salem
Arbitron Metro Market: New Boston, TX *Format:* Christian *Target Audience:* W 25 - 54
William Brothers, President

New Braunfels

KGNB
04-01-1950; 1420 khz AM *Hrs Open:* 24; 1 kw-D, ND1; 0.196 kw-N, ND1; N29 39 45 W98 10 29
1540 Loop 337 North, New Braunfels, TX 78130 US
(830) 625-7311, *Fax:* (830) 625-7336
www.kgnb.am
localnews@kgnb.com
License: New Braunfels, TX held by New Braunfels Communications Inc.
Nat'l Network: CNN Radio; Westwood One
Arbitron Metro Market: San Antonio, TX *Format:* Country, News *Hrs. of News Programming:* news progmg 26 hrs wkly *No. News Employees:* 3 *Target Audience:* 25-54; men
Bill Rainer, CEO
Mattson Rainer, Operations Dir
Stuart Wolfe, Advertising Sales Manager

KNBT
11-22-1968; 92.1 mhz FM *Hrs Open:* 24; 6 kw; 312 ft.; N29 43 50 W98 7 12
1540 Loop 337 North, New Braunfels, TX 78130 US
(830) 625-7311, *Fax:* (830) 625-7336
www.knbtfm.com
mattson@knbtfm.com
License: New Braunfels, Comal County, TX held by New Braunfels Communications Inc.
Arbitron Metro Market: San Antonio, TX *Format:* Triple A *Special Programming:* Relg 3 hrs wkly *Target Audience:* 25-54.
Mattson Rainer, General Manager

New Deal

KLZK
09-01-1961; 97.3 mhz FM *Hrs Open:* 24; 30.5 kw; 614 ft.; N33 30 8 W101 52 20
Mailing Address: P.O. Box 1118, Haskell, TX 79521 US
Second Address: 9800 University, Lubbock, TX 79423
(806) 745-3434, *Fax:* (806) 748-2470
www.stars1043.com
License: New Deal, Lubbock County, TX held by Ramar Communications II Ltd.
Group Owner: Ramar Communications II Ltd.; (acq 7-12-2002; $750,000)
Nat'l Reps: Univision Radio National Sales
Arbitron Metro Market: Lubbock, TX
Chuck Heinz, General Manager
Connie Hayes, General Sales Mgr
Eddie Moreno, Programming Director
Susie Gonsales, News Director
Lee Thomas, Chief Engineer
Gilbert Saldana, Music Director

New Ulm

KNRG
01-01-1999; 92.3 mhz FM; 6 kw; 328 ft.; N29 53 30 W96 38 22
P.O.Box 948, Houston, TX 77001 US
(979) 732-5766, *Fax:* (979) 732-6377
License: New Ulm, Austin County, TX held by New Ulm Broadcasting Co.
Format: Contemporary Hits/Top 40, Adult Contemp *Adv. Rates:* 12.50; 12.50; 12.50; 12.50
Carl Geisler, General Manager

Nolanville

KLFX
01-01-1994; 107.3 mhz FM; 1.35 kw; 548 ft.; N31 5 38 W97 34 51
Post Office 1996, Temple, TX 76502 US
(254) 699-5000, *Fax:* (254) 680-4212
1073rocks.com
klfx@klfx.com
License: Nolanville, Bell County, TX held by Clear Channel Broadcasting Licenses Inc.
Group Owner: Clear Channel Communications Inc.; (acq 1-15-2004; $2.6 million).
Arbitron Metro Market: Kileen, TX
Evan Armstrong, General Manager

Odem

KMJR
02-18-1985; 98.3 mhz FM *Hrs Open:* 24; 50 kw; Ant 433 ft; N27 47 26 W97 27 02
1300 Antelope, Corpus Christi, TX 78467
(361) 883-1600, *Fax:* (361) 883-9303
club983.com
johnnyo@johnnyoradio.com
License: Odem, San Patricio County, TX held by Tejas Broadcasting Ltd. LLP.
Group Owner: Tejas Broadcasting Ltd. LLP; (acq 11-15-2004; grpsl).
Population Served: 400,000 *Arbitron Metro Market:* Corpus Christi, TX *Target Audience:* 18-49; progsv, affluent, middle class Hispanics *Adv. Rates:* 85; 75; 85; 50
Bert Clark, Operations Dir
Paul Danitz, General Manager

Odessa

*KBMM
01-01-2004; 89.5 mhz FM; 25 kw; 535 ft.; N31 40 35 W102 21 32
P.O. Drawer2440, Tupelo, MS 38803 US
(662) 844-8888
afr.net
info@kbmmfm.com
License: Odessa, Ector County, TX held by American Family Association.
Group Owner: American Family Radio
Arbitron Metro Market: Odessa-Midland, TX *Format:* Christian
Marvin Sanders, General Manager

*KFLB
01-29-1947; 920 khz AM *Hrs Open:* 24
7355 N. Oracle Rd., Tucson, AZ 85704 US
(520) 742-6976, *Fax:* (520) 469-7312
www.myflr.org
kflb@flc.org
License: Odessa, TX held by Family Life Broadcasting System.
Group Owner: Family Life Communications Inc.; (acq 6-24-98; grpsl)
Arbitron Metro Market: Odessa-Midland, TX *Format:* Christian, Religious *Target Audience:* 34-59; females
Warren J. Bolthouse, Chairman
Randy L. Carlson, President
Dawn Bumstead, General Manager
Adam Biddell, Programming Director

KHKX
07-01-1977; 99.1 mhz FM *Hrs Open:* 24; 100 kw; 407 ft.; N32 3 9 W102 17 39
1425 N. Market Blvd, Suite 9, Sacramento, CA 95834 US
(432) 520-9912, *Fax:* (432) 520-0112
www.kicks99.net
morningkicks@aol.com
License: Odessa, Ector County, TX
Group Owner: Brazos Communications West LLC; (acq 2006; grpsl).
Nat'l Network: USA
Arbitron Metro Market: Odessa, TX *Format:* Country *Hrs. of News Programming:* News progmg one hr wkly *Target Audience:* 25-54; general
Terry Bond, CEO
Dana Carole, General Sales Mgr
Mike Lawrence, Programming Director

KMCM
01-01-1961; 96.9 mhz FM; 100 kw; 452 ft.; N32 5 8 W102 17 11
4101 East 42nd, Suite J2, Odessa, TX 79762 US
(432) 520-9912, *Fax:* (432) 520-0112
www.97gold.com
License: Odessa, Ector County, TX
Group Owner: Brazos Communications West LLC; (acq 2006; grpsl).
Nat'l Reps: Katz Radio
Arbitron Metro Market: Midland, TX *Format:* Contemporary Hits/Top 40, Adult Contemp *Hrs. of News Programming:* News progmg 2 hrs wkly *Target Audience:* 25-54; men *Adv. Rates:* 30; 25; 30; 15
Terry Bond, CEO

KMRK-FM
08-23-1991; 96.1 mhz FM *Hrs Open:* 24; 27.5 kw; 948 ft.; N32 5 11 W102 17 10
600 Congress Avenue, Suite 1400, Austin, TX 78701 US
(432) 563-9102, *Fax:* (432) 580-9102,
www.mycountry961.com
License: Odessa, Ector County, TX
Group Owner: ICA Radio Ltd.; (acq 10-1-2007; grpsl)
Nat'l Network: American Urban *Wire Services:* AP
Arbitron Metro Market: Odessa, TX *Format:* Country *Hrs. of News Programming:* news progmg 2 hrs wkly *No. News Employees:* 1 *Target Audience:* 18-34. *Adv. Rates:* 48; 40; 40; 18
Steve Driscoll, Operations Dir
Gloria Apolinario, General Manager

*KXWT
01-06-1964; 91.3 mhz FM *Hrs Open:* 6 AM-midnight; 5 kw; 300 ft; N31 51 30 W102 23 00
Odessa College, 201 W. University Blvd., Odessa, TX 79764
(432) 580-9130, *Fax:* (915) 337-0529
www.odessa.edu
cevan@odessa.edu
License: Odessa, Ector County, TX held by Odessa College.
Nat'l Network: NPR
Population Served: 78,380 *Arbitron Metro Market:* Odessa-Midland, TX *Special Programming:* Jazz 4 hrs, opera 4 hrs, folk 4 hrs, blues 4 hrs, bluegrass 2 hrs, Celtic 4 hrs wkly *Hrs. of News Programming:* news progmg 33hrs wkly *No. News Employees:* 1 *Target Audience:* 35 plus; educated, affluent adults
Carl Evans, Operations Dir

KODM
01-01-1965; 97.9 mhz FM *Hrs Open:* 24; 100 kw; 361 ft.; N31 47 39 W102 10 42
111 East Kilbourn Avenue, Suite 2700, Milwaukee, WI 53202 US
432) 563-5499, *Fax:* (432) 563-5330
www.kodm.com
spencer.bennett@cumulus.com
License: Odessa, Ector County, TX held by Cumulus Licensing Corp.
Group Owner: Cumulus Media Inc.; (acq 12-17-98; grpsl)
Nat'l Network: ABC
Arbitron Metro Market: Odessa-Midland, TX *Format:* Adult Contemp *Target Audience:* 25-54; women
John Moesch, Operations Dir
George DeMarco, General Manager
Aleese Fielder, General Sales Mgr
Tonya Calloway, Programming Director
Robbie Green, Chief Engineer

KOZA
01-20-1947; 1230 khz AM *Hrs Open:* 24
1100 South Grant, Odessa, TX 79763 US
(432) 332-1230, *Fax:* (432) 335-0064
License: Odessa, TX held by Stellar Media Inc.
Arbitron Metro Market: Odessa-Midland, TX *Target Audience:* 18-54.
Benjamin Velasquez, General Manager

KQLM
03-11-1996; 107.9 mhz FM *Hrs Open:* 24; 100 kw; 846 ft.; N32 5 51 W102 17 21
4350 North Fairfax Drive, Suite 900, Arlington, VA 22203 US
(432) 333-1227, *Fax:* (432) 335-0064
www.q108fm.com
benjaminv@kqlm.com
License: Odessa, Ector County, TX held by Stellar Media Inc.
Arbitron Metro Market: Odessa-Midland, TX *Format:* Spanish *Hrs. of News Programming:* News progmg 10 hrs wkly *Target Audience:* General; Hispanics/Latinos *Adv. Rates:* 27; 27; 27; na
Benjamin Velasquez, CEO
Belinda Carrasco, General Sales Mgr

KRIL
06-01-1946; 1410 khz AM *Rebroadcasts:* Rebroadcasts KMND(AM) Midland 100%
P. O. Box 4312, Odessa, TX 79760 US

(432) 563-5636, *Fax:* (432) 563-3823
www.1410kril.com
jmesher@aol.com
License: Odessa, TX held by Cumulus Licensing Corp.
Group Owner: Cumulus Media Inc.; (acq 8-10-99; $110,000)
Nat'l Network: ESPN Radio
Arbitron Metro Market: Odessa-Midland, *Format:* Country *Target Audience:* 25 plus; higher educ level, higher income level
George Demarco, General Manager
Robie Burns, Programming Director
Gary Vaugn, Chief Engineer

***KLVW**
01-01-2001; 90.5 mhz FM *Hrs Open:* 24; 86 kw; 614 ft.; N32 5 51 W102 17 21
7355 North Oracle Rd., Tucson, AZ 85704 US
(800) 525-5683, *Fax:* (916) 251-1650
www.klove.com
klove@klove.com
License: Odessa, Ector County, TX held by Educational Media Foundation.
Group Owner: EMF Broadcasting
Nat'l Network: K-Love
Arbitron Metro Market: Omaha, NE *Format:* Christian *No. News Employees:* 13 *Target Audience:* 25-44; Judeo Christian, female
Darrell Chambliss, Chairman
MIke Novak, President & CEO
David Pierce, Programming Director
Ed Lenane, News Director
Sam Wallington, Engineering Dir
Richard Hunt, News Reporter
Marya Morgan, News Reporter
Laura Daniels, NewsReporter
Tim Luttrell, News Reporter
Kenny Noble Cortes, News Reporter
Darren Vinson, News Reporter

Orange

KIOC
02-28-1977; 106.1 mhz FM *Hrs Open:* 24; 100 kw; 1070 ft.; N30 9 20 W93 59 10
600 Congress Avenue, Suite 1400, Austin, TX 78701 US
(409) 896-5555, *Fax:* (409) 896-5599
www.bigdog106.com
bigdog106@bigdog106.com
License: Orange, Orange County, TX held by Capstar TX L.P.
Group Owner: Clear Channel Communications Inc.; (acq 8-30-00; grpsl).
Arbitron Metro Market: Beaumont-Port Arthur, TX *Format:* Classic Rock *Target Audience:* 18-49; adults who have discretionary income *Adv. Rates:* 63; 63; 63; 63
Lowry Mays, Chairman
John Hogan, CEO
Mark Mays, President
Charlie Rahilly, Operations Dir
Vesta Brandt, General Manager
Elizabeth Blackstock, General Sales Mgr
Mike Davis, Programming Director
Randall Mays, CFO
Jim Love,Public Affairs Director
Mark Kopelman, Vice President

KKMY
01-01-1972; 104.5 mhz FM; 100 kw; 764 ft.; N30 9 20 W93 59 10
600 Congress Avenue, Suite 1400, Austin, TX 78701 US
(409) 896-5555, *Fax:* (409) 896-5500
www.mix1045.com
info@kkmyfm.com
License: Orange, Orange County, TX held by Capstar TX L.P.
Group Owner: Clear Channel Communications Inc.; (acq 8-30-00; grpsl).
Arbitron Metro Market: Beaumont, TX *Format:* Adult Contemp *Target Audience:* 25-54; at-work lstng audience *Adv. Rates:* 63; 63; 63; 63
Lowry Mays, Chairman
John Hogan, CEO
Mark Mays, President
Charlie Rahilly, Operations Dir
Vesta Brandt, General Manager
Elizabeth Blackstock, General Sales Mgr
Randall Mays, CFO
Trey Poston, Operations Director
Randall Mays,Vice President
Mark Kopelman

KOGT
01-01-1948; 1600 khz AM; 1 kw-D, DAN; 1 kw-N, DAN; N30 8 25 W93 45 11
Mailing Address: P.O. Box 1667, Orange, TX 77630 US
Second Address: 5304 Meeks Dr., Orange, TX 77632
(409) 883-4381, *Fax:* (409) 883-7996
www.kogt.com
news@kogt.com
License: Orange, TX held by G-CAP Communications Inc.
Regional Network: Texas State Networks
Arbitron Metro Market: Beaumont-Port Arthur, TX *Format:* News, Sports, 30 *Target Audience:* 25 plus.
Gary Stelly, President
Richard Corder, General Sales Mgr
Glenn Earle, News Director
Russ Ingram, Engineering Dir
Reg Russell, Disc Jockey
Clay Williams, Disc Jockey
Terry Lyons, Disc Jockey
Iva Odom, Traffic Manager

Ore City

KAZE
05-01-1991; 106.9 mhz FM; 8.2 kw; 502 ft.; N32 41 54 W94 37 4
P.O. Box 11196, College Station, TX 77842 US
(903) 581-5259, *Fax:* (903) 939-3473
www.theblaze.fm
chelle@theblaze.cc
License: Ore City, Upshur County, TX held by Reynolds Radio Inc.
Group Owner: Reynolds Radio Inc.; acq 1-9-97)
Arbitron Metro Market: Tyler, TX *Format:* Contemporary Hits/Top 40
Rusty Reynolds, President
Rick Reynolds, General Manager
Robin George, General Sales Mgr
Charlie O'Douglas, Programming Director
Chelle Wright-Peterson, News Director
James McWain, Engineering Dir
Marcus Love, Music Director

Overland

***KKVI**
01-01-2008; 89.9 mhz FM; 0.12 kw vert; 98 ft.; N33 4 0 W95 46 10
US
(469) 245-3604, *Fax:* (972) 414-8149
www.kkviradio.com
webmail@kkviradio.com
License: Overland, Hopkins County, TX held by Gospel American Network.
Arbitron Metro Market: Overland, TX *Format:* Christian
Bill Wright, General Manager

Overton

KPXI
10-08-1961; 100.7 mhz FM *Hrs Open:* 24; 8.1 kw; 571 ft.; N32 9 7 W95 3 27
1350 One Galleria Tower, 13355 Noel Rd, Dallas, TX 75240 US
(903) 655-1800, *Fax:* (903) 655-1808
www.mykpxi.com
info@mykpxi.com
License: Overton, Rusk County, TX held by Inspiration Media of Texas LLC.
Group Owner: Salem Communications Corp.; (acq 11-6-2000; with KWRD-FM Highland Village).
Arbitron Metro Market: Tyler-Longview *Format:* Country
Jerry Hanszen, President
David Jacobs, Operations Dir
David Chenault, General Manager
John McMillian, Programming Director

Ozona

KYXX
11-25-1976; 94.3 mhz FM; 3 kw; 394 ft.; N30 42 42.6 W101 7 28.7
Hc 65, Box 50, Sonora, TX 76950 US
(830) 896-1230, *Fax:* (830) 792-4142
www.revfmradio.com/
khoskyxx@verizon.net
License: Ozona, Crockett County, TX held by Foster Charitable Foundation Inc.
Group Owner: Revolution Broadcast Company of the West; (acq 5-31-2007)
Nat'l Network: ABC *Regional Network:* Texas State Networks
Arbitron Metro Market: Ozona, TX *Format:* Country *Target Audience:* 12-50 plus.
Marti Ashcraft, Operations Dir
Eddy Smith, Engineering Dir

Palacios

KROY
11-01-1996; 99.7 mhz FM; 50 kw; 331 ft.; N28 43 53 W96 5 26
13625 Pond Springs Rd, #105, Austin, TX 78729 US
(361) 572-0105, *Fax:* (361) 798-3798
License: Palacios, Matagorda County, TX held by Roy E. Henderson.
Group Owner: Fort Bend Broadcasting Co.; (acq 1-22-99)
Format: Country
Ryan Henderson, Operations Dir
Egon Barthels, General Manager
Lori Beusin, General Sales Mgr
Robi Austynn, Programming Director
Kim Brazil, News Director
Ray Nelson, Chief Engineer

Palestine

KNET
01-02-1936; 1450 khz AM *Hrs Open:* 24
Mailing Address: 5946 Club Oaks Dr., Dallas, TX 75248 US
Second Address: 800 W. Palestine Ave., Palestine, TX 75801
(903) 729-6077, *Fax:* (903) 729-4742
www.youreasttexas.com.com
lee@kyyk.com
License: Palestine, TX held by Tomlinson-Leis Communications L.P.
Nat'l Network: ESPN Radio
Format: News, Sports, 86 *Hrs. of News Programming:* news progmg 6 hrs wkly *No. News Employees:* 1 *Target Audience:* 35 plus. *Adv. Rates:* 10; 10; 10; 10
Edward Tomlinson II, President
Alana Andrews, Operations Dir
Lee Parkinson, General Manager
Buddy Jackson, Programming Director

***KYFP**
05-15-2000; 89.1 mhz FM *Hrs Open:* 24; 100 kw; 486 ft.; N32 0 12 W95 43 6
8030 Arrowridge Blvd., Charlotte, NC 28273 US
(704) 523-5555, *Fax:* (704) 522-1967
www.bbnradio.org
License: Palestine, Anderson County, TX held by Bible Broadcasting Network Inc.
Group Owner: Bible Broadcasting Network
Arbitron Metro Market: Charlotte, NC *Format:* Religious
Lowell Davey, President
Richard Johnson, Operations Dir
Hank Iarrior, Programming Director
Ron Muffley, Chief Engineer

KYYK
08-20-1976; 98.3 mhz FM *Hrs Open:* 24; 5 kw; Ant 728 ft; N31 55 33 W95 38 48
Mailing Address: Box 3649, Palestine, TX 75248
Second Address: 800 W. Palestine Ave., Palestine, TX 75801
(903) 729-6077, *Fax:* (903) 729-4742
www.youreasttexas.com
License: Palestine, Anderson County, TX
Group Owner: Tomlinson-Leis Communications LP
Population Served: 115,000*Hrs. of News Programming:* news progmg 1 hr wkly *No. News Employees:* 3 *Target Audience:* 18-54. *Adv. Rates:* 20; 20; 20; 20
Edward Tomlinson II, Chairman
Kent Burkhart, CEO/COO
Kent Burkhart, President
Alex Ward, Operations Dir
Lee Parkinson, General Manager
Michael McCulloch, Programming Director
Gary Richards, News Director

Pampa

***KAVO**
07-01-1998; 90.9 mhz FM; 17 kw; 364 ft.; N35 33 8 W101 2 42
Rebroadcasts: Rebroadcasts WAFR(FM) Tupelo, MS 100%
P O Drawer 2440, Tupelo, MS 38803 US
(662) 844-8888, *Fax:* (662) 842-6791
www.afr.net
comments@afr.net
License: Pampa, Gray County, TX held by American Family Association.
Group Owner: American Family Radio
Nat'l Network: American Family Radio
Arbitron Metro Market: Tupelo, MS *Format:* Christian, Religious
Marvin Sanders, General Manager

KGRO
01-01-1947; 1230 khz AM; 1 kw-U, ND1; N35 34 39 W100 57 8
P.O. Box 3121, Carlsbad, NM 88220 US

(806) 669-6809, *Fax:* (806) 669-0662
www.kgrokomxradio.com
production@kgrokomxradio.com
License: Pampa, TX held by Pampa Broadcasters Inc.
Nat'l Network: Jones Radio Networks; ABC
Format: Adult Contemp *Target Audience:* 18-45.
James Hughes, President
Darrell Sehorn, General Manager
Donny Hooper, News Director
Greg Campbell, Chief Engineer
Jimmy Story, Disc Jockey
Linda Sehorn, Traffic Manager

KOMX
05-18-1981; 100.3 mhz FM; 32 kw; Ant 300 ft; N35 34 39 W100 57 08
Box 1779, Pampa, TX 88220
(806) 669-6809, *Fax:* (806) 669-0662
License: Pampa, Gray County, TX held by Pampa Broadcasters Inc.
Nat'l Network: ABC; Jones Radio Networks *Regional Network:* Texas State Networks
Population Served: 125,000*Target Audience:* 20 plus.
James Hughes, President
Darrell Sahara, Operations Dir
Darrell Sahara, General Manager
Darrell Sahara, Station Manager
Jimmy Story, Programming Director
Linda Sehorn, News Director
Greg Campbell, Chief Engineer
Donny Hooper,Sports Commentator

Paris

***KHCP**
01-10-2001; 89.3 mhz FM *Hrs Open:* 24; 21 kw; 354 ft.; N33 49 36 W95 27 49
P O Drawer 2440, Tupelo, MS 38803 US
(713) 520-5200
www.khcb.org
email@khcb.org
License: Paris, Lamar County, TX held by Houston Christian Broadcasters Inc.
Group Owner: Houston Christian Broadcasters Inc.; acq 11-24-00; $3,500 for CP with CP of KKER(FM) Kerrville).
Nat'l Network: Moody
Arbitron Metro Market: Houston, TX *Format:* Christian
Bruce Munsterman, General Manager
Bonnie BeMent, Assistant General Manager

KBUS
06-03-1985; 101.9 mhz FM *Hrs Open:* 24; 50 kw; 492 ft.; N33 44 54 W95 24 52
PO Box 690, Paris, TX 75460 US
(903) 785-1068, *Fax:* (903) 785-7176
www.easttexasradio.com
jyoung@easttexasradio.com
License: Paris, Lamar County, TX held by East Texas Broadcasting Inc.
Group Owner: East Texas Broadcasting Inc.; acq 5-11-01; grpsl).
Format: Classic Rock, News *Special Programming:* Farm 6 hrs wkly *Hrs. of News Programming:* news progmg 20 hrs wkly *No. News Employees:* 1 *Target Audience:* 25-54.
Bud Kitchens, President
Trey Elliott, Operations Dir
Jimmy Young, General Manager
Jay James, Programming Director
Dave Johnson, News Director
Deanna Thorpe, Traffic Manager

KZHN
09-11-1950; 1250 khz AM *Hrs Open:* 24; 0.5 kw-D, ND1; 0.095 kw-N, ND1; N33 43 21 W95 32 50
Mailing Address: 2400 Clarksville Street, Paris, TX 75460 US
Second Address: 402 Munson Ave. Suite 111, Rockwall, TX 75087
(214) 499-1158, *Fax:* (972) 771-1775
www.txn1250.com
txn1250@gmail.com
License: Paris, TX held by Eiffel Tower Broadcasting
Nat'l Network: USA *Regional Network:* Agrinet *Regional Reps:* Eiffel Tower Broadcasting *Wire Services:* AP
Arbitron Metro Market: Dallas-Fort Worth *Format:* Country
Special Programming: Variety/diversified. *Hrs. of News Programming:* news progmg 24 hrs wkly *No. News Employees:* 4 *Target Audience:* 24-54+.*Adv. Rates:* 45; 45; 45; 45
Larry Ryan, CEO
Samantha Nicole, Operations Dir
B.J. Clayton, General Manager
MaryAnn Ryan, General Sales Mgr
Crystal Jewel, Programming Director
B.J.Clayton, Promotions Manager
Andy Jackson, News Director
Norm Laramie, ChiefEngineer
Dawn Mitchell, Local Sales Manager
Robert Ryan, Production Director

KOYN
10-06-1988; 93.9 mhz FM *Hrs Open:* 24; 50 kw; 492 ft.; N33 49 36 W95 27 49
Mailing Address: P.O. Box 690, Paris, TX 75461 US
Second Address: 2810 Pine Mill Rd., Paris, TX 75461
(903) 785-1068, *Fax:* (903) 785-7176
www.easttexasradio.com
jyoung@easttexasradio.com
License: Paris, Lamar County, TX held by East Texas Broadcasting Inc.
Group Owner: East Texas Broadcasting Inc.; acq 5-11-01; grpsl).
Nat'l Network: USA
Format: Country *Hrs. of News Programming:* news progmg 3 hrs wkly *No. News Employees:* 2 *Target Audience:* 12 plus.
Bud Kitchens, President
Trey Elliott, Operations Dir
Jimmy Young, General Manager
Jay James, Programming Director
Dave Johnson, News Director
Deanna Thorpe, Traffic Manager

KPLT
11-19-1936; 1490 khz AM *Hrs Open:* 24; 1 kw-U; N33 38 07 W95 33 14
Mailing Address: Box 9, Paris, TX 75461
Second Address: 2305 S.E. 3rd St., Paris, TX 75461
(903) 785-1068, *Fax:* (903) 785-7176
License: Paris, Lamar County, TX held by East Texas Broadcasting Inc.
Group Owner: East Texas Broadcasting Inc.; acq 5-11-01; grpsl).
Nat'l Network: FOX News
Population Served: 55,000*Special Programming:* Gospel 15 hrs wkly *Target Audience:* General.
John Mitchell, President
Dave Johnson, Operations Dir
Zeke Alexander, Promotions Manager
Dave Johnson, News Director
Bill Hughes, Engineering Dir
Bob Haschke, Executive Vice President
Dan Lewis, Public Affairs Director

KPLT-FM
08-14-1966; 107.7 mhz FM; 50 kw; 492 ft.; N33 44 55 W95 24 53
Mailing Address: P.O. Box 9, Paris, TX 75461 US
Second Address: 2305 S.E. 3rd St., Paris, TX 75461
(903) 785-1068, *Fax:* (903) 785-7176
www.easttexasradio.com
bobh@easttexasradio.com
License: Paris, Lamar County, TX
Nat'l Network: ABC
Arbitron Metro Market: Paris, TX *Format:* Adult Contemp *Target Audience:* 18-35; heavy female/listen at work
Bob Haschke, General Manager
Dave Johnson, Programming Director

Pasadena

***KFTG**
02-01-1981; 88.1 mhz FM *Hrs Open:* 24; 0.7 kw horiz, 0.658 kw vert; 187 ft.; N29 41 18 W95 12 7
8315 Cr 198, Alvin, TX 77511 US
(281) 393-3116, *Fax:* (281) 393-1652
License: Pasadena, Harris County, TX held by Aleluya Christian Broadcasting Inc.
Group Owner: Aleluya Christian Broadcasting Inc.; (acq 3-21-2003; $482,500)
Arbitron Metro Market: Pasadena, TX *Format:* Religious, Spanish
Target Audience: Christians
Roberto Villarreal, General Manager

KIKK
10-01-1957; 650 khz AM *Hrs Open:* Sunrise-sunset; 0.25 kw-D, NDD; N29 41 18 W95 10 29
600 New Hampshire Avenue, NW, Suite 1200, Washington, DC 20037 US
(713) 881-5100, *Fax:* (713) 881-5250
houston.cbslocal.com/station/talk-650
License: Pasadena, TX held by CBS Radio Partner I Inc.
Group Owner: CBS Radio; (acq 10-20-93;
Nat'l Network: CBS *Nat'l Reps:* CBS Radio
Arbitron Metro Market: Houston-Galvest *Format:* Talk *Special Programming:* Health 2 hrs wkly *Hrs. of News Programming:* news 60 hrs wkly *Target Audience:* 25-44.
Sherry Dollar, General Sales Mgr
Gavin Spittle, Programming Director
Maggie Wessel, Promotions Manager
Dan Woodard, Chief Engineer
Dan Blanchard, General Sales Manager
Richard Topper, Music Director
Dan Blanchard

KKBQ-FM
08-01-1962; 92.9 mhz FM *Hrs Open:* 24; 93.7 kw; 1919 ft.; N29 34 34 W95 30 36
510 Lovett Blvd., Houston, TX 77006 US
(713) 963-1200, *Fax:* (713) 622-5457
www.KKBQ.com
License: Pasadena, Harris County, TX held by Cox Radio Inc.
Group Owner: Cox Radio Inc.; (acq 8-7-2000; grpsl)
Arbitron Metro Market: Houston, TX *Format:* Country *Target Audience:* 25-54.
Johny Chiang, Operations Dir
Caroline Devine, General Manager
Judy Lakin, General Sales Mgr
Christi Brooks, Programming Director
Candy Mendez, Promotions Manager
Emily Gerald, News Director
Jed Wilkinson, Chief Engineer

KLVL
05-05-1950; 1480 khz AM
1302 N. Shepherd, Houston, TX 77008 US
(713) 868-5559, *Fax:* (713) 868-9631
www.klvl1480.com
diddierugalde@hotmail.com,docarango@houston.rr.com
License: Pasadena, TX held by SIGA Broadcasting Corp.
Group Owner: SIGA Broadcasting Corp.; acq 5-16-97; $1.25 million)
Arbitron Metro Market: Houston, TX *Format:* Christian, Sports, 86
Special Programming: Black 4 hrs wkly
Julian Arango, Operations Dir
Hector Guevara, General Manager
Dade Moore, Engineering Dir

Pearsall

KMFR
11-03-1962; 1280 khz AM; 500 w-D; N28 53 13 W99 06 40
Mailing Address: Box K, Pearsall, TX 78230
Second Address: 205 S. Walnut St., Pearsall, TX 78061
(830) 334-8900, *Fax:* (830) 334-3448
info@kvwg.com
License: Pearsall, Frio County, TX held by Pearsall Radio Works Ltd.
Population Served: 47,000
John Barger, President

KSAH-FM
08-04-2002; 104.1 mhz FM *Hrs Open:* 24; 100 kw; Ant 981 ft; N28 44 53 W98 50 14
4500 Eisenhauer Rd, San Antonio, TX 78217
(210) 654-5100, *Fax:* (210) 340-1775
License: Pearsall, Frio County, TX held by BMP San Antonio License Co. L.P.
Group Owner: Border Media Partners LLC; (acq 7-23-2004; $10.25 million)
Lance Hawkins, General Manager
Bob Brown, General Sales Mgr

KSAG
103.3 mhz FM; 6 kw; 328 ft.; N29 1 4 W99 9 25 US
(956) 489-1013
License: Pearsall, Frio County, TX held by Gary S. Hess
Arbitron Metro Market: Pearsall, TX
Gary Hess, General Manager

Pecan Grove

KREH
01-01-1952; 900 khz AM *Hrs Open:* Sunrise-sunset
P.O Box 60991, Palo Alto, CA 94306 US
(713) 917-0050, *Fax:* (713) 917-0213
www.radiosaigonhouston.com
info@daisaigon.com
License: Pecan Grove, TX held by Bustos Media Holdings LLC.
Group Owner: Bustos Media LLC; (acq 6-11-2002)
Arbitron Metro Market: Greater Houston *Format:* Japanese, Korean, 18
Thuy Vu, General Manager
Duong Phuc & Vu Thanh Thuy / FOUNDERS

Pecos

KIUN
10-23-1935; 1400 khz AM *Hrs Open:* 24; 1 kw-U, ND1; N31 26 9 W103 30 14
316 South Cedar St., Pecos, TX 79772 US

(432) 445-2497, *Fax:* (432) 445-4092
www.98xfm.com
kiun@valornet.com
License: Pecos, TX held by Pecos Radio Co.
Regional Network: Texas State Networks
Format: Country *Target Audience:* General.
Bill Cole, General Manager

KGEE
01-01-1999; 97.3 mhz FM; 0.3 kw; 70 ft.; N31 25 7 W103 30 58
Rebroadcasts: Simulcast with KZBT(FM) Midland 100%
Box 2537, Bay City, TX 77414 US
(432) 563-9300, *Fax:* (432) 563-3823
www.b93.net
License: Pecos, Reeves County, TX held by Cumulus Licensing LLC.
Group Owner: Cumulus Media Inc.; (acq 6-11-2002; $1 million)
Arbitron Metro Market: Odessa, TX *Format:* Blues
Jeff Stone, General Manager
Leo Caro, Programming Director

KPTX
08-03-1981; 98.3 mhz FM *Hrs Open:* 6 AM-10 PM; 9.5 kw; 423 ft.; N31 29 56 W103 19 50
P. O. Box 469, Pecos, TX 79772 US
(432) 445-2497, *Fax:* (432) 445-4092
www.98xfm.com
info@98xfm.com
License: Pecos, Reeves County, TX held by Parday Inc.
Nat'l Network: ABC
Arbitron Metro Market: Odessa-Midland *Format:* Adult Contemp
Target Audience: 25 plus; adult
Bill Randall, General Manager
Joe Bevilacqua, Programming Director

***KPKO**
91.3 mhz FM; 0.9 kw; 62 ft.; N31 25 6 W103 30 55
US
(662) 844-5036, *Fax:* (662) 842-6791
www.afr.net
contact@afa.net
License: Pecos, Reeves County, TX held by American Family Association.
Group Owner: American Family Radio
Nat'l Network: American Family Radio
Arbitron Metro Market: Pecos, TX *Format:* Christian
Donald E. Wildmon, Founder
Buster Wilson, General Manager
Jennifer Hagman, Programming Director

Perryton

KEYE
11-19-1948; 93.7 khz AM; 1 kw-U; N36 23 20 W100 49 37
Box 630, Perryton, TX 79070
(806) 435-5458, *Fax:* (806) 435-5393
www.keye.net
keye@ptsin.net
License: Perryton, Ochiltree County, TX held by Perryton Radio Inc.
Regional Network: Texas State Networks
Population Served: 40,000*Special Programming:* Farm 2 hrs, relg 3 hrs wkly
Chris Samples, General Manager
Lynlee Mullins, News Director

KEYE-FM
01-01-1978; 93.7 mhz FM; 8.5 kw; 402 ft.; N36 21 54 W100 46 45
7430 Colshire #4, McLean, VA 22102 US
(806) 435-5458, *Fax:* (806) 435-5393
www.keye.net
keye@keye.net
License: Perryton, Ochiltree County, TX held by Perryton Radio Inc.
Arbitron Metro Market: Perryton, TX *Format:* Oldies
Darin Clark, General Manager
David Schwalk, News Director

Pflugerville

KOKE
01-01-2001; 1600 khz AM
3 Asbury Court, Brownwood, TX 96801 US
(512) 453-1491, *Fax:* (512) 834-1491
License: Pflugerville, TX held by Encino Broadcasting LLC.
Group Owner: Encino Broadcasting LLC; (acq 2-15-2008; . grpsl)
Format: Tejano
Jose Garcia, General Manager

Pharr

KVJY
02-01-1985; 840 khz AM; 5 kw-D, DA2; 1 kw-N, DA2; N26 19 0 W98 6 16
P.O. Box 484, Austin, TX 78767 US
(956) 668-8585, *Fax:* (956) 668-9996
www.radiounica.com
info@radiounica.com
License: Pharr, TX held by BMP RGV License Co. L.P.
Group Owner: Border Media Partners LLC; (acq 3-31-2005; grpsl).
Arbitron Metro Market: McAllen-Brownsville-Harlingen, TX
Format: Country
Thomas Castro, President
Jeff Koch, Operations Dir
Jose Luis Munoz, General Manager

Pilot Point

KZMP-FM
10-17-1983; 104.9 mhz FM; 20.15 kw; 1755 ft.; N33 33 37 W96 57 34
17719 Cedar Creek, Canyon Drive, Dallas, TX 75252 US
(817) 868-2900, *Fax:* (817) 868-2929
www.funasia.net
License: Pilot Point, Denton County, TX held by Liberman Broadcasting of Dallas License LLC.
Group Owner: Liberman Broadcasting Inc.; (acq 11-2-2006; grpsl)
Arbitron Metro Market: Coleyville, TX *Format:* Ethnic
Rosa Cuellar, General Manager

Pittsburg

KSCN
03-01-1999; 96.9 mhz FM *Hrs Open:* 24; 14 kw; 390 ft; N33 00 31 W95 04 14
Mailing Address: Box 990, Mount Pleasant, TX 75456
Second Address: 1798 US Hwy. 67 W., Mount Pleasant, TX 75455
(903) 572-8726, *Fax:* (903) 572-7232
www.easttexasradio.com
bud@easttexasradio.com
License: Pittsburg, Camp County, TX held by East Texas Broadcasting Inc.
Group Owner: East Texas Broadcasting Inc.
Population Served: 68,000*Hrs. of News Programming:* news progmg 3 hrs wkly *No. News Employees:* 2 *Target Audience:* 25-54; general *Adv. Rates:* 26; 23; 26; 21
John Mitchell, Chairman
Bud Kitchens, President
Moose Morgan, Operations Dir
Bud Kitchens, General Manager
Bryan Friesth, General Sales Mgr
Moose Morgan, Programming Director
Clint Cooper, News Director
Bill Hughes, ChiefEngineer
Justice Thornburg, Traffic Manager

KMPA
12-15-1986; 103.1 mhz FM *Hrs Open:* 24; 10 kw; Ant 672 ft; N32 52 50 W94 58 13
Mailing Address: Box 1648, Jacksonville, TX 75644
Second Address: 402 S. Ragsdale, Jacksonville, TX 75766
(903) 586-2527, *Fax:* (903) 589-0677
dudleyw@wallerboradcasting.com
License: Pittsburg, Camp County, TX held by Waller Media LLC.
Group Owner: Waller Broadcasting; (acq 8-24-2005; $975,000 with KXAL-FM Tatum).
Population Served: 280,000*Hrs. of News Programming:* news progmg 6 hrs wkly *No. News Employees:* 1 *Adv. Rates:* 30; 24; 20; 10
Dudley Waller, General Manager

***KGWP**
01-01-2003; 91.1 mhz FM *Hrs Open:* 24; 1.1 kw vert; 194 ft.; N32 57 49.5 W94 55 10
US
(951) 737-1717, *Fax:* (903) 575-1984
www.radioimpacto.org
License: Pittsburg, Camp County, TX held by Andres Serranos Ministries Inc.
Arbitron Metro Market: Pittsburg, TX *Format:* Christian *Hrs. of News Programming:* news progmg 10 hrs wkly *No. News Employees:* 1 *Target Audience:* 30-55 plus. *Adv. Rates:* 10; 10; 10; 5
Rafael Garcia, President

***KPIT**
01-01-2008; 91.7 mhz FM; 0.45 kw vert; 131 ft.; N33 2 45.5 W95 3 23.2
US
(903) 466-6791
www.kpitradio.com
License: Pittsburg, Camp County, TX held by Millennium Broadcasting Corp.
Arbitron Metro Market: Pittsburg, TX *Format:* Tejano
James Furlow, President

Plains

***KPHS**
11-14-1977; 90.3 mhz FM *Hrs Open:* 8:30 AM-3:15 PM; 0.22 kw horiz; 135 ft.; N33 11 16 W102 49 20
P.O. Box 479, Plains, TX 79355 US
(806) 456-7445, *Fax:* (806) 456-4325
License: Plains, Yoakum County, TX held by Plains Independent School District.
Target Audience: High School Radio
Rennetta O'Quinn, General Manager

Plainview

***KBAH**
03-18-2004; 90.5 mhz FM; 75 kw; 427 ft.; N34 3 58 W101 42 16
P O Box 2440, Tupelo, MS 38803 US
(662) 844-8888
afr.net
info@kbahfm.com
License: Plainview, Hale County, TX held by American Family Association.
Group Owner: American Family Radio
Arbitron Metro Market: Tupelo, MS *Format:* Christian
Marvin Sanders, General Manager

KVOP
10-01-1974; 1090 khz AM *Hrs Open:* 24; 5 kw-D, DA2; 0.5 kw-N, DA2; N34 5 32 W101 38 26
Mailing Address: 2402 Broadmoor, Bldg D2, Suite 101, Bryan, TX 77802 US
Second Address: Box 147, Plainview, TX 79073
(806) 296-2771, *Fax:* (806) 293-5732
License: Plainview, TX held by Rhattigan Broadcasting (Texas) LP
Group Owner: Rhattigan Broadcasting (Texas) LP; (acq 8-19-2004; grpsl)
Nat'l Reps: Katz Radio
Arbitron Metro Market: Lubbock, TX *Format:* Sports, Talk *Special Programming:* Farm 12 hrs wkly *Hrs. of News Programming:* News progmg 10 hrs wkly *Target Audience:* Adults; 25-54 *Adv. Rates:* 20; 14; 18; 12
Tom Hall, Operations Dir
Dana Huggins, General Manager
Dimas Garcia, Programming Director
Michelle Johnson, Traffic Director

KKYN-FM
01-01-1987; 106.9 mhz FM *Hrs Open:* 24; 50 kw; 469 ft.; N34 15 47 W101 40 30
Mailing Address: 2402 Broadmoor, Building D-2, Suite #101, Bryan, TX 77802 US
Second Address: Box 147, Plainview, TX 79073
(806) 296-2771, *Fax:* (806) 293-5732
www.kkyn.net
License: Plainview, Hale County, TX held by Rhattigan Broadcasting (Texas) LP
Group Owner: Rhattigan Broadcasting (Texas) LP
Arbitron Metro Market: Lubbock, TX *Format:* Country *Hrs. of News Programming:* news progmg 5 hrs wkly *No. News Employees:* 1 *Target Audience:* 35 plus. *Adv. Rates:* 20; 14; 16; 12
Tom Hall, Operations Dir
Dana Huggins, General Manager
Jerry Larsen, Station Manager
Dimas Garcia, Programming Director

KREW
08-14-1944; 1400 khz AM *Hrs Open:* 24; 1 kw-U, ND1; N34 12 55 W101 43 25
Mailing Address: 2402 Broadmoor, Bldg, D-2, Suite 101, Bryan, TX 77802 US
Second Address: Box 1420, Plainview, TX 79072
(806) 293-2661, *Fax:* (806) 293-5732
License: Plainview, TX held by Rhattigan Broadcasting (Texas) LP
Group Owner: Rhattigan Broadcasting (Texas) LP; (acq 8-19-2004; grpsl)
Regional Network: Texas State Networks *Wire Services:* AP
Arbitron Metro Market: Plainview, TX *Format:* Oldies *Hrs. of News Programming:* News progmg 7 hrs wkly *Target Audience:* Adults 35+; baby boomers *Adv. Rates:* 14; 10; 12; 8
Michael Rhattigan, General Manager
Tom Hall, Station Manager

Brandy Haines, Programming Director
Dana Huggins, Traffic Manager

KRIA
01-01-1999; 103.9 mhz FM; 25 kw; 367 ft.; N34 15 47 W101 40 30
Mailing Address: 2402 Broadmoor, Bodg D-2, Suite 101, Bryan, TX 77802 US
Second Address: Box 1420, Plainview, TX 79073
(806) 293-2661, *Fax:* (806) 293-5732
License: Plainview, Hale County, TX held by Rhattigan Broadcasting (Texas) LP
Group Owner: Rhattigan Broadcasting (Texas) LP
Nat'l Network: CSN
Arbitron Metro Market: Plainview, TX *Format:* Classic Rock *Hrs. of News Programming:* News progmg 10 hrs wkly *Target Audience:* Hispanic; 18-49 *Adv. Rates:* 18; 14; 16; 10.
Tom Hall, Operations Dir
Michael Rhattigan, General Manager
Brandy Haines, Programming Director
Dana Huggins, Traffic Director

***KWLD**
01-01-1952; 91.5 mhz FM *Hrs Open:* 24; 0.37 kw; 105 ft.; N34 11 14 W101 43 32
1900 W. 7th St., Plainview, TX 79072 US
(806) 291-1091, *Fax:* (806) 291-1963
www.wbu.edu
kwld@wbu.edu
License: Plainview, Hale County, TX held by Wayland Baptist University.
Nat'l Network: USA
Arbitron Metro Market: Plainview, TX *Format:* Contemporary Hits/Top 40, Jazz, 20 *Hrs. of News Programming:* News progmg 14 hrs wkly *Target Audience:* 15-30; high school through college, young adult, afternoon & evening
Jim Smith, CFO
Paul Armes, President
Claude Lusk, Operations Dir
Steve Long, General Manager
Paul Sutton, Programming Director
David Carr, Chief Engineer
Bill Hardage, Executive Vice President
Betty Donaldson, Vice President

***KPMB**
88.5 mhz FM; 3 kw; 282 ft.; N34 13 14 W101 42 52
P.O. Box 252, McAllen, TX 78505 US
(956) 686-6382, *Fax:* (956) 686-2999
License: Plainview, Hale County, TX held by Paulino Bernal Evangelism.
Arbitron Metro Market: McAllen, TX *Format:* Religious
Larry Roberts, General Manager
Bryce Phillippy, General Sales Mgr
Kent Phillips, Programming Director
Jennifer Pirak, Promotions Manager
Lindsey Fields, News Director
John Barrett, Chief Engineer
Gary Greenberg, National SalesManager

Plano

KMKI
07-15-1999; 620 khz AM *Hrs Open:* 24; 5 kw-D, DA2; 4.5 kw-N, DA2; N33 14 34 W96 32 29
77 West 66th Street, 16th Floor, New York, NY 10023 US
(817) 695-1333, *Fax:* (817) 695-3556
www.radiodisney.com
License: Plano, TX held by Radio Disney Dallas LLC.
Group Owner: ABC Inc.; (acq 9-4-98; $12.1 million).
Nat'l Network: Radio Disney *Nat'l Reps:* Interep
Arbitron Metro Market: Dallas, TX *Format:* Contemporary Hits/Top 40 *Target Audience:* 6-12; 25-49; women adults *Adv. Rates:* Varies by inventory
Jamie Ramsey, Station Manager
Molly Bunker, Promotions Manager

Pleasant Valley

KZAM
01-01-2008; 98.7 mhz FM; 6 kw; 318 ft.; N34 2 54 W98 39 38 US
(956) 487-8015
License: Pleasant Valley, Wichita County, TX held by South Texas FM Investments LLC.
Group Owner: South Texas FM Investments LLC; (acq 9-16-2008; grpsl)
Arbitron Metro Market: Pleasant Valley, TX *Format:* Variety/Diverse
Eloy Vera, General Manager

Pleasanton

***KWMF**
02-08-1951; 1380 khz AM *Hrs Open:* 24 hrs
Mailing Address: 127 Mamanasco Road, Ridgefield, CT 06876 US
Second Address: 3308 Broadway, San Antonio, TX 78209
(432)682-5476, *Fax:* (432) 684-5588
www.grnonline.com
luisd@grnonline.com
License: Pleasanton, TX held by La Promesa Foundation.
Group Owner: La Promesa Foundation; (acq 12-13-2006; grpsl)
Nat'l Network: EWTN Radio
Arbitron Metro Market: Pleasanton, TX *Format:* Christian *Special Programming:* Vatican Radio 1 hr wkly *Target Audience:* Christian Families
Robert Dominguez, General Manager

Point Comfort

KJAZ
12-10-1998; 94.1 mhz FM *Hrs Open:* 24; 25 kw; 194 ft; N28 46 08 W96 42 39
102 Jason Plaza, Suite 2, Victoria, TX 78704
(361) 572-0105, *Fax:* (361) 798-3798
License: Point Comfort, Calhoun County, TX held by Roy E. Henderson.
Group Owner: Fort Bend Broadcasting Co.; (acq 4-13-2001; $400,000)
Target Audience: Baby boomers; active, affluent adults
Ryan Henderson, General Manager

Port Arthur

***KDEI**
08-01-1934; 1250 khz AM *Hrs Open:* 24
6420 Richmond Avenue, Suite 620, Houston, TX 77057 US
(888) 408-0201, *Fax:* (318) 449-9954
www.radiomaria.us
info.usa@radiomaria.org
License: Port Arthur, TX held by Radio Maria Inc.
Group Owner: Radio Maria Inc.; acq 9-20-99).
Nat'l Network: American Urban
Arbitron Metro Market: Alexandria, LA *Format:* Christian, Talk, 74 *Hrs. of News Programming:* News progmg 10.5 hrs wkly *Target Audience:* General; isolated and under-represented groups in society, sick, elderly etc
Duane Stenzel, General Manager
Dale DePerrodil, General Sales Mgr
Danny Brou, Chief Engineer

KOLE
01-01-1947; 1340 khz AM *Hrs Open:* 24; 1 kw-U, ND1; N29 54 15 W93 56 10
Post Office Box 22257, Beaumont, TX 77720 US
(409) 835-2222,(866) 835-1340, *Fax:* (409) 832-5686
www.birach.com/kole.htm
sima@birach.com
License: Port Arthur, TX held by Birach Broadcasting Corp.
Group Owner: Birach Broadcasting Corp.; (acq 3-20-2008; $450,000)
Nat'l Network: USA; Fox News Radio; Talk Radio Network
Regional Network: Texas State Networks
Arbitron Metro Market: Beaumont-Port Arthur, TX *Format:* News, News/Talk, 86 *Hrs. of News Programming:* news progmg 40 hrs wkly *No. News Employees:* 2 *Target Audience:* 25 plus. *Adv. Rates:* 24; 20; 22; 18
Sima Birach, President
Jeff Roberts, Operations Dir
Ralph McBride, General Manager
Brent Bobbitt, General Sales Mgr
Dominick Brascia, Programming Director
John St.John, News Director
Russ Ingram, Engineering Dir
JeanetteHarvey, Traffic Manager

KQBU-FM
07-04-1969; 93.3 mhz FM *Hrs Open:* 24; 97 kw; 1952 ft.; N30 3 5 W94 31 37
3102 Oak Lawn Ave., Suite 215, Dallas, TX 75219 US
(713) 965-2400, *Fax:* (713) 965-2401
License: Port Arthur, Jefferson County, TX held by Tichenor License Corp.
Group Owner: Univision Radio
Arbitron Metro Market: Houston-Galveston *Target Audience:* 18-34; urban/Latin audience
Mark Masepohl, Operations Dir

KTJM
04-15-1963; 98.5 mhz FM *Hrs Open:* 24; 100 kw; 1955 ft.; N30 1 1 W94 32 47
6420 Richmond Avenue, Suite 620, Houston, TX 77057 US
(713) 315-3400, *Fax:* (713) 315-3405
www.laraza.fm
License: Port Arthur, Jefferson County, TX held by Liberman Broadcasting of Houston License LLC.
Group Owner: Liberman Broadcasting Inc.; (acq 3-20-2001; grpsl)
Nat'l Network: Estrella TV *Nat'l Reps:* SMRT
Arbitron Metro Market: Houston-Galvest *TV Affiliate:* Estrella TV
Winter Horton, CEO/COO
Lenard Liberman, President
Winter Horton, General Manager
Wynette Ortiz, Station Manager
Wynette Ortiz, General Sales Mgr
Cheque Gonzalez, Programming Director
Raul Marquez, Promotions Manager
Mike Todd,Engineering Dir
Mike Todd, Chief Engineer

Port Isabel

KNVO-FM
01-01-1992; 101.1 mhz FM *Hrs Open:* 24; 50 kw; 486 ft.; N26 19 30 W97 25 25
13355 Noel Road, 1350 One Galleria Tower, Dallas, TX 75240 US
(956) 661-6000, *Fax:* (956) 661-6081
www.jose1011.com
msomonth@entravision.com
License: Port Isabel, Cameron County, TX held by Entravision Holdings L.L.C.
Group Owner: Entravision Communications Corp.; (acq 7-20-2000; grpsl)
Nat'l Network: Westwood One
Arbitron Metro Market: McAllen, TX *Format:* Spanish *Hrs. of News Programming:* news progmg one hr wkly *No. News Employees:* 1 *Target Audience:* 25-55.
Willie Rosales, General Manager
Mando Sanroman, Programming Director
Dora Borjas, News Director
Sonny Cabazos, Chief Engineer

Port Lavaca

KITE
08-01-1976; 93.3 mhz FM; 100 kw; 318 ft.; N28 42 22 W96 48 3
Mailing Address: 8023 Vantage Dr., Suite 840, San Antonio, TX 78230 US
Second Address: 3613 N. Main St., Victoria, TX 77903
(361) 576-6111, *Fax:* (361) 572-0014
License: Port Lavaca, Calhoun County, TX held by Victoria RadioWorks Ltd.
Group Owner: Victoria RadioWorks Ltd.; (acq 10-29-98; $500,000).
Nat'l Reps: McGavren Guild
Format: Oldies *Special Programming:* Farm one hr wkly
Cindy Cox, General Manager

Port Neches

KBPO
06-13-1959; 1150 khz AM
419 Stadium Road, Port Arthur, TX 77642 US
(409) 985-2323, *Fax:* (409) 983-5858
www.radiovida1150.com
info@kpbo.com
License: Port Neches, TX held by Vision Latina Broadcasting Inc.
Nat'l Network: Fox Sports
Arbitron Metro Market: Port Neches, TX *Format:* Sports
Eloy Castro, President
Marco Mata, General Sales Mgr
Patricia Montenegro, Programming Director
Richard Ryele, Chief Engineer
Lauri Grantham, Disc Jockey
Jeremy Ryan, Disc Jockey
Don Hebert, Disc Jockey

Port O'Connor

***KHPO**
01-01-2007; 91.9 mhz FM; 4 kw; 308 ft.; N28 25 44 W96 26 54
Rebroadcasts: Rebroadcasts KHCB-FM Houston 95%
2424 South Blvd, Houston, TX 77098 US
(713) 520-5200
www.khcb.org
email@khcb.org
License: Port O'Connor, Calhoun County, TX held by Houston Christian Broadcasters Inc.
Group Owner: Houston Christian Broadcasters Inc.
Nat'l Network: Moody
Arbitron Metro Market: Port O'Connor, TX *Format:* Christian *Hrs. of News Programming:* News progmg 6 hrs wkly

RADIO - U.S.

Bruce Munsterman, General Manager
Bonnie BeMent, News Director

Portland

KLHB

12-15-1979; 105.5 mhz FM *Hrs Open:* 24; 1.9 kw; 354 ft; N27 47 48 W97 23 51
1300 Antelope, Corpus Christi, TX 78729
(361) 883-1600, *Fax:* (361) 888-5685
License: Portland, San Patricio County, TX held by Tejas Broadcasting Ltd. LLP.
Group Owner: Tejas Broadcasting Ltd. LLP; (acq 11-15-2004; grpsl).
Arbitron Metro Market: Corpus Christi, TX *Target Audience:* 18-49; general
Eddie Alonzo, General Manager
Julie Garza, Programming Director
Lon Gonzalez, News Director
Henry Turner, Chief Engineer
Debbie Reid, Traffic Manager

*KSGR

10-01-2000; 91.1 mhz FM; 5.4 kw horiz, 25 kw vert; 328 ft.; N27 59 49 W97 14 46
30000 W. Macarthur Blvd., 3rd Floor, Santa Ana, CA 92704 US
(361) 814-7775, *Fax:* (361) 814-7779
www.ksgr.org
info@ksgr.org
License: Portland, San Patricio County, TX held by Coastlands Radio Inc.
Group Owner: CSN International; (acq 7-25-2008; $120,000)
Format: Christian
Jim Sheperd, General Manager

Post

KSSL

05-01-1991; 107.3 mhz FM *Hrs Open:* 24; 22 kw; Ant 748 ft; N33 13 23 W101 26 26 *Rebroadcasts:* Rebroadcasts KLRD(FM) Yucaipa, CA 100%
2351 Sunset Blvd., Suite 170-218, Rocklin, CA 74067
(916) 251-1600, (800) 464-5817, *Fax:* (916) 251-1650
www.godscountryradionetwork.com
info@happyjubilee.com
License: Post, Garza County, TX held by Educational Media Foundation.
Group Owner: EMF Broadcasting; (acq 5-21-2004; $550,000)
Population Served: 200,000
Mike Novak, President

Prairie View

*KPVU

11-26-1981; 91.3 mhz FM *Hrs Open:* 24; 31 kw; 421 ft.; N30 5 21 W95 59 46
P. O. Box 156, Prairie View, TX 77446 US
(936) 261-3750, *Fax:* (936) 261-3769
www.pvamu.edu/kpvu
kpvu_fm@pvamu.edu
License: Prairie View, Waller County, TX held by Prairie View A&M University.
Nat'l Network: NPR
Arbitron Metro Market: Houston-Galveston *Format:* Urban Contemporary, Variety/Diverse *Hrs. of News Programming:* News progmg 24 hrs daily *Target Audience:* 18 plus.
George LaBlanche, Operations Dir
Cheryl Granger Brooks, General Manager
Danielle Arriola, General Sales Mgr
Jeffrey Kelley, Programming Director
Leonard Moon, News Director
Dave Cassels, Chief Engineer

Premont

KMFM

01-01-1989; 100.7 mhz FM; 25 kw; 285 ft.; N27 28 30 W98 3 23
PO Box 252, McAllen, TX 78502 US
(956) 686-6382, *Fax:* (956) 686-2999
License: Premont, Jim Wells County, TX held by Radio Cristiana Network.
Format: Religious
Eloy Bernal, General Manager
Paulino Bernal Jr., Station Manager
John Ross, Chief Engineer

Ralls

KCLR

05-31-1963; 1530 khz AM; 1 kw-C, NDD; 5 kw-D, NDD; N33 40 0 W101 22 44
1112 W. 16th St., Plainview, TX 79072 US
(956) 686-6382, *Fax:* (956) 686-2999
www.laradiocristiana.com
paulinobernal@hotmail.com
License: Ralls, TX held by Paulino Bernal
Arbitron Metro Market: Lubbock, TX *Format:* Christian
Pete Guzman, Operations Dir
Paulino Bernal, General Manager
Eloy Bernal, Station Manager

Ranchitos Las Lomas

*KBAW

01-01-2001; 93.3 mhz FM; 25 kw; 328 ft.; N27 0 22 W99 22 53
2702 Pine At Louisiana, Laredo, TX 78043 US
(956) 726-4738
www.lacadenaradioluz.com/kbaw-93.htm
radiooluz@border.net
License: Ranchitos Las Lomas, Zapata County, TX held by La Nueva Cadena Radio Luz Inc.
Arbitron Metro Market: Laredo, TX *Format:* Christian
Isreal Tellez, Station Manager

Ranger

KWBY-FM

07-01-1990; 98.5 mhz FM *Hrs Open:* 24; 5.8 kw; Ant 335 ft; N32 20 48 W98 42 50
471 N. Harbin Dr., Suite 102, Stephenville, TX 59911
(254) 968-7459, *Fax:* (254) 968-6258
www.mandatoryfm.com
john@mandatoryfm.com
License: Ranger, Eastland County, TX held by Mandatory Broadcasting Inc.
Nat'l Network: Jones Radio Networks *Regional Network:* Texas State Networks
Target Audience: 20-65; all-important age group of today's buying public *Adv. Rates:* 22; 18; 18; 15
John Hollinger, General Manager
Jon Gibson, General Sales Mgr
Jim Rhodes, Chief Engineer

Raymondville

*KBIC

10-01-1996; 105.7 mhz FM *Hrs Open:* 24; 1.8 kw; 427 ft.; N26 26 37 W97 42 8
P.O. Box 1290, Weslaco, TX 78596 US
(956) 968-7777, *Fax:* (956) 968-5143
www.radiovida.com
informacion@radiovida.com
License: Raymondville, Willacy County, TX held by Christian Ministries of the Valley Inc.
Arbitron Metro Market: Weslaco, TX *Format:* Religious
Enrique Garza, General Manager

KBUC

01-01-1979; 102.1 mhz FM *Hrs Open:* 6 AM-midnight; 18 kw; 758 ft.; N26 38 9 W97 50 10
1 Paseo Del Prado, Bldg. 102, Edinburg, TX 78539 US
(956) 992-8895, *Fax:* (956) 992-8897
www.supertejano1021.com
License: Raymondville, Willacy County, TX held by BMP RGV License Company L.P.
Group Owner: Border Media Partners LLC; (acq 5-30-2003; $8 million with KBDR(FM) Mirando City).
Arbitron Metro Market: McAllen-Brownsv
Rogelio Rios, Operations Dir
Jose Munoz, General Manager
Maria Alvarez, General Sales Mgr
Angela Pina, News Director
Joe Espinoza, Chief Engineer

KSOX

06-01-1957; 1240 khz AM *Hrs Open:* 6 AM-midnight
1 Paseo Del Prado, Bldg. 102, Edinburg, TX 78539 US
(956) 383-2777, *Fax:* (956) 383-2570
License: Raymondville, TX held by BMP RGV License Co. L.P.
Group Owner: Border Media Partners LLC; (acq 2-6-2004; $7.5 million with KURV(AM) Edinburg)
Arbitron Metro Market: McAllen-Brownsville-Harlingen, TX
Format: Sports *Target Audience:* 25-55.
Angela Pina, News Director

Refugio

KOUL

05-20-1968; 103.7 mhz FM; 100 kw; 952 ft.; N28 2 7 W97 26 11
Mailing Address: 13625 Ponds Spring Road, #105, Austin, TX 78729 US
Second Address: 1300 Antelope, Corpus Christi, TX 78401
(361) 883-1600, *Fax:* (361) 883-9303
www.koul1037.com
License: Refugio, San Patricio County, TX held by Tejas Broadcasting Ltd. LLP.
Group Owner: Tejas Broadcasting Ltd. LLP; (acq 11-15-2004; grpsl).
Arbitron Metro Market: Corpus Christi, TX *Format:* Country
Target Audience: 25-49; general
Chuck Brooks, President
Clayton Allen, Operations Dir
Kent Cooper, General Manager
Shannon Mortenson, General Sales Mgr
KC Sheperd, Promotions Manager
Debra Reid, News Director
Russell Vaughan, Chief Engineer
Paul Danitz,Advertising Manager
Lisa Del Rey, Public Affairs Director

KYRK

10-05-1979; 106.1 mhz FM; 25 kw; Ant 328 ft; N28 08 15 W97 12 45
710 Buffalo St., Suite 608, Corpus Christi, TX 74876
(314) 345-1030,(361) 882-5749, *Fax:* (361) 884-1240
jim@koplar.com
License: Refugio, Refugio County, TX held by Pacific Broadcasting of Missouri L.L.C.
Population Served: 400,000 *Arbitron Metro Market:* Corpus Christi, TX
James Withers, General Manager

Reno

KLOW

06-01-2009; 98.9 mhz FM; 5.9 kw; 331 ft.; N33 38 54 W95 36 12 US
2526363333
bill@bigfishfm.com
License: Reno, Lamar County, TX held by Tower Investment Trust Inc.
Group Owner: Tower Investment Trust Inc.
Nat'l Reps: Salem
Arbitron Metro Market: Reno, TX *Format:* Christian *Target Audience:* Contempary Christian
William Brothers, President

Richardson

KKLF

01-01-1999; 1700 khz AM; 10 kw-D, 1 kw-N; N33 25 23 W96 39 45 *Rebroadcasts:* Rebroadcasts KTCK(AM) Dallas 100%
3500 Maple Ave., Suite 1310, Dallas, TX 17401
(214) 526-7400, *Fax:* (214) 525-2525
www.theticket.com
License: Richardson, Dallas County, TX held by Volt Radio LLC
Group Owner: Cumulus Media Partners LLC; (acq 4-30-98)
Arbitron Metro Market: Dallas-Fort Worth
Gordon Johnson, President

Rio Grande City

KQBO

04-01-1985; 107.5 mhz FM *Hrs Open:* 5 AM-midnight; 12 kw; 994 ft.; N26 31 1 W98 39 7
Rt 5, Box 103 Fm, Rio Grande City, TX 78582 US
(956) 487-8224, *Fax:* (815) 361-6185
www.kqbofm.com
info@kqbofm.com
License: Rio Grande City, Starr County, TX held by Gustavo Valadez Jr.
Arbitron Metro Market: McAllen-Brownsville-Harlingen, TX
Format: Ethnic *Hrs. of News Programming:* News progmg 5 hrs wkly *Target Audience:* 18-45.
Gustavo Valadez Jr., President

KRGX

95.1 mhz FM; 6 kw; 328 ft.; N26 26 4.9 W98 55 45.3 US
(956) 487-5621
www.exafm.com
exa95.1@gmail.com
License: Rio Grande City, Starr County, TX held by James Falcon.
Arbitron Metro Market: Rio Grande City, TX
James Falcon, General Manager

Robinson

KWPW

11-01-1972; 107.9 mhz FM *Hrs Open:* 24; 6 kw; Ant 328 ft; N31 30 33 W97 10 03
10801 N. Mopac Expwy. 2-250, Austin, TX 75219
(214) 525-0400,(512) 340-7100
www.univision.com

License: Robinson, McLennan County, TX held by KICI-FM License Corp.
Group Owner: Univision Radio; (acq 9-22-2003; grpsl).
Population Served: 35,000 *Arbitron Metro Market:* Waco, TX *Target Audience:* 18-54.
Tim McCoy, General Manager
Randall Garcia, General Sales Mgr
Alejandro Covarrubias, Programming Director
Samantha Martinez, News Director

Robstown

KROB
02-22-1963; 1510 khz AM
N. 9th Street, Robstown, TX 78380 US
(302) 566-5762, *Fax:* (361) 299-6002
www.krobradio.com
krobam1510@sbcglobal.net
License: Robstown, TX held by B Communications Joint Venture.
Group Owner: Claro Communications Ltd.; (acq 1-4-2002)
Arbitron Metro Market: Corpus-Christi, TX *Format:* Oldies, Spanish *Target Audience:* 25-54.
Jerry Benavides, President
Jerry Benevides, General Manager
Ben Benavides, General Sales Mgr
Bob Pena, Programming Director
Peter Hemphill, News Director
Gary Graham, Chief Engineer

*KLUX
03-17-1985; 89.5 mhz FM *Hrs Open:* 24; 60 kw; Ant 954 ft; N27 46 50 W97 38 03
1200 Lantana, Corpus Christi, TX 78407
(361) 289-2487, *Fax:* (361) 289-1420
www.klux.org
klux@goccn.org
License: Robstown, Nueces County, TX held by Diocesan Telecommunications Corp.
Nat'l Network: USA; IRN/USA
Population Served: 500,000 *Arbitron Metro Market:* Corpus Christi *Special Programming:* Sp 3 hrs wkly *Hrs. of News Programming:* news progmg 13 hrs wkly *No. News Employees:* 1 *Target Audience:* 35 plus;total persons
Rev. Msgr. Michael Howell, Chairman
Marty Wind, CEO/COO
Marty Wind, President
Russ Martin, Operations Dir
Marty Wind, General Manager
Marty Wind, Station Manager
Russ Martin, Programming Director
Russ Martin, PromotionsManager
Russ Martin, News Director
Marty Wind, Engineering Dir
Marty Wind, Chief Engineer
Russ Martin, Underwriting Director

KMIQ
07-23-1989; 104.9 mhz FM; 31 kw; 482 ft.; N27 46 35 W97 55 10
115 West Avenue D, Robstown, TX 78380 US
(361) 289-8877, *Fax:* (361) 289-7722
License: Robstown, Nueces County, TX held by Cotton Broadcasting.
Arbitron Metro Market: Corpus Christi, TX *Format:* Tejano *Special Programming:* Relg 6 hrs wkly *Target Audience:* 18 plus.
Carlo Lopez, General Manager
Santos Leal, Programming Director

KSAB
10-13-1966; 99.9 mhz FM; 100 kw; 932 ft.; N27 45 7 W97 38 17
600 Congress Ave., Suite 1400, Austin, TX 78701 US
(361) 289-0111, *Fax:* (361) 289-5035
www.ksabfm.com
ksabfm@aol.com
License: Robstown, Nueces County, TX held by Capstar TX L.P.
Group Owner: Clear Channel Communications Inc.; (acq 8-30-00; grpsl)
Arbitron Metro Market: Corpus Christi, TX *Format:* Tejano
Matt Martin, General Manager
Dan Pena, Promotions Manager

Rockdale

KRXT
02-27-1989; 98.5 mhz FM *Hrs Open:* 24 hrs; 6 kw; 328 ft.; N30 38 32 W97 2 13
P. O. Box 1560, Rockdale, TX 76567 US
(512) 446-6985, *Fax:* (512) 446-6987
www.krxt985.com
krxtl@farm-market.net
License: Rockdale, Milam County, TX held by KRXT Inc.
Regional Network: Texas State Networks
Arbitron Metro Market: Rockdale, TX *Format:* Country *Hrs. of News Programming:* news progmg 20 hrs wkly *No. News Employees:* 1 *Target Audience:* General. *Adv. Rates:* 11.50;11.50;11.50;11.50
Charles McGregor, President
Dave Gonnella, General Sales Mgr

Rockport

KKPN
10-01-1986; 102.3 mhz FM *Hrs Open:* 24; 50 kw; 446 ft.; N27 52 2 W97 13 7
7755 Carondelet Avenue, Clayton, MO 63105 US
(361) 814-3800, *Fax:* (361) 855-3770
www.planet1023.com
License: Rockport, Aransas County, TX held by Convergent Broadcasting Corpus Christi LP.
Group Owner: Convergent Broadcasting LP; (acq 1-12-2004; grpsl).
Arbitron Metro Market: Corpus Christi, TX *Format:* Contemporary Hits/Top 40 *Target Audience:* Adult; 18-49
Mark White, General Manager
Dallas Garcia, General Sales Mgr
Scott Holt, Programming Director
William Hooper, Chief Engineer

Rollingwood

KJCE
08-12-1958; 1370 khz AM
600 New Hampshire Ave., N.W., Suite 1200, Washington, DC 20037 US
(512) 327-9595, *Fax:* (512) 329-6255
www.talkradio137am.com
License: Rollingwood, TX held by Entercom Austin License LLC
Group Owner: Entercom Communications Corp.; .
Nat'l Network: Westwood One; ABC; Salem Radio Network
Regional Network: Texas State Networks
Arbitron Metro Market: Austin, TX *Format:* Talk *Hrs. of News Programming:* news progmg 10 hrs wkly *No. News Employees:* 1 *Target Audience:* Males 18-54.
Jenelle Schargios, General Manager

Roma

*KRIO-FM
04-30-1983; 97.7 mhz FM *Hrs Open:* 18; 3 kw; 298 ft; N26 24 22 W99 00 37
1201 N. Jackson Rd., Suite 900, McAllen, TX 50219
(956) 992-8895, *Fax:* (956) 992-8897
License: Roma, Starr County, TX held by Rio Grande Bible Institute
Nat'l Network: CNN Radio
Population Served: 50,000*Target Audience:* General; Sp speaking audience
Arturo Gonzalez, General Manager

Rosenburg-Richmond

KRTX
11-15-1948; 980 khz AM *Hrs Open:* 24
3102 Oak Lawn Ave., Suite 215, Dallas, TX 75219 US
(713) 589-1336, *Fax:* (713) 589-1335
www.radioaleluya.org
License: Rosenburg-Richmond, TX held by Aleluya Christian Broadcasting Inc.
Group Owner: Aleluya Christian Broadcasting Inc.; (acq 12-17-2008; $3 million)
Arbitron Metro Market: Pasadena, TX *Format:* Religious
Ruben Villarreal, General Manager

Round Rock

KFMK
10-01-1998; 105.9 mhz FM; 4.5 kw; 1302 ft.; N30 19 23 W97 47 58
600 Congress Ave., Ste 1400, Austin, TX 78701 US
(512) 329-4400, *Fax:* (512) 329-4380
www.spirit1059.com
info@spirit1059.com
License: Round Rock, Williamson County, TX held by Aloha Station Trust LLC
Arbitron Metro Market: Austin, TX *Format:* Christian
Mack Daniels, Operations Dir
Melody Caldwell, General Sales Mgr
Mel Jones, Programming Director
Pam McKay, Promotions Manager
Gil Garcia, Chief Engineer
Mitch Bordeno, Business Manager
Tracy Walker, Marketing Director

*KNLE-FM
08-17-1981; 88.1 mhz FM *Hrs Open:* 24; 3 kw; 233 ft.; N30 26 58 W97 39 44
Mailing Address: 12703 Research Blvd, Suite 222, Austin, TX 78759 US
Second Address: 12703 Research Dr., Suite 222, Austin, TX 78759
(512) 257-8881, *Fax:* (512) 257-8880
www.candle88.com
webmaster@candle88.com
License: Round Rock, Williamson County, TX held by Ixoye Productions Inc.
Arbitron Metro Market: Austin, TX *Format:* Adult Contemp *Special Programming:* Children 4 hrs wkly *Hrs. of News Programming:* News progmg 6 hrs wkly *Target Audience:* 18-49; primarily female
Sherland Priest, General Manager

Rudolph

*KTER
90.7 mhz FM *Hrs Open:* 24; 2.4 kw; 282 ft.; N26 41 13 W97 45 52
4501 West Expressway 83, Harlingen, TX 78552 US
(956) 412-5600, *Fax:* (956) 428-7556
License: Rudolph, Kenedy County, TX held by Faith Pleases God Church Corp.
Format: Christian *Special Programming:* Children 4 hrs wkly *Target Audience:* General.
Aracelis Ortiz, CEO
Clark Ortiz, President
Tonya Porter, Operations Dir
Ricardo Mejia, General Manager

Rusk

KTLU
01-01-1955; 1580 khz AM *Hrs Open:* 24; 0.84 kw-D, ND1; 0.165 kw-N, ND1; N31 49 12 W95 10 19
Mailing Address: P. O. Box 475, Rusk, TX 75785 US
Second Address: 618 N. Main St., Rusk, TX 75785
(903) 586-7771(903) 683-2257, *Fax:* (903) 683-5104
kwrw@mediactr.com
License: Rusk, TX held by E.H. Whitehead.
Nat'l Network: ABC *Regional Network:* Texas State Networks
Arbitron Metro Market: Tyler-Longview, TX *Format:* Oldies
Special Programming: Sp 10 hrs wkly *Hrs. of News Programming:* news progmg 3 hrs wkly *No. News Employees:* 1 *Target Audience:* 35-65.
Marie Whitehead, President
Robert Gonzalez, General Manager

KWRW
07-01-1981; 97.7 mhz FM *Hrs Open:* 24; 14.5 kw; 407 ft.; N31 49 12 W95 10 19
Mailing Address: Box 475, Rusk, TX 75785 US
Second Address: 618 N. Main St., Rusk, TX 75785
(903) 586-7771, *Fax:* (903) 683-5104
License: Rusk, Cherokee County, TX held by Marie Whitehead
Arbitron Metro Market: Rusk, TX *Special Programming:* Sp 10 hrs wkly *Target Audience:* 25-54. *Adv. Rates:* 9; 8; 9; 7.50
William Kling, President

San Angelo

KCRN
01-01-1947; 1340 khz AM *Hrs Open:* 24; 1 kw-U; N31 28 43 W100 27 50
Mailing Address: Box 32, San Angelo, TX 75261
Second Address: 17 S. Chadbourne, Suite 500, San Angelo, TX 76903
(325) 655-6917, *Fax:* (325) 655-7806
www.kcrn.org
License: San Angelo, Tom Green County, TX held by First Dallas Media Inc
Group Owner: Criswell Communications
Population Served: 100,000 *Arbitron Metro Market:* San Angelo, TX *Hrs. of News Programming:* News progmg 2 hrs wkly *Target Audience:* 35-54; adults with children in the home
John Grabie, President
Sharon Geiger, Operations Dir
Mark Mohr, General Manager
Mark Mohr, Programming Director
Keith Mayo, Chief Engineer

*KCRN-FM
02-01-1965; 93.9 mhz FM *Hrs Open:* 24; 100 kw; 650 ft.; N31 42 11 W100 19 20
Mailing Address: P.O. Box 619000, Dallas, TX 75261 US
Second Address: 17 S. Chadbourne, Suite 500, San Angelo, TX 76903

(325) 655-6917, *Fax:* (325) 655-7806
www.kcrn.org
mmohr@kcrn.org
License: San Angelo, Tom Green County, TX held by Criswell College
Group Owner: Criswell Communications; (acq 6-18-91; $350,000 with co-located AM;
Arbitron Metro Market: San Angelo, TX *Format:* Christian, Religious *Hrs. of News Programming:* News progmg 2 hrs wkly *Target Audience:* 25 plus.
Mark Mohr, Station Manager
Rachel Mohr, Administrative Assistant
Roland Nadeau, Business Underwriter
Steve Hayes, Production Director

KDCD

06-01-1980; 92.9 mhz FM; 100 kw; 600 ft.; N31 26 8 W100 34 8
3298 Sherwood Way, San Angelo, TX 76901 US
(325) 947-0899, *Fax:* (325) 947-0996
www.texaslonestarcountry.com
terry.radio@lonestarmix.com
License: San Angelo, Tom Green County, TX held by Four R Broadcasting Inc.
Arbitron Metro Market: San Angelo, TX *Format:* Country *Special Programming:* Relg 2 hrs wkly *Target Audience:* 18-49.
Frank De Francesco, President
Chris Ling, General Manager
Paul Gibson, Programming Director

KELI

11-01-1986; 98.7 mhz FM *Hrs Open:* 24; 93 kw; 1289 ft.; N31 22 1 W100 2 48
P.O. Box 3834, 910 W. 14th, San Angelo, TX 76902 US
(325) 655-7161, *Fax:* (325) 658-7377
www.bob987.com
License: San Angelo, Tom Green County, TX held by Double O Texas Corp.
Group Owner: Double O Radio L.L.C.; (acq 3-15-2006; grpsl)
Arbitron Metro Market: San Angelo, TX *Format:* Adult Contemp *Special Programming:* Relg 6 hrs wkly *Hrs. of News Programming:* news progmg 6 hrs wkly *No. News Employees:* 1 *Target Audience:* 25-54.
Dewey Weaver, General Manager
Randy Phair, General Sales Mgr
Boomer Kingston, Programming Director
Garry Vaughn, Engineering Dir

KGKL

12-04-1928; 960 khz AM
Mailing Address: P. O. Box 1878, San Angelo, TX 76902 US
Second Address: 1301 S. Abe, San Angelo, TX 76903
(325) 655-7161, *Fax:* (325) 658-7377
960kgkl.com
boomerkingston@townsquaremedia.com;
dewey.weaver@townsquaremedia.com;
ashley.haney@townsquaremedia.c
License: San Angelo, TX held by Double O Texas Corp.
Group Owner: Double O Radio L.L.C.; (acq 3-15-2006; grpsl)
Nat'l Reps: Katz Radio
Arbitron Metro Market: San Angelo, TX *Format:* News, Sports, 86 *Special Programming:* Farm 6 hrs wkly *Hrs. of News Programming:* News progmg 10 hrs wkly *Target Audience:* 35 plus.
Boomer Kingsten, Operations Dir
John Kerr, General Manager

KGKL-FM

12-24-1965; 97.5 mhz FM *Hrs Open:* 24; 100 kw; 410 ft.; N31 29 46 W100 24 50
Mailing Address: P. O. Box 1878, San Angelo, TX 76902 US
Second Address: 1301 S. Abe, San Angelo, TX 76903
(325) 655-7161, *Fax:* (325) 658-7377
www.975kgkl.com
boomerkingston@townsquaremedia.com;
dewey.weaver@townsquaremedia.com;
ashley.haney@townsquaremedia.c
License: San Angelo, Tom Green County, TX held by Double O Texas Corp.
Group Owner: Double O Radio L.L.C.
Nat'l Network: ABC
Arbitron Metro Market: San Angelo, TX *Format:* Country *Hrs. of News Programming:* News progmg 3 hrs wkly *Target Audience:* 25-54.
Boomer Kingston, Operations Dir
John Kerr, General Manager
Randy Phair, General Sales Mgr

KIXY-FM

10-01-1966; 94.7 mhz FM *Hrs Open:* 24; 100 kw; 358 ft.; N31 29 14 W100 26 57
2824 Sherwood Way, San Angelo, TX 76901 US
(325) 949-3333
www.kixyfm.com
kixy@kixyfm.com
License: San Angelo, Tom Green County, TX
Group Owner: Foster Communications Co. Inc.
Nat'l Network: CNN Radio *Nat'l Reps:* McGavren Guild
Arbitron Metro Market: San Angelo, TX *Format:* Adult Contemp, Contemporary Hits/Top 40 *No. News Employees:* 1 *Target Audience:* 18-49.
Shannon Roach, CFO
David Carr, Programming Director

KKSA

11-28-1954; 1260 khz AM *Hrs Open:* 24; 0.54 kw-D, ND2; 0.071 kw-N, ND2; N31 29 14 W100 26 57
Mailing Address: P.O. Box 2191, San Angelo, TX 76902 US
Second Address: KIXY Complex, 2824 Sherwood Way, San Angelo, TX 76902
(325) 949-2112, *Fax:* (325) 944-0851
www.kksa-am.com
kixy@kixyfm.com
License: San Angelo, TX held by Foster Communications Company Inc.
Group Owner: Foster Communications Co. Inc.; (acq 4-9-84).
Nat'l Network: Westwood One; CBS *Regional Network:* Texas State Networks *Nat'l Reps:* McGavren Guild *Wire Services:* UPI
Arbitron Metro Market: San Angelo, TX *Format:* News, News/Talk, 84, Talk *Hrs. of News Programming:* news progmg 20 hrs wkly *No. News Employees:* 1 *Target Audience:* 25-54.
Fred Key, CEO
Jay Michaels, Operations Dir
Doug Smith, General Sales Mgr

KMDX

12-05-1998; 106.1 mhz FM; 50 kw; 456 ft.; N31 26 8 W100 34 8
3298 Sherwood Way, San Angelo, TX 76901 US
(325) 947-0899, *Fax:* (325) 947-0996
www.themixonline.com
terry.radio@lonestarmix.com
License: San Angelo, Tom Green County, TX held by Four R Broadcasting Inc.
Nat'l Network: Jones Radio Networks *Nat'l Reps:* Interep
Arbitron Metro Market: San Angelo, TX *Format:* Adult Contemp *No. News Employees:* 1 *Target Audience:* 25-54.
Frank De Francesco, President
Aaron Harris, Operations Dir
Terry Hucks, General Manager
Biss Casey, News Director
Len Martinez, Engineering Dir
Debbie Smith, Traffic Manager

KSJT-FM

10-07-1985; 107.5 mhz FM *Hrs Open:* 24; 100 kw; 604 ft.; N31 26 19 W100 34 18
207 W Bearegard, San Angelo, TX 76903 US
(325) 655-1717, *Fax:* (325) 6557-0601
www.k107.net/K107-Guestbook.php
License: San Angelo, Tom Green County, TX held by La Unica Broadcasting Co.
Arbitron Metro Market: San Angelo, TX *Target Audience:* 18-55.
Louis Perez, President
Armando Martinez, Station Manager
Cody Austin, General Sales Mgr
Arturo Madrid, News Director
Dania Salas, Traffic Manager

*KNCH(FM)

04-01-1996; 90.1 mhz FM; 5 kw; 909 ft; N31 35 21 W100 31 00
Rebroadcasts: Rebroadcasts KUT(FM) Austin 100%
1 University Station A 0704, Univ. of Texas, Austin, TX 78712-1090
(512) 471-1631
kut@kut.org
License: San Angelo, Tom Green County, TX held by University of Texas at Austin.
Nat'l Network: NPR; PRI
Population Served: 100,000 *Arbitron Metro Market:* San Angelo, TX *Special Programming:* Folk 4 hrs, blues 6 hrs wkly *Target Audience:* 25-54; educated opinions, leaders and arts community
Stewart Vanderwilt, General Manager

KWFR

11-01-1995; 101.9 mhz FM *Hrs Open:* 24; 100 kw; 341 ft.; N31 29 29 W100 26 3
Mailing Address: 2824 Sherwood Way, San Angelo, TX 76901 US
Second Address: KIXY Complex, 2824 Sherwood Way, San Angelo, TX 76901
(325) 949-3333, *Fax:* (325) 944-0851
www.kwfrfm.com
kixy@kixyfm.com
License: San Angelo, Tom Green County, TX held by Foster Communications Co. Inc.
Group Owner: Foster Communications Co. Inc.; acq 12-1-94; $219,000 with KFXJ(FM) Abilene;
Nat'l Reps: McGavren Guild
Arbitron Metro Market: San Angelo, TX *Format:* Classic Rock *No. News Employees:* 1
Fred Key, President
Jay Michaels, Operations Dir
Doug Smith, General Sales Mgr
Chase O'Reily, Programming Director
Jeff Rottman, News Director
Adolph Ganza, Chief Engineer

KCLL

08-17-1995; 100.1 mhz FM *Hrs Open:* 24; 50 kw; 385 ft.; N31 31 49 W100 29 5
422 N. Van Buren St., San Angelo, TX 76901 US
(325) 949-3333, *Fax:* (325) 944-0851
www.kcll-fm.com
info@kcll-fm.com
License: San Angelo, Tom Green County, TX held by Foster Communications Co. Inc.
Group Owner: Foster Communications Co. Inc.; (acq 5-19-2004; $450,000).
Arbitron Metro Market: San Angelo, TX *Format:* Tejano *Target Audience:* 18-49; Hispanics, demographics
Fred M. Key, CEO/COO
Fred Key, President
Jay Michaels, General Manager
John Flynt, General Sales Mgr
Juan Vela, Programming Director
Freddy Maskill, Promotions Manager
Jeff Rottman, News Director

*KNAR

01-01-2006; 89.3 mhz FM; 1 kw; 801 ft.; N31 41 59 W100 26 30
Rebroadcasts: Rebroadcasts KLRD(FM) Yucaipa, CA 100%
188 South Bellevue, Suite 222, Memphis, TN 38104 US
(888) 937-2471, *Fax:* (916) 251-1650
www.air1.com
info@air1.com
License: San Angelo, Tom Green County, TX held by Educational Media Foundation.
Group Owner: EMF Broadcasting; (acq 9-22-2005; $40,000 for CP).
Nat'l Network: Air 1
Arbitron Metro Market: San Angelo, TX *Format:* Alternative, Christian
Darrell Chambliss, Chairman
Alan Mason, COO
Mike Novak, President and CEO
David Pierce, Programming Director
Ed Lenane, News Director
Sam Wallington, Engineering Dir
Marya Morgan, News Reporter
Richard Hunt, News Reporter
Eric Moser, Chief Financial Officer
Brian Burger, Vice President of Human Resources
D. Kevin Blair, Secretary and General Counsel
Larry Moody, Director

*KLTP

01-01-2008; 90.9 mhz FM; 2.915 kw; 627 ft.; N31 25 16 W100 32 36
US
(325) 673-3045, *Fax:* (325) 672-7938
www.kgnz.com
studio@kgnz.com
License: San Angelo, Tom Green County, TX held by Christian Broadcasting Co. Inc.
Arbitron Metro Market: San Angelo, TX *Format:* Christian
Gary Hill, General Manager

San Antonio

KAJA

01-01-1951; 97.3 mhz FM *Hrs Open:* 24; 98 kw; 984 ft.; N29 31 25 W98 43 25
200 Concord Plaza, Suite 600, San Antonio, TX 78216 US
(210) 736-9700, *Fax:* (210) 735 8811
www.kj97.com
pammckay@clearchannel.com
License: San Antonio, Bexar County, TX held by CCB Texas Licenses L.P.
Group Owner: Clear Channel Communications Inc.
Nat'l Reps: Clear Channel
Arbitron Metro Market: San Antonio, TX *Format:* Country *Hrs. of News Programming:* News progmg 2 hrs wkly *Target Audience:* 18-54.

Matt Martin, General Manager
Travis Moon, Programming Director
Jessica Fazende, Promotions Manager

KCHL

06-01-1960; 1480 khz AM *Hrs Open:* 15; 2.5 kw-D, DA2; 0.09 kw-N, DA2; N29 24 45 W98 24 52
4638 Decker Drive, Baytown, TX 77520 US
(210) 333-0050, *Fax:* (210) 333-0081
www.kchl.org
kchlradio@yahoo.com
License: San Antonio, TX held by Martin Broadcasting Inc.
Group Owner: Martin Broadcasting Inc.; acq 6-4-92;
Nat'l Reps: McGavren Guild
Arbitron Metro Market: San Antonio, TX *Format:* Gospel *No. News Employees:* 1 *Target Audience:* 25-54.
Darrel Martin, General Manager
Shouting Gail Barrett, Programming Director
Brett Huggins, Chief Engineer

KCOR

02-01-1946; 1350 khz AM; 5 kw-D, DAN; 5 kw-N, DAN; N29 31 27 W98 37 5
3102 Oak Lawn Ave., Suite 215, Dallas, TX 75219 US
(210) 821-6548, *Fax:* (210) 804-7825
www.univisionamerica.univision.com
License: San Antonio, TX held by Tichenor License Corp.
Group Owner: Univision Radio; (acq 9-22-2003; grpsl)
Arbitron Metro Market: San Antonio, TX *Format:* News, News/Talk, 86 *Target Audience:* 25-54; adults
Dan Wilson, General Manager

KCYY

06-25-1966; 100.3 mhz FM *Hrs Open:* 24; 98 kw; 984 ft.; N29 31 25 W98 43 25
3773 Howard Hughes Pwy, Suite 300n, Las Vegas, NV 89109 US
(210) 615-5400, *Fax:* (210) 615-5300
www.y100fm.com
License: San Antonio, Bexar County, TX
Group Owner: Cox Radio Inc.
Arbitron Metro Market: San Antonio, TX *No. News Employees:* 1 *Target Audience:* 25-54.
Alyce Ian, Operations Dir
Mark Bowka, General Sales Mgr
Randy Chase, Programming Director
Bill Jackson, Promotions Manager
Connye Rodriguez, News Director

KEDA

03-17-1966; 1540 khz AM; 5 kw-D, DA2; 1 kw-N, DA2; N29 21 30 W98 21 5
510 S. Flores, San Antonio, TX 78204 US
(210) 226-5254, *Fax:* (210) 227-7937
www.kedaradio.com
kedakid@aol.com
License: San Antonio, TX held by D & E Broadcasting Co.
Regional Network: Texas State Networks
Arbitron Metro Market: San Antonio, TX *Format:* Tejano *Special Programming:* Salsa 4 hrs wkly *Target Audience:* 25-54.
Madeline Davila, President
Alberto Davila, Operations Dir
Ricardo Davila, Programming Director
Susan Quijano, News Director
Bret Huggins, Chief Engineer
Eloy Espinoza, Disc Jockey

KRDY

11-13-1961; 1160 khz AM *Hrs Open:* 24; 10 kw-D, DA2; 1 kw-N, DA2; N29 32 11 W98 41 11
5400 Fredericksburg Rd., San Antonio, TX 78229 US
(210) 530-5360, *Fax:* (210) 530-5304
www.radio.disney.go.com
License: San Antonio, TX held by Radio Disney Group LLC.
Group Owner: ABC Inc.; (acq 5-30-2003; $3.2 million).
Nat'l Network: Radio Disney
Arbitron Metro Market: San Antonio, TX *Format:* Children
Fred Stockwell, General Manager

KFIT EXP S

01-01-1989; 1060 khz AM *Hrs Open:* 6 AM-8 PM; 1 kw-D, DA; N29 17 32 W98 31 57 *Rebroadcasts:* Rebroadcasts KFIT(AM) Lockhart
Mailing Address: 110 Wild Basin Rd., Box 160158, Lockhart, TX 78746
Second Address: 110 Wild Basin Rd., Suite 375, Austin, TX 78716
(512) 328-8400, *Fax:* (512) 328-8437
License: San Antonio, Bexar County, TX held by KFIT Inc.
Population Served: 500,000 *Arbitron Metro Market:* San Antonio, TX *Format:* Gospel

Rev. Darrell Martin, General Manager
Terri Lewis, Programming Director

KISS-FM

12-01-1946; 99.5 mhz FM; 97.7 kw; 1486 ft.; N29 16 29 W98 15 52
3773 Howard Hughes Pwy, Suite 300n, Las Vegas, NV 89109 US
(210) 646-0105, *Fax:* (210) 646-9711
www.kissrocks.com
virgil.thompson@cox.com
License: San Antonio, Bexar County, TX held by Cox Radio Inc.
Group Owner: Cox Radio Inc.; (acq 8-4-97; grpsl)
Nat'l Reps: Christal
Arbitron Metro Market: San Antonio, TX *Format:* Rock/AOR *Target Audience:* 18-44; men
Virgil Thompson, General Manager
Janis Maxymof, General Sales Mgr
Kevin Vargas, Programming Director
Jennifer Schultz, Promotions Manager
Steve Hahn, News Director
Richard Schuh, Chief Engineer
C.J. Cruz, Music Director

KKYX

01-01-1926; 680 khz AM *Hrs Open:* 24
3773 Howard Hughes Pwy, Suite 300n, Las Vegas, NV 89109 US
(210) 615-5400, *Fax:* (210) 615-5300
www.kkyx.com
License: San Antonio, TX held by Cox Radio Inc.
Group Owner: Cox Radio Inc.; (acq 3-28-97; grpsl)
Arbitron Metro Market: San Antonio, TX *Format:* Country *Special Programming:* Pub affrs 2 hrs wkly *Hrs. of News Programming:* news progmg 3 hrs wkly *No. News Employees:* 1 *Target Audience:* 35-64.
Bob Neil, CEO
Ben Reed, Operations Dir
Marty Choate, General Sales Mgr
George King, Programming Director
Julie Busse, Promotions Manager
Chrissie Murnin, News Director
Jim Bratt, National Sales Manager

KONO

01-01-1927; 860 khz AM *Hrs Open:* 24; 5 kw-D, 1 kw-N, DA-N; N29 26 14 W98 25 19
8122 Datapoint Dr., Suite 500, San Antonio, TX 89109
(210) 615-5400, *Fax:* (210) 615-5339
www.kono101.com
License: San Antonio, Bexar County, TX held by Cox Radio Inc.
Group Owner: Cox Radio Inc.; (acq 2-12-98; $23 million with KONO
Population Served: 1,300,000 *Arbitron Metro Market:* San Antonio, TX *Hrs. of News Programming:* news progmg one hr wkly *No. News Employees:* 1 *Target Audience:* 25-64; total audience appeal
Dan Lawrie, General Manager
Connie Tyra-Kremer, General Sales Mgr
Roger Allen, Programming Director
Sara Chadek, Promotions Manager
Chrissie Murrin, News Director
Paul Reynolds, Chief Engineer

*KPAC

11-07-1982; 88.3 mhz FM *Hrs Open:* 24; kw
8401 Datapoint Dr. #1050, San Antonio, TX 78229 US
(210) 614-8977, *Fax:* (210) 614-8983
www.tpr.org
info@tpr.org
License: San Antonio, Bexar County, TX held by Texas Public Radio.
Nat'l Network: PRI
Arbitron Metro Market: San Antonio, TX *Format:* Talk *Hrs. of News Programming:* News progmg 3 hrs wkly *Target Audience:* 25 plus; educated, upscale financially, mature, influential opinion leaders
Dan Skinner, President
Laverne Ditts, General Sales Mgr
Nathan Cone, Programming Director
Wayne Coble, Engineering Dir
Randy Anderson, Music Director
Janet Grojean, Sales

KQXT-FM

11-19-1967; 101.9 mhz FM *Hrs Open:* 24; 100 kw; 663 ft.; N29 25 6 W98 29 1
3305 W. Mountain Rd, #60, Las Vegas, NV 89102 US
(210) 736-9700, *Fax:* (210) 735-8811
www.q1019.com
License: San Antonio, Bexar County, TX held by CCB Texas Licenses L.P.

Group Owner: Clear Channel Communications Inc.; (acq 1-27-93; $8 million;
Regional Reps: Clear Channel.
Arbitron Metro Market: San Antonio, TX *Format:* Adult Contemp *Special Programming:* Contemp jazz 4 hrs, relg 2 hrs, pub affrs one hr w *Hrs. of News Programming:* news progmg 2 hrs wkly *No. News Employees:* 1 *Target Audience:* 25-54; core target is women 30-44
L. Lowry Mays, CEO
Tom Glade, General Manager
Mike McDonald, General Sales Mgr
Chase Murphy, Programming Director
Tim Kiesling, Promotions Manager
Randall Mays, CFO
Mark Mays, COO
Linda Hardy, General Sales Manager
SueNicholas, National Sales Manager
Marian Holdsworth, National Sales Manager
Bill Rohde, Promotions Director

KROM

06-01-1947; 92.9 mhz FM; 45 kw; 1352 ft.; N29 16 29 W98 15 52
3102 Oak Lawn Ave., Suite 215, Dallas, TX 75219 US
(210) 821-6548, *Fax:* (210) 804-7825
www.estereolatino929.univision.com/
License: San Antonio, Bexar County, TX held by Tichenor License Corp.
Group Owner: Univision Radio
Arbitron Metro Market: San Antonio, TX *Format:* Tejano *Target Audience:* 19-49; male
Jd Gonzalez, Operations Dir
Rosemary Scott, General Sales Mgr
Norma Perez, News Director

*KRTU-FM

01-22-1976; 91.7 mhz FM *Hrs Open:* 24; 8.9 kw; 118 ft.; N29 27 51 W98 28 56
715 Stadium Drive, San Antonio, TX 78284 US
(210) 999-8917, *Fax:* (210) 999-8355
www.krtu.org
krtu@trinity.edu
License: San Antonio, Bexar County, TX held by Trinity University
Arbitron Metro Market: San Antonio, TX *Format:* Jazz *Special Programming:* student alt-rock overnight *Target Audience:* well-connected, community-oriented opinion leaders; broad spectrum of ages, skewing 35-64;innovator *Adv. Rates:* 210-999-8337 - Kate Rawley-War
Rob Huesca, Operations Dir
William Christ, General Manager
Chris Karcher, General Sales Mgr
Ron Nirenberg, Programming Director
Kate Rawley-Warters, Director of Development
Alfredo Cruz, Music Director

KSLR

12-26-1926; 630 khz AM *Hrs Open:* 24; 5 kw-D, DA2; 4.3 kw-N, DA2; N29 23 29 W98 21 0; N29 31 50 W98 7 13
4880 Santa Rosa Rd #300, Camarillo, CA 93012 US
(210) 344-8481, *Fax:* (210) 340-1213
www.kslr.com
kslr@kslr.com
License: San Antonio, TX held by Salem Media of Texas Inc.
Group Owner: Salem Communications Corp.; (acq 8-6-94)
Nat'l Network: Salem Radio Network
Arbitron Metro Market: San Antonio, TX *Format:* Christian, Talk *Special Programming:* Sp 18 hrs wkly *No. News Employees:* 1 *Target Audience:* 18-54; women & families
Baron Wiley, Operations Dir
David Ziebell, General Manager
James Herring, General Sales Mgr

*KSTX

10-01-1988; 89.1 mhz FM *Hrs Open:* 24; kw
8401 Datapoint Drive, San Antonio, TX 78229 US
(210) 614-8977, *Fax:* (210) 614-8983
www.tpr.org
info@tpr.org
License: San Antonio, Bexar County, TX held by Texas Public Radio.
Nat'l Network: NPR; PRI *Wire Services:* AP
Arbitron Metro Market: San Antonio, TX *Format:* News *Special Programming:* Jazz 6 hrs, var talk 6 hrs, folk 5 hrs, blues 6 hrs wkly *Hrs. of News Programming:* news progmg 67 hrs wkly *No. News Employees:* 5 *Target Audience:* 25 plus; educated, upscale financially, influential opinion leaders
Pat MacGowan, Chairman
Dan Skinner, CEO/COO
Dan Skinner, President
Laverne Pitts, General Sales Mgr
Nathan Cone, Programming Director

RADIO - U.S.

Dave Davies, News Director
Wayne Coble, Engineering Dir
Janet Grojean, Sales

***KSYM-FM**
09-15-1966; 90.1 mhz FM *Hrs Open:* 24; 5.7 kw; 128 ft.; N29 26 50 W98 29 55
1300 San Pedro Avenue, San Antonio, TX 78212 US
(210) 733-2787, *Fax:* (210) 486-1373
www.ksym.org
ksym@accd.edu
License: San Antonio, Bexar County, TX held by San Antonio College.
Arbitron Metro Market: San Antonio, TX *Format:* Alternative, Triple A *Target Audience:* 12-54; depending on block format *Adv. Rates:* 15; 15; 20; 15
John Onderdonk, General Manager
Marlene Romo, General Sales Mgr
Charlie Castleman, Programming Director
Victor Pfau, Chief Engineer
Chelsea Owen-Music Director, Music Director

KJXK
01-01-1969; 102.7 mhz FM; 100 kw; 663 ft.; N29 25 6 W98 29 1
4050 Eisenhauer Road, San Antonio, TX 78218 US
(210) 528-5500, *Fax:* (210) 599-5588
www.1027krock.com
License: San Antonio, Bexar County, TX
Group Owner: Border Media Partners LLC
Arbitron Metro Market: San Antonio, TX *Format:* Contemporary Hits/Top 40 *Target Audience:* 12 plus.
John Cook, Programming Director

KTKR
05-10-1984; 760 khz AM *Hrs Open:* 24
3305 W. Mountain Rd, #60, Las Vegas, NV 89102 US
(210) 736-9700, *Fax:* (210) 735-8811
www.ticketsports.com
License: San Antonio, TX held by CCB Texas Licenses L.P.
Group Owner: Clear Channel Communications Inc.; (acq 6-16-93; $800,000;
Nat'l Network: Westwood One *Nat'l Reps:* Clear Channel
Arbitron Metro Market: San Antonio, TX *Format:* Sports *Target Audience:* 25-49; male
Matt Martin, General Manager
Tim Merryman, Programming Director
Abby Ferguson, Promotions Manager
Pam Mckay-Market Manager

KTSA
05-09-1922; 550 khz AM *Hrs Open:* 24
4050 Eisenhauer Road, San Antonio, TX 78218 US
(210) 528-5500, *Fax:* (210) 599-5588
www.ktsa.com
License: San Antonio, TX held by BMP San Antonio License Co. L.P.
Group Owner: Border Media Partners LLC; (acq 5-31-2007; $45 million with co-located FM)
Arbitron Metro Market: San Antonio, TX *Format:* News, News/Talk, 86 *Hrs. of News Programming:* news progmg 35 hrs wkly *No. News Employees:* 11 *Target Audience:* 25-54.
Lance Hawkins, General Manager
Christian Bove, News Director
Karen Clauss-AM News Anchor

KAHL
01-01-1948; 1310 khz AM *Hrs Open:* 24; 5 kw-D, DA2; 0.28 kw-N, DA2; N29 24 53 W98 20 36
3102 Oak Lawn Ave., Suite 215, Dallas, TX 75219 US
(210) 341-1310, *Fax:* (210) 341-1777
www.call1310.com
info@call1310.com
License: San Antonio, TX held by Pearsall RadioWorks Ltd.
Nat'l Reps: McGavren Guild
Arbitron Metro Market: San Antonio, TX *Format:* Adult Contemp
John Barger, President
John Barger, Sales Representative

KXTN-FM
12-31-1967; 107.5 mhz FM; 95.1 kw; 1486 ft.; N29 16 29 W98 15 52
3102 Oak Lawn Avenue, Suite 215, Dallas, TX 75219 US
(210) 829-1075, *Fax:* (210) 822-2372
www.kxtn.com
License: San Antonio, Bexar County, TX held by Tichenor License Corp.
Group Owner: Univision Radio
Arbitron Metro Market: San Antonio, TX *Format:* Tejano *Target Audience:* 25-49; contemp Sp, affluent, upscale
Kriby Kaden, Operations Dir
Kirby Kaden, General Sales Mgr

Norma Perez, News Director
Colleen Carnahan, Research Director

KXXM
05-05-1964; 96.1 mhz FM *Hrs Open:* 24; 99 kw; 597 ft.; N29 38 1 W98 37 54
200 Concord Plaza, Suite 600, San Antonio, TX 78216 US
(210) 736-9700, *Fax:* (210) 736-8811
www.mix961.com
tonytarvatto@clearchannel.com
License: San Antonio, Bexar County, TX held by CCB Texas Licenses L.P.
Group Owner: Clear Channel Communications Inc.; (acq 6-19-98; $15 million).
Arbitron Metro Market: San Antonio, TX *Format:* Contemporary Hits/Top 40 *Hrs. of News Programming:* news progmg 3 hrs wkly *No. News Employees:* 1 *Target Audience:* 18-34; females
Pam McKay, President
Tom Glade, Operations Dir
Mike Hall, General Sales Mgr
Chase Murphy, Programming Director
Abby Ferguson, Promotions Manager
Russell Rush, Asst. Program Director
Selena San Miguel, Digital ContentCoordinator

***KYFS**
11-07-1982; 90.9 mhz FM *Hrs Open:* 24; 100 kw; 476 ft.; N29 40 20 W98 14 43
8030 Arrowridge Blvd., Charlotte, NC 28273 US
(704) 523-5555, *Fax:* (704) 522-1967
www.bbnradio.org
bbn@bbnradio.org,info@kyzs.com
License: San Antonio, Bexar County, TX held by Bible Broadcasting Network Inc.
Group Owner: Bible Broadcasting Network; acq 11-20-91; $75,000;
Arbitron Metro Market: Charlotte, NC *Format:* Christian *Target Audience:* 2 plus.
John Woolery, General Manager

KZDC
01-01-1953; 1250 khz AM *Hrs Open:* 24
6290 Sunset Blvd, Suite 1600, Hollywood, CA 90028 US
(210) 654-5100, *Fax:* (210) 340-1775
www.espnsa.com/
License: San Antonio, TX held by BMP San Antonio License Co. L.P.
Group Owner: Border Media Partners LLC; (acq 3-312005; grpsl)
Nat'l Network: ESPN Radio
Arbitron Metro Market: San Antonio, TX *Format:* Sports
Lance Hawkins, General Manager
Bob Brown, General Sales Mgr

KZEP-FM
10-01-1966; 104.5 mhz FM *Hrs Open:* 24; 100 kw; 663 ft.; N29 25 6 W98 29 1
6290 Sunset Boulevard, Suite 1600, Hollywood, CA 90028 US
(210)736-9700, *Fax:* (210) 735-8811
www.kzep.com
staceybeigel@clearchannel.com
License: San Antonio, Bexar County, TX held by Citicasters Licenses L.P.
Group Owner: Clear Channel Communications Inc.; (acq 7-29-2008; exchange for KVMX(FM) Bakersfield, CA and KWID(FM) Las Vegas, NV)
Nat'l Reps: D & R Radio
Arbitron Metro Market: San Antonio, TX *Format:* Classic Rock *Hrs. of News Programming:* news progmg 3 hrs wkly *No. News Employees:* 1 *Target Audience:* 25-54; males
Jay Levine, President
Breanna Malik, General Sales Mgr
Craig Chambers, Programming Director
Abby Ferguson, Promotions Manager
Dave Delgado, News Director
Eddie Miles, Chief Engineer
Tom Scheppke, Music Director
BeckyTalamandes, Traffic Manager

WOAI
09-29-1922; 1200 khz AM; 50 kw-U, ND1; N29 30 7 W98 7 43
200 Concord Plaza, Suite 600, San Antonio, TX 78216 US
(210) 736-9700, *Fax:* (210) 735-8811
www.woai.com
License: San Antonio, TX held by CCB Texas Licenses L.P.
Group Owner: Clear Channel Communications Inc.; (acq 1975).
Nat'l Network: Fox News Radio *Regional Network:* Texas State Networks *Nat'l Reps:* Clear Channel *Wire Services:* AP
Arbitron Metro Market: San Antonio, TX *TV Affiliate:* Talk *Special Programming:* news progmg 20 hrs wkly *Hrs. of News Programming:* 13 *No. News Employees:* 35-64; general

Program Director, Gordie Taylor
Promotions Director, Jim Forsyth
News Director, News Director

San Augustine

KDET-FM
12-29-1993; 92.5 mhz FM *Hrs Open:* 24; 1.4 kw; Ant 220 ft; N31 31 44 W94 05 59 *Rebroadcasts:* Rebroadcasts KDET(AM) Center 100%
Box 930, Center, TX 75935
(936) 275-3242, *Fax:* (936) 598-9537
License: San Augustine, San Augustine County, TX held by Center Broadcasting Co. Inc.
Group Owner: Center Broadcasting Co. Inc.; acq 3-26-98; grpsl)
Nat'l Network: ABC *Regional Network:* Texas State Networks
Population Served: 25,000*No. News Employees:* 1 *Target Audience:* 35-65.
Barbara Harding, Operations Dir
Lori Alvis, General Sales Mgr
Rob Rockett, Programming Director
Rachel Shanz, News Director
Harlan Riley, Chief Engineer

San Benito

KHKZ
09-10-1982; 106.3 mhz FM *Hrs Open:* 24; 6.3 kw; 653 ft.; N26 8 33.3 W97 49 59.2
1050 McIntosh, Brownsville, TX 78521 US
(866) 973-1041, *Fax:* (956) 544-0311
www.kiss1063.net/pages/events.html
License: San Benito, Hidalgo County, TX held by Clear Channel Broadcasting Licenses Inc.
Group Owner: Clear Channel Communications Inc.; (acq 12-9-2003; grpsl).
Nat'l Network: USA
Arbitron Metro Market: McAllen-Brownsville-Harlingen, TX *Format:* Adult Contemp *Special Programming:* Black 3 hrs, southern gospel 2 hrs, Christian rock 3 hrs wkly *No. News Employees:* 3 *Target Audience:* General.
Billy Santiago, Operations Dir
Danny Fletcher, General Manager
Chris Aldrich, General Sales Mgr
J. Contu, Programming Director
Gloria Garcia, News Director
Ken Meek, Chief Engineer

San Diego

KUKA
07-14-1993; 105.9 mhz FM *Hrs Open:* 24; 10 kw; 413 ft.; N27 38 59 W98 7 44
P.O. Box 589, Alice, TX 78333 US
(361) 668-6666, *Fax:* (361) 668-6661
info@kuka.com
License: San Diego, Duval County, TX held by Claro Communications Ltd.
Group Owner: Claro Communications Ltd.; (acq 11-30-2007; $250,000)
Arbitron Metro Market: San Diego, TX *Hrs. of News Programming:* news progmg one hr wkly *No. News Employees:* 1 *Target Audience:* 18-34; middle to upper class *Adv. Rates:* 15; 10; 15; 10
Estela Nava, Operations Dir
Teo Pena, General Manager
Zulema Marroquin, General Sales Mgr
Pedro Vasquez, Programming Director
Tio Pena, Promotions Manager
Peter Vasquez, News Director
Armando Marroquin Jr., Marketing Manager
Javier Villanueva, Regional Sales Manager

San Isidro

***KMRV**
98.9 mhz FM; 3 kw; 23.7 meters; 26 42 N54 98 31 W50
License: San Isidro, TX held by Christian Ministries of the Valley Corp
Group Owner: Christian Ministries of the Valley Corp

San Juan

KUBR
01-01-1991; 1210 khz AM *Hrs Open:* 24; 10 kw-D, DA2; 5 kw-N, DA2; N26 14 41 W98 5 25; N26 14 38 W98 5 25
PO Box 252, McAllen, TX 78505 US
(956) 686-6382, *Fax:* (956) 686-2999
www.laradiocristiana.com
paylinobernal@hotmail.com
License: San Juan, TX held by Radio Christiana Network.

Arbitron Metro Market: San Juan, TX *Format:* Christian
Pete Guzman, Operations Dir
Paulino Bernal, General Manager
Eloy Bernal, Station Manager

San Marcos

KBPA
01-01-1971; 103.5 mhz FM *Hrs Open:* 24; 100 kw; 1257 ft.; N30 2 42 W97 52 50
200 Concord Plaza, # 600, San Antonio, TX 78216 US
(512) 832-4000, *Fax:* (512) 832-4081
www.1035bobfm.com
info@oldies103austin.com
License: San Marcos, Hays County, TX held by Emmis Austin Radio Broadcasting Co. L.P.
Group Owner: Emmis Communications Corp.; (acq 4-25-2003; grpsl).
Nat'l Reps: Clear Channel
Arbitron Metro Market: Austin, TX *Format:* Oldies *Hrs. of News Programming:* news progmg 4 hrs wkly *No. News Employees:* 1 *Target Audience:* 25-64.
Jeff Carrol, Operations Dir
Bruce Walden, General Manager
Tatjana Deegan, General Sales Mgr
Krash Kelly, Programming Director
Gary Weaver, Promotions Manager
Lisa Melton, News Director
Jim Henkle, Chief Engineer

*KTSW
04-15-1992; 89.9 mhz FM *Hrs Open:* 24; 10.5 kw; 213 ft.; N29 39 20 W98 7 59
601 University Drive, San Marcos, TX 78666 US
(512) 245-3485, *Fax:* (512) 245-3732
www.ktsw.net
ktsw@txstate.edu
License: San Marcos, Hays County, TX held by Texas State University-San Marcos.
Arbitron Metro Market: Austin, TX *Format:* Alternative, News, 62, Sports, Talk *Hrs. of News Programming:* News progmg 9 hrs wkly *Target Audience:* 18-24; college students & young adults
Dan Schumacher, General Manager
Jenn Kelly, Station Manager
Chris Green, Programming Director
Lauren Johnson, Promotions Manager
Greg Burnam, News Director
Tom Bruce, Engineering Dir
Jessie Clemons, Music Director
Taylor Wood,Office Manager
Taylor Wood, Production Director
Karl Schoening, Sports Director
Brandon Van Slyke, Webmaster

KUOL
01-01-1948; 1470 khz AM *Hrs Open:* 5:30 AM-midnight; 0.25 kw-D, DAN; 0.25 kw-N, DAN; N29 53 53 W97 54 44
P.O. Box 252, McAllen, TX 78502 US
(956) 686-6382, *Fax:* (956) 686-2999
www.laradiocristiana.com
paulinobernal@hotmail.com
License: San Marcos, TX held by Radio Christiana Network.
Arbitron Metro Market: San Marcos, TX *Format:* Christian
Pete Guzman, Operations Dir
Paulino Bernal, General Manager
Eloy Bernal, Station Manager

San Saba

KNUZ
01-01-1996; 106.1 mhz FM *Hrs Open:* 24; 3 kw; Ant 20 ft; N31 11 26 W98 42 55
PO Box 126, 705 South Live Oak, San Saba, TX 77802
(325) 372-5225, *Fax:* (325) 372-3817
License: San Saba, San Saba County, TX held by Roy E. Henderson
Regional Network: Texas State Networks
Target Audience: General.
Jeff Peterson, Operations Dir
Dan Seeman, General Manager
Bernie Laur, General Sales Mgr
Jon Blomstrand, Programming Director

KNVR
01-01-1954; 1410 khz AM *Hrs Open:* 24; 0.8 kw-D, ND1; 0.203 kw-N, ND1; N31 11 26 W98 42 55
2402 Broadmoor, Bldg, D-2, Suite 101, Bryan, TX 77802 US
(325) 372-5225, *Fax:* (325) 372-3817
www.sansabaradio.com
knuz@sansabaradio.com
License: San Saba, TX held by Roy E. Henderson
Regional Network: Texas State Networks
Arbitron Metro Market: San Saba, TX *Format:* Adult Contemp
Skeebo Norris, General Manager
Roy e. Henderson, Station Owner

Sanger

*KVRK
07-08-1999; 89.7 mhz FM *Hrs Open:* 24; 14 kw; 1,699 ft; N33 33 36 W96 57 35
11601 Shady Tr., Dallas, TX 75229
(214) 353-8970
www.kvrk.com
eddie@kvrk.com
License: Sanger, Denton County, TX held by Research Educational Foundation Inc.

Stanley Thomas, General Manager
Eddie Alcaraz, Station Manager
David Thomas, Operations Director
Chris Goodwin, Music Director
Dawn Henderson, Promotions Manager
Kent Loney, Chief Engineer

KTDK
12-01-1989; 104.1 mhz FM *Hrs Open:* 24; 6.2 kw; 630 ft.; N33 28 47 W97 3 22
140 East Market St, Dallas, TX 17401 US
(214) 526-2400, *Fax:* (214) 525-2525
www.theticket.com
License: Sanger, Denton County, TX held by KRBE Lico Inc.
Group Owner: Cumulus Media Partners LLC; (acq 4-30-98; $3.683 million).
Arbitron Metro Market: Dallas-Fort Worth, TX *Format:* Sports
Target Audience: 24-55; men & sports enthusiasts
Dan Bennett, Operations Dir
Dan Bennett, General Manager
Alec Drake, General Sales Mgr
Jeff Catlin, Programming Director
Marie Hompkins, Promotions Manager
Kimberly Jolly, News Director
Rob Chickering, Chief Engineer
KimRoberts, General Sales Manager
Tom Dailey, Human Resources
Rich Phillips, Asst. Program Director
Kimberly Jolly, Traffic Manager

Savoy

KQDR
01-01-2009; 107.3 mhz FM; 3.7 kw; 421 ft.; N33 42 31 W96 24 9 US
(903) 893-5625
www.1073docfm.com
License: Savoy, Fannin County, TX held by Prophecy Radio Group LLC.
Group Owner: William W. McCutchen III Stns
Arbitron Metro Market: Savoy, TX *Format:* Contemporary Hits/Top 40
Brad LaRock, General Manager

Schertz

KBBT
02-01-1976; 98.5 mhz FM *Hrs Open:* 24; 97 kw; 991 ft.; N29 31 25 W98 43 25
1428 Wiltshire, San Antonio, TX 78209 US
(210) 829-1075, *Fax:* (210) 804-7825
www.netmio.com,www.thebeatsa.com
info@netmio.com
License: Schertz, Guadalupe County, TX held by Univision Radio License Corp.
Group Owner: Univision Radio; (acq 9-22-2003; grpsl).
Arbitron Metro Market: San Antonio, TX *Format:* Urban Contemporary
Mac Tichenor, CEO
J. Gonzalez, Operations Dir
Dan Wilson, General Manager
Jeff Hinson, CFO

Scotland

KJKB
10-06-1996; 95.5 mhz FM *Hrs Open:* 24; 6 kw; 328 ft.; N33 19 43 W98 16 46
1776 East Tufts Avenue, Englewood, CO 80110 US
(940) 567-6600, *Fax:* (940) 567-6602
kjkb@boss9055.com
License: Scotland, Jack County, TX held by Hunt Broadcasting Inc.
Format: Classic Rock
Janice Hunt, CEO
Jim Hunt, President
Debbie Watts, Station Manager
Jerrod Knight, Programming Director

Seabrook

KROI
04-23-1984; 92.1 mhz FM *Hrs Open:* 24; 21.36 kw; 1726 ft.; N29 17 56 W95 14 11
Suite 5100, 1600 Smith Street, Houston, TX 77002 US
(713) 623-2108, *Fax:* (713) 623-8166
www.news92fm.com
License: Seabrook, Harris County, TX held by Radio One Licenses LLC.
Group Owner: Radio One Inc.; (acq 7-20-2004; $72.5 million).
Arbitron Metro Market: Houston, TX *Format:* Gospel *Target Audience:* General.
Alfred Liggins III, President
Doug Abernethy, General Manager
Denise Bishop, News Director
Scott Royster, Executive Vice President

Seadrift

KMAT
05-01-1999; 105.1 mhz FM *Hrs Open:* 24; 38.5 kw; Ant 456 ft; N28 26 17.1 W96 26 54.6
2424 South Blvd., Houston, TX 77079
(713) 520-7900, *Fax:* (713) 520-8104
License: Seadrift, Calhoun County, TX held by Cordell Communications Inc.
Population Served: 89,470*Hrs. of News Programming:* News progmg 2 hrs wkly *Target Audience:* 30-50.
Bill Cordell, President
Dolly Martin, Programming Director

Seguin

KSMG
09-09-1970; 105.3 mhz FM *Hrs Open:* 24; 97.5 kw; 1486 ft.; N29 16 29 W98 15 52
3773 Howard Hughes Pwy, Suite 300n, Las Vegas, NV 89109 US
(210) 615-5400, *Fax:* (210) 646-9711
www.magic1053.com
virgil.thompson@cox.com
License: Seguin, Guadalupe County, TX held by Cox Radio Inc.
Group Owner: Cox Radio Inc.; (acq 8-4-97; grpsl)
Nat'l Reps: Christal
Arbitron Metro Market: San Antonio, TX *Format:* Adult Contemp *Hrs. of News Programming:* news progmg 5 hrs wkly *No. News Employees:* 1 *Target Audience:* 25-49; females
Virgil Thompson, General Manager
Connie Kremer, General Sales Mgr
Doug Bennett, Programming Director
Karen Clauss, News Director
Richard Schuh, Chief Engineer
Katrina Curtiss, Music Director
Cathy Sheehan, Traffic Manager

KWED
09-09-1948; 1580 khz AM *Hrs Open:* 24; 1 kw-D, ND1; 0.253 kw-N, ND1; N29 34 48 W97 59 5
609 East Court Street, Seguin, TX 78155 US
(830) 379-2234, *Fax:* (830) 379-2238
www.seguintoday.com
contact@kwed1580.com
License: Seguin, TX held by Guadalupe Media, Ltd.
Nat'l Network: Westwood One; CNN Radio; Premiere Radio Networks *Nat'l Reps:* Rgnl Reps *Wire Services:* AP
Arbitron Metro Market: Seguin, TX *Format:* Country, News, 62, Talk *Special Programming:* Farm 6 hrs wkly *Hrs. of News Programming:* news progmg 30 hrs wkly *No. News Employees:* 5 *Target Audience:* 35-64.
Daeen Dunn, General Manager
Cindy Aguirre-Herrera, News Director
Richard Schuh, Chief Engineer
Rosie Pagan, Business office/Traffic Manager
Jessica Domel, Assistant News Director/ News Reporter
Georgia An Hester, AdvertisingConsultant
Priscilda Rios-Rodriguez, Classified Manager
Andie Rangel-Jenner, Print Production/ Photographer
Sennett Rockers, Sports Director

Seminole

KIKZ
04-15-1954; 1250 khz AM *Hrs Open:* 24; 1 kw-D, ND1; 0.25 kw-N, ND1; N32 41 58 W102 38 12
105 N.W. 11th Street, Seminol, TX 79360 US
(432) 758-5878, *Fax:* (432) 758-5474
License: Seminole, TX held by Gaines County Broadcasting LLC
Regional Network: Texas State Networks

Format: Country *Target Audience:* General.
Mike Elder, General Manager

KSEM
03-15-1985; 106.3 mhz FM *Hrs Open:* 24; 3 kw; Ant 174 ft; N32 41 58 W102 38 12
105 N.W. 11th St., Seminole, TX 79360
(432) 758-5878, *Fax:* (432) 758-5474
License: Seminole, Gaines County, TX held by Gaines County Broadcasting LLC.
Mike Elder, General Manager

Seymour

KSEY
10-26-1950; 1230 khz AM; 1 kw-U, ND1; N33 35 49 W99 16 42
P.O. Box 471, Seymour, TX 76380 US
(940) 889-2637, *Fax:* (940) 889-2665
fmksey@aol.com
License: Seymour, TX held by Mark Aulabaugh.
Wire Services: NWS (National Weather Service)
Arbitron Metro Market: Seymour, TX *Adv. Rates:* 18; 18; 18; 18
Mark Aulabaugh, General Manager
Orlando Jariez, Programming Director

KSEY-FM
06-26-1981; 94.3 mhz FM; 3 kw; 112 ft.; N33 35 49 W99 16 42
P.O. Box 471, Seymour, TX 76380 US
(940) 889-2637, *Fax:* (940) 889-2637
www.radioksey.com
info@ksey.com
License: Seymour, Baylor County, TX
Arbitron Metro Market: Seymour, TX *Format:* Variety/Diverse
Mark Aulabaugh, General Manager
Joe Gaither, Programming Director

Shanandoah

KRCM
07-01-1947; 1380 khz AM *Hrs Open:* 6 AM-6 PM; 1 kw-D, 127 w-N; N30 02 09 W94 08 31 *Rebroadcasts:* Rebroadcasts KOLE(AM) Port Arthur 50%
27 Sawyer St., Beaumont, TX 77070
(409) 835-1340,(409) 835-1340, *Fax:* (409) 832-5686
www.newsradiofox.com
manager@newsradiofox.com
License: Shanandoah, Jefferson County, TX held by Voice Broadcasting Inc.
Nat'l Network: Fox News Radio; Talk Radio Network; USA
Regional Network: Texas State Networks
Population Served: 115,917 *Arbitron Metro Market:* Beaumont-Port Arthur, TX *Hrs. of News Programming:* news progmg 40 hrs wkly *No. News Employees:* 2
Ralph McBride, President
Jeff Roberts, Operations Dir
Brent Bobbitt, General Sales Mgr
Dominick Brascia, Programming Director
Jeanette Harvey, News Director
Russ Ingram, Engineering Dir

Sherman

KJIM
12-19-1947; 1500 khz AM; 1 kw-D, DAD; N33 41 30 W96 33 29
Route 3 Box 176-K, Denison, TX 75020 US
(903) 893-1197
License: Sherman, TX held by Bob Mark Allen Productions Inc.
Nat'l Network: Westwood One; CBS
Format: News, Sports *Target Audience:* 40-65.
Bob Mark Allen, President

Silsbee

KAYD-FM
06-21-1980; 101.7 mhz FM; 10.5 kw; 503 ft.; N30 6 54 W93 59 56
103 Entrance Drive, Suite 1, Livingston, TX 77351 US
(409) 833-9421, *Fax:* (409) 833-9296
www.kayd.com
info@kayd.com
License: Silsbee, Hardin County, TX held by Cumulus Licensing LLC.
Group Owner: Cumulus Media Inc.; (acq 11-8-2004; $2.1 million).
Arbitron Metro Market: Beaumont-Port Arthur, TX *Format:* Country *Hrs. of News Programming:* News progmg 20 hrs wkly *Target Audience:* 25-54; persons *Adv. Rates:* 55; 50; 55; 40.
Jim West, Operations Dir
Zanetta Kelley, General Manager
Wes Matejka, General Sales Mgr
Mark Guzman, Promotions Manager

Liz Ferguson, News Director
J.P. White, Sports Commentator

Sinton

KDAE
01-01-1954; 1590 khz AM *Hrs Open:* 24; 1 kw-D, DA2; 0.5 kw-N, DA2; N28 1 16 W97 28 14
Mailing Address: P.O. Box 2010, Boerne, TX 78006 US
Second Address: 929 N. Padre Island Dr., Corpus Christi, TX 78406
(361) 299-1982, *Fax:* (361) 299-1049
www.radiolibertad.net
License: Sinton, TX held by The Worship Center of Kingsville.
Nat'l Network: ABC *Nat'l Reps:* McGavren Guild
Arbitron Metro Market: Corpus Christi, TX *Format:* Adult Contemp, Christian, 82 *Special Programming:* Farm 6 hrs wkly *Hrs. of News Programming:* news progmg 2 hrs wkly *No. News Employees:* 1 *Target Audience:* 35-64.
Rufino Sendejo, General Manager
A.J. Solis, Programming Director
George Sanders, Chief Engineer

KNCN
07-01-1972; 101.3 mhz FM *Hrs Open:* 24; 100 kw; 361 ft.; N27 55 24 W97 25 26
600 Congress Ave., Suite 1400, Austin, TX 78701 US
(361) 289-0111, *Fax:* (361) 289-5035
www.c101.com
c101@clearchannel.com
License: Sinton, San Patricio County, TX held by Capstar TX L.P.
Group Owner: Clear Channel Communications Inc.; (acq 8-30-00; grpsl).
Arbitron Metro Market: Corpus Christi, TX *Format:* Rock/AOR
Special Programming: Coastal Bend Forum one hr, In Concert 2 hrs, In th *Hrs. of News Programming:* News progmg one hr wkly
Target Audience: 18-49;active
Matt Martin, General Manager

Slaton

KJAK
02-12-1978; 92.7 mhz FM *Hrs Open:* 24; 100 kw; 584 ft.; N33 32 32 W101 50 14
P.O. Box 3890, Lubbock, TX 79452 US
(806) 745-6677, *Fax:* (806) 745-8140
www.kjak.com
kjak@kjak.com
License: Slaton, Lubbock County, TX held by G.O. Williams Oil Co. Inc. dba Williams Broadcasting Group
Arbitron Metro Market: Lubbock, TX *Format:* Christian *Special Programming:* Sports 5 hrs wkly *Target Audience:* General; Christians & those looking for answers to everyday problems
Woody Van Dyke, General Manager
Bob Howell, News Director
Roger Taylor, Chief Engineer

Snyder

KSNY
12-22-1949; 1450 khz AM *Hrs Open:* 24; 1 kw-U; N32 43 33 W100 56 30
Mailing Address: Box 1008, Snyder, TX 79550
Second Address: 2301 Ave. R, Snyder, TX 79549
(325) 573-9322, *Fax:* (325) 573-7445
lydia@ksnyradio.com
License: Snyder, Scurry County, TX held by Snyder Broadcasting Co.
Nat'l Network: ABC
Population Served: 11,171*Target Audience:* General.
Lydia Foree, Operations Dir
Dink Foree, General Manager
Alice Swiney, Programming Director

KSNY-FM
09-02-1980; 101.5 mhz FM *Hrs Open:* 24; 35 kw; 500 ft; N32 53 29 W101 06 29
Mailing Address: Box 1008, Snyder, TX 79550
Second Address: 2301 Ave. R, Snyder, TX 79550
(325) 573-9322, *Fax:* (325) 573-7445
lydia@ksnyradio.com
License: Snyder, Scurry County, TX held by Snyder Broadcasting Company
Nat'l Network: ABC
Hrs. of News Programming: news progmg 5 hrs wkly *No. News Employees:* 1 *Target Audience:* 25-54.
Lydia Foree, Operations Dir
Dink Foree, General Manager
Alice Swiney, Programming Director

KLYD
01-01-2003; 98.9 mhz FM *Hrs Open:* 24; 5.6 kw; 341 ft.; N32 45 23 W100 54 9
2800 34th Street, Snyder, TX 79549 US
(415) 975-5555, *Fax:* 415) 541-3087
www.wild949.com
tonyng@clearchannel.com?subject=Wild%2094.9%20Website
License: Snyder, Scurry County, TX held by Delbert Foree.
Arbitron Metro Market: San Francisco, CA *Format:* Rock/AOR
Dink Foree, General Manager
Anne Hudson, General Sales Mgr
Tony Ng, Promotions Manager
JayPlus, Assistant Promotion Director

***KGWB**
08-04-2008; 91.1 mhz FM; 0.24 kw; 36 ft.; N32 40 46 W100 54 51
US
(325) 573-8511, *Fax:* (325) 573-9321
wtc.edu/kgwb/
ifo@wtc.edu
License: Snyder, Scurry County, TX held by Scurry County Junior College District.
Arbitron Metro Market: Snyder, TX *Format:* Variety/Diverse
Mike Thornton, President
Bob Lewis, General Manager
Jim Palmer, Interim Vice President of Instruction
Patricia Claxton, Chief Financial Officer

Somerset

KYTY
03-01-1988; 810 khz AM *Hrs Open:* 24; 250 w-U, DA-2; N29 18 48 W98 30 29
Box 701582, San Antonio, TX 78270
(210) 545-0810, *Fax:* (210) 545-6713
www.star810.com
staram810@yahoo.com
License: Somerset, Bexar County, TX held by Maranatha Broadcasting Inc.
Population Served: 1,200,000 *Arbitron Metro Market:* San Antonio, TX *Target Audience:* 35-45; female
Mary Kaye, Operations Dir
Myron Wade, General Manager
Reuben Garcia, Programming Director

Sonora

KHOS-FM
05-01-1979; 92.1 mhz FM *Hrs Open:* 24; 3 kw; 299 ft.; N30 33 33 W100 37 54
Hc 65, Box 50, Sonora, TX 76950 US
(915) 387-3553, *Fax:* (915) 387-3554
khoskyxx@verizon.net
License: Sonora, Sutton County, TX held by Foster Charitable Foundation Inc.
Group Owner: Revolution Broadcast Company of the West; (acq 5-31-2007)
Nat'l Network: ABC *Regional Network:* Texas State Networks; Voice of Southwest Agriculture Radio
Format: Country *Target Audience:* 12-50 plus.
Marti Ashcraft, Operations Dir
Eddy Smith, Engineering Dir

South Padre Island

KESO
08-27-1996; 92.7 mhz FM *Hrs Open:* 24; 38 kw; 461 ft.; N26 3 12.8 W97 12 46.4
Mailing Address: P.O. Box 3907, South Padre Island, TX 78597 US
Second Address: PO Box 3907, McAllen, TX 78597
(956) 992-8895, *Fax:* (956) 992-8897
www.clubaley1025.com
License: South Padre Island, Cameron County, TX held by BMP RGV License Company L.P.
Group Owner: Border Media Partners LLC; (acq 1-28-2005; $6.6 million with KZSP(FM) South Padre Island)
Arbitron Metro Market: McAllen-Brownsville-Harlingen, TX
Format: Tejano
Terry Kimball, Station Manager
Jim Wilson, Programming Director

KZSP
07-27-1990; 95.3 mhz FM *Hrs Open:* 24; 2.9 kw; 421 ft.; N26 3 12.8 W97 12 46.4 *Rebroadcasts:* Simulcast with KURV(AM) Edinburg 100%
5009 Padre Blvd, Suite 16, South Padre Island, TX 78597 US
(956) 992-8895, *Fax:* (956) 992-8897
License: South Padre Island, Cameron County, TX held by BMP RGV License Company L.P.

Group Owner: Border Media Partners LLC; (acq 1-28-2005; $6.6 million with KESO(FM) South Padre Island)
Arbitron Metro Market: South Padre Island, TX *Format:* News, News/Talk, 86
Jose Munoz, General Manager

Spearman

KXDJ
12-16-1963; 98.3 mhz FM *Hrs Open:* 24; 17.5 kw; 837 ft.; N36 3 44 W101 1 56
P. O. Box 307, Spearman, TX 79081 US
(806) 648-2650, *Fax:* (806) 648-2652
www.kxdjradio.com
License: Spearman, Hansford County, TX held by Chris Samples Broadcasting
Nat'l Network: CBS Radio; AP Radio
Arbitron Metro Market: Amarillo, TX *Format:* Country *Hrs. of News Programming:* News progmg 25 hrs wkly *Adv. Rates:* 12; 12; 12; 12
Chris Samples, President
Chris Samples, General Manager

*KTOT
01-01-2003; 89.5 mhz FM *Hrs Open:* 24; 100 kw; 1066 ft.; N36 3 44 W101 1 56
207 N. 7th Street, Garden City, KS 67846 US
(620) 275-7444, *Fax:* (620) 275-7496
www.hppr.org
hppr@hppr.org
License: Spearman, Hansford County, TX held by Kanza Society Inc.
Nat'l Network: AP Radio; NPR; PRI
Arbitron Metro Market: Spearman, Texas *Format:* News *Target Audience:* 25-80; educated
Don Close, President
Richard Hicks, General Manager
Diana Gonzales, General Sales Mgr
Bob Kirby, Programming Director
Dean Yates, Promotions Manager
Chuck Springer, Chief Engineer
Rod Buchele, Vice President
Quentin Hope,Treasurer
Gary Pitner, Secretary
Barb Blevins, Community Donor Relations Assistant
Deb Oyler, Executive Director

Springtown

*KSQX
08-01-1985; 89.1 mhz FM *Hrs Open:* 24; 3 kw; 184 ft.; N32 58 53 W97 42 18
11061 Shady Trail, Dallas, TX 75229 US
(817) 341-2337, *Fax:* (817) 613-0230
www.kyqx.com
chb890@swbell.net
License: Springtown, Parker County, TX held by CSSI Non-Profit Educational Broadcasting Corp.
Format: Big Band, News, 64, Talk *Hrs. of News Programming:* news progmg 5 hrs wkly *No. News Employees:* 3
Charles Beard, CEO
Mindy Beard, President

Stamford

KLGD
02-22-1999; 106.9 mhz FM; 40 kw; 548 ft.; N32 56 16 W99 57 20
919 North Main, PO Box 1629, Cleburne, TX 76033 US
(915) 691-5400, *Fax:* (915) 691-5653
countrylegends.com
bruce@texas96.com
License: Stamford, Jones County, TX held by Texas Gulfwest Communications Corp.
Arbitron Metro Market: Abilene, TX *Format:* Country *Target Audience:* 35 plus; adults *Adv. Rates:* 25; 20; 25;15
Bill Hooten, CEO
Pete Garcia, Programming Director

KVRP
07-01-1947; 1400 khz AM *Hrs Open:* 24; 1 kw-U; N32 55 52 W99 47 00
Box 1118, 1406 N. First St., Haskell, TX 79521
(940) 864-8505, *Fax:* (940) 864-8001
www.kvrp.com
gary@kvrp.com
License: Stamford, Jones County, TX held by 1 Chronicles 14 L.P.
Group Owner: Weston Entertainment L.P.; (acq 8-4-2004; $700,000 with KVRP-F
Nat'l Network: Salem *Nat'l Reps:* Salem
Population Served: 50,000 *Arbitron Metro Market:* Abilene, TX *Target Audience:* 35+.
Gregg Weston, President
Gary Barrett, General Manager
Gary Barrett, General Sales Mgr
Dave Harrison, Programming Director
James Thompson, Chief Engineer

Stanton

*KFLB-FM
09-01-1989; 88.1 mhz FM *Hrs Open:* 24; 100 kw; 457 ft.; N32 5 44 W101 48 47
1425 N. Market Blvd, Suite 9, Sacramento, CA 95834 US
(520) 742-6976, *Fax:* (520) 469-7312
www.myflr.org
License: Stanton, Ector County, TX held by Family Life Broadcasting Inc.
Group Owner: Family Life Communications Inc.
Arbitron Metro Market: Odessa-Midland, TX *Format:* Christian, Religious
Warren J. Bolthouse, Chairman
Randy L. Carlson, President
Bart Jones, Operations Dir
Sharon Behl Brooks, General Manager
Tyler Maffitt, Station Manager
Adam Biddell, Programming Director

Stephenville

KSTV
01-01-1947; 1510 khz AM; 0.5 kw-D, NDD; N32 12 8 W98 14 54
P. O. Box 289, Stephenville, TX 76401 US
(254) 968-2141, *Fax:* (254) 968-6221
www.kstvfm.com
kstv@htcomp.net
License: Stephenville, TX held by CCR-Stephenville III LLC.
Group Owner: Cherry Creek Radio LLC; (acq 6-24-2004; grpsl).
Arbitron Metro Market: Stephenville, TX *Format:* Tejano *Special Programming:* Farm 5 hrs, relg 6 hrs wkly *Target Audience:* 54 plus; general
Robert Elliott, General Manager
Bob Haschke, General Sales Mgr
Jose Perez, Promotions Manager
Lorena Rodriquez, News Director
Justin McClure, Chief Engineer
Troy Stark, Traffic Manager

*KQXS
01-01-2004; 89.1 mhz FM; 1.2 kw vert; 424 ft.; N32 16 9 W98 18 51
206 Wiggs Lane, Weatherford, TX 76086 US
(817) 341-8950, *Fax:* (817) 596-9842
qxfmnews@yahoo.com
License: Stephenville, Erath County, TX held by CSSI Non-Profit Educational Broadcasting Corp.
Arbitron Metro Market: Abilene, TX *Format:* Big Band, News, 64 *No. News Employees:* 3
Jean Hudgens, General Manager

*KEQX
89.7 mhz FM *Hrs Open:* 24; 6 kw vert; 492 ft.; N32 7 24 W97 58 48
P.O. Box 801, Mansfield, TX 76063 US
(254) 445-2473, *Fax:* (254) 445-2765
www.keqx897.com
qxfmnews@yahoo.com
License: Stephenville, Erath County, TX held by CSSI Non-Profit Educational Broadcasting Corp.
Arbitron Metro Market: Stephenville, TX *Format:* Country
Jean Hudgens, General Manager
Sam Upshaw, Owner
Robert Webb, Production

Sterling City

KNRX
12-01-1998; 96.5 mhz FM *Hrs Open:* 24; 40 kw; 545 ft.; N31 35 56 W100 50 42
6999 East Highway 80, Odessa, TX 79762 US
(325) 655-7161, *Fax:* (325) 658-7377
965therock.com
License: Sterling City, Sterling County, TX held by Double O Texas Corp.
Group Owner: Double O Radio L.L.C.; (acq 3-15-2006; grpsl)
Arbitron Metro Market: San Angelo, TX *Format:* Classic Rock *Target Audience:* 25-64. *Adv. Rates:* 10; 10; 10; 10
Dewey Weaver, General Manager
Randy Phair, General Sales Mgr
Boomer Kingston, Programming Director
Garry Vaughn, Engineering Dir

Stockdale

KQQB
09-05-1979; 1520 khz AM *Hrs Open:* Sunrise-sunset; 2.5 kw-D; N29 26 38 W96 57 22
111 N. Main St., Hallettsville, TX 77965
(361) 798-4333, *Fax:* (361) 798-3798
texasthunderradio@yahoo.com
License: Stockdale, Lavaca County, TX held by Matthew Provenzano
Regional Network: Texas State Networks *Wire Services:* NWS (National Weather Service)
Special Programming: Farm 5 hrs, Czech 5 hrs, Ger 5 hrs wkly *Hrs. of News Programming:* news progmg 13 hrs wkly *No. News Employees:* 1 *Target Audience:* General.
Laura Kremling, General Manager
Travis Kremling, Programming Director

Stratford

*KOGW
91.1 mhz FM; 100 w horiz; Ant 118 ft; N36 19 31 W102 03 11
116 Hillcrest Dr., Seminole, OK
(405) 380-3516
www.bpba.us
info@bpba.us
License: Stratford, Sherman County, TX held by Better Public Broadcasting Association.
Dennis Burton, General Manager

Sulphur Bluff

KETE
99.7 mhz FM; 6 kw; Ant 318 ft; N33 27 29 W95 19 35
410 N. Jefferson Ave., Suite 298, Mt. Pleasant, TX
(903) 717-8305
License: Sulphur Bluff, Hopkins County, TX held by La Ke Manda Broadcasting.
Leo Ashcraft, General Manager

Sulphur Springs

KSCH
08-30-1982; 95.9 mhz FM *Hrs Open:* 24; 6 kw; 285 ft.; N33 9 7 W95 36 12 *Rebroadcasts:* Rebroadcasts KSCN(FM) Pittsburg 90%
P.O. Box 990, Mount Pleasant, TX 75456 US
(903) 885-1546, *Fax:* (903) 572-7232
www.easttexasradio.com
hitmusic@klake.net
License: Sulphur Springs, Hopkins County, TX held by East Texas Broadcasting Inc.
Group Owner: East Texas Broadcasting Inc.; acq 9-30-99).
Arbitron Metro Market: Sulphur Springs, TX *Format:* Country *Hrs. of News Programming:* news progmg 13 hrs wkly *No. News Employees:* 3 *Target Audience:* 18-60. *Adv. Rates:* 22.50; 21; 22.50; 17
J.R. Kitchens Jr., President
Daniel Osuna, General Manager

KSST
03-01-1947; 1230 khz AM *Hrs Open:* 24; 1 kw-U, ND1; N33 7 0 W95 35 5
Mailing Address: PO Box 284, Sulphur Springs, TX 75482 US
Second Address: 717 Shannon Rd. E., Sulphur Springs, TX 75482
(903) 885-3111, *Fax:* (903) 885-4160
www.ksstradio.com
ksst@neto.com
License: Sulphur Springs, TX held by Hopkins County Broadcasting Co.
Nat'l Network: ABC *Regional Network:* Texas State Networks
Arbitron Metro Market: Sulphur Spring, tx *Format:* Variety/Diverse, Adult Contemp *Hrs. of News Programming:* news progmg 30 hrs wkly *No. News Employees:* 2 *Target Audience:* 25-54.
William Bradford, CEO
Dwayne Grimes, Operations Dir
Enola Gay, Promotions Manager
Don Julian, News Director
Patsy Bradford, Advertising Director

Sweetwater

KXOX
11-01-1939; 1240 khz AM *Hrs Open:* 24; 1 kw-U, ND1; N32 29 16 W100 23 31
Mailing Address: P. O. Box 570, Sweetwater, TX 79556 US
Second Address: 1801 Hoyt Ln., Sweetwater, TX 79556
(325) 236-6655, *Fax:* (325) 235-4391
www.kxox.net
kxox@sweetwaternet.com

License: Sweetwater, TX held by Stein Broadcasting Inc.
Regional Network: Texas State Networks *Wire Services:* AP
Arbitron Metro Market: Sweetwater, TX *Format:* Country *Special Programming:* Farm 5 hrs, Sp 8 hrs, gospel 4 hrs wkly *Hrs. of News Programming:* News progmg 2 plus hrs wkly *Target Audience:* 25-54.
Jack Stein, President
Jeff Stein, General Manager
Rosie Tovar, General Sales Mgr
Richard Ferguson, Programming Director
Gary Graham, Chief Engineer

KXOX-FM
04-07-1976; 96.7 mhz FM *Hrs Open:* 18; 2.9 kw; Ant 154 ft; N32 29 16 W100 23 31
Mailing Address: Box 570, Sweetwater, TX 79556
Second Address: 1801 Hoyt Ln., Sweetwater, TX 79556
(325) 236-6655, *Fax:* (325) 235-4391
License: Sweetwater, Nolan County, TX held by Stein Broadcasting Co. Inc.
Wire Services: AP
No. News Employees: 1
Jeff Stein, Chairman
Jeff Stein, CEO/COO
Rosie Tovar, General Sales Mgr
Richard Ferguson, Programming Director
Jeff Stein, News Director
Gary Graham, Engineering Dir
Kyle Davian, Disc Jockey
Lillie Guttierez, SpanishDirector

Tahoka

KAMZ
01-01-2001; 103.5 mhz FM *Hrs Open:* 24; 20 kw; 328 ft.; N33 19 26 W101 48 15
4821 73rd Street, Lubbock, TX 79424 US
(806) 741-0701, *Fax:* (806) 741-0705
License: Tahoka, Lynn County, TX held by Albert Benavides.
Arbitron Metro Market: Lubbock, TX *Format:* Tejano
Rick Benavides, General Manager
Bob Benavides, Programming Director
Lou Gum, News Director
Bill Enloe, Chief Engineer

KMMX
08-13-1987; 100.3 mhz FM *Hrs Open:* 24; 100 kw; 883 ft.; N33 26 31 W101 52 40
1705 West Northwest Hgwy, Suite 275, Grapevine, TX 76051 US
(806) 762-3000, *Fax:* (806) 762-8419
www.kmmx.com
License: Tahoka, Lynn County, TX held by Wilks License Co.-Lubbock LLC.
Group Owner: Wilks Broadcast Group LLC; (acq 8-19-2005; grpsl).
Nat'l Network: ABC
Arbitron Metro Market: Lubbock, TX *Format:* Adult Contemp *Hrs. of News Programming:* news progmg 5 hrs wkly *No. News Employees:* 1 *Target Audience:* 25-54; females
Jeff Scott, Operations Dir
Scott Harris, General Manager
Jay Richards, General Sales Mgr
Damon Scott, Programming Director
Stacey James, News Director
Randy Hayes, Chief Engineer
Julie Aguilar, Traffic Manager

Tatum

KZQX
08-01-1965; 100.3 mhz FM *Hrs Open:* 24; 2.45 kw; Ant 518 ft; N32 22 37 W94 34 18
Mailing Address: Box 1648, Jacksonville, TX 80110
Second Address: 402 Ragsdale, Jacksonville, TX 75766
(903) 586-2527, *Fax:* (903) 589-0677
dudleyw@wallerbroadcasting.com
License: Tatum, Rusk County, TX held by Waller Media LLC.
Group Owner: Waller Broadcasting; (acq 8-24-2005; $975,000 with KDVE(FM) Pittsburg).
Population Served: 250,000 *Arbitron Metro Market:* Tyler-Longview, TX *Target Audience:* 25-54.
Dudley Waller, General Manager
Chris Ousley, General Sales Mgr
Victor Covarrubias, Programming Director

Taylor

KLQB
04-04-1975; 104.3 mhz FM *Hrs Open:* 24; 48 kw; 492 ft.; N30 26 4 W97 21 53
600 New Hampshire Ave., Suite 1200, Washington, DC 20037 US
(512) 381-1077, *Fax:* (512) 340-7100
www.laquebuena1043.univision.com
License: Taylor, Williamson County, TX held by Entercom Austin License Inc.
Group Owner: Entercom Communications Corp.; (acq 11-30-2007; grpsl)
Nat'l Reps: Katz Radio
Arbitron Metro Market: Austin, TX *Format:* Tejano
Clint Culp, Operations Dir
Rodney Brown, General Sales Mgr
Dusty Hayes, Programming Director
Carla Spears, Promotions Manager
Darell Heckendorf, Engineering Dir
John Hiatt, Marketing Manager

KWNX
04-01-1948; 1260 khz AM *Hrs Open:* 24
P.O. Box 484, Austin, TX 78767 US
(512) 346-8255, *Fax:* (512) 346-8262
www.espnaustin.com
controlroom@espnaustin.com
License: Taylor, TX held by Simmons-Austin, LS LLC.
Group Owner: Simmons Media Group; (acq 5-17-2004; $950,000).
Nat'l Network: ESPN Deportes
Arbitron Metro Market: Austin, TX *Format:* Sports
Steve Wilder, General Manager
Neil Parker, Promotions Manager
Flavia Chen, News Director
J. Cole McClellan, Chief Engineer

Temple

***KBDE**
01-01-2001; 89.9 mhz FM; 11.5 kw vert; 489 ft.; N31 16 5 W97 21 34
P.O. Drawer 2240, Tupelo, MS 38803 US
(254) 772-1900
License: Temple, Bell County, TX held by American Family Association.
Group Owner: American Family Radio
Arbitron Metro Market: Temple, TX *Format:* Christian
Marvin Sanders, General Manager

KLTD
01-01-1995; 101.7 mhz FM; 16.5 kw; 410 ft.; N31 16 24 W97 23 31
P. O. Box 1110, Temple, TX 76503 US
(254) 773-5252, *Fax:* (254) 547-2394
www.1017theticket.com
info@kltdfm.com
License: Temple, Bell County, TX held by Cumulus Licensing Corp.
Group Owner: Cumulus Media Inc.; (acq 4-20-01; $1.5 million including $50,000 noncompete agreement).
Arbitron Metro Market: Killeen, TX *Format:* Sports
Joyce Marshall, General Manager
Mikie Cummings, General Sales Mgr
Tom Rivers, Programming Director
Jamie Garrett, Promotions Manager
Chris Cummings, News Director
Doug Bernhardt, Chief Engineer
Thalesa Hector-Dixon, TrafficManager
John Medina, Brand manager

KTEM
11-25-1936; 1400 khz AM *Hrs Open:* 24
301 North Main, Temple, TX 76501 US
(254) 773-5252, *Fax:* (254) 773-0115
www.myktem.com
jamie.garrett@cumulus.com
License: Temple, TX held by Cumulus Licensing Corp.
Group Owner: Cumulus Media Inc.; (acq 3-12-01; $425,000).
Nat'l Network: CBS
Arbitron Metro Market: Temple, TX *Format:* News, News/Talk, 84, Talk *Special Programming:* Czech 3 hrs wkly *Hrs. of News Programming:* news progmg 30 hrs wkly *No. News Employees:* 1 *Target Audience:* 35-64;affluent, educated, politically active
Bourdon Wooten, General Manager
Bourdon Wooten, General Sales Mgr
Jamie Garrett, Programming Director
Brian Brown, Promotions Manager
Doug Bernhardt, Chief Engineer
Romeo Medina-Brand Manager

***KVLT**
05-01-2003; 88.5 mhz FM *Hrs Open:* 24; 5 kw vert; 617 ft.; N30 59 8 W97 37 56
Mailing Address: 1601 Belvedere Rd, 204 E, W Palm Beach, FL 33406 US
Second Address: 3411 Market Loop, Studio, Suite 108, Temple, TX 76502
(800) 525-5683, *Fax:* (916) 251-1650
www.klove.com
klove@klove.com
License: Temple, Bell County, TX held by American Educational Broadcasting Inc.
Nat'l Network: K-Love
Arbitron Metro Market: Temple, TX *Format:* Christian *No. News Employees:* 13
Darrell Chambliss, Chairman
Mike Novak, President and CEO
James Auel, General Manager
David Pierce, Chief Creative Officer and Programming Director
Ed Lenane, News Director
Sam Wallington, Engineering Dir
Alan Mason, ChiefOperating Officer
Dan Antonelli, Chief Business Development Officer
Eric Moser, Chief Financial Officer
Brian Burger, Vice President of Human Resources
D. Kevin Blair, Secretary and General Counsel
Tim Luttrell, News Reporter

Terrell

KPYK
10-01-1947; 1570 khz AM *Hrs Open:* 24
Mailing Address: P.O. Box 157, Terrell, TX 75160 US
Second Address: Town West Plaza, 1412-C W. Moore Ave., Terrell, TX 75160
(972) 524-5795, *Fax:* (972) 524-5795
www.kpyk.com
kpyk@broadcast.net
License: Terrell, TX held by Mohnkern Electronics Inc.
Nat'l Network: USA
Arbitron Metro Market: Dallas-Fort Worth *Format:* Big Band *Hrs. of News Programming:* news progmg 15 hrs wkly *No. News Employees:* 1 *Target Audience:* 40 plus; mature adults *Adv. Rates:* 15; 12.50; 15; na
Chuck Mohnkern, President
Susan Pinson, Promotions Manager
Liz Mohnkern, Assistant Music Director

Terrell Hills

KTKX
07-18-1979; 106.7 mhz FM *Hrs Open:* 24; 100 kw; Ant 1,017 ft; N29 11 03 W98 30 49
8122 Datapoint Dr., # 500, San Antonio, TX 89109
(210) 615-5400, *Fax:* (210) 615-5300
power1067fm.com
License: Terrell Hills, Bexar County, TX held by Cox Radio Inc.
Group Owner: Cox Radio Inc.; (acq 3-28-97; grpsl)
Wire Services: AP
Population Served: 1,300,000 *Arbitron Metro Market:* San Antonio, TX *No. News Employees:* 1 *Target Audience:* 18-34.
Bob Neil, CEO
Marty Choate, Operations Dir
Mark Bowka, General Sales Mgr
Doug Bennett, Programming Director
Adam Micheals, Promotions Manager
Paul Reynolds, Chief Engineer
Jeff Scott, National Sales Manager

KLUP
10-17-1947; 930 khz AM *Hrs Open:* 24; 5 kw-D, DAN; 1 kw-N, DAN; N29 31 6 W98 24 25
3773 Howard Hughes Pwy, Suite 300n, Las Vegas, NV 89109 US
(210) 344-8481, *Fax:* (210) 340-1213
www.klup.com
myopinion@klup.com
License: Terrell Hills, TX held by South Texas Broadcasting Inc.
Group Owner: Salem Communications Corp.; (acq 7-27-00; grpsl).
Nat'l Network: Salem Radio Network
Arbitron Metro Market: San Antonio, TX *Format:* News, News/Talk, 86 *Target Audience:* 35-64; upper & middle income, empty nesters
Baron Wiley, Operations Dir
Michael Payne, General Manager
Tim Gebhart, General Sales Mgr

Texarkana

KCMC
02-26-1932; 740 khz AM *Hrs Open:* 24; 1 kw-U, DA1; N33 26 17 W94 8 33
3227 Summerhill Road, Texarkana, TX 75503 US
(903) 793-4671, *Fax:* (903) 792-4261
www.kcmc740.com
scott@texarkanaradio.com
License: Texarkana, TX held by ArkLaTex LLC.

Group Owner: Arklatex LLC; (acq 1-3-2007; grpsl)
Nat'l Network: ESPN Radio *Nat'l Reps:* Interep
Arbitron Metro Market: Texarkana, TX *Format:* Sports *Target Audience:* 18 plus; sports fans
Harold Sudbury, CEO
John McCoy, Operations Dir
Scott Gray, General Manager
Roy Roane, General Sales Mgr
Scott Gray, CFO

KKTK
01-01-1946; 1400 khz AM *Hrs Open:* 24; 1 kw-U, ND1; N33 26 28 W94 3 16
1578 Boston Road, New Boston, TX 75570 US
(903) 255-7935, *Fax:* (903) 255-7942
www.foxsportstexarkana.com/kktk
License: Texarkana, TX held by American Media Investments Inc.
Group Owner: American Media Investments Inc.; (acq 2-17-2009; grpsl)
Nat'l Network: Fox News Radio
Arbitron Metro Market: Texarkana, TX-AR *Format:* Talk *Target Audience:* 35 plus.
Mike Basso, General Manager

KKYR-FM
07-15-1965; 102.5 mhz FM; 100 kw; 459 ft.; N33 25 48 W94 5 8
600 Congress Avenue, Suite 1400, Austin, TX 78701 US
(870) 772-3771, *Fax:* (870) 772-0364
www.kkyr.com
wesspicher@gapbroadcasting.com
License: Texarkana, Bowie County, TX held by GAP Broadcasting Texarkana License LLC.
Group Owner: GAP Broadcasting LLC; (acq 8-3-2007; grpsl)
Arbitron Metro Market: Texarkana, TX *Format:* Country *Target Audience:* General.
Ron Bird, General Manager
Mitzi Dowd, General Sales Mgr
Mario Garcia, Programming Director
John Williams, News Director
Wes Spicher, Chief Engineer

KTAL-FM
01-01-1945; 98.1 mhz FM *Hrs Open:* 24; 100 kw; 1362 ft.; N32 54 11 W94 0 20
3227 Summerhill Road, Texarkana, TX 75501 US
(318) 222-3122, *Fax:* (318) 459-1493
www.98rocks.fm
info@98rocks.fm
License: Texarkana, Bowie County, TX held by Access. 1 Louisiana Holding Co. LLC.
Group Owner: Access.1 Communications Corp.; (acq 12-20-02; grpsl).
Arbitron Metro Market: Shreveport, LA *Format:* Classic Rock *No. News Employees:* 1 *Target Audience:* 25-54.
Cary Camp, General Manager
Don Zimmerman, General Sales Mgr
Greg Hanson, Programming Director
Eddie Thurmand, Chief Engineer

KTFS
10-23-1961; 940 khz AM *Hrs Open:* 24; 2.5 kw-D, ND1; 0.011 kw-N, ND1; N33 24 28 W94 2 45
303 West Broad Street, Texarkana, TX 75501 US
(903) 793-4671, *Fax:* (903) 792-4261
www.940ktfs.com
License: Texarkana, TX held by ArkLaTex LLC.
Group Owner: Arklatex LLC; (acq 1-3-2007; grpsl)
Nat'l Network: Premiere Radio Networks; Radio America; Fox News Radio; Talk Radio Network *Nat'l Reps:* Interep
Arbitron Metro Market: Texarkana, TX *Format:* News, News/Talk, 86 *Hrs. of News Programming:* news progmg 25 hrs wkly *No. News Employees:* 1 *Target Audience:* 35 plus.
Harold Sudbury, CEO
Scott Gray, CFO/Vice President

***KTXK**
02-01-1984; 91.5 mhz FM *Hrs Open:* 24; 100 kw; 305 ft.; N33 23 33 W94 14 44
2500 N. Robinson Road, Texarkana, TX 75599 US
(903) 838-4541, *Fax:* (903) 832-5030
www.ktxk.org
steve@ktxk.org
License: Texarkana, Bowie County, TX held by Texarkana College.
Nat'l Network: PRI; NPR
Arbitron Metro Market: Texarkana, TX *Format:* News *Special Programming:* Jazz 15 hrs wkly *Hrs. of News Programming:* news progmg 35 hrs wkly *No. News Employees:* 1 *Target Audience:* 35 plus.
Steve Mitchell, President
Steve Mitchell, General Manager
Sabrina McCormick, News Director
Scott Williams, Chief Engineer
Frank Miller, Music Director
Alton Pettigrew, Classical Director

Texas City

KYST
11-01-1947; 920 khz AM; 5 kw-D, DA2; 1 kw-N, DA2; N29 25 3 W94 56 12
7322 S.W. Freeway #525, Houston, TX 77074 US
(713) 771-7995, *Fax:* (713) 779-1651
www.kyst920am.com
sales@kyst920am.com
License: Texas City, TX held by Hispanic Broadcasting Inc.
Arbitron Metro Market: Texas City, TX
Cruz Velasquez, General Manager

Thorndale

KOKE-FM
09-30-2005; 99.3 mhz FM *Hrs Open:* 24; 6 kw; Ant 328 ft; N30 29 23 W97 17 56
6633 E. Hwy 290, Austin, TX 77001
(512) 637-9300, *Fax:* (512) 637-0999
www.klgo.net
info@klgo.net
License: Thorndale, Milam County, TX held by Jackson Lake Broadcasting Co.
Nat'l Network: Moody; Salem Radio Network
Special Programming: Black 6 hrs wkly *Hrs. of News Programming:* News progmg 10 hrs wkly
Dean Clark, Operations Dir
Gene Bender, General Manager

Three Rivers

KEMA
01-01-2003; 94.5 mhz FM; 48 kw; 492 ft.; N28 43 10 W98 2 34
404 Woodbury Lane, Hiawatha, KS 66434 US
(512) 383-1112
License: Three Rivers, Live Oak County, TX held by Roy E. Henderson

Roy Henderson, General Manager

Tom Bean

KLAK
01-06-1984; 97.5 mhz FM *Hrs Open:* 24; 32 kw; 617 ft.; N33 28 30 W96 26 45
101 E. Main, Suite 255, Denison, TX 75020 US
(972) 542-9755, *Fax:* (972) 838-1330
www.975klak.com
webrequest@975klak.com
License: Tom Bean, Grayson County, TX held by NM Licensing LLC.
Group Owner: NextMedia Group Inc.; (acq 11-26-2001; grpsl).
Nat'l Network: ABC
Arbitron Metro Market: Dallas, TX *Format:* Adult Contemp *Hrs. of News Programming:* news progmg 7 hrs wkly *No. News Employees:* 1 *Target Audience:* 25-54; women
Steven Dinetz, CEO
Jeff Dinetz, President
Randy Friend, General Manager
Jennifer Isbell, Promotions Manager
Sean Stover, CFO

Tomball

KSEV
12-01-1986; 700 khz AM; 15 kw-D, DA2; 1 kw-N, DA2; N30 11 34 W95 35 40
3305 W. Spring Mtn Rd, Ste 60, Las Vegas, NV 89102 US
(281) 588-4800, *Fax:* (832) 358-9556
www.ksevradio.com
thevoice@ksevradio.com
License: Tomball, TX held by Liberman Broadcasting of Houston License LLC.
Group Owner: Liberman Broadcasting Inc.; (acq 3-20-2001; grpsl)
Arbitron Metro Market: Houston-Galveston *Format:* News, News/Talk, 86
Dan Patrick, General Manager
Bonny English, Station Manager
Chuck McLeod, Chief Engineer

Tulia

KBTE
04-01-1991; 104.9 mhz FM *Hrs Open:* 24; 96.6 kw; 978 ft.; N33 57 35 W101 35 20
3121 Magnolia Road, Ardmore, OK 73401 US
(806) 762-3000, *Fax:* (806) 770-5363
www.1049thebeat.com
License: Tulia, Swisher County, TX held by Wilks License Co.-Lubbock LLC.
Group Owner: Wilks Broadcast Group LLC; (acq 8-29-2005; $1,265,000)
Nat'l Network: ABC
Arbitron Metro Market: Lubbock, TX *Format:* Christian *Target Audience:* 18-34.
Jeff Scott, Operations Dir
Scott Harris, General Manager
Dee Brown, Programming Director
Julia Aguilar, News Director
Randy Hayes, Chief Engineer

Tye

KBCY
10-01-1983; 99.7 mhz FM *Hrs Open:* 24; 100 kw; 745 ft.; N32 24 39 W100 6 26
111 East Kilbourn Ave., Suite 2700, Milwaukee, WI 53202 US
(325) 793-9700, *Fax:* (325) 692-1576
www.kbcy.com
info@kbcy.com
License: Tye, Taylor County, TX held by Cumulus Licensing Corp.
Group Owner: Cumulus Media Inc.; (acq 2-13-98; grpsl)
Arbitron Metro Market: Abilene, TX *Format:* Country *Special Programming:* Relg 5 hrs wkly *Hrs. of News Programming:* News progmg 21 hrs wkly *Target Audience:* 25-49; upscale adults
John Scott, Operations Dir
Jim Christoferson, General Manager
Kelly Jay, Programming Director
Lori Barrett, News Director
Chris Andrews, Chief Engineer

KWFA
1030 khz AM; 5 kw-D, 370 w-N, DA-2; N32 27 37 W99 50 03
6720 Lakeview Dr., Carmichael, CA 95608
License: Tye, Taylor County, TX held by Marlene V. Borman.
Population Served: 61,762 *Arbitron Metro Market:* Carmichael, CA
Marlene Borman, General Manager

Tyler

KTBB-FM
11-01-1975; 92.1 mhz FM *Hrs Open:* 24; 9.6 kw; 443 ft.; N32 22 28 W95 16 24
928 N. N.E. Loop 323, Tyler, TX 75708 US
(903) 593-2519(903) 592-5200, *Fax:* (903) 597-4141
www.kdok.com
info@kdok.com
License: Tyler, Smith County, TX held by Gleiser Communications LLC
Group Owner: Gleiser Communications LLC; acq 11-21-2003; grpsl)
Arbitron Metro Market: Tyler-Longview, TX *Format:* Oldies *Special Programming:* Tyler Junior Collete football, Saturday Night Big Band Dance Party *Hrs. of News Programming:* news progmg 2 hrs wkly *No. NewsEmployees:* 1 *Target Audience:* 35 plus. *Adv. Rates:* 30; 25; 30; 15
Paul Gleiser, General Manager
Paul Berry, Programming Director
Mark Lavoux, Chief Engineer
Bill Davis, Disc Jockey
Barry Davis, News Reporter
Deborah Harrington, Traffic Manager

KGLD
07-05-2004; 1330 khz AM *Hrs Open:* 24; 1 kw-D, ND1; 0.077 kw-N, ND1; N32 22 35 W95 15 55
928 N. NELoop 323, Tyler, TX 75708 US
(903) 526-1330
www.kgld.org
kgldradio@yahoo.com
License: Tyler, TX held by Salt of the Earth Broadcasting Inc.
Format: Gospel *Special Programming:* Urban 3 hrs wkly *No. News Employees:* 2 *Target Audience:* African American
Darrell Martin, General Manager

***KGLY**
06-01-1988; 91.3 mhz FM *Hrs Open:* 24; 12 kw; 463 ft.; N32 21 6 W95 16 0

Mailing Address: 2721 E. Erwin, Tyler, TX 75701 US
Second Address: 2721 E. Erwin St., Tyler, TX 75708
(903) 593-5863, *Fax:* (903) 593-2663
www.kgly.com
kkgly@kgly.com
License: Tyler, Smith County, TX held by Educational Radio Foundation of East Texas Inc.
Nat'l Network: Moody; USA
Format: Religious *Hrs. of News Programming:* News progmg 3 hrs wkly *Target Audience:* 35 plus.
Dan Bolin, General Manager
Gary Lesniewski, Station Manager
Leah Coombs, Programming Director
Sans Hawkins, Chief Engineer

KKUS
01-01-1990; 104.1 mhz FM *Hrs Open:* 24; 50 kw; 492 ft.; N32 29 40 W95 28 55
Mailing Address: 3320 Ssw Loop #323, Tyler, TX 75701 US
Second Address: 210 S Broadway, Tyler, TX 75702
(903) 581-9966, *Fax:* (903) 534-5300
www.theranch.fm
kkus@etradiogroup.com
License: Tyler, Smith County, TX held by Access.1 Texas License Company LLC.
Group Owner: Access.1 Communications Corp.; (acq 1-7-2005; grpsl).
Nat'l Network: Fox News Radio *Nat'l Reps:* McGavren Guild
Arbitron Metro Market: Tyler, TX *Format:* Country *Target Audience:* 35+. *Adv. Rates:* 50; 50; 50; 50
Ginger Nimmons, General Manager
Carter Bentley, General Sales Mgr
Dru Laborde, Programming Director
Tara Holley, Local Sales Manager
Robert Taylor, National Sales Manager

KNUE
12-31-1964; 101.5 mhz FM *Hrs Open:* 24; 98 kw; 1073 ft.; N32 15 35 W94 57 2
600 Congress Avenue, Suite 1400, Austin, TX 78701 US
(903) 581-0606, *Fax:* (903) 581-2011
www.knue.com
craigreininger@gapbroadcasting.com
License: Tyler, Smith County, TX held by GAP Broadcasting Tyler License LLC.
Group Owner: GAP Broadcasting LLC; (acq 8-3-2007; grpsl)
Arbitron Metro Market: Tyler, TX *Format:* Country *Target Audience:* General.
Steve Joos, General Manager
Craig Reininger, General Sales Mgr
Michael Gibson, Programming Director
Chris Jones, Promotions Manager
Dave Goldman, News Director
Laura Conway, Traffic Manager

KTBB
08-28-1947; 600 khz AM *Hrs Open:* 24; 5 kw-D, DA2; 2.5 kw-N, DA2; N32 16 18 W95 12 23
928 N. NELoop 323, Tyler, TX 75708 US
(903) 593-2519, *Fax:* (903) 593-4918
www.ktbb.com
point@ktbb.com
License: Tyler, TX held by Gleiser Communications LLC
Group Owner: Gleiser Communications LLC; acq 11-21-2003; grpsl).
Regional Network: Texas State Networks
Arbitron Metro Market: Tyler-Longview, TX *Format:* News, News/Talk, 84, Talk *Special Programming:* Gospel 5 hrs wkly *Hrs. of News Programming:* news progmg 70 hrs wkly *No. News Employees:* 7 *Target Audience:* 35 plus.
Paul Gleiser, CEO
Paul Berry, Operations Dir
Paul Gleiser, General Manager
Garth Maier, Programming Director
Barry Davis, News Director
Mike LaRoux, Chief Engineer
Angie Mapes, Traffic Manager

KTYL-FM
02-01-1966; 93.1 mhz FM *Hrs Open:* 24; 82 kw; 938 ft.; N32 15 35 W94 57 2
600 Congress Avenue, Suite 1400, Austin, TX 78701 US
(413) 781-1011, *Fax:* (413) 734-4434
www.mix931.com
danielle@mix931.com
License: Tyler, Smith County, TX held by GAP Broadcasting Tyler License LLC.
Group Owner: GAP Broadcasting LLC; (acq 8-3-2007; grpsl)
Arbitron Metro Market: Tyler, TX *Format:* Adult Contemp *Target Audience:* 18-54.
Steve Joos, General Manager
Craig Reininger, General Sales Mgr
Jeff Evans, Programming Director
Danielle Veronesi, Promotions Manager
Chris Jones, General Sales Manager

***KVNE**
10-15-1983; 89.5 mhz FM *Hrs Open:* 24; 90 kw; 912 ft.; N32 32 21 W95 13 16
2721 East Erwin, Tyler, TX 75708 US
(903) 593-5863, *Fax:* (903) 593-2663
www.kvne.com
License: Tyler, Smith County, TX held by Educational Radio Foundation of East Texas Inc.
Arbitron Metro Market: Tyler-Longview, TX *Format:* Religious *Special Programming:* Gospel 4 hrs, children 4 hrs, Sp 2 hrs wkly *Hrs. of News Programming:* News progmg 6 hrs wkly *Target Audience:* 20-45; families
Jeff Strout, Chairman
Mike Harper, Station Manager
Dean Waskowiak, Vice Chairman
Lynn Roseman, Secretary/ Treasurer

KYZS
01-01-1930; 1490 khz AM *Hrs Open:* 24; 1 kw-U, ND1; N32 22 28 W95 16 24
928 N.E. Loop 323, Tyler, TX 75708 US
(903) 593-2519, *Fax:* (903) 597-8378
www.ktbb.com
point@ktbb.com
License: Tyler, TX held by Gleiser Communications LLC
Group Owner: Gleiser Communications LLC; acq 11-21-2003; grpsl).
Arbitron Metro Market: Tyler, TX *Format:* Sports
Paul Gleiser, General Manager
Garth Maier, Programming Director
Angie Mapes, News Director
Mike LaRoux, Chief Engineer

Umbarger

***KRBG**
01-01-2008; 88.7 mhz FM; 9.5 kw; Ant 374 ft; N34 53 50 W102 14 08
5331 Mt. Alifan Dr., San Diego, CA 95834
(858) 277-4991, *Fax:* (858) 277-1365
www.horizonsd.org, www.radiobygrace.com
contact@radiobygrace.com
License: Umbarger, Deaf Smith County, TX held by Horizon Christian Fellowship.
Group Owner: Horizon Christian Fellowship; (acq 4-7-2006; $150,000 for CP)

Mike MacIntosh, President

Universal City

KSAH
11-01-1986; 720 khz AM *Hrs Open:* 24; 10 kw-D, DA2; 0.89 kw-N, DA2; N29 31 51 W98 10 39
1777 N.E. Loop 410ste803, San Antonio, TX 78217 US
(210) 654-5100, *Fax:* (210) 340-1775
www.bmpradio.com
License: Universal City, TX held by BMP San Antonio License Co. L.P.
Group Owner: Border Media Partners LLC; (acq 4-28-2004; $24.4 million with KTFM(FM) Floresville)
Arbitron Metro Market: San Antonio, TX *Format:* Ethnic *Hrs. of News Programming:* news progmg 2 hrs wkly *No. News Employees:* 1 *Target Audience:* 18-49.
Lance Hawkins, General Manager
Bob Brown, General Sales Mgr

University Park

KTNO
01-01-1938; 1440 khz AM *Hrs Open:* 24
3270 Blazer Pkwy, Ste. 101600, Lexington, KY 40509 US
(214) 330-5866, *Fax:* (214) 330-9885
www.ktnoam.com
radiovida@ktno.com
License: University Park, TX held by Mortenson Broadcasting Co. of Texas Inc.
Group Owner: Mortenson Broadcasting Co.; (acq 8-8-97; $650,000).
Nat'l Network: ABC
Arbitron Metro Market: Dallas-Fort Worth *Format:* Christian, Talk *Hrs. of News Programming:* news progmg 40 hrs wkly *No. News Employees:* 2 *Target Audience:* 25 plus.
Jose Castillo, General Manager
Erica Garcia, News Director
Mike Benhauser, Chief Engineer

KZMP
01-01-1999; 1540 khz AM *Hrs Open:* 24; 32 kw-D, DA2; N32 48 45 W97 0 30
1436 Auburn Blvd., Sacramento, CA 95815 US
(214) 887-9107, *Fax:* (214) 841-4215
espndeportes.espn.go.com/radio/dallas-1540
License: University Park, TX held by Liberman Broadcasting of Dallas License LLC.
Group Owner: Liberman Broadcasting Inc.; (acq 11-2-2006; grpsl)
Nat'l Reps: Lotus Entravision Reps LLC
Arbitron Metro Market: University Park, TX *Format:* Tejano
Alex Sanchez, General Manager

Uvalde

KBNU
01-01-1996; 93.9 mhz FM *Hrs Open:* 24; 25 kw horiz, 14.3 kw vert; 292 ft.; N29 16 34 W99 41 44 *Rebroadcasts:* Rebroadcast KBLT(FM) Leakey 100%
8620 North New Braunfels, Suite 305, San Antonio, TX 78217 US
(830) 278-3693, *Fax:* (830) 278-2329
wwwkbnu.fm
kbradioranch@hotmail.com
License: Uvalde, Uvalde County, TX held by Radio Cactus Ltd.
Format: Country *Target Audience:* General; 18-49 *Adv. Rates:* 8; 8; 8; 5
John Furr, CEO
Regenia Tumbarello, General Manager
Paula Furr, CFO

KUVA
08-20-1984; 102.3 mhz FM *Hrs Open:* 24; 4 kw; 217 ft.; N29 11 16 W99 46 36
2402 Broadmoor, Bldg, D-2, Suite 101, Bryan, TX 77802 US
(830) 278-2555, *Fax:* (830) 278-9461
www.uvalderadio.com
joer@uvalderadio.com
License: Uvalde, Uvalde County, TX held by Rhattigan Broadcasting (Texas) LP
Group Owner: Rhattigan Broadcasting (Texas) LP; acq 6-3-2004; grpsl).
Nat'l Network: ABC *Regional Network:* Texas State Networks
Arbitron Metro Market: Uvalde, TX *Format:* Tejano *Hrs. of News Programming:* 6 hrs wkly *No. News Employees:* 1 *Target Audience:* 16-60; Hispanic
Glenn Tryon, General Manager
Jose Rodriguez, Station Manager
Hank Dicke, Sales
Elizabeth Zarate, Sales
Erica Uriegas, Office

KGWU
04-04-1947; 1400 khz AM *Hrs Open:* 24; 1 kw-U; N29 11 16 W99 46 36
Mailing Address: Box 758, Uvalde, TX 77802
Second Address: 1400 Batesville Rd., Uvalde, TX 78801
(830) 278-2555, *Fax:* (830) 278-9461
www.uvalderadio.com
production@uvalderadio.com
License: Uvalde, Uvalde County, TX held by Rhattigan Broadcasting (Texas) LP
Group Owner: Rhattigan Broadcasting (Texas) LP; (acq 8-19-2004; grpsl)
Regional Network: Texas State Networks
Population Served: 85,800*Special Programming:* Farm 12 hrs wkly *Hrs. of News Programming:* news progmg 15 hrs wkly *No. News Employees:* 1 *Target Audience:* 25-54; general
Glenn Tryon, General Manager

KVOU-FM
09-09-1976; 104.9 mhz FM *Hrs Open:* 24; 25 kw; 272 ft.; N29 11 16 W99 46 37
Mailing Address: 2402 Broadmoor, Bldg, D-2, Suite 101, Bryan, TX 77802 US
Second Address: 1400 Batesville Rd., Uvalde, TX 78801
(806) 853-9147, *Fax:* (815) 346-2084
www.uvalderadio.com
production@uvalderadio.com
License: Uvalde, Uvalde County, TX held by Rhattigan Broadcasting (Texas) LP
Group Owner: Rhattigan Broadcasting (Texas) LP; (acq 8-19-2004; grpsl)
Regional Network: Texas State Networks
Arbitron Metro Market: Uvalde, TX *Format:* Country *Special Programming:* High school play-by-play sports *Hrs. of News Programming:* 15+ hrs wkly *No. News Employees:* 1 *Target Audience:* 18-49.
Glenn Tryon, General Manager

Van Horn

*KVHR
91.5 mhz FM; 0.1 kw; -95 ft.; N31 2 2 W104 51 19 US
(662) 844-5036, *Fax:* (662) 842-7798
www.afr.net
contact@afa.net
License: Van Horn, Culberson County, TX held by American Family Association.
Group Owner: American Family Radio
Arbitron Metro Market: Van Horn, TX *Format:* Christian
Donald E. Wildmon, Founder
Buster Wilson, General Manager
Jennifer Hagman, Programming Director

Vernon

KVWC
07-01-1939; 1490 khz AM *Hrs Open:* 6 AM-10 PM; 1 kw-U; N34 09 12 W99 16 09
Mailing Address: Box 1419, Vernon, TX 76384
Second Address: 302 E. Wilbarger, Vernon, TX 76384
(940) 552-6221, *Fax:* (940) 553-4222
www.kvwc.com
kvwc@kvwc.com
License: Vernon, Wilbarger County, TX held by KVWC Inc.
Nat'l Reps: Riley
Population Served: 25,000*Special Programming:* Gospel 16 hrs wkly *Hrs. of News Programming:* news progmg 10 hrs wkly *No. News Employees:* 1 *Target Audience:* General; Wilbarger & surrounding counties
Mike Klappenbach, President

KVWC-FM
04-10-1972; 103.1 mhz FM *Hrs Open:* 6 AM-10 PM; 6 kw; Ant 141 ft; N34 09 12 W99 16 09
Mailing Address: Box 1419, Vernon, TX 76384
Second Address: 302 E. Wilbarger, Vernon, TX 76384
(940) 552-6221, *Fax:* (940) 553-4222
www.kvwc.com
License: Vernon, Wilbarger County, TX
Population Served: 100,000
Mike Klappenbach, General Manager

Victoria

KVNN
01-01-1940; 1340 khz AM *Hrs Open:* 24; 1 kw-U, ND1; N28 49 49 W97 0 33
Mailing Address: 8023 Vantage Dr., Suite 840, San Antonio, TX 78230 US
Second Address: 3613 N. Main St., Victoria, TX 77901
(361) 576-6113, *Fax:* (361) 572-0014
License: Victoria, TX held by Victoria RadioWorks Ltd.
Group Owner: Victoria RadioWorks Ltd.; (acq 10-26-98; $2.1 million with co-located FM).
Regional Network: Texas State Networks *Nat'l Reps:* McGavren Guild
Arbitron Metro Market: Victoria, TX *Format:* Country *Target Audience:* 25-54; adults
Cindy Cox, General Manager

*KAYK
10-01-2003; 88.5 mhz FM; 50 kw vert; 282 ft.; N28 46 43 W97 2 51
P O Drawer 2440, Tupelo, MS 38803 US
(662) 844-8888
www.afr.net
info@kaykfm.com
License: Victoria, Victoria County, TX held by American Family Association.
Group Owner: American Family Radio
Arbitron Metro Market: Tupelo, MS *Format:* Christian
Marvin Sanders, General Manager

KBAR-FM
02-02-1989; 100.9 mhz FM; 15 kw; 427 ft.; N28 46 55 W96 56 29
Mailing Address: 8023 Vantage Dr., Suite 840, San Antonio, TX 78230 US
Second Address: 8023 Vantage Drive, Suite 840, San Antonio, TX 78230
(361) 576-6111, *Fax:* (361) 572-0014
License: Victoria, Victoria County, TX held by Victoria RadioWorks Ltd.
Group Owner: Victoria RadioWorks Ltd.; (acq 1999; $27,500)
Arbitron Metro Market: San Antonio, TX *Format:* Rock/AOR
Cindy Cox, General Manager

KIXS
12-04-1980; 107.9 mhz FM; 100 kw; 505 ft.; N28 42 24 W96 50 6
Mailing Address: 600 Congress Avenue, Suite 1400, Austin, TX 78701 US
Second Address: 107 North Star Dr., Victoria, TX 77904
(361) 573-0777, *Fax:* (361) 578-0059
www.kixs.com
kixs@gapbroadcasting.com
License: Victoria, Victoria County, TX held by GAP Broadcasting Victoria License LLC.
Group Owner: GAP Broadcasting LLC; (acq 10-1-2007; grpsl)
Arbitron Metro Market: San Antonio, TX *Format:* Country *Target Audience:* 25-49; listeners in a growth & acquisition mode
Jeff Lyon, General Manager
Natalie Franz, General Sales Mgr
Eric Sharp, Programming Director
James Love, Promotions Manager
Charles Smithey, Chief Engineer
Mark Kingery, Disc Jockey
Joe Bob Burris, Music Director

KTXN-FM
12-01-1994; 98.7 mhz FM *Hrs Open:* 24; 100 kw; 253 ft.; N28 48 46 W97 3 45
P.O. Box 1363, Goliad, TX 77963 US
(361) 573-0777, *Fax:* (361) 578-0059
www.987jack.com
AdamWest@townsquaremedia.com
License: Victoria, Victoria County, TX held by Broadcast Equities Texas Inc.
Arbitron Metro Market: Victoria, TX *Format:* Adult Contemp
Target Audience: 18-54; general
Jeff Lyon, General Manager
Jeff Lyon, Director of Sales
Adam West, Brand Manager

KVIC
04-08-1976; 95.1 mhz FM *Hrs Open:* 24; 6.5 kw; 459 ft.; N28 46 55 W96 56 29
Mailing Address: 8023 Vantage Dr., Suite 840, San Antonio, TX 78230 US
Second Address: 3613 N. Main St., Victoria, TX 77901
(361) 576-6111, *Fax:* (361) 572-0014)
License: Victoria, Victoria County, TX
Group Owner: Victoria RadioWorks Ltd.
Arbitron Metro Market: Victoria, TX *Format:* Adult Contemp
Target Audience: 18-49.
Michael Cutchall, President
Jose Rodilles, General Manager
Ellen Cavanaugh, General Sales Mgr
Jaque Bosque Diaz, National Sales Manager

KQVT
12-01-1990; 92.3 mhz FM *Hrs Open:* 24; 6 kw; 299 ft.; N28 46 7 W96 59 10
2001 East Sabine, #208, Victoria, TX 77901 US
(361) 573-0777, *Fax:* (361) 578-0059
www.kqvt.com
AdamWest@townsquaremedia.com
License: Victoria, Victoria County, TX held by GAP Broadcasting Victoria License LLC.
Group Owner: GAP Broadcasting LLC; (acq 10-1-2007; grpsl)
Arbitron Metro Market: Victoria, TX *Format:* Adult Contemp
Jeff Lyon, General Manager
Natalie Franz, General Sales Mgr
Adam West, Programming Director
James Love, Promotions Manager
Charles Smithey, Chief Engineer
Jeff Lyon, Director of sales

*KVRT
01-01-1995; 90.7 mhz FM; 30 kw; 328 ft.; N28 46 55 W96 56 30
Rebroadcasts: Rebroadcasts KEDT-FM Corpus Christi 100%
4455 S.Padre Isl.Dr.#38, Corpus Christi, TX 78411 US
(361) 855-2213, *Fax:* (361) 855-3877
License: Victoria, Victoria County, TX held by South Texas Public Broadcasting System Inc.
Nat'l Network: NPR
Format: Jazz, News
Don Dunlap, President
Bob Scott, Programming Director
Myra Lombardo, Vice President

*KXGJ
09-01-1994; 89.3 mhz FM; 9.5 kw; 115 meters; N28 46 20 W96 57 17 *Rebroadcasts:* Rebroadcasts KSBJ(FM) Humble 100%
1600 Pasadena Blvd, Pasadena, TX 77347
(713) 589-1336, *Fax:* (713) 589-1335
www.radioaleluya.org
License: Victoria, Victoria County, TX held by Aleluya Broadcasting Network
Washington Law Firm: Dan J Alpert
Nat'l Network: USA
Population Served: 72,596*Target Audience:* 25-54.
Roberto Villarreal, President

KNAL
04-16-1948; 1410 khz AM *Hrs Open:* 24
Mailing Address: 8030 Arrowridge Boulevard, Charlotte, NC 28273 US
Second Address: 3613 N. Main St., Victoria, TX 77901
(361) 576-6111, *Fax:* (361) 572-0014
License: Victoria, TX held by Victoria RadioWorks Ltd.
Group Owner: Victoria RadioWorks Ltd.; (acq 2-1-2002; $100,000).
Arbitron Metro Market: San Antonio, TX *Format:* Adult Contemp
Cindy Cox, General Manager

Waco

KRZI
01-01-2001; 1660 khz AM
1018 N. Valley Mills Dr., Waco, TX 76710 US
(254) 772-0930, *Fax:* (254) 753-0499
www.1660espn.com
production@hot.rr.com
License: Waco, TX held by Simmons Austin, LS LLC.
Group Owner: Simmons Media Group; (acq 6-4-2004; grpsl)
Nat'l Network: ESPN Radio
Arbitron Metro Market: Waco, TX *Format:* Sports
Tom Barfield, Operations Dir
Daryl O'Neal, General Manager
Bill Le Grand, General Sales Mgr

KBBW
04-01-1953; 1010 khz AM
1019 Washington, Waco, TX 76701 US
(254) 757-1010, *Fax:* (254) 752-5339
www.kbbw.com
info@kbbw.com
License: Waco, TX held by Steve Williams dba American Broadcasting of Texas.
Arbitron Metro Market: Waco, TX *Format:* Christian *Target Audience:* 25-54.
Steve Williams, President
Ryan Williams, Operations Dir
Elizabeth Layne, Station Manager
Dave Fricker, Chief Engineer

KBCT
08-01-1996; 94.5 mhz FM *Hrs Open:* 24; 3.2 kw; 453 ft.; N31 30 31 W97 10 3
4701 West Waco Drive, Waco, TX 76710 US
(254) 388-5945
www.kbct.com
info@kbct.com
License: Waco, McLennan County, TX held by Kennelwood Broadcasting Co. Inc.
Arbitron Metro Market: Waco, TX *Format:* News, News/Talk, 86
Adv. Rates: 18; 18; 18; 10
Jerry Lenamon, President

KBGO
09-06-1959; 95.7 mhz FM *Hrs Open:* 24; 24 kw; 505 ft.; N31 30 51 W97 11 43
600 Congress Ave., Suite 1400, Austin, TX 78701 US
(254) 776-3900, *Fax:* (254) 761-6371
www.oldies95online.com
dewaynewells@clearchannel.com
License: Waco, McLennan County, TX held by Capstar TX L.P.
Group Owner: Clear Channel Communications Inc.; (acq 8-30-00; grpsl).
Arbitron Metro Market: Waco, TX *Format:* Oldies *Target Audience:* 35-64.
Zack Owen, Operations Dir
Evan Armstrong, General Manager
Vernon Riggs, General Sales Mgr
Dewayne Wells, Programming Director
Ron Davis, Chief Engineer
Scott Shafer, Production Director
Kathy Downs, Director of Sales
EvanArmstrong, Regional Market Manager

*KWBU-FM
03-15-1966; 103.3 mhz FM *Hrs Open:* 7-1 am; 2.75 kw; 492 ft.; N31 26 27 W97 10 41
B.U. Box 7368, Waco, TX 76798 US
(254) 710-3695, *Fax:* (254) 710-3874
www.baylor.edu/kwbu
kwbu@baylor.edu
License: Waco, McLennan County, TX held by Baylor University.
Nat'l Network: NPR; PRI
Arbitron Metro Market: Waco, TX *Format:* Variety/Diverse
Special Programming: Jazz 10 hrs wkly *Hrs. of News Programming:* news progmg 10 hrs wkly *No. News Employees:* 1 *Target Audience:* under 45; collegeage

Joe Railey, President and CEO
Brodie Bashaw, Station Manager
Lauren Lewis, News Director
Tony Poole, Chief Engineer
Derek Smith, News Director
Becky Fogel, Reporter
Carla Hervey, Business Affairs Manager
Loretta Howard,Membership Manager
Dave Ulman, Development Director

KWTX
05-01-1946; 1230 khz AM *Hrs Open:* 24; 1 kw-U, ND1; N31 31 42 W97 7 14
600 Congress Ave., Suite 1400, Austin, TX 78701 US
(254) 776-3900, *Fax:* (254) 761-6371
newstalk1230.com
info@newstalk1230.com
License: Waco, TX held by Capstar TX L.P.
Group Owner: Clear Channel Communications Inc.; (acq 8-30-2000; grpsl)
Nat'l Network: ABC *Nat'l Reps:* Clear Channel
Arbitron Metro Market: Waco, TX *Format:* News, News/Talk, 86 *Target Audience:* 35-64; adults
Zack Owen, Operations Dir
Michael Oppenheimer, General Manager
Evan Armstrong, General Sales Mgr
Max Watson, Programming Director
Steve Keating, Chief Engineer
Gloria Norris, National Sales Manager

KWTX-FM
12-01-1970; 97.5 mhz FM *Hrs Open:* 24; 100 kw; 1480 ft.; N31 20 15 W97 18 37
600 Congress Ave., Suite 1400, Austin, TX 78701 US
(254) 776-3900, *Fax:* (254) 761-6371
www.975online.com
info@975online.com
License: Waco, McLennan County, TX
Group Owner: Clear Channel Communications Inc.
Arbitron Metro Market: Waco, TX *Format:* Contemporary Hits/Top 40 *Target Audience:* 25-49; women
Jay Charles, Programming Director

WACO-FM
06-01-1960; 99.9 mhz FM; 90 kw; 1660 ft.; N31 20 15 W97 18 37
600 Congress Ave., Suite 1400, Austin, TX 78701 US
(406) 582-1045, *Fax:* (406) 582-0388
www.kbzm.com
sbalding@kbzm.com
License: Waco, McLennan County, TX held by Capstar TX L.P.
Group Owner: Clear Channel Communications Inc.; (acq 8-30-00; grpsl).
Arbitron Metro Market: Rocklin CA *Format:* Classic Rock, Adult Contemp *No. News Employees:* 2 *Target Audience:* 25-54.
John Radick, President

Wake Village

***KHTA**
09-22-2000; 92.5 mhz FM *Hrs Open:* 24; 25 kw; 328 ft.; N33 24 53 W93 58 12
2424 South Boulevard, Houston, TX 77098 US
(713) 520-5200
www.khcb.org
email@khcb.org
License: Wake Village, Bowie County, TX held by Houston Christian Broadcasters Inc.
Group Owner: Houston Christian Broadcasters Inc.
Nat'l Network: Moody
Arbitron Metro Market: Houston, TX *Format:* Religious *Target Audience:* General; all ages, families
Bruce Munsterman, General Manager
Bonnie BeMent, Assistant General Manager

Waskom

KQHN
01-01-1968; 97.3 mhz FM *Hrs Open:* 24; 42 kw; 533 ft.; N32 29 36 W93 45 55
Mailing Address: 131 South Jackson Street, Magnolia, AR 71753 US
Second Address: 270 Plaza Loop, Bossier City, TX 71111
(318) 549-8500, *Fax:* (318) 549-8545
mixfm973.com
License: Waskom, Harrison County, TX held by Cumulus Licensing LLC.
Group Owner: Cumulus Media Inc.; (acq 11-1-2002; $1.75 million).
Arbitron Metro Market: Bossier City, LA *Format:* Adult Contemp
Phil Robkin, General Manager
Gary Robinson, Promotions Manager
Dani Coate, News Director

Jasen Bragg, Engineering Dir
Danielle Kaiser, Regional Sales Manager

Waxahachie

KBEC
06-01-1955; 1390 khz AM *Hrs Open:* 24; 0.48 kw-D, DA2; 0.26 kw-N, DA2; N32 26 45 W96 48 15
711 Ferris Ave., Waxahachie, TX 75165 US
(972) 923-1390, *Fax:* (972) 935-0871
www.kbec.com
info@kbec.com
License: Waxahachie, TX held by Faye and Richard Tuck Inc.
Regional Network: Texas State Networks
Arbitron Metro Market: Waxahachie, TX *Format:* Country *Special Programming:* Farm 5 hrs *Hrs. of News Programming:* news progmg 15 hrs wkly *No. News Employees:* 1 *Target Audience:* 25-54.
Cristi Beaver, Operations Dir
Ken Roberts, General Manager
Barry Wolverton, General Sales Mgr
Richard Adams, News Director
Sylvia Smith, Business Manager
Coco Coco, PSA Director

Weatherford

***KYQX**
01-05-1986; 89.5 mhz FM *Hrs Open:* 24; 4.5 kw; 518 ft.; N32 51 5 W98 6 31
1101 North 81 Highway, Marlow, OK 73055 US
(817) 341-2337, *Fax:* (817) 598-1661
www.qxfm.com
robert@qxfm.com
License: Weatherford, Parker County, TX held by CSSI Non Profit Educational Broadcasting Corp.
Arbitron Metro Market: Weatherford, TX *Format:* Classic Rock *Hrs. of News Programming:* news progmg 7 hrs wkly *No. News Employees:* 3
Charles Beard, CEO
Mindy Beard, President
John Peterson, General Manager

KZEE
08-12-1956; 1220 khz AM
203 Eden Road, Weatherford, TX 76086 US
(817) 594-1220(817) 849-1971
www.radio1220am.com
License: Weatherford, TX held by Tarrant Radio Broadcasting Inc.
Arbitron Metro Market: Weatherford, TX *Format:* Christian, Gospel
Parvez Malik, President
Cima Hernandez, General Manager

***KMQX**
01-01-1995; 88.5 mhz FM *Hrs Open:* 24; 3.5 kw; 518 ft.; N32 51 5 W98 6 31
206 Wiggs Lane, Weatherford, TX 76086 US
(817) 341-2337, *Fax:* (817) 613-0230
www.qxfm.com
contact@qxfm.com
License: Weatherford, Parker County, TX held by CSSI Non-Profit Educational Broadcast Inc.
Arbitron Metro Market: Weatherford, TX *Format:* News, Oldies, 84 *No. News Employees:* 3
Charles Beard, CEO
Mindy Beard, Operations Dir

Wells

KVLL-FM
01-01-1993; 94.7 mhz FM *Hrs Open:* 24; 50 kw; 384 ft.; N31 6 47 W94 48 32
Mailing Address: 1470 Ben Sawyer Blvd, Suite 16, Mount Pleasant, SC 29464 US
Second Address: 1216 S. 1st St., Lufkin, TX 75901-4716
(936) 639-4455, *Fax:* (936) 632-5957
www.my947.com
License: Wells, Cherokee County, TX held by GAP Broadcasting Lufkin License LLC.
Group Owner: GAP Broadcasting LLC; (acq 10-2-2007; $750,000)
Arbitron Metro Market: Lufkin, TX *Format:* Oldies
Johnny Lathrop, General Manager

Weslaco

KRGE
01-01-1926; 1290 khz AM *Hrs Open:* 24; 5 kw-D, DAN; 5 kw-N, DAN; N26 12 36 W97 54 33
P.O. Box 1290, Weslaco, TX 78596 US
(956) 968-7777, *Fax:* (956) 968-5143
www.radiovida.com
egarza@radiovida.com
License: Weslaco, TX held by Christian Ministries of the Valley.
Arbitron Metro Market: McAllen-Brownsv *Format:* Christian *Hrs. of News Programming:* News progmg 3 hrs wkly *Target Audience:* 18-34.
Enrique Garza, General Manager

West Lake Hills

KTXZ
06-09-1982; 1560 khz AM *Hrs Open:* 24; 2.5 kw-D, DA2; 2.5 kw-N, DA2; N30 21 38 W97 39 11
7524 North Lamar Blvd., Suite 200, Austin, TX 78752 US
(512) 416-1100, *Fax:* (512) 453-6809
www.ktxz.com
License: West Lake Hills, TX held by Encino Broadcasting LLC.
Group Owner: Encino Broadcasting LLC; (acq 2-15-2008; grpsl)
Nat'l Network: CNN Radio; Westwood One
Arbitron Metro Market: Austin, TX *Format:* Tejano *Special Programming:* Christian mus 6 hrs wkly *Hrs. of News Programming:* News progmg 14 hrs wkly *Target Audience:* 18-54; bilingual, Hispanic, male & female
Paul Danitz, General Manager

West Odessa

***KFRI**
01-01-2005; 88.7 mhz FM *Hrs Open:* 24; 100 kw; 427 ft.; N31 50 53 W102 27 4 *Rebroadcasts:* Rebroadcasts KLRD(FM) Yucaipa, CA 100%
1425 North Market Blvd, Suite 9, Sacramento, CA 95834 US
(888) 937-2471, *Fax:* (916) 251-1650
www.air1.com
info@air1.com
License: West Odessa, Ector County, TX held by Educational Media Foundation.
Group Owner: EMF Broadcasting
Nat'l Network: Air 1
Arbitron Metro Market: West Odessa, TX *Format:* Alternative, Christian *No. News Employees:* 3 *Target Audience:* 18-35.
Darrell Chambliss, Chairman
Alan Mason, COO
Mike Novak, President and CEO
David Pierce, Programming Director
Ed Lenane, News Director
Sam Wallington, Engineering Dir
Richard Hunt, News Reporter
Marya Morgan, News Reporter
DanAntonelli, Chief Business Development Officer
Eric Moser, Chief Financial Officer
Brian Burger, Vice President of Human Resources
D. Kevin Blair, Secretary and General Counsel

Wharton

KANI
06-17-1962; 1500 khz AM; 0.5 kw-D, DAN; 0.5 kw-N, DAN; N29 19 22 W96 3 32
Mailing Address: 4638 Decker Drive, Baytown, TX 77520 US
Second Address: 215 E. Milam St., Wharton, TX 77488
(979) 532-3800, *Fax:* (979) 532-8510
kaniam1500@yahoo.com
License: Wharton, TX held by Martin Broadcasting Inc.
Group Owner: Martin Broadcasting Inc.
Regional Network: Texas State Networks
Arbitron Metro Market: Wharton, TX *Format:* Christian, Religious *Special Programming:* Sp 3 hrs, Pol 6 hrs wkly
Sandra Stewart, General Manager

Wheeler

***KPDR**
08-31-1986; 90.3 mhz FM *Hrs Open:* 24; 20 kw; 594 ft.; N35 31 6 W100 32 43
P.O. Box 8088, Amarillo, TX 79114 US
(806) 359-8855, *Fax:* (806) 354-2039
www.kingdomkeys.org
kjrt@kingdomkeys.org
License: Wheeler, Wheeler County, TX held by Top O' Texas Educational Broadcasting Foundation.
Nat'l Network: USA
Format: Religious *Special Programming:* Sp 5 hrs wkly *Target Audience:* General.
Ricky Pfeil, President
Jeremy Pfeil, Promotions Manager

***KOGC**
88.3 mhz FM; 100 w horiz; Ant 341 ft; N35 25 57 W100 16 31
116 Hillcrest Dr., Seminole, OK

(405) 380-3516
www.bpba.us
info@bpba.us
License: Wheeler, Wheeler County, TX held by Better Public Broadcasting Association.

Dennis Burton, General Manager

*KBDW
91.5 mhz FM; 3 kw horiz; 348 ft.; N35 31 6 W100 32 43 US
(806) 826-5202
License: Wheeler, Wheeler County, TX held by Solid Rock Foundation.
Arbitron Metro Market: Wheeler, TX
Gary Ware, President

Wheelock

KKEE
01-01-1950; 100.9 mhz FM *Hrs Open:* 24; kw US
(503) 861-6620, *Fax:* (503) 861-6630
kkee1230.com
tom.freel@nnbproduction.com?subject=My%2099.7%20FM
License: Wheelock, Clatsop County, TX held by New Northwest Broadcasters LLC
Group Owner: New Northwest Broadcasters LLC; acq 8-24-99; grpsl)
Arbitron Metro Market: Wheelock, TX *Format:* Talk *Hrs. of News Programming:* news progmg 7 hrs wkly *No. News Employees:* 1 *Target Audience:* 25-54; diverse
Kris Edwards, Operations Dir
Tom Freel, General Manager

White Oak

KZTK
05-17-2002; 99.3 mhz FM *Hrs Open:* 24; 34 kw; 541 ft.; N32 35 17 W94 58 53
P O Box 11196, College Station, TX 77842 US
(903) 581-5259, *Fax:* (903) 939-3473
www.993jackfm.com
chelle@theblaze.cc
License: White Oak, Gregg County, TX held by Reynolds Radio Inc.
Group Owner: Reynolds Radio Inc.
Arbitron Metro Market: Tyler-Longview, TX *Format:* Adult Contemp
Robin George, General Sales Mgr
Charlie O'Douglas, Programming Director
Chelle Wright-Peterson, News Director

Whitehouse

KISX
08-15-1982; 107.3 mhz FM *Hrs Open:* 24; 50 kw; 486 ft.; N32 17 19 W95 11 56
600 Congress Avenue, Suite 1400, Austin, TX 78701 US
(903) 581-0606, *Fax:* (903) 581-2011
kiss107i.com
craigreininger@gapbroadcasting.com
License: Whitehouse, Smith County, TX held by GAP Broadcasting Tyler License LLC.
Group Owner: GAP Broadcasting LLC; (acq 8-3-2007; grpsl)
Arbitron Metro Market: Tyler-Longview, TX *Format:* Contemporary Hits/Top 40 *Target Audience:* 18-44.
Steve Joos, General Manager
Craig Reininger, General Sales Mgr
Larry Thompson, Programming Director

Whitesboro

KMAD-FM
06-01-1985; 102.5 mhz FM *Hrs Open:* 24; 18 kw; 673 ft.; N33 41 31 W96 26 36
1913 West Elm Street, Durant, OK 74701 US
(903) 463-6800, *Fax:* (903) 463-9816
www.theclassicrockexperience.com
info@kmad.com
License: Whitesboro, Grayson County, TX held by NM Licensing LLC.
Group Owner: NextMedia Group Inc.; (acq 11-26-2001; grpsl).
Format: Classic Rock
David Smith, General Manager
David Macmullen, General Sales Mgr
Jason Taylor, Programming Director
Jennifer Isbell, Promotions Manager

Wichita Falls

KLUR
04-14-1963; 99.9 mhz FM; 100 kw; 808 ft.; N33 54 4 W98 32 21
111 East Kilbourn Ave., Suite 2700, Milwaukee, WI 53202 US
(940) 691-2311, *Fax:* (940) 696-2255
www.klur.com
info@klur.com
License: Wichita Falls, Wichita County, TX held by Cumulus Licensing Corp.
Group Owner: Cumulus Media Inc.; (acq 10-3-97; grpsl)
Arbitron Metro Market: Wichita Falls, *Format:* Country
Jim Marks, General Manager
Lindy Parr, General Sales Mgr
Zach Morton, Programming Director
Jeff Chancey, Chief Engineer
Andrea Lewis, Regional Sales Manager

*KMOC
07-09-1987; 89.5 mhz FM *Hrs Open:* 24 hours a day; 3 kw; 656 ft.; N33 53 23 W98 33 30
Mailing Address: P.O. Box 41, Wichita Falls, TX 76307 US
Second Address: 1040 W. Wenonah St., Wichita Falls, TX 76309
(940) 767-3303, *Fax:* (940) 723-5807
www.kmocfm.com
kmocfm@wf.net
License: Wichita Falls, Wichita County, TX held by Christian Service Foundation Inc.
Arbitron Metro Market: Wichita, TX *Format:* Christian *Target Audience:* 25-54.
Liz Sanderson, General Manager
Keith Sanderson, Station Manager
Daniel Boyd, Programming Director
Delvin Kinser, News Director

KNIN-FM
05-12-1975; 92.9 mhz FM *Hrs Open:* 24; 100 kw; 808 ft.; N33 54 4 W98 32 21
6 Whitefield Drive, Lafayette Hill, PA 19444 US
(940) 763-1111, *Fax:* (940) 322-3166
www.929nin.com
info@929nin.com
License: Wichita Falls, Wichita County, TX held by GAP Broadcasting Wichita Falls License LLC.
Group Owner: GAP Broadcasting LLC; (acq 8-3-2007; grpsl)
Nat'l Reps: McGavren Guild
Arbitron Metro Market: Wichita Falls, *Format:* Contemporary Hits/Top 40 *Target Audience:* 18-49. *Adv. Rates:* 35; 25; 25; 20
Chris Walters, Operations Dir
Kim Dodds, General Manager
Melissa Detrick, General Sales Mgr
Liz Ryan, Programming Director
Kara Tucker, Promotions Manager
Pamela Tracy, News Director
Scott Maingi, Chief Engineer
Vicki Vox,Assistant Music Director

KQXC-FM
01-07-1994; 103.9 mhz FM *Hrs Open:* 24; 19 kw; 807 ft.; N33 54 4 W98 32 21
111 East Kilbourn Ave., Suite 2700, Milwaukee, WI 53202 US
(940) 691-2311, *Fax:* (940) 696-2255
www.thehot1039.com
License: Wichita Falls, Wichita County, TX held by Cumulus Licensing Corp.
Group Owner: Cumulus Media Inc.; (acq 10-3-97; grpsl).
Nat'l Network: ABC
Arbitron Metro Market: Wichita Falls metro area *Format:* Contemporary Hits/Top 40 *Target Audience:* 18-45; males
Jim Marks, General Manager
Zach Morton, Programming Director
Susan Adkins, Promotions Manager
Jeff Chancey, Chief Engineer
Belda Holt, Regional Sales Manager

*KZKL
09-01-1993; 90.5 mhz FM *Hrs Open:* 24; 7 kw; 430 ft.; N33 53 50 W98 32 33
3700 Onaway Tr., Wichita Falls, TX 76309 US
(916) 251-1600, *Fax:* (916) 251-1650
www.klove.com
License: Wichita Falls, Wichita County, TX held by Educational Media Foundation.
Group Owner: EMF Broadcasting; (acq 10-20-2005; $600,000)
Nat'l Network: K-Love
Arbitron Metro Market: Rocklin, CA *Format:* Christian
Darrell Chambliss, Chairman
Mike Novak, CEO/COO
Mike Novak, President
David Pierce, Programming Director
Ed Lenane, News Director

Sam Wallington, Engineering Dir
Marya Morgan, News Reporter
Richard Hunt, News Reporter

KBZS
11-15-1984; 106.3 mhz FM *Hrs Open:* 24; 50 kw; 423 ft.; N33 53 18 W98 34 8
6 Whitefield Drive, Lafayette Hill, PA 19444 US
(940) 763-1111, *Fax:* (940) 322-3166
www.1063thebuzz.com
License: Wichita Falls, Wichita County, TX held by GAP Broadcasting Wichita Falls License LLC.
Group Owner: GAP Broadcasting LLC; (acq 8-3-2007; grpsl)
Nat'l Network: Westwood One *Nat'l Reps:* McGavren Guild
Arbitron Metro Market: Wichita Falls, TX *Format:* Adult Contemp, Rock/AOR *Target Audience:* 18-49. *Adv. Rates:* 30; 25; 25; 20
George Laughlin, President
Chris Walters, Operations Dir
Samantha Cole, General Manager
Melissa Detrick, General Sales Mgr
Liz Ryan, Programming Director
Kara Tucker, Promotions Manager
Scott Maingi, Chief Engineer
JohnnyThrash-Brand Manager

KWFS
01-01-1948; 1290 khz AM *Hrs Open:* 24; 5 kw-D, DAN; 0.073 kw-N, ND1; N33 57 38 W98 33 42
6 Whitefield Drive, Lafayette Hill, PA 19444 US
(940) 763-1111, *Fax:* (940) 322-3166
www.newstalk1290.com
info@newstalk1290.com
License: Wichita Falls, TX held by GAP Broadcasting Wichita Falls License LLC.
Group Owner: GAP Broadcasting LLC; (acq 8-3-2007; grpsl)
Regional Network: Texas State Networks *Nat'l Reps:* Clear Channel
Arbitron Metro Market: Wichita Falls, TX *Format:* News, News/Talk, 86 *Special Programming:* Sp 4 hrs wkly *Hrs. of News Programming:* news progmg 12 hrs wkly *No. News Employees:* 1 *Target Audience:* 25 plus.*Adv. Rates:* 15; 8; 8; 8;
Chris Walters, Operations Dir
Samantha Cole, General Manager
Melissa Detrick, General Sales Mgr
Mike Hendern, Programming Director
Kara Tucker, Promotions Manager
Joe White, News Director
Scott Maingi, Chief Engineer
Joe TomWhite, Farm Director

KWFS-FM
01-01-1961; 102.3 mhz FM *Hrs Open:* 24; 100 kw; 449 ft.; N33 53 51 W98 32 32
6 Whitefield Drive, Lafayette Hill, PA 19444 US
(940) 763-1111, *Fax:* (940) 322-3166
www.lonestar1023.com
info@lonestar1023.com
License: Wichita Falls, Wichita County, TX
Group Owner: GAP Broadcasting LLC
Arbitron Metro Market: Wichita Falls, TX *Format:* Country *Hrs. of News Programming:* News progmg one hr wkly *Target Audience:* 18-49. *Adv. Rates:* 30; 25; 25; 20
Samantha Cole, General Manager
Mike Hendern, Programming Director
Joe White, News Director

*KMCU
88.7 mhz FM *Hrs Open:* 24; 0.005 kw horiz, 3 kw vert; 253 ft.; N33 56 30 W98 34 6 *Rebroadcasts:* KCCU,KLW,KOCU,KYCU Lawton,Clinton,Ardmore,Altus, Oaklahoma, 90%
2800 West Gore Blvd, Lawton, OK 73505 US
(888) 454-7800, *Fax:* (580) 581-5571
www.kccu.org
kccu@cameron.edu
License: Wichita Falls, Wichita County, TX held by Cameron University.
Nat'l Network: NPR; PRI
Arbitron Metro Market: Wichita Falls, TX *Format:* Classical, Jazz, 60 *Hrs. of News Programming:* news progmg 36 hrs wkly *No. News Employees:* 2 *Target Audience:* 35 plus.
Ted Riley, General Manager, Director of Broadcasting
Doug Cole, Station Manager
Clinton Wieden, News Director
Cynthia Sosa, Production Director
Zach McGrew, Development Director

Willis

KVST
01-01-1998; 99.7 mhz FM; 2.9 kw; 482 ft.; N30 26 55 W95 31 48
1212 South Frazier, Conroe, TX 77301 US

(936) 788-1035, *Fax:* (936) 788-2525
www.kvst.com
dave@kstarcountry.com
License: Willis, Montgomery County, TX held by New Wavo Communication Group Inc.
Arbitron Metro Market: Willis, TX *Format:* Country
Ben Amato, President
William Boggs, General Sales Mgr
Larry Galla, Programming Director
Mike Shilo, News Director
Dade Moore, Engineering Dir
Linda Lott, Traffic Manager
John Erle, Traffic Manager
Christine Amato, AccountManager
Sherry Ingram, Account Manager
Karen White, Account Manager
Barbara Farr, Account Manager

Winfield

KALK
09-27-1987; 97.7 mhz FM *Hrs Open:* 24; 22.5 kw; 328 ft.; N33 11 1 W95 12 32
Mailing Address: 2201 Cantu Court, Suite 102a, Sarasota, FL 34232 US
Second Address: 1798 US Hwy. 67 W., Mount Pleasant, TX 75455
(903) 572-8726, *Fax:* (903) 572-7232
www.easttexasradio.com
bud@easttexasradio.com
License: Winfield, Titus County, TX held by East Texas Broadcasting Inc.
Group Owner: East Texas Broadcasting Inc.; acq 1999; $600,000).
Arbitron Metro Market: Mount Pleasant, TX *Format:* Adult Contemp *Special Programming:* Gospel one hr wkly *Hrs. of News Programming:* news progmg one hr wkly *No. News Employees:* 1 *Target Audience:* 18-54;younger, upwardly mobile, white collar *Adv. Rates:* 26; 23; 26; 21
John Mitchell, Chairman
Bud Kitchens, President
Craig Morgan, Operations Dir
Bud Kitchens, General Manager
Bryan Friesth, General Sales Mgr
Craig Morgan, Programming Director
Clint Cooper, News Director

Winnie

KPTY
11-01-1989; 105.3 mhz FM; 50 kw; 492 ft.; N29 49 31 W94 13 36
3102 Oak Lawn Avenue, Suite 215, Dallas, TX 75219 US
(713) 965-2400, *Fax:* (713) 965-2401
www.univision.com
tumusica1049@univision.com
License: Winnie, Chambers County, TX held by Tichenor License Corp.
Group Owner: Univision Radio; (acq 9-22-2003; grpsl)
Arbitron Metro Market: Beaumont, TX
Mark Masepohl, Operations Dir
Dave Burdette, General Sales Mgr
Raul Brindis, Programming Director
Nestor Enriquez, Promotions Manager

Winnsboro

KWNS
09-01-1983; 104.7 mhz FM *Hrs Open:* 24; 2.75 kw; 492 ft.; N33 4 17 W95 17 22
PO Box 54, 215 Market St., Winnsboro, TX 75494 US
(903) 342-3501
kwns-fm@cox-internet.com,kwns-fm@suddenlinkmail.com
License: Winnsboro, Wood County, TX held by Lottie L. Foster, executor of estate of Richard E. Foster.
Arbitron Metro Market: Winnsboro, TX *Format:* Gospel *No. News Employees:* 1 *Target Audience:* 35-70. *Adv. Rates:* 18; 18; 18; 18
Lottie Foster, President

Winona

KBLZ
102.7 mhz FM; 9.3 kw; 531 ft.; N32 23 9 W95 6 43
P.O. Box 11196, College Station, TX 77842 US
(903) 581-5259, *Fax:* (903) 939-3473
www.theblaze.fm
License: Winona, Smith County, TX held by S.O. 2,000 LLC.
Group Owner: Reynolds Radio Inc.; (acq 8-26-99)
Arbitron Metro Market: Tyler, TX *Format:* Urban Contemporary
Rick Reynolds, General Manager

Winters / Abilene

KORQ
11-01-1981; 96.1 mhz FM *Hrs Open:* 24; 50 kw; Ant 492 ft; N32 12 52 W99 53 22
1740 N. 1st St., Abilene, TX 73401
(325) 437-9596, *Fax:* (325) 673-1819
www.foxnewsabilene.com
doudmediagroup@aol.com
License: Winters / Abilene, Runnels County, TX held by Doud Media Group LLC
Nat'l Network: Fox News Radio *Nat'l Reps:* Local Focus
Population Served: 425,000 *Arbitron Metro Market:* Abilene, TX *Hrs. of News Programming:* news prgmg 10 hrs/week *No. News Employees:* 1 *Target Audience:* 25-54; 18-49.
Ryan Doud, Operations Dir
Richard Doud, General Manager
Martin Mims, General Sales Mgr
Panama, Programming Director
James Thompson, Engineering Dir
James Thompson, Chief Engineer

Wixon Valley

KBXT
11-07-1994; 101.9 mhz FM *Hrs Open:* 24; 2.5 kw; 156.2 meters; 30 48 05N 96 27 58W
Mailing Address: Box 3069, Bryan, TX 78729
Second Address: 1240 E Villa Maria Rd, Bryan, TX 77802
(979) 776-1240, *Fax:* (979) 776-0123
License: Wixon Valley, Brazos County, TX held by Brazos Valley Communications Ltd.
Group Owner: Brazos Valley Communications Ltd.; (acq 8-31-2006; grpsl)
Nat'l Network: American Urban *Nat'l Reps:* Katz Radio
Population Served: 150,000 *Arbitron Metro Market:* Bryan-College Station, TX *Special Programming:* Russ Parr AM Show
Dan Ginzel, Operations Dir
Chris Kiske, General Manager
Nathan Peacock, General Sales Mgr
Joseph Sanchez, Programming Director
Lance Parr, Chief Engineer

Wolfforth

KAIQ
01-01-2000; 95.5 mhz FM *Hrs Open:* 24; 100 kw; 676 ft.; N33 31 3 W101 51 24
3460 Torrance Blvd, #303, Torrance, CA 90503 US
(806) 763-6051, *Fax:* (806) 744-8363
www.tricolor955.com
ltrevino@entravision.com
License: Wolfforth, Lubbock County, TX held by Entravision Holdings LLC.
Group Owner: Entravision Communications Corp.; (acq 2-10-2005; $1.5 million).
Nat'l Reps: Lotus Entravision Reps LLC
Arbitron Metro Market: Lubbock, TX *Format:* Spanish *Target Audience:* Hispanic.
Leticia Flores, General Manager
Eric Segura, Promotions Manager
Lupe Trevino, Traffic Manager

Woodville

KWUD
01-04-1968; 1490 khz AM *Hrs Open:* 24; 1 kw-U, ND1; N30 44 52 W94 25 56
Mailing Address: 532 Magnolia Bend, League City, TX 77573 US
Second Address: 105 E Wheat, Woodville, TX 75979
(409) 283-8500, *Fax:* (409) 283-8500
www.kwud1490.com
production@kwudradio.com; press@kwudradio.com
License: Woodville, TX held by Carroll Texas Broadcasting Ltd.
Group Owner: Jimmy Ray Carroll Stns; (acq 10-5-2001)
Nat'l Network: ABC; Jones Radio Networks *Regional Network:* Texas State Networks
Arbitron Metro Market: Woodville, TX *Format:* Country *Special Programming:* Farm 2 hrs, gospel 6 hrs, relg 3 hrs wkly *Hrs. of News Programming:* news progmg 12 hrs wkly *No. News Employees:* 1 *Target Audience:* 18-55. *Adv. Rates:* 10; 10; 10; 6
Jim Carroll, General Manager
Richard McCullough, Programming Director
Carol Carroll, News Director
Chester Leediker, Chief Engineer

Wylie

KHSE
01-01-2004; 700 khz AM *Hrs Open:* 24; directional US
(972) 354-1990
www.funasia.net
License: Wylie, TX held by Bernard Dallas LLC
Group Owner: Bernard Radio LLC; (acq 1-31-2007; $9 million with KFCD(AM) Farmersville)
Arbitron Metro Market: Wylie, TX *Format:* Ethnic
Otter Miller, General Manager

Yoakum

KYKM
01-01-1982; 92.5 mhz FM *Hrs Open:* 24; 3 kw; 299 ft.; N29 21 3 W97 11 32
111 North Main, Hallettsville, TX 77964 US
(361) 798-4333, *Fax:* (361) 798-3798
www.texasthunderradio.com
texasthunderradio@yahoo.com
License: Yoakum, Lavaca County, TX held by Kremling Enterprises Inc.
Arbitron Metro Market: Hallettsville, TX *Format:* Country *Special Programming:* Polka 9 hrs wkly *Hrs. of News Programming:* news progmg 12 hrs wkly *No. News Employees:* 1 *Target Audience:* General.
Laura Kremling, General Manager
Travis Kremling, Programming Director

Yorktown

KGGB
01-01-2009; 96.3 mhz FM; 6 kw; 328 ft.; N29 2 43 W97 24 23 US
(361) 241-7944, *Fax:* (361) 241-7945
License: Yorktown, De Witt County, TX held by Gerald Benavides.
Group Owner: Claro Communications Ltd.
Arbitron Metro Market: Yorktown, TX
Gerald Benavides, General Manager

Zapata

KJJS
103.9 mhz FM; 4.5 kw; 377 ft.; N26 55 3 W99 15 0 US
(202) 429-8970, *Fax:* (202) 293-7783
License: Zapata, Zapata County, TX held by Hispanic Target Media Inc.
Group Owner: Hispanic Target Media Inc.
Arbitron Metro Market: Zapata, TX
Francisco San Millan, President
Meredith Senter, General Manager

Utah

Ballard

KFMR
95.5 mhz FM; 0.89 kw; 1660 ft.; N40 32 16 W109 41 57 US
(520) 797-4434
License: Ballard, Sublette County, UT held by Skywest Media L.L.C.
Group Owner: SkyWest Media L.L.C.
Arbitron Metro Market: Houston-Galveston
Ted Tucker, General Manager

Beaver

*KEZB
90.7 mhz FM; 0.1 kw; -509 ft.; N38 17 13.2 W112 38 18.5 US
(435) 438-2342
www.fbcbeaver.wordpress.com
License: Beaver, Beaver County, UT held by Christian Vision Inc.
Arbitron Metro Market: Beaver, UT *Format:* Religious
Lois McLario, President

Blanding

KBDX
92.7 mhz FM *Hrs Open:* 8am-5pm; 0.594 kw horiz, 0.255 kw vert; 3406 ft.; N37 50 24 W109 27 41
1632 South 2nd Street, Gallup, NM 87301 US
(808) 329-8090, *Fax:* (808) 769-5050
www.lava105.com
info@lava105.com
License: Blanding, San Juan County, UT held by Skynet, Hawaii LLC
Arbitron Metro Market: Kailua-Kona, HI *Format:* Oldies *Adv. Rates:* 10; 10; 10; 10
Thomas Troland, CEO
Chip Begay, Operations Dir
Joe Williams, General Manager

Bountiful

KJMY
03-15-1988; 99.5 mhz FM *Hrs Open:* 24; 39 kw; 2953 ft.; N40 36 29 W112 9 33
50 East Rivercenter Blvd, Suite 1200, Covington, KY 41011 US
(801) 908-1300, *Fax:* (801) 908-1449
www.my995fm.com
info@kjmy.com
License: Bountiful, Davis County, UT held by Citicasters Licenses L.P.
Group Owner: Clear Channel Communications Inc.; (acq 1999; grpsl).
Nat'l Reps: Clear Channel; Katz Radio
Arbitron Metro Market: Bountiful, UT *Format:* Alternative *Target Audience:* 18-49; adults
Bill Betts, Operations Dir
Stu Stanek, General Manager
Bill Matthews, General Sales Mgr
Mark Christiansen, Programming Director
Emily Hunt, General Sales Manager

Brian Head

KREC
11-14-1988; 98.1 mhz FM *Hrs Open:* 24; 54 kw; 2526 ft.; N37 32 32 W113 4 5
980 North Michigan Avenue, Suite 1880, Chicago, IL 60611 US
(435) 673-3579, *Fax:* (435) 673-8900
www.star98online.com
star98fm@bonnevillesg.com
License: Brian Head, Iron County, UT held by CCR-St. George IV LLC.
Group Owner: Cherry Creek Radio LLC; (acq 8-10-2006; grpsl)
Arbitron Metro Market: St. George *Format:* Adult Contemp *Target Audience:* 25-54. *Adv. Rates:* 25; 18; 18; 16
Chris McCarthy, General Sales Mgr
Rick Parrish, Promotions Manager
Dave Cory, Chief Engineer

Brigham City

KEGH
10-20-1972; 106.9 mhz FM; 5.2 kw; 2165 ft.; N41 47 3 W112 13 55
900 Oakmont Lane, Suite 210, Westmont, IL 60559 US
(801) 524-2600, *Fax:* (801) 908-4122
www.1015theeagle.com
License: Brigham City, Box Elder County, UT held by Simmons-SLC, LS LLC.
Group Owner: Simmons Media Group; (acq 4-19-2004; $3.95 million)
Arbitron Metro Market: Salt Lake City, UT *Format:* Country
Neica Kinney, General Manager

KXOL
07-01-1998; 1660 khz AM *Hrs Open:* 24
5777 South 3550 West, Roy, UT 84067 US
(801) 936-0706, *Fax:* (801) 936-0670
www.incacommunications.com
info@kxol.com
License: Brigham City, UT held by Simmons-SLC, LS, LLC.
Group Owner: Simmons Media Group; (acq 4-1-2003; $925,000 with KSOS(AM) Brigham City)
Arbitron Metro Market: Salt Lake City-Ogden-Provo, UT *Format:* Tejano
Jennifer Rodriguez, General Manager
Daniel Advincule, General Sales Mgr
Valentin Alvarez, Programming Director

Castle Dale

KEMR
102.1 mhz FM; 0.035 kw; 1736 ft.; N39 12 28 W111 8 32
US
(312) 204-9900
License: Castle Dale, Emery County, UT held by College Creek Media LLC.
Group Owner: College Creek Media LLC
Arbitron Metro Market: Castle Dale, UT *Format:* Religious
Neal Robinson, President

Cedar City

KOBY
01-01-1971; 940 khz AM; 10 kw-D, ND1; 0.039 kw-N, ND1; N37 45 51 W113 6 15
P.O. Box 858, Cedar City, UT 84720 US
(435) 628-1000, *Fax:* (435) 628-6636
License: Cedar City, UT held by Radio 940 LLC.
Group Owner: Legacy Media Corporation; (acq 2-9-2009; $150,000)
E. Morgan Skinner Jr., General Manager

KCIN
05-10-1974; 94.9 mhz FM; 55 kw; -121 ft.; N37 45 51 W113 6 15
P.O. Box 858, Cedar City, UT 84720 US
(435) 673-3579, *Fax:* (435) 673-8900
License: Cedar City, Iron County, UT held by CCR-St. George IV LLC.
Group Owner: Cherry Creek Radio LLC; (acq 5-3-2006; grpsl)
Format: Contemporary Hits/Top 40
Chris McCarthy, General Sales Mgr
Rick Parrish, Promotions Manager

KXBN
10-15-1976; 92.1 mhz FM *Hrs Open:* 24; 95 kw; 1745 ft.; N37 38 43 W113 22 22
6200 West, Highway 16, Cedar City, UT 84720 US
(435) 586-5900, *Fax:* (435) 673-8228
www.b92fmonline.com
License: Cedar City, Iron County, UT
Group Owner: Cherry Creek Radio LLC
Nat'l Network: Jones Radio Networks
Arbitron Metro Market: Cedar City, UT *Format:* Oldies *Hrs. of News Programming:* News progmg 5 hrs wkly
Ron Kurtis, CFO
Carl Gardner, President
Randy Bush, Operations Dir
Randy Bush, General Manager
Brian Gann, News Director
Ray Klotz, Engineering Dir
Ric Hampton, Operations Manager
April Sailsbury, General Manager

KSUB
07-04-1937; 590 khz AM *Hrs Open:* 24
6200 W. Highway 16, Cedar City, UT 84720 US
(435) 586-5900, *Fax:* (435) 673-8228
www.590ksub.com,www.mbmediagroup.com
License: Cedar City, UT held by CCR-St. George IV LLC.
Group Owner: Cherry Creek Radio LLC; (acq 5-3-2006; grpsl).
Nat'l Network: CBS *Regional Reps:* Target Radio.
Arbitron Metro Market: Saint George, UT *Format:* News, News/Talk, 86 *Special Programming:* Relg, loc talk, farm 6 hrs wkly *Hrs. of News Programming:* news progmg 15 hrs wkly *No. News Employees:* 1 *TargetAudience:* 35-65; adults
Brent Miner, General Manager
Steve Miner, Programming Director
Dan Hobson, Chief Engineer

*KSUU
10-01-1966; 91.1 mhz FM *Hrs Open:* 6 AM-midnight (winter); 10 AM-10 PM; 10 kw; -463 ft.; N37 38 55 W113 5 32
351 West Center Street, Department of Comm., Cedar City, UT 84720 US
(435) 865-8224, *Fax:* (435) 865-8352
www.suu.edu/ksuu
rollins@fuu.edu
License: Cedar City, Iron County, UT held by Southern Utah University.
Arbitron Metro Market: Cedar City, UT *Format:* Contemporary Hits/Top 40 *Special Programming:* News, class 3 hrs, rhythm and blues 4 hrs, rock 4 hrs wkly *Hrs. of News Programming:* News progmg 2 hrs wkly *TargetAudience:* 12-34; children, university students
Isacc madson, President
Cal Rollins, Station Manager
Luke Estes, Programming Director
Chris Holmes, News Director
Lance Jackson, Chief Engineer
Alisia Brooks, Music Director

*KCHG
88.9 mhz FM; 6.7 kw; 2605 ft.; N37 32 29 W113 4 4
US
(435) 867-8188
License: Cedar City, Iron County, UT held by Calvary Chapel Cedar City Inc.
Arbitron Metro Market: Cedar City, UT
Joe Carroll, President

Centerville

KTUB
12-01-1957; 1600 khz AM *Hrs Open:* 24; 5 kw-D, DAN; 1 kw-N, DAN; N40 54 8 W111 55 40
80 South Redwood Road, Suite 211, North Salt Lake City, UT 84054 US
(801) 908-8777, *Fax:* (801) 908-8782
www.mijuan.net
info@bustosmedia.com
License: Centerville, UT
Group Owner: Adelante Media Group LLC; (acq 9-1-2004; $1.5 million)
Nat'l Network: Ke-Buena
Arbitron Metro Market: Salt Lake City-Ogden-Provo, UT
Edward Distel, General Manager
Julieta Gil, Programming Director

Coalville

KLO-FM
01-01-2004; 103.1 mhz FM; 89 kw horiz; Ant 2,122 ft; N40 52 16 W110 59 43
Simmons Media Group, 515 South 700 East, Salt Lake City, UT 38104
(801) 524-2600, *Fax:* (801) 524-6002
www.simmonsmedia.com
reception@simonmedia.com
License: Coalville, Summit County, UT held by Simmons-SLC, LS LLC.
Group Owner: Simmons Media Group; (acq 5-20-2004; $4.4 million for CP)

G. Craig Hanson, General Manager

KZNSFM)
09-06-2005; 97.5 mhz FM; 89 kw horiz; Ant 2,122 ft; N40 52 16 W110 59 43
2835 East 3300 South, Salt Lake City, UT 84109
(801) 412-6040, *Fax:* (801) 412-6041
www.theblazeonline.com
License: Coalville, Summit County, UT held by 3 Point Media - Franklin L.L.C., debtor-in-possession
Group Owner: 3 Point Media; (acq 7-17-2007)
Arbitron Metro Market: Salt Lake City-Ogden-Provo, UT
Randy Rodgers, General Manager

Delta

KYAH
02-25-1974; 540 khz AM *Hrs Open:* 24; 1 kw-U; N39 20 12 W112 33 21
Mailing Address: Box 636, Delta, UT 84624
Second Address: 1259 N. 100 W., American Fork, UT 84003
(435) 864-5111, *Fax:* (801) 406-0067
www.radioforthefamily.com
info@knakam.com
License: Delta, Millard County, UT held by Accent Radio Inc.
Population Served: 50,000*Special Programming:* Farm 5 hrs wkly *Hrs. of News Programming:* News progmg 15 hrs wkly *Target Audience:* 20-50.
Jedidiah Harrison, President
Sam Bushman, General Manager
Curt Crosby, General Sales Mgr
Julie Bushman, Traffic Manager

KMGR
09-05-1989; 95.9 mhz FM *Hrs Open:* 24; 100 kw horiz; 961 ft.; N39 43 58 W111 56 34
P.O. Box 1450, 210 North 1000 East, St. George, UT 84771 US
(435) 835-7301, *Fax:* (435) 835-2250
www.midutahradio.com/kmgr
License: Delta, Millard County, UT held by 3 Point Media - Delta LLC.
Group Owner: 3 Point Media; (acq 8-1-2003; $1.25 million).
Arbitron Metro Market: Delta, UT
Bruce Buzil, General Manager

*KEYD
91.9 mhz FM; kw
US
(801) 374-5210, *Fax:* (801) 374-2910
www.keyy.com
mail@keyy.com
License: Delta, Millard County, UT held by Biblical Ministries Worldwide.
Arbitron Metro Market: Delta, UT *Format:* Religious
Mike Zander, General Manager
Karisa Clark, Public Relation Director

Elsinore

KWUT(FM)
01-01-1978; 97.7 mhz FM; 43 kw; Ant 2,883 ft; N38 32 30 W112 03 31
1600 West 500 North, PO Box 40, Manti, UT 84642
(435) 835-7301, *Fax:* (435) 835-2250
www.midutachradio.com
dougb@midutachradio.com
License: Elsinore, Sevier County, UT held by Mid-Utah Radio Inc.
Arbitron Metro Market: Central UT *Format:* Country

Douglas Barton, CEO/COO
Marianne Barton, President
Douglas Barton, General Manager
Michael Barton, Station Manager
Dave Gunderson, General Sales Mgr
J.D. Fox, Programming Director
Kirk Williams, Engineering Dir

Ephraim

*KAGJ
88.9 mhz FM; 0.38 kw; 2323 ft.; N39 19 18 W111 46 11
150 E. College Ave., Ephraim, UT 84627 US
(435) 283-7000
www.snow.edu/~kage
webmaster@snow.edu
License: Ephraim, Sanpete County, UT held by Snow College.
Arbitron Metro Market: Ephraim, UT *Format:* Classic Rock
Gary Chidester, General Manager

Huntington

KHUN
107.1 mhz FM; 0.36 kw; 1736 ft.; N39 12 28 W111 8 32 US
(312) 204-9900
License: Huntington, Emery County, UT held by College Creek Media LLC.
Group Owner: College Creek Media LLC
Arbitron Metro Market: Huntington, UT
Neal Robinson, President

Kanab

KPLD
01-01-1986; 105.1 mhz FM *Hrs Open:* 24; 100 kw; 600 meters; N36 43 18 W112 12 57
204 Playa Della Rosita, Washington, UT 60611
(435) 628-3643, *Fax:* (435) 673-1210
kony@infowest.com
License: Kanab, Kane County, UT held by Marathon Media Group L.L.C.
Adv. Rates: 40; 40; 40; 40
Carl Lamar, Operations Dir

Leeds

KCLS
11-01-1986; 101.5 mhz FM *Hrs Open:* 24; 40 kw; Ant 804 ft; N39 14 46 W114 55 39
College Creek Media LLC, 980 N. Michigan Ave., Chicago, IL 89301
(312) 204-9900
License: Leeds, Washington County, UT held by College Creek Media LLC.
Group Owner: College Creek Media LLC; (acq 10-25-2005; exchange for KOYT(FM) Elko)
Adv. Rates: 21; 18; 15; 13
Neal Robinson, President

Levan

KQMB
01-01-2001; 96.7 mhz FM; 67 kw horiz; 1919 ft.; N39 20 12 W111 27 6
P. O. Box 828, Orem, UT 84059 US
(801) 224-1400, *Fax:* (801) 224-1524
License: Levan, Juab County, UT held by Zeta Holdings LLC.
Arbitron Metro Market: Orem, UT *Format:* Adult Contemp
Robert Morey, General Manager

Logan

KBLQ-FM
08-01-1977; 92.9 mhz FM; 100 kw; 207 ft.; N41 52 18 W111 48 31
P. O. Box 570, Logan, UT 84321 US
(435) 752-1390, *Fax:* (435) 752-1392
www.q92.fm
License: Logan, Cache County, UT
Arbitron Metro Market: Logan, UT *Format:* Adult Contemp
Special Programming: Gospel 8 hrs, jazz 4 hrs wkly *Target Audience:* 25-54; general
Bill Walter, Programming Director
Laurie Gill, News Director
Michael Steel, Disc Jockey
Mindy Carey, Disc Jockey

KLGN
03-01-1968; 1390 khz AM; 5 kw-D, DAN; 0.5 kw-N, DAN; N41 44 4 W111 51 13
Mailing Address: P. O. Box 570, Logan, UT 84323 US
Second Address: 810 W. 200 N., Logan, UT 84321
(435) 752-1390, *Fax:* (435) 752-1392
www.1390.com
License: Logan, UT held by Sun Valley Radio Inc.
Group Owner: Sun Valley Radio Inc.; acq 12-27-91; $572,279 with co-located FM).
Nat'l Network: Westwood One; CBS
Arbitron Metro Market: Salt Lake City, UT *Format:* Adult Contemp
Special Programming: Talk *Target Audience:* 45 plus.
Kent Frandsen, President
Michael Carver, Operations Dir
Jay Eubanks, General Manager
Dan Baker, Chief Engineer

*KUSR
03-01-1999; 89.5 mhz FM *Hrs Open:* 24 hours; 0.82 kw; -571 ft.; N41 44 43 W111 48 16
8505 Old Main Hill, Logan, UT 84322 US
(435) 797-3138, *Fax:* (435)797-3150
www.upr.org
upr@upr.usu.edu
License: Logan, Cache County, UT held by Utah State University of Agricultural and Applied Science.
Nat'l Network: NPR
Arbitron Metro Market: Logan, UT *Format:* Classical, News, 62, Talk
Victor A. Hogstrom, General Manager
Tom Williams, Programming Director
Kerry Bringhurst, News Director
Friend Weller, Chief Engineer
April Ashland, Social Media Coordinator
Bryan Earl, Development Director
Jennifer Pemberton, WebContent Manager
Nora Zambreno, Development Specialist / Budget Officer
Shalayne Smith Needham, Production Specialist
Tamara Smith, Administrative Assistant

*KUSU-FM
04-01-1953; 91.5 mhz FM *Hrs Open:* 24; 90 kw; 1138 ft.; N41 53 11 W112 4 17
Utah Public Radio, 8505 Old Main Hill, Logan, UT 84322 US
(435) 797-3138, *Fax:* (435) 797-3150
www.upr.org
upr@upr.usu.edu
License: Logan, Cache County, UT held by Utah State University.
Nat'l Network: NPR; PRI
Arbitron Metro Market: Logan, UT *Format:* News, News/Talk, 86
No. News Employees: 2 *Target Audience:* General.
Nora Zambreno, Operations Dir
Victor A. Hogstrom, General Manager
Tom Williams, Programming Director
Kerry Bringhurst, News Director
Friend Weller, Chief Engineer
April Ashland, Social Media Coordinator
Bryan Earl, DevelopmentDirector
Jennifer Pemberton, Web Content Manager
Nora Zambreno, Development Specialist / Budget Officer
Shalayne Smith Needham, Production Specialist
Tamara Smith, Administrative Assistant

KVFX
11-11-1974; 94.5 mhz FM *Hrs Open:* 24; 94 kw; 1148 ft.; N41 53 50 W111 57 39
Mailing Address: P.O. Box 267, Logan, UT 84323 US
Second Address: 810 W. 200 N., Logan, UT 84321
(435) 752-5141, *Fax:* (435) 753-5555
www.utahsvfx.com
License: Logan, Cache County, UT
Arbitron Metro Market: Logan, UT *Format:* Contemporary Hits/Top 40 *Hrs. of News Programming:* News progmg 2 hrs wkly *Target Audience:* 18-35. *Adv. Rates:* 32; 32; 32; 25
Blair Carter, Programming Director
Kenton Frat Boy, Disc Jockey

KVNU
11-20-1938; 610 khz AM *Hrs Open:* 24
Mailing Address: P.O. Box 570, Logan, UT 84323 US
Second Address: 810 W. 200 N., Logan, UT 84321
(435) 752-5141, *Fax:* (435) 753-5555
610kvnu.com
kvnu@cvradio.com
License: Logan, UT held by Sun Valley Radio Inc.
Group Owner: Sun Valley Radio Inc.; acq 1996; $900,000 with co-located FM).
Nat'l Network: ABC
Arbitron Metro Market: Logan, UT *Format:* News, News/Talk, 86
Special Programming: Farm 2 hrs, relg 2 hrs wkly *Hrs. of News Programming:* news progmg 15 hrs wkly *No. News Employees:* 2 *Target Audience:* General. *Adv. Rates:* 36; 36; 36; 28
Al Lewis, General Manager
James Murdock, General Sales Mgr
Jennie Christensen, News Director
Bill Walter, Chief Engineer
Eric Frandsen, News Reporter
Heather Bailey, Reporter

*KUEU
01-01-2008; 90.5 mhz FM; 1 kw; Ant 367 ft; N41 36 41 W111 57 05
1971 West North Temple, Salt Lake City, UT 84101
(801) 363-1818, *Fax:* (801) 533-9136
License: Logan, Cache County, UT held by Listeners Community Radio of Utah Inc.

Donna Maldonado, General Manager

Manti

KMTI
06-07-1976; 650 khz AM *Hrs Open:* 24; 10 kw-D, DA2; 0.9 kw-N, DA2; N39 17 39 W111 38 13
Post Office Box 40, 500 North 1600 West, Manti, UT 84642 US
(435) 835-7301, *Fax:* (435) 835-2250
www.kmtiradio.com
License: Manti, UT held by Sanpete County Broadcasting Co.
Group Owner: Sanpete County Broadcasting Co.
Nat'l Network: ABC *Wire Services:* AP
Format: Country, News *Special Programming:* Farm 5 hrs wkly *Hrs. of News Programming:* news progmg 20 hrs wkly *No. News Employees:* 1 *Target Audience:* 25-60.
Douglas Barton, President
Willy Akers, General Sales Mgr
Larry Masco, Programming Director
Bruce Mehew, News Director
Beau Lund, Chief Engineer

KAUU
12-01-1978; 105.1 mhz FM *Hrs Open:* 24 hours; 48 kw horiz; 2244 ft.; N39 45 37 W111 34 38
Post Office Box 40, 500 North 1600 West, Manti, UT 84642 US
(801) 412-6040, *Fax:* (801) 412-6041
www.theblazeonline.com
License: Manti, Sanpete County, UT held by Millcreek Broadcasting L.L.C.
Group Owner: Millcreek Broadcasting L.L.C.; (acq 4-17-2001)

Randy Rodgers, General Manager

Midvale

KSL-FM
01-01-1995; 102.7 mhz FM *Hrs Open:* 24; 25 kw; 3740 ft.; N40 39 34 W112 12 5 *Rebroadcasts:* Rebroadcasts KSL(AM) Salt Lake City 100%
57 West South Temple, Suite 700, Salt Lake City, UT 84101 US
(801) 575-5555, *Fax:* (801) 526-1070
www.ksl.com
License: Midvale, Salt Lake County, UT held by Bonneville Holding Co.
Group Owner: Bonneville International Corporation; (acq 12-5-2003; grpsl).
Arbitron Metro Market: Salt Lake City-Ogden-Provo, UT *Format:* News, News/Talk, 84, Talk
Chris Redgrave, General Manager

Moab

KCYN
09-20-1998; 97.1 mhz FM *Hrs Open:* 24; 29 kw; 1293 ft.; N38 31 37 W109 18 21
Mailing Address: 1491 Thatcher Boulevard, Safford, AZ 85546 US
Second Address: 1030 S. Bowling Alley Ln. #3, Moab, UT 84532
(435) 259-1035, *Fax:* (435) 259-1037
www.kcynfm.com
kcyn@kcynfm.com
License: Moab, Grand County, UT held by Moab Communications LLC.
Group Owner: Carlson Communications International; (acq 8-15-97).
Nat'l Network: Fox News Radio; Jones Radio Networks *Nat'l Reps:* Rgnl Reps *Wire Services:* Metro Weather Service Inc.
Arbitron Metro Market: Moab, UT *Format:* Country *Hrs. of News Programming:* news progmg 12 hrs wkly *No. News Employees:* 1 *Target Audience:* 18-54.
Ralph J. Carlson, President
Phillip Mueller, General Manager
Phillip Mueller, Station Manager
Holly Wilson, News Director
Kenneth Meyer, Chief Engineer
Holly Wilson, Traffic Manager

***KZMU**
04-01-1992; 90.1 mhz FM *Hrs Open:* 24; 0.4 kw; 1280 ft.; N38 31 37 W109 18 21
Mailing Address: P. O. Box 1076, Moab, UT 84532 US
Second Address: 1734 Rocky Rd., Moab, UT 84532
(435) 259-5968(435) 259-8824, *Fax:* (435) 259-8763
www.kzmu.org
info@kzmu.org
License: Moab, Grand County, UT held by Moab Public Radio.
Arbitron Metro Market: Moab, UT *Format:* Variety/Diverse
Special Programming: Asian one hr, American Indian 5 hrs, Black 3 hrs, Sp one hr, folk 6 hrs, blues 19 hrs wkly *Hrs. of News Programming:* news progmg 8 hrswkly *No. News Employees:* 1
Target Audience: General.
Jeff Flanders, General Manager
Jeff Flanders, Station Manager
Christy Williams, Programming Director
Bob Owen, Engineering Dir
Bob Owen, Chief Engineer
Glen Peart, Music Director

Monroe

KMXD
08-01-2007; 100.5 mhz FM *Hrs Open:* 24; 33 kw; Ant 3,257 ft; N38 23 08 W112 19 57
Box 40, Monroe, UT
(435) 835-7301, *Fax:* (435) 835-2250
License: Monroe, Sevier County, UT held by Sanpete County Broadcasting Co.
Group Owner: Sanpete County Broadcasting Co.
Nat'l Network: ABC
Population Served: 3,297 *Arbitron Metro Market:* Monroe, UT
Target Audience: 30-65.
Douglas Barton, President

Murray

KJQS
11-08-1948; 1230 khz AM *Hrs Open:* 24; 1 kw-U, ND1; N40 39 57 W111 54 26
370 East South Temple, Suite 400, Salt Lake City, UT 84111 US
(801) 485-6700, *Fax:* (801) 487-5369
License: Murray, UT
Group Owner: Cumulus Media Inc.; (acq 2-29-00; $104,202).
Nat'l Network: ESPN Radio
Arbitron Metro Market: Salt Lake City-Ogden-Provo, UT *Format:* Sports
Eric Hauenstein, General Manager
Terry Mathis, General Sales Mgr
Scott Gerard, Programming Director
Liz Mills, News Director
Richard Bauer, Chief Engineer

Naples

KCUA
01-01-1993; 92.5 mhz FM; 0.84 kw; 1660 ft.; N40 32 16 W109 41 57
Box 1372, Park City, UT 84060 US
(801) 412-6080, *Fax:* (435) 645-0963
License: Naples, Uintah County, UT held by 3 Point Media - Coalville LLC.
Group Owner: 3 Point Media; (acq 5-28-2004; $1.7 million).
Format: Classic Rock
Joe Evans, Station Manager

Nephi

KUDE
05-09-1990; 103.9 mhz FM *Hrs Open:* 24; 74 kw horiz; 2244 ft.; N39 45 37 W111 34 38 *Rebroadcasts:* Rebroadcasts KUDD(FM) Roy 100%.
P O Box 165, Nephi, UT 84648 US
(801) 524-2600, *Fax:* (801) 412-6041
www.mix1079fm.com
License: Nephi, Juab County, UT held by Millcreek Broadcasting L.L.C.
Group Owner: Millcreek Broadcasting L.L.C.; (acq 4-17-2001).
Arbitron Metro Market: Salt Lake City, UT *Format:* Adult Contemp
Target Audience: 18-45.
Brian Michel, Operations Dir
Randy Rodgers, General Manager
Lutisha Merrill, General Sales Mgr
Scott St. John, Promotions Manager
Kevin Terry, Engineering Dir

***KBJF**
90.5 mhz FM; 75 kw; 2157 ft.; N39 45 37 W111 34 38 US
(800) 357-4226, *Fax:* (208) 736-1958
www.csnradio.com
License: Nephi, Juab County, UT held by First Baptist Church of Nephi, Utah.
Arbitron Metro Market: Nephi, UT
Mike Kestler, President
Daniel Davidson, Operations Dir
Keith South, General Manager
Don Mills, Music Director
Kelly Carlson, Engineering Dir
Jerry Johnson, Chief Engineer
Austin Morris, Accounting

North Ogden

***KNKL**
01-29-2004; 88.7 mhz FM *Hrs Open:* 24; 73 kw vert; 976 ft.; N41 35 30 W112 14 57
US
(800) 525-5683, *Fax:* (916) 251-1650
www.klove.com
klove@klove.com
License: North Ogden, Weber County, UT held by Educational Media Foundation.
Group Owner: EMF Broadcasting
Nat'l Network: K-Love
Arbitron Metro Market: North Ogden, UT *Format:* Christian *No. News Employees:* 3 *Target Audience:* 25-44; female-Judeo Christian
Darrell Chambliss, Chairman
Mike Novak, President and CEO
Mike Lee, Operations Dir
Eric Allen, General Sales Mgr
David Pierce, Programming Director
Ed Lenane, News Director
Sam Wallington, Engineering Dir
Marya Morgan, NewsReporter
Richard Hunt, News Reporter
Tracy Butler, Traffic Manager
Laura Daniels, News Reporter
Tim Luttrell, News Reporter
Kenny Noble Cortes, News Reporter

North Salt Lake City

KALL
09-22-1981; 700 khz AM *Hrs Open:* 24
50 East Rivercenter Boulevard, Suite 1200, Covington, KY 41011 US
(801) 727-2708, *Fax:* (801) 521-9234
www.kall700sports.com
reception@simmonsmedia.com
License: North Salt Lake City, UT held by Utah Radio Acquisition LLC
Nat'l Reps: Clear Channel
Arbitron Metro Market: Salt Lake City, UT *Format:* Sports, Talk
Hrs. of News Programming: news progmg 20 hrs wkly *No. News Employees:* 1 *Target Audience:* 18-49; men
David Glauser, Producer/Operations
Justin Weidauer, General Manager
Justin Weidauer, General Sales Mgr
John Kimball, Senior VP, Business Operations/General Manger
Bill Riley, Program Director/Afternoon Host
James Rust, ExecutiveProducer
Taylor James Cameron, Digital Content Manager

Oakley

KEGA
01-01-2003; 101.5 mhz FM; 89 kw horiz; 2123 ft.; N40 52 16 W110 59 43
57 West South Temple, Suite 700, Salt Lake City, UT 84101 US
(801) 524-2600, *Fax:* (801) 521-8100
www.1015theeagle.com
erika@1015theeagle.com
License: Oakley, Summit County, UT held by Simmons-SLC, LS LLC.
Group Owner: Simmons Media Group; (acq 4-4-2001; grpsl)
Arbitron Metro Market: Salt Lake City, UT *Format:* Country
Craig Hanson, President
Stephen Johnson, General Manager
Erika Hernandez, Promotions

Ogden

KBER
07-13-1976; 101.1 mhz FM *Hrs Open:* 24; 25 kw; 3740 ft.; N40 39 34 W112 12 5
140 South Ash Avenue, Tempe, AZ 85281 US
(801) 485-6700, *Fax:* (801) 487-5369
www.kber.com
info@kber.com
License: Ogden, Weber County, UT
Group Owner: Cumulus Media Inc.; (acq 1996; $7.7 million).
Nat'l Reps: Katz Radio
Arbitron Metro Market: Salt Lake City, UT *Format:* Rock/AOR *No. News Employees:* 1 *Target Audience:* 18-49; men
Eric Hauenstein, General Manager
Zandi Wilcox, General Sales Mgr
Kelly Hamer, Programming Director
Joel Smith, Promotions Manager
Richie Bauer, Engineering Dir
Diane Curtis, National Sales Manager

KBZN
01-01-1978; 97.9 mhz FM; 26 kw; 3770 ft.; N40 39 35 W112 12 5
257 E 2nd S. Suite 400, Salt Lake City, UT 84403 US
(801) 364-9836, *Fax:* (801) 364-8068
www.kbzn.com
comments@now979.com
License: Ogden, Weber County, UT held by Capitol Broadcasting Inc.
Arbitron Metro Market: Salt Lake City, UT *Format:* Adult Contemp
Adv. Rates: 50; 60; 60; 25
Rob Reisen, Operations Dir
John Webb, General Manager
Jan Bagley, General Sales Mgr
Rob Reisen, Programming Director

KENZ
08-01-1964; 101.9 mhz FM *Hrs Open:* 24; 25 kw; 3740 ft.; N40 39 34 W112 12 5
50 E River Center Blvd, Suite 1200, Covington, KY 41011 US
(801) 485-6700, *Fax:* (801) 412-6041
www.109theend.com
License: Ogden, Weber County, UT
Group Owner: Cumulus Media Inc.; (acq 7-30-2004; $16 million).
Nat'l Network: ABC
Arbitron Metro Market: Salt Lake City, UT *Format:* Country *Hrs. of News Programming:* news progmg 6 hrs wkly *No. News Employees:* 1 *Target Audience:* 25-54.
Randy Rodgers, General Manager
Biff Raff, Programming Director

KLO
01-01-1924; 1430 khz AM
257 East 200 South, Suite 400, Salt Lake City, UT 84111 US
(801) 627-1430, *Fax:* (801) 627-0317
www.kloradio.com
info@kloam.com
License: Ogden, UT held by KLO Broadcasting Co.
Arbitron Metro Market: Salt Lake City, UT *Format:* News, Sports, 86
John Webb, President
Dan Jessop, Operations Dir
Jan Bagley, General Sales Mgr
Sheri Jensen, News Director
Patrick Gleason, Chief Engineer

KSVN
01-01-1946; 730 khz AM *Hrs Open:* 24; 1 kw-D, ND1; 0.066 kw-N, ND1; N41 11 17 W112 4 52
323 East San Joaquin St., Tulare, CA 93274 US
(801) 292-1799, *Fax:* (801) 731-4445
www.aztecautah.com
info@aztecautah.com
License: Ogden, UT held by Azteca Broadcasting Corp.
Group Owner: Azteca Broadcasting Corp.; acq 2-1-86)
Arbitron Metro Market: West Haven, UT
Alex Collantes, President
Maria Coria, General Sales Mgr

***KWCR-FM**
05-21-1966; 88.1 mhz FM *Hrs Open:* 24; 2 kw; -315 ft.; N41 11 17 W111 56 43
1605 University Circle, Ogden, UT 84408 US
(801) 626-8800, *Fax:* (801) 626-6550
www.881weberfm.org
gm@881weberfml.org
License: Ogden, Weber County, UT held by Weber State University Board of Trustees.
Wire Services: UPI
Arbitron Metro Market: Ogden, UT *Format:* Contemporary Hits/Top 40, Classic Rock *Special Programming:* Relg 3 hrs, gospel 3 hrs, Sp 16 hrs wkly *Hrs. of News Programming:* News progmg 4 hrs wkly *Target Audience:* 18-26; college students, male & female *Adv. Rates:* 25; 25; 25; 25
Mark Howard, General Manager

KOGN
04-01-1948; 1490 khz AM *Hrs Open:* 24

8030 Arrow Ridge Blvd, Charlotte, NC 28273 US
(801) 395-5600, *Fax:* (801) 395-1490
License: Ogden, UT held by AM Radio 1490 Inc.
Group Owner: Legacy Media Corporation; (acq 4-10-2006; $520,000).
Nat'l Network: CNN Radio; Westwood One
Arbitron Metro Market: Salt Lake City-Ogden-Provo, UT *Format:* News, Adult Contemp
E. Morgan Skinner Jr., CEO
Dick Carter, Station Manager

***KYFO-FM**
06-01-1983; 95.5 mhz FM *Hrs Open:* 24; 100 kw; 719 ft.; N41 14 59 W112 14 11
8030 Arrowridge Blvd, Charlotte, NC 28273 US
704) 523-5555, *Fax:* (704) 522-1967
www.bbnradio.org
bbn@bbnradio.org
License: Ogden, Weber County, UT held by Bible Broadcasting Network.
Group Owner: Bible Broadcasting Network; (acq 1994).
Arbitron Metro Market: Charlotte, NC *Format:* Christian
Lowell Davey, President
Hank Crull, General Manager

Orem

***KKLV**
09-01-1999; 107.5 mhz FM; 43 kw; 2851 ft.; N40 16 48 W111 56 5
434 Bearcat Drive, Salt Lake City, UT 84115 US
(916) 251-1600, *Fax:* (916) 251-1650
www.klove.com
License: Orem, Crittenden County, UT held by Educational Media Foundation.
Group Owner: EMF Broadcasting; (acq 10-20-2000; grpsl).
Nat'l Network: K-Love
Arbitron Metro Market: Memphis, TN *Format:* Christian
Mike Novak, President
Glenn Goodwin, General Manager
David Pierce, Programming Director
Ed Lenane, News Director
Sam Wallington, Engineering Dir

KKAT
11-15-1978; 107.5 mhz FM *Hrs Open:* 24; 45 kw; Ant 2,850 ft; N40 16 48 W111 56 05
434 Bearcat Dr., Salt Lake City, UT 89128
(801) 485-6700, *Fax:* (801) 487-5369
www.1075.com
info@1075.com
License: Orem, Utah County, UT
Group Owner: Cumulus Media Inc.; (acq 12-18-96).
Arbitron Metro Market: Salt Lake City-Ogden-Provo, UT *Target Audience:* 25-54.
Eric Hauenstein, General Manager
Diane Curtis, General Sales Mgr
Bruce Jones, Programming Director
Kurt Johnson, Promotions Manager

***KOHS**
10-01-1994; 91.7 mhz FM; 1.75 kw; -869 ft.; N40 17 32 W111 40 58
175 South 400 East, Orem, UT 84058 US
(801) 224-9236, *Fax:* (801) 538-5690
License: Orem, Utah County, UT held by Orem HI. Sch.
Format: Alternative
Brenda Boyum, Operations Dir
Ed Matter, General Manager
Roger Lonnquist, General Sales Mgr
Brian Jackson, Programming Director

Paragonah

***KRRA**
91.3 mhz FM; kw
US
(580) 653-2777
License: Paragonah, Iron County, UT held by Ron Elmore Ministries Inc.
Arbitron Metro Market: Springer, OK *Format:* Religious
Ron Elmore, President

Park City

***KPCW**
07-02-1980; 91.9 mhz FM; 105 w; Ant -23 ft; N40 40 59 W111 31 22
Mailing Address: Box 1372, Park City, UT 84060
Second Address: KPCW City Hall Bldg., 445 Marsac, Park City, UT 84060
(435) 649-9004, *Fax:* (435) 645-9063
www.kpcw.org
letters@kpcw.org
License: Park City, Summit County, UT held by Community Wireless of Park City.
Population Served: 13,000*Special Programming:* Class 17 hrs, C&W 18 hrs, jazz 12 hrs wkly
Blair Feulner, General Manager
Karen Thomas, Programming Director
Leslie Thatcher, News Director
Dennis Silver, Chief Engineer

Parowan

KENT
10-06-2006; 1400 khz AM; 1 kw-U; N37 48 22 W112 56 40
2975 Valmont Road, #230, Boulder, CO
(435) 477-2000, *Fax:* (435) 477-1400
legacy1@infowest.com
License: Parowan, Iron County, UT held by US Capital Radio 1400 LLC
Group Owner: US Capital Inc; (acq 4-25-2011)
Population Served: 38,311
Lee Weinstein Esq., President

Payson

KTCE
11-01-1993; 92.1 mhz FM; 0.125 kw; 2156 ft.; N40 5 21 W111 49 15
P.O. Box 10, Provo, UT 84603 US
(801) 542-2600, *Fax:* (801) 364-1811
www.u92online.com/home
License: Payson, Utah County, UT held by Moenkopi Communications Inc.
Arbitron Metro Market: Salt Lake City-Ogden-Provo, UT *Format:* Adult Contemp *Adv. Rates:* 60; 30; 15; 7.50
Corey Sorenson, Station Manager
Kevin Cruise, Programming Director

Pleasant Grove

***KPGR**
05-01-1976; 88.1 mhz FM *Hrs Open:* 6:30 AM-10 PM; 0.115 kw; -1129 ft.; N40 21 48 W111 43 30
700 East 200 South, Pleasant Grove, UT 84062 US
(801) 785-5747, *Fax:* (801) 785-8744
www.kpgr.tripod.com
License: Pleasant Grove, Utah County, UT held by Alpine School District.
Format: Variety/Diverse *Special Programming:* All Pleasant Grove High football, basketball, base *Target Audience:* 12-18; students
Mike Basso, General Manager

Price

KARB
07-01-1977; 98.3 mhz FM; 7 kw; -105 ft.; N39 36 33 W110 48 50
Mailing Address: P.O. Box 875, Price, UT 84501 US
Second Address: 1899 North Carbonville Rd., Price, UT 84501
(435) 637-1167, *Fax:* (435) 637-1177
www.castlecountryradio.com
paul@koal.net
License: Price, Carbon County, UT held by Eastern Utah Broadcasting Co.
Arbitron Metro Market: Price, UT *Format:* Country
Tom Anderson, General Manager
Paul Anderson, General Sales Mgr
Amanda Holley, News Director

KOAL
10-01-1936; 750 khz AM; 10 kw-D, DAN; 6.8 kw-N, DAN; N39 34 2 W110 47 53
P.O. Box 875, Price, UT 84501 US
(435) 637-1167, *Fax:* (435) 637-1177
www.koal.net
koal@castlenet.com
License: Price, UT held by Eastern Utah Broadcasting Co.
Format: News, News/Talk, 84, Talk *Special Programming:* Farm 5 hrs wkly
Thomas Anderson, General Manager
Keith Mason, Programming Director

KWSA
12-01-1985; 100.1 mhz FM *Hrs Open:* 24; 3 kw; 135 ft.; N39 32 42 W110 48 57
Mailing Address: 163 East 100 North, Price, UT 84501 US
Second Address: 163 E. 100 N., Price, UT 84501
(435) 637-1080, *Fax:* (435) 637-8191
kwsa@preciscom.net
License: Price, Carbon County, UT
Format: Classic Rock
Paul Bjornstad, General Manager

KSLL
09-06-1980; 1080 khz AM; 5 kw-C, NDD; 10 kw-D, NDD; N39 33 43 W110 46 36
Mailing Address: 163 East, 100 North, Price, UT 84501 US
Second Address: 163 E. 100 N., Price, UT 84501
(435) 637-1080, *Fax:* (435) 637-8191
www.kusaonline.com
kwsa@preciscom.net
License: Price, UT held by Against the Wind Broadcasting Inc.
Arbitron Metro Market: Central UT *Format:* Country *Target Audience:* General.
Randy Timothy, President
David Smith, General Manager
Dennis Silver, Chief Engineer

***KCEU**
89.7 mhz FM; 0.44 kw; -164 ft.; N39 36 41 W110 48 36
US
(435) 613-5668, *Fax:* (435) 613-5042
www.theedge.ceu.edu
License: Price, Carbon County, UT held by College of Eastern Utah.
Arbitron Metro Market: Price, UT
Ryan Thomas, President
Troy Hunt, General Manager

***KEYP**
91.9 mhz FM; 0.1 kw; -423 ft.; N39 36 7.13 W110 48 15.43
US
(801) 374-5210, *Fax:* (801) 374-2910
www.keyy.com
mail@keyy.com
License: Price, Carbon County, UT held by Biblical Ministries Worldwide.
Arbitron Metro Market: Price, UT *Format:* Religious
Christopher Bauer, President
Mike Zander, General Manager
Karisa Clark, Public Relation Director

Provo

***KBYU-FM**
11-01-1960; 89.1 mhz FM *Hrs Open:* 24; 30 kw; 2976 ft.; N40 36 28 W112 9 33
C-302, Hfac, Provo, UT 84602 US
(801) 422-3552, *Fax:* (801) 422-0922
www.kbyu.org
kbyu@byu.edu
License: Provo, Utah County, UT held by Brigham Young University.
Nat'l Network: PRI; AP Radio; NPR
Arbitron Metro Market: Salt Lake City-Ogden-Provo, UT *TV Affiliate:* *KBYU-TV affil. *Format:* News, News/Talk, 86 *Hrs. of News Programming:* news progmg 5 hrs wkly *No. News Employees:* 2 *Target Audience:* 35plus.
Derek Marquis, CEO
Walter Rudolph, General Manager
Eric Glissmeyer, Programming Director
Daniel Hubbard, Promotions Manager
Wes Sims, News Director
Lynn Edwards, Engineering Dir
Christine Nokleby, Promotions Director

***KEYY**
12-01-1949; 1450 khz AM *Hrs Open:* 24; 1 kw-U; N40 13 49 W111 41 12
307 S. 1600 W., Provo, UT 22203
(801) 374-5210, *Fax:* (801) 374-2910
www.keyy.com
mail@keyy.com
License: Provo, Utah County, UT held by Biblical Ministries Worldwide.
Nat'l Network: Moody; Salem Radio Network
Population Served: 450,000 *Arbitron Metro Market:* Salt Lake City *Hrs. of News Programming:* news progmg 8 hrs wkly *Target Audience:* General.
Mike Zander, General Manager
Mike Zander, Programming Director
Chris Allinger, Engineering Dir

KOVO
09-12-1939; 960 khz AM *Hrs Open:* 24; 5 kw-D, DAN; 1 kw-N, DAN; N40 12 44 W111 40 13 *Rebroadcasts:* Rebroadcasts KZNS (AM) Salt Lake City 100%
15 North 100 East St., Library Pl, Suite 101, Provo, UT 84606 US
(801) 818-1074, *Fax:* (801) 818-3308
www.incacommunications.com
License: Provo, UT held by Simmons-SLC, LS LLC.

Group Owner: Simmons Media Group; (acq 4-19-2004; $1 million)
Nat'l Reps: D & R Radio
Arbitron Metro Market: Salt Lake City-Ogden-Provo, UT *Format:* Sports, Talk *Target Audience:* 35 plus; upper income affluent males & females 35-65
Craig Hanson, President
Stephen Johnson, General Manager
Kevin Graham, Programming Director

KSRR
11-24-1947; 1400 khz AM *Hrs Open:* 24; 1 kw-U, ND1; N40 15 29 W111 42 24
Mailing Address: 1240 East 800 North, P.O. Box 828, Orem, UT 84097 US
Second Address: 1454 W. Business Park Dr., Orem, UT 84058
(801) 224-1400, *Fax:* (801) 224-1524
License: Provo, UT held by Zeta Holdings LLC
Format: Adult Contemp *Hrs. of News Programming:* News progmg one hr wkly *Target Audience:* 18-54.
Robert Morey, General Manager

KXRK
02-14-1968; 96.3 mhz FM *Hrs Open:* 24; 25 kw; 3740 ft.; N40 39 34 W112 12 5
57 West South Temple, Suite 700, Salt Lake City, UT 84101 US
(801) 524-2600, *Fax:* (801) 521-9234
www.x96.com
xmail@x96.com
License: Provo, Utah County, UT held by Simmons-SLC, LS LLC.
Group Owner: Simmons Media Group; (acq 4-4-2001; grpsl)
Arbitron Metro Market: Salt Lake City-Ogden-Provo, UT *Format:* Alternative *Target Audience:* 18-34; young, affluent executives
Adv. Rates: 120; 120; 120; 100
Bruce Thomas, CFO
Craig Hanson, President
Alan Hague, Operations Dir
Stephen Johnson, General Manager
Mike Lund, General Sales Mgr
Todd Nukem, Programming Director
Natalie Divino, Promotions Manager
Scott Matthews, ChiefEngineer
Kris Burton, National Sales Manager

KHTB
11-01-1979; 94.9 mhz FM *Hrs Open:* 24; 47 kw; 2799 ft.; N40 16 58 W111 56 11
50 East Rivercenter Blvd, Suite 1200, Covington, KY 41011 US
(801) 485-6700, *Fax:* (801) 487-5369
949zrock.com
License: Provo, Utah County, UT
Group Owner: Cumulus Media Inc.; (acq 8-13-2008)
Arbitron Metro Market: Provo, UT
Judith Ellis, COO

Randolph

KDUT
01-01-2001; 102.3 mhz FM *Hrs Open:* 24; 89 kw horiz; 2123 ft.; N40 52 16 W110 59 43
980 North Michigan Avenue, Suite 1880, Chicago, IL 60611 US
(801) 908-8777, *Fax:* (801) 908-8782
www.bustosmedia.com
info@bustosmedia.com
License: Randolph, Rich County, UT
Group Owner: Adelante Media Group LLC; (acq 7-1-2004; $9 million).
Arbitron Metro Market: Salt Lake City, UT *Format:* Spanish, Christian
Edward Distel, General Manager

Richfield

KLGL
01-01-2000; 93.7 mhz FM *Hrs Open:* 24; 66 kw; 2356 ft.; N39 19 17 W111 46 11
P.O. Box 40, Manti, UT 84642 US
(435) 835-7301, *Fax:* (435) 835-2250
www.klgl.com
License: Richfield, Sevier County, UT held by Sanpete County Broadcasting Co.
Group Owner: Sanpete County Broadcasting Co.; (acq 3-1-2006; swap for KCYQ(FM) Elsinore).
Arbitron Metro Market: Manti, UT *Format:* Contemporary Hits/Top 40 *Hrs. of News Programming:* news progmg 11 hrs wkly *No. News Employees:* 1 *Target Audience:* General.
J.D. Fox, Programming Director

KSVC
09-01-1947; 980 khz AM *Hrs Open:* 24
P.O. Box 40, Manti, UT 84642 US
(435) 896-4456, *Fax:* (435) 896-9333
www.midutahradio.com
License: Richfield, UT held by Mid-Utah Radio Inc.
Arbitron Metro Market: Richfield, UT *Format:* News, News/Talk, 84, Talk *Special Programming:* Farm one hr wkly *Hrs. of News Programming:* News progmg 18 hrs wkly *Target Audience:* 18-54.
Kevin Kitchen, General Manager
Willy Akers, General Sales Mgr
Kathy Farneworth, Programming Director
Bruce Mehew, News Director
Kirk Williams, Chief Engineer

***KUSL**
89.3 mhz FM; 2 kw; 3192 ft.; N38 23 8 W112 19 57 US
(435) 797-3138, *Fax:* (435) 797-3150
www.upr.org
License: Richfield, Sevier County, UT held by Utah State University of Agriculture and Applied Science.
Arbitron Metro Market: Richfield, UT
Cathy Ives, General Manager

***KEYR**
91.7 mhz FM; 0.85 kw; 3136 ft.; N38 23 8 W112 19 56 US
(801) 374-5210, *Fax:* (801) 374-2910
www.keyy.com
mail@keyy.com
License: Richfield, Sevier County, UT held by Biblical Ministries Worldwide.
Arbitron Metro Market: Richfield, UT *Format:* Religious
Christopher Bauer, President
Mike Zander, General Manager
Karisa Clark, Public Relation Director

Roosevelt

KIFX
12-14-1987; 98.5 mhz FM *Hrs Open:* 24; 3.2 kw; 1690 ft.; N40 32 16 W109 41 57
Mailing Address: Rt.2, P.O. Box 2384, Roosevelt, UT 84066 US
Second Address: 2242 E. 1000 S., Roosevelt, UT 84066
(435) 722-5011, *Fax:* (435) 722-5012
www.hitsandfavorites.com
License: Roosevelt, Duchesne County, UT held by Evans Broadcasting Inc.
Regional Reps: Art Moore.
Format: Adult Contemp *Hrs. of News Programming:* news progmg 5 hrs wkly *No. News Employees:* 1 *Target Audience:* 21-45.
Joseph Evans, President
Vickie Reary, Operations Dir
Teena Christopherson, General Sales Mgr
Earl Hawkins, Programming Director
Jean Liddell, News Director
Steve Sprouce, Chief Engineer

KNEU
01-06-1978; 1250 khz AM *Hrs Open:* 5 AM-11 PM; 5 kw-D, ND1; 0.129 kw-N, ND1; N40 17 13 W109 57 32
Mailing Address: Route 2 Box 2384, Roosevelt, UT 84066 US
Second Address: 2242 E 1000 S, Roosevelt, UT 84066
(435) 722-5011, *Fax:* (435) 722-5012
www.realcountryonline.com
radio@ubtanet.com
License: Roosevelt, UT held by Country Gold Broadcasting.
Format: Country *Hrs. of News Programming:* news progmg 10 hrs wkly *No. News Employees:* 1 *Target Audience:* 25-54.
Joseph Evans, President
Teddie Evans, Operations Dir
Teena Christopherson, General Sales Mgr
Earl Hawkins, Programming Director
Jean Liddell, News Director
Jonathan Hawkins, Chief Engineer

KXRQ
12-18-1998; 94.3 mhz FM; 17.5 kw; 1864 ft.; N40 31 15 W109 42 25
3268 West Huntington Rd, Taylorsville, UT 84118 US
(435) 781-1100, *Fax:* (435) 781-1500
www.channelx94.com
cruise@channelx94.com
License: Roosevelt, Duchesne County, UT held by Uinta Broadcasting L.C.
Wire Services: Metro Weather Service Inc.
Arbitron Metro Market: Vernal, UT *Format:* Adult Contemp, Contemporary Hits/Top 40 *Special Programming:* Relg 8 hrs wkly *Target Audience:* 25-54. *Adv. Rates:* 22; 15; 22; 15
Charles Hall, Operations Dir
Charlie Hall, General Manager
Amy Jensen, Programming Director
Natasha Huber, News Director
Bradon Johnson, Local News Editor

Roy

***KANN**
09-01-1961; 1120 khz AM *Hrs Open:* 24
Mailing Address: 2201 South 6th Street, Las Vegas, NV 89104 US
Second Address: 2500 W. 3700 S., Syracuse, UT 84075
(702) 731-5452, *Fax:* (702) 731-1992
www.sosradio.net
info@sosradio.net
License: Roy, UT held by Faith Communications Corp.
Group Owner: Faith Communications Corp.
Arbitron Metro Market: Las Vegas, NV *Format:* Adult Contemp, Christian *Hrs. of News Programming:* News progmg 6 hrs wkly *Target Audience:* 25-44; young families
Brad Staley, President
Brad Staley, General Manager
Bob Alzugarat, Station Manager
Scott Herrold, Programming Director

KUDD
09-01-1986; 107.9 mhz FM *Hrs Open:* 24; 75 kw horiz; 2283 ft.; N41 15 27 W112 26 24 *Rebroadcasts:* Rebroadcasts KUDD(FM) Nephi.
450 E. 1000 North, Suite 200, N. Salt Lake, UT 84054 US
(801) 542-2600, *Fax:* (801) 412-6041
www.mix1079fm.com/home
License: Roy, Weber County, UT held by Millcreek Broadcasting L.L.C.
Group Owner: Millcreek Broadcasting L.L.C.; (acq 4-17-2001; grpsl).
Nat'l Reps: Interep
Arbitron Metro Market: Salt Lake City-Ogden-Provo, UT *Format:* Adult Contemp *Target Audience:* General.
Randy Rodgers, General Manager
Lutisha Merrill, General Sales Mgr
Brian Michel, Programming Director
Scott St. John, Promotions Manager
Kevin Terry, Chief Engineer

Saint George

KIYK
06-15-1973; 93.5 mhz FM; 3 kw; -125 ft; N37 06 54 W113 34 23
750 W. Ridgeview Dr., Suite 204, Saint George, UT 84101
(435) 673-3579, *Fax:* (435) 673-8900
License: Saint George, Washington County, UT held by CCR-St. George IV LLC.
Group Owner: Cherry Creek Radio LLC
Target Audience: 12-49.
Chris McCarthy, General Sales Mgr
Rick Parrish, Promotions Manager

***KSGU**
01-01-2005; 90.3 mhz FM; 2 kw; Ant 1,820 ft; N36 50 49 W113 29 28 *Rebroadcasts:* Rebroadcasts KNPR(FM) Las Vegas, NV 100%
1289 S. Torrey Pines Dr., Las Vegas, NV
(702) 258-9895, *Fax:* (702) 258-5646
www.ksgu.org
reception@knpr.org
License: Saint George, Washington County, UT held by Nevada Public Radio
Population Served: 120,000
Florence Rogers, General Manager
Christine Kiely, General Sales Mgr

Salt Lake City

KWDZ
01-01-1945; 910 khz AM *Hrs Open:* 24; 5 kw-D, 1 kw-N, DA-2; N40 30 48 W112 00 23
2801 S. Decker Lake Dr., Suite 100, Salt Lake City, UT 41011
(801) 908-5152, *Fax:* (801) 908-7844
www.radiodisney.com/saltlakecity
Steve.earnhart@disney.com
License: Salt Lake City, Salt Lake County, UT held by Radio Disney Group LLC.
Group Owner: ABC Inc.; (acq 4-30-03; $3.7 million).
Nat'l Network: Radio Disney
Population Served: 1,361,800 *Arbitron Metro Market:* Salt Lake City-Ogden-Provo, UT
Steve Earnhart, Station Manager
Valerie Walker, Promotions Manager
Barry McClellen, Chief Engineer

RADIO - U.S.

KKAT(AM)
11-15-1955; 860 khz AM; 10 kw-D, 195.8 w-N, 3 kw-CH; N40 42 47 W111 55 53
434 Bearcat Dr., Salt Lake City, UT 84115
(801) 485-6700, *Fax:* (801) 487-5369
www.b987.com
License: Salt Lake City, Salt Lake County, UT
Group Owner: Cumulus Media Inc.
Nat'l Reps: Christal
Arbitron Metro Market: Salt Lake City, UT *Format:* Country
Target Audience: 25-54.
Larry Wilson, CEO
Bob Proffitt, Operations Dir
Eric Hauenstein, General Manager
Susie Carlson, General Sales Mgr
Rusty Keys, Programming Director
Richie Bauer, Chief Engineer

KBEE
01-01-1947; 98.7 mhz FM; 34.5 kw; 2933 ft.; N40 36 30 W112 9 34
City Center West, 7201 W. Lake Mead Blvd, Las Vegas, NV 89128 US
(801) 485-6700, *Fax:* (801) 487-5369
www.b987.com
info@b987.com
License: Salt Lake City, Salt Lake County, UT
Group Owner: Cumulus Media Inc.; (acq 7-18-97; $2,873,027 with co-located AM).
Arbitron Metro Market: Salt Lake City, UT *Format:* Adult Contemp
Target Audience: General.
Ed Hill, Operations Dir
Eric Hauenstein, General Manager
Jim Bratt, General Sales Mgr
Rusty Keys, Programming Director
Jaelyn Carillo, Promotions Manager
Susan Wasescha, News Director
Richie Bauer, Chief Engineer

***KCPW-FM**
01-01-1992; 88.3 mhz FM *Hrs Open:* 24; 2.35 kw; -200 ft.; N40 45 48 W111 53 23
P.O. Box 1372, Park City, UT 84060 US
(801) 359-5279, *Fax:* (801) 355-1582
www.kcpw.org
news@kcpw.org
License: Salt Lake City, Salt Lake County, UT held by Community Wireless of Park City Inc.
Nat'l Network: NPR; PRI
Arbitron Metro Market: Salt Lake City-Ogden-Provo, UT *Format:* News, News/Talk, 86 *Target Audience:* 25 plus.
Ed Sweeney, CEO
Ed Sweeney, President
Jesse Ellis, Operations Dir
Eric Ray, Station Manager
Jeff Robinson, News Director
Tyler Ford, Production Manager
Cynthia Martinez, Development Manager

KZNS
02-01-1945; 1280 khz AM
57 West South Temple, Salt Lake City, UT 84101 US
(801) 524-2600, *Fax:* (801) 521-9234
www.1280thezone.com
reception@simmonsmedia.com
License: Salt Lake City, UT held by Simmons-SLC, LS LLC.
Group Owner: Simmons Media Group; (acq 4-4-2001; grpsl)
Nat'l Network: Westwood One; CNN Radio *Nat'l Reps:* CBS Radio
Arbitron Metro Market: Salt Lake City-Ogden-Provo, UT *Format:* Sports, Talk *Target Audience:* 35 plus; retired, affluent, responsible & loyal
David Simmons, Chairman
G. Craig Hanson, President
Stephen Johnson, General Manager
Kevin Graham, Programming Director
Scott Matthews, Chief Engineer

KFNZ
01-01-1923; 1320 khz AM; 5 kw-U, DA1; N40 38 36 W111 55 24
City Center West, 7201 W. Lake Mead Blvd, Las Vegas, NV 89128 US
(801) 485-6700, *Fax:* (801) 487-5369
License: Salt Lake City, UT
Group Owner: Cumulus Media Inc.
Arbitron Metro Market: Salt Lake City, UT *Format:* Sports
Zandi Wilcox, General Sales Mgr
Jeff Austin, Programming Director
Joel Smith, Promotions Manager
Julie Allen, News Director
Dave Coons, Sports Commentator
Steve Brown, Sports Commentator

KZHT
02-01-1961; 97.1 mhz FM *Hrs Open:* 24; 25 kw; 3740 ft.; N40 39 34 W112 12 5
900 Oakmont, Suite 210, Westmont, IL 60559 US
(801) 908-1300, *Fax:* (801) 908-1389
www.971zht.com
info@kzhfm.com
License: Salt Lake City, Salt Lake County, UT held by CC Licenses LLC.
Group Owner: Clear Channel Communications Inc.; (acq 7-10-2000).
Nat'l Reps: Katz Radio
Arbitron Metro Market: Salt Lake City-Ogden-Provo, UT *Format:* Contemporary Hits/Top 40 *Target Audience:* 18-49.
Bill Betts, Operations Dir
Bill Mathews, General Sales Mgr
Jeff McCartney, Programming Director
Stacy Sappenfield, Promotions Manager
Emily Hunt, General Sales Manager

KNRS
08-01-1938; 570 khz AM *Hrs Open:* 24; 5 kw-U, DA1; N40 49 9 W111 55 56
50 East Rivercenter Boulevard, Suite 1200, Covington, KY 41011 US
(801) 908-1300, *Fax:* (801) 908-1310
www.knrs.com
License: Salt Lake City, UT held by Citicasters Licenses L.P.
Group Owner: Clear Channel Communications Inc.; (acq 1999; grpsl).
Nat'l Reps: Clear Channel
Arbitron Metro Market: Salt Lake City, UT *TV Affiliate:* KTVX(TV) *Format:* News, News/Talk, 86 *Hrs. of News Programming:* news progmg 2 hrs wkly *No. News Employees:* 1 *Target Audience:* 25-54; adults
Jeff Cochran, Operations Dir
Stu Stanek, General Manager
Bill Mathews, General Sales Mgr
Greg Foster, Programming Director
Jim Vandiver, General Sales Manager

KODJ
12-01-1968; 94.1 mhz FM *Hrs Open:* 24; 21.5 kw; 3999 ft.; N40 39 35 W112 12 5
50 E River Center Blvd, Suite 1200, Covington, KY 41011 US
(801) 908-1300, *Fax:* (801) 908-1429
www.kodj.com
robboshard@clearchannel.com
License: Salt Lake City, Salt Lake County, UT held by Citicasters Licenses L.P.
Group Owner: Clear Channel Communications Inc.; (acq 5-4-99; grpsl).
Nat'l Reps: Clear Channel; Katz Radio
Arbitron Metro Market: Salt Lake City-Ogden-Provo, UT *TV Affiliate:* KUTV(TV) affil *Format:* Oldies *Hrs. of News Programming:* News progmg 2 hrs wkly *Target Audience:* 25-54; adults
Bill Betts, Operations Dir
Stu Stanek, General Manager
Kimberly Dickerson, General Sales Mgr
Rob Boshard, Programming Director

***KRCL**
12-03-1979; 90.9 mhz FM *Hrs Open:* 24; 25 kw; 3740 ft.; N40 39 34 W112 12 5 *Rebroadcasts:* Rebroadcasts KZMU(FM) Moab 50%
230 South 500, West Suite 105, Salt Lake City, UT 84101 US
(801) 363-1818, *Fax:* (801) 533-9136
www.krcl.org
mailman@krcl.org
License: Salt Lake City, Salt Lake County, UT held by Listeners Community Radio of Utah Inc.
Arbitron Metro Market: Salt Lake City-Ogden-Provo, UT *Format:* Talk *Special Programming:* Black 20 hrs, Sp 9 hrs, American Indian 4 hrs, A *Hrs. of News Programming:* news progmg 3 hrs wkly *No. News Employees:* 1 *Target Audience:* General.
Donna Maldonado, President
Tino Arana, Operations Dir
Vicki Mann, General Manager
Kami St. John, General Sales Mgr
Ebay Jamil Hamilton, Programming Director
Felix Gonzalez, Engineering Dir
Lewis Downey, Chief Engineer
DougYoung, Music Director
Gena Edualson, Public Affairs Director

KRSP-FM
08-21-1968; 103.5 mhz FM; 25 kw; 3740 ft.; N40 39 34 W112 12 5
57 West South Temple, Suite 700, Salt Lake City, UT 84101 US
(801) 575-5555, *Fax:* (801) 526-1070
www.arrow1035.com
License: Salt Lake City, Salt Lake County, UT held by Bonneville Holding Co.
Group Owner: Bonneville International Corporation; (acq 12-5-2003; grpsl).
Arbitron Metro Market: Salt Lake City-Ogden-Provo, UT *Format:* Classic Rock *Target Audience:* 18-34.
Chris Redgrave, General Manager

KSFI
12-26-1946; 100.3 mhz FM; 25 kw; 3740 ft.; N40 39 34 W112 12 5
57 West South Temple, Suite 700, Salt Lake City, UT 84101 US
(801) 575-5555, *Fax:* (801) 526-1070
www.fm100.com
License: Salt Lake City, Salt Lake County, UT held by Bonneville Holding Co.
Group Owner: Bonneville International Corporation; (acq 12-5-2003; grpsl).
Arbitron Metro Market: Salt Lake City-Ogden-Provo, UT *Format:* Adult Contemp *Target Audience:* 25-54; general
Chris Redgrave, General Manager
Paulette Cary, General Sales Mgr
Dain Craig, Programming Director
Peggy Ijams, News Director
Christa Durrant, Music Director
Trina Bodily, Traffic Manager

KSL
05-06-1922; 1160 khz AM *Hrs Open:* 24; 50 kw-U, ND1; N40 46 46 W112 5 56
David Redd, 55 N. 300 W, 8th Flr, Salt Lake City, UT 84180 US
(801) 575-5555, *Fax:* (801) 526-1070
www.ksl.com
License: Salt Lake City, UT held by Bonneville International Corp.
Group Owner: Bonneville International Corporation
Nat'l Network: CBS *Wire Services:* Reuters; UPI
Arbitron Metro Market: Salt Lake City-Ogden-Provo, UT *TV Affiliate:* KSL-TV affil. *Format:* News, News/Talk, 84, Talk *No. News Employees:* 12 *Target Audience:* 25-54.
Bruce Reese, CEO
Monica Leger, Operations Dir
Chris Redgrave, General Manager
Lora Woodbury, General Sales Mgr
Kevin Larue, Programming Director
Janet Johnson, News Director
John Dehnel, Chief Engineer
Robert Johnson, CFO
Paulette Cary, Regional Sales Manager
Greg Wrubell, Sports Commentator

KSOP-FM
12-10-1964; 104.3 mhz FM *Hrs Open:* 24; 25 kw; 3740 ft.; N40 39 34 W112 12 5
Mailing Address: P. O. Box 25548, Salt Lake City, UT 84125 US
Second Address: 1285 W. 2320 S., Salt Lake City, UT 84125
(801) 972-1043, *Fax:* (801) 974-0868
www.ksopcountry.com
License: Salt Lake City, Salt Lake County, UT held by KSOP Inc.
Nat'l Reps: McGavren Guild
Arbitron Metro Market: Salt Lake City-Ogden-Provo, UT *Format:* Country *No. News Employees:* 1 *Target Audience:* 18 plus.
Greg Hilton, General Manager
Phil Pond, Programming Director
John Greenwell, Disc Jockey
Bill Buckley, Disc Jockey

KUBL-FM
07-31-1965; 93.3 mhz FM; 25 kw; 3740 ft.; N40 39 34 W112 12 5
City Center West, 7201 W. Lake Blvd, Las Vegas, NV 89128 US
(801) 485-6700, *Fax:* (801) 464-8580
www.kbull93.com
License: Salt Lake City, Salt Lake County, UT held by Citadel Broadcasting Co.
Arbitron Metro Market: Salt Lake City, UT *Format:* Country
Terry Mathis, General Sales Mgr
Ed Hill, Programming Director
Randi P' Poll, Promotions Manager
Julie Johnson, News Director
Richie Bauer, Chief Engineer

***KUER-FM**
06-04-1960; 90.1 mhz FM; 38 kw; 2995 ft.; N40 36 30 W112 9 34
101 Wasatch Drive, Room 118, Salt Lake City, UT 84112 US
(801) 581-6625, *Fax:* (801) 581-6758
www.kuer.org
news@kuer.org
License: Salt Lake City, Salt Lake County, UT held by University of Utah.

Nat'l Network: NPR; PRI
Arbitron Metro Market: Salt Lake City, UT *Format:* Jazz, News
Michael Havey, Operations Dir
John Greene, General Manager
Susan Kropf, General Sales Mgr
Terry Gildea, News Director
Lewis Downey, Chief Engineer
Amy Fowler, Accountant
Becky Youkstetter, Manager of Individual and MajorGiving
Benjamin Bombard, Associate Producer for RadioWest
Chad L. Johnson, Web Site Producer
Elaine Clark, Senior Producer for RadioWest
Gayle Ewer, Marketing and Community Engagement Manager

*KUFR
12-14-1989; 91.7 mhz FM *Hrs Open:* 24; 0.22 kw; -318 ft.; N40 46 9 W111 53 12
4135 Northgate Blvd #1, Sacramento, CA 95834 US
(800) 543-1495, *Fax:* (916) 641-8238
www.familyradio.com
info@familyradio.com
License: Salt Lake City, Salt Lake County, UT held by Family Stations Inc.
Group Owner: Family Stations Inc.
Arbitron Metro Market: Salt Lake City, UT *Format:* Christian, Religious
Harold Camping, President
James Abrahamson, Operations Dir
Roger Crawford, Station Manager
Thad McKinney, General Sales Mgr

Sandy

KBJA
06-01-2001; 1640 khz AM *Hrs Open:* 24
10348 S. Redwood Rd, South Jordon, UT 84095 US
(801) 254-7699, *Fax:* (801) 254-7688
Super@kbja1640.com
License: Sandy, UT held by United Broadcasting Co. Inc.
Arbitron Metro Market: Salt Lake City-Ogden-Provo, UT *Format:* Spanish *Hrs. of News Programming:* news progmg 41.5 hrs wkly *No. News Employees:* 5 *Target Audience:* Hispanic adults; adult Hispanic market
Jose Rivera, General Manager
Karla Hernandez, General Sales Mgr
Daniel Rivera, Programming Director
Patricia Rivera, Promotions Manager
Carmen Vargas, News Director
Dennis Silver, Chief Engineer
Christian Rivera, PromotionsDirector

KTKK
05-13-1960; 630 khz AM *Hrs Open:* 24; 1 kw-D, DA2; 0.5 kw-N, DA2; N40 41 30 W111 55 30
10348 South Redwood Rd, South Jordan, UT 84095 US
(801) 253-4883, *Fax:* (801) 253-9085
www.k-talk.com
webmaster@k-talk.com
License: Sandy, UT held by United Broadcasting Co.
Arbitron Metro Market: Salt Lake City-Ogden-Provo, UT *Format:* Talk *Target Audience:* 35 plus.
Richard Perry, President
Janet Kelly, General Sales Mgr
Tom Draschil, Programming Director
Dennis Silver, Engineering Dir

Santa Clara

KRQX-FM
01-01-2002; 98.9 mhz FM; 14.5 kw; Ant 2,034 ft; N36 50 49 W113 29 28
515 S. 700 E., Suite 1C, Salt Lake City, UT 79714
(801) 524-2600
License: Santa Clara, Washington County, UT held by CBL Investments LLC

G. Craig Hanson, General Manager

*KXDS
91.3 mhz FM; 0.38 kw; 1854 ft.; N36 50 49 W113 29 28
US
(435) 319-0910
www.913thestorm.com
913TheStorm@Gmail.com
License: Santa Clara, Washington County, UT held by Dixie College.
Arbitron Metro Market: Saint George, UT *Format:* Alternative, Contemporary Hits/Top 40
Stan Plewe, President

Smithfield

KGNT
02-01-1983; 99.1 mhz FM; 3 kw; -131 ft.; N41 48 44 W111 47 31
P.O. Box 1450, 210 North 1000 East, St. George, UT 84771 US
(435) 752-1390, *Fax:* (435) 752-1392
www.koolfm.com
License: Smithfield, Cache County, UT held by Frandsen Media Co. LLC.
Group Owner: Sun Valley Radio Inc.; (acq 2-4-02; $775,000).
Nat'l Network: CBS; Westwood One
Arbitron Metro Market: Logan, UT *Format:* Oldies *Target Audience:* 18-49; 55% female, 45% male middle class *Adv. Rates:* 21; 18; 20; 14.50
Jay Eubanks, Station Manager
Lori Gill, General Sales Mgr
Paul Anderson, Chief Engineer
David Denton, Program Director

South Jordan

KUUU
09-01-1979; 92.5 mhz FM *Hrs Open:* 24; 0.5 kw; 3930 ft.; N40 39 35 W112 12 4
980 North Michigan Ave., Suite 1880, Chicago, IL 60611 US
(801) 524-2600, *Fax:* (801) 364-1811
www.u92online.com
License: South Jordan, Salt Lake County, UT held by Millcreek Broadcasting L.L.C.
Group Owner: Millcreek Broadcasting L.L.C.; (acq 4-17-2001; grpsl).
Nat'l Reps: Interep
Arbitron Metro Market: South Jordan, UT *Format:* Urban Contemporary, Blues *Hrs. of News Programming:* news progmg 15 hrs wkly *No. News Employees:* 1 *Target Audience:* General. *Adv. Rates:* 125; 125; 125;125
Brian Michel, Operations Dir
Randy Rodgers, General Manager
Lutisha Merrill, General Sales Mgr
Kevin Cruise, Programming Director
Jake Stone, Promotions Manager
Kevin Terry, Engineering Dir

South Salt Lake

KDYL
09-02-1967; 1060 khz AM *Hrs Open:* 24
Mailing Address: P.O. Box 57760, Salt Lake City, UT 84157 US
Second Address: 3606 South 500 West, Salt Lake City, UT 84115
(801) 262-5624, *Fax:* (801) 266-1510
www.kdylam.com
kdyl@kdylam.com
License: South Salt Lake, UT held by Holiday Broadcasting Co.
Group Owner: Carlson Communications International
Wire Services: CNN
Arbitron Metro Market: Salt Lake City, UT *Format:* Oldies *Hrs. of News Programming:* News progmg 13 hrs wkly *Target Audience:* 35-64; general *Adv. Rates:* 40; 40; 40; 40
Brent J. Carlson, Operations Dir
Ralph J. Carlson, General Manager
R. Steve Carlson, Vice President, Operations

KSOP
02-01-1955; 1370 khz AM *Hrs Open:* 24; 5 kw-D, DAN; 0.5 kw-N, DAN; N40 43 12 W111 55 42; N40 43 12 W111 55 41
Mailing Address: P.O. Box 25548, Salt Lake City, UT 84125 US
Second Address: 1285 W. 2320 S., Salt Lake City, UT 84125
(801) 972-1043, *Fax:* (801) 974-0868
www.goldcountryam1370.com
License: South Salt Lake, UT held by KSOP Inc.
Group Owner: 3 Daughters Media Inc.
Nat'l Reps: McGavren Guild
Arbitron Metro Market: Salt Lake City-Ogden-Provo, UT *Format:* Country *No. News Employees:* 1 *Target Audience:* 25-54+.
Greg Hilton, President
Don Hilton, Programming Director
Dick Jacobson, News Director
Bill Traue, Chief Engineer
Phil Pond, Disc Jockey
John Greenwell, Farm Director
Debbie Turpin, Music Director

Spanish Fork

KHQN
07-24-1960; 1480 khz AM; 1 kw-D, NDD; 0.133 kw-N, ND1; N40 4 30 W111 39 42
8628 South State, Spanish Fork, UT 84660 US
(801) 798-8610, *Fax:* (435) 864-3842
www.khqnradio.com
License: Spanish Fork, UT held by Robyn Howell
Arbitron Metro Market: Salt Lake City, UT *Format:* News, News/Talk, 84, Talk *Special Programming:* Sunday Accents 24 hrs wkly *Target Audience:* 25-54
Sam Bushman, General Manager

KOSY-FM
11-01-1967; 106.5 mhz FM *Hrs Open:* 24; 25 kw; 3740 ft.; N40 39 34 W112 12 5
900 Oakmont Lane, Suite 210, Westmont, IL 60559 US
(801) 908-1300, *Fax:* (801) 908-1459
www.kosy.com
License: Spanish Fork, Utah County, UT held by Citicasters Licenses L.P.
Group Owner: Clear Channel Communications Inc.; (acq 5-3-2004; $22 million with KXRV(FM) Centerville)
Nat'l Reps: Clear Channel; Katz Radio
Arbitron Metro Market: Salt Lake City-Ogden-Provo, UT *Format:* Adult Contemp *Target Audience:* 25-44; women
Bill Betts, Operations Dir
Stu Stanek, General Manager
Bill Matthews, General Sales Mgr
Steve Clem, Programming Director
Jim Vandiver, General Sales Manager

Spanish Valley

KCPX
06-15-2009; 1490 khz AM *Hrs Open:* 24
Mailing Address: US
Second Address: 1030 S. Bowling Alley Ln #3, Moab, UT 84532
(435) 259-1035, *Fax:* (435) 259-1037
License: Spanish Valley, UT held by Moab Communications LLC.
Group Owner: Carlson Communications International
Nat'l Network: Fox News Radio; Premiere Radio Networks *Nat'l Reps:* Rgnl Reps *Wire Services:* Metro Weather Service Inc.
Arbitron Metro Market: Spanish Valley, UT *Format:* Talk *Hrs. of News Programming:* 15 *No. News Employees:* 1
Ralph Carlson, President
Phillip Mueller, General Manager

St. George

KDXU
07-03-1957; 890 khz AM
57 West South Temple, Suite 700, Salt Lake City, UT 84101 US
(435) 673-3579, *Fax:* (435) 673-8900
www.newstalk890.com
License: St. George, UT held by CCR-St. George IV LLC.
Group Owner: Cherry Creek Radio LLC; (acq 8-10-2006; grpsl)
Arbitron Metro Market: Saint George, UT *Format:* News, News/Talk, 86 *Special Programming:* Relg 4 hrs wkly *Target Audience:* 25-54.
Joseph Schwartz, CEO
Debbie Calobeer, Operations Dir
Chris McCarthy, General Sales Mgr
Peter Gardner, Programming Director
Rick Parrish, Promotions Manager
Dave Cory, Chief Engineer

KONY
11-12-1994; 99.9 mhz FM *Hrs Open:* 24; 89 kw; 2034 ft.; N36 50 49 W113 29 28
Mailing Address: 210 North 1000 East, P. O. Box 1450, St. George, UT 84770 US
Second Address: 204 W Playa Della Rosita, Washington, UT 84780
(435) 628-3643, *Fax:* (435) 673-1210
www.999konycountry.com
kony@infowest.com
License: St. George, Washington County, UT held by Canyon Media Corp.
Nat'l Network: Fox News Radio *Nat'l Reps:* Katz Radio *Regional Reps:* Kathy Bingham
Arbitron Metro Market: Saint George, UT *Format:* Country *Target Audience:* 25-64; male & female *Adv. Rates:* 62; 55; 58; 47
M. Kent Frandsen, President
Marty Lane, Operations Dir
Carl Lamar, General Manager
Ben Lindquist, General Sales Mgr

KZNU
10-09-1957; 1450 khz AM *Hrs Open:* 24
Mailing Address: P O Box 1450, 210 North 1000 East, St. George, UT 84771 US
Second Address: 204 Playa Della Rosita, Washington, UT 84780
(435) 628-3643, *Fax:* (435) 673-1210
www.foxnews1450.com
info@1450newsradio.com
License: St. George, UT held by Canyon Media Corp..
Nat'l Network: Fox News Radio *Nat'l Reps:* Katz Radio *Regional Reps:* Kathy Bingham

RADIO - U.S.

Arbitron Metro Market: Saint George, UT *Format:* News, News/Talk, 86
Carl Lamar, General Manager
Ben Lindquist, General Sales Mgr
Dwight Goheen, Sales
Valorie Hansen, Sales
Chris Nelson, Sales
Nona Miller, Sales
Angie Watts, Sales
Cindy Watts, Sales

KZHK
01-01-1997; 95.9 mhz FM; 100 kw; 1952 ft.; N36 50 49 W113 29 28
P.O. Box 570, Logan, UT 84321 US
(435) 628-3643, *Fax:* (435) 673-1210
www.959thehawk.com
kony@infowest.com
License: St. George, Washington County, UT held by Marvin Kent Frandsen.
Group Owner: Sun Valley Radio Inc.
Arbitron Metro Market: St. George, UT *Format:* Classic Rock
Adv. Rates: 40; 40; 40; 40
M.K. Frandsen, President
Carl Lamar, General Manager
Marty Lane, Station Manager
Ben Lindquist, General Sales Mgr
Jon Smith, Programming Director
Aaronee Allen, Promotions Manager
Kelton Lloyd, Chief Engineer

Taylorsville

KUTR
05-09-2005; 820 khz AM
US
(336) 759-0363, *Fax:* (336) 759-0366
www.wtru.com
info@truthnetwork.com
License: Taylorsville, UT held by Julie Epperson
Arbitron Metro Market: Taylorsville, UT *Format:* Christian
Chris Redgrave, Operations Dir
Stuart Epperson, Jr., General Manager
Mike Carbone, Director of Sales / General Sales Manager
Beth Ann McBride, Programming Director
Mandel Owens, Chief Engineer
Rod Arquette, Vice President,Operations
Robby Dilmore, Sales
Anita Dean, Sales
Carol Allen, Business Manager
Joey Roberson, Assistant Network Program Director

Tremonton

KNFL
01-27-2006; 1470 khz AM *Hrs Open:* 24
US
(435) 628-1000
kognradio@comcast.net
License: Tremonton, UT held by AM Radio 1470 Inc.
Group Owner: Legacy Media Corporation; (acq 12-6-2004; grpsl).
Nat'l Network: CNN Radio; Westwood One
Arbitron Metro Market: Odgen, UT *Format:* News, Adult Contemp
Target Audience: 35 plus.
E. Morgan Skinner Jr., CEO
Richard Carter, Station Manager

Vernal

KLCY
05-01-1975; 105.5 mhz FM *Hrs Open:* 24; 3.3 kw; 1699 ft.; N40 32 16 W109 41 57
575 West Main Street, Vernal, UT 84078 US
(435) 789-0920, *Fax:* (435) 789-6977
kvel@ubtanet.com
License: Vernal, Uintah County, UT held by Ashley Communications Inc.
Nat'l Network: ABC; Jones Radio Networks
Arbitron Metro Market: Grand Junction, CO *Format:* Country *Hrs. of News Programming:* News progmg 2 hrs wkly *Target Audience:* 18-54; active
Rosanne Rybak, General Manager
Terry Lee, General Sales Mgr
Turner Williams, Programming Director
Kim David, News Director
Bill Davis, Chief Engineer

KRAM
12-01-1987; 1400 khz AM *Hrs Open:* Sunrise-sunset
US
(541) 884-8074, *Fax:* (541) 884-8226
License: Vernal, UT held by Scott D. MacArthur, Personal Rep., estate of Sandra A. Falk

Scott MacArthur, General Manager

KVEL
01-19-1947; 920 khz AM *Hrs Open:* 24; 5 kw-D, DAN; 1 kw-N, DAN; N40 29 30 W109 31 45
575 West Main Street, Vernal, UT 84078 US
(435) 789-0920, *Fax:* (435) 789-6977
www.920kvel.com
production@kvel.com
License: Vernal, UT held by Ashley Communications Inc.
Arbitron Metro Market: Vernal, UT *Format:* News, News/Talk, 84, Talk *Special Programming:* Farm 2 hrs, relg, Sp, pub affrs one hr wkly *Hrs. of News Programming:* news progmg 20 hrs wkly *No. News Employees:* 1 *Target Audience:* 35-64; affluent, upscale
Steve Evans, Owner/Manager
Lincon Brown, Programming Director
Steve Sprouse, Chief Engineer
Janet Crinklaw, Office Manager
Barry Johnson, Marketing Consultant
Malia Bascom, Marketing Consultant
Michael Evans, MarketingConsultant
Brian Baldwin, Marketing Consultant

***KEYV**
91.7 mhz FM; 910 w; Ant 1,637 ft; N40 32 16 W109 41 57
307 South 1600 West, Provo, UT
(801) 374-5210, *Fax:* (801) 374-2910
www.keyradio.org
mail@keyradio.org
License: Vernal, Uintah County, UT held by Biblical Ministries Worldwide.
Nat'l Network: Moody Broadcasting Network

Mike Zandler, General Manager

Washington

KUNF
06-06-1982; 1210 khz AM *Hrs Open:* 24; 10 kw-D, ND1; 0.25 kw-N, ND1; N37 8 38 W113 30 3
980 North Michigan Avenue, Suite 1880, Chicago, IL 60611 US
(435) 673-3579, *Fax:* (435) 673-8900
www.sportsradio1210.com
License: Washington, UT held by CCR-St. George IV LLC.
Group Owner: Cherry Creek Radio LLC; (acq 8-10-2006; grpsl)
Nat'l Network: ESPN Radio
Format: Sports, Talk *Target Audience:* 18-64. *Adv. Rates:* 22; 22; 22; 16
Debbie Calobeer, Operations Dir
Chris McCarthy, General Sales Mgr
Mike McGary, Programming Director
Rick Parrish, Promotions Manager
Michelle Matthews, News Director
Dave Cory, Chief Engineer

Wellington

KRPX
01-01-2006; 95.3 mhz FM; 6 kw; -138 ft.; N39 36 33 W110 48 50
US
(435) 637-1167, *Fax:* (435) 637-1177
koal@emerytelcom.net
License: Wellington, Carson County, UT held by College Creek Media LLC.
Group Owner: College Creek Media LLC
Arbitron Metro Market: San Antonio, TX *Format:* Light Rock
Neal Robinson, President
Tom Anderson, General Manager

West Jordan

KLLB
01-01-1982; 1510 khz AM; 1 kw-C, NDD; 10 kw-D, NDD; N40 33 6 W111 58 17
406 West S. Jordan Pkwy, Ste 100, South Jordan, UT 84107 US
(801) 487-0247, *Fax:* (801) 262-6200
kllbam@yahoo.com
License: West Jordan, UT held by United Security Financial Inc.
Arbitron Metro Market: Salt Lake City, UT *Format:* Gospel
Lois Johnson, General Manager
Joel Cosby, General Sales Mgr
D.J. Stone, Programming Director
Darrell Cosby, Chief Engineer

West Valley City

KMRI
11-16-1956; 1550 khz AM *Hrs Open:* 24; 10 kw-D, ND2; 0.34 kw-N, ND2; N40 43 16 W112 2 29
530 East 100 South, No. 204, Salt Lake City, UT 84102 US
(801) 886-1550, *Fax:* (801) 973-7145
www.exitos1550.com
License: West Valley City, UT held by Alpha & Omega Communications LLC
Arbitron Metro Market: Salt Lake City, UT *Format:* Christian *Hrs. of News Programming:* news progmg 40 hrs wkly *No. News Employees:* 2 *Target Audience:* 16-50. *Adv. Rates:* 40; 40; 40; 40
Pat Openshaw, President
Andy Acosta, General Manager

Woodruff

KYMV
06-01-2002; 100.7 mhz FM; 88 kw horiz; N40 52 16 W110 59 43
57 West South Temple, Suite 700, Salt Lake City, UT 84101 US
(801) 524-2600, *Fax:* (801) 521-9234
www.rewind1007.com
reception@simmonsmedia.com
License: Woodruff, Rich County, UT held by Simmons-SLC, LS LLC.
Group Owner: Simmons Media Group; (acq 4-4-2001; grpsl)
Arbitron Metro Market: Salt Lake City, UT *Format:* Adult Contemp
Stephen Johnson, General Manager
Jacquie Louie, General Sales Mgr
Alan Hague, Programming Director
Naziol Nazarina, Promotions Manager
Jennifer, Rewind Intern

Vermont

Addison

WIFY
01-01-1999; 93.7 mhz FM; 21 kw; Ant 354 ft; N44 13 15 W73 24 37
372 Dorset St., South Burlington, VT 05753
(802) 863-1010, *Fax:* (802) 861-7256
www.crusin937.com
License: Addison, Addison County, VT held by Addison Broadcasting Co. Inc.
Group Owner: Northeast Broadcasting Company Inc.; (acq 12-19-2000; $434,000)
Nat'l Network: Jones Radio Networks

Rich Delancy, General Manager
Rich Delancey, General Sales Mgr
J.J. Prieve, Programming Director
Chris Fells, News Director
Mike Raymond, Chief Engineer

Barre

***WCMD-FM**
08-01-1998; 89.9 mhz FM *Hrs Open:* 24; 0.94 kw; 591 ft.; N44 7 32 W72 28 36 *Rebroadcasts:* Rebroadcasts WCMK(FM) Bolton 99%
Mailing Address: P.O. Box 621, Essex Junction, VT 05453 US
Second Address: Box 8310, Essex, VT 05451-8310
(802) 878-8885, *Fax:* (802) 879-6835
thelightradio.net
cmi.radio@verizon.net
License: Barre, Washington County, VT held by Christian Ministries Inc.
Nat'l Network: Moody
Arbitron Metro Market: Essex,VT *Format:* Christian, Religious *Hrs. of News Programming:* News progmg 15 hrs wkly *Target Audience:* General; Christian, middle income
Mark Kinsley, President
Karlo Salminen, Operations Dir
Richard McClary, General Manager
Darlene Lamos, General Sales Mgr
Peter Morton, Chief Engineer

WORK
08-05-1974; 107.1 mhz FM; 3.9 kw; 410 ft.; N44 9 30 W72 28 46
2150 Washington Street, Suite 250, Newton, MA 02462 US
(802) 476-4168, *Fax:* (802) 479-5893
www.1071workfm.com
License: Barre, Washington County, VT
Group Owner: Nassau Broadcasting Partners L.P.
TV Affiliate: Classic hits

WSNO
10-13-1959; 1450 khz AM *Hrs Open:* 24; 1 kw-U, ND1; N44 11 40 W72 30 52
2150 Washington Street, Suite 250, Newton, MA 02462 US
(802) 476-4168, *Fax:* (802) 479-5893
www.wsno1450.net
License: Barre, VT held by Nassau Broadcasting III L.L.C.
Group Owner: Nassau Broadcasting Partners L.P.; (acq 8-2-2004; grpsl).
Nat'l Network: CBS
Format: News, News/Talk, 84, Talk
Ken Barlow, General Manager
Jim Severance, Programming Director

Barton

WQJQ
01-01-2008; 100.3 mhz FM; 100 w; Ant 525 ft; N44 45 57 W72 09 10
Box 97, Lyndonville, VT
(802) 626-9800, *Fax:* (802) 626-8500
wjpk@gmail.com
License: Barton, Orleans County, VT held by Vermont Broadcast Associates Inc.
Group Owner: Vermont Broadcast Associates Inc.
Bruce James, General Manager

Bellows Falls

WZLF
11-01-1981; 107.1 mhz FM *Hrs Open:* 24; 1.15 kw; 531 ft.; N43 12 33 W72 19 58 *Rebroadcasts:* Rebroadcasts WSSH(FM) Marlboro 100%
Post Office Box 1230, Route 12 and 103, Claremont, NH 03743 US
(603) 298-0332, *Fax:* (603) 727-0134
www.953thewolf.com
mtrombly@nassaubroadcasting.com
License: Bellows Falls, Windham County, VT held by Nassau Broadcasting III L.L.C.
Group Owner: Nassau Broadcasting Partners L.P.; (acq 8-2-2004; grpsl).
Nat'l Reps: Roslin
Arbitron Metro Market: West Lebanon, NH *Format:* Country *Special Programming:* Farm one hr wkly *Hrs. of News Programming:* news progmg 5 hrs wkly *No. News Employees:* 1 *Target Audience:* 25-54; general
Mike Trombly, General Manager
Matt Houseman, Programming Director
Brett Franklin, Public Service Director

Bennington

WBTN
09-23-1953; 1370 khz AM *Hrs Open:* 24/7; 1 kw-D, ND1; 0.085 kw-N, ND1; N42 54 19 W73 12 32
P. O. Box 560, Bennington, VT 05201 US
(802) 442-6321, *Fax:* (802) 442-3112
www.wbtnam.org
johnl@wbtnam.org
License: Bennington, VT held by Shires Media Partnership Inc (not-for-profit)
Nat'l Network: Westwood One *Wire Services:* AP
Arbitron Metro Market: Bennington, VT *Format:* News, News/Talk, 86 *Special Programming:* Red Sox/N.E. Patriots *Hrs. of News Programming:* 7-8 a.m.; 12-12:30 p.m. *Target Audience:* 24-54. *Adv. Rates:* Openrate: $15/30 second spot
Bov Howe, President
Ted Hollo, Sales Manager
Ken Norris, Programming Director
Brian Dempsey, Promotions Manager
John Likakis, Executive Director

***WBTN-FM**
11-04-1978; 94.3 mhz FM *Hrs Open:* 5:30 AM-midnight; 3 kw; 112 ft.; N42 56 52.9 W73 10 33.9
P. O. Box 560, Bennington, VT 05201 US
(802) 655-9451, *Fax:* (802) 655-2799
www.vpr.net
news@vpr.net.
License: Bennington, Bennington County, VT held by Vermont Public Radio.
Arbitron Metro Market: Colchester, VT *Format:* Classical *Hrs. of News Programming:* news progmg 4 hrs wkly *No. News Employees:* 1 *Target Audience:* 18-45.
Mark Vogelzang, President

Berlin

WWFY
04-02-1975; 100.9 mhz FM *Hrs Open:* 24; 4.5 kw; 778 ft.; N44 7 30.4 W72 28 27.9
3043 Lake Road West, Ashtabula, OH 44004 US
(802) 476-4168, *Fax:* (802) 479-5893
www.froggy1009.com
License: Berlin, Washington County, VT held by Nassau Broadcasting III L.L.C.
Group Owner: Nassau Broadcasting Partners L.P.; (acq 8-2-2004; grpsl).
Arbitron Metro Market: Middlebury, VT *Format:* Country *Target Audience:* 18-49; young professionals
John Gales, General Manager
Jim Severance, Programming Director

Bolton

***WGLY-FM**
01-01-1996; 91.5 mhz FM *Hrs Open:* 24; 1 kw; 935 ft.; N44 21 53 W72 55 52 *Rebroadcasts:* Rebroadcasts WCMD(FM) Barre 100%
Mailing Address: P.O. Box 583, Essex Jct., VT 05453 US
Second Address: Box 8310, Essex, VT 05451-8310
(802) 878-8885, *Fax:* (802) 879-6835
thelightradio.net
cmi.radio@verizon.net
License: Bolton, Chittenden County, VT held by Christian Ministries Inc.
Nat'l Network: Moody
Arbitron Metro Market: Burlington, VT *Format:* Religious
Mark Kinsley, President
Karlo Salminen, Operations Dir
Richard McClary, General Manager
Darlene Lamos, General Sales Mgr
Peter Morton, Chief Engineer

Brandon

WEXP
05-01-2000; 101.5 mhz FM *Hrs Open:* 24; 0.35 kw; 1306 ft.; N43 39 31 W73 6 26
9 Union Street, Waterbury, NH 95676 US
(802) 773-9264, *Fax:* (802) 747-0553
www.101thefox.com
License: Brandon, Rutland County, VT held by Nassau Broadcasting III L.L.C.
Group Owner: Nassau Broadcasting Partners L.P.; (acq 1-21-2005; $2.5 million with WTHK(FM) Wilmington)
Nat'l Network: Westwood One
Arbitron Metro Market: Brandon, VT *Format:* Classic Rock, Rock/AOR *Target Audience:* 25-54; male
John Gales, General Manager
Glenn Novak, General Sales Mgr
Kelly Kowalski, Programming Director
Kemy Chambers, Promotions Manager

Brattleboro

WKVT
11-29-1959; 1490 khz AM *Hrs Open:* 24; 1 kw-U, ND1; N42 50 51 W72 34 56
Stanhope Ave, P.O. Box 466, Keene, NH 03431 US
(802) 254-2343, *Fax:* (802) 254-6683
www.1490wkvt.com
pc@wkvt.com
License: Brattleboro, VT held by Saga Communications of New England LLC.
Group Owner: Saga Communications Inc.; (acq 5-1-2002; grpsl)
Nat'l Network: CBS *Wire Services:* AP
Format: News, News/Talk, 86 *Hrs. of News Programming:* news progmg 30 hrs wkly *No. News Employees:* 1 *Target Audience:* 35-64; news & info oriented adults *Adv. Rates:* 144; 120; 144; 120
Peter Case, Operations Dir
Dan Guin, General Manager

WKVT-FM
01-01-1980; 92.7 mhz FM *Hrs Open:* 24; 1.8 kw; 610 ft.; N42 53 45 W72 39 49
Stanhope Ave., P.O. Box 466, Keene, NH 03431 US
(802) 254-2343, *Fax:* (802) 254-6683
www.1490wkvt.com
pc@wkvt.com
License: Brattleboro, Windham County, VT
Group Owner: Saga Communications Inc.
Nat'l Network: AP Radio *Wire Services:* AP
Format: Contemporary Hits/Top 40, Adult Contemp *Hrs. of News Programming:* news progmg 8 hrs wkly *No. News Employees:* 1 *Target Audience:* 18-44.
Dan Guin, General Manager
Peter Case, Office Manager

WTSA
04-19-1950; 1450 khz AM *Hrs Open:* 24; 1 kw-U, ND1; N42 52 13 W72 33 35
Mailing Address: P.O. Box 819 Putney Road, Brattleboro, VT 05301 US
Second Address: 464 Putney Rd., Brattleboro, VT 5301
(802) 254-4577, *Fax:* (802) 257-4644
www.wtsa.net
news@wtsa.net.
License: Brattleboro, VT held by Tri-State Broadcasters Inc.
Nat'l Reps: D & R Radio
Arbitron Metro Market: Brattleboro, VT *Format:* Sports *No. News Employees:* 1 *Target Audience:* General.
John Kilduff, President
Kelli Corbell, General Manager
Steve Cormier, Station Manager
Stephanie Larson, Promotions Manager
Tim Johnson, News Director
Dan Taylor, Traffic Manager

WTSA-FM
12-15-1975; 96.7 mhz FM; 5.2 kw; 135 ft.; N42 53 21 W72 36 47
Mailing Address: P.O. Box 819 Putney Road, Brattleboro, VT 05302 US
Second Address: 464 Putney Rd., Brattleboro, VT 5301
(802) 254-4577, *Fax:* (802) 257-4644
www.wtsa.net
news@wtsa.net.
License: Brattleboro, Windham County, VT held by Tri-State Broadcasters Inc.
Arbitron Metro Market: Brattleboro, VT *Format:* Adult Contemp *Special Programming:* Oldies 16 hrs wkly *Target Audience:* 12 plus.
John Kilduff, President
Kelli Corbell, General Manager
Steve Cormier, Station Manager
Stephanie Larson, Promotions Manager
Tim Johnson, News Director
Dan Taylor, Traffic Manager

Brighton

***WVTI**
106.9 mhz FM; 1.42 kw; 694 ft.; N44 47 2 W71 53 13 US
(802) 655-9451, *Fax:* (802) 655-2799
www.vpr.net
License: Brighton, Essex County, VT held by Vermont Public Radio.
Arbitron Metro Market: Brighton, VT *Format:* Classical
Mark Vogelzang, President
Ross Sneyd, News Director
Kari Anderson, Board Operator

Bristol

WTNN
01-01-2007; 97.5 mhz FM; 8.7 kw; 518 ft.; N44 24 23.1 W73 8 12.8
US
(802) 864-9750, *Fax:* (802) 864-9777
www.eaglecountry975.com
info@eaglecountry975.com
License: Bristol, Addison County, VT held by Impact Radio Inc.
Arbitron Metro Market: Bristol, VT *Format:* Country
John J. Fuller, General Manager
Brian Ram, Vice President, Programming
Debbie Frenier, Traffic Manager
Rebecca Morse Whitten, Promotions Manager

***WXLQ**
01-01-2009; 90.5 mhz FM; 0.16 kw; 594 ft.; N44 13 24 W73 7 27 *Rebroadcasts:* Rebroadcasts WSLU(FM) Canton, NY 100%
US
(315) 229-5356, *Fax:* (315) 229-5373
www.ncpr.org
License: Bristol, Addison County, VT held by The St. Lawrence University.
Nat'l Network: NPR
Arbitron Metro Market: Bristol, VT *Format:* News
Ellen Rocco, General Manager

Burlington

WEZF
07-19-1968; 92.9 mhz FM *Hrs Open:* 24; 46 kw; 2703 ft.; N44 31 40 W72 48 58

Mailing Address: 600 Congress Ave., Suite 1400, Austin, TX 78701 US
Second Address: Box 1093, Burlington, VT 05402-1093
(802) 655-0093, *Fax:* (802) 655-0478
www.star929.com
JenniferFoxx@star929.com
License: Burlington, Chittenden County, VT held by Vox AM/FM LLC.
Group Owner: Vox AM/FM LLC; (acq 7-25-2008; grpsl)
Nat'l Reps: Clear Channel
Arbitron Metro Market: Burlington, VT *Format:* Adult Contemp *Hrs. of News Programming:* news progmg 7 hrs wkly *No. News Employees:* 1 *Target Audience:* 25-54.
Gale Parmalee, Operations Dir
Karen Marshall, General Manager
Jamie Dennis, Chief Engineer
Tara Madison, Webmaster

WJOY
09-14-1946; 1230 khz AM *Hrs Open:* 24; 1 kw-U, ND1; N44 27 3 W73 11 51
Mailing Address: P.O. Box 4368, Lancaster, PA 17604 US
Second Address: 70 Joy Dr., South Burlington, VT 5403
(802) 658-1230, *Fax:* (802) 862-0786
www.wjoy.com
wjoy@hallradio.com
License: Burlington, VT held by Hall Communications Inc.
Group Owner: Hall Communications Inc.; (acq 12-1-83;
Nat'l Network: Westwood One *Nat'l Reps:* D & R Radio
Arbitron Metro Market: Burlington-Plattsburgh, VT-NY *Format:* News *Hrs. of News Programming:* news progmg 4 hrs wkly *No. News Employees:* 1 *Target Audience:* General; affluent, empty nesters, well educated
Bonnie Rowbotham, Chairman
Arthur Rowbotham, President
Bill Baldwin, Operations Dir
Dan Dubonnet, General Manager
Lee Bodette, General Sales Mgr
Wendy Naylor, Promotions Manager
Ginny McGehee, News Director
Richard Reed,Executive Vice President
Steve Pelkey, Operations Director

WCAT
04-19-1954; 1390 khz AM *Hrs Open:* 24; 5 kw-D, DAN; 5 kw-N, DAN; N44 29 47 W73 12 49
9 Stowe Street, Waterbery, VT 05676 US
(802) 655-6753, *Fax:* (802) 860-4721
www.wcat1390.com
License: Burlington, VT held by Radio Broadcasting Services Inc.
Group Owner: Northeast Broadcasting Company Inc.; (acq 8-3-2006; $400,000).
Nat'l Network: ESPN Radio *Nat'l Reps:* McGavren Guild *Wire Services:* AP
Arbitron Metro Market: Burlington-Plattsburgh, VT-NY *Format:* Sports *Adv. Rates:* 25; 20; 22; 15
Steven Silberberg, President
Richard DeLancey Sr., General Manager
J.J. Prieve, Programming Director
Chris Fells, News Director

WOKO
06-26-1962; 98.9 mhz FM; 100 kw; 308 ft.; N44 27 3 W73 11 51
Mailing Address: P.O. Box 4368, Lancaster, PA 17604 US
Second Address: 70 Joy Dr., South Burlington, VT 5403
(802) 658-1230, *Fax:* (802) 862-0786
www.woko.com
License: Burlington, Chittenden County, VT held by Hall Communications Inc.
Group Owner: Hall Communications Inc.
Arbitron Metro Market: Burlington-Plat *TV Affiliate:* Country
Disc Jockey, Thom Richards
Disc Jockey, Cal Daniels
Disc Jockey, C.K. Coin
Disc Jockey, Ginny McGehee
Local News Editor

***WRUV**
10-03-1965; 90.1 mhz FM *Hrs Open:* 24; 0.46 kw; 131 ft.; N44 28 49 W73 12 7
Billings Student Center, 4th Floor, Burlington, VT 05405 US
(802) 656-4399, *Fax:* (802) 656-2281
www.wruv.org
wruv@wruv.org
License: Burlington, Chittenden County, VT held by University of Vermont & State Agricultural College.
Arbitron Metro Market: Burlington-Plat *Format:* Jazz, Variety/Diverse *Special Programming:* Non-commercial free format, progmg varies
Jenny Mudarri, Station Manager
Sadie Holliday, Programming Director
Sarah Attridge, Music Director
Kiley Schulze, PR Director

WVMT
05-20-1922; 620 khz AM *Hrs Open:* 24; 5 kw-D, DA2; 5 kw-N, DA2; N44 32 4 W73 13 15
Box 620 Malletts Bay Ave, Colchester, VT 05446 US
(802) 655-1620, *Fax:* (802) 655-1329
www.newstalk620wvmt.com
paulg@95triplex.com
License: Burlington, VT held by Sison Broadcasting Inc.
Nat'l Network: ABC Information & Entertainment *Nat'l Reps:* McGavren Guild
Arbitron Metro Market: Burlington, VT *Format:* News, News/Talk, 84, Talk *Hrs. of News Programming:* news progmg 14 hrs wkly *No. News Employees:* 2 *Target Audience:* 35-65.
Paul Goldman, President
Mark Esbjerg, Operations Dir

***WVPS**
10-15-1980; 107.9 mhz FM *Hrs Open:* 24; 48.8 kw; 2717 ft.; N44 31 32 W72 48 58
20 Troy Avenue, Colchester, VT 05446 US
(802) 655-9451, *Fax:* (802) 655-2799
www.vpr.net
contract@vpr.net
License: Burlington, Chittenden County, VT held by Vermont Public Radio.
Nat'l Network: NPR; PRI
Arbitron Metro Market: Burlington, VT *Format:* Jazz, News *Special Programming:* Switchboard call-in progmg 3 hrs, opera 5 hrs, fol *Hrs. of News Programming:* news progmg 43 hrs wkly *No. News Employees:* 9*Target Audience:* General.
Mark Vogelzang, CEO
Robin Turnau, President & CEO
Victoria St. John, Operations Dir
Anthony Hunt, Station Manager
Robin Turnau, General Sales Mgr
Cheryl Willoughby, Programming Director
Ross Sneyd, News Director
Richard Parker,Chief Engineer
Brian Donahue, VP For Finance & Operations/CFO
John Van Hoesen, VP for News & Programming
Brendan Kinney, VP for Development & Marketing

Castleton

***WIUV**
10-01-1976; 91.3 mhz FM; 0.23 kw horiz; -236 ft.; N43 36 29 W73 10 54
Castleton State College, Castleton, VT 05735 US
(802) 468-5611, *Fax:* (802) 468-5237
www.castleton.edu
License: Castleton, Rutland County, VT held by Board of Trustees.
Format: Alternative *Special Programming:* Jazz 10 hrs, reggae 6 hrs, rap-urban 5 hrs, folk 4 *Target Audience:* General; smart people
Robert Gershon, General Manager

Colchester

***WWPV-FM**
08-10-1973; 88.7 mhz FM *Hrs Open:* 8 AM-2 PM; 0.1 kw; 82 ft.; N44 29 38 W73 9 51
Box 1 Winooski Park, Colchester, VT 05439 US
(802) 654-2334, *Fax:* (802) 654-2336
www.wwpv.smcvt.edu
wwpv@smcvt.edu
License: Colchester, Chittenden County, VT held by Board of Trustees, St. Michaels College.
Arbitron Metro Market: Colchester, VT *Format:* Variety/Diverse *Target Audience:* 14-65; varies by time of day & progmg
Liam Connors, Station Manager
Diana Marchessault, Programming Director
Kate Lavelle, Promotions Manager
Dominic Wood, PSA & News Director
Dan Kuhn, Music Director
Lauren Mazzoleni, Business Manager
Derek Piette, TechnologyDirector
John Connors, Blues Music Director
Alexander Spinelli, Station Advisory Role

Danville

WDOT
01-01-1996; 95.7 mhz FM; 3.8 kw; 246 ft.; N44 24 58 W72 3 32
Rebroadcasts: Rebroadcasts WNCS(FM) Montpelier 90%
288 South River Road, Bedford, NJ 03110 US
(802) 223-2396, *Fax:* (802) 748-6939
www.pointfm.com
klm@pointfm.com
License: Danville, Caledonia County, VT held by Montpelier Broadcasting Inc.
Group Owner: Northeast Broadcasting Company Inc.; (acq 1996; $152,500 for CP)
Format: Variety/Diverse
Terry Lieberman, General Manager
Kim Buckminster, General Sales Mgr
Jamie Canfield, Programming Director
John Hosford, Chief Engineer

Derby Center

WMOO
04-01-1991; 92.1 mhz FM *Hrs Open:* 24; 2.25 kw horiz, 2.15 kw vert; 620 ft.; N44 58 23 W72 4 30
P.O. Box 92, Derby, VT 05829 US
(802) 766-9236, *Fax:* (802) 766-8067
http://www.moo92.com
dprudhomme@nassaubroadcasting.com
License: Derby Center, Orleans County, VT held by Nassau Broadcasting III L.L.C.
Group Owner: Nassau Broadcasting Partners L.P.; (acq 12-22-2004; $2.35 million with WIKE(AM) Newport).
Wire Services: AP
Arbitron Metro Market: Derby Center, VT *Format:* Adult Contemp *Special Programming:* Community events 8 hrs wkly *Hrs. of News Programming:* news progmg 16 hrs wkly *No. News Employees:* 1 *Target Audience:* General. *Adv. Rates:* 16; 14; 15; 12
Dawn Prudhomme, Operations Dir
Doug Weldon, Programming Director

Grand Isle

WIXM
04-01-1970; 102.3 mhz FM *Hrs Open:* 24; 20 w; Ant 364 ft; N44 45 53 W73 35 16
Box 712, 2 Main St., Saint Albans, VT 03110
(802) 524-2133, *Fax:* (802) 527-1450
www.purerock102.com
michaele@champlainradio.com
License: Grand Isle, Franklin County, VT held by Radio Broadcasting Services Inc.
Population Served: 270,000 *Arbitron Metro Market:* Burlington-Plattsburgh, VT-NY *Hrs. of News Programming:* news progmg 5 hrs wkly *No. News Employees:* 1 *Target Audience:* 18-49; men
Bob Rowe, General Manager
Carolyn Seifert, General Sales Mgr
J.J. Prieve, Programming Director

Hartford

WWOD
03-15-1992; 104.3 mhz FM *Hrs Open:* 24; 5.6 kw; 495 ft.; N43 39 15 W72 21 32
PO Box 8260, Essex, VT 05451 US
(603) 298-0332, *Fax:* (603) 727-0134
www.bestoldies104.com
info@bestoldies104.com
License: Hartford, Windsor County, VT held by Family Broadcasting Inc.
Group Owner: Nassau Broadcasting Partners L.P.; (acq 8-2-2004; grpsl).
Nat'l Network: USA
Format: Oldies *Special Programming:* Children 3 hrs, country gospel 2 hrs wkly *No. News Employees:* 1 *Target Audience:* 25 plus.
Mike Trombly, General Manager
Matt Houseman, Programming Director
Brett Franklin, Public Service Director

WXLF
02-01-1969; 95.3 mhz FM; 6 kw; 285 ft.; N43 39 14 W72 17 44
P.O.Box 1230, Claremont, NH 03743 US
(603) 298-0332, *Fax:* (603) 727-0134
www.953thewolf.com
mtrombly@nassaubroadcasting.com
License: Hartford, Windsor County, VT held by Nassau Broadcasting III LLC
Group Owner: Nassau Broadcasting Partners L.P.
Nat'l Network: Jones Radio Networks; Westwood One
Arbitron Metro Market: Hartford, VT *Format:* Country *Hrs. of News Programming:* News progmg one hr wkly *Target Audience:* 35-54.
Mike Trombly, General Manager
Matt Houseman, Programming Director
Brett Franklin, Public Service Director

Irasberg

WJJZ
94.5 mhz FM; 6 kw; 30.14 meters; N44 53.7 W72 14 13.2
PO Box 97, Lyndonville, VT
(802) 626-9800, *Fax:* (802) 626-8500
License: Irasberg, VT held by Vermont Broadcast Associates Inc
Group Owner: Vermont Broadcast Associates Inc.

Bruce A James, President

Johnson

***WJSC-FM**
07-16-1972; 90.7 mhz FM; 0.2 kw; -489 ft.; N44 38 29 W72 40 20
Johnson State College, Johnson, VT 05656 US
(802) 635-1355, *Fax:* (802) 635-1202
www.wjsc.findhere.org
wjsc907@hotmail.com
License: Johnson, Lamoille County, VT held by Board of Trustees, Vermont State College.
Format: Alternative, Variety/Diverse *Special Programming:* Class 3 hrs, C&W 3 hrs wkly
Andrew Frappier, General Manager

Killington

WJEN
08-04-1993; 105.3 mhz FM *Hrs Open:* 24; 1.25 kw; 2241 ft.; N43 38 22 W72 50 12
P O Box 282, Killington Rd., Killington, VT 05751 US
(802) 775-7500, *Fax:* (802) 775-7555
www.catcountryvermont.com
dgrembowicz@catamountradio.com
License: Killington, Rutland County, VT held by 6 Johnson Road Licenses Inc.
Group Owner: Pamal Broadcasting Ltd.; (acq 10-19-2001; grpsl).
Arbitron Metro Market: Killington, VT *Format:* Country *Target Audience:* 18-49; adult, income $35,000 plus, homeowners
Terry Jaye, Operations Dir
Debbie Grembowicz, General Manager
Brian Collamore, General Sales Mgr
Willie Clark, Programming Director
Chris O'Neil, Promotions Manager

Lunenburg

WOTX
05-05-2008; 93.7 mhz FM; 0.46 kw; 915 ft.; N44 23 39 W71 39 20
US
(603) 788-3636, *Fax:* (603) 788-3536
kiss102@together.net
License: Lunenburg, Essex County, VT held by Alexxon Corp.
Arbitron Metro Market: Lunenburg, VT *Format:* Classic Rock
Barry Lunderville, President

Lyndon

WGMT
05-19-1990; 97.7 mhz FM *Hrs Open:* 24; 0.6 kw; 1883 ft.; N44 34 15 W71 53 40
P. O. Box 97, Lyndonville, VT 05851 US
(802) 626-9800, *Fax:* (802) 626-8500
www.kingcon.com
wgmt@gmail.com
License: Lyndon, Caledonia County, VT held by Vermont Broadcast Associates Inc.
Group Owner: Vermont Broadcast Associates Inc.
Nat'l Network: CNN Radio *Nat'l Reps:* Roslin
Format: Adult Contemp *Hrs. of News Programming:* news progmg 5 hrs wkly *No. News Employees:* 2 *Target Audience:* 22-54; families, more female, disposable income, mobile
Bruce James, President
Steve Nichols, General Sales Mgr
Mike Barrett, Programming Director
Don Smith, Chief Engineer

Lyndonville

***WWLR**
02-04-1977; 91.5 mhz FM *Hrs Open:* 24 hrs; 2.75 kw; -75 ft.; N44 32 2 W72 1 45
Lyndon Stat College, College Road, Lyndonville, VT 05851 US
(802) 626-6413, *Fax:* (802) 626-4806
www.lsc.vsc.edu
impulse915@hotmail.com
License: Lyndonville, Caledonia County, VT held by Board of Trustees, Vermont State Colleges.
Arbitron Metro Market: Lyndonville, VT *Format:* Rock/AOR *Special Programming:* Class 2 hrs, jazz 3 hrs wkly *Target Audience:* Everyone.
Jim Champine, Operations Dir
P.J. Cioffi, General Manager

Manchester

WEQX
11-01-1984; 102.7 mhz FM *Hrs Open:* 24; 1.25 kw; 2490 ft.; N43 9 58 W73 6 59
Mailing Address: P.O. Box 1027, Manchester, VT 05254 US
Second Address: 161 Elm St., Manchester Center, VT 5255
(802) 362-4800, *Fax:* (802) 362-5555
www.weqx.com
eqx@weqx.com
License: Manchester, Bennington County, VT held by Northshire Communications Inc.
Nat'l Network: AP Radio
Arbitron Metro Market: Manchester, VT *Format:* Alternative *Special Programming:* Jazz 4 hrs, AAA 4 hrs, locl 2 hrs, new music 3 hrs wkly *Hrs. of News Programming:* News progmg 5 hrs wkly *Target Audience:* 25-44.
A. Brooks Brown, President
Melinda Brown, Operations Dir
Tim Bronson, Programming Director

***WVNK**
91.1 mhz FM; 0.115 kw; 317 ft.; N43 14 12 W73 1 44
US
(802) 655-9451, *Fax:* (802) 655-2799
www.vpr.net
License: Manchester, Bennington County, VT held by Vermont Public Radio.
Regional Network: Vermont Public Radio
Arbitron Metro Market: Manchester, VT *Format:* Classical *No. News Employees:* 6
Robin Turnau, CEO
Victoria St. John, Operations Dir
Franny Bastian, Production
Ross Sneyd, News Director
Rich Parker, Engineering Dir
Chris Albertine, Chief Engineer
Kari Anderson, Board Operator
Brian Donahue, Vice Presidentfor Finance & Operations/CFO
Brendan Kinney, Vice President for Development and Marketing
John Van Hoesen, Vice President for News & Programming
Lesli Blount, Director of Corporate Support
Sam Sanders, Senior Production Engineer

Marlboro

WRSY
07-01-1996; 101.5 mhz FM; 0.12 kw; 745 ft.; N42 50 46 W72 41 16 *Rebroadcasts:* Rebroadcasts WRSI(FM) Turners Falls, MA 100%
P.O. Box 1230, Claremont, NH 03743 US
(413) 586-7400, *Fax:* (413) 585-0927
www.wrsi.com
License: Marlboro, Windham County, VT held by Saga Communications of New England LLC.
Group Owner: Saga Communications Inc.; (acq 2-13-2004; grpsl).
Format: Triple A *Target Audience:* 35 plus; women
Sean O'Mealy, General Manager
Chris Belmonte, Programming Director
Scott Howard, Promotions Manager
Howard Frost, Chief Engineer

Middlebury

WFAD
12-24-1965; 1490 khz AM *Hrs Open:* 24; 1 kw-U, ND1; N43 59 57 W73 9 35
14 Lakeside Court, Plattsburgh, NY 12901 US
(802) 388-9000, *Fax:* (802) 388-3000
www.wtwk1070.com
sales@champlainradio.com
License: Middlebury, VT held by Addison Broadcasting Co. Inc.
Group Owner: Northeast Broadcasting Company Inc.; (acq 6-22-2001).
Nat'l Network: ESPN Radio
Arbitron Metro Market: Middlebury, VT *Format:* Sports
Bob Rowe, Operations Dir
Richard DeLancey Sr., General Manager
J.J. Prieve, Programming Director
Mike Raymond, Chief Engineer

***WRMC-FM**
05-01-1949; 91.1 mhz FM *Hrs Open:* 24; 2.9 kw; -30 ft.; N44 0 25 W73 10 40
Middlebury College, Middlebury, VT 05753 US
(802) 443-2471,(802) 443-6324, *Fax:* (802) 443-5108
www.wrmc.middlebury.edu
wrmc@wrmc.middlebury.edu
License: Middlebury, Addison County, VT held by President and Fellows of Middlebury College.
Nat'l Network: AP Radio
Format: Variety/Diverse *Special Programming:* Urban contemp 12 hrs, class 15 hrs, folk 15 hrs, relg one hr, blues 10 hrs, jazz 10 hrs, Sp one hr wkly *Hrs. of News Programming:* News progmg 8 hrs wkly *Target Audience:* General.
Ryan Abernnathey, General Manager

***WOXM**
90.1 mhz FM; 1.2 kw; 313 ft.; N44 1 34 W73 9 44
US
(802) 655-9451, *Fax:* (802) 655-2799
www.vpr.net
License: Middlebury, Addison County, VT held by Vermont Public Radio.
Arbitron Metro Market: Middlebury, VT *Format:* Classical *No. News Employees:* 6
Robin Turnau, CEO
Victoria St. John, Operations Dir
Franny Bastian, Production
Ross Sneyd, News Director
Rich Parker, Engineering Dir
Chris Albertine, Chief Engineer
Kari Anderson, Board Operator
Brian Donahue, Vice Presidentfor Finance & Operations/CFO
Brendan Kinney, Vice President for Development and Marketing
John Van Hoesen, Vice President for News & Programming
Lesli Blount, Director of Corporate Support
Sam Sanders, Senior Production Engineer

Montpelier

WNCS
06-13-1977; 104.7 mhz FM *Hrs Open:* 24; 1.9 kw; 2080 ft.; N44 25 14 W72 49 42
Box 551, Montpelier, VT 05601 US
(802) 223-2396, *Fax:* (802) 223-1520
www.pointfm.com
info@studiopointfm.com
License: Montpelier, Washington County, VT held by Montpelier Broadcasting Co. Inc.
Group Owner: Northeast Broadcasting Company Inc.; (acq 2-12-87).
Arbitron Metro Market: Montpelier, VT *Format:* Triple A *Special Programming:* Folk 4 hrs, jazz 5 hrs wkly *Target Audience:* 25-40; above-average income & educated, baby boomers
Steven Silberberg, President
Terry Lieberman, General Manager
Caroline Scribner, General Sales Mgr
Jamie Canfield, Programming Director
John Hosford, Chief Engineer

WSKI
12-07-1947; 1240 khz AM; 1 kw-U, ND1; N44 14 40 W72 32 47
288 South River Road, Bedford, NH 03110 US
(802) 223-2396, *Fax:* (802) 223-1520
www.pointfm.com
terry@pointfm.com
License: Montpelier, VT held by Galloway Communications Inc.
Group Owner: Northeast Broadcasting Company Inc.; (acq 5-2-00; grpsl).
Format: Oldies *Target Audience:* 35-64; 60% female, 40% male
Adv. Rates: 17.50; 12; 13.75; 10
Terry Lieberman, General Manager
Caroline Scribner, General Sales Mgr
Jamie Canfield, Programming Director
John Hosford, Chief Engineer

Morrisville

WLVB
08-01-1993; 93.9 mhz FM; 5.4 kw; 121 ft.; N44 34 42 W72 38 9
P.O. Box 550, Waterbury, VT 05676 US
(802) 888-4294, *Fax:* (802) 888-8523
wlvb@radiovermont.com
License: Morrisville, Lamoille County, VT held by Radio Vermont Inc.
Group Owner: Radio Vermont Group Inc.
Arbitron Metro Market: Morrisville, VT *Format:* Country
Ken Squier, President
Craig Ladd, Operations Dir
Eric Michaels, General Manager

Newport

WIKE
10-12-1952; 1490 khz AM *Hrs Open:* 24; 1 kw-U, ND1; N44 56 28 W72 13 35
Mailing Address: P.O. Box 92, Derby Center, VT 05829 US
Second Address: Derby Newport Rd., Derby, VT 5829
(802) 766-9236, *Fax:* (802) 766-8067
www.moo92.com
License: Newport, VT held by Nassau Broadcasting III L.L.C. *Group Owner:* Nassau Broadcasting Partners L.P.; (acq 12-22-2004; $2.35 million with WMOO(FM) Derby Center). *Format:* Country *Special Programming:* Loc info/entertainment 5 hrs wkly *Hrs. of News Programming:* news progmg 4 hrs wkly *No. News Employees:* 1 *Target Audience:* 18 plus. *Adv. Rates:* 14; 12; 13; 11
Dawn Prudhomme, Operations Dir
William Macek, General Manager

Northfield

***WNUB-FM**
12-08-1967; 88.3 mhz FM *Hrs Open:* 24; 0.285 kw; -387 ft.; N44 8 32 W72 39 31
65 South Main Street, Northfield, VT 05663 US
(802) 485-2483, *Fax:* (802) 485-2565
www.norwich.edu
wnub@norwich.edu
License: Northfield, Washington County, VT held by The Trustees of Norwich University.
Arbitron Metro Market: Northfield, VT *Format:* Rock/AOR, Triple A *Target Audience:* 15-40.
Doug Smith, General Manager

Norwich

***WNCH**
01-01-2004; 88.1 mhz FM *Hrs Open:* 24; 1.55 kw; 2251 ft.; N43 26 15 W72 27 8
Public Radio, 20 Troy Avenue, Colchester, VT 05446 US
(802) 655-9451, *Fax:* (802) 655-2799
www.vpr.net
vermontedition@vpr.net
License: Norwich, Windsor County, VT held by Vermont Public Radio.
Nat'l Network: NPR *Regional Network:* Vermont Public Radio
Arbitron Metro Market: Norwich, VT *Format:* Ethnic
Robin Turnau, President & CEO
Ross Sneyd, News Director
Peter Biello, Producer
Brian Donahue, Vice President for Finance & Operations/CFO
Brendan Kinney, Vice President for Development and Marketing
John Van Hoesen, Vice Presidentfor News & Programming

Plainfield

***WGDR**
05-11-1973; 91.1 mhz FM; 1.7 kw; -348 ft.; N44 17 4 W72 26 28
Box 336, Plainfield, VT 05667 US
(802) 454-7367, *Fax:* (802) 454-1451
www.wgdr.org
wgdr@goddard.edu
License: Plainfield, Washington County, VT held by Goddard College Corp.
Format: Talk, Variety/Diverse *Target Audience:* Multiple.
Bert Klunder, Operations Dir
Greg Hooker, General Manager
Jen Isaacs, Programming Director
Christine Farren, Special Events Coordinator

Poultney

WVNR
08-01-1981; 1340 khz AM *Hrs Open:* 5:30 AM-midnight; 1 kw-U, ND1; N43 30 16 W73 12 11
Mailing Address: P.O. Box 568, East Poultney, VT 05741 US
Second Address: 1214 Rt. 30 S., Poultney, VT 5764
(802) 287-9030
wvnrwnyv@yahoo.com
License: Poultney, VT held by Pine Tree Broadcasting Co.
Arbitron Metro Market: Poultney, VT *Format:* Adult Contemp, Country, 64 *Special Programming:* Big band 3 hrs, loc sports 6 hrs, swap shop one h *Hrs. of News Programming:* news progmg 3 hrs wkly *No. News Employees:* 1 *Target Audience:* 25-54; active, community oriented, working and professional, and families *Adv. Rates:* 10.25; 10.25; 10.25; 10.25
Michael Leech, President
Judith Leech, Executive Vice President

Putney

***WCMK**
01-01-2003; 91.9 mhz FM; 0.08 kw; 758 ft.; N42 58 28 W72 36 12
P O Box 583, Essex Jct, VT 05453 US
(866) 878-8885, *Fax:* (802) 879-6835
thelightradio.net
cmi.radio@verizon.net
License: Putney, Windham County, VT held by Christian Ministries Inc.
Arbitron Metro Market: Essex, VT *Format:* Christian
Ed Chase, President
Ric McClary, General Manager
Reverend Sean Troland, Vice President
Rachel Stringer, Secretary

Randolph

WVXR
10-25-1982; 102.1 mhz FM *Hrs Open:* 24; 11 kw; Ant 436 ft; N43 57 20 W72 36 10
62 Radio Dr., Randolph, VT 05061
(802) 728-4411, *Fax:* (802) 728-4013
www.champrocks.com
License: Randolph, Orange County, VT held by Vox AM/FM LLC. *Group Owner:* Vox AM/FM LLC; (acq 7-25-2008; grpsl)
Population Served: 315,000*Hrs. of News Programming:* News progmg 6 hrs wkly *Target Audience:* 25-54; 50% men & 50 % women *Adv. Rates:* 24; 18; 24; 16
Tom Barney, General Manager

WCVR(AM)
11-26-1968; 1320 khz AM; 1 kw-D, 66 w-N; N43 56 21 W72 38 13
Mailing Address: 62 Radio Dr., Randolph, VT 5060
Second Address: 265 Hegeman Ave., Colchester, VT 5446
(802) 728-4411, *Fax:* (802) 654-9381
randolphradio@clearchannel.com
License: Randolph, Orange County, VT held by Vox AM/FM LLC. *Group Owner:* Vox AM/FM LLC; (acq 7-25-2008; grpsl)
Population Served: 4,853 *Arbitron Metro Market:* Randolph, VT *Format:* News, News/Talk, 86 *Target Audience:* 18-49. *Adv. Rates:* 20; 10; 20; 12
Tom Barney, General Manager

Randolph Center

***WVTC**
08-29-1983; 90.7 mhz FM *Hrs Open:* 24; 0.3 kw; 210 ft.; N43 56 7 W72 36 10
Morey Hall, Vermont Technical Colleg, Randolph Center, VT 05061 US
(802) 728-1550, *Fax:* (802) 728-1550
www.wvtc.net
License: Randolph Center, Orange County, VT held by Vermont State Colleges Vermont Technical College.
Arbitron Metro Market: Randolph Center, VT *Format:* Alternative *Target Audience:* General.
Mike Collins, President
Aaron Minard, Operations Dir
Dan Andrews, Station Manager
Dan Hohmann, Programming Director
Steve Wichmann, Vice President
Kelley Herro, Music Director

Royalton

WRJT
01-01-1996; 103.1 mhz FM; 1.35 kw; 682 ft.; N43 46 28 W72 23 55 *Rebroadcasts:* Rebroadcasts WNCS(FM) Montpelier 90%
288 South River Rd, Bedford, NH 03110 US
(802) 223-2396, *Fax:* (802) 223-1520
www.pointfm.com
License: Royalton, Windsor County, VT held by Lisbon Communications Inc.
Group Owner: Northeast Broadcasting Company Inc.; (acq 11-30-01).
Format: Triple A
Ed Flanagan, General Manager
Mark Miller, Programming Director
Tanya Stepasiuk, Promotions Manager
Jon Hosford, Chief Engineer

Rupert

WMNV
04-10-1990; 104.1 mhz FM *Hrs Open:* 24; 4.3 kw horiz; 200 ft.; N43 16 1 W73 15 21 *Rebroadcasts:* Rebroadcasts WHAZ(AM) Troy, NY 100%
C/O Paul F. Lotters, 30 Park Avenue, Cohoes, NY 12047 US
(518) 237-1330, *Fax:* (518) 235-4468
www.aliveradionetwork.com
events@aliveradionetwork.com
License: Rupert, Bennington County, VT held by Capital Media Corp.
Group Owner: Capital Media Corp.; acq 4-15-97)
Arbitron Metro Market: Cohoes, NY *Format:* Christian *Special Programming:* Gospel, relg *Target Audience:* 25-75.
Paul Lotters, President
Steven Klob, Operations Dir
Rex Gregory, Programming Director
Bill Rosenfeld, Chief Engineer

Rutland

***WFTF**
01-10-1987; 90.5 mhz FM *Hrs Open:* 24; 0.72 kw; -561 ft.; N43 37 9 W72 59 4
2 Meadow Lane, Rutland, VT 05701 US
(802) 775-0358
www.cbcvt.org
cbcoffice@cbcvt.org
License: Rutland, Rutland County, VT held by Calvary Bible Church.
Nat'l Network: Moody
Format: Christian, Religious
Ronald Systo, President

WDVT
10-01-1988; 94.5 mhz FM *Hrs Open:* 24; 6 kw; 322 ft.; N43 34 4 W73 0 32
6 Johnson Road, Latham, NY 12110 US
(802) 775-7500, *Fax:* (802) 775-7555
www.945thedrive.com
catcountry@catamountradio.com
License: Rutland, Rutland County, VT held by 6 Johnson Road Licenses Inc.
Group Owner: Pamal Broadcasting Ltd.; (acq 10-19-2001; grpsl)
Format: Contemporary Hits/Top 40, Adult Contemp
Terry Jaye, Operations Dir
Debbie Grembowicz, General Manager
Brian Collamore, General Sales Mgr
Ed Kelly, Programming Director
Dave Tibbs, Promotions Manager
Carrie Allen, National Sales Manager

WJJR
03-25-1971; 98.1 mhz FM *Hrs Open:* 24; 1.15 kw; 2592 ft.; N43 36 17 W72 49 14
Mailing Address: 6 Johnson Road, Latham, NY 12110 US
Second Address: 67 Merchants Row, Ruthland, VT 5702
(802) 775-7500, *Fax:* (802) 775-7555
www.wjjr.net
wjjr@catamountradio.com
License: Rutland, Rutland County, VT held by 6 Johnson Road Licenses Inc.
Group Owner: Pamal Broadcasting Ltd.; (acq 10-19-2001; grpsl).
Format: Adult Contemp *Special Programming:* News, pub affrs one hr wkly *Hrs. of News Programming:* news progmg one hr wkly *No. News Employees:* 1 *Target Audience:* 25-54; in-office managerial, professional
Harry Weinhagen, General Manager
Debbie Grembowiez, General Sales Mgr
Terry Jayl, Programming Director
Ed Kelly, Promotions Manager

***WRVT**
01-10-1989; 88.7 mhz FM; 4 kw horiz, 4.8 kw vert; 1352 ft.; N43 39 31 W73 6 25 *Rebroadcasts:* Rebroadcasts WVPS(FM) Burlington 100%
20 Troy Avenue, Colchester, VT 05546 US
(802) 655-9451, *Fax:* (802) 655-2799,
www.vpr.net
contact@vpr.net
License: Rutland, Rutland County, VT held by Vermont Public Radio.
Nat'l Network: NPR; PRI *Regional Network:* Vermont Public Radio
Format: Jazz *Special Programming:* Switchboard call-in 3 hrs, folk 4 hrs wkly *Target Audience:* General.
Mark Vogelzang, President
Victoria St. John, Operations Dir
Robin Turnau, General Sales Mgr
Cheryl Willoughby, Programming Director
John VanHoesen, News Director
Rich Parker, Chief Engineer
Walter Parker, Music Director

WSYB
12-10-1930; 1380 khz AM; 5 kw-D, DAN; 1 kw-N, DAN; N43 35 35 W72 59 25

Mailing Address: 20 Stanford Drive, Farmington, CT 06032 US
Second Address: 250 Dorr Dr., Rutland, VT 5701
(802) 775-5597, *Fax:* (802) 775-6637
License: Rutland, VT held by 6 Johnson Road Licenses Inc.
Group Owner: Pamal Broadcasting Ltd.; (acq 4-1-2007; grpsl)
Nat'l Reps: McGavren Guild
Format: News, News/Talk, 86 *Target Audience:* 35-64.
Dave Ryeron, Programming Director
Glen Dudley, Chief Engineer

WZRT
01-01-1974; 97.1 mhz FM *Hrs Open:* 24; 1.15 kw; 2592 ft.; N43 36 17 W72 49 14
Mailing Address: 20 Stanford Drive, Farmington, CT 06032 US
Second Address: 250 Dorr Dr., Rutland, VT 5701
(802) 775-7500, *Fax:* (802) 775-7555
www.z971.com
dgrembowicz@catamountradio.com,
bcollamore@catamountradio.com
License: Rutland, Rutland County, VT
Group Owner: Pamal Broadcasting Ltd.
Arbitron Metro Market: Rutland, VT *Format:* Adult Contemp *Hrs. of News Programming:* news progmg 5 hrs wkly *No. News Employees:* 2 *Target Audience:* 18-49.
Dave Henderlite, CFO
Allen Dick, President
Debbie Grembowicz, General Manager
Brian Collamore, General Sales Mgr
Kwame Dankwa, Programming Director
Terry Jaye, Operations Manager
Glenda Hawley, Local/National Sales Manager

South Burlington

WXXX
11-16-1984; 95.5 mhz FM *Hrs Open:* 24; 25 kw; 236 ft.; N44 30 34 W73 10 59
Mailing Address: Box 9550 Malletts Bay Av, Colchester, VT 05446 US
Second Address: , Colchester, VT 5446
(802) 655-9550, *Fax:* (802) 655-1329
www.95triplex.com
paulg@95triplex.com
License: South Burlington, Chittenden County, VT held by Sison Broadcasting Inc.
Nat'l Reps: McGavren Guild
Arbitron Metro Market: Burlington, VT *Format:* Contemporary Hits/Top 40 *Hrs. of News Programming:* news progmg one hr wkly *No. News Employees:* 1 *Target Audience:* 18-49.
Mark Esbjerg, Operations Dir
Paul Goldman, General Manager
Ben Hamilton, Programming Director
Chantal Paulino, News Director

Springfield

WCFR
05-26-1954; 1480 khz AM *Hrs Open:* 24; 5 kw-D, NDD; N43 16 54 W72 29 21
52 Main Street, West Lebanon, NH 03784 US
(802) 885-1480
www.springfieldsvariety.com
ray@springfieldsvariety.com
License: Springfield, VT held by KOOR Communications Inc.
Group Owner: KOOR Communications Inc.; (acq 12-19-2001; $75,000).
Arbitron Metro Market: Springfield, VT *Format:* Contemporary Hits/Top 40, Adult Contemp *Hrs. of News Programming:* news progmg 7 hrs wkly *No. News Employees:* 1 *Target Audience:* 45 plus; 35-54
Bob Vinikoor, President
Ray Lemire, General Manager

St. Albans

WRSA
01-01-1930; 1420 khz AM *Hrs Open:* 24; 1 kw-D, ND1; 0.107 kw-N, ND1; N44 49 52 W73 5 25
288 S. River Rd., Bedford, NH 03110 US
(802) 524-2133, *Fax:* (802) 527-1450
www.cruisin937.com
michaele@champlainradio.net
License: St. Albans, VT held by Champlain Communications Corp.
Group Owner: Northeast Broadcasting Company Inc.; (acq 9-18-98; $500,000 with co-located FM).
Arbitron Metro Market: Saint Albans, VT *Format:* Sports, Talk *Hrs. of News Programming:* news progmg 20 hrs wkly *No. News Employees:* 1 *Target Audience:* General.
Mike Kmack, Operations Dir

St. Johnsbury

***WCKJ**
08-01-1998; 90.5 mhz FM; 1 kw; 738 ft.; N44 24 40 W71 58 13
Rebroadcasts: Rebroadcasts WGLY(FM) Bolton 100%
Mailing Address: P.O. Box 621, Essex Junction, VT 05453 US
Second Address: 140 Main St., Essec Junction, VT 5452
(802) 878-8885, *Fax:* (802) 879-6835
www.thelightradio.net
cmi.radio@verizon.net
License: St. Johnsbury, Caledonia County, VT held by Christian Ministries Inc.
Nat'l Network: Moody
Arbitron Metro Market: Essex,VT *Format:* Christian
Ric McClary, General Manager

WKXH
08-01-1985; 105.5 mhz FM *Hrs Open:* 24; 1.25 kw; 712 ft.; N44 24 38 W71 58 13
10 Church Street, P.O. Box 97, Lyndonville, VT 05851 US
(802) 748-2345, *Fax:* (802) 748-2361
www.kix1055.com
kix105@kix1055.com
License: St. Johnsbury, Caledonia County, VT held by Vermont Broadcast Associates Inc.
Group Owner: Vermont Broadcast Associates Inc.
Nat'l Network: ABC; Westwood One
Format: Country *No. News Employees:* 2 *Target Audience:* 24-55; families
Jim Stapleton, General Manager

WSTJ
07-10-1949; 1340 khz AM *Hrs Open:* 24; 1 kw-U, ND1; N44 25 6 W71 59 45
10 Church Street, P.O. Box 97, Lyndonville, VT 05851 US
(802) 748-1340, *Fax:* (802) 748-2361
kix105@kix1055.com
License: St. Johnsbury, VT held by Vermont Broadcast Associates Inc.
Group Owner: Vermont Broadcast Associates Inc.; (acq 4-3-98; $630,000 with co-located FM)
Nat'l Network: ABC; Jones Radio Networks
Format: Adult Contemp *Hrs. of News Programming:* news progmg 20 hrs wkly *No. News Employees:* 1 *Target Audience:* 35-75; adults and work places
Bruce James, President
Candis Leopold, Operations Dir
Dave Labounty, Programming Director
Don Smith, Chief Engineer

***WVPA**
01-01-1999; 88.5 mhz FM; 0.85 kw; 1867 ft.; N44 34 15 W71 53 38
20 Troy Ave, Colchester, VT 05446 US
(802) 655-9451, *Fax:* (802) 655-2799
www.vpr.net
mvogelzang@vpr.net
License: St. Johnsbury, Caledonia County, VT held by Vermont Public Radio.
Nat'l Network: NPR *Regional Network:* Vermont Public Radio
Arbitron Metro Market: St. Johnsbury, VT *Format:* Jazz, News
Robin Turnau, President & CEO
Victoria St. John, Operations Dir
Mark Vogelzang, General Manager
Robin Turnau, General Sales Mgr
Cheryl Willoughby, Programming Director
Ross Sneyd, News Director
Richard Parker, Chief Engineer
Walter Parker, Music Director
Brian Donahue, VP For Finance & Operations/CFO
John Van Hoesen, VP for News & Programming
Brendan Kinney, VP for Development & Marketing

Stowe

WCVT
02-28-1977; 101.7 mhz FM *Hrs Open:* 24; 1 kw; 2661 ft.; N44 31 32 W72 48 54
Mailing Address: P.O. Box 550, Waterbury, VT 05676 US
Second Address: 9 Stowe St., Waterbury, VT 5676
(802) 244-1764, *Fax:* (802) 244-1771
www.wcvtradio.com
wcvt@classicvermont.com
License: Stowe, Lamoille County, VT held by Radio Vermont Classics L.L.C.
Group Owner: Radio Vermont Group Inc.; (acq 6-19-97; $450,000)
Nat'l Reps: McGavren Guild
Arbitron Metro Market: Burlington-Plattsburgh, VT-NY *Format:* Classical *Special Programming:* Children one hr wkly *Target Audience:* 25-54; educated, upscale adults & families with active lifestyles *Adv. Rates:* 23; 21; 24; 19
Frankie Allen, Operations Dir
Eric Michaels, General Manager
Thomas Beardsley, Station Manager

Sunderland

***WVTQ**
05-01-1991; 95.1 mhz FM *Hrs Open:* 24; 0.096 kw; 2398 ft.; N43 9 58 W73 7 2 *Rebroadcasts:* Rebroadcasts WNCH(FM) Norwich 100%
6 Johnson Road, Latham, NY 12110 US
(802) 655-9451, *Fax:* (802) 655-2799
www.vpr.net
License: Sunderland, Bennington County, VT held by Vermont Public Radio
Nat'l Network: NPR *Regional Network:* Vermont Public Radio
Format: Classical *Target Audience:* 18-49.
Mark Vogelzang, President

Swanton

***WNGF**
89.9 mhz FM; 0.225 kw; -16 ft.; N44 55 2 W73 7 27
US
(518) 686-0975, *Fax:* (518) 686-0975
www.wngn.org
wngn@wngn.org
License: Swanton, Franklin County, VT held by Northeast Gospel Broadcasting Inc.
Arbitron Metro Market: Swanton, VT *Format:* Christian, Gospel
Bill Dagle, Vice President

Vergennes

WIZN
11-15-1983; 106.7 mhz FM *Hrs Open:* 24; 50 kw; 374 ft.; N44 18 40 W73 14 33
P.O. Box 1067, Burlington, VT 05402 US
(802) 860-2440, *Fax:* (802) 860-1818
www.wizn.com
wizn@wizn.com
License: Vergennes, Addison County, VT held by Hall Communications Inc.
Group Owner: Hall Communications Inc.; (acq 10-31-2005; $17 million)
Nat'l Reps: Katz Radio
Arbitron Metro Market: Burlington-Plattsburgh, VT-NY *Format:* Rock/AOR *Special Programming:* Oldies 3 hrs, reggae one hr, progsv one hr, blues *Target Audience:* 18-49.
Jennifer McCann, General Manager
Tracy Ovitt, General Sales Mgr
Matt Grasso, Programming Director

Warren

WDEV-FM
08-11-1989; 96.1 mhz FM *Hrs Open:* 24; 0.4 kw; 2277 ft.; N44 7 37 W72 55 43 *Rebroadcasts:* Rebroadcasts WDEV(AM) Waterbury 100%
Mailing Address: P.O. Box 550, Waterbury, VT 05676 US
Second Address: 9 Stowe St., Waterbury, VT 5676
(802) 244-7321, *Fax:* (802) 244-1771
www.wdevradio.com
wdev@radiovermont.com
License: Warren, Washington County, VT held by Radio Vermont Inc.
Group Owner: Radio Vermont Group Inc.; (acq 10-15-92; $643,000 with WKDR(AM) Burlington;
Nat'l Network: ABC
Arbitron Metro Market: Burlington-Plattsburgh, VT-NY *Format:* News, News/Talk, 84, Talk *Hrs. of News Programming:* news progmg 2 hrs wkly *No. News Employees:* 1 *Target Audience:* 25-54; affluent, upscale babyboomer generation
Ken Squier, President
Eric Michaels, General Manager
Tom Beardsley, General Sales Mgr
Jack Donovan, Programming Director
Rick Haskell, News Director
Tom Laffin, Chief Engineer

Waterbury

WDEV
07-16-1931; 550 khz AM
P.O. Box 550, Waterbury, VT 05676 US
(802) 244-7321, *Fax:* (802) 244-1771
www.wdevradio.com
wdev@radiovermont.com
License: Waterbury, VT held by Radio Vermont Inc.
Group Owner: Radio Vermont Group Inc.; (acq 1969)

Arbitron Metro Market: Waterbury, VT *Format:* News, Sports, 94 *Special Programming:* Class one hr wkly
Eric Michaels, General Manager
Tom Beardsley, General Sales Mgr
Jack Donovan, Programming Director
Rich Haskell, News Director
Tom Laffin, Chief Engineer

WWMP
02-14-1985; 103.3 mhz FM *Hrs Open:* 24; 2.85 kw; 932 ft.; N44 21 52 W72 55 53
P.O. Box 8260, Essex, VT 05451 US
(802) 863-1010, *Fax:* (802) 860-4721
www.mp103.com
License: Waterbury, Washington County, VT held by Radio Broadcasting Services Inc.
Group Owner: Northeast Broadcasting Company Inc.; (acq 5-4-2000).
Nat'l Network: USA
Arbitron Metro Market: Burlington-Plattsburgh, VT-NY *Format:* Variety/Diverse *Special Programming:* Children 3 hrs wkly *Hrs. of News Programming:* news progmg 16 hrs wkly *No. News Employees:* 1 *TargetAudience:* 25-54.
Rich Delancey, General Manager
J.J. Prieve, Programming Director
Mike Raymond, Chief Engineer

Wells River

WTWN
10-03-1976; 1100 khz AM *Hrs Open:* Sunrise-sunset; 2 kw-C, NDD; 5 kw-D, NDD; N44 8 55 W72 4 2
P.O. Box 1100, Wells River, VT 53865 US
(802) 757-3311, *Fax:* (802) 757-2774
www.wtwnradio.com
info@wtwnradio.com
License: Wells River, VT held by Puffer Broadcasting Inc.
Nat'l Network: Moody *Nat'l Reps:* Roslin
Arbitron Metro Market: Wells River, VT *Format:* Religious *Special Programming:* Children, gospel *Hrs. of News Programming:* News progmg 9 hrs wkly *Target Audience:* 25 plus.
Stephen Puffer, President
Teresa Puffer, Operations Dir
Glenn Hatch, Station Manager

Westminster

WKKN
01-01-1971; 101.9 mhz FM *Hrs Open:* 24; 1.05 kw; 774 ft.; N43 2 0 W72 22 3.7
31 Hanover St., Suite 4, Lebanon, NH 03766 US
(603) 283-1090
www.keenerocks.com
License: Westminster, Windham County, VT held by Great Eastern Radio LLC.
Group Owner: Great Eastern Radio LLC; (acq 10-30-2007; grpsl)
Nat'l Network: Westwood One
Arbitron Metro Market: Westminster, VT *No. News Employees:* 1 *Target Audience:* 25-54.
Tim Plante, General Manager

Wilmington

WTHK
06-01-1989; 100.7 mhz FM *Hrs Open:* 24; 0.13 kw; 1483 ft.; N42 57 33 W72 55 22 *Rebroadcasts:* Simulcast with WEXP(FM) Brandon 100%
Mailing Address: P.O. Box 1230, Claremont, NH 03743 US
Second Address: Box 850, West Dover, VT 5356
(802) 464-1350, *Fax:* (802) 747-0553
www.101thefox.com
License: Wilmington, Windham County, VT held by Nassau Broadcasting III L.L.C.
Group Owner: Nassau Broadcasting Partners L.P.; (acq 1-21-2005; $2.5 million with WEXP(FM) Brandon).
Nat'l Reps: McGavren Guild
Arbitron Metro Market: Wilmington, VT *Format:* Light Rock *Target Audience:* 25-54; residents, tourists, upscale Mt
John Gales, General Manager
Kelly Kowalski, Programming Director

Windsor

***WVPR**
08-13-1977; 89.5 mhz FM; 1.7 kw; 2277 ft.; N43 26 15 W72 27 8
Rebroadcasts: Rebroadcasts WVPS(FM) Burlington 100%
20 Troy Avenue, Colchester, VT 05446 US
(802) 655-9451, *Fax:* (802) 655-2799
www.vpr.net
mvogelzang@vpr.net
License: Windsor, Windsor County, VT held by Vermont Public Radio.
Nat'l Network: NPR; PRI
Arbitron Metro Market: Windsor, VT *Format:* Jazz, News *Special Programming:* Switchboard call-in 3 hrs, folk 6 hrs wkly *Target Audience:* General.
Mark Vogelzang, CEO
Robin Turnau, President & CEO
Michael Crane, Operations Dir
Anthony Hunt, Station Manager
Robin Turnau, General Sales Mgr
Cheryl Willoughby, Programming Director
Ross Sneyd, News Director
Wayne Perry, ChiefEngineer
Brian Donahue, VP For Finance & Operations/CFO
John Van Hoesen, VP for News & Programming
Brendan Kinney, VP for Development & Marketing

Woodstock

***WGLV**
01-01-2003; 91.7 mhz FM; 0.1 kw; 2277 ft.; N43 38 22 W72 50 12 *Rebroadcasts:* Rebroadcasts WGLY-FM Bolton 100%
Mailing Address: P O Box 583, Essex Junction, VT 05453 US
Second Address: 140 Main St., Essex Junction, VT 5452
(802) 878-8885, *Fax:* (802) 879-6835
www.thelightradio.net
cmi.radio@verizon.net
License: Woodstock, Windsor County, VT held by Christian Ministries Inc.
Nat'l Network: Salem Radio Network; Moody
Arbitron Metro Market: Essex, VT *Format:* Christian
Ric McClary, General Manager

WMXR
04-18-1989; 93.9 mhz FM *Hrs Open:* 24; 3.1 kw horiz, 2.98 kw vert; 456 ft.; N43 38 49 W72 21 49
52 Main Street, West Lebanon, NH 03784 US
(603) 448-1400, *Fax:* (603) 448-1755
www.maxx939.com
License: Woodstock, Windsor County, VT held by Great Eastern Radio LLC.
Group Owner: Great Eastern Radio LLC; (acq 10-30-2007; grpsl)
Arbitron Metro Market: Lebanon, NH *Format:* Contemporary Hits/Top 40
Tim Plante, General Manager
Chris Olsen, General Sales Mgr
Steven Smith, Programming Director

Virgin Islands

Charlotte Amalie

WGOD(AM)
01-01-1992; 1090 khz AM; 250 w-D; N18 18 57 W64 53 02
Box 305012, St. Thomas, VI 803
(340) 774-4498, *Fax:* (340) 777-9978
License: Charlotte Amalie, VI held by Three Angels Broadcasting Corp. Inc.
Charles Saunders, President

WGOD-FM
09-01-1980; 97.9 mhz FM; 50 kw; 1558 ft.; N18 21 25 W64 58 0
P.O. Box 5012, St. Thomas, VI 0803 US
(340) 774-4498, *Fax:* (340) 777-9978
License: Charlotte Amalie, VI
Format: Religious
Patricia Van Zandt, General Manager

***WIUJ**
10-05-1979; 102.9 mhz FM; 1.5 kw; 1427 ft.; N18 21 26 W64 56 50
P.O. Box 2477, St. Thomas, VI 0803 US
(340) 776-1029, *Fax:* (340) 774-0004
www.wiuj.com
info@wiuj.com
License: Charlotte Amalie, VI held by Virgin Islands Youth Development Radio.
Format: Adult Contemp, Big Band *Special Programming:* Class 5 hrs, jazz 6 hrs, Fr 4 hrs, Sp 4 hrs wkly *No. News Employees:* 1 *Target Audience:* General.
F. Ottley, Operations Dir
Leo Morone, General Manager
Greg Cyntje, Programming Director
Ron Hall, Chief Engineer

WIVI
04-26-1992; 96.1 mhz FM *Hrs Open:* 24; 2.4 kw horiz; 1499 ft.; N18 21 33 W64 58 18
P.O. Box 2179, Charlotte Amalie, VI 0801 US
(340) 774-1972, *Fax:* (340) 776-7060
www.amg.vi
License: Charlotte Amalie, VI held by Rox Radio Enterprises Inc.
Format: Classic Rock, Triple A *Hrs. of News Programming:* News progmg one hr wkly *Target Audience:* 25-54; general *Adv. Rates:* 15; 10; 15; 10
Lou Lambert, General Manager
Dorene Carle, General Sales Mgr

WSTA
08-01-1950; 1340 khz AM *Hrs Open:* 24; 1 kw-D, ND1; 1 kw-N, ND1; N18 20 10 W64 57 17
Mailing Address: P.O. Box 1340, St. Thomas, VI 0801 US
Second Address: 121 Sub Base, St. Thomas, VI 802
(340) 774-1340,(340) 777-4500, *Fax:* (340) 776-1316
www.WSTA.com or www.lucky13wsta.com
addie@wsta.com
License: Charlotte Amalie, VI held by Ottley Communications Corp.
Nat'l Network: ABC; CNN Radio
Format: Oldies, Variety/Diverse *Hrs. of News Programming:* news progmg 20 hrs wkly *No. News Employees:* 3 *Target Audience:* General.
Athneil Ottley, President
Peter Ottley, Operations Dir
Paula Smith, General Sales Mgr
Jean Forde, Traffic Manager

WVGN
01-01-2002; 107.3 mhz FM; 1.65 kw; 1440 ft.; N18 21 24 W64 57 59
P.O. Box 4084, Christiansted, St. Croix, VI 0822 US
(340) 774-2012, *Fax:* (340) 776-5362
www.wvgn.org
info@wvgn.org
License: Charlotte Amalie, VI held by LKK Group Corp.
Nat'l Network: NPR
Arbitron Metro Market: Charlotte Amalie, VI *Format:* News, News/Talk, 86
Patricia Bourne, Operations Dir
Victoria Squires, General Sales Mgr

WVJZ
03-15-1986; 105.3 mhz FM *Hrs Open:* 24; 30.2 kw; 1585 ft.; N18 21 33 W64 58 18
Mailing Address: P.O. Box 8209, P.O. Box 8209, St. Thomas, VI 0801 US
Second Address: Box 8209, Bluebeards's Castle, St. Thomas, VI 801
(340) 776-5260, *Fax:* (340) 776-5357
www.amg.vi
contact@kasvi.net
License: Charlotte Amalie, St. Thomas County, VI held by Gark LLC.
Group Owner: Gordon Ackley Stns; (acq 6-4-98)
Arbitron Metro Market: Charlotte Amalie, VI *Format:* Reggae *No. News Employees:* 2 *Target Audience:* 18-49; young adults, business professionals & college students
Randolph Knight, President
Jean Greaux Jr., Operations Dir
Mark Bastin, General Manager

WZIN
11-02-1976; 104.3 mhz FM; 44 kw; 1617 ft.; N18 21 35 W64 58 19
Post Office Box 4084, Christiansted, VI 0822 US
(340) 776-1043, *Fax:* (340) 775-3446
www.buzzrocks.com
info@buzzrocks.com
License: Charlotte Amalie, VI held by Pan Caribbean Broadcasting de P.R. Inc.
Arbitron Metro Market: Charlotte Amalie, VI *Format:* Alternative *Target Audience:* 18-34.
Alan Friedman, Operations Dir

WVWI
11-19-1962; 1000 khz AM *Hrs Open:* 24; 5 kw-D, ND1; 1 kw-N, ND1; N18 20 11 W64 56 41
#13 Crown Bay, P.O. Box 305678, St Thomas, VI 0803 US
(340) 776-1000, *Fax:* (340) 776-5357
www.amg.vi
License: Charlotte Amalie, VI held by Knight Communications of the Virgin Islands Inc.
Group Owner: Gordon Ackley Stns; (acq 1996; $250,000)
Nat'l Network: CBS; Westwood One
Arbitron Metro Market: Charlotte Amalie, VI *Format:* News, News/Talk, 84, Talk *Special Programming:* Relg 6 hrs, West Indian one hr, East Indian one hr *Hrs. of News Programming:* news progmg 25 hrs wkly *No. NewsEmployees:* 2 *Target Audience:* 25-54; middle/upper income professionals
Randolph Knight, President
Jean Greaux Jr., Operations Dir
Mark Bastin, General Manager

Christiansted

***WIVH**
07-01-1993; 89.9 mhz FM *Hrs Open:* 24; 1.4 kw; 997 ft.; N17 45 21 W64 47 56
Mailing Address: Rr #3, Hunlock Creek, PA 18621 US
Second Address: 5007 Estate Mt. Washington, Christiansted, VI 00820-4565
(570) 477-3688, *Fax:* (340) 719-3076
www.wrgn.org/wivh.htm
wrgn@epix.net
License: Christiansted, VI held by Gospel Media Institute Inc.
Format: Religious *Target Audience:* General.
Burl Updyke, President
Shirley Updyke, Programming Director

WJKC
10-29-1983; 95.1 mhz FM; 50 kw; 791 ft.; N17 44 7 W64 40 46
P.O. Box 4084, Christiansted St Cro, VI 0822 US
(340) 773-0995, *Fax:* (340) 773-9093
www.viradio.com
tom@visitcroix.com
License: Christiansted, VI held by Radio 95 Inc.
Format: Reggae *Target Audience:* General.
Jonathan Cohen, General Manager
Collin Hodge, General Sales Mgr
Tom Yarborough, Programming Director
Alvin Gee, News Director

WMNG
01-01-1997; 104.9 mhz FM; 15 kw; 755 ft.; N17 44 8 W64 40 47
P.O. Box 4084, Christiansted, VI 0822 US
(340) 773-0995, *Fax:* (340) 773-9093
www.viradio.com
tom@visitcroix.com
License: Christiansted, VI held by Clara Communications Corp.
Arbitron Metro Market: Christianstead, VI *Format:* Contemporary Hits/Top 40
Jonathan Cohen, General Manager
Amanda Cohen, General Sales Mgr
Tom Yarbaugh, Programming Director
Celia Jean, News Director
Herb Schoenbahm, Chief Engineer

WVIQ
05-17-1965; 99.5 mhz FM; 32 kw; 738 ft.; N17 44 7 W64 40 46
Post Office Box 4084, Christiansted, VI 0822 US
(340) 773-1180, *Fax:* (340) 773-9093
www.viradio.com
jkc95@aol.com
License: Christiansted, VI held by JKC Communications of the Virgin Islands Inc.
Arbitron Metro Market: St. Croix, VI *Format:* Adult Contemp *Adv. Rates:* 17; 10; 17; 10
Jonathan Cohen, General Manager
Tom Yarborough, Programming Director
Alvin Gee, News Director

WVVI-FM
02-26-1989; 93.5 mhz FM *Hrs Open:* 24; 9.6 kw; 807 ft.; N17 43 53 W64 41 17
Mailing Address: Carr. 167, Marginal #5, Bayamon, PR 0956 US
Second Address: 5027 Anchor Way, Christiansted, VI 820
(340) 773-3693, *Fax:* (340) 719-1800
paradise935fm@yahoo.com
License: Christiansted, VI held by The Rain Broadcasting Inc.
Arbitron Metro Market: Christiansted, VI *Format:* Country *Special Programming:* Relg 3 hrs wkly *Hrs. of News Programming:* News progmg one hr wkly *Target Audience:* General; affluent young adult permanentresidents
Roger Morgan, President
Herb Schoenbohm, Chief Engineer

WSTX
01-01-1952; 970 khz AM; 5 kw-D, ND1; 1 kw-N, ND1; N17 45 23 W64 41 38
P,O. Box 3279, St. Croix, VI 0822 US
(340) 773-0390, *Fax:* (340) 773-8515
vipn.vitelcom.net/herbs/
wstx@vitelcom.net
License: Christiansted, VI held by Family Broadcasting Inc.
Arbitron Metro Market: Christiansted, VI *Format:* Ethnic
Barbara James-Petersen, General Manager
Al Clarke, Programming Director
Arthur Bird, News Director
Herb Schoenbohm, Chief Engineer

WSTX-FM
09-01-1984; 100.3 mhz FM; 50 kw; Ant 1,030 ft; N17 45 20 W64 47 55
PO Box 3279, Christiansted, VI 822
(340) 773-0390, *Fax:* (340) 773-8515
License: Christiansted, VI
Format: Reggae
Brian Sands, General Manager

***WVSE**
91.9 mhz FM; 7400 watts; 274 meters; 17 44 N51 64 50 W11
License: Christiansted, VI
Group Owner: Crucial Educational Non-Profit

Cruz Bay

WWKS
02-03-1997; 101.3 mhz FM *Hrs Open:* 24; 50 kw; 1227 ft.; N18 20 30 W64 43 59
Mailing Address: P.O. Box 8209, St Thomas, VI 0801 US
Second Address: Box 8209, Bluebeard's Castle, St. Thomas, VI 801
(340) 776-4585, *Fax:* (340) 776-5357
www.amg.vi
License: Cruz Bay, VI held by Knight V.I. Radio Corp.
Group Owner: Gordon Ackley Stns; (acq 1996; $225,000)
Nat'l Network: ABC
Arbitron Metro Market: Cruz Bay, VI *Format:* Urban Contemporary *Special Programming:* West Indian/calypso 25 hrs wkly *Hrs. of News Programming:* news progmg 2 hrs wkly *No. News Employees:* 2 *Target Audience:* 25-54; middle/upper income professionals
Randolph Knight, President
Jean Greaux Jr., Operations Dir
Mark Bastin, General Manager

Frederiksted

WAXJ
01-01-1999; 103.5 mhz FM *Hrs Open:* 24; 6 kw; -33 ft.; N17 43 28 W64 53 3 *Rebroadcasts:* Rebroadcasts WDHP (AM) Frederiksted 50%
P.O. Box 755, St. Croix, VI 0851 US
(703) 527-1434
www.whdzx.com
radiobuxton@yahoo.com
License: Frederiksted, VI held by Reef Broadcasting Inc.

David Wilson, General Manager

WDHP
05-01-1999; 1620 khz AM
79-A Castle Coakley, Christiansted St. Cx, VI 0820 US
(340) 719-1620, *Fax:* (340) 778-1686
www.reefbroadcasting.com
wrra@islands.vi
License: Frederiksted, VI held by Reef Broadcasting Inc.
Arbitron Metro Market: St. Croix, U.S. Virgin Islands *Format:* Variety/Diverse
Hugh Pemberton, General Manager
Beverley Meyers, General Sales Mgr

WMYP
01-01-2002; 98.3 mhz FM *Hrs Open:* 24; 1.9 kw; 915 ft.; N17 44 51 W64 50 11
Dba Sky Broadcasting Co, P O Box 154, San German, PR 0683 US
(340) 772-0098, *Fax:* (340) 772-9852
latino98@viaccess.net
License: Frederiksted, VI held by Amanda Friedman
Format: Tejano *Target Audience:* 18-49.
Jose Martinez, General Manager

WEVI
01-01-2003; 101.7 mhz FM; 0.9 kw; 791 ft.; N17 43 15 W64 51 26
210 Church Avenue, High Point, NC 27260 US
(340) 719-1400, *Fax:* (340) 719-8783
www.frontlinemissions.org
info@frontlinemissions.org
License: Frederiksted, VI held by Frontline Missions International Inc.
Format: Christian
Antony Whitehead, General Manager

Virginia

Abingdon

WABN
12-10-1956; 1230 khz AM *Hrs Open:* 6 AM-midnight
P.O. Box 1067, Abingdon, VA 24210 US
(434) 220-2300, *Fax:* (434) 220-2304
www.wvax.com
License: Abingdon, VA held by Information Communication Corp.
Group Owner: Information Communications Corp.; (acq 1-1-2006; $250,000 with WHGG(AM) Kingsport, TN).
Arbitron Metro Market: Grand Junction CO *Format:* Talk *No. News Employees:* 4 *Target Audience:* 25-54; adult
John Kappes, General Sales Mgr
Jay James, Programming Director
Rob Graham, News Director

Accomac

WVES
08-13-1990; 99.3 mhz FM *Hrs Open:* 24; 22 kw; 344 ft.; N37 47 5 W75 36 16
P. O. Box 390, Accomac, VA 23301 US
(757) 665-6500, *Fax:* (757) 665-7178
www.shorecountry.net
hotcountry@tassnet.net
License: Accomac, Accomack County, VA held by Chincoteague Broadcasting Corp.
Nat'l Network: USA; Westwood One
Arbitron Metro Market: Parksley, VA *Format:* Country *Hrs. of News Programming:* News progmg 3 hrs wkly *Target Audience:* 25 plus.
Stephen Marks, President
Mark Dodds, General Manager
Dave Bralley, News Director
Tom Reynolds, Chief Engineer
Kelli Spragg, Public Affairs Director

Alberta

WWDW
01-01-2001; 107.7 mhz FM; 2.2 kw; 535 ft.; N36 52 2 W77 53 31
Rebroadcasts: Rebroadcasts WSMY(AM) Weldon, NC 100%
P O Box 539, C/O Putrese & Hunsaker, McLean, VA 22101 US
(252) 536-0209, *Fax:* (252) 538-0378
www.3wdfm.com/
Greg@Bestradioaround.com
License: Alberta, Brunswick County, VA held by First Media Radio LLC.
Group Owner: First Media Radio LLC; (acq 12-3-2003; grpsl)
Arbitron Metro Market: Alberta, VA *Format:* Gospel
CJ Riddick, Operations Dir
Al Haskins, General Manager
Greg Thrift, Station Manager

Alexandria

WTNT
12-10-1945; 730 khz AM *Hrs Open:* 24; 8 kw-D, 25 w-N; N38 44 43 W77 05 58
8121 Georgia Ave., Suite 1050, Silver Spring, MD 20910
(301) 562-5800, *Fax:* (301) 562-5850
espndeportes.espn.go.com
License: Alexandria, Alexandria City County, VA held by Red Zebra Broadcasting Licensee LLC.
Group Owner: Red Zebra Holdings LLC; (acq 5-9-2006; grpsl)
Nat'l Network: ESPN Deportes
Population Served: 55,500 *Arbitron Metro Market:* Washington, DC
Bruce Gilbert, CEO

Altavista

WKDE
04-29-1962; 1000 khz AM *Hrs Open:* Sunrise-sunset; 1 kw-D; N37 07 20 W79 17 20
Box 390, 200 Frazier Rd., Altavista, VA 24517
(434) 369-5588, *Fax:* (434) 369-1632
License: Altavista, Campbell County, VA held by DJ Broadcasting Corp.
Population Served: 250,000 *Arbitron Metro Market:* Roanoke-Lynchbu *Special Programming:* Southern gospel 5 hrs wkly *Hrs. of News Programming:* News progmg one hr wkly *Target Audience:* 25-54 yrs of age *Adv.Rates:* 12; 8; 12; na
Elizabeth Hoehne, President
Dave Haney, General Manager
Elizabeth Clancy, News Director

WKDE-FM
06-30-1969; 105.5 mhz FM *Hrs Open:* 24; 6 kw; 328 ft; N37 09 37 W79 13 28
Box 390, Altavista, VA 24517
(434) 369-1055, *Fax:* (434) 369-1632
www.kdcountry.com
info@kdcountry.com
License: Altavista, Campbell County, VA held by DJ Broadcasting Corp.
Nat'l Network: ABC
Population Served: 322,000 *Arbitron Metro Market:* Roanoke-Lynchburg *Special Programming:* Black gospel 5 hrs,

bluegrass 2 hrs wkly *No. News Employees:* 1 *Target Audience:* 25-54. *Adv. Rates:* 20; 15; 20;12
Elizabeth Hoehne, President
David Hoehne, General Manager
Joseph Aland, Programming Director
John Hart, Chief Engineer
Eleanor Haney, Traffic Manager

Amherst

WAMV
10-01-1976; 1420 khz AM; 2.2 kw-D, ND1; 0.047 kw-N, ND1; N37 32 23 W79 3 10; N37 32 23 W79 5 30
Mailing Address: P.O. Box 769, Amherst, VA 24521 US
Second Address: 132 School Rd., Amherst, VA 24521
(434) 946-9000, *Fax:* (434) 946-2201
www.wamvradio1420.com
WAMVradio@wamvradio1420.com
License: Amherst, VA held by Community First Broadcasters Inc.
Nat'l Network: USA
Arbitron Metro Market: Amherst, VA *Format:* Gospel *Target Audience:* 50+.
Robert Langstaff, President
Faron Tyree, General Sales Mgr
Mary Lu Gregg, Disc Jockey
Sterling Carter, Sales

WYYD
01-27-1981; 107.9 mhz FM *Hrs Open:* 24; 19 kw; 1801 ft.; N37 28 19 W79 22 28
600 Congress Avenue, Suite 1400, Austin, TX 78701 US
(434) 385-8298, *Fax:* (434) 385-8991
www.wyyd.cc
joeldearing@clearchannel.com
License: Amherst, Amherst County, VA held by Capstar TX L.P.
Group Owner: Clear Channel Communications Inc.; (acq 8-30-00; grpsl)
Nat'l Network: ABC *Nat'l Reps:* McGavren Guild
Arbitron Metro Market: Roanoke-Lynchbu *Format:* Country *No. News Employees:* 1 *Target Audience:* 25-54; those with moderate high expendable income
Ed Kilbane, Operations Dir
Dave Carwile, General Manager
Barry Holston, General Sales Mgr
Joel Dearing, Programming Director
Barry Michaels, Promotions Manager
Jeff Parker, Chief Engineer
Frank Smith, National Sales Manager

Appomattox

WJJX
05-17-1989; 102.7 mhz FM; 22 kw; 745 ft.; N37 28 7 W79 0 27
600 Congress Ave., Suite 1400, Austin, TX 78701 US
(434) 385-8298, *Fax:* (434) 385-8991
www.wjjs.com
stevencross@clearchannel.com
License: Appomattox, Appomattox County, VA held by Capstar TX L.P.
Group Owner: Clear Channel Communications Inc.; (acq 8-30-2000; grpsl)
Arbitron Metro Market: Roanoke-Lynchburg, VA *Format:* Contemporary Hits/Top 40 *Target Audience:* 35-54.
Chris Clendenen, General Manager
Dave Carwile, General Sales Mgr
Bill Cahill, Programming Director
Bobbi Crowder, Promotions Manager
Jeff Parker, Chief Engineer
Sarah Macomber, Advertising Director
Ron Gaylor, Vice President,Advertising
Tom Sweat, National Sales Manager
Steve Cross, Programming Director

*WTTX-FM
09-01-1976; 107.1 mhz FM; 1.7 kw; 427 ft.; N37 22 19 W78 50 6
P.O. Box 637, Appomattox, VA 24522 US
(336) 788-1155, *Fax:* (336) 788-7199
www.joyfm.org
office@joyfm.org
License: Appomattox, Appomattox County, VA held by Positive Alternative Radio Inc.
Group Owner: Positive Alternative Radio Inc.; (acq 1-11-2006; $1.8 million)
Arbitron Metro Market: Appomattox, VA *Format:* Gospel
Daniel Brit, Operations Dir
Adam McCain, Promotions Manager
Shelley Hicks, Office Manager
Candi Chandler, Music Director
Sam Stutts, Market Manager

WOWZ
06-01-1974; 1280 khz AM *Hrs Open:* 6 AM-8 PM; 1 kw-D, NDD; N37 22 19 W78 50 6
P.O. Box 637, Appomattox, VA 24522 US
(540) 343-7109, *Fax:* (540) 343-2306
License: Appomattox, VA held by Perception Media Inc.
Arbitron Metro Market: Roanoke, VA *Format:* News
Ben Peyton, President

Arlington

WAVA
11-07-1946; 780 khz AM *Hrs Open:* 6AM-6PM-or daylight hours
5545 Lee Highway, Arlington, VA 22207 US
(308) 632-5667, *Fax:* (308) 635-1905
License: Arlington, VA held by Salem Media of Virginia Inc.
Group Owner: Salem Communications Corp.; (acq 1-10-2000)
Nat'l Network: Salem Radio Network *Nat'l Reps:* Salem
Arbitron Metro Market: Glen Elder KS *Adv. Rates:* 50; 30; 40; na
Julie Marshall, General Manager

WAVA-FM
08-01-1948; 105.1 mhz FM; 33 kw; 604 ft.; N38 53 30 W77 7 55
4880 Santa Rosa Road, Suite 300, Camarillo, CA 93012 US
(330) 450-9250, *Fax:* (330) 821-0379
www.q92radio.com
radiosales@alliancelink.com
License: Arlington, Arlington County, VA held by Salem Media of Virginia Inc.
Group Owner: Salem Communications Corp.; (acq 2-13-92; $20 million;
Nat'l Network: Salem Radio Network *Nat'l Reps:* Salem
Arbitron Metro Market: Alliance OH *Format:* Adult Contemp *Hrs. of News Programming:* news progmg 4 hrs wkly *No. News Employees:* 2 *Target Audience:* 25-54. *Adv. Rates:* 250; 180; 200; 125
Don Peterson, General Manager
Mark O'Brian, General Sales Mgr
John Stewart, Programming Director
Clint M, News Director
Steve Hundt, Chief Engineer
Mark O'Brien, General Sales Manager
Dee Zink, Traffic Manager

WZHF
04-07-1947; 1390 khz AM; 5 kw-D, DA2; 5 kw-N, DA2; N38 54 15 W77 9 54
8121 Georgia Avenue, 10th Floor, Silver Spring, MD 20910 US
(301) 879-2422, *Fax:* (301) 879-9070
License: Arlington, VA held by Way Broadcasting Licensee LLC.
Group Owner: Multicultural Radio Broadcasting Inc.; (acq 5-30-00; grpsl).
Arbitron Metro Market: Washington, DC
Bill Parris, General Manager
Raoul Bastidas, General Sales Mgr
David Song, Chief Engineer

Ashland

WHAN
05-01-1962; 650 khz AM *Hrs Open:* Sunrise-sunset; 1 kw-D, ND1; 0.031 kw-N, ND1; N37 44 46 W77 29 44
Mailing Address: P.O. Box 148, Ashland, VA 23005 US
Second Address: 11337 Ashcake Rd, Ashland, VA 23005
(804) 798-1010, *Fax:* (804) 798-7933
www.whan1430.com
Bill@whan1430.com
License: Ashland, VA held by Fifth Estate Communications LLC
Nat'l Network: USA; Moody
Arbitron Metro Market: Richmond, VA *Format:* Talk *Hrs. of News Programming:* News progmg 7 hrs wkly *Target Audience:* 18-35; general *Adv. Rates:* 11.50; 10.50; 11.50; na
William Roberts, President
Skip Andrews, Programming Director
Arnold Meyer, News Director
Jim Grainger, Chief Engineer

*WYFJ
12-07-1967; 99.9 mhz FM *Hrs Open:* 24; 6 kw; 328 feet; N37 44 46 W77 29 44
Box 7300, Charlotte, NC 28273
(704) 523-5555
www.bbnradio.org
License: Ashland, Hanover County, VA held by Bible Broadcasting Network Inc.
Group Owner: Bible Broadcasting Network; acq 2-1-80)
Nat'l Network: Bible Bcstg Net
Hrs. of News Programming: News progmg 9 hrs wkly
Lowell Davey, President
Randy Adams, Station Manager

Bassett

WCBX
10-01-1960; 900 khz AM *Hrs Open:* 24; 1.1 kw-D, ND1; 0.18 kw-N, ND1; N36 42 36 W79 57 58
Mailing Address: P.O. Box 889, Blacksburg, VA 24063 US
Second Address: 1675 Grandview Dr., Martinsville, VA 24112
(276) 638-5235, *Fax:* (276) 638-6089
thesportsaddictnetwork.com
wcbxwodyfic@yahoo.com
License: Bassett, VA held by Base Communications Inc.
Nat'l Network: Fox Sports
Arbitron Metro Market: Blacksburg, VA *Format:* Sports *Hrs. of News Programming:* news progmg 12 hrs wkly *No. News Employees:* 1 *Target Audience:* 35-55.
Edward Baker, President
Steven Kuszlyk, Operations Dir
Aaron Marks, Station Manager

Bayside

WBVA
05-01-1999; 1450 khz AM *Rebroadcasts:* WPMH
Post Office Box 55387, Bayside, VA 23471 US
(757) 465-1603, *Fax:* (757) 488-7761
www.birach.com/wbva.htm
sima@BIRACH.Com
License: Bayside, VA held by Ronald W. Cowan Jr.
Arbitron Metro Market: Norfolk-Virginia Beach-Newport News, VA *Format:* News, News/Talk, 86
Ronald Cowan Jr., CEO
Henry Hoot, General Manager

Bedford

WZZK(FM)
10-20-1992; 106.9 mhz FM *Hrs Open:* 24; 290 w; Ant 1,276 ft; N37 19 14 W79 37 59
Mailing Address: Box 11798, Lynchburg, VA 24506
Second Address: 19-C Wadsworth St., Lynchburg, VA 24501
(434) 845-3698,(866) 431-5253, *Fax:* (434) 845-2063
www.rocktheplanet.fm
License: Bedford, Bedford County, VA held by Centennial Broadcasting LLC.
Group Owner: Centennial Broadcasting LLC; (acq 8-11-2005; $1.9 million)
Nat'l Network: ABC; Jones Radio Networks *Nat'l Reps:* McGavren Guild *Wire Services:* AP
Arbitron Metro Market: Roanoke-Lynchburg, VA *Hrs. of News Programming:* news progmg 14 hrs wkly *No. News Employees:* 3
Bob Abbott, Operations Dir
Ron Gaylor, General Sales Mgr
Kara Butterworth, News Director
Michael Williams, Business Manager
Sandi Conner, Production Director

WBLT
02-09-1950; 1350 khz AM
1201 Poplar Street, Bedford, VA 24523 US
(434) 534-6100, *Fax:* (434) 534-6101
www.espninva.com
wblt@inbox.com
License: Bedford, VA held by 3 Daughters Media Inc.
Group Owner: 3 Daughters Media Inc.; (acq 11-1-2005; $240,000)
Nat'l Network: ESPN Radio
Arbitron Metro Market: Eugene-Springfield, OR *Format:* Sports
Gary Burns, President
Devin Taylor, Operations Dir

Berryville

WXBN
05-19-1980; 105.5 mhz FM; 3 kw; Ant 300 ft; N39 07 03 W77 58 22 *Rebroadcasts:* Simulcast with WWRT(FM) Strasburg 100%
Mailing Address: Box 3300, Winchester, VA 22604
Second Address: 520 N. Pleasant Valley Rd., Winchester, VA 22601
(540) 667-2224, *Fax:* (540) 722-3295
www.everythingthatrocks.fm
License: Berryville, Clarke County, VA held by Mid Atlantic Network Inc.
Group Owner: Mid Atlantic Network; (acq 5-28-97; $850,000 with WWRT(FM) Strasburg).
Population Served: 280,000 *Arbitron Metro Market:* Winchester, VA *Target Audience:* 18 plus.
Allen Shaw, President
Jeff Adams, Operations Dir
Kathy Flerx, General Manager
Ron Baker, Programming Director

Robert Allen, News Director
Archie McKay, Chief Engineer

Big Island

WXCF-FM

11-20-1982; 103.9 mhz FM; 150 w; Ant 1,909 ft; N37 54 12 W79 52 15
Box 710 1047 Ingalls st., Clifton Forge, VA 24422
License: Big Island, Alleghany County, VA held by Quorum Radio Partners of Virginia Inc.
Population Served: 29,000*No. News Employees:* 1 *Target Audience:* 18-54; Targeting mostly women 25-54 *Adv. Rates:* 108; 108; 108; 90
Dennis Royer Jr., Programming Director

Big Stone Gap

WAXM

04-08-1975; 93.5 mhz FM *Hrs Open:* 24; 2.45 kw; 1883 ft.; N36 54 50 W82 53 40
Drawer W, Big Stone Gap, VA 24219 US
(800) 877-5600, *Fax:* (916) 251-1650
www.klove.com
License: Big Stone Gap, Wise County, VA held by Valley Broadcasting Inc.
Nat'l Network: CBS
Arbitron Metro Market: Winchendon MA *Format:* Christian
Darrell Chambliss, Chairman
Mike Novak, President
Glenn Goodwin, Operations Dir

WLSD

08-20-1953; 1220 khz AM; 1 kw-D, ND1; 0.045 kw-N, ND1; N36 50 26 W82 44 14
Drawer W, Big Stone Gap, VA 24219 US
(276) 523-1700, *Fax:* (276) 679-1198
93.5@waxm.com
License: Big Stone Gap, VA held by Valley Broadcasting and Communications Inc.
Nat'l Network: CBS
Format: Religious *Target Audience:* 19-60.
Greg Kress, President
William Stanley, General Manager
Rick Phillips, Programming Director
Jack Starnes, Chief Engineer
Paul Miller, Advertising Director

Blacksburg

WBRW

12-01-1964; 105.3 mhz FM *Hrs Open:* 24; 12 kw; 479 ft.; N37 11 12 W80 28 54
1930 Isaac Newton Square, #250, Reston, VA 20190 US
(540) 731-6000, *Fax:* (540) 731-6074
www.1053thebear.com
License: Blacksburg, Montgomery County, VA held by Cumulus Licensing LLC.
Group Owner: Cumulus Media Inc.; (acq 3-31-2004; grpsl).
Arbitron Metro Market: Radford, VA *Format:* Rock/AOR *Hrs. of News Programming:* News progmg 10 hrs wkly *Target Audience:* 18-49.
Scott Stevens, Operations Dir
Scott Claytons, General Sales Mgr
Courtney Quinn, Programming Director
Marty Gordon, News Director
Dave Dalesky, Chief Engineer

WFNR

01-01-1973; 710 khz AM
1930 Isaac Newton Square, #250, Reston, VA 20190 US
(540) 731-6000, *Fax:* (540) 731-6074
www.710wfnr.com
License: Blacksburg, VA held by Cumulus Licensing LLC.
Group Owner: Cumulus Media Inc.; (acq 3-31-2004; grpsl).
Regional Network: Va. News Net.
Format: News, News/Talk, 86 *Special Programming:* financial advise *Target Audience:* 25 plus; general
Scott Stevens, Operations Dir
Sarah Leftwich, General Manager

WKEX

07-10-1969; 1430 khz AM *Hrs Open:* 24; 1 kw-D, ND2; 0.062 kw-N, ND2; N37 13 57 W80 26 40
Mailing Address: P.O. Box 889, Blacksburg, VA 24063 US
Second Address: 145 Jackson St, Blacksburg, VA 24060
(540) 951-9791, *Fax:* (540) 961-2021
www.thesportsaddictnetwork.com
wkexam@yahoo.com
License: Blacksburg, VA held by Base Communications Inc.
Group Owner: Baker Family Stations; (acq 6-30-98; $60,000)
Nat'l Network: ESPN Radio
Format: Sports, Talk *Special Programming:* High School Sports, Redskins, MLB *Target Audience:* 35 plus; mature adults, all income levels
Amy Burnette, General Manager
Alison Baker, News Director
Sean Bielawski, Sports Director

*WUVT-FM

10-23-1969; 90.7 mhz FM *Hrs Open:* 24; 6.5 kw; 429 ft.; N37 11 12 W80 28 53.8
350 Squires Student, Center, Blacksburg, VA 24061 US
(540) 231-9880, *Fax:* (208) 692-5239
www.wuvt.vt.edu
wuvtamfm@vt.edu
License: Blacksburg, Montgomery County, VA held by Educational Media Corporation at Virginia Tech.
Arbitron Metro Market: Blacksburg, VA *Format:* Variety/Diverse *Special Programming:* American Indian 2 hrs, Greek 2 hrs, Chinese 2 hrs, *No. News Employees:* 1 *Target Audience:* general; college students
Mike Mosley, General Manager
Dustin East, General Sales Mgr
Amanda Dove, Programming Director
Linnea Morgan, Promotions Manager
Lauren Hickman, News Director
Kevin Sterne, Engineering Consultant
Ian Moore, Chief Engineer
Carlos Vializ, IT Director
Maddy Caddell, Business Manager
Angela Huang, Office Manager
Travis Brown, Traffic Director
Chris Guida, Music Director

Blackstone

WBBC-FM

11-17-1975; 93.5 mhz FM *Hrs Open:* 24; 17.5 kw; 394 ft.; N37 3 14 W78 1 15
P.O. Box 192, South 40 South, Blackstone, VA 23824 US
(416) 292-4059, *Fax:* (416) 292-4574
www.cmr24.com
info@cmr24.com
License: Blackstone, Nottoway County, VA
Nat'l Network: Westwood One
Arbitron Metro Market: Tyler-Longview TX *Format:* Ethnic *Adv. Rates:* 22; 22; 22; 22
Sivakumaran Sivapaphafundaram, General Manager

WKLV

01-01-1947; 1440 khz AM *Hrs Open:* Sunrise-sunset; 5 kw-D, ND1; 0.072 kw-N, ND1; N37 3 14 W78 1 15
P.O. Box 192, Highway 40 South, Blackstone, VA 23824 US
(434) 292-4146, *Fax:* (434) 292-7669
www.bobcatcountryradio.com
wbbc@bobcatcountryradio.com
License: Blackstone, VA held by Denbar Communications Inc.
Nat'l Network: ESPN Radio
Format: Sports *Target Audience:* 25-54. *Adv. Rates:* 15; 15; 15; 15
Dennis Royer, President
Dennis Royer, Station Manager
Dennis Royer Jr., General Sales Mgr
Shelly Allen, Sales
Ashley Barnes, Sales
Jack Daniels, Disc Jockey
Robbie Staylor, Disc Jockey

Bluefield

WHKX

12-01-1970; 106.3 mhz FM *Hrs Open:* 24; 0.33 kw; 1378 ft.; N37 15 5 W81 11 20
900 Bluefield Ave, #3, Bluefield, WV 24701 US
(304) 327-7114, *Fax:* (304) 325-7850
License: Bluefield, Tazewell County, VA
Nat'l Network: Westwood One
Arbitron Metro Market: Bluefield, WV *Format:* Country *Hrs. of News Programming:* News progmg 17 hrs wkly
Dave Crosier, Programming Director

Bon Air

WLES

09-01-1959; 590 khz AM *Hrs Open:* 24*Rebroadcasts:* Rebroadcasts WTRU(AM) Kernersville, NC 95%
Mailing Address: 2162 Plank Road, Lawrenceville, VA 23868 US
Second Address: 1001 E Main St, Level M, richmond, VA 23219
(804) 855-1524, *Fax:* (804) 855-1523
www.wtru.com
info@1010wpmh.com
License: Bon Air, VA held by Chesapeake-Portsmouth Broadcasting Corp.
Group Owner: Chesapeake-Portsmouth Broadcasting Corp.; (acq 7-19-2000)
Regional Network: Va. News Net.
Arbitron Metro Market: Richmond, VA *Format:* Christian
Nancy Epperson, President
Henry Hoot, Operations Dir

Bowling Green

WWUZ

01-01-1998; 96.9 mhz FM *Hrs Open:* 24; 2.95 kw; 472 ft.; N37 57 56 W77 22 19
P.O. Box 1306, Bowling Green, VA 22427 US
(540) 373-1500, *Fax:* (540) 374-5525
www.classicrock969.com
info@classicrock969.com
License: Bowling Green, Caroline County, VA held by The Free Lance-Star Publishing Co. of Fredericksburg, Virginia.
Group Owner: The Free Lance-Star Publishing Co.; (acq 8-23-01; $2.15 million).
Nat'l Network: AP Radio *Regional Reps:* RMR *Wire Services:* AP
Arbitron Metro Market: Bowling Green, VA *Format:* Classic Rock *Hrs. of News Programming:* news progmg 2.5 hours wkly *No. News Employees:* 1 *Target Audience:* 35 plus; male
Josiah Rowe III, President
Paul Johnson, Operations Dir
John Moen, General Manager
Jim Butler, General Sales Mgr
Jeff Beck, Programming Director
Sharon DeSouza, Promotions Manager
Frank Hammon, News Director
Chris Wilk, ChiefEngineer
Shel Bynum, Production Director
Sandy Ridgeway, Business Manager and Traffic Manager
Pat Covington, Traffic Assistant
Steve Johnson, Assistant Radio Engineer

Brandy Station

*WPRZ-FM

01-01-2008; 88.1 mhz FM; 10 kw; 449 ft.; N38 30 41.55 W78 3 22 *Rebroadcasts:* Rebroadcasts KLVR(FM) Middletown, CA 100%
US
(916) 251-1600, *Fax:* (916) 251-1650
www.klove.com
klove@klove.com
License: Brandy Station, Caldwell County, VA held by Educational Media Foundation.
Group Owner: EMF Broadcasting; (acq 5-22-2008; $299,600 for CP)
Nat'l Network: K-Love
Arbitron Metro Market: Brandy Station, VA *Format:* Christian
Darrell Chambliss, Chairman
Alan Mason, CEO/COO
Mike Novak, CEO
David Pierce, Chief Creative Officer
Dan Antonelli, Chief Business Development Officer
Eric Moser, Chief Financial Officer
Brian Burger, Vice President of HumanResources
D. Kevin Blair, Secretary and General Counsel

Bridgewater

WTGD

03-03-1989; 105.1 mhz FM *Hrs Open:* 24; 6 kw; 328 ft.; N38 27 8 W78 54 32
Mailing Address: 4850 Connecticut Ave NW, Suite 103, Washington, DC 20008 US
Second Address: 4850 Connecticut Ave NW, Suite 103, Washington, DC 20008
(540) 434-0331
www.1051bobrocks.com
License: Bridgewater, Rockingham County, VA held by M. Belmont VerStandig Inc.
Group Owner: VerStandig Broadcasting; (acq 1993; $10,000 with WHBG(AM) Harrisonburg;
Nat'l Network: La Gran D
Arbitron Metro Market: Harrisonburg, VA *No. News Employees:* 2 *Target Audience:* 24-54.
Susanne Myers, General Manager
Bill Phipps, Programming Director

Bristol

WFHG

01-01-1947; 980 khz AM *Hrs Open:* 24; 5 kw-D, DAN; 1 kw-N, DAN; N36 36 30 W82 9 36
Mailing Address: P.O. Box 1389, Bristol, VA 24203 US
Second Address: 901 E. Valley Dr., Bristol, VA 24201

(276) 669-8112, *Fax:* (276) 669-0541
www.supertalkwfhg.com
comments@supertalkwfhg.com
License: Bristol, VA held by Bristol Broadcasting Inc.
Group Owner: Bristol Broadcasting Co. Inc.; (acq 1972).
Nat'l Network: Fox Sports *Nat'l Reps:* McGavren Guild
Arbitron Metro Market: Bristol, VA *Format:* Sports
Lisa Hale, President
Bill Hagy, General Manager
Winnie Quaintance, General Sales Mgr
Roger Bouldin, Promotions Manager
Anna Honaker, News Director
Rick Perry, Chief Engineer
George Grant, Sports Commentator

WXBQ-FM
01-01-1945; 96.9 mhz FM; 75 kw; 2241 ft.; N36 25 59 W82 8 11
Mailing Address: 901 East Valley Drive, Bristol, VA 24201 US
Second Address: 901 E. Valley Dr., Bristol, VA 24201
(276) 669-8112, *Fax:* (276) 669-0541
www.wxbq.com
info@wxbq.com
License: Bristol, Sullivan County, VA held by Bristol Broadcasting Inc.
Group Owner: Bristol Broadcasting Co. Inc.
Nat'l Reps: McGavren Guild
Arbitron Metro Market: Bristol, VA *Format:* Country *Target Audience:* 25-54.
W.L. Nininger, President
Pete Nininger, General Manager
Winnie Quaintance, General Sales Mgr
Bill Hagy, Programming Director
Roger Bowldin, Promotions Manager
George Dixon, News Director
Chuck Lawson, Chief Engineer

WZAP
01-01-1946; 690 khz AM *Hrs Open:* 6 AM-midnight; 10 kw-D, 14 w-N; N36 37 51 W82 09 53
Mailing Address: Box 369, Bristol, VA 24203
Second Address: 11373 Wallace Pike, Bristol, VA 24202
(276) 669-6950, *Fax:* (276) 669-0794
www.wzapradio.com
wzapradio@aol.com
License: Bristol, Bristol County, VA held by RAM Communications Inc.
Nat'l Network: USA
Population Served: 502,000 *Arbitron Metro Market:* Johnson City-Ki *Hrs. of News Programming:* News progmg 8 hrs wkly *Target Audience:* General. *Adv. Rates:* 12; 10; 10; 9
R.A. Morris, President
Glen Harlow, Programming Director
Al Morris, News Director
Chuck Lawson, Chief Engineer
Matt Stevens, Disc Jockey
Dave Ray, Disc Jockey

Broadway

WJDV
12-18-1989; 96.1 mhz FM *Hrs Open:* 24; 2.6 kw; 1010 ft.; N38 33 50 W78 57 0
Mailing Address: P.O. Box 337, Broadway, VA 22815 US
Second Address: VA
(540) 434-0331
www.fresh961.com
smyers@valleyradio.com
License: Broadway, Rockingham County, VA held by HJV L.P.
Group Owner: VerStandig Broadcasting; (acq 3-12-2001; swap with WLTK(FM) New Market).
Arbitron Metro Market: Harrisonburg, VAA *Format:* Adult Contemp *Target Audience:* 25-44.
Susanne Meyers, General Manager
Kim Mitchell, General Sales Mgr
Ian Horne, Programming Director
Karl Magenhofer, News Director

Broadway-Timberville

WBTX
05-18-1972; 1470 khz AM *Hrs Open:* 6 AM-sunset; 5 kw-D, ND2; 0.036 kw-N, ND2; N38 37 24 W78 48 52
P.O. Box 337, Broadway, VA 22815 US
(540) 896-8933, *Fax:* (540) 896-1448
www.positive-radio.com
wbtx@positive-radio.com
License: Broadway-Timberville, VA held by Massanutten Broadcasting Co. Inc.
Nat'l Network: USA *Nat'l Reps:* Salem
Arbitron Metro Market: Harrisonburg, VA *Format:* Gospel *Special Programming:* Farm one hr wkly *Hrs. of News Programming:* News progmg 8 hrs wkly *Target Audience:* 35 plus. *Adv. Rates:* 16, 14 : 16, 14
David Eshleman, President
Christine Pompeo, General Sales Mgr
Jim Snavely, Programming Director
Christine Pompeo, Promotions Manager
Bill Fawcett, Chief Engineer
Judy Shafer, Traffic Manager

Brookneal

WODI
02-01-1997; 1230 khz AM; 1 kw-U, ND1; Rohn Guided; N37 2 17 W78 56 30
Mailing Address: 24 Belmont Avenue, Edison, NJ 08814 US
Second Address: 24 Belmont Ave., Edison, NJ
(434) 376-1230, *Fax:* (434) 376-9634
wodi@wodiradio.com
License: Brookneal, VA held by D & M Communications Inc.
Nat'l Network: CBS *Regional Network:* Va. News Net.
Arbitron Metro Market: Roanoke-Lynchbu *TV Affiliate:* Oldies
Special Programming: news progmg 6 hrs wkly *Hrs. of News Programming:* 3 *No. News Employees:* 25-54; general *Adv. Rates:* 12
Music Director, Dianne DeNicola
Promotions Manager

Buena Vista

WWZW
01-01-1981; 96.7 mhz FM; 2 kw; 1135 ft.; N37 43 37 W79 18 24
Mailing Address: P.O. Box 217, Sterling, VA 20167 US
Second Address: 392 E Midland Trail, Lexington, VA 24450
(540) 463-2161, *Fax:* (540) 463-9524
www.firstmediava.com
License: Buena Vista, Buena Vista County, VA held by First Media Radio LLC.
Group Owner: First Media Radio LLC; (acq 6-21-2004; $1.33 million with WREL(AM) Lexington)
Nat'l Network: NBC Radio
Format: Adult Contemp *Target Audience:* 25-54. *Adv. Rates:* 30; 20; 25; 15
Alex Kolobielski, President
Debra Reed, General Sales Mgr
Steve Williams, Programming Director

Buffalo Gap

WBOP
01-01-1988; 95.5 mhz FM *Hrs Open:* 24; 6 kw; 308 ft.; N38 10 55 W79 13 34
Mailing Address: P.O. Box 3206, Staunton, VA 24402 US
Second Address: 639 N. Main St., Mt. Crawford, VA 22841
(540) 432-1063, *Fax:* (540) 433-9267
www.zonesportsradio.com
race@rebel955.com
License: Buffalo Gap, Augusta County, VA held by Vox Communications Group LLC.
Group Owner: Vox Communications; (acq 8-31-2005; $900,000).
Nat'l Network: CNN Radio
Arbitron Metro Market: Harrisonburg, VA *Format:* Country
Race Ashlyn, General Manager

Cedar Bluff

WYRV
03-01-1985; 770 khz AM *Hrs Open:* Sunrise-sunset; 5 kw-D; N37 05 05 W81 46 07
Mailing Address: Box 70, Cedar Bluff, VA 24630
Second Address: 504 Middlecreek Rd., Cedar Bluff, VA 24609
(276) 964-9619,(276) 964-5167, *Fax:* (276) 964-9610
www.amen770.com
brad@wyrvam770.com
License: Cedar Bluff, Tazewell County, VA held by Faith Christian Music Broadcasting Ministries Inc.
Population Served: 285,000 *Arbitron Metro Market:* Bluefield, WV *Hrs. of News Programming:* news progmg 3 hrs wkly *No. News Employees:* 1 *Target Audience:* 30 plus.
Brad Ratliff, General Manager
Acie Rasnake, Chief Engineer
Greg Webb, Music Director

Charles City

***WAUQ**
01-01-2000; 89.7 mhz FM; 10 kw vert; 351 ft.; N37 25 58 W77 11 38
P O Drawer 2440, Tupelo, MS 38803 US
(662) 844-8888, *Fax:* (662 842-6791
www.afr.net
License: Charles City, Charles City County, VA held by American Family Association.
Group Owner: American Family Radio
Arbitron Metro Market: Visalia-Tulare-Hanford, CA *Format:* Christian, Religious
Marvin Sanders, General Manager

Charlottesville

WCHV
01-01-1930; 1260 khz AM *Hrs Open:* 24; 5 kw-D, DA2; 2.5 kw-N, DA2; N38 6 52 W78 27 18
1140 Rose Hill Drive, Charlottesville, VA 22903 US
(434) 978-4408, *Fax:* (434) 978-0723
www.wchv.com
joe@wchv.com
License: Charlottesville, VA held by Monticello Media LLC.
Group Owner: Monticello Media LLC; (acq 10-4-2007; grpsl)
Nat'l Network: Fox News Radio; Wall Street *Nat'l Reps:* Christal
Arbitron Metro Market: Charlottesville, VA *Format:* News, News/Talk, 86 *Hrs. of News Programming:* 20 hrs wkly *No. News Employees:* 4 *Target Audience:* Adults 35+. *Adv. Rates:* 20; 20; 20; 10
Vinnie Kice, Operations Dir
Dennis Mockler, General Manager
Mike Schneide, Sales manager
Joe Thomas, Programming Director
Mellissa Neeley, News Director
Joe Thomas, PD

WINA
09-01-1949; 1070 khz AM *Hrs Open:* 24; 5 kw-D, DAN; 5 kw-N, DAN; N38 5 22 W78 30 14
1140 Rose Hill Drive, Charlottesville, VA 22903 US
(434) 220-2300, *Fax:* (434) 220-2304
www.wina.com
rick@wina.com
License: Charlottesville, VA held by Saga Communications of Charlottesville LLC.
Group Owner: Saga Communications Inc.; (acq 1-6-2005; grpsl)
Nat'l Network: CBS *Nat'l Reps:* Katz Radio
Arbitron Metro Market: Charlottesville, VA *Format:* News, News/Talk, 84, Talk *Hrs. of News Programming:* news progmg 20 hrs wkly *No. News Employees:* 4 *Target Audience:* General. *Adv. Rates:* 55; 25; 35; 15
Rick Daniels, Operations Dir
Jim Principi, General Manager
John Kappes, General Sales Mgr
Rick Daniels, Programming Director
Rob Graham, News Director
Jay James, Sports Director

WKAV
10-01-1957; 1400 khz AM *Hrs Open:* 24; 1 kw-U, ND1; N38 1 49 W78 29 22
1140 Rose Hill Drive, Charlottesville, VA 22903 US
(434) 978-4408, *Fax:* (434) 978-0723
www.wkav.com
sportsradio1400@wkav.com
License: Charlottesville, VA held by Monticello Media LLC.
Group Owner: Monticello Media LLC; (acq 10-4-2007; grpsl)
Nat'l Network: Fox Sports *Nat'l Reps:* Christal
Arbitron Metro Market: Charlottesville, VA *Format:* Sports *Target Audience:* 18 - 54; Men *Adv. Rates:* 10; 10; 10; 7
Vinnie Kice, Operations Dir
Dennis Mockler, General Manager
Karen Cote, General Sales Mgr
Joe Thomas, Programming Director

***WNRN**
09-01-1996; 91.9 mhz FM *Hrs Open:* 24; 0.32 kw; 1066 ft.; N37 58 55 W78 29 3 *Rebroadcasts:* Rebroadcasts WNRS-FM Sweetbriar 85%
2125 Ivy Road, Suite ""L"", Charlottesville, VA 22903 US
(434) 971-4096, *Fax:* (434) 971-6562
www.wnrn.org
info@wnrn.org
License: Charlottesville, Charlottesville City County, VA held by Stu-Comm Inc.
Arbitron Metro Market: Charlottesville, VA *Format:* Alternative, Triple A *Special Programming:* Folk 19 hrs, techno 6 hrs, industrial 2 hrs, punk *Target Audience:* 18-49; educated, upscale young professionals andstudents *Adv. Rates:* 28; 22; 27; 19
Mike Friend, General Manager
Anne Williams, Promotions Manager
Steve Mendenhall, News Director
Mike Momson, Music Director

WQMZ
10-01-1954; 95.1 mhz FM; 6 kw; 325 ft.; N38 2 54 W78 28 12
1140 Rose Hill Drive, Charlottesville, VA 22903 US
(434) 220-2300, *Fax:* (434) 220-2304
www.literockz951.com

License: Charlottesville, Charlottesville City County, VA held by Saga Communications of Charlottesville LLC.
Group Owner: Saga Communications Inc.
Arbitron Metro Market: Charlottesville, VA *Format:* Adult Contemp *Adv. Rates:* 50; 50; 50; 20
Les Sinclair, Programming Director

***WTJU**
05-10-1957; 91.1 mhz FM *Hrs Open:* 24; 0.6 kw; 1066 ft.; N37 58 55 W78 29 3
Mailing Address: 711 Newcomb Hall Station, Charlottesville, VA 22904 US
Second Address: 2464 Lambeth Commons, 2nd Floor, Charlottesville, VA 22904
(434) 924-0885, *Fax:* (434) 924-8996
wtju.net
wtju@virginia.edu
License: Charlottesville, Charlottesville City County, VA held by Rector & Board of Visitors, University of Virginia
Nat'l Network: PRI
Arbitron Metro Market: Charlottesville, VA *Format:* Variety/Diverse *Special Programming:* Black 8 hrs, children 2 hrs, folk 20 hrs,gospel on *Hrs. of News Programming:* News progmg 6 hrs wkly *No. News Employees:* 1 *Target Audience:* General; from rural population to college educated *Adv. Rates:* underwriting (call)
Nathan Moore, General Manager
Robert Nowicki, Station Manager
Emma Potter, News Director
Pete Yadlowsky, Chief Engineer
Jane McDonald, Business Manager
Robert Nowicki, Underwriting Manager
Gayle Poirier, Office Administrator
Alan Williams, Contract Engineer
Morgan McLeod, Production Director
Peter Jones, Folk Director

WCHV-FM
01-01-1995; 107.5 mhz FM; 210 w; Ant 1,109 ft; N37 59 05 W78 28 49
1150 Pepsi Pl., Suite 300, Charlottesville, VA 22901
(434) 978-4408,(434) 964-1075, *Fax:* (978) 978-1190
www.1075tom.com
info@1075tom.com
License: Charlottesville, Charlottesville City County, VA held by Monticello Media LLC.
Group Owner: Monticello Media LLC; (acq 10-4-2007; grpsl)
Arbitron Metro Market: Charlottesville, VA
David Mitchel, General Manager
Kevin McCabe, General Sales Mgr
Kishore Persaud, Chief Engineer

WUVA
06-22-1979; 92.7 mhz FM *Hrs Open:* 24; 0.75 kw; 899 ft.; N37 59 8 W78 28 47
501 East Main Street, P.O. Box 498, Charlottesville, VA 22902 US
(434) 817-6880, *Fax:* (434) 817-6884
www.92.7kissfm.com
info@92.7kissfm.com
License: Charlottesville, Charlottesville City County, VA held by WUVA Inc.
Nat'l Reps: Katz Radio
Arbitron Metro Market: Charlottesville, VA *Format:* Urban Contemporary *Hrs. of News Programming:* news progmg 20 hrs wkly *No. News Employees:* 20 *Target Audience:* 18-54. *Adv. Rates:* 40; 40; 40; 40
Tanisha Thompson, Operations Dir
Sharon Sant, General Manager

***WVTU**
01-08-1991; 89.3 mhz FM; 0.195 kw horiz, 0.16 kw vert; 1696 ft.; N38 3 58 W78 47 54 *Rebroadcasts:* Rebroadcasts WVTF(FM) Roanoke 100%
4235 Electric Rd Sw, Suite 105, Roanoke, VA 24014 US
(540) 989-8900, *Fax:* (540) 776-2727
www.wvtf.org
info@wvtf.org
License: Charlottesville, Charlottesville City County, VA held by Virginia Tech. Foundation Inc.
Nat'l Network: NPR; PRI *Regional Network:* Va. News Net.
Arbitron Metro Market: Charlottesville, VA *Format:* Jazz
Glenn Gleixner, General Manager
Karen Dillon, General Sales Mgr
Rick Matttoni, Programming Director
Connie Stevens, News Director
Paxton Durham, Chief Engineer
Bart Prater, Traffic Director
Cynthia Gray, Development Director
Mary Grace Franchi, Business Manager
Brian Black, Administrative Assistant
Ben Martin, Operations Assistant & Producer/Radio Reading Serv

***WVTW**
01-01-1997; 88.5 mhz FM; 1 kw; 1040 ft.; N37 58 55 W78 29 3
Rebroadcasts: Rebroadcasts WVTF(FM) Roanoke 100%
315 Burruss Hall, Blacksburg, VA 24061 US
(540) 989-8900, *Fax:* (540) 776-2727
www.wvtf.org
info@wvtf.org
License: Charlottesville, Charlottesville City County, VA held by Virginia Tech Foundation Inc.
Nat'l Network: NPR
Arbitron Metro Market: Charlottesville, VA *Format:* Jazz
Glenn Gleixner, General Manager
Karen Dillon, General Sales Mgr
Rick Matttoni, Programming Director
Connie Stevens, News Director
Paxton Durham, Chief Engineer
Bart Prater, Traffic Director
Cynthia Gray, Development Director
Mary Grace Franchi, Business Manager
Brian Black, Administrative Assistant
Ben Martin, Operations Assistant & Producer/Radio Reading Serv

WWWV
01-01-1959; 97.5 mhz FM; 8.9 kw; 1132 ft.; N37 59 5 W78 28 49
1140 Rose Hill Drive, Charlottsville, VA 22903 US
(434) 220-2300, *Fax:* (434) 220-2304
www.3wv.com
pstone@3wv.com
License: Charlottesville, Charlottesville City County, VA held by Saga Communications of Charlottesville LLC.
Group Owner: Saga Communications Inc.; (acq 1-6-2005; grpsl)
Nat'l Reps: Katz Radio
Arbitron Metro Market: Charlottesville, VA *Target Audience:* 18-49. *Adv. Rates:* 50; 45; 45; 20
Rick Daniels, Operations Dir
John Kappes, General Sales Mgr
Perry Stone, Programming Director
Luke Church, Promotions Manager
John Spangler, Music Director

WVAX
04-01-2006; 1450 khz AM *Hrs Open:* 24
US
(434) 220-2300, *Fax:* (434) 220-2304
www.wvax.com
License: Charlottesville, VA held by Saga Communications of Charlottesville LLC.
Group Owner: Saga Communications Inc.; (acq 11-22-2005; $150,000 for CP)
Nat'l Network: CNN Radio *Nat'l Reps:* Katz Radio
Arbitron Metro Market: Grand Junction, CO *Format:* Talk *No. News Employees:* 4 *Target Audience:* 25-54; adult *Adv. Rates:* 25; 20; 25; 10
John Kappes, General Sales Mgr
Jay James, Programming Director
Rob Graham, News Director

Chase City

***WMVE**
10-10-2007; 90.1 mhz FM *Hrs Open:* 24; 8 kw; 371 ft.; N36 46 29 W78 20 41 *Rebroadcasts:* Rebroadcasts WCVE(FM) Richmond 100%
23 Sesame Street, Richmond, VA 23235 US
(804) 320-1301, *Fax:* (804) 320-8729
www.ideastations.org/radio
License: Chase City, Mecklenburg County, VA held by Commonwealth Public Broadcasting Corp.
Nat'l Network: NPR; PRI *Wire Services:* AP
Arbitron Metro Market: Chase City, VA *Format:* Classical, News, 62, Talk
Bill Miller, General Manager

WJYK
01-18-1959; 980 khz AM; 0.5 kw-D, NDD; N36 48 22 W78 26 22
P.O. Box 697, Chase City, VA 23924 US
(434) 372-0803
www.joyam980.com
wjyk@joyam980.com
License: Chase City, VA held by Stephen C. Battaglia Sr. & Janis G. Battaglia
Arbitron Metro Market: Chase City, VA *Format:* Christian, Religious *Adv. Rates:* 5; 5; 5; na
Stephen Battaglia Sr., General Manager

Chatham

WKBY
06-08-1966; 1080 khz AM; 1 kw-D, NDD; N36 46 54 W79 23 29
2341 E. Seven Mile Road, Detroit, MI 48234 US
(434) 432-8108, *Fax:* (434) 432-1523
wkby1080@gamewood.net
License: Chatham, VA held by William L. Bonner.
Format: Gospel *No. News Employees:* 1
William Bonner, President
Lois Stephens, General Manager
Lois B. Stephens, General Sales Mgr
Rodney Harper, Programming Director
Tim Walker, Chief Engineer

Cheriton

***WWIP**
01-01-2005; 89.1 mhz FM; 20 kw; Ant 449 ft; N37 10 53 W75 57 47
2202 Jolliff Rd., Chesapeake, VA 27104
(757) 465-1603, *Fax:* (757) 488-7761
www.wwip.org
info@wwip.org
License: Cheriton, Northampton County, VA held by Delmarva Educational Association.

Nancy Epperson, President
Henry Hoot, General Manager

Chesapeake

WCPK
01-01-1967; 1600 khz AM *Hrs Open:* 24; 4.2 kw-D, ND1; 0.023 kw-N, ND1; N36 48 10 W76 16 58
3780 Will Scarlet Road, Winston-Salem, NC 27104 US
(757) 488-1010, *Fax:* (757) 624-6515
www.wcpk.com
willisbroadcasting@yahoo.com
License: Chesapeake, VA held by Christian Broadcasting of Chesapeake Inc.
Group Owner: Willis Broadcasting Corp.; (acq 10-17-97; $200,000)
Arbitron Metro Market: Norfolk, VA *Format:* Gospel *No. News Employees:* 1 *Target Audience:* 45+; working class listeneres *Adv. Rates:* 40; 30; 40; 15
L. E. Willis, II, CEO
Hortense Willis, President
Walter Allen Brickhouse, General Manager
Julian Joyner, Programming Director
Terry Love, Chief Engineer
Ernestine Willis, Corporate Officer
Christine Willis, Corporate Officer
Celestine Willis, Corporate Officer
Lonnie Perry, Program Director

***WFOS**
09-14-1977; 88.7 mhz FM; 15.5 kw; 157 ft.; N36 43 18 W76 18 3
1617 Cedar Road, Chesapeake, VA 23320 US
(757) 547-1036, *Fax:* (757) 547-0160
www.cpschools.com
richard.babb@cpschools.com
License: Chesapeake, Chesapeake City County, VA held by Chesapeake School Board.
Arbitron Metro Market: Norfolk-Virginia Beach-Newport News, VA *Format:* Big Band, Blues, 64 *Target Audience:* High school.
W. Randolph Nichols, President
Richie Babb, General Manager
Richard Babb, Programming Director

WNOB
11-30-1973; 93.7 mhz FM *Hrs Open:* 24; 100 kw; 997 ft; N36 32 57 W76 11 21
500 Dominion Tower, 999 Waterside Dr., Norfolk, VA 23510
(757) 640-8500, *Fax:* (757) 640-8552
bob-fm.com
License: Chesapeake, Chesapeake City County, VA held by Commonwealth Radio L.L.C.
Group Owner: Sinclair Communications Inc.; (acq 1996; $8.1 million with WTAR(AM) Norfolk).
Nat'l Reps: McGavren Guild; Interep
Population Served: 1,400,000 *Arbitron Metro Market:* Norfolk-Virginia Beach-Newport News, VA *Hrs. of News Programming:* news progmg 2 hrs wkly *No. News Employees:* 1 *Target Audience:* 25-54.
Bob Sinclair, President
Dave Morgan, Operations Dir
Lisa Sinclair, General Manager
Luciana Varvarude, General Sales Mgr
Jay West, Programming Director
Donna Agresto, Promotions Manager
Ginger Power, National Sales Manager

Chester

WGGM
09-01-1964; 820 khz AM *Hrs Open:* 24; 10 kw-D, 1 kw-N, DA-2; N37 22 58 W77 25 21
4301 W. Hundred Rd., Chester, VA 22331
(804) 717-2000, *Fax:* (804) 717-2009
www.amen820.com
pscott.radio@qmail.com
License: Chester, Chesterfield County, VA
Group Owner: Delmarva Educational Association; (acq 12-2011).
Wire Services: Metro Weather Servic
Population Served: 900,000 *Arbitron Metro Market:* Richmond, VA *Target Audience:* 25-49. *Adv. Rates:* 20; 20; 20; 15
Nancy Epperson, President
Paul Scott, Operations Dir

Chincoteague

WCTG
01-01-2004; 96.5 mhz FM *Hrs Open:* 24; 5.3 kw; 344 ft.; N37 55 14 W75 23 7
6139 Franklin Park Road, McLean, VA 22101 US
(757) 336-1112, *Fax:* (757) 336-1805
www.albummusicsource.com
staff@wctg.fm
License: Chincoteague, Accomack County, VA held by Sebago Broadcasting Co. L.L.C.
Arbitron Metro Market: Chincoteague, VA *Format:* Triple A
A. Wray Fitch III, President

Christiansburg

WNMX
01-01-1990; 100.7 mhz FM *Hrs Open:* 17; 3 kw; 328 ft; N37 08 01 W80 21 17
7080 Lee Hwy., Radford, VA 20190
(540) 633-5330, *Fax:* (540) 633-2998
www.allthehitshot100.com
License: Christiansburg, Montgomery County, VA held by Cumulus Licensing LLC.
Group Owner: Cumulus Media Inc.; (acq 3-31-2004; grpsl).
Regional Network: Va. News Net.
Population Served: 561,000*Hrs. of News Programming:* News progmg 7 hrs wkly *Target Audience:* 25 plus.
Scott Stevens, Operations Dir
Sarah Leftwich, General Manager
Don Walker, Programming Director
Sam Parks, Chief Engineer

*WWVT
10-01-1954; 1260 khz AM *Hrs Open:* 6am-sunset*Rebroadcasts:* Rebroadcasts WWFC (FM) Ferrum 100%
4235 Electric Road, S.W., Suite 105, Roanoke, VA 24014 US
(540) 989-8900, *Fax:* (540) 776-2727
www.radioiq.org
info@radioiq.org
License: Christiansburg, VA held by Virginia Tech Foundation Inc.
Nat'l Network: NPR; PRI
Arbitron Metro Market: Christiansburg, VA *Format:* Talk *Hrs. of News Programming:* News progmg 60 hrs wkly *No. News Employees:* 8 *Target Audience:* 30-54; business professionals
Bart Pretor, Operations/Traffic Director
Glenn Gleixner, General Manager
Rick Mattioni, Programming Director
Connie Stevens, News Director
Paxton Durham, Chief Engineer
Mary Grace Franchi, MBA, Business Manager

Churchville

WNLR
03-09-1962; 1150 khz AM; 2.5 kw-D, ND1; 0.035 kw-N, ND1; N38 12 39 W79 7 53
Mailing Address: P.O. Box 400, Staunton, VA 24421 US
Second Address: Rt. 250 W., Churchville, VA
(540) 885-1150, *Fax:* (540) 886-8624
www.nlministries.org
wnlr@nlministries.org
License: Churchville, VA held by New Life Ministries Inc.
Nat'l Network: Moody; USA
Arbitron Metro Market: Churchville, VA *Format:* Adult Contemp, Religious *Target Audience:* 22-55; females with family size above average *Adv. Rates:* 9; 8; 9; 8
Bill Garvey, President
Russ Whitesell, Operations Dir
Tom Watson, General Manager

Claremont

WRJR
08-19-1997; 670 khz AM *Hrs Open:* Sunrise-sunset; 20 kw-D, 3 w-N, DA-2; N37 10 29 W76 53 49
2202 Jolliff Rd., Chesapeake, VA 23502
(757) 465-6700, *Fax:* (757) 488-7761
www.wpmhradio.com
info@wwip.org
License: Claremont, Surry County, VA held by Chesapeake-Portsmouth Broadcasting Corp.
Group Owner: Chesapeake-Portsmouth Broadcasting Corp.; (acq 3-2-2001; $950,000)

Henry Hoot, General Manager

Clarksville

WLUS-FM
01-01-1984; 98.3 mhz FM *Hrs Open:* 24; 17.5 kw; 390 ft.; N36 29 45 W78 33 16
Mailing Address: 1047 Evergreen Trail, Halifax, VA 24558 US
Second Address: 615 B Lewis St., Oxford, NC 27565
(919) 693-7900, *Fax:* (919) 693-9585
www.bestcountryaround.com
License: Clarksville, Mecklenburg County, VA held by Lakes Media Holding Company LLC.
Group Owner: Birch Broadcasting Corp.; (acq 2-1-2005; grpsl).
Nat'l Network: ABC
Format: Country *Hrs. of News Programming:* news progmg 2 hrs wkly *No. News Employees:* 3 *Target Audience:* 25-54; male & female *Adv. Rates:* 20; 18; 23; 15
Thomas Birch, President
Jerry Brown, Operations Dir
Melissa Wilkerson, General Sales Mgr
John Hart, Chief Engineer
Mike Elliott, Operations Manager

Clifton Forge

WXCF
10-19-1950; 1230 khz AM *Hrs Open:* 24; 1 kw-U, ND1; N37 49 18 W79 48 50
4 Professional Drive, Suite 145, Gaithersburg, MD 20877 US
(540) 862-5751, *Fax:* (540) 862-2120
wkeywigo@aol.com
License: Clifton Forge, VA held by Quorum Radio Partners of Virginia Inc.
Arbitron Metro Market: Clifton Forge, VA *Format:* Gospel *Hrs. of News Programming:* News progmg one hr wkly *Target Audience:* 40 & up. *Adv. Rates:* 84; 84; 84; 60
Michael Stone, President
Marcia Smith, General Sales Mgr
Lawrence Mason, Chief Engineer

*WVRI
90.9 mhz FM; 17.5 kw; ant -410 ft; N37 46 59 W80 00 00
282 Country Estate Dr., Springer, OK
(580) 653-2777
License: Clifton Forge, Alleghany County, VA held by Ron Elmore Ministries Inc.

Ron Elmore, President

Clinchco

WDIC
05-01-1961; 1430 khz AM *Hrs Open:* 24; 5 kw-D, ND2; N37 8 42 W82 23 22
Rte 1, Box 412, Clintwood, VA 24228 US
(276) 835-8626, *Fax:* (276) 835-8627
www.wdicradio.com/
wdic@wdicradio.com
License: Clinchco, VA held by Dickenson County Broadcasting Corp.
Nat'l Network: ABC *Regional Network:* Va. News Net. *Nat'l Reps:* Rgnl Reps *Regional Reps:* Rgnl Reps.
Arbitron Metro Market: Clinchco-Clintwood-Grundy, Virginia
Format: Country *Special Programming:* Trading Post - M-F 10:35 am *Hrs. of News Programming:* news progmg 8 hrs wkly *No. News Employees:* 3 *TargetAudience:* General. *Adv. Rates:* 8; 8; 8; 8
Richard Edwards, President
Betty Fleming, Operations Dir
Rufus Nickles, General Manager
Tammy Hill, Programming Director

WDIC-FM
07-02-1989; 92.1 mhz FM *Hrs Open:* 24; 2.5 kw; 505 ft.; N37 8 42 W82 23 22
Rt. 1, Box 412, Clintwood, VA 24228 US
(276) 835-8626, *Fax:* (276) 835_8627
www.wdicradio.com
wdic@wdicradio.com
License: Clinchco, Dickenson County, VA held by Dickenson County Broadcasting
Nat'l Network: ABC *Regional Network:* Va. News Net. *Nat'l Reps:* Rgnl Reps *Regional Reps:* Regnl Reps
Arbitron Metro Market: Clinchco-Clintwood-Grundy, Virginia
Format: News, Oldies, 84 *Special Programming:* On House Sunday 9 - 10:00 am *Hrs. of News Programming:* News progmg 3 hrs wkly *No. News Employees:* 3*Target Audience:* 25-55; baby boomers *Adv. Rates:* 10 - 10 - 10 - 10
Betty N. FLeming, Operations Dir
Rufus E. Nickles, General Manager

Coeburn

WGCK-FM
04-15-1991; 99.7 mhz FM; 1.95 kw; 1168 ft.; N37 3 15 W82 38 34
Mailing Address: P. O. Box 4026, Coeburn, VA 24293 US
Second Address: 32 Cowan St., Whitesburg, VA 41858
(800) 525-5683, *Fax:* (606) 633-3314
www.klove.com
info@klove.com
License: Coeburn, Wise County, VA held by Letcher County Broadcasting Inc.
Nat'l Network: K-Love
Arbitron Metro Market: Omaha, NE *Format:* Adult Contemp
Darrell Chambliss, Chairman
Mike Novak, President & CEO
G.C. Kincer, General Manager
Dr. David R. Ferry, Director
Mitch Barnhart, Director
Walter Golembeski, Director
David Pierce, Chief Creative Officer
Alan Mason, ChiefOperating Officer

Collinsville

WFIC
03-01-1970; 1530 khz AM; 0.25 kw-C, NDD; 1 kw-D, NDD; N36 42 56 W79 55 15
Mailing Address: P.O. Box 889, Blacksburg, VA 24063 US
Second Address: 1675 Grandview Dr., Martinsville, VA 24112
(276) 638-5235, *Fax:* (276) 638-6089
wcbxwodywfic@yahoo.com
License: Collinsville, VA held by BASE Communications Inc.
Group Owner: Baker Family Stations; (acq 9-3-97; $60,000).
Nat'l Network: USA
Arbitron Metro Market: Collinsville, VA *Format:* Gospel *Target Audience:* 35 plus; general *Adv. Rates:* 5; 5; 5; na
Steven Kuszlyk, Operations Dir
Brian Sanders, Station Manager
Wendell Minter, Programming Director

Colonial Heights

WDZY
01-01-1955; 1290 khz AM *Hrs Open:* 24; 25 kw-D, ND1; 0.041 kw-N, ND1; N37 15 30 W77 23 40
866 2nd Ave., 2nd Fl, New York, NY 10017 US
(804) 353-7200, *Fax:* (804) 353-2633
www.radiodisney.com/wdzy/1290
info@wdzy.com
License: Colonial Heights, VA held by Radio Disney Group LLC.
Group Owner: ABC Inc.; (acq 8-22-00; grpsl).
Arbitron Metro Market: Colonial Heights, VA *Format:* Children *Hrs. of News Programming:* News progmg 7 hrs wkly *Target Audience:* 2-12, 25-54; children & women
Laura Haemker, Station Manager
Amy Garelick, Promotions Manager

WKHK
11-17-1972; 95.3 mhz FM *Hrs Open:* 24; 47 kw; 512 ft.; N37 26 22 W77 26 1
600 Congress Ave., Suite 1400, Austin, TX 78701 US
(804) 330-5700, *Fax:* (804) 330-4079
www.k95country.com
info@k95country.com
License: Colonial Heights, Chesterfield County, VA held by Cox Radio Inc.
Group Owner: Cox Radio Inc.; (acq 8-31-00; grpsl)
Arbitron Metro Market: Richmond, VA *Format:* Country *Hrs. of News Programming:* news progmg 8 hrs wkly *No. News Employees:* 1 *Target Audience:* 25-54.
Bob Willoughby, General Manager
Buddy VanArsdale, Programming Director
Laura Kibler, Promotions Manager
Becky Wentworth, News Director
Gary Harrison, Chief Engineer

***WKYV**
90.1 mhz FM; 0.56 kw; 282 ft.; N37 15 2 W77 18 23
US
(916) 251-1600, *Fax:* (916) 251-1650
www.klove.com
License: Colonial Heights, Chesterfield County, VA held by Educational Media Foundation
Group Owner: EMF Broadcasting
Arbitron Metro Market: Colonial Heights, VA *Format:* Christian, Gospel
Mike Novak, President

Covington

WKEY
05-23-1941; 1340 khz AM *Hrs Open:* 24; 1 kw-U, ND1; N37 46 3 W79 59 6
Post Office Box 710, Covington, VA 24426 US
(540) 962-1133
www.big country101.com
info@bigcountry101.com
License: Covington, VA held by Quorum Radio Partners of Virginia Inc., debtor-in-possession
Group Owner: Quorum Radio Partners of Virginia Inc.; (acq 4-20-2005; with co-located FM).
Format: Oldies *Special Programming:* Black one hr, gospel 2 hrs wkly *Hrs. of News Programming:* news progmg 12 hrs wkly *No. News Employees:* 1 *Target Audience:* 25 plus; younger country listeners *Adv. Rates:* 6; 6; 6; 6
Michael Stone, President
Marcia Smith, General Sales Mgr
Dwight Rohr, News Director
Lawrence Mason, Chief Engineer

Crewe

WPZZ
06-09-1949; 104.7 mhz FM; 100 kw; 981 ft.; N37 10 15 W77 57 16
5900 Princess Garden Parkway, 8th Floor, Lanham, MD 20706 US
(804) 672-9299, *Fax:* (804) 672-9316
www.praise1047.com
lforem@radio-one.com
License: Crewe, Nottoway County, VA held by Radio One Licenses LLC.
Group Owner: Radio One Inc.; (acq 11-8-2001; grpsl).
Nat'l Reps: Eastman Radio
Arbitron Metro Market: Richmond, VA *Format:* Gospel *Target Audience:* 25-54; adults
Alfred Liggins, CFO
Reggie Baker, Operations Dir
Linda Forem, General Manager
Dennis Gettis, General Sales Mgr
Reggie Baker, Programming Director
Charles Taylor, Promotions Manager
Clovia Lawrence, News and Community AffairsDirector
Marsha Landess, Director of Sales
Chris Walker, Digital Sales Manager
Adam Drudge, Digital Support Coordinator
Terron Austin, Online Editor

WSVS
04-07-1947; 800 khz AM *Hrs Open:* 24
Route 45 North, Farmville, VA 23901 US
(434) 645-7734,(434) 645-7735, *Fax:* (434) 645-1701
www.wsvs800am.com
wsvsam@wsvs.com
License: Crewe, VA held by Colonial Broadcasting of Crewe Inc.
Nat'l Network: Family Radio
Format: Country *Hrs. of News Programming:* news progmg 7 hrs wkly *No. News Employees:* 1 *Target Audience:* 35 plus. *Adv. Rates:* 10; 10; 10; na
Hope Epperson, CFO
Steve Winn, Programming Director
John Hart, Chief Engineer

Crozet

***WMRY**
05-01-1995; 103.5 mhz FM *Hrs Open:* 24; 0.28 kw; 1463 ft.; N37 57 2 W78 43 46 *Rebroadcasts:* Rebroadcasts WMRA(FM) Harrisonburg 100%
821 South Main Street, Harrisonburg, VA 22807 US
(540) 568-6221, *Fax:* (540) 568-3814
www.wmra.org
wmra@jmu.edu
License: Crozet, Albemarle County, VA held by James Madison University Board of Visitors.
Nat'l Network: NPR; PRI
Arbitron Metro Market: Charlottesville, VA *Format:* News, Talk *Special Programming:* Folk 8 hrs, blues 5 hrs wkly *Hrs. of News Programming:* news progmg 80 hrs wkly *No. News Employees:* 2 *Target Audience:* 35-64; well educated *Adv. Rates:* 33; 17; 33; 15
Thomas DuVal, General Manager

WZGN
09-01-1980; 102.3 mhz FM; 4.9 kw; 354 ft.; N38 4 47 W78 44 22
200 Concord Plaza, Suite 600, San Antonio, TX 78216 US
(434) 978-4408, *Fax:* (434) 978-0723
www.generations1023.com
License: Crozet, Albemarle County, VA held by Monticello Media LLC.
Group Owner: Monticello Media LLC; (acq 10-4-2007; grpsl)
Nat'l Reps: Christal
Arbitron Metro Market: Charlottesville, VA *Format:* Contemporary Hits/Top 40, Adult Contemp *No. News Employees:* 1 *Target Audience:* 25 - 54/35 - 54; general *Adv. Rates:* 25; 22; 25; 10
Vinnie Kice, Operations Dir
Steve Gaines, General Manager
Mike Schneider, General Sales Mgr

Culpeper

***WARN**
01-01-1997; 91.5 mhz FM; 0.93 kw; 121 ft.; N38 27 15 W77 59 10
P.O. Drawer 2440, Tupelo, MS 38803 US
(662) 844-8888, *Fax:* (662) 842-6791
www.afr.net
faq@afr.net
License: Culpeper, Culpeper County, VA held by American Family Association.
Group Owner: American Family Radio
Arbitron Metro Market: Culpeper, VA *Format:* Christian, Religious
Marvin Sanders, General Manager

WJMA
12-04-1971; 103.1 mhz FM; 600 w; Ant 1,027 ft; N38 18 38 W78 00 12
Box 271, Orange, VA 22701
(540) 672-1000, *Fax:* (540) 672-0282
www.wjmafm.com
advertising@wjmafm.com
License: Culpeper, Culpeper County, VA held by Piedmont Communications Inc.
Group Owner: Piedmont Communications Inc.; 1993
Wire Services: AP
Population Served: 118,000*No. News Employees:* 1 *Target Audience:* 25-54; male & female
John Schick, President

WCVA
02-01-1949; 1490 khz AM *Hrs Open:* 24; 0.68 kw-U, ND1; N38 29 4 W77 59 22
P.O. Box 699, Culpeper, VA 22701 US
(540) 672-1000, *Fax:* (540) 672-0282
www.1055samfm.com
advertising@wjmafm.com
License: Culpeper, VA held by Piedmont Communications Inc.
Group Owner: Piedmont Communications Inc.; acq 11-21-2003; grpsl).
Nat'l Network: Westwood One; ABC
Arbitron Metro Market: Culpeper, VA *Format:* Adult Contemp *Hrs. of News Programming:* news progmg 10 hrs wkly *No. News Employees:* 1 *Target Audience:* 45 plus.
John Schick, President

***WPER**
01-01-1999; 89.9 mhz FM; 41 kw; 417 ft.; N38 40 42 W77 47 18
P. O. Box 889, Blacksburg, VA 24063 US
(540) 347-4825, *Fax:* (540) 347-3562
www.positivehits.org
info@positivehits.org
License: Culpeper, Culpeper County, VA held by Positive Alternative Radio Inc.
Group Owner: Positive Alternative Radio Inc.
Format: Christian
Frankie Morea, General Manager

Danville

WAKG
06-03-1968; 103.3 mhz FM *Hrs Open:* 24; 100 kw; 653 ft.; N36 44 28 W79 23 5
710 Grove Street, Danville, VA 24541 US
(434) 797-4290, *Fax:* (434) 797-3918
www.wakg.com
License: Danville, Danville City County, VA
Arbitron Metro Market: Danville, VA *Format:* Country *Target Audience:* 18-54.
Sherri Crowder, Programming Director
Carol Metz, Promotions Manager
Jimmy Allen, Disc Jockey
Alan Rowe, Disc Jockey
Carol Metz, Disc Jockey
Phil Watlington, Public Service Director

WBTM
05-24-1930; 1330 khz AM *Hrs Open:* 24; 5 kw-D, 1 kw-N, DA-N; N36 36 36 W79 25 47
Mailing Address: Box 1629, Danville, VA 24541
Second Address: 710 Grove St., Danville, VA 24541
(434) 793-4411, *Fax:* (434) 797-3918
www.wbtm1330.com
License: Danville, Danville City County, VA held by Piedmont Broadcasting Corp.
Population Served: 42,852 *Arbitron Metro Market:* Danville, VA *Hrs. of News Programming:* news progmg 5 hrs wkly *No. News Employees:* 2 *Target Audience:* 24 plus; young working adults
Bob Ashby, CEO
Mike Wimmer, General Sales Mgr
Alex Vardavas, Programming Director
Carol Metz, Promotions Manager
Chuck Vipperman, News Director
Johnny Cole, Chief Engineer

WDVA
06-29-1947; 1250 khz AM *Hrs Open:* 24; 5 kw-U, DA-N; N36 34 53 W79 26 33
One Radio Ln., Danville, VA 24501
(434) 797-1250, *Fax:* (434) 797-1255
wdvkradio@gmail.com
License: Danville, Danville City County, VA held by Mitchell Communications Inc.
Nat'l Network: CBS
Population Served: 1,900,000*Hrs. of News Programming:* News progmg 12 hrs wkly *No. News Employees:* 2 *Target Audience:* 18 plus. *Adv. Rates:* 30; 20; 60; 70
George Hairston, CEO/COO
C.G. Hairston, President
George Hairston, Operations Dir
George Hairston, General Manager
George Hairston, Station Manager
George Hairston, General Sales Mgr
George Hairston, Programming Director
GeorgeHairston, Promotions Manager
George Hairston, News Director

WWDN
08-25-1957; 1580 khz AM *Hrs Open:* Sunrise-sunset; 1 kw-D; N36 34 03 W79 22 50
Mailing Address: Box 3444, Danville, VA 24543
Second Address: 865 Industrial Ave., Danville, VA 24541
(434) 792-2133, *Fax:* (434) 792-2134
wilaradio@verizon.net
License: Danville, Danville City County, VA held by Tol-Tol Communications Inc.
Nat'l Network: American Urban
Population Served: 100,000*Target Audience:* General; ethnic (Black) and citizens who enjoy div progmg *Adv. Rates:* 9; 9; 9; 9
Lawrence Toller, President

***WOKD-FM**
01-01-1998; 91.1 mhz FM; 18 kw; 466 ft.; N36 44 30 W79 23 7
Rebroadcasts: Rebroadcasts WPAR(FM) Salem 100%
P O Box 889, Blacksburg, VA 20036 US
434-237-9798, *Fax:* 434-237-1025
www.spiritfm.com
mail@spiritfm.com
License: Danville, Danville City County, VA held by Positive Alternative Radio Inc.
Group Owner: Positive Alternative Radio Inc.
TV Affiliate: Relg

WMPW
970 khz AM *Hrs Open:* unlimited; 250 watts; 41 meters; 36 36 N41 79 23 W06
PO Box 3325, 1336 Piney Forest Road, Danville, VA 24543
(434) 799-1010, *Fax:* (800) 536-6194
www.countrylegends1037.com
info@lakesmediallc.com
License: Danville, VA held by Lakes Media LLC

Barbara Seamster, General Manager
Justin Lloyd, Operations Manager

Deltaville

WTYD
01-05-1999; 92.3 mhz FM *Hrs Open:* 24; 2.4 kw; 525 ft.; N37 29 37 W76 26 30

7203 University Drive, Richmond, VA 23229 US
(757) 565-1079, *Fax:* (757) 565-7094
www.tideradio.com
License: Deltaville, Middlesex County, VA held by Bullseye Broadcasting LLC
Wire Services: AP
Format: Triple A *No. News Employees:* 1 *Adv. Rates:* 26; 22; 26; 18
Tom Davis, President
Derek Mason, General Sales Mgr
Amy Miller, Promotions Manager
Barbara Warren, News Director

Dillwyn

WBNN-FM

07-01-2000; 105.3 mhz FM *Hrs Open:* 24; 6 kw; 328 ft.; N37 34 50 W78 37 18
Mailing Address: Post Office Box 889, Blacksburg, VA 24063 US
Second Address: 18498 N. Madison Hwy., Dillwyn, VA 23936
(434) 296-3300, *Fax:* (434) 983-6772
www.bigcountry1053.com
STUDIO@bigcountry1053.com
License: Dillwyn, Buckingham County, VA held by WKGM Inc.
Group Owner: Baker Family Stations
Nat'l Network: CNN Radio; Premiere Radio Networks *Regional Network:* Va. News Net.
Arbitron Metro Market: Charlottesville, VA *Format:* Country
Special Programming: Relg *Target Audience:* 18-49 and 25-54.
Adv. Rates: 28; 28; 28; 28.
Vernon Baker, CEO
Brian Sanders, Operations Dir
Greg Breeden, General Manager
Nancy McCaig, General Sales Mgr

Dublin

WPIN

01-01-1995; 810 khz AM; 4.2 kw-D, NDD; N37 7 55 W80 37 7
P.O. Box 889, Blacksburg, VA 24063 US
(540) 951-9791, *Fax:* (540) 961-2021
810wpin.com
License: Dublin, VA held by Dublin Radio.
Format: News, News/Talk, 86
Amy Burnette, General Manager

*WPIN-FM

01-01-1994; 91.5 mhz FM; 0.035 kw horiz, 0.085 kw vert; 1243 ft.; N37 1 29 W80 44 46 *Rebroadcasts:* Rebroadcasts WPAR(FM) Salem 100%
P.O. Box 889, Blacksburg, VA 24063 US
(540) 552-8073, *Fax:* (540) 951-5282
www.spiritfm.com
License: Dublin, Pulaski County, VA held by Positive Alternative Radio Inc.
Group Owner: Positive Alternative Radio Inc.
Format: Adult Contemp, Christian
Vernon Baker, Chairman
Edward Baker, President
Barry Armstrong, General Manager

Dumfries-Triangle

WPWC

12-22-1961; 1480 khz AM
214 S. Main, Dumfries, VA 22026 US
(703) 494-0100, *Fax:* (703) 490-1579
www.wpwcam.com
radiofiesta1480@yahoo.com
License: Dumfries-Triangle, VA held by JMK Communications Inc.
Arbitron Metro Market: Washington, DC
Grant Chang, President
Carlos Aragon, General Manager
Clara Marshall, General Sales Mgr
Emmanuel Szepeda, Programming Director
Dule Salinas, News Director

Earlysville

WKTR

02-17-1991; 840 khz AM *Hrs Open:* Daytime; 8.2 kw-D, DAD; N38 15 57 W78 24 53
Mailing Address: P.O. Box 889, Blacksburg, VA 24063 US
Second Address: 100 Business Park Circle, Quinque, VA 22965
(434) 985-8585, *Fax:* (434) 985-7369
www.espn840.com
aaron@espn840.com
License: Earlysville, VA held by Rural Radio Service.
Group Owner: Baker Family Stations
Nat'l Network: ESPN Radio
Arbitron Metro Market: Charlottesville, VA *Format:* Sports, Talk
Edward Baker, President
Brian Sanders, Operations Dir
Aaron Marks, General Manager

Eastville

WHRE

91.9 mhz FM; 4400 watts; 118 meters; 37 21 N32 75 56 W31
5200 Hampton Boulevard, Norfolk, VA
(757) 903-2302
www.whro.com
info@whro.com
License: Eastville, VA

Bert Schmidt, President

Edinburg

*WOTC

04-01-1994; 88.3 mhz FM; 1 kw; 404 ft.; N38 48 13 W78 41 21
Route 2, Box 30, Edinburg, VA 22824 US
(540) 984-8998, *Fax:* (540) 984-8977
www.valleybaptistchurch.net
wotcfm@shentel.net
License: Edinburg, Shenandoah County, VA held by Valley Baptist Church-Christian School.
Nat'l Network: USA
Format: News, Religious *Target Audience:* General; relg, children
Karl DeMay, General Manager

Elkton

WACL

03-06-1989; 98.5 mhz FM *Hrs Open:* 24; 0.9 kw; 1608 ft.; N38 23 36 W78 46 14
Mailing Address: P.O. Box 3300, Winchester, VA 22604 US
Second Address: 207 University Blvd., Harrisonburg, VA 22801
(512) 467-0643
License: Elkton, Rockingham County, VA held by Capstar TX L.P.
Group Owner: Clear Channel Communications Inc.; (acq 3-12-01; grpsl).
Arbitron Metro Market: Little Rock AR
Robert Walker, President

Elliston-Lafayette

WVBB(FM)

12-06-1983; 97.7 mhz FM *Hrs Open:* 24; 260 watts; 4710 meters; N37 47 54 W80 30 55
3934 Electyric Road SW, Roanoke, VA 24018
(540) 989-4591, *Fax:* (540) 744-5667
www.vibe100.com
License: Elliston-Lafayette, Greenbrier County, VA held by Mel Wheeler
Population Served: 75,000*Target Audience:* 25-60. *Adv. Rates:* 8; 8; 8; 4
Leonard Wheeler, President

WVBB

10-13-1968; 97.7 mhz FM; 0.26 kw; 1542 ft.; N37 18 30 W80 9 46
276 Seneca Trail North, Ronceverte, WV 24970 US
(260) 482-9288, *Fax:* (260) 482-8655
www.1063joefm.com
info@wvbbfm.com
License: Elliston-Lafayette, Whitley County, VA held by Oasis Radio 2 Corp.
Arbitron Metro Market: Fort Wayne, IN *Format:* Adult Contemp
Adv. Rates: 30; 20; 25; 10
Roger Diehm, General Manager
Phil Becker, Programming Director

Emory

*WEHC

11-15-1994; 90.7 mhz FM *Hrs Open:* 24; 8.7 kw; 374 ft.; N36 46 1 W81 50 18
Administration Building, Emory, VA 24327 US
(276) 944-6822(276) 944-6593, *Fax:* (276) 944-6934
www.ehc.edu/wehc
tdkeller@ehc.edu
License: Emory, Washington County, VA held by Emory and Henry College.
Arbitron Metro Market: Emory, VA *Format:* Variety/Diverse *Hrs. of News Programming:* News progmg 3 hrs wkly *Target Audience:* College community.
Dr. Teresa Keller, General Manager

Emporia

WEVA

11-04-1952; 860 khz AM *Hrs Open:* 24; 1 kw-D, NDD; N36 41 56 W77 32 55
Mailing Address: P. O. Box 1056, Emporia, VA 23847 US
Second Address: 705 Washington Street, Emporia, VA 23847
(434) 634-2133, *Fax:* (434) 634-5050
www.wevaradio.com
info@wevaradio.com
License: Emporia, VA held by Colonial Media Corp.
Nat'l Network: CBS; Westwood One *Regional Network:* Va. News Net.
Arbitron Metro Market: Emporia, VA *Format:* Adult Contemp, Talk
Special Programming: Beach Music *Hrs. of News Programming:* News progmg 14 hrs wkly *Target Audience:* 25 plus; Adults 25-64 *Adv. Rates:* 15;15; 15; 7.50
James Vautrot, CEO
Andy Lucy, Station Manager
Jim Wood, General Sales Mgr
Darrius Herring, Programming Director
Joseph Wetherbee, Chief Engineer

*WJYA

01-01-1999; 89.3 mhz FM *Hrs Open:* 24; 2 kw vert; 443 ft.; N36 46 4 W77 43 39
830 Gunnery Hill Road, Spotsylvania, VA 22553 US
(434) 237-9798, *Fax:* (434) 237-1025
www.spiritfm.com
office@spiritfm.com
License: Emporia, Greensville County, VA held by Positive Alternative Radio Inc.
Group Owner: Positive Alternative Radio Inc.; (acq 12-30-2005; grpsl)
Format: Christian
Barry Armstrong, General Manager

WYTT

01-01-2003; 99.5 mhz FM; 1.27 kw; 501 ft.; N36 39 20 W77 34 22
P.O. Box 910, Roanoke Rapids, NC 27870 US
(252) 538-0020, *Fax:* (252)538-0378
www.995jamz.com
al@bestradiosround.com
License: Emporia, Emporia City County, VA held by First Media Radio LLC.
Group Owner: First Media Radio LLC; (acq 12-3-2003; grpsl)
Arbitron Metro Market: Emporia, VA *Format:* Oldies
Alan Garrick, General Manager/Sales
CJ Riddick, Operations Manager/Program Director
Frank White, Chief Engineer
Marsha Collier, Business Manager

Ettrick

WLFV

01-01-2001; 93.1 mhz FM; 5.2 kw; 348 ft.; N37 16 21 W77 33 59
504 Baldwin Road, Richmond, VA 23229 US
(804) 327-9902, *Fax:* (804) 327-9911
www.931thewolf.com
info@thewolf.com
License: Ettrick, Chesterfield County, VA held by MLB-Richmond IV LLC.
Group Owner: Main Line Broadcasting LLC; (acq 12-13-2005; grpsl).
Arbitron Metro Market: Richmond, VA *Format:* Country
Troy Scott, General Sales Mgr
John McLeod, Promotions Manager
Elizabeth Gibbs, Market Controller

Exmore

WROX-FM

01-01-1986; 96.1 mhz FM *Hrs Open:* 24; 23 kw; 722 ft.; N37 15 45 W76 0 45
500 Dominion Tower, 999 Waterside Drive, Norfolk, VA 23510 US
(757) 640-8500, *Fax:* (757) 640-8552
www.96x.fm
License: Exmore, Northampton County, VA held by Sinclair Telecable Inc.
Group Owner: Sinclair Communications Inc.; (acq 9-28-93; $1.3 million;
Nat'l Reps: McGavren Guild; Interep
Arbitron Metro Market: Norfolk-Virginia Beach-Newport News, VA
Format: Rock/AOR *No. News Employees:* 1 *Target Audience:* 18-34; men
Bob Sinclair, President
Dave Morgan, Operations Dir
Lisa Sinclair, General Manager
Jeanette Xenakis, General Sales Mgr
Jay Michaels, Programming Director

Donna Agresto, Promotions Manager
Ginger Power, National Sales Manager

Fairfax

WDCT

09-25-1955; 1310 khz AM *Hrs Open:* 6 AM-midnight; 5 kw-D, DA2; 0.5 kw-N, DA2; N38 51 8 W77 18 57
Suite 506, 3251 Old Lee Hwy, Fairfax, VA 22030 US
(800) 543-1495, *Fax:* (916) 641-8238 (510) 633-7983
www.familyradio.com
familyradio@familyradio.org
License: Fairfax, VA held by Family Radio Ltd.
Nat'l Network: Moody
Arbitron Metro Market: Washington, DC *Format:* Korean *Target Audience:* 25-54; 60% female, 40% male
Kenneth Shin, General Manager
Ronnie Shin, Programming Director

Fairlawn

WKNV

01-01-1998; 890 khz AM; 10 kw-D, DAD; N37 7 55 W80 37 7
P. O. Box 889, Blacksburg, VA 24063 US
(540) 951-9791, *Fax:* (540) 961-2021
wknv@yahoo.com
License: Fairlawn, VA held by Base Communications Inc.
Group Owner: Baker Family Stations
Format: Christian, Religious
Amy Burnette, General Manager
Alison Baker, Programming Director
Winston Hawkins, Chief Engineer

Fairview Beach

WGRQ

05-03-1986; 95.9 mhz FM *Hrs Open:* 24; 1.9 kw; 595 ft.; N38 13 44 W77 7 28
4410-B Lafayette Blvd., Fredericksburg, VA 22408 US
(540) 891-9696, *Fax:* (540) 891-1656
www.959wgrq.com
tcooper@959wgrq.com
License: Fairview Beach, Westmoreland County, VA held by Telemedia Broadcasting Inc.
Nat'l Network: ABC *Nat'l Reps:* Roslin
Format: Oldies *Hrs. of News Programming:* news progmg 3 hrs wkly *No. News Employees:* 1 *Target Audience:* 25 plus; baby boomers *Adv. Rates:* 50; 45; 50; 30.
Carl Hurlebaus, President
Cathy Sato, Operations Dir
Thomas Cooper, General Manager
Edwin Pardue, General Sales Mgr
Jerome Hruska, Programming Director
Andi King, Promotions Manager
Keefe Coble, News Reporter
Paul Hayden,Special Events Coordinator

Falls Church

WFAX

09-15-1948; 1220 khz AM *Hrs Open:* 6 am-midnight; 5 kw-D, ND1; 0.048 kw-N, ND1; N38 52 47 W77 10 18
161-B Hillwood Avenue, Falls Church, VA 22046 US
(703) 532-1220, *Fax:* (703) 533-7572
www.wfax.com
wfax@wfaxam.com
License: Falls Church, VA held by Newcomb Broadcasting Corp.
Arbitron Metro Market: Falls Church, VA *Format:* Religious *Special Programming:* Black 15 hrs, It one hr wkly *Hrs. of News Programming:* News progmg one hr wkly *Target Audience:* 34-54.
Doris Newcomb, President and General Manager
R. C. Woolfenden, Operations Dir
Roy Martin, Programming Director
Henry Stewart, Chief Engineer

Falmouth

WGRX

05-17-2001; 104.5 mhz FM; 2.7 kw; 492 ft.; N38 16 31 W77 32 34
C/O Cary S. Tepper, Esq, 5101 Wisconsin Ave., NW, Suite 307, Washington, DC 20016 US
(540) 891-9696, *Fax:* (540) 891-1656
www.thunder1045.com
tcooper@959wgrq.com
License: Falmouth, Stafford County, VA held by Telemedia Broadcasting Inc.
Nat'l Reps: Roslin
Arbitron Metro Market: Falmouth, VA *Format:* Country *Hrs. of News Programming:* News progmg 3 hrs wkly *Target Audience:* 18-49; male audience, working class *Adv. Rates:* 50; 45; 50; 30.
Carl Hurlebaus, President
Cathy Sato, Operations Dir
Tom Cooper, General Manager
Edwin Pardue, Director of Sales & Marketing
Braden Smith, Programming Director
Andrea King, Promotions Manager
Sheila Quinn, News Director
KeefeCoble, News Reporter
Paul Hayden, Special Events Coordinator
Cathy Sato, Traffic Manager
Paul Hayden, Production Director
Braden Smith, Webmaster
Andrea King, Marketing Consultant

Farmville

WFLO

08-01-1947; 870 khz AM *Hrs Open:* Sunrise-sunset; 1 kw-D, NDD; N37 19 35 W78 23 9
P. O. Box 367, Farmville, VA 23901 US
(434) 392-4195, *Fax:* (434) 392-1823
www.wflo.net
programming@wflo.net
License: Farmville, VA held by Colonial Broadcasting Co. Inc.
Regional Network: Va. News Net. *Nat'l Reps:* Salem *Wire Services:* AP
Format: News, News/Talk, 86, Country *Special Programming:* Call Flo Radio Show, Relg 10 hrs wkly *Hrs. of News Programming:* news progmg 4 hrs wkly *No. News Employees:* 1 *Target Audience:* 25 plus. *Adv. Rates:* 9; 9; 9; 9
John Wilson, President
Henry Fulcher, Operations Dir
Francis Wood, General Manager
Polly A. Davis, General Sales Mgr
Christine C. Wood, Programming Director
Christopher Brochon, Promotions Manager
Henry M. Fulcher, SeniorPartner, Vice-President and Treasurer
David S. Jones, Sales Representative
T. Jordan Miles III, News Reporter
Jason Glenn, Radio Announcer
Dan Albus, Radio Announcer
William Lynn, Radio Announcer

WFLO-FM

05-01-1961; 95.7 mhz FM *Hrs Open:* 24; 50 kw; 492 ft.; N37 19 35 W78 23 9
P.O. Box 367, Farmville, VA 23901 US
(434) 392-4195, *Fax:* (434) 392-1823
www.wflo.net
programming@wflo.net
License: Farmville, Prince Edward County, VA
Nat'l Network: Jones Radio Networks; AP Radio *Regional Network:* Va. News Net. *Wire Services:* AP
Format: Adult Contemp *Hrs. of News Programming:* news progmg 4 hrs wkly *No. News Employees:* 1 *Target Audience:* 25 plus. *Adv. Rates:* 14; 14; 14; 14
John Wilson, President
Henry Fulcher, Operations Dir
Francis Wood, General Manager
Polly A. Davis, General Sales Mgr
Christine C. Wood, Programming Director
Christopher Brochon, Promotions Manager
Henry M. Fulcher, SeniorPartner, Vice-President and Treasurer
David S. Jones, Sales Representative
T. Jordan Miles III, News Reporter
Jason Glenn, Radio Announcer
Dan Albus, Radio Announcer
William Lynn, Radio Announcer

*WMLU

01-01-1988; 91.3 mhz FM *Hrs Open:* 24; 0.001 kw horiz, 0.15 kw vert; 72 ft.; N37 17 50 W78 23 42 *Rebroadcasts:* NPR
Longwood College, 201 High Street, Farmville, VA 23909 US
(434) 395-2792, *Fax:* (434) 395-2035
www.wmlu.org
wmlu@longwood.edu
License: Farmville, Prince Edward County, VA held by Longwood University.
Nat'l Network: NPR
Arbitron Metro Market: Richmond, VA *Format:* Variety/Diverse *Target Audience:* 18-23; div college students
Carly Bell, Operations Dir
Gerald Martin, General Manager
Brian Mandeville, Programming Director
Ben Jones, Chief Engineer
Olivia Planes, Music Director
Paul Gorman, News Director
Amy Jackson, Publicity Director
Courtney Jones,Remotes Director
Keenan Crump, Sports Director
William Guerrant, Webmaster

WPAK

06-15-1978; 1490 khz AM; 1 kw-U, ND1; N37 18 47 W78 23 41
1005 Richmond Road, Williamsburg, VA 23185 US
(434) 392-8114, *Fax:* (434) 392-8115
License: Farmville, VA held by Great Virginia Venture Inc.
Format: Religious *Special Programming:* Farm one hr, gospel 12 hrs wkly
George Granger, President
Mark Neimand, General Manager

WVHL

09-01-1997; 92.9 mhz FM *Hrs Open:* 24; 6 kw; 328 ft; N37 17 06 W78 29 39
Mailing Address: Drawer T, 116 North St., Farmville, VA 23901
Second Address: 116 North St., Farmville, VA 23901
(434) 392-6091, *Fax:* (434) 392-6091
www.wvhl.net
v93@wvhl.net
License: Farmville, Prince Edward County, VA held by The Farmville Herald Inc.
Nat'l Network: ABC
Population Served: 100,000*Target Audience:* General.
Larry Ames, Operations Dir
Steve Wall, General Manager
Doug McClure, General Sales Mgr

Ferrum

*WFFC

01-01-1989; 89.9 mhz FM *Hrs Open:* 16; 1.1 kw; 679 ft.; N36 54 50 W79 57 7
Route 40, Ferrum, VA 24088 US
(540) 989-8900, *Fax:* (540) 776-2727
www.radioiq.org
WVTF@vt.edu
License: Ferrum, Franklin County, VA held by Virginia Tech Foundation Inc.
Nat'l Network: NPR
Arbitron Metro Market: Ferrum, VA *Format:* Talk
Bart Prater, Operations/Traffic Director
Glenn Gleixner, General Manager
Rick Mattioni, Programming Director
Connie Stevens, News Director
Paxton Durham, Chief Engineer
Ben Martin, Operations Assistant & Producer/Radio ReadingServ
Joshua Day, Radio Reading Service Assistant/Producer
Jay Prater, Webmaster
Mary Grace Franchi, Business Manager
Brian Black, Administrative Assistant
Cynthia Gray, Director of Development

Fieldale

WODY

07-01-1993; 1160 khz AM; 5 kw-D, DAN; 0.25 kw-N, DAN; N36 42 36 W79 57 58
Mailing Address: P.O. Box 889, Blacksburg, VA 24063 US
Second Address: 1675 Grandview Dr, Martinsville, VA 24112
540-951-9791, *Fax:* 540-961-2021
http://espnblacksburg.com
wcbxwodywfic@yahoo.com
License: Fieldale, VA held by Base Communications Inc.
Group Owner: Baker Family Stations; (acq 4-17-98)
Nat'l Network: ESPN Radio
TV Affiliate: Sports *No. News Employees:* 25-54.
Executive Vice President

Floyd

WGFC

04-20-1985; 1030 khz AM *Hrs Open:* Sunrise-sunset; 1 kw-D, NDD; N36 55 33 W80 16 34
Mailing Address: State Rd, 860 PO Bx 495, Floyd, VA 24091 US
Second Address: 401 Shooting Creek Rd. S.E., Floyd, VA 24091
(276) 730-0704, *Fax:* (276) 730-0705
www.wgfcradio.com
wgfc@wgfcradio.com
License: Floyd, VA held by New Life Christian Communications Inc.
Format: Gospel *Hrs. of News Programming:* news progmg 10 hrs wkly *No. News Employees:* 2 *Target Audience:* General; loc community interest
R. Leon Goad, CEO
Jackie Goad, Operations Dir
Leon Goad, Chief Engineer

RADIO - U.S.

Forest

WIQO-FM

10-01-1964; 100.9 mhz FM *Hrs Open:* 24; 210 watts; 511 meters; N37 47 36 W79 55 57
Box 710, Covington, VA 24426
(540) 962-1133
www.bigcountry101.com
wkeywiqo@aol.com
License: Forest, Covington City County, VA held by Quorum Radio Partners of Virginia Inc., debtor-in-possession
Group Owner: Quorum Radio Partners of Virginia Inc.
Population Served: 85,000*Hrs. of News Programming:* news progmg 10 hrs wkly *No. News Employees:* 1 *Target Audience:* 25-54; general
Pat Pleasant, Programming Director

Fort Lee

WKLR

07-29-1963; 96.5 mhz FM *Hrs Open:* 24; 50 kw; 453 ft.; N37 20 22 W77 24 31
600 Congress Ave., Suite 1400, Austin, TX 78701 US
(804) 330-5700, *Fax:* (320) 330-4079
www.965theplanet.com
fisher@coxradio.com
License: Fort Lee, Prince George County, VA held by Cox Radio Inc.
Group Owner: Cox Radio Inc.; (acq 8-31-00; grpsl)
Arbitron Metro Market: Richmond, VA *Format:* Classic Rock *Hrs. of News Programming:* news progmg 5 hrs wkly *No. News Employees:* 1 *Target Audience:* 25-49.
James Kennedy, Chairman
Bob Willoughby, General Manager
Rene Clark, General Sales Mgr
Paul Cannell, Programming Director
Gary Harrison, Engineering Dir
Sam Giles, Disc Jockey
David Koye, National Sales Manager

Franklin

WLQM

10-13-1956; 1250 khz AM *Hrs Open:* 24; 1 kw-D, NDD; N36 40 57 W76 55 43
Mailing Address: 103 South Street, Franklin, VA 23851 US
Second Address: 320 N. Franklin St., Franklin, VA 23851
(757) 562-3135, *Fax:* (757) 562-2345
www.wlqmradio.com
wlqm@wlqmradio.com
License: Franklin, VA held by Franklin Broadcasting Corp.
Nat'l Network: American Urban
Format: Gospel *No. News Employees:* 3 *Target Audience:* 35-64.
Michael Clark, Operations Dir
Louise Morings, Programming Director
Mickel Pruden, Chief Engineer

WLQM-FM

01-01-1988; 101.7 mhz FM; 3 kw; 469 ft.; N36 41 17 W77 0 58
103 South Street, Franklin, VA 23851 US
(757) 562-3135, *Fax:* (757) 562-2345
www.wlqmradio.com
wlqm@wlqmradio.com
License: Franklin, Franklin City County, VA held by Franklin Broadcasting Corp.
Nat'l Network: Westwood One
Format: Country *No. News Employees:* 9 *Target Audience:* 35 plus; men & women
Michael Clark, Operations Dir
Tim Parsons, News Director
Mickel Pruden, Chief Engineer
Neal Steele, Assistant Vice President

Fredericksburg

WBQB

05-15-1960; 101.5 mhz FM *Hrs Open:* 24; 50 kw; 492 ft.; N38 19 57 W77 23 41
Mailing Address: P. O. Box 3300, Winchester, VA 22604 US
Second Address: 1914 Mimosa St., Fredericksburg, VA 22405
(540) 373-7721, *Fax:* (540) 899-3879
www.b1015.com
info@b1015.com
License: Fredericksburg, Fredericksburg City County, VA held by Mid Atlantic Network Inc.
Group Owner: Mid Atlantic Network
Nat'l Network: Westwood One
Arbitron Metro Market: Fredericksburg, VA *Format:* Adult Contemp *Hrs. of News Programming:* news progmg 8 hrs wkly *No. News Employees:* 3 *Target Audience:* 18-49.
Chuck Archer, Operations Dir
Shawn Sloan, General Manager
Ted Schubel, News Director
Tom Hamilton, Market Manager

WFLS-FM

06-12-1962; 93.3 mhz FM *Hrs Open:* 24; 50 kw; 492 ft.; N38 18 46 W77 26 20
616 Amelia St, Fredericksburg, VA 22401 US
(540) 373-1500, *Fax:* (540) 374-5525
www.wfls.com
info@wfls.com
License: Fredericksburg, Fredericksburg City County, VA held by The Free Lance-Star Publishing Co.
Group Owner: The Free Lance-Star Publishing Co.
Wire Services: AP
Format: Country *No. News Employees:* 4 *Target Audience:* 25-54; adults
Paul Johnson, Operations Dir
John Moen, General Manager
Paul Johnson, Programming Director
Sharon DeSouza, Promotions Manager
Chris Wilk, Chief Engineer
Shel Bynum, Production Director
Marion Weatherington, PromotionsCoordinator
Sandy Manager, Business Manager
Sharon Colleluore, Sales Assistant
Sandy Ridgeway, Traffic Manager
Pat Covington, Traffic Assistant

WFVA

09-08-1939; 1230 khz AM *Hrs Open:* 24; 1 kw-U, ND1; N38 16 50 W77 26 11
Mailing Address: P. O. Box 3300, Winchester, VA 22604 US
Second Address: 1914 Mimosa St., Fredericksburg, VA 22405
(540) 373-7721, *Fax:* (540) 899-3879
www.newstalk1230.net
info@newstalk1230.net
License: Fredericksburg, VA held by Mid-Atlantic Network Inc.
Group Owner: Mid Atlantic Network
Format: News, News/Talk, 86 *Hrs. of News Programming:* news progmg 15 hrs wkly *No. News Employees:* 3 *Target Audience:* 35 plus.
John Lewis, President
Chuck Archer, Operations Dir
Shawn Sloan, General Manager
Tom Hamilton, General Sales Mgr
Mark Clifford, Programming Director
Maureen Posillico, Promotions Manager
Ted Schubel, News Director
JohnDiamantis, Chief Engineer
Sean Quinn, Events Director

*WJYJ

05-06-1983; 90.5 mhz FM *Hrs Open:* 24; 26 kw; 409 ft.; N37 57 56 W77 22 19 *Rebroadcasts:* Simulcasts WPER(FM) Culpeper 100%
P.O. Box 905, Spotsylvania, VA 22553 US
(540) 347-4825, *Fax:* (540) 347-3562
www.positivehits.org
info@positivehits.org
License: Fredericksburg, Fredericksburg City County, VA held by Positive Alternative Radio Inc.
Group Owner: Positive Alternative Radio Inc.; (acq 12-30-2005; grpsl)
Format: Christian
Frankie Morea, General Manager

WNTX

07-15-1960; 1350 khz AM *Hrs Open:* 24; 1 kw-D, 37 w-N; N38 18 46 W77 26 20
616 Amelia St., Fredericksburg, VA 22401
(540) 373-1500, *Fax:* (540) 374-5525
www.wysk.com
info@wysk.com
License: Fredericksburg, Fredericksburg City County, VA held by The Free Lance-Star Publishing Co.
Group Owner: The Free Lance-Star Publishing Co.
Population Served: 85,000*Hrs. of News Programming:* news progmg 12 hrs wkly *No. News Employees:* 3 *Target Audience:* General.
John Moen, General Manager
Jim Butler, General Sales Mgr
Jo Anne Pope, Promotions Manager
Sandy Ridgeway, News Director
Chris Wilk, Chief Engineer

Front Royal

WFQX

01-17-1973; 99.3 mhz FM *Hrs Open:* 24; 6 kw; 328 ft.; N39 3 56 W78 22 58
600 Congress Avenue, Suite 1600, Austin, TX 78701 US
(540) 662-5101, *Fax:* (540) 662-8610
www.993thefox.com
License: Front Royal, Warren County, VA held by Capstar TX L.P.
Group Owner: Clear Channel Communications Inc.; (acq 8-30-00; grpsl).
Arbitron Metro Market: Winchester, VA *Format:* Rock/AOR *Hrs. of News Programming:* news progmg one hr wkly *No. News Employees:* 3 *Target Audience:* 25-49; men *Adv. Rates:* 30; 30; 28; 15
David Miller, Operations Dir
Chuck Peterson, General Manager
Marcella Vance, General Sales Mgr
Justin Maglione, Promotions Manager
Krissy Golden, News Director
Mark Kesner, Chief Engineer
Elwood King, Disc Jockey
Max James,Disc Jockey
Ben Gates, Public Affairs Director

WFTR

09-19-1948; 1450 khz AM *Hrs Open:* 24; 1 kw-U, ND1; N38 54 31 W78 10 37
Mailing Address: 57 West 57th Street, Suite 1204, Front Royal, NY 10019 US
Second Address: 1106 Elm St., Front Royal, VA 22630
(540) 635-4121, *Fax:* (540) 635-9387
sales@royalbroadcasting.net
License: Front Royal, VA held by Royal Broadcasting Inc.
Nat'l Network: ABC *Regional Reps:* Commercial Media Sales.
Arbitron Metro Market: Winchester, VA *Format:* Country *Hrs. of News Programming:* news progmg 20 hrs wkly *No. News Employees:* 1 *Target Audience:* 25-54. *Adv. Rates:* 10; 6; 8; 4.
Andrew Shearer, CEO
Lonnie Hill, Operations Dir
Kathy Willis, News Director
Mike O'Dell, COO

WZRV

01-01-1981; 95.3 mhz FM *Hrs Open:* 24; 6 kw; 299 ft.; N38 58 31 W78 12 6
Mailing Address: 1106 Elm Street, P. O. Box 192, Front Royal, NY 22630 US
Second Address: 1106 Elm St., Front Royal, VA 22630
(540) 665-9595, *Fax:* (540) 635-9387
www.oldiesradioonline.com
webmaster@greatestmojo.com
License: Front Royal, Warren County, VA
Nat'l Network: ABC
Format: Oldies *No. News Employees:* 1 *Target Audience:* 25-54. *Adv. Rates:* 24; 16; 20; 12
Mike O'Dell, General Sales Mgr
Randy Woodward, Programming Director
Mario Retrosi, News Director
Kathy Willis, Traffic Manager

Galax

WBRF

12-15-1961; 98.1 mhz FM *Hrs Open:* 24; 100 kw horiz, 96 kw vert; 1755 ft.; N36 33 34 W80 49 25
Mailing Address: 312 Robin Road, Mount Airy, NC 27030 US
Second Address: 325 Poplar Knob Rd., Galax, VA 24333
(276) 236-9273, *Fax:* (276) 236-7198
www.blueridgecountry98.com
debby@blueridgecountry98.com
License: Galax, Galax City County, VA held by Blue Ridge Radio Inc.
Group Owner: Blue Ridge Radio Inc.; (acq 4-19-85;
Nat'l Network: CBS; Motor Racing Net
Arbitron Metro Market: Galax,VA *Format:* Country *Target Audience:* General.
Earlene Epperson, President
Ray Bass, Operations Dir
Debby Stringer, General Manager
Deborah Epperson, General Sales Mgr
Betty Liddle, Programming Director
John Mullins, Chief Engineer
Jason Blevins, Music Director

WWWJ

02-01-1947; 1360 khz AM *Hrs Open:* 6 AM-10 PM; 5 kw-D, ND2; 0.031 kw-N, ND2; N36 39 48 W80 54 52
Mailing Address: P. O. Box 270, Galax, VA 24333 US
Second Address: 325 Poplar Knob Rd, Galax, VA 24333

(276) 236-2921, *Fax:* (276) 236-2922
www.wwwj1360.com
License: Galax, VA held by Twin County Broadcasting Corp.
Group Owner: Blue Ridge Radio Inc.; (acq 4-19-85; $200,000;
Nat'l Network: CBS *Regional Network:* Va. News Net.
Arbitron Metro Market: Caroll County, VA *Format:* Gospel *Special Programming:* Sp 20 hrs, farm one hr wkly *Hrs. of News Programming:* News progmg one hr wkly *Target Audience:* 18 plus. *Adv. Rates:* 6.45;6.45; 6.45; 6.45

Deborah Stringer, President & General Manager
J. Brice Parks, General Sales Mgr
Carole Bonn, Programming Director
Tony Phillips, Promotions Manager
John Mullins, Chief Engineer
Joel Bonn, Disc Jockey
Anthony Phillips, MusicDirector
Ray Bass, Production Manager
Carole Bonn, Office Manager
Michelle Lintecum, Account Executive & Marketing Director
Hal Epperson, Sports Director

*WOKG

01-01-2005; 90.3 mhz FM; 2.7 kw; 538 ft.; N36 39 27 W80 54 22
Post Office Box 889, Blacksburg, VA 24063 US
(434) 237-9798, *Fax:* (434) 237-1025
www.spiritfm.com
License: Galax, Galax City County, VA held by Positive Alternative Radio Inc.
Group Owner: Positive Alternative Radio Inc.
Arbitron Metro Market: Galax, VA *Format:* Christian

Paul Hunt, General Manager

Gate City

WGAT

07-24-1959; 1050 khz AM *Hrs Open:* 24; 1 kw-D, ND1; 0.267 kw-N, ND1; N36 37 59 W82 34 56
117 E. Jackson St., #2, Gate City, VA 24251 US
(276) 386-7025, *Fax:* (276) 386-7025
wgatradio@earthlink.com
License: Gate City, VA held by Tri-Cities Broadcasting Corp.
Nat'l Network: Salem Radio Network *Regional Network:* Va. News Net.
Arbitron Metro Market: Johnson City-Kingsport-Bristol, TN-VA *Format:* Gospel, Sports *Hrs. of News Programming:* news progmg 10 hrs wkly *No. News Employees:* 1 *Target Audience:* 25 plus. *Adv. Rates:* 16; 16;16; 16

Alan Giles, President
Mike Long, General Manager

Glade Spring

WFYE

01-01-2008; 100.5 mhz FM; 6 kw; -14 ft.; N36 48 45.38 W81 33 20.38
US
(317) 541-0417
y100wfye.com
asradio@aol.com
License: Glade Spring, Washington County, VA held by ASRadio LLC.
Arbitron Metro Market: Glade Spring, VA

Alan Sneed, General Manager

Glen Allen

WTOX

01-01-2004; 1480 khz AM *Hrs Open:* 24
US
(804) 643-0990, *Fax:* (804) 474-5070
www.lagrand.com
jjacobs@davidsonmediagroup.com
License: Glen Allen, VA held by Davidson Media Station WTOX Licensee LLC.
Group Owner: Davidson Media Group LLC; (acq 5-13-2005; grpsl)
Arbitron Metro Market: Glen Allen, VA *No. News Employees:* 1 *Target Audience:* 25 plus; Hispanic *Adv. Rates:* 50; 40; 45; 20

Felix Perez, President
Tim Hurley, Operations Dir
Jim Jacobs, General Manager
Carolyn Resendiz, General Sales Mgr
Selvin Paredes, Programming Director

Gloucester

WXGM

01-20-1957; 1420 khz AM *Hrs Open:* 24; 0.74 kw-D, ND1; 0.058 kw-N, ND1; N37 24 36 W76 32 52
P.O. Box 634, Main St., Gloucester, VA 23061 US
(804) 693-2105, *Fax:* (804) 693-2182
www.xtra99.com
noair@xtra99.com
License: Gloucester, VA held by WXGM Inc.
Nat'l Network: ABC *Regional Network:* Agrinet; Va. News Net.
Arbitron Metro Market: Gloucester, VA *Format:* Adult Contemp *Special Programming:* Farm 2 hrs, relg 2 hrs wkly *Hrs. of News Programming:* news progmg 7 hrs wkly *No. News Employees:* 1 *Target Audience:* 25-54. *Adv. Rates:* 23; 21; 23; 17

Thomas Robinson, President
Harvey King, Operations Dir
Iris Lassister, General Sales Mgr
Herman King, News Director
Bill Swartz, Chief Engineer
Pat Clemmer Collins, Advertising

WXGM-FM

07-29-1991; 99.1 mhz FM *Hrs Open:* 24; 6 kw; 328 ft.; N37 24 36 W76 32 52
P. O. Box 634, Main St., Gloucester, VA 23061 US
(804) 693-2105, *Fax:* (804) 693-2182
www.xtra99.com
License: Gloucester, Gloucester County, VA held by WXGM Inc.
Arbitron Metro Market: Gloucester, VA *Format:* Adult Contemp

Keith Lawless, Operations Dir
Shane Reeve, General Sales Mgr
Pat Clemmer Collins, Advertising

Gloucester Courthouse

WHRJ

89.9 mhz FM; 750 watts; 83.6 meters; 37 24 N36 76 32 W52
5200 Hampton Boulevard, Norfolk, VA
(757) 889-9400
www.whro.org
info@whro.org
License: Gloucester Courthouse, VA held by Hampton Roads Telecommunications

Bert Schmidt, President

Goochland

WZEZ

04-01-2001; 100.5 mhz FM *Hrs Open:* 24; 2.6 kw; 509 ft.; N37 47 37 W77 55 57
2461 Eisenhower Avenue, Alexandria, VA 22331 US
(804) 717-2000, *Fax:* (804) 717-2009
www.wzezradio.com
pscott@wggm-wzez.com
License: Goochland, Goochland County, VA held by Hubert N. Hoffman III, executor
Nat'l Network: CNN Radio *Wire Services:* Metro Weather Service Inc.
Arbitron Metro Market: Chester, VA *Format:* Oldies *Adv. Rates:* 30; 30; 30; 10

Jay Hoffman, President
Paul Scott, Operations Dir

Gretna

WMNA

08-11-1956; 730 khz AM *Hrs Open:* 6 AM-10 PM; 1 kw-D, DA2; 0.028 kw-N, DA2; N36 55 31 W79 19 50 *Rebroadcasts:* Rebroadcasts WLNI(FM) Lynchburg 80%
P. O. Box 730, Gretna, VA 24557 US
(434) 656-1234, *Fax:* (434) 847-5709
www.wlni.com
License: Gretna, VA held by 3 Daughters Media Inc.
Group Owner: 3 Daughters Media Inc.; (acq 11-14-2002; $300,000 with co-located FM).
Regional Network: Agrinet
Arbitron Metro Market: Gretna, VA *Format:* News, News/Talk, 86 *Special Programming:* Farm 8 hrs, Black 2 hrs, bluegrass 20 hrs, sports *Hrs. of News Programming:* news progmg 19 hrs wkly *No. News Employees:* 1*Target Audience:* 18-55; family groups *Adv. Rates:* 7; 7; 7; 7

Gary Burns, CEO
Mike Slenski, General Manager
Charlotte Wells, Programming Director
Melissa Eckhert, News Director
Dale Cook, Chief Engineer
Ron Franklin, Disc Jockey
Bob Haynes, Disc Jockey
Devin Taylor, Disc Jockey

WMNA-FM

02-28-1959; 106.3 mhz FM *Hrs Open:* 5:30 AM-10 PM; 6 kw; 259 ft.; N36 55 31 W79 19 50 *Rebroadcasts:* Rebroadcasts WLNI(FM) Lynchburg 85%
P. O. Box 730, Gretna, VA 24557 US
(434) 534-6100, *Fax:* (434) 534-6101
www.espninva.com
gary@espninva.com
License: Gretna, Pittsylvania County, VA held by 3 Daughters Media Inc
Group Owner: 3 Daughters Media Inc.
Regional Network: Agrinet
Arbitron Metro Market: Gretna, VA *Format:* Sports *Hrs. of News Programming:* News progmg 10 hrs wkly *Target Audience:* 24-54; active & mature

Gary Burns, CEO/COO
Ashley Schamerhorn, Operations Dir
Rich Roth, Programming Director
Melissa Eckhert, News Director
Brian Wegan, Disc Jockey
Dave Lewis, Disc Jockey
Mari White, Disc Jockey
Larry Richmond, Disc Jockey
Charlotte Wells, Disc Jockey

Grundy

WMJD

06-21-1965; 100.7 mhz FM *Hrs Open:* 24; 2.3 kw; 535 ft.; N37 18 8 W82 7 4
Box 2054, Grundy, VA 24614 US
(276) 935-7227, *Fax:* (276) 935-2587
www.wmjdfm.com
wmjd.fm@gmail.com
License: Grundy, Buchanan County, VA held by Peggy Sue Broadcasting Media Corp.
Group Owner: Peggy Sue Broadcasting Corp.
Nat'l Network: ABC
Arbitron Metro Market: Grundy, VA *Format:* Country *No. News Employees:* 5 *Target Audience:* 24-59.

Dirk Hall, Station Manager
Bink Rush, Programming Director

WNRG

11-16-1955; 940 khz AM; 5 kw-D, ND1; 0.014 kw-N, ND1; N37 18 8 W82 7 4
Mailing Address: P.O. Box 2045, Grundy, VA 24614 US
Second Address: Rt. 460 W., Grundy, VA 24614
(276) 935-7227, *Fax:* (276) 935-2587
wmjd.fm@gmail.com
License: Grundy, VA held by Peggy Sue Broadcasting Media Corp.
Group Owner: Peggy Sue Broadcasting Corp.; acq 3-29-2004; $200,000 with co-located FM).
Nat'l Network: ABC; Salem Radio Network
Arbitron Metro Market: Grundy, VA *Format:* Gospel *Special Programming:* Farm 5 hrs wkly *No. News Employees:* 2

Dirk Hall, General Manager

*WNBV

01-01-2009; 88.1 mhz FM; 0.1 kw vert; 148 ft.; N37 17 18 W82 5 9
US
(276) 979-9200
www.spotspitter.com
Support@SpotSpitter.com
License: Grundy, Buchanan County, VA held by New Beginning World Outreach Inc.
Arbitron Metro Market: Grundy, VA

John Dash, President
Harriett Dash, Station Manager

Hampden-Sydney

*WWHS-FM

10-11-1972; 92.1 mhz FM *Hrs Open:* 6 AM-2 AM; 0.01 kw horiz; 217 ft.; N37 14 23 W78 27 48
P. O. Box 128, Hampden-Sydney, VA 23943 US
(434) 223-6009, *Fax:* (434) 223-6009
www.wwhsfm.org
wwhs@wwhsfm.org
License: Hampden-Sydney, Prince Edward County, VA held by President & Board of Trustees of Hampden-Sydney College.
Arbitron Metro Market: Hampden Sydney, VA *Format:* Variety/Diverse *Special Programming:* Blues 2 hrs, class 2 hrs, jazz 6 hrs, reggae 4 hrs *Hrs. of News Programming:* News progmg 5 hrs wkly *Target Audience:* 18-25; college community

J. Andrew Craver, General Manager
Bill Anderson, General Sales Mgr
Christopher S. Pedraja, Programming Director
Henry Loehr, Music Director
Jared Christian, Technical Director
Dr. C. William Anderson, Advisor

Hampton

WXTG
07-01-1948; 1490 khz AM *Hrs Open:* 24
2845 N Armistead Ave, Hampton, VA 23666 US
(757) 747-1021, *Fax:* (757) 490-2755
www.1021thegame.com
decandidoj@redskins.com
License: Hampton, VA held by Red Zebra Broadcasting Licensee (Norfolk) LLC.
Group Owner: Red Zebra Holdings LLC; (acq 12-10-2007; $950,000)
Nat'l Network: Fox Sports
Arbitron Metro Market: Virginia Beach, VA *Format:* Sports
buck albritton, General Manager
John Decandido, Programming Director

***WHOV**
03-05-1964; 88.1 mhz FM *Hrs Open:* 17; 2 kw horiz, 8 kw vert; 194 ft.; N37 1 3 W76 20 13
607 Orchard Road, Hampton, VA 23668 US
(757) 727-5407, *Fax:* (757) 727-5084
www.whov.hamptonu.edu
info@whovfm.com
License: Hampton, Hampton City County, VA held by Hampton University.
Format: Variety/Diverse *Special Programming:* Sp 12 hrs, blues 3 hrs, reggae 4 hrs wkly *Hrs. of News Programming:* News progmg 2 hrs wkly *Target Audience:* 18-54.
Alvin Delk, Operations Dir
Robert Dixon, General Manager
Kevin Anderson, Station Manager

WWDE-FM
06-01-1962; 101.3 mhz FM; 50 kw; 499 ft.; N36 49 41 W76 15 5
10706 Beaver Dam Road, Cockeysville, MD 21030 US
(757) 497-2000, *Fax:* (757) 456-5458
www.2wd.com
info@2wd.com
License: Hampton, Hampton City County, VA held by Entercom Norfolk License LLC.
Group Owner: Entercom Communications Corp.; (acq 12-13-99; grpsl).
Nat'l Reps: D & R Radio
Arbitron Metro Market: Hampton, VA *Format:* Adult Contemp *Hrs. of News Programming:* News progmg one hr wkly
David Field, CEO
Steve Godofsky, Operations Dir
Jeff Brown, General Manager
Sandy Smith, General Sales Mgr
Kym Wollman, News Director
Steve Fisher, CFO
Don London, Operations Manager
Tim Robisch, Advertising

Harrisonburg

***WEMC**
01-01-1955; 91.7 mhz FM *Hrs Open:* 24; 1.85 kw; 190 ft.; N38 28 20 W78 52 57
1200 Park Rd, Harrisonburg, VA 22801 US
(540) 568-6221, *Fax:* (540) 568-3814
www.wmra.org/
License: Harrisonburg, Harrisonburg City County, VA held by Eastern Mennonite University.
Nat'l Network: NPR
Arbitron Metro Market: Harrisonburg, VA *Format:* Classical, News *Hrs. of News Programming:* news progmg 15 hrs wkly *No. News Employees:* 2 *Target Audience:* General.
Thomas DuVal, General Manager

WHBG
08-01-1956; 1360 khz AM *Hrs Open:* 24
Mailing Address: 4850 Connecticut Ave. NW, Suite 103, Washington, DC 20008 US
Second Address: VA
(540) 434-0331
License: Harrisonburg, VA held by M. Belmont VerStandig Inc.
Group Owner: VerStandig Broadcasting
Nat'l Network: ESPN Radio
Arbitron Metro Market: Harrisonburg, VA *Format:* Sports *Target Audience:* 24-50.
Susanne Myers, General Manager
Frank Wilt, Programming Director

WKCY
05-11-1967; 1300 khz AM
Mailing Address: P. O. Drawer 3300, Winchester, VA 22604 US
Second Address: 207 University Blvd., Harrisonburg, VA 22801
(540) 434-1777, *Fax:* (540) 432-9968
www.goodradio.com
stevekeupp@clearchannel.com
License: Harrisonburg, VA held by Capstar TX L.P.
Group Owner: Clear Channel Communications Inc.; (acq 3-12-01; grpsl).
Nat'l Network: USA
Arbitron Metro Market: Harrisonburg, VA *Format:* Talk *Special Programming:* Relg 2 hrs wkly *Target Audience:* 55 plus.
Steve Davis, General Manager
Susie Smith, General Sales Mgr
Steve Knupp, Programming Director
David Burman, News Director
Jeff Caudell, Chief Engineer

WKCY-FM
11-01-1980; 104.3 mhz FM *Hrs Open:* 24; 50 kw; 410 ft.; N38 23 47 W79 8 28
P.O. Box 3300, Winchester, VA 22604 US
(540) 434-1777, *Fax:* (540) 462-9968
www.goodradio.com
stevekeupp@clearchannel.com
License: Harrisonburg, Rockingham County, VA held by Capstar TX L.P.
Group Owner: Clear Channel Communications Inc.
Arbitron Metro Market: Harrisonburg, VA *Format:* Country *Target Audience:* 25-54.
Dennis Hughes, Programming Director

***WMRA**
06-18-1975; 90.7 mhz FM *Hrs Open:* 24; 10.5 kw; 1043 ft.; N38 33 50 W78 57 0
821 S. Main Street, Harrisonburg, VA 22807 US
(540) 568-6221, *Fax:* (540) 568-3814
www.wmra.org
wmra@jmu.edu
License: Harrisonburg, Harrisonburg City County, VA held by James Madison University Board of Visitors.
Nat'l Network: NPR; PRI
Arbitron Metro Market: Harrisonburg, VAA *Format:* News, Talk *Special Programming:* Folk 8 hrs, blues 5 hrs wkly *Hrs. of News Programming:* news progmg 80 hrs wkly *No. News Employees:* 2 *Target Audience:* 35-64; well-educated *Adv. Rates:* 33; 17; 33; 15
Thomas DuVal, General Manager
Diane Halke, General Sales Mgr
William Fawcett, Engineering Dir

WQPO
12-03-1946; 100.7 mhz FM *Hrs Open:* 24; 50 kw; 492 ft.; N38 27 8 W78 54 32
Mailing Address: 4850 Ct., Ave., Room 103, Washington, DC 20008 US
Second Address: VA
(540) 434-0331
q101online.com
License: Harrisonburg, Rockingham County, VA
Group Owner: VerStandig Broadcasting
Arbitron Metro Market: Harrisonburg, VA *Format:* Contemporary Hits/Top 40 *No. News Employees:* 3
John VerStandig, CEO
Susanne Myers, General Manager
Dennis Burchill, General Sales Mgr
Ryan O'Bryan, Programming Director

WSVA
06-09-1935; 550 khz AM *Hrs Open:* 24
Mailing Address: 4850 Connecticut Ave, NW, Suite 103, Washington, DC 20008 US
Second Address: VA
(540) 434-0331
wsvaonline.com
License: Harrisonburg, VA held by M. Belmont VerStandig Inc.
Group Owner: VerStandig Broadcasting; (acq 4-17-87).
Nat'l Network: ABC *Regional Network:* Va. News Net.
Arbitron Metro Market: Harrisonburg, VA *Format:* News, News/Talk, 86 *Special Programming:* Farm 8 hrs wkly *No. News Employees:* 5 *Target Audience:* 35 plus.
John VerStandig, President
Susanne Myers, General Manager
Dennis Burchill, General Sales Mgr
Frank Wilt, Programming Director

***WXJM**
09-01-1990; 88.7 mhz FM *Hrs Open:* 6 AM-2 AM; 0.39 kw; 62 ft.; N38 26 22 W78 52 21
821 S. Main Street, Harrisonburg, VA 22807 US
(540) 568-6878
orgs.jmu.edu/wxjm
wxjm@jmu.edu
License: Harrisonburg, Harrisonburg City County, VA held by James Madison University Board of Visitors.
Arbitron Metro Market: Harrisonburg, VA *Format:* Alternative *Special Programming:* Jazz 14 hrs, Sp 2 hrs wkly *Hrs. of News Programming:* News progmg 7 hrs wkly *Target Audience:* General.
Emily Wyman, General Manager
Thomas DuVal, General Sales Mgr
Tom Park, Programming Director
Michael Gears, Business Manager
Rachel Corson, Music Director
Derek Niver, Music Director
Tony Schaffner, Sports Director

Heathsville

***WCNV**
01-01-2007; 89.1 mhz FM; 0 kw horiz, 3.8 kw vert; 318 ft.; N37 54 22 W76 29 9
23 Sesame Street, Richmond, VA 23235 US
(804) 320-1301, *Fax:* (804) 320-8729
www.ideastations.org/radio
sjohnson@ideastations.org
License: Heathsville, Northumberland County, VA held by Commonwealth Public Broadcasting Corp.
Nat'l Network: NPR; PRI *Wire Services:* AP
Arbitron Metro Market: Heathsville, VA *Format:* News, News/Talk, 86
Bill Miller, General Manager

Highland Springs

WCLM
05-18-1959; 1450 khz AM *Hrs Open:* 24; 0.96 kw-U, ND1; N37 32 39 W77 20 47
1734 Tamarack Street NW, Washington, DC 20012 US
(804) 231-2186, *Fax:* (804) 231-2186
www.wclmradio.com
mrptbrown@aol.com
License: Highland Springs, VA held by World Media Broadcast Co.
Arbitron Metro Market: Richmond, VA *Format:* Variety/Diverse *Special Programming:* Gospel, blues 5 hrs wkly, country, Top 40 *Target Audience:* 25-65.
Preston Brown, CEO
George Lacey, General Sales Mgr
Jim Grainger, Chief Engineer
Jay Love, Disc Jockey
Curtis Bowman, Disc Jockey
Kimberly Osacio, General Sales Manager

***WHCE**
09-29-1980; 91.1 mhz FM; 3 kw horiz; 105 ft.; N37 32 18 W77 19 27
100 Tech Drive, Highland Springs, VA 23075 US
(804) 328-4079, *Fax:* (804) 328-4074
www.mix91.com
mix91@mix91.com
License: Highland Springs, Henrico County, VA held by Henrico County Schools.
Arbitron Metro Market: Highland Springs, VA *Format:* Contemporary Hits/Top 40 *Target Audience:* 12-20; teenagers, young adults
Bob Kaufman, General Manager

Hillsville

WHHV
09-16-1961; 1400 khz AM *Hrs Open:* 6 AM-midnight; 1 kw-U, ND1; N36 45 0 W80 43 20
Mailing Address: 915 Hwy. 109 North, Gallatin, TN 37066 US
Second Address: 343 Virginia St., Hillsville, VA 24343
(276) 728-9114, *Fax:* (276) 728-9968
www.whhvradio.com
whhv@whhvradio.com
License: Hillsville, VA held by New Life Christian Communications Inc.
Format: Gospel *Special Programming:* Farm one hr wkly *Hrs. of News Programming:* News progmg 20 hrs wkly *Target Audience:* General.
Leon Goad, President
Jackie Goad, Operations Dir
R. Leon Goad, General Manager

Hopewell

WHAP
01-16-1949; 1340 khz AM *Hrs Open:* 24; 1 kw-U, ND1; N37 17 46 W77 18 50
306 West Broad Street, Richmond, VA 23220 US
(804) 452-4999
License: Hopewell, VA held by P.T. Brown Broadcast Company Inc.
Arbitron Metro Market: Richmond, VA *Format:* Gospel, Oldies *Target Audience:* 25-65.

Preston Brown, CEO
Judy Brown, General Manager

Hot Springs

*WCHG
09-01-1995; 107.1 mhz FM *Hrs Open:* 6 AM-10 PM; 0.16 kw; 1407 ft.; N38 1 53 W79 46 52 *Rebroadcasts:* Rebroadcasts WVMR(AM) Frost, WV 50%
State Route, 28, Dunmore, WV 24934 US
(540) 839-5400, *Fax:* (540) 839-5403
www.alleghenymountainradio.org
wchg@tds.net
License: Hot Springs, Bath County, VA held by Pocahontas Communications Cooperative Corp.
Regional Network: Va. News Net.
Arbitron Metro Market: Hot Springs,VA *Format:* Variety/Diverse *Hrs. of News Programming:* News progmg 15 hrs wkly *Target Audience:* General.
Cheryl Kinderman, General Manager
Bonnie Gills, Station Manager
Heather Niday, News Director
Chuck Niday, Chief Engineer

Jonesville

WJNV
01-01-2000; 99.1 mhz FM; 4 kw; 404 ft.; N36 42 5 W83 10 14
Rt 2 Box 128b, Jonesville, VA 24263 US
(276) 346-2000, *Fax:* (276) 346-2049
www.wjnv.fm
wjnv-fm@verizon.net
License: Jonesville, Lee County, VA held by Regina Kay Moore.
Format: Country
Regina Moore, General Manager

Keswick

WCNR
03-02-1991; 106.1 mhz FM; 0.6 kw; 1024 ft.; N37 59 6 W78 28 48
1790-10 E. Market Street, Harrisonburg, VA 22801 US
(434) 220-2300, *Fax:* (434) 220-2304
www.1061thecorner.com
brad@1061thecorner.com
License: Keswick, Albemarle County, VA held by Saga Communications of Charlottesville LLC.
Group Owner: Saga Communications Inc.; (acq 11-2-2006; $2.9 million)
Arbitron Metro Market: Charlottesville, VA *Format:* Triple A *Adv. Rates:* 30; 25; 30; 15
Rick Dainels, Operations Dir
John Kappes, Station Manager
Michelle Conner, General Sales Mgr
Brad Savage, Programming Director

Kilmarnock

WKWI
09-01-1975; 101.7 mhz FM *Hrs Open:* 24; 2.2 kw; 400 ft.; N37 43 25 W76 23 28.8
Mailing Address: P.O. Box 819, Kilmarnock, VA 22482 US
Second Address: 101 Radio Rd, Kilmarnock, VA 22482
(804) 435-1414, *Fax:* (804) 435-0484
charlielassitor@1017bayfm.com
License: Kilmarnock, Lancaster County, VA held by Two Rivers Communications Inc.
Nat'l Network: AP Network News; CBS
Format: Adult Contemp *No. News Employees:* 1 *Target Audience:* 25-64.
William Sherard, President
Charlie Lassiter, General Manager
Syd Abel, General Sales Mgr
Tawne Hayes, Programming Director

Lakeside

WHTI(FM)
12-01-1968; 100.9 mhz FM; 15 kw; Ant 367 ft; N37 26 21 W77 25 57
812 Moorefield Park Dr., Suite 300, Richmond, VA 23236
(804) 330-5700, *Fax:* (804) 330-4079
y101rocks.com
info@y101rocks.com
License: Lakeside, Chesterfield County, VA held by Cox Radio Inc.
Group Owner: Cox Radio Inc.; (acq 2-1-2001; grpsl)
Wire Services: UPI
Arbitron Metro Market: Richmond, VA *Target Audience:* 18-34.
Rene Clark, General Sales Mgr
Mike Fisher, Programming Director
Gary Harrison, Chief Engineer

Lawrenceville

WHLQ
09-01-1991; 105.5 mhz FM; 6 kw; 154 ft; N36 45 10 W77 51 49
Mailing Address: Box 4, Lawrenceville, VA 23868
Second Address: 2162 Plank Rd., Lawrenceville, VA 23868
(434) 848-9433, *Fax:* (434) 848-9434
License: Lawrenceville, Brunswick County, VA held by Willis Broadcasting Corp.
Group Owner: Willis Broadcasting Corp.; acq 4-27-99; $350,000 with co-located AM)

Katrina Chase, General Manager

Lebanon

WLRV
10-28-1974; 1380 khz AM *Hrs Open:* 24; 1 kw-D, ND1; 0.063 kw-N, ND1; N36 55 18 W82 6 16
P. O. Box 1380, Lebanon, VA 24266 US
(276) 889-1380, *Fax:* (276) 889-1388
www.wlrv.com
wlrv@mounet.com
License: Lebanon, VA held by Gary W. Ward Broadcasting Corp.
Nat'l Network: USA
Format: Country, Gospel *Target Audience:* 25 plus.
Gary Ward, President
Mike Lowe, Operations Dir
Rick Lang, Chief Engineer

WXLZ-FM
02-01-1993; 107.3 mhz FM *Hrs Open:* 24; 1 kw; 774 ft.; N36 50 38 W82 11 4
Mailing Address: P. O. Box 1299, Lebanon, VA 24266 US
Second Address: 265 WXLZ Dr, Lebanon, VA 24266
(276) 889-1073, *Fax:* (276) 889-3677
www.wxlz.net
wxlz1073@bvu.net
License: Lebanon, Russell County, VA held by Yeary Broadcasting Inc.
Nat'l Network: CBS
Arbitron Metro Market: Saint Paul, VA *Format:* Country *Hrs. of News Programming:* news progmg 3 hrs wkly *No. News Employees:* 2 *Target Audience:* 18 plus; students, farmers, miners, executives & rural residents
Lannis Yeary, General Manager
Marshall Hendricks, Programming Director
Anthony Stevens, News Director
Don Linkous, Chief Engineer
Wilma Kiser, Office Manager
Richard Quillen, Music Director

Leesburg

WCRW(AM)
03-06-1958; 1190 khz AM *Hrs Open:* 24; 50 kw-D, DA; N39 02 28 W77 26 42 *Rebroadcasts:* (CP: 1190 khz; 50 kw-D, DA. TL: N39 02 28 W77 26 42)
711 Wage Dr. S.W., Leesburg, VA 20175
(703) 777-1200, *Fax:* (703) 777-7431
www.wage.com
wage@wage.com
License: Leesburg, Loudoun County, VA held by Potomac Radio LLC
Regional Network: Va. News Net.
Population Served: 100,000 *Arbitron Metro Market:* Washington, DC *Hrs. of News Programming:* news progmg 114 hrs wkly *No. News Employees:* 1 *Target Audience:* 25 plus; above average income, families, homeowners
Grenville Emmet III, President
Dene Hill, Station Manager
Chris King, Programming Director
Jeremy Huber, News Director
Ron Kitemiller, Sports Commentator

Lexington

*WLUR
02-27-1967; 91.5 mhz FM *Hrs Open:* 6:30 AM-2 AM; 0.175 kw; -167 ft.; N37 47 42 W79 26 49
P. O. Box 1153, Lexington, VA 24450 US
(540) 458-4017, *Fax:* (540) 458-4079
www.wlur.wlu.edu
wlur@wlu.edu
License: Lexington, Lexington City County, VA held by Washington & Lee University.
Format: Variety/Diverse *Hrs. of News Programming:* News progmg 2 hrs wkly *Target Audience:* General; college students, city and county residents
Tom Burish, President
Benjamin Losi, Operations Dir
Jeremy Franklin, General Manager
Jeremy Franklin, Programming Director
Angela Ernst, Promotions Manager
Derrick Barksdale, Music Director

*WMRL
06-01-1992; 89.9 mhz FM *Hrs Open:* 24; 0.1 kw; -266 ft.; N37 47 25 W79 26 5 *Rebroadcasts:* Rebroadcasts WMRA(FM) Harrisonburg 100%
821 South Main Street, Harrisonburg, VA 22807 US
(540) 568-6221, *Fax:* (540) 568-3814
www.wmra.org
wmra@jmu.edu
License: Lexington, Lexington City County, VA held by James Madison University Board of Visitors.
Nat'l Network: NPR; PRI
Arbitron Metro Market: Harrisonburg, VAA *Format:* News, Talk *Special Programming:* Folk 8 hrs, blues 5 hrs wkly *Hrs. of News Programming:* news progmg 80 hrs wkly *No. News Employees:* 2 *Target Audience:* 35-64; well-educated *Adv. Rates:* 33; 17; 33; 15
Thomas DuVal, General Manager
Diane Halke, General Sales Mgr

WREL
11-14-1948; 1450 khz AM *Hrs Open:* 24; 1 kw-U, ND1; N37 46 0 W79 25 56
Mailing Address: Postal Drawer 902, Lexington, VA 22101 US
Second Address: 392 E Midland Trail, Lexington, VA 24450
(540) 463-2161, *Fax:* (540) 463-9524
www.firstmediava.com
License: Lexington, VA held by First Media Radio LLC.
Group Owner: First Media Radio LLC; (acq 6-21-2004; $1.33 million with WWZW-FM Buena Vista)
Nat'l Reps: Keystone (unwired net)
Format: News, News/Talk, 84, Talk *Hrs. of News Programming:* news progmg 6 hrs wkly *No. News Employees:* 1 *Target Audience:* 35 plus. *Adv. Rates:* 12; 10; 12; 9
Debra Reed, General Sales Mgr
Steve Williams, Programming Director
Jim Bresnahan, News Director
Wayne Boone, Chief Engineer
Rebecca Rosson, Traffic Manager

*WRIQ
88.7 mhz FM; 3.9 kw; 259 ft.; N37 53 18 W79 17 50 US
(540) 989-8900, *Fax:* (540) 776-2727
www.wvtf.org
License: Lexington, Lexington City County, VA held by Virginia Tech Foundation Inc.
Arbitron Metro Market: Lexington, VA *Format:* Classical, Jazz *No. News Employees:* 8
Bart Prater, Traffic Director
Glenn Gleixner, General Manager
Rick Mattioni, Programming Director
Connie Stevens, News Director
Paxton Durham, Chief Engineer
Steve Brown, Music Director
Cynthia Gray, Director of Development
Mary Grace Franchi, MBA, Business Manager
Ben Martin, Operations Assistant & Producer/Radio Reading Serv

Louisa

WOJL
07-10-1980; 105.5 mhz FM *Hrs Open:* 24; 6 kw; 325 ft.; N38 1 37 W78 1 5
P.O. Box 277, Louisa, VA 23093 US
(540) 672-1000, *Fax:* (540) 672-0282
www.1055samfm.com
advertising@1055samfm.com
License: Louisa, Louisa County, VA held by Piedmont Communications Inc.
Group Owner: Piedmont Communications Inc.; (acq 5-27-2004)
Nat'l Network: Westwood One
Arbitron Metro Market: Charlottesville, VA *Format:* Adult Contemp *Hrs. of News Programming:* news progmg 2 hrs wkly *No. News Employees:* 1 *Target Audience:* 25-54.
John Schick, President

Luray

WMXH-FM
10-16-1979; 105.7 mhz FM; 0.15 kw; 1972 ft.; N38 35 59 W78 38 1
P. O. Box 387, Luray, VA 22835 US
(540) 801-1057, *Fax:* (540) 564-2873
License: Luray, Page County, VA
Regional Network: Va. News Net.

Arbitron Metro Market: Luray, VA *Format:* Adult Contemp *Special Programming:* Relg 5 hrs wkly *Target Audience:* 18-54; working people with disposable income interested in mus, news & sports
Mike DuBord, General Manager

WRAA
10-01-1962; 1330 khz AM
P. O. Box 387, Luray, VA 22835 US
(540) 801-1057, *Fax:* (540) 564-2873
production@easyradioinc.com
License: Luray, VA held by EZ Radio Inc.
Regional Network: Va. News Net.; Agrinet *Nat'l Reps:* Keystone (unwired net)
Format: Country *Special Programming:* Relg 7 hrs wkly *Target Audience:* 18-49; middle to upper income, mobile
Jason Cave, President
Joshua Cave, Operations Dir

***WYFT**
10-01-1986; 103.9 mhz FM; 6 kw; 302 ft.; N38 38 17 W78 24 6
8030 Arrowridge Blvd., Charlotte, NC 28273 US
(704) 523-5555, *Fax:* (704) 522-1967
www.bbnradio.org
bbn@bbnradio.org
License: Luray, Page County, VA held by Bible Broadcasting Network Inc.
Group Owner: Bible Broadcasting Network; (acq 12-22-86).
Arbitron Metro Market: Luray, VA *Format:* Religious *Hrs. of News Programming:* News progmg 13 hrs wkly *Target Audience:* General.
Lowell Davey, President

Lynchburg

WBRG
09-06-1956; 1050 khz AM *Hrs Open:* 24
Mailing Address: P. O. Box 1079, Lynchburg, VA 24505 US
Second Address: 239 Ragland Rd., Madison Heights, VA 24572
(434) 632-7204, *Fax:* (434) 401-0230
www.wbrgradio.com/
manager@wbrgradio.com
License: Lynchburg, VA held by Tri-County Broadcasting Inc.
Nat'l Network: ABC; Westwood One; Motor Racing Net *Regional Network:* Va. News Net.
Arbitron Metro Market: Lynchburg, VA *Format:* News, News/Talk, 84, Talk *Hrs. of News Programming:* news progmg 12 hrs. wkly *No. News Employees:* 2 *Target Audience:* 25-54; College educated,professional/management, high household income, married with children *Adv. Rates:* 28; 18; 28; 16
Brent Epperson, General Manager

WSNZ
08-01-1964; 101.7 mhz FM; 3.4 kw; 289 ft.; N37 25 37 W79 7 26
Rebroadcasts: Simulcast with WSNV(FM) Salem 100%
600 Congress Ave., Suite 1400, Austin, TX 78701 US
(540) 725-1220, *Fax:* (540) 725-1245
www.mysunnyfm.com
sunny@mysunnyfm.com
License: Lynchburg, Lynchburg City County, VA held by Aloha Station Trust LLC
Arbitron Metro Market: Roanoke-Lynchburg, VA *Format:* Adult Contemp *Target Audience:* 35-54.
Chris Clendenen, General Manager
Steve Cross, Programming Director

WKPA
07-07-1988; 1390 khz AM *Rebroadcasts:* Rebroadcasts WKBA (AM) Vinton 100%
PO Box 1092, Salem, VA 24153 US
(540) 343-5597, *Fax:* (540) 345-4064
www.radiowkba.com
ddurrett@radiowkba.com
License: Lynchburg, VA held by Seven Hills Media Inc.
Arbitron Metro Market: Roanoke-Lynchburg, VA *Format:* Religious *Target Audience:* General.
Dorothy Durrett, General Manager
Zeke Leonard, General Sales Mgr
Sharon Moran, Promotions Manager
Buddy Durrett, Music Director

WLLL
11-01-1963; 930 khz AM
Mailing Address: PO Box 11305, Lynchburg, VA 24506 US
Second Address: 105 Whitehall Rd., Lynchburg, VA 24501
(434) 385-9555, *Fax:* (434) 385-6073
www.wlllradio.com
wlllam930@aol.com
License: Lynchburg, VA held by Hubbards Advertising Agency Inc.
Arbitron Metro Market: Roanoke-Lynchburg, VA *Format:* Gospel
Fletcher Hubbard, President
Savannah Hubbard, News Director

WLNI
02-02-1994; 105.9 mhz FM *Hrs Open:* 24; 6 kw; 266 ft.; N37 25 37 W79 7 26
Mailing Address: P.O. Box 348, Forest, VA 24551 US
Second Address: 19-C Wadsworth St., Lynchburg, VA 24501
(434) 845-5463, *Fax:* (434) 845-2063
www.wlni.com
wlni@wlni.com
License: Lynchburg, Lynchburg City County, VA held by Centennial Broadcasting LLC.
Group Owner: Centennial Broadcasting LLC; (acq 1-7-2005; grpsl)
Nat'l Network: ABC; Westwood One; Fox News Radio; Talk Radio Network *Nat'l Reps:* McGavren Guild *Wire Services:* AP
Arbitron Metro Market: Roanoke-Lynchburg, VA *Format:* News, News/Talk, 86 *Hrs. of News Programming:* news progmg 20 hrs wkly *No. News Employees:* 3 *Target Audience:* 25-54.
Bob Abbott, Operations Dir
Ron Gaylor, General Manager
Mari White, News Director
Michael Williams, Business Manager
Sandi Conner, Production Director
Kara Butterworth, Traffic Manager

WLVA
04-21-1930; 580 khz AM *Hrs Open:* 24
4119 Boonsboro, #220, Lynchburg, VA 24503 US
(434) 534-0400, *Fax:* (434) 534-0401
License: Lynchburg, VA held by Chesapeake-Portsmouth Broadcasting Corp.
Group Owner: Chesapeake-Portsmouth Broadcasting Corp.; (acq 1-30-2009; $560,000)
Arbitron Metro Market: Lynchburg, VA *Format:* Religious *Target Audience:* 25-54
Vic Bosiger, General Manager

WVBE-FM
01-01-1948; 100.1 mhz FM *Hrs Open:* 24; 20 kw; 328 ft.; N37 27 0 W79 4 29 *Rebroadcasts:* Rebroadcasts WVBE(AM) Roanoke 90%
Mailing Address: 5009 South Hulen, Suite 101, Fort Worth, TX 76132 US
Second Address: 3934 Electric Rd. S.W., Roanoke, VA 24018
(434) 477-1000, *Fax:* (540) 774-5667
www.vibe100.com
info@vibe100.com
License: Lynchburg, Lynchburg City County, VA held by Mel Wheeler Inc.
Group Owner: Mel Wheeler Inc.; acq 3-12-97; $7.5 million with WXLK(FM) Roanoke).
Arbitron Metro Market: Lynchburg, VA *Format:* Urban Contemporary *Hrs. of News Programming:* News progmg one hr wkly *Target Audience:* 25-54; skew women, skew black
Leonard Wheeler, CEO
Kathy Rilee, General Sales Mgr

***WRVL**
06-19-1981; 88.3 mhz FM *Hrs Open:* 24; 50 kw horiz, 42 kw vert; 1083 ft.; N37 11 50 W79 21 7
3765 Candlers Mtn Rd, Lynchburg, VA 24502 US
(434) 582-3688, *Fax:* (434) 582-2994
www.wrvlfm.com
wrvl@liberty.edu
License: Lynchburg, Lynchburg City County, VA held by Liberty University.
Arbitron Metro Market: Roanoke-Lynchbu *Format:* Religious *Special Programming:* Liberty Univ. football & basketball *Hrs. of News Programming:* news progmg 8 hrs wkly *No. News Employees:* 1 *Target Audience:* 25 plus.
David Young, Operations Dir
Jerry Edwards, General Manager
Mark Edwards, Programming Director
Patti Silverthorn, Promotions Manager
Chris Wygal, Engineering Dir
Gina Willis, Public Affairs Director

WZZU
09-01-1970; 97.9 mhz FM *Hrs Open:* 24; 0.57 kw; 1926 ft.; N37 33 46 W79 11 38 *Rebroadcasts:* Simulcasts WZZI(FM) Vinton 100%
Mailing Address: 210 Fiest Street, Sw, Suite 240, Roanoke, VA 24011 US
Second Address: 19-C Wadsworth St., Lynchburg, VA 24501
(434) 845-3698, *Fax:* (434) 845-2063
www.rocktheplanet.fm
babbott@centennialbroadcasting.com
License: Lynchburg, Lynchburg City County, VA held by Centennial Broadcasting LLC.
Group Owner: Centennial Broadcasting LLC; (acq 11-23-2004; $4.15 million with WZZI(FM) Vinton)
Nat'l Network: Fox News Radio *Nat'l Reps:* McGavren Guild *Wire Services:* AP
Arbitron Metro Market: Roanoke-Lynchbu *Format:* Rock/AOR *Special Programming:* Relg one hr wkly *No. News Employees:* 3
Bob Abbott, Operations Dir
Mike Williams, General Manager
Bob Abbott, General Sales Mgr
Kara Butterworth, News Director
Michael Williams, Business Manager
Sandi Conner, Production Director

WVGM
02-22-1962; 1320 khz AM *Hrs Open:* 24; 1 kw-D, ND1; 0.024 kw-N, ND1; N37 25 37 W79 7 26
600 Congress Ave., Suite 1400, Austin, TX 78701 US
(434) 534-6100, *Fax:* (434) 534-6101
www.espninva.com
wblt@inbox.com
License: Lynchburg, VA held by 3 Daughters Media Inc.
Group Owner: 3 Daughters Media Inc.; (acq 6-22-2007; grpsl)
Nat'l Network: ESPN Radio *Nat'l Reps:* Katz Radio
Arbitron Metro Market: Roanoke, VA *Format:* Sports, Talk *Hrs. of News Programming:* News progmg 10 hrs wkly
Gary Burns, CEO
Randy Thompson, Vice President
Ashley Schamerhorn, Operations Dir
Melinda Schamerhorn, Business & Traffic Director
Jonny Fairplay, Account Executive

***WWMC**
02-01-1993; 90.9 mhz FM *Hrs Open:* 24; 100 w; 604 ft; N37 20 56 W79 10 05
1971 Univ. Blvd., Lynchburg, VA 24506
(434) 582-3691, *Fax:* (434) 582-7461
www.thelightonline.com
wwmcfm@liberty.edu
License: Lynchburg, Lynchburg City County, VA held by Liberty University Inc.
Arbitron Metro Market: Roanoke-Lynchburg, VA *Hrs. of News Programming:* News progmg 5 hrs wkly *Target Audience:* 12-45; high school, college & young adult
Jamie Hall, Station Manager
Chris Wygal, Chief Engineer

WKHF(FM)
93.7 mhz FM; 1600 watts; 197 meters; 37 20 56N 79 10 05W
1200 West Cornwalls, Greensboro, NC 27408 USA
License: Lynchburg, Amherst County, VA
Group Owner: United States CP LLC

Manassas

WJFK-FM
04-08-1968; 106.7 mhz FM *Hrs Open:* 24; 22.5 kw; 732 ft.; N38 52 28 W77 13 24
600 New Hampshire Avenue, Suite 1200, Washington, DC 20037 US
(703) 691-1900, *Fax:* (703) 934-9896
License: Manassas, Manassas City County, VA held by Infinity Broadcasting of Washington D.C. Inc.
Group Owner: CBS Radio; (acq 10-86; $13 million;
Arbitron Metro Market: Washington, DC *Format:* Sports *Hrs. of News Programming:* news progmg 3 hrs wkly *No. News Employees:* 1 *Target Audience:* 25-54.
Lisa Broyhill, Operations Dir
Michael Hughs, General Manager
Leo Donohoe, General Sales Mgr
Megan McCluskie, Promotions Manager
Buzz Burbank, News Director
Tony Diggs, Chief Engineer
Mike Elston, Public Affairs Director

WKDV
10-01-1957; 1460 khz AM *Hrs Open:* 24; 5 kw-D, DA2; 5 kw-N, DA2; N38 45 0 W77 30 49
8121 Georgia Ave, Silver Spring, MD 20910 US
(703) 330-8244, *Fax:* (703) 331-4706
www.metroradioinc.com
metroradioinc@aol.com
License: Manassas, VA held by Metro Radio Inc.
Group Owner: Metro Radio Inc.; (acq 8-1-2005; exchange for WFBR(AM) Glen Burnie, MD)
Arbitron Metro Market: Washington, DC *Format:* Talk
David Houston, CEO
Bruce Houston, President
Kelly Koonce, COO

WWWT-FM
03-28-1966; 107.7 mhz FM *Hrs Open:* 24; 29 kw; 646 ft.; N38 44 30 W77 50 8 *Rebroadcasts:* Rebroadcasts WTOP-FM Washington, DC 100%
P.O. Box 1160, Salt Lake City, UT 84110 US
(202) 895-5000, *Fax:* (202) 895-5016
www.wtop.com
info@wtop.com
License: Manassas, Manassas City County, VA held by Bonneville Holding Co.
Group Owner: Bonneville International Corporation; (acq 4-27-98)
Nat'l Network: CBS *Regional Network:* Va. News Net. *Nat'l Reps:* Katz Radio
Arbitron Metro Market: Washington, DC *Format:* News *No. News Employees:* 2 *Target Audience:* 25-54.
Bruce Reese, CEO
Joel Oxley, Senior Vice President and General Manager
Mitch Miller, Asst. News and Program Director
Mike McMearty, News Director
Ralph Renzi, Director of Federal Sales
John D. Meyer, Director of Digital Media
JimBattagliese, Director of Traffic and Transit Operations

Marion

WUKZ(AM)
12-12-1948; 1010 khz AM *Hrs Open:* 24; 1 kw-D, 30 w-N; N36 51 23 W81 30 21
1041 Radio Hill Rd., Marion, VA 24354
(276) 783-3151,(276) 783-9400 (STUDIO), *Fax:* (276) 783-3152
www.fm94.com
fm94@smyth.net
License: Marion, Smyth County, VA held by Holston Valley Broadcasting Corp.
Group Owner: Glenwood Communications Corp.; (acq 7-1-98; $1.65 million with co-located FM)
Nat'l Network: NBC; Motor Racing Network *Regional Reps:* Rgnl Reps
Population Served: 500,000 *Arbitron Metro Market:* Johnson City-Kingsport-Bristol, TN-VA *TV Affiliate:* WKPT-TV *Special Programming:* Gospel 2 hrs, relg 8 hrs wkly *Hrs. of News Programming:* News progmg 3 hrs wkly*Target Audience:* 18-54.
George DeVault Jr., President
Jim Mabe, Operations Dir
N. David Widener, General Manager
Tiffany Hickman, General Sales Mgr
Lynn Rutledge, Programming Director
Duane Nelson, News Director
Henry Thomas, Disc Jockey
Evelyn Payne,Traffic Manager

WMEV-FM
06-21-1961; 93.9 mhz FM; 100 kw; 1,480 ft; N36 54 08 W81 32 33
1041 Radio Hill Rd., Marion, VA 37662
(276) 783-3151, *Fax:* (276) 783-3152
fm94@smyth.net
License: Marion, Smyth County, VA held by Holston Valley Broadcasting Corp.
Group Owner: Glenwood Communications Corp.; 1-Jul-98
Nat'l Network: NBC; NASCAR-MRN *Wire Services:* AP
Arbitron Metro Market: Johnson City-Kingsport-Bristol, TN-VA *TV Affiliate:* WKPT-TV *Special Programming:* Nascar *No. News Employees:* 2 *Target Audience:* Persons 25-54
George Devault, President
Lynn Rutledge, Operations Dir
N. David Widener, General Manager
Tiffany Hickman, General Sales Mgr
Henry Thomas, Programming Director
Duane Nelson, News Director
Jim Mabe, Assistant Station Manager

WITM
04-25-1962; 1330 khz AM; 5 kw-D, ND2; 0.031 kw-N, ND2; N36 49 11 W81 28 12
P. O. Box 31, Marion, VA 24354 US
(423) 878-6279, *Fax:* (423) 878-6520
License: Marion, VA held by Appalachian Educational Communications Corp.
TV Affiliate: Relg

WOLD-FM
03-14-1968; 102.5 mhz FM; 0.44 kw; 1204 ft.; N36 54 10 W81 32 27
P. O. Box 31, Marion, VA 24354 US
(276) 783-7100
http://1025therenegade.com/
License: Marion, Smyth County, VA held by T.E.C. 2 Broadcasting Inc.
Nat'l Network: CNN Radio
TV Affiliate: Classic Rock

***WVTR**
11-22-1991; 91.9 mhz FM; 4.5 kw; 1490 ft.; N36 44 52 W81 18 15 *Rebroadcasts:* Rebroadcasts WVTF(FM) Roanoke 100%
4235 Electric Rd Sw, Suite 105, Roanoke, VA 24014 US
(540) 989-8900, *Fax:* (540) 776-2727
www.wvtf.org
info@wvtf.org
License: Marion, Smyth County, VA held by Virginia Tech Foundation Inc.
Nat'l Network: NPR
Format: Jazz
Glenn Gleixner, General Manager
Karen Dillon, General Sales Mgr

WZVA
09-02-1996; 103.5 mhz FM *Hrs Open:* 24; 3.7 kw; 423 ft.; N36 54 10 W81 22 56
113 N. Chestnut Street, Marion, VA 24354 US
(276) 783-4042, *Fax:* (276) 783-2120
www.1035thundercountry.com
info@1035thundercountry.com
License: Marion, Smyth County, VA held by T.E.C.O. Broadcasting Inc.
Arbitron Metro Market: Marion, VA *Format:* Adult Contemp, Contemporary Hits/Top 40 *Target Audience:* 18-49; women & men
Tom Copenhaver, CEO
Blake Frazier, Station Manager

Martinsville

WHEE
08-04-1954; 1370 khz AM; 5 kw-D, NDD; N36 41 9 W79 54 14
Mailing Address: P.O. Drawer 3551, 40 Franklin Street, Martinsville, VA 24112 US
Second Address: 40 Franklin St., Martinsville, VA 24115
(276) 632-9811, *Fax:* (276) 632-4500
martinsvillemedia.com
License: Martinsville, VA held by Martinsville Media Inc.
Nat'l Network: CBS
Format: Talk *Target Audience:* 17-60; agriculture & mfg area audience
Bill Wyatt, President
T.L. Walker, Chief Engineer

***WPIM**
01-01-1997; 90.5 mhz FM; 4 kw; 387 ft.; N36 42 16 W79 50 5
P.O. Box 889, Blacksburg, VA 24063 US
(540) 552-8073, *Fax:* (540) 951-5282
www.spiritfm.com
mail@spiritfm.com
License: Martinsville, Martinsville City County, VA held by Positive Alternative Radio Inc.
Group Owner: Positive Alternative Radio Inc.
Format: Adult Contemp, Christian
Vernon Baker, Chairman
Edward Baker, President
Barry Armstrong, General Manager

WROV-FM
01-01-1950; 96.3 mhz FM; 14 kw; 2077 ft.; N37 7 0 W80 0 58
600 Congress Avenue, Suite 1400, Austin, TX 78701 US
(540) 725-1220, *Fax:* (540) 725-1245
www.wrov.cc
License: Martinsville, Martinsville City County, VA held by Capstar TX L.P.
Group Owner: Clear Channel Communications Inc.; (acq 8-30-00; grpsl).
Nat'l Reps: D & R Radio
Arbitron Metro Market: Roanoke-Lynchburg, VA *Format:* Rock/AOR *Target Audience:* 18-49; general
Dave Carwile, General Manager
Tammy Cazad, General Sales Mgr
Jay Prayter, Programming Director
Ed Kilbane, News Director
Jeff Parker, Chief Engineer

WMVA
12-01-1941; 1450 khz AM; 1 kw-U, ND1; N36 42 0 W79 51 7
1129 Chatham Road, Martinsville, VA 24115 US
(276) 632-2152, *Fax:* (276) 632-4500
www.martinsvillemedia.com
93.5@waxm.com
License: Martinsville, VA held by Martinsville Media Inc.
Arbitron Metro Market: Lafayette, LA *Format:* Talk
Bill Wyatt, President

Mechanicsville

WCDX
10-07-1985; 92.1 mhz FM; 4.5 kw; 771 ft.; N37 36 52 W77 30 56
6158 Yellow Birch Court, Plainfield, IN 46168 US
(804) 672-9299, *Fax:* (804) 672-9316
www.ipowerrichmond.com/
License: Mechanicsville, Hanover County, VA held by Radio One Licenses LLC.
Group Owner: Radio One Inc.; (acq 11-8-2001; grpsl).
Nat'l Reps: Eastman Radio
Arbitron Metro Market: Richmond, VA *Format:* Urban Contemporary *Target Audience:* Ages 18-44.
Linda Forem, Operations Dir
Brian Robertson, General Sales Mgr
Reggie Baker, Programming Director
Dawna Covington, Promotions Manager
Chris Lawless, Chief Engineer
Bobby Walden, National Sales Manager
Al Payne, OperationsManager
Clovia Lawrence, Public Affairs Director

Midlothian

WWLB
11-22-1971; 98.9 mhz FM *Hrs Open:* 5 AM-midnight; 4.8 kw; 746 ft.; N37 36 52 W77 30 56
P.O. 271, Orange, VA 22960 US
(804) 327-9902, *Fax:* (804) 327-9911
www.989liberty.com
info@989liberty.com
License: Midlothian, Chesterfield County, VA held by MLB-Richmond IV LLC.
Group Owner: Main Line Broadcasting LLC; (acq 12-13-2005; grpsl).
Format: Variety/Diverse
Sandy Jimerson, General Sales Mgr

Minooka

01-01-2012; 88.5 mhz FM; 200 w; 32 meters; N41 29 47 W88 17 56
6139 Franklin Park Road, McLean, VA 22101
(703) 761-5013
License: Minooka, Grundy County, IL held by Silver Fish Broadcasting Inc

A Wray Fitch III, President

Moneta

WSLK
11-01-1991; 880 khz AM *Hrs Open:* 12; 0.9 kw-D, NDD; N37 10 0 W79 37 50
P.O. Box 880, 10 a Village Square, Moneta, WA 24121 US
(540) 297-7880, *Fax:* (540) 343-2306
wslk880.com
info@wslk880.com
License: Moneta, VA held by Smile Broadcasting LLC
Arbitron Metro Market: Roanoke, VA *Format:* Oldies *Target Audience:* 35 plus; mostly middle aged, affluent, cosmopolitan
Dale Cook, Chief Engineer
Martin Jeffrey, Sales

Monterey

***WVLS**
09-01-1995; 89.7 mhz FM *Hrs Open:* 6 AM-10 PM; 0.36 kw vert; 1460 ft.; N38 20 39 W79 35 47 *Rebroadcasts:* Rebroadcasts WVMR(AM) Frost, WV 60%
State Route 28, Dunmore, WV 24934 US
(304) 799-6004, *Fax:* (304) 799-7444
www.alleghenymountainradio.org
ewamr@frontier.com
License: Monterey, Highland County, VA held by Pocahontas Communications Cooperative Corp.
Arbitron Metro Market: Dunmore, WV *Format:* Variety/Diverse *Target Audience:* General.
Cheryl Kinderman, General Manager
Chuck Niday, Chief Engineer
Erin Will, Station Coordinator

Mount Jackson

WSIG
10-01-1988; 96.9 mhz FM *Hrs Open:* 24; 4.3 kw; 558 ft.; N38 36 31 W78 54 7
P.O. Box 425, Mt. Jackson, VA 22842 US
(540) 432-1063, *Fax:* (540) 433-9267
www.969wsig.com
race@realcountrywsig.com

License: Mount Jackson, Shenandoah County, VA held by Vox Communications Group LLC.
Group Owner: Vox Communications; (acq 8-31-2005; $2 million)
Nat'l Network: CNN Radio
Arbitron Metro Market: Harrisonburg, V *Format:* Country *Special Programming:* Bluegrass 6 hrs, gospel 4 hrs wkly
Race Ashlyn, General Manager

WSVG
04-23-1954; 790 khz AM *Hrs Open:* Sunrise-sunset; 1 kw-D, ND1; 0.04 kw-N, ND1; N38 46 15 W78 37 17
P.O. Box 425, Mt. Jackson, VA 22842 US
(540) 477-4443, *Fax:* (540) 477-4407
wsvg@chentil.net
License: Mount Jackson, VA held by Hometown Broadcasting of Mt. Jackson LLC
Arbitron Metro Market: Winchester, VA *Format:* Talk
Alan Arehart, General Manager
Patty Shaffer, General Manager

Narrows

WZFM
01-01-1992; 101.3 mhz FM; 0.21 kw; 1201 ft.; N37 17 54 W80 48 36
Mailing Address: 903 E. Main Street, Abingdon, VA 24210 US
Second Address: 145 Jackson St., Blacksburg, VA 24063
(540) 951-9791, *Fax:* (540) 961-2021
License: Narrows, Giles County, VA held by WZFM LLC..
Group Owner: Baker Family Stations; (acq 5-19-2006; $600,000).
Nat'l Network: ABC Music Radio
Arbitron Metro Market: Narrows, VA *Format:* Classic Rock, Oldies *Target Audience:* 30+
Amy Burnette, General Manager

Narrows-Pearisburg

WNRV
08-01-1953; 990 khz AM *Hrs Open:* 24; 5 kw-D, NDD; 0.01 kw-N, ND1; N37 20 39 W80 46 36 *Rebroadcasts:* Rebroadcast WWWR(AM) Roanoke 90%
1930 Isaac Newton Square, #250, Reston, VA 20190 US
(540) 343-7109, *Fax:* (540) 343-2306
www.wnrvbluegrassradio.com
info@wnrvbluegrassradio.com
License: Narrows-Pearisburg, VA held by Perception Media Group Inc.
Arbitron Metro Market: Narrows, VA *Format:* Blues
Terry Reed, President
Dennis Welch, Operations Dir
Dean Reed, General Manager

Nassawadox

*WHRX
01-01-2005; 90.1 mhz FM; 450 w vert; Ant 199 ft; N37 33 27 W75 49 44
5200 Hampton Blvd, Norfolk, VA 33487
(757) 889-9400, *Fax:* (757) 489-0007
www.whro.org
info@whro.org
License: Nassawadox, Northampton County, VA held by Hampton Roads Telecommunications Assoc Inc
Group Owner: Positive Alternative Radio Inc.; (acq 12-7-2012)

Bert Schmidt, President

New Market

WLTK
01-01-1997; 102.9 mhz FM *Hrs Open:* 24; 2.1 kw; 544 ft; N38 36 31 W78 54 07
PO Box 337, 166 N Main Street, Broadway, VA 22801
(540) 896-9585, *Fax:* (540) 896-1448
www.positive-radio.com
info@positive-radio.com
License: New Market, Shenandoah County, VA held by Massanutten Broadcasting Co.
Nat'l Network: USA *Nat'l Reps:* Salem
Population Served: 150,000 *Arbitron Metro Market:* Harrisonburg, VA *Hrs. of News Programming:* News progmg 9 hrs wkly *Target Audience:* 25-44. *Adv. Rates:* 20; 17; 20; 17
David Eshelman, President
David Eshleman, General Manager
Christine Pompeo, General Sales Mgr
Greg Crabtree, Programming Director
Judy Shafer, News Director
Dave Wyant, Disc Jockey
Karen Kenney, Disc Jockey

Newport News

WGH
10-01-1928; 1310 khz AM *Hrs Open:* 24
C/O Barnstable Broadcasting, Inc., Two Newton Executive Park, Newton, MA 02462 US
(757) 671-1000, *Fax:* (757) 671-1010
www.espnradio.com
info@espnradio.com
License: Newport News, VA held by MHR License LLC
Group Owner: MAX Media L.L.C.
Nat'l Network: ESPN Radio
Arbitron Metro Market: Norfolk-Virginia Beach-Newport News, VA *Format:* Sports, Talk *Target Audience:* General.
Eric Mastel, President
Vonneva Carter, General Manager
Anthony Mercurio, Promotions Manager
John Shomby, Programmign Director

WGH-FM
11-01-1948; 97.3 mhz FM; 74 kw; 394 ft.; N36 57 47 W76 24 42
C/O Barnstable Broadcasting, Inc., Two Newton Executive Park, Newton, MA 02462 US
(757) 671-1000, *Fax:* (757) 671-1010
www.eagle97.com
info@eagle97.com
License: Newport News, Newport News City County, VA held by MHR License LLC
Group Owner: MAX Media L.L.C.; (acq 3-24-2005; grpsl).
Arbitron Metro Market: Norfolk-Virginia Beach-Newport News, VA *Format:* Country *Target Audience:* Adults 25-54
Eric Mastel, President
Vonneva Carter, General Manager
John Shomby, Programming Director
Paul Campbell, Chief Engineer

WTJZ
11-01-1947; 1270 khz AM *Hrs Open:* 24
3780 Will Scarlet Road, Winston-Salem, NC 27104 US
(757) 723-1270, *Fax:* (757) 624-2307
www.lifestream.tv
wtjz1270@gmail.com
License: Newport News, VA held by Chesapeake-Portsmouth Broadcasting Corp.
Group Owner: Chesapeake-Portsmouth Broadcasting Corp.; (acq 1999; $380,000)
Arbitron Metro Market: Hampton, VA *Format:* Gospel *Special Programming:* 5 hrs wkly
Martin Culpepper, General Manager

Norfolk

WYRM
04-06-1976; 1110 khz AM *Hrs Open:* day; 50 kw-D, DAD; N36 56 34 W76 31 56
3801 Skillern Blvd, Flower Mound, TX 75028 US
(757) 622-9256, *Fax:* (757) 622-9253
www.wyrmradio.com
wyrm1110@hotmail.com
License: Norfolk, VA held by Word Broadcasting Network Inc.
Group Owner: Word Broadcasting Network Inc.; acq 7-29-2003; $1.25 million with WYMM(AM) Jacksonville, FL).
Arbitron Metro Market: Norfolk-Virginia Beach-Newport News, VA *Format:* Religious
Larry Cobb, General Manager
Paula Cobb, Office Manager

WVXX
07-01-1954; 1050 khz AM; 5 kw-D, DA2; 0.358 kw-N, DA2; N36 49 44 W76 12 26
900 Commonwealth Place, Virginia Beach, VA 23464 US
(757) 627-9899, *Fax:* (757) 627-0123
www.selecta1050.com
License: Norfolk, VA held by Davidson Media Station WVXX Licensee LLC.
Group Owner: Davidson Media Group LLC; (acq 2-10-2005; $975,000).
Arbitron Metro Market: Hampton Roads, VA *Format:* Spanish *Target Audience:* 18-54; Hispanic adults
Andy Hindlin, President

WVHT
04-29-2009; 100.5 mhz FM *Hrs Open:* 24; 50 kw; 499 ft.; N36 49 44 W76 12 26
900 Commonwealth Place, Virginia Beach, VA 23464 US
(757) 671-1000, *Fax:* (757) 490-8973
www.hot1005.com
theboss@hot1005.com
License: Norfolk, Norfolk City County, VA held by MHR License LLC.
Group Owner: MAX Media L.L.C.; (acq 3-24-2005; grpsl)
Nat'l Reps: Christal
Arbitron Metro Market: Hampton Roads, VA *Format:* Contemporary Hits/Top 40 *Target Audience:* Adults 18-49
Eric Martel, President
Michele Williams, Operations Dir
Vonneva Carter, General Manager
John Shomby, Programming Director
Paul Campbell, Chief Engineer
Paul McCoy, Program Director

*WHRO-FM
01-01-1990; 90.3 mhz FM *Hrs Open:* 20; kw
5200 Hampton Boulevard, Norfolk, VA 23508 US
(757) 889-9400, *Fax:* (757) 489-0007
www.whro.org
info@whro.org
License: Norfolk, Norfolk City County, VA held by Hampton Roads Educational Telecommunications Association Inc.
Nat'l Network: NPR; PRI *Wire Services:* AP
Arbitron Metro Market: Norfolk-Virginia Beach-Newport News, VA *TV Affiliate:* *WHRO-TV affil. *Format:* News *Target Audience:* 35 plus; well-educated, exec leaders
Bert Schmidt, CEO
John Heimerl, Operations Dir
Virginia Thumm, General Sales Mgr
Dwight Davis, Programming Director
Colleen Inghram, CFO

*WHRV
01-01-1974; 89.5 mhz FM *Hrs Open:* 24; 34 kw; 596 ft.; N36 48 32 W76 30 13
5200 Hampton Boulevard, Norfolk, VA 23508 US
(757) 889-9400, *Fax:* (757) 489-0007
www.whro.org
info@whro.org
License: Norfolk, Norfolk City County, VA held by Hampton Roads Educational Telecommunications Association, Inc.
Nat'l Network: NPR; PRI *Wire Services:* AP
Arbitron Metro Market: Norfolk-Virginia Beach-Newport News, VA *TV Affiliate:* *WHRO-TV affil. *Format:* Alternative, Jazz, 60, News/Talk, Talk *Special Programming:* Progsv 14 hrs, folk 7 hrs wkly *Hrs. of NewsProgramming:* news progmg 105 hrs wkly *No. News Employees:* 1 *Target Audience:* 35 plus.
Bert Schmidt, CEO
John Heimerl, Operations Dir
Virginia Thumm, General Sales Mgr
Heather Mazzon, Programming Director
Colleen Ingraham, CFO

WVMA(FM)
08-03-1962; 105.3 mhz FM; 50 kw; 499 ft; N36 48 43 W76 27 49
Clear Channel Communications, Inc., 1003 Norfolk Sq., Norfolk, VA 23502-4948
(757) 466-0009, *Fax:* (757) 466-4043
www.1053kiss.com
info@1053kiss.com
License: Norfolk, Norfolk City County, VA held by CC Licenses LLC.
Group Owner: Clear Channel Communications Inc.; (acq 1996; grpsl).
Nat'l Reps: Roslin
Arbitron Metro Market: Norfolk-Virginia Beach-Newport News, VA *Format:* Urban Contemporary *Target Audience:* 25-54.
Reggie Jordan, General Manager
Joi Jamison, Programming Director

WJOI
01-01-1949; 1230 khz AM
870 Greenbrier Circle, Suite 399, Chesapeake, VA 23320 US
(757) 366-9900, *Fax:* (757) 366-0022
www.1230wjoi.com
License: Norfolk, VA held by Tidewater Communications LLC.
Group Owner: Saga Communications Inc.; (acq 9-15-86)
Nat'l Reps: McGavren Guild
Arbitron Metro Market: Norfolk-Virginia Beach-Newport News, VA *Format:* Adult Contemp
Dave Paulus, President
Mike Beck, Operations Dir
Wayne Leland, General Manager
Dave Taylor, Promotions Manager
Don Crowder, Chief Engineer
Sonja Morrell, Marketing Director
Mike Anthony, Production Manager
Chuck Cooney,Production Manager
Laurie Bodner, Business Manager
Keri Credle, Traffic Manager

WNIS
09-21-1923; 790 khz AM *Hrs Open:* 24; 5 kw-U, DA1; N37 4 25 W76 17 31
500 Dominion Tower, 999 Waterside Drive, Norfolk, VA 23510 US

(757) 640-8500, *Fax:* (757) 640-8552
www.wnis.com
jaywest@sinclairstations.com
License: Norfolk, VA held by Sinclair Communications Inc.
Group Owner: Sinclair Communications Inc.
Nat'l Network: ABC; Westwood One *Regional Network:* Va. News Net. *Nat'l Reps:* McGavren Guild; Interep *Wire Services:* AP
Arbitron Metro Market: Norfolk, VA *Format:* News, News/Talk, 86 *Target Audience:* 25-54.
Bob Sinclair, CEO
Dave Morgan, Operations Dir
Lisa Sinclair, Station Manager
Juli Zobel, General Sales Mgr
Jay West, Programming Director
Donna Agresto, Promotions Manager
Ginger Power, National Sales Manager

WNOR
01-01-1961; 98.7 mhz FM; 46 kw; 518 ft.; N36 50 4 W76 16 11
73 Kercheval Avenue, Grosse Pointe Farms, MI 48236 US
(757) 366-9900, *Fax:* (757) 366-0022
www.fm99.com
info@fm99.com
License: Norfolk, Norfolk City County, VA held by Tidewater Communications LLC.
Group Owner: Saga Communications Inc.
Arbitron Metro Market: Norfolk, VA *Format:* Rock/AOR
Wayne Leland, General Manager
Harvey Najen, Programming Director

***WNSB**
03-22-1980; 91.1 mhz FM; 8.1 kw; 433 ft.; N36 46 32 W76 23 11
2401 Corprew Avenue, Norfolk, VA 23504 US
(757) 823-9672, *Fax:* (757) 823-2385
www.hot91online.com
wnsb@nsu.edu
License: Norfolk, Norfolk City County, VA held by Norfolk State University Board of Visitors.
Nat'l Network: NPR
Arbitron Metro Market: Norfolk, VA *Format:* Urban Contemporary *Target Audience:* 18-24.
Wanda Brockington, General Manager
Edward Turner, Station Manager

WNVZ
07-01-1967; 104.5 mhz FM; 49 kw; 479 ft.; N37 2 17.6 W76 18 28.7
10706 Beaver Dam Road, Cockeysville, MD 21030 US
(757) 497-2000, *Fax:* (757) 497-7158
www.z104.com
tias@entercom.com
License: Norfolk, Norfolk City County, VA held by Entercom Norfolk License LLC.
Group Owner: Entercom Communications Corp.; (acq 12-13-99; grpsl).
Nat'l Reps: D & R Radio
Arbitron Metro Market: Norfolk-Virgini *TV Affiliate:* Hip hop
Special Programming: News progmg one hr wkly *No. News Employees:* 18-34; females
CEO, CEO/COO
Operations Manager, Mike Klein
Program Director, Jade Kozup
Promotions Director, Promotions Manager
CFO, Cheri Pridgen
National Sales Manager, Don London
Operations Manager, Steve Godofsky
Vice President

WOWI
06-01-1948; 102.9 mhz FM; 50 kw; 472 ft.; N36 45 23 W76 23 6
200 Concord Plaza, Suite 600, San Antonio, TX 78216 US
(757) 466-0009, *Fax:* (757) 466-7043
www.103jamz.com
License: Norfolk, Norfolk City County, VA held by CC Licenses LLC.
Group Owner: Clear Channel Communications Inc.; (acq 1996; grpsl)
Nat'l Reps: McGavren Guild
Arbitron Metro Market: Norfolk-Virginia Beach-Newport News, VA *Format:* Urban Contemporary *Target Audience:* 18-34.
Lowery Mays, CEO
Travis Dylan, Operations Dir
Reggie Jordan, General Manager
Terry Ratliff, General Sales Mgr
D.J. Law, Programming Director
Toni Bailey Jones, Promotions Manager
Michael Mendelson, General Sales Manager
D.J.Fountz, Music Director

WTAR
09-01-1952; 850 khz AM *Hrs Open:* 24
999 Waterside Dr., Norfolk, VA 23510 US
(757) 640-8500, *Fax:* (757) 640-8552
www.wtar.com
License: Norfolk, VA held by Sinclair Communications Inc.
Group Owner: Sinclair Communications Inc.; (acq 9-87; $725,000;
Nat'l Reps: McGavren Guild; Interep
Arbitron Metro Market: Norfolk-Virginia Beach-Newport News, VA *Format:* Sports *Target Audience:* 25-54.
Bob Sinclair, CEO
Lisa Sinclair, General Manager
Juli Zobel, General Sales Mgr
Jay West, Programming Director
Donna Agresto, Promotions Manager
Ginger Power, National Sales Manager

WVKL
09-21-1961; 95.7 mhz FM; 40 kw; 879 ft.; N36 48 56 W76 28 0
10706 Beaver Dam Road, Cockeysville, MD 21030 US
(757) 497-2000, *Fax:* (757) 456-5458
www.957rnb.com
info@957rnb.com
License: Norfolk, Norfolk City County, VA held by Entercom Norfolk License LLC.
Group Owner: Entercom Communications Corp.; (acq 12-13-99; grpsl).
Arbitron Metro Market: Virginia Beach, VA *Format:* Blues
David Field, CEO
Steve Godofsky, Operations Dir
Jeff Brown, General Manager
Hope Angelone, General Sales Mgr
Karen Parker-Chesson, News Director
Steve Fisher, CFO
Don London, Operations Manager
Hope Angelone, AdvertisingContact

***WYFI**
10-02-1971; 99.7 mhz FM; 50 kw; 456 ft.; N36 49 41 W76 15 5
8030 Arrowridge Blvd., Charlotte, NC 28273 US
(704) 523-5555, *Fax:* (704) 522-1967
www.bbnradio.org
bbn@bbnradio.org
License: Norfolk, Norfolk City County, VA held by Bible Broadcasting Network Inc.
Group Owner: Bible Broadcasting Network; acq 12-24-70)
Arbitron Metro Market: Norfolk-Virgini *Format:* Religious
Lowell Davey, President
Dennis Gast, General Manager

Norton

WNVA
03-01-1946; 1350 khz AM; 5 kw-D, ND1; 0.037 kw-N, ND1; N36 57 58 W82 35 17
P.O. Box 500, Norton, VA 24273 US
540-328-2244, *Fax:* 540-328-0024
wnva@mounet.com
License: Norton, VA held by Radio-Wise Inc.
Regional Reps: Regnl Reps
TV Affiliate: Adult contemp *Format:* Gospel, Religious *Special Programming:* News progmg 2 hrs wkly *No. News Employees:* 25-65; adults & young adu *Adv. Rates:* 7; 6.50; 7; 6
Operations Director

WNVA-FM
07-25-1969; 106.3 mhz FM; 1.65 kw; 614 ft.; N36 57 58 W82 35 17
P.O. Box 500, Norton, VA 24273 US
540-328-2244, *Fax:* 540-328-0024
License: Norton, Norton City County, VA held by Radio-Wise Inc.
Nat'l Network: Jones Radio Networks *Regional Reps:* Regnl Reps
TV Affiliate: adult contemp *Special Programming:* News progmg 10 hrs wkly *No. News Employees:* 18-45; young adults *Adv. Rates:* 7; 6.50; 7; 5

Onley-Onancock

WESR
01-23-1958; 1330 khz AM; 5 kw-D, ND1; 0.051 kw-N, ND1; N37 43 2 W75 41 1
Mailing Address: Post Office Box 460, Onley, VA 23418 US
Second Address: 22479 Front St., Accomac, VA 23301
(757) 787-3200, *Fax:* (757) 787-3819
www.shoredailynews.com
crussell@wesr.net
License: Onley-Onancock, VA held by Eastern Shore Radio Inc.
Nat'l Network: ABC *Nat'l Reps:* Dome
Arbitron Metro Market: Onley, VA *Format:* Country, Talk
Charles Russell, General Manager and Owner
Bill LeCato, Programming Director

WESR-FM
01-01-1968; 103.3 mhz FM; 50 kw; 322 ft.; N37 43 2 W75 41 1
Mailing Address: Post Office Box 460, Onley, VA 23418 US
Second Address: 22479 Front St., Onley-Onancock, VA 23301
(757) 787-3200, *Fax:* (757) 787- 3819
www.shoredailynews.com
crussell@wesr.net
License: Onley-Onancock, Accomack County, VA
Nat'l Network: ABC
Arbitron Metro Market: Onley, VA *Format:* Adult Contemp
Misty Huff, Operations Dir
Charles Russell, General Manager and Owner
Bill Moody, General Sales Mgr
Jess Bailey, Programming Director
April Granger, News Director

Orange

WVCV
09-10-1949; 1340 khz AM; 1 kw-U, ND1; N38 15 14 W78 7 15
Rebroadcasts: Simulcasts WCVA (AM) Culpeper 100%
Mailing Address: P.O. Box 271, Orange, VA 22960 US
Second Address: 207 Spicers Mill Rd., Orange, VA 22960
(540) 672-1000, *Fax:* (540) 672-0282
www.wjmafm.com
advertising@wjmafm.com
License: Orange, VA held by Piedmont Communications Inc.
Group Owner: Piedmont Communications Inc.; acq 2-18-93; $30,000 with co-located FM;
Nat'l Network: Westwood One; ABC
Arbitron Metro Market: Orange, VA *Format:* Adult Contemp
Special Programming: Gospel 2 hrs, relg one hr, news 18 hrs wkly *No. News Employees:* 1 *Target Audience:* 45 plus.
John Schick, President
Kathy Campbell, Contact Rep
Elizabeth Duncan, Contact Rep

Pamplin City

***WEQP**
90.5 mhz FM; 0.08 kw; 410 ft.; N37 12 7 W78 41 31 US
(434)455-0306, *Fax:* (434) 239-6368
www.equipfm.org
info@equipfm.org
License: Pamplin City, Appomattox County, VA held by Airwaves for Jesus Inc.
Arbitron Metro Market: Pamplin, VA *Format:* Religious
Art Ramos, President
Scott Paulette, Station Manager

Pennington Gap

WSWV
06-01-1959; 1570 khz AM *Hrs Open:* 24; 2.3 kw-D, ND1; 0.191 kw-N, ND1; N36 44 2 W83 2 34
203 West Morgan Avenue, Pennington Gap, VA 24277 US
(276) 546-2520, *Fax:* (276) 546-1356
www.wswv.net
wswv@optidynamic.com
License: Pennington Gap, VA held by B C Broadcasting Co. Inc.
Nat'l Network: AP Network News *Nat'l Reps:* Rgnl Reps
Format: Gospel *Target Audience:* 24-54; young, working adults
Robert Wright, General Manager
Mike Cook, Chief Engineer

WSWV-FM
01-01-1973; 105.5 mhz FM *Hrs Open:* 24; 6 kw; 276 ft.; N36 44 2 W83 2 34
203 West Morgan Avenue, Pennington Gap, VA 24277 US
(276) 546-2520, *Fax:* (276) 546-1356
www.wswv.net
License: Pennington Gap, Lee County, VA
Format: Country
Robert Wright, General Manager

Petersburg

WTPS
05-07-1945; 1240 khz AM *Hrs Open:* 24; 1 kw-U, ND1; N37 14 1 W77 22 36
500 Dominion Tower, 999 Waterside Drive, Norfolk, VA 23510 US
(804) 672-9299, *Fax:* (804) 672-9314
www.newstalk1240WTPS.com
info@newstalk1240wtps.com
License: Petersburg, VA held by Radio One Licenses LLC.
Group Owner: Radio One Inc.; (acq 7-26-99; grpsl)
Nat'l Reps: McGavren Guild
Arbitron Metro Market: Richmond, VA *Format:* News, News/Talk, 86 *Target Audience:* 25-54.

Jeff Anderson, Operations Dir
Linda Forem, General Manager
Marsha Landess, General Sales Mgr
Jeff Anderson, Programming Director
Clovia Lawewnce, News Director
Chris Walker, Digital Sales Manager
Adam Drudge, Digital SupportCoordinator
Terron Austin, Online Editor

WKJM
10-01-1966; 99.3 mhz FM; 6 kw; 328 ft.; N37 14 1 W77 22 36
500 Dominion Tower, 999 Waterside Dr., Norfolk, VA 23510 US
(804) 672-9299, *Fax:* (804) 672-9314
www.yestokiss.com
info@yestokiss.com
License: Petersburg, Petersburg City County, VA
Group Owner: Radio One Inc.
Arbitron Metro Market: Richmond, VA *Format:* Adult Contemp
Target Audience: 25-54; Black adults *Adv. Rates:* 14; 14; 14; 14
Jeff Anderson, Operations Dir
Dennis Gettis, General Sales Mgr
Dawna Covington, Promotions Manager

WARV-FM
12-01-1992; 100.3 mhz FM; 4.5 kw; 381 ft.; N37 10 55 W77 24 1
Rebroadcasts: Simulcast with WBBT-FM Powhatan 100%
5900 Princess Garden Parkway, 8th Floor, Lanham, MD 20706 US
(804) 327-9902, *Fax:* (804) 327-9911
www.1073bbt.com
info@1073bbt.com
License: Petersburg, Petersburg City County, VA held by MLB-Richmond IV LLC.
Group Owner: Main Line Broadcasting LLC; (acq 12-13-2006; grpsl).
Arbitron Metro Market: Richmond, VA *Format:* Oldies
John Kolesa, General Sales Mgr
Mike Murphy, Programming Director
Michelle Prosser, Promotions Manager
Rob Astleford, Chief Engineer

***WVST-FM**
07-12-1987; 91.3 mhz FM *Hrs Open:* 19; 2.2 kw vert; 167 ft.; N37 14 15 W77 24 55
P.O. Box 9067, Harris Hall, Room 130, Petersburg, VA 23806 US
(804) 524-5000, *Fax:* (804) 524-5826
www.vsu.edu/wvst
License: Petersburg, Petersburg City County, VA held by Virginia State University.
Regional Network: Va. News Net.
Arbitron Metro Market: Richmond, VA *Format:* Jazz, Variety/Diverse *Special Programming:* Gospel 13 hrs wkly
Target Audience: 25 plus; general
Dr. Moadab, General Manager
Yolie Thomas, Station Manager
Hugh Mannah, Chief of Operations

Poquoson

WUSH
04-01-2001; 106.1 mhz FM *Hrs Open:* 24; 11 kw; 490 ft.; N36 51 39 W76 21 13
8280 Greensboro Drive, 7th Floor, McLean, VA 22102 US
(757) 640-8500, *Fax:* (757) 640-8552
www.us1061.com
brandon@us106.com
License: Poquoson, York County, VA held by Commonwealth Broadcasting L.L.C.
Group Owner: Sinclair Communications Inc.; (acq 8-24-2001; $1.883 million for CP)
Nat'l Reps: McGavren Guild; Interep
Arbitron Metro Market: Norfolk, VA *Format:* Country
Lisa Sinclair, General Manager
Jeanett Xenakis, General Sales Mgr
Brandon O'Brien, Program & Music Director
Donna Agresto-Seavey, Program & Music Director
Ginger Power, National Sales Manager
Dave Thompson, Website
Lisa Sapp,Website

Portsmouth

WGPL
01-01-1942; 1350 khz AM *Hrs Open:* 24; 5 kw-D, DA2; 5 kw-N, DA2; N36 53 0 W76 22 22
200 Concord Plaza, Suite 600, San Antonio, TX 78216 US
(757) 622-4600, *Fax:* (757) 624-6515
willisbroadcasting@yahoo.com
License: Portsmouth, VA held by Christian Broadcasting of Norfolk Inc.
Group Owner: Willis Broadcasting Corp.
Arbitron Metro Market: Norfolk-Virginia Beach-Newport News, VA
Format: Gospel *Hrs. of News Programming:* news progmg 6 hrs wkly *No. News Employees:* 2 *Target Audience:* W25-54.
L. E. Willis, II, CEO
Hortense Willis, President
Walter Allen Brickhouse, General Manager
Julian Joyner, Programming Director
Terry Love, Chief Engineer
Ernestine Willis, Corporate Officer
Christine Willis, Corporate Officer
Celestine Willis, Corporate Officer

WHKT
01-01-1999; 1650 khz AM
3780 Will Scarlet Rd, Winston-Salem, NC 27104 US
(757) 519-9171, *Fax:* (757) 519-9147
www.radio.disney.go.com
License: Portsmouth, VA held by Radio Disney Group LLC.
Group Owner: ABC Inc.; (acq 6-5-2002; $1.08 million with WRJR(AM) Portsmouth).
Arbitron Metro Market: Norfolk-Virginia Beach-Newport News, VA
Format: Children
Monica Ward, Operations Dir
Tom Winslow, Chief Engineer

WPCE
01-11-1964; 1400 khz AM *Hrs Open:* 24; 1 kw-U, ND1; N36 49 45 W76 19 23
645 Church St., Ste. 400, Norfolk, VA 23510 US
(757) 622-4600, *Fax:* (757) 624-6515
www.wpce1400.com
willisbroadcasting@yahoo.com
License: Portsmouth, VA held by Christian Broadcasting of Portsmouth Inc.
Group Owner: Willis Broadcasting Corp.; (acq 3-4-92; grpsl;
Arbitron Metro Market: Norfolk-Virginia Beach-Newport News, VA
Format: Gospel *Special Programming:* Block Programming
Target Audience: W 35+
L E Willis II, CEO
Hortense Willis, President
Walter Allen Brickhouse, General Manager
Julian Joyner, Programming Director
Terry Love, Chief Engineer
Ernestine Willis, Corporate Officer
Christine Willis, Corporate Officer
Celestine Willis, Corporate Officer
Shaye Southall, Program Director

WPMH
01-09-1972; 1010 khz AM; 5 kw-D, 449 w-N, DA-2; N36 49 20 W76 26 38
2202 Jolliff Rd., Chesapeake, VA 27104
(757) 488-1010, *Fax:* (757) 488-7761
www.wpmhradio.net
info@wwip.org
License: Portsmouth, Portsmouth City County, VA held by Radio Disney Group LLC.
Group Owner: ABC Inc.; (acq 6-5-2002; $1.08 million with WHKT(AM) Portsmouth).
Population Served: 75,000 *Arbitron Metro Market:* Norfolk-Virginia Beach-Newport News, VA
Henry Hoot, General Manager

Pound

WDXC
01-01-1990; 102.3 mhz FM *Hrs Open:* 24; 0.35 kw; 1316 ft.; N37 9 7 W82 38 41
P.O. Box 877, Pound, VA 24279 US
(276) 796-5411, *Fax:* (276) 796-5412
www.wdxcfm.com
wdxc102fm@windstream.net
License: Pound, Wise County, VA held by WDXC Radio Inc.
Arbitron Metro Market: Pound, VA *Format:* Country *Target Audience:* General.
Howard Cornett, President
M.K. Combs, Operations Dir
Jackie Cornett, Executive Vice President

Powhatan

WBBT-FM
01-01-1999; 107.3 mhz FM; 1.4 kw; 679 ft.; N37 30 16 W77 42 14
P.O. Box 910, Roanoke Rapids, NC 27870 US
(804) 327-9902, *Fax:* (804) 327-9911
www.1073bbt.com
info@1073bbt.com
License: Powhatan, Powhatan County, VA held by MLB-Richmond IV LLC.
Group Owner: Main Line Broadcasting LLC; (acq 12-13-2005; grpsl).
Arbitron Metro Market: Richmond, VA *Format:* Oldies
Jim Conlee, Operations Manager/Program Director
Troy Scott, General Sales Mgr
Mike Murphy, Programming Director
John McLeod, Promotions Manager
Rob Astleford, Chief Engineer

Pulaski

WPSK-FM
12-01-1967; 107.1 mhz FM *Hrs Open:* 24; 1.75 kw; 1207 ft.; N37 1 28 W80 44 47
1930 Isaac Newton Square, #250, Reston, VA 20190 US
(540) 633-5330, *Fax:* (540) 633-2998
www.wpsk107.com
License: Pulaski, Pulaski County, VA held by Cumulus Licensing LLC.
Group Owner: Cumulus Media Inc.; (acq 3-31-2004; grpsl).
Format: Country *Hrs. of News Programming:* news progmg 10 hrs wkly *No. News Employees:* 1 *Target Audience:* 25-54.
Scott Stevens, Operations Dir
Sarah Leftwich, General Manager
Sam Parks, Chief Engineer

Quantico

WURA
920 khz AM
US
(703) 490-0920, *Fax:* (202) 728-0354
www.radiounida920.com
License: Quantico, VA held by Prince William Broadcasting L.L.C.
Arbitron Metro Market: Quantico, VA
Matthew McCormick, General Manager
Second Amin, Programming Director

Radford

WWBU
01-01-1965; 101.7 mhz FM; 5.8 kw; 66 ft.; N37 8 33 W80 34 39
1930 Isaac Newton Square, #250, Reston, VA 20190 US
(540) 731-6000, *Fax:* (540) 731-6304
www.supersports1017.com
License: Radford, Montgomery County, VA
Arbitron Metro Market: Radford, VA *Format:* Talk
Sarah Leftwich, General Manager

WRAD
01-01-1950; 1460 khz AM *Hrs Open:* 5 AM-11 PM; 5 kw-D, DAN; 0.5 kw-N, DAN; N37 8 35 W80 34 38
Mailing Address: 1930 Isaac Newton Square, #250, Reston, VA 20190 US
Second Address: 7080 Lee Hwy., Radford, VA 24141
(540) 633-5330, *Fax:* (540) 633-6300
License: Radford, VA held by Cumulus Licensing LLC.
Group Owner: Cumulus Media Inc.; (acq 3-31-2004; grpsl).
Format: Sports, Oldies *Target Audience:* 25 plus.
Ron Walton, General Manager
Scott Stevens, General Sales Mgr
David Dalesky, Chief Engineer

***WVRU-FM**
10-09-1978; 89.9 mhz FM *Hrs Open:* 24; 0.5 kw; 16 ft.; N37 8 26 W80 33 11
Mailing Address: P.O. Box 6973, Radford, VA 24142 US
Second Address: 236 Porterfield, Radford, VA 24142
(540) 831-5171, *Fax:* (540) 831-5893
www.wvru.org
wvru@radford.edu
License: Radford, Montgomery County, VA held by Radford University.
Nat'l Network: PRI
Arbitron Metro Market: Radford, VA *Format:* Jazz, Triple A
Special Programming: Jazz 19 hrs, class 15 hrs, Black 6 hrs, folk one hr *Hrs. of News Programming:* News progmg 6 hrs wkly
Target Audience: General.
Jonathan Benfield, Operations Dir
Ashlee Claud, General Manager
Randy McCallister, Engineering Dir
Sandy Schronce, Office Manager

Richlands

WGTH
10-05-1951; 540 khz AM *Hrs Open:* 24; 1 kw-D, 97 w-N; N37 05 01 W81 46 58
Box 370, Richlands, VA 24641
(276) 964-2502, *Fax:* (276) 964-4500
License: Richlands, Tazewell County, VA held by High Knob Broadcasters Inc.
Nat'l Network: Salem Radio Network

Population Served: 50,000 *Arbitron Metro Market:* Bluefield, WV *Hrs. of News Programming:* News progmg 7 hrs wkly *Target Audience:* General. *Adv. Rates:* Same as FM
Ron Brown, General Manager

WGTH-FM
01-03-1977; 105.5 mhz FM *Hrs Open:* 24; 0.45 kw; 801 ft.; N37 9 20 W81 46 11
P.O. Drawer 370, Richlands, VA 24641 US
(276) 964-2502, *Fax:* (276) 964-4500
www.wgth.net
wgth@wgth.net
License: Richlands, Tazewell County, VA held by High Knob Broadcasters Inc.
Nat'l Network: Salem Radio Network
Arbitron Metro Market: Bluefield, WV *Format:* Gospel, Religious *Hrs. of News Programming:* News progmg 6 hrs wkly *Target Audience:* General. *Adv. Rates:* 10; 6; 10; 6
Ron Brown, President
Eric Miller, Operations Dir
Charlene Pinkerton, General Sales Mgr
Mike Luttrel, Chief Engineer

WRIC-FM
11-01-1989; 97.7 mhz FM *Hrs Open:* 24; 3.2 kw; 751 ft.; N37 9 4 W81 53 56
Mailing Address: 137 Oriole Ave., Princeton, WV 24740 US
Second Address: 201 Suffolk Ave, Suite 210, Richlands, VA 24641
(276) 964-4066,(276) 963-4400, *Fax:* (276) 963-4927
www.wric.net
wric@netscope.net
License: Richlands, Tazewell County, VA held by Peggy Sue Broadcasting Corp.
Group Owner: Peggy Sue Broadcasting Corp.; acq 12-1-98; $190,000).
Nat'l Network: USA *Regional Network:* Va. News Net.
Arbitron Metro Market: Bluefield, WV *Format:* Adult Contemp *Hrs. of News Programming:* news progmg 2 hrs wkly *No. News Employees:* 3 *Target Audience:* 24-54; young adult professionals *Adv. Rates:* 14; 12;12; 8
Dirk Hall, President
Sue Hall, Operations Dir
Matthew Caudill, Chief Engineer
Dave Mann, Chief of Operations

Richmond

***WCVE-FM**
05-06-1988; 88.9 mhz FM; 17.5 kw horiz; 840 ft.; N37 34 0 W77 28 36
23 Sesame Street, Richmond, VA 23235 US
(804) 320-1301, *Fax:* (804) 320-8729
www.ideastations.org/radio
mlloyd@ideastations.org
License: Richmond, Richmond City County, VA held by Commonwealth Public Broadcasting Corp.
Nat'l Network: NPR; PRI *Wire Services:* AP
Arbitron Metro Market: Richmond, VA *TV Affiliate:* *WCVE-TV affil. *Format:* Classical, News, 62, Talk *Special Programming:* Folk 6 hrs, blues 3 hrs, jazz 18 hrs wkly *Hrs. of News Programming:* news progmg 35 hrswkly *No. News Employees:* 1 *Target Audience:* 35 plus.
Bill Miller, Operations Dir
Lisa Tait, General Sales Mgr
Peter Solomon, Operations Manager

***WDCE**
09-07-1977; 90.1 mhz FM *Hrs Open:* 24; 0.1 kw; 85 ft.; N37 34 48 W77 32 35
Tyler Commons, Richmond, VA 23173 US
(804) 289-8698, *Fax:* (804) 289-8996
www.wdce.org
wdcefm@richmond.edu
License: Richmond, Richmond City County, VA held by University of Richmond.
Arbitron Metro Market: Richmond, VA *Format:* Variety/Diverse *Special Programming:* Class 3 hrs, jazz 9 hrs, relg 3 hrs wkly *Hrs. of News Programming:* News progmg 3 hrs wkly *Target Audience:* 15-30.
Andrew Brown, General Manager
Whitney Cavin, Programming Director

WFTH
06-16-1964; 1590 khz AM; 5 kw-D, ND1; 0.019 kw-N, ND1; N37 30 2 W77 27 28
P.O. Box 24625, Richmond, VA 23224 US
(804) 233-0765, *Fax:* (804) 233-3725
faithradio@verizon.net
License: Richmond, VA held by Tri-City Christian Radio Inc.
Arbitron Metro Market: Richmond, VA *Format:* Gospel
Jack Johnson, President
Mary Johnson, Operations Dir
Shawn Nicholson, General Manager

WKJS
01-01-1996; 105.7 mhz FM; 2.3 kw; 531 ft.; N37 30 52 W77 30 28 *Rebroadcasts:* 100% simulcast 99.3& 105.7(WKJM)
Suite 300, 2809 Emerywood Parkway, Richmond, VA 23294 US
(804) 672-9299, *Fax:* (804) 672-9314
www.wkjs-fm.firstmediaworks.com
info@wkjs-fm.firstmediaworks.com
License: Richmond, Richmond City County, VA held by Radio One Licenses LLC.
Group Owner: Radio One Inc.; (acq 11-8-2001; grpsl).
Nat'l Network: ABC *Nat'l Reps:* Eastman Radio
Arbitron Metro Market: Richmond, VA *Format:* Adult Contemp *Target Audience:* 25-54; general
Linda Forem, Operations Dir
Dennis Gettis, General Sales Mgr
Dottie Brooks, Promotions Manager
Chris Lawless, Chief Engineer
Bobby Walden, National Sales Manager
Al Payne, Operations Manager
Dawna Covington, PromotionsDirector
Clovia Lawrence, Public Affairs Director

WVNZ
09-01-1955; 1320 khz AM *Hrs Open:* 24; 5 kw-D, DA2; 0.008 kw-N, DA2; N37 28 0 W77 27 8
7450 Midlothian Turnpike, Richmond, VA 23225 US
(804) 643-0990, *Fax:* (804) 474-5070
www.selecta1320.com
jjacobs@davidsonmediagroup.com
License: Richmond, VA held by Davidson Media Station WVNZ Licensee LLC.
Group Owner: Davidson Media Group LLC; (acq 5-13-2005; grpsl)
Nat'l Network: ABC
Arbitron Metro Market: Richmond, VA *Hrs. of News Programming:* news progmg 15 hrs wkly *No. News Employees:* 3 *Target Audience:* 25 plus; Hispanic population *Adv. Rates:* 55; 45; 50; 20
Felix Perez, President
Tim Hurley, Operations Dir
Jim Jacobs, General Manager
Carolyn Resendiz, General Sales Mgr
Selvin Paredes, Programming Director

WURV(FM)
12-23-1961; 103.7 mhz FM *Hrs Open:* 24; 18.5 kw; 750 ft; N37 30 31 W77 34 37
812 Moorefield Park Dr., Suite 300, Richmond, VA 23236
(804) 330-5700, *Fax:* (804) 330-4079,(804) 323-1524 sls
www.mix1037.com
info@mix1037.com
License: Richmond, Richmond City County, VA held by Cox Radio Inc.
Group Owner: Cox Radio Inc.; (acq 8-00; grpsl).
Nat'l Network: ABC *Nat'l Reps:* McGavren Guild
Population Served: 766,100 *Arbitron Metro Market:* Richmond, VA *Hrs. of News Programming:* news progmg 8 hrs wkly *No. News Employees:* 1 *Target Audience:* 25-54; predominately female
James Kennedy, COO
Bob Willoughby, General Manager
Amy DeVries, General Sales Mgr
Fisher, Programming Director

WBTJ
05-01-1957; 106.5 mhz FM *Hrs Open:* 24; 14.5 kw; 919 ft.; N37 30 45 W77 36 5.7
600 Congress Ave., Suite 1400, Austin, TX 78701 US
(804) 474-0000, *Fax:* (804) 474-0167
www.1065thebeat.com
sheilahbelle@clearchannel.com
License: Richmond, Richmond City County, VA held by Capstar TX L.P.
Group Owner: Clear Channel Communications Inc.; (acq 8-30-00; grpsl).
Nat'l Reps: Christal
Arbitron Metro Market: Richmond, VA *Format:* Urban Contemporary, Blues *Hrs. of News Programming:* news progmg 5 hrs wkly *No. News Employees:* 1 *Target Audience:* 18-44. *Adv. Rates:* 85; 100; 75; 75
Mark Mays, President
Carrie Todd, General Sales Mgr
Aaron Maxwell, Programming Director
Ruth Jones, Promotions Manager
Sheilah Belle, News Director
Mike Flemming, Chief Engineer
Mike Street, Music Director
Mynette Eady,Promotions Director
Kim Hutcheson, Traffic Manager

WREJ
05-08-1964; 1540 khz AM *Hrs Open:* 24; 10 kw-D, DA2; 0.007 kw-N, DA2; N37 37 8 W77 25 27
6001 Wilkinson Road, Richmond, VA 23227 US
(804) 643-0990, *Fax:* (804) 474-5070
www.rejoice1540.com
jjacobs@davidsonmediagroup.com
License: Richmond, VA held by Davidson Media Station WREJ Licensee LLC.
Group Owner: Davidson Media Group LLC; (acq 5-13-2005; grpsl)
Nat'l Network: ABC
Arbitron Metro Market: Richmond, VA *Format:* Religious *No. News Employees:* 1 *Target Audience:* 35-64; African-American concerned about financial, civic & economic issues *Adv. Rates:* 40; 30; 30; 15
Felix Perez, President
Tim Hurley, Operations Dir
Jim Jacobs, General Manager
Bryan Hill, General Sales Mgr
B.L. Westbrook, Programming Director

WRNL
11-15-1937; 910 khz AM *Hrs Open:* 24; 5 kw-D, DAN; 1.5 kw-N, DAN; N37 36 50 W77 30 53
200 Concord Plaza, Suite 600, San Antonio, TX 78216 US
(804) 474-0000, *Fax:* (804) 474-0167
www.sportsradio910.com
info@sportsradio910.com
License: Richmond, VA held by CC Licenses LLC.
Group Owner: Clear Channel Communications Inc.; (acq 8-10-93; $9.75 million with co-located FM;
Regional Network: Va. News Net.
Arbitron Metro Market: Richmond, VA *Format:* Sports *Target Audience:* 25-54; men
Ruth Jones, Operations Dir
James Levy, General Sales Mgr
Mike Clifford, Programming Director
Kirby Oliveras, Promotions Manager

WRVA
11-02-1925; 1140 khz AM *Hrs Open:* 24; 50 kw-U, DA1; N37 24 13 W77 18 59
200 North 22nd Street, Richmond, VA 23223 US
(804) 474-0000, *Fax:* (804) 474-0167
www.wrva.com
jimmybarrett@clearchannel.com
License: Richmond, VA held by CC Licenses LLC.
Group Owner: Clear Channel Communications Inc.; (acq 6-26-92; grpsl;
Nat'l Network: ABC *Nat'l Reps:* Clear Channel
Arbitron Metro Market: Richmond, VA *Format:* News, News/Talk, 86 *Special Programming:* Relg 10 hrs, computers 2 hrs, gardening 3 hrs, hom *Hrs. of News Programming:* news progmg 24 hrs wkly *No. News Employees:* 10*Target Audience:* 35-54.
Ruth Jones, General Manager
Rhonda Reeser, General Sales Mgr
Jimmy Barrett, Programming Director
Aaron Sutten, Promotions Manager
Deanna Malone, News Director

WRVQ
08-04-1948; 94.5 mhz FM; 200 kw; 351 ft.; N37 24 13 W77 18 59
3305 W. Mountain Rd, #60, Las Vegas, NV 89102 US
(804) 474-0000, *Fax:* (804) 474-0090
www.q94radio.com
billcahill@clearchannel.com
License: Richmond, Richmond City County, VA held by CC Licenses LLC.
Group Owner: Clear Channel Communications Inc.
Nat'l Network: ABC
Arbitron Metro Market: Richmond, VA *Format:* Contemporary Hits/Top 40 *Target Audience:* 18-44; women
Dave Symonds, Operations Dir
Ruth Jones, General Manager
Tracy Driskill, General Sales Mgr
Dave Symonds, Programming Director
Virginia Rothwell, Promotions Manager
Mike Fleming, Chief Engineer

WRXL
03-04-1949; 102.1 mhz FM *Hrs Open:* 24; 20 kw; 791 ft.; N37 36 52 W77 30 56
3305 W. Mountain Rd, #60, Las Vegas, NV 89102 US
(804) 474-0000, *Fax:* (804) 474-0092
www.1021thex.com
License: Richmond, Richmond City County, VA held by CC Licenses LLC.

Group Owner: Clear Channel Communications Inc.
Arbitron Metro Market: Richmond, VA *Format:* Oldies, Rock/AOR
Target Audience: 25-44.
Dave Symonds, Operations Dir
Dave Carwile, General Manager
James Levy, General Sales Mgr
Dustin Fletcher, Programming Director
Virginia Rothwell, Promotions Manager

WBTK
09-01-1926; 1380 khz AM *Hrs Open:* 24 hrs/7 days a week; 5 kw-U, DA-2; N37 37 13 W77 26 57
2809 Emerywood Parkway, Suite 540, Richmond, VA 24011
(804) 353-8544, *Fax:* (804) 353-8549
www.wbtk.com
License: Richmond, Richmond City County, VA held by Mount Rich Media LLC.
Group Owner: Mountain Broadcasting Corp.; (acq 5-30-2006; $1.5 million).
Nat'l Network: CNN en Espanol
Population Served: 205,533 *Arbitron Metro Market:* Richmond, VA *Special Programming:* CNN en Espanol & local programming
Target Audience: Hispanic A25-54
Glen Motto, Operations Dir

WTVR-FM
02-01-1946; 98.1 mhz FM; 50 kw horiz; 840 ft.; N37 34 0 W77 28 36
401 - 3rd St, S.W., Roanoke, VA 24011 US
(804) 474-0000, *Fax:* (804) 474-0167
www.lite98.com
billcahill@clearchannel.com
License: Richmond, Richmond City County, VA held by CC Licenses LLC.
Group Owner: Clear Channel Communications Inc.; (acq 1996; $18 million with co-located AM).
Nat'l Reps: Clear Channel
Arbitron Metro Market: Richmond, VA *Format:* Adult Contemp
Bill Cahill, Operations Dir
Ruth Jones, General Manager
Rhonda Reeser, General Sales Mgr
Adam Stubbs, Promotions Manager
Mike Fleming, Chief Engineer

WLEE
05-04-1951; 990 khz AM *Hrs Open:* 24; 1 kw-D, ND1; 0.013 kw-N, ND1; N37 31 40 W77 22 48
3302 Old Dominion Blvd, Alexandria, VA 22305 US
(804) 643-0990, *Fax:* (804) 474-5070
www.wlee990.am
License: Richmond, VA held by Davidson Media Station WLEE Licensee LLC.
Group Owner: Davidson Media Group LLC; (acq 5-13-2005; grpsl)
Nat'l Network: CNN Radio; CBS
Arbitron Metro Market: Richmond, VA *Format:* News, News/Talk, 86 *Target Audience:* 25-64; white collar, upscale professionals
Adv. Rates: 40; 35; 40; 15
Felix Perez, President
Tim Hurley, Operations Dir
Jim Jacobs, General Manager
Bryan Hill, General Sales Mgr

WXGI
10-01-1947; 950 khz AM *Hrs Open:* 5:30 AM-midnight; 3.9 kw-D, ND1; 0.045 kw-N, ND1; N37 30 52 W77 30 28
701 German School Rd, Richmond, VA 23225 US
(804) 233-7666, *Fax:* (804) 233-7681
espn950am.com
info@espn950am.com
License: Richmond, VA held by Red Zebra Broadcasting Licensee (Richmond) LLC.
Group Owner: Red Zebra Holdings LLC; (acq 9-27-2006; $1.4 million)
Nat'l Network: ESPN Radio *Wire Services:* AP
Arbitron Metro Market: Richmond, VA *Format:* Sports *Target Audience:* 30 plus.
Bruce Gilbert, CEO
Mitchell Bradley, Operations, Production,& Program Director
Buck Albritton, General Manager
Mitchell Bradley, Programming Director
Walter Andes, Senior Sports Marketing Executive
Scott Hawthorne, Senior SportsMarketing Executive
John Fox, Senior Sports Marketing Executive
Sharon Eichenlaub, Business Manager

***WRIH**
01-01-2007; 88.1 mhz FM; 5 kw vert; 479 ft.; N37 42 54 W77 21 55 *Rebroadcasts:* Rebroadcasts WAFR(FM) Tupelo, MS 100%
P O Drawer 2440, Tupelo, MS 38803 US
(662) 844-8888, *Fax:* (662) 842-6791
www.afr.net
faq@afr.net
License: Richmond, Richmond City County, VA held by American Family Association.
Group Owner: American Family Radio
Nat'l Network: American Family Radio
Arbitron Metro Market: Richmond, VA *Format:* Christian
Marvin Sanders, General Manager

Roanoke

WFIR
06-20-1924; 960 khz AM *Hrs Open:* 24
Mailing Address: P. O. Box 150, Roanoke, VA 24002 US
Second Address: Box 92, Roanoke, VA 24022
(540) 345-1511, *Fax:* (504) 342-2270
www.wfir960.com
License: Roanoke, VA held by Mel Wheeler Inc.
Group Owner: Mel Wheeler Inc.; acq 3-31-00; with co-located FM).
Nat'l Network: ABC; Fox News Radio *Nat'l Reps:* Katz Radio
Arbitron Metro Market: Roanoke, VA *Format:* News, News/Talk, 86 *No. News Employees:* 4 *Target Audience:* 25-54; adult, skewed male 35-54
Anne Booze, General Sales Mgr
Jim Murphy, Programming Director
Jim Kent, News Director
Velvet Hall, Producer

WGMN
01-01-1946; 1240 khz AM; 1 kw-U, ND1; N37 16 12 W79 58 14
600 Congress Avenue, Suite 1400, Austin, TX 78701 US
(434) 534-6100, *Fax:* (434) 534-6101
www.espninva.com
wblt@inbox.com
License: Roanoke, VA held by 3 Daughters Media Inc.
Group Owner: 3 Daughters Media Inc.; (acq 6-22-2007; grpsl)
Nat'l Network: ESPN Radio *Regional Network:* Va. News Net.
Nat'l Reps: D & R Radio
Arbitron Metro Market: Roanoke-Lynchburg, VA *Format:* Sports
Target Audience: 25-54.
Gary Burns, CEO
Gary Burns, President
Ashley Schamerhorn, Operations Dir
Randy Thompson, Vice President
Melinda Schamerhorn, Business & Traffic Director
Jonny Fairplay, Account Executive

WSLC-FM
11-01-1948; 94.9 mhz FM *Hrs Open:* 24; 98 kw; 1982 ft.; N37 11 50 W80 9 11
Mailing Address: PO Box 150, Roanoke, VA 24002 US
Second Address: Box 92, Roanoke, VA 24022
(540) 774-0201, *Fax:* (540) 774-5667
www.949starcountry.com
License: Roanoke, Roanoke City County, VA
Group Owner: Mel Wheeler Inc.
Nat'l Reps: Katz Radio
Arbitron Metro Market: Roanoke-Lynchburg, VA *Format:* Country
Target Audience: 25-54.
Stan Reynolds, General Sales Mgr
Brett Sharp, Programming Director
Rachel Rodes, Promotions Manager

WJJS
11-01-1993; 104.9 mhz FM *Hrs Open:* 24; 14.5 kw; 925 ft.; N37 22 23 W79 55 40
600 Congress Ave., Suite 1400, Austin, TX 78701 US
(434) 385-8298, *Fax:* (434) 385-8991
www.wjjs.com
joeldearing@clearchannel.com
License: Roanoke, Roanoke City County, VA held by Capstar TX L.P.
Group Owner: Clear Channel Communications Inc.; (acq 8-30-2000; grpsl)
Arbitron Metro Market: Roanoke-Lynchburg, VA *Format:* Contemporary Hits/Top 40 *No. News Employees:* 2
Chris Clendenen, General Manager
Dave Carwile, General Sales Mgr
Joel Dearing, Programming Director

WRIS
02-28-1953; 1410 khz AM *Hrs Open:* 24; 5 kw-D, ND1; 0.072 kw-N, ND1; N37 16 47 W79 59 29
Mailing Address: 219 Luckett Street, NW, P.O. Box 6099, Roanoke, VA 24017 US
Second Address: 219 Luckett St. N.W., Roanoke, VA 24017
(540) 342-1410,(540) 342-7811, *Fax:* (540) 342-5952
www.wrisradio.com
info@wris.cc
License: Roanoke, VA held by WRIS L.L.C.
Regional Network: Va. News Net.
Arbitron Metro Market: Roanoke-Lynchburg, VA *Format:* Religious *No. News Employees:* 1 *Target Audience:* 35-75.
Lloyd Gochenour, President
Russ Brown, Operations Dir

***WRXT**
07-31-1994; 90.3 mhz FM; 5.5 kw; 1112 ft.; N37 23 9 W79 40 10
P.O. Box 20065, Roanoke, VA 24012 US
(434) 237-9798, *Fax:* (434) 237-1025
www.spiritfm.com
office@spiritfm.com
License: Roanoke, Roanoke City County, VA held by Positive Alternative Radio Inc.
Group Owner: Positive Alternative Radio Inc.; (acq 4-15-2002)
Arbitron Metro Market: Roanoke-Lynchbu *Format:* Religious
Barry Armstrong, General Manager
Brian Sumner, Programming Director

WVBE
10-01-1940; 610 khz AM *Hrs Open:* 24; 5 kw-D, DA2; 1 kw-N, DA2; N37 18 11 W80 2 33 *Rebroadcasts:* Rebroadcasts WVBE Lynchburg 100%
Mailing Address: 5009 South Hulen, Suite 101, Fort Worth, TX 76132 US
Second Address: Box 92, Roanoke, VA 24022
(540) 989-4591, *Fax:* (540) 774-5667
www.vibe100.com
info@vibe100.com
License: Roanoke, VA held by Mel Wheeler Inc.
Group Owner: Mel Wheeler Inc.; (acq 10-1-76).
Nat'l Reps: Katz Radio
Arbitron Metro Market: Roanoke-Lynchbu *Format:* Urban Contemporary *Target Audience:* Adult 25-54; skew female, skew black
Leonard Wheeler, President
Stan Reynolds, General Sales Mgr
Walt Ford, Programming Director

WSLQ
11-01-1947; 99.1 mhz FM *Hrs Open:* 24; 150 kw; 1991 ft.; N37 11 41 W80 9 22
Mailing Address: 5009 South Hulen, Suite 101, Fort Worth, TX 76132 US
Second Address: Box 92, Roanoke, VA 24018
(540) 387-0234, *Fax:* (540) 389-0837
www.q99fm.com
kscott@q99fm.com
License: Roanoke, Roanoke City County, VA held by Mel Wheeler Inc.
Group Owner: Mel Wheeler Inc.
Nat'l Reps: Katz Radio
Arbitron Metro Market: Roanoke-Lynchbu *Format:* Adult Contemp *Hrs. of News Programming:* News progmg 1 hr wkly
Target Audience: 25-54; skew female
Anne Booze, General Sales Mgr
Kevin Scott, Programming Director
Lauren Smith, Promotions Manager

***WVTF**
08-01-1973; 89.1 mhz FM *Hrs Open:* 24; 100 kw; 1969 ft.; N37 11 56 W80 9 2
4235 Electric Rd Sw, Suite 105, Roanoke, VA 24014 US
(540) 989-8900, *Fax:* (540) 776-2727
www.wvtf.org
info@wvtf.org
License: Roanoke, Roanoke City County, VA held by Virginia Tech Foundation Inc.
Nat'l Network: PRI; NPR *Regional Network:* Va. News Net.
Arbitron Metro Market: Roanoke, VA *Format:* Jazz *Hrs. of News Programming:* news progmg 39 hrs wkly *No. News Employees:* 8 *Target Audience:* General.
Glenn Gleixner, General Manager
Karen Dillon, General Sales Mgr
Rick Matttoni, Programming Director
Connie Stevens, News Director
Bart Prater, Traffic Director
Cynthia Gray, Development Director
Mary Grace Franchi, BusinessManager
Brian Black, Administrative Assistant
Ben Martin, Operations Assistant & Producer/Radio Reading Serv

WFJX
04-01-1957; 910 khz AM *Hrs Open:* 24; 1 kw-D, 84 w-N; N37 16 06 W79 54 46
1848 Clay St. S.E., Roanoke, VA 24013
(540) 343-7109, *Fax:* (540) 343-2306
www.3wradio.com
License: Roanoke, Roanoke City County, VA held by Perception Media Group Inc.
Nat'l Network: USA

Arbitron Metro Market: Roanoke-Lynchburg, VA *Target Audience:* 35-64.
Ben Peyton, President
Sharron Jeffrey, Station Manager
Martin Jeffrey, General Sales Mgr
Howie McKinney, Programming Director
Dale Cook, Chief Engineer

WXLK
12-17-1960; 92.3 mhz FM; 100 kw; 1985 ft.; N37 11 51 W80 9 10
Mailing Address: 5009 South Hulen, Suite 101, Fort Worth, TX 76132 US
Second Address: 3934 Electric Rd. S.W., Roanoke, VA 24018
(540) 774-9200, *Fax:* (540) 774-5667
www.k92radio.com
info@coronamediagroup.com
License: Roanoke, Roanoke City County, VA held by Mel Wheeler Inc.
Group Owner: Mel Wheeler Inc.; acq 3-12-97; $7.5 million with WVBE-FM Lynchburg).
Arbitron Metro Market: Roanoke, VA *Format:* Contemporary Hits/Top 40 *Target Audience:* 18-44; women
Leonard Wheeler, CEO
Kathy Rilee, Promotions Manager

Rocky Mount

WYTI
03-31-1957; 1570 khz AM *Hrs Open:* 6 AM-9 PM; 2.5 kw-D, 220 w-N; N36 58 37 W79 53 45
Mailing Address: Box430, Rocky Mount, VA 24151
Second Address: 275 Glenwood Dr, Rocky Mount, VA 24151
(540) 483-9955,(540) 483-2166, *Fax:* (540) 483-7802
www.wytiradio.com
wyti@wytiradio.com
License: Rocky Mount, Franklin County, VA held by WYTI Inc.
Nat'l Network: ABC
Population Served: 37,500*Special Programming:* NASCAR races, relg 10 hrs wkly *Target Audience:* 30 plus; general *Adv. Rates:* 11.29; 11.29; 11.29; 5.64
William Jefferson, President
Susan Mullins, Operations Dir
Susan Mullins, General Manager
Susan Mullins, Station Manager
Susan Mullins, General Sales Mgr
Bill Jefferson, Programming Director
Susan Mullins, Promotions Manager
Jesse Ramsey, News Director
Carl Castillo, Engineering Dir
Scott Gardener, Chief Engineer
Susan Mullins, Executive Vice President

Ruckersville

WHTE-FM
03-29-1990; 101.9 mhz FM *Hrs Open:* 24; 6 kw; 223 ft.; N38 18 5 W78 31 57
200 Concord Plaza, Suite 600, San Antonio, TX 78216 US
(434) 978-4408, *Fax:* (434) 978-0723
www.1019hot.com
License: Ruckersville, Greene County, VA held by Monticello Media LLC.
Group Owner: Monticello Media LLC; (acq 10-4-2007; grpsl)
Nat'l Reps: Christal
Arbitron Metro Market: Charlottesville, VA *Format:* Contemporary Hits/Top 40 *Hrs. of News Programming:* News progmg 5 hrs wkly *Target Audience:* 18-24.
Vinnie Kice, Operations Dir
Dennis Mockler, General Manager
Karen Cote, General Sales Mgr
P.J. Styles, Programming Director
Steve Gaines, Market Manager
Vinnie Kice, Operations Manager
Mike Chiumento, Sales Manager

Rural Retreat

WLOY
05-15-1985; 660 khz AM *Hrs Open:* Daytime; 0.55 kw-D, NDD; 90.2 meters; N36 55 17 W81 14 34
P.O. Box 660, Rural Retreat, VA 24368 US
(410) 617-1620, *Fax:* (276) 228-9261
www.wloy.com
wloy@loyola.edu
License: Rural Retreat, VA held by Three Rivers Media Corp.
Group Owner: Three Rivers Media Corp.; (acq 10-16-2006; $125,000)
Nat'l Reps: Rgnl Reps
Arbitron Metro Market: Rural Retreat-Wythe County, VA *Format:* News, Sports, 86 *No. News Employees:* 1 *Target Audience:* 25-54. *Adv. Rates:* 15; 15; 15; 15
Gary W.Hagerich, President
Christa Constantine, General Manager
Kate Marshall, Programming Director
Molly Dressel, Promotions Manager

WXBX
06-11-1992; 95.3 mhz FM *Hrs Open:* 24; 6 kw; 190 ft.; N36 55 17 W81 14 34
3006 Ben Venue Drive, Greensburg, PA 15601 US
(276) 228-3185, *Fax:* (276) 228-9261
www.wxbx.com
office@threeriversmedia.net
License: Rural Retreat, Wythe County, VA held by Three Rivers Media Corp.
Group Owner: Three Rivers Media Corp.; (acq 10-01-98; $200,000)
Nat'l Network: AP Network News; Jones Radio Networks
Regional Reps: Rgnl Reps
Arbitron Metro Market: Wytheville, VA *Format:* Oldies *Hrs. of News Programming:* news progmg 12 hrs wkly *No. News Employees:* 1 *Target Audience:* 25 plus. *Adv. Rates:* 24; 24; 24; 24
Gary Hagerich, CEO
Kristy Wrobel, News Director
Misty Pack, Sales and Office Staff
Deborah Crigger, Sales and Office Staff
Jerry Stone, Sales and Office Staff
Danny Gordon, Sales and Office Staff

Rustburg

***WWEM**
91.7 mhz FM; 1.15 kw; 748 ft.; N37 17 7 W79 5 26
830 Gunnery Hill Road, Spotsylvania, VA 22553 US
(540) 582-9700
www.wwedfm.org
License: Rustburg, Campbell County, VA held by Educational Media Corp.
Arbitron Metro Market: Rustburg, VA *Format:* Variety/Diverse
Peter Stover, President

Salem

WSNV
03-07-1969; 93.5 mhz FM *Hrs Open:* 24; 5.8 kw; 98 ft.; N37 16 47 W79 59 29
600 Congress Ave., Suite 1400, Austin, TX 78701 US
(540) 725-1220, *Fax:* (540) 725-1245
www.mysunnyfm.com
stevencross@clearchannel.com
License: Salem, Salem City County, VA held by Aloha Station Trust LLC
Nat'l Network: Westwood One
Arbitron Metro Market: Roanoke-Lynchburg, VA *Format:* Adult Contemp *Hrs. of News Programming:* News progmg one hr wkly *Target Audience:* 24 plus.
Dave Carwile, General Manager
Tammy Cazad, General Sales Mgr
Steve Cross, Programming Director
Ed Kilbane, News Director

***WPAR**
04-01-1994; 91.3 mhz FM *Hrs Open:* 24; 3.3 kw; 886 ft.; N37 22 23 W79 55 37
P.O. Box 889, Blacksburg, VA 24063 US
(540) 961-2377, *Fax:* (540) 951-5282
www.spiritfm.com
mail@spiritfm.com
License: Salem, Salem City County, VA held by Positive Alternative Radio Inc.
Group Owner: Positive Alternative Radio Inc.; (acq 5-90;
Nat'l Network: USA
Arbitron Metro Market: Roanoke-Lynchburg, VA *Format:* Adult Contemp, Christian *Target Audience:* 25-54; adults with families
Barry Armstrong, General Manager

WTOY
09-07-1956; 1480 khz AM; 5 kw-D, ND1; 0.02 kw-N, ND1; N37 16 21 W80 4 52
504 23rd St, N.W., Roanoke, VA 24017 US
(540) 344-9869, *Fax:* (540) 344-0976
www.roanokeradio.com
License: Salem, VA held by Ward Broadcasting Corp.
Arbitron Metro Market: Roanoke,VA *Format:* Urban Contemporary
Irving Ward Sr., Owner
Daniel Ellington, Programming Director

Saltville

WXMY
11-05-1981; 1600 khz AM *Hrs Open:* 6 AM-sunset; 5 kw-D; N36 51 43 W81 43 29
Box 5555, Chilhowie, VA 24228
(276) 685-1810, *Fax:* (641) 587-6242
www.heartofbluegrass.com
1600wxmy@gmail.com
License: Saltville, Smyth County, VA held by Continental Media Group LLC
Target Audience: 25-54.
Wendy Raynor, General Manager

Smithfield

WKGM
12-18-1974; 940 khz AM *Hrs Open:* 24
Mailing Address: P.O. Box 889, Blacksburg, VA 24603 US
Second Address: 13379 Great Spring Rd., Smithfield, VA 23430
(757) 357-9546, *Fax:* (757) 365-0412
wkgm@hotmail.com
License: Smithfield, VA held by WKGM Inc.
Group Owner: Baker Family Stations
Arbitron Metro Market: Norfolk-Virginia Beach-Newport News, VA *Format:* Religious *Special Programming:* Farm 2 hrs, Ger one hr, Sp one hr, gospel 5 hrs wk *Hrs. of News Programming:* News progmg one hr wkly *TargetAudience:* 25 plus.
Vernon Baker, President
T.R. Bumgardner, General Manager

South Boston

WHLF
09-01-1992; 95.3 mhz FM *Hrs Open:* 24; 6 kw; 246 ft.; N36 42 24 W78 55 28
Mailing Address: 1047 Evergreen Trail, Halifax, VA 24558 US
Second Address: 1210 Porter Ln, South Boston, VA 24592
(434) 572-2988, *Fax:* (434) 572-1662
www.whlf.com
whlf@whlf.com
License: South Boston, South Boston City County, VA held by JLC Properties Inc.
Nat'l Network: ABC *Wire Services:* AP
Format: Adult Contemp *Hrs. of News Programming:* news progmg 8 hrs wkly *No. News Employees:* 1 *Target Audience:* 25-54; those that have spendable income *Adv. Rates:* 15; 13; 15; 10
Tom Birch, President
Nick Long, General Manager
Kelly Redd, Programming Director

WSBV
01-01-1980; 1560 khz AM; 0.25 kw-C, NDD; 2.5 kw-D, NDD; N36 42 35 W78 52 28
P.O. Box 778, South Boston, VA 24592 US
(434) 572-4418, *Fax:* (434) 572-9245
www.wsbvsouthboston.com
wsbvgm@gcronline.com
License: South Boston, VA held by Linda Waller-Barton
Format: Religious *Special Programming:* Farm one hr wkly
Target Audience: 40 plus.
James Barton, Operations Dir
Linda Waller-Barton, General Manager
April Warf, Station Manager

WAJL
05-05-2010; 1400 khz AM *Hrs Open:* 24; 1 kw-U; N36 42 35 W78 52 28
PO Box 523, South Boston, VA
(434) 572-7608, *Fax:* (434) 572-9245
wajlradio@live.com
License: South Boston, Halifax County, VA held by Linda Waller-Barton.
Special Programming: Southern Gospel
Rhonda Powell, General Manager
Rhonda Powell, Station Manager
Rhonda Powell, General Sales Mgr
Rhonda Powell, Programming Director
Rhonda Powell, Promotions Manager
Rhonda Powell, News Director

South Hill

WSHV
11-01-1953; 1370 khz AM *Hrs Open:* 6 AM-6 PM
P.O. Box 216, South Hill, VA 23970 US
(434) 447-8997, *Fax:* (434) 447-4789
www.whsv.com
wshv@hotmail.com
License: South Hill, VA held by Lakes Media Holding Company LLC.

Group Owner: Birch Broadcasting Corp.; (acq 2-1-2005; grpsl).
Nat'l Network: ABC
Format: Black *No. News Employees:* 1 *Target Audience:* General.
Jerry Brown, Operations Dir
Greg Thirft, General Manager
Robert Wilson, Programming Director
Robby McMulian, News Director
John Hart, Chief Engineer
Jay Phillippi, Disc Jockey
Heather Skuggen, Disc Jockey
Paul Hoefler, DiscJockey

WKSK-FM
12-23-1966; 101.9 mhz FM; 6 kw horiz, 5.7 kw vert; 315 ft.; N36 44 39 W78 9 42
P. O. Box 216, South Hill, VA 23970 US
(434) 447-4007, *Fax:* (434) 447-4789
www.rewind1019.com
tombirch@lakesmediallc.com
License: South Hill, Mecklenburg County, VA
Group Owner: Birch Broadcasting Corp.
Nat'l Network: ABC
Format: Country *Hrs. of News Programming:* news progmg 2 hrs wkly *No. News Employees:* 1 *Target Audience:* General; adults 25-54
Melissa Wilkerson, General Sales Mgr
Robert Wilson, Disc Jockey
Ron Major, Disc Jockey
Greg Thrift, Disc Jockey

Spotsylvania

***WWED**
01-01-2005; 89.5 mhz FM; 8 kw; 495 ft.; N38 11 48 W77 33 45
P.O. Box 905, Spotsylvania, VA 22553 US
(540) 582-9700
www.bluegrassfm.org
License: Spotsylvania, Spotsylvania County, VA held by Educational Media Corp.
Nat'l Network: Moody
Arbitron Metro Market: Saint George, UT *Format:* Blues
Peter Stover, President

***WQIQ**
88.3 mhz FM; 3500 watts; 120 meters; 38 07 N47 77 42 W55 , Frederickson, VA
License: Spotsylvania, VA

Maureen Fiedler, Executive Producer
Laura Kwerel, Senior Producer

St. Paul

WXLZ
11-03-1981; 1140 khz AM *Hrs Open:* Sunrise-sunset; 1.1 kw-C, NDD; 2.5 kw-D, NDD; N36 52 15 W82 18 21 *Rebroadcasts:* Rebroadcasts WXLZ-FM Lebanon 80%
P.O. Box 250, Castlewood, VA 24224 US
(276) 889-1073, *Fax:* (276) 889-3677
www.wxlz.net
wxlz1073@bvu.net
License: St. Paul, VA held by Yeary Broadcasting Inc.
Nat'l Network: CBS
Arbitron Metro Market: Saint Paul, VA *Format:* Country, Religious *Special Programming:* Gospel 15 hrs wkly *Hrs. of News Programming:* news progmg 3 hrs wkly *No. News Employees:* 3 *Target Audience:* 25 plus;students, farmers, miners & rural area residents
Lannis Yeary, General Manager
Marshall Hendrix, Programming Director
Wilma Kiser, Office Manager

Stanleytown

WZBB
03-01-1989; 99.9 mhz FM *Hrs Open:* 24; 3.6 kw; 722 ft.; N36 54 50 W79 57 7
10899 Virginia Avenue, Bassett, VA 24055 US
(540) 489-9999, *Fax:* (276) 629-8399
www.wzbbfm.com
kristib@wzbbfm.com
License: Stanleytown, Henry County, VA held by WNLB Radio Inc.
Regional Network: Va. News Net.
Arbitron Metro Market: Stanleytown, VA *Format:* Country *Target Audience:* 21 plus.
Donny Brook, President
Glenn Lynch, Operations Dir
Kristi Banks, General Manager
Amy Coleman, Station Manager
Craig Richards, Programming Director
Lisa Layne, News Director

Staunton

WCYK-FM
09-01-1984; 99.7 mhz FM *Hrs Open:* 24; 3.3 kw; 1693 ft.; N38 3 52 W78 48 18
200 Concord Plaza, Suite 600, San Antonio, TX 78216 US
(434) 978-4408, *Fax:* (434) 978-0723
www.hitkicker997.com
jlopez@cvillestations.com
License: Staunton, Staunton City County, VA held by Monticello Media LLC.
Group Owner: Monticello Media LLC; (acq 10-4-2007; grpsl)
Nat'l Network: Motor Racing Net *Nat'l Reps:* Christal
Arbitron Metro Market: Charlottesville, VA *Format:* Country *Target Audience:* 25-54.
Vinnie Kice, Operations Dir
Steve Gaines, General Manager
Karen Cote, General Sales Mgr
Jay Lopez, Programming Director

WKDW
04-01-1954; 900 khz AM *Hrs Open:* 24
1150 Pepsi Place, Suite 300, Charlottesville, VA 22901 US
(540) 886-2376, *Fax:* (540) 885-8662
www.goodradio.com
wkdw@ntelos.net
License: Staunton, VA held by CC Licenses LLC.
Group Owner: Clear Channel Communications Inc.; (acq 11-15-2000; grpsl).
Format: Country *Special Programming:* Farm one hr, blue grass one hr wkly *Hrs. of News Programming:* news progmg 15 hrs wkly *No. News Employees:* 1 *Target Audience:* 25-54. *Adv. Rates:* 30; 30; 30; 10
Steve Davis, General Manager
Kris Losh, Programming Director
Jeff Caudell, Chief Engineer

WSVO
05-29-1959; 93.1 mhz FM; 2.8 kw; 338 ft.; N38 10 32 W79 4 12
1150 Pepsi Place, Suite 300, Charlottesville, VA 22901 US
(540) 886-2376, *Fax:* (540) 885-8662
www.goodradio.com
info@goodradio.com
License: Staunton, Staunton City County, VA held by CC Licenses LLC.
Group Owner: Clear Channel Communications Inc.
Format: Oldies *Hrs. of News Programming:* news progmg 15 hrs wkly *No. News Employees:* 1 *Target Audience:* 35-54.
Nancy Hall, CEO
Tom Barclay, Operations Dir
Bob Houghton, General Manager
Eric Nauert, Station Manager
Rob Maynard, Programming Director
Susanna Capelouto, News Director
Bonnie Bean, CFO
Orlando Montoya, News Reporter
RussellWells, Wsvh Operations manager

WTON
03-09-1946; 1240 khz AM *Hrs Open:* 24; 1 kw-U, ND1; N38 8 30 W79 2 33
Mailing Address: Box 1085, Staunton, VA 24402 US
Second Address: 304 W. Beverly St., Staunton, VA 24401
(540) 885-5188, *Fax:* (540) 885-1240
www.star94radio.com
License: Staunton, VA held by High Impact Communications Inc.
Nat'l Network: CBS; ESPN Radio
Arbitron Metro Market: Staunton,VA *Format:* Sports *Special Programming:* Virginia Tech SPorts *Hrs. of News Programming:* News progmg one hr wkly *Target Audience:* 18-49. *Adv. Rates:* 15; 10; 15; 7
J. Gary Ratcliff, President and Owner
Brenda Ratcliff, General Manager
Cass Johnson, Programming Director

WTON-FM
11-01-1990; 94.3 mhz FM *Hrs Open:* 24; 0.34 kw; 2231 ft.; N38 9 55 W79 18 51
Mailing Address: 304 W. Beverly St., Staunton, VA 24401 US
Second Address: 304 W. Beverly St., Staunton, VA
(540) 885-5188, *Fax:* (540) 885-1240
www.star94radio.com
License: Staunton, Staunton City County, VA held by High Impact Communications, INc.
Nat'l Network: CBS *Regional Reps:* Rgnl Reps
Arbitron Metro Market: Staunton,VA *Format:* Contemporary Hits/Top 40, Adult Contemp *Special Programming:* UVA Sports *Hrs. of News Programming:* News progmg 3 hrs wkly *Target Audience:* 25-54; 60% women, 40% men*Adv. Rates:* 30; 22; 28; na
J. Gary Ratcliff, President and Owner
Cass Johnson, Operations Dir
Brenda Ratcliff, General Manager

Stephens City

WKSI-FM
08-28-1966; 98.3 mhz FM *Hrs Open:* 24; 1.75 kw; 617 ft.; N39 10 38 W78 15 53
P.O. Box 700, Washington, DC 20036 US
(540) 662-5101, *Fax:* (540) 662-8610
www.983kissfm.com
DanielMartin@clearchannel.com
License: Stephens City, Frederick County, VA
Group Owner: Clear Channel Communications Inc.
Arbitron Metro Market: Stephens City, VA *Format:* Contemporary Hits/Top 40 *Target Audience:* 25-54.
David Miller, Operations Dir
Chuck Peterson, General Manager
Derrick Cole, Programming Director
Daniel Martin, Advertising

Stuart

WHEO
10-12-1959; 1270 khz AM *Hrs Open:* 6 AM-sunset; 5 kw-D, NDD; N36 37 25 W80 15 50
Rt. 1, Box 24, Stuart, VA 24171 US
(276) 694-3114, *Fax:* (276) 694-2241
www.wheo.net
wheo@sitesstar.net
License: Stuart, VA held by Mountain View Communications Inc.
Nat'l Network: CNN Radio *Regional Network:* Va. News Net.
Format: News, News/Talk, 86 *Special Programming:* Farm 4 hrs, relg 10 hrs, loc news 10 hrs wkly *Hrs. of News Programming:* news progmg 25 hrs wkly *No. News Employees:* 1 *Target Audience:* General. *Adv. Rates:* 156; 140; 156; na
Dean Goad, President
Jamie Clark, Operations Dir
La Vergne Collins, General Sales Mgr
Richard Rogers, Programming Director

Suffolk

WAFX
12-12-1983; 106.9 mhz FM; 100 kw; 984 ft.; N36 48 9 W76 45 19
Suite339, 870 Greenbriar Cir., Chesapeake, VA 23320 US
(757) 366-9900, *Fax:* (757) 366-0022
www.1069thefox.com
ehickman@tciradio.net
License: Suffolk, Suffolk City County, VA held by Tidewater Communications LLC.
Group Owner: Saga Communications Inc.; (acq 3-15-94; $4 million;
Nat'l Reps: McGavren Guild
Arbitron Metro Market: Norfolk-Virginia Beach-Newport News, VA
Format: Classic Rock *Target Audience:* 18-49.
Wayne Leland, General Manager
Barry Haugh, General Sales Mgr
Mike Beck, Programming Director
Leila Rice, News Director
Don Crowder, Chief Engineer

WVBW
12-01-1965; 92.9 mhz FM *Hrs Open:* 24; 50 kw; 486 ft.; N36 52 35 W76 23 28
C/O Barnstable Broadcasting, Inc., Two Newton Executive Park, Newton, MA 02462 US
(757) 671-1000, *Fax:* (757) 671-1010
www.929thewave.com
theboss@929thewave.com
License: Suffolk, Suffolk City County, VA held by MHR License LLC.
Group Owner: MAX Media L.L.C.; (acq 3-24-2005; grpsl).
Nat'l Reps: Christal
Arbitron Metro Market: Norfolk-Virginia Beach-Newport News, VA
Format: Adult Contemp *Special Programming:* Relg 2 hrs, Sunday Morning Magazine one hr wkly *Target Audience:* 25-54; women
Eric Mastel, President
Michele Williams, Operations Dir
Vonneva Carter, General Manager
Mike Allen, Programming Director
Jim Long, News Director
paul Campbell, Chief Engineer
John Shomby, Programmign Director

Sweet Briar

***WNRS-FM**
01-01-1980; 89.9 mhz FM *Hrs Open:* 24; 0.03 kw; 1942 ft.; N37 33 50 W79 11 34 *Rebroadcasts:* Rebroadcasts WNRN(FM) Charlottesville
Radio Station Wudz, P.O. Box 143, Sweet Briar, VA 24595 US
(434) 971-4096, *Fax:* (434) 971-6562
www.wnrn.org
info@wnrn.org
License: Sweet Briar, Amherst County, VA held by Sweet Briar College.
Arbitron Metro Market: Roanoke-Lynchbu *Format:* Rock/AOR *Target Audience:* General.
Maynard Sipe, President
Victoria Nelson, General Manager
Ashley Carroll, Station Manager
John Jaffe, General Sales Mgr
Allsion Bailey, Programming Director
Lauren Schein, Music Director
Jon Hall, Vice President
Paul Wright,Treasurer
John Jaffe, Secretary

Tappahannock

***WRAR**
11-01-1970; 1000 khz AM
P.O. Box 1023, Tappahannock, VA 22560 US
(804) 443-6572
License: Tappahannock, VA held by A.C.T.I.O.N. Inc.
Regional Reps: Virginia Broadcast SolutionsRegnl R
Format: Talk
Geoffrey Coleman, President
Rich Morgan, News Director

WRAR-FM
07-26-1971; 105.5 mhz FM *Hrs Open:* 24; 6 kw; 328 ft.; N37 52 27 W76 43 37
Mailing Address: P. O. Box 1023, Tappahannock, VA 22560 US
Second Address: 156 Prince St., Tappahannock, VA 22560
(804) 443-4321, *Fax:* (804) 443-1055
www.wrarfm.com
rich@wrarfm.com
License: Tappahannock, Essex County, VA held by Real Media Inc.
Nat'l Network: ABC *Nat'l Reps:* Rgnl Reps *Wire Services:* AP
Format: Adult Contemp
Billy Flynn, Programming Director
Tom Davis, News Director
Terry Brooks, Traffic Manager

Tazewell

WKQY
09-01-1968; 100.1 mhz FM *Hrs Open:* 24; 4.2 kw; 390 ft.; N37 8 1 W81 35 42
100 Bluefield Ave., Suite 3, Bluefield, WV 24701 US
(304) 327-7144, *Fax:* (304) 325-7850
www.theeaglefm.com
License: Tazewell, Tazewell County, VA
Arbitron Metro Market: Bluefield, WV *Format:* Oldies *No. News Employees:* 1 *Target Audience:* 25 plus.
Marv Nyren, Operations Dir
Lance Richard, General Sales Mgr
Mike Stern, Programming Director
Jennifer Welch, News Director
Patrick Berger, Chief Engineer

WTZE
04-22-1966; 1470 khz AM *Hrs Open:* 6 AM-sunset; 5 kw-D, NDD; N37 7 57 W81 33 21
100 Bluefield Ave., Suite 3, Bluefield, WV 24701 US
(304) 327-7114, *Fax:* (304) 325-7850
www.whistalkradio.com
License: Tazewell, VA held by Monterey Licenses LLC.
Group Owner: Triad Broadcasting Co. L.L.C.; (acq 7-18-00; grpsl)
Nat'l Network: Motor Racing Net
Arbitron Metro Market: Bluefield, WV *Format:* News, News/Talk, 86 *Special Programming:* Gospel 5 hrs wkly *Hrs. of News Programming:* News progmg 5 hrs wkly *Target Audience:* 21-54.
Dave Crosier, Operations Dir
John Halford, General Manager
Joseph Echoles, Programming Director
Keith Bowman, Chief Engineer

Vinton

WSFF
01-01-1994; 106.1 mhz FM; 6 kw; 95 ft.; N37 17 3 W79 59 14
600 Congress Ave., Suite 1400, Austin, TX 78701 US
(540) 725-1220, *Fax:* (540) 725-1245
www.1061stevefm.com
steve@1061stevefm.com
License: Vinton, Roanoke County, VA held by Aloha Station Trust LLC
Arbitron Metro Market: Roanoke-Lynchburg, VA *Format:* Adult Contemp
Chris Clendenen, General Manager
Ron Gaylor, General Sales Mgr
David Lee Michaels, Programming Director
Ed Kilbane, News Director
Jeff Parker, Chief Engineer
Sarah Leftwich, Advertising
Tammy Cazad, Advertizing
Lisa Layne,Advertizing

WKBA
10-09-1961; 1550 khz AM; 10 kw-D, DAD; N37 17 24 W79 55 22
P. O. Box 1092, Salem, VA 24153 US
(540) 343-5597, *Fax:* (540) 345-4064
www.radiowkba.com
ddurrett@radiowkba.com
License: Vinton, VA held by Tinker Creek Broadcasters Inc.
Arbitron Metro Market: Roanoke-Lynchburg, VA *Format:* Religious *Special Programming:* Black 10 hrs wkly *Target Audience:* General.
Dorothy Durrett, General Manager
Dale Cook, Chief Engineer

WVMP
12-12-1995; 101.5 mhz FM *Hrs Open:* 24; 630 w; Ant 705 ft; N37 21 57 W79 52 01 *Rebroadcasts:* Rebroadcasts WZZU(FM) Lynchburg 100%
210 1st St., Suite 240, Roanoke, VA 24179
(540) 344-2800, *Fax:* (540) 344-4001
www.rocktheplanet.fm
info@rocktheplanet.fm
License: Vinton, Roanoke County, VA held by Centennial Broadcasting LLC.
Group Owner: Centennial Broadcasting LLC; (acq 11-23-2004; $4.15 million with WZZU(FM) Lynchburg).
Nat'l Network: Fox News Radio *Nat'l Reps:* McGavren Guild
Arbitron Metro Market: Roanoke-Lynchburg, VA *Hrs. of News Programming:* news progmg 2 hrs wkly *No. News Employees:* 1
Allen B. Shaw, President
Gary Kirtley, General Sales Mgr
Dale Cook, Chief Engineer

Virginia Beach

WXTG-FM
01-01-2002; 102.1 mhz FM; 6 kw; 328 ft.; N36 45 7 W76 8 57
645 Church Street, Suite 400, Norfolk, VA 23510 US
(757) 747-1021, *Fax:* (757) 490-2755
www.1021fmthegame.com
buck@redskins.com
License: Virginia Beach, Virginia Beach County, VA held by Red Zebra Broadcasting Licensee (Norfolk) LLC.
Group Owner: Red Zebra Holdings LLC; (acq 12-4-2006; $4.25 million)
Nat'l Network: Fox Sports
Arbitron Metro Market: Virginia Beach, VA *Format:* Sports, Talk
buck albriton, General Manager
Buck Albritton, Station Manager
John Decandido, Programming Director
Joe Weatherbee, Chief Engineer

***WJLZ**
02-12-1989; 88.5 mhz FM; 1.2 kw; 118 ft.; N36 50 30.7 W76 5 37 *Rebroadcasts:* W279AD 103.7,W280CX 103.9, W250AE 97.9
3177 Va Beach Blvd., Suite B, Virginia Beach, VA 23452 US
(757) 498-9632, *Fax:* (757) 498-8609
www.currentfm.com
info@currentfm.com
License: Virginia Beach, Virginia Beach City County, VA held by Virginia Beach Educational Broadcasting Foundation Inc.
Arbitron Metro Market: Norfolk-Virgini *TV Affiliate:* Relg CHR *No. News Employees:* General.

WPTE
05-05-1984; 94.9 mhz FM *Hrs Open:* 24; 50 kw; 499 ft.; N36 48 37 W76 16 59
10706 Beaver Dam Road, Cockeysville, MD 21030 US
(757) 497-2000, *Fax:* (757) 456-5458
www.pointradio.com
info@pointradio.com
License: Virginia Beach, Virginia Beach City County, VA held by Entercom Norfolk License LLC.
Group Owner: Entercom Communications Corp.; (acq 12-13-99; grpsl).
Nat'l Reps: D & R Radio
Arbitron Metro Market: Norfolk-Virginia Beach-Newport News, VA *Format:* Rock/AOR *Hrs. of News Programming:* News progmg one hr wkly *Target Audience:* 18-49.
David Field, CEO
Jeff Brown, General Manager
Sandy Smith, General Sales Mgr
Barry McKay, Programming Director
Kym Wollman, News Director

WVAB
12-10-1954; 1550 khz AM *Rebroadcasts:* Simulcasts WWIP (FM) Cheriton 100%
1428 Franklin Drive, Virginia Beach, VA 23454 US
(757) 488-1010, *Fax:* (757) 488-7761
www.birach.com/wvab.htm
sima@BIRACH.Com
License: Virginia Beach, VA held by Ronald W. Cowan Jr.
Nat'l Network: CNN Radio
Arbitron Metro Market: Norfolk Virginia Beach, VA *Format:* Christian
Henry Hoot, General Manager

Warrenton

WKCW
12-07-1957; 1420 khz AM *Hrs Open:* 6 AM-sunset
P.O. Box 1726, Rockville, MD 20580 US
(703) 330-8244, *Fax:* (703) 331-4706
www.metroradioinc.com
metroradioinc@aol.com
License: Warrenton, VA held by Metro Radio Inc.
Group Owner: Metro Radio Inc.; (acq 1-2-2004; $400,000)
Format: Spanish *Special Programming:* Bluegrass, farm one hr, rel 6 hrs wkly *Hrs. of News Programming:* news progmg 2 hrs wkly *No. News Employees:* 1 *Target Audience:* 25-54; mature adults with discretionaryincome of $30,000 plus *Adv. Rates:* 20; 20; 20; 10
David Houston, CEO
Bruce Houston, President
Kelly Koonce, COO

WWXX
11-02-1978; 94.3 mhz FM *Hrs Open:* 24; 3 kw; Ant 397 ft; N38 40 42 W77 47 18
8121 Georgia Ave., Suite 1050, Silver Spring, VA 20109
(301) 562-5800, *Fax:* (301) 562-5850
www.espn980.com
License: Warrenton, Fauquier County, VA held by Red Zebra Broadcasting Licensee LLC.
Group Owner: Red Zebra Holdings LLC; (acq 5-9-2006; grpsl).
Nat'l Network: ESPN Radio
Population Served: 58,000 *Arbitron Metro Market:* Washington, DC
Bruce Gilbert, CEO
Tod Castleberry, General Manager

WKDL
11-21-1957; 1250 khz AM *Hrs Open:* 24
P. O. Box 3220, Warrenton, VA 20188 US
(703) 330-8244, *Fax:* (703) 331-4706
www.1250classiccountry.com
metroradioinc@aol.com
License: Warrenton, VA held by Metro Radio Inc.
Group Owner: Metro Radio Inc.; (acq 10-4-2007; $1.1 million)
Format: Country
David Houston, CEO
Bruce Houston, President
Kelly Koonce, COO

Warsaw

WNNT-FM
03-01-1967; 107.5 mhz FM; 6 kw; 328 ft.; N37 56 39 W76 45 5
Mailing Address: P.O. Box 1800, Raleigh, NC 27602 US
Second Address: 194 Islington Rd., Warsaw, VA 22572
(804) 333-4900, *Fax:* (804) 443-1055
www.wnntfm.com
contact@wnntfm.com
License: Warsaw, Richmond County, VA held by Northern Neck & Tidewater Communications Inc.
Arbitron Metro Market: Warsaw, VA *Format:* Country
Rich Morgan, General Manager
A.C. Walker, Programming Director
Frank Miner, Chief Engineer

Waynesboro

WKCI
03-10-1965; 970 khz AM *Hrs Open:* 24; 5 kw-D, DA2; 1 kw-N, DA2; N38 5 12 W78 54 42 *Rebroadcasts:* Rebroadcasts WKCY(AM) Harrisonburg 100%

Mailing Address: 1150 Pepsi Place, Sutie 300, Charlottesville, VA 22901 US
Second Address: 207 University Blvd., Harrisonburg, VA 22801
(540) 434-1777, *Fax:* (540) 432-9968
www.shenandoahradio.com
License: Waynesboro, VA held by CC Licenses LLC.
Group Owner: Clear Channel Communications Inc.; (acq 11-16-2000; grpsl).
Format: News, News/Talk, 86 *Special Programming:* Black 3 hrs, farm 2 hrs wkly *Hrs. of News Programming:* news progmg 2 hrs wkly *No. News Employees:* 1 *Target Audience:* 25-54.
Steve Knupp, Operations Dir
Steve Davis, General Manager
Mike Chiumento, General Sales Mgr
Mark Ness, Chief Engineer

***WPVA**
01-01-1999; 90.1 mhz FM; 2.5 kw; 961 ft.; N38 1 16 W78 52 38
P. O. Box 889, Blacksburg, VA 24063 US
(434) 237-9798, *Fax:* (434) 237-1025
www.spiritfm.com
office@spiritfm.com
License: Waynesboro, Waynesboro City County, VA held by Positive Alternative Radio Inc.
Group Owner: Positive Alternative Radio Inc.; (acq 12-30-2005; grpsl)
Format: Christian
Barry Armstrong, General Manager

Weber City

WVEK-FM
12-01-1994; 102.7 mhz FM *Hrs Open:* 24; 1.65 kw; Ant 1,233 ft; N36 31 36 W82 35 13
222 Commerce St., Kingsport, TN 40823
(423) 246-9578, *Fax:* (423) 247-9836
License: Weber City, Scott County, VA held by Holston Valley Broadcasting Corp.
Group Owner: Glenwood Communications Corp.; (acq 7-16-2008; $270,000)
Nat'l Reps: Eastman
Population Served: 150,000 *Arbitron Metro Market:* Johnson City-Kingsport-Bristol, TN-VA *TV Affiliate:* WKPT-TV
George Devault, President
David Widener, General Manager
Tim Loy, General Sales Mgr
Steve Mann, Programming Director
Brittany Moore, Promotions Manager
Duane Nelson, News Director

Welch

WKQB
02-01-1990; 102.9 mhz FM *Hrs Open:* 24; 1.8 kw; Ant 423 ft; N37 25 01 W81 36 58
Mailing Address: Box 949, Welch, WV 24801
Second Address: U.S. Rt. 52, Welch, WV 24801
(304) 436-2131, *Fax:* (304) 436-2132
www.welcamfm.com
License: Welch, McDowell County, WV
Wire Services: AP
Population Served: 50,000*No. News Employees:* 2 *Target Audience:* 25-54. *Adv. Rates:* 6.50; 6.50; 6.50; 6.50.
Laura Green, Operations Dir
Rick Lambert, Station Manager
Rod O'Dell, General Sales Mgr
Bob Spencer, Member/Manager

West Point

WBQK
07-01-1991; 107.9 mhz FM *Hrs Open:* 24; 4 kw; 328 ft.; N37 27 0 W76 48 46
10300 Attems Way, Glen Allen, VA 23060 US
(757) 565-1079, *Fax:* (757) 565-7094
www.wbach.net
License: West Point, King William County, VA held by Davis Media LLC
Format: Classical
Thomas Davis, President
Derek Mason, General Sales Mgr
Amy Miller, Promotions Manager
Barbara Warren, News Director

White Stone

WIGO-FM
09-01-1995; 104.9 mhz FM; 4.1 kw; 400 ft.; N37 43 25 W76 23 28.8
Mailing Address: P. O. Box 1049, White Stone, VA 22578 US
Second Address: 101 Radio Rd, Kilmarnock, VA 22482
(804)435-1414, *Fax:* (804) 435-0484
www.middlenecknews.com
dburchill@tworivers.net
License: White Stone, Lancaster County, VA held by Two Rivers Communications Inc.
Nat'l Network: Westwood One; AP Radio *Wire Services:* AP
Arbitron Metro Market: White Stone, VA *Format:* Country *No. News Employees:* 1 *Target Audience:* 25-54. *Adv. Rates:* 20; 18; 20; 15
Ron Jeffries, Operations Dir
Dennis Burchill, General Manager
Ron Jeffries, News Director
Charlie Lassiter, General Manager
Syd Abel, Managing Partner

Williamsburg

***WCWM**
09-28-1959; 90.9 mhz FM *Hrs Open:* 24; 13.5 kw; 269 ft.; N37 21 16 W76 59 58
% Kenneth E. Smith, Jr., PO Box 8795, Williamsburg, VA 23185 US
(757) 221-3287
www.wcwm.blogs.wm.edu
tcvanluling@email.wm.edu
License: Williamsburg, James City County, VA held by College of William & Mary.
Nat'l Network: Moody
Arbitron Metro Market: Williamsburg, VA *Format:* Alternative, Variety/Diverse *Special Programming:* Jazz 13 hrs, class 11 hrs, reggae 6 hrs, blues 3 hrs wkly *Hrs. of News Programming:* News progmg 3 hrs wkly *TargetAudience:* General.
Adam Burks, Station Manager
David Jordan, Programming Director

WMBG
01-01-1958; 740 khz AM *Hrs Open:* 24
302 Harrison Avenue, Williamsburg, VA 23185 US
(757) 229-7400, *Fax:* (757) 220-3074
www.wmbgradio.com
info@wmbgradio.com
License: Williamsburg, VA held by Williamsburg's Radio Station Inc.
Nat'l Network: AP Radio; Jones Radio Networks
Arbitron Metro Market: Norfolk, VA *Format:* Adult Contemp
Special Programming: Gospel 5 hrs wkly *Hrs. of News Programming:* news progmg one hr wkly *No. News Employees:* 1 *Target Audience:* 45 plus; wealthy& mature in Williamsburg
Adv. Rates: 120; 72; 96; 60
Greg Granger, President

Winchester

WINC
06-15-1941; 1400 khz AM *Hrs Open:* 24
Mailing Address: P. O. Box 3300, Winchester, VA 22601 US
Second Address: 520 N. Pleasant Valley Rd., Winchester, VA 22601
(540) 667-2224, *Fax:* (540) 722-3295
www.winc.fm
brian@rockthebone.com
License: Winchester, VA held by Mid-Atlantic Network Inc.
Group Owner: Mid Atlantic Network
Nat'l Network: Westwood One; CBS
Arbitron Metro Market: Winchester, VA *Format:* News, News/Talk, 84, Talk *Hrs. of News Programming:* news progmg 128 hrs wkly *No. News Employees:* 3 *Target Audience:* 25 plus; mid-to-upscale active adults
John Lewis, President
Jeff Adams, Operations Dir
Chris Lewis, General Manager
Brian Beddow, Programming Director
Steve Edwards, News Director
Archie McKay, Chief Engineer
Pam Christian, Traffic Manager

WINC-FM
10-01-1946; 92.5 mhz FM *Hrs Open:* 24; 22 kw; 1424 ft.; N38 57 21 W78 1 28
Mailing Address: P.O. Box 3300, Winchester, VA 22604 US
Second Address: 520 N. Pleasant Valley Rd., Winchester, VA 22601
(540) 667-2224, *Fax:* (540) 722-3295
www.winc.fm
brian@rockthebone.com
License: Winchester, Winchester City County, VA held by Mid-Atlantic Network Inc.
Group Owner: Mid Atlantic Network
Nat'l Network: Westwood One
Arbitron Metro Market: Winchester, VA *Format:* Adult Contemp *Hrs. of News Programming:* news progmg 6 hrs wkly *No. News Employees:* 4 *Target Audience:* 18-49; active, upscale listeners
Brian Beddow, Programming Director
Pam Christian, Promotions Manager

WXVA
01-27-1961; 610 khz AM *Hrs Open:* 24; 500 w-U, DA-2; N39 11 53 W78 13 13
510 Pegasus Ct., Winchester, VA 78701
(540) 662-5101, *Fax:* (540) 662-8610
License: Winchester, Winchester City County, VA held by Capstar TX L.P.
Group Owner: Clear Channel Communications Inc.; (acq 8-30-2000; grpsl)
Population Served: 127,500 *Arbitron Metro Market:* Winchester, VA
Jim Shea, President
Chuck Peterson, General Manager

***WTRM**
07-01-1986; 91.3 mhz FM *Hrs Open:* 24; 5.6 kw; 1401 ft.; N39 11 2 W78 23 15
P.O. Box 3438, Winchester, VA 22604 US
(540) 723-0123, *Fax:* (540) 723-0128
www.wtrm.org
office@southernlight.us
License: Winchester, Winchester City County, VA held by Timber Ridge Ministries Inc.
Nat'l Network: USA
Arbitron Metro Market: Winchester, VA *Format:* Gospel *Target Audience:* General.
Richard Choy, CEO
Leona Choy, President
Chris Petsko, General Manager
Cindy Hall, Promotions Manager
Rick Choy, Chief Engineer
Nathan Steele, Engineer
Roberta Varner, Office Manager

WUSQ-FM
12-10-1965; 102.5 mhz FM *Hrs Open:* 24; 32 kw; 630 ft.; N39 10 38 W78 15 53
600 Congress Avenue, Suite 1400, Austin, TX 78701 US
(540) 662-5101, *Fax:* (540) 662-8610
www.wusq.com
DanielMartin@clearchannel.com
License: Winchester, Winchester City County, VA
Arbitron Metro Market: Winchester, VA *Format:* Country *Hrs. of News Programming:* News progmg one hr wkly *Target Audience:* 25-54; males *Adv. Rates:* 125; 110; 110; 55
Chuck Peterson, General Manager
David Miller, Programming Director
Daniel Martin, Marketing

Wise

***WISE-FM**
08-01-1999; 90.5 mhz FM *Hrs Open:* 24; 0.22 kw; 669 ft.; N36 57 39 W82 30 56 *Rebroadcasts:* Rebroadcasts WVTF(FM) Roanoke 100%
College Relations, 1 College Avenue, Wise, VA 24293 US
(540) 989-8900, *Fax:* (540) 776-2727
www.wvtf.org
info@wvtf.org
License: Wise, Wise County, VA held by Clinch Valley College of the University of Virginia.
Nat'l Network: NPR; PRI *Regional Network:* Va. News Net.
Format: Jazz *Special Programming:* Jazz 9 hrs, Celtic 2 hrs wkly *Hrs. of News Programming:* News progmg 45 hrs wkly *Target Audience:* General.
Glenn Gleixner, General Manager

Woodbridge

WMAL-FM
12-25-1958; 105.9 mhz FM; 28 kw; Ant 648 ft; N38 52 28 W77 13 24
4400 Jenifer St. NW, Suite 400, Washington, DC 20015
(202) 686-3100, *Fax:* (202) 686-3064
www.trueoldies1059.com
info@trueoldies1059.com
License: Woodbridge, Prince William County, VA
Group Owner: Cumulus Media Inc.; (acq 6-12-2007; grpsl)
Population Served: 426,800 *Arbitron Metro Market:* Washington, DC
Kenny King, Operations Dir
Jeff Boden, General Manager
Cathy Whissel, General Sales Mgr
Steve Allan, Programming Director
Amy Kirberger, News Director

Woodstock

WAMM
10-09-1981; 1230 khz AM *Hrs Open:* 24; 1 kw-D, ND1; 0.25 kw-N, ND2; N38 51 11 W78 31 30
Box 542, 105 E. South St., Harrisonburg, VA 22664 US
(540) 477-4443, *Fax:* (540) 477-4407
www.wsvgradio.com
wsvgam@hotmail.com
License: Woodstock, VA held by Jason M. Rodriguez
Arbitron Metro Market: Woodstock, VA *Format:* Ethnic
Jason Rodriguez, General Manager

WAZR
10-18-1985; 93.7 mhz FM *Hrs Open:* 24; 8.5 kw; 420 ft.; N38 37 4 W78 42 39
Mailing Address: 123 East Court Street, Woodstock, VA 22664 US
Second Address: 207 University Blvd., Harrisonburg, VA 22801
(817) 641-3495
License: Woodstock, Shenandoah County, VA held by CC Licenses LLC.
Group Owner: Clear Channel Communications Inc.; (acq 6-3-2002; $1.35 million including five-year noncompete agreement).
Nat'l Network: Jones Radio Networks
Arbitron Metro Market: Tuscaloosa AL
Linda De Romanett, President

Wytheville

WYVE
09-21-1949; 1280 khz AM *Hrs Open:* 24; 2.5 kw-D, ND1; 0.164 kw-N, ND1; N36 57 54 W81 4 50
3006 Ben Venue Drive, Greensburg, PA 15601 US
(276) 228-3185, *Fax:* (276) 228-9261
www.wyve.com
trmedia@msn.com
License: Wytheville, VA held by Three Rivers Media Corp.
Group Owner: Three Rivers Media Corp.; (acq 10-1-98; $250,000).
Nat'l Network: AP Network News; Jones Radio Networks
Regional Reps: Rgnl Reps
Arbitron Metro Market: Wytheville, VA *Format:* News, Sports, 30
Special Programming: Gospel 4 hrs wkly *Hrs. of News Programming:* news progmg 10 hrs wkly *No. News Employees:* 1 *Target Audience:* 25 plus;general *Adv. Rates:* 20; 20; 20; 20
Gary W. Hagerich, CEO
Gary W. Hagerich, President
Danny Gordon, Operations Dir
Teresa Kingl, News Director

Yorktown

WVSP-FM
07-04-1975; 94.1 mhz FM *Hrs Open:* 24; 50 kw; 500 ft; N37 29 37 W76 26 30
5589 Greenwich Rd., Suite 200, Virginia Beach, VA 23692
(757) 671-1000, *Fax:* (757) 518-9364
www.wxez941.com
dmurray@wxez941.com
License: Yorktown, York County, VA held by MHR License LLC.
Group Owner: MAX Media L.L.C.; (acq 3-24-2005; grpsl).
Nat'l Reps: Christal
Arbitron Metro Market: Norfolk-Virginia Beach-Newport News, VA *No. News Employees:* 8 *Target Audience:* 35-64.
Eric Martel, President
Vonneva Carter, General Manager
Cynthia Weatherspoon, General Sales Mgr
Dale Murray, Programming Director
Mary Stott, Promotions Manager

***WYCS**
02-01-1966; 91.5 mhz FM *Hrs Open:* 24; 1.3 kw horiz, 20 kw vert; 331 ft.; N37 12 17 W76 30 7
Post Office Box 1924, Tulsa, OK 74101 US
(918) 455-5693, *Fax:* (757) 886-7491
www.oasisnetwork.org
mail@oasisnetwork.org
License: Yorktown, York County, VA held by Creative Educational Media Corp. Inc.
Arbitron Metro Market: Yorktown, VA *Format:* Religious *Target Audience:* General.
David Ingles, President
Greg Roth, General Manager

Washington

Aberdeen

KBKW
08-01-1949; 1450 khz AM *Hrs Open:* 24; 1 kw-U; N46 56 59 W123 49 13
Mailing Address: Box 1198, Aberdeen, WA 98005
Second Address: 1520 Simpson Ave., Aberdeen, WA 98520
(360) 533-3000, *Fax:* (360) 532-1456
www.jodesha.com
bossbill@jodesha.com
License: Aberdeen, Grays Harbor County, WA held by Jodesha Broadcasting Inc.
Group Owner: Jodesha Broadcasting Inc.; acq 2-28-03; $750,000 with KSWW(FM) Montesano).
Nat'l Network: ABC Information & Entertainment *Wire Services:* AP
Population Served: 52,200*Hrs. of News Programming:* 13 *No. News Employees:* 1 *Target Audience:* 25-54. *Adv. Rates:* 16; 12; 14; 12
Wm Wolfenbarger, President
Gabrielle Jordan, Operations Dir
Tony Halekakis, General Manager
Sally Miller, General Sales Mgr

KXRO
05-28-1928; 1320 khz AM *Hrs Open:* 24; 5 kw-D, DAN; 1 kw-N, DAN; N46 57 27 W123 48 33
725 Broad St., P.O. Box 936, Augusta, GA 30903 US
(360) 533-1320, *Fax:* (360) 532-0935
www.kxro.com
info@kxro.com
License: Aberdeen, WA held by Morris Communications Corp.
Group Owner: Morris Radio LLC; (acq 10-15-98; grpsl)
Nat'l Network: CBS *Nat'l Reps:* McGavren Guild
Arbitron Metro Market: Aberdeen, WA *Format:* News, News/Talk, 86 *Hrs. of News Programming:* news progmg 6 hrs wkly *No. News Employees:* 2 *Target Audience:* 35-64.
Pat Anderson, Operations Dir
Donna Rosi, General Manager
Liz Miller, News Director
Jay White, Chief Engineer
Ian Cope, Sports Commentator
Lorrie Larson, Traffic Manager

***KBSG**
90.3 mhz FM; kw
US
(360) 539-2233
License: Aberdeen, Lewis County, WA held by Samsno Educational Media.
Arbitron Metro Market: Tacoma, WA *Special Programming:* Soul
Jennifer Diane Reitz, President

Airway Heights

KXLX
10-01-1986; 700 khz AM; 10 kw-D, 600 w-N, DA-N; N47 36 31 W117 22 25
500 W. Boone Ave., Spokane, WA 83822
(509) 324-4000, *Fax:* (509) 324-8992
License: Airway Heights, Spokane County, WA held by QueenB Radio Inc.
Group Owner: Morgan Murphy Media (Evening Telegram Co); (acq 9-1-2005; $236,000)
Nat'l Network: ESPN Radio *Nat'l Reps:* Katz Radio

Brian Paul, VP/General Manager
Tery Garras, General Sales Mgr
Dennis Patchin, Program Director

Anacortes

KWLE
12-18-1957; 1340 khz AM *Hrs Open:* 24; 1 kw-U, ND1; N48 29 44 W122 36 15
P.O. Box 96, Anacortes, WA 98221 US
(360) 293-3141, *Fax:* (360) 293-9463
www.1340thewhale.com
info@kwleam.com
License: Anacortes, WA held by San Juan Communications Inc.
Nat'l Network: Westwood One; CBS; ABC
Arbitron Metro Market: Seattle, WA *Format:* Adult Contemp
Special Programming: Sp 6 hrs, relg one hr wkly *Hrs. of News Programming:* news progmg 30 hrs wkly *No. News Employees:* 3 *Target Audience:* 25-60.*Adv. Rates:* 21; 19; 21; 14
Jennifer Uteda, President
Lynn Mc Mullen, Operations Dir
William Berry, General Manager
Glen Harris, Programming Director
Dedrick Allen, Operations Manager

DKORC
07-01-1988; 820 khz AM
2104 North 30th, Tacoma, WA 98403 US
(541) 563-5100, *Fax:* (541) 563-5116
License: Anacortes, Lincoln County, WA held by Larry D. and Margaret E. Profitt, a General Partnership
Format: Easy Listening
Larry Profitt, General Manager

Asotin

KCLK
03-02-1971; 1430 khz AM *Hrs Open:* 24; 5 kw-D, DA2; 1 kw-N, DA2; N46 18 59 W117 2 24
P.O.Box 669, Clarkston, WA 99403 US
(208) 743-6564, *Fax:* (208) 798-0110
evanyeoman@pacempire.com
License: Asotin, WA
Group Owner: Pacific Empire Radio Corp.; (acq 9-12-2008; grpsl)
Arbitron Metro Market: Lewiston, ID *Format:* Sports, Talk *No. News Employees:* 1 *Target Audience:* 15 plus; sports interested
Mark Bolland, General Manager
Evan Yeoman, Programming Director
Leslie Gatherer, News Director

***KJCF**
01-01-2009; 89.3 mhz FM; 0.175 kw; -328 ft.; N46 19 56 W117 2 34 *Rebroadcasts:* Rebroadcasts KAWZ(FM) Twin Falls, ID 100%
US
(800) 357-4226, *Fax:* (208) 736-1958
www.csnradio.com
License: Asotin, Asotin County, WA held by CSN International.
Group Owner: CSN International
Arbitron Metro Market: Asotin, WA *Format:* Christian
Mike Kestler, President
Don Mills, Network Programming Director / Music Director
Kelly Carlson, Director of Engineering
Ray Gorney, Assistant Director of Engineering
Austin Morris, Accounting
Daniel Davidson, Operations Director

Auburn

***KGRG-FM**
12-01-1974; 89.9 mhz FM *Hrs Open:* 24; 0.25 kw; 367 ft.; N47 15 23 W122 13 7
12401 S.E. 320th Street, Auburn, WA 98002 US
(253) 833-9111, *Fax:* (253) 288-3439
www.kgrg.com
programming@kgrg.com
License: Auburn, King County, WA held by Green River Community College.
Arbitron Metro Market: Seattle-Tacoma, WA *Format:* Rock/AOR
Special Programming: Loc music 3 hrs, rap 3 hrs, metal 2 hrs, punk 4 hr *Hrs. of News Programming:* News progmg 2 hrs wkly *Target Audience:* 16-34.
Tom Evans Krause, General Manager
Matt Mikolas, Programming Director
Jeremy Hopkins, Promotions Manager
Salvador Arceo, News Director
Jon Kasprick, Chief Engineer
Anthony Androsko, Assistant Program Director

Auburn-Federal Way

KMIA
08-06-1958; 1210 khz AM *Hrs Open:* 24; 27.5 kw-D, 10 kw-N, DA-2; N47 18 20 W122 14 53
1400 W. Main St., Auburn, WA 19004
(253) 735-9700, *Fax:* (253) 735-7424
License: Auburn-Federal Way, King County, WA
Group Owner: Adelante Media Group LLC; (acq 1-21-2005; $6 million)
Nat'l Network: Ke-Buena
Population Served: 2,500,000 *Arbitron Metro Market:* Seattle-Tacoma, WA
Amador Bustos, President
Jose Diaz, General Manager
Cesar Valdiosera, Programming Director

Basin City

KOLW
02-01-1992; 97.5 mhz FM *Hrs Open:* 24; 50 kw; 620 ft.; N46 17 23 W119 25 28
P.O. Drawer K, Grande Coulee, WA 99133 US

(509) 547-9791, *Fax:* (509) 547-8509
www.975coolfm.com
barrylong@townsquaremedia.com
License: Basin City, Franklin County, WA held by GAP Broadcasting Tri-Cities License LLC.
Group Owner: GAPWEST Broadcasting; (acq 2-13-2008; grpsl)
Nat'l Network: Jones Radio Networks *Regional Reps:* Wheeler Broadcasting.
Arbitron Metro Market: Basin City, WA *Format:* Contemporary Hits/Top 40, Adult Contemp *Target Audience:* 25-49; 60% male, 40% female *Adv. Rates:* 12; 12; 12; 8
Cheryl Salomone, General Manager

Bellevue

***KASB**
03-22-1971; 89.9 mhz FM; 0.06 kw; 33 ft.; N47 36 15 W122 11 50
P.O. Box 90010, Bellevue, WA 98009 US
(425) 456-7101, *Fax:* (425) 456-7110
www.kasbfm.com
congerb@kasbfm.com
License: Bellevue, King County, WA held by Bellevue School District No. 405.
Arbitron Metro Market: Bellevue, WA *Special Programming:* Local School News and Events *Target Audience:* High School *Adv. Rates:* na
Wes Zujko, General Manager

***KBCS**
02-03-1973; 91.3 mhz FM *Hrs Open:* 24; 8 kw; 213 ft.; N47 35 9 W122 8 41
3000 Landerholm Cir Se, Bellevue, WA 98007 US
(425) 564-2427, *Fax:* (425) 564-5697
kbcs.fm
kbcs@ctc.edu
License: Bellevue, King County, WA held by Bellevue Community College.
Arbitron Metro Market: Bellevue, WA *Format:* Jazz *Hrs. of News Programming:* News progmg 4 hrs wkly *Target Audience:* General.
Bruce Wirth, Operations Dir
Steve Ramsey, General Manager
Sabrina Roach, General Sales Mgr
Robert Jefferson, Programming Director
Sam Roffe, Chief Engineer

KQMV
11-01-1964; 92.5 mhz FM; 56.8 kw; 2290 ft.; N47 30 17.3 W121 58 3.4
Newport Tower, Suite 550, 3650 131st Avenue, Se, Bellevue, WA 98006 US
(425) 653-9462, *Fax:* (425) 653-9464
www.movin925.fm
info@movin925.fm
License: Bellevue, King County, WA held by Bellevue Radio Inc.
Group Owner: Sandusky Radio
Nat'l Reps: Christal
Arbitron Metro Market: Seattle, WA *Format:* Adult Contemp *Hrs. of News Programming:* News progmg one hr wkly *Target Audience:* 25-49; working women & families *Adv. Rates:* 400; 300; 300; 100
Norman Rau, President
Marc Kaye, Operations Dir
Lois Mares, General Sales Mgr
Maynard Cohen, Programming Director
Annie O'Dell, Promotions Manager

KXPA
03-01-1958; 1540 khz AM; 5 kw-D, DAN; 5 kw-N, DAN; N47 35 29 W122 10 56
449 Broadway, New York, NY 10013 US
(206) 292-7800, *Fax:* (206) 292-2140
www.kxpa.com
info@kxpa.com
License: Bellevue, WA held by Multicultural Radio Broadcasting Licensee LLC.
Group Owner: Multicultural Radio Broadcasting Inc.; (acq 2-13-98; grpsl).
Arbitron Metro Market: Seattle-Tacoma, WA *Format:* Ethnic, Variety/Diverse
Arthur Liu, President
Dennis Hartley, Operations Dir
Lisa Shepherd, General Manager

Bellingham

KAFE
07-02-1965; 104.1 mhz FM *Hrs Open:* 24; 60 kw; 2300 ft.; N48 40 49.6 W122 50 26.3
73 Kercheval Avenue, Grosse Pointe Farms, MI 48236 US
(360) 734-9790, *Fax:* (360) 733-4551
www.kafe.com
michael@cascaderadiogroup.com
License: Bellingham, Whatcom County, WA
Arbitron Metro Market: Bellingham, WA *Format:* Adult Contemp
Michael O'Shea, General Manager
Don Kurtis, General Sales Mgr
Ken Richards, Programming Director
Scotty VanDryver, Promotions Manager
Bill Baker, News Director
Krista Kay, Disc Jockey
Like Caus, Disc Jockey
Lynn Roberts, DiscJockey
Jeff Nelson, Disc Jockey
Steve Sandmeyer, News Reporter
Mikelanne Burk, News Reporter

KGMI
01-01-1927; 790 khz AM; 5 kw-D, DAN; 1 kw-N, DAN; N48 43 9 W122 26 43
73 Kercheval Ave., Grosse Pointe Farms, MI 48236 US
(360) 734-9790, *Fax:* (360) 733-4551
www.kgmi.com
kgmi@kgmi.com
License: Bellingham, WA held by Saga Broadcasting LLC.
Group Owner: Saga Communications Inc.; (acq 9-24-98; $8 million with co-located FM)
Nat'l Reps: McGavren Guild
Format: News, News/Talk, 86 *Special Programming:* Home Improvement 2 hrs wkly *Hrs. of News Programming:* News 140 hrs wkly *Target Audience:* 35-64.
Ed Christian, President
Rick Staeb, General Manager
Brett Bonner, Programming Director
Krista Kay, Promotions Manager
Doug Lange, News Director
Will Vos, Chief Engineer
Steve Ricci, Women's Int Ed

KISM
03-01-1960; 92.9 mhz FM; 50 kw; 2441 ft.; N48 40 48 W122 50 24
73 Kercheval Ave., Grosse Pointe Farms, MI 48236 US
(360) 734-9790
www.kism.com
License: Bellingham, Whatcom County, WA held by Saga Broadcasting LLC.
Group Owner: Saga Communications Inc.
Format: Classic Rock *Target Audience:* 25-44.
Carol Dooley, Programming Director

KBAI
04-04-1958; 930 khz AM *Hrs Open:* 24
73 Kercheval Avenue, Grosse Pointe Farms, MI 48236 US
(360) 734-9790, *Fax:* (360) 733-4551
License: Bellingham, WA held by Saga Broadcasting LLC.
Group Owner: Saga Communications Inc.; (acq 3-8-99; $1 million).
Nat'l Reps: Tacher
Format: Alternative, Talk *Hrs. of News Programming:* news progmg 5 hrs wkly *No. News Employees:* 1
Ed Christian, President
Rick Staeb, General Manager

KPUG
02-29-1948; 1170 khz AM *Hrs Open:* 24
73 Kercheval Avenue, Grosse Pointe Farms, MI 48236 US
(360) 734-9790, *Fax:* (360) 733-4551
www.kpug1170.com
thezone@kpug1170.com
License: Bellingham, WA held by Saga Broadcasting LLC.
Group Owner: Saga Communications Inc.; (acq 10-30-98; $5,825,000 with co-located FM).
Nat'l Reps: McGavren Guild
Arbitron Metro Market: Whatcom County *Format:* Sports, Talk *Hrs. of News Programming:* news progmg 24 hrs wkly *No. News Employees:* 3 *Target Audience:* 25-54.
Ed Chrtistian, President
Rick Staeb, General Manager
Doug Lange, Programming Director
Will Vos, Chief Engineer

***KUGS**
01-29-1974; 89.3 mhz FM *Hrs Open:* 7 AM-12AM; 0.1 kw; 384 ft.; N48 44 11 W122 28 47
410 Viking Union, Bellingham, WA 98225 US
(360) 650-4771, *Fax:* (360) 650-2696
www.kugs.org
as.productions@wwu.edu
License: Bellingham, Whatcom County, WA held by Western Washington University.
Wire Services: AP
Arbitron Metro Market: Bellingham, WA *Format:* News, News/Talk, 86 *Special Programming:* Black 10 hrs, Hawaiian 2 hrs wkly *Hrs. of News Programming:* News progmg 17 hrs wkly *Target Audience:* 18-34; collegestudents & adults *Adv. Rates:* 10; 10; 10; 10
Ethan Glemaker, President
Nicholas Keefe, Operations Dir
Jamie Hoover, General Manager
Lauren Stelling, Programming Director
Casey Nolan, Promotions Manager
Jeff Emtman, News & Public Affairs Director
Matthew Eschbach, ChiefEngineer
Britt Barquist, Music Director
Kelsey Lorberau, Specialty Music Director
Daley Smith, Productions Director
Cathy Dang, Productions Assistant Director for Marketing & Ass
Cody Olsen, Films Coordinator
Megan Housekeeper, Pop MusicCoordinator

***KZAZ**
09-01-1991; 91.7 mhz FM *Hrs Open:* 24; 0.12 kw; 335 ft.; N48 48 4 W122 27 40 *Rebroadcasts:* Rebroadcasts KRFA-FM Pullman 95%
382 Murrow Center, Pullman, WA 99164 US
(509) 335-6500, *Fax:* (509) 335-6577
www.nwpr.org
nwpr@wsu.edu
License: Bellingham, Whatcom County, WA held by Washington State University.
Nat'l Network: NPR; PRI
Arbitron Metro Market: Bellingham, WA *Format:* Jazz, News *Special Programming:* Folk 8 hrs, world music 7 hrs wkly *Hrs. of News Programming:* News progmg 40 hrs wkly *Target Audience:* 25-54; general *Adv.Rates:* 160; 60; 160; 140
Kerry Swanson, Station Manager
Gillian Coldsnow, Programming Director
Robin Rilette, Music Director

Benton City

KMMG
08-01-1974; 96.7 mhz FM *Hrs Open:* 24; 0.82 kw; 889 ft.; N46 14 4 W119 19 13
P.O. Box 2888, Yakima, WA 98907 US
(509) 543-3334, *Fax:* (509) 452-0541
www.adelantemediagroup.com/station/kmmg-fm/
zorro@radiozorro.com
License: Benton City, Benton County, WA
Group Owner: Adelante Media Group LLC; (acq 11-18-2004; grpsl)
Arbitron Metro Market: Benton City, WA. *Hrs. of News Programming:* news progmg 22 hrs wkly *No. News Employees:* 1 *Target Audience:* 25 plus.
Bob Berry, General Manager
Bob Berrt, General Sales Mgr
Martin Ortiz, Programming Director
Keith Teske, Chief Engineer

Blaine

KARI
02-12-1960; 550 khz AM *Hrs Open:* 24; 5 kw-D, 2.5 kw-N, DA-2; N48 57 15 W122 44 36
4840 Lincoln Rd., Blaine, WA 98230
(360) 371-5500,(604) 536-7733, *Fax:* (360) 371-7617
www.kari55.com
kari@kari55.com
License: Blaine, Whatcom County, WA held by Way Broadcasting Licensee LLC
Population Served: 3,750,000*Special Programming:* Ger 2 hrs, Ukrainian one hr, Arabic one hr wkly *Target Audience:* 35 plus. *Adv. Rates:* 22; 22; 22; na
Arthur Liu, President
Yvonne Liu, Operations Dir
Gary Nawman, General Manager

KVRI
01-01-2001; 1600 khz AM
4840 Lincoln Road, Blaine, WA 98230 US
(360) 371-5500, *Fax:* (360) 371-7617
www.kari55.com
gary@kari55.com
License: Blaine, WA held by Way Broadcasting Licensee LLC
Arbitron Metro Market: Blaine, WA *Format:* Public Affairs
Arthur Liu, President
Yvonne Liu, Operations Dir
Gary Nawman, General Manager

Bremerton

KBRO
05-01-1947; 1490 khz AM *Hrs Open:* 6 AM-midnight; 1 kw-U, ND1; N47 33 52 W122 39 26
19939 Gatling Court, Katy, TX 77449 US
(303) 688-5162, *Fax:* (303) 660-4930
www.espndeportesseattle.com
o.ibarra@espndeportesseattle.com
License: Bremerton, WA held by Seattle Streaming Radio LLC.
Group Owner: Seattle Streaming Radio LLC; (acq 8-26-2005; $900,000 with KNTB(AM) Lakewood)
Nat'l Network: ESPN Deportes
Arbitron Metro Market: Seattle-Tacoma, WA *Format:* Sports
Oscar Ibarra, General Manager

KRWM
08-22-1964; 106.9 mhz FM *Hrs Open:* 24; 49 kw; 1299 ft.; N47 32 39 W122 6 29
3650 131st Avenue, Suite 550, Bellevue, WA 98006 US
(425) 373-5545, *Fax:* (425) 653-1188
www.warm1069.com
License: Bremerton, Kitsap County, WA held by Seascape Radio Inc.
Group Owner: Sandusky Radio; (acq 9-12-96; $29.25 million)
Nat'l Reps: Christal
Arbitron Metro Market: Bellevue, WA *Format:* Adult Contemp
Target Audience: 35-54; educated, upscale professionals, family oriented, white/blue collar *Adv. Rates:* 250; 300; 250; 75
Marc Kaye, Operations Dir
Marc Kaye, General Manager
Julie Judge, General Sales Mgr
Laura Dane, Programming Director
Heather Gardner, Promotions Manager

Burbank

KUJ-FM
01-01-1997; 99.1 mhz FM *Hrs Open:* 16; 52 kw; Ant 1,263 ft; N46 05 58 W119 07 40
830 N. Columbia Center Blvd., Suite B-2, Kennewick, WA 99362
(509) 783-0783, *Fax:* (509) 735-8627
www.power991fm.com
License: Burbank, Walla Walla County, WA held by James D Ingstad
Group Owner: James D. Ingstad Stns; (acq 6-22-2004; $1.68 million)
Arbitron Metro Market: Tri-Cities, WA (Richland-Kennewick-Pasco) *Target Audience:* 18-34.

KVAN
01-01-2007; 1560 khz AM
US
(509) 545-8836
www.laestaciondelafamilia.org
laestaciondelafamilia@gmail.com
License: Burbank, WA held by Compadres LC
Arbitron Metro Market: Burbank, WA *Format:* News
Angel Castaneda, General Manager

Burien-Seattle

KGNW
10-10-1970; 820 khz AM *Hrs Open:* 24; 50 kw-D, DA2; 5 kw-N, DA2; N47 26 0 W122 28 2
4880 Santa Rosa Rd, #300, Camarillo, CA 93012 US
(206) 443-8200, *Fax:* (206) 777-1133
www.kgnw.com
webmaster@kgnw.com
License: Burien-Seattle, WA held by Inspiration Media Inc.
Group Owner: Salem Communications Corp.; (acq 1984)
Nat'l Reps: Salem
Arbitron Metro Market: Seattle-Tacoma, WA *Format:* Christian, Talk, 74 *Special Programming:* Talk, women, loc affrs, health *Hrs. of News Programming:* News progmg 3 hrs wkly *Target Audience:* 35 plus.
Stuart Epperson, Chairman
Edward Atsinger III, President
Joshua Main, Operations Dir
Tim Harper, General Manager
Dave Drui, Programming Director
Rob Allyn, Engineering Dir
Monte Passmore, Chief Engineer
Marilyn Goggan, ProgramDirector

Camas

KNRK
11-01-1992; 94.7 mhz FM *Hrs Open:* 24; 6.3 kw; 1322 ft.; N45 29 20 W122 41 40
401 City Ave., Suite 409, Bala Cynwyd, PA 19004 US
(503) 223-1441, *Fax:* (503) 223-6909
www.947.fm
info@947.fm
License: Camas, Clark County, WA held by Entercom Portland License L.L.C.
Group Owner: Entercom Communications Corp.
Arbitron Metro Market: Portland, OR *Format:* Alternative *No. News Employees:* 1 *Target Audience:* 25-54.
David Field, President
Mark Hamilton, Station Manager
Jaime Cooley, Programming Director
Jack Hutchison, Executive Vice President

Cashmere

KWWX
01-01-1993; 106.7 mhz FM; 6 kw; -240 ft.; N47 30 21 W120 24 33
North 1212 Washington, Suite 307, Spokane, WA 99201 US
(509) 665-6565, *Fax:* (509) 663-1150
www.lasuperz.com/
License: Cashmere, Chelan County, WA held by CCR-Wenatchee IV LLC.
Group Owner: Cherry Creek Radio LLC; (acq 10-31-2006; grpsl)
Nat'l Reps: McGavren Guild
Arbitron Metro Market: Cashmere, WA *Format:* Classic Rock
Target Audience: 25-54.
Jim Senst, General Manager
Leona Frank, General Sales Mgr
Dave Keefer, Programming Director

Castle Rock

KRQT
01-01-1994; 107.1 mhz FM; 0.8 kw; 1716 ft.; N46 20 18 W123 5 45
401 City Ave., Suite 409, Bala Cynwyd, PA 19004 US
(360) 425-1500, *Fax:* (360) 423-1554
www.rocket107.com
License: Castle Rock, Cowlitz County, WA held by Bicoastal Media Licenses IV LLC.
Group Owner: Bicoastal Media L.L.C.; (acq 3-31-2005; grpsl)
Nat'l Network: ABC
Format: Light Rock *Hrs. of News Programming:* One
Kevin Taylor, Operations Dir
Julie Laird, Station Manager
Sam Lee, General Sales Mgr
Phil Blair, News Director
Dawn Crowe, Traffic Manager

Centralia

*KCED
02-17-1975; 91.3 mhz FM; 1 kw; -72 ft.; N46 42 56 W122 57 48
600 W. Locust, Centralia, WA 98531 US
(360) 736-9391 x343, *Fax:* (360) 330-7509,www.centralia.ctc.edu
info@kcedfm.com
License: Centralia, Lewis County, WA held by Board of Trustees, Centralia College.
Format: Variety/Diverse *Special Programming:* Sports 3 hrs wkly
Wade Fisher, General Manager

KNBQ
08-24-1965; 102.9 mhz FM *Hrs Open:* 24; 70 kw; 2192 ft.; N46 58 31 W123 8 16
50 East Rivercenter Blvd, Suite 1200, Covington, KY 41011 US
(206) 494-2000, *Fax:* (206) 286-2376
qcountry1029.com
info@qcountry1029.com
License: Centralia, Lewis County, WA held by Citicasters Licenses L.P.
Group Owner: Clear Channel Communications Inc.; (acq 5-4-99; grpsl)
Format: Country *Hrs. of News Programming:* news progmg 7 hrs wkly *No. News Employees:* 2 *Target Audience:* 18 plus.
Michele Grosenick, General Manager

Centralia-Chehalis

KELA
11-01-1937; 1470 khz AM *Hrs Open:* 24; 5 kw-D, ND1; 1 kw-N, ND1; N46 41 47 W122 57 23
1635 South Gold, Centralia, WA 98532 US
(360) 736-3321(360) 748-3321, *Fax:* (360) 736-0150
www.kelaam.com
johndimeoe@clearchannel.com
License: Centralia-Chehalis, WA held by Bicoastal Media Licenses IV LLC.
Group Owner: Bicoastal Media L.L.C.; (acq 12-1-2007; $4.175 milllion with KMNT(FM) Chehalis)
Nat'l Network: Fox News Radio *Nat'l Reps:* Tacher
Arbitron Metro Market: Centralia, WA *Format:* News, News/Talk, 84, Talk *Special Programming:* Home Improvement *Hrs. of News Programming:* news progmg 28 hrs wkly *No. News Employees:* 2 *Target Audience:* 35plus.
John DiMeo Jr., General Manager
Larry Miner, General Sales Mgr
Steve Richert, Programming Director
Steve B, Promotions Manager
Doug Adamson, News Director
Dan Smith, Chief Engineer

Chehalis

KMNT
01-01-2005; 104.3 mhz FM; 2.35 kw; 1056 ft.; N46 33 18 W123 3 27
US
(360) 330-0777, *Fax:* (360) 736-0150
www.kmnt.com
License: Chehalis, Lewis County, WA held by Bicoastal Media Licenses IV LLC.
Group Owner: Bicoastal Media L.L.C.; (acq 12-1-2007; $4.175 million with KELA(AM) Centralia-Chehalis)
Nat'l Reps: Tacher *Regional Reps:* Tacher
Arbitron Metro Market: Chehalis, WA *Format:* Country *Special Programming:* NFL Football *Hrs. of News Programming:* 60 minutes weekly *No. News Employees:* 1
John DiMeo Jr., General Manager

*KSWS
88.9 mhz FM; 1 kw; 1004 ft.; N46 33 16 W123 3 26
Ed Telcomm. & Tech, Murrow Communications, Pullman, WA 99164 US
(509) 335-6511
www.nwpr.org
nwpr@wsu.edu
License: Chehalis, Lewis County, WA held by Washington State University.
Arbitron Metro Market: Chehalis, WA *Format:* Classical
Dennis Haarsager, General Manager
Aki Wright, Development Coordinator
Gillian Coldsnow, Assistant Manager, Programming and Operations

Chehalis-Centralia

KITI
10-01-1954; 1420 khz AM *Hrs Open:* 24; 5 kw-U, DA-2; N46 42 08 W122 55 58
1133 Kresky, Centralia, WA 98531
(360) 736-1355, *Fax:* (360) 736-4761
www.1420kiti.com
mshannon@live95.com
License: Chehalis-Centralia, Lewis County, WA held by Premier Broadcasters Inc.
Group Owner: Premier Broadcasters; (acq 10-77)
Population Served: 60,000*Special Programming:* Elvis Only, Goddards Gold *Hrs. of News Programming:* news progmg 15 hrs wkly *No. News Employees:* 1 *Target Audience:* 35-64. *Adv. Rates:* 6am-7pm: $20
Rod Etherton, President
Rod Etherton, General Manager
Matt Shannon, Station Manager
Matt Shannon, General Sales Mgr
Matt Shannon, Programming Director
Miles McKnight, News Director
Ron Gallagher, Engineering Dir

Chelan

KOZI
03-01-1957; 1230 khz AM *Hrs Open:* 24
Mailing Address: 7375 Icicle Road, Leavenworth, WA 98826 US
Second Address: 123 E. Johnson, Chelan, WA 98816
(509) 682-4033, *Fax:* (509) 682-4035
www.kozi.com
info@kozi.com
License: Chelan, WA held by Icicle Broadcasting Co.
Group Owner: Icicle Broadcasting Inc.; (acq 8-26-99; grpsl)
Nat'l Reps: Target Broadcast Sales
Format: Adult Contemp, News, 62, Talk *Special Programming:* Farm 3 hrs, Sp 5 hrs wkly *Hrs. of News Programming:* news progmg 32 hrs wkly *No. News Employees:* 3 *Target Audience:* General.
Harriet Bullitt, President
Steve Byquist, Operations Dir
Gary Mathews, General Manager
Joe Fiala, Station Manager
Vicky Chandler, General Sales Mgr
Clint Strand, News Director
Michael Dickes, Music Director

KOZI-FM
08-26-1981; 93.5 mhz FM; 0.6 kw; 1037 ft.; N47 51 2 W119 52 26
Mailing Address: 7375 Icicle Road, Leavenworth, WA 98826 US
Second Address: 123 E. Johnson, Chelan, WA 98816
(509) 682-4033, *Fax:* (509) 682-4035
www.kozi.com
info@kozi.com
License: Chelan, Chelan County, WA
Group Owner: Icicle Broadcasting Inc.
Format: Adult Contemp, News, 62, Talk
Lee McVey, Programming Director

Cheney

***KEWU-FM**
04-03-1950; 89.5 mhz FM *Hrs Open:* 6 AM-12 AM (M-F); 9 AM-12 AM (S, Su; 10 kw; 1407 ft.; N47 34 43 W117 17 50
526 5th Street, Mail Stop 104, Cheney, WA 99004 US
(509) 359-6390, *Fax:* (509) 359-4841
www.kewu.ewu.edu
efarriss@mail.ewu.edu
License: Cheney, Spokane County, WA held by Eastern Washington University Board of Trustees.
Arbitron Metro Market: Cheney, WA *Format:* Jazz *Special Programming:* Latin,World,Ambient
Marvin Smith, General Manager
Elizabeth A. Farriss, Programming Director
Marvin Smith, Professor
Tom Mullin, Professor

KEYF-FM
05-04-1986; 101.1 mhz FM *Hrs Open:* 24; 100 kw; 1608 ft.; N47 35 35 W117 17 46
City Center West 7201 W. Lake Mead Blvd, Suite 400, Las Vegas, NV 89128 US
(509) 448-1000(509) 232-1011, *Fax:* (509) 448-7015
www.oldies1011.com
License: Cheney, Spokane County, WA held by Mapleton License of Spokane LLC.
Group Owner: Mapleton Communications LLC; (acq 12-3-2007; grpsl)
Arbitron Metro Market: Spokane, WA *Format:* Oldies *Hrs. of News Programming:* News progmg 15 hrs wkly *Target Audience:* 35-64.
Don Morin, General Manager
Mike Skot, Programming Director
Toby Howell, Promotions Manager
Larry Weir, News Director
Dave Ratener, Chief Engineer
Brenda Anderson, Traffic Manager
Promotion Coordinator

Clarkston

KCLK-FM
01-01-1974; 94.1 mhz FM *Hrs Open:* 24; 100 kw; 1234 ft.; N46 27 27 W117 6 3
P.O. Box 669, Clarkston, WA 99403 US
(208) 743-6564, *Fax:* (208) 798-0110
evanyeoman@pacempire.com
License: Clarkston, Asotin County, WA
Group Owner: Pacific Empire Radio Corp.; (acq 9-12-2008; grpsl)
Arbitron Metro Market: Lewiston, ID *Format:* Contemporary Hits/Top 40, Adult Contemp *Target Audience:* 25 plus.
Mark Bolland, President
Evan Yeoman, Programming Director
Dave Forsman, Chief Engineer

***KNWV**
07-11-1995; 90.5 mhz FM *Hrs Open:* 24; 0.42 kw; 1056 ft.; N46 27 26 W117 6 0 *Rebroadcasts:* Rebroadcasts KRFA-FM Moscow, ID 100%
PO Box 642530, Pullman, WA 99164 US
(509) 335-6500, *Fax:* (509) 335-3772
www.nwpr.org
nwpr@wsu.edu
License: Clarkston, Asotin County, WA held by Washington State University.
Format: News *Hrs. of News Programming:* news progmg 37 hrs wkly *No. News Employees:* 1
Karen Olstad, COO
Scott Weatherly, Operations Dir
Dennis Haarsager, General Manager
Roger Johnson, Station Manager
Sarah McDaniel, General Sales Mgr
Mary Hawkins, Programming Director
Rachael McDonald, News Director
RalphHogan, Engineering Dir
Robin Rilette, Music Director

KVAB
07-15-1997; 102.9 mhz FM *Hrs Open:* 24; 0.44 kw; 1171 ft.; N46 27 27 W117 6 3
P.O. Box 669, Clarkston, WA 99403 US
(509) 758-3361, *Fax:* (509) 758-4986
kvabfm.com
kvabfm@aol.com
License: Clarkston, Asotin County, WA held by Bolland Enterprises LLC.
Group Owner: Bolland Enterprises LLC; (acq 9-12-2008; grpsl)
Nat'l Network: Westwood One *Nat'l Reps:* Tacher
Arbitron Metro Market: Clarkston, WA *Format:* Classic Rock
Target Audience: 25-55.
Mark Bolland, CEO
Jay Mlazgar, General Manager
Mark Bone, Programming Director

***KUCC**
88.1 mhz FM; 0.24 kw; 453 ft.; N46 27 47 W116 54 25
P O Box 19039, Spokane, WA 99219 US
(509) 838-2761, *Fax:* (509) 456-4870
www.uccsda.org/communications
LidiaR@uccsda.org
License: Clarkston, Asotin County, WA held by Upper Columbia Media Association.
Arbitron Metro Market: Clarkston, WA *Format:* Religious
Bob Folkenberg, Jr., President
Lauren Adams, General Manager
Darin Patzer, Station Manager
Cindy Williams, Programming Director
Jay Wintermeyer, Communications Director/Media Relations
Randall Terry, VP for Finance
Doug Johnson,VP for Administration
Jay Wintermeyer, Director
Jon Dalrymple, Communications Assistant
Kathy Marson, Administrative Assistant

Cle Elum

KXAA
11-01-2002; 93.7 mhz FM *Hrs Open:* 24; 6 kw; 95 ft.; N47 9 6 W120 47 23
717 NE12th Street, East Wenatchee, WA 98802 US
(509) 662-3842, *Fax:* (509) 662-2482
www.kxa937.com
nwheeler@nwi.net
License: Cle Elum, Kittitas County, WA held by Wheeler Broadcasting Inc.
Group Owner: Wheeler Broadcasting Inc.; acq 5-28-2004; exercise of option).
Nat'l Network: Jones Radio Networks
Arbitron Metro Market: Cle Elum, WA *Format:* Contemporary Hits/Top 40, Adult Contemp
Jeri Trantham, Operations Dir
Mark Wheeler, General Sales Mgr
Nel Wheeler, National & Political Sales Manager
Bill Hansen, Local Sales

Colfax

KCLX
01-01-1950; 1450 khz AM
P.O. Box 710, Colfax, WA 99111 US
(509) 397-3441
www.palousecountry.com
info@palousecountry.com
License: Colfax, WA held by Inland Northwest Broadcasting LLC
Group Owner: Inland Northwest Broadcasting LLC
Nat'l Reps: Farmakis
Arbitron Metro Market: Spokane, WA *Format:* Country *Special Programming:* Farm 5 hrs, sports 7 hrs wkly *Target Audience:* 25 plus; agricultural-urban *Adv. Rates:* Same as FM
Gary Cummings, General Manager
Robert Hauser, General Sales Mgr
Steve Grubbs, Programming Director

KMAX
01-01-1998; 840 khz AM *Hrs Open:* 24; 10 kw-D, ND2; 0.28 kw-N, ND2; N46 54 50 W117 19 28
Post Office Box 710, Colfax, WA 99111 US
(208) 882-2551, *Fax:* (208) 883-3571
hauser@inlandradio.com
License: Colfax, WA held by Inland Northwest Broadcasting LLC.
Group Owner: Inland Northwest Broadcasting LLC; (acq 6-28-2005; grpsl)
Nat'l Network: Westwood One
Format: Talk *Hrs. of News Programming:* news progmg 15 hrs wkly *No. News Employees:* 2 *Target Audience:* 25-60; established professional aged people - young marrieds couples
Adv. Rates: 21; 19; 19; 15
Gary Cummings, General Manager
Ben Bonfield, General Sales Mgr
Darin Sievert, Programming Director
Glen Vaagen, News Director
Steve Franko, Chief Engineer

KRAO-FM
10-10-1994; 102.5 mhz FM *Hrs Open:* 24; 2.2 kw; 1079 ft.; N46 51 44 W117 10 20
P.O. Box 710, Colfax, WA 99111 US
(208) 882-2551, *Fax:* (208) 883-3571
License: Colfax, Whitman County, WA held by Inland Northwest Broadcasting LLC
Group Owner: Inland Northwest Broadcasting LLC; (acq 6-28-2005; grpsl)
Format: Adult Contemp *Target Audience:* 18-45. *Adv. Rates:* 23.80; 23.80; 23.80; 17
Gary Cummings, General Manager
Johnny Mann, Programming Director
Steve Franco, Chief Engineer

College Place

***KGTS**
10-05-1963; 91.3 mhz FM *Hrs Open:* 24; 7 kw; 1250 ft.; N45 59 20 W118 10 29
204 South College, College Place, WA 99324 US
(509) 527-2991, *Fax:* (509) 527-2611
www.plr.org
studio@plr.org
License: College Place, Walla Walla County, WA held by Walla Walla College.
Format: Christian *Special Programming:* Family 30 hrs wkly, church service varies *Target Audience:* 35-64.
Jon Dybdahl, President
Don Godman, Operations Dir
Kevin Krueger, General Manager
Elizabeth Nelson, Programming Director
Walter Cox, Chief Engineer

Colville

KCRK-FM
10-13-1981; 92.1 mhz FM *Hrs Open:* 24; 5.4 kw; 344 ft.; N48 34 30 W117 55 0
Mailing Address: Box 111, Colville, WA 99114 US
Second Address: 187 Mantz & Ricky Rd., Colville, WA 99114
(509) 684-5032, *Fax:* (509) 684-5034
www.kclv.com
License: Colville, Stevens County, WA held by North Country Broadcasting.
Nat'l Network: Westwood One
Format: Adult Contemp
Mike Newport, Operations Dir
Ruth Seymour, General Manager
Jennifer Ferro, Station Manager
David Kleinbart, General Sales Mgr

KCVL
11-15-1955; 1240 khz AM *Hrs Open:* 24; 1 kw-U, ND1; N48 31 15 W117 54 28
P.O. Box 111, Colville, WA 99114 US
(509) 684-5031, *Fax:* (509) 684-5034
www.kcvl.com
info@kcvl.com
License: Colville, WA held by North Country Broadcasting.
Arbitron Metro Market: Colville, WA *Format:* Country
Eric Carpenter, President
Mike Eakins, General Sales Mgr

Cosmopolis

KLSY
01-01-2008; 107.3 mhz FM; 0.79 kw; 906 ft.; N46 41 44 W123 46 17
US
(360) 918-9000, *Fax:* (360) 704-3146
License: Cosmopolis, Pacific County, WA held by South Sound Broadcasting LLC.
Arbitron Metro Market: Cosmopolis, WA *Format:* Classic Rock
Bill Bradley, General Manager

Covington

KMCQ
11-28-1968; 104.5 mhz FM *Hrs Open:* 24; 7.1 kw; 1273 ft.; N47 32 35 W122 6 25
P.O. Box 104, The Dalles, OR 97058 US
(541) 298-5116, *Fax:* (541) 298-5119
www.q104radio.com
q104@q104radio.com

License: Covington, Wasco County, WA held by First Broadcasting Capital Partners LLC.
Group Owner: First Broadcasting Operating Inc.; (acq 3-22-2007; $5.1 million)
Nat'l Network: CNN Radio *Nat'l Reps:* McGavren Guild
Format: Adult Contemp *Special Programming:* Blues 4 hrs, teen show 3 hrs wkly *Hrs. of News Programming:* news progmg 7 hrs wkly *No. News Employees:* 1 *Target Audience:* Females 25-49; mothers & family friendly*Adv. Rates:* 18; 18; 16
Gary Lawrence, President
John Huffman, Operations Dir
Linda Griswold, General Sales Mgr
Paula Fairclo, Operations Director

Davenport

***KKRS**
01-01-1998; 97.3 mhz FM *Hrs Open:* 24; 5.1 kw; 722 ft.; N47 35 14 W117 53 26
3000 West Macarthur, Third Floor, Santa Ana, CA 92704 US
(509) 244-5577, *Fax:* (509) 244-2232
kkrs@csnradio.com
License: Davenport, Lincoln County, WA held by CSN International.
Group Owner: CSN International; acq 1999; $111,425).
Format: Christian, Talk
Barney Dasovich, General Manager

Dayton

KZHR
08-01-1992; 92.5 mhz FM *Hrs Open:* 24; 54 kw; 1243 ft.; N45 59 19 W118 10 28
Mailing Address: Hc-11 Box N, Prescott, WA 99348 US
Second Address: 2823 W. Lewis St., Pasco, WA 99301
(509) 546-0313, *Fax:* (509) 546-2678
www.kzhr.com
gonzalo@kzhr.com
License: Dayton, Columbia County, WA held by CCR-Tri Cities IV LLC.
Group Owner: Cherry Creek Radio LLC; (acq 12-19-2003; grpsl).
Nat'l Reps: Interep; McGavren Guild
Arbitron Metro Market: Dayton, WA *Format:* Tejano *Hrs. of News Programming:* news progmg 7 hrs wkly *No. News Employees:* 1 *Target Audience:* 25-54; adult *Adv. Rates:* 23; 23; 16; na
Scott Smith, General Manager
Gonzalo Cortez, Station Manager
Daena Medina, News Director
Art Blum, Chief Engineer

Deer Park

KAZZ
09-01-1983; 107.1 mhz FM; 25 kw; Ant 328 ft; N48 01 45 W117 35 57
Box 28846, Spokane, WA 99006
(415) 729-5651
License: Deer Park, Spokane County, WA held by Spokane Broadcasting Co
Arbitron Metro Market: Spokane, WA

Dishman

KEYF
10-03-1984; 1050 khz AM *Hrs Open:* 24
City Center West 7201 W. Lake Mead Blvd, Suite 400, Las Vegas, NV 89128 US
(509) 448-1000, *Fax:* (509) 448-7015
License: Dishman, WA held by Mapleton License of Spokane LLC.
Group Owner: Mapleton Communications LLC; (acq 12-3-2007; grpsl)
Arbitron Metro Market: Spokane, WA *Format:* Adult Contemp *Hrs. of News Programming:* News progmg 15 hrs wkly *Target Audience:* 54 plus.
Don Morin, General Manager
Bob Castle, Programming Director
Larry Weir, News Director
Dave Ratener, Chief Engineer
Brenda Anderson, Traffic Manager

KSPO
01-01-1996; 106.5 mhz FM *Hrs Open:* 24; 2.25 kw; 528 ft.; N47 41 39 W117 20 3
P.O. Box 31000, Spokane, WA 99223 US
(509) 443-1000
www.kspo.com
acn@acn.cc
License: Dishman, Spokane County, WA held by Thomas W. Read dba Classical Broadcasting.
Nat'l Network: USA; Salem Radio Network
Arbitron Metro Market: Spokane, WA *Format:* Talk, Religious *Target Audience:* 35 plus.
Thomas Read, President
Melinda Read, Operations Dir

East Wenatchee

KYSN
12-25-1980; 97.7 mhz FM *Hrs Open:* 24; 6 kw; -98 ft.; N47 22 51 W120 17 15
N 1212 Washington, Suite 307, Spokane, WA 99201 US
(509) 663-1671, *Fax:* (509) 663-1150
www.kysn.com
production@nw-tel.net
License: East Wenatchee, Chelan County, WA held by CCR-Wenatchee IV LLC.
Group Owner: Cherry Creek Radio LLC; (acq 10-31-2006; grpsl)
Arbitron Metro Market: East Wenatchee, WA *Format:* Country *Special Programming:* Farm one hr, relg one hr wkly *Hrs. of News Programming:* news progmg 20 hrs wkly *No. News Employees:* 1 *Target Audience:* 25-54.
Todd Allen, Operations Dir
Steven Miller, General Manager
Leona Frank, General Sales Mgr
John Ross, Programming Director
Dave Bernstein, News Director
Manuel Garcia, Chief Engineer
Lisa Rodriguez, Traffic Manager

***KLUW**
01-01-2008; 88.1 mhz FM; 0.6 kw; -131 ft.; N47 22 52 W120 17 16 *Rebroadcasts:* Rebroadcasts KLVR(FM) Middletown, CA 100%
P.O. Box 31000, Spokane, WA 99223 US
(800) 877-5600, *Fax:* (916) 251-1650
www.klove.com
License: East Wenatchee, Chelan County, WA held by Educational Media Foundation.
Group Owner: EMF Broadcasting; (acq 2-11-2008; $100,000 for CP)
Nat'l Network: K-Love
Arbitron Metro Market: East Wenatchee, WA *Format:* Christian
Michael Novak, President

Eatonville

KKBW
01-01-1995; 104.9 mhz FM *Hrs Open:* 24; 17 kw; Ant 407 ft; N46 50 24 W122 15 27
351 Elliott Ave. W., 3rd Fl., Seattle, WA 98037
(206) 494-2000, *Fax:* (206) 286-2376
www.funkymonkey1049.fm
bobcase@clearchannel.com
License: Eatonville, Pierce County, WA held by Ackerley Broadcasting Operations LLC.
Group Owner: Clear Channel Communications Inc.; (acq 2-12-2003; $4.5 million).
Population Served: 250,000 *Arbitron Metro Market:* Seattle-Tacoma, WA
Bob Case, Operations Dir
Michele Grosenick, General Manager
Allison Hesse, General Sales Mgr
Jay Kelly, Programming Director
Steven Kilbreath, News Director
Doug Irwin, Chief Engineer

Edmonds

KCIS
01-01-1954; 630 khz AM *Hrs Open:* 24; 5 kw-D, 2.5 kw-N, DA-N; N47 46 06 W122 21 07
19303 Fremont Ave. N., Seattle, WA 98133
(206) 546-7350,(206) 546-7372
www.kcisradio.com
comments@kcisradio.com
License: Edmonds, Snohomish County, WA held by CRISTA Ministries
Group Owner: CRISTA Broadcasting
Nat'l Network: USA; Moody; AP Radio *Wire Services:* AP; U.S. Newswire
Population Served: 29,200 *Arbitron Metro Market:* Seattle-Tacoma, WA *Hrs. of News Programming:* news progmg 40 hrs wkly *No. News Employees:* 1 *Target Audience:* 45-64. *Adv. Rates:* Call for rates
Stan Mak, Vice President
Ann Marie Norman, Director of Sales
Mark Holland, Programming Director
Camille Birk, Promotions & Marketing Director
Keith Black, News Director
Bryan Hubert, Chief Engineer

KCMS
03-11-1960; 105.3 mhz FM *Hrs Open:* 24; 54 kw; Ant 1,263 ft; N47 32 40 W122 06 26
19303 Fremont Ave. N., Seattle, WA 98133
(206) 546-7350, *Fax:* (206) 546-7372
www.spirit1053.com
comments@spirit1053.com
License: Edmonds, Snohomish County, WA held by CRISTA Ministries
Group Owner: CRISTA Broadcasting
Wire Services: AP; U.S. Newswire
Population Served: 300,000 *Arbitron Metro Market:* Seattle-Tacoma, WA *Hrs. of News Programming:* News progmg one hr wkly *Target Audience:* 25-44. *Adv. Rates:* 300; 250; 275; 150
Stan Mak, Vice President/Crista Broadcasting
Ann Marie Mulholland, Sales Director
Camille Birk, Promotions and Marketing Director
Keith Black, News Director
Bryan Hubert, Chief Engineer

Ellensburg

***KCSH**
01-01-1998; 88.9 mhz FM; 0.38 kw; 548 ft.; N47 10 2 W120 45 50
402 E. Yakima Avenue, Suite 1320, Yakima, WA 98901 US
(509) 964-2061, *Fax:* (509) 964-2825
www.lifetalk.net
info@kcshfm.com
License: Ellensburg, Kittitas County, WA held by Lifetalk Broadcasting Association.
Arbitron Metro Market: Ellensburg, WA *Format:* Religious
Philip Follet, CEO
Kermit Netteburg, President
John Geli, Operations Dir
Don Zacharias, General Manager
Marcelo Vallado, Chief Engineer
Coleen Dolinsky, Treasurer
Connie Jeffery, Administration

***KCWU**
04-30-1999; 88.1 mhz FM *Hrs Open:* 24; 0.5 kw; -194 ft.; N47 0 21 W120 30 55
400 E 8th Avenue, Ellensburg, WA 98926 US
(509) 963-2283 2282, *Fax:* (509) 963-1688
www.881theburg.com
kcwu@cwu.edu
License: Ellensburg, Kittitas County, WA held by Trustees of Central Washington University.
Arbitron Metro Market: Ellensburg, WA *Format:* Alternative, Variety/Diverse *Hrs. of News Programming:* News progmg 5 hrs wkly *Target Audience:* 15-49; 18-34 core
Chris Hull, General Manager
John Cerney, Programming Director
Kurt Oberloh, Broadcast Technician

***KNWR**
06-01-1992; 90.7 mhz FM *Hrs Open:* 24; 4.6 kw; 2549 ft.; N47 15 48 W120 23 31 *Rebroadcasts:* Rebroadcasts KRFA-FM Moscow, ID 100%
PO Box 642530, Pullman, WA 99164 US
(509) 335-6500, *Fax:* (509) 335-3772
www.nwpr.org
nwpr@wsu.edu
License: Ellensburg, Kittitas County, WA held by Washington State University.
Nat'l Network: NPR; PRI
Format: News *Special Programming:* Jazz, folk *Hrs. of News Programming:* news progmg 37 hrs wkly *No. News Employees:* 1 *Target Audience:* General.
Karen Olstad, COO
Scott Weatherly, Operations Dir
Dennis Haarsager, General Manager
Roger Johnson, Station Manager
Sarah McDaniel, General Sales Mgr
Mary Hawkins, Programming Director
Rachael McDonald, News Director
RalphHogan, Engineering Dir
Robin Rilette, Music Director

KXLE
01-01-1946; 1240 khz AM *Hrs Open:* 24
2111 Sixth Ave N, Ste 200, Seattle, WA 98109 US
(509) 925-1488, *Fax:* (509) 962-7882
www.kxleradio.com
kxle@fairport.net
License: Ellensburg, WA held by KXLE Inc.
Nat'l Network: CBS *Nat'l Reps:* Tacher *Wire Services:* AP
Arbitron Metro Market: Ellensburg, WA *Format:* News, News/Talk, 84, Talk *Hrs. of News Programming:* news progmg

RADIO - U.S.

40 hrs wkly *No. News Employees:* 4 *Target Audience:* 25-54; adults *Adv. Rates:* 240; 240; 240;200
Sol Tacher, President
Brad Tacher, Operations Dir
Patti Burke, Promotions Manager
Dennis Leach, News Director
Kevin Whitaker, Engineering Dir
Frances Moen, Traffic Manager

Elma

KDDS-FM
01-01-1981; 99.3 mhz FM; 64 kw; 2434 ft.; N47 18 46 W123 22 15
13612 Northwest 37th Place, Bellevue, WA 98005 US
(253) 735-9700, *Fax:* (253) 735-7424
www.radiolagrand.com
License: Elma, Grays Harbor County, WA
Group Owner: Adelante Media Group LLC; (acq 9-28-2005; $20 million).
Arbitron Metro Market: Seattle, WA
Amador Bustos, President
Jose Diaz, General Manager
Cesar Valdiosera, Programming Director

Enumclaw

KGRG
03-01-1992; 1330 khz AM *Hrs Open:* 24; 0.5 kw-D, ND1; 0.026 kw-N, ND1; N47 12 53 W121 58 19
12401 S.E. 320th Street, Auburn, WA 98002 US
(253) 833-5004, *Fax:* (253) 288-3460
www.kgrg1.com
programing@kgrg.com
License: Enumclaw, WA held by Green River Foundation
Arbitron Metro Market: Auburn, WA *Format:* Alternative *Adv. Rates:* 21.25; 18.75; 20; 12
Tom Evans Krause, General Manager

Ephrata

KTAC
01-01-1998; 93.9 mhz FM *Hrs Open:* 24; 18 kw; 384 ft.; N47 19 13 W119 34 22 *Rebroadcasts:* Simulcast with KTBI(AM) Ephrata
P.O. Box 31000, Spokane, WA 99223 US
(509) 754-2000, *Fax:* (509) 448-3811
www.ktac.com
ktac@ktac.com
License: Ephrata, Grant County, WA held by TRMR Inc.
Arbitron Metro Market: Spokane, WA
Richard Bott II, President
Pat Rulon, General Sales Mgr
Candy Green, Programming Director
Rachel Moser, Promotions Manager
Jason Potocnik, News Director
John Tillman-Production Manager

KTBI
08-17-1950; 810 khz AM *Hrs Open:* Sunrise-sunset; 23 kw-C, NDD; 50 kw-D, NDD; N47 21 22 W119 28 56 *Rebroadcasts:* Simulcast with KTAC(FM) Ephrata
P.O. Box 31000, Spokane, WA 99223 US
(509) 754-2000, *Fax:* (509) 448-3811
www.ktbi.com
ktbi@ktbi.com
License: Ephrata, WA held by Tacoma Broadcasters Inc.
Arbitron Metro Market: Spokane, WA *Format:* Talk, Religious
Special Programming: Farm 15 hrs wkly *Target Audience:* 35 plus.
Thomas Read, President
Melinda Read, Operations Dir
George Frese, Engineering Dir
John Tillman, Operations Manager

KULE
01-01-1952; 730 khz AM
Mailing Address: 910 Basin Street, Sw, Ephrata, WA 98823 US
Second Address: 910 Basin S.W., Ephrata, WA 98823
(509) 457-1000, *Fax:* (509) 452-0541
www.radiozorro.com
zorro@radiozorro.com
License: Ephrata, WA
Group Owner: Adelante Media Group LLC; (acq 11-18-2004; grpsl).
Nat'l Network: Westwood One; CBS
Arbitron Metro Market: Ephrata, WA *Format:* News, News/Talk, 84, Talk *Special Programming:* Farm 1 hr wkly *Hrs. of News Programming:* news progmg 20 hrs wkly *No. News Employees:* 1 *Target Audience:* 25-54.*Adv. Rates:* 10; 10; 10; 10
Amador Bustos, President
Keith Teske, Operations Dir
Bob Berry, General Manager
Martin Ortiz, Programming Director
Judith McInnis, Promotions Manager

KULE-FM
12-25-1982; 92.3 mhz FM; 26 kw; 673 ft.; N47 18 18 W119 35 53
Mailing Address: 910 Basin Street, Sw, Ephrata, WA 98823 US
Second Address: 910 Basin S.W., Ephrata, WA 98823
(509) 457-1000, *Fax:* (509) 754-4110
www.radiozorro.com
kule@kule.com
License: Ephrata, Grant County, WA
Group Owner: Adelante Media Group LLC
Nat'l Network: CBS
Arbitron Metro Market: Ephrata, WA *Format:* Country
Keith Teske, Operations Dir
Bob Berry, General Manager
Tom Vinup, News Director

Everett

KRKO
08-01-1920; 1380 khz AM *Hrs Open:* 24; 5 kw-D, DAN; 5 kw-N, DAN; N47 55 32 W122 11 19
Suite 1380, 2707 Colby Avenue, Everett, WA 98201 US
(425) 304-1381, *Fax:* (425) 304-1382
www.krko.com
andrew.skotdal@krko.com
License: Everett, WA held by S - R Broadcasting Co., Inc.
Nat'l Network: Westwood One; Fox Sports
Arbitron Metro Market: Seattle Metro area *Format:* Sports *Hrs. of News Programming:* news progmg 24 hrs wkly *No. News Employees:* 1 *Target Audience:* Men 25-54; residents of Northern Puget Sound *Adv. Rates:* 80; 50; 50; 25
Andrew Skotdal, President
Andy Skotdal, Operations Dir
Melene Thompson, General Sales Mgr

*KSER
02-09-1991; 90.7 mhz FM *Hrs Open:* 24; 5.8 kw; 302 ft.; N48 1 28 W122 6 41
14920 Highway 99, # 150, Lynwood, WA 98037 US
(425) 303-9070, *Fax:* (425) 303-9075
www.kser.org
info@kser.com
License: Everett, Snohomish County, WA held by KSER Foundation.
Nat'l Network: PRI
Arbitron Metro Market: Everett, WA *Format:* Variety/Diverse
Special Programming: American Indian 2 hrs, folk 2 hrs, jazz 2 hrs, reggae 2 hrs, blues 6 hrs wkly *Hrs. of News Programming:* news progmg 17 hrs wkly *No.News Employees:* 1 *Target Audience:* General; public radio *Adv. Rates:* 25; 25; 25; 25
Bruce Wirth, General Manager
Tom Clendening, Station Manager
Chris Wartes, Chief Engineer

KWYZ
07-21-1957; 1230 khz AM; 1 kw-U, ND1; N47 58 6 W122 10 24
Rebroadcasts: Rebroadcasts KSUH(AM) Puyallup
15422 Third Place West, Lynnwood, WA 98037 US
(253) 815-1212, *Fax:* (253) 815-1913
www.radiohankook.com
License: Everett, WA held by Jean J. Suh dba Radio Hankook.
Nat'l Reps: Roslin
Arbitron Metro Market: Federal Way, WA *Format:* Korean
Sung Hong, General Manager

Ferndale

KRPI
05-01-1963; 1550 khz AM *Hrs Open:* 24; 50 kw-D, DA2; 10 kw-N, DA2; N48 50 35 W122 36 5
Mailing Address: PO Box 847, Ferndale, CA 98248 US
Second Address: 5538 Imhoff Rd., Ferndale, WA 98248
(360) 384-5117, *Fax:* (360) 380-4202
www.krpiradio.com
grace@krpiradio.com
License: Ferndale, WA held by BBC Broadcasting Inc.
Arbitron Metro Market: Ferndale, WA *Format:* Ethnic *Hrs. of News Programming:* News progmg 14 hrs wkly *Target Audience:* 35 plus; East Indian adults *Adv. Rates:* 21; 21; 25; 15
Suki Badh, General Manager
Grace Phelan, Station Manager

Forks

KBDB-FM
01-01-1985; 96.7 mhz FM; 6 kw; -75 ft.; N47 57 14 W124 23 20
PO Box 450, Forks, WA 98331 US
(360) 374-6233, *Fax:* (360) 374-6852
License: Forks, Clallam County, WA held by First Broadcasting Investment Partners LLC
Group Owner: First Broadcasting Operating Inc.
Format: Contemporary Hits/Top 40
Marvin Sanders, General Manager

KRKZ
10-01-1967; 1490 khz AM *Hrs Open:* 24; 1 kw-U; N47 57 16 W124 23 20
Mailing Address: Box 450, Forks, WA 98331
Second Address: 260 Cedar, Forks, WA 9833331
(360) 374-6233, *Fax:* (360) 374-6852
kllm@centurytel.net
License: Forks, Clallam County, WA held by First Broadcasting Investment Partners LLC.
Group Owner: First Broadcasting Operating Inc.; (acq 12-18-2003; $300,000 with co-located FM).
Regional Reps: Tacher.
Special Programming: NFL, Sonics, college & high school football, Mariners 20 hrs, gospel 6.5 hrs wkly *Hrs. of News Programming:* news progmg 2 hrs wkly *No. News Employees:* 2
Target Audience: 25-54; general
Gary Lawrence, President
Al Monroe, General Manager
Marcia Nearhoff, General Sales Mgr
Arthur George, Min Affairs Director

*KNWU
91.5 mhz FM; 0.17 kw; -7 ft.; N47 56 0 W124 23 41 US
(509) 335-6500, *Fax:* (509) 335-6577
www.nwpr.org
nwpr@wsu.edu
License: Forks, Clallam County, WA held by Washington State University.
Arbitron Metro Market: Forks, WA *Format:* Classical
Tony Wright, General Manager
Kerry Swanson, Station Manager
John Paxson, News Director
Aki Wright, Development Coordinator
Gillian Coldsnow, Assistant Manager of Programming and Operations
Kevin Rinker, Traffic Manager
SarahMcDaniel, Membership Director

Friday Harbor

*KSJU
91.9 mhz FM; 0.1 kw; 82 ft.; N48 31 21 W123 1 36 US
(360) 378-3779
License: Friday Harbor, San Juan County, WA held by San Juan Island Community Radio.
Arbitron Metro Market: Friday Harbor, WA
Michael Calhoun, President

Gig Harbor

*KGHP
08-30-1988; 89.9 mhz FM *Hrs Open:* 24; 1.35 kw horiz, 0.8 kw vert; 200 ft.; N47 14 27 W122 46 16
14015 62nd Ave., NW, Gig Harbor, WA 98332 US
(253) 857-3513, *Fax:* (253) 853-5841
www.kghp.wednet.edu
abersolds@psd401.net
License: Gig Harbor, Pierce County, WA held by Peninsula School District No. 401.
Format: Easy Listening *Special Programming:* jazz 5 hr wkly, reggae 5 hrs wkly, radio horror classics 2 hrs wkly, book club 2 hr wkly *Hrs. of News Programming:* News progmg 10 hrs wkly
Target Audience: General;diverse community audience *Adv. Rates:* 100; 75; 100; 50
Leland Smith, General Manager
Spencer Abersold, Station Manager
Theresa Evans, Programming Director
Keith Stiles, Chief Engineer

Glenoma

*KGHE
89.1 mhz FM; 225 watts; 94 meters; N46 32 37 W122 03 36
2200 Simpson Ave., Hoquiam, WA
(360) 705-0619
www.nwindy.org
License: Glenoma, Lewis County, WA held by Northwest Indy Radio.

Stephen Lepisto, President

Goldendale

KLCK
09-04-1984; 1400 khz AM
P. O. Box 305, Goldendale, WA 98620 US

(541) 296-9102, *Fax:* (541) 298-7775
www.klck1400.com
klck@gorge.net
License: Goldendale, WA held by Klickitat Valley Broadcasting Services Inc.
Arbitron Metro Market: Yakima, WA *Format:* Oldies
Danny Manciu, President
Jeanne Malcolm, General Sales Mgr
Kevin Malcolm, Programming Director
Julian Notestine, News Director
Cole Malcolm, Chief Engineer

KYYT
01-06-1992; 102.3 mhz FM; 2.1 kw; 1873 ft.; N45 40 53 W120 54 30
Mailing Address: P.O. Box 305, Goldendale, WA 98620 US
Second Address: 620 E. 3rd St., The Dalles, WA 97058
(541) 296-9102, *Fax:* (541) 298-7775
www.y102country.com
kyyt@gorge.net
License: Goldendale, Klickitat County, WA held by Haystack Broadcasting Inc.
Arbitron Metro Market: Goldendale, WA *Format:* Country
Danny Manciu, President
Betsy Hadden, General Sales Mgr
Kevin Malcolm, Programming Director

Grand Coulee

KEYG
01-01-1979; 1490 khz AM *Hrs Open:* 24
P.O. Drawer K, Grand Coulee, WA 99133 US
(509) 633-2020(509) 633-1490, *Fax:* (509) 633-1014
www.keyg985.com
keygfm@nwi.net
License: Grand Coulee, WA held by Wheeler Broadcasting Inc.
Group Owner: Wheeler Broadcasting Inc.; (acq 12-6-85)
Arbitron Metro Market: Grand Coulee, WA *Format:* Country
Special Programming: Class 4 hrs, mus to remember 4 hrs, big band 4 hrs wkly *Hrs. of News Programming:* news progmg 4 hrs wkly *No. News Employees:* 1*Target Audience:* 25 plus.
Verl Wheeler, CEO
Mark Wheeler, General Manager
Mark Wheeler, General Sales Mgr
Mike Helgerson, Chief Engineer
Nel Wheeler, National and Political Sales Manager

KEYG-FM
02-10-1984; 98.5 mhz FM *Hrs Open:* 24; 100 kw horiz, 85 kw vert; 994 ft.; N47 49 18 W118 55 59
Drawer K, Grand Coulee, WA 99133 US
(509) 633-2020(509) 633-1490, *Fax:* (509) 633-1014
www.keyg985.com
keygfm@nwi.net
License: Grand Coulee, Grant County, WA held by Wheeler Broadcasting Inc.
Group Owner: Wheeler Broadcasting Inc.
Arbitron Metro Market: Grand Coulee, WA *Format:* Contemporary Hits/Top 40, Adult Contemp
Don Morin, General Manager
Mark Wheeler, General Sales Mgr
Tim Cotter, Programming Director
Larry Weir, News Director
Dave Ratener, Chief Engineer
Brenda Anderson, Traffic Manager
National and Political Sales Manager

Grandview

KARY-FM
08-21-1989; 100.9 mhz FM *Hrs Open:* 24; 7.8 kw; Ant 1,210 ft; N46 29 12 W120 00 05
1200 Chesterly Dr., Suite 160, Yakima, WA 98006
(509) 248-2900, *Fax:* (509) 452-9661
cherryfm.com
info@cherryfm.com
License: Grandview, Yakima County, WA held by James D Ingstad
Group Owner: James D. Ingstad Stns; acq 10-20-98; grpsl).
Population Served: 140,000 *Arbitron Metro Market:* Yakima, WA
Special Programming: Relg 8 hrs wkly *Target Audience:* 25-54.
Adv. Rates: 28; 28; 28; 20
Pete Benedetti, CEO
Joe Benedetti, General Manager
Kevin Miskimins, General Sales Mgr
Dewey Boynton, Programming Director

Hamilton

***KSVU**
90.1 mhz FM; 0.33 kw; -522 ft.; N48 33 16 W121 47 40 US
(360) 416-7711, *Fax:* (360) 416-7822
www.ksvr.org
mail@ksvr.org
License: Hamilton, Skagit County, WA held by Board of Trustees of Skagit Valley College.
Arbitron Metro Market: Hamilton, WA
Rip Robbins, General Manager
Dave McConnell, Station Manager
Joseph C. McGuire, Production Manager

Hoquiam

KWOK
11-16-1961; 1490 khz AM *Hrs Open:* 24
120 State Ave N. E., Mb 95, Olympia, WA 98501 US
(360) 533-1320, *Fax:* (360) 532-0935
License: Hoquiam, WA held by Morris Communications Corp.
Group Owner: Morris Radio LLC; (acq 2-18-00; $650,000 with KXXK(FM) Hoquiam-Aberdeen)
Format: Sports, Talk *Target Audience:* 26-65.
Pat Anderson, Operations Dir
Donna Rosi, General Manager
Donna Rosa, General Sales Mgr
Harvey Brooks, Chief Engineer

KXXK
09-03-1965; 95.3 mhz FM *Hrs Open:* 24; 3.5 kw; 423 ft.; N46 55 55 W123 44 4
120 State Avenue, Ne, Mb 95, Olympia, WA 98501 US
(360) 533-1320, *Fax:* (360) 532-0935
1
License: Hoquiam, Grays Harbor County, WA held by Morris Communications Corp.
Group Owner: Morris Radio LLC; (acq 2-18-00; $650,000 with KWOK(AM) Hoquiam)
Format: Country *Target Audience:* 26-54.
Patrick Anderson, Operations Dir
Donna Rosi, General Manager
Ian Cope, News Director
Harvey Brooks, Chief Engineer

Ilwaco

KVAS-FM
01-01-2000; 103.9 mhz FM; 10 kw; Ant 171 ft; N46 18 51 W124 03 07
1006 W. Marine Dr., Astoria, OR 97210
(503) 325-2911, *Fax:* (503) 325-5570
www.kvasfm.com
kvas@newnw.com
License: Ilwaco, Pacific County, WA
Group Owner: Ohana Media Group LLC; acq 8-25-99; $250,000 for CP).
Tom Freel, Operations Dir
Paul Mitchell, General Manager
Brian Riffe, General Sales Mgr

Kelso

KLOG
10-08-1949; 1490 khz AM *Hrs Open:* 24; 1 kw-U, ND1; N46 7 0 W122 53 7
Mailing Address: P.O. Box 90, Kelso, WA 98626 US
Second Address: 506 Cowlitz Way W., Kelso, WA 98626
(360) 636-0110, *Fax:* (360) 577-6949
www.klog.com
info@klog.com
License: Kelso, WA held by Washington Interstate Broadcasting Co. Inc.
Arbitron Metro Market: Portland, OR *Format:* Adult Contemp *No. News Employees:* 2 *Target Audience:* 25-54.
Joel Hanson, General Manager
Bill Dodd, Programming Director

KLYK
08-07-1991; 94.5 mhz FM *Hrs Open:* 24; 3 kw; 476 ft.; N46 16 49 W122 52 34
P. O. Box 90, Kelso, WA 98626 US
(360) 425-1500, *Fax:* (360) 423-1554
www.todaysbesthits.com
License: Kelso, Cowlitz County, WA held by Bicoastal Media Licenses IV LLC.
Group Owner: Bicoastal Media L.L.C.; (acq 3-31-2005; grpsl)
Nat'l Network: Westwood One
Arbitron Metro Market: Kelso, WA *Format:* Adult Contemp *Hrs. of News Programming:* News progmg 2 hrs wkly *Target Audience:* 18-49.
Gayle Kessinger, Programming Director

***KTJC**
01-01-2004; 91.1 mhz FM; 0.017 kw horiz, 8 kw vert; 620 ft.; N46 19 46 W122 57 50
3000 West Macarthur Blvd, Santa Ana, CA 92704 US
(800) 357-4226, *Fax:* (208) 736-1958
www.csnradio.com
csn@csnradio.com
License: Kelso, Cowlitz County, WA held by CSN International
Group Owner: CSN International
Arbitron Metro Market: Portland, OR *Format:* Christian
Mike Kestler, President
Daniel Davidson, Operations Dir
Lee Flory, Station Manager
Don Mills, Network Programming Director / Music Director
Kelly Carlson, Engineering Dir
Jerry Johnson, Engineering Dir
Ray Gorney, AssistantDirector of Engineering
Dustin Pamplona, Engineer
Nolan Mather, Graphics / Website Maintenance
Mike Stocklin, National Underwriting
Austin Morris, Accounting
Lois Mills, FCC Applications / Translator Site Manager

Kennewick

***KBLD**
01-01-1998; 91.7 mhz FM; 1.8 kw; 971 ft.; N46 4 58 W119 9 39
3000 W. Macarthur Blvd., Santa Ana, CA 92704 US
(509) 736-2086, *Fax:* (509) 736-9599
www.kbld.com
kbld@csnradio.com
License: Kennewick, Benton County, WA held by CSN International
Group Owner: CSN International; acq 6-12-97; $14,120).
Arbitron Metro Market: Kennewick, WA *Format:* Christian
Marty Atkins, General Manager

KONA-FM
08-01-1969; 105.3 mhz FM *Hrs Open:* 24; 100 kw; 1138 ft.; N46 5 51 W119 11 30
Mailing Address: P.O. Box 2623, Tri-Cities, WA 99302 US
Second Address: Box 2623, Tri Cities, WA 99302
(509) 547-1618, *Fax:* (509) 546-2678
www.konaradio.com
kona@konaradio.com
License: Kennewick, Benton County, WA
Group Owner: Cherry Creek Radio LLC
Regional Reps: Allied Radio Partners.
Arbitron Metro Market: Tri-Cities, WA (Richland-Kennewick-Pasco) *Format:* Adult Contemp *Hrs. of News Programming:* news progmg 3 hrs wkly *No. News Employees:* 2 *Adv. Rates:* 25; 22; 25; 19
Dennis Goodman, COO
Scott Smith, General Sales Mgr
Todd Nevard, Programming Director
Linda Howard, News Director
Dennis Shannon, Local News Editor
Willy Contretas, Spanish Director
Mike McDonnal, Sports Commentator

KJOX
08-01-1945; 1340 khz AM; 1 kw-U; N46 13 16 W119 11 20
830 N. Columbia Ctr. Blvd., Suite B-2, Kennewick, WA 92101
(509) 783-0783, *Fax:* (509) 735-8627
www.ktcr.com
info@ktcr.com
License: Kennewick, Benton County, WA
Group Owner: James D. Ingstad Stns; acq 12-10-99; grpsl).
Nat'l Reps: Christal
Population Served: 125,000 *Arbitron Metro Market:* Tri-Cities, WA (Richland-Kennewick-Pasco) *Target Audience:* 25-64.

***KTCV**
12-10-1984; 88.1 mhz FM *Hrs Open:* 12; 3.5 kw vert; -92 ft.; N46 13 7 W119 12 1
5929 W Metaline, Kennewick, WA 99336 US
(509) 734-3621(509) 734-3622, *Fax:* (509) 734-3609
www.ktcv.net
dailed@ksd.org
License: Kennewick, Benton County, WA held by Kennewick School District No. 17.
Arbitron Metro Market: Kennewick, WA *Format:* Alternative
Ed Dailey, General Manager

Kennewick-Richland-P

KONA
01-01-1948; 610 khz AM *Hrs Open:* 24; 5 kw-D, DA2; 5 kw-N, DA2; N46 10 23 W119 4 7
Mailing Address: P. O. Box 2623, Tri-Cities, WA 99302 US
Second Address: Box 2623, Tri Cities, WA 99302

(509) 547-1618, *Fax:* (509) 546-2678
www.konaradio.com
kona@konaradio.com
License: Kennewick-Richland-P, WA held by CCR-Tri Cities IV LLC.
Group Owner: Cherry Creek Radio LLC; (acq 12-19-2003; grpsl).
Arbitron Metro Market: Tri-Cities, WA (Richland-Kennewick-Pasco) *Format:* News, News/Talk, 86 *Special Programming:* Farm 3 hrs, sports 8 hrs wkly *Hrs. of News Programming:* news progmg 25 hrs wkly *No. NewsEmployees:* 2 *Target Audience:* 25-54. *Adv. Rates:* 25; 22; 25; 19
Dennis Goodman, General Manager
Scott Smith, General Sales Mgr
Todd Nevard, Promotions Manager
Dennis Shannon, News Director
Art Blum, Chief Engineer
Michael McDonnal, Disc Jockey
Bob Martin, Disc Jockey
Rusty Faust, DiscJockey

Kirkland

*KARR
01-01-1964; 1460 khz AM *Hrs Open:* 24
Mailing Address: 4135 Northgate Blvd., #1, Sacramento, CA 95834 US
Second Address: 290 Hegenberger Rd., Oakland, CA 94621
(800) 543-1495
www.familyradio.com
info@familyradio.org
License: Kirkland, WA held by Family Stations Inc.
Group Owner: Family Stations Inc.; (acq 10-22-86; $50,000;
Arbitron Metro Market: Oakland, CA *Format:* Christian, Religious *Hrs. of News Programming:* News progmg 5 hrs wkly *Target Audience:* General; conservative Christians & evangelicals
Harold Camping, President
Thad McKinney, General Sales Mgr
Jim Dalke, Chief Engineer

Lacey

KBRD
06-01-1986; 680 khz AM *Hrs Open:* 6 AM-6 PM
Mailing Address: 125 N. Turner, Olympia, WA 98506 US
Second Address: 642 Cougar SE, Lacey, WA 98503
(360) 491-6800
www.hezzie.com/kbrd/
License: Lacey, WA held by BJ & Skip's for the Music
Nat'l Network: AP Radio
Arbitron Metro Market: Seattle-Tacoma, WA *Format:* Oldies *Special Programming:* Jazz one hr wkly *Target Audience:* General.
Adrian DeBee, General Manager

KLDY
09-22-1983; 1280 khz AM *Hrs Open:* 24; 1 kw-D, ND1; 0.5 kw-N, ND1; N47 3 44 W122 49 49
125 North Turner, Olympia, WA 98506 US
(303) 688-5162, *Fax:* (303) 660-4930
o.ibarra@espndeportesseattle.com
License: Lacey, WA held by Seattle Streaming Radio LLC.
Group Owner: Seattle Streaming Radio LLC; (acq 4-25-2007; $300,000)
Arbitron Metro Market: Seattle, WA
Oscar Ibarra, General Manager

Lakewood

KLAY
01-01-1991; 1180 khz AM *Hrs Open:* 24; 5 kw-D, DAN; 1 kw-N, DAN; N47 9 0 W122 24 38
10025 Lakewood Dr.,Sw #B, Tacoma, WA 98499 US
(253) 581-0324, *Fax:* (253) 581-0326
www.klay1180.com
klay11800@blarg.net
License: Lakewood, WA held by Clay Frank Huntington.
Nat'l Network: Westwood One
Arbitron Metro Market: Seattle, WA *Format:* Talk *Hrs. of News Programming:* news progmg 11 hrs wkly *No. News Employees:* 2 *Target Audience:* 30-65.
Clay Frank Huntington, President
Bruce Bond, Operations Dir
Bob McCluskey, General Sales Mgr
John Burton, Programming Director
Anna Winter, News Director
Nick Winter, Engineering Dir

KNTB
09-01-1978; 1480 khz AM *Hrs Open:* 6 AM-sunset; 1 kw-D, DAD; 0.111 kw-N, DA2; N47 9 56 W122 34 32
19939 Gatling Court, Katy, TX 77449 US
(303) 688-5162, *Fax:* (303) 660-4930
o.ibarra@espndeportesseattle.com
License: Lakewood, WA held by Seattle Streaming Radio LLC.
Group Owner: Seattle Streaming Radio LLC; (acq 8-26-2005; $900,000 with KBRO(AM) Bremerton)
Arbitron Metro Market: Seattle, WA
Oscar Ibarra, General Manager

Leavenworth

KOHO-FM
01-01-1998; 101.1 mhz FM; 0.93 kw; 2044 ft.; N47 36 7 W120 30 32
7375 Icicle Road, Leavenworth, WA 98826 US
(509) 548-1011, *Fax:* (509) 548-3222
www.kohoradio.com
esalmon@kohoradio.com
License: Leavenworth, Chelan County, WA held by Icicle Broadcasting Inc.
Group Owner: Icicle Broadcasting Inc.; acq 8-26-99; grpsl).
Arbitron Metro Market: Wenatchee-Wash *Format:* Triple A
Elliot Salmon, General Manager
Heather Winters, General Sales Mgr
Michael Dickes, Programming Director
Ian Dunn, News Director
Traci Ellingson, Traffic Manager

Longview

KBAM
08-15-1955; 1270 khz AM
401 City Ave., Suite 409, Bala Cynwyd, PA 19004 US
(360) 423-1210, *Fax:* (360) 423-1554
dcrowe@entercom.com
License: Longview, WA held by Bicoastal Media Licenses IV LLC.
Group Owner: Bicoastal Media L.L.C.; (acq 3-31-2005; grpsl)
Nat'l Network: CBS *Nat'l Reps:* McGavren Guild
Arbitron Metro Market: Longview, WA *Format:* Country
Julie Laird, General Manager
Phil Blair, News Director
Doug Fisher, Chief Engineer
Dawn Crowe, Traffic Manager

KEDO
05-01-1938; 1400 khz AM *Hrs Open:* 24
401 City Ave., Suite 409, Bala Cynwyd, PA 19004 US
(360) 425-1500, *Fax:* (360) 423-1554
www.oldiesradioonline.com
License: Longview, WA held by Bicoastal Media Licenses IV LLC.
Group Owner: Bicoastal Media L.L.C.; (acq 3-31-2005; grpsl)
Regional Reps: Art Moore.
Format: News, Oldies *Special Programming:* Pub affrs 2 hrs wkly *Hrs. of News Programming:* news progmg 15 hrs wkly *No. News Employees:* 1 *Target Audience:* 25-54.
Gayle Kessinger, General Manager
Doug Fisher, Chief Engineer

*KJVH
01-01-1988; 89.5 mhz FM; 0.1 kw vert; 781 ft.; N46 9 52 W122 51 13
4135 Northgate Blvd, Suite 1, Sacramento, CA 95834 US
(801) 359-3147, *Fax:* (801) 359-8112
www.familyradio.com
info@familyradio.com
License: Longview, Cowlitz County, WA held by Family Stations Inc.
Group Owner: Family Stations Inc.
Arbitron Metro Market: Salt Lake City, UT *Format:* Christian, Religious
Harold Camping, President
Roger Crawford, Station Manager

KUKN
07-07-1962; 105.5 mhz FM *Hrs Open:* 24; 0.7 kw; 860 ft.; N46 9 52 W122 51 13
Mailing Address: 401 City Ave., Suite 409, Bala Cynwyd, PA 19004 US
Second Address: 506 Cowlitz Way W., Longview, WA 98626
(360) 633-0110, *Fax:* (360) 577-6949
www.kukn.com
info@kukn.com
License: Longview, Cowlitz County, WA
Arbitron Metro Market: Portland, OR *Format:* Country *Hrs. of News Programming:* news progmg 2 hrs wkly *No. News Employees:* 2
Beth Jensen, Operations Dir
Joel Hanson, General Sales Mgr
John Mitchel, Programming Director
Jadd Curtis, Promotions Manager
Ray Byers, News Director
Bill Dodd, Disc Jockey
Ray Bartley, Bill Dodd
Kirc Rolland, SportsCommentator

*KLWO
10-22-1987; 90.3 mhz FM *Hrs Open:* 24; 400 w vert; Ant 892 ft; N46 09 47 W122 51 14
5700 West Oaks Blvd, Rocklin, CA 98632
(360) 578-1929, *Fax:* (360) 636-1357
wayfm.com
License: Longview, Cowlitz County, WA held by WAY-FM Media Group Inc.
Group Owner: WAY-FM Media Group Inc.; (acq 8-1-2003; with KWYA(FM) Astoria, OR)
Target Audience: 19-34.
Robert Augsburg, President
Danny Houle, General Manager

Lynden

KWPZ
11-08-1960; 106.5 mhz FM *Hrs Open:* 24; 63 kw; 2333 ft.; N48 40 46 W122 50 31
19303 Fremont Ave N, Seattle, WA 98133 US
(360) 354-5596, *Fax:* (360) 354-7517
www.praise1065.com
comment@praise1065.com
License: Lynden, Whatcom County, WA held by CRISTA Ministries Inc.
Group Owner: CRISTA Broadcasting; (acq 12-80).
Arbitron Metro Market: Lynden, WA *Format:* Christian, Religious *Target Audience:* 25-54; female *Adv. Rates:* 45; 40; 42; 28
James Gwinn, President
Melene Thompson, Operations Dir
Marvin Mickley, Station Manager
Roger Burke, General Sales Mgr
Lynette Schulz, Promotions Manager
Jim Bouma, Operations Manager

Mabton

KMNA
01-01-1997; 98.7 mhz FM; 11.5 kw; 874 ft.; N46 28 33 W120 8 37
361 West Monroe Street, Post Office Box 10, Mabton, WA 98935 US
(509) 895-0000, *Fax:* (509) 895-0005
License: Mabton, Yakima County, WA held by MBProsser Licensee LLC.
Group Owner: Moon Broadcasting; (acq 2-6-2004; $1.9 million).
Arbitron Metro Market: Richland, WA *Format:* Spanish
Carol Crider, General Manager

Manson

KZAL
01-01-2007; 94.7 mhz FM; 10.3 kw; 518 ft.; N47 51 16 W120 9 59
US
(509) 548-1011, *Fax:* (509) 548-3222
koho@kohoradio.com
License: Manson, Chelan County, WA held by Icicle Broadcasting Inc.
Group Owner: Icicle Broadcasting Inc.
Arbitron Metro Market: Commerce, TX *Format:* Jazz, Smooth Jazz
Harriet Bullitt, President
Gary Mathews, General Manager

*KHNW
88.3 mhz FM; 380 w; Ant 499 ft; N47 51 16 W120 09 59
12501 Park Avenue S., Tacoma, WA
(253) 535-7758, *Fax:* 253-535-8769
www.kplu.org
info@kplu.org
License: Manson, Chelan County, WA held by Pacific Lutheran University.

Paul Stankavich, General Manager
Jeff Bauman, Programming Director
Lowell Kiesow, Chief Engineer
Nick Francis, Music Director
Joey Cohn, Program Director

McCleary

KGY-FM
10-01-1992; 96.9 mhz FM *Hrs Open:* 24; 11 kw; 1053 ft.; N47 5 9 W123 11 17
1240 Washington St., Ne, Olympia, WA 98501 US

(360) 943-1240, *Fax:* (360) 352-1222
www.realcountryonline.com
kgysales@kgyradio.com
License: McCleary, Grays Harbor County, WA held by KGY Inc.
Format: Country *No. News Employees:* 2 *Target Audience:* 35 plus.
Dick Pust, General Manager
Darlene Kemery, General Sales Mgr
Jeanna Spain, News Director
Tom Trotzer, Chief Engineer

Medical Lake

*KTSL
03-07-1989; 101.9 mhz FM *Hrs Open:* 24; 28.5 kw; 650 ft.; N47 42 11 W117 44 26
10209 Southeast Division Street, Portland, OR 97266 US
(888) 937-2471, *Fax:* (916) 251-1650
www.air1.com
info@air1.com
License: Medical Lake, Spokane County, WA held by Educational Media Foundation.
Group Owner: EMF Broadcasting; (acq 5-23-2008; $2.15 million)
Arbitron Metro Market: Medical Lake, WA *Format:* Alternative, Christian
Darrell Chambliss, Chairman
Alan Mason, COO
Mike Novak, President and CEO
Tracy Butler, News Director
Sam Wallington, Engineering Dir
Marya Morgan, News Reporter
Richard Hunt, News Reporter
Larry Moody, Director
MitchBarnhart, Director
David R. Ferry, Director
Walter Golembeski, Director

Mercer Island

*KMIH
02-01-1970; 88.9 mhz FM *Hrs Open:* 24; 0.03 kw; 226 ft.; N47 34 21 W122 13 5
9100 S.E. 42nd Street, Mercer Island, WA 98040 US
(206) 236-3296, *Fax:* (206) 236-3342
hotjamz.org
pd@hotjamz.org
License: Mercer Island, King County, WA held by Mercer Island School District No. 400.
Arbitron Metro Market: Seattle, WA *Format:* Contemporary Hits/Top 40 *Target Audience:* 18-34; Female
Nathan Friend, General Manager
Bob Casserd, General Sales Mgr
Nic Alquist, Programming Director
John Van Oppen, Chief Engineer

Mercer Island/Seattl

KIXI
01-01-1947; 880 khz AM *Hrs Open:* 24
Newport Tower, 3650 131st Ave., S.E.550, Bellevue, WA 98006 US
(425) 562-8964, *Fax:* (425) 653-1088
www.kixi.com
danm@kixi.com
License: Mercer Island/Seattl, WA held by Bellevue Radio Inc.
Group Owner: Sandusky Radio; (acq 11-15-91; $3.5 million;
Nat'l Network: Music of Your Life *Nat'l Reps:* Christal
Arbitron Metro Market: Seattle-Tacoma, WA *Format:* Adult Contemp *Target Audience:* 35 plus; mature active adults
Marc Kaye, Operations Dir
Lois Mares, General Sales Mgr
Julie Judge, National Sales Manager
Dan Murphy, Operations Manager

Montesano

KANY
01-01-2008; 93.7 mhz FM; 14 kw; 400 ft.; N46 56 0 W123 43 57 US
(360) 533-3000, *Fax:* (360) 532-1456
www.jodesha.com
License: Montesano, Grays Harbor County, WA held by Jodesha Broadcasting Inc.
Group Owner: Jodesha Broadcasting Inc.; (acq 3-16-2007; $600,000 for CP)
Nat'l Network: Jones Radio Networks
Arbitron Metro Market: Waterloo-Cedar Falls, IA
Gabrielle Jordan, Operations Dir
Bill Wolfenbarger, General Manager
Sally Miller, General Sales Mgr

Moses Lake

KBSN
11-01-1947; 1470 khz AM *Hrs Open:* 24; 5 kw-D, DA2; 1 kw-N, DA2; N47 6 16 W119 17 32
Mailing Address: 1802 136th Place N.E., Bellevue, WA 98005 US
Second Address: 2241 W. Main, Moses Lake, WA 98837
(509) 765-3441, *Fax:* (509) 766-0273
jpl470@hotmail.com
License: Moses Lake, WA held by KSEM Inc.
Nat'l Network: ABC *Nat'l Reps:* McGavren Guild
Format: News, News/Talk, 84, Talk *Special Programming:* Sp 9 hrs wkly *No. News Employees:* 3 *Target Audience:* General.
Jim Davis, General Manager
Stacey Lehman, General Sales Mgr
Bill Ecret, Programming Director
Butch Bare, News Director
Will Vos, Chief Engineer
Dennis Clay, Outdoor Ed
Dave Heaverlo, Sports Commentator
Colleen Roth, TrafficManager

KDRM
10-01-1980; 99.3 mhz FM; 3 kw; 275 ft; N47 05 54 W119 17 47
2241 W. Main, Moses Lake, WA 98005
(509) 765-3441, *Fax:* (509) 766-0273
License: Moses Lake, Grant County, WA held by KSEM Inc.
Nat'l Reps: McGavren Guild
Hrs. of News Programming: 1 *Target Audience:* 18-34.
Bill Ecret, General Manager
Stacey Lehman-Garcia, General Sales Mgr
Bill Ecret, Programming Director
Butch Bare, News Director
Dale Roth, Public Service Director
Colleen Roth, Traffic Manager

*KLWS
04-10-1997; 91.5 mhz FM *Hrs Open:* 24; 7.2 kw; 686 ft.; N47 18 50 W119 34 55 *Rebroadcasts:* Rebroadcasts KWSU(AM) Pullman 100%
P.O. Box 642530, 382 Murrow Center, Pullman, WA 99165 US
(509) 335-6500, *Fax:* (509) 335-3772
www.nwpr.org
nwpr@wsu.edu
License: Moses Lake, Grant County, WA held by Washington State University.
Arbitron Metro Market: Washington *Format:* News
Scott Weatherly, Operations Dir
Dennis Haarsager, General Manager
Kerry Swanson, Station Manager
Mary Hawkins, Programming Director
John Paxson, News Director
Robin Rilette, Music Director

*KMLW
05-04-1997; 88.3 mhz FM; 4 kw; 817 ft; N46 56 31 W119 25 41
Rebroadcasts: Rebroadcasts KMBI-FM Spokane 100%
Mailing Address: 5408 S. Freya, Spokane, WA 60610
Second Address: 820 N. LaSalle Blvd., Chicago, IL 60610
(509) 448-2555,(312) 329-4301, *Fax:* (509 448-6855,(312) 329-4468
www.kmbi.fm
kmbi@moody.edu
License: Moses Lake, Grant County, WA held by Moody Bible Institute of Chicago.
Group Owner: The Moody Bible Institute of Chicago
Special Programming: Class one hr wkly *Target Audience:* 35-54; Christians
Rich Monteith, General Manager
Chris Wright, Programming Director
Gordon Canaday, Chief Engineer

KWIQ-FM
05-22-1968; 100.3 mhz FM *Hrs Open:* 24; 100 kw; 167 ft.; N47 6 9 W119 14 26
Mailing Address: 725 Broad St., P.O. Box 936, Augusta, GA 30903 US
Second Address: 11768 Kittleson Rd., Moses Lake, WA 98837
(509) 765-1761(509) 663-5186, *Fax:* (509) 765-8901
www.kkrt.com
info@kwiq.com
License: Moses Lake, Grant County, WA
Group Owner: Morris Radio LLC
Nat'l Reps: Katz Radio *Regional Reps:* Allied Radio Partners.
Arbitron Metro Market: Wenatchee, WA *Format:* Country *No. News Employees:* 1 *Adv. Rates:* Same as AM
Jeff Dahlstrom, General Sales Mgr
Dave Eichler, Sales Representative
Jennifer Heneghen, Sales Representative
Joe Oreb, Sales Representative
Todd Farrar, Sales Representatieve
Carol Arevalo, Sales Representative

Moses Lake North

KWIQ
02-20-1956; 1020 khz AM *Hrs Open:* 24
Mailing Address: 725 Broad St., P.O. Box 936, Augusta, GA 30903 US
Second Address: 11768 Kittleson Rd., Moses Lake, WA 98837
(509) 765-1761(509) 663-5186, *Fax:* (509) 765-8901
www.kkrt.com
info@kwiq.com
License: Moses Lake North, WA held by Morris Communications Corp.
Group Owner: Morris Radio LLC; (acq 10-15-98; grpsl)
Nat'l Network: ESPN Radio *Nat'l Reps:* Katz Radio
Arbitron Metro Market: Wenatchee, WA *Format:* Sports *Hrs. of News Programming:* news progmg 6 hrs wkly *No. News Employees:* 1 *Target Audience:* 18-49; men *Adv. Rates:* 18; 16; 18; 14
Gary Patrick, General Manager
Jeff Dahlstrom, General Sales Mgr
John Windus, Programming Director
Jay White, Chief Engineer
Dave Eichler, Sales Representative
Jennifer Heneghen, Sales Representative
Joe Oreb, SalesRepresentative
Todd Farrar, Sales Representatieve
Carol Arevalo, Sales Representative

Mount Vernon

KAPS
03-17-1963; 660 khz AM *Hrs Open:* 24; 10 kw-D, DA2; 1 kw-N, DA2; N48 26 19 W122 20 39
P.O. Box 70, Mount Vernon, WA 98273 US
(360) 424-7676, *Fax:* (360) 424-1660
www.kapsradio.com
kapsradio@gmail.com
License: Mount Vernon, WA held by Valley Broadcasters Inc.
Regional Reps: McGaven Guild
Arbitron Metro Market: Mount Vernon, WA *Format:* Country *Hrs. of News Programming:* news progmg hourly *No. News Employees:* 1 *Target Audience:* General.
Jim Keane, President
Jerry Keane, General Sales Mgr
Mike Yeoman, Programming Director

KBRC
12-11-1946; 1430 khz AM *Hrs Open:* 24; 5 kw-D, DAN; 1 kw-N, DAN; N48 25 22 W122 21 10
Mailing Address: P.O. Box 250, Mount Vernon, WA 98273 US
Second Address: 2029 Freeway Dr., Mount Vernon, WA 98273
(360) 424-4278, *Fax:* (360) 424-1660
kbrcradio.com
oldies@kbrcradio.com
License: Mount Vernon, WA held by Valley Broadcasting.
Nat'l Network: ABC *Regional Reps:* Tacher.
Format: Oldies *Special Programming:* Sp 3 hrs, farm 5 hrs wkly *No. News Employees:* 2 *Target Audience:* 25-54.
James Keane, President
Jerry Keane, General Sales Mgr
Mike Yoeman, Programming Director
Kirk Tollifson, News Director
Mike Gilbert, Chief Engineer
Julia Rasmussen, Traffic Manager

*KMWS
05-04-1973; 89.7 mhz FM *Hrs Open:* 24; 1.5 kw; 118 ft.; N48 32 30 W122 17 43 *Rebroadcasts:* Rebroadcasts KWSU(AM) Pullman 100%
2405 E. College Way, Mount Vernon, WA 98273 US
(509) 335-6536
www.nwpr.org
dahmen@wsu.edu
License: Mount Vernon, Skagit County, WA held by Washington State University
Arbitron Metro Market: Pullman. WA *Format:* News, News/Talk, 86
Dennis Haahnsager, General Manager
Kerry Swanson, Station Manager
John Paxon, News Director

*KSVR
01-01-2002; 91.7 mhz FM; 0.17 kw; 669 ft.; N48 23 49 W122 18 26
119 N Commercial, #270, Bellingham, WA 98225 US
(360) 416-7711, *Fax:* (360) 416-7822
www.ksvr.org
mail@ksvr.org

License: Mount Vernon, Skagit County, WA held by Board of Trustees of Skagit Valley College
Arbitron Metro Market: Mount Vernon, WA *Format:* News, News/Talk, 86
Rip Robbins, KSVR General Manager, Media Instructor
Dave McConnell, Station Manager
Bill McCuskey, Chief Engineer
Joseph C. McGuire, Production Manager

Naches

KIT-FM

11-01-2000; 99.3 mhz FM; 790 w; Ant 899 ft; N46 36 02 W120 52 06
4010 Summitview Ave., Yakima, WA 98901
(509) 972-3461, *Fax:* (509) 972-3540
www.my993fm.com
my993@live.com
License: Naches, Yakima County, WA held by GAP Broadcasting Yakima License LLC.
Group Owner: GAPWEST Broadcasting; (acq 2-13-2008; grpsl)

Larry Miner, General Manager
Connie Johnston, General Sales Mgr
Ron Harris, Programming Director
Lance Tormey, News Director
Bill Glenn, Chief Engineer

KZTA

10-25-1988; 96.9 mhz FM *Hrs Open:* 24; 14 kw; 935 ft.; N46 35 59 W120 52 8
Mailing Address: PO Box 2888, Yakima, WA 98907 US
Second Address: 706 Butterfield Rd., Yakima, WA 98901
(509) 457-1000, *Fax:* (509) 452-0541
www.adelantemediagroup.com/blog/station/kzta-fm/
kteske@bustosmedia.com
License: Naches, Yakima County, WA
Group Owner: Adelante Media Group LLC; (acq 11-18-2004; grpsl)
Nat'l Reps: Tacher
Arbitron Metro Market: Naches, WA *Hrs. of News Programming:* News progmg 3 hrs wkly *Target Audience:* 18-35; Hispanic *Adv. Rates:* 31; 28; 25; 21
Amador Bustos, President
Keith Teske, Operations Dir
Bob Berry, General Manager
Judith McInnes, Programming Director
Jesus Rosales, News Director

Newport

KGZG-FM

12-01-1989; 104.5 mhz FM; 87 kw hoirz; Ant 1,046 ft; N48 23 09 W117 14 15
1600 Gray Lynn Dr., Walla Walla, WA 83822
(509) 252-1000
License: Newport, Pend Oreille County, WA held by Radio Station KMJY LLC
Arbitron Metro Market: Spokane, WA *Target Audience:* 18-34.
Christa McDonald, General Manager

*KUBS

09-10-1973; 91.5 mhz FM; 0.15 kw horiz; 735 ft.; N48 10 42 W117 4 59
P.O. Box 70, 1400 West 5th Street, Newport, WA 99156 US
(509) 447-4931, *Fax:* (509) 447-4354
www.kubsradio.com
KUBS@newport.wednet.edu
License: Newport, Pend Oreille County, WA held by Newport Consolidated School District #56415.
Arbitron Metro Market: Newport, WA *Format:* Variety/Diverse
Hugo Morales, CEO
Maria Erana, Operations Dir
Maria Esana, Programming Director

KPWL

1370 khz AM
US
(213) 494-3377
License: Newport, WA held by Scott Powell.
Arbitron Metro Market: Newport, WA
Scott Powell, General Manager

Nile

*KSBC

01-01-2003; 88.3 mhz FM *Hrs Open:* 24; 0.2 kw; -1145 ft.; N46 50 2 W120 56 13
402 E Yakima Ave, Suite 1320, Yakima, WA 98901 US
(916) 251-1600, *Fax:* (916) 251-1650
www.klove.com
klove@klove.com
License: Nile, Yakima County, WA held by Educational Media Foundation.
Group Owner: EMF Broadcasting; (acq 10-2-2003; grpsl).
Nat'l Network: K-Love
Format: Christian *No. News Employees:* 3 *Target Audience:* 25-44; Judeo Christian female
Mike Novak, President
Mike Lee, Operations Dir
David Pierce, Programming Director
Ed Lenane, News Director
Sam Wallington, Engineering Dir
Marya Morgan, News Reporter

Oak Harbor

KRPA

12-14-1984; 1110 khz AM *Hrs Open:* 5:30 AM-6 PM; 500 w-D; N48 17 27 W122 42 28
3170 Heller Rd., Oak Harbor, WA 98277
(360) 240-1110, (360) 240-1520, *Fax:* (360) 675-0166
www.kwdb.com
kwdb@kwdb.com
License: Oak Harbor, Island County, WA held by Impact Directories of Northwest Washington, LLC
Nat'l Network: Fox News Radio
Population Served: 68,500 *Arbitron Metro Market:* Seattle-Tacoma, WA *Hrs. of News Programming:* 6 Hours A Week *No. News Employees:* 1 *Target Audience:* 20-60. *Adv. Rates:* 20; 15; 20; 15
David Lindsey, President
Joe Capitano, Station Manager
Stacia Doyle, General Sales Mgr

Oakville

KOMO-FM

10-26-1984; 97.7 mhz FM *Hrs Open:* 24; 63 kw; Ant 2,388 ft; N47 18 46 W123 22 15
Mailing Address: 4444 East 66th Street #208, Tacoma, OK 74136
Second Address: 1803 State Ave. N.E., Olympia, WA 98506
(918) 495-1079, *Fax:* (360) 236-8786
www.977theeagle.com
underwriting@kfmyradio.com; events@kfmyradio.com; feedback@kfmyradio.com; jason@kfmyradio.com
License: Oakville, Grays Harbor County, WA held by South Sound Broadcasting LLC
Nat'l Reps: McGavren Guild
Population Served: 2,600,000 *Arbitron Metro Market:* Tacoma, OK *Format:* Christian *Special Programming:* Live performance 10 hrs wkly, *Hrs. of News Programming:* News progmg 10 hrs wkly *Target Audience:* Christian Families
Bill Bradley, General Manager
Craig Sullivan, Programming Director
Jeff Turnbow, News Director

Ocean Park

*KWAO

01-01-2006; 88.1 mhz FM *Hrs Open:* 24; 550 w; Ant 1,044 ft; 46 41 46 W123 46 17 *Rebroadcasts:* Rebroadcasts KLVR(FM) Santa Rosa, CA 100%
2351 Sunset Blvd., Suite 170-218, Rocklin, CA
(916) 251-1600, *Fax:* (916) 251-1650
www.klove.com
klove@klove.com
License: Ocean Park, Pacific County, WA held by Educational Media Foundation.
Group Owner: EMF Broadcasting
Nat'l Network: K-Love
No. News Employees: 3 *Target Audience:* 25-44; Judeo Christian, female
Mike Novak, President
Mike Lee, Operations Dir
Eric Allen, General Sales Mgr
David Pierce, Programming Director
Ed Lenane, News Director
Sam Wallington, Engineering Dir
Scott Smith, Music Director
Marya Morgan, NewsReporter
Richard Hunt, News Reporter
Tracy Butler, Traffic Manager

Ocean Shores

KSWW

01-01-1998; 102.1 mhz FM *Hrs Open:* 24; 25 kw; 322 ft.; N46 57 31 W123 35 18
Mailing Address: 125 N. Turner, Olympia, WA 98506 US
Second Address: 1520 Simpson Ave., Aberdeen, WA 98520
(360) 533-3000, *Fax:* (360) 532-1456
www.jodesha.com
License: Ocean Shores, Grays Harbor County, WA held by Jodesha Broadcasting Inc.
Group Owner: Jodesha Broadcasting Inc.; acq 2-28-03; $750,000 with KBKW(AM) Aberdeen).
Nat'l Network: ABC *Regional Reps:* Tacher *Wire Services:* AP
Arbitron Metro Market: Aberdeen, WA *Format:* Adult Contemp
Hrs. of News Programming: 7 hrs wkly *No. News Employees:* 1
Target Audience: 25-54. *Adv. Rates:* 30; 26; 28; na
William Wolfenbarger, President
Gabrielle Jordan, Operations Dir
Gabrielle Jordan, General Manager
Sally Miller, General Sales Mgr
Tony Halekakis-vice president of sales

Olympia

*KAOS

01-01-1973; 89.3 mhz FM *Hrs Open:* 24; 1.5 kw; -19 ft; N47 04 22 W122 58 51
CAB 301, Olympia, WA 98505
(360) 867-6895, *Fax:* (360) 866-6797
www.kaosradio.org
kaos@evergreen.edu
License: Olympia, Thurston County, WA held by Evergreen State College.
Nat'l Network: PRI
Population Served: 100,000*Special Programming:* Folks 16 hrs, Asian 3 hrs, American Indian 3 hrs, *Hrs. of News Programming:* News progmg 5 hrs wkly *Target Audience:* 18-35. *Adv. Rates:* 20; 20; 20; 20
Ruth Brownstein, Operations Dir
Jerry Drummond, General Manager

KGTK

10-01-1956; 920 khz AM *Hrs Open:* 24*Rebroadcasts:* Rebroadcasts KITZ(AM) Silverdale 90%
Mailing Address: 120 State Ave N.E., Mb 95, Olympia, WA 98501 US
Second Address: 1700 Mile High Dr., Suite 201A, Port Orchard, WA 98366
(360) 876-1400, *Fax:* (360) 876-7920
www.kitz1400.com
info@kitz1400.com
License: Olympia, WA held by KITZ Radio Inc.
Nat'l Network: USA; Radio America *Regional Reps:* Tacher
Arbitron Metro Market: Seattle-Tacoma, WA *Format:* Talk *Hrs. of News Programming:* News progmg 7 hrs wkly *Target Audience:* 18-65; diversified adults *Adv. Rates:* 25; 15; 25; 10
Alan Gottlieb, President
Julie Versnel, Operations Dir
Conn Williamson, General Manager
Nichole Engelstad, General Sales Mgr
Kevin Corcoran, Operations Manager

KGY

04-15-1922; 1240 khz AM *Hrs Open:* 24
Mailing Address: 1240 Washington St, Ne, Olympia, WA 98507 US
Second Address: 1700 Marine Dr. N.E., Olympia, WA 98501
(360) 943-1240, *Fax:* (360) 352-1222
www.kgyradio.com
am1240@kgyradio.com
License: Olympia, WA held by KGY Inc.
Nat'l Network: CBS Radio *Wire Services:* AP
Arbitron Metro Market: Seattle-Tacoma, WA *Format:* Adult Contemp *No. News Employees:* 2 *Target Audience:* General. *Adv. Rates:* 372; 288; 288; 240
Dick Pust, General Manager
Darlene Kemery, General Sales Mgr
Kevin Huffer, Programming Director
Steve George, News Director
Tom Trotzer, Chief Engineer
Jeanna Spain, Traffic Manager

KXXO

01-16-1990; 96.1 mhz FM *Hrs Open:* 24; 85 kw; Ant 2,099 ft; N46 38 07 W122 28 01
Mailing Address: Box 7937, Olympia, WA 98507
Second Address: Rockway/Leland Bldg., 119 N. Washington Ave., Olympia, WA 98501
(360) 943-9937, *Fax:* (360) 352-3643
www.mixx96.com
admin@mixx96.com
License: Olympia, Thurston County, WA held by 3 Cities Inc.
Population Served: 1,325,000 *Arbitron Metro Market:* Seattle-Tacoma *Hrs. of News Programming:* news progmg one hr wkly *No. News Employees:* 1 *Target Audience:* 25-54; general
David Rauh, President
Toni Holm, Operations Dir
Toni Holm, Station Manager

Brian Butler, General Sales Mgr
John Foster, Programming Director
Ann D'Angelo, News Director
Tim Vik, Chief Engineer

***KPLI**
09-01-2006; 90.1 mhz FM; 100 w; Ant -59 ft; N47 02 20 W122 54 00 *Rebroadcasts:* Rebroadcasts KPLU-FM Tacoma 100%
12501 Park Avenue S., Tacoma, WA 98507
(253) 536-5009, *Fax:* 253-535-8769
License: Olympia, Thurston County, WA held by Pacific Lutheran University Inc.
Nat'l Network: NPR; PRI *Wire Services:* AP
Population Served: 60,000*Hrs. of News Programming:* news progmg 54 hrs wkly *No. News Employees:* 7
Jeff Bauman, Operations Dir
Paul Stankavich, General Manager
Joey Cohn, Programming Director
Brenda Goldstein-Young, Promotions Manager
Erin Hennessey, News Director
Lowell Kiesow, Chief Engineer
Nick Francis, Music Director
Jennifer Strchan, News Media Director

Omak

KNCW
04-10-1978; 92.7 mhz FM *Hrs Open:* 24; 4.1 kw; 942 ft.; N48 19 12 W119 32 18
P.O. Box 151, 320 Emery Street, Omak, WA 98841 US
(509) 826-0100, *Fax:* (509) 826-3929
www.komw.net
License: Omak, Okanogan County, WA
Format: Country *Target Audience:* General.
David Miller, President

KOMW
09-30-1947; 680 khz AM; 5 kw-D, NDD; N48 23 40 W119 32 0
Mailing Address: P.O. Box 151, Omak, WA 98841 US
Second Address: 320 Emery St., Omak, WA 98841
(509) 826-0100, *Fax:* (509) 826-3929
www.komw.net
License: Omak, WA held by North Cascades Broadcasting Inc.
Group Owner: North Cascades Broadcasting Inc.; acq 7-90)
Nat'l Network: ABC
Format: Talk, Adult Contemp *Special Programming:* Farm 2 hrs, Sp 2 hrs wkly *Target Audience:* 18-45.
John Andrist, CEO
Rick Duck, General Sales Mgr
Chris Schmidt, Programming Director
Steve Hardy, News Director
Rebecca Andrist, CFO

***KQWS**
01-06-1999; 90.1 mhz FM *Hrs Open:* 24; 3 kw; 2457 ft.; N48 44 37 W119 37 16 *Rebroadcasts:* Rebroadcasts KWSU(AM) Pullman 100%
PO Box 642530, 382 Murrow Center, Pullman, WA 99164 US
(509) 335-6500, *Fax:* (509)335-3772
www.nwpr.org
nwpr@wsu.edu
License: Omak, Okanogan County, WA held by Washington State University.
Format: News, News/Talk, 86 *Hrs. of News Programming:* news progmg 60 hrs wkly *No. News Employees:* 1
Scott Weatherly, Operations Dir
Dennis Haarsager, General Manager
Roger Johnson, Station Manager
Sarah McDaniel, General Sales Mgr
Mary Hawkins, Programming Director
John Paxson, News Director
Ralph Hogan, Chief Engineer

KZBE
06-22-1998; 104.3 mhz FM *Hrs Open:* 24; 3.5 kw; 981 ft.; N48 19 12 W119 32 18
320 Emery Street, Omak, WA 98841 US
(509) 826-0100, *Fax:* (509) 826-3929
www.komw.net
news@komw.net
License: Omak, Okanogan County, WA held by North Cascades Broadcasting Inc.
Group Owner: North Cascades Broadcasting Inc.; acq 10-14-97; $47,606)
Nat'l Network: ABC
Arbitron Metro Market: Omak, WA *Format:* Contemporary Hits/Top 40 *Hrs. of News Programming:* news progmg 3 hrs wkly *No. News Employees:* 2 *Target Audience:* 18 plus.
John Andrist, CEO
John Andrist, Station Manager
Rick Duck, General Sales Mgr
Chris Schmidt, Programming Director
Jerry Robinson, Chief Engineer
Rebecca Andrist, CFO

Opportunity

KTRW
11-01-1955; 630 khz AM *Hrs Open:* 24; 0.53 kw-D, ND1; 0.053 kw-N, ND1; N47 36 31 W117 22 25
500 West Boone Avenue, Spokane, WA 99201 US
(509) 443-1000
www.ktrw.com
ktw@fabulous.com
License: Opportunity, WA held by Mutual Broadcasting System LLC
Nat'l Network: Fox News Radio; Salem Radio Network; USA
Arbitron Metro Market: Spokane, WA *Format:* Big Band, Oldies, 86
Thomas Read, General Manager

KIXZ-FM
04-01-1961; 96.1 mhz FM; 64 kw; 2418 ft.; N47 34 14 W117 4 55
600 Congress Avenue, Suite 1400, Austin, TX 78701 US
(509) 242-2400, *Fax:* (509) 242-1160
www.kix961.com
License: Opportunity, Spokane County, WA held by Capstar TX L.P.
Group Owner: Clear Channel Communications Inc.; (acq 8-30-00; grpsl).
Arbitron Metro Market: Spokane, WA *Format:* Country *Target Audience:* 25-54.
Shannon Roach, CFO
David Carr, Programming Director

Othello

KRSC
09-01-1957; 1400 khz AM
180 Main St., Othello, WA 99344 US
(509) 488-0606, *Fax:* (509) 488-0909
License: Othello, WA held by Centro Familiar Cristiano
Arbitron Metro Market: Othello, WA
Betsy Gomez, General Manager

Pacific

KZIZ
01-01-1990; 1560 khz AM *Hrs Open:* 24
Mailing Address: 2600 S. Jackson Street, Seattle, WA 98144 US
Second Address: 2600 South Jackson Street, Seattle, WA 98144
(206) 323-3070, *Fax:* (206) 322-6518
www.ztwins.com
ztwins@aol.com
License: Pacific, WA held by KRIS Bennett Broadcasting Inc.
Nat'l Network: American Urban
Arbitron Metro Market: Pacific, WA. *Format:* Gospel *Special Programming:* Relg 18 hrs wkly *Target Audience:* 12 plus; African-American
Frank Barrow, Operations Dir
Christopher Bennett, General Manager
Gloria Bennett, Station Manager
Priscilla Hailey, Chief Engineer

Parachute

KDBL
01-01-2008; 101.1 mhz FM; 200 w; Ant -1,397 ft; N39 26 31 W108 01 15
315 Kennedy Ave., Grand Junction, CO 55409
(970) 242-7788, *Fax:* (970) 243-0567
License: Parachute, Garfield County, CO held by Cumulus Licensing LLC.
Group Owner: Cumulus Media Inc.

Mike Shafer, Operations Dir
Kevin Wodlinger, General Manager

Pasco

KEYW
06-30-1986; 98.3 mhz FM *Hrs Open:* 25; 12.5 kw; 997 ft.; N46 4 58 W119 9 39
City Center West, 7201 W. Lake Mead Blvd, Las Vegas, NV 89128 US
(509) 547-9791, *Fax:* (509) 547-8509
www.keyw.com
License: Pasco, Franklin County, WA held by GAP Broadcasting Tri-Cities License LLC.
Group Owner: GAPWEST Broadcasting; (acq 2-13-2008; grpsl)
Arbitron Metro Market: Tri-Cities, WA (Richland-Kennewick-Pasco) *Format:* Adult Contemp *Target Audience:* 18-49.
Eric Vanwinkle, General Manager
Grant Linnen, General Sales Mgr
Paul Drake, Programming Director
Bill Glenn, Chief Engineer

KFLD
07-28-1956; 870 khz AM *Hrs Open:* 24; 10 kw-D, ND1; 0.25 kw-N, ND1; N46 13 41 W119 7 32
Mailing Address: City Center West, 7201 W. Lake Mead Blvd, Las Vegas, NV 89128 US
Second Address: 2621 W.A. St., Pasco, WA 99301
(509) 547-9791, *Fax:* (509) 547-8509
www.newstalk870.am
License: Pasco, WA held by GAP Broadcasting Tri-Cities License LLC.
Group Owner: GAPWEST Broadcasting; (acq 2-13-2008; grpsl)
Regional Reps: Art Moore.
Arbitron Metro Market: Pasco, WA *Format:* News, News/Talk, 86 *Special Programming:* Travel 1 hr wkly, 5 hrs sports wkly *Hrs. of News Programming:* news progmg 140 hrs wkly *No. News Employees:* 1 *TargetAudience:* 18-64.
Eric Van Winkle, General Manager
Grant Linnen, General Sales Mgr
John McKay, Programming Director
Chuck Ince, Chief Engineer

KGDN
02-01-1992; 101.3 mhz FM *Hrs Open:* 24; 2.75 kw; 1001 ft.; N46 5 47 W119 11 36
Mailing Address: P.O. Box 31000, Spokane, WA 99223 US
Second Address: 830 N. Columbia Center Blvd., Suite B3, Pasco, WA 99336
(509) 783-8600, *Fax:* (509) 448-3811
www.kgdn.com
acn@acn.cc
License: Pasco, Franklin County, WA held by West Pasco Fine Arts Radio.
Arbitron Metro Market: Tri-Cities, WA *Format:* Christian *Target Audience:* 35 plus.
Thomas Read, General Manager
Bill Glenn, Station Manager
Melinda Read, General Sales Mgr
Joseph Spinelli, Programming Director

KRKG-FM
04-01-1997; 93.7 mhz FM *Hrs Open:* 24; 600 w; 958 ft; N46 04 59 W119 09 38
Box 2852, Pasco, WA 99301
(509) 547-5196, *Fax:* (509) 547-5203
www.kgsg.com
info@kgsg.com
License: Pasco, Franklin County, WA held by Gospel Music Broadcasting Corp.
Arbitron Metro Market: Tri-Cities, WA (Richland-Kennewick-Pasco)
Martin Gibbson, President
Sharon Harmon, Programming Director
Martin Gibbs, Chief Engineer

***KOLU**
09-01-1971; 90.1 mhz FM; 4.1 kw; 1001 ft.; N46 4 59 W119 9 38
4921 West Wernett Street, Pasco, WA 99301 US
(509) 547-2062, *Fax:* (509) 544-0340
www.riverviewbaptist.org
info@kolu.com
License: Pasco, Franklin County, WA held by Riverview Baptist Christian Schools.
Arbitron Metro Market: Tri-Cities, WA (Richland-Kennewick-Pasco) *Format:* Religious
John Paisley, General Manager

Port Angeles

***KNWP**
03-23-1998; 90.1 mhz FM *Hrs Open:* 24; 1.6 kw; 197 ft.; N48 9 3 W123 40 9 *Rebroadcasts:* Rebroadcasts KRFA-FM Moscow, ID 100%
PO Box 642530, 382 Murrow Center, Pullman, WA 99165 US
(509) 335-6500, *Fax:* (509) 335-3772
www.nwpr.org
nwpr@wsu.edu
License: Port Angeles, Clallam County, WA held by Washington State University.
Format: Classical, News *Hrs. of News Programming:* news progmg 37 hrs wkly *No. News Employees:* 1
Scott Weatherly, Operations Dir
Dennis Haarsager, General Manager
Roger Johnson, Station Manager
Sarah McDaniel, General Sales Mgr
Mary Hawkins, Programming Director
Ralph Hogan, Chief Engineer

RADIO - U.S.

KONP
01-01-1945; 1450 khz AM
P.O. Box 1450, Port Angeles, WA 98362 US
(360) 457-1450, *Fax:* (360) 457-9114
www.konp.com
info@konp.com
License: Port Angeles, WA held by Radio Pacific Inc.
Format: News, News/Talk, 86 *Target Audience:* 28-54.
Brown Maloney, Chairman
Todd Ortloff, General Manager
Stan Comeau, General Sales Mgr

***KVIX**
03-22-2005; 89.3 mhz FM; 0.6 kw; 489 ft.; N48 9 3 W123 40 9
Rebroadcasts: Rebroadcasts KPLU-FM Tacoma 100%
121st and Park, Tacoma, WA 98447 US
(253) 535-7758, *Fax:* (253) 535-8332
www.kplu.org
info@kplu.org
License: Port Angeles, Clallam County, WA held by Pacific Lutheran University Inc.
Nat'l Network: NPR; PRI *Wire Services:* AP
Arbitron Metro Market: Port Angeles, WA *Format:* Blues, Jazz, 60
Jeff Bauman, Operations Dir
Paul Stankavich, General Manager
Joey Cohn, Programming Director
Erin Hennessey, News Director
Lowell Kiesow, Chief Engineer
Nick Francis, Music Director
Jennifer Strachan, Assistant GM & Director ofPublic Media
Jeff Bauman, Assistant GM & Director of Support Services
Joey Cohn, Assistant GM & Director of Content

Port Townsend

***KPTZ**
91.9 mhz FM; 0.9 kw; 335 ft.; N48 7 42 W122 49 39 US
(360) 379-8122
www.olympus.net/community/radiopt/
info@kptz.org
License: Port Townsend, Jefferson County, WA held by Radio Port Townsend.
Arbitron Metro Market: Port Townsend, WA *Format:* Talk *No. News Employees:* 1
Sherry Jones, President
Kris Shapiro, Station Manager
Larry Stein, Programming Director
David Cunningham, News Director
Bill Putney, Chief Engineer

Prosser

KZXR
12-14-1956; 1310 khz AM; 5 kw-D, ND1; 0.066 kw-N, ND1; N46 14 3 W119 48 49
1227 Hillcrest Drive, Prosser, WA 99350 US
(509) 786-1209, *Fax:* (509) 786-1181
info@kzxr.com
License: Prosser, WA held by MBProsser Licensee LLC
Group Owner: Moon Broadcasting; (Acq 2-24-2000; $500,000).
Arbitron Metro Market: Prosser, WA *Format:* Tejano *Target Audience:* 25-54.
Frank Allec, General Manager

KLES
09-06-1962; 101.7 mhz FM; 3.5 kw; 869 ft.; N46 11 12 W119 45 13
1227 Hillcrest Drive, Prosser, WA 99350 US
(509) 786-1209, *Fax:* (509) 786-1181
License: Prosser, Benton County, WA held by MBProsser Licensee LLC
Group Owner: Moon Broadcasting; (acq 2-15-2000; $750,000).
Nat'l Reps: Target Broadcast Sales
Arbitron Metro Market: Prosser, WA *Format:* Spanish *Target Audience:* 18-49.
Carol Crider, General Manager

Pullman

KHTR
01-01-1967; 104.3 mhz FM; 24 kw; 1670 ft.; N46 48 40 W116 54 55
Mailing Address: P. O. Box 1, Pullman, WA 99163 US
Second Address: 801 Old Wawawai Rd., Pullman, WA 99163
(509) 334-6836, *Fax:* (509) 332-5151
www.border104.com
brynn@border104.com
License: Pullman, Whitman County, WA
Format: Contemporary Hits/Top 40 *Hrs. of News Programming:* news progmg 24 hrs wkly *No. News Employees:* 1 *Target Audience:* General.
Jeremy West, Programming Director

KQQQ
01-01-1938; 1150 khz AM *Hrs Open:* 24
Mailing Address: P. O. Box 1, Pullman, WA 99163 US
Second Address: Box 1, Pullman, WA 99163
(509) 332-6551, *Fax:* (509) 332-5151
www.pullmanradio.com
info@border104.com
License: Pullman, WA held by Radio Palouse Inc.
Group Owner: Radio Palouse Inc.; acq 12-74).
Regional Reps: Allied Radio Partners.
Arbitron Metro Market: Pullman-Moscow *Format:* News, News/Talk, 86 *Special Programming:* Farm 3 hrs, loc news 10 hrs wkly *Hrs. of News Programming:* news progmg 28 hrs wkly *No. News Employees:* 1 *TargetAudience:* General.
Larry Weir, Operations Dir
Bill Weed, General Manager
Rod Schwartz, General Sales Mgr
Evan Ellis, News Director
Steve Franko, Chief Engineer

***KRLF**
07-01-1991; 88.5 mhz FM *Hrs Open:* 24; 0.4 kw vert; 807 ft.; N46 38 4 W117 5 22
345 Sw Kimball, Pullman, WA 99163 US
(509) 332-3545, *Fax:* (509) 332-5433
www.krlf.org
krlf@krlf.org
License: Pullman, Whitman County, WA held by Living Faith Fellowship Educational Ministries.
Nat'l Network: Salem Radio Network
Arbitron Metro Market: Pullman-Moscow *Format:* Christian *Special Programming:* Alternative/CHR one hr, children 5 hrs—1 hr/weekd *Hrs. of News Programming:* News progmg 18 hrs wkly *Target Audience:* 13-52.*Adv. Rates:* underwriting $6/spot
Phillip Vance, President
Frank Younce, Station Manager
Ruth Younce, Programming Director

***KWSU**
06-01-1922; 1250 khz AM *Hrs Open:* 24; 5 kw-D, ND2; 5 kw-N, ND2; N46 41 47 W117 14 44
PO Box 642530, Pullman, WA 99164 US
(509) 335-6500, *Fax:* (509) 335-6577
www.nwpr.org
nwpr@wsu.edu
License: Pullman, WA held by Washington State University.
Nat'l Network: NPR
Arbitron Metro Market: Pullman, WA *TV Affiliate:* *KWSU-TV affil.
Format: News *Special Programming:* Jazz 14 hrs wkly *Hrs. of News Programming:* news progmg 60 hrs wkly *No. News Employees:* 1 *TargetAudience:* General.
Karen Olstad, COO
Scott Weatherly, Operations Dir
Tony Wright, General Manager
Warren Wright, Station Manager
Sarah McDaniel, General Sales Mgr
Mary Hawkins, Programming Director
Aki Wright, Development Coordinator
Andi Wilson,Music and Culture
Ashley Rockwell, Announcer
Courtney Flatt, Multimedia Journalist

***KZUU**
09-21-1979; 90.7 mhz FM *Hrs Open:* 24; 0.42 kw; 100 ft.; N46 43 51 W117 9 42
P.O. Box 642530, 382 Murrow Center, Pullman, WA 99165 US
(509) 335-2208, *Fax:* (509) 335-3772
www.kzuu.wsu.edu/
kzuu@wsu.edu
License: Pullman, Whitman County, WA held by Washington State University Board of Regents.
Arbitron Metro Market: Pullman, WA *Format:* Jazz, Variety/Diverse *Special Programming:* Jazz 12 hrs, Black 12 hrs, folk 4 hrs, Sp 3 hrs, new mus 10 hrs, environmental protection 2 hrs wkly *Hrs. of News Programming:* news progmg 5 hrs wkly *No. News Employees:* 1 *Target Audience:* 18-49; college students
Mike Guay, General Manager
Jackie Kaiser, Programming Director
Lori Stewart, Promotions Manager

KZZL-FM
11-01-1991; 99.5 mhz FM *Hrs Open:* 24; 77 kw; 1060 ft.; N46 40 52 W116 58 16
Post Office Box 710, Colfax, WA 99111 US
(509) 397-3441, *Fax:* (509) 397-4752
License: Pullman, Whitman County, WA held by Inland Northwest Broadcasting LLC.
Group Owner: Inland Northwest Broadcasting LLC; (acq 6-28-2005; grpsl)
Arbitron Metro Market: Pullman, WA *Format:* Country *Hrs. of News Programming:* news progmg 2 hrs wkly *No. News Employees:* 1 *Target Audience:* 25 plus.
Gary Cummings, General Manager
Ben Bonfield, General Sales Mgr
Ryan Chambers, Programming Director
Steve Franco, Chief Engineer

Puyallup

KSUH
12-01-1951; 1450 khz AM *Hrs Open:* 24; 1 kw-U, ND1; N47 10 41 W122 16 24
1336 South 336th Street, Federal Way, WA 98003 US
(253) 815-1212, *Fax:* (253) 815-1913
www.radiohankook.com
info@radiohankook.com
License: Puyallup, WA held by Jean J. Suh.
Arbitron Metro Market: Federal Way, WA *Format:* Korean, Variety/Diverse *No. News Employees:* 2 *Target Audience:* 25-65; working folks
Sung Hong, General Manager
Nancy Haan, Station Manager

Quincy

KZML
10-01-1998; 95.9 mhz FM *Hrs Open:* 24; 11 kw; 1050 ft.; N47 19 13 W119 47 59 *Rebroadcasts:* Rebroadcasts KZTA(FM) Naches 100%
Mailing Address: Post Office Box 31000, Spokane, WA 99223 US
Second Address: 706 Butterfield Rd., Yakima, WA 98901
(509) 457-1000, *Fax:* (509) 452-0541
www.bustosmedia.com
zorro@radiozorro.com
License: Quincy, Grant County, WA
Group Owner: Adelante Media Group LLC; (acq 11-18-2004; grpsl).
Regional Reps: Tacher
Format: Tejano *Hrs. of News Programming:* news progmg 3 hrs wkly *No. News Employees:* 1 *Target Audience:* 18-35; Hispanic *Adv. Rates:* 31; 28; 25; 21
Keith Teske, Operations Dir
Bob Berry, General Manager
Martin Ortiz, Programming Director
Judith McInnis, News Director

KWNC
09-10-1957; 1370 khz AM; 1 kw-D, ND1; 0.039 kw-N, ND1; N47 17 30 W119 51 10
32 North Mission, Wenatchee, WA 98802 US
(509) 787-5121, *Fax:* (509) 664-6799
info@cherrycreekradio.com
License: Quincy, WA held by Wescoast Broadcasting Co. Inc.
Arbitron Metro Market: Wenatchee, WA *Format:* News *Special Programming:* Farm 5 hrs wkly *Hrs. of News Programming:* news progmg 168 hrs wkly *No. News Employees:* 3 *Target Audience:* 35 plus; farm-oriented*Adv. Rates:* 10; 10; 10; na
Jim Wallace Jr., President
Debbie Capestrini, Operations Dir
Steve Hair, News Director

KWWW-FM
08-29-1985; 96.7 mhz FM *Hrs Open:* 24; 0.44 kw; 1033 ft.; N47 19 13 W119 48 0
N. 1212 Washington, Suite 307, Spokane, WA 99201 US
(509) 665-6565, *Fax:* (509) 663-1150
www.kw3.com
Lbradshaw@CherryCreekRadio.com
License: Quincy, Grant County, WA held by CCR-Wenatchee IV LLC.
Group Owner: Cherry Creek Radio LLC; (acq 10-31-2006; grpsl)
Nat'l Reps: McGavren Guild
Arbitron Metro Market: Wenatchee, WA *Format:* Christian *Target Audience:* 18-49.
Lisa Rodriguez, Operations Dir
Jim Senst, General Manager
Leona Frank, General Sales Mgr
Dale Roth, Promotions Manager
Dave Bernstein, News Director
Manuel Garcia, Chief Engineer
Dave Herald, National Sales Manager
JenniferBusboug, Research Director

Rainier

*KACS
08-18-1993; 90.5 mhz FM *Hrs Open:* 24; 6 kw; 187 ft.; N46 43 52 W123 1 28
2401 NEKresky Suite B, Chehalis, WA 98532 US
(360) 740-9436, *Fax:* (360) 740-9415
www.kacs.org
kacs@kacs.org
License: Rainier, Lewis County, WA held by Chehalis Valley Educational Foundation.
Arbitron Metro Market: Chehalis, WA *Format:* Religious *Hrs. of News Programming:* News progmg 6 hrs wkly *Target Audience:* 45-54. *Adv. Rates:* $10 ROS
Kerry O'Connor, Chairman
Cameron Beirle, General Manager

Raymond

KJET
07-01-1999; 105.7 mhz FM *Hrs Open:* 24; 58 kw; Ant 518 ft; N46 56 30 W123 47 07
Mailing Address: Box 1198, Aberdeen, WA 98577
Second Address: 1520 Simpson Ave., Aberdeen, WA 98520
(360) 538-3000, *Fax:* (360) 532-1456
www.jodesha.com
info@jodesha.com
License: Raymond, Pacific County, WA held by Jodesha Broadcasting Inc.
Group Owner: Jodesha Broadcasting Inc.
Nat'l Network: ABC *Nat'l Reps:* Tacher *Wire Services:* AP
Population Served: 85,000*Hrs. of News Programming:* news progmg 7 hrs wkly *No. News Employees:* 1 *Target Audience:* 18-49. *Adv. Rates:* 24; 20; 22; na
William Wolfenbarger, President
Gabrielle Jordan, Operations Dir
Tony Halekakis, General Sales Mgr

Renton

KRIZ
02-02-1982; 1420 khz AM *Hrs Open:* 24; 1 kw-D, DA2; 0.5 kw-N, DA2; N47 26 25 W122 12 9
Mailing Address: 2600 S. Jackson Street, Seattle, WA 98144 US
Second Address: Box 22462, Seattle, WA 98122-0462
(206) 323-3070, *Fax:* (206) 322-6518
www.ztwins.com UNDER CONSTRUCTION
ztwins@aol.com
License: Renton, WA held by KRIZ Broadcasting Inc.
Nat'l Network: American Urban
Arbitron Metro Market: Seattle *Format:* Adult Contemp, Blues
Special Programming: Relg 18 hrs wkly *Target Audience:* 18 plus.
Christopher Bennett, President
Gloria Bennett, Operations Dir
Frank Barrow, Chief of Operations

KYIZ
01-01-1998; 1620 khz AM
Mailing Address: P.O. Box 22462, Seattle, WA 98122 US
Second Address: Box 22462, Seattle, WA 98144
(206) 323-3070, *Fax:* (206) 322-6518
www.ztwins.com
ztwins@aol.com
License: Renton, WA held by KRIZ Broadcasting Inc.
Arbitron Metro Market: Seattle-Tacoma, WA *Format:* Blues
Christopher Bennett, President
Gloria Bennett, Operations Dir
Priscilla Hailey, News Director
Frank Barrow, Chief of Operations

Richland

KALE
04-01-1950; 960 khz AM *Hrs Open:* 24; 5 kw-D, 1 kw-N, DA-N; N46 14 34 W119 10 48
830 N. Columbia Center Blvd., Suite B-2, Kennewick, WA 92101
(509) 783-0783, *Fax:* (509) 735-8627
www.am960.com
info@am960.com
License: Richland, Benton County, WA held by James D Ingstad
Group Owner: James D. Ingstad Stns; acq 12-10-99; grpsl).
Nat'l Reps: D & R Radio
Population Served: 157,000 *Arbitron Metro Market:* Tri-Cities, WA (Richland-Kennewick-Pasco) *No. News Employees:* 1 *Target Audience:* 25 plus; general
Don Morin, General Manager

KEGX
06-10-1992; 106.5 mhz FM; 100 kw; Ant 1,392 ft; N46 05 58 W119 07 40
830 N. Columbia Ctr. Blvd., Suite B-2, Kennewick, WA 92101
(509) 783-0783, *Fax:* (509) 735-8627
www.kegx.com
info@kegx.com
License: Richland, Benton County, WA held by James D Ingstad
Group Owner: James D. Ingstad Stns
Population Served: 250,000 *Arbitron Metro Market:* Tri-Cities, WA (Richland-Kennewick-Pasco) *Target Audience:* 25-54.
Pat McMahon, Operations Dir
J.D. Freeman, General Manager

*KFAE-FM
07-01-1982; 89.1 mhz FM *Hrs Open:* 24; 100 kw horiz, 67 kw vert; 1148 ft.; N46 5 43 W119 11 41 *Rebroadcasts:* Rebroadcasts KRFA-FM Moscow, ID 100%
Mailing Address: PO Box 642530, Pullman, WA 99164 US
Second Address: Washington State Univ. at Tri-Cities, 100 Sprout Rd., Richland, WA 99164-2530
(509) 335-6500, *Fax:* (509) 335-3772
www.nwpr.org
nwpr@wsu.edu
License: Richland, Benton County, WA held by Washington State University.
Nat'l Network: PRI; NPR
Arbitron Metro Market: Tri-Cities, WA (Richland-Kennewick-Pasco) *TV Affiliate:* *KTNW(TV) affil.
Format: News *Special Programming:* Folk, jazz 15 hrs wkly *Hrs. of News Programming:* news progmg 37 hrs wkly *No.News Employees:* 1 *Target Audience:* General.
Scott Weatherly, Operations Dir
Dennis Haarsager, General Manager
Roger Johnson, Station Manager
Sarah McDaniel, General Sales Mgr
Mary Hawkins, Programming Director

KIOK
10-03-1978; 94.9 mhz FM; 100 kw; 1,250 ft; N46 05 47 W119 11 36
830 N. Columbia Center Blvd., Suite B-2, Kennewick, WA 92101
(509) 783-0783, *Fax:* (509) 735-8627
www.949thewolfpack.com
request@949thewolfpack.com
License: Richland, Benton County, WA held by James D Ingstad
Group Owner: James D. Ingstad Stns
Population Served: 250,000 *Arbitron Metro Market:* Tri-Cities, WA (Richland-Kennewick-Pasco)

KORD-FM
10-15-1965; 102.7 mhz FM; 100 kw; 1325 ft.; N46 5 58.4 W119 7 40.2
Mailing Address: City Center West, 7201 W. Lake Mead Blvd, Las Vegas, NV 89128 US
Second Address: 2621 West A. St., Pasco, WA 99301
(509) 547-9791, *Fax:* (509) 547-8509
www.1027kord.com
License: Richland, Benton County, WA held by GAP Broadcasting Tri-Cities License LLC.
Group Owner: GAPWEST Broadcasting; (acq 2-13-2008; grpsl)
Arbitron Metro Market: Tri-Cities, WA (Richland-Kennewick-Pasco) *Format:* Country *Target Audience:* 25-54.
Eric VanWinkle, General Manager
Grant Linnen, General Sales Mgr
Paul Drake, Programming Director

Rock Island

KAAP
09-19-1990; 99.5 mhz FM *Hrs Open:* 24; 5.3 kw; -82 ft.; N47 22 52 W120 17 15
N. 1212 Washington, Suite 307, Spokane, WA 99201 US
(509) 665-6565, *Fax:* (509) 663-1150
www.applefm.com
License: Rock Island, Douglas County, WA held by CCR-Wenatchee IV LLC.
Group Owner: Cherry Creek Radio LLC; (acq 10-31-2006; grpsl)
Nat'l Reps: McGavren Guild
Format: Adult Contemp *No. News Employees:* 1 *Target Audience:* 25-54.
Jim Senst, General Manager
Leona Frank, General Sales Mgr
Lisa Rodriguez, News Director
Joe Bowers, Engineering Dir
Manuel Garcia, Chief Engineer
Todd Johnson, Promotions Manager
Jennifer Busboug, Research Director
Jose LuisHigh, Spanish Director

Roy

*KWFJ
09-01-1995; 89.7 mhz FM; 1 kw horiz, 0.78 kw vert; 98 ft.; N46 57 59 W122 32 56
P.O. Box 401, Roy, WA 98580 US
(206) 843-1692, *Fax:* (360) 458-6649
www.bbnradio.org
License: Roy, Pierce County, WA held by Calvary Baptist Church.
Nat'l Network: Bible Bcstg Net
Arbitron Metro Market: Roy, WA *Format:* Christian
Walt Stowe, General Manager

Royal City

KRCW
01-01-1995; 96.3 mhz FM *Hrs Open:* 24; 19.5 kw; 791 ft.; N46 45 55 W119 16 51
P.O. Box 62, Keene, CA 93531 US
(509) 545-0700, *Fax:* (509) 543-4100
www.campesina.com
License: Royal City, Grant County, WA held by Farmworker Educational Radio Network.
Arbitron Metro Market: Tri-Cities, Washington *Format:* Tejano *Target Audience:* 25-54; Hispanic market
Raul Salvador, President
Paul Chavez, Operations Dir
Daniel Hernandez, General Manager
Gabriela Ramirez, Station Manager
David Whitehead, Chief Engineer

KWDR
93.5 mhz FM; 0.21 kw; 1667 ft.; N46 48 25 W119 33 20 US
(858) 277-4991, *Fax:* (858) 277-1365
www.horizonradio.org
License: Royal City, Grant County, WA held by Horizon Christian Fellowship.
Group Owner: Horizon Christian Fellowship
Arbitron Metro Market: Royal City, WA *Format:* Christian
Mike MacIntosh, President

Seattle

KNTS
03-31-2003; 1680 khz AM *Hrs Open:* 24
4880 Santa Rosa Rd, Camarillo, CA 93012 US
(206) 443-8200, *Fax:* (206) 777-1133
wilmerh@salemradioseattle.com
License: Seattle, WA held by Inspiration Media Inc.
Group Owner: Salem Communications Corp.
Arbitron Metro Market: Seattle-Tacoma, WA *Format:* Christian, Talk
Joshua Main, Operations Dir
Tim Harper, General Manager
Wilmer Herrera, General Sales Mgr

*KBLE
01-01-1948; 1050 khz AM *Hrs Open:* 6 AM-midnight; 5 kw-D, ND1; 0.44 kw-N, ND1; N47 33 41 W122 21 34
114 Lakeside Ave., Seattle, WA 98122 US
(425) 867-2340
www.sacredheartradio.org
info@sacredheartradio.org
License: Seattle, WA held by Sacred Heart Radio Inc.
Arbitron Metro Market: Kirkland, WA *Format:* Religious
Ron Belter, General Manager

*KEXP-FM
01-01-1972; 90.3 mhz FM *Hrs Open:* 24; 4.7 kw; 692 ft.; N47 36 58 W122 18 28
Box 353750, Ds-50, Seattle, WA 98195 US
(206) 520-5800, *Fax:* (206) 520-5899
www.kexp.org
info@kexp.org
License: Seattle, King County, WA held by Regents of University of Washington.
Nat'l Network: NPR
Arbitron Metro Market: Seattle, WA *Format:* Alternative, Variety/Diverse *Target Audience:* 18-44; educated, culturally interested, active outdoors, prof/mngr/tech positions
Jack Walters, Operations Dir
Tom Mara, General Manager
Kevin Cole, Programming Director
Courtney Miller, Promotions Manager
Jamie Alls, Chief Engineer
Mike McCormick, Public Affairs Director

*KING-FM
01-01-1947; 98.1 mhz FM *Hrs Open:* 24; 66 kw; 2320 ft.; N47 30 14 W121 58 29
333 Dexter Ave N, Suite # 400, Seattle, WA 98109 US
(206) 691-2981, *Fax:* (206) 691-2982
www.king.org
web@king.org
License: Seattle, King County, WA held by Classic Radio Inc.

Nat'l Reps: Katz Radio
Arbitron Metro Market: Seattle-Tacoma, WA *Format:* Contemporary Hits/Top 40 *Hrs. of News Programming:* News progmg 2 hrs wkly
Jennifer Ridewood, General Manager
Bob Goldfarb, Programming Director
Shawna Keen, Promotions Manager
Buzz Anderson, Chief Engineer

KIRO
01-01-1927; 710 khz AM *Hrs Open:* 24
401 City Ave., Suite 409, Bala Cynwyd, PA 19004 US
(206) 726-7000, *Fax:* (206) 726-5446
www.mynorthwest.com
info@710kiro.com
License: Seattle, WA held by Bonneville Holding Co.
Group Owner: Bonneville International Corporation; (acq 3-14-2008; grpsl)
Nat'l Network: ESPN Radio
Arbitron Metro Market: Seattle-Tacoma, WA *Format:* Sports *Target Audience:* 25-54.
David Pridemore, General Manager
Dennis McCormick, General Sales Mgr
Tom Lendening, Programming Director

KISW
01-01-1950; 99.9 mhz FM *Hrs Open:* 24; 67 kw; 2320 ft.; N47 30 14 W121 58 29
Suite 409, 401 City Avenue, Bala Cynwyd, PA 19004 US
(206) 285-7625, *Fax:* (206) 215-9355
www.kisw.com
rcastle@entercom.com
License: Seattle, King County, WA held by Entercom Seattle License LLC.
Group Owner: Entercom Communications Corp.; (acq 1996).
Nat'l Reps: D & R Radio
Arbitron Metro Market: Seattle-Tacoma, WA *Format:* Rock/AOR *Target Audience:* 18-49; men
David Field, President
Amy Griesheimer, Operations Dir
Ron Steinman, General Sales Mgr
Dave Richards, Programming Director
Joyce Jinka, News Director
Dwight Small, Chief Engineer

KJR
01-01-1921; 950 khz AM
1333 New Hampshire Avenue NW, Suite 1000, Washington, DC 20036 US
(206) 285-2295, *Fax:* (206) 286-2376
www.sportsradiokjr.com
info@kjram.com
License: Seattle, WA held by Ackerley Broadcasting Operations LLC.
Group Owner: Clear Channel Communications Inc.; (acq 6-14-2002; grpsl)
Nat'l Reps: D & R Radio
Arbitron Metro Market: Seattle, WA *Format:* Sports *Target Audience:* 25-54.
Michelle Grosnick, Operations Dir
Sean Shannon, General Sales Mgr
Rich Moore, Programming Director
Gus Swanson, Promotions Manager
Amy Spino, News Director
Doug Irwin, Chief Engineer
Gina Gray, Promotions Director
Tom Benton,Public Affairs Director
Gina Gray

KJR-FM
05-25-1960; 95.7 mhz FM; 98 kw; 1270 ft.; N47 32 40 W122 6 26
1333 New Hampshire Avenue NW, Suite 1000, Washington, DC 20036 US
(206) 494-2000, *Fax:* (206) 286-2376
www.957kjrfm.com
info@957kjrfm.com
License: Seattle, King County, WA held by Ackerley Broadcasting Operations LLC.
Group Owner: Clear Channel Communications Inc.
Arbitron Metro Market: Seattle, WA *Format:* Contemporary Hits/Top 40, Adult Contemp *Target Audience:* 30-44.
Andy Lohman, General Sales Mgr
John Peak, Programming Director
Valerie Koch, Promotions Manager
Stephen Kilbreath, News Director
Ric Hansen, Disc Jockey
Heidi May, Disc Jockey
Ric Hansen, Disc Jockey
Pat Cashman
Amy Spino

KKDZ
05-15-1993; 1250 khz AM *Hrs Open:* 24
200 First Ave. W. # 104, Attn: David Ebers, Seattle, WA 98119 US
(206) 281-5300, *Fax:* (206) 281-8881
www.radiodisney.com
info@kkdzam.com
License: Seattle, WA held by WMAL Inc.
Group Owner: ABC Inc.; (acq 1-21-98; $1.2 million)
Arbitron Metro Market: Seattle, WA *Format:* Children *No. News Employees:* 5 *Target Audience:* 6-14; Kids *Adv. Rates:* 125; 100; 125; 50
Bob Nordberg, General Manager
Laura Dunham, Promotions Manager

KKOL
01-01-1922; 1300 khz AM *Hrs Open:* 24
4880 Santa Rosa Road, Suite 300, Camarillo, CA 93012 US
(206) 443-8200, *Fax:* (206) 777-1133
www.kkol.com
License: Seattle, WA held by Inspiration Media Inc.
Group Owner: Salem Communications Corp.; (acq 4-17-97; $2 million)
Nat'l Reps: Salem
Arbitron Metro Market: Seattle, WA *Format:* News *Target Audience:* 35 plus; men & women
Joshua Main, Operations Dir
Andrew Adams, General Manager
Chad Gammage, General Sales Mgr
Dave Drui, Programming Director
Clara Hylarides, Promotions Manager
Monte Passmore, Chief Engineer
Wendy Bergsma-Passmore, BusinessManager

KLFE
09-10-1956; 1590 khz AM *Hrs Open:* 24; 5 kw-D, DAN; 5 kw-N, DAN; N47 39 19 W122 31 6
4880 Santa Rosa Rd, Ste 300, Camarillo, CA 93012 US
(206) 443-8200, *Fax:* (206) 777-1133
webmaster@kgnw.com
License: Seattle, WA held by Inspiration Media Inc.
Group Owner: Salem Communications Corp.; (acq 1994; $500,000)
Nat'l Reps: Salem
Arbitron Metro Market: Seattle, WA *Format:* Christian, Talk *Special Programming:* Russian 12 hrs *Target Audience:* 25-54.
Joshua Main, Operations Dir
Tim Harper, General Manager

KPTK
01-01-1927; 1090 khz AM *Hrs Open:* 24
600 New Hampshire Avenue, N.W., Suite 1200, Washington, DC 20037 US
(206) 805-1090, *Fax:* (206) 805-0911
www.am1090seattle.com
License: Seattle, WA held by Infinity Radio Holdings Inc.
Group Owner: CBS Radio; (acq 11-13-98; grpsl).
Arbitron Metro Market: Seattle, WA *Format:* Alternative, Talk
Dave McDonald, General Manager
Jim Trapp, Programming Director
Missy Wise, News Director
Tom McGinley, Chief Engineer

KMPS-FM
07-08-1961; 94.1 mhz FM; 69 kw; 2290 ft.; N47 30 17 W121 58 4
Mailing Address: 600 New Hampshire Avenue, N.W., Suite 1200, Washington, DC 20037 US
Second Address: 1000 Dexter Ave., N., Suite 100, Seattle, WA 98109
(206) 805-0941, *Fax:* (206) 805-0911
www.kmps.com
email@kmps.com
License: Seattle, King County, WA held by Infinity Radio Holdings Inc.
Group Owner: CBS Radio; (acq 11-13-98; grpsl).
Arbitron Metro Market: Seattle, WA *Format:* Country *Hrs. of News Programming:* one. *Target Audience:* General.
Becky Brenner, Operations Dir
Dave McDonald, General Manager
Rod Krebs, General Sales Mgr
Don Riggs, News Director
Tom McGinley, Chief Engineer

KNDD
03-09-1985; 107.7 mhz FM *Hrs Open:* 24; 67 kw; 2320 ft.; N47 30 14 W121 58 29
401 City Ave., Suite 409, Bala Cynwyd, PA 19004 US
(206) 622-3251, *Fax:* (206) 682-8349
www.1077theend.com
info@knddfm.com
License: Seattle, King County, WA held by Entercom Seattle License L.L.C.
Group Owner: Entercom Communications Corp.; (acq 1996)
Nat'l Reps: D & R Radio
Arbitron Metro Market: Seattle, WA *Format:* Alternative *No. News Employees:* 1 *Target Audience:* 18-34; well educated active adults
Amy Griesheimer, Operations Dir
Jennifer Wisbey, General Sales Mgr
Phil Manning, Programming Director
Dwight Smalls, Chief Engineer

*KNHC
01-25-1971; 89.5 mhz FM *Hrs Open:* 24; 8.5 kw; 1220 ft.; N47 32 35 W122 6 25
10750 30th Avenue, N. E., Seattle, WA 98125 US
(206) 252-3800, *Fax:* (206) 252-3805
www.c895worldwide.com
info@c895worldwide.com
License: Seattle, King County, WA held by Seattle Public Schools.
Wire Services: AP
Arbitron Metro Market: Seattle, WA *Format:* Contemporary Hits/Top 40 *Special Programming:* Black, gospel 6 hrs, gothic/industrial 6 hrs wkly *Hrs. of News Programming:* News progmg 9 hrs wkly *Target Audience:* 18-34; male & female
Richard Dalton, Operations Dir
Gregg Neilson, General Manager
Jon McDaniel, Programming Director

KTTH
01-01-1925; 770 khz AM *Hrs Open:* 24; 50 kw-D, DA2; 5 kw-N, DA2; N47 23 38 W122 25 25
401 City Ave., Suite 409, Bala Cynwyd, PA 19004 US
(206) 726-7000, *Fax:* (206) 726-5446
License: Seattle, WA held by Bonneville Holding Co.
Group Owner: Bonneville International Corporation; (acq 3-14-2008; grpsl)
Arbitron Metro Market: Seattle-Tacoma, WA *Format:* News *No. News Employees:* 6 *Target Audience:* 25-54; adults
David Pridemore, General Manager
Ken Berry, Station Manager

KOMO
01-01-1926; 1000 khz AM *Hrs Open:* 24; 50 kw-D, DAN; 50 kw-N, DAN; N47 27 49 W122 26 27
100 Fourth Avenue, North, Seattle, WA 98109 US
(206) 404-4000, *Fax:* (206) 404-3646
www.KOMO1000news.com
comments@KOMO1000news.com
License: Seattle, WA held by Fisher Broadcasting - Seattle Radio L.L.C.
Group Owner: Fisher Communications Inc.
Nat'l Network: ABC *Wire Services:* AP
Arbitron Metro Market: Seattle-Tacoma, WA *TV Affiliate:* KOMO-TV affil. *Format:* News *Hrs. of News Programming:* news progmg 168 hrs wkly *No. News Employees:* 50 *Target Audience:* 25-54.
Colleen Brown, CEO
Larry Roberts, General Manager
Joe Heslet, General Sales Mgr
Dennis Kelly, Programming Director
Jen Pivak, Promotions Manager
Brian Calvert, News Director
John Barrett, Chief Engineer
Gary Greenberg, NationalSales Manager
Charles Gouge, Regional Sales Manager
Julie Ross, Traffic Manager

KPLZ-FM
09-01-1959; 101.5 mhz FM *Hrs Open:* 24; 99 kw; 1263 ft.; N47 32 40 W122 6 26
100 - 4th Ave. North, Seattle, WA 98109 US
(206) 404-4000, *Fax:* (206) 404-3644
www.star1015.com
jclayton@komotv.com
License: Seattle, King County, WA held by Fisher Broadcasting - Seattle Radio L.L.C.
Group Owner: Fisher Communications Inc.; (acq 5-5-94; with co-located AM)
Nat'l Reps: Eastman Radio *Wire Services:* AP
Arbitron Metro Market: Seattle-Tacoma *Format:* Adult Contemp *Special Programming:* John Tesh at night *Hrs. of News Programming:* news progmg one hr wkly *No. News Employees:* 2 *Target Audience:* 25-54; women
Jim Clayton, General Manager
Bryce Phillipy, General Sales Mgr
Kent Phillips, Programming Director
Jennifer Pirak, Promotions Manager
Sheri Blatman, News Director

John Barrett, Chief Engineer
Gary Greenberg, National SalesManager

KKWF
01-01-1946; 100.7 mhz FM *Hrs Open:* 24; 67 kw; 2320 ft.; N47 30 14 W121 58 29
Suite 409, 401 City Avenue, Bala Cynwyd, PA 19004 US
(206) 285-7625, *Fax:* (206) 381-0997
www.seattlewolf.com
jemckenna@intercom.com
License: Seattle, King County, WA held by Entercom Seattle License LLC.
Group Owner: Entercom Communications Corp.
Arbitron Metro Market: Seattle-Tacoma, WA *Format:* Country *Hrs. of News Programming:* News progmg 15 hrs wkly
Steve Oshin, Operations Dir
Ron Steinman, General Sales Mgr
Lance Tidwell, Programming Director
Dwight Small, Chief Engineer
Melissa Forrest, Operations Manager

KKNW
01-01-1926; 1150 khz AM *Hrs Open:* 24
3650 131st Street, Se, Ste 550, Newport Tower, Bellevue, WA 98006 US
(425) 373-5536, *Fax:* (425) 373-5507
www.1150kknw.com
License: Seattle, WA held by Orca Radio Inc.
Group Owner: Sandusky Radio
Arbitron Metro Market: Belleuve, WA *Format:* News, News/Talk, 86 *Special Programming:* Loc sports 15 hrs, Russian 5 hrs wkly *Hrs. of News Programming:* news progmg 10 hrs wkly *No. News Employees:* 1 *TargetAudience:* 35-64; active, well educated adults with middle to upper income
Eric Burris, Operations Dir
Erik Krema, Station Manager
Alan Hines, News Director

KUBE
05-06-1964; 93.3 mhz FM *Hrs Open:* 24; 98 kw; 1270 ft.; N47 32 40 W122 6 26
1333 New Hampshire Avenue NW, Suite 1000, Washington, DC 20036 US
(206) 494-2000, *Fax:* (206) 286-2376
www.kube93.com
KarenHeric@ClearChannel.com
License: Seattle, King County, WA held by Ackerley Broadcasting Operations LLC.
Group Owner: Clear Channel Communications Inc.; (acq 6-14-2002; grpsl).
Arbitron Metro Market: Seattle, WA
Michele Grosenick, President
Shellie Hart, Operations Dir
Karen Heric, General Sales Mgr
Eric Powers, Programming Director
Amy Spino, News Director
Doug Irwin, Chief Engineer

***KUOW-FM**
01-16-1952; 94.9 mhz FM *Hrs Open:* 24; 100 kw; 735 ft.; N47 36 58 W122 18 28
Box 353750, Seattle, WA 98195 US
(206) 543-2710, *Fax:* (206) 616-9125
www.kuow.org
letters@kuow.org
License: Seattle, King County, WA held by University of Washington.
Nat'l Network: NPR; PRI
Arbitron Metro Market: Seattle, WA *Format:* News *Special Programming:* Sp 2 hrs, jazz 5 hrs wkly *Hrs. of News Programming:* news progmg 60 hrs wkly *No. News Employees:* 15 *Target Audience:* 25-54; highlyeducated, influential,decision makers
Dane Johnson, Operations Dir
Wayne Roth, General Manager
Marcia Scholl, General Sales Mgr
Jeff Hansen, Programming Director
Guy Nelson, News Director
Terry Denbrook, Chief Engineer

KVI
01-01-1926; 570 khz AM *Hrs Open:* 24; 5 kw-U, ND1; N47 25 19 W122 25 44
100 4th Avenue North, Seattle, WA 98109 US
(206) 404-4000, *Fax:* (206) 404-3648
www.570kvi.com
comment@kvi.com; 570KVI@fisherradio.com
License: Seattle, WA held by Fisher Broadcasting - Seattle Radio L.L.C.
Group Owner: Fisher Communications Inc.
Nat'l Network: Fox News Radio *Nat'l Reps:* Eastman Radio *Wire Services:* AP
Arbitron Metro Market: Seattle, WA *Format:* Talk *Hrs. of News Programming:* news progmg 20 hrs wkly *No. News Employees:* 2 *Target Audience:* 25-54.
Janene Drafs, General Manager
Joe Heslet, General Sales Mgr
Paul Duckworth, Programming Director
Jen Pirak, Promotions Manager
Anna Johnson, News Director
Gary Greenberg, National Sales Manager

KLCK-FM
11-01-1954; 98.9 mhz FM *Hrs Open:* 24; 63.9 kw; 698 meters; N47 32 41 W122 06 28
3650 131st Ave. S.E., Suite 550, Bellevue, WA 98006
(425) 373-5536, *Fax:* (425) 653-1133
www.kwjz.com
License: Seattle, King County, WA held by Orca Radio Inc.
Group Owner: Sandusky Radio; (acq 1996; $26 million with co-located AM)
Nat'l Network: Westwood One *Nat'l Reps:* Christal
Population Served: 3,084,700 *Arbitron Metro Market:* Seattle-Tacoma, WA *Hrs. of News Programming:* news progmg 9 hrs wkly *No. News Employees:* 2 *Target Audience:* 25-54; younger active, mid to upper income adults*Adv. Rates:* 250; 250; 250; 75
Marc Kaye, General Manager
Susan Hoffman, General Sales Mgr
Carol Handley, Programming Director
Cindy Gilsdorf, Promotions Manager
Alan Hines, News Director
George Bisso, Chief Engineer
Ann Mulholland, General Sales Manager
Dianna Rose, Music Director

KJAQ
01-01-1959; 96.5 mhz FM *Hrs Open:* 24; 49 kw; 2283 ft.; N47 30 17 W121 58 3
600 New Hampshire Avenue, N.W., Suite 1200, Washington, DC 20037 US
(206) 805-0965, *Fax:* (206) 805-0920
www.jackseattle.cbslocal.com
License: Seattle, King County, WA held by Infinity Radio Holdings Inc.
Group Owner: CBS Radio; (acq 11-13-98; grpsl).
Arbitron Metro Market: Seattle-Tacoma, WA *Target Audience:* 25-54.
Lisa McDonald, General Manager
Neah Flora, General Sales Mgr
Jim Trapp, Programming Director
Tom McGinley, Chief Engineer
Apryl Battin, Director of Marketing
Laura Hohnhaus, Promotion Coordinatior

KZOK-FM
12-01-1964; 102.5 mhz FM *Hrs Open:* 24; 68 kw; 2290 ft.; N47 30 17 W121 58 4
600 New Hampshire Ave., N.W., Suite 1200, Washington, DC 20037 US
(206) 805-1100, *Fax:* (206) 441-1411
www.kzok.cbslocal.com
julie.warner@cbsradio.com
License: Seattle, King County, WA held by Infinity Radio Holdings Inc.
Group Owner: CBS Radio; (acq 11-13-98; grpsl).
Arbitron Metro Market: Seattle, WA *Format:* Classic Rock *Target Audience:* 25-49. *Adv. Rates:* 300; 300; 275; 85
Dave McDonald, President
Carey Curelop, Operations Dir

Selah

KBBO
01-01-1955; 980 khz AM *Hrs Open:* 24; 5 kw-D, 500 w-N, DA-N; N46 36 46 W120 28 24
1200 Chesterley Dr., #160, Yakima, WA 98006
(509) 248-2900, *Fax:* (509) 452-9661
License: Selah, Yakima County, WA held by James D Ingstad
Group Owner: James D. Ingstad Stns; acq 12-1-98; grpsl).
Nat'l Network: ABC; USA *Regional Reps:* Allied Radio Partners.
Population Served: 193,000 *Arbitron Metro Market:* Yakima, WA *No. News Employees:* 1 *Target Audience:* 35-64.
Pete Benedetti, CEO
Brent Phillipy, Operations Dir
Kit Osborne, General Sales Mgr
Jenifer Wilde, Promotions Manager
Trila Bumstead, COO
Ron King, National Sales Manager
Lou Barfelli, Operations Director

***KYKV**
11-24-1983; 103.1 mhz FM; 5.4 kw; 1427 ft.; N46 38 27 W120 23 46 *Rebroadcasts:* Rebroadcasts KLVR(FM) Middletown, CA 100%
103 E. 4th, Ste 209, Ellensburg, WA 98926 US
(800) 525-5683, *Fax:* (916) 251-1650
www.klove.com
klove@klove.com
License: Selah, Kittitas County, WA held by Educational Media Foundation.
Group Owner: EMF Broadcasting; (acq 6-13-2008; $825,000)
Nat'l Network: K-Love
Arbitron Metro Market: Yakima, WA *Format:* Christian
Mike Novak, President

Sequim

***KSQM**
01-01-2009; 91.5 mhz FM; 0.7 kw; -276 ft.; N48 4 30 W123 11 32 US
(360) 681-0000
www.ksqmfm.com
radio@ksqmfm.com
License: Sequim, Clallam County, WA held by Sequim Community Broadcasting.
Arbitron Metro Market: Sequim, WA
Kent Welborn, Programming Director
Steve Kellmeyer, Music Director
Tama Bankston, Volunteer Coordinator and Underwriting Assistant

Shelton

KMAS
09-21-1962; 1030 khz AM *Hrs Open:* 24; 10 kw-D, 1 kw-N; N47 13 17 W123 04 46
Box 760, 210 W. Cota St., Shelton, WA 98584
(360) 426-1030, *Fax:* (360) 427-5268
www.kmas.com,www.masoncountydailynews.com
kmas1030@kmas.com
License: Shelton, Mason County, WA held by Olympic Broadcasting Inc.
Nat'l Network: ARNN *Regional Reps:* Tacher. *Wire Services:* AP
Population Served: 320,000*Special Programming:* Relg 1.5 hrs wkly *Hrs. of News Programming:* news progmg 70 hrs wkly *No. News Employees:* 3 *Target Audience:* 35-64. *Adv. Rates:* 30; 30; 30; 30
Dale Hubbard, President
Jerry Eckenrode, Operations Dir
Jeff Slakey, Programming Director
Carol Gardner, News Director
Jack Oronchek, Chief Engineer

KRXY
10-01-1998; 94.5 mhz FM *Hrs Open:* 24; 0.71 kw; 955 ft.; N47 8 18 W123 8 28
1133 Kresky Road, Centralia, WA 98531 US
(360) 236-1010, *Fax:* (360) 236-1133
www.945roxy.com
krxy@krxy.com
License: Shelton, Mason County, WA held by Premier Broadcasters Inc.
Group Owner: Premier Broadcasters
Arbitron Metro Market: Olympia, WA *Format:* Contemporary Hits/Top 40 *No. News Employees:* 1 *Adv. Rates:* 64; 47; 52; 29
Derek Shannon, General Manager
Bob Hart, Station Manager
Jerry Farmer, General Sales Mgr
Paul Walker, News Director

Silverdale

KITZ
10-26-1948; 1400 khz AM; 1 kw-D, ND1; 0.89 kw-N, ND1; N47 37 45 W122 39 52
10818 N.E. Coxley Drive, Vancouver, WA 98662 US
(360) 876-1400, *Fax:* (360) 876-7920
kitz1400.com
info@kittz1400.com
License: Silverdale, WA held by KITZ Radio Inc.
Nat'l Network: Westwood One
Arbitron Metro Market: Seattle-Tacoma, WA *Format:* Talk *Target Audience:* 25 plus; adults *Adv. Rates:* 20; 16; 18; 10
Alan Gottlieb, Chairman
Kevin Corcoran, Operations Dir
Paul Lyle, General Manager

Spokane

KZBD
11-08-1965; 105.7 mhz FM; 100 kw; 1909 ft.; N47 34 44 W117 17 46

City Center West, 7201 W. Lake Mead Blvd, Las Vegas, NV 89128 US
(509) 448-1000, *Fax:* (509) 448-7015
www.1057thebuzzard.com
ballison@radiospokane.com
License: Spokane, Spokane County, WA held by Mapleton License of Spokane LLC.
Group Owner: Mapleton Communications LLC; (acq 12-3-2007; grpsl)
Nat'l Network: ABC
Arbitron Metro Market: Spokane, WA *Format:* Alternative *Target Audience:* 18-49.
Ralph Cherry, Operations Dir
Paul Swint, General Manager
Phil Robken, General Sales Mgr
Toby Howell, Programming Director
Toby Howell, Promotions Manager
Allan Riley, Chief Engineer

*KAGU
03-16-1988; 88.7 mhz FM; 5 kw; 1529 ft.; N47 34 52 W117 17 47
East 502 Boone Avenue, Spokane, WA 99258 US
(509) 328-4220, *Fax:* (509) 324-5718
www.gonzaga.edu/kagu/
info@gonzaga.edu/kagu.com
License: Spokane, Spokane County, WA held by Gonzaga University Telecommunications Association.
Arbitron Metro Market: Spokane, WA *Format:* Adult Contemp
Special Programming: Class 2 hrs, jazz 2 hrs, folk 2 hrs, drama 2 hrs w
Fr. Robert Lyons, General Manager
Matt Caputo, Promotions Manager

KQNT
01-01-1922; 590 khz AM; 5 kw-U, ND1; N47 36 55 W117 14 57
600 Congress Avenue, Suite 1400, Austin, TX 78701 US
(509) 242-2400, *Fax:* (509) 242-1160
www.590kqnt.com
michaellacrosse@clearchannel.com
License: Spokane, WA held by Capstar TX L.P.
Group Owner: Clear Channel Communications Inc.; (acq 8-30-00; grpsl).
Wire Services: Reuters
Arbitron Metro Market: Spokane, WA *Format:* News, News/Talk, 86 *Target Audience:* 35-64.
Michael La Crosse, Operations Dir
Kosta Panidis, General Manager
Dean Allen, Programming Director
Matt Auclair, Promotions Manager
Kent Abendroth, Chief Engineer

KDRK-FM
01-01-1965; 93.7 mhz FM *Hrs Open:* 24; 60 kw; 2425 ft.; N47 34 14 W117 4 55
City Center West, 7201 W. Lake Mead Blvd, Las Vegas, NV 89128 US
(509) 448-1000, *Fax:* (509) 448-7015
www.catcountry94.com
License: Spokane, Spokane County, WA held by Mapleton License of Spokane LLC.
Group Owner: Mapleton Communications LLC; (acq 12-3-2007; grpsl)
Arbitron Metro Market: Spokane, WA *Format:* Country *Target Audience:* 25-54.
Sharon Bonds, Programming Director
Toby Howell, Promotions Manager

*KEEH
07-01-1991; 104.9 mhz FM *Hrs Open:* 24; 10.5 kw; 1549 ft.; N47 34 45 W117 17 51 *Rebroadcasts:* Rebroadcasts KGTS(FM) College Place 100%
Mailing Address: P.O. Box 19039, Spokane, WA 99219 US
Second Address: 3715 S. Grove Rd., Spokane, WA 99219
(509) 456-4870, *Fax:* (509) 838-4882
www.plr.org
keeh@plr.org
License: Spokane, Spokane County, WA held by Upper Columbia Media Association
Nat'l Network: USA
Arbitron Metro Market: Spokane, WA *Format:* Christian *Target Audience:* General.
John Dolrymple, General Manager

KEZE
12-25-1992; 96.9 mhz FM *Hrs Open:* 24; 8.2 kw; 1198 ft.; N47 43 33 W117 10 6
500 W. Boone Ave., Spokane, WA 99201 US
(509) 324-4000, *Fax:* (509) 324-8992
www.coyotecountry969.com
License: Spokane, Spokane County, WA held by QueenB Radio Inc.
Group Owner: Morgan Murphy Media (Evening Telegram Co)
Nat'l Network: USA *Nat'l Reps:* Katz Radio
Arbitron Metro Market: Spokane, WA *TV Affiliate:* KXLY-TV affil
Format: Country *Target Audience:* 25 plus; general
Elizabeth Burns, President
Ken Hopkins, Operations Dir
Teddie Gibbon, Station Manager
Maynard Cohen, Programming Director
Steve Herling, Executive Vice President

KGA
01-01-1926; 1510 khz AM *Hrs Open:* 24
City Center West, 7201 W. Lake Mead Blvd, Las Vegas, NV 89128 US
(509) 448-1000, *Fax:* (509) 448-7015
www.1510kga.com
License: Spokane, WA held by Mapleton License of Spokane LLC.
Group Owner: Mapleton Communications LLC; (acq 12-3-2007; grpsl)
Arbitron Metro Market: Spokane, WA *Format:* Sports, Talk
Special Programming: Farm one hr wkly *Target Audience:* 18-34.
Cary Rolfe, Operations Dir
Don Morin, General Manager
Regina Winkler, General Sales Mgr
Bob Castle, Programming Director
Dave Ratener, Chief Engineer

KISC
05-01-1966; 98.1 mhz FM; 92.1 kw; 2031 ft.; N47 34 52 W117 17 47
600 Congress Avenue, Suite 1400, Austin, TX 78701 US
(509) 242-3400, *Fax:* (509) 242-2581
www.literockkiss.com
info@literockkiss.com
License: Spokane, Spokane County, WA
Arbitron Metro Market: Spokane, WA *Format:* Adult Contemp
Rob Harder, Programming Director
Ian Richards, Disc Jockey
John Chrisopher Kowsky, Disc Jockey
Dawn Marcel, Disc Jockey
Stormy Morgan, Disc Jockey
Mark Holman, Disc Jockey

KJRB
01-01-1947; 790 khz AM *Hrs Open:* 24; 5 kw-D, DA2; 3.8 kw-N, DA2; N47 30 8 W117 23 6
City Center West, 7201 W. Lake Mead Blvd, Las Vegas, NV 89128 US
(509) 448-1000, *Fax:* (509) 448-7015
License: Spokane, WA held by Mapleton License of Spokane LLC.
Group Owner: Mapleton Communications LLC; (acq 12-3-2007; grpsl)
Arbitron Metro Market: Spokane, WA *Format:* News, Talk *Target Audience:* 25-54.
Cary Rolfe, Operations Dir
Don Morin, General Manager
Joe Via, General Sales Mgr
Bob Castle, Programming Director
Dave Ratener, Chief Engineer

KKZX
10-10-1975; 98.9 mhz FM *Hrs Open:* 24; 100 kw; 1608 ft.; N47 35 35 W117 17 46
600 Congress Avenue, Suite 1400, Austin, TX 78701 US
(509) 242-2400, *Fax:* (509) 242-2482
www.kkzx.com
info@kkzx.com
License: Spokane, Spokane County, WA
Group Owner: Clear Channel Communications Inc.
Arbitron Metro Market: Spokane, WA *Format:* Classic Rock
Special Programming: Blues 2 hrs wkly *Hrs. of News Programming:* News progmg one hr wkly *Target Audience:* 25-54.
Jon McGann, Programming Director

*KMBI
07-12-1959; 1330 khz AM *Hrs Open:* 6 AM-sunset; 5 kw-D, NDD; N47 36 17 W117 21 27
820 N Lasalle Blvd, Chicago, IL 60610 US
(509) 448-2555, *Fax:* (509) 448-6855
kmbi@moody.edu
License: Spokane, WA held by Moody Bible Institute
Group Owner: The Moody Bible Institute of Chicago; (Acq 6-74)
Arbitron Metro Market: Spokane, WA *Hrs. of News Programming:* News progmg 6 hrs wkly *Target Audience:* 35-54; Christian men & women
Steve Stewart, Operations Dir
D. Gary Leonard, Station Manager

*KMBI-FM
07-01-1974; 107.9 mhz FM *Hrs Open:* 24; 64 kw; 2379 ft.; N47 34 15 W117 5 0
820 N Lasalle Boulevard, Chicago, IL 60610 US
(509) 448-2555, *Fax:* (509) 448-6855
www.kmbi.org
kmbi@moody.edu
License: Spokane, Spokane County, WA held by Moody Bible Institute
Group Owner: The Moody Bible Institute of Chicago
Arbitron Metro Market: Spokane, WA *Format:* Religious *Hrs. of News Programming:* News progmg 9 hrs wkly *Target Audience:* 35-54; Christian men & women
Rich Monteith, Station Manager
Steve Stewart, Programming Director
Gordon Canaday, Chief Engineer
Shelly Hogeweide, Disc Jockey
Bret Bremberg, Shelly Hogeweide
Derek Cutlip, Disc Jockey

*KPBX-FM
01-01-1970; 91.1 mhz FM *Hrs Open:* 24; 56 kw; 2379 ft.; N47 34 13 W117 5 0
Mailing Address: 2319 N. Monroe Street, Spokane, WA 99205 US
Second Address: , Coeur d'Alene, ID
(509) 328-5729, *Fax:* (509) 328-5764
www.kpbx.org
rkunkel@kpbx.org
License: Spokane, Spokane County, WA held by Spokane Public Radio Inc.
Nat'l Network: NPR; PRI
Arbitron Metro Market: Spokane, WA *Format:* Jazz, News
Special Programming: Jazz, folk, world mus, new age/space, new mus *Hrs. of News Programming:* news progmg 50 hrs wkly *No. News Employees:* 3 *TargetAudience:* General; educated

KSBN
09-01-1921; 1230 khz AM *Hrs Open:* 24; 1 kw-U; N47 39 30 W117 25 08
7 South Howard, Suite 430, Spokane, WA 99202
(509) 838-4000, *Fax:* (509) 838-4800
www.ksbn.net
ksbn@ksbn.net
License: Spokane, Spokane County, WA held by KSBN Radio Inc.
Wire Services: Bloomberg Financial
Population Served: 400,000 *Arbitron Metro Market:* Spokane, WA *Hrs. of News Programming:* news progmg 24 hrs wkly *No. News Employees:* 1 *Target Audience:* 30-65; upscale; business owners *Adv. Rates:* 15;15;15;15
Alan Gottlieb, Chairman
Brad Kemmer, General Manager
Patrick Carey, General Sales Mgr
Conrad Agate, Chief Engineer

*KSFC
03-01-1973; 91.9 mhz FM *Hrs Open:* 24; 2.2 kw; 1098 ft.; N47 48 48 W117 30 23
2319 N. Monroe Street, Spokane, WA 99205 US
(509) 328-5729, *Fax:* (509) 328-5764
www.ksfc.org
rkunkel@kpbx.org
License: Spokane, Spokane County, WA held by Spokane Public Radio Inc.
Nat'l Network: NPR; PRI
Arbitron Metro Market: Spokane, WA *Format:* News *Special Programming:* American Indian 5 hrs, black 2 hrs wkly *Target Audience:* Curious.
Tom Parker, Chairman
Christie P. Anderson, Vice Chair

KTTO
01-01-1947; 970 khz AM *Hrs Open:* 24; 5 kw-D, DAN; 1 kw-N, DAN; N47 36 59 W117 21 55
500 W Boone Avenue, Spokane, WA 99201 US
(509) 327-3695, *Fax:* (509) 327-5171
www.spokanecatholicradio.com
License: Spokane, WA held by Sacred Heart Radio Inc.
Arbitron Metro Market: Spokane, WA *Format:* Christian
Sr. Patricia Proctor, General Manager

KPTQ
01-01-1965; 1280 khz AM *Hrs Open:* 6 AM-9 PM
600 Congress Avenue, Suite 1400, Austin, TX 78701 US
(509) 242-2400, *Fax:* (509) 459-9850
www.1280kptq.com
info@kaqq1280.com
License: Spokane, WA held by Capstar TX L.P.
Group Owner: Clear Channel Communications Inc.; (acq 8-30-2000; grpsl).

Nat'l Network: USA *Nat'l Reps:* D & R Radio *Regional Reps:* Tacher.
Arbitron Metro Market: Spokane, WA *Format:* News, News/Talk, 86 *Hrs. of News Programming:* News progmg one hr wkly *Target Audience:* General.
Michael La Crosse, Operations Dir
Kosta Panidis, General Manager
Paul Neumann, Programming Director
Matt Auclair, Promotions Manager
Garth Trimble, General Sales Manager
Dan Manella, Market Manager

KBBD
01-01-1988; 103.9 mhz FM *Hrs Open:* 24; 39 kw; 1417 ft.; N47 36 4 W117 17 53
City Center West 7201 W. Lake Mead Blvd., Suite 400, Las Vegas, NV 89128 US
(509) 448-1000, *Fax:* (509) 448-7015
www.1039bobfm.com
License: Spokane, Spokane County, WA held by Mapleton License of Spokane LLC.
Group Owner: Mapleton Communications LLC; (acq 12-3-2007; grpsl)
Nat'l Network: ABC
Arbitron Metro Market: Spokane, WA *Target Audience:* 25-49.
Cary Rolfe, Operations Dir
Don Morin, General Manager
Mike Skot, Programming Director
Toby Howell, Promotions Manager
Larry Weir, News Director
Dave Ratener, Chief Engineer
Brenda Anderson, Traffic Manager
Amanda Mellis,Promotions Coordinator

KXLY
10-01-1922; 920 khz AM *Hrs Open:* 24
500west Boone Avenue, Spokane, WA 99201 US
(509) 324-4000, *Fax:* (509) 324-8992
www.kxly.com
info@kxly.com
License: Spokane, WA held by QueenB Radio Inc.
Group Owner: Morgan Murphy Media (Evening Telegram Co); (acq 3-21-62)
Nat'l Network: CBS; Wall Street *Nat'l Reps:* Katz Radio
Arbitron Metro Market: Spokane, WA *Format:* News, News/Talk, 86 *Special Programming:* Sports talk 5 hrs, sports play-by-play 20 hrs, local talk 15 hrs wkly *Hrs. of News Programming:* news progmg 30 hrs wkly *No. NewsEmployees:* 25 *Target Audience:* Adults 35 plus; upper end education & income levels
Stephen Herling, Operations Dir
Chris Garras, General Manager
Teddie Gibbon, Station Manager
Roger Nelson, General Sales Mgr
Gina Mauro, Promotions Manager
Dick Brantley, Regional Sales Manager

KXLY-FM
09-01-1959; 99.9 mhz FM *Hrs Open:* 24; 37 kw; 2999 ft.; N47 55 18 W117 6 48
West 500 Boone Avenue, Spokane, WA 99201 US
(509) 324-4000, *Fax:* (509) 324-8992
www.kxly.com
info@kxly.com
License: Spokane, Spokane County, WA
Nat'l Network: Westwood One; Jones Radio Networks *Nat'l Reps:* Katz Radio
Arbitron Metro Market: Spokane, WA *Format:* Adult Contemp *Target Audience:* 25-64; adults, upper end income & education levels
Tery Garras, General Sales Mgr
Joe Via, Regional Sales Manager

KZZU-FM
09-01-1955; 92.9 mhz FM; 81 kw; 2080 ft.; N47 35 42 W117 17 53
500 W Boon Avenue, Spokane, WA 99201 US
(509) 324-4000, *Fax:* (509) 324-8992
www.929zzu.com/
License: Spokane, Spokane County, WA held by QueenB Radio Inc.
Group Owner: Morgan Murphy Media (Evening Telegram Co); (acq 4-1-96; $1.75 million with co-located AM).
Nat'l Reps: Katz Radio
Arbitron Metro Market: Spokane, WA *TV Affiliate:* KXLY-TV.
Format: Adult Contemp *Target Audience:* 18-49.
Brian, Operations Dir
Teddie Gibbon, Station Manager
Tery, General Sales Mgr
Ken, Programming Director
Sharleen, Promotions Manager
Jolene Longwill, News Director

Tim Anderson, Chief Engineer
Catherine Bruntlett, ResearchDirector

*KPBZ
90.3 mhz FM *Hrs Open:* 24; 0.55 kw; 1082 ft.; N47 48 48 W117 30 23
2319 N Monroe Street, Spokane, WA 99205 US
(509) 328-5729, *Fax:* (509) 328-5764
www.kpbx.org
kpbx@kpbx.org
License: Spokane, Spokane County, WA held by Spokane Public Radio Inc.
Arbitron Metro Market: Spokane, WA
Tom Parker, Chairman
Brian Flick, Operations Dir
Cary Boyce, General Manager
Verne Windham, Programming Director
Steve Jackson, News Director
Jerry Olson, Chief Engineer
Christie P. Anderson, Vice Chairman
Patrick Klausen,Production Director
Linda K. Stow, Business & Membership Director

Sunnyside

*KAYB
01-01-1998; 88.1 mhz FM; 0.25 kw; -190 ft.; N46 19 53 W120 0 51
P.O. Drawer 2440, Tupelo, MS 38803 US
(662) 844-8888, *Fax:* (662) 842-6791
www.afr.net
comments@afr.net
License: Sunnyside, Yakima County, WA held by American Family Association.
Group Owner: American Family Radio
Arbitron Metro Market: Tupelo, MS *Format:* Christian, Religious
Marvin Sanders, General Manager

KDYM
09-01-1950; 1230 khz AM *Hrs Open:* 24
Mailing Address: P.O. Box 2888, Yakima, WA 98907 US
Second Address: 706 Butterfield Rd., Yakima, WA 98901
(509) 457-1000, *Fax:* (509) 452-0541
www.adelantemediagroup.com
zorro@radiozorro.com
License: Sunnyside, WA held by Bustos Media of Eastern Washington License LLC.
Group Owner: Bustos Media LLC; (acq 11-18-2004; grpsl)
Nat'l Network: La Gran D *Nat'l Reps:* Tacher
Arbitron Metro Market: Yakima, WA *Format:* Oldies, Spanish *No. News Employees:* 1 *Target Audience:* 25-55; Hispanic *Adv. Rates:* 13; 13; 13; 11
Amador Bustos, President
Keith Teske, Operations Dir
Bob Berry, General Manager
Martin Ortiz, Programming Director
Lisa Gonzalez, News Director

Tacoma

KBKS-FM
05-01-1959; 106.1 mhz FM; 68 kw; 2290 ft.; N47 30 17 W121 58 4
600 New Hampshire Avenue, N.W., Suite 1200, Washington, DC 20037 US
(206) 494-2000, *Fax:* (206) 286-2376
www.kissfmseattle.com
karenheric@clearchannel.com
License: Tacoma, Pierce County, WA held by AMFM Texas Licenses L.P.
Group Owner: Clear Channel Communications Inc.; (acq 4-1-2009; grpsl)
Arbitron Metro Market: Seattle, WA *Format:* Contemporary Hits/Top 40 *Target Audience:* 25-54.
Michele Grosenick, General Manager
Karen Heric, General Sales Mgr

KIRO-FM
10-26-1948; 97.3 mhz FM *Hrs Open:* 24; 52 kw; 2392 ft.; N47 30 14 W121 58 29
Suite 409, 401 City Avenue, Bala Cynwyd, PA 19004 US
(206) 343-9700, *Fax:* (206) 623-7677
www.mynorthwest.com
kbsg@kbsg.com
License: Tacoma, Pierce County, WA held by Bonneville Holding Co.
Group Owner: Bonneville International Corporation; (acq 3-14-2008; grpsl)
Nat'l Reps: D & R Radio
Arbitron Metro Market: Seattle-Tacoma, WA *Format:* News, News/Talk, 84, Talk *Target Audience:* 25-54.

Bruce Reese, President
Kevin McCarthy, Operations Dir
Jerry McKenna, General Manager
Jerry Riley, General Sales Mgr
Brian Thomas, Programming Director
Gail Raisio, News Director
Tom Pierson, Chief Engineer

*KXOT
06-01-1949; 91.7 mhz FM *Hrs Open:* 24; 23 kw; 732 ft.; N47 18 14 W122 23 43
1101 South Yakima Avenue, Tacoma, WA 98405 US
(206) 543-2710, *Fax:* (206) 520-5899
www.kuow.org
letter@kuow.org
License: Tacoma, Pierce County, WA held by PRC Tacoma — I LLC
Nat'l Network: NPR
Arbitron Metro Market: Seattle-Tacoma, WA *TV Affiliate:* .
Format: News, News/Talk, 86 *Target Audience:* .
Tom Mara, General Manager
Gary Rubin, General Sales Mgr
Kevin Cole, Programming Director

KHHO
08-01-1942; 850 khz AM *Hrs Open:* 24
1333 New Hampshire Ave., Suite 1000, Washington, DC 20036 US
(206) 494-2000, *Fax:* (206) 286-2376
http://www.sportsradiokjr.com
dickfain@kjram.com
License: Tacoma, WA held by Ackerley Broadcasting Operations LLC.
Group Owner: Clear Channel Communications Inc.; (acq 6-14-2002; grpsl).
Arbitron Metro Market: Seattle-Tacoma, WA *Format:* Sports *Target Audience:* 25-55.
Michele Grosenick, President
Sean Shannon, General Sales Mgr
Rich Moore, Programming Director
Amy Spino, News Director
Doug Irwin, Chief Engineer

KKMO
01-01-1922; 1360 khz AM *Hrs Open:* 24; 5 kw-U, ND1; N47 18 19 W122 26 33
4880 Santa Rosa Road, Suite 300, Camarillo, CA 93012 US
(206) 443-8200, *Fax:* (206) 443-1561
www.kgnw.com
reception@inspirationradio.com
License: Tacoma, WA held by Inspiration Media Inc.
Group Owner: Salem Communications Corp.; (acq 8-12-98; $500,000)
Arbitron Metro Market: Seattle, WA *Target Audience:* 35 plus.
Chuck Olmstead, Operations Dir
Tim Harper, General Manager
Doug Rice, General Sales Mgr
Juanita Jasso, Promotions Manager
Monte Passmore, Chief Engineer

KMTT
06-02-1958; 103.7 mhz FM *Hrs Open:* 24; 67 kw; 2320 ft.; N47 30 14 W121 58 29
Suite 409, 401 City Avenue, Bala Cynwyd, PA 19004 US
(206) 233-1037, *Fax:* (206) 233-8979
www.kmtt.com
studio@kmtt.com
License: Tacoma, Pierce County, WA held by Entercom Seattle License L.L.C.
Group Owner: Entercom Communications Corp.; (acq 6-73; with co-located AM)
Nat'l Reps: D & R Radio
Arbitron Metro Market: Seattle, WA *Format:* Triple A *Hrs. of News Programming:* news progmg 3 hrs wkly *No. News Employees:* 1 *Target Audience:* 25-49.
David Field, President
Steve Oshin, General Manager
Traci Gregory, General Sales Mgr
Shaun Stewart, Programming Director
Jennifer Orr, Promotions Manager
Mike West, News Director
Dwight Smalls, Chief Engineer
Joyce Jinka,Traffic Manager

*KPLU-FM
11-01-1966; 88.5 mhz FM *Hrs Open:* 24; 64 kw; 2320 ft.; N47 30 14 W121 58 29
Mailing Address: 121st and Park Avenue, Tacoma, WA 98447 US
Second Address: 2601 4th Ave., Suite 150, Seattle, WA 98121

RADIO - U.S.

(253) 535-7758, *Fax:* (253) 535-8332
www.kplu.org
info@kplu.org
License: Tacoma, Pierce County, WA held by Pacific Lutheran University.
Nat'l Network: NPR; PRI *Wire Services:* AP
Arbitron Metro Market: Seattle-Tacoma, WA *Format:* Blues, Jazz, 60 *Hrs. of News Programming:* news progmg 54 hrs wkly *No. News Employees:* 7 *Target Audience:* 25-54; upscale, highly educated professionals
Jeff Bauman, Operations Dir
Paul Stankavich, General Manager
Joey Cohn, Programming Director
Brenda Goldstein-Young, Promotions Manager
Erin Hennessey, News Director
Lowell Kiesow, Chief Engineer
Nick Francis, Music Director

*KUPS

02-28-1978; 90.1 mhz FM *Hrs Open:* 24; 0.1 kw; 230 ft.; N47 15 48 W122 28 37
1500 North Warner St., Tacoma, WA 98416 US
(253) 879-3288
www.kups.net
thesound@ups.edu
License: Tacoma, Pierce County, WA held by University of Puget Sound.
Arbitron Metro Market: Tacoma, WA *Format:* Alternative *Special Programming:* Black 18 hrs, jazz 12 hrs, reggae 6 hrs, world mus 4 hrs, blues 6 hrs, metal 8 hrs wkly *Target Audience:* 18-45.
Doug Herstad, Operations Dir
Brenden Goetz, General Manager

*KVTI

11-15-1955; 90.9 mhz FM *Hrs Open:* 24; 51 kw; 364 ft; N47 09 39 W122 34 35
Northwest Public Radio
4500 Steilacoom Blvd. S.W., Lakewood, WA 98499
(253) 589-5884, *Fax:* (253) 589-5797
www.i91.ctc.edu
i-91fm@cptc.edu
License: Tacoma, Pierce County, WA held by Clover Park Technical College.
Wire Services: AP
Population Served: 2,500,000 *Arbitron Metro Market:* Seattle-Tacoma, WA *Special Programming:* Live mus 3 hrs, talk 4 hrs wkly *Hrs. of News Programming:* Northwest Public Radio
Target Audience: 12-34; youngadults & teens
John Mangan, General Manager
Al Bednarczyk, Chief Engineer
Beth Valiant, Music Director

Toppenish

KYNR

05-16-1954; 1490 khz AM *Hrs Open:* 24; 1 kw-U, ND1; N46 22 33 W120 19 18
Mailing Address: P. O. Box 350, Toppenish, WA 98948 US
Second Address: 711 King Ln., Toppenish, WA 98948
(509) 865-5363, *Fax:* (509) 865-2129
www.kynr.com
kyn@yakama.com
License: Toppenish, WA held by Confederated Tribes and Bands of the Yakama Nation
Arbitron Metro Market: Yakima, WA *Format:* Classic Rock, Country, 52, News, Oldies, Sports *Special Programming:* American Indian 20 hrs wkly *Hrs. of News Programming:* News progmg one hr wkly *Target Audience:* 18-58.
Lenny Abrams, General Manager
Reggie George, Programming Director

KDBL(FM)

10-31-1977; 92.9 mhz FM *Hrs Open:* 24; 17 kw; 843 ft; N46 30 15 W120 23 33
4010 Summitview Ave., Yakima, WA 98908
(509) 972-3461, *Fax:* (509) 972-3542
www.929thebull.com
cherylsalomone@townsquaremedia.com
License: Toppenish, Yakima County, WA held by GAP Broadcasting Yakima License LLC.
Group Owner: GAPWEST Broadcasting; (acq 2-13-2008; grpsl)
Nat'l Reps: McGavren Guild
Population Served: 190,000 *Arbitron Metro Market:* Yakima, WA *Format:* Country *No. News Employees:* 2 *Target Audience:* 18-49.
Gary Donovan, President
Ron Harris, Operations Dir
Cheryl Salomone, General Manager
Aimee Yoerger, General Sales Mgr
Rik Mikals, Programming Director

Tumwater

KUOW

08-01-1987; 1340 khz AM *Hrs Open:* 24*Rebroadcasts:* Rebroadcasts KUOW-FM Seattle 100%
6005 Capitol Blvd. S.E., Tumwater, WA 98501 US
(206) 543-2710, *Fax:* (206) 616-9125
www.kuow.org
letters@kuow.org
License: Tumwater, WA held by KUOW/Puget Sound Public Radio
Nat'l Network: NPR; PRI
Arbitron Metro Market: Seattle-Tacoma, WA *Format:* News
Wayne Roth, General Manager

Twisp

KCSY

06-01-1993; 106.3 mhz FM; 0.22 kw; 1637 ft.; N48 19 6 W120 6 46
P.O. Box 1130, Twisp, WA 98856 US
(509) 293-4397, *Fax:* (509) 997-5859
kcsyfm.com
sunnyfm@kcsyfm.com; teri@kcsyfm.com
License: Twisp, Okanogan County, WA held by Resort Radio LLC
Arbitron Metro Market: Wenatchee, WA *Format:* Oldies
Aaron Griffith, Operations Dir
David Herald, General Manager/ Partner
Debbie Griggs, General Sales Mgr
Lonnie England, Chief Engineer
Teri Moore, Executive Office Manager
Mike Moore, Account Executive

Union Gap

KDYK

09-13-1983; 1020 khz AM *Hrs Open:* 24
Mailing Address: P.O. Box 2888, Yakima, WA 98907 US
Second Address: 706 Butterfield Rd., Union Gap, WA 98907
(509) 457-1000, *Fax:* (509) 452-0541
www.bustosmedia.com
zorro@radiozorro.com
License: Union Gap, WA
Group Owner: Adelante Media Group LLC; (acq 11-18-2004; grpsl)
Nat'l Network: La Gran D *Regional Reps:* Tacher.
Arbitron Metro Market: Union Gap, WA *Target Audience:* 25-49; Hispanic adults *Adv. Rates:* 25; 20; 25; 15
Keith Teske, Operations Dir
Bob Berry, General Manager
Martin Ortiz, Programming Director

Vancouver

KBMS

01-01-1955; 1480 khz AM *Hrs Open:* 24; 1 kw-D, DAN; 2.5 kw-N, DAN; N45 36 6 W122 43 6
601 Main Street, Suite 400, Vancouver, WA 98660 US
(360) 699-1881
avjkbms@aol.com
License: Vancouver, WA held by Christopher H. Bennett Broadcasting Co. of WA Inc.
Nat'l Network: ABC
Arbitron Metro Market: Portland, OR *Format:* Talk *Target Audience:* 54; male & female *Adv. Rates:* 65; 65; 65; 65
Chris Bennett, General Manager
Angela Jenkins, Station Manager

KKSN

09-01-1946; 910 khz AM *Hrs Open:* 24; 5 kw-U, DA-2; N45 33 28 W122 30 09
6400 S.E. Lake Rd., Suite 350, Portland, OR 10004
(503) 786-0600, *Fax:* (503) 786-1551
www.espndeportesradio.com
License: Vancouver, Clark County, WA held by Entercom Portland License LLC.
Group Owner: Entercom Communications Corp.; (acq 4-23-98; grpsl)
Nat'l Network: ESPN Deportes *Nat'l Reps:* D & R Radio
Population Served: 230,600 *Arbitron Metro Market:* Portland, OR
Dennis Hayes, General Manager
Justin Mansfield, Programming Director
Jordan Smith, Promotions Manager

KKOV

08-10-1963; 1550 khz AM *Hrs Open:* 24; 50 kw-D, 12 kw-N, DA-N; N45 38 47 W122 30 51
6605 S.E. Lake Rd., Portland, OR 97266
(503) 223-4321, *Fax:* (503) 294-0074
www.sunny1550kkad.com
markail@kpam.com
License: Vancouver, Clark County, WA held by Pamplin Broadcasting-Washington Inc.
Group Owner: Pamplin Broadcasting; (acq 11-20-98; $1.65 million)
Nat'l Network: AP Network News *Nat'l Reps:* Tacher *Regional Reps:* The Tacher Co.; INc. *Wire Services:* AP
Arbitron Metro Market: Portland, OR *Special Programming:* Portland Beaver baseball 18 hrs wkly *Hrs. of News Programming:* news progmg 5.6 hrs wkly *No. News Employees:* 2 *Target Audience:* 35-64.
Mark Ail, Operations Dir
Paul Clithero, General Manager
Margaret Evans, General Sales Mgr
Paul Duckworth, Programming Director
Misty Osko, Promotions Manager
Bill Gallagher, News Director
Dave Bischoff, Chief Engineer
JeanneWinters, National Sales Manager
Paul Blanding, Traffic Manager

Walla Walla

KGDC

12-06-1956; 1320 khz AM *Hrs Open:* 24; 1 kw-D, ND1; 0.066 kw-N, ND1; N46 1 25 W118 21 17
P.O. Box 941, Walla Walla, WA 99362 US
(509) 525-7878, *Fax:* (509) 522-2046
comments@kgdcradio.com
License: Walla Walla, WA held by Two Hearts Communications LLC
Format: News, News/Talk, 86 *Hrs. of News Programming:* News progmg 5 hrs wkly *Target Audience:* General. *Adv. Rates:* 9; 8; 8; 8
Rod Fazzari, President

KKSR

01-01-1980; 95.7 mhz FM; 100 kw; Ant 1,401 ft; N45 59 04 W118 10 08
830 N. Columbia Center Blvd., Suite B-2, Kennewick, WA 99336
(509) 783-0783, *Fax:* (509) 735-8627
www.957starfm.com
rik.mikals@nnbradio.com
License: Walla Walla, Walla Walla County, WA held by James R Ingstad
Group Owner: James D. Ingstad Stns; (acq 1999)
Nat'l Reps: Christal
Arbitron Metro Market: Tri-Cities, WA (Richland-Kennewick-Pasco) *Target Audience:* 25-54.
Lisa Perez, News Director

KTEL

10-01-1946; 1490 khz AM *Hrs Open:* 24; 1 kw-U, ND1; N46 2 33 W118 20 0
112 N.E. 5th Avenue, Milton-Freewater, OR 97862 US
(509) 522-1383, *Fax:* (509) 522-0211
www.1490ktel.com
License: Walla Walla, WA held by WW2 L.L.C.
Group Owner: Capps Broadcast Group; (acq 6-2-03)
Nat'l Network: Jones Radio Networks; ABC *Regional Reps:* Tacher
Arbitron Metro Market: Walla Walla, WA *Format:* Oldies *Special Programming:* Farm 5 hrs wkly *Target Audience:* 25 plus; general *Adv. Rates:* 23; 19; 21; 17
Dave Capps, President
Randy McKone, Operations Dir
Liz Halley, General Sales Mgr
Joe Oertel-Sports Director

*KRKL

05-10-1977; 93.3 mhz FM *Hrs Open:* 24; 42 kw; 1378 ft.; N45 59 19 W118 10 28
112 N. E. 5th Street, Milton-Freewater, OR 97862 US
(800) 525-5683, *Fax:* (916) 251-1650
www.klove.com
klove@klove.com
License: Walla Walla, Walla Walla County, WA held by Educational Media Foundation.
Group Owner: EMF Broadcasting; (acq 4-1-02; $1 million).
Nat'l Network: K-Love
Arbitron Metro Market: Walla Walla, WA *Format:* Christian *No. News Employees:* 13 *Target Audience:* 25-44; Judeo Christian, female
Darrell Chambliss, Chairman
Mike Novak, President and CEO
Mike Lee, Operations Dir
David Pierce, Programming Director
David Pierce, Chief Creative Officer
Ed Lenane, News Director

Sam Wallington, Engineering Dir
Marya Morgan,News Reporter
Richard Hunt, News Reporter
Alan Mason, Chief Operating Officer
Dan Antonelli, Chief Business Development Officer
Eric Moser, Chief Financial Officer
Brian Burger, Vice President of Human Resources

KUJ
01-01-1928; 1420 khz AM *Hrs Open:* 24
Rt 5, Box 513, Walla Walla, WA 99362 US
(509) 527-1000, *Fax:* (509) 529-5534
www.kujam.com
kujam@bmi.net,info@power991fm.com
License: Walla Walla, WA held by Alexandra Communications Inc.
Group Owner: Alexandra Communications Inc.; (acq 4-13-2001).
Nat'l Network: Westwood One *Regional Reps:* Tacher.
Arbitron Metro Market: Walla Walla, WA *Format:* News, News/Talk, 84, Talk *Hrs. of News Programming:* news progmg 15 hrs wkly *No. News Employees:* 1 *Target Audience:* 25 plus. *Adv. Rates:* 16; 12; 16; 10
Tom Hodgins, CEO
Cheryl Hodgins, President

***KWCW**
01-01-1971; 90.5 mhz FM *Hrs Open:* 24; 0.16 kw; -52 ft.; N46 4 11 W118 19 51
200 Boyer Avenue, Walla Walla, WA 99362 US
(509) 527-5285
www.kwcw.net
License: Walla Walla, Walla Walla County, WA held by The Associated Students of Whitman College Radio Committee.
Arbitron Metro Market: Walla Walla, WA *Format:* Variety/Diverse *Hrs. of News Programming:* news progmg 2.5 hrs wkly *No. News Employees:* 1
Brian Kilgore, General Manager

***KWWS**
03-06-1997; 89.7 mhz FM; 3.2 kw; 1345 ft.; N45 59 4 W118 10 8
Rebroadcasts: Rebroadcasts KWSU(AM) Pullman 100%
382 Murrow Center, Pullman, WA 99164 US
(509) 335-6500, *Fax:* (509) 335-6577
www.nwpr.org
nwpr@wsu.edu
License: Walla Walla, Walla Walla County, WA held by Washington State University.
Arbitron Metro Market: Pullman, WA *Format:* News, News/Talk, 86
Karen Olstad, COO
Scott Weatherly, Operations Dir
Dennis Haarsager, General Manager
Roger Johnson, Station Manager
Sarah McDaniel, General Sales Mgr
Mary Hawkins, Programming Director
Aki Wright, Development Coordinator
AndiWilson, Music and Culture

KXRX
08-01-1977; 97.1 mhz FM *Hrs Open:* 24; 100 kw; 1329 ft.; N45 59 4 W118 10 9
Mailing Address: City Center West, 7201 W. Lake Mead Blvd, Las Vegas, NV 89128 US
Second Address: 2621 West A. St., Pasco, WA 99301
(509) 547-9791, *Fax:* (509) 547-8509
www.97rock.fm
cherylsalomone@townsquaremedia.com
License: Walla Walla, Walla Walla County, WA held by GAP Broadcasting Tri-Cities License LLC.
Group Owner: GAPWEST Broadcasting; (acq 2-13-2008; grpsl)
Arbitron Metro Market: Paso, WA *Hrs. of News Programming:* news progmg one hr wkly *No. News Employees:* 1 *Target Audience:* 25 plus; middle to upper income level listeners
CherylSalomone@townsquaremedia.com, General Manager
Grant Linnen, General Sales Mgr
Scott Stele, Programming Director
Adam Lamberd, Brand Manager

Wapato

***KSOH**
03-06-1992; 89.5 mhz FM; 9.5 kw; 974 ft.; N46 31 42 W120 31 16
402 E. Yakima Avenue, #1320, Yakima, WA 98901 US
(800) 775-4673, *Fax:* (615) 216-7266
www.lifetalk.net
ksoh@lifetalk.net
License: Wapato, Yakima County, WA held by Life Talk Broadcasting Association.
Arbitron Metro Market: Wapato, WA *Format:* Religious *Target Audience:* 25-50; families, singles needing courage, hope & answers to societal ills

Steve Gallmore, General Manager

Wenatchee

KKRT
11-17-1956; 900 khz AM *Hrs Open:* 24; 1 kw-D, NDD; 0.072 kw-N, ND1; N47 27 44 W120 21 28
725 Broad St., P.O. Box 936, Augusta, GA 30903 US
(509) 663-5186, *Fax:* (509) 663-8779
www.kkrt.com
info@kkrt.com
License: Wenatchee, WA held by Morris Communications Corp.
Group Owner: Morris Radio LLC; (acq 10-15-98; grpsl)
Nat'l Network: ESPN Radio *Nat'l Reps:* Katz Radio
Arbitron Metro Market: Yakima, WA *Format:* Sports *Target Audience:* 18-54; men
William Morris III, CEO
Michael Osterhont, President
Gary Patrick, General Manager
Jeff Dahlstrom, General Sales Mgr
John Windus, Programming Director
Jay White, Chief Engineer

KKRV
05-01-1976; 104.7 mhz FM *Hrs Open:* 24; 6.5 kw; 1322 ft.; N47 28 44 W120 12 49
725 Broad St., P.O. Box 936, Augusta, GA 30903 US
(509) 663-5186, *Fax:* (509) 663- 8779
www.kkrv.com
info@kkrv.com
License: Wenatchee, Chelan County, WA held by Morris Communications Corp.
Arbitron Metro Market: Yakima, WA *Format:* Country *Target Audience:* 25-54; women
Shari Alexander, News Director

***KPLW**
01-01-1996; 89.9 mhz FM *Hrs Open:* 24; 5 kw; 1391 ft.; N47 19 25 W120 13 56
606 North Western Ave., Wenatchee, WA 98801 US
(509) 665-6641, *Fax:* (509) 665-3126
www.plr.org
kplw@plr.org
License: Wenatchee, Chelan County, WA held by Growing Christian Foundation.
Format: Christian, News, 74 *Hrs. of News Programming:* News progmg 2 hrs wkly *Target Audience:* 35-54; female
Kevin Krueger, President
Sean Ruud, General Manager

KPQ
12-01-1929; 560 khz AM *Hrs Open:* 24; 5 kw-D, DAN; 5 kw-N, DAN; N47 27 12 W120 19 43
Mailing Address: 32 N. Misssion Street, Wenatchee, WA 98801 US
Second Address: 231 North Wenatchee Ave, Wenatchee, WA 98801
(509) 665-6565, *Fax:* (509) 663-1150
www.kpq.com
info@cherrycreekradio.com
License: Wenatchee, WA held by Wescoast Broadcasting Co.
Nat'l Reps: Tacher
Arbitron Metro Market: Wenatchee *Format:* News, News/Talk, 86
Special Programming: Farm 3 hrs wkly *Hrs. of News Programming:* News progmg 165 hrs wkly *Target Audience:* 35 plus.
Jim Wallace Jr., President
Debi Campestrini, Operations Dir
Greg McEwen, General Sales Mgr
Steve Hair, News Director
Pete Peterson, Chief Engineer
Tom Cashman, News Reporter
Eric Granstrom, Sports Commentator
Janette Morris,Traffic Manager

KPQ-FM
12-01-1967; 102.1 mhz FM *Hrs Open:* 24; 35 kw; 2654 ft.; N47 16 28 W120 25 30
Mailing Address: 32 North Mission Street, Wenatchee, WA 98801 US
Second Address: 231 North Wenatchee Ave, Wenatchee, WA 98807

www.thequake1021.com
info@cherrycreekradio.com
License: Wenatchee, Chelan County, WA
Arbitron Metro Market: Wenatchee, Yakima *Format:* Classic Rock *Hrs. of News Programming:* News progmg one hr wkly *Target Audience:* 25 plus.
Janette Morris, News Director
Kelly Hart, Local News Editor

Tom Cashman, News Reporter
Eric Granstrom, Sports Commentator

KZNW
01-01-1948; 1340 khz AM *Hrs Open:* 24
N. 1212 Washington, Suite 307, Spokane, WA 99201 US
(509) 665-6565, *Fax:* (509) 663-1150
www.lasuperz.com
License: Wenatchee, WA held by CCR-Wenatchee IV LLC.
Group Owner: Cherry Creek Radio LLC; (acq 10-31-2006; grpsl)
Nat'l Reps: McGavren Guild
Arbitron Metro Market: Wenatchee, WA *Hrs. of News Programming:* news progmg 10 hrs wkly *No. News Employees:* 1 *Target Audience:* General; Hispanic *Adv. Rates:* 14; 14; 14; 14
Steve Miller, General Manager
Leona Frank, General Sales Mgr
Elsa Esparza, Programming Director
Manuel Garcia, Chief Engineer

West Clarkston

***KAUC**
89.7 mhz FM; 0.5 kw; -607 ft.; N46 26 20 W117 0 31
P.O. Box 19039, Spokane, WA 99219 US
License: West Clarkston, Asotin County, WA held by Upper Columbia Media Corp.
Arbitron Metro Market: Spokane, WA
Tommy Austin, Operations Dir
Dennis Lamme, General Manager
Beth Davis, General Sales Mgr
John Helmkamp, Promotions Manager
Dan Sullivan, General Sales Manager

Westport

***KLWA**
101.3 mhz FM; 1.2 kw; -6 meters; N46 53 04 W124 00 44
Rebroadcasts: KLVR(FM) Middletown, Ca
5700 West Oaks Blvd, Rocklin, CA
(916) 251-1600, *Fax:* (916) 251-1650
www.klove.com
License: Westport, Grays Harbor County, WA held by Educational Media Foundation LLC
Group Owner: College Creek Media LLC

Mike Novak, President

***KCFL**
91.1 mhz FM; 4 kw horiz; 26 meters; N47 00 35 W124 09 09
717 Lincoln Street, Hoquiam, WA
(360) 580-4001
www.ghinstitute.org
License: Westport, WA held by Grays Harbor Institute

Gary Murrell, President

White Salmon

***KBNO-FM**
01-01-2001; 89.3 mhz FM; 0 kw horiz, 0.016 kw vert; 1102 ft.; N45 43 23 W121 26 42
Box 3765, McAllen, TX 78502 US
(956) 787-9788
www.hcjb.org/wrn
License: White Salmon, Klickitat County, WA held by World Radio Network Inc.
Arbitron Metro Market: McAllen, TX *Format:* Religious
Dr. Abelardo Limn, Chairman
Glenn Lafitte, CEO
John Estey, General Manager
Kitty Stinson, Chief Operations Officer
James Gamblin, Director of Broadcast Operations
Jamie Sepulveda, Director of Finance and Administration
DwightLind, Western Regional Coordinator
David Soper, Vice Chairman
Glenn Lafitte, Secretary

Wilson Creek

KWLN
11-01-1994; 103.3 mhz FM *Hrs Open:* 24; 25 kw; 243 ft.; N47 16 40 W119 0 0
725 Broad St., P.O. Box 936, Augusta, GA 30903 US
(509) 663-5186, *Fax:* (509) 663-8779
www.lanuevaradio.com
info@lanuevaradio.com
License: Wilson Creek, Grant County, WA held by Morris Communications Corp.
Group Owner: Morris Radio LLC; (acq 10-15-98; grpsl).
Nat'l Reps: Katz Radio
Arbitron Metro Market: Augusta, GA *Target Audience:* 15 plus.

Gary Patrick, General Manager
Jeff Dahlstrom, General Sales Mgr
Jose Luis High, Programming Director

Winlock

KITI-FM
08-15-1995; 95.1 mhz FM *Hrs Open:* 24; 380 w; Ant 879 ft; N46 32 35 W123 01 14
1133 Kresky Rd., Centralia, WA 98531
(360) 736-1355, *Fax:* (360) 736-4761
www.live95.com
live95@live95.com
License: Winlock, Lewis County, WA held by Premier Broadcasters Inc.
Group Owner: Premier Broadcasters Inc.
Regional Reps: Allide
Population Served: 76,000*No. News Employees:* 1 *Target Audience:* 21-49. *Adv. Rates:* Enquire with station.
Rod Etherton, President
Rod Etherton, General Manager
Matt Shannon, Station Manager
Matt Shannon, General Sales Mgr
Matt Shannon, Programming Director
Miles McKnight, News Director
Rong Gallagher, Engineering Dir
Harvey Brooks,Chief Engineer

Winthrop

KTRT
01-01-2008; 97.5 mhz FM; 0.33 kw; 1650 ft.; N48 19 6 W120 6 47
US
(509) 341-4230
License: Winthrop, Okanogan County, WA held by Tin Can Communications LLC.
Arbitron Metro Market: Barling, AR *Format:* Triple A
Don Ashford, General Manager

Yakima

KATS
12-15-1968; 94.5 mhz FM *Hrs Open:* 24; 100 kw; 909 ft.; N46 31 59 W120 30 14
4701 E. Lake Harriet Pkw, Minneapolis, MN 55409 US
(509) 972-3461, *Fax:* (509) 972-3540
www.katsfm.com
KATSFM@GMail.com
License: Yakima, Yakima County, WA held by GAP Broadcasting Yakima License LLC.
Group Owner: GAPWEST Broadcasting; (acq 2-13-2008; grpsl)
Arbitron Metro Market: Yakima, WA *Format:* Rock/AOR *No. News Employees:* 1 *Target Audience:* 20-45.
Cheryl Salomone, General Manager
Aimee Yoerger, General Sales Mgr
Todd Lyons, Programming Director
Lance Tormey, News Director

KTCR
01-01-1947; 1390 khz AM *Hrs Open:* 24; 5 kw-D, 500 w-N, DA-2; N46 34 17 W120 27 15
1200 Chesterly Dr., Suite 160, Yakima, WA 98006
(509) 248-2990, *Fax:* (509) 452-9661
License: Yakima, Yakima County, WA held by James D Ingstad
Group Owner: James D. Ingstad Stns; (acq 10-20-98; grpsl)
Nat'l Network: USA
Population Served: 140,000 *Arbitron Metro Market:* Yakima, WA *Special Programming:* Black 2 hrs, gospel 2 hrs wkly *Hrs. of News Programming:* news progmg 12 hrs wkly *No. News Employees:* 2 *Target Audience:* 35-64; family oriented *Adv. Rates:* 20; 20; 20; 12
Pete Benedetti, CEO
Brent Phillipy, Operations Dir
Kit Osborne, General Sales Mgr
Lou Bartelli, Programming Director
Jenifer Wilde, Promotions Manager
Trila Houston, CFO
Trila Bumstead, COO
Ron King, National Sales Manager

*KDNA
12-19-1979; 91.9 mhz FM *Hrs Open:* 6 AM-midnight; 18.5 kw; 919 ft.; N46 31 42 W120 31 3
P.O. Box 800, 121 Sunnyside Avenue, Granger, WA 98932 US
(509) 854-1900(509) 854-1900, *Fax:* (509) 854-2223
www.kdna.org
info@kdna.org
License: Yakima, Yakima County, WA held by Northwest Communities Educational Center.
Arbitron Metro Market: Yakima, WA *Format:* Spanish *Special Programming:* Relg 4 hrs, children 5 hrs, Sp 106 hrs wkly *Hrs. of News Programming:* news progmg 8 hrs wkly *No. News Employees:* 1 *Target Audience:* General; Sp speaking farm workers
Irma Jimenez de Prieto, Chairman
Pat McMahon, Operations Dir
J.D. Freeman, General Manager
Gabriel Martinez, Station Manager
Jeff Mitchell, General Sales Mgr
Saida Rodruguez, Programming Director
Steve Lee, Promotions Manager
Francisco Rios, News Director
Louis Sutton, Engineering Dir

KFFM
08-31-1970; 107.3 mhz FM *Hrs Open:* 24; 100 kw; 1512 ft.; N46 38 26 W120 23 45
P.O. Box 1248, Minnetonka, MN 55345 US
(509) 972-3461, *Fax:* (509) 972-3540
www.kffm.com
jessicastuckel@gapbroadcasting.com
License: Yakima, Yakima County, WA held by GAP Broadcasting Yakima License LLC.
Group Owner: GAPWEST Broadcasting; (acq 2-13-2008; grpsl)
Nat'l Reps: McGavren Guild
Arbitron Metro Market: Yakima, WA *Format:* Contemporary Hits/Top 40 *Hrs. of News Programming:* news progmg one hr wkly *No. News Employees:* 1 *Target Audience:* 18-34.
Cheryl Salomone, General Manager
Aimee Yoerger, General Sales Mgr
Rik Mikals, Programming Director
Esther Johnson, News Director

KHHK
12-01-1984; 99.7 mhz FM *Hrs Open:* 5 AM-midnight; 4.1 kw; 804 ft.; N46 31 20 W120 20 8
5455 Highland Drive, Bellevue, WA 98006 US
(509) 248-2900, *Fax:* (509) 452-9661
newhot997.com
info@newhot997.com
License: Yakima, Yakima County, WA
Group Owner: James D. Ingstad Stns; acq 12-1-98; grpsl).
Arbitron Metro Market: Yakima, WA *Format:* Urban Contemporary *Target Audience:* 18-34.
Pete Benedetti, CEO
Dewey Boynton, Operations Dir
Don Morin, General Manager

KIT
04-08-1929; 1280 khz AM *Hrs Open:* 24; 5 kw-D, ND1; 1 kw-N, ND1; N46 34 19 W120 29 41
Post Office Box 1248, Minnetonka, MN 55345 US
(509) 972-3461, *Fax:* (509) 972-3540,(509) 972-3542
www.1280kit.com
jessicastuckel@gapbroadcasting.com
License: Yakima, WA held by GAP Broadcasting Yakima License LLC.
Group Owner: GAPWEST Broadcasting; (acq 2-13-2008; grpsl)
Nat'l Network: CBS *Nat'l Reps:* McGavren Guild
Arbitron Metro Market: Yakima, WA *Format:* News, News/Talk, 86 *Special Programming:* Farm 6 hrs wkly *No. News Employees:* 2 *Target Audience:* 25-64; professional, mature
Gary Donovan, President
Ron Harris, Operations Dir
Cheryl Salomone, General Manager
Connie Johnston, General Sales Mgr
Dave Ettl, Programming Director
Lance Tormey, News Director
John Wilbanks, Chief Engineer

KUTI
10-19-1944; 1460 khz AM *Hrs Open:* 24; 5 kw-D, DAN; 3.7 kw-N, DAN; N46 33 29 W120 27 2
4701 E. Lake Hariet Pywy, Minneapolis, MN 55409 US
(509) 972-3461, *Fax:* (509) 972-3540
www.1460kuti.com
AM1460KUTI@yahoo.com
License: Yakima, WA held by GAP Broadcasting Yakima License LLC.
Group Owner: GAPWEST Broadcasting; (acq 2-13-2008; grpsl)
Nat'l Reps: McGavren Guild
Arbitron Metro Market: Yakima, WA *Format:* Country *Hrs. of News Programming:* news progmg 2 hrs wkly *No. News Employees:* 1 *Target Audience:* 35 plus.
Gary Donavan, President
Ron Harris, Operations Dir
Cheryl Salomone, General Manager
Jack Balzer, Programming Director
Lance Tormey, News Director
John Wilbanks, Chief Engineer
Lueta Bishop, Traffic Manager

*KNWY
02-20-1993; 90.3 mhz FM *Hrs Open:* 24; 1.9 kw; 843 ft.; N46 31 57 W120 30 37 *Rebroadcasts:* Rebroadcasts KFAE-FM Richland 100%
PO Box 642530, Pullman, WA 99164 US
(509) 335-6500, *Fax:* (509) 335-3772
www.nwpr.org
nwpr@wsu.edu
License: Yakima, Yakima County, WA held by Washington State University.
Arbitron Metro Market: Yakima, WA *Format:* News *Hrs. of News Programming:* news progmg 37 hrs wkly *No. News Employees:* 1
Karen Olstad, COO
Scott Weatherly, Operations Dir
Dennis Haarsager, General Manager
Roger Johnson, Station Manager
Sarah McDaniel, General Sales Mgr
Mary Hawkins, Programming Director

KRSE
08-18-1977; 105.7 mhz FM *Hrs Open:* 24; 100 kw; Ant 584 ft; N46 42 45 W120 37 46
1200 Chesterly Dr., Suite 160, Yakima, WA 98006
(509) 248-2990, *Fax:* (509) 452-9661
k105.com
info@k105.com
License: Yakima, Yakima County, WA held by James D Ingstad
Group Owner: James D. Ingstad Stns
Arbitron Metro Market: Yakima, WA *Target Audience:* 25-64; upscale listener, primarily women *Adv. Rates:* 34; 34; 34; 20
Kendall Weaver, Programming Director
Gail Dahl, News Director

KXDD
07-01-1971; 104.1 mhz FM *Hrs Open:* 24 hrs; 61 kw; 781 ft; N46 30 48 W120 24 05
1200 Chesterley Dr., #160, Yakima, WA 98006
(509) 248-2900, *Fax:* (509) 452-9661
License: Yakima, Yakima County, WA held by James D Ingstad
Group Owner: James D. Ingstad Stns; 2012
Nat'l Reps: The Teacher Company
Arbitron Metro Market: Yakima, WA *Target Audience:* 18-54.
Nancy Odney, COO
James Ingstad, President
Dewey Boynton, Operations Dir
Kelly Gasseling, Station Manager
Kelly Gasseling, General Sales Mgr
Charlie Brooks, Promotions Manager
Lou Bartelli, News Director

KYAK
10-17-1962; 930 khz AM *Hrs Open:* 24
P.O. Box 31000, Spokane, WA 99223 US
(509) 452-5925
kyak.com
kyak@kyak.com
License: Yakima, WA held by Thomas W. Read dba Yakima Christian Broadcasting.
Nat'l Network: Salem Radio Network; USA
Arbitron Metro Market: Yakima, WA *Format:* Christian
Melinda Read, General Manager
Bill Glenn, Station Manager

*KYPL
10-15-1997; 91.1 mhz FM *Hrs Open:* 24; 26 kw; 794 ft.; N46 30 48 W120 24 3 *Rebroadcasts:* Rebroadcasts KGTS(FM) College Place 95%
P.O. Box 602, College Place, WA 99324 US
(509) 457-0725, *Fax:* (509) 457-0658
www.plr.org
studio@plr.org
License: Yakima, Yakima County, WA held by Growing Christian Foundation.
Arbitron Metro Market: Yakima, WA *Format:* Christian *Hrs. of News Programming:* News progmg 8 hrs wkly *Target Audience:* 35-64; family-oriented, Christian
Kevin Krueger, General Manager
Harry Watts, General Sales Mgr
Elizabeth Nelson, Programming Director
Walter Cox, Chief Engineer

*KYVT
09-01-1980; 88.5 mhz FM *Hrs Open:* 24; 3 kw; -256 ft.; N46 35 6 W120 31 41
1116 South 15th Ave., Yakima, WA 98902 US
(509) 573-5022, *Fax:* (509) 573-5023
www.kyvtfm.com
885kyvt@ysdmail.org
License: Yakima, Yakima County, WA held by Yakima School District No. 7.

Arbitron Metro Market: Yakima, WA *Format:* Alternative *Special Programming:* Urban alternative 3 hrs wkly *Hrs. of News Programming:* news progmg 2 hrs wkly *No. News Employees:* 1 *Target Audience:* 18-25;student & working people
John Schieche, President
Randy Beckstead, General Manager
Andy Ward, Promotions Manager

West Virginia

Barrackville

WFGM-FM
07-01-1993; 93.1 mhz FM *Hrs Open:* 24; 2.6 kw; 495 ft.; N39 26 40 W79 59 10 *Rebroadcasts:* Rebroadcasts WBTQ-FM Buckhannon 100%
Mailing Address: Wbuc Road, Buckhannon, WV 26201 US
Second Address: WBUC Rd., Buckhannon, WV 26201
(304) 284-2030, *Fax:* (304) 296-0029
www.931wfgm.com
jcopen@ajradio.com
License: Barrackville, Marion County, WV held by Descendants Trust, Lauren M. Kelley, trustee
Nat'l Network: ABC *Regional Reps:* Dome.
Arbitron Metro Market: Morgantown, WV *Format:* Oldies *No. News Employees:* 1 *Target Audience:* 25-54; active adults *Adv. Rates:* 27; 27; 27; 27
Ryan Elliott, General Manager
David Collett, General Sales Mgr
Brad Allen, News Director
Dick McGraw, Chief Engineer

Beckley

WCIR-FM
06-01-1971; 103.7 mhz FM *Hrs Open:* 24; 5 kw; 1483 ft.; N37 56 51 W81 18 32
P.O. Box 1037, Beaver, WV 25813 US
(304) 253-7000, *Fax:* (304) 255-1044
www.103cir.com
jayq@radiocitywv.com
License: Beckley, Raleigh County, WV held by Southern Communications Corp.
Group Owner: Southern Communications Corp.
Nat'l Reps: Katz Radio
Arbitron Metro Market: Beckley, WV *Format:* Contemporary Hits/Top 40 *Hrs. of News Programming:* news progmg 2 hrs wkly *No. News Employees:* 2 *Target Audience:* 25-54.
Quesenberry, Jay, General Manager
Rhonda Pritt, News Director

WBKW(AM)
11-14-1966; 1070 khz AM; 10 kw-D; N37 45 18 W81 14 12
306 S. Karawha St., Beckley, WV 25801-5619
(304) 253-7000, *Fax:* (304) 255-1044
License: Beckley, Raleigh County, WV held by Southern Communications Corp.
Group Owner: Southern Communications Corp.; (acq 1976)
Population Served: 70,000 *Arbitron Metro Market:* Beckley, WV *Target Audience:* 18-54; traveling motorists
Jay Quesenberry, General Manager
Rennolt Madrazo, General Sales Mgr
Rick Pizer, Promotions Manager
Rhonda Pritt, News Director
Randy Kerbawy, Chief Engineer

WJLS
03-05-1939; 560 khz AM *Hrs Open:* 24
Mailing Address: P.O. Box Ab, Beckley, WV 25802 US
Second Address: WJLS Bldg., 102 N. Kanawha St., Beckley, WV 25801

www.wjls.com
stacie@wjls.com
License: Beckley, WV held by First Media Radio LLC
Group Owner: First Media Radio LLC
Nat'l Network: CNN Radio *Nat'l Reps:* Dome; Rgnl Reps
Arbitron Metro Market: Beckley, WV *Format:* Gospel, Religious
Special Programming: Sports 3 hrs wkly *Hrs. of News Programming:* news progmg 4 hrs wkly *No. News Employees:* 5 *Target Audience:* 25-54.
Stacie Buckland, Operations Dir
Jeffrey Joe Buckland, Programming Director
Gary Hosey, Music Director
Mark Reid, Advertising
Stacie Buckland, Webmaster

WJLS-FM
11-06-1946; 99.5 mhz FM *Hrs Open:* 24; 34 kw; 1050 ft.; N37 35 23 W81 6 51
Mailing Address: P.O. Box Ab, Beckley, WV 25802 US
Second Address: WJLS Bldg., 102 N. Kanawha St., Beckley, WV 25801
(304) 253-7311, *Fax:* (304) 253-3466
www.wjls.com
dawg@wjls.com
License: Beckley, Raleigh County, WV held by First Media Radio LLC
Group Owner: First Media Radio LLC; (acq 2-1-2002; $3.6 million with co-located AM)
Nat'l Network: CNN Radio *Regional Reps:* Dome; Rgnl Reps.
Wire Services: AP
Arbitron Metro Market: Beckley, WV *Format:* Country *Hrs. of News Programming:* news progmg 10 hrs wkly *No. News Employees:* 15 *Target Audience:* 25-54.
Mark Reid, General Manager
Darrell Ramsay, Programming Director
Bob Cannon, News Director
Charles Marlow, Chief Engineer
Maria Marvin, Traffic Manager

*WVPB
05-01-1974; 91.7 mhz FM *Hrs Open:* 24; 10.4 kw; 919 ft.; N37 53 46 W80 59 21
600 Capitol Street, Charleston, WV 25301 US
(304) 556-4900, *Fax:* (304) 556-4960
www.wvpubcast.org
feedback@wvpubcast.org
License: Beckley, Raleigh County, WV held by West Virginia Educational Broadcasting Authority.
Nat'l Network: NPR; PRI
Arbitron Metro Market: Beckley, WV *Format:* Jazz, News
Rita Ray, General Manager
Marilyn DiVita, General Sales Mgr
Craig Lanham, Programming Director
Beth Vorhees, Director of News and Public Affairs
Dennis Adkins, Executive Director
Bill Acker, Director of Broadcasting &Technology
Marilyn DiVita, Director of Development
Michael L. Meador, Director of Finance
Shawn Patterson, Director of Marketing

WWNR
08-09-1946; 620 khz AM *Hrs Open:* 5 AM-midnight
PO Box 757, Daniels, WV 25832 US
(304) 253-7000, *Fax:* (304) 255-1044
www.newstalk620.com
wwnr@radiocitywv.com
License: Beckley, WV held by Southern Communications Corp.
Group Owner: Southern Communications Corp.; acq 1-26-2004).
Nat'l Network: CBS Radio
Arbitron Metro Market: Beckley, WV *Format:* News, Sports, 86 *Hrs. of News Programming:* news progmg 35 hrs wkly *No. News Employees:* 2 *Target Audience:* 25-54. *Adv. Rates:* 30; 25; 30; 20
R. Shane Southern, President
Jay Quesenberry, General Manager
Rennold Madrazo, General Sales Mgr
Rick Rizer, Promotions Manager
Warren Ellison, News Director
Randy Kerbawy, Chief Engineer
Shane Sothern, General Sales Manager
Rhonda Pritt, Traffic Manager

*WBKW
1070 khz AM; Ant 679 ft
P.O. Box 1037, Beaver, WV 25813 US
(203) 268-9667
www.wmnr.org
License: Beckley, WV held by Monroe Board of Education.
Arbitron Metro Market: Beckley, WV
Jane Stadler, Operations Dir
Kurt Anderson, General Manager

*WJJJ
10-30-2007; 88.1 mhz FM; 0.84 kw; 1142 ft.; N37 35 24 W81 6 54
118 McGovran Road, Charleston, WV 25314 US
(888) 382-0881
www.wjjjfm.org
wjjfm@soddenlinkmail,com
License: Beckley, Raleigh County, WV held by Shofar Broadcasting Corp.
Arbitron Metro Market: Beckley, WV *Format:* Religious
James Jenkins, General Manager

Berkeley Springs

WCST
09-07-1958; 1010 khz AM
1010 Radio Station Road, Berkeley Springs, WV 25411 US
(304) 258-1010, *Fax:* (304) 258-1976
c929@comcast.net
License: Berkeley Springs, WV held by Capper Broadcasting Co.
Arbitron Metro Market: Berkeley Springs, WV *Format:* News, Talk
Laura Haber, General Manager
Shari Leadman, General Sales Mgr
Lee Bohrer, Programming Director
Mike Hurst, Chief Engineer

WDHC
12-01-1965; 92.9 mhz FM; 3.2 kw; 456 ft.; N39 37 0 W78 13 3
6321 St. James Drive, West Bloomfield, MI 48322 US
(304) 258-1010, *Fax:* (304) 258-1976
www.wdhc.com
stacydrake@yahoo.com
License: Berkeley Springs, Morgan County, WV
Arbitron Metro Market: Berkeley Springs, WV
Laura Haber, General Manager
Shari Leadman, General Sales Mgr
Lee Bohrer, Programming Director

Bethany

*WVBC
01-01-1967; 88.1 mhz FM; 1.1 kw; 410 ft.; N40 12 58 W80 33 31
Renner Union, Bethany, WV 26032 US
(304) 829-7853
www.bethanywv.edu
admission@bethanywv.edu
License: Bethany, Brooke County, WV held by Bethany College.
Nat'l Network: AP Radio *Wire Services:* AP
Arbitron Metro Market: Bethany, WV *Format:* Variety/Diverse
Special Programming: Christian rock 4 hrs, folk 2 hrs, classic rock 8 h *Hrs. of News Programming:* News progmg one hr wkly
Target Audience: 18-34;high school & college students
Patrick Sutherland, General Manager

Bethlehem

WUKL
02-27-2004; 105.5 mhz FM *Hrs Open:* 6 am-midnight; 13.5 kw; 312 ft.; N40 3 17 W80 42 26
600 Congress Avenue, Suite 1400, Austin, TX 78701 US
(800) 833-9211, *Fax:* (740) 676-2742
oldiesradioonline.com
webmaster@greatestmojo.com
License: Bethlehem, Ohio County, WV held by Keymarket Licenses LLC
Group Owner: Keymarket Communications LLC; (acq 2-4-2004; $1.35 million).
Nat'l Network: ABC
Arbitron Metro Market: Dallas, TX *Format:* Oldies *No. News Employees:* 1 *Target Audience:* 35-54.
Gerald Getz, President

Blennerhassett

*WPJY
01-01-2008; 88.7 mhz FM; 10 kw; 341 ft.; N39 14 0 W81 53 26
P. O. Box 889, Blacksburg, VA 24063 US
(540) 552-4252, *Fax:* (540) 951-5282
www.walkfm.org
License: Blennerhassett, Wood County, WV held by Positive Alternative Radio Inc.
Group Owner: Positive Alternative Radio Inc.
Arbitron Metro Market: Blennerhassett, WV *Format:* Christian
Vernon Baker, President
Adam McDowell, Operations Dir
Jeremy Wolfe, Operations Manager
Elisha Dorsey, Production Assistant
Mike Nelson, Underwriting Representative/Sales Dept
Mel Mendoza, Marketing & Creative Manager

Bluefield

WHAJ
04-23-1963; 104.5 mhz FM; 93 kw horiz, 62 kw vert; 1549 ft.; N37 15 5 W81 11 20
100 Bluefield Ave, Suite 3, Bluefield, WV 24701 US
(304) 327-7114, *Fax:* (304) 325-7850
License: Bluefield, Mercer County, WV held by Monterey Licenses LLC.
Group Owner: Triad Broadcasting Co. L.L.C.
Arbitron Metro Market: Bluefield, WV *Format:* Adult Contemp
Target Audience: 25-54.
Dave Harris, Programming Director
Jackie White, News Director

WHIS
06-27-1929; 1440 khz AM; 5 kw-D, ND1; 0.5 kw-N, ND1; N37 16 33 W81 15 6
900 Bluefield Ave., Bluefield, WV 24701 US

(304) 327-7114, *Fax:* (304) 325-7850
www.wihsradio.org
wihs@snet.net
License: Bluefield, WV held by Monterey Licenses LLC.
Group Owner: Triad Broadcasting Co. L.L.C.; (acq 7-18-2000; grpsl)
Arbitron Metro Market: Bluefield, WV *Format:* News, News/Talk, 86, Religious *Target Audience:* 35 plus; upper income, leaders of the community
John Halford, General Manager
Danny Clemons, General Sales Mgr
Joseph Echles, Programming Director
Keith Bowman, Chief Engineer

WKEZ
05-18-1948; 1240 khz AM *Hrs Open:* 24; 1 kw-U, ND1; N37 15 57 W81 11 20
100 Bluefield Avenue, Suite 3, Bluefield, WV 24701 US
(304) 327-7114, *Fax:* (304) 325-7850
www.kez999.com
License: Bluefield, WV held by Monterey Licenses LLC.
Group Owner: Triad Broadcasting Co. L.L.C.; (acq 7-18-2000; grpsl)
Arbitron Metro Market: Bluefield, WV *Format:* Sports *Special Programming:* Relg 5 hrs wkly
David Benjamin, CEO
John Halford, General Manager
Danny Clemons, General Sales Mgr
Ed Weiland, Programming Director
Patty Davis, News Director
Keith Bowman, Engineering Dir

***WPIB**
09-01-1995; 91.1 mhz FM; 12 kw; 1184 ft.; N37 15 26 W81 10 43
P. O. Box 889, Blacksburg, VA 24063 US
, *Fax:* (540) 951-5282
www.spiritfm.com
office@spiritfm.com
License: Bluefield, Mercer County, WV held by Positive Alternative Radio Inc.
Group Owner: Positive Alternative Radio Inc.; (acq 4-22-92)
Nat'l Network: USA
Format: Adult Contemp, Christian
Edward Baker, President

Bridgeport

WETT
06-29-1991; 104.1 mhz FM *Hrs Open:* 24; 3 kw; 328 ft; N39 17 59 W80 17 30
Box 360, Bridgeport, WV 43812
(304) 842-8644, *Fax:* (304) 842-8653
rtgresak@aol.com
License: Bridgeport, Harrison County, WV held by WDCI Radio Inc.
Nat'l Network: Jones Radio Networks *Regional Reps:* Dome.
Population Served: 125,000 *Arbitron Metro Market:* Morgantown-Clarksburg-Fairmont, WV *Target Audience:* 25-54.
Bruce Wallace, President
Tom Thompson, General Sales Mgr
Tina Grefak, Programming Director
Hank Vest, Chief Engineer

Buckhannon

WBRB
06-16-1990; 101.3 mhz FM *Hrs Open:* 24; 50 kw; 492 ft.; N38 56 40 W80 10 46
Drawer C, Wbuc Road, Buckhannon, WV 26201 US
(304) 623-6546, *Fax:* (304) 472-1528
www.1013thebear.com/
prinehart@wvradio.com
License: Buckhannon, Upshur County, WV held by West Virginia Radio Corp. of Buckhannon.
Group Owner: West Virginia Radio Corp.; (acq 10-18-2005; $4,267,900 with WBUC(AM) Buckhannon)
Arbitron Metro Market: MOUNT CLAIRE,WV *Format:* Country *Hrs. of News Programming:* news progmg 4 hrs wkly *No. News Employees:* 1 *Target Audience:* 25-54; upper middle class, white collar, craftsman *Adv. Rates:* 27; 27; 27; 27
Jan Harr, News Director

WBTQ
01-01-1984; 93.5 mhz FM *Hrs Open:* 24; 16 kw; 417 ft.; N38 58 11 W80 1 58
228 Randolph Ave, Elkins, WV 26241 US
(304) 636-1300, *Fax:* (304) 472-1528
www.935btq.com
ballen@wvradio.com
License: Buckhannon, Upshur County, WV held by West Virginia Radio Corp. of Elkins.
Group Owner: West Virginia Radio Corp.; (acq 5-15-2008; $1.25 million)
Nat'l Network: ABC *Regional Reps:* Dome.
Arbitron Metro Market: Elkins,WV *Format:* Adult Contemp *Hrs. of News Programming:* news progmg 3 hrs wkly *No. News Employees:* 1 *Target Audience:* 18-49. *Adv. Rates:* 25; 20; 23; 18
Brian Elliott, General Manager
Wendy Dogas, News Director
Richard McGraw, Engineering Dir

WBUC
12-13-1959; 1460 khz AM *Hrs Open:* Sunrise-sunset
%Fisher Wayland Et Al, 2001 Penn. Ave, NW #400, Washington, DC 20006 US
(304) 472-1460, *Fax:* (304) 472-1528
License: Buckhannon, WV held by West Virginia Radio Corp. of Buckhannon.
Group Owner: West Virginia Radio Corp.; (acq 10-18-2005; $4,267,900 with WBRB(FM) Buckhannon)
Format: Talk *Special Programming:* Relg 7 hrs wkly *No. News Employees:* 1 *Target Audience:* General.
Harry Elliott, CFO
Dale Miller, President
Todd Elliott, Operations Dir
Brian Elliott, General Sales Mgr
Ron Roth, Promotions Manager
Nancy Boyce, News Director
Tamara Cicogna, Advertising Manager

***WVPW**
09-01-1968; 88.9 mhz FM *Hrs Open:* 24; 14 kw; 850 ft.; N39 2 4 W80 33 47
600 Capitol Street, Charleston, WV 25301 US
(304) 556-4900, *Fax:* (304) 556-4960
www.wvpubcast.org
feedback@wvpubcast.org
License: Buckhannon, Upshur County, WV held by West Virginia Education Broadcasting Authority.
Nat'l Network: NPR; PRI
Arbitron Metro Market: Buckhannon, WV *Format:* Jazz, News
Rita Ray, General Manager
Marilyn DiVita, General Sales Mgr
Craig Lanham, Programming Director
Beth Vorhees, Director of News and Public Affairs
Dennis Adkins, Executive Director
Bill Acker, Director of Broadcasting &Technology
Marilyn DiVita, Director of Development
Michael L. Meador, Director of Finance
Shawn Patterson, Director of Marketing

***WVWC**
09-15-1997; 92.1 mhz FM; 0.013 kw horiz; -69 ft.; N38 59 24 W80 13 10
Box 167, Wvwc, Buckhannon, WV 26201 US
(304) 473-8292, *Fax:* (304) 472-2571
www.wvwc.edu/c92
c92@wvwc.edu
License: Buckhannon, Upshur County, WV held by West Virginia Wesleyan College.
Arbitron Metro Market: Buckhannon, WV *Format:* Classic Rock, Variety/Diverse *Special Programming:* Black 4 hrs, class 2 hrs, jazz 8 hrs, relg 4 hrs, *Target Audience:* 12-25; high school & college audience
Liz Short, General Manager
Marybeth Yoder, Programming Director
Whitney Law, Promotions Manager
Brian Schooley, Sports Director
Travis Rexroad, Training Director
Amanda Jones, Training Director
Sarah Carr, Music Director
MicahOsborne, Music Director

Charleston

WKAZ
01-01-1946; 680 khz AM *Hrs Open:* 24; 10 kw-D, DAN; 0.221 kw-N, DAN; N38 19 7 W81 32 28
1251 Earl Core Road, Morgantown, WV 26505 US
(304) 342-8131, *Fax:* (304) 344-4745
License: Charleston, WV held by West Virginia Radio Corp. of Charleston.
Group Owner: West Virginia Radio Corp.; (acq 7-14-93; $1.1 million with co-located FM;
Nat'l Network: ABC
Arbitron Metro Market: Morgantown, WV *Format:* Country *No. News Employees:* 1 *Target Audience:* 25-54.
Gregg Smith, Programming Director

WCHS
09-15-1927; 580 khz AM; 5 kw-D, DAN; 5 kw-N, DAN; N38 21 51 W81 46 5
Greer Building, Rte. 7, Morgantown, WV 26505 US
(304) 342-8131, *Fax:* (304) 344-4745
www.58wchs.com
58live@wvradio.com
License: Charleston, WV held by West Virginia Radio Corp. of Charleston.
Group Owner: West Virginia Radio Corp.; (acq 6-1-92; $1.74 million with co-located FM;
Nat'l Network: CBS *Nat'l Reps:* McGavren Guild
Arbitron Metro Market: Charleston, WV *Format:* News, News/Talk, 84, Talk *No. News Employees:* 2 *Target Audience:* 25-54.
Dale Miller, President
Rick Johnson, Operations Dir
Sean Banks, General Manager
Sara Shingleyon, News Director
Noel Richardson, Chief Engineer

WKWS
09-16-1969; 96.1 mhz FM; 45 kw; 515 ft.; N38 21 54 W81 46 6
1251 Earl L. Core Road, Morgantown, WV 26505 US
(304) 342-8131, *Fax:* (304) 344-4745
www.kick96.com
info@kick96.com
License: Charleston, Kanawha County, WV
Group Owner: West Virginia Radio Corp.
Arbitron Metro Market: Charleston, WV *Format:* Country
Rick Johnson, Operations Dir
Christian Miller, General Sales Mgr
John Anthony, Programming Director
Sara Shingleton, News Director

WBES
02-16-1957; 950 khz AM; 5 kw-D, 1 kw-N, DA-N; N38 23 00 W81 42 52
Box 871, 4250 Washington St. W., Charleston, WV 24203
(304) 744-7020, *Fax:* (304) 744-8562
License: Charleston, Kanawha County, WV held by Bristol Broadcasting Co. Inc.
Group Owner: Bristol Broadcasting Co. Inc.; acq 5-1-64).
Nat'l Reps: McGavren Guild
Population Served: 640,500 *Arbitron Metro Market:* Charleston, WV
Mike Robinson, General Manager
John Gush, General Sales Mgr
Dan King, Regional Sales Manager

WQBE-FM
02-16-1957; 97.5 mhz FM; 50 kw; 499 ft.; N38 24 22 W81 43 26
P.O. Box 1389, Bristol, VA 24203 US
(304) 744-7020, *Fax:* (304) 744-8562
www.wqbe.com
info@wqbe.com
License: Charleston, Kanawha County, WV
Arbitron Metro Market: Charleston, WV
Scott Collins, President
J. Scott Collins, General Manager
John Meaney, Station Manager
Fran Dingman, General Sales Mgr
Amanda Albright, Promotions Manager

WSWW
01-01-1939; 1490 khz AM *Hrs Open:* 24; 1 kw-U, ND1; N38 21 28 W81 37 0
1251 Earl L. Core Road, Morgantown, WV 26505 US
(304) 342-8131, *Fax:* (304) 344-4745
License: Charleston, WV held by West Virginia Radio Corp.
Group Owner: West Virginia Radio Corp.; (acq 6-5-97; $2.15 million with WKAZ-FM Miami)
Nat'l Network: ESPN Radio *Nat'l Reps:* D & R Radio
Arbitron Metro Market: Charleston, WV *Format:* Sports, Talk
John Raese, Chairman
Dale Miller, President
Mike Buxser, General Manager
Vince Wardell, General Sales Mgr
Dave Harmon, Programming Director
Sarah Shingleton, News Director
Noel Richardson, Chief Engineer

WVAF
02-01-1965; 99.9 mhz FM; 24.5 kw; 705 ft.; N38 16 25 W81 31 27
1111 Virginia Street, E, Charleston, WV 25301 US
(304) 342-8131, *Fax:* (304) 344-4745
www.v100.fm
info@100radio.com
License: Charleston, Kanawha County, WV held by West Virginia Radio Corp. of Charleston.
Group Owner: West Virginia Radio Corp.
Arbitron Metro Market: Charleston, WV *Format:* Adult Contemp *Target Audience:* Female skew.

Nikki Walters, Operations Dir
Dale Miller, General Sales Mgr
Rich Johnson, Programming Director
Doug Daniels, News Director
Greg Johnson, Assistant Music Director
Noel Richardson, Disc Jockey
Denise Daniels, Disc Jockey

***WVPN**
05-08-1979; 88.5 mhz FM *Hrs Open:* 24; 44 kw; 440 ft.; N38 22 34.3 W81 39 24
600 Capitol Street, Charleston, WV 25301 US
(304) 556-4900, *Fax:* (304) 556-4960
www.wvpubcast.org
feedback@wvpubcast.org
License: Charleston, Kanawha County, WV held by West Virginia Educational Broadcasting Authority.
Nat'l Network: NPR; PRI
Arbitron Metro Market: Charleston, WV *Format:* Jazz, News
Rita Ray, General Manager
Marilyn DiVita, General Sales Mgr
Craig Lanham, Programming Director
Beth Vorhees, Director of News and Public Affairs
Dennis Adkins, Executive Director
Bill Acker, Director of Broadcasting &Technology
Marilyn DiVita, Director of Development
Michael L. Meador, Director of Finance
Shawn Patterson, Director of Marketing

WVSR-FM
09-01-1964; 102.7 mhz FM; 50 kw; 404 ft.; N38 21 26 W81 40 5
Mailing Address: P.O Box 1389, Bristol, VA 24203 US
Second Address: 4250 Washington St., Charleston, WV 25313
(304) 342-3136, *Fax:* (304) 342-3118
www.electric102.com
info@electric102.com
License: Charleston, Kanawha County, WV
Arbitron Metro Market: Charleston, WV *Format:* Contemporary Hits/Top 40
Candis Isberner, CEO
Mike Zelten, Operations Dir
Jeff Williams, Station Manager
Renee Dillard, General Sales Mgr
Brandy Thomas-Ray, Local Sales Manager

***WXAF**
01-01-1994; 90.9 mhz FM; 0.8 kw; 623 ft.; N38 16 25 W81 31 27
P. O. Box 7575, Huntington, WV 25777 US
(740) 867-5333
www.wjjjfm.org
WJJJFM@Suddenlinkmail.com
License: Charleston, Kanawha County, WV held by Maranatha Broadcasting Inc.
Arbitron Metro Market: Charleston, WV *Format:* Religious
Paul Warren, President

WVTS(AM)
1240 khz AM; 1000 watts; non-directional; 38 23 08N 81 42 51W
PO Box 1389, Bristol, VA 24203 USA
(304) 744-7020, *Fax:* (304) 744-8562
License: Charleston, Kanawha County, WV
Group Owner: Bristol Broadcasting Inc

Charlestown

WMRE
05-28-1962; 1550 khz AM *Hrs Open:* Sunrise-sunset; 5 kw-D, ND2; 0.006 kw-N, ND2; N39 16 23 W77 51 56
Rural Route 1, Box 325-A, Charles Town, WV 25414 US
(540) 662-5101, *Fax:* (540) 662-8610
www.sportstalk1550.com
Davidmiller@clearchannel.com
License: Charlestown, WV held by AMFM Radio Licenses LLC.
Group Owner: Clear Channel Communications Inc.; (acq 2-16-2001; $1.525 million with co-located FM)
Nat'l Network: Fox Sports *Nat'l Reps:* Roslin
Arbitron Metro Market: Winchester, VA *Format:* Sports *No. News Employees:* 2
David Miller, Operations Dir
Chuck Peterson, General Manager
Marcella Vance, General Sales Mgr
Justin Maglione, Promotions Manager
Krissy Groves, News Director
Maark Kesner, Chief Engineer

Clarksburg

WWLW
01-01-1973; 106.5 mhz FM *Hrs Open:* 24; 28 kw; 653 ft.; N39 15 44 W80 28 1
1065 Radio Park Drive, Mount Clare, WV 26408 US
(304) 623-6546, *Fax:* (304) 623-6547
www.wvmagic.com
jacklogar@wvradio.com
License: Clarksburg, Harrison County, WV held by West Virginia Radio Corp. of Clarksburg.
Group Owner: West Virginia Radio Corp.; (acq 3-2-93; $1.2 million;
Arbitron Metro Market: Clarksburg, WV *Format:* Adult Contemp *Hrs. of News Programming:* news progmg 2 hrs wkly *No. News Employees:* 1
Dale Miller, President
Chad Perry, Operations Dir
Christian Miller, Station Manager
Tim Brady, News Director
Steve Lough, Chief Engineer
Donna Tubolino, Traffic Manager

WXKX
11-28-1946; 1340 khz AM *Hrs Open:* 24; 1 kw-U, ND1; N39 17 27 W80 18 56
P.O. Box 2423, Clarksburg, WV 26302 US
(304) 624-1400, *Fax:* (304) 624-1402
License: Clarksburg, WV held by Burbach of DE LLC.
Group Owner: Burbach Broadcasting Group; (acq 11-2-00; $435,000 cash with co-located FM).
Nat'l Network: ESPN Radio *Nat'l Reps:* Roslin; Rgnl Reps
Arbitron Metro Market: Morgantown-Clarksburg-Fairmont, WV *Format:* Sports *Special Programming:* Pittsburgh Pirates, Alderson-Broadus College baske *Hrs. of News Programming:* News progmg 14 hrs wkly *Target Audience:* 35 plus; office workers, retirees, upper income *Adv. Rates:* 17.50; 14.50; 17.50; 14.50
Nick Galli, President
Dan Barham, General Manager
David Branham, General Sales Mgr
Greg Bolgard, Promotions Manager
Debbie Southern, News Director
Larry Smith, Chief Engineer

***WKJL**
10-01-1992; 88.1 mhz FM *Hrs Open:* 19; 19 kw horiz, 32 kw vert; 489 ft.; N39 17 59 W80 17 30 *Rebroadcasts:* Rebroadcasts WAIJ(FM) Grantsville, Md. 100%
Mailing Address: 34 Springs Road, P.O. Box 540, Clarksburg, WV 26301 US
Second Address: He's Alive Corp. Offices, 34 Springs Rd., Grantsville, WV 21536
(301) 895-3292, *Fax:* (301) 895-3293
www.hesalive.net
hesalive@hesalive.net
License: Clarksburg, Harrison County, WV held by He's Alive Inc.
Nat'l Network: USA
Arbitron Metro Market: Morgantown-Clarksburg-Fairmont, WV *Format:* Christian, Gospel *Target Audience:* 18-35.
Sharon Johnson, President
Melissa Flores, General Manager
Tim Eutin, Programming Director
Brandon Hutzell, News Director
Hank Vest, Chief Engineer

WPDX
08-19-1947; 750 khz AM; 1 kw-D, NDD; N39 14 40 W80 23 5
15 Campbell Street, Luray, VA 22835 US
(304) 363-3851, *Fax:* (304) 363-3852
wpdx@iolinc.net
License: Clarksburg, WV held by Tschudy Broadcasting Corp.
Nat'l Network: AP Radio *Regional Reps:* Commercial Media Sales
Arbitron Metro Market: Morgantown-Clarksburg-Fairmont, WV *Format:* Country *Target Audience:* 35-54; blue collar *Adv. Rates:* 15; 15; 15; 12
Mike Oberg, President
Lyric Klaske, General Manager
Robert Hoffer, General Sales Mgr
Susann Gamble, Programming Director
Wendy Oberg, Executive Vice President

WPDX-FM
08-19-1974; 104.9 mhz FM *Hrs Open:* 24; 7.4 kw; Ant 597 ft; N39 15 22 W80 06 46
7013 Mountains Park Dr., Fairmont, WV 22835
(304) 363-3851, *Fax:* (304) 363-3852
License: Clarksburg, Harrison County, WV held by Tschudy Broadcasting Corp.
Nat'l Network: AP Radio *Regional Reps:* Commercial Media Sales
Population Served: 400,000 *Arbitron Metro Market:* Morgantown-Clarksburg-Fairmont, WV *Hrs. of News Programming:* News progmg 5 hrs wkly *Target Audience:* 35-54; blue collar *Adv. Rates:* 15; 15; 15; 12
Tony Gee, Programming Director

WGIE
01-01-1975; 92.7 mhz FM *Hrs Open:* 24; 0.62 kw; 669 ft.; N39 17 27 W80 18 56 *Rebroadcasts:* Rebroadcasts WGYE(FM) Fairmont 100%
P.O. Box 2423, Clarksburg, WV 26301 US
(304) 367-0823
www.froggycountry.net
License: Clarksburg, Harrison County, WV held by Burbach of DE LLC
Group Owner: Burbach Broadcasting Group
Arbitron Metro Market: Morgantown, WV *Format:* Country *Hrs. of News Programming:* News progmg 3 hrs wkly *Target Audience:* 25-45; young professionals
Laura Candell, Office Manager

***WCKU**
01-01-1993; 90.1 mhz FM; 4 kw; 705 ft.; N39 19 9 W80 23 31
P.O. Box 7575, Huntington, WV 25777 US
(916) 251-1600, *Fax:* (916) 251-1650
www.klove.com
klove@klove.com
License: Clarksburg, Harrison County, WV held by Educational Media Foundation.
Group Owner: EMF Broadcasting; (acq 2-29-2008; $900,000 with WHKU(FM) Proctorville, OH)
Nat'l Network: K-Love
Arbitron Metro Market: Clarksburg, WV *Format:* Christian
Darrell Chambliss, Chairman
Alan Mason, CEO/COO
Mike Novak, CEO
David Pierce, Chief Creative Officer
Dan Antonelli, Chief Business Development Officer
Eric Moser, Chief Financial Officer
Brian Burger, Vice President of HumanResources
D. Kevin Blair, Secretary and General Counsel

Cowen

WKQV
01-01-2007; 105.5 mhz FM *Hrs Open:* 24; 3.5 kw; 883 ft.; N38 21 35 W80 38 51
US
(304) 765-7373, *Fax:* (304) 765-7836
www.105kqv.com
info@105kqv.com
License: Cowen, Webster County, WV held by Summit Media Broadcasting LLC.
Group Owner: Summit Media Broadcasting LLC; (acq 3-15-2006; $482,500 for CP)
Nat'l Network: CNN Radio *Nat'l Reps:* Rgnl Reps
Arbitron Metro Market: Cowen, WV *Format:* Classic Rock *Target Audience:* 18-49. *Adv. Rates:* 20; 16; 20; 13
Al Sergi, President

Craigsville

WSWW-FM
01-01-2008; 95.7 mhz FM; 25 kw; Ant 325 ft; N38 24 56 W80 31 49
812 Northside Dr., Suite 1, Summersville, WV
(304) 872-6403, *Fax:* (304) 872-6816
License: Craigsville, Nicholas County, WV held by West Virginia Radio Corp. of Charleston.
Group Owner: West Virginia Radio Corp.; (acq 9-11-2007)

Dale Miller, President
Greg Carter, Programming Director

Danville

WZAC-FM
10-09-1989; 92.5 mhz FM; 0.61 kw; 696 ft.; N38 5 1 W81 48 17
Mailing Address: P. O. Box 87, Danville, WV 25053 US
Second Address: 457 Main St., Madison, WV 25130
(304) 369-5200, *Fax:* (304) 369-5200
License: Danville, Boone County, WV held by Price Broadcasting Co.
Arbitron Metro Market: Danville, WV *Format:* Country *Target Audience:* General.
Wayne Price, General Manager

Dunbar

WVTS-FM
10-13-1988; 94.5 mhz FM *Hrs Open:* 24; 9.6 kw; Ant 525 ft; N38 25 11 W81 43 24
Mailing Address: Box 871, Charleston, WV 24201
Second Address: 4250 Washington St., Charleston, WV 25313
(304) 744-7020, *Fax:* (304) 744-8562
www.mix945online.com
info@mix945online.com

RADIO - U.S.

License: Dunbar, Kanawha County, WV held by Bristol Broadcasting Co. Inc.
Group Owner: Bristol Broadcasting Co. Inc.; acq 1996; grpsl).
Nat'l Network: Moody; Westwood One *Nat'l Reps:* Dome; Rgnl Reps; Katz Radio
Arbitron Metro Market: Charleston, WV *Special Programming:* Class 2 hrs wkly
Mike Robinson, General Manager
Dave Evans, Programming Director
Barrie Hamm, Promotions Manager
Randy Justice, Chief Engineer

WVTS
11-04-1946; 1240 khz AM; 1 kw-U; N38 23 08 W81 42 51
Mailing Address: Box 871, Charleston, WV 24203
Second Address: 4250 Washington St., Charleston, WV 25313
(304) 744-7020, *Fax:* (304) 744-8562
95thesportsfox.com
MSH@95thesportsfox.com
License: Dunbar, Kanawha County, WV held by Bristol Broadcasting Co. Inc.
Group Owner: Bristol Broadcasting Co. Inc.; acq 8-90; grpsl).
Population Served: 51,177 *Arbitron Metro Market:* Charleston, WV *Target Audience:* 18-49.
Mike Robinson, General Manager
John Gush, General Sales Mgr
Brandy Thomas-Ray, Local Sales Manager

WLUX
1450 khz AM; 1 kw-U; N38 23 08 W81 42 52
Mailing Address: Box 3744, Charleston, WV
Second Address: 1114 Virginia St E., Charleston, WV 25301
(304) 345-2000, *Fax:* (304) 343-7999
License: Dunbar, Kanawha County, WV held by St. Paul Radio Co.
Arbitron Metro Market: Charleston, WV *Adv. Rates:* N/A
Mark Sadd, President
Ronald J Tenfel, Chief Engineer

Elizabeth

WXIL
09-01-1975; 95.1 mhz FM *Hrs Open:* 24; 50 kw; 499 ft.; N39 14 47 W81 28 19
104 Broadway Ave., Carnegie, PA 15106 US
(304) 485-7425, *Fax:* (304) 424-6955
www.95xil.com
questions@95xil.com
License: Elizabeth, Wood County, WV held by PBBC Inc.
Group Owner: Burbach Broadcasting Group; (acq 9-1-80; $1 million;
Nat'l Reps: Katz Radio
Arbitron Metro Market: Parkersburg, WV *Format:* Adult Contemp *Hrs. of News Programming:* news progmg 6 hrs wkly *No. News Employees:* 1 *Target Audience:* 25-54; women
Nicholas Galli, Chairman
Don Staats, Operations Dir
Chuck Helmick, Local Sales Manager
Luke Woytowich, News Director
Larry Smith, Chief Engineer
Chuck Martin, Local Sales Manager

Elkins

***WBHZ**
01-01-1999; 91.9 mhz FM; 0.275 kw; 1119 ft.; N38 52 18 W79 55 39
P O Box Drawer 2440, Tupelo, MS 38803 US
(662) 844-8888, *Fax:* (662) 842-6791
www.afa.net
License: Elkins, Randolph County, WV held by American Family Association.
Group Owner: American Family Radio
Arbitron Metro Market: Elkins, WV *Format:* Christian
Marvin Sanders, General Manager

WDNE
02-01-1948; 1240 khz AM *Hrs Open:* 21
1251 Earl L. Core Road, Morgantown, WV 26505 US
(304) 636-1300, *Fax:* (304) 636-2200
www.wdnefm.com
wdne@wvradio.com,scooper@wvradio.com
License: Elkins, WV held by West Virginia Radio Corp. of Elkins.
Group Owner: West Virginia Radio Corp.; (acq 6-17-97; $750,000 with co-located FM)
Arbitron Metro Market: Elkins-Randolph County, WV *Format:* Adult Contemp *No. News Employees:* 1 *Target Audience:* 18 plus. *Adv. Rates:* 18; 18; 18; 18
Rick Cooper, General Manager
Roger Taylor, Programming Director
Howard Swick, Promotions Manager
Fay Cowgill, News Director
Noel Richardson, Chief Engineer
Joe Gaynor, Music Director

WDNE-FM
06-15-1985; 98.9 mhz FM *Hrs Open:* 21; 5.1 kw; 725 ft.; N38 54 36 W79 47 18
Putbrese, Hunsaker, Tren, P.O Box 217, Sterling, VA 20167 US
(304) 636-1300, *Fax:* (304) 636-2200
www.wdnefm.com
info@wdnefm.com
License: Elkins, Randolph County, WV
Group Owner: West Virginia Radio Corp.
Arbitron Metro Market: Elkins-Randolph County, WV *Format:* Country *Adv. Rates:* Same as AM
Fay Cowgill, News Director

WELK
10-17-1982; 94.7 mhz FM *Hrs Open:* 24; 5 kw; 728 ft.; N38 54 43 W79 47 19
228 Randolph Ave., Elkins, WV 26241 US
(304) 636-1300, *Fax:* (304) 636-2200
www.947welk.com/
radiosales@3wlogic.net
License: Elkins, Randolph County, WV held by West Virginia Radio Corp. of Elkins.
Group Owner: West Virginia Radio Corp.; (acq 5-15-2008; $1.05 million)
Nat'l Network: CNN Radio
Arbitron Metro Market: Elkins, WV. *Format:* Adult Contemp, Contemporary Hits/Top 40 *Hrs. of News Programming:* news progmg 3 hrs wkly *No. News Employees:* 1 *Target Audience:* 18-49; female
Harry Elliot, CFO
Dale Miller, President
Todd Elliott, Operations Dir
Brian Elliott, General Sales Mgr
Brad Elliott, Programming Director
Jane Birdsong, News Director
Bill Davisson, Chief Engineer

Fairmont

WKKW
10-01-1975; 97.9 mhz FM; 29 kw; 640 ft.; N39 25 4 W80 3 44
P.O. Box 1549, Fairmont, WV 26555 US
(304) 296-0029, *Fax:* (304) 296-3876
www.wkkwfm.com
jshaffer@wvradio.com
License: Fairmont, Marion County, WV held by Descendants Trust, Lauren M. Kelley, trustee.
Arbitron Metro Market: Morgantown-Clarksburg-Fairmont, WV *Format:* Country *Target Audience:* 25-54; young professionals
Dave Jecklin, General Manager
Christian Miller, General Sales Mgr
John Thomas, Programming Director

WMMN
12-22-1928; 920 khz AM; 5 kw-D, ND1; 0.2 kw-N, ND1; N39 28 3 W80 12 20
P.O. Box 1549, Fairmont, WV 26555 US
(304) 366-3700, *Fax:* (304) 366-3706
www.920wmmn.com
License: Fairmont, WV held by Fantasia Broadcasting Inc.
Group Owner: Fantasia Broadcasting Inc.
Nat'l Network: Fox Sports *Regional Reps:* Commercial Media Sales.
Arbitron Metro Market: Morgantown, WV *Format:* Sports *Target Audience:* 18 plus.
Nick Fantasia, President
Bill Dunn, Operations Dir

WRLF
08-26-1989; 94.3 mhz FM *Hrs Open:* 24; 3.6 kw; 249 ft.; N39 28 19 W80 8 26
Mailing Address: P.O. Box 1549, Fairmont, WV 26554 US
Second Address: 450 Leonard Ave., Fairmont, WV 26554
(304) 366-3700, *Fax:* (304) 366-3706
www.wrlf.com
License: Fairmont, Marion County, WV held by Fairmont Broadcasting Co.
Group Owner: Fantasia Broadcasting Inc.
Arbitron Metro Market: Morgantown-Clarksburg-Fairmont, WV *Format:* Classic Rock *Target Audience:* 25-55; 60% male, 40% female
Bill Dunn, Operations Dir
Nick Fantasia, General Manager

WTCS
01-01-1948; 1490 khz AM *Hrs Open:* 24; 1 kw-U, ND1; N39 28 19 W80 8 26
Mailing Address: P. O. Box 1549, Fairmont, WV 26555 US
Second Address: 450 Leonard Ave., Fairmont, WV 26554
(304) 366-3700, *Fax:* (304) 366-3706
www.1490wtcs.com
License: Fairmont, WV held by Fairmont Broadcasting Co.
Group Owner: Fantasia Broadcasting Inc.; (acq 5-1-56)
Nat'l Network: CNN Radio *Regional Network:* W. Va. MetroNews Network *Regional Reps:* Commercial Media Sales.
Arbitron Metro Market: Morgantown, WV *Format:* News, News/Talk, 86 *Special Programming:* It 3 hrs wkly *Target Audience:* 35 plus.
Nick Fantasia, General Manager
Bill Dunn, General Sales Mgr
Bob Ice, Chief Engineer

Fayetteville

WVBD
100.7 mhz FM; 0.48 kw; 1125 ft.; N37 55 40.4 W80 58 11.5 US
(304) 765-7373, *Fax:* (304)765-7836
www.wvbigdaddy.com
info@wsgdfm.com
License: Fayetteville, Fayette County, WV held by Daniel W. Finch Jr.
Arbitron Metro Market: Fayetteville, WV *Format:* Country
Daniel Finch Jr., General Manager

Fisher

WELD
08-01-1956; 690 khz AM *Hrs Open:* 24
Rt.1, Kessel Road, Fisher, WV 26818 US
(304) 538-6062, *Fax:* (304) 538-7032
weldamfm.com
WELD@hardynet.com
License: Fisher, WV held by Thunder Associates LLC
Nat'l Network: ABC *Regional Network:* W. Va. MetroNews Network *Nat'l Reps:* Dome
Arbitron Metro Market: Fisher, WV *Format:* Contemporary Hits/Top 40, Adult Contemp *Hrs. of News Programming:* News progmg 3 hrs wkly *No. News Employees:* 1 *Target Audience:* 25+; 25+ *Adv. Rates:* 14; 14;14; 14
Curtis Durst, President
Alan Yokum, General Manager
Sandra Durst, Executive Vice President

WQWV
07-01-1998; 103.7 mhz FM *Hrs Open:* 24; 0.31 kw; 1385 ft.; N39 2 16 W79 5 23
Mailing Address: 103 Raleigh Place, Westover, WV 26501 US
Second Address: 2 Alt Ave., Petersburg, WV 26847
(304) 257-4432, *Fax:* (304) 257-9733
www.wqwv.com
V103@V103.NewCountry.com
License: Fisher, Hardy County, WV held by McGuire Broadcasting L.L.C.
Nat'l Network: CNN Radio
Format: Contemporary Hits/Top 40, Variety/Diverse
Kevin Spencer, Operations Dir
Eric McGuire, General Manager
Angel Blizzard, General Sales Mgr

Fort Gay

***WFGH**
06-04-1973; 90.7 mhz FM *Hrs Open:* 24; 7.8 kw; 203 ft.; N38 7 58 W82 35 37
P.O. Box 410, Fort Gay, WV 25514 US
(304) 648-5752, *Fax:* (304) 648-5447
www.wfghfm.com
wfgh907@radio.com
License: Fort Gay, Wayne County, WV held by Wayne County Board of Education.
Wire Services: AP
Arbitron Metro Market: Fort Gay, WV *Format:* Country, Gospel, 64 *Special Programming:* Oldies *Hrs. of News Programming:* news progmg 15 hrs wkly *No. News Employees:* 2 *Target Audience:* General.
Vernon Stanfill, General Manager
Hazel Damron, Programming Director

Franklin

***WVPC**
91.1 mhz FM; kw
US
(304) 799-6004, *Fax:* (304) 799-7444
www.alleghenymountainradio.org
License: Franklin, Pendleton County, WV held by Pocahontas Communications Cooperative Corp.
Arbitron Metro Market: Franklin, WV
Cheryl Kinderman, General Manager

Frost

***WVMR**
08-17-1981; 1370 khz AM; 5 kw-D, NDD; N38 17 25 W79 55 52
Route 2, Box 39, Dunmore, WV 24934 US
(304) 799-6004, *Fax:* (304) 799-7444
www.alleghenymountainradio.org
amrinet@starband.net
License: Frost, WV held by Pocahontas Communications Cooperative Corp.
Arbitron Metro Market: Dunmore, WV *Format:* Country *Special Programming:* Farm 5 hrs, relg 10 hrs, big band 3 hrs, bluegrass *Target Audience:* General.
Bill Ellenburg, Operations Dir
Dave Smithson, Station Manager

Gary

WHQX
01-01-1989; 107.7 mhz FM *Hrs Open:* 24; 8.6 kw; 564 ft.; N37 8 1 W81 35 42
100 Bluefield Avenue, Suite 3, Bluefield, WV 24701 US
(304) 327-7114, *Fax:* (304) 325-7850
www.kickscountry.com
License: Gary, Tazewell County, WV held by Monterey Licenses LLC.
Group Owner: Triad Broadcasting Co. L.L.C.; (acq 7-18-00; grpsl)
Arbitron Metro Market: Bluefield, WV *Format:* Country *No. News Employees:* 1
John Halford, General Manager
Dave Crouiser, Programming Director
Keith Bowman, Chief Engineer

Glenville

WVRW
01-01-2008; 107.7 mhz FM; 1.7 kw; Ant 623 ft; N38 54 29 W80 49 48
303 Harrison Ave., Weston, WV
(304) 269-5555, *Fax:* (304) 269-4800
www.wvrwfm.com
info@wvrwfm.com
License: Glenville, Gilmer County, WV held by Della Jane Woofter.
Nat'l Network: Cumlus
Arbitron Metro Market: Metro Clarksbur *Hrs. of News Programming:* 11:55am 4:50pm *Target Audience:* 35+ *Adv. Rates:* 8.25; 30; 10.25; 60
Della Jane Woofter, General Manager

Grafton

WVUS
01-01-1948; 1190 khz AM *Hrs Open:* 24 hrs
P.O. Box 2, Grafton, WV 26354 US
(304) 265-2200, *Fax:* (304) 265-0972
www.1190wvus.com
wtbz@go.com,mail@wtbz.com
License: Grafton, WV held by Appalachian Radio LLC
Arbitron Metro Market: Grafton, WV *Format:* Adult Contemp *Hrs. of News Programming:* News progmg 15 hrs wkly *Target Audience:* 18-65.
Melanie Tocco, General Manager

***WDKL**
09-10-1979; 95.9 mhz FM *Hrs Open:* 24; 6 kw; 299 ft.; N39 21 16 W80 1 27
P.O. Box 2, Grafton, WV 26354 US
(916) 251-1600, *Fax:* (916) 251-1650
www.klove.com
klove@klove.com
License: Grafton, Taylor County, WV held by Educational Media Foundation
Group Owner: EMF Broadcasting; (acq 5-28-02).
Nat'l Network: K-Love
Arbitron Metro Market: Grafton, WV *Format:* Christian *No. News Employees:* 3 *Target Audience:* 25-44; female-Judeo Christian
Darrell Chambliss, Chairman
Mike Novak, CEO
Mike Novak, President
Pam Patrick-Thompson, Operations Dir
David Pierce, Programming Director
Ed Lenane, News Director
Sam Wallington, Engineering Dir
Marya Morgan, News Reporter
Richard Hunt, News Reporter
Mitch Barnhart, Director
Larry Moody, Director
Dr.David.R.Ferry, Director

Green Valley

WAMN
01-01-1987; 1050 khz AM *Hrs Open:* 24 hours a day; 1.43 kw-D, ND1; 0.2 kw-N, ND1; N37 18 20 W81 7 30
Mailing Address: P. O. Box 889, Blacksburg, VA 24063 US
Second Address: 4415 Blue Prince Road, Bluefield, WV 24701
(304) 327-9266 (304) 327-9140, *Fax:* (304) 325-8058
www.mywillie.com
espn1050@yahoo.com
License: Green Valley, WV held by WAMN Inc.
Group Owner: Baker Family Stations; (acq 2-8-89)
Nat'l Network: ESPN Radio
Arbitron Metro Market: Bluefield, WV *Format:* Sports
Vernon Baker, President
Amy Burnette, General Manager

Hillsboro

***WVMR-FM**
91.9 mhz FM; 0.55 kw; -35 ft.; N38 11 30 W80 11 44 US
(304) 799-6004, *Fax:* (304) 799-7444
www.alleghenymountainradio.org
dsamr@frontier.com
License: Hillsboro, Pocahontas County, WV held by Pocahontas Communications Cooperative Corp.
Arbitron Metro Market: Hillsboro, WV *Format:* Country *No. News Employees:* 1
Cheryl Kinderman, General Manager
Bonnie Ralston, Station Manager
Heather Niday, Programming Director
Geoff Hamill, News Director
Chuck Niday, Chief Engineer
Gibbs Kinderman, Director of Special Projects

Hinton

WMTD
01-11-1963; 1380 khz AM *Hrs Open:* 24*Rebroadcasts:* Rebroadcasts WAXS(FM) Oak Hill 75%
95 Pleasant Street, Hinton, WV 25951 US
(304) 466-1380, *Fax:* (304) 466-8082
www.radioam1380.com
License: Hinton, WV held by Southern Communications Corp.
Group Owner: Southern Communications Corp.; (acq 4-19-2000; $107,000 with co-located FM).
Nat'l Network: CBS
Arbitron Metro Market: Beckley, WV *Format:* Contemporary Hits/Top 40 *Hrs. of News Programming:* news progmg 9 hrs wkly *No. News Employees:* 3 *Target Audience:* General. *Adv. Rates:* 75; 50; 50; 40
R. Shane Southern, President
Jay Quesenberry, General Manager
Rennold Madrazo, General Sales Mgr
Rick Rizer, Programming Director
Rhonda Pritt, News Director
Randy Kerbawy, Engineering Dir
Steve Coleman, Regional Sales Manager

WMTD-FM
10-01-1985; 102.3 mhz FM *Hrs Open:* 24; 0.37 kw; 1273 ft.; N37 42 53 W80 57 9
Box 820, Hinton, WV 25951 US
(304) 253-7000, *Fax:* (304) 255-1044
www.theticket102.com
kthompson@radiocitywv.com
License: Hinton, Summers County, WV held by Southern Communications Corp.
Group Owner: Southern Communications Corp.
Arbitron Metro Market: Beckley, WV *Format:* Sports *Hrs. of News Programming:* news progmg 1 hr wkly *No. News Employees:* 1 *Target Audience:* Adults 18-49. *Adv. Rates:* 70; 50; 60; 40
Lisa Elkins, General Sales Mgr
Rhonda Pritt, News Director

Huntington

WEMM-FM
09-06-1971; 107.9 mhz FM *Hrs Open:* 24; 50 kw; 499 ft.; N38 28 37 W82 15 20
3270 Blazer Prkwy, Suite 101, Lexington, KY 40509 US
(304) 525-5141(304) 525-9366, *Fax:* (304) 525-0748
www.wemmfm.com
License: Huntington, Cabell County, WV held by Mortenson Broadcasting Co.
Group Owner: Mortenson Broadcasting Co.
Nat'l Network: USA
Arbitron Metro Market: Huntington, WV *Format:* Christian, Gospel *Hrs. of News Programming:* News progmg 4 hrs wkly *Target Audience:* 35 plus; responsive, loyal, family oriented
Jack Mortenson, President
Anita Jones, General Manager
Alicia Vance, News Director

WEMM
01-01-1946; 1200 khz AM *Hrs Open:* 24; 5 kw-D, 72 w-N; N38 24 17 W82 29 21
703 3rd Ave., Huntington, WV 29928
(304) 525-5141, *Fax:* (304) 525-0748
License: Huntington, Cabell County, WV held by Mortenson Broadcasting Co. of West Virginia LLC.
Group Owner: Mortenson Broadcasting Co.; (acq 1-30-2004; $200,000)
Arbitron Metro Market: Huntington-Ashland, WV-KY *Target Audience:* 25-50; general
Jack Mortenson, President
Anita Jones, General Manager

WVHU
07-01-1947; 800 khz AM; 5 kw-D, ND1; 0.185 kw-N, ND1; N38 23 35 W82 28 24
Mailing Address: 600 Congress Avenue, Suite 1400, Austin, TX 78701 US
Second Address: 134 4th Ave., Huntington, WV 25701
(304) 525-7788, *Fax:* (304) 525-6281
www.800wvhu.com
paulswann@clearchanneler
License: Huntington, WV held by Capstar TX L.P.
Group Owner: Clear Channel Communications Inc.; (acq 8-30-2000; grpsl)
Arbitron Metro Market: Huntington-Ashland, WV-KY *Format:* News, News/Talk, 86 *Target Audience:* 25-54; older, professional, higher income
Judy Cornett, General Manager
Matt Tweel, General Sales Mgr
Paul Swann, Programming Director
Truezy Robinette, Promotions Manager
Bill Cornwell, News Director
Scott Hensley, Chief Engineer
Kym Blake, National Sales Manager

WKEE-FM
11-01-1947; 100.5 mhz FM; 53 kw; 561 ft.; N38 23 35 W82 28 24
Mailing Address: 600 Congress Avenue, Suite 1400, Austin, TX 78701 US
Second Address: 134 4th Ave., Huntington, WV 25701
(304) 525-7788, *Fax:* (304) 525-6281
www.wkee.com
License: Huntington, Cabell County, WV held by Capstar TX L.P.
Group Owner: Clear Channel Communications Inc.; (acq 8-30-2000; grpsl)
Arbitron Metro Market: Huntington-Ashland, WV-KY *Format:* Contemporary Hits/Top 40 *Target Audience:* 18-42.
Judy Cornett, Operations Dir
Gloria Ward, General Sales Mgr
Jim Davis, Programming Director
Gary Miller, Music Director

***WMUL**
11-01-1961; 88.1 mhz FM *Hrs Open:* 6 AM-3 AM; 1.15 kw; -56 ft.; N38 25 26 W82 25 39
400 Hal Greer Boulevard, Huntington, WV 25755 US
(304) 696-6640, *Fax:* (304) 696-3232
www.marshall.edu/wmul
wmul@marshall.edu
License: Huntington, Cabell County, WV held by Marshall University Board of Governors
Wire Services: AP
Arbitron Metro Market: Huntington, WV *Format:* Variety/Diverse *Hrs. of News Programming:* News progmg 7 hrs wkly *Target Audience:* General.
Dr. Stephen Kopp, President
Michael Stanley, Operations Dir
Dr. Chuck G. Bailey, General Manager
Adam Cavalier, Station Manager
Jessie Kirk, Programming Director
Jason van Meter, Promotions Manager
Leannda Carey, NewsDirector
Chuck Cook, Chief Engineer
Delaney McLemore, Production Director
Ryan Epling, Sports Commentator

WRVC
10-23-1923; 930 khz AM *Hrs Open:* 24
Mailing Address: 401 11th St, Suite 200, Huntington, WV 25701 US
Second Address: 401 11th St., Suite 200, Huntington, WV 25701
(304) 523-8401, *Fax:* (304) 523-4848
www.supertalk941.com
studio@huntingtonsupertalk.com
License: Huntington, WV held by Fifth Avenue Broadcasting Co. Inc.

Group Owner: Kindred Communications Inc.; (acq 6-1-70)
Nat'l Network: ESPN Radio; ABC; CBS Radio; Motor Racing Net; Westwood One *Regional Network:* W. Va. MetroNews Network
Nat'l Reps: McGavren Guild *Wire Services:* AP; Accu-Weather; ESPN/SportsTicker
Arbitron Metro Market: Huntington-Ashl *Format:* Sports *Special Programming:* Relg 3 hrs wkly *Hrs. of News Programming:* news progmg 40 hrs wkly *No. News Employees:* 1
Tom Wolf, CEO
Mike Kirtner, President
Rae Ann Parsons, General Sales Mgr
Cameron Smith, Engineering Dir
Rich Myhrwold, Regional Sales Manager

WTCR-FM
05-01-1966; 103.3 mhz FM; 50 kw; 492 ft.; N38 25 11 W82 24 6
600 Congress Avenue, Suite 1400, Austin, TX 78701 US
(606) 739-8427, *Fax:* (606) 739-6009
wtcr.com
wtcr@clearchannel.com
License: Huntington, Cabell County, WV held by Capstar TX L.P.
Group Owner: Clear Channel Communications Inc.; (acq 8-30-00; grpsl)
Nat'l Network: ABC *Nat'l Reps:* Rgnl Reps; Katz Radio
Arbitron Metro Market: Huntington, WV *Format:* Country
Jim Davis, Operations Dir
Judy Jennings, General Manager
Judy Eaton, Programming Director

*WVWV
11-28-1977; 89.9 mhz FM *Hrs Open:* 24; 8.1 kw; 1165 ft.; N38 29 41 W82 12 3
600 Capitol Street, Charleston, WV 25301 US
(304) 556-4900, *Fax:* (304) 556-4981
www.wvpubcast.org
feedback@wvpubcast.org
License: Huntington, Cabell County, WV held by West Virginia Educational Broadcasting Authority.
Nat'l Network: NPR; PRI
Arbitron Metro Market: Huntington, WV *Format:* Jazz, News
Rita Ray, General Manager
Marilyn DiVita, General Sales Mgr
Craig Lanham, Programming Director
Beth Vorhees, Director of News and Public Affairs
Dennis Adkins, Executive Director
Bill Acker, Director of Broadcasting &Technology
Marilyn DiVita, Director of Development
Michael L. Meador, Director of Finance
Shawn Patterson, Director of Marketing

Hurricane

WMUX
07-02-1971; 1110 khz AM *Hrs Open:* 10; 1 kw-D; N38 26 41 W82 00 54 *Rebroadcasts:* Simulcast with WOKT(AM) Cannonsburg, KY 100%
3006 Mt. Vernon Rd., Suite 1080, Hurricane, WV 24063
(304) 757-9661, *Fax:* (304) 757-9620
www.i64country.com
info@i64country.com
License: Hurricane, Putnam County, WV held by Big River Radio Inc.
Group Owner: Baker Family Stations; (acq 1996; $20,000)
Population Served: 800,000 *Arbitron Metro Market:* Charleston, WV
Vernon Baker, President
Matt Curry, Operations Dir
Randy Parsons, General Manager
Winston Hawkins, Chief Engineer

*WPJW
01-01-2009; 91.5 mhz FM; 3 kw; 302 ft.; N38 26 41 W82 0 54
Post Office Box 889, Blacksburg, VA 24063 US
(540) 552-4252
www.walkfm.org
License: Hurricane, Putnam County, WV held by Positive Alternative Radio Inc.
Group Owner: Positive Alternative Radio Inc.
Arbitron Metro Market: Hurricane, WV
Vernon Baker, President
Adam McDowell, Operations Dir
Jeremy Wolfe, Operations Manager
Elisha Dorsey, Production Assistant
Mike Nelson, Underwriting Representative/Sales Dept
Mel Mendoza, Marketing & Creative Manager

Kenova

WTCR
08-01-1954; 1420 khz AM; 5 kw-D, DAN; 0.5 kw-N, DAN; N38 24 42 W82 36 13
600 Congress Avenue, Suite 1400, Austin, TX 78701 US
(304) 525-7788
wtcr.com
wtcr@clearchannel.com
License: Kenova, WV held by Capstar TX L.P.
Group Owner: Clear Channel Communications Inc.; (acq 8-30-00; grpsl)
Nat'l Reps: Rgnl Reps; Katz Radio
Arbitron Metro Market: Huntington, WV *Format:* Blues *Target Audience:* 35 plus.
Jim Davis, Operations Dir
Judy Jennings, General Manager
Judy Eaton, Programming Director

WMGA
01-01-2006; 97.9 mhz FM; 3.5 kw; 436 ft.; N38 25 26 W82 32 8
Mailing Address: US
Second Address: 919 Fifth Ave., Suite 210, Huntington, WV 25701
(304) 399-9603, *Fax:* (304) 399-9608
www.magic979.com
License: Kenova, Wayne County, WV held by Connoisseur Media LLC.
Group Owner: Connoisseur Media LLC
Arbitron Metro Market: Oakland, CA *Format:* Adult Contemp
Newman Adkins, General Manager

Keyser

WCBC-FM
01-01-1990; 107.1 mhz FM; 0.48 kw; 830 ft.; N39 31 30 W78 51 43
P.O. Box 1290, Cumberland, MD 21502 US
(301) 724-5000, *Fax:* (301) 722-8336
www.wcbcradio.com
News@WCBCRadio.com
License: Keyser, Mineral County, WV held by Prosperitas Broadcasting System.
Arbitron Metro Market: Cumberland, MD *Format:* Oldies
David Aydelotte, General Manager
Mary Clites, General Sales Mgr
Bryan Gowans, News Director
Martin White, Chief Engineer

WKLP
08-31-1965; 1390 khz AM *Hrs Open:* 24; 1 kw-D, ND1; 0.074 kw-N, ND1; N39 26 12 W78 57 21
P.O. Box F, Keyser, WV 26726 US
(301) 759-1005, *Fax:* (301) 759-3124
www.1230espnam.com
License: Keyser, WV held by Starcast Systems Inc.
Group Owner: West Virginia Radio Corp.; (acq 12-29-2006; with co-located FM)
Format: Adult Contemp *Special Programming:* Big band *Target Audience:* 35 plus.
Jerry Hannahs, General Manager
Jack Mullen III, Programming Director
Pat Sullivan, News Director
Mark Allen, Music Director

WQZK-FM
09-15-1973; 94.1 mhz FM *Hrs Open:* 24; 13 kw; 928 ft.; N39 25 7 W78 57 15
P.O. Drawer F, Keyser, WV 26726 US
(304) 759-1005, *Fax:* (304) 759-3124
www.941qzk.com
License: Keyser, Mineral County, WV held by Starcast Systems Inc.
Group Owner: West Virginia Radio Corp.
Format: Classic Rock *Target Audience:* 18-49.
Jerry Hannahs, General Manager

Kingwood

WFSP
08-25-1967; 1560 khz AM; 0.25 kw-C, NDD; 1 kw-D, NDD; N39 28 50 W79 43 11
Mailing Address: P. O. Box 567, Kingwood, WV 26537 US
Second Address: Rt. 7, W., Kingwood, WV 26537
(304) 329-1780, *Fax:* (304) 329-1781
www.prestoncounty.com/wfsp
wfsp@wvdsl.net
License: Kingwood, WV held by WFSP Inc.
Nat'l Network: CBS *Nat'l Reps:* Dome
Format: News, Talk *No. News Employees:* 1 *Target Audience:* 20 plus. *Adv. Rates:* 12; 12; 12; 12
Arthur George, President
Donna Nestor, Operations Dir
Dave Wills, Programming Director
Kathy Casseday, News Director
Chuck Clemence, Chief Engineer
Kathy Casseday, Public Affairs Director
Art George, Radio Announcer
Dave Price,Sales
Donna Nestor, Office Manager

WFSP-FM
06-10-1991; 107.7 mhz FM *Hrs Open:* 24; 1.6 kw; 449 ft.; N39 28 50 W79 43 11
Mailing Address: Post Office Box 567, Kingwood, WV 26537 US
Second Address: Rt. 7, W., Kingwood, WV 26537
(304) 329-1780, *Fax:* (304) 329-1781
www.prestoncounty.com/wfsp
wfsp@wvdsl.net
License: Kingwood, Preston County, WV
Nat'l Network: Westwood One *Nat'l Reps:* Dome
Format: Oldies, Religious *Hrs. of News Programming:* news progmg 25 hrs wkly *No. News Employees:* 1 *Target Audience:* 18-45. *Adv. Rates:* 12; 12; 12; 12
Kathy Cassedy, Operations Dir
Arthur George, General Sales Mgr
Donna Nestor, Programming Director
Dave Wills, Disc Jockey
Mike Barnett, Disc Jockey

WKMM
12-01-1986; 96.7 mhz FM *Hrs Open:* 24; 0.3 kw; 797 ft.; N39 27 29 W79 35 18
106 E Main Street, Kingwood, WV 26537 US
(304) 329-0967, *Fax:* (304) 329-2131
www.wkmmfm.com
wkmmfm@yahoo.com
License: Kingwood, Preston County, WV held by MarPat Corp.
Nat'l Network: Westwood One; CNN Radio
Format: Country *Target Audience:* 25-55.
Greg Bolyard, Operations Dir
Neil Waldeck, General Manager
Tina Waldeck, News Director
Marty White, Chief Engineer

Lewisburg

WRON-FM
10-01-1981; 103.1 mhz FM *Hrs Open:* 24; 3.3 kw; 896 ft.; N37 47 54 W80 30 56
Mailing Address: P.O. Box 610, White Sulphur Spring, WV 24986 US
Second Address: 276 Seneca Trail, Ronceverte, WV 24970
(304) 536-1310, *Fax:* (304) 536-1311
www.wron.com
radio@wron.com
License: Lewisburg, Greenbrier County, WV held by Michael J. Kidd dba Greenbrier Radio
Nat'l Network: ABC *Nat'l Reps:* Rgnl Reps
Format: Country *Special Programming:* Gospel 6 hrs, relg 4 hrs, farm 3 hrs wkly *Hrs. of News Programming:* News progmg 12 hrs wkly *Target Audience:* 25-55. *Adv. Rates:* 7.25; 7.25; 7.25; 7.25
Joyce Tucker, General Manager
Marcia Smith, General Sales Mgr
Chuck Harper, Programming Director

Lindside

*WHFI
09-01-1990; 106.7 mhz FM *Hrs Open:* 24; 6 kw; 121 ft.; N37 28 56 W80 39 40
P. O. Box 330, Union, WV 24983 US
(304) 753-9971, *Fax:* (304) 753-9792
www.whfi-fm.com
License: Lindside, Monroe County, WV held by Monroe County Board of Education
Format: Adult Contemp
James Higginbotham, General Manager

Logan

WVOW
05-01-1954; 1290 khz AM *Hrs Open:* 24
Mailing Address: P.O. Box 1776, Logan, WV 25601 US
Second Address: 204 Main St., Suite 201, Logan, WV 25601
(304) 752-5080, *Fax:* (304) 752-5711
www.wvowradio.com
advertise@wvowradio.com
License: Logan, WV held by Logan Broadcasting Corp.
Arbitron Metro Market: Logan, WV *Format:* Adult Contemp *No. News Employees:* 2 *Target Audience:* General.
Martha Jane Becker, President
Larry Bevins, General Manager
Bill France, Programming Director
Bob Weisner, News Director
Terry Bucklew, Chief Engineer
Rhonda Bryant, Traffic Manager

WVOW-FM
08-01-1969; 101.9 mhz FM *Hrs Open:* 24; 15 kw horiz, 13.5 kw vert; 830 ft.; N37 51 24 W81 58 18
Mailing Address: P.O. Box 1776, Logan, WV 25601 US
Second Address: 204 Main St., Suite 201, Logan, WV 25601
(304) 752-5080, *Fax:* (304) 752-5711
www.wvowradio.com
advertise@wvowradio.com
License: Logan, Logan County, WV
Arbitron Metro Market: Logan, WV *Format:* Adult Contemp
Rhonda Bryant, News Director

Lost Creek

WHAW
02-14-1948; 980 khz AM *Hrs Open:* 24; 1 kw-D, 50 w-N; N39 02 25 W80 27 16
300 Harrison Ave., Weston, WV 26452
(304) 269-5555, *Fax:* (304) 269-4800
www.whawradio.com
whaw@aol.com
License: Lost Creek, Lewis County, WV held by Stephen R. Peters.
Nat'l Network: CUMULUS
Special Programming: Bluegrass 8 hrs, folk 4 hrs, gospel 18 hrs wkly *Hrs. of News Programming:* news progmg 2 hrs wkly *No. News Employees:* 1 *Target Audience:* General. *Adv. Rates:* 10; 10; 10; 10
Stephen Peters, General Manager

WOTR(FM)
12-09-1991; 96.3 mhz FM *Hrs Open:* 8 AM-10 PM; 6 kw horiz; 302 ft; N39 08 43 W80 19 40
Box 505, Lost Creek, WV 26385
(304) 745-4243
License: Lost Creek, Harrison County, WV held by James W. Allman.
Population Served: 50,000*Format:* Gospel, Religious *Target Audience:* 25-99.
James Allman, CEO
Bill Allman, General Manager

Mannington

WGYE
12-01-1992; 102.7 mhz FM *Hrs Open:* 24; 3.2 kw; 453 ft.; N39 28 3 W80 12 20
104 Broadway Avenue, Carnegie, PA 15106 US
(304) 363-8888, *Fax:* (304) 367-1885
www.froggycountry.net
laura@froggycountry.net
License: Mannington, Marion County, WV held by Burbach of DE LLC.
Group Owner: Burbach Broadcasting Group; (acq 6-20-2000; grpsl).
Arbitron Metro Market: Morgantown, WV *Format:* Country *Hrs. of News Programming:* news progmg 4 hrs wkly *No. News Employees:* 1 *Target Audience:* 25-54. *Adv. Rates:* 17; 13; 15; 10
Nicholas Galli, President
David Bronham, General Manager
Greg Bolyard, Programming Director
Larry Smith, Chief Engineer
Laura Candell, Office Manager

Marlinton

***WNMP**
88.5 mhz FM; 1 kw; -216 ft.; N38 13 40 W80 4 40
US
(304) 799-6004, *Fax:* (304) 799-7444
www.alleghenymountainradio.org
dsamr@frontier.com
License: Marlinton, Pocahontas County, WV held by Pocahontas Communications Cooperative Corp.
Arbitron Metro Market: Marlinton, WV *No. News Employees:* 1
Cheryl Kinderman, General Manager
Bonnie Ralston, Station Manager
Heather Niday, Programming Director
Geoff Hamill, News Director
Chuck Niday, Chief Engineer
Gibbs Kinderman, Director of Special Projects

Marmet

***WKVW**
06-30-1995; 93.3 mhz FM *Hrs Open:* 24; 1.7 kw; 620 ft.; N38 16 25 W81 31 27
2925 East Exposition Avenue, Denver, CO 80209 US
(800) 525-5683, *Fax:* (916) 251-1650
www.klove.com
klove@klove.com
License: Marmet, Kanawha County, WV held by Educational Media Foundation
Group Owner: EMF Broadcasting; (acq 7-1-2002; $500,000)
Nat'l Network: K-Love
Arbitron Metro Market: Marmet, WV *Format:* Christian *No. News Employees:* 13 *Target Audience:* 25-44; Judeo Christian, female
Darrell Chambliss, Chairman
MIke Novak, President & CEO
Pam Patrick-Thompson, Operations Dir
Eric Allen, General Sales Mgr
David Pierce, Programming Director
Ed Lenane, News Director
Sam Wallington, Engineering Dir
MaryaMorgan, News Reporter
Richard Hunt, News Reporter
Laura Daniels, News Reporter
Tim Luttrell, News Reporter
Kenny Noble Cortes, News Reporter
Darren Vinson, News Reporter

Martinsburg

WEPM
10-13-1946; 1340 khz AM; 1 kw-U, ND1; N39 27 48 W77 59 11
5393 Royal Mile Blvd, Salisbury, MD 21801 US
(304) 263-8868, *Fax:* (304) 263-8906
www.wepm.com
mikem@prettymanbroadcasting.com
License: Martinsburg, WV held by Prettyman Broadcasting Co.
Group Owner: Prettyman Broadcasting Co.; (acq 1-1-87; $2 million;
Nat'l Network: CBS *Nat'l Reps:* Katz Radio
Arbitron Metro Market: Martinsburg, WV *Format:* News, News/Talk, 84, Talk *Special Programming:* Relg 6 hrs wkly *Target Audience:* 35 plus.
Mike McGough, General Manager/Sales Inquiries
Chuck Thornton, General Sales Mgr
Fred Persinger II, Programming and Content
Susan Grissinger, News Director
Rodney Rockwell, Chief Engineer

WLTF
01-01-1949; 97.5 mhz FM *Hrs Open:* 24; 11.4 kw; 1037 ft.; N39 27 33 W78 3 48
5393 Royal Mile Blvd., Salisbury, MD 21801 US
(304) 263-8868, *Fax:* (304) 263-8906
www.lite975.com
marc@prettymanbroadcasting.com
License: Martinsburg, Berkeley County, WV
Group Owner: Prettyman Broadcasting Co.
Arbitron Metro Market: Hagerstown-Chambersburg-Waynesboro, MD-PA *Format:* Adult Contemp *Target Audience:* 30-49.
Norm Slemenda, General Manager
Marc Richards, Programming Director
Norm Slemenda, Sales

WRNR
04-16-1976; 740 khz AM *Hrs Open:* 24; 0.5 kw-D, DA2; 0.021 kw-N, DA2; N39 28 25 W77 55 57
P.O. Box 709, Martinsburg, VA 25401 US
(304) 263-6586, *Fax:* (304) 263-3082
info@talkradiowrnr.com
License: Martinsburg, WV held by Shenandoah Communications Inc.
Nat'l Network: Westwood One; CBS; CNN Radio *Nat'l Reps:* Rgnl Reps
Format: News, News/Talk, 84, Talk *Hrs. of News Programming:* news progmg 28 hrs wkly *No. News Employees:* 3 *Target Audience:* 35 plus; middle to upper age & income *Adv. Rates:* 26.05; 25.05; 26.05; 25.05
Richard Wachtel, President
Matt Miller, Operations Dir
Tom Tucker, Promotions Manager
Fran Little, Chief Engineer
Gregg Wachtel, Executive Vice President

***WVEP**
02-11-1987; 88.9 mhz FM *Hrs Open:* 24; 3.6 kw horiz; 1624 ft.; N39 8 38 W78 26 9
600 Capitol Street, Charleston, WV 25301 US
(304) 556-4900, *Fax:* (304) 556-4981
www.wvpubcast.org
feedback@wvpubcast.org
License: Martinsburg, Berkeley County, WV held by West Virginia Educational Broadcasting Authority.
Nat'l Network: NPR; PRI
Arbitron Metro Market: Charleston, WV *Format:* Jazz, News
Craig Lanham, Programming Director
Beth Vorhees, Director of News and Public Affairs
Dennis Adkins, Executive Director
Bill Acker, Director of Broadcasting & Technology
Marilyn DiVita, Director of Development
Michael L. Meador,Director of Finance
Shawn Patterson, Director of Marketing

Matewan

WHJC
12-02-1951; 1360 khz AM; 1 kw-D, NDD; N37 37 2 W82 10 4
Mailing Address: 156 Radio Hill, McCarr, KY 41544 US
Second Address: 156 Radio Hill, McCarr, KY 41544
(606) 427-7261, *Fax:* (606) 427-7260
pwr1067@bellsouth.net
License: Matewan, WV held by Three States Broadcasting Co. Inc.
Format: Gospel
George Warren, President
Evelyn Warren, General Manager
Melissa White, Programming Director
Russell Laferty, Chief Engineer

WVKM
08-30-1989; 106.7 mhz FM *Hrs Open:* 24; 4.3 kw; 751 ft.; N37 36 49 W82 11 22
Mailing Address: P.O. Box 68, Matewan, WV 25678 US
Second Address: 156 Radio Hill, McCarr, KY 41544

kixx1067@yahoo.com
License: Matewan, Mingo County, WV held by Three States Broadcasting Co. Inc.
Arbitron Metro Market: Matewan, WV *Format:* Classic Rock *Adv. Rates:* 25; 12; 12; 12
Melissa White, News Director

Miami

WKAZ-FM
11-01-1985; 107.3 mhz FM *Hrs Open:* 24; 23.5 kw; 676 ft.; N38 16 25 W81 31 27
1251 Earl L. Core Road, Morgantown, WV 26505 US
(304) 342-8131, *Fax:* (304) 344-4745
www.1073krock.com
License: Miami, Kanawha County, WV held by West Virginia Radio Corp of Charleston.
Group Owner: West Virginia Radio Corp.; (acq 6-5-97; $2.15 million with WCZR(AM) Charleston)
Nat'l Reps: D & R Radio
Arbitron Metro Market: Charleston, WV *Format:* Oldies *Target Audience:* 25-54.
Sean Banks, General Manager
Max Wulf, Programming Director
Noel Richardson, Chief Engineer

Middlebourne

***WRSG**
01-01-2001; 91.5 mhz FM *Hrs Open:* 24; 0.9 kw; 157 ft.; N39 30 59 W80 54 0
P. O. Box 25, Middlebourne, WV 26149 US
(304) 758-9007, *Fax:* (304) 758-9006
tchs.tyle.k12.wv.us/ths/wrsg/wrsg.htm
wrsgfm@yahoo.com
License: Middlebourne, Tyler County, WV held by Tyler County Board of Education.
Arbitron Metro Market: Sistersville, WV *Format:* Variety/Diverse
Tom Charity, Operations Dir
John Maloney, General Sales Mgr
Ray Hall, Programming Director
Jerry Barco, News Director

Milton

WAMX
10-01-1980; 106.3 mhz FM *Hrs Open:* 24; 1.65 kw; 1109 ft.; N38 30 21 W82 12 33
600 Congress Avenue, Suite 1400, Austin, TX 78701 US
(304) 525-7788, *Fax:* (304) 525-6281
www.x1063.com
judyjennings@clearchannel.com
License: Milton, Cabell County, WV held by Capstar TX L.P.
Group Owner: Clear Channel Communications Inc.; (acq 8-30-00; grpsl)
Arbitron Metro Market: Milton, WV *Format:* Rock/AOR *Hrs. of News Programming:* news progmg 4 hrs wkly *No. News Employees:* 1 *Target Audience:* 25-49; males in their late teens to late '40s
Jim Davis, Operations Dir
Judy Cornett, General Manager
Kevin Beller, General Sales Mgr
Erik Raines, Programming Director
Robin Wilds, Promotions Manager

RADIO - U.S.

WZZW
06-26-1973; 1600 khz AM; 5 kw-D, ND1; 0.026 kw-N, ND1; N38 25 46 W82 6 21
600 Congress Avenue, Suite 1400, Austin, TX 78701 US
(304) 525-7788, *Fax:* (304) 525-6281
www.800wvhu.com
judyjennings@clearchannel.com
License: Milton, WV held by Aloha Station Trust LLC
Arbitron Metro Market: Huntington, WV *Format:* Christian *Target Audience:* 25-44; adult, upscale baby boomers
Judy Jennings, Operations Dir
Kym York-Blake, General Sales Mgr
Jim Davis, Operations Manager/Program Director
Dixie McDavid, News Director
Judy Jennings, General Market Manager

Montgomery

WMON
07-14-1946; 1340 khz AM; 1 kw-U, ND1; N38 10 38 W81 18 51
2925 East Exposition Avenue, Denver, CO 80209 US
(304) 722-3308, *Fax:* (304) 727-1300
www.wklc.com
news@wklc.com
License: Montgomery, WV held by L.M. Communications of Kentucky LLC.
Group Owner: L M Communications Inc.; (acq 4-1-03; grpsl).
Nat'l Network: Salem Radio Network
Arbitron Metro Market: Montgomery, WV *Target Audience:* 25 plus.
Ron Walton, General Manager
Chris Colagrosso, Programming Director
Emma Allen, News Director
Fred Francis, Chief Engineer

Moorefield

WELD-FM
02-06-1987; 101.7 mhz FM *Hrs Open:* 24; 0.285 kw; 1493 ft.; N38 58 58 W78 54 30
Route 1 Kessel Road, Fisher, WV 26818 US
(304) 538-6062, *Fax:* (304) 538-7032
www.weldamfm.com
weld@chardynet.com
License: Moorefield, Hardy County, WV held by Thunder Associates LLC
Nat'l Network: ABC *Nat'l Reps:* Dome; Keystone (unwired net)
Arbitron Metro Market: Fisher, WV *Format:* Country, Religious
Special Programming: Gospel 3 hrs wkly/contemporary christian/talk 6hrs wkly *Hrs. of News Programming:* news progmg 10 hrs wkly *No. News Employees:* 1 *Target Audience:* 25 plus. *Adv. Rates:* 14; 14; 14; 12
Curtis Durst, President
Alan Yokum, General Manager
Sandra Durst, Executive Vice President

Morgantown

WAJR
12-07-1940; 1440 khz AM *Hrs Open:* 24; 5 kw-D, DA2; 0.5 kw-N, DA2; N39 40 34 W80 0 12
1251 Earl Core Road, Morgantown, WV 26505 US
(304) 296-0029, *Fax:* (304) 296-3876
www.wajr.com
wajr@wvradio.com
License: Morgantown, WV held by West Virginia Radio Corp.
Group Owner: West Virginia Radio Corp.
Nat'l Network: ABC
Arbitron Metro Market: Morgantown, WV *Format:* News, News/Talk, 86 *Hrs. of News Programming:* news progmg 15 hrs wkly *No. News Employees:* 7 *Target Audience:* 25+.
Dale Miller, GM
Hoppy Kercheval, V.P. Of Operations
Gary Mertins, General Sales Mgr
Jim Stallings, Programming Director
Tim Loughry, Promotions Manager
Shawm Falkenstein, News Director
Noel Richardson, Engineering Dir
RalphMesser, Chief Engineer
Kay Murray, Public Affairs Director

WCLG
12-01-1954; 1300 khz AM; 2.5 kw-D, ND1; 0.044 kw-N, ND1; N39 37 40 W79 58 11
Mailing Address: 343 High Street, Morgantown, WV 26505 US
Second Address: 343 High St., Morgantown, WV 26505
(304) 292-2222, *Fax:* (304) 292-2224
www.wclg.com
debbie@wclg.com
License: Morgantown, WV held by Bowers Broadcasting Corp.
Nat'l Reps: Dome
Arbitron Metro Market: Morgantown, WV *Format:* Oldies
Garry Bowers, President
Debbie Lofstead, Sales Manager
Jeffrey Miller, Programming Director
Lucinda Funk, News Director
Ken Tennant, Chief Engineer

WCLG-FM
09-28-1974; 100.1 mhz FM; 6 kw; 299 ft.; N39 37 40 W79 58 11
Mailing Address: Po.Box 885, Morgantown, WV 26505 US
Second Address: 343 High St., Morgantown, WV 26505
(304) 292-2222, *Fax:* (304) 292-2224
www.wclg.com
debbie@wclg.com
License: Morgantown, Monongalia County, WV
Arbitron Metro Market: Morgantown, WV *Format:* Classic Rock
Debbie Lofstead, Sales Manager
Lucinda Funk, News Director

WVAQ
01-01-1948; 101.9 mhz FM *Hrs Open:* 24; 50 kw; 499 ft.; N39 36 30 W79 59 7
1251 Earl L Core Road, Morgantown, WV 26505 US
(304) 296-0029, *Fax:* (304) 296-3876
www.wvaq.com
License: Morgantown, Monongalia County, WV
Group Owner: West Virginia Radio Corp.
Arbitron Metro Market: Morgantown, WV *Format:* Contemporary Hits/Top 40 *Hrs. of News Programming:* news progmg one hr wkly *No. News Employees:* 2 *Target Audience:* 18-49.
Hoppy Kercheval, Operations Dir
Lacy Neff, Programming Director
Eric McGuire, Disc Jockey
Meghan Dunt, Disc Jockey

***WVPM**
05-27-1981; 90.9 mhz FM *Hrs Open:* 24; 5 kw; 1440 ft.; N39 41 45 W79 45 45
600 Capitol Street, Charleston, WV 25301 US
(304) 556-4900, *Fax:* (304) 556-4960
www.wvpubcast.org
feedback@wvpubcast.org
License: Morgantown, Monongalia County, WV held by West Virginia Educational Broadcasting Authority.
Nat'l Network: NPR; PRI
Arbitron Metro Market: Morgantown, WV *Format:* Jazz, News
Marilyn DiVita, General Manager
Marilyn DiVita, General Sales Mgr
Craig Lanham, Programming Director
Beth Vorhees, Director of News and Public Affairs
Dennis Adkins, Executive Director
Bill Acker, Director of Broadcasting &Technology
Marilyn DiVita, Director of Development
Michael L. Meador, Director of Finance
Shawn Patterson, Director of Marketing

***WWVU-FM**
08-20-1982; 91.7 mhz FM *Hrs Open:* 24; 2.6 kw; 180 ft.; N39 38 9 W79 56 38
Mountainlair, Pob 6446, Morgantown, WV 26506 US
(304) 293-3329, *Fax:* (304) 293-7363
u92.wvu.edu
u92@mail.wvu.edu
License: Morgantown, Monongalia County, WV held by West Virginia University Board of Governors
Arbitron Metro Market: Morgantown, WV *Format:* Variety/Diverse
Special Programming: New age 6 hrs, reggae 4 hrs, metal 6 hrs, bluegras *Hrs. of News Programming:* News progmg 2 hrs wkly *Target Audience:* 18-35;mostly college & high school students
Alex Gavula, General Manager

Moundsville

WVLY
10-01-1950; 1370 khz AM *Hrs Open:* 24; 5 kw-D, ND1; 0.02 kw-N, ND1; N39 54 20 W80 46 42
1401 Wheeling Avenue, Glen Dale, WV 26038 US
(304) 233-9859, *Fax:* (304) 214-9859
www.talkradio1370.com
wvlyradio@aol.com
License: Moundsville, WV held by Monroe Communications LLC
Nat'l Network: CNN Radio *Regional Network:* W. Va. MetroNews Network
Arbitron Metro Market: Wheeling, WV *Format:* News, News/Talk, 86 *Hrs. of News Programming:* News progmg 14 hrs wkly *Target Audience:* 25-54; adults
Howard Monroe, President

WBGI-FM
01-15-1990; 96.5 mhz FM *Hrs Open:* 24; 2.5 kw; 138 meters; N39 50 51 W80 45 23
56325 High Ridge Road, Bellaire, OH 15301
(740) 676-5661, *Fax:* (740) 676-2742
www.biggie965.com
License: Moundsville, Marshall County, WV held by Keymart Licenses LICdation.
Group Owner: EMF Broadcasting; (acq 12-15-2011)
Arbitron Metro Market: Wheeling, WV
Scott Miller, Marketing Director

Mount Hope

WTNJ
06-01-1980; 105.9 mhz FM *Hrs Open:* 24; 4.4 kw; 1532 ft.; N37 56 51 W81 18 29
P.O. Box 1127, Beckley, WV 25801 US
(304) 253-9865, *Fax:* (304) 255-1044
www.wtnjfm.com
License: Mount Hope, Fayette County, WV held by Southern Communications
Group Owner: Southern Communications Corp.; (acq 3-12-01; $2.375 million).
Arbitron Metro Market: Beckley, WV *Format:* Country *Special Programming:* NASCAR races, West Virginia Univ. sports *Hrs. of News Programming:* news progmg 12 hrs wkly *No. News Employees:* 1 *Target Audience:* 25-54.
Rick Reiser, Operations Dir
Jay Quesenberry, General Manager
Rick Peiser, Programming Director
Warren Ellison, News Director
Randy Kerbawy, Chief Engineer
Bill Wise, Traffic Manager

Mullens

WKQR(FM)
09-30-1981; 92.7 mhz FM; 1.65 kw; 443 ft; N37 35 39 W81 23 49
213 Howard Ave., Mullens, WV 25882
(304) 294-4405, *Fax:* (304) 294-5616
www.c92radio.com
ranny@c92.com
License: Mullens, Wyoming County, WV held by West Virginia-Virginia Holding Co. LLC
Nat'l Network: ABC
Format: Classic Rock
Ranny Parks, General Manager
Debra Toler, General Sales Mgr
Jeff Halsey, Programming Director

New Martinsville

WETZ
05-25-1953; 1330 khz AM *Hrs Open:* 24; 1 kw-D, ND2; 0.059 kw-N, ND2; N39 39 27 W80 51 34
Mailing Address: 325 Main Street, P.O. Box 249, New Martinsville, WV 26155 US
Second Address: 325 N.Main St., New Martinsville, WV 26155
(304) 455-1111, *Fax:* (304) 455-1170
wetz@verizon.net
License: New Martinsville, WV held by Dailey Corp.
Group Owner: Dailey Corp.; (acq 2-1-2001; grpsl).
Nat'l Network: ABC
Arbitron Metro Market: Wheeling, WV *Format:* Classic Rock *Hrs. of News Programming:* News progmg 10 hrs wkly *Target Audience:* 25-64. *Adv. Rates:* 12; 12; 12; 8.
Calvin Dailey Jr., President
Dennis Gage, General Manager

WETZ(FM)
12-01-1977; 103.9 mhz FM *Hrs Open:* 24; 2.5 kw; Ant 502 ft; N39 39 10 W80 54 47
Mailing Address: Box 10, New Martinsville, WV 26155
Second Address: 325 N.Main St., New Martinsville, WV 26155
(304) 455-1111, *Fax:* (304) 455-1170
www.powercountry104.com
wetz@verizon.net
License: New Martinsville, Wetzel County, WV
Nat'l Network: ABC
Population Served: 28,355 *Arbitron Metro Market:* Wheeling, WV *Hrs. of News Programming:* News progmg 10 hrs wkly *Target Audience:* 25-54; country *Adv. Rates:* 22; 22; 22; 14
Paul Stanton, President
Wayne Winkler, General Manager
Larry Mayer, Programming Director
Mitch Sandidge, Chief Engineer
Jim Blalock, Music Director
Susan Lachmann, Women's Int Ed

WXCR
01-01-2002; 92.3 mhz FM *Hrs Open:* 24; 3.2 kw; 453 ft.; N39 40 16 W80 53 4
Mailing Address: P O Box 374, Greens Run Rd, Saint Marys, WV 26170 US
Second Address: Box 374, Saints Marys, WV 26170

(800) 296-2617, *Fax:* (304) 684-9241
www.wxcr.com
lisa.wilson@literock93r.com
License: New Martinsville, Wetzel County, WV held by Seven Ranges Radio Co. Inc.
Arbitron Metro Market: New Martinsville, WV *Format:* Classic Rock *Target Audience:* 25-54; 70% men, 30% women *Adv. Rates:* 6.50; 6; 6; 5
Sam Yoho, President
Lou Petronio, Operations Dir

WYMJ
12-01-2002; 99.5 mhz FM *Hrs Open:* 24; 2.7 kw; 482 ft.; N39 39 10 W80 54 47
P O Box 83, Proctor, WV 26055 US
(800) 833-9211, *Fax:* (304) 455-1170
www.oldiesradioonline.com
webmaster@greatestmojo.com
License: New Martinsville, Wetzel County, WV held by Dailey Corp.
Group Owner: Dailey Corp.; acq 2-6-2001; grpsl).
Arbitron Metro Market: Dallas, TX *Format:* Adult Contemp *No. News Employees:* 3
Dex Gage, General Manager
Ed Wilhelm, Chief Engineer

Oak Hill

WAXS
01-01-1948; 94.1 mhz FM *Hrs Open:* 24; 25.5 kw; 650 ft.; N37 57 30 W81 9 3
609 Main Street, Mount Hope, WV 25880 US
License: Oak Hill, Fayette County, WV held by Plateau Broadcasting Inc.
Group Owner: Southern Communications Corp.; (acq 3-12-01; $875,000).
Nat'l Network: ABC
Arbitron Metro Market: South Park WY
Ted Tucker, General Manager

WOAY
02-22-1947; 860 khz AM; 5 kw-C, ND1; 10 kw-D, ND1; ND1; 0.011 kw; N37 57 30 W81 9 3
Mailing Address: Rt. 1, Box 185f, Fayetteville, WV 25840 US
Second Address: 300 N. Kanawha St., Suite 100, Beckley, WV 25801
(304) 465-0534, *Fax:* (304) 465-1486
www.woayradio.com
info@woayradio.com
License: Oak Hill, WV held by Mountaineer Media Inc.
Arbitron Metro Market: Beckley, WV *TV Affiliate:* Relg *No. News Employees:* General.
Operations Director, Vernon Drumheller
General Manager, General Manager

Parkersburg

WADC
04-09-1954; 1050 khz AM *Hrs Open:* 24; 5 kw-D, ND2; 0.144 kw-N, ND2; N39 15 29 W81 33 49
104 Broadway Ave., Carnegie, PA 15106 US
(386) 437-1992
wnzf.com
newsradio@wnzf.com
License: Parkersburg, WV held by Burbach of Delaware, LLC.
Group Owner: Burbach Broadcasting Group; (acq 3-19-98; $1.775 million with co-located FM).
Nat'l Network: CNN Radio
Format: News, News/Talk, 86 *Adv. Rates:* 20; 20; 20; 20
David Ayers, General Manager
Ron Charles, News Director

WHBR-FM
03-01-1967; 103.1 mhz FM *Hrs Open:* 24; 2.1 kw; 561 ft.; N39 21 0 W81 33 56
104 Broadway Ave., Carnegie, PA 15106 US
(304) 485-4565, *Fax:* (304) 424-6955
www.1031thebear.net
License: Parkersburg, Wood County, WV
Group Owner: Burbach Broadcasting Group
Arbitron Metro Market: Parkersburg-Marietta, WV-OH *Format:* Rock/AOR *Hrs. of News Programming:* news progmg 6 hrs wkly *No. News Employees:* 1 *Target Audience:* 18-49; active/modern rock listeners *Adv. Rates:* 25; 25; 25; 25
Donald Biggs, General Manager

WVNT
09-01-1947; 1230 khz AM *Hrs Open:* 24
104 Broadway Avenue, Carnegie, PA 15106 US
(304) 485-4565, *Fax:* (304) 424-6955
www.nvnt.net
License: Parkersburg, WV held by Burbach of Delaware, LLC.
Group Owner: Burbach Broadcasting Group; (acq 1-1-97; grpsl).
Nat'l Network: CNN Radio *Nat'l Reps:* McGavren Guild
Arbitron Metro Market: Parkersburg-Marietta, WV-OH *Format:* News, News/Talk, 86 *Special Programming:* Gospel 4 hrs wkly *No. News Employees:* 1 *Target Audience:* 30-50. *Adv. Rates:* 12; 12; 12; 12
Don Staats, General Manager

WHNK
07-12-1935; 1450 khz AM *Hrs Open:* 24; 1 kw-U, ND1; N39 17 23 W81 31 36
6006 Grand Central Ave, Vienna, WV 26105 US
(304) 295-6070, *Fax:* (304) 295-4389
www.whnk.com
johnchalfant@clearchannel.com
License: Parkersburg, WV held by CC Licenses LLC.
Group Owner: Clear Channel Communications Inc.; (acq 4-17-2001).
Nat'l Reps: Clear Channel
Arbitron Metro Market: Parkersburg, WV *Format:* Country *Hrs. of News Programming:* news progmg 3 hrs wkly *No. News Employees:* 1 *Target Audience:* 25-54; middle-aged, middle to upper income *Adv. Rates:* 12;10; 12; 6
John Chalfant, Operations Dir
Chuck Poet, General Manager
Kirk McCall, General Sales Mgr
Rodney Ortiz, Programming Director
Doug Hess, News Director
Jerry Kuhn, Chief Engineer
Belinda Marcinko, Traffic Manager

WRZZ
01-01-1986; 106.1 mhz FM *Hrs Open:* 24; 3.3 kw; 453 ft.; N39 14 47 W81 28 19
Box 474a, Route 4, Jewell Road, Parkersburg, WV 26101 US
(304) 485-4565, *Fax:* (304) 424-6955
www.z106.net
info@classicrockz106.com
License: Parkersburg, Wirt County, WV held by Burbach of DE LLC.
Group Owner: Burbach Broadcasting Group; (acq 8-8-2005; $750,000)
Nat'l Network: Westwood One
Arbitron Metro Market: Parkersburg-Mar *Format:* Classic Rock *Target Audience:* 25-54; baby boomer rock listeners
Brian Guthrie, Operations Dir
Don Staats, General Manager
Chuck Helmick, General Sales Mgr
Mike Cameron, Programming Director
Elista Burneisen, Promotions Manager
Shawn Jones, News Director

***WVPG**
04-04-1985; 90.3 mhz FM *Hrs Open:* 24; 9 kw; 322 ft.; N39 12 44 W81 35 30
600 Capitol Street, Charleston, WV 25301 US
(304) 556-4900, *Fax:* (304) 556-4960
www.wvpubcast.org
feedback@wvpubcast.org
License: Parkersburg, Wood County, WV held by West Virginia Educational Broadcasting Authority.
Nat'l Network: NPR; PRI
Arbitron Metro Market: Parkersburg, WV *Format:* Jazz, News *Special Programming:* Mountain Stage 2 hrs, children one hr wkly *No. News Employees:* 2
Rita Ray, CEO
Marilyn DiVita, General Manager
Peggy Dorsey, General Sales Mgr
Craig Lanham, Programming Director
Beth Vorhees, Director of News and Public Affairs
Dennis Adkins, Executive Director
Bill Acker, Director ofBroadcasting & Technology
Marilyn DiVita, Director of Development
Michael L. Meador, Director of Finance
Shawn Patterson, Director of Marketing

WGGE
09-01-1965; 99.1 mhz FM; 11.5 kw; 486 ft.; N39 17 15 W81 39 25
104 Broadway Ave., Carnegie, PA 15106 US
(304) 485-4565, *Fax:* (304) 424-6955
www.froggy99.net
info@froggy99.net
License: Parkersburg, Wood County, WV
Group Owner: Burbach Broadcasting Group
Arbitron Metro Market: Parkersburg, WV *Format:* Country *Special Programming:* Farm 2 hrs, NASCAR 5 hrs wkly *Target Audience:* 25-54; loyal modern country listeners
Bill Evans, General Manager
Darrin Evans, Station Manager

Petersburg

***WAUA**
12-01-1997; 89.5 mhz FM *Hrs Open:* 24; 10 kw; 1056 ft.; N39 12 7 W79 16 31
600 Capitol Street, Charleston, WV 25301 US
(304) 556-4900, *Fax:* (304) 556-4981
www.wvpubcast.org
feedback@wvpubcast.org
License: Petersburg, Grant County, WV held by West Virginia Educational Broadcasting Authority.
Nat'l Network: NPR; PRI
Arbitron Metro Market: Petersburg, WV *Format:* News
Rita Ray, General Manager
Marilyn DeVita, General Sales Mgr
James Muhammad, Programming Director
Greg Collard, News Director
Jack Wells, Chief Engineer
Teresa Wills, Traffic Manager

Philippi

***WQAB**
10-01-1975; 91.3 mhz FM *Hrs Open:* 8 AM-10 PM; 7.2 kw; 180 ft.; N39 9 52 W80 2 57
P.O. Box 1428, Philippi, WV 26416 US
(304) 457-6281,(304) 457-2916, *Fax:* (304) 457-6239
License: Philippi, Barbour County, WV held by Alderson-Broaddus College.
Nat'l Network: AP Radio
Format: Adult Contemp, Variety/Diverse *Special Programming:* Jazz 4 hrs, Black 2 hrs, radio drama 2 hrs, children's 2 hrs wkly *Hrs. of News Programming:* News progmg 5 hrs wkly *Target Audience:* 15-40; collegestudents
Harry Hancock, Station Manager
George Sommer, Engineering Dir

Pineville

WWYO
01-01-1949; 970 khz AM; 1 kw-D, ND2; 0.026 kw-N, ND2; N37 35 20 W81 32 25
Mailing Address: P. O. Box 647, Bluefield, WV 24701 US
Second Address: Rt. 10, One Radio Rd., Pineville, WV 24701
(304) 327-5651, *Fax:* (304) 327-5651
www.am970wwyo.bizland.com
am970wwyo@citlink.net
License: Pineville, WV held by MRJ Inc.
Arbitron Metro Market: Pineville, WV *Format:* Variety/Diverse *Special Programming:* Folk one hr, sports 18 hrs, educ 2 hrs, community *Target Audience:* 25-65; housewives *Adv. Rates:* 5.15; 5.15; 5.15; na
Rudolph Jennings, President

Pocatalico

WRVZ
01-01-1995; 98.7 mhz FM; 0.63 kw; 617 ft.; N38 23 53 W81 41 6
1235 Fletcher Ave, Dunbar, WV 25301 US
(304) 342-8131, *Fax:* (304) 344-4745
www.987thebeat.com
mbuxser@wvradio.com
License: Pocatalico, Kanawha County, WV held by West Virginia Radio Corp. of Charleston.
Group Owner: West Virginia Radio Corp.; (acq 3-12-2001; $800,000)
Arbitron Metro Market: Charleston, WV *Format:* Contemporary Hits/Top 40
Dale Miller, President
Woody Woods, Operations Dir
Mike Buxser, General Manager
Courtney Patrick, Promotions Manager
Jeff Jenkins, News Director
Noel Richardson, Chief Engineer

Point Pleasant

WBGS
01-01-1994; 1030 khz AM; 2.9 kw-C, DAD; 10 kw-D, DAD; N38 48 42 W82 5 59
P.O. Box 889, Blacksburg, VA 24060 US
(304) 675-2763, *Fax:* (304) 675-2771
cruzin1030wbgs@gmail.com
License: Point Pleasant, WV held by Big River Radio Inc.
Group Owner: Baker Family Stations
Arbitron Metro Market: Point Pleasant,VA *Format:* News, News/Talk, 86
Vernon Baker, CEO
Edward Baker, Operations Dir
Kevin Nott, General Manager
Shari Cochron, General Sales Mgr
Kathy Wise, News Director

RADIO - U.S.

Winston Hawkins, Chief Engineer
Tom Payne, Music Director

WBYG

01-01-1994; 99.5 mhz FM; 4.7 kw; Ant 328 ft; N38 50 49 W82 07 50
303 8th St., Point Pleasant, WV 24063
(304) 675-2763, *Fax:* (304) 675-2771
www.wbyg.com
License: Point Pleasant, Mason County, WV
Shari Cochran, Station Manager
Shari Cochran, General Sales Mgr
Tim Payne, News Director
Winston Hawkins, Chief Engineer
Kathy Wise, Office Manager

*WPCN(FM)

12-21-2000; 88.1 mhz FM *Hrs Open:* 24; 3 kw; Ant 289 ft; N38 50 49 W82 07 50
303 8th Street, Point Pleasant, WV 25550
(304) 675-2727, *Fax:* (304) 675-2771
www.joyfm881.com
joyfm881@yahoo.com
License: Point Pleasant, Mason County, WV held by Positive Alternative Radio Inc.
Group Owner: Positive Alternative Radio Inc.
Format: Gospel
Randy Parson, General Manager

Princeton

WAEY

12-01-1947; 1490 khz AM *Hrs Open:* 24; 1 kw-U, ND1; N37 23 23 W81 5 58
Mailing Address: 1345 Mercer Street, Princeton, WV 24740 US
Second Address: Lilly Grove Addition, 1 Radio Ln., Princeton, WV 24740
(304) 425-2151, *Fax:* (304) 487-2016
www.star95.com
progeam@star95.com
License: Princeton, WV held by Princeton Broadcasting Inc.
Arbitron Metro Market: Princeton, WV *Format:* Gospel *Hrs. of News Programming:* news progmg 14 hrs wkly *No. News Employees:* 1 *Target Audience:* 25 plus; blue collar
Linda Witt, President
Pat Tolley, Operations Dir
Bob Spencer, General Manager
Ron Witt, Programming Director
Amy Mills, News Director
Wayne Boone, Chief Engineer
Patricia Tolley, Min Affairs Director
Jason Reed, OperationsManager

WKOY-FM

04-01-1983; 100.9 mhz FM *Hrs Open:* 24; 0.34 kw; 1342 ft.; N37 15 5 W81 11 20
100 Bluefield Avenue, Suite 3, Bluefield, WV 24701 US
(304) 327-7114, *Fax:* (304) 325-7850
www.theeaglefm.com
License: Princeton, Mercer County, WV held by Monterey Licenses LLC.
Group Owner: Triad Broadcasting Co. L.L.C.; (acq 7-18-00; grpsl)
Nat'l Network: ABC *Nat'l Reps:* Katz Radio; Rgnl Reps
Arbitron Metro Market: Bluefield, WV *Format:* Classic Rock *No. News Employees:* 1 *Target Audience:* 25 plus.
Ken Deitz, Operations Dir
John Halford, General Manager
Danny Clemmon, General Sales Mgr
P.J. Toler, News Director
Keith Bowman, Chief Engineer

WSTG

04-01-1973; 95.9 mhz FM *Hrs Open:* 24; 0.48 kw; 1142 ft.; N37 15 30 W81 10 37
Mailing Address: 1345 Mercer Street, Princeton, WV 24740 US
Second Address: Lilly Grove Addition, 1Radio Ln, Princeton, WV 24740
(304) 425-2151, *Fax:* (304) 487-2016
www.star95.com
program@star95.com
License: Princeton, Mercer County, WV held by L & P Broadcasting Inc.
Arbitron Metro Market: Bluefield, WV *Format:* Contemporary Hits/Top 40 *No. News Employees:* 1
Linda Witt, General Sales Mgr
Jeff Davis, Programming Director
Amy Mills, News Director
Jason Reed, Disc Jockey
Bob Spencer, Disc Jockey
Charlie Brown, Local News Editor
Jim Nelson, Sports Commentator

*WPWV

09-01-2003; 90.1 mhz FM; 2.5 kw vert; 1040 ft.; N37 30 35 W81 12 55
P.O. Drawer 2440, Tupelo, MS 38801 US
(662) 844-8888, *Fax:* (662) 842-6791
www.afr.net
faq@afr.net
License: Princeton, Mercer County, WV held by American Family Association.
Group Owner: American Family Radio
Arbitron Metro Market: Princeton, WV *Format:* Christian
Marvin Sanders, General Manager

Rainelle

WRLB

02-01-1977; 95.3 mhz FM *Hrs Open:* 24; 13 kw; 456 ft.; N37 57 28 W80 45 45
P.O. Box 1450, Lewisburg, WV 24901 US
(304) 647-3606
www.wrlb.com
License: Rainelle, Greenbrier County, WV held by Faith Communications Network Inc.
Format: Christian, Religious *Target Audience:* 25-54.
Norma Mnich, Chairman
Matthew Mnich, CEO
Mark Jividen, Operations Dir
Jim Pontius, General Sales Mgr
Hal Fish, Programming Director
Greg Moebius, Promotions Manager
Eric Feucht, General Sales Manager
Ronni Hunter, MusicDirector

WRRL

01-01-1973; 1130 khz AM; 1 kw-D, NDD; N37 57 28 W80 45 45
507 Main Street, Rainelle, WV 25962 US
(304) 438-8537 phone/fax
wrrlam@mountain.net
License: Rainelle, WV held by Faith Mountain Communications Inc.
Regional Network: W. Va. MetroNews Network
Format: Christian, Gospel, 60, News/Talk, Talk *Target Audience:* 35 plus. *Adv. Rates:* 3; 3; 3; 3
Nancy Whitt, CEO
Allen Whitt, President

Ravenswood

WMOV

01-01-1953; 1360 khz AM *Hrs Open:* 24 hours
P. O. Box 647, Ravenswood, WV 26164 US
(304) 273-2544, *Fax:* (304) 868-1360
http://www.wmov1360.com
contact@wmov1360.com
License: Ravenswood, WV held by Allen Media Stations
Nat'l Network: CBS Radio; Westwood One; Jones Radio Networks *Regional Network:* W. Va. MetroNews Network; Radio Sound Net.
Arbitron Metro Market: Charleston, WV *Format:* News, Talk
Special Programming: Cincinnati Reds baseball; Cincinnati Bengal footba *Hrs. of News Programming:* news programming 12 hrs weekly *No. News Employees:* 1*Target Audience:* 35 plus
Adv. Rates: 6.50; 6.50; 6.50; 2.50
Burke Allen, President
Greg Gack, General Manager

Richwood

WVAR

01-01-1956; 600 khz AM *Hrs Open:* 6 AM-sunset; 1 kw-D, NDD; 0.055 kw-N, NDD; N38 13 50 W80 32 49 *Rebroadcasts:* Rebroadcasts WSGB(AM) Sutton 100%
713 Main Street, Summerville, WV 26651 US
(304) 765-7373, *Fax:* (304) 765-7836
www.theboss97fm.com
al@summitmediawv.com
License: Richwood, WV held by Summit Media Inc.
Group Owner: Summit Media Broadcasting LLC; (acq 3-8-2007; $1.24 million with WAFD(FM) Webster Springs)
Nat'l Network: ABC *Regional Network:* W. Va. MetroNews Network *Nat'l Reps:* Rgnl Reps
Arbitron Metro Market: Sutton, WV *Format:* Contemporary Hits/Top 40, Adult Contemp *Hrs. of News Programming:* News progmg 5 hrs wkly *Target Audience:* 35-64; male and female
Adv. Rates: 9; 7; 9; 6
Al Sergi, General Sales Mgr
Lisa Mace Godwin, Programming Director
Danny Finch, Office Manager

Ridgeley

WDYK

01-01-2006; 100.5 mhz FM; 6 kw; 328 ft.; N39 42 49.6 W78 42 56.5
US
(301) 759-1005, *Fax:* (301) 759-3124
www.cumberlandsmagic.com
License: Ridgeley, Mineral County, WV held by Radioactive LLC.
Group Owner: Radioactive LLC
Arbitron Metro Market: Spencer, IA *Format:* Adult Contemp
Dale Miller, President
Jerry Hannahs, Promotions Manager

Ripley

WCEF

02-24-1981; 98.3 mhz FM *Hrs Open:* 24; 6 kw; 308 ft.; N38 46 4 W81 41 9
P.O. Box 798, Ripley, WV 25271 US
(304) 372-9800, *Fax:* (304) 372-9811
www.c98.com
studio@thebull983.com
License: Ripley, Jackson County, WV held by Big River Radio Inc.
Group Owner: Baker Family Stations; (acq 1-31-2003; $762,500).
Nat'l Network: ABC
Arbitron Metro Market: Ripley, WV *Format:* Country *Target Audience:* 25-54.
Ric Shannon, General Manager
Rich Lacey, Programming Director
Charmin McCarty, News Director
Larry Koenig, Chief Engineer

*WLKV

03-26-1994; 90.7 mhz FM; 3 kw; 328 ft.; N38 51 44 W81 41 27
P.O. Box 568, Belpre, OH 45714 US
(916) 251-1600, *Fax:* (916) 251-1650
www.klove.com
klove@klove.com
License: Ripley, Jackson County, WV held by Educational Media Foundation.
Group Owner: EMF Broadcasting; (acq 3-31-2005; $700,000 with WLKP(FM) Belpre, OH).
Nat'l Network: K-Love
Arbitron Metro Market: Ripley, WV *Format:* Christian *No. News Employees:* 3 *Target Audience:* 25-44; female-Judeo Christian
Darrell Chambliss, Chairman
Mike Novak, CEO
Mike Novak, President
Pam Patrick-Thompson, Operations Dir
Eric Allen, General Sales Mgr
David Pierce, Programming Director
Ed Lenane, News Director
Sam Wallington, EngineeringDir
Marya Morgan, News Reporter
Richard Hunt, News Reporter
Mitch Barnhart, Director
Larry Moody, Director
Dr.David.R.Ferry, Director

Romney

*WVSB

03-30-1973; 104.1 mhz FM *Hrs Open:* 24; 0.1 kw; 781 ft.; N39 18 56 W78 43 4
301 East Main Street, Romney, WV 26757 US
(304) 822-4838, *Fax:* (304) 822-4896
wvsdb.state.k12.wv.us/radio_station.htm
gpark@access.k12.wv.us
License: Romney, Hampshire County, WV held by West Virginia Schools for the Deaf & Blind.
Format: Country *Target Audience:* General.
Jane McBride, President
Connie Newhouse, Operations Dir
George Park, General Manager

WVMD

01-01-2008; 100.1 mhz FM; 0.9 kw; 823 ft.; N39 25 20 W78 47 25
76 Baltimore Street, Cumberland, MD 21502 US
(301) 759-1005, *Fax:* (301) 759-3124
www.tristateswolf.com
treed@wvradio.com
License: Romney, Allegany County, WV held by West Virginia Radio Corp. of the Alleghenies.
Group Owner: West Virginia Radio Corp.; (acq 1-18-2007; $375,000 for CP)
Arbitron Metro Market: Romney, WV *Format:* Country

Dale Miller, President
Jerry Hannahs, General Sales Mgr
Brian Mo, Programming Director

Ronceverte

WRON
01-01-1947; 1400 khz AM *Hrs Open:* 24; 1 kw-U, ND1; N37 45 36 W80 27 18
276 Seneca Trail North, Ronceverte, WV 24970 US
(304) 645-1400,(304) 645-1327, *Fax:* (304) 647-4802
www.wron.com
radio@wron.net
License: Ronceverte, WV held by Radio Greenbrier LLC.
Nat'l Network: Premiere Radio Networks; Westwood One; Talk Radio Network *Nat'l Reps:* Dome; Rgnl Reps *Wire Services:* AP *Format:* News, Talk *Special Programming:* Relg 2 hrs wkly *Hrs. of News Programming:* News progmg 21 hrs wkly *Target Audience:* 35; & under *Adv. Rates:* 6.90; 6.90; 6.90; 3.00
Roy Jarrell, Operations Dir
Michael Kidd, General Manager
Larry Carver, Chief Engineer
Jeff Campbell, Sports Commentator

Rupert

WYKM
12-09-1981; 1250 khz AM *Hrs Open:* 6 AM-sunset; 5 kw-D, NDD; N37 59 35 W80 41 3
Mailing Address: Box 627, Rupert, WV 25984 US
Second Address: 714 Nicholas St., Rupert, WV 25984
(304) 392-6003, *Fax:* (304) 392-5352
www.todaysbestcountryonline.com
License: Rupert, WV held by Mountain State Broadcasting Co.
Nat'l Network: CBS
Arbitron Metro Market: Rupert, WV *Format:* Country, Gospel *Hrs. of News Programming:* News progmg 7 hrs wkly *Adv. Rates:* 5.50; 5.50; 5.50; 5.50
Betty Crookshanks, President
Donald Crookshanks, Executive Vice President

Salem

WOBG-FM
11-01-1990; 105.7 mhz FM; 1.95 kw; 581 ft.; N39 19 6 W80 26 18
104 Broadway Avenue, Carnegie, PA 15106 US
(304) 624-1400, *Fax:* (304) 624-1402
License: Salem, Harrison County, WV held by Burbach of DE LLC.
Group Owner: Burbach Broadcasting Group; (acq 5-17-00; grpsl).
Regional Reps: Commercial Media Sales.
Arbitron Metro Market: Morgantown-Clar *TV Affiliate:* Classic rock *No. News Employees:* 25-54.

WAJR-FM
01-01-1999; 103.3 mhz FM; 1.8 kw; 590 ft.; N39 15 44 W80 28 1
C/O Putbrese & Hunsaker, P. O. Box 217, Sterling, VA 20167 US
(304) 296-0029, *Fax:* (304) 296-3876
www.wajrfm.com
info@wajrfm.com
License: Salem, Harrison County, WV held by West Virginia Radio Corp. of Salem.
Group Owner: West Virginia Radio Corp.
Arbitron Metro Market: Morgantown, WV *Format:* News, News/Talk, 86
Dale Miller, General Manager
Travis Jones, Programming Director
Reuben Perdue, News Director
Hoppy Kercheval, V.P. Of Operations
Kay Murray, Public Affairs Director

Shepherdstown

*WSHC
01-01-1974; 89.7 mhz FM *Hrs Open:* 24; 0.95 kw; -10 ft.; N39 25 53 W77 48 18
Knutti Hall Shepard Col., Shepherdstown, WV 25443 US
(304) 876-5134, *Fax:* (304) 876-5405
www.897wshc.org
wshc@shepherd.edu
License: Shepherdstown, Jefferson County, WV held by Shepherd College Board of Governors
Nat'l Network: ABC
Format: Variety/Diverse *Hrs. of News Programming:* News progmg 7 hrs wkly *Target Audience:* 18-24; college/young adult
Buck Lam, General Manager

South Charleston

WMXE
07-29-1985; 100.9 mhz FM *Hrs Open:* 24; 3 kw; 299 ft.; N38 22 34 W81 42 13
P. O. Box 8600, South Charleston, WV 25303 US
(304) 722-3308, *Fax:* (304) 727-1300
www.wmxe.net
mixstudio@wmxe.com
License: South Charleston, Kanawha County, WV
Group Owner: L M Communications Inc.
Arbitron Metro Market: Charleston, WV *Format:* Adult Contemp, Religious *Target Audience:* 25-54.
Mark Atkinson, Programming Director

WSCW
12-13-1963; 1410 khz AM
6815 Shallowford Road, Chattanooga, TN 37421 US
(304) 722-3308, *Fax:* (304) 727-1300
www.ccrnonline.com
news@wklc.com
License: South Charleston, WV held by L.M. Communications of Kentucky LLC.
Group Owner: L M Communications Inc.; (acq 4-1-03; grpsl).
Arbitron Metro Market: Charleston, WV *Format:* Country *Target Audience:* 25-64.
Ron Walton, General Manager
Chris Colagrasso, Programming Director
Emma Allen, News Director
Fred Francis, Chief Engineer

*WWLA
89.3 mhz FM; 2.3 kw; 207 ft.; N38 23 47 W81 35 28
188 South Belleuve, Suite 222, Memphis, TN 38104 US
(901) 726-8970, *Fax:* (901) 375-0041
mail@flinn.com
License: South Charleston, Kanawha County, WV held by Broadcasting for the Challenged Inc.
Arbitron Metro Market: Charleston, WV
George Flinn Jr., President

Spencer

WVRC
09-12-1961; 1400 khz AM; 1 kw-U, ND1; N38 48 23 W81 21 40
106 Radio Street, Spencer, WV 25276 US
(304) 927-3760, *Fax:* (304) 927-2877
www.wvrcfm.com
mail@wvrcradio.com
License: Spencer, WV held by Star Communications Inc.
Nat'l Reps: Rgnl Reps
Arbitron Metro Market: Spencer, WV *Format:* Gospel
Larry Koenig, President
Bob Edwards, Operations Dir
Kim Parrish, News Director

WVRC-FM
10-01-1992; 104.7 mhz FM; 4.8 kw; 367 ft.; N38 47 40 W81 17 36
106 Radio Street, Spencer, WV 25276 US
(304) 927-3760, *Fax:* (304) 927-2877
www.wvrcfm.com
info@wcrvradio.com
License: Spencer, Roane County, WV
Arbitron Metro Market: Spencer, WV *Format:* Country
Keith Whipple, General Manager
Kim Parrish, News Director

St. Albans

WJYP
01-14-1956; 1300 khz AM *Hrs Open:* 24
100 Kanawha Terrace, St. Albans, WV 25177 US
(304) 722-3308, *Fax:* (304) 727-1300
www.wjypam.com
chris@wjypam.com
License: St. Albans, WV held by WKLC Inc.
Group Owner: L M Communications Inc.; (acq 2-23-80).
Arbitron Metro Market: Kanawha County-Putnam County, WV *Format:* Talk, Religious *Target Audience:* 18-49.
Ron Walton, General Manager
Chris Colagrasso, Programming Director
Emma Allen, News Director
Fred Francis, Chief Engineer

WKLC-FM
01-01-1966; 105.1 mhz FM *Hrs Open:* 24; 3.6 kw; 1663 ft.; N38 25 15 W81 55 27
100 Kanawha Terrace, St. Albans, WV 25177 US
(304) 722-3308, *Fax:* (304) 727-1300
www.wklc.com
news@wkcl.com
License: St. Albans, Kanawha County, WV
Group Owner: L M Communications Inc.
Nat'l Network: ABC
Arbitron Metro Market: Charleston, WV *Format:* Rock/AOR
Jay Nunley, Programming Director
Dawn Cox, Music Director

St. Marys

WRRR-FM
11-16-1983; 93.9 mhz FM; 17 kw; 390 ft.; N39 22 49 W81 11 36
Box 374, Greens Run Road, St. Marys, WV 26170 US
(304) 684-3400, *Fax:* (304) 684-9241
License: St. Marys, Pleasants County, WV held by Seven Ranges Radio Co. Inc.
Arbitron Metro Market: Parkersburg-Marietta, WV-OH *Format:* Adult Contemp *Hrs. of News Programming:* news progmg 9 hrs wkly *No. News Employees:* 1 *Target Audience:* 25-49. *Adv. Rates:* 15; 14; 14; 12
Sam Yoho, President
Lou Petronio, Operations Dir

WJAW
10-01-1984; 630 khz AM *Hrs Open:* 24; 1 kw-D, ND1; 0.037 kw-N, ND1; N39 23 42 W81 13 49
Box 374 Greens Run Road, St. Marys, WV 26170 US
(740) 373-1490, *Fax:* (740) 373-1717
www.wmoa1490.com
kwenzel@wmoa1490.com
License: St. Marys, WV held by JAWCO Inc.
Nat'l Network: ESPN Radio
Arbitron Metro Market: St.Marys, WV *Format:* Sports *No. News Employees:* 3
John Wharf III, President
Jamey Styer, Operations Dir
Stephanie Wiles, Station Manager
Andy Rex, Programming Director
Ralph Matheny, Chief Engineer
Jamey Styer, Chief Operator
Kyle Wenzel, Public Service Director
TomHushion, Account Executive
Chris Wharff, Account Executive
Andy Rex, Automation Director

Star City

*WLOL-FM
89.7 mhz FM; 0.08 kw; 185 ft.; N39 40 9.3 W80 0 11 US
(304) 879-5752
www.wvlol.org
License: Star City, Monongalia County, WV held by Light of Life Community Inc.
Nat'l Network: EWTN Radio
Arbitron Metro Market: Star City, WV
Robert Carubia, President

Summersville

WCWV
03-13-1983; 92.9 mhz FM *Hrs Open:* 24; 11 kw; 899 ft.; N38 21 37 W80 38 49
713 Main Street, Summerville, WV 26651 US
(304) 872-5202, *Fax:* (304) 872-6904
www.wcwv929.com
wcwv@wcwv92.9.com
License: Summersville, Nicholas County, WV held by R-S Broadcasting Co. Inc.
Nat'l Network: Westwood One *Nat'l Reps:* Dome
Arbitron Metro Market: Summersville WV *Format:* Adult Contemp *Special Programming:* Gospel 15 hrs, relg 18 hrs wkly *Hrs. of News Programming:* News progmg 23 hrs wkly *Target Audience:* 18-54. *Adv. Rates:* 15; 15; 15; 10
Michael Brown, Operations Dir
Wes Brown, General Manager
Wes Brown, General Sales Mgr
Cassy Holcomb, News Director
Fred Francis, Chief Engineer

*WMLJ
01-01-1993; 90.5 mhz FM *Hrs Open:* 24; 11 kw; 1033 ft.; N38 6 42 W80 35 52 *Rebroadcasts:* Rebroadcasts WOTJ(FM) Morehead City, NC 90%
4723 Country Club Road, Morehead City, NC 28557 US
(304) 872-4612, *Fax:* (252) 223-2201
License: Summersville, Nicholas County, WV held by Grace Missionary Baptist Church
Arbitron Metro Market: Summersville, WV *Format:* Children, Gospel *Special Programming:* Sp one hr wkly *Target Audience:* General.

RADIO - U.S.

Clyde Ebron, President
Chris Brown, General Manager
Mike Tyler, Chief Engineer

***WSJE**
91.3 mhz FM; 0.24 kw; 819 ft.; N38 21 38.5 W80 38 50.4 US
(304) 872-4968
License: Summersville, Nicholas County, WV held by Kesan Inc.
Arbitron Metro Market: Summersville, WV
Gary Criste, President

Sutton

WDBS
04-25-1987; 97.1 mhz FM *Hrs Open:* 24; 22 kw; 751 ft.; N38 27 5 W80 27 14
189a Main St., Sutton, WV 26601 US
(304) 765-7373, *Fax:* (304) 765-7836
theboss97fm.com
al@summitmediawv.com
License: Sutton, Braxton County, WV held by Summit Media Broadcasting LLC
Group Owner: Summit Media Broadcasting LLC; (acq 12-30-99)
Nat'l Network: Dial Global Mainstream Country; AP Radio
Regional Network: WV MetroNews *Nat'l Reps:* Rgnl Reps
Arbitron Metro Market: Sutton, WV *Format:* Country *Hrs. of News Programming:* News progmg 9 hrs wkly *Target Audience:* 18-49; young adults females/males *Adv. Rates:* 25; 20; 25; 15
Al Sergi, General Manager
Al Sergi, General Sales Mgr
Lisa Mace-Godwin, Programming Director
Danny Finch, Office Manager/ Traffic / Billing

WSGB
01-22-1964; 1490 khz AM *Hrs Open:* 24
189 a Main Street, Sutton, WV 26601 US
(304) 765-7373, *Fax:* (304) 765-7836
www.theboss97fm.com
mail@wsgbam.com
License: Sutton, WV held by Summit Media Broadcasting L.L.C.
Group Owner: Summit Media Broadcasting LLC; (acq 12-30-99; $250,000 with co-located FM)
Nat'l Network: ABC *Regional Network:* W. Va. MetroNews Network *Nat'l Reps:* Rgnl Reps *Regional Reps:* Dome; Regnl Reps
Format: Contemporary Hits/Top 40, Adult Contemp *Hrs. of News Programming:* News prgmg 5 hrs per week *Target Audience:* 35-64; male and female *Adv. Rates:* 9; 7; 9; 6
Al Sergi, President
Al Sergi, Station Manager
Lisa Mace-Godwin, Programming Director

Vienna

WDMX
05-22-1989; 100.1 mhz FM *Hrs Open:* 24; 1.65 kw; 440 ft.; N39 20 18 W81 30 1
6006 Grand Central Ave, Vienna, WV 26105 US
(304) 295-6070(304) 375-6558, *Fax:* (304) 295-4389
www.mymix100.com
oldies@radio1.netassoc.net
License: Vienna, Wood County, WV held by CC Licenses LLC.
Group Owner: Clear Channel Communications Inc.; (acq 4-17-2001; grpsl).
Nat'l Network: ABC *Nat'l Reps:* Clear Channel
Arbitron Metro Market: Parkersburg-Marietta, WV-OH *Format:* Oldies *Hrs. of News Programming:* news progmg 2 hrs wkly *No. News Employees:* 2 *Target Audience:* 25-54. *Adv. Rates:* 35; 30; 35; 18
Jim Grywalsky, Operations Dir
Chuck Poet, General Manager
Kurt McCall, General Sales Mgr
Jim Grywalsky, Programming Director
Doug Hess, News Director
Jerry Kuhn, Chief Engineer
Belinda Marcinko, Traffic Manager

Wardenville

WTCF(FM)
103.3 mhz FM; 350 watts; 410 meters; non directional
25 East 86th Street, Apt 13B, New York, NY 10028 USA
(517) 752-3456, *Fax:* (517) 754-5046
License: Wardenville, Hardy County, WV
Group Owner: Alex Media Corp

Webster Springs

WAFD
02-01-1996; 100.3 mhz FM *Hrs Open:* 24; 26 kw; 682 ft.; N38 27 5 W80 27 14
200 Back Fork Street, Webster Springs, WV 26288 US
(304) 765-7373, *Fax:* (304) 765-7836
www.theboss97fm.com
al@summitmediawv.com
License: Webster Springs, Webster County, WV held by Summit Media Inc.
Group Owner: Summit Media Broadcasting LLC; (acq 3-8-2007; $1.24 million with WVAR(AM) Richwood)
Nat'l Network: CNN Radio *Nat'l Reps:* Rgnl Reps
Arbitron Metro Market: Webster Springs, WV *Format:* Adult Contemp *Hrs. of News Programming:* News prgrmg 3 hrs/week *Target Audience:* M-F/18-49. *Adv. Rates:* 20; 16; 20; 13
Al Sergi, President
Al Sergi, General Manager
Lisa Mace-Godwin, Programming Director

Weirton

WEIR
09-15-1950; 1430 khz AM *Hrs Open:* 24; 1 kw-D, DA2; 1 kw-N, DA2; N40 26 42 W80 37 41
51 West Long Beach Avenue, Du Bois, PA 15801 US
(304) 723-1444, *Fax:* (304) 723-1688
www.weirsports.net/
jvavrek@1063theriver.com
License: Weirton, WV held by Priority Communications Ohio L.L.C.
Group Owner: Priority Communications; (acq 12-4-98; $475,000 with WCDK(FM) Cadiz, OH)
Nat'l Network: Westwood One *Regional Reps:* Dome
Arbitron Metro Market: Weirton, WV *Format:* Adult Contemp, Talk *Special Programming:* It 3 hrs, Gr 1 hr wkly *Hrs. of News Programming:* news progmg 25 hrs wkly *No. News Employees:* 1 *Target Audience:* General.
Jay Philippone, President
Tammie Beagle, Operations Dir
Judy Vavrek, Station Manager
Dave Whalen, General Sales Mgr
Jude Sheets, Programming Director
Hank Siegle, Chief Engineer

Welch

WELC
08-19-1950; 1150 khz AM *Hrs Open:* 6 AM- Sunset; 5 kw-D, NDD; N37 25 1 W81 36 58
Mailing Address: P. O. Box 949, Welch, WV 24801 US
Second Address: U.S. Rt. 52, Welch, WV 24801
(304) 436-2131, *Fax:* (304) 436-2132
www.welcamfm.com
mail@welcamfm.com
License: Welch, WV held by Pocahontas Broadcasting Co.
Nat'l Network: AP Radio *Regional Reps:* Rgnl Reps. *Wire Services:* AP
Arbitron Metro Market: Welch, WV *Format:* Adult Contemp
Special Programming: Relg 15 hrs wkly *No. News Employees:* 2 *Target Audience:* 21-54. *Adv. Rates:* 6.50; 6.50; 6.50; 6.50
Laura Green, Operations Dir
Rick Lambert, Station Manager
Rod O'dell, General Sales Mgr
Bob Spencer, Member/Manager

West Liberty

***WGLZ**
09-04-1990; 91.5 mhz FM; 0.15 kw; 213 ft.; N40 9 49 W80 36 6
West Liberty State Coll., West Liberty, WV 26074 US
(304) 336-8045, *Fax:* (304) 336-8286
www.wglzradio.com
wglz@westliberty.edu
License: West Liberty, Ohio County, WV held by West Liberty State College.
Format: Alternative
Christian Lee, Station Manager

West Union

***WVGV**
89.7 mhz FM; 2.35 kw; 395 ft.; N39 17 22 W80 48 16 US
(304) 873-2225
www.wvgvradio.com
License: West Union, Doddridge County, WV held by Araiza Revival Ministries Inc.
Arbitron Metro Market: West Union, WV *Format:* Gospel
Oliver Araiza, President

Weston

WFBY
08-29-1972; 102.3 mhz FM *Hrs Open:* 24; 10 kw; 509 ft.; N39 1 27 W80 19 16
1065 Radio Park Drive, Mount Clare, WV 26408 US
(304) 623-6546, *Fax:* (304) 623-6547
www.wfby.com
License: Weston, Lewis County, WV held by AJG Corporation
Group Owner: West Virginia Radio Corp.; (acq 1994; $250,000)
Format: Classic Rock *Target Audience:* 25-44.
Dale Miller, President
Harvey Kercheval, Operations Dir
Christian Miller, Station Manager
Max Wurf, Programming Director
Stan Fa, Chief Engineer
Mark Rogers, Music Director

Westover

WZST
01-05-1983; 100.9 mhz FM; 3 kw; 266 ft.; N39 32 44 W79 55 58
15 Campbell Street, Luray, VA 22835 US
(304) 292-1101, *Fax:* (304) 366-3706
www.variety101fm.com
star100radio@aol.com
License: Westover, Monongalia County, WV held by Fantasia Broadcasting Inc.
Group Owner: Fantasia Broadcasting Inc.; (acq 6-27-2008; $750,000)
Arbitron Metro Market: Fairmont, WV *Format:* Adult Contemp
Special Programming: Relg mus 2 hrs wkly
Nick Fantasia, President
Dick Yoder, General Manager
Bill Dunn, Sales Manager
Mike Donota, Programming Director

Wheeling

WBBD
05-02-1941; 1400 khz AM *Hrs Open:* 24; 1 kw-U, ND1; N40 5 49 W80 42 6
600 Congress Avenue, Suite 1400, Austin, TX 78701 US
(318) 550-2000, *Fax:* 318-550-2002
miracle891.org
info@miracle891.org
License: Wheeling, WV held by Capstar TX L.P.
Group Owner: Clear Channel Communications Inc.; (acq 8-30-00; grpsl).
Arbitron Metro Market: Dallas-Fort Worth *Format:* Religious
A.T. Moore, President
Dan Perkins, Operations Dir
Donna Cole, General Manager
Joe Miot, Programming Director

WEGW
10-01-1966; 107.5 mhz FM *Hrs Open:* 24; 16 kw; 883 ft.; N40 3 41 W80 45 9
600 Congress Avenue, Suite 1400, Austin, TX 78701 US
(304) 232-1170, *Fax:* (304) 234-0067
www.eagle1075.com/
License: Wheeling, Ohio County, WV held by Capstar TX L.P.
Group Owner: Clear Channel Communications Inc.; (acq 8-30-00; grpsl).
Arbitron Metro Market: Wheeling, WV *Format:* Rock/AOR *Target Audience:* 25-54.
Mark Mays, President
Scott Miller, Operations Dir
Karen Hardy, General Sales Mgr
Chad Tyson, Programming Director
Minda Moticker, Promotions Manager
Jonathan Nixon, News Director
Jack Rees, Chief Engineer

WKWK-FM
03-17-1948; 97.3 mhz FM *Hrs Open:* 24; 50 kw; 420 ft.; N40 5 49 W80 42 6
600 Congress Avenue, Suite 1400, Austin, TX 78701 US
(304) 232-1170, *Fax:* (304) 234-0041
www.wk973.com
License: Wheeling, Ohio County, WV
Group Owner: Clear Channel Communications Inc.
Arbitron Metro Market: Wheeling, WV *Format:* Variety/Diverse
Target Audience: 25-54.
Jim Connor, Programming Director
Steve Novotry, News Director

WKKX
04-07-1963; 1600 khz AM; 5 kw-D, ND1; 0.033 kw-N, ND1; N40 5 26 W80 42 11
104 Broadway Avenue, Carnegie, PA 15106 US
(304) 214-1610, *Fax:* 304-214-1610

License: Wheeling, WV held by RCK 1 Group LLC
Nat'l Network: ESPN Radio *Nat'l Reps:* Christal
Arbitron Metro Market: Wheeling, WV *TV Affiliate:* Sports talk *No. News Employees:* 25-54; men

WOVK
09-01-1947; 98.7 mhz FM; 50 kw; 390 ft.; N40 4 58 W80 46 18
600 Congress Avenue, Suite 1400, Austin, TX 78701 US

www.wovk.com
License: Wheeling, Ohio County, WV held by Capstar TX L.P.
Arbitron Metro Market: Wheeling, WV *Format:* Country
Jim Elliott, Programming Director
Molly Kilgore, News Director

***WPHP**
04-04-1977; 91.9 mhz FM; 0.1 kw horiz; 259 ft.; N40 4 7 W80 39 4
2203 National Road, Wheeling, WV 26003 US
(304) 243-0400, *Fax:* (304) 243-0449
License: Wheeling, Ohio County, WV held by Ohio County Board of Education.
Arbitron Metro Market: Wheeling, WV *Format:* Contemporary Hits/Top 40 *Special Programming:* Black 4 hrs, jazz one hr wkly
Carolyn Ihlenfeld, General Manager

***WVNP**
10-07-1981; 89.9 mhz FM *Hrs Open:* 24; 25 kw; 499 ft.; N40 12 58 W80 33 31
600 Capitol Street, Charleston, WV 25301 US
(304) 556-4900, *Fax:* (304) 556-4960
www.wvpubcast.org
feedback@wvpubcast.org
License: Wheeling, Ohio County, WV held by West Virginia Educational Broadcasting Authority.
Nat'l Network: NPR; PRI
Arbitron Metro Market: Wheeling, WV *Format:* Jazz, News
Rita Ray, General Manager
Craig Lanham, Programming Director
Beth Vorhees, Director of News and Public Affairs
Dennis Adkins, Executive Director
Bill Acker, Director of Broadcasting & Technology
Marilyn DiVita, Director ofDevelopment
Michael L. Meador, Director of Finance
Shawn Patterson, Director of Marketing

WWVA
12-01-1926; 1170 khz AM; 50 kw-D, DAN; 50 kw-N, DAN; N40 6 7 W80 52 2
600 Congress Avenue, Suite 1400, Austin, TX 78701 US
(304) 232-1170, *Fax:* (304) 234-0041
www.wwva.com
License: Wheeling, WV held by Capstar TX L.P.
Group Owner: Clear Channel Communications Inc.; (acq 8-30-00; grpsl)
Nat'l Reps: McGavren Guild
Arbitron Metro Market: Wheeling, WV *Format:* News, News/Talk, 86 *Special Programming:* Farm 2 hrs wkly *Target Audience:* 25-54.
Scott Miller, General Manager
Scott Peel, General Sales Mgr
Jim Harrington, Programming Director
Tammie Beagle, News Director
Barb Vaughn, Traffic Manager

White Sulphur Spring

WSLW
01-01-1971; 1310 khz AM *Hrs Open:* 6 AM-sunset; 5 kw-D, NDD; N37 48 17 W80 21 3
Mailing Address: P.O. Box 610, White Sulphur Spring, WV 24986 US
Second Address: Rt. 60 W. Harts Run, Ronceverte, WV 24986
(304) 536-1310, *Fax:* (304) 536-1311
www.wron.com
radio@wkcjwslw.com
License: White Sulphur Spring, WV held by Quorum Radio Partners of Virginia Inc., debtor-in-possession.
Group Owner: Quorum Radio Partners of Virginia Inc.; (acq 4-20-2005; grpsl).
Nat'l Reps: Rgnl Reps
Format: Sports *Hrs. of News Programming:* News progmg 8 hrs wkly *Target Audience:* 16-25 (60 plus). *Adv. Rates:* 6.50; 6.50; 6.50; na
Joyce Tucker, General Manager
Mike Kidd, Station Manager
Larry Carver, Chief Engineer
Roy Jarrell, Production Manager

Williamson

WBTH
04-19-1939; 1400 khz AM; 1 kw-U; N37 40 09 W82 16 09
Box 2200, Pikeville, KY 25661
(606) 235-3600,(606) 437-4051, *Fax:* (606) 432-2809
info@ekbradio.com
License: Williamson, Mingo County, WV held by East Kentucky Radio Network Inc.
Group Owner: East Kentucky Radio Network Inc.; acq 4-4-00; $630,000 with co-located FM).
Population Served: 70,000*Target Audience:* 25-54.
Walter E May, Chairman
Cindy May Johnson, General Manager
Andrew Joyce, Programming Director
Homer Owens, News Director
Paul Manuel, Chief Engineer

WXCC
10-27-1978; 96.5 mhz FM; 75 kw; 1112 ft.; N37 30 48 W82 15 20
P O Box 261, Williamson, WV 25661 US
(606) 235-3600, *Fax:* (606) 432-2809
www.wxccfm.com
wxcc@mikrotec.com
License: Williamson, Mingo County, WV
Regional Network: Ky. News Net
Arbitron Metro Market: Williamson, WV *Format:* Country
Walter.E.May, Owner & CEO
Cindy May Johnson, President/General Manager
Kim Little, Sales Manager
Walt May, VP/Programming Director
Debbie Lawson, Office Manager

Williamstown

WVVV
01-01-2000; 96.9 mhz FM; 3.5 kw; 423 ft.; N39 20 18 W81 30 1
305 Ohio Street, Marietta, OH 45750 US
(304) 295-3100, *Fax:* (304) 684-9241
www.v969radio.net
samyoho@v969radio.net
License: Williamstown, Wood County, WV held by Bennco Inc.
Arbitron Metro Market: Parkersburg, WV *Format:* Variety/Diverse
Sam Yoho, General Manager
Jack Horton, Programming Director
Shelia Britton, News Director
Tom Taggart, Chief Engineer
Scott Northcraft, Production Director

Wisconsin

Adams

WDKM
10-08-1993; 106.1 mhz FM *Hrs Open:* 24; 6 kw; 328 ft.; N43 57 29 W89 49 43
Mailing Address: 408 Hillwood Lane, Friendship, WI 53934 US
Second Address: 1040 W. Center St., Adams, WI 53910
(608) 339-3221, *Fax:* (608) 339-2403
www.wdkmfm.com
info@wdkmfm.com
License: Adams, Adams County, WI held by Roche-A-Cri Broadcasting.
Arbitron Metro Market: Wisconsin Dells, WI *Format:* Contemporary Hits/Top 40, Adult Contemp *Special Programming:* Polka 14 hrs wkly
Heidi Roekle, General Manager
Drew Smith, Station Manager

***WHAA**
89.1 mhz FM; 28.5 kw; 581 ft.; N44 1 13 W89 33 31
3319 W. Beltline Highway, Madison, WI 53713 US
(608) 263-3970, *Fax:* (608) 263-9763
www.wpr.org
License: Adams, Adams County, WI held by State of Wisconsin-Educational Communications Board.
Arbitron Metro Market: Adams, WI *Format:* Talk
Tim Allen, Operations Dir
Phil Corriveau, General Manager
Michael Leland, News Director
Mike Crane, Director of Radio
Michael Arnold, Associate Director
Mary Kay Dadisman, Director of Development
Steve Johnston, Director ofEngineering & Operations

Algoma

WBDK
11-12-1986; 96.7 mhz FM *Hrs Open:* 24; 8 kw; 538 ft.; N44 42 26 W87 24 26
4400 Hilltop Ave, Wausau, WI 54401 US
(215) 721-2141, *Fax:* (215) 721-9811
www.wordfm.org
wordfm@wordfm.org
License: Algoma, Kewaunee County, WI held by Nicolet Broadcasting Inc.
Group Owner: Nicolet Broadcasting Inc.; acq 9-3-93;
Arbitron Metro Market: Le Grande OR *Format:* Christian
Charles Loughery, President

WRLU
08-01-1999; 104.1 mhz FM; 2.4 kw; 518 ft.; N44 42 26 W87 24 26
4400 Hilltop Avenue, Wausau, WI 54401 US
(920) 746-9430, *Fax:* (920) 746-9433
www.doorradio.com
info@doorradio.com
License: Algoma, Kewaunee County, WI held by Nicolet Broadcasting Inc.
Group Owner: Nicolet Broadcasting Inc.
Format: Country *Hrs. of News Programming:* News progmg 3 hrs wkly
Roger Utnehmer, President
Karen Leitzinger, Operations Dir
Miles Knuteson, General Manager
John Focke, News Director
Kathy Robinson, Traffic Manager

Allouez

WKRU
01-01-1996; 106.7 mhz FM *Hrs Open:* 24; 25 kw; Ant 328 ft; N44 29 03 W87 56 12
810 Victoria St., Green Bay, WI 53202
(920) 468-4100, *Fax:* (920) 468-0250
www.1067thezone.com
ted.bare@cumulus.com
License: Allouez, Brown County, WI held by WI Radio LLC, as trustee
Nat'l Network: Talk Radio Network *Nat'l Reps:* Katz Radio
Population Served: 832,000 *Arbitron Metro Market:* Green Bay, WI *Hrs. of News Programming:* news progmg 5 hrs wkly *No. News Employees:* 1 *Target Audience:* 18-49; educated, 65/35 male skew *Adv. Rates:* 50;50; 50; 20
Greg Jessen, Operations Dir
Buck Hein, General Sales Mgr
Ted Bare, Programming Director
Mark Heller, Chief Engineer
Jimmy Clark, Operations Manager

Altoona

WISM-FM
11-15-1991; 98.1 mhz FM *Hrs Open:* 24; 25 kw; 276 ft.; N44 46 38 W91 28 29
1819 Mitchell Ave, Eau Claire, WI 54701 US
(715) 830-4000, *Fax:* (715) 835-9680
www.themix981.com
rickhencley@clearchannel.com
License: Altoona, Eau Claire County, WI held by Aloha Station Trust LLC, as Trustee
Nat'l Reps: Clear Channel
Arbitron Metro Market: Eau Claire, WI *Format:* Adult Contemp *No. News Employees:* 2 *Target Audience:* 25-54. *Adv. Rates:* 25; 25; 25; 15
Dave Deville, Operations Dir
Rick Hencley, General Manager
Steve Potter, General Sales Mgr
Jim Finn, Programming Director
Rick Hencley, Promotions Manager
Keith Edwards, News Director
Paul Orth, Chief Engineer
Geri Feldhausen,Promotions Director
Theresa Nelson, Taffic Manager

Amery

WXCE
01-23-1978; 1260 khz AM *Hrs Open:* 5 AM-noon; 5 kw-D, DA2; 5 kw-N, DA2; N45 15 25 W92 22 0
1031 West Grace Street, St. Peter, MN 56082 US
(715) 268-7185, *Fax:* (715) 268-7187
www.wxce1260.com
wxce@spacestar.net
License: Amery, WI held by Lake Country Broadcasting Corp.
Nat'l Network: ABC *Regional Network:* Tribune Radio Networks; Wisconsin Radio Net.
Format: News, News/Talk, 86 *Hrs. of News Programming:* news progmg 20 hrs wkly *No. News Employees:* 1 *Target Audience:* 35 plus. *Adv. Rates:* 9.50; 9.50; 9.50; na
Darren Van Blaricom, General Manager
Greg Marsten, News Director
Julie Measner, Traffic Manager

RADIO - U.S.

Antigo

WACD

01-01-1998; 106.1 mhz FM; 10 kw; 276 ft.; N45 6 23 W89 9 9
101 West Grand, Chicago, IL 60601 US
(907) 283-8700, *Fax:* (907) 283-9177
info@radiokenai.com
License: Antigo, Langlade County, WI held by Results Broadcasting Inc.
Group Owner: Results Broadcasting; (acq 4-29-2005; $500,000 with WATK(AM) Antigo).
Arbitron Metro Market: Medford-Ashland OR
John Davis, President
Cherie Curry, General Manager

WATK

03-15-1948; 900 khz AM *Hrs Open:* 24; 0.25 kw-D, ND1; 0.195 kw-N, ND1; N45 6 23 W89 9 9
980 North Michigan Ave., Suite 1880, Chicago, IL 60611 US
(715) 623-4124, *Fax:* (715) 627-4497
www.watkantigo.com/
wrlo@marathonmedianorth.net
License: Antigo, WI held by Results Broadcasting Inc.
Group Owner: Results Broadcasting; (acq 4-29-2005; $500,000 with WACD(FM) Antigo).
Nat'l Network: Jones Radio Networks
Arbitron Metro Market: Antigo,WI *Format:* Adult Contemp *Special Programming:* Gospel 2 hrs wkly *Hrs. of News Programming:* news progmg 12 hrs wkly *No. News Employees:* 2 *Target Audience:* 25-59; two-incomefamilies
Duff Damos, Operations Dir
Tom Hopfensperger, General Manager
Shaughn Novy, General Sales Mgr
Dave St. Peter, Programming Director
Cliff Groth, Chief Engineer

WRLO-FM

11-11-1973; 105.3 mhz FM *Hrs Open:* 24; 100 kw; 541 ft.; N45 22 4 W89 8 20
980 North Michigan Ave., Suite 1880, Chicago, IL 60611 US
(715) 362-1975, *Fax:* (715) 362-1973
www.wrlo.com
License: Antigo, Langlade County, WI held by NRG License Sub. LLC.
Group Owner: NRG Media LLC; (acq 10-31-2005; grpsl)
Format: Classic Rock *Target Audience:* 18-54. *Adv. Rates:* 33; 30; 32; 11
Duff Damos, Operations Dir
Steve Albertson, General Sales Mgr

Appleton

WAPL

12-24-1965; 105.7 mhz FM *Hrs Open:* 24; 100 kw; 1175 ft.; N44 21 32 W87 59 7
Mailing Address: 7601 Ganser Wy, Madison, WI 53719 US
Second Address: 2800 E. College Ave., Appleton, WI 54915
(920) 734-9226, *Fax:* (920) 733-3291
www.wapl.com
wapl@wcinet.com
License: Appleton, Outagamie County, WI held by Woodward Communications Inc.
Group Owner: Woodward Communications Inc.; (acq 3-75)
Nat'l Reps: McGavren Guild *Wire Services:* AP
Arbitron Metro Market: Appleton, WI *Format:* Rock/AOR *Hrs. of News Programming:* News progmg 2 hrs wkly *Target Audience:* 20-plus; professional & semi-professional adults
Greg Bell, General Manager
Greg Lawrence, General Sales Mgr
Joe Calgaro, Programming Director
Kay Taylor, News Director
Steve Brown, Chief Engineer
Elwood, Disc Jockey
Len Nelson, Disc Jockey
Rick McNeal, Disc Jockey

*WEMI

01-01-1994; 91.9 mhz FM *Hrs Open:* 24; 3.1 kw; Ant 328 ft; N44 15 17 W88 26 13
1909 W. 2nd St., Appleton, WI 54914
(920) 749-WEMI, *Fax:* (920) 749-0474
christianfamilyradio.net
www.thefamily.net
License: Appleton, Outagamie County, WI held by Evangel Ministries Inc.
Group Owner: Evangel Ministries Inc.
Nat'l Network: Moody; Salem Radio Network
Population Served: 300,000 *Arbitron Metro Market:* Appleton-Oshkosh, WI *Hrs. of News Programming:* News progmg 10 hrs wkly *No. News Employees:* 14 *Target Audience:* 25-54; women *Adv. Rates:* 240; 204; 240;204
Peggy Ament, Chairman
Paul Cameron, General Manager
Andy Kilgar, General Sales Mgr
Terry Michaels, Programming Director
Bill Moede, Chief Engineer
Andy Kilgas, Sales Director

*WOVM

03-10-1956; 91.1 mhz FM *Hrs Open:* 5 AM-midnight; 3.6 kw; 417 ft.; N44 15 37 W88 22 0
420 E. College Ave., Appleton, WI 54911 US
(920) 965-9696, *Fax:* (920) 965-9697
wovmfm.com
License: Appleton, Outagamie County, WI held by Starboard Media Foundation Inc.
Group Owner: Relevant Radio; (acq 9-20-2005; $300,000)
Arbitron Metro Market: Appleton-Oshkosh, WI *Format:* Adult Contemp
Mike Watts, General Manager

WSCO

01-01-1952; 1570 khz AM *Hrs Open:* 24 hrs; 1 kw-D, ND1; 0.331 kw-N, ND1; N44 13 4 W88 24 33
2145 South Memorial Dr., P.O. Box 4056, Appleton, WI 54915 US
(920) 733-6639, *Fax:* (920) 739-0494
License: Appleton, WI held by Woodward Communications Inc.
Group Owner: Woodward Communications Inc.; acq 12-3-01; $450,000).
Nat'l Network: Fox Sports; Sporting News Radio Network
Arbitron Metro Market: Appleton-Oshkosh, WI *Format:* Sports *Target Audience:* 25-54; Male
Greg Bell, General Manager
John Wanie, Station Manager
Mary Anne Drewer, General Sales Mgr
Dave Edwards, Programming Director
Steve Brown, Chief Engineer

Ashland

WATW

05-01-1940; 1400 khz AM *Hrs Open:* 24; 0.78 kw-U, ND1; N46 34 25 W90 51 56
Rt. 2 Box 63, 2320 Ellis Avenue, Ashland, WI 54806 US
(715) 682-2727(715) 682-2728, *Fax:* (715) 682-9338
www.watwam.com
productionash@charter.net
License: Ashland, WI held by Heartland Communications License LLC.
Group Owner: Heartland Communications Group LLC; (acq 4-23-2004; grpsl).
Nat'l Network: ABC
Arbitron Metro Market: Ashland, WI *Format:* News *Special Programming:* Relg 5 hrs wkly *Hrs. of News Programming:* news progmg 17 hrs wkly *No. News Employees:* 1 *Target Audience:* 40 plus; middle to upperincome adults
Rich Cannata, Operations Dir
Scott Jaeger, General Manager
Skip Hunter, Chief Engineer

WBSZ

07-25-1994; 93.3 mhz FM *Hrs Open:* 24; 71 kw; 246 ft.; N46 34 25 W90 51 56
222 11th Street West, Ashland, WI 54806 US
(715) 682-2727, *Fax:* (715) 682-9338
www.wbszfm.com
productionash@charter.net
License: Ashland, Ashland County, WI held by Heartland Communications License LLC.
Group Owner: Heartland Communications Group LLC; (acq 4-23-2004; grpsl).
Nat'l Network: ABC; Westwood One
Arbitron Metro Market: Ashland, WI *Format:* Country *Target Audience:* 18-49.
Rich Canatta, Operations Dir
Scott Jaeger, General Manager
Skip Hunter, Programming Director

WJJH

08-01-1970; 96.7 mhz FM *Hrs Open:* 24; 50 kw; 246 ft.; N46 34 25 W90 51 56
Route 2, Box 63, Ashland, WI 54806 US
(715) 682-2727, *Fax:* (715) 682-9338
www.wjjhfm.com
License: Ashland, Ashland County, WI
Group Owner: Heartland Communications Group LLC
Nat'l Network: ABC
Format: Classic Rock *Target Audience:* 25-45.
Rich Cannata, Operations Dir
Scott Jaeger, General Manager
Skip Hunter, Programming Director

*WUWS

90.9 mhz FM; 24.5 kw; 231 ft.; N46 36 28 W90 50 13 US
(608) 263-3970, *Fax:* (608) 263-9763
www.wpr.org
Listener@wpr.org
License: Ashland, Ashland County, WI held by Board of Regents of the University of Wisconsin System.
Arbitron Metro Market: Ashland, OR
Steve Johnston, Director of Engineering & Operations
Phil Corriveau, General Manager
Michael Leland, News Director
Mike Crane, Director of Radio
Michael Arnold, Associate Director
Sarah Jacobs, Audience Services Manager
JeffreyPotter, Marketing Director
Rebecca Dopart, Membership and Corporate Support

Auburndale

*WLBL

01-01-1922; 930 khz AM *Hrs Open:* Sunrise-sunset
3319 W. Beltline Hwy., Madison, WI 53713 US
(715) 261-6298, *Fax:* (715) 848-28
www.wpr.org
listener@wpr.org
License: Auburndale, WI held by State of Wisconsin, Education Communications Board.
Nat'l Network: NPR; PRI
Format: Adult Contemp, News, 62, Talk *No. News Employees:* 4
Phil Corriveau, General Manager
Rick Reyer, Station Manager

Baileys Harbor

WLGE

04-26-2008; 106.9 mhz FM; 6 kw; 184 ft.; N45 3 14 W87 8 37 US
(920) 854-3400, *Fax:* (800) 799-7143
www.fm1069thelodge.com
contact@fm1069thelodge.com
License: Baileys Harbor, Door County, WI held by Michael J. Mesic.
Arbitron Metro Market: Baileys Harbor, WI *Format:* Triple A
Mike Mesic, President
Michael Mesic, General Manager
Carrie Mesic, Vice President
Martha Scully Beller, Business Development Manager
Jaime Forest, Marketing Advisor and Creative Director
Chrystal Kugle, Marketing Advisor
MeghanHolly, Office Manager/Promotions Manager

Baldwin

WDMO

10-24-1973; 95.7 mhz FM; 4 kw; 407 ft.; N44 56 33 W92 24 59
114 W. Main, Durand, WI 54736 US
(715) 231-9500, *Fax:* (715) 231-9505
www.thunder959.com
License: Baldwin, Pepin County, WI held by Zoe Communications Inc.
Group Owner: Zoe Communications Inc.; (acq 7-31-2001; with co-located AM).
Format: Country
Bo Landry, Operations Dir
Wendy Oberg, General Manager
Mike Oberg, Chief Engineer

Balsam Lake

WLMX-FM

02-14-1997; 104.9 mhz FM; 22 kw; 348 ft.; N45 29 27 W92 11 32
1859 21st Ave., Rice Lake, WI 54868 US
(715) 268-7185, *Fax:* (715) 268-7187
mix105.ws
studio@mix105.ws
License: Balsam Lake, Polk County, WI held by Red Rock Radio Corp.
Group Owner: Red Rock Radio Corp.; (acq 9-1-2006; grpsl)
Nat'l Network: ABC *Regional Network:* Wisconsin Radio Net.
Arbitron Metro Market: Balsam Lake, WI *Format:* Country *Hrs. of News Programming:* News progmg 5 hrs wkly *Target Audience:* 18-49; adults
Ron Revere, General Manager

Baraboo

WOLX-FM

03-03-1946; 94.9 mhz FM; 37 kw; 1299 ft.; N43 25 40 W89 39 14
7601 Ganser Wy, Madison, WI 53719 US

(608) 826-0077, *Fax:* 608-826-1245
www.wolx.com
info@wolx.com
License: Baraboo, Sauk County, WI held by Entercom Madison Licensee LLP.
Group Owner: Entercom Communications Corp.; (acq 7-10-00; grpsl)
Nat'l Reps: Christal
Arbitron Metro Market: Madison, WI *TV Affiliate:* Oldies *Special Programming:* news progmg 2 hrs wkly *Hrs. of News Programming:* 2 *No. News Employees:* 25-54.
Operations Manager

WRPQ
06-01-1967; 740 khz AM *Hrs Open:* 24; 0.25 kw-D, ND1; 0.006 kw-N, ND1; N43 27 19 W89 45 13
Mailing Address: 613 S. La Grange Road, La Grange, IL 60525 US
Second Address: 407 Oak St., Baraboo, WI 53913
(608) 356-3974, *Fax:* (608) 355-9952
www.wrpq.com
jeffsmith@wrpq.com
License: Baraboo, WI held by Baraboo Broadcasting Co.
Nat'l Network: CNN Radio *Regional Network:* Wisconsin Radio Net.
TV Affiliate: W43BR *Format:* Adult Contemp *Special Programming:* Relg 5 hrs wkly *Hrs. of News Programming:* news progmg 8 hrs wkly *No. News Employees:* 1 *Target Audience:* 25-54. *Adv. Rates:* 8; 8;8; 8
Jeff Smith, President
Gregory Buchwald, Operations Dir
Annette Koberstein, News Director

Barron

WAQE-FM
01-01-1999; 97.7 mhz FM; 15.5 kw; 289 ft.; N45 32 16 W91 45 50
1859 21st Avenue, Rice Lake, WI 54868 US
(715) 234-9059, *Fax:* (715) 234-6942
www.waqe.com
info@waqe.com
License: Barron, Barron County, WI held by TKC Inc.
Hrs. of News Programming: news progmg 5 hrs wkly *No. News Employees:* 1 *Target Audience:* 25-54; general *Adv. Rates:* 12; 8; 10; 6
Tom Koser, General Manager
Brian Schultz, Station Manager
Sondra Maanum, News Director

Beaver Dam

WBEV
03-21-1951; 1430 khz AM *Hrs Open:* 24; 1 kw-D, DAN; 1 kw-N, DAN; N43 25 43 W88 53 33
Mailing Address: 18 Upper Brook Drive, North Brunswick, NJ 08902 US
Second Address: 100 Stoddart St., Beaver Dam, WI 533916
(920) 885-4442, *Fax:* (920) 885-2152
www.wbevradio.com
License: Beaver Dam, WI held by Good Karma Broadcasting L.L.C.
Group Owner: Good Karma Broadcasting L.L.C.; acq 12-2-97; grpsl).
Wire Services: Wheeler News Service
Arbitron Metro Market: Beaver Dam, WI *Format:* Adult Contemp, News, 62, Talk *Special Programming:* Farm 8 hrs, sports 18 hrs wkly *Hrs. of News Programming:* news progmg 20 hrs wkly *No. News Employees:* 3*Target Audience:* 30 plus; general
Craig Karmazin, President
Rick Armon, Operations Dir
John Moser, General Sales Mgr
Warren Jorgenson, Chief Engineer
Deb Iamers, Traffic Manager
Laura Slosser, Marketing Consultant
Zach Heilprin, AM News Anchor/Reporter
JohnKraft, Air Announcer
Brenda Murphy, Host
Karen Kuhn, Marketing Consultant

WXRO
07-15-1968; 95.3 mhz FM *Hrs Open:* 24; 6 kw; 328 ft.; N43 28 9 W88 49 32
Mailing Address: 18 Upper Brook Drive, North Brunswick, NJ 08902 US
Second Address: 100 Stoddart St., Beaver Dam, WI 533916
(920) 885-4442, *Fax:* (920) 885-2152
www.wbevradio.com
License: Beaver Dam, Dodge County, WI
Group Owner: Good Karma Broadcasting L.L.C.
Wire Services: Wheeler News Service
Arbitron Metro Market: Beaver Dam, WI *Format:* Country *Special Programming:* Farm 6 hrs wkly *Hrs. of News Programming:* news progmg 10 hrs wkly *No. News Employees:* 3 *Target Audience:* 25-54; general
Craig Karmazin, Chairman
John Moser, General Sales Mgr
Rick Armon, Promotions Manager
John Kraft, Farm Director

Beloit

*WBCR-FM
11-30-1965; 90.3 mhz FM; 0.13 kw; 59 ft.; N42 30 13 W89 1 55
700 College St., Beloit, WI 53511 US
(870) 238-8141, *Fax:* (870) 238-5997
License: Beloit, Rock County, WI held by Beloit College.
Arbitron Metro Market: Las Vegas NV *Format:* Adult Contemp
Bradford Caldwell, General Manager

WGEZ
09-26-1948; 1490 khz AM *Hrs Open:* 24; 1 kw-U, ND1; N42 29 45 W89 1 3
Mailing Address: 622 Public Avenue, P.O. Box 416, Beloit, WI 53511 US
Second Address: 622 Public Ave., Beloit, WI 53511
(608) 365-8865, *Fax:* (608) 365-8867
www.1490trueoldies.com
wgezam@hotmail.com
License: Beloit, WI held by Alliance Communications Inc.
Nat'l Network: ABC Music Radio; AP Network News *Regional Network:* Brownfield; Wisconsin Radio Net.
Arbitron Metro Market: Rockford, IL *Format:* Oldies *No. News Employees:* 1 *Target Audience:* 25-54; baby boomers
Alan Kearns, General Manager
Keith Salerno, General Sales Mgr
Carla Cornell, News Director

Berlin

WBJZ
07-31-1972; 104.7 mhz FM *Hrs Open:* 24; 5.2 kw; 351 ft.; N43 53 57 W88 53 37
476 South National Ave, Fond Du Lac, WI 54935 US
(920) 230-1047, *Fax:* (208)906-8536
www.b104online.com/
Marty@b104online.com
License: Berlin, Green Lake County, WI held by Caxambas Corp.
Arbitron Metro Market: Oshkosh, WI *Format:* Adult Contemp *Target Audience:* 35-54; upscale, adults *Adv. Rates:* 15; 15; 15; 12
Marty Schibbelhut, President
Mike Enfelt, General Manager
Jason Mansmith, Programming Director
Amber Sanders, Marketing Consultant
Lynne Schibbelhut, Vice President

WISS
06-28-1971; 1100 khz AM *Hrs Open:* Sunrise-sunset
Mailing Address: 470 South National Ave, Fond Du Lac, WI 54935 US
Second Address: 112 N. Pearl St., Berlin, WI 54923
(920) 361-3551, *Fax:* (920) 361-3737
www.wissradio.com
production@hometownbroadcasting.com
License: Berlin, WI held by Hometown Broadcasting LLC
Format: Country, Oldies *Hrs. of News Programming:* news progmg 10 hrs wkly *No. News Employees:* 1 *Target Audience:* 25-54; local community
Tom Boyson, General Manager
Margaret Corrente, General Sales Mgr
Bernie Phillips, Programming Director
Andrew Disterhaft, News Director
Bill Denkert, General Sales Manager

Birnamwood

WYNW
01-01-2003; 92.9 mhz FM; 6 kw; 328 ft.; N44 59 50 W89 22 7
1456 E Green Bay Street, Shawano, WI 54166 US
(920) 884-1460, *Fax:* (920) 465-9986
www.relevantradio.com
info@relevantradio.com
License: Birnamwood, Shawano County, WI held by Starboard Media Foundation Inc.
Group Owner: Relevant Radio; (acq 7-9-2002).
Arbitron Metro Market: Green Bay, WI *Format:* Christian
Thomas Vorpahl, Chairman
Trish Leurck, Chief Development Officer
Mike Strub, Station Manager
Rev. Francis J. Hoffman, JCD, Executive Director
Amy Vanden Langenberg, Chief Financial Officer
Nancy Jensen, Chief Marketing Officer
Mike Kendall, Chief Programming Officer
Bob Benes, Chief Sales Officer

Black River Falls

WWIS
08-23-1958; 1260 khz AM *Hrs Open:* 6 AM-sunset; 0.58 kw-D, NDD; N44 19 11 W90 53 31
Route 1, Box 279a, Black River Falls, WI 54615 US
(715) 284-4391, *Fax:* (715) 284-9740
www.wwisradio.com
wwis@wwisradio.com
License: Black River Falls, WI held by WWIS Radio Inc.
Nat'l Network: CBS Radio *Regional Network:* Brownfield *Wire Services:* Wheeler News Service
Arbitron Metro Market: Black River Falls, WI *Format:* Oldies *Hrs. of News Programming:* News progmg 6 hrs wkly *Target Audience:* General. *Adv. Rates:* 8.50; 6.50; 6.50, na
Robert E. Smith, President
Nelson Lent, Operations Dir
Bob Gabrielson, Vice President & General Manager
Tony Hart, News Director
Brian B, Sports Director
Dick Deno, Sales Associate
Angel Graf, Sales Associate
Natalie Oppelt,Administrative Assistant

WWIS-FM
01-21-1991; 99.7 mhz FM *Hrs Open:* 24; 25 kw; 328 ft.; N44 19 11 W90 53 31
Route 1 Box 279a, Black River Falls, WI 54615 US
(715) 284-4391, *Fax:* (715) 284-9740
www.wwisradio.com
wwis@cuttingedge.net
License: Black River Falls, Jackson County, WI held by WWIS Radio Inc.
Nat'l Network: CBS *Wire Services:* Wheeler News Service
Arbitron Metro Market: Black River Falls, WI *Format:* Adult Contemp *Hrs. of News Programming:* News progmg 12 hrs wkly *Target Audience:* 25-55. *Adv. Rates:* 13; 13; 13; 12
Robert Smith, President
Nelson Lent, Operations Dir
Bob Gabrielson, Vice President & General Manager
Tony Hart, News Director
Brian B, Sports Director
Dick Deno, Sales Associate
Angel Graf, Sales Associate
Natalie Oppelt,Administrative Assistant

Bloomer

WQRB
01-01-1993; 95.1 mhz FM *Hrs Open:* 24; 8.9 kw; 545 ft.; N44 55 44 W91 32 31
111 East Kilbourn Avenue, Suite 2700, Milwaukee, WI 53202 US
(715) 830-4000, *Fax:* (715) 835-9680
www.b95radio.com
License: Bloomer, Chippewa County, WI held by Capstar TX L.P.
Group Owner: Clear Channel Communications Inc.; (acq 2000; grpsl)
Nat'l Reps: Clear Channel
Arbitron Metro Market: Eau Claire, WI *Format:* Country *No. News Employees:* 2 *Target Audience:* 25-54.
Jare Jordan, Operations Dir
Steve Potter, General Sales Mgr
Mike McKay, Programming Director
Rick Hencley, Promotions Manager
Keith Edwards, News Director
Paul Orth, Chief Engineer
Bobby Tripp, Disc Jockey
Trina Butak, TrafficManager

Brillion

WDUZ-FM
03-01-1993; 107.5 mhz FM *Hrs Open:* 24; 3.6 kw; 879 ft.; N44 21 32 W87 59 7
111 East Kilbourn Ave, Suite 2700, Milwaukee, WI 53202 US
(920) 468-4100, *Fax:* (920) 468-0250
www.thefan1075.com
thefan@cumulus.com
License: Brillion, Calumet County, WI held by Jacor Broadcasting Corp.
Group Owner: Clear Channel Communications Inc.; (acq 4-10-2009; grpsl)
Nat'l Network: ABC; ESPN Radio; Premiere Radio Networks
Arbitron Metro Market: Green Bay, WI *Format:* Sports, Talk *Target Audience:* 18-49; educated, affluent, upper-income *Adv. Rates:* 70; 70; 70; 10
Greg Jessen, Operations Dir
Buck Hein, General Sales Mgr
Mark Heller, Engineering Dir

Jimmy Clark, Operations Manager
Brian Stenzel, Promotions Director

Brookfield

WJZX(FM)

08-18-1995; 106.9 mhz FM; 4.4 kw; Ant 380 ft; N43 02 49 W87 58 52
5407 W. McKinley Ave., Milwaukee, WI 53208
(414) 978-9000, *Fax:* (414) 978-9001
License: Brookfield, Waukesha County, WI held by Saga Communications of Milwaukee LLC.
Group Owner: Saga Communications Inc.; (acq 5-9-97; $5 million with WJMR-FM Menomonee Falls)
Nat'l Reps: Katz Radio
Arbitron Metro Market: Milwaukee-Racine, WI *No. News Employees:* 1 *Target Audience:* 35-64.
Thomas Joerres, President
Traci Northrop, General Sales Mgr
Lauri Jones, Programming Director
Cris Ruid, News Director
Phil Longenecker, Chief Engineer
LaTonya Lucas, Promotions Director

Brule

*WHSA

09-14-1952; 89.9 mhz FM *Hrs Open:* 24; 38 kw; 551 ft.; N46 27 59 W91 33 56
3319 W. Beltline Hwy., Madison, WI 53713 US
(715) 394-8530, *Fax:* (715) 394-8404
www.wpr.org
listener@wpr.org
License: Brule, Douglas County, WI held by State of Wisconsin Educational Communications Board.
Nat'l Network: NPR *Regional Network:* Wis. Public Radio
Arbitron Metro Market: Duluth-Superior, MN-WI *Format:* News, News/Talk, 86 *Special Programming:* Folk 3 hrs, jazz 6 hrs wkly *Hrs. of News Programming:* news progmg 39 hrs wkly *No. News Employees:* 1 *TargetAudience:* 34 plus.
John Munson, General Manager

Burlington

*WBSD

04-07-1975; 89.1 mhz FM *Hrs Open:* 24; 0.21 kw; 92 ft.; N42 40 14 W88 16 18
225 Robert Street, Burlington, WI 53105 US
(262) 763-0195, *Fax:* (262) 763-0207
www.wbsdfm.com
tom@wbsdfm.com
License: Burlington, Racine County, WI held by Burlington Area School District.
Arbitron Metro Market: Burlington,WI *Format:* Alternative *Special Programming:* Jazz 8 hrs, reggae 3 hrs, ska/punk 2 hrs, metal one hr, blues 4 hrs, folk 5 hrs wkly *Hrs. of News Programming:* One *Target Audience:* 25-54.
Kevin Fay, Operations Dir
Terry Havel, General Manager
Alex Nazarkewich, Production Director
Nigel Reed, Assistant to the General Manager

Chetek

WATQ

05-17-1997; 106.7 mhz FM *Hrs Open:* 24; 35 kw; 584 ft.; N45 11 4 W91 43 52
111 East Kilbourn Avenue, Suite 2700, Milwaukee, WI 53202 US
(715) 830-4000, *Fax:* (715) 835-9680
www.moose106.com
rickhencley@clearchannel.com
License: Chetek, Barron County, WI held by Capstar TX L.P.
Group Owner: Clear Channel Communications Inc.; (acq 2000; grpsl)
Nat'l Network: CNN Radio *Regional Network:* Brownfield *Nat'l Reps:* Clear Channel
Arbitron Metro Market: Eau Claire, WI *Format:* Country *No. News Employees:* 2 *Target Audience:* 35-64.
Jare Jordan, Operations Dir
Steve Potter, General Sales Mgr
Jay Moore, Programming Director
Rick Hencley, Promotions Manager
Keith Edwards, News Director
Paul Orth, Engineering Dir
Theresa Nelson, Traffic Manager

Chippewa Falls

WCFW

10-20-1968; 105.7 mhz FM *Hrs Open:* 24; 25 kw; 305 ft.; N44 52 18 W91 17 11
P.O. Box 16, Eau Claire, WI 54702 US
(715) 723-2257, *Fax:* (715) 723-8276
wcfwradio@clearwire.net
License: Chippewa Falls, Chippewa County, WI held by Roland L. Bushland dba Bushland Radio/WCFW.
Wire Services: AP
Arbitron Metro Market: Eau Claire, WI *Format:* Adult Contemp *Special Programming:* Relg 2 hrs wkly *Hrs. of News Programming:* News progmg 8 hrs wkly *Target Audience:* 35 plus; upscale *Adv. Rates:* 15; 15;15; 10
Roland Bushland, General Manager
Patricia Bushland, General Sales Mgr

WEAQ

09-07-1958; 1150 khz AM; 5 kw-D, ND1; 0.046 kw-N, ND1; N44 53 5 W91 23 25
Mailing Address: 944 Harlam, Altoona, WI 54720 US
Second Address: 944 Harlem St., Altoona, WI 54720
(715) 832-1530, *Fax:* (715) 832-5329
www.espn1150.com
webmaster@espn1150.com
License: Chippewa Falls, WI held by Maverick Media of Eau Claire License LLC.
Group Owner: Maverick Media LLC; (acq 6-13-2003; grpsl).
Nat'l Reps: Katz Radio
Arbitron Metro Market: Eau Claire, WI *Format:* Sports, Talk *Special Programming:* Sportsvue, Bill Scott sports from Green Bay *Target Audience:* 40 plus; general
Gary Rozynek, President
George Roberts, Operations Dir
Bruce Butler, General Manager
Dave Craig, Station Manager
Bill Holden, Chief Engineer

Cleveland

WLKN

04-25-1985; 98.1 mhz FM *Hrs Open:* 24; 5.8 kw; Ant 292 ft; N43 59 03 W87 45 55
Box 26, 1050 Linden St., Cleveland, WI 53015
(920) 693-3103, *Fax:* (920) 693-3104
www.wlkn.com
manager@wlkn.com
License: Cleveland, Manitowoc County, WI held by Seehafer Broadcasting Corp
Wire Services: AP
Population Served: 225,000 *Arbitron Metro Market:* Sheboygan, WI *Hrs. of News Programming:* news progmg 7 hrs wkly *No. News Employees:* 1 *Target Audience:* 25-54; active, upscale *Adv. Rates:* 21; 20; 21; 14
Jack Taddeo, CEO
Don Seehafer, President
Mark Seehafer, Vice President
David Jetzer, Station Manager
Sandi Davis, News Director

Clintonville

WOTE

02-28-1983; 1380 khz AM *Hrs Open:* 24
33 East 3rd Street, P.O. Box 269, Clintonville, WI 54929 US
(715) 524-2194, *Fax:* (715) 524-9980
www.1380thelounge.com
License: Clintonville, WI held by Results Broadcasting Inc.
Group Owner: Results Broadcasting; (acq 1996)
Nat'l Network: ABC *Regional Network:* Wisconsin Radio Net.
Arbitron Metro Market: Clintonville, WI *Format:* Oldies *Special Programming:* Farm 8 hrs wkly *Hrs. of News Programming:* news progmg 12 hrs wkly *No. News Employees:* 1 *Target Audience:* 25-54. *Adv.Rates:* 23; 23; 23; 23
Eric Voight, General Manager
Walt Baldwin, Chief Engineer

WJMQ

10-27-1986; 92.3 mhz FM *Hrs Open:* 24; 6 kw; 299 ft.; N44 34 1 W88 44 33
33 East 3rd Street, P.O. Box 269, Clintonville, WI 54929 US
(715) 524-2194, *Fax:* (715) 524-9980
www.frogcountry923.com
resultsbroadcasting@gmail.com
License: Clintonville, Waupaca County, WI held by Results Broadcasting Inc.
Group Owner: Results Broadcasting
Arbitron Metro Market: Appleton-Oshkosh, WI *Format:* Country *Hrs. of News Programming:* news progmg 12 hrs wkly *No. News Employees:* 1 *Target Audience:* 12-plus. *Adv. Rates:* 23; 23; 23; 23
Eric Voight, Station Manager

Columbus

WTTN

04-02-1950; 1580 khz AM *Hrs Open:* 24
100 Stoddart Street, Beaver Dam, WI 53916 US
(920) 261-1580, *Fax:* (920) 261-0624
jmoser@gkbradio.com
License: Columbus, WI held by Good Karma Broadcasting L.L.C.
Group Owner: Good Karma Broadcasting L.L.C.; acq 8-26-99; $525,000)
Nat'l Network: CNN Radio *Wire Services:* Wheeler News Service
Arbitron Metro Market: Madison, WI *Format:* Oldies *Special Programming:* Relg 4 hrs wkly *Hrs. of News Programming:* news progmg 15 hrs wkly *No. News Employees:* 2 *Target Audience:* 25-64. *Adv. Rates:* 18; 15; 15; 15
Craig Karmazin, CEO
Rick Armon, Operations Dir
Scott Trentadue, General Manager
John Moser, General Sales Mgr
Warren Jorgensen, Chief Engineer

Cornell

WDRK

01-01-2001; 99.9 mhz FM; 25 kw; 328 ft.; N45 7 22 W91 24 23
141 East Michigan Ave., Suite 300, Kalamazoo, MI 49007 US
(715) 832-1530, *Fax:* (715) 832-5329
www.bobfm999.com
License: Cornell, Chippewa County, WI held by Maverick Media of Eau Claire License LLC.
Group Owner: Maverick Media LLC; (acq 6-13-2003; grpsl).
Arbitron Metro Market: Eau Claire, WI *Hrs. of News Programming:* news progmg one hr wkly *No. News Employees:* 1
George Roberts, Operations Dir
Rick Roberts, Station Manager
Lynn Bieritz, General Sales Mgr
Al Shannon, Operations Manager
Kris Cooper, Promotions Director
Dan Gainey, Regional Sales Manager

Cross Plains

WMAD

09-18-1964; 96.3 mhz FM *Hrs Open:* 24; 5.1 kw; 699 ft.; N43 12 44 W89 35 59
600 Congress Ave., Suite 1400, Austin, TX 78701 US
(608) 274-5450, *Fax:* (608) 274-5521
www.wmad.com
info@wmad.com
License: Cross Plains, Sauk County, WI held by Capstar TX L.P.
Group Owner: Clear Channel Communications Inc.; (acq 8-30-2000; grpsl).
Nat'l Reps: Christal
Arbitron Metro Market: Madison, WI *Format:* Country *Hrs. of News Programming:* news progmg one hr wkly *No. News Employees:* 1 *Target Audience:* 25-49.
Jeff Tyler, General Manager
Hugh Garret, General Sales Mgr
Brad Savage, Programming Director
Joshua Wescott, News Director
Cliff Groth, Chief Engineer
Jacqueline Forney, Traffic Manager

De Forest

WJQM

01-01-2003; 93.1 mhz FM; 6 kw horiz, 5.4 kw vert; 322 ft.; N43 9 34 W89 12 55
Mailing Address: 908 West Mohawk Trail, Deforest, WI 53532 US
Second Address: 730 Rayovc Dr., De Forest, WI 53711
(608) 273-1000, *Fax:* (608) 273-3588
www.madisonjams.com
info@madisonjamz.com
License: De Forest, Dane County, WI held by Mid-West Management Inc.
Group Owner: The Mid-West Family Broadcast Group; (acq 8-13-2002)
Arbitron Metro Market: Madison, WI *Format:* Contemporary Hits/Top 40
Randy Hawke, Operations Dir
Tom Walker, General Manager
Ted Waldbillig, General Sales Mgr
J.D. Garfield, Programming Director

De Pere

WKSZ

10-01-1984; 95.9 mhz FM *Hrs Open:* 24; 4.5 kw; 774 ft.; N44 21 32 W87 59 7
Mailing Address: 7601 Ganser Wy, Madison, WI 53719 US
Second Address: 1263 main St., Suite #225, Green Bay, WI 54301
(920) 431-0959, *Fax:* (920) 739-0494
www.959kissfm.com

License: De Pere, Brown County, WI held by Woodward Communications Inc.
Group Owner: Woodward Communications Inc.; acq 1995).
Nat'l Reps: McGavren Guild
Arbitron Metro Market: Green Bay, WI *Format:* Contemporary Hits/Top 40 *Target Audience:* 18-34; females
Greg Bell, Operations Dir
Kelly Radandt, General Sales Mgr
Dayton Kane, Programming Director
Steve Brown, Chief Engineer

Delafield

*WHAD

05-30-1948; 90.7 mhz FM *Hrs Open:* 24; 72 kw; 682 ft.; N43 1 42 W88 23 32 *Rebroadcasts:* Rebroadcasts WHA(AM) Madison 60%
3319 W. Beltline Hwy., Madison, WI 53713 US
(414) 227-2040, *Fax:* (414) 227-2043
www.wpr.org
whad@wpr.org
License: Delafield, Waukesha County, WI held by State of Wisconsin Educational Communications Board.
Nat'l Network: NPR
Arbitron Metro Market: Milwaukee-Racine, WI *Format:* News, News/Talk, 86 *Hrs. of News Programming:* news progmg 11 hrs wkly *No. News Employees:* 1 *Target Audience:* 35-55; general
Lisa Nalbandian, Station Manager
Shavonn Brown, General Sales Mgr
Chuck Quirmbach, News Director

Denmark

WPCK

09-01-1969; 104.9 mhz FM *Hrs Open:* 24; 10 kw; 515 ft.; N44 29 17 W87 45 40
2401 W. Waukau Avenue, P.O. Box 3450, Oshkosh, WI 54903 US
(920) 468-4100, *Fax:* (920) 468-0250
www.kicks1049.com
dylan.fletcher@cumulus.com
License: Denmark, Brown County, WI held by Citicasters Licenses Inc.
Group Owner: Clear Channel Communications Inc.; (acq 4-10-2009; grpsl)
Nat'l Reps: Katz Radio
Arbitron Metro Market: Green Bay, WI *Format:* Country *Target Audience:* 25-54; adults *Adv. Rates:* 55; 55; 55; 10
Greg Jessen, Operations Dir
Chris Moreau, General Sales Mgr
Dylan Fletcher, Programming Director
Mark Heller, Chief Engineer
Jimmy Clark, Operations Manager

WGBW

10-29-1951; 1590 khz AM *Hrs Open:* 24; 10 kw-D, 500 w-N; N44 18 50 W87 47 16.3
1414 16th St., Two Rivers, WI 54241
(920) 863-1234, *Fax:* (920) 794-1800
wgbwradio.com
wgbw@lsol.net
License: Denmark, Brown County, WI held by WTRW Inc.
Nat'l Network: ABC Radio Network News; Westwood One
Population Served: 330,000*Hrs. of News Programming:* news progmg 10 hrs wkly *No. News Employees:* 1 *Target Audience:* 35-54; baby boomers & professionals *Adv. Rates:* 24; 24; 24; 24
Mark Heller, President

Dickeyville

WVRE

02-01-2003; 101.1 mhz FM *Hrs Open:* 24; 3.7 kw; 423 ft.; N42 31 44 W90 36 58
961 Whispering Lane, Hazel Green, WI 53811 US
(563) 690-0800, *Fax:* (563) 588-5688
www.1011theriver.com
mbaumgartner@1011theriver.com
License: Dickeyville, Grant County, WI held by Radio Dubuque Inc.
Group Owner: Radio Dubuque Inc.; acq 8-1-01).
Nat'l Reps: International Media; Katz Radio
Arbitron Metro Market: Dickeyville, WI *Format:* Country *No. News Employees:* 1 *Target Audience:* Adults; 25-54
Thomas Parsley, General Manager

Dodgeville

WDMP

11-01-1968; 810 khz AM *Hrs Open:* 24
Mailing Address: P. O. Box 58, Dodgeville, WI 53533 US
Second Address: 2163 Hwy. 151 S., Dodgeville, WI 53523
(608) 935-2302, *Fax:* (608) 935-3464
www.d99point3.com
KREINICKE@CHARTER.NET
License: Dodgeville, WI held by Dodge-Point Broadcasting Co.
Arbitron Metro Market: Madison, WI *Format:* Country *Hrs. of News Programming:* news progmg 5 hrs wkly *No. News Employees:* 1 *Target Audience:* General.
Louise Hamlin, President
Kurt Reinicke, General Manager
Michael Anthony, Programming Director
Robert Brainerd, News Director
Melanie Rae, Disc Jockey
Jon Satterlee, Disc Jockey

WDMP-FM

11-01-1968; 99.3 mhz FM *Hrs Open:* 24; 1.55 kw; 459 ft.; N42 55 10 W90 8 6
Mailing Address: P. O. Box 58, Dodgeville, WI 53533 US
Second Address: 2163 Hwy. 151 S., Dodgeville, WI 53523
(608) 935-2302, *Fax:* (608) 935-3464
www.d99point3.com
KREINICKE@CHARTER.NET
License: Dodgeville, Iowa County, WI
Arbitron Metro Market: Madison, WI *No. News Employees:* 1
Kurt Reinicke, General Manager
Michael Anthony, Programming Director
Jon Satterlee, Disc Jockey
Melanie Rae, Disc Jockey
Robert Brainerd, Disc Jockey

Durand

WRDN

11-21-1968; 1430 khz AM *Hrs Open:* 18; 2 kw-D, 152 w-N; N44 38 28 W91 55 22
313 Main St., Menomonie, WI 54736
(715) 231-9500, *Fax:* (715) 231-9505
License: Durand, Pepin County, WI held by Zoe Communications Inc.
Group Owner: Zoe Communications Inc.
Population Served: 2,103 *Arbitron Metro Market:* Eau Claire, WI
C. Williams, President
Tom Moran, General Manager

Eagle River

WERL

05-23-1961; 950 khz AM *Hrs Open:* 24; 1 kw-D, ND1; 0.051 kw-N, ND1; N45 58 32 W89 14 44
P.O. Box 309, Eagle River, WI 54521 US
(715) 479-4451, *Fax:* (715) 479-6511
www.wrjo.com
jim@wrjo.com
License: Eagle River, WI held by Heartland Communications License LLC.
Group Owner: Heartland Communications Group LLC; (acq 12-7-2004; $2.2 million with co-located FM).
Arbitron Metro Market: Eagle River, WI *Format:* Adult Contemp *Hrs. of News Programming:* news progmg 7 hrs wkly *No. News Employees:* 1 *Target Audience:* General. *Adv. Rates:* 11; 11; 11; na
Mary Jo Berner, President
Jim Hodges, General Manager
Mike Wolf, Corporate Program Director
Jeff Litscher, Corporate Program Director
Bruce Marcus, News/Sports Director
Del Dayton, Chief Engineer
Lynn Weiland, Traffic Manager

WRJO

07-31-1971; 94.5 mhz FM *Hrs Open:* 24; 50 kw; 492 ft.; N46 9 57 W89 21 57
P.O. Box 309, Eagle River, WI 54521 US
(715) 479-4451, *Fax:* (715) 479-6511
www.wrjo.com
info@wrjo.com
License: Eagle River, Vilas County, WI
Group Owner: Heartland Communications Group LLC
Format: Oldies *Adv. Rates:* 21; 21; 21; 16
Jo French, General Manager
Amy Holland, Programming Director

Eau Claire

WAXX

02-01-1965; 104.5 mhz FM *Hrs Open:* 24; 100 kw; 1801 ft.; N44 39 50 W90 57 40
944 Harlam St., Altoona, WI 54720 US
(701) 852-7449, *Fax:* (701) 837-6925
pbiminot@srt.com
License: Eau Claire, Eau Claire County, WI held by Maverick Media of Eau Claire License LLC.
Group Owner: Maverick Media LLC; (acq 6-13-2003; grpsl).
Arbitron Metro Market: Burlington ND *Format:* Adult Contemp *Hrs. of News Programming:* News progmg 5 hrs wkly *Target Audience:* 18-49.
John Kircher, President
Jean Kircher, Operations Dir
Jean Schemmp, Station Manager
J. Davis, General Sales Mgr
Jeff Bliss, Chief Engineer

WAYY

05-01-1937; 790 khz AM *Hrs Open:* 24; 5 kw-D, DAN; 5 kw-N, DAN; N44 49 51 W91 26 58
P.O. Box 1, Eau Claire, WI 54702 US
(800) 877-5600, *Fax:* (916) 251-1650
www.klove.com
License: Eau Claire, WI held by Maverick Media of Eau Claire License LLC.
Group Owner: Maverick Media LLC; (acq 6-13-2003; grpsl).
Regional Network: Wisconsin Radio Net.
Arbitron Metro Market: Tehachapi CA *Format:* Christian
Mike Novak, President
David Pierce, Programming Director
Ed Lenane, News Director
Sam Wallington, Engineering Dir
Marya Morgan, News Reporter
Richard Hunt, News Reporter

WBIZ

11-11-1947; 1400 khz AM *Hrs Open:* 24
111 East Kilbourn Avenue, Suite 2700, Milwaukee, WI 53202 US
(715) 830-4000, *Fax:* (715) 835-9680
www.sportsradio1400.com
jameskaska@clearchannel.com
License: Eau Claire, WI held by Capstar TX L.P.
Group Owner: Clear Channel Communications Inc.; (acq 2000; grpsl)
Nat'l Network: CBS *Nat'l Reps:* Clear Channel
Arbitron Metro Market: Eau Claire, WI *Format:* Sports *Target Audience:* 25-54.
Dave Deville, Operations Dir
Steve Potter, General Sales Mgr
Jimmie Kaska, Programming Director
Rick Hencley, Promotions Manager
Keith Edwards, News Director
Paul Orth, Chief Engineer
Theresa Nelson, Traffic Manager
RickHencley, Market Manager

WBIZ-FM

12-01-1967; 100.7 mhz FM; 100 kw; 482 ft.; N44 55 44 W91 32 31
111 East Kilbourn Avenue, Suite 2700, Milwaukee, WI 53202 US
(715) 830-4000, *Fax:* (715) 835-9680
www.z100radio.com
dave@z100radio.com
License: Eau Claire, Eau Claire County, WI held by Capstar Limited Partnership
Group Owner: Clear Channel Communications Inc.
Nat'l Reps: Clear Channel
Arbitron Metro Market: Eau Claire, WI *Format:* Contemporary Hits/Top 40 *Hrs. of News Programming:* 2 *Target Audience:* 18 - 49.
Rick Hencley, Operations Dir
Keith Edwards, News Director
Paul Orth, Engineering Dir
Jare Jordan, Operations Manager
Theresa Nelson, Traffic Manager
Rick Hencley, Market Manager
Dave Deville, Operations Manager

*WDVM

04-01-1948; 1050 khz AM
1819 Mitchell Ave, Eau Claire, WI 54701 US
(715) 855-1439(715) 577-0943, *Fax:* (715) 855-1471
www.relevantradio.com
wdvm@relevantradio.com
License: Eau Claire, WI held by Starboard Media Foundation Inc.
Group Owner: Relevant Radio; (acq 7-6-2001).
Arbitron Metro Market: Eau Claire, WI *Format:* Talk, Religious *No. News Employees:* 1 *Target Audience:* 35 plus; mature adults *Adv. Rates:* 6; 6; 6; 6
Mark Follett, CEO
Sherry Brownrigg, President
Martin Jury, Operations Dir
Raymond Jay, Station Manager

*WHEM

08-22-1995; 91.3 mhz FM *Hrs Open:* 24; 0.3 kw; 285 ft.; N44 45 50 W91 31 6
228 E. Lowes Creek Rd, Eau Claire, WI 54701 US

RADIO - U.S.

(715) 838-9595
www.whem.com
whem@discover-net.net
License: Eau Claire, Eau Claire County, WI held by Fourth Dimension Inc.
Arbitron Metro Market: Eau Claire, WI *Format:* Christian
Harlan Reinders, General Manager
Phyllis Reinders, Programming Director

WIAL
01-01-1948; 94.1 mhz FM *Hrs Open:* 24; 84 kw; 351 ft.; N44 49 48 W91 26 48
944 Harlam St., Altoona, WI 54720 US
(715) 832-1530, *Fax:* (715) 832-5329
www.i94online.com
License: Eau Claire, Eau Claire County, WI
Group Owner: Maverick Media LLC
Arbitron Metro Market: Eau Claire, WI *Format:* Adult Contemp
No. News Employees: 1 *Target Audience:* 18-54.
Gary Rozynek, President
George Roberts, General Manager
Rick Roberts, Station Manager
Lynn Bieritz, General Sales Mgr
Luc Anthony, Promotions Manager
Bill Holden, Chief Engineer
Curt St ohn, Disc Jockey
Sue Kelly, DiscJockey

***WUEC**
10-27-1975; 89.7 mhz FM *Hrs Open:* 24; 5.2 kw; 630 ft; N44 47 58 W91 27 59
Wisconsin Public Radio, 1221 W. Clairemont Ave., Eau Claire, WI 53706
(715) 839-3868, *Fax:* (715) 839-2939
www.wpr.org
kallenbach@wpr.org
License: Eau Claire, Eau Claire County, WI held by Board of Regents, University of Wisconsin.
Nat'l Network: NPR *Regional Network:* Wis. Public Radio
Population Served: 168,000 *Arbitron Metro Market:* Eau Claire, WI *Special Programming:* Folk 3 hrs, blues 3 hrs wkly *Hrs. of News Programming:* News progmg 24 hrs wkly *Target Audience:* General.
Dean Kallenbach, Station Manager
Marvin Spielman, General Sales Mgr
Rick Kremer, News Director
Stev Johnston, Chief Engineer

***WVCF**
01-01-1997; 90.5 mhz FM *Hrs Open:* 24; 1600 w; 112 m; N44 58 57 W91 25 47
VCY/America Inc., 3434 W. Kilbourn Ave., Milwaukee, WI 53208
(414) 935-3000, *Fax:* (414) 935-3015
www.vcyamerica.org
wvcf@vcyamerica.org
License: Eau Claire, Eau Claire County, WI held by VCY America Inc.
Group Owner: VCY America Inc.
Nat'l Network: IRN/USA; Moody
Arbitron Metro Market: Eau Claire, WI *Target Audience:* All ages
Dr. Randall Melchert, President
Vic Eliason, General Manager
Jim Schneider, Programming Director
Andy Eliason, Chief Engineer
Gordon Morris, Operations Manager

Elk Mound

WECL
03-01-2004; 92.9 mhz FM *Hrs Open:* 24; 3.3 kw; 446 ft.; N44 53 4 W91 35 4
944 Harlam St., Altoona, WI 54720 US
(715) 832-1530, *Fax:* (715) 832-5329
www.929thebigcheese.com
License: Elk Mound, Dunn County, WI held by Maverick Media of Eau Claire License LLC.
Group Owner: Maverick Media LLC; (acq 6-13-2003; grpsl).
Arbitron Metro Market: Elk Mound, WI *Special Programming:* Flashback 4 hrs wkly *Target Audience:* 35-54; adults
Gary Rozynek, President
Dan Lea, Operations Dir
George Roberts, General Manager
Rick Roberts, Station Manager
Lynn Bieritz, General Sales Mgr
Kris Cooper, Programming Director
Scott driver, Promotions Manager
Bill Holden, ChiefEngineer
Dan Gainey, Regional Sales Manager

Elm Grove

WGLB
12-06-1963; 1560 khz AM *Hrs Open:* 24
900 E Green Bay Road, Port Washington, WI 53074 US
(414) 527-4365, *Fax:* (414) 527-4367
www.wglbam1560.com
wglb@wglbam1560.com
License: Elm Grove, WI held by Joel J. Kinlow
Arbitron Metro Market: Milwaukee-Racine, WI *Format:* Gospel
Target Audience: African American
Joel Kinlow, CEO
Joel Kinlow, President
Willis Payne Jr., Station Manager

Evansville

WWHG
08-17-1989; 105.9 mhz FM *Hrs Open:* 24; 1.7 kw; 482 ft.; N42 43 38 W89 15 2
Suite 485, 1 Parker Place, Janesville, WI 53545 US
(608) 758-9025, *Fax:* (608) 758-9550
www.hot1059.net
production@gkbradio.com
License: Evansville, Rock County, WI held by Good Karma Broadcasting L.L.C.
Group Owner: Good Karma Broadcasting L.L.C.; (acq 10-2-97; $1.5 million)
Hrs. of News Programming: news progmg 3 hrs wkly *No. News Employees:* 1 *Adv. Rates:* 40; 35; 45; 30
Craig Karmazin, CEO
Rick Armon, Operations Dir
Keith Williams, Station Manager
Dan Hunt, Programming Director
Kyle Jacob, News Director
Warren Jorgensen, Chief Engineer
Deb Lamers, Traffic Manager

Fond Du Lac

KFIZ
07-06-1922; 1450 khz AM; 1 kw-U, ND1; N43 47 28 W88 28 16
Mailing Address: 254 Winnebago Drive, Fond Du Lac, WI 54935 US
Second Address: 254 Winnebago Dr., Fond du Lac, WI 54935
(920) 921-1071, *Fax:* (920) 921-0757
www.kfiz.com
info@kfiz.com
License: Fond Du Lac, WI held by RBH Enterprises Inc.
Group Owner: Mountain Dog Media; (acq 1-23-97; $1 plus assumption of liabilities with co-located FM).
Arbitron Metro Market: Fond du Lac, WI *Format:* News, News/Talk, 84, Talk *Special Programming:* Farm 10 hrs wkly *Hrs. of News Programming:* news progmg 10 hrs wkly *Target Audience:* 35-64; Men & Women
R.B. Hopper, President
Anne Schaefer, General Sales Mgr
Wade Bates, Programming Director
Bob Nelson, News Director

WFON
10-05-1967; 107.1 mhz FM *Hrs Open:* 24; 6 kw; 299 ft.; N43 50 20 W88 22 8
254 Winnebago Drive, Fond Du Lac, WI 54935 US
(920) 921-1071, *Fax:* (920) 921-0757
www.k107.com
License: Fond Du Lac, Fond Du Lac County, WI held by RBH Enterprises Inc.
Group Owner: Mountain Dog Media; (acq 1-23-97).
Arbitron Metro Market: Fond du Lac, WI *Format:* Adult Contemp *Hrs. of News Programming:* news progmg 1 hr wkly *No. News Employees:* 1 *Target Audience:* Women 25-54.
Randy Hopper, General Manager

***WDKV**
01-01-2005; 91.7 mhz FM; 20 kw vert; 357 ft.; N43 39 35 W88 26 26
600 W. Mason St., Springfield, IL 62702 US
(800) 525-5683, *Fax:* (916) 251-1650
www.klove.com
klove@klove.com
License: Fond Du Lac, Fond Du Lac County, WI held by Educational Media Foundation.
Group Owner: EMF Broadcasting; (acq 2-21-2006; $350,000)
Nat'l Network: K-Love
Arbitron Metro Market: Fond du Lac, WI *Format:* Christian *No. News Employees:* 13
Darrell Chambliss, Chairman
Mike Novak, President and CEO
John Clements, Operations Dir
David Pierce, Chief Creative Officer and Programming Director
Ed Lenane, News Director
Sam Wallington, Engineering Dir
Richard Hunt, NewsReporter
Alan Mason, Chief Operating Officer
Dan Antonelli, Chief Business Development Officer
Eric Moser, Chief Financial Officer
Brian Burger, Vice President of Human Resources
D. Kevin Blair, Secretary and General Counsel

***WVFL**
01-01-2007; 89.9 mhz FM; 1 kw vert; 384 ft.; N43 48 9 W88 20 18 *Rebroadcasts:* Rebroadcasts WVCY-FM Milwaukee 100%
3434 W Kilbourn Avenue, Milwaukee, WI 53208 US
(414) 935-3000, *Fax:* (414) 935-3015
www.vcyamerica.org
vcy@vcyamerica.org
License: Fond Du Lac, Fond du Lac County, WI held by VCY America Inc.
Group Owner: VCY America Inc.
Nat'l Network: USA
Arbitron Metro Market: Fond Du Lac, WI *Format:* Christian, Religious
Vic Eliason, Operations Dir
Jim Schneider, Programming Director
Andy Eliason, Chief Engineer

WIWN
01-02-2000; ; 700 watts; 43 26 20 3N 88 31 29 1W
823 West Center Avenue, Visalia, CA 93291 USA
(559) 733-7800
License: Fond Du Lac, Fond Du Lac County, WI held by WWAZ License LLC

Forestville

WRKU
08-01-1999; 102.1 mhz FM; 2.6 kw; 499 ft.; N44 42 26 W87 24 26
4400 Hilltop Avenue, Wausau, WI 54001 US
(920) 746-9430, *Fax:* (920) 746-9433
www.doorradio.com
info@doorradio.com
License: Forestville, Door County, WI held by Nicolet Broadcasting Inc.
Group Owner: Nicolet Broadcasting Inc.
Format: Oldies *Hrs. of News Programming:* News progmg 3 hrs wkly
Roger Utnehmer, President
Karen Leitzinger, Operations Dir
Miles Knuteson, General Manager
John Focke, News Director
Kathy Robinson, Traffic Manager

Fort Atkinson

WFAW
01-24-1963; 940 khz AM; 500 w-D, 550 w-N, DA-2; N42 54 24 W88 45 06
Box 94, Fort Atkinson, WI 60611
(920) 563-9329, *Fax:* (920) 563-0315
License: Fort Atkinson, Jefferson County, WI held by NRG License Sub. LLC.
Group Owner: NRG Media LLC; (acq 10-31-2005; grpsl)
Nat'l Reps: Regional Reps
Population Served: 9,782*No. News Employees:* 1 *Adv. Rates:* 25; 24; 24; 22
Mary Quass, CEO
Gary Douglas, Operations Dir
Jim Vriezen, General Manager
Shane Sparks, General Sales Mgr
Michael Clish, News Director
George Nichols, Engineering Dir
Ernie Swanson, Chief Engineer
Jim Smith, CFO
Chuck DuCoty,COO
Lynette Furley, Traffic Manager

WSJY
09-04-1959; 107.3 mhz FM *Hrs Open:* 24; 26 kw; 676 ft.; N42 48 2 W89 3 16
980 North Michigan Avenue, Suite 1880, Chicago, IL 60611 US
(608) 756-0747, *Fax:* (608) 563-0315
www.lite1073.com
jvriezen@nrgmedia.com
License: Fort Atkinson, Jefferson County, WI
Group Owner: NRG Media LLC
Nat'l Reps: McGavren Guild
Arbitron Metro Market: Madison, WI *Format:* Adult Contemp *No. News Employees:* 1 *Target Audience:* 25-54. *Adv. Rates:* 30; 29; 29; 27
Gary Douglas Lundberg, Operations Dir
James Vriezen, General Manager

Shane Sparks, General Sales Mgr
Jennifer Maxwell, Programming Director
Sonja Untz, News Director
Polly Peterson, Disc Jockey
Eric Stone, Disc Jockey
MichaelClish, Local News Editor

Goodman

***WMVM**
05-03-1993; 90.7 mhz FM; 7 kw; 285 ft.; N45 46 23 W88 24 38
No. 1 Falconcrest Dr., Goodman-Armstrong H.S, Goodman, WI 54125 US
(920) 842-2900, *Fax:* (920) 842-2704
www.wrvm.org
wrvm@wrvm.org
License: Goodman, Marinette County, WI held by WRVM Inc.
Format: Christian
Michael Cornell, General Manager
Bryan Hay, General Sales Mgr
Dennis Jones, Programming Director
Alan Kilgore, Chief Engineer

Green Bay

WDUZ
06-19-1947; 1400 khz AM *Hrs Open:* 24; 1 kw-U, ND1; N44 29 36 W87 59 13
810 Victoria, Green Bay, WI 54301 US
(920) 468-4100, *Fax:* (920) 468-0250
www.thefan1075.com
thefan@cumulus.com
License: Green Bay, WI held by Jacor Broadcasting Corp.
Group Owner: Clear Channel Communications Inc.; (acq 4-10-2009; grpsl)
Nat'l Network: ESPN Radio; ABC; Premiere Radio Networks
Nat'l Reps: Katz Radio
Arbitron Metro Market: Green Bay, WI *Format:* Sports *Target Audience:* 18-54; high income, male skew *Adv. Rates:* 70; 70; 70; 15
Jimmy Clark, Operations Dir
Greg Jessen, General Manager
Buck Hein, General Sales Mgr
Bob Watts, Programming Director
Mark Heller, Chief Engineer

***WEMY**
08-26-1974; 91.5 mhz FM *Hrs Open:* 24; 710 w; 741 ft; N44 21 32 W87 59 07 *Rebroadcasts:* Rebroadcasts WEMI(FM) Appleton 95%
1909 W. 2nd St., Appleton, WI 53706
(920) 499-9957, *Fax:* (920) 749-0474
www.christianfamilyradio.net
www.thefamily.net
License: Green Bay, Brown County, WI held by Evangel Ministries Inc.
Group Owner: Evangel Ministries Inc.; acq 3-10-98).
Nat'l Network: Salem Radio Network; USA
Population Served: 200,000 *Arbitron Metro Market:* Green Bay, WI *Hrs. of News Programming:* News progmg 10 hr wkly *No. News Employees:* 5 *Target Audience:* 25-54; women *Adv. Rates:* 21; 21; 21; 21
Peggy Ament, Chairman
Paul Cameron, General Manager
Andy Kilgar, General Sales Mgr
Terry Michaels, Programming Director
Bill Moede, Chief Engineer
Andy Kilgas, Sales Director

WTAQ
04-06-1925; 1360 khz AM
Mailing Address: 904 Grand Avenue, Wausau, WI 54403 US
Second Address: 115 South Jefferson St., Green Bay, WI 54301
(902) 435-3771, *Fax:* (920) 321-2300
www.wtaq.com
License: Green Bay, WI held by Midwest Communications Inc.
Group Owner: Midwest Communications Inc.; acq 1975).
Nat'l Network: CBS *Nat'l Reps:* Christal
Arbitron Metro Market: Green Bay, WI *Format:* News, News/Talk, 86 *Special Programming:* Farm 5 hrs wkly *No. News Employees:* 4 *Target Audience:* 30 plus.
D.E. Wright, President
Shelley LuKasik, General Sales Mgr
Jerry Bader, Programming Director
Aaron Vorass, Promotions Manager
Daniell Binna, News Director
Tim Laes, Chief Engineer
Gary Tesch, Executive Vice President
MikeAustin, Farm Director

***WHID**
04-01-1997; 88.1 mhz FM *Hrs Open:* 24; 17 kw; 1014 ft.; N44 21 32 W87 59 7
1220 Linden Drive, Madison, WI 53706 US
(920) 465-2444, *Fax:* (920) 465-2576
www.wpr.org
nalbandian@wpr.org
License: Green Bay, Brown County, WI held by Board of Regents of University of Wisconsin Systems.
Nat'l Network: NPR; PRI
Arbitron Metro Market: Green Bay, WI *Format:* Talk *Special Programming:* Hmong Public Radio, 2 hrs wkly *Hrs. of News Programming:* news progmg 18 hrs wkly *No. News Employees:* 1 *Target Audience:* 35 plus;socially active, life-long learners *Adv. Rates:* 45; 30; 40; 25
Lisa Nalbandian, General Sales Mgr
Patty Murray, News Director

WIXX
11-01-1960; 101.1 mhz FM; 96 kw; 1079 ft.; N44 24 35 W88 0 5
Mailing Address: 904 Grand Ave., Wausau, WI 54403 US
Second Address: 115 South Jefferson St., Green Bay, WI 54301
(414) 435-3771, *Fax:* (414) 455-1155
www.wixx.com
License: Green Bay, Brown County, WI
Group Owner: Midwest Communications Inc.
Arbitron Metro Market: Green Bay, WI *Format:* Contemporary Hits/Top 40
Mary Wright, General Sales Mgr
Jeff McCarthy, Programming Director
Tony Wailckus, Programming Director

WNFL
12-12-1947; 1440 khz AM *Hrs Open:* 24; 5 kw-D, DA2; 0.5 kw-N, DA2; N44 28 40 W88 0 0
Mailing Address: 904 Grand Avenue, Wausau, WI 54403 US
Second Address: Box 23333, Green Bay, WI 54305
(920) 435-3771, *Fax:* (920) 321-2300
www.wnflam.com
License: Green Bay, WI held by Midwest Communications Inc.
Group Owner: Midwest Communications Inc.; acq 12-10-96; grpsl).
Nat'l Network: Fox Sports; Westwood One *Nat'l Reps:* Christal
Wire Services: AP
Arbitron Metro Market: Green Bay, WI *Format:* Sports *Hrs. of News Programming:* news progmg 10 hrs wkly *No. News Employees:* 4 *Target Audience:* 35-64; people in upper-income level with above average education
Duke Wright, President
Shelley Lukasik, General Sales Mgr
Mark Daniels, Programming Director
Jerry Bader, News Director
Tim Laes, Chief Engineer
Gary Tesch, Executive Vice President

***WORQ**
02-01-1994; 90.1 mhz FM; 11 kw; 646 ft.; N44 21 32 W87 59 7
1075 Brookwood Drive, Green Bay, WI 54304 US
(920) 494-9010, *Fax:* (920) 494-7602
www.q90fm.com
email@q90fm.com
License: Green Bay, Brown County, WI held by Lakeshore Communications Inc.
Nat'l Network: USA
Arbitron Metro Market: Green Bay, WI *TV Affiliate:* Relg *Special Programming:* News progmg 7 hrs wkly *No. News Employees:* 30; & under, rock and rol *Adv. Rates:* 9; 9; 7; 5

***WPNE-FM**
01-15-1973; 89.3 mhz FM *Hrs Open:* 24; 100 kw; 940 ft; N44 24 35 W88 00 05
2420 Nicolet Dr., Green Bay, WI 54311-7001
(920) 465-2444, *Fax:* (920) 465-2576
www.wpr.org
License: Green Bay, Brown County, WI held by State of Wisconsin Educational Communications Board.
Nat'l Network: NPR; PRI
Population Served: 300,000 *Arbitron Metro Market:* Green Bay, WI *Format:* Classical, News *Special Programming:* Jazz 10 hrs, folk 3 hrs, Native American 2 hrs, blues 2 hrs, experimental 2 hrs, wkly *Hrs. of NewsProgramming:* news progmg 29 hrs wkly *No. News Employees:* 2 *Target Audience:* 35 plus; socially aware, artistically stimulated *Adv. Rates:* 55; 40; 50; 35
Lisa Nalbandian, General Sales Mgr
Patty Murray, News Director

WQLH
07-01-1967; 98.5 mhz FM; 100 kw; 499 ft.; N44 38 41 W88 8 13
810 Victoria, Green Bay, WI 54301 US
(920) 468-4100, *Fax:* (920) 468-0250
www.star98.net
jimmy.clark@cumulus.com
License: Green Bay, Brown County, WI held by Citicasters Licenses Inc.
Group Owner: Clear Channel Communications Inc.; (acq 4-10-2009; grpsl)
Nat'l Reps: Katz Radio
Arbitron Metro Market: Green Bay, WI *Format:* Adult Contemp *Target Audience:* Adults 25-54. *Adv. Rates:* 110; 110; 110; 25.
Greg Jessen, Operations Dir
Buck Hein, General Sales Mgr
Mark Heller, Chief Engineer
Jimmy Clark, Operations Manager
Brian Stenzel, Promotions Director

Greenfield

WMCS
04-27-1947; 1290 khz AM *Hrs Open:* 24; 5 kw-D, DA2; 5 kw-N, DA2; N42 55 11 W87 59 17
Mailing Address: 2979 North Mayfair Road, Milwaukee, WI 53222 US
Second Address: N72 W12922 Good Hope Road, Menomonee Falls, WI 53051
(414) 444-1290, *Fax:* (414) 444-1409
www.1290wmcs.com
cspinks@1290wmcs.com
License: Greenfield, WI held by Milwaukee Radio Alliance L.L.C.
Group Owner: Milwaukee Radio Alliance L.L.C.; (acq 9-23-97; grpsl)
Arbitron Metro Market: Milwaukee, WI *Format:* Talk *Special Programming:* Blues 6 hrs, gospel 5 hrs, Sp 5 hrs, church 3.25 h *Hrs. of News Programming:* news progmg 7 hrs wkly *No. News Employees:* 1 *TargetAudience:* 25-54; upwardly mobile Blacks *Adv. Rates:* 31; 21; 21; 17
Tyrene Jackson, Operations Dir
Robbie Fulton, General Sales Mgr
John Church, Chief Engineer

Hallie

WOGO
06-01-1985; 680 khz AM; 2.5 kw-D, DA2; 0.5 kw-N, DA2; N44 53 22 W91 23 3
2396 St Hwy 53, Suite 1, Chippewa Falls, WI 54729 US
(715) 723-1037, *Fax:* (715) 723-1348
www.wwib.com
wwib@wwib.com
License: Hallie, WI held by Stewards of Sound Inc.
Nat'l Network: USA
Arbitron Metro Market: Eau Claire, WI *TV Affiliate:* Talk *Special Programming:* news progmg 16 hrs wkly *Hrs. of News Programming:* 1 *No. News Employees:* 25-54.
General Manager, General Manager
Program Director, Programming Director

WWIB
12-30-1972; 103.7 mhz FM *Hrs Open:* 24; 100 kw; 679 ft.; N45 6 7 W91 9 33
2396 St Hwy 53, Suite 1, Chippewa Falls, WI 54729 US
(715) 723-1037, *Fax:* (715) 723-1348
www.wwib.com
wwib@wwib.com
License: Hallie, Chippewa County, WI held by Stewards of Sound Inc.
Nat'l Network: USA
Arbitron Metro Market: Hallie, WI *Format:* Christian *Hrs. of News Programming:* news progmg 16 hrs wkly *No. News Employees:* 1 *Target Audience:* 25-54.
Terri Steward, General Manager
Steven Slater, General Sales Mgr
Greg Steward, Programming Director
Pat Wahl, News Director
Mark Halvorsen, News Contact
Steve Flater, Advertising Sales Manager
Dave Staszcuk, AdvertisingSales
Molly Lee, Traffic Manager
Sue Steward, Accounting

Hartford

WTKM
01-01-1951; 1540 khz AM *Hrs Open:* Sunrise-sunset; 500 w-D; N43 16 48 W88 23 02
Mailing Address: Box 270526, Hartford, WI 53027
Second Address: 27 N. Main St., Hartford, WI 53027
(262) 673-7500
wtkm@nconnect.com
License: Hartford, Washington County, WI held by Tomsun Media LLC
Regional Network: Agrinet *Nat'l Reps:* Farmakis

Arbitron Metro Market: Milwaukee-Racin *Adv. Rates:* same as FM
David M. Stout, General Manager
Connie Stout, General Sales Mgr
Susan Tupper, Promotions Manager
Richard Feutz, Engineering Dir

WTKM-FM
10-01-1973; 104.9 mhz FM *Hrs Open:* 24; 5.8 kw; Ant 300 ft; N43 16 48 W88 23 02
Box 270526, Hartford, WI 53207
(262) 673-7800, *Fax:* (262) 673-5472
www.wtkm.com
wtkm@nconnect.net
License: Hartford, Washington County, WI held by Tomsun Media LLC
Wire Services: AP
Population Served: 1,500,000 *Arbitron Metro Market:* Milwaukee-Racin *Hrs. of News Programming:* news progmg 20 hrs wkly *No. News Employees:* 2 *Target Audience:* 35 plus.
Adv. Rates: 30; 30; 30; 25
David M. Stout, President
David M. Stout, General Manager
Connie Stout, General Sales Mgr
Susan Tupper, Promotions Manager
Richard Feutz, Engineering Dir

Hayward

WHSM
12-21-1957; 910 khz AM *Hrs Open:* 24; 5 kw-D, 75 w-N; N45 59 07 W91 32 21
16880 W. US Hwy. 63, Hayward, WI 55720
(715) 634-4836, *Fax:* (715) 634-8256
www.whsm.com
radio@whsm.com
License: Hayward, Sawyer County, WI held by Red Rock Radio Corp.
Group Owner: Red Rock Radio Corp.; (acq 9-1-2006; grpsl)
Nat'l Network: Dial Global
Population Served: 40,000 *Arbitron Metro Market:* Duluth/Superior *Hrs. of News Programming:* news progmg 2 hrs wkly *No. News Employees:* 1 *Target Audience:* 34-70.
Ro Grignon, President
Jon DeTray, News Director
Brent Christenson, Chief Engineer
Don Welch, Executive Vice President
Bobi Hopp, Operations Manager

WHSM-FM
06-21-1980; 101.1 mhz FM *Hrs Open:* 24; 1.45 kw; Ant 410 ft; N45 59 07 W91 32 23
16880 W. US Hwy. 63, Hayward, WI 55720
(715) 634-4836, *Fax:* (715) 634-8256
www.whsm.com
radio@whsm.com
License: Hayward, Sawyer County, WI held by Red Rock Radio Corp.
Group Owner: Red Rock Radio Corp.; (acq 9-1-2006; grpsl)
Nat'l Network: Dial Global
Arbitron Metro Market: Duluth/Superior *No. News Employees:* 1 *Target Audience:* 24-60.
Ro Grignon, President
Don Welch, General Manager
Jon DeTray, News Director
Brent Christensen, Chief Engineer
Bobi Hopp, Operations Manager

WRLS-FM
04-16-1968; 92.3 mhz FM *Hrs Open:* 24; 6 kw; 322 ft.; N46 1 14 W91 30 41
P.O. Box 1008, Hayward, WI 54843 US
(715) 634-4871, *Fax:* (715) 634-3025
www.wrlsfm.com
wrls@cheqnet.net
License: Hayward, Sawyer County, WI held by Vacationland Broadcasting Inc.
Nat'l Network: CNN Radio; AP Radio *Regional Network:* Wisconsin Radio Net. *Wire Services:* AP
Format: Adult Contemp *Hrs. of News Programming:* news progrmg 10 hrs wkly *No. News Employees:* 1 *Target Audience:* 25 plus; general
Tom Koser, President
Robert Koser, Operations Dir
Steve Kaner, General Manager
Grant Turpin, Operations Manager

Highland

***WHHI**
09-14-1952; 91.3 mhz FM *Hrs Open:* 24; 100 kw; 559 ft.; N43 2 55.6 W90 22 7.5 *Rebroadcasts:* Rebroadcasts WHA(AM) Madison 100%
3319 W. Beltline Hwy., Madison, WI 53713 US
(608) 263-3970, *Fax:* (608) 263-9763
www.wpr.org
schnirring@wpr.org
License: Highland, Iowa County, WI held by State of Wisconsin Educational Communications Board.
Nat'l Network: NPR; PRI
Format: News, News/Talk, 86 *No. News Employees:* 9 *Target Audience:* 35-54; Skews female: issue oriented talk-variety of perspectives
Phil Corriveau, General Manager
Mary Sherer, General Sales Mgr
Steve Jorhnston, Chief Engineer

Holmen

WKBH
07-28-1984; 1570 khz AM *Hrs Open:* 24; 1 kw-D, ND1; 0.36 kw-N, ND1; N43 55 32 W91 16 2
1407 2nd Avenue North, Onalaska, WI 54602 US
(608) 779-4418, *Fax:* (608) 779-4419
www.relevantradio.com
WKBH@relevantradio.com
License: Holmen, WI held by Starboard Media Foundation Inc.
Group Owner: Relevant Radio; (acq 1-17-2003; $210,000).
Format: Talk, Christian *Hrs. of News Programming:* news progmg 35 hrs wkly *No. News Employees:* 1 *Target Audience:* 40 plus; those interested in Catholic news, talk & opinion
Mike Strub, Operations Dir
Jim DeSchepper, Station Manager

Hudson

WDGY
12-14-1983; 740 khz AM *Hrs Open:* 6 AM-7 PM
P.O. Box 25130, St. Paul, MN 55125 US
(651) 436-4000, *Fax:* (651) 436-6770
www.wdgyradio.com
License: Hudson, WI held by WRPX Inc.
Arbitron Metro Market: Minneapolis, MN *Format:* Oldies *Target Audience:* 25-54.
Gregory Borgen, President
Jeff Borgen, General Sales Mgr
Tom Witschen, Programming Director
Paul Orth, Chief Engineer

Hurley

WHRY
03-01-1985; 1450 khz AM; 1 kw-U, ND1; N46 24 56 W90 9 34
209 Harrison Street, Ironwood, MI 49938 US
(906) 932-5234, *Fax:* (906) 932-1548
www.wupm-whry.com
License: Hurley, WI held by Big G Little O Inc.
Format: Oldies
Charles Gervasio, President
Norma Rigoni, Operations Dir
Laura Keller, Programming Director

Iron River

WNXR
11-01-1994; 107.3 mhz FM; 21 kw; 361 ft.; N46 32 49 W91 24 50
P.O. Box 10, Iron River, WI 54847 US
(715) 372-5400, *Fax:* (715) 682-9338
www.wnxrfm.com
productionash@charter.net
License: Iron River, Bayfield County, WI held by Heartland Communications License LLC.
Group Owner: Heartland Communications Group LLC; (acq 4-23-2004; grpsl).
Nat'l Network: Westwood One
Arbitron Metro Market: Duluth-Superior *TV Affiliate:* Hits of the 50s, 60s & 70s

Jackson

WAUK
05-01-1964; 540 khz AM *Hrs Open:* 24
8910 University Center Lane, #130, San Diego, CA 92122 US
(414) 273-3776, *Fax:* (414) 291-3776
www.espnmilwaukee.com
www.wauksportsradio@msn.com
License: Jackson, WI held by Good Karma Broadcasting LLC.
Group Owner: Good Karma Broadcasting L.L.C.; (acq 3-28-2008; $3.8 million)
Nat'l Network: ESPN Radio
Arbitron Metro Market: Milwaukee-Racin *Format:* Sports *Adv. Rates:* 28; 28; 28; 24
Craig Karmazin, General Manager

Janesville

WCLO
07-01-1930; 1230 khz AM *Hrs Open:* 24; 1 kw-U, ND1; N42 39 35 W89 2 32
Mailing Address: Box 5001, One South Parker Dr., Janesville, WI 53547 US
Second Address: One S. Parker Dr., Janesville, WI 53545
(608) 752-7895, *Fax:* (608) 752-4438
www.wclo.com
programming@wclo.com
License: Janesville, WI held by Southern Wisconsin Broadcasting L.L.C.
Group Owner: Bliss Communications Inc.
Nat'l Network: CNN Radio; Talk Radio Network; Premiere Radio Networks; Westwood One *Regional Network:* Brownfield; Wisconsin Radio Net.
Arbitron Metro Market: Janesville, WI *Format:* News, News/Talk, 86 *Hrs. of News Programming:* news progmg 9 hrs wkly *No. News Employees:* 3 *Target Audience:* 30+ years
Robert Dailey, Operations Dir
Mike O'Brien, General Manager
Tim Bremel, Programming Director

WJVL
10-01-1947; 99.9 mhz FM; 11 kw; 502 ft.; N42 43 47 W89 10 10
Mailing Address: 1 S. Parker Dr.,Box 5001, Janesville, WI 53545 US
Second Address: One S. Parker Dr., Janesville, WI 53545
(608) 752-7895, *Fax:* (608) 752-4438
www.wjvl.com
tbremel@wclo.com
License: Janesville, Rock County, WI
Format: Country *Target Audience:* 25 plus.
Tim Bremel, Operations Dir
Mike O'Brien, General Sales Mgr
Ken Scott, Programming Director
Tim Bremel, Promotions Manager
Stan Stricker, News Director
Rob West, Assistant Program Director
Ken Scott, Music Director
Al Fagerli,Sports Director

Kaukauna

WJOK
09-25-1965; 1050 khz AM *Hrs Open:* 24; 1 kw-D, DA2; 0.5 kw-N, DA2; N44 14 51 W88 18 0
1296 Marian Lane, Green Bay, WI 54304 US
(920) 469-3021, *Fax:* (920) 469-3023
www.1050am.org
License: Kaukauna, WI held by Starboard Media Foundation Inc.
Group Owner: Relevant Radio; (acq 8-28-2001; $500,000).
Nat'l Network: USA; Moody
Arbitron Metro Market: Appleton-Oshkosh, WI *Format:* Christian
Special Programming: Relg 2 hrs wkly *Target Audience:* 35-54.
Adv. Rates: 11; 11; 11; 11
Dave Nier, General Manager

WOGB
01-01-1996; 103.1 mhz FM; 3.6 kw; 879 ft.; N44 21 32 W87 59 7
111 East Kilbourn Avenue, Suite 2700, Milwaukee, WI 53202 US
(920) 468-4100, *Fax:* (920) 468-0250
www.wogb.fm
wogb@cumulus.com
License: Kaukauna, Outagamie County, WI held by Jacor Broadcasting Corp.
Group Owner: Clear Channel Communications Inc.; (acq 4-10-2009; grpsl)
Nat'l Reps: Katz Radio *Wire Services:* AP
Arbitron Metro Market: Appleton-Oshkos *TV Affiliate:* classic hits
No. News Employees: 35-54; affluent baby-boom *Adv. Rates:* 90; 90; 90; 25
Operations Manager

Kenosha

***WGTD**
12-23-1975; 91.1 mhz FM; 3.2 kw; 203 ft.; N42 36 32 W87 50 56
3520 - 30th Avenue, Kenosha, WI 53140 US
(262) 564-3800, *Fax:* (262) 564-3801
wgtd.org
coled@gtc.edu
License: Kenosha, Kenosha County, WI held by Gateway Technical College.
Nat'l Network: NPR *Regional Network:* Wis. Public Radio *Wire Services:* AP

Format: Classical, News *Special Programming:* Ger one hr wkly *No. News Employees:* 2 *Target Audience:* General.
David Cole, General Manager

WLIP
05-11-1947; 1050 khz AM *Hrs Open:* 24; 0.25 kw-D, ND1; 0.25 kw-N, ND1; N42 33 10 W87 53 38
8800 Route 14, Crystal Lake, IL 60012 US
(262) 694-7800, *Fax:* (262) 694-7767
www.wlip.com
info@wlip.com
License: Kenosha, WI held by NM Licensing LLC.
Group Owner: NextMedia Group Inc.; (acq 11-26-00; grpsl).
Regional Network: Wisconsin Radio Net.
Arbitron Metro Market: Chicago, IL *Format:* Talk *No. News Employees:* 2 *Target Audience:* 35 plus.
John Perry, Operations Dir
Kara Lafond, General Manager
Rory Fraley, General Sales Mgr
Stewart Wattles, News Director
Lisa Sladek, Traffic Manager

Kewaunee

WAUN-FM
01-01-1973; 92.7 mhz FM *Hrs Open:* 5 AM-10 PM; 6 kw; 328 ft.; N44 29 50 W87 35 12
1021 North Superior Ave., Suite 205, Tomah, WI 54660 US
(920) 388-9286, *Fax:* (920) 743-9183
info@waun.com
License: Kewaunee, Kewaunee County, WI held by Magnum Broadcasting Inc.
Wire Services: AP
Arbitron Metro Market: Durango, CO *Format:* Jazz, Smooth Jazz *Special Programming:* Czech one hr, farm 10 hrs, relg 3 hrs wkly *Hrs. of News Programming:* news progmg 15 hrs wkly *No. News Employees:* 1 *TargetAudience:* 25-54.
Dave Magnum, President
Rick Jensen, Operations Dir
Frank Devillers, General Manager
Debbie Doyle, News Director

Kiel

***WSTM**
91.3 mhz FM; 1.1 kw; 473 ft.; N43 43 23 W88 3 51.7
N5569 State Rd 57, Plymouth, WI 53073 US
(920) 893-2661, *Fax:* (920) 892-2706
www.wstmfm.org
wstm@jmiradio.org
License: Kiel, Manitowoc County, WI held by Jubilation Ministries Inc.
Arbitron Metro Market: Kiel, WI *Format:* Christian
Rachel Knight & Darcie Laack, Operations Coordinators
Bill Horsch, General Manager
Susan Noordyk, Programming Director
Dave Hendrickson, News Director
Suzy Noordyk, Director of FM Operations
Christopher Holycross, AccountExecutive

Kimberly

WHBY
12-01-1925; 1150 khz AM *Hrs Open:* 24
Mailing Address: 2306 West Badger Road, Madison, WI 53713 US
Second Address: 2800 E. College Ave., Appleton, WI 54915
(920) 733-6639, *Fax:* (920) 739-0494
www.whby.com
whby@wcinet.com
License: Kimberly, WI held by Woodward Communications Inc.
Group Owner: Woodward Communications Inc.; (acq 3-75).
Regional Network: Wisconsin Radio Net. *Nat'l Reps:* McGavren Guild *Wire Services:* AP
Arbitron Metro Market: Appleton-Oshkosh, WI *Format:* News, News/Talk, 86 *Hrs. of News Programming:* news progmg 25 hrs wkly *No. News Employees:* 3 *Target Audience:* 35 plus; upper middle class, educated
Greg Bell, General Manager
John Wanie, Station Manager
Mary Ann Drewek, General Sales Mgr
Dave Edwards, Programming Director
Steve Brown, Chief Engineer

La Crosse

***WHLA**
11-21-1950; 90.3 mhz FM *Hrs Open:* 24; 97 kw; 1007 ft.; N43 48 17 W91 22 6 *Rebroadcasts:* Rebroadcasts WHA(AM) Madison 95%
3319 W. Beltline Hwy., Madison, WI 53713 US
(608) 785-8380, *Fax:* (608) 785-5005
www.wpr.org/whla
listener@wpr.org
License: La Crosse, La Crosse County, WI held by State of Wis. Educational Communications Board.
Nat'l Network: NPR; PRI *Wire Services:* AP
Format: Talk *No. News Employees:* 3 *Target Audience:* 35-54; skews female: issue oriented talk-var of perspectives
John Gaddo, General Manager
Marv Spielman, General Sales Mgr
Sheryl Gasser, Programming Director
John Davis, News Director
Steve Bauder, Chief Engineer

WIZM
01-02-1923; 1410 khz AM *Hrs Open:* 24
PO Box 99, Lacrosse, WI 54602 US
(608) 782-1230, *Fax:* (608) 782-1170
www.1410wizm.com
License: La Crosse, WI held by Family Radio Inc.
Group Owner: The Mid-West Family Broadcast Group; (acq 7-12-71; $500,000)
Nat'l Network: Westwood One; CBS *Nat'l Reps:* Christal *Wire Services:* AP
Format: News, News/Talk, 84, Talk *Special Programming:* Asian 2 hrs wkly *Hrs. of News Programming:* news progmg 18 hrs wkly *No. News Employees:* 5 *Target Audience:* 35 plus. *Adv. Rates:* 49; 44; 45; 32
Dick Record, President
Keith Carr, Operations Dir
Howard Gloede, General Sales Mgr
Scott Robert Shaw, Programming Director
Mike Hayes, Promotions Manager
Chris O'Hearn, Chief Engineer
Theresa Timm, General Sales Manager
PeggySchelbe, Traffic Manager
Mike Hayes, Disc Jockey
Brad Williams, News Reporter

WIZM-FM
01-01-1966; 93.3 mhz FM *Hrs Open:* 24; 100 kw; 1020 ft.; N43 48 23 W91 22 4
Mailing Address: P.O. Box 99, 432 Cass Street, Lacrosse, WI 54602 US
Second Address: 201 State St., La Crosse, WI 54601-3246
(608) 782-1230, *Fax:* (608) 782-1170
www.1410wizm.com
License: La Crosse, La Crosse County, WI held by Family Radio Inc.
Group Owner: The Mid-West Family Broadcast Group; (acq 6-15-76)
Wire Services: AP
Format: Contemporary Hits/Top 40 *Hrs. of News Programming:* news progmg 2 hrs wkly *No. News Employees:* 5 *Target Audience:* 18-49. *Adv. Rates:* 102; 92; 94; 78
Jen O'Brien, Programming Director
Peggy Schelbe, News Director
Brittany Styles, Disc Jockey
Scott Robert Shaw, Local News Editor
Brad Williams, News Reporter
Mitch Reynolds, Reporter

WKTY
05-01-1948; 580 khz AM *Hrs Open:* 24; 5 kw-D, DA2; 0.74 kw-N, DA2; N43 44 25 W91 12 21
PO Box 99, 432 Cass Street, Lacrosse, WI 54602 US
(608) 782-1230, *Fax:* (608) 782-1170
midwestfamilybroadcasting.com
dickr@mwfbroadcasting.com
License: La Crosse, WI held by Family Radio Inc.
Group Owner: The Mid-West Family Broadcast Group; (acq 1996; $1.3 million)
Nat'l Network: ABC *Nat'l Reps:* Christal *Wire Services:* AP
Format: Sports, Talk *Special Programming:* Farm 5 hrs wkly *Hrs. of News Programming:* news progmg 18 hrs wkly *No. News Employees:* 5 *Target Audience:* 25-54. *Adv. Rates:* 45; 43; 44; 37
Dick Record, President
Keith Carr, Operations Dir
Howard Gloede, General Sales Mgr
Scott Robert Shaw, Programming Director
Mike Kearns, Promotions Manager
Chris O'Hearn, Chief Engineer
Theresa Timm, General Sales Manager
PeggySchelbe, Traffic Manager

WLFN
05-01-1947; 1490 khz AM *Hrs Open:* 24; 1 kw-U, ND1; N43 49 42 W91 14 27
Mailing Address: P.O. Box 2017, La Crosse, WI 54602 US
Second Address: 1407 Second Ave. N., Onalaska, WI 54650
(608) 782-8335, *Fax:* (608) 782-8340
www.1490wlfn.com
License: La Crosse, WI held by Mississippi Valley Broadcasters L.L.C.
Group Owner: La Crosse Radio Group
Format: Contemporary Hits/Top 40 *Hrs. of News Programming:* news progmg 5 hrs wkly *No. News Employees:* 1 *Target Audience:* 35 plus.
Pat Smith, General Manager
Mike Schmitz, General Sales Mgr
Pete Schreier, Programming Director
Lucy Lemar, News Director
Patrick Delaney, Chief Engineer
Laurie Lane, Traffic Manager

***WLSU**
01-04-1971; 88.9 mhz FM *Hrs Open:* 24; 8.2 kw; 928 ft.; N43 48 17 W91 22 6
1220 Linden Drive, Madison, WI 53706 US
(608) 785-8380, *Fax:* (608) 785-5005
www.wpr.org/wlsu
Listener@wpr.org
License: La Crosse, La Crosse County, WI held by University of Wisconsin System.
Nat'l Network: NPR; PRI *Wire Services:* AP
Arbitron Metro Market: La Crosse, WI *Format:* Jazz, News *Hrs. of News Programming:* news progmg 40 hrs wkly *No. News Employees:* 3 *Target Audience:* General.
Tim Allen, Operations Dir
John Gaddo, General Manager
Marvin Spielman, General Sales Mgr
Michael Leland, News Director
Steve Johnston, Engineering Dir

WLXR-FM
03-01-1975; 104.9 mhz FM; 0.8 kw; 659 ft.; N43 43 17 W91 17 24
Mailing Address: 201 Main Street, Suite 400, Lacrosse, WI 54601 US
Second Address: 1407 Second Ave. N., La Crosse, WI 54650
(608) 782-8335, *Fax:* (608) 782-8340
www.wlxr.com
License: La Crosse, La Crosse County, WI
Group Owner: La Crosse Radio Group
Arbitron Metro Market: La Crosse, WI *Format:* Adult Contemp *Target Audience:* 18-49.
Debbie Brague, Programming Director

WQCC
03-31-1994; 106.3 mhz FM *Hrs Open:* 24; 18 kw; 387 ft.; N43 51 2 W91 12 8
201 Main St., Suite 400, La Crosse, WI 54601 US
(608) 782-1063,(608) 782-8335, *Fax:* (608) 779-5945
wlxr/wqcc@aol.com
License: La Crosse, La Crosse County, WI held by Mississippi Valley Broadcasters L.L.C.
Group Owner: La Crosse Radio Group; (acq 12-31-96).
Format: Country
Pat Smith, General Manager
Mike Schmitz, General Sales Mgr
John Stevenson, Programming Director
Lucy Lemar, News Director
Patrick Delaney, Chief Engineer

WRQT
01-01-1972; 95.7 mhz FM; 50 kw; 492 ft.; N43 37 57 W91 17 6
704 La Crosse Street, La Crosse, WI 54601 US
(608) 782-1230, *Fax:* (608) 782-1170
License: La Crosse, La Crosse County, WI held by Family Radio Inc.
Group Owner: The Mid-West Family Broadcast Group; (acq 1996)
Format: Rock/AOR *Hrs. of News Programming:* News progmg 5 hrs wkly *Target Audience:* 18-49. *Adv. Rates:* 50; 45; 48; 41
Jean Taylor, Programming Director
Peggy Schelbe, News Director
Scott Robert Shaw, News Director
Brad Williams, News Reporter
Bill Black, Reporter

Ladysmith

WJBL
10-01-1984; 93.1 mhz FM *Hrs Open:* 24; 4.9 kw; 358 ft.; N45 27 59 W91 7 23
Mailing Address: P. O. Box 351, Ladysmith, WI 54848 US
Second Address: W8746 Hwy. 8, Ladysmith, WI 54848
(715) 532-5588, *Fax:* (715) 532-7357
wldy@centurytel.net
License: Ladysmith, Rusk County, WI
Nat'l Network: ABC

RADIO - U.S.

Format: Oldies *Hrs. of News Programming:* news progmg 10 hrs wkly *No. News Employees:* 1 *Target Audience:* 25-54.
Robert Krejcarek, General Sales Mgr
Sandy Zajec, Programming Director
Tom Costello, News Director

WLDY
09-01-1948; 1340 khz AM *Hrs Open:* 24; 1 kw-U, ND1; N45 27 59 W91 7 23
Mailing Address: W 8746 Highway 8, Ladysmith, WI 54848 US
Second Address: W8746 Hwy. 8, Ladysmith, WI 54848
(715) 532-5588, *Fax:* (715) 532-7357
wldy@centurytel.net
License: Ladysmith, WI held by Roth Broadcasting Inc.
Nat'l Network: ABC *Wire Services:* UPI
Format: Country, News, 62, Talk *Special Programming:* Polka 3 hrs wkly *Hrs. of News Programming:* news progmg 15 hrs wkly
No. News Employees: 1 *Target Audience:* 35 plus; mature audience *Adv. Rates:* 10;10; 10; 2
Sandra Roth, President
David Roth, General Sales Mgr
Jocelyn Kilmer, Programming Director
Tom Costello, News Director
Del Dayton, Chief Engineer
Robert Krejcarek, Farm Director
Judi Novak, Traffic Manager

Lake Geneva

WLKG
06-06-1994; 96.1 mhz FM *Hrs Open:* 24; 6 kw; 328 ft.; N42 36 34 W88 26 36
500 Interchange North, Box 9610, Lake Geneva, WI 53147 US
(262) 249-9600, *Fax:* (262) 249-9630
www.wlkg.com
lake96@wlkg.com
License: Lake Geneva, Walworth County, WI held by CTJ Communications Ltd.
Format: Adult Contemp *Special Programming:* Hits of the 70s 10 hrs, sports 2 hrs wkly *Hrs. of News Programming:* News progmg 15 hrs wkly *Target Audience:* 25-54; mainly female
Tom Kwiatkowski, President
Barb Kwiatkowski, Operations Dir
Nancy Douglass, General Manager

Lancaster

WGLR
09-09-1977; 1280 khz AM; 500 w-D; N42 50 22 W90 40 19
51 Means Drive, Platteville, WI 53744
(608) 349-2000, *Fax:* (608) 349-2002
License: Lancaster, Grant County, WI held by QueenB Radio Wisconsin Inc.
Group Owner: Morgan Murphy Media (Evening Telegram Co); (acq 3-18-98; $1.66 million with co
Nat'l Network: ESPN; Agri-Talk
Arbitron Metro Market: Dubuque, IA *Special Programming:* 5 hrs wkly
Doug Wagen, Operations Dir
Danny Sullivan, General Manager
Rick Sanson, General Sales Mgr
Doug Wagen, Programming Director

WGLR-FM
09-09-1982; 97.7 mhz FM *Hrs Open:* 24; 11.5 kw; 482 ft.; N42 51 48 W90 42 11
7025 Raymond Road, Madison, WI 53744 US
(608) 349-2000, *Fax:* (608) 349-2002
www.wglr.com
wglrsales@queenbradio.com
License: Lancaster, Grant County, WI held by QueenB Radio Wisconsin Inc.
Group Owner: Morgan Murphy Media (Evening Telegram Co); (acq 1998)
Nat'l Network: ABC; Premiere Radio Networks *Regional Network:* Radio Iowa; Wisconsin Radio Net. *Regional Reps:* Local Focus
Arbitron Metro Market: Dubuque, IA *Format:* Country *Special Programming:* News, Sports and Agriculture *Hrs. of News Programming:* News prgmg 2 hrs per day *Target Audience:* 25-64. *Adv. Rates:* 25; 20; 25;15
Rob Spangler, Programming Director

***WJTY**
03-12-1983; 88.1 mhz FM *Hrs Open:* 24; 7 kw horiz, 50 kw vert; 476 ft.; N42 57 8 W90 25 47
341 S. Washington Street, Lancaster, WI 53813 US
(608) 723-7888, *Fax:* (608) 723-4557
www.wjty.org
info@wjty.org
License: Lancaster, Grant County, WI held by Family Life Broadcasting Inc.
Group Owner: Family Life Communications Inc.; (acq 5-23-2007; grpsl)
Nat'l Network: Moody; USA
Arbitron Metro Market: Dubuque, IA *Format:* Adult Contemp, Religious *Hrs. of News Programming:* news progmg 11 hrs wkly
No. News Employees: 1 *Target Audience:* 30-90; families
Tom Bush, General Manager
Dennis Baldridge, Chief Engineer

Lomira

WFDL-FM
04-01-1993; 97.7 mhz FM *Hrs Open:* 24; 17.5 kw; 400 ft.; N43 39 14 W88 26 25
210 South Main Street, Fond Du Lac, WI 54935 US
(920) 924-9697, *Fax:* (920) 929-8865
www.wfdl.com
info@sunny97-7.com
License: Lomira, Dodge County, WI held by Radio Plus of Fond du Lac Inc.
Arbitron Metro Market: Fond du Lac, WI *Format:* Adult Contemp
No. News Employees: 1 *Target Audience:* 25-54. *Adv. Rates:* 25; 20; 22; 15
Chris Bernier, President
Terry Davis, Operations Dir
Keith Heisler, Programming Director
Kimberly King, Promotions Manager
Greg Stensland, News Director
Mike Enfelt, Operations Manager
Kerry Longrie, Traffic Manager
PaulMillard, Assistant Web Master and Project Manager
Terry Davis, Sales and Advertising

Madison

***WERN**
03-30-1947; 88.7 mhz FM *Hrs Open:* 24; 20.5 kw; 1263 ft.; N43 3 21 W89 32 6
3319 West Beltline Hwy., Madison, WI 53713 US
(800) 747-7444, *Fax:* (847) 888-0272
www.wpr.org
Listener@wpr.org
License: Madison, Dane County, WI held by State of Wisconsin Educational Communications Board.
Nat'l Network: NPR; PRI *Regional Network:* Wis. Public Radio
Arbitron Metro Market: Madison, WI *Format:* Classical, News
Hrs. of News Programming: news progmg 29 hrs wkly *No. News Employees:* 9 *Target Audience:* 25-64; persons seeking quality music & intellectualstimulation
Steve Johnston, Director of Engineering & Operations
Phil Corriveau, General Manager
Ben Spindler, General Sales Mgr
Anders Yokum, Programming Director
Michael Leland, News Director
Mike Crane, Director of Radio
Michael Arnold,Associate Director
Sarah Jacobs, Audience Services Manager
Jeffrey Potter, Marketing Director
Rebecca Dopart, Membership and Corporate Support
Mary Kay Dadisman, Director of Development

***WHA**
01-01-1922; 970 khz AM *Hrs Open:* 24; 5 kw-D, ND1; 0.051 kw-N, ND1; N43 2 30 W89 24 31
1220 Linden Drive, Madison, WI 53706 US
(608) 263-3970, *Fax:* (608) 263-9763
www.wpr.org
listener@wpr.org
License: Madison, WI held by Regents of University of Wisconsin System.
Nat'l Network: NPR; PRI *Regional Network:* Wis. Public Radio
Wire Services: NOAA Weather
Arbitron Metro Market: Madison, WI *TV Affiliate:* *WHA-TV affil
Format: News, Talk *No. News Employees:* 9 *Target Audience:* 35-54; male/female, educated, skews female: issue oriented talk-variety of perspectives
Tom Martin-Erickson, Operations Dir
Phil Corriveau, General Manager
Ben Spindler, General Sales Mgr
Anders Yokum, Programming Director
Vicki Nonn, Music Director

WHIT
08-14-1964; 1550 khz AM *Hrs Open:* 24
Mailing Address: P.O. Box 253, Madison, WI 53701 US
Second Address: 730 Rayovac Dr., Madison, WI 53711
(608) 273-1000, *Fax:* (608) 271-0400
www.wtux.com
License: Madison, WI held by Mid-West Management Inc.
Group Owner: The Mid-West Family Broadcast Group; (acq 8-12-97; $6.4 million with WWQM-FM Middleton)
Nat'l Network: ABC *Nat'l Reps:* McGavren Guild
Arbitron Metro Market: Madison, WI *Format:* Oldies *Target Audience:* 25-54.
Tom Walker, President
Ted Waldbillig, General Sales Mgr
Amy Ziebel, Programming Director

WIBA
04-02-1925; 1310 khz AM; 5 kw-D, DAN; 5 kw-N, DAN; N42 59 58 W89 25 47
600 Congress Ave., Suite 1400, Austin, TX 78701 US
(608) 274-5450, *Fax:* (608) 274-5521
www.wiba.com
info@wiba.com
License: Madison, WI held by Capstar TX L.P.
Group Owner: Clear Channel Communications Inc.; (acq 8-30-2000; grpsl)
Nat'l Network: CBS; Wall Street
Arbitron Metro Market: Madison, WI *Format:* News, News/Talk, 86 *Target Audience:* 25-64.
Jeff Tyler, General Manager
Kurt Peterson, General Sales Mgr
Tim Scott, Programming Director
Josh Wescott, News Director
Tim Wagner, Chief Engineer
Marta Keller, Traffic Manager

WMGN
09-01-1948; 98.1 mhz FM *Hrs Open:* 24; 36 kw; 577 ft.; N42 57 46 W89 22 47
P.O. Box 253, 2934 Fish Hatchery Rd, Madison, WI 53701 US
(608) 321-0098, *Fax:* (608) 441-0098
www.magic98.com
dj@magic98.com
License: Madison, Dane County, WI held by Mid-West Management Inc.
Group Owner: The Mid-West Family Broadcast Group
Nat'l Reps: McGavren Guild
Arbitron Metro Market: Madison, WI *Format:* Adult Contemp
Target Audience: 25-54.
Tom Walker, General Manager
Ted Waldbillig, General Sales Mgr
Pat O'Neill, Programming Director
Amy Ziebel, Assistant Programming Director

***WNWC-FM**
04-30-1959; 102.5 mhz FM; 50 kw; 492 ft.; N43 2 8 W89 30 25
3003 North Snelling Ave., St. Paul, MN 55113 US
(608) 271-1025, *Fax:* (608) 271-1150
www.life1025.com
wnwc@nwc.edu
License: Madison, Dane County, WI held by Northwestern College.
Group Owner: Northwestern College & Radio; (acq 1-19-73).
Nat'l Network: AP Radio *Wire Services:* AP
Arbitron Metro Market: Madison, WI *TV Affiliate:* Contemp Christian Music *Special Programming:* news progmg 20 hrs wkly
Hrs. of News Programming: 1 *No. News Employees:* 35-45.

***WORT**
12-01-1975; 89.9 mhz FM; 2 kw; 938 ft.; N43 3 3 W89 29 13
118 South Bedford Street, Madison, WI 53703 US
(608) 256-2695, *Fax:* (608) 256-3704
www.wort-fm.org
wort@wort-fm.org
License: Madison, Dane County, WI held by Back Porch Radio Broadcasting Inc.
Arbitron Metro Market: Madison, WI *TV Affiliate:* Div, class
Format: Jazz, Spanish *Special Programming:* news progmg 20 hrs wkly *Hrs. of News Programming:* 1 *No. News Employees:* all *Adv. Rates:* non-comm - underwriting
Operations Coordinator, Operations Dir

***WSUM**
01-01-2003; 91.7 mhz FM *Hrs Open:* 24; 5.5 kw; 338 ft.; N42 54 16 W89 33 20
1220 Linden Drive, Madison, WI 53706 US
(608) 262-1864
www.wsum.org
License: Madison, Dane County, WI held by Board of Regents of the University of Wisconsin.
Arbitron Metro Market: Madison, WI
Dave Black, General Manager

WLMV
09-01-1948; 1480 khz AM *Hrs Open:* 24; 5 kw-D, DA2; 5 kw-N, DA2; N43 1 30 W89 23 48
Mailing Address: P.O. Box 253, Madison, WI 53701 US
Second Address: 2740 Ski Ln., Madison, WI 53713
(608) 273-1000, *Fax:* (608) 271-0400
License: Madison, WI held by Mid-West Management Inc.
Group Owner: The Mid-West Family Broadcast Group

Nat'l Reps: Christal Radio
Arbitron Metro Market: Madison, WI *Target Audience:* General; Latino community
Thomas Walker, President
Rick Melloy, Operations Dir
Ted Waldbillig, General Sales Mgr
Luis Montoto, Programming Director
Tara Arnold, News Director
John Bauer, Chief Engineer

WTDY
01-01-1998; 1670 khz AM *Hrs Open:* 24
Mailing Address: 2001 Penn. Ave., NW, Ste 400, Washington, DC 20006 US
Second Address: 730 Rayovac Dr., Madison, WI 53711
(608) 273-1000, *Fax:* (608) 271-8182
www.wtdy.com
glen@wtdy.com
License: Madison, WI held by Mid-West Management Inc.
Group Owner: The Mid-West Family Broadcast Group
Nat'l Reps: McGavren Guild
Arbitron Metro Market: Madison, WI *Format:* News, News/Talk, 86 *Hrs. of News Programming:* news progmg 15 hrs wkly *No. News Employees:* 6 *Target Audience:* 25-54; young to middle aged males
Tom Walker, President
Ted Waldbillig, General Sales Mgr
Glen Gardner, Programming Director
Tara Arnold, News Director
John Bauer, Chief Engineer

WTSO
01-01-1948; 1070 khz AM *Hrs Open:* 24; 10 kw-D, DA2; 5 kw-N, DA2; N42 59 45 W89 18 50
600 Congress Ave., Suite 1400, Austin, TX 78701 US
(608) 274-5450, *Fax:* (608) 274-5521
www.espn1070.com
info@espn1070.com
License: Madison, WI held by Capstar TX L.P.
Group Owner: Clear Channel Communications Inc.; (acq 8-30-2000; grpsl)
Regional Network: Wisconsin Radio Net.
Arbitron Metro Market: Madison, WI *Format:* Sports *Special Programming:* Farm 20 hrs wkly *No. News Employees:* 6 *Target Audience:* 25-54.
Jeff Tyler, General Manager
Kurt Peterson, General Sales Mgr
Tim Scott, Programming Director
Jennie Hibbard, News Director
Tim Wagner, Chief Engineer

WZEE
01-01-1948; 104.1 mhz FM *Hrs Open:* 24; 12 kw; 1004 ft.; N43 3 3 W89 29 13
600 Congress Ave., Suite 1400, Austin, TX 78701 US
(608) 274-5450, *Fax:* (608) 274-5521
www.z104fm.com
info@z104fm.com
License: Madison, Dane County, WI
Arbitron Metro Market: Madison, WI *Format:* Adult Contemp *Hrs. of News Programming:* news progmg one hr wkly *No. News Employees:* 2
Tommy Bodean, Programming Director

Manitowoc

WLTU
09-01-1966; 92.1 mhz FM *Hrs Open:* 24; 3.7 kw; 420 ft.; N44 7 31 W87 37 41
Mailing Address: P.O. Box 1990, Manitowoc, WI 54221 US
Second Address: 1915 Mirro Dr., Manitowoc, WI 54220
(920) 683-6800, *Fax:* (920) 683-6807
www.cubradio.com
License: Manitowoc, Manitowoc County, WI
Nat'l Reps: Katz Radio
Arbitron Metro Market: Manitowoc, WI *Format:* Oldies *No. News Employees:* 1 *Target Audience:* 25-64.
Lee Davis, General Manager
Dean Lester, Programming Director
Bryan Lundberg, News Director
Joel Nelson, Engineering Dir

WOMT
11-08-1926; 1240 khz AM; 0.992 kw-U, ND1; N44 7 31 W87 37 41
P.O. Box 1385, Manitowoc, WI 54221 US
(920) 682-0351, *Fax:* (920) 682-1008
www.womtradio.com
info@womtradio.com
License: Manitowoc, WI held by Seehafer Broadcasting Corp.
Group Owner: Seehafer Broadcasting Corp.; (acq 1-1-70).
Nat'l Network: CBS *Regional Network:* Wisconsin Radio Net.
Wire Services: AP
TV Affiliate: Adult Contemp, Sports *Format:* News *Special Programming:* news progmg 45 hrs wkly *Hrs. of News Programming:* 2 *No. News Employees:* 25-64; business executive *Adv. Rates:* 52.75; 52.75; 52.75;40.60
Local News Editor

WQTC-FM
11-19-1965; 102.3 mhz FM *Hrs Open:* 24; 3 kw; 328 ft; N44 07 31 W87 37 41
Box 1385, 3730 Mangin St., Manitowoc, WI 54220
(920) 682-0351, *Fax:* (920) 682-1008
www.womtradio.com
License: Manitowoc, Manitowoc County, WI held by Seehafer Broadcasting Corp.
Group Owner: Seehafer Broadcasting Corp.
Nat'l Network: CUMULU *Regional Network:* Wisconsin Radio Net. *Wire Services:* AP
Population Served: 150,000*Hrs. of News Programming:* news progmg 8 hrs wkly *No. News Employees:* 8 *Target Audience:* 18-49. *Adv. Rates:* 40; 40; 40; 30.80
Don Seehafer, President
Courtny Hermson, Operations Dir
Russ Matan, General Sales Mgr
Tim Strews, Programming Director
Russ Matan, Promotions Manager
Damon Ryan, News Director
Joel Nelson, Chief Engineer
Mark Seehafer, VicePresident

Marathon

WKQH
01-01-1988; 104.9 mhz FM; 21 kw; 358 ft.; N44 50 13 W89 45 57
2600 Stewart Ave., Suite 272, Wausau, WI 54401 US
(715) 341-9800, *Fax:* (715) 341-0000
www.b1049.com
rmuzzy@1010wspt.com
License: Marathon, Marathon County, WI held by RLM Communications Inc.
Group Owner: Muzzy Broadcasting L.L.C.; (acq 1994; $150,000)
Arbitron Metro Market: Wausau-Stevens Point, WI (Central Wisconsin) *Format:* Country *No. News Employees:* 3 *Target Audience:* 25-54; adult
Richard Muzzy, General Manager
Rob West, Programming Director
Scott Krueger, News Director
Jim Zastnow, Chief Engineer
Geri Butler, Traffic Manager

Marinette

WLST
09-01-1976; 95.1 mhz FM *Hrs Open:* 24; 100 kw; 436 ft.; N45 3 48 W87 39 26
68 Bay Point Drive, San Rafael, CA 94901 US
(906) 863-5551, *Fax:* (906) 863-5679
www.baycitiesradio.net/whyb/
License: Marinette, Marinette County, WI held by Armada Media - Menominee Inc.
Group Owner: Armada Media Corp.
Wire Services: AP
Format: Country *No. News Employees:* 1 *Target Audience:* 25-54
Jim Callow, Operations Dir
Chris Bernier, General Manager
Barb VanDeHei, General Sales Mgr
Ken Conners, News Director

WMAM
10-08-1939; 570 khz AM *Hrs Open:* 24; 0.25 kw-D, ND1; 0.1 kw-N, ND1; N45 6 2 W87 37 30
68 Bay Point Drive, San Rafael, CA 94901 US
906-863-5551, *Fax:* 906-863-5679
www.espn570.com
jimcallow@baycitiesradio.net
License: Marinette, WI held by Armada Media - Menominee Inc.
Group Owner: Armada Media Corp.; (acq 12-19-2006; grpsl)
Nat'l Network: NBC Radio; ESPN Radio *Regional Network:* Wisconsin Radio Net. *Nat'l Reps:* Michigan Spot Sales *Wire Services:* AP
Format: Sports *Special Programming:* Milwaukee Brewers, Green Bay Packers, Wisconsin Ba *Hrs. of News Programming:* news progmg 4 hrs wkly *No. News Employees:* 1 *Target Audience:* 18+
Jim Callow, Operations Dir
Chris Bernier, General Manager
Barb VanDeHi, General Sales Mgr
Ken Conners, News Director

Marshall

***WJWD**
01-01-2003; 90.3 mhz FM; 0.051 kw horiz, 9.9 kw vert; 312 ft.; N43 20 40 W89 6 10
30000 W. Macarthur Blvd, Santa Ana, CA 92704 US
(920) 484-6220, *Fax:* (920) 484-3753
www.calvaryradionetwork.com/contact.htm
wjwd@centurytel.net
License: Marshall, Dane County, WI held by CSN International
Group Owner: CSN International
Arbitron Metro Market: Fall River, WI *Format:* Religious
Patrick Lannoye, General Manager

Marshfield

WDLB
02-02-1947; 1450 khz AM *Hrs Open:* 24; 1 kw-U; N44 41 49 W90 09 20
1714 N. Central Ave., Marshfield, WI 60611
(715) 384-2191, *Fax:* (715) 387-3588
wdlbwosq.com
License: Marshfield, Wood County, WI held by Seehafer Broadcasting Corp.
Group Owner: Seehafer Broadcasting Corp.; (acq 6-1-2006; swap with WOSQ(FM) Spencer and WFHR(AM) Wisconsin Rapids for WBCV(FM) Wausau)
Nat'l Network: ABC; Westwood One *Regional Network:* Brownfield
Population Served: 150,000 *Arbitron Metro Market:* Wausau-Stevens Point, WI (Central Wisconsin) *No. News Employees:* 2 *Target Audience:* 25-54
Don Seehafer, President
Jon Albrecht, Operations Dir
Mike Warren, News Director
Chuck Gennaro, Engineering Dir

WYTE
12-01-1965; 106.5 mhz FM; 100 kw; 801 ft.; N44 38 39 W89 51 12
980 North Michigan Avenue, Suite 1880, Chicago, IL 60611 US
(715) 341-8838, *Fax:* (715) 341-9744
www.wyte.com
info@wyte.com
License: Marshfield, Wood County, WI held by NRG License Sub, LLC.
Group Owner: NRG Media LLC; (acq 10-31-2005; grpsl)
Nat'l Reps: McGavren Guild
Arbitron Metro Market: Wausau-Stevens Point, WI (Central Wisconsin) *Format:* Country *Target Audience:* 25-54.
Mark Skibba, Operations Dir
Benjamin Rosenthal, General Manager
Bob Jung, General Sales Mgr

Mauston

WRJC
01-04-1962; 1270 khz AM *Hrs Open:* 24; 0.5 kw-D, ND1; 0.027 kw-N, ND1; N43 49 52 W90 4 51 *Rebroadcasts:* translator FM 92.9 FM
Fairway Lane Box 200, Mauston, WI 53948 US
(608) 847-6565, *Fax:* (608) 847-6249
wrjc.com
deb@wrjc.com
License: Mauston, WI held by WRJC Broadcasting Co.
Nat'l Network: CBS *Nat'l Reps:* Rgnl Reps *Wire Services:* AP
Format: Oldies *Hrs. of News Programming:* news progmg 8 hrs wkly *No. News Employees:* 1 *Target Audience:* 35 plus; general *Adv. Rates:* 25; 25; 25; 25
Rick Charles, President
Greg Lawrence, Promotions Manager
June Gill, News Director
Ken Ebneter, Chief Engineer

WRJC-FM
01-01-1976; 92.1 mhz FM *Hrs Open:* 24; 2 kw; 571 ft.; N43 47 16 W90 11 52
P.O. Box 200, Fairway Lane, Mauston, WI 53948 US
(608) 847-6565, *Fax:* (608) 847-6249
www.wrjc.com
deb@wrjc.com
License: Mauston, Juneau County, WI held by WRJC Inc.
Nat'l Network: CBS Radio *Nat'l Reps:* Rgnl Reps *Wire Services:* AP
Format: Adult Contemp *Hrs. of News Programming:* news progmg 10 hrs wkly *No. News Employees:* 1 *Target Audience:* 18 plus; adults *Adv. Rates:* Same as AM
Rick Charles, CEO

Mayville

WMDC

10-31-1998; 98.7 mhz FM *Hrs Open:* 24; 6 kw; 328 ft.; N43 26 17 W88 31 35
200 Fillmore St., Kaukauna, WI 54130 US
(920) 387-0000, *Fax:* (920) 387-2222
www.great98.com
bigsky@wmdcfm.com
License: Mayville, Dodge County, WI held by Radio Plus Inc.
Arbitron Metro Market: Mayville, WI *Format:* Contemporary Hits/Top 40 *No. News Employees:* 1 *Target Audience:* 25-54. *Adv. Rates:* 20; 20; 20; 12
Tom Biolo, General Manager
Norm Grey, General Sales Mgr

Medford

WIGM

10-26-1941; 1490 khz AM *Hrs Open:* 24
Mailing Address: P. O. Box 59, Medford, WI 54451 US
Second Address: 630 S. 8th, Medford, WI 54451
(715) 748-2566
www.k99wigm.com
k99@k99wigm.com
License: Medford, WI held by WIGM Inc.
Nat'l Network: ESPN Radio *Wire Services:* AP
Format: Sports *Special Programming:* Farm 10 hrs wkly *Hrs. of News Programming:* news progmg 14 hrs wkly *No. News Employees:* 1 *Target Audience:* 21 plus.
Brad Dahlvig, President
Karen Dahlvig, General Sales Mgr
Paula Liske, News Director
Del Dayton, Chief Engineer

WKEB

09-01-1967; 99.3 mhz FM *Hrs Open:* 24; 23 kw; 341 ft.; N45 9 51 W90 20 28
Mailing Address: P. O. Box 59, Medford, WI 54451 US
Second Address: 630 S. 8th, Medford, WI 54451
(715) 748-2566
www.k99wigm.com
k99@k99wigm.com
License: Medford, Taylor County, WI held by WIGM Inc.
Nat'l Network: ABC *Wire Services:* AP
Format: Contemporary Hits/Top 40
Brad Dahlvig, CEO
Karen Dahlvig, Operations Dir
Del Dayton, Engineering Dir

Menomonee Falls

WJMR-FM

06-26-1956; 98.3 mhz FM *Hrs Open:* 24; 4.9 kw; 364 ft.; N43 2 49 W87 58 52
5407 West McKinley Ave, Milwaukee, WI 53208 US
(414) 978-9000, *Fax:* (414) 978-9001
www.wjmr.com,jammin983.com
atopel@jammin983.com
License: Menomonee Falls, Waukesha County, WI held by Lakefront Communications LLC.
Group Owner: Saga Communications Inc.; (acq 4-24-97; $5 million with WJZX(FM) Brookfield)
Nat'l Reps: Katz Radio
Arbitron Metro Market: Milwaukee-Racine, WI *Format:* Urban Contemporary *Hrs. of News Programming:* news progmg 4 hrs wkly *No. News Employees:* 1 *Target Audience:* 25 plus. *Adv. Rates:* 85; 100; 90; 50
Tom Joerres, President
Annmarie Topel, General Manager
Traci Northrop, General Sales Mgr
Lauri Jones, Programming Director
LaTonya Lucas, Promotions Manager
Cris Ruid, News Director
Phil Longenecker, Chief Engineer

Menomonie

*WHWC

06-28-1950; 88.3 mhz FM *Hrs Open:* 24; 70 kw; 1050 ft.; N45 2 49 W91 51 47 *Rebroadcasts:* Rebroadcasts WHAD(FM) Delafield 90%
Mailing Address: 3319 W. Beltline Hwy., Madison, WI 53713 US
Second Address: 821 University Ave., Madison, WI 53706-1496
(715) 839-3868, *Fax:* (715) 839-2939
www.wpr.org
info@wpr.org
License: Menomonie, Dunn County, WI held by State of Wisconsin Educational Communications Board.
Nat'l Network: NPR; PRI *Regional Network:* Wis. Public Radio
Format: Talk *Special Programming:* Folk 7 hrs wkly *Target Audience:* 35-54.
Dean Kallenbach, General Manager
Mary Jo Wagner, News Director

WMEQ

05-01-1951; 880 khz AM *Hrs Open:* 24; 10 kw-D, DAN; 0.21 kw-N, DAN; N44 50 44 W91 50 45
111 East Kilbourn Avenue, Suite 2700, Milwaukee, WI 53202 US
(715) 830-4000, *Fax:* (715) 835-9680
www.wmeq.com
License: Menomonie, WI held by Capstar TX L.P.
Group Owner: Clear Channel Communications Inc.; (acq 2000; grpsl)
Nat'l Network: CBS Radio *Nat'l Reps:* Clear Channel
Arbitron Metro Market: Eau Claire, WI *Format:* News, News/Talk, 84, Talk *No. News Employees:* 2 *Target Audience:* 25 plus.
Dave Deville, Operations Dir
Rick Hencley, General Sales Mgr
Rick Hencley, Promotions Manager
Trina Butak, News Director
Paul Orth, Chief Engineer

WMEQ-FM

07-19-1967; 92.1 mhz FM *Hrs Open:* 24; 17.5 kw; 719 ft.; N44 54 59 W91 41 55
111 East Kilbourn Avenue, Suite 2700, Milwaukee, WI 53202 US
(715) 830-4000, *Fax:* (715) 835-9680
www.rock921.com
License: Menomonie, Dunn County, WI held by Capstar TX LP
Group Owner: Clear Channel Communications Inc.
Nat'l Reps: Clear Channel
Arbitron Metro Market: Eau Claire, WI *Format:* Light Rock *No. News Employees:* 2 *Target Audience:* 25-54.
Dave Deville, Operations Dir
Rick Hencley, General Sales Mgr
Rick Hencley, Promotions Manager
Trina Butak, News Director
Paul Orth, Chief Engineer

*WVSS

04-22-1969; 90.7 mhz FM *Hrs Open:* 24; 0.59 kw; 427 ft.; N44 54 56 W92 4 34 *Rebroadcasts:* Rebroadcasts WERN(FM) Madison 90%
1220 Linden Drive, Madison, WI 53706 US
(715) 839-3868, *Fax:* (715) 839-2939
License: Menomonie, Dunn County, WI held by Board of Regents, University of Wisconsin Systems.
Regional Network: Wis. Public Radio
Arbitron Metro Market: Menomonie, WI *Format:* News, News/Talk, 86 *Special Programming:* Folk 6 hrs, jazz 5 hrs wkly *Target Audience:* 45-64.
Dean Kallenbach, General Manager

Merrill

WJMT

05-10-1960; 730 khz AM *Hrs Open:* 24; 1 kw-D, ND1; 0.127 kw-N, ND1; N45 10 45 W89 38 20
120 S. Mill Street, Merrill, WI 54452 US
(715) 536-6262, *Fax:* (715) 536-6208
www.wjmt.com
License: Merrill, WI held by Quicksilver Broadcasting LLC.
Nat'l Reps: D & R Radio
Format: Adult Contemp, Talk *Special Programming:* Relg 3 hrs, farm 7 hrs, Pol 3 hrs wkly *No. News Employees:* 1 *Target Audience:* 35-59.
David Winters, President
Steven Resnick, General Manager
Christine Vorpagel, General Sales Mgr
Nick Summers, Programming Director
Joe Weniger, News Director
Chuck Genarro, Chief Engineer

WMZK

08-25-1968; 104.1 mhz FM *Hrs Open:* 24; 24 kw; 617 ft.; N45 6 14 W89 43 5
120 S. Mill Street, Merrill, WI 54452 US
(715) 536-6262, *Fax:* (715) 536-0583
www.z104rocks.com
advertising@z104rocks.com
License: Merrill, Lincoln County, WI held by Quicksilver Broadcasting LLC.
Arbitron Metro Market: Wausau, WI *Format:* Rock/AOR *No. News Employees:* 1 *Target Audience:* 18-49.
James Hoge, President

*WHJL

88.1 mhz FM; 63 kw; 620 ft.; N45 21 7.6 W89 39 12.7 US
(920) 842-2900, *Fax:* (920) 842-2704
www.wrvm.org
wrvm@wrvm.org
License: Merrill, Lincoln County, WI held by WRVM Inc.
Arbitron Metro Market: Merrill, WI *Format:* Christian, Religious
Elwood Anderson, President
Michael Cornell, General Manager
Dennis Jones, Programming Director
Alan Kilgore, Chief Engineer
Brian Hay, Music Director
Rich Frischkorn, Public Service Coordinator
Michael Fletcher, PromotionsDirector

Middleton

WWQM-FM

10-20-1970; 106.3 mhz FM *Hrs Open:* 24; 4.5 kw; 374 ft.; N43 3 3 W89 29 13
2740 Ski Lane, Madison, WI 53713 US
(608) 273-1000, *Fax:* (608) 271-8182
www.q106.com
fletch@Q106.com
License: Middleton, Dane County, WI held by Mid-West Management Inc.
Group Owner: The Mid-West Family Broadcast Group; (acq 8-15-97; $6.4 million with WHIT(AM) Madison)
Nat'l Reps: McGavren Guild
Arbitron Metro Market: Madison, WI *Format:* Country *Target Audience:* 25-54; general
Thomas Walker, President
Ted Waldbillig, General Sales Mgr
Fletcher Keyes, Programming Director
Dave Ogden, Promotions Manager
John Bauer, Chief Engineer
Sara Freeman, Music Director

Milladore

*WGNV

02-13-1986; 88.5 mhz FM *Hrs Open:* 24; 50 kw; 584 ft.; N44 38 37 W89 50 48 *Rebroadcasts:* 94.1 Antigo
Box 88, Country Rd. N., Milladore, WI 54914
(715) 457-2988, *Fax:* (715) 457-2987
christianfamilyradio.net
wgnv@christianfamilyradio.net
License: Milladore, Wood County, WI held by Evangel Ministries Inc.
Group Owner: Evangel Ministries Inc.
Nat'l Network: Moody; Salem Radio Network
Arbitron Metro Market: Wausau-Stevens Point, WI (Central Wisconsin) *Special Programming:* Children 4 hrs wkly *Hrs. of News Programming:* News progmg 10 hrs wkly *Target Audience:* Women; 35-49 *Adv. Rates:* 15.40;15.40; 15.40; 14
Karen Bencke, Operations Dir
Paul Cameron, General Manager
Bill Schumacher, General Sales Mgr
Mark Bystrom, Programming Director
Vicky Hofkens, News Director
Todd Christopher, Music Director

Milwaukee

WSSP

10-14-1935; 1250 khz AM *Hrs Open:* 24
10706 Beaver Dam Road, Cockeysville, MD 21030 US
(414) 529-1250, *Fax:* (414) 529-2122
www.sportsradio1250.com/
License: Milwaukee, WI held by Entercom Milwaukee License LLC.
Group Owner: Entercom Communications Corp.; (acq 12-13-99; grpsl).
Arbitron Metro Market: Milwaukee, WI *Format:* Christian *Special Programming:* Relg 3 hrs, Ger 8 hrs, Sp 3 hrs wkly *Target Audience:* 25-49.
Craig Hodgson, General Manager
Alan Kirshbom, General Sales Mgr
Glenn Redd, Programming Director
Jim Morales, Promotions Manager
Michael Clemens, News Director
Chris Tarr, Chief Engineer
Andrea Biebel, National Sales Manager

WISN

01-01-1922; 1130 khz AM *Hrs Open:* 24; 50 kw-D, DA2; 10 kw-N, DA2; N42 45 18 W88 4 53
600 Congress Ave, Suite 1400, Austin, TX 78701 US
(414) 545-8900, *Fax:* (414) 327-3200
www.newstalk1130.com
info@newstalk1130.com
License: Milwaukee, WI held by Capstar TX L.P.
Group Owner: Clear Channel Communications Inc.; (acq 8-30-2000; grpsl)
Nat'l Network: Fox News Radio; Premiere Radio Networks
Arbitron Metro Market: Milwaukee-Racine, WI *Format:* News, Talk *No. News Employees:* 4 *Target Audience:* 25-54.

Cindy McDowell, General Manager
Jay Daily, General Sales Mgr
Jerry Bott, Programming Director
Harold Mester, News Director
Al Hajny, Chief Engineer
Phil Kurth, General Sales Manager
Shannon Lippert, Taffic Manager

WJYI
01-01-1955; 1340 khz AM *Hrs Open:* 24
5407 W. McKinley Ave., Milwaukee, WI 53233 US
(414) 978-9000, *Fax:* (414) 978-9001
www.joy1340.com
ryansalzer@joy1340.com
License: Milwaukee, WI held by Lakefront Communications LLC.
Group Owner: Saga Communications Inc.; (acq 2-23-94; $7 million with co-located FM;
Nat'l Network: CBS
Arbitron Metro Market: Milwaukee-Racine, WI *Format:* Christian *Target Audience:* 18-54.
Tom Joerres, President
Ryan Salzer, Operations Dir
Stacey Kolterjahn, News Director
Phil Longenecken, Chief Engineer

WLDB
06-01-1958; 93.3 mhz FM *Hrs Open:* 24; 16 kw; 886 ft.; N43 5 46 W87 54 15
2979 North Mayfair Rd, Milwaukee, WI 53222 US
(414) 778-1933, *Fax:* (414) 771-3036
www.b933fm.com
info@b933fm.com
License: Milwaukee, Milwaukee County, WI held by Milwaukee Radio Alliance L.L.C.
Group Owner: Milwaukee Radio Alliance L.L.C.; (acq 9-23-97; grpsl)
Arbitron Metro Market: Milwaukee-Racine, WI *Format:* Classic Rock *Target Audience:* 25-54; general *Adv. Rates:* 100; 90; 100; 70
Willie Davis, Chairman
William Lynett, President
Bill Hurwitz, General Manager
Traci Northrup, General Sales Mgr
Stan Atkinson, Programming Director
John Church, Chief Engineer
Tiffany Dlugi, Traffic Manager

WKLH
01-01-1958; 96.5 mhz FM *Hrs Open:* 24; 20 kw; 810 ft.; N43 5 48 W87 54 19
5407 W. McKinley Ave, Milwaukee, WI 53208 US
(414) 978-9000, *Fax:* (414) 978-9001
www.wklh.com
klhstudio@wklh.com
License: Milwaukee, Milwaukee County, WI held by Lakefront Communications LLC.
Group Owner: Saga Communications Inc.; (acq 7-18-90).
Nat'l Reps: Katz Radio
Arbitron Metro Market: Milwaukee-Racine, WI *Format:* Contemporary Hits/Top 40, Adult Contemp *No. News Employees:* 1 *Target Audience:* 35-54; baby boomers
Tom Joerres, President
Annmarie Topel, Programming Director
Scott Schubert, Promotions Manager
Carole Caine, News Director
Phil Longenecker, Chief Engineer
Bob Bellini, Programming Director
Stacey Kolterjahn, Traffic Manager

WLWK-FM
06-01-1959; 94.5 mhz FM *Hrs Open:* 24; 14 kw; 955 ft.; N43 5 29 W87 54 7
Mailing Address: 3355 S. Valley View Blvd, Las Vegas, NV 89102 US
Second Address: Box 693, Milwaukee, WI 53201
(414) 332-9611, *Fax:* (414) 967-5266
www.945lakefm.com
info@wkti.com
License: Milwaukee, Milwaukee County, WI held by Journal Broadcast Corp.
Group Owner: Journal Communications Inc.
Arbitron Metro Market: Milwaukee-Racine, WI *TV Affiliate:* WTMJ-TV affil *Format:* Adult Contemp *No. News Employees:* 1 *Target Audience:* 25-54.
Jon Schweitzer, Station Manager
Bob Walker, Programming Director
Lisa Letterman, Promotions Manager

WRNW
01-01-1961; 97.3 mhz FM *Hrs Open:* 24; 15.5 kw; Ant 980 ft; N43 06 41 W87 55 38
12100 W. Howard Ave., Greenfield, WI 78701
(414) 545-8900, *Fax:* (414) 327-3200
www.l973thebrew.com
info@1973thebrew.com
License: Milwaukee, Milwaukee County, WI held by Capstar TX L.P.
Group Owner: Clear Channel Communications Inc.
Nat'l Network: ABC
Population Served: 717,099 *Arbitron Metro Market:* Milwaukee-Racine, WI
Randy Wanek, General Sales Mgr
Jeff Lynn, Programming Director

WLUM-FM
09-01-1960; 102.1 mhz FM; 8.8 kw; 843 ft.; N43 6 42 W87 55 50
2979 North Mayfair Road, Milwaukee, WI 53222 US
(414) 771-1021, *Fax:* (414) 771-3036
www.fm1021milwaukee.com
info@fm1021milwaukee.com
License: Milwaukee, Milwaukee County, WI held by Milwaukee Radio Alliance LLC
Group Owner: Milwaukee Radio Alliance L.L.C.
Wire Services: CBS
Arbitron Metro Market: Milwaukee, WI *Format:* Alternative *Target Audience:* 18-49; teens & adults
Bill Hurwitz, General Manager
Traci Northrop, General Sales Mgr
Tommy Wilde, Programming Director
Stan Atkinson, News Director
John Church, Chief Engineer
Jerry Arndt, National Sales Manager
Tiffany Dlugi, Traffic Manager

WHQG
10-01-1960; 102.9 mhz FM *Hrs Open:* 24; 50 kw; 427 ft.; N43 2 49 W87 58 52
5407 W. McKinley Ave, Miwaukee, WI 53233 US
(414) 978-9000, *Fax:* (414) 978-9001
www.1029thehog.com
headhog@1029thehog.com
License: Milwaukee, Milwaukee County, WI
Group Owner: Saga Communications Inc.
Arbitron Metro Market: Milwaukee, WI *Format:* Rock/AOR
Tom Joerres, President
Stacey Kolterjahn, Operations Dir
Annmarie Topel, Programming Director
Scott Schubert, Promotions Manager
Keith Hastings, Programming Director

***WMSE**
03-14-1981; 91.7 mhz FM *Hrs Open:* 24; 3.2 kw; 131 ft.; N43 2 44 W87 54 28
1025 N. Broadway Street, Milwaukee, WI 53202 US
(414) 277-7247, *Fax:* (414) 277-7149
www.wmse.org
wmse@msoe.edu
License: Milwaukee, Milwaukee County, WI held by Milwaukee School of Engineering.
Arbitron Metro Market: Milwaukee, WI *Format:* Alternative
Special Programming: Black 13 hrs, jazz 15 hrs, lt 3 hrs, Sp 3 hrs, cla *Target Audience:* 18-35; young adults
Tom Crawford, General Manager
Tom Crawford, Station Manager
Ryan Schleicher, Promotions Manager
Julie Cudahy, Chief Engineer
Justin Shoman, Development Director/Member Support
Erin Wolf, Music Director

***WMWK**
12-07-1990; 88.1 mhz FM *Hrs Open:* 24; 1.1 kw; 906 ft.; N43 5 26 W87 53 50
Mailing Address: 4135 Northgate Blvd, Suite 1, Sacramento, CA 95834 US
Second Address: 290 Hegenberger Rd., Oakland, CA 94621
(916) 641-8191, *Fax:* (916) 641-8238
www.familyradio.com
info@familyradio.com
License: Milwaukee, Milwaukee County, WI held by Family Stations Inc.
Group Owner: Family Stations Inc.
Arbitron Metro Market: Milwaukee, CA *Format:* Christian, Religious
Harold Camping, President
John Rorvik, Operations Dir

WMYX-FM
11-01-1962; 99.1 mhz FM; 50 kw; 449 ft.; N42 56 44 W88 3 39
10706 Beaver Dam Road, Cockeysville, MD 21030 US
(414) 529-1250, *Fax:* (414) 529-2122
www.991wmyx.com
License: Milwaukee, Milwaukee County, WI
Group Owner: Entercom Communications Corp.
Nat'l Network: Westwood One *Nat'l Reps:* D & R Radio
Arbitron Metro Market: Milwaukee, WI *Format:* Adult Contemp
Special Programming: Relg one hr wkly *Target Audience:* 25-49; women
Jane Matenaer, Operations Dir
Tom Gjerdrum, Programming Director

WNOV
08-15-1946; 860 khz AM; 0.25 kw-D, NDD; 0.005 kw-N, ND1; N43 4 20 W87 57 7
38 15 N. Teutonia Ave., Milwaukee, WI 53206 US
(414) 449-9668, *Fax:* (414) 449-9945
www.wnovmusic.com
info@wnovmusic.com
License: Milwaukee, WI held by Courier Communications Corp.
Arbitron Metro Market: Milwaukee, WI *Format:* Urban Contemporary
Jerrel Jones, CEO
Sandra Robinson, General Manager
Homer Blow, Programming Director
Amari Brown, News Director

WOKY
01-01-1947; 920 khz AM; 5 kw-D, DA2; 1 kw-N, DA2; N42 58 32 W88 3 56
200 Concord Plaza, Suite 600, San Antonio, TX 78216 US
(414) 545-8900, *Fax:* (414) 327-3200
www.am920thewolf.com
License: Milwaukee, WI held by Clear Channel Radio Licenses Inc.
Group Owner: Clear Channel Communications Inc.; (acq 3-17-97; $40 million with WMIL(FM) Waukesha)
Nat'l Network: CBS Radio *Nat'l Reps:* Clear Channel *Wire Services:* AP
Arbitron Metro Market: Milwaukee-Racin *TV Affiliate:* Classic country *Special Programming:* news progmg 15 hrs wkly *Hrs. of News Programming:* 3 *No. News Employees:* 35-64.
Program Director, Brad Wallace
Promotions Director, Promotions Manager
General Sales Manager, Barb Fagnat
Traffic Manager

WTMJ
07-25-1927; 620 khz AM; 50 kw-D, DA2; 10 kw-N, DA2; N42 42 28 W88 3 57
Mailing Address: P.O. Box 693, 720 East Capitol Drive, Milwaukee, WI 53212 US
Second Address: Box 693, Milwaukee, WI 53201
(414) 799-1620, *Fax:* (414) 967-5561
www.620wtmj.com
tsheridan@620wtmj.com
License: Milwaukee, WI held by Journal Broadcast Corp.
Group Owner: Journal Communications Inc.
Nat'l Network: ABC *Nat'l Reps:* Christal
Arbitron Metro Market: Milwaukee-Racin *Format:* News, News/Talk, 84, Talk *Special Programming:* Relg 2 hrs wkly *Target Audience:* General.
Doug Kiel, CEO
Rick Belcher, Operations Dir
Jon Schweitzer, General Manager
Tom Sheridan, General Sales Mgr
Joe Scialfa, Programming Director
Helen Kosterman, Promotions Manager
Jon Byman, News Director
Randy Price, EngineeringDir
Susan Petropoullis, Traffic Manager
Carl Moll, Director of Network Operations
James Conigliaro, Director, Interactive Technology

***WUWM**
09-24-1964; 89.7 mhz FM *Hrs Open:* 24; 15 kw; 871 ft; N43 05 24 W87 53 47
Mailing Address: Milwaukee Public Radio, Box 413, Milwaukee, WI 53706
Second Address: John Plankinton Bldg., 161 W. Wisconsin Ave., Suite LL1000, Milwaukee, WI 53202
(414) 227-3355, *Fax:* (414) 270-1297
www.wuwm.com
wuwm@uwm.edu
License: Milwaukee, Milwaukee County, WI held by Board of Regents of University of Wisconsin.
Nat'l Network: PRI; NPR
Arbitron Metro Market: Milwaukee-Racine, WI *No. News Employees:* 12 *Target Audience:* General.
Dave Edwards, Programming Director
Tom May, Chief Engineer
Noel Skarpmoen, Development Director
Bruce Winter, Program Director

***WVCY-FM**
01-01-1961; 107.7 mhz FM *Hrs Open:* 24; 43 kw; 528 ft.; N42 57 46 W88 4 23

RADIO - U.S.

3434 West Kilbourn Ave, Milwaukee, WI 53208 US
(414) 935-3000, *Fax:* (414) 935-3015
www.vcyamerica.org
wvcyfm@vcyamerica.org
License: Milwaukee, Milwaukee County, WI held by VCY/America Inc.
Group Owner: VCY America Inc.; (acq 1-70)
Nat'l Network: USA; Moody
Arbitron Metro Market: Milwaukee, WI *Format:* Christian, Religious
Dr. Randall Melchert, President
Victor Eliason, Operations Dir
Jim Schneider, Programming Director
Gordon Morris, Operations Manager

***WYMS**
03-05-1973; 88.9 mhz FM *Hrs Open:* 24; 1.45 kw; 948 ft.; N43 5 26 W87 53 50
5225 West Vliet Street, Milwaukee, WI 53208 US
(414) 475-8890, *Fax:* (414) 475-8413
www.radioformilwaukee.org
info@radiomilwaukee.org
License: Milwaukee, Milwaukee County, WI held by Milwaukee Board of School Directors.
Wire Services: AP
Arbitron Metro Market: Milwaukee-Racin *Format:* Triple A *Target Audience:* 20-40.
Dex Gage, General Manager
Ed Wilhelm, Chief Engineer

WRIT-FM
05-10-1961; 95.7 mhz FM; 34 kw; 610 ft.; N43 5 24 W87 54 55
12100 W. Howard Avenue, Greenfield, WI 53228 US
(414) 545-8900, *Fax:* (414) 546-9654
www.milwaukeeoldies.com/main.html
contactus@milwaukeeoldies.com%20?subject=Contact%20Oldies%2095.7
License: Milwaukee, Milwaukee County, WI held by Clear Channel Radio Licenses Inc.
Group Owner: Clear Channel Communications Inc.; (acq 10-97; $14.5 million)
Nat'l Reps: Clear Channel
Arbitron Metro Market: Greenfield, WI *Format:* Adult Contemp *Target Audience:* 25-54; baby boomers
Kerry Wolfe, Operations Dir
Cindy McDowell, General Manager
Jeff Lynn, Station Manager
Keith Bratel, General Sales Mgr
Dave Adams, Programming Director
Brad Wallace, Promotions Manager
Harold Mester, News Director
Al Hajny,Chief Engineer
Marvy Quesnell, Traffic Manager
Colleen Kurth, Advertising Contact
Dave Murphy, Assistant Program Director
Hannah Kultgen, On the Streets/Contest Manager

Minocqua

WLKD
08-01-1978; 1570 khz AM *Hrs Open:* 24; 5 kw-D, ND1; 0.5 kw-N, ND1; N45 49 13 W89 43 27
PO Bx 96- 7380 Hwy 51 S., Minocqua, WI 54548 US
(715) 362-1975, *Fax:* (715) 362-1973
License: Minocqua, WI held by Raven License Sub. LLC.
Group Owner: NRG Media LLC; (acq 10-31-2005; grpsl)
Nat'l Network: Fox News Radio *Nat'l Reps:* Katz Radio *Wire Services:* Wheeler News Service
Format: Contemporary Hits/Top 40 *No. News Employees:* 1 *Target Audience:* 35 plus. *Adv. Rates:* 8; 6; 6; 3
Duff Damos, Operations Dir
Steve Albertson, Station Manager

WMQA-FM
04-03-1975; 95.9 mhz FM *Hrs Open:* 24; 22 kw; 351 ft.; N45 49 19 W89 43 16
7380 Hwy 51 South Box 96, Minocqua, WI 54548 US
(715) 362-1975, *Fax:* (715) 362-1973
www.wmqa.com
License: Minocqua, Oneida County, WI
Group Owner: NRG Media LLC
Nat'l Network: Fox News Radio *Nat'l Reps:* Katz Radio
Arbitron Metro Market: Rhinelander, WI *Format:* Adult Contemp *No. News Employees:* 1 *Target Audience:* 35-64 *Adv. Rates:* 23; 20; 21; 8
Duff Damos, Operations Dir
Steve Albertson, General Sales Mgr
Dave Imlah, Programming Director

Mishicot

WZOR
12-17-1994; 94.7 mhz FM *Hrs Open:* 24; 21.5 kw; 354 ft.; N44 20 30 W87 47 10
Mailing Address: Bel-Mart Centre, Ste 8b, 2733 Manitowoc Road, Green Bay, WI 54311 US
Second Address: 2727 E. Radio Rd., Appleton, WI 54915
(920) 734-9226, *Fax:* (920) 733-2391
www.razor947.com
razor@wcinet.com
License: Mishicot, Manitowoc County, WI held by Woodward Communications Inc.
Group Owner: Woodward Communications Inc.; acq 1-27-00).
Nat'l Reps: McGavren Guild
Arbitron Metro Market: Green Bay, WI *Format:* Rock/AOR *Target Audience:* 18-34; men
Greg Bell, General Manager
Kelly Radandt, General Sales Mgr
Joe Calgaro, Programming Director
Roxanne Steele, Promotions Manager
Borna Velic, Music Director

Monona

WTLX
07-16-1990; 100.5 mhz FM *Hrs Open:* 24; 6 kw; 180 ft.; N43 8 4 W89 23 56
Mailing Address: 2000 K Street, NW, Suite 600, Washington, DC 20006 US
Second Address: 5315 Wall St., Suite 135, Madison, WI 53718
(608) 245-9859, *Fax:* (608) 245-1720
www.espnmadison.com
License: Monona, Columbia County, WI held by Good Karma Broadcasting L.L.C.
Group Owner: Good Karma Broadcasting L.L.C.; (acq 12-2-97; grpsl)
Nat'l Network: ESPN Radio
Arbitron Metro Market: Madison, WI *Format:* Sports, Talk *Target Audience:* 25-54; males
Craig Karmazin, President
Ken Rovak, General Manager
Jim Rutledge, Programming Director
Laura Mizer, Promotions Manager
Brittany Rhett, Sports Marketing Consultant
Andrew Klein, Sports Marketing Consultant

Monroe

WEKZ
07-27-1951; 1260 khz AM *Hrs Open:* 24; 1 kw-D, ND1; 0.019 kw-N, ND1; N42 35 40 W89 35 34
D/B/A Green Country B/C, 916 17th Avenue, Monroe, WI 53566 US
(608) 325-2161, *Fax:* (608) 325-2164
www.wekz.com
wekz@wekz.com
License: Monroe, WI held by Scott A. Thompson dba Big Radio
Nat'l Network: ABC
Arbitron Metro Market: Monroe, WI *Format:* Country *Special Programming:* Ger 3 hrs, Swiss 3 hrs wkly *Hrs. of News Programming:* news progmg 16 hrs wkly *No. News Employees:* 4 *Target Audience:* 35 plus.*Adv. Rates:* 12; 12; 12; 12
Kent McConnell, Operations Dir
Wyatt Herrmann, Programming Director
Don Jacobson, News Director
Todd Hausser, Chief Engineer
Becky Koester, Traffic Manager

WEKZ-FM
06-01-1959; 93.7 mhz FM *Hrs Open:* 24; 36 kw; 581 ft.; N42 34 35 W89 41 35
D/B/A Green Country B/C, 916 17th Ave., Monroe, WI 53566 US
(608) 325-2161, *Fax:* (608) 325-2164
www.wekz.com
License: Monroe, Green County, WI held by Scott A. Thompson dba Big Radio.
Nat'l Network: ABC
Arbitron Metro Market: Monroe, WI *Format:* Adult Contemp *Hrs. of News Programming:* news progmg 10 hrs wkly *No. News Employees:* 4 *Target Audience:* 35-55. *Adv. Rates:* 14; 14; 14; 14
Kent McConnell, Operations Dir
Wyatt Herrmann, Programming Director
Don Jacobson, News Director
Todd Hausser, Chief Engineer
Becky Koester, Traffic Manager

Mosinee

WOZZ
10-07-1991; 94.7 mhz FM *Hrs Open:* 24; 50 kw; Ant 492 ft; N44 59 18 W89 59 42 *Rebroadcasts:* Simulcast with WIZD(FM) Rudolph 100%
557 Scott St., Wausau, WI 54403
(715) 842-1672, *Fax:* (715) 848-3158
www.lovethevalley.com
info@947thepeak.com
License: Mosinee, Marathon County, WI held by WRIG Inc.
Group Owner: Midwest Communications Inc.; (acq 9-24-97; $35,000 for 70%)
Nat'l Reps: Christal
Population Served: 212,000 *Arbitron Metro Market:* Wausau-Stevens Point, WI (Central Wisconsin) *Hrs. of News Programming:* news progmg 2 hrs wkly *No. News Employees:* 1 *Target Audience:* 25-54; upscale babyboomers
Duke Wright, President
Brett Lucht, General Manager
Jim Schroeder, General Sales Mgr
Chad Edwards, Programming Director
Melanie Comeau, News Director
Frank Zastrow, Chief Engineer
Gary Tesch, Executive Vice President

Mount Horeb

WTDY-FM
10-01-2004; 106.7 mhz FM; 2.9 kw; Ant 479 ft; N43 00 19 W89 52 25 *Rebroadcasts:* Simulcast with WWQM-FM Middleton 100%
Box 2058, Madison, WI 54660
(608) 273-1000, *Fax:* (608) 271-8182
www.q106.com
License: Mount Horeb, Dane County, WI held by Mid-West Management Inc.
Group Owner: The Mid-West Family Broadcast Group; (acq 3-20-2003; $2,166,000 for CP)
Nat'l Reps: McGavren Guild
Arbitron Metro Market: Madison, WI *Target Audience:* 25-54; general
Tom Walker, General Manager
Ted Waldbillig, General Sales Mgr
Brad Austin, Programming Director
John Bauer, Chief Engineer

Mukwonago

***WLVE**
01-01-2002; 105.3 mhz FM *Hrs Open:* 24; 1.65 kw; Ant 633 ft; N42 58 05 W88 11 20
2351 Sunset Blvd., Suite 170-218, Rocklin, CA 85737
(916) 251-1600, *Fax:* (916) 251-1650
www.klove.com
License: Mukwonago, Waukesha County, WI held by Educational Media Foundation.
Group Owner: EMF Broadcasting; (acq 5-30-2008; $8.05 million)
Nat'l Network: K-Love
Arbitron Metro Market: Milwaukee-Racine, WI
Mike Novak, President

Neenah-Menasha

WNAM
05-23-1947; 1280 khz AM *Hrs Open:* 24; 5 kw-D, DA2; 5 kw-N, DA2; N44 6 1 W88 32 2
111 East Kilbourn Ave., Suite 2700, Milwaukee, WI 53202 US
(920) 426-3239, *Fax:* (920) 231-0145
www.1280wnam.com
info@1280wnam.com
License: Neenah-Menasha, WI held by Cumulus Broadcasting L.L.C.
Group Owner: Cumulus Media Inc.; (acq 6-30-97; grpsl)
Arbitron Metro Market: Appleton, WI *Format:* Adult Contemp *Hrs. of News Programming:* news progmg 13 hrs wkly *No. News Employees:* 3 *Target Audience:* 35 plus.
Guy Dark, Operations Dir
Jeffrey Schmidt, General Manager
Jason Davis, General Sales Mgr
Sarah Van Straten, Programming Director

WNCY-FM
09-09-1977; 100.3 mhz FM *Hrs Open:* 24; 45 kw; 489 ft.; N44 15 27 W88 11 41
Mailing Address: 904 Grand Ave., Wausau, WI 54403 US
Second Address: 115 S. Jefferson St., Green Bay, WI 54301
(920) 435-3771, *Fax:* (920) 321-2300
www.wncy.com
info@wncy.com
License: Neenah-Menasha, Winnebago County, WI held by Midwest Communications Inc.

Group Owner: Midwest Communications Inc.; acq 12-10-96; grpsl)
Arbitron Metro Market: Appleton, WI *Format:* Country
D.E. Wright, President
Jeff McCarthy, Operations Dir
Craig Von Able, General Sales Mgr
Dan Stone, Programming Director
Jerry Bader, News Director
Tim Laes, Chief Engineer

WYDR
11-01-1971; 94.3 mhz FM; 13 kw; 459 ft; N44 09 30 W88 17 03
Box 23333, Green Bay, WI 54403
(920) 435-3771, *Fax:* (920) 444-1155
www.mci.fm
info@mci.fm
License: Neenah-Menasha, Winnebago County, WI held by Midwest Communications Inc.
Group Owner: Midwest Communications Inc.; acq 12-10-96; grpsl)
Population Served: 27,600 *Arbitron Metro Market:* Appleton-Oshkosh, WI *Target Audience:* 25-54.
Duke Wright, CEO
David Fries, General Sales Mgr
Jenny Lawrence, Programming Director
Jerry Bader, News Director
Tim Laes, Chief Engineer

Neillsville

WCCN
09-22-1957; 1370 khz AM *Hrs Open:* 24
1201 E. Division Street, Neillsville, WI 54456 US
(715) 743-3333, *Fax:* (715) 743-2288
www.cwbradio.com
1075therock@tds.net
License: Neillsville, WI held by Central Wisconsin Broadcasting Inc.
Group Owner: Central Wisconsin Broadcasting Inc.; acq 12-87;
Nat'l Network: ABC *Regional Network:* Wisconsin Radio Net.
Arbitron Metro Market: Neillsville,WI *Format:* Big Band, Oldies
Special Programming: Farm 19 hrs, Polka 2 hrs wkly *Hrs. of News Programming:* news progmg 20 hrs wkly *No. News Employees:* 1 *Target Audience:* 45 plus. *Adv. Rates:* 19; 17; 16; 13
J. Kevin Grap, President
Margaret Grap, Operations Dir

WCCN-FM
07-01-1964; 107.5 mhz FM *Hrs Open:* 24; 100 kw; 577 ft.; N44 35 30 W90 37 9
1201 E Division Street, Neillsville, WI 54456 US
(715) 743-3333, *Fax:* (715) 743-2288
www.cwbradio.com
1075therock@tds.net
License: Neillsville, Clark County, WI
Group Owner: Central Wisconsin Broadcasting Inc.
Arbitron Metro Market: Neillsville,WI *No. News Employees:* 1 *Target Audience:* 25-40. *Adv. Rates:* 27; 25; 24; 20
Nick Ferrara, General Manager

WPKG
02-01-2004; 92.7 mhz FM *Hrs Open:* 24; 3.4 kw; 440 ft.; N44 35 30 W90 37 9
W4798 Moonlite Road, Neillsville, WI 54456 US
(715) 743-3333, *Fax:* (715) 743-2288
www.todaysbesthits.com
License: Neillsville, Clark County, WI held by Central Wisconsin Broadcasting Inc.
Group Owner: Central Wisconsin Broadcasting Inc.
Nat'l Network: ABC
Arbitron Metro Market: Neillsville, WI *Format:* Adult Contemp
Target Audience: 18+; Females *Adv. Rates:* 22.50; 18; 17; 15
J. Kevin Grap, General Manager

Nekoosa

WMMA
01-01-2002; 93.9 mhz FM *Hrs Open:* 24; 18 kw; 367 ft.; N44 13 23 W89 49 46
Mailing Address: 2470 Crooks Ave., Kaukauna, WI 54130 US
Second Address: 645 25th Ave N, Wisconsin Rapids, WI 54495
(920) 884-1460, *Fax:* (920) 465-9986
www.relevantradio.com
wmma@relevantradio.com
License: Nekoosa, Wood County, WI held by Starboard Media Foundation Inc.
Group Owner: Relevant Radio; (acq 12-20-2001; $2.3 million with WIBU(AM) Wisconsin Dells).
Arbitron Metro Market: Nekoosa, WI *Format:* Religious
Thomas Vorpahl, Chairman
Jack O'Keefe, General Manager
Mike Kendall, Chief Programming Officer
Amy Vanden Langenberg, Chief Financial Officer
Trish Leurck, Chief Development Officer
Nancy Jensen, Chief Marketing Officer

WRCW
01-01-2003; 105.5 mhz FM; 6 kw; 279 ft.; N44 21 45 W90 3 58
Gammon & Grange Pc, 8280 Greensboro Dr, McLean, VA 22102 US
(715) 424-1300, *Fax:* (715) 424-1347
www.wrcwfm.com
blocked@northwoodstech.com
License: Nekoosa, Wood County, WI held by Seehafer Broadcasting Corp.
Group Owner: Seehafer Broadcasting Corp.; 3/5/2008
Arbitron Metro Market: Nekoosa, WI *Format:* Oldies
Donald Seehafer, President
Kent Reeves, Operations Dir
Jeff Sigler, General Sales Mgr

New Holstein

WLWB
05-25-1984; 1530 khz AM *Hrs Open:* Sunrise-sunset; 250 w-D; N44 01 10 W88 09 32
Mailing Address: Box 1450, Fond du Lac, WI 53014
Second Address: 354 Winnebago Dr., Fond du Lac, WI 54935
(920) 921-1071, *Fax:* (920) 921-0757
www.espnradio1530.com
info@espnradio1530.com
License: New Holstein, Calumet County, WI held by Maszka-Pacer Radio Inc.
Nat'l Network: USA
Arbitron Metro Market: Appleton-Oshkosh, WI *No. News Employees:* 2 *Target Audience:* 18-54; male sports fans *Adv. Rates:* 36; 36; 36; 36
R.B. Hopper, General Manager
Mark Kastein, General Sales Mgr
Shawn Kiser, Programming Director
Cindy Konen, News Director
Stu Muck, Engineering Dir

New London

WRQE
10-06-1967; 93.5 mhz FM *Hrs Open:* 24; 50 kw; 528 ft; N44 21 35 W88 42 46
1500 N. Casaloma Dr., Suite 307, Appleton, WI 54403
(920) 733-4990, *Fax:* (920) 733-5507
www.wozz.com
License: New London, Outagamie County, WI held by Midwest Communications of Iowa Inc.
Group Owner: Midwest Communications Inc.; (acq 6-30-93; $1.85 million with WZBY(FM) Sturgeon Bay;
Population Served: 837,000 *Arbitron Metro Market:* Appleton-Oshkosh, WI *Hrs. of News Programming:* news progmg 8 hrs wkly *No. News Employees:* 2 *Target Audience:* 25-44.
David Fries, General Manager
David Louis, Programming Director

New Richmond

WIXK
09-29-1960; 1590 khz AM *Hrs Open:* 24
Mailing Address: 125 E. 3rd St., New Richmond, WI 54017 US
Second Address: 125 East 3rd St., New Richmond, WI
(715) 246-2254, *Fax:* (715) 246-7090
wixk.com
jpetersen@hbi.com
License: New Richmond, WI held by WIXK-AM LLC.
Group Owner: Hubbard Broadcasting Inc.; (acq 5-18-2000; with co-located FM)
Nat'l Network: ABC *Regional Network:* Wisconsin Radio Net.
Arbitron Metro Market: Minneapolis-St. Paul, MN *TV Affiliate:* KSTP *Format:* Country *Hrs. of News Programming:* news progmg 9 hrs wkly *No. News Employees:* 1 *Target Audience:* 25-54.
Stanley Hubbard, CEO
Virginia Morris, President
Todd Fisher, General Manager

Oconto

WOCO
03-11-1966; 1260 khz AM; 1 kw-D, ND1; 0.029 kw-N, ND1; N44 53 31 W87 57 18
P.O. Box 197, Oconto, WI 54153 US
(920) 834-3540, *Fax:* (920) 834-3532
wocoamfm@bayland.net
License: Oconto, WI held by Lamardo Inc.
TV Affiliate: Country *No. News Employees:* 29 plus.
Regional Sales Manager

WOCO-FM
08-01-1968; 107.1 mhz FM; 3 kw; 210 ft.; N44 53 31 W87 57 18
PO Box 197, Oconto, WI 54153 US
(920) 834-3540, *Fax:* (920) 834-3532
wocoamfm@bayland.net
License: Oconto, Oconto County, WI held by Lamardo Inc.
TV Affiliate: Nostalgia
Sports Commentator

Omro

WPKR
07-12-1990; 99.5 mhz FM *Hrs Open:* 24; 25 kw; 495 ft.; N43 49 44 W88 40 6
P.O. Box 3450, Osh Kosh, WI 54903 US
(920) 426-3239, *Fax:* (920) 231-0145
wpkr.com
info@wpkr.com
License: Omro, Winnebago County, WI held by Cumulus Licensing LLC.
Group Owner: Cumulus Media Inc.; (acq 11-10-2003; $8.1 million with WPCK(FM) Denmark).
Arbitron Metro Market: Appleton-Oshkosh, WI *Format:* Country
Special Programming: Farm one hr wkly *Hrs. of News Programming:* news progmg 2 hrs wkly *No. News Employees:* 1
Target Audience: 25-54. *Adv.Rates:* 60; 54; 60; 48
Jeff Schmidt, General Manager

Oshkosh

WOSH
12-31-1941; 1490 khz AM
111 East Kilbourn Ave., Suite 2700, Milwaukee, WI 53202 US
(920) 426-3239, *Fax:* (920) 231-0145
www.cumulus.com
woshnews@cumulus.com
License: Oshkosh, WI held by Cumulus Broadcasting Inc.
Group Owner: Cumulus Media Inc.; (acq 9-1-97; grpsl)
Nat'l Reps: D & R Radio
Arbitron Metro Market: Appleton-Oshkosh, WI *Format:* News, News/Talk, 84, Talk *Target Audience:* 25 plus.
Jeffrey Schmidt, General Manager
Larry Phillip, General Sales Mgr
Bob Burnell, Programming Director
John Stiloski, Promotions Manager
Jonathan Krause, News Director
Steve Griesbach, Chief Engineer
Alexandra Marohn, TrafficManager

*WRST-FM
04-20-1966; 90.3 mhz FM; 960 w; 125 ft; N44 01 45 W88 33 08
800 Algoma Blvd., Oshkosh, WI 53706
(920) 424-3113, *Fax:* (920) 424-1279
License: Oshkosh, Winnebago County, WI held by Board of Regents, University of Wisconsin System.
Nat'l Network: NPR *Regional Network:* Wis. Public Radio *Wire Services:* Wheeler News Service
Population Served: 60,000 *Arbitron Metro Market:* Appleton-Oshkos *Target Audience:* General.
Ben Jarman, General Manager
Kelly Bougneit, Station Manager

*WVCY
07-01-1969; 690 khz AM *Hrs Open:* 24; 0.25 kw-D, DA1; 0.077 kw-N, DA1; N44 4 51 W88 33 53
3434 West Kilbourne Ave., Milwaukee, WI 53208 US
(414) 935-3000, *Fax:* (414) 935-3015
www.vcyamerica.org
wvcyam@vcyamerica.org
License: Oshkosh, WI held by VCY/America Inc.
Group Owner: VCY America Inc.; acq 1-19-95)
Nat'l Network: USA
Arbitron Metro Market: Oshkos, WI *Format:* Religious
Dr. Randall Melchert, President
Vic Eliason, Operations Dir

WWWX
01-30-1967; 96.9 mhz FM; 6 kw; 328 ft.; N44 6 1 W88 32 2
111 East Kilbourn Ave., Suite 2700, Milwaukee, WI 53202 US
(920) 426-3239, *Fax:* (920) 231-0145
www.fox969.com
info@fox969.com
License: Oshkosh, Winnebago County, WI held by WI Radio LLC, as trustee
Nat'l Network: ABC *Wire Services:* UPI
Arbitron Metro Market: Oshkosh, WI *Target Audience:* 25-54.
Jeff Schmidt, General Manager
Guy Dark, Programming Director

Owen

*WVCS
90.1 mhz FM; 1.9 kw; 502 ft.; N45 1 11 W90 29 48 US
(414) 935-3000, *Fax:* (414) 935-3015
www.vcyamerica.org
vcy@vcyamerica.org
License: Owen, Clark County, WI held by VCY America Inc.
Group Owner: VCY America Inc.; (acq 12-30-2008; $7,000 for CP)
Arbitron Metro Market: Owen, WI *Format:* Christian
Vic Eliason, President

Park Falls

WCQM
04-13-1968; 98.3 mhz FM *Hrs Open:* 24; 100 kw; 440 ft.; N45 52 56 W90 26 15
P.O. Box 339, Luxemburg, WI 54217 US
(715) 762-3221, *Fax:* (715) 762-2358
www.wcqm.com
wcqm@wcqm.com
License: Park Falls, Price County, WI held by Heartland Communications License LLC
Group Owner: Heartland Communications Group LLC
Nat'l Network: ABC
Arbitron Metro Market: Luxemburg, WI *Format:* Country *Hrs. of News Programming:* news progmg 6 hrs wkly *No. News Employees:* 1 *Target Audience:* 20-70. *Adv. Rates:* 19.95; 19.95; 19.95; 19.95
Kirk Knoll, News Director

*WHBM
11-11-1988; 90.3 mhz FM *Hrs Open:* 24; 35 kw; 712 ft.; N45 56 43 W90 16 22 *Rebroadcasts:* Rebroadcasts WHA (AM) Madison 100%
3319 W. Beltline Highway, Madison, WI 53713 US
(715) 261-6298, *Fax:* (715) 848-2890
www.wpr.org
reyer@wpr.org
License: Park Falls, Price County, WI held by State of Wisconsin Educational Communications Board.
Regional Network: Wis. Public Radio
Format: News, News/Talk, 86 *No. News Employees:* 9 *Target Audience:* 35-54; skews female: Issue oriented talk-var of perspectives
Wendy Wink, CEO
Tom Martin-Erickson, Operations Dir
Phil Corriveau, General Manager
Rick Reyer, General Sales Mgr
Allen Rieland, Chief Engineer
Ted Tobie, CFO

WPFP
01-01-1953; 980 khz AM *Hrs Open:* 24; 1 kw-D, 105 w-N; N45 55 04 W90 26 58
Mailing Address: Box 309, Park Falls, WI 54217
Second Address: Hwy. 13 S., Park Falls, WI 54552
(715) 762-3221, *Fax:* (715) 762-2358
wnbi@pctcnet.net
License: Park Falls, Price County, WI held by Heartland Comunications License LLC.
Group Owner: Heartland Communications Group LLC; (acq 7-30-2002; $850,000 with co-located FM).
Nat'l Network: ABC
Population Served: 18,000*Special Programming:* Relg one hr, loc community talk 5 hrs wkly *Hrs. of News Programming:* news progmg 12 hrs wkly *No. News Employees:* 2 *Target Audience:* 25-54; adults withdisposable income *Adv. Rates:* 12; 12; 12; 12
Joel Karnick, Operations Dir
James Gregori, General Manager
Darla Isham, General Sales Mgr
Arthur Dunham, Chief Engineer
Kirk Knoll, Traffic Manager

Peshtigo

WSFQ
08-05-1996; 96.3 mhz FM *Hrs Open:* 24; 49 kw; 482 ft.; N45 7 19 W87 51 7
413 10th Ave., Menominee, MI 49858 US
906-863-5551, *Fax:* 906-863-5679
baycitiesradio.net
License: Peshtigo, Marinette County, WI held by Armada Media - Menominee Inc.
Group Owner: Armada Media Corp.; (acq 12-19-2006; grpsl)
Format: Oldies *No. News Employees:* 1 *Target Audience:* 35-54
Jim Callow, Operations Dir
Chris Bernier, General Manager
Barb VanDeHei, General Sales Mgr
Ken Conners, News Director

Platteville

WPVL
02-22-1955; 1590 khz AM *Hrs Open:* 24; 1 kw-D, DAN; 0.5 kw-N, DAN; N42 44 46 W90 28 28
7025 Raymond Road, Madison, WI 53744 US
(608) 349-2000, *Fax:* (608) 349-2002
www.wpvl.com
info@wpvl.com
License: Platteville, WI held by QueenB Radio Wisconsin Inc.
Group Owner: Morgan Murphy Media (Evening Telegram Co); (acq 3-18-98; $825,000 with co-located FM)
Nat'l Network: ABC; ESPN Radio
Arbitron Metro Market: Dubuque, IA *Format:* Sports *Special Programming:* Farm 12 hrs, sports 15 hrs wkly *Hrs. of News Programming:* news progmg 10 hrs wkly *No. News Employees:* 2 *Target Audience:* 35 plus.*Adv. Rates:* 15; 12; 14; 11
Dan Sullivan, General Manager

WPVL-FM
09-01-1966; 107.1 mhz FM *Hrs Open:* 24; 4.2 kw; 394 ft.; N42 41 27 W90 37 26
7025 Raymond Road, Madison, WI 53744 US
(608) 349-2000, *Fax:* (608) 349-2002
www.wpvl.com
info@wpvl.com
License: Platteville, Grant County, WI held by QueenB Radio Wisconsin Inc.
Group Owner: Morgan Murphy Media (Evening Telegram Co)
Arbitron Metro Market: Dubuque, IA *Format:* Oldies *Hrs. of News Programming:* news progmg 10 hrs wkly *No. News Employees:* 1 *Target Audience:* 30 plus; general adults
Rick Samson, Station Manager

*WSUP
02-25-1964; 90.5 mhz FM *Hrs Open:* 20; 1 kw; 148 ft.; N42 43 57 W90 29 9
1220 Linden Drive, Madison, WI 53706 US
(608) 342-1165,(608) 342-1291, *Fax:* (608) 342-1290
ums.www.uwplatt.edu/~wsup/
wsup@uwplatt.edu
License: Platteville, Grant County, WI held by Board of Regents, University of Wisconsin System.
Arbitron Metro Market: Dubuque, IA *Format:* Rock/AOR *Special Programming:* Class 4 hrs, jazz 3 hrs, alternative 6 hrs, metal 6 hrs, dance 4 hrs wkly *Hrs. of News Programming:* News progmg 10 hrs wkly *TargetAudience:* 18-24; college-age
George Smith, General Manager
Laura Lohfink, Station Manager

*WSSW
02-01-2007; 89.1 mhz FM; 0.06 kw; 561 ft.; N42 45 50.7 W90 24 19.7 *Rebroadcasts:* Rebroadcasts WERN(FM) Madison 100%
3319 W Beltline Highway, Madison, WI 53713 US
(608) 263-3970, *Fax:* (608) 263-9763
www.wpr.org
License: Platteville, Grant County, WI held by State of Wisconsin-Educational Communications Board.
Nat'l Network: NPR *Regional Network:* Wis. Public Radio
Arbitron Metro Market: Platteville, WI *Format:* Classical
Tim Allen, Operations Dir
Phil Corniveau, General Manager
Michael Leland, News Director
Mike Crane, Director of Radio
Michael Arnold, Associate Director
Mary Kay Dadisman, Director of Development
Steve Johnston, Director ofEngineering & Operations

Plymouth

WJUB
04-01-1954; 1420 khz AM *Hrs Open:* 24; 0.5 kw-D, ND1; 0.062 kw-N, ND1; N43 44 33 W87 56 21
N5569 Sth 57, Plymouth, WI 53073 US
(920) 893-2661, *Fax:* (920) 892-2706
www.1420thebreeze.com
1420amthebreeze@jmiradio.org
License: Plymouth, WI held by Jubilation Ministries Inc.
Nat'l Network: USA
Arbitron Metro Market: Sheboygan, WI *Format:* Adult Contemp *Special Programming:* Farm 5 hrs wkly *Hrs. of News Programming:* News progmg 11 hrs wkly *Target Audience:* 25-54.
Gerry Krebsbach, President
William Horsch, General Manager
David Hendrickson, Programming Director

WXER
10-03-2000; 104.5 mhz FM *Hrs Open:* 24; 5.1 kw; 354 ft.; N43 43 32 W88 3 7
1102 Fond Du Lac Avenue, Sheboygan Falls, WI 53085 US
(920) 458-2107, *Fax:* (920) 458-9775
www.wxerfm.com
studio@wxerfm.com
License: Plymouth, Sheboygan County, WI held by Midwest Communications Inc.
Group Owner: Midwest Communications Inc.; (acq 11-1-2005; $2.3 million)
Arbitron Metro Market: Sheboygan, WI *Format:* Adult Contemp *Special Programming:* Ger 3 hrs wkly *Target Audience:* 29-54.
Duke Wright, President
Steve Schouten, Operations Dir
Randall Hopper, Station Manager
Dave Riley, Programming Director
Patrick Pendergrast, Promotions Manager
Karen Branch, News Director
Stewart Muck, Chief Engineer

Port Washington

WPJP
10-01-1969; 100.1 mhz FM *Hrs Open:* 24; 6 kw; 318 ft.; N43 25 14 W87 59 40
900 East Green Bay Road, Port Washington, WI 53074 US
(920) 469-3021, *Fax:* (262) 784-2149
www.live365.com
License: Port Washington, Ozaukee County, WI held by Starboard Media Foundation Inc.
Group Owner: Relevant Radio; (acq 5-15-2003; $900,000).
Arbitron Metro Market: Milwaukee-Racine, WI
Mark Follett, CEO
Neil Robbins, Station Manager

Portage

WBKY
01-01-1998; 95.9 mhz FM *Hrs Open:* 24; 5.4 kw; 322 ft.; N43 38 17 W89 34 16
Mailing Address: 1021 North Superior Ave., Suite 5, Tomah, WI 54660 US
Second Address: 1420 E. Wisconsin St., Portage, WI 53901
(608) 742-1001, *Fax:* (608) 635-7343
www.buckycountry959.com
License: Portage, Columbia County, WI held by Magnum Communications Inc.
Group Owner: Magnum Communications Inc.
Nat'l Network: AP Radio
Arbitron Metro Market: Portage, WI *Format:* Country *Hrs. of News Programming:* news progmg 7 hrs wkly *No. News Employees:* 2
Rick Jensen, Operations Dir
Dave Magnum, General Manager
Doug Steele, General Sales Mgr
Steve Paterson, Programming Director
Pete Holliday, News Director
Jon Zecherle, Chief Engineer
Deb Doyle, Traffic Manager

WDDC
11-08-1966; 100.1 mhz FM *Hrs Open:* 24; 3.1 kw; 374 ft.; N43 31 42 W89 26 1
Mailing Address: P. O. Box 300, Portage, WI 53901 US
Second Address: N6912 Hwy. 51, Portage, WI 53901
(608) 742-1001, *Fax:* (608) 742-1688
www.thunder100fm.com
License: Portage, Columbia County, WI held by Zoe Communications
Arbitron Metro Market: Madison, WI *Format:* Country *No. News Employees:* 2 *Target Audience:* 25-45; office workers, young adults
Kevin Todryk, Programming Director

WPDR
07-31-1952; 1350 khz AM *Hrs Open:* 24; 1 kw-D, ND1; 0.041 kw-N, ND1; N43 31 42 W89 26 1
Mailing Address: P. O. Box 300, Portage, WI 53901 US
Second Address: N6912 Hwy. 51, Portage, WI 53901
(608) 742-1001, *Fax:* (608) 742-1688
wpdr@jvlnet.com
License: Portage, WI held by Zoe Communications Inc.
Group Owner: Zoe Communications Inc.; acq 2003; $1.1 million with co-located FM).
Format: Adult Contemp, News, 62, Talk *Special Programming:* Farm 6 hrs wkly *Hrs. of News Programming:* news progmg 14 hrs wkly *No. News Employees:* 2 *Target Audience:* 35 plus.
Adv. Rates: 12; 12; 12; 6
Mike Oberg, President
Lyric Klaske, General Manager
Robert Hoffer, General Sales Mgr
Susann Gamble, Programming Director
Wendy Oberg, Executive Vice President

Poynette

WHFA
07-01-1925; 1240 khz AM *Hrs Open:* 24; 1 kw-U, ND1; N43 21 38 W89 24 8
1021 N. Superior Ave., Suite 5, Tomah, WI 54660 US
(920) 469-3021, *Fax:* (608) 833-7117
www.relevantradio.com
whfa@relevantradio.com
License: Poynette, WI held by Starboard Media Foundation Inc.
Group Owner: Relevant Radio; (acq 6-28-2001; $1 million).
Nat'l Network: ABC *Regional Network:* Tribune Radio Networks; Wisconsin Radio Net.
Arbitron Metro Market: Madison, WI *Format:* Christian *Hrs. of News Programming:* News progmg 3 hrs wkly *Target Audience:* 35-64.
Martin Jury, Operations Dir

Prairie Du Chien

WPRE
12-11-1952; 980 khz AM *Hrs Open:* 24
Mailing Address: Rt. 4 Box 6a, Viroqua, WI 54665 US
Second Address: 640 North Villa Louis Rd., Prairie du Chien, WI 53821
(608) 326-2411, *Fax:* (608) 326-2412
www.wpreradio.com
wqpcwpre@mwt.net
License: Prairie Du Chien, WI held by Robinson Corp.
Group Owner: Robinson Corporation; (acq 1-7-98; with co-located FM).
Nat'l Network: Westwood One
Format: Oldies *No. News Employees:* 1
David Robinson, President
Jeff Robinson, Operations Dir

WQPC
01-01-1968; 94.3 mhz FM *Hrs Open:* 24; 36 kw; 525 ft.; N43 3 35 W91 6 2
Mailing Address: Rt. 4 Box 6a, Viroqua, WI 54665 US
Second Address: 640 North Villa Rd., Prairie du Chien, WI 53821
(608) 326-2411, *Fax:* (608) 326-2412
www.wqpcradio.com
wqpcwpre@mwt.net
License: Prairie Du Chien, Crawford County, WI held by Robinson Corp.
Group Owner: Robinson Corporation
Format: Country
Derek Wagner, General Manager
Paul Gubala, Programming Director
Derick McMillan, Chief Engineer
Chris Malone, Assistant Music Director
Sherman Austin, Public Affairs Director

Racine

WEZY
08-06-1962; 92.1 mhz FM *Hrs Open:* 24; 2.7 kw; 492 ft.; N42 45 36 W87 57 53
One South Parker Drive, Janesville, WI 53545 US
(262) 634-3311, *Fax:* 92620 634-6515
www.literock921.com
cmoreau@racineradio.com
License: Racine, Racine County, WI
Arbitron Metro Market: Racine, WI *Format:* Easy Listening *Hrs. of News Programming:* news progmg 4 hrs wkly *No. News Employees:* 2 *Target Audience:* 25-54.
Chris Moreau, Vice President and General Manager
Don Rosen, Programming Director
Lew Turner, Promotions Manager
Tom Karkow, News Director

WKKV-FM
08-01-1948; 100.7 mhz FM *Hrs Open:* 24; 50 kw; 499 ft.; N42 48 18 W88 2 54
200 Concord Plaza, Suite 600, San Antonio, TX 78216 US
(414) 321-1007, *Fax:* (414) 327-3200
www.v100.com
info@v100.com
License: Racine, Racine County, WI held by Clear Channel Radio Licenses Inc.
Group Owner: Clear Channel Communications Inc.; (acq 1996; grpsl)
Nat'l Network: Premiere Radio Networks; Superadio *Nat'l Reps:* Clear Channel
Arbitron Metro Market: Milwaukee-Racine, WI *Format:* Blues
Special Programming: Gospel 6 hrs wkly *Target Audience:* 18-44; general
L. Lowry Mays, CEO
Mark Mays, President
Kerry Wolfe, Operations Dir
Cindy McDowell, General Manager
Randy Wanek, General Sales Mgr
Bailey Coleman, Programming Director
Sean John, Promotions Manager
Terry James, NewsDirector
Al Hajny, Chief Engineer
Karen Mason, Traffic Manager

WRJN
12-01-1926; 1400 khz AM *Hrs Open:* 24; 1 kw-U, ND1; N42 42 38 W87 49 49
One South Parker Drive, Janesville, WI 53547 US
(262) 634-3311, *Fax:* (262) 634-6515
wrjn@wi.net
License: Racine, WI held by Racine Broadcasting L.L.C.
Group Owner: Bliss Communications Inc.; (acq 7-11-97; $5 million with co-located FM)
Nat'l Reps: Christal
Arbitron Metro Market: Milwaukee-Racine, WI *Format:* News, News/Talk, 86 *Special Programming:* Class 2 hrs, lt 2.5, Serbian 2 hrs wkly *Hrs. of News Programming:* news progmg 40 hrs wkly *No. News Employees:* 2*Target Audience:* 35 plus.
Rob Lisser, CFO
Skip Bliss, President
Tim Etes, Operations Dir
Leo Edelstein, General Sales Mgr
Don Rosen, Programming Director
Lew Turner, Promotions Manager
Bob Dailey, Executive Vice President
Ron Richards, OperationsDirector

Reedsburg

WBDL
01-01-1997; 102.9 mhz FM; 3.6 kw; 423 ft.; N43 35 32 W90 0 42
980 North Michigan Avenue, Suite 1880, Chicago, IL 60611 US
(256) 497-4502, *Fax:* NA
varietyrock@hotmail.com
License: Reedsburg, Sauk County, WI held by Magnum Communications Inc.
Group Owner: Magnum Communications Inc.; (acq 10-18-2007; grpsl)
Nat'l Network: ABC
Arbitron Metro Market: Mesquite TX *Format:* Variety/Diverse, Rock/AOR *Target Audience:* 18-54.
Richard Dabney, General Manager

WNFM
07-16-1967; 104.9 mhz FM *Hrs Open:* 24; 3.2 kw; 449 ft.; N43 35 32 W90 0 42
980 North Michigan Avenue, Suite 1880, Chicago, IL 60611 US
(608) 524-1400, *Fax:* (608) 524-2474
www.wnfmcountry.com
License: Reedsburg, Sauk County, WI
Group Owner: Magnum Communications Inc.
Arbitron Metro Market: Reedsburh, WI *Format:* Country *Hrs. of News Programming:* news progmg 10 hrs wkly *No. News Employees:* 1 *Target Audience:* 25 plus.
Bob Hendrickson, General Manager
Keith Conway, Programming Director

WRDB
02-06-1953; 1400 khz AM *Hrs Open:* 24; 1 kw-U, ND1; N43 32 30 W90 2 5
980 North Michigan Avenue, Suite 1880, Chicago, IL 60611 US
(608) 524-1400,(608) 524-1049, *Fax:* (608) 524-2474
saukbroad@mwt.net
License: Reedsburg, WI held by Magnum Communications Inc.
Group Owner: Magnum Communications Inc.; (acq 10-18-2007; grpsl)
Format: News, Oldies *Hrs. of News Programming:* news progmg 14 hrs wkly *No. News Employees:* 1 *Target Audience:* 25-54.
Tommy Lee Bychinski, General Manager
Amber Selje, News Director

Reserve

***WOJB**
04-01-1982; 88.9 mhz FM; 100 kw; 604 ft; N45 52 16 W91 20 56
13386 W. Trepania Rd., Hayward, WI 54843
(715) 634-4070, *Fax:* (715) 634-4070
www.wojb.org
generalmanager@wojb.org
License: Reserve, WI held by Lac Courte Oreilles Ojibwe Public Broadcasting Corp.
Nat'l Network: NPR; PRI
Special Programming: Indian 15 hrs, country 15 hrs, jazz 10 hrs, bluegrass 2 hrs wkly
Sid Kellar, General Manager

Rhinelander

WHDG
09-01-1994; 97.3 mhz FM *Hrs Open:* 24; 100 kw; 551 ft.; N45 22 50 W89 11 22
P. O. Box 96, 7380 Hwy 51 South, Minocqua, WI 54548 US
(715) 362-1975, *Fax:* (715) 362-1973
www.whdg.com
whdg@whdg.com
License: Rhinelander, Oneida County, WI held by Raven License Sub. LLC.
Group Owner: NRG Media LLC; (acq 10-31-2005; grpsl)
Wire Services: Wheeler News Service
Format: Country *Hrs. of News Programming:* news progmg 10 hrs wkly *No. News Employees:* 1 *Target Audience:* 25-54. *Adv. Rates:* 45; 42; 44; 15
Duff Damos, Operations Dir
Steve Albertson, General Manager
Bill Mitchell, Programming Director
Mary Spatz, News Director
Al Johnson, Chief Engineer

WOBT
03-09-1947; 1240 khz AM
980 North Michigan Ave, Ste. 1880, Chicago, IL 60611 US
715-362-6140, *Fax:* 715-362-4200
License: Rhinelander, WI held by NRG License Sub. LLC.
Group Owner: NRG Media LLC; (acq 10-31-2005; grpsl)
TV Affiliate: Sports *Special Programming:* news progmg 10 hrs wkly *Hrs. of News Programming:* 1 *No. News Employees:* 18+.

WRHN
01-26-1966; 100.1 mhz FM *Hrs Open:* 24; 100 kw; 292 ft.; N45 37 42 W89 23 38
980 North Michigan Ave, Ste. 1880, Chicago, IL 60611 US
(715) 362-1975, *Fax:* (715) 362-1973
www.wrhn.com
License: Rhinelander, Oneida County, WI held by NRG License Sub. LLC.
Group Owner: NRG Media LLC
Format: Adult Contemp *Target Audience:* 18-49. *Adv. Rates:* 30; 27; 29; 9
Duff Damos, Operations Dir
Steve Albertson, General Sales Mgr

***WXPR**
04-24-1983; 91.7 mhz FM *Hrs Open:* 5 AM-midnight; 100 kw; 420 ft.; N45 46 28 W89 14 54
303 W. Prospect St., Rhinelander, WI 54501 US
(715) 362-6000, *Fax:* (715) 362-6007
www.wxpr.org
wxpr@wxpr.org
License: Rhinelander, Oneida County, WI held by White Pine Community Broadcasting Inc.
Nat'l Network: NPR
Arbitron Metro Market: Rhinelander, WI *Format:* Variety/Diverse
Special Programming: Jazz 8 hrs wkly
Mick Fiocchi, President
Walt Gander, Operations Dir
Peg Arnold, Station Manager
Ken Krall, News Director
Elmer Goetsch, Chief Engineer
Mick Fiocchi, Executive Advisor
Becky Tegen, Membership Director
Marcia Barkus, MusicDirector
Cara Kulhanek, Database Manager
Jessie Dick, Development Director

***KSPP**
89.1 mhz FM; 8.5 kw vert; 89.9 meters; N45 46 30.5 W89 14 55.1
1980 Moraine Terrace, Suite 9, Green Bay, WI
(262) 349-3254
www.familyradio.org
familyradio@familyradio.org
License: Rhinelander, WI held by Northwoods Catholic Radio

WHOH
96.5 mhz FM; 2.45 kw; 318 m; N45 40 03 W89 12 29
1528 S. Koeller Road, Oshkosh, WI
(920) 987-5566
License: Rhinelander, Oneida County, WI held by Multi-Cultural Diversity Radio Inc.

Samir Abumayyaleh, President

Rice Lake

WAQE
08-06-1979; 1090 khz AM; 5 kw-D, NDD; N45 32 16 W91 45 50
1859 21st Avenue, Rice Lake, WI 54868 US

(715) 234-9059, *Fax:* (715) 234-6942
www.waqe.com
info@wage.com
License: Rice Lake, WI held by TKC Inc.
Group Owner: Koser Radio Group; (acq 1999)
Arbitron Metro Market: Rice Lake, WI *Format:* Country *Hrs. of News Programming:* news progmg 5 hrs wkly *No. News Employees:* 1 *Target Audience:* 24-59; traditional country mus listeners *Adv. Rates:* 12; 8;10; na
Tom Koser, General Manager
Brian Schultz, Station Manager
Dane Jensen, General Sales Mgr
Mike Bigner, Programming Director
John Roberts, News Director
Mike Murrey, Chief Engineer

WKFX
11-20-1980; 97.7 mhz FM *Hrs Open:* 24; 44 kw; 522 ft.; N45 22 23 W91 55 22
1859 21st Avenue, Rice Lake, WI 54868 US
(715) 234-9059, *Fax:* (715) 234-6942
www.fox99.com
info@fox99.com
License: Rice Lake, Barron County, WI held by TKC Inc.
Arbitron Metro Market: Rice Lake, WI *Format:* Contemporary Hits/Top 40, Adult Contemp *Hrs. of News Programming:* news progmg 3 hrs wkly *No. News Employees:* 1 *Target Audience:* 18-49; young, upscale adults*Adv. Rates:* 12; 8; 10; 6
Tom Koser, CEO
Peter Neuser, Station Manager

WJMC
01-01-1938; 1240 khz AM *Hrs Open:* 24; 1 kw-U, ND1; N45 30 31 W91 46 26
1859 21st Ave., Rice Lake, WI 54868 US
(715) 234-2131, *Fax:* (715) 234-6942
www.wjmcradio.com
info@wjmc.com
License: Rice Lake, WI held by TKC Inc.
Group Owner: Koser Radio Group; (acq 1-1-89)
Regional Network: Wisconsin Radio Net.
Format: Adult Contemp, News, 62, Talk *Target Audience:* 25-54.
Thomas Koser, President
Dane Jensen, Station Manager
Mike Bigner, Programming Director
Ken DeNucci, News Director
Mike Murrey, Chief Engineer
John Roberts, Traffic Manager

WJMC-FM
01-01-1947; 96.1 mhz FM *Hrs Open:* 24; 50 kw; 482 ft.; N45 37 14 W91 44 44
Mailing Address: 1859 21st Ave, Rice Lake, WI 54868 US
Second Address: 1859 21st Ave., Rice Lake, WI 54868
(715) 234-2131, *Fax:* (715) 234-6942
www.wjmcradio.com
info@wjmc.com
License: Rice Lake, Barron County, WI held by TKC Inc.
Group Owner: Koser Radio Group
Format: Country *Target Audience:* 25-54.
Dane Jensen, Station Manager
Mike Bigner, Programming Director
Ken DeNucci, News Director
Don Tobias, Sports Commentator

Richland Center

WRCO
10-18-1949; 1450 khz AM *Hrs Open:* 24; 1 kw-U, ND1; N43 18 58 W90 22 31
P.O. Box 529, 2111 Bohmann Drive, Richland Center, WI 53581 US
(608) 647-2111, *Fax:* (608) 647-8025
www.wrco.com
wrconews@wrco.com
License: Richland Center, WI held by Fruit Broadcasting LLC.
Nat'l Network: CBS; Westwood One *Wire Services:* AP; Wheeler News Service
Format: Adult Contemp *Special Programming:* Farm 2.hrs wkly *Hrs. of News Programming:* news progmg 20 hrs wkly *No. News Employees:* 1 *Target Audience:* 25-54; general *Adv. Rates:* 6; 5; 5; 3
Ron Fruit, President
Alice Schulte, General Sales Mgr
Phil Nee, Programming Director
Aaron Joyce, News Director
Dennis Baldridge, Chief Engineer
Amy Cook, Traffic Manager

WRCO-FM
08-01-1965; 100.9 mhz FM *Hrs Open:* 24; 8.4 kw; 559 ft.; N43 18 55.5 W90 25 34.6
2111 Bohmann Drive, PO Box 529, Richland Center, WI 53581 US
(608) 647-21111, *Fax:* (608) 647-8025
www.wrco.com
wrconews@wrco.com
License: Richland Center, Richland County, WI
Nat'l Network: CBS Radio *Regional Network:* Wisconsin Radio Net. *Wire Services:* AP; Wheeler News Service
Format: Country, News *Special Programming:* Farm 18 hrs, Gospel 6 hrs wkly *Hrs. of News Programming:* news progmg 45 hrs wkly *No. News Employees:* 2 *Target Audience:* General; adult *Adv. Rates:* 12; 10;12; 8
Ron Fruit, Operations Dir
Alice Schulte, General Sales Mgr
Phil Nee, Programming Director
Dennis Baldridge, Chief Engineer
Ray Schroeder, Disc Jockey
Tammy Dotson, Disc Jockey
Adam Hess, Disc Jockey

Ripon

***WRPN-FM**
09-15-1957; 90.1 mhz FM *Hrs Open:* 24; 0.23 kw horiz; 144 ft.; N43 50 37 W88 50 31
300 Seward Street, Ripon, WI 54971 US
(920) 748-8147,(920) 748-8115 (college), *Fax:* (920) 748-7243
www.homestead.com
wrpnfm@yahoo.com
License: Ripon, WI held by Board of Trustees of Ripon College.
Nat'l Network: CBS; ABC *Nat'l Reps:* Farmakis *Wire Services:* Wheeler News Service
Format: Classic Rock, Variety/Diverse *Special Programming:* Pol 2 hrs, sports 15 hrs wkly *Hrs. of News Programming:* news progmg 25 hrs wkly *No. News Employees:* 4
Joe Laedtke, Operations Dir
Guy McHendry, General Manager

WTCX
02-01-1965; 96.1 mhz FM *Hrs Open:* 24; 4 kw; 404 ft.; N43 49 10 W88 43 20
6 Western Avenue, Fond Du Lac, WI 54935 US
(920) 924-9697, *Fax:* (920) 929-8865
www.961tcx.com
License: Ripon, Fond du Lac County, WI
Arbitron Metro Market: Ripon, WI *Format:* Adult Contemp, Rock/AOR *Hrs. of News Programming:* news progmg 3 hrs wkly *No. News Employees:* 1 *Target Audience:* 25-54; women
Terry Davis, Operations Dir
Gregg Owens, Programming Director
Kimberley Kings, Promotions Manager
Greg Stensland, News Director
Mike Enfelt, Operations Manager

WRPN
09-15-1957; 1600 khz AM *Hrs Open:* 24; 5 kw-D, DA2; 5 kw-N, DA2; N43 49 1 W88 50 49
6 Western Avenue, Fond Du Lac, WI 54935 US
(920) 748-5111, *Fax:* (920) 748-5530
www.wrpnam.com
wrpn@wrpnam.com
License: Ripon, WI held by Radio Broadcasting L.P.
Nat'l Network: CBS; ABC *Nat'l Reps:* Farmakis *Wire Services:* Wheeler News Service
Arbitron Metro Market: Ripon, WI *Format:* News, News/Talk, 86 *Hrs. of News Programming:* news progmg 25 hrs wkly *No. News Employees:* 4 *Target Audience:* 25 plus.
Mike Enfelt, President & CEO
Mike Enfelt, General Manager
Jason Marsmith, Programming Director
Sarah Kesich, News and Producer / Traffic & Billing
Jean Hoffmann, Traffic & Billing

River Falls

WEVR
09-14-1969; 1550 khz AM *Hrs Open:* 6 AM-sunset; 0.92 kw-D, ND1; 0.004 kw-N, ND1; N44 53 19 W92 39 2
178 Radio Road, River Falls, WI 54022 US
(715) 425-1111(612) 381-1111
License: River Falls, WI held by Hanten Broadcasting Co. Inc.
Nat'l Network: USA *Wire Services:* Wheeler News Service
Arbitron Metro Market: River Falls, WI *Format:* Adult Contemp, Sports *Special Programming:* Farm 18 hrs wkly *Hrs. of News Programming:* News progmg 5 hrs wkly *Target Audience:* General.
Carol Hanten, President

WEVR-FM
09-30-1970; 106.3 mhz FM *Hrs Open:* 6 AM-11 PM; 6 kw; 328 ft.; N44 53 19 W92 39 2
178 Radio Road, River Falls, WI 54022 US
(715) 425-1111, *Fax:* (715) 381-1111
License: River Falls, Pierce County, WI held by Hanten Broadcasting Co. Inc.
Wire Services: Wheeler News Service
Arbitron Metro Market: River Falls, WI *Format:* Adult Contemp, News, 84 *Hrs. of News Programming:* News progmg 18 hrs wkly *Target Audience:* General.
Carol Hanten, President

***WRFW**
11-02-1968; 88.7 mhz FM *Hrs Open:* 24; 3 kw; 82 ft.; N44 53 8 W92 39 20
1220 Linden Drive, Madison, WI 53706 US
(715) 425-3886/3887
www.uwrf.edu/wrfw
urfw@uwrf.edu
License: River Falls, Pierce County, WI held by University of Wisconsin System.
Nat'l Network: NPR *Regional Reps:* Wisconsin Public Radio
Arbitron Metro Market: Minneapolis-St. Paul, MN *Format:* Variety/Diverse *Special Programming:* Farm 10 hrs wkly
Rick Burgsteiner, General Manager
Adam Lee, Programming Director
Nick Hassel, Promotions Manager
Tara Sowle, News Director
Paul Karklus, Music Director

Rothschild

WDTX
100.5 mhz FM; 25 kw; 276 ft.; N44 50 13 W89 45 57 US
(715) 845-8218, *Fax:* (715) 845-6582
www.espn1005.com
License: Rothschild, Marathon County, WI held by JER Licenses LLC.
Group Owner: JER Licenses LLC
Arbitron Metro Market: Rothschild, WI *Format:* Sports, Talk
Jon Robinson, General Manager

Rudolph

WSAU-FM
09-30-1990; 99.9 mhz FM *Hrs Open:* 24; 13 kw; Ant 453 ft; N44 20 19 W89 38 55 *Rebroadcasts:* Simulcast with WOFM(FM) Mosinee 100%
Box 850, 2460 Plover Rd., Plover, WI 54467
(715) 344-6050,(715) 421-4040, *Fax:* (715) 341-8070
www.lovethevalley.com
info@lovethevalley.com
License: Rudolph, Wood County, WI held by WRIG Inc.
Group Owner: Midwest Communications Inc.; (acq 1999; $1.4 million)
Nat'l Network: Fox News Radio *Nat'l Reps:* Christal
Arbitron Metro Market: Wausau-Stevens Point, WI (Central Wisconsin) *Hrs. of News Programming:* news progmg 3 hrs wkly *No. News Employees:* 3 *Target Audience:* 35 plus; upper income
Duke Wright, President
Brett Lucht, General Manager
Dawn Prudhomme, General Sales Mgr
Bill Phillips, Programming Director
John Flesch, News Director
Frank Zastrow, Chief Engineer

Sarona

WPLT
01-01-2003; 106.3 mhz FM *Hrs Open:* 24; 3.4 kw; 440 ft.; N45 40 28 W91 58 52
Pob 85-104 Donovan Cove, Shell Lake, WI 54871 US
(715) 468-9500, *Fax:* (715) 468-9505
www.king1063.com
spots@95gmo.com
License: Sarona, Washburn County, WI held by Zoe Communications Inc.
Group Owner: Zoe Communications Inc.; acq 12-6-00; $439,000 for CP).
Arbitron Metro Market: Shell Lake, WI *Format:* Country
Wendy Oberg, General Manager
Tasha Hagberg, General Sales Mgr
Bo Landry, Programming Director
Mike Oberg, Chief Engineer

Sauk City

WIBA-FM
03-01-1947; 101.5 mhz FM; 12 kw; 1014 ft.; N43 3 21 W89 32 6
600 Congress Ave., Suite 1400, Austin, TX 78701 US
(608) 274-5450, *Fax:* (608) 274-5521
www.wibafm.com
info@wibafm.com

License: Sauk City, Dane County, WI held by Capstar TX L.P.
Group Owner: Clear Channel Communications Inc.
Arbitron Metro Market: Madison, WI *Format:* Classic Rock
Mike Ferris, Programming Director
Jennie Hibbard, News Director

Schofield

WRIG

08-01-1958; 1390 khz AM *Hrs Open:* 24
Mailing Address: 904 Grand Avenue, Wausau, WI 54403 US
Second Address: 557 Scott St., Wausau, WI 54403
(715) 842-1672, *Fax:* (715) 848-3158
www.bigwrig.com
ken@bigwrig.com
License: Schofield, WI held by WRIG Inc.
Group Owner: Midwest Communications Inc.
Arbitron Metro Market: Wausau-Stevens Point, WI (Central Wisconsin) *Format:* Oldies *Hrs. of News Programming:* news progmg 2 hrs wkly *No. News Employees:* 2
D.E. Wright, President
Brett Lucht, General Manager
Samantha Milanowski, General Sales Mgr
Ken Clark, Programming Director
John Flesch, News Director
Frank Zastrow, Chief Engineer
Gary Tesch, Executive Vice President

Seymour

WCHK-FM

05-01-1998; 104.3 mhz FM; 5.6 kw; Ant 341 ft; N44 31 26 W88 19 56
Box 1519, Appleton, WI 54165
(920) 734-9226, *Fax:* (920) 739-0494
www.1043thebreeze.com
License: Seymour, Outagamie County, WI held by Woodward Communications Inc.
Group Owner: Woodward Communications Inc.; acq 6-23-2003; $1.75 million).
Population Served: 152,069 *Arbitron Metro Market:* Green Bay, WI
Greg Bell, General Manager
Kelly Radandt, General Sales Mgr
Dayton Kane, Programming Director
Steve Brown, Chief Engineer

Shawano

WOWN

12-01-1966; 99.3 mhz FM *Hrs Open:* 24; 14 kw; 440 ft.; N44 45 14 W88 20 1
1456 East Green Bay St., Shawano, WI 54166 US
(715) 524-2194, *Fax:* (715) 524-9980
License: Shawano, Shawano County, WI
Group Owner: Results Broadcasting
Nat'l Network: ABC
Arbitron Metro Market: Green Bay, WI *Format:* Contemporary Hits/Top 40, Adult Contemp *Hrs. of News Programming:* news progmg 13 hrs wkly *No. News Employees:* 1 *Target Audience:* 20-45.
Bruce Grassman, CEO

WTCH

09-03-1948; 960 khz AM *Hrs Open:* 24
1456 East Green Bay St., Shawano, WI 54166 US
(715) 524-2194, *Fax:* (715) 524-9980
www.wtcham960.com
ResultsBroadcasting@gmail.com
License: Shawano, WI held by Results Broadcasting Inc.
Group Owner: Results Broadcasting; (acq 12-23-96; $2,704,670 for 50% of stock with co-located FM).
Nat'l Network: CBS
Arbitron Metro Market: Green Bay, WI *Format:* Country *Special Programming:* Farm 21 hrs wkly *Hrs. of News Programming:* news progmg 25 hrs wkly *No. News Employees:* 1 *Target Audience:* 25-54; northeastWisconsin adults
Bruce Grassman, Chairman
Trisha Peterson, Operations Dir

Sheboygan

WBFM

03-01-1977; 93.7 mhz FM; 6 kw; 253 ft.; N43 43 12 W87 44 4
1626 Prospect Avenue, #2310, Milwaukee, IL 53202 US
(920) 451-2310, *Fax:* (920) 458-9775
www.b93radio.com
randy.shannon@b93radio.com
License: Sheboygan, Sheboygan County, WI held by Midwest Communications Inc.
Group Owner: Midwest Communications Inc.
Nat'l Network: Fox News Radio *Regional Reps:* Rgnl Reps
Arbitron Metro Market: Sheboygan, WI *Format:* Country *Hrs. of News Programming:* news progmg 24 hrs wkly *No. News Employees:* 2 *Target Audience:* 25-54; adults in Sheboygan county/Northern Milwaukee metro area*Adv. Rates:* 50; 50; 50; 20
Eddie Ybarra, Programming Director
Steve Schouten, Promotions Manager
Tim Laes, Chief Engineer

WCLB

01-01-1956; 950 khz AM *Hrs Open:* 18; 0.5 kw-D, DA2; 0.011 kw-N, DA2; N43 44 33 W87 49 0
1102 Fond Du Lac Avenue, Sheboygan Falls, WI 53085 US
(920) 921-1071, *Fax:* (920) 467-4300
www.950thegame.com
info@950thegame.com
License: Sheboygan, WI held by RBH Enterprises Inc. dba Yellow Dog Broadcasting.
Group Owner: Mountain Dog Media; (acq 6-23-00; $700,000 with WXER(FM) Plymouth).
Nat'l Network: Westwood One
Arbitron Metro Market: Sheboygan, WI *Format:* Sports *Hrs. of News Programming:* news progmg 8 hrs wkly *No. News Employees:* 2 *Target Audience:* 35-64. *Adv. Rates:* 22; 20; 22
Randy Hopper, General Manager

WHBL

01-01-1926; 1330 khz AM *Hrs Open:* 24; 5 kw-D, DA2; 1 kw-N, DA2; N43 43 14 W87 44 4
Mailing Address: 1626 Prospect Avenue, #2310, Milwaukee, WI 53202 US
Second Address: 2100 Washington Ave., Sheboygan, WI 53082
(920) 458-2107, *Fax:* (920) 458-9775
www.whbl.com
studio@whbl.com
License: Sheboygan, WI held by Midwest Communications Inc.
Group Owner: Midwest Communications Inc.; (acq 8-8-2000; grpsl)
Nat'l Network: Fox News Radio *Regional Network:* Wisconsin Radio Net. *Nat'l Reps:* Rgnl Reps
Arbitron Metro Market: Sheboygan, WI *Format:* News, News/Talk, 86 *Special Programming:* Farm 10 hrs wkly *Hrs. of News Programming:* news progmg 24 hrs wkly *No. News Employees:* 2 *Target Audience:* 35-64*Adv. Rates:* 50; 50; 50; 20
Kelly Meyer, Programming Director
Steve Schouten, Promotions Manager
Tim Laes, Chief Engineer
Mike Kinzel, News Director

*WSHS

11-19-1971; 91.7 mhz FM *Hrs Open:* 24; 0.175 kw vert; 85 ft.; N43 46 32 W87 43 4
830 Virginia Avenue, Sheboygan, WI 53081 US
(920) 459-3500, *Fax:* (920) 803-7612
www.sheboygan.k12.wi.us
wshs@sheboygan.k12.wi.us
License: Sheboygan, Sheboygan County, WI held by Sheboygan Area School District.
Nat'l Network: NPR *Regional Network:* Wis. Public Radio
Regional Reps: Glenn Slatts
Arbitron Metro Market: Sheboygan, WI *Format:* Adult Contemp, Rock/AOR *Special Programming:* Hmong 3 hrs, Sp 3 hrs wkly
Target Audience: 18-45; young adults & teens
Ron Rindfleish, President
Jon Etter, General Manager

Sheboygan Falls

WHBZ

04-01-1997; 106.5 mhz FM; 6 kw; 240 ft.; N43 43 16 W87 44 3
1625 Prospect Avenue, #2310, Milwaukee, WI 53201 US
(920) 458-2107, *Fax:* (920) 458-9775
www.whbz.fm
thebuzz@whbz.fm
License: Sheboygan Falls, Sheboygan County, WI held by Midwest Communications Inc.
Group Owner: Midwest Communications Inc.; acq 8-8-00; grpsl).
Nat'l Network: Fox News Radio *Nat'l Reps:* Rgnl Reps
Arbitron Metro Market: Sheboygan, WI *Hrs. of News Programming:* News progmg 10 hrs wkly *No. News Employees:* 2 *Target Audience:* Males 18-49 *Adv. Rates:* 65; 65; 65; 65
Dave Nelson, Programming Director
Steve Schouten, Promotions Manager
Tim Laes, Chief Engineer
Mike Kinzel, News Director

Shell Lake

WCSW

12-30-1967; 940 khz AM; 1 kw-D, NDD; N45 41 36 W91 57 57
Mailing Address: PO Box 190, Shell Lake, WI 54871 US
Second Address: 345 Hwy. 63 S., Shell Lake, WI 54871
(715) 468-9500, *Fax:* (715) 468-9505
info@wcsw.com
License: Shell Lake, WI held by Zoe Communications Inc.
Group Owner: Zoe Communications Inc.; acq 1-1-00; with co-located FM)
Nat'l Network: ABC
Arbitron Metro Market: Eau Claire WI *Format:* Talk *Special Programming:* Farm 3 hrs wkly *Target Audience:* General.
Wendy Oberg, General Manager
Loren Miller, General Sales Mgr
Mike Oberg, Programming Director
Stephanie Butenhoff, Traffic Manager

Siren

WXCX

01-01-2000; 105.7 mhz FM *Hrs Open:* 24; 6 kw; 328 ft.; N45 49 43 W92 28 41
Mailing Address: 3750 Us 27, North Suite 1, Sebring, FL 33870 US
Second Address: 2547 Hwy. 35, Suite 3, Luck, WI 54853
(715)-825-4240, *Fax:* (715)-825-4244
www.redrockonair.com/wxcx/
jesselogan@redrockonair.com.
License: Siren, Burnett County, WI held by Red Rock Radio Corp.
Group Owner: Red Rock Radio Corp.; (acq 9-1-2006; grpsl)
Nat'l Network: Jones Radio Networks *Nat'l Reps:* Midwest Radio
Regional Reps: MidwestRadio
Arbitron Metro Market: Sebring, FL *Format:* News, Sports *No. News Employees:* 1 *Target Audience:* 35-64.
Ro Grignon, President
Don Welch, Operations Dir
Ron Revere, General Manager

Sister Bay

*WHDI

01-01-2000; 91.9 mhz FM; 3.4 kw; 476 ft.; N45 14 19 W87 5 27
3319 West Beltline Hwy, Madison, WI 53713 US
(608) 264-9600, *Fax:* (608) 264-9664
www.ecb.org
info@ecb.org
License: Sister Bay, Door County, WI held by State of Wisconsin-Educational Communications Board.
Nat'l Network: NPR *Regional Network:* Wis. Public Radio
Format: Talk
Gene Purcell, General Manager
Phil Corriveau, Station Manager

*WHND

09-16-1999; 89.7 mhz FM *Hrs Open:* 24; 3.4 kw; 538 ft.; N45 14 19 W87 5 27
Mailing Address: 3319 West Beltline Hwy, Madison, WI 53713 US
Second Address: 821 University Ave., Madison, WI 53706
(920) 465-2444, *Fax:* (920) 465-2576
www.wpr.org
listener@wpr.org
License: Sister Bay, Door County, WI held by State of Wisconsin Educational Communications Board.
Nat'l Network: NPR; PRI
Format: Classical, News *Special Programming:* Native American 2 hrs, blues 2 hrs, folk 2 hrs, ja *Hrs. of News Programming:* news progmg 29 hrs wkly *No. News Employees:* 1 *Target Audience:* 35 plus; sociallyaware, educated & financially secure *Adv. Rates:* 55; 40; 50; 35
Lisa Nalbandian, General Sales Mgr
Patty Murray, News Director

WSBW

01-01-2007; 105.1 mhz FM *Hrs Open:* 24; 3.1 kw; 466 ft.; N45 14 5 W87 5 27
US
(920) 746-9430, *Fax:* (920) 746-9433
info@dailynews.com
License: Sister Bay, Door County, WI held by Nicolet Broadcasting Inc.
Group Owner: Nicolet Broadcasting Inc.
Arbitron Metro Market: Sister Bay, WI *Format:* Oldies *Hrs. of News Programming:* news prgmg 10 hrs wkly *No. News Employees:* 2
Roger Utnehmer, President

Soldiers Grove

WKPO

06-03-2009; 105.9 mhz FM *Hrs Open:* 24; 25 kw; 328 ft.; N43 34 26 W90 48 55
US

(608) 637-7200, *Fax:* (608) 637-7299
License: Soldiers Grove, Crawford County, WI held by Robinson Corp.
Group Owner: Robinson Corporation; (acq 6-5-2008; $250,000)
Arbitron Metro Market: Soldiers Grove, WI *Format:* Adult Contemp *No. News Employees:* 1
David Robinson, President
Jeff Robinson, General Manager

Sparta

WCOW-FM

03-01-1960; 97.1 mhz FM *Hrs Open:* 24; 100 kw; 587 ft.; N43 58 6 W90 51 35
P.O. Box 539, Sparta, WI 54656 US
(608) 269-3100, *Fax:* (608) 269-5170
www.cow97.com
info@cow97.com
License: Sparta, Monroe County, WI held by Sparta-Tomah Broadcasting Co. Inc.
Group Owner: Sparta-Tomah Broadcasting Co. Inc.
Nat'l Reps: Rgnl Reps *Wire Services:* CNN
Arbitron Metro Market: La Crosse,WI *Format:* Country *Special Programming:* Green Bay Packers *Hrs. of News Programming:* news progmg 15 hrs wkly *Target Audience:* 25 plus; rural & city residents
Shelly Holen, President
William Hoffman, General Manager
Jake Preston, Programming Director
Clary Harris, News Director
Arnie Andrews, Music Director

WKLJ

06-01-1951; 1290 khz AM *Hrs Open:* 6 AM-6 PM; 5 kw-D, ND1; 0.059 kw-N, ND1; N43 58 6 W90 51 35
P.O. Box 539, Sparta, WI 54656 US
(608) 269-3100, *Fax:* (608) 269-5170
www.espnlacrosse.com
info@espnlacrosse.com
License: Sparta, WI held by Sparta-Tomah Broadcasting Co. Inc.
Group Owner: Sparta-Tomah Broadcasting Co. Inc.; (Acq 1-19-89)
Nat'l Network: ESPN Radio *Nat'l Reps:* Rgnl Reps
Format: Sports
Shelly Holen, President
William Hoffman, General Manager

Spencer

WOSQ

09-20-1984; 92.3 mhz FM *Hrs Open:* 24; 6 kw; 299 ft.; N44 48 32 W90 21 41
980 North Michigan Avenue, Suite 1880, Chicago, IL 60611 US
(715) 384-2191, *Fax:* (715) 387-3588
www.wdlbwosq.com
License: Spencer, Marathon County, WI held by Seehafer Broadcasting Corp.
Group Owner: Seehafer Broadcasting Corp.; (acq 6-1-2006; swap with WDLB(AM) Marshfield and WFHR(AM) Wisconsin Rapids for WBCV(FM) Wausau)
Nat'l Network: ESPN Radio *Regional Network:* Brownfield *Wire Services:* Wheeler News Service
Arbitron Metro Market: Wausau-Stevens Point, WI (Central Wisconsin) *Format:* Sports *Hrs. of News Programming:* news progmg 7 hrs wkly *No. News Employees:* 2 *Target Audience:* 25-54.
Don Seehafer, President
Kent Reeves, Operations Dir
Mike Warren, News Director
Chuck Gennaro, Chief Engineer

Spooner

WGMO

12-01-1974; 95.3 mhz FM *Hrs Open:* 24; 7.1 kw; 499 ft.; N45 40 28 W91 58 52
Mailing Address: P. O. Box 190, Shell Lake, WI 54871 US
Second Address: 345 Hwy. 63 S., Shell Lake, WI 54871
(715) 468-9500, *Fax:* (715) 468-9505
www.95gmo.com
info@95gmo.com
License: Spooner, Washburn County, WI
Nat'l Network: Westwood One
Format: Classic Rock *No. News Employees:* 1
Donna Nelson, News Director

Stevens Point

WPCN

01-01-1948; 1010 khz AM; 1 kw-D; N44 32 17 W89 35 43
500 Division St., Stevens Point, WI 54481
(715) 341-9800, *Fax:* (715) 341-0000
1010wspt.com
rmuzzy@1010wspt.com
License: Stevens Point, Portage County, WI held by Americus Communications L.L.C.
Group Owner: Muzzy Broadcasting L.L.C.; (acq 1996; $1.2 million with co-located FM)
Nat'l Network: Fox News Radio
Population Served: 23,631 *Arbitron Metro Market:* Wausau-Stevens Point, WI (Central Wisconsin) *Special Programming:* Pol one hr wkly *Target Audience:* 25-54; upscale, male-orientated
Richard Muzzy, President

WSPT

05-01-1961; 97.9 mhz FM; 100 kw; Ant 338 ft; N44 32 17 W89 35 43
500 Division St., Stevens Point, WI 54481
(715) 341-9800, *Fax:* (715) 341-0000
979jackfm.com
License: Stevens Point, Portage County, WI
Group Owner: Muzzy Broadcasting L.L.C.
Population Served: 210,600 *Arbitron Metro Market:* Wausau-Stevens Point, WI (Central Wisconsin) *Target Audience:* 25-54; adult
David Harvey, General Manager
Glenn Reider, Station Manager

*WWSP

09-28-1968; 89.9 mhz FM *Hrs Open:* 6 AM-2 AM; 30 kw; 321 ft.; N44 28 55 W89 40 35
1220 Linden Drive, Madison, WI 53706 US
(715) 346-3755, *Fax:* (715) 346-4012
License: Stevens Point, Portage County, WI held by Board of Regents, University of Wisconsin System.
Wire Services: Wheeler News Service; UPI
Arbitron Metro Market: Stevens Point, WI *Format:* Jazz *Special Programming:* Hmong one hr, pub affrs 5 hrs, sports 3 hrs, blues *Target Audience:* College students.
Mark Tolstedt, General Manager
Courtney Sikorski, Station Manager
Cynthia Atchison, General Sales Mgr
Jesse Hinze, Programming Director
Dana Scheffen, News Director
Dan Neckar, Production Director
Taylor Christian, MusicDirector
Andrew Quaschnick, Computer Operations Director
Matthew Pagel, Business Director
Nicole Allee, Underwriting/Sponsorship Director
Megan Turbin, PR Director

Sturgeon Bay

WDOR

09-08-1951; 910 khz AM *Hrs Open:* 6 AM-sunset; 1 kw-D; N44 49 38 W87 21 27
Box 549, 800 S. 15th Ave., Sturgeon Bay, WI 54235
(920) 487-2822,(920) 743-4411, *Fax:* (920) 743-2334
wdor.com
email@wdor.com
License: Sturgeon Bay, Door County, WI held by Door County Broadcasting Co. Inc.
Nat'l Network: ABC
Population Served: 50,000*Hrs. of News Programming:* news progmg 23 hrs wkly *No. News Employees:* 1 *Target Audience:* 21-50; general *Adv. Rates:* 12.50; 9.40; 9.40; na
Edward Allen III, President
Edward Allen, General Sales Mgr
Edward Allen IV, Programming Director
Roger Levendusky, News Director
Steve Konopka, Engineering Dir
Dan Allen, Music Director
Peggy Pfister, Traffic Manager

WDOR-FM

12-12-1966; 93.9 mhz FM *Hrs Open:* 5 AM-midnight; 77 kw; 640 ft; N44 54 23 W87 22 15
Box 549, 800 S. 15th Ave., Sturgeon Bay, WI 54235
(920) 487-2822, *Fax:* (920) 743-4411,(920) 743-2334
wdor.com
email@wdor.com
License: Sturgeon Bay, Door County, WI held by Door County Broadcasting Co. Inc.
Nat'l Network: ABC; Milwaukee Brewers Network *Wire Services:* Wheeler News Service
Population Served: 100,000*Special Programming:* Farm 3 hrs wkly *Hrs. of News Programming:* News progmg 25 hrs wkly *No. News Employees:* 1.5 *Target Audience:* 20-40; general
Edward Allen, General Manager

WZDR(FM)

03-04-1982; 99.7 mhz FM *Hrs Open:* 24; 46 kw; 512 ft; N44 38 08 W87 37 37
Mailing Address: 1420 Bellevue St, Green Bay, WI 54311
Second Address: 115 S. Jefferson St., Green Bay, WI 54301
(920) 435-3771, *Fax:* (920) 321-2300
www.wydrthedrive.com
studio@wlyd997.com
License: Sturgeon Bay, Door County, WI held by Midwest Communications Inc.
Group Owner: Midwest Communications Inc.; (acq 6-18-93; $3.5 million with WOZZ(FM) New London;
Nat'l Reps: Christal
Population Served: 867,000 *Arbitron Metro Market:* Green Bay, WI *Format:* Light Rock *Hrs. of News Programming:* news progmg 3 hrs wkly *No. News Employees:* 4 *Target Audience:* 21-54 *Adv. Rates:* 25;25; 50; 25
Duke Wright, President
Jennifer Kalies, General Sales Mgr
Jenny Lawrence, Programming Director
Jerry Bader, News Director
Tim Laes, Chief Engineer

*WPFF

08-01-1991; 90.5 mhz FM *Hrs Open:* 24; 100 kw; 640 ft.; N44 54 14 W87 22 13
1723 Michigan Street, PO Box 444, Sturgeon Bay, WI 54235 US
(920) 743-7443
www.wpff.com
wpff@wpff.com
License: Sturgeon Bay, Door County, WI held by Bethesda Christian Broadcasting.
Group Owner: Bethesda Christian Broadcasting; (acq 12-31-2007; $1.7 million with WNLI(FM) Sturgeon Bay)
Nat'l Network: USA
Format: Christian *Hrs. of News Programming:* News progmg 12 hrs wkly *Target Audience:* 25-49; baby boomers
Mark Schwarzbauer, General Manager
Andy King, Station Manager

*WNLI

07-01-1998; 88.5 mhz FM *Hrs Open:* 24; 50 kw; 518 ft.; N44 54 14 W87 22 13
Mailing Address: 1723 Michigan Street, Sturgeon Bay, WI 54235 US
Second Address: 1723 Michigan St., Sturgeon Bay, WI 54235
(920) 743-7443, *Fax:* (920) 743-7543
www.wrgx.com
wrgx@wrgx.com
License: Sturgeon Bay, Door County, WI held by Bethesda Christian Broadcasting.
Group Owner: Bethesda Christian Broadcasting; (acq 12-31-2007; $1.7 million with WPFF(FM) Sturgeon Bay)
Format: Christian, Rock/AOR *Target Audience:* 13-35; teens & generation x listeners
Mark Pluimer, President
Dr. Mark Schwarzbaur, General Manager

WSRG

04-18-1988; 97.7 mhz FM *Hrs Open:* 24; 1.85 kw; 597 ft.; N44 54 14 W87 22 13
C/O David R. Magnum,#105, 1021 N. Superior Ave, Tomah, WI 54660 US
(920) 743-6677, *Fax:* (920) 743-9183
info@wsrc.com
License: Sturgeon Bay, Door County, WI held by Al Johnson Broadcasting LLC
Nat'l Network: Jones Radio Networks
Format: Adult Contemp *No. News Employees:* 2 *Target Audience:* 25-54. *Adv. Rates:* 18; 14; 14; 12
Rick Jensen, Operations Dir
Dave Magnum, General Sales Mgr

Sturtevant

WDDW

06-18-1993; 104.7 mhz FM *Hrs Open:* 24; 4.2 kw; 338 ft.; N42 51 20 W87 50 41
8800 Route 14, Crystal Lake, IL 60012 US
(262) 694-7800, *Fax:* (262) 694-7767
papimio@sbcglobal.net
License: Sturtevant, Racine County, WI
Group Owner: Adelante Media Group LLC; (acq 1-6-2006; $10.2 million).
Arbitron Metro Market: Milwaukee, WI *Target Audience:* 18-49.
John Perry, Operations Dir
Kira LaFond, General Manager
Jerod Bast, General Sales Mgr
Lisa Tyler, News Director

Mark Anthony, Chief Engineer
Lisa Sladek, Traffic Manager

Sun Prairie

WXXM
04-12-1972; 92.1 mhz FM; 3.7 kw; 410 ft.; N43 10 10 W89 15 38
600 Congress Ave., Suite 1400, Austin, TX 78701 US
(608) 274-5450, *Fax:* (608) 274-5521
www.themic921.com
info@themic921.com
License: Sun Prairie, Dane County, WI held by Capstar TX L.P.
Group Owner: Clear Channel Communications Inc.; (acq 8-30-2000; grpsl)
Nat'l Network: Fox Sports
Arbitron Metro Market: Madison, WI *Format:* Talk *Target Audience:* General, progsv people
Tim Scott, Operations Dir
Jeff Tyler, General Manager
Sue Garret, General Sales Mgr
Ryan Turany, Programming Director
Josh Westscott, News Director
Cliff Groth, Chief Engineer
Jacqueline Forney, Traffic Manager

***WNWC**
01-12-1982; 1190 khz AM
3003 Snelling Avenue North, St. Paul, MN 55113 US
651-631-5000, *Fax:* (608) 271-1150
www.faith1190.com
feedback@faithradionet.com
License: Sun Prairie, WI held by Northwestern College.
Group Owner: Northwestern College & Radio; (acq 12-19-96; $250,000).
Arbitron Metro Market: Madison, WI *TV Affiliate:* Relg, talk

Superior

KDWZ
09-09-1979; 102.5 mhz FM *Hrs Open:* 24; 100 kw; Ant 600 ft; N46 47 21 W92 07 09
715 E. Central Entrance, Duluth, WI 53713
(218) 722-4321, *Fax:* (218) 722-5423
www.krbr.com
License: Superior, Douglas County, WI held by Midwest Communications Inc.
Group Owner: Midwest Communications Inc.
Arbitron Metro Market: Duluth-Superior, MN-WI *Hrs. of News Programming:* News progmg 3 hrs wkly *Target Audience:* 18-49.
Duke Wright, CEO
Jack Lawson, Operations Dir
Mike Rasmusson, General Sales Mgr
John Talcott, Chief Engineer

***KUWS**
01-31-1966; 91.3 mhz FM *Hrs Open:* 24; 83 kw; 646 ft.; N46 47 21 W92 6 51
1220 Linden Drive #1866, Madison, WI 53706 US
(715) 394-8530, *Fax:* (715) 394-8404
www.kuws.fm
jmunson@uwsuper.edu
License: Superior, Douglas County, WI held by Board of Regents, University of Wisconsin System.
Nat'l Network: NPR *Regional Network:* Wis. Public Radio
Arbitron Metro Market: Superior, WI *Format:* News, News/Talk, 86, Variety/Diverse *Special Programming:* Alternative 16 hrs, jazz 15 hrs, *Hrs. of News Programming:* news progmg 20 hrs wkly *No. News Employees:* 1 *Target Audience:* 12 plus; above average income & education
John Munson, Station Manager and WPR Northern Regional Manager
Mike Simonson, News Director and WPR Northern Bureau Corresponden
Rudy Listing, Chief Engineer
Kim Gustafson, Office Manager
Sara Broshofske, Jazz Director
John Munson,Sports Director
Patrick Lilja, Sports Director
Crystal Detlefsen, Deans List Director
Walt Dizzo, Deans List Director

WGEE
06-18-1959; 970 khz AM *Hrs Open:* 24; 1 kw-D, ND1; 0.026 kw-N, ND1; N46 43 28 W92 7 11
5727 Tokay Blvd., Madison, WI 53719 US
(218) 722-4321, *Fax:* (218) 722-5423
fleisch@mwcradio.com
License: Superior, WI held by Midwest Communications Inc.
Group Owner: Midwest Communications Inc.; (acq 8-1-2001; grpsl)
Nat'l Network: Music of Your Life *Regional Reps:* Hyett/Ramsland.
Arbitron Metro Market: Duluth-Superior, MN-WI *Format:* Adult Contemp *Target Audience:* 18-44.
Duke Wright, CEO
Jack Lawson, Operations Dir
Mike Rasmusson, General Sales Mgr
Bruce Ciskie, Programming Director
John Talcott, Chief Engineer

WDSM
10-01-1939; 710 khz AM *Hrs Open:* 24; 10 kw-D, DAN; 5 kw-N, DAN; N46 39 13 W92 8 50
5727 Tokay Blvd., Madison, WI 53719 US
(218) 722-4321, *Fax:* (218) 722-5423
wdsm710.com/
License: Superior, WI held by Midwest Communications Inc.
Group Owner: Midwest Communications Inc.; (acq 8-1-2001; grpsl)
Nat'l Network: ABC; Talk Radio Network; Salem Radio Network; Premiere Radio Networks; CNN Radio *Regional Network:* MNN; Wisconsin Radio Net. *Wire Services:* AP
Arbitron Metro Market: Superior, WI *Format:* Talk *Target Audience:* 25-54.
Roxanne Charles, CEO
Jack Lawson, Operations Dir
Mike Rasmusson, General Sales Mgr
Bruce Ciskie, Programming Director
John Talcott, Chief Engineer

Suring

***WRVM**
09-17-1967; 102.7 mhz FM *Hrs Open:* 24; 98 kw; 981 ft.; N44 59 50 W88 23 49
Mailing Address: P. O. Box 212, Suring, WI 54174 US
Second Address: Hwy. 32 N., Suring, WI 54174
(920) 842-2900, *Fax:* (920) 842-2704
www.wrvm.org
wrvm@wrvm.org
License: Suring, Oconto County, WI held by WRVM Inc.
Nat'l Network: Moody
Format: Religious *Target Audience:* General; family stn with children's programs
Michael Cornell, General Manager
Brian Hay, General Sales Mgr
Dennis Jones, Programming Director
Michael Fletcher, Promotions Manager
Alan Kilgore, Chief Engineer
Dave Ogren, Assistant to Engineer

Sussex

WKSH
11-01-2002; 1640 khz AM *Hrs Open:* 24
18501 Follett Dr., Brookfield, WI 53045 US
(262) 695-9500, *Fax:* (262) 691-2378
www.radiodisney.com
debra.l.bratel@disney.com
License: Sussex, WI held by Radio Disney Group LLC.
Group Owner: ABC Inc.; (acq 9-26—02; $2.6 million).
Nat'l Network: Radio Disney *Nat'l Reps:* McGavren Guild
Arbitron Metro Market: Milwaukee-Racine, WI *Format:* Children *Target Audience:* Kids 6-14 & Women 25-49. *Adv. Rates:* 70; 70; 70; 25
Debra Bratel, Station Manager
Melissa Schumacher, General Sales Mgr
Patricia Schultz, Promotions Manager

Three Lakes

WCYE
08-01-1994; 93.7 mhz FM *Hrs Open:* 24; 100 kw; 407 ft.; N45 46 30 W89 14 55
980 North Michigan Ave, Ste. 1880, Chicago, IL 60611 US
(715) 369-9575, *Fax:* (715) 369-9475
www.mycoyoteradio.com
wcyeginger@newnorth.net
License: Three Lakes, Oneida County, WI held by Results Broadcasting of Rhinelander Inc.
Group Owner: Results Broadcasting; (acq 3-10-2000; $500,000)
Nat'l Network: Premiere Radio Networks
Format: Country *Hrs. of News Programming:* news progmg 4 hrs wkly *No. News Employees:* 1 *Target Audience:* 25-54.
Bruce Grassman, CEO
Ben Rosenthal, General Manager
Ben Merritt, Disc Jockey
Brian Douglas, Disc Jockey
Jeff Young, Disc Jockey

Tomah

WTMB
07-11-1990; 94.5 mhz FM *Hrs Open:* 24; 8.3 kw; 564 ft.; N43 53 56 W90 29 23
1021 North Superior Ave., Suite 5, Tomah, WI 54660 US
(608) 372-9600, *Fax:* (608) 372-7566
www.classicrockwtmb.com
info@buzzcountry.com
License: Tomah, Monroe County, WI
Group Owner: Magnum Radio Inc.
Arbitron Metro Market: Tomah, WI *Format:* Classic Rock *Hrs. of News Programming:* news progmg 6 hrs wkly *No. News Employees:* 2 *Target Audience:* 25-54
Floyd Evans, General Manager
Eugene Brown, Programming Director

WBOG
04-19-1959; 1460 khz AM *Hrs Open:* 24; 1 kw-D, NDD; N43 58 7 W90 30 50
1021 North Superior Ave., Suite 5, Tomah, WI 54660 US
(608) 372-9600, *Fax:* (608) 372-7566
www.koolgold1460.com
info@magnumbroadcasting.com
License: Tomah, WI held by Magnum Radio Inc.
Group Owner: Magnum Radio Inc.; acq 1994; $275,000 with co-located FM).
Nat'l Network: Jones Radio Networks *Regional Network:* Wisconsin Radio Net.
Arbitron Metro Market: Tomah, WI *Format:* Oldies *Hrs. of News Programming:* news progmg 10 hrs wkly *No. News Employees:* 2 *Target Audience:* 35 plus. *Adv. Rates:* 19; 19; 19; 18
Dave Magnum, President
Brian Winnekins, Operations Dir
Steve Peterson, General Manager
Diane Pergande, General Sales Mgr
Clary Harris, News Director
Darrell Sanders, Chief Engineer

WXYM
03-11-1992; 96.1 mhz FM *Hrs Open:* 24; 44 kw; 525 ft.; N44 1 32 W90 48 58
1021 North Superior Ave., Tomah, WI 54660 US
(608) 372-9600, *Fax:* (608) 372-7566
www.magnumradiogroup.net
info@mixwxym.com
License: Tomah, Monroe County, WI held by Magnum Radio Inc.
Group Owner: Magnum Radio Inc.; (acq 9-27-91;
Regional Network: Wisconsin Radio Net.
Arbitron Metro Market: Tomah, WI *Format:* Adult Contemp *Hrs. of News Programming:* news progmg 6 hrs wkly *No. News Employees:* 2 *Target Audience:* 25-54. *Adv. Rates:* 19; 19; 19; 18
Dave Magnum, President
Debbie Doyle, Operations Dir
Steve Peterson, General Manager

***WVCX**
01-29-1965; 98.9 mhz FM *Hrs Open:* 24; 100 kw; 984 ft.; N43 51 10 W90 27 36
3434 West Kilbourn Ave., Milwaukee, WI 53208 US
(414) 935-3000, *Fax:* (414) 935-3015
www.vcyamerica.org
wvcx@vcyamerica.org
License: Tomah, Monroe County, WI held by VCY/America Inc.
Group Owner: VCY America Inc.; acq 1984)
Nat'l Network: USA; Moody
Arbitron Metro Market: Milwaukee, WI *Format:* Christian, Talk, 74
Dr. Randall Melchert, President
Victor Eliason, Operations Dir
Jim Schneider, Programming Director
Gordon Morris, News Director
Andy Eliason, Chief Engineer

Tomahawk

WJJQ
08-01-1968; 810 khz AM *Hrs Open:* 24
Mailing Address: D/B/A Albert B/Casting, P.O. Box 10, Tomahawk, WI 54487 US
Second Address: 81 E. Mohawk Dr., Tomahawk, WI 54487
(715) 453-4482, *Fax:* (715) 453-7169
www.wjjq.com
wjjq@wjjq.com
License: Tomahawk, WI held by Albert Broadcasting II LLC
Nat'l Network: CBS; ESPN Radio; Westwood One *Regional Network:* Wisconsin Radio Net. *Nat'l Reps:* Rgnl Reps *Wire Services:* AP
Format: Sports *Hrs. of News Programming:* news progmg 15 hrs wkly *No. News Employees:* 1 *Target Audience:* 25 plus. *Adv. Rates:* 7; 7; 5; 5

RADIO - U.S.

Gregg Albert, President
Margaruite Albert, Operations Dir
Tim Albert, Programming Director

WJJQ-FM
10-15-1984; 92.5 mhz FM *Hrs Open:* 24; 25 kw; 259 ft.; N45 29 27 W89 43 36
Mailing Address: D/B/A Albert B/Casting, P.O. Box 10, Tomahawk, WI 54487 US
Second Address: 81 E. Mohawk Dr., Tomahawk, WI 54487
(715) 453-4482, *Fax:* (715) 453-7169
www.wjjq.com
galbert@wjjq.com
License: Tomahawk, Lincoln County, WI held by Albert Broadcasting II LLC.
Nat'l Network: CBS Radio *Regional Network:* Wisconsin Radio Net. *Nat'l Reps:* Rgnl Reps *Regional Reps:* Regional Reps *Wire Services:* AP
Format: News, Oldies, 84 *Hrs. of News Programming:* news progmg 30 hrs wkly *No. News Employees:* 1 *Target Audience:* 25 plus. *Adv. Rates:* 15; 15; 12; 12
Gregg Albert, President
Mary Lu Voermans, General Sales Mgr
Tim Albert, Programming Director
Mark Everett, Disc Jockey
Michael McGovern, Disc Jockey

Trempealeau

WFBZ
11-24-1984; 105.5 mhz FM *Hrs Open:* 24; 2.1 kw; 531 ft.; N43 56 33 W91 26 3
1407 2nd Avenue North, Onalaska, WI 54650 US
(608) 269-3100, *Fax:* (608) 269-5170
www.espnlacrosse.com
info@espnlacrosse.com
License: Trempealeau, Trempealeau County, WI held by Sparta-Tomah Broadcasting Co. Inc.
Group Owner: Sparta-Tomah Broadcasting Co. Inc.; (acq 10-19-2006; $850,000)
Nat'l Network: ESPN Radio *Nat'l Reps:* Rgnl Reps *Wire Services:* ESPN/SportsTicker
Arbitron Metro Market: Trempealeau, WI *Format:* Sports
Shelly Holen, President
William Hoffman, General Manager

Two Rivers

WCUB
11-01-1952; 980 khz AM *Hrs Open:* 24; 5 kw-D, DA2; 5 kw-N, DA2; N44 3 50 W87 41 49
Mailing Address: P.O. Box 1990, Manitowoc, WI 54221 US
Second Address: 1915 Mirro Dr., Manitowoc, WI 54220
(920) 683-6800, *Fax:* (920)683-6807
www.cubradio.com
License: Two Rivers, WI held by Cub Radio Inc.
Nat'l Reps: Katz Radio
Format: Country *Hrs. of News Programming:* news progmg 16 hrs wkly *No. News Employees:* 2 *Target Audience:* 35 plus.
Lee Davis, President
Dean Lester, Programming Director
Bryan Lundberg, News Director

Union Grove

WIIL
01-01-1961; 95.1 mhz FM; 50 kw; 384 ft.; N42 33 10 W87 53 38
8800 Route 14, Crystal Lake, IL 60012 US
(262) 694-7800, *Fax:* (262) 694-7767
www.95wiil.com
info@95wiil.com
License: Union Grove, Kenosha County, WI held by NM Licensing LLC
Arbitron Metro Market: Chicago, IL *Target Audience:* 18-54.
Chris Allinger, Operations Dir
Susan Johnston, General Manager

Verona

WMMM-FM
07-04-1991; 105.5 mhz FM; 2 kw; 574 ft.; N42 57 32 W89 29 25
7601 Ganser Wy, Madison, WI 53719 US
(608) 826-0077, *Fax:* (608) 826-1244
www.1055triplem.com
demoore@entercom.com
License: Verona, Dane County, WI held by Entercom Madison Licensee LLP.
Group Owner: Entercom Communications Corp.; (acq 7-10-00; grpsl)
Arbitron Metro Market: Madison, WI *Format:* Triple A *Target Audience:* 25-44; upscale, college educated adults
Steve Fisher, CFO
David Field, President
David Moore, Operations Dir
Lindsay Wood Davis, Promotions Manager

Viroqua

WVRQ
02-25-1958; 1360 khz AM *Hrs Open:* 24; 1 kw-D, 23 w-N; N43 32 04 W90 52 23
E7601A County Rd. SS, Viroqua, WI 54665
(608) 637-7200, *Fax:* (608) 637-7299
www.wvrq.com
wvrq@mwt.net
License: Viroqua, Vernon County, WI held by Robinson Corp.
Group Owner: Robinson Corporation
Nat'l Network: ABC *Regional Network:* Wisconsin Radio Net.
Wire Services: AP
Population Served: 43,762*Special Programming:* Farm one hr, relg 6 hrs, polka 6 hrs wkly *Hrs. of News Programming:* news progmg 14 hrs wkly *No. News Employees:* 1 *Target Audience:* 25 plus.
Tim Hundt, President
Jeff Robinson, General Manager
Jeff Robinson, General Sales Mgr

WVRQ-FM
10-06-1967; 102.3 mhz FM *Hrs Open:* 24; 3.3 kw; 299 ft.; N43 31 27 W90 51 51
Rt. 4 Box 6a, Viroqua, WI 54665 US
(608) 637-7200, *Fax:* (608) 637-7299
www.wvrq.com
wvrq@mwt.net
License: Viroqua, Vernon County, WI held by Robinson Corp.
Group Owner: Robinson Corporation
Wire Services: AP
Arbitron Metro Market: La Crosse, WI *Format:* Country *Special Programming:* Bluegrass 2 hrs, farm one hr wkly *Hrs. of News Programming:* News progmg 20 hrs wkly *No. News Employees:* 1 *Target Audience:* 25-54.
David Robinson, President
Jeff Robinson, General Sales Mgr
Tim Hundt, News Director
Gary Gilbertson, Sports Director
Linda Mayns, Traffic Director

***WDRT**
91.9 mhz FM; 0.48 kw; 435 ft.; N43 36 28 W90 53 24 US
(608) 638-9378
www.wdrt.org
info@wdrt.org
License: Viroqua, Vernon County, WI held by Driftless Community Radio Inc.
Arbitron Metro Market: Viroqua, WI *Format:* Variety/Diverse
Bob Hill, President
Eddy Nix, Vice President
Jane Even, Secretary
Charlie Knower, Treasurer
John Tully

Washburn

***WEGZ**
10-05-1981; 105.9 mhz FM *Hrs Open:* 24; 98 kw; 741 ft.; N46 41 31 W90 59 27
115 Candlestick Road, North Andover, MA 01845 US
(715) 373-5151, *Fax:* (715) 373-5805
www.vcyamerica.org
wegz@vcyamerica.org
License: Washburn, Bayfield County, WI held by Keweenaw Bay Broadcasting Inc.
Group Owner: VCY America Inc.; (acq 4-19-2002).
Nat'l Network: USA
Arbitron Metro Market: Washburn, WI *Format:* Christian, Religious, 86
Dr. Randall Melchert, President
Victor Eliason, Operations Dir
Jim Schneider, Programming Director
Gordon Morris, Operations Director

Watertown

WJJO
08-01-1961; 94.1 mhz FM *Hrs Open:* 24; 50 kw; 492 ft; N43 11 43 W88 45 17
Mailing Address: Box 44408, Madison, WI 53701
Second Address: 730 Rayovac Dr., Madison, WI 53711
(608) 273-1000, *Fax:* (608) 271-8182
www.wjjo.com
License: Watertown, Jefferson County, WI held by Mid-West Management Inc.
Group Owner: The Mid-West Family Broadcast Group; (acq 6-18-93; $1.6 million;
Nat'l Reps: McGavren Guild
Population Served: 450,000 *Arbitron Metro Market:* Madison, WI *Target Audience:* 21-49; male
Tom Walker, President
Rick Malloy, General Manager
Ted Waldbillig, General Sales Mgr
Randy Hawke, Programming Director
John Bauer, Chief Engineer
Blake Patton, Music Director

Waukesha

WRRD
03-27-1947; 1510 khz AM *Hrs Open:* 6 AM-8:30 PM
1801 Coral Drive, Waukesha, WI 53186 US
(414) 273-3776, *Fax:* (414) 291-3776
www.wauksportsradio@msn.com
License: Waukesha, WI held by Good Karma Broadcasting L.L.C.
Group Owner: Good Karma Broadcasting L.L.C.; (acq 4-30-2004; $2 million)
Nat'l Network: ESPN Deportes
Arbitron Metro Market: Eugene-Springfield, OR *Format:* Sports
Craig Karmazin, President
C.J. Knee, Operations Dir
Bill Johnson, Programming Director
Warren Jorgenson, News Director

***WCCX**
09-01-1978; 104.5 mhz FM *Hrs Open:* 24; 0.013 kw; 49 ft.; N43 0 16 W88 13 39
221 North East Avenue, Waukesha, WI 53186 US
(262) 524-7355, *Fax:* (262) 650-4950
www.wccx.carrollu.edu
wccx@carrollu.edu
License: Waukesha, Waukesha County, WI held by Trustees Carroll College.
Arbitron Metro Market: Waukesha, WI *Format:* Variety/Diverse
Special Programming: Sp 8 hrs, metal 3 hrs, rap 3 hrs wkly
Target Audience: General; high school & college students
Ed Tuten, President
Howard Tuten, General Manager

WMIL-FM
01-01-1982; 106.1 mhz FM *Hrs Open:* 24; 12 kw; 997 ft.; N43 5 46 W87 54 15
200 Concord Plaza, Suite 600, San Antonio, TX 78216 US
(414) 545-8900, *Fax:* (414) 327-3200
www.fm106.com
License: Waukesha, Waukesha County, WI held by Clear Channel Broadcasting Inc.
Group Owner: Clear Channel Communications Inc.; (acq 3-17-97; $40 million with WOKY(AM) Milwaukee)
Nat'l Reps: Clear Channel
Arbitron Metro Market: Milwaukee, WI *Format:* Country *Hrs. of News Programming:* news progmg 1.5 hrs wkly *No. News Employees:* 4 *Target Audience:* 25-54; middle America *Adv. Rates:* 210; 200; 200; 55
L. Lowry Mays, CEO
Mark Mays, President
Cindy McDowell, General Manager
Keith Bratel, General Sales Mgr
Kerry Wolfe, Programming Director
Enid Parkinson, Promotions Manager
Mitch Morgan, Music Director
Colleen Kurth, NationalSales Manager
Jean Kemp, Regional Sales Manager

Waunakee

WCHY
04-20-1992; 105.1 mhz FM; 6 kw; 243 ft.; N43 13 20 W89 18 1
7601 Ganser Wy, Madison, WI 53719 US
(608) 826-0077, *Fax:* (608) 826-1244
www.y105.com
info@wchy.com
License: Waunakee, Dane County, WI held by Entercom Madison Licensee LLP.
Group Owner: Entercom Communications Corp.; (acq 7-10-2000; grpsl)
Arbitron Metro Market: Madison, WI *Format:* Classic Rock *Target Audience:* 18-49.
Steve Fisher, CFO
David Field, President
Ed Schulz, General Manager

Waupaca

WDUX
04-29-1956; 800 khz AM *Hrs Open:* 24 hours; 5 kw-D, DA2; 0.5 kw-N, DA2; N44 21 15 W89 3 29
Mailing Address: P.O. Box 310, Green Bay, WI 54305 US
Second Address: 200 Tower Rd., Waupaca, WI 54981
(715) 258-5528, *Fax:* (715) 258-7711
www.wdux.net/
mail@wdux.net
License: Waupaca, WI held by Laird Broadcasting Co.
Nat'l Network: Jones Radio Networks; ABC *Regional Network:* Brownfield; Wisconsin Radio Net. *Nat'l Reps:* Katz Radio *Wire Services:* AP
Arbitron Metro Market: Waupaca, WI *Format:* Country *Special Programming:* Farm 1 hr wkly *Hrs. of News Programming:* news progmg 20 hrs wkly *No. News Employees:* 1 *Target Audience:* 35 plus. *Adv. Rates:* 18; 16; 16; 12
William Laird, President
Jack Barry, Operations Dir
Tina Grenlie, Station Manager
Ann Myer, Traffic Manager

WDUX-FM
01-29-1967; 92.7 mhz FM *Hrs Open:* 24; 6 kw; 243 ft; N44 21 14 W89 03 44
Mailing Address: Box 247, Waupaca, WI 54305
Second Address: 200 Tower Rd., Waupaca, WI 54981
(715) 258-5528, *Fax:* (715) 258-7711
www.wduxradio.com
License: Waupaca, Waupaca County, WI held by Laird Broadcasting Co.
Nat'l Network: ABC; Westwood One *Regional Network:* Wisconsin Radio Net. *Nat'l Reps:* Katz Radio *Wire Services:* AP
Arbitron Metro Market: Green Bay, WI *Special Programming:* Sports 15 hrs wkly *No. News Employees:* 1 *Target Audience:* 25-54. *Adv. Rates:* 18; 16; 16; 12
Tina Grenlie, General Manager
Tina Grenlie, Station Manager
Larry Stevens, General Sales Mgr
Rick Winters, Programming Director
Jack Barry, News Director
Jack Barry, News Director

Waupun

WFDL
05-26-1966; 1170 khz AM *Hrs Open:* Sunrise to sunset; 1 kw-D, NDD; N43 38 30 W88 43 22
609 Home Avenue, Waupun, WI 53963 US
(920) 324-4441, *Fax:* (920) 324-3139
www.am1170.com,www.wfdl.com
nickr@wfdl.com
License: Waupun, WI held by Radio Plus Inc.
Nat'l Network: CBS Radio
Arbitron Metro Market: Waupun, WI *Format:* Adult Contemp *Special Programming:* Farm 5 hrs wkly *Target Audience:* 35 plus; mature adults *Adv. Rates:* 15; 12; 12; n/a
Chris Bernier, President
Mike Enfelt, Operations Dir
Terry Davis, General Manager
Todd Dehring, Programming Director
Greg Stensland, News Director
Kerry Longrie, Traffic Manager

Wausau

*WCLQ
05-23-1988; 89.5 mhz FM *Hrs Open:* 24; 90 kw; 607 ft.; N44 55 11 W89 40 45
536 Grand Ave., Schofield, WI 54476 US
(715) 355-5151, *Fax:* (715) 359-3128
www.89q.org
coy@89q.org
License: Wausau, Marathon County, WI held by Christian Life Communications Inc.
Nat'l Network: USA
Arbitron Metro Market: Wausau-Stevens Point, WI *Format:* Contemporary Hits/Top 40 *Hrs. of News Programming:* News progmg 9 hrs wkly *Target Audience:* 18-35; Christian/young family
Coy Sawyer, CFO
Coy Sawyer, General Manager
Scott Michaels, Programming Director
Frank Zastrow, Chief Engineer

WDEZ
03-27-1964; 101.9 mhz FM *Hrs Open:* 24; 100 kw; 489 ft; N44 58 58 W89 36 06
Mailing Address: 557 Scott Street, Wausau, WI 54403
Second Address: PO Box 2048, Wausau, WI 54402-2048
(715) 842-1672, *Fax:* (715) 848-3158
www.wdez.com
wdez@wdez.com
License: Wausau, Marathon County, WI held by WRIG Inc.
Group Owner: Midwest Communications Inc.
Nat'l Reps: Christal *Wire Services:* Wheeler News Service; UPI
Population Served: 212,000 *Arbitron Metro Market:* Wausau-Stevens Point, WI (Central Wisconsin) *Special Programming:* Farm 4 hrs wkly *Hrs. of News Programming:* news progmg 4 hrs wkly *No. News Employees:* 1*Target Audience:* 25-54.
D.E. Wright, President
Gary Tesch, Operations Dir
Brett Lucht, General Manager
Bob Jung, General Sales Mgr
Joe Cassady, Programming Director
Chris Conley, News Director
Frank Zastrow, Chief Engineer
Mike Austin, FarmDirector
Bryan Scott, Mornings
Nikki Montgomery, Mornings
Vanessa Ryan, Middays
Joe Cassady, Afternoons
Terry Stevens, Nights

*WHRM
06-10-1949; 90.9 mhz FM *Hrs Open:* 24; 81 kw; 1079 ft.; N44 55 14 W89 41 28
3319 W. Beltline Hwy., Madison, WI 53713 US
(715) 848-1978, *Fax:* (715) 848-2890
www.wpr.org
listener@wpr.org
License: Wausau, Marathon County, WI held by State of Wisconsin Educational Communications Board.
Nat'l Network: NPR; PRI
Arbitron Metro Market: Wausau-Stevens Point, WI (Central Wisconsin) *Format:* News *Hrs. of News Programming:* News progmg 29 hrs wkly *Target Audience:* 25-64; male/female
Wendy Wink, CEO
Maru Nonn, Operations Dir
Phil Corriveau, General Manager
Rick Reyer, Station Manager
Allen Rieland, Chief Engineer
Ted Tobie, CFO
Tom Martin-Erickson, Chief of Operations

WIFC
01-01-1947; 95.5 mhz FM *Hrs Open:* 24; 98.6 kw; 1079 ft.; N44 55 14 W89 41 28
Mailing Address: 904 Grand Ave., Wausau, WI 54403 US
Second Address: 557 Scott St., Wausau, WI 54403
(715) 842-1672, *Fax:* (715) 848-3158
www.wifc.com
wifc@wifc.com
License: Wausau, Marathon County, WI
Group Owner: Midwest Communications
Arbitron Metro Market: Wausau-Stevens Point, WI (Central Wisconsin) *Format:* Contemporary Hits/Top 40 *No. News Employees:* 2 *Target Audience:* 18-49.
Brett Lucht, General Sales Mgr
Chris Pickett, Programming Director

*WLBL-FM
11-01-1995; 91.9 mhz FM *Hrs Open:* 5 AM-midnight (M-F); 6 AM-midnight; 0.054 kw; 837 ft.; N44 55 14 W89 41 28
3319 West Beltline Hwy, Madison, WI 53713 US
(715) 848-1978, *Fax:* (715) 848-2890
www.wpr.org
rick.reyer@wpr.org
License: Wausau, Marathon County, WI held by State of Wisconsin-Educational Communications Board.
Nat'l Network: NPR *Regional Network:* Wisconsin Radio Net.
Arbitron Metro Market: Wausau-Stevens Point, WI (Central Wisconsin) *Format:* Talk *Special Programming:* Folk 3 hrs wkly
Wendy Wink, CEO
Phil Corriveau, General Manager
Rick Reyer, Station Manager
Allen Rieland, Chief Engineer

WSAU
01-30-1937; 550 khz AM *Hrs Open:* 24
Mailing Address: 904 Grand Avenue, Wausau, WI 54403 US
Second Address: 557 Scott St., Wausau, WI 54403
(715) 842-1672, *Fax:* (715) 842-7061
www.wsau.com
wsau@wsau.com
License: Wausau, WI held by WRIG Inc.
Group Owner: Midwest Communications Inc.; (acq 1996; $3.5 million with co-located FM)
Nat'l Reps: Christal
Arbitron Metro Market: Wausau-Stevens *Format:* News, News/Talk, 86 *Special Programming:* Farm 5 hrs, Polish 3 hrs, religious 3 hrs wkly *No. News Employees:* 2 *Target Audience:* 35-64.
Patrick Snyder, Operations Dir
Brett Lucht, General Manager
Samantha Milanwwski, General Sales Mgr
Carrie Van Deraa, Promotions Manager
Frank Zastrow, Chief Engineer

WXCO
08-01-1953; 1230 khz AM *Hrs Open:* 24; 1 kw-U, ND1; N44 58 10 W89 36 25
1110 E. Wausau Avenue, Wausau, WI 54402 US
(715) 845-8218, *Fax:* (715) 845-6582
www.1230wxco.com
chadh@1230wxco.com
License: Wausau, WI held by Seehafer Broadcasting Corp.
Group Owner: Seehafer Broadcasting Corp.; (acq 9-26-73).
Nat'l Network: CBS; Westwood One; ESPN Radio
Arbitron Metro Market: Wausau, WI *Format:* Sports, Talk *No. News Employees:* 1 *Target Audience:* 25 plus; professionals/business *Adv. Rates:* 14; 13; 13; 7
Chad Holmes, Operations Dir
Steve Resnick, General Manager
Ken Rajek, General Sales Mgr
Chad Holmes, Programming Director
Kim Weyers, News Director
Charles Gennaro, Chief Engineer
Roger Bertram, Account Executive
Jamie Potter,Account Executive
Cole Corrigan, Account Executive
Kim Weyers, Traffic Manager

*WXPW
02-01-1996; 91.9 mhz FM; 0.054 kw; 837 ft.; N44 55 14 W89 41 28 *Rebroadcasts:* Rebroadcasts WXPR(FM) Rhinelander
303 W. Prospect Street, Rhinelander, WI 54501 US
(715) 362-6000, *Fax:* (715) 362-6007
www.wxpr.org
wxpr@wxpr.org
License: Wausau, Marathon County, WI held by White Pine Community Broadcasting Inc.
Arbitron Metro Market: Wausau, WI *Format:* News
Mick Fiocchi, President
Walt Gander, Operations Dir
Jessie Dick, General Sales Mgr
Ken Krall, News Director
Elmer Goetsch, Chief Engineer

WBCV
02-01-1985; 107.9 mhz FM; 100 kw; 1030 ft.; N45 3 33 W89 26 10
1110 E. Wausau Ave, Wausau, WI 54401 US
1-866-967-9983, *Fax:* (715) 341-9744
www.bigcheese1079.net
License: Wausau, Marathon County, WI held by NRG License Sub, LLC.
Group Owner: NRG Media LLC; (acq 5-31-2006; swap for WDLB(AM) Marshfield, WOSQ(FM) Spencer and WFHR(AM) Wisconsin Rapids)
Nat'l Reps: McGavren Guild
Arbitron Metro Market: Wausau, WI *Format:* Rock/AOR
Ben Rosenthal, General Manager
Jon Albrecht, General Sales Mgr
Panama Jack, Programming Director

Wautoma

WAUH
01-01-2001; 102.3 mhz FM; 5.3 kw; 349 ft.; N44 1 54 W89 9 7
6161 N Santa Monica Blvd, Whitefish Bay, WI 53217 US
(902) 787-7720, *Fax:* (866) 594-4698
www.wauhradio.com
thebug@wauhradio.com
License: Wautoma, Waushara County, WI held by Hometown Broadcasting LLC
Arbitron Metro Market: Wautoma, WI *Format:* Contemporary Hits/Top 40, Adult Contemp
JoAnn Boyson, CEO
Bernie Phillips, General Manager
Bill Denkert, General Sales Mgr
JoAnn Boyson, Co-Owner
Mark Melby, Account Executive
John Peck, Account Executive
Joshua Werner, IT & Webmaster
Jean Hoffmann, Traffic &Billing

Wauwatosa

WXSS
01-01-1961; 103.7 mhz FM *Hrs Open:* 24; 19.5 kw; 843 ft.; N43 5 48 W87 54 18
10706 Beaver Dam Road, Cockeysville, MD 21030 US
(414) 529-1250, *Fax:* (414) 529-2122
www.1037kissfm.com
License: Wauwatosa, Milwaukee County, WI held by Entercom Milwaukee License LLC.
Group Owner: Entercom Communications Corp.; (acq 12-13-99; grpsl).
Arbitron Metro Market: Milwaukee, WI *Format:* Contemporary Hits/Top 40 *No. News Employees:* 1 *Target Audience:* 18-44; women
Alan Kirshbon, General Sales Mgr
Brian Kelly, Programming Director
Jane Matenaer, News Director
Chris Tarr, Chief Engineer
Andrea Biebel, National Sales Manager

Wentworth

***WWEN**
88.1 mhz FM; 0.85 kw vert; 456 ft.; N46 32 8 W92 4 7
P O Drawer 2440, Tupelo, MS 38803 US
(662) 844-5036, *Fax:* (662) 842-7798
www.afr.net
contact@afa.net
License: Wentworth, Douglas County, WI held by American Family Association.
Group Owner: American Family Radio
Arbitron Metro Market: Wentworth, WI *Format:* Christian
Donald E. Wildmon, Founder
Buster Wilson, General Manager
Jennifer Hagman, Programming Director

West Allis

WJTI
06-04-1950; 1460 khz AM *Hrs Open:* 24; 500 w-D, 65 w-N; N42 45 06 W87 49 55
1530 N Cass St., Suite A, Milwaukee, WI 60085
(414) 899-9902
License: West Allis, Racine County, WI held by El Sol Broadcasting LLC
Population Served: 1,300,000 *Arbitron Metro Market:* Milwaukee-Racine, WI *No. News Employees:* 3 *Target Audience:* Sp all ages *Adv. Rates:* 50; 50; 50; 50
John Torres, General Manager

West Bend

WBKV
11-01-1950; 1470 khz AM *Hrs Open:* 24
Mailing Address: P. O. Box 933, West Bend, WI 53095 US
Second Address: 2410 S. Main St., Suite A, West Bend, WI 53095
(262) 334-2344, *Fax:* (262) 334-1512
wbkvam.com
jhodges@westbendradio.com
License: West Bend, WI held by West Bend Broadcasting Inc.
Group Owner: Bliss Communications Inc.; (acq 10-18-70)
Nat'l Network: CNN Radio *Nat'l Reps:* Rgnl Reps
Arbitron Metro Market: West Bend, WI *Format:* Country *Hrs. of News Programming:* news progmg 20 hrs wkly *No. News Employees:* 1 *Target Audience:* 35-64; info-hungry adults interested in loc events & classiccountry music
Rob Lisser, CFO
Skip Bliss, President
James Hodges, Operations Dir
Ken Scott, General Manager
Paul Clements, General Sales Mgr
Bob Bonenfant, Programming Director
Mark Morris, News Director
Jason Mielke, Chief Engineer

WBWI-FM
09-01-1958; 92.5 mhz FM *Hrs Open:* 24; 17.5 kw; 538 ft.; N43 25 46 W88 18 2
Mailing Address: PO Box 933, West Bend, WI 53095 US
Second Address: 2410 S. Main St., Suite A, West Bend, WI 53095
(262) 334-2344, *Fax:* (262) 334-1512
wbwifm.com
License: West Bend, Washington County, WI
Group Owner: Bliss Communications Inc.
Nat'l Reps: Rgnl Reps
Arbitron Metro Market: West Bend, WI *Hrs. of News Programming:* news progmg 2 hrs wkly *No. News Employees:* 1 *Target Audience:* 25-54; country music listeners with disposable income
Fuzz Martin, Programming Director

West Salem

WKBH-FM
03-15-1982; 100.1 mhz FM *Hrs Open:* 24; 3.6 kw; 427 ft.; N43 51 2 W91 12 8
1407 2nd Avenue North, Onalaska, WI 54650 US
(608) 782-8335, *Fax:* (608) 782-8340
www.classicrock1001.com
License: West Salem, La Crosse County, WI held by Mississippi Valley Broadcasters LLC.
Group Owner: La Crosse Radio Group; (acq 12-16-2000).
Format: Classic Rock *No. News Employees:* 1 *Target Audience:* 25-54.
Lee Norman, President
Todd Wohlert, Station Manager

Westby

WTPN
103.9 mhz FM; 2.75 kw; Ant 477 ft; N43 37 36 W90 41 57
5331 Mount Alifan Dr., San Diego, CA
(858) 277-4991, *Fax:* (858) 277-1365
License: Westby, Vernon County, WI held by Horizon Christian Fellowship.
Group Owner: Horizon Christian Fellowship
Michael MacIntosh, President

Whitehall

WHTL-FM
09-10-1981; 102.3 mhz FM *Hrs Open:* 24; 1.55 kw; 400 ft.; N44 24 45 W91 16 53
Hwy 53 South, P.O. Box 66, Whitehall, WI 54773 US
(715) 538-4341, *Fax:* (715) 538-4360
www.whtlradio.com
whtl@centurytel.net
License: Whitehall, Trempealeau County, WI held by The WHTL Group L.L.C.
Nat'l Network: Jones Radio Networks *Regional Network:* Wisconsin Radio Net.
Format: Contemporary Hits/Top 40 *Hrs. of News Programming:* news progmg 24 hrs wkly *No. News Employees:* 1 *Target Audience:* 25 plus; adult fans who make household buying decisions *Adv. Rates:* 15; 15; 16; 12
Barb Semb, Operations Dir
Butch Halama, General Manager
Mary Little, Programming Director
Marty Little, News Director

Whitewater

WKCH
01-02-1998; 106.5 mhz FM; 6 kw; 200 ft.; N42 54 20 W88 45 5
980 North Michigan Avenue, Suite 1880, Chicago, IL 60611 US
(920) 563-9329, *Fax:* (920) 563-0315
fortproduction@nrgmedia.com
License: Whitewater, Walworth County, WI held by NRG License Sub. LLC.
Group Owner: NRG Media LLC; (acq 10-31-2005; grpsl)
Format: Oldies
Mary Quass, CEO
Gary Douglas, Operations Dir
James Vriezen, General Manager
Shane Sparks, General Sales Mgr
Michael Clish, News Director
George Nicholas, Chief Engineer
Tami Billmore, CFO
Jaimie Flom, Traffic Manager

WSLD
11-16-1992; 104.5 mhz FM *Hrs Open:* 24; 6 kw; 328 ft.; N42 43 38 W88 44 54
P.O. Box 885, Monmouth, IL 61462 US
(608) 883-6677, *Fax:* (608) 883-2054
www.1045wsld.com
wsld@starband.net
License: Whitewater, Walworth County, WI held by WPW Broadcasting Inc.
Group Owner: Prairie Radio Communications; (acq 8-4-99; $700,000)
Format: Country *Hrs. of News Programming:* news progmg 10 hrs wkly *No. News Employees:* 1 *Target Audience:* General.
Don Davis, CEO
Nora Karbash, General Manager
Reggie Michaels, Programming Director
Ryan O'Brien, News Director
Aaron Winski, Chief Engineer
Trish Donovan, Traffic Manager

***WSUW**
01-10-1965; 91.7 mhz FM *Hrs Open:* 6 AM-2 AM; 1.3 kw; 180 ft.; N42 50 10 W88 44 36
1220 Linden Drive, Madison, WI 53706 US
(262) 472-1323,(262) 472-1314, *Fax:* (262) 472-5029
www.wsuw.org
wsuw@uww.edu
License: Whitewater, Walworth County, WI held by Board of Regents University of Wisconsin System.
Format: Alternative *Special Programming:* Heavy metal 14 hrs, jazz/world beat 6 hrs, urban contemp 14 hrs wkly *Target Audience:* 18-44.
Wilfred Tremblay, General Manager
Kelly O'Brien, Programming Director
Mark Neilsen, Promotions Manager

Winneconne

WVBO
09-01-1966; 103.9 mhz FM; 24.95 kw; 328 ft.; N44 8 23 W88 29 2 *Rebroadcasts:* Rebroadcasts WOGB(FM) Kaukauna 80%
111 East Kilbourn Ave., Suite 2700, Milwaukee, WI 53202 US
(920) 426-3239, *Fax:* (920) 231-1040
www.1039wvbo.com
info@1039vbo.com
License: Winneconne, Winnebago County, WI held by Cumulus Broadcasting Inc.
Nat'l Network: Westwood One
Arbitron Metro Market: Oshkosh, WI *Format:* Oldies *Target Audience:* 35-54.
Guy Dark, Operations Dir
Jason Davis, General Sales Mgr
Jim Franklin, Program Director/Brand Manager
Steve Edwards, Program Director/Brand Manager
Jonathan Krause, News Director
Steve Griesbach, Chief Engineer
Ellie Jackson,Business Manager

Wisconsin Dells

WDLS
05-01-1969; 900 khz AM *Hrs Open:* 24; 1 kw-D, ND1; 0.22 kw-N, ND1; N43 38 23 W89 43 14
Box 444, Wisconsin Dells, WI 53965 US
(608) 742-1001, *Fax:* (608) 742-1688
wdlsam.com
info@magnumbroadcasting.com
License: Wisconsin Dells, WI held by Magnum Communications Inc.
Group Owner: Magnum Communications Inc.; (acq 2-10-99; $775,000 with co-located FM)
Nat'l Network: Jones Radio Networks; AP Radio
Arbitron Metro Market: Wisconsin Dells, WI *Format:* Country *Special Programming:* Medical 5 hrs wkly *Hrs. of News Programming:* news progmg 6 hrs wlky *No. News Employees:* 1 *Target Audience:* 35-54
Dave Magnum, Chairman
JIm Coursole, General Manager

WNNO-FM
05-01-1974; 106.9 mhz FM *Hrs Open:* 24; 6 kw; 322 ft.; N43 38 23 W89 43 14
Box 444, Wisconsin Dells, WI 53965 US
(608) 745-0959, *Fax:* (608) 745-5771
www.mix106wnno.com
rick@magnumradiogroup.net
License: Wisconsin Dells, Columbia County, WI
Group Owner: Magnum Communications Inc.
Arbitron Metro Market: Columbia, WI *Format:* Adult Contemp *Hrs. of News Programming:* news progmg 7 hrs wkly *No. News Employees:* 1 *Target Audience:* 18-40.
Cy Young, Operations Dir
Gary Weiss, General Manager
Kim Gattis, General Sales Mgr
Jerry Smith, Programming Director
Steven Walker, General Sales Manager
Jodi Luke, National Sales Manager

Wisconsin Rapids

WFHR
11-05-1940; 1320 khz AM; 5 kw-D, DAN; 0.5 kw-N, DAN; N44 24 56 W89 50 6
P.O. Box 8022, Wisconsin Rapids, WI 54495 US
(715) 424-1300, *Fax:* (715) 424-1347
www.wfhr.com
otbf@wfhr.com
License: Wisconsin Rapids, WI held by Seehafer Broadcasting Corp.

Group Owner: Seehafer Broadcasting Corp.; (acq 6-1-2006; swap with WDLB(AM) Marshfield and WOSQ(FM) Spencer for WBCV(FM) Wausau)
Nat'l Network: CBS
Arbitron Metro Market: Wisconsin Rapids, WI *Format:* News, News/Talk, 86
Donald Seehafer, President
Kent Reeves, Operations Dir
Jeff Seigler, Sales Manager
Bob Look, Programming Director
Carl Hilke, News Director
Renee Sievers, Chief Engineer
Car Hilke, News Reporter
Pam Hilke, Traffic Director

WGLX-FM
08-01-1946; 103.3 mhz FM; 65 kw; 801 ft.; N44 38 39 W89 51 12
PO Box 8022, Wisconsin Rapids, WI 54495 US
(715) 341-8838, *Fax:* (715) 341-9744
www.wglx.com
onradio@wglx.com
License: Wisconsin Rapids, Wood County, WI held by NRG License Sub, LLC.
Group Owner: NRG Media LLC; (acq 10-31-2005; grpsl)
Arbitron Metro Market: Wausau-Stevens Point, WI (Central Wisconsin) *Format:* Classic Rock *Target Audience:* 25-49.
Benjamin Rosenthal, General Manager
John Albrecht, General Sales Mgr
Panama Jack, Programming Director

***WRAO**
91.9 mhz FM; kw
Mailing Address: US
Second Address: 611 24th St. N., Wisconsin Rapids, WI 54494-5509
(715) 325-3486
License: Wisconsin Rapids, Wood County, WI held by Wisconsin Rapids Seventh-Day Adventist Church.
Arbitron Metro Market: Wisconsin Rapids, WI
Fred Miller, General Manager

Wittenberg

***WVRN**
12-27-2007; 88.9 mhz FM; 25 kw; Ant 482 ft; N44 57 54 W89 00 18
3434 W. Kilbourn Ave., Milwaukee, WI 53208
(800) 729-9829, *Fax:* (414) 935-3015
www.vcyamerica.org
License: Wittenberg, Shawano County, WI held by VCY America Inc.
Group Owner: VCY America Inc.
Population Served: 1,077 *Arbitron Metro Market:* Wittenberg, WI
Vic Eliason, Operations Dir
Jim Schneider, Programming Director
Andy Eliason, Chief Engineer

Wyoming

Afton

KRSV
08-13-1985; 1210 khz AM; 5 kw-D, ND1; 0.25 kw-N, ND1; N42 43 22 W110 57 39
P. O. Box 1210, Afton, WY 83110 US
(307) 885-5778
hansenjw@silverstar.com
License: Afton, WY held by Western Wyoming Radio Inc.
Nat'l Network: ABC
Arbitron Metro Market: Afton, WY *Format:* Country, News, 84
Adv. Rates: 10; 8; 9; na
Jerry Hansen, President
Jennie Hansen, General Sales Mgr
Dan Dockstader, News Director

KRSV-FM
11-13-1985; 98.7 mhz FM; 3 kw; -289 ft.; N42 51 2 W110 58 46
P. O. Box 1210, Afton, WY 83110 US
(307) 885-5778, *Fax:* (307) 885-3678
License: Afton, Lincoln County, WY
Arbitron Metro Market: Afton, WY *Format:* Country
Jerry Hansen, General Manager

***KUWA**
07-01-1998; 91.3 mhz FM *Hrs Open:* 24; 0.4 kw; -312 ft.; N42 51 2 W110 58 46 *Rebroadcasts:* Rebroadcasts KUWR(FM) Laramie 100%
P.O. Box 3984, Laramie, WY 82071 US
(307) 766-4240, *Fax:* (307) 766-6184
www.wyomingpublicradio.net
onair@uwyo.edu
License: Afton, Lincoln County, WY held by University of Wyoming.
Nat'l Network: NPR; PRI *Wire Services:* AP
Arbitron Metro Market: Afton, WY *Format:* News, News/Talk, 86
Special Programming: Folk 5 hrs, jazz 5 hrs wkly *Hrs. of News Programming:* News progmg 4 hrs wkly *Target Audience:* 25-54 plus; demographic, highincome, education
Roger Adams, Operations Dir
Christina Kuzmych, General Manager
Hank Arnold, General Sales Mgr
Grady Kirkpatrick, Interim Program Director/ Music Director
Bob Beck, News Director
Ben Slater, Engineer
Reid Fletcher, ChiefEngineer
Diana Denison, Office Assistant, Senior
Kathy Dempsey, Accountant
Sarah Brown Mathews, Major Gifts
Valerie Hansen, Underwriting Representative
Shane Toven, Coordinator Engineer
Erin O'Doherty, Development Analyst

Albin

KKAW
01-01-2001; 107.3 mhz FM; 9.3 kw; 531 ft.; N41 29 31 W104 5 7
Rebroadcasts: Rebroadcasts KZDR(FM) Cheyenne 100%
C/O Brill Media Co., P.O. Box 3353, Evansville, IN 47732 US
(307) 638-8921, *Fax:* (307) 638-8922
License: Albin, Laramie County, WY held by Chisholm Trail Broadcasting LLC
Format: Country
Eric Hauenstein, General Manager
Diane Curtis, General Sales Mgr
Bruce Jones, Programming Director
Kurt Johnson, Promotions Manager

Antelope Valley Crestview

KLED
93.3 mhz FM; 13.5 kw; 136.2 meters; N44 14 35 W105 32 19
1121 Fort Street, Buffalo, WY
(307) 684-5126, *Fax:* (307) 684-7676
License: Antelope Valley Crestview, Weston County, WY held by Legend Communications of Wyoming LLC
Group Owner: Horizon Christian Fellowship

Tom Phillips, Chief Operating Officer

Bar Nunn

KDAD
01-01-2007; 92.5 mhz FM; 3.1 kw; 521 meters; N42 16 05 W105 26 33
2109 E. 10th St., Cheyenne, WY
(307) 638-8921, *Fax:* (307) 638-8922
License: Bar Nunn, Converse County, WY held by White Park Broadcasting Inc.
Group Owner: Northeast Broadcasting Company Inc.

Steven Silberberg, President
Roger Ingram, General Manager

Basin

KBHM
107.9 mhz FM; 100 kw; 418 meters; N44 34 11 W108 49 07
PO Box 5086, Sheriden, WY
(307) 672-7421, *Fax:* (307) 672-2933
www.sheridanmedia.com
License: Basin, WY held by Lovecom Inc
W K Love, President

Buffalo

KBBS
04-17-1956; 1450 khz AM *Hrs Open:* 24; 1 kw-U, ND1; N44 20 33 W106 40 54
1221 Fort Street, Buffalo, WY 82834 US
(307) 684-5126, *Fax:* (307) 684-7676
www.bighornmountainradio.com
kbbs@vcn.com
License: Buffalo, WY held by Legend Communications of Wyoming L.L.C.
Group Owner: Legend Communications L.L.C.; (acq 9-1-2000; $1.05 million with KLGT(FM) Buffalo)
Nat'l Reps: McGavren Guild
Arbitron Metro Market: Buffalo, WY *Format:* News, News/Talk, 64, Sports, Talk *Hrs. of News Programming:* News progmg 10 hrs wkly *Target Audience:* 35-64; age group with the most money to spend *Adv. Rates:* 10.50;10.50; 10.50; 9.50
Larry Patrick, CEO
Larry Patrick, President
Dave Wooten, General Manager
Steve Lawrence, Station Manager
Ed Cwiklin, Programming Director
Justin Wolfing, News Director
Charles Dozier, Chief Engineer

***KBUW**
01-01-2000; 90.5 mhz FM; 0.43 kw; -197 ft.; N44 20 50 W106 43 25
P O Box 3984, Laramie, WY 82071 US
(307) 766-4240, *Fax:* (307) 766-6184
uwadmnweb.uwyo.edu/WPR
rgriscom@uwyo.edu
License: Buffalo, Johnson County, WY held by University of Wyoming.
Format: News, Triple A
Jon Schwartz, General Manager
Peg Arnold, General Sales Mgr
Bob Beck, News Director
Larry Dean, Chief Engineer
Roger Adams, Advertising Director

KLGT
03-07-1983; 96.5 mhz FM *Hrs Open:* 24; 100 kw; 333 ft.; N44 34 31.9 W106 52 21.7
1221 Fort Street, Buffalo, WY 82834 US
(307) 684-5126, *Fax:* (307) 684-7676
klgt@vcn.com
License: Buffalo, Johnson County, WY held by Legend Communications of Wyoming L.L.C.
Group Owner: Legend Communications L.L.C.; (acq 9-1-2000)
Nat'l Network: Jones Radio Networks *Nat'l Reps:* McGavren Guild
Arbitron Metro Market: Casper, WY *Format:* Country *Special Programming:* Relg one hr wkly *Hrs. of News Programming:* news progmg 9 hrs wkly *No. News Employees:* 1 *Target Audience:* 24-54; those withspendable income *Adv. Rates:* 16; 16; 16; 13
Larry Patrick, CEO
Ed Cwiklin, Operations Dir
Smokey Wildeman, General Manager
Zach Morton, Chief Engineer
Nicki Williams, CFO

Burns

KIGN
09-26-1990; 101.9 mhz FM *Hrs Open:* 24; 50 kw; 492 ft.; N41 7 1 W104 40 7
1513 Carey Avenue, Cheyenne, WY 82001 US
(307) 632-4400, *Fax:* (307) 632-1818
www.kingfm.com
License: Burns, Laramie County, WY held by GAP Broadcasting Cheyenne License LLC.
Group Owner: GAPWEST Broadcasting; (acq 2-13-2008; grpsl)
Arbitron Metro Market: Cheyenne, WY *Format:* Rock/AOR *Hrs. of News Programming:* news progmg 3 hrs wkly *No. News Employees:* 1 *Target Audience:* 25-54.
Rick Darcy, Operations Dir
Craig Cochran, General Manager
Geoff Gundy, Programming Director
Amy Richards, News Director
Jim Mross, Chief Engineer

***KIHI**
01-01-2008; 88.9 mhz FM; 600 w; Ant 118 ft; N41 09 45 W104 30 16
87 Jasper Lake Rd., Loveland, CO
(970) 669-9200, *Fax:* (970) 669-0800
License: Burns, Laramie County, WY held by Cedar Cove Broadcasting Inc.
Group Owner: Cedar Cove Broadcasting Inc.
Victor Michael Jr., President

Casper

KASS
10-15-1990; 106.9 mhz FM *Hrs Open:* 24; 94 kw; 1765 ft.; N42 44 37 W106 18 31
218 N. Wolcott, Casper, WY 82602 US
(307) 265-1984, *Fax:* (307) 473-7461
License: Casper, Natrona County, WY held by Mount Rushmore Broadcasting Inc.
Group Owner: Mt. Rushmore Broadcasting Inc.; (acq 1995; $150,000).
Arbitron Metro Market: Casper, WY *Format:* Classic Rock
Roger Arndt, General Manager
Donny Rood, Programming Director
Jenniey Lyman, News Director
Steve Fritz, Chief Engineer

***KCSP-FM**
01-01-1992; 90.3 mhz FM *Hrs Open:* 24; 100 kw; 1,922 ft; N42 44 24 W106 18 23
6363 Hwy. 50 E., Carson City, NV 89701
(775) 883-5647
www.pilgrimradio.com
info@pilgrimradio.com
License: Casper, Natrona County, WY held by Western Inspirational Broadcasters Inc.
Group Owner: Western Inspirational Broadcasters Inc.; (acq 10-3-90).
Population Served: 330,000 *Arbitron Metro Market:* Casper, WY *No. News Employees:* 1 *Target Audience:* General.
Tim Weidemann, Operations Dir
Tom Hesse, General Manager
Bill Feltner, Programming Director
Ian Perry, Engineering Dir

KHOC
01-01-1998; 102.5 mhz FM *Hrs Open:* 24; 100 kw; 1696 ft.; N42 44 37 W106 18 31
218 N. Wolcott, Casper, WY 82601 US
(307) 265-1984, *Fax:* (307) 266-3295
www.wyomingradio.com
mrbnews@wyoming.com
License: Casper, Natrona County, WY held by Mount Rushmore Broadcasting Inc.
Group Owner: Mt. Rushmore Broadcasting Inc.; (acq 10-29-98; $300,000).
Arbitron Metro Market: Casper, WY *Format:* Adult Contemp *No. News Employees:* 1 *Target Audience:* m/f 18-45
Kevin Gray, General Manager
Glenna Hunter, Programming Director
Michelle Reynolds, News Director
Steve Fritz, Engineering Dir

KKTL
01-01-1999; 1400 khz AM; 1 kw-U, ND1; N42 51 22 W106 21 41
555 13th Street, N.W., Washington, DC 20004 US
(307) 266-5252, *Fax:* (307) 235-9143
kktl@thegapbroadcasting.com
License: Casper, WY held by GAP Broadcasting Casper License LLC.
Group Owner: GAPWEST Broadcasting; (acq 2-13-2008; grpsl)
Arbitron Metro Market: Casper, WY *Format:* Sports
Donovan Short, Operations Dir
Robert Price, General Manager
Walter Hawn, General Sales Mgr
Dave Borino, News Director
Dave Nutter, Chief Engineer

KMLD
10-01-1967; 94.5 mhz FM; 63 kw; 1909 ft.; N42 44 3 W106 20 0
200 Concord Plaza, Suite 600, San Antonio, TX 78216 US
(307) 265-1984, *Fax:* (307) 473-7461
www.wyomingradio.com
kmld@wyomingradio.com
License: Casper, Natrona County, WY held by Mt. Rushmore Broadcasting Inc.
Group Owner: Mt. Rushmore Broadcasting Inc.; (acq 3-12-2001; grpsl).
Arbitron Metro Market: Casper, WY *Format:* Oldies *Target Audience:* 35-64.
Roger Arndt, General Manager
Donny Rood, Programming Director
Jenniey Lyman, News Director
Steve Fritz, Chief Engineer

KRNK
01-01-1998; 96.7 mhz FM; 2.85 kw; Ant 1,771 ft; N42 44 37 W106 18 26
150 N. Nichols Ave., Casper, WY 82601
(307) 266-5252, *Fax:* (307) 235-9143
www.rock967online.com
License: Casper, Natrona County, WY held by GAP Broadcasting Casper License LLC.
Group Owner: GAPWEST Broadcasting; (acq 2-13-2008; grpsl)
Arbitron Metro Market: Casper, WY
Donovan Short, Operations Dir
Bob Price, General Manager
Trisha Berry, Promotions Manager

KQLT
10-07-1983; 103.7 mhz FM *Hrs Open:* 24; 97 kw; 1860 ft.; N42 44 37 W106 18 31
218 No Wolcott, Casper, WY 82602 US
(307) 265-1984, *Fax:* (307) 473-7461
www.wyomingradio.com
kqlt@wyomingradio.com
License: Casper, Natrona County, WY held by Mount Rushmore Broadcasting Inc.
Group Owner: Mt. Rushmore Broadcasting Inc.; (acq 8-17-94; $230,000;
Nat'l Reps: McGavren Guild
Arbitron Metro Market: Casper, WY *Format:* Country *Target Audience:* General.
Jan Charles Gray, President
Don Rood, Operations Dir
Roger Arndt, General Manager
Donny Rood, Programming Director
Jenniey Lyman, News Director
Steve Fritz, Chief Engineer

KTRS-FM
01-01-1997; 104.7 mhz FM; 18 kw; 1818 ft.; N42 44 37 W106 18 24
6807 Foxglove Drive, Cheyenne, WY 82009 US
(307) 266-5252, *Fax:* (307) 235-9143
kisscasper.com
ktrs@clearchannel.com
License: Casper, Natrona County, WY held by GAP Broadcasting Casper License LLC.
Group Owner: GAPWEST Broadcasting; (acq 2-13-2008; grpsl)
Arbitron Metro Market: Casper, WY *Format:* Contemporary Hits/Top 40 *Target Audience:* 12-24.
Donovan Short, Operations Dir
Bob Price, General Manager
Bob Price, General Sales Mgr
Dave Borino, News Director
Dave Nutter, Chief Engineer
Donovan Short-Brand Manager

KTWO
01-02-1930; 1030 khz AM
50 East Rivercenter Blvd., Suite 1200, Covington, KY 41011 US
(307) 266-5252, *Fax:* (307) 235-9143
www.k2radio.com
ktwo@clearchanel.com
License: Casper, WY held by GAP Broadcasting Casper License LLC.
Group Owner: GAPWEST Broadcasting; (acq 2-13-2008; grpsl)
Nat'l Network: CBS
Arbitron Metro Market: Casper, WY *Format:* Talk *Target Audience:* 25-54.
Bob Price, General Manager and Director of Sales
Donovan Short, Programming Director
Vicki Daniels, News Director
David Nutter, Chief Engineer
Dave Borino, Traffic Manager

***KUWC**
01-01-2000; 91.3 mhz FM; 0.53 kw; 1785 ft.; N42 44 26 W106 21 34
P O Box 3434, Laramie, WY 82071 US
(307) 766-4240, *Fax:* (307) 766-6184
www.wyomingpublicradio.net
onair@uwyo.edu
License: Casper, Natrona County, WY held by University of Wyoming.
Arbitron Metro Market: Casper, WY *Format:* News, Triple A
Christina Kuzmych, General Manager
Grady Kirkpatrick, Interim Program Director/ Music Director
Peg Arnold, Interim Program Director/ Music Director
Bob Beck, News Director
Ben Slater, Engineer
Reid Fletcher, Chief Engineer
DianaDenison, Office Assistant, Senior
Kathy Dempsey, Accountant
Sarah Brown Mathews, Major Gifts
Valerie Hansen, Underwriting Representative
Shane Toven, Coordinator Engineer
Erin O'Doherty, Development Analyst

KVOC
09-29-1946; 1230 khz AM; 1 kw-U, ND1; N42 50 5 W106 17 44
212 North Wolcott, Casper, WY 82601 US
(307) 265-1984, *Fax:* (307) 473-7461
mtrushmore@mrbradio.com
License: Casper, WY held by Mount Rushmore Broadcasting Inc.
Group Owner: Mt. Rushmore Broadcasting Inc.; (acq 6-12-97; $105,000).
Nat'l Network: ESPN Radio
Arbitron Metro Market: Casper, WY *Format:* Sports
Jan Charles Gray, President
Roger Arndt, General Manager
Donny Rood, Programming Director
Jenniey Lyman, News Director
Steve Fritz, Chief Engineer

***KLWC**
01-01-2005; 89.1 mhz FM; 2.7 kw vert; 1850 ft.; N42 44 3 W106 20 0 *Rebroadcasts:* Rebroadcasts KLVR(FM) Santa Rosa, CA).
188 South Bellevue, Suite 222, Memphis, TN 38104 US
(800) 525-5683, *Fax:* (916) 251-1650
www.klove.com
klove@klove.com
License: Casper, Natrona County, WY held by Educational Media Foundation.
Group Owner: EMF Broadcasting; (acq 1-11-2005; $100,000 for CP with CP for KLRV(FM) Billings, MT).
Nat'l Network: K-Love
Arbitron Metro Market: Casper, WY *Format:* Christian
Darrell Chambliss, Chairman
Mike Novak, President and CEO
Jennifer Lohman, Operations Dir
David Pierce, Programming Director
Ed Lenane, News Director
Sam Wallington, Engineering Dir
Marya Morgan, News Reporter
Richard Hunt,News Reporter
Laura Daniels, News Reporter
Tim Luttrell, News Reporter
Kenny Noble Cortes, News Reporter
Darren Vinson, News Reporter

KWYX
93.5 mhz FM; 3.8 kw; 1739 ft.; N42 44 28 W106 18 31 US
(703) 812-0482
www.kwyx.com
License: Casper, Natrona County, WY held by Cochise Broadcasting LLC.
Group Owner: Cochise Broadcasting LLC
Arbitron Metro Market: Casper, WY
Ted Tucker, General Manager

***KKRR**
01-01-2008; 88.3 mhz FM; 0.5 kw vert; 1726 ft.; N42 44 26 W106 21 34
2232 Dell Range Blvd., Suite 306, Cheyenne, WY 82009 US
(307) 637-7777
License: Casper, Natrona County, WY held by WCN Inc.
Arbitron Metro Market: Casper, WY *Format:* Oldies
Robert Rule, President

Cheyenne

KFBC
01-01-1940; 1240 khz AM *Hrs Open:* 24; 0.7 kw-U, ND1; N41 7 17 W104 50 22
5101 Timberline Road, Cheyenne, WY 82009 US
(307) 634-4461, *Fax:* (307) 632-8586
www.kfbcradio.com
info@kfbcam.com
License: Cheyenne, WY held by Montgomery Broadcasting L.L.C.
Nat'l Network: ABC
Arbitron Metro Market: Cheyenne, WY *Format:* News, Sports *Hrs. of News Programming:* news progmg 25 hrs wkly *No. News Employees:* 5 *Target Audience:* 35-54. *Adv. Rates:* 12; 8; 12; 5
Dave Montgomery, President
J.D. Harris, Station Manager

KXBG
09-01-1968; 97.9 mhz FM *Hrs Open:* 24; 100 kw; 541 ft.; N41 6 1 W105 0 23
50 East Rivercenter Blvd, Suite 1200, Covington, KY 41011 US
(970) 461-2560, *Fax:* (970) 461-0118
www.bigcountry979.com
stuhaskell@clearchannel.com; chriskelly@clearchannel.com; kathyarias@clearchannel.com
License: Cheyenne, Laramie County, WY held by Citicasters Licenses L.P.
Group Owner: Clear Channel Communications Inc.; (acq 1999; grpsl)
Arbitron Metro Market: Cheyenne, WY *Format:* Country *Hrs. of News Programming:* news progmg 2 hrs wkly *No. News Employees:* 3 *Target Audience:* 25-54.
Stu Haskell, General Manager
Scott James, Programming Director
Mike Sanchez, Promotions Manager
Kathy Arias, News Director
Dave Agnew, Chief Engineer
Chris Kelly, Program Director
Rob Austin, Asst. Program Director

KJUA
01-01-1952; 1380 khz AM *Hrs Open:* 24
110 East 17th Street, Suite 205, Cheyenne, WY 82001 US
(307) 635-8787, *Fax:* (307) 635-8788
www.kjjl.com
kjjl@kjjl.com
License: Cheyenne, WY held by Christus Broadcasting Inc.
Nat'l Network: CNN Radio

Arbitron Metro Market: Cheyenne, WY *Format:* Adult Contemp *Special Programming:* Gospel one hr wkly *Hrs. of News Programming:* news progmg 22 hrs wkly *No. News Employees:* 2 *Target Audience:* 35 plus;mature adults *Adv. Rates:* 18; 16; 18; 14
Paul Montoya, President

KLEN
09-26-1983; 106.3 mhz FM *Hrs Open:* 24; 6 kw; 325 ft.; N41 3 9 W104 49 55
50 East Rivercenter Blvd, Suite 1200, Covington, KY 41011 US
(307) 632-4400, *Fax:* (307) 632-1818
www.1063klen.com
cheyenneaudio@clearchannel.com
License: Cheyenne, Laramie County, WY held by GAP Broadcasting Cheyenne License LLC.
Group Owner: GAPWEST Broadcasting; (acq 2-13-2008; grpsl)
Arbitron Metro Market: Cheyenne, WY *Format:* Country *No. News Employees:* 3 *Target Audience:* 25-54.
Rick Darcy, Operations Dir
Craig Cochran, General Manager
Amy Richards, News Director
Jim Mross, Chief Engineer
Lesley Martin, Traffic Manager

KOLZ
08-01-1961; 100.7 mhz FM; 100 kw; 663 ft.; N41 2 55 W104 53 28
50 East Rivercenter Blvd, Suite 1200, Covington, KY 41011 US
(307) 632-4400, *Fax:* (307) 632-1818
www.kolz.com
License: Cheyenne, Laramie County, WY held by Citicasters Licenses L.P.
Group Owner: Clear Channel Communications Inc.
Arbitron Metro Market: Cheyenne, WY *Format:* Country
Jeff Brown, Programming Director

KRAE
04-29-1961; 1480 khz AM
P. O. Box 189, Cheyenne, WY 82001 US
(307) 638-8921, *Fax:* (307) 638-8922
news@1049krrr.com
License: Cheyenne, WY held by Brahmin Broadcasting Corp.
Group Owner: Northeast Broadcasting Company Inc.; (acq 5-10-2004; grpsl).
Nat'l Network: ESPN Radio
Arbitron Metro Market: Cheyenne, WY *Format:* Sports *Special Programming:* Sp 2 hrs wkly *Adv. Rates:* 144; 132; 120; 96
Larry Proietti, General Manager
Jessica Cooper, General Sales Mgr
Larry Proeitti, Programming Director
R.J. Fox, News Director
Rob Thomas, Chief Engineer
Sandra Cooper, Traffic Manager

KKPL
01-01-1997; 99.9 mhz FM; 50 kw; Ant 492 ft; N40 59 22 W105 03 47
600 Main St., Windsor, CO 82009
(970) 674-2700, *Fax:* (970) 686-7491
www.999thepoint.com
info@999thepoint.com
License: Cheyenne, Laramie County, WY held by Townsquare Media of Fort Collins Inc
Group Owner: Townsquare Media; (acq 11-15-2004; $7.75 million with KARS-FM Laramie)
Arbitron Metro Market: Cheyenne, WY
Mark Callaghan, Operations Dir
Cal Hall, General Manager
Miles Schallert, General Sales Mgr
Mark Callaghan, Programming Director
Susan Moore, News Director
Kerry Richards, Chief Engineer

KRRR
01-01-1997; 104.9 mhz FM; 25.5 kw; 115 ft.; N41 8 4 W104 41 32
2109 E 10th Street, Cheyenne, WY 82001 US
(307) 638-8921, *Fax:* (307) 638-8922
www.1049krrr.com/
sales@radiowyo.com
License: Cheyenne, Laramie County, WY
Arbitron Metro Market: Cheyenne, WY *Format:* Oldies *Target Audience:* 25-54.
Roger Ingram, General Manager

***KWYC**
01-01-2005; 90.3 mhz FM *Hrs Open:* 24; 20.5 kw; 426 ft.; N41 13 1 W104 26 53
1425 N Market Blvd., Suite 9, Sacramento, CA 95834 US
(800) 357-4226, *Fax:* (208) 736-1958
www.csnradio.com
csn@csnradio.com
License: Cheyenne, Laramie County, WY held by CSN International.
Group Owner: CSN International; (acq 1-9-2004; $1 for CP).
Arbitron Metro Market: Cheyenne, WY *Format:* Talk
Mike Kestler, President
Daniel Davidson, Operations Dir
Mike Stockland, General Manager
Don Mills, Programming Director
Kelly Carlson, Engineering Dir
Jerry Johnson, Engineering Dir
Don Mills, Network Programming Director / MusicDirector
Ray Gorney, Assistant Director of Engineering
Nolan Mather, Graphics / Website Maintenance
Mike Stocklin, National Underwriting
Austin Morris, Accounting
Austin Morris, Accounting

***KAIX**
01-01-2006; 88.1 mhz FM; 1.9 kw; 207 ft.; N41 9 37 W104 42 13
Rebroadcasts: Rebroadcasts KLRD(FM) Yucaipa, CA 100%
P O Drawer 2440, Tupelo, MS 38803 US
(888) 937-2471, *Fax:* (916) 251-1650
www.air1.com
info@air1.com
License: Cheyenne, Laramie County, WY held by Educational Media Foundation.
Group Owner: EMF Broadcasting; (acq 3-23-2007; grpsl)
Nat'l Network: Air 1
Arbitron Metro Market: Cheyenne, WY *Format:* Alternative, Christian
Darrell Chambliss, Chairman
Alan Mason, COO
Mike Novak, President and CEO
Ed Lenane, News Director
Sam Wallington, Engineering Dir
Eric Moser, Chief Financial Officer
Brian Burger, Vice President of Human Resources
D. KevinBlair, Secretary and General Counsel
Larry Moody, Director
Mitch Barnhart, Director

KAZY
06-15-2006; 93.7 mhz FM; 25 kw; 115 ft.; N41 8 4 W104 41 32 US
(307) 638-8921, *Fax:* (307) 638-8922
License: Cheyenne, Laramie County, WY held by White Park Broadcasting Inc.
Group Owner: Northeast Broadcasting Company Inc.
Arbitron Metro Market: Auburn, WA *Format:* Rock/AOR
Steven Silberberg, President
Roger Ingram, General Manager

Chugwater

***KLWV**
01-01-2004; 90.9 mhz FM *Hrs Open:* 24; 100 kw; 1183 ft.; N41 18 39 W105 27 12
16075 West Belleview Ave, Morrison, CO 80465 US
(800) 525-5683, *Fax:* (916) 251-1650
www.klove.com
klove@klove.com
License: Chugwater, Platte County, WY held by Educational Media Foundation.
Group Owner: EMF Broadcasting; (acq 10-2-03; grpsl).
Nat'l Network: K-Love
Arbitron Metro Market: Cheyenne, WY *Format:* Christian *No. News Employees:* 3 *Target Audience:* 25-44; Judeo Christian, female
Darrell Chambliss, Chairman
Mike Novak, President and CEO
Jennifer Lohman, Operations Dir
David Pierce, Programming Director
Ed Lenane, News Director
Sam Wallington, Engineering Dir
Marya Morgan, News Reporter
Richard Hunt,News Reporter
Tracy Butler, Traffic Manager
Laura Daniels, News Reporter
Tim Luttrell, News Reporter
Kenny Noble Cortes, News Reporter

Clearmont

KLQQ
01-01-2006; 104.9 mhz FM; 100 kw; 1207 ft.; N44 37 20 W107 6 57
US
(307) 672-7421, *Fax:* (307) 672-2933
www.sheridanmedia.com
info@sheridanmedia.com
License: Clearmont, Sheridan County, WY held by Lovcom Inc.
Group Owner: Lovcom Inc.
Arbitron Metro Market: Clearmont, WY *Format:* Contemporary Hits/Top 40
Bob Rolston, President
Bob Grammens, General Manager
Jim Schellinger, General Sales Mgr
Ed Cwik, Programming Director
Trevor Jackson, Sports Director
Ted Wenckus, Marketing Specialist
Julie Chadwick, Marketing Specialist
GrantToth, Webmaster / Assistant Director of Operations
Gay Higley, Marketing Specialist

Cody

KODI
03-01-1947; 1400 khz AM *Hrs Open:* 6 AM-midnight
2001 Mountain View Drive, Post Office Box 1210, Cody, WY 82414 US
(307) 578-5000, *Fax:* (307) 527-5045
www.bighornradio.com
ckary@bhrnwy.com
License: Cody, WY held by Legend Communications of Wyoming LLC.
Group Owner: Legend Communications L.L.C.; (acq 6-29-99; $890,000 with co-located FM)
Wire Services: NWS (National Weather Service)
Format: News, News/Talk, 84, Talk *Hrs. of News Programming:* news progmg 20 hrs wkly *No. News Employees:* 1 *Target Audience:* 35 plus.
Larry Patrick, President
Carol Kary, Operations Dir
Cory Ostermiller, General Sales Mgr
Tom Morrison, Programming Director
Wendy Corr, News Director
Charles Dozier, Chief Engineer
Roger Gelder, Executive Vice President

KTAG
11-30-1981; 97.9 mhz FM *Hrs Open:* 6 AM-midnight; 100 kw; 1890 ft.; N44 29 42 W109 9 10
P.O. Box 1210, Cody, WY 82414 US
(307) 578-5000, *Fax:* (307) 527-5045
bighornradio.com
ckary@bhrnwy.com
License: Cody, Park County, WY
Group Owner: Legend Communications L.L.C.
Arbitron Metro Market: Cody, WY *Format:* Adult Contemp *Hrs. of News Programming:* News progmg 6 hrs wkly *Target Audience:* 25-39; upper middle class, young families, suburban w/some college, 60% female
Larry Patrick, CEO
Carol Kary, General Manager
Cory Ostermiller, General Sales Mgr
Wendy Corr, News Director
Roger Gelder, COO

KROW
96.7 mhz FM; 2.4 kw; Ant 1,831 ft; N44 29 49 W109 09 19
288 S. River Rd., Bedford, NH
(603) 668-6400, *Fax:* (603) 668-6470
License: Cody, Park County, WY held by White Park Broadcasting Inc.
Group Owner: Northeast Broadcasting Company Inc.
Steven Silberberg, President

***KOFG**
91.1 mhz FM; 8.7 kw; 1795 ft.; N44 29 46 W109 9 9
US
(903) 503-0304
www.oldfashiongospel.org
License: Cody, Park County, WY held by Tres Hermanas Educational Media Foundation of Texas Inc.
Arbitron Metro Market: Cody, WY *Format:* Gospel
Lonnie Horton, President

Cowley

KBEN-FM
103.3 mhz FM; 100 kw; 1401 ft.; N44 34 13 W108 49 9
US
(603) 668-6400, *Fax:* (603) 668-6470
License: Cowley, WY held by White Park Broadcasting Inc.
Group Owner: Northeast Broadcasting Company Inc.
Steven Silberberg, President

Daniel

KYPT
104.3 mhz FM; kw
US
(206) 805-0965, *Fax:* (206) 805-0932
License: Daniel, Sweetwater County, WY held by Martin Dirst
Arbitron Metro Market: Daniel, WY
Martin Dirst, General Manager

Dayton

KOWY
102.3 mhz FM; 2100 watts; 343 meters; 44 37 N20 107 06 W57
1716 Kroe Lane, PO Box 5086, Sheridan, WY
(307) 672-7421, *Fax:* (307) 672-2933
www.sheridanmedia.com/magic-1023
info@sheridanmedia.com
License: Dayton, WY

Kim Love, President/Owner
Steve Sisson, Operations Dir
Bob Grammens, General Manager
Jim Schellinger, General Sales Mgr
Tracee Davis, News Director

Diamondville

KDWY
01-01-2000; 105.3 mhz FM; 16 kw; 886 ft.; N41 50 18 W110 30 11
36 Cross Highway, Redding, CT 06896 US
(307) 877-4422, *Fax:* (307) 877-5537
kmer@onewest.net
License: Diamondville, Lincoln County, WY held by Simmons-SLC, LS LLC.
Group Owner: Simmons Media Group; (acq 4-19-2004; grpsl)
Nat'l Network: ABC
Arbitron Metro Market: Kemmerer, WY *Format:* Country *Hrs. of News Programming:* news progmg one hr wkly *No. News Employees:* 1 *Target Audience:* 25-55. *Adv. Rates:* 12; 12; 12; 12
Jim Thoeny, Operations Dir
Jim Carroll, General Manager

Douglas

KKTY
06-22-1957; 1470 khz AM *Hrs Open:* 24; 1 kw-D, ND2; 0.5 kw-N, ND2; N42 45 48 W105 23 32
112 North 2nd St., Douglas, WY 82633 US
(307) 358-3636, *Fax:* (307) 358-4010
www.kktyonline.com
kkty@netcommander.com
License: Douglas, WY held by Douglas Broadcasting Inc.
Nat'l Network: Westwood One; CNN Radio *Regional Reps:* Regnl Reps *Wire Services:* AP
Arbitron Metro Market: Casper, WY *Format:* Oldies *Hrs. of News Programming:* News progmg 28 hrs wkly *Target Audience:* Adults 18+ *Adv. Rates:* 9.25; 9.25; 9.25; na
Dennis Switzer, General Manager

KKTS-FM
12-06-1982; 99.3 mhz FM *Hrs Open:* 24; 813 w; 530 ft; N42 43 42 W105 31 46
Box 135, 247 Russell Ave., Douglas, WY 82633
(307) 358-3636, *Fax:* (307) 358-4010
www.kktyonline.com
kkty@netcommander.com
License: Douglas, Converse County, WY
Nat'l Network: Jones Radio Networks; CNN Radio
Hrs. of News Programming: news progmg 28 hrs wkly *No. News Employees:* 1 *Target Audience:* General. *Adv. Rates:* Same as AM
Becky Heidt, News Director

***KDUW**
01-01-2000; 91.7 mhz FM; 0.45 kw; 312 ft.; N42 43 24 W105 18 21
P.O. Box 3984, Laramie, WY 82071 US
(307) 766-4240, *Fax:* (307) 766-6184
www.wyomingpublicmedia.org
onair@uwyo.edu
License: Douglas, Converse County, WY held by University of Wyoming.
Arbitron Metro Market: Laramie, WY *Format:* News
Jon Schwartz, General Manager
Roger Adams, Programming Director
Bob Beck, News Director
Reid Fletcher, Chief Engineer
Peg Arnold, Programming Director
Tristan Ahtone, Reporter
Willow Belden, Reporter
Diana Denison, OfficeAssistant, Senior
Kathy Dempsey, Accountant
Valerie Hansen, Underwriting Representative

***KKWY**
88.7 mhz FM; 7 kw; 240 ft.; N42 51 29 W105 14 3
US
(307) 460-4224
License: Douglas, Converse County, WY held by Wren Communications Inc.
Arbitron Metro Market: Douglas, WY
Tara Parker, President

Elk Mountain

***KGCV**
88.1 mhz FM; 0.1 kw; -105 ft.; N41 41 39 W106 24 2
US
(703) 761-5013
License: Elk Mountain, Carbon County, WY held by Ocean Side Broadcasting Inc.
Arbitron Metro Market: Elk Mountain, WY
A. Wray Fitch III, President

Esterbrook

***KQCO**
89.5 mhz FM; 320 watts; Ant 3,165 ft; N42 16 06 W105 26 31
87 Jasper Lake Rd., Loveland, CO
(970) 669-9200
License: Esterbrook, Converse County, WY held by Cedar Cove Broadcasting Inc.
Group Owner: Cedar Cove Broadcasting Inc.
Victor Michael, President

Ethete

***KWRR**
01-01-2000; 89.5 mhz FM; 85 kw; 1821 ft.; N43 27 30 W108 11 39
P. O. Box 396, Fort Washakie, WY 82514 US
(307) 335-8659, *Fax:* (307) 335-8740
www.nv1.org
etheteroad@yahoo.com
License: Ethete, Fremont County, WY held by Business Council of the Northern Arapaho Tribe.
Arbitron Metro Market: Kinnear, WY *Format:* Native American
Steven White, General Manager
Jason Foskey, Programming Director
Lincoln Scott, Chief Engineer
Lisa Yawakia, Air Personality
Big Joe Antelope, Air Personality

Evanston

KEVA
06-27-1953; 1240 khz AM *Hrs Open:* 24; 0.88 kw-U, ND1; N41 15 29 W111 0 51
P. O. Box 190, Evanston, WY 82930 US
(307) 789-9101(307) 789-9102, *Fax:* (307) 789-8521
1240keva,com
keva@vcn.com
License: Evanston, WY held by Sagebrush Broadcasting Co. Inc.
Group Owner: Jimmy Ray Carroll Stns; (acq 1-23-2001).
Arbitron Metro Market: Evanston, WY *Format:* Country *Target Audience:* 25-54.
Linda Burris, General Manager
Linda Burns, General Sales Mgr
Bill Smith, Programming Director
J.C. Jewett, News Director
Michael Richard, Chief Engineer

KBMG
06-01-1982; 106.1 mhz FM; 89 kw horiz; 2123 ft.; N40 52 16 W110 59 43
P.O. Box 190, Evanston, WY 82931 US
(801) 908-8777, *Fax:* (801) 908-8782
License: Evanston, Uinta County, WY
Group Owner: Adelante Media Group LLC; (acq 7-1-2004; $3 million).
Edward Distel, General Manager

KADQ-FM
01-01-2008; 98.3 mhz FM; 1.2 kw; 1490 ft.; N41 21 10 W110 54 31
US
(312) 204-9900
License: Evanston, Uinta County, WY held by College Creek Media LLC.
Group Owner: College Creek Media LLC
Arbitron Metro Market: Evanston, WY
David Stout, General Manager

Evansville

KUYO
08-23-1985; 830 khz AM *Hrs Open:* Sunrise-sunset
Mailing Address: 40 South Curtis, Evansville, WY 82636 US
Second Address: 1423 S. Beverly, Casper, WY 82609
(307) 577-5896, *Fax:* (307) 577-0850
www.kuyo.com
joy@kuyo.com
License: Evansville, WY held by Wyoming Christian Broadcasting Co.
Arbitron Metro Market: Evansville, WY *Format:* Christian, Talk
Target Audience: 35-65; general
Steve Stumbo, President
Aaron Remington, Operations Dir

KTED
01-01-2008; 100.5 mhz FM; 10 kw; 1434 ft.; N42 45 30 W106 19 23
US
(307) 232-2155
www.kted1005.com
License: Evansville, Converse County, WY held by White Park Broadcasting Inc.
Group Owner: Northeast Broadcasting Company Inc.
Arbitron Metro Market: Evansville, WY
Steven Silberberg, President
Rood Dogg, Programming Director
Courtney Williams, Sales Representative

Fort Bridger

KNYN
01-01-2001; 103.9 mhz FM; 27.5 kw; 1604 ft.; N41 21 10 W110 54 26
P.O. Box 570, Logan, UT 84321 US
(307) 789-9101, *Fax:* (307) 789-8521
info@keva.com
License: Fort Bridger, Uinta County, WY held by M. Kent Frandsen.
Format: Adult Contemp
Linda Burris, General Manager
Bill Smith, Programming Director
J.C. Jewett, News Director
Michael Richard, Chief Engineer

Fort Washakie

***KRKM**
91.7 mhz FM; 6 kw horiz; 1309 ft.; N42 34 42 W108 42 46
US
(800) 525-5683
www.klove.com
License: Fort Washakie, Summit County, WY held by Wren Communications Inc.
Arbitron Metro Market: Fort Washakie, WY *Format:* Christian, Gospel
Darrell Chambliss, Chairman
Mike Novak, CEO
Alan Mason, Operations Dir
David Pierce, Chief Creative Officer
Dan Antonelli, Chief Business Development Officer
Eric Moser, Chief Financial Officer
Brian Burger, Vice President ofHuman Resources
D. Kevin Blair, Secretary and General Counsel

***KFTW**
90.9 mhz FM; 8 kw; 495 ft.; N42 54 27 W108 44 50
US
(307) 332-5983, *Fax:* (307) 332-7267
www.radioftw.com
License: Fort Washakie, Fremont County, WY held by Fremont County School District #21.
Arbitron Metro Market: Fort Washakie, WY
Gregory Cox, General Manager

Fox Farm

KRND
01-01-1998; 1630 khz AM *Hrs Open:* 24
110 E. 17th Street, Ste 205, Cheyenne, WY 82001 US
(307) 635-8787, *Fax:* (307) 635-8788
www.kwyradio.com
kwy@kwyradio.com
License: Fox Farm, WY held by Christus Broadcasting Inc.
Nat'l Network: AP Network News
Arbitron Metro Market: Cheyenne, WY *Format:* Country *Hrs. of News Programming:* news progmg 22 hrs wkly *No. News Employees:* 1 *Target Audience:* 35 plus; mature adults *Adv. Rates:* 18; 16; 18; 16

Paul Montoya, President

Gillette

KAML-FM

05-01-1976; 97.3 mhz FM *Hrs Open:* 24; 100 kw; 1098 ft.; N43 59 57 W105 15 15
400 East Third Avenue, Gillette, WY 82717 US
(307) 686-2242, *Fax:* (307) 686-7736
www.basinsradio.com
License: Gillette, Campbell County, WY held by Legend Communications of Wyoming LLC.
Group Owner: Legend Communications L.L.C.; (acq 1-16-2007; $300,000 with KIML(AM) Gillette)
Arbitron Metro Market: Gillette, WY *Format:* Adult Contemp *Hrs. of News Programming:* news progmg one hr wkly *Target Audience:* 25-54. *Adv. Rates:* 18; 16; 17; 14
Don Clonch, General Manager
Terry Michael, Programming Director

*KAXG

03-27-2003; 89.7 mhz FM *Hrs Open:* 24; 0.4 kw vert; 449 ft.; N44 12 34 W105 28 4 *Rebroadcasts:* Rebroadcasts KXEI(FM) Havre, MT 100%
P O Drawer 2440, Tupelo, MS 38803 US
(406) 265-5845, *Fax:* (406) 265-8860
www.ynopradio.org
ynop@ynopradio.org
License: Gillette, Campbell County, WY held by Hi-Line Radio Fellowship Inc.
Nat'l Network: Salem Radio Network *Wire Services:* AP
Arbitron Metro Market: Havre, MT *Format:* Christian, Religious
Target Audience: General; those looking for inpriprational Christian music & progmg
Roger Lonnquist, General Manager
Brenda Boyum, Station Manager
Brian Jackson, Programming Director

KGWY

01-05-1983; 100.7 mhz FM *Hrs Open:* 24; 98 kw; 620 ft.; N44 14 35 W105 32 19
Mailing Address: Box 1179, Gillette, WY 82716 US
Second Address: 2810 Southern Dr., Gillette, WY 82718
(307) 686-2242, *Fax:* (307) 686-7736
www.basinsradio.com
thefox@basinsradio.com
License: Gillette, Campbell County, WY held by Legend Communications of Wyoming LLC.
Group Owner: Legend Communications L.L.C.; (acq 5-29-2001; $1.9 million)
Format: Country *No. News Employees:* 1 *Target Audience:* 20-45.
Larry Patrick, President
Terry Michael, Operations Dir
Don Clonch, General Manager

KIML

09-13-1957; 1270 khz AM *Hrs Open:* 24; 5 kw-D, DAN; 1 kw-N, DAN; N44 18 12 W105 29 52
P. O. Box 1009, Gillette, WY 82716 US
(307) 686-2242, *Fax:* (307) 686-7736
www.basinsradio.com
License: Gillette, WY held by Legend Communications of Wyoming LLC.
Group Owner: Legend Communications L.L.C.; (acq 1-16-2007; $300,000 with KAML-FM Gillette)
Nat'l Network: Fox News Radio; Fox Sports *Wire Services:* AP
Format: News, News/Talk, 84, Talk *Hrs. of News Programming:* news progmg 40 hrs wkly *No. News Employees:* 1 *Target Audience:* 25 plus. *Adv. Rates:* 16; 15; 16; 12
Terry Michael, Operations Dir
Don Clonch, General Manager
Mark Warren, General Sales Mgr
Paul Wallem, News Director

*KLWD

01-01-2001; 91.9 mhz FM *Hrs Open:* 24; 1 kw; 318 ft.; N44 13 50 W105 27 45
P.O. Box 1492, Gillette, WY 82717 US
(800) 682-9253, *Fax:* (307) 682-8509
klwd.vcn.com
calvarycom@vcn.com
License: Gillette, Campbell County, WY held by CSN International
Group Owner: CSN International; acq 5-8-00; $10,000 for CP).
Format: Christian
Don Wight, President

*KUWG

01-01-1997; 90.9 mhz FM; 0.45 kw; 413 ft.; N44 12 34 W105 28 4 *Rebroadcasts:* Rebroadcasts KUWR(FM) Laramie 100%
P.O. Box 3984, Laramie, WY 82071 US
(307) 766-4240, *Fax:* (307) 766-6184
www.wyomingpublicradio.net
onair@uwyo.edu
License: Gillette, Campbell County, WY held by University of Wyoming.
Arbitron Metro Market: Gillette, WY *Format:* News
Christina Kuzmych, General Manager
Hank Arnold, General Sales Mgr
Grady Kirkpatrick, Interim Program Director/ Music Director
Bob Beck, News Director
Ben Slater, Engineer
Reid Fletcher, Chief Engineer
Diana Denison, OfficeAssistant, Senior
Kathy Dempsey, Accountant
Sarah Brown Mathews, Major Gifts
Valerie Hansen, Underwriting Representative
Shane Toven, Coordinator Engineer
Erin O'Doherty, Development Analyst

KGCC

01-01-2004; 99.9 mhz FM; 51 kw; 114 meters; N44 13 50 W105 27 45
Box 2230, Gillette, WY 60611
(307) 687-1003, *Fax:* (307) 687-1006
koaal1039@collinscom.net
License: Gillette, Campbell County, WY held by Keyhole Broadcasting LLC.
Deborah Semple, General Manager
Rob Olsen, Programming Director

*KLOF

01-01-2000; 88.9 mhz FM; 0.44 kw; 397 ft.; N44 12 34 W105 28 4
1500 N 30th Street, Billings, MT 59101 US
(916) 251-1600, *Fax:* (916) 251-1650
www.klove.com
klove@klove.com
License: Gillette, Campbell County, WY held by Educational Media Foundation.
Group Owner: EMF Broadcasting; (acq 3-29-2007; $55,000)
Nat'l Network: K-Love
Arbitron Metro Market: Gillette, WY *Format:* Christian
Darrell Chambliss, Chairman
Alan Mason, CEO/COO
Mike Novak, CEO
David Pierce, Chief Creative Officer
Dan Antonelli, Chief Business Development Officer
Eric Moser, Chief Financial Officer
Brian Burger, Vice President of HumanResources
D. Kevin Blair, Secretary and General Counsel

*KGLL

88.1 mhz FM; 0.2 kw vert; 279 ft.; N44 13 50 W105 27 45 US
(662) 844-5036, *Fax:* (662) 842-7798
www.afr.net
contact@afa.net
License: Gillette, Campbell County, WY held by Solid Rock Broadcasting Inc.
Arbitron Metro Market: Gillette, WY *Format:* Christian
Donald E. Wildmon, Founder
Barbara Coggin, President
Buster Wilson, General Manager
Jennifer Hagman, Programming Director

Glendo

KKTY-FM

07-10-1999; 100.1 mhz FM *Hrs Open:* 24; 100 kw; Ant 456 ft; N42 46 13 W105 13 21
1837 Madora Ave., Suite B, Douglas, WY 82009
(307) 358-6177, *Fax:* (307) 358-0978
www.kyod.com
kyod@netcommander.com
License: Glendo, Platte County, WY held by Canned Ham Communications LLC
Nat'l Network: Westwood One; CBS Radio
Population Served: 50,000 *Arbitron Metro Market:* Casper, WY
Special Programming: Religious, 3hrs wkly *Hrs. of News Programming:* news progmg one hr wkly *No. News Employees:* 1 *Target Audience:* 25-54.*Adv. Rates:* 9; 7; 9; 5
Darrell Woolsey, General Manager
Mary Woolsey, Station Manager

Glenrock

KGRK

01-01-2007; 98.5 mhz FM; 3.5 kw; 1699 ft.; N42 44 28 W106 18 31
7901 Stonridge Drive, Cheyenne, WY 82009 US
(970) 669-9200
ted@silvercityradio.com
License: Glenrock, Converse County, WY held by Michael Radio Group LLC.
Group Owner: Michael Radio Group
Arbitron Metro Market: Glenrock, WY
Victor Michael Jr., General Manager

Green River

KFRZ

09-23-1999; 92.1 mhz FM *Hrs Open:* 24; 90 kw; 1138 ft.; N41 29 47 W109 20 44
Mailing Address: P O Box 970, Green River, WY 82935 US
Second Address: 40 Shoshone Ave., Green River, WY 82935
(307) 875-6666, *Fax:* (307) 875-5847
www.theradionetwork.net
mail@theradionetwork.net
License: Green River, Sweetwater County, WY
Group Owner: Wagonwheel Communications Corp.
Nat'l Network: Westwood One
Arbitron Metro Market: Green River, WY *Format:* Country *Hrs. of News Programming:* news progmg 3 hrs wkly *No. News Employees:* 1 *Target Audience:* General. *Adv. Rates:* Same as AM
Jeff Driggs, General Sales Mgr
Steve Core, News Director

KUGR

06-18-1976; 1490 khz AM *Hrs Open:* 24; 1 kw-U, ND1; N41 30 56 W109 26 11
Mailing Address: 40 Shoshone, Green River, WY 82935 US
Second Address: 40 Shoshone Ave., Green River, WY 82935
(307) 875-6666, *Fax:* (307) 875-5847
www.theradionetwork.net
alankugr@hotmail.com
License: Green River, WY held by Wagon Wheel Communications Corp.
Group Owner: Wagonwheel Communications Corp.; (acq 1-1-79).
Nat'l Network: CBS; Westwood One
Arbitron Metro Market: Green River, WY *Format:* Adult Contemp
Special Programming: Sp 5 hrs wkly *Hrs. of News Programming:* news progmg 4 hrs wkly *No. News Employees:* 1 *Target Audience:* 30 plus. *Adv.Rates:* 13.60; 11.90; 13.60; 10.20
Al Harris, CEO
Steve Core, General Manager
Jeff Driggs, General Sales Mgr
Jasmine Weaver, Programming Director
Jon Schade, News Director
Teresa Warren, Traffic Manager
Faith Harris
Dave Arambel, Sales
Joe Martinez, Sales
Leah Lassise, Sales
Ryan Claxton, Sales

KZWB

01-01-2005; 97.9 mhz FM *Hrs Open:* 24; 10.5 kw; 1073 ft.; N41 29 47 W109 20 44
US
(307) 875-6666, *Fax:* (307) 875-5847
theradionetwork.net
mail@theradionetwork.net
License: Green River, Sweetwater County, WY held by Wagonwheel Communications Corp.
Group Owner: Wagonwheel Communications Corp.
Arbitron Metro Market: Green River, WY *Format:* Contemporary Hits/Top 40, Adult Contemp *No. News Employees:* 1
Alan Harris, President
Steve Core, General Manager

Greybull

KZMQ-FM

02-21-1986; 100.3 mhz FM; 53 kw; 2444 ft.; N44 48 41 W107 55 6
PO Box 352, Greybull, WY 82426 US
(307) 578-5000, *Fax:* (307) 527-5045
ckary@bhmwy.com
License: Greybull, Big Horn County, WY
Group Owner: Legend Communications L.L.C.
Arbitron Metro Market: Greybull, WY *Format:* Country
Carol Kary, General Manager

Guernsey

KANT

01-01-2008; 104.1 mhz FM; 36 kw; 564 ft.; N42 20 46.6 W105 2 3.9
US
(307) 638-8921, *Fax:* (307) 638-8922
1049krrr.com

RADIO - U.S.

License: Guernsey, Platte County, WY held by Brahmin Broadcasting Corp.
Group Owner: Northeast Broadcasting Company Inc.
Arbitron Metro Market: Guernsey, WY *Format:* Oldies
Steven Silberberg, President
Roger Ingram, General Manager

Hanna

KBDY
01-01-2009; 102.1 mhz FM; 0.63 kw; 3445 ft.; N41 38 0.9 W106 31 32.1
US
(307) 326-8642
License: Hanna, Carbon County, WY held by Toga Radio LLC
Arbitron Metro Market: Hanna, WY *Format:* Country
Don Day Jr., General Manager

Hillsdale

KYOY
01-01-1999; 92.3 mhz FM *Hrs Open:* 24; 12 kw; 144 ft.; N41 14 55 W104 27 46
P.O. Box 532, Scottsbluff, NE 69363 US
(308) 632-5667, *Fax:* (308) 635-1905
www.kyoy.net
propshop@kyoy.net
License: Hillsdale, Kimball County, WY held by Kimball Radio LLC.
Group Owner: Michael Radio Group; (acq 4-2-2007; $300,000 with KIMB(AM) Kimball)
Nat'l Network: AP Radio
Arbitron Metro Market: Kimball, NB *Format:* Oldies *No. News Employees:* 2
Larry Swikard, General Manager

Hudson

KTUG
105.1 mhz FM; 12.5 kw horiz; 262 ft.; N43 2 32 W108 26 28
US
(307) 855-4002, *Fax:* (307) 855-4005
www.ledge105.com
License: Hudson, Fremont County, WY held by White Park Broadcasting Inc.
Group Owner: Northeast Broadcasting Company Inc.
Arbitron Metro Market: Hudson, WY *Format:* Christian
Steven Silberberg, President
Shane Haynes, Station Manager

Jackson

KJAX
01-01-2000; 93.3 mhz FM; 100 kw; 1070 ft.; N43 27 40 W110 45 9
P. O. Box 291, Jackson, WY 83001 US
(307) 733-2120, *Fax:* (307) 733-4760
www.kjaxfm.com
mornings@kjaxfm.com
License: Jackson, Teton County, WY held by Chaparral Broadcasting Inc.
Group Owner: Chaparral Communications; (acq 3-29-2000; $393,787 for stock).
Arbitron Metro Market: Jackson, WY *Format:* Country
Scott Anderson, General Manager

KMTN
12-16-1974; 96.9 mhz FM; 50 kw; 1060 ft.; N43 27 42 W110 45 10
Mailing Address: P.O. Box 100, Jackson, WY 83001 US
Second Address: 645 S. Cache St., Jackson, WY 83001
(307) 733-2120, *Fax:* (307) 733-4760
www.jacksonholeradio.com
License: Jackson, Teton County, WY
Group Owner: Chaparral Communications
Nat'l Network: ABC
Format: Rock/AOR *Target Audience:* 18-54.
Mark Fishman, Programming Director
Lynda John, News Director

KSGT
07-20-1962; 1340 khz AM
Mailing Address: P.O. Box 100, Jackson, WY 83001 US
Second Address: 645 S. Cache St., Jackson, WY 83001
(307) 733-2120, *Fax:* (307) 733-4760
www.jacksonholeradio.com
License: Jackson, WY held by Chaparral Broadcasting Inc.
Group Owner: Chaparral Communications; (acq 11-30-92; $215,000 with KMER(AM) Kemmerer;
Arbitron Metro Market: Jackson, WY *Format:* Country *Target Audience:* 25 plus.
Scott Anderson, General Manager
Del Ray, Programming Director
Tom Ninneman, News Director

*KUWJ
11-01-1992; 90.3 mhz FM *Hrs Open:* 5 AM-midnight; 3 kw; 1106 ft.; N43 27 40 W110 45 9 *Rebroadcasts:* Rebroadcasts KUWR(FM) Laramie 100%
P.O. Box 3984, Laramie, WY 82071 US
(307) 766-4240, *Fax:* (307) 766-6184
www.wyomingpublicradio.net
onair@uwyo.edu
License: Jackson, Teton County, WY held by University of Wyoming.
Nat'l Network: NPR; PRI
Arbitron Metro Market: Jackson, WY *Format:* News *Special Programming:* Folk 10 hrs, jazz 6 hrs, state news 3 hrs wkly *Hrs. of News Programming:* news progmg 42 hrs wkly *No. News Employees:* 3 *Target Audience:* 25-54; educated, upper-income professionals *Adv. Rates:* 14; 10; 14; 10
Christina Kuzmych, General Manager
Hank Arnold, General Sales Mgr
Grady Kirkpatrick, Interim Program Director/ Music Director
Bob Beck, News Director
Ben Slater, Engineer
Reid Fletcher, Chief Engineer
Diana Denison, OfficeAssistant, Senior
Kathy Dempsey, Accountant
Sarah Brown Mathews, Major Gifts
Valerie Hansen, Underwriting Representative
Shane Toven, Coordinator Engineer
Erin O'Doherty, Development Analyst

KZJH
07-13-1989; 95.3 mhz FM *Hrs Open:* 24; 100 kw; 1056 ft.; N43 27 40 W110 45 9
P.O. Box 2158, Ketchum, ID 83340 US
(307) 733-1770, *Fax:* (307) 733-4760
www.jacksonholeradio.com
acksonholeradionews@gmail.com
License: Jackson, Teton County, WY held by Chaparral Broadcasting Co.
Group Owner: Chaparral Communications; (acq 8-25-00; $1.1 million).
Nat'l Network: ABC
Arbitron Metro Market: Jackson, WY *Format:* Classic Rock *No. News Employees:* 1 *Target Audience:* 18-55.
Scott Anderson, General Manager
Jay Martin, Programming Director
Patricia Karnik, Promotions Manager
Dee Dee Dudley, News Director

*KHOL
04-04-2008; 89.1 mhz FM; 2.2 kw; Ant 1,102 ft; N43 27 40 W110 45 09
Box 8639, Jackson, WY 38104
(307) 733-4030
www.jhcr.org
info@jhcr.org
License: Jackson, Teton County, WY held by Jackson Hole Community Radio Inc.
Jim Tallichet, General Manager

*KMLT
01-01-2008; 88.3 mhz FM; 0.3 kw; 938 ft.; N43 27 43 W110 45 12 *Rebroadcasts:* Rebroadcasts KLVR(FM) Middletown, CA 100%
188 South Bellevue, Suite 222, Memphis, TN 38104 US
(800) 877-5600, *Fax:* (916) 251-1650
www.klove.com
License: Jackson, Teton County, WY held by Educational Media Foundation.
Group Owner: EMF Broadcasting; (acq 7-23-2007; grpsl)
Nat'l Network: K-Love
Arbitron Metro Market: Jackson, WY *Format:* Christian
Darrell Chambliss, Chairman
Mike Novak, President

*KMWY
91.1 mhz FM; 0.35 kw; 1024 ft.; N43 27 40 W110 45 9
US
(509) 448-2555, *Fax:* (509) 448-6855
www.moodyradionorthwest.fm
kmbi@moody.edu
License: Jackson, Teton County, WY held by The Moody Bible Institute of Chicago.
Group Owner: The Moody Bible Institute of Chicago
Arbitron Metro Market: Jackson, WY *Format:* Christian
Robert Neff, Operations Dir
Rich Monteith, Station Manager
Gordon Canaday, Chief Engineer
Jodi Murphy, Office Administrator

Kemmerer

KAOX
10-01-1999; 107.3 mhz FM *Hrs Open:* 24; 13.5 kw; 948 ft.; N41 50 18 W110 30 11
Mailing Address: 1510 Canyon Road, Kemmerer, WY 83101 US
Second Address: 436 Fossil Butte, Kemmerer, WY 83101
(307) 877-4422, *Fax:* (307) 877-5527
kmer@onewest.net
License: Kemmerer, Lincoln County, WY held by Simmons-SLC, LS LLC.
Group Owner: Simmons Media Group; (acq 4-19-2004; grpsl)
Nat'l Network: CBS
Arbitron Metro Market: Kemmerer, WY *Format:* Adult Contemp *Hrs. of News Programming:* news progmg 2 hrs wkly *No. News Employees:* 1 *Target Audience:* 35 plus; male / female *Adv. Rates:* 12; 12; 12; 12
Jim Thoeny, Operations Dir
Jim Carroll, General Manager

KMER
12-07-1962; 940 khz AM
Mailing Address: P.O. Box 100, Jackson, WY 83001 US
Second Address: 436 Fossil Butte Dr., Kemmerer, WY 83101
(307) 877-4422, *Fax:* (307) 877-5537
kmer@onewest.net
License: Kemmerer, WY held by Simmons-SLC, LS LLC.
Group Owner: Simmons Media Group; (acq 5-20-2004; grpsl)
Format: Oldies *Special Programming:* News/talk 7 hrs, farm 3 hrs wkly *Hrs. of News Programming:* news progmg one hr wkly *No. News Employees:* 1 *Target Audience:* 25-54. *Adv. Rates:* 12; 12; 12; 12
Jim Thoeny, Operations Dir
Jim Carroll, General Manager

Kirby

*KKBY
90.5 mhz FM; kw
US
License: Kirby, Hot Springs County, WY held by Union Valley Baptist Church Inc.
Arbitron Metro Market: Kirby, WY
Steve Vandegrift, President

La Barge

*KRBR
88.9 mhz FM; 40 watts; 425 meters; 42 19 N30 110 19 W12
PO Box 1096, Mount Vernon, TX
(888) 732-3599, *Fax:* (214) 231-9325
www.wma1.viastreaming.net
License: La Barge, WY held by Nexxus Broadcast

Lander

KDLY
01-01-1975; 97.5 mhz FM *Hrs Open:* 24; 62 kw; -364 ft.; N42 49 15 W108 45 53
1530 Main Street, Lander, WY 82520 US
(307) 332-5683, *Fax:* (307) 332-5548
www.kdlykove.com
radio1@wyoming.com
License: Lander, Fremont County, WY held by Fremont Broadcasting Inc.
Nat'l Network: Fox News Radio *Nat'l Reps:* Commercial Media Sales *Wire Services:* AP
Arbitron Metro Market: Lander, WY *Format:* Classic Rock *Hrs. of News Programming:* news progmg 5 hrs wkly *No. News Employees:* 1 *Target Audience:* 18-49; general *Adv. Rates:* 24; 11.75; 9.75; 11.75
Joe Kenney, President
Andrea Kenney, Operations Dir
Joe Kenney, General Manager
Bryce House, General Sales Mgr

KOVE
01-01-1947; 1330 khz AM
1530 Main Street, Lander, WY 82520 US
(307) 332-5683, *Fax:* (307) 332-5548
www.kdlykove.com
radio1@wyoming.com
License: Lander, WY held by Fremont Broadcasting Inc.
Nat'l Network: Fox News Radio *Nat'l Reps:* Commercial Media Sales *Wire Services:* AP
Format: Country *Special Programming:* Talk 15 hrs wkly *Hrs. of News Programming:* one. *Target Audience:* 25 plus.
Joe Kenney, President
Andrea Kenney, Operations Dir
Glenn Lemons, News Director
Lincoln Scott, Chief Engineer
Krista Perez, Traffic Manager

Laramie

KCGY
11-07-1983; 95.1 mhz FM *Hrs Open:* 24; 100 kw; 1070 ft.; N41 18 34 W105 27 11
Mailing Address: 3525 Soldier Springs Rd., Laramie, WY 82070 US
Second Address: 3525 Soldier Springs Rd., Laramie, WY 82070
(307) 745-4888, *Fax:* (307) 742-4576
www.y95country.com
andyhoefer@gapbroadcasting.com
License: Laramie, Albany County, WY held by GAP Broadcasting Laramie License LLC.
Group Owner: GAPWEST Broadcasting; (acq 2-13-2008; grpsl)
Nat'l Network: Jones Radio Networks *Nat'l Reps:* Katz Radio
Wire Services: AP
Arbitron Metro Market: Cheyenne, WY *Format:* Country *Target Audience:* 25-54. *Adv. Rates:* 22; 22; 22; 22
Andrew Hoefer, General Manager
Eric Henderson, General Sales Mgr
Dave Shannon, Programming Director
Jim Mross, Chief Engineer

KHAT
02-27-1962; 1210 khz AM; 10 kw-D, DAN; 1 kw-N, DAN; N41 15 19 W105 33 1
36 Cross Hwy, Rd #4, West Redding, CT 06896 US
(307) 745-5208, *Fax:* (307) 745-8570
mix967@fiberpipe.net
License: Laramie, WY held by Appaloosa Broadcasting Co.
Group Owner: Northeast Broadcasting Company Inc.; (acq 3-2-2004; $160,000)
Nat'l Network: ESPN Radio
Arbitron Metro Market: Cheyenne, WY *Format:* Sports *Special Programming:* Farm one hr wkly
Mike Schutta, General Manager

KOWB
02-20-1948; 1290 khz AM *Hrs Open:* 24; 5 kw-D, DA2; 1 kw-N, DA2; N41 17 2 W105 34 51
Mailing Address: 3525 Soldier Springs Rd, Laramie, WY 82070 US
Second Address: 3525 Soldier Springs Rd., Laramie, WY 82070
(307) 745-4888, *Fax:* (307) 742-4576
www.kowb1290.com
andyhoefer@gapbroadcasting.com
License: Laramie, WY held by GAP Broadcasting Laramie License LLC.
Group Owner: GAPWEST Broadcasting; (acq 2-13-2008; grpsl)
Nat'l Network: Fox News Radio *Nat'l Reps:* Katz Radio *Wire Services:* AP
Format: News, News/Talk, 84, Talk *Hrs. of News Programming:* news progmg 7 hrs wkly *No. News Employees:* 1 *Target Audience:* 25-54. *Adv. Rates:* 20; 20; 20; 20
David Settle, Operations Dir
Andrew Hoefer, General Manager
Eric Henderson, General Sales Mgr
Jim Mross, Chief Engineer

KARS-FM
09-23-1974; 102.9 mhz FM; 100 kw; Ant 1,220 ft; N41 18 39 W105 27 12
600 Main St., Windsor, CO 06896
(970) 674-2700, *Fax:* (970) 686-7491
www.rock1029.com
License: Laramie, Albany County, WY held by The Fort Collins/Layfayette Devestiture Trust
Group Owner: Townsquare Media; (acq 11-15-2004; $7.75 million with KKPL(FM) Cheyenne).
Wire Services: CBS
Population Served: 80,000 *Arbitron Metro Market:* Cheyenne, WY *Target Audience:* 18-44. *Adv. Rates:* 11; 10; 11; 6
Shawn Steinmetz, General Manager

***KUWR**
09-10-1966; 91.9 mhz FM *Hrs Open:* 5 AM-midnight; 100 kw; 1099 ft.; N41 18 36 W105 27 17
P.O. Box 3984, Laramie, WY 82071 US
(307) 766-4240, *Fax:* (307) 766-6184
www.wyomingpublicradio.org
onair@uwyo.edu
License: Laramie, Albany County, WY held by University of Wyoming.
Nat'l Network: NPR; PRI
Arbitron Metro Market: Laramie, WY *Format:* News *Special Programming:* Folk 10 hrs, jazz 6 hrs, state news 3 hrs wkly *Hrs. of News Programming:* news progmg 42 hrs wkly *No. News Employees:* 3 *Target Audience:* 25-54; educated, college graduates, professionals, upper income
Christina Kuzmych, General Manager
Don Woods, General Sales Mgr
Grady Kirkpatrick, Interim Program Director/ Music Director
Bob Beck, News Director
Ben Slater, Engineer
Reid Fletcher, Chief Engineer
Diana Denison, OfficeAssistant, Senior
Kathy Dempsey, Accountant
Sarah Brown Mathews, Major Gifts
Valerie Hansen, Underwriting Representative
Shane Toven, Coordinator Engineer
Erin O'Doherty, Development Analyst

KAAZ
01-01-2006; 98.7 mhz FM; 110 w; Ant 1,073 ft; N41 18 39 W105 27 12
302 S. 2nd St., Suite 204, Laramie, WY 82604
(307) 745-5208, *Fax:* (307) 745-8570
mix967@fiberpipe.net
License: Laramie, Albany County, WY held by Murray Grey Broadcasting Inc.
Group Owner: Northeast Broadcasting Company Inc.; (acq 12-21-2005; $750,000 with KVUW(FM) Wendover, NV)

Steven Silberberg, President
Jim O'Reilly, General Manager

***KAIW**
01-01-2006; 88.9 mhz FM; 1.15 kw; 645 ft.; N41 17 46 W105 53 30
1425 North Market Blvd, Suite 9, Sacramento, CA 95834 US
(800) 877-5600, *Fax:* (916) 251-1650
www.air1.com
info@air1.com
License: Laramie, Albany County, WY held by Educational Media Foundation.
Group Owner: EMF Broadcasting
Nat'l Network: Air 1
Arbitron Metro Market: Laramie, WY *Format:* Alternative, Christian
Darrell Chambliss, Chairman
Mike Novak, President
Alan Mason, Operations Dir
David Pierce, Programming Director
Ed Lenane, News Director
Sam Wallington, Engineering Dir
Marya Morgan, News Reporter
Richard Hunt, News Reporter

***KUWY**
01-01-2008; 88.5 mhz FM *Hrs Open:* 24; 0.135 kw; 978 ft.; N41 18 36 W105 27 17
P O Box 3984, Laramie, WY 82071 US
(307) 766-4240, *Fax:* (307) 766-6184
www.wyomingpublicmedia.org
onair@uwyo.edu
License: Laramie, Albany County, WY held by University of Wyoming.
Regional Network: Wyoming Public Radio
Arbitron Metro Market: Laramie, WY *Format:* Jazz
Christina Kuzmych, General Manager
Grady Kirkpatrick, Programming Director
Bob Beck, News Director
Reid Fletcher, Chief Engineer
Diana Denison, Office Assistant, Senior
Kathy Dempsey, Accountant
Erin O'Doherty, DevelopmentAnalyst

***KUWL**
01-01-2008; 90.1 mhz FM *Hrs Open:* 24; 0.11 kw; 968 ft.; N41 18 36 W105 27 17
P.O.Box 3984, Laramie, WY 82071 US
(307) 766-4240, *Fax:* (307) 766-6184
www.wyomingpublicmedia.org
onair@uwyo.edu
License: Laramie, Albany County, WY held by University of Wyoming.
Regional Network: Wyoming Public Radio
Arbitron Metro Market: Laramie, WY *Format:* Jazz
Christina Kuzmych, General Manager
Grady Kirkpatrick, Programming Director
Bob Beck, News Director
Reid Fletcher, Chief Engineer
Diana Denison, Office Assistant, Senior
Kathy Dempsey, Accountant
Erin O'Doherty, DevelopmentAnalyst

***KTDX**
01-01-2008; 89.3 mhz FM; 0.45 kw; 1138 ft.; N41 18 39 W105 27 12 *Rebroadcasts:* Rebroadcasts KTLF(FM) Colorado Springs, CO 100%
1665 Briargate Blvd, Colorado Springs, CO 80920 US
(719) 593-0600, *Fax:* (719) 593-2399
www.ktlf.org
lightpraise@ktlf.org
License: Laramie, Albany County, WY held by Educational Communications of Colorado Springs Inc.
Arbitron Metro Market: Laramie, WY *Format:* Christian *Target Audience:* 45-60; Christian
Ron Johnson, Chairman
Tom Sullivan, General Manager
Sharick Wade, Programming Director
Robert Mumm, Chief Engineer
Skip Rice, Sonrise Host
James Felix, Operations Manager & Sonrise Co-Host
Marge Wallace, Office Manager
AlleenWagnon, Office Assistant

Lost Cabin

KWYW
01-01-2001; 99.1 mhz FM; 50 kw; 1896 ft.; N43 26 18 W107 59 37
3565 Standish Avenue, Santa Rosa, CA 95407 US
(307) 864-2119, *Fax:* (307) 864-3937
www.mykwyw.com
kthe@directairnet.com
License: Lost Cabin, Fremont County, WY held by Jimmy Ray Carroll.
Group Owner: Jimmy Ray Carroll Stns; (acq 6-25-2001; $30,000 for CP).
Arbitron Metro Market: Thermopolis, WY *Format:* Country
Jimmy Carroll, President
Cheerie Dorris, General Manager
Jeremy James, Programming Director
Amanda Plant, Promotions Manager
Mike St. Clair, News Director

Lovell

KWHO
107.1 mhz FM; 64 kw; Ant 2,375 ft; N44 48 38 W107 55 18
288 S. River Rd., Bedford, NH
(603) 668-6470
License: Lovell, Big Horn County, WY held by White Park Broadcasting Inc.
Group Owner: Northeast Broadcasting Company Inc.

Steven Silberberg, President

Lusk

KQWY
96.3 mhz FM; kw
US
(202) 251-7589
License: Lusk, Niobrara County, WY held by Alma Corp.
Group Owner: Alma Corp.
Arbitron Metro Market: Lusk, WY
Dennis Wallace, President

Lyman

KNIV
07-01-1983; 104.7 mhz FM *Hrs Open:* 24; 89 kw horiz; Ant 2,122 ft; N40 52 16 W110 59 43
Box 3369, Logan, WY 84771
(435) 752-1390, *Fax:* (435) 752-1392
License: Lyman, Uinta County, WY held by 3 Point Media - Utah LLC, debtor-in-possession
Group Owner: 3 Point Media; (acq 11-28-2001; $1.73 million)
Nat'l Network: CBS
Population Served: 300,000 *Arbitron Metro Market:* Salt Lake City-Ogden-Provo, UT *Target Audience:* 35-54.
Kent Frandsen, President
Jay Eubanks, General Manager
Lori Gill, News Director
Paul Anderson, Chief Engineer

Manderson

KYTS
105.7 mhz FM; 75 kw; 492 ft.; N44 3 34 W107 51 13
US
(410) 799-1740
License: Manderson, Washakie County, WY held by Legend Communications of Wyoming LLC.
Group Owner: Legend Communications L.L.C.
Arbitron Metro Market: Manderson, WY
W. Lawrence Patrick, President

Medicine Bow

KRQU

01-01-2007; 99.7 mhz FM; 9.6 kw; Ant 239 ft; N41 46 04 W104 49 00
2109 E. 10th St., Cheyenne, WY
(307) 638-8921, *Fax:* (307) 638-8922
License: Medicine Bow, Platte County, WY held by Brahmin Broadcasting Corp.
Group Owner: Northeast Broadcasting Company Inc.
Steven Silberberg, President
Roger Ingram, General Manager

Midwest

KWYY

11-30-1981; 95.5 mhz FM; 100 kw; 1939 ft.; N42 44 37 W106 18 24
251 West First Street, Casper, WY 82601 US
(307) 266-5252, *Fax:* (307) 235-9143
www.mycountry955.com
donovanshort@townsquaremedia.com
License: Midwest, Natrona County, WY held by GAP Broadcasting Casper License LLC.
Group Owner: GAPWEST Broadcasting; (acq 2-13-2008; grpsl)
Arbitron Metro Market: Casper, WY *Format:* Country *Target Audience:* 25-54.
Donovan Short, Operations Dir
Bob Price, General Manager
Bob Price, General Sales Mgr
Dave Borino, News Director
Dave Nutter, Chief Engineer
Donovan Short, Brand Manager

Mills

KZQL

01-01-2008; 105.5 mhz FM; 5 kw; 1699 ft.; N42 44 30 W106 18 23
US
(603) 668-6470
License: Mills, Natrona County, WY held by White Park Broadcasting Inc.
Group Owner: Northeast Broadcasting Company Inc.
Arbitron Metro Market: Mills, WY *Format:* Adult Contemp
Steven Silberberg, President

Moorcroft

KXXL

01-01-2008; 106.1 mhz FM; 100 kw; 392 ft.; N44 13 50 W105 27 45
US
(602) 248-9116
License: Moorcroft, Crook County, WY held by Family Voice Communications LLC.
Arbitron Metro Market: Moorcroft, WY *Format:* Classic Rock
Robert Olson Jr., General Manager

Moose Wilson Road

KXJN

98.5 mhz FM; 25 watts; 804 meters; N43 35 50 W110 52 12
Box 11060, Jackson, WY
License: Moose Wilson Road, Fremont County, WY held by Cochise Media Licenses LLC
Ted Tucker, General Manager

Newcastle

KASL

07-10-1953; 1240 khz AM *Hrs Open:* 24; 1 kw-U, ND1; N43 50 47 W104 12 45
227 S. Seneca, Newcastle, WY 82701 US
(307) 746-4433
www.am1240kasl.com
kasl@vcn.com
License: Newcastle, WY held by Val Rasmuson Cook
Arbitron Metro Market: Newcastle, WY *Format:* Country *Special Programming:* Farm 5 hrs, relg 2 hrs wkly *Hrs. of News Programming:* news progmg 35 hrs wkly *No. News Employees:* 1 *Target Audience:* General;town & county residents, children through adults *Adv. Rates:* 7.55; 7.55; 7.55; 6.55
Val Cook, CEO
Pam Pendield, General Sales Mgr
Ed Schlup, Programming Director

*KUWN

01-01-1998; 90.5 mhz FM; 0.4 kw; 203 ft.; N43 49 57 W104 13 8
Rebroadcasts: Rebroadcasts KUWR(FM) Laramie 100%
P.O. Box 3984, Laramie, WI 82071 US
(307) 766-4240, *Fax:* (307) 766-6184
www.wyomingpublicradio.net
onair@uwyo.edu
License: Newcastle, Weston County, WY held by University of Wyoming.
Arbitron Metro Market: Newcastle, WY *Format:* News
Christina Kuzmych, General Manager
Peg Arnold, General Sales Mgr
Grady Kirkpatrick, Interim Program Director/ Music Director
Bob Beck, News Director
Ben Slater, Engineer
Reid Fletcher, Chief Engineer
Diana Denison, OfficeAssistant, Senior
Kathy Dempsey, Accountant
Sarah Brown Mathews, Major Gifts
Valerie Hansen, Underwriting Representative
Shane Toven, Coordinator Engineer
Erin O'Doherty, Development Analyst

Orchard Valley

KGAB

01-01-1952; 650 khz AM *Hrs Open:* 24
50 East Rivercenter Blvd, Suite 1200, Covington, KY 41011 US
(307) 632-4400, *Fax:* (307) 632-1818
www.kgab.com
davechaffin@townsquaremedia.com;
craigcochran@townsquaremedia.com;
michealmartin@townsquaremedia.com
License: Orchard Valley, WY held by GAP Broadcasting Cheyenne License LLC.
Group Owner: GAPWEST Broadcasting; (acq 2-13-2008; grpsl)
Arbitron Metro Market: Cheyenne, WY *Format:* News, News/Talk, 86 *No. News Employees:* 3 *Target Audience:* 25-64.
Dave Chaffin, Operations Dir
Craig Cochran, General Manager
Amy Richards, News Director
Jim Mross, Chief Engineer

Pine Bluffs

KREO

12-01-2000; 105.3 mhz FM *Hrs Open:* 24; 6 kw; 249 ft.; N41 17 17 W104 0 21 *Rebroadcasts:* Simulcast with KRRR(FM) Cheyenne
P.O. Box 532, Scotts Bluff, NE 69363 US
(307) 638-8921, *Fax:* (307) 638-8922
www.1049krrr.com
sales@radiowyo.com
License: Pine Bluffs, Laramie County, WY held by Chisholm Trail Broadcasting LLC
Arbitron Metro Market: Cheyenne, WY *Format:* Oldies *Target Audience:* 25-54. *Adv. Rates:* 192; 192; 180; 144
Larry Proietti, General Manager
Dan Conway, General Sales Mgr
Ron Krob, Chief Engineer

Pine Haven

KYDT

11-01-1997; 103.1 mhz FM *Hrs Open:* 24; 25 kw; 1650 ft.; N44 28 35 W104 26 54 *Rebroadcasts:* Rebroadcasts KBFS(AM) Belle Fourche 99.9%
Mailing Address: P.O. Box 787, Belle Fourche, SD 57717 US
Second Address: PO Box 1128, Sundance, WY 82729
(605) 892-2571, *Fax:* (605) 892-2573
www.kydt.com
karl@kbfs.com
License: Pine Haven, Crook County, WY held by Ultimate Caps Inc.
Nat'l Network: ESPN Radio; Westwood One; AP Network News; Radio America; Jones Radio Networks *Wire Services:* AP
Arbitron Metro Market: Belle Fourche, SD *Format:* Country, News, 84, Talk *Hrs. of News Programming:* News progmg 25 hrs wkly *Target Audience:* General; rural, suburban, country mus, sports fans
Karl Grimmelmann, President

KWAP(FM)

99.1 mhz FM; 100 kw; Ant 308 ft; N44 19 04 W104 46 31
PO Box 36717, Tucson, AZ 85740-6717
(520) 797-1008
License: Pine Haven, Crook County, WY held by Davao LLC.
Population Served: 8,092 *Arbitron Metro Market:* Wasilla, AK
Hursel Adkins Jr., CEO

Pinedale

KPIN

12-01-1997; 101.1 mhz FM *Hrs Open:* 24 Hours; 4 kw; 476 ft.; N42 50 39 W109 55 23
Rule Communications, 2232 Dell Range Blvd, Cheyenne, WY 82009 US
(307) 367-2000, *Fax:* (307) 367-3300
www.pinedaleonline.com/b-radio.htm
kpin@wyoming.com
License: Pinedale, Sublette County, WY held by Robert R. Rule dba Rule Communications.
Wire Services: AP
Format: Country *Special Programming:* Heavy local events coverage *Hrs. of News Programming:* Weekday mornings 5 7 9 10 AM *No. News Employees:* 1 *Target Audience:* Everyone in the county *Adv. Rates:* $11.50/30 Sec $19.95/60 Sec Al
Bob Rule, CEO

*KUWX

01-01-2000; 90.9 mhz FM; 0.45 kw; 440 ft.; N42 50 40 W109 55 24
P.O. Box 3984, Laramie, WI 82071 US
(307) 766-4240, *Fax:* (307) 766-6184
www.wyomingpublicmedia.org
onair@uwyo.edu
License: Pinedale, Sublette County, WY held by University of Wyoming.
Arbitron Metro Market: Laramie, WY *Format:* News
Jon Schwartz, General Manager
Peg Arnold, General Sales Mgr
Roger Adams, Programming Director
Bob Beck, News Director
Reid Fletcher, Chief Engineer
Don Woods, Music Director
Tristan Ahtone, Reporter
Willow Belden, Reporter
Diana Denison, Office Assistant, Senior
Kathy Dempsey, Accountant
Valerie Hansen, Underwriting Representative

KWCN

89.9 mhz FM; 1.25 kw; 128 meters; N42 50 39.2 W109 55 29.44
970 West Broadway, Suite 371, Jackson Hole, WY
(480) 282-8545
License: Pinedale, WY held by W S Educational Broadcasting

Powell

KPOW

03-30-1941; 1260 khz AM *Hrs Open:* 6 AM-1 AM; 5 kw-D, DAN; 1 kw-N, DAN; N44 42 0 W108 46 0
Mailing Address: P.O. Box 100, Jackson, WY 83001 US
Second Address: 912 Ln. 11 1/2, Powell, WY 82435
(307) 754-5183, *Fax:* (307) 754-9667
www.1260kpow.com (COMING SOON)
kpow@tritel.net
License: Powell, WY held by Chaparral Broadcasting Inc.
Group Owner: Chaparral Communications; (acq 11-30-92; $215,000 with co-located FM;
Format: Country, News, 86 *Special Programming:* Farm 19 hrs wkly *Hrs. of News Programming:* News progmg 38 hrs wkly
Target Audience: 29-64. *Adv. Rates:* 13.50; 13.50;13.50; 13.50
Scott Anderson, General Manager
Scott Mangold, General Sales Mgr

*KUWP

01-01-2000; 90.1 mhz FM; 0.43 kw; 1624 ft.; N44 35 14 W108 51 8
P. O. Box 3984, Laramine, WY 82071 US
(307) 766-4240, *Fax:* (307) 766-6184(
www.wyomingpublicmedia.org
onair@uwyo.edu
License: Powell, Park County, WY held by University of Wyoming.
Arbitron Metro Market: Laramie WY *Format:* News
Jon Schwartz, General Manager
Peg Arnold, General Sales Mgr
Roger Adams, Programming Director
Bob Beck, News Director
Reid Fletcher, Chief Engineer
Don Woods, Music Director
Tristan Ahtone, Reporter
Willow Belden, Reporter
Diana Denison, Office Assistant, Senior
Kathy Dempsey, Accountant
Valerie Hansen, Underwriting Representative

KCGL

11-26-2001; 104.1 mhz FM *Hrs Open:* 24; 100 kw; 1795 ft.; N44 29 42 W109 9 10
Mailing Address: P O Box 2515, Casper, WY 82602 US
Second Address: 1949 Mountain View Dr., Cody, WY 82414
(307) 578-5000, *Fax:* (307) 527-5045
www.mybighornbasin.com
rgelder@bhrnwy.com

License: Powell, Park County, WY held by Legend Communications of Wyoming LLC.
Group Owner: Legend Communications L.L.C.; (acq 4-3-02; $450,000).
Arbitron Metro Market: Cody, WY *Format:* Classic Rock
Larry Patrick, President
Carol Kary, Operations Dir
Roger Gelder, Executive VP/General Manager
Wes Baumstarck, Station Manager
Cory Ostermiller, Sales Manager
Tom Morrison, Programming Director
David Koch, News Director
CharlesDozier, Chief Engineer
Roger Gelder, Executive VP/General Manager
Karla McMillen, Traffic Manager
Rita Conners, VP of Business Affairs
Mike Fell, Sales Director
Jed Burns, Development & Sales
Paulette Bagnell, Sales

Ranchester

KHRW
92.7 mhz FM; 2.3 kw; 1135 ft.; N44 37 20 W107 6 57
US
(307) 672-2690, *Fax:* (307) 672-1722
www.bighornmountainradio.com
License: Ranchester, Campbell County, WY held by Horizon Christian Fellowship.
Group Owner: Horizon Christian Fellowship
Arbitron Metro Market: Ranchester, WY *Format:* Contemporary Hits/Top 40, Adult Contemp
Mike MacIntosh, President
Dave Wooten, General Manager
Brenna Mack, Programming Director
Justin Wolffing, News Director
April Link, Web Design/Administration
Debbie McMahon, Admistrative Assistant
Jeff Rickett, SportsProgramming
Jonna Nimick, Account Executive

Rawlins

KIQZ
11-12-1981; 92.7 mhz FM; 3 kw; 299 ft.; N41 46 16 W107 14 15
218 No Wolcott, Casper, WY 82601 US
(307) 324-3315, *Fax:* (307) 324-3509
www.kiqz-kral.com
License: Rawlins, Carbon County, WY
Group Owner: Mt. Rushmore Broadcasting Inc.
Allen Brill, Chairman
Ward Holmes, Operations Dir
Kristin Dills, Business Manager

KRAL
02-01-1947; 1240 khz AM *Hrs Open:* 24; 1 kw-U, ND1; N41 46 55 W107 15 40
218 No Wolcott, Casper, WY 82601 US
(307) 324-3315, *Fax:* (307) 324-3509
www.kiqz.net
jackmorgan@vcn.com
License: Rawlins, WY held by Mount Rushmore Broadcasting Inc.
Group Owner: Mt. Rushmore Broadcasting Inc.; (acq 8-6-93; $80,000 with co-located FM;
Nat'l Network: ABC *Wire Services:* UPI
Format: Adult Contemp *Target Audience:* 14 plus. *Adv. Rates:* 12.95; 10.95; 12.95; 10.95
Jack Morgan, Programming Director

KPAD
107.5 mhz FM; 0.53 kw; 1093 ft.; N41 49 0 W105 3 48
US
(307) 638-8921, *Fax:* (307)638-8922
www.1049krrr.com
sales@radiowyo.com
License: Rawlins, Platte County, WY held by Brahmin Broadcasting Corp.
Group Owner: Northeast Broadcasting Company Inc.
Arbitron Metro Market: Rawlins, WY *Format:* Oldies
Steven Silberberg, President

*KUWI
89.9 mhz FM; 2 kw; 986 ft.; N41 40 46 W107 14 8
US
(307) 766-4240, *Fax:* (307) 766-6184
www.wyomingpublicradio.net
onair@uwyo.edu
License: Rawlins, Carbon County, WY held by University of Wyoming.
Regional Network: Wyoming Public Radio
Arbitron Metro Market: Rawlins, WY
Christina Kuzmych, General Manager
Grady Kirkpatrick, Music Director
Bob Beck, News Director
Ben Slater, Engineering Dir
Reid Fletcher, Chief Engineer
Tristan Ahtone, Reporter
Willow Belden, Reporter
Erin O'Doherty, DevelopmentAnalyst

*KRWY
89.3 mhz FM; kw
US
(940) 668-7971
License: Rawlins, Carbon County, WY held by 1 A Chord Inc.
Arbitron Metro Market: Gainesville, TX
Mary Fay Jackson, General Manager

Reliance

KWXR
98.7 mhz FM; 0.25 kw; 509 ft.; N41 39 24 W109 9 32
US
License: Reliance, Sweetwater County, WY held by Cochise Broadcasting LLC.
Group Owner: Cochise Broadcasting LLC
Arbitron Metro Market: Reliance, WY *Format:* Variety/Diverse
Ted Tucker, General Manager

*KZUW
88.5 mhz FM; 0.26 kw; 1550 ft.; N41 25 39 W109 7 17
Rebroadcasts: Rebroadcasts KUWYFM) Laramie 100%
US
(307) 766-4240, *Fax:* (307) 766-6184
www.wyomingpublicradio.org
onair@uwyo.edu
License: Reliance, Sweetwater County, WY held by University of Wyoming.
Arbitron Metro Market: Reliance, WY *Format:* Classical *No. News Employees:* 4
Christina Kuzmych, General Manager
Grady Kirkpatrick, Programming Director
Bob Beck, News Director
Reid Fletcher, Chief Engineer

Riverton

*KCWC-FM
03-01-1974; 88.1 mhz FM *Hrs Open:* 24; 3 kw; 1450 ft.; N42 34 59 W108 42 36
2660 Peck Avenue, Riverton, WY 82501 US
(307) 855-2000, *Fax:* (307) 856-3893
www.cwc.edu
jgabriel@cwc.edu
License: Riverton, Fremont County, WY held by Central Wyoming College.
Arbitron Metro Market: Riverton, WY *Format:* Jazz
JoAnne McFarland, President
Dale Smith, Station Manager

KTAK
12-15-1976; 93.9 mhz FM; 50 kw; 951 ft.; N42 43 10 W108 8 45
125 Eagles Nest Drive, Seneca, SC 29678 US
(307) 856-2251, *Fax:* (307) 856-0252
www.ktakradio.com
edward@rivertonradio.com
License: Riverton, Fremont County, WY
Group Owner: Edwards Communications L.C.
Arbitron Metro Market: Riverton, WY *Format:* Country
Rumaldo Juarez, President

KTRZ
12-04-1984; 93.1 mhz FM *Hrs Open:* 24; 100 kw; 883 ft.; N42 43 10 W108 8 41
Mailing Address: Box 808, 1002 N. 8th West, Riverton, WY 82501 US
Second Address: 1002 N. 8th West, Riverton, WY 82501
(307) 856-2922, *Fax:* (307) 856-7552
www.ktrzfm.com
ktrz@tcinc.net
License: Riverton, Fremont County, WY held by Jimmy Ray Carroll.
Group Owner: Jimmy Ray Carroll Stns; (acq 4-1-02).
Nat'l Network: AP Network News *Wire Services:* AP
Arbitron Metro Market: Riverton, WY *Format:* Adult Contemp *Hrs. of News Programming:* news progmg 2 hrs wkly *No. News Employees:* 1 *Target Audience:* 25 plus; rgnl/loc tourists, agribusiness, core population*Adv. Rates:* 11.50; 10.50; 11.50; 10.50
Jim Carroll, CEO
Jim Hockett, General Manager

KVOW
07-02-1948; 1450 khz AM; 1 kw-U, ND1; N43 1 35 W108 20 45
125 Eagles Nest Drive, Seneca, SC 29678 US
(307) 856-2251, *Fax:* (307) 856-0252
www.rivertonradio.com
edward@rivertonradio.com
License: Riverton, WY held by Edwards Communications L.C.
Group Owner: Edwards Communications L.C.; (acq 6-22-99; $875,000 with co-located FM).
Arbitron Metro Market: Riverton, WY *Format:* Oldies *Special Programming:* Farm 5 hrs wkly
Larry Cross, General Manager
Jeff Kehl, Programming Director
Lonnie Fairfield, Chief Engineer
John Gabrielsen, Sports Commentator
Tracy Coston, Traffic Manager

Rock River

KLMI
01-01-2008; 106.1 mhz FM; 25 kw; 171 ft.; N41 29 5 W106 3 6
US
(307) 745-4888, *Fax:* (307) 742-4576
www.1061theriver.com
klmi@myhits106.com
License: Rock River, Albany County, WY held by Greeley Broadcasting Corp.
Group Owner: Greeley Broadcasting Corp.; (acq 4-18-2008; $250,000 for CP)
Arbitron Metro Market: Rock River, WY *Format:* Contemporary Hits/Top 40
Andy Hoefer, General Manager
Eric Henderson, General Sales Mgr

Rock Springs

KSIT
10-01-1981; 99.7 mhz FM *Hrs Open:* 24; 99 kw; 1619 ft.; N41 26 0 W109 7 2
Mailing Address: 2727 Yellowstone Road, Rock Springs, WY 82901 US
Second Address: 2717 Yellowstone Rd., Rock Springs, WY 82902
(307) 362-7034, *Fax:* (307) 362-8727
www.wyoradio.com
wyoradio@wyoradio.com
License: Rock Springs, Sweetwater County, WY held by Big Thicket Broadcasting Co. of Wyoming Inc.
Group Owner: Communications Corp. of the Americas Inc.; (acq 12-2-2005; grpsl)
Format: Classic Rock *Hrs. of News Programming:* news progmg 10 hrs wkly *No. News Employees:* 1 *Target Audience:* 18-45; general
Bill Luzmoor, President
Jon Collins, General Manager
Tom Ellis, General Sales Mgr
John Collins, Programming Director
Doug Randall, News Director
Kim Walker, Traffic Manager

KQSW
01-01-1977; 96.5 mhz FM; 98 kw; 1621 ft.; N41 25 54 W109 7 1
Mailing Address: P.O. Box 2128, Rock Springs, WY 82902 US
Second Address: 2717 Yellowstone Rd., Rock Springs, WY 82902
(307) 362-3793, *Fax:* (307) 362-8727
wyoradio@wyoradio.com
License: Rock Springs, Sweetwater County, WY held by Big Thicket Broadcasting Co. of Wyoming Inc.
Group Owner: Communications Corp. of the Americas Inc.
Format: Country
W. Grant Hafley, President
Dave Kessel, General Manager
Mike Puetz, General Sales Mgr
John Herring, Programming Director

KRKK
01-01-1938; 1360 khz AM; 5 kw-D, DAN; 1 kw-N, DAN; N41 37 12 W109 14 20
Mailing Address: P.O. Box 2128, Rock Springs, WY 82902 US
Second Address: 2717 Yellowstone Rd., Rock Springs, WY 82901
(307) 362-3793, *Fax:* (307) 362-8727
www.wyoradio.com
wyoradio@wyoradio.com
License: Rock Springs, WY held by Big Thicket Broadcasting Co. of Wyoming Inc.
Group Owner: Communications Corp. of the Americas Inc.; (acq 12-2-2005; grpsl)
Arbitron Metro Market: Southwestern WY *Format:* Talk

Bill Luzmoor, President
Jon Collins, General Manager
Tom Ellis, General Sales Mgr
Doug Randall, News Director
Tim Walker, Traffic Manager

***KUWZ**
11-01-1994; 90.5 mhz FM *Hrs Open:* Sunrise-sunset; 35 kw; 1680 ft.; N41 25 39 W109 7 17 *Rebroadcasts:* Rebroadcasts KUWR(FM) Laramie 100%
P.O. Box 3984, Laramie, WY 82071 US
(307) 766-4240, *Fax:* (307) 766-6184
www.wyomingpublicradio.net
onair@uwyo.edu
License: Rock Springs, Sweetwater County, WY held by University of Wyoming.
Nat'l Network: NPR; PRI
Arbitron Metro Market: Rock Springs, WY *Format:* News *Special Programming:* Folk 10 hrs, jazz 6 hrs, state news 3 hrs wkly *Hrs. of News Programming:* news progmg 52 hrs wkly *No. News Employees:* 3 *TargetAudience:* 25-54; college graduates, professionals, mgrs, upper income
Christina Kuzmych, General Manager
Peg Arnold, General Sales Mgr
Grady Kirkpatrick, Interim Program Director/ Music Director
Bob Beck, News Director
Ben Slater, Engineer
Reid Fletcher, Chief Engineer
Diana Denison, OfficeAssistant, Senior
Kathy Dempsey, Accountant
Sarah Brown Mathews, Major Gifts
Valerie Hansen, Underwriting Representative
Shane Toven, Coordinator Engineer
Erin O'Doherty, Development Analyst

KYCS
10-01-1986; 95.1 mhz FM *Hrs Open:* 24; 94 kw; 1165 ft.; N41 29 50 W109 20 36
PO Box 2046, Rock Springs, WY 82901 US
(307) 362-6746, *Fax:* (307) 875-5847
www.theradionetwork.net
mail@theradionetwork.net
License: Rock Springs, Sweetwater County, WY held by Faith Broadcasting Corporation.
Group Owner: Wagonwheel Communications Corp.
Arbitron Metro Market: Green River, WY *Format:* Contemporary Hits/Top 40 *No. News Employees:* 1
Faith Harris, President
Steve Core, General Manager
Jeff Driggs, General Sales Mgr
Jasmine Weaver, Programming Director
Ron Krob, Chief Engineer

Rozet

KLSX
01-01-1954; 99.1 mhz FM; 25 kw; 315 ft.; N44 17 33 W105 26 10 US
(323) 971-9710, *Fax:* (323) 954-0971
www.ampradio.com
info@klsxfm.com
License: Rozet, Los Angeles County, WY held by Infinity Broadcasting East Inc.
Group Owner: CBS Radio; (acq 7-23-97).
Nat'l Reps: CBS Radio
Arbitron Metro Market: Los Angeles, CA *Format:* Contemporary Hits/Top 40 *Target Audience:* 25-54; adults
Ron Escarsega, Operations Dir
Bob Moore, General Manager
David Severino, General Sales Mgr
Jack Silver, Programming Director
Michael Olson, Promotions Manager

Saratoga

KTGA
01-01-2008; 99.3 mhz FM *Hrs Open:* 24; 18 kw; 1063 ft.; N41 40 46 W107 14 8
Mailing Address: US
Second Address: 106 N. First St., Saratoga, WY 82331
(307) 326-8642, *Fax:* (307) 326-8340
www.bigfoot99.com
bigfoot@bigfoot99.com
License: Saratoga, Carbon County, WY held by Toga Radio LLC
Arbitron Metro Market: Saratoga, WY *Format:* Country *No. News Employees:* 3
Jim O'Reilly, General Manager

Sheridan

KROE
03-18-1961; 930 khz AM *Hrs Open:* 24; 5 kw-D, ND1; 0.117 kw-N, ND1; N44 47 54 W106 55 51
Mailing Address: Box N, Sheridan, WY 82801 US
Second Address: 1716 KROE Ln., Sheridan, WY 82801
(307) 672-7421, *Fax:* (307) 672-2933
www.sheridanmedia.com
info@sheridanmedia.com
License: Sheridan, WY held by Lovcom Inc.
Group Owner: Lovcom Inc.
Nat'l Network: CBS *Wire Services:* AP
Format: News, News/Talk, 86 *No. News Employees:* 3 *Target Audience:* 25-54; general *Adv. Rates:* 14.50; 14; 11.75; 10
Kim Love, President
Steve Sisson, Operations Dir
Bob Grammens, General Manager
Jim Schellinger, General Sales Mgr
Russ Davidson, Programming Director
Mary Johnson, News Director
Trevor Jackson, Sports Commentator
Liz Reynolds,Traffic Manager

***KSUW**
01-01-1998; 91.3 mhz FM; 0.45 kw; 1132 ft.; N44 36 9 W106 55 51 *Rebroadcasts:* Rebroadcasts KUWR(FM) Laramie 100%
P O Box 3984, Laramie, WY 82071 US
(307) 766-4240, *Fax:* (307) 766-6184
www.wyomingpublicradio.net
wpr@uwyo.edu
License: Sheridan, Sheridan County, WY held by University of Wyoming.
Arbitron Metro Market: Laramie, WY *Format:* News
Christina Kuzmych, General Manager
Peg Arnold, General Sales Mgr
Roger Adams, Programming Director
Bob Beck, News Director
Reid Fletcher, Chief Engineer
Don Woods, Music Director

KWYO
07-09-1934; 1410 khz AM *Hrs Open:* 24
Mailing Address: 11 North Main Street, Suite 100, Buffalo, WY 82834 US
Second Address: 1716 Kroe Ln, Sheridan, WY 82801
(307) 672-7421, *Fax:* (307) 672-2933
www.sheridanmedia.com
info@sheridanmedia.com
License: Sheridan, WY held by Lovcom Inc.
Group Owner: Lovcom Inc.; acq 9-11-03).
Arbitron Metro Market: Sheridan, WY *Format:* Adult Contemp *Hrs. of News Programming:* news progmg 20 hrs wkly *No. News Employees:* 1 *Target Audience:* 25-54. *Adv. Rates:* 10.75; 10.75; 10.75; 10.75.
Steve Sisson, Operations Dir
Bob Grammens, General Manager, Account Executive, Announcer
Jim Schellinger, General Sales Mgr
Russ Davidson, Programming Director
Ace Young, News Director
Tony Questa, Chief Engineer
Kim Love,Owner
Liz Reynolds, Grant Toth
Webmaster, Margo Heck
Account Executive, Gay Higley
Jerry Walker, Account Executive
Tracee Davis, News

KYTI
09-01-1978; 93.7 mhz FM *Hrs Open:* 24; 75 kw; 1207 ft.; N44 37 20 W107 6 57
PO Box N, Sheridan, WY 82801 US
(307) 672-7421, *Fax:* (307) 672-2933
www.sheridanmedia.com
info@sheridanmedia.com
License: Sheridan, Sheridan County, WY held by Lovcom Inc.
Group Owner: Lovcom Inc.; acq 5-15-97).
Nat'l Network: ABC
Arbitron Metro Market: Sheridan, WY *Format:* Country *Hrs. of News Programming:* News progmg 4 hrs wkly *Target Audience:* 25-50. *Adv. Rates:* 14.50; 14; 11.75; 10
Steve Sisson, Operations Dir
Bob Grammens, General Manager
Jim Schellinger, General Sales Mgr
Russ Davidson, Programming Director
Ace Young, News Director
Tony Questa, Chief Engineer

KZWY
12-01-1977; 94.9 mhz FM *Hrs Open:* 24; 75 kw; 1207 ft.; N44 37 20 W107 6 57
Mailing Address: Box N, Sheridan, WY 82801 US
Second Address: 1716 KROE Ln., Sheridan, WY 82801
(307) 672-7421, *Fax:* (307) 672-7421
www.sheridanmedia.com
info@sheridanmedia.com
License: Sheridan, Sheridan County, WY
Group Owner: Lovcom Inc.
Arbitron Metro Market: Sheridan, WY *Format:* Classic Rock
Target Audience: 18-49; general *Adv. Rates:* Same as AM
Steve Sisson, Operations Dir
Bob Grammens, General Manager
Jim Schellinger, General Sales Mgr
Liz Reynolds, News Director
Trevor Jackson, Sports Commentator

***KOHR**
01-01-2004; 88.9 mhz FM *Hrs Open:* 24; 0.425 kw vert; 72 ft.; N44 47 54 W106 55 51 *Rebroadcasts:* Rebroadcasts KXEI(FM) Havre, MT 100%
P O Drawer 2440, Tupelo, MS 38803 US
(406) 265-5845, *Fax:* (406) 265-8860
www.ynop.org
info@ynop.org
License: Sheridan, Sheridan County, WY held by Hi-Line Radio Fellowship Inc.
Wire Services: AP
Arbitron Metro Market: Sheridan, WY *Format:* Christian, Religious
Brenda Boyum, Operations Dir
Roger Lonnquist, General Manager
Brenda Boyum, Station Manager
Clark Berg, General Sales Mgr
David Brown, Programming Director
Nicholas Tobiason, Music/IT Director
Ron Huckeby, Chief Engineer
MarySue Amundgaard, Office Staff
Joanna Baer, Office Assistant
Elizabeth McClenahan, Office Manager at KXEI/Webmaster
Joe McGee, Account Executive
Carlene Prince, Associate Network Manager
Dan Shepherd, Account Executive

***KWCF**
01-01-2005; 89.3 mhz FM; 0.85 kw; 959 ft.; N44 36 10 W106 55 42
Mailing Address: 3000 W. Macarthur Blvd., Santa Ana, CA 92704 US
Second Address: CSN International, 3232 W. MacArthur Blvd., Santa Ana, CA 92704-6802
(800) 357-4226, *Fax:* (208) 736-1958
www.csnradio.com
csn@csnradio.com
License: Sheridan, Sheridan County, WY held by CSN International
Group Owner: CSN International
Arbitron Metro Market: Sheridan, WY *Format:* Religious
Mike Kestler, President
Daniel Davidson, Operations Dir
Paul Orlando, General Manager
Don Mills, Network Programming Director / Music Director
Kelly Carlson, Engineering Dir
Jerry Johnson, Engineering Dir
Ray Gorney, AssistantDirector of Engineering
Dustin Pamplona, Engineer
Nolan Mather, Graphics / Website Maintenance
Mike Stocklin, National Underwriting
Austin Morris, Accounting
Lois Mills, FCC Applications / Translator Site Manager

***KPRQ**
01-01-2006; 88.1 mhz FM; 0.45 kw; 1119 ft.; N44 37 26 W107 7 2
1500 North 30th Street, Billings, MT 59101 US
(406) 657-2941, *Fax:* (406) 657-2977
www.yellowstonepublicradio.org
License: Sheridan, Sheridan County, WY held by Montana State University-Billings.
Nat'l Network: NPR
Format: Classical, Jazz, 60
Lois Bent, General Manager

***KVLZ**
01-01-2009; 90.3 mhz FM; 0.15 kw; -138 ft.; N44 47 54 W106 55 51 *Rebroadcasts:* Rebroadcasts KLVR(FM) Middletown, CA 100&
P.O. Box 1452, Washington, DC 20013 US

(916) 251-1600, *Fax:* (916) 251-1650
www.klove.com
klove@klove.com
License: Sheridan, Sheridan County, WY held by Educational Media Foundation.
Group Owner: EMF Broadcasting; (acq 3-23-2007; grpsl)
Nat'l Network: K-Love
Arbitron Metro Market: Sheridan, WY *Format:* Christian
Darrell Chambliss, Chairman
Alan Mason, CEO/COO
Mike Novak, CEO
David Pierce, Chief Creative Officer
Dan Antonelli, Chief Business Development Officer
Eric Moser, Chief Financial Officer
Brian Burger, Vice President of HumanResources
D. Kevin Blair, Secretary and General Counsel

Sleepy Hollow

KQOL
01-01-2001; 105.3 mhz FM *Hrs Open:* Unlimited; 51 kw; 374 ft.; N44 17 33 W105 26 10
US
(503) 226-0100, *Fax:* (503) 802-1640
www.kool1059.com
info@kqolfm.com
License: Sleepy Hollow, Clark County, WY held by Citicasters Licenses L.P.
Group Owner: Clear Channel Communications Inc.; (acq 1999; grpsl)
Arbitron Metro Market: Portland, OR *Format:* Oldies
Tony Coles, Operations Dir
Robert Dove, General Manager

South Greeley

*KDNR
12-23-2003; 88.7 mhz FM *Hrs Open:* 24; 0.5 kw; 423 ft.; N41 6 2 W105 1 29.1
1425 N. Market Blvd.#9, Sacramento, CA 95834 US
(775) 883-5647
www.pilgrimradio.com
info@pilgrimradio.com
License: South Greeley, Laramie County, WY held by Western Inspirational Broadcasters, Inc.
Arbitron Metro Market: South Greeley, WY *Format:* Christian *No. News Employees:* 1
Robert Hesse, General Manager

South Park

KJXN
01-01-2008; 105.1 mhz FM; 0.15 kw; 1076 ft.; N43 29 34 W110 57 19
US
License: South Park, Teton County, WY held by Cochise Media Licenses LLC
Arbitron Metro Market: South Park, WY
Ted Tucker, General Manager

Story

KZZS
11-13-2003; 98.3 mhz FM *Hrs Open:* 24; 100 kw; 249 ft.; N44 34 31.9 W106 52 21.7
Mailing Address: 3565 Standish Avenue, Santa Rosa, CA 95407 US
Second Address: 610 Illinois St., Buffalo, WY 82834
(307) 684-7070, *Fax:* (307) 684-7676
kbbs@vcn.com
License: Story, Sheridan County, WY held by Legend Communications of Wyoming L.L.C.
Group Owner: Legend Communications L.L.C.; (acq 5-31-00; $200,000 for CP).
Arbitron Metro Market: Santa Rosa, CA *Format:* Contemporary Hits/Top 40 *Hrs. of News Programming:* news progmg 6 hrs wkly *No. News Employees:* 1 *Target Audience:* 18-35. *Adv. Rates:* 15; 15; 15; 12
Larry Patrick, CEO
Ed Cwik, Operations Dir
Smokey Wildeman, General Manager
Rita Conners, News Director
Charles Dozier, Chief Engineer

Sundance

*KUWD
01-01-2000; 91.5 mhz FM; 0.43 kw; 1591 ft.; N44 28 35 W104 26 54
P.O. Box 3984, Laramie, WY 82071 US
(307) 766-4240, *Fax:* (307) 766-6184
www.wyomingpublicmedia.org
onair@uwyo.edu
License: Sundance, Cibola County, WY held by University of Wyoming.
Arbitron Metro Market: Laramie, WY *Format:* News
Jon Schwartz, General Manager
Peg Arnold, General Sales Mgr
Roger Adams, Programming Director
Bob Beck, News Director
Reid Fletcher, Chief Engineer
Don Woods, Music Director
Tristan Ahtone, Reporter
Willow Belden, Reporter
Diana Denison, Office Assistant, Senior
Kathy Dempsey, Accountant
Valerie Hansen, Underwriting Representative

Superior

KMRZ-FM
07-15-2008; 106.7 mhz FM; 7 kw; 1581 ft.; N41 25 28 W109 7 54
US
(307) 362-3793, *Fax:* (307) 362-8727
www.wyoradio.com
License: Superior, Sweetwater County, WY held by Big Thicket Broadcasting Co. of Wyoming Inc.
Group Owner: Communications Corp. of the Americas Inc.; (acq 8-1-2008; $400,000)
Wiliam Luzmoor III, President
Jon Collins, General Manager

Ten Sleep

KZMQ
05-20-1979; 1140 khz AM; 10 kw-D; N44 06 12 W107 28 50
Box 1210, 1949 Mountain View Dr., Cody, WY 82426
(307) 578-5000, *Fax:* (307) 527-5045
www.bighornradio.com
rgelder@bhrnway.com
License: Ten Sleep, Big Horn County, WY held by Legend Communications of Wyoming L.L.C.
Group Owner: Legend Communications L.L.C.; (acq 1-27-98; $1.5 million with co-located FM)
Population Served: 50,000*Target Audience:* 25-49.
Larry Patrick, President
Rita Conners, Operations Dir
Carol Kary, Station Manager
Barbara Greene, General Sales Mgr
Jerry Dunning, Programming Director
Mack Frost, News Director
Charlie Dozier, Chief Engineer
Roger Gelder,Executive Vice President

Thayne

*KTYN
91.9 mhz FM; 0.077 kw; 2329 ft.; N43 6 18 W111 7 17
P. O. Box 156, Thayne, WY 83127 US
(801) 580-4339
License: Thayne, Lincoln County, WY held by Intermountain Public Radio.
Arbitron Metro Market: Thayne, WY
Carolyn Ashauer, President

Thermopolis

KDNO
08-30-2001; 101.7 mhz FM; 16.25 kw; 1902 ft.; N43 26 18 W107 59 37
Mailing Address: P O Box 866, Thermopolis, WY 82443 US
Second Address: 420 Arapahoe, Thermopolis, WY 82443
(307) 864-2119, *Fax:* (307) 864-3937
kthe@directairnet.com
License: Thermopolis, Hot Springs County, WY held by Carjim LLC.
Group Owner: Jimmy Ray Carroll Stns; (acq 9-13-2001; $20,000 for CP).
Arbitron Metro Market: Thermopolis, WY *Format:* Country
Jim Carroll, President
Dick Howe, General Manager
Dennis Silver, Chief Engineer

KTHE
04-01-1957; 1240 khz AM
Mailing Address: P.O. Box 591, Thermopolis, WY 82443 US
Second Address: 420 Arapahoe, Thermopolis, WY 82443
(307) 864-2119, *Fax:* (307) 864-3937
kthe@directairnet.com
License: Thermopolis, WY held by Carjim LLC.
Group Owner: Jimmy Ray Carroll Stns; (acq 5-7-2002).
Arbitron Metro Market: Thermopolis, WY *Format:* Adult Contemp, Oldies *Target Audience:* 25-54; varied
Jim Carroll, President
Dick Howe, General Manager

*KUWT
01-01-2001; 91.3 mhz FM; 2 kw; 1962 ft.; N43 26 16 W107 59 48
Rebroadcasts: Rebroadcasts KUWR(FM) Laramie 100%
P. O. Box 3984, Laramie, WY 82071 US
(307) 766-4240, *Fax:* (307) 766-6184
www.wyomingpublicmedia.org
onair@uwyo.edu
License: Thermopolis, Hot Springs County, WY held by University of Wyoming.
Arbitron Metro Market: Laramie, WY *Format:* News
Jon Schwartz, General Manager
Bob Beck, News Director
Reid Fletcher, Chief Engineer
Tristan Ahtone, Reporter
Willow Belden, Reporter
Diana Denison, Office Assistant, Senior
Kathy Dempsey, Accountant
Valerie Hansen, UnderwritingRepresentative

Torrington

KERM
12-15-1976; 98.3 mhz FM; 3 kw; 299 ft.; N41 59 41 W104 12 5
218 North Wolcott, Casper, WY 82602 US
(307) 532-2158, *Fax:* (307) 532-2641
www.kgoskerm.com
License: Torrington, Goshen County, WY held by Mount Rushmore Broadcasting Inc.
Group Owner: Mt. Rushmore Broadcasting Inc.
Arbitron Metro Market: Torrington, WY *Format:* Country
Barger Tygart, Chairman
Kevin Martin, COO
Jeff Luchsinger, Station Manager
Patricia Lyons, General Sales Mgr
Shane Viktorin, Programming Director

KGOS
05-15-1950; 1490 khz AM *Hrs Open:* 5:30 AM-10:15 PM; 1 kw-U; N42 04 20 W104 13 40
760 Radio Rd., Torrington, WY 82601
(307) 532-2158, *Fax:* (307) 532-2641
License: Torrington, Goshen County, WY held by Kath Broadcasting
Group Owner: Mt. Rushmore Broadcasting Inc.
Regional Reps: Art Moore.
Population Served: 30,000*Target Audience:* 20 plus; general
Grant Kath, General Manager

Upton

KHAD
104.5 mhz FM; 28.5 kw; 1572 ft.; N44 28 29 W104 26 27
US
(603) 668-6400, *Fax:* (603) 668-6470
License: Upton, Weston County, WY held by White Park Broadcasting Inc.
Group Owner: Northeast Broadcasting Company Inc.
Steven Silberberg, President

Vista West

KRVK
01-01-2001; 107.9 mhz FM; 15.5 kw; 1939 ft.; N42 44 37 W106 18 24
33 Hale Street, Pittston, PA 18640 US
(307) 266-5252, *Fax:* (307) 235-9143
theriver1079.com
krvk@clearchannel.com
License: Vista West, Natrona County, WY held by GAP Broadcasting Casper License LLC.
Group Owner: GAPWEST Broadcasting; (acq 2-13-2008; grpsl)
Arbitron Metro Market: Casper, WY *Format:* Classic Rock
Bob Price, General Manager
Bob Price, General Sales Mgr
Donovan Short, Programming Director
Dave Borino, News Director
Dave Nutter, Chief Engineer

Wamsutter

KHNA
104.9 mhz FM; 0.12 kw; 52 ft.; N41 39 56 W107 58 11
US
(307) 638-8921, *Fax:* (307) 638-8922
www.1049krrr.com
sales@radiowyo.com

License: Wamsutter, Sweetwater County, WY held by White Park Broadcasting Inc.
Group Owner: Northeast Broadcasting Company Inc.
Arbitron Metro Market: Wamsutter, WY *Format:* Oldies
Steven Silberberg, President

Warren Afb

KOLT-FM
08-04-1978; 92.9 mhz FM *Hrs Open:* 24; 33 kw; 607 ft.; N41 4 35 W105 12 10
P. O. Box 532, Scottsbluff, NE 69361 US
(720) 685-0757, *Fax:* (720) 685-0756
www.lapantera929.com
stracy@lapantera929.com
License: Warren Afb, Laramie County, WY held by Tracy Broadcasting Corp.
Arbitron Metro Market: Cheyenne, WY
Michael Tracy, General Manager
Beto Gaytan, Programming Director

KRAN
103.3 mhz FM; 37 kw; 256 ft.; N41 9 34 W104 43 19
US
(603) 668-6400
www.1033therange.com
License: Warren Afb, Laramie County, WY held by White Park Broadcasting Inc.
Group Owner: Northeast Broadcasting Company Inc.
Arbitron Metro Market: Warren AFB, WY *Format:* Country
Steven Silberberg, President

Wheatland

KYCN
11-16-1960; 1340 khz AM *Hrs Open:* 24; 0.25 kw-U, ND1; N42 2 44 W104 56 47
Mailing Address: P. O. Box 248, Wheatland, WY 82201 US
Second Address: 450 E. Cole, Wheatland, WY 82201
(307) 322-5926(307) 322-5927, *Fax:* (307) 322-9300
www.kycn-kzew.com
info@kycn-kzew.com
License: Wheatland, WY held by Smith Broadcasting Inc.
Nat'l Network: ABC *Nat'l Reps:* Target Broadcast Sales
Format: Country *Special Programming:* Farm 7 hrs wkly *Hrs. of News Programming:* news progmg 14 hrs wkly *No. News Employees:* 1 *Target Audience:* General. *Adv. Rates:* 8.50; 8.50; 8.50; 8
Kent Smith, President
Catherine Smith, General Sales Mgr
Derek Barton, News Director

KZEW
02-01-1985; 101.7 mhz FM *Hrs Open:* 24; 3 kw; 125 ft.; N42 2 44 W104 56 47
Mailing Address: P. O. Box 248, Wheatland, WY 82201 US
Second Address: 450 E. Cole, Wheatland, WY 82201
(307) 322-5926(307) 322-5927, *Fax:* (307) 322-9300
www.wheatlandradio.com
kzew@wheatlandradio.com
License: Wheatland, Platte County, WY
Nat'l Network: Jones Radio Networks
Arbitron Metro Market: Wheatland,WY *Format:* Adult Contemp
Adv. Rates: 8.75; 8.75; 8.75; 8
Kent Smith, Operations Dir

KRKU
106.5 mhz FM; 100 watts; 423 feet; N41 56 13 W104 55 50
911 Colonial Dr., Cheyenne, WY
(307) 638-1345
License: Wheatland, Platte County, WY held by Lorenz E. Proietti.

Lorenz Proietti, General Manager

Worland

KKLX
12-01-1980; 96.1 mhz FM; 63 kw; 576 ft.; N44 3 33.6 W107 51 12.7
1340 Radio Drive, Worland, WY 82401 US
(307) 347-3231, *Fax:* (307) 347-4880
License: Worland, Washakie County, WY
Group Owner: Legend Communications L.L.C.
Arbitron Metro Market: Casper, WY *Format:* Oldies
Bill Harrington, General Manager
Nancy Harrington, News Director

KWOR
03-07-1946; 1340 khz AM; 1 kw-U, ND1; N44 1 2 W107 58 14
1340 Radio Drive, Route 2, Worland, WY 82401 US
(307) 347-3231, *Fax:* (307) 347-4880
www.mybighornbasin.com
dnutt@bhrnwy.com
License: Worland, WY held by Legend Communications of Wyoming LLC.
Group Owner: Legend Communications L.L.C.; (acq 12-31-2007; $750,000 with co-located FM)
Arbitron Metro Market: Worland, WY *Format:* Oldies *Target Audience:* General.
Bill Harrington, General Manager
Wes Baumstarck, Station Manager
Tess Vigil, General Sales Mgr
Nancy Harrington, News Director
Tony Cuesta, Chief Engineer
Darren Nutt, News and Sports

Wright

KDDV-FM
01-01-2008; 101.5 mhz FM; 100 kw; 1098 ft.; N43 59 57 W105 15 15
US
(307) 686-2242, *Fax:* (307) 686-7736
www.basinradio.com
License: Wright, Campbell County, WY held by Legend Communications of Wyoming LLC.
Group Owner: Legend Communications L.L.C.
Format: Contemporary Hits/Top 40, Adult Contemp
Don Clonch, General Manager

US-Based International Radio

Adventist World Radio
12501 Old Columbia Pike, Silver Spring, MD 20904-6600
(301) 680-6304, *Fax:* (301) 680-6303
www.awr.org
info@awr.org
Benjamin D. Schoun, President
AWR has 70 production studios bcstg worldwide in over 75 languages thousands of hours daily via AM/FM, shortwave & internet.

American Forces Radio & Television Service (AFRTS)
Department of Defense, American Forces Info Service, 601 N. Fairfax St., Alexandria, VA 22314
(703) 428-0616, *Fax:* (703) 428-0624
www.afrts.osd.mil
afrtdir@hq.afis.osd.mil
Andreas I. Friedrich, General Manager
AFRTS has radio & TV svc 177 countries & on bd U.S. Navy ships. AFRTS stns operate in 15 countries providing rgnl & loc info to large concentrations of U.S. forces. All of the entertainment progmg, U.S sporting events, & natl. &international news is provided to the outlets either directly via international satellites from the AFRTS Broadcast Center at March Air Reserve Base, CA., or through the AFRTS operated stns which insert their rgnl & loc radio drive-time programs &radio & TV news & spot announcements. A rgnl AFRTS svc in Europe delivers the AFRTS fed progmg & rgnl news & info via EUTELSAT to affils located in seven nations as well as directly to cable head-ends, remote transmitters, homes throughout Europe &the Middle East. The worldwide AFRTS-TV progmg consists of: an entertainment svc time shifted for the various parts of the globe & providing the best of U.S. net TV progmg; a news svc providing natl & international news from CNN, Fox News, MSNB,major U.S. networks; a sports ch providing sports news & sporting events from ESPN, ESPN2 & the major U.S. nets & a fourth svc devoted to alternative entertainment progmg primarily oriented on family-type programs from PBS & from U.S.cable TV chs. Afifth & sixth svc were added in 2005 for family entertainmnet & full-time movies. A seventh svc began in 2006 providing additional sporting events. Finally, the Pentagon Channel is also carried by AFRTS.
AFRTS Broadcast Center
1363 Z St, Bldg. 2730, March Air Reserve Base, CA 92518-2077
(909) 413-2201;
Tom Weber, Industry Liaison
Larry Sichter, Mgr Affiliate Rel

Blue Ridge Communications Inc.
Shortwave Radio Station WWRB, c/o Airline Transport Communications, Box 7, Manchester, TN 37349-0007
(931) 841-0492, (931) 728-6087
www.wwrb.org
WWRB Manchester, TN. Worldwide bcstg utilizing 5 shortwave transmitters & 6 major antenna systems (azimuths); more than 10 years of well established global audience.

Broadcasting Board of Governors
330 Independence Ave. S.W., Rm. 3360, Washington, DC 20237
(202) 203-4545, *Fax:* (202) 203-4585
www.bbg.gov/
The bd makes & supervises grants to Radio Free Europe, Radio Liberty, & Radio Free Asia, the Middle East Bcstg Networks & assures that funds are applied consistently with the broad foreign policy objectives of the U.S. govt. The BBG servesas the governing body for all non-military U.S. bcstg including VOA, OCB, RFE/RL, RFA, & MBN.

EWTN Global Catholic Network
5817 Old Leeds Rd., Irondale, AL 35210-2164
(205) 271-2900, *Fax:* (205) 271-2926
www.ewtn.com
radio@ewtn.com
Willaim Stelemeier, Chairman
Global Catholic Radio Networks available in English & Sp 24 hours a day, satellite delivered, free of charge.

Family Stations Inc.
10400 N.W. 240th St., Okeechobee, FL 34972
(863) 763-0281, *Fax:* (863) 763-8867
www.familyradio.com
fsiyfr@okeechobee.com
Harold Camping, President
David Hoff, General Manager
Dan Elyea, Engineering Dir
WYFR Okeechobee, Fla. Twelve 100 kw transmitters & two 50 kw transmitters in Florida. Bcstg on various frequencies, in English to Europe, Africa & the Americas (including Caribbean area), in German to Europe, in Russian to East Europe,in Arabic to West Africa, in French to Europe, North Africa & the Americas & in Sp to Southern Europe, Central & South America, in Portuguese to Europe, South America & West Africa, in It to Europe. Format: Relg.

Far East Broadcasting Co. Inc.
Box 1, La Mirada, CA 90637
(562) 947-4651, *Fax:* (310) 943-0160
www.febc.org
febc@febc.org
Dr. Robert S. Fortner, Chairman
Broadcasts 560 hrs of progmg in 150 languages, to a potential audience of more than 2.5 billion people. FEBC's broadcasts are heard in many countries with limited access to Christian ministry, or where there is tremendous political andcultural opposition to the gospel.

Fundamental Broadcasting Network
c/o Grace Missionary Baptist Church, 520 Roberts Rd., Newport, NC 28570
(252) 223-4600, *Fax:* (252) 223-2201
www.fbnradio.com
fbn@fbnradio.com
WBOH Newport, NC, Broadcasts on 5.920 mhz 24 hrs a day.
WTJC Newport, NC, Broadcasts on 9.370 mhz 24 hrs a day.

Good News World Outreach
WRNO Worldwide, Box 895, Fort Worth, TX 76101-0895
(817) 850-9990, *Fax:* (817) 850-9994
www.wrnoworldwide.org
wrnoradio@mailup.net
Dr. Robert E. Mawire, CEO
WRNO New Orleans. 50 kw shortwave transmitter reaching North America, Central America, Europe, & Far East. Format: news, talk (educational, Christian), sports, music.

Hill Radio International
5920 Oak Manor Dr., Milton, FL 32570-7704
CP for New International HF Broadcast Station in MIlton, FL.

International Fellowship of Churches Inc.
Div/DBA: dba IMF World Missions
Radio Station KIMF, 9746 6th St., Rancho Cucamonga, CA 91730
(909) 466-4793
www.tvspotnet.com
earlcant@comcast.net
Earl F. Reilly, President
Bcst rep, representing U.S. TV stns in Canada. Also licensed bcst stn brokers.
Box 1300, Freeland, WA 98249-1300
(206) 331-7223; *Fax:* (206) 331-7223

La Voz de Restauracion Broadcasting Inc.
Box 56320, Los Angeles, CA 90056
(323) 766-2454, *Fax:* (323) 766-2458
www.restauracion.com
info@restauracion.com
Rene F. Molina, General Manager
KVOH Rancho Simi, CAFormat: Sp.

Leap of Faith Inc.
661 Ormond Dr., Nashville, TN 37205
New international HF broadcast stn in Lebanon, TN.

Radio Free Asia
2025 M Street NW, Suite 300, Washington, DC 20036
(202) 530-4900, *Fax:* (202) 530-7797
www.rfa.org
contact@rfa.org
Libby Liu, President
Norman Thompson, Treasurer
Bernadette Burns, Secretary
Provides info, news & commentary about events in the respective countries of Asia & elsewhere. The svc is intended to be a forum for a var of opinions & voices from within Asian nations whose people do not fully enjoy freedom of expression.

Radio Free Europe/Radio Liberty
Div/DBA: (RFE/RL Inc.)
1201 Connecticut Ave. N.W., Suite 400, Washington, DC 20036
(202) 457-6900, *Fax:* (202) 457-6992
www.rferl.org
Through bcsts in 28 languages to 20 countries, RFE/RL provides news, info, responsible dicussion of domestic & international issues to countries where free & ind media are not permitted, or not yet fully established.

Radio Miami International
175 Fontainebleau Blvd., Suite 1N4, Miami, FL 33172
(305) 559-9764, *Fax:* (305) 559-8186
www.wrmi.net
info@wrmi.net
Jeff White, General Manager
WRMI Miami. Stn sells block airtime for $1/minute to organizations wanting to reach any part of the Americas in any language. 7,385 & 9,955 & 15,725 khz shortwave, 50 kw power.

Trans World Radio
Box 8700, Cary, NC 27512-8700
(919) 460-3700, *Fax:* (919) 460-3702
www.twr.org
info@twr.org
Thomas Lowell, CEO
KTWR Agana, Guam. Guam E-mail: twrguamk@twr.hafa.net.gu
Four 100-kw shortwave transmitters to bcst to Australia, Bali, China, the eastern & central part of the Commonwealth of Independent States, Far East, India, Indonesia, Japan, Korea,Myanmar, Southeast Asia. Format: Relg (more than 30 languages).

Trinity Broadcasting Network
Attn Superpower KTBN Radio QSL Mgr., Tustin, CA 92780
(801) 250-4111 (office)
www.tbn.org
Johnny Mitchell, General Manager
TBN, is the worlds largest religious net offering 24 hours commerical-free inspiration progmg that appeals to a wide variety of denominations.

Two If By Sea Broadcasting Corp.
1784 W. Northfield Blvd., Suite 305, Murfreesboro, TN 37129-1702

www.sound4film-tv.com
senator@sound4film-tv.com
Mike Michaels, President
Stringers, crew news, sports, features, remote bcsts, engrs, announcers, reporters, equipment for radio, TV, film & video.
8715 Waikiki Stn., Honolulu, HI
(888) 389-7372; *Fax:* (213) 389-3299
www.sound4film-tv.com
senator@sound4film-tv.com

United Nations
Div/DBA: Audio-Visual Promotion & Distribution
405 E. 42nd St., Rm. S-805, HQ-Secretariat Bldg., New York, NY 10017
(212) 963-6982, (212) 963-7318, *Fax:* (212) 963-6869
www.unmultimedia.org
audio-visual@un.org
Antonio Carlos Da Silva, Promotions Manager
TV coverage of UN meetings events, the production, promotion & distribution of UN TV radio progmg, photo & footage. All major UN events are also recorded on audio for radio distribution. Offices in 63 countries of 192 member countries.

Voice of America
330 Independence Ave. S.W., Washington, DC 20237
(202) 203-4959, *Fax:* (202) 203-4960
www.voanews.com
publicrelations@voanews.com
Danforth W. Austin, General Manager
Went on the air in 1942, is a multimedia international bcstg svc funded by the U.S govt through Bcstg Bd of Governors. Bcsts more than 1,000 hrs of news, info, educ, & cultural progmg every week to an estimated worldwide audience of morethan 138 million people. Programs are produced in 45 languages. AM/FM & shortwave transmitters are located at over 30 transmitting sites world-wide.

The Voice of the OAS
17th & Constitution N.W., Washington, DC 20006
(202) 458-3000, *Fax:* (202) 458-3930
www.oas.org
informacion-publica@oas.org
Claudio Lessa, Programming Director
Radio programs with news, interviews, info & music from Latin America. Concentrating on the acitivities of the Organization of American States.

WBCQ Radio
274 Britton Rd., Monticello, ME 04760-3110
(207) 538-9180
www.wbcq.com
wbcq@wbcq.com
Allan H. Weiner, General Manager
WBCQ Monticello, Me. International bcst shortwave stn. Lease & program time available. 5.105 mhz, 7.415 mhz, 9.330 mhz & 17.495 mhz. Serves North, Central, South America & the Carribean.

WJIE International Shortwave
Box 197309, Louisville, KY 40259
(502) 968-1220, *Fax:* (502) 964-3304
www.wjiesw.com
wjiesw@hotmail.com
Robert W. Rodgers, President
Greg Holt, Operations Dir
Doug Rumsey, General Manager
WJIE Millerstown, Ky. On two sw frequencies operating 24 hours daily. Target areas: Europe & Asia. Also operates WJIE-FM on 88.5 mhz with 24.5 kw horiz, 18.5 kw vert in Okolona, Ky.

WMLK Radio
Assemblies of Yahweh, Box C, Bethel, PA 19507
(717) 933-4518, (800) 523-3827
www.assembliesofyahweh.com
Elder Jacob O. Meyer, President
Branch offices in Metro-Manila, Phillippines; San Juan, Port of Spain, Trinidad & Tobago; Leeds, England. WMLK Bethel, PA. Bcstg to Europe & the Middle East 5 hours, five days a week, Mon-Fri, with relg instruction content.

WNQM Inc.
Div/DBA: Group owner: F.W. Robbert Broadcasting Inc.
1300 WWCR Ave., Nashville, TN 37218
(615) 255-1300, (800) 238-5576, *Fax:* (615) 255-1311
www.wwcr.com
wwcr@wwcr.com
Eric Westenberger, CEO
WWCR Nashville. Frequencies: 3.210 mhz, 5.070 mhz, 5.935 mhz, 7.465 mhz, 9.475 mhz, 12.160 mhz, 15.825 mhz.

World Christian Broadcasting Corp.
Operations Center, 605 Bradley Court, Franklin, TN 37067-8200
(615) 371-8707, *Fax:* (615) 371-8791
www.knls.org
gcrowe@worldchristian.org
Charles Caudill, CEO
KNLS Anchor Point, Alaska (transmission facilities): Relg & secular progmg beamed to Asia, eastern Europe & the Pacific Rim on the international shortwave bands.
KNLS
Box 473, Anchor Point, AK 99556-0473
(907) 235-8262, (907) 235-8462;
Kevin Chambers, Chief Eng

World Harvest Radio International
61300 Ironwood Rd., South Bend, IN 46614
(574) 291-8200, *Fax:* (574) 291-9043
www.whr.org
whr@lesea.com
Pete Sumarall, President
Joe Hill, General Sales Mgr
Douglas Garlinger, Chief Engineer
WHRI Indianapolis. Two 100 kw transmitters serving Europe, Russia, North, Central & South America. KWHR Naalehu, Hawaii. Two 100 kw transmitters serving primarily Asia, & also Oceania & Australia/New Zealand. WHRA Greenbush, Me.One 250 kw transmitter serving Africa & the Middle East. Shortwave transmitters are available for lease (time sls).

World International Broadcasters Inc.
Box 88, Red Lion, PA 17356
(717) 246-1681, EXT. 140, *Fax:* (717) 244-9316
www.wgcbtv.com
businessoffice@wgctv.com
John H. Norris, President
Patricia Norris-Slaughter, Operations Dir
Fred Wise, General Manager
WINB Red Lion, Pa. Shortwave progmg of programs to Western Europe, the Mediterranean, North Africa, Mexico, Philippines, Guam, Formosa & Australia. Format: Relg.

US-Based Satellite Radio

Sirius Radio (XM), United States
1221 Avenue of the Americas, 49th Street, New York, NY 10020
(888) 539-7474
www.siriusxm.xom
care@siriusxm.com
Mel Karmazin, CEO
Scott Greenstein, President/Chief Content Officer
James Meyer, President/Operations/Sales
Dora Altman, EVP
Patrick Donnelly, EVP/General Counsel
David Frear, EVP/CFO
Canada Office
135 Liberty Street, 4th Floor, Toronto, ON M6K 1A7; Tel: (416) 408-6000; wwww.siriusxm.ca; care@siriusxm.ca.

US AM Radio Stations by Call Letters

CFVM-1 Causapscal, Quebec
DKCPC Rancho Mirage, California
DKEZD Windsor, California
DKORC Anacortes, Washington
DWKEL Myrtle Beach, South Carolina
KAAA Kingman, Arizona
KAAB Batesville, Arkansas
KAAM Garland, Texas
KAAN Bethany, Missouri
KAAY Little Rock, Arkansas
KABC Los Angeles, California
KABI Abilene, Kansas
KABQ Albuquerque, New Mexico
KACH Preston, Idaho
KACI The Dalles, Oregon
KACT Andrews, Texas
KADA Ada, Oklahoma
KADI Springfield, Missouri
KADR Elkader, Iowa
KADS Elk City, Oklahoma
KAFF Flagstaff, Arizona
KAFY Bakersfield, California
KAGC Bryan, Texas
KAGE Winona, Minnesota
KAGH Crossett, Arkansas
KAGI Grants Pass, Oregon
KAGO Klamath Falls, Oregon
KAGV Big Lake, Alaska
KAGY Port Sulphur, Louisiana
KAHI Auburn, California
KAHL San Antonio, Texas
KAHS El Dorado, Kansas
KAHZ Pomona, California
KAIR Atchison, Kansas
KAJO Grants Pass, Oregon
KAKC Tulsa, Oklahoma
KAKK Walker, Minnesota
KALE Richland, Washington
KALI West Covina, California
KALL North Salt Lake City, Utah
KALM Thayer, Missouri
KALV Alva, Oklahoma
KALY Los Ranchos De Albuquerque, New Mexico
KAMA El Paso, Texas
KAMI Cozad, Nebraska
KAML Kenedy-Karnes City, Texas
KAMQ Carlsbad, New Mexico
KANA Anaconda, Montana
KAND Corsicana, Texas
KANE New Iberia, Louisiana
KANI Wharton, Texas
KANN Roy, Utah
KAOI Kihei, Hawaii
KAOK Lake Charles, Louisiana
KAOL Carrollton, Missouri
KAPE Cape Girardeau, Missouri
KAPL Phoenix, Oregon
KAPR Douglas, Arizona
KAPS Mount Vernon, Washington
KARI Blaine, Washington
KARN Little Rock, Arkansas
KARR Kirkland, Washington
KARS Belen, New Mexico
KART Jerome, Idaho
KARV Russellville, Arkansas
KASA Phoenix, Arizona
KASI Ames, Iowa
KASL Newcastle, Wyoming
KASM Albany, Minnesota
KASO Minden, Louisiana
KAST Astoria, Oregon
KATA Arcata, California
KATD Pittsburg, California
KATE Albert Lea, Minnesota
KATH Frisco, Texas
KATK Carlsbad, New Mexico
KATL Miles City, Montana
KATO Safford, Arizona
KATQ Plentywood, Montana
KATZ St. Louis, Missouri
KAUS Austin, Minnesota
KAVA Pueblo, Colorado
KAVL Lancaster, California
KAVP Colona, Colorado
KAWC Yuma, Arizona
KAWL York, Nebraska
KAWW Heber Springs, Arkansas
KAYL Storm Lake, Iowa
KAYS Hays, Kansas
KAZA Gilroy, California
KAZG Scottsdale, Arizona
KAZM Sedona, Arizona
KAZN Pasadena, California
KBAD Las Vegas, Nevada
KBAI Bellingham, Washington
KBAM Longview, Washington
KBAR Burley, Idaho
KBBI Homer, Alaska
KBBO Selah, Washington
KBBR North Bend, Oregon
KBBS Buffalo, Wyoming
KBBW Waco, Texas
KBCH Lincoln City, Oregon
KBCK Deer Lodge, Montana
KBCL Bossier City, Louisiana
KBCQ Roswell, New Mexico
KBCR Steamboat Springs, Colorado
KBCV Hollister, Missouri
KBEC Waxahachie, Texas
KBED Nederland, Texas
KBEN Carrizo Springs, Texas
KBEW Blue Earth, Minnesota
KBFI Bonners Ferry, Idaho
KBFL Springfield, Missouri
KBFP Bakersfield, California
KBFS Belle Fourche, South Dakota
KBGG Des Moines, Iowa
KBGN Caldwell, Idaho
KBHB Sturgis, South Dakota
KBHC Nashville, Arkansas
KBHS Hot Springs, Arkansas
KBIB Marion, Texas
KBIF Fresno, California
KBIM Roswell, New Mexico
KBIX Muskogee, Oklahoma
KBIZ Ottumwa, Iowa
KBJA Sandy, Utah
KBJD Denver, Colorado
KBJM Lemmon, South Dakota
KBJT Fordyce, Arkansas
KBKB Fort Madison, Iowa
KBKR Baker, Oregon
KBKW Aberdeen, Washington
KBLA Santa Monica, California
KBLE Seattle, Washington
KBLF Red Bluff, California
KBLG Billings, Montana
KBLI Blackfoot, Idaho
KBLJ La Junta, Colorado
KBLL Helena, Montana
KBLU Yuma, Arizona
KBLY Idaho Falls, Idaho
KBMB Black Canyon City, Arizona
KBME Houston, Texas
KBMO Benson, Minnesota
KBMR Bismarck, North Dakota
KBMS Vancouver, Washington
KBMW Breckenridge, Minnesota
KBND Bend, Oregon
KBNN Lebanon, Missouri
KBNO Denver, Colorado
KBNP Portland, Oregon
KBNW Bend, Oregon
KBOA Kennett, Missouri
KBOE Oskaloosa, Iowa
KBOI Boise, Idaho
KBOK Malvern, Arkansas
KBOV Bishop, California
KBOW Butte, Montana
KBOZ Bozeman, Montana
KBPO Port Neches, Texas
KBPS Portland, Oregon
KBQX Big Spring, Texas
KBRB Ainsworth, Nebraska
KBRC Mount Vernon, Washington
KBRD Lacey, Washington
KBRF Fergus Falls, Minnesota
KBRH Baton Rouge, Louisiana
KBRI Brinkley, Arkansas
KBRK Brookings, South Dakota
KBRL McCook, Nebraska
KBRN Boerne, Texas
KBRO Bremerton, Washington
KBRT Avalon, California
KBRV Soda Springs, Idaho
KBRW Barrow, Alaska
KBRX O'Neill, Nebraska
KBRZ Missouri City, Texas
KBSN Moses Lake, Washington
KBSR Laurel, Montana
KBST Big Spring, Texas
KBSU-FM Boise, Idaho
KBSZ Apache Junction, Arizona
KBTA Batesville, Arkansas
KBTC Houston, Missouri
KBTM Jonesboro, Arkansas
KBTN Neosho, Missouri
KBUF Holcomb, Kansas
KBUL Billings, Montana
KBUN Bemidji, Minnesota
KBUR Burlington, Iowa
KBUY Ruidoso, New Mexico
KBWD Brownwood, Texas
KBXD Dallas, Texas
KBYG Big Spring, Texas
KBYO Tallulah, Louisiana
KBYR Anchorage, Alaska
KBZO Lubbock, Texas
KBZY Salem, Oregon
KBZZ Sparks, Nevada
KCAA Loma Linda, California
KCAB Dardanelle, Arkansas
KCAL(AM) Redlands, California
KCAM Glennallen, Alaska
KCAP Helena, Montana
KCAR Clarksville, Texas
KCAT Pine Bluff, Arkansas
KCBC Manteca, California
KCBF Fairbanks, Alaska
KCBL Fresno, California
KCBQ San Diego, California
KCBR Monument, Colorado
KCBS San Francisco, California
KCCB Corning, Arkansas
KCCC Carlsbad, New Mexico
KCCR Pierre, South Dakota
KCCT Corpus Christi, Texas
KCCV Overland Park, Kansas
KCCY(AM) Pueblo, Colorado
KCEE Tucson, Arizona
KCEO Vista, California
KCFC Boulder, Colorado
KCFI(AM) Cedar Falls, Iowa
KCFJ Alturas, California
KCFM(AM) Florence, Oregon
KCFO Tulsa, Oklahoma
KCGS Marshall, Arkansas
KCHA Charles City, Iowa
KCHE Cherokee, Iowa
KCHI Chillicothe, Missouri
KCHJ Delano, California
KCHK New Prague, Minnesota
KCHL San Antonio, Texas
KCHN Brookshire, Texas
KCHR Charleston, Missouri
KCHS Truth or Consequences, New Mexico
KCHU Valdez, Alaska
KCID Caldwell, Idaho
KCII Washington, Iowa
KCIM Carroll, Iowa
KCIS Edmonds, Washington
KCJB Minot, North Dakota
KCJJ Iowa City, Iowa
KCKK Littleton, Colorado
KCKM Monahans, Texas
KCKN Roswell, New Mexico
KCKX Stayton, Oregon
KCKY Coolidge, Arizona
KCLE Burleson, Texas
KCLF New Roads, Louisiana
KCLI Clinton, Oklahoma
KCLK Asotin, Washington
KCLN Clinton, Iowa
KCLR Ralls, Texas
KCLU Santa Barbara, California
KCLV Clovis, New Mexico
KCLW Hamilton, Texas
KCLX Colfax, Washington
KCMC Texarkana, Texas
KCMO Kansas City, Missouri
KCMX Phoenix, Oregon
KCMY Carson City, Nevada
KCNI Broken Bow, Nebraska
KCNR Shasta, California
KCNW Fairway, Kansas
KCNZ Cedar Falls, Iowa
KCOB Newton, Iowa
KCOG Centerville, Iowa
KCOH Houston, Texas
KCOL Wellington, Colorado
KCOM Comanche, Texas
KCOR San Antonio, Texas
KCOW Alliance, Nebraska
KCOX Jasper, Texas
KCPS Burlington, Iowa
KCPX Spanish Valley, Utah
KCQL Aztec, New Mexico
KCRC Enid, Oklahoma
KCRN San Angelo, Texas
KCRO Omaha, Nebraska
KCRS Midland, Texas
KCRT Trinidad, Colorado
KCRV Caruthersville, Missouri
KCRX Roswell, New Mexico
KCSF Colorado Springs, Colorado
KCSJ Pueblo, Colorado
KCSP Kansas City, Missouri
KCSR Chadron, Nebraska
KCTA Corpus Christi, Texas
KCTC West Sacramento, California
KCTE Independence, Missouri
KCTI Gonzales, Texas
KCTO Cleveland, Missouri
KCTX Childress, Texas
KCUB Tucson, Arizona
KCUE Red Wing, Minnesota
KCUL Marshall, Texas
KCUP Toledo, Oregon
KCUZ Clifton, Arizona
KCVL Colville, Washington
KCVR Lodi, California
KCWJ Blue Springs, Missouri
KCWM Hondo, Texas
KCXL Liberty, Missouri
KCYK Yuma, Arizona
KCYL Lampasas, Texas
KCZZ Mission, Kansas
KDAC Fort Bragg, California
KDAE Sinton, Texas
KDAK Carrington, North Dakota
KDAL Duluth, Minnesota
KDAO Marshalltown, Iowa
KDAP Douglas, Arizona
KDAV Lubbock, Texas
KDAZ Albuquerque, New Mexico
KDBM Dillon, Montana
KDBS Alexandria, Louisiana
KDBV Salinas, California
KDCC Dodge City, Kansas
KDCE Espanola, New Mexico
KDDD Dumas, Texas
KDDR Oakes, North Dakota
KDDZ Arvada, Colorado
KDEB(AM) Estes Park, Colorado
KDEC Decorah, Iowa
KDEF Albuquerque, New Mexico
KDEI Port Arthur, Texas
KDET Center, Texas
KDEX Dexter, Missouri
KDFN Doniphan, Missouri
KDFT Ferris, Texas
KDGO Durango, Colorado
KDHL Faribault, Minnesota
KDHN Dimmitt, Texas
KDIA Vallejo, California
KDIL Jerome, Idaho
KDIO Ortonville, Minnesota
KDIS Pasadena, California
KDIX Dickinson, North Dakota
KDIZ Golden Valley, Minnesota
KDJI Holbrook, Arizona
KDJS Willmar, Minnesota
KDJW Amarillo, Texas
KDKA Pittsburgh, Pennsylvania
KDKD Clinton, Missouri
KDKT Beulah, North Dakota
KDLA De Ridder, Louisiana
KDLG Dillingham, Alaska
KDLM Detroit Lakes, Minnesota
KDLR Devils Lake, North Dakota
KDLS Perry, Iowa
KDMA Montevideo, Minnesota
KDMO Carthage, Missouri
KDMS El Dorado, Arkansas
KDOM Windom, Minnesota

KDOW Palo Alto, California
KDQN De Queen, Arkansas
KDRO Sedalia, Missouri
KDRS Paragould, Arkansas
KDRY Alamo Heights, Texas
KDSJ Deadwood, South Dakota
KDSN Denison, Iowa
KDTA Delta, Colorado
KDTD Kansas City, Kansas
KDTH Dubuque, Iowa
KDUN Reedsport, Oregon
KDUS Tempe, Arizona
KDUZ Hutchinson, Minnesota
KDWA Hastings, Minnesota
KDWN Las Vegas, Nevada
KDXE North Little Rock, Arkansas
KDXU St. George, Utah
KDYA Vallejo, California
KDYK Union Gap, Washington
KDYL South Salt Lake, Utah
KDYM Sunnyside, Washington
KDYN Ozark, Arkansas
KDZR Lake Oswego, Oregon
KEAR San Francisco, California
KEBC Del City, Oklahoma
KEBE Jacksonville, Texas
KEBR Rocklin, California
KECR El Cajon, California
KEDA San Antonio, Texas
KEDO Longview, Washington
KEEL Shreveport, Louisiana
KEES Gladewater, Texas
KEIN Great Falls, Montana
KEJO Corvallis, Oregon
KEJY Eureka, California
KELA Centralia-Chehalis, Washington
KELD El Dorado, Arkansas
KELE Mountain Grove, Missouri
KELG Manor, Texas
KELK Elko, Nevada
KELO Sioux Falls, South Dakota
KELP El Paso, Texas
KELY Ely, Nevada
KENA Fort Smith, Arkansas
KENI Anchorage, Alaska
KENN Farmington, New Mexico
KENO Las Vegas, Nevada
KENT Parowan, Utah
KEOR Catoosa, Oklahoma
KEPN Lakewood, Colorado
KEPS Eagle Pass, Texas
KERB Kermit, Texas
KERI Bakersfield, California
KERN Wasco-Greenacres, California
KERR Polson, Montana
KERV Kerrville, Texas
KESM Eldorado Springs, Missouri
KESP Modesto, California
KESQ Indio, California
KEST San Francisco, California
KETX Livingston, Texas
KEUN Eunice, Louisiana
KEVA Evanston, Wyoming
KEVT Sahuarita, Arizona
KEWE Oroville, California
KEWI Benton, Arkansas
KEX Portland, Oregon
KEXO Grand Junction, Colorado
KEXS Excelsior Springs, Missouri
KEYE Perryton, Texas
KEYF Dishman, Washington
KEYG Grand Coulee, Washington
KEYH Houston, Texas
KEYL Long Prairie, Minnesota
KEYQ Fresno, California
KEYS Corpus Christi, Texas
KEYY Provo, Utah
KEYZ Williston, North Dakota
KEZJ Twin Falls, Idaho
KEZL(AM) Visalia, California
KEZM Sulphur, Louisiana
KEZW Aurora, Colorado
KEZX Medford, Oregon
KEZY San Bernardino, California
KFAB Omaha, Nebraska
KFAL Fulton, Missouri
KFAN Rochester, Minnesota
KFAQ Tulsa, Oklahoma
KFAR Fairbanks, Alaska
KFAX San Francisco, California
KFAY Farmington, Arkansas
KFBC Cheyenne, Wyoming
KFBK Sacramento, California
KFBX Fairbanks, Alaska
KFCD Farmersville, Texas
KFCR Custer, South Dakota
KFEL Pueblo, Colorado
KFEQ St. Joseph, Missouri
KFFA Helena, Arkansas
KFFF(AM) Boone, Iowa
KFFK Rogers, Arkansas
KFFN Tucson, Arizona
KFGO Fargo, North Dakota
KFH Wichita, Kansas
KFI Los Angeles, California
KFIA Carmichael, California
KFIG Fresno, California
KFIL Preston, Minnesota
KFIR Sweet Home, Oregon
KFIT Lockhart, Texas
KFIT EXP S San Antonio, Texas
KFIV Modesto, California
KFIZ Fond Du Lac, Wisconsin
KFJB Marshalltown, Iowa
KFJL Central Point, Oregon
KFJZ Fort Worth, Texas
KFKA Greeley, Colorado
KFLB Odessa, Texas
KFLC Fort Worth, Texas
KFLD Pasco, Washington
KFLG Bullhead City, Arizona
KFLN Baker, Montana
KFLP Floydada, Texas
KFLS Klamath Falls, Oregon
KFLT Tucson, Arizona
KFMB San Diego, California
KFMO Park Hills, Missouri
KFMZ Brookfield, Missouri
KFMZ(AM) Brookfield, Missouri
KFNN Mesa, Arizona
KFNS Wood River, Illinois
KFNW West Fargo, North Dakota
KFNX Cave Creek, Arizona
KFNZ Salt Lake City, Utah
KFOR Lincoln, Nebraska
KFOX Torrance, California
KFPT Clovis, California
KFPW Fort Smith, Arkansas
KFQD Anchorage, Alaska
KFRA Franklin, Louisiana
KFRM Salina, Kansas
KFRN Long Beach, California
KFRO Longview, Texas
KFRU Columbia, Missouri
KFSA Fort Smith, Arkansas
KFSD Escondido, California
KFSG Roseville, California
KFST Fort Stockton, Texas
KFTA Rupert, Idaho
KFTM Fort Morgan, Colorado
KFUN Las Vegas, New Mexico
KFUO Clayton, Missouri
KFUT Thousand Palms, California
KFVR Crescent City, California
KFWB Los Angeles, California
KFXD Boise, Idaho
KFXN Minneapolis, Minnesota
KFXR Dallas, Texas
KFXX Portland, Oregon
KFXY Enid, Oklahoma
KFXZ Lafayette, Louisiana
KFYI Phoenix, Arizona
KFYN Bonham, Texas
KFYO Lubbock, Texas
KFYR Bismarck, North Dakota
KGA Spokane, Washington
KGAB Orchard Valley, Wyoming
KGAF Gainesville, Texas
KGAK Gallup, New Mexico
KGAL Lebanon, Oregon
KGAS Carthage, Texas
KGBA Heber, California
KGBC Galveston, Texas
KGBT Harlingen, Texas
KGDC Walla Walla, Washington
KGDD Oregon City, Oregon
KGED Fresno, California
KGEM Boise, Idaho
KGEN Tulare, California
KGEO Bakersfield, California
KGEZ Kalispell, Montana
KGFF Shawnee, Oklahoma
KGFK East Grand Forks, Minnesota
KGFL Clinton, Arkansas
KGFW Kearney, Nebraska
KGFX Pierre, South Dakota
KGGF Coffeyville, Kansas
KGGN Gladstone, Missouri
KGGR Dallas, Texas
KGHL Billings, Montana
KGHM Midwest City, Oklahoma
KGHS International Falls, Minnesota
KGIM Aberdeen, South Dakota
KGIR Cape Girardeau, Missouri
KGIW Alamosa, Colorado
KGKL San Angelo, Texas
KGLA Gretna, Louisiana
KGLD Tyler, Texas
KGLE Glendive, Montana
KGLN Glenwood Springs, Colorado
KGLO Mason City, Iowa
KGME Phoenix, Arizona
KGMI Bellingham, Washington
KGMS Tucson, Arizona
KGMT Fairbury, Nebraska
KGMY Springfield, Missouri
KGNB New Braunfels, Texas
KGNC Amarillo, Texas
KGND Vinita, Oklahoma
KGNM St. Joseph, Missouri
KGNO Dodge City, Kansas
KGNU Denver, Colorado
KGNW Burien-Seattle, Washington
KGO San Francisco, California
KGOE Eureka, California
KGOL Humble, Texas
KGOS Torrington, Wyoming
KGOW Bellaire, Texas
KGOW(AM) Bellaire, Hawaii
KGRE Greeley, Colorado
KGRG Enumclaw, Washington
KGRN Grinnell, Iowa
KGRO Pampa, Texas
KGRV Winston, Oregon
KGRZ Missoula, Montana
KGSO Wichita, Kansas
KGST Fresno, California
KGTK Olympia, Washington
KGTL Homer, Alaska
KGTL(AM) Homer, Alaska
KGTO Tulsa, Oklahoma
KGU Honolulu, Hawaii
KGUM Hagatna, Guam
KGVL Greenville, Texas
KGVO Missoula, Montana
KGVW Belgrade, Montana
KGVY Green Valley, Arizona
KGWA Enid, Oklahoma
KGWU Uvalde, Texas
KGY Olympia, Washington
KGYM Cedar Rapids, Iowa
KGYN Guymon, Oklahoma
KHAC Tse Bonito, New Mexico
KHAR Anchorage, Alaska
KHAS Hastings, Nebraska
KHAT Laramie, Wyoming
KHBM Monticello, Arkansas
KHBR Hillsboro, Texas
KHCB League City, Texas
KHCH Huntsville, Texas
KHCM Honolulu, Hawaii
KHDN Hardin, Montana
KHEY El Paso, Texas
KHFX Cleburne, Texas
KHGG Van Buren, Arkansas
KHHO Tacoma, Washington
KHIL Willcox, Arizona
KHIT Reno, Nevada
KHJ Los Angeles, California
KHLO Hilo, Hawaii
KHMO Hannibal, Missouri
KHNC Johnstown, Colorado
KHND Harvey, North Dakota
KHNR Honolulu, Hawaii
KHNU Hilo, Hawaii
KHNU(AM) Hilo, Hawaii
KHOB Hobbs, New Mexico
KHOJ St. Charles, Missouri
KHOT Madera, California
KHOW Denver, Colorado
KHOZ Harrison, Arkansas
KHPP(AM) Waukon, Iowa
KHPY Moreno Valley, California
KHQN Spanish Fork, Utah
KHRA Honolulu, Hawaii
KHRO El Paso, Texas
KHRT Minot, North Dakota
KHSE Wylie, Texas
KHSN Coos Bay, Oregon
KHTK Sacramento, California
KHTS Canyon Country, California
KHTY Bakersfield, California
KHUB Fremont, Nebraska
KHVH Honolulu, Hawaii
KHVL Huntsville, Texas
KHVN Fort Worth, Texas
KHWG Fallon, Nevada
KIAM Nenana, Alaska
KIBL Beeville, Texas
KICA Clovis, New Mexico
KICD Spencer, Iowa
KICE Bend, Oregon
KICS Hastings, Nebraska
KICY Nome, Alaska
KID Idaho Falls, Idaho
KIDD Monterey, California
KIDO Nampa, Idaho
KIDR Phoenix, Arizona
KIEV Burbank, California
KIFG Iowa Falls, Iowa
KIFW Sitka, Alaska
KIGO St. Anthony, Idaho
KIGS Hanford, California
KIHH Eureka, California
KIHM Reno, Nevada
KIHN Hugo, Oklahoma
KIHP Mesa, Arizona
KIHR Hood River, Oregon
KIID Sacramento, California
KIIK Waynesville, Missouri
KIIX Fort Collins, Colorado
KIJN Farwell, Texas
KIJV Huron, South Dakota
KIKC Forsyth, Montana
KIKI(AM) Honolulu, Hawaii
KIKK Pasadena, Texas
KIKO Miami, Arizona
KIKR Beaumont, Texas
KIKZ Seminole, Texas
KILJ Mount Pleasant, Iowa
KILR Estherville, Iowa
KILT Houston, Texas
KIMB Kimball, Nebraska
KIML Gillette, Wyoming
KIMM Rapid City, South Dakota
KIMP Mount Pleasant, Texas
KINA Salina, Kansas
KIND Independence, Kansas
KINE Kingsville, Texas
KINN Alamogordo, New Mexico
KINO Winslow, Arizona
KINY Juneau, Alaska
KIOL Iola, Kansas
KION Salinas, California
KIOU Shreveport, Louisiana
KIPA Hilo, Hawaii
KIQI San Francisco, California
KIQQ Barstow, California
KIQS Willows, California
KIRN Simi Valley, California
KIRO Seattle, Washington
KIRT Mission, Texas
KIRV Fresno, California
KIRX Kirksville, Missouri
KIT Yakima, Washington
KITI Chehalis-Centralia, Washington
KITZ Silverdale, Washington
KIUL Garden City, Kansas
KIUN Pecos, Texas
KIUP Durango, Colorado
KIVA Albuquerque, New Mexico
KIVY Crockett, Texas
KIWA Sheldon, Iowa
KIXI Mercer Island/Seattl, Washington
KIXL Del Valle, Texas
KIXW Apple Valley, California
KIXZ Amarillo, Texas
KIYU Galena, Alaska
KJAA Globe, Arizona
KJAL Tafuna, American Samoa
KJAM Madison, South Dakota
KJAN Atlantic, Iowa
KJAY Sacramento, California
KJBN Little Rock, Arkansas

KJCB Lafayette, Louisiana
KJCE Rollingwood, Texas
KJCK Junction City, Kansas
KJDJ San Luis Obispo, California
KJDL Lubbock, Texas
KJDY John Day, Oregon
KJEF Jennings, Louisiana
KJFF Festus, Missouri
KJFK Reno, Nevada
KJIM Sherman, Texas
KJIN Houma, Louisiana
KJJD Windsor, Colorado
KJJK Fergus Falls, Minnesota
KJJQ Volga, South Dakota
KJJR Whitefish, Montana
KJLT North Platte, Nebraska
KJME Fountain, Colorado
KJMJ Alexandria, Louisiana
KJMP Pierce, Colorado
KJMU Sand Springs, Oklahoma
KJNO Juneau, Alaska
KJNP North Pole, Alaska
KJOC Davenport, Iowa
KJOL Grand Junction, Colorado
KJON Carrollton, Texas
KJOP Lemoore, California
KJOX Kennewick, Washington
KJOZ Conroe, Texas
KJPG Frazier Park, California
KJPR Shasta Lake City, California
KJPW Waynesville, Missouri
KJQS Murray, Utah
KJR Seattle, Washington
KJRB Spokane, Washington
KJRG Newton, Kansas
KJSK Columbus, Nebraska
KJSL St. Louis, Missouri
KJTV Lubbock, Texas
KJUA Cheyenne, Wyoming
KJUG Tulare, California
KJXX Jackson, Missouri
KKAA Aberdeen, South Dakota
KKAM Lubbock, Texas
KKAN Phillipsburg, Kansas
KKAQ Thief River Falls, Minnesota
KKAT(AM) Salt Lake City, Utah
KKAY White Castle, Louisiana
KKBJ Bemidji, Minnesota
KKCQ Fosston, Minnesota
KKDA Grand Prairie, Texas
KKDD San Bernardino, California
KKDZ Seattle, Washington
KKEA Honolulu, Hawaii
KKGM Fort Worth, Texas
KKGR East Helena, Montana
KKIM Albuquerque, New Mexico
KKIN Aitkin, Minnesota
KKJL San Luis Obispo, California
KKLE Winfield, Kansas
KKLF Richardson, Texas
KKLL Webb City, Missouri
KKLO Leavenworth, Kansas
KKLS Rapid City, South Dakota
KKMC Gonzales, California
KKMO Tacoma, Washington
KKMS Richfield, Minnesota
KKNE Waipahu, Hawaii
KKNO Gretna, Louisiana
KKNS Corrales, New Mexico
KKNT Phoenix, Arizona
KKNW Seattle, Washington
KKNX Eugene, Oregon
KKOB Albuquerque, New Mexico
KKOB Exp S Santa Fe, New Mexico
KKOH Reno, Nevada
KKOJ Jackson, Minnesota
KKOL Seattle, Washington
KKON Kealakekua, Hawaii
KKOV Vancouver, Washington
KKOW Pittsburg, Kansas
KKOY Chanute, Kansas
KKOZ Ava, Missouri
KKPC Pueblo, Colorado
KKPZ Portland, Oregon
KKRT Wenatchee, Washington
KKRX Lawton, Oklahoma
KKSA San Angelo, Texas
KKSF Oakland, California
KKSM Oceanside, California
KKSN Vancouver, Washington
KKTK Texarkana, Texas

KKTL Casper, Wyoming
KKTX Corpus Christi, Texas
KKTY Douglas, Wyoming
KKUB Brownfield, Texas
KKVV Las Vegas, Nevada
KKXL Grand Forks, North Dakota
KKXX Paradise, California
KKYX San Antonio, Texas
KKZN Thornton, Colorado
KKZZ Santa Paula, California
KLAA Orange, California
KLAC Los Angeles, California
KLAD Klamath Falls, Oregon
KLAM Cordova, Alaska
KLAR Laredo, Texas
KLAT Houston, Texas
KLAV Las Vegas, Nevada
KLAY Lakewood, Washington
KLBB Stillwater, Minnesota
KLBJ Austin, Texas
KLBM La Grande, Oregon
KLBS Los Banos, California
KLBW New Boston, Texas
KLCB Libby, Montana
KLCK Goldendale, Washington
KLCL Lake Charles, Louisiana
KLCN Blytheville, Arkansas
KLDC Denver, Colorado
KLDS Falfurrias, Texas
KLDY Lacey, Washington
KLEA Lovington, New Mexico
KLEB Golden Meadow, Louisiana
KLEE Ottumwa, Iowa
KLEM Le Mars, Iowa
KLER Orofino, Idaho
KLEX Lexington, Missouri
KLEY Wellington, Kansas
KLFD Litchfield, Minnesota
KLFE Seattle, Washington
KLFF Arroyo Grande, California
KLFJ Springfield, Missouri
KLGA Algona, Iowa
KLGN Logan, Utah
KLGO Austin, Texas
KLGR Redwood Falls, Minnesota
KLHC Bakersfield, California
KLHT Honolulu, Hawaii
KLIB Roseville, California
KLIC Richwood, Louisiana
KLID Poplar Bluff, Missouri
KLIF Dallas, Texas
KLIK Jefferson City, Missouri
KLIM Black Forest, Colorado
KLIN Lincoln, Nebraska
KLIO Wichita, Kansas
KLIV San Jose, California
KLIX Twin Falls, Idaho
KLIZ Brainerd, Minnesota
KLKC Parsons, Kansas
KLLA Leesville, Louisiana
KLLB West Jordan, Utah
KLLK Willits, California
KLLV Breen, Colorado
KLMR Lamar, Colorado
KLMS Lincoln, Nebraska
KLMX Clayton, New Mexico
KLNG Council Bluffs, Iowa
KLNT Laredo, Texas
KLO Ogden, Utah
KLOA Ridgecrest, California
KLOC Turlock, California
KLOE Goodland, Kansas
KLOG Kelso, Washington
KLOH Pipestone, Minnesota
KLOK San Jose, California
KLOO Corvallis, Oregon
KLPF Midland, Texas
KLPL(AM) Lake Providence, Louisiana
KLPW Union, Missouri
KLPZ Parker, Arizona
KLRK Mexia, Texas
KLSD San Diego, California
KLSQ Whitney, Nevada
KLTC Dickinson, North Dakota
KLTF Little Falls, Minnesota
KLTI Macon, Missouri
KLTK Centerton, Arkansas
KLTO Del Rio, Texas
KLTT Commerce City, Colorado
KLTX Long Beach, California
KLTZ Glasgow, Montana

KLUP Terrell Hills, Texas
KLVI Beaumont, Texas
KLVL Pasadena, Texas
KLVQ Athens, Texas
KLVT Levelland, Texas
KLVZ Brighton, Colorado
KLWJ(AM) Umatilla, Oregon
KLWN Lawrence, Kansas
KLWT Lebanon, Missouri
KLXR Redding, California
KLXX Bismarck-Mandan, North Dakota
KLYC McMinnville, Oregon
KLYQ Hamilton, Montana
KLYR Clarksville, Arkansas
KLZ Denver, Colorado
KLZN Susanville, California
KLZS Eugene, Oregon
KMA Shenandoah, Iowa
KMAD Madill, Oklahoma
KMAJ Topeka, Kansas
KMAL Malden, Missouri
KMAM Butler, Missouri
KMAN Manhattan, Kansas
KMAQ Maquoketa, Iowa
KMAS Shelton, Washington
KMAX Colfax, Washington
KMBD(AM) Tillamook, Oregon
KMBI Spokane, Washington
KMBL Junction, Texas
KMBS West Monroe, Louisiana
KMBX Soledad, California
KMBZ Kansas City, Missouri
KMCD Fairfield, Iowa
KMCL(AM) Donnelly, Idaho
KMDO Fort Scott, Kansas
KMED Medford, Oregon
KMER Kemmerer, Wyoming
KMET Banning, California
KMFR Pearsall, Texas
KMFS Guthrie, Oklahoma
KMHI Mountain Home, Idaho
KMHL Marshall, Minnesota
KMHR(AM) Boise, Idaho
KMHS Coos Bay, Oregon
KMHT Marshall, Texas
KMIA Auburn-Federal Way, Washington
KMIC Houston, Texas
KMIK Tempe, Arizona
KMIN Grants, New Mexico
KMIS Portageville, Missouri
KMJ Fresno, California
KMJC Mount Shasta, California
KMJM Cedar Rapids, Iowa
KMKI Plano, Texas
KMKY Oakland, California
KMLB Monroe, Louisiana
KMMJ Grand Island, Nebraska
KMMM Pratt, Kansas
KMMO Marshall, Missouri
KMMQ Plattsmouth, Nebraska
KMMS Bozeman, Montana
KMND Midland, Texas
KMNQ Brooklyn Park, Minnesota
KMNS Sioux City, Iowa
KMNV St. Paul, Minnesota
KMNY Hurst, Texas
KMOG Payson, Arizona
KMON Great Falls, Montana
KMOX St. Louis, Missouri
KMOZ Rolla, Missouri
KMPC Los Angeles, California
KMPG Hollister, California
KMPH Modesto, California
KMPT East Missoula, Montana
KMRB San Gabriel, California
KMRC Morgan City, Louisiana
KMRF Marshfield, Missouri
KMRI West Valley City, Utah
KMRN Cameron, Missouri
KMRS Morris, Minnesota
KMRY Cedar Rapids, Iowa
KMSD Mibank, South Dakota
KMSR Mayville, North Dakota
KMTA Miles City, Montana
KMTI Manti, Utah
KMTL Sherwood, Arkansas
KMTX Helena, Montana
KMUL Farwell, Texas
KMUS Sperry, Oklahoma
KMVI Wailuku, Hawaii
KMVL Madisonville, Texas

KMVP Phoenix, Arizona
KMXA Aurora, Colorado
KMXO Merkel, Texas
KMYC Marysville, California
KMZQ Las Vegas, Nevada
KNAB Burlington, Colorado
KNAF Fredericksburg, Texas
KNAL Victoria, Texas
KNAX McCook, Nebraska
KNBR San Francisco, California
KNBY Newport, Arkansas
KNCB Vivian, Louisiana
KNCK Concordia, Kansas
KNCO Grass Valley, California
KNCR Fortuna, California
KNCY Nebraska City, Nebraska
KNDC Hettinger, North Dakota
KNDI Honolulu, Hawaii
KNDK Langdon, North Dakota
KNDN Farmington, New Mexico
KNDY Marysville, Kansas
KNEA Jonesboro, Arkansas
KNEB Scottsbluff, Nebraska
KNED McAlester, Oklahoma
KNEK Washington, Louisiana
KNEL Brady, Texas
KNEM Nevada, Missouri
KNET Palestine, Texas
KNEU Roosevelt, Utah
KNEW Oakland, California
KNEW(AM) Oakland, California
KNFL Tremonton, Utah
KNFT Bayard, New Mexico
KNGL McPherson, Kansas
KNGN McCook, Nebraska
KNGR Daingerfield, Texas
KNHD Camden, Arkansas
KNIA Knoxville, Iowa
KNIM Maryville, Missouri
KNIR New Iberia, Louisiana
KNLV Ord, Nebraska
KNML Albuquerque, New Mexico
KNMX Las Vegas, New Mexico
KNND Cottage Grove, Oregon
KNNR Sparks, Nevada
KNNS Larned, Kansas
KNOC Natchitoches, Louisiana
KNOM Nome, Alaska
KNOT Prescott, Arizona
KNOX Grand Forks, North Dakota
KNPT Newport, Oregon
KNRO Redding, California
KNRS Salt Lake City, Utah
KNRV Englewood, Colorado
KNRY Monterey Bay, California
KNSA Unalakleet, Alaska
KNSI St. Cloud, Minnesota
KNSN San Diego, California
KNSP Staples, Minnesota
KNSS Wichita, Kansas
KNST Tucson, Arizona
KNTB Lakewood, Washington
KNTH Houston, Texas
KNTR Lake Havasu City, Arizona
KNTS Seattle, Washington
KNTX Bowie, Texas
KNUI Kahului, Hawaii
KNUJ New Ulm, Minnesota
KNUS Denver, Colorado
KNUU Paradise, Nevada
KNUV Tolleson, Arizona
KNVR San Saba, Texas
KNWA Bellefonte, Arkansas
KNWC Sioux Falls, South Dakota
KNWH Yucca Valley, California
KNWQ Palm Springs, California
KNWS Waterloo, Iowa
KNWZ Coachella, California
KNX Los Angeles, California
KNXN Sierra Vista, Arizona
KNZR Bakersfield, California
KNZZ Grand Junction, Colorado
KOA Denver, Colorado
KOAC Corvallis, Oregon
KOAI Van Buren, Arkansas
KOAK Red Oak, Iowa
KOAL Price, Utah
KOAQ Terrytown, Nebraska
KOAZ Isleta, New Mexico
KOBB Bozeman, Montana
KOBE Las Cruces, New Mexico

KOBO Yuba City, California
KOBY Cedar City, Utah
KODI Cody, Wyoming
KODL The Dalles, Oregon
KODY North Platte, Nebraska
KOEL Oelwein, Iowa
KOFC Fayetteville, Arkansas
KOFE St. Maries, Idaho
KOFI Kalispell, Montana
KOFO Ottawa, Kansas
KOGA Ogallala, Nebraska
KOGN Ogden, Utah
KOGO San Diego, California
KOGT Orange, Texas
KOHI St. Helens, Oregon
KOHU Hermiston, Oregon
KOIL Omaha, Nebraska
KOJM Havre, Montana
KOKA Shreveport, Louisiana
KOKB Blackwell, Oklahoma
KOKC Oklahoma City, Oklahoma
KOKE Pflugerville, Texas
KOKK Huron, South Dakota
KOKL Okmulgee, Oklahoma
KOKO Warrensburg, Missouri
KOKP Perry, Oklahoma
KOKX Keokuk, Iowa
KOLE Port Arthur, Texas
KOLM Rochester, Minnesota
KOLT Scottsbluff, Nebraska
KOLY Mobridge, South Dakota
KOMC Branson, Missouri
KOMJ Omaha, Nebraska
KOMO Seattle, Washington
KOMW Omak, Washington
KOMY La Selva Beach, California
KONA Kennewick-Richland-P, Washington
KONO San Antonio, Texas
KONP Port Angeles, Washington
KOOQ North Platte, Nebraska
KOOR Milwaukie, Oregon
KOPB Eugene, Oregon
KOPY Alice, Texas
KORE Springfield-Eugene, Oregon
KORL Honolulu, Hawaii
KORN Mitchell, South Dakota
KORT(AM/FM) Grangeville, Idaho
KOSE Wilson, Arkansas
KOSS Lancaster, California
KOSY Texarkana, Arkansas
KOTA Rapid City, South Dakota
KOTC Memphis, Tennessee
KOTK Omaha, Nebraska
KOTS Deming, New Mexico
KOTZ Kotzebue, Alaska
KOUU Pocatello, Idaho
KOVC Valley City, North Dakota
KOVE Lander, Wyoming
KOVO Provo, Utah
KOWB Laramie, Wyoming
KOWL South Lake Tahoe, California
KOXR Oxnard, California
KOY Phoenix, Arizona
KOZA Odessa, Texas
KOZE Lewiston, Idaho
KOZI Chelan, Washington
KOZN Bellevue, Nebraska
KOZY Grand Rapids, Minnesota
KPAM Troutdale, Oregon
KPAN Hereford, Texas
KPAY Chico, California
KPBL Hemphill, Texas
KPDQ Portland, Oregon
KPEL Lafayette, Louisiana
KPET Lamesa, Texas
KPGE Page, Arizona
KPGM Pawhuska, Oklahoma
KPHI Honolulu, Hawaii
KPHN Kansas City, Missouri
KPHX Phoenix, Arizona
KPIO Loveland, Colorado
KPIR Granbury, Texas
KPJC Salem, Oregon
KPKE Gunnison, Colorado
KPLT Paris, Texas
KPLY Reno, Nevada
KPMO Mendocino, California
KPNP Watertown, Minnesota
KPNS Duncan, Oklahoma
KPNW Eugene, Oregon
KPOC Pocahontas, Arkansas
KPOD Crescent City, California
KPOF Denver, Colorado
KPOJ Portland, Oregon
KPOK Bowman, North Dakota
KPOW Powell, Wyoming
KPQ Wenatchee, Washington
KPRC Houston, Texas
KPRK Livingston, Montana
KPRL Paso Robles, California
KPRM Park Rapids, Minnesota
KPRO Riverside, California
KPRT Kansas City, Missouri
KPRV Poteau, Oklahoma
KPRZ San Marcos-Poway, California
KPSI Palm Springs, California
KPSZ Des Moines, Iowa
KPTK Seattle, Washington
KPTO Pocatello, Idaho
KPTQ Spokane, Washington
KPTR Palm Springs, California
KPUA Hilo, Hawaii
KPUG Bellingham, Washington
KPUR Amarillo, Texas
KPWB Piedmont, Missouri
KPWL Newport, Washington
KPXQ Glendale, Arizona
KPYK Terrell, Texas
KPYN Atlanta, Texas
KPZK Little Rock, Arkansas
KQAB(AM) Lake Isabella, California
KQAD Luverne, Minnesota
KQAM Wichita, Kansas
KQAQ Austin, Minnesota
KQBU El Paso, Texas
KQBZ Brownwood, Texas
KQCV Oklahoma City, Oklahoma
KQDI Great Falls, Montana
KQDJ Jamestown, North Dakota
KQDS Duluth, Minnesota
KQEN Roseburg, Oregon
KQEQ Fowler, California
KQIK Lakeview, Oregon
KQJZ Evergreen, Montana
KQKD Redfield, South Dakota
KQLL Henderson, Nevada
KQLO Sun Valley, Nevada
KQLX Lisbon, North Dakota
KQMG Independence, Iowa
KQMS Redding, California
KQNA Prescott Valley, Arizona
KQNG Lihue, Hawaii
KQNK Norton, Kansas
KQNM Milan, New Mexico
KQNT Spokane, Washington
KQPN West Memphis, Arkansas
KQQB Stockdale, Texas
KQQQ Pullman, Washington
KQQZ Fairview Heights, Missouri
KQRR(AM) Mount Angel, Oregon
KQSP Shakopee, Minnesota
KQTY Borger, Texas
KQUE Houston, Texas
KQV Pittsburgh, Pennsylvania
KQWB West Fargo, North Dakota
KQWC Webster City, Iowa
KQYX Galena, Kansas
KRAC Quincy, California
KRAE Cheyenne, Wyoming
KRAI Craig, Colorado
KRAK Hesperia, California
KRAL Rawlins, Wyoming
KRAM Vernal, Utah
KRBA Lufkin, Texas
KRBT Eveleth, Minnesota
KRCM Shanandoah, Texas
KRCN Longmont, Colorado
KRCO Prineville, Oregon
KRDD Roswell, New Mexico
KRDM Redmond, Oregon
KRDO Colorado Springs, Colorado
KRDU Dinuba, California
KRDY San Antonio, Texas
KRDZ Wray, Colorado
KREA Honolulu, Hawaii
KREB Bentonville-Bella, Arkansas
KREF Norman, Oklahoma
KREH Pecan Grove, Texas
KREI Farmington, Missouri
KREL Colorado Springs, Colorado
KREW Plainview, Texas
KRFE Lubbock, Texas
KRFO Owatonna, Minnesota
KRFS Superior, Nebraska
KRGE Weslaco, Texas
KRGI Grand Island, Nebraska
KRGS Rifle, Colorado
KRHW Sikeston, Missouri
KRIB Mason City, Iowa
KRIL Odessa, Texas
KRIO McAllen, Texas
KRIZ Renton, Washington
KRJO Monroe, Louisiana
KRKC King City, California
KRKE Milan, New Mexico
KRKK Rock Springs, Wyoming
KRKO Everett, Washington
KRKS Denver, Colorado
KRKY Granby, Colorado
KRKZ Forks, Washington
KRLA Glendale, California
KRLC Lewiston-Clarkston, Idaho
KRLD Dallas, Texas
KRLL California, Missouri
KRLN Canon City, Colorado
KRLV Las Vegas, Nevada
KRLW Walnut Ridge, Arkansas
KRMD Shreveport, Louisiana
KRMG Tulsa, Oklahoma
KRML Carmel, California
KRMO Cassville, Missouri
KRMP Oklahoma City, Oklahoma
KRMS Osage Beach, Missouri
KRMY Killeen, Texas
KRND Fox Farm, Wyoming
KRNI Mason City, Iowa
KRNT Des Moines, Iowa
KROB Robstown, Texas
KROC Rochester, Minnesota
KROD El Paso, Texas
KROE Sheridan, Wyoming
KROF Abbeville, Louisiana
KROO Breckenridge, Texas
KROP Brawley, California
KROS Clinton, Iowa
KROX Crookston, Minnesota
KRPA Oak Harbor, Washington
KRPI Ferndale, Washington
KRPL Moscow, Idaho
KRRP Coushatta, Louisiana
KRRS Santa Rosa, California
KRRZ Minot, North Dakota
KRSA Petersburg, Alaska
KRSC Othello, Washington
KRSL Russell, Kansas
KRSN Los Alamos, New Mexico
KRSV Afton, Wyoming
KRSY Alamogordo, New Mexico
KRTA Medford, Oregon
KRTK Chubbuck, Idaho
KRTN Raton, New Mexico
KRTR Honolulu, Hawaii
KRTX Rosenburg-Richmond, Texas
KRUE Waseca, Minnesota
KRUI Ruidoso Downs, New Mexico
KRUN Ballinger, Texas
KRUS Ruston, Louisiana
KRVA Cockrell Hill, Texas
KRVM Eugene, Oregon
KRVN Lexington, Nebraska
KRVT Claremore, Oklahoma
KRVZ Springerville, Arizona
KRWB Roseau, Minnesota
KRWC Buffalo, Minnesota
KRWZ Parker, Colorado
KRXA Carmel Valley, California
KRXK Rexburg, Idaho
KRXR Gooding, Idaho
KRYN(AM) Gresham, Oregon
KRZI Waco, Texas
KRZR Visalia, California
KRZY Albuquerque, New Mexico
KSAH Universal City, Texas
KSAL Salina, Kansas
KSAM Whitefish, Montana
KSAZ Marana, Arizona
KSBN Spokane, Washington
KSBQ Santa Maria, California
KSCB Liberal, Kansas
KSCJ Sioux City, Iowa
KSCO Santa Cruz, California
KSCR Eugene, Oregon
KSDN Aberdeen, South Dakota
KSDO San Diego, California
KSDP Sand Point, Alaska
KSDR Watertown, South Dakota
KSDT Hemet, California
KSEI Pocatello, Idaho
KSEK Pittsburg, Kansas
KSEL Portales, New Mexico
KSEN Shelby, Montana
KSEO Durant, Oklahoma
KSET Lumberton, Texas
KSEV Tomball, Texas
KSEW Seward, Alaska
KSEY Seymour, Texas
KSFA Nacogdoches, Texas
KSFB San Francisco, California
KSFN(AM) Piedmont, California
KSFO San Francisco, California
KSFT(AM) Saint Joseph, Missouri
KSGF Springfield, Missouri
KSGL Wichita, Kansas
KSGM Chester, Illinois
KSGT Jackson, Wyoming
KSHO Lebanon, Oregon
KSHP North Las Vegas, Nevada
KSIB Creston, Iowa
KSID Sidney, Nebraska
KSIG Crowley, Louisiana
KSIM Sikeston, Missouri
KSIR Brush, Colorado
KSIS Sedalia, Missouri
KSIV Clayton, Missouri
KSIW Woodward, Oklahoma
KSIX Corpus Christi, Texas
KSJB Jamestown, North Dakota
KSJK Talent, Oregon
KSJX San Jose, California
KSKE Buena Vista, Colorado
KSKR Roseburg, Oregon
KSKY Balch Springs, Texas
KSL Salt Lake City, Utah
KSLD Soldotna, Alaska
KSLI Abilene, Texas
KSLL Price, Utah
KSLO Opelousas, Louisiana
KSLR San Antonio, Texas
KSLV Monte Vista, Colorado
KSMA Lompoc, California
KSMH West Sacramento, California
KSML Diboll, Texas
KSMM Liberal, Kansas
KSMO Salem, Missouri
KSMX Santa Maria, California
KSNM Las Cruces, New Mexico
KSNY Snyder, Texas
KSOK Arkansas City, Kansas
KSOO Sioux Falls, South Dakota
KSOP South Salt Lake, Utah
KSOU Sioux Center, Iowa
KSOX Raymondville, Texas
KSPA Ontario, California
KSPD Boise, Idaho
KSPI Stillwater, Oklahoma
KSPN Los Angeles, California
KSPT Sandpoint, Idaho
KSPZ Ammon, Idaho
KSQB(AM) Sioux Falls, South Dakota
KSRA Salmon, Idaho
KSRM Soldotna, Alaska
KSRO Santa Rosa, California
KSRR Provo, Utah
KSRV Ontario, Oregon
KSSK Honolulu, Hawaii
KSST Sulphur Springs, Texas
KSTA Coleman, Texas
KSTC Sterling, Colorado
KSTE Rancho Cordova, California
KSTL St. Louis, Missouri
KSTN Stockton, California
KSTP St. Paul, Minnesota
KSTV Stephenville, Texas
KSUB Cedar City, Utah
KSUE Susanville, California
KSUH Puyallup, Washington
KSUM Fairmont, Minnesota
KSVA Albuquerque, New Mexico
KSVC Richfield, Utah
KSVE El Paso, Texas
KSVN Ogden, Utah
KSVP Artesia, New Mexico
KSWA Graham, Texas
KSWB Seaside, Oregon

KSWM Aurora, Missouri
KSWV Santa Fe, New Mexico
KSYB Shreveport, Louisiana
KSYC Yreka, California
KSYL Alexandria, Louisiana
KSZL Barstow, California
KSZN(AM) Gresham, Oregon
KTAE Cameron, Texas
KTAM Bryan, Texas
KTAN Sierra Vista, Arizona
KTAP Santa Maria, California
KTAR Phoenix, Arizona
KTAT Frederick, Oklahoma
KTBA Tuba City, Arizona
KTBB Tyler, Texas
KTBI Ephrata, Washington
KTBL Los Ranchos, New Mexico
KTBR Roseburg, Oregon
KTBZ Tulsa, Oklahoma
KTCH Wayne, Nebraska
KTCK Dallas, Texas
KTCN Minneapolis, Minnesota
KTCR Yakima, Washington
KTCS Fort Smith, Arkansas
KTCT San Mateo, California
KTDD San Bernardino, California
KTEK Alvin, Texas
KTEL Walla Walla, Washington
KTEM Temple, Texas
KTFI Wendell, Idaho
KTFJ Dakota City, Nebraska
KTFS Texarkana, Texas
KTGE Salinas, California
KTGG Okemos, Michigan
KTGO Tioga, North Dakota
KTGR Columbia, Missouri
KTHE Thermopolis, Wyoming
KTHH Albany, Oregon
KTHO South Lake Tahoe, California
KTHS Berryville, Arkansas
KTIB Thibodaux, Louisiana
KTIC West Point, Nebraska
KTIE San Bernardino, California
KTIK Nampa, Idaho
KTIP Porterville, California
KTIQ Merced, California
KTIS Minneapolis, Minnesota
KTIX Pendleton, Oregon
KTJS Hobart, Oklahoma
KTKC Springhill, Louisiana
KTKK Sandy, Utah
KTKN Ketchikan, Alaska
KTKR San Antonio, Texas
KTKT Tucson, Arizona
KTKZ Sacramento, California
KTLK Los Angeles, California
KTLO Mountain Home, Arkansas
KTLQ Tahlequah, Oklahoma
KTLR Oklahoma City, Oklahoma
KTLU Rusk, Texas
KTLV Midwest City, Oklahoma
KTMC McAlester, Oklahoma
KTMM Grand Junction, Colorado
KTMR Converse, Texas
KTMS Santa Barbara, California
KTNC Falls City, Nebraska
KTNF St. Louis Park, Minnesota
KTNM Tucumcari, New Mexico
KTNN Window Rock, Arizona
KTNO University Park, Texas
KTNQ Los Angeles, California
KTNS Oakhurst, California
KTNZ Amarillo, Texas
KTOB Petaluma, California
KTOE Mankato, Minnesota
KTOK Oklahoma City, Oklahoma
KTOP Topeka, Kansas
KTOQ Rapid City, South Dakota
KTOX Needles, California
KTPA Prescott, Arkansas
KTPI Mojave, California
KTRB San Francisco, California
KTRC Santa Fe, New Mexico
KTRF Thief River Falls, Minnesota
KTRH Houston, Texas
KTRP Weiser, Idaho
KTRS St. Louis, Missouri
KTRW Opportunity, Washington
KTSA San Antonio, Texas
KTSM El Paso, Texas
KTSN Elko, Nevada
KTTH Seattle, Washington
KTTN Trenton, Missouri
KTTO Spokane, Washington
KTTP Pineville, Louisiana
KTTR Rolla, Missouri
KTTT Columbus, Nebraska
KTUB Centerville, Utah
KTUC Tucson, Arizona
KTUI Sullivan, Missouri
KTUV Little Rock, Arkansas
KTWG Agana, Guam
KTWN Glencoe, Minnesota
KTWO Casper, Wyoming
KTXV Mabank, Texas
KTXW Manor, Texas
KTXZ West Lake Hills, Texas
KTYM Inglewood, California
KTZN Anchorage, Alaska
KTZR Tucson, Arizona
KUAI Eleele, Hawaii
KUAM Agana, Guam
KUAU Haiku, Hawaii
KUAZ Tucson, Arizona
KUBA Yuba City, California
KUBC Montrose, Colorado
KUBR San Juan, Texas
KUDL Kansas City, Kansas
KUDO Anchorage, Alaska
KUGN Eugene, Oregon
KUGR Green River, Wyoming
KUHL Santa Maria, California
KUIK Hillsboro, Oregon
KUJ Walla Walla, Washington
KUKI Ukiah, California
KUKU Willow Springs, Missouri
KULE Ephrata, Washington
KULF Bellville, Texas
KULP El Campo, Texas
KULY Ulysses, Kansas
KUMA Pendleton, Oregon
KUMU(AM) Honolulu, Hawaii
KUNF Washington, Utah
KUNO Corpus Christi, Texas
KUNX Ventura, California
KUOA Siloam Springs, Arkansas
KUOL San Marcos, Texas
KUOM Minneapolis, Minnesota
KUOW Tumwater, Washington
KUPA Pearl City, Hawaii
KURL Billings, Montana
KURM Rogers, Arkansas
KURS San Diego, California
KURV Edinburg, Texas
KURY Brookings, Oregon
KUSH Cushing, Oklahoma
KUTI Yakima, Washington
KUTR Taylorsville, Utah
KUTY Palmdale, California
KUVR Holdrege, Nebraska
KUYO Evansville, Wyoming
KUZZ Bakersfield, California
KVAK Valdez, Alaska
KVAN Burbank, Washington
KVBR Brainerd, Minnesota
KVCE Highland Park, Texas
KVCK Wolf Point, Montana
KVCU Boulder, Colorado
KVDW England, Arkansas
KVEC San Luis Obispo, California
KVEL Vernal, Utah
KVEN Ventura, California
KVET Austin, Texas
KVFC Cortez, Colorado
KVFD Fort Dodge, Iowa
KVGB Great Bend, Kansas
KVI Seattle, Washington
KVIN Ceres, California
KVIP Redding, California
KVIS Miami, Oklahoma
KVIV El Paso, Texas
KVJY Pharr, Texas
KVKK Verndale, Minnesota
KVLE Vail, Colorado
KVLF Alpine, Texas
KVLG La Grange, Texas
KVLV Fallon, Nevada
KVMA Magnolia, Arkansas
KVMC Colorado City, Texas
KVML Sonora, California
KVNA Flagstaff, Arizona
KVNI Coeur D'Alene, Idaho
KVNN Victoria, Texas
KVNR Santa Ana, California
KVNS Brownsville, Texas
KVNU Logan, Utah
KVOC Casper, Wyoming
KVOE Emporia, Kansas
KVOG Agana, Guam
KVOI Cortaro, Arizona
KVOK Kodiak, Alaska
KVOL Lafayette, Louisiana
KVOM Morrilton, Arkansas
KVON Napa, California
KVOP Plainview, Texas
KVOQ(AM) Denver, Colorado
KVOR Colorado Springs, Colorado
KVOT Taos, New Mexico
KVOW Riverton, Wyoming
KVOX Fargo, North Dakota
KVOZ Del Mar Hills, Texas
KVPI Ville Platte, Louisiana
KVRC Arkadelphia, Arkansas
KVRH Salida, Colorado
KVRI Blaine, Washington
KVRP Stamford, Texas
KVSA McGehee, Arkansas
KVSF Santa Fe, New Mexico
KVSH Valentine, Nebraska
KVSI Montpelier, Idaho
KVSL Show Low, Arizona
KVSO Ardmore, Oklahoma
KVSV Beloit, Kansas
KVTA Port Hueneme, California
KVTK Vermillion, South Dakota
KVTO Berkeley, California
KVTT Mineral Wells, Texas
KVVN Santa Clara, California
KVWC Vernon, Texas
KVWM Show Low, Arizona
KVXR Moorhead, Minnesota
KWAC Bakersfield, California
KWAD Wadena, Minnesota
KWAI Honolulu, Hawaii
KWAK Stuttgart, Arkansas
KWAL Wallace, Idaho
KWAM Memphis, Tennessee
KWAP Wasilla, Alaska
KWAT Watertown, South Dakota
KWAY Waverly, Iowa
KWBC Navasota, Texas
KWBE Beatrice, Nebraska
KWBG Boone, Iowa
KWBW Hutchinson, Kansas
KWBY Woodburn, Oregon
KWCK Searcy, Arkansas
KWDF Ball, Louisiana
KWDJ Ridgecrest, California
KWDZ Salt Lake City, Utah
KWED Seguin, Texas
KWEI Notus, Idaho
KWEI(AM) Payette, Idaho
KWEL Midland, Texas
KWES Ruidoso, New Mexico
KWEY Weatherford, Oklahoma
KWFA Tye, Texas
KWFM South Tucson, Arizona
KWFS Wichita Falls, Texas
KWG Stockton, California
KWHI Brenham, Texas
KWHN Fort Smith, Arkansas
KWHW Altus, Oklahoma
KWIK Pocatello, Idaho
KWIL Albany, Oregon
KWIP Dallas, Oregon
KWIQ Moses Lake North, Washington
KWIX Moberly, Missouri
KWJB Canton, Texas
KWKA Clovis, New Mexico
KWKC Abilene, Texas
KWKH Shreveport, Louisiana
KWKU Pomona, California
KWKW Los Angeles, California
KWKY Des Moines, Iowa
KWLC Decorah, Iowa
KWLE Anacortes, Washington
KWLM Willmar, Minnesota
KWLO Waterloo, Iowa
KWMC Del Rio, Texas
KWMF Pleasanton, Texas
KWMO Washington, Missouri
KWMT Fort Dodge, Iowa
KWNA Winnemucca, Nevada
KWNC Quincy, Washington
KWNO Winona, Minnesota
KWNX Taylor, Texas
KWOA Worthington, Minnesota
KWOC Poplar Bluff, Missouri
KWOK Hoquiam, Washington
KWON Bartlesville, Oklahoma
KWOR Worland, Wyoming
KWOS Jefferson City, Missouri
KWPC Muscatine, Iowa
KWPM West Plains, Missouri
KWPN(AM) Moore, Oklahoma
KWRD Henderson, Texas
KWRE Warrenton, Missouri
KWRF Warren, Arkansas
KWRM Corona, California
KWRN Apple Valley, California
KWRO Coquille, Oregon
KWRT Boonville, Missouri
KWRU Fresno, California
KWSH Wewoka, Oklahoma
KWSL Sioux City, Iowa
KWSN Sioux Falls, South Dakota
KWST El Centro, California
KWSU Pullman, Washington
KWSW Eureka, California
KWSW(AM) Eureka, California
KWSX Stockton, California
KWTL Grand Forks, North Dakota
KWTO Springfield, Missouri
KWTX Waco, Texas
KWUD Woodville, Texas
KWUF Pagosa Springs, Colorado
KWVE(AM) Oildale, California
KWVR Enterprise, Oregon
KWWJ Baytown, Texas
KWWN Las Vegas, Nevada
KWXI Glenwood, Arkansas
KWXT Dardanelle, Arkansas
KWYN Wynne, Arkansas
KWYO Sheridan, Wyoming
KWYR Winner, South Dakota
KWYS West Yellowstone, Montana
KWYZ Everett, Washington
KXAR Hope, Arkansas
KXBX Lakeport, California
KXCA Lawton, Oklahoma
KXEG Phoenix, Arizona
KXEL Waterloo, Iowa
KXEN St. Louis, Missouri
KXEO Mexico, Missouri
KXEQ Reno, Nevada
KXET(AM) Portland, Oregon
KXEW South Tucson, Arizona
KXEX Fresno, California
KXFN Saint Louis, Missouri
KXGF Great Falls, Montana
KXGN Glendive, Montana
KXIC Iowa City, Iowa
KXIQ(AM) Turrell, Arkansas
KXIT Dalhart, Texas
KXJK Forrest City, Arkansas
KXKS Albuquerque, New Mexico
KXLE Ellensburg, Washington
KXLO Lewistown, Montana
KXLQ Indianola, Iowa
KXLX Airway Heights, Washington
KXLY Spokane, Washington
KXMR Bismarck, North Dakota
KXNO Des Moines, Iowa
KXNT North Las Vegas, Nevada
KXO El Centro, California
KXOI Crane, Texas
KXOL Brigham City, Utah
KXOR Junction City, Oregon
KXOX Sweetwater, Texas
KXPA Bellevue, Washington
KXPD Tigard, Oregon
KXPL El Paso, Texas
KXPN Kearney, Nebraska
KXPO Grafton, North Dakota
KXPS Thousand Palms, California
KXRA Alexandria, Minnesota
KXRB Sioux Falls, South Dakota
KXRE Manitou Springs, Colorado
KXRO Aberdeen, Washington
KXSP Omaha, Nebraska
KXSS Waite Park, Minnesota
KXTD Wagoner, Oklahoma
KXTG Portland, Oregon
KXTG(AM) Portland, Oregon

KXTK Arroyo Grande, California
KXTL Butte, Montana
KXTO Reno, Nevada
KXXA(AM) Conway, Arkansas
KXXJ Juneau, Alaska
KXXT Tolleson, Arizona
KXXX Colby, Kansas
KXYZ Houston, Texas
KXZZ Lake Charles, Louisiana
KYAA Soquel, California
KYAH Delta, Utah
KYAK Yakima, Washington
KYAL Sapulpa, Oklahoma
KYBC Cottonwood, Arizona
KYCA Prescott, Arizona
KYCN Wheatland, Wyoming
KYCR Golden Valley, Minnesota
KYDZ North Las Vegas, Nevada
KYES Rockville, Minnesota
KYET Golden Valley, Arizona
KYFR Shenandoah, Iowa
KYHN Ft. Smith, Arkansas
KYIZ Renton, Washington
KYKK Humble City, New Mexico
KYKN Keizer, Oregon
KYLS Fredericktown, Missouri
KYLT Missoula, Montana
KYLW Lockwood, Montana
KYMN Northfield, Minnesota
KYMO East Prairie, Missouri
KYND Cypress, Texas
KYNG Springdale, Arkansas
KYNO Fresno, California
KYNR Toppenish, Washington
KYNS San Luis Obispo, California
KYNT Yankton, South Dakota
KYOK Conroe, Texas
KYOO Bolivar, Missouri
KYOS Merced, California
KYPA Los Angeles, California
KYRO Troy, Missouri
KYSM Mankato, Minnesota
KYST Texas City, Texas
KYTY Somerset, Texas
KYUK Bethel, Alaska
KYUL Scott City, Kansas
KYVA Gallup, New Mexico
KYW Philadelphia, Pennsylvania
KYYS Kansas City, Kansas
KYYW Abilene, Texas
KYZS Tyler, Texas
KZDC San Antonio, Texas
KZDG(AM) San Francisco, California
KZEE Weatherford, Texas
KZER Santa Barbara, California
KZHN Paris, Texas
KZHS Hot Springs, Arkansas
KZIM Cape Girardeau, Missouri
KZIP Amarillo, Texas
KZIZ Pacific, Washington
KZLI Catoosa, Oklahoma
KZMP University Park, Texas
KZMQ Ten Sleep, Wyoming
KZMX Hot Springs, South Dakota
KZNE College Station, Texas
KZNG Hot Springs, Arkansas
KZNS Salt Lake City, Utah
KZNT Colorado Springs, Colorado
KZNU St. George, Utah
KZNW Wenatchee, Washington
KZNX Creedmoor, Texas
KZOO Honolulu, Hawaii
KZOT Bellevue, Nebraska
KZPA Fort Yukon, Alaska
KZQQ Abilene, Texas
KZQZ St. Louis, Missouri
KZRG Joplin, Missouri
KZRK Canyon, Texas
KZSB Santa Barbara, California
KZSF San Jose, California
KZSJ San Martin, California
KZTD Cabot, Arkansas
KZUE El Reno, Oklahoma
KZXR Prosser, Washington
KZYM Joplin, Missouri
KZZB Beaumont, Texas
KZZJ Rugby, North Dakota
KZZN Littlefield, Texas
KZZZ Bullhead City, Arizona
WAAM Ann Arbor, Michigan
WAAV Leland, North Carolina
WAAX Gadsden, Alabama
WABA Aguadilla, Puerto Rico
WABB Mobile, Alabama
WABC New York, New York
WABF Fairhope, Alabama
WABG Greenwood, Mississippi
WABH Bath, New York
WABJ Adrian, Michigan
WABL Amite, Louisiana
WABN Abingdon, Virginia
WABO Waynesboro, Mississippi
WABQ Painesville, Ohio
WABV Abbeville, South Carolina
WABY Mechanicville, New York
WACA Wheaton, Maryland
WACB Taylorsville, North Carolina
WACC Hialeah, Florida
WACE Chicopee, Massachusetts
WACK Newark, New York
WACM West Springfield, Massachusetts
WACQ(AM) Tuskegee, Alabama
WACT Tuscaloosa, Alabama
WADB(AM) Asbury Park, New Jersey
WADC Parkersburg, West Virginia
WADE Wadesboro, North Carolina
WADK Newport, Rhode Island
WADO New York, New York
WADS Ansonia, Connecticut
WADV Lebanon, Pennsylvania
WAEB Allentown, Pennsylvania
WAEC Atlanta, Georgia
WAEI Bangor, Maine
WAEW Crossville, Tennessee
WAEY Princeton, West Virginia
WAFC Clewiston, Florida
WAFS Atlanta, Georgia
WAFZ Immokalee, Florida
WAGF Dothan, Alabama
WAGG Birmingham, Alabama
WAGL Lancaster, South Carolina
WAGN Menominee, Michigan
WAGR Lumberton, North Carolina
WAGS Bishopville, South Carolina
WAGY Forest City, North Carolina
WAHT Clemson, South Carolina
WAIK Galesburg, Illinois
WAIM Anderson, South Carolina
WAIN Columbia, Kentucky
WAIS Buchtel, Ohio
WAIT Crystal Lake, Illinois
WAIZ Hickory, North Carolina
WAJD Gainesville, Florida
WAJL South Boston, Virginia
WAJR Morgantown, West Virginia
WAKE Valparaiso, Indiana
WAKI McMinnville, Tennessee
WAKK McComb, Mississippi
WAKM Franklin, Tennessee
WAKO Lawrenceville, Illinois
WAKR Akron, Ohio
WAKV Otsego, Michigan
WALD Johnsonville, South Carolina
WALE Greenville, Rhode Island
WALG Albany, Georgia
WALH Mountain City, Georgia
WALK Patchogue, New York
WALL Middletown, New York
WALO Humacao, Puerto Rico
WALQ Carrville, Alabama
WALT Meridian, Mississippi
WAMA Tampa, Florida
WAMB Nashville, Tennessee
WAMC Albany, New York
WAMD Aberdeen, Maryland
WAME Statesville, North Carolina
WAMG Dedham, Massachusetts
WAMI Opp, Alabama
WAML Laurel, Mississippi
WAMM Woodstock, Virginia
WAMN Green Valley, West Virginia
WAMO Wilkinsburg, Pennsylvania
WAMS(AM) Ocean City, Maryland
WAMT Pine Castle Sky Lake, Florida
WAMV Amherst, Virginia
WAMW Washington, Indiana
WAMY Amory, Mississippi
WANB Waynesburg, Pennsylvania
WANG Havelock, North Carolina
WANI Opelika, Alabama
WANO Pineville, Kentucky
WANS Anderson, South Carolina
WANY Albany, Kentucky
WAOC Saint Augustine, Florida
WAOK Atlanta, Georgia
WAOS Austell, Georgia
WAOV Vincennes, Indiana
WAPA San Juan, Puerto Rico
WAPF McComb, Mississippi
WAPI Birmingham, Alabama
WAQE Rice Lake, Wisconsin
WAQI Miami, Florida
WARD Petoskey, Michigan
WARE Ware, Massachusetts
WARF Akron, Ohio
WARK Hagerstown, Maryland
WARL Attleboro, Massachusetts
WARM Scranton, Pennsylvania
WARR Warrenton, North Carolina
WARU Peru, Indiana
WARV Warwick, Rhode Island
WASB Brockport, New York
WASC Spartanburg, South Carolina
WASG Daphne, Alabama
WASK Lafayette, Indiana
WASN Youngstown, Ohio
WASR Wolfeboro, New Hampshire
WATA Boone, North Carolina
WATB Decatur, Georgia
WATH Athens, Ohio
WATK Antigo, Wisconsin
WATN Watertown, New York
WATR Waterbury, Connecticut
WATS Sayre, Pennsylvania
WATT Cadillac, Michigan
WATV Birmingham, Alabama
WATW Ashland, Wisconsin
WATX Algood, Tennessee
WATZ Alpena, Michigan
WAUB Auburn, New York
WAUC Wauchula, Florida
WAUD Auburn, Alabama
WAUG New Hope, North Carolina
WAUK Jackson, Wisconsin
WAUR Sandwich, Illinois
WAVA Arlington, Virginia
WAVL Apollo, Pennsylvania
WAVN Southaven, Mississippi
WAVO Rock Hill, South Carolina
WAVQ Jacksonville, North Carolina
WAVS Davie, Florida
WAVU Albertville, Alabama
WAVZ New Haven, Connecticut
WAWK Kendallville, Indiana
WAWO Alma, Georgia
WAXB Ridgefield, Connecticut
WAXO Lewisburg, Tennessee
WAXY South Miami, Florida
WAYE Birmingham, Alabama
WAYN Rockingham, North Carolina
WAYR Orange Park, Florida
WAYS Macon, Georgia
WAYY Eau Claire, Wisconsin
WAZL Hazleton, Pennsylvania
WAZN Watertown, Massachusetts
WAZS Summerville, South Carolina
WAZX Smyrna, Georgia
WAZZ Fayetteville, North Carolina
WBAA West Lafayette, Indiana
WBAC Cleveland, Tennessee
WBAE Portland, Maine
WBAF Barnesville, Georgia
WBAG Burlington-Graham, North Carolina
WBAJ Blythewood, South Carolina
WBAL Baltimore, Maryland
WBAP Fort Worth, Texas
WBAT Marion, Indiana
WBAX Wilkes-Barre, Pennsylvania
WBBD Wheeling, West Virginia
WBBF Buffalo, New York
WBBM Chicago, Illinois
WBBP Memphis, Tennessee
WBBR New York, New York
WBBT Lyons, Georgia
WBBW Youngstown, Ohio
WBBX Kingston, Tennessee
WBBZ Ponca City, Oklahoma
WBCB Levittown, Pennsylvania
WBCE Wickliffe, Kentucky
WBCF Florence, Alabama
WBCH Hastings, Michigan
WBCK Battle Creek, Michigan
WBCN Charlotte, North Carolina
WBCN(AM) Charlotte, North Carolina
WBCO Bucyrus, Ohio
WBCP Urbana, Illinois
WBCR Alcoa, Tennessee
WBCU Union, South Carolina
WBEC Pittsfield, Massachusetts
WBEJ Elizabethton, Tennessee
WBEN Buffalo, New York
WBES Charleston, West Virginia
WBET Sturgis, Michigan
WBEV Beaver Dam, Wisconsin
WBEX Chillicothe, Ohio
WBFC Stanton, Kentucky
WBFD Bedford, Pennsylvania
WBFJ Winston-Salem, North Carolina
WBFN Battle Creek, Michigan
WBGC Chipley, Florida
WBGG Pittsburgh, Pennsylvania
WBGN Bowling Green, Kentucky
WBGS Point Pleasant, West Virginia
WBGX Harvey, Illinois
WBGZ Alton, Illinois
WBHA Wabasha, Minnesota
WBHB Fitzgerald, Georgia
WBHF Cartersville, Georgia
WBHN Bryson City, North Carolina
WBHP Huntsville, Alabama
WBHR Sauk Rapids, Minnesota
WBHY Mobile, Alabama
WBIB Centreville, Alabama
WBIG Aurora, Illinois
WBIN Benton, Tennessee
WBIP Booneville, Mississippi
WBIW Bedford, Indiana
WBIZ Eau Claire, Wisconsin
WBKK Wilton, Minnesota
WBKV West Bend, Wisconsin
WBKW Beckley, West Virginia
WBKW(AM) Beckley, West Virginia
WBLA Elizabethtown, North Carolina
WBLC Lenoir City, Tennessee
WBLF Bellefonte, Pennsylvania
WBLJ Dalton, Georgia
WBLL Bellefontaine, Ohio
WBLO Thomasville, North Carolina
WBLQ(AM) Westerly, Rhode Island
WBLR Batesburg, South Carolina
WBLT Bedford, Virginia
WBMC McMinnville, Tennessee
WBMD Baltimore, Maryland
WBMJ San Juan, Puerto Rico
WBML Macon, Georgia
WBMQ Savannah, Georgia
WBNC Conway, New Hampshire
WBNL Boonville, Indiana
WBNM Alexander City, Alabama
WBNR Beacon, New York
WBNS Columbus, Ohio
WBNW Concord, Massachusetts
WBOB Jacksonville, Florida
WBOB(AM) Jacksonville, Florida
WBOG Tomah, Wisconsin
WBOK New Orleans, Louisiana
WBOL Bolivar, Tennessee
WBOW Terre Haute, Indiana
WBOX Bogalusa, Louisiana
WBPZ Lock Haven, Pennsylvania
WBQH Silver Spring, Maryland
WBQH(AM) Silver Spring, Maryland
WBQN Barceloneta-Manati, Puerto Rico
WBRD Palmetto, Florida
WBRG Lynchburg, Virginia
WBRI Indianapolis, Indiana
WBRK Pittsfield, Massachusetts
WBRM Marion, North Carolina
WBRN Big Rapids, Michigan
WBRT Bardstown, Kentucky
WBRV Boonville, New York
WBSA Boaz, Alabama
WBSC Bennettsville, South Carolina
WBSG Lajas, Puerto Rico
WBSM New Bedford, Massachusetts
WBSR Pensacola, Florida
WBSS Pleasantville, New Jersey
WBSS(AM) Pleasantville, New Jersey
WBT Charlotte, North Carolina
WBTA Batavia, New York
WBTC Uhrichsville, Ohio
WBTE Windsor, North Carolina
WBTG Sheffield, Alabama
WBTH Williamson, West Virginia

WBTK Richmond, Virginia
WBTM Danville, Virginia
WBTN Bennington, Vermont
WBTX Broadway-Timberville, Virginia
WBUC Buckhannon, West Virginia
WBUR West Yarmouth, Massachusetts
WBUT Butler, Pennsylvania
WBVA Bayside, Virginia
WBVP Beaver Falls, Pennsylvania
WBWX(AM) Berwick, Pennsylvania
WBXR Hazel Green, Alabama
WBYN Lehighton, Pennsylvania
WBYS Canton, Illinois
WBZ Boston, Massachusetts
WBZI Xenia, Ohio
WBZK York, South Carolina
WBZQ Huntington, Indiana
WBZR Robertsdale, Alabama
WBZT West Palm Beach, Florida
WBZU Scranton, Pennsylvania
WCAB Rutherfordton, North Carolina
WCAM Camden, South Carolina
WCAO Baltimore, Maryland
WCAP Lowell, Massachusetts
WCAR Livonia, Michigan
WCAT Burlington, Vermont
WCAZ Carthage, Illinois
WCBA Corning, New York
WCBC Cumberland, Maryland
WCBG Waynesboro, Pennsylvania
WCBL Benton, Kentucky
WCBM Baltimore, Maryland
WCBQ Oxford, North Carolina
WCBR Richmond, Kentucky
WCBS New York, New York
WCBT Roanoke Rapids, North Carolina
WCBX Bassett, Virginia
WCBY Cheboygan, Michigan
WCCC West Hartford, Connecticut
WCCD Parma, Ohio
WCCF Punta Gorda, Florida
WCCM Salem, New Hampshire
WCCN Neillsville, Wisconsin
WCCO Minneapolis, Minnesota
WCCS Homer City, Pennsylvania
WCCW Traverse City, Michigan
WCCY Houghton, Michigan
WCDL Carbondale, Pennsylvania
WCDO Sidney, New York
WCDS Glasgow, Kentucky
WCDT Winchester, Tennessee
WCEC Haverhill, Massachusetts
WCED Du Bois, Pennsylvania
WCEH Hawkinsville, Georgia
WCEM Cambridge, Maryland
WCEO Columbia, South Carolina
WCEV Cicero, Illinois
WCFJ Chicago Heights, Illinois
WCFO East Point, Georgia
WCFR Springfield, Vermont
WCGA Woodbine, Georgia
WCGB Juana Diaz, Puerto Rico
WCGC Belmont, North Carolina
WCGL Jacksonville, Florida
WCGO Evanston, Illinois
WCGR Canandaigua, New York
WCGW Nicholasville, Kentucky
WCHA Chambersburg, Pennsylvania
WCHB Taylor, Michigan
WCHE West Chester, Pennsylvania
WCHI Chillicothe, Ohio
WCHJ Brookhaven, Mississippi
WCHK Canton, Georgia
WCHL Chapel Hill, North Carolina
WCHM Clarkesville, Georgia
WCHN Norwich, New York
WCHO Washington Ct House, Ohio
WCHP Champlain, New York
WCHR Trenton, New Jersey
WCHS Charleston, West Virginia
WCHT Escanaba, Michigan
WCHV Charlottesville, Virginia
WCHZ Augusta, Georgia
WCIL Carbondale, Illinois
WCIS Morganton, North Carolina
WCIT(AM) Lima, Ohio
WCJU Columbia, Mississippi
WCJW Warsaw, New York
WCKA Jacksonville, Alabama
WCKB Dunn, North Carolina
WCKI Greer, South Carolina
WCKL Catskill, New York
WCKW Garyville, Louisiana
WCKY Cincinnati, Ohio
WCLA Claxton, Georgia
WCLB Sheboygan, Wisconsin
WCLC Jamestown, Tennessee
WCLD Cleveland, Mississippi
WCLE Cleveland, Tennessee
WCLG Morgantown, West Virginia
WCLM Highland Springs, Virginia
WCLN Clinton, North Carolina
WCLO Janesville, Wisconsin
WCLT Newark, Ohio
WCLU Glasgow, Kentucky
WCLW Eden, North Carolina
WCLY Raleigh, North Carolina
WCMA(AM) Bayamon, Puerto Rico
WCMC Wildwood, New Jersey
WCMD Cumberland, Maryland
WCME(AM) Brunswick, Maine
WCMI Ashland, Kentucky
WCMN Arecibo, Puerto Rico
WCMP Pine City, Minnesota
WCMR Elkhart, Indiana
WCMT Martin, Tennessee
WCMX Leominster, Massachusetts
WCMY Ottawa, Illinois
WCNC Elizabeth City, North Carolina
WCND Shelbyville, Kentucky
WCNF Dothan, Alabama
WCNL Newport, New Hampshire
WCNN North Atlanta, Georgia
WCNS Latrobe, Pennsylvania
WCNW Fairfield, Ohio
WCNZ Marco Island, Florida
WCOA Pensacola, Florida
WCOC Dora, Alabama
WCOG Greensboro, North Carolina
WCOH Newnan, Georgia
WCOJ Coatesville, Pennsylvania
WCOK Sparta, North Carolina
WCON Cornelia, Georgia
WCOR Lebanon, Tennessee
WCOS Columbia, South Carolina
WCPA Clearfield, Pennsylvania
WCPC Houston, Mississippi
WCPH Etowah, Tennessee
WCPK Chesapeake, Virginia
WCPM Cumberland, Kentucky
WCPR Coamo, Puerto Rico
WCPS Tarboro, North Carolina
WCPT Willow Springs, Illinois
WCRA Effingham, Illinois
WCRE Cheraw, South Carolina
WCRI(AM) Hope Valley, Rhode Island
WCRK Morristown, Tennessee
WCRL Oneonta, Alabama
WCRM Fort Myers, Florida
WCRN Worcester, Massachusetts
WCRO Johnstown, Pennsylvania
WCRS Greenwood, South Carolina
WCRT Donelson, Tennessee
WCRU Dallas, North Carolina
WCRV Collierville, Tennessee
WCRW(AM) Leesburg, Virginia
WCSA Ripley, Mississippi
WCSI Columbus, Indiana
WCSJ Morris, Illinois
WCSL Cherryville, North Carolina
WCSM Celina, Ohio
WCSR Hillsdale, Michigan
WCSS Amsterdam, New York
WCST Berkeley Springs, West Virginia
WCSV Crossville, Tennessee
WCSW Shell Lake, Wisconsin
WCSZ Sans Souci, South Carolina
WCTA Alamo, Tennessee
WCTC New Brunswick, New Jersey
WCTF Vernon, Connecticut
WCTN Potomac-Cabin John, Maryland
WCTR Chestertown, Maryland
WCTS Maplewood, Minnesota
WCTT Corbin, Kentucky
WCUB Two Rivers, Wisconsin
WCUE Cuyahoga Falls, Ohio
WCUM Bridgeport, Connecticut
WCVA Culpeper, Virginia
WCVC Tallahassee, Florida
WCVG Covington, Kentucky
WCVL Crawfordsville, Indiana
WCVP Murphy, North Carolina
WCVR(AM) Randolph, Vermont
WCVX Cincinnati, Ohio
WCWA Toledo, Ohio
WCWC Williamsburg, Kentucky
WCXI Fenton, Michigan
WCXN Claremont, North Carolina
WCXZ Harrogate, Tennessee
WCYN Cynthiana, Kentucky
WCZZ Greenwood, South Carolina
WDAD Indiana, Pennsylvania
WDAE St. Petersburg, Florida
WDAK Columbus, Georgia
WDAL Dalton, Georgia
WDAN Danville, Illinois
WDAO Dayton, Ohio
WDAY Fargo, North Dakota
WDBC Escanaba, Michigan
WDBL Springfield, Tennessee
WDBO Orlando, Florida
WDBQ Dubuque, Iowa
WDBZ Cincinnati, Ohio
WDCF Dade City, Florida
WDCT Fairfax, Virginia
WDCX Rochester, New York
WDCY Douglasville, Georgia
WDDO Macon, Georgia
WDDV Venice, Florida
WDDY Albany, New York
WDDZ Pittsburgh, Pennsylvania
WDEA Ellsworth, Maine
WDEB Jamestown, Tennessee
WDEF Chattanooga, Tennessee
WDEH Sweetwater, Tennessee
WDEK(AM) Lexington, South Carolina
WDEL Wilmington, Delaware
WDEO Ypsilanti, Michigan
WDEP Ponce, Puerto Rico
WDER Derry, New Hampshire
WDEV Waterbury, Vermont
WDEX Monroe, North Carolina
WDFB Junction City, Kentucky
WDFN Detroit, Michigan
WDGR Dahlonega, Georgia
WDGY Hudson, Wisconsin
WDHP Frederiksted, Virgin Islands
WDIA Memphis, Tennessee
WDIC Clinchco, Virginia
WDIG Steubenville, Ohio
WDIS Norfolk, Massachusetts
WDIZ Panama City, Florida
WDJA Delray Beach, Florida
WDJL Huntsville, Alabama
WDJO(AM) Florence, Kentucky
WDJS Mount Olive, North Carolina
WDJZ Bridgeport, Connecticut
WDKD Kingstree, South Carolina
WDKN Dickson, Tennessee
WDLA Walton, New York
WDLB Marshfield, Wisconsin
WDLC Port Jervis, New York
WDLK Dadeville, Alabama
WDLM East Moline, Illinois
WDLR Delaware, Ohio
WDLS Wisconsin Dells, Wisconsin
WDLW Lorain, Ohio
WDLX Washington, North Carolina
WDMC Melbourne, Florida
WDMG Douglas, Georgia
WDMJ Marquette, Michigan
WDMP Dodgeville, Wisconsin
WDMV Walkersville, Maryland
WDNC Durham, North Carolina
WDND South Bend, Indiana
WDNE Elkins, West Virginia
WDNG Anniston, Alabama
WDNO Quebradillas, Puerto Rico
WDNT Dayton, Tennessee
WDNY Dansville, New York
WDOC Prestonsburg, Kentucky
WDOE Dunkirk, New York
WDOG Barnwell, South Carolina
WDOR Sturgeon Bay, Wisconsin
WDOS Oneonta, New York
WDOV Dover, Delaware
WDPC Dallas, Georgia
WDPN Alliance, Ohio
WDQN Duquoin, Illinois
WDRC Hartford, Connecticut
WDRJ Inkster, Michigan
WDRU Creedmore, North Carolina
WDSC Dillon, South Carolina
WDSL Mocksville, North Carolina
WDSM Superior, Wisconsin
WDSP De Funiak Springs, Florida
WDSR Lake City, Florida
WDTK Detroit, Michigan
WDTM Selmer, Tennessee
WDTW Dearborn, Michigan
WDUN Gainesville, Georgia
WDUR Durham, North Carolina
WDUX Waupaca, Wisconsin
WDUZ Green Bay, Wisconsin
WDVA Danville, Virginia
WDVH Gainesville, Florida
WDVM Eau Claire, Wisconsin
WDWD Atlanta, Georgia
WDWR Pensacola, Florida
WDWS Champaign, Illinois
WDXE Lawrenceburg, Tennessee
WDXI Jackson, Tennessee
WDXL Lexington, Tennessee
WDXQ Cochran, Georgia
WDXR Paducah, Kentucky
WDXY Sumter, South Carolina
WDYN Rossville, Georgia
WDYT Kings Mountain, North Carolina
WDYZ Orlando, Florida
WDZ Decatur, Illinois
WDZY Colonial Heights, Virginia
WEAF Saint Stephen, South Carolina
WEAL Greensboro, North Carolina
WEAQ Chippewa Falls, Wisconsin
WEAV Plattsburgh, New York
WEBC Duluth, Minnesota
WEBJ Brewton, Alabama
WEBO Owego, New York
WEBQ Harrisburg, Illinois
WEBS Calhoun, Georgia
WEBY Milton, Florida
WECK Cheektowaga, New York
WECO Wartburg, Tennessee
WECR Newland, North Carolina
WECU Winterville, North Carolina
WECZ Punxsutawney, Pennsylvania
WEDI Eaton, Ohio
WEDM(AM) Fort Walton Beach, Florida
WEDO McKeesport, Pennsylvania
WEEB Southern Pines, North Carolina
WEED Rocky Mount, North Carolina
WEEF Deerfield, Illinois
WEEI Boston, Massachusetts
WEEN Lafayette, Tennessee
WEEO Shippensburg, Pennsylvania
WEEU Reading, Pennsylvania
WEEX Easton, Pennsylvania
WEFL Tequesta, Florida
WEGA Vega Baja, Puerto Rico
WEGG Rose Hill, North Carolina
WEGI Fort Campbell, Kentucky
WEGO(AM) Winston-Salem, North Carolina
WEGP Presque Isle, Maine
WEHH Elmira Hts-Horsehds, New York
WEIR Weirton, West Virginia
WEIS Centre, Alabama
WEJL Scranton, Pennsylvania
WEKB Elkhorn City, Kentucky
WEKC Williamsburg, Kentucky
WEKG Jackson, Kentucky
WEKO Morovis, Puerto Rico
WEKR Fayetteville, Tennessee
WEKT Elkton, Kentucky
WEKY Richmond, Kentucky
WEKZ Monroe, Wisconsin
WELB Elba, Alabama
WELC Welch, West Virginia
WELD Fisher, West Virginia
WELE Ormond Beach, Florida
WELI New Haven, Connecticut
WELM Elmira, New York
WELO Tupelo, Mississippi
WELP Easley, South Carolina
WELR Roanoke, Alabama
WELS Kinston, North Carolina
WELW Willoughby, Ohio
WELY Ely, Minnesota
WELZ Belzoni, Mississippi
WEMB Erwin, Tennessee
WEMG Camden, New Jersey
WEMJ Laconia, New Hampshire
WEMM Huntington, West Virginia
WENA Yauco, Puerto Rico
WENC Whiteville, North Carolina

WENE Endicott, New York
WENG Englewood, Florida
WENI Corning, New York
WENJ Atlantic City, New Jersey
WENK Union City, Tennessee
WENN Birmingham, Alabama
WENO Nashville, Tennessee
WENR Englewood, Tennessee
WENT Gloversville, New York
WENU South Glen Falls, New York
WENY Elmira, New York
WEOA Evansville, Indiana
WEOK Poughkeepsie, New York
WEOL Elyria, Ohio
WEPG South Pittsburg, Tennessee
WEPM Martinsburg, West Virginia
WEPN New York, New York
WERC Birmingham, Alabama
WERE Cleveland Heights, Ohio
WERH Hamilton, Alabama
WERL Eagle River, Wisconsin
WERT Van Wert, Ohio
WESB Bradford, Pennsylvania
WESO Southbridge, Massachusetts
WESR Onley-Onancock, Virginia
WEST Easton, Pennsylvania
WESX Nahant, Massachusetts
WESY Leland, Mississippi
WETB Johnson City, Tennessee
WETC Wendell-Zebulon, North Carolina
WETR Knoxville, Tennessee
WETZ New Martinsville, West Virginia
WEUP Huntsville, Alabama
WEUV Moulton, Alabama
WEVA Emporia, Virginia
WEVG Evergreen, Alabama
WEVR River Falls, Wisconsin
WEW St. Louis, Missouri
WEWC Callahan, Florida
WEWO Laurinburg, North Carolina
WEXL Royal Oak, Michigan
WEXS Patillas, Puerto Rico
WEXY Wilton Manors, Florida
WEZE Boston, Massachusetts
WEZO Augusta, Georgia
WEZR Lewiston, Maine
WEZS Laconia, New Hampshire
WEZZ Brantley, Alabama
WFAB Ceiba, Puerto Rico
WFAD Middlebury, Vermont
WFAI Salem, New Jersey
WFAM Augusta, Georgia
WFAN New York, New York
WFAS White Plains, New York
WFAU Gardiner, Maine
WFAW Fort Atkinson, Wisconsin
WFAX Falls Church, Virginia
WFAY Fayetteville, North Carolina
WFBG Altoona, Pennsylvania
WFBL Syracuse, New York
WFBR Glen Burnie, Maryland
WFBX Spring Lake, North Carolina
WFCM Smyrna, Tennessee
WFCV Fort Wayne, Indiana
WFDF Farmington Hills, Michigan
WFDL Waupun, Wisconsin
WFDR Manchester, Georgia
WFEA Manchester, New Hampshire
WFEB Sylacauga, Alabama
WFED Washington, District of Columbia
WFER Iron River, Michigan
WFFF Columbia, Mississippi
WFFG Marathon, Florida
WFFX(AM) East St. Louis, Illinois
WFGL Fitchburg, Massachusetts
WFGN Gaffney, South Carolina
WFGW Black Mountain, North Carolina
WFHG Bristol, Virginia
WFHK Pell City, Alabama
WFHR Wisconsin Rapids, Wisconsin
WFHT Avon Park, Florida
WFIA Louisville, Kentucky
WFIC Collinsville, Virginia
WFIF Milford, Connecticut
WFIL Philadelphia, Pennsylvania
WFIN Findlay, Ohio
WFIR Roanoke, Virginia
WFIS Fountain Inn, South Carolina
WFIW Fairfield, Illinois
WFJS Trenton, New Jersey
WFJX Roanoke, Virginia
WFKJ Cashtown, Pennsylvania
WFKN Franklin, Kentucky
WFLA Tampa, Florida
WFLE Flemingsburg, Kentucky
WFLF Pine Hills, Florida
WFLI Lookout Mountain, Tennessee
WFLL Fort Lauderdale, Florida
WFLN Arcadia, Florida
WFLO Farmville, Virginia
WFLR Dundee, New York
WFLT Flint, Michigan
WFLW Monticello, Kentucky
WFMB Springfield, Illinois
WFMC Goldsboro, North Carolina
WFMD Frederick, Maryland
WFMH Cullman, Alabama
WFMO Fairmont, North Carolina
WFMW Madisonville, Kentucky
WFNC Fayetteville, North Carolina
WFNI Indianapolis, Indiana
WFNL Raleigh, North Carolina
WFNN Erie, Pennsylvania
WFNO Norco, Louisiana
WFNR Blacksburg, Virginia
WFNS Blackshear, Georgia
WFNT Flint, Michigan
WFNW Naugatuck, Connecticut
WFNX Coral Springs, Florida
WFNY Gloversville, New York
WFNZ Charlotte, North Carolina
WFOB Fostoria, Ohio
WFOM Marietta, Georgia
WFOR Hattiesburg, Mississippi
WFOY St. Augustine, Florida
WFPA Fort Payne, Alabama
WFPB Orleans, Massachusetts
WFPR Hammond, Louisiana
WFQY Brandon, Mississippi
WFRA Franklin, Pennsylvania
WFRB Frostburg, Maryland
WFRF Tallahassee, Florida
WFRL Freeport, Illinois
WFRM Coudersport, Pennsylvania
WFRX West Frankfort, Illinois
WFSC Franklin, North Carolina
WFSI Baltimore, Maryland
WFSP Kingwood, West Virginia
WFSR Harlan, Kentucky
WFST Caribou, Maine
WFTD Marietta, Georgia
WFTG London, Kentucky
WFTH Richmond, Virginia
WFTL West Palm Beach, Florida
WFTM Maysville, Kentucky
WFTN Franklin, New Hampshire
WFTR Front Royal, Virginia
WFTU Riverhead, New York
WFTW Fort Walton Beach, Florida
WFUN Ashtabula, Ohio
WFUR Grand Rapids, Michigan
WFVA Fredericksburg, Virginia
WFWL Camden, Tennessee
WFXH(AM) Hilton Head Island, South Carolina
WFXJ Jacksonville, Florida
WFXN Moline, Illinois
WFXY Middlesboro, Kentucky
WFYC Alma, Michigan
WFYL King of Prussia, Pennsylvania
WGAB Newburgh, Indiana
WGAC Augusta, Georgia
WGAD Gadsden, Alabama
WGAI Elizabeth City, North Carolina
WGAM Manchester, New Hampshire
WGAM(AM) Manchester, New Hampshire
WGAN Portland, Maine
WGAP Maryville, Tennessee
WGAS South Gastonia, North Carolina
WGAT Gate City, Virginia
WGAU Athens, Georgia
WGAW Gardner, Massachusetts
WGBB Freeport, New York
WGBF Evansville, Indiana
WGBN New Kensington, Pennsylvania
WGBR Goldsboro, North Carolina
WGBW Denmark, Wisconsin
WGCD Chester, South Carolina
WGCH Greenwich, Connecticut
WGCL Bloomington, Indiana
WGCM Gulfport, Mississippi
WGCR Pisgah Forest, North Carolina
WGCV Cayce, South Carolina
WGDJ Rensselaer, New York
WGDL Lares, Puerto Rico
WGDN Gladwin, Michigan
WGEA Geneva, Alabama
WGEE Superior, Wisconsin
WGEM Quincy, Illinois
WGES St. Petersburg, Florida
WGET Gettysburg, Pennsylvania
WGEZ Beloit, Wisconsin
WGFA Watseka, Illinois
WGFC Floyd, Virginia
WGFP Webster, Massachusetts
WGFS Covington, Georgia
WGFT Campbell, Ohio
WGFY Charlotte, North Carolina
WGGA Gainesville, Georgia
WGGG Gainesville, Florida
WGGH Marion, Illinois
WGGM Chester, Virginia
WGGO Salamanca, New York
WGH Newport News, Virginia
WGHB Farmville, North Carolina
WGHC Clayton, Georgia
WGHC(AM) Clayton, Georgia
WGHM Nashua, New Hampshire
WGHN Grand Haven, Michigan
WGHQ Kingston, New York
WGHT Pompton Lakes, New Jersey
WGIG Brunswick, Georgia
WGIL Galesburg, Illinois
WGIR Manchester, New Hampshire
WGIT Canovanas, Puerto Rico
WGIV Pineville, North Carolina
WGJK Rome, Georgia
WGKA Atlanta, Georgia
WGL Fort Wayne, Indiana
WGLB Elm Grove, Wisconsin
WGLD Manchester Township, Pennsylvania
WGLL Auburn, Indiana
WGLM Greenville, Michigan
WGLR Lancaster, Wisconsin
WGMA Spindale, North Carolina
WGMI Bremen, Georgia
WGML Hinesville, Georgia
WGMN Roanoke, Virginia
WGMP Montgomery, Alabama
WGN(AM) Chicago, Illinois
WGNC Gastonia, North Carolina
WGNQ Bridgeport, Alabama
WGNR Anderson, Indiana
WGNS Murfreesboro, Tennessee
WGNU Granite City, Illinois
WGNY Newburgh, New York
WGNZ Fairborn, Ohio
WGOC Kingsport, Tennessee
WGOD(AM) Charlotte Amalie, Virgin Islands
WGOH Grayson, Kentucky
WGOK Mobile, Alabama
WGOL Russellville, Alabama
WGOP Pocomoke City, Maryland
WGOS High Point, North Carolina
WGOV Valdosta, Georgia
WGOW Chattanooga, Tennessee
WGPA Bethlehem, Pennsylvania
WGPC Albany, Georgia
WGPL Portsmouth, Virginia
WGR Buffalo, New York
WGRA Cairo, Georgia
WGRB Chicago, Illinois
WGRK Jeffersontown, Kentucky
WGRM Greenwood, Mississippi
WGRO Lake City, Florida
WGRP Greenville, Pennsylvania
WGRV Greeneville, Tennessee
WGRY Grayling, Michigan
WGSB Mebane, North Carolina
WGSF Memphis, Tennessee
WGSO New Orleans, Louisiana
WGSP Charlotte, North Carolina
WGST Atlanta, Georgia
WGSV Guntersville, Alabama
WGTA Summerville, Georgia
WGTH Richlands, Virginia
WGTJ Murrayville, Georgia
WGTK Louisville, Kentucky
WGTN Georgetown, South Carolina
WGTO Cassopolis, Michigan
WGUL Dunedin, Florida
WGUN Atlanta, Georgia
WGVA Geneva, New York
WGVL Greenville, South Carolina
WGVM Greenville, Mississippi
WGVS Muskegon, Michigan
WGVU Kentwood, Michigan
WGWM London, Kentucky
WGY Schenectady, New York
WGYM Hammonton, New Jersey
WGYV Greenville, Alabama
WHA Madison, Wisconsin
WHAG Halfway, Maryland
WHAK Rogers City, Michigan
WHAL Phenix City/Columbus, Alabama
WHAM Rochester, New York
WHAN Ashland, Virginia
WHAP Hopewell, Virginia
WHAS Louisville, Kentucky
WHAT Philadelphia, Pennsylvania
WHAW Lost Creek, West Virginia
WHAZ Troy, New York
WHB Kansas City, Missouri
WHBB Selma, Alabama
WHBC Canton, Ohio
WHBE Newburg, Kentucky
WHBG Harrisonburg, Virginia
WHBK Marshall, North Carolina
WHBL Sheboygan, Wisconsin
WHBN Harrodsburg, Kentucky
WHBO Pinellas Park, Florida
WHBQ Memphis, Tennessee
WHBT Tallahassee, Florida
WHBU Anderson, Indiana
WHBY Kimberly, Wisconsin
WHCG Metter, Georgia
WHCO Sparta, Illinois
WHCU Ithaca, New York
WHDD Sharon, Connecticut
WHDL Olean, New York
WHDM McKenzie, Tennessee
WHEE Martinsville, Virginia
WHEN Syracuse, New York
WHEO Stuart, Virginia
WHEP Foley, Alabama
WHFA Poynette, Wisconsin
WHFB Benton Harbor-St. Jo, Michigan
WHFS(AM) Seffner, Florida
WHGB Harrisburg, Pennsylvania
WHGG Kingsport, Tennessee
WHGS Hampton, South Carolina
WHGT Maugansville, Maryland
WHHV Hillsville, Virginia
WHIC Rochester, New York
WHIE Griffin, Georgia
WHIM Coral Gables, Florida
WHIM(AM) Coral Gables, Florida
WHIN Gallatin, Tennessee
WHIO Dayton, Ohio
WHIP Mooresville, North Carolina
WHIR Danville, Kentucky
WHIS Bluefield, West Virginia
WHIT Madison, Wisconsin
WHIY Huntsville, Alabama
WHJA Laurel, Mississippi
WHJB Bedford, Pennsylvania
WHJC Matewan, West Virginia
WHJD Hazlehurst, Georgia
WHJJ Providence, Rhode Island
WHK Cleveland, Ohio
WHKP Hendersonville, North Carolina
WHKT Portsmouth, Virginia
WHKW Cleveland, Ohio
WHKY Hickory, North Carolina
WHKZ Warren, Ohio
WHLD Niagara Falls, New York
WHLI Hempstead, New York
WHLJ(AM) Moultrie, Georgia
WHLL Springfield, Massachusetts
WHLM Bloomsburg, Pennsylvania
WHLN Harlan, Kentucky
WHLO Akron, Ohio
WHLS Port Huron, Michigan
WHLX Marine City, Michigan
WHLY South Bend, Indiana
WHMA Anniston, Alabama
WHMP Northampton, Massachusetts
WHMQ Greenfield, Massachusetts
WHMT(AM) Tullahoma, Tennessee
WHNC Henderson, North Carolina
WHNK Parkersburg, West Virginia
WHNP East Longmeadow, Massachusetts
WHNR Cypress Gardens, Florida
WHNZ Tampa, Florida
WHO Des Moines, Iowa

WHOC Philadelphia, Mississippi
WHOG Hobson City, Alabama
WHOL Allentown, Pennsylvania
WHON Centerville, Indiana
WHOO Kissimmee, Florida
WHOP Hopkinsville, Kentucky
WHOS Decatur, Alabama
WHOW Clinton, Illinois
WHOY Salinas, Puerto Rico
WHP Harrisburg, Pennsylvania
WHPY Clayton, North Carolina
WHRY Hurley, Wisconsin
WHSC Conway, South Carolina
WHSC(AM) Conway, South Carolina
WHSL(AM) Butler, Alabama
WHSM Hayward, Wisconsin
WHSR Pompano Beach, Florida
WHSY Hattiesburg, Mississippi
WHTB Fall River, Massachusetts
WHTC Holland, Michigan
WHTG Eatontown, New Jersey
WHTH Heath, Ohio
WHTK Rochester, New York
WHTX Warren, Ohio
WHTY Riviera Beach, Florida
WHTY(AM) Riviera Beach, Florida
WHUB Cookeville, Tennessee
WHUC Hudson, New York
WHVN Charlotte, North Carolina
WHVO Hopkinsville, Kentucky
WHVR Hanover, Pennsylvania
WHVW Hyde Park, New York
WHWH Princeton, New Jersey
WHYF(AM) Shiremanstown, Pennsylvania
WHYL Carlisle, Pennsylvania
WHYM Lake City, South Carolina
WHYN Springfield, Massachusetts
WHYP(AM) Corry, Pennsylvania
WIAC San Juan, Puerto Rico
WIAM Williamston, North Carolina
WIAN Ishpeming, Michigan
WIBA Madison, Wisconsin
WIBB Macon, Georgia
WIBG Ocean City/Somers Po, New Jersey
WIBH Anna, Illinois
WIBM Jackson, Michigan
WIBR Baton Rouge, Louisiana
WIBS Guayama, Puerto Rico
WIBW Topeka, Kansas
WIBX Utica, New York
WICC Bridgeport, Connecticut
WICH Norwich, Connecticut
WICK Scranton, Pennsylvania
WICO Salisbury, Maryland
WICY Malone, New York
WIDA Carolina, Puerto Rico
WIDG St. Ignace, Michigan
WIDS Russell Springs, Kentucky
WIDU Fayetteville, North Carolina
WIEL Elizabethtown, Kentucky
WIEZ Lewistown, Pennsylvania
WIFA Knoxville, Tennessee
WIFE Connersville, Indiana
WIFI Florence, New Jersey
WIFN Atlanta, Georgia
WIGM Medford, Wisconsin
WIGN Bristol, Tennessee
WIGO Morrow, Georgia
WIHM Taylorville, Illinois
WIIN Ridgeland, Mississippi
WIJD Prichard, Alabama
WIJR Highland, Illinois
WIKE Newport, Vermont
WILB Canton, Ohio
WILC Laurel, Maryland
WILD Boston, Massachusetts
WILE Cambridge, Ohio
WILI Willimantic, Connecticut
WILK Wilkes-Barre, Pennsylvania
WILL Urbana, Illinois
WILM Wilmington, Delaware
WILO Frankfort, Indiana
WILS Lansing, Michigan
WILY Centralia, Illinois
WIMA Lima, Ohio
WIMG Ewing, New Jersey
WIMO Winder, Georgia
WIMS Michigan City, Indiana
WINA Charlottesville, Virginia
WINC Winchester, Virginia
WIND Chicago, Illinois
WINE Brookfield, Connecticut
WING Dayton, Ohio
WINI Murphysboro, Illinois
WINK Pine Island Center, Florida
WINR Binghamton, New York
WINS New York, New York
WINU Shelbyville, Illinois
WINW Canton, Ohio
WINY Putnam, Connecticut
WINZ Miami, Florida
WIOD Miami, Florida
WIOI New Boston, Ohio
WIOL Columbus, Georgia
WION Ionia, Michigan
WIOO Carlisle, Pennsylvania
WIOS Tawas City-East Tawa, Michigan
WIOU Kokomo, Indiana
WIOV Reading, Pennsylvania
WIOZ Pinehurst, North Carolina
WIP Philadelphia, Pennsylvania
WIPC Lake Wales, Florida
WIPR San Juan, Puerto Rico
WIQR Prattville, Alabama
WIRA Fort Pierce, Florida
WIRB Level Plains, Alabama
WIRD Lake Placid, New York
WIRJ Humboldt, Tennessee
WIRL Peoria, Illinois
WIRO Ironton, Ohio
WIRV Irvine, Kentucky
WIRY Plattsburgh, New York
WISA Isabela, Puerto Rico
WISE Asheville, North Carolina
WISK Lawrenceville, Georgia
WISN Milwaukee, Wisconsin
WISO Ponce, Puerto Rico
WISP Doylestown, Pennsylvania
WISR Butler, Pennsylvania
WISS Berlin, Wisconsin
WIST New Orleans, Louisiana
WISW Columbia, South Carolina
WITA Knoxville, Tennessee
WITK Pittston, Pennsylvania
WITM Marion, Virginia
WITS Sebring, Florida
WITZ Jasper, Indiana
WIVV Island of Vieques, Puerto Rico
WIWA St. Cloud, Florida
WIXC Titusville, Florida
WIXE Monroe, North Carolina
WIXI Jasper, Alabama
WIXK New Richmond, Wisconsin
WIXN Dixon, Illinois
WIXT Little Falls, New York
WIYD Palatka, Florida
WIZD Neon, Kentucky
WIZE Springfield, Ohio
WIZK Bay Springs, Mississippi
WIZM La Crosse, Wisconsin
WIZR Johnstown, New York
WIZS Henderson, North Carolina
WIZZ Greenfield, Massachusetts
WJAG Norfolk, Nebraska
WJAK Jackson, Tennessee
WJAM Selma, Alabama
WJAS Pittsburgh, Pennsylvania
WJAT Swainsboro, Georgia
WJAW St. Marys, West Virginia
WJAX Jacksonville, Florida
WJAY Mullins, South Carolina
WJBC Bloomington, Illinois
WJBD Salem, Illinois
WJBI Batesville, Mississippi
WJBM Jerseyville, Illinois
WJBO Baton Rouge, Louisiana
WJBS Holly Hill, South Carolina
WJBW Jupiter, Florida
WJBY Rainbow City, Alabama
WJCM Sebring, Florida
WJCP North Vernon, Indiana
WJCV Jacksonville, North Carolina
WJCW Johnson City, Tennessee
WJDA Quincy, Massachusetts
WJDB Thomasville, Alabama
WJDJ Hartsville, South Carolina
WJDM Elizabeth, New Jersey
WJDX Jackson, Mississippi
WJDY Salisbury, Maryland
WJEH Gallipolis, Ohio
WJEJ Hagerstown, Maryland
WJEM Valdosta, Georgia
WJER Dover-New Philadelphia, Ohio
WJET Erie, Pennsylvania
WJFC Jefferson City, Tennessee
WJFJ Tryon, North Carolina
WJHX Lexington, Alabama
WJIB Cambridge, Massachusetts
WJIL Jacksonville, Illinois
WJIM Lansing, Michigan
WJIP Ellenville, New York
WJIT Sabana, Puerto Rico
WJJC Commerce, Georgia
WJJG Elmhurst, Illinois
WJJL Niagara Falls, New York
WJJM Lewisburg, Tennessee
WJJQ Tomahawk, Wisconsin
WJJT Jellico, Tennessee
WJKB Moncks Corner, South Carolina
WJKN Jackson, Michigan
WJKY Jamestown, Kentucky
WJLD(AM) Fairfield, Alabama
WJLE Smithville, Tennessee
WJLG Savannah, Georgia
WJLS Beckley, West Virginia
WJLX Jasper, Alabama
WJMC Rice Lake, Wisconsin
WJML Petoskey, Michigan
WJMO Cleveland, Ohio
WJMP Kent, Ohio
WJMS Ironwood, Michigan
WJMT Merrill, Wisconsin
WJMX Florence, South Carolina
WJNC Jacksonville, North Carolina
WJNL Kingsley, Michigan
WJNO West Palm Beach, Florida
WJNT Pearl, Mississippi
WJNX Fort Pierce, Florida
WJOB Hammond, Indiana
WJOC Chattanooga, Tennessee
WJOE Lake City, Florida
WJOI Norfolk, Virginia
WJOK Kaukauna, Wisconsin
WJOL Joliet, Illinois
WJON St. Cloud, Minnesota
WJOT Wabash, Indiana
WJOY Burlington, Vermont
WJPA Washington, Pennsylvania
WJPF Herrin, Illinois
WJQS Jackson, Mississippi
WJR Detroit, Michigan
WJRD Tuscaloosa, Alabama
WJRI Lenoir, North Carolina
WJRM Troy, North Carolina
WJSA Jersey Shore, Pennsylvania
WJSB Crestview, Florida
WJSS Havre De Grace, Maryland
WJST New Castle, Pennsylvania
WJTB North Ridgeville, Ohio
WJTH Calhoun, Georgia
WJTI West Allis, Wisconsin
WJTN Jamestown, New York
WJTO Bath, Maine
WJTP Lithia Springs, Georgia
WJUB Plymouth, Wisconsin
WJUL Hiawassee, Georgia
WJUN Mexico, Pennsylvania
WJUS Marion, Alabama
WJWF Columbus, Mississippi
WJWK Seaford, Delaware
WJWL Georgetown, Delaware
WJXL Jacksonville Beach, Florida
WJYI Milwaukee, Wisconsin
WJYK Chase City, Virginia
WJYM Bowling Green, Ohio
WJYP St. Albans, West Virginia
WJYZ Albany, Georgia
WJZ Baltimore, Maryland
WJZI Decatur, Indiana
WJZI(AM) Decatur, Indiana
WJZM Clarksville, Tennessee
WJZN Augusta, Maine
WKAC Athens, Alabama
WKAL Rome, New York
WKAM Goshen, Indiana
WKAN Kankakee, Illinois
WKAQ San Juan, Puerto Rico
WKAR East Lansing, Michigan
WKAT North Miami, Florida
WKAV Charlottesville, Virginia
WKAX Russellville, Alabama
WKAZ Charleston, West Virginia
WKBA Vinton, Virginia
WKBC North Wilkesboro, North Carolina
WKBF Rock Island, Illinois
WKBH Holmen, Wisconsin
WKBI St. Marys, Pennsylvania
WKBK Keene, New Hampshire
WKBL Covington, Tennessee
WKBN Youngstown, Ohio
WKBO Harrisburg, Pennsylvania
WKBV Richmond, Indiana
WKBY Chatham, Virginia
WKBZ Muskegon, Michigan
WKCB Hindman, Kentucky
WKCE Maryville, Tennessee
WKCI Waynesboro, Virginia
WKCM Hawesville, Kentucky
WKCT Bowling Green, Kentucky
WKCU Corinth, Mississippi
WKCW Warrenton, Virginia
WKCY Harrisonburg, Virginia
WKDA Lebanon, Tennessee
WKDE Altavista, Virginia
WKDG Sumiton, Alabama
WKDI Denton, Maryland
WKDK Newberry, South Carolina
WKDL Warrenton, Virginia
WKDM New York, New York
WKDO Liberty, Kentucky
WKDP Corbin, Kentucky
WKDR Berlin, New Hampshire
WKDV Manassas, Virginia
WKDW Staunton, Virginia
WKDX Hamlet, North Carolina
WKDZ Cadiz, Kentucky
WKEI Kewanee, Illinois
WKEU Griffin, Georgia
WKEW Greensboro, North Carolina
WKEX Blacksburg, Virginia
WKEY Covington, Virginia
WKEZ Bluefield, West Virginia
WKFB Jeannette, Pennsylvania
WKFE Yauco, Puerto Rico
WKFI Wilmington, Ohio
WKFL Bushnell, Florida
WKFN Clarksville, Tennessee
WKGC Southport, Florida
WKGE Johnstown, Pennsylvania
WKGM Smithfield, Virginia
WKGN Knoxville, Tennessee
WKGX Lenoir, North Carolina
WKHB Irwin, Pennsylvania
WKHM Jackson, Michigan
WKHZ Easton, Maryland
WKIC(AM) Hazard, Kentucky
WKII Solana, Florida
WKIK La Plata, Maryland
WKIP Poughkeepsie, New York
WKIQ Eustis, Florida
WKIZ Key West, Florida
WKJB Mayaguez, Puerto Rico
WKJG Fort Wayne, Indiana
WKJK Louisville, Kentucky
WKJR Rantoul, Illinois
WKKP McDonough, Georgia
WKKS Vanceburg, Kentucky
WKKX Wheeling, West Virginia
WKLA Ludington, Michigan
WKLB Manchester, Kentucky
WKLJ Sparta, Wisconsin
WKLK Cloquet, Minnesota
WKLP Keyser, West Virginia
WKLQ Whitehall, Michigan
WKLV Blackstone, Virginia
WKLY Hartwell, Georgia
WKMB Stirling, New Jersey
WKMC Roaring Spring, Pennsylvania
WKMG Newberry, South Carolina
WKMI Kalamazoo, Michigan
WKMQ Tupelo, Mississippi
WKND Windsor, Connecticut
WKNG Tallapoosa, Georgia
WKNR Cleveland, Ohio
WKNV Fairlawn, Virginia
WKNW Sault Sainte Marie, Michigan
WKNY Kingston, New York
WKOK Sunbury, Pennsylvania
WKOR Starkville, Mississippi
WKOX Everett, Massachusetts
WKPA Lynchburg, Virginia
WKPR Kalamazoo, Michigan
WKPT Kingsport, Tennessee
WKQW Oil City, Pennsylvania

WKRA Holly Springs, Mississippi
WKRC Cincinnati, Ohio
WKRD Louisville, Kentucky
WKRK Murphy, North Carolina
WKRM Columbia, Tennessee
WKRO Cairo, Illinois
WKRS Waukegan, Illinois
WKSC Kershaw, South Carolina
WKSH Sussex, Wisconsin
WKSK West Jefferson, North Carolina
WKSN Jamestown, New York
WKSR Pulaski, Tennessee
WKST New Castle, Pennsylvania
WKTA Evanston, Illinois
WKTE King, North Carolina
WKTF Vienna, Georgia
WKTI Powell, Tennessee
WKTP Jonesborough, Tennessee
WKTQ South Paris, Maine
WKTR Earlysville, Virginia
WKTX Cortland, Ohio
WKTY La Crosse, Wisconsin
WKUN Monroe, Georgia
WKVA Lewistown, Pennsylvania
WKVG Jenkins, Kentucky
WKVI Knox, Indiana
WKVL Knoxville, Tennessee
WKVM San Juan, Puerto Rico
WKVQ Eatonton, Georgia
WKVT Brattleboro, Vermont
WKVX Wooster, Ohio
WKWF Key West, Florida
WKWL Florala, Alabama
WKWN Trenton, Georgia
WKXG Greenwood, Mississippi
WKXL Concord, New Hampshire
WKXM Winfield, Alabama
WKXO Berea, Kentucky
WKXR Asheboro, North Carolina
WKXV Knoxville, Tennessee
WKY Oklahoma City, Oklahoma
WKYH Paintsville, Kentucky
WKYK Burnsville, North Carolina
WKYO Caro, Michigan
WKYW Frankfort, Kentucky
WKYX Paducah, Kentucky
WKZD Priceville, Alabama
WKZI Casey, Illinois
WKZK North Augusta, South Carolina
WKZN West Hazleton, Pennsylvania
WKZO Kalamazoo, Michigan
WKZV Washington, Pennsylvania
WLAA Winter Garden, Florida
WLAC Nashville, Tennessee
WLAD Danbury, Connecticut
WLAF La Follette, Tennessee
WLAG La Grange, Georgia
WLAM Lewiston, Maine
WLAN Lancaster, Pennsylvania
WLAP Lexington, Kentucky
WLAQ Rome, Georgia
WLAR Athens, Tennessee
WLAT New Britain, Connecticut
WLAY Muscle Shoals, Alabama
WLBA Gainesville, Georgia
WLBB Carrollton, Georgia
WLBE Leesburg-Eustis, Florida
WLBG Laurens, South Carolina
WLBH Mattoon, Illinois
WLBK Dekalb, Illinois
WLBL Auburndale, Wisconsin
WLBN Lebanon, Kentucky
WLBQ Morgantown, Kentucky
WLBR Lebanon, Pennsylvania
WLBY Saline, Michigan
WLCC Brandon, Florida
WLCK Scottsville, Kentucky
WLCM Holt, Michigan
WLCO Lapeer, Michigan
WLCR Mt Washington, Kentucky
WLDS Jacksonville, Illinois
WLDX Fayette, Alabama
WLDY Ladysmith, Wisconsin
WLEA Hornell, New York
WLEC Sandusky, Ohio
WLEE Richmond, Virginia
WLEM Emporium, Pennsylvania
WLEO Ponce, Puerto Rico
WLES Bon Air, Virginia
WLEW Bad Axe, Michigan
WLEY Cayey, Puerto Rico

WLFJ Greenville, South Carolina
WLFN La Crosse, Wisconsin
WLFP Braddock, Pennsylvania
WLFP(AM) Braddock, Pennsylvania
WLGC Greenup, Kentucky
WLGN Logan, Ohio
WLIB New York, New York
WLIE Islip, New York
WLIJ Shelbyville, Tennessee
WLIK Newport, Tennessee
WLIL Lenoir City, Tennessee
WLIM Patchogue, New York
WLIP Kenosha, Wisconsin
WLIQ Quincy, Illinois
WLIS Old Saybrook, Connecticut
WLIV Livingston, Tennessee
WLJN Elmwood Township, Michigan
WLJW Cadillac, Michigan
WLKD Minocqua, Wisconsin
WLKF Lakeland, Florida
WLKR Norwalk, Ohio
WLKS West Liberty, Kentucky
WLKW West Warwick, Rhode Island
WLLH Lowell, Massachusetts
WLLI Huntingdon, Pennsylvania
WLLI(AM) Huntingdon, Pennsylvania
WLLL Lynchburg, Virginia
WLLM Lincoln, Illinois
WLLN Lillington, North Carolina
WLLQ Chapel Hill, North Carolina
WLLV Louisville, Kentucky
WLLY Wilson, North Carolina
WLMC Georgetown, South Carolina
WLMR Chattanooga, Tennessee
WLMV Madison, Wisconsin
WLNC Laurinburg, North Carolina
WLNL Horseheads, New York
WLNO New Orleans, Louisiana
WLNR Kinston, North Carolina
WLOA Farrell, Pennsylvania
WLOB Portland, Maine
WLOC Munfordville, Kentucky
WLOD Loudon, Tennessee
WLOE Eden, North Carolina
WLOH Lancaster, Ohio
WLOI La Porte, Indiana
WLOK Memphis, Tennessee
WLOL Minneapolis, Minnesota
WLON Lincolnton, North Carolina
WLOP Jesup, Georgia
WLOR Huntsville, Alabama
WLOU Louisville, Kentucky
WLOV Washington, Georgia
WLOY Rural Retreat, Virginia
WLPA Lancaster, Pennsylvania
WLPO Lasalle, Illinois
WLPR Prichard, Alabama
WLQH Chiefland, Florida
WLQM Franklin, Virginia
WLQR Toledo, Ohio
WLQV Detroit, Michigan
WLQY Hollywood, Florida
WLRB Macomb, Illinois
WLRC Walnut, Mississippi
WLRM Millington, Tennessee
WLRO Denham Springs, Louisiana
WLRP San Sebastian, Puerto Rico
WLRV Lebanon, Virginia
WLS Chicago, Illinois
WLSB Copper Hill, Tennessee
WLSC Loris, South Carolina
WLSD Big Stone Gap, Virginia
WLSG Wilmington, North Carolina
WLSH Lansford, Pennsylvania
WLSI Pikeville, Kentucky
WLSS Sarasota, Florida
WLSV Wellsville, New York
WLTA Alpharetta, Georgia
WLTG Panama City, Florida
WLTH Gary, Indiana
WLTI(AM) New Castle, Indiana
WLTN Littleton, New Hampshire
WLTP Marietta, Ohio
WLTQ Charleston, South Carolina
WLUE Eminence, Kentucky
WLUV Loves Park, Illinois
WLUX Dunbar, West Virginia
WLVA Lynchburg, Virginia
WLVJ Boynton Beach, Florida
WLVL Lockport, New York
WLVP Gorham, Maine

WLW Cincinnati, Ohio
WLWB New Holstein, Wisconsin
WLWI Montgomery, Alabama
WLWL Rockingham, North Carolina
WLXE Rockville, Maryland
WLXG Lexington, Kentucky
WLXN Lexington, North Carolina
WLYC Williamsport, Pennsylvania
WLYN Lynn, Massachusetts
WLYV Fort Wayne, Indiana
WLZR(AM) Melbourne, Florida
WMAC Macon, Georgia
WMAF Madison, Florida
WMAL Washington, District of Columbia
WMAM Marinette, Wisconsin
WMAN Mansfield, Ohio
WMAX Bay City, Michigan
WMAY Springfield, Illinois
WMBA Ambridge, Pennsylvania
WMBD Peoria, Illinois
WMBG Williamsburg, Virginia
WMBH Joplin, Missouri
WMBI Chicago, Illinois
WMBM Miami Beach, Florida
WMBN Petoskey, Michigan
WMBS Uniontown, Pennsylvania
WMC Memphis, Tennessee
WMCA New York, New York
WMCH Church Hill, Tennessee
WMCJ Cullman, Alabama
WMCL McLeansboro, Illinois
WMCP Columbia, Tennessee
WMCR Oneida, New York
WMCS Greenfield, Wisconsin
WMCT Mountain City, Tennessee
WMDB Nashville, Tennessee
WMDD Fajardo, Puerto Rico
WMDR Augusta, Maine
WMEL Cocoa Beach, Florida
WMEN Royal Palm Beach, Florida
WMEQ Menomonie, Wisconsin
WMER Meridian, Mississippi
WMET Gaithersburg, Maryland
WMFA Raeford, North Carolina
WMFC(AM) Monroeville, Alabama
WMFD Wilmington, North Carolina
WMFG Hibbing, Minnesota
WMFJ Daytona Beach, Florida
WMFN Zeeland, Michigan
WMFR High Point, North Carolina
WMGC Murfreesboro, Tennessee
WMGG Egypt Lake, Florida
WMGJ Gadsden, Alabama
WMGO Canton, Mississippi
WMGR Bainbridge, Georgia
WMGW Meadville, Pennsylvania
WMGY Montgomery, Alabama
WMIA Arecibo, Puerto Rico
WMIC Sandusky, Michigan
WMID Atlantic City, New Jersey
WMIK Middlesboro, Kentucky
WMIN Sauk Rapids, Minnesota
WMIQ Iron Mountain, Michigan
WMIR Atlantic Beach, South Carolina
WMIS Natchez, Mississippi
WMIX Mount Vernon, Illinois
WMIZ Vineland, New Jersey
WMJH Rockford, Michigan
WMJL Marion, Kentucky
WMJR Nicholasville, Kentucky
WMKI Boston, Massachusetts
WMKT Charlevoix, Michigan
WMLB Avondale Estates, Georgia
WMLC Monticello, Mississippi
WMLM St. Louis, Michigan
WMLP Milton, Pennsylvania
WMLR Hohenwald, Tennessee
WMLT Dublin, Georgia
WMMB Melbourne, Florida
WMMG Brandenburg, Kentucky
WMMI Shepherd, Michigan
WMML Glens Falls, New York
WMMN Fairmont, West Virginia
WMMV Cocoa, Florida
WMMW Meriden, Connecticut
WMNA Gretna, Virginia
WMNC Morganton, North Carolina
WMNI Columbus, Ohio
WMNT Manati, Puerto Rico
WMNY McKeesport, Pennsylvania
WMNZ Montezuma, Georgia

WMOA Marietta, Ohio
WMOB Mobile, Alabama
WMOG Brunswick, Georgia
WMOH Hamilton, Ohio
WMOK Metropolis, Illinois
WMON Montgomery, West Virginia
WMOP Ocala, Florida
WMOR Morehead, Kentucky
WMOU Berlin, New Hampshire
WMOV Ravenswood, West Virginia
WMOX Meridian, Mississippi
WMPC Lapeer, Michigan
WMPL Hancock, Michigan
WMPM Smithfield, North Carolina
WMPO Middleport-Pomeroy, Ohio
WMPS Bartlett, Tennessee
WMPW Danville, Virginia
WMPX Midland, Michigan
WMQM Lakeland, Tennessee
WMRB Columbia, Tennessee
WMRC Milford, Massachusetts
WMRD Middletown, Connecticut
WMRE Charlestown, West Virginia
WMRI Marion, Indiana
WMRN Marion, Ohio
WMRO Gallatin, Tennessee
WMSA Massena, New York
WMSG Oakland, Maryland
WMSK Morganfield, Kentucky
WMSP Montgomery, Alabama
WMSR Manchester, Tennessee
WMST Mt. Sterling, Kentucky
WMSW Hatillo, Puerto Rico
WMSX Brockton, Massachusetts
WMT Cedar Rapids, Iowa
WMTA Central City, Kentucky
WMTC Vancleve, Kentucky
WMTD Hinton, West Virginia
WMTE Manistee, Michigan
WMTL Leitchfield, Kentucky
WMTM Moultrie, Georgia
WMTN Morristown, Tennessee
WMTR Morristown, New Jersey
WMTY Farragut, Tennessee
WMUX Hurricane, West Virginia
WMVA Martinsville, Virginia
WMVB Millville, New Jersey
WMVG Milledgeville, Georgia
WMVO Mount Vernon, Ohio
WMVP Chicago, Illinois
WMXB Tuscaloosa, Alabama
WMXF Waynesville, North Carolina
WMYF Portsmouth, New Hampshire
WMYJ Martinsville, Indiana
WMYM Miami, Florida
WMYN Mayodan, North Carolina
WMYR Fort Myers, Florida
WNAE Warren, Pennsylvania
WNAH Nashville, Tennessee
WNAM Neenah-Menasha, Wisconsin
WNAP Norristown, Pennsylvania
WNAT Natchez, Mississippi
WNAU New Albany, Mississippi
WNAV Annapolis, Maryland
WNAW North Adams, Massachusetts
WNAX Yankton, South Dakota
WNBF Binghamton, New York
WNBH New Bedford, Massachusetts
WNBN Meridian, Mississippi
WNBP Newburyport, Massachusetts
WNBS Murray, Kentucky
WNBT Wellsboro, Pennsylvania
WNBY Newberry, Michigan
WNBZ Saranac Lake, New York
WNCA Siler City, North Carolina
WNCC Barnesboro, Pennsylvania
WNCO Ashland, Ohio
WNCT Greenville, North Carolina
WNDA New Albany, Indiana
WNDB Daytona Beach, Florida
WNDE Indianapolis, Indiana
WNDI Sullivan, Indiana
WNDZ Portage, Indiana
WNEA Newnan, Georgia
WNEB Worcester, Massachusetts
WNED Buffalo, New York
WNEG Toccoa, Georgia
WNEL Caguas, Puerto Rico
WNEM Bridgeport, Michigan
WNER Watertown, New York
WNES Central City, Kentucky

WNEW Morningside, Maryland
WNEX Macon, Georgia
WNEZ Manchester, Connecticut
WNFL Green Bay, Wisconsin
WNFO Sun City-Hilton Head, South Carolina
WNGL Mobile, Alabama
WNGO Mayfield, Kentucky
WNIK Arecibo, Puerto Rico
WNIL Niles, Michigan
WNIO Youngstown, Ohio
WNIS Norfolk, Virginia
WNIV Atlanta, Georgia
WNIX Greenville, Mississippi
WNJC Vineland, New Jersey
WNJE Flemington, New Jersey
WNKX Lobelville, Tennessee
WNLA Indianola, Mississippi
WNLK Norwalk, Connecticut
WNLR Churchville, Virginia
WNLS Tallahassee, Florida
WNMA Miami Springs, Florida
WNMB North Myrtle Beach, South Carolina
WNML Knoxville, Tennessee
WNMT Nashwauk, Minnesota
WNNC Newton, North Carolina
WNNR Jacksonville, Florida
WNNW Lawrence, Massachusetts
WNNZ Westfield, Massachusetts
WNOG Naples, Florida
WNOO Chattanooga, Tennessee
WNOP Newport, Kentucky
WNOS New Bern, North Carolina
WNOV Milwaukee, Wisconsin
WNOW Mint Hill, North Carolina
WNPL Golden Gate, Florida
WNPV Lansdale, Pennsylvania
WNPZ Knoxville, Tennessee
WNQM Nashville, Tennessee
WNRA Eufaula, Alabama
WNRG Grundy, Virginia
WNRI Woonsocket, Rhode Island
WNRP Gulf Breeze, Florida
WNRR North Augusta, South Carolina
WNRS Herkimer, New York
WNRV Narrows-Pearisburg, Virginia
WNSH Beverly, Massachusetts
WNSR Brentwood, Tennessee
WNST Towson, Maryland
WNSW Newark, New Jersey
WNTA Rockford, Illinois
WNTD Chicago, Illinois
WNTF Bithlo, Florida
WNTJ Johnstown, Pennsylvania
WNTM Mobile, Alabama
WNTN Newton, Massachusetts
WNTP Philadelphia, Pennsylvania
WNTS Beech Grove, Indiana
WNTT Tazewell, Tennessee
WNTW Somerset, Pennsylvania
WNTX Fredericksburg, Virginia
WNVA Norton, Virginia
WNVL Nashville, Tennessee
WNVR Vernon Hills, Illinois
WNVY Cantonment, Florida
WNWC Sun Prairie, Wisconsin
WNWF Destin, Florida
WNWI Oak Lawn, Illinois
WNWN Portage, Michigan
WNWR Philadelphia, Pennsylvania
WNWS Brownsville, Tennessee
WNWT Rossford, Ohio
WNWZ Grand Rapids, Michigan
WNXT Portsmouth, Ohio
WNYC New York, New York
WNYG Medford, New York
WNYH Huntington, New York
WNYM Hackensack, New Jersey
WNYY Ithaca, New York
WNZF Bunnell, Florida
WNZK Dearborn Heights, Michigan
WNZS Veazie, Maine
WNZZ Montgomery, Alabama
WOAD Jackson, Mississippi
WOAI San Antonio, Texas
WOAM Peoria, Illinois
WOAP Owosso, Michigan
WOAY Oak Hill, West Virginia
WOBL Oberlin, Ohio
WOBM Lakewood Township, New Jersey
WOBT Rhinelander, Wisconsin
WOBX Wanchese, North Carolina
WOC Davenport, Iowa
WOCA Ocala, Florida
WOCC Corydon, Indiana
WOCN Miami, Florida
WOCO Oconto, Wisconsin
WOCV Oneida, Tennessee
WODI Brookneal, Virginia
WODJ Big Rapids, Michigan
WODT New Orleans, Louisiana
WODY Fieldale, Virginia
WOEG Hazlehurst, Mississippi
WOEN Olean, New York
WOFC Murray, Kentucky
WOFX Troy, New York
WOGO Hallie, Wisconsin
WOGR Charlotte, North Carolina
WOHI East Liverpool, Ohio
WOHS Shelby, North Carolina
WOI Ames, Iowa
WOIC Columbia, South Carolina
WOIR Homestead, Florida
WOIZ Guayanilla, Puerto Rico
WOKA Douglas, Georgia
WOKB Winter Garden, Florida
WOKC Okeechobee, Florida
WOKS Columbus, Georgia
WOKY Milwaukee, Wisconsin
WOL Washington, District of Columbia
WOLA Barranquitas, Puerto Rico
WOLB Baltimore, Maryland
WOLF Syracuse, New York
WOLH Florence, South Carolina
WOLI Spartanburg, South Carolina
WOMI Owensboro, Kentucky
WOMN Franklinton, Louisiana
WOMP Bellaire, Ohio
WOMT Manitowoc, Wisconsin
WONA Winona, Mississippi
WOND Pleasantville, New Jersey
WONE Dayton, Ohio
WONG Canton, Mississippi
WONN Lakeland, Florida
WONQ Oviedo, Florida
WONW Defiance, Ohio
WOOD Grand Rapids, Michigan
WOOF Dothan, Alabama
WOON Woonsocket, Rhode Island
WOPI Bristol, Tennessee
WOPP Opp, Alabama
WOQI Adjuntas, Puerto Rico
WOR New York, New York
WORA Mayaguez, Puerto Rico
WORC Worcester, Massachusetts
WORD Spartanburg, South Carolina
WORL Altamonte Springs, Florida
WORM Savannah, Tennessee
WORV Hattiesburg, Mississippi
WOSH Oshkosh, Wisconsin
WOSO San Juan, Puerto Rico
WOSW Fulton, New York
WOTE Clintonville, Wisconsin
WOTS Kissimmee, Florida
WOUB Athens, Ohio
WOWO Fort Wayne, Indiana
WOWW Germantown, Tennessee
WOWZ Appomattox, Virginia
WOYK York, Pennsylvania
WOZK Ozark, Alabama
WPAB Ponce, Puerto Rico
WPAD Paducah, Kentucky
WPAK Farmville, Virginia
WPAM Pottsville, Pennsylvania
WPAQ Mount Airy, North Carolina
WPAT Paterson, New Jersey
WPAX Thomasville, Georgia
WPBC Decatur, Georgia
WPBQ Flowood, Mississippi
WPBR Lantana, Florida
WPBS Conyers, Georgia
WPCC Clinton, South Carolina
WPCE Portsmouth, Virginia
WPCF Panama City Beach, Florida
WPCI Greenville, South Carolina
WPCM Burlington-Graham, North Carolina
WPCN Stevens Point, Wisconsin
WPDC Elizabethtown, Pennsylvania
WPDM Potsdam, New York
WPDR Portage, Wisconsin
WPDX Clarksburg, West Virginia
WPEH Louisville, Georgia
WPEK Fairview, North Carolina
WPEL Montrose, Pennsylvania
WPEN Philadelphia, Pennsylvania
WPEO Peoria, Illinois
WPET Greensboro, North Carolina
WPFB Middletown, Ohio
WPFC Baton Rouge, Louisiana
WPFJ Franklin, North Carolina
WPFP Park Falls, Wisconsin
WPFR Terre Haute, Indiana
WPGA Perry, Georgia
WPGM Danville, Pennsylvania
WPGR Monroeville, Pennsylvania
WPGS Mims, Florida
WPGW Portland, Indiana
WPGY Ellijay, Georgia
WPHB Philipsburg, Pennsylvania
WPHE Phoenixville, Pennsylvania
WPHM Port Huron, Michigan
WPHT Philadelphia, Pennsylvania
WPIC Sharon, Pennsylvania
WPID Piedmont, Alabama
WPIE Trumansburg, New York
WPIN Dublin, Virginia
WPIP Winston-Salem, North Carolina
WPIT Pittsburgh, Pennsylvania
WPJF Greenville, South Carolina
WPJK Orangeburg, South Carolina
WPJL Raleigh, North Carolina
WPJM Greer, South Carolina
WPJS Conway, South Carolina
WPJX Zion, Illinois
WPKE Pikeville, Kentucky
WPKX(AM) Rochester, New Hampshire
WPKY Princeton, Kentucky
WPKZ Fitchburg, Massachusetts
WPLA Dry Branch, Georgia
WPLA(AM) Dry Branch, Georgia
WPLK Palatka, Florida
WPLM Plymouth, Massachusetts
WPLN Madison, Tennessee
WPLO Grayson, Georgia
WPLV West Point, Georgia
WPLY Mount Pocono, Pennsylvania
WPMB Vandalia, Illinois
WPMH Portsmouth, Virginia
WPMO Pascagoula-Moss Point, Mississippi
WPMZ East Providence, Rhode Island
WPNA Oak Park, Illinois
WPNH Plymouth, New Hampshire
WPNI Amherst, Massachusetts
WPNN Pensacola, Florida
WPNW Zeeland, Michigan
WPOG St. Matthews, South Carolina
WPOL Winston-Salem, North Carolina
WPON Walled Lake, Michigan
WPOP Hartford, Connecticut
WPPA Pottsville, Pennsylvania
WPPC Penuelas, Puerto Rico
WPRA Mayaguez, Puerto Rico
WPRD Winter Park, Florida
WPRE Prairie Du Chien, Wisconsin
WPRO Providence, Rhode Island
WPRP Ponce, Puerto Rico
WPRR Ada, Michigan
WPRS Paris, Illinois
WPRT Prestonsburg, Kentucky
WPRV Providence, Rhode Island
WPRX Bristol, Connecticut
WPRY Perry, Florida
WPSE Erie, Pennsylvania
WPSL Port St. Lucie, Florida
WPSN Honesdale, Pennsylvania
WPSO New Port Richey, Florida
WPSP Royal Palm Beach, Florida
WPTB Statesboro, Georgia
WPTF Raleigh, North Carolina
WPTK(AM) Raleigh, North Carolina
WPTL Canton, North Carolina
WPTN Cookeville, Tennessee
WPTR(AM) Schenectady, New York
WPTW Piqua, Ohio
WPTX Lexington Park, Maryland
WPUL South Daytona, Florida
WPUT Brewster, New York
WPVL Platteville, Wisconsin
WPWA Chester, Pennsylvania
WPWC Dumfries-Triangle, Virginia
WPWT Colonial Heights, Tennessee
WPYB Benson, North Carolina
WPYR Baton Rouge, Louisiana
WQAL(AM) Pikesville, Maryland
WQAM Miami, Florida
WQBA Miami, Florida
WQBC Vicksburg, Mississippi
WQBN Temple Terrace, Florida
WQBQ Leesburg, Florida
WQBS San Juan, Puerto Rico
WQCH La Fayette, Georgia
WQCR Alabaster, Alabama
WQCT Bryan, Ohio
WQEW New York, New York
WQFX Gulfport, Mississippi
WQHC Hanceville, Alabama
WQHL Live Oak, Florida
WQII San Juan, Puerto Rico
WQIZ St. George, South Carolina
WQKC Jeffersonville, Indiana
WQKR Portland, Tennessee
WQLA La Follette, Tennessee
WQLX Chillicothe, Ohio
WQMS Quitman, Mississippi
WQMV Waverly, Tennessee
WQNT Charleston, South Carolina
WQOH Irondale, Alabama
WQOM Natick, Massachusetts
WQOP Jacksonville, Florida
WQOR Olyphant, Pennsylvania
WQPM Princeton, Minnesota
WQRX Valley Head, Alabama
WQSC Charleston, South Carolina
WQSE White Bluff, Tennessee
WQST Forest, Mississippi
WQSV Ashland City, Tennessee
WQTM Fair Bluff, North Carolina
WQTT Marysville, Ohio
WQTW Latrobe, Pennsylvania
WQUL Woodruff, South Carolina
WQUL(AM) Woodruff, South Carolina
WQUN Hamden, Connecticut
WQWK(AM) State College, Pennsylvania
WQXI Atlanta, Georgia
WQXL Columbia, South Carolina
WQXM Bartow, Florida
WQXO Munising, Michigan
WQXY Hazard, Kentucky
WQZQ Goodlettsville, Tennessee
WRAA Luray, Virginia
WRAB Arab, Alabama
WRAD Radford, Virginia
WRAK Williamsport, Pennsylvania
WRAM Monmouth, Illinois
WRAR Tappahannock, Virginia
WRAW Reading, Pennsylvania
WRAY Princeton, Indiana
WRBS Baltimore, Maryland
WRBZ Wetumpka, Alabama
WRCA Watertown, Massachusetts
WRCE Watkins Glen, New York
WRCG Columbus, Georgia
WRCI Three Rivers, Michigan
WRCK Remsen, New York
WRCO Richland Center, Wisconsin
WRCR Ramapo, New York
WRCS Ahoskie, North Carolina
WRCY Mt. Vernon, Indiana
WRDB Reedsburg, Wisconsin
WRDD Ebensburg, Pennsylvania
WRDN Durand, Wisconsin
WRDT Monroe, Michigan
WRDW Augusta, Georgia
WRDZ La Grange, Illinois
WREC Memphis, Tennessee
WRED Westbrook, Maine
WREJ Richmond, Virginia
WREL Lexington, Virginia
WREV Reidsville, North Carolina
WREY St. Paul, Minnesota
WRFC Athens, Georgia
WRFD Columbus-Worthington, Ohio
WRFM Muncie, Indiana
WRFV Valdosta, Georgia
WRGA Rome, Georgia
WRGC Sylva, North Carolina
WRGM Ontario, Ohio
WRGS Rogersville, Tennessee
WRHA(AM) Spring City, Tennessee
WRHC Coral Gables, Florida
WRHI Rock Hill, South Carolina
WRHL Rochelle, Illinois
WRIE Erie, Pennsylvania
WRIG Schofield, Wisconsin
WRIN Rensselaer, Indiana

WRIS Roanoke, Virginia
WRIV Riverhead, New York
WRIX Homeland Park, South Carolina
WRJC Mauston, Wisconsin
WRJD Durham, North Carolina
WRJE Dover, Delaware
WRJM(AM) Charleston, Illinois
WRJN Racine, Wisconsin
WRJR Claremont, Virginia
WRJW Picayune, Mississippi
WRJX Jackson, Alabama
WRJZ Knoxville, Tennessee
WRKB Kannapolis, North Carolina
WRKD Rockland, Maine
WRKK Hughesville, Pennsylvania
WRKL New City, New York
WRKM Carthage, Tennessee
WRKO Boston, Massachusetts
WRKQ Madisonville, Tennessee
WRLA West Point, Georgia
WRLL Cicero, Illinois
WRLV Salyersville, Kentucky
WRLZ Eatonville, Florida
WRME Hampden, Maine
WRMG Red Bay, Alabama
WRMN Elgin, Illinois
WRMQ Orlando, Florida
WRMS Beardstown, Illinois
WRMT Rocky Mount, North Carolina
WRNA China Grove, North Carolina
WRNE Gulf Breeze, Florida
WRNI Providence, Rhode Island
WRNJ Hackettstown, New Jersey
WRNL Richmond, Virginia
WRNN Myrtle Beach, South Carolina
WRNR Martinsburg, West Virginia
WRNS Kinston, North Carolina
WRNY Rome, New York
WROA Gulfport, Mississippi
WROC Rochester, New York
WROD Daytona Beach, Florida
WROK Rockford, Illinois
WROL Boston, Massachusetts
WROM Rome, Georgia
WRON Ronceverte, West Virginia
WROP Belton, South Carolina
WROS Jacksonville, Florida
WROW Albany, New York
WROX Clarksdale, Mississippi
WROY Carmi, Illinois
WRPM Poplarville, Mississippi
WRPN Ripon, Wisconsin
WRPQ Baraboo, Wisconsin
WRQR(AM) Paris, Tennessee
WRRD Waukesha, Wisconsin
WRRE Juncos, Puerto Rico
WRRL Rainelle, West Virginia
WRRZ Clinton, North Carolina
WRSA St. Albans, Vermont
WRSB Canandaigua, New York
WRSC State College, Pennsylvania
WRSJ Bayamon, Puerto Rico
WRSL Corbin, Kentucky
WRSO(AM) Orlovista, Florida
WRSS San Sebastian, Puerto Rico
WRSW Warsaw, Indiana
WRTA Altoona, Pennsylvania
WRTG Garner, North Carolina
WRTO Chicago, Illinois
WRUF Gainesville, Florida
WRUS Russellville, Kentucky
WRVA Richmond, Virginia
WRVC Huntington, West Virginia
WRVK Mount Vernon, Kentucky
WRVP Mount Kisco, New York
WRWH Cleveland, Georgia
WRWR Warner Robins, Georgia
WRXB St. Petersburg Beach, Florida
WRXO Roxboro, North Carolina
WRYM New Britain, Connecticut
WRYT Edwardsville, Illinois
WRZN Hernando, Florida
WSAI Cincinnati, Ohio
WSAL Logansport, Indiana
WSAM Saginaw, Michigan
WSAN Allentown, Pennsylvania
WSAO Senatobia, Mississippi
WSAR Fall River, Massachusetts
WSAT Salisbury, North Carolina
WSAU Wausau, Wisconsin
WSB Atlanta, Georgia
WSBA York, Pennsylvania
WSBB New Smyrna Beach, Florida
WSBC Chicago, Illinois
WSBI Static, Tennessee
WSBM Florence, Alabama
WSBR Boca Raton, Florida
WSBS Great Barrington, Massachusetts
WSBT South Bend, Indiana
WSBV South Boston, Virginia
WSBX Ochlocknee, Georgia
WSCO Appleton, Wisconsin
WSCP Sandy Creek-Pulaski, New York
WSCR Chicago, Illinois
WSCW South Charleston, West Virginia
WSDE Cobleskill, New York
WSDK Bloomfield, Connecticut
WSDO Sanford, Florida
WSDQ Dunlap, Tennessee
WSDR Sterling, Illinois
WSDS Salem Township, Michigan
WSDT Soddy-Daisy, Tennessee
WSDV Sarasota, Florida
WSDX Brazil, Indiana
WSDZ Belleville, Illinois
WSEG Savannah, Georgia
WSEL Pontotoc, Mississippi
WSEM Donalsonville, Georgia
WSEN Baldwinsville, New York
WSEV Sevierville, Tennessee
WSEZ Paoli, Indiana
WSFB Quitman, Georgia
WSFC Somerset, Kentucky
WSFE Burnside, Kentucky
WSFM Carolina Beach, North Carolina
WSFN Brunswick, Georgia
WSFW Seneca Falls, New York
WSFZ Jackson, Mississippi
WSGB Sutton, West Virginia
WSGC Elberton, Georgia
WSGH Lewisville, North Carolina
WSGI Springfield, Tennessee
WSGO Oswego, New York
WSGW Saginaw, Michigan
WSHE Columbus, Georgia
WSHO New Orleans, Louisiana
WSHU Westport, Connecticut
WSHV South Hill, Virginia
WSHY Lafayette, Indiana
WSIC Statesville, North Carolina
WSIP Paintsville, Kentucky
WSIR Winter Haven, Florida
WSIV E. Syracuse, New York
WSJC Magee, Mississippi
WSJM St. Joseph, Michigan
WSJS Winston-Salem, North Carolina
WSKI Montpelier, Vermont
WSKN San Juan, Puerto Rico
WSKO Syracuse, New York
WSKW Skowhegan, Maine
WSKY Asheville, North Carolina
WSLA Slidell, Louisiana
WSLB Ogdensburg, New York
WSLK Moneta, Virginia
WSLM Salem, Indiana
WSLW White Sulphur Spring, West Virginia
WSM Nashville, Tennessee
WSME Camp Lejeune, North Carolina
WSMG Greeneville, Tennessee
WSMI Litchfield, Illinois
WSML Graham, North Carolina
WSMN Nashua, New Hampshire
WSMT Sparta, Tennessee
WSMX Winston-Salem, North Carolina
WSMY Weldon, North Carolina
WSNG Torrington, Connecticut
WSNJ Bridgeton, New Jersey
WSNL Flint, Michigan
WSNO Barre, Vermont
WSNR Jersey City, New Jersey
WSNT Sandersville, Georgia
WSNW Seneca, South Carolina
WSOK Savannah, Georgia
WSOL San German, Puerto Rico
WSOM Salem, Ohio
WSON Henderson, Kentucky
WSOO Sault Ste. Marie, Michigan
WSOS St. Augustine Beach, Florida
WSOY Decatur, Illinois
WSPC Albemarle, North Carolina
WSPD Toledo, Ohio
WSPG Spartanburg, South Carolina
WSPL Streator, Illinois
WSPO Charleston, South Carolina
WSPQ Springville, New York
WSPR Springfield, Massachusetts
WSPY Geneva, Illinois
WSPZ(AM) Birmingham, Alabama
WSQL Brevard, North Carolina
WSQR Sycamore, Illinois
WSRA Albany, Georgia
WSRF Fort Lauderdale, Florida
WSRO Ashland, Massachusetts
WSRP Jacksonville, North Carolina
WSRQ Sarasota, Florida
WSRY Elkton, Maryland
WSSC Sumter, South Carolina
WSSG Goldsboro, North Carolina
WSSO Starkville, Mississippi
WSSP Milwaukee, Wisconsin
WSTA Charlotte Amalie, Virgin Islands
WSTC Stamford, Connecticut
WSTJ St. Johnsbury, Vermont
WSTL Providence, Rhode Island
WSTP Salisbury, North Carolina
WSTT Thomasville, Georgia
WSTU Stuart, Florida
WSTV Steubenville, Ohio
WSTX Christiansted, Virgin Islands
WSUA Miami, Florida
WSUI Iowa City, Iowa
WSVA Harrisonburg, Virginia
WSVG Mount Jackson, Virginia
WSVM Valdese, North Carolina
WSVS Crewe, Virginia
WSVU North Palm Beach, Florida
WSVX Shelbyville, Indiana
WSWI Evansville, Indiana
WSWN Belle Glade, Florida
WSWV Pennington Gap, Virginia
WSWW Charleston, West Virginia
WSYA(AM) Anniston, Alabama
WSYB Rutland, Vermont
WSYD Mount Airy, North Carolina
WSYL Sylvania, Georgia
WSYR Syracuse, New York
WSYW Indianapolis, Indiana
WSYY Millinocket, Maine
WTAB Tabor City, North Carolina
WTAD Quincy, Illinois
WTAG Worcester, Massachusetts
WTAL Tallahassee, Florida
WTAM Cleveland, Ohio
WTAN Clearwater, Florida
WTAQ Green Bay, Wisconsin
WTAR Norfolk, Virginia
WTAW College Station, Texas
WTAX Springfield, Illinois
WTAY Robinson, Illinois
WTBC Tuscaloosa, Alabama
WTBF Troy, Alabama
WTBI Pickens, South Carolina
WTBN Pinellas Park, Florida
WTBO Cumberland, Maryland
WTBQ Warwick, New York
WTCA Plymouth, Indiana
WTCH Shawano, Wisconsin
WTCJ Tell City, Indiana
WTCL Chattahoochee, Florida
WTCM Traverse City, Michigan
WTCO Campbellsville, Kentucky
WTCR Kenova, West Virginia
WTCS Fairmont, West Virginia
WTCW Whitesburg, Kentucky
WTDY Madison, Wisconsin
WTEL Red Springs, North Carolina
WTEM Washington, District of Columbia
WTGA Thomaston, Georgia
WTGM Salisbury, Maryland
WTHB Augusta, Georgia
WTHE Mineola, New York
WTHQ Brookport, Illinois
WTHU Thurmont, Maryland
WTHV Hahira, Georgia
WTIC Hartford, Connecticut
WTIF Tifton, Georgia
WTIG Massillon, Ohio
WTIK Durham, North Carolina
WTIL Mayaguez, Puerto Rico
WTIQ Manistique, Michigan
WTIS Tampa, Florida
WTIV Titusville, Pennsylvania
WTJH East Point, Georgia
WTJK South Beloit, Illinois
WTJS Jackson, Tennessee
WTJV Deland, Florida
WTJZ Newport News, Virginia
WTKA Ann Arbor, Michigan
WTKG Grand Rapids, Michigan
WTKI Huntsville, Alabama
WTKM Hartford, Wisconsin
WTKN Corinth, Mississippi
WTKS Savannah, Georgia
WTKT Harrisburg, Pennsylvania
WTKY Tompkinsville, Kentucky
WTKZ Allentown, Pennsylvania
WTLA North Syracuse, New York
WTLB Utica, New York
WTLC Indianapolis, Indiana
WTLK Taylorsville, North Carolina
WTLM Opelika, Alabama
WTLN Orlando, Florida
WTLO Somerset, Kentucky
WTLS Tallassee, Alabama
WTMA Charleston, South Carolina
WTMC Wilmington, Delaware
WTME Rumford, Maine
WTMJ Milwaukee, Wisconsin
WTMN Gainesville, Florida
WTMP Egypt Lake, Florida
WTMR Camden, New Jersey
WTMY Sarasota, Florida
WTMZ Dorchester Terrace-Brentwood, South Carolina
WTNE Trenton, Tennessee
WTNI Biloxi, Mississippi
WTNK Hartsville, Tennessee
WTNL Reidsville, Georgia
WTNS Coshocton, Ohio
WTNT Alexandria, Virginia
WTNY Watertown, New York
WTOB Winston-Salem, North Carolina
WTOC Newton, New Jersey
WTOE Spruce Pine, North Carolina
WTOF Bay Minette, Alabama
WTON Staunton, Virginia
WTOR Youngstown, New York
WTOT Marianna, Florida
WTOX Glen Allen, Virginia
WTOY Salem, Virginia
WTPR Paris, Tennessee
WTPS Petersburg, Virginia
WTQS Cameron, South Carolina
WTRB Ripley, Tennessee
WTRC Elkhart, Indiana
WTRE Greensburg, Indiana
WTRI Brunswick, Maryland
WTRN Tyrone, Pennsylvania
WTRO Dyersburg, Tennessee
WTRP La Grange, Georgia
WTRU Kernersville, North Carolina
WTRX Flint, Michigan
WTSA Brattleboro, Vermont
WTSB Selma, North Carolina
WTSK Tuscaloosa, Alabama
WTSL Hanover, New Hampshire
WTSN Dover, New Hampshire
WTSO Madison, Wisconsin
WTSV Claremont, New Hampshire
WTTB Vero Beach, Florida
WTTC Towanda, Pennsylvania
WTTF Tiffin, Ohio
WTTI Dalton, Georgia
WTTL Madisonville, Kentucky
WTTM Lindenwold, New Jersey
WTTN Columbus, Wisconsin
WTTR Westminster, Maryland
WTUP Tupelo, Mississippi
WTUV Louisville, Kentucky
WTVB Coldwater, Michigan
WTVL Waterville, Maine
WTVN Columbus, Ohio
WTWA Thomson, Georgia
WTWB Auburndale, Florida
WTWD Plant City, Florida
WTWG Columbus, Mississippi
WTWK Plattsburgh, New York
WTWN Wells River, Vermont
WTWZ Clinton, Mississippi
WTXK Pike Road, Alabama
WTXY Whiteville, North Carolina
WTYL Tylertown, Mississippi
WTYM Kittanning, Pennsylvania
WTYS Marianna, Florida

WTZE Tazewell, Virginia
WTZN Troy, Pennsylvania
WTZQ Hendersonville, North Carolina
WTZX Sparta, Tennessee
WUAM Watervliet, New York
WUAT Pikeville, Tennessee
WUBR Baton Rouge, Louisiana
WUFE Baxley, Georgia
WUFF Eastman, Georgia
WUFL Sterling Heights, Michigan
WUFO Amherst, New York
WUKQ Ponce, Puerto Rico
WUKZ(AM) Marion, Virginia
WULM Springfield, Ohio
WUMP Madison, Alabama
WUNA Ocoee, Florida
WUNN Mason, Michigan
WUNO San Juan, Puerto Rico
WUNR Brookline, Massachusetts
WUPE Pittsfield, Massachusetts
WUPR Utuado, Puerto Rico
WURA Quantico, Virginia
WURD Philadelphia, Pennsylvania
WURL Moody, Alabama
WURN Kendall, Florida
WUSP Utica, New York
WUST Washington, District of Columbia
WUTI Utica, New York
WUVR Lebanon, New Hampshire
WVAB Virginia Beach, Virginia
WVAE Biddeford, Maine
WVAL Sauk Rapids, Minnesota
WVAM Altoona, Pennsylvania
WVAR Richwood, West Virginia
WVAX Charlottesville, Virginia
WVBE Roanoke, Virginia
WVBF Middleborough Center, Massachusetts
WVBG Vicksburg, Mississippi
WVBS Burgaw, North Carolina
WVCB Shallotte, North Carolina
WVCC Hogansville, Georgia
WVCD Bamberg-Denmark, South Carolina
WVCH Chester, Pennsylvania
WVCV Orange, Virginia
WVCY Oshkosh, Wisconsin
WVEI Worcester, Massachusetts
WVEL Pekin, Illinois
WVFN East Lansing, Michigan
WVGB Beaufort, South Carolina
WVGG Lucedale, Mississippi
WVGM Lynchburg, Virginia
WVHF Kentwood, Michigan
WVHI Evansville, Indiana
WVHU Huntington, West Virginia
WVJP Caguas, Puerto Rico
WVJS Owensboro, Kentucky
WVKO Columbus, Ohio
WVLD Valdosta, Georgia
WVLG Wildwood, Florida
WVLK Lexington, Kentucky
WVLN Olney, Illinois
WVLY Moundsville, West Virginia
WVLZ Knoxville, Tennessee
WVMR Frost, West Virginia
WVMT Burlington, Vermont
WVNA Tuscumbia, Alabama
WVNE Leicester, Massachusetts
WVNJ Oakland, New Jersey
WVNN Athens, Alabama
WVNR Poultney, Vermont
WVNT Parkersburg, West Virginia
WVNZ Richmond, Virginia
WVOE Chadbourn, North Carolina
WVOG New Orleans, Louisiana
WVOI Marco Island, Florida
WVOJ Fernandina Beach, Florida
WVOK Oxford, Alabama
WVOL Berry Hill, Tennessee
WVON Berwyn, Illinois
WVOP Vidalia, Georgia
WVOS Liberty, New York
WVOT Wilson, North Carolina
WVOW Logan, West Virginia
WVOX New Rochelle, New York
WVOZ San Juan, Puerto Rico
WVPO Stroudsburg, Pennsylvania
WVRC Spencer, West Virginia
WVRQ Viroqua, Wisconsin
WVSA Vernon, Alabama
WVSG Columbus, Ohio
WVSL(AM) Selinsgrove, Pennsylvania
WVSM Rainsville, Alabama
WVTJ Pensacola, Florida
WVTL Amsterdam, New York
WVTS Dunbar, West Virginia
WVTS(AM) Charleston, West Virginia
WVUS Grafton, West Virginia
WVWI Charlotte Amalie, Virgin Islands
WVXX Norfolk, Virginia
WVZN Columbia, Pennsylvania
WWAB Lakeland, Florida
WWBA Largo, Florida
WWBC Cocoa, Florida
WWBF Bartow, Florida
WWBG Greensboro, North Carolina
WWBJ Martinsburg, Pennsylvania
WWCA Gary, Indiana
WWCD Baltimore, Ohio
WWCH Clarion, Pennsylvania
WWCK Flint, Michigan
WWCL Lehigh Acres, Florida
WWCN North Fort Myers, Florida
WWCO Waterbury, Connecticut
WWCS Canonsburg, Pennsylvania
WWDB Philadelphia, Pennsylvania
WWDJ Boston, Massachusetts
WWDN Danville, Virginia
WWDR Murfreesboro, North Carolina
WWDX Huntingdon, Tennessee
WWFD Frederick, Maryland
WWFE Miami, Florida
WWFL Clermont, Florida
WWGA(AM) Waycross, Georgia
WWGB Indian Head, Maryland
WWGC Albertville, Alabama
WWGE Loretto, Pennsylvania
WWGK Cleveland, Ohio
WWGP Sanford, North Carolina
WWHM Sumter, South Carolina
WWHN Joliet, Illinois
WWIC Scottsboro, Alabama
WWIL Wilmington, North Carolina
WWIN Baltimore, Maryland
WWIO St. Marys, Georgia
WWIS Black River Falls, Wisconsin
WWJ Detroit, Michigan
WWJB Brooksville, Florida
WWJC Duluth, Minnesota
WWJZ Mount Holly, New Jersey
WWKB Buffalo, New York
WWKU Plum Springs, Kentucky
WWL New Orleans, Louisiana
WWLE Cornwall, New York
WWLF Auburn, New York
WWLX Lawrenceburg, Tennessee
WWLZ Horseheads, New York
WWMI St. Petersburg, Florida
WWMK Cleveland, Ohio
WWNA Aguadilla, Puerto Rico
WWNB New Bern, North Carolina
WWNC Asheville, North Carolina
WWNH Madbury, New Hampshire
WWNL Pittsburgh, Pennsylvania
WWNN Pompano Beach, Florida
WWNR Beckley, West Virginia
WWNS Statesboro, Georgia
WWNT Dothan, Alabama
WWNZ Veazie, Maine
WWOL Forest City, North Carolina
WWON Waynesboro, Tennessee
WWOW Conneaut, Ohio
WWPA Williamsport, Pennsylvania
WWPR Bradenton, Florida
WWRC Washington, District of Columbia
WWRF Lake Worth, Florida
WWRK Darlington, South Carolina
WWRL New York, New York
WWRU Jersey City, New Jersey
WWRV New York, New York
WWSC Glens Falls, New York
WWSF Sanford, Maine
WWSJ St. Johns, Michigan
WWSM Annville-Cleona, Pennsylvania
WWTC Minneapolis, Minnesota
WWTF Georgetown, Kentucky
WWTK Lake Placid, Florida
WWTM Decatur, Alabama
WWTR Bridgewater, New Jersey
WWTX Wilmington, Delaware
WWVA Wheeling, West Virginia
WWVT Christiansburg, Virginia
WWWC Wilkesboro, North Carolina
WWWE Hapeville, Georgia
WWWH Haleyville, Alabama
WWWI Baxter, Minnesota
WWWJ Galax, Virginia
WWWL New Orleans, Louisiana
WWWS Buffalo, New York
WWXL Manchester, Kentucky
WWYC Toledo, Ohio
WWYO Pineville, West Virginia
WWZN Boston, Massachusetts
WWZQ Aberdeen, Mississippi
WXAG Athens, Georgia
WXAL Demopolis, Alabama
WXAM Buffalo, Kentucky
WXBD Biloxi, Mississippi
WXBR Brockton, Massachusetts
WXBT Columbia, South Carolina
WXBT(AM) Columbia, South Carolina
WXCE Amery, Wisconsin
WXCF Clifton Forge, Virginia
WXCO Wausau, Wisconsin
WXCT Southington, Connecticut
WXEM Buford, Georgia
WXEW Yabucoa, Puerto Rico
WXEX Exeter, New Hampshire
WXFN Muncie, Indiana
WXFO Royston, Georgia
WXGI Richmond, Virginia
WXGM Gloucester, Virginia
WXGO Madison, Indiana
WXIC Waverly, Ohio
WXIT Blowing Rock, North Carolina
WXJC Birmingham, Alabama
WXJO Douglasville, Georgia
WXKL Sanford, North Carolina
WXKO Fort Valley, Georgia
WXKS Newton, Massachusetts
WXKX Clarksburg, West Virginia
WXLA Dimondale, Michigan
WXLI Dublin, Georgia
WXLM Groton, Connecticut
WXLW Indianapolis, Indiana
WXLZ St. Paul, Virginia
WXMC Parsippany-Troy Hill, New Jersey
WXME Monticello, Maine
WXMY Saltville, Virginia
WXNC Monroe, North Carolina
WXNH Jaffrey, New Hampshire
WXNT Indianapolis, Indiana
WXOK Port Allen, Louisiana
WXQW Fairhope, Alabama
WXRF Guayama, Puerto Rico
WXRL Lancaster, New York
WXRQ Mount Pleasant, Tennessee
WXRS Swainsboro, Georgia
WXSM Blountville, Tennessee
WXTG Hampton, Virginia
WXTN Benton, Mississippi
WXVA Winchester, Virginia
WXVI Montgomery, Alabama
WXXI Rochester, New York
WXYB Indian Rocks Beach, Florida
WXYG Sauk Rapids, Minnesota
WXYT Detroit, Michigan
WYAC Cabo Rojo, Puerto Rico
WYAL Scotland Neck, North Carolina
WYAM Hartselle, Alabama
WYBC New Haven, Connecticut
WYBG Massena, New York
WYBT Blountstown, Florida
WYBY Cortland, New York
WYCB Washington, District of Columbia
WYCK Plains, Pennsylvania
WYCL Niles, Ohio
WYCV Granite Falls, North Carolina
WYDE Birmingham, Alabama
WYEA Sylacauga, Alabama
WYEL Mayaguez, Puerto Rico
WYFN Nashville, Tennessee
WYFQ Charlotte, North Carolina
WYGH Paris, Kentucky
WYGM Orlando, Florida
WYGR Wyoming, Michigan
WYHL Meridian, Mississippi
WYHM Rockwood, Tennessee
WYHY Cannonsburg, Kentucky
WYIS McRae, Georgia
WYKM Rupert, West Virginia
WYKO Sabana Grande, Puerto Rico
WYLD New Orleans, Louisiana
WYLF Penn Yan, New York
WYLL Chicago, Illinois
WYLS York, Alabama
WYMB Manning, South Carolina
WYMC Mayfield, Kentucky
WYMM Jacksonville, Florida
WYNC Yanceyville, North Carolina
WYND Deland, Florida
WYNE North East, Pennsylvania
WYNF Augusta, Georgia
WYNN Florence, South Carolina
WYNY(AM) Ontario, New York
WYNY(AM) Milford, Pennsylvania
WYNY(AM) Milford, New York
WYOS Binghamton, New York
WYPC Wellston, Ohio
WYRD Greenville, South Carolina
WYRE Annapolis, Maryland
WYRM Norfolk, Virginia
WYRN Louisburg, North Carolina
WYRV Cedar Bluff, Virginia
WYSE Canton, North Carolina
WYSH Clinton, Tennessee
WYSL Avon, New York
WYSR High Point, North Carolina
WYTH Madison, Georgia
WYTI Rocky Mount, Virginia
WYTS Columbus, Ohio
WYUS Milford, Delaware
WYVE Wytheville, Virginia
WYWY Barbourville, Kentucky
WYXC Cartersville, Georgia
WYXE Gallatin, Tennessee
WYXI Athens, Tennessee
WYYC York, Pennsylvania
WYYZ Jasper, Georgia
WYZD Dobson, North Carolina
WYZE Atlanta, Georgia
WZAB Sweetwater, Florida
WZAM Ishpeming, Michigan
WZAN Portland, Maine
WZAP Bristol, Virginia
WZAZ Jacksonville, Florida
WZBK Keene, New Hampshire
WZBO Edenton, North Carolina
WZCC Cross City, Florida
WZCT Scottsboro, Alabama
WZEP De Funiak Springs, Florida
WZFG Dilworth, Minnesota
WZGM Black Mountain, North Carolina
WZGV Cramerton, North Carolina
WZGX Bessemer, Alabama
WZHF Arlington, Virginia
WZHR Zephyrhills, Florida
WZJY Mount Pleasant, South Carolina
WZKY Albemarle, North Carolina
WZMF(AM) Nanticoke, Pennsylvania
WZMG Pepperell, Alabama
WZNA Moca, Puerto Rico
WZNG Shelbyville, Tennessee
WZNH Fitzwilliam Depot, New Hampshire
WZNZ Atlantic Beach, Florida
WZOB Fort Payne, Alabama
WZOE Princeton, Illinois
WZON Bangor, Maine
WZOO Asheboro, North Carolina
WZOT Rockmart, Georgia
WZQZ Trion, Georgia
WZRC New York, New York
WZRK Northbrook, Illinois
WZSK Everett, Pennsylvania
WZTA Vero Beach, Florida
WZTQ Centre, Alabama
WZUM Carnegie, Pennsylvania
WZYX Cowan, Tennessee
WZZA Tuscumbia, Alabama
WZZB Seymour, Indiana
WZZQ(AM) Gaffney, South Carolina
WZZW Milton, West Virginia
WZZX Lineville, Alabama
XETRA Tijuana, Mexico

US FM Radio Stations by Call Letters

Minooka, Virginia
CJTT-FM New Liskeard, Ontario
CJWV-FM Petersburgh, Ontario
DKEAU Hilo, Hawaii
KAAI Palisade, Colorado
KAAK Great Falls, Montana
KAAN-FM Bethany, Missouri
KAAP Rock Island, Washington
KAAQ Alliance, Nebraska
KAAR Butte, Montana
KAAT Oakhurst, California
KAAX Avenal, California
KAAZ Laramie, Wyoming
KABA Louise, Texas
KABD Ipswich, South Dakota
KABF Little Rock, Arkansas
KABG Los Alamos, New Mexico
KABN-FM Kasilof, Alaska
KABQ-FM Bosque Farms, New Mexico
KABR Alamo Community, New Mexico
KABU Fort Totten, North Dakota
KABW Baird / Abilene, Texas
KABX-FM Merced, California
KABZ Little Rock, Arkansas
KACC Alvin, Texas
KACI-FM The Dalles, Oregon
KACL Bismarck, North Dakota
KACO Apache, Oklahoma
KACQ Lometa, Texas
KACS Rainier, Washington
KACT-FM Andrews, Texas
KACU Abilene, Texas
KACV-FM Amarillo, Texas
KACY Arkansas City, Kansas
KACZ Riley, Kansas
KADA-FM Ada, Oklahoma
KADD Logandale, Nevada
KADE Salida, Colorado
KADI-FM Republic, Missouri
KADL Imperial, Nebraska
KADQ-FM Evanston, Wyoming
KADU Hibbing, Minnesota
KADV Modesto, California
KAEH Beaumont, California
KAER Mesquite, Nevada
KAFC Anchorage, Alaska
KAFE Bellingham, Washington
KAFF-FM Flagstaff, Arizona
KAFH Great Falls, Montana
KAFM Grand Junction, Colorado
KAFR Conroe, Texas
KAFX-FM Diboll, Texas
KAGB Waimea, Hawaii
KAGE-FM Winona, Minnesota
KAGG Madisonville, Texas
KAGH-FM Crossett, Arkansas
KAGJ Ephraim, Utah
KAGL El Dorado, Arkansas
KAGM Los Lunas, New Mexico
KAGO-FM Klamath Falls, Oregon
KAGT Abilene, Texas
KAGU Spokane, Washington
KAGZ(FM) Lufkin, Texas
KAHE Dodge City, Kansas
KAHL-FM Hondo, Texas
KAHM Prescott, Arizona
KAHR Poplar Bluff, Missouri
KAHU Pahala, Hawaii
KAIA Bloomfield, Missouri
KAIB Shafter, California
KAIC Tucson, Arizona
KAIG Dodge City, Kansas
KAIH Lake Havasu City, Arizona
KAIK Tillamook, Oregon
KAIM-FM Honolulu, Hawaii
KAIO Idaho Falls, Idaho
KAIP Wapello, Iowa
KAIQ Wolfforth, Texas
KAIR-FM Horton, Kansas
KAIS(FM) Tracy, California
KAIW Laramie, Wyoming
KAIX Cheyenne, Wyoming
KAIZ Mesquite, Nevada
KAJA San Antonio, Texas
KAJC Salem, Oregon
KAJM Camp Verde, Arizona
KAJN-FM Crowley, Louisiana
KAJP Carrizo Springs, Texas
KAJR Indian Wells, California
KAJT Ada, Oklahoma
KAJX Aspen, Colorado
KAJZ Llano, Texas
KAKA Salina, Kansas
KAKI Juneau, Alaska
KAKJ Marianna, Arkansas
KAKL Anchorage, Alaska
KAKN Naknek, Alaska
KAKO Ada, Oklahoma
KAKQ-FM Fairbanks, Alaska
KAKS Huntsville, Arkansas
KAKT Phoenix, Oregon
KAKV El Dorado, Arkansas
KAKX Mendocino, California
KALA Davenport, Iowa
KALC Denver, Colorado
KALF Red Bluff, California
KALG Kaltag, Alaska
KALI-FM Santa Ana, California
KALK Winfield, Texas
KALN Dexter, New Mexico
KALP Alpine, Texas
KALQ-FM Alamosa, Colorado
KALR Hot Springs, Arkansas
KALS Kalispell, Montana
KALT-FM Alturas, California
KALU Langston, Oklahoma
KALW San Francisco, California
KALX Berkeley, California
KALZ Fowler, California
KAMA-FM Deer Park, Texas
KAMB Merced, California
KAMD-FM Camden, Arkansas
KAMF Tulare, South Dakota
KAMJ Gosnell, Arkansas
KAML-FM Gillette, Wyoming
KAMO-FM Rogers, Arkansas
KAMS Mammoth Spring, Arkansas
KAMU-FM College Station, Texas
KAMX Luling, Texas
KAMY Lubbock, Texas
KAMZ Tahoka, Texas
KANC Baker, Oregon
KANH Emporia, Kansas
KANJ Giddings, Texas
KANL Baker, Oregon
KANO Hilo, Hawaii
KANQ Chanute, Kansas
KANR Belle Plaine, Kansas
KANS Emporia, Kansas
KANT Guernsey, Wyoming
KANU Lawrence, Kansas
KANV Olsburg, Kansas
KANW Albuquerque, New Mexico
KANX Sheridan, Arkansas
KANY Montesano, Washington
KANZ Garden City, Kansas
KAOC Cavalier, North Dakota
KAOD Babbitt, Minnesota
KAOG Jonesboro, Arkansas
KAOI-FM Wailuku, Hawaii
KAOR Vermillion, South Dakota
KAOS Olympia, Washington
KAOW Fort Smith, Arkansas
KAOX Kemmerer, Wyoming
KAOY Kealakekua, Hawaii
KAPA Hilo, Hawaii
KAPB-FM Marksville, Louisiana
KAPC Butte, Montana
KAPG Bentonville, Arkansas
KAPI Ruston, Louisiana
KAPK Grants Pass, Oregon
KAPM Alexandria, Louisiana
KAPN Caldwell, Texas
KAQA Kilauea, Hawaii
KAQD Abilene, Texas
KAQF Clovis, New Mexico
KARA Williams, California
KARB Price, Utah
KARF Independence, Kansas
KARG Poteau, Oklahoma
KARH Forrest City, Arkansas
KARJ Kuna, Idaho
KARL Tracy, Minnesota
KARM Visalia, California
KARN-FM Sheridan, Arkansas
KARO Nyssa, Oregon
KARP-FM Dassel, Minnesota
KARQ San Andreas, California
KARS-FM Laramie, Wyoming
KARU Cache, Oklahoma
KARV-FM Ola, Arkansas
KARX Claude, Texas
KARY-FM Grandview, Washington
KARZ Marshall, Minnesota
KASB Bellevue, Washington
KASD Rapid City, South Dakota
KASE-FM Austin, Texas
KASF Alamosa, Colorado
KASH-FM Anchorage, Alaska
KASK Fairfield, California
KASR Vilonia, Arkansas
KASS Casper, Wyoming
KASU Jonesboro, Arkansas
KASV Borger, Texas
KATB Anchorage, Alaska
KATC-FM Colorado Springs, Colorado
KATF Dubuque, Iowa
KATG Elkhart, Texas
KATI California, Missouri
KATJ-FM George, California
KATK-FM Carlsbad, New Mexico
KATM Modesto, California
KATO-FM New Ulm, Minnesota
KATP Amarillo, Texas
KATQ-FM Plentywood, Montana
KATR-FM Wray, Colorado
KATS Yakima, Washington
KATT-FM Oklahoma City, Oklahoma
KATW Lewiston, Idaho
KATX Eastland, Texas
KATY-FM Idyllwild, California
KAUC West Clarkston, Washington
KAUD Mexico, Missouri
KAUF Kennett, Missouri
KAUG Anchorage, Alaska
KAUJ Grafton, North Dakota
KAUM Colorado City, Texas
KAUR Sioux Falls, South Dakota
KAUS-FM Austin, Minnesota
KAUU Manti, Utah
KAVB Hawthorne, Nevada
KAVE Oakridge, Oregon
KAVH Eudora, Arkansas
KAVK Many, Louisiana
KAVO Pampa, Texas
KAVV Benson, Arizona
KAVW Amarillo, Texas
KAVX Lufkin, Texas
KAWC-FM Yuma, Arizona
KAWK Custer, South Dakota
KAWN Winslow, Arizona
KAWO Boise, Idaho
KAWS Marsing, Idaho
KAWZ Twin Falls, Idaho
KAXA Mountain Home, Texas
KAXE Grand Rapids, Minnesota
KAXG Gillette, Wyoming
KAXL Greenacres, California
KAXR Arkansas City, Kansas
KAXV Bastrop, Louisiana
KAYA Hubbard, Nebraska
KAYB Sunnyside, Washington
KAYC Durant, Oklahoma
KAYD-FM Silsbee, Texas
KAYE-FM Tonkawa, Oklahoma
KAYF Bayfield, Colorado
KAYG Camp Wood, Texas
KAYH Fayetteville, Arkansas
KAYK Victoria, Texas
KAYL-FM Storm Lake, Iowa
KAYM Weatherford, Oklahoma
KAYO Wasilla, Alaska
KAYP Burlington, Iowa
KAYQ Warsaw, Missouri
KAYT Jena, Louisiana
KAYW Meeker, Colorado
KAYX Richmond, Missouri
KAZC Healdton, Oklahoma
KAZE Ore City, Texas
KAZF Hebbronville, Texas
KAZI Austin, Texas
KAZR Pella, Iowa
KAZU Pacific Grove, California
KAZX Kirtland, New Mexico
KAZY Cheyenne, Wyoming
KAZZ Deer Park, Washington
KBAA Grass Valley, California
KBAC Las Vegas, New Mexico
KBAH Plainview, Texas
KBAJ Deer River, Minnesota
KBAN De Ridder, Louisiana
KBAQ Phoenix, Arizona
KBAR-FM Victoria, Texas
KBAT Monahans, Texas
KBAW Ranchitos Las Lomas, Texas
KBAY Gilroy, California
KBAZ Hamilton, Montana
KBBB(FM) Billings, Montana
KBBC Tishomingo, Oklahoma
KBBD Spokane, Washington
KBBE McPherson, Kansas
KBBF Calistoga, California
KBBG Waterloo, Iowa
KBBK Lincoln, Nebraska
KBBM Jefferson City, Missouri
KBBN-FM Broken Bow, Nebraska
KBBO-FM Houston, Alaska
KBBQ-FM Van Buren, Arkansas
KBBT Schertz, Texas
KBBU Modesto, California
KBBX-FM Nebraska City, Nebraska
KBBY-FM Ventura, California
KBBZ Kalispell, Montana
KBCE Boyce, Louisiana
KBCM Blytheville, Arkansas
KBCN-FM Marshall, Arkansas
KBCO Boulder, Colorado
KBCQ-FM Roswell, New Mexico
KBCR-FM Steamboat Springs, Colorado
KBCS Bellevue, Washington
KBCT Waco, Texas
KBCU North Newton, Kansas
KBCW-FM McAlester, Oklahoma
KBCX Big Spring, Texas
KBCY Tye, Texas
KBDA Great Bend, Kansas
KBDB-FM Forks, Washington
KBDC Mason City, Iowa
KBDD Winfield, Kansas
KBDE Temple, Texas
KBDG Turlock, California
KBDK Leakey, Texas
KBDN Bandon, Oregon
KBDO Des Arc, Arkansas
KBDR Mirando City, Texas
KBDS Taft, California
KBDV Leesville, Louisiana
KBDW Wheeler, Texas
KBDX Blanding, Utah
KBDY Hanna, Wyoming
KBDZ Perryville, Missouri
KBEA-FM Muscatine, Iowa
KBEE Salt Lake City, Utah
KBEF Gibsland, Louisiana
KBEK Mora, Minnesota
KBEL-FM Idabel, Oklahoma
KBEM-FM Minneapolis, Minnesota
KBEN-FM Cowley, Wyoming
KBEQ-FM Kansas City, Missouri
KBER Ogden, Utah
KBES Ceres, California
KBEV-FM Dillon, Montana
KBEW-FM Blue Earth, Minnesota
KBEY Burnet, Texas
KBEZ Tulsa, Oklahoma
KBFB Dallas, Texas
KBFL-FM Buffalo, Missouri
KBFM Edinburg, Texas
KBFO Aberdeen, South Dakota
KBFP-FM Delano, California
KBFR Bismarck, North Dakota
KBFX Anchorage, Alaska
KBGA Missoula, Montana
KBGL Larned, Kansas
KBGM Park Hills, Missouri
KBGO Waco, Texas
KBGX Keaau, Hawaii
KBGY Faribault, Minnesota
KBGZ Spring Creek, Nevada
KBHE-FM Rapid City, South Dakota
KBHG Alexandria, Minnesota
KBHH Kerman, California
KBHI Miner, Missouri
KBHL Osakis, Minnesota
KBHM Basin, Wyoming
KBHN Booneville, Arkansas

KBHP Bemidji, Minnesota
KBHR Big Bear City, California
KBHT Crockett, Texas
KBHU-FM Spearfish, South Dakota
KBHW International Falls, Minnesota
KBHZ Willmar, Minnesota
KBIA Columbia, Missouri
KBIC Raymondville, Texas
KBIG-FM Los Angeles, California
KBIJ Guymon, Oklahoma
KBIK Independence, Kansas
KBIL Park City, Montana
KBIM-FM Roswell, New Mexico
KBIO Natchitoches, Louisiana
KBIQ Manitou Springs, Colorado
KBIU Lake Charles, Louisiana
KBIY Van Buren, Missouri
KBJF Nephi, Utah
KBJQ Bronson, Kansas
KBJS Jacksonville, Texas
KBKB-FM Fort Madison, Iowa
KBKC Moberly, Missouri
KBKG Corning, Arkansas
KBKK Ball, Louisiana
KBKL Grand Junction, Colorado
KBKN Lamesa, Texas
KBKO Kodiak, Alaska
KBKS-FM Tacoma, Washington
KBKY Merced, California
KBKZ Raton, New Mexico
KBLB Nisswa, Minnesota
KBLC Fredericksburg, Texas
KBLD Kennewick, Washington
KBLL-FM Helena, Montana
KBLO Corcoran, California
KBLP Lindsay, Oklahoma
KBLQ-FM Logan, Utah
KBLR-FM Blair, Nebraska
KBLS North Fort Riley, Kansas
KBLT Leakey, Texas
KBLV Tehachapi, California
KBLW Billings, Montana
KBLX-FM Berkeley, California
KBLZ Winona, Texas
KBMB(FM) Sacramento, California
KBMC Bozeman, Montana
KBMD Marble Falls, Texas
KBMG Evanston, Wyoming
KBMH Holbrook, Arizona
KBMJ Heber Springs, Arkansas
KBMK Bismarck, North Dakota
KBMM Odessa, Texas
KBMP Enterprise, Kansas
KBMQ Monroe, Louisiana
KBMV-FM Birch Tree, Missouri
KBMX Proctor, Minnesota
KBNA-FM El Paso, Texas
KBNJ Corpus Christi, Texas
KBNL Laredo, Texas
KBNO-FM White Salmon, Washington
KBNR Brownsville, Texas
KBNU Uvalde, Texas
KBNV Fayetteville, Arkansas
KBOA-FM Piggott, Arkansas
KBOB-FM De Witt, Iowa
KBOC Bridgeport, Texas
KBOE-FM Oskaloosa, Iowa
KBOM Socorro, New Mexico
KBON Mamou, Louisiana
KBOO Portland, Oregon
KBOQ Seaside, California
KBOS-FM Tulare, California
KBOT Pelican Rapids, Minnesota
KBOX Lompoc, California
KBOY-FM Medford, Oregon
KBOZ-FM Bozeman, Montana
KBPA San Marcos, Texas
KBPB Harrison, Arkansas
KBPG Montevideo, Minnesota
KBPI Denver, Colorado
KBPK Buena Park, California
KBPN Brainerd, Minnesota
KBPR Brainerd, Minnesota
KBPU De Queen, Arkansas
KBPW Hampton, Arkansas
KBQB Chico, California
KBQC Independence, Kansas
KBQF McFarland, California
KBQI Albuquerque, New Mexico
KBQL Las Vegas, New Mexico
KBRB-FM Ainsworth, Nebraska
KBRE Atwater, California
KBRG San Jose, California
KBRJ Anchorage, Alaska
KBRK-FM Brookings, South Dakota
KBRQ Hillsboro, Texas
KBRU Oklahoma City, Oklahoma
KBRW-FM Barrow, Alaska
KBRX-FM O'Neill, Nebraska
KBSA El Dorado, Arkansas
KBSB Bemidji, Minnesota
KBSG Aberdeen, Washington
KBSJ Jackpot, Nevada
KBSK McCall, Idaho
KBSM McCall, Idaho
KBSO Corpus Christi, Texas
KBSQ McCall, Idaho
KBSS Sun Valley, Idaho
KBST-FM Big Spring, Texas
KBSU-FM Boise, Idaho
KBSW Twin Falls, Idaho
KBSX Boise, Idaho
KBSY Burley, Idaho
KBTA-FM Batesville, Arkansas
KBTE Tulia, Texas
KBTK(FM) Kachina Village, Arizona
KBTL El Dorado, Kansas
KBTN-FM Neosho, Missouri
KBTO Bottineau, North Dakota
KBTQ Harlingen, Texas
KBTS Big Spring, Texas
KBTT Haughton, Louisiana
KBTW Lenwood, California
KBUA San Fernando, California
KBUB Brownwood, Texas
KBUC Raymondville, Texas
KBUD Sardis, Mississippi
KBUE Long Beach, California
KBUK La Grange, Texas
KBUL-FM Carson City, Nevada
KBUS Paris, Texas
KBUT Crested Butte, Colorado
KBUW Buffalo, Wyoming
KBUX Quartzsite, Arizona
KBUZ Topeka, Kansas
KBVA Bella Vista, Arkansas
KBVB Barnesville, Minnesota
KBVC Buena Vista, Colorado
KBVM Portland, Oregon
KBVR Corvallis, Oregon
KBVU-FM Alta, Iowa
KBWA Brush, Colorado
KBWC Marshall, Texas
KBWS-FM Sisseton, South Dakota
KBWW Broken Bow, Oklahoma
KBXB Sikeston, Missouri
KBXJ Los Ybanez, Texas
KBXL Caldwell, Idaho
KBXR Columbia, Missouri
KBXT Wixon Valley, Texas
KBXX Houston, Texas
KBYB Hope, Arkansas
KBYI Rexburg, Idaho
KBYN Arnold, California
KBYO-FM Farmerville, Louisiana
KBYR-FM Rexburg, Idaho
KBYU-FM Provo, Utah
KBYZ Bismarck, North Dakota
KBZC Sacramento, California
KBZD Amarillo, Texas
KBZE Berwick, Louisiana
KBZM Big Sky, Montana
KBZN Ogden, Utah
KBZQ Lawton, Oklahoma
KBZR Billings, Montana
KBZS Wichita Falls, Texas
KBZT San Diego, California
KBZU Albuquerque, New Mexico
KCAC Camden, Arkansas
KCAD Dickinson, North Dakota
KCAI Lodi, California
KCAJ-FM Roseau, Minnesota
KCAL-FM Redlands, California
KCAQ Oxnard, California
KCAR-FM Baxter Springs, Kansas
KCAS McCook, Texas
KCAV Marshall, Arkansas
KCAW Sitka, Alaska
KCBI Dallas, Texas
KCBS-FM Los Angeles, California
KCBW Grandin, Missouri
KCBX San Luis Obispo, California
KCCD Moorhead, Minnesota
KCCK-FM Cedar Rapids, Iowa
KCCL Placerville, California
KCCM-FM Moorhead, Minnesota
KCCN-FM Honolulu, Hawaii
KCCQ Ames, Iowa
KCCS Starkville, Colorado
KCCU Lawton, Oklahoma
KCCV-FM Olathe, Kansas
KCCY-FM Pueblo, Colorado
KCDA Post Falls, Idaho
KCDD Hamlin, Texas
KCDQ Douglas, Arizona
KCDU Carmel, California
KCDV Cordova, Alaska
KCDX Florence, Arizona
KCDY Carlsbad, New Mexico
KCDZ Twentynine Palms, California
KCEA Atherton, California
KCEC-FM Wellton, Arizona
KCED Centralia, Washington
KCEI Red River, New Mexico
KCEL Mojave, California
KCEP Las Vegas, Nevada
KCEU Price, Utah
KCEY Ranchos De Taos, New Mexico
KCEZ Los Molinos, California
KCFA Arnold, California
KCFB St. Cloud, Minnesota
KCFD Crawford, Nebraska
KCFL Westport, Washington
KCFN Wichita, Kansas
KCFP Pueblo, Colorado
KCFR-FM Denver, Colorado
KCFS Sioux Falls, South Dakota
KCFV Ferguson, Missouri
KCFX Harrisonville, Missouri
KCFY Yuma, Arizona
KCGB-FM Hood River, Oregon
KCGL Powell, Wyoming
KCGM Scobey, Montana
KCGN-FM Ortonville, Minnesota
KCGQ-FM Gordonville, Missouri
KCGR Oran, Missouri
KCGY Laramie, Wyoming
KCHA-FM Charles City, Iowa
KCHB Kaibito, Arizona
KCHE-FM Cherokee, Iowa
KCHG Cedar City, Utah
KCHI-FM Chillicothe, Missouri
KCHO Chico, California
KCHQ Driggs, Idaho
KCHT Childress, Texas
KCHX Midland, Texas
KCHZ Ottawa, Kansas
KCIC Grand Junction, Colorado
KCIE Dulce, New Mexico
KCIF Hilo, Hawaii
KCII-FM Washington, Iowa
KCIJ Atlanta, Louisiana
KCIL Gray, Louisiana
KCIN Cedar City, Utah
KCIR Twin Falls, Idaho
KCIV Mount Bullion, California
KCIX Garden City, Idaho
KCJC Dardanelle, Arkansas
KCJF Earle, Arkansas
KCJH Livingston, California
KCJK Garden City, Missouri
KCJX Carbondale, Colorado
KCKC Kansas City, Missouri
KCKJ Sarcoxie, Missouri
KCKL Malakoff, Texas
KCKR Church Point, Louisiana
KCKS Hamilton City, California
KCKT Crockett, Texas
KCKV Kirksville, Missouri
KCLB-FM Coachella, California
KCLC St. Charles, Missouri
KCLD-FM St. Cloud, Minnesota
KCLH Caledonia, Minnesota
KCLI-FM Cordell, Oklahoma
KCLK-FM Clarkston, Washington
KCLL San Angelo, Texas
KCLQ Lebanon, Missouri
KCLR-FM Boonville, Missouri
KCLS Leeds, Utah
KCLT West Helena, Arkansas
KCLU-FM Thousand Oaks, California
KCLV-FM Clovis, New Mexico
KCLY Clay Center, Kansas
KCMB Baker City, Oregon
KCMC-FM Viola, Arkansas
KCMD Grants Pass, Oregon
KCME Manitou Springs, Colorado
KCMF Fergus Falls, Minnesota
KCMH Mountain Home, Arkansas
KCMI Terrytown, Nebraska
KCML St. Joseph, Minnesota
KCMM Belgrade, Montana
KCMO-FM Shawnee, Kansas
KCMP Northfield, Minnesota
KCMQ Columbia, Missouri
KCMR Mason City, Iowa
KCMS Edmonds, Washington
KCMT Oro Valley, Arizona
KCMX-FM Ashland, Oregon
KCNA Cave Junction, Oregon
KCNB Chadron, Nebraska
KCND Bismarck, North Dakota
KCNE-FM Chadron, Nebraska
KCNO Alturas, California
KCNP Ada, Oklahoma
KCNQ Kernville, California
KCNT Hastings, Nebraska
KCNV Las Vegas, Nevada
KCNY Greenbrier, Arkansas
KCOB-FM Newton, Iowa
KCOI Clovis, New Mexico
KCOL-FM Groves, Texas
KCOO Dunkerton, Iowa
KCOU Columbia, Missouri
KCOZ Point Lookout, Missouri
KCPB-FM Warrenton, Oregon
KCPI Albert Lea, Minnesota
KCPR San Luis Obispo, California
KCPW-FM Salt Lake City, Utah
KCQQ Davenport, Iowa
KCRB-FM Bemidji, Minnesota
KCRE-FM Crescent City, California
KCRF-FM Lincoln City, Oregon
KCRH Hayward, California
KCRI Indio, California
KCRK-FM Colville, Washington
KCRL Sunrise Beach, Missouri
KCRN-FM San Angelo, Texas
KCRR Grundy Center, Iowa
KCRS-FM Midland, Texas
KCRT-FM Trinidad, Colorado
KCRU Oxnard, California
KCRV-FM Caruthersville, Missouri
KCRW Santa Monica, California
KCRX-FM Seaside, Oregon
KCRY Mojave, California
KCRZ Tipton, California
KCSB-FM Santa Barbara, California
KCSC Edmond, Oklahoma
KCSD Sioux Falls, South Dakota
KCSH Ellensburg, Washington
KCSI Villisca, Iowa
KCSM San Mateo, California
KCSN Northridge, California
KCSP-FM Casper, Wyoming
KCSS Turlock, California
KCST-FM Florence, Oregon
KCSU-FM Fort Collins, Colorado
KCSY Twisp, Washington
KCTN Garnavillo, Iowa
KCTR-FM Billings, Montana
KCTT-FM Yellville, Arkansas
KCTX-FM Childress, Texas
KCTY Emerson, Nebraska
KCUA Naples, Utah
KCUK Chevak, Alaska
KCUL-FM Marshall, Texas
KCUR-FM Kansas City, Missouri
KCVI Blackfoot, Idaho
KCVJ Osceola, Missouri
KCVK Otterville, Missouri
KCVM Hudson, Iowa
KCVN Cozad, Nebraska
KCVO-FM Camdenton, Missouri
KCVQ Knob Noster, Missouri
KCVR-FM Columbia, California
KCVS Salina, Kansas
KCVT Silver Lake, Kansas
KCVW Kingman, Kansas
KCVX Salem, Missouri
KCVY Cabool, Missouri
KCVZ Dixon, Missouri
KCWC-FM Riverton, Wyoming
KCWD Harrison, Arkansas

KCWH Weed, California
KCWN New Sharon, Iowa
KCWR Bakersfield, California
KCWU Ellensburg, Washington
KCWW Battle Mountain, Nevada
KCXR Taft, Oklahoma
KCXX Lake Arrowhead, California
KCXY East Camden, Arkansas
KCYE Boulder City, Nevada
KCYN Moab, Utah
KCYS Seaside, Oregon
KCYY San Antonio, Texas
KCZE New Hampton, Iowa
KCZO Carrizo Springs, Texas
KCZQ Cresco, Iowa
KDAA Rolla, Missouri
KDAB Central City, Colorado
KDAD Bar Nunn, Wyoming
KDAG Farmington, New Mexico
KDAI Scottsbluff, Nebraska
KDAL-FM Duluth, Minnesota
KDAO-FM Eldora, Iowa
KDAQ Shreveport, Louisiana
KDAR Oxnard, California
KDAT Cedar Rapids, Iowa
KDAY Redondo Beach, California
KDB Santa Barbara, California
KDBB Bonne Terre, Missouri
KDBH-FM Natchitoches, Louisiana
KDBI Emmett, Idaho
KDBL Parachute, Washington
KDBL(FM) Toppenish, Washington
KDBQ Rattan, Oklahoma
KDBR Kalispell, Montana
KDBX Clear Lake, South Dakota
KDBZ Anchorage, Alaska
KDCD San Angelo, Texas
KDCQ Coos Bay, Oregon
KDCR Sioux Center, Iowa
KDCV-FM Blair, Nebraska
KDCZ Eyota, Minnesota
KDDB Waipahu, Hawaii
KDDD-FM Dumas, Texas
KDDG Albany, Minnesota
KDDK Franklin, Louisiana
KDDL Chino Valley, Arizona
KDDQ Comanche, Oklahoma
KDDS-FM Elma, Washington
KDDV-FM Wright, Wyoming
KDDX Spearfish, South Dakota
KDEC-FM Decorah, Iowa
KDEL-FM Arkadelphia, Arkansas
KDEM Deming, New Mexico
KDEP Garibaldi, Oregon
KDES-FM Cathedral City, California
KDET-FM San Augustine, Texas
KDEW-FM De Witt, Arkansas
KDEX-FM Dexter, Missouri
KDEY(FM) Ontario, California
KDEZ Brandon, South Dakota
KDFC Angwin, California
KDFM Falfurrias, Texas
KDFO Delano, California
KDFR Des Moines, Iowa
KDGE Fort Worth-Dallas, Texas
KDGL Yucca Valley, California
KDGS Andover, Kansas
KDHX Saint Louis, Missouri
KDIM Coweta, Oklahoma
KDIS-FM Little Rock, Arkansas
KDJC Baker, Oregon
KDJE Jacksonville, Arkansas
KDJF Ester, Alaska
KDJK Mariposa, California
KDJM Lindsborg, Kansas
KDJR De Soto, Missouri
KDJS-FM Willmar, Minnesota
KDKB Mesa, Arizona
KDKD-FM Clinton, Missouri
KDKK Park Rapids, Minnesota
KDKL Coalinga, California
KDKN Ellington, Missouri
KDKR Decatur, Texas
KDKS-FM Blanchard, Louisiana
KDLD Santa Monica, California
KDLE Newport Beach, California
KDLG-FM Dillingham, Alaska
KDLI Del Rio, Texas
KDLK-FM Del Rio, Texas
KDLL Kenai, Alaska
KDLO-FM Watertown, South Dakota
KDLS-FM Perry, Iowa
KDLW Los Alamos, New Mexico
KDLX Makawao, Hawaii
KDLY Lander, Wyoming
KDMG Burlington, Iowa
KDMX Dallas, Texas
KDNA Yakima, Washington
KDND Sacramento, California
KDNE Crete, Nebraska
KDNG Durango, Colorado
KDNI Duluth, Minnesota
KDNK Glenwood Springs, Colorado
KDNN Honolulu, Hawaii
KDNO Thermopolis, Wyoming
KDNR South Greeley, Wyoming
KDNS Downs, Kansas
KDNW Duluth, Minnesota
KDOE Antlers, Oklahoma
KDOG North Mankato, Minnesota
KDOM-FM Windom, Minnesota
KDON-FM Salinas, California
KDOT Reno, Nevada
KDOV Medford, Oregon
KDPR Dickinson, North Dakota
KDQN-FM De Queen, Arkansas
KDRB Des Moines, Iowa
KDRE Sterling, Colorado
KDRF Albuquerque, New Mexico
KDRH King City, California
KDRI Grants, New Mexico
KDRK-FM Spokane, Washington
KDRM Moses Lake, Washington
KDRS-FM Paragould, Arkansas
KDRX Laughlin Afb, Texas
KDSC Thousand Oaks, California
KDSD-FM Pierpont, South Dakota
KDSK Grants, New Mexico
KDSN-FM Denison, Iowa
KDSP(FM) Greenwood Village, Colorado
KDSR Williston, North Dakota
KDSS Ely, Nevada
KDST Dyersville, Iowa
KDSU Fargo, North Dakota
KDTR Florence, Montana
KDUC Barstow, California
KDUK-FM Florence, Oregon
KDUP Cedarville, California
KDUQ Ludlow, California
KDUR Durango, Colorado
KDUT Randolph, Utah
KDUV Visalia, California
KDUW Douglas, Wyoming
KDVA Buckeye, Arizona
KDVB Effingham, Kansas
KDVC Loma, Colorado
KDVI Devils Lake, North Dakota
KDVL Devils Lake, North Dakota
KDVS Davis, California
KDVV Topeka, Kansas
KDWB-FM Richfield, Minnesota
KDWG Dillon, Montana
KDWY Diamondville, Wyoming
KDWZ Superior, Wisconsin
KDXL St. Louis Park, Minnesota
KDXN South Heart, North Dakota
KDXT Lolo, Montana
KDXX Denton, Texas
KDXY Lake City, Arkansas
KDYN-FM Ozark, Arkansas
KDZA-FM Pueblo, Colorado
KDZN Glendive, Montana
KDZY McCall, Idaho
KDZZ St. Charles, Minnesota
KEAF Fort Smith, Arkansas
KEAG Anchorage, Alaska
KEAL Taft, California
KEAN-FM Abilene, Texas
KEAR-FM Sacramento, California
KEAZ Heber Springs, Arkansas
KEBN Garden Grove, California
KEBT Lost Hills, California
KECC La Junta, Colorado
KECG El Cerrito, California
KECH-FM Sun Valley, Idaho
KECK Eckley, Colorado
KECO Elk City, Oklahoma
KECU Kaibito, Arizona
KEDB Chariton, Iowa
KEDC Hearne, Texas
KEDG Alexandria, Louisiana
KEDM Monroe, Louisiana
KEDP Las Vegas, New Mexico
KEDR Bay City, Texas
KEDR(FM) Butte, Montana
KEDT-FM Corpus Christi, Texas
KEEA Aberdeen, South Dakota
KEEH Spokane, Washington
KEEP Bandera, Texas
KEEY-FM St. Paul, Minnesota
KEEZ-FM Mankato, Minnesota
KEFH Clarendon, Texas
KEFR Le Grand, California
KEFS North Powder, Oregon
KEFX Twin Falls, Idaho
KEGA Oakley, Utah
KEGE Pocatello, Idaho
KEGH Brigham City, Utah
KEGI Jonesboro, Arkansas
KEGK Wahpeton, North Dakota
KEGL Fort Worth, Texas
KEGR Fort Dodge, Iowa
KEGX Richland, Washington
KEGY(FM) San Diego, California
KEHK Brownsville, Oregon
KEIS York, Nebraska
KEJA Cale, Arkansas
KEJJ Gunnison, Colorado
KEJL Eunice, New Mexico
KEJS Lubbock, Texas
KEKA-FM Eureka, California
KEKB Fruita, Colorado
KEKL Mesquite, Nevada
KEKO Hebbronville, Texas
KEKS Olpe, Kansas
KELC Hawthorne, Nevada
KELD-FM Hampton, Arkansas
KELE-FM Mountain Grove, Missouri
KELI San Angelo, Texas
KELN North Platte, Nebraska
KELO-FM Sioux Falls, South Dakota
KELP-FM Mesquite, New Mexico
KELU Clovis, New Mexico
KEMA Three Rivers, Texas
KEMC Billings, Montana
KEMR Castle Dale, Utah
KEMX Locust Grove, Oklahoma
KENA-FM Mena, Arkansas
KEND Roswell, New Mexico
KENM Tucumcari, New Mexico
KENR Superior, Montana
KENU Des Moines, New Mexico
KENW-FM Portales, New Mexico
KENZ Ogden, Utah
KEOJ Caney, Kansas
KEOK Tahlequah, Oklahoma
KEOL La Grande, Oregon
KEOM Mesquite, Texas
KEOS College Station, Texas
KEPC Colorado Springs, Colorado
KEPI Eagle Pass, Texas
KEPX Eagle Pass, Texas
KEQX Stephenville, Texas
KERA Dallas, Texas
KERB-FM Kermit, Texas
KERL Cotton Plant, Arkansas
KERM Torrington, Wyoming
KERP Ingalls, Kansas
KERX Paris, Arkansas
KESA Eureka Springs, Arkansas
KESC Morro Bay, California
KESD Brookings, South Dakota
KESG Sayre, Oklahoma
KESM-FM El Dorado Springs, Missouri
KESN Allen, Texas
KESO South Padre Island, Texas
KESR Shasta Lake City, California
KESS-FM Lewisville, Texas
KESY Baker City, Oregon
KESZ Phoenix, Arizona
KETE Sulphur Bluff, Texas
KETP Enterprise, Oregon
KETR Commerce, Texas
KETT Mitchell, Nebraska
KETX-FM Livingston, Texas
KEUG Veneta, Oregon
KEUL Girdwood, Alaska
KEUN-FM Eunice, Louisiana
KEWB Anderson, California
KEWF(FM) Billings, Colorado
KEWL-FM New Boston, Texas
KEWS(FM) Sac City, Iowa
KEWU-FM Cheney, Washington
KEXA King City, California
KEXL Pierce, Nebraska
KEXP-FM Seattle, Washington
KEXS-FM Ravenwood, Missouri
KEXX(FM) Gilbert, Arizona
KEYA Belcourt, North Dakota
KEYB Altus, Oklahoma
KEYD Delta, Utah
KEYE-FM Perryton, Texas
KEYF-FM Cheney, Washington
KEYG-FM Grand Coulee, Washington
KEYJ-FM Abilene, Texas
KEYN-FM Wichita, Kansas
KEYP Price, Utah
KEYR Richfield, Utah
KEYV Vernal, Utah
KEYW Pasco, Washington
KEZA Fayetteville, Arkansas
KEZB Beaver, Utah
KEZE Spokane, Washington
KEZJ-FM Twin Falls, Idaho
KEZK-FM St. Louis, Missouri
KEZN Palm Desert, California
KEZO-FM Omaha, Nebraska
KEZP Bunkie, Louisiana
KEZQ West Yellowstone, Montana
KEZR San Jose, California
KEZS-FM Cape Girardeau, Missouri
KEZZ Phippsburg, Colorado
KFAE-FM Richland, Washington
KFAI Minneapolis, Minnesota
KFAN-FM Johnson City, Texas
KFAT Anchorage, Alaska
KFAV Warrenton, Missouri
KFBD-FM Waynesville, Missouri
KFBK-FM Sacramento, California
KFBN Fargo, North Dakota
KFBR Gerlach, Nevada
KFBZ Haysville, Kansas
KFCF Fresno, California
KFCM Ash Flat, Arkansas
KFDC Shiprock, New Mexico
KFDI-FM Wichita, Kansas
KFEB Campbell, Missouri
KFEG Klamath Falls, Oregon
KFER Santa Cruz, California
KFEZ(FM) Walsenburg, Colorado
KFFA-FM Helena, Arkansas
KFFB Fairfield Bay, Arkansas
KFFF Bennington, Nebraska
KFFF-FM Boone, Iowa
KFFG Los Altos, California
KFFM Yakima, Washington
KFFX Emporia, Kansas
KFGE Milford, Nebraska
KFGI Crosby, Minnesota
KFGY Healdsburg, California
KFH-FM Clearwater, Kansas
KFHC Ponca, Nebraska
KFHL Wasco, California
KFIL-FM Chatfield, Minnesota
KFIN Jonesboro, Arkansas
KFIS Scappoose, Oregon
KFIX Plainville, Kansas
KFJC Los Altos, California
KFJM Grand Forks, North Dakota
KFJS North Platte, Nebraska
KFKF-FM Kansas City, Kansas
KFKX Hastings, Nebraska
KFLB-FM Stanton, Texas
KFLF Somers, Montana
KFLG-FM Big River, California
KFLI Des Arc, Arkansas
KFLO-FM Blanchard, Louisiana
KFLP-FM Floydada, Texas
KFLQ Albuquerque, New Mexico
KFLR-FM Phoenix, Arizona
KFLS-FM Tulelake, California
KFLT-FM Tucson, Arizona
KFLV Wilber, Nebraska
KFLW St. Robert, Missouri
KFLY Corvallis, Oregon
KFMA Green Valley, Arizona
KFMB-FM San Diego, California
KFMC-FM Fairmont, Minnesota
KFMF Chico, California
KFMH Belle Fourche, South Dakota
KFMI Eureka, California
KFMJ Ketchikan, Alaska
KFMK Round Rock, Texas
KFML Little Falls, Minnesota

KFMM Thatcher, Arizona
KFMN Lihue, Hawaii
KFMQ Gallup, New Mexico
KFMR Ballard, Utah
KFMT-FM Fremont, Nebraska
KFMU-FM Oak Creek, Colorado
KFMW Waterloo, Iowa
KFMX-FM Lubbock, Texas
KFNC Mont Belvieu, Texas
KFNF Oberlin, Kansas
KFNL Kindred, North Dakota
KFNO Fresno, California
KFNS-FM Troy, Missouri
KFNV-FM Ferriday, Louisiana
KFNW-FM Fargo, North Dakota
KFOG San Francisco, California
KFON Menard, Texas
KFPR Redding, California
KFPW-FM Barling, Arkansas
KFRB Bakersfield, California
KFRC-FM San Francisco, California
KFRD Butte, Montana
KFRG San Bernardino, California
KFRH North Las Vegas, Nevada
KFRI West Odessa, Texas
KFRJ China Lake, California
KFRO-FM Gilmer, Texas
KFRP Coalinga, California
KFRQ Harlingen, Texas
KFRR Woodlake, California
KFRS Soledad, California
KFRW Great Falls, Montana
KFRX Lincoln, Nebraska
KFRY Pueblo, Colorado
KFRZ Green River, Wyoming
KFSE Kasilof, Alaska
KFSH-FM La Mirada, California
KFSI Rochester, Minnesota
KFSK Petersburg, Alaska
KFSO-FM Visalia, California
KFSR Fresno, California
KFST-FM Fort Stockton, Texas
KFSZ Munds Park, Arizona
KFTE Abbeville, Louisiana
KFTG Pasadena, Texas
KFTI-FM Newton, Kansas
KFTK Florissant, Missouri
KFTT Bagdad, Arizona
KFTW Fort Washakie, Wyoming
KFTX Kingsville, Texas
KFTZ Idaho Falls, Idaho
KFVR-FM Beulah, Colorado
KFWA(FM) Weldona, Colorado
KFWR Jacksboro, Texas
KFXH Marlow, Oklahoma
KFXI Marlow, Oklahoma
KFXJ Augusta, Kansas
KFXN-FM Minneapolis, Minnesota
KFXR-FM Chinle, Arizona
KFXS Rapid City, South Dakota
KFXT Sulphur, Oklahoma
KFXU Chickasha, Oklahoma
KFXX-FM Hugoton, Kansas
KFXZ-FM Opelousas, Louisiana
KFYV Ojai, California
KFYX(FM) Texarkana, Arkansas
KFZX Gardendale, Texas
KGAC Saint Peter, Minnesota
KGAM Merced, California
KGAM(FM) Merced, California
KGAP Clarksville, Texas
KGAS-FM Carthage, Texas
KGB-FM San Diego, California
KGBA-FM Holtville, California
KGBB Edwards, California
KGBI-FM Omaha, Nebraska
KGBM Randsburg, California
KGBR Gold Beach, Oregon
KGBT-FM McAllen, Texas
KGBX-FM Nixa, Missouri
KGCB Prescott, Arizona
KGCC Gillette, Wyoming
KGCD Wray, Colorado
KGCL Jordan Valley, Oregon
KGCM Belgrade, Montana
KGCN Roswell, New Mexico
KGCO Fort Collins, Colorado
KGCR Goodland, Kansas
KGCU Port Alsworth, Alaska
KGCV Elk Mountain, Wyoming
KGCX Sidney, Montana
KGDN Pasco, Washington
KGDP-FM Santa Maria, California
KGEE Pecos, Texas
KGEN-FM Hanford, California
KGFA Great Falls, Montana
KGFC Great Falls, Montana
KGFJ Belt, Montana
KGFM Bakersfield, California
KGFT Pueblo, Colorado
KGFX-FM Pierre, South Dakota
KGFY Stillwater, Oklahoma
KGGA Gallup, New Mexico
KGGB Yorktown, Texas
KGGF-FM Fredonia, Kansas
KGGI Riverside, California
KGGL Missoula, Montana
KGGM Delhi, Louisiana
KGGO Des Moines, Iowa
KGHE Glenoma, Washington
KGHL(FM) Billings, Montana
KGHP Gig Harbor, Washington
KGHR Tuba City, Arizona
KGHT El Jebel, Colorado
KGHT(FM) El Jebel, Colorado
KGHT-FM El Jebel, Alaska
KGHY Beaumont, Texas
KGIL Johannesburg, California
KGIM-FM Redfield, South Dakota
KGIO Astoria, Oregon
KGJX Fruita, Colorado
KGKL-FM San Angelo, Texas
KGKS Scott City, Missouri
KGLC Miami, Oklahoma
KGLF Doss, Texas
KGLI Sioux City, Iowa
KGLL Gillette, Wyoming
KGLM-FM Anaconda, Montana
KGLP Gallup, New Mexico
KGLT Bozeman, Montana
KGLU Gideon, Missouri
KGLV Manhattan, Kansas
KGLX Gallup, New Mexico
KGLY Tyler, Texas
KGMN Kingman, Arizona
KGMO Cape Girardeau, Missouri
KGMX Lancaster, California
KGMZ(FM) San Francisco, California
KGNA-FM Arnold, Missouri
KGNC-FM Amarillo, Texas
KGNN-FM Cuba, Missouri
KGNT Smithfield, Utah
KGNU-FM Boulder, Colorado
KGNV Washington, Missouri
KGNX Ballwin, Missouri
KGNZ Abilene, Texas
KGON Portland, Oregon
KGOR Omaha, Nebraska
KGOT Anchorage, Alaska
KGOU Norman, Oklahoma
KGOZ Gallatin, Missouri
KGPQ Monticello, Arkansas
KGPR Great Falls, Montana
KGPZ Coleraine, Minnesota
KGRA Jefferson, Iowa
KGRB(FM) Jackson, California
KGRC Hannibal, Missouri
KGRD Orchard, Nebraska
KGRG-FM Auburn, Washington
KGRI Lebanon, Oregon
KGRK Glenrock, Wyoming
KGRM Grambling, Louisiana
KGRP Grand Rapids, Minnesota
KGRR Epworth, Iowa
KGRS Burlington, Iowa
KGRT-FM Las Cruces, New Mexico
KGRW Friona, Texas
KGSF Green Forest, Arkansas
KGSP Parkville, Missouri
KGSR Cedar Park, Texas
KGSX Comfort, Texas
KGTM Rexburg, Idaho
KGTR Albany, Missouri
KGTS College Place, Washington
KGTW Ketchikan, Alaska
KGUA Gualala, California
KGUD Longmont, Colorado
KGUM-FM Dededo, Guam
KGVA Fort Belknap Agency, Montana
KGVB Holliday, Texas
KGVE Grove, Oklahoma
KGVO-FM Frenchtown, Montana
KGVV Goltry, Oklahoma
KGWB Snyder, Texas
KGWP Pittsburg, Texas
KGWT George West, Texas
KGWY Gillette, Wyoming
KGY-FM McCleary, Washington
KGZG-FM Newport, Washington
KGZO Shafter, California
KHAD Upton, Wyoming
KHAI Wahiawa, Hawaii
KHAK Cedar Rapids, Iowa
KHAL Cedarville, California
KHAM Britt, Iowa
KHAN(FM) Kensett, Arkansas
KHAP Chico, California
KHAQ Maxwell, Nebraska
KHAY Ventura, California
KHAZ Hays, Kansas
KHBC Hilo, Hawaii
KHBM-FM Monticello, Arkansas
KHBT Humboldt, Iowa
KHBW(FM) Brownwood, Texas
KHCA Wamego, Kansas
KHCB-FM Houston, Texas
KHCC-FM Hutchinson, Kansas
KHCD Salina, Kansas
KHCJ Jefferson, Texas
KHCL Arcadia, Louisiana
KHCM-FM Honolulu, Hawaii
KHCO Hayden, Colorado
KHCP Paris, Texas
KHCR Bismarck, Missouri
KHCS Palm Desert, California
KHCT Great Bend, Kansas
KHDC Chualar, California
KHDK New London, Iowa
KHDR Lenwood, California
KHDV Darby, Montana
KHDX Conway, Arkansas
KHEB Granite, Oklahoma
KHEC Crescent City, California
KHED Arkadelphia, Arkansas
KHEI-FM Kihei, Hawaii
KHER Crystal City, Texas
KHEV Fairview, Oklahoma
KHEW Rocky Boy's Reserv., Montana
KHEY-FM El Paso, Texas
KHFI-FM Georgetown, Texas
KHFM Santa Fe, New Mexico
KHFR Santa Maria, California
KHGE Fresno, California
KHGG-FM Waldron, Arkansas
KHGO Homer, Alaska
KHHG Hico, Texas
KHHK Yakima, Washington
KHHL Karnes City, Texas
KHHT Los Angeles, California
KHHZ Gridley, California
KHIB Bastrop, Texas
KHID McAllen, Texas
KHIH Estes Park, Colorado
KHII Cloudcroft, New Mexico
KHIM Mangum, Oklahoma
KHIP Gonzales, California
KHIS Jackson, Missouri
KHIT-FM Madera, California
KHIX Carlin, Nevada
KHJC Lihue, Hawaii
KHJJ Shaniko, Oregon
KHJK La Porte, Texas
KHJL(FM) Thousand Oaks, California
KHKC-FM Atoka, Oklahoma
KHKE Cedar Falls, Iowa
KHKI Des Moines, Iowa
KHKK Modesto, California
KHKL Laytonville, California
KHKN Maumelle, Arkansas
KHKR-FM East Helena, Montana
KHKS Denton, Texas
KHKV Kerrville, Texas
KHKX Odessa, Texas
KHKY Akiachak, Alaska
KHKZ San Benito, Texas
KHLA Jennings, Louisiana
KHLB Mason, Texas
KHLE Kempner, Texas
KHLL Richwood, Louisiana
KHLR Benton, Arkansas
KHLS Blytheville, Arkansas
KHLV Helena, Montana
KHLX Pollock Pines, California
KHMB Hamburg, Arkansas
KHMC Goliad, Texas
KHMD Mansfield, Louisiana
KHME Winona, Minnesota
KHMG Barrigada, Guam
KHML Madisonville, Texas
KHMR Lovelady, Texas
KHMS Victorville, California
KHMX Houston, Texas
KHMY Pratt, Kansas
KHNA Wamsutter, Wyoming
KHNE-FM Hastings, Nebraska
KHNK Columbia Falls, Montana
KHNS Haines, Alaska
KHNW Manson, Washington
KHOC Casper, Wyoming
KHOE Fairfield, Iowa
KHOI Story City, Iowa
KHOK Hoisington, Kansas
KHOL Jackson, Wyoming
KHOM Salem, Arkansas
KHOP Oakdale, California
KHOS-FM Sonora, Texas
KHOT-FM Paradise Valley, Arizona
KHOV-FM Wickenburg, Arizona
KHOY Laredo, Texas
KHOZ-FM Harrison, Arkansas
KHPA Hope, Arkansas
KHPE Albany, Oregon
KHPO Port O'Connor, Texas
KHPQ Clinton, Arkansas
KHPR Honolulu, Hawaii
KHPT Conroe, Texas
KHQT Las Cruces, New Mexico
KHRD Weaverville, California
KHRI Hollister, California
KHRQ Baker, California
KHRS Winthrop, Minnesota
KHRT-FM Minot, North Dakota
KHRV Hood River, Oregon
KHRW Ranchester, Wyoming
KHSK Allen, Nebraska
KHSL-FM Paradise, California
KHSR Crescent City, California
KHSS Athena, Oregon
KHST Lamar, Missouri
KHSU Arcata, California
KHTA Wake Village, Texas
KHTB Provo, Utah
KHTC(FM) Lake Jackson, Texas
KHTE-FM England, Arkansas
KHTN Planada, California
KHTQ Hayden, Idaho
KHTR Pullman, Washington
KHTS-FM El Cajon, California
KHTT Muskogee, Oklahoma
KHTZ Ganado, Texas
KHUI Alamosa, Colorado
KHUM Cutten, California
KHUN Huntington, Utah
KHUT Hutchinson, Kansas
KHVT Bloomington, Texas
KHWG-FM Crystal, Nevada
KHWI Holualoa, Hawaii
KHWK Tonopah, Nevada
KHWY Essex, California
KHWZ Ludlow, California
KHXS Merkel, Texas
KHXT Erath, Louisiana
KHYI Howe, Texas
KHYL Auburn, California
KHYM Copeland, Kansas
KHYS Hays, Kansas
KHYT Tucson, Arizona
KHYY Minatare, Nebraska
KHYZ Mountain Pass, California
KHZK Kotzebue, Alaska
KHZR Potosi, Missouri
KHZY Overton, Nebraska
KHZZ Sargent, Nebraska
KIAD Dubuque, Iowa
KIAI Mason City, Iowa
KIAK-FM Fairbanks, Alaska
KIAM-FM North Nenana, Alaska
KIAQ Clarion, Iowa
KIBB Haven, Kansas
KIBC Burney, California
KIBG Bigfork, Montana
KIBR Sandpoint, Idaho
KIBS Bishop, California
KIBT Fountain, Colorado

RADIO - U.S.

KIBX Bonners Ferry, Idaho
KIBZ Crete, Nebraska
KICA-FM Farwell, Texas
KICB Fort Dodge, Iowa
KICD-FM Spencer, Iowa
KICJ(FM) Mitchellville, Iowa
KICK-FM Palmyra, Missouri
KICL(FM) Pleasantville, Iowa
KICM Healdton, Oklahoma
KICO Rico, Colorado
KICR Coeur D'Alene, Idaho
KICT-FM Wichita, Kansas
KICX-FM McCook, Nebraska
KICY-FM Nome, Alaska
KID-FM Idaho Falls, Idaho
KIDE Hoopa, California
KIDI-FM Lompoc, California
KIDN-FM Burns, Colorado
KIDS Grants, New Mexico
KIDX Ruidoso, New Mexico
KIFG-FM Iowa Falls, Iowa
KIFM San Diego, California
KIFR Alice, Texas
KIFS Ashland, Oregon
KIFT(FM) Kremmling, Colorado
KIFX Roosevelt, Utah
KIGC Oskaloosa, Iowa
KIGL Seligman, Missouri
KIGN Burns, Wyoming
KIHI Burns, Wyoming
KIHK Rock Valley, Iowa
KIHS Adel, Iowa
KIHT St. Louis, Missouri
KIIC Albia, Iowa
KIIM-FM Tucson, Arizona
KIIS-FM Los Angeles, California
KIIZ-FM Killeen, Texas
KIJI Tumon, Guam
KIJN-FM Farwell, Texas
KIKC-FM Forsyth, Montana
KIKD Lake City, Iowa
KIKF Cascade, Montana
KIKG Licking, Missouri
KIKL Lafayette, Louisiana
KIKN-FM Salem, South Dakota
KIKO-FM Claypool, Arizona
KIKS-FM Iola, Kansas
KIKT Greenville, Texas
KIKV-FM Sauk Centre, Minnesota
KIKX Ketchum, Idaho
KILE-FM Woodland Park, Colorado
KILI Porcupine, South Dakota
KILJ-FM Mount Pleasant, Iowa
KILO Colorado Springs, Colorado
KILR-FM Estherville, Iowa
KILT-FM Houston, Texas
KILV Castana, Iowa
KILX Hatfield, Arkansas
KIMN Denver, Colorado
KIMX Nunn, Colorado
KIMY Watonga, Oklahoma
KINB Kingfisher, Oklahoma
KIND-FM Elk City, Kansas
KINE-FM Honolulu, Hawaii
KING-FM Seattle, Washington
KINI Crookston, Nebraska
KINK Portland, Oregon
KINL Eagle Pass, Texas
KINT-FM El Paso, Texas
KINU Kotzebue, Alaska
KINX Fairfield, Montana
KINZ Humboldt, Kansas
KIOA Des Moines, Iowa
KIOC Orange, Texas
KIOD McCook, Nebraska
KIOI San Francisco, California
KIOK Richland, Washington
KIOO Porterville, California
KIOS-FM Omaha, Nebraska
KIOT Los Lunas, New Mexico
KIOW Forest City, Iowa
KIOX-FM Edna, Texas
KIOZ San Diego, California
KIPO Honolulu, Hawaii
KIPR Pine Bluff, Arkansas
KIQK Rapid City, South Dakota
KIQN-FM Pueblo, Colorado
KIQO Atascadero, California
KIQQ-FM Newberry Springs, California
KIQX Durango, Colorado
KIQZ Rawlins, Wyoming
KIRC Seminole, Oklahoma
KIRK Macon, Missouri
KIRL Osage Beach, Missouri
KIRO-FM Tacoma, Washington
KIRQ Twin Falls, Idaho
KISC Spokane, Washington
KISD Pipestone, Minnesota
KISF Las Vegas, Nevada
KISH Agana, Guam
KISL Avalon, California
KISM Bellingham, Washington
KISN Belgrade, Montana
KISO Omaha, Nebraska
KISQ San Francisco, California
KISR Fort Smith, Arkansas
KISS-FM San Antonio, Texas
KIST-FM Carpinteria, California
KISU-FM Pocatello, Idaho
KISV Bakersfield, California
KISW Seattle, Washington
KISX Whitehouse, Texas
KISZ-FM Cortez, Colorado
KIT-FM Naches, Washington
KITA Iota, Louisiana
KITE Port Lavaca, Texas
KITF International Falls, Minnesota
KITH Kapaa, Hawaii
KITI-FM Winlock, Washington
KITN Worthington, Minnesota
KITO-FM Vinita, Oklahoma
KITS San Francisco, California
KITT Soda Springs, Idaho
KITX Hugo, Oklahoma
KITY Llano, Texas
KIVY-FM Crockett, Texas
KIWA-FM Sheldon, Iowa
KIWI McFarland, California
KIWR Council Bluffs, Iowa
KIXA Lucerne Valley, California
KIXB El Dorado, Arkansas
KIXF Baker, California
KIXN Hobbs, New Mexico
KIXO Sulphur, Oklahoma
KIXQ Joplin, Missouri
KIXR Ponca City, Oklahoma
KIXS Victoria, Texas
KIXT(FM) Bay City, Oregon
KIXV(FM) Malvern, Arkansas
KIXW-FM Lenwood, California
KIXX Watertown, South Dakota
KIXY-FM San Angelo, Texas
KIXZ-FM Opportunity, Washington
KIYK Saint George, Utah
KIYS Walnut Ridge, Arkansas
KIYS-FM Walnut Ridge, Arkansas
KIYU-FM Galena, Alaska
KIYX Sageville, Iowa
KIZN Boise, Idaho
KIZS Collinsville, Oklahoma
KIZZ Minot, North Dakota
KJAB-FM Mexico, Missouri
KJAC Timnath, Colorado
KJAE Leesville, Louisiana
KJAK Slaton, Texas
KJAM-FM Madison, South Dakota
KJAQ Seattle, Washington
KJAS Jasper, Texas
KJAV Alamo, Texas
KJAX Jackson, Wyoming
KJAZ Point Comfort, Texas
KJBB(FM) Watertown, South Dakota
KJBI Fort Pierre, South Dakota
KJBL Julesburg, Colorado
KJBR Marked Tree, Arkansas
KJBX Cash, Arkansas
KJBZ Laredo, Texas
KJCC Carnegie, Oklahoma
KJCD Fort Benton, Montana
KJCF Asotin, Washington
KJCG Missoula, Montana
KJCH Coos Bay, Oregon
KJCK-FM Junction City, Kansas
KJCM Snyder, Oklahoma
KJCQ Westwood, California
KJCS Nacogdoches, Texas
KJCU Fort Bragg, California
KJCV-FM Country Club, Missouri
KJCY St. Ansgar, Iowa
KJDL-FM Levelland, Texas
KJDX Susanville, California
KJDY-FM Canyon City, Oregon
KJEE Montecito, California
KJEL Lebanon, Missouri
KJET Raymond, Washington
KJEZ Poplar Bluff, Missouri
KJFA Santa Fe, New Mexico
KJFM Louisiana, Missouri
KJFT Arlee, Montana
KJFX Fresno, California
KJGS Aurora, Nebraska
KJHA Houston, Alaska
KJHK Lawrence, Kansas
KJHL Boise City, Oklahoma
KJIA Spirit Lake, Iowa
KJIH Manhattan, Kansas
KJIK Duncan, Arizona
KJIL Copeland, Kansas
KJIR Hannibal, Missouri
KJIV Reno, Nevada
KJIW-FM Helena, Arkansas
KJJJ Laughlin, Nevada
KJJK-FM Fergus Falls, Minnesota
KJJM Baker, Montana
KJJP Amarillo, Texas
KJJS Zapata, Texas
KJJY West Des Moines, Iowa
KJJZ Indio, California
KJKB Scotland, Texas
KJKE Newcastle, Oklahoma
KJKJ Grand Forks, North Dakota
KJKK Dallas, Texas
KJKL Selma, Oregon
KJKS Kahului, Hawaii
KJKT Spearfish, South Dakota
KJLC(FM) Susanville, California
KJLC-FM Needles, California
KJLF Butte, Montana
KJLG Emporia, Kansas
KJLH Compton, California
KJLJ Scott City, Kansas
KJLL(FM) Fountain Valley, California
KJLO-FM Monroe, Louisiana
KJLP Palmer, Alaska
KJLS Hays, Kansas
KJLT-FM North Platte, Nebraska
KJLU Jefferson City, Missouri
KJLV Hoxie, Arkansas
KJLY Blue Earth, Minnesota
KJMA Floresville, Texas
KJMB-FM Blythe, California
KJMC Des Moines, Iowa
KJMD Pukalani, Hawaii
KJMG Bastrop, Louisiana
KJMH Lake Arthur, Louisiana
KJMK Webb City, Missouri
KJML Columbus, Kansas
KJML(FM) Columbus, Kansas
KJMM Bixby, Oklahoma
KJMN Castle Rock, Colorado
KJMO Linn, Missouri
KJMQ Lihue, Hawaii
KJMS Olive Branch, Mississippi
KJMT Calico Rock, Arkansas
KJMX Reedsport, Oregon
KJMY Bountiful, Utah
KJMZ Cache, Oklahoma
KJNA-FM Jena, Louisiana
KJND-FM Williston, North Dakota
KJNP-FM North Pole, Alaska
KJNZ Hereford, Texas
KJOE Slayton, Minnesota
KJOG Cleveland, Oklahoma
KJOJ-FM Freeport, Texas
KJOK Hollis, Oklahoma
KJOL-FM Montrose, Colorado
KJOR Windsor, California
KJOT Boise, Idaho
KJOV Woodward, Oklahoma
KJOY Stockton, California
KJQY Colorado City, Colorado
KJR-FM Seattle, Washington
KJRF Lawton, Oklahoma
KJRL Herington, Kansas
KJRN Keene, Texas
KJRT Amarillo, Texas
KJRV Wessington Springs, South Dakota
KJSB Jonesboro, Arkansas
KJSM-FM Augusta, Arkansas
KJSN Modesto, California
KJSR Tulsa, Oklahoma
KJTA Flagstaff, Arizona
KJTH Ponca City, Oklahoma
KJTW Jamestown, North Dakota
KJTX Jefferson, Texas
KJTY Topeka, Kansas
KJUG-FM Tulare, California
KJUL Moapa Valley, Nevada
KJVC Mansfield, Louisiana
KJVH Longview, Washington
KJWA Trinidad, Colorado
KJWL Fresno, California
KJWR Windom, Minnesota
KJXJ Franklin, Texas
KJXK San Antonio, Texas
KJXN South Park, Wyoming
KJYL Eagle Grove, Iowa
KJYO Oklahoma City, Oklahoma
KJZA Drake, Arizona
KJZK Kingman, Arizona
KJZN San Joaquin, California
KJZP Prescott, Arizona
KJZY Sebastopol, California
KJZZ Phoenix, Arizona
KKAC Vandalia, Missouri
KKAJ-FM Davis, Oklahoma
KKAL Paso Robles, California
KKAT Orem, Utah
KKAW Albin, Wyoming
KKBA Kingsville, Texas
KKBB Bakersfield, California
KKBC-FM Baker, Oregon
KKBD Sallisaw, Oklahoma
KKBG Hilo, Hawaii
KKBI Broken Bow, Oklahoma
KKBJ-FM Bemidji, Minnesota
KKBL Monett, Missouri
KKBN Twain Harte, California
KKBO Flasher, North Dakota
KKBQ-FM Pasadena, Texas
KKBR Billings, Montana
KKBS Guymon, Oklahoma
KKBW Eatonville, Washington
KKBY Kirby, Wyoming
KKBZ Auberry, California
KKCB Duluth, Minnesota
KKCD Omaha, Nebraska
KKCH Glenwood Springs, Colorado
KKCI Goodland, Kansas
KKCJ Cannon Afb, New Mexico
KKCK Marshall, Minnesota
KKCL Lorenzo, Texas
KKCM Thermal, California
KKCN Ballinger, Texas
KKCQ-FM Bagley, Minnesota
KKCR Hanalei, Hawaii
KKCS(FM) Calhan, Colorado
KKCT Bismarck, North Dakota
KKCV Rozel, Kansas
KKCW Beaverton, Oregon
KKCY Colusa, California
KKDA-FM Dallas, Texas
KKDC Dolores, Colorado
KKDL Dilley, Texas
KKDM Des Moines, Iowa
KKDQ Thief River Falls, Minnesota
KKDT Burdett, Kansas
KKDV Walnut Creek, California
KKDY West Plains, Missouri
KKED Fairbanks, Alaska
KKEE Wheelock, Texas
KKEG Bentonville, Arkansas
KKEN Duncan, Oklahoma
KKER Kerrville, Texas
KKEX Preston, Idaho
KKEZ Fort Dodge, Iowa
KKFC Hart, Texas
KKFD-FM Fairfield, Iowa
KKFG Bloomfield, New Mexico
KKFI Kansas City, Missouri
KKFM Colorado Springs, Colorado
KKFN Longmont, Colorado
KKFR Mayer, Arizona
KKFS Lincoln, California
KKFT Gardnerville-Minden, Nevada
KKGB Sulphur, Louisiana
KKGL Nampa, Idaho
KKGO Los Angeles, California
KKHA Markham, Texas
KKHB Eureka, California
KKHH Houston, Texas
KKHI Kihei, Hawaii
KKHJ-FM Pago Pago, American Samoa
KKHK Carmel, California

KKHQ-FM Oelwein, Iowa
KKHR Abilene, Texas
KKHT-FM Lumberton, Texas
KKIA Ida Grove, Iowa
KKID Salem, Missouri
KKIK Horseshoe Bend, Arkansas
KKIM-FM Santa Fe, New Mexico
KKIN-FM Aitkin, Minnesota
KKIQ Livermore, California
KKIS-FM Soldotna, Alaska
KKIT Taos, New Mexico
KKIX Fayetteville, Arkansas
KKJA Redmond, Oregon
KKJD Borrego Springs, California
KKJG San Luis Obispo, California
KKJK Ravenna, Nebraska
KKJM St. Joseph, Minnesota
KKJO-FM St. Joseph, Missouri
KKJQ Garden City, Kansas
KKJZ Long Beach, California
KKKJ Merrill, Oregon
KKLA-FM Los Angeles, California
KKLC Fall River Mills, California
KKLD Cottonwood, Arizona
KKLG Newton, Iowa
KKLH Marshfield, Missouri
KKLI Widefield, Colorado
KKLJ Klamath Falls, Oregon
KKLM Corpus Christi, Texas
KKLN Atwater, Minnesota
KKLP La Pine, Oregon
KKLQ Harwood, North Dakota
KKLR-FM Poplar Bluff, Missouri
KKLS-FM Sioux Falls, South Dakota
KKLT Texarkana, Arkansas
KKLU Lubbock, Texas
KKLV Orem, Utah
KKLW Willmar, Minnesota
KKLX Worland, Wyoming
KKLY El Paso, Texas
KKLZ Las Vegas, Nevada
KKMA Le Mars, Iowa
KKMG Pueblo, Colorado
KKMI Burlington, Iowa
KKMJ-FM Austin, Texas
KKMK Rapid City, South Dakota
KKMR Arizona City, Arizona
KKMT Pablo, Montana
KKMV Rupert, Idaho
KKMX Tri City, Oregon
KKMY Orange, Texas
KKND Belle Chasse, Louisiana
KKNG-FM Blanchard, Oklahoma
KKNI Sterling, Alaska
KKNL Valentine, Nebraska
KKNM Bovina, Texas
KKNN Delta, Colorado
KKNU Springfield-Eugene, Oregon
KKOA Volcano, Hawaii
KKOB-FM Albuquerque, New Mexico
KKOK-FM Morris, Minnesota
KKOL-FM Aiea, Hawaii
KKOR Waseca, Minnesota
KKOT Columbus, Nebraska
KKOW-FM Pittsburg, Kansas
KKOY-FM Chanute, Kansas
KKOZ-FM Ava, Missouri
KKPK Colorado Springs, Colorado
KKPL Cheyenne, Wyoming
KKPN Rockport, Texas
KKPR-FM Kearney, Nebraska
KKPS Brownsville, Texas
KKPT Little Rock, Arkansas
KKQQ Volga, South Dakota
KKQX Manhattan, Montana
KKQY Hill City, Kansas
KKRB Klamath Falls, Oregon
KKRC Granite Falls, Minnesota
KKRD Enid, Oklahoma
KKRE Hollis, Oklahoma
KKRF Stuart, Iowa
KKRG Albuquerque, New Mexico
KKRH Grangeville, Idaho
KKRI Pocola, Oklahoma
KKRK Coffeyville, Kansas
KKRL Carroll, Iowa
KKRN Bella Vista, California
KKRO Red Bluff, California
KKRQ Iowa City, Iowa
KKRR Casper, Wyoming
KKRS Davenport, Washington
KKRV Wenatchee, Washington
KKRW Houston, Texas
KKRZ Portland, Oregon
KKSD Milbank, South Dakota
KKSI Eddyville, Iowa
KKSP Bryant, Arkansas
KKSR Walla Walla, Washington
KKSS Santa Fe, New Mexico
KKST Oakdale, Louisiana
KKSW Lawrence, Kansas
KKSY-FM Cedar Rapids, Iowa
KKTC Angel Fire, New Mexico
KKTO Tahoe City, California
KKTR Kirksville, Missouri
KKTS-FM Douglas, Wyoming
KKTU-FM Fallon, Nevada
KKTV Fallon, Nevada
KKTX-FM Kilgore, Texas
KKTY-FM Glendo, Wyoming
KKTZ Lakeview, Arkansas
KKUA Wailuku, Hawaii
KKUP Cupertino, California
KKUS Tyler, Texas
KKUU Indio, California
KKVI Overland, Texas
KKVO Altus, Oklahoma
KKVR Kerrville, Texas
KKVS Truth or Consequences, New Mexico
KKVT(FM) Grand Junction, Colorado
KKVU Stevensville, Montana
KKWB Kelliher, Minnesota
KKWD Bethany, Oklahoma
KKWD(FM) Bethany, Colorado
KKWF Seattle, Washington
KKWK Cameron, Missouri
KKWQ Warroad, Minnesota
KKWS Wadena, Minnesota
KKWV Aransas Pass, Texas
KKWW Shelbina, Missouri
KKWY Douglas, Wyoming
KKXK Montrose, Colorado
KKXL-FM Grand Forks, North Dakota
KKXS Shingletown, California
KKXX-FM Shafter, California
KKYA Yankton, South Dakota
KKYC Clovis, New Mexico
KKYN-FM Plainview, Texas
KKYR-FM Texarkana, Texas
KKYS Bryan, Texas
KKYY Whiting, Iowa
KKYZ Sierra Vista, Arizona
KKZQ Tehachapi, California
KKZX Spokane, Washington
KKZY Bemidji, Minnesota
KLAA-FM Tioga, Louisiana
KLAD-FM Klamath Falls, Oregon
KLAI Laytonville, California
KLAK Tom Bean, Texas
KLAL Wrightsville, Arkansas
KLAN Glasgow, Montana
KLAP Gerlach, Nevada
KLAQ El Paso, Texas
KLAW Lawton, Oklahoma
KLAX-FM East Los Angeles, California
KLAZ Hot Springs, Arkansas
KLBC Durant, Oklahoma
KLBD(FM) Fremont, Texas
KLBJ-FM Austin, Texas
KLBL Pearcy, Arkansas
KLBN Fresno, California
KLBQ El Dorado, Arkansas
KLBR Bend, Oregon
KLBT Beaumont, Texas
KLBU Pecos, New Mexico
KLBV Steamboat Springs, Colorado
KLBZ Bozeman, Montana
KLCA Tahoe City, California
KLCC Eugene, Oregon
KLCD Decorah, Iowa
KLCE Blackfoot, Idaho
KLCH Lake City, Minnesota
KLCI Elk River, Minnesota
KLCK-FM Seattle, Washington
KLCM Lewistown, Montana
KLCO Newport, Oregon
KLCR Lakeview, Oregon
KLCU Ardmore, Oklahoma
KLCV Lincoln, Nebraska
KLCY Vernal, Utah
KLCZ Lewiston, Idaho
KLDD McCloud, California
KLDE Eldorado, Texas
KLDG Liberal, Kansas
KLDJ Duluth, Minnesota
KLDN Lufkin, Texas
KLDR Harbeck-Fruitdale, Oregon
KLDV Morrison, Colorado
KLDZ Medford, Oregon
KLEA-FM Lovington, New Mexico
KLED Antelope Valley Crestview, Wyoming
KLEF Anchorage, Alaska
KLEJ Rayne, Louisiana
KLEN Cheyenne, Wyoming
KLEO Kahaluu, Hawaii
KLER-FM Orofino, Idaho
KLES Prosser, Washington
KLEU Lewistown, Montana
KLEY-FM Jourdanton, Texas
KLFC Branson, Missouri
KLFF-FM San Luis Obispo, California
KLFH Ojai, California
KLFM Great Falls, Montana
KLFN Sunburg, Minnesota
KLFO Florence, Oregon
KLFR Reedsport, Oregon
KLFS Van Buren, Arkansas
KLFV Grand Junction, Colorado
KLFX Nolanville, Texas
KLGA-FM Algona, Iowa
KLGD Stamford, Texas
KLGL Richfield, Utah
KLGS College Station, Texas
KLGT Buffalo, Wyoming
KLHB Portland, Texas
KLHI-FM Kahului, Hawaii
KLIF-FM Haltom City, Texas
KLIL Moreauville, Louisiana
KLIP Monroe, Louisiana
KLIQ Hastings, Nebraska
KLIR Columbus, Nebraska
KLIT Del Rio, Texas
KLIX-FM Twin Falls, Idaho
KLIZ-FM Brainerd, Minnesota
KLJA(FM) Georgetown, Texas
KLJA(FM) Georgetown, North Dakota
KLJC Kansas City, Missouri
KLJH Bayfield, Colorado
KLJR-FM Santa Paula, California
KLJT Jacksonville, Texas
KLJV Scottsbluff, Nebraska
KLJY Clayton, Missouri
KLJZ Yuma, Arizona
KLKA Globe, Arizona
KLKC-FM Parsons, Kansas
KLKI Dolan Springs, Arizona
KLKK Clear Lake, Iowa
KLKL Minden, Louisiana
KLKM Kalispell, Montana
KLKO Elko, Nevada
KLKS Pequot Lakes, Minnesota
KLKX(FM) Rosamond, California
KLKY Stanfield, Oregon
KLLC San Francisco, California
KLLE North Fork, California
KLLL-FM Lubbock, Texas
KLLN Newark, Arkansas
KLLP Chubbuck, Idaho
KLLR Dripping Springs, Texas
KLLT Spencer, Iowa
KLLU Gallup, New Mexico
KLLY Oildale, California
KLLZ-FM Walker, Minnesota
KLMA Hobbs, New Mexico
KLMB Roundup, Montana
KLMF Klamath Falls, Oregon
KLMG Esparto, California
KLMI Rock River, Wyoming
KLMI(FM) Rocky River, Oregon
KLMJ Hampton, Iowa
KLMK Marvell, Arkansas
KLMM Oceano, California
KLMO-FM Dilley, Texas
KLMP Rapid City, South Dakota
KLMR-FM Lamar, Colorado
KLMT Billings, Montana
KLNB Grand Island, Nebraska
KLNC Lincoln, Nebraska
KLND Little Eagle, South Dakota
KLNE-FM Lexington, Nebraska
KLNI Decorah, Iowa
KLNN Questa, New Mexico
KLNO Fort Worth, Texas
KLNR Panaca, Nevada
KLNV San Diego, California
KLNZ Glendale, Arizona
KLO-FM Coalville, Utah
KLOA(FM) Ridgecrest, California
KLOB Thousand Palms, California
KLOF Gillette, Wyoming
KLOK-FM Greenfield, California
KLOL Houston, Texas
KLON Rockaway Beach, Oregon
KLOO-FM Corvallis, Oregon
KLOQ-FM Winton, California
KLOR-FM Ponca City, Oklahoma
KLOS Los Angeles, California
KLOU St. Louis, Missouri
KLOV Winchester, Oregon
KLOW Reno, Texas
KLOX Creston, Iowa
KLOY Astoria, Oregon
KLOZ Eldon, Missouri
KLPI Ruston, Louisiana
KLPL(FM) Lake Providence, Louisiana
KLPR Kearney, Nebraska
KLPW-FM Steelville, Missouri
KLPX Tucson, Arizona
KLQB Taylor, Texas
KLQL Luverne, Minnesota
KLQP Madison, Minnesota
KLQQ Clearmont, Wyoming
KLQT Corrales, New Mexico
KLQV San Diego, California
KLRB Stuart, Oklahoma
KLRC Siloam Springs, Arkansas
KLRD Yucaipa, California
KLRE-FM Little Rock, Arkansas
KLRF Milton-Freewater, Oregon
KLRH Sparks, Nevada
KLRI Rigby, Idaho
KLRJ Aberdeen, South Dakota
KLRM Melbourne, Arkansas
KLRO Hot Springs, Arkansas
KLRQ Clinton, Missouri
KLRR Redmond, Oregon
KLRV Billings, Montana
KLRW Byrne, Texas
KLRX Lee's Summit, Missouri
KLRY Gypsum, Colorado
KLRZ Larose, Louisiana
KLSA Alexandria, Louisiana
KLSB Norfolk, Nebraska
KLSC Malden, Missouri
KLSE Rochester, Minnesota
KLSI Thousand Oaks, California
KLSK Great Falls, Montana
KLSM Tallulah, Louisiana
KLSN Adelanto, California
KLSP Angola, Louisiana
KLSR-FM Memphis, Texas
KLSS-FM Mason City, Iowa
KLSU Baton Rouge, Louisiana
KLSX Rozet, Wyoming
KLSY Cosmopolis, Washington
KLSZ-FM Fort Smith, Arkansas
KLTA Breckenridge, Minnesota
KLTD Temple, Texas
KLTE Kirksville, Missouri
KLTG Corpus Christi, Texas
KLTH Lake Oswego, Oregon
KLTI-FM Ames, Iowa
KLTN Houston, Texas
KLTP San Angelo, Texas
KLTQ New England, North Dakota
KLTR Brenham, Texas
KLTU Mammoth, Arizona
KLTW-FM Prineville, Oregon
KLTY Arlington, Texas
KLUA Kailua Kona, Hawaii
KLUB Bloomington, Texas
KLUC-FM Las Vegas, Nevada
KLUE Poplar Bluff, Missouri
KLUH Poplar Bluff, Missouri
KLUK Needles, California
KLUN Paso Robles, California
KLUR Wichita Falls, Texas
KLUU Jamestown, North Dakota
KLUV Dallas, Texas
KLUW East Wenatchee, Washington
KLUX Robstown, Texas
KLVA Maricopa, Arizona
KLVB Citrus Heights, California
KLVC Magalia, California

KLVE Los Angeles, California
KLVF Las Vegas, New Mexico
KLVG Garberville, California
KLVH San Luis Obispo, California
KLVJ Julian, California
KLVK Fountain Hills, Arizona
KLVM Prunedale, California
KLVN Livingston, California
KLVO Belen, New Mexico
KLVP Sandy, Oregon
KLVR Middletown, California
KLVS Livermore, California
KLVU Sweet Home, Oregon
KLVV Ponca City, Oklahoma
KLVW Odessa, Texas
KLVY Fairmead, California
KLWA Westport, Washington
KLWC Casper, Wyoming
KLWD Gillette, Wyoming
KLWG Lompoc, California
KLWL Chillicothe, Missouri
KLWO Longview, Washington
KLWS Moses Lake, Washington
KLWV Chugwater, Wyoming
KLXA Alexandria, Louisiana
KLXD Springfield, Colorado
KLXK Breckenridge, Texas
KLXO Beaver, Oklahoma
KLXQ Mountain Pine, Arkansas
KLXS-FM Pierre, South Dakota
KLXV Glenwood Springs, Colorado
KLYD Snyder, Texas
KLYK Kelso, Washington
KLYR-FM Clarksville, Arkansas
KLYT Albuquerque, New Mexico
KLYV Dubuque, Iowa
KLYY Riverside, California
KLZA Falls City, Nebraska
KLZK New Deal, Texas
KLZR Westcliffe, Colorado
KLZV Brush, Colorado
KLZX Weston, Idaho
KLZY Honokaa, Hawaii
KLZZ Waite Park, Minnesota
KMA-FM Clarinda, Iowa
KMAC Gainesville, Missouri
KMAD-FM Whitesboro, Texas
KMAG Fort Smith, Arkansas
KMAJ-FM Carbondale, Kansas
KMAK Orange Cove, California
KMAP Fleming, Colorado
KMAQ-FM Maquoketa, Iowa
KMAR-FM Winnsboro, Louisiana
KMAT Seadrift, Texas
KMAV-FM Mayville, North Dakota
KMAX-FM Wellington, Colorado
KMBH-FM Harlingen, Texas
KMBI-FM Spokane, Washington
KMBM Polson, Montana
KMBN Las Cruces, New Mexico
KMBQ-FM Wasilla, Alaska
KMBR Butte, Montana
KMBV Valentine, Nebraska
KMBZ-FM Kansas City, Kansas
KMCG McGrath, Alaska
KMCH Manchester, Iowa
KMCJ Colstrip, Montana
KMCK-FM Prarie Grove, Arkansas
KMCM Odessa, Texas
KMCN Clinton, Iowa
KMCO Wilburton, Oklahoma
KMCQ Covington, Washington
KMCR Montgomery City, Missouri
KMCS Muscatine, Iowa
KMCU Wichita Falls, Texas
KMCV High Point, Missouri
KMCX-FM Ogallala, Nebraska
KMDL Kaplan, Louisiana
KMDR McKinleyville, California
KMDX San Angelo, Texas
KMDY Keokuk, Iowa
KMDZ Las Vegas, New Mexico
KMEL San Francisco, California
KMEM-FM Memphis, Missouri
KMEN Mendota, California
KMEO Mertzon, Texas
KMEZ Port Sulphur, Louisiana
KMFA Austin, Texas
KMFB(FM) Mendocino, California
KMFC Centralia, Missouri
KMFG Nashwauk, Minnesota
KMFM Premont, Texas
KMFX-FM Lake City, Minnesota
KMFY Grand Rapids, Minnesota
KMGC Camden, Arkansas
KMGE Eugene, Oregon
KMGI Pocatello, Idaho
KMGJ Grand Junction, Colorado
KMGK Glenwood, Minnesota
KMGL Oklahoma City, Oklahoma
KMGM Montevideo, Minnesota
KMGN Flagstaff, Arizona
KMGO Centerville, Iowa
KMGQ(FM) Goleta, California
KMGR Delta, Utah
KMGT Circle, Montana
KMGV Fresno, California
KMGX Bend, Oregon
KMGZ Lawton, Oklahoma
KMHA Four Bears, North Dakota
KMHD Gresham, Oregon
KMHK Billings, Montana
KMHM Lutesville, Missouri
KMHS-FM Coos Bay, Oregon
KMHT-FM Marshall, Texas
KMHX Rohnert Park, California
KMIH Mercer Island, Washington
KMIL Cameron, Texas
KMIQ Robstown, Texas
KMIT Mitchell, South Dakota
KMIX Tracy, California
KMIY Tucson, Arizona
KMJ-FM Fresno, California
KMJE Woodland, California
KMJG Homer, Alaska
KMJI Ashdown, Arkansas
KMJJ-FM Shreveport, Louisiana
KMJK North Kansas City, Missouri
KMJM-FM Columbia, Illinois
KMJO Hope, North Dakota
KMJQ Houston, Texas
KMJR Odem, Texas
KMJV Soledad, California
KMJX Conway, Arkansas
KMKF Manhattan, Kansas
KMKK-FM Kaunakakai, Hawaii
KMKL North Branch, Minnesota
KMKO-FM Lake Crystal, Minnesota
KMKR Canyonville, Oregon
KMKS Bay City, Texas
KMKT Bells, Texas
KMKX Willits, California
KMKZ(FM) Red Feather Lakes, Colorado
KMLA El Rio, California
KMLD Casper, Wyoming
KMLE Chandler, Arizona
KMLK El Dorado, Arkansas
KMLL Marysville, Kansas
KMLO Lowry, South Dakota
KMLR Gonzales, Texas
KMLT Jackson, Wyoming
KMLV Ralston, Nebraska
KMLW Moses Lake, Washington
KMME(FM) Cottage Grove, Oregon
KMMG Benton City, Washington
KMML Cimarron, Kansas
KMMO-FM Marshall, Missouri
KMMR Malta, Montana
KMMS-FM Bozeman, Montana
KMMT Mammoth Lakes, California
KMMX Tahoka, Texas
KMMY Soper, Oklahoma
KMMZ Crane, Texas
KMNA Mabton, Washington
KMNB Minneapolis, Minnesota
KMNE-FM Bassett, Nebraska
KMNO Wailuku, Hawaii
KMNR Rolla, Missouri
KMNT Chehalis, Washington
KMOA Nu'uuli, American Samoa
KMOC Wichita Falls, Texas
KMOD-FM Tulsa, Oklahoma
KMOE Butler, Missouri
KMOJ Minneapolis, Minnesota
KMOK Lewiston, Idaho
KMOM Roscoe, South Dakota
KMON-FM Great Falls, Montana
KMOO-FM Mineola, Texas
KMOQ Columbus, Kansas
KMOR Gering, Nebraska
KMOU Roswell, New Mexico
KMOZ-FM Grand Junction, Colorado
KMPA Pittsburg, Texas
KMPB Breckenridge, Colorado
KMPO Modesto, California
KMPQ Roseburg, Oregon
KMPR Minot, North Dakota
KMPS-FM Seattle, Washington
KMPZ Salida, Colorado
KMQA East Porterville, California
KMQX Weatherford, Texas
KMRJ Rancho Mirage, California
KMRK-FM Odessa, Texas
KMRL Buras, Louisiana
KMRO Camarillo, California
KMRQ Riverbank, California
KMRV San Isidro, Texas
KMRX El Dorado, Arkansas
KMRZ-FM Superior, Wyoming
KMSA Grand Junction, Colorado
KMSC Sioux City, Iowa
KMSE Rochester, Minnesota
KMSI Moore, Oklahoma
KMSK Austin, Minnesota
KMSL Mansfield, Louisiana
KMSM-FM Butte, Montana
KMSO Missoula, Montana
KMST Rolla, Missouri
KMSU Mankato, Minnesota
KMSW The Dalles, Oregon
KMTB Murfreesboro, Arkansas
KMTC Russellville, Arkansas
KMTG San Jose, California
KMTH Maljamar, New Mexico
KMTK Bend, Oregon
KMTN Jackson, Wyoming
KMTS Glenwood Springs, Colorado
KMTT Tacoma, Washington
KMTX-FM Helena, Montana
KMTY Gibbon, Nebraska
KMTZ Three Forks, Montana
KMUD Garberville, California
KMUE Eureka, California
KMUL-FM Muleshoe, Texas
KMUN Astoria, Oregon
KMUW Wichita, Kansas
KMUZ Turner, Oregon
KMVA Dewey-Humboldt, Arizona
KMVC Marshall, Missouri
KMVE California City, California
KMVK Fort Worth, Texas
KMVL-FM Madisonville, Texas
KMVN Palmer, Alaska
KMVQ-FM San Francisco, California
KMVR Mesilla Park, New Mexico
KMVV Meadow Lakes, Alaska
KMWB Captain Cook, Hawaii
KMWR Brookings, Oregon
KMWS Mount Vernon, Washington
KMWX Abilene, Texas
KMWY Jackson, Wyoming
KMXA-FM Minot, North Dakota
KMXB Henderson, Nevada
KMXC Sioux Falls, South Dakota
KMXD Monroe, Utah
KMXE-FM Red Lodge, Montana
KMXF Lowell, Arkansas
KMXG Clinton, Iowa
KMXH Alexandria, Louisiana
KMXI Chico, California
KMXJ-FM Amarillo, Texas
KMXK Cold Spring, Minnesota
KMXL Carthage, Missouri
KMXM(FM) Helena Valley N, Montana
KMXN Osage City, Kansas
KMXP Phoenix, Arizona
KMXQ Socorro, New Mexico
KMXR Corpus Christi, Texas
KMXS Anchorage, Alaska
KMXT Kodiak, Alaska
KMXV Kansas City, Missouri
KMXW Sparks, Nevada
KMXX Imperial, California
KMXY Grand Junction, Colorado
KMXZ-FM Tucson, Arizona
KMYI San Diego, California
KMYK Osage Beach, Missouri
KMYT Temecula, California
KMYX-FM Arvin, California
KMYY Rayville, Louisiana
KMYZ-FM Pryor, Oklahoma
KMZA Seneca, Kansas
KMZE Woodward, Oklahoma
KMZK Clifton, Colorado
KMZL Missoula, Montana
KMZO Hamilton, Montana
KMZQ-FM Payson, Arizona
KMZT-FM Big Sur, California
KMZU Carrollton, Missouri
KMZZ Bishop, Texas
KNAA Show Low, Arizona
KNAB-FM Burlington, Colorado
KNAC Earlimart, California
KNAD Page, Arizona
KNAF-FM Fredericksburg, Texas
KNAG Grand Canyon, Arizona
KNAI Phoenix, Arizona
KNAN Nanakuli, Hawaii
KNAQ Prescott, Arizona
KNAR San Angelo, Texas
KNAS Nashville, Arkansas
KNAU Flagstaff, Arizona
KNBA Anchorage, Alaska
KNBB Dubach, Louisiana
KNBE Beatrice, Nebraska
KNBJ Bemidji, Minnesota
KNBQ Centralia, Washington
KNBT New Braunfels, Texas
KNBU Baldwin City, Kansas
KNBX San Ardo, California
KNBZ Redfield, South Dakota
KNCA Burney, California
KNCB-FM Vivian, Louisiana
KNCC Elko, Nevada
KNCH(FM) San Angelo, Texas
KNCI Sacramento, California
KNCM Appleton, Minnesota
KNCN Sinton, Texas
KNCO-FM Grass Valley, California
KNCQ Redding, California
KNCT-FM Killeen, Texas
KNCU Newport, Oregon
KNCW Omak, Washington
KNCY-FM Auburn, Nebraska
KNDA Alice, Texas
KNDD Seattle, Washington
KNDE College Station, Texas
KNDH Hettinger, North Dakota
KNDK-FM Langdon, North Dakota
KNDL(FM) Angwin, California
KNDN-FM Teec Nos Pos, Arizona
KNDR Mandan, North Dakota
KNDW Williston, North Dakota
KNDY-FM Marysville, Kansas
KNDZ McKinleyville, California
KNEB-FM Scottsbluff, Nebraska
KNEC Yuma, Colorado
KNEI-FM Waukon, Iowa
KNEK-FM Washington, Louisiana
KNEL-FM Brady, Texas
KNEN Norfolk, Nebraska
KNEO Neosho, Missouri
KNES Fairfield, Texas
KNEV Reno, Nevada
KNEX Laredo, Texas
KNFA Grand Island, Nebraska
KNFM Midland, Texas
KNFO Basalt, Colorado
KNFT-FM Bayard, New Mexico
KNFX-FM Bryan, Texas
KNGA Saint Peter, Minnesota
KNGM Guymon, Oklahoma
KNGS Coalinga, California
KNGT Lake Charles, Louisiana
KNGW Juneau, Alaska
KNHC Seattle, Washington
KNHM Bayside, California
KNHT Rio Dell, California
KNID North Enid, Oklahoma
KNIN-FM Wichita Falls, Texas
KNIS Carson City, Nevada
KNIT Humboldt, Nebraska
KNIV Lyman, Wyoming
KNIX-FM Phoenix, Arizona
KNJT Coldwater, Kansas
KNKI Pinetop, Arizona
KNKK Needles, California
KNKL North Ogden, Utah
KNKN(FM) Pueblo, Colorado
KNKT Armijo, New Mexico
KNLB Lake Havasu City, Arizona
KNLE-FM Round Rock, Texas
KNLF Quincy, California
KNLG New Bloomfield, Missouri

KNLH Cedar Hill, Missouri
KNLK Santa Rosa, New Mexico
KNLL Nashville, Arkansas
KNLM Marshfield, Missouri
KNLN Vienna, Missouri
KNLP Potosi, Missouri
KNLQ Cuba, Missouri
KNLR Bend, Oregon
KNLT Anchorage, Alaska
KNLT(FM) Palmer, Alaska
KNLV-FM Ord, Nebraska
KNLX Prineville, Oregon
KNMA Tularosa, New Mexico
KNMB Cloudcroft, New Mexico
KNMC Havre, Montana
KNMI Farmington, New Mexico
KNMO-FM Nevada, Missouri
KNMZ Alamogordo, New Mexico
KNNB Whiteriver, Arizona
KNNG Sterling, Colorado
KNNK Dimmitt, Texas
KNNN(FM) Shasta Lake City, California
KNOB Healdsburg, California
KNOD Harlan, Iowa
KNOE-FM Monroe, Louisiana
KNOF St. Paul, Minnesota
KNOG Nogales, Arizona
KNOM-FM Nome, Alaska
KNON Dallas, Texas
KNOR Krum, Texas
KNOW-FM Minneapolis-St. Paul, Minnesota
KNPQ Hershey, Nebraska
KNPR Las Vegas, Nevada
KNRB Atlanta, Texas
KNRG New Ulm, Texas
KNRI Bismarck, North Dakota
KNRJ Cordes Lakes, Arizona
KNRK Camas, Washington
KNRQ-FM Aloha, Oregon
KNRX Sterling City, Texas
KNSB(FM) Bettendorf, Iowa
KNSC(FM) Carroll, Iowa
KNSE Austin, Minnesota
KNSG Springfield, Minnesota
KNSH(FM) Fort Dodge, Iowa
KNSL(FM) Lamoni, Iowa
KNSM(FM) Mason City, Iowa
KNSQ Mount Shasta, California
KNSR Collegeville, Minnesota
KNST-FM Green Valley, Arizona
KNSU Thibodaux, Louisiana
KNSW Worthington-Marshall, Minnesota
KNSX(FM) Moville, Iowa
KNSY(FM) Dubuque, Iowa
KNSZ(FM) Ottumwa, Iowa
KNTE Bay City, Texas
KNTI Lakeport, California
KNTK Firth, Nebraska
KNTN Thief River Falls, Minnesota
KNTO Chowchilla, California
KNTU McKinney, Texas
KNTY Shingle Springs, California
KNUE Tyler, Texas
KNUJ-FM Sleepy Eye, Minnesota
KNUL Nulato, Alaska
KNUQ Paauilo, Hawaii
KNUT Tamuning, Guam
KNUW Santa Clara, New Mexico
KNUZ San Saba, Texas
KNVO-FM Port Isabel, Texas
KNWB Hilo, Hawaii
KNWC-FM Sioux Falls, South Dakota
KNWD Natchitoches, Louisiana
KNWF Fergus Falls, Minnesota
KNWI Osceola, Iowa
KNWJ Leone, American Samoa
KNWM Madrid, Iowa
KNWO Cottonwood, Idaho
KNWP Port Angeles, Washington
KNWR Ellensburg, Washington
KNWS-FM Waterloo, Iowa
KNWU Forks, Washington
KNWV Clarkston, Washington
KNWY Yakima, Washington
KNXR Rochester, Minnesota
KNYD Broken Arrow, Oklahoma
KNYE Pahrump, Nevada
KNYN Fort Bridger, Wyoming
KNYR Yreka, California
KNZA Hiawatha, Kansas
KNZS Arlington, Kansas

KOAB-FM Bend, Oregon
KOAP Lakeview, Oregon
KOAR Beebe, Arkansas
KOAS Dolan Springs, Arizona
KOAY(FM) Middleton, Idaho
KOBB-FM Bozeman, Montana
KOBC Joplin, Missouri
KOBH Hobbs, New Mexico
KOBK Baker City, Oregon
KOBN Burns, Oregon
KOCN Pacific Grove, California
KOCP Camarillo, California
KOCU Altus, Oklahoma
KODA Houston, Texas
KODJ Salt Lake City, Utah
KODM Odessa, Texas
KODS Carnelian Bay, California
KODV Barstow, California
KODZ Eugene, Oregon
KOEA Doniphan, Missouri
KOEL-FM Cedar Falls, Iowa
KOFG Cody, Wyoming
KOFH Nogales, Arizona
KOFM Enid, Oklahoma
KOFX El Paso, Texas
KOGA-FM Ogallala, Nebraska
KOGB McGrath, Alaska
KOGC Wheeler, Texas
KOGJ Kenai, Alaska
KOGL Gleneden Beach, Oregon
KOGM Opelousas, Louisiana
KOGW Stratford, Texas
KOHL Fremont, California
KOHN Sells, Arizona
KOHO-FM Leavenworth, Washington
KOHR Sheridan, Wyoming
KOHS Orem, Utah
KOHT Marana, Arizona
KOIA Storm Lake, Iowa
KOIR Edinburg, Texas
KOIT San Francisco, California
KOJB Cass Lake, Minnesota
KOJD John Day, Oregon
KOJI Okoboji, Iowa
KOJO Lake Charles, Louisiana
KOKE-FM Thorndale, Texas
KOKF Edmond, Oklahoma
KOKN Oketo, Kansas
KOKO-FM Kerman, California
KOKR Newport, Arkansas
KOKS Poplar Bluff, Missouri
KOKU Hagatna, Guam
KOKX-FM Keokuk, Iowa
KOKY Sherwood, Arkansas
KOKZ Waterloo, Iowa
KOLA San Bernardino, California
KOLI Electra, Texas
KOLJ-FM Warroad, Minnesota
KOLL Lonoke, Arkansas
KOLT-FM Warren Afb, Wyoming
KOLU Pasco, Washington
KOLV Olivia, Minnesota
KOLW Basin City, Washington
KOLY-FM Mobridge, South Dakota
KOLZ Cheyenne, Wyoming
KOMA Oklahoma City, Oklahoma
KOMB Fort Scott, Kansas
KOMC-FM Kimberling City, Missouri
KOME-FM Meridian, Texas
KOMG Willard, Missouri
KOMH Marshall, Minnesota
KOMO-FM Oakville, Washington
KOMP Las Vegas, Nevada
KOMR Sun City, Arizona
KOMS Poteau, Oklahoma
KOMT Mountain Home, Arkansas
KOMX Pampa, Texas
KONA-FM Kennewick, Washington
KOND Clovis, California
KONE Lubbock, Texas
KONI Lanai City, Hawaii
KONN-FM Bennett, Colorado
KONO-FM Helotes, Texas
KONQ Dodge City, Kansas
KONY St. George, Utah
KOOI Jacksonville, Texas
KOOK Junction, Texas
KOOL-FM Phoenix, Arizona
KOOO La Vista, Nebraska
KOOP Hornsby, Texas
KOOS North Bend, Oregon

KOOT Hurley, New Mexico
KOOU Hardy, Arkansas
KOOZ Myrtle Point, Oregon
KOPA(FM) Pala, California
KOPB-FM Portland, Oregon
KOPJ Sebeka, Minnesota
KOPN Columbia, Missouri
KOPR Butte, Montana
KOPW Plattsmouth, Nebraska
KOPY-FM Alice, Texas
KOQL Ashland, Missouri
KORA-FM Bryan, Texas
KORB Hopland, California
KORC(FM) Burns, Oregon
KORD-FM Richland, Washington
KORQ Winters / Abilene, Texas
KORR American Falls, Idaho
KORT-FM Grangeville, Idaho
KORV Lakeview, Oregon
KORV-FM Lakeview, Oregon
KOSB Perry, Oklahoma
KOSG Pawhuska, Oklahoma
KOSI Denver, Colorado
KOSN Ketchum, Oklahoma
KOSO Patterson, California
KOSP Ozark, Missouri
KOST Los Angeles, California
KOSU Stillwater, Oklahoma
KOSY-FM Spanish Fork, Utah
KOTD The Dalles, Oregon
KOTE Eureka, Kansas
KOTM-FM Ottumwa, Iowa
KOTN Gould, Arkansas
KOTN(FM) Gould, Arkansas
KOTO Telluride, Colorado
KOTY Mason, Texas
KOUI Louisville, Mississippi
KOUL Refugio, Texas
KOUT Rapid City, South Dakota
KOVA Bovina, Texas
KOVE-FM Galveston, Texas
KOWY Dayton, Wyoming
KOWZ-FM Blooming Prairie, Minnesota
KOXE Brownwood, Texas
KOYA Rosebud, South Dakota
KOYE Frankston, Texas
KOYN Paris, Texas
KOYT(FM) Alberton, Montana
KOYT(FM) Montana City, Montana
KOYU Koyukuk, Alaska
KOZB Livingston, Montana
KOZE-FM Lewiston, Idaho
KOZI-FM Chelan, Washington
KOZO Branson, Missouri
KOZQ-FM Waynesville, Missouri
KOZT Fort Bragg, California
KOZX Cabool, Missouri
KOZY-FM Bridgeport, Nebraska
KOZZ-FM Reno, Nevada
KPAC San Antonio, Texas
KPAD Rawlins, Wyoming
KPAE Erwinville, Louisiana
KPAK Alva, Oklahoma
KPAN-FM Hereford, Texas
KPAQ Plaquemine, Louisiana
KPAS Fabens, Texas
KPAT Orcutt, California
KPAU Center, Colorado
KPAW Fort Collins, Colorado
KPBB Brownfield, Texas
KPBE Brownwood, Texas
KPBM McCamey, Texas
KPBN Freer, Texas
KPBQ-FM Pine Bluff, Arkansas
KPBR Poplar Bluff, Missouri
KPBS-FM San Diego, California
KPBX-FM Spokane, Washington
KPBZ Spokane, Washington
KPCC Pasadena, California
KPCH Ruston, Louisiana
KPCL Farmington, New Mexico
KPCP New Roads, Louisiana
KPCR Fowler, Colorado
KPCS Princeton, Minnesota
KPCV Portales, New Mexico
KPCW Park City, Utah
KPDA-FM Gooding, Idaho
KPDB Big Lake, Texas
KPDO Pescadero, California
KPDQ-FM Portland, Oregon
KPDR Wheeler, Texas

KPEK Albuquerque, New Mexico
KPEL-FM Breaux Bridge, Louisiana
KPEN-FM Soldotna, Alaska
KPER Hobbs, New Mexico
KPEZ Austin, Texas
KPFA Berkeley, California
KPFB Berkeley, California
KPFC Callisburg, Texas
KPFK Los Angeles, California
KPFM Mountain Home, Arkansas
KPFR Pine Grove, Oregon
KPFT Houston, Texas
KPFX Fargo, North Dakota
KPFZ-FM Lakeport, California
KPGA Morton, Texas
KPGB Pryor, Montana
KPGG Ashdown, Arkansas
KPGR Pleasant Grove, Utah
KPGS Pagosa Springs, Colorado
KPHD Elko, Nevada
KPHF Phoenix, Arizona
KPHR Ortonville, Minnesota
KPHS Plains, Texas
KPHT Rocky Ford, Colorado
KPHW Kaneohe, Hawaii
KPIG-FM Freedom, California
KPIJ Junction City, Oregon
KPIN Pinedale, Wyoming
KPIO-FM Pleasanton, Kansas
KPIT Pittsburg, Texas
KPJH Polson, Montana
KPJP Greenville, California
KPKJ Mentmore, New Mexico
KPKK Amargosa Valley, Nevada
KPKO Pecos, Texas
KPKP Harts Bluff, Texas
KPKR Parker, Arizona
KPKX Phoenix, Arizona
KPKY Pocatello, Idaho
KPLA Columbia, Missouri
KPLD Kanab, Utah
KPLG Plains, Montana
KPLI Olympia, Washington
KPLM Palm Springs, California
KPLN Lockwood, Montana
KPLO-FM Reliance, South Dakota
KPLT-FM Paris, Texas
KPLU-FM Tacoma, Washington
KPLV Las Vegas, Nevada
KPLW Wenatchee, Washington
KPLX Fort Worth, Texas
KPLZ-FM Seattle, Washington
KPMB Plainview, Texas
KPMW Haliimaile, Hawaii
KPMX Sterling, Colorado
KPNC Ponca City, Oklahoma
KPND Sandpoint, Idaho
KPNE-FM North Platte, Nebraska
KPNO Norfolk, Nebraska
KPNT Collinsville, Illinois
KPNY Alliance, Nebraska
KPOA Lahaina, Hawaii
KPOC-FM Pocahontas, Arkansas
KPOD-FM Crescent City, California
KPOI-FM Honolulu, Hawaii
KPOO San Francisco, California
KPOR Emporia, Kansas
KPOS Fouke, Arkansas
KPOW-FM La Monte, Missouri
KPOY(FM) Fraser, Colorado
KPPD Devils Lake, North Dakota
KPPK Rainier, Oregon
KPPL Poplar Bluff, Missouri
KPPR Williston, North Dakota
KPPT-FM Depoe Bay, Oregon
KPPV Prescott Valley, Arizona
KPQ-FM Wenatchee, Washington
KPQX Havre, Montana
KPRA Ukiah, California
KPRB Brush, Colorado
KPRC-FM Salinas, California
KPRD Hays, Kansas
KPRE Vail, Colorado
KPRF Amarillo, Texas
KPRG Agana, Guam
KPRH Montrose, Colorado
KPRI Encinitas, California
KPRJ Jamestown, North Dakota
KPRN Grand Junction, Colorado
KPRQ Sheridan, Wyoming
KPRR El Paso, Texas

RADIO - U.S.

KPRS Kansas City, Missouri
KPRU Delta, Colorado
KPRV-FM Heavener, Oklahoma
KPRW Perham, Minnesota
KPRX Bakersfield, California
KPSA-FM Lordsburg, New Mexico
KPSC Palm Springs, California
KPSD-FM Faith, South Dakota
KPSH Coachella, California
KPSI-FM Palm Springs, California
KPSL-FM Bakersfield, California
KPSM Brownwood, Texas
KPSO-FM Falfurrias, Texas
KPSU Goodwell, Oklahoma
KPTE Durango, Colorado
KPTL Ankeny, Iowa
KPTT Denver, Colorado
KPTX Pecos, Texas
KPTY Winnie, Texas
KPTZ Port Townsend, Washington
KPUB Flagstaff, Arizona
KPUL Winterset, Iowa
KPUR-FM Canyon, Texas
KPUS Gregory, Texas
KPVL Postville, Iowa
KPVR Bowling Green, Missouri
KPVS Hilo, Hawaii
KPVU Prairie View, Texas
KPVW Aspen, Colorado
KPWB-FM Piedmont, Missouri
KPWJ(FM) Madisonville, Texas
KPWR Los Angeles, California
KPWW Hooks, Texas
KPXI Overton, Texas
KPYG Cayucos, California
KPYR Craig, Colorado
KPZA-FM Jal, New Mexico
KPZE-FM Carlsbad, New Mexico
KPZK-FM Cabot, Arkansas
KQAC Portland, Oregon
KQAI Roswell, New Mexico
KQAK Bend, Oregon
KQAL Winona, Minnesota
KQAY-FM Tucumcari, New Mexico
KQAZ Springerville, Arizona
KQBA Los Alamos, New Mexico
KQBB Center, Texas
KQBK Booneville, Arkansas
KQBO Rio Grande City, Texas
KQBR Lubbock, Texas
KQBU-FM Port Arthur, Texas
KQCH Omaha, Nebraska
KQCL Faribault, Minnesota
KQCO Esterbrook, Wyoming
KQCR-FM Parkersburg, Iowa
KQCS Bettendorf, Iowa
KQCV-FM Shawnee, Oklahoma
KQDI-FM Great Falls, Montana
KQDJ-FM Valley City, North Dakota
KQDL Hines, Oregon
KQDR Savoy, Texas
KQDS-FM Duluth, Minnesota
KQDY Bismarck, North Dakota
KQED-FM San Francisco, California
KQEG La Crescent, Minnesota
KQEI-FM North Highlands, California
KQEL Alamogordo, New Mexico
KQEO Idaho Falls, Idaho
KQEW Fordyce, Arkansas
KQEZ(FM) Shelley, Idaho
KQFC Boise, Idaho
KQFE Springfield, Oregon
KQFM Hermiston, Oregon
KQFR Rapid City, South Dakota
KQFX Borger, Texas
KQHK McCook, Nebraska
KQHN Waskom, Texas
KQHR The Dalles, Oregon
KQHT Crookston, Minnesota
KQIB Idabel, Oklahoma
KQIC Willmar, Minnesota
KQID-FM Alexandria, Louisiana
KQIZ-FM Amarillo, Texas
KQJK Roseville, California
KQKI-FM Bayou Vista, Louisiana
KQKK Walker, Minnesota
KQKL Selma, California
KQKQ-FM Council Bluffs, Iowa
KQKS Lakewood, Colorado
KQKX Norfolk, Nebraska
KQKY Kearney, Nebraska
KQLA Ogden, Kansas
KQLB Los Banos, California
KQLK De Ridder, Louisiana
KQLM Odessa, Texas
KQLN Alamo, Nevada
KQLP Leupp, Arizona
KQLQ Columbia, Louisiana
KQLR Whitehall, Montana
KQLT Casper, Wyoming
KQLV(FM) Bosque Farms, New Mexico
KQLX-FM Lisbon, North Dakota
KQLZ(FM) Mt Home, Idaho
KQMA Phillipsburg, Kansas
KQMB Levan, Utah
KQMC Hawthorne, Nevada
KQMG-FM Independence, Iowa
KQMJ(FM) Osceola, Arkansas
KQMN Thief River Falls, Minnesota
KQMO Shell Knob, Missouri
KQMQ-FM Honolulu, Hawaii
KQMR Globe, Arizona
KQMT Denver, Colorado
KQMV Bellevue, Washington
KQMX Lost Hills, California
KQNC Quincy, California
KQNG-FM Lihue, Hawaii
KQNK-FM Norton, Kansas
KQNO Coalinga, California
KQNU(FM) Onawa, Iowa
KQNV Fallon, Nevada
KQNY Quincy, California
KQOB Enid, Oklahoma
KQOC Gleneden Beach, Oregon
KQOD Stockton, California
KQOL Sleepy Hollow, Wyoming
KQOR Mena, Arkansas
KQPD Ardmore, Oklahoma
KQPI Aberdeen, Idaho
KQPM Ukiah, California
KQPR Albert Lea, Minnesota
KQPT Colusa, California
KQQK Beaumont, Texas
KQQL Anoka, Minnesota
KQQX Hermann, Missouri
KQRA Brookline, Missouri
KQRB Windom, Minnesota
KQRC-FM Leavenworth, Kansas
KQRI Bosque Farms, New Mexico
KQRK Ronan, Montana
KQRN Mitchell, South Dakota
KQRQ Rapid City, South Dakota
KQRS-FM Golden Valley, Minnesota
KQRT Las Vegas, Nevada
KQRV Deer Lodge, Montana
KQRX Midland, Texas
KQSC Santa Barbara, California
KQSD-FM Lowry, South Dakota
KQSE Gypsum, Colorado
KQSK Chadron, Nebraska
KQSM-FM Fayetteville, Arkansas
KQSR Yuma, Arizona
KQSS Miami, Arizona
KQST Sedona, Arizona
KQSW Rock Springs, Wyoming
KQTA Homedale, Idaho
KQTH Tucson, Arizona
KQTM Rio Rancho, New Mexico
KQTY-FM Borger, Texas
KQTZ Hobart, Oklahoma
KQUL Lake Ozark, Missouri
KQUR Laredo, Texas
KQUS-FM Hot Springs, Arkansas
KQVO Calexico, California
KQVT Victoria, Texas
KQWB-FM Moorhead, Minnesota
KQWC-FM Webster City, Iowa
KQWS Omak, Washington
KQWY Lusk, Wyoming
KQXB Breckenridge, Texas
KQXB(FM) Belton, Texas
KQXC-FM Wichita Falls, Texas
KQXE Eastland, Texas
KQXL-FM New Roads, Louisiana
KQXR Payette, Idaho
KQXS Stephenville, Texas
KQXT-FM San Antonio, Texas
KQXX-FM Mission, Texas
KQXY-FM Beaumont, Texas
KQYB Spring Grove, Minnesota
KQZB Troy, Idaho
KQZQ Kiowa, Kansas
KQZR Hayden, Colorado
KQZZ Devils Lake, North Dakota
KRAB Greenacres, California
KRAI-FM Craig, Colorado
KRAJ Johannesburg, California
KRAN Warren Afb, Wyoming
KRAO-FM Colfax, Washington
KRAQ Jackson, Minnesota
KRAR Espanola, New Mexico
KRAT(FM) Altamont, Oregon
KRAV-FM Tulsa, Oklahoma
KRAW Kasilof, Alaska
KRAY-FM Salinas, California
KRAZ Santa Ynez, California
KRBB Wichita, Kansas
KRBD Ketchikan, Alaska
KRBE Houston, Texas
KRBG Umbarger, Texas
KRBI-FM St. Peter, Minnesota
KRBL Idalou, Texas
KRBM Pendleton, Oregon
KRBO(FM) Millers Ranch, California
KRBP Rock Creek, California
KRBR La Barge, Wyoming
KRBW Ottawa, Kansas
KRBY Ruby, Alaska
KRBZ Kansas City, Missouri
KRCB-FM Windsor, California
KRCC Colorado Springs, Colorado
KRCD Inglewood, California
KRCH Rochester, Minnesota
KRCI Pinetop-Lakeside, Arizona
KRCK-FM Mecca, California
KRCL Salt Lake City, Utah
KRCQ Detroit Lakes, Minnesota
KRCS Sturgis, South Dakota
KRCU Cape Girardeau, Missouri
KRCV West Covina, California
KRCW Royal City, Washington
KRCX-FM Marysville, California
KRCY-FM Lake Havasu City, Arizona
KRDA Hanford, California
KRDE Globe, Arizona
KRDG Shingletown, California
KRDJ New Iberia, Louisiana
KRDO-FM Security, Colorado
KRDQ Colby, Kansas
KRDS-FM New Prague, Minnesota
KRDX Vail, Arizona
KREC Brian Head, Utah
KRED-FM Eureka, California
KREJ Medicine Lodge, Kansas
KREK Bristow, Oklahoma
KREO Pine Bluffs, Wyoming
KREP Belleville, Kansas
KRES Moberly, Missouri
KREU Roland, Oklahoma
KREV Alameda, California
KREZ Chaffee, Missouri
KRFA-FM Moscow, Idaho
KRFC Fort Collins, Colorado
KRFD(FM) Merino, Colorado
KRFG Glenwood, Minnesota
KRFH Marshalltown, Iowa
KRFI Redwood Falls, Minnesota
KRFM Show Low, Arizona
KRFO-FM Owatonna, Minnesota
KRFS-FM Superior, Nebraska
KRFX Denver, Colorado
KRGI-FM Grand Island, Nebraska
KRGM Marshall, Minnesota
KRGN Amarillo, Texas
KRGO Alton, Iowa
KRGT Indian Springs, Nevada
KRGX Rio Grande City, Texas
KRGY Aurora, Nebraska
KRHS Overland, Missouri
KRHV Big Pine, California
KRIA Plainview, Texas
KRIG-FM Nowata, Oklahoma
KRIO-FM Roma, Texas
KRIT Parker, Arizona
KRJA Lamesa, Texas
KRJB Ada, Minnesota
KRJC Elko, Nevada
KRJM Mahnomen, Minnesota
KRJT Elgin, Oregon
KRJY Truth or Consequence, New Mexico
KRKC-FM King City, California
KRKG-FM Pasco, Washington
KRKH Wailea-Makena, Hawaii
KRKI Keystone, South Dakota
KRKL Walla Walla, Washington
KRKM Fort Washakie, Wyoming
KRKN Eldon, Iowa
KRKQ Mountain Village, Colorado
KRKR Waverly, Nebraska
KRKS-FM Lafayette, Colorado
KRKT-FM Albany, Oregon
KRKU Wheatland, Wyoming
KRKV Las Animas, Colorado
KRKX Billings, Montana
KRKY-FM Estes Park, Colorado
KRLD-FM Dallas, Texas
KRLE Oberlin, Kansas
KRLF Pullman, Washington
KRLH Hereford, Texas
KRLI Malta Bend, Missouri
KRLP Fairmont, Minnesota
KRLQ Hodge, Louisiana
KRLR Sulphur, Louisiana
KRLS Knoxville, Iowa
KRLT South Lake Tahoe, California
KRLU Roswell, New Mexico
KRLX Northfield, Minnesota
KRMB Bisbee, Arizona
KRMC Douglas, Arizona
KRMD-FM Oil City, Louisiana
KRMG-FM Sand Springs, Oklahoma
KRMH Red Mesa, Arizona
KRMQ-FM Clovis, New Mexico
KRMR Hays, Kansas
KRMX Marlin, Texas
KRMX(FM) Marlin, Texas
KRNA Iowa City, Iowa
KRNB Decatur, Texas
KRNC Steamboat Springs, Colorado
KRNE-FM Merriman, Nebraska
KRNF Montezuma, Iowa
KRNG Fallon, Nevada
KRNH Kerrville, Texas
KRNK Casper, Wyoming
KRNL-FM Mount Vernon, Iowa
KRNN Juneau, Alaska
KRNO Incline Village, Nevada
KRNP Sutherland, Nebraska
KRNQ Keokuk, Iowa
KRNU Lincoln, Nebraska
KRNV-FM Reno, Nevada
KRNW Chillicothe, Missouri
KRNY Kearney, Nebraska
KRNZ Gonzales, Texas
KROA Grand Island, Nebraska
KROC-FM Rochester, Minnesota
KROG Grants Pass, Oregon
KROI Seabrook, Texas
KROK South Fort Polk, Louisiana
KROM San Antonio, Texas
KROQ-FM Pasadena, California
KROR Hastings, Nebraska
KROU Spencer, Oklahoma
KROW Cody, Wyoming
KROX-FM Buda, Texas
KROY Palacios, Texas
KRPH Morristown, Arizona
KRPM Billings, Montana
KRPR Rochester, Minnesota
KRPS Pittsburg, Kansas
KRPT Devine, Texas
KRPW(FM) Coarsegold, California
KRPX Wellington, Utah
KRQB San Jacinto, California
KRQK Lompoc, California
KRQN Vinton, Iowa
KRQQ Tucson, Arizona
KRQR Orland, California
KRQT Castle Rock, Washington
KRQU Medicine Bow, Wyoming
KRQX-FM Santa Clara, Utah
KRQZ Lompoc, California
KRRA Paragonah, Utah
KRRC Portland, Oregon
KRRE Las Vegas, New Mexico
KRRG Laredo, Texas
KRRK Desert Hills, Arizona
KRRM Rogue River, Oregon
KRRN Moapa Valley, Nevada
KRRO Sioux Falls, South Dakota
KRRQ Lafayette, Louisiana
KRRR Cheyenne, Wyoming
KRRT Arroyo Seco, New Mexico
KRRV-FM Alexandria, Louisiana

KRRW St. James, Minnesota
KRRX Burney, California
KRRY Canton, Missouri
KRSB-FM Roseburg, Oregon
KRSC-FM Claremore, Oklahoma
KRSD Sioux Falls, South Dakota
KRSE Yakima, Washington
KRSF Ridgecrest, California
KRSH Healdsburg, California
KRSJ Durango, Colorado
KRSK Molalla, Oregon
KRSL-FM Russell, Kansas
KRSP-FM Salt Lake City, Utah
KRSQ Laurel, Montana
KRSS Tarkio, Missouri
KRST Albuquerque, New Mexico
KRSU Appleton, Minnesota
KRSV-FM Afton, Wyoming
KRSW Worthington, Minnesota
KRSX-FM Twentynine Palms, California
KRSY-FM La Luz, New Mexico
KRTH Los Angeles, California
KRTI Grinnell, Iowa
KRTM Yucca Valley, California
KRTN-FM Raton, New Mexico
KRTO Guadalupe, California
KRTR-FM Kailua, Hawaii
KRTS Marfa, Texas
KRTT Great Bend, Kansas
KRTU-FM San Antonio, Texas
KRTY Los Gatos, California
KRTZ Cortez, Colorado
KRUA Anchorage, Alaska
KRUC Las Cruces, New Mexico
KRUF Shreveport, Louisiana
KRUI-FM Iowa City, Iowa
KRUP Dillingham, Alaska
KRUX Las Cruces, New Mexico
KRUZ Santa Barbara, California
KRVA-FM Campbell, Texas
KRVB Nampa, Idaho
KRVC Hornbrook, California
KRVE Brusly, Louisiana
KRVF Kerens, Texas
KRVG Glenwood Springs, Colorado
KRVH Rio Vista, California
KRVI Mount Vernon, Missouri
KRVK Vista West, Wyoming
KRVL Kerrville, Texas
KRVM-FM Eugene, Oregon
KRVN-FM Lexington, Nebraska
KRVO Columbia Falls, Montana
KRVQ-FM Lake Isabella, California
KRVR Copperopolis, California
KRVS Lafayette, Louisiana
KRVV Bastrop, Louisiana
KRVX Wimbledon, North Dakota
KRVY-FM Starbuck, Minnesota
KRWA Rye, Colorado
KRWG Las Cruces, New Mexico
KRWK Fargo, North Dakota
KRWM Bremerton, Washington
KRWN Farmington, New Mexico
KRWP Stockton, Missouri
KRWQ Gold Hill, Oregon
KRWY Rawlins, Wyoming
KRXB Beeville, Texas
KRXF Bend, Oregon
KRXL Kirksville, Missouri
KRXO Oklahoma City, Oklahoma
KRXP Pueblo West, Colorado
KRXQ Sacramento, California
KRXT Rockdale, Texas
KRXV Yermo, California
KRXW Roseau, Minnesota
KRXX Kodiak, Alaska
KRXY Shelton, Washington
KRYD Norwood, Colorado
KRYE Olney Springs, Colorado
KRYK Chinook, Montana
KRYL(FM) Haiku, Hawaii
KRYP Gladstone, Oregon
KRYS-FM Corpus Christi, Texas
KRZA Alamosa, Colorado
KRZK Branson, Missouri
KRZN Billings, Montana
KRZS Hunt, Texas
KRZU Batesville, Texas
KRZX Redlands, Colorado
KRZY-FM Santa Fe, New Mexico
KRZZ San Francisco, California
KSAB Robstown, Texas
KSAC-FM Dunnigan, California
KSAG Pearsall, Texas
KSAH-FM Pearsall, Texas
KSAJ-FM Abilene, Kansas
KSAK Walnut, California
KSAL-FM Salina, Kansas
KSAM-FM Huntsville, Texas
KSAN San Mateo, California
KSAQ Charlotte, Texas
KSAR Thayer, Missouri
KSAS-FM Caldwell, Idaho
KSAU Nacogdoches, Texas
KSAY Ft. Bragg, California
KSBA Coos Bay, Oregon
KSBC Nile, Washington
KSBH Coushatta, Louisiana
KSBJ Humble, Texas
KSBL Isla Vista, California
KSBR Mission Viejo, California
KSBS-FM Pago Pago, American Samoa
KSBV Salida, Colorado
KSBX Santa Barbara, California
KSBZ Sitka, Alaska
KSCA Glendale, California
KSCB-FM Liberal, Kansas
KSCH Sulphur Springs, Texas
KSCL Shreveport, Louisiana
KSCN Pittsburg, Texas
KSCQ Silver City, New Mexico
KSCR-FM Benson, Minnesota
KSCS Fort Worth, Texas
KSCU Santa Clara, California
KSCV Springfield, Missouri
KSCY Four Corners, Montana
KSD St. Louis, Missouri
KSDA-FM Agat, Guam
KSDB-FM Manhattan, Kansas
KSDJ Brookings, South Dakota
KSDL Sedalia, Missouri
KSDM International Falls, Minnesota
KSDN-FM Aberdeen, South Dakota
KSDQ Moberly, Missouri
KSDR-FM Watertown, South Dakota
KSDS San Diego, California
KSDZ Gordon, Nebraska
KSEA Greenfield, California
KSEC Bentonville, Arkansas
KSED Sedona, Arizona
KSEF Ste. Genevieve, Missouri
KSEG Sacramento, California
KSEH Brawley, California
KSEK-FM Girard, Kansas
KSEL-FM Portales, New Mexico
KSEM Seminole, Texas
KSEQ Visalia, California
KSER Everett, Washington
KSES-FM Seaside, California
KSEY-FM Seymour, Texas
KSEZ Sioux City, Iowa
KSFC Spokane, Washington
KSFH Mountain View, California
KSFI Salt Lake City, Utah
KSFM Woodland, California
KSFR White Rock, New Mexico
KSFS Sioux Falls, South Dakota
KSFT-FM South Sioux City, Nebraska
KSFX Roswell, New Mexico
KSGF-FM Ash Grove, Missouri
KSGG Carson City, Nevada
KSGN Riverside, California
KSGR Portland, Texas
KSGU Saint George, Utah
KSHA Redding, California
KSHE Crestwood, Missouri
KSHI Zuni, New Mexico
KSHK Kekaha, Hawaii
KSHL Coburg, Oregon
KSHN Liberty, Texas
KSHR-FM Coquille, Oregon
KSHU Huntsville, Texas
KSIB-FM Creston, Iowa
KSID-FM Sidney, Nebraska
KSIH Belcourt, North Dakota
KSII El Paso, Texas
KSIL Rincon, New Mexico
KSIT Rock Springs, Wyoming
KSIV-FM St. Louis, Missouri
KSJD Cortez, Colorado
KSJE Farmington, New Mexico
KSJI Saint Joseph, Missouri
KSJJ Redmond, Oregon
KSJL Strasburg, Colorado
KSJN Minneapolis, Minnesota
KSJO San Jose, California
KSJP(FM) Ipswich, South Dakota
KSJQ Savannah, Missouri
KSJR-FM Collegeville, Minnesota
KSJS San Jose, California
KSJT-FM San Angelo, Texas
KSJU Friday Harbor, Washington
KSJV Fresno, California
KSJY St. Martinville, Louisiana
KSJZ Jamestown, North Dakota
KSKA Anchorage, Alaska
KSKB Brooklyn, Iowa
KSKD Livingston, California
KSKE-FM Eagle, Colorado
KSKF Klamath Falls, Oregon
KSKG Salina, Kansas
KSKI-FM Sun Valley, Idaho
KSKK Staples, Minnesota
KSKL Scott City, Kansas
KSKR-FM Sutherlin, Oregon
KSKS Fresno, California
KSKU Sterling, Kansas
KSKX Chemult, Oregon
KSKZ Copeland, Kansas
KSL-FM Midvale, Utah
KSLC McMinnville, Oregon
KSLE Wewoka, Oklahoma
KSLG-FM Hydesville, California
KSLK Visalia, California
KSLO-FM Simmesport, Louisiana
KSLQ-FM Washington, Missouri
KSLT Spearfish, South Dakota
KSLU Hammond, Louisiana
KSLV-FM Del Norte, Colorado
KSLX-FM Scottsdale, Arizona
KSLY-FM San Luis Obispo, California
KSLZ St. Louis, Missouri
KSMA-FM Osage, Iowa
KSMB Lafayette, Louisiana
KSMC Moraga, California
KSMD Pangburn, Arkansas
KSME Greeley, Colorado
KSMF Ashland, Oregon
KSMG Seguin, Texas
KSMJ Shafter, California
KSML-FM Huntington, Texas
KSMM-FM Liberal, Kansas
KSMR Winona, Minnesota
KSMS-FM Point Lookout, Missouri
KSMT Breckenridge, Colorado
KSMU Springfield, Missouri
KSMW West Plains, Missouri
KSMX-FM Clovis, New Mexico
KSMY Lompoc, California
KSNA Idaho Falls, Idaho
KSNB Norton, Kansas
KSND Monmouth, Oregon
KSNE-FM Las Vegas, Nevada
KSNI-FM Santa Maria, California
KSNN-FM Ridgway, Colorado
KSNO-FM Snowmass Village, Colorado
KSNP Burlington, Kansas
KSNQ Twin Falls, Idaho
KSNR Fisher, Minnesota
KSNS Medicine Lodge, Kansas
KSNX(FM) Show Low, Arizona
KSNY-FM Snyder, Texas
KSOB Larned, Kansas
KSOC Gainesville, Texas
KSOF Dinuba, California
KSOH Wapato, Washington
KSOK-FM Winfield, Kansas
KSOL San Francisco, California
KSOM Audubon, Iowa
KSON San Diego, California
KSOO-FM Lennox, South Dakota
KSOP-FM Salt Lake City, Utah
KSOQ-FM Escondido, California
KSOR Ashland, Oregon
KSOS Las Vegas, Nevada
KSOU-FM Sioux Center, Iowa
KSPB Pebble Beach, California
KSPC Claremont, California
KSPE-FM Ellwood, California
KSPI-FM Stillwater, Oklahoma
KSPK-FM Walsenburg, Colorado
KSPL Kalispell, Montana
KSPM Sand Point, Alaska
KSPN-FM Aspen, Colorado
KSPO Dishman, Washington
KSPP Rhinelander, Wisconsin
KSPQ West Plains, Missouri
KSPW Sparta, Missouri
KSQB-FM Dell Rapids, South Dakota
KSQL Santa Cruz, California
KSQM Sequim, Washington
KSQQ Morgan Hill, California
KSQS Ririe, Idaho
KSQX Springtown, Texas
KSQY Deadwood, South Dakota
KSRA-FM Salmon, Idaho
KSRC Loup City, Nebraska
KSRD St. Joseph, Missouri
KSRF Poipu, Hawaii
KSRG Ashland, Oregon
KSRH San Rafael, California
KSRI Santa Cruz, California
KSRN Kings Beach, California
KSRQ Thief River Falls, Minnesota
KSRS Roseburg, Oregon
KSRT Cloverdale, California
KSRV-FM Ontario, Oregon
KSRW Independence, California
KSRX Sterling, Colorado
KSRY Tehachapi, California
KSRZ Omaha, Nebraska
KSSA Ingalls, Kansas
KSSB Calipatria, California
KSSC Ventura, California
KSSD Fallbrook, California
KSSE Arcadia, California
KSSH Shubert, Nebraska
KSSI China Lake, California
KSSJ(FM) Fair Oaks, California
KSSK-FM Waipahu, Hawaii
KSSL Post, Texas
KSSM Copperas Cove, Texas
KSSN Little Rock, Arkansas
KSSO Norman, Oklahoma
KSSR-FM Santa Rosa, New Mexico
KSSS Bismarck, North Dakota
KSSU Durant, Oklahoma
KSSW Nashville, Arkansas
KSSZ Fayette, Missouri
KSTB Crystal Beach, Texas
KSTH Holyoke, Colorado
KSTK Wrangell, Alaska
KSTM Indianola, Iowa
KSTN-FM Redding, California
KSTO Agana, Guam
KSTP-FM St. Paul, Minnesota
KSTQ(FM) Brownfield, Texas
KSTR-FM Montrose, Colorado
KSTT-FM Los Osos-Baywood Par, California
KSTV-FM Dublin, Texas
KSTX San Antonio, Texas
KSTY Canon City, Colorado
KSTZ Des Moines, Iowa
KSUA Fairbanks, Alaska
KSUI Iowa City, Iowa
KSUL Port Sulphur, Louisiana
KSUP Juneau, Alaska
KSUR Mart, Texas
KSUT Ignacio, Colorado
KSUU Cedar City, Utah
KSUW Sheridan, Wyoming
KSUX Winnebago, Nebraska
KSVL Smith, Nevada
KSVR Mount Vernon, Washington
KSVU Hamilton, Washington
KSVY Sonoma, California
KSWC Winfield, Kansas
KSWD Los Angeles, California
KSWF Aurora, Missouri
KSWG Wickenburg, Arizona
KSWH-FM Arkadelphia, Arkansas
KSWI Atlantic, Iowa
KSWN McCook, Nebraska
KSWP Lufkin, Texas
KSWS Chehalis, Washington
KSWW Ocean Shores, Washington
KSXY Forestville, California
KSYC-FM Yreka, California
KSYD Reedsport, Oregon
KSYE Frederick, Oklahoma
KSYM-FM San Antonio, Texas
KSYN Joplin, Missouri
KSYR Benton, Louisiana
KSYV Solvang, California

KSYY Ingram, Texas
KSYZ-FM Grand Island, Nebraska
KSZR Oro Valley, Arizona
KTAA Big Sandy, Texas
KTAC Ephrata, Washington
KTAD Sterling, Colorado
KTAG Cody, Wyoming
KTAI Kingsville, Texas
KTAK Riverton, Wyoming
KTAL-FM Texarkana, Texas
KTAO Taos, New Mexico
KTAR-FM Glendale, Arizona
KTAW Walsenburg, Colorado
KTBB-FM Tyler, Texas
KTBG Warrensburg, Missouri
KTBH-FM Kurtistown, Hawaii
KTBJ Festus, Missouri
KTBQ Nacogdoches, Texas
KTBT Broken Arrow, Oklahoma
KTBZ-FM Houston, Texas
KTCB Tillamook, Oregon
KTCC Colby, Kansas
KTCE Payson, Utah
KTCF Dolores, Colorado
KTCL Wheat Ridge, Colorado
KTCM Madison, Missouri
KTCO Duluth, Minnesota
KTCS-FM Fort Smith, Arkansas
KTCU-FM Fort Worth, Texas
KTCV Kennewick, Washington
KTCX Beaumont, Texas
KTCY Azle, Texas
KTCZ-FM Minneapolis, Minnesota
KTDA Dalhart, Texas
KTDB Ramah, New Mexico
KTDE Gualala, California
KTDK Sanger, Texas
KTDL Trinidad, Colorado
KTDR Del Rio, Texas
KTDU Durango, Colorado
KTDV State Center, Iowa
KTDX Laramie, Wyoming
KTDY Lafayette, Louisiana
KTDZ College, Alaska
KTEC Klamath Falls, Oregon
KTED Evansville, Wyoming
KTEE North Bend, Oregon
KTEG Santa Fe, New Mexico
KTEI Placerville, Colorado
KTEP El Paso, Texas
KTER Rudolph, Texas
KTEX Mercedes, Texas
KTEZ Zwolle, Louisiana
KTFC Sioux City, Iowa
KTFG Sioux Rapids, Iowa
KTFM Floresville, Texas
KTFR Chelsea, Oklahoma
KTFW-FM Glen Rose, Texas
KTFX-FM Warner, Oklahoma
KTFY Buhl, Idaho
KTGA Saratoga, Wyoming
KTGL Beatrice, Nebraska
KTGR-FM Fulton, Missouri
KTGS Tishomingo, Oklahoma
KTGV Oracle, Arizona
KTGW Fruitland, New Mexico
KTGX Owasso, Oklahoma
KTHC Sidney, Montana
KTHF Hammon, Oklahoma
KTHI Caldwell, Idaho
KTHK Idaho Falls, Idaho
KTHL Altus, Oklahoma
KTHM Red Bluff, California
KTHN La Junta, Colorado
KTHP Hemphill, Texas
KTHQ Eagar, Arizona
KTHR Wichita, Kansas
KTHS-FM Berryville, Arkansas
KTHT Cleveland, Texas
KTHU Corning, California
KTHX-FM Dayton, Nevada
KTIC-FM West Point, Nebraska
KTIG Pequot Lakes, Minnesota
KTIJ Elk City, Oklahoma
KTIL-FM Bay City, Oregon
KTIS-FM Minneapolis, Minnesota
KTJC Kelso, Washington
KTJJ Farmington, Missouri
KTJM Port Arthur, Texas
KTJO-FM Ottawa, Kansas
KTJZ Tallulah, Louisiana
KTKC-FM Springhill, Louisiana
KTKE Truckee, California
KTKL Stigler, Oklahoma
KTKO Beeville, Texas
KTKS Versailles, Missouri
KTKU Juneau, Alaska
KTKX Terrell Hills, Texas
KTLB Twin Lakes, Iowa
KTLC Canon City, Colorado
KTLF Colorado Springs, Colorado
KTLI El Dorado, Kansas
KTLN Thibodaux, Louisiana
KTLO-FM Mountain Home, Arkansas
KTLS-FM Holdenville, Oklahoma
KTLT Anson, Texas
KTLW Lancaster, California
KTLX Columbus, Nebraska
KTLZ Cuero, Texas
KTMC-FM McAlester, Oklahoma
KTMG Prescott, Arizona
KTMH Montrose, Colorado
KTMK Tillamook, Oregon
KTML South Fork, Colorado
KTMO New Madrid, Missouri
KTMQ Temecula, California
KTMT-FM Medford, Oregon
KTMU Muenster, Texas
KTMX York, Nebraska
KTMY Coon Rapids, Minnesota
KTNA Talkeetna, Alaska
KTNE-FM Alliance, Nebraska
KTNR Kenedy, Texas
KTNT Eufaula, Oklahoma
KTNX Arcadia, Missouri
KTNY Libby, Montana
KTOC-FM Jonesboro, Louisiana
KTOH Kalaheo, Hawaii
KTOL Leadville, Colorado
KTOM-FM Marina, California
KTOO Juneau, Alaska
KTOP-FM Saint Marys, Kansas
KTOR Gerber, California
KTOT Spearman, Texas
KTOY Texarkana, Arkansas
KTOZ-FM Pleasant Hope, Missouri
KTPF Salida, Colorado
KTPH Tonopah, Nevada
KTPI-FM Mojave, California
KTPK Topeka, Kansas
KTPL Pueblo, Colorado
KTPO Kootenai, Idaho
KTPS Pagosa Springs, Colorado
KTPT Rapid City, South Dakota
KTPZ Hazelton, Idaho
KTQM-FM Clovis, New Mexico
KTQQ Elko, Nevada
KTQX Bakersfield, California
KTRA-FM Farmington, New Mexico
KTRI-FM Mansfield, Missouri
KTRM Kirksville, Missouri
KTRN White Hall, Arkansas
KTRQ Colt, Arkansas
KTRR Loveland, Colorado
KTRS-FM Casper, Wyoming
KTRT Winthrop, Washington
KTRU(FM) Houston, Texas
KTRX Dickson, Oklahoma
KTRY(FM) Cazadero, California
KTRZ Riverton, Wyoming
KTSC-FM Pueblo, Colorado
KTSD-FM Reliance, South Dakota
KTSE-FM Patterson, California
KTSG Steamboat Springs, Colorado
KTSL Medical Lake, Washington
KTSM-FM El Paso, Texas
KTSO Glenpool, Oklahoma
KTSR De Quincy, Louisiana
KTST Oklahoma City, Oklahoma
KTSU Houston, Texas
KTSW San Marcos, Texas
KTSY Caldwell, Idaho
KTTA(FM) Jackson, California
KTTG Mena, Arkansas
KTTI Yuma, Arizona
KTTK Lebanon, Missouri
KTTN-FM Trenton, Missouri
KTTR-FM St. James, Missouri
KTTS-FM Springfield, Missouri
KTTX Brenham, Texas
KTTY New Boston, Texas
KTTZ-FM Lubbock, Texas
KTUF Kirksville, Missouri
KTUG Hudson, Wyoming
KTUH Honolulu, Hawaii
KTUI-FM Sullivan, Missouri
KTUM Tatum, New Mexico
KTUN New Castle, Colorado
KTUN(FM) New Castle, Nebraska
KTUT Frankfort, South Dakota
KTUX Carthage, Texas
KTUZ-FM Okarche, Oklahoma
KTVR-FM La Grande, Oregon
KTWA Ottumwa, Iowa
KTWB Sioux Falls, South Dakota
KTWD Wallace, Idaho
KTWL Hempstead, Texas
KTWN-FM Edina, Minnesota
KTWS Bend, Oregon
KTWV Los Angeles, California
KTXB Beaumont, Texas
KTXC Lamesa, Texas
KTXG Greenville, Texas
KTXI Ingram, Texas
KTXJ-FM Jasper, Texas
KTXK Texarkana, Texas
KTXM Hallettsville, Texas
KTXN-FM Victoria, Texas
KTXO Goldsmith, Texas
KTXP Bushland, Texas
KTXR Springfield, Missouri
KTXT-FM Lubbock, Texas
KTXX-FM Dripping Springs, Texas
KTXY Jefferson City, Missouri
KTYD Santa Barbara, California
KTYL-FM Tyler, Texas
KTYN Thayne, Wyoming
KTZA Artesia, New Mexico
KTZU Velva, North Dakota
KTZZ Conrad, Montana
KUAC Fairbanks, Alaska
KUAD-FM Windsor, Colorado
KUAF Fayetteville, Arkansas
KUAL-FM Brainerd, Minnesota
KUAM-FM Hagatna, Guam
KUAP Pine Bluff, Arkansas
KUAR Little Rock, Arkansas
KUAT-FM Tucson, Arizona
KUAZ-FM Tucson, Arizona
KUBB Mariposa, California
KUBE Seattle, Washington
KUBJ Brenham, Texas
KUBL-FM Salt Lake City, Utah
KUBO Calexico, California
KUBQ La Grande, Oregon
KUBS Newport, Washington
KUCA Conway, Arkansas
KUCB Unalaska, Alaska
KUCC Clarkston, Washington
KUCD Pearl City, Hawaii
KUCI Irvine, California
KUCR Riverside, California
KUCV Lincoln, Nebraska
KUDD Roy, Utah
KUDE Nephi, Utah
KUDI Choteau, Montana
KUDU Tok, Alaska
KUEL(FM) Fort Dodge, Iowa
KUER-FM Salt Lake City, Utah
KUEU Logan, Utah
KUFL Libby, Montana
KUFM Missoula, Montana
KUFN Hamilton, Montana
KUFO-FM Portland, Oregon
KUFR Salt Lake City, Utah
KUFX San Jose, California
KUGS Bellingham, Washington
KUHB-FM St. Paul, Alaska
KUHC Clayton, New Mexico
KUHF Houston, Texas
KUHM Helena, Montana
KUHN Golden Meadow, Louisiana
KUIC Vacaville, California
KUJ-FM Burbank, Washington
KUJZ Creswell, Oregon
KUKA San Diego, Texas
KUKI-FM Ukiah, California
KUKL Kalispell, Montana
KUKN Longview, Washington
KUKU-FM Willow Springs, Missouri
KUKY Wellton, Arizona
KULE-FM Ephrata, Washington
KULH Wheeling, Missouri
KULL Abilene, Texas
KULM-FM Columbus, Texas
KULO Alexandria, Minnesota
KULV Ukiah, California
KUMA-FM Pilot Rock, Oregon
KUMD-FM Duluth, Minnesota
KUMM Morris, Minnesota
KUMR Doolittle, Missouri
KUMU-FM Honolulu, Hawaii
KUMX North Fort Polk, Louisiana
KUNA-FM La Quinta, California
KUNC Greeley, Colorado
KUND-FM Grand Forks, North Dakota
KUNI Cedar Falls, Iowa
KUNM Albuquerque, New Mexico
KUNQ Houston, Missouri
KUNR Reno, Nevada
KUNV Las Vegas, Nevada
KUOI-FM Moscow, Idaho
KUOM-FM St. Louis Park, Minnesota
KUOO Spirit Lake, Iowa
KUOP Stockton, California
KUOR-FM Redlands, California
KUOW-FM Seattle, Washington
KUPD Tempe, Arizona
KUPH Mountain View, Missouri
KUPI-FM Rexburg, Idaho
KUPL Portland, Oregon
KUPR Alamogordo, New Mexico
KUPS Tacoma, Washington
KUQL Ethan, South Dakota
KUQQ Milford, Iowa
KURB Little Rock, Arkansas
KURE Ames, Iowa
KURK Reno, Nevada
KURL(FM) Billings, Montana
KURM-FM Gravette, Arkansas
KURQ Grover Beach, California
KURR Indian Springs, Nevada
KURY-FM Brookings, Oregon
KUSB Hazelton, North Dakota
KUSC Los Angeles, California
KUSD Vermillion, South Dakota
KUSJ Harker Heights, Texas
KUSL Richfield, Utah
KUSN Dearing, Kansas
KUSO Albion, Nebraska
KUSP Santa Cruz, California
KUSQ Worthington, Minnesota
KUSQ-FM Worthington, Minnesota
KUSR Logan, Utah
KUSS(FM) Carlsbad, California
KUSU-FM Logan, Utah
KUSW Flora Vista, New Mexico
KUSZ Olathe, Colorado
KUT Austin, Texas
KUTE Ignacio, Colorado
KUUB Sun Valley, Nevada
KUUL East Moline, Illinois
KUUR Carbondale, Colorado
KUUT Farmington, New Mexico
KUUU South Jordan, Utah
KUUZ Lake Village, Arkansas
KUVA Uvalde, Texas
KUVO Denver, Colorado
KUWA Afton, Wyoming
KUWC Casper, Wyoming
KUWD Sundance, Wyoming
KUWG Gillette, Wyoming
KUWI Rawlins, Wyoming
KUWJ Jackson, Wyoming
KUWL Laramie, Wyoming
KUWN Newcastle, Wyoming
KUWP Powell, Wyoming
KUWR Laramie, Wyoming
KUWS Superior, Wisconsin
KUWT Thermopolis, Wyoming
KUWX Pinedale, Wyoming
KUWY Laramie, Wyoming
KUWZ Rock Springs, Wyoming
KUYI Hotevilla, Arizona
KUYY Emmetsburg, Iowa
KUZN Centerville, Texas
KUZZ-FM Bakersfield, California
KVAB Clarkston, Washington
KVAK-FM Valdez, Alaska
KVAL Cal-Nev-Ari, Nevada
KVAM Kimball, Nebraska
KVAR Pine Ridge, South Dakota
KVAS-FM Ilwaco, Washington
KVAY Lamar, Colorado

KVAZ Henryetta, Oklahoma
KVCF Freeman, South Dakota
KVCH Huron, South Dakota
KVCK-FM Wolf Point, Montana
KVCL-FM Winnfield, Louisiana
KVCM Helena, Montana
KVCO Concordia, Kansas
KVCR San Bernardino, California
KVCS Spring Valley, Minnesota
KVCX Gregory, South Dakota
KVCY Fort Scott, Kansas
KVDG Midland, Texas
KVDP Dry Prong, Louisiana
KVDU Houma, Louisiana
KVEG Mesquite, Nevada
KVER El Paso, Texas
KVET-FM Austin, Texas
KVFG Victorville, California
KVFL Pierre, South Dakota
KVFM Beeville, Texas
KVFX Logan, Utah
KVGB-FM Great Bend, Kansas
KVGG Salome, Arizona
KVGO Spring Valley, Minnesota
KVGQ Overton, Nevada
KVGS Meadview, Arizona
KVHR Van Horn, Texas
KVHS Concord, California
KVHT Vermillion, South Dakota
KVHU Judsonia, Arkansas
KVIB Sun City West, Arizona
KVIC Victoria, Texas
KVIL Highland Park-Dallas, Texas
KVIP-FM Redding, California
KVIR Bullhead City, Arizona
KVIX Port Angeles, Washington
KVJC Globe, Arizona
KVJM Hearne, Texas
KVJZ Vail, Colorado
KVKI-FM Shreveport, Louisiana
KVKL Las Vegas, Nevada
KVKR Pine Ridge, South Dakota
KVLB Bend, Oregon
KVLC Hatch, New Mexico
KVLD Atkins, Arkansas
KVLE-FM Gunnison, Colorado
KVLI(FM) Lake Isabella, California
KVLK Milan, New Mexico
KVLL-FM Wells, Texas
KVLO Humnoke, Arkansas
KVLP Tucumcari, New Mexico
KVLR Elgin, Texas
KVLT Temple, Texas
KVLU Beaumont, Texas
KVLW Gatesville, Texas
KVLY Edinburg, Texas
KVLZ Sheridan, Wyoming
KVMA-FM Shreveport, Louisiana
KVMI Arthur, North Dakota
KVMN Cave City, Arkansas
KVMR Nevada City, California
KVMT Montrose, Colorado
KVMV Mc Allen, Texas
KVMX Bakersfield, California
KVMZ Waldo, Arkansas
KVNA-FM Flagstaff, Arizona
KVNE Tyler, Texas
KVNF Paonia, Colorado
KVNO Omaha, Nebraska
KVOB Lindsborg, Kansas
KVOD Lakewood, Colorado
KVOE-FM Emporia, Kansas
KVOM-FM Morrilton, Arkansas
KVOO-FM Tulsa, Oklahoma
KVOU-FM Uvalde, Texas
KVOV Carbondale, Colorado
KVOX-FM Moorhead, Minnesota
KVPI-FM Ville Platte, Louisiana
KVPR Fresno, California
KVPW Kingsburg, California
KVRA Sisters, Oregon
KVRD-FM Cottonwood, Arizona
KVRE Hot Springs Village, Arkansas
KVRG Victor, Idaho
KVRH-FM Salida, Colorado
KVRK Sanger, Texas
KVRO Stillwater, Oklahoma
KVRP-FM Haskell, Texas
KVRS Lawton, Oklahoma
KVRT Victoria, Texas
KVRV Monte Rio, California
KVRW Lawton, Oklahoma
KVRX Austin, Texas
KVRZ Libby, Montana
KVSC St. Cloud, Minnesota
KVSF-FM Pecos, New Mexico
KVSP Anadarko, Oklahoma
KVSR Kirksville, Missouri
KVSS Omaha, Nebraska
KVST Willis, Texas
KVSV-FM Beloit, Kansas
KVTI Tacoma, Washington
KVTY Lewiston, Idaho
KVUH Laytonville, California
KVUU Pueblo, Colorado
KVUW Wendover, Nevada
KVVA-FM Apache Junction, Arizona
KVVF Santa Clara, California
KVVL Maryville, Missouri
KVVP Leesville, Louisiana
KVVR Dutton, Montana
KVVS Rosamond, California
KVVZ San Rafael, California
KVWC-FM Vernon, Texas
KVWF Augusta, Kansas
KVWG-FM Dilley, Texas
KVXX Quincy, California
KVYB Santa Barbara, California
KVYL Mohave Valley, Arizona
KVYN St. Helena, California
KWAK-FM Stuttgart, Arkansas
KWAO Ocean Park, Washington
KWAP(FM) Pine Haven, Wyoming
KWAR Waverly, Iowa
KWAV Monterey, California
KWAX Eugene, Oregon
KWAY-FM Waverly, Iowa
KWBI Great Bend, Kansas
KWBT Mexia, Texas
KWBU-FM Waco, Texas
KWBX Salem, Oregon
KWBY-FM Ranger, Texas
KWBZ Monroe City, Missouri
KWCA Palo Cedro, California
KWCD Bisbee, Arizona
KWCF Sheridan, Wyoming
KWCK-FM Searcy, Arkansas
KWCL-FM Oak Grove, Louisiana
KWCN Pinedale, Wyoming
KWCO-FM Chickasha, Oklahoma
KWCR-FM Ogden, Utah
KWCW Walla Walla, Washington
KWCX-FM Tanque Verde, Arizona
KWDD(FM) Fairbanks, Alaska
KWDI Idalia, Colorado
KWDM West Des Moines, Iowa
KWDQ Woodward, Oklahoma
KWDR Royal City, Washington
KWDS Kettleman City, California
KWEN Tulsa, Oklahoma
KWES-FM Ruidoso, New Mexico
KWEY-FM Clinton, Oklahoma
KWFA(FM) Limon, Colorado
KWFB Holliday, Texas
KWFC Springfield, Missouri
KWFH Parker, Arizona
KWFJ Roy, Washington
KWFL Roswell, New Mexico
KWFP Sparks, Nevada
KWFR San Angelo, Texas
KWFS-FM Wichita Falls, Texas
KWFX Woodward, Oklahoma
KWGB Colby, Kansas
KWGL Ouray, Colorado
KWGO Burlington, North Dakota
KWGS Tulsa, Oklahoma
KWHF Harrisburg, Arkansas
KWHK Hutchinson, Kansas
KWHL Anchorage, Alaska
KWHO Lovell, Wyoming
KWHQ-FM Kenai, Alaska
KWHT Pendleton, Oregon
KWHW-FM Altus, Oklahoma
KWIC Topeka, Kansas
KWID Las Vegas, Nevada
KWIM Window Rock, Arizona
KWIN Lodi, California
KWIQ-FM Moses Lake, Washington
KWIS Plummer, Idaho
KWIT Sioux City, Iowa
KWIZ Santa Ana, California
KWJC Liberty, Missouri
KWJG Kasilof, Alaska
KWJJ-FM Portland, Oregon
KWJK Boonville, Missouri
KWKJ Windsor, Missouri
KWKK Russellville, Arkansas
KWKL Grandfield, Oklahoma
KWKM St. Johns, Arizona
KWKQ Graham, Texas
KWKR Leoti, Kansas
KWKZ Charleston, Missouri
KWLD Plainview, Texas
KWLF Fairbanks, Alaska
KWLN Wilson Creek, Washington
KWLR Maumelle, Arkansas
KWLS Winfield, Kansas
KWLT North Crossett, Arkansas
KWLU Chester, California
KWLV Many, Louisiana
KWLZ-FM West Linn, Oregon
KWMD Sterling, Alaska
KWME Wellington, Kansas
KWMR Point Reyes Station, California
KWMU St. Louis, Missouri
KWMW Maljamar, New Mexico
KWMX Williams, Arizona
KWMY Joliet, Montana
KWMZ-FM Empire, Louisiana
KWNA-FM Winnemucca, Nevada
KWND Springfield, Missouri
KWNE Ukiah, California
KWNG Red Wing, Minnesota
KWNM Winnemucca, Nevada
KWNN Turlock, California
KWNO-FM Rushford, Minnesota
KWNR Henderson, Nevada
KWNS Winnsboro, Texas
KWNZ Lovelock, Nevada
KWOF Broomfield, Colorado
KWOL-FM Whitefish, Montana
KWOP(FM) Fort Dodge, North Carolina
KWOW Clifton, Texas
KWOX Woodward, Oklahoma
KWOZ Mountain View, Arkansas
KWPK-FM Sisters, Oregon
KWPR Lund, Nevada
KWPT Fortuna, California
KWPW Robinson, Texas
KWPZ Lynden, Washington
KWQW Boone, Iowa
KWRB Bisbee, Arizona
KWRC Hermosa, South Dakota
KWRD-FM Highland Village, Texas
KWRF-FM Warren, Arkansas
KWRI Bartlesville, Oklahoma
KWRK Window Rock, Arizona
KWRL La Grande, Oregon
KWRQ Clifton, Arizona
KWRR Ethete, Wyoming
KWRV Sun Valley, Idaho
KWRW Rusk, Texas
KWRX Redmond, Oregon
KWSA Price, Utah
KWSB-FM Gunnison, Colorado
KWSC Wayne, Nebraska
KWSO Warm Springs, Oregon
KWTD Ridgecrest, California
KWTG Vidalia, Louisiana
KWTH Barstow, California
KWTM June Lake, California
KWTO-FM Springfield, Missouri
KWTS Canyon, Texas
KWTU Tulsa, Oklahoma
KWTW Bishop, California
KWTX-FM Waco, Texas
KWTY Cartago, California
KWUF-FM Pagosa Springs, Colorado
KWUP Navasota, Texas
KWUR Clayton, Missouri
KWUT(FM) Elsinore, Utah
KWUZ Poncha Springs, Colorado
KWVA Eugene, Oregon
KWVE-FM San Clemente, California
KWVI Waverly, Iowa
KWVR-FM Enterprise, Oregon
KWVV-FM Homer, Alaska
KWVZ Florence, Oregon
KWWC-FM Columbia, Missouri
KWWK Rochester, Minnesota
KWWR Mexico, Missouri
KWWS Walla Walla, Washington
KWWV Santa Margarita, California
KWWW-FM Quincy, Washington
KWWX Cashmere, Washington
KWXC Grove, Oklahoma
KWXD Asbury, Missouri
KWXR Reliance, Wyoming
KWXX-FM Hilo, Hawaii
KWXY(FM) Cathedral City, California
KWYC Cheyenne, Wyoming
KWYD Parma, Idaho
KWYE Fresno, California
KWYI Kawaihae, Hawaii
KWYK-FM Aztec, New Mexico
KWYL South Lake Tahoe, California
KWYN-FM Wynne, Arkansas
KWYR-FM Winner, South Dakota
KWYS(FM) Island Park, Idaho
KWYW Lost Cabin, Wyoming
KWYX Casper, Wyoming
KWYY Midwest, Wyoming
KXAA Cle Elum, Washington
KXAC St. James, Minnesota
KXAZ Page, Arizona
KXBA Nikiski, Alaska
KXBC Garberville, California
KXBG Cheyenne, Wyoming
KXBJ El Campo, Texas
KXBL Henryetta, Oklahoma
KXBN Cedar City, Utah
KXBR International Falls, Minnesota
KXBT Leander, Texas
KXBX-FM Lakeport, California
KXBZ Manhattan, Kansas
KXCI Tucson, Arizona
KXCL Westcliffe, Colorado
KXCM Joshua Tree, California
KXCS(FM) Coahoma, Texas
KXCV Maryville, Missouri
KXDD Yakima, Washington
KXDG Webb City, Missouri
KXDI Belfield, North Dakota
KXDJ Spearman, Texas
KXDL Browerville, Minnesota
KXDR Pinedale, Montana
KXDR(FM) Pinesdale, Montana
KXDS Santa Clara, Utah
KXDZ Templeton, California
KXEI Havre, Montana
KXEZ Farmersville, Texas
KXFC Coalgate, Oklahoma
KXFE Dumas, Arkansas
KXFF Colorado City, Arizona
KXFG Sun City, California
KXFM Santa Maria, California
KXFR Socorro, New Mexico
KXFT Manson, Iowa
KXGA Glennallen, Alaska
KXGE Dubuque, Iowa
KXGJ Victoria, Texas
KXGL Amarillo, Texas
KXGM-FM Hiawatha, Iowa
KXGO Arcata, California
KXGR Loveland, Colorado
KXGT Carrington, North Dakota
KXHT Marion, Arkansas
KXIA Marshalltown, Iowa
KXIM Sanborn, Iowa
KXIO Clarksville, Arkansas
KXIT-FM Dalhart, Texas
KXIX Sunriver, Oregon
KXJM Banks, Oregon
KXJN Moose Wilson Road, Wyoming
KXJO St. Maries, Idaho
KXJS Sutter, California
KXJZ Sacramento, California
KXKC New Iberia, Louisiana
KXKK Park Rapids, Minnesota
KXKL-FM Denver, Colorado
KXKM McCarthy, Alaska
KXKQ Safford, Arizona
KXKS-FM Shreveport, Louisiana
KXKT Glenwood, Iowa
KXKU Lyons, Kansas
KXKX Knob Noster, Missouri
KXKZ Ruston, Louisiana
KXLB Livingston, Montana
KXLC La Crescent, Minnesota
KXLG Milbank, South Dakota
KXLI Moapa, Nevada
KXLL Juneau, Alaska
KXLM Oxnard, California
KXLP Eagle Lake, Minnesota

KXLR Fairbanks, Alaska
KXLS Lahoma, Oklahoma
KXLT-FM Eagle, Idaho
KXLU Los Angeles, California
KXLV Amarillo, Texas
KXLW Houston, Alaska
KXLY-FM Spokane, Washington
KXMG Jean Lafitte, Louisiana
KXML Fairfield, Idaho
KXMO-FM Owensville, Missouri
KXMS Joplin, Missouri
KXMT Taos, New Mexico
KXMX Muldrow, Oklahoma
KXMZ Box Elder, South Dakota
KXNA Springdale, Arkansas
KXNC Ness City, Kansas
KXNE-FM Norfolk, Nebraska
KXNM Encino, New Mexico
KXNP North Platte, Nebraska
KXNT-FM Henderson, Nevada
KXNV Sun Valley, Nevada
KXO-FM El Centro, California
KXOJ-FM Sapulpa, Oklahoma
KXOL-FM Los Angeles, California
KXOO Elk City, Oklahoma
KXOQ Kennett, Missouri
KXOR-FM Thibodaux, Louisiana
KXOT Tacoma, Washington
KXOX-FM Sweetwater, Texas
KXPC-FM Harrisburg, Oregon
KXPK Evergreen, Colorado
KXPR Sacramento, California
KXPT Las Vegas, Nevada
KXPZ Las Cruces, New Mexico
KXQL Flandreau, South Dakota
KXRA-FM Alexandria, Minnesota
KXRD Victorville, California
KXRI Amarillo, Texas
KXRJ Russellville, Arkansas
KXRK Provo, Utah
KXRL Cherry Valley, Arkansas
KXRQ Roosevelt, Utah
KXRR Monroe, Louisiana
KXRS Hemet, California
KXRT Idabel, Oklahoma
KXRV Cannon Ball, North Dakota
KXRX Walla Walla, Washington
KXRZ Alexandria, Minnesota
KXSA-FM Dermott, Arkansas
KXSB Big Bear Lake, California
KXSC(FM) Sunnyvale, California
KXSE Davis, California
KXSM Hollister, California
KXSR Groveland, California
KXSS-FM Amarillo, Texas
KXTC Thoreau, New Mexico
KXTE Pahrump, Nevada
KXTH Seminole, Oklahoma
KXTN-FM San Antonio, Texas
KXTQ-FM Lubbock, Texas
KXTS Geyserville, California
KXTT Maricopa, California
KXTZ Pismo Beach, California
KXUA Fayetteville, Arkansas
KXUL Monroe, Louisiana
KXUS Springfield, Missouri
KXWA Centennial, Colorado
KXWT Odessa, Texas
KXXI Gallup, New Mexico
KXXK Hoquiam, Washington
KXXL Moorcroft, Wyoming
KXXM San Antonio, Texas
KXXN Iowa Park, Texas
KXXO Olympia, Washington
KXXQ Milan, New Mexico
KXXR Minneapolis, Minnesota
KXXS Menard, Texas
KXXY-FM Oklahoma City, Oklahoma
KXXZ Barstow, California
KXYL-FM Coleman, Texas
KXZK Vail, Arizona
KXZM Felton, California
KXZS Wall, South Dakota
KXZT Newell, South Dakota
KYAF Firebaugh, California
KYAI McKee, Kentucky
KYAL-FM Muskogee, Oklahoma
KYAR Lorena, Texas
KYAT Gallup, New Mexico
KYBA Stewartville, Minnesota
KYBB Canton, South Dakota
KYBE Frederick, Oklahoma
KYBG Basile, Louisiana
KYBI Lufkin, Texas
KYBJ Lake Jackson, Texas
KYBR Espanola, New Mexico
KYCC Stockton, California
KYCH-FM Portland, Oregon
KYCI Firebaugh, California
KYCJ Camino, California
KYCK Crookston, Minnesota
KYCM Alamogordo, New Mexico
KYCO Limon, Colorado
KYCS Rock Springs, Wyoming
KYCT Ruidoso, New Mexico
KYCU Clinton, Oklahoma
KYDL(FM) Hot Springs, Arkansas
KYDN Monte Vista, Colorado
KYDS Sacramento, California
KYDT Pine Haven, Wyoming
KYEE Alamogordo, New Mexico
KYEL Danville, Arkansas
KYEN Severance, Colorado
KYEZ Salina, Kansas
KYFB Denison, Texas
KYFL Monroe, Louisiana
KYFM Bartlesville, Oklahoma
KYFO-FM Ogden, Utah
KYFP Palestine, Texas
KYFS San Antonio, Texas
KYFW Wichita, Kansas
KYGL Texarkana, Arkansas
KYGO-FM Denver, Colorado
KYGR Alamo, New Mexico
KYIS Oklahoma City, Oklahoma
KYIX South Oroville, California
KYJC Commerce, Texas
KYJK Missoula, Montana
KYKC Byng, Oklahoma
KYKD Bethel, Alaska
KYKM Yoakum, Texas
KYKR Beaumont, Texas
KYKS Lufkin, Texas
KYKV Selah, Washington
KYKX Longview, Texas
KYKY St. Louis, Missouri
KYKZ Lake Charles, Louisiana
KYLA Homer, Louisiana
KYLC Lake Charles, Louisiana
KYLD San Francisco, California
KYLF Adrian, Missouri
KYLI Bunkerville, Nevada
KYLK Okemah, Oklahoma
KYLR Hutto, Texas
KYLS-FM Ironton, Missouri
KYLV Oklahoma City, Oklahoma
KYME Rockford, Iowa
KYMG Anchorage, Alaska
KYMK-FM Maurice, Louisiana
KYMS Rathdrum, Idaho
KYMV Woodruff, Utah
KYMX Sacramento, California
KYNU Jamestown, North Dakota
KYNZ Lone Grove, Oklahoma
KYOE Point Arena, California
KYOO-FM Half Way, Missouri
KYOR Newport, Oregon
KYOT-FM Phoenix, Arizona
KYOX Comanche, Texas
KYOY Hillsdale, Wyoming
KYPB Big Timber, Montana
KYPC Colstrip, Montana
KYPF Stanford, Montana
KYPL Yakima, Washington
KYPM Livingston, Montana
KYPR Miles City, Montana
KYPT Daniel, Wyoming
KYPW Wolf Point, Montana
KYPY Donaldsonville, Louisiana
KYQQ Arkansas City, Kansas
KYQX Weatherford, Texas
KYRK Refugio, Texas
KYRM Yuma, Arizona
KYRN Socorro, New Mexico
KYRQ Natalia, Texas
KYRT Hunt, Texas
KYRV Concordia, Missouri
KYRX Marble Hill, Missouri
KYSC Fairbanks, Alaska
KYSE El Paso, Texas
KYSF Bonanza, Oregon
KYSJ Coos Bay, Oregon
KYSL Frisco, Colorado
KYSM-FM Mankato, Minnesota
KYSN East Wenatchee, Washington
KYSR Los Angeles, California
KYSS-FM Missoula, Montana
KYSX(FM) Billings, Montana
KYTC Northwood, Iowa
KYTE Newport, Oregon
KYTI Sheridan, Wyoming
KYTM Corrigan, Texas
KYTN(FM) Union City, Tennessee
KYTS Manderson, Wyoming
KYTT-FM Coos Bay, Oregon
KYTZ Walhalla, North Dakota
KYUN Hailey, Idaho
KYUS-FM Miles City, Montana
KYVA-FM Church Rock, New Mexico
KYVT Yakima, Washington
KYWA Wichita, Kansas
KYWH Lockwood, Montana
KYXK Gurdon, Arkansas
KYXX Ozona, Texas
KYXY San Diego, California
KYYI Burkburnett, Texas
KYYK Palestine, Texas
KYYT Goldendale, Washington
KYYX Minot, North Dakota
KYYY Bismarck, North Dakota
KYYZ Williston, North Dakota
KYZK Sun Valley, Idaho
KYZQ Mount Pleasant, Texas
KYZZ Salinas, California
KZAI Superior, Arizona
KZAL Manson, Washington
KZAM Pleasant Valley, Texas
KZAN Hays, Kansas
KZAP Paradise, California
KZAR McQueeney, Texas
KZAT-FM Belle Plaine, Iowa
KZAZ Bellingham, Washington
KZBB Poteau, Oklahoma
KZBD Spokane, Washington
KZBE Omak, Washington
KZBG Lapwai, Idaho
KZBI Elko, Nevada
KZBJ Bay City, Texas
KZBK Brookfield, Missouri
KZBL Natchitoches, Louisiana
KZBQ Pocatello, Idaho
KZBR La Jara, Colorado
KZBS Granite, Oklahoma
KZBT Midland, Texas
KZCD Lawton, Oklahoma
KZCH Derby, Kansas
KZCR Fergus Falls, Minnesota
KZCU Woodward, Oklahoma
KZDX Burley, Idaho
KZDY Cawker City, Kansas
KZEL-FM Eugene, Oregon
KZEN Central City, Nebraska
KZEP-FM San Antonio, Texas
KZET Cortez, Colorado
KZEW Wheatland, Wyoming
KZFM Corpus Christi, Texas
KZFN Moscow, Idaho
KZFO(FM) Benbrook, Texas
KZFR Chico, California
KZFT Fannett, Texas
KZGF Grand Forks, North Dakota
KZGL Flagstaff, Arizona
KZGM Cabool, Missouri
KZGZ Hagatna, Guam
KZHE Stamps, Arkansas
KZHK St. George, Utah
KZHR Dayton, Washington
KZHT Salt Lake City, Utah
KZIA Cedar Rapids, Iowa
KZID Culdesac, Idaho
KZII-FM Lubbock, Texas
KZIN-FM Shelby, Montana
KZIO Two Harbors, Minnesota
KZIQ-FM Ridgecrest, California
KZIU-FM Weston, Oregon
KZJB Pocatello, Idaho
KZJF Jefferson City, Missouri
KZJH Jackson, Wyoming
KZJK St. Louis Park, Minnesota
KZJZ St. Regis, Montana
KZKE Seligman, Arizona
KZKK Huron, South Dakota
KZKL Wichita Falls, Texas
KZKR Jonesville, Louisiana
KZKS Rifle, Colorado
KZKX Seward, Nebraska
KZKY(FM) Ucon, Idaho
KZKZ-FM Greenwood, Arkansas
KZLA Riverdale, California
KZLE Batesville, Arkansas
KZLG Mansura, Louisiana
KZLK Rapid City, South Dakota
KZLO Kilgore, Texas
KZLS Mustang, Oklahoma
KZLT-FM East Grand Forks, Minnesota
KZLU Inyokern, California
KZLV Lytle, Texas
KZLZ Casas Adobes, Arizona
KZMA Naylor, Missouri
KZMC McCook, Nebraska
KZME Brightwood, Oregon
KZMK Sierra Vista, Arizona
KZML Quincy, Washington
KZMN Kalispell, Montana
KZMP-FM Pilot Point, Texas
KZMQ-FM Greybull, Wyoming
KZMT Helena, Montana
KZMU Moab, Utah
KZMX-FM Hot Springs, South Dakota
KZMY Bozeman, Montana
KZMZ Alexandria, Louisiana
KZNA Hill City, Kansas
KZND-FM Houston, Alaska
KZNN Rolla, Missouri
KZNO (FM) Jerome, Idaho
KZNSFM) Coalville, Utah
KZOC Bourbon, Missouri
KZOK-FM Seattle, Washington
KZON Phoenix, Arizona
KZOQ-FM Missoula, Montana
KZOZ San Luis Obispo, California
KZPE Ford City, California
KZPI Deming, New Mexico
KZPK Paynesville, Minnesota
KZPO Lindsay, California
KZPR Minot, North Dakota
KZPS Dallas, Texas
KZPT Kansas City, Missouri
KZQD Liberal, Kansas
KZQL Mills, Wyoming
KZQX Tatum, Texas
KZRB New Boston, Texas
KZRC Bennington, Oklahoma
KZRD Dodge City, Kansas
KZRI Welches, Oregon
KZRK-FM Canyon, Texas
KZRM Chama, New Mexico
KZRO Dunsmuir, California
KZRR Albuquerque, New Mexico
KZRS Great Bend, Kansas
KZRV Sartell, Minnesota
KZRX Dickinson, North Dakota
KZRZ West Monroe, Louisiana
KZSC Santa Cruz, California
KZSD-FM Martin, South Dakota
KZSE Rochester, Minnesota
KZSN Hutchinson, Kansas
KZSP South Padre Island, Texas
KZSQ-FM Sonora, California
KZST Santa Rosa, California
KZSU Stanford, California
KZTA Naches, Washington
KZTB Milton-Freewater, Oregon
KZTH Piedmont, Oklahoma
KZTI(FM) Fallon Station, Pennsylvania
KZTK White Oak, Texas
KZTL Paxton, Nebraska
KZTQ Sun Valley, Nevada
KZTW Tioga, North Dakota
KZUA Holbrook, Arizona
KZUH Minneapolis, Kansas
KZUL-FM Lake Havasu City, Arizona
KZUM Lincoln, Nebraska
KZUU Pullman, Washington
KZUW Reliance, Wyoming
KZWA Moss Bluff, Louisiana
KZWB Green River, Wyoming
KZWV Eldon, Missouri
KZWY Sheridan, Wyoming
KZXK Doney Park, Arizona
KZXL Hudson, Texas
KZXQ Lake of the Woods, Arizona
KZXT Eureka, Montana
KZXY-FM Apple Valley, California

KZXZ Wyola, Montana
KZYR Avon, Colorado
KZYX Philo, California
KZYZ Willits, California
KZZA Muenster, Texas
KZZE Eagle Point, Oregon
KZZI Belle Fourche, South Dakota
KZZK New London, Missouri
KZZL-FM Pullman, Washington
KZZO Sacramento, California
KZZP Mesa, Arizona
KZZR Government Camp, Oregon
KZZS Story, Wyoming
KZZT Moberly, Missouri
KZZU-FM Spokane, Washington
KZZX Alamogordo, New Mexico
KZZY Devils Lake, North Dakota
WAAC Valdosta, Georgia
WAAE New Bern, North Carolina
WAAF Westborough, Massachusetts
WAAG Galesburg, Illinois
WAAI Hurlock, Maryland
WAAJ Benton, Kentucky
WAAL Binghamton, New York
WAAO-FM Andalusia, Alabama
WAAW Williston, South Carolina
WAAZ-FM Crestview, Florida
WABE Atlanta, Georgia
WABK-FM Gardiner, Maine
WABO-FM Waynesboro, Mississippi
WABR Tifton, Georgia
WABT(FM) Lehman Township, Pennsylvania
WABX Evansville, Indiana
WABZ Sherman, Illinois
WACD Antigo, Wisconsin
WACF Young Harris, Georgia
WACG-FM Augusta, Georgia
WACL Elkton, Virginia
WACO-FM Waco, Texas
WACR-FM Columbus Afb, Mississippi
WACV Coosada, Alabama
WADI Corinth, Mississippi
WAEB-FM Allentown, Pennsylvania
WAEF Cordele, Georgia
WAEG Evans, Georgia
WAEL-FM Maricao, Puerto Rico
WAER Syracuse, New York
WAES Lincolnshire, Illinois
WAEV Savannah, Georgia
WAEZ Greeneville, Tennessee
WAFC-FM Okeechobee, Florida
WAFD Webster Springs, West Virginia
WAFJ Belvedere, South Carolina
WAFL Milford, Delaware
WAFM Amory, Mississippi
WAFN-FM Arab, Alabama
WAFR Tupelo, Mississippi
WAFT Valdosta, Georgia
WAFX Suffolk, Virginia
WAFY Middletown, Maryland
WAFZ-FM Immokalee, Florida
WAGF-FM Dothan, Alabama
WAGH Smiths, Alabama
WAGO Snow Hill, North Carolina
WAGP Beaufort, South Carolina
WAGR-FM Lexington, Mississippi
WAGX Manchester, Ohio
WAHR Huntsville, Alabama
WAHS Auburn Hills, Michigan
WAIC Springfield, Massachusetts
WAID Clarksdale, Mississippi
WAIH Potsdam, New York
WAII Hattiesburg, Mississippi
WAIJ Grantsville, Maryland
WAIL Key West, Florida
WAIN-FM Columbia, Kentucky
WAIR Lake City, Michigan
WAIV Cape May, New Jersey
WAJI Fort Wayne, Indiana
WAJJ McKenzie, Tennessee
WAJK La Salle, Illinois
WAJM Atlantic City, New Jersey
WAJQ-FM Alma, Georgia
WAJR-FM Salem, West Virginia
WAJS Tupelo, Mississippi
WAJV Brooksville, Mississippi
WAJZ Voorheesville, New York
WAKB Hephzibah, Georgia
WAKD Sheffield, Alabama
WAKG Danville, Virginia
WAKH McComb, Mississippi
WAKJ Defuniak Springs, Florida
WAKL Flint, Michigan
WAKO-FM Lawrenceville, Illinois
WAKP Smithboro, Georgia
WAKQ Paris, Tennessee
WAKS Akron, Ohio
WAKT-FM Callaway, Florida
WAKU Crawfordville, Florida
WAKW Cincinnati, Ohio
WAKY Radcliff, Kentucky
WAKZ Sharpsville, Pennsylvania
WALC Charleston, South Carolina
WALF Alfred, New York
WALI Walterboro, South Carolina
WALK-FM Patchogue, New York
WALN Carrollton, Alabama
WALR-FM Palmetto, Georgia
WALS Oglesby, Illinois
WALT-FM Meridian, Mississippi
WALV-FM Lakesite, Tennessee
WALX Orrville, Alabama
WALY Bellwood, Pennsylvania
WALZ-FM Machias, Maine
WAMC-FM Albany, New York
WAMH Amherst, Massachusetts
WAMI-FM Opp, Alabama
WAMJ Roswell, Georgia
WAMK Kingston, New York
WAMP Jackson, Tennessee
WAMQ Great Barrington, Massachusetts
WAMR-FM Miami, Florida
WAMS-FM Snow Hill, Maryland
WAMU Washington, District of Columbia
WAMW-FM Washington, Indiana
WAMX Milton, West Virginia
WAMZ Louisville, Kentucky
WANC Ticonderoga, New York
WANH Meredith, New Hampshire
WANM Tallahassee, Florida
WANT Lebanon, Tennessee
WANV Annville, Kentucky
WANY-FM Albany, Kentucky
WAOA-FM Melbourne, Florida
WAOB-FM Beaver Falls, Pennsylvania
WAOL Ripley, Ohio
WAOQ Goshen, Alabama
WAOR(FM) Nappanee, Indiana
WAOX Staunton, Illinois
WAOY Gulfport, Mississippi
WAPB Madison, Florida
WAPD Campbellsville, Kentucky
WAPE-FM Jacksonville, Florida
WAPI-FM Northport, Alabama
WAPJ Torrington, Connecticut
WAPL Appleton, Wisconsin
WAPN Holly Hill, Florida
WAPO Mount Vernon, Illinois
WAPR Selma, Alabama
WAPS Akron, Ohio
WAPX-FM Clarksville, Tennessee
WAQB Tupelo, Mississippi
WAQE-FM Barron, Wisconsin
WAQG Ozark, Alabama
WAQL McComb, Mississippi
WAQU Selma, Alabama
WAQV Crystal River, Florida
WAQX-FM Manlius, New York
WAQY Springfield, Massachusetts
WARA New Washington, Indiana
WARC Meadville, Pennsylvania
WARG Summit, Illinois
WARH Granite City, Illinois
WARM-FM York, Pennsylvania
WARN Culpeper, Virginia
WARO Naples, Florida
WARQ Columbia, South Carolina
WARU-FM Roann, Indiana
WARV-FM Petersburg, Virginia
WARW Dorsey, Illinois
WARX Lewiston, Maine
WARY Valhalla, New York
WASH Washington, District of Columbia
WASJ Panama City Beach, Florida
WASK-FM Battle Ground, Indiana
WASL Dyersburg, Tennessee
WASM Natchez, Mississippi
WASU-FM Boone, North Carolina
WASW Waycross, Georgia
WATD-FM Marshfield, Massachusetts
WATG Trion, Georgia
WATI Vincennes, Indiana
WATP Laurel, Mississippi
WATQ Chetek, Wisconsin
WATU Port Gibson, Mississippi
WATY Folkston, Georgia
WATZ-FM Alpena, Michigan
WAUA Petersburg, West Virginia
WAUH Wautoma, Wisconsin
WAUI Shelby, Ohio
WAUM Duck Hill, Mississippi
WAUN-FM Kewaunee, Wisconsin
WAUO Hohenwald, Tennessee
WAUQ Charles City, Virginia
WAUS Berrien Springs, Michigan
WAUV Ripley, Tennessee
WAUZ Greensburg, Indiana
WAVA-FM Arlington, Virginia
WAVC Mio, Michigan
WAVD Ocean Pines, Maryland
WAVF Hanahan, South Carolina
WAVH Daphne, Alabama
WAVI Oxford, Mississippi
WAVJ Princeton, Kentucky
WAVK Marathon, Florida
WAVM Maynard, Massachusetts
WAVR Waverly, New York
WAVT-FM Pottsville, Pennsylvania
WAVV Naples Park, Florida
WAVW Stuart, Florida
WAWC Syracuse, Indiana
WAWF Kankakee, Illinois
WAWH Dublin, Georgia
WAWI Lawrenceburg, Tennessee
WAWJ Marion, Illinois
WAWN Franklin, Pennsylvania
WAWZ Zarephath, New Jersey
WAXG Mount Sterling, Kentucky
WAXI Rockville, Indiana
WAXJ Frederiksted, Virgin Islands
WAXL Santa Claus, Indiana
WAXM Big Stone Gap, Virginia
WAXQ New York, New York
WAXR Geneseo, Illinois
WAXS Oak Hill, West Virginia
WAXU Troy, Alabama
WAXX Eau Claire, Wisconsin
WAXY-FM West Palm Beach, Florida
WAYA-FM Ridgeville, South Carolina
WAYB-FM Graysville, Tennessee
WAYC-FM Bedford, Pennsylvania
WAYD Auburn, Kentucky
WAYF West Palm Beach, Florida
WAYG Grand Rapids, Michigan
WAYH Harvest, Alabama
WAYI Charlestown, Indiana
WAYI(FM) Sellersville, Indiana
WAYJ Naples, Florida
WAYJ(FM) Naples, Florida
WAYK Kalamazoo, Michigan
WAYL St. Augustine, Florida
WAYM Spring Hill, Tennessee
WAYO Benton Harbor, Michigan
WAYP Marianna, Florida
WAYQ Clarksville, Tennessee
WAYR-FM Brunswick, Georgia
WAYT Thomasville, Georgia
WAYU Steele, Alabama
WAYV Atlantic City, New Jersey
WAYW New Johnsonville, Tennessee
WAYZ Hagerstown, Maryland
WAZA Liberty, Mississippi
WAZD Savannah, Tennessee
WAZO Southport, North Carolina
WAZP Munising, Michigan
WAZQ Islamorada, Florida
WAZR Woodstock, Virginia
WAZS(FM) McClellanville, South Carolina
WAZU Peoria, Illinois
WAZX-FM Cleveland, Georgia
WAZY-FM Lafayette, Indiana
WBAA-FM West Lafayette, Indiana
WBAB Babylon, New York
WBAD Leland, Mississippi
WBAI New York, New York
WBAK Belfast, Maine
WBAM-FM Montgomery, Alabama
WBAP-FM Flower Mound, Texas
WBAR-FM Lake Luzerne, New York
WBAV-FM Gastonia, North Carolina
WBAW-FM Pembroke, Georgia
WBAZ Bridgehampton, New York
WBBA-FM Pittsfield, Illinois
WBBB Raleigh, North Carolina
WBBC-FM Blackstone, Virginia
WBBE Heyworth, Illinois
WBBG Niles, Ohio
WBBI Endwell, New York
WBBK-FM Blakely, Georgia
WBBM-FM Chicago, Illinois
WBBN Taylorsville, Mississippi
WBBO(FM) Ocean Acres, New Jersey
WBBQ-FM Augusta, Georgia
WBBS Fulton, New York
WBBT-FM Powhatan, Virginia
WBBV Vicksburg, Mississippi
WBCG Murdock, Florida
WBCH-FM Hastings, Michigan
WBCI Bath, Maine
WBCJ Spencerville, Ohio
WBCK-FM Battle Creek, Michigan
WBCL Fort Wayne, Indiana
WBCM Boyne City, Michigan
WBCQ-FM Monticello, Maine
WBCR-FM Beloit, Wisconsin
WBCT Grand Rapids, Michigan
WBCV Wausau, Wisconsin
WBCX Gainesville, Georgia
WBCY Archbold, Ohio
WBDC Huntingburg, Indiana
WBDG Indianapolis, Indiana
WBDK Algoma, Wisconsin
WBDL Reedsburg, Wisconsin
WBDR Copenhagen, New York
WBDX Trenton, Georgia
WBEA Southold, New York
WBEB Philadelphia, Pennsylvania
WBEC-FM Pittsfield, Massachusetts
WBEE-FM Rochester, New York
WBEI Reform, Alabama
WBEL Cairo, Illinois
WBEN-FM Philadelphia, Pennsylvania
WBEQ Morris, Illinois
WBER Rochester, New York
WBET-FM Sturgis, Michigan
WBEW Chesterton, Indiana
WBEY-FM Crisfield, Maryland
WBEZ Chicago, Illinois
WBFA Fort Mitchell, Alabama
WBFB Bangor, Maine
WBFG Parker's Crossroads, Tennessee
WBFH Bloomfield Hills, Michigan
WBFI McDaniels, Kentucky
WBFJ-FM Winston-Salem, North Carolina
WBFK Smiths Grove, Kentucky
WBFM Sheboygan, Wisconsin
WBFO Buffalo, New York
WBFR Birmingham, Alabama
WBFX Grand Rapids, Michigan
WBFY Pinehurst, North Carolina
WBGA St. Simons Island, Georgia
WBGE Bainbridge, Georgia
WBGF Belle Glade, Florida
WBGG-FM Fort Lauderdale, Florida
WBGI-FM Moundsville, West Virginia
WBGK Newport Village, New York
WBGL Champaign, Illinois
WBGM New Berlin, Pennsylvania
WBGO Newark, New Jersey
WBGQ Bulls Gap, Tennessee
WBGU Bowling Green, Ohio
WBGV Marlette, Michigan
WBGW Fort Branch, Indiana
WBGY Everglades City, Florida
WBHB-FM Waynesboro, Pennsylvania
WBHC-FM Hampton, South Carolina
WBHD Olyphant, Pennsylvania
WBHJ Midfield, Alabama
WBHK Warrior, Alabama
WBHL Harrison, Michigan
WBHM Birmingham, Alabama
WBHQ Beverly Beach, Florida
WBHT Mountain Top, Pennsylvania
WBHV-FM State College, Pennsylvania
WBHW Loogootee, Indiana
WBHX Tuckerton, New Jersey
WBHY-FM Mobile, Alabama
WBHZ Elkins, West Virginia
WBIA Shelbyville, Tennessee
WBIB-FM Forsyth, Georgia
WBIE Delphos, Ohio
WBIG-FM Washington, District of Columbia
WBIK Pleasant City, Ohio
WBIL Union Springs, Alabama

WBIM-FM Bridgewater, Massachusetts
WBIO Philpot, Kentucky
WBIY La Belle, Florida
WBIZ-FM Eau Claire, Wisconsin
WBJB-FM Lincroft, New Jersey
WBJC Baltimore, Maryland
WBJD Atlantic Beach, North Carolina
WBJI Blackduck, Minnesota
WBJV Steubenville, Ohio
WBJW Albion, Illinois
WBJY Americus, Georgia
WBJZ Berlin, Wisconsin
WBKE-FM North Manchester, Indiana
WBKG Macon, Georgia
WBKL Clinton, Louisiana
WBKN Brookhaven, Mississippi
WBKR Owensboro, Kentucky
WBKS Columbus Grove, Ohio
WBKT Norwich, New York
WBKU Ahoskie, North Carolina
WBKX Fredonia, New York
WBKY Portage, Wisconsin
WBLD Orchard Lake, Michigan
WBLE Batesville, Mississippi
WBLH Black River, New York
WBLI Patchogue, New York
WBLJ-FM Shamokin, Pennsylvania
WBLK Depew, New York
WBLM Portland, Maine
WBLS New York, New York
WBLU-FM Grand Rapids, Michigan
WBLV Twin Lake, Michigan
WBLW Gaylord, Michigan
WBLX-FM Mobile, Alabama
WBMF Crete, Illinois
WBMH Grove Hill, Alabama
WBMI West Branch, Michigan
WBMK Morehead, Kentucky
WBMR Telford, Pennsylvania
WBMT Boxford, Massachusetts
WBMV Mount Vernon, Illinois
WBMW Pawcatuck, Connecticut
WBMX Boston, Massachusetts
WBMZ Metter, Georgia
WBNB Equality, Alabama
WBNE Wrightsville Beach, North Carolina
WBNH Pekin, Illinois
WBNI-FM Roanoke, Indiana
WBNJ Barnegat, New Jersey
WBNK Pine Knoll Shores, North Carolina
WBNN-FM Dillwyn, Virginia
WBNO-FM Bryan, Ohio
WBNQ Bloomington, Illinois
WBNS-FM Columbus, Ohio
WBNT-FM Oneida, Tennessee
WBNV Barnesville, Ohio
WBNY Buffalo, New York
WBNZ Frankfort, Michigan
WBOI Fort Wayne, Indiana
WBOJ Lumpkin, Georgia
WBON Westhampton, New York
WBOO Morganfield, Kentucky
WBOP Buffalo Gap, Virginia
WBOQ Gloucester, Massachusetts
WBOR Brunswick, Maine
WBOS Brookline, Massachusetts
WBOX-FM Varnado, Louisiana
WBOZ Woodbury, Tennessee
WBPC Ebro, Florida
WBPE Brookston, Indiana
WBPM Saugerties, New York
WBPR Worcester, Massachusetts
WBPT Homewood, Alabama
WBPW Presque Isle, Maine
WBQB Fredericksburg, Virginia
WBQI Bar Harbor, Maine
WBQK West Point, Virginia
WBQQ Kennebunk, Maine
WBQW Kennebunkport, Maine
WBQX Thomaston, Maine
WBRB Buckhannon, West Virginia
WBRF Galax, Virginia
WBRH Baton Rouge, Louisiana
WBRK-FM Pittsfield, Massachusetts
WBRO Marengo, Indiana
WBRP Baker, Louisiana
WBRQ La Grange, Georgia
WBRR Bradford, Pennsylvania
WBRS Waltham, Massachusetts
WBRU Providence, Rhode Island
WBRV-FM Boonville, New York
WBRW Blacksburg, Virginia
WBRX Cresson, Pennsylvania
WBSB Anderson, Indiana
WBSD Burlington, Wisconsin
WBSH Hagerstown, Indiana
WBSJ Portland, Indiana
WBSL-FM Sheffield, Massachusetts
WBSN-FM New Orleans, Louisiana
WBST Muncie, Indiana
WBSU Brockport, New York
WBSW Marion, Indiana
WBSX Hazleton, Pennsylvania
WBSZ Ashland, Wisconsin
WBT-FM Chester, South Carolina
WBTF Midway, Kentucky
WBTG-FM Sheffield, Alabama
WBTI Lexington, Michigan
WBTJ Richmond, Virginia
WBTN-FM Bennington, Vermont
WBTO-FM Petersburg, Indiana
WBTP Clearwater, Florida
WBTQ Buckhannon, West Virginia
WBTR-FM Carrollton, Georgia
WBTT Naples Park, Florida
WBTU Kendallville, Indiana
WBTY Homerville, Georgia
WBTZ Plattsburgh, New York
WBUF Buffalo, New York
WBUG-FM Fort Plain, New York
WBUK Ottawa, Ohio
WBUL-FM Lexington, Kentucky
WBUQ Bloomsburg, Pennsylvania
WBUR-FM Boston, Massachusetts
WBUS Boalsburg, Pennsylvania
WBUV Moss Point, Mississippi
WBUX Buxton, North Carolina
WBUZ La Vergne, Tennessee
WBVB Coal Grove, Ohio
WBVC Pomfret, Connecticut
WBVE Bedford, Pennsylvania
WBVI Fostoria, Ohio
WBVM Tampa, Florida
WBVN Carrier Mills, Illinois
WBVR-FM Auburn, Kentucky
WBVV Guntown, Mississippi
WBVX Carlisle, Kentucky
WBWB Bloomington, Indiana
WBWC Berea, Ohio
WBWI-FM West Bend, Wisconsin
WBWN Le Roy, Illinois
WBWR Hilliard, Ohio
WBWZ New Paltz, New York
WBXB Edenton, North Carolina
WBXE Baxter, Tennessee
WBXL Baldwinsville, New York
WBXQ Patton, Pennsylvania
WBXX Marshall, Michigan
WBXY La Crosse, Florida
WBYA Islesboro, Maine
WBYG Point Pleasant, West Virginia
WBYH Hawley, Pennsylvania
WBYL Salladasburg, Pennsylvania
WBYN-FM Boyertown, Pennsylvania
WBYO Sellersville, Pennsylvania
WBYP Belzoni, Mississippi
WBYR Woodburn, Indiana
WBYT Elkhart, Indiana
WBYW(FM) Lynn Haven, Florida
WBYX Stroudsburg, Pennsylvania
WBYY Somersworth, New Hampshire
WBYZ Baxley, Georgia
WBZA Rochester, New York
WBZC Pemberton, New Jersey
WBZD-FM Muncy, Pennsylvania
WBZE Tallahassee, Florida
WBZF Hartsville, South Carolina
WBZG Peru, Illinois
WBZL(FM) Greenwood, Mississippi
WBZN Old Town, Maine
WBZO Bay Shore, New York
WBZV Hudson, Michigan
WBZY Bowdon, Georgia
WBZZ(FM) New Kensington, Pennsylvania
WCAD San Juan, Puerto Rico
WCAI Woods Hole, Massachusetts
WCAL California, Pennsylvania
WCAN Canajoharie, New York
WCAT-FM Carlisle, Pennsylvania
WCBC-FM Keyser, West Virginia
WCBE Columbus, Ohio
WCBH Casey, Illinois
WCBJ Campton, Kentucky
WCBK-FM Martinsville, Indiana
WCBL-FM Grand Rivers, Kentucky
WCBN-FM Ann Arbor, Michigan
WCBS-FM New York, New York
WCBU Peoria, Illinois
WCBW-FM East St. Louis, Illinois
WCCC-FM Hartford, Connecticut
WCCE Buies Creek, North Carolina
WCCG Hope Mills, North Carolina
WCCH Holyoke, Massachusetts
WCCI Savanna, Illinois
WCCK Calvert City, Kentucky
WCCL Central City, Pennsylvania
WCCN-FM Neillsville, Wisconsin
WCCP-FM Clemson, South Carolina
WCCQ Crest Hill, Illinois
WCCR Clarion, Pennsylvania
WCCV Cartersville, Georgia
WCCW-FM Traverse City, Michigan
WCCX Waukesha, Wisconsin
WCDA Versailles, Kentucky
WCDB Albany, New York
WCDD Canton, Illinois
WCDG(FM) Moyock, North Carolina
WCDK Cadiz, Ohio
WCDO-FM Sidney, New York
WCDQ Crawfordsville, Indiana
WCDW Susquehanna, Pennsylvania
WCDX Mechanicsville, Virginia
WCDZ Dresden, Tennessee
WCEF Ripley, West Virginia
WCEI-FM Easton, Maryland
WCEL Plattsburgh, New York
WCEM-FM Cambridge, Maryland
WCEN-FM Hemlock, Michigan
WCEZ Carthage, Illinois
WCFB Daytona Beach, Florida
WCFF Urbana, Illinois
WCFG Springfield, Michigan
WCFL Morris, Illinois
WCFL(FM) Nashville, Tennessee
WCFM Williamstown, Massachusetts
WCFS-FM Elmwood Park, Illinois
WCFW Chippewa Falls, Wisconsin
WCFX Clare, Michigan
WCGQ Columbus, Georgia
WCGX Dublin, Ohio
WCHC Worcester, Massachusetts
WCHG Hot Springs, Virginia
WCHK-FM Seymour, Wisconsin
WCHO-FM Washington Court Hou, Ohio
WCHR-FM Manahawkin, New Jersey
WCHV-FM Charlottesville, Virginia
WCHW-FM Bay City, Michigan
WCHX Lewistown, Pennsylvania
WCHY Waunakee, Wisconsin
WCHZ-FM Warrenton, Georgia
WCIB Falmouth, Massachusetts
WCIC Pekin, Illinois
WCID Friendship, New York
WCIE New Port Richey, Florida
WCIF Melbourne, Florida
WCIG Dallas, Pennsylvania
WCIH Elmira, New York
WCII Spencer, New York
WCIJ Unadilla, New York
WCIL-FM Carbondale, Illinois
WCIM Shenandoah, Pennsylvania
WCIR-FM Beckley, West Virginia
WCIT-FM Trout Run, Pennsylvania
WCIY Canandaigua, New York
WCIZ-FM Watertown, New York
WCJC Van Buren, Indiana
WCJK Murfreesboro, Tennessee
WCJL Morgantown, Indiana
WCJM-FM West Point, Georgia
WCJO Jackson, Ohio
WCJU-FM Prentiss, Mississippi
WCJX Five Points, Florida
WCKC Cadillac, Michigan
WCKF Ashland, Alabama
WCKJ St. Johnsbury, Vermont
WCKM-FM Lake George, New York
WCKQ Campbellsville, Kentucky
WCKR Hornell, New York
WCKS Fruithurst, Alabama
WCKT Lehigh Acres, Florida
WCKU Clarksburg, West Virginia
WCKX Columbus, Ohio
WCKY-FM Pemberville, Ohio
WCKZ Orland, Indiana
WCLC-FM Jamestown, Tennessee
WCLD-FM Cleveland, Mississippi
WCLE-FM Calhoun, Tennessee
WCLG-FM Morgantown, West Virginia
WCLH Wilkes-Barre, Pennsylvania
WCLI-FM Enon, Ohio
WCLK Atlanta, Georgia
WCLN-FM Clinton, North Carolina
WCLQ Wausau, Wisconsin
WCLR Arlington Heights, Illinois
WCLS Spencer, Indiana
WCLT-FM Newark, Ohio
WCLU-FM Munfordville, Kentucky
WCLV Lorain, Ohio
WCLX Westport, New York
WCLZ North Yarmouth, Maine
WCMB-FM Oscoda, Michigan
WCMC-FM Holly Springs, North Carolina
WCMD-FM Barre, Vermont
WCMF-FM Rochester, New York
WCMG Latta, South Carolina
WCMI-FM Catlettsburg, Kentucky
WCMJ Cambridge, Ohio
WCMK Putney, Vermont
WCML-FM Alpena, Michigan
WCMM Gulliver, Michigan
WCMN-FM Arecibo, Puerto Rico
WCMO Marietta, Ohio
WCMP-FM Pine City, Minnesota
WCMQ-FM Hialeah, Florida
WCMS-FM Hatteras, North Carolina
WCMT-FM Martin, Tennessee
WCMU-FM Mount Pleasant, Michigan
WCMW-FM Harbor Springs, Michigan
WCMZ-FM Sault Ste. Marie, Michigan
WCNA Potts Camp, Mississippi
WCNB Dayton, Indiana
WCNG Murphy, North Carolina
WCNI New London, Connecticut
WCNK Key West, Florida
WCNO Palm City, Florida
WCNR Keswick, Virginia
WCNV Heathsville, Virginia
WCNY-FM Syracuse, New York
WCOA-FM Pensacola, Florida
WCOD-FM Hyannis, Massachusetts
WCOE La Porte, Indiana
WCOF Arcade, New York
WCOG-FM Galeton, Pennsylvania
WCOH-FM Du Bois, Pennsylvania
WCOL-FM Columbus, Ohio
WCOM-FM Silver Creek, New York
WCON-FM Cornelia, Georgia
WCOO Kiawah Island, South Carolina
WCOP Farmington Township, Pennsylvania
WCOQ Colquitt, Georgia
WCOS-FM Columbia, South Carolina
WCOT Jamestown, New York
WCOU Attica, New York
WCOV-FM Clyde, New York
WCOW-FM Sparta, Wisconsin
WCOY Quincy, Illinois
WCOZ Laceyville, Pennsylvania
WCPE Raleigh, North Carolina
WCPI McMinnville, Tennessee
WCPN Cleveland, Ohio
WCPQ Park Forest, Illinois
WCPR-FM Wiggins, Mississippi
WCPT-FM Arlington Heights, Illinois
WCPV Essex, New York
WCPY Dekalb, Illinois
WCPZ Sandusky, Ohio
WCQL Queensbury, New York
WCQM Park Falls, Wisconsin
WCQR-FM Kingsport, Tennessee
WCQS Asheville, North Carolina
WCRB Lowell, Massachusetts
WCRC Effingham, Illinois
WCRF-FM Cleveland, Ohio
WCRG Williamsport, Pennsylvania
WCRH Williamsport, Maryland
WCRI-FM Block Island, Rhode Island
WCRJ Jacksonville, Florida
WCRP Guayama, Puerto Rico
WCRQ Dennysville, Maine
WCRT-FM Terre Haute, Indiana
WCRX Chicago, Illinois
WCRZ Flint, Michigan
WCSB Cleveland, Ohio
WCSF Joliet, Illinois

WCSG Grand Rapids, Michigan
WCSJ-FM Morris, Illinois
WCSK Kingsport, Tennessee
WCSM-FM Celina, Ohio
WCSN-FM Orange Beach, Alabama
WCSO Columbus, Mississippi
WCSP-FM Washington, District of Columbia
WCSR-FM Hillsdale, Michigan
WCSU-FM Wilberforce, Ohio
WCSX Birmingham, Michigan
WCSY-FM South Haven, Michigan
WCTB Fairfield, Maine
WCTG Chincoteague, Virginia
WCTH Plantation Key, Florida
WCTK New Bedford, Massachusetts
WCTL Union City, Pennsylvania
WCTO Easton, Pennsylvania
WCTP Gagetown, Michigan
WCTQ Sarasota, Florida
WCTT-FM Corbin, Kentucky
WCTW Catskill, New York
WCTY Norwich, Connecticut
WCUC-FM Clarion, Pennsylvania
WCUP L'Anse, Michigan
WCUR West Chester, Pennsylvania
WCUW Worcester, Massachusetts
WCUZ Bear Lake, Michigan
WCVE-FM Richmond, Virginia
WCVF-FM Fredonia, New York
WCVH Flemington, New Jersey
WCVJ Jefferson, Ohio
WCVK Bowling Green, Kentucky
WCVM Bronson, Michigan
WCVO Gahanna, Ohio
WCVP-FM Robbinsville, North Carolina
WCVQ Fort Campbell, Kentucky
WCVS-FM Virden, Illinois
WCVT Stowe, Vermont
WCVU Solana, Florida
WCVV Belpre, Ohio
WCVY Coventry, Rhode Island
WCWM Williamsburg, Virginia
WCWP Brookville, New York
WCWS-FM Wooster, Ohio
WCWT-FM Centerville, Ohio
WCWV Summersville, West Virginia
WCXL Kill Devil Hills, North Carolina
WCXR Lewisburg, Pennsylvania
WCXT Hartford, Michigan
WCXU Caribou, Maine
WCXV Van Buren, Maine
WCXX Madawaska, Maine
WCYE Three Lakes, Wisconsin
WCYJ-FM Waynesburg, Pennsylvania
WCYK-FM Staunton, Virginia
WCYN-FM Cynthiana, Kentucky
WCYO Irvine, Kentucky
WCYQ Karns, Tennessee
WCYT Lafayette Township, Indiana
WCYY Biddeford, Maine
WCZE Harbor Beach, Michigan
WCZQ Monticello, Illinois
WCZR Vero Beach, Florida
WCZT Villas, New Jersey
WCZW Charlevoix, Michigan
WCZX Hyde Park, New York
WCZY-FM Mount Pleasant, Michigan
WDAC Lancaster, Pennsylvania
WDAF-FM Liberty, Missouri
WDAI Pawleys Island, South Carolina
WDAQ Danbury, Connecticut
WDAR-FM Darlington, South Carolina
WDAS-FM Philadelphia, Pennsylvania
WDAV Davidson, North Carolina
WDAY-FM Fargo, North Dakota
WDBK Blackwood, New Jersey
WDBM East Lansing, Michigan
WDBN Wrightsville, Georgia
WDBQ-FM Galena, Illinois
WDBR Springfield, Illinois
WDBS Sutton, West Virginia
WDBT Geneva, Alabama
WDBX Carbondale, Illinois
WDBY Patterson, New York
WDCB Glen Ellyn, Illinois
WDCC Sanford, North Carolina
WDCD-FM Clifton Park, New York
WDCE Richmond, Virginia
WDCG Durham, North Carolina
WDCL-FM Somerset, Kentucky
WDCR Oreana, Illinois
WDCV-FM Carlisle, Pennsylvania
WDCX-FM Buffalo, New York
WDDC Portage, Wisconsin
WDDD-FM Johnston City, Illinois
WDDH St. Marys, Pennsylvania
WDDJ Paducah, Kentucky
WDDK Greensboro, Georgia
WDDQ Adel, Georgia
WDDW Sturtevant, Wisconsin
WDEB-FM Jamestown, Tennessee
WDEC-FM Americus, Georgia
WDEE-FM Reed City, Michigan
WDEF-FM Chattanooga, Tennessee
WDEN-FM Macon, Georgia
WDEO-FM San Carlos Park, Florida
WDEQ-FM De Graff, Ohio
WDER-FM Peterborough, New Hampshire
WDET-FM Detroit, Michigan
WDEV-FM Warren, Vermont
WDEZ Wausau, Wisconsin
WDFB-FM Danville, Kentucky
WDFH Ossining, New York
WDFM Defiance, Ohio
WDFX Cleveland, Mississippi
WDGC-FM Downers Grove, Illinois
WDGG Ashland, Kentucky
WDGL Baton Rouge, Louisiana
WDGM Greensboro, Alabama
WDHA-FM Dover, New Jersey
WDHC Berkeley Springs, West Virginia
WDHI Delhi, New York
WDHR Pikeville, Kentucky
WDHT Urbana, Ohio
WDIC-FM Clinchco, Virginia
WDIH Salisbury, Maryland
WDIN Camuy, Puerto Rico
WDIY Allentown, Pennsylvania
WDJC-FM Birmingham, Alabama
WDJM-FM Framingham, Massachusetts
WDJQ Alliance, Ohio
WDJR Enterprise, Alabama
WDJW Somers, Connecticut
WDJX Louisville, Kentucky
WDKB Dekalb, Illinois
WDKC Covington, Pennsylvania
WDKL Grafton, West Virginia
WDKM Adams, Wisconsin
WDKR Maroa, Illinois
WDKS Newburgh, Indiana
WDKV Fond Du Lac, Wisconsin
WDKX Rochester, New York
WDLA-FM Walton, New York
WDLD Halfway, Maryland
WDLG Thomasville, Alabama
WDLJ Breese, Illinois
WDLL Dillon, South Carolina
WDLM-FM East Moline, Illinois
WDLT-FM Atmore, Alabama
WDLZ Murfreesboro, North Carolina
WDMG-FM Ambrose, Georgia
WDMK Detroit, Michigan
WDML Woodlawn, Illinois
WDMO Baldwin, Wisconsin
WDMP-FM Dodgeville, Wisconsin
WDMS Greenville, Mississippi
WDMT Pittston, Pennsylvania
WDMX Vienna, West Virginia
WDNA Miami, Florida
WDNB Jeffersonville, New York
WDNE-FM Elkins, West Virginia
WDNH-FM Honesdale, Pennsylvania
WDNJ Hopatcong, New Jersey
WDNL Danville, Illinois
WDNR Chester, Pennsylvania
WDNS Bowling Green, Kentucky
WDNX Olive Hill, Tennessee
WDNY-FM Dansville, New York
WDOD-FM Chattanooga, Tennessee
WDOG-FM Allendale, South Carolina
WDOH Delphos, Ohio
WDOK Cleveland, Ohio
WDOM Providence, Rhode Island
WDOR-FM Sturgeon Bay, Wisconsin
WDOT Danville, Vermont
WDPG Greenville, Ohio
WDPR Dayton, Ohio
WDPS Dayton, Ohio
WDPW Greenville, Michigan
WDQN-FM Duquoin, Illinois
WDQX Morton, Illinois
WDRC-FM Hartford, Connecticut
WDRK Cornell, Wisconsin
WDRM Decatur, Alabama
WDRQ Detroit, Michigan
WDRR Martinez, Georgia
WDRT Viroqua, Wisconsin
WDRV Chicago, Illinois
WDSD Dover, Delaware
WDSJ Greenville, Ohio
WDSN Reynoldsville, Pennsylvania
WDSO Chesterton, Indiana
WDST Woodstock, New York
WDSV Greenville, Mississippi
WDSY-FM Pittsburgh, Pennsylvania
WDTR Imlay City, Michigan
WDTW-FM Detroit, Michigan
WDTX Rothschild, Wisconsin
WDUB Granville, Ohio
WDUK Havana, Illinois
WDUN-FM Clarkesville, Georgia
WDUV New Port Richey, Florida
WDUX-FM Waupaca, Wisconsin
WDUZ-FM Brillion, Wisconsin
WDVD Detroit, Michigan
WDVE Pittsburgh, Pennsylvania
WDVI Rochester, New York
WDVR Delaware Township, New Jersey
WDVT Rutland, Vermont
WDVV Wilmington, North Carolina
WDVW(FM) LaPlace, Louisiana
WDVW(FM) Humboldt, Tennessee
WDVX Clinton, Tennessee
WDVY Mount Kisco, New York
WDWG Rocky Mount, North Carolina
WDWN Auburn, New York
WDWZ Andalusia, Alabama
WDXB Jasper, Alabama
WDXC Pound, Virginia
WDXE-FM Lawrenceburg, Tennessee
WDXO Hazlehurst, Mississippi
WDYF Dothan, Alabama
WDYK Ridgeley, West Virginia
WDZH Detroit, Michigan
WDZN Midland, Maryland
WDZQ Decatur, Illinois
WDZZ-FM Flint, Michigan
WEAA Baltimore, Maryland
WEAI Lynnville, Illinois
WEAM-FM Buena Vista, Georgia
WEAN-FM Wakefield-Peacedale, Rhode Island
WEAS-FM Springfield, Georgia
WEAT West Palm Beach, Florida
WEAX Angola, Indiana
WEBB Waterville, Maine
WEBE Westport, Connecticut
WEBF Lerose, Kentucky
WEBK Society Hill, South Carolina
WEBN Cincinnati, Ohio
WEBQ-FM Eldorado, Illinois
WEBT Langdale, Alabama
WEBZ Mexico Beach, Florida
WECB Headland, Alabama
WECC-FM Folkston, Georgia
WECI Richmond, Indiana
WECL Elk Mound, Wisconsin
WECO-FM Wartburg, Tennessee
WECQ(FM) Destin, Florida
WECR-FM Beech Mountain, North Carolina
WECS Willimantic, Connecticut
WECV-FM Nashville, Tennessee
WECW Elmira, New York
WEDB East Dublin, Georgia
WEDG Buffalo, New York
WEDJ Danville, Indiana
WEDM Indianapolis, Indiana
WEDR Miami, Florida
WEDW-FM Stamford, Connecticut
WEEC Springfield, Ohio
WEEI(FM) Lawrence, Massachusetts
WEEI-FM Lawrence, Massachusetts
WEEM-FM Pendleton, Indiana
WEEO-FM McConnellsburg, Pennsylvania
WEER Montauk, New York
WEEY Swanzey, New Hampshire
WEFI Effingham, Illinois
WEFM Michigan City, Indiana
WEFR Erie, Pennsylvania
WEFT Champaign, Illinois
WEFX Henderson, New York
WEGB Napeague, New York
WEGC Sasser, Georgia
WEGE Lima, Ohio
WEGH Northumberland, Pennsylvania
WEGI-FM Oak Grove, Kentucky
WEGL Auburn, Alabama
WEGM San German, Puerto Rico
WEGN Kankakee, Illinois
WEGR Arlington, Tennessee
WEGS Milton, Florida
WEGW Wheeling, West Virginia
WEGX Dillon, South Carolina
WEGZ Washburn, Wisconsin
WEHA(FM) Port Republic, New Jersey
WEHC Emory, Virginia
WEHM Manorville, New York
WEHN East Hampton, New York
WEIB Northampton, Massachusetts
WEII Dennis, Massachusetts
WEIO(FM) Huntingdon, Tennessee
WEIU Charleston, Illinois
WEJC White Star, Michigan
WEJF Palm Bay, Florida
WEJK Boonville, Indiana
WEJT Shelbyville, Illinois
WEJZ Jacksonville, Florida
WEKF Corbin, Kentucky
WEKH Hazard, Kentucky
WEKL Augusta, Georgia
WEKS Zebulon, Georgia
WEKU Richmond, Kentucky
WEKV South Webster, Ohio
WEKX Jellico, Tennessee
WEKZ-FM Monroe, Wisconsin
WELD-FM Moorefield, West Virginia
WELH Providence, Rhode Island
WELJ Montauk, New York
WELK Elkins, West Virginia
WELL-FM Waverly, Alabama
WELR-FM Roanoke, Alabama
WELS-FM Kinston, North Carolina
WELX Isabela, Puerto Rico
WELY-FM Ely, Minnesota
WEMC Harrisonburg, Virginia
WEMI Appleton, Wisconsin
WEMM-FM Huntington, West Virginia
WEMR Pleasant Gap, Pennsylvania
WEMU Ypsilanti, Michigan
WEMX Kentwood, Louisiana
WEMY Green Bay, Wisconsin
WEND Salisbury, North Carolina
WENI-FM Big Flats, New York
WENS Wadesville, Indiana
WENY-FM Elmira, New York
WENZ Cleveland, Ohio
WEOS Geneva, New York
WEOW Key West, Florida
WEPC Belton, South Carolina
WEPN-FM New York, New York
WEPR Greenville, South Carolina
WEPS Elgin, Illinois
WEQP Pamplin City, Virginia
WEQR Walnut Creek, North Carolina
WEQX Manchester, Vermont
WERB Berlin, Connecticut
WERG Erie, Pennsylvania
WERH-FM Hamilton, Alabama
WERK Muncie, Indiana
WERN Madison, Wisconsin
WERO Washington, North Carolina
WERQ-FM Baltimore, Maryland
WERR Vega Alta, Puerto Rico
WERS Boston, Massachusetts
WERU-FM Blue Hill, Maine
WERV-FM Aurora, Illinois
WERX-FM Columbia, North Carolina
WERZ Exeter, New Hampshire
WESA Pittsburgh, Pennsylvania
WESC-FM Greenville, South Carolina
WESE Baldwyn, Mississippi
WESM Princess Anne, Maryland
WESN Bloomington, Illinois
WESP Dothan, Alabama
WESR-FM Onley-Onancock, Virginia
WESS East Stroudsburg, Pennsylvania
WESU Middletown, Connecticut
WETA Washington, District of Columbia
WETD Alfred, New York
WETL South Bend, Indiana
WETN Wheaton, Illinois
WETS-FM Johnson City, Tennessee
WETT Bridgeport, West Virginia
WETZ(FM) New Martinsville, West Virginia
WEUC Morganfield, Kentucky

WEUL Kingsford, Michigan
WEUP-FM Moulton, Alabama
WEUZ Minor Hill, Tennessee
WEVE-FM Eveleth, Minnesota
WEVH Hanover, New Hampshire
WEVI Frederiksted, Virgin Islands
WEVJ Jackson, New Hampshire
WEVL Memphis, Tennessee
WEVN Keene, New Hampshire
WEVO Concord, New Hampshire
WEVO(FM) Concord, New Hampshire
WEVR-FM River Falls, Wisconsin
WEVS Nashua, New Hampshire
WEXP Brandon, Vermont
WEXR Stonewall, Mississippi
WEXT Amsterdam, New York
WEYE Surgoinsville, Tennessee
WEYY Tallapoosa, Georgia
WEZB New Orleans, Louisiana
WEZC Clinton, Illinois
WEZF Burlington, Vermont
WEZJ-FM Williamsburg, Kentucky
WEZL Charleston, South Carolina
WEZN-FM Bridgeport, Connecticut
WEZQ Bangor, Maine
WEZV North Myrtle Beach, South Carolina
WEZW Wildwood Crest, New Jersey
WEZX Scranton, Pennsylvania
WEZY Racine, Wisconsin
WFAE Charlotte, North Carolina
WFAN-FM New York, New York
WFAR Danbury, Connecticut
WFAS-FM Bronxville, New York
WFAV Gilman, Illinois
WFAZ Goodwater, Alabama
WFBC-FM Greenville, South Carolina
WFBE Flint, Michigan
WFBF Buffalo, New York
WFBK Fort Mill, South Carolina
WFBQ Indianapolis, Indiana
WFBY Weston, West Virginia
WFBZ Trempealeau, Wisconsin
WFCA Ackerman, Mississippi
WFCC-FM Chatham, Massachusetts
WFCF St. Augustine, Florida
WFCG Tylertown, Mississippi
WFCH Charleston, South Carolina
WFCI Franklin, Indiana
WFCJ Miamisburg, Ohio
WFCM-FM Murfreesboro, Tennessee
WFCO Lancaster, Ohio
WFCR Amherst, Massachusetts
WFCS New Britain, Connecticut
WFCT Apalachicola, Florida
WFCX Leland, Michigan
WFDD Winston-Salem, North Carolina
WFDL-FM Lomira, Wisconsin
WFDM-FM Franklin, Indiana
WFDR-FM Woodbury, Georgia
WFDT Aguada, Puerto Rico
WFDU Teaneck, New Jersey
WFDX Atlanta, Michigan
WFDZ Perry, Florida
WFEN Rockford, Illinois
WFEZ(FM) Miami, Florida
WFFC Ferrum, Virginia
WFFF-FM Columbia, Mississippi
WFFG-FM Corinth, New York
WFFH Smyrna, Tennessee
WFFI Kingston Springs, Tennessee
WFFL Panama City, Florida
WFFM Ashburn, Georgia
WFFN Coaling, Alabama
WFFX Hattiesburg, Mississippi
WFGA Hicksville, Ohio
WFGB Kingston, New York
WFGE Tyrone, Pennsylvania
WFGF Wapakoneta, Ohio
WFGH Fort Gay, West Virginia
WFGI-FM Johnstown, Pennsylvania
WFGM-FM Barrackville, West Virginia
WFGR Grand Rapids, Michigan
WFGS Murray, Kentucky
WFGY Altoona, Pennsylvania
WFHB Bloomington, Indiana
WFHE Hickory, North Carolina
WFHG-FM Bluff City, Tennessee
WFHL New Bedford, Massachusetts
WFHM-FM Cleveland, Ohio
WFHN Fairhaven, Massachusetts
WFHU Henderson, Tennessee
WFIA-FM New Albany, Indiana
WFID Rio Piedras, Puerto Rico
WFIT Melbourne, Florida
WFIU Bloomington, Indiana
WFIV-FM Loudon, Tennessee
WFIW-FM Fairfield, Illinois
WFIX Florence, Alabama
WFIZ Odessa, New York
WFJA Sanford, North Carolina
WFJO Jacksonville Beach, Florida
WFJS-FM Freehold, New Jersey
WFKL Fairport, New York
WFKS Melbourne, Florida
WFKS(FM) Melbourne, Florida
WFKX Henderson, Tennessee
WFKY Frankfort, Kentucky
WFKZ Plantation Key, Florida
WFLA-FM Midway, Florida
WFLB Laurinburg, North Carolina
WFLC Miami, Florida
WFLE-FM Flemingsburg, Kentucky
WFLF-FM Parker, Florida
WFLK Geneva, New York
WFLM White City, Florida
WFLO-FM Farmville, Virginia
WFLQ French Lick, Indiana
WFLS-FM Fredericksburg, Virginia
WFLY Troy, New York
WFLZ-FM Tampa, Florida
WFMB-FM Springfield, Illinois
WFME Newark, New Jersey
WFMF Baton Rouge, Louisiana
WFMG Richmond, Indiana
WFMH-FM Hackleburg, Alabama
WFMI Southern Shores, North Carolina
WFMK East Lansing, Michigan
WFML Vincennes, Indiana
WFMM Sumrall, Mississippi
WFMN Flora, Mississippi
WFMQ Lebanon, Tennessee
WFMR Orleans, Massachusetts
WFMS Fishers, Indiana
WFMT Chicago, Illinois
WFMU East Orange, New Jersey
WFMV South Congaree, South Carolina
WFMX Skowhegan, Maine
WFMZ Hertford, North Carolina
WFNK Lewiston, Maine
WFNM Lancaster, Pennsylvania
WFNP Rosendale, New York
WFNQ Nashua, New Hampshire
WFOF Covington, Indiana
WFON Fond Du Lac, Wisconsin
WFOS Chesapeake, Virginia
WFOT Lexington, Ohio
WFOX Norwalk, Connecticut
WFPB-FM Falmouth, Massachusetts
WFPG Atlantic City, New Jersey
WFPK Louisville, Kentucky
WFPL Louisville, Kentucky
WFPS Freeport, Illinois
WFQS Franklin, North Carolina
WFQX Front Royal, Virginia
WFRB-FM Frostburg, Maryland
WFRC Columbus, Georgia
WFRD Hanover, New Hampshire
WFRE Frederick, Maryland
WFRF-FM Monticello, Florida
WFRG-FM Utica, New York
WFRH Kingston, New York
WFRI Winamac, Indiana
WFRJ Johnstown, Pennsylvania
WFRN-FM Elkhart, Indiana
WFRO-FM Fremont, Ohio
WFRP Americus, Georgia
WFRR Walton, Indiana
WFRS Smithtown, New York
WFRU Quincy, Florida
WFRW Webster, New York
WFRY-FM Watertown, New York
WFSE Edinboro, Pennsylvania
WFSH-FM Athens, Georgia
WFSK-FM Nashville, Tennessee
WFSL Thomasville, Georgia
WFSO Olivebridge, New York
WFSP-FM Kingwood, West Virginia
WFSQ Tallahassee, Florida
WFSS Fayetteville, North Carolina
WFSU-FM Tallahassee, Florida
WFSW Panama City, Florida
WFSX-FM Estero, Florida
WFSY Panama City, Florida
WFTA Fulton, Mississippi
WFTE Mount Cobb, Pennsylvania
WFTF Rutland, Vermont
WFTI-FM St. Petersburg, Florida
WFTK Lebanon, Ohio
WFTM-FM Maysville, Kentucky
WFTN-FM Franklin, New Hampshire
WFTZ Manchester, Tennessee
WFUM(FM) Flint, Michigan
WFUN-FM Bethalto, Illinois
WFUR-FM Grand Rapids, Michigan
WFUS Gulfport, Florida
WFUV New York, New York
WFVL Lumberton, North Carolina
WFWM Frostburg, Maryland
WFWO Medina, New York
WFWR Attica, Indiana
WFXA-FM Augusta, Georgia
WFXC Durham, North Carolina
WFXD Marquette, Michigan
WFXE Columbus, Georgia
WFXH-FM Hilton Head Island, South Carolina
WFXJ-FM North Kingsville, Ohio
WFXK Bunn, North Carolina
WFXM Gordon, Georgia
WFXN-FM Galion, Ohio
WFXO Southside, Alabama
WFXX Georgiana, Alabama
WFYE Glade Spring, Virginia
WFYI-FM Indianapolis, Indiana
WFYR Elmwood, Illinois
WFYV-FM Atlantic Beach, Florida
WFYX Walpole, New Hampshire
WFYY Bloomsburg, Pennsylvania
WGAC-FM Harlem, Georgia
WGAO Franklin, Massachusetts
WGAR-FM Cleveland, Ohio
WGBE Bryan, Ohio
WGBF-FM Henderson, Kentucky
WGBG Seaford, Delaware
WGBH(FM) Boston, Massachusetts
WGBJ Auburn, Indiana
WGBK Glenview, Illinois
WGBQ Lynchburg, Tennessee
WGCA-FM Quincy, Illinois
WGCC-FM Batavia, New York
WGCF Paducah, Kentucky
WGCI-FM Chicago, Illinois
WGCK-FM Coeburn, Virginia
WGCM-FM Gulfport, Mississippi
WGCN Nashville, Georgia
WGCO Midway, Georgia
WGCP Cadillac, Michigan
WGCQ Hayti, Missouri
WGCS Goshen, Indiana
WGCU-FM Fort Myers, Florida
WGCY Gibson City, Illinois
WGDE Defiance, Ohio
WGDN-FM Gladwin, Michigan
WGDQ Sumrall, Mississippi
WGDR Plainfield, Vermont
WGEL Greenville, Illinois
WGEM-FM Quincy, Illinois
WGER Saginaw, Michigan
WGEX Bainbridge, Georgia
WGFA-FM Watseka, Illinois
WGFB Rockton, Illinois
WGFG Branchville, South Carolina
WGFM Cheboygan, Michigan
WGFN Glen Arbor, Michigan
WGFR Glens Falls, New York
WGFX Gallatin, Tennessee
WGGC Bowling Green, Kentucky
WGGE Parkersburg, West Virginia
WGGI Benton, Pennsylvania
WGGL-FM Houghton, Michigan
WGGN Castalia, Ohio
WGGY Scranton, Pennsylvania
WGH-FM Newport News, Virginia
WGHN-FM Grand Haven, Michigan
WGHW Lockwoods Folly Town, North Carolina
WGIB Birmingham, Alabama
WGIC Cookeville, Tennessee
WGIE Clarksburg, West Virginia
WGIR-FM Manchester, New Hampshire
WGIW Pilot Mountain, North Carolina
WGKC Mahomet, Illinois
WGKL Gladstone, Michigan
WGKR Grand Gorge, New York
WGKS Paris, Kentucky
WGKV Pulaski, New York
WGKX Memphis, Tennessee
WGKY Wickliffe, Kentucky
WGL-FM Huntington, Indiana
WGLC-FM Mendota, Illinois
WGLE Lima, Ohio
WGLF Tallahassee, Florida
WGLI Hancock, Michigan
WGLM-FM Lakeview, Michigan
WGLO Pekin, Illinois
WGLQ Escanaba, Michigan
WGLR-FM Lancaster, Wisconsin
WGLS-FM Glassboro, New Jersey
WGLT Normal, Illinois
WGLV Woodstock, Vermont
WGLX-FM Wisconsin Rapids, Wisconsin
WGLY-FM Bolton, Vermont
WGLZ West Liberty, West Virginia
WGMC Greece, New York
WGMD Rehoboth Beach, Delaware
WGMG Crawford, Georgia
WGMI(FM) Thomasville, Georgia
WGMK Donalsonville, Georgia
WGMM Corning, New York
WGMO Spooner, Wisconsin
WGMR Effingham, Illinois
WGMS Hagerstown, Maryland
WGMT Lyndon, Vermont
WGMX Marathon, Florida
WGMY Thomasville, Georgia
WGMZ Glencoe, Alabama
WGNA-FM Albany, New York
WGNB Zeeland, Michigan
WGNE-FM Middleburg, Florida
WGNG Tchula, Mississippi
WGNI Wilmington, North Carolina
WGNJ St. Joseph, Illinois
WGNK Pennsuco, Florida
WGNL Greenwood, Mississippi
WGNN Fisher, Illinois
WGNR-FM Anderson, Indiana
WGNV Milladore, Wisconsin
WGNX Colchester, Illinois
WGOD-FM Charlotte Amalie, Virgin Islands
WGOG Walhalla, South Carolina
WGOJ Conneaut, Ohio
WGOV-FM Valdosta, Georgia
WGOW-FM Soddy-Daisy, Tennessee
WGPB Rome, Georgia
WGPH Vidalia, Georgia
WGPR Detroit, Michigan
WGQR Rennert, North Carolina
WGRC Lewisburg, Pennsylvania
WGRD-FM Grand Rapids, Michigan
WGRE Greencastle, Indiana
WGRF Buffalo, New York
WGRH Hinckley, Minnesota
WGRK-FM Greensburg, Kentucky
WGRM-FM Greenwood, Mississippi
WGRQ Fairview Beach, Virginia
WGRR Hamilton, Ohio
WGRS Guilford, Connecticut
WGRT Port Huron, Michigan
WGRW Anniston, Alabama
WGRX Falmouth, Virginia
WGRY-FM Grayling, Michigan
WGSG Mayo, Florida
WGSK South Kent, Connecticut
WGSL Loves Park, Illinois
WGSN Newport, Tennessee
WGSP-FM Pageland, South Carolina
WGSQ Cookeville, Tennessee
WGSU Geneseo, New York
WGSY Phenix City, Alabama
WGTD Kenosha, Wisconsin
WGTE-FM Toledo, Ohio
WGTF Dothan, Alabama
WGTH-FM Richlands, Virginia
WGTI Winfall, North Carolina
WGTN-FM Andrews, South Carolina
WGTR Bucksport, South Carolina
WGTS Takoma Park, Maryland
WGTT Emeralda, Florida
WGTX Truro, Massachusetts
WGTY Gettysburg, Pennsylvania
WGTZ Eaton, Ohio
WGUC Cincinnati, Ohio
WGUF Marco, Florida
WGUR Milledgeville, Georgia
WGUS-FM New Ellenton, South Carolina
WGVE-FM Gary, Indiana

WGVS-FM Whitehall, Michigan
WGVU-FM Allendale, Michigan
WGVX Lakeville, Minnesota
WGVY Cambridge, Minnesota
WGVZ Eden Prarie, Minnesota
WGWD Gretna, Florida
WGWG Boiling Springs, North Carolina
WGWR Liberty, New York
WGWS St. Mary's City, Maryland
WGXC Acra, New York
WGXL Hanover, New Hampshire
WGY-FM Albany, New York
WGYE Mannington, West Virginia
WGYI Oil City, Pennsylvania
WGYL Vero Beach, Florida
WGYY Meadville, Pennsylvania
WGZB-FM Lanesville, Indiana
WGZO Parris Island, South Carolina
WGZR Bluffton, Michigan
WGZS Cloquet, Minnesota
WGZZ Waverly, Alabama
WHAA Adams, Wisconsin
WHAB Acton, Massachusetts
WHAD Delafield, Wisconsin
WHAI Greenfield, Massachusetts
WHAJ Bluefield, West Virginia
WHAK-FM Rogers City, Michigan
WHAL-FM Horn Lake, Mississippi
WHAY Whitley City, Kentucky
WHAZ-FM Hoosick Falls, New York
WHBA Lynn, Massachusetts
WHBC-FM Canton, Ohio
WHBJ Barnwell, South Carolina
WHBM Park Falls, Wisconsin
WHBP Harbor Springs, Michigan
WHBQ-FM Germantown, Tennessee
WHBR-FM Parkersburg, West Virginia
WHBX Tallahassee, Florida
WHBZ Sheboygan Falls, Wisconsin
WHCB Bristol, Tennessee
WHCC Ellettsville, Indiana
WHCE Highland Springs, Virginia
WHCF Bangor, Maine
WHCJ Savannah, Georgia
WHCL-FM Clinton, New York
WHCM Palatine, Illinois
WHCN Hartford, Connecticut
WHCR-FM New York, New York
WHCY Blairstown, New Jersey
WHDD-FM Sharon, Connecticut
WHDG Rhinelander, Wisconsin
WHDI Sister Bay, Wisconsin
WHDQ Claremont, New Hampshire
WHDX Buxton, North Carolina
WHDZ Buxton, North Carolina
WHEB Portsmouth, New Hampshire
WHEM Eau Claire, Wisconsin
WHEY North Muskegon, Michigan
WHFB-FM Benton Harbor, Michigan
WHFC Bel Air, Maryland
WHFG Broussard, Louisiana
WHFH Flossmoor, Illinois
WHFI Lindside, West Virginia
WHFM Southampton, New York
WHFR Dearborn, Michigan
WHFX Darien, Georgia
WHGL-FM Canton, Pennsylvania
WHGN Crystal River, Florida
WHGO Hertford, North Carolina
WHHB Holliston, Massachusetts
WHHD Clearwater, South Carolina
WHHH Indianapolis, Indiana
WHHI Highland, Wisconsin
WHHL Hazelwood, Missouri
WHHM-FM Henderson, Tennessee
WHHN Hollidaysburg, Pennsylvania
WHHR Vienna, Georgia
WHHS Havertown, Pennsylvania
WHHT Horse Cave, Kentucky
WHHT(FM) Cave City, Kentucky
WHHY-FM Montgomery, Alabama
WHHZ Newberry, Florida
WHID Green Bay, Wisconsin
WHIF Palatka, Florida
WHIJ Ocala, Florida
WHIL-FM Mobile, Alabama
WHIO-FM Pleasant Hill, Ohio
WHIZ(FM) South Zanesville, Ohio
WHIZ-FM South Zanesville, Ohio
WHJE Carmel, Indiana
WHJL Merrill, Wisconsin
WHJM Anna, Ohio
WHJT Clinton, Mississippi
WHJY Providence, Rhode Island
WHKB Houghton, Michigan
WHKC Columbus, Ohio
WHKF Harrisburg, Pennsylvania
WHKL Crenshaw, Mississippi
WHKN Millen, Georgia
WHKO Dayton, Ohio
WHKR Rockledge, Florida
WHKS Port Allegany, Pennsylvania
WHKU Proctorville, Ohio
WHKV Sylvester, Georgia
WHKX Bluefield, Virginia
WHLA La Crosse, Wisconsin
WHLC Highlands, North Carolina
WHLF South Boston, Virginia
WHLG Port St. Lucie, Florida
WHLH Jackson, Mississippi
WHLJ-FM Statenville, Georgia
WHLK Cleveland, Ohio
WHLM-FM Berwick, Pennsylvania
WHLP Hanna, Indiana
WHLQ Lawrenceville, Virginia
WHLW Luverne, Alabama
WHLZ Marion, South Carolina
WHMA-FM Hobson City, Alabama
WHMC-FM Conway, South Carolina
WHMD Hammond, Louisiana
WHME South Bend, Indiana
WHMF Marianna, Florida
WHMH-FM Sauk Rapids, Minnesota
WHMI-FM Howell, Michigan
WHMJ Franklin, Pennsylvania
WHMO Madison, Indiana
WHMS-FM Champaign, Illinois
WHMX Lincoln, Maine
WHND Sister Bay, Wisconsin
WHNN Bay City, Michigan
WHOD Jackson, Alabama
WHOF North Canton, Ohio
WHOG-FM Ormond-By-The-Sea, Florida
WHOH Rhinelander, Wisconsin
WHOJ Terre Haute, Indiana
WHOK-FM Lancaster, Ohio
WHOM Mount Washington, New Hampshire
WHOP-FM Hopkinsville, Kentucky
WHOT-FM Youngstown, Ohio
WHOU-FM Houlton, Maine
WHOV Hampton, Virginia
WHPC Garden City, New York
WHPD Dowagiac, Michigan
WHPE-FM High Point, North Carolina
WHPF Pittston Farm, Maine
WHPH Jemison, Alabama
WHPI Glasford, Illinois
WHPK-FM Chicago, Illinois
WHPL West Lafayette, Indiana
WHPO Hoopeston, Illinois
WHPR-FM Highland Park, Michigan
WHPT Sarasota, Florida
WHPY-FM Lobelville, Tennessee
WHPZ Bremen, Indiana
WHQC Shelby, North Carolina
WHQG Milwaukee, Wisconsin
WHQQ Neoga, Illinois
WHQR Wilmington, North Carolina
WHQT Coral Gables, Florida
WHQX Gary, West Virginia
WHRB Cambridge, Massachusetts
WHRE Eastville, Virginia
WHRJ Gloucester Courthouse, Virginia
WHRK Memphis, Tennessee
WHRM Wausau, Wisconsin
WHRO-FM Norfolk, Virginia
WHRP Gurley, Alabama
WHRS Cookeville, Tennessee
WHRV Norfolk, Virginia
WHRW Binghamton, New York
WHRX Nassawadox, Virginia
WHSA Brule, Wisconsin
WHSB Alpena, Michigan
WHSD Hinsdale, Illinois
WHSL Lisman, Alabama
WHSM-FM Hayward, Wisconsin
WHSN Bangor, Maine
WHSS Hamilton, Ohio
WHST Tawas City, Michigan
WHSX Edmonton, Kentucky
WHTA Hampton, Georgia
WHTE-FM Ruckersville, Virginia
WHTF Havana, Florida
WHTI(FM) Lakeside, Virginia
WHTL-FM Whitehall, Wisconsin
WHTO Iron Mountain, Michigan
WHTQ(FM) Orlando, Florida
WHTS Coopersville, Michigan
WHTT-FM Buffalo, New York
WHTZ Newark, New Jersey
WHUD Peekskill, New York
WHUG Jamestown, New York
WHUR-FM Washington, District of Columbia
WHUS Storrs, Connecticut
WHUZ(FM) Cole, Indiana
WHVE Russell Springs, Kentucky
WHVP Hudson, New York
WHVT Clyde, Ohio
WHWC Menomonie, Wisconsin
WHWG Trout Lake, Michigan
WHWK Binghamton, New York
WHWL Marquette, Michigan
WHWT New Hope, Alabama
WHXR Scarborough, Maine
WHXT Orangeburg, South Carolina
WHYA(FM) Mashpee, Massachusetts
WHYB Menominee, Michigan
WHYI-FM Fort Lauderdale, Florida
WHYN-FM Springfield, Massachusetts
WHYT Goodland Township, Michigan
WHYY-FM Philadelphia, Pennsylvania
WHYZ Palm Coast, Florida
WHYZ(FM) Palm Bay, Florida
WHZN New Whiteland, Indiana
WHZR Royal Center, Indiana
WHZT Williamston, South Carolina
WHZZ Lansing, Michigan
WIAA Interlochen, Michigan
WIAB Mackinaw City, Michigan
WIAD Bethesda, Maryland
WIAL Eau Claire, Wisconsin
WIBA-FM Sauk City, Wisconsin
WIBB-FM Fort Valley, Georgia
WIBC Indianapolis, Indiana
WIBG-FM Avalon, New Jersey
WIBI Carlinville, Illinois
WIBL(FM) Fairbury, Illinois
WIBN Earl Park, Indiana
WIBQ Paris, Illinois
WIBT Indianola, Mississippi
WIBV Mount Vernon, Illinois
WIBW-FM Topeka, Kansas
WIBZ Wedgefield, South Carolina
WICA Traverse City, Michigan
WICB Ithaca, New York
WICL Williamsport, Maryland
WICN Worcester, Massachusetts
WICO-FM Pocomoke City, Maryland
WICR Indianapolis, Indiana
WICV East Jordan, Michigan
WIDA-FM Carolina, Puerto Rico
WIDI Quebradillas, Puerto Rico
WIDL Caro, Michigan
WIDR Kalamazoo, Michigan
WIFC Wausau, Wisconsin
WIFE-FM Rushville, Indiana
WIFF Windsor, New York
WIFM-FM Elkin, North Carolina
WIFO-FM Jesup, Georgia
WIFX-FM Jenkins, Kentucky
WIFY Addison, Vermont
WIGH Jackson, Tennessee
WIGO-FM White Stone, Virginia
WIGW Eustis, Florida
WIGX Smithtown, New York
WIGY Madison, Maine
WIHC Newberry, Michigan
WIHG Rockwood, Tennessee
WIHG(FM) Rockwood, Tennessee
WIHN Normal, Illinois
WIHS Middletown, Connecticut
WIHT Washington, District of Columbia
WIII Cortland, New York
WIIL Union Grove, Wisconsin
WIIS Key West, Florida
WIIT Chicago, Illinois
WIIZ Blackville, South Carolina
WIJV Harriman, Tennessee
WIKB-FM Iron River, Michigan
WIKI Carrollton, Kentucky
WIKK Newton, Illinois
WIKL(FM) Elwood, Indiana
WIKQ Tusculum, Tennessee
WIKS New Bern, North Carolina
WIKV Plymouth, Indiana
WIKX Charlotte Harbor, Florida
WIKY-FM Evansville, Indiana
WIKZ Chambersburg, Pennsylvania
WIL-FM St. Louis, Missouri
WILA Live Oak, Florida
WILE-FM Byesville, Ohio
WILI-FM Willimantic, Connecticut
WILK-FM Avoca, Pennsylvania
WILL-FM Urbana, Illinois
WILN Panama City, Florida
WILQ Williamsport, Pennsylvania
WILT Wilmington, North Carolina
WILV Chicago, Illinois
WILZ Saginaw, Michigan
WIMC Crawfordsville, Indiana
WIMI Ironwood, Michigan
WIMK Iron Mountain, Michigan
WIMT Lima, Ohio
WIMX Gibsonburg, Ohio
WIMZ-FM Knoxville, Tennessee
WINC-FM Winchester, Virginia
WINK-FM Fort Myers, Florida
WINL Linden, Alabama
WINN Columbus, Indiana
WINO Odessa, New York
WINQ Winchester, New Hampshire
WINX-FM St. Michaels, Maryland
WIOA San Juan, Puerto Rico
WIOB Mayaguez, Puerto Rico
WIOC Ponce, Puerto Rico
WIOG Bay City, Michigan
WIOK Falmouth, Kentucky
WIOL-FM Waverly Hall, Georgia
WIOQ Philadelphia, Pennsylvania
WIOT Toledo, Ohio
WIOV-FM Ephrata, Pennsylvania
WIOX Roxbury, New York
WIOZ-FM Southern Pines, North Carolina
WIPA Pittsfield, Illinois
WIPR-FM San Juan, Puerto Rico
WIQH Concord, Massachusetts
WIQO-FM Forest, Virginia
WIQQ Leland, Mississippi
WIRC Ely, Minnesota
WIRE Lebanon, Indiana
WIRK Indiantown, Florida
WIRK(FM) Indiantown, Florida
WIRN Buhl, Minnesota
WIRQ Rochester, New York
WIRR Virginia-Hibbing, Minnesota
WIRX St. Joseph, Michigan
WISE-FM Wise, Virginia
WISH-FM Galatia, Illinois
WISK-FM Americus, Georgia
WISM-FM Altoona, Wisconsin
WISU Terre Haute, Indiana
WISX Philadelphia, Pennsylvania
WITC Cazenovia, New York
WITF-FM Harrisburg, Pennsylvania
WITH Ithaca, New York
WITL-FM Lansing, Michigan
WITR Henrietta, New York
WITT Zionsville, Indiana
WITZ-FM Jasper, Indiana
WIUJ Charlotte Amalie, Virgin Islands
WIUM Macomb, Illinois
WIUP-FM Indiana, Pennsylvania
WIUS Macomb, Illinois
WIUV Castleton, Vermont
WIUW Warsaw, Illinois
WIVA-FM Aguadilla, Puerto Rico
WIVG Tunica, Mississippi
WIVH Christiansted, Virgin Islands
WIVI Charlotte Amalie, Virgin Islands
WIVK-FM Knoxville, Tennessee
WIVL Jasper, Georgia
WIVQ Spring Valley, Illinois
WIVR Kentland, Indiana
WIVY Morehead, Kentucky
WIWC Kokomo, Indiana
WIWF Charleston, South Carolina
WIXM Grand Isle, Vermont
WIXO Peoria, Illinois
WIXQ Millersville, Pennsylvania
WIXV Savannah, Georgia
WIXX Green Bay, Wisconsin
WIXY Champaign, Illinois
WIYN Deposit, New York
WIYY Baltimore, Maryland

WIZB Abbeville, Alabama
WIZF Erlanger, Kentucky
WIZM-FM La Crosse, Wisconsin
WIZN Vergennes, Vermont
WJAA Austin, Indiana
WJAB Huntsville, Alabama
WJAD Leesburg, Georgia
WJAI Pearl, Mississippi
WJAQ Marianna, Florida
WJAW-FM McConnelsville, Ohio
WJAZ Summerdale, Pennsylvania
WJBC-FM Pontiac, Illinois
WJBD-FM Salem, Illinois
WJBE Five Points, Alabama
WJBL Ladysmith, Wisconsin
WJBP Red Bank, Tennessee
WJBQ Portland, Maine
WJBR-FM Wilmington, Delaware
WJBT Callahan, Florida
WJBX Fort Myers Beach, Florida
WJBZ-FM Seymour, Tennessee
WJCA Albion, New York
WJCB Clewiston, Florida
WJCF-FM Morristown, Indiana
WJCH Joliet, Illinois
WJCK Piedmont, Alabama
WJCL-FM Savannah, Georgia
WJCO Montpelier, Indiana
WJCR-FM Upton, Kentucky
WJCS Allentown, Pennsylvania
WJCT-FM Jacksonville, Florida
WJCU University Heights, Ohio
WJCX Pittsfield, Maine
WJCY Cicero, Indiana
WJCZ Milford, Illinois
WJDB-FM Thomasville, Alabama
WJDD Carrollton, Ohio
WJDF Orange, Massachusetts
WJDK-FM Seneca, Illinois
WJDQ Meridian, Mississippi
WJDR Prentiss, Mississippi
WJDS Sparta, Georgia
WJDT Rogersville, Tennessee
WJDV Broadway, Virginia
WJDX-FM Kosciusko, Mississippi
WJDZ Pastillo, Puerto Rico
WJEC Vernon, Alabama
WJED Dogwood Lakes Estate, Florida
WJEF Lafayette, Indiana
WJEK(FM) Rantoul, Illinois
WJEL Indianapolis, Indiana
WJEN Killington, Vermont
WJEQ Macomb, Illinois
WJEZ Dwight, Illinois
WJFD-FM New Bedford, Massachusetts
WJFF Jeffersonville, New York
WJFH Sebring, Florida
WJFK-FM Manassas, Virginia
WJFL Tennille, Georgia
WJFM Baton Rouge, Louisiana
WJFP Fort Pierce, Florida
WJFR Jacksonville, Florida
WJFX New Haven, Indiana
WJGA-FM Jackson, Georgia
WJGK(FM) Newburgh, New York
WJGL Jacksonville, Florida
WJGM(FM) Baldwin, Florida
WJGO Tice, Florida
WJHD Portsmouth, Rhode Island
WJHM Daytona Beach, Florida
WJHO Alexander City, Alabama
WJHS Columbia City, Indiana
WJHT Johnstown, Pennsylvania
WJIA Guntersville, Alabama
WJIC Zanesville, Ohio
WJIE-FM Okolona, Kentucky
WJIF Opp, Alabama
WJIK Fulton, Alabama
WJIM-FM Lansing, Michigan
WJIR Key West, Florida
WJIS Bradenton, Florida
WJIV Cherry Valley, New York
WJIW Greenville, Mississippi
WJIZ-FM Albany, Georgia
WJJB-FM Gray, Maine
WJJE Delaware, Ohio
WJJH Ashland, Wisconsin
WJJJ Beckley, West Virginia
WJJK Noblesville, Indiana
WJJM-FM Lewisburg, Tennessee
WJJN Columbia, Alabama
WJJO Watertown, Wisconsin
WJJQ-FM Tomahawk, Wisconsin
WJJR Rutland, Vermont
WJJS Roanoke, Virginia
WJJW North Adams, Massachusetts
WJJX Appomattox, Virginia
WJJY-FM Brainerd, Minnesota
WJJZ Irasberg, Vermont
WJKA Jacksonville, North Carolina
WJKC Christiansted, Virgin Islands
WJKD Vero Beach, Florida
WJKE(FM) Stillwater, New York
WJKI Bethany Beach, Delaware
WJKK Vicksburg, Mississippi
WJKL Glendale Heights, Illinois
WJKN-FM Spring Arbor, Michigan
WJKR Upper Arlington, Ohio
WJKS Canton, New Jersey
WJKW Athens, Ohio
WJKX Ellisville, Mississippi
WJKZ Hanover, Michigan
WJLB Detroit, Michigan
WJLE-FM Smithville, Tennessee
WJLF Gainesville, Florida
WJLH Flagler Beach, Florida
WJLK Asbury Park, New Jersey
WJLR Seymour, Indiana
WJLS-FM Beckley, West Virginia
WJLT Evansville, Indiana
WJLU New Smyrna Beach, Florida
WJLV Jackson, Mississippi
WJLY Ramsey, Illinois
WJLZ Virginia Beach, Virginia
WJMA Culpeper, Virginia
WJMC-FM Rice Lake, Wisconsin
WJMD Hazard, Kentucky
WJMF Smithfield, Rhode Island
WJMG Hattiesburg, Mississippi
WJMH Reidsville, North Carolina
WJMI Jackson, Mississippi
WJMJ Hartford, Connecticut
WJMK Chicago, Illinois
WJMM-FM Keene, Kentucky
WJMN Boston, Massachusetts
WJMQ Clintonville, Wisconsin
WJMR-FM Menomonee Falls, Wisconsin
WJMU Decatur, Illinois
WJMX-FM Cheraw, South Carolina
WJMZ-FM Anderson, South Carolina
WJNG Johnsonburg, Pennsylvania
WJNI Ladson, South Carolina
WJNR-FM Iron Mountain, Michigan
WJNS-FM Bentonia, Mississippi
WJNV Jonesville, Virginia
WJNY Watertown, New York
WJOD Asbury, Iowa
WJOG Good Hart, Michigan
WJOH Raco, Michigan
WJOJ Rust Township, Michigan
WJOM Eagle, Michigan
WJOT-FM Wabash, Indiana
WJOU Huntsville, Alabama
WJOX-FM Birmingham, Alabama
WJPA-FM Washington, Pennsylvania
WJPD Ishpeming, Michigan
WJPG Cape May Court House, New Jersey
WJPH Woodbine, New Jersey
WJPR Jasper, Indiana
WJPT Fort Myers Villas, Florida
WJPZ-FM Syracuse, New York
WJQB Spring Hill, Florida
WJQK Zeeland, Michigan
WJQM De Forest, Wisconsin
WJQZ Wellsville, New York
WJRC Lewistown, Pennsylvania
WJRE Galva, Illinois
WJRF Duluth, Minnesota
WJRH Easton, Pennsylvania
WJRL-FM Fort Rucker, Alabama
WJRR Cocoa Beach, Florida
WJRS Jamestown, Kentucky
WJRV(FM) Oliver Springs, Tennessee
WJRZ-FM Manahawkin, New Jersey
WJSA-FM Jersey Shore, Pennsylvania
WJSC-FM Johnson, Vermont
WJSE North Cape May, New Jersey
WJSG Hamlet, North Carolina
WJSH Folsom, Louisiana
WJSJ Fernandina Beach, Florida
WJSM-FM Martinsburg, Pennsylvania
WJSN-FM Jackson, Kentucky
WJSO Pikeville, Kentucky
WJSP-FM Warm Springs, Georgia
WJSQ Athens, Tennessee
WJSR Birmingham, Alabama
WJSU-FM Jackson, Mississippi
WJSV Morristown, New Jersey
WJSZ Ashley, Michigan
WJTF Panama City, Florida
WJTG Fort Valley, Georgia
WJTK Columbia City, Florida
WJTL Lancaster, Pennsylvania
WJTT Red Bank, Tennessee
WJTY Lancaster, Wisconsin
WJUC Swanton, Ohio
WJUF Inverness, Florida
WJUN-FM Mexico, Pennsylvania
WJUX Monticello, New York
WJVC Center Moriches, New York
WJVK Owensboro, Kentucky
WJVL Janesville, Wisconsin
WJVO South Jacksonville, Illinois
WJVP Culebra, Puerto Rico
WJWD Marshall, Wisconsin
WJWJ-FM Beaufort, South Carolina
WJWR Bloomington, Illinois
WJWT Gardner, Massachusetts
WJWV Fort Gaines, Georgia
WJWZ Wetumpka, Alabama
WJXA Nashville, Tennessee
WJXB-FM Knoxville, Tennessee
WJXM De Kalb, Mississippi
WJXN-FM Utica, Mississippi
WJXQ Charlotte, Michigan
WJXR Macclenny, Florida
WJXY-FM Conway, South Carolina
WJYA Emporia, Virginia
WJYE Buffalo, New York
WJYJ Fredericksburg, Virginia
WJYO Fort Myers, Florida
WJYW Union City, Indiana
WJYY Concord, New Hampshire
WJZ-FM Catonsville, Maryland
WJZB Starkville, Mississippi
WJZD-FM Long Beach, Mississippi
WJZE Oak Harbor, Ohio
WJZJ Glen Arbor, Michigan
WJZQ Cadillac, Michigan
WJZR Rochester, New York
WJZS Block Island, Rhode Island
WJZX(FM) Brookfield, Wisconsin
WJZZ North Salem, New York
WJZZ(FM) North Salem, New York
WKAA Willacoochee, Georgia
WKAD Harrietta, Michigan
WKAF Brockton, Massachusetts
WKAI Macomb, Illinois
WKAK Albany, Georgia
WKAO Ashland, Kentucky
WKAQ-FM San Juan, Puerto Rico
WKAR-FM East Lansing, Michigan
WKAY Knoxville, Illinois
WKAZ-FM Miami, West Virginia
WKBB Mantee, Mississippi
WKBC-FM North Wilkesboro, North Carolina
WKBE Warrensburg, New York
WKBH-FM West Salem, Wisconsin
WKBI-FM St. Marys, Pennsylvania
WKBQ Covington, Tennessee
WKBU New Orleans, Louisiana
WKBX Kingsland, Georgia
WKCA Salt Lick, Kentucky
WKCB-FM Hindman, Kentucky
WKCC Kankakee, Illinois
WKCH Whitewater, Wisconsin
WKCI-FM Hamden, Connecticut
WKCL Ladson, South Carolina
WKCN Fort Benning South, Georgia
WKCO Gambier, Ohio
WKCP Miami, Florida
WKCQ Saginaw, Michigan
WKCR-FM New York, New York
WKCS Knoxville, Tennessee
WKCY-FM Harrisonburg, Virginia
WKDB Laurel, Delaware
WKDC-FM Cedarville, Ohio
WKDD Munroe Falls, Ohio
WKDE-FM Altavista, Virginia
WKDF Nashville, Tennessee
WKDJ-FM Clarksdale, Mississippi
WKDL-FM Brockport, New York
WKDN(FM) State College, Pennsylvania
WKDO-FM Liberty, Kentucky
WKDP-FM Corbin, Kentucky
WKDQ Henderson, Kentucky
WKDS Kalamazoo, Michigan
WKDU Philadelphia, Pennsylvania
WKDZ-FM Cadiz, Kentucky
WKEA-FM Scottsboro, Alabama
WKEB Medford, Wisconsin
WKEE-FM Huntington, West Virginia
WKEK Gunflint Lake, Minnesota
WKEQ Somerset, Kentucky
WKES Lakeland, Florida
WKET Kettering, Ohio
WKEU-FM The Rock, Georgia
WKEY-FM Key West, Florida
WKEZ-FM Tavernier, Florida
WKFA St. Catherine, Florida
WKFC North Corbin, Kentucky
WKFM Huron, Ohio
WKFP(FM) Navarre, Florida
WKFR-FM Battle Creek, Michigan
WKFS Milford, Ohio
WKFX Rice Lake, Wisconsin
WKGA Goodwater, Alabama
WKGB-FM Conklin, New York
WKGC-FM Panama City, Florida
WKGL-FM Loves Park, Illinois
WKGO Cumberland, Maryland
WKGR Wellington, Florida
WKGS Irondequoit, New York
WKGV Swansboro, North Carolina
WKHF(FM) Lynchburg, Virginia
WKHG Leitchfield, Kentucky
WKHI Fruitland, Maryland
WKHJ Mountain Lake Park, Maryland
WKHK Colonial Heights, Virginia
WKHL West Lafayette, Indiana
WKHM-FM Brooklyn, Michigan
WKHQ-FM Charlevoix, Michigan
WKHR Bainbridge, Ohio
WKHS Worton, Maryland
WKHT Knoxville, Tennessee
WKHX-FM Marietta, Georgia
WKHY Lafayette, Indiana
WKIB Anna, Illinois
WKIC Hyden, Kentucky
WKID Vevay, Indiana
WKIF Kankakee, Illinois
WKIK-FM California, Maryland
WKIM Munford, Tennessee
WKIS Boca Raton, Florida
WKIT-FM Brewer, Maine
WKIV Westerly, Rhode Island
WKIW Ironwood, Michigan
WKIX-FM Raleigh, North Carolina
WKJA Brunswick, Ohio
WKJC Tawas City, Michigan
WKJD Columbus, Indiana
WKJL Clarksburg, West Virginia
WKJM Petersburg, Virginia
WKJN Centreville, Mississippi
WKJQ-FM Parsons, Tennessee
WKJS Richmond, Virginia
WKJT Teutopolis, Illinois
WKJX Elizabeth City, North Carolina
WKJY Hempstead, New York
WKJZ Hillman, Michigan
WKKB Middletown, Rhode Island
WKKC Chicago, Illinois
WKKF Ballston Spa, New York
WKKG Columbus, Indiana
WKKI Celina, Ohio
WKKJ Chillicothe, Ohio
WKKL West Barnstable, Massachusetts
WKKN Westminster, Vermont
WKKO Toledo, Ohio
WKKQ Barbourville, Kentucky
WKKR Auburn, Alabama
WKKS-FM Vanceburg, Kentucky
WKKT Statesville, North Carolina
WKKV-FM Racine, Wisconsin
WKKW Fairmont, West Virginia
WKKY Geneva, Ohio
WKKZ Dublin, Georgia
WKLA-FM Ludington, Michigan
WKLB-FM Waltham, Massachusetts
WKLC-FM St. Albans, West Virginia
WKLG Rock Harbor, Florida
WKLH Milwaukee, Wisconsin
WKLI-FM Albany, New York
WKLK-FM Cloquet, Minnesota

WKLL Frankfort, New York
WKLM Millersburg, Ohio
WKLN Wilmington, Ohio
WKLO Hardinsburg, Indiana
WKLR Fort Lee, Virginia
WKLT Kalkaska, Michigan
WKLU Brownsburg, Indiana
WKLV-FM Port Chester, New York
WKLW-FM Paintsville, Kentucky
WKLX Brownsville, Kentucky
WKLZ-FM Petoskey, Michigan
WKMD Madisonville, Kentucky
WKMJ-FM Hancock, Michigan
WKMK Eatontown, New Jersey
WKML Lumberton, North Carolina
WKMM Kingwood, West Virginia
WKMO Lebanon Junction, Kentucky
WKMS-FM Murray, Kentucky
WKMT Fulton, Kentucky
WKMV Muncie, Indiana
WKMX Enterprise, Alabama
WKMY Winchendon, Massachusetts
WKNA Logan, Ohio
WKNB Clarendon, Pennsylvania
WKNC-FM Raleigh, North Carolina
WKNE Keene, New Hampshire
WKNG-FM Heflin, Alabama
WKNH Keene, New Hampshire
WKNJ-FM Union Township, New Jersey
WKNK(FM) Callaway, Florida
WKNL New London, Connecticut
WKNN-FM Pascagoula, Mississippi
WKNO-FM Memphis, Tennessee
WKNP Jackson, Tennessee
WKNS Kinston, North Carolina
WKNU Brewton, Alabama
WKNZ Harrington, Delaware
WKOA Lafayette, Indiana
WKOL Plattsburgh, New York
WKOM Columbia, Tennessee
WKOR-FM Columbus, Mississippi
WKOS Kingsport, Tennessee
WKOV-FM Wellston, Ohio
WKOY-FM Princeton, West Virginia
WKOZ-FM Carthage, Mississippi
WKPB Henderson, Kentucky
WKPE-FM South Yarmouth, Massachusetts
WKPK Michigamme, Michigan
WKPL Ellwood City, Pennsylvania
WKPO Soldiers Grove, Wisconsin
WKPQ Hornell, New York
WKPS State College, Pennsylvania
WKPW Knightstown, Indiana
WKPX Sunrise, Florida
WKQB Welch, Virginia
WKQC Charlotte, North Carolina
WKQH Marathon, Wisconsin
WKQI Detroit, Michigan
WKQK Germantown, Tennessee
WKQL Brookville, Pennsylvania
WKQQ Winchester, Kentucky
WKQR(FM) Mullens, West Virginia
WKQS-FM Negaunee, Michigan
WKQV Cowen, West Virginia
WKQW-FM Oil City, Pennsylvania
WKQX Watseka, Illinois
WKQY Tazewell, Virginia
WKQZ Midland, Michigan
WKRA-FM Holly Springs, Mississippi
WKRB Brooklyn, New York
WKRF Tobyhanna, Pennsylvania
WKRH Minetto, New York
WKRI Cokesbury, South Carolina
WKRJ New Philadelphia, Ohio
WKRK-FM Cleveland Heights, Ohio
WKRL-FM North Syracuse, New York
WKRO-FM Port Orange, Florida
WKRQ Cincinnati, Ohio
WKRR Asheboro, North Carolina
WKRU Allouez, Wisconsin
WKRV Vandalia, Illinois
WKRW Wooster, Ohio
WKRX Roxboro, North Carolina
WKRY Versailles, Indiana
WKRZ Freeland, Pennsylvania
WKSB Williamsport, Pennsylvania
WKSC-FM Chicago, Illinois
WKSD Paulding, Ohio
WKSE Niagara Falls, New York
WKSF Old Fort, North Carolina
WKSG Cedar Creek, Florida
WKSI-FM Stephens City, Virginia
WKSJ-FM Mobile, Alabama
WKSK-FM South Hill, Virginia
WKSL Cary, North Carolina
WKSM Fort Walton Beach, Florida
WKSO Natchez, Mississippi
WKSP Aiken, South Carolina
WKSQ Ellsworth, Maine
WKSR-FM Loretto, Tennessee
WKSS Hartford-Meriden, Connecticut
WKST-FM Pittsburgh, Pennsylvania
WKST-FM Pittsburgh, New Hampshire
WKSU-FM Kent, Ohio
WKSV Thompson, Ohio
WKSX-FM Johnston, South Carolina
WKSZ De Pere, Wisconsin
WKTG Madisonville, Kentucky
WKTJ-FM Farmington, Maine
WKTK Crystal River, Florida
WKTL Struthers, Ohio
WKTM Soperton, Georgia
WKTN Kenton, Ohio
WKTO Edgewater, Florida
WKTS Kingston, Tennessee
WKTT Salisbury, Maryland
WKTU Lake Success, New York
WKTZ-FM Jacksonville, Florida
WKUA Moundville, Alabama
WKUB Blackshear, Georgia
WKUE Elizabethtown, Kentucky
WKUL Cullman, Alabama
WKUZ Wabash, Indiana
WKVB Port Matilda, Pennsylvania
WKVC North Myrtle Beach, South Carolina
WKVE Mount Pleasant, Pennsylvania
WKVF Bartlett, Tennessee
WKVH Monticello, Florida
WKVI-FM Knox, Indiana
WKVJ Dannemora, New York
WKVK Semora, North Carolina
WKVN Morganfield, Kentucky
WKVO Georgetown, Kentucky
WKVP Cherry Hill, New Jersey
WKVR-FM Huntingdon, Pennsylvania
WKVS Lenoir, North Carolina
WKVT-FM Brattleboro, Vermont
WKVU Utica, New York
WKVV Searsport, Maine
WKVW Marmet, West Virginia
WKVY Somerset, Kentucky
WKVZ Dexter, Maine
WKWC Owensboro, Kentucky
WKWH Liberty, Indiana
WKWI Kilmarnock, Virginia
WKWK-FM Wheeling, West Virginia
WKWM Marathon, Florida
WKWR Key West, Florida
WKWS Charleston, West Virginia
WKWV Watertown, New York
WKWX Savannah, Tennessee
WKWY Tompkinsville, Kentucky
WKWZ Syosset, New York
WKXA-FM Findlay, Ohio
WKXB Boiling Spring Lakes, North Carolina
WKXC-FM Aiken, South Carolina
WKXD-FM Monterey, Tennessee
WKXH St. Johnsbury, Vermont
WKXI-FM Magee, Mississippi
WKXK Pine Hill, Alabama
WKXM-FM Winfield, Alabama
WKXN Fort Deposit, Alabama
WKXP Kingston, New York
WKXQ Rushville, Illinois
WKXS-FM Leland, North Carolina
WKXW Trenton, New Jersey
WKXX Attalla, Alabama
WKXY Merigold, Mississippi
WKXZ Norwich, New York
WKYA Greenville, Kentucky
WKYB Burgin, Kentucky
WKYE Johnstown, Pennsylvania
WKYJ Rouses Point, New York
WKYL Lawrenceburg, Kentucky
WKYM Monticello, Kentucky
WKYN Owingsville, Kentucky
WKYP Ledbetter, Kentucky
WKYQ Paducah, Kentucky
WKYR-FM Burkesville, Kentucky
WKYS Washington, District of Columbia
WKYU-FM Bowling Green, Kentucky
WKYV Colonial Heights, Virginia
WKYX-FM Golconda, Illinois
WKYZ Key Colony Beach, Florida
WKZA Lakewood, New York
WKZB Marion, Mississippi
WKZC Scottville, Michigan
WKZE-FM Salisbury, Connecticut
WKZJ Eufaula, Alabama
WKZL Winston-Salem, North Carolina
WKZM Sarasota, Florida
WKZO-FM Portage, Michigan
WKZP Bethany Beach, Delaware
WKZQ-FM Forestbrook, South Carolina
WKZR Milledgeville, Georgia
WKZS Thomasboro, Illinois
WKZU Iuka, Mississippi
WKZW Sandersville, Mississippi
WKZX-FM Lenoir City, Tennessee
WKZY Cross City, Florida
WKZZ Tifton, Georgia
WLAB Fort Wayne, Indiana
WLAI Wilmore, Kentucky
WLAK Huntingdon, Pennsylvania
WLAN-FM Lancaster, Pennsylvania
WLAU Heidelberg, Mississippi
WLAV-FM Grand Rapids, Michigan
WLAW Newaygo, Michigan
WLAY-FM Littleville, Alabama
WLAZ Kissimmee, Florida
WLBC-FM Muncie, Indiana
WLBF Montgomery, Alabama
WLBH-FM Mattoon, Illinois
WLBL-FM Wausau, Wisconsin
WLBS Bristol, Pennsylvania
WLBW Fenwick Island, Delaware
WLCA Godfrey, Illinois
WLCE Petersburg, Illinois
WLCH Lancaster, Pennsylvania
WLCN Atlanta, Illinois
WLCS North Muskegon, Michigan
WLCT Lafayette, Tennessee
WLCU Campbellsville, Kentucky
WLCY Blairsville, Pennsylvania
WLDA Slocomb, Alabama
WLDB Milwaukee, Wisconsin
WLDE Fort Wayne, Indiana
WLDI Juno Beach, Florida
WLDR-FM Traverse City, Michigan
WLEG Ligonier, Indiana
WLEL Ellaville, Georgia
WLEN Adrian, Michigan
WLER-FM Butler, Pennsylvania
WLEV Allentown, Pennsylvania
WLEW-FM Bad Axe, Michigan
WLEY-FM Aurora, Illinois
WLFA Asheville, North Carolina
WLFC North Baltimore, Ohio
WLFE-FM Key Largo, Florida
WLFF Georgetown, South Carolina
WLFJ-FM Greenville, South Carolina
WLFK Gouverneur, New York
WLFR Pomona, New Jersey
WLFS Port Wentworth, Georgia
WLFV Ettrick, Virginia
WLFW Chandler, Indiana
WLFX Berea, Kentucky
WLGC-FM Greenup, Kentucky
WLGE Baileys Harbor, Wisconsin
WLGH Leroy Township, Michigan
WLGI Hemingway, South Carolina
WLGP Harkers Island, North Carolina
WLGT Washington, North Carolina
WLGX Louisville, Kentucky
WLGZ-FM Webster, New York
WLHC Robbins, North Carolina
WLHH(FM) Ridgeland, South Carolina
WLHK Shelbyville, Indiana
WLHR-FM Lavonia, Georgia
WLHS West Chester, Ohio
WLHT-FM Grand Rapids, Michigan
WLHW Casey, Illinois
WLIC Frostburg, Maryland
WLIF Baltimore, Maryland
WLIH Whitneyville, Pennsylvania
WLIN-FM Durant, Mississippi
WLIR-FM Hampton Bays, New York
WLIT-FM Chicago, Illinois
WLIV-FM Monterey, Tennessee
WLJA-FM Ellijay, Georgia
WLJC Beattyville, Kentucky
WLJE Valparaiso, Indiana
WLJH Glens Falls, New York
WLJI Summerton, South Carolina
WLJK Aiken, South Carolina
WLJN-FM Traverse City, Michigan
WLJP Monroe, New York
WLJR Birmingham, Alabama
WLJS-FM Jacksonville, Alabama
WLJZ Mackinaw City, Michigan
WLKA Tafton, Pennsylvania
WLKB Bay City, Michigan
WLKC Campton, New Hampshire
WLKE Bar Harbor, Maine
WLKG Lake Geneva, Wisconsin
WLKH Somerset, Pennsylvania
WLKI Angola, Indiana
WLKJ Portage, Pennsylvania
WLKK Wethersfield Twnshp, New York
WLKL Mattoon, Illinois
WLKM-FM Three Rivers, Michigan
WLKN Cleveland, Wisconsin
WLKO Hickory, North Carolina
WLKP Belpre, Ohio
WLKQ-FM Buford, Georgia
WLKR-FM Norwalk, Ohio
WLKS-FM West Liberty, Kentucky
WLKT Lexington-Fayette, Kentucky
WLKU Rock Island, Illinois
WLKV Ripley, West Virginia
WLKX-FM Forest Lake, Minnesota
WLKZ Wolfeboro, New Hampshire
WLLD Lakeland, Florida
WLLD(FM) Lakeland, Florida
WLLE Mayfield, Kentucky
WLLF Mercer, Pennsylvania
WLLG Lowville, New York
WLLJ Etowah, Tennessee
WLLK-FM Somerset, Kentucky
WLLR-FM Davenport, Iowa
WLLT Polo, Illinois
WLLW Seneca Falls, New York
WLLX Lawrenceburg, Tennessee
WLMD Bushnell, Illinois
WLME Lewisport, Kentucky
WLMG New Orleans, Louisiana
WLMI(FM) Kane/Bradford, Pennsylvania
WLMN Manistee, Michigan
WLMU Harrogate, Tennessee
WLMW Manchester, New Hampshire
WLMX-FM Balsam Lake, Wisconsin
WLND Signal Mountain, Tennessee
WLNF Rapids, New York
WLNG Sag Harbor, New York
WLNH-FM Laconia, New Hampshire
WLNI Lynchburg, Virginia
WLNJ Lakehurst, New Jersey
WLNK Charlotte, North Carolina
WLNQ White Pine, Tennessee
WLNQ-FM Newport, Tennessee
WLNX Lincoln, Illinois
WLNZ Lansing, Michigan
WLOF Elma, New York
WLOG Markleysburg, Pennsylvania
WLOL-FM Star City, West Virginia
WLOQ Indian Lakes Estates, Florida
WLPE Augusta, Georgia
WLPF Ocilla, Georgia
WLPG Florence, South Carolina
WLPR-FM Lowell, Indiana
WLPS-FM Lumberton, North Carolina
WLPT Jesup, Georgia
WLPW Lake Placid, New York
WLQB Ocean Isle Beach, North Carolina
WLQC Sharpsburg, North Carolina
WLQI Rensselaer, Indiana
WLQK Livingston, Tennessee
WLQM-FM Franklin, Virginia
WLQR-FM Delta, Ohio
WLQT Englewood, Ohio
WLRA Lockport, Illinois
WLRD Willard, Ohio
WLRH Huntsville, Alabama
WLRK Greenville, Mississippi
WLRN-FM Miami, Florida
WLRR Milledgeville, Georgia
WLRS Shepherdsville, Kentucky
WLRW Champaign, Illinois
WLRX Ironton, Ohio
WLRY Rushville, Ohio
WLS-FM Chicago, Illinois
WLSK Lebanon, Kentucky
WLSM-FM Louisville, Mississippi
WLSN Grand Marais, Minnesota

WLSO Sault Ste. Marie, Michigan
WLSR Galesburg, Illinois
WLST Marinette, Wisconsin
WLSU La Crosse, Wisconsin
WLSW Scottdale, Pennsylvania
WLTB Johnson City, New York
WLTC Cusseta, Georgia
WLTF Martinsburg, West Virginia
WLTJ Pittsburgh, Pennsylvania
WLTK New Market, Virginia
WLTL La Grange, Illinois
WLTM Greenville, Mississippi
WLTN-FM Lisbon, New Hampshire
WLTO Nicholasville, Kentucky
WLTQ-FM Venice, Florida
WLTR Columbia, South Carolina
WLTT Bolivia, North Carolina
WLTU Manitowoc, Wisconsin
WLTW New York, New York
WLTY Cayce, South Carolina
WLUJ Springfield, Illinois
WLUM-FM Milwaukee, Wisconsin
WLUN Pinconning, Michigan
WLUP-FM Chicago, Illinois
WLUR Lexington, Virginia
WLUS-FM Clarksville, Virginia
WLUW Chicago, Illinois
WLUZ Levittown, Puerto Rico
WLVB Morrisville, Vermont
WLVE Mukwonago, Wisconsin
WLVF-FM Haines City, Florida
WLVG Havelock, North Carolina
WLVH Hardeeville, South Carolina
WLVK Fort Knox, Kentucky
WLVM(FM) Mobile, Alabama
WLVQ Columbus, Ohio
WLVR-FM Bethlehem, Pennsylvania
WLVS-FM Clifton, Tennessee
WLVU Belle Meade, Tennessee
WLVV Midland, Maryland
WLVW Salisbury, Maryland
WLVW(FM) Trenton, Florida
WLVX(FM) Greenville, Pennsylvania
WLVY Elmira, New York
WLVZ Collins, Mississippi
WLWF(FM) Marseilles, Illinois
WLWI-FM Montgomery, Alabama
WLWJ Petersburg, Illinois
WLWK-FM Milwaukee, Wisconsin
WLXC Columbia, South Carolina
WLXO Stamping Ground, Kentucky
WLXP Savannah, Georgia
WLXR-FM La Crosse, Wisconsin
WLXT Petoskey, Michigan
WLXV Cadillac, Michigan
WLXX Lexington, Kentucky
WLYE-FM Glasgow, Kentucky
WLYF Miami, Florida
WLYK Cape Vincent, New York
WLYT(FM) Norris, Tennessee
WLYU Lyons, Georgia
WLZA Eupora, Mississippi
WLZK Paris, Tennessee
WLZL Annapolis, Maryland
WLZN Macon, Georgia
WLZS Beaver Springs, Pennsylvania
WLZW Utica, New York
WLZX Northampton, Massachusetts
WMAB-FM Mississippi State, Mississippi
WMAD Cross Plains, Wisconsin
WMAE-FM Booneville, Mississippi
WMAG High Point, North Carolina
WMAH-FM Biloxi, Mississippi
WMAJ-FM Centre Hall, Pennsylvania
WMAL-FM Woodbridge, Virginia
WMAN-FM Fredericktown, Ohio
WMAO-FM Greenwood, Mississippi
WMAS-FM Enfield, Connecticut
WMAU-FM Bude, Mississippi
WMAV-FM Oxford, Mississippi
WMAW-FM Meridian, Mississippi
WMAX-FM Holland, Michigan
WMBI-FM Chicago, Illinois
WMBJ Murrells Inlet, South Carolina
WMBL Mitchell, Indiana
WMBR Cambridge, Massachusetts
WMBU Forest, Mississippi
WMBV Dixons Mills, Alabama
WMBW Chattanooga, Tennessee
WMBX Jensen Beach, Florida
WMC-FM Memphis, Tennessee
WMCD Claxton, Georgia
WMCE Erie, Pennsylvania
WMCG Milan, Georgia
WMCI Neoga B, Illinois
WMCM Rockland, Maine
WMCN St. Paul, Minnesota
WMCO New Concord, Ohio
WMCQ Muskegon, Michigan
WMCR-FM Oneida, New York
WMCX West Long Branch, New Jersey
WMDC Mayville, Wisconsin
WMDH-FM New Castle, Indiana
WMDJ-FM Allen, Kentucky
WMDM Lexington Park, Maryland
WMDR-FM Oakland, Maine
WMEA Portland, Maine
WMEB-FM Orono, Maine
WMED Calais, Maine
WMEE Fort Wayne, Indiana
WMEF Fort Kent, Maine
WMEG Guayama, Puerto Rico
WMEH Bangor, Maine
WMEK Kennebunkport, Maine
WMEM Presque Isle, Maine
WMEP Camden, Maine
WMEQ-FM Menomonie, Wisconsin
WMEV-FM Marion, Virginia
WMEW Waterville, Maine
WMEZ Pensacola, Florida
WMFC Monroeville, Alabama
WMFE-FM Orlando, Florida
WMFG-FM Hibbing, Minnesota
WMFL Florida City, Florida
WMFM Key West, Florida
WMFO Medford, Massachusetts
WMFQ Ocala, Florida
WMFS-FM Bartlett, Tennessee
WMFT Tuscaloosa, Alabama
WMFU(FM) Mount Hope, New York
WMFX St. Andrews, South Carolina
WMGA Kenova, West Virginia
WMGB Montezuma, Georgia
WMGC-FM Detroit, Michigan
WMGE Miami Beach, Florida
WMGF Mount Dora, Florida
WMGH-FM Tamaqua, Pennsylvania
WMGI Terre Haute, Indiana
WMGK Philadelphia, Pennsylvania
WMGL Ravenel, South Carolina
WMGM Atlantic City, New Jersey
WMGN Madison, Wisconsin
WMGP Hogansville, Georgia
WMGQ New Brunswick, New Jersey
WMGS Wilkes-Barre, Pennsylvania
WMGU Southern Pines, North Carolina
WMGV Newport, North Carolina
WMGX Portland, Maine
WMGZ Eatonton, Georgia
WMHB Waterville, Maine
WMHC South Hadley, Massachusetts
WMHD-FM Terre Haute, Indiana
WMHI Cape Vincent, New York
WMHK Columbia, South Carolina
WMHN Webster, New York
WMHQ Malone, New York
WMHR Syracuse, New York
WMHS Pike Creek, Delaware
WMHT-FM Schenectady, New York
WMHU(FM) Cold Brook, New York
WMHW-FM Mount Pleasant, Michigan
WMHX(FM) Hershey, Pennsylvania
WMIA-FM Miami Beach, Florida
WMIE-FM Cocoa, Florida
WMIK-FM Middlesboro, Kentucky
WMIL-FM Waukesha, Wisconsin
WMIM Luna Pier, Michigan
WMIO Cabo Rojo, Puerto Rico
WMIS-FM Blackduck, Minnesota
WMIT Black Mountain, North Carolina
WMIX-FM Mount Vernon, Illinois
WMJC Richland, Michigan
WMJD Grundy, Virginia
WMJI Cleveland, Ohio
WMJJ Birmingham, Alabama
WMJK Clyde, Ohio
WMJL-FM Marion, Kentucky
WMJM Jeffersontown, Kentucky
WMJO Essexville, Michigan
WMJT McMillan, Michigan
WMJU Bude, Mississippi
WMJW Rosedale, Mississippi
WMJX Boston, Massachusetts
WMJY Biloxi, Mississippi
WMJZ-FM Gaylord, Michigan
WMKB Earlville, Illinois
WMKC Indian River, Michigan
WMKD Pickford, Michigan
WMKL Hammocks, Florida
WMKO Marco, Florida
WMKR Pana, Illinois
WMKS Clemmons, North Carolina
WMKV Reading, Ohio
WMKW Crossville, Tennessee
WMKX Brookville, Pennsylvania
WMKY Morehead, Kentucky
WMKZ Monticello, Kentucky
WMLJ Summersville, West Virginia
WMLL Bedford, New Hampshire
WMLN-FM Milton, Massachusetts
WMLQ Manistee, Michigan
WMLS Grand Marais, Minnesota
WMLU Farmville, Virginia
WMLV Butler, Alabama
WMLX St. Marys, Ohio
WMMA Nekoosa, Wisconsin
WMMC Marshall, Illinois
WMME-FM Augusta, Maine
WMMG-FM Brandenburg, Kentucky
WMMJ Bethesda, Maryland
WMMM-FM Verona, Wisconsin
WMMO Orlando, Florida
WMMQ East Lansing, Michigan
WMMR Philadelphia, Pennsylvania
WMMS Cleveland, Ohio
WMMT Whitesburg, Kentucky
WMMX Dayton, Ohio
WMMY Jefferson, North Carolina
WMNA-FM Gretna, Virginia
WMNC-FM Morganton, North Carolina
WMNF Tampa, Florida
WMNG Christiansted, Virgin Islands
WMNI-FM Westerville, Ohio
WMNR Monroe, Connecticut
WMNV Rupert, Vermont
WMNX Wilmington, North Carolina
WMOC Lumber City, Georgia
WMOD Bolivar, Tennessee
WMOI Monmouth, Illinois
WMOJ-FM Norwood, Ohio
WMOM Pentwater, Michigan
WMOO Derby Center, Vermont
WMOQ Bostwick, Georgia
WMOR-FM Morehead, Kentucky
WMOS Stonington, Connecticut
WMOT Murfreesboro, Tennessee
WMOZ Moose Lake, Minnesota
WMPG Gorham, Maine
WMPH Wilmington, Delaware
WMPI Scottsburg, Indiana
WMPN-FM Jackson, Mississippi
WMPR Jackson, Mississippi
WMPZ Harrison, Tennessee
WMQA-FM Minocqua, Wisconsin
WMQT-FM Ishpeming, Michigan
WMQZ Colchester, Illinois
WMRA Harrisonburg, Virginia
WMRF-FM Lewistown, Pennsylvania
WMRK-FM Shorter, Alabama
WMRL Lexington, Virginia
WMRN-FM Marion, Ohio
WMRQ-FM) Waterbury, Connecticut
WMRR Muskegon Heights, Michigan
WMRS Monticello, Indiana
WMRT Marietta, Ohio
WMRV-FM Endicott, New York
WMRX-FM Beaverton, Michigan
WMRY Crozet, Virginia
WMRZ Dawson, Georgia
WMSB Byhalia, Mississippi
WMSC Upper Montclair, New Jersey
WMSD Rose Township, Michigan
WMSE Milwaukee, Wisconsin
WMSI-FM Jackson, Mississippi
WMSJ Freeport, Maine
WMSK-FM Sturgis, Kentucky
WMSL Athens, Georgia
WMSO Quitman, Mississippi
WMSR-FM Collinwood, Tennessee
WMSS Middletown, Pennsylvania
WMSU Starkville, Mississippi
WMSV Starkville, Mississippi
WMTB-FM Emmitsburg, Maryland
WMTC-FM Vancleve, Kentucky
WMTD-FM Hinton, West Virginia
WMTE-FM Manistee, Michigan
WMTH Park Ridge, Illinois
WMTI Picayune, Mississippi
WMTK Littleton, New Hampshire
WMTM-FM Moultrie, Georgia
WMTR-FM Archbold, Ohio
WMTS-FM Murfreesboro, Tennessee
WMTT Tioga, Pennsylvania
WMTU-FM Houghton, Michigan
WMTX Tampa, Florida
WMTY-FM Sweetwater, Tennessee
WMUA Amherst, Massachusetts
WMUB Oxford, Ohio
WMUC-FM College Park, Maryland
WMUF Henry, Tennessee
WMUH Allentown, Pennsylvania
WMUI(FM) Rushville, Indiana
WMUK Kalamazoo, Michigan
WMUL Huntington, West Virginia
WMUM-FM Cochran, Georgia
WMUS Muskegon, Michigan
WMUT Grenada, Mississippi
WMUU-FM Greenville, South Carolina
WMUV Brunswick, Georgia
WMUW Columbus, Mississippi
WMUZ Detroit, Michigan
WMVE Chase City, Virginia
WMVL Linesville, Pennsylvania
WMVM Goodman, Wisconsin
WMVN Sylvan Beach, New York
WMVR-FM Sidney, Ohio
WMVV Griffin, Georgia
WMVW Peachtree City, Georgia
WMVY Tisbury, Massachusetts
WMWI Demopolis, Alabama
WMWK Milwaukee, Wisconsin
WMWM Salem, Massachusetts
WMWV Conway, New Hampshire
WMWX Miamitown, Ohio
WMXA Opelika, Alabama
WMXC Mobile, Alabama
WMXD Detroit, Michigan
WMXE South Charleston, West Virginia
WMXG Stephenson, Michigan
WMXH-FM Luray, Virginia
WMXI Laurel, Mississippi
WMXJ Pompano Beach, Florida
WMXK Morristown, Tennessee
WMXL Lexington, Kentucky
WMXM Lake Forest, Illinois
WMXN-FM Stevenson, Alabama
WMXO Olean, New York
WMXR Woodstock, Vermont
WMXS Montgomery, Alabama
WMXT Pamplico, South Carolina
WMXU Starkville, Mississippi
WMXV St. Joseph, Tennessee
WMXW Vestal, New York
WMXX-FM Jackson, Tennessee
WMXY Youngstown, Ohio
WMXZ Isle of Palms, South Carolina
WMYB Myrtle Beach, South Carolina
WMYE Fort Myers, Florida
WMYI Hendersonville, North Carolina
WMYJ-FM Oolitic, Indiana
WMYK Peru, Indiana
WMYL Halls Crossroads, Tennessee
WMYP Frederiksted, Virgin Islands
WMYQ South Whitley, Indiana
WMYT Carolina Beach, North Carolina
WMYX-FM Milwaukee, Wisconsin
WMYY Schoharie, New York
WMYZ Clermont, Florida
WMZK Merrill, Wisconsin
WMZQ-FM Washington, District of Columbia
WNAA Greensboro, North Carolina
WNAN Nantucket, Massachusetts
WNAS New Albany, Indiana
WNAX-FM Yankton, South Dakota
WNBB Bayboro, North Carolina
WNBK Whitmire, South Carolina
WNBQ Mansfield, Pennsylvania
WNBR-FM Bethel, North Carolina
WNBT-FM Wellsboro, Pennsylvania
WNBU(FM) Oriental, North Carolina
WNBV Grundy, Virginia
WNBY-FM Newberry, Michigan
WNCC-FM Franklin, North Carolina
WNCD Youngstown, Ohio

WNCH Norwich, Vermont
WNCI Columbus, Ohio
WNCK Nantucket, Massachusetts
WNCL Milford, Delaware
WNCO-FM Ashland, Ohio
WNCQ-FM Canton, New York
WNCS Montpelier, Vermont
WNCT-FM Greenville, North Carolina
WNCU Durham, North Carolina
WNCV Shalimar, Florida
WNCW Spindale, North Carolina
WNCX Cleveland, Ohio
WNCY-FM Neenah-Menasha, Wisconsin
WNDD Silver Springs, Florida
WNDH Napoleon, Ohio
WNDI-FM Sullivan, Indiana
WNDN Chiefland, Florida
WNDT Alachua, Florida
WNDV-FM South Bend, Indiana
WNDY Crawfordsville, Indiana
WNEC-FM Henniker, New Hampshire
WNED-FM Buffalo, New York
WNEE Patterson, Georgia
WNEF Newburyport, Massachusetts
WNEK-FM Springfield, Massachusetts
WNEV Friars Point, Mississippi
WNEW(FM) Bowie, Maryland
WNFA Port Huron, Michigan
WNFB Lake City, Florida
WNFC Paducah, Kentucky
WNFK Perry, Florida
WNFM Reedsburg, Wisconsin
WNFN Millersville, Tennessee
WNFR Sandusky, Michigan
WNFZ Powell, Tennessee
WNGA Clermont, Georgia
WNGB Petersham, Massachusetts
WNGC Arcade, Georgia
WNGE Negaunee, Michigan
WNGF Swanton, Vermont
WNGH-FM Chatsworth, Georgia
WNGM(FM) Tallulah Falls, Georgia
WNGM(FM) Tallulah Falls, Georgia
WNGN Argyle, New York
WNGU Dahlonega, Georgia
WNGZ Montour Falls, New York
WNHI Farmington, New Hampshire
WNHT Churubusco, Indiana
WNHU West Haven, Connecticut
WNHW Belmont, New Hampshire
WNIC Dearborn, Michigan
WNIE Freeport, Illinois
WNIJ Dekalb, Illinois
WNIK-FM Arecibo, Puerto Rico
WNIN-FM Evansville, Indiana
WNIQ Sterling, Illinois
WNIR Kent, Ohio
WNIU Rockford, Illinois
WNIW La Salle, Illinois
WNJA Jamestown, New York
WNJB-FM Bridgeton, New Jersey
WNJM Manahawkin, New Jersey
WNJN-FM Atlantic City, New Jersey
WNJO Toms River, New Jersey
WNJP Sussex, New Jersey
WNJR Washington, Pennsylvania
WNJS-FM Berlin, New Jersey
WNJT-FM Trenton, New Jersey
WNJY Netcong, New Jersey
WNJZ Cape May Court House, New Jersey
WNKE New Boston, Ohio
WNKI Corning, New York
WNKJ Hopkinsville, Kentucky
WNKK Circleville, Ohio
WNKL Wauseon, Ohio
WNKN Middletown, Ohio
WNKO New Albany, Ohio
WNKR Williamstown, Kentucky
WNKS Charlotte, North Carolina
WNKT Eastover, South Carolina
WNKU Highland Heights, Kentucky
WNKV Norco, Louisiana
WNKX-FM Centerville, Tennessee
WNKZ Dushore, Pennsylvania
WNLC East Lyme, Connecticut
WNLF Macomb, Illinois
WNLI Sturgeon Bay, Wisconsin
WNLT Delhi Hills, Ohio
WNMC-FM Traverse City, Michigan
WNML-FM Friendsville, Tennessee
WNMP Marlinton, West Virginia
WNMQ Columbus, Mississippi
WNMR Dannemora, New York
WNMU-FM Marquette, Michigan
WNMX Christiansburg, Virginia
WNND Pickerington, Ohio
WNNF Cincinnati, Ohio
WNNG-FM Unadilla, Georgia
WNNH Henniker, New Hampshire
WNNJ Newton, New Jersey
WNNK-FM Harrisburg, Pennsylvania
WNNL Fuquay-Varina, North Carolina
WNNO-FM Wisconsin Dells, Wisconsin
WNNP Richwood, Ohio
WNNS Springfield, Illinois
WNNT-FM Warsaw, Virginia
WNNV San German, Puerto Rico
WNNX College Park, Georgia
WNNZ-FM Deerfield, Massachusetts
WNOB Chesapeake, Virginia
WNOC Bowling Green, Ohio
WNOD Mayaguez, Puerto Rico
WNOE-FM New Orleans, Louisiana
WNOI Flora, Illinois
WNOK Columbia, South Carolina
WNON Warfield, Kentucky
WNOR Norfolk, Virginia
WNOU Speedway, Indiana
WNOW-FM Gaffney, South Carolina
WNOX Oak Ridge, Tennessee
WNPQ New Philadelphia, Ohio
WNPR Meriden, Connecticut
WNPT-FM Marion, Alabama
WNQS Dillsboro, North Carolina
WNRK Norwalk, Ohio
WNRN Charlottesville, Virginia
WNRQ Nashville, Tennessee
WNRS-FM Sweet Briar, Virginia
WNRT Manati, Puerto Rico
WNRW(FM) Salem, Indiana
WNRX Jefferson City, Tennessee
WNRZ Dickson, Tennessee
WNSB Norfolk, Virginia
WNSC-FM Rock Hill, South Carolina
WNSL Laurel, Mississippi
WNSN South Bend, Indiana
WNSP Bay Minette, Alabama
WNSV Nashville, Illinois
WNSX Winter Harbor, Maine
WNSY Talking Rock, Georgia
WNTB Topsail Beach, North Carolina
WNTC Drakesboro, Kentucky
WNTE Mansfield, Pennsylvania
WNTH Winnetka, Illinois
WNTI Hackettstown, New Jersey
WNTK-FM New London, New Hampshire
WNTO Racine, Ohio
WNTQ Syracuse, New York
WNTR Indianapolis, Indiana
WNUA Chicago, Illinois
WNUB-FM Northfield, Vermont
WNUE-FM Deltona, Florida
WNUQ Sylvester, Georgia
WNUR-FM Evanston, Illinois
WNUS Belpre, Ohio
WNUZ Mercersburg, Pennsylvania
WNVA-FM Norton, Virginia
WNVE Culebra, Puerto Rico
WNVM Cidra, Puerto Rico
WNVZ Norfolk, Virginia
WNWC-FM Madison, Wisconsin
WNWN-FM Coldwater, Michigan
WNWS-FM Jackson, Tennessee
WNWV Elyria, Ohio
WNXR Iron River, Wisconsin
WNXT-FM Portsmouth, Ohio
WNXX Jackson, Louisiana
WNYC-FM New York, New York
WNYE New York, New York
WNYK Nyack, New York
WNYN-FM Whitefield, New Hampshire
WNYO Oswego, New York
WNYQ Hudson Falls, New York
WNYR-FM Waterloo, New York
WNYU-FM New York, New York
WNYV Whitehall, New York
WNZN Lorain, Ohio
WNZR Mount Vernon, Ohio
WOAB Ozark, Alabama
WOAH Glennville, Georgia
WOAK La Grange, Georgia
WOAR South Vienna, Ohio
WOAS Ontonagon, Michigan
WOBB Tifton, Georgia
WOBC-FM Oberlin, Ohio
WOBE Crystal Falls, Michigan
WOBG-FM Salem, West Virginia
WOBM-FM Toms River, New Jersey
WOBN Westerville, Ohio
WOBO Batavia, Ohio
WOBR-FM Wanchese, North Carolina
WOBX-FM Manteo, North Carolina
WOCE Ringgold, Georgia
WOCL Deland, Florida
WOCM Selbyville, Delaware
WOCN-FM Orleans, Massachusetts
WOCO-FM Oconto, Wisconsin
WOCQ Berlin, Maryland
WOCR Olivet, Michigan
WOCY Carrabelle, Florida
WODA Bayamon, Puerto Rico
WODC Ashville, Ohio
WODE-FM Easton, Pennsylvania
WODR Fair Bluff, North Carolina
WODS Boston, Massachusetts
WODX South Bristol Township, New York
WODZ-FM Rome, New York
WOEL-FM Elkton, Maryland
WOES Ovid-Elsie, Michigan
WOFN Beach City, Ohio
WOFR Schoolcraft, Michigan
WOFX-FM Cincinnati, Ohio
WOGB Kaukauna, Wisconsin
WOGG Oliver, Pennsylvania
WOGH Burgettstown, Pennsylvania
WOGI(FM) Moon Township, Pennsylvania
WOGK Ocala, Florida
WOGL Philadelphia, Pennsylvania
WOGR-FM Salisbury, North Carolina
WOGT East Ridge, Tennessee
WOGY Jackson, Tennessee
WOHC Chillicothe, Ohio
WOHF Bellevue, Ohio
WOHT Grenada, Mississippi
WOI-FM Ames, Iowa
WOJB Reserve, Wisconsin
WOJC Crothersville, Indiana
WOJG Bolivar, Tennessee
WOJL Louisa, Virginia
WOJO Evanston, Illinois
WOKA-FM Douglas, Georgia
WOKD-FM Danville, Virginia
WOKE Garrison, Kentucky
WOKG Galax, Virginia
WOKI Oliver Springs, Tennessee
WOKK Meridian, Mississippi
WOKL Troy, Ohio
WOKN Southport, New York
WOKO Burlington, Vermont
WOKQ Dover, New Hampshire
WOKR Remsen, New York
WOKV-FM Ponte Vedra Beach, Florida
WOKW Curwensville, Pennsylvania
WOKZ Fairfield, Illinois
WOLC Princess Anne, Maryland
WOLD-FM Marion, Virginia
WOLF-FM DeRuyter, New York
WOLF-FM DeRuyter, New York
WOLG Carlinville, Illinois
WOLI-FM Easley, South Carolina
WOLL Hobe Sound, Florida
WOLN Olean, New York
WOLR Lake City, Florida
WOLS Waxhaw, North Carolina
WOLT Greer, South Carolina
WOLV Houghton, Michigan
WOLW Cadillac, Michigan
WOLX-FM Baraboo, Wisconsin
WOLZ Fort Myers, Florida
WOMC Detroit, Michigan
WOMG Lexington, South Carolina
WOMR Provincetown, Massachusetts
WOMX-FM Orlando, Florida
WONA-FM Winona, Mississippi
WONB Ada, Ohio
WONC Naperville, Illinois
WONE-FM Akron, Ohio
WONU Kankakee, Illinois
WONY Oneonta, New York
WOOD-FM Muskegon, Michigan
WOOF-FM Dothan, Alabama
WOOZ-FM Harrisburg, Illinois
WORC-FM Webster, Massachusetts
WORD-FM Pittsburgh, Pennsylvania
WORG Elloree, South Carolina
WORI Harrison, Ohio
WORK Barre, Vermont
WORM-FM Savannah, Tennessee
WORO Corozal, Puerto Rico
WORQ Green Bay, Wisconsin
WORT Madison, Wisconsin
WORW Port Huron, Michigan
WORX-FM Madison, Indiana
WOSA Grove City, Ohio
WOSB Marion, Ohio
WOSE Coshocton, Ohio
WOSM Ocean Springs, Mississippi
WOSN Indian River Shores, Florida
WOSP Portsmouth, Ohio
WOSQ Spencer, Wisconsin
WOSR Middletown, New York
WOSS Ossining, New York
WOSU-FM Columbus, Ohio
WOSV Mansfield, Ohio
WOTC Edinburg, Virginia
WOTJ Morehead City, North Carolina
WOTL Toledo, Ohio
WOTR(FM) Lost Creek, West Virginia
WOTT Calcium, New York
WOTW Monee, Illinois
WOTX Lunenburg, Vermont
WOUB-FM Athens, Ohio
WOUC-FM Cambridge, Ohio
WOUF Beulah, Michigan
WOUH-FM Chillicothe, Ohio
WOUL-FM Ironton, Ohio
WOUR Utica, New York
WOUZ-FM Zanesville, Ohio
WOVI Novi, Michigan
WOVK Wheeling, West Virginia
WOVM Appleton, Wisconsin
WOVO Glasgow, Kentucky
WOVV Ocracoke, North Carolina
WOWB Brewton, Alabama
WOWC Morrison, Tennessee
WOWE Vassar, Michigan
WOWF Crossville, Tennessee
WOWI Norfolk, Virginia
WOWL Burnsville, Mississippi
WOWN Shawano, Wisconsin
WOWO-FM Fort Wayne, Indiana
WOWQ Du Bois, Pennsylvania
WOWY University Park, Pennsylvania
WOXD Oxford, Mississippi
WOXL-FM Biltmore Forest, North Carolina
WOXM Middlebury, Vermont
WOXO-FM Norway, Maine
WOXR Schuyler Falls, New York
WOXY Mason, Ohio
WOYE Rio Grande, Puerto Rico
WOYS Apalachicola, Florida
WOZI Presque Isle, Maine
WOZQ Northampton, Massachusetts
WOZZ Mosinee, Wisconsin
WPAC Ogdensburg, New York
WPAE Centreville, Mississippi
WPAI Nanty Glo, Pennsylvania
WPAL Laporte, Pennsylvania
WPAL(FM) Laporte, Pennsylvania
WPAP-FM Panama City, Florida
WPAR Salem, Virginia
WPAS Pascagoula, Mississippi
WPAT-FM Paterson, New Jersey
WPAW Winston-Salem, North Carolina
WPAZ Pottstown, Pennsylvania
WPBD Lewes, Delaware
WPBG Peoria, Illinois
WPBI(FM) West Palm Beach, Florida
WPBK Crab Orchard, Kentucky
WPBX Crossville, Tennessee
WPCD Champaign, Illinois
WPCH Gray, Georgia
WPCJ Pittsford, Michigan
WPCK Denmark, Wisconsin
WPCL Northern Cambria, Pennsylvania
WPCN(FM) Point Pleasant, West Virginia
WPCR-FM Plymouth, New Hampshire
WPCS Pensacola, Florida
WPCV Winter Haven, Florida
WPDA Jeffersonville, New York
WPDH Poughkeepsie, New York
WPDI Hazlet, New Jersey
WPDT Coward, South Carolina
WPDX-FM Clarksburg, West Virginia

WPEA Exeter, New Hampshire
WPEB Philadelphia, Pennsylvania
WPEF Kentwood, Louisiana
WPEG Concord, North Carolina
WPEH-FM Louisville, Georgia
WPEI Saco, Maine
WPEL-FM Montrose, Pennsylvania
WPEN-FM Burlington, New Jersey
WPER Culpeper, Virginia
WPEZ Jeffersonville, Georgia
WPFF Sturgeon Bay, Wisconsin
WPFL Century, Florida
WPFM-FM Panama City, Florida
WPFR-FM Clinton, Indiana
WPFT Pigeon Forge, Tennessee
WPFW Washington, District of Columbia
WPFX-FM Luckey, Ohio
WPGA-FM Perry, Georgia
WPGB Pittsburgh, Pennsylvania
WPGC-FM Morningside, Maryland
WPGI Horseheads, New York
WPGL Pattersonville, New York
WPGM-FM Danville, Pennsylvania
WPGU Urbana, Illinois
WPGW-FM Portland, Indiana
WPHD South Waverly, Pennsylvania
WPHI-FM Pennsauken, New Jersey
WPHK Blountstown, Florida
WPHN Gaylord, Michigan
WPHP Wheeling, West Virginia
WPHS Warren, Michigan
WPHZ Orleans, Indiana
WPIA Eureka, Illinois
WPIB Bluefield, West Virginia
WPIG Olean, New York
WPIK Summerland Key, Florida
WPIL Heflin, Alabama
WPIM Martinsville, Virginia
WPIN-FM Dublin, Virginia
WPIO Titusville, Florida
WPIQ Manistique, Michigan
WPIR Hickory, North Carolina
WPJC Pontiac, Illinois
WPJN Jemison, Alabama
WPJP Port Washington, Wisconsin
WPJW Hurricane, West Virginia
WPJY Blennerhassett, West Virginia
WPKE-FM Coal Run, Kentucky
WPKF Poughkeepsie, New York
WPKG Neillsville, Wisconsin
WPKL Uniontown, Pennsylvania
WPKN Bridgeport, Connecticut
WPKO-FM Bellefontaine, Ohio
WPKQ North Conway, New Hampshire
WPKR Omro, Wisconsin
WPKT Norwich, Connecticut
WPLB Plattsburgh West, New York
WPLH Tifton, Georgia
WPLJ New York, New York
WPLM-FM Plymouth, Massachusetts
WPLN-FM Nashville, Tennessee
WPLR New Haven, Connecticut
WPLT Sarona, Wisconsin
WPLW Hillsborough, North Carolina
WPLZ Ooltewah, Tennessee
WPMA Buckhead, Georgia
WPMJ Chillicothe, Illinois
WPMW Bayview, Massachusetts
WPMX Statesboro, Georgia
WPNC-FM Plymouth, North Carolina
WPNE-FM Green Bay, Wisconsin
WPNG Pearson, Georgia
WPNH-FM Plymouth, New Hampshire
WPNR-FM Utica, New York
WPOB Plainview, New York
WPOC Baltimore, Maryland
WPOI St. Petersburg, Florida
WPOR Portland, Maine
WPOS-FM Holland, Ohio
WPOW Miami, Florida
WPOZ Union Park, Florida
WPPB Southampton, New York
WPPG Repton, Alabama
WPPI Topsham, Maine
WPPL Blue Ridge, Georgia
WPPN Des Plaines, Illinois
WPPR Demorest, Georgia
WPPZ-FM Jenkintown, Pennsylvania
WPRB Princeton, New Jersey
WPRC Sheffield, Illinois
WPRF Reserve, Louisiana
WPRG Columbia, Mississippi
WPRH Paris, Tennessee
WPRJ Coleman, Michigan
WPRK Winter Park, Florida
WPRL Lorman, Mississippi
WPRM-FM San Juan, Puerto Rico
WPRO-FM Providence, Rhode Island
WPRS-FM Waldorf, Maryland
WPRT-FM Pegram, Tennessee
WPRW-FM Martinez, Georgia
WPRZ-FM Brandy Station, Virginia
WPSC-FM Wayne, New Jersey
WPSF Clewiston, Florida
WPSK-FM Pulaski, Virginia
WPSM Fort Walton Beach, Florida
WPSR Evansville, Indiana
WPST Trenton, New Jersey
WPSU State College, Pennsylvania
WPSX Kane, Pennsylvania
WPTC Williamsport, Pennsylvania
WPTE Virginia Beach, Virginia
WPTH Olney, Illinois
WPTI Eden, North Carolina
WPTJ Paris, Kentucky
WPTM Roanoke Rapids, North Carolina
WPTS-FM Pittsburgh, Pennsylvania
WPTY Calverton-Roanoke, New York
WPUB-FM Camden, South Carolina
WPUC-FM Ponce, Puerto Rico
WPUM Rensselaer, Indiana
WPUP Watkinsville, Georgia
WPUR Atlantic City, New Jersey
WPVA Waynesboro, Virginia
WPVL-FM Platteville, Wisconsin
WPVQ Greenfield, Massachusetts
WPWB Byron, Georgia
WPWQ Mount Sterling, Illinois
WPWV Princeton, West Virginia
WPWX Hammond, Indiana
WPWZ Pinetops, North Carolina
WPXC Hyannis, Massachusetts
WPXN Paxton, Illinois
WPXY-FM Rochester, New York
WPXZ-FM Punxsutawney, Pennsylvania
WPYO Maitland, Florida
WPYX Albany, New York
WPZE Mableton, Georgia
WPZR Mount Clemens, Michigan
WPZS Harrisburg, North Carolina
WPZX Pocono Pines, Pennsylvania
WPZZ Crewe, Virginia
WQAB Philippi, West Virginia
WQAC Alma, Michigan
WQAH-FM Addison, Alabama
WQAI Thomson, Georgia
WQAK Union City, Tennessee
WQAL Cleveland, Ohio
WQAQ Hamden, Connecticut
WQBE-FM Charleston, West Virginia
WQBJ Cobleskill, New York
WQBK-FM Rensselaer, New York
WQBR Avis, Pennsylvania
WQBT Savannah, Georgia
WQBU-FM Garden City, New York
WQBW Honeoye Falls, New York
WQBX Fowler, Michigan
WQBZ Fort Valley, Georgia
WQCB Brewer, Maine
WQCC La Crosse, Wisconsin
WQCK(FM) Philipsburg, Pennsylvania
WQCM Greencastle, Pennsylvania
WQCS Fort Pierce, Florida
WQCY Quincy, Illinois
WQDK Gatesville, North Carolina
WQDR-FM Raleigh, North Carolina
WQDY-FM Calais, Maine
WQED-FM Pittsburgh, Pennsylvania
WQEJ Johnstown, Pennsylvania
WQEL Bucyrus, Ohio
WQEM Columbiana, Alabama
WQEN Trussville, Alabama
WQFL Rockford, Illinois
WQFM Forest City, Pennsylvania
WQFN(FM) Forest City, Pennsylvania
WQFS Greensboro, North Carolina
WQFX-FM Russell, Pennsylvania
WQGA Waycross, Georgia
WQGN-FM Groton, Connecticut
WQHH Dewitt, Michigan
WQHK-FM Huntertown, Indiana
WQHL-FM Live Oak, Florida
WQHQ Ocean City-Salisbury, Maryland
WQHR Presque Isle, Maine
WQHT New York, New York
WQHY Prestonsburg, Kentucky
WQHZ Erie, Pennsylvania
WQIC Lebanon, Pennsylvania
WQIK-FM Jacksonville, Florida
WQIL Chauncey, Georgia
WQIO Mount Vernon, Ohio
WQIQ Spotsylvania, Virginia
WQJB State College, Mississippi
WQJK Maryville, Tennessee
WQJQ Barton, Vermont
WQJU Mifflintown, Pennsylvania
WQKE Plattsburgh, New York
WQKI-FM Orangeburg, South Carolina
WQKK(FM) Renovo, Pennsylvania
WQKL Ann Arbor, Michigan
WQKO Howe, Indiana
WQKQ Carthage, Illinois
WQKS-FM Montgomery, Alabama
WQKT Wooster, Ohio
WQKV Rochester, Indiana
WQKX Sunbury, Pennsylvania
WQKY Emporium, Pennsylvania
WQKZ Ferdinand, Indiana
WQLB Tawas City, Michigan
WQLC Watertown, Florida
WQLF Lena, Illinois
WQLH Green Bay, Wisconsin
WQLI Meigs, Georgia
WQLJ Oxford, Mississippi
WQLK Richmond, Indiana
WQLN-FM Erie, Pennsylvania
WQLT-FM Florence, Alabama
WQLV Millersburg, Pennsylvania
WQLZ Taylorville, Illinois
WQME Anderson, Indiana
WQMF Jeffersonville, Indiana
WQMG Greensboro, North Carolina
WQMJ Forsyth, Georgia
WQMU Indiana, Pennsylvania
WQMX Medina, Ohio
WQMZ Charlottesville, Virginia
WQNA Springfield, Illinois
WQNC Indian Trail, North Carolina
WQNQ Fletcher, North Carolina
WQNR Tallassee, Alabama
WQNS Waynesville, North Carolina
WQNU Lyndon, Kentucky
WQNY Ithaca, New York
WQNZ Natchez, Mississippi
WQOK Carrboro, North Carolina
WQOL Vero Beach, Florida
WQON Roscommon, Michigan
WQOX Memphis, Tennessee
WQPC Prairie Du Chien, Wisconsin
WQPO Harrisonburg, Virginia
WQPR Muscle Shoals, Alabama
WQPW Valdosta, Georgia
WQQB Rantoul, Illinois
WQQK Goodlettsville, Tennessee
WQQL Springfield, Illinois
WQQQ Sharon, Connecticut
WQQR Clinton, Kentucky
WQRA Greencastle, Indiana
WQRB Bloomer, Wisconsin
WQRC Barnstable, Massachusetts
WQRI Bristol, Rhode Island
WQRK Bedford, Indiana
WQRL Benton, Illinois
WQRN Cook, Minnesota
WQRP Dayton, Ohio
WQRS Salamanca, New York
WQRV Meridianville, Alabama
WQRW Wellsville, New York
WQSB Albertville, Alabama
WQSG Lafayette, Indiana
WQSH Malta, New York
WQSI Tuskegee, Alabama
WQSL Jacksonville, North Carolina
WQSM Fayetteville, North Carolina
WQSO Rochester, New Hampshire
WQSR Baltimore, Maryland
WQSS Camden, Maine
WQST-FM Forest, Mississippi
WQSU Selinsgrove, Pennsylvania
WQTC-FM Manitowoc, Wisconsin
WQTE Adrian, Michigan
WQTK Ogdensburg, New York
WQTL Tallahassee, Florida
WQTQ Hartford, Connecticut
WQTU Rome, Georgia
WQTX Saint Johns, Michigan
WQTY Linton, Indiana
WQUA Citronelle, Alabama
WQUB Quincy, Illinois
WQUE-FM New Orleans, Louisiana
WQUS Lapeer, Michigan
WQUT Johnson City, Tennessee
WQVE Albany, Georgia
WQVI Madison, Mississippi
WQWV Fisher, West Virginia
WQXA-FM York, Pennsylvania
WQXB Grenada, Mississippi
WQXC-FM Otsego, Michigan
WQXE Elizabethtown, Kentucky
WQXJ Blackduck, Minnesota
WQXK Salem, Ohio
WQXQ Central City, Kentucky
WQXR-FM Newark, New Jersey
WQXZ Hawkinsville, Georgia
WQYK-FM St. Petersburg, Florida
WQYX Clearfield, Pennsylvania
WQYZ Ocean Springs, Mississippi
WQZK-FM Keyser, West Virginia
WQZL Belhaven, North Carolina
WQZS Meyersdale, Pennsylvania
WQZX Greenville, Alabama
WQZY Dublin, Georgia
WQZZ Boligee, Alabama
WRAC Georgetown, Ohio
WRAE Raeford, North Carolina
WRAF Toccoa Falls, Georgia
WRAL Raleigh, North Carolina
WRAN Tower Hill, Illinois
WRAO Wisconsin Rapids, Wisconsin
WRAR-FM Tappahannock, Virginia
WRAS Atlanta, Georgia
WRAT Point Pleasant, New Jersey
WRAU Ocean City, Maryland
WRAX Lake Isabella, Michigan
WRAY-FM Princeton, Indiana
WRAZ-FM Leisure City, Florida
WRBA Springfield, Florida
WRBB Boston, Massachusetts
WRBC Lewiston, Maine
WRBE-FM Lucedale, Mississippi
WRBF Plainville, Georgia
WRBH New Orleans, Louisiana
WRBI Batesville, Indiana
WRBJ-FM Brandon, Mississippi
WRBK Richburg, South Carolina
WRBN Clayton, Georgia
WRBO Como, Mississippi
WRBP Hubbard, Ohio
WRBQ-FM Tampa, Florida
WRBR-FM South Bend, Indiana
WRBS-FM Baltimore, Maryland
WRBT Harrisburg, Pennsylvania
WRBV Warner Robins, Georgia
WRBX Reidsville, Georgia
WRCC Dibrell, Tennessee
WRCD Canton, New York
WRCH New Britain, Connecticut
WRCJ-FM Detroit, Michigan
WRCL Frankenmuth, Michigan
WRCM Wingate, North Carolina
WRCN-FM Riverhead, New York
WRCO-FM Richland Center, Wisconsin
WRCQ Dunn, North Carolina
WRCT Pittsburgh, Pennsylvania
WRCT(FM) Pittsburgh, Pennsylvania
WRCU-FM Hamilton, New York
WRCV Dixon, Illinois
WRCW Nekoosa, Wisconsin
WRDK Bladenboro, North Carolina
WRDL Ashland, Ohio
WRDO Fitzgerald, Georgia
WRDR Freehold Township, New Jersey
WRDU Knightdale, North Carolina
WRDV Warminster, Pennsylvania
WRDW-FM Philadelphia, Pennsylvania
WRDX Smyrna, Delaware
WRDZ-FM Plainfield, Indiana
WREB Greencastle, Indiana
WREH Cypress Quarters, Florida
WREK Atlanta, Georgia
WREM Canton, New York
WREO-FM Ashtabula, Ohio
WREZ Metropolis, Illinois
WRFE Chesterfield, South Carolina

WRFF Philadelphia, Pennsylvania
WRFG Atlanta, Georgia
WRFI Watkins Glen, New York
WRFL Lexington, Kentucky
WRFQ Mount Pleasant, South Carolina
WRFT Indianapolis, Indiana
WRFW River Falls, Wisconsin
WRFX Kannapolis, North Carolina
WRFY-FM Reading, Pennsylvania
WRGC-FM Milledgeville, Georgia
WRGF Greenfield, Indiana
WRGN Sweet Valley, Pennsylvania
WRGO Cedar Key, Florida
WRGP Homestead, Florida
WRGR Tupper Lake, New York
WRGZ Rogers City, Michigan
WRHD Farmville, North Carolina
WRHK Danville, Illinois
WRHL-FM Rochelle, Illinois
WRHM Lancaster, South Carolina
WRHN Rhinelander, Wisconsin
WRHO Oneonta, New York
WRHQ Richmond Hill, Georgia
WRHT Morehead City, North Carolina
WRHU Hempstead, New York
WRHV Poughkeepsie, New York
WRIC-FM Richlands, Virginia
WRIF Detroit, Michigan
WRIH Richmond, Virginia
WRIJ Masontown, Pennsylvania
WRIK-FM Metropolis, Illinois
WRIL Pineville, Kentucky
WRIO Ponce, Puerto Rico
WRIP Windham, New York
WRIQ Lexington, Virginia
WRIT-FM Milwaukee, Wisconsin
WRIU Kingston, Rhode Island
WRIX-FM Honea Path, South Carolina
WRJA-FM Sumter, South Carolina
WRJB Camden, Tennessee
WRJC-FM Mauston, Wisconsin
WRJJ La Center, Kentucky
WRJL-FM Eva, Alabama
WRJO Eagle River, Wisconsin
WRJT Royalton, Vermont
WRJY Brunswick, Georgia
WRKA Louisville, Kentucky
WRKC Wilkes-Barre, Pennsylvania
WRKF Baton Rouge, Louisiana
WRKH Mobile, Alabama
WRKI Brookfield, Connecticut
WRKJ Westbrook, Maine
WRKR Portage, Michigan
WRKS Pickens, Mississippi
WRKT North East, Pennsylvania
WRKU Forestville, Wisconsin
WRKW Ebensburg, Pennsylvania
WRKX Ottawa, Illinois
WRKY-FM Hollidaysburg, Pennsylvania
WRKZ Columbus, Ohio
WRLB Rainelle, West Virginia
WRLC Williamsport, Pennsylvania
WRLD Valley, Alabama
WRLF Fairmont, West Virginia
WRLI-FM Southampton, New York
WRLO-FM Antigo, Wisconsin
WRLS-FM Hayward, Wisconsin
WRLT Franklin, Tennessee
WRLU Algoma, Wisconsin
WRLV-FM Salyersville, Kentucky
WRLX West Palm Beach, Florida
WRMA Fort Lauderdale, Florida
WRMB Boynton Beach, Florida
WRMC-FM Middlebury, Vermont
WRMF Palm Beach, Florida
WRMJ Aledo, Illinois
WRMM-FM Rochester, New York
WRMO Milbridge, Maine
WRMR(FM) Jacksonville, North Carolina
WRMS-FM Beardstown, Illinois
WRMU-FM Alliance, Ohio
WRNB Media, Pennsylvania
WRNF Selma, Alabama
WRNI-FM Narragansett Pier, Rhode Island
WRNN-FM Socastee, South Carolina
WRNO-FM New Orleans, Louisiana
WRNQ Poughkeepsie, New York
WRNR-FM Grasonville, Maryland
WRNS-FM Kinston, North Carolina
WRNW Milwaukee, Wisconsin
WRNX Amherst, Massachusetts
WRNZ Lancaster, Kentucky
WROI Rochester, Indiana
WROK-FM Macon, Georgia
WRON-FM Lewisburg, West Virginia
WROQ Anderson, South Carolina
WROR-FM Framingham, Massachusetts
WROU-FM West Carrollton, Ohio
WROV-FM Martinsville, Virginia
WROX-FM Exmore, Virginia
WROZ Lancaster, Pennsylvania
WRPB Benedicta, Maine
WRPI Troy, New York
WRPJ Port Jervis, New York
WRPN-FM Ripon, Wisconsin
WRPR Mahwah, New Jersey
WRPS Rockland, Massachusetts
WRPW Colfax, Illinois
WRQC(FM) East Tawas, Michigan
WRQE New London, Wisconsin
WRQK-FM Canton, Ohio
WRQM Rocky Mount, North Carolina
WRQN Bowling Green, Ohio
WRQO Monticello, Mississippi
WRQQ(FM) Hammond, Louisiana
WRQT La Crosse, Wisconsin
WRQX Washington, District of Columbia
WRR Dallas, Texas
WRRB Arlington, New York
WRRC Lawrenceville, New Jersey
WRRG River Grove, Illinois
WRRH Hormigueros, Puerto Rico
WRRK Braddock, Pennsylvania
WRRM Cincinnati, Ohio
WRRN Warren, Pennsylvania
WRRQ Port Dickinson, New York
WRRR-FM St. Marys, West Virginia
WRRV Middletown, New York
WRRX Gulf Breeze, Florida
WRSA-FM Holly Pond, Alabama
WRSD Folsom, Pennsylvania
WRSE Elmhurst, Illinois
WRSF Columbia, North Carolina
WRSG Middlebourne, West Virginia
WRSH Rockingham, North Carolina
WRSI Turners Falls, Massachusetts
WRSN Lebanon, Tennessee
WRSR Owosso, Michigan
WRST-FM Oshkosh, Wisconsin
WRSU-FM New Brunswick, New Jersey
WRSV Elm City, North Carolina
WRSW-FM Warsaw, Indiana
WRSY Marlboro, Vermont
WRTB Winnebago, Illinois
WRTC-FM Hartford, Connecticut
WRTE Chicago, Illinois
WRTI Philadelphia, Pennsylvania
WRTJ Coatesville, Pennsylvania
WRTK Paxton, Illinois
WRTL Ephrata, Pennsylvania
WRTM-FM Sharon, Mississippi
WRTO-FM Goulds, Florida
WRTP Franklinton, North Carolina
WRTQ Ocean City, New Jersey
WRTR Brookwood, Alabama
WRTS Erie, Pennsylvania
WRTT-FM Huntsville, Alabama
WRTU San Juan, Puerto Rico
WRTW Crown Point, Indiana
WRTX Dover, Delaware
WRTY Jackson Township, Pennsylvania
WRUC Schenectady, New York
WRUF-FM Gainesville, Florida
WRUL Carmi, Illinois
WRUM Orlando, Florida
WRUN Remsen, New York
WRUO Mayaguez, Puerto Rico
WRUP Palmer, Michigan
WRUR-FM Rochester, New York
WRUV Burlington, Vermont
WRUW-FM Cleveland, Ohio
WRVA-FM Wake Forest, North Carolina
WRVB Marietta, Ohio
WRVD Syracuse, New York
WRVE Schenectady, New York
WRVF Toledo, Ohio
WRVH Clayton, New York
WRVJ Watertown, New York
WRVL Lynchburg, Virginia
WRVM Suring, Wisconsin
WRVN Utica, New York
WRVO Oswego, New York
WRVQ Richmond, Virginia
WRVR Memphis, Tennessee
WRVS-FM Elizabeth City, North Carolina
WRVT Rutland, Vermont
WRVV Harrisburg, Pennsylvania
WRVW Lebanon, Tennessee
WRVX Cameron, Missouri
WRVY-FM Henry, Illinois
WRVZ Pocatalico, West Virginia
WRWA Dothan, Alabama
WRWB-FM Ellenville, New York
WRWD-FM Highland, New York
WRWJ Murrysville, Pennsylvania
WRWM(FM) Lawrence, Indiana
WRWM(FM) Lawrence, Indiana
WRWR-FM Cochran, Georgia
WRWV Beech Creek, Pennsylvania
WRXC Shelton, Connecticut
WRXD Fajardo, Puerto Rico
WRXK-FM Bonita Springs, Florida
WRXL Richmond, Virginia
WRXQ Coal City, Illinois
WRXR-FM Rossville, Georgia
WRXT Roanoke, Virginia
WRXV State College, Pennsylvania
WRXX Centralia, Illinois
WRXZ Briarcliff Acres, South Carolina
WRYN Hickory, North Carolina
WRYP Wellfleet, Massachusetts
WRYV Milroy, Pennsylvania
WRZE Kingstree, South Carolina
WRZI Hodgenville, Kentucky
WRZK Colonial Heights, Tennessee
WRZQ-FM Greensburg, Indiana
WRZR Loogootee, Indiana
WRZX Indianapolis, Indiana
WRZZ Parkersburg, West Virginia
WSAA Benton, Tennessee
WSAG Linwood, Michigan
WSAJ-FM Grove City, Pennsylvania
WSAK Hampton, New Hampshire
WSAQ Port Huron, Michigan
WSAU-FM Rudolph, Wisconsin
WSB-FM Atlanta, Georgia
WSBF-FM Clemson, South Carolina
WSBG Stroudsburg, Pennsylvania
WSBH Satellite Beach, Florida
WSBW Sister Bay, Wisconsin
WSBY-FM Salisbury, Maryland
WSBZ Miramar Beach, Florida
WSCB Springfield, Massachusetts
WSCC-FM Goose Creek, South Carolina
WSCD-FM Duluth, Minnesota
WSCF-FM Vero Beach, Florida
WSCH Aurora, Indiana
WSCI Charleston, South Carolina
WSCL Salisbury, Maryland
WSCN Cloquet, Minnesota
WSCS New London, New Hampshire
WSCT Springfield, Illinois
WSCY Moultonborough, New Hampshire
WSCZ(FM) Saint Matthews, South Carolina
WSDH Sandwich, Massachusetts
WSDL Ocean City, Maryland
WSDM-FM Brazil, Indiana
WSDP Plymouth, Michigan
WSEA Atlantic Beach, South Carolina
WSEB Englewood, Florida
WSEI Olney, Illinois
WSEK Burnside, Kentucky
WSEL-FM Pontotoc, Mississippi
WSEN-FM Baldwinsville, New York
WSEO Nelsonville, Ohio
WSEV-FM Gatlinburg, Tennessee
WSEW Sanford, Maine
WSEY Oregon, Illinois
WSFF Vinton, Virginia
WSFL-FM New Bern, North Carolina
WSFP Harrisville, Michigan
WSFQ Peshtigo, Wisconsin
WSFR Corydon, Indiana
WSFX Nanticoke, Pennsylvania
WSGA Hinesville, Georgia
WSGC-FM Elberton, Georgia
WSGE Dallas, North Carolina
WSGG Norfolk, Connecticut
WSGL Naples, Florida
WSGM Coalmont, Tennessee
WSGN Gadsden, Alabama
WSGP Glasgow, Kentucky
WSGR-FM Port Huron, Michigan
WSGS Hazard, Kentucky
WSGW-FM Carrollton, Michigan
WSHA Raleigh, North Carolina
WSHC Shepherdstown, West Virginia
WSHD Eastport, Maine
WSHE-FM Fort Lauderdale, Florida
WSHH Pittsburgh, Pennsylvania
WSHJ Southfield, Michigan
WSHK Kittery, Maine
WSHL-FM Easton, Massachusetts
WSHM Wixom, Michigan
WSHP Attica, Indiana
WSHR Lake Ronkonkoma, New York
WSHS Sheboygan, Wisconsin
WSHU-FM Fairfield, Connecticut
WSHW Frankfort, Indiana
WSIA Staten Island, New York
WSIB Selmer, Tennessee
WSIE Edwardsville, Illinois
WSIF Wilkesboro, North Carolina
WSIG Mount Jackson, Virginia
WSIM Lamar, South Carolina
WSIP-FM Paintsville, Kentucky
WSIS Riverside, Michigan
WSIU Carbondale, Illinois
WSIX-FM Nashville, Tennessee
WSIZ-FM Jacksonville, Georgia
WSJD Princeton, Indiana
WSJE Summersville, West Virginia
WSJK(FM) Tuscola, Illinois
WSJL Bessemer, Alabama
WSJM-FM Benton Harbor, Michigan
WSJO Egg Harbor City, New Jersey
WSJR Dallas, Pennsylvania
WSJY Fort Atkinson, Wisconsin
WSJZ-FM Sebastian, Florida
WSKB Westfield, Massachusetts
WSKE Everett, Pennsylvania
WSKG-FM Binghamton, New York
WSKK Ripley, Mississippi
WSKL Veedersburg, Indiana
WSKQ-FM New York, New York
WSKS Whitesboro, New York
WSKU Little Falls, New York
WSKV-FM Stanton, Kentucky
WSKX York Center, Maine
WSKY-FM Micanopy, Florida
WSKZ Chattanooga, Tennessee
WSLC-FM Roanoke, Virginia
WSLD Whitewater, Wisconsin
WSLE Salem, Illinois
WSLG Gouverneur, New York
WSLI Belding, Michigan
WSLJ Watertown, New York
WSLL Saranac Lake, New York
WSLM-FM Salem, Indiana
WSLO Malone, New York
WSLP Saranac Lake, New York
WSLQ Roanoke, Virginia
WSLT Statesboro, Georgia
WSLU Canton, New York
WSLX New Canaan, Connecticut
WSLY York, Alabama
WSLZ Cape Vincent, New York
WSM-FM Nashville, Tennessee
WSMA Scituate, Massachusetts
WSMB Harbor Beach, Michigan
WSMC-FM Collegedale, Tennessee
WSMD-FM Mechanicsville, Maryland
WSMF Monroe, Michigan
WSMI-FM Litchfield, Illinois
WSMJ(FM) Wilkinson, Indiana
WSMK Buchanan, Michigan
WSMM New Carlisle, Indiana
WSMP New Hebron, Mississippi
WSMR Sarasota, Florida
WSMS Artesia, Mississippi
WSMW Greensboro, North Carolina
WSNC Winston-Salem, North Carolina
WSND-FM Notre Dame, Indiana
WSNE-FM Taunton, Massachusetts
WSNI Keene, New Hampshire
WSNN Potsdam, New York
WSNQ Cape May Court House, New Jersey
WSNT-FM Sandersville, Georgia
WSNV Salem, Virginia
WSNX-FM Muskegon, Michigan
WSNY Columbus, Ohio
WSNZ Lynchburg, Virginia
WSOC-FM Charlotte, North Carolina
WSOE Elon College, North Carolina

WSOF-FM Madisonville, Kentucky
WSOG Spring Valley, Illinois
WSOL-FM Brunswick, Georgia
WSOR Naples, Florida
WSOS-FM Fruit Cove, Florida
WSOU South Orange, New Jersey
WSOX Red Lion, Pennsylvania
WSOY-FM Decatur, Illinois
WSPA-FM Spartanburg, South Carolina
WSPI Ellsworth, Illinois
WSPK Poughkeepsie, New York
WSPM Cloverdale, Indiana
WSPN Saratoga Springs, New York
WSPS Concord, New Hampshire
WSPT Stevens Point, Wisconsin
WSPX Bowman, South Carolina
WSPY-FM Plano, Illinois
WSQA Hornell, New York
WSQC-FM Oneonta, New York
WSQE Corning, New York
WSQG-FM Ithaca, New York
WSQH Decatur, Mississippi
WSQV(FM) Lock Haven, Pennsylvania
WSQX-FM Binghamton, New York
WSRB Lansing, Illinois
WSRC(FM) Waynetown, Indiana
WSRG Sturgeon Bay, Wisconsin
WSRI Sugar Grove, Illinois
WSRJ Honor, Michigan
WSRK Oneonta, New York
WSRM Coosa, Georgia
WSRN-FM Swarthmore, Pennsylvania
WSRS Worcester, Massachusetts
WSRT Gaylord, Michigan
WSRU Slippery Rock, Pennsylvania
WSRV Gainesville, Georgia
WSRW-FM Grand Rapids, Michigan
WSRZ-FM Coral Cove, Florida
WSSB(FM) Doraville, Georgia
WSSB-FM Orangeburg, South Carolina
WSSD Chicago, Illinois
WSSJ Rincon, Georgia
WSSK Saratoga Springs, New York
WSSL-FM Gray Court, South Carolina
WSSM(FM) Goshen, Indiana
WSSQ Sterling, Illinois
WSSR Joliet, Illinois
WSSW Platteville, Wisconsin
WSSX-FM Charleston, South Carolina
WSSY Pinehurst, Georgia
WSTB Streetsboro, Ohio
WSTF Andalusia, Alabama
WSTG Princeton, West Virginia
WSTH-FM Alexander City, Alabama
WSTI-FM Quitman, Georgia
WSTK Aurora, North Carolina
WSTM Kiel, Wisconsin
WSTO Owensboro, Kentucky
WSTQ Streator, Illinois
WSTR Smyrna, Georgia
WSTS Fairmont, North Carolina
WSTV-FM Frankfort, Kentucky
WSTW Wilmington, Delaware
WSTX-FM Christiansted, Virgin Islands
WSTZ-FM Vicksburg, Mississippi
WSUC-FM Cortland, New York
WSUE Sault Ste. Marie, Michigan
WSUF Noyack, New York
WSUL Monticello, New York
WSUM Madison, Wisconsin
WSUN-FM Holiday, Florida
WSUP Platteville, Wisconsin
WSUS Franklin, New Jersey
WSUW Whitewater, Wisconsin
WSVH Savannah, Georgia
WSVO Staunton, Virginia
WSWR Shelby, Ohio
WSWS(FM) Smithboro, Illinois
WSWT Peoria, Illinois
WSWV-FM Pennington Gap, Virginia
WSWW-FM Craigsville, West Virginia
WSYC-FM Shippensburg, Pennsylvania
WSYE Houston, Mississippi
WSYI Valley Station, Kentucky
WSYN Surfside Beach, South Carolina
WSYR-FM Gifford, Florida
WSYY-FM Millinocket, Maine
WTAC Burton, Michigan
WTAI Union City, Tennessee
WTAK-FM Hartselle, Alabama
WTAO-FM Herrin, Illinois
WTAW-FM Buffalo, Texas
WTBB Gadsden, Alabama
WTBD-FM Delhi, New York
WTBF-FM Brundidge, Alabama
WTBG Brownsville, Tennessee
WTBI-FM Greenville, South Carolina
WTBJ Oxford, Alabama
WTBK Manchester, Kentucky
WTBM Mexico, Maine
WTBX Hibbing, Minnesota
WTCB Orangeburg, South Carolina
WTCC Springfield, Massachusetts
WTCD Indianola, Mississippi
WTCF(FM) Wardenville, West Virginia
WTCJ-FM Cannelton, Indiana
WTCK Charlevoix, Michigan
WTCM-FM Traverse City, Michigan
WTCQ Vidalia, Georgia
WTCR-FM Huntington, West Virginia
WTCX Ripon, Wisconsin
WTDK Federalsburg, Maryland
WTDR-FM Talladega, Alabama
WTDY-FM Mount Horeb, Wisconsin
WTEB New Bern, North Carolina
WTFH Helen, Georgia
WTFM Kingsport, Tennessee
WTFX-FM Clarksville, Indiana
WTGA-FM Thomaston, Georgia
WTGD Bridgewater, Virginia
WTGE Baton Rouge, Louisiana
WTGG Amite, Louisiana
WTGN Lima, Ohio
WTGR Union City, Ohio
WTGV-FM Sandusky, Michigan
WTGY Charleston, Mississippi
WTGZ Union Springs, Alabama
WTHB-FM Wrens, Georgia
WTHD Lagrange, Indiana
WTHG Hinesville, Georgia
WTHI-FM Terre Haute, Indiana
WTHK Wilmington, Vermont
WTHL Somerset, Kentucky
WTHN Sault Ste. Marie, Michigan
WTHO-FM Thomson, Georgia
WTHP Gibson, Georgia
WTHS Holland, Michigan
WTHT Auburn, Maine
WTHX Vine Grove, Kentucky
WTIB Williamston, North Carolina
WTIC-FM Hartford, Connecticut
WTID Thomaston, Alabama
WTIF-FM Omega, Georgia
WTIM-FM Taylorville, Illinois
WTIP Grand Marais, Minnesota
WTIX-FM Galliano, Louisiana
WTJB Columbus, Georgia
WTJJ Dyer, Tennessee
WTJT Baker, Florida
WTJU Charlottesville, Virginia
WTJY Asheboro, North Carolina
WTKB-FM Atwood, Tennessee
WTKC Findlay, Ohio
WTKE-FM Niceville, Florida
WTKF Atlantic, North Carolina
WTKK Boston, Massachusetts
WTKL North Dartmouth, Massachusetts
WTKM-FM Hartford, Wisconsin
WTKS-FM Cocoa Beach, Florida
WTKU-FM Petersburg, New Jersey
WTKV Oswego, New York
WTKW Bridgeport, New York
WTKX-FM Pensacola, Florida
WTKY-FM Tompkinsville, Kentucky
WTLC-FM Greenwood, Indiana
WTLD Jesup, Georgia
WTLG Starke, Florida
WTLI Bear Creek Township, Michigan
WTLP Braddock Heights, Maryland
WTLQ-FM Punta Rassa, Florida
WTLR State College, Pennsylvania
WTLT Sanibel, Florida
WTLX Monona, Wisconsin
WTLZ Saginaw, Michigan
WTMB Tomah, Wisconsin
WTMD Towson, Maryland
WTMG Williston, Florida
WTMK Wanatah, Indiana
WTML Tullahoma, Tennessee
WTMM-FM Mechanicville, New York
WTMP-FM Dade City, Florida
WTMT Weaverville, North Carolina
WTMX Skokie, Illinois
WTMY(FM) Coon Rapids, Minnesota
WTNJ Mount Hope, West Virginia
WTNM Water Valley, Mississippi
WTNN Bristol, Vermont
WTNQ La Follette, Tennessee
WTNR Holland, Michigan
WTNS-FM Coshocton, Ohio
WTNT-FM Tallahassee, Florida
WTNV Tiptonville, Tennessee
WTOJ Carthage, New York
WTOK-FM San Juan, Puerto Rico
WTON-FM Staunton, Virginia
WTOP-FM Washington, District of Columbia
WTOS-FM Skowhegan, Maine
WTOT-FM Graceville, Florida
WTPA Palmyra, Pennsylvania
WTPG Whitehouse, Ohio
WTPL Hillsboro, New Hampshire
WTPM Aguadilla, Puerto Rico
WTPN Westby, Wisconsin
WTPO New Albany, Mississippi
WTPR-FM McKinnon, Tennessee
WTPT Forest City, North Carolina
WTQR Winston-Salem, North Carolina
WTQX Boothbay Harbor, Maine
WTRC-FM Niles, Michigan
WTRE(FM) Greensburg, Indiana
WTRG Gaston, North Carolina
WTRH Ramsey, Illinois
WTRK Freeland, Michigan
WTRM Winchester, Virginia
WTRS Dunnellon, Florida
WTRT Benton, Kentucky
WTRV Walker, Michigan
WTRW Carbondale, Pennsylvania
WTRW(FM) Carbondale, Pennsylvania
WTRY-FM Rotterdam, New York
WTRZ Spencer, Tennessee
WTSA-FM Brattleboro, Vermont
WTSC-FM Potsdam, New York
WTSE Benton, Tennessee
WTSG Carlinville, Illinois
WTSH-FM Aragon, Georgia
WTSM(FM) Woodville, Florida
WTSR Trenton, New Jersey
WTSS Buffalo, New York
WTSU Montgomery-Troy, Alabama
WTTC-FM Towanda, Pennsylvania
WTTH Margate City, New Jersey
WTTL-FM Madisonville, Kentucky
WTTS Bloomington, Indiana
WTTU Cookeville, Tennessee
WTTX-FM Appomattox, Virginia
WTUA Pinopolis, South Carolina
WTUE Dayton, Ohio
WTUF Boston, Georgia
WTUG-FM Northport, Alabama
WTUK Harlan, Kentucky
WTUL New Orleans, Louisiana
WTUR Upland, Indiana
WTUV-FM Eminence, Kentucky
WTUZ Uhrichsville, Ohio
WTVR-FM Richmond, Virginia
WTVY-FM Dothan, Alabama
WTWF Fairview, Pennsylvania
WTWS Houghton Lake, Michigan
WTWT Bradford, Pennsylvania
WTWX-FM Guntersville, Alabama
WTXO Ashland, Alabama
WTXR Toccoa Falls, Georgia
WTXT Fayette, Alabama
WTYB Bluffon, South Carolina
WTYD Deltaville, Virginia
WTYE Robinson, Illinois
WTYG Sparr, Florida
WTYJ Fayette, Mississippi
WTYL-FM Tylertown, Mississippi
WTYS-FM Marianna, Florida
WTZB Englewood, Florida
WTZI Rosemont, Illinois
WTZR Elizabethton, Tennessee
WUAG Greensboro, North Carolina
WUAL-FM Tuscaloosa, Alabama
WUAW Erwin, North Carolina
WUBA High Springs, Florida
WUBE-FM Cincinnati, Ohio
WUBJ Jamestown, New York
WUBK(FM) Enoree, South Carolina
WUBL Atlanta, Georgia
WUBS South Bend, Indiana
WUBT Russellville, Kentucky
WUBU South Bend, Indiana
WUCF-FM Orlando, Florida
WUCL Newton, Mississippi
WUCS Windsor Locks, Connecticut
WUCX-FM Bay City, Michigan
WUCZ Carthage, Tennessee
WUDR Dayton, Ohio
WUEC Eau Claire, Wisconsin
WUEV Evansville, Indiana
WUEZ Carterville, Illinois
WUFF-FM Eastman, Georgia
WUFM Columbus, Ohio
WUFN Albion, Michigan
WUFR Bedford, Pennsylvania
WUFT-FM Gainesville, Florida
WUGA Athens, Georgia
WUGN Midland, Michigan
WUGO Grayson, Kentucky
WUHT Birmingham, Alabama
WUHU Smiths Grove, Kentucky
WUIL Arcola, Illinois
WUIN Oak Island, North Carolina
WUIS Springfield, Illinois
WUJC St. Marks, Florida
WUJM Gulfport, Mississippi
WUKL Bethlehem, West Virginia
WUKQ-FM Mayaguez, Puerto Rico
WUKS St. Pauls, North Carolina
WUKV Portsmouth, Ohio
WUKY Lexington, Kentucky
WULF Hardinsburg, Kentucky
WULS Broxton, Georgia
WUMB-FM Boston, Massachusetts
WUMC Elizabethton, Tennessee
WUMD North Dartmouth, Massachusetts
WUME-FM Paoli, Indiana
WUMI Newberry, Michigan
WUMJ Fayetteville, Georgia
WUML Lowell, Massachusetts
WUMM Machias, Maine
WUMR Memphis, Tennessee
WUMS University, Mississippi
WUMX Rome, New York
WUNC Chapel Hill, North Carolina
WUND-FM Manteo, North Carolina
WUNH Durham, New Hampshire
WUNV Albany, Georgia
WUNY Utica, New York
WUOG Athens, Georgia
WUOL-FM Louisville, Kentucky
WUOM Ann Arbor, Michigan
WUOT Knoxville, Tennessee
WUOW Milford, New York
WUPE-FM North Adams, Massachusetts
WUPF Powers, Michigan
WUPG Republic, Michigan
WUPI Presque Isle, Maine
WUPJ Escanaba, Michigan
WUPK Marquette, Michigan
WUPM Ironwood, Michigan
WUPN Paradise, Michigan
WUPS Houghton Lake, Michigan
WUPT Gwinn, Michigan
WUPX Marquette, Michigan
WUPY Ontonagon, Michigan
WUPZ Chocolay Township, Michigan
WURB Cross City, Florida
WURC Holly Springs, Mississippi
WURI Manteo, North Carolina
WURV(FM) Richmond, Virginia
WUSB Stony Brook, New York
WUSC-FM Columbia, South Carolina
WUSF Tampa, Florida
WUSH Poquoson, Virginia
WUSI Olney, Illinois
WUSJ Madison, Mississippi
WUSL Philadelphia, Pennsylvania
WUSM-FM Hattiesburg, Mississippi
WUSN Chicago, Illinois
WUSO Springfield, Ohio
WUSQ-FM Winchester, Virginia
WUSR Scranton, Pennsylvania
WUSY Cleveland, Tennessee
WUSZ Virginia, Minnesota
WUTC Chattanooga, Tennessee
WUTK-FM Knoxville, Tennessee
WUTM Martin, Tennessee
WUTQ-FM Utica, New York
WUTS Sewanee, Tennessee
WUUB Jupiter, Florida

WUUF Sodus, New York
WUUQ South Pittsburg, Tennessee
WUUU Franklinton, Louisiana
WUUZ Cooperstown, Pennsylvania
WUVA Charlottesville, Virginia
WUVT-FM Blacksburg, Virginia
WUWF Pensacola, Florida
WUWG Carrollton, Georgia
WUWM Milwaukee, Wisconsin
WUWS Ashland, Wisconsin
WUZR Bicknell, Indiana
WUZZ Saegertown, Pennsylvania
WVAC-FM Adrian, Michigan
WVAF Charleston, West Virginia
WVAQ Morgantown, West Virginia
WVAS Montgomery, Alabama
WVAZ Oak Park, Illinois
WVBB Elliston-Lafayette, Virginia
WVBB(FM) Elliston-Lafayette, Virginia
WVBC Bethany, West Virginia
WVBD Fayetteville, West Virginia
WVBE-FM Lynchburg, Virginia
WVBG-FM Redwood, Mississippi
WVBH Beach Haven West, New Jersey
WVBO Winneconne, Wisconsin
WVBR-FM Ithaca, New York
WVBU-FM Lewisburg, Pennsylvania
WVBV Medford Lakes, New Jersey
WVBW Suffolk, Virginia
WVBZ High Point, North Carolina
WVCF Eau Claire, Wisconsin
WVCM Iron Mountain, Michigan
WVCN Baraga, Michigan
WVCO Loris, South Carolina
WVCP Gallatin, Tennessee
WVCR-FM Loudonville, New York
WVCS Owen, Wisconsin
WVCT Keavy, Kentucky
WVCX Tomah, Wisconsin
WVCY-FM Milwaukee, Wisconsin
WVDA Valdosta, Georgia
WVEE Atlanta, Georgia
WVEK-FM Weber City, Virginia
WVEP Martinsburg, West Virginia
WVES Accomac, Virginia
WVEZ St. Matthews, Kentucky
WVFA Lebanon, New Hampshire
WVFB Celina, Tennessee
WVFJ-FM Manchester, Georgia
WVFL Fond Du Lac, Wisconsin
WVFM Kalamazoo, Michigan
WVFS Tallahassee, Florida
WVGA Lakeland, Georgia
WVGN Charlotte Amalie, Virgin Islands
WVGR Grand Rapids, Michigan
WVGS Statesboro, Georgia
WVGV West Union, West Virginia
WVHC Herkimer, New York
WVHL Farmville, Virginia
WVHM Benton, Kentucky
WVHT Norfolk, Virginia
WVIA-FM Scranton, Pennsylvania
WVIB Holton, Michigan
WVIC Jackson, Michigan
WVIJ Port Charlotte, Florida
WVIK Rock Island, Illinois
WVIL Virginia, Illinois
WVIM-FM Coldwater, Mississippi
WVIN-FM Bath, New York
WVIP New Rochelle, New York
WVIQ Christiansted, Virgin Islands
WVIS Vieques, Puerto Rico
WVIV-FM Highland Park, Illinois
WVIX Lemont, Illinois
WVJC Mount Carmel, Illinois
WVJP-FM Caguas, Puerto Rico
WVJZ Charlotte Amalie, Virgin Islands
WVKC Galesburg, Illinois
WVKF Shadyside, Ohio
WVKL Norfolk, Virginia
WVKM Matewan, West Virginia
WVKO-FM Johnstown, Ohio
WVKR-FM Poughkeepsie, New York
WVKS Toledo, Ohio
WVKV Nashville, Georgia
WVKX Irwinton, Georgia
WVKY Shelbyville, Kentucky
WVKY(FM) Shelbyville, Kentucky
WVLC Mannsville, Kentucky
WVLE Scottsville, Kentucky
WVLF Norwood, New York
WVLI Kankakee, Illinois
WVLK-FM Richmond, Kentucky
WVLO Cridersville, Ohio
WVLS Monterey, Virginia
WVLT Vineland, New Jersey
WVLY-FM Milton, Pennsylvania
WVMA(FM) Norfolk, Virginia
WVMC-FM Mansfield, Ohio
WVMD Romney, West Virginia
WVME Meadville, Pennsylvania
WVMJ Conway, New Hampshire
WVML Millersburg, Ohio
WVMM Grantham, Pennsylvania
WVMN New Castle, Pennsylvania
WVMP Vinton, Virginia
WVMR-FM Hillsboro, West Virginia
WVMS Sandusky, Ohio
WVMW-FM Scranton, Pennsylvania
WVMX Westerville, Ohio
WVNA-FM Muscle Shoals, Alabama
WVNH Concord, New Hampshire
WVNI Nashville, Indiana
WVNK Manchester, Vermont
WVNL Vandalia, Illinois
WVNN-FM Trinity, Alabama
WVNO-FM Mansfield, Ohio
WVNP Wheeling, West Virginia
WVNU Greenfield, Ohio
WVNV Malone, New York
WVNW Burnham, Pennsylvania
WVOA-FM Mexico, New York
WVOB Dothan, Alabama
WVOD Manteo, North Carolina
WVOF Fairfield, Connecticut
WVOH-FM Nicholls, Georgia
WVOK-FM Oxford, Alabama
WVOM Howland, Maine
WVOR Canandaigua, New York
WVOS-FM Liberty, New York
WVOW-FM Logan, West Virginia
WVOZ-FM Carolina, Puerto Rico
WVPA St. Johnsbury, Vermont
WVPB Beckley, West Virginia
WVPC Franklin, West Virginia
WVPE Elkhart, Indiana
WVPG Parkersburg, West Virginia
WVPH Piscataway, New Jersey
WVPL Dozier, Alabama
WVPM Morgantown, West Virginia
WVPN Charleston, West Virginia
WVPR Windsor, Vermont
WVPS Burlington, Vermont
WVPW Buckhannon, West Virginia
WVQM Augusta, Maine
WVRA Enfield, North Carolina
WVRB Wilmore, Kentucky
WVRC-FM Spencer, West Virginia
WVRD Zebulon, North Carolina
WVRE Dickeyville, Wisconsin
WVRH Norlina, North Carolina
WVRI Clifton Forge, Virginia
WVRK Columbus, Georgia
WVRL Elizabeth City, North Carolina
WVRN Wittenberg, Wisconsin
WVRP Roanoke Rapids, North Carolina
WVRQ-FM Viroqua, Wisconsin
WVRT Mill Hall, Pennsylvania
WVRU-FM Radford, Virginia
WVRV Pine Level, Alabama
WVRW Glenville, West Virginia
WVRY Waverly, Tennessee
WVRZ Mount Carmel, Pennsylvania
WVSB Romney, West Virginia
WVSD Itta Bena, Mississippi
WVSE Christiansted, Virgin Islands
WVSH Huntington, Indiana
WVSI Mt. Vernon, Illinois
WVSL-FM Riverside, Pennsylvania
WVSP-FM Yorktown, Virginia
WVSR-FM Charleston, West Virginia
WVSS Menomonie, Wisconsin
WVST-FM Petersburg, Virginia
WVSU-FM Birmingham, Alabama
WVSZ Chesterfield, South Carolina
WVTC Randolph Center, Vermont
WVTF Roanoke, Virginia
WVTI Brighton, Vermont
WVTK Port Henry, New York
WVTQ Sunderland, Vermont
WVTR Marion, Virginia
WVTS-FM Dunbar, West Virginia
WVTT Portville, New York
WVTU Charlottesville, Virginia
WVTW Charlottesville, Virginia
WVUA-FM Tuscaloosa, Alabama
WVUB Vincennes, Indiana
WVUD Newark, Delaware
WVUM Coral Gables, Florida
WVUR-FM Valparaiso, Indiana
WVUV-FM Fagaitua, American Samoa
WVVE Panama City Beach, Florida
WVVI-FM Christiansted, Virgin Islands
WVVL Elba, Alabama
WVVR Hopkinsville, Kentucky
WVVS-FM Valdosta, Georgia
WVVV Williamstown, West Virginia
WVWC Buckhannon, West Virginia
WVWV Huntington, West Virginia
WVXG Mount Gilead, Ohio
WVXR Randolph, Vermont
WVXU Cincinnati, Ohio
WVYA Williamsport, Pennsylvania
WVYB Holly Hill, Florida
WVYC York, Pennsylvania
WVYN Bluford, Illinois
WVZA Murphysboro, Illinois
WWAC Ocean City, New Jersey
WWAG McKee, Kentucky
WWAV Santa Rosa Beach, Florida
WWAX Hermantown, Minnesota
WWBB Providence, Rhode Island
WWBD Sumter, South Carolina
WWBE Mifflinburg, Pennsylvania
WWBL Washington, Indiana
WWBN Tuscola, Michigan
WWBR Big Rapids, Michigan
WWBU Radford, Virginia
WWCF McConnellsburg, Pennsylvania
WWCJ Cape May, New Jersey
WWCK-FM Flint, Michigan
WWCM Standish, Michigan
WWCT Bartonville, Illinois
WWCU Cullowhee, North Carolina
WWDC Washington, District of Columbia
WWDE-FM Hampton, Virginia
WWDL Plainfield, Indiana
WWDM Sumter, South Carolina
WWDV Zion, Illinois
WWDW Alberta, Virginia
WWEB Wallingford, Connecticut
WWED Spotsylvania, Virginia
WWEG Myersville, Maryland
WWEI Easthampton, Massachusetts
WWEL London, Kentucky
WWEM Rustburg, Virginia
WWEN Wentworth, Wisconsin
WWES Mount Kisco, New York
WWET Valdosta, Georgia
WWEV-FM Cumming, Georgia
WWFA St. Florian, Alabama
WWFF-FM New Market, Alabama
WWFG Ocean City, Maryland
WWFJ East Fayetteville, North Carolina
WWFM Trenton, New Jersey
WWFN-FM Lake City, South Carolina
WWFP Brigantine, New Jersey
WWFR Stuart, Florida
WWFS New York, New York
WWFX Southbridge, Massachusetts
WWFY Berlin, Vermont
WWGF Donalsonville, Georgia
WWGM Alamo, Tennessee
WWGN Ottawa, Illinois
WWGO Charleston, Illinois
WWGR Fort Myers, Florida
WWGV Grove City, Ohio
WWGY Grove City, Pennsylvania
WWHC Oakland, Maryland
WWHG Evansville, Wisconsin
WWHI Muncie, Indiana
WWHK Concord, New Hampshire
WWHP Farmer City, Illinois
WWHQ Meredith, New Hampshire
WWHR Bowling Green, Kentucky
WWHS-FM Hampden-Sydney, Virginia
WWHT Syracuse, New York
WWIB Hallie, Wisconsin
WWIL-FM Wilmington, North Carolina
WWIN-FM Glen Burnie, Maryland
WWIO-FM Brunswick, Georgia
WWIP Cheriton, Virginia
WWIQ Camden, New Jersey
WWIS-FM Black River Falls, Wisconsin
WWIZ West Middlesex, Pennsylvania
WWJD Pippa Passes, Kentucky
WWJM New Lexington, Ohio
WWJO St. Cloud, Minnesota
WWKA Orlando, Florida
WWKC Caldwell, Ohio
WWKF Fulton, Kentucky
WWKI Kokomo, Indiana
WWKL Mechanicsburg, Pennsylvania
WWKM Rochelle, Georgia
WWKN Morgantown, Kentucky
WWKR Hart, Michigan
WWKS Cruz Bay, Virgin Islands
WWKT-FM Kingstree, South Carolina
WWKX Woonsocket, Rhode Island
WWKY Providence, Kentucky
WWKZ Okolona, Mississippi
WWL-FM Kenner, Louisiana
WWLA South Charleston, West Virginia
WWLB Midlothian, Virginia
WWLC Cross City, Florida
WWLD Cairo, Georgia
WWLF-FM Oswego, New York
WWLG Peachtree City, Georgia
WWLI Providence, Rhode Island
WWLL Sebring, Florida
WWLN Lincoln, Maine
WWLR Lyndonville, Vermont
WWLT Manchester, Kentucky
WWLU Lincoln University, Pennsylvania
WWLV(FM) Lexington, North Carolina
WWLW Clarksburg, West Virginia
WWMC Lynchburg, Virginia
WWMG Millbrook, Alabama
WWMJ Ellsworth, Maine
WWMP Waterbury, Vermont
WWMR Saltillo, Mississippi
WWMS Oxford, Mississippi
WWMX Baltimore, Maryland
WWNJ Toms River Township, New Jersey
WWNO New Orleans, Louisiana
WWNQ Forest Acres, South Carolina
WWNU Irmo, South Carolina
WWNW New Wilmington, Pennsylvania
WWOD Hartford, Vermont
WWOF(FM) Tallahassee, Florida
WWOG Cookeville, Tennessee
WWOJ Avon Park, Florida
WWOT Altoona, Pennsylvania
WWOZ New Orleans, Louisiana
WWPG Eutaw, Alabama
WWPH Princeton Junction, New Jersey
WWPJ Pen Argyl, Pennsylvania
WWPL Smithfield, North Carolina
WWPN Westernport, Maryland
WWPR-FM New York, New York
WWPT Westport, Connecticut
WWPV-FM Colchester, Vermont
WWPW(FM) Atlanta, Georgia
WWQA North Granby, Connecticut
WWQM-FM Middleton, Wisconsin
WWQQ-FM Wilmington, North Carolina
WWQW(FM) Wartburg, Tennessee
WWQY Yadkin, North Carolina
WWQZ Baptist Village, Massachusetts
WWRA Clinton, Louisiana
WWRM Tampa, Florida
WWRQ-FM Valdosta, Georgia
WWRR Scranton, Pennsylvania
WWRW Mt. Sterling, Kentucky
WWRX Ledyard, Connecticut
WWRZ Fort Meade, Florida
WWSE Jamestown, New York
WWSL Philadelphia, Mississippi
WWSN Whitehall, Michigan
WWSP Stevens Point, Wisconsin
WWSR Lima, Ohio
WWSS Tuscarora Township, Michigan
WWST Sevierville, Tennessee
WWSU Fairborn, Ohio
WWSW-FM Pittsburgh, Pennsylvania
WWTA Marion, Massachusetts
WWTG Carpentersville, Illinois
WWTH Oscoda, Michigan
WWTN Hendersonville, Tennessee
WWUF Waycross, Georgia
WWUH West Hartford, Connecticut
WWUN-FM Friar's Point, Mississippi
WWUS Big Pine Key, Florida
WWUU Washington, Mississippi

WWUZ Bowling Green, Virginia
WWVA-FM Canton, Georgia
WWVO Albany, Georgia
WWVR West Terre Haute, Indiana
WWVU-FM Morgantown, West Virginia
WWVY Waverly, Ohio
WWWA Winslow, Maine
WWWD Bolingbroke, Georgia
WWWH-FM Haleyville, Alabama
WWWI-FM Pillager, Minnesota
WWWK Islamorada, Florida
WWWM-FM Sylvania, Ohio
WWWQ Atlanta, Georgia
WWWT-FM Manassas, Virginia
WWWV Charlottesville, Virginia
WWWW-FM Ann Arbor, Michigan
WWWX Oshkosh, Wisconsin
WWWY North Vernon, Indiana
WWWZ Summerville, South Carolina
WWXM Garden City, South Carolina
WWXT Prince Frederick, Maryland
WWXX Warrenton, Virginia
WWYL Chenango Bridge, New York
WWYN McKenzie, Tennessee
WWYW Dundee, Illinois
WWYY Belvidere, New Jersey
WWYZ Waterbury, Connecticut
WWZD-FM New Albany, Mississippi
WWZW Buena Vista, Virginia
WWZY Long Branch, New Jersey
WXAC Reading, Pennsylvania
WXAF Charleston, West Virginia
WXAJ Hillsboro, Illinois
WXAN Ava, Illinois
WXBA Brentwood, New York
WXBB Erie, Pennsylvania
WXBC Hardinsburg, Kentucky
WXBE Beaufort, North Carolina
WXBM-FM Milton, Florida
WXBN Berryville, Virginia
WXBP Corinth, Maine
WXBQ-FM Bristol, Virginia
WXBW Gallipolis, Ohio
WXBX Rural Retreat, Virginia
WXCC Williamson, West Virginia
WXCF-FM Big Island, Virginia
WXCH Columbus, Indiana
WXCI Danbury, Connecticut
WXCL Pekin, Illinois
WXCM Whitesville, Kentucky
WXCR New Martinsville, West Virginia
WXCV Homosassa Springs, Florida
WXCX Siren, Wisconsin
WXCY Havre De Grace, Maryland
WXDE Lewes, Delaware
WXDJ North Miami Beach, Florida
WXDU Durham, North Carolina
WXDX-FM Pittsburgh, Pennsylvania
WXEF Effingham, Illinois
WXEG Beavercreek, Ohio
WXER Plymouth, Wisconsin
WXEX-FM Sanford, Maine
WXFL Florence, Alabama
WXFM-FM Mount Zion, Illinois
WXFX Prattville, Alabama
WXGL St. Petersburg, Florida
WXGM-FM Gloucester, Virginia
WXGN Egg Harbor Township, New Jersey
WXHB Richton, Mississippi
WXHC Homer, New York
WXHL-FM Christiana, Delaware
WXHM Middletown, Delaware
WXHT Madison, Florida
WXIL Elizabeth, West Virginia
WXIV Lumpkin, Georgia
WXIZ Waverly, Ohio
WXJC-FM Cordova, Alabama
WXJM Harrisonburg, Virginia
WXJY Georgetown, South Carolina
WXJZ Gainesville, Florida
WXKB Cape Coral, Florida
WXKC Erie, Pennsylvania
WXKE Fort Wayne, Indiana
WXKQ-FM Whitesburg, Kentucky
WXKR Port Clinton, Ohio
WXKS-FM Medford, Massachusetts
WXKT Maysville, Georgia
WXKU-FM Austin, Indiana
WXKV Selmer, Tennessee
WXKY-FM Stanford, Kentucky
WXKZ-FM Prestonsburg, Kentucky
WXLB Boonville, New York
WXLC Waukegan, Illinois
WXLF Hartford, Vermont
WXLG North Creek, New York
WXLH Blue Mountain Lake, New York
WXLK Roanoke, Virginia
WXLO Fitchburg, Massachusetts
WXLP Moline, Illinois
WXLQ Bristol, Vermont
WXLR Harold, Kentucky
WXLS Tupper Lake, New York
WXLT Christopher, Illinois
WXLU Peru, New York
WXLV Schnecksville, Pennsylvania
WXLX Lajas, Puerto Rico
WXLY North Charleston, South Carolina
WXLZ-FM Lebanon, Virginia
WXMA Louisville, Kentucky
WXMF Marion, Ohio
WXMG London, Ohio
WXMJ Cambridge Springs, Pennsylvania
WXMK Dock Junction, Georgia
WXML Upper Sandusky, Ohio
WXMT Smethport, Pennsylvania
WXMX Millington, Tennessee
WXMZ Hartford, Kentucky
WXNR Grifton, North Carolina
WXNU St. Anne, Illinois
WXNY-FM New York, New York
WXOF Yankeetown, Florida
WXOQ Selmer, Tennessee
WXOS East St. Louis, Illinois
WXOU Auburn Hills, Michigan
WXPH Middletown, Pennsylvania
WXPK Briarcliff Manor, New York
WXPL Fitchburg, Massachusetts
WXPN Philadelphia, Pennsylvania
WXPR Rhinelander, Wisconsin
WXPW Wausau, Wisconsin
WXPZ Clyde Township, Michigan
WXQR-FM Jacksonville, North Carolina
WXRA Inglis, Florida
WXRB Dudley, Massachusetts
WXRC Hickory, North Carolina
WXRD Crown Point, Indiana
WXRG Athol, Massachusetts
WXRI Winston-Salem, North Carolina
WXRK New York, New York
WXRO Beaver Dam, Wisconsin
WXRR Hattiesburg, Mississippi
WXRS-FM Portal, Georgia
WXRT Chicago, Illinois
WXRV Andover, Massachusetts
WXRX Belvidere, Illinois
WXRZ Corinth, Mississippi
WXSH Pocomoke City, Maryland
WXSR Quincy, Florida
WXSS Wauwatosa, Wisconsin
WXST Hollywood, South Carolina
WXTA Edinboro, Pennsylvania
WXTB Clearwater, Florida
WXTC Greenville, Pennsylvania
WXTG-FM Virginia Beach, Virginia
WXTK West Yarmouth, Massachusetts
WXTL Syracuse, New York
WXTP North Windham, Maine
WXTQ Athens, Ohio
WXTS-FM Toledo, Ohio
WXTU Philadelphia, Pennsylvania
WXUR Herkimer, New York
WXUT Toledo, Ohio
WXVS Waycross, Georgia
WXVU Villanova, Pennsylvania
WXWX Marietta, Mississippi
WXXB Delphi, Indiana
WXXC Marion, Indiana
WXXE Fenner, New York
WXXF Loudonville, Ohio
WXXF(FM) Pittsburgh, Pennsylvania
WXXI-FM Rochester, New York
WXXJ Jacksonville, Florida
WXXK Lebanon, New Hampshire
WXXL Tavares, Florida
WXXM Sun Prairie, Wisconsin
WXXQ Freeport, Illinois
WXXR(FM) Seelyville, Indiana
WXXS Lancaster, New Hampshire
WXXX South Burlington, Vermont
WXXY Houghton, New York
WXXY(FM) Houghton, New York
WXXZ Grand Marais, Minnesota
WXYC Chapel Hill, North Carolina
WXYK Gulfport, Mississippi
WXYM Tomah, Wisconsin
WXYT-FM Detroit, Michigan
WXYX Bayamon, Puerto Rico
WXYY(FM) Port Royal, South Carolina
WXZO Willsboro, New York
WXZQ Piketon, Ohio
WXZZ Georgetown, Kentucky
WYAB Flora, Mississippi
WYAD Benton, Mississippi
WYAI Scotia, New York
WYAJ Sudbury, Massachusetts
WYAR Yarmouth, Maine
WYAS Luquillo, Puerto Rico
WYAV Myrtle Beach, South Carolina
WYAY Gainesville, Georgia
WYAZ Yazoo City, Mississippi
WYBA Coldwater, Michigan
WYBB Folly Beach, South Carolina
WYBC-FM New Haven, Connecticut
WYBF Radnor Township, Pennsylvania
WYBH Fayetteville, North Carolina
WYBJ Newton Grove, North Carolina
WYBK(FM) Chattanooga, Tennessee
WYBL Ashtabula, Ohio
WYBP Fort Lauderdale, Florida
WYBR Big Rapids, Michigan
WYBV Wakarusa, Indiana
WYBX(FM) Key West, Florida
WYBZ Crooksville, Ohio
WYCA Crete, Illinois
WYCD Detroit, Michigan
WYCE Wyoming, Michigan
WYCM Charlton, Massachusetts
WYCR York-Hanover, Pennsylvania
WYCS Yorktown, Virginia
WYCT Pensacola, Florida
WYCY Hawley, Pennsylvania
WYDE-FM Cullman, Alabama
WYDK Eufaula, Alabama
WYDL Middleton, Tennessee
WYDM Monroe, Michigan
WYDR Neenah-Menasha, Wisconsin
WYDS Decatur, Illinois
WYEC Cambridge, Illinois
WYEP-FM Pittsburgh, Pennsylvania
WYER Carmi, Illinois
WYEZ Murrells Inlet, South Carolina
WYFA Waynesboro, Georgia
WYFB Gainesville, Florida
WYFC Clinton, Tennessee
WYFD Decatur, Alabama
WYFE Tarpon Springs, Florida
WYFG Gaffney, South Carolina
WYFH North Charleston, South Carolina
WYFI Norfolk, Virginia
WYFJ Ashland, Virginia
WYFK Columbus, Georgia
WYFL Henderson, North Carolina
WYFM Sharon, Pennsylvania
WYFO Lakeland, Florida
WYFP Harpswell, Maine
WYFQ-FM Wadesboro, North Carolina
WYFS Savannah, Georgia
WYFT Luray, Virginia
WYFU Masontown, Pennsylvania
WYFV Cayce, South Carolina
WYFW Winder, Georgia
WYFX Mount Vernon, Indiana
WYFY Cambridge, Ohio
WYFZ Belleview, Florida
WYGB Edinburgh, Indiana
WYGC High Springs, Florida
WYGE London, Kentucky
WYGG Asbury Park, New Jersey
WYGL-FM Elizabethville, Pennsylvania
WYGO Madisonville, Tennessee
WYGS Hope, Indiana
WYGY Fort Thomas, Kentucky
WYGY(FM) Fort Thomas, Kentucky
WYHT Mansfield, Ohio
WYJB Albany, New York
WYJC Greenville, Florida
WYJK-FM Bellaire, Ohio
WYJZ Fearsville, Kentucky
WYKE(FM) Inglis, Florida
WYKL Crestline, Ohio
WYKR-FM Haverhill, New Hampshire
WYKS Gainesville, Florida
WYKT Wilmington, Illinois
WYKV Ravena, New York
WYKX Escanaba, Michigan
WYKY Science Hill, Kentucky
WYKZ Beaufort, South Carolina
WYLC Jackson, Kentucky
WYLD-FM New Orleans, Louisiana
WYLJ(FM) Tullahoma, Tennessee
WYLK Lacombe, Louisiana
WYLV Maynardville, Tennessee
WYLV(FM) Maynardville, Tennessee
WYMG Chatham, Illinois
WYMJ New Martinsville, West Virginia
WYMS Milwaukee, Wisconsin
WYMX Greenwood, Mississippi
WYMY Goldsboro, North Carolina
WYNA Calabash, North Carolina
WYND-FM Hatteras, North Carolina
WYNG Mount Carmel, Illinois
WYNJ Blackduck, Minnesota
WYNK-FM Baton Rouge, Louisiana
WYNN-FM Florence, South Carolina
WYNR Waycross, Georgia
WYNS Waynesville, Ohio
WYNT Caledonia, Ohio
WYNU Milan, Tennessee
WYNW Birnamwood, Wisconsin
WYNZ South Portland, Maine
WYOO Springfield, Florida
WYOR Republic, Ohio
WYOY Gluckstadt, Mississippi
WYPF Frederick, Maryland
WYPL Memphis, Tennessee
WYPO Ocean City, Maryland
WYPR Baltimore, Maryland
WYQE Naguabo, Puerto Rico
WYQS Mars Hill, North Carolina
WYRB Genoa, Illinois
WYRD-FM Simpsonville, South Carolina
WYRE-FM Saint Augustine Beach, Florida
WYRK Buffalo, New York
WYRO McArthur, Ohio
WYRQ-FM Little Falls, Minnesota
WYRR Lakewood, New York
WYRS Manahawkin, New Jersey
WYRY Hinsdale, New Hampshire
WYSA Wauseon, Ohio
WYSB Springfield, Kentucky
WYSM Lima, Ohio
WYSO Yellow Springs, Ohio
WYSP Dushore, Pennsylvania
WYSS Sault Ste. Marie, Michigan
WYSU Youngstown, Ohio
WYSX Morristown, New York
WYSZ Maumee, Ohio
WYTE Marshfield, Wisconsin
WYTF Indianola, Mississippi
WYTJ Linton, Indiana
WYTK Rogersville, Alabama
WYTL Wyomissing, Pennsylvania
WYTM-FM Fayetteville, Tennessee
WYTN Youngstown, Ohio
WYTT Emporia, Virginia
WYTZ Bridgman, Michigan
WYUL Chateaugay, New York
WYUM Mount Vernon, Georgia
WYUU Safety Harbor, Florida
WYVK Middleport, Ohio
WYVL(FM) Youngsville, Pennsylvania
WYVN Saugatuck, Michigan
WYVS Spectacular, New York
WYXB Indianapolis, Indiana
WYXL Ithaca, New York
WYXY(FM) Danville, Illinois
WYYD Amherst, Virginia
WYYS Streator, Illinois
WYYU Dalton, Georgia
WYYX Bonifay, Florida
WYYY Syracuse, New York
WYZB Mary Esther, Florida
WYZO-FM Portage, Michigan
WYZY Saranac, New York
WZAC-FM Danville, West Virginia
WZAD Wurtsboro, New York
WZAE Wadley, Georgia
WZAI Brewster, Massachusetts
WZAK Cleveland, Ohio
WZAQ Louisa, Kentucky
WZAR Ponce, Puerto Rico
WZAT Tybee Island, Georgia
WZAX Nashville, North Carolina
WZBA Westminster, Maryland

WZBB Stanleytown, Virginia
WZBC Newton, Massachusetts
WZBD Berne, Indiana
WZBG Litchfield, Connecticut
WZBH Georgetown, Delaware
WZBN Camilla, Georgia
WZBQ Carrollton, Alabama
WZBT Gettysburg, Pennsylvania
WZBX Rocky Ford, Georgia
WZBZ Pleasantville, New Jersey
WZCA Quebradillas, Puerto Rico
WZCH Warner Robins, Georgia
WZCP Chillicothe, Ohio
WZCR Hudson, New York
WZDB Sykesville, Pennsylvania
WZDG Scotts Hill, North Carolina
WZDM Vincennes, Indiana
WZDQ Humboldt, Tennessee
WZDR(FM) Sturgeon Bay, Wisconsin
WZEB Ocean View, Delaware
WZEC Strasburg, Mississippi
WZEE Madison, Wisconsin
WZET Hormigueros, Puerto Rico
WZEV Lineville, Alabama
WZEW Fairhope, Alabama
WZEZ Goochland, Virginia
WZFJ(FM) Breezy Point, Minnesota
WZFM Narrows, Virginia
WZFT Baltimore, Maryland
WZFX Whiteville, North Carolina
WZGC Atlanta, Georgia
WZGL Charleston, Illinois
WZGN Crozet, Virginia
WZGO Aurora, North Carolina
WZHL New Augusta, Mississippi
WZHT Troy, Alabama
WZID Manchester, New Hampshire
WZIM(FM) Lexington, Illinois
WZIN Charlotte Amalie, Virgin Islands
WZIP Akron, Ohio
WZIQ Smithville, Georgia
WZJS Banner Elk, North Carolina
WZJZ Port Charlotte, Florida
WZKB Wallace, North Carolina
WZKL Woodstock, Illinois
WZKM Waynesboro, Mississippi
WZKN(FM) Ridgebury, Pennsylvania
WZKR Collinsville, Mississippi
WZKS Union, Mississippi
WZKV Dyersburg, Tennessee
WZKX Bay St. Louis, Mississippi
WZKZ Alfred, New York
WZKZ(FM) Alfred, New York
WZLA-FM Abbeville, South Carolina
WZLD Petal, Mississippi
WZLF Bellows Falls, Vermont
WZLK Virgie, Kentucky
WZLQ Tupelo, Mississippi
WZLR Xenia, Ohio
WZLT Lexington, Tennessee
WZLX Boston, Massachusetts
WZLY Wellesley, Massachusetts
WZMB Greenville, North Carolina
WZMJ Batesburg, South Carolina
WZMR Altamont, New York
WZMT Ponce, Puerto Rico
WZMX Hartford, Connecticut
WZNB New Bern, North Carolina
WZNE Brighton, New York
WZNF Lumberton, Mississippi
WZNJ Demopolis, Alabama
WZNL Norway, Michigan
WZNP Newark, Ohio
WZNS Fort Walton Beach, Florida
WZNT San Juan, Puerto Rico
WZNX Sullivan, Illinois
WZNY Augusta, Georgia
WZOC Plymouth, Indiana
WZOE-FM Princeton, Illinois
WZOK Rockford, Illinois
WZOL Vieques, Puerto Rico
WZOM Defiance, Ohio
WZOO-FM Edgewood, Ohio
WZOR Mishicot, Wisconsin
WZOZ Oneonta, New York
WZPE Bath, North Carolina
WZPL Greenfield, Indiana
WZPN Farmington, Illinois
WZPR Nags Head, North Carolina
WZPW Peoria, Illinois
WZRD Chicago, Illinois
WZRG(FM) Kulpmont, Pennsylvania
WZRI Spring Lake, North Carolina
WZRN Norlina, North Carolina
WZRR Birmingham, Alabama
WZRT Rutland, Vermont
WZRU Garysburg, North Carolina
WZRV Front Royal, Virginia
WZRX-FM Fort Shawnee, Ohio
WZSN Greenwood, South Carolina
WZSP Nocatee, Florida
WZSR Woodstock, Illinois
WZST Westover, West Virginia
WZTF Scranton, South Carolina
WZTH Tusculum, Tennessee
WZTK Burlington, North Carolina
WZTR Dahlonega, Georgia
WZUN Phoenix, New York
WZUP La Grange, North Carolina
WZUS Macon, Illinois
WZUU Mattawan, Michigan
WZVA Marion, Virginia
WZVN Lowell, Indiana
WZWP West Union, Ohio
WZWW Bellefonte, Pennsylvania
WZWZ Kokomo, Indiana
WZXE East Nottingham, Pennsylvania
WZXH Hagerstown, Maryland
WZXL Wildwood, New Jersey
WZXM Harrisburg, Pennsylvania
WZXP Au Sable, New York
WZXQ Chambersburg, Pennsylvania
WZXR South Williamsport, Pennsylvania
WZXV Palmyra, New York
WZXX Lawrenceburg, Tennessee
WZYP Athens, Alabama
WZYZ Spencer, Tennessee
WZZD Warwick, Pennsylvania
WZZE Glen Mills, Pennsylvania
WZZG Toomsboro, Georgia
WZZH Honesdale, Pennsylvania
WZZK(FM) Bedford, Virginia
WZZK-FM Birmingham, Alabama
WZZL Reidland, Kentucky
WZZN Oneonta, Alabama
WZZO Bethlehem, Pennsylvania
WZZP Hopkinsville, Kentucky
WZZR Riviera Beach, Florida
WZZS Zolfo Springs, Florida
WZZT Morrison, Illinois
WZZU Lynchburg, Virginia
WZZY Winchester, Indiana
WZZZ Portsmouth, Ohio
XETRAFM Tijuana, Mexico
XHRMFM Tijuana, Mexico

US AM Stations by Frequency

1000 khz

KBIB Marion, Texas
KCEO Vista, California
KFLG Bullhead City, Arizona
KKIM Albuquerque, New Mexico
KOMO Seattle, Washington
KSTA Coleman, Texas
KTOK Oklahoma City, Oklahoma
KXRB Sioux Falls, South Dakota
WCCD Parma, Ohio
WCMX Leominster, Massachusetts
WJBW Jupiter, Florida
WDJL Huntsville, Alabama
WIOO Carlisle, Pennsylvania
WKDE Altavista, Virginia
WKVG Jenkins, Kentucky
WLNL Horseheads, New York
WRQR(AM) Paris, Tennessee
WMVP Chicago, Illinois
WRAR Tappahannock, Virginia
WRTG Garner, North Carolina
WVWI Charlotte Amalie, Virgin Islands
WXTN Benton, Mississippi
WBZR Robertsdale, Alabama
WYBT Blountstown, Florida

1010 khz

KBBW Waco, Texas
KCHI Chillicothe, Missouri
KCHJ Delano, California
KDLA De Ridder, Louisiana
KIND Independence, Kansas
KIQI San Francisco, California
KLAT Houston, Texas
KXPS Thousand Palms, California
KRNI Mason City, Iowa
KSIR Brush, Colorado
KTNZ Amarillo, Texas
KXXT Tolleson, Arizona
KXEN St. Louis, Missouri
KOOR Milwaukie, Oregon
WCKW Garyville, Louisiana
WCSI Columbus, Indiana
WCST Berkeley Springs, West Virginia
WELS Kinston, North Carolina
WFGW Black Mountain, North Carolina
WGUN Atlanta, Georgia
WHIN Gallatin, Tennessee
WINS New York, New York
WIOI New Boston, Ohio
WJXL Jacksonville Beach, Florida
WUKZ(AM) Marion, Virginia
WMOX Meridian, Mississippi
WCNL Newport, New Hampshire
WOLB Baltimore, Maryland
WORM Savannah, Tennessee
WPMH Portsmouth, Virginia
WCOC Dora, Alabama
WHFS(AM) Seffner, Florida
WSPC Albemarle, North Carolina
WPCN Stevens Point, Wisconsin
WMIN Sauk Rapids, Minnesota

1020 khz

KCKN Roswell, New Mexico
KDKA Pittsburgh, Pennsylvania
KJJK Fergus Falls, Minnesota
KOKP Perry, Oklahoma
KMMQ Plattsmouth, Nebraska
KTNQ Los Angeles, California
KWIQ Moses Lake North, Washington
KDYK Union Gap, Washington
WCIL Carbondale, Illinois
WIBG Ocean City/Somers Po, New Jersey
WSBX Ochlocknee, Georgia
WHDD Sharon, Connecticut
WPEO Peoria, Illinois
WOQI Adjuntas, Puerto Rico
WURN Kendall, Florida
WRIX Homeland Park, South Carolina

1030 khz

KBUF Holcomb, Kansas
KCTA Corpus Christi, Texas
KCWJ Blue Springs, Missouri
KFAY Farmington, Arkansas
KJDJ San Luis Obispo, California
KDUN Reedsport, Oregon
KMAS Shelton, Washington
KTWO Casper, Wyoming
KVOI Cortaro, Arizona
WBGS Point Pleasant, West Virginia
WBZ Boston, Massachusetts
WCTS Maplewood, Minnesota
WEBS Calhoun, Georgia
WDRU Creedmore, North Carolina
WGFC Floyd, Virginia
WNOW Mint Hill, North Carolina
WNVR Vernon Hills, Illinois
WONQ Oviedo, Florida
WOSO San Juan, Puerto Rico
WQSE White Bluff, Tennessee
WGSF Memphis, Tennessee
WUFL Sterling Heights, Michigan
WWGB Indian Head, Maryland
KWFA Tye, Texas

1040 khz

KCBR Monument, Colorado
KGGR Dallas, Texas
KLHT Honolulu, Hawaii
KXPD Tigard, Oregon
KURS San Diego, California
WHO Des Moines, Iowa
WNJE Flemington, New Jersey
WLVJ Boynton Beach, Florida
WJTB North Ridgeville, Ohio
WLCR Mt Washington, Kentucky
WPBS Conyers, Georgia
WKTI Powell, Tennessee
WSGH Lewisville, North Carolina
WZSK Everett, Pennsylvania
WHBO Pinellas Park, Florida
WYSL Avon, New York
WZNA Moca, Puerto Rico

1050 khz

KCAA Loma Linda, California
KBLE Seattle, Washington
KCHN Brookshire, Texas
KEYF Dishman, Washington
KGTO Tulsa, Oklahoma
KJBN Little Rock, Arkansas
KKRX Lawton, Oklahoma
KLOH Pipestone, Minnesota
KLPL(AM) Lake Providence, Louisiana
KMIS Portageville, Missouri
KMTA Miles City, Montana
KTBL Los Ranchos, New Mexico
KORE Springfield-Eugene, Oregon
KRMY Killeen, Texas
KSIS Sedalia, Missouri
KTCT San Mateo, California
KJPG Frazier Park, California
KVPI Ville Platte, Louisiana
WTWG Columbus, Mississippi
WADC Parkersburg, West Virginia
WAMN Green Valley, West Virginia
WBNC Conway, New Hampshire
WBRG Lynchburg, Virginia
WBUT Butler, Pennsylvania
WVXX Norfolk, Virginia
WDZ Decatur, Illinois
WDVM Eau Claire, Wisconsin
WEPN New York, New York
WFAM Augusta, Georgia
WSEN Baldwinsville, New York
WFSC Franklin, North Carolina
WGAT Gate City, Virginia
WHSC Conway, South Carolina
WJCM Sebring, Florida
WJOK Kaukauna, Wisconsin
WJSB Crestview, Florida
WHSC(AM) Conway, South Carolina
WBQH(AM) Silver Spring, Maryland
WLIP Kenosha, Wisconsin
WLON Lincolnton, North Carolina
WLYC Williamsport, Pennsylvania
WMNZ Montezuma, Georgia
WMSG Oakland, Maryland
WNES Central City, Kentucky
WBNM Alexander City, Alabama
WROS Jacksonville, Florida
WSMT Sparta, Tennessee
WTCA Plymouth, Indiana
WTKA Ann Arbor, Michigan
WCVX Cincinnati, Ohio
WWGP Sanford, North Carolina
WWIC Scottsboro, Alabama
WYBG Massena, New York
WBQH Silver Spring, Maryland

1060 khz

KOAI Van Buren, Arkansas
KBGN Caldwell, Idaho
KDUS Tempe, Arizona
KFIL Preston, Minnesota
KFIT Lockhart, Texas
KFIT EXP S San Antonio, Texas
KXPL El Paso, Texas
KGFX Pierre, South Dakota
KIJN Farwell, Texas
KDYL South Salt Lake, Utah
KKVV Las Vegas, Nevada
KRCN Longmont, Colorado
KNLV Ord, Nebraska
KTNS Oakhurst, California
KBFL Springfield, Missouri
KYW Philadelphia, Pennsylvania
WIXC Titusville, Florida
WCGB Juana Diaz, Puerto Rico
WCOK Sparta, North Carolina
WFLE Flemingsburg, Kentucky
WGSB Mebane, North Carolina
WHFB Benton Harbor-St. Jo, Michigan
WJKY Jamestown, Kentucky
WQOM Natick, Massachusetts
WKNG Tallapoosa, Georgia
WXNC Monroe, North Carolina
WLNO New Orleans, Louisiana
WMCL McLeansboro, Illinois
WKMQ Tupelo, Mississippi
WQMV Waverly, Tennessee
WILB Canton, Ohio
WRHL Rochelle, Illinois
KIPA Hilo, Hawaii

1070 khz

KATQ Plentywood, Montana
KBCL Bossier City, Louisiana
KNTH Houston, Texas
KLIO Wichita, Kansas
KHMO Hannibal, Missouri
KILR Estherville, Iowa
KNX Los Angeles, California
KOPY Alice, Texas
KWEL Midland, Texas
WAPI Birmingham, Alabama
WDIA Memphis, Tennessee
WTWK Plattsburgh, New York
WEKT Elkton, Maryland
WFLI Lookout Mountain, Tennessee
WFRF Tallahassee, Florida
WGOS High Point, North Carolina
WCSZ Sans Souci, South Carolina
WFNI Indianapolis, Indiana
WINA Charlottesville, Virginia
WBKW(AM) Beckley, West Virginia
WKII Solana, Florida
WKMB Stirling, New Jersey
WKOK Sunbury, Pennsylvania
WMIA Arecibo, Puerto Rico
WNCT Greenville, North Carolina
WNVY Cantonment, Florida
WSCP Sandy Creek-Pulaski, New York
WTSO Madison, Wisconsin
KVKK Verndale, Minnesota
WBKW Beckley, West Virginia

1080 khz

KUDO Anchorage, Alaska
KGVY Green Valley, Arizona
KNDK Langdon, North Dakota
KOAK Red Oak, Iowa
KFXX Portland, Oregon
KRLD Dallas, Texas
KSLL Price, Utah
KSCO Santa Cruz, California
KVNI Coeur D'Alene, Idaho
KWAI Honolulu, Hawaii
KYMN Northfield, Minnesota
KYMO East Prairie, Missouri
WALD Johnsonville, South Carolina
WHOO Kissimmee, Florida
WFTD Marietta, Georgia
WHIM Coral Gables, Florida
WKAC Athens, Alabama
WKBY Chatham, Virginia
WKGX Lenoir, North Carolina
WKJK Louisville, Kentucky
WLEY Cayey, Puerto Rico
WNWI Oak Lawn, Illinois
WOAP Owosso, Michigan
WYHY Cannonsburg, Kentucky
WWNL Pittsburgh, Pennsylvania
WRYT Edwardsville, Illinois
WTIC Hartford, Connecticut
WUFO Amherst, New York
WHIM(AM) Coral Gables, Florida
WWDR Murfreesboro, North Carolina

1090 khz

KAAY Little Rock, Arkansas
KBOZ Bozeman, Montana
KEXS Excelsior Springs, Missouri
KVOP Plainview, Texas
KLWJ(AM) Umatilla, Oregon
KPTK Seattle, Washington
KMXA Aurora, Colorado
KNCR Fortuna, California
KULF Bellville, Texas
KNWS Waterloo, Iowa
KSOU Sioux Center, Iowa
KTGO Tioga, North Dakota
WAQE Rice Lake, Wisconsin
WBAF Barnesville, Georgia
WBAL Baltimore, Maryland
WTSB Selma, North Carolina
WCAR Livonia, Michigan
WCRA Effingham, Illinois
WENR Englewood, Tennessee
WFCV Fort Wayne, Indiana
WGOD(AM) Charlotte Amalie, Virgin Islands
WILD Boston, Massachusetts
WTNK Hartsville, Tennessee
WHGG Kingsport, Tennessee
WKFI Wilmington, Ohio
WKTE King, North Carolina
WCZZ Greenwood, South Carolina
WKBZ Muskegon, Michigan
WSOL San German, Puerto Rico
WWGC Albertville, Alabama

1100 khz

KRKE Milan, New Mexico
KDRY Alamo Heights, Texas
KFAX San Francisco, California
KFNX Cave Creek, Arizona
KKLL Webb City, Missouri
KNZZ Grand Junction, Colorado
KQNM Milan, New Mexico
KAFY Bakersfield, California
WCGA Woodbine, Georgia
WGPA Bethlehem, Pennsylvania
WHLI Hempstead, New York
WISS Berlin, Wisconsin
WSGI Springfield, Tennessee
WTAM Cleveland, Ohio
WTWN Wells River, Vermont
WWWE Hapeville, Georgia
KWWN Las Vegas, Nevada
WZFG Dilworth, Minnesota

1110 khz

KAOI Kihei, Hawaii
KBND Bend, Oregon
KFAB Omaha, Nebraska
KGFL Clinton, Arkansas
KRPA Oak Harbor, Washington
KLIB Roseville, California
KDIS Pasadena, California
KTEK Alvin, Texas
KTTP Pineville, Louisiana
KYKK Humble City, New Mexico
WTOF Bay Minette, Alabama
WBIB Centreville, Alabama
WBT Charlotte, North Carolina
WCBR Richmond, Kentucky
WYRM Norfolk, Virginia
WOMN Franklinton, Louisiana
WGNZ Fairborn, Ohio
WJML Petoskey, Michigan

WWBJ Martinsburg, Pennsylvania
WKDZ Cadiz, Kentucky
WKRA Holly Springs, Mississippi
WKZV Washington, Pennsylvania
WMBI Chicago, Illinois
WNAP Norristown, Pennsylvania
WCCM Salem, New Hampshire
WMUX Hurricane, West Virginia
WPMZ East Providence, Rhode Island
WSFW Seneca Falls, New York
WTBQ Warwick, New York
WTIS Tampa, Florida
WUAT Pikeville, Tennessee
WUPE Pittsfield, Massachusetts
WUNN Mason, Michigan
WVJP Caguas, Puerto Rico
KAGV Big Lake, Alaska

1120 khz

KANN Roy, Utah
KEOR Catoosa, Oklahoma
KVTT Mineral Wells, Texas
KLIM Black Forest, Colorado
KMOX St. Louis, Missouri
KPNW Eugene, Oregon
KZSJ San Martin, California
WEAF Saint Stephen, South Carolina
WXJO Douglasville, Georgia
WBNW Concord, Massachusetts
WNWF Destin, Florida
WHOG Hobson City, Alabama
WKCE Maryville, Tennessee
WKQW Oil City, Pennsylvania
WBBF Buffalo, New York
WMSW Hatillo, Puerto Rico
WPRX Bristol, Connecticut
WTWZ Clinton, Mississippi
WUST Washington, District of Columbia
WSME Camp Lejeune, North Carolina
KTXW Manor, Texas
WFNX Coral Springs, Florida

1130 khz

KAAB Batesville, Arkansas
KBMR Bismarck, North Dakota
KTCN Minneapolis, Minnesota
KILJ Mount Pleasant, Iowa
KLEY Wellington, Kansas
KQNA Prescott Valley, Arizona
KQRR(AM) Mount Angel, Oregon
KRDU Dinuba, California
KSDO San Diego, California
KTMR Converse, Texas
KWKH Shreveport, Louisiana
WALQ Carrville, Alabama
WBBR New York, New York
WCLW Eden, North Carolina
WEDI Eaton, Ohio
WDFN Detroit, Michigan
WECR Newland, North Carolina
WFXH(AM) Hilton Head Island, South Carolina
WISN Milwaukee, Wisconsin
WLBA Gainesville, Georgia
WOIZ Guayanilla, Puerto Rico
WPYB Benson, North Carolina
WQFX Gulfport, Mississippi
WRRL Rainelle, West Virginia
WSDX Brazil, Indiana
WOFC Murray, Kentucky
WWBF Bartow, Florida
WYXE Gallatin, Tennessee
KPHI Honolulu, Hawaii

1140 khz

KYOK Conroe, Texas
KHFX Cleburne, Texas
KNWQ Palm Springs, California
KCXL Liberty, Missouri
KGEM Boise, Idaho
KHTK Sacramento, California
KLTK Centerton, Arkansas
KNAB Burlington, Colorado
KPWB Piedmont, Missouri
KQAB(AM) Lake Isabella, California
KYDZ North Las Vegas, Nevada
KSLD Soldotna, Alaska
KSOO Sioux Falls, South Dakota
KRMP Oklahoma City, Oklahoma
KZMQ Ten Sleep, Wyoming
WAPF McComb, Mississippi

WAWK Kendallville, Indiana
WBXR Hazel Green, Alabama
WCJW Warsaw, New York
WVHF Kentwood, Michigan
WLOD Loudon, Tennessee
WMMG Brandenburg, Kentucky
WQBA Miami, Florida
WQII San Juan, Puerto Rico
WRLV Salyersville, Kentucky
WRMQ Orlando, Florida
WRNA China Grove, North Carolina
WRVA Richmond, Virginia
WSAO Senatobia, Mississippi
WVEL Pekin, Illinois
WXLZ St. Paul, Virginia

1150 khz

KAGO Klamath Falls, Oregon
KASM Albany, Minnesota
KCCT Corpus Christi, Texas
KCKY Coolidge, Arizona
KCPS Burlington, Iowa
KNRV Englewood, Colorado
KDEF Albuquerque, New Mexico
KIMM Rapid City, South Dakota
KLPF Midland, Texas
KNED McAlester, Oklahoma
KQQQ Pullman, Washington
KRMS Osage Beach, Missouri
KSAL Salina, Kansas
KSEN Shelby, Montana
KKNW Seattle, Washington
KHRO El Paso, Texas
KBPO Port Neches, Texas
KWKY Des Moines, Iowa
KTLK Los Angeles, California
WAVO Rock Hill, South Carolina
WBAG Burlington-Graham, North Carolina
WCRK Morristown, Tennessee
WCUE Cuyahoga Falls, Ohio
WDEL Wilmington, Delaware
WDTM Selmer, Tennessee
WEAQ Chippewa Falls, Wisconsin
WELC Welch, West Virginia
WGBN New Kensington, Pennsylvania
WGBR Goldsboro, North Carolina
WGEA Geneva, Alabama
WGGH Marion, Illinois
WGOW Chattanooga, Tennessee
WHBY Kimberly, Wisconsin
WLLI Huntingdon, Pennsylvania
WLLI(AM) Huntingdon, Pennsylvania
WIMA Lima, Ohio
WJBO Baton Rouge, Louisiana
WLOC Munfordville, Kentucky
WMRD Middletown, Connecticut
WMST Mt. Sterling, Kentucky
WNDB Daytona Beach, Florida
WWDJ Boston, Massachusetts
WNLR Churchville, Virginia
WONG Canton, Mississippi
WUTI Utica, New York
WSNW Seneca, South Carolina
WJRD Tuscaloosa, Alabama
KZNE College Station, Texas
WTMP Egypt Lake, Florida
WXKO Fort Valley, Georgia
WJEM Valdosta, Georgia
KXET(AM) Portland, Oregon

1160 khz

KVCE Highland Park, Texas
KRDY San Antonio, Texas
KSL Salt Lake City, Utah
WCRT Donelson, Tennessee
WDJO(AM) Florence, Kentucky
WBQN Barceloneta-Manati, Puerto Rico
WCCS Homer City, Pennsylvania
WEWC Callahan, Florida
WJFJ Tryon, North Carolina
WKCM Hawesville, Kentucky
WCFO East Point, Georgia
WMET Gaithersburg, Maryland
WABY Mechanicville, New York
WOBM Lakewood Township, New Jersey
WODY Fieldale, Virginia
WPIE Trumansburg, New York
WYLL Chicago, Illinois
WSKW Skowhegan, Maine
WTEL Red Springs, North Carolina
WVNJ Oakland, New Jersey

WCXI Fenton, Michigan
WBYN Lehighton, Pennsylvania
WIWA St. Cloud, Florida
KCTO Cleveland, Missouri
KHPP(AM) Waukon, Iowa

1170 khz

KCBQ San Diego, California
KJNP North Pole, Alaska
KJOC Davenport, Iowa
KLOK San Jose, California
KRUE Waseca, Minnesota
KPUG Bellingham, Washington
KJXX Jackson, Missouri
KFAQ Tulsa, Oklahoma
KJJD Windsor, Colorado
KYET Golden Valley, Arizona
WGMP Montgomery, Alabama
WAVS Davie, Florida
WCLN Clinton, North Carolina
WCTF Vernon, Connecticut
WCXN Claremont, North Carolina
WDFB Junction City, Kentucky
WDIS Norfolk, Massachusetts
WFPB Orleans, Massachusetts
WKFL Bushnell, Florida
WSOS St. Augustine Beach, Florida
WLBH Mattoon, Illinois
WDEK(AM) Lexington, South Carolina
WFDL Waupun, Wisconsin
WRPM Poplarville, Mississippi
WWLE Cornwall, New York
WWTR Bridgewater, New Jersey
WWVA Wheeling, West Virginia
WQHC Hanceville, Alabama
WLEO Ponce, Puerto Rico

1180 khz

KERN Wasco-Greenacres, California
KGOL Humble, Texas
KLAY Lakewood, Washington
KOFI Kalispell, Montana
KORL Honolulu, Hawaii
KZOT Bellevue, Nebraska
WFGN Gaffney, South Carolina
WGAB Newburgh, Indiana
WHAM Rochester, New York
WVLZ Knoxville, Tennessee
WCRI(AM) Hope Valley, Rhode Island
WJNT Pearl, Mississippi
WLDS Jacksonville, Illinois
WFYL King of Prussia, Pennsylvania
WSFM Carolina Beach, North Carolina
KXIQ(AM) Turrell, Arkansas
WZQZ Trion, Georgia
WSQR Sycamore, Illinois
WXLA Dimondale, Michigan
KYES Rockville, Minnesota

1190 khz

KDAO Marshalltown, Iowa
KDYA Vallejo, California
KREB Bentonville-Bella, Arkansas
KEX Portland, Oregon
KQQZ Fairview Heights, Missouri
KKOJ Jackson, Minnesota
KFXR Dallas, Texas
WBHA Wabasha, Minnesota
KNUV Tolleson, Arizona
KNEK Washington, Louisiana
KPHN Kansas City, Missouri
KVCU Boulder, Colorado
KVSV Beloit, Kansas
KXKS Albuquerque, New Mexico
WCRW(AM) Leesburg, Virginia
WAMT Pine Castle Sky Lake, Florida
WBMJ San Juan, Puerto Rico
WWIO St. Marys, Georgia
WAFS Atlanta, Georgia
WEUV Moulton, Alabama
WIXE Monroe, North Carolina
WLIB New York, New York
WNWC Sun Prairie, Wisconsin
WOWO Fort Wayne, Indiana
WPSP Royal Palm Beach, Florida
WSDQ Dunlap, Tennessee
WVUS Grafton, West Virginia
WSDE Cobleskill, New York

1200 khz

KFNW West Fargo, North Dakota
KYAA Soquel, California
KYOO Bolivar, Missouri
WGRK Jeffersontown, Kentucky
WBCE Wickliffe, Kentucky
WKST New Castle, Pennsylvania
WCHB Taylor, Michigan
WGDL Lares, Puerto Rico
WEMM Huntington, West Virginia
WINK Pine Island Center, Florida
WAMB Nashville, Tennessee
WXKS Newton, Massachusetts
WRTO Chicago, Illinois
WMIR Atlantic Beach, South Carolina
WOAI San Antonio, Texas
WRKK Hughesville, Pennsylvania
WSML Graham, North Carolina
WTLA North Syracuse, New York
WXIT Blowing Rock, North Carolina
DKCPC Rancho Mirage, California

1210 khz

KMIA Auburn-Federal Way, Washington
KEBR Rocklin, California
KGYN Guymon, Oklahoma
KHAT Laramie, Wyoming
KOKK Huron, South Dakota
KUNF Washington, Utah
KPRZ San Marcos-Poway, California
KQEQ Fowler, California
KEVT Sahuarita, Arizona
KRSV Afton, Wyoming
KUBR San Juan, Texas
KZOO Honolulu, Hawaii
WANB Waynesburg, Pennsylvania
WDAO Dayton, Ohio
WDGR Dahlonega, Georgia
WMPS Bartlett, Tennessee
WHOY Salinas, Puerto Rico
WILY Centralia, Illinois
WJNL Kingsley, Michigan
WNMA Miami Springs, Florida
WPHT Philadelphia, Pennsylvania
WTXK Pike Road, Alabama
WSBI Static, Tennessee
WLRO Denham Springs, Louisiana

1220 khz

KHTS Canyon Country, California
KLDC Denver, Colorado
KDOW Palo Alto, California
KPJC Salem, Oregon
KDDR Oakes, North Dakota
KGIR Cape Girardeau, Missouri
KJAN Atlantic, Iowa
KLPW Union, Missouri
KMVL Madisonville, Texas
KOFO Ottawa, Kansas
KOMC Branson, Missouri
KQMG Independence, Iowa
KTLV Midwest City, Oklahoma
KVSA McGehee, Arkansas
KWKU Pomona, California
KZEE Weatherford, Texas
WABF Fairhope, Alabama
WAXO Lewisburg, Tennessee
WAYE Birmingham, Alabama
WBCH Hastings, Michigan
WCPH Etowah, Tennessee
WENC Whiteville, North Carolina
WERT Van Wert, Ohio
KLBB Stillwater, Minnesota
WFAX Falls Church, Virginia
WFKN Franklin, Kentucky
WFWL Camden, Tennessee
WGNY Newburgh, New York
WJAX Jacksonville, Florida
WJUN Mexico, Pennsylvania
WZBK Keene, New Hampshire
WDYT Kings Mountain, North Carolina
WHKW Cleveland, Ohio
WKRS Waukegan, Illinois
WLPO Lasalle, Illinois
WLSD Big Stone Gap, Virginia
WOEG Hazlehurst, Mississippi
WOTS Kissimmee, Florida
WSRQ Sarasota, Florida
WQUN Hamden, Connecticut
WREV Reidsville, North Carolina

WSTL Providence, Rhode Island
WSLM Salem, Indiana
WWSF Sanford, Maine
WZOT Rockmart, Georgia

1230 khz

KAAA Kingman, Arizona
KADA Ada, Oklahoma
KATO Safford, Arizona
KBAR Burley, Idaho
KBCR Steamboat Springs, Colorado
KBOV Bishop, California
KBTM Jonesboro, Arkansas
KJFK Reno, Nevada
KDAC Fort Bragg, California
KDIX Dickinson, North Dakota
KELY Ely, Nevada
KERV Kerrville, Texas
KEXO Grand Junction, Colorado
KFJB Marshalltown, Iowa
KFPW Fort Smith, Arkansas
KFUN Las Vegas, New Mexico
KGEO Bakersfield, California
KGHS International Falls, Minnesota
KGRO Pampa, Texas
KHAS Hastings, Nebraska
KHDN Hardin, Montana
KHSN Coos Bay, Oregon
KIFW Sitka, Alaska
KINO Winslow, Arizona
KKPC Pueblo, Colorado
KLAV Las Vegas, Nevada
KLCB Libby, Montana
KLIC Richwood, Louisiana
KLVT Levelland, Texas
KLWT Lebanon, Missouri
KLXR Redding, California
KMRS Morris, Minnesota
KSZN(AM) Gresham, Oregon
KRSY Alamogordo, New Mexico
KOBB Bozeman, Montana
KORT(AM/FM) Grangeville, Idaho
KOTS Deming, New Mexico
KOY Phoenix, Arizona
KOZA Odessa, Texas
KOZI Chelan, Washington
KCUP Toledo, Oregon
KPRL Paso Robles, California
KQIK Lakeview, Oregon
KQUE Houston, Texas
KDYM Sunnyside, Washington
KBCQ Roswell, New Mexico
KRXK Rexburg, Idaho
KSBN Spokane, Washington
KSEY Seymour, Texas
KSIX Corpus Christi, Texas
KSJK Talent, Oregon
KSLO Opelousas, Louisiana
KSST Sulphur Springs, Texas
KSTC Sterling, Colorado
KSZL Barstow, California
KYVA Gallup, New Mexico
KLTO Del Rio, Texas
KTNC Falls City, Nebraska
KTRF Thief River Falls, Minnesota
KVAK Valdez, Alaska
KVOC Casper, Wyoming
KZYM Joplin, Missouri
KWG Stockton, California
KWIX Moberly, Missouri
KWNO Winona, Minnesota
KWSN Sioux Falls, South Dakota
KWTX Waco, Texas
KJQS Murray, Utah
KWYZ Everett, Washington
KXLO Lewistown, Montana
KXO El Centro, California
KYPA Los Angeles, California
KYSM Mankato, Minnesota
WABN Abingdon, Virginia
WAIM Anderson, South Carolina
WAKI McMinnville, Tennessee
WAMM Woodstock, Virginia
WANO Pineville, Kentucky
WAUD Auburn, Alabama
WBBZ Ponca City, Oklahoma
WBHP Huntsville, Alabama
WBLJ Dalton, Georgia
WBOK New Orleans, Louisiana
WBPZ Lock Haven, Pennsylvania
WBVP Beaver Falls, Pennsylvania
WCBT Roanoke Rapids, North Carolina
WCLO Janesville, Wisconsin
WTKN Corinth, Mississippi
WCMC Wildwood, New Jersey
WCRO Johnstown, Pennsylvania
WCWA Toledo, Ohio
WECK Cheektowaga, New York
WEEX Easton, Pennsylvania
WENY Elmira, New York
WESX Nahant, Massachusetts
WFAY Fayetteville, North Carolina
WFAS White Plains, New York
WYTS Columbus, Ohio
WFOM Marietta, Georgia
WFVA Fredericksburg, Virginia
WGGG Gainesville, Florida
WGRY Grayling, Michigan
WHCO Sparta, Illinois
WHIR Danville, Kentucky
WRJX Jackson, Alabama
WHOP Hopkinsville, Kentucky
WHUC Hudson, New York
WFER Iron River, Michigan
WIRO Ironton, Ohio
WRBS Baltimore, Maryland
WWWH Haleyville, Alabama
WJBC Bloomington, Illinois
WBZT West Palm Beach, Florida
WJOB Hammond, Indiana
WJOI Norfolk, Virginia
WJOY Burlington, Vermont
WKBO Harrisburg, Pennsylvania
WEZO Augusta, Georgia
WKLK Cloquet, Minnesota
WKWL Florala, Alabama
WVNT Parkersburg, West Virginia
WNEZ Manchester, Connecticut
WIXT Little Falls, New York
WFXN Moline, Illinois
WLNR Kinston, North Carolina
WMAF Madison, Florida
WMFR High Point, North Carolina
WMLR Hohenwald, Tennessee
WMML Glens Falls, New York
WMOU Berlin, New Hampshire
WMPC Lapeer, Michigan
WBET Sturgis, Michigan
WNAW North Adams, Massachusetts
WNEB Worcester, Massachusetts
WNIK Arecibo, Puerto Rico
WNNC Newton, North Carolina
WCMD Cumberland, Maryland
WODI Brookneal, Virginia
WOIC Columbia, South Carolina
WOLH Florence, South Carolina
WONN Lakeland, Florida
WSAL Logansport, Indiana
WSBB New Smyrna Beach, Florida
WSKY Asheville, North Carolina
WSOK Savannah, Georgia
WSOO Sault Ste. Marie, Michigan
WSSO Starkville, Mississippi
WTBC Tuscaloosa, Alabama
WTCJ Tell City, Indiana
WTIV Titusville, Pennsylvania
WTKG Grand Rapids, Michigan
WTSV Claremont, New Hampshire
WDBZ Cincinnati, Ohio
WXCF Clifton Forge, Virginia
WXCO Wausau, Wisconsin
WXLI Dublin, Georgia
WBLQ(AM) Westerly, Rhode Island
WDWR Pensacola, Florida
WWGA(AM) Waycross, Georgia
WCDS Glasgow, Kentucky
WJUL Hiawassee, Georgia
KRYN(AM) Gresham, Oregon

1240 khz

KADS Elk City, Oklahoma
KALY Los Ranchos De Albuquerque, New Mexico
KAMQ Carlsbad, New Mexico
KANE New Iberia, Louisiana
KASL Newcastle, Wyoming
KASO Minden, Louisiana
KBIZ Ottumwa, Iowa
KBLL Helena, Montana
KCCR Pierre, South Dakota
KCLV Clovis, New Mexico
KCRT Trinidad, Colorado
KCVL Colville, Washington
KDEC Decorah, Iowa
KDGO Durango, Colorado
KDLR Devils Lake, North Dakota
KEJO Corvallis, Oregon
KELK Elko, Nevada
KEVA Evanston, Wyoming
KFBC Cheyenne, Wyoming
KFMO Park Hills, Missouri
KFOR Lincoln, Nebraska
KGY Olympia, Washington
KICD Spencer, Iowa
KIUL Garden City, Kansas
KJAA Globe, Arizona
KJOP Lemoore, California
KEZY San Bernardino, California
KLOA Ridgecrest, California
KLTZ Glasgow, Montana
KLYQ Hamilton, Montana
KMCL(AM) Donnelly, Idaho
KMHI Mountain Home, Idaho
KNEM Nevada, Missouri
KNRY Monterey Bay, California
KFH Wichita, Kansas
KODY North Platte, Nebraska
KOFE St. Maries, Idaho
KOKL Okmulgee, Oklahoma
KPBL Hemphill, Texas
KPOD Crescent City, California
KQEN Roseburg, Oregon
KRAL Rawlins, Wyoming
KRDO Colorado Springs, Colorado
KSLV Monte Vista, Colorado
KSMX Santa Maria, California
KNSN San Diego, California
KSOX Raymondville, Texas
KSUE Susanville, California
KTAM Bryan, Texas
KTHE Thermopolis, Wyoming
KTIX Pendleton, Oregon
KTLO Mountain Home, Arkansas
KVLF Alpine, Texas
KVRC Arkadelphia, Arkansas
KVSO Ardmore, Oklahoma
KWAK Stuttgart, Arkansas
KWIK Pocatello, Idaho
KWLC Decorah, Iowa
KLIK Jefferson City, Missouri
KXIT Dalhart, Texas
KXLE Ellensburg, Washington
KXOX Sweetwater, Texas
KQBZ Brownwood, Texas
WALO Humacao, Puerto Rico
WJLX Jasper, Alabama
WATN Watertown, New York
WATT Cadillac, Michigan
WAVN Southaven, Mississippi
WBAX Wilkes-Barre, Pennsylvania
WBBW Youngstown, Ohio
WBCF Florence, Alabama
WBEJ Elizabethton, Tennessee
WBGC Chipley, Florida
WBHB Fitzgerald, Georgia
WBUR West Yarmouth, Massachusetts
WCBY Cheboygan, Michigan
WCEM Cambridge, Maryland
WCNC Elizabeth City, North Carolina
WDDO Macon, Georgia
WZCC Cross City, Florida
WDNE Elkins, West Virginia
WDXY Sumter, South Carolina
WEBJ Brewton, Alabama
WEBQ Harrisburg, Illinois
WEKR Fayetteville, Tennessee
WENK Union City, Tennessee
WFOY St. Augustine, Florida
WFTM Maysville, Kentucky
WFTN Franklin, New Hampshire
WGBB Freeport, New York
WGCM Gulfport, Mississippi
WTPS Petersburg, Virginia
WGGA Gainesville, Georgia
WGMN Roanoke, Virginia
WGRM Greenwood, Mississippi
WGVA Geneva, New York
WHMQ Greenfield, Massachusetts
WHBU Anderson, Indiana
WWCD Baltimore, Ohio
WHVN Charlotte, North Carolina
WIAN Ishpeming, Michigan
WHFA Poynette, Wisconsin
WIFA Knoxville, Tennessee
WIOV Reading, Pennsylvania
WJEJ Hagerstown, Maryland
WJIM Lansing, Michigan
WJMC Rice Lake, Wisconsin
WJNC Jacksonville, North Carolina
WJON St. Cloud, Minnesota
WJTN Jamestown, New York
WKDK Newberry, South Carolina
WKEZ Bluefield, West Virginia
WKIQ Eustis, Florida
WLAG La Grange, Georgia
WLLV Louisville, Kentucky
WLSC Loris, South Carolina
WMFG Hibbing, Minnesota
WMGJ Gadsden, Alabama
WMIS Natchez, Mississippi
WMMB Melbourne, Florida
WNBZ Saranac Lake, New York
WNVL Nashville, Tennessee
WOBT Rhinelander, Wisconsin
WOMT Manitowoc, Wisconsin
WOON Woonsocket, Rhode Island
WPAX Thomasville, Georgia
WPBQ Flowood, Mississippi
WPJL Raleigh, North Carolina
WPKE Pikeville, Kentucky
WRTA Altoona, Pennsylvania
WSBC Chicago, Illinois
WSDR Sterling, Illinois
WSDT Soddy-Daisy, Tennessee
WSFC Somerset, Kentucky
WSKI Montpelier, Vermont
WSNJ Bridgeton, New Jersey
WSQL Brevard, North Carolina
WSYY Millinocket, Maine
WTAX Springfield, Illinois
WEZR Lewiston, Maine
WTON Staunton, Virginia
WTWA Thomson, Georgia
WNRA Eufaula, Alabama
WPTR(AM) Schenectady, New York
WVOS Liberty, New York
WVTS Dunbar, West Virginia
WWCO Waterbury, Connecticut
WWNS Statesboro, Georgia
WWWC Wilkesboro, North Carolina
WWZQ Aberdeen, Mississippi
WVSL(AM) Selinsgrove, Pennsylvania
KRDM Redmond, Oregon
KSAM Whitefish, Montana
WVTS(AM) Charleston, West Virginia

1250 khz

KDEI Port Arthur, Texas
KBRF Fergus Falls, Minnesota
KBTC Houston, Missouri
KCFI(AM) Cedar Falls, Iowa
KCFM(AM) Florence, Oregon
KCUE Red Wing, Minnesota
KZER Santa Barbara, California
KZHN Paris, Texas
KHIL Willcox, Arizona
KHOT Madera, California
KIKC Forsyth, Montana
KIKZ Seminole, Texas
KKDZ Seattle, Washington
KPZK Little Rock, Arkansas
KLLK Willits, California
KNEU Roosevelt, Utah
KOFC Fayetteville, Arkansas
KNWH Yucca Valley, California
KTFJ Dakota City, Nebraska
KWSU Pullman, Washington
KZDC San Antonio, Texas
WSRA Albany, Georgia
WRBZ Wetumpka, Alabama
WARE Ware, Massachusetts
WBRM Marion, North Carolina
WCHO Washington Ct House, Ohio
WHNZ Tampa, Florida
WDVA Danville, Virginia
WSSP Milwaukee, Wisconsin
WGHB Farmville, North Carolina
WGL Fort Wayne, Indiana
WSPL Streator, Illinois
WJIT Sabana, Puerto Rico
WKBL Covington, Tennessee
WGAM Manchester, New Hampshire
WKDX Hamlet, North Carolina
WNEM Bridgeport, Michigan

WLCK Scottsville, Kentucky
WLEM Emporium, Pennsylvania
WDDZ Pittsburgh, Pennsylvania
WLQM Franklin, Virginia
WMTR Morristown, New Jersey
WNTT Tazewell, Tennessee
WKDL Warrenton, Virginia
WQHL Live Oak, Florida
WYYC York, Pennsylvania
WRAY Princeton, Indiana
KYYS Kansas City, Kansas
WRKQ Madisonville, Tennessee
WTMA Charleston, South Carolina
WYKM Rupert, West Virginia
WYTH Madison, Georgia
WZOB Fort Payne, Alabama
WGAM(AM) Manchester, New Hampshire

1260 khz

KBHC Nashville, Arkansas
KBRH Baton Rouge, Louisiana
KBSZ Apache Junction, Arizona
KCCB Corning, Arkansas
KDUZ Hutchinson, Minnesota
KFFF(AM) Boone, Iowa
KBLY Idaho Falls, Idaho
KIMB Kimball, Nebraska
KKSA San Angelo, Texas
KLDS Falfurrias, Texas
KLYC McMinnville, Oregon
KSFB San Francisco, California
KPOW Powell, Wyoming
KROX Crookston, Minnesota
KSML Diboll, Texas
KWNX Taylor, Texas
KSGF Springfield, Missouri
KTRC Santa Fe, New Mexico
KWSH Wewoka, Oklahoma
KWYR Winner, South Dakota
WBNR Beacon, New York
WFJS Trenton, New Jersey
WCHV Charlottesville, Virginia
WCLC Jamestown, Tennessee
WCSA Ripley, Mississippi
WYDE Birmingham, Alabama
WDKN Dickson, Tennessee
WEKZ Monroe, Wisconsin
WFTW Fort Walton Beach, Florida
WWRC Washington, District of Columbia
WGVM Greenville, Mississippi
WHYM Lake City, South Carolina
WISO Ponce, Puerto Rico
WIYD Palatka, Florida
WKXR Asheboro, North Carolina
WMCH Church Hill, Tennessee
WSHU Westport, Connecticut
WPJF Greenville, South Carolina
WNDE Indianapolis, Indiana
WNOO Chattanooga, Tennessee
WSKO Syracuse, New York
WNXT Portsmouth, Ohio
WOCO Oconto, Wisconsin
WPHB Philipsburg, Pennsylvania
WMKI Boston, Massachusetts
WRIE Erie, Pennsylvania
WSDZ Belleville, Illinois
WSUA Miami, Florida
WTJH East Point, Georgia
WUFE Baxley, Georgia
WWIS Black River Falls, Wisconsin
WPNW Zeeland, Michigan
WWMK Cleveland, Ohio
WWVT Christiansburg, Virginia
WXCE Amery, Wisconsin
WZBO Edenton, North Carolina
KTRP Weiser, Idaho

1270 khz

KAJO Grants Pass, Oregon
KBAM Longview, Washington
KDJI Holbrook, Arizona
KEPS Eagle Pass, Texas
KFLC Fort Worth, Texas
KGNM St. Joseph, Missouri
KIML Gillette, Wyoming
KINN Alamogordo, New Mexico
KJUG Tulare, California
KLXX Bismarck-Mandan, North Dakota
KNDI Honolulu, Hawaii
KNWC Sioux Falls, South Dakota
KIIK Waynesville, Missouri
KBZZ Sparks, Nevada
KSCB Liberal, Kansas
KRVT Claremore, Oklahoma
KFAN Rochester, Minnesota
KXBX Lakeport, California
KFUT Thousand Palms, California
WAIN Columbia, Kentucky
WHGS Hampton, South Carolina
WCBC Cumberland, Maryland
WCGC Belmont, North Carolina
WDLA Walton, New York
WRJM(AM) Charleston, Illinois
WCMR Elkhart, Indiana
WGSV Guntersville, Alabama
WHEO Stuart, Virginia
WHLD Niagara Falls, New York
WILE Cambridge, Ohio
WJJC Commerce, Georgia
WKBF Rock Island, Illinois
WIJD Prichard, Alabama
WLBR Lebanon, Pennsylvania
WLIK Newport, Tennessee
WMIZ Vineland, New Jersey
WMKT Charlevoix, Michigan
WSHE Columbus, Georgia
WMPM Smithfield, North Carolina
WNLS Tallahassee, Florida
WNOG Naples, Florida
WQKR Portland, Tennessee
WRJC Mauston, Wisconsin
WRLZ Eatonville, Florida
WSPR Springfield, Massachusetts
WTJZ Newport News, Virginia
WTSN Dover, New Hampshire
WQTT Marysville, Ohio
WWCA Gary, Indiana
WWWI Baxter, Minnesota
WXGO Madison, Indiana
WXYT Detroit, Michigan
WYXC Cartersville, Georgia
WMLC Monticello, Mississippi

1280 khz

KCNI Broken Bow, Nebraska
KCOB Newton, Iowa
KDKD Clinton, Missouri
KQLL Henderson, Nevada
KZNS Salt Lake City, Utah
KFRN Long Beach, California
KSLI Abilene, Texas
KIT Yakima, Washington
KWSX Stockton, California
KXTK Arroyo Grande, California
KLDY Lacey, Washington
KNBY Newport, Arkansas
KPRV Poteau, Oklahoma
KRVM Eugene, Oregon
KSOK Arkansas City, Kansas
KXEG Phoenix, Arizona
KPTQ Spokane, Washington
KBNO Denver, Colorado
KVXR Moorhead, Minnesota
KMFR Pearsall, Texas
KWHI Brenham, Texas
KYRO Troy, Missouri
WADO New York, New York
WANS Anderson, South Carolina
WBIG Aurora, Illinois
WCMN Arecibo, Puerto Rico
WCPM Cumberland, Kentucky
WDNT Dayton, Tennessee
WPKZ Fitchburg, Massachusetts
WFAU Gardiner, Maine
WFYC Alma, Michigan
WGBF Evansville, Indiana
WGLR Lancaster, Wisconsin
WDSP De Funiak Springs, Florida
WHTK Rochester, New York
WHVR Hanover, Pennsylvania
WIPC Lake Wales, Florida
WJAY Mullins, South Carolina
WJWK Seaford, Delaware
WJST New Castle, Pennsylvania
WIBB Macon, Georgia
WMCP Columbia, Tennessee
WNAM Neenah-Menasha, Wisconsin
WODT New Orleans, Louisiana
WONW Defiance, Ohio
WPID Piedmont, Alabama
WSAT Salisbury, North Carolina
WBWX(AM) Berwick, Pennsylvania
WTMY Sarasota, Florida
WOWZ Appomattox, Virginia
WMXB Tuscaloosa, Alabama
WWTC Minneapolis, Minnesota
WYAL Scotland Neck, North Carolina
WYVE Wytheville, Virginia

1290 khz

KALM Thayer, Missouri
KAZA Gilroy, California
KCUB Tucson, Arizona
KDMS El Dorado, Arkansas
KGVO Missoula, Montana
KIVY Crockett, Texas
KJEF Jennings, Louisiana
KOIL Omaha, Nebraska
KKDD San Bernardino, California
KOUU Pocatello, Idaho
KOWB Laramie, Wyoming
KPAY Chico, California
KRGE Weslaco, Texas
KBMO Benson, Minnesota
KUMA Pendleton, Oregon
KUOA Siloam Springs, Arkansas
KWFS Wichita Falls, Texas
KMMM Pratt, Kansas
KZSB Santa Barbara, California
WBTG Sheffield, Alabama
WJNO West Palm Beach, Florida
WCBL Benton, Kentucky
WCCC West Hartford, Connecticut
WCHK Canton, Georgia
WTKS Savannah, Georgia
WLBY Saline, Michigan
WPCF Panama City Beach, Florida
WDZY Colonial Heights, Virginia
WFBG Altoona, Pennsylvania
WHIO Dayton, Ohio
WHKY Hickory, North Carolina
WIRL Peoria, Illinois
WJBI Batesville, Mississippi
WWTX Wilmington, Delaware
WJCV Jacksonville, North Carolina
WKLB Manchester, Kentucky
WKLJ Sparta, Wisconsin
WKBK Keene, New Hampshire
WMCS Greenfield, Wisconsin
WNBF Binghamton, New York
WNBN Meridian, Mississippi
WNIL Niles, Michigan
WOMP Bellaire, Ohio
WOPP Opp, Alabama
WWHM Sumter, South Carolina
WRNI Providence, Rhode Island
WTYL Tylertown, Mississippi
WVOW Logan, West Virginia
WXKL Sanford, North Carolina
WYEA Sylacauga, Alabama

1300 khz

KACI The Dalles, Oregon
KAKC Tulsa, Oklahoma
KAPL Phoenix, Oregon
KAZN Pasadena, California
KBRL McCook, Nebraska
KSYB Shreveport, Louisiana
KGLO Mason City, Iowa
KSET Lumberton, Texas
KKOL Seattle, Washington
KROP Brawley, California
KKUB Brownfield, Texas
KLAR Laredo, Texas
KLER Orofino, Idaho
KMMO Marshall, Missouri
KOLY Mobridge, South Dakota
KPMO Mendocino, California
KCMY Carson City, Nevada
KCSF Colorado Springs, Colorado
KVET Austin, Texas
KWCK Searcy, Arkansas
KYNO Fresno, California
WAVZ New Haven, Connecticut
WBSA Boaz, Alabama
WBZQ Huntington, Indiana
WCKI Greer, South Carolina
WCLG Morgantown, West Virginia
WJYP St. Albans, West Virginia
WJMO Cleveland, Ohio
WFFG Marathon, Florida
WFRX West Frankfort, Illinois
WIBR Baton Rouge, Louisiana
WKZN West Hazleton, Pennsylvania
WIMG Ewing, New Jersey
WIMO Winder, Georgia
WJDA Quincy, Massachusetts
WJZ Baltimore, Maryland
WBOW Terre Haute, Indiana
WKCY Harrisonburg, Virginia
WKSC Kershaw, South Carolina
WKXM Winfield, Alabama
WLNC Laurinburg, North Carolina
WLXG Lexington, Kentucky
WMTM Moultrie, Georgia
WMTN Morristown, Tennessee
WMVO Mount Vernon, Ohio
WNEA Newnan, Georgia
WNQM Nashville, Tennessee
WOAD Jackson, Mississippi
WOOD Grand Rapids, Michigan
WPNH Plymouth, New Hampshire
WQBN Temple Terrace, Florida
WQPM Princeton, Minnesota
WRDZ La Grange, Illinois
WSYD Mount Airy, North Carolina
WTIL Mayaguez, Puerto Rico
WTLS Tallassee, Alabama
WGDJ Rensselaer, New York
WWCH Clarion, Pennsylvania
WXRL Lancaster, New York
WMEL Cocoa Beach, Florida
WOSW Fulton, New York
WSSG Goldsboro, North Carolina

1310 khz

KBOK Malvern, Arkansas
KDLS Perry, Iowa
KEIN Great Falls, Montana
KEZM Sulphur, Louisiana
KFKA Greeley, Colorado
KYUL Scott City, Kansas
KFVR Crescent City, California
KGMT Fairbury, Nebraska
KIQQ Barstow, California
KKNS Corrales, New Mexico
KLIX Twin Falls, Idaho
KMBS West Monroe, Louisiana
KMKY Oakland, California
KNOX Grand Forks, North Dakota
KNPT Newport, Oregon
KZRG Joplin, Missouri
KOKX Keokuk, Iowa
KTWN Glencoe, Minnesota
KTCK Dallas, Texas
KIHP Mesa, Arizona
KAHL San Antonio, Texas
KZIP Amarillo, Texas
KZXR Prosser, Washington
WADB(AM) Asbury Park, New Jersey
WAUC Wauchula, Florida
WCCW Traverse City, Michigan
WDCT Fairfax, Virginia
WDKD Kingstree, South Carolina
WDOC Prestonsburg, Kentucky
WDPN Alliance, Ohio
WDXI Jackson, Tennessee
WGH Newport News, Virginia
WGSP Charlotte, North Carolina
WHEP Foley, Alabama
WTZN Troy, Pennsylvania
WIBA Madison, Wisconsin
WICH Norwich, Connecticut
WISE Asheville, North Carolina
WKZD Priceville, Alabama
WJUS Marion, Alabama
WLOB Portland, Maine
WNAE Warren, Pennsylvania
WOCV Oneida, Tennessee
WOKA Douglas, Georgia
WBFD Bedford, Pennsylvania
WORC Worcester, Massachusetts
WPBC Decatur, Georgia
WPLV West Point, Georgia
WRSB Canandaigua, New York
WSLW White Sulphur Spring, West Virginia
WEMG Camden, New Jersey
WTIK Durham, North Carolina
WTLB Utica, New York
WTLC Indianapolis, Indiana
WTTL Madisonville, Kentucky
WRVP Mount Kisco, New York
WXMC Parsippany-Troy Hill, New Jersey
WYND Deland, Florida

RADIO - U.S.

WDTW Dearborn, Michigan

1320 khz

KAWC Yuma, Arizona
KCLI Clinton, Oklahoma
KCTC West Sacramento, California
KELO Sioux Falls, South Dakota
KFNZ Salt Lake City, Utah
KGDC Walla Walla, Washington
KHRT Minot, North Dakota
KKSM Oceanside, California
KLWN Lawrence, Kansas
KMAQ Maquoketa, Iowa
KNCB Vivian, Louisiana
KNIA Knoxville, Iowa
KSCR Eugene, Oregon
KOLT Scottsbluff, Nebraska
KOZY Grand Rapids, Minnesota
KRDD Roswell, New Mexico
KRLW Walnut Ridge, Arkansas
KSDT Hemet, California
KSIV Clayton, Missouri
KVMC Colorado City, Texas
KWHN Fort Smith, Arkansas
KXRO Aberdeen, Washington
KXYZ Houston, Texas
WAGF Dothan, Alabama
WDDV Venice, Florida
WATR Waterbury, Connecticut
WBRT Bardstown, Kentucky
WCOG Greensboro, North Carolina
WCVG Covington, Kentucky
WDER Derry, New Hampshire
WDMJ Marquette, Michigan
WENN Birmingham, Alabama
WFHR Wisconsin Rapids, Wisconsin
WGET Gettysburg, Pennsylvania
WHIE Griffin, Georgia
WICO Salisbury, Maryland
WILS Lansing, Michigan
WISW Columbia, South Carolina
WNGO Mayfield, Kentucky
WJAS Pittsburgh, Pennsylvania
WARL Attleboro, Massachusetts
WKAN Kankakee, Illinois
WGOC Kingsport, Tennessee
WKRK Murphy, North Carolina
WVNZ Richmond, Virginia
WLOH Lancaster, Ohio
WLQY Hollywood, Florida
WMSR Manchester, Tennessee
WOBL Oberlin, Ohio
WRJW Picayune, Mississippi
WTKZ Allentown, Pennsylvania
WSKN San Juan, Puerto Rico
WVGM Lynchburg, Virginia
WCVR(AM) Randolph, Vermont
WAGY Forest City, North Carolina

1330 khz

KGRG Enumclaw, Washington
KNSS Wichita, Kansas
KGAK Gallup, New Mexico
KGLD Tyler, Texas
KINE Kingsville, Texas
KWFM South Tucson, Arizona
KKPZ Portland, Oregon
KCKM Monahans, Texas
KLBS Los Banos, California
KMBI Spokane, Washington
KTAE Cameron, Texas
KOVE Lander, Wyoming
KSWA Graham, Texas
KXXA(AM) Conway, Arkansas
KUKU Willow Springs, Missouri
KVOL Lafayette, Louisiana
KWKW Los Angeles, California
KWLO Waterloo, Iowa
WAEW Crossville, Tennessee
WANG Havelock, North Carolina
WJSS Havre De Grace, Maryland
WGFT Campbell, Ohio
WBTM Danville, Virginia
WLBB Carrollton, Georgia
WCVC Tallahassee, Florida
WEBO Owego, New York
WEBY Milton, Florida
WELW Willoughby, Ohio
WENA Yauco, Puerto Rico
WESR Onley-Onancock, Virginia
WETZ New Martinsville, West Virginia
WFIN Findlay, Ohio
WFNN Erie, Pennsylvania
WHAZ Troy, New York
WHBL Sheboygan, Wisconsin
WJNX Fort Pierce, Florida
WKDP Corbin, Kentucky
WKTA Evanston, Illinois
WGTJ Murrayville, Georgia
WMLT Dublin, Georgia
WLOL Minneapolis, Minnesota
WMOR Morehead, Kentucky
WNIX Greenville, Mississippi
WNTA Rockford, Illinois
WITM Marion, Virginia
WPJS Conway, South Carolina
WHSL(AM) Butler, Alabama
WRAA Luray, Virginia
WRAM Monmouth, Illinois
WRCA Watertown, Massachusetts
WSPQ Springville, New York
WTRE Greensburg, Indiana
WTRX Flint, Michigan
WVHI Evansville, Indiana
WWAB Lakeland, Florida
WWRV New York, New York
WYPC Wellston, Ohio
WYRD Greenville, South Carolina
WZCT Scottsboro, Alabama
KJPR Shasta Lake City, California
KXXJ Juneau, Alaska

1340 khz

KACH Preston, Idaho
KVNN Victoria, Texas
KAND Corsicana, Texas
KATA Arcata, California
KTPI Mojave, California
KBBR North Bend, Oregon
KBTA Batesville, Arkansas
KCAP Helena, Montana
KCAT Pine Bluff, Arkansas
KCBL Fresno, California
KCQL Aztec, New Mexico
KCRN San Angelo, Texas
KDLM Detroit Lakes, Minnesota
KGHM Midwest City, Oklahoma
KDTD Kansas City, Kansas
KGFW Kearney, Nebraska
KYNS San Luis Obispo, California
KHUB Fremont, Nebraska
KADI Springfield, Missouri
KIHN Hugo, Oklahoma
KIHR Hood River, Oregon
KIJV Huron, South Dakota
KEWE Oroville, California
KKAM Lubbock, Texas
KVOQ(AM) Denver, Colorado
KLID Poplar Bluff, Missouri
KWLE Anacortes, Washington
KLOO Corvallis, Oregon
KOLE Port Arthur, Texas
KOMY La Selva Beach, California
KPGE Page, Arizona
KPOK Bowman, North Dakota
KPRK Livingston, Montana
KTMM Grand Junction, Colorado
KRBA Lufkin, Texas
KRBT Eveleth, Minnesota
KRLV Las Vegas, Nevada
KRMD Shreveport, Louisiana
KROC Rochester, Minnesota
KROS Clinton, Iowa
KSEK Pittsburg, Kansas
KSGT Jackson, Wyoming
KSID Sidney, Nebraska
KSMO Salem, Missouri
KJOX Kennewick, Washington
KTFI Wendell, Idaho
KJMU Sand Springs, Oklahoma
KTOQ Rapid City, South Dakota
KTOX Needles, California
KTSN Elko, Nevada
KVBR Brainerd, Minnesota
KVIV El Paso, Texas
KVRH Salida, Colorado
KUOW Tumwater, Washington
KWKC Abilene, Texas
KWLM Willmar, Minnesota
KWOR Worland, Wyoming
KWVR Enterprise, Oregon
KZNW Wenatchee, Washington
KXEO Mexico, Missouri
KXEQ Reno, Nevada
KXPO Grafton, North Dakota
KCLU Santa Barbara, California
KYCN Wheatland, Wyoming
KYLT Missoula, Montana
KZNG Hot Springs, Arkansas
WADE Wadesboro, North Carolina
WAGN Menominee, Michigan
WAGR Lumberton, North Carolina
WLSG Wilmington, North Carolina
WALH Mountain City, Georgia
WALL Middletown, New York
WIFN Atlanta, Georgia
WAML Laurel, Mississippi
WBAC Cleveland, Tennessee
WYNF Augusta, Georgia
WBBT Lyons, Georgia
WBGN Bowling Green, Kentucky
WBIW Bedford, Indiana
WBRK Pittsfield, Massachusetts
WCBQ Oxford, North Carolina
WCDT Winchester, Tennessee
WCMI Ashland, Kentucky
WCSR Hillsdale, Michigan
WDSR Lake City, Florida
WEKY Richmond, Kentucky
WENT Gloversville, New York
WEPM Martinsburg, West Virginia
WEXL Royal Oak, Michigan
WFEB Sylacauga, Alabama
WGAU Athens, Georgia
WGAW Gardner, Massachusetts
WGRV Greeneville, Tennessee
WHAP Hopewell, Virginia
WXKX Clarksburg, West Virginia
WHAT Philadelphia, Pennsylvania
WIRY Plattsburgh, New York
WITS Sebring, Florida
WIZE Springfield, Ohio
WJOL Joliet, Illinois
WJPF Herrin, Illinois
WJRI Lenoir, North Carolina
WJYI Milwaukee, Wisconsin
WKCB Hindman, Kentucky
WKEY Covington, Virginia
WWLF Auburn, New York
WKGN Knoxville, Tennessee
WKRM Columbia, Tennessee
WKSN Jamestown, New York
WLDY Ladysmith, Wisconsin
WLEW Bad Axe, Michigan
WLOK Memphis, Tennessee
WLVL Lockport, New York
WMBN Petoskey, Michigan
WMDR Augusta, Maine
WMID Atlantic City, New Jersey
WMON Montgomery, West Virginia
WJAM Selma, Alabama
WMSA Massena, New York
WMTE Manistee, Michigan
WNBH New Bedford, Massachusetts
WNBS Murray, Kentucky
WNCO Ashland, Ohio
WWNA Aguadilla, Puerto Rico
WOKS Columbus, Georgia
WOUB Athens, Ohio
WPBR Lantana, Florida
WPOL Winston-Salem, North Carolina
WQSC Charleston, South Carolina
WRAW Reading, Pennsylvania
WRHI Rock Hill, South Carolina
WROD Daytona Beach, Florida
WSBM Florence, Alabama
WSOY Decatur, Illinois
WSSC Sumter, South Carolina
WSTA Charlotte Amalie, Virgin Islands
WSTJ St. Johnsbury, Vermont
WSTV Steubenville, Ohio
WTAN Clearwater, Florida
WTIF Tifton, Georgia
WTRC Elkhart, Indiana
WTRN Tyrone, Pennsylvania
WTYS Marianna, Florida
WVCV Orange, Virginia
WVNR Poultney, Vermont
WWFL Clermont, Florida
WWNH Madbury, New Hampshire
WWPA Williamsport, Pennsylvania
WXFN Muncie, Indiana
WFMH Cullman, Alabama
WYBC New Haven, Connecticut
WYCB Washington, District of Columbia
WYCK Plains, Pennsylvania
WNZS Veazie, Maine
KVOT Taos, New Mexico
KQJZ Evergreen, Montana
KBNW Bend, Oregon

1350 khz

KABQ Albuquerque, New Mexico
KZTD Cabot, Arkansas
KLHC Bakersfield, California
KBRX O'Neill, Nebraska
KCAR Clarksville, Texas
KCHK New Prague, Minnesota
KCHR Charleston, Missouri
KTDD San Bernardino, California
KCOR San Antonio, Texas
KDIO Ortonville, Minnesota
KCCY(AM) Pueblo, Colorado
KPNS Duncan, Oklahoma
KMAN Manhattan, Kansas
KRLC Lewiston-Clarkston, Idaho
KRNT Des Moines, Iowa
KSRO Santa Rosa, California
KTIK Nampa, Idaho
KTLQ Tahlequah, Oklahoma
KCOX Jasper, Texas
KWMO Washington, Missouri
WCBA Corning, New York
WCHI Chillicothe, Ohio
WCMP Pine City, Minnesota
WRWR Warner Robins, Georgia
WCRM Fort Myers, Florida
WCSM Celina, Ohio
WDCF Dade City, Florida
WEGA Vega Baja, Puerto Rico
WELB Elba, Alabama
WEZS Laconia, New Hampshire
WGAD Gadsden, Alabama
WGDN Gladwin, Michigan
WFNS Blackshear, Georgia
WGPL Portsmouth, Virginia
WHIP Mooresville, North Carolina
WHWH Princeton, New Jersey
WINY Putnam, Connecticut
WIOU Kokomo, Indiana
WJBD Salem, Illinois
WKCU Corinth, Mississippi
WLLY Wilson, North Carolina
WLOU Louisville, Kentucky
WMMV Cocoa, Florida
WNLK Norwalk, Connecticut
WNVA Norton, Virginia
WOAM Peoria, Illinois
WOYK York, Pennsylvania
WPDR Portage, Wisconsin
WRKM Carthage, Tennessee
WRNY Rome, New York
WRWH Cleveland, Georgia
WWWL New Orleans, Louisiana
WARF Akron, Ohio
WZGM Black Mountain, North Carolina
WNTX Fredericksburg, Virginia
WBLT Bedford, Virginia

1360 khz

KACT Andrews, Texas
KMNY Hurst, Texas
KBKB Fort Madison, Iowa
KBUY Ruidoso, New Mexico
KBYO Tallulah, Louisiana
KDJW Amarillo, Texas
KELE Mountain Grove, Missouri
KPXQ Glendale, Arizona
KFFA Helena, Arkansas
KFIV Modesto, California
KHNC Johnstown, Colorado
KKBJ Bemidji, Minnesota
KKMO Tacoma, Washington
KLYR Clarksville, Arkansas
KMRN Cameron, Missouri
KNGN McCook, Nebraska
KNIR New Iberia, Louisiana
KOHU Hermiston, Oregon
KLSD San Diego, California
KRKK Rock Springs, Wyoming
KRWC Buffalo, Minnesota
KKTX Corpus Christi, Texas
KSCJ Sioux City, Iowa
KAHS El Dorado, Kansas

KMJM Cedar Rapids, Iowa
KUIK Hillsboro, Oregon
KWWJ Baytown, Texas
KWDJ Ridgecrest, California
WBLC Lenoir City, Tennessee
WCGL Jacksonville, Florida
WCHL Chapel Hill, North Carolina
WSAI Cincinnati, Ohio
WDRC Hartford, Connecticut
WELP Easley, South Carolina
WELR Roanoke, Alabama
WFFF Columbia, Mississippi
WFLW Monticello, Kentucky
WTAQ Green Bay, Wisconsin
WGFA Watseka, Illinois
WHBG Harrisonburg, Virginia
WHCG Metter, Georgia
WHJC Matewan, West Virginia
WHNR Cypress Gardens, Florida
WKAT North Miami, Florida
WKMI Kalamazoo, Michigan
WYOS Binghamton, New York
WKYO Caro, Michigan
WLBK Dekalb, Illinois
WLYN Lynn, Massachusetts
WMFC(AM) Monroeville, Alabama
WOEN Olean, New York
WMOB Mobile, Alabama
WMOV Ravenswood, West Virginia
WNAH Nashville, Tennessee
WNJC Vineland, New Jersey
WTOC Newton, New Jersey
WPPA Pottsville, Pennsylvania
WMNY McKeesport, Pennsylvania
WGJK Rome, Georgia
WVRQ Viroqua, Wisconsin
WWOW Conneaut, Ohio
WWWJ Galax, Virginia
WIXI Jasper, Alabama

1370 khz

KIOL Iola, Kansas
KAST Astoria, Oregon
KAWL York, Nebraska
KAWW Heber Springs, Arkansas
KCRV Caruthersville, Missouri
KDTH Dubuque, Iowa
KFRO Longview, Texas
KGEN Tulare, California
KGNO Dodge City, Kansas
KUPA Pearl City, Hawaii
KJCE Rollingwood, Texas
KRAC Quincy, California
KSOP South Salt Lake, Utah
KSUM Fairmont, Minnesota
KTPA Prescott, Arkansas
KWTL Grand Forks, North Dakota
KWNC Quincy, Washington
KWRM Corona, California
KWRT Boonville, Missouri
KXTL Butte, Montana
KZSF San Jose, California
WEGI Fort Campbell, Kentucky
WALK Patchogue, New York
WZTA Vero Beach, Florida
WBTN Bennington, Vermont
WCCN Neillsville, Wisconsin
WCOA Pensacola, Florida
WDEA Ellsworth, Maine
WDEF Chattanooga, Tennessee
WDXE Lawrenceburg, Tennessee
WJIP Ellenville, New York
WFDR Manchester, Georgia
WFEA Manchester, New Hampshire
WGCL Bloomington, Indiana
WGHN Grand Haven, Michigan
WGOH Grayson, Kentucky
WHEE Martinsville, Virginia
WIVV Island of Vieques, Puerto Rico
WSHV South Hill, Virginia
WLJW Cadillac, Michigan
WKMC Roaring Spring, Pennsylvania
WLLM Lincoln, Illinois
WLLN Lillington, North Carolina
WLOP Jesup, Georgia
WLOV Washington, Georgia
WGIV Pineville, North Carolina
WLTH Gary, Indiana
WMGO Canton, Mississippi
WVLY Moundsville, West Virginia
WOCA Ocala, Florida

WRGS Rogersville, Tennessee
WSPD Toledo, Ohio
WTAB Tabor City, North Carolina
WTKY Tompkinsville, Kentucky
WVMR Frost, West Virginia
WHYP(AM) Corry, Pennsylvania
WQAL(AM) Pikesville, Maryland
WXXI Rochester, New York
KPWL Newport, Washington

1380 khz

KAGE Winona, Minnesota
KBWD Brownwood, Texas
KCII Washington, Iowa
KCIM Carroll, Iowa
KCNW Fairway, Kansas
KWMF Pleasanton, Texas
KOSS Lancaster, California
KJUA Cheyenne, Wyoming
KLIZ Brainerd, Minnesota
KLPZ Parker, Arizona
KMUS Sperry, Oklahoma
KOTA Rapid City, South Dakota
KQKD Redfield, South Dakota
KRCM Shanandoah, Texas
KRKO Everett, Washington
KDXE North Little Rock, Arkansas
KSRV Ontario, Oregon
KTKZ Sacramento, California
KHEY El Paso, Texas
KUVR Holdrege, Nebraska
KXCA Lawton, Oklahoma
KXFN Saint Louis, Missouri
WABH Bath, New York
WAGS Bishopville, South Carolina
WTMC Wilmington, Delaware
WAOK Atlanta, Georgia
WDLW Lorain, Ohio
WELE Ormond Beach, Florida
WOTE Clintonville, Wisconsin
WPYR Baton Rouge, Louisiana
WFNW Naugatuck, Connecticut
WNRR North Augusta, South Carolina
WGYV Greenville, Alabama
WCBG Waynesboro, Pennsylvania
WKJG Fort Wayne, Indiana
WKDM New York, New York
WLRV Lebanon, Virginia
WWRF Lake Worth, Florida
WMJR Nicholasville, Kentucky
WMLP Milton, Pennsylvania
WMTA Central City, Kentucky
WMTD Hinton, West Virginia
WMYF Portsmouth, New Hampshire
WNLA Indianola, Mississippi
WNRI Woonsocket, Rhode Island
WOLA Barranquitas, Puerto Rico
WLRM Millington, Tennessee
WPHM Port Huron, Michigan
WGLM Greenville, Michigan
WRAB Arab, Alabama
WSYB Rutland, Vermont
WTJK South Beloit, Illinois
WTOB Winston-Salem, North Carolina
WBTK Richmond, Virginia
WTYM Kittanning, Pennsylvania
WVSA Vernon, Alabama
WWMI St. Petersburg, Florida
WYSH Clinton, Tennessee

1390 khz

KTCR Yakima, Washington
KBEC Waxahachie, Texas
KCLN Clinton, Iowa
KCRC Enid, Oklahoma
KDQN De Queen, Arkansas
KENN Farmington, New Mexico
KFRA Franklin, Louisiana
KHOB Hobbs, New Mexico
KJAM Madison, South Dakota
KGNU Denver, Colorado
KJPW Waynesville, Missouri
KLGN Logan, Utah
KLTX Long Beach, California
KNCK Concordia, Kansas
KFFK Rogers, Arkansas
KRFO Owatonna, Minnesota
KRRZ Minot, North Dakota
KULP El Campo, Texas
KLOC Turlock, California
KXSS Waite Park, Minnesota

WOHS Shelby, North Carolina
WAJD Gainesville, Florida
WANY Albany, Kentucky
WFHT Avon Park, Florida
WBLL Bellefontaine, Ohio
WFBL Syracuse, New York
WEED Rocky Mount, North Carolina
WEGP Presque Isle, Maine
WEOK Poughkeepsie, New York
WFIW Fairfield, Illinois
WGRB Chicago, Illinois
WHMA Anniston, Alabama
WROP Belton, South Carolina
WISA Isabela, Puerto Rico
WJRM Troy, North Carolina
WCAT Burlington, Vermont
WKIC(AM) Hazard, Kentucky
WKLP Keyser, West Virginia
WKPA Lynchburg, Virginia
WLAN Lancaster, Pennsylvania
WLCM Holt, Michigan
WMCT Mountain City, Tennessee
WMER Meridian, Mississippi
WMPO Middleport-Pomeroy, Ohio
WPLM Plymouth, Massachusetts
WRIG Schofield, Wisconsin
WRIV Riverhead, New York
WROA Gulfport, Mississippi
WRSC State College, Pennsylvania
WNIO Youngstown, Ohio
WTJS Jackson, Tennessee
WTNL Reidsville, Georgia
WSPO Charleston, South Carolina
WYXI Athens, Tennessee
WZHF Arlington, Virginia
WZZB Seymour, Indiana

1400 khz

KADR Elkader, Iowa
KAOK Lake Charles, Louisiana
KART Jerome, Idaho
KAYS Hays, Kansas
KBCH Lincoln City, Oregon
KBJM Lemmon, South Dakota
KBRB Ainsworth, Nebraska
KBYG Big Spring, Texas
KBLJ La Junta, Colorado
KCHS Truth or Consequences, New Mexico
KCOG Centerville, Iowa
KCOW Alliance, Nebraska
KBCK Deer Lodge, Montana
KDTA Delta, Colorado
KEBE Jacksonville, Texas
KEDO Longview, Washington
KELD El Dorado, Arkansas
KESQ Indio, California
KKTK Texarkana, Texas
KEYL Long Prairie, Minnesota
KFRU Columbia, Missouri
KFTM Fort Morgan, Colorado
KGMY Springfield, Missouri
KGVL Greenville, Texas
KHCB League City, Texas
KITZ Silverdale, Washington
KIUN Pecos, Texas
KJDY John Day, Oregon
KJFF Festus, Missouri
KCYK Yuma, Arizona
KKJL San Luis Obispo, California
KKTL Casper, Wyoming
KKZZ Santa Paula, California
KMNV St. Paul, Minnesota
KLCK Goldendale, Washington
KLIN Lincoln, Nebraska
KMHL Marshall, Minnesota
KNND Cottage Grove, Oregon
KREF Norman, Oklahoma
KODI Cody, Wyoming
KQDJ Jamestown, North Dakota
KQMS Redding, California
KRAM Vernal, Utah
KRLN Canon City, Colorado
KRPL Moscow, Idaho
KRSC Othello, Washington
KRUN Ballinger, Texas
KRVZ Springerville, Arizona
KRZR Visalia, California
KSHP North Las Vegas, Nevada
KSIM Sikeston, Missouri
KSPT Sandpoint, Idaho
KSRR Provo, Utah

KTEM Temple, Texas
KTMC McAlester, Oklahoma
KTNM Tucumcari, New Mexico
KVSF Santa Fe, New Mexico
KTUC Tucson, Arizona
KUKI Ukiah, California
KUNO Corpus Christi, Texas
KEZL(AM) Visalia, California
KVFD Fort Dodge, Iowa
KVOE Emporia, Kansas
KREW Plainview, Texas
KGWU Uvalde, Texas
KVRP Stamford, Texas
KVTO Berkeley, California
KWNA Winnemucca, Nevada
KWON Bartlesville, Oklahoma
KWUF Pagosa Springs, Colorado
KWYN Wynne, Arkansas
KXGF Great Falls, Montana
KXGN Glendive, Montana
WAMC Albany, New York
WAWO Alma, Georgia
WANI Opelika, Alabama
WATW Ashland, Wisconsin
WBAT Marion, Indiana
WBBD Wheeling, West Virginia
WBIP Booneville, Mississippi
WBIZ Eau Claire, Wisconsin
WBTH Williamson, West Virginia
WCCY Houghton, Michigan
WCOH Newnan, Georgia
WCOS Columbia, South Carolina
WCYN Cynthiana, Kentucky
WDNY Dansville, New York
WDUZ Green Bay, Wisconsin
WDWS Champaign, Illinois
WWGE Loretto, Pennsylvania
WEOA Evansville, Indiana
WEST Easton, Pennsylvania
WJZN Augusta, Maine
WEDM(AM) Fort Walton Beach, Florida
WFOR Hattiesburg, Mississippi
WFPR Hammond, Louisiana
WFTG London, Kentucky
WFLL Fort Lauderdale, Florida
WGAP Maryville, Tennessee
WGHC(AM) Clayton, Georgia
WGIL Galesburg, Illinois
WGTN Georgetown, South Carolina
WMXF Waynesville, North Carolina
WHHV Hillsville, Virginia
WHMP Northampton, Massachusetts
WHTB Fall River, Massachusetts
WHUB Cookeville, Tennessee
WICK Scranton, Pennsylvania
WIDA Carolina, Puerto Rico
WVAE Biddeford, Maine
WIEL Elizabethtown, Kentucky
WILI Willimantic, Connecticut
WINC Winchester, Virginia
WIRA Fort Pierce, Florida
WJLD(AM) Fairfield, Alabama
WJWF Columbus, Mississippi
WJZM Clarksville, Tennessee
WKAV Charlottesville, Virginia
WKBI St. Marys, Pennsylvania
WSPG Spartanburg, South Carolina
WKEW Greensboro, North Carolina
WKNW Sault Sainte Marie, Michigan
WKPT Kingsport, Tennessee
WJQS Jackson, Mississippi
WLJN Elmwood Township, Michigan
WJET Erie, Pennsylvania
WLLH Lowell, Massachusetts
WLSB Copper Hill, Tennessee
WLTA Alpharetta, Georgia
WLTN Littleton, New Hampshire
WMAN Mansfield, Ohio
WMFA Raeford, North Carolina
WFPA Fort Payne, Alabama
WNEX Macon, Georgia
WOND Pleasantville, New Jersey
WPCE Portsmouth, Virginia
WWRK Darlington, South Carolina
WPRY Perry, Florida
WDTK Detroit, Michigan
WQXO Munising, Michigan
WRAK Williamsport, Pennsylvania
WBFN Battle Creek, Michigan
WRDB Reedsburg, Wisconsin
WRJN Racine, Wisconsin

WRON Ronceverte, West Virginia
WSAM Saginaw, Michigan
WSEG Savannah, Georgia
WSIC Statesville, North Carolina
WSJM St. Joseph, Michigan
WSLB Ogdensburg, New York
WSMY Weldon, North Carolina
WSTC Stamford, Connecticut
WHGB Harrisburg, Pennsylvania
WSDO Sanford, Florida
WTSL Hanover, New Hampshire
WVRC Spencer, West Virginia
WWIN Baltimore, Maryland
WSGC Elberton, Georgia
WWWS Buffalo, New York
WXAL Demopolis, Alabama
WZAZ Jacksonville, Florida
WZHR Zephyrhills, Florida
WZNG Shelbyville, Tennessee
KENT Parowan, Utah
WHLJ(AM) Moultrie, Georgia
WWNZ Veazie, Maine
KNNR Sparks, Nevada
WWTM Decatur, Alabama
WAJL South Boston, Virginia
KIHH Eureka, California
WGHC Clayton, Georgia
WYNY(AM) Milford, New York
WAVQ Jacksonville, North Carolina
KFJL Central Point, Oregon

1410 khz

KBNP Portland, Oregon
KCAL(AM) Redlands, California
KIIX Fort Collins, Colorado
KCUL Marshall, Texas
KDBS Alexandria, Louisiana
KERI Bakersfield, California
KGRN Grinnell, Iowa
KHCH Huntsville, Texas
KDKT Beulah, North Dakota
KKLO Leavenworth, Kansas
KLEM Le Mars, Iowa
KLFD Litchfield, Minnesota
KLVQ Athens, Texas
KMYC Marysville, California
KGSO Wichita, Kansas
KOOQ North Platte, Nebraska
KQV Pittsburgh, Pennsylvania
KRIL Odessa, Texas
KNTX Bowie, Texas
KRML Carmel, California
KRWB Roseau, Minnesota
KTCS Fort Smith, Arkansas
KSMA Lompoc, California
KWYO Sheridan, Wyoming
KNAL Victoria, Texas
WSHY Lafayette, Indiana
WBBX Kingston, Tennessee
WENU South Glen Falls, New York
WCMT Martin, Tennessee
WDOE Dunkirk, New York
WDOV Dover, Delaware
WELM Elmira, New York
WHAG Halfway, Maryland
WHBT Tallahassee, Florida
WHLN Harlan, Kentucky
WHTG Eatontown, New Jersey
WHTM Taylorville, Illinois
WING Dayton, Ohio
WIQR Prattville, Alabama
WIZM La Crosse, Wisconsin
WKKP McDonough, Georgia
WLAQ Rome, Georgia
WLSH Lansford, Pennsylvania
WNGL Mobile, Alabama
WMSX Brockton, Massachusetts
WMYR Fort Myers, Florida
WNWZ Grand Rapids, Michigan
WPCC Clinton, South Carolina
WPOP Hartford, Connecticut
WQBQ Leesburg, Florida
WRIS Roanoke, Virginia
WRMN Elgin, Illinois
WRSS San Sebastian, Puerto Rico
WSCW South Charleston, West Virginia
WRJD Durham, North Carolina
WNER Watertown, New York
WVCB Shallotte, North Carolina
WYIS McRae, Georgia
WZZA Tuscumbia, Alabama
KNVR San Saba, Texas

1420 khz

KOTK Omaha, Nebraska
KBTN Neosho, Missouri
KKEA Honolulu, Hawaii
KFYN Bonham, Texas
KGIM Aberdeen, South Dakota
KGNB New Braunfels, Texas
KIGO St. Anthony, Idaho
KITI Chehalis-Centralia, Washington
KJCK Junction City, Kansas
KJDL Lubbock, Texas
KMHS Coos Bay, Oregon
KMOG Payson, Arizona
KPIR Granbury, Texas
KPEL Lafayette, Louisiana
KPOC Pocahontas, Arkansas
KRLL California, Missouri
KRIZ Renton, Washington
KSTN Stockton, California
KTAN Sierra Vista, Arizona
KTJS Hobart, Oklahoma
KTOE Mankato, Minnesota
KUJ Walla Walla, Washington
KULY Ulysses, Kansas
KBHS Hot Springs, Arkansas
WACK Newark, New York
WACT Tuscaloosa, Alabama
WVOT Wilson, North Carolina
WAMV Amherst, Virginia
WAOC Saint Augustine, Florida
WASR Wolfeboro, New Hampshire
WATB Decatur, Georgia
WBEC Pittsfield, Massachusetts
WBRD Palmetto, Florida
WBSM New Bedford, Massachusetts
WCED Du Bois, Pennsylvania
WCOJ Coatesville, Pennsylvania
WCRE Cheraw, South Carolina
WDJA Delray Beach, Florida
WEMB Erwin, Tennessee
WUKQ Ponce, Puerto Rico
WFLT Flint, Michigan
WGAS South Gastonia, North Carolina
WHBN Harrodsburg, Kentucky
WHK Cleveland, Ohio
WIMS Michigan City, Indiana
WINI Murphysboro, Illinois
WJUB Plymouth, Wisconsin
WKCW Warrenton, Virginia
WKSR Pulaski, Tennessee
WKWN Trenton, Georgia
WLIS Old Saybrook, Connecticut
WMYN Mayodan, North Carolina
WNRS Herkimer, New York
WOC Davenport, Iowa
WPEH Louisville, Georgia
WQBC Vicksburg, Mississippi
WRCG Columbus, Georgia
WTCR Kenova, West Virginia
WVJS Owensboro, Kentucky
WRSA St. Albans, Vermont
WXGM Gloucester, Virginia

1430 khz

KALV Alva, Oklahoma
KWST El Centro, California
KAOL Carrollton, Missouri
KASI Ames, Iowa
KBRC Mount Vernon, Washington
KBRK Brookings, South Dakota
KCLK Asotin, Washington
KCOH Houston, Texas
KCRX Roswell, New Mexico
KEES Gladewater, Texas
KEZW Aurora, Colorado
KFIG Fresno, California
KHBM Monticello, Arkansas
KJAY Sacramento, California
KKOZ Ava, Missouri
KLO Ogden, Utah
KMRB San Gabriel, California
KMRC Morgan City, Louisiana
KNSP Staples, Minnesota
KTBZ Tulsa, Oklahoma
KRGI Grand Island, Nebraska
KROO Breckenridge, Texas
KVVN Santa Clara, California
KYKN Keizer, Oregon
WBEV Beaver Dam, Wisconsin
WBLR Batesburg, South Carolina
WCLT Newark, Ohio
WCMY Ottawa, Illinois
WDAL Dalton, Georgia
WDEX Monroe, North Carolina
WDIC Clinchco, Virginia
WDJS Mount Olive, North Carolina
WEEF Deerfield, Illinois
WEIR Weirton, West Virginia
WENE Endicott, New York
WCWC Williamsburg, Kentucky
WFHK Pell City, Alabama
WFOB Fostoria, Ohio
WGFS Covington, Georgia
WION Ionia, Michigan
WKEX Blacksburg, Virginia
WLKF Lakeland, Florida
WLTG Panama City, Florida
WPLN Madison, Tennessee
WMNC Morganton, North Carolina
WXNT Indianapolis, Indiana
WNAV Annapolis, Maryland
WNEL Caguas, Puerto Rico
WNFO Sun City-Hilton Head, South Carolina
WNSW Newark, New Jersey
WOIR Homestead, Florida
WOWW Germantown, Tennessee
WRDN Durand, Wisconsin
WRMG Red Bay, Alabama
KZQZ St. Louis, Missouri
WRXO Roxboro, North Carolina
WPNI Amherst, Massachusetts
WVAM Altoona, Pennsylvania
WTMN Gainesville, Florida
WXAM Buffalo, Kentucky
WKOX Everett, Massachusetts
WYMC Mayfield, Kentucky
KWAP Wasilla, Alaska

1440 khz

KCHE Cherokee, Iowa
KDIZ Golden Valley, Minnesota
KELG Manor, Texas
KETX Livingston, Texas
KEYS Corpus Christi, Texas
KTUV Little Rock, Arkansas
KKXL Grand Forks, North Dakota
KMAJ Topeka, Kansas
KMED Medford, Oregon
KODL The Dalles, Oregon
KPUR Amarillo, Texas
KRDZ Wray, Colorado
KAZG Scottsdale, Arizona
KTNO University Park, Texas
KUHL Santa Maria, California
KVON Napa, California
WAJR Morgantown, West Virginia
WBLA Elizabethtown, North Carolina
WGEM Quincy, Illinois
WGIG Brunswick, Georgia
WGMI Bremen, Georgia
WGVL Greenville, South Carolina
WHDM McKenzie, Tennessee
WLWI Montgomery, Alabama
WHIS Bluefield, West Virginia
WIBH Anna, Illinois
WRED Westbrook, Maine
WJBS Holly Hill, South Carolina
WJJL Niagara Falls, New York
WCDL Carbondale, Pennsylvania
WKLV Blackstone, Virginia
WKPR Kalamazoo, Michigan
WLXN Lexington, North Carolina
WMAX Bay City, Michigan
WDRJ Inkster, Michigan
WMVB Millville, New Jersey
WNFL Green Bay, Wisconsin
WNPV Lansdale, Pennsylvania
WNYG Medford, New York
WPGW Portland, Indiana
WPRD Winter Park, Florida
WPRS Paris, Illinois
WVGG Lucedale, Mississippi
WHKZ Warren, Ohio
WRGM Ontario, Ohio
WROK Rockford, Illinois
WSEL Pontotoc, Mississippi
WSGO Oswego, New York
WGLD Manchester Township, Pennsylvania
WDXQ Cochran, Georgia
WWCL Lehigh Acres, Florida
WVEI Worcester, Massachusetts
WYGH Paris, Kentucky
WZYX Cowan, Tennessee
WFNY Gloversville, New York
KPTO Pocatello, Idaho

1450 khz

KATE Albert Lea, Minnesota
KAVP Colona, Colorado
KBBS Buffalo, Wyoming
KBEN Carrizo Springs, Texas
KBFI Bonners Ferry, Idaho
KBFS Belle Fourche, South Dakota
KBKW Aberdeen, Washington
KBMW Breckenridge, Minnesota
KBPS Portland, Oregon
KBUN Bemidji, Minnesota
KCLX Colfax, Washington
KCTI Gonzales, Texas
KCYL Lampasas, Texas
KDAP Douglas, Arizona
KSKE Buena Vista, Colorado
KENA Fort Smith, Arkansas
KEST San Francisco, California
KEYY Provo, Utah
KEZJ Twin Falls, Idaho
KFIZ Fond Du Lac, Wisconsin
KFLS Klamath Falls, Oregon
KGFF Shawnee, Oklahoma
KGIW Alamosa, Colorado
KGRE Greeley, Colorado
KGRZ Missoula, Montana
KHIT Reno, Nevada
KIKR Beaumont, Texas
KWEI(AM) Payette, Idaho
KIRX Kirksville, Missouri
KLZS Eugene, Oregon
KLAM Cordova, Alaska
KLBM La Grande, Oregon
KLMX Clayton, New Mexico
KMBL Junction, Texas
KMHT Marshall, Texas
KMMS Bozeman, Montana
KMRY Cedar Rapids, Iowa
KNET Palestine, Texas
KNHD Camden, Arkansas
KNOC Natchitoches, Louisiana
KNOT Prescott, Arizona
KNSI St. Cloud, Minnesota
KOBE Las Cruces, New Mexico
KOBO Yuba City, California
KOKO Warrensburg, Missouri
KONP Port Angeles, Washington
KQDI Great Falls, Montana
KRZY Albuquerque, New Mexico
KSEL Portales, New Mexico
KSIG Crowley, Louisiana
KSIW Woodward, Oklahoma
KSNY Snyder, Texas
KFSD Escondido, California
KSUH Puyallup, Washington
KTIP Porterville, California
KZNU St. George, Utah
KTZR Tucson, Arizona
KVCK Wolf Point, Montana
KVEN Ventura, California
KVML Sonora, California
KVOW Riverton, Wyoming
KVSI Montpelier, Idaho
KVSL Show Low, Arizona
KWBE Beatrice, Nebraska
KWBW Hutchinson, Kansas
KWEI Notus, Idaho
KWHW Altus, Oklahoma
KWPM West Plains, Missouri
KPTR Palm Springs, California
KYLS Fredericktown, Missouri
KYNT Yankton, South Dakota
KZZJ Rugby, North Dakota
WAOV Vincennes, Indiana
WASK Lafayette, Indiana
WATA Boone, North Carolina
WATZ Alpena, Michigan
WQKC Jeffersonville, Indiana
WBHF Cartersville, Georgia
WBSR Pensacola, Florida
WBVA Bayside, Virginia
WJOE Lake City, Florida
WWKU Plum Springs, Kentucky
WCEV Cicero, Illinois
WFBX Spring Lake, North Carolina

WCJU Columbia, Mississippi
WENI Corning, New York
WCLM Highland Springs, Virginia
WCON Cornelia, Georgia
WCPR Coamo, Puerto Rico
WCRS Greenwood, South Carolina
WCTC New Brunswick, New Jersey
WCUM Bridgeport, Connecticut
WDAD Indiana, Pennsylvania
WDLB Marshfield, Wisconsin
WDLK Dadeville, Alabama
WDNG Anniston, Alabama
WDXR Paducah, Kentucky
WLKW West Warwick, Rhode Island
WELY Ely, Minnesota
WYHL Meridian, Mississippi
WFMB Springfield, Illinois
WENJ Atlantic City, New Jersey
WFRA Franklin, Pennsylvania
WFTR Front Royal, Virginia
WGNC Gastonia, North Carolina
WGNS Murfreesboro, Tennessee
WGPC Albany, Georgia
WHDL Olean, New York
WHKP Hendersonville, North Carolina
WHLS Port Huron, Michigan
WHRY Hurley, Wisconsin
WHTC Holland, Michigan
WIBM Jackson, Michigan
WILM Wilmington, Delaware
WIZS Henderson, North Carolina
WJER Dover-New Philadelphia, Ohio
WJPA Washington, Pennsylvania
WKEI Kewanee, Illinois
WKEU Griffin, Georgia
WKIP Poughkeepsie, New York
WKLA Ludington, Michigan
WKTQ South Paris, Maine
WKXL Concord, New Hampshire
WRNN Myrtle Beach, South Carolina
WLAF La Follette, Tennessee
WLAR Athens, Tennessee
WLAY Muscle Shoals, Alabama
WLEC Sandusky, Ohio
WLKS West Liberty, Kentucky
WLMR Chattanooga, Tennessee
WHNK Parkersburg, West Virginia
WLYV Fort Wayne, Indiana
WQWK(AM) State College, Pennsylvania
WHLL Springfield, Massachusetts
KQYX Galena, Kansas
WMFJ Daytona Beach, Florida
WMIQ Iron Mountain, Michigan
WMOH Hamilton, Ohio
WMVG Milledgeville, Georgia
WNAT Natchez, Mississippi
WNBP Newburyport, Massachusetts
WNBY Newberry, Michigan
WNOS New Bern, North Carolina
WOCN Miami, Florida
CFVM-1 Causapscal, Quebec
WOL Washington, District of Columbia
WPAM Pottsville, Pennsylvania
WPSE Erie, Pennsylvania
WQNT Charleston, South Carolina
WRCO Richland Center, Wisconsin
WREL Lexington, Virginia
WRKD Rockland, Maine
WROX Clarksdale, Mississippi
WSMG Greeneville, Tennessee
WZGX Bessemer, Alabama
WSNO Barre, Vermont
WSDV Sarasota, Florida
WSTU Stuart, Florida
WTAL Tallahassee, Florida
WTBO Cumberland, Maryland
WTCO Campbellsville, Kentucky
WTKI Huntsville, Alabama
WTRO Dyersburg, Tennessee
WTSA Brattleboro, Vermont
WVLD Valdosta, Georgia
WRLL Cicero, Illinois
WWJB Brooksville, Florida
WWNT Dothan, Alabama
WWSC Glens Falls, New York
WWXL Manchester, Kentucky
WKAL Rome, New York
KYLW Lockwood, Montana
WMVA Martinsville, Virginia
WVAX Charlottesville, Virginia
WYNY(AM) Ontario, New York
KWES Ruidoso, New Mexico
DWKEL Myrtle Beach, South Carolina
WTHU Thurmont, Maryland
WYNY(AM) Milford, Pennsylvania
WLUX Dunbar, West Virginia

1460 khz

KARR Kirkland, Washington
KBRZ Missouri City, Texas
KTKC Springhill, Louisiana
KBZO Lubbock, Texas
KCKX Stayton, Oregon
KCWM Hondo, Texas
KDMA Montevideo, Minnesota
KXNO Des Moines, Iowa
KDWA Hastings, Minnesota
KENO Las Vegas, Nevada
KHRA Honolulu, Hawaii
KHOJ St. Charles, Missouri
KKAQ Thief River Falls, Minnesota
KZNT Colorado Springs, Colorado
KKOY Chanute, Kansas
KXPN Kearney, Nebraska
KCLE Burleson, Texas
KLTC Dickinson, North Dakota
KCNR Shasta, California
KUTI Yakima, Washington
KRRS Santa Rosa, California
KION Salinas, California
KTYM Inglewood, California
KZUE El Reno, Oklahoma
WQXM Bartow, Florida
WBCU Union, South Carolina
WXBR Brockton, Massachusetts
WJTI West Allis, Wisconsin
WABQ Painesville, Ohio
WBNS Columbus, Ohio
WEKB Elkhorn City, Kentucky
WBRN Big Rapids, Michigan
WBUC Buckhannon, West Virginia
WKHZ Easton, Maryland
WDOG Barnwell, South Carolina
WEEN Lafayette, Tennessee
WELZ Belzoni, Mississippi
WEWO Laurinburg, North Carolina
WMCJ Cullman, Alabama
WDDY Albany, New York
WHBK Marshall, North Carolina
WIFI Florence, New Jersey
WIXN Dixon, Illinois
WJAK Jackson, Tennessee
WKJR Rantoul, Illinois
WKAM Goshen, Indiana
WKDV Manassas, Virginia
WLRP San Sebastian, Puerto Rico
WMBA Ambridge, Pennsylvania
WJCP North Vernon, Indiana
WHAL Phenix City/Columbus, Alabama
WPON Walled Lake, Michigan
WQOP Jacksonville, Florida
WRAD Radford, Virginia
WRKB Kannapolis, North Carolina
WROY Carmi, Illinois
WRRE Juncos, Puerto Rico
WRVK Mount Vernon, Kentucky
WBOG Tomah, Wisconsin
WVOX New Rochelle, New York
WTKT Harrisburg, Pennsylvania
WHIC Rochester, New York
WXEM Buford, Georgia
WXOK Port Allen, Louisiana
WXRQ Mount Pleasant, Tennessee
WZEP De Funiak Springs, Florida
WNPL Golden Gate, Florida

1470 khz

KAIR Atchison, Kansas
KYYW Abilene, Texas
KBSN Moses Lake, Washington
KDHN Dimmitt, Texas
KELA Centralia-Chehalis, Washington
KDEB(AM) Estes Park, Colorado
KHND Harvey, North Dakota
KGND Vinita, Oklahoma
KKTY Douglas, Wyoming
KLCL Lake Charles, Louisiana
KNXN Sierra Vista, Arizona
KIID Sacramento, California
KMAL Malden, Missouri
KUOL San Marcos, Texas
KUTY Palmdale, California
KWAY Waverly, Iowa
KWRD Henderson, Texas
KWSL Sioux City, Iowa
KSMM Liberal, Kansas
KFMZ Brookfield, Missouri
WBCR Alcoa, Tennessee
WBFC Stanton, Kentucky
WBKV West Bend, Wisconsin
WBTX Broadway-Timberville, Virginia
WCFJ Chicago Heights, Illinois
WCHJ Brookhaven, Mississippi
WCLA Claxton, Georgia
WFNT Flint, Michigan
WGNR Anderson, Indiana
WEVG Evergreen, Alabama
WJDY Salisbury, Maryland
WSAN Allentown, Pennsylvania
WLMC Georgetown, South Carolina
KMNQ Brooklyn Park, Minnesota
WLQR Toledo, Ohio
WMBD Peoria, Illinois
WMMW Meriden, Connecticut
WNAU New Albany, Mississippi
WLOA Farrell, Pennsylvania
WPDM Potsdam, New York
WQXL Columbia, South Carolina
WRGA Rome, Georgia
WAZN Watertown, Massachusetts
WMGG Egypt Lake, Florida
WNYY Ithaca, New York
WTOE Spruce Pine, North Carolina
WTTR Westminster, Maryland
WTZE Tazewell, Virginia
WVBS Burgaw, North Carolina
WVOL Berry Hill, Tennessee
WWBG Greensboro, North Carolina
WWNN Pompano Beach, Florida
WXAG Athens, Georgia
WLAM Lewiston, Maine
KNFL Tremonton, Utah
KFMZ(AM) Brookfield, Missouri

1480 khz

KAUS Austin, Minnesota
KAVA Pueblo, Colorado
KBMS Vancouver, Washington
KCHL San Antonio, Texas
KBXD Dallas, Texas
KGOE Eureka, California
KHQN Spanish Fork, Utah
KIOU Shreveport, Louisiana
KKCQ Fosston, Minnesota
KLEE Ottumwa, Iowa
KLMS Lincoln, Nebraska
KLVL Pasadena, Texas
KNTB Lakewood, Washington
KPHX Phoenix, Arizona
KQAM Wichita, Kansas
KRAE Cheyenne, Wyoming
KRXR Gooding, Idaho
KSBQ Santa Maria, California
KSDR Watertown, South Dakota
KTHS Berryville, Arkansas
KCZZ Mission, Kansas
KVNR Santa Ana, California
KYOS Merced, California
WABB Mobile, Alabama
WRCK Remsen, New York
WBBP Memphis, Tennessee
WCNS Latrobe, Pennsylvania
WIZD Neon, Kentucky
WSPY Geneva, Illinois
WGFY Charlotte, North Carolina
WGVU Kentwood, Michigan
WHBC Canton, Ohio
WIOS Tawas City-East Tawa, Michigan
WJBM Jerseyville, Illinois
WJFC Jefferson City, Tennessee
WJLE Smithville, Tennessee
WGNQ Bridgeport, Alabama
WKGC Southport, Florida
WKND Windsor, Connecticut
WLEA Hornell, New York
WQOH Irondale, Alabama
WMDD Fajardo, Puerto Rico
WCFR Springfield, Vermont
WQTM Fair Bluff, North Carolina
WVOI Marco Island, Florida
WPFJ Franklin, North Carolina
WPWC Dumfries-Triangle, Virginia
WHVO Hopkinsville, Kentucky
WCHZ Augusta, Georgia
WRSW Warsaw, Indiana
WSAR Fall River, Massachusetts
WSDS Salem Township, Michigan
WEEO Shippensburg, Pennsylvania
WLMV Madison, Wisconsin
WPFR Terre Haute, Indiana
WTLO Somerset, Kentucky
WTOY Salem, Virginia
WUNA Ocoee, Florida
WYRN Louisburg, North Carolina
WYZE Atlanta, Georgia
WZJY Mount Pleasant, South Carolina
WZRC New York, New York
WFLN Arcadia, Florida
WTOX Glen Allen, Virginia

1490 khz

KZZZ Bullhead City, Arizona
KBIX Muskogee, Oklahoma
KBKR Baker, Oregon
KBLF Red Bluff, California
KBRO Bremerton, Washington
KBSR Laurel, Montana
KBST Big Spring, Texas
KBUR Burlington, Iowa
KBZY Salem, Oregon
KCID Caldwell, Idaho
KCUZ Clifton, Arizona
KDBM Dillon, Montana
KDMO Carthage, Missouri
KDRO Sedalia, Missouri
KDRS Paragould, Arkansas
KYNR Toppenish, Washington
KEUN Eunice, Louisiana
KEYG Grand Coulee, Washington
KFCR Custer, South Dakota
KFFN Tucson, Arizona
KLGO Austin, Texas
KWOK Hoquiam, Washington
KGOS Torrington, Wyoming
KIBL Beeville, Texas
KGBA Heber, California
KJIN Houma, Louisiana
KKAN Phillipsburg, Kansas
KLGR Redwood Falls, Minnesota
KLNT Laredo, Texas
KLOG Kelso, Washington
KMET Banning, California
KNDC Hettinger, North Dakota
KNEL Brady, Texas
KMFS Guthrie, Oklahoma
KORN Mitchell, South Dakota
KOMJ Omaha, Nebraska
KOVC Valley City, North Dakota
KPKE Gunnison, Colorado
KPLT Paris, Texas
KQDS Duluth, Minnesota
KQTY Borger, Texas
KRIB Mason City, Iowa
KRKC King City, California
KSKR Roseburg, Oregon
KRSN Los Alamos, New Mexico
KRTK Chubbuck, Idaho
KRTN Raton, New Mexico
KRUI Ruidoso Downs, New Mexico
KRUS Ruston, Louisiana
KHVL Huntsville, Texas
KSYC Yreka, California
KTEL Walla Walla, Washington
KTOB Petaluma, California
KTOP Topeka, Kansas
KTTR Rolla, Missouri
KUGR Green River, Wyoming
KRKZ Forks, Washington
KWUD Woodville, Texas
KVWC Vernon, Texas
KCFC Boulder, Colorado
KWAC Bakersfield, California
KWMC Del Rio, Texas
KWXT Dardanelle, Arkansas
KXAR Hope, Arkansas
KXLQ Indianola, Iowa
KXRA Alexandria, Minnesota
KXRE Manitou Springs, Colorado
KYCA Prescott, Arizona
KOGN Ogden, Utah
KYZS Tyler, Texas
KZZN Littlefield, Texas
WABJ Adrian, Michigan
WACM West Springfield, Massachusetts

WAEY Princeton, West Virginia
WAFZ Immokalee, Florida
WSYA(AM) Anniston, Alabama
WARK Hagerstown, Maryland
WAZL Hazleton, Pennsylvania
WAZZ Fayetteville, North Carolina
WBAE Portland, Maine
WBCB Levittown, Pennsylvania
WBEX Chillicothe, Ohio
WBTA Batavia, New York
WXTG Hampton, Virginia
WCDO Sidney, New York
WCHM Clarkesville, Georgia
WCLD Cleveland, Mississippi
WCLU Glasgow, Kentucky
WCSS Amsterdam, New York
WCSV Crossville, Tennessee
WCVA Culpeper, Virginia
WDAN Danville, Illinois
WDBQ Dubuque, Iowa
WDLC Port Jervis, New York
WDUR Durham, North Carolina
WRLA West Point, Georgia
WDXL Lexington, Tennessee
WEMJ Laconia, New Hampshire
WESB Bradford, Pennsylvania
WFFX(AM) East St. Louis, Illinois
WFAD Middlebury, Vermont
WKYW Frankfort, Kentucky
WFXY Middlesboro, Kentucky
WGCD Chester, South Carolina
WGCH Greenwich, Connecticut
WGEZ Beloit, Wisconsin
WRCE Watkins Glen, New York
WBSS(AM) Pleasantville, New Jersey
WCEC Haverhill, Massachusetts
WHBB Selma, Alabama
WHOC Philadelphia, Mississippi
WIGM Medford, Wisconsin
WIKE Newport, Vermont
WITA Knoxville, Tennessee
WJJM Lewisburg, Tennessee
WERE Cleveland Heights, Ohio
WJOC Chattanooga, Tennessee
WKBV Richmond, Indiana
WKNY Kingston, New York
WKRO Cairo, Illinois
WKUN Monroe, Georgia
WKVT Brattleboro, Vermont
WDEP Ponce, Puerto Rico
WLFN La Crosse, Wisconsin
WLOE Eden, North Carolina
WLPA Lancaster, Pennsylvania
WMBM Miami Beach, Florida
WMGW Meadville, Pennsylvania
WMOA Marietta, Ohio
WMOG Brunswick, Georgia
WMPX Midland, Michigan
WMRC Milford, Massachusetts
WMRN Marion, Ohio
WNBT Wellsboro, Pennsylvania
WNTJ Johnstown, Pennsylvania
WKLQ Whitehall, Michigan
WOHI East Liverpool, Ohio
WOLF Syracuse, New York
WOMI Owensboro, Kentucky
WOPI Bristol, Tennessee
WOSH Oshkosh, Wisconsin
WPAK Farmville, Virginia
WPCI Greenville, South Carolina
WPNA Oak Park, Illinois
WBSS Pleasantville, New Jersey
WRMT Rocky Mount, North Carolina
WVBG Vicksburg, Mississippi
WSFB Quitman, Georgia
WSGB Sutton, West Virginia
WSIP Paintsville, Kentucky
WSIR Winter Haven, Florida
WSTP Salisbury, North Carolina
WSVM Valdese, North Carolina
WSWW Charleston, West Virginia
WSYL Sylvania, Georgia
WTCS Fairmont, West Virginia
WTIQ Manistique, Michigan
WJDJ Hartsville, South Carolina
WTTB Vero Beach, Florida
WTUP Tupelo, Mississippi
WTVL Waterville, Maine
WVGB Beaufort, South Carolina
WWIL Wilmington, North Carolina
WWNB New Bern, North Carolina
WWPR Bradenton, Florida
WXBD Biloxi, Mississippi
WTJV Deland, Florida
WYYZ Jasper, Georgia
WZOE Princeton, Illinois
WCOR Lebanon, Tennessee
WIRB Level Plains, Alabama
KOWL South Lake Tahoe, California
WUVR Lebanon, New Hampshire
KLZN Susanville, California
KCPX Spanish Valley, Utah
WKDR Berlin, New Hampshire
WTQS Cameron, South Carolina
WSNT Sandersville, Georgia

1500 khz

KANI Wharton, Texas
KBRN Boerne, Texas
KDFN Doniphan, Missouri
KJIM Sherman, Texas
KPGM Pawhuska, Oklahoma
KIEV Burbank, California
KSJX San Jose, California
KSTP St. Paul, Minnesota
KUMU(AM) Honolulu, Hawaii
WAKE Valparaiso, Indiana
WQMS Quitman, Mississippi
WBRI Indianapolis, Indiana
WBZI Xenia, Ohio
WPJX Zion, Illinois
WDEB Jamestown, Tennessee
WAYS Macon, Georgia
WDPC Dallas, Georgia
WZZQ(AM) Gaffney, South Carolina
WFIF Milford, Connecticut
WASN Youngstown, Ohio
WGHT Pompton Lakes, New Jersey
WQCR Alabaster, Alabama
WICY Malone, New York
WKAX Russellville, Alabama
WKIZ Key West, Florida
WKXO Berea, Kentucky
WLQV Detroit, Michigan
WMJL Marion, Kentucky
WMNT Manati, Puerto Rico
WPMB Vandalia, Illinois
WPSO New Port Richey, Florida
WSEM Donalsonville, Georgia
WSMX Winston-Salem, North Carolina
WTNE Trenton, Tennessee
WFED Washington, District of Columbia
WVSM Rainsville, Alabama
KMXO Merkel, Texas
KCLF New Roads, Louisiana

1510 khz

KOAZ Isleta, New Mexico
KAGC Bryan, Texas
KAGY Port Sulphur, Louisiana
KCTE Independence, Missouri
KCTX Childress, Texas
KCKK Littleton, Colorado
KFNN Mesa, Arizona
KGA Spokane, Washington
KROB Robstown, Texas
KIFG Iowa Falls, Iowa
KIRV Fresno, California
KSFN(AM) Piedmont, California
KLLB West Jordan, Utah
KMND Midland, Texas
KMRF Marshfield, Missouri
KMSD Mibank, South Dakota
KSPA Ontario, California
KNNS Larned, Kansas
KBED Nederland, Texas
KSTV Stephenville, Texas
KTTT Columbus, Nebraska
KWJB Canton, Texas
WRRD Waukesha, Wisconsin
WBSG Lajas, Puerto Rico
WEAL Greensboro, North Carolina
WJKN Jackson, Michigan
WJOT Wabash, Indiana
WLAC Nashville, Tennessee
WLGN Logan, Ohio
WLRB Macomb, Illinois
WFAI Salem, New Jersey
WWZN Boston, Massachusetts
WPUT Brewster, New York
WQUL Woodruff, South Carolina
WRNJ Hackettstown, New Jersey
WLKR Norwalk, Ohio
WWBC Cocoa, Florida
WWHN Joliet, Illinois
WWSM Annville-Cleona, Pennsylvania
WPGR Monroeville, Pennsylvania
WQUL(AM) Woodruff, South Carolina

1520 khz

KFXZ Lafayette, Louisiana
KQQB Stockdale, Texas
KGDD Oregon City, Oregon
KMSR Mayville, North Dakota
KMPG Hollister, California
KOLM Rochester, Minnesota
KOKC Oklahoma City, Oklahoma
KRHW Sikeston, Missouri
KSQB(AM) Sioux Falls, South Dakota
KSIB Creston, Iowa
KVTA Port Hueneme, California
KYND Cypress, Texas
WARR Warrenton, North Carolina
WCHE West Chester, Pennsylvania
WDCY Douglasville, Georgia
WNWT Rossford, Ohio
WDSL Mocksville, North Carolina
WEXY Wilton Manors, Florida
WIZZ Greenfield, Massachusetts
WGMA Spindale, North Carolina
WHOW Clinton, Illinois
WINW Canton, Ohio
WJMP Kent, Ohio
WKMG Newberry, South Carolina
WKVI Knox, Indiana
WLGC Greenup, Kentucky
WRCI Three Rivers, Michigan
WLUV Loves Park, Illinois
WMLM St. Louis, Michigan
WNWS Brownsville, Tennessee
WSVX Shelbyville, Indiana
WQCT Bryan, Ohio
WTHE Mineola, New York
WTLM Opelika, Alabama
WTRI Brunswick, Maryland
WVOZ San Juan, Puerto Rico
WWKB Buffalo, New York
WXYB Indian Rocks Beach, Florida

1530 khz

KCLR Ralls, Texas
KDSN Denison, Iowa
KFBK Sacramento, California
KGBT Harlingen, Texas
KVDW England, Arkansas
KMAM Butler, Missouri
KLBW New Boston, Texas
WLIQ Quincy, Illinois
KQNK Norton, Kansas
KZNX Creedmoor, Texas
KQSP Shakopee, Minnesota
KXTD Wagoner, Oklahoma
WASC Spartanburg, South Carolina
WCTR Chestertown, Maryland
WWDX Huntingdon, Tennessee
WDJZ Bridgeport, Connecticut
WENG Englewood, Florida
WYNE North East, Pennsylvania
WFIC Collinsville, Virginia
WJDM Elizabeth, New Jersey
WJJG Elmhurst, Illinois
WLCO Lapeer, Michigan
WLWB New Holstein, Wisconsin
WOBX Wanchese, North Carolina
WYMM Jacksonville, Florida
WLLQ Chapel Hill, North Carolina
WCKY Cincinnati, Ohio
WUPR Utuado, Puerto Rico
WVBF Middleborough Center, Massachusetts
WYGR Wyoming, Michigan
KVOG Agana, Guam
WTTI Dalton, Georgia

1540 khz

KASA Phoenix, Arizona
KBOA Kennett, Missouri
KMPC Los Angeles, California
KDYN Ozark, Arkansas
KEDA San Antonio, Texas
KGBC Galveston, Texas
KGLA Gretna, Louisiana
KREA Honolulu, Hawaii
KLKC Parsons, Kansas
KNGL McPherson, Kansas
KTGG Okemos, Michigan
KXEL Waterloo, Iowa
KXPA Bellevue, Washington
KZMP University Park, Texas
WWGK Cleveland, Ohio
WACA Wheaton, Maryland
WADK Newport, Rhode Island
WJZI(AM) Decatur, Indiana
WBCO Bucyrus, Ohio
WBIN Benton, Tennessee
WBNL Boonville, Indiana
WBTC Uhrichsville, Ohio
WECZ Punxsutawney, Pennsylvania
WXEX Exeter, New Hampshire
WIBS Guayama, Puerto Rico
WJJT Jellico, Tennessee
WKVQ Eatonton, Georgia
WKXG Greenwood, Mississippi
WLOI La Porte, Indiana
WMYJ Martinsville, Indiana
WNWR Philadelphia, Pennsylvania
WOGR Charlotte, North Carolina
WREJ Richmond, Virginia
WKDG Sumiton, Alabama
WSIV E. Syracuse, New York
WSMI Litchfield, Illinois
WTBI Pickens, South Carolina
WTKM Hartford, Wisconsin
WTXY Whiteville, North Carolina
WYCL Niles, Ohio
WYNC Yanceyville, North Carolina
WJZI Decatur, Indiana

1550 khz

KAPE Cape Girardeau, Missouri
KRPI Ferndale, Washington
KCOM Comanche, Texas
KDCC Dodge City, Kansas
KICS Hastings, Nebraska
KIWA Sheldon, Iowa
KKLE Winfield, Kansas
KLFJ Springfield, Missouri
KMAD Madill, Oklahoma
KMRI West Valley City, Utah
KSFT(AM) Saint Joseph, Missouri
KUAZ Tucson, Arizona
KKOV Vancouver, Washington
KWBC Navasota, Texas
KWRN Apple Valley, California
KXEX Fresno, California
KYAL Sapulpa, Oklahoma
KXTO Reno, Nevada
KZDG(AM) San Francisco, California
KZRK Canyon, Texas
WAMA Tampa, Florida
WZRK Northbrook, Illinois
WAZX Smyrna, Georgia
WIGN Bristol, Tennessee
WBFJ Winston-Salem, North Carolina
WBSC Bennettsville, South Carolina
WCGR Canandaigua, New York
WCLY Raleigh, North Carolina
WCSJ Morris, Illinois
WCVL Crawfordsville, Indiana
WLFP Braddock, Pennsylvania
WDLR Delaware, Ohio
WSDK Bloomfield, Connecticut
WEVR River Falls, Wisconsin
WHIT Madison, Wisconsin
WIRV Irvine, Kentucky
WJIL Jacksonville, Illinois
WKBA Vinton, Virginia
WKFE Yauco, Puerto Rico
WITK Pittston, Pennsylvania
WLOR Huntsville, Alabama
WLTI(AM) New Castle, Indiana
WMRE Charlestown, West Virginia
WNDI Sullivan, Indiana
WNTN Newton, Massachusetts
WOCC Corydon, Indiana
WPFC Baton Rouge, Louisiana
WRHC Coral Gables, Florida
WSRY Elkton, Maryland
WTHB Augusta, Georgia
WTTC Towanda, Pennsylvania
WUSP Utica, New York
WVAB Virginia Beach, Virginia
WKTF Vienna, Georgia
WMSK Morganfield, Kentucky

WNZF Bunnell, Florida
WLFP(AM) Braddock, Pennsylvania

1560 khz

KABI Abilene, Kansas
KBEW Blue Earth, Minnesota
KNGR Daingerfield, Texas
KHBR Hillsboro, Texas
KGOW Bellaire, Texas
KIQS Willows, California
KKAA Aberdeen, South Dakota
KLNG Council Bluffs, Iowa
KLTI Macon, Missouri
KZQQ Abilene, Texas
KNZR Bakersfield, California
WMBH Joplin, Missouri
KTUI Sullivan, Missouri
KTXZ West Lake Hills, Texas
KEBC Del City, Oklahoma
KZIZ Pacific, Washington
WZTQ Centre, Alabama
WAGL Lancaster, South Carolina
WAHT Clemson, South Carolina
WBOL Bolivar, Tennessee
WBYS Canton, Illinois
WCNW Fairfield, Ohio
WFSP Kingwood, West Virginia
WGLB Elm Grove, Wisconsin
WKDO Liberty, Kentucky
WKIK La Plata, Maryland
WMRO Gallatin, Tennessee
WNWN Portage, Michigan
WPAD Paducah, Kentucky
WQEW New York, New York
WQXY Hazard, Kentucky
WRIN Rensselaer, Indiana
WRSJ Bayamon, Puerto Rico
WSBV South Boston, Virginia
WSEZ Paoli, Indiana
WSLA Slidell, Louisiana
WLZR(AM) Melbourne, Florida
WTNS Coshocton, Ohio
WWYC Toledo, Ohio
WYZD Dobson, North Carolina
KVAN Burbank, Washington
KGOW(AM) Bellaire, Hawaii

1570 khz

KBRI Brinkley, Arkansas
KCVR Lodi, California
KPIO Loveland, Colorado
KLEX Lexington, Missouri
KLLA Leesville, Louisiana
KAKK Walker, Minnesota
KMCD Fairfield, Iowa
KZLI Catoosa, Oklahoma
KNDY Marysville, Kansas
KVTK Vermillion, South Dakota
KPRO Riverside, California
KPYK Terrell, Texas
KQWC Webster City, Iowa
KTAT Frederick, Oklahoma
KTGE Salinas, California
KUAU Haiku, Hawaii
KVLG La Grange, Texas
KYCR Golden Valley, Minnesota
WABL Amite, Louisiana
WHTX Warren, Ohio
WBGX Harvey, Illinois
WBGZ Alton, Illinois
WVTL Amsterdam, New York
WCLE Cleveland, Tennessee
WCRL Oneonta, Alabama
WFLR Dundee, New York
WFRL Freeport, Illinois
WFUR Grand Rapids, Michigan
WGLL Auburn, Indiana
WVOJ Fernandina Beach, Florida
WILO Frankfort, Indiana
WISP Doylestown, Pennsylvania
WIZK Bay Springs, Mississippi
WKBH Holmen, Wisconsin
WKKS Vanceburg, Kentucky
WLBQ Morgantown, Kentucky
WLKD Minocqua, Wisconsin
WNCA Siler City, North Carolina
WNKX Lobelville, Tennessee
WNSH Beverly, Massachusetts
WNST Towson, Maryland
WOKC Okeechobee, Florida
WONA Winona, Mississippi
WPGM Danville, Pennsylvania
WPPC Penuelas, Puerto Rico
WPTW Piqua, Ohio
WQTW Latrobe, Pennsylvania
WFTU Riverhead, New York
WSCO Appleton, Wisconsin
WIGO Morrow, Georgia
WSWV Pennington Gap, Virginia
WTAY Robinson, Illinois
WTLK Taylorsville, North Carolina
WTRB Ripley, Tennessee
WTWB Auburndale, Florida
WWCK Flint, Michigan
WNDA New Albany, Indiana
WYTI Rocky Mount, Virginia
KBCV Hollister, Missouri
WECU Winterville, North Carolina

1580 khz

KAMI Cozad, Nebraska
KBLA Santa Monica, California
KCHA Charles City, Iowa
KDOM Windom, Minnesota
KESM Eldorado Springs, Missouri
KHGG Van Buren, Arkansas
KGAF Gainesville, Texas
KGAL Lebanon, Oregon
KIRT Mission, Texas
KMIK Tempe, Arizona
KNIM Maryville, Missouri
KOKB Blackwell, Oklahoma
KTGR Columbia, Missouri
KTLU Rusk, Texas
KREL Colorado Springs, Colorado
KWED Seguin, Texas
KXZZ Lake Charles, Louisiana
WNPZ Knoxville, Tennessee
WAMW Washington, Indiana
WAMY Amory, Mississippi
WBCP Urbana, Illinois
WCCF Punta Gorda, Florida
WIFE Connersville, Indiana
WDQN Duquoin, Illinois
WIOL Columbus, Georgia
WESY Leland, Mississippi
WWDN Danville, Virginia
WHLY South Bend, Indiana
WLIJ Shelbyville, Tennessee
WLIM Patchogue, New York
WPGY Ellijay, Georgia
WEKO Morovis, Puerto Rico
WNTF Bithlo, Florida
WGYM Hammonton, New Jersey
WORV Hattiesburg, Mississippi
WVOK Oxford, Alabama
WNEW Morningside, Maryland
WPJK Orangeburg, South Carolina
WPKY Princeton, Kentucky
WRDD Ebensburg, Pennsylvania
WSRF Fort Lauderdale, Florida
WTCL Chattahoochee, Florida
WWTF Georgetown, Kentucky
WTTN Columbus, Wisconsin
WVKO Columbus, Ohio
WVZN Columbia, Pennsylvania
WWSJ St. Johns, Michigan
WZKY Albemarle, North Carolina
WPMO Pascagoula-Moss Point, Mississippi
DKEZD Windsor, California

1590 khz

KBJT Fordyce, Arkansas
KGFK East Grand Forks, Minnesota
KDAE Sinton, Texas
KDAV Lubbock, Texas
KDEX Dexter, Missouri
KDJS Willmar, Minnesota
KELP El Paso, Texas
KGAS Carthage, Texas
KKAY White Castle, Louisiana
KLFE Seattle, Washington
KLIV San Jose, California
KMBD(AM) Tillamook, Oregon
KMOZ Rolla, Missouri
KPRT Kansas City, Missouri
KQLO Sun Valley, Nevada
KLRK Mexia, Texas
KTCH Wayne, Nebraska
KUNX Ventura, California
KVGB Great Bend, Kansas
KWBG Boone, Iowa
KWEY Weatherford, Oklahoma
KMIC Houston, Texas
KYNG Springdale, Arkansas
WABV Abbeville, South Carolina
WAIK Galesburg, Illinois
WAKR Akron, Ohio
WALG Albany, Georgia
WARV Warwick, Rhode Island
WASB Brockport, New York
WAUB Auburn, New York
WBHN Bryson City, North Carolina
WCAM Camden, South Carolina
WCSL Cherryville, North Carolina
WDBL Springfield, Tennessee
WAMS(AM) Ocean City, Maryland
WFTH Richmond, Virginia
WGGO Salamanca, New York
WHPY Clayton, North Carolina
WHLX Marine City, Michigan
WIXK New Richmond, Wisconsin
WFBR Glen Burnie, Maryland
WKTP Jonesborough, Tennessee
WLBN Lebanon, Kentucky
WNTS Beech Grove, Indiana
WYSR High Point, North Carolina
WCGO Evanston, Illinois
WRCY Mt. Vernon, Indiana
WPSL Port St. Lucie, Florida
WPUL South Daytona, Florida
WPVL Platteville, Wisconsin
WPWA Chester, Pennsylvania
WQCH La Fayette, Georgia
WRXB St. Petersburg Beach, Florida
WSMN Nashua, New Hampshire
WQLX Chillicothe, Ohio
WTGA Thomaston, Georgia
WGBW Denmark, Wisconsin
WTVB Coldwater, Michigan
WODJ Big Rapids, Michigan
WVNA Tuscumbia, Alabama
WVOE Chadbourn, North Carolina
WPSN Honesdale, Pennsylvania
WXRF Guayama, Puerto Rico
WXRS Swainsboro, Georgia
WZUM Carnegie, Pennsylvania
WHGT Maugansville, Maryland

1600 khz

KATZ St. Louis, Missouri
KVRI Blaine, Washington
KEPN Lakewood, Colorado
KGYM Cedar Rapids, Iowa
KDAK Carrington, North Dakota
KIVA Albuquerque, New Mexico
KOPB Eugene, Oregon
KGST Fresno, California
KLEB Golden Meadow, Louisiana
KLGA Algona, Iowa
KMDO Fort Scott, Kansas
KAHZ Pomona, California
KNCY Nebraska City, Nebraska
KNWA Bellefonte, Arkansas
KOGT Orange, Texas
KOHI St. Helens, Oregon
KOKE Pflugerville, Texas
KRFS Superior, Nebraska
KRVA Cockrell Hill, Texas
KTUB Centerville, Utah
KTAP Santa Maria, California
KTTN Trenton, Missouri
KUBA Yuba City, California
KPNP Watertown, Minnesota
KXEW South Tucson, Arizona
KYBC Cottonwood, Arizona
WAAM Ann Arbor, Michigan
WAOS Austell, Georgia
WARU Peru, Indiana
WATX Algood, Tennessee
WHJB Bedford, Pennsylvania
WULM Springfield, Ohio
WCPK Chesapeake, Virginia
WEHH Elmira Hts-Horsehds, New York
WHIY Huntsville, Alabama
WFIS Fountain Inn, South Carolina
WHOL Allentown, Pennsylvania
WHTY Riviera Beach, Florida
WIDU Fayetteville, North Carolina
WLXE Rockville, Maryland
WJSA Jersey Shore, Pennsylvania
WMQM Lakeland, Tennessee
WKWF Key West, Florida
WLUE Eminence, Kentucky
WKZK North Augusta, South Carolina
WCMA(AM) Bayamon, Puerto Rico
WMCR Oneida, New York
WKKX Wheeling, West Virginia
WLAA Winter Garden, Florida
WPDC Elizabethtown, Pennsylvania
WHNP East Longmeadow, Massachusetts
WHTY(AM) Riviera Beach, Florida
WRSL Corbin, Kentucky
WTTF Tiffin, Ohio
WTZQ Hendersonville, North Carolina
WUNR Brookline, Massachusetts
WWRL New York, New York
WXMY Saltville, Virginia
WXVI Montgomery, Alabama
WZNZ Atlantic Beach, Florida
WZZW Milton, West Virginia
WRPN Ripon, Wisconsin
KUSH Cushing, Oklahoma
WRJE Dover, Delaware

1620 khz

KOZN Bellevue, Nebraska
WTAW College Station, Texas
KSMH West Sacramento, California
KYIZ Renton, Washington
WDHP Frederiksted, Virgin Islands
WDND South Bend, Indiana
WNRP Gulf Breeze, Florida

1630 khz

KCJJ Iowa City, Iowa
KRND Fox Farm, Wyoming
KKGM Fort Worth, Texas
WRDW Augusta, Georgia

1640 khz

KFXY Enid, Oklahoma
KBJA Sandy, Utah
KDIA Vallejo, California
KDZR Lake Oswego, Oregon
WKSH Sussex, Wisconsin
WTNI Biloxi, Mississippi

1650 khz

KSVE El Paso, Texas
KBJD Denver, Colorado
KCNZ Cedar Falls, Iowa
KFOX Torrance, California
KYHN Ft. Smith, Arkansas
WHKT Portsmouth, Virginia

1660 khz

KTIQ Merced, California
KRZI Waco, Texas
KUDL Kansas City, Kansas
KQWB West Fargo, North Dakota
KXOL Brigham City, Utah
WBCN Charlotte, North Carolina
WBCN(AM) Charlotte, North Carolina
WCNZ Marco Island, Florida
WWRU Jersey City, New Jersey
WGIT Canovanas, Puerto Rico

1670 khz

KNRO Redding, California
KHPY Moreno Valley, California
WPLA(AM) Dry Branch, Georgia
WPLA Dry Branch, Georgia
WTDY Madison, Wisconsin

1680 khz

KGED Fresno, California
KNTS Seattle, Washington
KRJO Monroe, Louisiana
WPRR Ada, Michigan
WOKB Winter Garden, Florida
WTTM Lindenwold, New Jersey

1690 khz

KDDZ Arvada, Colorado
KFSG Roseville, California
WMLB Avondale Estates, Georgia
WVON Berwyn, Illinois
WPTX Lexington Park, Maryland

1700 khz

KBGG Des Moines, Iowa
KVNS Brownsville, Texas

KKLF Richardson, Texas
WRCR Ramapo, New York
WEUP Huntsville, Alabama

540 khz

KDFT Ferris, Texas
KRXA Carmel Valley, California
KYAH Delta, Utah
KNMX Las Vegas, New Mexico
KMLB Monroe, Louisiana
KVIP Redding, California
KWMT Fort Dodge, Iowa
WASG Daphne, Alabama
WDAK Columbus, Georgia
WGOP Pocomoke City, Maryland
WKFN Clarksville, Tennessee
WETC Wendell-Zebulon, North Carolina
WGTH Richlands, Virginia
WLIE Islip, New York
WFLF Pine Hills, Florida
WRGC Sylva, North Carolina
WWCS Canonsburg, Pennsylvania
WYNN Florence, South Carolina
WAUK Jackson, Wisconsin
WXNH Jaffrey, New Hampshire
WXYG Sauk Rapids, Minnesota

550 khz

KARI Blaine, Washington
KBOW Butte, Montana
KCRS Midland, Texas
KFRM Salina, Kansas
KFYR Bismarck, North Dakota
KFYI Phoenix, Arizona
KMVI Wailuku, Hawaii
KOAC Corvallis, Oregon
KRAI Craig, Colorado
KTRS St. Louis, Missouri
KTSA San Antonio, Texas
KTZN Anchorage, Alaska
KUZZ Bakersfield, California
WAYR Orange Park, Florida
WDEV Waterbury, Vermont
WDUN Gainesville, Georgia
WGR Buffalo, New York
WIOZ Pinehurst, North Carolina
WAME Statesville, North Carolina
WKRC Cincinnati, Ohio
WPAB Ponce, Puerto Rico
WSAU Wausau, Wisconsin
WSVA Harrisonburg, Virginia
KLLV Breen, Colorado

560 khz

KBLU Yuma, Arizona
KLVI Beaumont, Texas
KLZ Denver, Colorado
KMON Great Falls, Montana
KPQ Wenatchee, Washington
KSFO San Francisco, California
KVOK Kodiak, Alaska
KWTO Springfield, Missouri
WCKL Catskill, New York
WEBC Duluth, Minnesota
WFIL Philadelphia, Pennsylvania
WFRB Frostburg, Maryland
WGAI Elizabeth City, North Carolina
WGAN Portland, Maine
WHBQ Memphis, Tennessee
WHYN Springfield, Massachusetts
WIND Chicago, Illinois
WJLS Beckley, West Virginia
WRDT Monroe, Michigan
WMIK Middlesboro, Kentucky
WNSR Brentwood, Tennessee
WOOF Dothan, Alabama
WQAM Miami, Florida
WXBT Columbia, South Carolina
WXBT(AM) Columbia, South Carolina

567 khz

KGUM Hagatna, Guam

570 khz

KSNM Las Cruces, New Mexico
KCFJ Alturas, California
KLAC Los Angeles, California
KLIF Dallas, Texas
KNRS Salt Lake City, Utah
KQNG Lihue, Hawaii
KVI Seattle, Washington
WAAX Gadsden, Alabama
WTBN Pinellas Park, Florida
WIDS Russell Springs, Kentucky
WKBN Youngstown, Ohio
WKYX Paducah, Kentucky
WMAM Marinette, Wisconsin
WMCA New York, New York
WNAX Yankton, South Dakota
WFNL Raleigh, North Carolina
WSYR Syracuse, New York
WWNC Asheville, North Carolina

580 khz

KIDO Nampa, Idaho
KJMJ Alexandria, Louisiana
KMJ Fresno, California
KRFE Lubbock, Texas
KRSA Petersburg, Alaska
KSAZ Marana, Arizona
KUBC Montrose, Colorado
KZMX Hot Springs, South Dakota
WACQ(AM) Tuskegee, Alabama
WCHS Charleston, West Virginia
WDBO Orlando, Florida
WELO Tupelo, Mississippi
WGAC Augusta, Georgia
WHP Harrisburg, Pennsylvania
WIBW Topeka, Kansas
WILL Urbana, Illinois
WKAQ San Juan, Puerto Rico
WKSK West Jefferson, North Carolina
WKTY La Crosse, Wisconsin
WLVA Lynchburg, Virginia
WYHM Rockwood, Tennessee
WTAG Worcester, Massachusetts
WTCM Traverse City, Michigan
KANA Anaconda, Montana

585 khz

KJAL Tafuna, American Samoa

590 khz

KQNT Spokane, Washington
KZHS Hot Springs, Arkansas
KCSJ Pueblo, Colorado
KFNS Wood River, Illinois
KGLE Glendive, Montana
KHAR Anchorage, Alaska
KID Idaho Falls, Idaho
KLBJ Austin, Texas
KSSK Honolulu, Hawaii
KSUB Cedar City, Utah
KTIE San Bernardino, California
KTHO South Lake Tahoe, California
KUGN Eugene, Oregon
WAFC Clewiston, Florida
WARM Scranton, Pennsylvania
WCAB Rutherfordton, North Carolina
WDIZ Panama City, Florida
WDWD Atlanta, Georgia
WEZE Boston, Massachusetts
WJMS Ironwood, Michigan
WKZO Kalamazoo, Michigan
WLES Bon Air, Virginia
WMBS Uniontown, Pennsylvania
KXSP Omaha, Nebraska
WROW Albany, New York
WVLK Lexington, Kentucky
WWLX Lawrenceburg, Tennessee

600 khz

KERB Kermit, Texas
KGEZ Kalispell, Montana
KCOL Wellington, Colorado
KOGO San Diego, California
KROD El Paso, Texas
KSJB Jamestown, North Dakota
KTBB Tyler, Texas
KVNA Flagstaff, Arizona
WYEL Mayaguez, Puerto Rico
WBOB(AM) Jacksonville, Florida
WCAO Baltimore, Maryland
WCHT Escanaba, Michigan
WCVP Murphy, North Carolina
WFRM Coudersport, Pennsylvania
WFST Caribou, Maine
WICC Bridgeport, Connecticut
WBOB Jacksonville, Florida
WKYH Paintsville, Kentucky
WMT Cedar Rapids, Iowa
WREC Memphis, Tennessee
WSJS Winston-Salem, North Carolina
WSNL Flint, Michigan
WSOM Salem, Ohio
WVAR Richwood, West Virginia
WVOG New Orleans, Louisiana

610 khz

KARV Russellville, Arkansas
KAVL Lancaster, California
KCSR Chadron, Nebraska
KDAL Duluth, Minnesota
KEAR San Francisco, California
KNML Albuquerque, New Mexico
KILT Houston, Texas
KOJM Havre, Montana
KONA Kennewick-Richland-P, Washington
KRTA Medford, Oregon
KVLE Vail, Colorado
KVNU Logan, Utah
WAGG Birmingham, Alabama
WCEH Hawkinsville, Georgia
KCSP Kansas City, Missouri
WEXS Patillas, Puerto Rico
WFNZ Charlotte, North Carolina
WGIR Manchester, New Hampshire
WIOD Miami, Florida
WIP Philadelphia, Pennsylvania
WXVA Winchester, Virginia
WPLO Grayson, Georgia
WRUS Russellville, Kentucky
WVBE Roanoke, Virginia
WSNG Torrington, Connecticut
WTVN Columbus, Ohio
WVTJ Pensacola, Florida

620 khz

KPOJ Portland, Oregon
KGTL Homer, Alaska
KIGS Hanford, California
KHNU Hilo, Hawaii
KMJC Mount Shasta, California
KMKI Plano, Texas
KMNS Sioux City, Iowa
KJOL Grand Junction, Colorado
KTAR Phoenix, Arizona
KWAL Wallace, Idaho
WDNC Durham, North Carolina
WHEN Syracuse, New York
WJDX Jackson, Mississippi
WSNR Jersey City, New Jersey
WJHX Lexington, Alabama
WKHB Irwin, Pennsylvania
WRJZ Knoxville, Tennessee
WDAE St. Petersburg, Florida
WGCV Cayce, South Carolina
WTMJ Milwaukee, Wisconsin
WTUV Louisville, Kentucky
WTRP La Grange, Georgia
WVMT Burlington, Vermont
WWNR Beckley, West Virginia
WZON Bangor, Maine
KHNU(AM) Hilo, Hawaii
KGTL(AM) Homer, Alaska

630 khz

KCIS Edmonds, Washington
KHOW Denver, Colorado
KIAM Nenana, Alaska
KIDD Monterey, California
KFXD Boise, Idaho
KJNO Juneau, Alaska
KJSL St. Louis, Missouri
KTRW Opportunity, Washington
KLEA Lovington, New Mexico
KPLY Reno, Nevada
KSLR San Antonio, Texas
KTKK Sandy, Utah
KUAM Agana, Guam
KVMA Magnolia, Arkansas
KWRO Coquille, Oregon
WAVU Albertville, Alabama
WBMQ Savannah, Georgia
WREY St. Paul, Minnesota
WEJL Scranton, Pennsylvania
WAIZ Hickory, North Carolina
WJDB Thomasville, Alabama
WLAP Lexington, Kentucky
WMAL Washington, District of Columbia
WMFD Wilmington, North Carolina
WNEG Toccoa, Georgia
WPRO Providence, Rhode Island
WUNO San Juan, Puerto Rico
WJAW St. Marys, West Virginia

640 khz

KFI Los Angeles, California
KGVW Belgrade, Montana
KTIB Thibodaux, Louisiana
KYUK Bethel, Alaska
WCRV Collierville, Tennessee
WFNC Fayetteville, North Carolina
WXSM Blountville, Tennessee
WGST Atlanta, Georgia
WHLO Akron, Ohio
WVLG Wildwood, Florida
WMEN Royal Palm Beach, Florida
WMFN Zeeland, Michigan
WNNZ Westfield, Massachusetts
WOI Ames, Iowa
WWJZ Mount Holly, New Jersey
KWPN(AM) Moore, Oklahoma

650 khz

KENI Anchorage, Alaska
KGAB Orchard Valley, Wyoming
KRTR Honolulu, Hawaii
KIKK Pasadena, Texas
KMTI Manti, Utah
KSTE Rancho Cordova, California
WHAN Ashland, Virginia
WNMT Nashwauk, Minnesota
WSRO Ashland, Massachusetts
WSM Nashville, Tennessee

660 khz

KAPS Mount Vernon, Washington
KCRO Omaha, Nebraska
KEYZ Williston, North Dakota
KFAR Fairbanks, Alaska
KWVE(AM) Oildale, California
KSKY Balch Springs, Texas
KTNN Window Rock, Arizona
KXOR Junction City, Oregon
WAMO Wilkinsburg, Pennsylvania
WBHR Sauk Rapids, Minnesota
WLOY Rural Retreat, Virginia
WXQW Fairhope, Alabama
WLFJ Greenville, South Carolina
WFAN New York, New York
WMIC Sandusky, Michigan
WORL Altamonte Springs, Florida
WXIC Waverly, Ohio

670 khz

KBOI Boise, Idaho
KDLG Dillingham, Alaska
KLTT Commerce City, Colorado
KPUA Hilo, Hawaii
KIRN Simi Valley, California
KWXI Glenwood, Arkansas
WIEZ Lewistown, Pennsylvania
WMTY Farragut, Tennessee
WSCR Chicago, Illinois
WRJR Claremont, Virginia
WWFE Miami, Florida
WYLS York, Alabama
KMZQ Las Vegas, Nevada

680 khz

KBRD Lacey, Washington
KBRW Barrow, Alaska
KFEQ St. Joseph, Missouri
KKGR East Helena, Montana
KKYX San Antonio, Texas
KNBR San Francisco, California
KOMW Omak, Washington
KWKA Clovis, New Mexico
WAPA San Juan, Puerto Rico
WKAZ Charleston, West Virginia
WCBM Baltimore, Maryland
WCNN North Atlanta, Georgia
WCTT Corbin, Kentucky
WDBC Escanaba, Michigan
WINR Binghamton, New York
WISR Butler, Pennsylvania
WHBE Newburg, Kentucky
WOGO Hallie, Wisconsin
WPTF Raleigh, North Carolina

WRKO Boston, Massachusetts
WGES St. Petersburg, Florida

690 khz

KBLI Blackfoot, Idaho
KCEE Tucson, Arizona
KEWI Benton, Arkansas
KFXN Minneapolis, Minnesota
KGGF Coffeyville, Kansas
KTSM El Paso, Texas
KOAQ Terrytown, Nebraska
KPET Lamesa, Texas
KHNR Honolulu, Hawaii
KRCO Prineville, Oregon
KRGS Rifle, Colorado
KSTL St. Louis, Missouri
WADS Ansonia, Connecticut
WELD Fisher, West Virginia
WSPZ(AM) Birmingham, Alabama
WNZK Dearborn Heights, Michigan
WPHE Phoenixville, Pennsylvania
WIST New Orleans, Louisiana
WVCY Oshkosh, Wisconsin
WZAP Bristol, Virginia
XETRA Tijuana, Mexico

700 khz

KBYR Anchorage, Alaska
KGRV Winston, Oregon
KXLX Airway Heights, Washington
KSEV Tomball, Texas
KMBX Soledad, California
KALL North Salt Lake City, Utah
WCNF Dothan, Alabama
WLW Cincinnati, Ohio
WDMV Walkersville, Maryland
KHSE Wylie, Texas
KNAX McCook, Nebraska

710 khz

KCMO Kansas City, Missouri
KSPN Los Angeles, California
KEEL Shreveport, Louisiana
KFIA Carmichael, California
KGNC Amarillo, Texas
KIRO Seattle, Washington
KNUS Denver, Colorado
KBMB Black Canyon City, Arizona
KURV Edinburg, Texas
KXMR Bismarck, North Dakota
WAQI Miami, Florida
WDSM Superior, Wisconsin
WEGG Rose Hill, North Carolina
WEKC Williamsburg, Kentucky
WFCM Smyrna, Tennessee
WFNR Blacksburg, Virginia
WKJB Mayaguez, Puerto Rico
WNTM Mobile, Alabama
WOR New York, New York
WPOG St. Matthews, South Carolina
WROM Rome, Georgia
WTPR Paris, Tennessee
WUFF Eastman, Georgia
WZOO Asheboro, North Carolina

720 khz

KDWN Las Vegas, Nevada
KFIR Sweet Home, Oregon
KOTZ Kotzebue, Alaska
KSAH Universal City, Texas
KUAI Eleele, Hawaii
WGCR Pisgah Forest, North Carolina
WGN(AM) Chicago, Illinois
WVCC Hogansville, Georgia
WRZN Hernando, Florida
WHYF(AM) Shiremanstown, Pennsylvania

730 khz

KBSU-FM Boise, Idaho
KDAZ Albuquerque, New Mexico
KKDA Grand Prairie, Texas
KLOE Goodland, Kansas
KEZX Medford, Oregon
KQPN West Memphis, Arkansas
KSVN Ogden, Utah
KULE Ephrata, Washington
KURL Billings, Montana
KWOA Worthington, Minnesota
KWRE Warrenton, Missouri
WACE Chicopee, Massachusetts
WTNT Alexandria, Virginia
WDOS Oneonta, New York
WFMC Goldsboro, North Carolina
WFMW Madisonville, Kentucky
WJMT Merrill, Wisconsin
WJTO Bath, Maine
WJYM Bowling Green, Ohio
WLIL Lenoir City, Tennessee
WMNA Gretna, Virginia
WMTC Vancleve, Kentucky
WZMF(AM) Nanticoke, Pennsylvania
WZGV Cramerton, North Carolina
WPIT Pittsburgh, Pennsylvania
WLTQ Charleston, South Carolina
WSTT Thomasville, Georgia
WUMP Madison, Alabama
WVFN East Lansing, Michigan
WWTK Lake Placid, Florida
KBQX Big Spring, Texas

740 khz

KATK Carlsbad, New Mexico
KBOE Oskaloosa, Iowa
KBRT Avalon, California
KCBS San Francisco, California
KCMC Texarkana, Texas
KIDR Phoenix, Arizona
KRMG Tulsa, Oklahoma
KTRH Houston, Texas
KVFC Cortez, Colorado
KVOR Colorado Springs, Colorado
WNYH Huntington, New York
WIAC San Juan, Puerto Rico
WIRJ Humboldt, Tennessee
WJIB Cambridge, Massachusetts
WHMT(AM) Tullahoma, Tennessee
WMBG Williamsburg, Virginia
WDGY Hudson, Wisconsin
WMSP Montgomery, Alabama
WNOP Newport, Kentucky
WPAQ Mount Airy, North Carolina
WRNR Martinsburg, West Virginia
WRPQ Baraboo, Wisconsin
WCXZ Harrogate, Tennessee
WSBR Boca Raton, Florida
WVCH Chester, Pennsylvania
WVLN Olney, Illinois
WYGM Orlando, Florida
KVOX Fargo, North Dakota

750 khz

KAMA El Paso, Texas
KBNN Lebanon, Missouri
KERR Polson, Montana
KFQD Anchorage, Alaska
KKNO Gretna, Louisiana
KMMJ Grand Island, Nebraska
KOAL Price, Utah
KSEO Durant, Oklahoma
KXTG Portland, Oregon
KXTG(AM) Portland, Oregon
WQOR Olyphant, Pennsylvania
WAUG New Hope, North Carolina
WBMD Baltimore, Maryland
WARD Petoskey, Michigan
WNDZ Portage, Indiana
WPDX Clarksburg, West Virginia
WTHQ Brookport, Illinois
WSB Atlanta, Georgia
KHWG Fallon, Nevada
WRME Hampden, Maine

760 khz

KCCV Overland Park, Kansas
KFMB San Diego, California
KGU Honolulu, Hawaii
KMTL Sherwood, Arkansas
KTBA Tuba City, Arizona
KTKR San Antonio, Texas
KKZN Thornton, Colorado
WEFL Tequesta, Florida
WCHP Champlain, New York
WCIS Morganton, North Carolina
WCPS Tarboro, North Carolina
WENO Nashville, Tennessee
WJR Detroit, Michigan
WLCC Brandon, Florida
WETR Knoxville, Tennessee
WORA Mayaguez, Puerto Rico
WURL Moody, Alabama
WVNE Leicester, Massachusetts

770 khz

KATL Miles City, Montana
KCBC Manteca, California
KCHU Valdez, Alaska
KJCB Lafayette, Louisiana
KKOB Albuquerque, New Mexico
KKOB Exp S Santa Fe, New Mexico
KTTH Seattle, Washington
KAAM Garland, Texas
KUOM Minneapolis, Minnesota
WABC New York, New York
WAIS Buchtel, Ohio
WKFB Jeannette, Pennsylvania
WCGW Nicholasville, Kentucky
WEW St. Louis, Missouri
WLWL Rockingham, North Carolina
WTOR Youngstown, New York
WVNN Athens, Alabama
WWCN North Fort Myers, Florida
WYRV Cedar Bluff, Virginia

780 khz

KAZM Sedona, Arizona
KKOH Reno, Nevada
KNOM Nome, Alaska
KSPI Stillwater, Oklahoma
WAVA Arlington, Virginia
WBBM Chicago, Illinois
WCKB Dunn, North Carolina
WIIN Ridgeland, Mississippi
WJAG Norfolk, Nebraska
WTME Rumford, Maine
WPTN Cookeville, Tennessee
WXME Monticello, Maine
WWOL Forest City, North Carolina
WZZX Lineville, Alabama

790 khz

KABC Los Angeles, California
KBME Houston, Texas
KBRV Soda Springs, Idaho
KCAM Glennallen, Alaska
KFGO Fargo, North Dakota
KFYO Lubbock, Texas
KGHL Billings, Montana
KGMI Bellingham, Washington
KJRB Spokane, Washington
KKON Kealakekua, Hawaii
KOSY Texarkana, Arkansas
KNST Tucson, Arizona
KFPT Clovis, California
KSPD Boise, Idaho
KURM Rogers, Arkansas
KWIL Albany, Oregon
KXXX Colby, Kansas
WAEB Allentown, Pennsylvania
WAXY South Miami, Florida
WAYY Eau Claire, Wisconsin
WETB Johnson City, Tennessee
WGRA Cairo, Georgia
WHTH Heath, Ohio
WLBE Leesburg-Eustis, Florida
WLSV Wellsville, New York
WMC Memphis, Tennessee
WNIS Norfolk, Virginia
WPIC Sharon, Pennsylvania
WQSV Ashland City, Tennessee
WQXI Atlanta, Georgia
WVCD Bamberg-Denmark, South Carolina
WRMS Beardstown, Illinois
WSFN Brunswick, Georgia
WSGW Saginaw, Michigan
WPRV Providence, Rhode Island
WSVG Mount Jackson, Virginia
WPNN Pensacola, Florida
WBLO Thomasville, North Carolina
WTNY Watertown, New York
WTSK Tuscaloosa, Alabama
WKRD Louisville, Kentucky
KEJY Eureka, California

800 khz

KAGH Crossett, Arkansas
KDDD Dumas, Texas
KBFP Bakersfield, California
KINY Juneau, Alaska
KPDQ Portland, Oregon
KQAD Luverne, Minnesota
KQCV Oklahoma City, Oklahoma
KREI Farmington, Missouri
KVOM Morrilton, Arkansas
KXIC Iowa City, Iowa
WNNW Lawrence, Massachusetts
WCHA Chambersburg, Pennsylvania
WDEH Sweetwater, Tennessee
WDSC Dillon, South Carolina
WDUX Waupaca, Wisconsin
WHOS Decatur, Alabama
WJAT Swainsboro, Georgia
WKBC North Wilkesboro, North Carolina
WVHU Huntington, West Virginia
WKZI Casey, Illinois
WLAD Danbury, Connecticut
WMGY Montgomery, Alabama
WPEL Montrose, Pennsylvania
WPJM Greer, South Carolina
WPLK Palatka, Florida
WSHO New Orleans, Louisiana
WSVS Crewe, Virginia
WTMR Camden, New Jersey
WVAL Sauk Rapids, Minnesota

801 khz

KTWG Agana, Guam

810 khz

KBHB Sturgis, South Dakota
KGO San Francisco, California
KLVZ Brighton, Colorado
KYTY Somerset, Texas
KSWV Santa Fe, New Mexico
KTBI Ephrata, Washington
KXOI Crane, Texas
WXFO Royston, Georgia
WCTA Alamo, Tennessee
WDMP Dodgeville, Wisconsin
WEDO McKeesport, Pennsylvania
WEKG Jackson, Kentucky
WGY Schenectady, New York
WHB Kansas City, Missouri
WJJQ Tomahawk, Wisconsin
WKVM San Juan, Puerto Rico
WMGC Murfreesboro, Tennessee
WMJH Rockford, Michigan
WCKA Jacksonville, Alabama
WPIN Dublin, Virginia
WQIZ St. George, South Carolina
WSJC Magee, Mississippi
WSYW Indianapolis, Indiana
WTHV Hahira, Georgia
WYRE Annapolis, Maryland
WRSO(AM) Orlovista, Florida

820 khz

KCBF Fairbanks, Alaska
KGNW Burien-Seattle, Washington
DKORC Anacortes, Washington
WBAP Fort Worth, Texas
WGGM Chester, Virginia
WNYC New York, New York
WVSG Columbus, Ohio
WSWI Evansville, Indiana
WWLZ Horseheads, New York
WWFD Frederick, Maryland
WCPT Willow Springs, Illinois
WWBA Largo, Florida
KUTR Taylorsville, Utah
WBKK Wilton, Minnesota

830 khz

KFLT Tucson, Arizona
KHVH Honolulu, Hawaii
KMUL Farwell, Texas
KNCO Grass Valley, California
KOTC Memphis, Tennessee
KLAA Orange, California
KSDP Sand Point, Alaska
KUYO Evansville, Wyoming
WACC Hialeah, Florida
WCCO Minneapolis, Minnesota
WCRN Worcester, Massachusetts
WQZQ Goodlettsville, Tennessee
WEEU Reading, Pennsylvania
WFNO Norco, Louisiana
WKTX Cortland, Ohio
WMMI Shepherd, Michigan
WTRU Kernersville, North Carolina

840 khz

KKNX Eugene, Oregon
KMAX Colfax, Washington
KSWB Seaside, Oregon
KTIC West Point, Nebraska
KVJY Pharr, Texas
KWDF Ball, Louisiana
KXNT North Las Vegas, Nevada
WBHY Mobile, Alabama
WCEO Columbia, South Carolina
WHAS Louisville, Kentucky
WKDI Denton, Maryland
WKTR Earlysville, Virginia
WPGS Mims, Florida
WRYM New Britain, Connecticut
WVPO Stroudsburg, Pennsylvania
WXEW Yabucoa, Puerto Rico
KMPH Modesto, California

850 khz

KEYH Houston, Texas
KFUO Clayton, Missouri
KHHO Tacoma, Washington
KHLO Hilo, Hawaii
KICY Nome, Alaska
KJON Carrollton, Texas
KOA Denver, Colorado
WABA Aguadilla, Puerto Rico
WAIT Crystal Lake, Illinois
WFTL West Palm Beach, Florida
WEEI Boston, Massachusetts
WGVS Muskegon, Michigan
WKGE Johnstown, Pennsylvania
WKVL Knoxville, Tennessee
WLRC Walnut, Mississippi
WXJC Birmingham, Alabama
WPTB Statesboro, Georgia
WQST Forest, Mississippi
WPTK(AM) Raleigh, North Carolina
WAXB Ridgefield, Connecticut
WKNR Cleveland, Ohio
WRUF Gainesville, Florida
WTAR Norfolk, Virginia
WWJC Duluth, Minnesota
WYLF Penn Yan, New York

860 khz

KARS Belen, New Mexico
KKAT(AM) Salt Lake City, Utah
KFST Fort Stockton, Texas
KKOW Pittsburg, Kansas
KMVP Phoenix, Arizona
KNUJ New Ulm, Minnesota
KONO San Antonio, Texas
KOSE Wilson, Arkansas
KPAM Troutdale, Oregon
KPAN Hereford, Texas
KSFA Nacogdoches, Texas
KTRB San Francisco, California
KWPC Muscatine, Iowa
KWRF Warren, Arkansas
WACB Taylorsville, North Carolina
WAEC Atlanta, Georgia
WAMI Opp, Alabama
WFSI Baltimore, Maryland
WDMG Douglas, Georgia
WEVA Emporia, Virginia
WFMO Fairmont, North Carolina
WMRI Marion, Indiana
WGUL Dunedin, Florida
WLBG Laurens, South Carolina
WNOV Milwaukee, Wisconsin
WOAY Oak Hill, West Virginia
WSBS Great Barrington, Massachusetts
WSON Henderson, Kentucky
WTZX Sparta, Tennessee
WWDB Philadelphia, Pennsylvania

870 khz

KAAN Bethany, Missouri
KFJZ Fort Worth, Texas
KFLD Pasco, Washington
KRLA Glendale, California
KLSQ Whitney, Nevada
KPRM Park Rapids, Minnesota
WINU Shelbyville, Illinois
WFLO Farmville, Virginia
WHCU Ithaca, New York
WKAR East Lansing, Michigan
WLVP Gorham, Maine
WMTL Leitchfield, Kentucky
WPWT Colonial Heights, Tennessee
WQBS San Juan, Puerto Rico
WQRX Valley Head, Alabama
WWL New Orleans, Louisiana
KJMP Pierce, Colorado
WZNH Fitzwilliam Depot, New Hampshire

880 khz

KHCM Honolulu, Hawaii
KCMX Phoenix, Oregon
KHAC Tse Bonito, New Mexico
KIXI Mercer Island/Seattl, Washington
KJJR Whitefish, Montana
KJOZ Conroe, Texas
KKMC Gonzales, California
KRVN Lexington, Nebraska
KWIP Dallas, Oregon
WCBS New York, New York
WIJR Highland, Illinois
WMDB Nashville, Tennessee
WMEQ Menomonie, Wisconsin
WPIP Winston-Salem, North Carolina
WRFD Columbus-Worthington, Ohio
WRRZ Clinton, North Carolina
WPEK Fairview, North Carolina
WSLK Moneta, Virginia
WYKO Sabana Grande, Puerto Rico
WZAB Sweetwater, Florida

890 khz

KBBI Homer, Alaska
KTLR Oklahoma City, Oklahoma
KDXU St. George, Utah
KGGN Gladstone, Missouri
KQLX Lisbon, North Dakota
KVOZ Del Mar Hills, Texas
WBAJ Blythewood, South Carolina
WAMG Dedham, Massachusetts
WHJA Laurel, Mississippi
WFAB Ceiba, Puerto Rico
WFKJ Cashtown, Pennsylvania
WJTP Lithia Springs, Georgia
WHNC Henderson, North Carolina
WKNV Fairlawn, Virginia
WLS Chicago, Illinois
WYAM Hartselle, Alabama
KLFF Arroyo Grande, California
KTXV Mabank, Texas
KJME Fountain, Colorado

900 khz

KALI West Covina, California
KPYN Atlanta, Texas
KBIF Fresno, California
KCLW Hamilton, Texas
KFAL Fulton, Missouri
KFLP Floydada, Texas
KHOZ Harrison, Arkansas
KJSK Columbus, Nebraska
KKRT Wenatchee, Washington
KNUI Kahului, Hawaii
KREH Pecan Grove, Texas
KSGL Wichita, Kansas
KTIS Minneapolis, Minnesota
KZPA Fort Yukon, Alaska
WATK Antigo, Wisconsin
WATV Birmingham, Alabama
WAYN Rockingham, North Carolina
WBML Macon, Georgia
WBRV Boonville, New York
WCBX Bassett, Virginia
WKDA Lebanon, Tennessee
WCPA Clearfield, Pennsylvania
WDLS Wisconsin Dells, Wisconsin
WURD Philadelphia, Pennsylvania
WFIA Louisville, Kentucky
WGOK Mobile, Alabama
WNMB North Myrtle Beach, South Carolina
WIAM Williamston, North Carolina
WILC Laurel, Maryland
WCME(AM) Brunswick, Maine
WJLG Savannah, Georgia
WJTH Calhoun, Georgia
WJWL Georgetown, Delaware
WUAM Watervliet, New York
WKDW Staunton, Virginia
WKXV Knoxville, Tennessee
WLSI Pikeville, Kentucky
WMOP Ocala, Florida
WGHM Nashua, New Hampshire
WOZK Ozark, Alabama
WSWN Belle Glade, Florida
WYCV Granite Falls, North Carolina

910 khz

KWDZ Salt Lake City, Utah
KBIM Roswell, New Mexico
KBLG Billings, Montana
KCJB Minot, North Dakota
KECR El Cajon, California
KKSN Vancouver, Washington
KGME Phoenix, Arizona
KINA Salina, Kansas
KIYU Galena, Alaska
KJJQ Volga, South Dakota
KKSF Oakland, California
KLCN Blytheville, Arkansas
KNAF Fredericksburg, Texas
KOXR Oxnard, California
KPOF Denver, Colorado
KRIO McAllen, Texas
KURY Brookings, Oregon
KVIS Miami, Oklahoma
KRAK Hesperia, California
KATH Frisco, Texas
WAEI Bangor, Maine
WAKO Lawrenceville, Illinois
WALT Meridian, Mississippi
WAVL Apollo, Pennsylvania
WDOR Sturgeon Bay, Wisconsin
WEPG South Pittsburg, Tennessee
WFDF Farmington Hills, Michigan
WRFV Valdosta, Georgia
WBZU Scranton, Pennsylvania
WGTO Cassopolis, Michigan
WHSM Hayward, Wisconsin
WJCW Johnson City, Tennessee
WSFE Burnside, Kentucky
WMRB Columbia, Tennessee
WUBR Baton Rouge, Louisiana
WLAT New Britain, Connecticut
WOLI Spartanburg, South Carolina
WPFB Middletown, Ohio
WPRP Ponce, Puerto Rico
WRKL New City, New York
WRNL Richmond, Virginia
WSBA York, Pennsylvania
WSRP Jacksonville, North Carolina
WSUI Iowa City, Iowa
WTWD Plant City, Florida
WTMZ Dorchester Terrace-Brentwood, South Carolina
WFJX Roanoke, Virginia
WLTP Marietta, Ohio
WZMG Pepperell, Alabama

920 khz

KARN Little Rock, Arkansas
KGTK Olympia, Washington
KBAD Las Vegas, Nevada
KQBU El Paso, Texas
KDHL Faribault, Minnesota
KFLB Odessa, Texas
KIHM Reno, Nevada
KKLS Rapid City, South Dakota
KLMR Lamar, Colorado
KVIN Ceres, California
KPSI Palm Springs, California
KSHO Lebanon, Oregon
KSRM Soldotna, Alaska
KSVA Albuquerque, New Mexico
KVEC San Luis Obispo, California
KVEL Vernal, Utah
KWAD Wadena, Minnesota
KWYS West Yellowstone, Montana
KXLY Spokane, Washington
KYFR Shenandoah, Iowa
KYST Texas City, Texas
WGKA Atlanta, Georgia
WBOX Bogalusa, Louisiana
WCHR Trenton, New Jersey
WGHQ Kingston, New York
WGNU Granite City, Illinois
WGOL Russellville, Alabama
WHJJ Providence, Rhode Island
WIRD Lake Placid, New York
WYBY Cortland, New York
WKVA Lewistown, Pennsylvania
WLIV Livingston, Tennessee
WDMC Melbourne, Florida
WMMN Fairmont, West Virginia
WMNI Columbus, Ohio
WMOK Metropolis, Illinois
WMPL Hancock, Michigan
WOKY Milwaukee, Wisconsin
WPCM Burlington-Graham, North Carolina
WPTL Canton, North Carolina
WTCW Whitesburg, Kentucky
WHJD Hazlehurst, Georgia
WYMB Manning, South Carolina
WEZZ Brantley, Alabama
WBAA West Lafayette, Indiana
WURA Quantico, Virginia

93.7 khz

KEYE Perryton, Texas

930 khz

KAFF Flagstaff, Arizona
KAGI Grants Pass, Oregon
KAPR Douglas, Arizona
KCCC Carlsbad, New Mexico
KDET Center, Texas
KIUP Durango, Colorado
KBAI Bellingham, Washington
KHJ Los Angeles, California
KKIN Aitkin, Minnesota
KKXX Paradise, California
KMPT East Missoula, Montana
KLUP Terrell Hills, Texas
KNSA Unalakleet, Alaska
KOGA Ogallala, Nebraska
KRKY Granby, Colorado
KROE Sheridan, Wyoming
KSDN Aberdeen, South Dakota
KSEI Pocatello, Idaho
KTKN Ketchikan, Alaska
KWOC Poplar Bluff, Missouri
KYAK Yakima, Washington
WAUR Sandwich, Illinois
WBCK Battle Creek, Michigan
WBEN Buffalo, New York
WHLM Bloomsburg, Pennsylvania
WDLX Washington, North Carolina
WYAC Cabo Rojo, Puerto Rico
WEOL Elyria, Ohio
WFMD Frederick, Maryland
WPKX(AM) Rochester, New Hampshire
WHON Centerville, Indiana
WIZR Johnstown, New York
WJBY Rainbow City, Alabama
WKCT Bowling Green, Kentucky
WLSS Sarasota, Florida
WKY Oklahoma City, Oklahoma
WLBL Auburndale, Wisconsin
WLLL Lynchburg, Virginia
WMGR Bainbridge, Georgia
WFXJ Jacksonville, Florida
WPAT Paterson, New Jersey
WRVC Huntington, West Virginia
WSEV Sevierville, Tennessee
WSFZ Jackson, Mississippi
WTAD Quincy, Illinois
WWON Waynesboro, Tennessee
WYFQ Charlotte, North Carolina
WYUS Milford, Delaware

940 khz

KOBY Cedar City, Utah
KGMS Tucson, Arizona
KWRU Fresno, California
KIXZ Amarillo, Texas
KKNE Waipahu, Hawaii
KMER Kemmerer, Wyoming
KSWM Aurora, Missouri
KTFS Texarkana, Texas
KVSH Valentine, Nebraska
KWBY Woodburn, Oregon
KPSZ Des Moines, Iowa
KICE Bend, Oregon
WADV Lebanon, Pennsylvania
WCND Shelbyville, Kentucky
WCPC Houston, Mississippi
WCSW Shell Lake, Wisconsin
WECO Wartburg, Tennessee
WFAW Fort Atkinson, Wisconsin
WGFP Webster, Massachusetts
WGRP Greenville, Pennsylvania
WIDG St. Ignace, Michigan
WINE Brookfield, Connecticut

WINZ Miami, Florida
WIPR San Juan, Puerto Rico
WKGM Smithfield, Virginia
WKYK Burnsville, North Carolina
WCIT(AM) Lima, Ohio
WLQH Chiefland, Florida
WMAC Macon, Georgia
WMIX Mount Vernon, Illinois
WNRG Grundy, Virginia
WYLD New Orleans, Louisiana
KDIL Jerome, Idaho

950 khz

KAHI Auburn, California
KDCE Espanola, New Mexico
KFSA Fort Smith, Arkansas
KJR Seattle, Washington
KJRG Newton, Kansas
KRWZ Parker, Colorado
KMHR(AM) Boise, Idaho
KWOS Jefferson City, Missouri
KMTX Helena, Montana
KNFT Bayard, New Mexico
KOEL Oelwein, Iowa
KOZE Lewiston, Idaho
KPRC Houston, Texas
KTNF St. Louis Park, Minnesota
KSEW Seward, Alaska
KTBR Roseburg, Oregon
KWAT Watertown, South Dakota
KXJK Forrest City, Arkansas
KJTV Lubbock, Texas
WAKM Franklin, Tennessee
WHSY Hattiesburg, Mississippi
WCLB Sheboygan, Wisconsin
WCTN Potomac-Cabin John, Maryland
WDIG Steubenville, Ohio
WERL Eagle River, Wisconsin
WROC Rochester, New York
WGOV Valdosta, Georgia
WGTA Summerville, Georgia
WHVW Hyde Park, New York
WIBX Utica, New York
WJKB Moncks Corner, South Carolina
WNCC Barnesboro, Pennsylvania
WNTD Chicago, Illinois
WNZZ Montgomery, Alabama
WPEN Philadelphia, Pennsylvania
WPET Greensboro, North Carolina
WBES Charleston, West Virginia
WROL Boston, Massachusetts
WORD Spartanburg, South Carolina
WTLN Orlando, Florida
WWJ Detroit, Michigan
WXGI Richmond, Virginia
WXLW Indianapolis, Indiana
WYWY Barbourville, Kentucky
KRRP Coushatta, Louisiana

960 khz

KNEW(AM) Oakland, California
KALE Richland, Washington
KCGS Marshall, Arkansas
KFLN Baker, Montana
KGKL San Angelo, Texas
KGWA Enid, Oklahoma
KIMP Mount Pleasant, Texas
KIXW Apple Valley, California
KLAD Klamath Falls, Oregon
KLTF Little Falls, Minnesota
KMA Shenandoah, Iowa
KNDN Farmington, New Mexico
KNEB Scottsbluff, Nebraska
KNEW Oakland, California
KOVO Provo, Utah
KKNT Phoenix, Arizona
KROF Abbeville, Louisiana
KSRA Salmon, Idaho
KZIM Cape Girardeau, Missouri
WCRU Dallas, North Carolina
WABG Greenwood, Mississippi
WATS Sayre, Pennsylvania
WBMC McMinnville, Tennessee
WDLM East Moline, Illinois
WEAV Plattsburgh, New York
WELI New Haven, Connecticut
WERC Birmingham, Alabama
WFGL Fitchburg, Massachusetts
WFIR Roanoke, Virginia
WQLA La Follette, Tennessee
WGRO Lake City, Florida
WHAK Rogers City, Michigan
WHYL Carlisle, Pennsylvania
WPLY Mount Pocono, Pennsylvania
WJYZ Albany, Georgia
WDNO Quebradillas, Puerto Rico
WKVX Wooster, Ohio
WLPR Prichard, Alabama
WPRT Prestonsburg, Kentucky
WRFC Athens, Georgia
WRNS Kinston, North Carolina
WSBT South Bend, Indiana
WTCH Shawano, Wisconsin
WTGM Salisbury, Maryland
WSVU North Palm Beach, Florida

97.3 mhz

KIKO Miami, Arizona

970 khz

KHTY Bakersfield, California
KESP Modesto, California
KFTA Rupert, Idaho
KBUL Billings, Montana
KCFO Tulsa, Oklahoma
KNWZ Coachella, California
KFEL Pueblo, Colorado
KHVN Fort Worth, Texas
KFBX Fairbanks, Alaska
KIXL Del Valle, Texas
KJLT North Platte, Nebraska
KNEA Jonesboro, Arkansas
KQAQ Austin, Minnesota
KNUU Paradise, Nevada
KSYL Alexandria, Louisiana
KTTO Spokane, Washington
KVWM Show Low, Arizona
WGEE Superior, Wisconsin
WAMD Aberdeen, Maryland
WATH Athens, Ohio
WBLF Bellefonte, Pennsylvania
WCHN Norwich, New York
WDAY Fargo, North Dakota
WERH Hamilton, Alabama
WESO Southbridge, Massachusetts
WFLA Tampa, Florida
WFSR Harlan, Kentucky
WFUN Ashtabula, Ohio
WHA Madison, Wisconsin
WKCI Waynesboro, Virginia
WJMX Florence, South Carolina
WKHM Jackson, Michigan
WGTK Louisville, Kentucky
WMAY Springfield, Illinois
WNED Buffalo, New York
WNIV Atlanta, Georgia
WRCS Ahoskie, North Carolina
WFQY Brandon, Mississippi
WTBF Troy, Alabama
WNNR Jacksonville, Florida
WVOP Vidalia, Georgia
WNYM Hackensack, New Jersey
WYSE Canton, North Carolina
WBGG Pittsburgh, Pennsylvania
WWYO Pineville, West Virginia
WRHA(AM) Spring City, Tennessee
WZAM Ishpeming, Michigan
WZAN Portland, Maine
WSTX Christiansted, Virgin Islands
WMPW Danville, Virginia

980 khz

KNTR Lake Havasu City, Arizona
KCAB Dardanelle, Arkansas
KDBV Salinas, California
KDSJ Deadwood, South Dakota
KEYQ Fresno, California
KFWB Los Angeles, California
KGLN Glenwood Springs, Colorado
KICA Clovis, New Mexico
KWSW(AM) Eureka, California
KBBO Selah, Washington
KKMS Richfield, Minnesota
KMBZ Kansas City, Missouri
KMIN Grants, New Mexico
KOKA Shreveport, Louisiana
KRTX Rosenburg-Richmond, Texas
KSGM Chester, Illinois
KSVC Richfield, Utah
KSPZ Ammon, Idaho
KVLV Fallon, Nevada
KWSW Eureka, California
WEGO(AM) Winston-Salem, North Carolina
WAAV Leland, North Carolina
WAKV Otsego, Michigan
WAKK McComb, Mississippi
WAZS Summerville, South Carolina
WBZK York, South Carolina
WCAP Lowell, Massachusetts
WCUB Two Rivers, Wisconsin
WGWM London, Kentucky
WHAW Lost Creek, West Virginia
WHSR Pompano Beach, Florida
WILK Wilkes-Barre, Pennsylvania
WKLY Hartwell, Georgia
WKOR Starkville, Mississippi
WDYN Rossville, Georgia
WDVH Gainesville, Florida
WPFP Park Falls, Wisconsin
WONE Dayton, Ohio
WPGA Perry, Georgia
WPRE Prairie Du Chien, Wisconsin
WRNE Gulf Breeze, Florida
WXLM Groton, Connecticut
WTEM Washington, District of Columbia
WTOT Marianna, Florida
WOFX Troy, New York
WFHG Bristol, Virginia
WYFN Nashville, Tennessee
WJYK Chase City, Virginia

990 khz

KAML Kenedy-Karnes City, Texas
KATD Pittsburg, California
KAYL Storm Lake, Iowa
KIKI(AM) Honolulu, Hawaii
KRKS Denver, Colorado
KTHH Albany, Oregon
KRMO Cassville, Missouri
KRSL Russell, Kansas
KSVP Artesia, New Mexico
KTKT Tucson, Arizona
KTMS Santa Barbara, California
KFCD Farmersville, Texas
KWAM Memphis, Tennessee
KZZB Beaumont, Texas
WABO Waynesboro, Mississippi
WALE Greenville, Rhode Island
WBTE Windsor, North Carolina
WCAZ Carthage, Illinois
WDCX Rochester, New York
WEEB Southern Pines, North Carolina
WEIS Centre, Alabama
WMYM Miami, Florida
WGML Hinesville, Georgia
WGSO New Orleans, Louisiana
WDYZ Orlando, Florida
WISK Lawrenceville, Georgia
WITZ Jasper, Indiana
WJEH Gallipolis, Ohio
WLDX Fayette, Alabama
WRFM Muncie, Indiana
WNML Knoxville, Tennessee
WNRV Narrows-Pearisburg, Virginia
WXCT Southington, Connecticut
WPRA Mayaguez, Puerto Rico
WTIG Massillon, Ohio
WLEE Richmond, Virginia
WNTW Somerset, Pennsylvania
WDEO Ypsilanti, Michigan
WNTP Philadelphia, Pennsylvania

US FM Stations by Frequency

100.1 mhz

KATQ-FM Plentywood, Montana
KCTN Garnavillo, Iowa
KDJR De Soto, Missouri
KUYY Emmetsburg, Iowa
KITT Soda Springs, Idaho
KGBA-FM Holtville, California
KGMN Kingman, Arizona
KHWZ Ludlow, California
KBBM Jefferson City, Missouri
KKZQ Tehachapi, California
KVNA-FM Flagstaff, Arizona
KLVJ Julian, California
KMMR Malta, Montana
KMXT Kodiak, Alaska
KNGS Coalinga, California
KKWK Cameron, Missouri
KOLV Olivia, Minnesota
KOMC-FM Kimberling City, Missouri
KWSA Price, Utah
KNRB Atlanta, Texas
KQFM Hermiston, Oregon
KQOD Stockton, California
KRVV Bastrop, Louisiana
KTHX-FM Dayton, Nevada
KYBI Lufkin, Texas
KKTY-FM Glendo, Wyoming
KWFX Woodward, Oklahoma
KWHQ-FM Kenai, Alaska
KYFM Bartlesville, Oklahoma
KYKC Byng, Oklahoma
KYKD Bethel, Alaska
KCLL San Angelo, Texas
KZOQ-FM Missoula, Montana
KZRO Dunsmuir, California
KZST Santa Rosa, California
WASL Dyersburg, Tennessee
WBCH-FM Hastings, Michigan
WBRR Bradford, Pennsylvania
WBRS Waltham, Massachusetts
WBXB Edenton, North Carolina
WCLG-FM Morgantown, West Virginia
WDDC Portage, Wisconsin
WDMX Vienna, West Virginia
WDST Woodstock, New York
WFLQ French Lick, Indiana
WFRI Winamac, Indiana
WQMJ Forsyth, Georgia
WPJP Port Washington, Wisconsin
WGLC-FM Mendota, Illinois
WGSY Phenix City, Alabama
WHOU-FM Houlton, Maine
WJBD-FM Salem, Illinois
WJRZ-FM Manahawkin, New Jersey
WKAI Macomb, Illinois
WKBH-FM West Salem, Wisconsin
WKQQ Winchester, Kentucky
WKQY Tazewell, Virginia
WVBE-FM Lynchburg, Virginia
WSSJ Rincon, Georgia
WMDJ-FM Allen, Kentucky
WUPE-FM North Adams, Massachusetts
WNIR Kent, Ohio
WNSY Talking Rock, Georgia
WZJZ Port Charlotte, Florida
WVVE Panama City Beach, Florida
WPNH-FM Plymouth, New Hampshire
WWOT Altoona, Pennsylvania
WQFM Forest City, Pennsylvania
WQIC Lebanon, Pennsylvania
WQXB Grenada, Mississippi
WRHN Rhinelander, Wisconsin
WRLT Franklin, Tennessee
WVIB Holton, Michigan
WCUZ Bear Lake, Michigan
WSWR Shelby, Ohio
WWFN-FM Lake City, South Carolina
WWFX Southbridge, Massachusetts
WPUP Watkinsville, Georgia
WXZQ Piketon, Ohio
WQFN(FM) Forest City, Pennsylvania
KLKS Pequot Lakes, Minnesota
WVMD Romney, West Virginia
KJBI Fort Pierre, South Dakota
KDEZ Brandon, South Dakota
KHWG-FM Crystal, Nevada
WILA Live Oak, Florida

100.3 mhz

KBRG San Jose, California
KCCN-FM Honolulu, Hawaii
KSWD Los Angeles, California
KCVJ Osceola, Missouri
KCYY San Antonio, Texas
KQMR Globe, Arizona
KZQX Tatum, Texas
KDVV Topeka, Kansas
KFXS Rapid City, South Dakota
KCXR Taft, Oklahoma
KAPA Hilo, Hawaii
KICY-FM Nome, Alaska
KILT-FM Houston, Texas
KIMN Denver, Colorado
KJCM Snyder, Oklahoma
KJMB-FM Blythe, California
KJNP-FM North Pole, Alaska
KKRZ Portland, Oregon
KLRZ Larose, Louisiana
KMAK Orange Cove, California
KMMX Tahoka, Texas
KDRB Des Moines, Iowa
KOKU Hagatna, Guam
KOMX Pampa, Texas
KPEK Albuquerque, New Mexico
KDJE Jacksonville, Arkansas
KWPT Fortuna, California
KRDQ Colby, Kansas
KQXR Payette, Idaho
KJKK Dallas, Texas
KRQK Lompoc, California
KRRV-FM Alexandria, Louisiana
KRWQ Gold Hill, Oregon
KSFI Salt Lake City, Utah
KVXX Quincy, California
KSNR Fisher, Minnesota
KSWC Winfield, Kansas
KNZS Arlington, Kansas
KTEX Mercedes, Texas
KUKU-FM Willow Springs, Missouri
KWIQ-FM Moses Lake, Washington
KURM-FM Gravette, Arkansas
KZEN Central City, Nebraska
KZMQ-FM Greybull, Wyoming
WAFD Webster Springs, West Virginia
WAOQ Goshen, Alabama
WYDL Middleton, Tennessee
WMVN Sylvan Beach, New York
WBIG-FM Washington, District of Columbia
WCCI Savanna, Illinois
WCLT-FM Newark, Ohio
WCTH Plantation Key, Florida
WDHI Delhi, New York
WGRY-FM Grayling, Michigan
WHEB Portsmouth, New Hampshire
WHGL-FM Canton, Pennsylvania
WKKB Middletown, Rhode Island
WVBZ High Point, North Carolina
WHTZ Newark, New Jersey
WMOJ-FM Norwood, Ohio
WIVA-FM Aguadilla, Puerto Rico
WIXY Champaign, Illinois
WKBE Warrensburg, New York
WKIT-FM Brewer, Maine
WLGP Harkers Island, North Carolina
WLKI Angola, Indiana
WNCY-FM Neenah-Menasha, Wisconsin
WNIC Dearborn, Michigan
WILV Chicago, Illinois
WNSL Laurel, Mississippi
WOBB Tifton, Georgia
WNOX Oak Ridge, Tennessee
WORG Elloree, South Carolina
KFXN-FM Minneapolis, Minnesota
WSEA Atlantic Beach, South Carolina
WRUM Orlando, Florida
WRNB Media, Pennsylvania
WARV-FM Petersburg, Virginia
WTKE-FM Niceville, Florida
WQRV Meridianville, Alabama
WVVR Hopkinsville, Kentucky
WYGB Edinburgh, Indiana
WGYY Meadville, Pennsylvania
KLSK Great Falls, Montana
WQJQ Barton, Vermont
WSTX-FM Christiansted, Virgin Islands
WUPT Gwinn, Michigan

100.5 mhz

KATT-FM Oklahoma City, Oklahoma
KBDR Mirando City, Texas
KBFX Anchorage, Alaska
KMME(FM) Cottage Grove, Oregon
KDEC-FM Decorah, Iowa
KQBB Center, Texas
KEGI Jonesboro, Arkansas
KGHT El Jebel, Colorado
KSWF Aurora, Missouri
KIKN-FM Salem, South Dakota
KJJM Baker, Montana
KTGR-FM Fulton, Missouri
KMEM-FM Memphis, Missouri
KMQA East Porterville, California
KMVL-FM Madisonville, Texas
KXNT-FM Henderson, Nevada
KNNK Dimmitt, Texas
KPSI-FM Palm Springs, California
KRSJ Durango, Colorado
KSFX Roswell, New Mexico
KTDE Gualala, California
KXAC St. James, Minnesota
KZHE Stamps, Arkansas
KZZO Sacramento, California
WALC Charleston, South Carolina
WBLE Batesville, Mississippi
WCDW Susquehanna, Pennsylvania
WVHT Norfolk, Virginia
WHLZ Marion, South Carolina
WNNX College Park, Georgia
WJNG Johnsonburg, Pennsylvania
WKEE-FM Huntington, West Virginia
WKXA-FM Findlay, Ohio
WAPI-FM Northport, Alabama
WYJK-FM Bellaire, Ohio
WOYS Apalachicola, Florida
WRCH New Britain, Connecticut
WHHZ Newberry, Florida
WRTM-FM Sharon, Mississippi
WRVY-FM Henry, Illinois
WSCN Cloquet, Minnesota
WSJD Princeton, Indiana
WSSL-FM Gray Court, South Carolina
WSGW-FM Carrollton, Michigan
WLGX Louisville, Kentucky
WTLX Monona, Wisconsin
WTRV Walker, Michigan
WDVI Rochester, New York
WWKI Kokomo, Indiana
WXRS-FM Portal, Georgia
WLDA Slocomb, Alabama
WXXK Lebanon, New Hampshire
WYGL-FM Elizabethville, Pennsylvania
WYMG Chatham, Illinois
KMEN Mendota, California
WZEZ Goochland, Virginia
KXDZ Templeton, California
KTED Evansville, Wyoming
WDYK Ridgeley, West Virginia
KGHT(FM) El Jebel, Colorado
KQZB Troy, Idaho
KVWF Augusta, Kansas
WFYE Glade Spring, Virginia
KMXD Monroe, Utah
WDTX Rothschild, Wisconsin
KGHT-FM El Jebel, Alaska

100.7 mhz

KSNA Idaho Falls, Idaho
KXLL Juneau, Alaska
KASE-FM Austin, Texas
KATJ-FM George, California
KEAZ Heber Springs, Arkansas
KLSZ-FM Fort Smith, Arkansas
KTHU Corning, California
KFMB-FM San Diego, California
KGBI-FM Omaha, Nebraska
KGFT Pueblo, Colorado
KGMO Cape Girardeau, Missouri
KGWY Gillette, Wyoming
KHAY Ventura, California
KHOK Hoisington, Kansas
KHSS Athena, Oregon
KIBS Bishop, California
KMGX Bend, Oregon
KIKV-FM Sauk Centre, Minnesota
KVVZ San Rafael, California
KJYL Eagle Grove, Iowa
KKHI Kihei, Hawaii
KKRQ Iowa City, Iowa
KLVF Las Vegas, New Mexico
KMFM Premont, Texas
KMLO Lowry, South Dakota
KPDA-FM Gooding, Idaho
KMZU Carrollton, Missouri
KOLZ Cheyenne, Wyoming
KULL Abilene, Texas
KPNC Ponca City, Oklahoma
KPPT-FM Depoe Bay, Oregon
KPXI Overton, Texas
KKWF Seattle, Washington
KXXQ Milan, New Mexico
KWRD-FM Highland Village, Texas
KKLQ Harwood, North Dakota
KRRK Desert Hills, Arizona
KKHT-FM Lumberton, Texas
KIBG Bigfork, Montana
KSLX-FM Scottsdale, Arizona
KMOZ-FM Grand Junction, Colorado
KTFR Chelsea, Oklahoma
KPRC-FM Salinas, California
KZBL Natchitoches, Louisiana
KFNS-FM Troy, Missouri
WMTX Tampa, Florida
WBGQ Bulls Gap, Tennessee
WBIZ-FM Eau Claire, Wisconsin
WRXQ Coal City, Illinois
WBYT Elkhart, Indiana
WNMX Christiansburg, Virginia
WWTH Oscoda, Michigan
WCOG-FM Galeton, Pennsylvania
WCYO Irvine, Kentucky
WDMS Greenville, Mississippi
WEEC Springfield, Ohio
WZBA Westminster, Maryland
WGTN-FM Andrews, South Carolina
WHUD Peekskill, New York
WHYI-FM Fort Lauderdale, Florida
WITL-FM Lansing, Michigan
WFLA-FM Midway, Florida
WKKV-FM Racine, Wisconsin
WKLX Brownsville, Kentucky
WLEV Allentown, Pennsylvania
WLRR Milledgeville, Georgia
WMGI Terre Haute, Indiana
WMJD Grundy, Virginia
WMMS Cleveland, Ohio
WEAM-FM Buena Vista, Georgia
WTHK Wilmington, Vermont
WOBE Crystal Falls, Michigan
WEFX Henderson, New York
WQPO Harrisonburg, Virginia
WTBM Mexico, Maine
WRVA-FM Wake Forest, North Carolina
WUSY Cleveland, Tennessee
WUTQ-FM Utica, New York
WCOA-FM Pensacola, Florida
WMUV Brunswick, Georgia
WTGE Baton Rouge, Louisiana
WXYX Bayamon, Puerto Rico
WZJS Banner Elk, North Carolina
WZLX Boston, Massachusetts
WBZZ(FM) New Kensington, Pennsylvania
WZXL Wildwood, New Jersey
KXLB Livingston, Montana
KYMV Woodruff, Utah
KJIK Duncan, Arizona
WVBD Fayetteville, West Virginia
WCKF Ashland, Alabama
KRNP Sutherland, Nebraska
WPLB Plattsburgh West, New York

100.9 mhz

KAEH Beaumont, California
KAKN Naknek, Alaska
KARY-FM Grandview, Washington
KCDV Cordova, Alaska
KCLY Clay Center, Kansas
KDEL-FM Arkadelphia, Arkansas
KEJL Eunice, New Mexico
KBAR-FM Victoria, Texas
KFSK Petersburg, Alaska
KGLC Miami, Oklahoma
KSXY Forestville, California
KHLL Richwood, Louisiana

KWFB Holliday, Texas
KMIX Tracy, California
KNEC Yuma, Colorado
KOWZ-FM Blooming Prairie, Minnesota
KXGL Amarillo, Texas
KRAJ Johannesburg, California
KRRY Canton, Missouri
KMXW Sparks, Nevada
KHOM Salem, Arkansas
KSSB Calipatria, California
KESA Eureka Springs, Arkansas
KKEE Wheelock, Texas
KWKK Russellville, Arkansas
KXOJ-FM Sapulpa, Oklahoma
KAUJ Grafton, North Dakota
KQSR Yuma, Arizona
KZMK Sierra Vista, Arizona
WAAI Hurlock, Maryland
WQNC Indian Trail, North Carolina
WAKB Hephzibah, Georgia
WALX Orrville, Alabama
WAYA-FM Ridgeville, South Carolina
WAYC-FM Bedford, Pennsylvania
WBDC Huntingburg, Indiana
WBNO-FM Bryan, Ohio
WWBR Big Rapids, Michigan
WCDO-FM Sidney, New York
WCJM-FM West Point, Georgia
WCMP-FM Pine City, Minnesota
WMJK Clyde, Ohio
WHTI(FM) Lakeside, Virginia
WHPO Hoopeston, Illinois
WIFM-FM Elkin, North Carolina
WIQO-FM Forest, Virginia
WICV East Jordan, Michigan
WJAQ Marianna, Florida
WJAW-FM McConnelsville, Ohio
WJXN-FM Utica, Mississippi
WMXE South Charleston, West Virginia
WKBB Mantee, Mississippi
WKLI-FM Albany, New York
WKOY-FM Princeton, West Virginia
WKRL-FM North Syracuse, New York
WBZG Peru, Illinois
WLSK Lebanon, Kentucky
WLYU Lyons, Georgia
WPGA-FM Perry, Georgia
WPGI Horseheads, New York
WPGW-FM Portland, Indiana
WQFL Rockford, Illinois
WQXC-FM Otsego, Michigan
WRCO-FM Richland Center, Wisconsin
WRKT North East, Pennsylvania
WRNX Amherst, Massachusetts
WSTS Fairmont, North Carolina
WKNL New London, Connecticut
WEIO(FM) Huntingdon, Tennessee
WVLY-FM Milton, Pennsylvania
WWFY Berlin, Vermont
WXIZ Waverly, Ohio
WZUS Macon, Illinois
WXJZ Gainesville, Florida
WNOU Speedway, Indiana
WLUN Pinconning, Michigan
WYNZ South Portland, Maine
WZST Westover, West Virginia
WFMI Southern Shores, North Carolina
KHSK Allen, Nebraska
KAYO Wasilla, Alaska
KXXS Menard, Texas

101.1 mhz

KAKQ-FM Fairbanks, Alaska
KSKR-FM Sutherlin, Oregon
KBER Ogden, Utah
KBHP Bemidji, Minnesota
KNUT Tamuning, Guam
KBON Mamou, Louisiana
KCFX Harrisonville, Missouri
KDDX Spearfish, South Dakota
KDSR Williston, North Dakota
KEOJ Caney, Kansas
KNRJ Cordes Lakes, Arizona
KEYF-FM Cheney, Washington
KFNF Oberlin, Kansas
KHME Winona, Minnesota
KHYL Auburn, California
KJMS Olive Branch, Mississippi
KLIR Columbus, Nebraska
KLOL Houston, Texas
KLQL Luverne, Minnesota
KLRC Siloam Springs, Arkansas
KOHO-FM Leavenworth, Washington
KWYD Parma, Idaho
KONE Lubbock, Texas
KONO-FM Helotes, Texas
KOSI Denver, Colorado
KPIN Pinedale, Wyoming
KQDJ-FM Valley City, North Dakota
KRMD-FM Oil City, Louisiana
KRTH Los Angeles, California
KRXX Kodiak, Alaska
KSFR White Rock, New Mexico
KUFO-FM Portland, Oregon
KVLC Hatch, New Mexico
KNVO-FM Port Isabel, Texas
KVRO Stillwater, Oklahoma
KWYE Fresno, California
KWOX Woodward, Oklahoma
KXIA Marshalltown, Iowa
KZMT Helena, Montana
WAFT Valdosta, Georgia
WQZL Belhaven, North Carolina
WAVV Naples Park, Florida
WHPI Glasford, Illinois
WBEB Philadelphia, Pennsylvania
WBUG-FM Fort Plain, New York
WCBS-FM New York, New York
WGIR-FM Manchester, New Hampshire
WFGE Tyrone, Pennsylvania
WHOT-FM Youngstown, Ohio
WHSM-FM Hayward, Wisconsin
WIXX Green Bay, Wisconsin
WIZF Erlanger, Kentucky
WJRR Cocoa Beach, Florida
WUBT Russellville, Kentucky
WZTK Burlington, North Carolina
WLIN-FM Durant, Mississippi
WLJA-FM Ellijay, Georgia
WLVH Hardeeville, South Carolina
WMYQ South Whitley, Indiana
WNOE-FM New Orleans, Louisiana
WQON Roscommon, Michigan
WRIF Detroit, Michigan
WRIO Ponce, Puerto Rico
WROQ Anderson, South Carolina
WRR Dallas, Texas
WYDE-FM Cullman, Alabama
WSGS Hazard, Kentucky
WTGA-FM Thomaston, Georgia
WUPY Ontonagon, Michigan
WXOS East St. Louis, Illinois
WOSA Grove City, Ohio
WWDC Washington, District of Columbia
WHYA(FM) Mashpee, Massachusetts
WWPN Westernport, Maryland
WPPG Repton, Alabama
WYOO Springfield, Florida
WVVL Elba, Alabama
WAMS-FM Snow Hill, Maryland
KPKK Amargosa Valley, Nevada
KWCA Palo Cedro, California
WVRE Dickeyville, Wisconsin
KDBL Parachute, Washington

101.3 mhz

KARV-FM Ola, Arkansas
KATY-FM Idyllwild, California
KOZY-FM Bridgeport, Nebraska
KDWB-FM Richfield, Minnesota
KFDI-FM Wichita, Kansas
KGDN Pasco, Washington
KGOT Anchorage, Alaska
KIKC-FM Forsyth, Montana
KIOI San Francisco, California
KIQX Durango, Colorado
KKYY Whiting, Iowa
KKGB Sulphur, Louisiana
KMMZ Crane, Texas
KLAW Lawton, Oklahoma
KLZA Falls City, Nebraska
KMCO Wilburton, Oklahoma
KNCN Sinton, Texas
KOXE Brownwood, Texas
KPBQ-FM Pine Bluff, Arkansas
KRNG Fallon, Nevada
KKRG Albuquerque, New Mexico
KRYK Chinook, Montana
KSIB-FM Creston, Iowa
KSTT-FM Los Osos-Baywood Par, California
KTXR Springfield, Missouri
KUUL East Moline, Illinois
WAGF-FM Dothan, Alabama
WAGX Manchester, Ohio
WBBV Vicksburg, Mississippi
WAGH Smiths, Alabama
WBRB Buckhannon, West Virginia
WBRV-FM Boonville, New York
WCMT-FM Martin, Tennessee
WCPV Essex, New York
WBFX Grand Rapids, Michigan
WECO-FM Wartburg, Tennessee
WFMG Richmond, Indiana
WGGY Scranton, Pennsylvania
WHLG Port St. Lucie, Florida
WJDQ Meridian, Mississippi
WVQM Augusta, Maine
WKCI-FM Hamden, Connecticut
WMCI Neoga B, Illinois
WMJM Jeffersontown, Kentucky
WNCO-FM Ashland, Ohio
WJKE(FM) Stillwater, New York
WQIL Chauncey, Georgia
WRMM-FM Rochester, New York
WROZ Lancaster, Pennsylvania
WSUE Sault Ste. Marie, Michigan
WTMG Williston, Florida
WVIL Virginia, Illinois
WWDE-FM Hampton, Virginia
WWDM Sumter, South Carolina
WWKS Cruz Bay, Virgin Islands
WWQQ-FM Wilmington, North Carolina
WNCL Milford, Delaware
WYKR-FM Haverhill, New Hampshire
WMUT Grenada, Mississippi
WMSK-FM Sturgis, Kentucky
KLWA Westport, Washington
KFEZ(FM) Walsenburg, Colorado
WZFM Narrows, Virginia
WBAA-FM West Lafayette, Indiana
KPWJ(FM) Madisonville, Texas

101.5 mhz

KAMB Merced, California
KAOY Kealakekua, Hawaii
KATW Lewiston, Idaho
KAVH Eudora, Arkansas
KCGN-FM Ortonville, Minnesota
KCLS Leeds, Utah
KCVI Blackfoot, Idaho
KEKA-FM Eureka, California
KFLY Corvallis, Oregon
KGB-FM San Diego, California
KGFM Bakersfield, California
KMLK El Dorado, Arkansas
KIKS-FM Iola, Kansas
KIXV(FM) Malvern, Arkansas
KIXF Baker, California
KKSI Eddyville, Iowa
KMJE Woodland, California
KMKF Manhattan, Kansas
KIZS Collinsville, Oklahoma
KNUE Tyler, Texas
KOAR Beebe, Arkansas
KPLA Columbia, Missouri
KPLZ-FM Seattle, Washington
KROR Hastings, Nebraska
KROX-FM Buda, Texas
KRRW St. James, Minnesota
KSMM-FM Liberal, Kansas
KSNY-FM Snyder, Texas
KSSS Bismarck, North Dakota
KSTB Crystal Beach, Texas
KFGI Crosby, Minnesota
KVCX Gregory, South Dakota
KZON Phoenix, Arizona
WBHB-FM Waynesboro, Pennsylvania
WBGW Fort Branch, Indiana
WWHQ Meredith, New Hampshire
WBNQ Bloomington, Illinois
WBQB Fredericksburg, Virginia
WCIL-FM Carbondale, Illinois
WDKC Covington, Pennsylvania
WEXP Brandon, Vermont
WPOI St. Petersburg, Florida
WFTZ Manchester, Tennessee
WIBA-FM Sauk City, Wisconsin
WJNR-FM Iron Mountain, Michigan
WMXV St. Joseph, Tennessee
WKHX-FM Marietta, Georgia
WKKG Columbus, Indiana
WELX Isabela, Puerto Rico
WCLI-FM Enon, Ohio
WKXW Trenton, New Jersey
WVLK-FM Richmond, Kentucky
WLYF Miami, Florida
WMJZ-FM Gaylord, Michigan
WMXO Olean, New York
WNSN South Bend, Indiana
WNWS-FM Jackson, Tennessee
WORD-FM Pittsburgh, Pennsylvania
WPDH Poughkeepsie, New York
WQEM Columbiana, Alabama
WQUT Johnson City, Tennessee
WRAL Raleigh, North Carolina
WRCD Canton, New York
WRVF Toledo, Ohio
WXBW Gallipolis, Ohio
WTHX Vine Grove, Kentucky
WSOL-FM Brunswick, Georgia
WRSY Marlboro, Vermont
WTKX-FM Pensacola, Florida
WVFB Celina, Tennessee
WWBB Providence, Rhode Island
WWBN Tuscola, Michigan
WWUN-FM Friar's Point, Mississippi
WXHC Homer, New York
WXSR Quincy, Florida
WMTE-FM Manistee, Michigan
WYNK-FM Baton Rouge, Louisiana
WVMP Vinton, Virginia
KIDX Ruidoso, New Mexico
KEGA Oakley, Utah
KRJM Mahnomen, Minnesota
KVSF-FM Pecos, New Mexico
KRMQ-FM Clovis, New Mexico
KTKE Truckee, California
WHDZ Buxton, North Carolina
KQLP Leupp, Arizona
WTPO New Albany, Mississippi
KDDV-FM Wright, Wyoming
KGVO-FM Frenchtown, Montana
KGJX Fruita, Colorado

101.7 mhz

KAYL-FM Storm Lake, Iowa
KDNO Thermopolis, Wyoming
KBKB-FM Fort Madison, Iowa
KCDU Carmel, California
KCKS Hamilton City, California
KCTT-FM Yellville, Arkansas
KEKO Hebbronville, Texas
KGOZ Gallatin, Missouri
KHST Lamar, Missouri
KIYS Walnut Ridge, Arkansas
KKIQ Livermore, California
KVLO Humnoke, Arkansas
KKYZ Sierra Vista, Arizona
KLDJ Duluth, Minnesota
KLEA-FM Lovington, New Mexico
KLRR Redmond, Oregon
KLTD Temple, Texas
KPEN-FM Soldotna, Alaska
KQAZ Springerville, Arizona
KRCH Rochester, Minnesota
KREJ Medicine Lodge, Kansas
KSAM-FM Huntsville, Texas
KSBL Isla Vista, California
KSKE-FM Eagle, Colorado
KSTK Wrangell, Alaska
KTFX-FM Warner, Oklahoma
KTNY Libby, Montana
KVOE-FM Emporia, Kansas
KVOM-FM Morrilton, Arkansas
KAYD-FM Silsbee, Texas
KBYB Hope, Arkansas
KNTE Bay City, Texas
KXSB Big Bear Lake, California
KZEW Wheatland, Wyoming
KQTM Rio Rancho, New Mexico
KTCY Azle, Texas
KLES Prosser, Washington
WBEA Southold, New York
WCZR Vero Beach, Florida
WBRK-FM Pittsfield, Massachusetts
WWBU Radford, Virginia
WKVV Searsport, Maine
WCVT Stowe, Vermont
WLVW(FM) Trenton, Florida
WELD-FM Moorefield, West Virginia
WNYQ Hudson Falls, New York
WFLK Geneva, New York
WHBA Lynn, Massachusetts
WGEL Greenville, Illinois

RADIO - U.S.

WHMH-FM Sauk Rapids, Minnesota
WHZZ Lansing, Michigan
WRCV Dixon, Illinois
WHOF North Canton, Ohio
WSNZ Lynchburg, Virginia
WJKS Canton, New Jersey
WJLE-FM Smithville, Tennessee
WJSQ Athens, Tennessee
WKOM Columbia, Tennessee
WKWI Kilmarnock, Virginia
WKYM Monticello, Kentucky
WKYZ Key Colony Beach, Florida
WAVF Hanahan, South Carolina
WLDE Fort Wayne, Indiana
WLQM-FM Franklin, Virginia
WLTB Johnson City, New York
WMRR Muskegon Heights, Michigan
WMXN-FM Stevenson, Alabama
WNKO New Albany, Ohio
WQVE Albany, Georgia
WORM-FM Savannah, Tennessee
WPRJ Coleman, Michigan
WZEB Ocean View, Delaware
WRBV Warner Robins, Georgia
WGKV Pulaski, New York
WCCL Central City, Pennsylvania
WTHO-FM Thomson, Georgia
WVKY(FM) Shelbyville, Kentucky
WBEI Reform, Alabama
WTPR-FM McKinnon, Tennessee
WTYE Robinson, Illinois
WVKY Shelbyville, Kentucky
WIKL(FM) Elwood, Indiana
WMVL Linesville, Pennsylvania
WLOF Elma, New York
WTOT-FM Graceville, Florida
WYOY Gluckstadt, Mississippi
WYUM Mount Vernon, Georgia
WIVR Kentland, Indiana
WEVI Frederiksted, Virgin Islands
WZHL New Augusta, Mississippi
KMXM(FM) Helena Valley N, Montana
KDJM Lindsborg, Kansas
KXCL Westcliffe, Colorado

101.9 mhz

KACQ Lometa, Texas
KATP Amarillo, Texas
KBTO Bottineau, North Dakota
KBUS Paris, Texas
KCMX-FM Ashland, Oregon
KRWK Fargo, North Dakota
KWID Las Vegas, Nevada
KINK Portland, Oregon
KDBI Emmett, Idaho
KENZ Ogden, Utah
KKQY Hill City, Kansas
KIGN Burns, Wyoming
KMXF Lowell, Arkansas
KNOE-FM Monroe, Louisiana
KNWS-FM Waterloo, Iowa
KLBN Fresno, California
KQKK Walker, Minnesota
KQSS Miami, Arizona
KQXT-FM San Antonio, Texas
KNTY Shingle Springs, California
KRSQ Laurel, Montana
KSCA Glendale, California
KTAO Taos, New Mexico
KTSL Medical Lake, Washington
KTST Oklahoma City, Oklahoma
KTWB Sioux Falls, South Dakota
KUCD Pearl City, Hawaii
KWFR San Angelo, Texas
KSML-FM Huntington, Texas
KLXQ Mountain Pine, Arkansas
KOOO La Vista, Nebraska
KBXT Wixon Valley, Texas
KZIU-FM Weston, Oregon
WAVT-FM Pottsville, Pennsylvania
WAZX-FM Cleveland, Georgia
WBAV-FM Gastonia, North Carolina
WARU-FM Roann, Indiana
WRBP Hubbard, Ohio
WCIB Falmouth, Massachusetts
WDET-FM Detroit, Michigan
WDEZ Wausau, Wisconsin
WFTA Fulton, Mississippi
WHHY-FM Montgomery, Alabama
WHUG Jamestown, New York
WIKS New Bern, North Carolina
WJFL Tennille, Georgia
WJHM Daytona Beach, Florida
WJIV Cherry Valley, New York
WKLU Brownsburg, Indiana
WKQS-FM Negaunee, Michigan
WKRQ Cincinnati, Ohio
WLDR-FM Traverse City, Michigan
WLIF Baltimore, Maryland
WLMG New Orleans, Louisiana
WOZI Presque Isle, Maine
WPNG Pearson, Georgia
WPOR Portland, Maine
WFAN-FM New York, New York
WQQL Springfield, Illinois
WQXQ Central City, Kentucky
WOCE Ringgold, Georgia
WKSK-FM South Hill, Virginia
WTMX Skokie, Illinois
WVAQ Morgantown, West Virginia
WVOW-FM Logan, West Virginia
WKKN Westminster, Vermont
WHTE-FM Ruckersville, Virginia
WWGR Fort Myers, Florida
WZAR Ponce, Puerto Rico
WZKZ Alfred, New York
WBGE Bainbridge, Georgia
KFMH Belle Fourche, South Dakota
KXWA Centennial, Colorado
KZWV Eldon, Missouri
WKFC North Corbin, Kentucky
KVGG Salome, Arizona
WZKZ(FM) Alfred, New York

102.1 mhz

KAHM Prescott, Arizona
KBMC Bozeman, Montana
KCAJ-FM Roseau, Minnesota
KEEY-FM St. Paul, Minnesota
KENA-FM Mena, Arkansas
KEOK Tahlequah, Oklahoma
KFZX Gardendale, Texas
KHKC-FM Atoka, Oklahoma
KBUC Raymondville, Texas
KJFM Louisiana, Missouri
KDBZ Anchorage, Alaska
KMJQ Houston, Texas
KOKY Sherwood, Arkansas
KPNY Alliance, Nebraska
KPQ-FM Wenatchee, Washington
KPRR El Paso, Texas
KYBG Basile, Louisiana
KRKC-FM King City, California
KRKY-FM Estes Park, Colorado
KRNV-FM Reno, Nevada
KDKS-FM Blanchard, Louisiana
KSMT Breckenridge, Colorado
KCKC Kansas City, Missouri
KSWW Ocean Shores, Washington
KCEZ Los Molinos, California
KTRA-FM Farmington, New Mexico
KTUI-FM Sullivan, Missouri
KDGE Fort Worth-Dallas, Texas
KUQQ Milford, Iowa
KPRI Encinitas, California
KZPE Ford City, California
KZSN Hutchinson, Kansas
WIBV Mount Vernon, Illinois
WALS Oglesby, Illinois
WXTG-FM Virginia Beach, Virginia
WAQY Springfield, Massachusetts
WJCA Albion, New York
WLLE Mayfield, Kentucky
WVXR Randolph, Vermont
WDNL Danville, Illinois
WDOK Cleveland, Ohio
WDRM Decatur, Alabama
WGMG Crawford, Georgia
WKVZ Dexter, Maine
WIMT Lima, Ohio
WIOQ Philadelphia, Pennsylvania
WJMH Reidsville, North Carolina
WKLG Rock Harbor, Florida
WKYL Lawrenceburg, Kentucky
WLCT Lafayette, Tennessee
WLEW-FM Bad Axe, Michigan
WLJC Beattyville, Kentucky
WLUM-FM Milwaukee, Wisconsin
WALT-FM Meridian, Mississippi
WMUK Kalamazoo, Michigan
WMXT Pamplico, South Carolina
WWST Sevierville, Tennessee
WOWQ Du Bois, Pennsylvania
WQLC Watertown, Florida
WQUA Citronelle, Alabama
WZUN Phoenix, New York
WRGR Tupper Lake, New York
WRKU Forestville, Wisconsin
WRQO Monticello, Mississippi
WRVB Marietta, Ohio
WRXL Richmond, Virginia
WWAV Santa Rosa Beach, Florida
WDNB Jeffersonville, New York
WNUQ Sylvester, Georgia
WSAK Hampton, New Hampshire
WNVE Culebra, Puerto Rico
WZAT Tybee Island, Georgia
KCMT Oro Valley, Arizona
KBUD Sardis, Mississippi
WQLF Lena, Illinois
KQRA Brookline, Missouri
KCHQ Driggs, Idaho
WWWD Bolingbroke, Georgia
KTBH-FM Kurtistown, Hawaii
KIRQ Twin Falls, Idaho
KZMC McCook, Nebraska
KBDY Hanna, Wyoming
KEMR Castle Dale, Utah
KYRN Socorro, New Mexico
KAXA Mountain Home, Texas

102.3 mhz

KDSP(FM) Greenwood Village, Colorado
KDUT Randolph, Utah
KBCE Boyce, Louisiana
KICR Coeur D'Alene, Idaho
KKPN Rockport, Texas
KBXR Columbia, Missouri
KCJC Dardanelle, Arkansas
KCZQ Cresco, Iowa
KDEX-FM Dexter, Missouri
KEHK Brownsville, Oregon
KHNS Haines, Alaska
KJJJ Laughlin, Nevada
KJJZ Indio, California
KJLH Compton, California
KOZQ-FM Waynesville, Missouri
KJSN Modesto, California
KKQQ Volga, South Dakota
KKYC Clovis, New Mexico
KLJT Jacksonville, Texas
KPEZ Austin, Texas
KQEW Fordyce, Arkansas
KRCQ Detroit Lakes, Minnesota
KRNY Kearney, Nebraska
KRMG-FM Sand Springs, Oklahoma
KSPK-FM Walsenburg, Colorado
KTRQ Colt, Arkansas
KCRX-FM Seaside, Oregon
KUVA Uvalde, Texas
KVLE-FM Gunnison, Colorado
KWDQ Woodward, Oklahoma
KWFS-FM Wichita Falls, Texas
KCWH Weed, California
KWRQ Clifton, Arizona
KXGE Dubuque, Iowa
KXYL-FM Coleman, Texas
KYYT Goldendale, Washington
KQNU(FM) Onawa, Iowa
KZXY-FM Apple Valley, California
WAMI-FM Opp, Alabama
WAVR Waverly, New York
WBAB Babylon, New York
WCBK-FM Martinsville, Indiana
WGTX Truro, Massachusetts
WGBJ Auburn, Indiana
WCLU-FM Munfordville, Kentucky
WCXX Madawaska, Maine
WCYN-FM Cynthiana, Kentucky
WDXC Pound, Virginia
WEBQ-FM Eldorado, Illinois
WECR-FM Beech Mountain, North Carolina
WZNY Augusta, Georgia
WELR-FM Roanoke, Alabama
WWPL Smithfield, North Carolina
WFVL Lumberton, North Carolina
WBTO-FM Petersburg, Indiana
WGCM-FM Gulfport, Mississippi
WFXN-FM Galion, Ohio
WGOW-FM Soddy-Daisy, Tennessee
WGRT Port Huron, Michigan
WSMM New Carlisle, Indiana
WHKB Houghton, Michigan
WHTL-FM Whitehall, Wisconsin
WCAT-FM Carlisle, Pennsylvania
WIQQ Leland, Mississippi
WVOR Canandaigua, New York
WQHZ Erie, Pennsylvania
WAIV Cape May, New Jersey
WKJT Teutopolis, Illinois
WWHK Concord, New Hampshire
WKZR Milledgeville, Georgia
WSKK Ripley, Mississippi
WIXM Grand Isle, Vermont
WLKQ-FM Buford, Georgia
WLLK-FM Somerset, Kentucky
WXMA Louisville, Kentucky
WMBX Jensen Beach, Florida
WMFX St. Andrews, South Carolina
WMIO Cabo Rojo, Puerto Rico
WMMJ Bethesda, Maryland
WMTD-FM Hinton, West Virginia
WPOS-FM Holland, Ohio
WPTM Roanoke Rapids, North Carolina
WQTC-FM Manitowoc, Wisconsin
WQTU Rome, Georgia
WRHL-FM Rochelle, Illinois
WRMJ Aledo, Illinois
WGSP-FM Pageland, South Carolina
WDMT Pittston, Pennsylvania
WWLD Cairo, Georgia
WFBY Weston, West Virginia
WSUS Franklin, New Jersey
WKLN Wilmington, Ohio
WDQX Morton, Illinois
WTRS Dunnellon, Florida
WUGO Grayson, Kentucky
WZGN Crozet, Virginia
WVRQ-FM Viroqua, Wisconsin
WMOS Stonington, Connecticut
WWSL Philadelphia, Mississippi
WKKF Ballston Spa, New York
WXLC Waukegan, Illinois
WXXS Lancaster, New Hampshire
WYCA Crete, Illinois
WYBR Big Rapids, Michigan
WZDQ Humboldt, Tennessee
WAUH Wautoma, Wisconsin
KVUW Wendover, Nevada
WTHN Sault Ste. Marie, Michigan
KYOE Point Arena, California
KBLO Corcoran, California
KDOE Antlers, Oklahoma
KMKK-FM Kaunakakai, Hawaii
KSAQ Charlotte, Texas
KNDH Hettinger, North Dakota
WSIZ-FM Jacksonville, Georgia
KOWY Dayton, Wyoming

102.5 mhz

KOTN(FM) Gould, Arkansas
KPZK-FM Cabot, Arkansas
KBLS North Fort Riley, Kansas
KBRQ Hillsboro, Texas
KCNQ Kernville, California
KDON-FM Salinas, California
KDUQ Ludlow, California
KDVL Devils Lake, North Dakota
KEZK-FM St. Louis, Missouri
KHOC Casper, Wyoming
KIAK-FM Fairbanks, Alaska
KIBR Sandpoint, Idaho
KIOT Los Lunas, New Mexico
KIXQ Joplin, Missouri
KKCI Goodland, Kansas
KKDY West Plains, Missouri
KKYR-FM Texarkana, Texas
KACY Arkansas City, Kansas
KMAD-FM Whitesboro, Texas
KMFX-FM Lake City, Minnesota
KMGI Pocatello, Idaho
KMKS Bay City, Texas
KMSO Missoula, Montana
KNIX-FM Phoenix, Arizona
KOTN Gould, Arkansas
KQIC Willmar, Minnesota
KRAO-FM Colfax, Washington
KDWZ Superior, Wisconsin
KSFM Woodland, California
KSNI-FM Santa Maria, California
KSTZ Des Moines, Iowa
KTCX Beaumont, Texas
KTNT Eufaula, Oklahoma
KTRR Loveland, Colorado

KZII-FM Lubbock, Texas
KZOK-FM Seattle, Washington
KZSD-FM Martin, South Dakota
WAGR-FM Lexington, Mississippi
WPZE Mableton, Georgia
WYNR Waycross, Georgia
WBAZ Bridgehampton, New York
WCMM Gulliver, Michigan
WKLB-FM Waltham, Massachusetts
WDVE Pittsburgh, Pennsylvania
WERX-FM Columbia, North Carolina
WESP Dothan, Alabama
WGNN Fisher, Illinois
WJRE Galva, Illinois
WPLW Hillsborough, North Carolina
WHPT Sarasota, Florida
WTOK-FM San Juan, Puerto Rico
WIOG Bay City, Michigan
WIOZ-FM Southern Pines, North Carolina
WJKX Ellisville, Mississippi
WZCH Warner Robins, Georgia
WFMF Baton Rouge, Louisiana
WLTO Nicholasville, Kentucky
WMDH-FM New Castle, Indiana
WTSS Buffalo, New York
WBZV Hudson, Michigan
WMYI Hendersonville, North Carolina
WNWC-FM Madison, Wisconsin
WOLC Princess Anne, Maryland
WOLD-FM Marion, Virginia
WDXB Jasper, Alabama
WOWF Crossville, Tennessee
WPIK Summerland Key, Florida
WQSS Camden, Maine
WPRT-FM Pegram, Tennessee
WRFY-FM Reading, Pennsylvania
WUMX Rome, New York
WUSQ-FM Winchester, Virginia
WPHZ Orleans, Indiana
WXLY North Charleston, South Carolina
WZOO-FM Edgewood, Ohio
KHLB Mason, Texas
KQSE Gypsum, Colorado
KKCV Rozel, Kansas
KDVC Loma, Colorado
KKWB Kelliher, Minnesota

102.7 mhz

KRNN Juneau, Alaska
KHGE Fresno, California
KBIQ Manitou Springs, Colorado
KBLZ Winona, Texas
KCNA Cave Junction, Oregon
KHXS Merkel, Texas
KIIS-FM Los Angeles, California
KJNA-FM Jena, Louisiana
KCYE Boulder City, Nevada
KJYO Oklahoma City, Oklahoma
KDDB Waipahu, Hawaii
KLDG Liberal, Kansas
KBBQ-FM Van Buren, Arkansas
KNTN Thief River Falls, Minnesota
KORD-FM Richland, Washington
KQEG La Crescent, Minnesota
KSL-FM Midvale, Utah
KQUL Lake Ozark, Missouri
KSSI China Lake, California
KJXK San Antonio, Texas
KTIG Pequot Lakes, Minnesota
KVSS Omaha, Nebraska
KWLT North Crossett, Arkansas
KTXJ-FM Jasper, Texas
KYBB Canton, South Dakota
KYTC Northwood, Iowa
KYTE Newport, Oregon
WGUS-FM New Ellenton, South Carolina
WRNI-FM Narragansett Pier, Rhode Island
WYSB Springfield, Kentucky
WLYK Cape Vincent, New York
WBDX Trenton, Georgia
WCKS Fruithurst, Alabama
WCNG Murphy, North Carolina
WLGZ-FM Webster, New York
WPZR Mount Clemens, Michigan
WEBN Cincinnati, Ohio
WEGR Arlington, Tennessee
WEKX Jellico, Tennessee
WEQX Manchester, Vermont
WGNI Wilmington, North Carolina
WHKR Rockledge, Florida
WJEQ Macomb, Illinois
WWAC Ocean City, New Jersey
WKSB Williamsport, Pennsylvania
WJJX Appomattox, Virginia
WLME Lewisport, Kentucky
WLEG Ligonier, Indiana
WMJL-FM Marion, Kentucky
WMOM Pentwater, Michigan
WCPZ Sandusky, Ohio
WMXJ Pompano Beach, Florida
WWFS New York, New York
WPHK Blountstown, Florida
WPMA Buckhead, Georgia
WPUB-FM Camden, South Carolina
WRGO Cedar Key, Florida
WRVM Suring, Wisconsin
WVEK-FM Weber City, Virginia
WGYE Mannington, West Virginia
WVAZ Oak Park, Illinois
WVSR-FM Charleston, West Virginia
WXBM-FM Milton, Florida
WQSR Baltimore, Maryland
WXHT Madison, Florida
KINX Fairfield, Montana
KKRO Red Bluff, California
WKWY Tompkinsville, Kentucky
WWFA St. Florian, Alabama
KXMZ Box Elder, South Dakota
KJOK Hollis, Oklahoma

102.9 mhz

KAJN-FM Crowley, Louisiana
KAZX Kirtland, New Mexico
KVMA-FM Shreveport, Louisiana
KBLX-FM Berkeley, California
KBRX-FM O'Neill, Nebraska
KBWS-FM Sisseton, South Dakota
KCTR-FM Billings, Montana
KDMX Dallas, Texas
KEZS-FM Cape Girardeau, Missouri
KHOZ-FM Harrison, Arkansas
KHUT Hutchinson, Kansas
KBIK Independence, Kansas
KIXN Hobbs, New Mexico
KLQV San Diego, California
KLTN Houston, Texas
KKND Belle Chasse, Louisiana
KMMO-FM Marshall, Missouri
KNBQ Centralia, Washington
KZNO (FM) Jerome, Idaho
KNDA Alice, Texas
KNFT-FM Bayard, New Mexico
KQIB Idabel, Oklahoma
KQST Sedona, Arizona
KTOP-FM Saint Marys, Kansas
KRGN Amarillo, Texas
KARS-FM Laramie, Wyoming
KSJJ Redmond, Oregon
KIWI McFarland, California
KTFG Sioux Rapids, Iowa
KLBU Pecos, New Mexico
KVAB Clarkston, Washington
KARN-FM Sheridan, Arkansas
KWYS(FM) Island Park, Idaho
KXLM Oxnard, California
KYSF Bonanza, Oregon
KZIA Cedar Rapids, Iowa
KWYL South Lake Tahoe, California
WJGO Tice, Florida
WBDL Reedsburg, Wisconsin
WLTK New Market, Virginia
WBLM Portland, Maine
WCLX Westport, New York
WCRQ Dennysville, Maine
WDIN Camuy, Puerto Rico
WDRC-FM Hartford, Connecticut
WKQB Welch, Virginia
WELS-FM Kinston, North Carolina
WGL-FM Huntington, Indiana
WFUR-FM Grand Rapids, Michigan
WQKI-FM Orangeburg, South Carolina
WDHT Urbana, Ohio
WWWW-FM Ann Arbor, Michigan
WIUJ Charlotte Amalie, Virgin Islands
WKIK-FM California, Maryland
WKXX Attalla, Alabama
WLKS-FM West Liberty, Kentucky
KMNB Minneapolis, Minnesota
WLKO Hickory, North Carolina
WHQG Milwaukee, Wisconsin
WMGK Philadelphia, Pennsylvania
WMHR Syracuse, New York
WDUN-FM Clarkesville, Georgia
WMKC Indian River, Michigan
WMSI-FM Jackson, Mississippi
WXXJ Jacksonville, Florida
WXXB Delphi, Indiana
WNPT-FM Marion, Alabama
WOKW Curwensville, Pennsylvania
WOWI Norfolk, Virginia
WPMX Statesboro, Georgia
WPXC Hyannis, Massachusetts
WSOY-FM Decatur, Illinois
WZTF Scranton, South Carolina
WNCQ-FM Canton, New York
WVRK Columbus, Georgia
WKIX-FM Raleigh, North Carolina
WXCH Columbus, Indiana
WYFM Sharon, Pennsylvania
WBUZ La Vergne, Tennessee
KMFG Nashwauk, Minnesota
WMKB Earlville, Illinois
KADL Imperial, Nebraska
KITY Llano, Texas
KISH Agana, Guam
KWGO Burlington, North Dakota
KLZY Honokaa, Hawaii
WWMR Saltillo, Mississippi
WPBK Crab Orchard, Kentucky

103.1 mhz

KAAT Oakhurst, California
KDLD Santa Monica, California
KWFA(FM) Limon, Colorado
KHRD Weaverville, California
KDLE Newport Beach, California
KLUN Paso Robles, California
KCDA Post Falls, Idaho
KCDX Florence, Arizona
KQLQ Columbia, Louisiana
KDAA Rolla, Missouri
KDMG Burlington, Iowa
KEEP Bandera, Texas
KEZN Palm Desert, California
KFFA-FM Helena, Arkansas
KFIL-FM Chatfield, Minnesota
KVFG Victorville, California
KJAM-FM Madison, South Dakota
KKCN Ballinger, Texas
KKCY Colusa, California
KMUL-FM Muleshoe, Texas
KMXS Anchorage, Alaska
KNCY-FM Auburn, Nebraska
KOFM Enid, Oklahoma
KSSM Copperas Cove, Texas
KPAS Fabens, Texas
KYKV Selah, Washington
KRSB-FM Roseburg, Oregon
KHGG-FM Waldron, Arkansas
KSBZ Sitka, Alaska
KSPN-FM Aspen, Colorado
KSRY Tehachapi, California
KVCM Helena, Montana
KVJM Hearne, Texas
KVWC-FM Vernon, Texas
KMPA Pittsburg, Texas
KHQT Las Cruces, New Mexico
KXSA-FM Dermott, Arkansas
KYDT Pine Haven, Wyoming
WAFY Middletown, Maryland
WWOF(FM) Tallahassee, Florida
WAKO-FM Lawrenceville, Illinois
WKVE Mount Pleasant, Pennsylvania
WBZO Bay Shore, New York
WJMA Culpeper, Virginia
WLLJ Etowah, Tennessee
WFKZ Plantation Key, Florida
WFXA-FM Augusta, Georgia
WGBF-FM Henderson, Kentucky
WGDN-FM Gladwin, Michigan
WJGK(FM) Newburgh, New York
WGZO Parris Island, South Carolina
WHBR-FM Parkersburg, West Virginia
WHME South Bend, Indiana
WGY-FM Albany, New York
WIRK Indiantown, Florida
WRON-FM Lewisburg, West Virginia
WNMQ Columbus, Mississippi
WMXX-FM Jackson, Tennessee
WNDH Napoleon, Ohio
WOGB Kaukauna, Wisconsin
WLXC Columbia, South Carolina
WOSM Ocean Springs, Mississippi
WIRK(FM) Indiantown, Florida
WPKE-FM Coal Run, Kentucky
WPLH Tifton, Georgia
WRAC Georgetown, Ohio
WRIX-FM Honea Path, South Carolina
WRJT Royalton, Vermont
WQNU Lyndon, Kentucky
WQFX-FM Russell, Pennsylvania
WRNR-FM Grasonville, Maryland
WGFB Rockton, Illinois
WQUS Lapeer, Michigan
WIKQ Tusculum, Tennessee
WVKO-FM Johnstown, Ohio
WTOJ Carthage, New York
WUAG Greensboro, North Carolina
WILK-FM Avoca, Pennsylvania
WWLT Manchester, Kentucky
WEUP-FM Moulton, Alabama
WVIV-FM Highland Park, Illinois
WSYN Surfside Beach, South Carolina
WCSJ-FM Morris, Illinois
WZOZ Oneonta, New York
KLO-FM Coalville, Utah
KHHL Karnes City, Texas
WLHC Robbins, North Carolina
KKJK Ravenna, Nebraska
KRVX Wimbledon, North Dakota
WVUV-FM Fagaitua, American Samoa
KRVO Columbia Falls, Montana
KEKS Olpe, Kansas
KURR Indian Springs, Nevada
WLQC Sharpsburg, North Carolina
KFWA(FM) Weldona, Colorado

103.3 mhz

KSAS-FM Caldwell, Idaho
KATM Modesto, California
KAZR Pella, Iowa
KBIU Lake Charles, Louisiana
KCRS-FM Midland, Texas
KDFM Falfurrias, Texas
KESN Allen, Texas
KFTZ Idaho Falls, Idaho
KIXB El Dorado, Arkansas
KJCS Nacogdoches, Texas
KJLS Hays, Kansas
KJOJ-FM Freeport, Texas
KJSR Tulsa, Oklahoma
KKCW Beaverton, Oregon
KLOU St. Louis, Missouri
KPRS Kansas City, Missouri
KPRU Delta, Colorado
KVYB Santa Barbara, California
KSCU Santa Clara, California
KSHK Kekaha, Hawaii
KDRF Albuquerque, New Mexico
KTFC Sioux City, Iowa
KUKI-FM Ukiah, California
KUMD-FM Duluth, Minnesota
KWLN Wilson Creek, Washington
KWBU-FM Waco, Texas
KWOZ Mountain View, Arkansas
KZCR Fergus Falls, Minnesota
KZKE Seligman, Arizona
KZPO Lindsay, California
WIVQ Spring Valley, Illinois
WAKG Danville, Virginia
WARM-FM York, Pennsylvania
WAXL Santa Claus, Indiana
WKQL Brookville, Pennsylvania
WRQQ(FM) Hammond, Louisiana
WCRF-FM Cleveland, Ohio
WEDG Buffalo, New York
WESR-FM Onley-Onancock, Virginia
WFXD Marquette, Michigan
WGLX-FM Wisconsin Rapids, Wisconsin
WWMP Waterbury, Vermont
WJMX-FM Cheraw, South Carolina
WJOD Asbury, Iowa
WKDF Nashville, Tennessee
WKFR-FM Battle Creek, Michigan
WKVS Lenoir, North Carolina
WKZS Thomasboro, Illinois
WMCM Rockland, Maine
WMGV Newport, North Carolina
WMLX St. Marys, Ohio
WMXS Montgomery, Alabama
WMXW Vestal, New York
WODS Boston, Massachusetts
WOLT Greer, South Carolina
WPRB Princeton, New Jersey

WQLB Tawas City, Michigan
WQQQ Sharon, Connecticut
WRZX Indianapolis, Indiana
WTCR-FM Huntington, West Virginia
WVEE Atlanta, Georgia
WVJP-FM Caguas, Puerto Rico
WVYB Holly Hill, Florida
WQGA Waycross, Georgia
WXZZ Georgetown, Kentucky
WZKR Collinsville, Mississippi
KTMQ Temecula, California
KBAA Grass Valley, California
KDTR Florence, Montana
KUSB Hazelton, North Dakota
KSAG Pearsall, Texas
KRAN Warren Afb, Wyoming
KBEN-FM Cowley, Wyoming
KJQY Colorado City, Colorado
WAJR-FM Salem, West Virginia
WBZL(FM) Greenwood, Mississippi
WTCF(FM) Wardenville, West Virginia

103.5 mhz

KAMZ Tahoka, Texas
KBMB(FM) Sacramento, California
KBPA San Marcos, Texas
KUAL-FM Brainerd, Minnesota
KJNZ Hereford, Texas
KHSL-FM Paradise, California
KISF Las Vegas, Nevada
KLAA-FM Tioga, Louisiana
KLDZ Medford, Oregon
KLNZ Glendale, Arizona
KNEI-FM Waukon, Iowa
KOST Los Angeles, California
KQLA Ogden, Kansas
KRAY-FM Salinas, California
KRFX Denver, Colorado
KVSP Anadarko, Oklahoma
KRSP-FM Salt Lake City, Utah
KWHT Pendleton, Oregon
KWVV-FM Homer, Alaska
KWXD Asbury, Missouri
KXNP North Platte, Nebraska
KYSM-FM Mankato, Minnesota
KLUE Poplar Bluff, Missouri
KZRB New Boston, Texas
KZZY Devils Lake, North Dakota
WAKY Radcliff, Kentucky
WAWC Syracuse, Indiana
WAXJ Frederiksted, Virgin Islands
WCCH Holyoke, Massachusetts
WEZL Charleston, South Carolina
WTOP-FM Washington, District of Columbia
WGRR Hamilton, Ohio
WIKK Newton, Illinois
WIMZ-FM Knoxville, Tennessee
WJAD Leesburg, Georgia
WJQZ Wellsville, New York
WJKI Bethany Beach, Delaware
WNND Pickerington, Ohio
WHLM-FM Berwick, Pennsylvania
WLAY-FM Littleville, Alabama
WKTU Lake Success, New York
WLAK Huntingdon, Pennsylvania
WMRY Crozet, Virginia
WMUZ Detroit, Michigan
WAKT-FM Callaway, Florida
WUUF Sodus, New York
WSHE-FM Fort Lauderdale, Florida
WQBJ Cobleskill, New York
WRBO Como, Mississippi
WRCQ Dunn, North Carolina
WOGH Burgettstown, Pennsylvania
WFUS Gulfport, Florida
WTCM-FM Traverse City, Michigan
WKSC-FM Chicago, Illinois
WXLT Christopher, Illinois
WZSN Greenwood, South Carolina
WZVA Marion, Virginia
KZMY Bozeman, Montana
KHAI Wahiawa, Hawaii
KRXW Roseau, Minnesota
WHWT New Hope, Alabama
KPAU Center, Colorado
WTAW-FM Buffalo, Texas
WKNK(FM) Callaway, Florida

103.7 mhz

KIQQ-FM Newberry Springs, California
KBBB(FM) Billings, Montana
KSNN-FM Ridgway, Colorado
KCDD Hamlin, Texas
KBTT Haughton, Louisiana
KEYN-FM Wichita, Kansas
KGIM-FM Redfield, South Dakota
KJEL Lebanon, Missouri
KKBJ-FM Bemidji, Minnesota
KLKK Clear Lake, Iowa
KLVG Garberville, California
KLZZ Waite Park, Minnesota
KMHK Billings, Montana
KMLA El Rio, California
KMTT Tacoma, Washington
KNUQ Paauilo, Hawaii
KODS Carnelian Bay, California
KOUL Refugio, Texas
KEGY(FM) San Diego, California
KNMZ Alamogordo, New Mexico
KPZA-FM Jal, New Mexico
KQLT Casper, Wyoming
KRRO Sioux Falls, South Dakota
KSKI-FM Sun Valley, Idaho
KABZ Little Rock, Arkansas
KVIL Highland Park-Dallas, Texas
KHJK La Porte, Texas
KXKT Glenwood, Iowa
KXPC-FM Harrisburg, Oregon
KYVA-FM Church Rock, New Mexico
WAAO-FM Andalusia, Alabama
WCBJ Campton, Kentucky
WTIB Williamston, North Carolina
WCIR-FM Beckley, West Virginia
WCKY-FM Pemberville, Ohio
WCXR Lewisburg, Pennsylvania
WDBR Springfield, Illinois
WEEO-FM McConnellsburg, Pennsylvania
WFGS Murray, Kentucky
WFIU Bloomington, Indiana
WHYB Menominee, Michigan
WHZR Royal Center, Indiana
WSTV-FM Frankfort, Kentucky
WKNE Keene, New Hampshire
WLLR-FM Davenport, Iowa
WBNE Wrightsville Beach, North Carolina
WMGM Atlantic City, New Jersey
WURV(FM) Richmond, Virginia
WNNJ Newton, New Jersey
WPKQ North Conway, New Hampshire
WHHT(FM) Cave City, Kentucky
WXKT Maysville, Georgia
WQEN Trussville, Alabama
WQNY Ithaca, New York
WQOL Vero Beach, Florida
WQWV Fisher, West Virginia
WRTS Erie, Pennsylvania
WRUF-FM Gainesville, Florida
WSOC-FM Charlotte, North Carolina
WULS Broxton, Georgia
WFFX Hattiesburg, Mississippi
WVKX Irwinton, Georgia
WWIB Hallie, Wisconsin
WXCY Havre De Grace, Maryland
WXLX Lajas, Puerto Rico
WXSS Wauwatosa, Wisconsin
WCSY-FM South Haven, Michigan
KYLK Okemah, Oklahoma
WCZE Harbor Beach, Michigan
KVRG Victor, Idaho
KLNN Questa, New Mexico
WFAV Gilman, Illinois
KZGL Flagstaff, Arizona
WLTC Cusseta, Georgia
KXZK Vail, Arizona

103.9 mhz

KRCD Inglewood, California
KBHL Osakis, Minnesota
KVAS-FM Ilwaco, Washington
KBEY Burnet, Texas
KOSG Pawhuska, Oklahoma
KCXX Lake Arrowhead, California
KDJK Mariposa, California
KGBB Edwards, California
KGRT-FM Las Cruces, New Mexico
KJXJ Franklin, Texas
KPGG Ashdown, Arkansas
KHYM Copeland, Kansas
KBOQ Seaside, California
KKIX Fayetteville, Arkansas
KMCR Montgomery City, Missouri
KMSM-FM Butte, Montana
KBDS Taft, California
KNLV-FM Ord, Nebraska
KNYN Fort Bridger, Wyoming
KNZA Hiawatha, Kansas
KVMI Arthur, North Dakota
KZMN Kalispell, Montana
KOMB Fort Scott, Kansas
KEXX(FM) Gilbert, Arizona
KQXC-FM Wichita Falls, Texas
KRFS-FM Superior, Nebraska
KRLI Malta Bend, Missouri
KSNO-FM Snowmass Village, Colorado
KSYC-FM Yreka, California
KUOO Spirit Lake, Iowa
KTDZ College, Alaska
KRIA Plainview, Texas
KBBD Spokane, Washington
KKFS Lincoln, California
KUDE Nephi, Utah
KRXP Pueblo West, Colorado
KMHT-FM Marshall, Texas
WWKZ Okolona, Mississippi
WALY Bellwood, Pennsylvania
WANC Ticonderoga, New York
WTID Thomaston, Alabama
WCLD-FM Cleveland, Mississippi
WCMW-FM Harbor Springs, Michigan
WDDK Greensboro, Georgia
WDEB-FM Jamestown, Tennessee
WDKX Rochester, New York
WMNI-FM Westerville, Ohio
WETZ(FM) New Martinsville, West Virginia
WFAS-FM Bronxville, New York
WHXT Orangeburg, South Carolina
WIMC Crawfordsville, Indiana
WLEN Adrian, Michigan
WLMI(FM) Kane/Bradford, Pennsylvania
WLSW Scottdale, Pennsylvania
WYAB Flora, Mississippi
WRKA Louisville, Kentucky
WQCY Quincy, Illinois
WNNL Fuquay-Varina, North Carolina
WNOI Flora, Illinois
WNTC Drakesboro, Kentucky
WKPE-FM South Yarmouth, Massachusetts
WOCQ Berlin, Maryland
WOLI-FM Easley, South Carolina
WPPZ-FM Jenkintown, Pennsylvania
WPPL Blue Ridge, Georgia
WQBK-FM Rensselaer, New York
WJRL-FM Fort Rucker, Alabama
WQXZ Hawkinsville, Georgia
WRBI Batesville, Indiana
WRBR-FM South Bend, Indiana
WRCN-FM Riverhead, New York
WNKZ Dushore, Pennsylvania
WRSR Owosso, Michigan
WTYB Bluffon, South Carolina
WSRK Oneonta, New York
WVBO Winneconne, Wisconsin
WVOM Howland, Maine
WVOA-FM Mexico, New York
WWEL London, Kentucky
WWIZ West Middlesex, Pennsylvania
WTLP Braddock Heights, Maryland
WXAN Ava, Illinois
WXCF-FM Big Island, Virginia
WXEG Beavercreek, Ohio
WXKB Cape Coral, Florida
WXKE Fort Wayne, Indiana
WXKQ-FM Whitesburg, Kentucky
WXRD Crown Point, Indiana
WYFT Luray, Virginia
WWYW Dundee, Illinois
KCJF Earle, Arkansas
KTHP Hemphill, Texas
KTNX Arcadia, Missouri
KGLU Gideon, Missouri
KHZK Kotzebue, Alaska
KCOO Dunkerton, Iowa
WTPN Westby, Wisconsin
KBGZ Spring Creek, Nevada
KYEN Severance, Colorado
KDCZ Eyota, Minnesota
KJJS Zapata, Texas
KQHK McCook, Nebraska
WWUU Washington, Mississippi

104.1 mhz

KAFE Bellingham, Washington
KBFM Edinburg, Texas
KILX Hatfield, Arkansas
KBOT Pelican Rapids, Minnesota
KBOX Lompoc, California
KBRJ Anchorage, Alaska
KBVC Buena Vista, Colorado
KCDY Carlsbad, New Mexico
WNAX-FM Yankton, South Dakota
KFMU-FM Oak Creek, Colorado
KFRR Woodlake, California
KGGF-FM Fredonia, Kansas
KHKK Modesto, California
KHKR-FM East Helena, Montana
KIQK Rapid City, South Dakota
KJLO-FM Monroe, Louisiana
KFIS Scappoose, Oregon
KIBZ Crete, Nebraska
KKUS Tyler, Texas
KTEG Santa Fe, New Mexico
KLTI-FM Ames, Iowa
KMGL Oklahoma City, Oklahoma
KMHM Lutesville, Missouri
KJOR Windsor, California
KNAB-FM Burlington, Colorado
KORR American Falls, Idaho
KPOC-FM Pocahontas, Arkansas
KWPK-FM Sisters, Oregon
KRBE Houston, Texas
KSDM International Falls, Minnesota
KVDU Houma, Louisiana
KWOW Clifton, Texas
KXDD Yakima, Washington
KTDK Sanger, Texas
KQTH Tucson, Arizona
KSGF-FM Ash Grove, Missouri
WAEB-FM Allentown, Pennsylvania
WBMX Boston, Massachusetts
WBWN Le Roy, Illinois
WCKQ Campbellsville, Kentucky
WCLE-FM Calhoun, Tennessee
WCXL Kill Devil Hills, North Carolina
WETT Bridgeport, West Virginia
WERR Vega Alta, Puerto Rico
WGLF Tallahassee, Florida
WHTT-FM Buffalo, New York
WIKY-FM Evansville, Indiana
WVSB Romney, West Virginia
WALR-FM Palmetto, Georgia
WLBC-FM Muncie, Indiana
WMNV Rupert, Vermont
WMQZ Colchester, Illinois
WMRQ-FM) Waterbury, Connecticut
WMZK Merrill, Wisconsin
WNNK-FM Harrisburg, Pennsylvania
WNKE New Boston, Ohio
WPXZ-FM Punxsutawney, Pennsylvania
WQAL Cleveland, Ohio
WRBN Clayton, Georgia
WRBX Reidsville, Georgia
WRLU Algoma, Wisconsin
WRJY Brunswick, Georgia
WTKS-FM Cocoa Beach, Florida
WOGY Jackson, Tennessee
WTQR Winston-Salem, North Carolina
WUCZ Carthage, Tennessee
WVGR Grand Rapids, Michigan
WWUS Big Pine Key, Florida
WPRS-FM Waldorf, Maryland
KZJK St. Louis Park, Minnesota
WHHL Hazelwood, Missouri
WYAV Myrtle Beach, South Carolina
WDLT-FM Atmore, Alabama
WWYL Chenango Bridge, New York
WZEE Madison, Wisconsin
WZKS Union, Mississippi
WKGV Swansboro, North Carolina
KZJF Jefferson City, Missouri
KCGL Powell, Wyoming
WSAG Linwood, Michigan
KSAH-FM Pearsall, Texas
KANT Guernsey, Wyoming
KCHT Childress, Texas
KZTW Tioga, North Dakota

104.3 mhz

KBCN-FM Marshall, Arkansas
KBEQ-FM Kansas City, Missouri
KCAR-FM Baxter Springs, Kansas
KBIG-FM Los Angeles, California
KBLT Leakey, Texas
KAJM Camp Verde, Arizona
KKFN Longmont, Colorado

KDBB Bonne Terre, Missouri
KEZP Bunkie, Louisiana
KGAS-FM Carthage, Texas
KHTR Pullman, Washington
KXSE Davis, California
KKMX Tri City, Oregon
KKSD Milbank, South Dakota
WZFJ(FM) Breezy Point, Minnesota
KPOS Fouke, Arkansas
KAWO Boise, Idaho
KSTQ(FM) Brownfield, Texas
KHIP Gonzales, California
KMXY Grand Junction, Colorado
KLQB Taylor, Texas
KQFX Borger, Texas
KRKN Eldon, Iowa
KSHA Redding, California
KSOP-FM Salt Lake City, Utah
KFRH North Las Vegas, Nevada
KTOO Juneau, Alaska
KVGB-FM Great Bend, Kansas
KVGO Spring Valley, Minnesota
KPHW Kaneohe, Hawaii
KXOQ Kennett, Missouri
KZBE Omak, Washington
KZIO Two Harbors, Minnesota
KZLT-FM East Grand Forks, Minnesota
WABK-FM Gardiner, Maine
WAJQ-FM Alma, Georgia
WAXQ New York, New York
WBBQ-FM Augusta, Georgia
WAYI Charlestown, Indiana
WVCN Baraga, Michigan
WCBH Casey, Illinois
WCZY-FM Mount Pleasant, Michigan
WCHK-FM Seymour, Wisconsin
WOGI(FM) Moon Township, Pennsylvania
WEYE Surgoinsville, Tennessee
WEZJ-FM Williamsburg, Kentucky
WFRG-FM Utica, New York
WFXK Bunn, North Carolina
WWOD Hartford, Vermont
WGNL Greenwood, Mississippi
WYKE(FM) Inglis, Florida
WJMK Chicago, Illinois
WJSG Hamlet, North Carolina
WKCY-FM Harrisonburg, Virginia
WZTR Dahlonega, Georgia
WKNB Clarendon, Pennsylvania
WKZM Sarasota, Florida
WMJU Bude, Mississippi
WQNQ Fletcher, North Carolina
WNLT Delhi Hills, Ohio
WZFT Baltimore, Maryland
WOMC Detroit, Michigan
WHLW Luverne, Alabama
WWPG Eutaw, Alabama
WSKE Everett, Pennsylvania
WZIN Charlotte Amalie, Virgin Islands
WXBC Hardinsburg, Kentucky
WNNP Richwood, Ohio
WZYP Athens, Alabama
KKAC Vandalia, Missouri
KIJI Tumon, Guam
KMNT Chehalis, Washington
KYPT Daniel, Wyoming
KBQF McFarland, California
WBYW(FM) Lynn Haven, Florida
KHMR Lovelady, Texas
KZBS Granite, Oklahoma
WRJJ La Center, Kentucky
WAXY-FM West Palm Beach, Florida

104.5 mhz

CJTT-FM New Liskeard, Ontario
KCVN Cozad, Nebraska
KBEF Gibsland, Louisiana
KCEC-FM Wellton, Arizona
KWMZ-FM Empire, Louisiana
KBTW Lenwood, California
KLSM Tallulah, Louisiana
KDAT Cedar Rapids, Iowa
KDOT Reno, Nevada
KFOG San Francisco, California
KIQO Atascadero, California
KJLY Blue Earth, Minnesota
KJTX Jefferson, Texas
KKDA-FM Dallas, Texas
KKFG Bloomfield, New Mexico
KKMY Orange, Texas
KPUS Gregory, Texas
KFXJ Augusta, Kansas
KMCQ Covington, Washington
KMGC Camden, Arkansas
KGZG-FM Newport, Washington
KMYZ-FM Pryor, Oklahoma
KZXQ Lake of the Woods, Arizona
KSLQ-FM Washington, Missouri
KSRZ Omaha, Nebraska
KSTY Canon City, Colorado
KTRN White Hall, Arkansas
KVLI(FM) Lake Isabella, California
KLBL Pearcy, Arkansas
KZEP-FM San Antonio, Texas
KZUL-FM Lake Havasu City, Arizona
WTMM-FM Mechanicville, New York
WXMJ Cambridge Springs, Pennsylvania
WAXX Eau Claire, Wisconsin
WNXX Jackson, Louisiana
WVMJ Conway, New Hampshire
WBVN Carrier Mills, Illinois
WCCG Hope Mills, North Carolina
WCCX Waukesha, Wisconsin
WGRX Falmouth, Virginia
WFMB-FM Springfield, Illinois
WSTK Aurora, North Carolina
WFYV-FM Atlantic Beach, Florida
WGFX Gallatin, Tennessee
WJJK Noblesville, Indiana
WHAJ Bluefield, West Virginia
WHLC Highlands, North Carolina
WILZ Saginaw, Michigan
WKAK Albany, Georgia
WKHJ Mountain Lake Park, Maryland
WLKT Lexington-Fayette, Kentucky
WNBT-FM Wellsboro, Pennsylvania
WNVZ Norfolk, Virginia
WKHT Knoxville, Tennessee
WQKT Wooster, Ohio
WRFQ Mount Pleasant, South Carolina
WILT Wilmington, North Carolina
WRVR Memphis, Tennessee
WSLD Whitewater, Wisconsin
WSNX-FM Muskegon, Michigan
WXER Plymouth, Wisconsin
WXLO Fitchburg, Massachusetts
WXRR Hattiesburg, Mississippi
WRFF Philadelphia, Pennsylvania
WYYU Dalton, Georgia
WQJB State College, Mississippi
KRVQ-FM Lake Isabella, California
KKVU Stevensville, Montana
KHAD Upton, Wyoming
KUMR Doolittle, Missouri
KZKY(FM) Ucon, Idaho
WQXJ Blackduck, Minnesota
KCBW Grandin, Missouri

104.7 mhz

KBZM Big Sky, Montana
KJUL Moapa Valley, Nevada
KCAQ Oxnard, California
KCAW Sitka, Alaska
KCLD-FM St. Cloud, Minnesota
KCMB Baker City, Oregon
KDUK-FM Florence, Oregon
KABQ-FM Bosque Farms, New Mexico
KQBK Booneville, Arkansas
KNWJ Leone, American Samoa
KHTN Planada, California
KHUM Cutten, California
KIKX Ketchum, Idaho
KIXR Ponca City, Oklahoma
KKED Fairbanks, Alaska
KKLH Marshfield, Missouri
KKLS-FM Sioux Falls, South Dakota
KKRV Wenatchee, Washington
KKYS Bryan, Texas
KMOU Roswell, New Mexico
KNDR Mandan, North Dakota
KNEK-FM Washington, Louisiana
KNIV Lyman, Wyoming
KNNG Sterling, Colorado
KONI Lanai City, Hawaii
KOOU Hardy, Arkansas
KHMD Mansfield, Louisiana
KRES Moberly, Missouri
KTRS-FM Casper, Wyoming
KTXC Lamesa, Texas
KVCY Fort Scott, Kansas
KWNS Winnsboro, Texas
KSLE Wewoka, Oklahoma
KXBZ Manhattan, Kansas
KREZ Chaffee, Missouri
KYYI Burkburnett, Texas
KHTZ Ganado, Texas
KZZP Mesa, Arizona
WAAZ-FM Crestview, Florida
WFSH-FM Athens, Georgia
WBBS Fulton, New York
WELJ Montauk, New York
WBAK Belfast, Maine
WBJZ Berlin, Wisconsin
WZUP La Grange, North Carolina
WCFL Morris, Illinois
WPDI Hazlet, New Jersey
WDDW Sturtevant, Wisconsin
WFLM White City, Florida
WFRN-FM Elkhart, Indiana
WTHG Hinesville, Georgia
WIOT Toledo, Ohio
WITZ-FM Jasper, Indiana
WPGB Pittsburgh, Pennsylvania
WJMD Hazard, Kentucky
WKAQ-FM San Juan, Puerto Rico
WKJC Tawas City, Michigan
WPZZ Crewe, Virginia
WKKY Geneva, Ohio
WOCN-FM Orleans, Massachusetts
WLIV-FM Monterey, Tennessee
WLMD Bushnell, Illinois
WMUF Henry, Tennessee
WNCS Montpelier, Vermont
WNOK Columbia, South Carolina
WNSV Nashville, Illinois
WQBX Fowler, Michigan
WBQW Kennebunkport, Maine
WQHQ Ocean City-Salisbury, Maryland
WRBQ-FM Tampa, Florida
WSGL Naples, Florida
WSGM Coalmont, Tennessee
WSPK Poughkeepsie, New York
WKQC Charlotte, North Carolina
WTUE Dayton, Ohio
WVRC-FM Spencer, West Virginia
WAYZ Hagerstown, Maryland
WYKX Escanaba, Michigan
WJSH Folsom, Louisiana
WZZK-FM Birmingham, Alabama
KFEG Klamath Falls, Oregon
KMJO Hope, North Dakota
KFLI Des Arc, Arkansas
WJIW Greenville, Mississippi
KTOY Texarkana, Arkansas
KXNC Ness City, Kansas
WLNQ White Pine, Tennessee
KWTG Vidalia, Louisiana
KEWS(FM) Sac City, Iowa
KKCS(FM) Calhan, Colorado

104.9 mhz

KAGH-FM Crossett, Arkansas
KTXX-FM Dripping Springs, Texas
KBOE-FM Oskaloosa, Iowa
KXNA Springdale, Arkansas
KBUK La Grange, Texas
KCLT West Helena, Arkansas
KXSC(FM) Sunnyvale, California
KCRZ Tipton, California
KDXY Lake City, Arkansas
KEEH Spokane, Washington
KFFX Emporia, Kansas
KHPA Hope, Arkansas
KLLT Spencer, Iowa
KJAV Alamo, Texas
KYPY Donaldsonville, Louisiana
KKBW Eatonville, Washington
KBTE Tulia, Texas
KLMJ Hampton, Iowa
KLOA(FM) Ridgecrest, California
KMIQ Robstown, Texas
KMJM-FM Columbia, Illinois
KMVR Mesilla Park, New Mexico
KKWD Bethany, Oklahoma
KAMA-FM Deer Park, Texas
KPWB-FM Piedmont, Missouri
KBOB-FM De Witt, Iowa
KREK Bristow, Oklahoma
KRFO-FM Owatonna, Minnesota
KRIG-FM Nowata, Oklahoma
KMHX Rohnert Park, California
KRYD Norwood, Colorado
KCTY Emerson, Nebraska
KZMP-FM Pilot Point, Texas
KTMX York, Nebraska
KTOC-FM Jonesboro, Louisiana
KWCX-FM Tanque Verde, Arizona
KWIM Window Rock, Arizona
KWBT Mexia, Texas
KYIX South Oroville, California
KVOU-FM Uvalde, Texas
KSAL-FM Salina, Kansas
KRRR Cheyenne, Wyoming
KZWA Moss Bluff, Louisiana
WEGE Lima, Ohio
WAVJ Princeton, Kentucky
WAXI Rockville, Indiana
WCJU-FM Prentiss, Mississippi
WBMZ Metter, Georgia
WBOQ Gloucester, Massachusetts
WBOZ Woodbury, Tennessee
WZEC Strasburg, Mississippi
WCCP-FM Clemson, South Carolina
WCVO Gahanna, Ohio
WCVU Solana, Florida
WBUV Moss Point, Mississippi
WSJO Egg Harbor City, New Jersey
WERK Muncie, Indiana
WFIW-FM Fairfield, Illinois
WFMZ Hertford, North Carolina
WFXE Columbus, Georgia
WKZU Iuka, Mississippi
WLHH(FM) Ridgeland, South Carolina
WHTF Havana, Florida
WIHS Middletown, Connecticut
WJRH Easton, Pennsylvania
WJRS Jamestown, Kentucky
WKHG Leitchfield, Kentucky
WKKS-FM Vanceburg, Kentucky
WKOS Kingsport, Tennessee
WKQH Marathon, Wisconsin
WFKY Frankfort, Kentucky
WLKZ Wolfeboro, New Hampshire
WLXR-FM La Crosse, Wisconsin
WMCG Milan, Georgia
WMNG Christiansted, Virgin Islands
WRKY-FM Hollidaysburg, Pennsylvania
WIGO-FM White Stone, Virginia
WNFM Reedsburg, Wisconsin
WNGZ Montour Falls, New York
WOAB Ozark, Alabama
WPCK Denmark, Wisconsin
WPDX-FM Clarksburg, West Virginia
WPXN Paxton, Illinois
WTNQ La Follette, Tennessee
WQNS Waynesville, North Carolina
WRBB Boston, Massachusetts
WJJS Roanoke, Virginia
WKDL-FM Brockport, New York
WSKV-FM Stanton, Kentucky
WSLY York, Alabama
WTKM-FM Hartford, Wisconsin
WWRR Scranton, Pennsylvania
WWKC Caldwell, Ohio
WBXX Marshall, Michigan
WLMX-FM Balsam Lake, Wisconsin
WINN Columbus, Indiana
WXCL Pekin, Illinois
WYGC High Springs, Florida
WXLR Harold, Kentucky
WXRX Belvidere, Illinois
WYNA Calabash, North Carolina
WYRY Hinsdale, New Hampshire
KYTN(FM) Union City, Tennessee
WCLV Lorain, Ohio
WZMR Altamont, New York
KIKF Cascade, Montana
WAIR Lake City, Michigan
KRYE Olney Springs, Colorado
WKJN Centreville, Mississippi
KNLX Prineville, Oregon
KLQQ Clearmont, Wyoming
KHNA Wamsutter, Wyoming
KLDE Eldorado, Texas
KVAL Cal-Nev-Ari, Nevada
WRBF Plainville, Georgia
KMVV Meadow Lakes, Alaska
KKWD(FM) Bethany, Colorado

105.1 mhz

KAKT Phoenix, Oregon
KAOC Cavalier, North Dakota
KIDI-FM Lompoc, California
KARL Tracy, Minnesota

RADIO - U.S.

KAWK Custer, South Dakota
KYSX(FM) Billings, Montana
KBLP Lindsay, Oklahoma
KCCQ Ames, Iowa
KJFA Santa Fe, New Mexico
KEAN-FM Abilene, Texas
KXMX Muldrow, Oklahoma
KBTK(FM) Kachina Village, Arizona
KCJK Garden City, Missouri
KGUM-FM Dededo, Guam
KMIL Cameron, Texas
KINE-FM Honolulu, Hawaii
KJOT Boise, Idaho
KKCB Duluth, Minnesota
KKGO Los Angeles, California
KKBZ Auberry, California
KCRV-FM Caruthersville, Missouri
KLTA Breckenridge, Minnesota
KMAT Seadrift, Texas
KMJX Conway, Arkansas
KAUU Manti, Utah
KNCI Sacramento, California
KOCN Pacific Grove, California
KPLD Kanab, Utah
KOSB Perry, Oklahoma
KOMG Willard, Missouri
KFTE Abbeville, Louisiana
KRSK Molalla, Oregon
KTKU Juneau, Alaska
KTMC-FM McAlester, Oklahoma
KZKR Jonesville, Louisiana
KQRT Las Vegas, Nevada
KVTY Lewiston, Idaho
KWMW Maljamar, New Mexico
KXKL-FM Denver, Colorado
KYKS Lufkin, Texas
KZKK Huron, South Dakota
WGVX Lakeville, Minnesota
KZQD Liberal, Kansas
WASJ Panama City Beach, Florida
WTGD Bridgewater, Virginia
WAMQ Great Barrington, Massachusetts
WLVG Havelock, North Carolina
WAVA-FM Arlington, Virginia
WCLC-FM Jamestown, Tennessee
WDCG Durham, North Carolina
WALV-FM Lakesite, Tennessee
WEJT Shelbyville, Illinois
WHCC Ellettsville, Indiana
WGEM-FM Quincy, Illinois
WGFM Cheboygan, Michigan
WNGA Clermont, Georgia
WHQT Coral Gables, Florida
WILQ Williamsport, Pennsylvania
WIOC Ponce, Puerto Rico
WIOV-FM Ephrata, Pennsylvania
WKLC-FM St. Albans, West Virginia
WKOL Plattsburgh, New York
WKUB Blackshear, Georgia
WNEK-FM Springfield, Massachusetts
WOJO Evanston, Illinois
WOMX-FM Orlando, Florida
WPDT Coward, South Carolina
WPFL Century, Florida
WQHK-FM Huntertown, Indiana
WJDX-FM Kosciusko, Mississippi
WQSB Albertville, Alabama
WQXK Salem, Ohio
WRNZ Lancaster, Kentucky
WWPR-FM New York, New York
WTOS-FM Skowhegan, Maine
WTUK Harlan, Kentucky
WUBE-FM Cincinnati, Ohio
WOLF-FM DeRuyter, New York
WVRY Waverly, Tennessee
WVZA Murphysboro, Illinois
WWLI Providence, Rhode Island
WMGC-FM Detroit, Michigan
WLRS Shepherdsville, Kentucky
WCHY Waunakee, Wisconsin
KJXN South Park, Wyoming
KWOL-FM Whitefish, Montana
WSBW Sister Bay, Wisconsin
KTTY New Boston, Texas
KTUG Hudson, Wyoming
WOLF-FM DeRuyter, New York

105.3 mhz

KAKJ Marianna, Arkansas
KREO Pine Bluffs, Wyoming
KDWY Diamondville, Wyoming
KQOR Mena, Arkansas
KCMS Edmonds, Washington
KDDQ Comanche, Oklahoma
KEDB Chariton, Iowa
KTWL Hempstead, Texas
KGRD Orchard, Nebraska
KIOD McCook, Nebraska
KIOZ San Diego, California
KITS San Francisco, California
KIWA-FM Sheldon, Iowa
KMOQ Columbus, Kansas
KJMM Bixby, Oklahoma
KBFP-FM Delano, California
KQOL Sleepy Hollow, Wyoming
KLNC Lincoln, Nebraska
KLIP Monroe, Louisiana
KLSR-FM Memphis, Texas
KPTY Winnie, Texas
KJDL-FM Levelland, Texas
KLYV Dubuque, Iowa
KMTX-FM Helena, Montana
KHOV-FM Wickenburg, Arizona
KNCB-FM Vivian, Louisiana
KNOD Harlan, Iowa
KJLV Hoxie, Arkansas
KONA-FM Kennewick, Washington
KKNI Sterling, Alaska
KRBD Ketchikan, Alaska
KRDG Shingletown, California
KSMG Seguin, Texas
KFBZ Haysville, Kansas
KYBA Stewartville, Minnesota
KRSX-FM Twentynine Palms, California
KRLD-FM Dallas, Texas
KZKS Rifle, Colorado
KZLZ Casas Adobes, Arizona
KZNN Rolla, Missouri
WGVY Cambridge, Minnesota
KZPR Minot, North Dakota
KZZX Alamogordo, New Mexico
WNOW-FM Gaffney, South Carolina
WAOX Staunton, Illinois
WECB Headland, Alabama
WKAY Knoxville, Illinois
WBNN-FM Dillwyn, Virginia
WBRW Blacksburg, Virginia
WHTS Coopersville, Michigan
WDAS-FM Philadelphia, Pennsylvania
WJEN Killington, Vermont
WSGC-FM Elberton, Georgia
WFIV-FM Loudon, Tennessee
WFRB-FM Frostburg, Maryland
WGFG Branchville, South Carolina
WGKR Grand Gorge, New York
WVMA(FM) Norfolk, Virginia
WKHM-FM Brooklyn, Michigan
WKOA Lafayette, Indiana
WKPQ Hornell, New York
WDVW(FM) Humboldt, Tennessee
WWL-FM Kenner, Louisiana
WMPI Scottsburg, Indiana
WOVO Glasgow, Kentucky
WRHQ Richmond Hill, Georgia
WRLO-FM Antigo, Wisconsin
WOWC Morrison, Tennessee
WSTI-FM Quitman, Georgia
WVJZ Charlotte Amalie, Virgin Islands
WACR-FM Columbus Afb, Mississippi
WSHK Kittery, Maine
WXKZ-FM Prestonsburg, Kentucky
WPTY Calverton-Roanoke, New York
WBZY Bowdon, Georgia
WYCY Hawley, Pennsylvania
WYHT Mansfield, Ohio
WYKS Gainesville, Florida
WJLT Evansville, Indiana
WZSP Nocatee, Florida
WJSJ Fernandina Beach, Florida
WODR Fair Bluff, North Carolina
WLVE Mukwonago, Wisconsin
KINB Kingfisher, Oklahoma
KBGX Keaau, Hawaii
KSLO-FM Simmesport, Louisiana
KZTI(FM) Fallon Station, Pennsylvania

105.5 mhz

KACT-FM Andrews, Texas
KXFC Coalgate, Oklahoma
KBAJ Deer River, Minnesota
KBOA-FM Piggott, Arkansas
KBUE Long Beach, California
KCGB-FM Hood River, Oregon
KDDG Albany, Minnesota
KDEP Garibaldi, Oregon
KDLS-FM Perry, Iowa
KESM-FM El Dorado Springs, Missouri
KEUG Veneta, Oregon
KFMT-FM Fremont, Nebraska
KDDK Franklin, Louisiana
KGFY Stillwater, Oklahoma
KBKK Ball, Louisiana
KILJ-FM Mount Pleasant, Iowa
KJAC Timnath, Colorado
KEUN-FM Eunice, Louisiana
KFYV Ojai, California
KKHB Eureka, California
KKJO-FM St. Joseph, Missouri
KKOY-FM Chanute, Kansas
KLCY Vernal, Utah
KSAC-FM Dunnigan, California
KLVA Maricopa, Arizona
KUKN Longview, Washington
KMAV-FM Mayville, North Dakota
KMGM Montevideo, Minnesota
KNAS Nashville, Arkansas
KVVS Rosamond, California
KTHK Idaho Falls, Idaho
KPFM Mountain Home, Arkansas
KPMW Haliimaile, Hawaii
KQLV(FM) Bosque Farms, New Mexico
KLHB Portland, Texas
KRBI-FM St. Peter, Minnesota
KRVR Copperopolis, California
KRDO-FM Security, Colorado
KQXX-FM Mission, Texas
KWCO-FM Chickasha, Oklahoma
KJZN San Joaquin, California
KVSV-FM Beloit, Kansas
KWAK-FM Stuttgart, Arkansas
KWRF-FM Warren, Arkansas
KUSJ Harker Heights, Texas
KZZT Moberly, Missouri
WABO-FM Waynesboro, Mississippi
WSRJ Honor, Michigan
WAKQ Paris, Tennessee
WXBN Berryville, Virginia
WWWK Islamorada, Florida
WDBY Patterson, New York
WBYA Islesboro, Maine
WWEI Easthampton, Massachusetts
WBMI West Branch, Michigan
WBNT-FM Oneida, Tennessee
WCHO-FM Washington Court Hou, Ohio
WCHX Lewistown, Pennsylvania
WCOO Kiawah Island, South Carolina
WCZQ Monticello, Illinois
WDAR-FM Darlington, South Carolina
WROK-FM Macon, Georgia
WDHA-FM Dover, New Jersey
WSEV-FM Gatlinburg, Tennessee
WDUV New Port Richey, Florida
WFBZ Trempealeau, Wisconsin
WFJA Sanford, North Carolina
WGKL Gladstone, Michigan
WGOG Walhalla, South Carolina
WGOJ Conneaut, Ohio
WGTH-FM Richlands, Virginia
WHLQ Lawrenceville, Virginia
WIFO-FM Jesup, Georgia
WYRE-FM Saint Augustine Beach, Florida
WJVO South Jacksonville, Illinois
WJYY Concord, New Hampshire
WKDE-FM Altavista, Virginia
WKXH St. Johnsbury, Vermont
WKYA Greenville, Kentucky
WVNA-FM Muscle Shoals, Alabama
WLJE Valparaiso, Indiana
WRXR-FM Rossville, Georgia
WLPW Lake Placid, New York
WTNM Water Valley, Mississippi
WOJL Louisa, Virginia
WLVK Fort Knox, Kentucky
WLVW Salisbury, Maryland
WMGH-FM Tamaqua, Pennsylvania
WMKX Brookville, Pennsylvania
WMMM-FM Verona, Wisconsin
WWRW Mt. Sterling, Kentucky
WMVR-FM Sidney, Ohio
WIBT Indianola, Mississippi
WFDT Aguada, Puerto Rico
WNSP Bay Minette, Alabama
WOLL Hobe Sound, Florida
WSKU Little Falls, New York
WQGN-FM Groton, Connecticut
WBTT Naples Park, Florida
WQRK Bedford, Indiana
WZBN Camilla, Georgia
WRAR-FM Tappahannock, Virginia
WREZ Metropolis, Illinois
WSWV-FM Pennington Gap, Virginia
WTHD Lagrange, Indiana
WTKV Oswego, New York
WWCK-FM Flint, Michigan
WWVR West Terre Haute, Indiana
WWWM-FM Sylvania, Ohio
WFCT Apalachicola, Florida
WXOQ Selmer, Tennessee
WXQR-FM Jacksonville, North Carolina
WXTQ Athens, Ohio
WYKT Wilmington, Illinois
WYTM-FM Fayetteville, Tennessee
WYZB Mary Esther, Florida
WSNQ Cape May Court House, New Jersey
WUKL Bethlehem, West Virginia
WZSR Woodstock, Illinois
KYEL Danville, Arkansas
WMKD Pickford, Michigan
KQRI Bosque Farms, New Mexico
WRCW Nekoosa, Wisconsin
KSIL Rincon, New Mexico
WVBG-FM Redwood, Mississippi
KZQL Mills, Wyoming
WKQV Cowen, West Virginia
KOYT(FM) Alberton, Montana
KXCS(FM) Coahoma, Texas
KMOM Roscoe, South Dakota
KKKJ Merrill, Oregon

105.7 mhz

KZBD Spokane, Washington
KJJP Amarillo, Texas
KVVF Santa Clara, California
KBIC Raymondville, Texas
KJRL Herington, Kansas
KOAS Dolan Springs, Arizona
KHCB-FM Houston, Texas
KJET Raymond, Washington
KMCK-FM Prarie Grove, Arkansas
KNLT Anchorage, Alaska
KOKZ Waterloo, Iowa
KOZZ-FM Reno, Nevada
KPMX Sterling, Colorado
KPNT Collinsville, Illinois
KQAK Bend, Oregon
KRAQ Jackson, Minnesota
KRBL Idalou, Texas
KRNB Decatur, Texas
KROU Spencer, Oklahoma
KRSE Yakima, Washington
KSUX Winnebago, Nebraska
KTKO Beeville, Texas
KVAY Lamar, Colorado
KVRD-FM Cottonwood, Arizona
KVVP Leesville, Louisiana
KWGL Ouray, Colorado
KXKX Knob Noster, Missouri
KXRS Hemet, California
KYKX Longview, Texas
WGVZ Eden Prarie, Minnesota
WAKH McComb, Mississippi
WAPL Appleton, Wisconsin
WXCX Siren, Wisconsin
WCAD San Juan, Puerto Rico
WCFW Chippewa Falls, Wisconsin
WCHR-FM Manahawkin, New Jersey
WCSN-FM Orange Beach, Alabama
WCUP L'Anse, Michigan
WFFM Ashburn, Georgia
WLKJ Portage, Pennsylvania
WMKS Clemmons, North Carolina
WGQR Rennert, North Carolina
WGRK-FM Greensburg, Kentucky
WWVA-FM Canton, Georgia
WHMX Lincoln, Maine
WKJS Richmond, Virginia
WJXM De Kalb, Mississippi
WLGC-FM Greenup, Kentucky
WMJI Cleveland, Ohio
WMRV-FM Endicott, New York
WMXH-FM Luray, Virginia
WQSH Malta, New York
WOBG-FM Salem, West Virginia
WIHG Rockwood, Tennessee

WSRW-FM Grand Rapids, Michigan
WQAK Union City, Tennessee
WJZ-FM Catonsville, Maryland
WQXA-FM York, Pennsylvania
WROR-FM Framingham, Massachusetts
WRSF Columbia, North Carolina
WTBK Manchester, Kentucky
WYXB Indianapolis, Indiana
WUZR Bicknell, Indiana
WLKC Campton, New Hampshire
WFRF-FM Monticello, Florida
WIXO Peoria, Illinois
WWLL Sebring, Florida
WTUV-FM Eminence, Kentucky
WJGM(FM) Baldwin, Florida
WQAH-FM Addison, Alabama
WBWR Hilliard, Ohio
WZHT Troy, Alabama
WEKL Augusta, Georgia
WZOM Defiance, Ohio
WTCJ-FM Cannelton, Indiana
KNAF-FM Fredericksburg, Texas
KKQX Manhattan, Montana
KHAN(FM) Kensett, Arkansas
KQMX Lost Hills, California
KYTS Manderson, Wyoming
WIHG(FM) Rockwood, Tennessee
KRMR Hays, Kansas
KDXN South Heart, North Dakota

105.9 mhz

KAAQ Alliance, Nebraska
KUZN Centerville, Texas
KALC Denver, Colorado
KBZE Berwick, Louisiana
KCIX Garden City, Idaho
KFMK Round Rock, Texas
KGBX-FM Nixa, Missouri
KHOT-FM Paradise Valley, Arizona
KIRC Seminole, Oklahoma
KKCD Omaha, Nebraska
KKWS Wadena, Minnesota
KLAZ Hot Springs, Arkansas
KKSW Lawrence, Kansas
KWMY Joliet, Montana
KMIT Mitchell, South Dakota
KPOI-FM Honolulu, Hawaii
KPWR Los Angeles, California
KQKY Kearney, Nebraska
KQPM Ukiah, California
KQTZ Hobart, Oklahoma
KRAZ Santa Ynez, California
KAHL-FM Hondo, Texas
KMJ-FM Fresno, California
KRZY-FM Santa Fe, New Mexico
KSEL-FM Portales, New Mexico
KSSA Ingalls, Kansas
KTLB Twin Lakes, Iowa
KUKA San Diego, Texas
KULH Wheeling, Missouri
KFXZ-FM Opelousas, Louisiana
KWNG Red Wing, Minnesota
KYSJ Coos Bay, Oregon
KZZK New London, Missouri
WBCI Bath, Maine
WBGG-FM Fort Lauderdale, Florida
WQXR-FM Newark, New Jersey
WCFS-FM Elmwood Park, Illinois
WTMT Weaverville, North Carolina
WDMK Detroit, Michigan
WEGZ Washburn, Wisconsin
WGKC Mahomet, Illinois
WGKX Memphis, Tennessee
WHCN Hartford, Connecticut
WVGA Lakeland, Georgia
WILN Panama City, Florida
WJOT-FM Wabash, Indiana
WJZR Rochester, New York
WMAL-FM Woodbridge, Virginia
WKHQ-FM Charlevoix, Michigan
WWHG Evansville, Wisconsin
WLNI Lynchburg, Virginia
WXTL Syracuse, New York
WMMC Marshall, Illinois
WEZV North Myrtle Beach, South Carolina
WNRQ Nashville, Tennessee
WOCL Deland, Florida
WOKZ Fairfield, Illinois
WNKN Middletown, Ohio
WFXO Southside, Alabama
WRTR Brookwood, Alabama
WSYI Valley Station, Kentucky
WTNJ Mount Hope, West Virginia
WTUA Pinopolis, South Carolina
WQCK(FM) Philipsburg, Pennsylvania
WXDX-FM Pittsburgh, Pennsylvania
WXDE Lewes, Delaware
WXMK Dock Junction, Georgia
WTZB Englewood, Florida
WPZX Pocono Pines, Pennsylvania
KYJK Missoula, Montana
KRJT Elgin, Oregon
KHRS Winthrop, Minnesota
WKYB Burgin, Kentucky
WKPO Soldiers Grove, Wisconsin
KKBO Flasher, North Dakota
WRKS Pickens, Mississippi

106.0 mhz

KLMI(FM) Rocky River, Oregon

106.1 mhz

KNUZ San Saba, Texas
KPZE-FM Carlsbad, New Mexico
KBKS-FM Tacoma, Washington
KCFA Arnold, California
KCII-FM Washington, Iowa
KFFB Fairfield Bay, Arkansas
KFLP-FM Floydada, Texas
KFMQ Gallup, New Mexico
KHKS Denton, Texas
KIOC Orange, Texas
KIXO Sulphur, Oklahoma
KIYX Sageville, Iowa
KJOE Slayton, Minnesota
KWWV Santa Margarita, California
KKBI Broken Bow, Oklahoma
KKMV Rupert, Idaho
KLCI Elk River, Minnesota
KLEO Kahaluu, Hawaii
KLSS-FM Mason City, Iowa
KMDX San Angelo, Texas
KMEL San Francisco, California
KXRR Monroe, Louisiana
KNEX Laredo, Texas
KNFO Basalt, Colorado
KOQL Ashland, Missouri
KBMG Evanston, Wyoming
KPLM Palm Springs, California
KQDI-FM Great Falls, Montana
KTGX Owasso, Oklahoma
KQLX-FM Lisbon, North Dakota
KRAB Greenacres, California
KRRX Burney, California
KYRK Refugio, Texas
KTTX Brenham, Texas
KWKZ Charleston, Missouri
KXKU Lyons, Kansas
KZFN Moscow, Idaho
WACD Antigo, Wisconsin
WAFC-FM Okeechobee, Florida
WMMY Jefferson, North Carolina
WBLI Patchogue, New York
WCNR Keswick, Virginia
WCOD-FM Hyannis, Massachusetts
WDKM Adams, Wisconsin
WDKS Newburgh, Indiana
WBMH Grove Hill, Alabama
WFXH-FM Hilton Head Island, South Carolina
WHDQ Claremont, New Hampshire
WHST Tawas City, Michigan
WWWY North Vernon, Indiana
WSFF Vinton, Virginia
WISX Philadelphia, Pennsylvania
WJXQ Charlotte, Michigan
WKGO Cumberland, Maryland
WXSH Pocomoke City, Maryland
WMTI Picayune, Mississippi
WKTM Soperton, Georgia
WLZS Beaver Springs, Pennsylvania
WMEM Presque Isle, Maine
WMIL-FM Waukesha, Wisconsin
WMOR-FM Morehead, Kentucky
WMXU Starkville, Mississippi
WBBG Niles, Ohio
WNKI Corning, New York
WOLS Waxhaw, North Carolina
WPDA Jeffersonville, New York
WRDU Knightdale, North Carolina
WRRH Hormigueros, Puerto Rico
WHKV Sylvester, Georgia
WRZZ Parkersburg, West Virginia
WSMI-FM Litchfield, Illinois
WNGC Arcade, Georgia
WSTH-FM Alexander City, Alabama
WTAK-FM Hartselle, Alabama
WVNO-FM Mansfield, Ohio
WQTL Tallahassee, Florida
WYYS Streator, Illinois
WRRX Gulf Breeze, Florida
WUSH Poquoson, Virginia
KLMI Rock River, Wyoming
KFSZ Munds Park, Arizona
KRZX Redlands, Colorado
KKVR Kerrville, Texas
WVIS Vieques, Puerto Rico
WYKY Science Hill, Kentucky
KXXL Moorcroft, Wyoming
KEXS-FM Ravenwood, Missouri
WJRV(FM) Oliver Springs, Tennessee
WCOP Farmington Township, Pennsylvania

106.3 mhz

KALI-FM Santa Ana, California
KQEZ(FM) Shelley, Idaho
KQTA Homedale, Idaho
KMLR Gonzales, Texas
KDBR Kalispell, Montana
KOMR Sun City, Arizona
KERB-FM Kermit, Texas
KYMK-FM Maurice, Louisiana
KGAM Merced, California
KTGV Oracle, Arizona
KGMX Lancaster, California
KGOU Norman, Oklahoma
KOLL Lonoke, Arkansas
KGAM(FM) Merced, California
KFRX Lincoln, Nebraska
KJBX Cash, Arkansas
KKHR Abilene, Texas
KKLI Widefield, Colorado
KMGQ(FM) Goleta, California
KLBC Durant, Oklahoma
KLEN Cheyenne, Wyoming
KLOO-FM Corvallis, Oregon
KMJV Soledad, California
KVPW Kingsburg, California
KQXB(FM) Belton, Texas
KPAN-FM Hereford, Texas
KPHR Ortonville, Minnesota
KPRB Brush, Colorado
KPSO-FM Falfurrias, Texas
KIFT(FM) Kremmling, Colorado
KIYS-FM Walnut Ridge, Arkansas
KRZK Branson, Missouri
KSEM Seminole, Texas
KSUP Juneau, Alaska
KHKZ San Benito, Texas
KBZS Wichita Falls, Texas
KVHT Vermillion, South Dakota
KCSY Twisp, Washington
KWUF-FM Pagosa Springs, Colorado
KXOR-FM Thibodaux, Louisiana
KYGL Texarkana, Arkansas
KAGM Los Lunas, New Mexico
KPTL Ankeny, Iowa
KZKZ-FM Greenwood, Arkansas
KZZE Eagle Point, Oregon
WAMX Milton, West Virginia
WANY-FM Albany, Kentucky
WHXR Scarborough, Maine
WBTG-FM Sheffield, Alabama
WLTT Bolivia, North Carolina
WCDA Versailles, Kentucky
WCDK Cadiz, Ohio
WCEM-FM Cambridge, Maryland
WCIF Melbourne, Florida
WCTL Union City, Pennsylvania
WXMG London, Ohio
WYRD-FM Simpsonville, South Carolina
WEIB Northampton, Massachusetts
WEVR-FM River Falls, Wisconsin
WGCY Gibson City, Illinois
WGER Saginaw, Michigan
WGMK Donalsonville, Georgia
WGNG Tchula, Mississippi
WJQB Spring Hill, Florida
WHCY Blairstown, New Jersey
WHKX Bluefield, Virginia
WFNQ Nashua, New Hampshire
WKMK Eatontown, New Jersey
WJNI Ladson, South Carolina
WJSE North Cape May, New Jersey
WJPT Fort Myers Villas, Florida
WKBX Kingsland, Georgia
WOAH Glennville, Georgia
WKLA-FM Ludington, Michigan
WKNU Brewton, Alabama
WLCY Blairsville, Pennsylvania
WMCR-FM Oneida, New York
WMFG-FM Hibbing, Minnesota
WZLD Petal, Mississippi
WMNA-FM Gretna, Virginia
WMTK Littleton, New Hampshire
WNVA-FM Norton, Virginia
WYRB Genoa, Illinois
WGLM-FM Lakeview, Michigan
WQBZ Fort Valley, Georgia
WQCC La Crosse, Wisconsin
WQRL Benton, Illinois
WXMT Smethport, Pennsylvania
WBUK Ottawa, Ohio
WRIL Pineville, Kentucky
WSBZ Miramar Beach, Florida
WYZY Saranac, New York
WTUF Boston, Georgia
WUBU South Bend, Indiana
WCDQ Crawfordsville, Indiana
WMXG Stephenson, Michigan
WWJM New Lexington, Ohio
WWKX Woonsocket, Rhode Island
WWQM-FM Middleton, Wisconsin
WSRB Lansing, Illinois
WYNN-FM Florence, South Carolina
WRAZ-FM Leisure City, Florida
WDVY Mount Kisco, New York
KZLK Rapid City, South Dakota
WPLT Sarona, Wisconsin
WPFT Pigeon Forge, Tennessee
KWNZ Lovelock, Nevada
WUUB Jupiter, Florida
KFON Menard, Texas
KTRY(FM) Cazadero, California

106.5 mhz

KALT-FM Alturas, California
KBVA Bella Vista, Arkansas
KKMR Arizona City, Arizona
WDAF-FM Liberty, Missouri
KCQQ Davenport, Iowa
KDXL St. Louis Park, Minnesota
KEGX Richland, Washington
KEJS Lubbock, Texas
KEND Roswell, New Mexico
KEZR San Jose, California
KFMC-FM Fairmont, Minnesota
KIXA Lucerne Valley, California
KLNV San Diego, California
KMCX-FM Ogallala, Nebraska
KTMO New Madrid, Missouri
KMMT Mammoth Lakes, California
KOOI Jacksonville, Texas
KOSY-FM Spanish Fork, Utah
KOVE-FM Galveston, Texas
KQXL-FM New Roads, Louisiana
KRJB Ada, Minnesota
KUSZ Olathe, Colorado
KSNE-FM Las Vegas, Nevada
KSPO Dishman, Washington
KTLS-FM Holdenville, Oklahoma
KWHL Anchorage, Alaska
KBZC Sacramento, California
KWPZ Lynden, Washington
KYQQ Arkansas City, Kansas
WAID Clarksdale, Mississippi
WAVH Daphne, Alabama
WOKV-FM Ponte Vedra Beach, Florida
WDSJ Greenville, Ohio
WBMW Pawcatuck, Connecticut
WLQR-FM Delta, Ohio
WCJX Five Points, Florida
WCTQ Sarasota, Florida
WDSN Reynoldsville, Pennsylvania
WEND Salisbury, North Carolina
WWLW Clarksburg, West Virginia
WHHT Horse Cave, Kentucky
WFYY Bloomsburg, Pennsylvania
WJDT Rogersville, Tennessee
WJEC Vernon, Alabama
WKCH Whitewater, Wisconsin
WKDZ-FM Cadiz, Kentucky
WARH Granite City, Illinois
WKRH Minetto, New York
WYTE Marshfield, Wisconsin

WMEF Fort Kent, Maine
WHLK Cleveland, Ohio
WNIK-FM Arecibo, Puerto Rico
WOCY Carrabelle, Florida
WPYX Albany, New York
WQCB Brewer, Maine
WVFM Kalamazoo, Michigan
WBTJ Richmond, Virginia
WRLV-FM Salyersville, Kentucky
WSFL-FM New Bern, North Carolina
WSKZ Chattanooga, Tennessee
WLFF Georgetown, South Carolina
WWBL Washington, Indiana
WHBZ Sheboygan Falls, Wisconsin
WWMX Baltimore, Maryland
WYRK Buffalo, New York
WZBX Rocky Ford, Georgia
WNHI Farmington, New Hampshire
WZIQ Smithville, Georgia
WZNJ Demopolis, Alabama
WLVS-FM Clifton, Tennessee
KLFN Sunburg, Minnesota
KCIJ Atlanta, Louisiana
KUOM-FM St. Louis Park, Minnesota
KKIK Horseshoe Bend, Arkansas
KEAL Taft, California
WXNU St. Anne, Illinois
KRYL(FM) Haiku, Hawaii
KRKU Wheatland, Wyoming

106.7 mhz

KSMY Lompoc, California
KAOD Babbitt, Minnesota
KYTZ Walhalla, North Dakota
KDKN Ellington, Missouri
KBFO Aberdeen, South Dakota
KDLW Los Alamos, New Mexico
KBPI Denver, Colorado
KCHX Midland, Texas
KUMX North Fort Polk, Louisiana
KTKX Terrell Hills, Texas
KTUZ-FM Okarche, Oklahoma
KQKX Norfolk, Nebraska
KFXX-FM Hugoton, Kansas
KGTW Ketchikan, Alaska
KRVI Mount Vernon, Missouri
KIKD Lake City, Iowa
KJUG-FM Tulare, California
KLTH Lake Oswego, Oregon
KMEZ Port Sulphur, Louisiana
KLEJ Rayne, Louisiana
KHLR Benton, Arkansas
KPPV Prescott Valley, Arizona
KQNK-FM Norton, Kansas
KQTY-FM Borger, Texas
KROQ-FM Pasadena, California
KRQR Orland, California
KRTI Grinnell, Iowa
KXDR Pinesdale, Montana
KZZA Muenster, Texas
KYLA Homer, Louisiana
KWWX Cashmere, Washington
WAOB-FM Beaver Falls, Pennsylvania
WATQ Chetek, Wisconsin
WLYT(FM) Norris, Tennessee
WTLC-FM Greenwood, Indiana
WYFX Mount Vernon, Indiana
WDXE-FM Lawrenceburg, Tennessee
WKHL West Lafayette, Indiana
WHFI Lindside, West Virginia
WIZN Vergennes, Vermont
WJFK-FM Manassas, Virginia
WJJY-FM Brainerd, Minnesota
WKRU Allouez, Wisconsin
WKGS Irondequoit, New York
WKMX Enterprise, Alabama
WSRT Gaylord, Michigan
WLFX Berea, Kentucky
WXTP North Windham, Maine
WMYT Carolina Beach, North Carolina
WPWQ Mount Sterling, Illinois
WLTW New York, New York
WMJX Boston, Massachusetts
WCGX Dublin, Ohio
WNKR Williamstown, Kentucky
WNFN Millersville, Tennessee
WOKA-FM Douglas, Georgia
WKVK Semora, North Carolina
WMHX(FM) Hershey, Pennsylvania
WRMA Fort Lauderdale, Florida
WSTZ-FM Vicksburg, Mississippi
WTCB Orangeburg, South Carolina
WVKM Matewan, West Virginia
WBDR Copenhagen, New York
WWZD-FM New Albany, Mississippi
WXXL Tavares, Florida
WYAY Gainesville, Georgia
WPPN Des Plaines, Illinois
WZNX Sullivan, Illinois
WZZL Reidland, Kentucky
WFGA Hicksville, Ohio
WDTW-FM Detroit, Michigan
KXDR(FM) Pinesdale, Montana
WHTO Iron Mountain, Michigan
KTPO Kootenai, Idaho
WTDY-FM Mount Horeb, Wisconsin
KPLN Lockwood, Montana
KYUN Hailey, Idaho
WRRQ Port Dickinson, New York
KNAN Nanakuli, Hawaii
KMRZ-FM Superior, Wyoming
KNKI Pinetop, Arizona

106.9 mhz

KAAX Avenal, California
KASS Casper, Wyoming
WMOZ Moose Lake, Minnesota
KBGL Larned, Kansas
KMVE California City, California
KCST-FM Florence, Oregon
KFRC-FM San Francisco, California
KEDG Alexandria, Louisiana
KMZZ Bishop, Texas
KEGK Wahpeton, North Dakota
KHLE Kempner, Texas
KHTT Muskogee, Oklahoma
KIHK Rock Valley, Iowa
KHPT Conroe, Texas
KARP-FM Dassel, Minnesota
KAZE Ore City, Texas
KKRB Klamath Falls, Oregon
KKYN-FM Plainview, Texas
KLUB Bloomington, Texas
KDVA Buckeye, Arizona
KMOK Lewiston, Idaho
KMZK Clifton, Colorado
KNKN(FM) Pueblo, Colorado
KLGD Stamford, Texas
KOPW Plattsmouth, Nebraska
KQLB Los Banos, California
KEGH Brigham City, Utah
KRNO Incline Village, Nevada
KROC-FM Rochester, Minnesota
KRWM Bremerton, Washington
KTIJ Elk City, Oklahoma
KTPK Topeka, Kansas
KTXY Jefferson City, Missouri
KWYI Kawaihae, Hawaii
KXFE Dumas, Arkansas
KXIO Clarksville, Arkansas
KDGL Yucca Valley, California
KYXK Gurdon, Arkansas
KRVF Kerens, Texas
WAFX Suffolk, Virginia
WWEG Myersville, Maryland
WBQX Thomaston, Maine
WCCC-FM Hartford, Connecticut
WDML Woodlawn, Illinois
WEZX Scranton, Pennsylvania
WHKL Crenshaw, Mississippi
WJZX(FM) Brookfield, Wisconsin
WWIQ Camden, New Jersey
WMGU Southern Pines, North Carolina
WKXD-FM Monterey, Tennessee
WKZY Cross City, Florida
WZZK(FM) Bedford, Virginia
WMEG Guayama, Puerto Rico
WMIT Black Mountain, North Carolina
WEXR Stonewall, Mississippi
WXXC Marion, Indiana
WOOD-FM Muskegon, Michigan
WNNO-FM Wisconsin Dells, Wisconsin
WBPT Homewood, Alabama
WRBE-FM Lucedale, Mississippi
WRIJ Masontown, Pennsylvania
WRQK-FM Canton, Ohio
WYPO Ocean City, Maryland
WSCY Moultonborough, New Hampshire
WSWT Peoria, Illinois
WUPM Ironwood, Michigan
WVEZ St. Matthews, Kentucky
WWSU Fairborn, Ohio
WGZR Bluffton, Michigan
WWYN McKenzie, Tennessee
WTTL-FM Madisonville, Kentucky
WQKK(FM) Renovo, Pennsylvania
WZZS Zolfo Springs, Florida
WKZA Lakewood, New York
KHRT-FM Minot, North Dakota
KSCY Four Corners, Montana
KHYY Minatare, Nebraska
KFSE Kasilof, Alaska
KVGQ Overton, Nevada
KDRX Laughlin Afb, Texas
WVTI Brighton, Vermont
WLGE Baileys Harbor, Wisconsin
KIQN-FM Pueblo, Colorado

107.1 mhz

KAUM Colorado City, Texas
KAZZ Deer Park, Washington
KDBX Clear Lake, South Dakota
KBHI Miner, Missouri
KBMV-FM Birch Tree, Missouri
KSRT Cloverdale, California
KTHI Caldwell, Idaho
KCWR Bakersfield, California
KDRS-FM Paragould, Arkansas
KDSN-FM Denison, Iowa
KZFO(FM) Benbrook, Texas
WFON Fond Du Lac, Wisconsin
KFNV-FM Ferriday, Louisiana
KESR Shasta Lake City, California
KNWI Osceola, Iowa
KELD-FM Hampton, Arkansas
KCNY Greenbrier, Arkansas
KLVU Sweet Home, Oregon
KSSE Arcadia, California
KMGK Glenwood, Minnesota
KHIT-FM Madera, California
KJML(FM) Columbus, Kansas
KNKT Armijo, New Mexico
KOGM Opelousas, Louisiana
KPUR-FM Canyon, Texas
KRQT Castle Rock, Washington
KSFT-FM South Sioux City, Nebraska
KONN-FM Bennett, Colorado
KSSD Fallbrook, California
KTHS-FM Berryville, Arkansas
KFYX(FM) Texarkana, Arkansas
KTMY Coon Rapids, Minnesota
KSES-FM Seaside, California
KVVA-FM Apache Junction, Arizona
KSSC Ventura, California
KWLV Many, Louisiana
KXHT Marion, Arkansas
KYNZ Lone Grove, Oklahoma
KRXB Beeville, Texas
KRVA-FM Campbell, Texas
WFXM Gordon, Georgia
WAOA-FM Melbourne, Florida
WNKK Circleville, Ohio
WUHU Smiths Grove, Kentucky
WEJK Boonville, Indiana
WBYP Belzoni, Mississippi
WCBC-FM Keyser, West Virginia
WCHG Hot Springs, Virginia
WCKC Cadillac, Michigan
WCKT Lehigh Acres, Florida
WDOH Delphos, Ohio
WEAI Lynnville, Illinois
WERZ Exeter, New Hampshire
WLVX(FM) Greenville, Pennsylvania
WFHN Fairhaven, Massachusetts
WFXC Durham, North Carolina
WLRX Ironton, Ohio
WLAI Wilmore, Kentucky
WHMD Hammond, Louisiana
WFFG-FM Corinth, New York
WIIS Key West, Florida
WIRX St. Joseph, Michigan
WTMY(FM) Coon Rapids, Minnesota
WKCB-FM Hindman, Kentucky
WKFS Milford, Ohio
WLVZ Collins, Mississippi
WKRV Vandalia, Illinois
WLIH Whitneyville, Pennsylvania
WLSM-FM Louisville, Mississippi
WNUS Belpre, Ohio
WOCO-FM Oconto, Wisconsin
WGMI(FM) Thomasville, Georgia
WORK Barre, Vermont
WPGU Urbana, Illinois
WPSK-FM Pulaski, Virginia
WPVL-FM Platteville, Wisconsin
WQJU Mifflintown, Pennsylvania
WQKL Ann Arbor, Michigan
WRHM Lancaster, South Carolina
WSAQ Port Huron, Michigan
WSPY-FM Plano, Illinois
WEDJ Danville, Indiana
WTDK Federalsburg, Maryland
WTKF Atlantic, North Carolina
WTLZ Saginaw, Michigan
WTSH-FM Aragon, Georgia
WTTX-FM Appomattox, Virginia
WRXZ Briarcliff Acres, South Carolina
WLIR-FM Hampton Bays, New York
WWYY Belvidere, New Jersey
WWZY Long Branch, New Jersey
WXYK Gulfport, Mississippi
WYFA Waynesboro, Georgia
WXPK Briarcliff Manor, New York
WZLF Bellows Falls, Vermont
WZVN Lowell, Indiana
KLJH Bayfield, Colorado
KTUM Tatum, New Mexico
KQEO Idaho Falls, Idaho
KNKK Needles, California
KPVW Aspen, Colorado
KRQN Vinton, Iowa
KWHO Lovell, Wyoming
WGMY Thomasville, Georgia
KHUN Huntington, Utah
WNMR Dannemora, New York
KNID North Enid, Oklahoma
KJML Columbus, Kansas

107.3 mhz

KOOS North Bend, Oregon
KAOX Kemmerer, Wyoming
KQZR Hayden, Colorado
KXFF Colorado City, Arizona
KBBK Lincoln, Nebraska
KFFM Yakima, Washington
KFXR-FM Chinle, Arizona
KGRS Burlington, Iowa
KIOW Forest City, Iowa
KISX Whitehouse, Texas
KIXW-FM Lenwood, California
KJAS Jasper, Texas
KKAW Albin, Wyoming
KTHR Wichita, Kansas
KLFX Nolanville, Texas
KLPW-FM Steelville, Missouri
KAPN Caldwell, Texas
KLVS Livermore, California
KNHT Rio Dell, California
KMJK North Kansas City, Missouri
KNUJ-FM Sleepy Eye, Minnesota
KSSL Post, Texas
KOMS Poteau, Oklahoma
KQMJ(FM) Osceola, Arkansas
KURQ Grover Beach, California
KQRN Mitchell, South Dakota
KSLT Spearfish, South Dakota
KVRW Lawton, Oklahoma
WAAF Westborough, Massachusetts
WBZN Old Town, Maine
WCGQ Columbus, Georgia
WMCD Claxton, Georgia
WCLN-FM Clinton, North Carolina
WCMN-FM Arecibo, Puerto Rico
WXGL St. Petersburg, Florida
WCTT-FM Corbin, Kentucky
WCWT-FM Centerville, Ohio
WCOH-FM Du Bois, Pennsylvania
WDDD-FM Johnston City, Illinois
WDKR Maroa, Illinois
WEGH Northumberland, Pennsylvania
WJMZ-FM Anderson, South Carolina
WJUC Swanton, Ohio
WKAZ-FM Miami, West Virginia
WRZI Hodgenville, Kentucky
WODX South Bristol Township, New York
WMGL Ravenel, South Carolina
WNWV Elyria, Ohio
WNXR Iron River, Wisconsin
WPUR Atlantic City, New Jersey
WQLT-FM Florence, Alabama
WKVU Utica, New York
WRQX Washington, District of Columbia
WRSW-FM Warsaw, Indiana
WRWD-FM Highland, New York

WRZQ-FM Greensburg, Indiana
WSJY Fort Atkinson, Wisconsin
WBRP Baker, Louisiana
WVGN Charlotte Amalie, Virgin Islands
WVSZ Chesterfield, South Carolina
WTRZ Spencer, Tennessee
WXLZ-FM Lebanon, Virginia
WBBT-FM Powhatan, Virginia
WYBZ Crooksville, Ohio
WFCG Tylertown, Mississippi
KRKV Las Animas, Colorado
WVRA Enfield, North Carolina
KLSY Cosmopolis, Washington
WUPF Powers, Michigan
KQDR Savoy, Texas
KNPQ Hershey, Nebraska
WQZZ Boligee, Alabama

107.5 mhz

KKLV Orem, Utah
KARZ Marshall, Minnesota
KASH-FM Anchorage, Alaska
KXJM Banks, Oregon
KBGY Faribault, Minnesota
KXMG Jean Lafitte, Louisiana
KQBO Rio Grande City, Texas
KWBZ Monroe City, Missouri
KQBA Los Alamos, New Mexico
KKAT Orem, Utah
KFEB Campbell, Missouri
KOSN Ketchum, Oklahoma
KHYT Tucson, Arizona
KJKJ Grand Forks, North Dakota
KKDM Des Moines, Iowa
KIFS Ashland, Oregon
KOMT Mountain Home, Arkansas
KLIZ-FM Brainerd, Minnesota
KLVE Los Angeles, California
KILV Castana, Iowa
KRDA Hanford, California
KMVK Fort Worth, Texas
KPIG-FM Freedom, California
KQPT Colusa, California
KQKS Lakewood, Colorado
KJMH Lake Arthur, Louisiana
KENR Superior, Montana
KSCB-FM Liberal, Kansas
KSED Sedona, Arizona
KSJT-FM San Angelo, Texas
KSMX-FM Clovis, New Mexico
KHTC(FM) Lake Jackson, Texas
KXKZ Ruston, Louisiana
KXO-FM El Centro, California
KXTE Pahrump, Nevada
KXTN-FM San Antonio, Texas
WABX Evansville, Indiana
WAMJ Roswell, Georgia
WAMR-FM Miami, Florida
WBBI Endwell, New York
WBLS New York, New York
WZRX-FM Fort Shawnee, Ohio
WBYN-FM Boyertown, Pennsylvania
WCCN-FM Neillsville, Wisconsin
WCCW-FM Traverse City, Michigan
WCKX Columbus, Ohio
WDBQ-FM Galena, Illinois
WEGW Wheeling, West Virginia
WFCC-FM Chatham, Massachusetts
WGCI-FM Chicago, Illinois
WGPR Detroit, Michigan
WIOK Falmouth, Kentucky
WHBQ-FM Germantown, Tennessee
WKXI-FM Magee, Mississippi
WKZL Winston-Salem, North Carolina
WMJW Rosedale, Mississippi
WNKT Eastover, South Carolina
WNNT-FM Warsaw, Virginia
WRVW Lebanon, Tennessee
WAZO Southport, North Carolina
WFNK Lewiston, Maine
WTIF-FM Omega, Georgia
WCHV-FM Charlottesville, Virginia
WBVE Bedford, Pennsylvania
WWGF Donalsonville, Georgia
WDUZ-FM Brillion, Wisconsin
WZLK Virgie, Kentucky
WFXJ-FM North Kingsville, Ohio
WZZZ Portsmouth, Ohio
KRPM Billings, Montana
KYZK Sun Valley, Idaho
KPAD Rawlins, Wyoming
KHEI-FM Kihei, Hawaii
KXZS Wall, South Dakota
KXRV Cannon Ball, North Dakota
KABR Alamo Community, New Mexico

107.7 mhz

KLJA(FM) Georgetown, Texas
KFTT Bagdad, Arizona
KCDZ Twentynine Palms, California
KGCR Goodland, Kansas
KSRN Kings Beach, California
KICD-FM Spencer, Iowa
KIST-FM Carpinteria, California
KKOA Volcano, Hawaii
KLAL Wrightsville, Arkansas
KDZZ St. Charles, Minnesota
KMAJ-FM Carbondale, Kansas
KNDD Seattle, Washington
KCVK Otterville, Missouri
KPLT-FM Paris, Texas
KRWP Stockton, Missouri
KRXO Oklahoma City, Oklahoma
KSAN San Mateo, California
KSLZ St. Louis, Missouri
KSYZ-FM Grand Island, Nebraska
KTBQ Nacogdoches, Texas
KBMX Proctor, Minnesota
WWDW Alberta, Virginia
WAZA Liberty, Mississippi
WXXF Loudonville, Ohio
WECW Elmira, New York
WEGC Sasser, Georgia
WFCS New Britain, Connecticut
WFSP-FM Kingwood, West Virginia
WFXX Georgiana, Alabama
WGNA-FM Albany, New York
WGTY Gettysburg, Pennsylvania
WHHM-FM Henderson, Tennessee
WHQX Gary, West Virginia
WHSB Alpena, Michigan
WPFX-FM Luckey, Ohio
WIVK-FM Knoxville, Tennessee
WKYN Owingsville, Kentucky
WWRX Ledyard, Connecticut
WKHI Fruitland, Maryland
WLLT Polo, Illinois
WBQI Bar Harbor, Maine
WMGF Mount Dora, Florida
WMMX Dayton, Ohio
WMQT-FM Ishpeming, Michigan
WMRS Monticello, Indiana
WLKK Wethersfield Twnshp, New York
WHSL Lisman, Alabama
WUHT Birmingham, Alabama
WTPL Hillsboro, New Hampshire
WRKR Portage, Michigan
WRRC Lawrenceville, New Jersey
WSEO Nelsonville, Ohio
WSFR Corydon, Indiana
WWWT-FM Manassas, Virginia
WUKS St. Pauls, North Carolina
WPRW-FM Martinez, Georgia
WVCY-FM Milwaukee, Wisconsin
WVOZ-FM Carolina, Puerto Rico
WHFX Darien, Georgia
WUUZ Cooperstown, Pennsylvania
WIBL(FM) Fairbury, Illinois
WCIG Dallas, Pennsylvania
KMTZ Three Forks, Montana
KABD Ipswich, South Dakota
WVRW Glenville, West Virginia
KLJA(FM) Georgetown, North Dakota
KHHG Hico, Texas

107.9 mhz

KLLE North Fork, California
KBKL Grand Junction, Colorado
KCLQ Lebanon, Missouri
KDND Sacramento, California
KESS-FM Lewisville, Texas
KWPW Robinson, Texas
KDZA-FM Pueblo, Colorado
KEYB Altus, Oklahoma
KEYJ-FM Abilene, Texas
KEZA Fayetteville, Arkansas
KFAN-FM Johnson City, Texas
KFIN Jonesboro, Arkansas
KFMW Waterloo, Iowa
KKOL-FM Aiea, Hawaii
KHPE Albany, Oregon
KIXS Victoria, Texas
KKRF Stuart, Iowa
KLTE Kirksville, Missouri
KVGS Meadview, Arizona
KMBI-FM Spokane, Washington
KKLC Fall River Mills, California
KMLE Chandler, Arizona
KPAW Fort Collins, Colorado
KPFX Fargo, North Dakota
KQLM Odessa, Texas
KQQL Anoka, Minnesota
KRVK Vista West, Wyoming
KHXT Erath, Louisiana
KSEA Greenfield, California
KUDD Roy, Utah
KWLS Winfield, Kansas
KXQL Flandreau, South Dakota
KBQI Albuquerque, New Mexico
KUZZ-FM Bakersfield, California
KVLY Edinburg, Texas
KTIC-FM West Point, Nebraska
KWVE-FM San Clemente, California
KXLT-FM Eagle, Idaho
KQQK Beaumont, Texas
KZRS Great Bend, Kansas
KZRK-FM Canyon, Texas
WAMW-FM Washington, Indiana
WBTF Midway, Kentucky
WCDD Canton, Illinois
WCRZ Flint, Michigan
WCVQ Fort Campbell, Kentucky
WDBN Wrightsville, Georgia
WDSY-FM Pittsburgh, Pennsylvania
WEAT West Palm Beach, Florida
WEBE Westport, Connecticut
WEMM-FM Huntington, West Virginia
WENZ Cleveland, Ohio
WFCA Ackerman, Mississippi
WLZL Annapolis, Maryland
WGTR Bucksport, South Carolina
WFMX Skowhegan, Maine
WMRK-FM Shorter, Alabama
WJFX New Haven, Indiana
WKRF Tobyhanna, Pennsylvania
WKYR-FM Burkesville, Kentucky
WLEY-FM Aurora, Illinois
WPFM-FM Panama City, Florida
WLNK Charlotte, North Carolina
WXYY(FM) Port Royal, South Carolina
WNDN Chiefland, Florida
WKVB Port Matilda, Pennsylvania
WNCT-FM Greenville, North Carolina
WOGT East Ridge, Tennessee
WHTA Hampton, Georgia
WPHI-FM Pennsauken, New Jersey
WBQK West Point, Virginia
WMUS Muskegon, Michigan
WSRZ-FM Coral Cove, Florida
WNTR Indianapolis, Indiana
WVAC-FM Adrian, Michigan
WMFM Key West, Florida
WVPS Burlington, Vermont
WWAG McKee, Kentucky
WWHT Syracuse, New York
WWPH Princeton Junction, New Jersey
WWRQ-FM Valdosta, Georgia
WUIL Arcola, Illinois
WXKS-FM Medford, Massachusetts
WVMX Westerville, Ohio
WBCV Wausau, Wisconsin
WYYD Amherst, Virginia
WZKX Bay St. Louis, Mississippi
WCZW Charlevoix, Michigan
KQEL Alamogordo, New Mexico
KHDV Darby, Montana
KXZT Newell, South Dakota
KBHM Basin, Wyoming

74.5 mhz

KTUN(FM) New Castle, Nebraska

87.9 mhz

KSFH Mountain View, California

88.1 mhz

KAFM Grand Junction, Colorado
KARH Forrest City, Arkansas
KAYB Sunnyside, Washington
KAYT Jena, Louisiana
KBBG Waterloo, Iowa
KBCU North Newton, Kansas
KBTL El Dorado, Kansas
KCEP Las Vegas, Nevada
KCFY Yuma, Arizona
KCNT Hastings, Nebraska
KCOU Columbia, Missouri
KCRY Mojave, California
KCUK Chevak, Alaska
KCWC-FM Riverton, Wyoming
KCWU Ellensburg, Washington
KDHX Saint Louis, Missouri
KECG El Cerrito, California
KEAR-FM Sacramento, California
KFLB-FM Stanton, Texas
KFCF Fresno, California
KFTG Pasadena, Texas
KGNZ Abilene, Texas
KGVA Fort Belknap Agency, Montana
KHID McAllen, Texas
KHMG Barrigada, Guam
KHOY Laredo, Texas
KHPR Honolulu, Hawaii
KICB Fort Dodge, Iowa
KJTY Topeka, Kansas
KLFC Branson, Missouri
KLFO Florence, Oregon
KKJZ Long Beach, California
KMLV Ralston, Nebraska
KMSI Moore, Oklahoma
KMUE Eureka, California
KNLE-FM Round Rock, Texas
KNNB Whiteriver, Arizona
KNSQ Mount Shasta, California
KNTU McKinney, Texas
KPGR Pleasant Grove, Utah
KRLX Northfield, Minnesota
KRSD Sioux Falls, South Dakota
KRTM Yucca Valley, California
KRUA Anchorage, Alaska
KSRH San Rafael, California
KTCV Kennewick, Washington
KTXT-FM Lubbock, Texas
KUYI Hotevilla, Arizona
KVSC St. Cloud, Minnesota
KWCR-FM Ogden, Utah
KWVA Eugene, Oregon
KYRV Concordia, Missouri
KZSC Santa Cruz, California
WAES Lincolnshire, Illinois
WAMP Jackson, Tennessee
WARY Valhalla, New York
WAXG Mount Sterling, Kentucky
WAXR Geneseo, Illinois
WAYF West Palm Beach, Florida
WAZD Savannah, Tennessee
WBCJ Spencerville, Ohio
WBFH Bloomfield Hills, Michigan
WBGM New Berlin, Pennsylvania
WBGU Bowling Green, Ohio
WBGY Everglades City, Florida
WKIV Westerly, Rhode Island
WBLW Gaylord, Michigan
WBMF Crete, Illinois
WCHC Worcester, Massachusetts
WCQS Asheville, North Carolina
WCRP Guayama, Puerto Rico
WCRX Chicago, Illinois
WCWP Brookville, New York
WUBA High Springs, Florida
WDFB-FM Danville, Kentucky
WDIY Allentown, Pennsylvania
WDPR Dayton, Ohio
WEFR Erie, Pennsylvania
WELH Providence, Rhode Island
WESN Bloomington, Illinois
WESU Middletown, Connecticut
WETN Wheaton, Illinois
WFRW Webster, New York
WFSK-FM Nashville, Tennessee
WGWR Liberty, New York
WHID Green Bay, Wisconsin
WHIJ Ocala, Florida
WHOV Hampton, Virginia
WHPR-FM Highland Park, Michigan
WYPR Baltimore, Maryland
WJIS Bradenton, Florida
WJSP-FM Warm Springs, Georgia
WYPF Frederick, Maryland
WJTY Lancaster, Wisconsin
WKJL Clarksburg, West Virginia
WKNC-FM Raleigh, North Carolina
WLGH Leroy Township, Michigan

WLRA Lockport, Illinois
WLTL La Grange, Illinois
WLXP Savannah, Georgia
WMAW-FM Meridian, Mississippi
WMBR Cambridge, Massachusetts
WMNR Monroe, Connecticut
WMUC-FM College Park, Maryland
WMUL Huntington, West Virginia
WMWK Milwaukee, Wisconsin
WNAS New Albany, Indiana
WCRJ Jacksonville, Florida
WNJS-FM Berlin, New Jersey
WNJT-FM Trenton, New Jersey
WNTH Winnetka, Illinois
WPCN(FM) Point Pleasant, West Virginia
WPEB Philadelphia, Pennsylvania
WPIR Hickory, North Carolina
WPTC Williamsport, Pennsylvania
WPTH Olney, Illinois
WRFL Lexington, Kentucky
WRGN Sweet Valley, Pennsylvania
WRGP Homestead, Florida
WRJA-FM Sumter, South Carolina
WSRU Slippery Rock, Pennsylvania
WRWJ Murrysville, Pennsylvania
WSBF-FM Clemson, South Carolina
WSDP Plymouth, Michigan
WSSD Chicago, Illinois
WTRT Benton, Kentucky
WUBJ Jamestown, New York
WURC Holly Springs, Mississippi
WUTC Chattanooga, Tennessee
WUWF Pensacola, Florida
WVBC Bethany, West Virginia
WVPE Elkhart, Indiana
WVYC York, Pennsylvania
WXBA Brentwood, New York
WXLU Peru, New York
WZXM Harrisburg, Pennsylvania
WXTC Greenville, Pennsylvania
WYCE Wyoming, Michigan
WYGG Asbury Park, New Jersey
WYSP Dushore, Pennsylvania
WZIP Akron, Ohio
KBPW Hampton, Arkansas
WMHS Pike Creek, Delaware
WZZD Warwick, Pennsylvania
WSMF Monroe, Michigan
WJCF-FM Morristown, Indiana
WKRY Versailles, Indiana
WLWJ Petersburg, Illinois
KQHR The Dalles, Oregon
WMBL Mitchell, Indiana
KKRI Pocola, Oklahoma
WSOG Spring Valley, Illinois
KDNK Glenwood Springs, Colorado
KEDR(FM) Butte, Montana
WAYH Harvest, Alabama
WFHL New Bedford, Massachusetts
KAPG Bentonville, Arkansas
WAYT Thomasville, Georgia
KVOD Lakewood, Colorado
KGLF Doss, Texas
WAYD Auburn, Kentucky
KDJC Baker, Oregon
KTFY Buhl, Idaho
KGRI Lebanon, Oregon
WKVY Somerset, Kentucky
WHYT Goodland Township, Michigan
KDIM Coweta, Oklahoma
KLBT Beaumont, Texas
KVLW Gatesville, Texas
KQNC Quincy, California
WNCH Norwich, Vermont
KWAO Ocean Park, Washington
KMPQ Roseburg, Oregon
WJPG Cape May Court House, New Jersey
KEDR Bay City, Texas
KPAQ Plaquemine, Louisiana
KAIX Cheyenne, Wyoming
WRIH Richmond, Virginia
KLTU Mammoth, Arizona
KLWG Lompoc, California
KRNZ Gonzales, Texas
KLUW East Wenatchee, Washington
WSJL Bessemer, Alabama
KPRQ Sheridan, Wyoming
KNMA Tularosa, New Mexico
WGHW Lockwoods Folly Town, North Carolina
KPGS Pagosa Springs, Colorado
KGGA Gallup, New Mexico
KLBR Bend, Oregon
KATG Elkhart, Texas
KIDS Grants, New Mexico
KKWV Aransas Pass, Texas
WPRZ-FM Brandy Station, Virginia
KRLP Fairmont, Minnesota
KUSW Flora Vista, New Mexico
WSFP Harrisville, Michigan
KQOC Gleneden Beach, Oregon
DKEAU Hilo, Hawaii
WSRC(FM) Waynetown, Indiana
WJJJ Beckley, West Virginia
WWGV Grove City, Ohio
WWTG Carpentersville, Illinois
KFHC Ponca, Nebraska
WZGL Charleston, Illinois
WTZI Rosemont, Illinois
KZGM Cabool, Missouri
KGLL Gillette, Wyoming
KGCV Elk Mountain, Wyoming
WDNJ Hopatcong, New Jersey
WWEN Wentworth, Wisconsin
KSRC Loup City, Nebraska
KRFI Redwood Falls, Minnesota
KOYA Rosebud, South Dakota
KPFZ-FM Lakeport, California
KDUP Cedarville, California
WHHN Hollidaysburg, Pennsylvania
KMPZ Salida, Colorado
WNEE Patterson, Georgia
WGWS St. Mary's City, Maryland
WHUZ(FM) Cole, Indiana
KGFJ Belt, Montana
WSLZ Cape Vincent, New York
WUBK(FM) Enoree, South Carolina
WWFJ East Fayetteville, North Carolina
KAKI Juneau, Alaska
WNBV Grundy, Virginia
KCOI Clovis, New Mexico
WHJL Merrill, Wisconsin
WRSN Lebanon, Tennessee
KYGR Alamo, New Mexico
KRTT Great Bend, Kansas
KOOT Hurley, New Mexico
KOIA Storm Lake, Iowa
KUCC Clarkston, Washington
KCFD Crawford, Nebraska
WHPF Pittston Farm, Maine
KLBD(FM) Fremont, Texas
WYFY Cambridge, Ohio
KTQQ Elko, Nevada
KLWL Chillicothe, Missouri
KOGJ Kenai, Alaska

88.3 mhz

KABF Little Rock, Arkansas
KAPI Ruston, Louisiana
KAFR Conroe, Texas
KAXL Greenacres, California
KDKL Coalinga, California
KTGS Tishomingo, Oklahoma
KBCM Blytheville, Arkansas
KBJQ Bronson, Kansas
KBNR Brownsville, Texas
KBVM Portland, Oregon
KCCK-FM Cedar Rapids, Iowa
KCLU-FM Thousand Oaks, California
KCPW-FM Salt Lake City, Utah
KESD Brookings, South Dakota
KJAB-FM Mexico, Missouri
KJRN Keene, Texas
KJRT Amarillo, Texas
KSBC Nile, Washington
KLVC Magalia, California
KLVN Livingston, California
KLYT Albuquerque, New Mexico
KMLW Moses Lake, Washington
KNAI Phoenix, Arizona
KPAC San Antonio, Texas
KPHF Phoenix, Arizona
KPRH Montrose, Colorado
KSDS San Diego, California
KSRG Ashland, Oregon
KUCR Riverside, California
KVCO Concordia, Kansas
KWND Springfield, Missouri
KXUA Fayetteville, Arkansas
KYFW Wichita, Kansas
WAER Syracuse, New York
WAFJ Belvedere, South Carolina
WAFR Tupelo, Mississippi
WAPR Selma, Alabama
WYLV(FM) Maynardville, Tennessee
WAUI Shelby, Ohio
WAWF Kankakee, Illinois
WAWH Dublin, Georgia
WAYK Kalamazoo, Michigan
WBGO Newark, New Jersey
WBIA Shelbyville, Tennessee
WBIY La Belle, Florida
WBMT Boxford, Massachusetts
WBWC Berea, Ohio
WCBN-FM Ann Arbor, Michigan
WCOU Attica, New York
WCQR-FM Kingsport, Tennessee
WDCV-FM Carlisle, Pennsylvania
WDGC-FM Downers Grove, Illinois
WDSO Chesterton, Indiana
WEAX Angola, Indiana
WEJC White Star, Michigan
WFEN Rockford, Illinois
WFSO Olivebridge, New York
WGAO Franklin, Massachusetts
WGWG Boiling Springs, North Carolina
WMBJ Murrells Inlet, South Carolina
WHWC Menomonie, Wisconsin
WIQH Concord, Massachusetts
WGNK Pennsuco, Florida
WIUS Macomb, Illinois
WJCK Piedmont, Alabama
WJLY Ramsey, Illinois
WAYP Marianna, Florida
WLAB Fort Wayne, Indiana
WLFC North Baltimore, Ohio
WLPT Jesup, Georgia
WMRT Marietta, Ohio
WMTS-FM Murfreesboro, Tennessee
WIVL Jasper, Georgia
WNFA Port Huron, Michigan
WNIN-FM Evansville, Indiana
WNUB-FM Northfield, Vermont
WUKV Portsmouth, Ohio
WOTC Edinburg, Virginia
WPPB Southampton, New York
WPOZ Union Park, Florida
WPPR Demorest, Georgia
WQNA Springfield, Illinois
WQRI Bristol, Rhode Island
WRBH New Orleans, Louisiana
WRCT Pittsburgh, Pennsylvania
WRPS Rockland, Massachusetts
WRUO Mayaguez, Puerto Rico
WRVL Lynchburg, Virginia
WSHJ Southfield, Michigan
WARA New Washington, Indiana
WEBF Lerose, Kentucky
WTLG Starke, Florida
WUAW Erwin, North Carolina
WVCR-FM Loudonville, New York
WXOU Auburn Hills, Michigan
WXTS-FM Toledo, Ohio
WXUT Toledo, Ohio
WYAR Yarmouth, Maine
WYLV Maynardville, Tennessee
WZRD Chicago, Illinois
KPGB Pryor, Montana
WVBH Beach Haven West, New Jersey
WLKA Tafton, Pennsylvania
WPJC Pontiac, Illinois
WHCM Palatine, Illinois
WCLR Arlington Heights, Illinois
WVRL Elizabeth City, North Carolina
WAYQ Clarksville, Tennessee
KBPN Brainerd, Minnesota
KGCO Fort Collins, Colorado
KTPL Pueblo, Colorado
KLNB Grand Island, Nebraska
WYBX(FM) Key West, Florida
KARJ Kuna, Idaho
KLJV Scottsbluff, Nebraska
WZXQ Chambersburg, Pennsylvania
KKLG Newton, Iowa
WSGP Glasgow, Kentucky
WXBE Beaufort, North Carolina
KBMK Bismarck, North Dakota
KPYR Craig, Colorado
KLRH Sparks, Nevada
WEVS Nashua, New Hampshire
KLMP Rapid City, South Dakota
WOAR South Vienna, Ohio
KMLT Jackson, Wyoming
WKMV Muncie, Indiana
WKIW Ironwood, Michigan
KYCJ Camino, California
WKDN(FM) State College, Pennsylvania
WKPK Michigamme, Michigan
WHZN New Whiteland, Indiana
KIFR Alice, Texas
KJCG Missoula, Montana
WRAU Ocean City, Maryland
KPCP New Roads, Louisiana
KJSB Jonesboro, Arkansas
WRCC Dibrell, Tennessee
KITF International Falls, Minnesota
WYAD Benton, Mississippi
KVAM Kimball, Nebraska
WSHM Wixom, Michigan
KYZQ Mount Pleasant, Texas
KGUA Gualala, California
KKRR Casper, Wyoming
WZXE East Nottingham, Pennsylvania
KOGC Wheeler, Texas
WRGC-FM Milledgeville, Georgia
KLMB Roundup, Montana
KVKR Pine Ridge, South Dakota
WXLS Tupper Lake, New York
WMEK Kennebunkport, Maine
KBWW Broken Bow, Oklahoma
WLVV Midland, Maryland
KWIS Plummer, Idaho
KHNW Manson, Washington
KYPW Wolf Point, Montana
KBKO Kodiak, Alaska
WQIQ Spotsylvania, Virginia
WRCT(FM) Pittsburgh, Pennsylvania

88.5 mhz

KAKA Salina, Kansas
KALA Davenport, Iowa
KAYK Victoria, Texas
KBDC Mason City, Iowa
KBEM-FM Minneapolis, Minnesota
KBMD Marble Falls, Texas
KBSY Burley, Idaho
KCIC Grand Junction, Colorado
KCRB-FM Bemidji, Minnesota
KCSN Northridge, California
KDCR Sioux Center, Iowa
KEOM Mesquite, Texas
KEYA Belcourt, North Dakota
KBZR Billings, Montana
KGNU-FM Boulder, Colorado
KHMS Victorville, California
KLCV Lincoln, Nebraska
KLJC Kansas City, Missouri
KLRF Milton-Freewater, Oregon
KLVH San Luis Obispo, California
KRSU Appleton, Minnesota
KOIR Edinburg, Texas
KPBB Brownfield, Texas
KPLU-FM Tacoma, Washington
KPSC Palm Springs, California
KQED-FM San Francisco, California
KRLF Pullman, Washington
KSBA Coos Bay, Oregon
KSBR Mission Viejo, California
KTEP El Paso, Texas
KMST Rolla, Missouri
KURE Ames, Iowa
KWTW Bishop, California
KHIB Bastrop, Texas
KYVT Yakima, Washington
WIAB Mackinaw City, Michigan
WAMU Washington, District of Columbia
WYLJ(FM) Tullahoma, Tennessee
WYOR Republic, Ohio
WBEL Cairo, Illinois
WBHY-FM Mobile, Alabama
WBMK Morehead, Kentucky
WBNH Pekin, Illinois
WCII Spencer, New York
WCRT-FM Terre Haute, Indiana
WEDW-FM Stamford, Connecticut
WEPC Belton, South Carolina
WFCF St. Augustine, Florida
WFCH Charleston, South Carolina
WFCR Amherst, Massachusetts
WFDD Winston-Salem, North Carolina
WGBK Glenview, Illinois
WGCA-FM Quincy, Illinois
WGNV Milladore, Wisconsin
WGVU-FM Allendale, Michigan
WHCF Bangor, Maine

WHFH Flossmoor, Illinois
WHPK-FM Chicago, Illinois
WHSD Hinsdale, Illinois
WJFM Baton Rouge, Louisiana
WJIA Guntersville, Alabama
WJIE-FM Okolona, Kentucky
WJSU-FM Jackson, Mississippi
WKPX Sunrise, Florida
WLUZ Levittown, Puerto Rico
WKWZ Syosset, New York
WLJR Birmingham, Alabama
WMCE Erie, Pennsylvania
WMFL Florida City, Florida
WMNF Tampa, Florida
WMUB Oxford, Ohio
WNJP Sussex, New Jersey
WOAS Ontonagon, Michigan
WJLZ Virginia Beach, Virginia
WPOB Plainview, New York
WQOX Memphis, Tennessee
WRAS Atlanta, Georgia
WNLI Sturgeon Bay, Wisconsin
WRKC Wilkes-Barre, Pennsylvania
WRUR-FM Rochester, New York
WYVL(FM) Youngsville, Pennsylvania
WTTU Cookeville, Tennessee
WUSM-FM Hattiesburg, Mississippi
WVCP Gallatin, Tennessee
WVOF Fairfield, Connecticut
WVPA St. Johnsbury, Vermont
WVPN Charleston, West Virginia
WVTW Charlottesville, Virginia
WHYZ(FM) Palm Bay, Florida
WWTA Marion, Massachusetts
WXPN Philadelphia, Pennsylvania
WYFU Masontown, Pennsylvania
WYFV Cayce, South Carolina
WYSA Wauseon, Ohio
WYSU Youngstown, Ohio
WRTP Franklinton, North Carolina
KPMB Plainview, Texas
KBQC Independence, Kansas
KCKT Crockett, Texas
WJCB Clewiston, Florida
KIHS Adel, Iowa
KWRX Redmond, Oregon
WZXX Lawrenceburg, Tennessee
KVUH Laytonville, California
KQKL Selma, California
KTKL Stigler, Oklahoma
KTDU Durango, Colorado
WBOJ Lumpkin, Georgia
KAKL Anchorage, Alaska
WZNB New Bern, North Carolina
KLMF Klamath Falls, Oregon
KMQX Weatherford, Texas
WVDA Valdosta, Georgia
KVLT Temple, Texas
WWLC Cross City, Florida
WTMK Wanatah, Indiana
KLRW Byrne, Texas
WEKF Corbin, Kentucky
KRNC Steamboat Springs, Colorado
WJOM Eagle, Michigan
KJCQ Westwood, California
KAIK Tillamook, Oregon
KAVE Oakridge, Oregon
KEKL Mesquite, Nevada
KFLT-FM Tucson, Arizona
KIAD Dubuque, Iowa
KLKA Globe, Arizona
KZLU Inyokern, California
KPIJ Junction City, Oregon
KPKJ Mentmore, New Mexico
WCTP Gagetown, Michigan
WMUW Columbus, Mississippi
WZDG Scotts Hill, North Carolina
KUWY Laramie, Wyoming
KGHY Beaumont, Texas
KZTH Piedmont, Oklahoma
KVJZ Vail, Colorado
WJBE Five Points, Alabama
KECU Kaibito, Arizona
WWVY Waverly, Ohio
WSLT Statesboro, Georgia
KKRN Bella Vista, California
WRKJ Westbrook, Maine
KMUZ Turner, Oregon
WGRH Hinckley, Minnesota
WNMP Marlinton, West Virginia
KZUW Reliance, Wyoming
KJLJ Scott City, Kansas
KHEW Rocky Boy's Reserv., Montana
KEDC Hearne, Texas
WPMW Bayview, Massachusetts
KENU Des Moines, New Mexico
WKUA Moundville, Alabama
WUOW Milford, New York
Minooka, Virginia

88.7 mhz

KAGU Spokane, Washington
KASV Borger, Texas
KAZI Austin, Texas
KKER Kerrville, Texas
KBMQ Monroe, Louisiana
KBPU De Queen, Arkansas
KBVR Corvallis, Oregon
KCME Manitou Springs, Colorado
KDCV-FM Blair, Nebraska
KEPI Eagle Pass, Texas
KQSC Santa Barbara, California
KFBN Fargo, North Dakota
KKLM Corpus Christi, Texas
KIGC Oskaloosa, Iowa
KISL Avalon, California
KJHA Houston, Alaska
KLNE-FM Lexington, Nebraska
KLNI Decorah, Iowa
KLVP Sandy, Oregon
KLVV Ponca City, Oklahoma
KMPO Modesto, California
KMSE Rochester, Minnesota
KNAU Flagstaff, Arizona
KRVS Lafayette, Louisiana
KRZA Alamosa, Colorado
KSPC Claremont, California
KTCU-FM Fort Worth, Texas
KZLO Kilgore, Texas
KTRM Kirksville, Missouri
KUBO Calexico, California
KUHF Houston, Texas
KUNR Reno, Nevada
KWDM West Des Moines, Iowa
KWPR Lund, Nevada
KXMS Joplin, Missouri
WAGO Snow Hill, North Carolina
WAGP Beaufort, South Carolina
WAYM Spring Hill, Tennessee
WBFO Buffalo, New York
WBHW Loogootee, Indiana
WBYX Stroudsburg, Pennsylvania
WCSF Joliet, Illinois
WELL-FM Waverly, Alabama
WERN Madison, Wisconsin
WFNP Rosendale, New York
WFOS Chesapeake, Virginia
WGVE-FM Gary, Indiana
WHCL-FM Clinton, New York
WIAA Interlochen, Michigan
WICR Indianapolis, Indiana
WIGH Jackson, Tennessee
WJCU University Heights, Ohio
WJFR Jacksonville, Florida
WJMF Smithfield, Rhode Island
WJZB Starkville, Mississippi
WMYZ Clermont, Florida
WWLU Lincoln University, Pennsylvania
WLOQ Indian Lakes Estates, Florida
WLUW Chicago, Illinois
WMMT Whitesburg, Kentucky
WMOC Lumber City, Georgia
WNCW Spindale, North Carolina
WNHU West Haven, Connecticut
WNYK Nyack, New York
WOBO Batavia, Ohio
WOFN Beach City, Ohio
WPCD Champaign, Illinois
WPSC-FM Wayne, New Jersey
WQPR Muscle Shoals, Alabama
WRFW River Falls, Wisconsin
WRHU Hempstead, New York
WRHV Poughkeepsie, New York
WRSE Elmhurst, Illinois
WRSU-FM New Brunswick, New Jersey
WRVT Rutland, Vermont
WRWA Dothan, Alabama
WSEW Sanford, Maine
WSIE Edwardsville, Illinois
WSQA Hornell, New York
WSYC-FM Shippensburg, Pennsylvania
WUFM Columbus, Ohio
WWPV-FM Colchester, Vermont
WXDU Durham, North Carolina
WXJM Harrisonburg, Virginia
WJDS Sparta, Georgia
WEHA(FM) Port Republic, New Jersey
WMLS Grand Marais, Minnesota
KOAP Lakeview, Oregon
KMCU Wichita Falls, Texas
WSRI Sugar Grove, Illinois
KJKL Selma, Oregon
KDNR South Greeley, Wyoming
WFRP Americus, Georgia
KNKL North Ogden, Utah
WPRC Sheffield, Illinois
KFRI West Odessa, Texas
KXJS Sutter, California
KLKM Kalispell, Montana
KAJT Ada, Oklahoma
KWTU Tulsa, Oklahoma
WYTF Indianola, Mississippi
WQKV Rochester, Indiana
WXPH Middletown, Pennsylvania
KLOY Astoria, Oregon
WWCF McConnellsburg, Pennsylvania
WEER Montauk, New York
WRAE Raeford, North Carolina
WKYJ Rouses Point, New York
KORB Hopland, California
KBLV Tehachapi, California
KGSF Green Forest, Arkansas
KRBG Umbarger, Texas
KMPB Breckenridge, Colorado
WPJY Blennerhassett, West Virginia
WHJM Anna, Ohio
KRFH Marshalltown, Iowa
KOAY(FM) Middleton, Idaho
KBOM Socorro, New Mexico
KETP Enterprise, Oregon
WEGN Kankakee, Illinois
KVCH Huron, South Dakota
WLCU Campbellsville, Kentucky
WEYY Tallapoosa, Georgia
KMKZ(FM) Red Feather Lakes, Colorado
KFXH Marlow, Oklahoma
KSDQ Moberly, Missouri
WREM Canton, New York
WKNZ Harrington, Delaware
WEUC Morganfield, Kentucky
KESG Sayre, Oklahoma
KXNM Encino, New Mexico
WRIQ Lexington, Virginia
KHIH Estes Park, Colorado
KUDI Choteau, Montana
WSIS Riverside, Michigan
KKWY Douglas, Wyoming
KTMU Muenster, Texas
KOKN Oketo, Kansas
WMWI Demopolis, Alabama
WRYV Milroy, Pennsylvania
KWOP(FM) Fort Dodge, North Carolina

88.9 mhz

KAOW Fort Smith, Arkansas
KAWC-FM Yuma, Arizona
KHII Cloudcroft, New Mexico
KCSH Ellensburg, Washington
KDUV Visalia, California
KEFX Twin Falls, Idaho
KETR Commerce, Texas
KEUL Girdwood, Alaska
KFPR Redding, California
KGFC Great Falls, Montana
KJLU Jefferson City, Missouri
KLDN Lufkin, Texas
KLCZ Lewiston, Idaho
KMBH-FM Harlingen, Texas
KMIH Mercer Island, Washington
KMPR Minot, North Dakota
KNMI Farmington, New Mexico
KNSR Collegeville, Minnesota
KPRD Hays, Kansas
KQFE Springfield, Oregon
KRNW Chillicothe, Missouri
KRUC Las Cruces, New Mexico
KSTM Indianola, Iowa
KTJO-FM Ottawa, Kansas
KTLW Lancaster, California
KTNA Talkeetna, Alaska
KUCI Irvine, California
KUSP Santa Cruz, California
KXPR Sacramento, California
KXLU Los Angeles, California
KYLV Oklahoma City, Oklahoma
WAJM Atlantic City, New Jersey
WARG Summit, Illinois
WBJV Steubenville, Ohio
WBKG Macon, Georgia
WBLU-FM Grand Rapids, Michigan
WBYO Sellersville, Pennsylvania
WBZC Pemberton, New Jersey
WCIY Canandaigua, New York
WCSU-FM Wilberforce, Ohio
WCVE-FM Richmond, Virginia
WCVF-FM Fredonia, New York
WDBM East Lansing, Michigan
WDCR Oreana, Illinois
WDNA Miami, Florida
WEAA Baltimore, Maryland
WEIU Charleston, Illinois
WEKU Richmond, Kentucky
WEPS Elgin, Illinois
WERS Boston, Massachusetts
WPUC-FM Ponce, Puerto Rico
WFRJ Johnstown, Pennsylvania
WFRS Smithtown, New York
WFSE Edinboro, Pennsylvania
WFSU-FM Tallahassee, Florida
WAKL Flint, Michigan
WITC Cazenovia, New York
WOTW Monee, Illinois
WJMJ Hartford, Connecticut
WJYW Union City, Indiana
WKEU-FM The Rock, Georgia
WMSB Byhalia, Mississippi
WKTO Edgewater, Florida
WKYU-FM Bowling Green, Kentucky
WLNX Lincoln, Illinois
WLRY Rushville, Ohio
WLSU La Crosse, Wisconsin
WMAU-FM Bude, Mississippi
WMBW Chattanooga, Tennessee
WMCX West Long Branch, New Jersey
WKVC North Myrtle Beach, South Carolina
WMSL Athens, Georgia
WMXM Lake Forest, Illinois
WNSC-FM Rock Hill, South Carolina
WNYO Oswego, New York
WOJB Reserve, Wisconsin
WIIT Chicago, Illinois
WQCS Fort Pierce, Florida
WQSU Selinsgrove, Pennsylvania
WRDL Ashland, Ohio
WRPJ Port Jervis, New York
WRRG River Grove, Illinois
WSHA Raleigh, North Carolina
WSIA Staten Island, New York
WSLJ Watertown, New York
WSND-FM Notre Dame, Indiana
WSTB Streetsboro, Ohio
WVEP Martinsburg, West Virginia
WVPW Buckhannon, West Virginia
WWGN Ottawa, Illinois
WWIO-FM Brunswick, Georgia
WWNW New Wilmington, Pennsylvania
WYFE Tarpon Springs, Florida
WYMS Milwaukee, Wisconsin
KAGJ Ephraim, Utah
KHJC Lihue, Hawaii
KMJG Homer, Alaska
KJIA Spirit Lake, Iowa
WVSI Mt. Vernon, Illinois
WUND-FM Manteo, North Carolina
KAKV El Dorado, Arkansas
KARU Cache, Oklahoma
KRFC Fort Collins, Colorado
WTAI Union City, Tennessee
KAIP Wapello, Iowa
WMYJ-FM Oolitic, Indiana
KKLJ Klamath Falls, Oregon
KNPR Las Vegas, Nevada
KOHR Sheridan, Wyoming
KJLP Palmer, Alaska
KOBK Baker City, Oregon
KABN-FM Kasilof, Alaska
KYWH Lockwood, Montana
KSEF Ste. Genevieve, Missouri
KCJX Carbondale, Colorado
KICJ(FM) Mitchellville, Iowa
WMFT Tuscaloosa, Alabama
KAIC Tucson, Arizona
WMDR-FM Oakland, Maine
KFRD Butte, Montana

WVRN Wittenberg, Wisconsin
KAIW Laramie, Wyoming
KYOR Newport, Oregon
KWXC Grove, Oklahoma
KWVI Waverly, Iowa
KLLU Gallup, New Mexico
KSUR Mart, Texas
KNBE Beatrice, Nebraska
KGLV Manhattan, Kansas
WMWX Miamitown, Ohio
KLOF Gillette, Wyoming
KSWS Chehalis, Washington
WWES Mount Kisco, New York
WHEY North Muskegon, Michigan
KVRZ Libby, Montana
KSJP(FM) Ipswich, South Dakota
KIHI Burns, Wyoming
WQRN Cook, Minnesota
KNGM Guymon, Oklahoma
KNGW Juneau, Alaska
KUHN Golden Meadow, Louisiana
KENM Tucumcari, New Mexico
KCHG Cedar City, Utah
WYRR Lakewood, New York
KDAB Central City, Colorado
WTPG Whitehouse, Ohio
WCIJ Unadilla, New York
KRJA Lamesa, Texas
KRBR La Barge, Wyoming
KYLF Adrian, Missouri

89.1 mhz

KANW Albuquerque, New Mexico
KLFR Reedsport, Oregon
KAUR Sioux Falls, South Dakota
KBBF Calistoga, California
KBHU-FM Spearfish, South Dakota
KLVK Fountain Hills, Arizona
KBYU-FM Provo, Utah
KCEA Atherton, California
KCLC St. Charles, Missouri
KCRU Oxnard, California
KEOS College Station, Texas
KFAE-FM Richland, Washington
KHAP Chico, California
KHNE-FM Hastings, Nebraska
KXLV Amarillo, Texas
KLPI Ruston, Louisiana
KMHD Gresham, Oregon
KSQX Springtown, Texas
KMUW Wichita, Kansas
KTTZ-FM Lubbock, Texas
KHUI Alamosa, Colorado
KPRX Bakersfield, California
KSMF Ashland, Oregon
KSTX San Antonio, Texas
KTLC Canon City, Colorado
KUAR Little Rock, Arkansas
KUAZ-FM Tucson, Arizona
KUFM Missoula, Montana
KVDP Dry Prong, Louisiana
KVMT Montrose, Colorado
KWFC Springfield, Missouri
KCJH Livingston, California
KYFP Palestine, Texas
WAUZ Greensburg, Indiana
WBCX Gainesville, Georgia
WBOI Fort Wayne, Indiana
WBSD Burlington, Wisconsin
WBSN-FM New Orleans, Louisiana
WBSU Brockport, New York
WCID Friendship, New York
WDNX Olive Hill, Tennessee
WDWN Auburn, New York
WEMU Ypsilanti, Michigan
WGMS Hagerstown, Maryland
WEVO(FM) Concord, New Hampshire
WFDU Teaneck, New Jersey
WFNM Lancaster, Pennsylvania
WFSW Panama City, Florida
WGLT Normal, Illinois
WHAB Acton, Massachusetts
WIDR Kalamazoo, Michigan
WJPZ-FM Syracuse, New York
WKSV Thompson, Ohio
WLBF Montgomery, Alabama
WLJK Aiken, South Carolina
WMBU Forest, Mississippi
WMHT-FM Schenectady, New York
WECV-FM Nashville, Tennessee
WNIE Freeport, Illinois
WPKT Norwich, Connecticut
WNYU-FM New York, New York
WNZN Lorain, Ohio
WOCR Olivet, Michigan
WONC Naperville, Illinois
WOUC-FM Cambridge, Ohio
WOUL-FM Ironton, Ohio
WPAZ Pottstown, Pennsylvania
WPHS Warren, Michigan
WSFX Nanticoke, Pennsylvania
WSMR Sarasota, Florida
WLKB Bay City, Michigan
WUFT-FM Gainesville, Florida
WUSO Springfield, Ohio
WVJC Mount Carmel, Illinois
WVTF Roanoke, Virginia
WWCJ Cape May, New Jersey
WWFM Trenton, New Jersey
WLAZ Kissimmee, Florida
WXHL-FM Christiana, Delaware
WEVO Concord, New Hampshire
WXVU Villanova, Pennsylvania
WYBF Radnor Township, Pennsylvania
KECC La Junta, Colorado
KJBB(FM) Watertown, South Dakota
WBYH Hawley, Pennsylvania
WDTR Imlay City, Michigan
KXTH Seminole, Oklahoma
KWRI Bartlesville, Oklahoma
KYCU Clinton, Oklahoma
WLOG Markleysburg, Pennsylvania
WPAS Pascagoula, Mississippi
KQXS Stephenville, Texas
KLWC Casper, Wyoming
KXGM-FM Hiawatha, Iowa
WSPM Cloverdale, Indiana
WJJE Delaware, Ohio
WRXV State College, Pennsylvania
WCNV Heathsville, Virginia
WWIP Cheriton, Virginia
KQAI Roswell, New Mexico
KAWS Marsing, Idaho
WKNG-FM Heflin, Alabama
KBWA Brush, Colorado
KHOL Jackson, Wyoming
KRLR Sulphur, Louisiana
KDAI Scottsbluff, Nebraska
KODV Barstow, California
KFLO-FM Blanchard, Louisiana
KLUU Jamestown, North Dakota
KVFL Pierre, South Dakota
WLPR-FM Lowell, Indiana
KXBC Garberville, California
WSSW Platteville, Wisconsin
KUOR-FM Redlands, California
WHAA Adams, Wisconsin
WRYN Hickory, North Carolina
KVCS Spring Valley, Minnesota
KPVL Postville, Iowa
KNSZ(FM) Ottumwa, Iowa
WBIB-FM Forsyth, Georgia
KGHE Glenoma, Washington
WSMJ(FM) Wilkinson, Indiana
KYCO Limon, Colorado
KQDL Hines, Oregon
KPKP Harts Bluff, Texas
WAKP Smithboro, Georgia
WGZS Cloquet, Minnesota
KHOI Story City, Iowa
KXNV Sun Valley, Nevada
KSPP Rhinelander, Wisconsin
WKEK Gunflint Lake, Minnesota
KKWW Shelbina, Missouri

89.3 mhz

KAKX Mendocino, California
KALU Langston, Oklahoma
KAOS Olympia, Washington
KATB Anchorage, Alaska
KAVK Many, Louisiana
KAYH Fayetteville, Arkansas
KHCP Paris, Texas
KBHE-FM Rapid City, South Dakota
KCCU Lawton, Oklahoma
KCRI Indio, California
KCUR-FM Kansas City, Missouri
KQEI-FM North Highlands, California
KIPO Honolulu, Hawaii
KJMC Des Moines, Iowa
KMTG San Jose, California
KLFF-FM San Luis Obispo, California
KLOV Winchester, Oregon
KNON Dallas, Texas
KOHL Fremont, California
KPBE Brownwood, Texas
KPCC Pasadena, California
KPFB Berkeley, California
KPRG Agana, Guam
KNAQ Prescott, Arizona
KRSW Worthington, Minnesota
KSBJ Humble, Texas
KTBJ Festus, Missouri
KUGS Bellingham, Washington
KUND-FM Grand Forks, North Dakota
KUOI-FM Moscow, Idaho
KUVO Denver, Colorado
KVPR Fresno, California
KXGJ Victoria, Texas
KXNE-FM Norfolk, Nebraska
KZUM Lincoln, Nebraska
WAII Hattiesburg, Mississippi
WALN Carrollton, Alabama
WAMH Amherst, Massachusetts
WATU Port Gibson, Mississippi
WBFJ-FM Winston-Salem, North Carolina
WBJY Americus, Georgia
WBLD Orchard Lake, Michigan
KCMP Northfield, Minnesota
WCSB Cleveland, Ohio
WDLM-FM East Moline, Illinois
WECC-FM Folkston, Georgia
WFPL Louisville, Kentucky
WGCF Paducah, Kentucky
WGNB Zeeland, Michigan
WGNJ St. Joseph, Illinois
WGSU Geneseo, New York
WHFR Dearborn, Michigan
WHSN Bangor, Maine
WIPA Pittsfield, Illinois
WSMB Harbor Beach, Michigan
WJCS Allentown, Pennsylvania
WJEL Indianapolis, Indiana
WJVP Culebra, Puerto Rico
WJYA Emporia, Virginia
WKKC Chicago, Illinois
WKRW Wooster, Ohio
WLFJ-FM Greenville, South Carolina
WLJP Monroe, New York
WLRH Huntsville, Alabama
WMHN Webster, New York
WMKV Reading, Ohio
WMKW Crossville, Tennessee
WMSJ Freeport, Maine
WNJB-FM Bridgeton, New Jersey
WNKJ Hopkinsville, Kentucky
WNUR-FM Evanston, Illinois
WPFW Washington, District of Columbia
WPIO Titusville, Florida
WPNE-FM Green Bay, Wisconsin
WQED-FM Pittsburgh, Pennsylvania
WRDV Warminster, Pennsylvania
WRFG Atlanta, Georgia
WRKF Baton Rouge, Louisiana
WRMB Boynton Beach, Florida
WRTC-FM Hartford, Connecticut
WSCI Charleston, South Carolina
WRVH Clayton, New York
WSKG-FM Binghamton, New York
WSOE Elon College, North Carolina
WTEB New Bern, North Carolina
WTLI Bear Creek Township, Michigan
WVTU Charlottesville, Virginia
WZCP Chillicothe, Ohio
WXYC Chapel Hill, North Carolina
WYPL Memphis, Tennessee
WYSZ Maumee, Ohio
KBNO-FM White Salmon, Washington
WAJJ McKenzie, Tennessee
WYSM Lima, Ohio
KELP-FM Mesquite, New Mexico
WSGG Norfolk, Connecticut
KARQ San Andreas, California
KLMT Billings, Montana
KLBV Steamboat Springs, Colorado
KKLT Texarkana, Arkansas
WIKV Plymouth, Indiana
WYTJ Linton, Indiana
WJKN-FM Spring Arbor, Michigan
WZRI Spring Lake, North Carolina
KWCF Sheridan, Wyoming
KPJP Greenville, California
KAER Mesquite, Nevada
KPDO Pescadero, California
WKFA St. Catherine, Florida
KVIX Port Angeles, Washington
KOPJ Sebeka, Minnesota
KAIH Lake Havasu City, Arizona
KNAR San Angelo, Texas
WRFE Chesterfield, South Carolina
KYAI McKee, Kentucky
KLBZ Bozeman, Montana
WWLA South Charleston, West Virginia
KSSO Norman, Oklahoma
KVRA Sisters, Oregon
KTAW Walsenburg, Colorado
KOGL Gleneden Beach, Oregon
KJCF Asotin, Washington
KNDZ McKinleyville, California
WUMD North Dartmouth, Massachusetts
WJIK Fulton, Alabama
WRTJ Coatesville, Pennsylvania
KDNG Durango, Colorado
KUSL Richfield, Utah
KKNL Valentine, Nebraska
WZNP Newark, Ohio
KRSF Ridgecrest, California
WNJY Netcong, New Jersey
KIRL Osage Beach, Missouri
KTDX Laramie, Wyoming
WPJN Jemison, Alabama
WIRC Ely, Minnesota
WAZQ Islamorada, Florida
WRWV Beech Creek, Pennsylvania
KTHL Altus, Oklahoma
WYNS Waynesville, Ohio
KRWY Rawlins, Wyoming
KAZC Healdton, Oklahoma
WRPB Benedicta, Maine
KKFC Hart, Texas
KYPB Big Timber, Montana
WFJS-FM Freehold, New Jersey
WCOM-FM Silver Creek, New York
WDWZ Andalusia, Alabama
KRBO(FM) Millers Ranch, California

89.5 mhz

KBAQ Phoenix, Arizona
KBES Ceres, California
KBHG Alexandria, Minnesota
KBMJ Heber Springs, Arkansas
KBMM Odessa, Texas
KBPG Montevideo, Minnesota
KCAC Camden, Arkansas
KCFV Ferguson, Missouri
KENW-FM Portales, New Mexico
KEPX Eagle Pass, Texas
KEWU-FM Cheney, Washington
KHCD Salina, Kansas
KHKE Cedar Falls, Iowa
KJVH Longview, Washington
KLCD Decorah, Iowa
KLND Little Eagle, South Dakota
KLUX Robstown, Texas
KMFA Austin, Texas
KMOC Wichita Falls, Texas
KNHC Seattle, Washington
KNLH Cedar Hill, Missouri
KCNV Las Vegas, Nevada
KOKS Poplar Bluff, Missouri
KOPN Columbia, Missouri
KPBS-FM San Diego, California
KPOO San Francisco, California
KPPR Williston, North Dakota
KPRA Ukiah, California
KPRN Grand Junction, Colorado
KQAL Winona, Minnesota
KSMC Moraga, California
KSOH Wapato, Washington
KTEC Klamath Falls, Oregon
KCNP Ada, Oklahoma
KTSC-FM Pueblo, Colorado
KTSY Caldwell, Idaho
KUSR Logan, Utah
KVMR Nevada City, California
KVNE Tyler, Texas
KWGS Tulsa, Oklahoma
KWRR Ethete, Wyoming
KKLY El Paso, Texas
KXRD Victorville, California
KYFL Monroe, Louisiana
KYQX Weatherford, Texas
WAHS Auburn Hills, Michigan
WBEW Chesterton, Indiana

WAUA Petersburg, West Virginia
WAWN Franklin, Pennsylvania
WAYJ Naples, Florida
WBCY Archbold, Ohio
WBFR Birmingham, Alabama
WBKE-FM North Manchester, Indiana
WBSB Anderson, Indiana
WCLQ Wausau, Wisconsin
WCMU-FM Mount Pleasant, Michigan
WCVV Belpre, Ohio
WDNR Chester, Pennsylvania
WDPS Dayton, Ohio
WETS-FM Johnson City, Tennessee
WFCI Franklin, Indiana
WFIT Melbourne, Florida
WGSG Mayo, Florida
WGTF Dothan, Alabama
WHRV Norfolk, Virginia
WHSS Hamilton, Ohio
WITF-FM Harrisburg, Pennsylvania
WIUW Warsaw, Illinois
WJMU Decatur, Illinois
WKPB Henderson, Kentucky
WKSG Cedar Creek, Florida
WMAE-FM Booneville, Mississippi
WMOT Murfreesboro, Tennessee
WJRF Duluth, Minnesota
WNGU Dahlonega, Georgia
WNIJ Dekalb, Illinois
WNTE Mansfield, Pennsylvania
WOVI Novi, Michigan
WPCS Pensacola, Florida
WPKN Bridgeport, Connecticut
WQRP Dayton, Ohio
WSCL Salisbury, Maryland
WKVP Cherry Hill, New Jersey
WSKB Westfield, Massachusetts
WSLU Canton, New York
WSOU South Orange, New Jersey
WAYJ(FM) Naples, Florida
WTJY Asheboro, North Carolina
WUNY Utica, New York
WVMS Sandusky, Ohio
WVPR Windsor, Vermont
WZWP West Union, Ohio
WYFK Columbus, Georgia
WYFS Savannah, Georgia
WYFW Winder, Georgia
WOFR Schoolcraft, Michigan
WWPJ Pen Argyl, Pennsylvania
KJZA Drake, Arizona
WPRG Columbia, Mississippi
WNCK Nantucket, Massachusetts
KTOT Spearman, Texas
WCOF Arcade, New York
KEGR Fort Dodge, Iowa
KPFR Pine Grove, Oregon
KTCF Dolores, Colorado
KLRI Rigby, Idaho
KSBX Santa Barbara, California
KJCC Carnegie, Oklahoma
KLFH Ojai, California
WARW Dorsey, Illinois
KZBJ Bay City, Texas
WYAZ Yazoo City, Mississippi
KAIB Shafter, California
KVLK Milan, New Mexico
KTCB Tillamook, Oregon
KITA Iota, Louisiana
KEFS North Powder, Oregon
WRNF Selma, Alabama
WWED Spotsylvania, Virginia
WEFI Effingham, Illinois
WQAI Thomson, Georgia
WLPS-FM Lumberton, North Carolina
WFOT Lexington, Ohio
KJIV Reno, Nevada
KICO Rico, Colorado
KQCO Esterbrook, Wyoming
WKMT Fulton, Kentucky
KLAP Gerlach, Nevada
WYNJ Blackduck, Minnesota
KCKJ Sarcoxie, Missouri
WSPI Ellsworth, Illinois
KSKX Chemult, Oregon
KILE-FM Woodland Park, Colorado
KPJH Polson, Montana
WWQZ Baptist Village, Massachusetts
KTUT Frankfort, South Dakota
KRCI Pinetop-Lakeside, Arizona
KYPF Stanford, Montana
KCEY Ranchos De Taos, New Mexico

89.7 mhz

KACC Alvin, Texas
KACU Abilene, Texas
KARM Visalia, California
KAXG Gillette, Wyoming
KBDA Great Bend, Kansas
KBIO Natchitoches, Louisiana
KMBN Las Cruces, New Mexico
KKTR Kirksville, Missouri
KBSB Bemidji, Minnesota
KCVQ Knob Noster, Missouri
KEPC Colorado Springs, Colorado
KFJC Los Altos, California
KIWR Council Bluffs, Iowa
KLCC Eugene, Oregon
KLVM Prunedale, California
KMNR Rolla, Missouri
KMSU Mankato, Minnesota
KNBU Baldwin City, Kansas
KNCA Burney, California
KNLP Potosi, Missouri
KOZO Branson, Missouri
KRMH Red Mesa, Arizona
KRNL-FM Mount Vernon, Iowa
KRUI-FM Iowa City, Iowa
KSGN Riverside, California
KMWS Mount Vernon, Washington
KTDB Ramah, New Mexico
KVRK Sanger, Texas
KTXB Beaumont, Texas
KUAP Pine Bluff, Arkansas
KUMM Morris, Minnesota
KUSD Vermillion, South Dakota
KJMA Floresville, Texas
KWFJ Roy, Washington
KWWS Walla Walla, Washington
KXKM McCarthy, Alaska
KGNX Ballwin, Missouri
WAAJ Benton, Kentucky
WALF Alfred, New York
WAUQ Charles City, Virginia
WAUV Ripley, Tennessee
WAWI Lawrenceburg, Tennessee
WAZP Munising, Michigan
WBMV Mount Vernon, Illinois
WCBW-FM East St. Louis, Illinois
WCPE Raleigh, North Carolina
WDCL-FM Somerset, Kentucky
WMUM-FM Cochran, Georgia
WDJW Somers, Connecticut
WDVR Delaware Township, New Jersey
WDVV Wilmington, North Carolina
WYBK(FM) Chattanooga, Tennessee
WEOS Geneva, New York
WFGB Kingston, New York
WGBH(FM) Boston, Massachusetts
WGLS-FM Glassboro, New Jersey
WHND Sister Bay, Wisconsin
WISU Terre Haute, Indiana
WITR Henrietta, New York
WJLU New Smyrna Beach, Florida
WKSU-FM Kent, Ohio
WLUJ Springfield, Illinois
WLNZ Lansing, Michigan
WKCP Miami, Florida
WMED Calais, Maine
WMHB Waterville, Maine
WMHK Columbia, South Carolina
WJOJ Rust Township, Michigan
WNJA Jamestown, New York
WNJN-FM Atlantic City, New Jersey
WNKU Highland Heights, Kentucky
WONU Kankakee, Illinois
WOSU-FM Columbus, Ohio
WPAE Centreville, Mississippi
WRDR Freehold Township, New Jersey
WQEJ Johnstown, Pennsylvania
WRGF Greenfield, Indiana
WRHO Oneonta, New York
WRTU San Juan, Puerto Rico
WRUC Schenectady, New York
WSHC Shepherdstown, West Virginia
WSSK Saratoga Springs, New York
WTMD Towson, Maryland
WTUR Upland, Indiana
WTXR Toccoa Falls, Georgia
WUBS South Bend, Indiana
WUEC Eau Claire, Wisconsin
WUSF Tampa, Florida
WUWM Milwaukee, Wisconsin
WVFS Tallahassee, Florida
WVLS Monterey, Virginia
WLSN Grand Marais, Minnesota
WZKM Waynesboro, Mississippi
KCMF Fergus Falls, Minnesota
WVYA Williamsport, Pennsylvania
KGBM Randsburg, California
KANH Emporia, Kansas
KJCV-FM Country Club, Missouri
KBIL Park City, Montana
KTPS Pagosa Springs, Colorado
KHFR Santa Maria, California
WOJC Crothersville, Indiana
KEQX Stephenville, Texas
WKVJ Dannemora, New York
KNRI Bismarck, North Dakota
KJTH Ponca City, Oklahoma
KBHN Booneville, Arkansas
KNSY(FM) Dubuque, Iowa
KJWA Trinidad, Colorado
KQLR Whitehall, Montana
WTKC Findlay, Ohio
KUUT Farmington, New Mexico
KUBJ Brenham, Texas
KRLE Oberlin, Kansas
KHYS Hays, Kansas
KGRP Grand Rapids, Minnesota
KCAI Lodi, California
WTAC Burton, Michigan
KPCS Princeton, Minnesota
WJHO Alexander City, Alabama
KCEU Price, Utah
KDBQ Rattan, Oklahoma
KOTD The Dalles, Oregon
KUCB Unalaska, Alaska
KWNM Winnemucca, Nevada
WKWH Liberty, Indiana
WLMN Manistee, Michigan
WGIW Pilot Mountain, North Carolina
KRNF Montezuma, Iowa
KOJD John Day, Oregon
WLOL-FM Star City, West Virginia
WVGV West Union, West Virginia
WNOC Bowling Green, Ohio
KAUC West Clarkston, Washington
KMOA Nu'uuli, American Samoa
KADE Salida, Colorado
WFWO Medina, New York
WYLC Jackson, Kentucky
KXGR Loveland, Colorado
WNQS Dillsboro, North Carolina

89.9 mhz

KACV-FM Amarillo, Texas
KSJY St. Martinville, Louisiana
KASB Bellevue, Washington
KAUF Kennett, Missouri
KAWZ Twin Falls, Idaho
KAYP Burlington, Iowa
KBDE Temple, Texas
KBGA Missoula, Montana
KMCV High Point, Missouri
KBNL Laredo, Texas
KBSK McCall, Idaho
KQAC Portland, Oregon
KCRH Hayward, California
KCRW Santa Monica, California
KGNA-FM Arnold, Missouri
KDAQ Shreveport, Louisiana
KDFC Angwin, California
KDPR Dickinson, North Dakota
KEFR Le Grand, California
KFER Santa Cruz, California
KFLV Wilber, Nebraska
KFRS Soledad, California
KGHP Gig Harbor, Washington
KGNV Washington, Missouri
KGPR Great Falls, Montana
KGRG-FM Auburn, Washington
KJTA Flagstaff, Arizona
KMOJ Minneapolis, Minnesota
KNDL(FM) Angwin, California
KLXA Alexandria, Louisiana
KPLW Wenatchee, Washington
KPRE Vail, Colorado
KRPR Rochester, Minnesota
KRPS Pittsburg, Kansas
KTSW San Marcos, Texas
KUAC Fairbanks, Alaska
KUNM Albuquerque, New Mexico
KVMN Cave City, Arkansas
WAKD Sheffield, Alabama
WAPJ Torrington, Connecticut
WATI Vincennes, Indiana
WAYG Grand Rapids, Michigan
WCBU Peoria, Illinois
WCMD-FM Barre, Vermont
WCNO Palm City, Florida
WDAV Davidson, North Carolina
WDPG Greenville, Ohio
WDVX Clinton, Tennessee
WERU-FM Blue Hill, Maine
WEVL Memphis, Tennessee
WFBF Buffalo, New York
WFFC Ferrum, Virginia
WHPL West Lafayette, Indiana
WHSA Brule, Wisconsin
WHWG Trout Lake, Michigan
WIVH Christiansted, Virgin Islands
WJCT-FM Jacksonville, Florida
WJPH Woodbine, New Jersey
WJTF Panama City, Florida
WJWJ-FM Beaufort, South Carolina
WKCR-FM New York, New York
WKDS Kalamazoo, Michigan
WBRO Marengo, Indiana
WLCA Godfrey, Illinois
WLHS West Chester, Ohio
WLJN-FM Traverse City, Michigan
WLKL Mattoon, Illinois
WMAB-FM Mississippi State, Mississippi
WMRL Lexington, Virginia
WMTB-FM Emmitsburg, Maryland
WNJM Manahawkin, New Jersey
WOEL-FM Elkton, Maryland
WORT Madison, Wisconsin
WPER Culpeper, Virginia
WQTQ Hartford, Connecticut
WKVO Georgetown, Kentucky
WRVO Oswego, New York
WRVS-FM Elizabeth City, North Carolina
WSCB Springfield, Massachusetts
WSOF-FM Madisonville, Kentucky
WSUF Noyack, New York
WTBB Gadsden, Alabama
WTFH Helen, Georgia
WTHS Holland, Michigan
WTLR State College, Pennsylvania
WTSU Montgomery-Troy, Alabama
WUCF-FM Orlando, Florida
WVIA-FM Scranton, Pennsylvania
WVNP Wheeling, West Virginia
WVRU-FM Radford, Virginia
WVWV Huntington, West Virginia
WWEB Wallingford, Connecticut
WWNO New Orleans, Louisiana
WWSP Stevens Point, Wisconsin
WXLG North Creek, New York
WNRS-FM Sweet Briar, Virginia
WAYW New Johnsonville, Tennessee
KQRB Windom, Minnesota
KCVY Cabool, Missouri
KWKL Grandfield, Oklahoma
WHLP Hanna, Indiana
KTLZ Cuero, Texas
KLRB Stuart, Oklahoma
KTMH Montrose, Colorado
KQFR Rapid City, South Dakota
KJCU Fort Bragg, California
KTAD Sterling, Colorado
KYMS Rathdrum, Idaho
KZAI Superior, Arizona
KFRY Pueblo, Colorado
WVFL Fond Du Lac, Wisconsin
KAIG Dodge City, Kansas
KKJA Redmond, Oregon
KWDS Kettleman City, California
WYBV Wakarusa, Indiana
KLGS College Station, Texas
KDVI Devils Lake, North Dakota
KVIR Bullhead City, Arizona
KDLI Del Rio, Texas
KYCM Alamogordo, New Mexico
KJTW Jamestown, North Dakota
KWAR Waverly, Iowa
WAYO Benton Harbor, Michigan
KAUG Anchorage, Alaska
KINU Kotzebue, Alaska
WSWS(FM) Smithboro, Illinois
KGTR Albany, Missouri
KANC Baker, Oregon

RADIO - U.S.

KDLG-FM Dillingham, Alaska
KKVI Overland, Texas
KQXB Breckenridge, Texas
KJIH Manhattan, Kansas
KUWI Rawlins, Wyoming
KQNV Fallon, Nevada
KHGO Homer, Alaska
WNGF Swanton, Vermont
KTHF Hammon, Oklahoma
KRGM Marshall, Minnesota
WINO Odessa, New York
KYPC Colstrip, Montana
WWQA North Granby, Connecticut
KWCN Pinedale, Wyoming
WHRJ Gloucester Courthouse, Virginia
KHIS Jackson, Missouri
WTRE(FM) Greensburg, Indiana

90.1 mhz

KSCV Springfield, Missouri
KAMY Lubbock, Texas
KBKC Moberly, Missouri
KBNV Fayetteville, Arkansas
KBPK Buena Park, California
KCBX San Luis Obispo, California
KCFR-FM Denver, Colorado
KYCC Stockton, California
KCSC Edmond, Oklahoma
KERA Dallas, Texas
KFKX Hastings, Nebraska
KHCC-FM Hutchinson, Kansas
KKFI Kansas City, Missouri
KLRD Yucaipa, California
KNMC Havre, Montana
KNWO Cottonwood, Idaho
KNWP Port Angeles, Washington
KOLU Pasco, Washington
KPFT Houston, Texas
KQWS Omak, Washington
KCEI Red River, New Mexico
KRHS Overland, Missouri
KRMB Bisbee, Arizona
KSAK Walnut, California
KSAU Nacogdoches, Texas
KLRO Hot Springs, Arkansas
KSJR-FM Collegeville, Minnesota
KSOR Ashland, Oregon
KSRQ Thief River Falls, Minnesota
KSYM-FM San Antonio, Texas
KTQX Bakersfield, California
KTRU(FM) Houston, Texas
KTXI Ingram, Texas
KUER-FM Salt Lake City, Utah
KUKL Kalispell, Montana
KUPS Tacoma, Washington
KUTE Ignacio, Colorado
KNCH(FM) San Angelo, Texas
KZFR Chico, California
KZMU Moab, Utah
KZSU Stanford, California
WABE Atlanta, Georgia
WAWJ Marion, Illinois
WCAI Woods Hole, Massachusetts
WCCE Buies Creek, North Carolina
WCSP-FM Washington, District of Columbia
WDCE Richmond, Virginia
WECS Willimantic, Connecticut
WEFT Champaign, Illinois
WEPR Greenville, South Carolina
WFYI-FM Indianapolis, Indiana
WGCU-FM Fort Myers, Florida
WGMC Greece, New York
WGSK South Kent, Connecticut
WZRU Garysburg, North Carolina
WHMC-FM Conway, South Carolina
WIUP-FM Indiana, Pennsylvania
WJCR-FM Upton, Kentucky
WIFF Windsor, New York
WJSO Pikeville, Kentucky
WJUF Inverness, Florida
WORI Harrison, Ohio
WKNP Jackson, Tennessee
WLSO Sault Ste. Marie, Michigan
WMBI-FM Chicago, Illinois
WMEA Portland, Maine
WMPR Jackson, Mississippi
WNAA Greensboro, North Carolina
WNMU-FM Marquette, Michigan
WJOU Huntsville, Alabama
WOHC Chillicothe, Ohio
WOI-FM Ames, Iowa
WORQ Green Bay, Wisconsin
WOUZ-FM Zanesville, Ohio
WPSX Kane, Pennsylvania
WPVA Waynesboro, Virginia
WRCU-FM Hamilton, New York
WRPN-FM Ripon, Wisconsin
WRTI Philadelphia, Pennsylvania
WRUV Burlington, Vermont
WRXC Shelton, Connecticut
WTJT Baker, Florida
WTSG Carlinville, Illinois
WUCX-FM Bay City, Michigan
WUSB Stony Brook, New York
WVMN New Castle, Pennsylvania
WMFU(FM) Mount Hope, New York
WXML Upper Sandusky, Ohio
WXVS Waycross, Georgia
KUWP Powell, Wyoming
WKWV Watertown, New York
WKTS Kingston, Tennessee
WCIT-FM Trout Run, Pennsylvania
WZYZ Spencer, Tennessee
KOCU Altus, Oklahoma
WPWV Princeton, West Virginia
KBLW Billings, Montana
WENS Wadesville, Indiana
KKLP La Pine, Oregon
KNSE Austin, Minnesota
WMHQ Malone, New York
WKYP Ledbetter, Kentucky
KHCO Hayden, Colorado
KAJC Salem, Oregon
WHRX Nassawadox, Virginia
WKWR Key West, Florida
KHLV Helena, Montana
WJDZ Pastillo, Puerto Rico
KWMD Sterling, Alaska
KQMC Hawthorne, Nevada
WRYP Wellfleet, Massachusetts
WYCM Charlton, Massachusetts
KRLU Roswell, New Mexico
KPLI Olympia, Washington
KADU Hibbing, Minnesota
WZPE Bath, North Carolina
WMVE Chase City, Virginia
WJKA Jacksonville, North Carolina
KSFS Sioux Falls, South Dakota
WXPZ Clyde Township, Michigan
KXRL Cherry Valley, Arkansas
WYBA Coldwater, Michigan
KILI Porcupine, South Dakota
WDLG Thomasville, Alabama
KUWL Laramie, Wyoming
WFRU Quincy, Florida
WITH Ithaca, New York
KOBN Burns, Oregon
KEEA Aberdeen, South Dakota
WCKU Clarksburg, West Virginia
WOVV Ocracoke, North Carolina
KHRV Hood River, Oregon
WJZZ North Salem, New York
WHBP Harbor Springs, Michigan
KSIH Belcourt, North Dakota
WXIV Lumpkin, Georgia
KSVU Hamilton, Washington
KYPM Livingston, Montana
WOXM Middlebury, Vermont
WKYV Colonial Heights, Virginia
KCHB Kaibito, Arizona
WJZZ(FM) North Salem, New York
KNIT Humboldt, Nebraska
WVCS Owen, Wisconsin
KJZP Prescott, Arizona
KOJB Cass Lake, Minnesota
KFJS North Platte, Nebraska

90.3 mhz

KABA Louise, Texas
KAZU Pacific Grove, California
KBJS Jacksonville, Texas
KBMH Holbrook, Arizona
KBSU-FM Boise, Idaho
KBUB Brownwood, Texas
KBUT Crested Butte, Colorado
KBUZ Topeka, Kansas
KCCD Moorhead, Minnesota
KCIF Hilo, Hawaii
KEXP-FM Seattle, Washington
KCRL Sunrise Beach, Missouri
KCSP-FM Casper, Wyoming
KDVS Davis, California
KEDM Monroe, Louisiana
KEDT-FM Corpus Christi, Texas
KFAI Minneapolis, Minnesota
KFLR-FM Phoenix, Arizona
KFNO Fresno, California
KGNN-FM Cuba, Missouri
KLFV Grand Junction, Colorado
KLCU Ardmore, Oklahoma
KLUH Poplar Bluff, Missouri
KMNE-FM Bassett, Nebraska
KMRO Camarillo, California
KNBA Anchorage, Alaska
KNLG New Bloomfield, Missouri
KNWY Yakima, Washington
KPDR Wheeler, Texas
KPHS Plains, Texas
KRNU Lincoln, Nebraska
KSLC McMinnville, Oregon
KTUH Honolulu, Hawaii
KUWJ Jackson, Wyoming
KVRS Lawton, Oklahoma
KWFH Parker, Arizona
KWIT Sioux City, Iowa
KWUR Clayton, Missouri
KLWO Longview, Washington
WAEF Cordele, Georgia
WYBP Fort Lauderdale, Florida
WAIH Potsdam, New York
WAIJ Grantsville, Maryland
WAMC-FM Albany, New York
WARC Meadville, Pennsylvania
WBCL Fort Wayne, Indiana
WBCR-FM Beloit, Wisconsin
WBFY Pinehurst, North Carolina
WBHM Birmingham, Alabama
WBLV Twin Lake, Michigan
WBRH Baton Rouge, Louisiana
WKDC-FM Cedarville, Ohio
WCIH Elmira, New York
WCPN Cleveland, Ohio
WCSK Kingsport, Tennessee
WDFH Ossining, New York
WDIH Salisbury, Maryland
WEJF Palm Bay, Florida
WESS East Stroudsburg, Pennsylvania
WFHE Hickory, North Carolina
WFOF Covington, Indiana
WHBM Park Falls, Wisconsin
WHCJ Savannah, Georgia
WHCR-FM New York, New York
WHLA La Crosse, Wisconsin
WHPC Garden City, New York
WHRO-FM Norfolk, Virginia
WJLH Flagler Beach, Florida
WXXY(FM) Houghton, New York
WJTL Lancaster, Pennsylvania
WKNJ-FM Union Township, New Jersey
WKNS Kinston, North Carolina
WKRB Brooklyn, New York
WKWC Owensboro, Kentucky
WLVF-FM Haines City, Florida
WMAH-FM Biloxi, Mississippi
WMAV-FM Oxford, Mississippi
WMKY Morehead, Kentucky
WMSC Upper Montclair, New Jersey
WNJZ Cape May Court House, New Jersey
WOTL Toledo, Ohio
WPLN-FM Nashville, Tennessee
WQUB Quincy, Illinois
WXXY Houghton, New York
WRBK Richburg, South Carolina
WRIU Kingston, Rhode Island
WRPR Mahwah, New Jersey
WRST-FM Oshkosh, Wisconsin
WRVD Syracuse, New York
WRXT Roanoke, Virginia
WSSB-FM Orangeburg, South Carolina
WUSI Olney, Illinois
WUTK-FM Knoxville, Tennessee
WUTM Martin, Tennessee
WVIK Rock Island, Illinois
WVPG Parkersburg, West Virginia
WVPH Piscataway, New Jersey
WWPT Westport, Connecticut
WXLV Schnecksville, Pennsylvania
WZBC Newton, Massachusetts
KYLC Lake Charles, Louisiana
KZRI Welches, Oregon
WDYF Dothan, Alabama
KNAG Grand Canyon, Arizona
KMKL North Branch, Minnesota
WJWD Marshall, Wisconsin
KSMW West Plains, Missouri
KWBX Salem, Oregon
KLFS Van Buren, Arkansas
WOKG Galax, Virginia
KTVR-FM La Grande, Oregon
KWYC Cheyenne, Wyoming
KZJB Pocatello, Idaho
WYJC Greenville, Florida
KGCD Wray, Colorado
KLON Rockaway Beach, Oregon
KELU Clovis, New Mexico
KSGU Saint George, Utah
KJFT Arlee, Montana
KLAI Laytonville, California
KASD Rapid City, South Dakota
KDRI Grants, New Mexico
WKJD Columbus, Indiana
KVLZ Sheridan, Wyoming
WRUN Remsen, New York
WJWR Bloomington, Illinois
WFTE Mount Cobb, Pennsylvania
KSPM Sand Point, Alaska
KMCG McGrath, Alaska
WBOO Morganfield, Kentucky
KYRQ Natalia, Texas
KGCU Port Alsworth, Alaska
WUMI Newberry, Michigan
WWQW(FM) Wartburg, Tennessee
KEIS York, Nebraska
WNJO Toms River, New Jersey
WNGM(FM) Tallulah Falls, Georgia
KPOY(FM) Fraser, Colorado
KBSG Aberdeen, Washington
KPBZ Spokane, Washington
KHEV Fairview, Oklahoma
KANQ Chanute, Kansas
KNJT Coldwater, Kansas
KMGT Circle, Montana
WIGW Eustis, Florida
KCAV Marshall, Arkansas
WXBP Corinth, Maine
WWQY Yadkin, North Carolina

90.5 mhz

KACS Rainier, Washington
KADV Modesto, California
KAOG Jonesboro, Arkansas
KAYM Weatherford, Oklahoma
KBAH Plainview, Texas
KBMP Enterprise, Kansas
KBUW Buffalo, Wyoming
KCIE Dulce, New Mexico
KCND Bismarck, North Dakota
KCSU-FM Fort Collins, Colorado
KDNI Duluth, Minnesota
KVOV Carbondale, Colorado
KNGA Saint Peter, Minnesota
KGSP Parkville, Missouri
KHOE Fairfield, Iowa
KHSU Arcata, California
KIBC Burney, California
KSOS Las Vegas, Nevada
KKTO Tahoe City, California
KLCO Newport, Oregon
KLRE-FM Little Rock, Arkansas
KNWV Clarkston, Washington
KNYD Broken Arrow, Oklahoma
KRBW Ottawa, Kansas
KSHU Huntsville, Texas
KSJS San Jose, California
KSMS-FM Point Lookout, Missouri
KZKL Wichita Falls, Texas
KTLF Colorado Springs, Colorado
KTLN Thibodaux, Louisiana
KUAT-FM Tucson, Arizona
KUT Austin, Texas
KUWN Newcastle, Wyoming
KUWZ Rock Springs, Wyoming
KVHS Concord, California
KWCW Walla Walla, Washington
KWMR Point Reyes Station, California
KWWC-FM Columbia, Missouri
KXCV Maryville, Missouri
KXGA Glennallen, Alaska
KZNA Hill City, Kansas
WVRD Zebulon, North Carolina
WANM Tallahassee, Florida
WAPO Mount Vernon, Illinois
WAQL McComb, Mississippi
WASU-FM Boone, North Carolina

WBER Rochester, New York
WBJB-FM Lincroft, New Jersey
WTLD Jesup, Georgia
WBVM Tampa, Florida
WBXL Baldwinsville, New York
WCBE Columbus, Ohio
WCKJ St. Johnsbury, Vermont
WCRH Williamsport, Maryland
WCVH Flemington, New Jersey
WDCC Sanford, North Carolina
WESA Pittsburgh, Pennsylvania
WERG Erie, Pennsylvania
WFRC Columbus, Georgia
WFTF Rutland, Vermont
WHRW Binghamton, New York
WHVT Clyde, Ohio
WICN Worcester, Massachusetts
WIDA-FM Carolina, Puerto Rico
WISE-FM Wise, Virginia
WJFF Jeffersonville, New York
WJSV Morristown, New Jersey
WJYJ Fredericksburg, Virginia
WKAR-FM East Lansing, Michigan
WKHS Worton, Maryland
WMLJ Summersville, West Virginia
WMTH Park Ridge, Illinois
WRTK Paxton, Illinois
WNIU Rockford, Illinois
WPEA Exeter, New Hampshire
WPFF Sturgeon Bay, Wisconsin
WPHN Gaylord, Michigan
WPIM Martinsville, Virginia
WNPR Meriden, Connecticut
WPWB Byron, Georgia
WRTE Chicago, Illinois
WSCT Springfield, Illinois
WSLL Saranac Lake, New York
WSMC-FM Collegedale, Tennessee
WSNC Winston-Salem, North Carolina
WSPS Concord, New Hampshire
WSUC-FM Cortland, New York
WSUP Platteville, Wisconsin
WTHL Somerset, Kentucky
WUMC Elizabethton, Tennessee
WUOG Athens, Georgia
WUOL-FM Louisville, Kentucky
WUSC-FM Columbia, South Carolina
WVBU-FM Lewisburg, Pennsylvania
WVCF Eau Claire, Wisconsin
WVHM Benton, Kentucky
WYQS Mars Hill, North Carolina
WVUM Coral Gables, Florida
WWCU Cullowhee, North Carolina
WWIL-FM Wilmington, North Carolina
WXGN Egg Harbor Township, New Jersey
WXXE Fenner, New York
WYFB Gainesville, Florida
WMEP Camden, Maine
KLVW Odessa, Texas
WREH Cypress Quarters, Florida
WVFA Lebanon, New Hampshire
WVML Millersburg, Ohio
KVLB Bend, Oregon
WZRN Norlina, North Carolina
KAGT Abilene, Texas
KZFT Fannett, Texas
WVBV Medford Lakes, New Jersey
WQVI Madison, Mississippi
WQRA Greencastle, Indiana
WGCN Nashville, Georgia
KRAW Kasilof, Alaska
WBUX Buxton, North Carolina
WSMA Scituate, Massachusetts
KGDP-FM Santa Maria, California
WWFP Brigantine, New Jersey
KGIO Astoria, Oregon
WCSO Columbus, Mississippi
KTXG Greenville, Texas
KVCF Freeman, South Dakota
KUEU Logan, Utah
WXKV Selmer, Tennessee
KAIO Idaho Falls, Idaho
KFXU Chickasha, Oklahoma
KNLL Nashville, Arkansas
KJLF Butte, Montana
WDLL Dillon, South Carolina
KLIT Del Rio, Texas
WRTW Crown Point, Indiana
KRFG Glenwood, Minnesota
WCOQ Colquitt, Georgia
KYCI Firebaugh, California
KCGR Oran, Missouri
WYER Carmi, Illinois
WSLG Gouverneur, New York
WXLQ Bristol, Vermont
WEQP Pamplin City, Virginia
KUFL Libby, Montana
KUHC Clayton, New Mexico
WLNF Rapids, New York
WCOZ Laceyville, Pennsylvania
KBJF Nephi, Utah
WWLN Lincoln, Maine
WTWT Bradford, Pennsylvania
KGVV Goltry, Oklahoma
KKBY Kirby, Wyoming
KFDC Shiprock, New Mexico
KZET Cortez, Colorado
KAUD Mexico, Missouri
WVPL Dozier, Alabama
WZEV Lineville, Alabama

90.7 mhz

KABU Fort Totten, North Dakota
KALX Berkeley, California
KAVW Amarillo, Texas
KAYE-FM Tonkawa, Oklahoma
KTAA Big Sandy, Texas
KBOO Portland, Oregon
KTER Rudolph, Texas
KBPR Brainerd, Minnesota
KGUD Longmont, Colorado
KCIR Twin Falls, Idaho
KYPR Miles City, Montana
KFJM Grand Forks, North Dakota
KFSR Fresno, California
KFXT Sulphur, Oklahoma
KVSR Kirksville, Missouri
KJHK Lawrence, Kansas
KJOV Woodward, Oklahoma
KKUA Wailuku, Hawaii
KLSA Alexandria, Louisiana
KSRI Santa Cruz, California
KNAA Show Low, Arizona
KNOG Nogales, Arizona
KNWR Ellensburg, Washington
KOBC Joplin, Missouri
KPFK Los Angeles, California
KPOR Emporia, Kansas
KRWG Las Cruces, New Mexico
KSDJ Brookings, South Dakota
KSER Everett, Washington
KVNO Omaha, Nebraska
KLMK Marvell, Arkansas
KVRT Victoria, Texas
KWMU St. Louis, Missouri
KLSE Rochester, Minnesota
KZUU Pullman, Washington
KZYX Philo, California
KYWA Wichita, Kansas
WACG-FM Augusta, Georgia
WAUO Hohenwald, Tennessee
WAUS Berrien Springs, Michigan
WAYR-FM Brunswick, Georgia
WCLH Wilkes-Barre, Pennsylvania
WCVK Bowling Green, Kentucky
WEHC Emory, Virginia
WETD Alfred, New York
WEVN Keene, New Hampshire
WFAE Charlotte, North Carolina
WFGH Fort Gay, West Virginia
WFUV New York, New York
WMVM Goodman, Wisconsin
WGCC-FM Batavia, New York
WGLE Lima, Ohio
WWVO Albany, Georgia
WGRW Anniston, Alabama
WHAD Delafield, Wisconsin
WJHD Portsmouth, Rhode Island
WJSC-FM Johnson, Vermont
WKGC-FM Panama City, Florida
WKKL West Barnstable, Massachusetts
WZKV Dyersburg, Tennessee
WKPS State College, Pennsylvania
WKPW Knightstown, Indiana
WKTL Struthers, Ohio
WLJH Glens Falls, New York
WLMW Manchester, New Hampshire
WMCO New Concord, Ohio
WMFE-FM Orlando, Florida
WMHD-FM Terre Haute, Indiana
WMRA Harrisonburg, Virginia
WMVV Griffin, Georgia
WNCU Durham, North Carolina
WNFR Sandusky, Michigan
WNMC-FM Traverse City, Michigan
WOTJ Morehead City, North Carolina
WPGL Pattersonville, New York
WPNR-FM Utica, New York
WPSR Evansville, Indiana
WSDL Ocean City, Maryland
WTCC Springfield, Massachusetts
WTIP Grand Marais, Minnesota
WUVT-FM Blacksburg, Virginia
WVAS Montgomery, Alabama
WVKC Galesburg, Illinois
WVMC-FM Mansfield, Ohio
WVMM Grantham, Pennsylvania
WLKV Ripley, West Virginia
WVSS Menomonie, Wisconsin
WVTC Randolph Center, Vermont
WVUA-FM Tuscaloosa, Alabama
WUWG Carrollton, Georgia
WWOZ New Orleans, Louisiana
WPBI(FM) West Palm Beach, Florida
WYFH North Charleston, South Carolina
WYRS Manahawkin, New Jersey
KBSQ McCall, Idaho
WPTJ Paris, Kentucky
KHRI Hollister, California
KAIS(FM) Tracy, California
WCRG Williamsport, Pennsylvania
WRTL Ephrata, Pennsylvania
KOJI Okoboji, Iowa
KMWR Brookings, Oregon
KNSC(FM) Carroll, Iowa
KANL Baker, Oregon
KTEI Placerville, Colorado
KMZO Hamilton, Montana
WFSL Thomasville, Georgia
WBEQ Morris, Illinois
WNRK Norwalk, Ohio
KFRP Coalinga, California
KDRE Sterling, Colorado
KTTK Lebanon, Missouri
WQSG Lafayette, Indiana
KKCJ Cannon Afb, New Mexico
KGFA Great Falls, Montana
KPBN Freer, Texas
WPAI Nanty Glo, Pennsylvania
KNFA Grand Island, Nebraska
KLRM Melbourne, Arkansas
KTDL Trinidad, Colorado
KEAF Fort Smith, Arkansas
KJKT Spearfish, South Dakota
WYBJ Newton Grove, North Carolina
KTHM Red Bluff, California
WAZU Peoria, Illinois
WGSN Newport, Tennessee
KEZB Beaver, Utah
KOMH Marshall, Minnesota
WRDK Bladenboro, North Carolina
WBHL Harrison, Michigan
WEGB Napeague, New York
KMBV Valentine, Nebraska
WGXC Acra, New York
KOUI Louisville, Mississippi
KJND-FM Williston, North Dakota
KJZK Kingman, Arizona
KMBM Polson, Montana
KRZU Batesville, Texas
KJLC-FM Needles, California
KRBP Rock Creek, California

90.9 mhz

KAMU-FM College Station, Texas
KASF Alamosa, Colorado
KAVO Pampa, Texas
KBDG Turlock, California
KBSA El Dorado, Arkansas
KCBI Dallas, Texas
KTBG Warrensburg, Missouri
KCSD Sioux Falls, South Dakota
KDSD-FM Pierpont, South Dakota
KGCB Prescott, Arizona
KGZO Shafter, California
KHCT Great Bend, Kansas
KHDC Chualar, California
KWTM June Lake, California
KKCR Hanalei, Hawaii
KKVO Altus, Oklahoma
KLLN Newark, Arkansas
KMDY Keokuk, Iowa
KOKF Edmond, Oklahoma
KPNO Norfolk, Nebraska
KRBM Pendleton, Oregon
KRCL Salt Lake City, Utah
KRCU Cape Girardeau, Missouri
KSHI Zuni, New Mexico
KSJE Farmington, New Mexico
KIKL Lafayette, Louisiana
KSKF Klamath Falls, Oregon
KSLU Hammond, Louisiana
KSPL Kalispell, Montana
KSWP Lufkin, Texas
KTSU Houston, Texas
KUNI Cedar Falls, Iowa
KUWG Gillette, Wyoming
KVNF Paonia, Colorado
KVTI Tacoma, Washington
KWRB Bisbee, Arizona
KXJZ Sacramento, California
KYFS San Antonio, Texas
KKLU Lubbock, Texas
WAMK Kingston, New York
WAQB Tupelo, Mississippi
WAQV Crystal River, Florida
WATP Laurel, Mississippi
WBDG Indianapolis, Indiana
WBSW Marion, Indiana
WBUR-FM Boston, Massachusetts
WCDB Albany, New York
WCNI New London, Connecticut
WCOT Jamestown, New York
WCVJ Jefferson, Ohio
WCWM Williamsburg, Virginia
WCWS-FM Wooster, Ohio
WDCB Glen Ellyn, Illinois
WRCJ-FM Detroit, Michigan
WEKH Hazard, Kentucky
WETA Washington, District of Columbia
WFCO Lancaster, Ohio
WGBE Bryan, Ohio
WGUC Cincinnati, Ohio
WHRM Wausau, Wisconsin
WHYY-FM Philadelphia, Pennsylvania
WILL-FM Urbana, Illinois
WIRQ Rochester, New York
WIRR Virginia-Hibbing, Minnesota
WJAB Huntsville, Alabama
WJIR Key West, Florida
WJNY Watertown, New York
WJRC Lewistown, Pennsylvania
WJWV Fort Gaines, Georgia
WKTZ-FM Jacksonville, Florida
WKUE Elizabethtown, Kentucky
WLGI Hemingway, South Carolina
WMAO-FM Greenwood, Mississippi
WMEH Bangor, Maine
WMPG Gorham, Maine
WNZR Mount Vernon, Ohio
WOAK La Grange, Georgia
WONY Oneonta, New York
WOWB Brewton, Alabama
WQAC Alma, Michigan
WQFS Greensboro, North Carolina
WRAF Toccoa Falls, Georgia
WRQM Rocky Mount, North Carolina
WSCS New London, New Hampshire
WSIF Wilkesboro, North Carolina
WSLO Malone, New York
WSOR Naples, Florida
WSQG-FM Ithaca, New York
WVPM Morgantown, West Virginia
WVVS-FM Valdosta, Georgia
WWMC Lynchburg, Virginia
WWOG Cookeville, Tennessee
KNLN Vienna, Missouri
KUWX Pinedale, Wyoming
KXRT Idabel, Oklahoma
WMSD Rose Township, Michigan
WURI Manteo, North Carolina
KDWG Dillon, Montana
WLFE-FM Key Largo, Florida
WTRK Freeland, Michigan
KLWV Chugwater, Wyoming
KLRV Billings, Montana
KGCL Jordan Valley, Oregon
KAIZ Mesquite, Nevada
KKLW Willmar, Minnesota
KJCH Coos Bay, Oregon
KLOX Creston, Iowa
WCJL Morgantown, Indiana
KPSH Coachella, California
WTCK Charlevoix, Michigan

WOXR Schuyler Falls, New York
KWRC Hermosa, South Dakota
KLTP San Angelo, Texas
KRWA Rye, Colorado
KGCM Belgrade, Montana
WZZH Honesdale, Pennsylvania
KCPB-FM Warrenton, Oregon
KTOL Leadville, Colorado
WCFG Springfield, Michigan
KVDG Midland, Texas
KRLH Hereford, Texas
WSLI Belding, Michigan
WPRH Paris, Tennessee
KRRT Arroyo Seco, New Mexico
KKRH Grangeville, Idaho
KGVB Holliday, Texas
KJLC(FM) Susanville, California
KJWR Windom, Minnesota
KHJJ Shaniko, Oregon
WKMD Madisonville, Kentucky
WNBK Whitmire, South Carolina
WJKZ Hanover, Michigan
WXAF Charleston, West Virginia
WJDD Carrollton, Ohio
WVYN Bluford, Illinois
KJHL Boise City, Oklahoma
KZXZ Wyola, Montana
KOVA Bovina, Texas
WVRI Clifton Forge, Virginia
WUWS Ashland, Wisconsin
KFTW Fort Washakie, Wyoming
WUPJ Escanaba, Michigan

91.1 mhz

KANJ Giddings, Texas
KANO Hilo, Hawaii
KANX Sheridan, Arkansas
KANZ Garden City, Kansas
KAOR Vermillion, South Dakota
KAPK Grants Pass, Oregon
KAQF Clovis, New Mexico
KAYC Durant, Oklahoma
KBGM Park Hills, Missouri
KKRD Enid, Oklahoma
KBWC Marshall, Texas
KCCM-FM Moorhead, Minnesota
KCFN Wichita, Kansas
KDSC Thousand Oaks, California
KCSM San Mateo, California
KEDP Las Vegas, New Mexico
KISU-FM Pocatello, Idaho
KHKV Kerrville, Texas
KLPR Kearney, Nebraska
KLSU Baton Rouge, Louisiana
KLVY Fairmead, California
KMTC Russellville, Arkansas
KMUD Garberville, California
KMZL Missoula, Montana
KNLB Lake Havasu City, Arizona
KXUL Monroe, Louisiana
KNOW-FM Minneapolis-St. Paul, Minnesota
KOJO Lake Charles, Louisiana
KPBX-FM Spokane, Washington
KRCB-FM Windsor, California
KSGR Portland, Texas
KSKA Anchorage, Alaska
KSMU Springfield, Missouri
KRJY Truth or Consequence, New Mexico
KSUU Cedar City, Utah
KSWH-FM Arkadelphia, Arkansas
KTAI Kingsville, Texas
KTNE-FM Alliance, Nebraska
KNSH(FM) Fort Dodge, Iowa
KTSD-FM Reliance, South Dakota
KUCV Lincoln, Nebraska
KVER El Paso, Texas
KWAX Eugene, Oregon
KLDV Morrison, Colorado
KWSB-FM Gunnison, Colorado
KWTS Canyon, Texas
KXLC La Crescent, Minnesota
KYBJ Lake Jackson, Texas
KYPL Yakima, Washington
WABR Tifton, Georgia
WAQU Selma, Alabama
WASM Natchez, Mississippi
WAXU Troy, Alabama
WBOR Brunswick, Maine
WBSH Hagerstown, Indiana
WBUQ Bloomsburg, Pennsylvania
WBVC Pomfret, Connecticut
WCYT Lafayette Township, Indiana
WDBX Carbondale, Illinois
WDUB Granville, Ohio
WEDM Indianapolis, Indiana
WEGL Auburn, Alabama
WFMU East Orange, New Jersey
WFUM(FM) Flint, Michigan
WGCS Goshen, Indiana
WGDR Plainfield, Vermont
WGGL-FM Houghton, Michigan
WGSL Loves Park, Illinois
WGTD Kenosha, Wisconsin
WHFC Bel Air, Maryland
WHVP Hudson, New York
WIBI Carlinville, Illinois
WIRE Lebanon, Indiana
WJED Dogwood Lakes Estate, Florida
WJFP Fort Pierce, Florida
WJJW North Adams, Massachusetts
WJSR Birmingham, Alabama
WKCS Knoxville, Tennessee
WKES Lakeland, Florida
WKNO-FM Memphis, Tennessee
WOVM Appleton, Wisconsin
WMSS Middletown, Pennsylvania
WMSV Starkville, Mississippi
WMUA Amherst, Massachusetts
WNAN Nantucket, Massachusetts
WNSB Norfolk, Virginia
WOKD-FM Danville, Virginia
WOLW Cadillac, Michigan
WOSB Marion, Ohio
WOSE Coshocton, Ohio
WOSS Ossining, New York
WPCJ Pittsford, Michigan
WPIB Bluefield, West Virginia
WPSM Fort Walton Beach, Florida
WREK Atlanta, Georgia
WRMC-FM Middlebury, Vermont
WRMU-FM Alliance, Ohio
WRSH Rockingham, North Carolina
WRTY Jackson Township, Pennsylvania
WRUW-FM Cleveland, Ohio
WCFL(FM) Nashville, Tennessee
WSAJ-FM Grove City, Pennsylvania
WSHU-FM Fairfield, Connecticut
WTKL North Dartmouth, Massachusetts
WSPN Saratoga Springs, New York
WSQE Corning, New York
WSVH Savannah, Georgia
WTJU Charlottesville, Virginia
WKCC Kankakee, Illinois
WTSC-FM Potsdam, New York
WVNH Concord, New Hampshire
WVSU-FM Birmingham, Alabama
WVUB Vincennes, Indiana
WWNJ Toms River Township, New Jersey
WVRP Roanoke Rapids, North Carolina
WYFG Gaffney, South Carolina
WZBT Gettysburg, Pennsylvania
XETRAFM Tijuana, Mexico
KJRF Lawton, Oklahoma
KQPD Ardmore, Oklahoma
KLEU Lewistown, Montana
KBSS Sun Valley, Idaho
KFRJ China Lake, California
KTJC Kelso, Washington
WUJC St. Marks, Florida
KGWP Pittsburg, Texas
WYGS Hope, Indiana
KTMK Tillamook, Oregon
WHCE Highland Springs, Virginia
WTSE Benton, Tennessee
WNKV Norco, Louisiana
WKMY Winchendon, Massachusetts
KVKL Las Vegas, Nevada
WUFR Bedford, Pennsylvania
KQXE Eastland, Texas
WZGO Aurora, North Carolina
WYBH Fayetteville, North Carolina
WKAO Ashland, Kentucky
KNSB(FM) Bettendorf, Iowa
KMWY Jackson, Wyoming
WFAZ Goodwater, Alabama
WVPC Franklin, West Virginia
WHMO Madison, Indiana
KHEC Crescent City, California
KZME Brightwood, Oregon
KOFG Cody, Wyoming
KGWB Snyder, Texas
KJOG Cleveland, Oklahoma
WEBK Society Hill, South Carolina
KSJI Saint Joseph, Missouri
WAYU Steele, Alabama
WHYZ Palm Coast, Florida
WVNK Manchester, Vermont
KIKG Licking, Missouri
KOGW Stratford, Texas
WZTH Tusculum, Tennessee
WKST-FM Pittsburgh, New Hampshire
WHMF Marianna, Florida
WBFK Smiths Grove, Kentucky
KCFL Westport, Washington
WMHU(FM) Cold Brook, New York

91.3 mhz

KAPC Butte, Montana
KAQD Abilene, Texas
KAXR Arkansas City, Kansas
KAYA Hubbard, Nebraska
KDRH King City, California
KBCS Bellevue, Washington
KBIA Columbia, Missouri
KBIY Van Buren, Missouri
KBKN Lamesa, Texas
KCED Centralia, Washington
KCPR San Luis Obispo, California
KDFR Des Moines, Iowa
KDKR Decatur, Texas
KFRB Bakersfield, California
KGHR Tuba City, Arizona
KGLY Tyler, Texas
KGTS College Place, Washington
KIDE Hoopa, California
KMHA Four Bears, North Dakota
KMSA Grand Junction, Colorado
KMSK Austin, Minnesota
KNBJ Bemidji, Minnesota
KNCT-FM Killeen, Texas
KNIS Carson City, Nevada
KOAB-FM Bend, Oregon
KXWT Odessa, Texas
KPVU Prairie View, Texas
KRSC-FM Claremore, Oklahoma
KNCM Appleton, Minnesota
KSCL Shreveport, Louisiana
KSUT Ignacio, Colorado
KSUW Sheridan, Wyoming
KUAF Fayetteville, Arkansas
KUCA Conway, Arkansas
KUOP Stockton, California
KUWA Afton, Wyoming
KUWC Casper, Wyoming
KUWS Superior, Wisconsin
KVFM Beeville, Texas
KVLU Beaumont, Texas
KXCI Tucson, Arizona
KZLV Lytle, Texas
WAKJ Defuniak Springs, Florida
WAPS Akron, Ohio
WATY Folkston, Georgia
WFIX Florence, Alabama
WBNY Buffalo, New York
WCHW-FM Bay City, Michigan
WCNY-FM Syracuse, New York
WCPI McMinnville, Tennessee
WCSG Grand Rapids, Michigan
WCUW Worcester, Massachusetts
WDJM-FM Framingham, Massachusetts
WDOM Providence, Rhode Island
WESM Princess Anne, Maryland
WEVH Hanover, New Hampshire
WFHB Bloomington, Indiana
WFQS Franklin, North Carolina
WGRC Lewisburg, Pennsylvania
WGTE-FM Toledo, Ohio
WHEM Eau Claire, Wisconsin
WHHI Highland, Wisconsin
WHIF Palatka, Florida
WHIL-FM Mobile, Alabama
WHJE Carmel, Indiana
WHQR Wilmington, North Carolina
WIPR-FM San Juan, Puerto Rico
WIUM Macomb, Illinois
WIUV Castleton, Vermont
WJTG Fort Valley, Georgia
WKMS-FM Murray, Kentucky
WKNH Keene, New Hampshire
WLCH Lancaster, Pennsylvania
WMLU Farmville, Virginia
WLFA Asheville, North Carolina
WLMU Harrogate, Tennessee
WLRN-FM Miami, Florida
WLTR Columbia, South Carolina
WLVR-FM Bethlehem, Pennsylvania
WMEW Waterville, Maine
WMPN-FM Jackson, Mississippi
WNDY Crawfordsville, Indiana
WNIW La Salle, Illinois
WOES Ovid-Elsie, Michigan
WOLN Olean, New York
WOLR Lake City, Florida
WOUB-FM Athens, Ohio
WPAR Salem, Virginia
WQAB Philippi, West Virginia
WQLN-FM Erie, Pennsylvania
WRLI-FM Southampton, New York
WRTQ Ocean City, New Jersey
WSEB Englewood, Florida
WSGR-FM Port Huron, Michigan
WSHL-FM Easton, Massachusetts
WTBJ Oxford, Alabama
WTRM Winchester, Virginia
WTSR Trenton, New Jersey
WUKY Lexington, Kentucky
WUNH Durham, New Hampshire
WUTS Sewanee, Tennessee
WVKR-FM Poughkeepsie, New York
WVOB Dothan, Alabama
WVST-FM Petersburg, Virginia
WVUD Newark, Delaware
WWHI Muncie, Indiana
WYFZ Belleview, Florida
WWUH West Hartford, Connecticut
WXAC Reading, Pennsylvania
WXLH Blue Mountain Lake, New York
WXPL Fitchburg, Massachusetts
WHGO Hertford, North Carolina
WXRI Winston-Salem, North Carolina
WYEP-FM Pittsburgh, Pennsylvania
WYSO Yellow Springs, Ohio
WZMB Greenville, North Carolina
KBSJ Jackpot, Nevada
WCKZ Orland, Indiana
KUWT Thermopolis, Wyoming
KANV Olsburg, Kansas
WJCO Montpelier, Indiana
WJCZ Milford, Illinois
WSTM Kiel, Wisconsin
KNYR Yreka, California
KLZV Brush, Colorado
KWTH Barstow, California
KYJC Commerce, Texas
WJOG Good Hart, Michigan
WSLE Salem, Illinois
KLRY Gypsum, Colorado
KSVY Sonoma, California
KAKO Ada, Oklahoma
WRQC(FM) East Tawas, Michigan
WHFG Broussard, Louisiana
KTPF Salida, Colorado
WWDL Plainfield, Indiana
KYCT Ruidoso, New Mexico
WFMR Orleans, Massachusetts
KQLN Alamo, Nevada
KFLF Somers, Montana
KAWN Winslow, Arizona
WNON Warfield, Kentucky
KMHS-FM Coos Bay, Oregon
WIOX Roxbury, New York
WSJE Summersville, West Virginia
WBNB Equality, Alabama
KOGB McGrath, Alaska
KPKO Pecos, Texas
WNGB Petersham, Massachusetts
KSSH Shubert, Nebraska
KRRA Paragonah, Utah
KXDS Santa Clara, Utah
KOPA(FM) Pala, California
WGMR Effingham, Illinois
KKJD Borrego Springs, California
WBIL Union Springs, Alabama

91.5 mhz

KAJX Aspen, Colorado
KALR Hot Springs, Arkansas
KANU Lawrence, Kansas
KARF Independence, Kansas
KASK Fairfield, California
KBAN De Ridder, Louisiana
KBCX Big Spring, Texas
KBSX Boise, Idaho
KCAS McCook, Texas

KCFB St. Cloud, Minnesota
KCMH Mountain Home, Arkansas
KFLQ Albuquerque, New Mexico
KGRM Grambling, Louisiana
KIOS-FM Omaha, Nebraska
KJZZ Phoenix, Arizona
KKUP Cupertino, California
KLWS Moses Lake, Washington
KNCC Elko, Nevada
KGAC Saint Peter, Minnesota
KNSU Thibodaux, Louisiana
KOPB-FM Portland, Oregon
KPAE Erwinville, Louisiana
KPLG Plains, Montana
KPRJ Jamestown, North Dakota
KQMN Thief River Falls, Minnesota
KRCC Colorado Springs, Colorado
KRNE-FM Merriman, Nebraska
KRUX Las Cruces, New Mexico
KRVH Rio Vista, California
KSIV-FM St. Louis, Missouri
KSJD Cortez, Colorado
KSJV Fresno, California
KSNS Medicine Lodge, Kansas
KSRS Roseburg, Oregon
KSTN-FM Redding, California
KSUA Fairbanks, Alaska
KSYE Frederick, Oklahoma
KTXK Texarkana, Texas
KUBS Newport, Washington
KUNC Greeley, Colorado
KUNV Las Vegas, Nevada
KNSM(FM) Mason City, Iowa
KUSC Los Angeles, California
KUSU-FM Logan, Utah
KVAZ Henryetta, Oklahoma
KBYR-FM Rexburg, Idaho
KWJG Kasilof, Alaska
KWLD Plainview, Texas
KWVZ Florence, Oregon
KYDS Sacramento, California
KNHM Bayside, California
KZYZ Willits, California
WAPN Holly Hill, Florida
WARN Culpeper, Virginia
WAVI Oxford, Mississippi
WJBP Red Bank, Tennessee
WBEZ Chicago, Illinois
WBFI McDaniels, Kentucky
WBIE Delphos, Ohio
WBIM-FM Bridgewater, Massachusetts
WBJC Baltimore, Maryland
WBJD Atlantic Beach, North Carolina
WCIC Pekin, Illinois
WGLY-FM Bolton, Vermont
WCVY Coventry, Rhode Island
WDBK Blackwood, New Jersey
WEBT Langdale, Alabama
WECI Richmond, Indiana
WEMY Green Bay, Wisconsin
WFHU Henderson, Tennessee
WFMQ Lebanon, Tennessee
WFSQ Tallahassee, Florida
WGLZ West Liberty, West Virginia
WGPH Vidalia, Georgia
WGRE Greencastle, Indiana
WGRS Guilford, Connecticut
WHCB Bristol, Tennessee
WICA Traverse City, Michigan
WJHS Columbia City, Indiana
WJLR Seymour, Indiana
WUML Lowell, Massachusetts
WJYO Fort Myers, Florida
WKCL Ladson, South Carolina
WKHR Bainbridge, Ohio
WKRJ New Philadelphia, Ohio
WCIE New Port Richey, Florida
WLUR Lexington, Virginia
WMFO Medford, Massachusetts
WMHC South Hadley, Massachusetts
WMHW-FM Mount Pleasant, Michigan
WMIE-FM Cocoa, Florida
WMLN-FM Milton, Massachusetts
WNIQ Sterling, Illinois
WNRZ Dickson, Tennessee
WNYE New York, New York
WOBC-FM Oberlin, Ohio
WOSP Portsmouth, Ohio
WPIN-FM Dublin, Virginia
WPRK Winter Park, Florida
WPSU State College, Pennsylvania

WRBC Lewiston, Maine
WRFT Indianapolis, Indiana
WRPI Troy, New York
WSDH Sandwich, Massachusetts
WSGN Gadsden, Alabama
WSQX-FM Binghamton, New York
WSRN-FM Swarthmore, Pennsylvania
WSTF Andalusia, Alabama
WTBI-FM Greenville, South Carolina
WTUL New Orleans, Louisiana
WUAL-FM Tuscaloosa, Alabama
WUEV Evansville, Indiana
WUNC Chapel Hill, North Carolina
WUPX Marquette, Michigan
WVCT Keavy, Kentucky
WVHC Herkimer, New York
WWEV-FM Cumming, Georgia
WWLR Lyndonville, Vermont
WXXI-FM Rochester, New York
WYCS Yorktown, Virginia
WZLY Wellesley, Massachusetts
KUWD Sundance, Wyoming
WVCM Iron Mountain, Michigan
WFWR Attica, Indiana
WTML Tullahoma, Tennessee
KRQZ Lompoc, California
KNWF Fergus Falls, Minnesota
WRSG Middlebourne, West Virginia
KTXP Bushland, Texas
WJCY Cicero, Indiana
KAIA Bloomfield, Missouri
KHVT Bloomington, Texas
WLRK Greenville, Mississippi
KSUL Port Sulphur, Louisiana
WJOH Raco, Michigan
WLHW Casey, Illinois
KAFH Great Falls, Montana
KHML Madisonville, Texas
WHKC Columbus, Ohio
WKWM Marathon, Florida
WCIM Shenandoah, Pennsylvania
WGTT Emeralda, Florida
KBLC Fredericksburg, Texas
KYFB Denison, Texas
WPJW Hurricane, West Virginia
WJFH Sebring, Florida
WPSF Clewiston, Florida
WCNB Dayton, Indiana
KRGO Alton, Iowa
KVHR Van Horn, Texas
KSNB Norton, Kansas
WFBK Fort Mill, South Carolina
KNWU Forks, Washington
KSQM Sequim, Washington
WANH Meredith, New Hampshire
KBDW Wheeler, Texas
WPEF Kentwood, Louisiana
WTYG Sparr, Florida
KTML South Fork, Colorado
WPBD Lewes, Delaware
KFBR Gerlach, Nevada

91.7 mhz

KALW San Francisco, California
KAPM Alexandria, Louisiana
KARG Poteau, Oklahoma
KAXE Grand Rapids, Minnesota
KNBX San Ardo, California
KBDO Des Arc, Arkansas
KBLD Kennewick, Washington
KBNJ Corpus Christi, Texas
KBSM McCall, Idaho
KBSW Twin Falls, Idaho
KXOT Tacoma, Washington
KCHO Chico, California
KCOZ Point Lookout, Missouri
KCVO-FM Camdenton, Missouri
KCVS Salina, Kansas
KDOV Medford, Oregon
KEMC Billings, Montana
KEOL La Grande, Oregon
KGLP Gallup, New Mexico
KHCS Palm Desert, California
KHBW(FM) Brownwood, Texas
KJIR Hannibal, Missouri
KLNR Panaca, Nevada
KZSE Rochester, Minnesota
KLSP Angola, Louisiana
KMVC Marshall, Missouri
KNAD Page, Arizona
KPUB Flagstaff, Arizona

KNEO Neosho, Missouri
KNWD Natchitoches, Louisiana
KOHS Orem, Utah
KOOP Hornsby, Texas
KOSU Stillwater, Oklahoma
KOTO Telluride, Colorado
KPNE-FM North Platte, Nebraska
KPSU Goodwell, Oklahoma
KRFA-FM Moscow, Idaho
KRMC Douglas, Arizona
KRTU-FM San Antonio, Texas
KSUI Iowa City, Iowa
KTPH Tonopah, Nevada
KUFR Salt Lake City, Utah
KUHM Helena, Montana
KUPR Alamogordo, New Mexico
KVRX Austin, Texas
KXSR Groveland, California
KZAZ Bellingham, Washington
KZPI Deming, New Mexico
WAJS Tupelo, Mississippi
WAOY Gulfport, Mississippi
WAPD Campbellsville, Kentucky
WAQG Ozark, Alabama
WAVM Maynard, Massachusetts
WBGL Champaign, Illinois
WBJW Albion, Illinois
WBKU Ahoskie, North Carolina
WBMR Telford, Pennsylvania
WBSJ Portland, Indiana
WBSL-FM Sheffield, Massachusetts
WCCV Cartersville, Georgia
WGLV Woodstock, Vermont
WCML-FM Alpena, Michigan
WCUC-FM Clarion, Pennsylvania
WCUR West Chester, Pennsylvania
WDEQ-FM De Graff, Ohio
WEEM-FM Pendleton, Indiana
WEGS Milton, Florida
WEMC Harrisonburg, Virginia
WETL South Bend, Indiana
WFCM-FM Murfreesboro, Tennessee
WFRH Kingston, New York
WFTI-FM St. Petersburg, Florida
WNNZ-FM Deerfield, Massachusetts
WHRS Cookeville, Tennessee
WHUS Storrs, Connecticut
WICB Ithaca, New York
WIWC Kokomo, Indiana
WIXQ Millersville, Pennsylvania
WJAZ Summerdale, Pennsylvania
WJIC Zanesville, Ohio
WJLF Gainesville, Florida
WKDU Philadelphia, Pennsylvania
WLBS Bristol, Pennsylvania
WLFR Pomona, New Jersey
WLPE Augusta, Georgia
WLPG Florence, South Carolina
WMCN St. Paul, Minnesota
WMKO Marco, Florida
WMPH Wilmington, Delaware
WMSE Milwaukee, Wisconsin
WMUH Allentown, Pennsylvania
WMWM Salem, Massachusetts
WNEC-FM Henniker, New Hampshire
WOSR Middletown, New York
WOSV Mansfield, Ohio
WPAL Laporte, Pennsylvania
WPCR-FM Plymouth, New Hampshire
WPRL Lorman, Mississippi
WRLC Williamsport, Pennsylvania
WRTX Dover, Delaware
WRVJ Watertown, New York
WSGE Dallas, North Carolina
WSHD Eastport, Maine
WSHS Sheboygan, Wisconsin
WSQC-FM Oneonta, New York
WSUM Madison, Wisconsin
WSUW Whitewater, Wisconsin
WTJB Columbus, Georgia
WUGA Athens, Georgia
WUMR Memphis, Tennessee
WUNV Albany, Georgia
WUOM Ann Arbor, Michigan
WVIJ Port Charlotte, Florida
WVMW-FM Scranton, Pennsylvania
WVPB Beckley, West Virginia
WVSD Itta Bena, Mississippi
WVXU Cincinnati, Ohio
WWET Valdosta, Georgia
WWFR Stuart, Florida

WWHR Bowling Green, Kentucky
WWJD Pippa Passes, Kentucky
WWVU-FM Morgantown, West Virginia
WXCI Danbury, Connecticut
WNJR Washington, Pennsylvania
WXPR Rhinelander, Wisconsin
WYFD Decatur, Alabama
WYTN Youngstown, Ohio
WNNV San German, Puerto Rico
KTGW Fruitland, New Mexico
KDUW Douglas, Wyoming
KSVR Mount Vernon, Washington
WMCQ Muskegon, Michigan
WVNL Vandalia, Illinois
WNEF Newburyport, Massachusetts
KCVX Salem, Missouri
KZAN Hays, Kansas
KBFR Bismarck, North Dakota
WAPB Madison, Florida
WPIL Heflin, Alabama
WJVK Owensboro, Kentucky
WDKV Fond Du Lac, Wisconsin
WSQH Decatur, Mississippi
KPCV Portales, New Mexico
KFHL Wasco, California
WJWT Gardner, Massachusetts
WYTL Wyomissing, Pennsylvania
WJPR Jasper, Indiana
KNSW Worthington-Marshall, Minnesota
KMSL Mansfield, Louisiana
WFFL Panama City, Florida
KTSG Steamboat Springs, Colorado
KSQS Ririe, Idaho
KPBR Poplar Bluff, Missouri
KVLP Tucumcari, New Mexico
KTDA Dalhart, Texas
WZXH Hagerstown, Maryland
KOBH Hobbs, New Mexico
WWEM Rustburg, Virginia
WMVW Peachtree City, Georgia
KGCN Roswell, New Mexico
KCCS Starkville, Colorado
WYJZ Fearsville, Kentucky
KPIT Pittsburg, Texas
KAHU Pahala, Hawaii
KMLL Marysville, Kansas
KRKM Fort Washakie, Wyoming
KNDW Williston, North Dakota
WNFC Paducah, Kentucky
KLXD Springfield, Colorado
KOLJ-FM Warroad, Minnesota
WXLB Boonville, New York
WZKL Woodstock, Illinois
WNGM(FM) Tallulah Falls, Georgia
WUMM Machias, Maine
KEJA Cale, Arkansas
KLSB Norfolk, Nebraska
KAMF Tulare, South Dakota
WRVX Cameron, Missouri
WPAL(FM) Laporte, Pennsylvania
KEYV Vernal, Utah
KEYR Richfield, Utah
WLNJ Lakehurst, New Jersey
KPPD Devils Lake, North Dakota
WZCA Quebradillas, Puerto Rico
KMNO Wailuku, Hawaii

91.9 mhz

KAQA Kilauea, Hawaii
KASU Jonesboro, Arkansas
KAVX Lufkin, Texas
KAXV Bastrop, Louisiana
KAZF Hebbronville, Texas
KBCW-FM McAlester, Oklahoma
KBDD Winfield, Kansas
KBHZ Willmar, Minnesota
KXBR International Falls, Minnesota
KBPB Harrison, Arkansas
KBRW-FM Barrow, Alaska
KCFP Pueblo, Colorado
KCNE-FM Chadron, Nebraska
KCSB-FM Santa Barbara, California
KCSS Turlock, California
KDLL Kenai, Alaska
KDNA Yakima, Washington
KDNE Crete, Nebraska
KLXV Glenwood Springs, Colorado
KDSU Fargo, North Dakota
KDUR Durango, Colorado
KGLT Bozeman, Montana
KHSR Crescent City, California

KLVR Middletown, California
KLWD Gillette, Wyoming
KMRL Buras, Louisiana
KMUN Astoria, Oregon
KJLG Emporia, Kansas
KNLM Marshfield, Missouri
KONQ Dodge City, Kansas
KPCW Park City, Utah
KPFC Callisburg, Texas
KRVM-FM Eugene, Oregon
KSDA-FM Agat, Guam
KSDB-FM Manhattan, Kansas
KSFC Spokane, Washington
KSPB Pebble Beach, California
KQSD-FM Lowry, South Dakota
KSSU Durant, Oklahoma
KTCC Colby, Kansas
KTLX Columbus, Nebraska
KUDU Tok, Alaska
KUFN Hamilton, Montana
KUHB-FM St. Paul, Alaska
KUWR Laramie, Wyoming
KVCR San Bernardino, California
KWJC Liberty, Missouri
KWRV Sun Valley, Idaho
KWSC Wayne, Nebraska
KWSO Warm Springs, Oregon
KXRJ Russellville, Arkansas
KXRI Amarillo, Texas
KYRM Yuma, Arizona
WAAE New Bern, North Carolina
WAIC Springfield, Massachusetts
WHOJ Terre Haute, Indiana
WAPX-FM Clarksville, Tennessee
WASW Waycross, Georgia
WAUM Duck Hill, Mississippi
WLFS Port Wentworth, Georgia
WAYL St. Augustine, Florida
WBHZ Elkins, West Virginia
WBPR Worcester, Massachusetts
WCEL Plattsburgh, New York
WCLK Atlanta, Georgia
WEMI Appleton, Wisconsin
WFPB-FM Falmouth, Massachusetts
WFPK Louisville, Kentucky
WFSS Fayetteville, North Carolina
WFWM Frostburg, Maryland
WGDE Defiance, Ohio
WGIB Birmingham, Alabama
WGTS Takoma Park, Maryland
WHDI Sister Bay, Wisconsin
WJCH Joliet, Illinois
WJEF Lafayette, Indiana
WJIF Opp, Alabama
WKCO Gambier, Ohio
WLBL-FM Wausau, Wisconsin
WLJS-FM Jacksonville, Alabama
WLKP Belpre, Ohio
WMBV Dixons Mills, Alabama
WMEB-FM Orono, Maine
WHKU Proctorville, Ohio
WMKL Hammocks, Florida
WMTU-FM Houghton, Michigan
WNGN Argyle, New York
WNRN Charlottesville, Virginia
WNTI Hackettstown, New Jersey
WORW Port Huron, Michigan
WOUH-FM Chillicothe, Ohio
WOWL Burnsville, Mississippi
WOZQ Northampton, Massachusetts
WPHP Wheeling, West Virginia
WQKO Howe, Indiana
WRCM Wingate, North Carolina
WRVN Utica, New York
WSCF-FM Vero Beach, Florida
WSHR Lake Ronkonkoma, New York
WSIU Carbondale, Illinois
WSLX New Canaan, Connecticut
WUIS Springfield, Illinois
WUMB-FM Boston, Massachusetts
WUOT Knoxville, Tennessee
WCAL California, Pennsylvania
WVGS Statesboro, Georgia
WVSH Huntington, Indiana
WVTR Marion, Virginia
WHGN Crystal River, Florida
WXPW Wausau, Wisconsin
WYFO Lakeland, Florida
WYFP Harpswell, Maine
WVME Meadville, Pennsylvania
WCMK Putney, Vermont
KOHN Sells, Arizona
KWBI Great Bend, Kansas
KESY Baker City, Oregon
KSRD St. Joseph, Missouri
KHKL Laytonville, California
KHCJ Jefferson, Texas
WKVH Monticello, Florida
KWTD Ridgecrest, California
KNLK Santa Rosa, New Mexico
KVJC Globe, Arizona
KNLQ Cuba, Missouri
KFRW Great Falls, Montana
KLLR Dripping Springs, Texas
KMEO Mertzon, Texas
WCFM Williamstown, Massachusetts
WDPW Greenville, Michigan
KCKR Church Point, Louisiana
KTDV State Center, Iowa
WMJC Richland, Michigan
KXFR Socorro, New Mexico
KHPO Port O'Connor, Texas
KLKI Dolan Springs, Arizona
WITT Zionsville, Indiana
KHED Arkadelphia, Arkansas
WXMF Marion, Ohio
KRRE Las Vegas, New Mexico
WBNJ Barnegat, New Jersey
KRAR Espanola, New Mexico
KPGA Morton, Texas
KTYN Thayne, Wyoming
WMYE Fort Myers, Florida
WWRA Clinton, Louisiana
WHDD-FM Sharon, Connecticut
KIAM-FM North Nenana, Alaska
KJOL-FM Montrose, Colorado
WKJA Brunswick, Ohio
WRAO Wisconsin Rapids, Wisconsin
KLXO Beaver, Oklahoma
WBRQ La Grange, Georgia
WZRG(FM) Kulpmont, Pennsylvania
KELC Hawthorne, Nevada
WVMR-FM Hillsboro, West Virginia
KLDD McCloud, California
WRFI Watkins Glen, New York
WXHM Middletown, Delaware
WKRI Cokesbury, South Carolina
KPTZ Port Townsend, Washington
KCKV Kirksville, Missouri
KQNY Quincy, California
WGCP Cadillac, Michigan
WGBQ Lynchburg, Tennessee
KEYD Delta, Utah
WMUI(FM) Rushville, Indiana
KEYP Price, Utah
WZZG Toomsboro, Georgia
WSMP New Hebron, Mississippi
KSJU Friday Harbor, Washington
KHEB Granite, Oklahoma
WDRT Viroqua, Wisconsin
WDSV Greenville, Mississippi
WHRE Eastville, Virginia
WVSE Christiansted, Virgin Islands
KJGS Aurora, Nebraska
KCWW Battle Mountain, Nevada
KLZR Westcliffe, Colorado

92.1 mhz

KHWI Holualoa, Hawaii
KATK-FM Carlsbad, New Mexico
KMKR Canyonville, Oregon
KTHN La Junta, Colorado
KCHE-FM Cherokee, Iowa
KCRK-FM Colville, Washington
KCZO Carrizo Springs, Texas
KKCM Thermal, California
KTBB-FM Tyler, Texas
KDQN-FM De Queen, Arkansas
KQSM-FM Fayetteville, Arkansas
KKDV Walnut Creek, California
KFMA Green Valley, Arizona
KFRZ Green River, Wyoming
KSOQ-FM Escondido, California
KFXI Marlow, Oklahoma
KHOS-FM Sonora, Texas
KHPQ Clinton, Arkansas
KJMN Castle Rock, Colorado
KKOZ-FM Ava, Missouri
KVMX Bakersfield, California
KLIL Moreauville, Louisiana
KSYR Benton, Louisiana
KLQP Madison, Minnesota
KMFC Centralia, Missouri
KMOE Butler, Missouri
KMZA Seneca, Kansas
KMZE Woodward, Oklahoma
KNBT New Braunfels, Texas
KTBT Broken Arrow, Oklahoma
KOPY-FM Alice, Texas
KBBO-FM Houston, Alaska
KYLR Hutto, Texas
KREP Belleville, Kansas
KRLS Knoxville, Iowa
KTSR De Quincy, Louisiana
KROI Seabrook, Texas
KKOR Waseca, Minnesota
KSBS-FM Pago Pago, American Samoa
KWFP Sparks, Nevada
KXBN Cedar City, Utah
KSYD Reedsport, Oregon
KTCE Payson, Utah
KTFW-FM Glen Rose, Texas
KTNR Kenedy, Texas
KUEL(FM) Fort Dodge, Iowa
KUMA-FM Pilot Rock, Oregon
KVCL-FM Winnfield, Louisiana
KWVR-FM Enterprise, Oregon
KXEZ Farmersville, Texas
KOND Clovis, California
KZRX Dickinson, North Dakota
KCCL Placerville, California
KZUA Holbrook, Arizona
WBHC-FM Hampton, South Carolina
WBIK Pleasant City, Ohio
WBKN Brookhaven, Mississippi
WBST Muncie, Indiana
WBTR-FM Carrollton, Georgia
WXEX-FM Sanford, Maine
WCDX Mechanicsville, Virginia
WCKR Hornell, New York
WCSR-FM Hillsdale, Michigan
WDDQ Adel, Georgia
WLTQ-FM Venice, Florida
WDIC-FM Clinchco, Virginia
WDLA-FM Walton, New York
WZET Hormigueros, Puerto Rico
WERH-FM Hamilton, Alabama
WEUZ Minor Hill, Tennessee
WEZY Racine, Wisconsin
WFGF Wapakoneta, Ohio
WFPS Freeport, Illinois
WAFZ-FM Immokalee, Florida
WGHN-FM Grand Haven, Michigan
WJHT Johnstown, Pennsylvania
WIDL Caro, Michigan
WWNU Irmo, South Carolina
WJGA-FM Jackson, Georgia
WJJN Columbia, Alabama
WJMG Hattiesburg, Mississippi
WJNS-FM Bentonia, Mississippi
WJXR Macclenny, Florida
WMYB Myrtle Beach, South Carolina
WTWS Houghton Lake, Michigan
WKPL Ellwood City, Pennsylvania
WKUL Cullman, Alabama
WLBW Fenwick Island, Delaware
WLNG Sag Harbor, New York
WLTU Manitowoc, Wisconsin
WXXM Sun Prairie, Wisconsin
WMEQ-FM Menomonie, Wisconsin
WECQ(FM) Destin, Florida
WMNC-FM Morganton, North Carolina
WMOO Derby Center, Vermont
WYVK Middleport, Ohio
WMSU Starkville, Mississippi
WNFK Perry, Florida
WDER-FM Peterborough, New Hampshire
WQKQ Carthage, Illinois
WOHF Bellevue, Ohio
WNUZ Mercersburg, Pennsylvania
WOMR Provincetown, Massachusetts
WPEH-FM Louisville, Georgia
WPTS-FM Pittsburgh, Pennsylvania
WQQK Goodlettsville, Tennessee
WRJC-FM Mauston, Wisconsin
WRLX West Palm Beach, Florida
WRNQ Poughkeepsie, New York
WROI Rochester, Indiana
WROU-FM West Carrollton, Ohio
WRSV Elm City, North Carolina
WSEN-FM Baldwinsville, New York
WSQV(FM) Lock Haven, Pennsylvania
WBVX Carlisle, Kentucky
WCDG(FM) Moyock, North Carolina
WTKY-FM Tompkinsville, Kentucky
WTPA Palmyra, Pennsylvania
WUMS University, Mississippi
WUPI Presque Isle, Maine
WHPD Dowagiac, Michigan
WVLT Vineland, New Jersey
WVWC Buckhannon, West Virginia
WWAX Hermantown, Minnesota
WQTX Saint Johns, Michigan
WWGO Charleston, Illinois
WWHS-FM Hampden-Sydney, Virginia
WLHR-FM Lavonia, Georgia
WVTK Port Henry, New York
WYRQ-FM Little Falls, Minnesota
WZDM Vincennes, Indiana
WZEW Fairhope, Alabama
KIBX Bonners Ferry, Idaho
KCVZ Dixon, Missouri
KEGE Pocatello, Idaho
WYAS Luquillo, Puerto Rico
WKXY Merigold, Mississippi
KHZZ Sargent, Nebraska
WHHR Vienna, Georgia
WMIS-FM Blackduck, Minnesota
KXJO St. Maries, Idaho

92.3 mhz

KYOY Hillsdale, Wyoming
KCCV-FM Olathe, Kansas
KCUL-FM Marshall, Texas
KETX-FM Livingston, Texas
KEZO-FM Omaha, Nebraska
KGON Portland, Oregon
KIIZ-FM Killeen, Texas
KIJN-FM Farwell, Texas
KIPR Pine Bluff, Arkansas
KRNH Kerrville, Texas
KIZN Boise, Idaho
KKVT(FM) Grand Junction, Colorado
KHHT Los Angeles, California
KTAR-FM Glendale, Arizona
KYUS-FM Miles City, Montana
KSTH Holyoke, Colorado
KNRG New Ulm, Texas
KNFM Midland, Texas
KKHQ-FM Oelwein, Iowa
KFTI-FM Newton, Kansas
KOFX El Paso, Texas
KOMP Las Vegas, Nevada
KQRK Ronan, Montana
KRED-FM Eureka, California
KREU Roland, Oklahoma
KRST Albuquerque, New Mexico
KSDL Sedalia, Missouri
KSJO San Jose, California
KSSK-FM Waipahu, Hawaii
KSVL Smith, Nevada
KMYY Rayville, Louisiana
KTTN-FM Trenton, Missouri
KULE-FM Ephrata, Washington
KQVT Victoria, Texas
KVRH-FM Salida, Colorado
KWCD Bisbee, Arizona
KXRA-FM Alexandria, Minnesota
WAEG Evans, Georgia
WZPW Peoria, Illinois
WBNZ Frankfort, Michigan
WDVW(FM) LaPlace, Louisiana
WCMQ-FM Hialeah, Florida
WCOL-FM Columbus, Ohio
WDEF-FM Chattanooga, Tennessee
WERQ-FM Baltimore, Maryland
WFLY Troy, New York
WOWO-FM Fort Wayne, Indiana
WGXL Hanover, New Hampshire
WIL-FM St. Louis, Missouri
WJMQ Clintonville, Wisconsin
WJPD Ishpeming, Michigan
WKRR Asheboro, North Carolina
WKVR-FM Huntingdon, Pennsylvania
WVSL-FM Riverside, Pennsylvania
WLWI-FM Montgomery, Alabama
WMME-FM Augusta, Maine
WMOQ Bostwick, Georgia
WMXD Detroit, Michigan
WNBQ Mansfield, Pennsylvania
WZPR Nags Head, North Carolina
WOSQ Spencer, Wisconsin
WLZN Macon, Georgia
WPRO-FM Providence, Rhode Island

WQSL Jacksonville, North Carolina
WRLS-FM Hayward, Wisconsin
WRRN Warren, Pennsylvania
WZAQ Louisa, Kentucky
WSGA Hinesville, Georgia
WTYD Deltaville, Virginia
WTTS Bloomington, Indiana
WWHC Oakland, Maryland
WWKA Orlando, Florida
WXLK Roanoke, Virginia
WXRK New York, New York
WPWX Hammond, Indiana
WYGE London, Kentucky
WYNU Milan, Tennessee
WKRK-FM Cleveland Heights, Ohio
WXCR New Martinsville, West Virginia
WQLI Meigs, Georgia
KSAR Thayer, Missouri
WOHT Grenada, Mississippi
KQRQ Rapid City, South Dakota

92.5 mhz

KAAR Butte, Montana
KAYX Richmond, Missouri
KMYX-FM Arvin, California
KHTA Wake Village, Texas
KDET-FM San Augustine, Texas
KCRT-FM Trinidad, Colorado
KCUA Naples, Utah
KCVT Silver Lake, Kansas
KSRW Independence, California
KKAL Paso Robles, California
KWOF Broomfield, Colorado
KELE-FM Mountain Grove, Missouri
KELO-FM Sioux Falls, South Dakota
KFBK-FM Sacramento, California
KKHA Markham, Texas
KJJY West Des Moines, Iowa
KBRE Atwater, California
KVLR Elgin, Texas
KKWQ Warroad, Minnesota
KLAD-FM Klamath Falls, Oregon
KQMV Bellevue, Washington
KWUP Navasota, Texas
KOMA Oklahoma City, Oklahoma
KPQX Havre, Montana
KPRV-FM Heavener, Oklahoma
KQMA Phillipsburg, Kansas
KQRS-FM Golden Valley, Minnesota
KRPT Devine, Texas
KSMR Winona, Minnesota
KSYN Joplin, Missouri
KCOL-FM Groves, Texas
KTHQ Eagar, Arizona
KMWX Abilene, Texas
KUUU South Jordan, Utah
KVPI-FM Ville Platte, Louisiana
KWYN-FM Wynne, Arkansas
KXKK Park Rapids, Minnesota
KYKM Yoakum, Texas
KZHR Dayton, Washington
KZPS Dallas, Texas
WBEE-FM Rochester, New York
WBGV Marlette, Michigan
WBKR Owensboro, Kentucky
WBWI-FM West Bend, Wisconsin
WFDX Atlanta, Michigan
WCPY Dekalb, Illinois
WEKS Zebulon, Georgia
WESC-FM Greenville, South Carolina
WESE Baldwyn, Mississippi
WINC-FM Winchester, Virginia
WIRN Buhl, Minnesota
WJJQ-FM Tomahawk, Wisconsin
WJSZ Ashley, Michigan
WJUN-FM Mexico, Pennsylvania
WKGB-FM Conklin, New York
WCFF Urbana, Illinois
WKXQ Rushville, Illinois
WKZZ Tifton, Georgia
WNDT Alachua, Florida
WOFX-FM Cincinnati, Ohio
WFJO Jacksonville Beach, Florida
WORO Corozal, Puerto Rico
WPAP-FM Panama City, Florida
WQMU Indiana, Pennsylvania
WQST-FM Forest, Mississippi
WQYZ Ocean Springs, Mississippi
WVKS Toledo, Ohio
WFSX-FM Estero, Florida
WVNN-FM Trinity, Alabama
WWYZ Waterbury, Connecticut
WXRV Andover, Massachusetts
WXTU Philadelphia, Pennsylvania
WYFL Henderson, North Carolina
WYUU Safety Harbor, Florida
WZAC-FM Danville, West Virginia
WXJC-FM Cordova, Alabama
WDJQ Alliance, Ohio
WZUU Mattawan, Michigan
WZWZ Kokomo, Indiana
XHRMFM Tijuana, Mexico
WICO-FM Pocomoke City, Maryland
KHCL Arcadia, Louisiana
KPPL Poplar Bluff, Missouri
WLAW Newaygo, Michigan
KKRE Hollis, Oklahoma
KDAD Bar Nunn, Wyoming
KLHI-FM Kahului, Hawaii
KAYF Bayfield, Colorado
WBLH Black River, New York

92.7 mhz

KHBC Hilo, Hawaii
KDSK Grants, New Mexico
KALP Alpine, Texas
KASR Vilonia, Arkansas
KNCU Newport, Oregon
KBRB-FM Ainsworth, Nebraska
KDSS Ely, Nevada
KESO South Padre Island, Texas
KGBR Gold Beach, Oregon
KGFX-FM Pierre, South Dakota
KHWK Tonopah, Nevada
KZUH Minneapolis, Kansas
KINL Eagle Pass, Texas
KIQZ Rawlins, Wyoming
KIVY-FM Crockett, Texas
KJAK Slaton, Texas
KJBZ Laredo, Texas
KJVC Mansfield, Louisiana
KKBA Kingsville, Texas
KKBS Guymon, Oklahoma
KKCH Glenwood Springs, Colorado
KKUU Indio, California
KLGA-FM Algona, Iowa
KJLL(FM) Fountain Valley, California
KLOZ Eldon, Missouri
KLPL(FM) Lake Providence, Louisiana
KBQB Chico, California
KLYR-FM Clarksville, Arkansas
KMFB(FM) Mendocino, California
KHJL(FM) Thousand Oaks, California
KNCW Omak, Washington
KORT-FM Grangeville, Idaho
KFNL Kindred, North Dakota
KRSY-FM La Luz, New Mexico
KQAY-FM Tucumcari, New Mexico
KORC(FM) Burns, Oregon
KRRN Moapa Valley, Nevada
KTOM-FM Marina, California
KSJQ Savannah, Missouri
KSRA-FM Salmon, Idaho
KTWA Ottumwa, Iowa
KUSO Albion, Nebraska
KVCK-FM Wolf Point, Montana
KBYO-FM Farmerville, Louisiana
KWME Wellington, Kansas
KWNA-FM Winnemucca, Nevada
KREV Alameda, California
KZIQ-FM Ridgecrest, California
KZSQ-FM Sonora, California
WAFN-FM Arab, Alabama
WAUN-FM Kewaunee, Wisconsin
WPZS Harrisburg, North Carolina
WCCR Clarion, Pennsylvania
WHIZ(FM) South Zanesville, Ohio
WDUX-FM Waupaca, Wisconsin
WDZZ-FM Flint, Michigan
WENY-FM Elmira, New York
WEOW Key West, Florida
WYVN Saugatuck, Michigan
WTDR-FM Talladega, Alabama
WGFR Glens Falls, New York
WGMD Rehoboth Beach, Delaware
WBGA St. Simons Island, Georgia
WHIZ-FM South Zanesville, Ohio
WHVE Russell Springs, Kentucky
WKZJ Eufaula, Alabama
WWWH-FM Haleyville, Alabama
WBHQ Beverly Beach, Florida
WXKU-FM Austin, Indiana
WJSM-FM Martinsburg, Pennsylvania
WCPT-FM Arlington Heights, Illinois
WKIF Kankakee, Illinois
WKKZ Dublin, Georgia
WKRA-FM Holly Springs, Mississippi
WKSX-FM Johnston, South Carolina
WKVT-FM Brattleboro, Vermont
WQBU-FM Garden City, New York
WLSR Galesburg, Illinois
WMIK-FM Middlesboro, Kentucky
WWXT Prince Frederick, Maryland
WMVY Tisbury, Massachusetts
WOBM-FM Toms River, New Jersey
WOXO-FM Norway, Maine
WQTK Ogdensburg, New York
WKQR(FM) Mullens, West Virginia
WBKL Clinton, Louisiana
WQDY-FM Calais, Maine
WQEL Bucyrus, Ohio
WQLZ Taylorville, Illinois
WRRV Middletown, New York
WCMI-FM Catlettsburg, Kentucky
WSDM-FM Brazil, Indiana
WTAO-FM Herrin, Illinois
WIJV Harriman, Tennessee
WUVA Charlottesville, Virginia
WGIE Clarksburg, West Virginia
WXUR Herkimer, New York
WZBD Berne, Indiana
WAVW Stuart, Florida
WPKG Neillsville, Wisconsin
KMSW The Dalles, Oregon
KBDX Blanding, Utah
KTRX Dickson, Oklahoma
WPIQ Manistique, Michigan
KLSI Thousand Oaks, California
KTPZ Hazelton, Idaho
KHRW Ranchester, Wyoming
KHKY Akiachak, Alaska
WBNK Pine Knoll Shores, North Carolina
KBQL Las Vegas, New Mexico
KBDV Leesville, Louisiana
KLSN Adelanto, California

92.9 mhz

KAFF-FM Flagstaff, Arizona
KMXN Osage City, Kansas
KATF Dubuque, Iowa
KBEZ Tulsa, Oklahoma
KBLQ-FM Logan, Utah
KOSP Ozark, Missouri
KDCD San Angelo, Texas
KDCQ Coos Bay, Oregon
KRMX(FM) Marlin, Texas
KEZQ West Yellowstone, Montana
KFAT Anchorage, Alaska
KFGY Healdsburg, California
KFSI Rochester, Minnesota
KFSO-FM Visalia, California
KGRC Hannibal, Missouri
KISM Bellingham, Washington
KJEE Montecito, California
KHLA Jennings, Louisiana
KKBQ-FM Pasadena, Texas
KKIA Ida Grove, Iowa
KKID Salem, Missouri
KKJM St. Joseph, Minnesota
KKXL-FM Grand Forks, North Dakota
KLFM Great Falls, Montana
KLSC Malden, Missouri
KOLT-FM Warren Afb, Wyoming
KMSC Sioux City, Iowa
KMXQ Socorro, New Mexico
KURK Reno, Nevada
KNIN-FM Wichita Falls, Texas
KOSO Patterson, California
KDBL(FM) Toppenish, Washington
KRMX Marlin, Texas
KROM San Antonio, Texas
KRWN Farmington, New Mexico
KSCQ Silver City, New Mexico
KSDR-FM Watertown, South Dakota
KKPK Colorado Springs, Colorado
KTGL Beatrice, Nebraska
KTKC-FM Springhill, Louisiana
KTZA Artesia, New Mexico
KVRE Hot Springs Village, Arkansas
KMIY Tucson, Arizona
KXFG Sun City, California
KYBR Espanola, New Mexico
KYYY Bismarck, North Dakota
KZZU-FM Spokane, Washington
WAAC Valdosta, Georgia
WFHG-FM Bluff City, Tennessee
WBLX-FM Mobile, Alabama
WBOS Brookline, Massachusetts
WBOX-FM Varnado, Louisiana
WCWV Summersville, West Virginia
WDHC Berkeley Springs, West Virginia
WRDX Smyrna, Delaware
WDXO Hazlehurst, Mississippi
WECL Elk Mound, Wisconsin
WEGX Dillon, South Carolina
WEZF Burlington, Vermont
WEZQ Bangor, Maine
WVBW Suffolk, Virginia
WGTZ Eaton, Ohio
WIKX Charlotte Harbor, Florida
WJXA Nashville, Tennessee
WJZQ Cadillac, Michigan
WBUF Buffalo, New York
WLTJ Pittsburgh, Pennsylvania
WMFQ Ocala, Florida
WMFS-FM Bartlett, Tennessee
WMGS Wilkes-Barre, Pennsylvania
WNDV-FM South Bend, Indiana
WLNQ-FM Newport, Tennessee
WBPM Saugerties, New York
WSCD-FM Duluth, Minnesota
WSEI Olney, Illinois
WSKL Veedersburg, Indiana
WRPW Colfax, Illinois
WTPM Aguadilla, Puerto Rico
WTUG-FM Northport, Alabama
WVHL Farmville, Virginia
WLXX Lexington, Kentucky
WYQE Naguabo, Puerto Rico
WZGC Atlanta, Georgia
WZLA-FM Abbeville, South Carolina
WYNW Birnamwood, Wisconsin
WEHM Manorville, New York
KRXF Bend, Oregon
KMML Cimarron, Kansas
KYME Rockford, Iowa

93.1 mhz

KRYP Gladstone, Oregon
KBDZ Perryville, Missouri
KWJK Boonville, Missouri
KCBS-FM Los Angeles, California
KXSM Hollister, California
KKXX-FM Shafter, California
KHMY Pratt, Kansas
KHDX Conway, Arkansas
KKHJ-FM Pago Pago, American Samoa
KHLX Pollock Pines, California
KKYA Yankton, South Dakota
KLJZ Yuma, Arizona
KMKT Bells, Texas
KQID-FM Alexandria, Louisiana
KMGJ Grand Junction, Colorado
KQIZ-FM Amarillo, Texas
KQMQ-FM Honolulu, Hawaii
KPLV Las Vegas, Nevada
KRCS Sturgis, South Dakota
KRVN-FM Lexington, Nebraska
KSII El Paso, Texas
KSTV-FM Dublin, Texas
KTRZ Riverton, Wyoming
KTYL-FM Tyler, Texas
KMCS Muscatine, Iowa
KXGO Arcata, California
KATO-FM New Ulm, Minnesota
KZLE Batesville, Arkansas
WBBK-FM Blakely, Georgia
WEZW Wildwood Crest, New Jersey
WDHR Pikeville, Kentucky
WDRQ Detroit, Michigan
WEAS-FM Springfield, Georgia
WGMZ Glencoe, Alabama
WHYN-FM Springfield, Massachusetts
WIMK Iron Mountain, Michigan
WJBL Ladysmith, Wisconsin
WKRO-FM Port Orange, Florida
WMGX Portland, Maine
WMKZ Monticello, Kentucky
WNTO Racine, Ohio
WPAW Winston-Salem, North Carolina
WIBC Indianapolis, Indiana
WNTQ Syracuse, New York
WSAA Benton, Tennessee
WPAT-FM Paterson, New Jersey

RADIO - U.S.

WPOC Baltimore, Maryland
WTFX-FM Clarksville, Indiana
WQYX Clearfield, Pennsylvania
WCHZ-FM Warrenton, Georgia
WSVO Staunton, Virginia
WFEZ(FM) Miami, Florida
WFGM-FM Barrackville, West Virginia
WWGM Alamo, Tennessee
WCYQ Karns, Tennessee
WXRT Chicago, Illinois
WYDS Decatur, Illinois
WZAK Cleveland, Ohio
WZMJ Batesburg, South Carolina
WWSR Lima, Ohio
WJQM De Forest, Wisconsin
KGCX Sidney, Montana
WGDQ Sumrall, Mississippi
WLFV Ettrick, Virginia
KBDK Leakey, Texas
KMWB Captain Cook, Hawaii
WACV Coosada, Alabama
WWKM Rochelle, Georgia

93.3 mhz

KAGL El Dorado, Arkansas
KMJI Ashdown, Arkansas
KZBT Midland, Texas
KBAW Ranchitos Las Lomas, Texas
KJAX Jackson, Wyoming
KBHR Big Bear City, California
KBLB Nisswa, Minnesota
KDKB Mesa, Arizona
KGGL Missoula, Montana
KJDX Susanville, California
KHTS-FM El Cajon, California
KIOA Des Moines, Iowa
KIGL Seligman, Missouri
KJKE Newcastle, Oklahoma
KKNU Springfield-Eugene, Oregon
KKOB-FM Albuquerque, New Mexico
KLIF-FM Haltom City, Texas
KGSR Cedar Park, Texas
KKSP Bryant, Arkansas
KMXV Kansas City, Missouri
KQQX Hermann, Missouri
KMOR Gering, Nebraska
KQBU-FM Port Arthur, Texas
KITE Port Lavaca, Texas
KRHV Big Pine, California
KSJZ Jamestown, North Dakota
KNTO Chowchilla, California
KTCL Wheat Ridge, Colorado
KFFF Bennington, Nebraska
KRKL Walla Walla, Washington
KUBE Seattle, Washington
KUBL-FM Salt Lake City, Utah
KVAK-FM Valdez, Alaska
KXAZ Page, Arizona
KXBA Nikiski, Alaska
KRZZ San Francisco, California
KURL(FM) Billings, Montana
KZOZ San Luis Obispo, California
WAKW Cincinnati, Ohio
WNCD Youngstown, Ohio
WBSZ Ashland, Wisconsin
WBTU Kendallville, Indiana
WBWZ New Paltz, New York
WCAN Canajoharie, New York
WCIZ-FM Watertown, New York
WDNS Bowling Green, Kentucky
WERO Washington, North Carolina
WFAR Danbury, Connecticut
WFLS-FM Fredericksburg, Virginia
WFLZ-FM Tampa, Florida
WGWD Gretna, Florida
WBZD-FM Muncy, Pennsylvania
WIZM-FM La Crosse, Wisconsin
WLDB Milwaukee, Wisconsin
WODC Ashville, Ohio
WKQZ Midland, Michigan
WKYQ Paducah, Kentucky
WMMR Philadelphia, Pennsylvania
WNHW Belmont, New Hampshire
WOGR-FM Salisbury, North Carolina
WPBG Peoria, Illinois
WNCV Shalimar, Florida
WJBT Callahan, Florida
WPUM Rensselaer, Indiana
WWFF-FM New Market, Alabama
WFKL Fairport, New York
WQTY Linton, Indiana
WQUE-FM New Orleans, Louisiana
WQZS Meyersdale, Pennsylvania
WSNE-FM Taunton, Massachusetts
WSYE Houston, Mississippi
WTPT Forest City, North Carolina
WTRH Ramsey, Illinois
WVFJ-FM Manchester, Georgia
WWSE Jamestown, New York
WWWZ Summerville, South Carolina
WKVW Marmet, West Virginia
WZMT Ponce, Puerto Rico
KKDC Dolores, Colorado
KJRV Wessington Springs, South Dakota
WSLP Saranac Lake, New York
KLED Antelope Valley Crestview, Wyoming
WZAE Wadley, Georgia

93.5 mhz

KADD Logandale, Nevada
KALQ-FM Alamosa, Colorado
KKTZ Lakeview, Arkansas
KBHT Crockett, Texas
KBKG Corning, Arkansas
KCVM Hudson, Iowa
KDAY Redondo Beach, California
KGGM Delhi, Louisiana
KIKT Greenville, Texas
KITN Worthington, Minnesota
KJAE Leesville, Louisiana
KKBN Twain Harte, California
KKMI Burlington, Iowa
KKOT Columbus, Nebraska
KLAN Glasgow, Montana
KLKC-FM Parsons, Kansas
KLKX(FM) Rosamond, California
KMKX Willits, California
KLXK Breckenridge, Texas
KNAC Earlimart, California
KOOK Junction, Texas
KQCS Bettendorf, Iowa
KOTE Eureka, Kansas
KOZI-FM Chelan, Washington
KPOA Lahaina, Hawaii
KORV-FM Lakeview, Oregon
KQNG-FM Lihue, Hawaii
KDEY(FM) Ontario, California
KWHW-FM Altus, Oklahoma
KMYK Osage Beach, Missouri
KRSS Tarkio, Missouri
KSCR-FM Benson, Minnesota
KLMR-FM Lamar, Colorado
KIYK Saint George, Utah
KSNX(FM) Show Low, Arizona
KWES-FM Ruidoso, New Mexico
WAIN-FM Columbia, Kentucky
WARQ Columbia, South Carolina
WAXM Big Stone Gap, Virginia
WBBC-FM Blackstone, Virginia
WBCM Boyne City, Michigan
WBGF Belle Glade, Florida
WBNV Barnesville, Ohio
WBTQ Buckhannon, West Virginia
WEEY Swanzey, New Hampshire
WCTB Fairfield, Maine
WDOG-FM Allendale, South Carolina
WLQB Ocean Isle Beach, North Carolina
WSJK(FM) Tuscola, Illinois
WHJT Clinton, Mississippi
WHMI-FM Howell, Michigan
WSNV Salem, Virginia
WLFW Chandler, Indiana
WVIX Lemont, Illinois
WKBQ Covington, Tennessee
WKHY Lafayette, Indiana
WKEY-FM Key West, Florida
WKWX Savannah, Tennessee
WMLV Butler, Alabama
WKZX-FM Lenoir City, Tennessee
WMMG-FM Brandenburg, Kentucky
WKMJ-FM Hancock, Michigan
WMPZ Harrison, Tennessee
WMWV Conway, New Hampshire
WWKL Mechanicsburg, Pennsylvania
WRQE New London, Wisconsin
WOKR Remsen, New York
WRQN Bowling Green, Ohio
WVIP New Rochelle, New York
WSBG Stroudsburg, Pennsylvania
WZCR Hudson, New York
WVBR-FM Ithaca, New York
WVOH-FM Nicholls, Georgia
WVVI-FM Christiansted, Virgin Islands
WYFQ-FM Wadesboro, North Carolina
WZBH Georgetown, Delaware
WSRM Coosa, Georgia
KDJF Ester, Alaska
KZXT Eureka, Montana
KWYX Casper, Wyoming
KWDR Royal City, Washington
WQRW Wellsville, New York
KRTS Marfa, Texas
KZTL Paxton, Nebraska
KKDT Burdett, Kansas
WFDZ Perry, Florida
KGWT George West, Texas
KORV Lakeview, Oregon
KAJP Carrizo Springs, Texas

93.7 mhz

KAFC Anchorage, Alaska
KAIR-FM Horton, Kansas
KZTQ Sun Valley, Nevada
KBRK-FM Brookings, South Dakota
KCLB-FM Coachella, California
KLGL Richfield, Utah
KDB Santa Barbara, California
KDRK-FM Spokane, Washington
KTZZ Conrad, Montana
KEYE-FM Perryton, Texas
KRKG-FM Pasco, Washington
KHBM-FM Monticello, Arkansas
KXZM Felton, California
KNOR Krum, Texas
KISR Fort Smith, Arkansas
KXKS-FM Shreveport, Louisiana
KIZZ Minot, North Dakota
KJBR Marked Tree, Arkansas
KJZY Sebastopol, California
KKRL Carroll, Iowa
KKRW Houston, Texas
KLBJ-FM Austin, Texas
KLKO Elko, Nevada
KOBB-FM Bozeman, Montana
KRDJ New Iberia, Louisiana
KRAI-FM Craig, Colorado
KRQQ Tucson, Arizona
KSD St. Louis, Missouri
KSKS Fresno, California
KSPI-FM Stillwater, Oklahoma
KTMT-FM Medford, Oregon
KTUF Kirksville, Missouri
KWYR-FM Winner, South Dakota
KQJK Roseville, California
KXTQ-FM Lubbock, Texas
KXXI Gallup, New Mexico
KXXR Minneapolis, Minnesota
KYEZ Salina, Kansas
KYTI Sheridan, Wyoming
KZBQ Pocatello, Idaho
WALI Walterboro, South Carolina
WAZR Woodstock, Virginia
WBCT Grand Rapids, Michigan
WBFM Sheboygan, Wisconsin
WBLK Depew, New York
WBUS Boalsburg, Pennsylvania
WBXE Baxter, Tennessee
WXXF(FM) Pittsburgh, Pennsylvania
WSJR Dallas, Pennsylvania
WDAY-FM Fargo, North Dakota
WDGG Ashland, Kentucky
WDJC-FM Birmingham, Alabama
WEKZ-FM Monroe, Wisconsin
WFBC-FM Greenville, South Carolina
WFCJ Miamisburg, Ohio
WFRR Walton, Indiana
WGYL Vero Beach, Florida
WCYE Three Lakes, Wisconsin
WSIM Lamar, South Carolina
WNOB Chesapeake, Virginia
WCOV-FM Clyde, New York
WPEZ Jeffersonville, Georgia
WMJY Biloxi, Mississippi
WJBC-FM Pontiac, Illinois
WOGK Ocala, Florida
WPFR-FM Clinton, Indiana
WQIO Mount Vernon, Ohio
WQLJ Oxford, Mississippi
WEEI(FM) Lawrence, Massachusetts
WDBT Geneva, Alabama
WIFY Addison, Vermont
WSTW Wilmington, Delaware
WTKB-FM Atwood, Tennessee
WTLT Sanibel, Florida
WEEI-FM Lawrence, Massachusetts
WXJY Georgetown, South Carolina
WFFI Kingston Springs, Tennessee
WZMX Hartford, Connecticut
WZNT San Juan, Puerto Rico
WYAI Scotia, New York
KXAA Cle Elum, Washington
WNTB Topsail Beach, North Carolina
KSBV Salida, Colorado
WRCL Frankenmuth, Michigan
WKAD Harrietta, Michigan
WRMO Milbridge, Maine
KAZY Cheyenne, Wyoming
KVAR Pine Ridge, South Dakota
KANY Montesano, Washington
WOTX Lunenburg, Vermont
KNTK Firth, Nebraska
KKDL Dilley, Texas
KVYL Mohave Valley, Arizona
KPIO-FM Pleasanton, Kansas
WKHF(FM) Lynchburg, Virginia

93.9 mhz

KAMJ Gosnell, Arkansas
KBNU Uvalde, Texas
KCRN-FM San Angelo, Texas
KDGS Andover, Kansas
KBBU Modesto, California
KMXH Alexandria, Louisiana
KFMF Chico, California
KGKS Scott City, Missouri
KIAI Mason City, Iowa
KIMY Watonga, Oklahoma
KINT-FM El Paso, Texas
KJMK Webb City, Missouri
KKMK Rapid City, South Dakota
KKRC Granite Falls, Minnesota
KSSZ Fayette, Missouri
KLUA Kailua Kona, Hawaii
KMGN Flagstaff, Arizona
KMXR Corpus Christi, Texas
KOYN Paris, Texas
KPDQ-FM Portland, Oregon
KRLT South Lake Tahoe, California
KZRD Dodge City, Kansas
KRTN-FM Raton, New Mexico
KSOU-FM Sioux Center, Iowa
KSPQ West Plains, Missouri
KSWN McCook, Nebraska
KTAC Ephrata, Washington
KTAK Riverton, Wyoming
KUAM-FM Hagatna, Guam
KYSL Frisco, Colorado
KEXA King City, California
WAVC Mio, Michigan
WARX Lewiston, Maine
WDNY-FM Dansville, New York
WDOR-FM Sturgeon Bay, Wisconsin
WYTK Rogersville, Alabama
WDRR Martinez, Georgia
WRWM(FM) Lawrence, Indiana
WGRM-FM Greenwood, Mississippi
WYEC Cambridge, Illinois
WJXY-FM Conway, South Carolina
WKBI-FM St. Marys, Pennsylvania
WKTG Madisonville, Kentucky
WKXZ Norwich, New York
WKYS Washington, District of Columbia
WLIT-FM Chicago, Illinois
WLVB Morrisville, Vermont
WMIA-FM Miami Beach, Florida
WMEV-FM Marion, Virginia
WMTM-FM Moultrie, Georgia
WMXR Woodstock, Vermont
WNBY-FM Newberry, Michigan
WNYC-FM New York, New York
WRSI Turners Falls, Massachusetts
WAYI(FM) Sellersville, Indiana
WQKE Plattsburgh, New York
WSCZ(FM) Saint Matthews, South Carolina
WRRR-FM St. Marys, West Virginia
WKSL Cary, North Carolina
WTGZ Union Springs, Alabama
WSIB Selmer, Tennessee
WTBX Hibbing, Minnesota
WJAI Pearl, Mississippi
WSEK Burnside, Kentucky
WMMA Nekoosa, Wisconsin
WABZ Sherman, Illinois
WCEZ Carthage, Illinois

WTWF Fairview, Pennsylvania
WBKS Columbus Grove, Ohio
KRIT Parker, Arizona
KAGZ(FM) Lufkin, Texas
WRWM(FM) Lawrence, Indiana
KXDI Belfield, North Dakota

94.1 mhz

KJAZ Point Comfort, Texas
KSLG-FM Hydesville, California
KBKY Merced, California
KMXJ-FM Amarillo, Texas
KBXL Caldwell, Idaho
KLMM Oceano, California
KTSO Glenpool, Oklahoma
KCLK-FM Clarkston, Washington
KDLK-FM Del Rio, Texas
KDNS Downs, Kansas
KFKF-FM Kansas City, Kansas
KFML Little Falls, Minnesota
KISV Bakersfield, California
KMYI San Diego, California
KKLN Atwater, Minnesota
KKPT Little Rock, Arkansas
KKXK Montrose, Colorado
KTFM Floresville, Texas
KLNO Fort Worth, Texas
KMPS-FM Seattle, Washington
KMXB Henderson, Nevada
KNCO-FM Grass Valley, California
KNEB-FM Scottsbluff, Nebraska
KODJ Salt Lake City, Utah
KOPR Butte, Montana
KPVR Bowling Green, Missouri
KPFA Berkeley, California
KQXY-FM Beaumont, Texas
KRKX Billings, Montana
KRNA Iowa City, Iowa
KRDE Globe, Arizona
KSDN-FM Aberdeen, South Dakota
KOOZ Myrtle Point, Oregon
KLTR Brenham, Texas
KXIX Sunriver, Oregon
KXKQ Safford, Arizona
KZCD Lawton, Oklahoma
KZRR Albuquerque, New Mexico
WAKU Crawfordville, Florida
WAXS Oak Hill, West Virginia
WTYS-FM Marianna, Florida
WEMX Kentwood, Louisiana
WFTN-FM Franklin, New Hampshire
WLYE-FM Glasgow, Kentucky
WGFA-FM Watseka, Illinois
WRZE Kingstree, South Carolina
WHBC-FM Canton, Ohio
WHJY Providence, Rhode Island
WIAL Eau Claire, Wisconsin
WJJO Watertown, Wisconsin
WLLD Lakeland, Florida
WLZK Paris, Tennessee
WMEZ Pensacola, Florida
WMIX-FM Mount Vernon, Illinois
WMXK Morristown, Tennessee
WNBU(FM) Oriental, North Carolina
WNYV Whitehall, New York
WKQK Germantown, Tennessee
KQCH Omaha, Nebraska
WNOD Mayaguez, Puerto Rico
WQKX Sunbury, Pennsylvania
WQZK-FM Keyser, West Virginia
WFFH Smyrna, Tennessee
WQBT Savannah, Georgia
WLLD(FM) Lakeland, Florida
WSOS-FM Fruit Cove, Florida
WSTR Smyrna, Georgia
WUPK Marquette, Michigan
WNNF Cincinnati, Ohio
WWLV(FM) Lexington, North Carolina
WWKR Hart, Michigan
WVSP-FM Yorktown, Virginia
WVIC Jackson, Michigan
WHRP Gurley, Alabama
WBNI-FM Roanoke, Indiana
WZBQ Carrollton, Alabama
WZNE Brighton, New York
KWDI Idalia, Colorado
WOTT Calcium, New York
KRLQ Hodge, Louisiana
KEZZ Phippsburg, Colorado
KXLP Eagle Lake, Minnesota
KZOC Bourbon, Missouri

94.3 mhz

KAMO-FM Rogers, Arkansas
KATI California, Missouri
KBTS Big Spring, Texas
KBUA San Fernando, California
KBUX Quartzsite, Arizona
KCRE-FM Crescent City, California
KCVW Kingman, Kansas
KDEM Deming, New Mexico
KDLX Makawao, Hawaii
KDOM-FM Windom, Minnesota
KDUC Barstow, California
KFST-FM Fort Stockton, Texas
KHER Crystal City, Texas
KEBN Garden Grove, California
KILO Colorado Springs, Colorado
KKIN-FM Aitkin, Minnesota
KOKO-FM Kerman, California
KULO Alexandria, Minnesota
KTTA(FM) Jackson, California
KDDL Chino Valley, Arizona
KBYI Rexburg, Idaho
KRVL Kerrville, Texas
KSEY-FM Seymour, Texas
KXOO Elk City, Oklahoma
KXRQ Roosevelt, Utah
KYEE Alamogordo, New Mexico
KYOX Comanche, Texas
KYXX Ozona, Texas
KZZR Government Camp, Oregon
WBAD Leland, Mississippi
WVRH Norlina, North Carolina
WKXP Kingston, New York
WBXQ Patton, Pennsylvania
WBTN-FM Bennington, Vermont
WFCX Leland, Michigan
WQCM Greencastle, Pennsylvania
WCMG Latta, South Carolina
WTRW(FM) Carbondale, Pennsylvania
WCYY Biddeford, Maine
WIBG-FM Avalon, New Jersey
WEGI-FM Oak Grove, Kentucky
WMRN-FM Marion, Ohio
WKYX-FM Golconda, Illinois
WINX-FM St. Michaels, Maryland
WKKJ Chillicothe, Ohio
WPMJ Chillicothe, Illinois
WGMX Marathon, Florida
WRHD Farmville, North Carolina
WIFX-FM Jenkins, Kentucky
WIZB Abbeville, Alabama
WJJM-FM Lewisburg, Tennessee
WJKL Glendale Heights, Illinois
WJLK Asbury Park, New Jersey
WJTT Red Bank, Tennessee
WKKI Celina, Ohio
WKZW Sandersville, Mississippi
WTJJ Dyer, Tennessee
WLVY Elmira, New York
WUZZ Saegertown, Pennsylvania
WIGX Smithtown, New York
WMKR Pana, Illinois
WNFB Lake City, Florida
WNFZ Powell, Tennessee
WWXX Warrenton, Virginia
WQPC Prairie Du Chien, Wisconsin
WQZX Greenville, Alabama
WIFE-FM Rushville, Indiana
WREB Greencastle, Indiana
WRLF Fairmont, West Virginia
WRMS-FM Beardstown, Illinois
WYDR Neenah-Menasha, Wisconsin
WSCC-FM Goose Creek, South Carolina
WSSQ Sterling, Illinois
WTIX-FM Galliano, Louisiana
WTON-FM Staunton, Virginia
WULF Hardinsburg, Kentucky
WZZR Riviera Beach, Florida
WXRZ Corinth, Mississippi
WYBC-FM New Haven, Connecticut
WZKB Wallace, North Carolina
WGZZ Waverly, Alabama
WZNL Norway, Michigan
WZOC Plymouth, Indiana
KMAX-FM Wellington, Colorado
WWNQ Forest Acres, South Carolina
WZAI Brewster, Massachusetts
WTHP Gibson, Georgia
WTRW Carbondale, Pennsylvania
KCMC-FM Viola, Arkansas
WLEL Ellaville, Georgia
KWDD(FM) Fairbanks, Alaska
KGRB(FM) Jackson, California

94.5 mhz

KATS Yakima, Washington
KBAY Gilroy, California
KBCT Waco, Texas
KLIQ Hastings, Nebraska
KEMA Three Rivers, Texas
KCFS Sioux Falls, South Dakota
KCNO Alturas, California
KSOC Gainesville, Texas
KEMX Locust Grove, Oklahoma
KFMX-FM Lubbock, Texas
KFRQ Harlingen, Texas
KGEN-FM Hanford, California
KHTQ Hayden, Idaho
KUUB Sun Valley, Nevada
KJDY-FM Canyon City, Oregon
KJIW-FM Helena, Arkansas
KKEZ Fort Dodge, Iowa
KKLR-FM Poplar Bluff, Missouri
KYAT Gallup, New Mexico
KTBZ-FM Houston, Texas
KMGE Eugene, Oregon
KMLD Casper, Wyoming
KMON-FM Great Falls, Montana
KFPW-FM Barling, Arkansas
KOOL-FM Phoenix, Arizona
KPLO-FM Reliance, South Dakota
KQDY Bismarck, North Dakota
KRUF Shreveport, Louisiana
KRXL Kirksville, Missouri
KRXY Shelton, Washington
KSKL Scott City, Kansas
KSMB Lafayette, Louisiana
KSPE-FM Ellwood, California
KSTP-FM St. Paul, Minnesota
KTUN New Castle, Colorado
KLYK Kelso, Washington
KVFX Logan, Utah
KWNE Ukiah, California
KSEH Brawley, California
KWTY Cartago, California
WKXS-FM Leland, North Carolina
WYKV Ravena, New York
WARO Naples, Florida
WVTS-FM Dunbar, West Virginia
WTMB Tomah, Wisconsin
WBYZ Baxley, Georgia
WCEN-FM Hemlock, Michigan
WCFB Daytona Beach, Florida
WDAC Lancaster, Pennsylvania
WELY-FM Ely, Minnesota
WERB Berlin, Connecticut
WBHV-FM State College, Pennsylvania
WHPY-FM Lobelville, Tennessee
WHOD Jackson, Alabama
WIBW-FM Topeka, Kansas
WDVT Rutland, Vermont
WJMN Boston, Massachusetts
WJZD-FM Long Beach, Mississippi
WTNR Holland, Michigan
WKSQ Ellsworth, Maine
WLWK-FM Milwaukee, Wisconsin
WLJZ Mackinaw City, Michigan
WLQT Englewood, Ohio
WLRW Champaign, Illinois
WMUU-FM Greenville, South Carolina
WMXL Lexington, Kentucky
WNED-FM Buffalo, New York
WPST Trenton, New Jersey
WFLF-FM Parker, Florida
WRJO Eagle River, Wisconsin
WYEZ Murrells Inlet, South Carolina
WRVQ Richmond, Virginia
WRZR Loogootee, Indiana
WSPX Bowman, South Carolina
WCMS-FM Hatteras, North Carolina
WWSW-FM Pittsburgh, Pennsylvania
WXKR Port Clinton, Ohio
WPTI Eden, North Carolina
WJOX-FM Birmingham, Alabama
WYYY Syracuse, New York
KMYT Temecula, California
KZBI Elko, Nevada
KXLI Moapa, Nevada
WFDR-FM Woodbury, Georgia
KRPW(FM) Coarsegold, California
KRFD(FM) Merino, Colorado
WJJZ Irasberg, Vermont

94.7 mhz

KZND-FM Houston, Alaska
KYAF Firebaugh, California
KAMX Luling, Texas
KYSE El Paso, Texas
KBSO Corpus Christi, Texas
KEWB Anderson, California
KSKU Sterling, Kansas
KGRW Friona, Texas
KIXY-FM San Angelo, Texas
KFVR-FM Beulah, Colorado
KLOB Thousand Palms, California
KMCH Manchester, Iowa
KNEN Norfolk, Nebraska
KZGF Grand Forks, North Dakota
KNRK Camas, Washington
KNSG Springfield, Minnesota
KBRU Oklahoma City, Oklahoma
KRKS-FM Lafayette, Colorado
KRRM Rogue River, Oregon
KCLH Caledonia, Minnesota
KSHE Crestwood, Missouri
KSKK Staples, Minnesota
KSSJ(FM) Fair Oaks, California
KTTS-FM Springfield, Missouri
KTWV Los Angeles, California
KUMU-FM Honolulu, Hawaii
KVLL-FM Wells, Texas
KWKQ Graham, Texas
KWXX-FM Hilo, Hawaii
KMCN Clinton, Iowa
KKIM-FM Santa Fe, New Mexico
KFLG-FM Big River, California
WAAW Williston, South Carolina
WIAD Bethesda, Maryland
WSYR-FM Gifford, Florida
WBAR-FM Lake Luzerne, New York
WBIO Philpot, Kentucky
WBRX Cresson, Pennsylvania
WODA Bayamon, Puerto Rico
WCSX Birmingham, Michigan
WCVM Bronson, Michigan
WDEC-FM Americus, Georgia
WELK Elkins, West Virginia
WFBQ Indianapolis, Indiana
WXBB Erie, Pennsylvania
WFME Newark, New Jersey
WZOR Mishicot, Wisconsin
WGSQ Cookeville, Tennessee
WWBD Sumter, South Carolina
WQQR Clinton, Kentucky
WIYN Deposit, New York
WKLW-FM Paintsville, Kentucky
WFIA-FM New Albany, Indiana
WMAS-FM Enfield, Connecticut
WMHI Cape Vincent, New York
WOZZ Mosinee, Wisconsin
WOJG Bolivar, Tennessee
WMTT Tioga, Pennsylvania
WQDR-FM Raleigh, North Carolina
WDSD Dover, Delaware
WSNY Columbus, Ohio
WTBF-FM Brundidge, Alabama
WJLV Jackson, Mississippi
WLS-FM Chicago, Illinois
WYLK Lacombe, Louisiana
WYUL Chateaugay, New York
KZAL Manson, Washington
KTXO Goldsmith, Texas
KCNB Chadron, Nebraska
WBCQ-FM Monticello, Maine

94.9 mhz

KBIM-FM Roswell, New Mexico
KBOS-FM Tulare, California
KCIN Cedar City, Utah
KBZT San Diego, California
KCMO-FM Shawnee, Kansas
KCPI Albert Lea, Minnesota
KHKN Maumelle, Arkansas
KRVB Nampa, Idaho
KGGO Des Moines, Iowa
KIOK Richland, Washington
KJLT-FM North Platte, Nebraska
KMXK Cold Spring, Minnesota
KMXZ-FM Tucson, Arizona
KOLI Electra, Texas
KTEE North Bend, Oregon
KPYG Cayucos, California

KQUR Laredo, Texas
KPKY Pocatello, Idaho
KLRJ Aberdeen, South Dakota
KQDS-FM Duluth, Minnesota
KSBH Coushatta, Louisiana
KUOW-FM Seattle, Washington
KLTY Arlington, Texas
KWYK-FM Aztec, New Mexico
KYLD San Francisco, California
KYSS-FM Missoula, Montana
KHTB Provo, Utah
KZWY Sheridan, Wyoming
WAAG Galesburg, Illinois
WPRF Reserve, Louisiana
WOGG Oliver, Pennsylvania
WSJM-FM Benton Harbor, Michigan
WDKB Dekalb, Illinois
WHKN Millen, Georgia
WHKS Port Allegany, Pennsylvania
WHOM Mount Washington, New Hampshire
WAEZ Greeneville, Tennessee
WKJZ Hillman, Michigan
WKLL Frankfort, New York
WKOR-FM Columbus, Mississippi
WKSJ-FM Mobile, Alabama
WKZC Scottville, Michigan
WMMQ East Lansing, Michigan
WMSR-FM Collinwood, Tennessee
WOLX-FM Baraboo, Wisconsin
WONB Ada, Ohio
WUBL Atlanta, Georgia
WPTE Virginia Beach, Virginia
WSLC-FM Roanoke, Virginia
WQMX Medina, Ohio
WRBT Harrisburg, Pennsylvania
WRHK Danville, Illinois
WRSD Folsom, Pennsylvania
WSYY-FM Millinocket, Maine
WTNT-FM Tallahassee, Florida
WYNG Mount Carmel, Illinois
WVCO Loris, South Carolina
WWRM Tampa, Florida
WKVF Bartlett, Tennessee
WEKV South Webster, Ohio
WMGE Miami Beach, Florida
KLCH Lake City, Minnesota
KHRQ Baker, California
KTZU Velva, North Dakota
KXTT Maricopa, California
WUPZ Chocolay Township, Michigan
KIND-FM Elk City, Kansas

95.1 mhz

KAMS Mammoth Spring, Arkansas
KAOI-FM Wailuku, Hawaii
KABW Baird / Abilene, Texas
KBBY-FM Ventura, California
KCGY Laramie, Wyoming
KCZE New Hampton, Iowa
KEWL-FM New Boston, Texas
KBVB Barnesville, Minnesota
KVIB Sun City West, Arizona
KFRG San Bernardino, California
KHOP Oakdale, California
KICT-FM Wichita, Kansas
KITI-FM Winlock, Washington
KKNN Delta, Colorado
KLER-FM Orofino, Idaho
KMAQ-FM Maquoketa, Iowa
KMMS-FM Bozeman, Montana
KMXI Chico, California
KMXL Carthage, Missouri
KNUW Santa Clara, New Mexico
KQCV-FM Shawnee, Oklahoma
KQRX Midland, Texas
KATC-FM Colorado Springs, Colorado
KRKR Waverly, Nebraska
KGSX Comfort, Texas
KSND Monmouth, Oregon
KSQY Deadwood, South Dakota
KLQT Corrales, New Mexico
KTHC Sidney, Montana
KTKS Versailles, Missouri
KNDE College Station, Texas
KTTI Yuma, Arizona
KVIC Victoria, Texas
KUSQ-FM Worthington, Minnesota
KXEI Havre, Montana
KYCS Rock Springs, Wyoming
KYKR Beaumont, Texas
WAJI Fort Wayne, Indiana
WAPE-FM Jacksonville, Florida
WAYV Atlantic City, New Jersey
WFKS(FM) Melbourne, Florida
WCDZ Dresden, Tennessee
WGAC-FM Harlem, Georgia
WEGM San German, Puerto Rico
WDZQ Decatur, Illinois
WFBE Flint, Michigan
WFLE-FM Flemingsburg, Kentucky
WFKS Melbourne, Florida
WGGC Bowling Green, Kentucky
WWGY Grove City, Pennsylvania
WIIL Union Grove, Wisconsin
WIKZ Chambersburg, Pennsylvania
WVTQ Sunderland, Vermont
WJKC Christiansted, Virgin Islands
WLST Marinette, Wisconsin
WRTT-FM Huntsville, Alabama
WNKS Charlotte, North Carolina
WXRB Dudley, Massachusetts
WQBW Honeoye Falls, New York
WONA-FM Winona, Mississippi
WQMZ Charlottesville, Virginia
WQNZ Natchez, Mississippi
WQRB Bloomer, Wisconsin
WRBS-FM Baltimore, Maryland
WRKI Brookfield, Connecticut
WRNS-FM Kinston, North Carolina
WSSX-FM Charleston, South Carolina
WVLI Kankakee, Illinois
WVNI Nashville, Indiana
WVUR-FM Valparaiso, Indiana
WVXG Mount Gilead, Ohio
WXFX Prattville, Alabama
WXIL Elizabeth, West Virginia
WUEZ Carterville, Illinois
WXTK West Yarmouth, Massachusetts
WKZB Marion, Mississippi
WZZO Bethlehem, Pennsylvania
WZZT Morrison, Illinois
WMGB Montezuma, Georgia
KNYE Pahrump, Nevada
WBPC Ebro, Florida
WACF Young Harris, Georgia
KMDR McKinleyville, California
KUSQ Worthington, Minnesota
WUPN Paradise, Michigan
KRGX Rio Grande City, Texas

95.3 mhz

KAGE-FM Winona, Minnesota
KBBN-FM Broken Bow, Nebraska
KBHH Kerman, California
KCSI Villisca, Iowa
KCXY East Camden, Arkansas
KDJS-FM Willmar, Minnesota
KDKD-FM Clinton, Missouri
KCDQ Douglas, Arizona
KECH-FM Sun Valley, Idaho
KERX Paris, Arkansas
KFRO-FM Gilmer, Texas
KXXK Hoquiam, Washington
KHCA Wamego, Kansas
KHYI Howe, Texas
KIFG-FM Iowa Falls, Iowa
KINZ Humboldt, Kansas
KKBC-FM Baker, Oregon
KLCR Lakeview, Oregon
KLLY Oildale, California
KLXS-FM Pierre, South Dakota
KMGZ Lawton, Oklahoma
KDDD-FM Dumas, Texas
KNEL-FM Brady, Texas
KNOF St. Paul, Minnesota
KUJZ Creswell, Oregon
KOKX-FM Keokuk, Iowa
KOZT Fort Bragg, California
KPBM McCamey, Texas
KPND Sandpoint, Idaho
KQKI-FM Bayou Vista, Louisiana
KQMG-FM Independence, Iowa
KRJC Elko, Nevada
KRTY Los Gatos, California
KYDN Monte Vista, Colorado
KUIC Vacaville, California
KURY-FM Brookings, Oregon
KVWG-FM Dilley, Texas
KXTZ Pismo Beach, California
KZJH Jackson, Wyoming
KZSP South Padre Island, Texas
WADI Corinth, Mississippi
WPLZ Ooltewah, Tennessee
WALZ-FM Machias, Maine
WTRC-FM Niles, Michigan
WBKT Norwich, New York
WBCK-FM Battle Creek, Michigan
WCFX Clare, Michigan
WDNH-FM Honesdale, Pennsylvania
WFFN Coaling, Alabama
WFMV South Congaree, South Carolina
WZRV Front Royal, Virginia
WLFK Gouverneur, New York
WGMO Spooner, Wisconsin
WGUR Milledgeville, Georgia
WGVS-FM Whitehall, Michigan
WHFM Southampton, New York
WHLF South Boston, Virginia
WHRB Cambridge, Massachusetts
WIKI Carrollton, Kentucky
WBLJ-FM Shamokin, Pennsylvania
WKDB Laurel, Delaware
WJPA-FM Washington, Pennsylvania
WVKV Nashville, Georgia
WKHK Colonial Heights, Virginia
WKLM Millersburg, Ohio
WRTB Winnebago, Illinois
WKTN Kenton, Ohio
WBPE Brookston, Indiana
WLKR-FM Norwalk, Ohio
WZNF Lumberton, Mississippi
WKVN Morganfield, Kentucky
WNDI-FM Sullivan, Indiana
WOBR-FM Wanchese, North Carolina
WOLZ Fort Myers, Florida
WPYO Maitland, Florida
WQTE Adrian, Michigan
WRKX Ottawa, Illinois
WRLB Rainelle, West Virginia
WRLD Valley, Alabama
WPVQ Greenfield, Massachusetts
WRXX Centralia, Illinois
WTBG Brownsville, Tennessee
WTTC-FM Towanda, Pennsylvania
WSKX York Center, Maine
WUME-FM Paoli, Indiana
WVIM-FM Coldwater, Mississippi
WVRB Wilmore, Kentucky
WXLF Hartford, Vermont
WWWA Winslow, Maine
WXBX Rural Retreat, Virginia
WXCV Homosassa Springs, Florida
WXRO Beaver Dam, Wisconsin
WXXZ Grand Marais, Minnesota
WYFC Clinton, Tennessee
WZLR Xenia, Ohio
WJEK(FM) Rantoul, Illinois
WZWW Bellefonte, Pennsylvania
KXMO-FM Owensville, Missouri
KRPX Wellington, Utah
KVHU Judsonia, Arkansas
KOME-FM Meridian, Texas
KECK Eckley, Colorado
WWSS Tuscarora Township, Michigan

95.5 mhz

KAAN-FM Bethany, Missouri
KAFX-FM Diboll, Texas
KAIM-FM Honolulu, Hawaii
KBEK Mora, Minnesota
KKHK Carmel, California
KRDS-FM New Prague, Minnesota
KGLI Sioux City, Iowa
KJCY St. Ansgar, Iowa
KJEZ Poplar Bluff, Missouri
KJKB Scotland, Texas
KKMJ-FM Austin, Texas
KKZY Bemidji, Minnesota
KLAQ El Paso, Texas
KLOS Los Angeles, California
KMBR Butte, Montana
KHFM Santa Fe, New Mexico
KNDY-FM Marysville, Kansas
KNEV Reno, Nevada
KAHE Dodge City, Kansas
KPHT Rocky Ford, Colorado
KWEY-FM Clinton, Oklahoma
KVOB Lindsborg, Kansas
KRRQ Lafayette, Louisiana
KSDZ Gordon, Nebraska
KSTO Agana, Guam
KTOZ-FM Pleasant Hope, Missouri
KWEN Tulsa, Oklahoma
KWNR Henderson, Nevada
KWYY Midwest, Wyoming
KYNU Jamestown, North Dakota
KYFO-FM Ogden, Utah
KYOT-FM Phoenix, Arizona
KZAT-FM Belle Plaine, Iowa
KZFM Corpus Christi, Texas
KMVN Palmer, Alaska
WHMA-FM Hobson City, Alabama
WBRU Providence, Rhode Island
WFHM-FM Cleveland, Ohio
WFIZ Odessa, New York
WFMH-FM Hackleburg, Alabama
WFMS Fishers, Indiana
WFUN-FM Bethalto, Illinois
WGLO Pekin, Illinois
WHOK-FM Lancaster, Ohio
WHPE-FM High Point, North Carolina
WIBZ Wedgefield, South Carolina
WIFC Wausau, Wisconsin
WIXV Savannah, Georgia
WJDB-FM Thomasville, Alabama
WJZJ Glen Arbor, Michigan
WKQI Detroit, Michigan
WPWZ Pinetops, North Carolina
WHLH Jackson, Mississippi
WFGI-FM Johnstown, Pennsylvania
WLDI Juno Beach, Florida
WBYL Salladasburg, Pennsylvania
WNDD Silver Springs, Florida
WSSB(FM) Doraville, Georgia
WNUA Chicago, Illinois
WOXD Oxford, Mississippi
WPGC-FM Morningside, Maryland
WPLJ New York, New York
WQHY Prestonsburg, Kentucky
WSM-FM Nashville, Tennessee
WTVY-FM Dothan, Alabama
WPPI Topsham, Maine
WXXX South Burlington, Vermont
WYJB Albany, New York
WBOP Buffalo Gap, Virginia
KRVG Glenwood Springs, Colorado
KAIQ Wolfforth, Texas
KHAL Cedarville, California
KFMR Ballard, Utah
KRKQ Mountain Village, Colorado
KITX Hugo, Oklahoma
KNLT(FM) Palmer, Alaska

95.7 mhz

KALF Red Bluff, California
KARX Claude, Texas
KLEY-FM Jourdanton, Texas
KBOY-FM Medford, Oregon
KBST-FM Big Spring, Texas
KCGM Scobey, Montana
KCHZ Ottawa, Kansas
KBGO Waco, Texas
KDAL-FM Duluth, Minnesota
KEZJ-FM Twin Falls, Idaho
KPTT Denver, Colorado
KLTW-FM Prineville, Oregon
KKHH Houston, Texas
KJFX Fresno, California
KJR-FM Seattle, Washington
KKAJ-FM Davis, Oklahoma
KKOK-FM Morris, Minnesota
KXLS Lahoma, Oklahoma
KUSS(FM) Carlsbad, California
KNDK-FM Langdon, North Dakota
KKSR Walla Walla, Washington
KPAT Orcutt, California
KPCL Farmington, New Mexico
KPER Hobbs, New Mexico
KQWC-FM Webster City, Iowa
KROA Grand Island, Nebraska
KSQB-FM Dell Rapids, South Dakota
KSSN Little Rock, Arkansas
KLKL Minden, Louisiana
KWKM St. Johns, Arizona
KWWR Mexico, Missouri
KGMZ(FM) San Francisco, California
WAFM Amory, Mississippi
WAQX-FM Manlius, New York
WATG Trion, Georgia
WAYB-FM Graysville, Tennessee
WBHJ Midfield, Alabama
WCCK Calvert City, Kentucky
WHIO-FM Pleasant Hill, Ohio
WCMB-FM Oscoda, Michigan

WCRC Effingham, Illinois
WVKF Shadyside, Ohio
WFID Rio Piedras, Puerto Rico
WFKX Henderson, Tennessee
WFLO-FM Farmville, Virginia
WSHP Attica, Indiana
WKFP(FM) Navarre, Florida
WHOG-FM Ormond-By-The-Sea, Florida
WHWL Marquette, Michigan
WIMX Gibsonburg, Ohio
WJDK-FM Seneca, Illinois
WKML Lumberton, North Carolina
WKSS Hartford-Meriden, Connecticut
WKXN Fort Deposit, Alabama
WIOL-FM Waverly Hall, Georgia
WLHT-FM Grand Rapids, Michigan
WAOR(FM) Nappanee, Indiana
WMRF-FM Lewistown, Pennsylvania
WHAL-FM Horn Lake, Mississippi
WPIG Olean, New York
WQMF Jeffersonville, Indiana
WQPW Valdosta, Georgia
WDMO Baldwin, Wisconsin
WRQT La Crosse, Wisconsin
WSEY Oregon, Illinois
WDOT Danville, Vermont
WBTP Clearwater, Florida
WTGY Charleston, Mississippi
WKBU New Orleans, Louisiana
WQJK Maryville, Tennessee
WVKL Norfolk, Virginia
WWMJ Ellsworth, Maine
WBHD Olyphant, Pennsylvania
WXDJ North Miami Beach, Florida
WXRC Hickory, North Carolina
WBEN-FM Philadelphia, Pennsylvania
WZID Manchester, New Hampshire
WRIT-FM Milwaukee, Wisconsin
KSWI Atlantic, Iowa
KSEC Bentonville, Arkansas
KOTY Mason, Texas
KROK South Fort Polk, Louisiana
KMKO-FM Lake Crystal, Minnesota
KLTQ New England, North Dakota
WSWW-FM Craigsville, West Virginia

95.9 mhz

KSOK-FM Winfield, Kansas
WWWI-FM Pillager, Minnesota
KBYN Arnold, California
KRSL-FM Russell, Kansas
KCHA-FM Charles City, Iowa
KCKL Malakoff, Texas
KCOB-FM Newton, Iowa
KZML Quincy, Washington
KHMC Goliad, Texas
KIDN-FM Burns, Colorado
KKFD-FM Fairfield, Iowa
KILR-FM Estherville, Iowa
KKBL Monett, Missouri
KWHF Harrisburg, Arkansas
KHNK Columbia Falls, Montana
KLCM Lewistown, Montana
KMAR-FM Winnsboro, Louisiana
KZCU Woodward, Oklahoma
KKBD Sallisaw, Oklahoma
KNLF Quincy, California
KSKD Livingston, California
KOCP Camarillo, California
KPVS Hilo, Hawaii
KPWW Hooks, Texas
KQCL Faribault, Minnesota
KSSR-FM Santa Rosa, New Mexico
KSCH Sulphur Springs, Texas
KSRF Poipu, Hawaii
KRSH Healdsburg, California
KTIL-FM Bay City, Oregon
KTRI-FM Mansfield, Missouri
KUUZ Lake Village, Arkansas
KXLR Fairbanks, Alaska
KFSH-FM La Mirada, California
KXXZ Barstow, California
KYBE Frederick, Oklahoma
KYLS-FM Ironton, Missouri
KFWR Jacksboro, Texas
KMGR Delta, Utah
KKLD Cottonwood, Arizona
KZHK St. George, Utah
KZZI Belle Fourche, South Dakota
WATD-FM Marshfield, Massachusetts
WBBN Taylorsville, Mississippi

WSJZ-FM Sebastian, Florida
WBKY Portage, Wisconsin
WCNA Potts Camp, Mississippi
WCQL Queensbury, New York
WCRI-FM Block Island, Rhode Island
WCVP-FM Robbinsville, North Carolina
WDQN-FM Duquoin, Illinois
WEFM Michigan City, Indiana
WFOX Norwalk, Connecticut
WFTM-FM Maysville, Kentucky
WGGI Benton, Pennsylvania
WGKY Wickliffe, Kentucky
WGRQ Fairview Beach, Virginia
WEZC Clinton, Illinois
WJKW Athens, Ohio
WKID Vevay, Indiana
WERV-FM Aurora, Illinois
WKQX Watseka, Illinois
WKSZ De Pere, Wisconsin
WKUZ Wabash, Indiana
WLKM-FM Three Rivers, Michigan
WLKX-FM Forest Lake, Minnesota
WMQA-FM Minocqua, Wisconsin
WMXZ Isle of Palms, South Carolina
WNPQ New Philadelphia, Ohio
WOLG Carlinville, Illinois
WKZP Bethany Beach, Delaware
WPNC-FM Plymouth, North Carolina
WFDM-FM Franklin, Indiana
WQZY Dublin, Georgia
WRAT Point Pleasant, New Jersey
WRBA Springfield, Florida
WPEI Saco, Maine
WRJB Camden, Tennessee
WRZK Colonial Heights, Tennessee
WSTG Princeton, West Virginia
WDKL Grafton, West Virginia
WQSI Tuskegee, Alabama
WXXR(FM) Seelyville, Indiana
WAKZ Sharpsville, Pennsylvania
WTWX-FM Guntersville, Alabama
WBEC-FM Pittsfield, Massachusetts
WLQK Livingston, Tennessee
WVOS-FM Liberty, New York
WWIN-FM Glen Burnie, Maryland
WICL Williamsport, Maryland
WYNT Caledonia, Ohio
KLZX Weston, Idaho
KZLG Mansura, Louisiana
WNLF Macomb, Illinois
KIXT(FM) Bay City, Oregon
KKIT Taos, New Mexico
KWHK Hutchinson, Kansas
KAJR Indian Wells, California
WZDB Sykesville, Pennsylvania
KJCD Fort Benton, Montana
KMAP Fleming, Colorado
KUKY Wellton, Arizona
KMZT-FM Big Sur, California

96.1 mhz

KAGG Madisonville, Texas
KORQ Winters / Abilene, Texas
KKXS Shingletown, California
KMRX El Dorado, Arkansas
KCWD Harrison, Arkansas
KISO Omaha, Nebraska
KZRC Bennington, Oklahoma
KSME Greeley, Colorado
KGPZ Coleraine, Minnesota
KIOX-FM Edna, Texas
KICX-FM McCook, Nebraska
KID-FM Idaho Falls, Idaho
KINI Crookston, Nebraska
KITO-FM Vinita, Oklahoma
KBTQ Harlingen, Texas
KIXX Watertown, South Dakota
KKLX Worland, Wyoming
KKTX-FM Kilgore, Texas
KLPX Tucson, Arizona
KLRQ Clinton, Missouri
KNWM Madrid, Iowa
KMRK-FM Odessa, Texas
KMXG Clinton, Iowa
KIXZ-FM Opportunity, Washington
KNOM-FM Nome, Alaska
KIBT Fountain, Colorado
KQHT Crookston, Minnesota
KQPR Albert Lea, Minnesota
KRVE Brusly, Louisiana
KANS Emporia, Kansas

KSLK Visalia, California
KSLY-FM San Luis Obispo, California
KSQQ Morgan Hill, California
KSRV-FM Ontario, Oregon
KCTX-FM Childress, Texas
KSTR-FM Montrose, Colorado
KWRK Window Rock, Arizona
KRQB San Jacinto, California
KXXM San Antonio, Texas
KXXO Olympia, Washington
KXXY-FM Oklahoma City, Oklahoma
KZRM Chama, New Mexico
KYKZ Lake Charles, Louisiana
KYMX Sacramento, California
KYYZ Williston, North Dakota
KZEL-FM Eugene, Oregon
WAEL-FM Maricao, Puerto Rico
WKZQ-FM Forestbrook, South Carolina
WVLF Norwood, New York
WBBB Raleigh, North Carolina
WCTO Easton, Pennsylvania
WDEV-FM Warren, Vermont
WEJZ Jacksonville, Florida
WHBX Tallahassee, Florida
WHNN Bay City, Michigan
WIVI Charlotte Amalie, Virgin Islands
WJMC-FM Rice Lake, Wisconsin
WJYE Buffalo, New York
WKFM Huron, Ohio
WWPW(FM) Atlanta, Georgia
WKWS Charleston, West Virginia
WLXO Stamping Ground, Kentucky
WLKG Lake Geneva, Wisconsin
WJDV Broadway, Virginia
WJVC Center Moriches, New York
WLZA Eupora, Mississippi
WTMP-FM Dade City, Florida
WIVG Tunica, Mississippi
WMTR-FM Archbold, Ohio
WODZ-FM Rome, New York
WKST-FM Pittsburgh, Pennsylvania
WQHR Presque Isle, Maine
WQKS-FM Montgomery, Alabama
WQLK Richmond, Indiana
WQQB Rantoul, Illinois
WRKH Mobile, Alabama
WROX-FM Exmore, Virginia
WRXK-FM Bonita Springs, Florida
WSOX Red Lion, Pennsylvania
WSRS Worcester, Massachusetts
WSTO Owensboro, Kentucky
WTCX Ripon, Wisconsin
WPKF Poughkeepsie, New York
WTTH Margate City, New Jersey
WXYM Tomah, Wisconsin
WMAX-FM Holland, Michigan
WHQC Shelby, North Carolina
WXFL Florence, Alabama
WKKQ Barbourville, Kentucky
WPHD South Waverly, Pennsylvania
KLKY Stanfield, Oregon
KCEL Mojave, California
KALN Dexter, New Mexico

96.3 mhz

KTWN-FM Edina, Minnesota
KERP Ingalls, Kansas
KBAZ Hamilton, Montana
KRZN Billings, Montana
KFMI Eureka, California
KXOL-FM Los Angeles, California
KHEY-FM El Paso, Texas
KBZU Albuquerque, New Mexico
KHLS Blytheville, Arkansas
KIHT St. Louis, Missouri
KXCM Joshua Tree, California
KKLZ Las Vegas, Nevada
KLLL-FM Lubbock, Texas
KRCW Royal City, Washington
KRNQ Keokuk, Iowa
KRTR-FM Kailua, Hawaii
KZCH Derby, Kansas
KSCS Fort Worth, Texas
KSWG Wickenburg, Arizona
KTDR Del Rio, Texas
KTTG Mena, Arkansas
KUBB Mariposa, California
KWLZ-FM West Linn, Oregon
KXIT-FM Dalhart, Texas
KXRK Provo, Utah
KZDY Cawker City, Kansas

WAJZ Voorheesville, New York
WBBM-FM Chicago, Illinois
WNHT Churubusco, Indiana
WHHH Indianapolis, Indiana
WHUR-FM Washington, District of Columbia
WIVY Morehead, Kentucky
WJAA Austin, Indiana
WJBZ-FM Seymour, Tennessee
WJIZ-FM Albany, Georgia
WJSA-FM Jersey Shore, Pennsylvania
WKQW-FM Oil City, Pennsylvania
WUSJ Madison, Mississippi
WJJB-FM Gray, Maine
WLVQ Columbus, Ohio
WLXT Petoskey, Michigan
WMAD Cross Plains, Wisconsin
WLCN Atlanta, Illinois
WOTR(FM) Lost Creek, West Virginia
WDVD Detroit, Michigan
WXNY-FM New York, New York
WRHT Morehead City, North Carolina
WCJK Murfreesboro, Tennessee
WROV-FM Martinsville, Virginia
WXKY-FM Stanford, Kentucky
WKSP Aiken, South Carolina
WEII Dennis, Massachusetts
WSFQ Peshtigo, Wisconsin
WXOF Yankeetown, Florida
KXLW Houston, Alaska
KAJZ Llano, Texas
WFYX Walpole, New Hampshire
KZXL Hudson, Texas
KACZ Riley, Kansas
KGGB Yorktown, Texas
KXXN Iowa Park, Texas
KQWY Lusk, Wyoming
KICL(FM) Pleasantville, Iowa
WXWX Marietta, Mississippi

96.5 mhz

KBDN Bandon, Oregon
KBKZ Raton, New Mexico
KBYZ Bismarck, North Dakota
KNRX Sterling City, Texas
KCYS Seaside, Oregon
KDZN Glendive, Montana
KECO Elk City, Oklahoma
KFLS-FM Tulelake, California
KPEL-FM Breaux Bridge, Louisiana
KHMX Houston, Texas
KPSL-FM Bakersfield, California
KJJK-FM Fergus Falls, Minnesota
KKIS-FM Soldotna, Alaska
KLCA Tahoe City, California
KHTE-FM England, Arkansas
KLGT Buffalo, Wyoming
KLIX-FM Twin Falls, Idaho
KLMA Hobbs, New Mexico
KLTG Corpus Christi, Texas
KSPW Sparta, Missouri
KNWC-FM Sioux Falls, South Dakota
KOIT San Francisco, California
KOZE-FM Lewiston, Idaho
KQSW Rock Springs, Wyoming
KRAV-FM Tulsa, Oklahoma
KRFM Show Low, Arizona
KRGI-FM Grand Island, Nebraska
KSOM Audubon, Iowa
KVKI-FM Shreveport, Louisiana
KWWK Rochester, Minnesota
KXPK Evergreen, Colorado
KRBZ Kansas City, Missouri
KJAQ Seattle, Washington
KYXY San Diego, California
WAZY-FM Lafayette, Indiana
WBFG Parker's Crossroads, Tennessee
WCMF-FM Rochester, New York
WBKX Fredonia, New York
WDOD-FM Chattanooga, Tennessee
WRXD Fajardo, Puerto Rico
WKZO-FM Portage, Michigan
WFLB Laurinburg, North Carolina
WGZB-FM Lanesville, Indiana
WHTQ(FM) Orlando, Florida
WJCL-FM Savannah, Georgia
WZPN Farmington, Illinois
WAKS Akron, Ohio
WKDJ-FM Clarksdale, Mississippi
WKIB Anna, Illinois
WKLH Milwaukee, Wisconsin
WKLK-FM Cloquet, Minnesota

WKLR Fort Lee, Virginia
WLWF(FM) Marseilles, Illinois
WMJJ Birmingham, Alabama
WKYE Johnstown, Pennsylvania
WPEL-FM Montrose, Pennsylvania
WPOW Miami, Florida
WQHH Dewitt, Michigan
WMLL Bedford, New Hampshire
WYZO-FM Portage, Michigan
WBGI-FM Moundsville, West Virginia
WPCH Gray, Georgia
WTGG Amite, Louisiana
WTIC-FM Hartford, Connecticut
WVNV Malone, New York
WRDW-FM Philadelphia, Pennsylvania
WXCC Williamson, West Virginia
WXHB Richton, Mississippi
WFTK Lebanon, Ohio
WZNS Fort Walton Beach, Florida
WOXL-FM Biltmore Forest, North Carolina
WCTG Chincoteague, Virginia
KJBL Julesburg, Colorado
KMMY Soper, Oklahoma
WJTK Columbia City, Florida
KSYY Ingram, Texas
KKSY-FM Cedar Rapids, Iowa
KSLV-FM Del Norte, Colorado
KKNM Bovina, Texas
KNDN-FM Teec Nos Pos, Arizona
WYVS Spectacular, New York
WHOH Rhinelander, Wisconsin

96.7 mhz

KAHR Poplar Bluff, Missouri
KRCY-FM Lake Havasu City, Arizona
KBBE McPherson, Kansas
KBEL-FM Idabel, Oklahoma
KQMB Levan, Utah
KCAL-FM Redlands, California
KCMQ Columbia, Missouri
KCRF-FM Lincoln City, Oregon
KLJR-FM Santa Paula, California
KDOG North Mankato, Minnesota
KDYN-FM Ozark, Arkansas
KALZ Fowler, California
KCIL Gray, Louisiana
KSOB Larned, Kansas
KHFI-FM Georgetown, Texas
KHIX Carlin, Nevada
KKCQ-FM Bagley, Minnesota
KKEX Preston, Idaho
KMRQ Riverbank, California
KZRV Sartell, Minnesota
KIIC Albia, Iowa
KOYE Frankston, Texas
KBDB-FM Forks, Washington
KYDL(FM) Hot Springs, Arkansas
WBAP-FM Flower Mound, Texas
KRNK Casper, Wyoming
KOKR Newport, Arkansas
KQZZ Devils Lake, North Dakota
KISN Belgrade, Montana
KSYV Solvang, California
KUNA-FM La Quinta, California
KWCL-FM Oak Grove, Louisiana
KWIZ Santa Ana, California
KWMX Williams, Arizona
KWWW-FM Quincy, Washington
KXOX-FM Sweetwater, Texas
KZAP Paradise, California
KZIN-FM Shelby, Montana
KZMX-FM Hot Springs, South Dakota
KMMG Benton City, Washington
WBDK Algoma, Wisconsin
WBVI Fostoria, Ohio
WBVR-FM Auburn, Kentucky
WBWB Bloomington, Indiana
WCEI-FM Easton, Maryland
WTQX Boothbay Harbor, Maine
WCMJ Cambridge, Ohio
WCOE La Porte, Indiana
WCSM-FM Celina, Ohio
WCVS-FM Virden, Illinois
WDCD-FM Clifton Park, New York
WFFF-FM Columbia, Mississippi
WFML Vincennes, Indiana
WIHN Normal, Illinois
WJJH Ashland, Wisconsin
WKLV-FM Port Chester, New York
WKJX Elizabeth City, North Carolina
WKMM Kingwood, West Virginia
WKOV-FM Wellston, Ohio
WKRX Roxboro, North Carolina
WKXK Pine Hill, Alabama
WLLF Mercer, Pennsylvania
WSSR Joliet, Illinois
WUJM Gulfport, Mississippi
WLTN-FM Lisbon, New Hampshire
WLTY Cayce, South Carolina
WKGL-FM Loves Park, Illinois
WLXV Cadillac, Michigan
WWLG Peachtree City, Georgia
WMOD Bolivar, Tennessee
WMXA Opelika, Alabama
WYSX Morristown, New York
WNKX-FM Centerville, Tennessee
WWLF-FM Oswego, New York
WORX-FM Madison, Indiana
WPGM-FM Danville, Pennsylvania
WDLD Halfway, Maryland
WQSO Rochester, New Hampshire
WWZW Buena Vista, Virginia
WNCC-FM Franklin, North Carolina
WSEL-FM Pontotoc, Mississippi
WTSA-FM Brattleboro, Vermont
WABT(FM) Lehman Township, Pennsylvania
WUFN Albion, Michigan
WRWR-FM Cochran, Georgia
WVNW Burnham, Pennsylvania
WRGZ Rogers City, Michigan
WMYL Halls Crossroads, Tennessee
WXZO Willsboro, New York
WGOV-FM Valdosta, Georgia
KMDZ Las Vegas, New Mexico
KNMB Cloudcroft, New Mexico
KNOB Healdsburg, California
KUUR Carbondale, Colorado
WANV Annville, Kentucky
WMJT McMillan, Michigan
KROW Cody, Wyoming
WUPG Republic, Michigan
WGNX Colchester, Illinois
KYLI Bunkerville, Nevada
CJWV-FM Petersburgh, Ontario
WVTT Portville, New York

96.9 mhz

KBCR-FM Steamboat Springs, Colorado
KIMX Nunn, Colorado
KCCY-FM Pueblo, Colorado
KCMI Terrytown, Nebraska
KDAG Farmington, New Mexico
KDLO-FM Watertown, South Dakota
KEZE Spokane, Washington
KFIX Plainville, Kansas
KFMN Lihue, Hawaii
KGY-FM McCleary, Washington
KIAQ Clarion, Iowa
KXBJ El Campo, Texas
KKGL Nampa, Idaho
KKOW-FM Pittsburg, Kansas
KMCM Odessa, Texas
KMFY Grand Rapids, Minnesota
KXSS-FM Amarillo, Texas
KMTN Jackson, Wyoming
KMXP Phoenix, Arizona
KQOB Enid, Oklahoma
KQRV Deer Lodge, Montana
KROG Grants Pass, Oregon
KSCN Pittsburg, Texas
KSEG Sacramento, California
KUPH Mountain View, Missouri
KVMV Mc Allen, Texas
KWAV Monterey, California
KWLR Maumelle, Arkansas
KEBT Lost Hills, California
KZBK Brookfield, Missouri
KZKX Seward, Nebraska
KZMZ Alexandria, Louisiana
KZTA Naches, Washington
WTHB-FM Wrens, Georgia
WBPW Presque Isle, Maine
WBTI Lexington, Michigan
WDDJ Paducah, Kentucky
WDJR Enterprise, Alabama
WRRB Arlington, New York
WEHN East Hampton, New York
WFPG Atlantic City, New Jersey
WGKS Paris, Kentucky
WGRF Buffalo, New York
WHPZ Bremen, Indiana
WINK-FM Fort Myers, Florida
WKEZ-FM Tavernier, Florida
WYMY Goldsboro, North Carolina
WKKT Statesville, North Carolina
WJGL Jacksonville, Florida
WLAN-FM Lancaster, Pennsylvania
WLAV-FM Grand Rapids, Michigan
WLBH-FM Mattoon, Illinois
WLRD Willard, Ohio
WWDV Zion, Illinois
WNRT Manati, Puerto Rico
WOUR Utica, New York
WRDO Fitzgerald, Georgia
WZKN(FM) Ridgebury, Pennsylvania
WOKL Troy, Ohio
WRRK Braddock, Pennsylvania
WRSA-FM Holly Pond, Alabama
WSIG Mount Jackson, Virginia
WTKK Boston, Massachusetts
WWCM Standish, Michigan
WIWF Charleston, South Carolina
WTCD Indianola, Mississippi
WWUZ Bowling Green, Virginia
WWWX Oshkosh, Wisconsin
WXBQ-FM Bristol, Virginia
WXLP Moline, Illinois
WVVV Williamstown, West Virginia
WNKL Wauseon, Ohio
WKLO Hardinsburg, Indiana
KYSC Fairbanks, Alaska
KSSW Nashville, Arkansas
KHDR Lenwood, California
KDVB Effingham, Kansas

97.1 mhz

KALS Kalispell, Montana
KAMD-FM Camden, Arkansas
KAYQ Warsaw, Missouri
KBCQ-FM Roswell, New Mexico
KCYN Moab, Utah
KEGL Fort Worth, Texas
KELN North Platte, Nebraska
KNST-FM Green Valley, Arizona
KRTO Guadalupe, California
KZHT Salt Lake City, Utah
KKBR Billings, Montana
KKEN Duncan, Oklahoma
KYCH-FM Portland, Oregon
KTHT Cleveland, Texas
KYAL-FM Muskogee, Oklahoma
KVVL Maryville, Missouri
KNWB Hilo, Hawaii
KPSD-FM Faith, South Dakota
KSEQ Visalia, California
KIBB Haven, Kansas
KTCZ-FM Minneapolis, Minnesota
KVRP-FM Haskell, Texas
KFTK Florissant, Missouri
KXPT Las Vegas, Nevada
KXRX Walla Walla, Washington
KYCK Crookston, Minnesota
KYYX Minot, North Dakota
KTSE-FM Patterson, California
WASH Washington, District of Columbia
WBHT Mountain Top, Pennsylvania
WBNS-FM Columbus, Ohio
WBVB Coal Grove, Ohio
WDBS Sutton, West Virginia
WCOW-FM Sparta, Wisconsin
WLHK Shelbyville, Indiana
WEZB New Orleans, Louisiana
WSRV Gainesville, Georgia
WGLQ Escanaba, Michigan
WHRK Memphis, Tennessee
WXYT-FM Detroit, Michigan
WLIC Frostburg, Maryland
WWMG Millbrook, Alabama
WDRV Chicago, Illinois
WOKK Meridian, Mississippi
WOSN Indian River Shores, Florida
WQHT New York, New York
WAVD Ocean Pines, Maryland
WQMG Greensboro, North Carolina
WOWY University Park, Pennsylvania
WREO-FM Ashtabula, Ohio
WKEQ Somerset, Kentucky
WSUN-FM Holiday, Florida
WBFB Bangor, Maine
WXCM Whitesville, Kentucky
WYND-FM Hatteras, North Carolina
WZRT Rutland, Vermont
KULV Ukiah, California
KJMT Calico Rock, Arkansas
WLVU Belle Meade, Tennessee
KZBR La Jara, Colorado
KIYU-FM Galena, Alaska
KNSX(FM) Moville, Iowa

97.3 mhz

KAJA San Antonio, Texas
KAML-FM Gillette, Wyoming
KRVY-FM Starbuck, Minnesota
KBCO Boulder, Colorado
KYRX Marble Hill, Missouri
KIRO-FM Tacoma, Washington
KLRX Lee's Summit, Missouri
KDEW-FM De Witt, Arkansas
KDNW Duluth, Minnesota
KEAG Anchorage, Alaska
KGRR Epworth, Iowa
KLZK New Deal, Texas
KHKI Des Moines, Iowa
KIKO-FM Claypool, Arizona
KJMG Bastrop, Louisiana
KKJQ Garden City, Kansas
KGEE Pecos, Texas
KKRS Davenport, Washington
KKSS Santa Fe, New Mexico
KLCE Blackfoot, Idaho
KLLC San Francisco, California
KRGY Aurora, Nebraska
KMDL Kaplan, Louisiana
KMXC Sioux Falls, South Dakota
KNCQ Redding, California
KSHR-FM Coquille, Oregon
KSON San Diego, California
KQHN Waskom, Texas
KKNG-FM Blanchard, Oklahoma
KSGG Carson City, Nevada
KXUS Springfield, Missouri
WAEV Savannah, Georgia
WDEE-FM Reed City, Michigan
WMJO Essexville, Michigan
WFLC Miami, Florida
WFMM Sumrall, Mississippi
WFMN Flora, Mississippi
WFYR Elmwood, Illinois
WGH-FM Newport News, Virginia
WHDG Rhinelander, Wisconsin
WJDF Orange, Massachusetts
WJFD-FM New Bedford, Massachusetts
WJSN-FM Jackson, Kentucky
WJZE Oak Harbor, Ohio
WKBC-FM North Wilkesboro, North Carolina
WKJQ-FM Parsons, Tennessee
WKWK-FM Wheeling, West Virginia
WUUQ South Pittsburg, Tennessee
WRNW Milwaukee, Wisconsin
WMEE Fort Wayne, Indiana
WGEX Bainbridge, Georgia
WMNX Wilmington, North Carolina
WYGY Fort Thomas, Kentucky
WMYY Schoharie, New York
WPCL Northern Cambria, Pennsylvania
WRUL Carmi, Illinois
WRVV Harrisburg, Pennsylvania
WSKY-FM Micanopy, Florida
WTIM-FM Taylorville, Illinois
WKSO Natchez, Mississippi
WYGY(FM) Fort Thomas, Kentucky
WYXL Ithaca, New York
WZAD Wurtsboro, New York
WZBG Litchfield, Connecticut
WZZE Glen Mills, Pennsylvania
WOYE Rio Grande, Puerto Rico
KHDK New London, Iowa
KBLR-FM Blair, Nebraska
WTNV Tiptonville, Tennessee
KQNO Coalinga, California
KTCM Madison, Missouri
KPKR Parker, Arizona
KRKH Wailea-Makena, Hawaii

97.5 mhz

KABX-FM Merced, California
KFNC Mont Belvieu, Texas
KVEG Mesquite, Nevada
KBNA-FM El Paso, Texas
KBVU-FM Alta, Iowa
KDBH-FM Natchitoches, Louisiana
KDKK Park Rapids, Minnesota
KDLY Lander, Wyoming
KFTX Kingsville, Texas

KGKL-FM San Angelo, Texas
KJCK-FM Junction City, Kansas
KKCT Bismarck, North Dakota
KLAK Tom Bean, Texas
KRUZ Santa Barbara, California
KMOD-FM Tulsa, Oklahoma
KNLR Bend, Oregon
KNMO-FM Nevada, Missouri
KNXR Rochester, Minnesota
KSZR Oro Valley, Arizona
KOEA Doniphan, Missouri
KOZB Livingston, Montana
KHCM-FM Honolulu, Hawaii
KQSK Chadron, Nebraska
KQUS-FM Hot Springs, Arkansas
KTWD Wallace, Idaho
KLYY Riverside, California
KMVA Dewey-Humboldt, Arizona
KWTX-FM Waco, Texas
KZGZ Hagatna, Guam
KOLW Basin City, Washington
WLVM(FM) Mobile, Alabama
WALK-FM Patchogue, New York
WAMZ Louisville, Kentucky
WBBA-FM Pittsfield, Illinois
WCOS-FM Columbia, South Carolina
WWSN Whitehall, Michigan
WYDM Monroe, Michigan
WFRY-FM Watertown, New York
WHLJ-FM Statenville, Georgia
WHMS-FM Champaign, Illinois
WUMJ Fayetteville, Georgia
WKTT Salisbury, Maryland
WIGY Madison, Maine
WIOB Mayaguez, Puerto Rico
WJIM-FM Lansing, Michigan
WJXB-FM Knoxville, Tennessee
WKLT Kalkaska, Michigan
WLTF Martinsburg, West Virginia
WLLX Lawrenceburg, Tennessee
WOBN Westerville, Ohio
WOKQ Dover, New Hampshire
WONE-FM Akron, Ohio
WPCV Winter Haven, Florida
WDDH St. Marys, Pennsylvania
WPEN-FM Burlington, New Jersey
WQBE-FM Charleston, West Virginia
WQOK Carrboro, North Carolina
WKGA Goodwater, Alabama
WTGR Union City, Ohio
WUFF-FM Eastman, Georgia
WVNU Greenfield, Ohio
WWMS Oxford, Mississippi
WWWV Charlottesville, Virginia
WYTZ Bridgman, Michigan
WHAZ-FM Hoosick Falls, New York
WZOK Rockford, Illinois
WDLJ Breese, Illinois
WZZP Hopkinsville, Kentucky
KPAK Alva, Oklahoma
KZNSFM) Coalville, Utah
KTJZ Tallulah, Louisiana
KTRT Winthrop, Washington
KPHD Elko, Nevada
KWUZ Poncha Springs, Colorado
KJMO Linn, Missouri
WTNN Bristol, Vermont
KSRX Sterling, Colorado
WTBD-FM Delhi, New York
WVRV Pine Level, Alabama
KEXL Pierce, Nebraska

97.7 mhz

KJSM-FM Augusta, Arkansas
KACI-FM The Dalles, Oregon
KALK Winfield, Texas
KAPB-FM Marksville, Louisiana
KTPI-FM Mojave, California
KAVV Benson, Arizona
KRIO-FM Roma, Texas
KCRR Grundy Center, Iowa
KATX Eastland, Texas
KFFG Los Altos, California
KOMO-FM Oakville, Washington
KGLM-FM Anaconda, Montana
KICM Healdton, Oklahoma
KHBT Humboldt, Iowa
KHZR Potosi, Missouri
KHIM Mangum, Oklahoma
KLVO Belen, New Mexico
KVRV Monte Rio, California
KMTY Gibbon, Nebraska
KNBZ Redfield, South Dakota
KOTM-FM Ottumwa, Iowa
KNBB Dubach, Louisiana
KPOW-FM La Monte, Missouri
KBBX-FM Nebraska City, Nebraska
KQMO Shell Knob, Missouri
KQVO Calexico, California
KRAT(FM) Altamont, Oregon
KRCK-FM Mecca, California
KWUT(FM) Elsinore, Utah
KSMJ Shafter, California
KSHL Coburg, Oregon
KSNP Burlington, Kansas
KZAR McQueeney, Texas
KWIN Lodi, California
KWRW Rusk, Texas
KYSN East Wenatchee, Washington
KHHZ Gridley, California
KZYR Avon, Colorado
WAFL Milford, Delaware
WNSX Winter Harbor, Maine
WKFX Rice Lake, Wisconsin
WKCA Salt Lick, Kentucky
WEXT Amsterdam, New York
WNVM Cidra, Puerto Rico
WKAF Brockton, Massachusetts
WTLQ-FM Punta Rassa, Florida
WCJO Jackson, Ohio
WCTY Norwich, Connecticut
WCXU Caribou, Maine
WCZX Hyde Park, New York
WHPH Jemison, Alabama
WFDL-FM Lomira, Wisconsin
WGGN Castalia, Ohio
WGLR-FM Lancaster, Wisconsin
WENI-FM Big Flats, New York
WGMT Lyndon, Vermont
WWKY Providence, Kentucky
WILE-FM Byesville, Ohio
WSNI Keene, New Hampshire
WGPB Rome, Georgia
WAQE-FM Barron, Wisconsin
WKKR Auburn, Alabama
WZZN Oneonta, Alabama
WAVK Marathon, Florida
WKXM-FM Winfield, Alabama
WLER-FM Butler, Pennsylvania
WLQI Rensselaer, Indiana
WLCE Petersburg, Illinois
WMDM Lexington Park, Maryland
WMGZ Eatonton, Georgia
WMOI Monmouth, Illinois
WMRX-FM Beaverton, Michigan
WOLV Houghton, Michigan
WOXY Mason, Ohio
WRIC-FM Richlands, Virginia
WRBJ-FM Brandon, Mississippi
WVBB(FM) Elliston-Lafayette, Virginia
WLKH Somerset, Pennsylvania
WVBB Elliston-Lafayette, Virginia
WCLS Spencer, Indiana
WSRG Sturgeon Bay, Wisconsin
WSTQ Streator, Illinois
WTCQ Vidalia, Georgia
WTGN Lima, Ohio
WTGV-FM Sandusky, Michigan
WTYJ Fayette, Mississippi
WTYL-FM Tylertown, Mississippi
WGTI Winfall, North Carolina
WVRT Mill Hall, Pennsylvania
WMLQ Manistee, Michigan
WWUF Waycross, Georgia
WWXM Garden City, South Carolina
WYAJ Sudbury, Massachusetts
WYYX Bonifay, Florida
WEQR Walnut Creek, North Carolina
WSSM(FM) Goshen, Indiana
KZBG Lapwai, Idaho
KSJL Strasburg, Colorado
WURB Cross City, Florida

97.9 mhz

KBFB Dallas, Texas
KBXB Sikeston, Missouri
KBXX Houston, Texas
KBZN Ogden, Utah
KCMR Mason City, Iowa
KQLK De Ridder, Louisiana
KFBD-FM Waynesville, Missouri
KFNW-FM Fargo, North Dakota
KGNC-FM Amarillo, Texas
KICK-FM Palmyra, Missouri
KXBG Cheyenne, Wyoming
KNSL(FM) Lamoni, Iowa
KISZ-FM Cortez, Colorado
KJMZ Cache, Oklahoma
KKBG Hilo, Hawaii
KNRQ-FM Aloha, Oregon
KLAX-FM East Los Angeles, California
KVVR Dutton, Montana
KTPT Rapid City, South Dakota
KYZZ Salinas, California
KMGV Fresno, California
KLUK Needles, California
KODM Odessa, Texas
KPOD-FM Crescent City, California
KQFC Boise, Idaho
KPSA-FM Lordsburg, New Mexico
KRBB Wichita, Kansas
KRRC Portland, Oregon
KSEZ Sioux City, Iowa
KTAG Cody, Wyoming
KZTB Milton-Freewater, Oregon
KTLO-FM Mountain Home, Arkansas
KLMG Esparto, California
KUPD Tempe, Arizona
KWGB Colby, Kansas
KXDG Webb City, Missouri
KZBB Poteau, Oklahoma
WLTM Greenville, Mississippi
WBEY-FM Crisfield, Maryland
WNBB Bayboro, North Carolina
WCPR-FM Wiggins, Mississippi
WYDK Eufaula, Alabama
WEVE-FM Eveleth, Minnesota
WGNR-FM Anderson, Indiana
WGOD-FM Charlotte Amalie, Virgin Islands
WGRD-FM Grand Rapids, Michigan
WIBB-FM Fort Valley, Georgia
WIHC Newberry, Michigan
WIIZ Blackville, South Carolina
WIYY Baltimore, Maryland
WJBQ Portland, Maine
WJLB Detroit, Michigan
WJWZ Wetumpka, Alabama
WDMG-FM Ambrose, Georgia
WKKW Fairmont, West Virginia
WTRG Gaston, North Carolina
WLUP-FM Chicago, Illinois
WUCL Newton, Mississippi
WNCI Columbus, Ohio
WSKS Whitesboro, New York
WPEG Concord, North Carolina
WUCS Windsor Locks, Connecticut
WPXY-FM Rochester, New York
WRIP Windham, New York
WRMF Palm Beach, Florida
WZZU Lynchburg, Virginia
WSIX-FM Nashville, Tennessee
WSKQ-FM New York, New York
WSLM-FM Salem, Indiana
WSPT Stevens Point, Wisconsin
WVOK-FM Oxford, Alabama
WBSX Hazleton, Pennsylvania
WXEF Effingham, Illinois
WXTA Edinboro, Pennsylvania
WXTB Clearwater, Florida
WKIC Hyden, Kentucky
WTSM(FM) Woodville, Florida
KZWB Green River, Wyoming
WBBE Heyworth, Illinois
WMGA Kenova, West Virginia
KDXT Lolo, Montana
WZXP Au Sable, New York
KYRT Hunt, Texas

98.1 mhz

KJMQ Lihue, Hawaii
KAYW Meeker, Colorado
KBAC Las Vegas, New Mexico
KBEW-FM Blue Earth, Minnesota
KBUL-FM Carson City, Nevada
KFGE Milford, Nebraska
KTLT Anson, Texas
KGTM Rexburg, Idaho
KHAK Cedar Rapids, Iowa
KIFM San Diego, California
KING-FM Seattle, Washington
KISC Spokane, Washington
KISQ San Francisco, California
KKCL Lorenzo, Texas
KKFM Colorado Springs, Colorado
KKJG San Luis Obispo, California
KUSN Dearing, Kansas
KLEF Anchorage, Alaska
KOZX Cabool, Missouri
KREC Brian Head, Utah
KRRG Laredo, Texas
KRXV Yermo, California
KTAL-FM Texarkana, Texas
KMBZ-FM Kansas City, Kansas
KVET-FM Austin, Texas
KVIP-FM Redding, California
KWLF Fairbanks, Alaska
KSKZ Copeland, Kansas
KYKY St. Louis, Missouri
WOBX-FM Manteo, North Carolina
WBRF Galax, Virginia
WBUL-FM Lexington, Kentucky
WCTK New Bedford, Massachusetts
WDFM Defiance, Ohio
WDGL Baton Rouge, Louisiana
WEDB East Dublin, Georgia
WEUL Kingsford, Michigan
WFGY Altoona, Pennsylvania
WGFN Glen Arbor, Michigan
WNUE-FM Deltona, Florida
WKDD Munroe Falls, Ohio
WHWK Binghamton, New York
WIBN Earl Park, Indiana
WISM-FM Altoona, Wisconsin
WJJR Rutland, Vermont
WKCQ Saginaw, Michigan
WLKN Cleveland, Wisconsin
WKZE-FM Salisbury, Connecticut
WLND Signal Mountain, Tennessee
WMGN Madison, Wisconsin
WMXI Laurel, Mississippi
WOGL Philadelphia, Pennsylvania
WHZT Williamston, South Carolina
WQAQ Hamden, Connecticut
WQHL-FM Live Oak, Florida
WQSM Fayetteville, North Carolina
WRAY-FM Princeton, Indiana
WOCM Selbyville, Delaware
WXMX Millington, Tennessee
WTVR-FM Richmond, Virginia
WTXT Fayette, Alabama
WWJO St. Cloud, Minnesota
WYBB Folly Beach, South Carolina
WMGP Hogansville, Georgia
WZOE-FM Princeton, Illinois
WMRZ Dawson, Georgia
WUDR Dayton, Ohio
WCXV Van Buren, Maine
KRBY Ruby, Alaska
KALG Kaltag, Alaska
KOYU Koyukuk, Alaska

98.3 mhz

KARB Price, Utah
KATR-FM Wray, Colorado
KBEV-FM Dillon, Montana
KBOC Bridgeport, Texas
KDAR Oxnard, California
KDZY McCall, Idaho
KEJJ Gunnison, Colorado
KERM Torrington, Wyoming
KEYW Pasco, Washington
KFCM Ash Flat, Arkansas
KUQL Ethan, South Dakota
KICA-FM Farwell, Texas
KKEG Bentonville, Arkansas
KKFR Mayer, Arizona
KLDR Harbeck-Fruitdale, Oregon
KMJR Odem, Texas
KJMD Pukalani, Hawaii
KOHT Marana, Arizona
KORA-FM Bryan, Texas
KPTX Pecos, Texas
KQYB Spring Grove, Minnesota
KXDJ Spearman, Texas
KWQW Boone, Iowa
KRCV West Covina, California
KYAR Lorena, Texas
KTWS Bend, Oregon
KULM-FM Columbus, Texas
KWNN Turlock, California
KXBX-FM Lakeport, California
KZRZ West Monroe, Louisiana
KXGT Carrington, North Dakota
KYYK Palestine, Texas

WBFA Fort Mitchell, Alabama
WTXO Ashland, Alabama
WUIN Oak Island, North Carolina
WBJI Blackduck, Minnesota
WCCQ Crest Hill, Illinois
WCEF Ripley, West Virginia
WCMZ-FM Sault Ste. Marie, Michigan
WCQM Park Falls, Wisconsin
WCXT Hartford, Michigan
WLGT Washington, North Carolina
WDAQ Danbury, Connecticut
WMTY-FM Sweetwater, Tennessee
WDFX Cleveland, Mississippi
WDLZ Murfreesboro, North Carolina
WJMR-FM Menomonee Falls, Wisconsin
WGCO Midway, Georgia
WHAI Greenfield, Massachusetts
WHAY Whitley City, Kentucky
WRUP Palmer, Michigan
WILI-FM Willimantic, Connecticut
WJDR Prentiss, Mississippi
WLUS-FM Clarksville, Virginia
WKEA-FM Scottsboro, Alabama
WKET Kettering, Ohio
WKJY Hempstead, New York
WSSY Pinehurst, Georgia
WKSR-FM Loretto, Tennessee
WLCS North Muskegon, Michigan
WKNA Logan, Ohio
WLJI Summerton, South Carolina
WLNH-FM Laconia, New Hampshire
WMGQ New Brunswick, New Jersey
WOKE Garrison, Kentucky
WPKO-FM Bellefontaine, Ohio
WIDI Quebradillas, Puerto Rico
WQRS Salamanca, New York
WQXE Elizabethtown, Kentucky
WRAN Tower Hill, Illinois
WMYP Frederiksted, Virgin Islands
WRIK-FM Metropolis, Illinois
WRTO-FM Goulds, Florida
WHHD Clearwater, South Carolina
WSMD-FM Mechanicsville, Maryland
WKOZ-FM Carthage, Mississippi
WSUL Monticello, New York
WTKU-FM Petersburg, New Jersey
WTRY-FM Rotterdam, New York
WMIM Luna Pier, Michigan
WVIN-FM Bath, New York
WWBE Mifflinburg, Pennsylvania
WMAN-FM Fredericktown, Ohio
WWHP Farmer City, Illinois
WWRZ Fort Meade, Florida
WRDZ-FM Plainfield, Indiana
WKSI-FM Stephens City, Virginia
WZZY Winchester, Indiana
KPDB Big Lake, Texas
KZZS Story, Wyoming
KSNQ Twin Falls, Idaho
WYBL Ashtabula, Ohio
KPPK Rainier, Oregon
KZLA Riverdale, California
KADQ-FM Evanston, Wyoming
KQZQ Kiowa, Kansas
KXIM Sanborn, Iowa

98.5 mhz

KABG Los Alamos, New Mexico
KACO Apache, Oklahoma
KBBZ Kalispell, Montana
KBBT Schertz, Texas
KCHI-FM Chillicothe, Missouri
KWBY-FM Ranger, Texas
KDES-FM Cathedral City, California
KEYG-FM Grand Coulee, Washington
KGAP Clarksville, Texas
KGBT-FM McAllen, Texas
KGIL Johannesburg, California
KGHL(FM) Billings, Montana
KIFX Roosevelt, Utah
KOEL-FM Cedar Falls, Iowa
KDNN Honolulu, Hawaii
KLLP Chubbuck, Idaho
KLUC-FM Las Vegas, Nevada
KQKQ-FM Council Bluffs, Iowa
KRXQ Sacramento, California
KRXT Rockdale, Texas
KSAJ-FM Abilene, Kansas
KSAY Ft. Bragg, California
KDFO Delano, California
KTIS-FM Minneapolis, Minnesota
KTJJ Farmington, Missouri
KTJM Port Arthur, Texas
KUFX San Jose, California
KURB Little Rock, Arkansas
KVOO-FM Tulsa, Oklahoma
KWXY(FM) Cathedral City, California
KYGO-FM Denver, Colorado
KBXJ Los Ybanez, Texas
KRDX Vail, Arizona
WIBQ Paris, Illinois
WACL Elkton, Virginia
WMYK Peru, Indiana
WBBO(FM) Ocean Acres, New Jersey
WBZF Hartsville, South Carolina
WCKM-FM Lake George, New York
WCMO Marietta, Ohio
WCTW Catskill, New York
WDAI Pawleys Island, South Carolina
WBON Westhampton, New York
WDEO-FM San Carlos Park, Florida
WEBB Waterville, Maine
WPIA Eureka, Illinois
WFSY Panama City, Florida
WGBG Seaford, Delaware
WGIC Cookeville, Tennessee
WINL Linden, Alabama
WKRZ Freeland, Pennsylvania
WKSE Niagara Falls, New York
WKTK Crystal River, Florida
WLPF Ocilla, Georgia
WOMG Lexington, South Carolina
WNCX Cleveland, Ohio
WNWN-FM Coldwater, Michigan
WNYR-FM Waterloo, New York
WGYI Oil City, Pennsylvania
WPRM-FM San Juan, Puerto Rico
WQKZ Ferdinand, Indiana
WQLH Green Bay, Wisconsin
WRRM Cincinnati, Ohio
WDWG Rocky Mount, North Carolina
WSB-FM Atlanta, Georgia
WTFM Kingsport, Tennessee
WUPS Houghton Lake, Michigan
WXXQ Freeport, Illinois
WYCR York-Hanover, Pennsylvania
WYLD-FM New Orleans, Louisiana
WZLQ Tupelo, Mississippi
KHAQ Maxwell, Nebraska
KWKJ Windsor, Missouri
KZID Culdesac, Idaho
KGRK Glenrock, Wyoming
WSBH Satellite Beach, Florida
KAAI Palisade, Colorado
KOYT(FM) Montana City, Montana
KXJN Moose Wilson Road, Wyoming
KEWF(FM) Billings, Colorado

98.7 mhz

KACL Bismarck, North Dakota
KFH-FM Clearwater, Kansas
KBEE Salt Lake City, Utah
KELI San Angelo, Texas
KARO Nyssa, Oregon
KISD Pipestone, Minnesota
KPKX Phoenix, Arizona
KKST Oakdale, Louisiana
KLBQ El Dorado, Arkansas
KMNA Mabton, Washington
KLOQ-FM Winton, California
KLUV Dallas, Texas
KMGO Centerville, Iowa
KMTH Maljamar, New Mexico
KPRF Amarillo, Texas
KOUT Rapid City, South Dakota
KQWB-FM Moorhead, Minnesota
KXTS Geyserville, California
KRSV-FM Afton, Wyoming
KRTZ Cortez, Colorado
KSID-FM Sidney, Nebraska
KKVS Truth or Consequences, New Mexico
KTXN-FM Victoria, Texas
KUBQ La Grande, Oregon
KUPL Portland, Oregon
KSMA-FM Osage, Iowa
KWTO-FM Springfield, Missouri
KYSR Los Angeles, California
KYTT-FM Coos Bay, Oregon
WASK-FM Battle Ground, Indiana
WYCT Pensacola, Florida
WBHK Warrior, Alabama
WBTY Homerville, Georgia
WBYY Somersworth, New Hampshire
WGMM Corning, New York
WCNK Key West, Florida
WEMR Pleasant Gap, Pennsylvania
WFGR Grand Rapids, Michigan
WFMT Chicago, Illinois
WHOP-FM Hopkinsville, Kentucky
WISK-FM Americus, Georgia
WJKK Vicksburg, Mississippi
WYRO McArthur, Ohio
WKDO-FM Liberty, Kentucky
WKGR Wellington, Florida
WRMR(FM) Jacksonville, North Carolina
WSMW Greensboro, North Carolina
WLZW Utica, New York
WMDC Mayville, Wisconsin
WMZQ-FM Washington, District of Columbia
WNLC East Lyme, Connecticut
WNNS Springfield, Illinois
WNOR Norfolk, Virginia
WOVK Wheeling, West Virginia
WQME Anderson, Indiana
WEPN-FM New York, New York
WRVZ Pocatalico, West Virginia
WOKI Oliver Springs, Tennessee
WGCQ Hayti, Missouri
WDZH Detroit, Michigan
WCZT Villas, New Jersey
WINQ Winchester, New Hampshire
WYKZ Beaufort, South Carolina
WPAC Ogdensburg, New York
WYKL Crestline, Ohio
WGLI Hancock, Michigan
KAAZ Laramie, Wyoming
WNEV Friars Point, Mississippi
KZAM Pleasant Valley, Texas
KAVB Hawthorne, Nevada
KWXR Reliance, Wyoming

98.9 mhz

KAAK Great Falls, Montana
KITH Kapaa, Hawaii
KWLU Chester, California
KRQX-FM Santa Clara, Utah
KFLW St. Robert, Missouri
KGRA Jefferson, Iowa
KHWY Essex, California
KXBT Leander, Texas
KKMG Pueblo, Colorado
KKPR-FM Kearney, Nebraska
KKZX Spokane, Washington
KQRC-FM Leavenworth, Kansas
KSOF Dinuba, California
KSOL San Francisco, California
KTCO Duluth, Minnesota
KCVR-FM Columbia, California
WKIM Munford, Tennessee
KTUX Carthage, Texas
KKRK Coffeyville, Kansas
KLCK-FM Seattle, Washington
KYIS Oklahoma City, Oklahoma
KYMG Anchorage, Alaska
KZPK Paynesville, Minnesota
WAJV Brooksville, Mississippi
WANT Lebanon, Tennessee
WBAM-FM Montgomery, Alabama
WBZA Rochester, New York
WBYR Woodburn, Indiana
WBZE Tallahassee, Florida
WCLZ North Yarmouth, Maine
WDNE-FM Elkins, West Virginia
WNBR-FM Bethel, North Carolina
WUUU Franklinton, Louisiana
WGUF Marco, Florida
WBCG Murdock, Florida
WNRW(FM) Salem, Indiana
WHQQ Neoga, Illinois
WLKU Rock Island, Illinois
WWLB Midlothian, Virginia
WMXY Youngstown, Ohio
WKLZ-FM Petoskey, Michigan
WJEZ Dwight, Illinois
WMMO Orlando, Florida
WOKO Burlington, Vermont
WORC-FM Webster, Massachusetts
WOWE Vassar, Michigan
WQKY Emporium, Pennsylvania
WQLV Millersburg, Pennsylvania
WNGH-FM Chatsworth, Georgia
WZOL Vieques, Puerto Rico
WSBY-FM Salisbury, Maryland
WSIP-FM Paintsville, Kentucky
WSPA-FM Spartanburg, South Carolina
WUSL Philadelphia, Pennsylvania
WVCX Tomah, Wisconsin
WAZS(FM) McClellanville, South Carolina
WJKR Upper Arlington, Ohio
WMSO Quitman, Mississippi
KQCR-FM Parkersburg, Iowa
KLMO-FM Dilley, Texas
WISH-FM Galatia, Illinois
KLYD Snyder, Texas
KLOW Reno, Texas
KRVC Hornbrook, California
WRAX Lake Isabella, Michigan
KZXK Doney Park, Arizona
KMRV San Isidro, Texas

99.1 mhz

KAGB Waimea, Hawaii
KAYG Camp Wood, Texas
KCAD Dickinson, North Dakota
KCLV-FM Clovis, New Mexico
KEEZ-FM Mankato, Minnesota
KFMM Thatcher, Arizona
KLJY Clayton, Missouri
KGGI Riverside, California
KGLX Gallup, New Mexico
KGNT Smithfield, Utah
KKFT Gardnerville-Minden, Nevada
KDXX Denton, Texas
KXMT Taos, New Mexico
KJIL Copeland, Kansas
KMA-FM Clarinda, Iowa
KLLZ-FM Walker, Minnesota
KLSX Rozet, Wyoming
KHKX Odessa, Texas
KMAG Fort Smith, Arkansas
KMTS Glenwood Springs, Colorado
KNES Fairfield, Texas
KTMG Prescott, Arizona
KODA Houston, Texas
KODZ Eugene, Oregon
KOFH Nogales, Arizona
KRUP Dillingham, Alaska
KRYS-FM Corpus Christi, Texas
KSEK-FM Girard, Kansas
KSKB Brooklyn, Iowa
KQLZ(FM) Mt Home, Idaho
KTLI El Dorado, Kansas
KUAD-FM Windsor, Colorado
KUJ-FM Burbank, Washington
KUPI-FM Rexburg, Idaho
KXFM Santa Maria, California
KXKC New Iberia, Louisiana
KYOO-FM Half Way, Missouri
KXLG Milbank, South Dakota
KSQL Santa Cruz, California
WAAL Binghamton, New York
WAHR Huntsville, Alabama
WAWZ Zarephath, New Jersey
WDEN-FM Macon, Georgia
WCBL-FM Grand Rivers, Kentucky
WEDR Miami, Florida
WFMK East Lansing, Michigan
WFRO-FM Fremont, Ohio
WNEW(FM) Bowie, Maryland
WHKO Dayton, Ohio
WYXY(FM) Danville, Illinois
WIKB-FM Iron River, Michigan
WJMM-FM Keene, Kentucky
WJNV Jonesville, Virginia
WHSX Edmonton, Kentucky
WKNN-FM Pascagoula, Mississippi
WLKE Bar Harbor, Maine
WMYX-FM Milwaukee, Wisconsin
WNNH Henniker, New Hampshire
WNML-FM Friendsville, Tennessee
WPLM-FM Plymouth, Massachusetts
WPLR New Haven, Connecticut
WQIK-FM Jacksonville, Florida
WRKW Ebensburg, Pennsylvania
WSLQ Roanoke, Virginia
WSMK Buchanan, Michigan
WUKQ-FM Mayaguez, Puerto Rico
WVOD Manteo, North Carolina
WWOJ Avon Park, Florida
WXGM-FM Gloucester, Virginia
WGGE Parkersburg, West Virginia
WYMX Greenwood, Mississippi
WZFX Whiteville, North Carolina
KWYW Lost Cabin, Wyoming

KCMM Belgrade, Montana
WDGM Greensboro, Alabama
KVMZ Waldo, Arkansas
KARA Williams, California
KSMD Pangburn, Arkansas
KZJZ St. Regis, Montana
KWAP(FM) Pine Haven, Wyoming
WNYN-FM Whitefield, New Hampshire
WWKN Morgantown, Kentucky
KSOO-FM Lennox, South Dakota
KNUL Nulato, Alaska
WHBJ Barnwell, South Carolina

99.3 mhz

KADA-FM Ada, Oklahoma
KDDS-FM Elma, Washington
KCLI-FM Cordell, Oklahoma
KCGQ-FM Gordonville, Missouri
KCLR-FM Boonville, Missouri
KDRM Moses Lake, Washington
KDST Dyersville, Iowa
KEFH Clarendon, Texas
KFFF-FM Boone, Iowa
KGVE Grove, Oklahoma
KZTK White Oak, Texas
KJOY Stockton, California
KJWL Fresno, California
KKBB Bakersfield, California
KKDQ Thief River Falls, Minnesota
KKTS-FM Douglas, Wyoming
KLOR-FM Ponca City, Oklahoma
KMXE-FM Red Lodge, Montana
KMXX Imperial, California
KPCH Ruston, Louisiana
KNNN(FM) Shasta Lake City, California
KPSM Brownwood, Texas
KRGT Indian Springs, Nevada
KIT-FM Naches, Washington
KVLD Atkins, Arkansas
KXRZ Alexandria, Minnesota
KUNQ Houston, Missouri
KCMD Grants Pass, Oregon
KVYN St. Helena, California
KWAY-FM Waverly, Iowa
KWFL Roswell, New Mexico
KWIC Topeka, Kansas
KWNO-FM Rushford, Minnesota
WTZR Elizabethton, Tennessee
WAJK La Salle, Illinois
WATZ-FM Alpena, Michigan
WBAW-FM Pembroke, Georgia
WBVV Guntown, Mississippi
WBQQ Kennebunk, Maine
WBT-FM Chester, South Carolina
WOUF Beulah, Michigan
WCJC Van Buren, Indiana
WCON-FM Cornelia, Georgia
WDMP-FM Dodgeville, Wisconsin
WDUK Havana, Illinois
WJZS Block Island, Rhode Island
WNRX Jefferson City, Tennessee
WFQX Front Royal, Virginia
WHMJ Franklin, Pennsylvania
WFRD Hanover, New Hampshire
WLAU Heidelberg, Mississippi
WLZX Northampton, Massachusetts
WJBX Fort Myers Beach, Florida
WJQK Zeeland, Michigan
WKCN Fort Benning South, Georgia
WKEB Medford, Wisconsin
WKTJ-FM Farmington, Maine
WKVI-FM Knox, Indiana
WLLG Lowville, New York
WMFC Monroeville, Alabama
WBET-FM Sturgis, Michigan
WNXT-FM Portsmouth, Ohio
WKMO Lebanon Junction, Kentucky
WOWN Shawano, Wisconsin
WKJM Petersburg, Virginia
WPKL Uniontown, Pennsylvania
WQDK Gatesville, North Carolina
WZBZ Pleasantville, New Jersey
WSCH Aurora, Indiana
WLLW Seneca Falls, New York
WEBZ Mexico Beach, Florida
WSNN Potsdam, New York
WRWB-FM Ellenville, New York
WTNS-FM Coshocton, Ohio
WVES Accomac, Virginia
WVLE Scottsville, Kentucky
WWKF Fulton, Kentucky
WHKF Harrisburg, Pennsylvania
WWKT-FM Kingstree, South Carolina
WXFM-FM Mount Zion, Illinois
WPBX Crossville, Tennessee
WZAX Nashville, North Carolina
WZLT Lexington, Tennessee
WZXR South Williamsport, Pennsylvania
KOKE-FM Thorndale, Texas
KTGA Saratoga, Wyoming
KMZQ-FM Payson, Arizona
KERL Cotton Plant, Arkansas
KETT Mitchell, Nebraska
KHZY Overton, Nebraska
WXRA Inglis, Florida
KPCR Fowler, Colorado
KYTM Corrigan, Texas
WVLO Cridersville, Ohio
KKTU-FM Fallon, Nevada

99.5 mhz

KADI-FM Republic, Missouri
KAGO-FM Klamath Falls, Oregon
KBHW International Falls, Minnesota
KBLL-FM Helena, Montana
KNFX-FM Bryan, Texas
KBTA-FM Batesville, Arkansas
KBZQ Lawton, Oklahoma
KXBL Henryetta, Oklahoma
KQBR Lubbock, Texas
KDAO-FM Eldora, Iowa
KLVB Citrus Heights, California
KHAZ Hays, Kansas
KNGT Lake Charles, Louisiana
KHMB Hamburg, Arkansas
KIIM-FM Tucson, Arizona
KISS-FM San Antonio, Texas
KQMT Denver, Colorado
KKLA-FM Los Angeles, California
KKMA Le Mars, Iowa
KKPS Brownsville, Texas
KLOK-FM Greenfield, California
KMRJ Rancho Mirage, California
KMTB Murfreesboro, Arkansas
KNTI Lakeport, California
KOLY-FM Mobridge, South Dakota
KPLX Fort Worth, Texas
KPRW Perham, Minnesota
KJMX Reedsport, Oregon
KAKS Huntsville, Arkansas
KXPZ Las Cruces, New Mexico
KSJN Minneapolis, Minnesota
KJMY Bountiful, Utah
KKTV Fallon, Nevada
KWJJ-FM Portland, Oregon
KAAP Rock Island, Washington
KDIS-FM Little Rock, Arkansas
KZZL-FM Pullman, Washington
KPUL Winterset, Iowa
WAIL Key West, Florida
WAOL Ripley, Ohio
WBAI New York, New York
WBXY La Crosse, Florida
WBYG Point Pleasant, West Virginia
WCYJ-FM Waynesburg, Pennsylvania
WDCX-FM Buffalo, New York
WKAA Willacoochee, Georgia
WDZN Midland, Maryland
WGAR-FM Cleveland, Ohio
WJBR-FM Wilmington, Delaware
WJCX Pittsfield, Maine
WJLS-FM Beckley, West Virginia
WIHT Washington, District of Columbia
WKDP-FM Corbin, Kentucky
WKDQ Henderson, Kentucky
WCRB Lowell, Massachusetts
WKSM Fort Walton Beach, Florida
WKXC-FM Aiken, South Carolina
WMAG High Point, North Carolina
WRNN-FM Socastee, South Carolina
WNGE Negaunee, Michigan
WOKN Southport, New York
WPKR Omro, Wisconsin
WCOY Quincy, Illinois
WQYK-FM St. Petersburg, Florida
WRNO-FM New Orleans, Louisiana
WRVE Schenectady, New York
WTKW Bridgeport, New York
WUSN Chicago, Illinois
WUSR Scranton, Pennsylvania
WVIQ Christiansted, Virgin Islands
WMAJ-FM Centre Hall, Pennsylvania
WXNR Grifton, North Carolina
WYCD Detroit, Michigan
WYGO Madisonville, Tennessee
WYSS Sault Ste. Marie, Michigan
WZPL Greenfield, Indiana
WZRR Birmingham, Alabama
KMCJ Colstrip, Montana
KRKI Keystone, South Dakota
WYMJ New Martinsville, West Virginia
WZIM(FM) Lexington, Illinois
WEVJ Jackson, New Hampshire
WYTT Emporia, Virginia
KHAM Britt, Iowa
KHCR Bismarck, Missouri
KBIJ Guymon, Oklahoma
KQPI Aberdeen, Idaho
KRPH Morristown, Arizona

99.7 mhz

KANR Belle Plaine, Kansas
KBCY Tye, Texas
KBEA-FM Muscatine, Iowa
KBTN-FM Neosho, Missouri
KBZD Amarillo, Texas
KMVQ-FM San Francisco, California
KHHK Yakima, Washington
KHYZ Mountain Pass, California
KIOO Porterville, California
KKCK Marshall, Minnesota
KROY Palacios, Texas
KMAC Gainesville, Missouri
KMBQ-FM Wasilla, Alaska
KMJJ-FM Shreveport, Louisiana
KSIT Rock Springs, Wyoming
KOGA-FM Ogallala, Nebraska
KPTE Durango, Colorado
KTTR-FM St. James, Missouri
KVST Willis, Texas
KESC Morro Bay, California
KXDL Browerville, Minnesota
KZLS Mustang, Oklahoma
KZPT Kansas City, Missouri
WBGK Newport Village, New York
WBHX Tuckerton, New Jersey
WRKZ Columbus, Ohio
WCYK-FM Staunton, Virginia
WDJX Louisville, Kentucky
WXST Hollywood, South Carolina
WIMI Ironwood, Michigan
WJMI Jackson, Mississippi
WJUX Monticello, New York
WKSD Paulding, Ohio
WZDR(FM) Sturgeon Bay, Wisconsin
WMC-FM Memphis, Tennessee
WWWQ Atlanta, Georgia
WNTK-FM New London, New Hampshire
WOOF-FM Dothan, Alabama
WJKD Vero Beach, Florida
WRFX Kannapolis, North Carolina
WSHH Pittsburgh, Pennsylvania
WSHW Frankfort, Indiana
WVRZ Mount Carmel, Pennsylvania
WUGN Midland, Michigan
WWIS-FM Black River Falls, Wisconsin
WWTN Hendersonville, Tennessee
WXAJ Hillsboro, Illinois
WEAN-FM Wakefield-Peacedale, Rhode Island
WYFI Norfolk, Virginia
WGCK-FM Coeburn, Virginia
WZXV Palmyra, New York
KMTK Bend, Oregon
KTOR Gerber, California
KRQU Medicine Bow, Wyoming
KKMT Pablo, Montana
KXFT Manson, Iowa
KETE Sulphur Bluff, Texas
KBBC Tishomingo, Oklahoma

99.9 mhz

KAUS-FM Austin, Minnesota
KTOH Kalaheo, Hawaii
KBFL-FM Buffalo, Missouri
KCIV Mount Bullion, California
KCML St. Joseph, Minnesota
KCWN New Sharon, Iowa
KEKB Fruita, Colorado
KONY St. George, Utah
KESZ Phoenix, Arizona
KFAV Warrenton, Missouri
KFMJ Ketchikan, Alaska
KBAT Monahans, Texas
KGOR Omaha, Nebraska
KGPQ Monticello, Arkansas
KTEZ Zwolle, Louisiana
KIRK Macon, Missouri
KISW Seattle, Washington
KKTC Angel Fire, New Mexico
KLUR Wichita Falls, Texas
KMOO-FM Mineola, Texas
KMXA-FM Minot, North Dakota
KJKS Kahului, Hawaii
KOLA San Bernardino, California
KRCX-FM Marysville, California
KRKT-FM Albany, Oregon
KKPL Cheyenne, Wyoming
KSAB Robstown, Texas
KSHN Liberty, Texas
KSKG Salina, Kansas
KWKR Leoti, Kansas
KTCS-FM Fort Smith, Arkansas
KTDY Lafayette, Louisiana
KTQM-FM Clovis, New Mexico
KTSM-FM El Paso, Texas
KTXM Hallettsville, Texas
KTYD Santa Barbara, California
KVOX-FM Moorhead, Minnesota
KVUU Pueblo, Colorado
KWCK-FM Searcy, Arkansas
KWRL La Grande, Oregon
KXLY-FM Spokane, Washington
KXTC Thoreau, New Mexico
KZDX Burley, Idaho
KBOZ-FM Bozeman, Montana
WACO-FM Waco, Texas
WQNR Tallassee, Alabama
WNNG-FM Unadilla, Georgia
WBTZ Plattsburgh, New York
WXRG Athol, Massachusetts
WEZN-FM Bridgeport, Connecticut
WGNE-FM Middleburg, Florida
WFRE Frederick, Maryland
WCMC-FM Holly Springs, North Carolina
WHAK-FM Rogers City, Michigan
WHFB-FM Benton Harbor, Michigan
WHHB Holliston, Massachusetts
WHHS Havertown, Pennsylvania
WIII Cortland, New York
WIOA San Juan, Puerto Rico
WWCT Bartonville, Illinois
WSAU-FM Rudolph, Wisconsin
WJVL Janesville, Wisconsin
WKIS Boca Raton, Florida
WKKO Toledo, Ohio
WKSF Old Fort, North Carolina
WKXB Boiling Spring Lakes, North Carolina
WMTC-FM Vancleve, Kentucky
WTHT Auburn, Maine
WMXC Mobile, Alabama
WODE-FM Easton, Pennsylvania
WOOZ-FM Harrisburg, Illinois
WQBR Avis, Pennsylvania
WQRC Barnstable, Massachusetts
WRJL-FM Eva, Alabama
WCPQ Park Forest, Illinois
WTHI-FM Terre Haute, Indiana
WTUZ Uhrichsville, Ohio
WUSZ Virginia, Minnesota
WVAF Charleston, West Virginia
WVLC Mannsville, Kentucky
WWFG Ocean City, Maryland
WXKC Erie, Pennsylvania
WXMZ Hartford, Kentucky
WYFJ Ashland, Virginia
WZBB Stanleytown, Virginia
WDRK Cornell, Wisconsin
KGCC Gillette, Wyoming
WSMS Artesia, Mississippi
KZMA Naylor, Missouri
WHDX Buxton, North Carolina
WSNT-FM Sandersville, Georgia
KXML Fairfield, Idaho
KRZS Hunt, Texas

Radio Formats Defined

Following these format definitions are indexes of both U.S. and Canadian radio stations by these program format headings. Special Programming typically refers to 1 to 4 hour segments on specific days, of the listed program format.

AAA (or Triple A)—Adult Album Alternative. Eclectic choice of music ranging from hard rock to folk music.

Adult Contemporary—Recent popular songs, with a few oldies. The songs tend to be upbeat and soft. News and talk segments are prominent during rush hour "drive times." Also known as Light Rock.

Agriculture & Farm—News, weather and features of interest to farmers and others involved in agriculture.

Album-Oriented Rock—Popular rock music from past and present rock albums. Also see Rock/AOR.

Alternative—Rock music first popularized in the late 80s and early 90s. Also known as Progressive.

American Indian—Programming for North American Indians; includes native language (i.e. Navajo) broadcasts.

Arabic.

Beautiful Music—Uninterrupted, instrumental soft music. There is usually very little talk and few commercials. Also known as Easy Listening.

Big Band—Popular music from the 30s and 40s. Primarily instrumental works by bands such as Glen Miller's Orchestra and Tommy Dorsey.

Black—Music, talk and news targeted at Black listeners. Music at these stations is similar to Urban Contemporary stations, but this format caters more directly to the interests and tastes of Black audiences.

Bluegrass—Related formats are Country and Folk.

Blues—Some Jazz and Progressive stations also program blues music.

Children—Programming for children, usually for educational purposes. Includes music, informational programming, and news presented for young people.

Chinese.

Christian.

Classic Rock—Popular rock music of the 60s, 70s and 80s. Also see Rock/AOR.

Classical—Classical music, often long pieces played without interruption. Announcers provide extended commentary and criticism on the pieces. Special features, such as live concerts, are common. Primarily a noncommercial FM format.

Comedy—Recorded stand-up comics and/or old radio comedy series. A rare format.

Contemporary Hit/Top-40—Current hot selling records. Usually a playlist of 20 to 40 songs continuously played throughout the day. DJs are often upbeat "personalities." News and information are given light coverage.

Country—Country music, ranging from older traditional country and western to today's "Hit Country" sounds. The amount of news and talk on country stations varies widely from station to station.

Disco—High-energy dance music first popular in the 70s. Also see Black and Urban Contemporary.

Diversified—See Variety/Diverse.

Easy Listening—Similar to Beautiful Music, but may include some soft rock.

Ethnic—Programming for ethnic minorities, mostly in foreign languages.

Farsi.

Filipino.

Folk—Played full-time on very few stations, American folk music is also heard on noncommercial Variety stations. Also see Bluegrass.

Foreign Language/Ethnic—In addition to the specific language categories (i.e. French, German), this format denotes multilingual stations and others catering to ethnic minorities.

French.

Golden Oldies—Hit songs of the 50s. Also see Oldies.

Gospel—Especially popular in the South, evangelical music is programmed on many Religious format stations.

Greek.

Italian.

Japanese.

Jazz—Primarily a noncommercial FM format. Some Classical stations program jazz music features.

Korean.

Light Rock—See Adult Contemporary.

MOR (Middle-of-the-Road)—Traditional AM format featuring a balanced mix of music, news and talk. Songs are usually popular standards. Announcers are often personalities who try to keep the listener interested and informed. News, both local and national, plays an important role at most MOR stations; coverage of sporting events and other features of interest to the community is common.

Native American.

News—Continous coverage of local, national and international news, including sports, weather forecasts and features.

News/Talk—Combination of news and talk formats. One of these elements may receive more emphasis. Also see News and Talk.

Oldies—Hit songs from the 50s, 60s and 70s. Usually played by upbeat DJs, with news, talk and special features (chart countdowns, trivia contests, etc.) playing an important role.

Polish.

Polka—Music for the traditional dance. Most polka format stations are located in Wisconsin.

Portuguese.

Public Affairs—Community interest programming (i.e. broadcasts of city council meetings.) Many noncommercial, News, and Talk stations cover local issues on news features or talk shows.

Reggae—Jamaican music. Often played on Alternative stations.

Religious—Inspirational/spiritual talk and music. Most religious stations air Christian sermons or songs. Also see Gospel.

Rock/AOR—Rock music from the 60s to the present. Album-oriented rock features music "sweeps" or uninterrrupted sets. News plays a secondary role. Also see Classic Rock.

Russian.

Spanish.

Sports—Play-by-play and taped coverage, sports news, interviews, discussion.

Talk—Topical programs on various subjects. Includes health, finance, and community issues. Listener call-in and interview shows are common, and the host's personality tends to be an important element. Many talk stations air national satellite-delivered talk programs. News, sports and weather are usually emphasized during "drive times." Also see News and News/Talk.

Tejano—Bicultural programming including Spanish programming, popular in Texas, particularly near the Mexican border. Interest surged in this type of Spanish music during the early 90s.

Top-40—See Contemporary Hit/Top-40.

Urban Contemporary—Dance music, often from a variety of genres (i.e. rhythm & blues, rap). Most Urban Contemporary stations emphasize music by Black artists. Also see Black and Disco.

Variety/Diverse—A station listing four or more formats. Typical of noncommerical stations.

Vietnamese.

Programming on Radio Stations in the U.S.

Adult Contemp

KDBZ Anchorage, Alaska
KHAR Anchorage, Alaska
KMXS Anchorage, Alaska
KYMG Anchorage, Alaska
KBRW-FM Barrow, Alaska
KTDZ College, Alaska
KCDV Cordova, Alaska
KDLG Dillingham, Alaska
KYSC Fairbanks, Alaska
KGTL Homer, Alaska
KWVV-FM Homer, Alaska
KBBO-FM Houston, Alaska
KINY Juneau, Alaska
KTKN Ketchikan, Alaska
KMVV Meadow Lakes, Alaska
KAKN Naknek, Alaska
KMVN Palmer, Alaska
KIFW Sitka, Alaska
KKIS-FM Soldotna, Alaska
KUHB-FM St. Paul, Alaska
KVAK-FM Valdez, Alaska
WSTF Andalusia, Alabama
WDLT-FM Atmore, Alabama
WKXX Attalla, Alabama
WAYE Birmingham, Alabama
WMJJ Birmingham, Alabama
WQZZ Boligee, Alabama
WMLV Butler, Alabama
WYDE-FM Cullman, Alabama
WAGF-FM Dothan, Alabama
WDYF Dothan, Alabama
WKZJ Eufaula, Alabama
WFIX Florence, Alabama
WQLT-FM Florence, Alabama
WHEP Foley, Alabama
WBFA Fort Mitchell, Alabama
WCKS Fruithurst, Alabama
WFXX Georgiana, Alabama
WAHR Huntsville, Alabama
WHOD Jackson, Alabama
WWMG Millbrook, Alabama
WMXC Mobile, Alabama
WLBF Montgomery, Alabama
WMXS Montgomery, Alabama
WEUP-FM Moulton, Alabama
WMXA Opelika, Alabama
WTLM Opelika, Alabama
WCSN-FM Orange Beach, Alabama
WALX Orrville, Alabama
WOZK Ozark, Alabama
WGSY Phenix City, Alabama
WPID Piedmont, Alabama
WJAM Selma, Alabama
WLDA Slocomb, Alabama
WAGH Smiths, Alabama
WWFA St. Florian, Alabama
WQNR Tallassee, Alabama
KMJI Ashdown, Arkansas
KBTA-FM Batesville, Arkansas
KHLR Benton, Arkansas
KJBX Cash, Arkansas
KBKG Corning, Arkansas
KDMS El Dorado, Arkansas
KLBQ El Dorado, Arkansas
KMLK El Dorado, Arkansas
KMRX El Dorado, Arkansas
KESA Eureka Springs, Arkansas
KFFB Fairfield Bay, Arkansas
KEZA Fayetteville, Arkansas
KOTN Gould, Arkansas
KCNY Greenbrier, Arkansas
KHMB Hamburg, Arkansas
KOOU Hardy, Arkansas
KILX Hatfield, Arkansas
KEAZ Heber Springs, Arkansas
KFFA-FM Helena, Arkansas
KBYB Hope, Arkansas
KBHS Hot Springs, Arkansas
KLAZ Hot Springs, Arkansas
KYDL(FM) Hot Springs, Arkansas
KVRE Hot Springs Village, Arkansas
KVLO Humnoke, Arkansas
KHAN(FM) Kensett, Arkansas
KKTZ Lakeview, Arkansas
KKPT Little Rock, Arkansas
KURB Little Rock, Arkansas
KOLL Lonoke, Arkansas
KGPQ Monticello, Arkansas
KHBM-FM Monticello, Arkansas
KOMT Mountain Home, Arkansas
KTLO-FM Mountain Home, Arkansas
KNAS Nashville, Arkansas
KQMJ(FM) Osceola, Arkansas
KBOA-FM Piggott, Arkansas
KPOC Pocahontas, Arkansas
KPOC-FM Pocahontas, Arkansas
KWKK Russellville, Arkansas
KTOY Texarkana, Arkansas
KKHJ-FM Pago Pago, American Samoa
KFTT Bagdad, Arizona
KIKO-FM Claypool, Arizona
KWRQ Clifton, Arizona
KYBC Cottonwood, Arizona
KJIK Duncan, Arizona
KVNA-FM Flagstaff, Arizona
KZUL-FM Lake Havasu City, Arizona
KESZ Phoenix, Arizona
KMXP Phoenix, Arizona
KPKX Phoenix, Arizona
KTMG Prescott, Arizona
KPPV Prescott Valley, Arizona
KRFM Show Low, Arizona
KZMK Sierra Vista, Arizona
KQAZ Springerville, Arizona
KWKM St. Johns, Arizona
KTBA Tuba City, Arizona
KMXZ-FM Tucson, Arizona
KTUC Tucson, Arizona
KWIM Window Rock, Arizona
KLJZ Yuma, Arizona
KQSR Yuma, Arizona
XETRA Tijuana, Mexico
XHRMFM Tijuana, Mexico
KLSN Adelanto, California
KZXY-FM Apple Valley, California
KHYL Auburn, California
KBLX-FM Berkeley, California
KJMB-FM Blythe, California
KBPK Buena Park, California
KCDU Carmel, California
KWXY(FM) Cathedral City, California
KVIN Ceres, California
KBQB Chico, California
KMXI Chico, California
KXSE Davis, California
KBFP-FM Delano, California
KGBB Edwards, California
KXO-FM El Centro, California
KFSD Escondido, California
KHWY Essex, California
KEJY Eureka, California
KFMI Eureka, California
KSXY Forestville, California
KWPT Fortuna, California
KJLL(FM) Fountain Valley, California
KALZ Fowler, California
KSAY Ft. Bragg, California
KBAY Gilroy, California
KMGQ(FM) Goleta, California
KNCO-FM Grass Valley, California
KTDE Gualala, California
KRDA Hanford, California
KCRH Hayward, California
KNOB Healdsburg, California
KATY-FM Idyllwild, California
KSRW Independence, California
KAJR Indian Wells, California
KRCD Inglewood, California
KRKC-FM King City, California
KNTI Lakeport, California
KXBX Lakeport, California
KXBX-FM Lakeport, California
KGMX Lancaster, California
KKIQ Livermore, California
KCJH Livingston, California
KSKD Livingston, California
KBOX Lompoc, California
KBIG-FM Los Angeles, California
KLVE Los Angeles, California
KOST Los Angeles, California
KYSR Los Angeles, California
KSTT-FM Los Osos-Baywood Par, California
KMMT Mammoth Lakes, California
KMDR McKinleyville, California
KBKY Merced, California
KJSN Modesto, California
KWAV Monterey, California
KHYZ Mountain Pass, California
KTNS Oakhurst, California
KLMM Oceano, California
KLLY Oildale, California
KFYV Ojai, California
KSPA Ontario, California
KXLM Oxnard, California
KEZN Palm Desert, California
KKAL Paso Robles, California
KXTZ Pismo Beach, California
KLXR Redding, California
KSHA Redding, California
KMHX Rohnert Park, California
KQJK Roseville, California
KBZC Sacramento, California
KYMX Sacramento, California
KZZO Sacramento, California
KEGY(FM) San Diego, California
KFMB-FM San Diego, California
KMYI San Diego, California
KIOI San Francisco, California
KLLC San Francisco, California
KMVQ-FM San Francisco, California
KOIT San Francisco, California
KEZR San Jose, California
KKJL San Luis Obispo, California
KVYB Santa Barbara, California
KLJR-FM Santa Paula, California
KZST Santa Rosa, California
KKXX-FM Shafter, California
KESR Shasta Lake City, California
KIRN Simi Valley, California
KSYV Solvang, California
KWYL South Lake Tahoe, California
KVYN St. Helena, California
KJOY Stockton, California
KYCC Stockton, California
KLZN Susanville, California
KXDZ Templeton, California
KHJL(FM) Thousand Oaks, California
KLSI Thousand Oaks, California
KCRZ Tipton, California
KFOX Torrance, California
KCDZ Twentynine Palms, California
KWNE Ukiah, California
KUIC Vacaville, California
KBBY-FM Ventura, California
KHMS Victorville, California
KKDV Walnut Creek, California
KCWH Weed, California
KMJE Woodland, California
KRXV Yermo, California
KDGL Yucca Valley, California
KGIW Alamosa, Colorado
KEZW Aurora, Colorado
KPRB Brush, Colorado
KNAB Burlington, Colorado
KKPK Colorado Springs, Colorado
KRTZ Cortez, Colorado
KALC Denver, Colorado
KIMN Denver, Colorado
KOSI Denver, Colorado
KPTT Denver, Colorado
KIQX Durango, Colorado
KPTE Durango, Colorado
KFTM Fort Morgan, Colorado
KDSP(FM) Greenwood Village, Colorado
KSTH Holyoke, Colorado
KBLJ La Junta, Colorado
KTRR Loveland, Colorado
KBIQ Manitou Springs, Colorado
KAYW Meeker, Colorado
KIMX Nunn, Colorado
KWUF-FM Pagosa Springs, Colorado
KWUZ Poncha Springs, Colorado
KVUU Pueblo, Colorado
KVRH-FM Salida, Colorado
KPMX Sterling, Colorado
KKLI Widefield, Colorado
KNEC Yuma, Colorado
WEZN-FM Bridgeport, Connecticut
WMAS-FM Enfield, Connecticut
WTIC-FM Hartford, Connecticut
WZBG Litchfield, Connecticut
WRCH New Britain, Connecticut
WBMW Pawcatuck, Connecticut
WINY Putnam, Connecticut
WQQQ Sharon, Connecticut

RADIO - U.S.

WMRQ-FM) Waterbury, Connecticut
WEBE Westport, Connecticut
WILI Willimantic, Connecticut
WASH Washington, District of Columbia
WHUR-FM Washington, District of Columbia
WRQX Washington, District of Columbia
WKDB Laurel, Delaware
WAFL Milford, Delaware
WZEB Ocean View, Delaware
WRDX Smyrna, Delaware
WJBR-FM Wilmington, Delaware
WSTW Wilmington, Delaware
WFCT Apalachicola, Florida
WWUS Big Pine Key, Florida
WJIS Bradenton, Florida
WKSG Cedar Creek, Florida
WBTP Clearwater, Florida
WWFL Clermont, Florida
WHQT Coral Gables, Florida
WKZY Cross City, Florida
WAQV Crystal River, Florida
WKTK Crystal River, Florida
WCFB Daytona Beach, Florida
WROD Daytona Beach, Florida
WTMP Egypt Lake, Florida
WWRZ Fort Meade, Florida
WINK-FM Fort Myers, Florida
WSOS-FM Fruit Cove, Florida
WTOT-FM Graceville, Florida
WRZN Hernando, Florida
WCMQ-FM Hialeah, Florida
WVYB Holly Hill, Florida
WOSN Indian River Shores, Florida
WYKE(FM) Inglis, Florida
WAZQ Islamorada, Florida
WEJZ Jacksonville, Florida
WJAX Jacksonville, Florida
WJGL Jacksonville, Florida
WKEY-FM Key West, Florida
WNFB Lake City, Florida
WQHL Live Oak, Florida
WAVK Marathon, Florida
WGMX Marathon, Florida
WAMR-FM Miami, Florida
WLYF Miami, Florida
WMIA-FM Miami Beach, Florida
WSBZ Miramar Beach, Florida
WMGF Mount Dora, Florida
WBCG Murdock, Florida
WSGL Naples, Florida
WCIE New Port Richey, Florida
WDUV New Port Richey, Florida
WHIJ Ocala, Florida
WMFQ Ocala, Florida
WMMO Orlando, Florida
WHIF Palatka, Florida
WEJF Palm Bay, Florida
WRMF Palm Beach, Florida
WCNO Palm City, Florida
WFSY Panama City, Florida
WVVE Panama City Beach, Florida
WBSR Pensacola, Florida
WMEZ Pensacola, Florida
WPRY Perry, Florida
WHLG Port St. Lucie, Florida
WKLG Rock Harbor, Florida
WTLT Sanibel, Florida
WWAV Santa Rosa Beach, Florida
WSDV Sarasota, Florida
WITS Sebring, Florida
WNCV Shalimar, Florida
WCVU Solana, Florida
WKII Solana, Florida
WXGL St. Petersburg, Florida
WRXB St. Petersburg Beach, Florida
WBZE Tallahassee, Florida
WMTX Tampa, Florida
WWRM Tampa, Florida
WEFL Tequesta, Florida
WJGO Tice, Florida
WDDV Venice, Florida
WGYL Vero Beach, Florida
WJKD Vero Beach, Florida
WEAT West Palm Beach, Florida
WTMG Williston, Florida
WDEC-FM Americus, Georgia
WSB-FM Atlanta, Georgia
WRDW Augusta, Georgia
WBGE Bainbridge, Georgia
WBAF Barnesville, Georgia
WMCD Claxton, Georgia
WGHC(AM) Clayton, Georgia
WRBN Clayton, Georgia
WGMG Crawford, Georgia
WYYU Dalton, Georgia
WXMK Dock Junction, Georgia
WGMK Donalsonville, Georgia
WKVQ Eatonton, Georgia
WMGZ Eatonton, Georgia
WLEL Ellaville, Georgia
WRDO Fitzgerald, Georgia
WSRV Gainesville, Georgia
WPCH Gray, Georgia
WSGA Hinesville, Georgia
WMGP Hogansville, Georgia
WBTY Homerville, Georgia
WJGA-FM Jackson, Georgia
WIVL Jasper, Georgia
WBKG Macon, Georgia
WYTH Madison, Georgia
WDRR Martinez, Georgia
WQLI Meigs, Georgia
WBMZ Metter, Georgia
WLRR Milledgeville, Georgia
WALR-FM Palmetto, Georgia
WPNG Pearson, Georgia
WPGA-FM Perry, Georgia
WSSY Pinehurst, Georgia
WSFB Quitman, Georgia
WQTU Rome, Georgia
WEGC Sasser, Georgia
WSEG Savannah, Georgia
WPMX Statesboro, Georgia
WTGA Thomaston, Georgia
WGMY Thomasville, Georgia
WTWA Thomson, Georgia
WKZZ Tifton, Georgia
WNEG Toccoa, Georgia
WRAF Toccoa Falls, Georgia
WNNG-FM Unadilla, Georgia
WQPW Valdosta, Georgia
WTCQ Vidalia, Georgia
WZCH Warner Robins, Georgia
WWUF Waycross, Georgia
WYFW Winder, Georgia
KSTO Agana, Guam
KUAM Agana, Guam
KMWB Captain Cook, Hawaii
KUAI Eleele, Hawaii
KKBG Hilo, Hawaii
KNWB Hilo, Hawaii
KWXX-FM Hilo, Hawaii
KHWI Holualoa, Hawaii
KSSK Honolulu, Hawaii
KUMU-FM Honolulu, Hawaii
KLEO Kahaluu, Hawaii
KJKS Kahului, Hawaii
KRTR-FM Kailua, Hawaii
KLUA Kailua Kona, Hawaii
KTOH Kalaheo, Hawaii
KMKK-FM Kaunakakai, Hawaii
KWYI Kawaihae, Hawaii
KAOY Kealakekua, Hawaii
KTBH-FM Kurtistown, Hawaii
KPOA Lahaina, Hawaii
KAOI-FM Wailuku, Hawaii
KSSK-FM Waipahu, Hawaii
KLGA Algona, Iowa
KLTI-FM Ames, Iowa
KJAN Atlantic, Iowa
KSWI Atlantic, Iowa
KZAT-FM Belle Plaine, Iowa
KSKB Brooklyn, Iowa
KAYP Burlington, Iowa
KBUR Burlington, Iowa
KGRS Burlington, Iowa
KKMI Burlington, Iowa
KDAT Cedar Rapids, Iowa
KMRY Cedar Rapids, Iowa
KCOG Centerville, Iowa
KEDB Chariton, Iowa
KCHA Charles City, Iowa
KCHA-FM Charles City, Iowa
KCHE-FM Cherokee, Iowa
KMA-FM Clarinda, Iowa
KMCN Clinton, Iowa
KMXG Clinton, Iowa
KQKQ-FM Council Bluffs, Iowa
KCZQ Cresco, Iowa
KLOX Creston, Iowa
KDSN Denison, Iowa
KDSN-FM Denison, Iowa
KRNT Des Moines, Iowa
KSTZ Des Moines, Iowa
KATF Dubuque, Iowa
KDAO-FM Eldora, Iowa
KADR Elkader, Iowa
KUYY Emmetsburg, Iowa
KGRR Epworth, Iowa
KIOW Forest City, Iowa
KKEZ Fort Dodge, Iowa
KLMJ Hampton, Iowa
KCVM Hudson, Iowa
KHBT Humboldt, Iowa
KIFG Iowa Falls, Iowa
KOKX Keokuk, Iowa
KRLS Knoxville, Iowa
KLEM Le Mars, Iowa
KMCH Manchester, Iowa
KDAO Marshalltown, Iowa
KBDC Mason City, Iowa
KLSS-FM Mason City, Iowa
KCWN New Sharon, Iowa
KSMA-FM Osage, Iowa
KTWA Ottumwa, Iowa
KQCR-FM Parkersburg, Iowa
KYME Rockford, Iowa
KSOU-FM Sioux Center, Iowa
KGLI Sioux City, Iowa
KUOO Spirit Lake, Iowa
KTDV State Center, Iowa
KAYL-FM Storm Lake, Iowa
KRQN Vinton, Iowa
KCII Washington, Iowa
KNWS-FM Waterloo, Iowa
KOKZ Waterloo, Iowa
KWAY-FM Waverly, Iowa
KORR American Falls, Idaho
KLCE Blackfoot, Idaho
KLLP Chubbuck, Idaho
KXLT-FM Eagle, Idaho
KCIX Garden City, Idaho
KQEO Idaho Falls, Idaho
KATW Lewiston, Idaho
KLER-FM Orofino, Idaho
KBYR-FM Rexburg, Idaho
KGTM Rexburg, Idaho
KSQS Ririe, Idaho
KSRA Salmon, Idaho
KOFE St. Maries, Idaho
WERV-FM Aurora, Illinois
WSDZ Belleville, Illinois
WKRO Cairo, Illinois
WYEC Cambridge, Illinois
WCDD Canton, Illinois
WIBI Carlinville, Illinois
WUEZ Carterville, Illinois
WCEZ Carthage, Illinois
WHMS-FM Champaign, Illinois
WLRW Champaign, Illinois
WILV Chicago, Illinois
WLIT-FM Chicago, Illinois
WNUA Chicago, Illinois
WEZC Clinton, Illinois
KMJM-FM Columbia, Illinois
WDNL Danville, Illinois
WDKB Dekalb, Illinois
WDQN Duquoin, Illinois
WJEZ Dwight, Illinois
WXEF Effingham, Illinois
WEBQ-FM Eldorado, Illinois
WCFS-FM Elmwood Park, Illinois
WIBL(FM) Fairbury, Illinois
WNOI Flora, Illinois
WISH-FM Galatia, Illinois
WDBQ-FM Galena, Illinois
WAIK Galesburg, Illinois
WSPY Geneva, Illinois
WLDS Jacksonville, Illinois
WSSR Joliet, Illinois
WAJK La Salle, Illinois
WAKO Lawrenceville, Illinois
WQLF Lena, Illinois
WKAI Macomb, Illinois
WLWF(FM) Marseilles, Illinois
WLBH Mattoon, Illinois
WLBH-FM Mattoon, Illinois
WREZ Metropolis, Illinois
WRIK-FM Metropolis, Illinois
WMOI Monmouth, Illinois
WCSJ Morris, Illinois
WCSJ-FM Morris, Illinois
WYNG Mount Carmel, Illinois

WBMV Mount Vernon, Illinois
WMIX Mount Vernon, Illinois
WVZA Murphysboro, Illinois
WNSV Nashville, Illinois
WVAZ Oak Park, Illinois
WCMY Ottawa, Illinois
WRKX Ottawa, Illinois
WCIC Pekin, Illinois
WPBG Peoria, Illinois
WSWT Peoria, Illinois
WBBA-FM Pittsfield, Illinois
WLLT Polo, Illinois
WZOE-FM Princeton, Illinois
WLIQ Quincy, Illinois
WTAY Robinson, Illinois
WRHL-FM Rochelle, Illinois
WGFB Rockton, Illinois
WJBD-FM Salem, Illinois
WJDK-FM Seneca, Illinois
WEJT Shelbyville, Illinois
WABZ Sherman, Illinois
WTMX Skokie, Illinois
WIVQ Spring Valley, Illinois
WNNS Springfield, Illinois
WAOX Staunton, Illinois
WSSQ Sterling, Illinois
WSQR Sycamore, Illinois
WRAN Tower Hill, Illinois
WKRV Vandalia, Illinois
WXLC Waukegan, Illinois
WRTB Winnebago, Illinois
WZSR Woodstock, Illinois
WQME Anderson, Indiana
WLKI Angola, Indiana
WZBD Berne, Indiana
WBNL Boonville, Indiana
WBPE Brookston, Indiana
WINN Columbus, Indiana
WIMC Crawfordsville, Indiana
WEOA Evansville, Indiana
WIKY-FM Evansville, Indiana
WVHI Evansville, Indiana
WAJI Fort Wayne, Indiana
WGL Fort Wayne, Indiana
WLAB Fort Wayne, Indiana
WLDE Fort Wayne, Indiana
WMEE Fort Wayne, Indiana
WSHW Frankfort, Indiana
WKAM Goshen, Indiana
WZPL Greenfield, Indiana
WRZQ-FM Greensburg, Indiana
WPWX Hammond, Indiana
WKLO Hardinsburg, Indiana
WGL-FM Huntington, Indiana
WNTR Indianapolis, Indiana
WITZ-FM Jasper, Indiana
WKVI Knox, Indiana
WZWZ Kokomo, Indiana
WLOI La Porte, Indiana
WIRE Lebanon, Indiana
WLEG Ligonier, Indiana
WSAL Logansport, Indiana
WZVN Lowell, Indiana
WXXC Marion, Indiana
WEFM Michigan City, Indiana
WMRS Monticello, Indiana
WAOR(FM) Nappanee, Indiana
WPHZ Orleans, Indiana
WTCA Plymouth, Indiana
WPGW Portland, Indiana
WLQI Rensselaer, Indiana
WRIN Rensselaer, Indiana
WFMG Richmond, Indiana
WARU-FM Roann, Indiana
WAYI(FM) Sellersville, Indiana
WHME South Bend, Indiana
WNSN South Bend, Indiana
WUBU South Bend, Indiana
WMYQ South Whitley, Indiana
WCLS Spencer, Indiana
WVUB Vincennes, Indiana
WZDM Vincennes, Indiana
WRSW-FM Warsaw, Indiana
WAMW Washington, Indiana
WAMW-FM Washington, Indiana
WZZY Winchester, Indiana
KABI Abilene, Kansas
KVSV Beloit, Kansas
KKDT Burdett, Kansas
KMAJ-FM Carbondale, Kansas
KZDY Cawker City, Kansas
KKOY-FM Chanute, Kansas
KCLY Clay Center, Kansas
KRDQ Colby, Kansas
KSKZ Copeland, Kansas
KONQ Dodge City, Kansas
KTLI El Dorado, Kansas
KFFX Emporia, Kansas
KVOE Emporia, Kansas
KOMB Fort Scott, Kansas
KKJQ Garden City, Kansas
KKCI Goodland, Kansas
KZRS Great Bend, Kansas
KIBB Haven, Kansas
KJLS Hays, Kansas
KFBZ Haysville, Kansas
KIND Independence, Kansas
KSCB-FM Liberal, Kansas
KBLS North Fort Riley, Kansas
KQLA Ogden, Kansas
KHMY Pratt, Kansas
KRSL Russell, Kansas
KRSL-FM Russell, Kansas
KWIC Topeka, Kansas
KHCA Wamego, Kansas
KRBB Wichita, Kansas
WANV Annville, Kentucky
WKKQ Barbourville, Kentucky
WLJC Beattyville, Kentucky
WTRT Benton, Kentucky
WCVK Bowling Green, Kentucky
WKLX Brownsville, Kentucky
WCKQ Campbellsville, Kentucky
WBVX Carlisle, Kentucky
WQXQ Central City, Kentucky
WCTT Corbin, Kentucky
WCTT-FM Corbin, Kentucky
WQXE Elizabethtown, Kentucky
WIZF Erlanger, Kentucky
WCVQ Fort Campbell, Kentucky
WEGI Fort Campbell, Kentucky
WSTV-FM Frankfort, Kentucky
WSON Henderson, Kentucky
WHHT Horse Cave, Kentucky
WMJM Jeffersontown, Kentucky
WKHG Leitchfield, Kentucky
WLME Lewisport, Kentucky
WMXL Lexington, Kentucky
WXMA Louisville, Kentucky
WYMC Mayfield, Kentucky
WBFI McDaniels, Kentucky
WFXY Middlesboro, Kentucky
WCLU-FM Munfordville, Kentucky
WEGI-FM Oak Grove, Kentucky
WGCF Paducah, Kentucky
WKLW-FM Paintsville, Kentucky
WGKS Paris, Kentucky
WWJD Pippa Passes, Kentucky
WHVE Russell Springs, Kentucky
WYKY Science Hill, Kentucky
WUHU Smiths Grove, Kentucky
WKEQ Somerset, Kentucky
WLLK-FM Somerset, Kentucky
WYSB Springfield, Kentucky
WVEZ St. Matthews, Kentucky
WCDA Versailles, Kentucky
WABL Amite, Louisiana
KCIJ Atlanta, Louisiana
KJMG Bastrop, Louisiana
KBZE Berwick, Louisiana
KDKS-FM Blanchard, Louisiana
KRVE Brusly, Louisiana
KQLK De Ridder, Louisiana
KBYO-FM Farmerville, Louisiana
KFNV-FM Ferriday, Louisiana
KHLA Jennings, Louisiana
KTDY Lafayette, Louisiana
KBIU Lake Charles, Louisiana
KBDV Leesville, Louisiana
KZLG Mansura, Louisiana
KYMK-FM Maurice, Louisiana
KASO Minden, Louisiana
KLIP Monroe, Louisiana
KMRC Morgan City, Louisiana
WLMG New Orleans, Louisiana
WYLD-FM New Orleans, Louisiana
KPCP New Roads, Louisiana
KUMX North Fort Polk, Louisiana
KOGM Opelousas, Louisiana
KAGY Port Sulphur, Louisiana
KVKI-FM Shreveport, Louisiana
KLSM Tallulah, Louisiana
KNEK-FM Washington, Louisiana
KZRZ West Monroe, Louisiana
KTEZ Zwolle, Louisiana
WXRV Andover, Massachusetts
WQRC Barnstable, Massachusetts
WBMX Boston, Massachusetts
WMJX Boston, Massachusetts
WJIB Cambridge, Massachusetts
WCIB Falmouth, Massachusetts
WXLO Fitchburg, Massachusetts
WROR-FM Framingham, Massachusetts
WSBS Great Barrington, Massachusetts
WHAI Greenfield, Massachusetts
WCOD-FM Hyannis, Massachusetts
WATD-FM Marshfield, Massachusetts
WMRC Milford, Massachusetts
WMLN-FM Milton, Massachusetts
WNBP Newburyport, Massachusetts
WNAW North Adams, Massachusetts
WJDF Orange, Massachusetts
WBEC-FM Pittsfield, Massachusetts
WBRK-FM Pittsfield, Massachusetts
WPLM Plymouth, Massachusetts
WPLM-FM Plymouth, Massachusetts
WRPS Rockland, Massachusetts
WHYN-FM Springfield, Massachusetts
WSNE-FM Taunton, Massachusetts
WSRS Worcester, Massachusetts
WNAV Annapolis, Maryland
WLIF Baltimore, Maryland
WWMX Baltimore, Maryland
WMMJ Bethesda, Maryland
WCEM-FM Cambridge, Maryland
WCEI-FM Easton, Maryland
WLIC Frostburg, Maryland
WILC Laurel, Maryland
WSMD-FM Mechanicsville, Maryland
WAFY Middletown, Maryland
WKHJ Mountain Lake Park, Maryland
WWEG Myersville, Maryland
WQHQ Ocean City-Salisbury, Maryland
WGOP Pocomoke City, Maryland
WTTR Westminster, Maryland
WJTO Bath, Maine
WVAE Biddeford, Maine
WQSS Camden, Maine
WCXU Caribou, Maine
WCRQ Dennysville, Maine
WKSQ Ellsworth, Maine
WWMJ Ellsworth, Maine
WABK-FM Gardiner, Maine
WHOU-FM Houlton, Maine
WALZ-FM Machias, Maine
WCXX Madawaska, Maine
WRMO Milbridge, Maine
WMGX Portland, Maine
WFMX Skowhegan, Maine
WCXV Van Buren, Maine
WHSB Alpena, Michigan
WJSZ Ashley, Michigan
WFDX Atlanta, Michigan
WIOG Bay City, Michigan
WMRX-FM Beaverton, Michigan
WYBR Big Rapids, Michigan
WBCM Boyne City, Michigan
WKHM-FM Brooklyn, Michigan
WSMK Buchanan, Michigan
WLXV Cadillac, Michigan
WIDL Caro, Michigan
WPRJ Coleman, Michigan
WNIC Dearborn, Michigan
WDRQ Detroit, Michigan
WDVD Detroit, Michigan
WMGC-FM Detroit, Michigan
WMXD Detroit, Michigan
WFMK East Lansing, Michigan
WGLQ Escanaba, Michigan
WMJO Essexville, Michigan
WCRZ Flint, Michigan
WQBX Fowler, Michigan
WSRT Gaylord, Michigan
WGHN-FM Grand Haven, Michigan
WLHT-FM Grand Rapids, Michigan
WUPT Gwinn, Michigan
WKMJ-FM Hancock, Michigan
WCXT Hartford, Michigan
WBCH Hastings, Michigan
WCSR Hillsdale, Michigan
WMAX-FM Holland, Michigan
WCCY Houghton, Michigan
WHMI-FM Howell, Michigan

RADIO - U.S.

WIKB-FM Iron River, Michigan
WIMI Ironwood, Michigan
WUPM Ironwood, Michigan
WMQT-FM Ishpeming, Michigan
WVFM Kalamazoo, Michigan
WHZZ Lansing, Michigan
WFCX Leland, Michigan
WBTI Lexington, Michigan
WKLA-FM Ludington, Michigan
WMLQ Manistee, Michigan
WHLX Marine City, Michigan
WBXX Marshall, Michigan
WMJT McMillan, Michigan
WMPX Midland, Michigan
WCZY-FM Mount Pleasant, Michigan
WZNL Norway, Michigan
WWTH Oscoda, Michigan
WMOM Pentwater, Michigan
WLXT Petoskey, Michigan
WQON Roscommon, Michigan
WGER Saginaw, Michigan
WTGV-FM Sandusky, Michigan
WYVN Saugatuck, Michigan
WSOO Sault Ste. Marie, Michigan
WLKM-FM Three Rivers, Michigan
WTRV Walker, Michigan
KDDG Albany, Minnesota
KATE Albert Lea, Minnesota
KCPI Albert Lea, Minnesota
KQQL Anoka, Minnesota
KAUS Austin, Minnesota
KKBJ-FM Bemidji, Minnesota
KKZY Bemidji, Minnesota
KSCR-FM Benson, Minnesota
KOWZ-FM Blooming Prairie, Minnesota
WJJY-FM Brainerd, Minnesota
WZFJ(FM) Breezy Point, Minnesota
KXDL Browerville, Minnesota
KRWC Buffalo, Minnesota
KCLH Caledonia, Minnesota
WKLK-FM Cloquet, Minnesota
KMXK Cold Spring, Minnesota
KBAJ Deer River, Minnesota
KDLM Detroit Lakes, Minnesota
KZLT-FM East Grand Forks, Minnesota
WEVE-FM Eveleth, Minnesota
WLKX-FM Forest Lake, Minnesota
KQRS-FM Golden Valley, Minnesota
WTIP Grand Marais, Minnesota
KMFY Grand Rapids, Minnesota
WWAX Hermantown, Minnesota
WMFG-FM Hibbing, Minnesota
KLCH Lake City, Minnesota
KFML Little Falls, Minnesota
KQAD Luverne, Minnesota
KEEZ-FM Mankato, Minnesota
KKCK Marshall, Minnesota
KTCZ-FM Minneapolis, Minnesota
KMRS Morris, Minnesota
KDOG North Mankato, Minnesota
KCGN-FM Ortonville, Minnesota
KBMX Proctor, Minnesota
KWNG Red Wing, Minnesota
KFSI Rochester, Minnesota
WMIN Sauk Rapids, Minnesota
KNUJ-FM Sleepy Eye, Minnesota
KNSG Springfield, Minnesota
KKJM St. Joseph, Minnesota
KSTP-FM St. Paul, Minnesota
KRBI-FM St. Peter, Minnesota
KRVY-FM Starbuck, Minnesota
KYBA Stewartville, Minnesota
KLBB Stillwater, Minnesota
KTRF Thief River Falls, Minnesota
KQKK Walker, Minnesota
KQIC Willmar, Minnesota
KAGE-FM Winona, Minnesota
KITN Worthington, Minnesota
KBMV-FM Birch Tree, Missouri
KWJK Boonville, Missouri
KFMZ Brookfield, Missouri
KZBK Brookfield, Missouri
KOZX Cabool, Missouri
KNLH Cedar Hill, Missouri
KREZ Chaffee, Missouri
KPLA Columbia, Missouri
KLOZ Eldon, Missouri
KZWV Eldon, Missouri
KCFV Ferguson, Missouri
KCJK Garden City, Missouri
KGLU Gideon, Missouri
KYOO-FM Half Way, Missouri
KTXY Jefferson City, Missouri
KCKC Kansas City, Missouri
KCXL Liberty, Missouri
KIRK Macon, Missouri
KLSC Malden, Missouri
KTRI-FM Mansfield, Missouri
KXEO Mexico, Missouri
KZZT Moberly, Missouri
KMCR Montgomery City, Missouri
KUPH Mountain View, Missouri
KZMA Naylor, Missouri
KGBX-FM Nixa, Missouri
KTOZ-FM Pleasant Hope, Missouri
KAHR Poplar Bluff, Missouri
KNLP Potosi, Missouri
KADI-FM Republic, Missouri
KDAA Rolla, Missouri
KGKS Scott City, Missouri
KSDL Sedalia, Missouri
KBFL Springfield, Missouri
KWND Springfield, Missouri
KGNM St. Joseph, Missouri
KKJO-FM St. Joseph, Missouri
KEZK-FM St. Louis, Missouri
KIHT St. Louis, Missouri
KYKY St. Louis, Missouri
KFLW St. Robert, Missouri
KTTN Trenton, Missouri
KBIY Van Buren, Missouri
KSLQ-FM Washington, Missouri
KFBD-FM Waynesville, Missouri
KULH Wheeling, Missouri
WJBI Batesville, Mississippi
WMJY Biloxi, Mississippi
WMJU Bude, Mississippi
WOWL Burnsville, Mississippi
WFFF-FM Columbia, Mississippi
WTWG Columbus, Mississippi
WLIN-FM Durant, Mississippi
WFTA Fulton, Mississippi
WGNL Greenwood, Mississippi
WUJM Gulfport, Mississippi
WKRA-FM Holly Springs, Mississippi
WSYE Houston, Mississippi
WJMI Jackson, Mississippi
WIQQ Leland, Mississippi
WJZD-FM Long Beach, Mississippi
WLSM-FM Louisville, Mississippi
WKSO Natchez, Mississippi
WOXD Oxford, Mississippi
WQLJ Oxford, Mississippi
WHOC Philadelphia, Mississippi
WWSL Philadelphia, Mississippi
WSKK Ripley, Mississippi
WKZW Sandersville, Mississippi
WZLQ Tupelo, Mississippi
WUMS University, Mississippi
WJKK Vicksburg, Mississippi
WVBG Vicksburg, Mississippi
KGLM-FM Anaconda, Montana
KBBB(FM) Billings, Montana
KOBB Bozeman, Montana
KZMY Bozeman, Montana
KOPR Butte, Montana
KRYK Chinook, Montana
KVVR Dutton, Montana
KJCD Fort Benton, Montana
KLAN Glasgow, Montana
KXGN Glendive, Montana
KAAK Great Falls, Montana
KEIN Great Falls, Montana
KHDN Hardin, Montana
KOJM Havre, Montana
KMTX-FM Helena, Montana
KWMY Joliet, Montana
KALS Kalispell, Montana
KBBZ Kalispell, Montana
KLCM Lewistown, Montana
KPLN Lockwood, Montana
KMMR Malta, Montana
KKQX Manhattan, Montana
KATL Miles City, Montana
KYUS-FM Miles City, Montana
KMSO Missoula, Montana
KMZL Missoula, Montana
KYJK Missoula, Montana
KKMT Pablo, Montana
KTHC Sidney, Montana
KKVU Stevensville, Montana
KEZQ West Yellowstone, Montana
WECR-FM Beech Mountain, North Carolina
WSQL Brevard, North Carolina
WBHN Bryson City, North Carolina
WYNA Calabash, North Carolina
WKSL Cary, North Carolina
WLNK Charlotte, North Carolina
WMKS Clemmons, North Carolina
WKJX Elizabeth City, North Carolina
WZRU Garysburg, North Carolina
WSMW Greensboro, North Carolina
WMYI Hendersonville, North Carolina
WFMZ Hertford, North Carolina
WHGO Hertford, North Carolina
WMAG High Point, North Carolina
WQSL Jacksonville, North Carolina
WCXL Kill Devil Hills, North Carolina
WFLB Laurinburg, North Carolina
WLNC Laurinburg, North Carolina
WWLV(FM) Lexington, North Carolina
WDLZ Murfreesboro, North Carolina
WCVP Murphy, North Carolina
WIKS New Bern, North Carolina
WNNC Newton, North Carolina
WIOZ Pinehurst, North Carolina
WPNC-FM Plymouth, North Carolina
WRAL Raleigh, North Carolina
WJMH Reidsville, North Carolina
WLHC Robbins, North Carolina
WAYN Rockingham, North Carolina
WIOZ-FM Southern Pines, North Carolina
WUKS St. Pauls, North Carolina
WEQR Walnut Creek, North Carolina
WMXF Waynesville, North Carolina
WGNI Wilmington, North Carolina
WILT Wilmington, North Carolina
WWIL-FM Wilmington, North Carolina
WRCM Wingate, North Carolina
KYYY Bismarck, North Dakota
KWGO Burlington, North Dakota
KXRV Cannon Ball, North Dakota
KXGT Carrington, North Dakota
KQZZ Devils Lake, North Dakota
KDIX Dickinson, North Dakota
KKBO Flasher, North Dakota
KKXL Grand Forks, North Dakota
KHND Harvey, North Dakota
KMJO Hope, North Dakota
KSJZ Jamestown, North Dakota
KNDK-FM Langdon, North Dakota
KNDR Mandan, North Dakota
KIZZ Minot, North Dakota
KMXA-FM Minot, North Dakota
KRRZ Minot, North Dakota
KYTZ Walhalla, North Dakota
KBRB Ainsworth, Nebraska
KBRB-FM Ainsworth, Nebraska
KRGY Aurora, Nebraska
KWBE Beatrice, Nebraska
KCNB Chadron, Nebraska
KLIR Columbus, Nebraska
KINI Crookston, Nebraska
KMTY Gibbon, Nebraska
KHAS Hastings, Nebraska
KLIQ Hastings, Nebraska
KBBK Lincoln, Nebraska
KSRC Loup City, Nebraska
KSWN McCook, Nebraska
KELN North Platte, Nebraska
KJLT-FM North Platte, Nebraska
KOMJ Omaha, Nebraska
KQCH Omaha, Nebraska
KSRZ Omaha, Nebraska
KSID-FM Sidney, Nebraska
KRFS Superior, Nebraska
KRKR Waverly, Nebraska
KTMX York, Nebraska
WKDR Berlin, New Hampshire
WMOU Berlin, New Hampshire
WBNC Conway, New Hampshire
WVMJ Conway, New Hampshire
WFTN-FM Franklin, New Hampshire
WSAK Hampton, New Hampshire
WGXL Hanover, New Hampshire
WNEC-FM Henniker, New Hampshire
WKNE Keene, New Hampshire
WSNI Keene, New Hampshire
WLNH-FM Laconia, New Hampshire
WXXS Lancaster, New Hampshire
WLTN-FM Lisbon, New Hampshire
WWNH Madbury, New Hampshire
WFEA Manchester, New Hampshire

WZID Manchester, New Hampshire
WHOM Mount Washington, New Hampshire
WFNQ Nashua, New Hampshire
WBYY Somersworth, New Hampshire
WNYN-FM Whitefield, New Hampshire
WASR Wolfeboro, New Hampshire
WLKZ Wolfeboro, New Hampshire
WJLK Asbury Park, New Jersey
WFPG Atlantic City, New Jersey
WVBH Beach Haven West, New Jersey
WHCY Blairstown, New Jersey
WAIV Cape May, New Jersey
WSJO Egg Harbor City, New Jersey
WIMG Ewing, New Jersey
WSUS Franklin, New Jersey
WWZY Long Branch, New Jersey
WJRZ-FM Manahawkin, New Jersey
WTTH Margate City, New Jersey
WMGQ New Brunswick, New Jersey
WPAT-FM Paterson, New Jersey
WBZC Pemberton, New Jersey
WBHX Tuckerton, New Jersey
WCZT Villas, New Jersey
WCMC Wildwood, New Jersey
WEZW Wildwood Crest, New Jersey
KYCM Alamogordo, New Mexico
KDEF Albuquerque, New Mexico
KKOB-FM Albuquerque, New Mexico
KPEK Albuquerque, New Mexico
KWYK-FM Aztec, New Mexico
KAMQ Carlsbad, New Mexico
KATK Carlsbad, New Mexico
KCDY Carlsbad, New Mexico
KSMX-FM Clovis, New Mexico
KTQM-FM Clovis, New Mexico
KDEM Deming, New Mexico
KLVF Las Vegas, New Mexico
KMVR Mesilla Park, New Mexico
KQNM Milan, New Mexico
KLBU Pecos, New Mexico
KLNN Questa, New Mexico
KRTN Raton, New Mexico
KBIM-FM Roswell, New Mexico
KSFX Roswell, New Mexico
KYCT Ruidoso, New Mexico
KKOB Exp S Santa Fe, New Mexico
KSCQ Silver City, New Mexico
KKIT Taos, New Mexico
KVAL Cal-Nev-Ari, Nevada
KHIX Carlin, Nevada
KELK Elko, Nevada
KMXB Henderson, Nevada
KRNO Incline Village, Nevada
KKLZ Las Vegas, Nevada
KKVV Las Vegas, Nevada
KSNE-FM Las Vegas, Nevada
KXPT Las Vegas, Nevada
KADD Logandale, Nevada
KJUL Moapa Valley, Nevada
KFRH North Las Vegas, Nevada
KNEV Reno, Nevada
WKLI-FM Albany, New York
WYJB Albany, New York
WSEN-FM Baldwinsville, New York
WVIN-FM Bath, New York
WINR Binghamton, New York
WBAZ Bridgehampton, New York
WFAS-FM Bronxville, New York
WHTT-FM Buffalo, New York
WJYE Buffalo, New York
WVOR Canandaigua, New York
WTOJ Carthage, New York
WCTW Catskill, New York
WRVH Clayton, New York
WGMM Corning, New York
WNKI Corning, New York
WDNY-FM Dansville, New York
WOLF-FM DeRuyter, New York
WENY-FM Elmira, New York
WLVY Elmira, New York
WEHH Elmira Hts-Horsehds, New York
WHPC Garden City, New York
WHLI Hempstead, New York
WKJY Hempstead, New York
WXUR Herkimer, New York
WKPQ Hornell, New York
WHUC Hudson, New York
WNYQ Hudson Falls, New York
WCZX Hyde Park, New York
WYXL Ithaca, New York
WWSE Jamestown, New York
WLTB Johnson City, New York
WIZR Johnstown, New York
WKNY Kingston, New York
WMSA Massena, New York
WSUL Monticello, New York
WBWZ New Paltz, New York
WLTW New York, New York
WPLJ New York, New York
WKXZ Norwich, New York
WMXO Olean, New York
WSRK Oneonta, New York
WALK-FM Patchogue, New York
WHUD Peekskill, New York
WYLF Penn Yan, New York
WZUN Phoenix, New York
WKOL Plattsburgh, New York
WRRQ Port Dickinson, New York
WPDM Potsdam, New York
WRNQ Poughkeepsie, New York
WRCR Ramapo, New York
WRIV Riverhead, New York
WDVI Rochester, New York
WRMM-FM Rochester, New York
WSLP Saranac Lake, New York
WBPM Saugerties, New York
WRVE Schenectady, New York
WCDO Sidney, New York
WCDO-FM Sidney, New York
WHFM Southampton, New York
WSPQ Springville, New York
WYYY Syracuse, New York
WRGR Tupper Lake, New York
WLZW Utica, New York
WTLB Utica, New York
WMXW Vestal, New York
WFAS White Plains, New York
WIFF Windsor, New York
WDJQ Alliance, Ohio
WNCO Ashland, Ohio
WREO-FM Ashtabula, Ohio
WATH Athens, Ohio
WJKW Athens, Ohio
WOUB-FM Athens, Ohio
WXTQ Athens, Ohio
WBNV Barnesville, Ohio
WPKO-FM Bellefontaine, Ohio
WBNO-FM Bryan, Ohio
WBCO Bucyrus, Ohio
WILE-FM Byesville, Ohio
WCDK Cadiz, Ohio
WYNT Caledonia, Ohio
WCMJ Cambridge, Ohio
WHBC-FM Canton, Ohio
WGGN Castalia, Ohio
WKRQ Cincinnati, Ohio
WNNF Cincinnati, Ohio
WRRM Cincinnati, Ohio
WFHM-FM Cleveland, Ohio
WQAL Cleveland, Ohio
WZAK Cleveland, Ohio
WNCI Columbus, Ohio
WSNY Columbus, Ohio
WTNS-FM Coshocton, Ohio
WMMX Dayton, Ohio
WDFM Defiance, Ohio
WGTZ Eaton, Ohio
WLQT Englewood, Ohio
WKXA-FM Findlay, Ohio
WBVI Fostoria, Ohio
WFRO-FM Fremont, Ohio
WCVO Gahanna, Ohio
WXBW Gallipolis, Ohio
WIMX Gibsonburg, Ohio
WVNU Greenfield, Ohio
WKTN Kenton, Ohio
WVNO-FM Mansfield, Ohio
WYHT Mansfield, Ohio
WMOA Marietta, Ohio
WKLM Millersburg, Ohio
WQIO Mount Vernon, Ohio
WKDD Munroe Falls, Ohio
WIOI New Boston, Ohio
WWJM New Lexington, Ohio
WHOF North Canton, Ohio
WLKR-FM Norwalk, Ohio
WMOJ-FM Norwood, Ohio
WNTO Racine, Ohio
WAOL Ripley, Ohio
WCPZ Sandusky, Ohio
WMVR-FM Sidney, Ohio
WHIZ-FM South Zanesville, Ohio
WMLX St. Marys, Ohio
WKTL Struthers, Ohio
WJUC Swanton, Ohio
WWWM-FM Sylvania, Ohio
WRVF Toledo, Ohio
WERT Van Wert, Ohio
WCHO Washington Ct House, Ohio
WVMX Westerville, Ohio
WZLR Xenia, Ohio
WMXY Youngstown, Ohio
KKWD Bethany, Oklahoma
KZLI Catoosa, Oklahoma
KXOO Elk City, Oklahoma
KTSO Glenpool, Oklahoma
KQTZ Hobart, Oklahoma
KQIB Idabel, Oklahoma
KXLS Lahoma, Oklahoma
KMGZ Lawton, Oklahoma
KVRW Lawton, Oklahoma
KMGL Oklahoma City, Oklahoma
KOMA Oklahoma City, Oklahoma
KYIS Oklahoma City, Oklahoma
KXTH Seminole, Oklahoma
KJCM Snyder, Oklahoma
KSPI-FM Stillwater, Oklahoma
KBEZ Tulsa, Oklahoma
KGTO Tulsa, Oklahoma
KRAV-FM Tulsa, Oklahoma
KMZE Woodward, Oklahoma
KCMX-FM Ashland, Oregon
KTIL-FM Bay City, Oregon
KKCW Beaverton, Oregon
KMGX Bend, Oregon
KNLR Bend, Oregon
KEHK Brownsville, Oregon
KORC(FM) Burns, Oregon
KCNA Cave Junction, Oregon
KDCQ Coos Bay, Oregon
KMGE Eugene, Oregon
KODZ Eugene, Oregon
KCST-FM Florence, Oregon
KAJO Grants Pass, Oregon
KLDR Harbeck-Fruitdale, Oregon
KQFM Hermiston, Oregon
KCGB-FM Hood River, Oregon
KWRL La Grande, Oregon
KORV Lakeview, Oregon
KSHO Lebanon, Oregon
KTMT-FM Medford, Oregon
KKKJ Merrill, Oregon
KOOR Milwaukie, Oregon
KRSK Molalla, Oregon
KSND Monmouth, Oregon
KSRV-FM Ontario, Oregon
KUMA-FM Pilot Rock, Oregon
KYCH-FM Portland, Oregon
KPPK Rainier, Oregon
KLRR Redmond, Oregon
KWPK-FM Sisters, Oregon
KODL The Dalles, Oregon
KKMX Tri City, Oregon
KEUG Veneta, Oregon
KWSO Warm Springs, Oregon
WLEV Allentown, Pennsylvania
WFBG Altoona, Pennsylvania
WNCC Barnesboro, Pennsylvania
WHLM-FM Berwick, Pennsylvania
WFYY Bloomsburg, Pennsylvania
WBYN-FM Boyertown, Pennsylvania
WRRK Braddock, Pennsylvania
WXMJ Cambridge Springs, Pennsylvania
WTRW(FM) Carbondale, Pennsylvania
WIKZ Chambersburg, Pennsylvania
WCCR Clarion, Pennsylvania
WQYX Clearfield, Pennsylvania
WUUZ Cooperstown, Pennsylvania
WBRX Cresson, Pennsylvania
WNKZ Dushore, Pennsylvania
WQKY Emporium, Pennsylvania
WXBB Erie, Pennsylvania
WXKC Erie, Pennsylvania
WRSD Folsom, Pennsylvania
WQFM Forest City, Pennsylvania
WQFN(FM) Forest City, Pennsylvania
WFRA Franklin, Pennsylvania
WHMJ Franklin, Pennsylvania
WGET Gettysburg, Pennsylvania
WMHX(FM) Hershey, Pennsylvania
WRKY-FM Hollidaysburg, Pennsylvania
WCCS Homer City, Pennsylvania
WDNH-FM Honesdale, Pennsylvania

WLAK Huntingdon, Pennsylvania
WQMU Indiana, Pennsylvania
WCRO Johnstown, Pennsylvania
WKYE Johnstown, Pennsylvania
WLAN Lancaster, Pennsylvania
WROZ Lancaster, Pennsylvania
WLSH Lansford, Pennsylvania
WQTW Latrobe, Pennsylvania
WQIC Lebanon, Pennsylvania
WGRC Lewisburg, Pennsylvania
WMRF-FM Lewistown, Pennsylvania
WSQV(FM) Lock Haven, Pennsylvania
WNBQ Mansfield, Pennsylvania
WRIJ Masontown, Pennsylvania
WLLF Mercer, Pennsylvania
WMSS Middletown, Pennsylvania
WVRT Mill Hall, Pennsylvania
WQLV Millersburg, Pennsylvania
WVLY-FM Milton, Pennsylvania
WBZZ(FM) New Kensington, Pennsylvania
WPCL Northern Cambria, Pennsylvania
WEGH Northumberland, Pennsylvania
WKQW-FM Oil City, Pennsylvania
WBEN-FM Philadelphia, Pennsylvania
WDAS-FM Philadelphia, Pennsylvania
WISX Philadelphia, Pennsylvania
WJAS Pittsburgh, Pennsylvania
WLTJ Pittsburgh, Pennsylvania
WSHH Pittsburgh, Pennsylvania
WWSW-FM Pittsburgh, Pennsylvania
WHKS Port Allegany, Pennsylvania
WPPA Pottsville, Pennsylvania
WPXZ-FM Punxsutawney, Pennsylvania
WDSN Reynoldsville, Pennsylvania
WKMC Roaring Spring, Pennsylvania
WATS Sayre, Pennsylvania
WLSW Scottdale, Pennsylvania
WWRR Scranton, Pennsylvania
WYFM Sharon, Pennsylvania
WKBI St. Marys, Pennsylvania
WQKX Sunbury, Pennsylvania
WMGH-FM Tamaqua, Pennsylvania
WTTC-FM Towanda, Pennsylvania
WTRN Tyrone, Pennsylvania
WCTL Union City, Pennsylvania
WMBS Uniontown, Pennsylvania
WCYJ-FM Waynesburg, Pennsylvania
WNBT Wellsboro, Pennsylvania
WNBT-FM Wellsboro, Pennsylvania
WMGS Wilkes-Barre, Pennsylvania
WKSB Williamsport, Pennsylvania
WARM-FM York, Pennsylvania
WYCR York-Hanover, Pennsylvania
WFDT Aguada, Puerto Rico
WABA Aguadilla, Puerto Rico
WTPM Aguadilla, Puerto Rico
WVJP Caguas, Puerto Rico
WVOZ-FM Carolina, Puerto Rico
WCPR Coamo, Puerto Rico
WALO Humacao, Puerto Rico
WISA Isabela, Puerto Rico
WIVV Island of Vieques, Puerto Rico
WTIL Mayaguez, Puerto Rico
WEXS Patillas, Puerto Rico
WPPC Penuelas, Puerto Rico
WIOC Ponce, Puerto Rico
WPUC-FM Ponce, Puerto Rico
WZAR Ponce, Puerto Rico
WFID Rio Piedras, Puerto Rico
WBMJ San Juan, Puerto Rico
WIOA San Juan, Puerto Rico
WLRP San Sebastian, Puerto Rico
WERR Vega Alta, Puerto Rico
WVIS Vieques, Puerto Rico
WXEW Yabucoa, Puerto Rico
WENA Yauco, Puerto Rico
WJZS Block Island, Rhode Island
WWBB Providence, Rhode Island
WGTN-FM Andrews, South Carolina
WYKZ Beaufort, South Carolina
WEPC Belton, South Carolina
WSSX-FM Charleston, South Carolina
WDAR-FM Darlington, South Carolina
WWNQ Forest Acres, South Carolina
WFBC-FM Greenville, South Carolina
WCRS Greenwood, South Carolina
WZSN Greenwood, South Carolina
WMXZ Isle of Palms, South Carolina
WDKD Kingstree, South Carolina
WKCL Ladson, South Carolina
WMYB Myrtle Beach, South Carolina
WKDK Newberry, South Carolina
WTCB Orangeburg, South Carolina
WMGL Ravenel, South Carolina
WSNW Seneca, South Carolina
WSPA-FM Spartanburg, South Carolina
WWBD Sumter, South Carolina
KBFO Aberdeen, South Dakota
KBRK-FM Brookings, South Dakota
KFCR Custer, South Dakota
KSQB-FM Dell Rapids, South Dakota
KJBI Fort Pierre, South Dakota
KZKK Huron, South Dakota
KQRN Mitchell, South Dakota
KGFX-FM Pierre, South Dakota
KLXS-FM Pierre, South Dakota
KKMK Rapid City, South Dakota
KQRQ Rapid City, South Dakota
KNBZ Redfield, South Dakota
KELO-FM Sioux Falls, South Dakota
KMXC Sioux Falls, South Dakota
KIXX Watertown, South Dakota
KWAT Watertown, South Dakota
KWYR-FM Winner, South Dakota
KYNT Yankton, South Dakota
WBGQ Bulls Gap, Tennessee
WCLE-FM Calhoun, Tennessee
WRJB Camden, Tennessee
WDEF-FM Chattanooga, Tennessee
WKRM Columbia, Tennessee
WGIC Cookeville, Tennessee
WPBX Crossville, Tennessee
WDNT Dayton, Tennessee
WLLJ Etowah, Tennessee
WMRO Gallatin, Tennessee
WSEV-FM Gatlinburg, Tennessee
WMPZ Harrison, Tennessee
WHHM-FM Henderson, Tennessee
WIFA Knoxville, Tennessee
WAWI Lawrenceburg, Tennessee
WDXE-FM Lawrenceburg, Tennessee
WZLT Lexington, Tennessee
WYGO Madisonville, Tennessee
WFTZ Manchester, Tennessee
WCMT-FM Martin, Tennessee
WMC-FM Memphis, Tennessee
WQOX Memphis, Tennessee
WRVR Memphis, Tennessee
WKIM Munford, Tennessee
WCJK Murfreesboro, Tennessee
WAMB Nashville, Tennessee
WJXA Nashville, Tennessee
WNRQ Nashville, Tennessee
WBNT-FM Oneida, Tennessee
WLZK Paris, Tennessee
WPRT-FM Pegram, Tennessee
WSEV Sevierville, Tennessee
WUUQ South Pittsburg, Tennessee
WAYM Spring Hill, Tennessee
WTNE Trenton, Tennessee
WQAK Union City, Tennessee
KACU Abilene, Texas
KGNZ Abilene, Texas
KJAV Alamo, Texas
KMXJ-FM Amarillo, Texas
KPRF Amarillo, Texas
KLTY Arlington, Texas
KKMJ-FM Austin, Texas
KQXB(FM) Belton, Texas
KBTS Big Spring, Texas
KROO Breckenridge, Texas
KLTR Brenham, Texas
KSTQ(FM) Brownfield, Texas
KBWD Brownwood, Texas
KKYS Bryan, Texas
KAPN Caldwell, Texas
KETR Commerce, Texas
KSSM Copperas Cove, Texas
KLTG Corpus Christi, Texas
KDMX Dallas, Texas
KJKK Dallas, Texas
KTDR Del Rio, Texas
KAFX-FM Diboll, Texas
KVLY Edinburg, Texas
KINT-FM El Paso, Texas
KSII El Paso, Texas
KTSM-FM El Paso, Texas
KFST Fort Stockton, Texas
KMVK Fort Worth, Texas
KGAF Gainesville, Texas
KSOC Gainesville, Texas
KTWL Hempstead, Texas
KHMX Houston, Texas
KODA Houston, Texas
KSYY Ingram, Texas
KLJT Jacksonville, Texas
KOOI Jacksonville, Texas
KJAS Jasper, Texas
KKVR Kerrville, Texas
KQUR Laredo, Texas
KAJZ Llano, Texas
KHMR Lovelady, Texas
KONE Lubbock, Texas
KYBI Lufkin, Texas
KAMX Luling, Texas
KZLV Lytle, Texas
KMVL Madisonville, Texas
KKHA Markham, Texas
KBWC Marshall, Texas
KCHX Midland, Texas
KCRS-FM Midland, Texas
KQRX Midland, Texas
KLBW New Boston, Texas
KZRB New Boston, Texas
KNRG New Ulm, Texas
KMCM Odessa, Texas
KODM Odessa, Texas
KKMY Orange, Texas
KGRO Pampa, Texas
KPLT-FM Paris, Texas
KPTX Pecos, Texas
KNLE-FM Round Rock, Texas
KELI San Angelo, Texas
KIXY-FM San Angelo, Texas
KMDX San Angelo, Texas
KAHL San Antonio, Texas
KQXT-FM San Antonio, Texas
KHKZ San Benito, Texas
KNVR San Saba, Texas
KSMG Seguin, Texas
KDAE Sinton, Texas
KSST Sulphur Springs, Texas
KMMX Tahoka, Texas
KLAK Tom Bean, Texas
KTYL-FM Tyler, Texas
KNAL Victoria, Texas
KQVT Victoria, Texas
KTXN-FM Victoria, Texas
KVIC Victoria, Texas
WACO-FM Waco, Texas
KQHN Waskom, Texas
KZTK White Oak, Texas
KBZS Wichita Falls, Texas
KALK Winfield, Texas
KREC Brian Head, Utah
KQMB Levan, Utah
KBLQ-FM Logan, Utah
KLGN Logan, Utah
KUDE Nephi, Utah
KBZN Ogden, Utah
KOGN Ogden, Utah
KTCE Payson, Utah
KSRR Provo, Utah
KIFX Roosevelt, Utah
KXRQ Roosevelt, Utah
KANN Roy, Utah
KUDD Roy, Utah
KBEE Salt Lake City, Utah
KSFI Salt Lake City, Utah
KOSY-FM Spanish Fork, Utah
KNFL Tremonton, Utah
KYMV Woodruff, Utah
WAVA-FM Arlington, Virginia
WJDV Broadway, Virginia
WWZW Buena Vista, Virginia
WQMZ Charlottesville, Virginia
WNLR Churchville, Virginia
WGCK-FM Coeburn, Virginia
WZGN Crozet, Virginia
WCVA Culpeper, Virginia
WPIN-FM Dublin, Virginia
WVBB Elliston-Lafayette, Virginia
WEVA Emporia, Virginia
WFLO-FM Farmville, Virginia
WBQB Fredericksburg, Virginia
WXGM Gloucester, Virginia
WXGM-FM Gloucester, Virginia
WWDE-FM Hampton, Virginia
WKWI Kilmarnock, Virginia
WOJL Louisa, Virginia
WMXH-FM Luray, Virginia
WSNZ Lynchburg, Virginia
WZVA Marion, Virginia

WPIM Martinsville, Virginia
WJOI Norfolk, Virginia
WESR-FM Onley-Onancock, Virginia
WVCV Orange, Virginia
WKJM Petersburg, Virginia
WRIC-FM Richlands, Virginia
WKJS Richmond, Virginia
WTVR-FM Richmond, Virginia
WSLQ Roanoke, Virginia
WPAR Salem, Virginia
WSNV Salem, Virginia
WHLF South Boston, Virginia
WTON-FM Staunton, Virginia
WVBW Suffolk, Virginia
WRAR-FM Tappahannock, Virginia
WSFF Vinton, Virginia
WMBG Williamsburg, Virginia
WINC-FM Winchester, Virginia
WIUJ Charlotte Amalie, Virgin Islands
WVIQ Christiansted, Virgin Islands
WKVT-FM Brattleboro, Vermont
WTSA-FM Brattleboro, Vermont
WEZF Burlington, Vermont
WMOO Derby Center, Vermont
WGMT Lyndon, Vermont
WVNR Poultney, Vermont
WDVT Rutland, Vermont
WJJR Rutland, Vermont
WZRT Rutland, Vermont
WCFR Springfield, Vermont
WSTJ St. Johnsbury, Vermont
KWLE Anacortes, Washington
KOLW Basin City, Washington
KQMV Bellevue, Washington
KAFE Bellingham, Washington
KRWM Bremerton, Washington
KOZI Chelan, Washington
KOZI-FM Chelan, Washington
KCLK-FM Clarkston, Washington
KXAA Cle Elum, Washington
KRAO-FM Colfax, Washington
KCRK-FM Colville, Washington
KMCQ Covington, Washington
KEYF Dishman, Washington
KEYG-FM Grand Coulee, Washington
KLOG Kelso, Washington
KLYK Kelso, Washington
KONA-FM Kennewick, Washington
KIXI Mercer Island/Seattl, Washington
KSWW Ocean Shores, Washington
KGY Olympia, Washington
KOMW Omak, Washington
KEYW Pasco, Washington
KRIZ Renton, Washington
KAAP Rock Island, Washington
KJR-FM Seattle, Washington
KPLZ-FM Seattle, Washington
KAGU Spokane, Washington
KISC Spokane, Washington
KXLY-FM Spokane, Washington
KZZU-FM Spokane, Washington
WDKM Adams, Wisconsin
WISM-FM Altoona, Wisconsin
WATK Antigo, Wisconsin
WOVM Appleton, Wisconsin
WLBL Auburndale, Wisconsin
WRPQ Baraboo, Wisconsin
WBEV Beaver Dam, Wisconsin
WBCR-FM Beloit, Wisconsin
WBJZ Berlin, Wisconsin
WWIS-FM Black River Falls, Wisconsin
WCFW Chippewa Falls, Wisconsin
WERL Eagle River, Wisconsin
WAXX Eau Claire, Wisconsin
WIAL Eau Claire, Wisconsin
WFON Fond Du Lac, Wisconsin
WSJY Fort Atkinson, Wisconsin
WQLH Green Bay, Wisconsin
WRLS-FM Hayward, Wisconsin
WLXR-FM La Crosse, Wisconsin
WLKG Lake Geneva, Wisconsin
WJTY Lancaster, Wisconsin
WFDL-FM Lomira, Wisconsin
WMGN Madison, Wisconsin
WZEE Madison, Wisconsin
WRJC-FM Mauston, Wisconsin
WJMT Merrill, Wisconsin
WKLH Milwaukee, Wisconsin
WLWK-FM Milwaukee, Wisconsin
WMYX-FM Milwaukee, Wisconsin
WRIT-FM Milwaukee, Wisconsin
WMQA-FM Minocqua, Wisconsin
WEKZ-FM Monroe, Wisconsin
WNAM Neenah-Menasha, Wisconsin
WPKG Neillsville, Wisconsin
WJUB Plymouth, Wisconsin
WXER Plymouth, Wisconsin
WPDR Portage, Wisconsin
WRHN Rhinelander, Wisconsin
WJMC Rice Lake, Wisconsin
WKFX Rice Lake, Wisconsin
WRCO Richland Center, Wisconsin
WTCX Ripon, Wisconsin
WEVR River Falls, Wisconsin
WEVR-FM River Falls, Wisconsin
WOWN Shawano, Wisconsin
WSHS Sheboygan, Wisconsin
WKPO Soldiers Grove, Wisconsin
WSRG Sturgeon Bay, Wisconsin
WGEE Superior, Wisconsin
WXYM Tomah, Wisconsin
WFDL Waupun, Wisconsin
WAUH Wautoma, Wisconsin
WNNO-FM Wisconsin Dells, Wisconsin
WHAJ Bluefield, West Virginia
WPIB Bluefield, West Virginia
WBTQ Buckhannon, West Virginia
WVAF Charleston, West Virginia
WWLW Clarksburg, West Virginia
WXIL Elizabeth, West Virginia
WDNE Elkins, West Virginia
WELK Elkins, West Virginia
WELD Fisher, West Virginia
WVUS Grafton, West Virginia
WMGA Kenova, West Virginia
WKLP Keyser, West Virginia
WHFI Lindside, West Virginia
WVOW Logan, West Virginia
WVOW-FM Logan, West Virginia
WLTF Martinsburg, West Virginia
WYMJ New Martinsville, West Virginia
WQAB Philippi, West Virginia
WVAR Richwood, West Virginia
WDYK Ridgeley, West Virginia
WMXE South Charleston, West Virginia
WRRR-FM St. Marys, West Virginia
WCWV Summersville, West Virginia
WSGB Sutton, West Virginia
WAFD Webster Springs, West Virginia
WEIR Weirton, West Virginia
WELC Welch, West Virginia
WZST Westover, West Virginia
KHOC Casper, Wyoming
KJUA Cheyenne, Wyoming
KTAG Cody, Wyoming
KNYN Fort Bridger, Wyoming
KAML-FM Gillette, Wyoming
KUGR Green River, Wyoming
KZWB Green River, Wyoming
KAOX Kemmerer, Wyoming
KZQL Mills, Wyoming
KHRW Ranchester, Wyoming
KRAL Rawlins, Wyoming
KTRZ Riverton, Wyoming
KWYO Sheridan, Wyoming
KTHE Thermopolis, Wyoming
KZEW Wheatland, Wyoming
KDDV-FM Wright, Wyoming

Agriculture

KSIR Brush, Colorado
WOC Davenport, Iowa
WHOW Clinton, Illinois
WORX-FM Madison, Indiana
KNDY Marysville, Kansas
KSUM Fairmont, Minnesota
KQLX Lisbon, North Dakota
KNEB-FM Scottsbluff, Nebraska
WCJW Warsaw, New York
KWHW Altus, Oklahoma
KBHB Sturgis, South Dakota
KFLP-FM Floydada, Texas

Alternative

KRUA Anchorage, Alaska
KSUA Fairbanks, Alaska
KXLL Juneau, Alaska
KUHB-FM St. Paul, Alaska
WAAO-FM Andalusia, Alabama
WEGL Auburn, Alabama
WZEW Fairhope, Alabama
WVUA-FM Tuscaloosa, Alabama
KCAC Camden, Arkansas
KPOS Fouke, Arkansas
KALR Hot Springs, Arkansas
KJBR Marked Tree, Arkansas
KXNA Springdale, Arkansas
KFMA Green Valley, Arizona
KAIH Lake Havasu City, Arizona
KZAI Superior, Arizona
KAIC Tucson, Arizona
XETRAFM Tijuana, Mexico
KSPC Claremont, California
KKUP Cupertino, California
KHRI Hollister, California
KDRH King City, California
KTLK Los Angeles, California
KPTR Palm Springs, California
KOSO Patterson, California
KSPB Pebble Beach, California
KGBM Randsburg, California
KKRO Red Bluff, California
KUCR Riverside, California
KARQ San Andreas, California
KBZT San Diego, California
KITS San Francisco, California
KSJO San Jose, California
KYNS San Luis Obispo, California
KSCU Santa Clara, California
KSRI Santa Cruz, California
KAIB Shafter, California
KYIX South Oroville, California
KKZQ Tehachapi, California
KSRY Tehachapi, California
KXRD Victorville, California
KARA Williams, California
KFRR Woodlake, California
KLRD Yucaipa, California
KCSU-FM Fort Collins, Colorado
KMSA Grand Junction, Colorado
KHCO Hayden, Colorado
KAAI Palisade, Colorado
KDRE Sterling, Colorado
KKZN Thornton, Colorado
KTCL Wheat Ridge, Colorado
WXCI Danbury, Connecticut
WQAQ Hamden, Connecticut
WDJW Somers, Connecticut
WVUM Coral Gables, Florida
WTZB Englewood, Florida
WJBX Fort Myers Beach, Florida
WSUN-FM Holiday, Florida
WIRK(FM) Indiantown, Florida
WIIS Key West, Florida
WAYJ Naples, Florida
WAYR Orange Park, Florida
WUWF Pensacola, Florida
WXSR Quincy, Florida
WKPX Sunrise, Florida
WVFS Tallahassee, Florida
WUOG Athens, Georgia
WVGS Statesboro, Georgia
WQAI Thomson, Georgia
WPLH Tifton, Georgia
WVDA Valdosta, Georgia
WVVS-FM Valdosta, Georgia
KUCD Pearl City, Hawaii
KHAI Wahiawa, Hawaii
KBVU-FM Alta, Iowa
KIWR Council Bluffs, Iowa
KICB Fort Dodge, Iowa
KSTM Indianola, Iowa
KIGC Oskaloosa, Iowa
KMSC Sioux City, Iowa
KAIP Wapello, Iowa
KWDM West Des Moines, Iowa
KAIO Idaho Falls, Idaho
KARJ Kuna, Idaho
KCDA Post Falls, Idaho
KSKI-FM Sun Valley, Idaho
WCLR Arlington Heights, Illinois
WCPT-FM Arlington Heights, Illinois
WPCD Champaign, Illinois
WRTE Chicago, Illinois
WXRT Chicago, Illinois
WJMU Decatur, Illinois
WCPY Dekalb, Illinois
WARW Dorsey, Illinois
WRSE Elmhurst, Illinois
WGBK Glenview, Illinois
WIUS Macomb, Illinois
WVJC Mount Carmel, Illinois

WONC Naperville, Illinois
WRRG River Grove, Illinois
WSRI Sugar Grove, Illinois
WARG Summit, Illinois
WSJK(FM) Tuscola, Illinois
WPGU Urbana, Illinois
WKQX Watseka, Illinois
WCPT Willow Springs, Illinois
WEAX Angola, Indiana
WHJE Carmel, Indiana
WJHS Columbia City, Indiana
WSWI Evansville, Indiana
WGRE Greencastle, Indiana
WQRA Greencastle, Indiana
WCYT Lafayette Township, Indiana
WARA New Washington, Indiana
KAIG Dodge City, Kansas
KSDB-FM Manhattan, Kansas
WYGY(FM) Fort Thomas, Kentucky
WFPK Louisville, Kentucky
WVRB Wilmore, Kentucky
KSLU Hammond, Louisiana
KITA Iota, Louisiana
WNXX Jackson, Louisiana
KXUL Monroe, Louisiana
WTUL New Orleans, Louisiana
KLPI Ruston, Louisiana
KSCL Shreveport, Louisiana
KROK South Fort Polk, Louisiana
KNSU Thibodaux, Louisiana
WDJM-FM Framingham, Massachusetts
WZBC Newton, Massachusetts
WKKL West Barnstable, Massachusetts
WCHC Worcester, Massachusetts
WMTB-FM Emmitsburg, Maryland
WRNR-FM Grasonville, Maryland
WHSN Bangor, Maine
WQAC Alma, Michigan
WDTW Dearborn, Michigan
WDBM East Lansing, Michigan
WTRK Freeland, Michigan
WGRD-FM Grand Rapids, Michigan
WUPX Marquette, Michigan
WMHW-FM Mount Pleasant, Michigan
WOVI Novi, Michigan
WYCE Wyoming, Michigan
KDAL-FM Duluth, Minnesota
KUMM Morris, Minnesota
KVSC St. Cloud, Minnesota
KSRQ Thief River Falls, Minnesota
KAIA Bloomfield, Missouri
KWUR Clayton, Missouri
KCOU Columbia, Missouri
KQQX Hermann, Missouri
KTRM Kirksville, Missouri
KMVC Marshall, Missouri
KZZK New London, Missouri
KGSP Parkville, Missouri
WMSV Starkville, Mississippi
WUMS University, Mississippi
WABO-FM Waynesboro, Mississippi
WCPR-FM Wiggins, Mississippi
KMSM-FM Butte, Montana
KRVO Columbia Falls, Montana
KMPT East Missoula, Montana
KGFA Great Falls, Montana
KBAZ Hamilton, Montana
KBIL Park City, Montana
KSAM Whitefish, Montana
WASU-FM Boone, North Carolina
WSOE Elon College, North Carolina
WZMB Greenville, North Carolina
WEND Salisbury, North Carolina
WDCC Sanford, North Carolina
WZDG Scotts Hill, North Carolina
WZRI Spring Lake, North Carolina
KNRI Bismarck, North Dakota
KDNE Crete, Nebraska
KDAI Scottsbluff, Nebraska
KWSC Wayne, Nebraska
WUNH Durham, New Hampshire
WKNH Keene, New Hampshire
WPNH-FM Plymouth, New Hampshire
WADB(AM) Asbury Park, New Jersey
WDBK Blackwood, New Jersey
WLFR Pomona, New Jersey
WTSR Trenton, New Jersey
WPSC-FM Wayne, New Jersey
KABQ Albuquerque, New Mexico
KGGA Gallup, New Mexico
KQAI Roswell, New Mexico
KTEG Santa Fe, New Mexico
KTRC Santa Fe, New Mexico
KAER Mesquite, Nevada
KAIZ Mesquite, Nevada
KXTE Pahrump, Nevada
KJFK Reno, Nevada
KHWK Tonopah, Nevada
WRRB Arlington, New York
WZNE Brighton, New York
WBNY Buffalo, New York
WWKB Buffalo, New York
WITC Cazenovia, New York
WEHN East Hampton, New York
WGSU Geneseo, New York
WNYH Huntington, New York
WNYY Ithaca, New York
WRRV Middletown, New York
WKRH Minetto, New York
WBAI New York, New York
WWRL New York, New York
WDBY Patterson, New York
WBTZ Plattsburgh, New York
WQKE Plattsburgh, New York
WTSC-FM Potsdam, New York
WBER Rochester, New York
WYAI Scotia, New York
WDST Woodstock, New York
WXEG Beavercreek, Ohio
WCSB Cleveland, Ohio
WKRK-FM Cleveland Heights, Ohio
WLQR-FM Delta, Ohio
WCVJ Jefferson, Ohio
WOXY Mason, Ohio
WOAR South Vienna, Ohio
WUSO Springfield, Ohio
WXUT Toledo, Ohio
KPAK Alva, Oklahoma
KWRI Bartlesville, Oklahoma
KARU Cache, Oklahoma
KRSC-FM Claremore, Oklahoma
KOKF Edmond, Oklahoma
KKRD Enid, Oklahoma
KKRI Pocola, Oklahoma
WBBZ Ponca City, Oklahoma
KMYZ-FM Pryor, Oklahoma
KNRQ-FM Aloha, Oregon
KBVR Corvallis, Oregon
KGRI Lebanon, Oregon
KSLC McMinnville, Oregon
KARO Nyssa, Oregon
KVRA Sisters, Oregon
KAIK Tillamook, Oregon
KZRI Welches, Oregon
WBUQ Bloomsburg, Pennsylvania
WESS East Stroudsburg, Pennsylvania
WFSE Edinboro, Pennsylvania
WERG Erie, Pennsylvania
WZBT Gettysburg, Pennsylvania
WARC Meadville, Pennsylvania
WXPH Middletown, Pennsylvania
WPAI Nanty Glo, Pennsylvania
WKDU Philadelphia, Pennsylvania
WXPN Philadelphia, Pennsylvania
WQCK(FM) Philipsburg, Pennsylvania
WXDX-FM Pittsburgh, Pennsylvania
WUSR Scranton, Pennsylvania
WVMW-FM Scranton, Pennsylvania
WCHE West Chester, Pennsylvania
WCLH Wilkes-Barre, Pennsylvania
WRLC Williamsport, Pennsylvania
WBRU Providence, Rhode Island
WDOM Providence, Rhode Island
WJMF Smithfield, Rhode Island
WSBF-FM Clemson, South Carolina
KSDJ Brookings, South Dakota
KAUR Sioux Falls, South Dakota
KBHU-FM Spearfish, South Dakota
WTTU Cookeville, Tennessee
WTZR Elizabethton, Tennessee
WBBP Memphis, Tennessee
WNFZ Powell, Tennessee
WTAI Union City, Tennessee
KAGT Abilene, Texas
KEYJ-FM Abilene, Texas
KACV-FM Amarillo, Texas
KXRI Amarillo, Texas
KTLT Anson, Texas
KKWV Aransas Pass, Texas
KVRX Austin, Texas
KROX-FM Buda, Texas
KDGE Fort Worth-Dallas, Texas
KYAR Lorena, Texas
KPGA Morton, Texas
KNAR San Angelo, Texas
KSYM-FM San Antonio, Texas
KTSW San Marcos, Texas
KFRI West Odessa, Texas
KJMY Bountiful, Utah
KOHS Orem, Utah
KXRK Provo, Utah
KXDS Santa Clara, Utah
WNRN Charlottesville, Virginia
WXJM Harrisonburg, Virginia
WHRV Norfolk, Virginia
WCWM Williamsburg, Virginia
WZIN Charlotte Amalie, Virgin Islands
WIUV Castleton, Vermont
WJSC-FM Johnson, Vermont
WEQX Manchester, Vermont
WVTC Randolph Center, Vermont
KBAI Bellingham, Washington
KNRK Camas, Washington
KCWU Ellensburg, Washington
KGRG Enumclaw, Washington
KTCV Kennewick, Washington
KTSL Medical Lake, Washington
KEXP-FM Seattle, Washington
KNDD Seattle, Washington
KPTK Seattle, Washington
KZBD Spokane, Washington
KUPS Tacoma, Washington
KYVT Yakima, Washington
WBSD Burlington, Wisconsin
WLUM-FM Milwaukee, Wisconsin
WMSE Milwaukee, Wisconsin
WSUW Whitewater, Wisconsin
WGLZ West Liberty, West Virginia
KAIX Cheyenne, Wyoming
KAIW Laramie, Wyoming

Arabic

KXMX Muldrow, Oklahoma

Big Band

KBRW-FM Barrow, Alaska
WAUD Auburn, Alabama
KCEA Atherton, California
KEZW Aurora, Colorado
KCLN Clinton, Iowa
WAIK Galesburg, Illinois
WPMB Vandalia, Illinois
WFRX West Frankfort, Illinois
WICN Worcester, Massachusetts
WYAR Yarmouth, Maine
WCBY Cheboygan, Michigan
WZFJ(FM) Breezy Point, Minnesota
KRLI Malta Bend, Missouri
KBFL Springfield, Missouri
WELO Tupelo, Mississippi
WPAQ Mount Airy, North Carolina
WPNH Plymouth, New Hampshire
KNCC Elko, Nevada
WABY Mechanicville, New York
WADO New York, New York
WNYC New York, New York
WNYV Whitehall, New York
WKHR Bainbridge, Ohio
WMKV Reading, Ohio
WJAS Pittsburgh, Pennsylvania
KSQX Springtown, Texas
KQXS Stephenville, Texas
KPYK Terrell, Texas
WFOS Chesapeake, Virginia
WIUJ Charlotte Amalie, Virgin Islands
KTRW Opportunity, Washington
WCCN Neillsville, Wisconsin

Black

WATV Birmingham, Alabama
WXAL Demopolis, Alabama
WOOF Dothan, Alabama
WRJX Jackson, Alabama
WEUV Moulton, Alabama
WOPP Opp, Alabama
WZZA Tuscumbia, Alabama
WBHK Warrior, Alabama
KABF Little Rock, Arkansas
KAKJ Marianna, Arkansas
KTYM Inglewood, California
KSRH San Rafael, California

KJQY Colorado City, Colorado
WOCA Ocala, Florida
WYZE Atlanta, Georgia
WFXA-FM Augusta, Georgia
WBHB Fitzgerald, Georgia
WJGA-FM Jackson, Georgia
WDDO Macon, Georgia
WIBB Macon, Georgia
WIGO Morrow, Georgia
KIGC Oskaloosa, Iowa
WFUN-FM Bethalto, Illinois
WYRB Genoa, Illinois
WSRB Lansing, Illinois
WVAZ Oak Park, Illinois
WLLV Louisville, Kentucky
KXZZ Lake Charles, Louisiana
KRUS Ruston, Louisiana
KTKC-FM Springhill, Louisiana
WOMR Provincetown, Massachusetts
WCAO Baltimore, Maryland
WPRS-FM Waldorf, Maryland
WFLT Flint, Michigan
WELZ Belzoni, Mississippi
WCHJ Brookhaven, Mississippi
WCLD Cleveland, Mississippi
WACR-FM Columbus Afb, Mississippi
WRBO Como, Mississippi
WCPC Houston, Mississippi
WNLA Indianola, Mississippi
WFMO Fairmont, North Carolina
WIDU Fayetteville, North Carolina
WQMG Greensboro, North Carolina
WTEL Red Springs, North Carolina
WEGG Rose Hill, North Carolina
WARR Warrenton, North Carolina
WWIL Wilmington, North Carolina
WNEC-FM Henniker, New Hampshire
KCEP Las Vegas, Nevada
WXXY Houghton, New York
WTHE Mineola, New York
WBLS New York, New York
WHCR-FM New York, New York
WLIB New York, New York
WNYU-FM New York, New York
WNYK Nyack, New York
WBGU Bowling Green, Ohio
WOHC Chillicothe, Ohio
WXTC Greenville, Pennsylvania
WIXQ Millersville, Pennsylvania
WNAP Norristown, Pennsylvania
WDAS-FM Philadelphia, Pennsylvania
WAMO Wilkinsburg, Pennsylvania
WPRM-FM San Juan, Puerto Rico
WOON Woonsocket, Rhode Island
WDOG Barnwell, South Carolina
WPJS Conway, South Carolina
WWRK Darlington, South Carolina
WYNN Florence, South Carolina
WBZF Hartsville, South Carolina
WLGI Hemingway, South Carolina
WKZK North Augusta, South Carolina
WASC Spartanburg, South Carolina
WQZQ Goodlettsville, Tennessee
WFKX Henderson, Tennessee
WDIA Memphis, Tennessee
KGGR Dallas, Texas
KCOH Houston, Texas
WSHV South Hill, Virginia

Blues

WUHT Birmingham, Alabama
WJLD(AM) Fairfield, Alabama
WZEW Fairhope, Alabama
WKXN Fort Deposit, Alabama
WHIY Huntsville, Alabama
WJAB Huntsville, Alabama
WBHJ Midfield, Alabama
WKXK Pine Hill, Alabama
WZZA Tuscumbia, Alabama
WBHK Warrior, Alabama
KAJM Camp Verde, Arizona
KOHT Marana, Arizona
KPKR Parker, Arizona
KJLH Compton, California
KKUP Cupertino, California
KPIG-FM Freedom, California
KPAT Orcutt, California
KQNY Quincy, California
KSFM Woodland, California
KTSC-FM Pueblo, Colorado
WKND Windsor, Connecticut
WKYS Washington, District of Columbia
WSHE-FM Fort Lauderdale, Florida
WWAB Lakeland, Florida
WFLC Miami, Florida
WFLM White City, Florida
WMRZ Dawson, Georgia
WUMJ Fayetteville, Georgia
WIBB-FM Fort Valley, Georgia
WVKX Irwinton, Georgia
WAMJ Roswell, Georgia
WNUQ Sylvester, Georgia
WGOV Valdosta, Georgia
WRBV Warner Robins, Georgia
KBBG Waterloo, Iowa
WFUN-FM Bethalto, Illinois
WSSD Chicago, Illinois
WFFX(AM) East St. Louis, Illinois
WYRB Genoa, Illinois
WSRB Lansing, Illinois
WGLT Normal, Illinois
WTLC-FM Greenwood, Indiana
WHHH Indianapolis, Indiana
KBRH Baton Rouge, Louisiana
KRVS Lafayette, Louisiana
WWOZ New Orleans, Louisiana
KTJZ Tallulah, Louisiana
WATD-FM Marshfield, Massachusetts
WESM Princess Anne, Maryland
WUCX-FM Bay City, Michigan
WDMK Detroit, Michigan
WLNZ Lansing, Michigan
WNWN Portage, Michigan
WTLZ Saginaw, Michigan
WNMC-FM Traverse City, Michigan
WEMU Ypsilanti, Michigan
KMVC Marshall, Missouri
KCOZ Point Lookout, Missouri
WELZ Belzoni, Mississippi
WTWZ Clinton, Mississippi
WACR-FM Columbus Afb, Mississippi
WNEV Friars Point, Mississippi
WURC Holly Springs, Mississippi
WHJA Laurel, Mississippi
WESY Leland, Mississippi
WNBN Meridian, Mississippi
WQYZ Ocean Springs, Mississippi
WQZL Belhaven, North Carolina
WQMG Greensboro, North Carolina
WNCT Greenville, North Carolina
WCCG Hope Mills, North Carolina
WGIV Pineville, North Carolina
WENC Whiteville, North Carolina
WPHI-FM Pennsauken, New Jersey
KCEP Las Vegas, Nevada
WJZR Rochester, New York
WDAO Dayton, Ohio
WRBP Hubbard, Ohio
WYOR Republic, Ohio
WJUC Swanton, Ohio
KROU Spencer, Oklahoma
KMHD Gresham, Oregon
WUSR Scranton, Pennsylvania
WAMO Wilkinsburg, Pennsylvania
WKSP Aiken, South Carolina
WYNN Florence, South Carolina
WVOL Berry Hill, Tennessee
WBOL Bolivar, Tennessee
WEVL Memphis, Tennessee
WEUZ Minor Hill, Tennessee
KNDA Alice, Texas
KKDA Grand Prairie, Texas
KGEE Pecos, Texas
KUUU South Jordan, Utah
WFOS Chesapeake, Virginia
WNRV Narrows-Pearisburg, Virginia
WVKL Norfolk, Virginia
WBTJ Richmond, Virginia
WWED Spotsylvania, Virginia
KVIX Port Angeles, Washington
KRIZ Renton, Washington
KYIZ Renton, Washington
KPLU-FM Tacoma, Washington
WKKV-FM Racine, Wisconsin
WTCR Kenova, West Virginia

Children

KDIS-FM Little Rock, Arkansas
KIDR Phoenix, Arizona
KMIK Tempe, Arizona
KMKY Oakland, California
KDIS Pasadena, California
KIID Sacramento, California
KKDD San Bernardino, California
KDDZ Arvada, Colorado
WSDK Bloomfield, Connecticut
WAJD Gainesville, Florida
WBOB(AM) Jacksonville, Florida
WDYZ Orlando, Florida
WHTY(AM) Riviera Beach, Florida
WDWD Atlanta, Georgia
WPGA Perry, Georgia
WRDZ La Grange, Illinois
WYLC Jackson, Kentucky
WMKI Boston, Massachusetts
WDZN Midland, Maryland
WFDF Farmington Hills, Michigan
KDIZ Golden Valley, Minnesota
KPHN Kansas City, Missouri
WGFY Charlotte, North Carolina
WCOG Greensboro, North Carolina
KMMQ Plattsmouth, Nebraska
WYRS Manahawkin, New Jersey
WWJZ Mount Holly, New Jersey
KALY Los Ranchos De Albuquerque, New Mexico
KYDZ North Las Vegas, Nevada
WDDY Albany, New York
WWLF Auburn, New York
WALL Middletown, New York
WQEW New York, New York
WWMK Cleveland, Ohio
KMUS Sperry, Oklahoma
KDZR Lake Oswego, Oregon
KBPS Portland, Oregon
WWCS Canonsburg, Pennsylvania
WWCF McConnellsburg, Pennsylvania
WDDZ Pittsburgh, Pennsylvania
WOWW Germantown, Tennessee
KMIC Houston, Texas
KRDY San Antonio, Texas
WDZY Colonial Heights, Virginia
WHKT Portsmouth, Virginia
KKDZ Seattle, Washington
WKSH Sussex, Wisconsin
WMLJ Summersville, West Virginia

Chinese

KVTO Berkeley, California
KBIF Fresno, California
KAZN Pasadena, California
KAHZ Pomona, California
KNSN San Diego, California
KMRB San Gabriel, California
KALI-FM Santa Ana, California
KHCM Honolulu, Hawaii
KFXN Minneapolis, Minnesota
WKDM New York, New York
WZRC New York, New York
KGBC Galveston, Texas
KREH Pecan Grove, Texas

Christian

KHKY Akiachak, Alaska
KAFC Anchorage, Alaska
KAKL Anchorage, Alaska
KFAT Anchorage, Alaska
KAGV Big Lake, Alaska
KNGW Juneau, Alaska
KHZK Kotzebue, Alaska
KAKN Naknek, Alaska
KIAM Nenana, Alaska
KICY-FM Nome, Alaska
KIAM-FM North Nenana, Alaska
KJLP Palmer, Alaska
WIZB Abbeville, Alabama
WAAO-FM Andalusia, Alabama
WGRW Anniston, Alabama
WBFR Birmingham, Alabama
WDJC-FM Birmingham, Alabama
WGIB Birmingham, Alabama
WGNQ Bridgeport, Alabama
WALN Carrollton, Alabama
WQUA Citronelle, Alabama
WAVH Daphne, Alabama
WKWL Florala, Alabama
WBCF Florence, Alabama
WFIX Florence, Alabama
WJIA Guntersville, Alabama
WAYH Harvest, Alabama
WBXR Hazel Green, Alabama

WQOH Irondale, Alabama
WIXI Jasper, Alabama
WBHY Mobile, Alabama
WBAM-FM Montgomery, Alabama
WXVI Montgomery, Alabama
WAQG Ozark, Alabama
WIJD Prichard, Alabama
WAQU Selma, Alabama
WAKD Sheffield, Alabama
WAYU Steele, Alabama
WYEA Sylacauga, Alabama
WTID Thomaston, Alabama
WDLG Thomasville, Alabama
WMFT Tuscaloosa, Alabama
WELL-FM Waverly, Alabama
KJSM-FM Augusta, Arkansas
KOAR Beebe, Arkansas
KAPG Bentonville, Arkansas
KBCM Blytheville, Arkansas
KBHN Booneville, Arkansas
KKSP Bryant, Arkansas
KEJA Cale, Arkansas
KXRL Cherry Valley, Arkansas
KWXT Dardanelle, Arkansas
KBPU De Queen, Arkansas
KAKV El Dorado, Arkansas
KAYH Fayetteville, Arkansas
KBNV Fayetteville, Arkansas
KOFC Fayetteville, Arkansas
KEAF Fort Smith, Arkansas
KPOS Fouke, Arkansas
KGSF Green Forest, Arkansas
KZKZ-FM Greenwood, Arkansas
KBPW Hampton, Arkansas
KBPB Harrison, Arkansas
KBMJ Heber Springs, Arkansas
KALR Hot Springs, Arkansas
KLRO Hot Springs, Arkansas
KJLV Hoxie, Arkansas
KJSB Jonesboro, Arkansas
KJBR Marked Tree, Arkansas
KLMK Marvell, Arkansas
KLRM Melbourne, Arkansas
KNLL Nashville, Arkansas
KLRC Siloam Springs, Arkansas
KKLT Texarkana, Arkansas
KLFS Van Buren, Arkansas
KNWJ Leone, American Samoa
KJAL Tafuna, American Samoa
KRMB Bisbee, Arizona
KWRB Bisbee, Arizona
KVIR Bullhead City, Arizona
KCKY Coolidge, Arizona
KJTA Flagstaff, Arizona
KLVK Fountain Hills, Arizona
KLKA Globe, Arizona
KVJC Globe, Arizona
KBMH Holbrook, Arizona
KAIH Lake Havasu City, Arizona
KNLB Lake Havasu City, Arizona
KLTU Mammoth, Arizona
KLVA Maricopa, Arizona
KFLR-FM Phoenix, Arizona
KPHF Phoenix, Arizona
KXEG Phoenix, Arizona
KNXN Sierra Vista, Arizona
KZAI Superior, Arizona
KAIC Tucson, Arizona
KFLT Tucson, Arizona
KFLT-FM Tucson, Arizona
KGMS Tucson, Arizona
KWIM Window Rock, Arizona
KAWN Winslow, Arizona
KCFY Yuma, Arizona
KYRM Yuma, Arizona
KNDL(FM) Angwin, California
KERI Bakersfield, California
KFRB Bakersfield, California
KWTH Barstow, California
KWTW Bishop, California
KWLU Chester, California
KHAP Chico, California
KFRJ China Lake, California
KLVB Citrus Heights, California
KPSH Coachella, California
KDKL Coalinga, California
KFRP Coalinga, California
KRDU Dinuba, California
KLMG Esparto, California
KIHH Eureka, California
KLVY Fairmead, California
KKLC Fall River Mills, California
KSSD Fallbrook, California
KJCU Fort Bragg, California
KJPG Frazier Park, California
KGED Fresno, California
KIRV Fresno, California
KLVG Garberville, California
KXBC Garberville, California
KKMC Gonzales, California
KGBA Heber, California
KSDT Hemet, California
KHRI Hollister, California
KORB Hopland, California
KZLU Inyokern, California
KRAJ Johannesburg, California
KLVJ Julian, California
KWTM June Lake, California
KWDS Kettleman City, California
KDRH King City, California
KVPW Kingsburg, California
KFSH-FM La Mirada, California
KHKL Laytonville, California
KEFR Le Grand, California
KJOP Lemoore, California
KKFS Lincoln, California
KLVS Livermore, California
KLVN Livingston, California
KRQZ Lompoc, California
KFRN Long Beach, California
KKLA-FM Los Angeles, California
KLVC Magalia, California
KAMB Merced, California
KTIQ Merced, California
KLVR Middletown, California
KCIV Mount Bullion, California
KWVE(AM) Oildale, California
KDAR Oxnard, California
KHCS Palm Desert, California
KLVM Prunedale, California
DKCPC Rancho Mirage, California
KGBM Randsburg, California
KKRO Red Bluff, California
KWTD Ridgecrest, California
KPRO Riverside, California
KSGN Riverside, California
KDBV Salinas, California
KARQ San Andreas, California
KWVE-FM San Clemente, California
KEAR San Francisco, California
KSFB San Francisco, California
KYLD San Francisco, California
KLFF-FM San Luis Obispo, California
KLVH San Luis Obispo, California
KPRZ San Marcos-Poway, California
KSRI Santa Cruz, California
KGDP-FM Santa Maria, California
KHFR Santa Maria, California
KSBQ Santa Maria, California
KBLA Santa Monica, California
KQKL Selma, California
KAIB Shafter, California
KFRS Soledad, California
KYIX South Oroville, California
KWG Stockton, California
KBLV Tehachapi, California
KAIS(FM) Tracy, California
KBOS-FM Tulare, California
KPRA Ukiah, California
KULV Ukiah, California
KHMS Victorville, California
KXRD Victorville, California
KARM Visalia, California
KDUV Visalia, California
KSAK Walnut, California
KFHL Wasco, California
KALI West Covina, California
KARA Williams, California
KIQS Willows, California
KLRD Yucaipa, California
KRTM Yucca Valley, California
KLJH Bayfield, Colorado
KLLV Breen, Colorado
KLVZ Brighton, Colorado
KBWA Brush, Colorado
KLZV Brush, Colorado
KTLC Canon City, Colorado
KXWA Centennial, Colorado
KMZK Clifton, Colorado
KTLF Colorado Springs, Colorado
KLZ Denver, Colorado
KPOF Denver, Colorado
KRKS Denver, Colorado
KTCF Dolores, Colorado
KTDU Durango, Colorado
KMAP Fleming, Colorado
KGCO Fort Collins, Colorado
KLXV Glenwood Springs, Colorado
KJOL Grand Junction, Colorado
KLFV Grand Junction, Colorado
KLRY Gypsum, Colorado
KHCO Hayden, Colorado
KRKS-FM Lafayette, Colorado
KTOL Leadville, Colorado
KPIO Loveland, Colorado
KXGR Loveland, Colorado
KBIQ Manitou Springs, Colorado
KTMH Montrose, Colorado
KCBR Monument, Colorado
KLDV Morrison, Colorado
KTPS Pagosa Springs, Colorado
KAAI Palisade, Colorado
KTEI Placerville, Colorado
KFRY Pueblo, Colorado
KGFT Pueblo, Colorado
KTPL Pueblo, Colorado
KRWA Rye, Colorado
KTPF Salida, Colorado
KTML South Fork, Colorado
KLBV Steamboat Springs, Colorado
KTSG Steamboat Springs, Colorado
KDRE Sterling, Colorado
KTAD Sterling, Colorado
KJWA Trinidad, Colorado
KTDL Trinidad, Colorado
KTAW Walsenburg, Colorado
WADS Ansonia, Connecticut
WAVZ New Haven, Connecticut
WSGG Norfolk, Connecticut
WXCT Southington, Connecticut
WXHL-FM Christiana, Delaware
WZNZ Atlantic Beach, Florida
WTWB Auburndale, Florida
WTJT Baker, Florida
WJIS Bradenton, Florida
WKSG Cedar Creek, Florida
WMYZ Clermont, Florida
WPSF Clewiston, Florida
WHIM Coral Gables, Florida
WHIM(AM) Coral Gables, Florida
WAKU Crawfordville, Florida
WAQV Crystal River, Florida
WHGN Crystal River, Florida
WREH Cypress Quarters, Florida
WJHM Daytona Beach, Florida
WAKJ Defuniak Springs, Florida
WYND Deland, Florida
WECQ(FM) Destin, Florida
WVOJ Fernandina Beach, Florida
WJLH Flagler Beach, Florida
WMFL Florida City, Florida
WCRM Fort Myers, Florida
WJYO Fort Myers, Florida
WMYE Fort Myers, Florida
WPSM Fort Walton Beach, Florida
WJLF Gainesville, Florida
WSYR-FM Gifford, Florida
WYJC Greenville, Florida
WMKL Hammocks, Florida
WXRA Inglis, Florida
WCRJ Jacksonville, Florida
WROS Jacksonville, Florida
WLFE-FM Key Largo, Florida
WJIR Key West, Florida
WKWR Key West, Florida
WYBX(FM) Key West, Florida
WLAZ Kissimmee, Florida
WBIY La Belle, Florida
WYFO Lakeland, Florida
WWCL Lehigh Acres, Florida
WAYP Marianna, Florida
WTOT Marianna, Florida
WDMC Melbourne, Florida
WEGS Milton, Florida
WKVH Monticello, Florida
WAYJ Naples, Florida
WAYJ(FM) Naples, Florida
WSOR Naples, Florida
WBTT Naples Park, Florida
WKFP(FM) Navarre, Florida
WCIE New Port Richey, Florida
WHIJ Ocala, Florida
WAYR Orange Park, Florida

WTLN Orlando, Florida
WHIF Palatka, Florida
WEJF Palm Bay, Florida
WHYZ(FM) Palm Bay, Florida
WCNO Palm City, Florida
WHYZ Palm Coast, Florida
WFFL Panama City, Florida
WGNK Pennsuco, Florida
WDWR Pensacola, Florida
WTBN Pinellas Park, Florida
WTWD Plant City, Florida
WOKV-FM Ponte Vedra Beach, Florida
WDEO-FM San Carlos Park, Florida
WSMR Sarasota, Florida
WJFH Sebring, Florida
WTLG Starke, Florida
WWFR Stuart, Florida
WFRF Tallahassee, Florida
WTAL Tallahassee, Florida
WBVM Tampa, Florida
WPOZ Union Park, Florida
WZTA Vero Beach, Florida
WBJY Americus, Georgia
WFRP Americus, Georgia
WFFM Ashburn, Georgia
WFSH-FM Athens, Georgia
WMSL Athens, Georgia
WAEC Atlanta, Georgia
WNIV Atlanta, Georgia
WBBQ-FM Augusta, Georgia
WLPE Augusta, Georgia
WBBK-FM Blakely, Georgia
WGMI Bremen, Georgia
WULS Broxton, Georgia
WPMA Buckhead, Georgia
WPWB Byron, Georgia
WCHM Clarkesville, Georgia
WPBS Conyers, Georgia
WAEF Cordele, Georgia
WTTI Dalton, Georgia
WWGF Donalsonville, Georgia
WECC-FM Folkston, Georgia
WBIB-FM Forsyth, Georgia
WTHP Gibson, Georgia
WPLO Grayson, Georgia
WMVV Griffin, Georgia
WTFH Helen, Georgia
WLPT Jesup, Georgia
WDEN-FM Macon, Georgia
WVFJ-FM Manchester, Georgia
WGTJ Murrayville, Georgia
WVKV Nashville, Georgia
WLPF Ocilla, Georgia
WTIF-FM Omega, Georgia
WMVW Peachtree City, Georgia
WWLG Peachtree City, Georgia
WLFS Port Wentworth, Georgia
WLXP Savannah, Georgia
WYFS Savannah, Georgia
WAYT Thomasville, Georgia
WQAI Thomson, Georgia
WTXR Toccoa Falls, Georgia
WBDX Trenton, Georgia
WVDA Valdosta, Georgia
WGPH Vidalia, Georgia
WKTF Vienna, Georgia
WASW Waycross, Georgia
WFDR-FM Woodbury, Georgia
KSDA-FM Agat, Guam
KCIF Hilo, Hawaii
KAIM-FM Honolulu, Hawaii
KGU Honolulu, Hawaii
KHAI Wahiawa, Hawaii
KIHS Adel, Iowa
KRGO Alton, Iowa
KSKB Brooklyn, Iowa
KAYP Burlington, Iowa
KILV Castana, Iowa
KLNG Council Bluffs, Iowa
KLOX Creston, Iowa
KPSZ Des Moines, Iowa
KWKY Des Moines, Iowa
KIAD Dubuque, Iowa
KJYL Eagle Grove, Iowa
KXGM-FM Hiawatha, Iowa
KMDY Keokuk, Iowa
KNWM Madrid, Iowa
KCWN New Sharon, Iowa
KKLG Newton, Iowa
KNWI Osceola, Iowa
KYFR Shenandoah, Iowa
KSOU Sioux Center, Iowa
KJIA Spirit Lake, Iowa
KJCY St. Ansgar, Iowa
KTDV State Center, Iowa
KAIP Wapello, Iowa
KNWS Waterloo, Iowa
KNWS-FM Waterloo, Iowa
KWVI Waverly, Iowa
KPUL Winterset, Iowa
KGEM Boise, Idaho
KSPD Boise, Idaho
KTFY Buhl, Idaho
KBGN Caldwell, Idaho
KBXL Caldwell, Idaho
KTSY Caldwell, Idaho
KRTK Chubbuck, Idaho
KKRH Grangeville, Idaho
KTPZ Hazelton, Idaho
KAIO Idaho Falls, Idaho
KARJ Kuna, Idaho
KAWS Marsing, Idaho
KZJB Pocatello, Idaho
KLRI Rigby, Idaho
KSQS Ririe, Idaho
KAWZ Twin Falls, Idaho
KCIR Twin Falls, Idaho
KEFX Twin Falls, Idaho
KTWD Wallace, Idaho
WUIL Arcola, Illinois
WCLR Arlington Heights, Illinois
WRMS Beardstown, Illinois
WIBI Carlinville, Illinois
WBVN Carrier Mills, Illinois
WCBH Casey, Illinois
WLHW Casey, Illinois
WZGL Charleston, Illinois
WMBI Chicago, Illinois
WBMF Crete, Illinois
WYCA Crete, Illinois
WAIT Crystal Lake, Illinois
WARW Dorsey, Illinois
WDQN-FM Duquoin, Illinois
WEFI Effingham, Illinois
WGMR Effingham, Illinois
WSPI Ellsworth, Illinois
WJKL Glendale Heights, Illinois
WGNU Granite City, Illinois
WBGX Harvey, Illinois
WIJR Highland, Illinois
WKAY Knoxville, Illinois
WLLM Lincoln, Illinois
WAWJ Marion, Illinois
WJCZ Milford, Illinois
WOTW Monee, Illinois
WAPO Mount Vernon, Illinois
WBMV Mount Vernon, Illinois
WPTH Olney, Illinois
WRTK Paxton, Illinois
WCIC Pekin, Illinois
WLWJ Petersburg, Illinois
WPJC Pontiac, Illinois
WGCA-FM Quincy, Illinois
WJLY Ramsey, Illinois
WLKU Rock Island, Illinois
WFEN Rockford, Illinois
WQFL Rockford, Illinois
WSLE Salem, Illinois
WAUR Sandwich, Illinois
WPRC Sheffield, Illinois
WINU Shelbyville, Illinois
WSOG Spring Valley, Illinois
WLUJ Springfield, Illinois
WGNJ St. Joseph, Illinois
WSRI Sugar Grove, Illinois
WIHM Taylorville, Illinois
WVNL Vandalia, Illinois
WETN Wheaton, Illinois
WGNR Anderson, Indiana
WGNR-FM Anderson, Indiana
WQME Anderson, Indiana
WHPZ Bremen, Indiana
WNHT Churubusco, Indiana
WJCY Cicero, Indiana
WOJC Crothersville, Indiana
WRTW Crown Point, Indiana
WCMR Elkhart, Indiana
WFRN-FM Elkhart, Indiana
WFCV Fort Wayne, Indiana
WLAB Fort Wayne, Indiana
WLYV Fort Wayne, Indiana
WQRA Greencastle, Indiana
WAUZ Greensburg, Indiana
WQKO Howe, Indiana
WBDG Indianapolis, Indiana
WAWK Kendallville, Indiana
WAZY-FM Lafayette, Indiana
WQSG Lafayette, Indiana
WSHY Lafayette, Indiana
WBAT Marion, Indiana
WJCO Montpelier, Indiana
WCJL Morgantown, Indiana
WJCF-FM Morristown, Indiana
WKMV Muncie, Indiana
WVNI Nashville, Indiana
WARA New Washington, Indiana
WHZN New Whiteland, Indiana
WGAB Newburgh, Indiana
WRDZ-FM Plainfield, Indiana
WIKV Plymouth, Indiana
WQKV Rochester, Indiana
WAXI Rockville, Indiana
WJLR Seymour, Indiana
WHLY South Bend, Indiana
WHME South Bend, Indiana
WHOJ Terre Haute, Indiana
WMGI Terre Haute, Indiana
WJYW Union City, Indiana
WTUR Upland, Indiana
WATI Vincennes, Indiana
WENS Wadesville, Indiana
WYBV Wakarusa, Indiana
WFRR Walton, Indiana
WKHL West Lafayette, Indiana
WFRI Winamac, Indiana
KAXR Arkansas City, Kansas
KAIR Atchison, Kansas
KEOJ Caney, Kansas
KHYM Copeland, Kansas
KJIL Copeland, Kansas
KAIG Dodge City, Kansas
KTLI El Dorado, Kansas
KBMP Enterprise, Kansas
KCNW Fairway, Kansas
KVCY Fort Scott, Kansas
KGCR Goodland, Kansas
KBDA Great Bend, Kansas
KWBI Great Bend, Kansas
KHYS Hays, Kansas
KARF Independence, Kansas
KBQC Independence, Kansas
KCVW Kingman, Kansas
KKLO Leavenworth, Kansas
KZQD Liberal, Kansas
KGLV Manhattan, Kansas
KMLL Marysville, Kansas
KSNS Medicine Lodge, Kansas
KJRG Newton, Kansas
KSNB Norton, Kansas
KRLE Oberlin, Kansas
KCCV-FM Olathe, Kansas
KRBW Ottawa, Kansas
KTJO-FM Ottawa, Kansas
KCCV Overland Park, Kansas
KPIO-FM Pleasanton, Kansas
KCVS Salina, Kansas
KJLJ Scott City, Kansas
KCVT Silver Lake, Kansas
KHCA Wamego, Kansas
KCFN Wichita, Kansas
KYFW Wichita, Kansas
KYWA Wichita, Kansas
KBDD Winfield, Kansas
WAYD Auburn, Kentucky
WTRT Benton, Kentucky
WCVK Bowling Green, Kentucky
WAPD Campbellsville, Kentucky
WKCB Hindman, Kentucky
WJMM-FM Keene, Kentucky
WDJX Louisville, Kentucky
WFIA Louisville, Kentucky
WSOF-FM Madisonville, Kentucky
WWLT Manchester, Kentucky
WBFI McDaniels, Kentucky
WBTF Midway, Kentucky
WBMK Morehead, Kentucky
WEUC Morganfield, Kentucky
WKVN Morganfield, Kentucky
WAXG Mount Sterling, Kentucky
WNOP Newport, Kentucky
WJIE-FM Okolona, Kentucky
WJVK Owensboro, Kentucky
WWJD Pippa Passes, Kentucky

RADIO - U.S.

WAVJ Princeton, Kentucky
WKVY Somerset, Kentucky
WXKY-FM Stanford, Kentucky
WMTC Vancleve, Kentucky
WMTC-FM Vancleve, Kentucky
WBCE Wickliffe, Kentucky
WVRB Wilmore, Kentucky
KAPM Alexandria, Louisiana
KJMJ Alexandria, Louisiana
KLXA Alexandria, Louisiana
KHCL Arcadia, Louisiana
KAXV Bastrop, Louisiana
WJFM Baton Rouge, Louisiana
WPYR Baton Rouge, Louisiana
KBCL Bossier City, Louisiana
WBKL Clinton, Louisiana
KBAN De Ridder, Louisiana
KVDP Dry Prong, Louisiana
KBEF Gibsland, Louisiana
KKNO Gretna, Louisiana
KYLA Homer, Louisiana
KITA Iota, Louisiana
KTOC-FM Jonesboro, Louisiana
WYLK Lacombe, Louisiana
KIKL Lafayette, Louisiana
KOJO Lake Charles, Louisiana
KYLC Lake Charles, Louisiana
KHMD Mansfield, Louisiana
KMSL Mansfield, Louisiana
KAVK Many, Louisiana
KBMQ Monroe, Louisiana
KYFL Monroe, Louisiana
KBIO Natchitoches, Louisiana
KNIR New Iberia, Louisiana
WBSN-FM New Orleans, Louisiana
WLNO New Orleans, Louisiana
WVOG New Orleans, Louisiana
WNKV Norco, Louisiana
KUMX North Fort Polk, Louisiana
KPAQ Plaquemine, Louisiana
KHLL Richwood, Louisiana
KAPI Ruston, Louisiana
KSYB Shreveport, Louisiana
KSJY St. Martinville, Louisiana
KRLR Sulphur, Louisiana
WPMW Bayview, Massachusetts
WROL Boston, Massachusetts
WWDJ Boston, Massachusetts
WYCM Charlton, Massachusetts
WFGL Fitchburg, Massachusetts
WVNE Leicester, Massachusetts
WCMX Leominster, Massachusetts
WXKS-FM Medford, Massachusetts
WTKL North Dartmouth, Massachusetts
WNGB Petersham, Massachusetts
WBEC Pittsfield, Massachusetts
WSMA Scituate, Massachusetts
WRYP Wellfleet, Massachusetts
WKMY Winchendon, Massachusetts
WKDI Denton, Maryland
WLIC Frostburg, Maryland
WAIJ Grantsville, Maryland
WWGB Indian Head, Maryland
WHGT Maugansville, Maryland
WDIH Salisbury, Maryland
WWPN Westernport, Maryland
WHCF Bangor, Maine
WRPB Benedicta, Maine
WFST Caribou, Maine
WKVZ Dexter, Maine
WMSJ Freeport, Maine
WARX Lewiston, Maine
WRBC Lewiston, Maine
WHMX Lincoln, Maine
WMDR-FM Oakland, Maine
WJCX Pittsfield, Maine
WHPF Pittston Farm, Maine
WBAE Portland, Maine
WKVV Searsport, Maine
WWWA Winslow, Maine
WUFN Albion, Michigan
WAAM Ann Arbor, Michigan
WVCN Baraga, Michigan
WBFN Battle Creek, Michigan
WLKB Bay City, Michigan
WMAX Bay City, Michigan
WTLI Bear Creek Township, Michigan
WSLI Belding, Michigan
WAYO Benton Harbor, Michigan
WCVM Bronson, Michigan
WTAC Burton, Michigan
WLJW Cadillac, Michigan
WTCK Charlevoix, Michigan
WCFX Clare, Michigan
WPRJ Coleman, Michigan
WMUZ Detroit, Michigan
WHPD Dowagiac, Michigan
WJOM Eagle, Michigan
WRQC(FM) East Tawas, Michigan
WAKL Flint, Michigan
WSNL Flint, Michigan
WRCL Frankenmuth, Michigan
WTRK Freeland, Michigan
WBLW Gaylord, Michigan
WPHN Gaylord, Michigan
WHYT Goodland Township, Michigan
WCSG Grand Rapids, Michigan
WCZE Harbor Beach, Michigan
WSFP Harrisville, Michigan
WVCM Iron Mountain, Michigan
WAYK Kalamazoo, Michigan
WAIR Lake City, Michigan
WLGH Leroy Township, Michigan
WCAR Livonia, Michigan
WKPK Michigamme, Michigan
WUGN Midland, Michigan
WRDT Monroe, Michigan
WMCQ Muskegon, Michigan
WHEY North Muskegon, Michigan
WPCJ Pittsford, Michigan
WJOH Raco, Michigan
WSIS Riverside, Michigan
WJOJ Rust Township, Michigan
WTHN Sault Ste. Marie, Michigan
WOFR Schoolcraft, Michigan
WJKN-FM Spring Arbor, Michigan
WCFG Springfield, Michigan
WIDG St. Ignace, Michigan
WUFL Sterling Heights, Michigan
WHST Tawas City, Michigan
WLJN-FM Traverse City, Michigan
WEJC White Star, Michigan
WDEO Ypsilanti, Michigan
WJQK Zeeland, Michigan
KBHG Alexandria, Minnesota
WYNJ Blackduck, Minnesota
WQRN Cook, Minnesota
KDNW Duluth, Minnesota
WJRF Duluth, Minnesota
KRLP Fairmont, Minnesota
KBGY Faribault, Minnesota
WLKX-FM Forest Lake, Minnesota
KRFG Glenwood, Minnesota
KADU Hibbing, Minnesota
KBHW International Falls, Minnesota
KXBR International Falls, Minnesota
WCTS Maplewood, Minnesota
KTIS Minneapolis, Minnesota
WLOL Minneapolis, Minnesota
KVXR Moorhead, Minnesota
KMKL North Branch, Minnesota
KCGN-FM Ortonville, Minnesota
KBHL Osakis, Minnesota
KKMS Richfield, Minnesota
KFSI Rochester, Minnesota
KYES Rockville, Minnesota
KKJM St. Joseph, Minnesota
KKLW Willmar, Minnesota
KJWR Windom, Minnesota
KQRB Windom, Minnesota
KUSQ Worthington, Minnesota
KHCR Bismarck, Missouri
KAIA Bloomfield, Missouri
KCWJ Blue Springs, Missouri
KPVR Bowling Green, Missouri
KCVY Cabool, Missouri
KCVO-FM Camdenton, Missouri
KSIV Clayton, Missouri
KLRQ Clinton, Missouri
KCVZ Dixon, Missouri
KEXS Excelsior Springs, Missouri
KTBJ Festus, Missouri
KMCV High Point, Missouri
KBCV Hollister, Missouri
KOBC Joplin, Missouri
KLJC Kansas City, Missouri
KAUF Kennett, Missouri
KLTE Kirksville, Missouri
KCVQ Knob Noster, Missouri
KTTK Lebanon, Missouri
KLRX Lee's Summit, Missouri
KNLM Marshfield, Missouri
KBKC Moberly, Missouri
KCGR Oran, Missouri
KCVJ Osceola, Missouri
KCVK Otterville, Missouri
KBGM Park Hills, Missouri
KHZR Potosi, Missouri
KADI-FM Republic, Missouri
KAYX Richmond, Missouri
KCVX Salem, Missouri
KSCV Springfield, Missouri
KWFC Springfield, Missouri
KWND Springfield, Missouri
KGNM St. Joseph, Missouri
KSRD St. Joseph, Missouri
KJSL St. Louis, Missouri
KSIV-FM St. Louis, Missouri
KCRL Sunrise Beach, Missouri
KRSS Tarkio, Missouri
KKLL Webb City, Missouri
KULH Wheeling, Missouri
WXTN Benton, Mississippi
WMSB Byhalia, Mississippi
WDFX Cleveland, Mississippi
WLVZ Collins, Mississippi
WPRG Columbia, Mississippi
WCSO Columbus, Mississippi
WKCU Corinth, Mississippi
WSQH Decatur, Mississippi
WMBU Forest, Mississippi
WQST-FM Forest, Mississippi
WWUN-FM Friar's Point, Mississippi
WLRK Greenville, Mississippi
WABG Greenwood, Mississippi
WAOY Gulfport, Mississippi
WCPC Houston, Mississippi
WYTF Indianola, Mississippi
WBAD Leland, Mississippi
WAZA Liberty, Mississippi
WQVI Madison, Mississippi
WPAS Pascagoula, Mississippi
WAFR Tupelo, Mississippi
WAJS Tupelo, Mississippi
WJXN-FM Utica, Mississippi
WLRC Walnut, Mississippi
WABO-FM Waynesboro, Mississippi
WYAZ Yazoo City, Mississippi
KJFT Arlee, Montana
KCMM Belgrade, Montana
KBZR Billings, Montana
KLMT Billings, Montana
KLRV Billings, Montana
KLBZ Bozeman, Montana
KEDR(FM) Butte, Montana
KFRD Butte, Montana
KJLF Butte, Montana
KUDI Choteau, Montana
KMCJ Colstrip, Montana
KAFH Great Falls, Montana
KFRW Great Falls, Montana
KGFA Great Falls, Montana
KGFC Great Falls, Montana
KMZO Hamilton, Montana
KXEI Havre, Montana
KHLV Helena, Montana
KVCM Helena, Montana
KALS Kalispell, Montana
KLKM Kalispell, Montana
KLEU Lewistown, Montana
KMZL Missoula, Montana
KBIL Park City, Montana
KQLR Whitehall, Montana
WBKU Ahoskie, North Carolina
WZGO Aurora, North Carolina
WXBE Beaufort, North Carolina
WFGW Black Mountain, North Carolina
WMIT Black Mountain, North Carolina
WVBS Burgaw, North Carolina
WYFQ Charlotte, North Carolina
WCSL Cherryville, North Carolina
WHPY Clayton, North Carolina
WCLN-FM Clinton, North Carolina
WWFJ East Fayetteville, North Carolina
WYBH Fayetteville, North Carolina
WRTP Franklinton, North Carolina
WSSG Goldsboro, North Carolina
WJSG Hamlet, North Carolina
WLGP Harkers Island, North Carolina
WRYN Hickory, North Carolina
WJKA Jacksonville, North Carolina
WTRU Kernersville, North Carolina
WGHW Lockwoods Folly Town, North Carolina

WDJS Mount Olive, North Carolina
WWDR Murfreesboro, North Carolina
WBNK Pine Knoll Shores, North Carolina
WBFY Pinehurst, North Carolina
WRAE Raeford, North Carolina
WCLY Raleigh, North Carolina
WPJL Raleigh, North Carolina
WXKL Sanford, North Carolina
WZDG Scotts Hill, North Carolina
WKVK Semora, North Carolina
WNCA Siler City, North Carolina
WMPM Smithfield, North Carolina
WAGO Snow Hill, North Carolina
WZRI Spring Lake, North Carolina
WKGV Swansboro, North Carolina
WJRM Troy, North Carolina
WJFJ Tryon, North Carolina
WDVV Wilmington, North Carolina
WWIL-FM Wilmington, North Carolina
WVOT Wilson, North Carolina
WRCM Wingate, North Carolina
WBFJ Winston-Salem, North Carolina
WBFJ-FM Winston-Salem, North Carolina
WPIP Winston-Salem, North Carolina
KBFR Bismarck, North Dakota
KBMK Bismarck, North Dakota
KNRI Bismarck, North Dakota
KDVI Devils Lake, North Dakota
KFNW-FM Fargo, North Dakota
KWTL Grand Forks, North Dakota
KKLQ Harwood, North Dakota
KJTW Jamestown, North Dakota
KLUU Jamestown, North Dakota
KNDR Mandan, North Dakota
KHRT-FM Minot, North Dakota
KNDW Williston, North Dakota
KNBE Beatrice, Nebraska
KAMI Cozad, Nebraska
KCVN Cozad, Nebraska
KLNB Grand Island, Nebraska
KMMJ Grand Island, Nebraska
KNFA Grand Island, Nebraska
KAYA Hubbard, Nebraska
KLCV Lincoln, Nebraska
KJLT North Platte, Nebraska
KCRO Omaha, Nebraska
KGBI-FM Omaha, Nebraska
KGRD Orchard, Nebraska
KHZY Overton, Nebraska
KFHC Ponca, Nebraska
KMLV Ralston, Nebraska
KHZZ Sargent, Nebraska
KDAI Scottsbluff, Nebraska
KLJV Scottsbluff, Nebraska
KKNL Valentine, Nebraska
KRKR Waverly, Nebraska
KFLV Wilber, Nebraska
KEIS York, Nebraska
WVNH Concord, New Hampshire
WNHI Farmington, New Hampshire
WADB(AM) Asbury Park, New Jersey
WWFP Brigantine, New Jersey
WXGN Egg Harbor Township, New Jersey
WRDR Freehold Township, New Jersey
WDNJ Hopatcong, New Jersey
WVBV Medford Lakes, New Jersey
WFME Newark, New Jersey
WNSW Newark, New Jersey
WIBG Ocean City/Somers Po, New Jersey
WKMB Stirling, New Jersey
WFJS Trenton, New Jersey
KKIM Albuquerque, New Mexico
KLYT Albuquerque, New Mexico
KSVA Albuquerque, New Mexico
KXKS Albuquerque, New Mexico
KQLV(FM) Bosque Farms, New Mexico
KQRI Bosque Farms, New Mexico
KKCJ Cannon Afb, New Mexico
KAMQ Carlsbad, New Mexico
KAQF Clovis, New Mexico
KCOI Clovis, New Mexico
KELU Clovis, New Mexico
KZPI Deming, New Mexico
KNMI Farmington, New Mexico
KPCL Farmington, New Mexico
KTGW Fruitland, New Mexico
KGGA Gallup, New Mexico
KLLU Gallup, New Mexico
KOBH Hobbs, New Mexico
KMBN Las Cruces, New Mexico
KELP-FM Mesquite, New Mexico
KVLK Milan, New Mexico
KXXQ Milan, New Mexico
KGCN Roswell, New Mexico
KQAI Roswell, New Mexico
KRLU Roswell, New Mexico
KKIM-FM Santa Fe, New Mexico
KXFR Socorro, New Mexico
KHAC Tse Bonito, New Mexico
KVLP Tucumcari, New Mexico
KNMA Tularosa, New Mexico
KNIS Carson City, Nevada
KQRT Las Vegas, Nevada
KAER Mesquite, Nevada
KAIZ Mesquite, Nevada
KEKL Mesquite, Nevada
KIHM Reno, Nevada
KLRH Sparks, Nevada
WAMC Albany, New York
WJCA Albion, New York
WCOF Arcade, New York
WNGN Argyle, New York
WCOU Attica, New York
WABH Bath, New York
WAAL Binghamton, New York
WXBA Brentwood, New York
WASB Brockport, New York
WKDL-FM Brockport, New York
WDCX-FM Buffalo, New York
WFBF Buffalo, New York
WCIY Canandaigua, New York
WRSB Canandaigua, New York
WLYK Cape Vincent, New York
WCOV-FM Clyde, New York
WKVJ Dannemora, New York
WCIH Elmira, New York
WBBI Endwell, New York
WCID Friendship, New York
WBBS Fulton, New York
WLJH Glens Falls, New York
WGKR Grand Gorge, New York
WHAZ-FM Hoosick Falls, New York
WHVP Hudson, New York
WCOT Jamestown, New York
WFGB Kingston, New York
WGWR Liberty, New York
WMHQ Malone, New York
WLJP Monroe, New York
WRVP Mount Kisco, New York
WAXQ New York, New York
WBAI New York, New York
WBBR New York, New York
WMCA New York, New York
WWRV New York, New York
WZXV Palmyra, New York
WDBY Patterson, New York
WPGL Pattersonville, New York
WRPJ Port Jervis, New York
WPKF Poughkeepsie, New York
WDCX Rochester, New York
WHIC Rochester, New York
WKYJ Rouses Point, New York
WSSK Saratoga Springs, New York
WMYY Schoharie, New York
WYAI Scotia, New York
WFRS Smithtown, New York
WCII Spencer, New York
WMHR Syracuse, New York
WHAZ Troy, New York
WCIJ Unadilla, New York
WAJZ Voorheesville, New York
WKWV Watertown, New York
WIFF Windsor, New York
WHJM Anna, Ohio
WJKW Athens, Ohio
WCVV Belpre, Ohio
WLKP Belpre, Ohio
WILB Canton, Ohio
WGGN Castalia, Ohio
WZCP Chillicothe, Ohio
WAKW Cincinnati, Ohio
WFHM-FM Cleveland, Ohio
WHKW Cleveland, Ohio
WVKO Columbus, Ohio
WGOJ Conneaut, Ohio
WYKL Crestline, Ohio
WQRP Dayton, Ohio
WTKC Findlay, Ohio
WCVO Gahanna, Ohio
WWGV Grove City, Ohio
WPOS-FM Holland, Ohio
WCVJ Jefferson, Ohio
WFCO Lancaster, Ohio
WFOT Lexington, Ohio
WTGN Lima, Ohio
WXMF Marion, Ohio
WYSZ Maumee, Ohio
WFCJ Miamisburg, Ohio
WZNP Newark, Ohio
WCCD Parma, Ohio
WHKU Proctorville, Ohio
WNWT Rossford, Ohio
WLRY Rushville, Ohio
WVMS Sandusky, Ohio
WAUI Shelby, Ohio
WOAR South Vienna, Ohio
WEKV South Webster, Ohio
WEEC Springfield, Ohio
WULM Springfield, Ohio
WBJV Steubenville, Ohio
WOKL Troy, Ohio
WHKZ Warren, Ohio
WNKL Wauseon, Ohio
WYSA Wauseon, Ohio
WWVY Waverly, Ohio
WKLN Wilmington, Ohio
WJIC Zanesville, Ohio
KAKO Ada, Oklahoma
KKVO Altus, Oklahoma
KQPD Ardmore, Oklahoma
KVSO Ardmore, Oklahoma
KWRI Bartlesville, Oklahoma
KKWD(FM) Bethany, Colorado
KJHL Boise City, Oklahoma
KARU Cache, Oklahoma
KJCC Carnegie, Oklahoma
KTFR Chelsea, Oklahoma
KAYC Durant, Oklahoma
KSEO Durant, Oklahoma
KOKF Edmond, Oklahoma
KXOO Elk City, Oklahoma
KKRD Enid, Oklahoma
KWKL Grandfield, Oklahoma
KBIJ Guymon, Oklahoma
KXRT Idabel, Oklahoma
KJRF Lawton, Oklahoma
KVRS Lawton, Oklahoma
KEMX Locust Grove, Oklahoma
KTLV Midwest City, Oklahoma
KQCV Oklahoma City, Oklahoma
KYLV Oklahoma City, Oklahoma
KPGM Pawhuska, Oklahoma
KZTH Piedmont, Oklahoma
KKRI Pocola, Oklahoma
KJTH Ponca City, Oklahoma
KLVV Ponca City, Oklahoma
WBBZ Ponca City, Oklahoma
KARG Poteau, Oklahoma
KXOJ-FM Sapulpa, Oklahoma
KXTH Seminole, Oklahoma
KTKL Stigler, Oklahoma
KLRB Stuart, Oklahoma
KCXR Taft, Oklahoma
KAYM Weatherford, Oklahoma
KJOV Woodward, Oklahoma
KHPE Albany, Oregon
KWIL Albany, Oregon
KLOY Astoria, Oregon
KHSS Athena, Oregon
KANC Baker, Oregon
KANL Baker, Oregon
KNLR Bend, Oregon
KVLB Bend, Oregon
KYTT-FM Coos Bay, Oregon
KAPK Grants Pass, Oregon
KGCL Jordan Valley, Oregon
KPIJ Junction City, Oregon
KKLJ Klamath Falls, Oregon
KKLP La Pine, Oregon
KGRI Lebanon, Oregon
KYOR Newport, Oregon
KTEE North Bend, Oregon
KEFS North Powder, Oregon
KARO Nyssa, Oregon
KAPL Phoenix, Oregon
KPFR Pine Grove, Oregon
KKPZ Portland, Oregon
KPDQ Portland, Oregon
KPDQ-FM Portland, Oregon
KNLX Prineville, Oregon
KKJA Redmond, Oregon
KLON Rockaway Beach, Oregon
KPJC Salem, Oregon

KWBX Salem, Oregon
KLVP Sandy, Oregon
KFIS Scappoose, Oregon
KJKL Selma, Oregon
KVRA Sisters, Oregon
KQFE Springfield, Oregon
KORE Springfield-Eugene, Oregon
KLVU Sweet Home, Oregon
KAIK Tillamook, Oregon
KLWJ(AM) Umatilla, Oregon
KZRI Welches, Oregon
KLOV Winchester, Oregon
KGRV Winston, Oregon
WAEB-FM Allentown, Pennsylvania
WJCS Allentown, Pennsylvania
WTWT Bradford, Pennsylvania
WPWA Chester, Pennsylvania
WVCH Chester, Pennsylvania
WCOJ Coatesville, Pennsylvania
WCIG Dallas, Pennsylvania
WCOH-FM Du Bois, Pennsylvania
WEFR Erie, Pennsylvania
WCOP Farmington Township, Pennsylvania
WCOG-FM Galeton, Pennsylvania
WVMM Grantham, Pennsylvania
WLVX(FM) Greenville, Pennsylvania
WKBO Harrisburg, Pennsylvania
WHHN Hollidaysburg, Pennsylvania
WFRJ Johnstown, Pennsylvania
WDAC Lancaster, Pennsylvania
WPAL Laporte, Pennsylvania
WBYN Lehighton, Pennsylvania
WBCB Levittown, Pennsylvania
WGRC Lewisburg, Pennsylvania
WJRC Lewistown, Pennsylvania
WLOG Markleysburg, Pennsylvania
WRIJ Masontown, Pennsylvania
WYFU Masontown, Pennsylvania
WQJU Mifflintown, Pennsylvania
WRYV Milroy, Pennsylvania
WPGR Monroeville, Pennsylvania
WPAI Nanty Glo, Pennsylvania
WBGM New Berlin, Pennsylvania
WPCL Northern Cambria, Pennsylvania
WPIT Pittsburgh, Pennsylvania
WWNL Pittsburgh, Pennsylvania
WITK Pittston, Pennsylvania
WKVB Port Matilda, Pennsylvania
WLKJ Portage, Pennsylvania
WRAW Reading, Pennsylvania
WZKN(FM) Ridgebury, Pennsylvania
WCIM Shenandoah, Pennsylvania
WHYF(AM) Shiremanstown, Pennsylvania
WBHV-FM State College, Pennsylvania
WRXV State College, Pennsylvania
WTLR State College, Pennsylvania
WLKA Tafton, Pennsylvania
WCIT-FM Trout Run, Pennsylvania
WCTL Union City, Pennsylvania
WLIH Whitneyville, Pennsylvania
WYVL(FM) Youngsville, Pennsylvania
WABA Aguadilla, Puerto Rico
WNIK-FM Arecibo, Puerto Rico
WNVM Cidra, Puerto Rico
WNVE Culebra, Puerto Rico
WMEG Guayama, Puerto Rico
WRRH Hormigueros, Puerto Rico
WNRT Manati, Puerto Rico
WAEL-FM Maricao, Puerto Rico
WZNA Moca, Puerto Rico
WJDZ Pastillo, Puerto Rico
WNNV San German, Puerto Rico
WERR Vega Alta, Puerto Rico
WSTL Providence, Rhode Island
WKIV Westerly, Rhode Island
WWKX Woonsocket, Rhode Island
WZMJ Batesburg, South Carolina
WEPC Belton, South Carolina
WAFJ Belvedere, South Carolina
WALC Charleston, South Carolina
WMHK Columbia, South Carolina
WDLL Dillon, South Carolina
WELP Easley, South Carolina
WLPG Florence, South Carolina
WKZQ-FM Forestbrook, South Carolina
WYFG Gaffney, South Carolina
WLMC Georgetown, South Carolina
WMBJ Murrells Inlet, South Carolina
DWKEL Myrtle Beach, South Carolina
WYFH North Charleston, South Carolina
WTBI Pickens, South Carolina
WAYA-FM Ridgeville, South Carolina
WQIZ St. George, South Carolina
WAZS Summerville, South Carolina
WSSC Sumter, South Carolina
WBZK York, South Carolina
KEEA Aberdeen, South Dakota
KKAA Aberdeen, South Dakota
KLRJ Aberdeen, South Dakota
KVCF Freeman, South Dakota
KWRC Hermosa, South Dakota
KVFL Pierre, South Dakota
KASD Rapid City, South Dakota
KQFR Rapid City, South Dakota
KTPT Rapid City, South Dakota
KQKD Redfield, South Dakota
KNWC-FM Sioux Falls, South Dakota
KSFS Sioux Falls, South Dakota
WWGM Alamo, Tennessee
WATX Algood, Tennessee
WTKB-FM Atwood, Tennessee
WKVF Bartlett, Tennessee
WLVU Belle Meade, Tennessee
WFHG-FM Bluff City, Tennessee
WHCB Bristol, Tennessee
WIGN Bristol, Tennessee
WJOC Chattanooga, Tennessee
WLMR Chattanooga, Tennessee
WAYQ Clarksville, Tennessee
WYFC Clinton, Tennessee
WCRV Collierville, Tennessee
WNRZ Dickson, Tennessee
WCRT Donelson, Tennessee
WZKV Dyersburg, Tennessee
WUMC Elizabethton, Tennessee
WLLJ Etowah, Tennessee
WIJV Harriman, Tennessee
WAUO Hohenwald, Tennessee
WAMP Jackson, Tennessee
WIGH Jackson, Tennessee
WCQR-FM Kingsport, Tennessee
WKTS Kingston, Tennessee
WFFI Kingston Springs, Tennessee
WIFA Knoxville, Tennessee
WITA Knoxville, Tennessee
WRJZ Knoxville, Tennessee
WZXX Lawrenceburg, Tennessee
WRSN Lebanon, Tennessee
WBLC Lenoir City, Tennessee
WAXO Lewisburg, Tennessee
WHPY-FM Lobelville, Tennessee
WGBQ Lynchburg, Tennessee
WYLV Maynardville, Tennessee
WYLV(FM) Maynardville, Tennessee
WAJJ McKenzie, Tennessee
WBBP Memphis, Tennessee
WMXK Morristown, Tennessee
WECV-FM Nashville, Tennessee
WENO Nashville, Tennessee
WAYW New Johnsonville, Tennessee
WDNX Olive Hill, Tennessee
WPRH Paris, Tennessee
WJBP Red Bank, Tennessee
WDTM Selmer, Tennessee
WXKV Selmer, Tennessee
WBIA Shelbyville, Tennessee
WFFH Smyrna, Tennessee
WDBL Springfield, Tennessee
WHMT(AM) Tullahoma, Tennessee
WTAI Union City, Tennessee
WBOZ Woodbury, Tennessee
KAGT Abilene, Texas
KAQD Abilene, Texas
KGNZ Abilene, Texas
KAVW Amarillo, Texas
KJJP Amarillo, Texas
KTNZ Amarillo, Texas
KXLV Amarillo, Texas
KXRI Amarillo, Texas
KKWV Aransas Pass, Texas
KNRB Atlanta, Texas
KPYN Atlanta, Texas
KPEZ Austin, Texas
KHIB Bastrop, Texas
KLBT Beaumont, Texas
KTXB Beaumont, Texas
KIBL Beeville, Texas
KPDB Big Lake, Texas
KTAA Big Sandy, Texas
KBCX Big Spring, Texas
KBQX Big Spring, Texas
KHVT Bloomington, Texas
KUBJ Brenham, Texas
KPBB Brownfield, Texas
KBUB Brownwood, Texas
KHBW(FM) Brownwood, Texas
KPBE Brownwood, Texas
KPSM Brownwood, Texas
KAGC Bryan, Texas
KLRW Byrne, Texas
KAYG Camp Wood, Texas
KCZO Carrizo Springs, Texas
KJON Carrollton, Texas
KXCS(FM) Coahoma, Texas
KLGS College Station, Texas
KYJC Commerce, Texas
KAFR Conroe, Texas
KKLM Corpus Christi, Texas
KCKT Crockett, Texas
KTLZ Cuero, Texas
KTDA Dalhart, Texas
KCBI Dallas, Texas
KDLI Del Rio, Texas
KIXL Del Valle, Texas
KYFB Denison, Texas
KGLF Doss, Texas
KLLR Dripping Springs, Texas
KEPI Eagle Pass, Texas
KEPX Eagle Pass, Texas
KELP El Paso, Texas
KKLY El Paso, Texas
KLDS Falfurrias, Texas
KZFT Fannett, Texas
KIJN Farwell, Texas
KIJN-FM Farwell, Texas
KDFT Ferris, Texas
KJMA Floresville, Texas
KTFM Floresville, Texas
KBLC Fredericksburg, Texas
KPBN Freer, Texas
KLJA(FM) Georgetown, Texas
KANJ Giddings, Texas
KMLR Gonzales, Texas
KTXG Greenville, Texas
KEDC Hearne, Texas
KAZF Hebbronville, Texas
KEKO Hebbronville, Texas
KRLH Hereford, Texas
KWRD-FM Highland Village, Texas
KHCB-FM Houston, Texas
KSBJ Humble, Texas
KHCH Huntsville, Texas
KYLR Hutto, Texas
KXXN Iowa Park, Texas
KBJS Jacksonville, Texas
KCOX Jasper, Texas
KHCJ Jefferson, Texas
KJTX Jefferson, Texas
KERB Kermit, Texas
KHKV Kerrville, Texas
KKER Kerrville, Texas
KZLO Kilgore, Texas
KBKN Lamesa, Texas
KLAR Laredo, Texas
KBLT Leakey, Texas
KFRO Longview, Texas
KYAR Lorena, Texas
KAMY Lubbock, Texas
KKLU Lubbock, Texas
KSWP Lufkin, Texas
KKHT-FM Lumberton, Texas
KZLV Lytle, Texas
KHML Madisonville, Texas
KBMD Marble Falls, Texas
KSUR Mart, Texas
KVMV Mc Allen, Texas
KRIO McAllen, Texas
KMXO Merkel, Texas
KMEO Mertzon, Texas
KLPF Midland, Texas
KBRZ Missouri City, Texas
KPGA Morton, Texas
KYRQ Natalia, Texas
KLBW New Boston, Texas
KTTY New Boston, Texas
KBMM Odessa, Texas
KFLB Odessa, Texas
KLVW Odessa, Texas
KKVI Overland, Texas
KAVO Pampa, Texas
KHCP Paris, Texas
KLVL Pasadena, Texas
KPKO Pecos, Texas

KGWP Pittsburg, Texas
KBAH Plainview, Texas
KWLD Plainview, Texas
KWMF Pleasanton, Texas
KDEI Port Arthur, Texas
KHPO Port O'Connor, Texas
KSGR Portland, Texas
KCLR Ralls, Texas
KBAW Ranchitos Las Lomas, Texas
KLOW Reno, Texas
KFMK Round Rock, Texas
KTER Rudolph, Texas
KCRN-FM San Angelo, Texas
KLTP San Angelo, Texas
KNAR San Angelo, Texas
KSLR San Antonio, Texas
KYFS San Antonio, Texas
KUBR San Juan, Texas
KUOL San Marcos, Texas
KDAE Sinton, Texas
KJAK Slaton, Texas
KFLB-FM Stanton, Texas
KBDE Temple, Texas
KVLT Temple, Texas
KBTE Tulia, Texas
KTNO University Park, Texas
KVHR Van Horn, Texas
KAYK Victoria, Texas
KBBW Waco, Texas
KZEE Weatherford, Texas
KRGE Weslaco, Texas
KFRI West Odessa, Texas
KANI Wharton, Texas
KMOC Wichita Falls, Texas
KZKL Wichita Falls, Texas
KNKL North Ogden, Utah
KYFO-FM Ogden, Utah
KKLV Orem, Utah
KDUT Randolph, Utah
KANN Roy, Utah
KUFR Salt Lake City, Utah
KUTR Taylorsville, Utah
KMRI West Valley City, Utah
WAXM Big Stone Gap, Virginia
WLES Bon Air, Virginia
WPRZ-FM Brandy Station, Virginia
WAUQ Charles City, Virginia
WJYK Chase City, Virginia
WKYV Colonial Heights, Virginia
WARN Culpeper, Virginia
WPER Culpeper, Virginia
WPIN-FM Dublin, Virginia
WJYA Emporia, Virginia
WKNV Fairlawn, Virginia
WJYJ Fredericksburg, Virginia
WOKG Galax, Virginia
WPIM Martinsville, Virginia
WRIH Richmond, Virginia
WPAR Salem, Virginia
WVAB Virginia Beach, Virginia
WPVA Waynesboro, Virginia
WEVI Frederiksted, Virgin Islands
WCMD-FM Barre, Vermont
WCMK Putney, Vermont
WMNV Rupert, Vermont
WFTF Rutland, Vermont
WCKJ St. Johnsbury, Vermont
WNGF Swanton, Vermont
WGLV Woodstock, Vermont
KJCF Asotin, Washington
KGNW Burien-Seattle, Washington
KGTS College Place, Washington
KKRS Davenport, Washington
KLUW East Wenatchee, Washington
KTJC Kelso, Washington
KBLD Kennewick, Washington
KARR Kirkland, Washington
KJVH Longview, Washington
KWPZ Lynden, Washington
KTSL Medical Lake, Washington
KSBC Nile, Washington
KOMO-FM Oakville, Washington
KGDN Pasco, Washington
KRLF Pullman, Washington
KWWW-FM Quincy, Washington
KWFJ Roy, Washington
KWDR Royal City, Washington
KLFE Seattle, Washington
KNTS Seattle, Washington
KYKV Selah, Washington
KEEH Spokane, Washington
KTTO Spokane, Washington
KAYB Sunnyside, Washington
KRKL Walla Walla, Washington
KPLW Wenatchee, Washington
KYAK Yakima, Washington
KYPL Yakima, Washington
WBDK Algoma, Wisconsin
WYNW Birnamwood, Wisconsin
WAYY Eau Claire, Wisconsin
WHEM Eau Claire, Wisconsin
WDKV Fond Du Lac, Wisconsin
WVFL Fond Du Lac, Wisconsin
WMVM Goodman, Wisconsin
WWIB Hallie, Wisconsin
WKBH Holmen, Wisconsin
WJOK Kaukauna, Wisconsin
WSTM Kiel, Wisconsin
WHJL Merrill, Wisconsin
WJYI Milwaukee, Wisconsin
WMWK Milwaukee, Wisconsin
WSSP Milwaukee, Wisconsin
WVCY-FM Milwaukee, Wisconsin
WVCS Owen, Wisconsin
WHFA Poynette, Wisconsin
WNLI Sturgeon Bay, Wisconsin
WPFF Sturgeon Bay, Wisconsin
WVCX Tomah, Wisconsin
WEGZ Washburn, Wisconsin
WWEN Wentworth, Wisconsin
WPJY Blennerhassett, West Virginia
WPIB Bluefield, West Virginia
WCKU Clarksburg, West Virginia
WKJL Clarksburg, West Virginia
WBHZ Elkins, West Virginia
WDKL Grafton, West Virginia
WEMM-FM Huntington, West Virginia
WKVW Marmet, West Virginia
WZZW Milton, West Virginia
WPWV Princeton, West Virginia
WRLB Rainelle, West Virginia
WRRL Rainelle, West Virginia
WLKV Ripley, West Virginia
KLWC Casper, Wyoming
KAIX Cheyenne, Wyoming
KLWV Chugwater, Wyoming
KUYO Evansville, Wyoming
KRKM Fort Washakie, Wyoming
KAXG Gillette, Wyoming
KGLL Gillette, Wyoming
KLOF Gillette, Wyoming
KLWD Gillette, Wyoming
KTUG Hudson, Wyoming
KMLT Jackson, Wyoming
KMWY Jackson, Wyoming
KAIW Laramie, Wyoming
KTDX Laramie, Wyoming
KOHR Sheridan, Wyoming
KVLZ Sheridan, Wyoming
KDNR South Greeley, Wyoming

Classic Rock

KBFX Anchorage, Alaska
KLAM Cordova, Alaska
KXLR Fairbanks, Alaska
KSUP Juneau, Alaska
KSLD Soldotna, Alaska
KUHB-FM St. Paul, Alaska
WJSR Birmingham, Alabama
WZRR Birmingham, Alabama
WERH-FM Hamilton, Alabama
WTAK-FM Hartselle, Alabama
WRKH Mobile, Alabama
WVNA-FM Muscle Shoals, Alabama
WPPG Repton, Alabama
KDEL-FM Arkadelphia, Arkansas
KKEG Bentonville, Arkansas
KCCB Corning, Arkansas
KAGL El Dorado, Arkansas
KXJK Forrest City, Arkansas
KCWD Harrison, Arkansas
KHKN Maumelle, Arkansas
KLXQ Mountain Pine, Arkansas
KWLT North Crossett, Arkansas
KYGL Texarkana, Arkansas
KWRF Warren, Arkansas
KTRN White Hall, Arkansas
KCUZ Clifton, Arizona
KMGN Flagstaff, Arizona
KCDX Florence, Arizona
KZUL-FM Lake Havasu City, Arizona
KPKR Parker, Arizona
KSLX-FM Scottsdale, Arizona
KLPX Tucson, Arizona
KWMX Williams, Arizona
KALT-FM Alturas, California
KKBZ Auberry, California
KHRQ Baker, California
KGFM Bakersfield, California
KVMX Bakersfield, California
KRHV Big Pine, California
KOCP Camarillo, California
KWTY Cartago, California
KTHU Corning, California
KDFO Delano, California
KSOF Dinuba, California
KZRO Dunsmuir, California
KJFX Fresno, California
KJWL Fresno, California
KTOR Gerber, California
KHIP Gonzales, California
KRVQ-FM Lake Isabella, California
KHDR Lenwood, California
KFFG Los Altos, California
KLOS Los Angeles, California
KIXA Lucerne Valley, California
KDJK Mariposa, California
KHKK Modesto, California
KVRV Monte Rio, California
KLUK Needles, California
KKSF Oakland, California
KIOO Porterville, California
KMRJ Rancho Mirage, California
KRVH Rio Vista, California
KLKX(FM) Rosamond, California
KSEG Sacramento, California
KGB-FM San Diego, California
KYXY San Diego, California
KFOG San Francisco, California
KUFX San Jose, California
KZOZ San Luis Obispo, California
KSAN San Mateo, California
KXFM Santa Maria, California
KTMQ Temecula, California
KHRD Weaverville, California
KKFM Colorado Springs, Colorado
KQMT Denver, Colorado
KRFX Denver, Colorado
KKDC Dolores, Colorado
KPAW Fort Collins, Colorado
KRVG Glenwood Springs, Colorado
KVLE-FM Gunnison, Colorado
KQZR Hayden, Colorado
KLMR-FM Lamar, Colorado
KTUN New Castle, Colorado
KCCY(AM) Pueblo, Colorado
KSBV Salida, Colorado
KYEN Severance, Colorado
KCRT-FM Trinidad, Colorado
KMAX-FM Wellington, Colorado
WRKI Brookfield, Connecticut
WFOX Norwalk, Connecticut
WJKI Bethany Beach, Delaware
WGBG Seaford, Delaware
WFYV-FM Atlantic Beach, Florida
WRXK-FM Bonita Springs, Florida
WCJX Five Points, Florida
WBGG-FM Fort Lauderdale, Florida
WXCV Homosassa Springs, Florida
WKYZ Key Colony Beach, Florida
WAIL Key West, Florida
WARO Naples, Florida
WSVU North Palm Beach, Florida
WHTQ(FM) Orlando, Florida
WHOG-FM Ormond-By-The-Sea, Florida
WHTY Riviera Beach, Florida
WRBA Springfield, Florida
WGLF Tallahassee, Florida
WLTQ-FM Venice, Florida
WKGR Wellington, Florida
WAYF West Palm Beach, Florida
WXOF Yankeetown, Florida
WDMG-FM Ambrose, Georgia
WEKL Augusta, Georgia
WVRK Columbus, Georgia
WZTR Dahlonega, Georgia
WQBZ Fort Valley, Georgia
WTHG Hinesville, Georgia
WSIZ-FM Jacksonville, Georgia
WYYZ Jasper, Georgia
WPEZ Jeffersonville, Georgia
WBAW-FM Pembroke, Georgia

RADIO - U.S.

WRBF Plainville, Georgia
WZBX Rocky Ford, Georgia
WIXV Savannah, Georgia
WKEU-FM The Rock, Georgia
WWRQ-FM Valdosta, Georgia
WLOV Washington, Georgia
WPUP Watkinsville, Georgia
KIPA Hilo, Hawaii
KPOI-FM Honolulu, Hawaii
KRKH Wailea-Makena, Hawaii
KLKK Clear Lake, Iowa
KCQQ Davenport, Iowa
KXGE Dubuque, Iowa
KKSI Eddyville, Iowa
KGRR Epworth, Iowa
KKFD-FM Fairfield, Iowa
KCRR Grundy Center, Iowa
KKRQ Iowa City, Iowa
KGRA Jefferson, Iowa
KUQQ Milford, Iowa
KSEZ Sioux City, Iowa
KJOT Boise, Idaho
KWYS(FM) Island Park, Idaho
KTPO Kootenai, Idaho
KKGL Nampa, Idaho
KRVB Nampa, Idaho
KMGI Pocatello, Idaho
KPKY Pocatello, Idaho
KQEZ(FM) Shelley, Idaho
KECH-FM Sun Valley, Idaho
KSNQ Twin Falls, Idaho
KLZX Weston, Idaho
WDLJ Breese, Illinois
WWGO Charleston, Illinois
WYMG Chatham, Illinois
WRXQ Coal City, Illinois
WRHK Danville, Illinois
WYXY(FM) Danville, Illinois
KUUL East Moline, Illinois
WMXM Lake Forest, Illinois
WKGL-FM Loves Park, Illinois
WJEQ Macomb, Illinois
WGKC Mahomet, Illinois
WXLP Moline, Illinois
WZZT Morrison, Illinois
WIKK Newton, Illinois
WGLO Pekin, Illinois
WBZG Peru, Illinois
WABZ Sherman, Illinois
WSHP Attica, Indiana
WJAA Austin, Indiana
WTCJ-FM Cannelton, Indiana
WHJE Carmel, Indiana
WXRD Crown Point, Indiana
WOWO-FM Fort Wayne, Indiana
WXKE Fort Wayne, Indiana
WSSM(FM) Goshen, Indiana
WRGF Greenfield, Indiana
WFBQ Indianapolis, Indiana
WYXB Indianapolis, Indiana
WQMF Jeffersonville, Indiana
WKHY Lafayette, Indiana
WRZR Loogootee, Indiana
WSMM New Carlisle, Indiana
WMYK Peru, Indiana
WBTO-FM Petersburg, Indiana
WTCJ Tell City, Indiana
WWVR West Terre Haute, Indiana
KNZS Arlington, Kansas
KFXJ Augusta, Kansas
KCAR-FM Baxter Springs, Kansas
KKRK Coffeyville, Kansas
KANS Emporia, Kansas
KOTE Eureka, Kansas
KSEK-FM Girard, Kansas
KVGB-FM Great Bend, Kansas
KINZ Humboldt, Kansas
KWKR Leoti, Kansas
KTHR Wichita, Kansas
WLFX Berea, Kentucky
WDNS Bowling Green, Kentucky
WCBJ Campton, Kentucky
WHHT(FM) Cave City, Kentucky
WQQR Clinton, Kentucky
WWEL London, Kentucky
WTBK Manchester, Kentucky
WFTM-FM Maysville, Kentucky
WKYM Monticello, Kentucky
WKQQ Winchester, Kentucky
WDGL Baton Rouge, Louisiana
WKBU New Orleans, Louisiana
KKGB Sulphur, Louisiana
WXRG Athol, Massachusetts
WZLX Boston, Massachusetts
WGAO Franklin, Massachusetts
WOCN-FM Orleans, Massachusetts
WAQY Springfield, Massachusetts
WKGO Cumberland, Maryland
WDLD Halfway, Maryland
WZBA Westminster, Maryland
WKIT-FM Brewer, Maine
WQDY-FM Calais, Maine
WCTB Fairfield, Maine
WFNK Lewiston, Maine
WNSX Winter Harbor, Maine
WCSX Birmingham, Michigan
WCKC Cadillac, Michigan
WGFM Cheboygan, Michigan
WMMQ East Lansing, Michigan
WBNZ Frankfort, Michigan
WGFN Glen Arbor, Michigan
WBFX Grand Rapids, Michigan
WLAV-FM Grand Rapids, Michigan
WGLI Hancock, Michigan
WWKR Hart, Michigan
WKJZ Hillman, Michigan
WSRJ Honor, Michigan
WBZV Hudson, Michigan
WIMK Iron Mountain, Michigan
WSAG Linwood, Michigan
WUPK Marquette, Michigan
WIHC Newberry, Michigan
WOVI Novi, Michigan
WRSR Owosso, Michigan
WRUP Palmer, Michigan
WRKR Portage, Michigan
WUPF Powers, Michigan
WILZ Saginaw, Michigan
WSUE Sault Ste. Marie, Michigan
WQLB Tawas City, Michigan
KAOD Babbitt, Minnesota
KLIZ-FM Brainerd, Minnesota
KFGI Crosby, Minnesota
KXLP Eagle Lake, Minnesota
KFMC-FM Fairmont, Minnesota
KMGK Glenwood, Minnesota
WXXZ Grand Marais, Minnesota
KOZY Grand Rapids, Minnesota
KARZ Marshall, Minnesota
KMGM Montevideo, Minnesota
KQWB-FM Moorhead, Minnesota
KMFG Nashwauk, Minnesota
KPHR Ortonville, Minnesota
KRCH Rochester, Minnesota
KRWB Roseau, Minnesota
KDXL St. Louis Park, Minnesota
KLFN Sunburg, Minnesota
KLZZ Waite Park, Minnesota
KLLZ-FM Walker, Minnesota
KHME Winona, Minnesota
KHRS Winthrop, Minnesota
KGMO Cape Girardeau, Missouri
KSHE Crestwood, Missouri
KCFX Harrisonville, Missouri
KRXL Kirksville, Missouri
KKLH Marshfield, Missouri
KZZK New London, Missouri
KJEZ Poplar Bluff, Missouri
KIGL Seligman, Missouri
KXUS Springfield, Missouri
KXDG Webb City, Missouri
KSPQ West Plains, Missouri
WXRR Hattiesburg, Mississippi
WZNF Lumberton, Mississippi
WCNA Potts Camp, Mississippi
WSTZ-FM Vicksburg, Mississippi
KFLN Baker, Montana
KJJM Baker, Montana
KBZM Big Sky, Montana
KURL(FM) Billings, Montana
KMBR Butte, Montana
KTZZ Conrad, Montana
KGVO-FM Frenchtown, Montana
KZMT Helena, Montana
KZMN Kalispell, Montana
KOZB Livingston, Montana
KKQX Manhattan, Montana
KMTA Miles City, Montana
WKRR Asheboro, North Carolina
WZJS Banner Elk, North Carolina
WTZQ Hendersonville, North Carolina
WRFX Kannapolis, North Carolina
WCNG Murphy, North Carolina
WMGV Newport, North Carolina
WNTB Topsail Beach, North Carolina
WRVA-FM Wake Forest, North Carolina
WQNS Waynesville, North Carolina
WBNE Wrightsville Beach, North Carolina
KBYZ Bismarck, North Dakota
KSSS Bismarck, North Dakota
KPFX Fargo, North Dakota
KRWK Fargo, North Dakota
KZPR Minot, North Dakota
KTZU Velva, North Dakota
KTGL Beatrice, Nebraska
KBBN-FM Broken Bow, Nebraska
KKOT Columbus, Nebraska
KCFD Crawford, Nebraska
KLZA Falls City, Nebraska
KFMT-FM Fremont, Nebraska
KQHK McCook, Nebraska
KNEN Norfolk, Nebraska
KBRX O'Neill, Nebraska
KKCD Omaha, Nebraska
WMLL Bedford, New Hampshire
WHDQ Claremont, New Hampshire
WWHQ Meredith, New Hampshire
WDHA-FM Dover, New Jersey
WCHR-FM Manahawkin, New Jersey
WBSS Pleasantville, New Jersey
WZXL Wildwood, New Jersey
KZRM Chama, New Mexico
KEJL Eunice, New Mexico
KDAG Farmington, New Mexico
KRWN Farmington, New Mexico
KXXI Gallup, New Mexico
KMDZ Las Vegas, New Mexico
KPSA-FM Lordsburg, New Mexico
KIOT Los Lunas, New Mexico
KIDX Ruidoso, New Mexico
KTUM Tatum, New Mexico
KOZZ-FM Reno, Nevada
KURK Reno, Nevada
WPYX Albany, New York
WBNR Beacon, New York
WTKW Bridgeport, New York
WGRF Buffalo, New York
WSDE Cobleskill, New York
WKGB-FM Conklin, New York
WIII Cortland, New York
WNMR Dannemora, New York
WECW Elmira, New York
WCPV Essex, New York
WLPW Lake Placid, New York
WNGZ Montour Falls, New York
WWFS New York, New York
WCHN Norwich, New York
WRHO Oneonta, New York
WTKV Oswego, New York
WPDH Poughkeepsie, New York
WRCN-FM Riverhead, New York
WCMF-FM Rochester, New York
WQRS Salamanca, New York
WLLW Seneca Falls, New York
WRGR Tupper Lake, New York
WLKK Wethersfield Twnshp, New York
WQEL Bucyrus, Ohio
WCWT-FM Centerville, Ohio
WDOK Cleveland, Ohio
WLVQ Columbus, Ohio
WDOH Delphos, Ohio
WFXN-FM Galion, Ohio
WDUB Granville, Ohio
WGRR Hamilton, Ohio
WBWR Hilliard, Ohio
WKET Kettering, Ohio
WEGE Lima, Ohio
WXXF Loudonville, Ohio
WYRO McArthur, Ohio
WMWX Miamitown, Ohio
WVXG Mount Gilead, Ohio
WYCL Niles, Ohio
WFXJ-FM North Kingsville, Ohio
WBUK Ottawa, Ohio
WBIK Pleasant City, Ohio
WXKR Port Clinton, Ohio
WZZZ Portsmouth, Ohio
WBCJ Spencerville, Ohio
WKTL Struthers, Ohio
KFXU Chickasha, Oklahoma
KDDQ Comanche, Oklahoma
KTRX Dickson, Oklahoma
KTLS-FM Holdenville, Oklahoma

KTMC McAlester, Oklahoma
KTMC-FM McAlester, Oklahoma
KRXO Oklahoma City, Oklahoma
KLOR-FM Ponca City, Oklahoma
KKBD Sallisaw, Oklahoma
KJSR Tulsa, Oklahoma
KTWS Bend, Oregon
KLOO-FM Corvallis, Oregon
KZEL-FM Eugene, Oregon
KDEP Garibaldi, Oregon
KAGO-FM Klamath Falls, Oregon
KFEG Klamath Falls, Oregon
KUBQ La Grande, Oregon
KLCR Lakeview, Oregon
KBOY-FM Medford, Oregon
KGON Portland, Oregon
KJMX Reedsport, Oregon
KCRX-FM Seaside, Oregon
KMSW The Dalles, Oregon
WBVE Bedford, Pennsylvania
WBUS Boalsburg, Pennsylvania
WHYP(AM) Corry, Pennsylvania
WQHZ Erie, Pennsylvania
WQCM Greencastle, Pennsylvania
WKVR-FM Huntingdon, Pennsylvania
WJNG Johnsonburg, Pennsylvania
WCXR Lewisburg, Pennsylvania
WRKT North East, Pennsylvania
WHAT Philadelphia, Pennsylvania
WPZX Pocono Pines, Pennsylvania
WPAM Pottsville, Pennsylvania
WQKK(FM) Renovo, Pennsylvania
WQFX-FM Russell, Pennsylvania
WYFM Sharon, Pennsylvania
WSRU Slippery Rock, Pennsylvania
WXMT Smethport, Pennsylvania
WZXR South Williamsport, Pennsylvania
WMTT Tioga, Pennsylvania
WBAX Wilkes-Barre, Pennsylvania
WVJP-FM Caguas, Puerto Rico
WROQ Anderson, South Carolina
WVGB Beaufort, South Carolina
WBAJ Blythewood, South Carolina
WSIM Lamar, South Carolina
WRFQ Mount Pleasant, South Carolina
WYAV Myrtle Beach, South Carolina
WQKI-FM Orangeburg, South Carolina
WMFX St. Andrews, South Carolina
WQUL Woodruff, South Carolina
KSDN-FM Aberdeen, South Dakota
KYBB Canton, South Dakota
KDBX Clear Lake, South Dakota
KFXS Rapid City, South Dakota
KRRO Sioux Falls, South Dakota
KJRV Wessington Springs, South Dakota
WEGR Arlington, Tennessee
WKOM Columbia, Tennessee
WFHU Henderson, Tennessee
WEKX Jellico, Tennessee
WQUT Johnson City, Tennessee
WIMZ-FM Knoxville, Tennessee
WKHT Knoxville, Tennessee
WQLA La Follette, Tennessee
WLQK Livingston, Tennessee
WYNU Milan, Tennessee
WOWC Morrison, Tennessee
WKTI Powell, Tennessee
KQQK Beaumont, Texas
KRXB Beeville, Texas
KLUB Bloomington, Texas
KYYI Burkburnett, Texas
KARX Claude, Texas
KZPS Dallas, Texas
KATX Eastland, Texas
KICA-FM Farwell, Texas
KFZX Gardendale, Texas
KWKQ Graham, Texas
KPUS Gregory, Texas
KBRQ Hillsboro, Texas
KKRW Houston, Texas
KKTX-FM Kilgore, Texas
KONE Lubbock, Texas
KHXS Merkel, Texas
KTBQ Nacogdoches, Texas
KIOC Orange, Texas
KBUS Paris, Texas
KRIA Plainview, Texas
KWFR San Angelo, Texas
KZEP-FM San Antonio, Texas
KJKB Scotland, Texas
KNRX Sterling City, Texas
KTAL-FM Texarkana, Texas
WACO-FM Waco, Texas
KYQX Weatherford, Texas
KMAD-FM Whitesboro, Texas
KAGJ Ephraim, Utah
KCUA Naples, Utah
KWCR-FM Ogden, Utah
KWSA Price, Utah
KRSP-FM Salt Lake City, Utah
KZHK St. George, Utah
WWUZ Bowling Green, Virginia
WKLR Fort Lee, Virginia
WZFM Narrows, Virginia
WAFX Suffolk, Virginia
WIVI Charlotte Amalie, Virgin Islands
WEXP Brandon, Vermont
WOTX Lunenburg, Vermont
KISM Bellingham, Washington
KWWX Cashmere, Washington
KVAB Clarkston, Washington
KLSY Cosmopolis, Washington
KZOK-FM Seattle, Washington
KKZX Spokane, Washington
KYNR Toppenish, Washington
KPQ-FM Wenatchee, Washington
WRLO-FM Antigo, Wisconsin
WJJH Ashland, Wisconsin
WLDB Milwaukee, Wisconsin
WRPN-FM Ripon, Wisconsin
WIBA-FM Sauk City, Wisconsin
WGMO Spooner, Wisconsin
WTMB Tomah, Wisconsin
WCHY Waunakee, Wisconsin
WKBH-FM West Salem, Wisconsin
WGLX-FM Wisconsin Rapids, Wisconsin
WVWC Buckhannon, West Virginia
WKQV Cowen, West Virginia
WRLF Fairmont, West Virginia
WQZK-FM Keyser, West Virginia
WVKM Matewan, West Virginia
WCLG-FM Morgantown, West Virginia
WKQR(FM) Mullens, West Virginia
WETZ New Martinsville, West Virginia
WXCR New Martinsville, West Virginia
WRZZ Parkersburg, West Virginia
WKOY-FM Princeton, West Virginia
WFBY Weston, West Virginia
KASS Casper, Wyoming
KZJH Jackson, Wyoming
KDLY Lander, Wyoming
KXXL Moorcroft, Wyoming
KCGL Powell, Wyoming
KSIT Rock Springs, Wyoming
KZWY Sheridan, Wyoming
KRVK Vista West, Wyoming

Classical

WHIL-FM Mobile, Alabama
WTSU Montgomery-Troy, Alabama
KBSA El Dorado, Arkansas
KASU Jonesboro, Arkansas
KJZP Prescott, Arizona
KUAT-FM Tucson, Arizona
KGIL Johannesburg, California
KLDD McCloud, California
KESC Morro Bay, California
KPSC Palm Springs, California
KNHT Rio Dell, California
KXPR Sacramento, California
KVOV Carbondale, Colorado
KMPZ Salida, Colorado
WJUF Inverness, Florida
WKAT North Miami, Florida
WWIO-FM Brunswick, Georgia
WUWG Carrollton, Georgia
WNGH-FM Chatsworth, Georgia
WAZX-FM Cleveland, Georgia
WMUM-FM Cochran, Georgia
WNGU Dahlonega, Georgia
WGPB Rome, Georgia
WWIO St. Marys, Georgia
WXVS Waycross, Georgia
KHOE Fairfield, Iowa
KIBX Bonners Ferry, Idaho
WAXR Geneseo, Illinois
WNIW La Salle, Illinois
WCBU Peoria, Illinois
WNIU Rockford, Illinois
WETN Wheaton, Illinois
WBST Muncie, Indiana
WSND-FM Notre Dame, Indiana
WCKZ Orland, Indiana
WBNI-FM Roanoke, Indiana
WBAA-FM West Lafayette, Indiana
WEKF Corbin, Kentucky
KLSA Alexandria, Louisiana
KEDM Monroe, Louisiana
KDAQ Shreveport, Louisiana
WFCC-FM Chatham, Massachusetts
WCRB Lowell, Massachusetts
WBJC Baltimore, Maryland
WFWM Frostburg, Maryland
WICV East Jordan, Michigan
WIAA Interlochen, Michigan
WSCD-FM Duluth, Minnesota
WMLS Grand Marais, Minnesota
WVAL Sauk Rapids, Minnesota
KQMN Thief River Falls, Minnesota
KRCU Cape Girardeau, Missouri
KAUD Mexico, Missouri
KSMS-FM Point Lookout, Missouri
KSMU Springfield, Missouri
KSEF Ste. Genevieve, Missouri
WWSL Philadelphia, Mississippi
KAPC Butte, Montana
KUFN Hamilton, Montana
KUHM Helena, Montana
KUKL Kalispell, Montana
WZPE Bath, North Carolina
WBUX Buxton, North Carolina
WURI Manteo, North Carolina
WCPE Raleigh, North Carolina
WWCJ Cape May, New Jersey
WWNJ Toms River Township, New Jersey
WWFM Trenton, New Jersey
KSJE Farmington, New Mexico
KQMC Hawthorne, Nevada
KBSJ Jackpot, Nevada
KTPH Tonopah, Nevada
WEXT Amsterdam, New York
WOXR Schuyler Falls, New York
WCNY-FM Syracuse, New York
WCLV Lorain, Ohio
WOSV Mansfield, Ohio
WOSP Portsmouth, Ohio
KOCU Altus, Oklahoma
KLCU Ardmore, Oklahoma
KYCU Clinton, Oklahoma
KCCU Lawton, Oklahoma
KWTU Tulsa, Oklahoma
KSRG Ashland, Oregon
KWVZ Florence, Oregon
KQOC Gleneden Beach, Oregon
KQDL Hines, Oregon
KQAC Portland, Oregon
KWRX Redmond, Oregon
KQHR The Dalles, Oregon
WRTJ Coatesville, Pennsylvania
WRTL Ephrata, Pennsylvania
WQLN-FM Erie, Pennsylvania
WQEJ Johnstown, Pennsylvania
WWPJ Pen Argyl, Pennsylvania
WJAZ Summerdale, Pennsylvania
KQSD-FM Lowry, South Dakota
KZSD-FM Martin, South Dakota
KBHE-FM Rapid City, South Dakota
KTSD-FM Reliance, South Dakota
KUSD Vermillion, South Dakota
WFHU Henderson, Tennessee
WKNP Jackson, Tennessee
WUOT Knoxville, Tennessee
WKNO-FM Memphis, Tennessee
WTML Tullahoma, Tennessee
WRR Dallas, Texas
KLDN Lufkin, Texas
KMCU Wichita Falls, Texas
KUSR Logan, Utah
WMVE Chase City, Virginia
WEMC Harrisonburg, Virginia
WRIQ Lexington, Virginia
WCVE-FM Richmond, Virginia
WBQK West Point, Virginia
WBTN-FM Bennington, Vermont
WVTI Brighton, Vermont
WVNK Manchester, Vermont
WOXM Middlebury, Vermont
WCVT Stowe, Vermont
WVTQ Sunderland, Vermont
KSWS Chehalis, Washington
KNWU Forks, Washington
KNWP Port Angeles, Washington

WPNE-FM Green Bay, Wisconsin
WGTD Kenosha, Wisconsin
WERN Madison, Wisconsin
WSSW Platteville, Wisconsin
WHND Sister Bay, Wisconsin
KZUW Reliance, Wyoming
KPRQ Sheridan, Wyoming

Comedy

WMVP Chicago, Illinois
WNTA Rockford, Illinois
KTHH Albany, Oregon

Contemporary Hits/Top 40

KGOT Anchorage, Alaska
KAKQ-FM Fairbanks, Alaska
KWLF Fairbanks, Alaska
KSUP Juneau, Alaska
KUHB-FM St. Paul, Alaska
WZYP Athens, Alabama
WZBQ Carrollton, Alabama
WKMX Enterprise, Alabama
WHHY-FM Montgomery, Alabama
WWFA St. Florian, Alabama
WMXN-FM Stevenson, Alabama
WQNR Tallassee, Alabama
WJDB-FM Thomasville, Alabama
WQEN Trussville, Alabama
KLBQ El Dorado, Arkansas
KHTE-FM England, Arkansas
KISR Fort Smith, Arkansas
KKPT Little Rock, Arkansas
KMXF Lowell, Arkansas
KHBM Monticello, Arkansas
KHBM-FM Monticello, Arkansas
KQMJ(FM) Osceola, Arkansas
KFYX(FM) Texarkana, Arkansas
KBBQ-FM Van Buren, Arkansas
KIYS Walnut Ridge, Arkansas
KIYS-FM Walnut Ridge, Arkansas
KCDQ Douglas, Arizona
KZZP Mesa, Arizona
KFSZ Munds Park, Arizona
KOFH Nogales, Arizona
KXAZ Page, Arizona
KQST Sedona, Arizona
KRQQ Tucson, Arizona
KREV Alameda, California
KEWB Anderson, California
KWRN Apple Valley, California
KISV Bakersfield, California
KDUC Barstow, California
KXSB Big Bear Lake, California
KQPT Colusa, California
KHTS-FM El Cajon, California
KWPT Fortuna, California
KOHL Fremont, California
KWYE Fresno, California
KRTO Guadalupe, California
KRVC Hornbrook, California
KNTI Lakeport, California
KWIN Lodi, California
KIIS-FM Los Angeles, California
KPWR Los Angeles, California
KDUQ Ludlow, California
KRCK-FM Mecca, California
KSMC Moraga, California
KNKK Needles, California
KHOP Oakdale, California
KLFH Ojai, California
KSPA Ontario, California
KCAQ Oxnard, California
KXTZ Pismo Beach, California
KHTN Planada, California
KGGI Riverside, California
KVVS Rosamond, California
KDND Sacramento, California
KYZZ Salinas, California
KMEL San Francisco, California
KWWV Santa Margarita, California
KRLT South Lake Tahoe, California
KLCA Tahoe City, California
KXDZ Templeton, California
KWNN Turlock, California
KSEQ Visalia, California
KCWH Weed, California
KDGL Yucca Valley, California
KASF Alamosa, Colorado
KONN-FM Bennett, Colorado
KIDN-FM Burns, Colorado
KPTE Durango, Colorado
KIBT Fountain, Colorado
KMGJ Grand Junction, Colorado
KSME Greeley, Colorado
KIFT(FM) Kremmling, Colorado
KBLJ La Junta, Colorado
KQKS Lakewood, Colorado
KWUZ Poncha Springs, Colorado
KKMG Pueblo, Colorado
KRDZ Wray, Colorado
WNLC East Lyme, Connecticut
WQGN-FM Groton, Connecticut
WKCI-FM Hamden, Connecticut
WKSS Hartford-Meriden, Connecticut
WWRX Ledyard, Connecticut
WILI-FM Willimantic, Connecticut
WIHT Washington, District of Columbia
WZBH Georgetown, Delaware
WRDX Smyrna, Delaware
WWUS Big Pine Key, Florida
WXKB Cape Coral, Florida
WLQH Chiefland, Florida
WROD Daytona Beach, Florida
WHYI-FM Fort Lauderdale, Florida
WZNS Fort Walton Beach, Florida
WRUF-FM Gainesville, Florida
WYKS Gainesville, Florida
WHTF Havana, Florida
WAPE-FM Jacksonville, Florida
WJGL Jacksonville, Florida
WMBX Jensen Beach, Florida
WLDI Juno Beach, Florida
WEOW Key West, Florida
WQHL Live Oak, Florida
WXHT Madison, Florida
WAOA-FM Melbourne, Florida
WFKS Melbourne, Florida
WFKS(FM) Melbourne, Florida
WMYM Miami, Florida
WPOW Miami, Florida
WILN Panama City, Florida
WPFM-FM Panama City, Florida
WPRY Perry, Florida
WMXJ Pompano Beach, Florida
WWMI St. Petersburg, Florida
WXGL St. Petersburg, Florida
WFLZ-FM Tampa, Florida
WXXL Tavares, Florida
WQVE Albany, Georgia
WWWQ Atlanta, Georgia
WCGQ Columbus, Georgia
WXMK Dock Junction, Georgia
WKKZ Dublin, Georgia
WEDB East Dublin, Georgia
WLEL Ellaville, Georgia
WSRV Gainesville, Georgia
WPCH Gray, Georgia
WMGP Hogansville, Georgia
WBTY Homerville, Georgia
WDRR Martinez, Georgia
WBMZ Metter, Georgia
WMGB Montezuma, Georgia
WMTM-FM Moultrie, Georgia
WSFB Quitman, Georgia
WAEV Savannah, Georgia
WSEG Savannah, Georgia
WSTR Smyrna, Georgia
WJFL Tennille, Georgia
WPAX Thomasville, Georgia
WZAT Tybee Island, Georgia
WKTF Vienna, Georgia
WZCH Warner Robins, Georgia
WWUF Waycross, Georgia
KOKU Hagatna, Guam
KMWB Captain Cook, Hawaii
KPMW Haliimaile, Hawaii
KNWB Hilo, Hawaii
KINE-FM Honolulu, Hawaii
KLHI-FM Kahului, Hawaii
KTOH Kalaheo, Hawaii
KPHW Kaneohe, Hawaii
KSHK Kekaha, Hawaii
KJMQ Lihue, Hawaii
KQNG-FM Lihue, Hawaii
KJMD Pukalani, Hawaii
KDDB Waipahu, Hawaii
KCCQ Ames, Iowa
KSWI Atlantic, Iowa
KZAT-FM Belle Plaine, Iowa
KKDM Des Moines, Iowa
KRTI Grinnell, Iowa
KIFG Iowa Falls, Iowa
KXFT Manson, Iowa
KBEA-FM Muscatine, Iowa
KHDK New London, Iowa
KOTM-FM Ottumwa, Iowa
KIYX Sageville, Iowa
KRQN Vinton, Iowa
KOKZ Waterloo, Iowa
KWAR Waverly, Iowa
KSAS-FM Caldwell, Idaho
KFTZ Idaho Falls, Idaho
KQEO Idaho Falls, Idaho
KSNA Idaho Falls, Idaho
KVTY Lewiston, Idaho
KZFN Moscow, Idaho
KWYD Parma, Idaho
KGTM Rexburg, Idaho
KOFE St. Maries, Idaho
WKIB Anna, Illinois
WERV-FM Aurora, Illinois
WSDZ Belleville, Illinois
WBNQ Bloomington, Illinois
WCDD Canton, Illinois
WCIL-FM Carbondale, Illinois
WKSC-FM Chicago, Illinois
WRPW Colfax, Illinois
WSOY-FM Decatur, Illinois
WPIA Eureka, Illinois
WISH-FM Galatia, Illinois
WDBQ-FM Galena, Illinois
WFAV Gilman, Illinois
WXAJ Hillsboro, Illinois
WVLI Kankakee, Illinois
WQLF Lena, Illinois
WLRB Macomb, Illinois
WLWF(FM) Marseilles, Illinois
WPBG Peoria, Illinois
WZPW Peoria, Illinois
WZOE-FM Princeton, Illinois
WQQB Rantoul, Illinois
WRRG River Grove, Illinois
WZOK Rockford, Illinois
WEJT Shelbyville, Illinois
WIVQ Spring Valley, Illinois
WDBR Springfield, Illinois
WSTQ Streator, Illinois
WKRV Vandalia, Illinois
WRTB Winnebago, Illinois
WBWB Bloomington, Indiana
WINN Columbus, Indiana
WIMC Crawfordsville, Indiana
WXXB Delphi, Indiana
WLDE Fort Wayne, Indiana
WFCI Franklin, Indiana
WVSH Huntington, Indiana
WEDM Indianapolis, Indiana
WXXC Marion, Indiana
WNAS New Albany, Indiana
WJFX New Haven, Indiana
WDKS Newburgh, Indiana
WUME-FM Paoli, Indiana
WTCA Plymouth, Indiana
WLQI Rensselaer, Indiana
WNRW(FM) Salem, Indiana
WAYI(FM) Sellersville, Indiana
WDND South Bend, Indiana
WNDV-FM South Bend, Indiana
WNOU Speedway, Indiana
WCLS Spencer, Indiana
WMGI Terre Haute, Indiana
WRSW-FM Warsaw, Indiana
WAMW-FM Washington, Indiana
KDGS Andover, Kansas
KTCC Colby, Kansas
KMOQ Columbus, Kansas
KZCH Derby, Kansas
KOMB Fort Scott, Kansas
KRMR Hays, Kansas
KJCK-FM Junction City, Kansas
KXNC Ness City, Kansas
KQNK Norton, Kansas
KQNK-FM Norton, Kansas
KACZ Riley, Kansas
KRSL Russell, Kansas
KRSL-FM Russell, Kansas
KSAL-FM Salina, Kansas
KSKU Sterling, Kansas
KWIC Topeka, Kansas
WANV Annville, Kentucky
WBVX Carlisle, Kentucky
WWKF Fulton, Kentucky

WLKT Lexington-Fayette, Kentucky
WFTM Maysville, Kentucky
WLTO Nicholasville, Kentucky
WEGI-FM Oak Grove, Kentucky
WSTO Owensboro, Kentucky
WDDJ Paducah, Kentucky
WQHY Prestonsburg, Kentucky
WKEQ Somerset, Kentucky
WKKS-FM Vanceburg, Kentucky
WZLK Virgie, Kentucky
WXKQ-FM Whitesburg, Kentucky
KQID-FM Alexandria, Louisiana
WABL Amite, Louisiana
KCIJ Atlanta, Louisiana
WFMF Baton Rouge, Louisiana
KTSR De Quincy, Louisiana
KFNV-FM Ferriday, Louisiana
KHLA Jennings, Louisiana
KLIP Monroe, Louisiana
KNOE-FM Monroe, Louisiana
WEZB New Orleans, Louisiana
KRUF Shreveport, Louisiana
WJMN Boston, Massachusetts
WFHN Fairhaven, Massachusetts
WCIB Falmouth, Massachusetts
WROR-FM Framingham, Massachusetts
WPGC-FM Morningside, Maryland
WWEG Myersville, Maryland
WTTR Westminster, Maryland
WMME-FM Augusta, Maine
WWMJ Ellsworth, Maine
WALZ-FM Machias, Maine
WSKX York Center, Maine
WFDX Atlanta, Michigan
WAHS Auburn Hills, Michigan
WKFR-FM Battle Creek, Michigan
WKHQ-FM Charlevoix, Michigan
WUPZ Chocolay Township, Michigan
WHTS Coopersville, Michigan
WKQI Detroit, Michigan
WWCK-FM Flint, Michigan
WGRY Grayling, Michigan
WUPT Gwinn, Michigan
WHMI-FM Howell, Michigan
WJIM-FM Lansing, Michigan
WFCX Leland, Michigan
WSNX-FM Muskegon, Michigan
WKQS-FM Negaunee, Michigan
WSDP Plymouth, Michigan
WYVN Saugatuck, Michigan
WYSS Sault Ste. Marie, Michigan
WMXG Stephenson, Michigan
WLKM-FM Three Rivers, Michigan
KKIN Aitkin, Minnesota
KBSB Bemidji, Minnesota
KBMO Benson, Minnesota
KSCR-FM Benson, Minnesota
KCLH Caledonia, Minnesota
WKLK Cloquet, Minnesota
KQHT Crookston, Minnesota
WMFG-FM Hibbing, Minnesota
WTBX Hibbing, Minnesota
KDKK Park Rapids, Minnesota
KWNG Red Wing, Minnesota
KDWB-FM Richfield, Minnesota
KROC-FM Rochester, Minnesota
KCAJ-FM Roseau, Minnesota
KCLD-FM St. Cloud, Minnesota
KCML St. Joseph, Minnesota
KTNX Arcadia, Missouri
KOQL Ashland, Missouri
KOZX Cabool, Missouri
KRRY Canton, Missouri
KGRC Hannibal, Missouri
KSYN Joplin, Missouri
KMXV Kansas City, Missouri
KBOA Kennett, Missouri
KWJC Liberty, Missouri
KZZT Moberly, Missouri
KDAA Rolla, Missouri
KSPW Sparta, Missouri
KIHT St. Louis, Missouri
KSLZ St. Louis, Missouri
WHJT Clinton, Mississippi
WYOY Gluckstadt, Mississippi
WROA Gulfport, Mississippi
WXYK Gulfport, Mississippi
WNSL Laurel, Mississippi
WOXD Oxford, Mississippi
WSKK Ripley, Mississippi
KBUD Sardis, Mississippi
WIVG Tunica, Mississippi
WBBV Vicksburg, Mississippi
WVBG Vicksburg, Mississippi
KISN Belgrade, Montana
KMXM(FM) Helena Valley N, Montana
KWMY Joliet, Montana
KRSQ Laurel, Montana
KLCM Lewistown, Montana
KPLN Lockwood, Montana
KKMT Pablo, Montana
KXDR Pinesdale, Montana
KENR Superior, Montana
WKXB Boiling Spring Lakes, North Carolina
WBHN Bryson City, North Carolina
WNKS Charlotte, North Carolina
WDCG Durham, North Carolina
WQSM Fayetteville, North Carolina
WFMZ Hertford, North Carolina
WHGO Hertford, North Carolina
WRHT Morehead City, North Carolina
WZPR Nags Head, North Carolina
WKBC-FM North Wilkesboro, North Carolina
WDCC Sanford, North Carolina
WAZO Southport, North Carolina
WERO Washington, North Carolina
WKZL Winston-Salem, North Carolina
KKCT Bismarck, North Dakota
KXRV Cannon Ball, North Dakota
WDAY-FM Fargo, North Dakota
KKXL-FM Grand Forks, North Dakota
KMJO Hope, North Dakota
KQDJ Jamestown, North Dakota
KQDJ-FM Valley City, North Dakota
KCNT Hastings, Nebraska
KQKY Kearney, Nebraska
KFRX Lincoln, Nebraska
KGOR Omaha, Nebraska
KOPW Plattsmouth, Nebraska
WJYY Concord, New Hampshire
WERZ Exeter, New Hampshire
WFTN Franklin, New Hampshire
WSAK Hampton, New Hampshire
WKNE Keene, New Hampshire
WMTK Littleton, New Hampshire
WLKZ Wolfeboro, New Hampshire
WSNQ Cape May Court House, New Jersey
WHTG Eatontown, New Jersey
WRPR Mahwah, New Jersey
WJRZ-FM Manahawkin, New Jersey
WHTZ Newark, New Jersey
WPST Trenton, New Jersey
KYEE Alamogordo, New Mexico
KDRF Albuquerque, New Mexico
KKYC Clovis, New Mexico
KAZX Kirtland, New Mexico
KHQT Las Cruces, New Mexico
KLEA Lovington, New Mexico
KBCQ-FM Roswell, New Mexico
KSFX Roswell, New Mexico
KKSS Santa Fe, New Mexico
KXTC Thoreau, New Mexico
KKLZ Las Vegas, Nevada
KLUC-FM Las Vegas, Nevada
KPLV Las Vegas, Nevada
KXPT Las Vegas, Nevada
KVEG Mesquite, Nevada
WBXL Baldwinsville, New York
WSEN-FM Baldwinsville, New York
WKKF Ballston Spa, New York
WYUL Chateaugay, New York
WWYL Chenango Bridge, New York
WBDR Copenhagen, New York
WDNY Dansville, New York
WDHI Delhi, New York
WECW Elmira, New York
WLVY Elmira, New York
WMRV-FM Endicott, New York
WITR Henrietta, New York
WXUR Herkimer, New York
WKGS Irondequoit, New York
WKTU Lake Success, New York
WKZA Lakewood, New York
WSKU Little Falls, New York
WYSX Morristown, New York
WXRK New York, New York
WKSE Niagara Falls, New York
WFIZ Odessa, New York
WMCR-FM Oneida, New York
WOSS Ossining, New York
WBLI Patchogue, New York
WKOL Plattsburgh, New York
WSPK Poughkeepsie, New York
WPXY-FM Rochester, New York
WYZY Saranac, New York
WBPM Saugerties, New York
WENU South Glen Falls, New York
WJPZ-FM Syracuse, New York
WNTQ Syracuse, New York
WWHT Syracuse, New York
WFLY Troy, New York
WKBE Warrensburg, New York
WQRW Wellsville, New York
WAKS Akron, Ohio
WZIP Akron, Ohio
WOHF Bellevue, Ohio
WBNO-FM Bryan, Ohio
WCDK Cadiz, Ohio
WMJI Cleveland, Ohio
WOSU-FM Columbus, Ohio
WUFM Columbus, Ohio
WKXA-FM Findlay, Ohio
WJEH Gallipolis, Ohio
WWSR Lima, Ohio
WRVB Marietta, Ohio
WYVK Middleport, Ohio
WKFS Milford, Ohio
WNKO New Albany, Ohio
WJZE Oak Harbor, Ohio
WXZQ Piketon, Ohio
WVKF Shadyside, Ohio
WVKS Toledo, Ohio
WZWP West Union, Ohio
WZLR Xenia, Ohio
KTBT Broken Arrow, Oklahoma
KXFC Coalgate, Oklahoma
KTIJ Elk City, Oklahoma
KTSO Glenpool, Oklahoma
KGLC Miami, Oklahoma
KHTT Muskogee, Oklahoma
KJYO Oklahoma City, Oklahoma
KOMA Oklahoma City, Oklahoma
KZBB Poteau, Oklahoma
KAYE-FM Tonkawa, Oklahoma
KIFS Ashland, Oregon
KQAK Bend, Oregon
KZME Brightwood, Oregon
KMKR Canyonville, Oregon
KCNA Cave Junction, Oregon
KDCQ Coos Bay, Oregon
KMHS-FM Coos Bay, Oregon
KMME(FM) Cottage Grove, Oregon
KCFM(AM) Florence, Oregon
KDUK-FM Florence, Oregon
KEOL La Grande, Oregon
KORV-FM Lakeview, Oregon
KLDZ Medford, Oregon
KOOS North Bend, Oregon
KKRZ Portland, Oregon
KLKY Stanfield, Oregon
KXIX Sunriver, Oregon
WHOL Allentown, Pennsylvania
WWOT Altoona, Pennsylvania
WAYC-FM Bedford, Pennsylvania
WHLM-FM Berwick, Pennsylvania
WBYN-FM Boyertown, Pennsylvania
WLER-FM Butler, Pennsylvania
WCUC-FM Clarion, Pennsylvania
WUUZ Cooperstown, Pennsylvania
WRTS Erie, Pennsylvania
WKRZ Freeland, Pennsylvania
WZZE Glen Mills, Pennsylvania
WHKF Harrisburg, Pennsylvania
WNNK-FM Harrisburg, Pennsylvania
WJHT Johnstown, Pennsylvania
WNTE Mansfield, Pennsylvania
WWKL Mechanicsburg, Pennsylvania
WNUZ Mercersburg, Pennsylvania
WVRZ Mount Carmel, Pennsylvania
WBHT Mountain Top, Pennsylvania
WEGH Northumberland, Pennsylvania
WBHD Olyphant, Pennsylvania
WIOQ Philadelphia, Pennsylvania
WRDW-FM Philadelphia, Pennsylvania
WKST-FM Pittsburgh, Pennsylvania
WWSW-FM Pittsburgh, Pennsylvania
WXXF(FM) Pittsburgh, Pennsylvania
WRFY-FM Reading, Pennsylvania
WWRR Scranton, Pennsylvania
WAKZ Sharpsville, Pennsylvania
WKRF Tobyhanna, Pennsylvania
WTTC-FM Towanda, Pennsylvania
WYCR York-Hanover, Pennsylvania

WCMN-FM Arecibo, Puerto Rico
WBQN Barceloneta-Manati, Puerto Rico
WODA Bayamon, Puerto Rico
WXYX Bayamon, Puerto Rico
WMIO Cabo Rojo, Puerto Rico
WNOD Mayaguez, Puerto Rico
WPRA Mayaguez, Puerto Rico
WUKQ-FM Mayaguez, Puerto Rico
WEGM San German, Puerto Rico
WKAQ-FM San Juan, Puerto Rico
WCVY Coventry, Rhode Island
WPRO-FM Providence, Rhode Island
WWBB Providence, Rhode Island
WSEA Atlantic Beach, South Carolina
WSSX-FM Charleston, South Carolina
WJMX-FM Cheraw, South Carolina
WHHD Clearwater, South Carolina
WNOK Columbia, South Carolina
WHSC Conway, South Carolina
WWNQ Forest Acres, South Carolina
WWXM Garden City, South Carolina
WOMG Lexington, South Carolina
WYMB Manning, South Carolina
WAVO Rock Hill, South Carolina
WWBD Sumter, South Carolina
KXMZ Box Elder, South Dakota
KSQB-FM Dell Rapids, South Dakota
KJBI Fort Pierre, South Dakota
KQRQ Rapid City, South Dakota
KKLS-FM Sioux Falls, South Dakota
KRCS Sturgis, South Dakota
WMPS Bartlett, Tennessee
WDOD-FM Chattanooga, Tennessee
WMSR-FM Collinwood, Tennessee
WUMC Elizabethton, Tennessee
WHBQ-FM Germantown, Tennessee
WAYB-FM Graysville, Tennessee
WAEZ Greeneville, Tennessee
WRVW Lebanon, Tennessee
WUTM Martin, Tennessee
WBMC McMinnville, Tennessee
WCRK Morristown, Tennessee
WAKQ Paris, Tennessee
WWST Sevierville, Tennessee
WUUQ South Pittsburg, Tennessee
WTRZ Spencer, Tennessee
WQAK Union City, Tennessee
KQIZ-FM Amarillo, Texas
KXSS-FM Amarillo, Texas
KGHY Beaumont, Texas
KQXY-FM Beaumont, Texas
KVNS Brownsville, Texas
KPFC Callisburg, Texas
KNDE College Station, Texas
KZFM Corpus Christi, Texas
KMMZ Crane, Texas
KHKS Denton, Texas
KBFM Edinburg, Texas
KPRR El Paso, Texas
KYSE El Paso, Texas
KCDD Hamlin, Texas
KPWW Hooks, Texas
KKHH Houston, Texas
KRBE Houston, Texas
KKVR Kerrville, Texas
KKBA Kingsville, Texas
KNEX Laredo, Texas
KHMR Lovelady, Texas
KZII-FM Lubbock, Texas
KKHA Markham, Texas
KZBT Midland, Texas
KNRG New Ulm, Texas
KMCM Odessa, Texas
KAZE Ore City, Texas
KWLD Plainview, Texas
KMKI Plano, Texas
KKPN Rockport, Texas
KIXY-FM San Angelo, Texas
KJXK San Antonio, Texas
KXXM San Antonio, Texas
KQDR Savoy, Texas
KWTX-FM Waco, Texas
KISX Whitehouse, Texas
KNIN-FM Wichita Falls, Texas
KQXC-FM Wichita Falls, Texas
KCIN Cedar City, Utah
KSUU Cedar City, Utah
KVFX Logan, Utah
KWCR-FM Ogden, Utah
KLGL Richfield, Utah
KXRQ Roosevelt, Utah
KZHT Salt Lake City, Utah
KXDS Santa Clara, Utah
WJJX Appomattox, Virginia
WZGN Crozet, Virginia
WQPO Harrisonburg, Virginia
WHCE Highland Springs, Virginia
WZVA Marion, Virginia
WVHT Norfolk, Virginia
WRVQ Richmond, Virginia
WJJS Roanoke, Virginia
WXLK Roanoke, Virginia
WHTE-FM Ruckersville, Virginia
WTON-FM Staunton, Virginia
WKSI-FM Stephens City, Virginia
WMNG Christiansted, Virgin Islands
WKVT-FM Brattleboro, Vermont
WDVT Rutland, Vermont
WXXX South Burlington, Vermont
WCFR Springfield, Vermont
WMXR Woodstock, Vermont
KOLW Basin City, Washington
KCLK-FM Clarkston, Washington
KXAA Cle Elum, Washington
KBDB-FM Forks, Washington
KEYG-FM Grand Coulee, Washington
KMIH Mercer Island, Washington
KZBE Omak, Washington
KHTR Pullman, Washington
KING-FM Seattle, Washington
KJR-FM Seattle, Washington
KNHC Seattle, Washington
KRXY Shelton, Washington
KBKS-FM Tacoma, Washington
KFFM Yakima, Washington
WDKM Adams, Wisconsin
WJQM De Forest, Wisconsin
WKSZ De Pere, Wisconsin
WBIZ-FM Eau Claire, Wisconsin
WIXX Green Bay, Wisconsin
WIZM-FM La Crosse, Wisconsin
WLFN La Crosse, Wisconsin
WMDC Mayville, Wisconsin
WKEB Medford, Wisconsin
WKLH Milwaukee, Wisconsin
WLKD Minocqua, Wisconsin
WKFX Rice Lake, Wisconsin
WOWN Shawano, Wisconsin
WCLQ Wausau, Wisconsin
WIFC Wausau, Wisconsin
WAUH Wautoma, Wisconsin
WXSS Wauwatosa, Wisconsin
WHTL-FM Whitehall, Wisconsin
WCIR-FM Beckley, West Virginia
WVSR-FM Charleston, West Virginia
WELK Elkins, West Virginia
WELD Fisher, West Virginia
WQWV Fisher, West Virginia
WMTD Hinton, West Virginia
WKEE-FM Huntington, West Virginia
WVAQ Morgantown, West Virginia
WRVZ Pocatalico, West Virginia
WSTG Princeton, West Virginia
WVAR Richwood, West Virginia
WSGB Sutton, West Virginia
WPHP Wheeling, West Virginia
KTRS-FM Casper, Wyoming
KLQQ Clearmont, Wyoming
KZWB Green River, Wyoming
KHRW Ranchester, Wyoming
KLMI Rock River, Wyoming
KYCS Rock Springs, Wyoming
KLSX Rozet, Wyoming
KZZS Story, Wyoming
KDDV-FM Wright, Wyoming

Country

KASH-FM Anchorage, Alaska
KBRJ Anchorage, Alaska
KLAM Cordova, Alaska
KDLG Dillingham, Alaska
KIAK-FM Fairbanks, Alaska
KJHA Houston, Alaska
KTKU Juneau, Alaska
KWHQ-FM Kenai, Alaska
KGTW Ketchikan, Alaska
KVOK Kodiak, Alaska
KJNP North Pole, Alaska
KSEW Seward, Alaska
KPEN-FM Soldotna, Alaska
KVAK Valdez, Alaska
KAYO Wasilla, Alaska
WQAH-FM Addison, Alabama
WQSB Albertville, Alabama
WSTH-FM Alexander City, Alabama
WSYA(AM) Anniston, Alabama
WRAB Arab, Alabama
WKKR Auburn, Alabama
WZZK-FM Birmingham, Alabama
WKNU Brewton, Alabama
WEIS Centre, Alabama
WBIB Centreville, Alabama
WAVH Daphne, Alabama
WDRM Decatur, Alabama
WTVY-FM Dothan, Alabama
WELB Elba, Alabama
WVVL Elba, Alabama
WDJR Enterprise, Alabama
WABF Fairhope, Alabama
WLDX Fayette, Alabama
WTXT Fayette, Alabama
WKWL Florala, Alabama
WXFL Florence, Alabama
WZOB Fort Payne, Alabama
WGEA Geneva, Alabama
WKGA Goodwater, Alabama
WAOQ Goshen, Alabama
WQZX Greenville, Alabama
WBMH Grove Hill, Alabama
WTWX-FM Guntersville, Alabama
WFMH-FM Hackleburg, Alabama
WERH Hamilton, Alabama
WPIL Heflin, Alabama
WHMA-FM Hobson City, Alabama
WCKA Jacksonville, Alabama
WINL Linden, Alabama
WZZX Lineville, Alabama
WNPT-FM Marion, Alabama
WQRV Meridianville, Alabama
WKSJ-FM Mobile, Alabama
WLWI-FM Montgomery, Alabama
WWFF-FM New Market, Alabama
WFHK Pell City, Alabama
WRMG Red Bay, Alabama
WELR-FM Roanoke, Alabama
WGOL Russellville, Alabama
WKEA-FM Scottsboro, Alabama
WWIC Scottsboro, Alabama
WYEA Sylacauga, Alabama
WJDB-FM Thomasville, Alabama
WGZZ Waverly, Alabama
KPGG Ashdown, Arkansas
KEWI Benton, Arkansas
KTHS-FM Berryville, Arkansas
KHLS Blytheville, Arkansas
KLYR Clarksville, Arkansas
KLYR-FM Clarksville, Arkansas
KXIO Clarksville, Arkansas
KHPQ Clinton, Arkansas
KMJX Conway, Arkansas
KAGH Crossett, Arkansas
KAGH-FM Crossett, Arkansas
KYEL Danville, Arkansas
KCJC Dardanelle, Arkansas
KWXT Dardanelle, Arkansas
KDQN-FM De Queen, Arkansas
KDEW-FM De Witt, Arkansas
KXSA-FM Dermott, Arkansas
KIXB El Dorado, Arkansas
KKIX Fayetteville, Arkansas
KQSM-FM Fayetteville, Arkansas
KMAG Fort Smith, Arkansas
KTCS-FM Fort Smith, Arkansas
KOTN(FM) Gould, Arkansas
KYXK Gurdon, Arkansas
KWHF Harrisburg, Arkansas
KHOZ Harrison, Arkansas
KHOZ-FM Harrison, Arkansas
KFFA Helena, Arkansas
KHPA Hope, Arkansas
KFIN Jonesboro, Arkansas
KSSN Little Rock, Arkansas
KVMA Magnolia, Arkansas
KBOK Malvern, Arkansas
KAMS Mammoth Spring, Arkansas
KENA-FM Mena, Arkansas
KVOM-FM Morrilton, Arkansas
KPFM Mountain Home, Arkansas
KTLO Mountain Home, Arkansas
KWOZ Mountain View, Arkansas
KMTB Murfreesboro, Arkansas
KOKR Newport, Arkansas

KDYN Ozark, Arkansas
KLBL Pearcy, Arkansas
KPBQ-FM Pine Bluff, Arkansas
KHOM Salem, Arkansas
KWCK-FM Searcy, Arkansas
KZHE Stamps, Arkansas
KOSY Texarkana, Arkansas
KVMZ Waldo, Arkansas
KWYN-FM Wynne, Arkansas
KWCD Bisbee, Arizona
KFLG Bullhead City, Arizona
KMLE Chandler, Arizona
KFXR-FM Chinle, Arizona
KDDL Chino Valley, Arizona
KVRD-FM Cottonwood, Arizona
KTHQ Eagar, Arizona
KZUA Holbrook, Arizona
KGMN Kingman, Arizona
KSAZ Marana, Arizona
KQSS Miami, Arizona
KPGE Page, Arizona
KLPZ Parker, Arizona
KMOG Payson, Arizona
KNIX-FM Phoenix, Arizona
KNOT Prescott, Arizona
KBUX Quartzsite, Arizona
KSED Sedona, Arizona
KIIM-FM Tucson, Arizona
KSWG Wickenburg, Arizona
KHIL Willcox, Arizona
KTNN Window Rock, Arizona
KWRK Window Rock, Arizona
KINO Winslow, Arizona
KTTI Yuma, Arizona
KCNO Alturas, California
KBYN Arnold, California
KIXF Baker, California
KCWR Bakersfield, California
KUZZ-FM Bakersfield, California
KFLG-FM Big River, California
KIBS Bishop, California
KROP Brawley, California
KKHK Carmel, California
KKCY Colusa, California
KWST El Centro, California
KSOQ-FM Escondido, California
KEKA-FM Eureka, California
KRED-FM Eureka, California
KPIG-FM Freedom, California
KHGE Fresno, California
KSKS Fresno, California
KATJ-FM George, California
KFGY Healdsburg, California
KXCM Joshua Tree, California
KCNQ Kernville, California
KRKC King City, California
KIXW-FM Lenwood, California
KKGO Los Angeles, California
KRTY Los Gatos, California
KTOM-FM Marina, California
KUBB Mariposa, California
KGAM(FM) Merced, California
KATM Modesto, California
KTPI-FM Mojave, California
KSMC Moraga, California
KPLM Palm Springs, California
KHSL-FM Paradise, California
KYOE Point Arena, California
KALF Red Bluff, California
KNCQ Redding, California
KLOA(FM) Ridgecrest, California
KZIQ-FM Ridgecrest, California
KFBK-FM Sacramento, California
KNCI Sacramento, California
KFRG San Bernardino, California
KTDD San Bernardino, California
KSON San Diego, California
KGMZ(FM) San Francisco, California
KKJG San Luis Obispo, California
KSLY-FM San Luis Obispo, California
KSNI-FM Santa Maria, California
KRAZ Santa Ynez, California
KNNN(FM) Shasta Lake City, California
KNTY Shingle Springs, California
KXFG Sun City, California
KJDX Susanville, California
KJUG Tulare, California
KJUG-FM Tulare, California
KFLS-FM Tulelake, California
KKBN Twain Harte, California
KQPM Ukiah, California
KUKI-FM Ukiah, California
KHAY Ventura, California
KSYC-FM Yreka, California
KALQ-FM Alamosa, Colorado
KWOF Broomfield, Colorado
KBVC Buena Vista, Colorado
KNAB-FM Burlington, Colorado
KSTY Canon City, Colorado
KAVP Colona, Colorado
KATC-FM Colorado Springs, Colorado
KCSF Colorado Springs, Colorado
KREL Colorado Springs, Colorado
KISZ-FM Cortez, Colorado
KRAI Craig, Colorado
KPRU Delta, Colorado
KYGO-FM Denver, Colorado
KRSJ Durango, Colorado
KSKE-FM Eagle, Colorado
KMTS Glenwood Springs, Colorado
KRKY Granby, Colorado
KMOZ-FM Grand Junction, Colorado
KPKE Gunnison, Colorado
KJBL Julesburg, Colorado
KTHN La Junta, Colorado
KLMR Lamar, Colorado
KVAY Lamar, Colorado
KSLV Monte Vista, Colorado
KYDN Monte Vista, Colorado
KKXK Montrose, Colorado
KRYD Norwood, Colorado
KWGL Ouray, Colorado
KWUF Pagosa Springs, Colorado
KCCY-FM Pueblo, Colorado
KADE Salida, Colorado
KNNG Sterling, Colorado
KCRT Trinidad, Colorado
KSPK-FM Walsenburg, Colorado
KUAD-FM Windsor, Colorado
KATR-FM Wray, Colorado
KGCD Wray, Colorado
WCTY Norwich, Connecticut
WWYZ Waterbury, Connecticut
WMZQ-FM Washington, District of Columbia
WDSD Dover, Delaware
WWOJ Avon Park, Florida
WQXM Bartow, Florida
WPHK Blountstown, Florida
WKIS Boca Raton, Florida
WAKT-FM Callaway, Florida
WIKX Charlotte Harbor, Florida
WJSB Crestview, Florida
WZCC Cross City, Florida
WDSP De Funiak Springs, Florida
WTRS Dunnellon, Florida
WBGY Everglades City, Florida
WWGR Fort Myers, Florida
WGWD Gretna, Florida
WFUS Gulfport, Florida
WYGC High Springs, Florida
WIRK Indiantown, Florida
WWWK Islamorada, Florida
WQIK-FM Jacksonville, Florida
WCNK Key West, Florida
WGRO Lake City, Florida
WCKT Lehigh Acres, Florida
WQHL-FM Live Oak, Florida
WMAF Madison, Florida
WJAQ Marianna, Florida
WTYS Marianna, Florida
WYZB Mary Esther, Florida
WGNE-FM Middleburg, Florida
WXBM-FM Milton, Florida
WWKA Orlando, Florida
WIYD Palatka, Florida
WPAP-FM Panama City, Florida
WPCF Panama City Beach, Florida
WYCT Pensacola, Florida
WNFK Perry, Florida
WCTH Plantation Key, Florida
WKRO-FM Port Orange, Florida
WHKR Rockledge, Florida
WCTQ Sarasota, Florida
WQYK-FM St. Petersburg, Florida
WAVW Stuart, Florida
WTNT-FM Tallahassee, Florida
WWOF(FM) Tallahassee, Florida
WLVW(FM) Trenton, Florida
WQLC Watertown, Florida
WPCV Winter Haven, Florida
WZZS Zolfo Springs, Florida
WKAK Albany, Georgia
WAJQ-FM Alma, Georgia
WISK-FM Americus, Georgia
WUBL Atlanta, Georgia
WKUB Blackshear, Georgia
WPPL Blue Ridge, Georgia
WTUF Boston, Georgia
WMOQ Bostwick, Georgia
WMUV Brunswick, Georgia
WRJY Brunswick, Georgia
WBTR-FM Carrollton, Georgia
WNGA Clermont, Georgia
WCON Cornelia, Georgia
WCON-FM Cornelia, Georgia
WZTR Dahlonega, Georgia
WPLA Dry Branch, Georgia
WQZY Dublin, Georgia
WXLI Dublin, Georgia
WUFF Eastman, Georgia
WLJA-FM Ellijay, Georgia
WPGY Ellijay, Georgia
WKCN Fort Benning South, Georgia
WXKO Fort Valley, Georgia
WYAY Gainesville, Georgia
WHIE Griffin, Georgia
WKLY Hartwell, Georgia
WIFO-FM Jesup, Georgia
WKBX Kingsland, Georgia
WPEH Louisville, Georgia
WLYU Lyons, Georgia
WKHX-FM Marietta, Georgia
WKKP McDonough, Georgia
WMCG Milan, Georgia
WKZR Milledgeville, Georgia
WHKN Millen, Georgia
WMNZ Montezuma, Georgia
WYUM Mount Vernon, Georgia
WALH Mountain City, Georgia
WGCN Nashville, Georgia
WXRS-FM Portal, Georgia
WJCL-FM Savannah, Georgia
WKNG Tallapoosa, Georgia
WTHO-FM Thomson, Georgia
WABR Tifton, Georgia
WTIF Tifton, Georgia
WAAC Valdosta, Georgia
WYNR Waycross, Georgia
WCJM-FM West Point, Georgia
WKAA Willacoochee, Georgia
WEKS Zebulon, Georgia
KUAI Eleele, Hawaii
KDLX Makawao, Hawaii
KKOA Volcano, Hawaii
KKNE Waipahu, Hawaii
KIIC Albia, Iowa
WJOD Asbury, Iowa
KSOM Audubon, Iowa
KDMG Burlington, Iowa
KOEL-FM Cedar Falls, Iowa
KHAK Cedar Rapids, Iowa
KKSY-FM Cedar Rapids, Iowa
KMGO Centerville, Iowa
KSIB Creston, Iowa
KSIB-FM Creston, Iowa
WLLR-FM Davenport, Iowa
KDSN Denison, Iowa
KDST Dyersville, Iowa
KRKN Eldon, Iowa
KILR Estherville, Iowa
KILR-FM Estherville, Iowa
KMCD Fairfield, Iowa
KIOW Forest City, Iowa
KWMT Fort Dodge, Iowa
KBKB Fort Madison, Iowa
KBKB-FM Fort Madison, Iowa
KCTN Garnavillo, Iowa
KXKT Glenwood, Iowa
KLMJ Hampton, Iowa
KKIA Ida Grove, Iowa
KNIA Knoxville, Iowa
KIKD Lake City, Iowa
KMCH Manchester, Iowa
KMAQ Maquoketa, Iowa
KXIA Marshalltown, Iowa
KIAI Mason City, Iowa
KRNF Montezuma, Iowa
KILJ Mount Pleasant, Iowa
KILJ-FM Mount Pleasant, Iowa
KMCS Muscatine, Iowa
KCZE New Hampton, Iowa
KCOB Newton, Iowa
KCOB-FM Newton, Iowa

KBOE Oskaloosa, Iowa
KBOE-FM Oskaloosa, Iowa
KLEE Ottumwa, Iowa
KICL(FM) Pleasantville, Iowa
KOAK Red Oak, Iowa
KIHK Rock Valley, Iowa
KICD-FM Spencer, Iowa
KKRF Stuart, Iowa
KCSI Villisca, Iowa
KNEI-FM Waukon, Iowa
KWAY Waverly, Iowa
KKYY Whiting, Iowa
KQPI Aberdeen, Idaho
KAWO Boise, Idaho
KIZN Boise, Idaho
KQFC Boise, Idaho
KICR Coeur D'Alene, Idaho
KYUN Hailey, Idaho
KID-FM Idaho Falls, Idaho
KTHK Idaho Falls, Idaho
KART Jerome, Idaho
KZBG Lapwai, Idaho
KMOK Lewiston, Idaho
KRLC Lewiston-Clarkston, Idaho
KDZY McCall, Idaho
KVSI Montpelier, Idaho
KMHI Mountain Home, Idaho
KLER Orofino, Idaho
KOUU Pocatello, Idaho
KZBQ Pocatello, Idaho
KKEX Preston, Idaho
KUPI-FM Rexburg, Idaho
KKMV Rupert, Idaho
KSRA Salmon, Idaho
KIBR Sandpoint, Idaho
KBRV Soda Springs, Idaho
KITT Soda Springs, Idaho
KEZJ-FM Twin Falls, Idaho
KVRG Victor, Idaho
KWAL Wallace, Idaho
WRMJ Aledo, Illinois
WIBH Anna, Illinois
WLCN Atlanta, Illinois
WRMS-FM Beardstown, Illinois
WLMD Bushnell, Illinois
WRUL Carmi, Illinois
WIXY Champaign, Illinois
KSGM Chester, Illinois
WUSN Chicago, Illinois
WCCQ Crest Hill, Illinois
WDZQ Decatur, Illinois
WRCV Dixon, Illinois
WDQN Duquoin, Illinois
WCRC Effingham, Illinois
WFYR Elmwood, Illinois
WFPS Freeport, Illinois
WXXQ Freeport, Illinois
WAAG Galesburg, Illinois
WJRE Galva, Illinois
WGEL Greenville, Illinois
WEBQ Harrisburg, Illinois
WDUK Havana, Illinois
WRVY-FM Henry, Illinois
WHPO Hoopeston, Illinois
WDDD-FM Johnston City, Illinois
WAKO Lawrenceville, Illinois
WBWN Le Roy, Illinois
WSMI Litchfield, Illinois
WLUV Loves Park, Illinois
WGGH Marion, Illinois
WMCL McLeansboro, Illinois
WGLC-FM Mendota, Illinois
WMOK Metropolis, Illinois
WFXN Moline, Illinois
WRAM Monmouth, Illinois
WIBV Mount Vernon, Illinois
WMIX-FM Mount Vernon, Illinois
WALS Oglesby, Illinois
WSEI Olney, Illinois
WMKR Pana, Illinois
WXCL Pekin, Illinois
WIRL Peoria, Illinois
WCOY Quincy, Illinois
WJEK(FM) Rantoul, Illinois
WJBD Salem, Illinois
WCCI Savanna, Illinois
WJVO South Jacksonville, Illinois
WFMB-FM Springfield, Illinois
WXNU St. Anne, Illinois
WKJT Teutopolis, Illinois
WKZS Thomasboro, Illinois

WSCH Aurora, Indiana
WXKU-FM Austin, Indiana
WUZR Bicknell, Indiana
WLFW Chandler, Indiana
WKKG Columbus, Indiana
WXCH Columbus, Indiana
WCDQ Crawfordsville, Indiana
WYGB Edinburgh, Indiana
WBYT Elkhart, Indiana
WHCC Ellettsville, Indiana
WQKZ Ferdinand, Indiana
WFMS Fishers, Indiana
WFLQ French Lick, Indiana
WREB Greencastle, Indiana
WTRE Greensburg, Indiana
WQHK-FM Huntertown, Indiana
WBTU Kendallville, Indiana
WIVR Kentland, Indiana
WKPW Knightstown, Indiana
WCOE La Porte, Indiana
WKOA Lafayette, Indiana
WTHD Lagrange, Indiana
WRCY Mt. Vernon, Indiana
WLTI(AM) New Castle, Indiana
WMDH-FM New Castle, Indiana
WARU Peru, Indiana
WPGW-FM Portland, Indiana
WRAY-FM Princeton, Indiana
WECI Richmond, Indiana
WQLK Richmond, Indiana
WHZR Royal Center, Indiana
WIFE-FM Rushville, Indiana
WMPI Scottsburg, Indiana
WLHK Shelbyville, Indiana
WNDI Sullivan, Indiana
WTHI-FM Terre Haute, Indiana
WLJE Valparaiso, Indiana
WCJC Van Buren, Indiana
WKID Vevay, Indiana
WFML Vincennes, Indiana
WWBL Washington, Indiana
KVWF Augusta, Kansas
KREP Belleville, Kansas
KSNP Burlington, Kansas
KWGB Colby, Kansas
KXXX Colby, Kansas
KNCK Concordia, Kansas
KUSN Dearing, Kansas
KDNS Downs, Kansas
KIND-FM Elk City, Kansas
KVOE-FM Emporia, Kansas
KOTE Eureka, Kansas
KKJQ Garden City, Kansas
KLOE Goodland, Kansas
KNZA Hiawatha, Kansas
KKQY Hill City, Kansas
KHOK Hoisington, Kansas
KBUF Holcomb, Kansas
KAIR-FM Horton, Kansas
KHUT Hutchinson, Kansas
KZSN Hutchinson, Kansas
KERP Ingalls, Kansas
KIKS-FM Iola, Kansas
KFKF-FM Kansas City, Kansas
KQZQ Kiowa, Kansas
KLDG Liberal, Kansas
KDJM Lindsborg, Kansas
KXKU Lyons, Kansas
KXBZ Manhattan, Kansas
KNDY Marysville, Kansas
KNDY-FM Marysville, Kansas
KFTI-FM Newton, Kansas
KFNF Oberlin, Kansas
KKOW Pittsburg, Kansas
KKOW-FM Pittsburg, Kansas
KSKG Salina, Kansas
KYEZ Salina, Kansas
KMZA Seneca, Kansas
KTPK Topeka, Kansas
WIBW-FM Topeka, Kansas
KULY Ulysses, Kansas
KFDI-FM Wichita, Kansas
KWLS Winfield, Kansas
WANY Albany, Kentucky
WANY-FM Albany, Kentucky
WMDJ-FM Allen, Kentucky
WDGG Ashland, Kentucky
WBVR-FM Auburn, Kentucky
WGGC Bowling Green, Kentucky
WMMG Brandenburg, Kentucky
WKYR-FM Burkesville, Kentucky

WSEK Burnside, Kentucky
WKDZ-FM Cadiz, Kentucky
WCCK Calvert City, Kentucky
WIKI Carrollton, Kentucky
WAIN-FM Columbia, Kentucky
WKDP-FM Corbin, Kentucky
WCPM Cumberland, Kentucky
WCYN-FM Cynthiana, Kentucky
WHSX Edmonton, Kentucky
WFLE Flemingsburg, Kentucky
WLVK Fort Knox, Kentucky
WYGY Fort Thomas, Kentucky
WFKY Frankfort, Kentucky
WFKN Franklin, Kentucky
WLYE-FM Glasgow, Kentucky
WGOH Grayson, Kentucky
WGRK-FM Greensburg, Kentucky
WLGC-FM Greenup, Kentucky
WULF Hardinsburg, Kentucky
WXBC Hardinsburg, Kentucky
WTUK Harlan, Kentucky
WXLR Harold, Kentucky
WHBN Harrodsburg, Kentucky
WKCM Hawesville, Kentucky
WSGS Hazard, Kentucky
WKDQ Henderson, Kentucky
WVVR Hopkinsville, Kentucky
WCYO Irvine, Kentucky
WJSN-FM Jackson, Kentucky
WJKY Jamestown, Kentucky
WJRS Jamestown, Kentucky
WGRK Jeffersontown, Kentucky
WMTL Leitchfield, Kentucky
WBUL-FM Lexington, Kentucky
WLXX Lexington, Kentucky
WKDO Liberty, Kentucky
WZAQ Louisa, Kentucky
WAMZ Louisville, Kentucky
WRKA Louisville, Kentucky
WQNU Lyndon, Kentucky
WFMW Madisonville, Kentucky
WKLB Manchester, Kentucky
WVLC Mannsville, Kentucky
WLLE Mayfield, Kentucky
WWAG McKee, Kentucky
WMKZ Monticello, Kentucky
WMOR Morehead, Kentucky
WLBQ Morgantown, Kentucky
WRVK Mount Vernon, Kentucky
WLOC Munfordville, Kentucky
WFGS Murray, Kentucky
WKFC North Corbin, Kentucky
WBKR Owensboro, Kentucky
WKYN Owingsville, Kentucky
WKYQ Paducah, Kentucky
WSIP-FM Paintsville, Kentucky
WBIO Philpot, Kentucky
WDHR Pikeville, Kentucky
WRIL Pineville, Kentucky
WRLV Salyersville, Kentucky
WRLV-FM Salyersville, Kentucky
WVLE Scottsville, Kentucky
WKWY Tompkinsville, Kentucky
WTKY Tompkinsville, Kentucky
WTKY-FM Tompkinsville, Kentucky
WKKS Vanceburg, Kentucky
WLKS-FM West Liberty, Kentucky
WTCW Whitesburg, Kentucky
WEZJ-FM Williamsburg, Kentucky
WNKR Williamstown, Kentucky
KRRV-FM Alexandria, Louisiana
KBKK Ball, Louisiana
WYNK-FM Baton Rouge, Louisiana
KQKI-FM Bayou Vista, Louisiana
WBOX Bogalusa, Louisiana
KSBH Coushatta, Louisiana
KEUN-FM Eunice, Louisiana
WOMN Franklinton, Louisiana
KLEB Golden Meadow, Louisiana
WFPR Hammond, Louisiana
WHMD Hammond, Louisiana
KRLQ Hodge, Louisiana
KJNA-FM Jena, Louisiana
KMDL Kaplan, Louisiana
KNGT Lake Charles, Louisiana
KYKZ Lake Charles, Louisiana
KJAE Leesville, Louisiana
KLLA Leesville, Louisiana
KVVP Leesville, Louisiana
KBON Mamou, Louisiana
KJVC Mansfield, Louisiana

KWLV Many, Louisiana
KAPB-FM Marksville, Louisiana
KJLO-FM Monroe, Louisiana
KDBH-FM Natchitoches, Louisiana
WNOE-FM New Orleans, Louisiana
KSLO Opelousas, Louisiana
KMYY Rayville, Louisiana
KXKZ Ruston, Louisiana
KWKH Shreveport, Louisiana
KXKS-FM Shreveport, Louisiana
KLAA-FM Tioga, Louisiana
WBOX-FM Varnado, Louisiana
KWTG Vidalia, Louisiana
KNCB Vivian, Louisiana
KNCB-FM Vivian, Louisiana
KVCL-FM Winnfield, Louisiana
KMAR-FM Winnsboro, Louisiana
WPVQ Greenfield, Massachusetts
WESO Southbridge, Massachusetts
WKLB-FM Waltham, Massachusetts
WGFP Webster, Massachusetts
WPOC Baltimore, Maryland
WTRI Brunswick, Maryland
WKIK-FM California, Maryland
WBEY-FM Crisfield, Maryland
WFRE Frederick, Maryland
WFRB-FM Frostburg, Maryland
WKHI Fruitland, Maryland
WAYZ Hagerstown, Maryland
WXCY Havre De Grace, Maryland
WAAI Hurlock, Maryland
WKIK La Plata, Maryland
WWHC Oakland, Maryland
WWFG Ocean City, Maryland
WKTT Salisbury, Maryland
WINX-FM St. Michaels, Maryland
WTHT Auburn, Maine
WLKE Bar Harbor, Maine
WQCB Brewer, Maine
WTBM Mexico, Maine
WBCQ-FM Monticello, Maine
WOXO-FM Norway, Maine
WMDR-FM Oakland, Maine
WPOR Portland, Maine
WMCM Rockland, Maine
WSKW Skowhegan, Maine
WQTE Adrian, Michigan
WATZ-FM Alpena, Michigan
WWWW-FM Ann Arbor, Michigan
WLEW Bad Axe, Michigan
WCUZ Bear Lake, Michigan
WHFB-FM Benton Harbor, Michigan
WOUF Beulah, Michigan
WWBR Big Rapids, Michigan
WYTZ Bridgman, Michigan
WDTW-FM Detroit, Michigan
WYCD Detroit, Michigan
WYKX Escanaba, Michigan
WCXI Fenton, Michigan
WGDN-FM Gladwin, Michigan
WGRY-FM Grayling, Michigan
WCMM Gulliver, Michigan
WCEN-FM Hemlock, Michigan
WTNR Holland, Michigan
WHKB Houghton, Michigan
WTWS Houghton Lake, Michigan
WMKC Indian River, Michigan
WJNR-FM Iron Mountain, Michigan
WJMS Ironwood, Michigan
WJPD Ishpeming, Michigan
WCUP L'Anse, Michigan
WGLM-FM Lakeview, Michigan
WITL-FM Lansing, Michigan
WLCO Lapeer, Michigan
WLJZ Mackinaw City, Michigan
WBGV Marlette, Michigan
WFXD Marquette, Michigan
WLAW Newaygo, Michigan
WNBY Newberry, Michigan
WUPY Ontonagon, Michigan
WARD Petoskey, Michigan
WSAQ Port Huron, Michigan
WYZO-FM Portage, Michigan
WHAK Rogers City, Michigan
WRGZ Rogers City, Michigan
WKCQ Saginaw, Michigan
WMIC Sandusky, Michigan
WKZC Scottville, Michigan
WMLM St. Louis, Michigan
WKJC Tawas City, Michigan
WRCI Three Rivers, Michigan
WLDR-FM Traverse City, Michigan
WTCM-FM Traverse City, Michigan
KRJB Ada, Minnesota
KKIN-FM Aitkin, Minnesota
KASM Albany, Minnesota
KAUS-FM Austin, Minnesota
KQAQ Austin, Minnesota
KKCQ-FM Bagley, Minnesota
KBVB Barnesville, Minnesota
KBHP Bemidji, Minnesota
KBMW Breckenridge, Minnesota
KRWC Buffalo, Minnesota
KFIL-FM Chatfield, Minnesota
KGPZ Coleraine, Minnesota
KARP-FM Dassel, Minnesota
KRCQ Detroit Lakes, Minnesota
KTCO Duluth, Minnesota
KLCI Elk River, Minnesota
KJJK-FM Fergus Falls, Minnesota
KSNR Fisher, Minnesota
KGRP Grand Rapids, Minnesota
KKOJ Jackson, Minnesota
KKWB Kelliher, Minnesota
KMFX-FM Lake City, Minnesota
KEYL Long Prairie, Minnesota
KLQL Luverne, Minnesota
KYSM-FM Mankato, Minnesota
KDMA Montevideo, Minnesota
KVOX-FM Moorhead, Minnesota
KKOK-FM Morris, Minnesota
KATO-FM New Ulm, Minnesota
KNUJ New Ulm, Minnesota
KBLB Nisswa, Minnesota
KOLV Olivia, Minnesota
KDIO Ortonville, Minnesota
KRFO-FM Owatonna, Minnesota
KPRM Park Rapids, Minnesota
KXKK Park Rapids, Minnesota
KZPK Paynesville, Minnesota
KBOT Pelican Rapids, Minnesota
KFIL Preston, Minnesota
WQPM Princeton, Minnesota
KCUE Red Wing, Minnesota
KLGR Redwood Falls, Minnesota
KWWK Rochester, Minnesota
KWNO-FM Rushford, Minnesota
KIKV-FM Sauk Centre, Minnesota
WVAL Sauk Rapids, Minnesota
KJOE Slayton, Minnesota
KQYB Spring Grove, Minnesota
WWJO St. Cloud, Minnesota
KRRW St. James, Minnesota
KEEY-FM St. Paul, Minnesota
KNSP Staples, Minnesota
KKDQ Thief River Falls, Minnesota
KARL Tracy, Minnesota
KVKK Verndale, Minnesota
WUSZ Virginia, Minnesota
KKWS Wadena, Minnesota
KWAD Wadena, Minnesota
KKWQ Warroad, Minnesota
KDOM Windom, Minnesota
KDOM-FM Windom, Minnesota
KAGE Winona, Minnesota
KSWF Aurora, Missouri
KAAN Bethany, Missouri
KYOO Bolivar, Missouri
KCLR-FM Boonville, Missouri
KWRT Boonville, Missouri
KMAM Butler, Missouri
KATI California, Missouri
KRLL California, Missouri
KEZS-FM Cape Girardeau, Missouri
KAOL Carrollton, Missouri
KCRV Caruthersville, Missouri
KRMO Cassville, Missouri
KWKZ Charleston, Missouri
KDKD-FM Clinton, Missouri
KDEX Dexter, Missouri
KDEX-FM Dexter, Missouri
KOEA Doniphan, Missouri
KESM Eldorado Springs, Missouri
KTJJ Farmington, Missouri
KFAL Fulton, Missouri
KGOZ Gallatin, Missouri
WGCQ Hayti, Missouri
KUNQ Houston, Missouri
KYLS-FM Ironton, Missouri
KZJF Jefferson City, Missouri
KIXQ Joplin, Missouri
KBEQ-FM Kansas City, Missouri
KCSP Kansas City, Missouri
KTUF Kirksville, Missouri
KXKX Knob Noster, Missouri
KHST Lamar, Missouri
KCLQ Lebanon, Missouri
KJEL Lebanon, Missouri
KLWT Lebanon, Missouri
KJFM Louisiana, Missouri
KLTI Macon, Missouri
KMMO-FM Marshall, Missouri
KMEM-FM Memphis, Missouri
KWWR Mexico, Missouri
KRES Moberly, Missouri
KELE Mountain Grove, Missouri
KELE-FM Mountain Grove, Missouri
KBTN Neosho, Missouri
KBTN-FM Neosho, Missouri
KNEM Nevada, Missouri
KTMO New Madrid, Missouri
KICK-FM Palmyra, Missouri
KBDZ Perryville, Missouri
KPWB-FM Piedmont, Missouri
KKLR-FM Poplar Bluff, Missouri
KPBR Poplar Bluff, Missouri
KPPL Poplar Bluff, Missouri
KZNN Rolla, Missouri
KKID Salem, Missouri
KSMO Salem, Missouri
KSJQ Savannah, Missouri
KDRO Sedalia, Missouri
KBXB Sikeston, Missouri
KRHW Sikeston, Missouri
KTTS-FM Springfield, Missouri
KSD St. Louis, Missouri
WIL-FM St. Louis, Missouri
KLPW-FM Steelville, Missouri
KTUI-FM Sullivan, Missouri
KSAR Thayer, Missouri
KTTN-FM Trenton, Missouri
KKAC Vandalia, Missouri
KTKS Versailles, Missouri
KFAV Warrenton, Missouri
KWRE Warrenton, Missouri
KAYQ Warsaw, Missouri
KKDY West Plains, Missouri
KWKJ Windsor, Missouri
WBLE Batesville, Mississippi
WIZK Bay Springs, Mississippi
WZKX Bay St. Louis, Mississippi
WBYP Belzoni, Mississippi
WBKN Brookhaven, Mississippi
WKJN Centreville, Mississippi
WKDJ-FM Clarksdale, Mississippi
WVIM-FM Coldwater, Mississippi
WZKR Collinsville, Mississippi
WFFF Columbia, Mississippi
WKOR-FM Columbus, Mississippi
WDMS Greenville, Mississippi
WQXB Grenada, Mississippi
WGCM Gulfport, Mississippi
WCPC Houston, Mississippi
WKZU Iuka, Mississippi
WMSI-FM Jackson, Mississippi
WAGR-FM Lexington, Mississippi
WRBE-FM Lucedale, Mississippi
WUSJ Madison, Mississippi
WKXY Merigold, Mississippi
WQNZ Natchez, Mississippi
WWZD-FM New Albany, Mississippi
WWMS Oxford, Mississippi
WKNN-FM Pascagoula, Mississippi
WJDR Prentiss, Mississippi
WMJW Rosedale, Mississippi
WQJB State College, Mississippi
WBBN Taylorsville, Mississippi
WTYL Tylertown, Mississippi
KGCM Belgrade, Montana
KCTR-FM Billings, Montana
KGHL(FM) Billings, Montana
KRKX Billings, Montana
KBOZ-FM Bozeman, Montana
KAAR Butte, Montana
KIKF Cascade, Montana
KHNK Columbia Falls, Montana
KQRV Deer Lodge, Montana
KDBM Dillon, Montana
KHKR-FM East Helena, Montana
KIKC-FM Forsyth, Montana
KSCY Four Corners, Montana
KLTZ Glasgow, Montana
KDZN Glendive, Montana

KMON Great Falls, Montana
KMON-FM Great Falls, Montana
KPQX Havre, Montana
KBLL-FM Helena, Montana
KDBR Kalispell, Montana
KXLO Lewistown, Montana
KLCB Libby, Montana
KXLB Livingston, Montana
KDXT Lolo, Montana
KMMR Malta, Montana
KGGL Missoula, Montana
KYSS-FM Missoula, Montana
KATQ Plentywood, Montana
KATQ-FM Plentywood, Montana
KERR Polson, Montana
KCGM Scobey, Montana
KZIN-FM Shelby, Montana
KVCK-FM Wolf Point, Montana
WKXR Asheboro, North Carolina
WNBB Bayboro, North Carolina
WPYB Benson, North Carolina
WKYK Burnsville, North Carolina
WSME Camp Lejeune, North Carolina
WPTL Canton, North Carolina
WSOC-FM Charlotte, North Carolina
WRSF Columbia, North Carolina
WAGY Forest City, North Carolina
WNCC-FM Franklin, North Carolina
WQDK Gatesville, North Carolina
WJSG Hamlet, North Carolina
WCMS-FM Hatteras, North Carolina
WYND-FM Hatteras, North Carolina
WIZS Henderson, North Carolina
WMMY Jefferson, North Carolina
WKTE King, North Carolina
WRNS Kinston, North Carolina
WRNS-FM Kinston, North Carolina
WRDU Knightdale, North Carolina
WKGX Lenoir, North Carolina
WKVS Lenoir, North Carolina
WKML Lumberton, North Carolina
WBRM Marion, North Carolina
WDSL Mocksville, North Carolina
WIXE Monroe, North Carolina
WMNC Morganton, North Carolina
WMNC-FM Morganton, North Carolina
WKRK Murphy, North Carolina
WECR Newland, North Carolina
WKBC North Wilkesboro, North Carolina
WLQB Ocean Isle Beach, North Carolina
WKSF Old Fort, North Carolina
WPTM Roanoke Rapids, North Carolina
WCVP-FM Robbinsville, North Carolina
WDWG Rocky Mount, North Carolina
WRXO Roxboro, North Carolina
WCAB Rutherfordton, North Carolina
WWGP Sanford, North Carolina
WTSB Selma, North Carolina
WCOK Sparta, North Carolina
WAME Statesville, North Carolina
WKKT Statesville, North Carolina
WTAB Tabor City, North Carolina
WWQQ-FM Wilmington, North Carolina
WPAW Winston-Salem, North Carolina
WTQR Winston-Salem, North Carolina
KVMI Arthur, North Dakota
KEYA Belcourt, North Dakota
KBMR Bismarck, North Dakota
KQDY Bismarck, North Dakota
KBTO Bottineau, North Dakota
KPOK Bowman, North Dakota
KDAK Carrington, North Dakota
KAOC Cavalier, North Dakota
KDLR Devils Lake, North Dakota
KZZY Devils Lake, North Dakota
KCAD Dickinson, North Dakota
KLTC Dickinson, North Dakota
KXPO Grafton, North Dakota
KUSB Hazelton, North Dakota
KNDC Hettinger, North Dakota
KSJB Jamestown, North Dakota
KYNU Jamestown, North Dakota
KNDK Langdon, North Dakota
KQLX-FM Lisbon, North Dakota
KCJB Minot, North Dakota
KDDR Oakes, North Dakota
KZZJ Rugby, North Dakota
KDXN South Heart, North Dakota
KTGO Tioga, North Dakota
KOVC Valley City, North Dakota
KEYZ Williston, North Dakota
KYYZ Williston, North Dakota
KBRB Ainsworth, Nebraska
KUSO Albion, Nebraska
KAAQ Alliance, Nebraska
KNCY-FM Auburn, Nebraska
KBLR-FM Blair, Nebraska
KCNI Broken Bow, Nebraska
KZEN Central City, Nebraska
KCSR Chadron, Nebraska
KSDZ Gordon, Nebraska
KRGI-FM Grand Island, Nebraska
KNPQ Hershey, Nebraska
KRNY Kearney, Nebraska
KICX-FM McCook, Nebraska
KFGE Milford, Nebraska
KHYY Minatare, Nebraska
KXNP North Platte, Nebraska
KMCX-FM Ogallala, Nebraska
KZTL Paxton, Nebraska
KNEB Scottsbluff, Nebraska
KNEB-FM Scottsbluff, Nebraska
KSID Sidney, Nebraska
KRFS-FM Superior, Nebraska
KMBV Valentine, Nebraska
KVSH Valentine, Nebraska
KTIC West Point, Nebraska
KTIC-FM West Point, Nebraska
KSUX Winnebago, Nebraska
WNHW Belmont, New Hampshire
WYKR-FM Haverhill, New Hampshire
WYRY Hinsdale, New Hampshire
WXXK Lebanon, New Hampshire
WSCY Moultonborough, New Hampshire
WCNL Newport, New Hampshire
WPKQ North Conway, New Hampshire
WINQ Winchester, New Hampshire
WPUR Atlantic City, New Jersey
WCVH Flemington, New Jersey
KUPR Alamogordo, New Mexico
KZZX Alamogordo, New Mexico
KBQI Albuquerque, New Mexico
KRST Albuquerque, New Mexico
KKTC Angel Fire, New Mexico
KTZA Artesia, New Mexico
KNFT-FM Bayard, New Mexico
KARS Belen, New Mexico
KABQ-FM Bosque Farms, New Mexico
KATK-FM Carlsbad, New Mexico
KLMX Clayton, New Mexico
KNMB Cloudcroft, New Mexico
KCLV-FM Clovis, New Mexico
KOTS Deming, New Mexico
KTRA-FM Farmington, New Mexico
KGLX Gallup, New Mexico
KYVA Gallup, New Mexico
KIXN Hobbs, New Mexico
KPER Hobbs, New Mexico
KRSY-FM La Luz, New Mexico
KGRT-FM Las Cruces, New Mexico
KFUN Las Vegas, New Mexico
KQBA Los Alamos, New Mexico
KAGM Los Lunas, New Mexico
KMWW Maljamar, New Mexico
KSEL-FM Portales, New Mexico
KTDB Ramah, New Mexico
KBKZ Raton, New Mexico
KCKN Roswell, New Mexico
KMOU Roswell, New Mexico
KWES-FM Ruidoso, New Mexico
KMXQ Socorro, New Mexico
KQAY-FM Tucumcari, New Mexico
KTNM Tucumcari, New Mexico
KCYE Boulder City, Nevada
KBUL-FM Carson City, Nevada
KCMY Carson City, Nevada
KRJC Elko, Nevada
KDSS Ely, Nevada
KHWG Fallon, Nevada
KVLV Fallon, Nevada
KLAP Gerlach, Nevada
KWNR Henderson, Nevada
KJJJ Laughlin, Nevada
KJUL Moapa Valley, Nevada
KWNA-FM Winnemucca, Nevada
WGNA-FM Albany, New York
WZKZ Alfred, New York
WHWK Binghamton, New York
WBRV Boonville, New York
WYRK Buffalo, New York
WFFG-FM Corinth, New York
WFLR Dundee, New York
WBUG-FM Fort Plain, New York
WBKX Fredonia, New York
WFLK Geneva, New York
WRWD-FM Highland, New York
WCKR Hornell, New York
WPGI Horseheads, New York
WQNY Ithaca, New York
WHUG Jamestown, New York
WDNB Jeffersonville, New York
WKXP Kingston, New York
WXRL Lancaster, New York
WVOS Liberty, New York
WLLG Lowville, New York
WVNV Malone, New York
WBGK Newport Village, New York
WBKT Norwich, New York
WPIG Olean, New York
WDOS Oneonta, New York
WDLC Port Jervis, New York
WSNN Potsdam, New York
WOKR Remsen, New York
WBZA Rochester, New York
WUUF Sodus, New York
WSPQ Springville, New York
WFRG-FM Utica, New York
WCJW Warsaw, New York
WFRY-FM Watertown, New York
WRCE Watkins Glen, New York
WAVR Waverly, New York
WLSV Wellsville, New York
WZAD Wurtsboro, New York
WNCO-FM Ashland, Ohio
WNUS Belpre, Ohio
WWKC Caldwell, Ohio
WKKJ Chillicothe, Ohio
WUBE-FM Cincinnati, Ohio
WGAR-FM Cleveland, Ohio
WMJK Clyde, Ohio
WCOL-FM Columbus, Ohio
WHKO Dayton, Ohio
WZOM Defiance, Ohio
WEDI Eaton, Ohio
WRAC Georgetown, Ohio
WDSJ Greenville, Ohio
WKFM Huron, Ohio
WCJO Jackson, Ohio
WHOK-FM Lancaster, Ohio
WIMT Lima, Ohio
WKNA Logan, Ohio
WMRN-FM Marion, Ohio
WQMX Medina, Ohio
WPFB Middletown, Ohio
WSEO Nelsonville, Ohio
WCKY-FM Pemberville, Ohio
WQXK Salem, Ohio
WTUZ Uhrichsville, Ohio
WTGR Union City, Ohio
WFGF Wapakoneta, Ohio
WCHO-FM Washington Court Hou, Ohio
WXIZ Waverly, Ohio
WKFI Wilmington, Ohio
WQKT Wooster, Ohio
WBZI Xenia, Ohio
KADA-FM Ada, Oklahoma
KEYB Altus, Oklahoma
KWHW Altus, Oklahoma
KACO Apache, Oklahoma
KHKC-FM Atoka, Oklahoma
KREK Bristow, Oklahoma
KKBI Broken Bow, Oklahoma
KWEY-FM Clinton, Oklahoma
KKAJ-FM Davis, Oklahoma
KKEN Duncan, Oklahoma
KLBC Durant, Oklahoma
KECO Elk City, Oklahoma
KOFM Enid, Oklahoma
KTNT Eufaula, Oklahoma
KYBE Frederick, Oklahoma
KGVE Grove, Oklahoma
KGYN Guymon, Oklahoma
KICM Healdton, Oklahoma
KPRV-FM Heavener, Oklahoma
KXBL Henryetta, Oklahoma
KTJS Hobart, Oklahoma
KKRE Hollis, Oklahoma
KITX Hugo, Oklahoma
KBEL-FM Idabel, Oklahoma
KLAW Lawton, Oklahoma
KBLP Lindsay, Oklahoma
KMAD Madill, Oklahoma
KFXI Marlow, Oklahoma

KNED McAlester, Oklahoma
KZLS Mustang, Oklahoma
KNID North Enid, Oklahoma
KRIG-FM Nowata, Oklahoma
KTST Oklahoma City, Oklahoma
KXXY-FM Oklahoma City, Oklahoma
KOKL Okmulgee, Oklahoma
KPNC Ponca City, Oklahoma
KOMS Poteau, Oklahoma
KPRV Poteau, Oklahoma
KIRC Seminole, Oklahoma
KGFY Stillwater, Oklahoma
KLRB Stuart, Oklahoma
KIXO Sulphur, Oklahoma
KEOK Tahlequah, Oklahoma
KTLQ Tahlequah, Oklahoma
KVOO-FM Tulsa, Oklahoma
KWEN Tulsa, Oklahoma
KITO-FM Vinita, Oklahoma
KTFX-FM Warner, Oklahoma
KWEY Weatherford, Oklahoma
KWSH Wewoka, Oklahoma
KMCO Wilburton, Oklahoma
KWFX Woodward, Oklahoma
KRKT-FM Albany, Oregon
KESY Baker City, Oregon
KBDN Bandon, Oregon
KMTK Bend, Oregon
KJDY-FM Canyon City, Oregon
KSHL Coburg, Oregon
KMHS Coos Bay, Oregon
KSHR-FM Coquille, Oregon
KNND Cottage Grove, Oregon
KWVR-FM Enterprise, Oregon
KCST-FM Florence, Oregon
KRWQ Gold Hill, Oregon
KZZR Government Camp, Oregon
KCMD Grants Pass, Oregon
KXPC-FM Harrisburg, Oregon
KOHU Hermiston, Oregon
KIHR Hood River, Oregon
KJDY John Day, Oregon
KLAD-FM Klamath Falls, Oregon
KQIK Lakeview, Oregon
KSRV Ontario, Oregon
KWHT Pendleton, Oregon
KAKT Phoenix, Oregon
KUPL Portland, Oregon
KWJJ-FM Portland, Oregon
KRCO Prineville, Oregon
KSJJ Redmond, Oregon
KRSB-FM Roseburg, Oregon
KKNU Springfield-Eugene, Oregon
KCKX Stayton, Oregon
WFGY Altoona, Pennsylvania
WWSM Annville-Cleona, Pennsylvania
WGGI Benton, Pennsylvania
WLCY Blairsville, Pennsylvania
WVNW Burnham, Pennsylvania
WBUT Butler, Pennsylvania
WHGL-FM Canton, Pennsylvania
WCAT-FM Carlisle, Pennsylvania
WIOO Carlisle, Pennsylvania
WKNB Clarendon, Pennsylvania
WWCH Clarion, Pennsylvania
WFRM Coudersport, Pennsylvania
WDKC Covington, Pennsylvania
WSJR Dallas, Pennsylvania
WOWQ Du Bois, Pennsylvania
WCTO Easton, Pennsylvania
WXTA Edinboro, Pennsylvania
WYGL-FM Elizabethville, Pennsylvania
WLEM Emporium, Pennsylvania
WIOV-FM Ephrata, Pennsylvania
WSKE Everett, Pennsylvania
WTWF Fairview, Pennsylvania
WLOA Farrell, Pennsylvania
WGTY Gettysburg, Pennsylvania
WGRP Greenville, Pennsylvania
WWGY Grove City, Pennsylvania
WHVR Hanover, Pennsylvania
WRBT Harrisburg, Pennsylvania
WLLI Huntingdon, Pennsylvania
WFGI-FM Johnstown, Pennsylvania
WLMI(FM) Kane/Bradford, Pennsylvania
WGYY Meadville, Pennsylvania
WJUN-FM Mexico, Pennsylvania
WWBE Mifflinburg, Pennsylvania
WKVE Mount Pleasant, Pennsylvania
WGYI Oil City, Pennsylvania
WOGG Oliver, Pennsylvania
WQOR Olyphant, Pennsylvania
WBXQ Patton, Pennsylvania
WXTU Philadelphia, Pennsylvania
WPHB Philipsburg, Pennsylvania
WDSY-FM Pittsburgh, Pennsylvania
WVSL-FM Riverside, Pennsylvania
WBYL Salladasburg, Pennsylvania
WGGY Scranton, Pennsylvania
WVSL(AM) Selinsgrove, Pennsylvania
WBLJ-FM Shamokin, Pennsylvania
WEEO Shippensburg, Pennsylvania
WDDH St. Marys, Pennsylvania
WFGE Tyrone, Pennsylvania
WKZV Washington, Pennsylvania
WCBG Waynesboro, Pennsylvania
WILQ Williamsport, Pennsylvania
WKXC-FM Aiken, South Carolina
WDOG Barnwell, South Carolina
WGTR Bucksport, South Carolina
WEZL Charleston, South Carolina
WIWF Charleston, South Carolina
WVSZ Chesterfield, South Carolina
WCOS-FM Columbia, South Carolina
WEGX Dillon, South Carolina
WNOW-FM Gaffney, South Carolina
WZZQ(AM) Gaffney, South Carolina
WSSL-FM Gray Court, South Carolina
WESC-FM Greenville, South Carolina
WJDJ Hartsville, South Carolina
WWNU Irmo, South Carolina
WWKT-FM Kingstree, South Carolina
WHYM Lake City, South Carolina
WRHM Lancaster, South Carolina
WHLZ Marion, South Carolina
WJKB Moncks Corner, South Carolina
WSYN Surfside Beach, South Carolina
WGOG Walhalla, South Carolina
WALI Walterboro, South Carolina
KBFS Belle Fourche, South Dakota
KZZI Belle Fourche, South Dakota
KZMX Hot Springs, South Dakota
KZMX-FM Hot Springs, South Dakota
KOKK Huron, South Dakota
KBJM Lemmon, South Dakota
KMLO Lowry, South Dakota
KJAM-FM Madison, South Dakota
KXLG Milbank, South Dakota
KMIT Mitchell, South Dakota
KGFX Pierre, South Dakota
KIQK Rapid City, South Dakota
KOUT Rapid City, South Dakota
KGIM-FM Redfield, South Dakota
KPLO-FM Reliance, South Dakota
KMOM Roscoe, South Dakota
KIKN-FM Salem, South Dakota
KTWB Sioux Falls, South Dakota
KXRB Sioux Falls, South Dakota
KBWS-FM Sisseton, South Dakota
KKQQ Volga, South Dakota
KDLO-FM Watertown, South Dakota
KSDR-FM Watertown, South Dakota
KWYR Winner, South Dakota
KKYA Yankton, South Dakota
WNAX-FM Yankton, South Dakota
WJSQ Athens, Tennessee
WLAR Athens, Tennessee
WMOD Bolivar, Tennessee
WTBG Brownsville, Tennessee
WFWL Camden, Tennessee
WUCZ Carthage, Tennessee
WVFB Celina, Tennessee
WNKX-FM Centerville, Tennessee
WUSY Cleveland, Tennessee
WLVS-FM Clifton, Tennessee
WYSH Clinton, Tennessee
WMCP Columbia, Tennessee
WGSQ Cookeville, Tennessee
WHUB Cookeville, Tennessee
WLSB Copper Hill, Tennessee
WZYX Cowan, Tennessee
WOWF Crossville, Tennessee
WSDQ Dunlap, Tennessee
WEMB Erwin, Tennessee
WEKR Fayetteville, Tennessee
WYTM-FM Fayetteville, Tennessee
WAKM Franklin, Tennessee
WHIN Gallatin, Tennessee
WGRV Greeneville, Tennessee
WMYL Halls Crossroads, Tennessee
WLMU Harrogate, Tennessee
WMUF Henry, Tennessee
WMLR Hohenwald, Tennessee
WEIO(FM) Huntingdon, Tennessee
WWDX Huntingdon, Tennessee
WOGY Jackson, Tennessee
WDEB Jamestown, Tennessee
WDEB-FM Jamestown, Tennessee
WJFC Jefferson City, Tennessee
WCYQ Karns, Tennessee
WIVK-FM Knoxville, Tennessee
WTNQ La Follette, Tennessee
WLCT Lafayette, Tennessee
WDXE Lawrenceburg, Tennessee
WLLX Lawrenceburg, Tennessee
WWLX Lawrenceburg, Tennessee
WANT Lebanon, Tennessee
WLIL Lenoir City, Tennessee
WJJM-FM Lewisburg, Tennessee
WKSR-FM Loretto, Tennessee
WGAP Maryville, Tennessee
WWYN McKenzie, Tennessee
WBMC McMinnville, Tennessee
WGKX Memphis, Tennessee
WLIV-FM Monterey, Tennessee
WMTN Morristown, Tennessee
WMCT Mountain City, Tennessee
WKDF Nashville, Tennessee
WSIX-FM Nashville, Tennessee
WSM Nashville, Tennessee
WSM-FM Nashville, Tennessee
WBNT-FM Oneida, Tennessee
WRQR(AM) Paris, Tennessee
WKJQ-FM Parsons, Tennessee
WUAT Pikeville, Tennessee
WTRB Ripley, Tennessee
WJDT Rogersville, Tennessee
WAZD Savannah, Tennessee
WKWX Savannah, Tennessee
WXOQ Selmer, Tennessee
WLIJ Shelbyville, Tennessee
WLND Signal Mountain, Tennessee
WJLE Smithville, Tennessee
WJLE-FM Smithville, Tennessee
WTZX Sparta, Tennessee
WMXV St. Joseph, Tennessee
WSBI Static, Tennessee
WEYE Surgoinsville, Tennessee
WNTT Tazewell, Tennessee
WTNV Tiptonville, Tennessee
WIKQ Tusculum, Tennessee
KYTN(FM) Union City, Tennessee
WECO-FM Wartburg, Tennessee
WLNQ White Pine, Tennessee
WBOZ Woodbury, Tennessee
KEAN-FM Abilene, Texas
KSLI Abilene, Texas
KYYW Abilene, Texas
KOPY Alice, Texas
KALP Alpine, Texas
KATP Amarillo, Texas
KDJW Amarillo, Texas
KGNC-FM Amarillo, Texas
KACT-FM Andrews, Texas
KASE-FM Austin, Texas
KVET-FM Austin, Texas
KRUN Ballinger, Texas
KMKS Bay City, Texas
KYKR Beaumont, Texas
KTKO Beeville, Texas
KMKT Bells, Texas
KBST-FM Big Spring, Texas
KNEL-FM Brady, Texas
KLXK Breckenridge, Texas
KTTX Brenham, Texas
KWHI Brenham, Texas
KKUB Brownfield, Texas
KOXE Brownwood, Texas
KORA-FM Bryan, Texas
KCLE Burleson, Texas
KMIL Cameron, Texas
KTAE Cameron, Texas
KPUR-FM Canyon, Texas
KGAS-FM Carthage, Texas
KCTX-FM Childress, Texas
KCAR Clarksville, Texas
KHFX Cleburne, Texas
KTHT Cleveland, Texas
KSTA Coleman, Texas
KAUM Colorado City, Texas
KVMC Colorado City, Texas
KULM-FM Columbus, Texas
KCOM Comanche, Texas

KYOX Comanche, Texas
KRYS-FM Corpus Christi, Texas
KBHT Crockett, Texas
KIVY-FM Crockett, Texas
KSTB Crystal Beach, Texas
KNGR Daingerfield, Texas
KXIT Dalhart, Texas
KRPT Devine, Texas
KDHN Dimmitt, Texas
KSTV-FM Dublin, Texas
KDDD Dumas, Texas
KIOX-FM Edna, Texas
KULP El Campo, Texas
KHEY-FM El Paso, Texas
KOLI Electra, Texas
KNES Fairfield, Texas
KXEZ Farmersville, Texas
KFLP Floydada, Texas
KFST-FM Fort Stockton, Texas
KPLX Fort Worth, Texas
KSCS Fort Worth, Texas
KNAF Fredericksburg, Texas
KNAF-FM Fredericksburg, Texas
KHTZ Ganado, Texas
KGWT George West, Texas
KTFW-FM Glen Rose, Texas
KCTI Gonzales, Texas
KSWA Graham, Texas
KPIR Granbury, Texas
KTXM Hallettsville, Texas
KCLW Hamilton, Texas
KUSJ Harker Heights, Texas
KPBL Hemphill, Texas
KTHP Hemphill, Texas
KHBR Hillsboro, Texas
KILT-FM Houston, Texas
KHYI Howe, Texas
KSAM-FM Huntsville, Texas
KFWR Jacksboro, Texas
KEBE Jacksonville, Texas
KMBL Junction, Texas
KOOK Junction, Texas
KAML Kenedy-Karnes City, Texas
KRNH Kerrville, Texas
KFTX Kingsville, Texas
KVLG La Grange, Texas
KPET Lamesa, Texas
KCYL Lampasas, Texas
KRRG Laredo, Texas
KDRX Laughlin Afb, Texas
KJDL-FM Levelland, Texas
KLVT Levelland, Texas
KZZN Littlefield, Texas
KETX Livingston, Texas
KETX-FM Livingston, Texas
KACQ Lometa, Texas
KYKX Longview, Texas
KLLL-FM Lubbock, Texas
KQBR Lubbock, Texas
KRBA Lufkin, Texas
KYKS Lufkin, Texas
KAGG Madisonville, Texas
KCKL Malakoff, Texas
KRMX Marlin, Texas
KCUL Marshall, Texas
KMHT-FM Marshall, Texas
KHLB Mason, Texas
KLSR-FM Memphis, Texas
KTEX Mercedes, Texas
KNFM Midland, Texas
KMOO-FM Mineola, Texas
KMUL-FM Muleshoe, Texas
KJCS Nacogdoches, Texas
KGNB New Braunfels, Texas
KHKX Odessa, Texas
KMRK-FM Odessa, Texas
KRIL Odessa, Texas
KOGT Orange, Texas
KPXI Overton, Texas
KYXX Ozona, Texas
KROY Palacios, Texas
KOYN Paris, Texas
KZHN Paris, Texas
KKBQ-FM Pasadena, Texas
KIUN Pecos, Texas
KVJY Pharr, Texas
KKYN-FM Plainview, Texas
KOUL Refugio, Texas
KRXT Rockdale, Texas
KDCD San Angelo, Texas
KGKL-FM San Angelo, Texas
KAJA San Antonio, Texas
KKYX San Antonio, Texas
KWED Seguin, Texas
KIKZ Seminole, Texas
KAYD-FM Silsbee, Texas
KHOS-FM Sonora, Texas
KXDJ Spearman, Texas
KLGD Stamford, Texas
KEQX Stephenville, Texas
KSCH Sulphur Springs, Texas
KXOX Sweetwater, Texas
KKYR-FM Texarkana, Texas
KBCY Tye, Texas
KKUS Tyler, Texas
KNUE Tyler, Texas
KBNU Uvalde, Texas
KVOU-FM Uvalde, Texas
KIXS Victoria, Texas
KVNN Victoria, Texas
KBEC Waxahachie, Texas
KLUR Wichita Falls, Texas
KWFS-FM Wichita Falls, Texas
KVST Willis, Texas
KWUD Woodville, Texas
KYKM Yoakum, Texas
KEGH Brigham City, Utah
KWUT(FM) Elsinore, Utah
KMTI Manti, Utah
KCYN Moab, Utah
KEGA Oakley, Utah
KENZ Ogden, Utah
KARB Price, Utah
KSLL Price, Utah
KNEU Roosevelt, Utah
KKAT(AM) Salt Lake City, Utah
KSOP-FM Salt Lake City, Utah
KUBL-FM Salt Lake City, Utah
KSOP South Salt Lake, Utah
KONY St. George, Utah
KLCY Vernal, Utah
WVES Accomac, Virginia
WYYD Amherst, Virginia
WHKX Bluefield, Virginia
WXBQ-FM Bristol, Virginia
WBOP Buffalo Gap, Virginia
WLUS-FM Clarksville, Virginia
WDIC Clinchco, Virginia
WKHK Colonial Heights, Virginia
WSVS Crewe, Virginia
WAKG Danville, Virginia
WBNN-FM Dillwyn, Virginia
WLFV Ettrick, Virginia
WGRX Falmouth, Virginia
WFLO Farmville, Virginia
WLQM-FM Franklin, Virginia
WFLS-FM Fredericksburg, Virginia
WFTR Front Royal, Virginia
WBRF Galax, Virginia
WMJD Grundy, Virginia
WKCY-FM Harrisonburg, Virginia
WJNV Jonesville, Virginia
WLRV Lebanon, Virginia
WXLZ-FM Lebanon, Virginia
WRAA Luray, Virginia
WSIG Mount Jackson, Virginia
WGH-FM Newport News, Virginia
WESR Onley-Onancock, Virginia
WSWV-FM Pennington Gap, Virginia
WUSH Poquoson, Virginia
WDXC Pound, Virginia
WPSK-FM Pulaski, Virginia
WSLC-FM Roanoke, Virginia
WKSK-FM South Hill, Virginia
WXLZ St. Paul, Virginia
WZBB Stanleytown, Virginia
WCYK-FM Staunton, Virginia
WKDW Staunton, Virginia
WKDL Warrenton, Virginia
WNNT-FM Warsaw, Virginia
WIGO-FM White Stone, Virginia
WUSQ-FM Winchester, Virginia
WYVE Wytheville, Virginia
WVVI-FM Christiansted, Virgin Islands
WZLF Bellows Falls, Vermont
WWFY Berlin, Vermont
WTNN Bristol, Vermont
WXLF Hartford, Vermont
WJEN Killington, Vermont
WLVB Morrisville, Vermont
WIKE Newport, Vermont
WVNR Poultney, Vermont
WKXH St. Johnsbury, Vermont
KNBQ Centralia, Washington
KMNT Chehalis, Washington
KCLX Colfax, Washington
KCVL Colville, Washington
KYSN East Wenatchee, Washington
KULE-FM Ephrata, Washington
KYYT Goldendale, Washington
KEYG Grand Coulee, Washington
KXXK Hoquiam, Washington
KBAM Longview, Washington
KUKN Longview, Washington
KGY-FM McCleary, Washington
KWIQ-FM Moses Lake, Washington
KAPS Mount Vernon, Washington
KNCW Omak, Washington
KIXZ-FM Opportunity, Washington
KZZL-FM Pullman, Washington
KORD-FM Richland, Washington
KKWF Seattle, Washington
KMPS-FM Seattle, Washington
KDRK-FM Spokane, Washington
KEZE Spokane, Washington
KDBL(FM) Toppenish, Washington
KYNR Toppenish, Washington
KKRV Wenatchee, Washington
KUTI Yakima, Washington
WRLU Algoma, Wisconsin
WBSZ Ashland, Wisconsin
WDMO Baldwin, Wisconsin
WLMX-FM Balsam Lake, Wisconsin
WXRO Beaver Dam, Wisconsin
WISS Berlin, Wisconsin
WQRB Bloomer, Wisconsin
WATQ Chetek, Wisconsin
WJMQ Clintonville, Wisconsin
WMAD Cross Plains, Wisconsin
WPCK Denmark, Wisconsin
WVRE Dickeyville, Wisconsin
WDMP Dodgeville, Wisconsin
WJVL Janesville, Wisconsin
WQCC La Crosse, Wisconsin
WLDY Ladysmith, Wisconsin
WGLR-FM Lancaster, Wisconsin
WKQH Marathon, Wisconsin
WLST Marinette, Wisconsin
WYTE Marshfield, Wisconsin
WWQM-FM Middleton, Wisconsin
WEKZ Monroe, Wisconsin
WNCY-FM Neenah-Menasha, Wisconsin
WIXK New Richmond, Wisconsin
WPKR Omro, Wisconsin
WCQM Park Falls, Wisconsin
WBKY Portage, Wisconsin
WDDC Portage, Wisconsin
WQPC Prairie Du Chien, Wisconsin
WNFM Reedsburg, Wisconsin
WHDG Rhinelander, Wisconsin
WAQE Rice Lake, Wisconsin
WJMC-FM Rice Lake, Wisconsin
WRCO-FM Richland Center, Wisconsin
WPLT Sarona, Wisconsin
WTCH Shawano, Wisconsin
WBFM Sheboygan, Wisconsin
WCOW-FM Sparta, Wisconsin
WCYE Three Lakes, Wisconsin
WCUB Two Rivers, Wisconsin
WVRQ-FM Viroqua, Wisconsin
WMIL-FM Waukesha, Wisconsin
WDUX Waupaca, Wisconsin
WBKV West Bend, Wisconsin
WSLD Whitewater, Wisconsin
WDLS Wisconsin Dells, Wisconsin
WJLS-FM Beckley, West Virginia
WBRB Buckhannon, West Virginia
WKAZ Charleston, West Virginia
WKWS Charleston, West Virginia
WGIE Clarksburg, West Virginia
WPDX Clarksburg, West Virginia
WZAC-FM Danville, West Virginia
WDNE-FM Elkins, West Virginia
WKKW Fairmont, West Virginia
WVBD Fayetteville, West Virginia
WFGH Fort Gay, West Virginia
WVMR Frost, West Virginia
WHQX Gary, West Virginia
WVMR-FM Hillsboro, West Virginia
WTCR-FM Huntington, West Virginia
WKMM Kingwood, West Virginia
WRON-FM Lewisburg, West Virginia
WGYE Mannington, West Virginia

WELD-FM Moorefield, West Virginia
WTNJ Mount Hope, West Virginia
WGGE Parkersburg, West Virginia
WHNK Parkersburg, West Virginia
WCEF Ripley, West Virginia
WVMD Romney, West Virginia
WVSB Romney, West Virginia
WYKM Rupert, West Virginia
WSCW South Charleston, West Virginia
WVRC-FM Spencer, West Virginia
WDBS Sutton, West Virginia
WOVK Wheeling, West Virginia
WXCC Williamson, West Virginia
KRSV Afton, Wyoming
KRSV-FM Afton, Wyoming
KKAW Albin, Wyoming
KLGT Buffalo, Wyoming
KQLT Casper, Wyoming
KLEN Cheyenne, Wyoming
KOLZ Cheyenne, Wyoming
KXBG Cheyenne, Wyoming
KDWY Diamondville, Wyoming
KEVA Evanston, Wyoming
KRND Fox Farm, Wyoming
KGWY Gillette, Wyoming
KFRZ Green River, Wyoming
KZMQ-FM Greybull, Wyoming
KBDY Hanna, Wyoming
KJAX Jackson, Wyoming
KSGT Jackson, Wyoming
KOVE Lander, Wyoming
KCGY Laramie, Wyoming
KWYW Lost Cabin, Wyoming
KWYY Midwest, Wyoming
KASL Newcastle, Wyoming
KYDT Pine Haven, Wyoming
KPIN Pinedale, Wyoming
KPOW Powell, Wyoming
KTAK Riverton, Wyoming
KQSW Rock Springs, Wyoming
KTGA Saratoga, Wyoming
KYTI Sheridan, Wyoming
KDNO Thermopolis, Wyoming
KERM Torrington, Wyoming
KRAN Warren Afb, Wyoming
KYCN Wheatland, Wyoming

Disco

KUHB-FM St. Paul, Alaska

Easy Listening

KIXV(FM) Malvern, Arkansas
KAHM Prescott, Arizona
KGBA-FM Holtville, California
KIDE Hoopa, California
KGNU Denver, Colorado
KRKQ Mountain Village, Colorado
WYBC New Haven, Connecticut
WKTZ-FM Jacksonville, Florida
WKGC Southport, Florida
WKEZ-FM Tavernier, Florida
WGPC Albany, Georgia
WRFG Atlanta, Georgia
WGCY Gibson City, Illinois
WLLM Lincoln, Illinois
KVSV-FM Beloit, Kansas
WJEJ Hagerstown, Maryland
WBCH-FM Hastings, Michigan
WCZY-FM Mount Pleasant, Michigan
WSAM Saginaw, Michigan
KUMR Doolittle, Missouri
KYMO East Prairie, Missouri
KTXR Springfield, Missouri
WGCM-FM Gulfport, Mississippi
KZJZ St. Regis, Montana
WHLC Highlands, North Carolina
KTAT Frederick, Oklahoma
KMUN Astoria, Oregon
WSBG Stroudsburg, Pennsylvania
WFID Rio Piedras, Puerto Rico
WDAR-FM Darlington, South Carolina
WMUU-FM Greenville, South Carolina
WEZV North Myrtle Beach, South Carolina
KDEZ Brandon, South Dakota
WCPH Etowah, Tennessee
DKORC Anacortes, Washington
KGHP Gig Harbor, Washington
WEZY Racine, Wisconsin

Ethnic

KDVA Buckeye, Arizona
KCFA Arnold, California
KTQX Bakersfield, California
KSEH Brawley, California
KUBO Calexico, California
KBES Ceres, California
KHDC Chualar, California
KSJV Fresno, California
KVUH Laytonville, California
KMPO Modesto, California
KSQQ Morgan Hill, California
KFSG Roseville, California
KLIB Roseville, California
KLOK San Jose, California
KYAA Soquel, California
KOBO Yuba City, California
KHUI Alamosa, Colorado
WDJZ Bridgeport, Connecticut
WUST Washington, District of Columbia
WRMA Fort Lauderdale, Florida
WLQY Hollywood, Florida
WXYB Indian Rocks Beach, Florida
WURN Kendall, Florida
WMGE Miami Beach, Florida
WHSR Pompano Beach, Florida
WPIK Summerland Key, Florida
WTIS Tampa, Florida
WREK Atlanta, Georgia
WATB Decatur, Georgia
KISH Agana, Guam
KKCR Hanalei, Hawaii
KAPA Hilo, Hawaii
KHBC Hilo, Hawaii
KCCN-FM Honolulu, Hawaii
KDNN Honolulu, Hawaii
KINE-FM Honolulu, Hawaii
KNDI Honolulu, Hawaii
KORL Honolulu, Hawaii
KPHI Honolulu, Hawaii
KITH Kapaa, Hawaii
KHEI-FM Kihei, Hawaii
KAQA Kilauea, Hawaii
KNUQ Paauilo, Hawaii
KAHU Pahala, Hawaii
KSRF Poipu, Hawaii
KAGB Waimea, Hawaii
WEEF Deerfield, Illinois
WPNA Oak Park, Illinois
WPJX Zion, Illinois
KJEF Jennings, Louisiana
KLCL Lake Charles, Louisiana
KLRZ Larose, Louisiana
KANE New Iberia, Louisiana
WUNR Brookline, Massachusetts
WHTB Fall River, Massachusetts
WESX Nahant, Massachusetts
WJFD-FM New Bedford, Massachusetts
WJDA Quincy, Massachusetts
WRCA Watertown, Massachusetts
WORC-FM Webster, Massachusetts
KCCM-FM Moorhead, Minnesota
KPNP Watertown, Minnesota
WEW St. Louis, Missouri
WKRA Holly Springs, Mississippi
WABO Waynesboro, Mississippi
WWTR Bridgewater, New Jersey
WTTM Lindenwold, New Jersey
KKRG Albuquerque, New Mexico
WLIE Islip, New York
WOBO Batavia, Ohio
WOMP Bellaire, Ohio
KCHN Brookshire, Texas
KRVA Cockrell Hill, Texas
KYND Cypress, Texas
KGOL Humble, Texas
KZZA Muenster, Texas
KZMP-FM Pilot Point, Texas
KQBO Rio Grande City, Texas
KSAH Universal City, Texas
KHSE Wylie, Texas
WBBC-FM Blackstone, Virginia
WAMM Woodstock, Virginia
WSTX Christiansted, Virgin Islands
WNCH Norwich, Vermont
KXPA Bellevue, Washington
KRPI Ferndale, Washington

Farsi

KIRN Simi Valley, California

Filipino

KNDI Honolulu, Hawaii

Gospel

KJHA Houston, Alaska
KICY Nome, Alaska
WBNM Alexander City, Alabama
WJHO Alexander City, Alabama
WHMA Anniston, Alabama
WRAB Arab, Alabama
WAGG Birmingham, Alabama
WBSA Boaz, Alabama
WEIS Centre, Alabama
WBIB Centreville, Alabama
WQEM Columbiana, Alabama
WXJC-FM Cordova, Alabama
WMCJ Cullman, Alabama
WDLK Dadeville, Alabama
WXAL Demopolis, Alabama
WAGF Dothan, Alabama
WOOF Dothan, Alabama
WVOB Dothan, Alabama
WRJL-FM Eva, Alabama
WJLD(AM) Fairfield, Alabama
WXQW Fairhope, Alabama
WKWL Florala, Alabama
WGEA Geneva, Alabama
WERH Hamilton, Alabama
WQHC Hanceville, Alabama
WKNG-FM Heflin, Alabama
WPIL Heflin, Alabama
WDJL Huntsville, Alabama
WEUP Huntsville, Alabama
WRJX Jackson, Alabama
WIXI Jasper, Alabama
WJLX Jasper, Alabama
WEBT Langdale, Alabama
WIRB Level Plains, Alabama
WHLW Luverne, Alabama
WGOK Mobile, Alabama
WMGY Montgomery, Alabama
WURL Moody, Alabama
WEUV Moulton, Alabama
WJIF Opp, Alabama
WOPP Opp, Alabama
WKXK Pine Hill, Alabama
WLPR Prichard, Alabama
WVSM Rainsville, Alabama
WRMG Red Bay, Alabama
WKAX Russellville, Alabama
WZCT Scottsboro, Alabama
WZZA Tuscumbia, Alabama
WACQ(AM) Tuskegee, Alabama
WJEC Vernon, Alabama
WYLS York, Alabama
KNWA Bellefonte, Arkansas
KBRI Brinkley, Arkansas
KPZK-FM Cabot, Arkansas
KEJA Cale, Arkansas
KNHD Camden, Arkansas
KWXT Dardanelle, Arkansas
KVDW England, Arkansas
KENA Fort Smith, Arkansas
KTCS Fort Smith, Arkansas
KWXI Glenwood, Arkansas
KBPB Harrison, Arkansas
KJIW-FM Helena, Arkansas
KNEA Jonesboro, Arkansas
KAAY Little Rock, Arkansas
KABF Little Rock, Arkansas
KJBN Little Rock, Arkansas
KPZK Little Rock, Arkansas
KCGS Marshall, Arkansas
KLLN Newark, Arkansas
KCAT Pine Bluff, Arkansas
KTPA Prescott, Arkansas
KOSE Wilson, Arkansas
KLTU Mammoth, Arizona
KIBC Burney, California
KYCJ Camino, California
KYCI Firebaugh, California
KCJH Livingston, California
KYCC Stockton, California
KDYA Vallejo, California
KLLV Breen, Colorado
KLDC Denver, Colorado
KGHT El Jebel, Colorado
KGCD Wray, Colorado
WDJZ Bridgeport, Connecticut
WQTQ Hartford, Connecticut

WYCB Washington, District of Columbia
WTJT Baker, Florida
WSWN Belle Glade, Florida
WTCL Chattahoochee, Florida
WJCB Clewiston, Florida
WWBC Cocoa, Florida
WJED Dogwood Lakes Estate, Florida
WIRA Fort Pierce, Florida
WTMN Gainesville, Florida
WRNE Gulf Breeze, Florida
WLVF-FM Haines City, Florida
WZAZ Jacksonville, Florida
WGRO Lake City, Florida
WTYS-FM Marianna, Florida
WRMQ Orlando, Florida
WBRD Palmetto, Florida
WPUL South Daytona, Florida
WHBT Tallahassee, Florida
WEXY Wilton Manors, Florida
WOKB Winter Garden, Florida
WZHR Zephyrhills, Florida
WJYZ Albany, Georgia
WXAG Athens, Georgia
WAFS Atlanta, Georgia
WYZE Atlanta, Georgia
WTHB Augusta, Georgia
WGMI Bremen, Georgia
WULS Broxton, Georgia
WEAM-FM Buena Vista, Georgia
WQIL Chauncey, Georgia
WSHE Columbus, Georgia
WCON Cornelia, Georgia
WDPC Dallas, Georgia
WOKA-FM Douglas, Georgia
WMLT Dublin, Georgia
WXLI Dublin, Georgia
WTJH East Point, Georgia
WUFF-FM Eastman, Georgia
WLJA-FM Ellijay, Georgia
WBHB Fitzgerald, Georgia
WJTG Fort Valley, Georgia
WKLY Hartwell, Georgia
WGML Hinesville, Georgia
WVKX Irwinton, Georgia
WTLD Jesup, Georgia
WMOC Lumber City, Georgia
WDDO Macon, Georgia
WNEX Macon, Georgia
WFDR Manchester, Georgia
WHCG Metter, Georgia
WKUN Monroe, Georgia
WMNZ Montezuma, Georgia
WIGO Morrow, Georgia
WMTM Moultrie, Georgia
WALH Mountain City, Georgia
WGCN Nashville, Georgia
WRBX Reidsville, Georgia
WTNL Reidsville, Georgia
WSSJ Rincon, Georgia
WZOT Rockmart, Georgia
WROM Rome, Georgia
WSOK Savannah, Georgia
WSTT Thomasville, Georgia
WIMO Winder, Georgia
WTHB-FM Wrens, Georgia
KTFC Sioux City, Iowa
KTFG Sioux Rapids, Iowa
KBBG Waterloo, Iowa
WXAN Ava, Illinois
WTSG Carlinville, Illinois
WRJM(AM) Charleston, Illinois
WGRB Chicago, Illinois
WSSD Chicago, Illinois
WFFX(AM) East St. Louis, Illinois
WWHN Joliet, Illinois
WRTK Paxton, Illinois
WVEL Pekin, Illinois
WJBC-FM Pontiac, Illinois
WAUZ Greensburg, Indiana
WYGS Hope, Indiana
WTLC Indianapolis, Indiana
WMYJ Martinsville, Indiana
WRFM Muncie, Indiana
WMYJ-FM Oolitic, Indiana
WYWY Barbourville, Kentucky
WAAJ Benton, Kentucky
WVHM Benton, Kentucky
WCVG Covington, Kentucky
WEKT Elkton, Kentucky
WIOK Falmouth, Kentucky
WFLE Flemingsburg, Kentucky
WFSR Harlan, Kentucky
WHBN Harrodsburg, Kentucky
WEKG Jackson, Kentucky
WKVG Jenkins, Kentucky
WVCT Keavy, Kentucky
WGWM London, Kentucky
WLLV Louisville, Kentucky
WLOU Louisville, Kentucky
WMIK Middlesboro, Kentucky
WFLW Monticello, Kentucky
WRVK Mount Vernon, Kentucky
WLOC Munfordville, Kentucky
WCGW Nicholasville, Kentucky
WYGH Paris, Kentucky
WDOC Prestonsburg, Kentucky
WCBR Richmond, Kentucky
WIDS Russell Springs, Kentucky
WBFC Stanton, Kentucky
WJCR-FM Upton, Kentucky
WEKC Williamsburg, Kentucky
KWDF Ball, Louisiana
WPFC Baton Rouge, Louisiana
KDLA De Ridder, Louisiana
KGGM Delhi, Louisiana
KGRM Grambling, Louisiana
KKNO Gretna, Louisiana
KJCB Lafayette, Louisiana
WBOK New Orleans, Louisiana
WYLD New Orleans, Louisiana
KTTP Pineville, Louisiana
KRUS Ruston, Louisiana
KIOU Shreveport, Louisiana
KOKA Shreveport, Louisiana
KSYB Shreveport, Louisiana
KTKC-FM Springhill, Louisiana
KTJZ Tallulah, Louisiana
KNCB Vivian, Louisiana
WNGB Petersham, Massachusetts
WSMA Scituate, Massachusetts
WCAO Baltimore, Maryland
WWIN Baltimore, Maryland
WLIC Frostburg, Maryland
WAIJ Grantsville, Maryland
WPRS-FM Waldorf, Maryland
WHCF Bangor, Maine
WFST Caribou, Maine
WFLT Flint, Michigan
WCTP Gagetown, Michigan
WJOG Good Hart, Michigan
WUNN Mason, Michigan
WEXL Royal Oak, Michigan
WWSJ St. Johns, Michigan
WCHB Taylor, Michigan
KNOF St. Paul, Minnesota
KGNA-FM Arnold, Missouri
KCWJ Blue Springs, Missouri
KNLH Cedar Hill, Missouri
KYRV Concordia, Missouri
KGNN-FM Cuba, Missouri
KNLQ Cuba, Missouri
KGGN Gladstone, Missouri
KJIR Hannibal, Missouri
WGCQ Hayti, Missouri
KPRT Kansas City, Missouri
KMHM Lutesville, Missouri
KMRF Marshfield, Missouri
KJAB-FM Mexico, Missouri
KNLG New Bloomfield, Missouri
KPWB Piedmont, Missouri
KNLP Potosi, Missouri
KATZ St. Louis, Missouri
KSTL St. Louis, Missouri
KALM Thayer, Missouri
KBIY Van Buren, Missouri
KGNV Washington, Missouri
WBYP Belzoni, Mississippi
WELZ Belzoni, Mississippi
WXTN Benton, Mississippi
WCHJ Brookhaven, Mississippi
WAJV Brooksville, Mississippi
WCLD Cleveland, Mississippi
WFFF Columbia, Mississippi
WAUM Duck Hill, Mississippi
WQST Forest, Mississippi
WNEV Friars Point, Mississippi
WJIW Greenville, Mississippi
WGRM Greenwood, Mississippi
WGRM-FM Greenwood, Mississippi
WQFX Gulfport, Mississippi
WURC Holly Springs, Mississippi
WHAL-FM Horn Lake, Mississippi
WCPC Houston, Mississippi
WNLA Indianola, Mississippi
WVSD Itta Bena, Mississippi
WHLH Jackson, Mississippi
WESY Leland, Mississippi
WAKK McComb, Mississippi
WMER Meridian, Mississippi
WNBN Meridian, Mississippi
WYHL Meridian, Mississippi
WOSM Ocean Springs, Mississippi
WXHB Richton, Mississippi
WBBN Taylorsville, Mississippi
WAQB Tupelo, Mississippi
KGCM Belgrade, Montana
WRCS Ahoskie, North Carolina
WTJY Asheboro, North Carolina
WZOO Asheboro, North Carolina
WPYB Benson, North Carolina
WZGM Black Mountain, North Carolina
WVOE Chadbourn, North Carolina
WRNA China Grove, North Carolina
WYZD Dobson, North Carolina
WCKB Dunn, North Carolina
WRJD Durham, North Carolina
WBXB Edenton, North Carolina
WFMO Fairmont, North Carolina
WSTS Fairmont, North Carolina
WIDU Fayetteville, North Carolina
WWOL Forest City, North Carolina
WNNL Fuquay-Varina, North Carolina
WYCV Granite Falls, North Carolina
WEAL Greensboro, North Carolina
WKEW Greensboro, North Carolina
WNAA Greensboro, North Carolina
WPET Greensboro, North Carolina
WKDX Hamlet, North Carolina
WHNC Henderson, North Carolina
WPIR Hickory, North Carolina
WRKB Kannapolis, North Carolina
WKTE King, North Carolina
WELS Kinston, North Carolina
WEWO Laurinburg, North Carolina
WAGR Lumberton, North Carolina
WLPS-FM Lumberton, North Carolina
WHBK Marshall, North Carolina
WDSL Mocksville, North Carolina
WDEX Monroe, North Carolina
WIXE Monroe, North Carolina
WCIS Morganton, North Carolina
WSYD Mount Airy, North Carolina
WWDR Murfreesboro, North Carolina
WCVP Murphy, North Carolina
WAUG New Hope, North Carolina
WCBQ Oxford, North Carolina
WGIW Pilot Mountain, North Carolina
WMFA Raeford, North Carolina
WCLY Raleigh, North Carolina
WTEL Red Springs, North Carolina
WGQR Rennert, North Carolina
WEGG Rose Hill, North Carolina
WXKL Sanford, North Carolina
WYAL Scotland Neck, North Carolina
WVCB Shallotte, North Carolina
WGAS South Gastonia, North Carolina
WFMI Southern Shores, North Carolina
WTAB Tabor City, North Carolina
WTLK Taylorsville, North Carolina
WJRM Troy, North Carolina
WZKB Wallace, North Carolina
WARR Warrenton, North Carolina
WLGT Washington, North Carolina
WENC Whiteville, North Carolina
WIAM Williamston, North Carolina
WLSG Wilmington, North Carolina
WWIL Wilmington, North Carolina
WLLY Wilson, North Carolina
WBTE Windsor, North Carolina
WPOL Winston-Salem, North Carolina
WSMX Winston-Salem, North Carolina
WXRI Winston-Salem, North Carolina
WECU Winterville, North Carolina
WYNC Yanceyville, North Carolina
KHRT Minot, North Dakota
KTFJ Dakota City, Nebraska
KJLT-FM North Platte, Nebraska
KEIS York, Nebraska
WIMG Ewing, New Jersey
WEHA(FM) Port Republic, New Jersey
WFAI Salem, New Jersey
WNJC Vineland, New Jersey
KUPR Alamogordo, New Mexico

KYCM Alamogordo, New Mexico
KHII Cloudcroft, New Mexico
KYCT Ruidoso, New Mexico
KRJY Truth or Consequence, New Mexico
KEKL Mesquite, Nevada
WUFO Amherst, New York
WXXY Houghton, New York
WBAR-FM Lake Luzerne, New York
WFWO Medina, New York
WTHE Mineola, New York
WLIB New York, New York
WHLD Niagara Falls, New York
WOKR Remsen, New York
WKYJ Rouses Point, New York
WINW Canton, Ohio
WDBZ Cincinnati, Ohio
WJMO Cleveland, Ohio
WBIE Delphos, Ohio
WGNZ Fairborn, Ohio
WCNW Fairfield, Ohio
WRAC Georgetown, Ohio
WJTB North Ridgeville, Ohio
WABQ Painesville, Ohio
WCCD Parma, Ohio
WXIC Waverly, Ohio
WLRD Willard, Ohio
KAJT Ada, Oklahoma
KZBS Granite, Oklahoma
KPRV-FM Heavener, Oklahoma
KVAZ Henryetta, Oklahoma
KVIS Miami, Oklahoma
KTLV Midwest City, Oklahoma
KOSG Pawhuska, Oklahoma
KPRV Poteau, Oklahoma
KLRB Stuart, Oklahoma
KFXT Sulphur, Oklahoma
KTGS Tishomingo, Oklahoma
KIMY Watonga, Oklahoma
WPWA Chester, Pennsylvania
WXTC Greenville, Pennsylvania
WADV Lebanon, Pennsylvania
WJSM-FM Martinsburg, Pennsylvania
WRIJ Masontown, Pennsylvania
WPEL Montrose, Pennsylvania
WNAP Norristown, Pennsylvania
WPCL Northern Cambria, Pennsylvania
WOON Woonsocket, Rhode Island
WBSC Bennettsville, South Carolina
WSPX Bowman, South Carolina
WGCV Cayce, South Carolina
WGCD Chester, South Carolina
WRFE Chesterfield, South Carolina
WPJS Conway, South Carolina
WWRK Darlington, South Carolina
WDSC Dillon, South Carolina
WOLH Florence, South Carolina
WYNN Florence, South Carolina
WNOW-FM Gaffney, South Carolina
WLMC Georgetown, South Carolina
WTBI-FM Greenville, South Carolina
WCZZ Greenwood, South Carolina
WPJM Greer, South Carolina
WJDJ Hartsville, South Carolina
WLGI Hemingway, South Carolina
WJBS Holly Hill, South Carolina
WALD Johnsonville, South Carolina
WRZE Kingstree, South Carolina
WKCL Ladson, South Carolina
WAGL Lancaster, South Carolina
WJAY Mullins, South Carolina
WGUS-FM New Ellenton, South Carolina
WKZK North Augusta, South Carolina
WPJK Orangeburg, South Carolina
WSSB-FM Orangeburg, South Carolina
WTUA Pinopolis, South Carolina
WCSZ Sans Souci, South Carolina
WPOG St. Matthews, South Carolina
WIBZ Wedgefield, South Carolina
WWGM Alamo, Tennessee
WTKB-FM Atwood, Tennessee
WJOC Chattanooga, Tennessee
WNOO Chattanooga, Tennessee
WHUB Cookeville, Tennessee
WWOG Cookeville, Tennessee
WBEJ Elizabethton, Tennessee
WENR Englewood, Tennessee
WEMB Erwin, Tennessee
WEKR Fayetteville, Tennessee
WQZQ Goodlettsville, Tennessee
WJAK Jackson, Tennessee
WDEB-FM Jamestown, Tennessee
WJJT Jellico, Tennessee
WETB Johnson City, Tennessee
WKGN Knoxville, Tennessee
WKXV Knoxville, Tennessee
WLAF La Follette, Tennessee
WEEN Lafayette, Tennessee
WDXL Lexington, Tennessee
WFLI Lookout Mountain, Tennessee
WGBQ Lynchburg, Tennessee
WBMC McMinnville, Tennessee
WXRQ Mount Pleasant, Tennessee
WMDB Nashville, Tennessee
WNAH Nashville, Tennessee
WUAT Pikeville, Tennessee
WJBZ-FM Seymour, Tennessee
WLIJ Shelbyville, Tennessee
WSMT Sparta, Tennessee
WMXV St. Joseph, Tennessee
WDEH Sweetwater, Tennessee
WECO Wartburg, Tennessee
WQSE White Bluff, Tennessee
WBOZ Woodbury, Tennessee
KAZI Austin, Texas
KWWJ Baytown, Texas
KGHY Beaumont, Texas
KZZB Beaumont, Texas
KCOM Comanche, Texas
KYJC Commerce, Texas
KYOK Conroe, Texas
KDKR Decatur, Texas
KVOZ Del Mar Hills, Texas
KHVN Fort Worth, Texas
KKGM Fort Worth, Texas
KTXJ-FM Jasper, Texas
KJTX Jefferson, Texas
KRMY Killeen, Texas
KZZN Littlefield, Texas
KFIT Lockhart, Texas
KCHL San Antonio, Texas
KFIT EXP S San Antonio, Texas
KROI Seabrook, Texas
KGLD Tyler, Texas
KZEE Weatherford, Texas
KWNS Winnsboro, Texas
KLLB West Jordan, Utah
WWDW Alberta, Virginia
WAMV Amherst, Virginia
WTTX-FM Appomattox, Virginia
WBTX Broadway-Timberville, Virginia
WKBY Chatham, Virginia
WCPK Chesapeake, Virginia
WXCF Clifton Forge, Virginia
WFIC Collinsville, Virginia
WKYV Colonial Heights, Virginia
WPZZ Crewe, Virginia
WGFC Floyd, Virginia
WLQM Franklin, Virginia
WWWJ Galax, Virginia
WGAT Gate City, Virginia
WNRG Grundy, Virginia
WHHV Hillsville, Virginia
WHAP Hopewell, Virginia
WLRV Lebanon, Virginia
WLLL Lynchburg, Virginia
WTJZ Newport News, Virginia
WNVA Norton, Virginia
WSWV Pennington Gap, Virginia
WGPL Portsmouth, Virginia
WPCE Portsmouth, Virginia
WGTH-FM Richlands, Virginia
WFTH Richmond, Virginia
WTRM Winchester, Virginia
WNGF Swanton, Vermont
KZIZ Pacific, Washington
WGLB Elm Grove, Wisconsin
WJLS Beckley, West Virginia
WKJL Clarksburg, West Virginia
WFGH Fort Gay, West Virginia
WEMM-FM Huntington, West Virginia
WOTR(FM) Lost Creek, West Virginia
WHJC Matewan, West Virginia
WPCN(FM) Point Pleasant, West Virginia
WAEY Princeton, West Virginia
WRRL Rainelle, West Virginia
WYKM Rupert, West Virginia
WVRC Spencer, West Virginia
WMLJ Summersville, West Virginia
WVGV West Union, West Virginia
KOFG Cody, Wyoming
KRKM Fort Washakie, Wyoming

Greek

WXYB Indian Rocks Beach, Florida
WPSO New Port Richey, Florida
WCGO Evanston, Illinois
WNTN Newton, Massachusetts

Japanese

KVTO Berkeley, California
KBIF Fresno, California
KMRB San Gabriel, California
KALI-FM Santa Ana, California
KZOO Honolulu, Hawaii
KFXN Minneapolis, Minnesota
KREH Pecan Grove, Texas

Jazz

WAUD Auburn, Alabama
WAAX Gadsden, Alabama
WJAB Huntsville, Alabama
WVAS Montgomery, Alabama
WQPR Muscle Shoals, Alabama
WAPR Selma, Alabama
WUAL-FM Tuscaloosa, Alabama
WZZA Tuscumbia, Alabama
KBSA El Dorado, Arkansas
KUAF Fayetteville, Arkansas
KASU Jonesboro, Arkansas
KABF Little Rock, Arkansas
KUAR Little Rock, Arkansas
KUAP Pine Bluff, Arkansas
KXRJ Russellville, Arkansas
KOAS Dolan Springs, Arizona
KJZA Drake, Arizona
KJZZ Phoenix, Arizona
KYOT-FM Phoenix, Arizona
KJZP Prescott, Arizona
KUAZ Tucson, Arizona
KUAZ-FM Tucson, Arizona
KAWC-FM Yuma, Arizona
KNCA Burney, California
KRML Carmel, California
KCHO Chico, California
KSPC Claremont, California
KECG El Cerrito, California
KSSJ(FM) Fair Oaks, California
KFSR Fresno, California
KMGQ(FM) Goleta, California
KJJZ Indio, California
KKJZ Long Beach, California
KTWV Los Angeles, California
KNSQ Mount Shasta, California
KQNC Quincy, California
KFPR Redding, California
KXJZ Sacramento, California
KIFM San Diego, California
KCBX San Luis Obispo, California
KCSM San Mateo, California
KSBX Santa Barbara, California
KJZY Sebastopol, California
KKXS Shingletown, California
KXJS Sutter, California
KMYT Temecula, California
KRZA Alamosa, Colorado
KAJX Aspen, Colorado
KCJX Carbondale, Colorado
KUVO Denver, Colorado
WQTQ Hartford, Connecticut
WDJW Somers, Connecticut
WPFW Washington, District of Columbia
WRTX Dover, Delaware
WUFT-FM Gainesville, Florida
WXJZ Gainesville, Florida
WLOQ Indian Lakes Estates, Florida
WJUF Inverness, Florida
WLLD(FM) Lakeland, Florida
WCNZ Marco Island, Florida
WDNA Miami, Florida
WUCF-FM Orlando, Florida
WZJZ Port Charlotte, Florida
WUSF Tampa, Florida
WGYL Vero Beach, Florida
WTSM(FM) Woodville, Florida
WCLK Atlanta, Georgia
WAZX-FM Cleveland, Georgia
WSVH Savannah, Georgia
KPRG Agana, Guam
KIPO Honolulu, Hawaii
KKHI Kihei, Hawaii
KCCK-FM Cedar Rapids, Iowa

KALA Davenport, Iowa
KJMC Des Moines, Iowa
KBSU-FM Boise, Idaho
KIBX Bonners Ferry, Idaho
KBSK McCall, Idaho
KISU-FM Pocatello, Idaho
KYZK Sun Valley, Idaho
KQZB Troy, Idaho
KEZJ Twin Falls, Idaho
WBEZ Chicago, Illinois
WHPK-FM Chicago, Illinois
WNUA Chicago, Illinois
WNIJ Dekalb, Illinois
WSIE Edwardsville, Illinois
WNUR-FM Evanston, Illinois
WARH Granite City, Illinois
WBEQ Morris, Illinois
WGLT Normal, Illinois
WIPA Pittsfield, Illinois
WQUB Quincy, Illinois
WUIS Springfield, Illinois
WFIU Bloomington, Indiana
WBEW Chesterton, Indiana
WVPE Elkhart, Indiana
WUEV Evansville, Indiana
WBOI Fort Wayne, Indiana
WBDC Huntingburg, Indiana
WICR Indianapolis, Indiana
WBAA West Lafayette, Indiana
KANH Emporia, Kansas
KKCI Goodland, Kansas
KANU Lawrence, Kansas
KJHK Lawrence, Kansas
KANV Olsburg, Kansas
KMUW Wichita, Kansas
WKYL Lawrenceburg, Kentucky
KLSA Alexandria, Louisiana
WBRH Baton Rouge, Louisiana
WJSH Folsom, Louisiana
KRVS Lafayette, Louisiana
KEDM Monroe, Louisiana
WWNO New Orleans, Louisiana
WWOZ New Orleans, Louisiana
KDAQ Shreveport, Louisiana
KTLN Thibodaux, Louisiana
WGBH(FM) Boston, Massachusetts
WHRB Cambridge, Massachusetts
WEIB Northampton, Massachusetts
WICN Worcester, Massachusetts
WEAA Baltimore, Maryland
WYPR Baltimore, Maryland
WFWM Frostburg, Maryland
WYPO Ocean City, Maryland
WESM Princess Anne, Maryland
WMEH Bangor, Maine
WMED Calais, Maine
WMEP Camden, Maine
WMEF Fort Kent, Maine
WMEM Presque Isle, Maine
WMEW Waterville, Maine
WGVU-FM Allendale, Michigan
WCML-FM Alpena, Michigan
WUCX-FM Bay City, Michigan
WJZQ Cadillac, Michigan
WRCJ-FM Detroit, Michigan
WBLU-FM Grand Rapids, Michigan
WCMW-FM Harbor Springs, Michigan
WMUK Kalamazoo, Michigan
WLNZ Lansing, Michigan
WNMU-FM Marquette, Michigan
WCMU-FM Mount Pleasant, Michigan
WCMB-FM Oscoda, Michigan
WSGR-FM Port Huron, Michigan
WCMZ-FM Sault Ste. Marie, Michigan
WWCM Standish, Michigan
WNMC-FM Traverse City, Michigan
WBLV Twin Lake, Michigan
WGVS-FM Whitehall, Michigan
WEMU Ypsilanti, Michigan
KBEM-FM Minneapolis, Minnesota
KRCU Cape Girardeau, Missouri
KWWC-FM Columbia, Missouri
KZWV Eldon, Missouri
KJLU Jefferson City, Missouri
WDAF-FM Liberty, Missouri
KRLI Malta Bend, Missouri
KXCV Maryville, Missouri
KCOZ Point Lookout, Missouri
KSEF Ste. Genevieve, Missouri
WURC Holly Springs, Mississippi
WVSD Itta Bena, Mississippi
WJSU-FM Jackson, Mississippi
KEMC Billings, Montana
KBMC Bozeman, Montana
KAPC Butte, Montana
KQJZ Evergreen, Montana
KUFN Hamilton, Montana
KNMC Havre, Montana
KUHM Helena, Montana
KUKL Kalispell, Montana
KUFM Missoula, Montana
WCQS Asheville, North Carolina
WCCE Buies Creek, North Carolina
WNCU Durham, North Carolina
WFSS Fayetteville, North Carolina
WFQS Franklin, North Carolina
WNAA Greensboro, North Carolina
WSHA Raleigh, North Carolina
WSNC Winston-Salem, North Carolina
KCND Bismarck, North Dakota
KPPD Devils Lake, North Dakota
KDPR Dickinson, North Dakota
KFJM Grand Forks, North Dakota
KPRJ Jamestown, North Dakota
KMPR Minot, North Dakota
KLPR Kearney, Nebraska
KZUM Lincoln, Nebraska
KIOS-FM Omaha, Nebraska
WNEC-FM Henniker, New Hampshire
WBGO Newark, New Jersey
WRTQ Ocean City, New Jersey
WPRB Princeton, New Jersey
WNJO Toms River, New Jersey
KSJE Farmington, New Mexico
KRWG Las Cruces, New Mexico
KNCC Elko, Nevada
KBSJ Jackpot, Nevada
KUNV Las Vegas, Nevada
KUNR Reno, Nevada
WSQX-FM Binghamton, New York
WCWP Brookville, New York
WBFO Buffalo, New York
WEOS Geneva, New York
WGMC Greece, New York
WRCU-FM Hamilton, New York
WVHC Herkimer, New York
WSQA Hornell, New York
WUBJ Jamestown, New York
WADO New York, New York
WHCR-FM New York, New York
WKCR-FM New York, New York
WNYC-FM New York, New York
WJZR Rochester, New York
WAER Syracuse, New York
WRMU-FM Alliance, Ohio
WBGU Bowling Green, Ohio
WCPN Cleveland, Ohio
WDPS Dayton, Ohio
WMRT Marietta, Ohio
WOBC-FM Oberlin, Ohio
WMUB Oxford, Ohio
WXTS-FM Toledo, Ohio
WCSU-FM Wilberforce, Ohio
KALU Langston, Oklahoma
KROU Spencer, Oklahoma
KSMF Ashland, Oregon
KSBA Coos Bay, Oregon
KYSJ Coos Bay, Oregon
KBVR Corvallis, Oregon
KMHD Gresham, Oregon
KSKF Klamath Falls, Oregon
KLCO Newport, Oregon
KZIU-FM Weston, Oregon
WAEB Allentown, Pennsylvania
WRTJ Coatesville, Pennsylvania
WRTL Ephrata, Pennsylvania
WQLN-FM Erie, Pennsylvania
WRTY Jackson Township, Pennsylvania
WRTI Philadelphia, Pennsylvania
WXAC Reading, Pennsylvania
WUSR Scranton, Pennsylvania
WVIA-FM Scranton, Pennsylvania
WJAZ Summerdale, Pennsylvania
WVYA Williamsport, Pennsylvania
WOLA Barranquitas, Puerto Rico
WELH Providence, Rhode Island
WOLH Florence, South Carolina
WSSB-FM Orangeburg, South Carolina
KPSD-FM Faith, South Dakota
KQSD-FM Lowry, South Dakota
KZSD-FM Martin, South Dakota
KDSD-FM Pierpont, South Dakota
KBHE-FM Rapid City, South Dakota
KTSD-FM Reliance, South Dakota
KAUR Sioux Falls, South Dakota
KUSD Vermillion, South Dakota
WBOL Bolivar, Tennessee
WFHU Henderson, Tennessee
WUOT Knoxville, Tennessee
WFMQ Lebanon, Tennessee
WUMR Memphis, Tennessee
WMOT Murfreesboro, Tennessee
WFSK-FM Nashville, Tennessee
KVLU Beaumont, Texas
KAMU-FM College Station, Texas
KETR Commerce, Texas
KEDT-FM Corpus Christi, Texas
KTEP El Paso, Texas
KMBH-FM Harlingen, Texas
KTSU Houston, Texas
KERV Kerrville, Texas
KLDN Lufkin, Texas
KHID McAllen, Texas
KNTU McKinney, Texas
KSAU Nacogdoches, Texas
KWLD Plainview, Texas
KRTU-FM San Antonio, Texas
KVRT Victoria, Texas
KMCU Wichita Falls, Texas
KUER-FM Salt Lake City, Utah
WVTU Charlottesville, Virginia
WVTW Charlottesville, Virginia
WRIQ Lexington, Virginia
WVTR Marion, Virginia
WHRV Norfolk, Virginia
WVST-FM Petersburg, Virginia
WVRU-FM Radford, Virginia
WVTF Roanoke, Virginia
WISE-FM Wise, Virginia
WRUV Burlington, Vermont
WVPS Burlington, Vermont
WRVT Rutland, Vermont
WVPA St. Johnsbury, Vermont
WVPR Windsor, Vermont
KBCS Bellevue, Washington
KZAZ Bellingham, Washington
KEWU-FM Cheney, Washington
KZAL Manson, Washington
KVIX Port Angeles, Washington
KZUU Pullman, Washington
KPBX-FM Spokane, Washington
KPLU-FM Tacoma, Washington
KYNR Toppenish, Washington
WAUN-FM Kewaunee, Wisconsin
WLSU La Crosse, Wisconsin
WORT Madison, Wisconsin
WWSP Stevens Point, Wisconsin
WVPB Beckley, West Virginia
WVPW Buckhannon, West Virginia
WVPN Charleston, West Virginia
WVWV Huntington, West Virginia
WVEP Martinsburg, West Virginia
WVPM Morgantown, West Virginia
WVPG Parkersburg, West Virginia
WVNP Wheeling, West Virginia
KUWL Laramie, Wyoming
KUWY Laramie, Wyoming
KCWC-FM Riverton, Wyoming
KPRQ Sheridan, Wyoming

Korean

KVTO Berkeley, California
KBIF Fresno, California
KMPC Los Angeles, California
KYPA Los Angeles, California
KMRB San Gabriel, California
KALI-FM Santa Ana, California
KFOX Torrance, California
KHRA Honolulu, Hawaii
KREA Honolulu, Hawaii
WKTA Evanston, Illinois
KFXN Minneapolis, Minnesota
WWRU Jersey City, New Jersey
KXMX Muldrow, Oklahoma
KREH Pecan Grove, Texas
WDCT Fairfax, Virginia
KWYZ Everett, Washington
KSUH Puyallup, Washington

Light Rock

KRRK Desert Hills, Arizona
WNDT Alachua, Florida

WHPT Sarasota, Florida
WNDD Silver Springs, Florida
KRNQ Keokuk, Iowa
KLLT Spencer, Iowa
WDRV Chicago, Illinois
WMKB Earlville, Illinois
WQCY Quincy, Illinois
WZLK Virgie, Kentucky
WMDM Lexington Park, Maryland
WMRR Muskegon Heights, Michigan
KQPR Albert Lea, Minnesota
KQDS-FM Duluth, Minnesota
KQCL Faribault, Minnesota
KRVY-FM Starbuck, Minnesota
KMYK Osage Beach, Missouri
WWKZ Okolona, Mississippi
WOXL-FM Biltmore Forest, North Carolina
KEXL Pierce, Nebraska
WHOM Mount Washington, New Hampshire
WFPG Atlantic City, New Jersey
WNCX Cleveland, Ohio
WMKX Brookville, Pennsylvania
WZMF(AM) Nanticoke, Pennsylvania
WUZZ Saegertown, Pennsylvania
WWLI Providence, Rhode Island
WMXT Pamplico, South Carolina
KNFX-FM Bryan, Texas
KVIL Highland Park-Dallas, Texas
KRPX Wellington, Utah
WTHK Wilmington, Vermont
KRQT Castle Rock, Washington
WMEQ-FM Menomonie, Wisconsin
WZDR(FM) Sturgeon Bay, Wisconsin

Native American

KOHN Sells, Arizona
KGHR Tuba City, Arizona
KSUT Ignacio, Colorado
KOJB Cass Lake, Minnesota
KHEW Rocky Boy's Reserv., Montana
KINI Crookston, Nebraska
KNDN Farmington, New Mexico
KUSW Flora Vista, New Mexico
KGAK Gallup, New Mexico
KWSO Warm Springs, Oregon
KILI Porcupine, South Dakota
KWRR Ethete, Wyoming

News

KBYR Anchorage, Alaska
KFQD Anchorage, Alaska
KSKA Anchorage, Alaska
KAGV Big Lake, Alaska
KLAM Cordova, Alaska
KFAR Fairbanks, Alaska
KFBX Fairbanks, Alaska
KUAC Fairbanks, Alaska
KTOO Juneau, Alaska
KTKN Ketchikan, Alaska
KMXT Kodiak, Alaska
KIAM Nenana, Alaska
KNOM Nome, Alaska
KFSK Petersburg, Alaska
KCAW Sitka, Alaska
KIFW Sitka, Alaska
KSRM Soldotna, Alaska
KUHB-FM St. Paul, Alaska
KTNA Talkeetna, Alaska
KUCB Unalaska, Alaska
WDNG Anniston, Alabama
WVNN Athens, Alabama
WAPI Birmingham, Alabama
WBHM Birmingham, Alabama
WERC Birmingham, Alabama
WYDE Birmingham, Alabama
WACV Coosada, Alabama
WFMH Cullman, Alabama
WXAL Demopolis, Alabama
WRWA Dothan, Alabama
WWNT Dothan, Alabama
WHEP Foley, Alabama
WFPA Fort Payne, Alabama
WSGN Gadsden, Alabama
WGEA Geneva, Alabama
WGYV Greenville, Alabama
WGSV Guntersville, Alabama
WLRH Huntsville, Alabama
WNTM Mobile, Alabama
WLWI Montgomery, Alabama
WTSU Montgomery-Troy, Alabama
WQPR Muscle Shoals, Alabama
WAPR Selma, Alabama
WHBB Selma, Alabama
WFEB Sylacauga, Alabama
WVNN-FM Trinity, Alabama
WTBC Tuscaloosa, Alabama
WUAL-FM Tuscaloosa, Alabama
WVNA Tuscumbia, Alabama
KVRC Arkadelphia, Arkansas
KEWI Benton, Arkansas
KLCN Blytheville, Arkansas
KJMT Calico Rock, Arkansas
KCAB Dardanelle, Arkansas
KBSA El Dorado, Arkansas
KFAY Farmington, Arkansas
KUAF Fayetteville, Arkansas
KBJT Fordyce, Arkansas
KQEW Fordyce, Arkansas
KXJK Forrest City, Arkansas
KFPW Fort Smith, Arkansas
KWHN Fort Smith, Arkansas
KYHN Ft. Smith, Arkansas
KOTN Gould, Arkansas
KURM-FM Gravette, Arkansas
KELD-FM Hampton, Arkansas
KAWW Heber Springs, Arkansas
KZHS Hot Springs, Arkansas
KZNG Hot Springs, Arkansas
KASU Jonesboro, Arkansas
KBTM Jonesboro, Arkansas
KARN Little Rock, Arkansas
KUAR Little Rock, Arkansas
KBOK Malvern, Arkansas
KNBY Newport, Arkansas
KARV-FM Ola, Arkansas
KSMD Pangburn, Arkansas
KFFK Rogers, Arkansas
KARN-FM Sheridan, Arkansas
KWAK Stuttgart, Arkansas
KVOI Cortaro, Arizona
KAPR Douglas, Arizona
KNAU Flagstaff, Arizona
KPUB Flagstaff, Arizona
KVNA Flagstaff, Arizona
KTAR-FM Glendale, Arizona
KJAA Globe, Arizona
KNAG Grand Canyon, Arizona
KDJI Holbrook, Arizona
KUYI Hotevilla, Arizona
KAAA Kingman, Arizona
KNTR Lake Havasu City, Arizona
KFNN Mesa, Arizona
KNAD Page, Arizona
KLPZ Parker, Arizona
KBAQ Phoenix, Arizona
KFYI Phoenix, Arizona
KJZZ Phoenix, Arizona
KKNT Phoenix, Arizona
KNAQ Prescott, Arizona
KYCA Prescott, Arizona
KQNA Prescott Valley, Arizona
KNAA Show Low, Arizona
KVWM Show Low, Arizona
KTAN Sierra Vista, Arizona
KNST Tucson, Arizona
KQTH Tucson, Arizona
KUAZ Tucson, Arizona
KUAZ-FM Tucson, Arizona
KAWC Yuma, Arizona
KAWC-FM Yuma, Arizona
KBLU Yuma, Arizona
KHSU Arcata, California
KGEO Bakersfield, California
KNZR Bakersfield, California
KPRX Bakersfield, California
KSZL Barstow, California
KNCA Burney, California
KCHO Chico, California
KPAY Chico, California
KZFR Chico, California
KHSR Crescent City, California
KGOE Eureka, California
KWSW(AM) Eureka, California
KMJ Fresno, California
KVPR Fresno, California
KRLA Glendale, California
KNCO Grass Valley, California
KCRI Indio, California
KQAB(AM) Lake Isabella, California
KOSS Lancaster, California
KCAA Loma Linda, California
KSMA Lompoc, California
KFRN Long Beach, California
KFWB Los Angeles, California
KNX Los Angeles, California
KPFK Los Angeles, California
KTNQ Los Angeles, California
KLDD McCloud, California
KPMO Mendocino, California
KGAM Merced, California
KYOS Merced, California
KFIV Modesto, California
KMPH Modesto, California
KCRY Mojave, California
KNRY Monterey Bay, California
KSMC Moraga, California
KMJC Mount Shasta, California
KNSQ Mount Shasta, California
KVON Napa, California
KTOX Needles, California
KQEI-FM North Highlands, California
KNEW Oakland, California
KLAA Orange, California
KCRU Oxnard, California
KAZU Pacific Grove, California
KNWQ Palm Springs, California
KPSI Palm Springs, California
KDOW Palo Alto, California
KKXX Paradise, California
KPRL Paso Robles, California
KZYX Philo, California
KAHZ Pomona, California
KWKU Pomona, California
KVTA Port Hueneme, California
KTIP Porterville, California
KQNC Quincy, California
KFPR Redding, California
KQMS Redding, California
KWDJ Ridgecrest, California
KNHT Rio Dell, California
KLKX(FM) Rosamond, California
KFBK Sacramento, California
KXJZ Sacramento, California
KION Salinas, California
KTIE San Bernardino, California
KVCR San Bernardino, California
KCBQ San Diego, California
KFMB San Diego, California
KOGO San Diego, California
KPBS-FM San Diego, California
KCBS San Francisco, California
KFRC-FM San Francisco, California
KGO San Francisco, California
KSFO San Francisco, California
KLIV San Jose, California
KCBX San Luis Obispo, California
KVEC San Luis Obispo, California
KYNS San Luis Obispo, California
KCLU Santa Barbara, California
KZSB Santa Barbara, California
KSCO Santa Cruz, California
KSMX Santa Maria, California
KUHL Santa Maria, California
KCRW Santa Monica, California
KKZZ Santa Paula, California
KSRO Santa Rosa, California
KSMJ Shafter, California
KJPR Shasta Lake City, California
KIRN Simi Valley, California
KOWL South Lake Tahoe, California
KUOP Stockton, California
KSUE Susanville, California
KXJS Sutter, California
KKTO Tahoe City, California
KCLU-FM Thousand Oaks, California
KUNX Ventura, California
KVFG Victorville, California
KERN Wasco-Greenacres, California
KZYZ Willits, California
KRCB-FM Windsor, California
KNYR Yreka, California
KUBA Yuba City, California
KNWH Yucca Valley, California
KRZA Alamosa, Colorado
KAJX Aspen, Colorado
KNFO Basalt, Colorado
KCFC Boulder, Colorado
KRLN Canon City, Colorado
KCJX Carbondale, Colorado
KRDO Colorado Springs, Colorado
KVOR Colorado Springs, Colorado
KZNT Colorado Springs, Colorado

KVFC Cortez, Colorado
KPYR Craig, Colorado
KRAI Craig, Colorado
KCFR-FM Denver, Colorado
KNUS Denver, Colorado
KOA Denver, Colorado
KVOQ(AM) Denver, Colorado
KDGO Durango, Colorado
KFTM Fort Morgan, Colorado
KDNK Glenwood Springs, Colorado
KNZZ Grand Junction, Colorado
KPRN Grand Junction, Colorado
KFKA Greeley, Colorado
KUNC Greeley, Colorado
KHNC Johnstown, Colorado
KECC La Junta, Colorado
KPRH Montrose, Colorado
KVMT Montrose, Colorado
KWUF Pagosa Springs, Colorado
KVNF Paonia, Colorado
KCFP Pueblo, Colorado
KCSJ Pueblo, Colorado
KGFT Pueblo, Colorado
KKPC Pueblo, Colorado
KRDO-FM Security, Colorado
KRNC Steamboat Springs, Colorado
KPRE Vail, Colorado
KCOL Wellington, Colorado
WPRX Bristol, Connecticut
WSHU-FM Fairfield, Connecticut
WGCH Greenwich, Connecticut
WQAQ Hamden, Connecticut
WQUN Hamden, Connecticut
WDRC Hartford, Connecticut
WTIC Hartford, Connecticut
WZBG Litchfield, Connecticut
WNEZ Manchester, Connecticut
WMMW Meriden, Connecticut
WELI New Haven, Connecticut
WNLK Norwalk, Connecticut
WHDD-FM Sharon, Connecticut
WEDW-FM Stamford, Connecticut
WSTC Stamford, Connecticut
WSNG Torrington, Connecticut
WATR Waterbury, Connecticut
WWCO Waterbury, Connecticut
WSHU Westport, Connecticut
WILI Willimantic, Connecticut
WAMU Washington, District of Columbia
WFED Washington, District of Columbia
WMAL Washington, District of Columbia
WPFW Washington, District of Columbia
WTOP-FM Washington, District of Columbia
WDOV Dover, Delaware
WGMD Rehoboth Beach, Delaware
WDEL Wilmington, Delaware
WILM Wilmington, Delaware
WFLN Arcadia, Florida
WTWB Auburndale, Florida
WWJB Brooksville, Florida
WNZF Bunnell, Florida
WKFL Bushnell, Florida
WTAN Clearwater, Florida
WMMV Cocoa, Florida
WMEL Cocoa Beach, Florida
WJTK Columbia City, Florida
WNDB Daytona Beach, Florida
WTJV Deland, Florida
WYND Deland, Florida
WNWF Destin, Florida
WENG Englewood, Florida
WMYR Fort Myers, Florida
WJNX Fort Pierce, Florida
WQCS Fort Pierce, Florida
WFTW Fort Walton Beach, Florida
WDVH Gainesville, Florida
WRUF Gainesville, Florida
WNRP Gulf Breeze, Florida
WXYB Indian Rocks Beach, Florida
WJUF Inverness, Florida
WBOB Jacksonville, Florida
WJCT-FM Jacksonville, Florida
WJBW Jupiter, Florida
WYBX(FM) Key West, Florida
WBXY La Crosse, Florida
WLKF Lakeland, Florida
WPBR Lantana, Florida
WWBA Largo, Florida
WFFG Marathon, Florida
WKWM Marathon, Florida
WGUF Marco, Florida
WMMB Melbourne, Florida
WAQI Miami, Florida
WIOD Miami, Florida
WLRN-FM Miami, Florida
WQBA Miami, Florida
WSUA Miami, Florida
WSKY-FM Micanopy, Florida
WEBY Milton, Florida
WNOG Naples, Florida
WPSO New Port Richey, Florida
WKAT North Miami, Florida
WDBO Orlando, Florida
WMFE-FM Orlando, Florida
WELE Ormond Beach, Florida
WFSW Panama City, Florida
WKGC-FM Panama City, Florida
WLTG Panama City, Florida
WFLF-FM Parker, Florida
WCOA Pensacola, Florida
WCOA-FM Pensacola, Florida
WUWF Pensacola, Florida
WAMT Pine Castle Sky Lake, Florida
WFLF Pine Hills, Florida
WINK Pine Island Center, Florida
WPSL Port St. Lucie, Florida
WCCF Punta Gorda, Florida
WDEO-FM San Carlos Park, Florida
WSDO Sanford, Florida
WLSS Sarasota, Florida
WSRQ Sarasota, Florida
WFOY St. Augustine, Florida
WIWA St. Cloud, Florida
WSTU Stuart, Florida
WZAB Sweetwater, Florida
WANM Tallahassee, Florida
WFSU-FM Tallahassee, Florida
WTAL Tallahassee, Florida
WFLA Tampa, Florida
WHNZ Tampa, Florida
WUSF Tampa, Florida
WIXC Titusville, Florida
WJNO West Palm Beach, Florida
WPBI(FM) West Palm Beach, Florida
WPRD Winter Park, Florida
WALG Albany, Georgia
WUNV Albany, Georgia
WLTA Alpharetta, Georgia
WUGA Athens, Georgia
WAOK Atlanta, Georgia
WGKA Atlanta, Georgia
WGST Atlanta, Georgia
WSB Atlanta, Georgia
WGAC Augusta, Georgia
WGIG Brunswick, Georgia
WWIO-FM Brunswick, Georgia
WGRA Cairo, Georgia
WLBB Carrollton, Georgia
WUWG Carrollton, Georgia
WBHF Cartersville, Georgia
WYXC Cartersville, Georgia
WNGH-FM Chatsworth, Georgia
WGHC Clayton, Georgia
WRBN Clayton, Georgia
WAZX-FM Cleveland, Georgia
WMUM-FM Cochran, Georgia
WDAK Columbus, Georgia
WRCG Columbus, Georgia
WTJB Columbus, Georgia
WSRM Coosa, Georgia
WNGU Dahlonega, Georgia
WBLJ Dalton, Georgia
WPPR Demorest, Georgia
WSEM Donalsonville, Georgia
WCFO East Point, Georgia
WUFF-FM Eastman, Georgia
WSGC Elberton, Georgia
WJWV Fort Gaines, Georgia
WDUN Gainesville, Georgia
WHIE Griffin, Georgia
WKEU Griffin, Georgia
WCEH Hawkinsville, Georgia
WVCC Hogansville, Georgia
WSIZ-FM Jacksonville, Georgia
WTRP La Grange, Georgia
WVGA Lakeland, Georgia
WMAC Macon, Georgia
WMVG Milledgeville, Georgia
WMTM Moultrie, Georgia
WCNN North Atlanta, Georgia
WGPB Rome, Georgia
WLAQ Rome, Georgia
WRGA Rome, Georgia
WBMQ Savannah, Georgia
WSVH Savannah, Georgia
WTKS Savannah, Georgia
WWIO St. Marys, Georgia
WWNS Statesboro, Georgia
WJAT Swainsboro, Georgia
WNEG Toccoa, Georgia
WKWN Trenton, Georgia
WWET Valdosta, Georgia
WVOP Vidalia, Georgia
WJSP-FM Warm Springs, Georgia
WWGA(AM) Waycross, Georgia
WXVS Waycross, Georgia
WCGA Woodbine, Georgia
KGUM Hagatna, Guam
KHNU Hilo, Hawaii
KPUA Hilo, Hawaii
KHPR Honolulu, Hawaii
KHVH Honolulu, Hawaii
KIKI(AM) Honolulu, Hawaii
KIPO Honolulu, Hawaii
KRTR Honolulu, Hawaii
KWAI Honolulu, Hawaii
KNUI Kahului, Hawaii
KAOI Kihei, Hawaii
KQNG Lihue, Hawaii
KKUA Wailuku, Hawaii
KASI Ames, Iowa
KJAN Atlantic, Iowa
KWBG Boone, Iowa
KBUR Burlington, Iowa
KUNI Cedar Falls, Iowa
WMT Cedar Rapids, Iowa
KLNI Decorah, Iowa
WHO Des Moines, Iowa
WDBQ Dubuque, Iowa
KIOW Forest City, Iowa
KVFD Fort Dodge, Iowa
KGRN Grinnell, Iowa
KXIC Iowa City, Iowa
WSUI Iowa City, Iowa
KIFG-FM Iowa Falls, Iowa
KOKX Keokuk, Iowa
KLEM Le Mars, Iowa
KFJB Marshalltown, Iowa
KRNI Mason City, Iowa
KICJ(FM) Mitchellville, Iowa
KCOB Newton, Iowa
KOEL Oelwein, Iowa
KOJI Okoboji, Iowa
KBIZ Ottumwa, Iowa
KLEE Ottumwa, Iowa
KPVL Postville, Iowa
KIWA Sheldon, Iowa
KMA Shenandoah, Iowa
KSCJ Sioux City, Iowa
KWIT Sioux City, Iowa
KCII Washington, Iowa
KCII-FM Washington, Iowa
KXEL Waterloo, Iowa
KBOI Boise, Idaho
KBSU-FM Boise, Idaho
KBSX Boise, Idaho
KBFI Bonners Ferry, Idaho
KIBX Bonners Ferry, Idaho
KBSY Burley, Idaho
KVNI Coeur D'Alene, Idaho
KNWO Cottonwood, Idaho
KID Idaho Falls, Idaho
KIKX Ketchum, Idaho
KBSM McCall, Idaho
KBSQ McCall, Idaho
KRFA-FM Moscow, Idaho
KIDO Nampa, Idaho
KWEI Notus, Idaho
KEGE Pocatello, Idaho
KISU-FM Pocatello, Idaho
KSEI Pocatello, Idaho
KWIK Pocatello, Idaho
KSPT Sandpoint, Idaho
KBSS Sun Valley, Idaho
KEZJ Twin Falls, Idaho
KLIX Twin Falls, Idaho
WRMJ Aledo, Illinois
WBGZ Alton, Illinois
WBIG Aurora, Illinois
WBYS Canton, Illinois
WCIL Carbondale, Illinois
WDWS Champaign, Illinois
KSGM Chester, Illinois

WBEZ Chicago, Illinois
WCRX Chicago, Illinois
WGN(AM) Chicago, Illinois
WIND Chicago, Illinois
WLS Chicago, Illinois
WRTO Chicago, Illinois
WHOW Clinton, Illinois
WDAN Danville, Illinois
WSOY Decatur, Illinois
WLBK Dekalb, Illinois
WNIJ Dekalb, Illinois
WIXN Dixon, Illinois
WCRA Effingham, Illinois
WRMN Elgin, Illinois
WFIW Fairfield, Illinois
WGNN Fisher, Illinois
WNIE Freeport, Illinois
WGIL Galesburg, Illinois
WKYX-FM Golconda, Illinois
WJPF Herrin, Illinois
WJIL Jacksonville, Illinois
WLDS Jacksonville, Illinois
WKIF Kankakee, Illinois
WKEI Kewanee, Illinois
WNIW La Salle, Illinois
WLPO Lasalle, Illinois
WSMI Litchfield, Illinois
WIUM Macomb, Illinois
WGGH Marion, Illinois
WLBH Mattoon, Illinois
WBEQ Morris, Illinois
WCSJ Morris, Illinois
WCSJ-FM Morris, Illinois
WVSI Mt. Vernon, Illinois
WINI Murphysboro, Illinois
WUSI Olney, Illinois
WCMY Ottawa, Illinois
WPRS Paris, Illinois
WCBU Peoria, Illinois
WMBD Peoria, Illinois
WIPA Pittsfield, Illinois
WZOE Princeton, Illinois
WGEM Quincy, Illinois
WGEM-FM Quincy, Illinois
WQUB Quincy, Illinois
WTAD Quincy, Illinois
WRHL Rochelle, Illinois
WVIK Rock Island, Illinois
WROK Rockford, Illinois
WJBD-FM Salem, Illinois
WCCI Savanna, Illinois
WHCO Sparta, Illinois
WMAY Springfield, Illinois
WTAX Springfield, Illinois
WUIS Springfield, Illinois
WNIQ Sterling, Illinois
WSDR Sterling, Illinois
WSPL Streator, Illinois
WTIM-FM Taylorville, Illinois
WILL Urbana, Illinois
WIUW Warsaw, Illinois
WKRS Waukegan, Illinois
WFRX West Frankfort, Illinois
WBSB Anderson, Indiana
WHBU Anderson, Indiana
WBIW Bedford, Indiana
WZBD Berne, Indiana
WFHB Bloomington, Indiana
WFIU Bloomington, Indiana
WGCL Bloomington, Indiana
WHON Centerville, Indiana
WBEW Chesterton, Indiana
WCSI Columbus, Indiana
WTRC Elkhart, Indiana
WVPE Elkhart, Indiana
WGBF Evansville, Indiana
WNIN-FM Evansville, Indiana
WBOI Fort Wayne, Indiana
WOWO Fort Wayne, Indiana
WLTH Gary, Indiana
WREB Greencastle, Indiana
WTRE Greensburg, Indiana
WBSH Hagerstown, Indiana
WJOB Hammond, Indiana
WFYI-FM Indianapolis, Indiana
WIBC Indianapolis, Indiana
WXNT Indianapolis, Indiana
WIOU Kokomo, Indiana
WSAL Logansport, Indiana
WLPR-FM Lowell, Indiana
WXGO Madison, Indiana
WBSW Marion, Indiana
WBST Muncie, Indiana
WLBC-FM Muncie, Indiana
WFIA-FM New Albany, Indiana
WNDA New Albany, Indiana
WBSJ Portland, Indiana
WRAY Princeton, Indiana
WZZB Seymour, Indiana
WSBT South Bend, Indiana
WAKE Valparaiso, Indiana
WAOV Vincennes, Indiana
WBAA West Lafayette, Indiana
WBAA-FM West Lafayette, Indiana
KGGF Coffeyville, Kansas
KDCC Dodge City, Kansas
KGNO Dodge City, Kansas
KVOE Emporia, Kansas
KIUL Garden City, Kansas
KLOE Goodland, Kansas
KHCT Great Bend, Kansas
KVGB Great Bend, Kansas
KZAN Hays, Kansas
KZNA Hill City, Kansas
KHCC-FM Hutchinson, Kansas
KJCK Junction City, Kansas
KLWN Lawrence, Kansas
KSCB Liberal, Kansas
KMAN Manhattan, Kansas
KKAN Phillipsburg, Kansas
KHCD Salina, Kansas
KINA Salina, Kansas
KSAL Salina, Kansas
KYUL Scott City, Kansas
KMAJ Topeka, Kansas
WIBW Topeka, Kansas
KLEY Wellington, Kansas
KMUW Wichita, Kansas
KNSS Wichita, Kansas
KQAM Wichita, Kansas
WKXO Berea, Kentucky
WKCT Bowling Green, Kentucky
WKYU-FM Bowling Green, Kentucky
WCTT Corbin, Kentucky
WEKF Corbin, Kentucky
WKDP Corbin, Kentucky
WCPM Cumberland, Kentucky
WHIR Danville, Kentucky
WKUE Elizabethtown, Kentucky
WEKH Hazard, Kentucky
WKPB Henderson, Kentucky
WNKU Highland Heights, Kentucky
WHOP Hopkinsville, Kentucky
WLAP Lexington, Kentucky
WUKY Lexington, Kentucky
WVLK Lexington, Kentucky
WFPL Louisville, Kentucky
WGTK Louisville, Kentucky
WHAS Louisville, Kentucky
WTTL Madisonville, Kentucky
WNGO Mayfield, Kentucky
WMST Mt. Sterling, Kentucky
WKMS-FM Murray, Kentucky
WNBS Murray, Kentucky
WVJS Owensboro, Kentucky
WKYX Paducah, Kentucky
WKYH Paintsville, Kentucky
WEKU Richmond, Kentucky
WEKY Richmond, Kentucky
WVKY Shelbyville, Kentucky
WDCL-FM Somerset, Kentucky
KLSA Alexandria, Louisiana
WJBO Baton Rouge, Louisiana
WRKF Baton Rouge, Louisiana
KEUN Eunice, Louisiana
WWL-FM Kenner, Louisiana
KVOL Lafayette, Louisiana
KAOK Lake Charles, Louisiana
KEDM Monroe, Louisiana
KMLB Monroe, Louisiana
KNOC Natchitoches, Louisiana
WGSO New Orleans, Louisiana
WRBH New Orleans, Louisiana
WRNO-FM New Orleans, Louisiana
WWL New Orleans, Louisiana
WWNO New Orleans, Louisiana
KSLO Opelousas, Louisiana
KDAQ Shreveport, Louisiana
KEEL Shreveport, Louisiana
KTLN Thibodaux, Louisiana
KNCB Vivian, Louisiana
WHAB Acton, Massachusetts
WPNI Amherst, Massachusetts
WARL Attleboro, Massachusetts
WBUR-FM Boston, Massachusetts
WBZ Boston, Massachusetts
WGBH(FM) Boston, Massachusetts
WILD Boston, Massachusetts
WXBR Brockton, Massachusetts
WBNW Concord, Massachusetts
WHNP East Longmeadow, Massachusetts
WSAR Fall River, Massachusetts
WGAW Gardner, Massachusetts
WBOQ Gloucester, Massachusetts
WAMQ Great Barrington, Massachusetts
WCAP Lowell, Massachusetts
WVBF Middleborough Center, Massachusetts
WMLN-FM Milton, Massachusetts
WNAN Nantucket, Massachusetts
WBSM New Bedford, Massachusetts
WDIS Norfolk, Massachusetts
WESO Southbridge, Massachusetts
WHYN Springfield, Massachusetts
WGTX Truro, Massachusetts
WBUR West Yarmouth, Massachusetts
WXTK West Yarmouth, Massachusetts
WNNZ Westfield, Massachusetts
WCAI Woods Hole, Massachusetts
WTAG Worcester, Massachusetts
WEAA Baltimore, Maryland
WYPR Baltimore, Maryland
WTLP Braddock Heights, Maryland
WCBC Cumberland, Maryland
WFMD Frederick, Maryland
WWFD Frederick, Maryland
WYPF Frederick, Maryland
WHAG Halfway, Maryland
WJSS Havre De Grace, Maryland
WPTX Lexington Park, Maryland
WSDL Ocean City, Maryland
WYPO Ocean City, Maryland
WICO Salisbury, Maryland
WBQH(AM) Silver Spring, Maryland
WVQM Augusta, Maine
WMEH Bangor, Maine
WMED Calais, Maine
WMEP Camden, Maine
WCXU Caribou, Maine
WMEF Fort Kent, Maine
WVOM Howland, Maine
WCXX Madawaska, Maine
WJCX Pittsfield, Maine
WGAN Portland, Maine
WMEA Portland, Maine
WEGP Presque Isle, Maine
WMEM Presque Isle, Maine
WCXV Van Buren, Maine
WNZS Veazie, Maine
WMEW Waterville, Maine
WABJ Adrian, Michigan
WGVU-FM Allendale, Michigan
WCML-FM Alpena, Michigan
WUOM Ann Arbor, Michigan
WBCK-FM Battle Creek, Michigan
WUCX-FM Bay City, Michigan
WSJM-FM Benton Harbor, Michigan
WHFB Benton Harbor-St. Jo, Michigan
WBRN Big Rapids, Michigan
WMKT Charlevoix, Michigan
WDET-FM Detroit, Michigan
WDTK Detroit, Michigan
WJR Detroit, Michigan
WICV East Jordan, Michigan
WKAR East Lansing, Michigan
WKAR-FM East Lansing, Michigan
WCHT Escanaba, Michigan
WWCK Flint, Michigan
WBLU-FM Grand Rapids, Michigan
WVGR Grand Rapids, Michigan
WGLM Greenville, Michigan
WMPL Hancock, Michigan
WCMW-FM Harbor Springs, Michigan
WHTC Holland, Michigan
WGGL-FM Houghton, Michigan
WIAA Interlochen, Michigan
WMIQ Iron Mountain, Michigan
WIAN Ishpeming, Michigan
WKHM Jackson, Michigan
WKMI Kalamazoo, Michigan
WKZO Kalamazoo, Michigan
WMUK Kalamazoo, Michigan
WGVU Kentwood, Michigan
WJNL Kingsley, Michigan

WILS Lansing, Michigan
WJIM Lansing, Michigan
WKLA Ludington, Michigan
WLMN Manistee, Michigan
WMTE Manistee, Michigan
WPIQ Manistique, Michigan
WDMJ Marquette, Michigan
WNMU-FM Marquette, Michigan
WAVC Mio, Michigan
WCMU-FM Mount Pleasant, Michigan
WAZP Munising, Michigan
WGVS Muskegon, Michigan
WKBZ Muskegon, Michigan
WCMB-FM Oscoda, Michigan
WPHM Port Huron, Michigan
WSGW Saginaw, Michigan
WMIC Sandusky, Michigan
WKNW Sault Sainte Marie, Michigan
WCMZ-FM Sault Ste. Marie, Michigan
WSJM St. Joseph, Michigan
WWCM Standish, Michigan
WICA Traverse City, Michigan
WTCM Traverse City, Michigan
WBLV Twin Lake, Michigan
WGVS-FM Whitehall, Michigan
WEMU Ypsilanti, Michigan
WPNW Zeeland, Michigan
KASM Albany, Minnesota
KATE Albert Lea, Minnesota
KAUS Austin, Minnesota
KNSE Austin, Minnesota
WWWI Baxter, Minnesota
KNBJ Bemidji, Minnesota
KBPN Brainerd, Minnesota
KRWC Buffalo, Minnesota
WIRN Buhl, Minnesota
WSCN Cloquet, Minnesota
KNSR Collegeville, Minnesota
KDLM Detroit Lakes, Minnesota
KDAL Duluth, Minnesota
WEBC Duluth, Minnesota
WIRC Ely, Minnesota
KSUM Fairmont, Minnesota
KDHL Faribault, Minnesota
KBRF Fergus Falls, Minnesota
KNWF Fergus Falls, Minnesota
WLSN Grand Marais, Minnesota
KDWA Hastings, Minnesota
WGRH Hinckley, Minnesota
KDUZ Hutchinson, Minnesota
KXLC La Crescent, Minnesota
KLTF Little Falls, Minnesota
KTOE Mankato, Minnesota
KMHL Marshall, Minnesota
KTIS Minneapolis, Minnesota
WCCO Minneapolis, Minnesota
WWTC Minneapolis, Minnesota
KNOW-FM Minneapolis-St. Paul, Minnesota
KCCD Moorhead, Minnesota
KMRS Morris, Minnesota
WNMT Nashwauk, Minnesota
KCHK New Prague, Minnesota
WWWI-FM Pillager, Minnesota
WCMP Pine City, Minnesota
WCMP-FM Pine City, Minnesota
KLOH Pipestone, Minnesota
KRFI Redwood Falls, Minnesota
KROC Rochester, Minnesota
KRXW Roseau, Minnesota
KNSI St. Cloud, Minnesota
WJON St. Cloud, Minnesota
KKAQ Thief River Falls, Minnesota
KNTN Thief River Falls, Minnesota
KTRF Thief River Falls, Minnesota
KWLM Willmar, Minnesota
KDOM Windom, Minnesota
KDOM-FM Windom, Minnesota
KWNO Winona, Minnesota
KWOA Worthington, Minnesota
KNSW Worthington-Marshall, Minnesota
KGNA-FM Arnold, Missouri
KSGF-FM Ash Grove, Missouri
KSWM Aurora, Missouri
KKOZ-FM Ava, Missouri
KAAN Bethany, Missouri
KYOO Bolivar, Missouri
KBFL-FM Buffalo, Missouri
KAPE Cape Girardeau, Missouri
KRCU Cape Girardeau, Missouri
KZIM Cape Girardeau, Missouri
KCHI Chillicothe, Missouri
KRNW Chillicothe, Missouri
KBIA Columbia, Missouri
KFRU Columbia, Missouri
KOPN Columbia, Missouri
KGNN-FM Cuba, Missouri
KREI Farmington, Missouri
KSSZ Fayette, Missouri
KJFF Festus, Missouri
KHMO Hannibal, Missouri
KLIK Jefferson City, Missouri
KWOS Jefferson City, Missouri
KCUR-FM Kansas City, Missouri
KKFI Kansas City, Missouri
KMBZ Kansas City, Missouri
KLWT Lebanon, Missouri
KMAL Malden, Missouri
KNIM Maryville, Missouri
KXCV Maryville, Missouri
KXEO Mexico, Missouri
KRMS Osage Beach, Missouri
KFMO Park Hills, Missouri
KBDZ Perryville, Missouri
KCOZ Point Lookout, Missouri
KSMS-FM Point Lookout, Missouri
KWOC Poplar Bluff, Missouri
KMIS Portageville, Missouri
KMST Rolla, Missouri
KTTR Rolla, Missouri
KSMO Salem, Missouri
KSIS Sedalia, Missouri
KQMO Shell Knob, Missouri
KSIM Sikeston, Missouri
KLFJ Springfield, Missouri
KSGF Springfield, Missouri
KSMU Springfield, Missouri
KWTO Springfield, Missouri
KTTR-FM St. James, Missouri
KFEQ St. Joseph, Missouri
KMOX St. Louis, Missouri
KTRS St. Louis, Missouri
KWMU St. Louis, Missouri
KSEF Ste. Genevieve, Missouri
KTUI Sullivan, Missouri
KSAR Thayer, Missouri
KTTN-FM Trenton, Missouri
KGNV Washington, Missouri
KSMW West Plains, Missouri
KWPM West Plains, Missouri
KUKU Willow Springs, Missouri
WAMY Amory, Mississippi
WMAH-FM Biloxi, Mississippi
WTNI Biloxi, Mississippi
WMAE-FM Booneville, Mississippi
WMAU-FM Bude, Mississippi
WCJU Columbia, Mississippi
WADI Corinth, Mississippi
WMAO-FM Greenwood, Mississippi
WHSY Hattiesburg, Mississippi
WURC Holly Springs, Mississippi
WTCD Indianola, Mississippi
WJQS Jackson, Mississippi
WJSU-FM Jackson, Mississippi
WMPN-FM Jackson, Mississippi
WMXI Laurel, Mississippi
WJZD-FM Long Beach, Mississippi
WKBB Mantee, Mississippi
WALT Meridian, Mississippi
WMAW-FM Meridian, Mississippi
WMOX Meridian, Mississippi
WMAB-FM Mississippi State, Mississippi
WBUV Moss Point, Mississippi
WNAT Natchez, Mississippi
WNAU New Albany, Mississippi
WMAV-FM Oxford, Mississippi
WJNT Pearl, Mississippi
WFMM Sumrall, Mississippi
KGVW Belgrade, Montana
KBLG Billings, Montana
KBUL Billings, Montana
KEMC Billings, Montana
KBMC Bozeman, Montana
KMMS Bozeman, Montana
KAPC Butte, Montana
KGVA Fort Belknap Agency, Montana
KGPR Great Falls, Montana
KQDI Great Falls, Montana
KLYQ Hamilton, Montana
KUFN Hamilton, Montana
KHDN Hardin, Montana
KBLL Helena, Montana
KCAP Helena, Montana
KUHM Helena, Montana
KGEZ Kalispell, Montana
KOFI Kalispell, Montana
KUKL Kalispell, Montana
KBSR Laurel, Montana
KYPF Stanford, Montana
KJJR Whitefish, Montana
WSPC Albemarle, North Carolina
WZKY Albemarle, North Carolina
WCQS Asheville, North Carolina
WWNC Asheville, North Carolina
WTKF Atlantic, North Carolina
WBJD Atlantic Beach, North Carolina
WXIT Blowing Rock, North Carolina
WLTT Bolivia, North Carolina
WATA Boone, North Carolina
WCHL Chapel Hill, North Carolina
WUNC Chapel Hill, North Carolina
WBT Charlotte, North Carolina
WFAE Charlotte, North Carolina
WNCU Durham, North Carolina
WGAI Elizabeth City, North Carolina
WFNC Fayetteville, North Carolina
WFSS Fayetteville, North Carolina
WIDU Fayetteville, North Carolina
WFQS Franklin, North Carolina
WFSC Franklin, North Carolina
WGBR Goldsboro, North Carolina
WSML Graham, North Carolina
WHKY Hickory, North Carolina
WJNC Jacksonville, North Carolina
WTRU Kernersville, North Carolina
WKNS Kinston, North Carolina
WJRI Lenoir, North Carolina
WLXN Lexington, North Carolina
WOBX-FM Manteo, North Carolina
WUND-FM Manteo, North Carolina
WYQS Mars Hill, North Carolina
WCVP Murphy, North Carolina
WTEB New Bern, North Carolina
WZNB New Bern, North Carolina
WAUG New Hope, North Carolina
WGCR Pisgah Forest, North Carolina
WPTF Raleigh, North Carolina
WRQM Rocky Mount, North Carolina
WCAB Rutherfordton, North Carolina
WSTP Salisbury, North Carolina
WNCA Siler City, North Carolina
WEEB Southern Pines, North Carolina
WNCW Spindale, North Carolina
WSIC Statesville, North Carolina
WTXY Whiteville, North Carolina
WHQR Wilmington, North Carolina
WFDD Winston-Salem, North Carolina
WSJS Winston-Salem, North Carolina
WSNC Winston-Salem, North Carolina
KCND Bismarck, North Dakota
KFYR Bismarck, North Dakota
KLXX Bismarck-Mandan, North Dakota
KDAK Carrington, North Dakota
KDLR Devils Lake, North Dakota
KDPR Dickinson, North Dakota
KFBN Fargo, North Dakota
KFGO Fargo, North Dakota
WDAY Fargo, North Dakota
KKXL Grand Forks, North Dakota
KNOX Grand Forks, North Dakota
KPRJ Jamestown, North Dakota
KNDK Langdon, North Dakota
KQLX Lisbon, North Dakota
KHRT Minot, North Dakota
KMPR Minot, North Dakota
KDDR Oakes, North Dakota
KOVC Valley City, North Dakota
KEYZ Williston, North Dakota
KCOW Alliance, Nebraska
KNCY-FM Auburn, Nebraska
KWBE Beatrice, Nebraska
KJSK Columbus, Nebraska
KGMT Fairbury, Nebraska
KHUB Fremont, Nebraska
KRGI Grand Island, Nebraska
KGFW Kearney, Nebraska
KFOR Lincoln, Nebraska
KLIN Lincoln, Nebraska
WJAG Norfolk, Nebraska
KODY North Platte, Nebraska
KFAB Omaha, Nebraska
KIOS-FM Omaha, Nebraska
KNEB Scottsbluff, Nebraska
KTIC West Point, Nebraska

WEVO(FM) Concord, New Hampshire
WKXL Concord, New Hampshire
WTSN Dover, New Hampshire
WXEX Exeter, New Hampshire
WEVH Hanover, New Hampshire
WTSL Hanover, New Hampshire
WTPL Hillsboro, New Hampshire
WEVJ Jackson, New Hampshire
WEVN Keene, New Hampshire
WKBK Keene, New Hampshire
WZBK Keene, New Hampshire
WUVR Lebanon, New Hampshire
WGIR Manchester, New Hampshire
WEVS Nashua, New Hampshire
WSMN Nashua, New Hampshire
WNTK-FM New London, New Hampshire
WPKX(AM) Rochester, New Hampshire
WCCM Salem, New Hampshire
WASR Wolfeboro, New Hampshire
WNJN-FM Atlantic City, New Jersey
WNJS-FM Berlin, New Jersey
WNJB-FM Bridgeton, New Jersey
WNJZ Cape May Court House, New Jersey
WNYM Hackensack, New Jersey
WRNJ Hackettstown, New Jersey
WBJB-FM Lincroft, New Jersey
WNJM Manahawkin, New Jersey
WNJY Netcong, New Jersey
WVNJ Oakland, New Jersey
WIBG Ocean City/Somers Po, New Jersey
WVPH Piscataway, New Jersey
WNJP Sussex, New Jersey
WNJT-FM Trenton, New Jersey
KINN Alamogordo, New Mexico
KDEF Albuquerque, New Mexico
KKOB Albuquerque, New Mexico
KUNM Albuquerque, New Mexico
KRRT Arroyo Seco, New Mexico
KWKA Clovis, New Mexico
KENN Farmington, New Mexico
KSJE Farmington, New Mexico
KUSW Flora Vista, New Mexico
KGLP Gallup, New Mexico
KYKK Humble City, New Mexico
KPZA-FM Jal, New Mexico
KOBE Las Cruces, New Mexico
KRWG Las Cruces, New Mexico
KSNM Las Cruces, New Mexico
KNMX Las Vegas, New Mexico
KRSN Los Alamos, New Mexico
KTBL Los Ranchos, New Mexico
KMTH Maljamar, New Mexico
KSEL Portales, New Mexico
KBIM Roswell, New Mexico
KRUI Ruidoso Downs, New Mexico
KKIM-FM Santa Fe, New Mexico
KTRC Santa Fe, New Mexico
KNCC Elko, Nevada
KTSN Elko, Nevada
KDWN Las Vegas, Nevada
KWPR Lund, Nevada
KXNT North Las Vegas, Nevada
KLNR Panaca, Nevada
KNUU Paradise, Nevada
KKOH Reno, Nevada
KUNR Reno, Nevada
KBZZ Sparks, Nevada
KQLO Sun Valley, Nevada
KTPH Tonopah, Nevada
KWNA Winnemucca, Nevada
WAMC-FM Albany, New York
WROW Albany, New York
WVTL Amsterdam, New York
WYSL Avon, New York
WBTA Batavia, New York
WINR Binghamton, New York
WNBF Binghamton, New York
WSKG-FM Binghamton, New York
WSQX-FM Binghamton, New York
WCWP Brookville, New York
WBEN Buffalo, New York
WNED Buffalo, New York
WCAN Canajoharie, New York
WCGR Canandaigua, New York
WENI Corning, New York
WSQE Corning, New York
WWLE Cornwall, New York
WFLR Dundee, New York
WDOE Dunkirk, New York
WENY Elmira, New York
WGSU Geneseo, New York
WEOS Geneva, New York
WGVA Geneva, New York
WWSC Glens Falls, New York
WLEA Hornell, New York
WSQA Hornell, New York
WWLZ Horseheads, New York
WHCU Ithaca, New York
WSQG-FM Ithaca, New York
WJTN Jamestown, New York
WUBJ Jamestown, New York
WJFF Jeffersonville, New York
WAMK Kingston, New York
WGHQ Kingston, New York
WLVL Lockport, New York
WLLG Lowville, New York
WOSR Middletown, New York
WCBS New York, New York
WFUV New York, New York
WINS New York, New York
WSUF Noyack, New York
WOEN Olean, New York
WMCR Oneida, New York
WSQC-FM Oneonta, New York
WNYO Oswego, New York
WEBO Owego, New York
WCEL Plattsburgh, New York
WKIP Poughkeepsie, New York
WRCR Ramapo, New York
WBEE-FM Rochester, New York
WHAM Rochester, New York
WNBZ Saranac Lake, New York
WGY Schenectady, New York
WRLI-FM Southampton, New York
WUSB Stony Brook, New York
WAER Syracuse, New York
WSYR Syracuse, New York
WANC Ticonderoga, New York
WIBX Utica, New York
WCJW Warsaw, New York
WTNY Watertown, New York
WUAM Watervliet, New York
WAKR Akron, Ohio
WHLO Akron, Ohio
WYBL Ashtabula, Ohio
WATH Athens, Ohio
WOUB Athens, Ohio
WBLL Bellefontaine, Ohio
WCVV Belpre, Ohio
WGBE Bryan, Ohio
WAIS Buchtel, Ohio
WOUC-FM Cambridge, Ohio
WBEX Chillicothe, Ohio
WOUH-FM Chillicothe, Ohio
WKRC Cincinnati, Ohio
WLW Cincinnati, Ohio
WVXU Cincinnati, Ohio
WCPN Cleveland, Ohio
WTAM Cleveland, Ohio
WERE Cleveland Heights, Ohio
WCBE Columbus, Ohio
WMNI Columbus, Ohio
WTVN Columbus, Ohio
WWOW Conneaut, Ohio
WHIO Dayton, Ohio
WGDE Defiance, Ohio
WEOL Elyria, Ohio
WFIN Findlay, Ohio
WMOH Hamilton, Ohio
WIRO Ironton, Ohio
WOUL-FM Ironton, Ohio
WFCO Lancaster, Ohio
WGLE Lima, Ohio
WIMA Lima, Ohio
WMAN Mansfield, Ohio
WMOA Marietta, Ohio
WMRT Marietta, Ohio
WMRN Marion, Ohio
WMVO Mount Vernon, Ohio
WKRJ New Philadelphia, Ohio
WCLT Newark, Ohio
WMUB Oxford, Ohio
WCWA Toledo, Ohio
WGTE-FM Toledo, Ohio
WSPD Toledo, Ohio
WBTC Uhrichsville, Ohio
WYSO Yellow Springs, Ohio
WASN Youngstown, Ohio
WKBN Youngstown, Ohio
WYSU Youngstown, Ohio
WOUZ-FM Zanesville, Ohio
KOCU Altus, Oklahoma
KWHW Altus, Oklahoma
KWON Bartlesville, Oklahoma
KCLI Clinton, Oklahoma
KYCU Clinton, Oklahoma
KUSH Cushing, Oklahoma
KCRC Enid, Oklahoma
KGWA Enid, Oklahoma
KTJS Hobart, Oklahoma
KIHN Hugo, Oklahoma
KOSN Ketchum, Oklahoma
KCCU Lawton, Oklahoma
KGOU Norman, Oklahoma
KOKC Oklahoma City, Oklahoma
KQCV Oklahoma City, Oklahoma
KTOK Oklahoma City, Oklahoma
KOKL Okmulgee, Oklahoma
KPGM Pawhuska, Oklahoma
KRMG-FM Sand Springs, Oklahoma
KOSU Stillwater, Oklahoma
KSPI Stillwater, Oklahoma
KRMG Tulsa, Oklahoma
KWGS Tulsa, Oklahoma
KSMF Ashland, Oregon
KSOR Ashland, Oregon
KAST Astoria, Oregon
KBKR Baker, Oregon
KOBK Baker City, Oregon
KBND Bend, Oregon
KBNW Bend, Oregon
KOAB-FM Bend, Oregon
KSBA Coos Bay, Oregon
KWRO Coquille, Oregon
KLOO Corvallis, Oregon
KOAC Corvallis, Oregon
KNND Cottage Grove, Oregon
KWVR Enterprise, Oregon
KOPB Eugene, Oregon
KPNW Eugene, Oregon
KUGN Eugene, Oregon
KOGL Gleneden Beach, Oregon
KZZR Government Camp, Oregon
KAGI Grants Pass, Oregon
KAJO Grants Pass, Oregon
KUIK Hillsboro, Oregon
KAGO Klamath Falls, Oregon
KFLS Klamath Falls, Oregon
KLMF Klamath Falls, Oregon
KSKF Klamath Falls, Oregon
KLBM La Grande, Oregon
KTVR-FM La Grande, Oregon
KOAP Lakeview, Oregon
KGAL Lebanon, Oregon
KDOV Medford, Oregon
KMED Medford, Oregon
KOOZ Myrtle Point, Oregon
KLCO Newport, Oregon
KBBR North Bend, Oregon
KSRV Ontario, Oregon
KRBM Pendleton, Oregon
KUMA Pendleton, Oregon
KAPL Phoenix, Oregon
KCMX Phoenix, Oregon
KBNP Portland, Oregon
KEX Portland, Oregon
KOPB-FM Portland, Oregon
KPOJ Portland, Oregon
KXTG(AM) Portland, Oregon
KDUN Reedsport, Oregon
KQEN Roseburg, Oregon
KSRS Roseburg, Oregon
KTBR Roseburg, Oregon
KOHI St. Helens, Oregon
KSJK Talent, Oregon
KACI The Dalles, Oregon
KMBD(AM) Tillamook, Oregon
KTMK Tillamook, Oregon
KCUP Toledo, Oregon
KPAM Troutdale, Oregon
KLWJ(AM) Umatilla, Oregon
KWLZ-FM West Linn, Oregon
WDIY Allentown, Pennsylvania
WJCS Allentown, Pennsylvania
WRTA Altoona, Pennsylvania
WILK-FM Avoca, Pennsylvania
WBVP Beaver Falls, Pennsylvania
WBLF Bellefonte, Pennsylvania
WGPA Bethlehem, Pennsylvania
WHLM Bloomsburg, Pennsylvania
WISR Butler, Pennsylvania
WHYL Carlisle, Pennsylvania
WZUM Carnegie, Pennsylvania

WCHA Chambersburg, Pennsylvania
WWCH Clarion, Pennsylvania
WFRM Coudersport, Pennsylvania
WCED Du Bois, Pennsylvania
WRDD Ebensburg, Pennsylvania
WJET Erie, Pennsylvania
WPSE Erie, Pennsylvania
WQLN-FM Erie, Pennsylvania
WZSK Everett, Pennsylvania
WFRA Franklin, Pennsylvania
WGET Gettysburg, Pennsylvania
WHP Harrisburg, Pennsylvania
WITF-FM Harrisburg, Pennsylvania
WAZL Hazleton, Pennsylvania
WRKK Hughesville, Pennsylvania
WLLI(AM) Huntingdon, Pennsylvania
WKGE Johnstown, Pennsylvania
WNTJ Johnstown, Pennsylvania
WNPV Lansdale, Pennsylvania
WLBR Lebanon, Pennsylvania
WIEZ Lewistown, Pennsylvania
WWGE Loretto, Pennsylvania
WJSM-FM Martinsburg, Pennsylvania
WWBJ Martinsburg, Pennsylvania
WMGW Meadville, Pennsylvania
WPLY Mount Pocono, Pennsylvania
KYW Philadelphia, Pennsylvania
WPHB Philipsburg, Pennsylvania
KDKA Pittsburgh, Pennsylvania
KQV Pittsburgh, Pennsylvania
WDVE Pittsburgh, Pennsylvania
WPGB Pittsburgh, Pennsylvania
WEMR Pleasant Gap, Pennsylvania
WPAZ Pottstown, Pennsylvania
WECZ Punxsutawney, Pennsylvania
WYBF Radnor Township, Pennsylvania
WEEU Reading, Pennsylvania
WBZU Scranton, Pennsylvania
WVIA-FM Scranton, Pennsylvania
WPIC Sharon, Pennsylvania
WNTW Somerset, Pennsylvania
WRSC State College, Pennsylvania
WKOK Sunbury, Pennsylvania
WTIV Titusville, Pennsylvania
WKZN West Hazleton, Pennsylvania
WLIH Whitneyville, Pennsylvania
WILK Wilkes-Barre, Pennsylvania
WRAK Williamsport, Pennsylvania
WVYA Williamsport, Pennsylvania
WWPA Williamsport, Pennsylvania
WSBA York, Pennsylvania
WCMN Arecibo, Puerto Rico
WYAC Cabo Rojo, Puerto Rico
WLEY Cayey, Puerto Rico
WRXD Fajardo, Puerto Rico
WMSW Hatillo, Puerto Rico
WALO Humacao, Puerto Rico
WMNT Manati, Puerto Rico
WKJB Mayaguez, Puerto Rico
WEKO Morovis, Puerto Rico
WEXS Patillas, Puerto Rico
WDEP Ponce, Puerto Rico
WISO Ponce, Puerto Rico
WPAB Ponce, Puerto Rico
WPRP Ponce, Puerto Rico
WUKQ Ponce, Puerto Rico
WSOL San German, Puerto Rico
WAPA San Juan, Puerto Rico
WIAC San Juan, Puerto Rico
WIPR San Juan, Puerto Rico
WKAQ San Juan, Puerto Rico
WSKN San Juan, Puerto Rico
WUNO San Juan, Puerto Rico
WUPR Utuado, Puerto Rico
WENA Yauco, Puerto Rico
WKFE Yauco, Puerto Rico
WCRI(AM) Hope Valley, Rhode Island
WRNI-FM Narragansett Pier, Rhode Island
WHJJ Providence, Rhode Island
WPRO Providence, Rhode Island
WRNI Providence, Rhode Island
WEAN-FM Wakefield-Peacedale, Rhode Island
WBLQ(AM) Westerly, Rhode Island
WNRI Woonsocket, Rhode Island
WAIM Anderson, South Carolina
WZMJ Batesburg, South Carolina
WBT-FM Chester, South Carolina
WXBT(AM) Columbia, South Carolina
WGTN Georgetown, South Carolina
WYRD Greenville, South Carolina
WCRS Greenwood, South Carolina
WHGS Hampton, South Carolina
WFXH(AM) Hilton Head Island, South Carolina
WRIX-FM Honea Path, South Carolina
WRHM Lancaster, South Carolina
WRHI Rock Hill, South Carolina
WSNW Seneca, South Carolina
WYRD-FM Simpsonville, South Carolina
WORD Spartanburg, South Carolina
WSPG Spartanburg, South Carolina
WRJA-FM Sumter, South Carolina
WGOG Walhalla, South Carolina
KBFS Belle Fourche, South Dakota
KESD Brookings, South Dakota
KDSJ Deadwood, South Dakota
KPSD-FM Faith, South Dakota
KSOO-FM Lennox, South Dakota
KQSD-FM Lowry, South Dakota
KJAM Madison, South Dakota
KJAM-FM Madison, South Dakota
KZSD-FM Martin, South Dakota
KMSD Mibank, South Dakota
KORN Mitchell, South Dakota
KDSD-FM Pierpont, South Dakota
KCCR Pierre, South Dakota
KBHE-FM Rapid City, South Dakota
KOTA Rapid City, South Dakota
KTSD-FM Reliance, South Dakota
KELO Sioux Falls, South Dakota
KNWC Sioux Falls, South Dakota
KRSD Sioux Falls, South Dakota
KSOO Sioux Falls, South Dakota
KUSD Vermillion, South Dakota
KWAT Watertown, South Dakota
WNAX Yankton, South Dakota
WCTA Alamo, Tennessee
WTBG Brownsville, Tennessee
WGOW Chattanooga, Tennessee
WJZM Clarksville, Tennessee
WBAC Cleveland, Tennessee
WCLE Cleveland, Tennessee
WSMC-FM Collegedale, Tennessee
WHRS Cookeville, Tennessee
WPTN Cookeville, Tennessee
WMKW Crossville, Tennessee
WTJJ Dyer, Tennessee
WCPH Etowah, Tennessee
WAKM Franklin, Tennessee
WWTN Hendersonville, Tennessee
WDXI Jackson, Tennessee
WKNP Jackson, Tennessee
WETS-FM Johnson City, Tennessee
WETR Knoxville, Tennessee
WNML Knoxville, Tennessee
WUOT Knoxville, Tennessee
WCOR Lebanon, Tennessee
WLIV Livingston, Tennessee
WLOD Loudon, Tennessee
WPLN Madison, Tennessee
WRKQ Madisonville, Tennessee
WCMT Martin, Tennessee
WAKI McMinnville, Tennessee
KWAM Memphis, Tennessee
WKNO-FM Memphis, Tennessee
WREC Memphis, Tennessee
WYPL Memphis, Tennessee
WGNS Murfreesboro, Tennessee
WLAC Nashville, Tennessee
WPLN-FM Nashville, Tennessee
WFCM Smyrna, Tennessee
WGOW-FM Soddy-Daisy, Tennessee
WRHA(AM) Spring City, Tennessee
WNTT Tazewell, Tennessee
WTML Tullahoma, Tennessee
KACU Abilene, Texas
KWKC Abilene, Texas
KIXZ Amarillo, Texas
KACT Andrews, Texas
KLBJ Austin, Texas
KUT Austin, Texas
KSKY Balch Springs, Texas
KLVI Beaumont, Texas
KVLU Beaumont, Texas
KBST-FM Big Spring, Texas
KWHI Brenham, Texas
KTXP Bushland, Texas
KXYL-FM Coleman, Texas
KAMU-FM College Station, Texas
WTAW College Station, Texas
KETR Commerce, Texas
KEDT-FM Corpus Christi, Texas
KEYS Corpus Christi, Texas
KKTX Corpus Christi, Texas
KHER Crystal City, Texas
KERA Dallas, Texas
KFXR Dallas, Texas
KLIF Dallas, Texas
KRLD Dallas, Texas
KURV Edinburg, Texas
KULP El Campo, Texas
KTEP El Paso, Texas
KTSM El Paso, Texas
KXPL El Paso, Texas
KFLP-FM Floydada, Texas
KFLC Fort Worth, Texas
KGAF Gainesville, Texas
KMBH-FM Harlingen, Texas
KLAT Houston, Texas
KNTH Houston, Texas
KPFT Houston, Texas
KPRC Houston, Texas
KTRH Houston, Texas
KUHF Houston, Texas
KTXI Ingram, Texas
KAML Kenedy-Karnes City, Texas
KNCT-FM Killeen, Texas
KFYO Lubbock, Texas
KJDL Lubbock, Texas
KJTV Lubbock, Texas
KRFE Lubbock, Texas
KLDN Lufkin, Texas
KCUL Marshall, Texas
KHID McAllen, Texas
KCRS Midland, Texas
KWEL Midland, Texas
KSFA Nacogdoches, Texas
KWBC Navasota, Texas
KGNB New Braunfels, Texas
KOGT Orange, Texas
KNET Palestine, Texas
KBUS Paris, Texas
KOLE Port Arthur, Texas
KGKL San Angelo, Texas
KKSA San Angelo, Texas
KCOR San Antonio, Texas
KSTX San Antonio, Texas
KTSA San Antonio, Texas
KTSW San Marcos, Texas
KWED Seguin, Texas
KJIM Sherman, Texas
KZSP South Padre Island, Texas
KTOT Spearman, Texas
KSQX Springtown, Texas
KQXS Stephenville, Texas
KTEM Temple, Texas
KLUP Terrell Hills, Texas
KTFS Texarkana, Texas
KTXK Texarkana, Texas
KSEV Tomball, Texas
KTBB Tyler, Texas
KVRT Victoria, Texas
KBCT Waco, Texas
KWTX Waco, Texas
KMQX Weatherford, Texas
KMCU Wichita Falls, Texas
KWFS Wichita Falls, Texas
KSUB Cedar City, Utah
KUSR Logan, Utah
KUSU-FM Logan, Utah
KVNU Logan, Utah
KMTI Manti, Utah
KSL-FM Midvale, Utah
KLO Ogden, Utah
KOGN Ogden, Utah
KOAL Price, Utah
KBYU-FM Provo, Utah
KSVC Richfield, Utah
KCPW-FM Salt Lake City, Utah
KNRS Salt Lake City, Utah
KSL Salt Lake City, Utah
KUER-FM Salt Lake City, Utah
KHQN Spanish Fork, Utah
KDXU St. George, Utah
KZNU St. George, Utah
KNFL Tremonton, Utah
KVEL Vernal, Utah
WOWZ Appomattox, Virginia
WBVA Bayside, Virginia
WFNR Blacksburg, Virginia
WCHV Charlottesville, Virginia
WINA Charlottesville, Virginia
WMVE Chase City, Virginia
WDIC-FM Clinchco, Virginia

WMRY Crozet, Virginia
WPIN Dublin, Virginia
WOTC Edinburg, Virginia
WFLO Farmville, Virginia
WFVA Fredericksburg, Virginia
WMNA Gretna, Virginia
WEMC Harrisonburg, Virginia
WMRA Harrisonburg, Virginia
WSVA Harrisonburg, Virginia
WCNV Heathsville, Virginia
WMRL Lexington, Virginia
WREL Lexington, Virginia
WBRG Lynchburg, Virginia
WLNI Lynchburg, Virginia
WWWT-FM Manassas, Virginia
WHRO-FM Norfolk, Virginia
WHRV Norfolk, Virginia
WNIS Norfolk, Virginia
WTPS Petersburg, Virginia
WCVE-FM Richmond, Virginia
WLEE Richmond, Virginia
WRVA Richmond, Virginia
WFIR Roanoke, Virginia
WLOY Rural Retreat, Virginia
WHEO Stuart, Virginia
WTZE Tazewell, Virginia
WKCI Waynesboro, Virginia
WINC Winchester, Virginia
WYVE Wytheville, Virginia
WVGN Charlotte Amalie, Virgin Islands
WVWI Charlotte Amalie, Virgin Islands
WSNO Barre, Vermont
WBTN Bennington, Vermont
WKVT Brattleboro, Vermont
WXLQ Bristol, Vermont
WJOY Burlington, Vermont
WVMT Burlington, Vermont
WVPS Burlington, Vermont
WCVR(AM) Randolph, Vermont
WSYB Rutland, Vermont
WVPA St. Johnsbury, Vermont
WDEV-FM Warren, Vermont
WDEV Waterbury, Vermont
WVPR Windsor, Vermont
KXRO Aberdeen, Washington
KGMI Bellingham, Washington
KUGS Bellingham, Washington
KZAZ Bellingham, Washington
KVAN Burbank, Washington
KELA Centralia-Chehalis, Washington
KOZI Chelan, Washington
KOZI-FM Chelan, Washington
KNWV Clarkston, Washington
KNWR Ellensburg, Washington
KXLE Ellensburg, Washington
KULE Ephrata, Washington
KONA Kennewick-Richland-P, Washington
KEDO Longview, Washington
KBSN Moses Lake, Washington
KLWS Moses Lake, Washington
KMWS Mount Vernon, Washington
KSVR Mount Vernon, Washington
KQWS Omak, Washington
KFLD Pasco, Washington
KNWP Port Angeles, Washington
KONP Port Angeles, Washington
KVIX Port Angeles, Washington
KQQQ Pullman, Washington
KWSU Pullman, Washington
KWNC Quincy, Washington
KFAE-FM Richland, Washington
KKNW Seattle, Washington
KKOL Seattle, Washington
KOMO Seattle, Washington
KTTH Seattle, Washington
KUOW-FM Seattle, Washington
KJRB Spokane, Washington
KPBX-FM Spokane, Washington
KPTQ Spokane, Washington
KQNT Spokane, Washington
KSFC Spokane, Washington
KXLY Spokane, Washington
KIRO-FM Tacoma, Washington
KPLU-FM Tacoma, Washington
KXOT Tacoma, Washington
KYNR Toppenish, Washington
KUOW Tumwater, Washington
KGDC Walla Walla, Washington
KUJ Walla Walla, Washington
KWWS Walla Walla, Washington
KPLW Wenatchee, Washington
KPQ Wenatchee, Washington
KIT Yakima, Washington
KNWY Yakima, Washington
WXCE Amery, Wisconsin
WATW Ashland, Wisconsin
WLBL Auburndale, Wisconsin
WBEV Beaver Dam, Wisconsin
WHSA Brule, Wisconsin
WHAD Delafield, Wisconsin
KFIZ Fond Du Lac, Wisconsin
WPNE-FM Green Bay, Wisconsin
WTAQ Green Bay, Wisconsin
WHHI Highland, Wisconsin
WCLO Janesville, Wisconsin
WGTD Kenosha, Wisconsin
WHBY Kimberly, Wisconsin
WIZM La Crosse, Wisconsin
WLSU La Crosse, Wisconsin
WLDY Ladysmith, Wisconsin
WERN Madison, Wisconsin
WHA Madison, Wisconsin
WIBA Madison, Wisconsin
WTDY Madison, Wisconsin
WOMT Manitowoc, Wisconsin
WMEQ Menomonie, Wisconsin
WVSS Menomonie, Wisconsin
WISN Milwaukee, Wisconsin
WTMJ Milwaukee, Wisconsin
WOSH Oshkosh, Wisconsin
WHBM Park Falls, Wisconsin
WPDR Portage, Wisconsin
WRJN Racine, Wisconsin
WRDB Reedsburg, Wisconsin
WJMC Rice Lake, Wisconsin
WRCO-FM Richland Center, Wisconsin
WRPN Ripon, Wisconsin
WEVR-FM River Falls, Wisconsin
WHBL Sheboygan, Wisconsin
WXCX Siren, Wisconsin
WHND Sister Bay, Wisconsin
KUWS Superior, Wisconsin
WJJQ-FM Tomahawk, Wisconsin
WHRM Wausau, Wisconsin
WSAU Wausau, Wisconsin
WXPW Wausau, Wisconsin
WFHR Wisconsin Rapids, Wisconsin
WVPB Beckley, West Virginia
WWNR Beckley, West Virginia
WCST Berkeley Springs, West Virginia
WHIS Bluefield, West Virginia
WVPW Buckhannon, West Virginia
WCHS Charleston, West Virginia
WVPN Charleston, West Virginia
WTCS Fairmont, West Virginia
WVHU Huntington, West Virginia
WVWV Huntington, West Virginia
WFSP Kingwood, West Virginia
WEPM Martinsburg, West Virginia
WRNR Martinsburg, West Virginia
WVEP Martinsburg, West Virginia
WAJR Morgantown, West Virginia
WVPM Morgantown, West Virginia
WVLY Moundsville, West Virginia
WADC Parkersburg, West Virginia
WVNT Parkersburg, West Virginia
WVPG Parkersburg, West Virginia
WAUA Petersburg, West Virginia
WBGS Point Pleasant, West Virginia
WRRL Rainelle, West Virginia
WMOV Ravenswood, West Virginia
WRON Ronceverte, West Virginia
WAJR-FM Salem, West Virginia
WVNP Wheeling, West Virginia
WWVA Wheeling, West Virginia
KRSV Afton, Wyoming
KUWA Afton, Wyoming
KBBS Buffalo, Wyoming
KBUW Buffalo, Wyoming
KUWC Casper, Wyoming
KFBC Cheyenne, Wyoming
KODI Cody, Wyoming
KDUW Douglas, Wyoming
KIML Gillette, Wyoming
KUWG Gillette, Wyoming
KUWJ Jackson, Wyoming
KOWB Laramie, Wyoming
KUWR Laramie, Wyoming
KUWN Newcastle, Wyoming
KGAB Orchard Valley, Wyoming
KYDT Pine Haven, Wyoming
KUWX Pinedale, Wyoming
KPOW Powell, Wyoming
KUWP Powell, Wyoming
KUWZ Rock Springs, Wyoming
KPRQ Sheridan, Wyoming
KROE Sheridan, Wyoming
KSUW Sheridan, Wyoming
KUWD Sundance, Wyoming
KUWT Thermopolis, Wyoming

News/Talk

KBYR Anchorage, Alaska
KFQD Anchorage, Alaska
KAGV Big Lake, Alaska
KFAR Fairbanks, Alaska
KUAC Fairbanks, Alaska
KBBI Homer, Alaska
KTKN Ketchikan, Alaska
KIAM Nenana, Alaska
KNOM Nome, Alaska
KFSK Petersburg, Alaska
KIFW Sitka, Alaska
KSRM Soldotna, Alaska
KTNA Talkeetna, Alaska
WDNG Anniston, Alabama
WVNN Athens, Alabama
WAPI Birmingham, Alabama
WERC Birmingham, Alabama
WYDE Birmingham, Alabama
WACV Coosada, Alabama
WFMH Cullman, Alabama
WXAL Demopolis, Alabama
WHEP Foley, Alabama
WFPA Fort Payne, Alabama
WGEA Geneva, Alabama
WGYV Greenville, Alabama
WGSV Guntersville, Alabama
WNTM Mobile, Alabama
WLWI Montgomery, Alabama
WHBB Selma, Alabama
WFEB Sylacauga, Alabama
WVNN-FM Trinity, Alabama
WTBC Tuscaloosa, Alabama
WUAL-FM Tuscaloosa, Alabama
WVNA Tuscumbia, Alabama
KVRC Arkadelphia, Arkansas
KLCN Blytheville, Arkansas
KJMT Calico Rock, Arkansas
KCAB Dardanelle, Arkansas
KFAY Farmington, Arkansas
KBJT Fordyce, Arkansas
KXJK Forrest City, Arkansas
KWHN Fort Smith, Arkansas
KYHN Ft. Smith, Arkansas
KOTN Gould, Arkansas
KURM-FM Gravette, Arkansas
KELD-FM Hampton, Arkansas
KAWW Heber Springs, Arkansas
KZHS Hot Springs, Arkansas
KZNG Hot Springs, Arkansas
KBTM Jonesboro, Arkansas
KARN Little Rock, Arkansas
KUAR Little Rock, Arkansas
KNBY Newport, Arkansas
KARV-FM Ola, Arkansas
KSMD Pangburn, Arkansas
KFFK Rogers, Arkansas
KAPR Douglas, Arizona
KVNA Flagstaff, Arizona
KTAR-FM Glendale, Arizona
KJAA Globe, Arizona
KDJI Holbrook, Arizona
KAAA Kingman, Arizona
KNTR Lake Havasu City, Arizona
KFNN Mesa, Arizona
KLPZ Parker, Arizona
KFYI Phoenix, Arizona
KKNT Phoenix, Arizona
KNKI Pinetop, Arizona
KYCA Prescott, Arizona
KQNA Prescott Valley, Arizona
KVWM Show Low, Arizona
KTAN Sierra Vista, Arizona
KNST Tucson, Arizona
KUAZ-FM Tucson, Arizona
KAWC Yuma, Arizona
KBLU Yuma, Arizona
KGEO Bakersfield, California
KNZR Bakersfield, California
KPAY Chico, California
KZFR Chico, California

RADIO - U.S.

KGOE Eureka, California
KWSW(AM) Eureka, California
KMJ Fresno, California
KRLA Glendale, California
KNCO Grass Valley, California
KOSS Lancaster, California
KSMA Lompoc, California
KPFK Los Angeles, California
KTNQ Los Angeles, California
KPMO Mendocino, California
KGAM Merced, California
KYOS Merced, California
KFIV Modesto, California
KMPH Modesto, California
KNRY Monterey Bay, California
KMJC Mount Shasta, California
KVON Napa, California
KTOX Needles, California
KNEW Oakland, California
KNWQ Palm Springs, California
KPSC Palm Springs, California
KKXX Paradise, California
KPRL Paso Robles, California
KAHZ Pomona, California
KWKU Pomona, California
KVTA Port Hueneme, California
KTIP Porterville, California
KQMS Redding, California
KFBK Sacramento, California
KION Salinas, California
KTIE San Bernardino, California
KCBQ San Diego, California
KFMB San Diego, California
KOGO San Diego, California
KPBS-FM San Diego, California
KGO San Francisco, California
KVEC San Luis Obispo, California
KYNS San Luis Obispo, California
KCLU Santa Barbara, California
KZSB Santa Barbara, California
KSCO Santa Cruz, California
KSMX Santa Maria, California
KUHL Santa Maria, California
KKZZ Santa Paula, California
KSRO Santa Rosa, California
KSMJ Shafter, California
KIRN Simi Valley, California
KOWL South Lake Tahoe, California
KSUE Susanville, California
KUNX Ventura, California
KVFG Victorville, California
KERN Wasco-Greenacres, California
KRCB-FM Windsor, California
KUBA Yuba City, California
KNWH Yucca Valley, California
KRLN Canon City, Colorado
KRCC Colorado Springs, Colorado
KRDO Colorado Springs, Colorado
KVOR Colorado Springs, Colorado
KZNT Colorado Springs, Colorado
KVFC Cortez, Colorado
KCFR-FM Denver, Colorado
KNUS Denver, Colorado
KOA Denver, Colorado
KDGO Durango, Colorado
KFTM Fort Morgan, Colorado
KNZZ Grand Junction, Colorado
KFKA Greeley, Colorado
KHNC Johnstown, Colorado
KWUF Pagosa Springs, Colorado
KCSJ Pueblo, Colorado
KGFT Pueblo, Colorado
KRDO-FM Security, Colorado
KCOL Wellington, Colorado
WPRX Bristol, Connecticut
WQAQ Hamden, Connecticut
WDRC Hartford, Connecticut
WTIC Hartford, Connecticut
WNEZ Manchester, Connecticut
WELI New Haven, Connecticut
WNLK Norwalk, Connecticut
WEDW-FM Stamford, Connecticut
WSTC Stamford, Connecticut
WATR Waterbury, Connecticut
WWCO Waterbury, Connecticut
WSHU Westport, Connecticut
WAMU Washington, District of Columbia
WMAL Washington, District of Columbia
WPFW Washington, District of Columbia
WDOV Dover, Delaware
WGMD Rehoboth Beach, Delaware
WJWK Seaford, Delaware
WDEL Wilmington, Delaware
WILM Wilmington, Delaware
WFLN Arcadia, Florida
WTWB Auburndale, Florida
WWJB Brooksville, Florida
WNZF Bunnell, Florida
WKFL Bushnell, Florida
WMMV Cocoa, Florida
WMEL Cocoa Beach, Florida
WJTK Columbia City, Florida
WNDB Daytona Beach, Florida
WTJV Deland, Florida
WYND Deland, Florida
WNWF Destin, Florida
WENG Englewood, Florida
WJNX Fort Pierce, Florida
WFTW Fort Walton Beach, Florida
WDVH Gainesville, Florida
WRUF Gainesville, Florida
WNRP Gulf Breeze, Florida
WXYB Indian Rocks Beach, Florida
WBOB Jacksonville, Florida
WJCT-FM Jacksonville, Florida
WJBW Jupiter, Florida
WYBX(FM) Key West, Florida
WLKF Lakeland, Florida
WPBR Lantana, Florida
WWBA Largo, Florida
WFFG Marathon, Florida
WKWM Marathon, Florida
WGUF Marco, Florida
WMMB Melbourne, Florida
WAQI Miami, Florida
WIOD Miami, Florida
WLRN-FM Miami, Florida
WQBA Miami, Florida
WSUA Miami, Florida
WSKY-FM Micanopy, Florida
WNOG Naples, Florida
WPSO New Port Richey, Florida
WKAT North Miami, Florida
WDBO Orlando, Florida
WELE Ormond Beach, Florida
WLTG Panama City, Florida
WFLF-FM Parker, Florida
WCOA Pensacola, Florida
WCOA-FM Pensacola, Florida
WAMT Pine Castle Sky Lake, Florida
WFLF Pine Hills, Florida
WINK Pine Island Center, Florida
WPSL Port St. Lucie, Florida
WCCF Punta Gorda, Florida
WDEO-FM San Carlos Park, Florida
WSDO Sanford, Florida
WLSS Sarasota, Florida
WSRQ Sarasota, Florida
WFOY St. Augustine, Florida
WIWA St. Cloud, Florida
WSTU Stuart, Florida
WZAB Sweetwater, Florida
WFSU-FM Tallahassee, Florida
WTAL Tallahassee, Florida
WFLA Tampa, Florida
WHNZ Tampa, Florida
WIXC Titusville, Florida
WJNO West Palm Beach, Florida
WPRD Winter Park, Florida
WALG Albany, Georgia
WAOK Atlanta, Georgia
WGKA Atlanta, Georgia
WGST Atlanta, Georgia
WSB Atlanta, Georgia
WGAC Augusta, Georgia
WGIG Brunswick, Georgia
WGRA Cairo, Georgia
WLBB Carrollton, Georgia
WRCG Columbus, Georgia
WSRM Coosa, Georgia
WBLJ Dalton, Georgia
WCFO East Point, Georgia
WDUN Gainesville, Georgia
WHIE Griffin, Georgia
WVCC Hogansville, Georgia
WVGA Lakeland, Georgia
WMAC Macon, Georgia
WLAQ Rome, Georgia
WRGA Rome, Georgia
WBMQ Savannah, Georgia
WWNS Statesboro, Georgia
WKWN Trenton, Georgia
WWGA(AM) Waycross, Georgia
WCGA Woodbine, Georgia
KGUM Hagatna, Guam
KHVH Honolulu, Hawaii
KIKI(AM) Honolulu, Hawaii
KWAI Honolulu, Hawaii
KNUI Kahului, Hawaii
KQNG Lihue, Hawaii
KASI Ames, Iowa
KWBG Boone, Iowa
KBUR Burlington, Iowa
WMT Cedar Rapids, Iowa
WHO Des Moines, Iowa
KGRN Grinnell, Iowa
WSUI Iowa City, Iowa
KOKX Keokuk, Iowa
KFJB Marshalltown, Iowa
KOEL Oelwein, Iowa
KOJI Okoboji, Iowa
KBIZ Ottumwa, Iowa
KLEE Ottumwa, Iowa
KIWA Sheldon, Iowa
KMA Shenandoah, Iowa
KSCJ Sioux City, Iowa
KWIT Sioux City, Iowa
KXEL Waterloo, Iowa
KBOI Boise, Idaho
KBSU-FM Boise, Idaho
KBFI Bonners Ferry, Idaho
KBSY Burley, Idaho
KID Idaho Falls, Idaho
KRFA-FM Moscow, Idaho
KWEI Notus, Idaho
KWIK Pocatello, Idaho
KSPT Sandpoint, Idaho
KEZJ Twin Falls, Idaho
KLIX Twin Falls, Idaho
WBGZ Alton, Illinois
WBIG Aurora, Illinois
WBYS Canton, Illinois
WCIL Carbondale, Illinois
WDWS Champaign, Illinois
KSGM Chester, Illinois
WGN(AM) Chicago, Illinois
WIND Chicago, Illinois
WLS Chicago, Illinois
WRTO Chicago, Illinois
WHOW Clinton, Illinois
WDAN Danville, Illinois
WSOY Decatur, Illinois
WLBK Dekalb, Illinois
WCRA Effingham, Illinois
WRMN Elgin, Illinois
WFIW Fairfield, Illinois
WGNN Fisher, Illinois
WGIL Galesburg, Illinois
WKYX-FM Golconda, Illinois
WJPF Herrin, Illinois
WJIL Jacksonville, Illinois
WLDS Jacksonville, Illinois
WKEI Kewanee, Illinois
WLPO Lasalle, Illinois
WSMI Litchfield, Illinois
WGGH Marion, Illinois
WLBH Mattoon, Illinois
WBEQ Morris, Illinois
WCSJ Morris, Illinois
WCSJ-FM Morris, Illinois
WINI Murphysboro, Illinois
WCMY Ottawa, Illinois
WMBD Peoria, Illinois
WZOE Princeton, Illinois
WGEM Quincy, Illinois
WGEM-FM Quincy, Illinois
WTAD Quincy, Illinois
WRHL Rochelle, Illinois
WROK Rockford, Illinois
WHCO Sparta, Illinois
WMAY Springfield, Illinois
WTAX Springfield, Illinois
WNIQ Sterling, Illinois
WSPL Streator, Illinois
WTIM-FM Taylorville, Illinois
WILL Urbana, Illinois
WKRS Waukegan, Illinois
WHBU Anderson, Indiana
WGCL Bloomington, Indiana
WHON Centerville, Indiana
WCSI Columbus, Indiana
WTRC Elkhart, Indiana
WVPE Elkhart, Indiana

WGBF Evansville, Indiana
WBOI Fort Wayne, Indiana
WOWO Fort Wayne, Indiana
WLTH Gary, Indiana
WTRE Greensburg, Indiana
WJOB Hammond, Indiana
WFYI-FM Indianapolis, Indiana
WIBC Indianapolis, Indiana
WXNT Indianapolis, Indiana
WIOU Kokomo, Indiana
WSAL Logansport, Indiana
WLPR-FM Lowell, Indiana
WNDA New Albany, Indiana
WSBT South Bend, Indiana
WAOV Vincennes, Indiana
WBAA West Lafayette, Indiana
KGGF Coffeyville, Kansas
KIUL Garden City, Kansas
KLOE Goodland, Kansas
KZAN Hays, Kansas
KZNA Hill City, Kansas
KJCK Junction City, Kansas
KLWN Lawrence, Kansas
KSCB Liberal, Kansas
KMAN Manhattan, Kansas
KINA Salina, Kansas
KSAL Salina, Kansas
KYUL Scott City, Kansas
KMAJ Topeka, Kansas
WIBW Topeka, Kansas
KNSS Wichita, Kansas
KQAM Wichita, Kansas
WKXO Berea, Kentucky
WKCT Bowling Green, Kentucky
WCTT Corbin, Kentucky
WKDP Corbin, Kentucky
WHIR Danville, Kentucky
WHOP Hopkinsville, Kentucky
WVLK Lexington, Kentucky
WFPL Louisville, Kentucky
WGTK Louisville, Kentucky
WHAS Louisville, Kentucky
WNGO Mayfield, Kentucky
WMST Mt. Sterling, Kentucky
WKYX Paducah, Kentucky
WKYH Paintsville, Kentucky
WEKY Richmond, Kentucky
WVKY Shelbyville, Kentucky
WRKF Baton Rouge, Louisiana
KEUN Eunice, Louisiana
KAOK Lake Charles, Louisiana
KNOC Natchitoches, Louisiana
WGSO New Orleans, Louisiana
WRNO-FM New Orleans, Louisiana
WWL New Orleans, Louisiana
KNCB Vivian, Louisiana
WPNI Amherst, Massachusetts
WARL Attleboro, Massachusetts
WBZ Boston, Massachusetts
WILD Boston, Massachusetts
WXBR Brockton, Massachusetts
WHNP East Longmeadow, Massachusetts
WSAR Fall River, Massachusetts
WGAW Gardner, Massachusetts
WAMQ Great Barrington, Massachusetts
WMLN-FM Milton, Massachusetts
WNAN Nantucket, Massachusetts
WBSM New Bedford, Massachusetts
WDIS Norfolk, Massachusetts
WESO Southbridge, Massachusetts
WHYN Springfield, Massachusetts
WGTX Truro, Massachusetts
WBUR West Yarmouth, Massachusetts
WXTK West Yarmouth, Massachusetts
WCAI Woods Hole, Massachusetts
WTAG Worcester, Massachusetts
WEAA Baltimore, Maryland
WYPR Baltimore, Maryland
WCBC Cumberland, Maryland
WFMD Frederick, Maryland
WYPF Frederick, Maryland
WHAG Halfway, Maryland
WJSS Havre De Grace, Maryland
WPTX Lexington Park, Maryland
WYPO Ocean City, Maryland
WICO Salisbury, Maryland
WVQM Augusta, Maine
WVOM Howland, Maine
WJCX Pittsfield, Maine
WGAN Portland, Maine
WNZS Veazie, Maine

WABJ Adrian, Michigan
WUOM Ann Arbor, Michigan
WBCK-FM Battle Creek, Michigan
WSJM-FM Benton Harbor, Michigan
WHFB Benton Harbor-St. Jo, Michigan
WBRN Big Rapids, Michigan
WMKT Charlevoix, Michigan
WDTK Detroit, Michigan
WJR Detroit, Michigan
WKAR East Lansing, Michigan
WCHT Escanaba, Michigan
WWCK Flint, Michigan
WVGR Grand Rapids, Michigan
WHTC Holland, Michigan
WMIQ Iron Mountain, Michigan
WIAN Ishpeming, Michigan
WKHM Jackson, Michigan
WKMI Kalamazoo, Michigan
WKZO Kalamazoo, Michigan
WILS Lansing, Michigan
WKLA Ludington, Michigan
WMTE Manistee, Michigan
WPIQ Manistique, Michigan
WDMJ Marquette, Michigan
WAVC Mio, Michigan
WAZP Munising, Michigan
WPHM Port Huron, Michigan
WSGW Saginaw, Michigan
WMIC Sandusky, Michigan
WKNW Sault Sainte Marie, Michigan
WSJM St. Joseph, Michigan
WTCM Traverse City, Michigan
KATE Albert Lea, Minnesota
KAUS Austin, Minnesota
WWWI Baxter, Minnesota
KRWC Buffalo, Minnesota
KDLM Detroit Lakes, Minnesota
KDAL Duluth, Minnesota
WEBC Duluth, Minnesota
KBRF Fergus Falls, Minnesota
KLTF Little Falls, Minnesota
KTOE Mankato, Minnesota
KMHL Marshall, Minnesota
WCCO Minneapolis, Minnesota
WWTC Minneapolis, Minnesota
KMRS Morris, Minnesota
WNMT Nashwauk, Minnesota
KCHK New Prague, Minnesota
WWWI-FM Pillager, Minnesota
KROC Rochester, Minnesota
KNSI St. Cloud, Minnesota
WJON St. Cloud, Minnesota
KQMN Thief River Falls, Minnesota
KWLM Willmar, Minnesota
KDOM Windom, Minnesota
KDOM-FM Windom, Minnesota
KWNO Winona, Minnesota
KWOA Worthington, Minnesota
KNSW Worthington-Marshall, Minnesota
KGNA-FM Arnold, Missouri
KSWM Aurora, Missouri
KKOZ-FM Ava, Missouri
KBFL-FM Buffalo, Missouri
KZIM Cape Girardeau, Missouri
KRNW Chillicothe, Missouri
KFRU Columbia, Missouri
KOPN Columbia, Missouri
KGNN-FM Cuba, Missouri
KREI Farmington, Missouri
KSSZ Fayette, Missouri
KJFF Festus, Missouri
KHMO Hannibal, Missouri
KLIK Jefferson City, Missouri
KWOS Jefferson City, Missouri
KLWT Lebanon, Missouri
KMAL Malden, Missouri
KRMS Osage Beach, Missouri
KFMO Park Hills, Missouri
KCOZ Point Lookout, Missouri
KWOC Poplar Bluff, Missouri
KTTR Rolla, Missouri
KSMO Salem, Missouri
KSIS Sedalia, Missouri
KSIM Sikeston, Missouri
KSGF Springfield, Missouri
KWTO Springfield, Missouri
KTTR-FM St. James, Missouri
KFEQ St. Joseph, Missouri
KMOX St. Louis, Missouri
KTRS St. Louis, Missouri
KTUI Sullivan, Missouri

KGNV Washington, Missouri
KWPM West Plains, Missouri
KUKU Willow Springs, Missouri
WTNI Biloxi, Mississippi
WCJU Columbia, Mississippi
WURC Holly Springs, Mississippi
WTCD Indianola, Mississippi
WMXI Laurel, Mississippi
WJZD-FM Long Beach, Mississippi
WKBB Mantee, Mississippi
WALT Meridian, Mississippi
WBUV Moss Point, Mississippi
WNAT Natchez, Mississippi
WJNT Pearl, Mississippi
WFMM Sumrall, Mississippi
KGVW Belgrade, Montana
KBLG Billings, Montana
KMMS Bozeman, Montana
KGVA Fort Belknap Agency, Montana
KQDI Great Falls, Montana
KLYQ Hamilton, Montana
KBLL Helena, Montana
KCAP Helena, Montana
KGEZ Kalispell, Montana
KOFI Kalispell, Montana
KJJR Whitefish, Montana
WSPC Albemarle, North Carolina
WWNC Asheville, North Carolina
WTKF Atlantic, North Carolina
WXIT Blowing Rock, North Carolina
WLTT Bolivia, North Carolina
WCHL Chapel Hill, North Carolina
WBT Charlotte, North Carolina
WFAE Charlotte, North Carolina
WNCU Durham, North Carolina
WGAI Elizabeth City, North Carolina
WFNC Fayetteville, North Carolina
WIDU Fayetteville, North Carolina
WGBR Goldsboro, North Carolina
WSML Graham, North Carolina
WFHE Hickory, North Carolina
WHKY Hickory, North Carolina
WJNC Jacksonville, North Carolina
WJRI Lenoir, North Carolina
WLXN Lexington, North Carolina
WYQS Mars Hill, North Carolina
WAUG New Hope, North Carolina
WPTF Raleigh, North Carolina
WCAB Rutherfordton, North Carolina
WSTP Salisbury, North Carolina
WNCA Siler City, North Carolina
WEEB Southern Pines, North Carolina
WTXY Whiteville, North Carolina
KFYR Bismarck, North Dakota
KLXX Bismarck-Mandan, North Dakota
KFGO Fargo, North Dakota
WDAY Fargo, North Dakota
KNOX Grand Forks, North Dakota
KNDK Langdon, North Dakota
KQLX Lisbon, North Dakota
KHRT Minot, North Dakota
KEYZ Williston, North Dakota
KCOW Alliance, Nebraska
KWBE Beatrice, Nebraska
KJSK Columbus, Nebraska
KHUB Fremont, Nebraska
KRGI Grand Island, Nebraska
KGFW Kearney, Nebraska
KFOR Lincoln, Nebraska
KLIN Lincoln, Nebraska
WJAG Norfolk, Nebraska
KODY North Platte, Nebraska
KFAB Omaha, Nebraska
KNEB Scottsbluff, Nebraska
WEVO(FM) Concord, New Hampshire
WKXL Concord, New Hampshire
WTSN Dover, New Hampshire
WXEX Exeter, New Hampshire
WEVH Hanover, New Hampshire
WTSL Hanover, New Hampshire
WTPL Hillsboro, New Hampshire
WEVJ Jackson, New Hampshire
WEVN Keene, New Hampshire
WZBK Keene, New Hampshire
WUVR Lebanon, New Hampshire
WGIR Manchester, New Hampshire
WEVS Nashua, New Hampshire
WSMN Nashua, New Hampshire
WPKX(AM) Rochester, New Hampshire
WCCM Salem, New Hampshire
WNJN-FM Atlantic City, New Jersey

RADIO - U.S.

WNJS-FM Berlin, New Jersey
WNJB-FM Bridgeton, New Jersey
WNJZ Cape May Court House, New Jersey
WNYM Hackensack, New Jersey
WRNJ Hackettstown, New Jersey
WNJM Manahawkin, New Jersey
WNJY Netcong, New Jersey
WNJP Sussex, New Jersey
WNJT-FM Trenton, New Jersey
KINN Alamogordo, New Mexico
KKOB Albuquerque, New Mexico
KUNM Albuquerque, New Mexico
KRRT Arroyo Seco, New Mexico
KWKA Clovis, New Mexico
KENN Farmington, New Mexico
KYKK Humble City, New Mexico
KOBE Las Cruces, New Mexico
KNMX Las Vegas, New Mexico
KTBL Los Ranchos, New Mexico
KSEL Portales, New Mexico
KBIM Roswell, New Mexico
KKIM-FM Santa Fe, New Mexico
KDWN Las Vegas, Nevada
KXNT North Las Vegas, Nevada
KNUU Paradise, Nevada
KKOH Reno, Nevada
KBZZ Sparks, Nevada
KWNA Winnemucca, Nevada
WROW Albany, New York
WBTA Batavia, New York
WINR Binghamton, New York
WNBF Binghamton, New York
WBEN Buffalo, New York
WNED Buffalo, New York
WCGR Canandaigua, New York
WENI Corning, New York
WWLE Cornwall, New York
WFLR Dundee, New York
WDOE Dunkirk, New York
WENY Elmira, New York
WEOS Geneva, New York
WGVA Geneva, New York
WWSC Glens Falls, New York
WLEA Hornell, New York
WWLZ Horseheads, New York
WHCU Ithaca, New York
WJFF Jeffersonville, New York
WAMK Kingston, New York
WGHQ Kingston, New York
WLVL Lockport, New York
WSUF Noyack, New York
WOEN Olean, New York
WMCR Oneida, New York
WNYO Oswego, New York
WKIP Poughkeepsie, New York
WBEE-FM Rochester, New York
WHAM Rochester, New York
WNBZ Saranac Lake, New York
WGY Schenectady, New York
WRLI-FM Southampton, New York
WUSB Stony Brook, New York
WSYR Syracuse, New York
WIBX Utica, New York
WHLO Akron, Ohio
WATH Athens, Ohio
WOUB Athens, Ohio
WBLL Bellefontaine, Ohio
WAIS Buchtel, Ohio
WOUC-FM Cambridge, Ohio
WBEX Chillicothe, Ohio
WOUH-FM Chillicothe, Ohio
WKRC Cincinnati, Ohio
WLW Cincinnati, Ohio
WTAM Cleveland, Ohio
WERE Cleveland Heights, Ohio
WTVN Columbus, Ohio
WWOW Conneaut, Ohio
WHIO Dayton, Ohio
WEOL Elyria, Ohio
WFIN Findlay, Ohio
WMOH Hamilton, Ohio
WIRO Ironton, Ohio
WOUL-FM Ironton, Ohio
WFCO Lancaster, Ohio
WIMA Lima, Ohio
WMAN Mansfield, Ohio
WMRT Marietta, Ohio
WMRN Marion, Ohio
WMVO Mount Vernon, Ohio
WCLT Newark, Ohio
WMUB Oxford, Ohio
WCWA Toledo, Ohio
WSPD Toledo, Ohio
WBTC Uhrichsville, Ohio
WKBN Youngstown, Ohio
WOUZ-FM Zanesville, Ohio
KWHW Altus, Oklahoma
KWON Bartlesville, Oklahoma
KUSH Cushing, Oklahoma
KGWA Enid, Oklahoma
KTJS Hobart, Oklahoma
KOSN Ketchum, Oklahoma
KGOU Norman, Oklahoma
KOKC Oklahoma City, Oklahoma
KTOK Oklahoma City, Oklahoma
KOKL Okmulgee, Oklahoma
KRMG-FM Sand Springs, Oklahoma
KSPI Stillwater, Oklahoma
KRMG Tulsa, Oklahoma
KAST Astoria, Oregon
KBKR Baker, Oregon
KOBK Baker City, Oregon
KBNW Bend, Oregon
KWRO Coquille, Oregon
KLOO Corvallis, Oregon
KOAC Corvallis, Oregon
KNND Cottage Grove, Oregon
KWVR Enterprise, Oregon
KOPB Eugene, Oregon
KPNW Eugene, Oregon
KUGN Eugene, Oregon
KAJO Grants Pass, Oregon
KUIK Hillsboro, Oregon
KAGO Klamath Falls, Oregon
KFLS Klamath Falls, Oregon
KLBM La Grande, Oregon
KDOV Medford, Oregon
KMED Medford, Oregon
KBBR North Bend, Oregon
KRBM Pendleton, Oregon
KAPL Phoenix, Oregon
KPOJ Portland, Oregon
KXTG(AM) Portland, Oregon
KACI The Dalles, Oregon
KMBD(AM) Tillamook, Oregon
KTMK Tillamook, Oregon
KPAM Troutdale, Oregon
KLWJ(AM) Umatilla, Oregon
KWLZ-FM West Linn, Oregon
WJCS Allentown, Pennsylvania
WRTA Altoona, Pennsylvania
WILK-FM Avoca, Pennsylvania
WBLF Bellefonte, Pennsylvania
WGPA Bethlehem, Pennsylvania
WISR Butler, Pennsylvania
WHYL Carlisle, Pennsylvania
WCHA Chambersburg, Pennsylvania
WWCH Clarion, Pennsylvania
WFRM Coudersport, Pennsylvania
WCED Du Bois, Pennsylvania
WRDD Ebensburg, Pennsylvania
WJET Erie, Pennsylvania
WZSK Everett, Pennsylvania
WHP Harrisburg, Pennsylvania
WITF-FM Harrisburg, Pennsylvania
WAZL Hazleton, Pennsylvania
WRKK Hughesville, Pennsylvania
WLLI(AM) Huntingdon, Pennsylvania
WKGE Johnstown, Pennsylvania
WNTJ Johnstown, Pennsylvania
WNPV Lansdale, Pennsylvania
WLBR Lebanon, Pennsylvania
WWGE Loretto, Pennsylvania
WJSM-FM Martinsburg, Pennsylvania
WMGW Meadville, Pennsylvania
WPHB Philipsburg, Pennsylvania
KDKA Pittsburgh, Pennsylvania
WEMR Pleasant Gap, Pennsylvania
WPAZ Pottstown, Pennsylvania
WYBF Radnor Township, Pennsylvania
WEEU Reading, Pennsylvania
WBZU Scranton, Pennsylvania
WPIC Sharon, Pennsylvania
WNTW Somerset, Pennsylvania
WRSC State College, Pennsylvania
WKOK Sunbury, Pennsylvania
WTIV Titusville, Pennsylvania
WKZN West Hazleton, Pennsylvania
WILK Wilkes-Barre, Pennsylvania
WRAK Williamsport, Pennsylvania
WWPA Williamsport, Pennsylvania
WSBA York, Pennsylvania
WCMN Arecibo, Puerto Rico
WYAC Cabo Rojo, Puerto Rico
WMSW Hatillo, Puerto Rico
WALO Humacao, Puerto Rico
WMNT Manati, Puerto Rico
WKJB Mayaguez, Puerto Rico
WDEP Ponce, Puerto Rico
WISO Ponce, Puerto Rico
WPAB Ponce, Puerto Rico
WPRP Ponce, Puerto Rico
WUKQ Ponce, Puerto Rico
WAPA San Juan, Puerto Rico
WKAQ San Juan, Puerto Rico
WSKN San Juan, Puerto Rico
WUNO San Juan, Puerto Rico
WUPR Utuado, Puerto Rico
WENA Yauco, Puerto Rico
WKFE Yauco, Puerto Rico
WRNI-FM Narragansett Pier, Rhode Island
WHJJ Providence, Rhode Island
WPRO Providence, Rhode Island
WRNI Providence, Rhode Island
WEAN-FM Wakefield-Peacedale, Rhode Island
WNRI Woonsocket, Rhode Island
WAIM Anderson, South Carolina
WBT-FM Chester, South Carolina
WXBT(AM) Columbia, South Carolina
WORG Elloree, South Carolina
WGTN Georgetown, South Carolina
WYRD Greenville, South Carolina
WCRS Greenwood, South Carolina
WRIX-FM Honea Path, South Carolina
WRHI Rock Hill, South Carolina
WYRD-FM Simpsonville, South Carolina
WORD Spartanburg, South Carolina
WSPG Spartanburg, South Carolina
KSOO-FM Lennox, South Dakota
KJAM Madison, South Dakota
KMSD Mibank, South Dakota
KORN Mitchell, South Dakota
KCCR Pierre, South Dakota
KOTA Rapid City, South Dakota
KELO Sioux Falls, South Dakota
KSOO Sioux Falls, South Dakota
WNAX Yankton, South Dakota
WTBG Brownsville, Tennessee
WGOW Chattanooga, Tennessee
WJZM Clarksville, Tennessee
WBAC Cleveland, Tennessee
WCLE Cleveland, Tennessee
WPTN Cookeville, Tennessee
WMKW Crossville, Tennessee
WTJJ Dyer, Tennessee
WCPH Etowah, Tennessee
WAKM Franklin, Tennessee
WWTN Hendersonville, Tennessee
WETS-FM Johnson City, Tennessee
WETR Knoxville, Tennessee
WNML Knoxville, Tennessee
WCOR Lebanon, Tennessee
WLOD Loudon, Tennessee
WPLN Madison, Tennessee
WRKQ Madisonville, Tennessee
WCMT Martin, Tennessee
WAKI McMinnville, Tennessee
WREC Memphis, Tennessee
WGNS Murfreesboro, Tennessee
WLAC Nashville, Tennessee
WFCM Smyrna, Tennessee
WGOW-FM Soddy-Daisy, Tennessee
WRHA(AM) Spring City, Tennessee
KWKC Abilene, Texas
KIXZ Amarillo, Texas
KLBJ Austin, Texas
KLVI Beaumont, Texas
KBST-FM Big Spring, Texas
KWHI Brenham, Texas
KXYL-FM Coleman, Texas
WTAW College Station, Texas
KEYS Corpus Christi, Texas
KKTX Corpus Christi, Texas
KHER Crystal City, Texas
KERA Dallas, Texas
KLIF Dallas, Texas
KURV Edinburg, Texas
KULP El Campo, Texas
KTSM El Paso, Texas
KFLC Fort Worth, Texas
KGAF Gainesville, Texas
KLAT Houston, Texas
KNTH Houston, Texas

KPRC Houston, Texas
KFYO Lubbock, Texas
KJDL Lubbock, Texas
KJTV Lubbock, Texas
KRFE Lubbock, Texas
KCRS Midland, Texas
KSFA Nacogdoches, Texas
KWBC Navasota, Texas
KOLE Port Arthur, Texas
KKSA San Angelo, Texas
KCOR San Antonio, Texas
KTSA San Antonio, Texas
KTSW San Marcos, Texas
KWED Seguin, Texas
KZSP South Padre Island, Texas
KTEM Temple, Texas
KLUP Terrell Hills, Texas
KTFS Texarkana, Texas
KSEV Tomball, Texas
KTBB Tyler, Texas
KBCT Waco, Texas
KWTX Waco, Texas
KWFS Wichita Falls, Texas
KSUB Cedar City, Utah
KUSR Logan, Utah
KUSU-FM Logan, Utah
KVNU Logan, Utah
KSL-FM Midvale, Utah
KOAL Price, Utah
KBYU-FM Provo, Utah
KSVC Richfield, Utah
KCPW-FM Salt Lake City, Utah
KNRS Salt Lake City, Utah
KSL Salt Lake City, Utah
KHQN Spanish Fork, Utah
KDXU St. George, Utah
KZNU St. George, Utah
KVEL Vernal, Utah
WBVA Bayside, Virginia
WFNR Blacksburg, Virginia
WCHV Charlottesville, Virginia
WINA Charlottesville, Virginia
WMVE Chase City, Virginia
WPIN Dublin, Virginia
WFLO Farmville, Virginia
WFVA Fredericksburg, Virginia
WMNA Gretna, Virginia
WSVA Harrisonburg, Virginia
WCNV Heathsville, Virginia
WREL Lexington, Virginia
WBRG Lynchburg, Virginia
WLNI Lynchburg, Virginia
WHRV Norfolk, Virginia
WNIS Norfolk, Virginia
WTPS Petersburg, Virginia
WCVE-FM Richmond, Virginia
WLEE Richmond, Virginia
WRVA Richmond, Virginia
WFIR Roanoke, Virginia
WHEO Stuart, Virginia
WTZE Tazewell, Virginia
WKCI Waynesboro, Virginia
WINC Winchester, Virginia
WVGN Charlotte Amalie, Virgin Islands
WVWI Charlotte Amalie, Virgin Islands
WSNO Barre, Vermont
WBTN Bennington, Vermont
WKVT Brattleboro, Vermont
WVMT Burlington, Vermont
WCVR(AM) Randolph, Vermont
WSYB Rutland, Vermont
WDEV-FM Warren, Vermont
KXRO Aberdeen, Washington
KGMI Bellingham, Washington
KUGS Bellingham, Washington
KELA Centralia-Chehalis, Washington
KOZI Chelan, Washington
KOZI-FM Chelan, Washington
KXLE Ellensburg, Washington
KULE Ephrata, Washington
KONA Kennewick-Richland-P, Washington
KBSN Moses Lake, Washington
KMWS Mount Vernon, Washington
KSVR Mount Vernon, Washington
KQWS Omak, Washington
KFLD Pasco, Washington
KONP Port Angeles, Washington
KQQQ Pullman, Washington
KKNW Seattle, Washington
KPTQ Spokane, Washington
KQNT Spokane, Washington
KXLY Spokane, Washington
KIRO-FM Tacoma, Washington
KXOT Tacoma, Washington
KGDC Walla Walla, Washington
KUJ Walla Walla, Washington
KWWS Walla Walla, Washington
KPQ Wenatchee, Washington
KIT Yakima, Washington
WXCE Amery, Wisconsin
WLBL Auburndale, Wisconsin
WBEV Beaver Dam, Wisconsin
WHSA Brule, Wisconsin
WHAD Delafield, Wisconsin
KFIZ Fond Du Lac, Wisconsin
WTAQ Green Bay, Wisconsin
WHHI Highland, Wisconsin
WCLO Janesville, Wisconsin
WHBY Kimberly, Wisconsin
WIZM La Crosse, Wisconsin
WLDY Ladysmith, Wisconsin
WIBA Madison, Wisconsin
WTDY Madison, Wisconsin
WMEQ Menomonie, Wisconsin
WVSS Menomonie, Wisconsin
WTMJ Milwaukee, Wisconsin
WOSH Oshkosh, Wisconsin
WHBM Park Falls, Wisconsin
WPDR Portage, Wisconsin
WRJN Racine, Wisconsin
WJMC Rice Lake, Wisconsin
WRPN Ripon, Wisconsin
WHBL Sheboygan, Wisconsin
KUWS Superior, Wisconsin
WSAU Wausau, Wisconsin
WFHR Wisconsin Rapids, Wisconsin
WHIS Bluefield, West Virginia
WCHS Charleston, West Virginia
WTCS Fairmont, West Virginia
WVHU Huntington, West Virginia
WEPM Martinsburg, West Virginia
WRNR Martinsburg, West Virginia
WAJR Morgantown, West Virginia
WVLY Moundsville, West Virginia
WADC Parkersburg, West Virginia
WVNT Parkersburg, West Virginia
WBGS Point Pleasant, West Virginia
WRRL Rainelle, West Virginia
WAJR-FM Salem, West Virginia
WWVA Wheeling, West Virginia
KUWA Afton, Wyoming
KBBS Buffalo, Wyoming
KODI Cody, Wyoming
KIML Gillette, Wyoming
KOWB Laramie, Wyoming
KGAB Orchard Valley, Wyoming
KROE Sheridan, Wyoming

Oldies

KEAG Anchorage, Alaska
KMJG Homer, Alaska
KWJG Kasilof, Alaska
KFMJ Ketchikan, Alaska
KXBA Nikiski, Alaska
KIFW Sitka, Alaska
WAFN-FM Arab, Alabama
WKAC Athens, Alabama
WATV Birmingham, Alabama
WEBJ Brewton, Alabama
WTBF-FM Brundidge, Alabama
WHOS Decatur, Alabama
WZNJ Demopolis, Alabama
WGMZ Glencoe, Alabama
WGYV Greenville, Alabama
WLOR Huntsville, Alabama
WHPH Jemison, Alabama
WLAY-FM Littleville, Alabama
WMFC Monroeville, Alabama
WMFC(AM) Monroeville, Alabama
WQKS-FM Montgomery, Alabama
WVOK Oxford, Alabama
WPID Piedmont, Alabama
WKZD Priceville, Alabama
WJDB Thomasville, Alabama
WRLD Valley, Alabama
WKXM-FM Winfield, Alabama
KFCM Ash Flat, Arkansas
KVLD Atkins, Arkansas
KEWI Benton, Arkansas
KQBK Booneville, Arkansas
KTRQ Colt, Arkansas
KBKG Corning, Arkansas
KFLI Des Arc, Arkansas
KLSZ-FM Fort Smith, Arkansas
KKIK Horseshoe Bend, Arkansas
KQOR Mena, Arkansas
KAMO-FM Rogers, Arkansas
KWAK-FM Stuttgart, Arkansas
KRLW Walnut Ridge, Arkansas
KCTT-FM Yellville, Arkansas
KXFF Colorado City, Arizona
KKLD Cottonwood, Arizona
KMVA Dewey-Humboldt, Arizona
KGVY Green Valley, Arizona
KRCY-FM Lake Havasu City, Arizona
KVYL Mohave Valley, Arizona
KOOL-FM Phoenix, Arizona
KOY Phoenix, Arizona
KBUX Quartzsite, Arizona
KAZG Scottsdale, Arizona
KZKE Seligman, Arizona
KSNX(FM) Show Low, Arizona
KVSL Show Low, Arizona
KKYZ Sierra Vista, Arizona
KCEE Tucson, Arizona
XHRMFM Tijuana, Mexico
KIQO Atascadero, California
KCEA Atherton, California
KHYL Auburn, California
KKBB Bakersfield, California
KBOV Bishop, California
KUSS(FM) Carlsbad, California
KODS Carnelian Bay, California
KDES-FM Cathedral City, California
KCHJ Delano, California
KZRO Dunsmuir, California
KXO El Centro, California
KSPE-FM Ellwood, California
KKHB Eureka, California
KYAF Firebaugh, California
KMGV Fresno, California
KAZA Gilroy, California
KRAK Hesperia, California
KOKO-FM Kerman, California
KOMY La Selva Beach, California
KVLI(FM) Lake Isabella, California
KXBX Lakeport, California
KZPO Lindsay, California
KRTH Los Angeles, California
KCEZ Los Molinos, California
KABX-FM Merced, California
KOCN Pacific Grove, California
KHLX Pollock Pines, California
KBLF Red Bluff, California
KLOA Ridgecrest, California
KZLA Riverdale, California
KOLA San Bernardino, California
KURS San Diego, California
KALW San Francisco, California
KISQ San Francisco, California
KZDG(AM) San Francisco, California
KRDG Shingletown, California
KTHO South Lake Tahoe, California
KWYL South Lake Tahoe, California
KQOD Stockton, California
KSTN Stockton, California
KVEN Ventura, California
KRCV West Covina, California
KJOR Windsor, California
KEZW Aurora, Colorado
KLIM Black Forest, Colorado
KXKL-FM Denver, Colorado
KEJJ Gunnison, Colorado
KUSZ Olathe, Colorado
KRWZ Parker, Colorado
KPHT Rocky Ford, Colorado
KVRH Salida, Colorado
KSTC Sterling, Colorado
KSJL Strasburg, Colorado
WKNL New London, Connecticut
WATR Waterbury, Connecticut
WBIG-FM Washington, District of Columbia
WLBW Fenwick Island, Delaware
WNCL Milford, Delaware
WMHS Pike Creek, Delaware
WWBF Bartow, Florida
WYBT Blountstown, Florida
WRGO Cedar Key, Florida
WPFL Century, Florida
WSRZ-FM Coral Cove, Florida
WAVS Davie, Florida
WMGG Egypt Lake, Florida

WFSX-FM Estero, Florida
WMYR Fort Myers, Florida
WEDM(AM) Fort Walton Beach, Florida
WDSR Lake City, Florida
WJOE Lake City, Florida
WEBZ Mexico Beach, Florida
WPLK Palatka, Florida
WDIZ Panama City, Florida
WYRE-FM Saint Augustine Beach, Florida
WJCM Sebring, Florida
WJQB Spring Hill, Florida
WAYL St. Augustine, Florida
WPOI St. Petersburg, Florida
WRBQ-FM Tampa, Florida
WLTQ-FM Venice, Florida
WQOL Vero Beach, Florida
WMGR Bainbridge, Georgia
WEBS Calhoun, Georgia
WBHF Cartersville, Georgia
WCLA Claxton, Georgia
WCOQ Colquitt, Georgia
WGFS Covington, Georgia
WMRZ Dawson, Georgia
WXJO Douglasville, Georgia
WSGC Elberton, Georgia
WDDK Greensboro, Georgia
WKEU Griffin, Georgia
WQXZ Hawkinsville, Georgia
WISK Lawrenceville, Georgia
WJTP Lithia Springs, Georgia
WPEH Louisville, Georgia
WPZE Mableton, Georgia
WAYS Macon, Georgia
WYIS McRae, Georgia
WGCO Midway, Georgia
WMNZ Montezuma, Georgia
WAZX Smyrna, Georgia
WXRS Swainsboro, Georgia
WJFL Tennille, Georgia
WNEG Toccoa, Georgia
WATG Trion, Georgia
WVOP Vidalia, Georgia
WRLA West Point, Georgia
KIJI Tumon, Guam
KKOL-FM Aiea, Hawaii
KBGX Keaau, Hawaii
KONI Lanai City, Hawaii
KASI Ames, Iowa
KCIM Carroll, Iowa
KKRL Carroll, Iowa
KCHE Cherokee, Iowa
KJOC Davenport, Iowa
KIOA Des Moines, Iowa
KJMC Des Moines, Iowa
KVFD Fort Dodge, Iowa
KLMJ Hampton, Iowa
KNOD Harlan, Iowa
KOKX-FM Keokuk, Iowa
KKMA Le Mars, Iowa
KRIB Mason City, Iowa
KWPC Muscatine, Iowa
KIGC Oskaloosa, Iowa
KWSL Sioux City, Iowa
KTLB Twin Lakes, Iowa
KCII-FM Washington, Iowa
KWLO Waterloo, Iowa
KHPP(AM) Waukon, Iowa
KBAR Burley, Idaho
KCID Caldwell, Idaho
KTHI Caldwell, Idaho
KVNI Coeur D'Alene, Idaho
KQLZ(FM) Mt Home, Idaho
KLIX-FM Twin Falls, Idaho
KTFI Wendell, Idaho
WQRL Benton, Illinois
WROY Carmi, Illinois
WILY Centralia, Illinois
WJMK Chicago, Illinois
WLS-FM Chicago, Illinois
WMQZ Colchester, Illinois
WPPN Des Plaines, Illinois
WIXN Dixon, Illinois
WWYW Dundee, Illinois
WRSE Elmhurst, Illinois
WAIK Galesburg, Illinois
WJBM Jerseyville, Illinois
WEAI Lynnville, Illinois
WDKR Maroa, Illinois
WMMC Marshall, Illinois
WPWQ Mount Sterling, Illinois
WHQQ Neoga, Illinois
WSEY Oregon, Illinois
WPXN Paxton, Illinois
WTRH Ramsey, Illinois
WKXQ Rushville, Illinois
WQQL Springfield, Illinois
WYYS Streator, Illinois
WBCP Urbana, Illinois
WCFF Urbana, Illinois
WYKT Wilmington, Illinois
WASK-FM Battle Ground, Indiana
WQRK Bedford, Indiana
WKLU Brownsburg, Indiana
WIFE Connersville, Indiana
WCVL Crawfordsville, Indiana
WIBN Earl Park, Indiana
WIKL(FM) Elwood, Indiana
WJLT Evansville, Indiana
WILO Frankfort, Indiana
WTLC-FM Greenwood, Indiana
WBZQ Huntington, Indiana
WJPR Jasper, Indiana
WJEF Lafayette, Indiana
WQTY Linton, Indiana
WXGO Madison, Indiana
WMRI Marion, Indiana
WEFM Michigan City, Indiana
WERK Muncie, Indiana
WSEZ Paoli, Indiana
WZOC Plymouth, Indiana
WNDZ Portage, Indiana
WSJD Princeton, Indiana
WROI Rochester, Indiana
WSKL Veedersburg, Indiana
WJOT-FM Wabash, Indiana
KSAJ-FM Abilene, Kansas
KCAR-FM Baxter Springs, Kansas
KAHE Dodge City, Kansas
KVOE Emporia, Kansas
KMDO Fort Scott, Kansas
KGGF-FM Fredonia, Kansas
KQYX Galena, Kansas
KAYS Hays, Kansas
KWHK Hutchinson, Kansas
KIOL Iola, Kansas
KBGL Larned, Kansas
KSOB Larned, Kansas
KBBE McPherson, Kansas
KLKC-FM Parsons, Kansas
KMMM Pratt, Kansas
KSKL Scott City, Kansas
KCMO-FM Shawnee, Kansas
KWME Wellington, Kansas
KEYN-FM Wichita, Kansas
WMDJ-FM Allen, Kentucky
WAIN Columbia, Kentucky
WCTT Corbin, Kentucky
WCYN Cynthiana, Kentucky
WEKB Elkhorn City, Kentucky
WDJO(AM) Florence, Kentucky
WKYW Frankfort, Kentucky
WOVO Glasgow, Kentucky
WCBL-FM Grand Rivers, Kentucky
WKYA Greenville, Kentucky
WQXY Hazard, Kentucky
WHVO Hopkinsville, Kentucky
WIRV Irvine, Kentucky
WLBN Lebanon, Kentucky
WMJL-FM Marion, Kentucky
WIVY Morehead, Kentucky
WSIP Paintsville, Kentucky
WPKE Pikeville, Kentucky
WANO Pineville, Kentucky
WXKZ-FM Prestonsburg, Kentucky
WWKY Providence, Kentucky
WCND Shelbyville, Kentucky
WTLO Somerset, Kentucky
WLKS West Liberty, Kentucky
WGKY Wickliffe, Kentucky
WTGG Amite, Louisiana
KSIG Crowley, Louisiana
WTIX-FM Galliano, Louisiana
KLEB Golden Meadow, Louisiana
KLKL Minden, Louisiana
KLIL Moreauville, Louisiana
KZBL Natchitoches, Louisiana
WIST New Orleans, Louisiana
KWCL-FM Oak Grove, Louisiana
KPCH Ruston, Louisiana
WXRB Dudley, Massachusetts
WIZZ Greenfield, Massachusetts
WATD-FM Marshfield, Massachusetts
WAVM Maynard, Massachusetts
WUPE-FM North Adams, Massachusetts
WUPE Pittsfield, Massachusetts
WARE Ware, Massachusetts
WAMD Aberdeen, Maryland
WCTR Chestertown, Maryland
WTBO Cumberland, Maryland
WTDK Federalsburg, Maryland
WMSG Oakland, Maryland
WCTN Potomac-Cabin John, Maryland
WJDY Salisbury, Maryland
WICL Williamsport, Maryland
WCXU Caribou, Maine
WKTJ-FM Farmington, Maine
WLVP Gorham, Maine
WLAM Lewiston, Maine
WCXX Madawaska, Maine
WCXV Van Buren, Maine
WTVL Waterville, Maine
WYAR Yarmouth, Maine
WHNN Bay City, Michigan
WMRX-FM Beaverton, Michigan
WKYO Caro, Michigan
WGTO Cassopolis, Michigan
WCBY Cheboygan, Michigan
WTVB Coldwater, Michigan
WDBC Escanaba, Michigan
WFNT Flint, Michigan
WGKL Gladstone, Michigan
WAYG Grand Rapids, Michigan
WFGR Grand Rapids, Michigan
WHPR-FM Highland Park, Michigan
WHTO Iron Mountain, Michigan
WMTE-FM Manistee, Michigan
WTIQ Manistique, Michigan
WHLX Marine City, Michigan
WHYB Menominee, Michigan
WMPX Midland, Michigan
WQXO Munising, Michigan
WKQS-FM Negaunee, Michigan
WNGE Negaunee, Michigan
WNBY-FM Newberry, Michigan
WLCS North Muskegon, Michigan
WHLS Port Huron, Michigan
WDEE-FM Reed City, Michigan
WHAK-FM Rogers City, Michigan
WCSY-FM South Haven, Michigan
WSHJ Southfield, Michigan
WCCW-FM Traverse City, Michigan
WPON Walled Lake, Michigan
WBMI West Branch, Michigan
KULO Alexandria, Minnesota
KAUS Austin, Minnesota
WQXJ Blackduck, Minnesota
KUAL-FM Brainerd, Minnesota
KRWC Buffalo, Minnesota
WGVY Cambridge, Minnesota
KLDJ Duluth, Minnesota
WGVZ Eden Prarie, Minnesota
KJJK Fergus Falls, Minnesota
KKCQ Fosston, Minnesota
KKRC Granite Falls, Minnesota
KDUZ Hutchinson, Minnesota
KGHS International Falls, Minnesota
KRAQ Jackson, Minnesota
KQEG La Crescent, Minnesota
WGVX Lakeville, Minnesota
KRJM Mahnomen, Minnesota
WMOZ Moose Lake, Minnesota
KBEK Mora, Minnesota
KRDS-FM New Prague, Minnesota
KRFO Owatonna, Minnesota
KISD Pipestone, Minnesota
KVGO Spring Valley, Minnesota
KXAC St. James, Minnesota
KZJK St. Louis Park, Minnesota
KAKK Walker, Minnesota
KWNO Winona, Minnesota
KBFL-FM Buffalo, Missouri
KCRV-FM Caruthersville, Missouri
KCHR Charleston, Missouri
KDKD Clinton, Missouri
KWWC-FM Columbia, Missouri
KDFN Doniphan, Missouri
KESM Eldorado Springs, Missouri
KXOQ Kennett, Missouri
KIRX Kirksville, Missouri
KQUL Lake Ozark, Missouri
KJMO Linn, Missouri
KRLI Malta Bend, Missouri
KYRX Marble Hill, Missouri

KBHI Miner, Missouri
KWBZ Monroe City, Missouri
KXMO-FM Owensville, Missouri
KLID Poplar Bluff, Missouri
KSFT(AM) Saint Joseph, Missouri
KBFL Springfield, Missouri
KLOU St. Louis, Missouri
KZQZ St. Louis, Missouri
KOKO Warrensburg, Missouri
KUKU-FM Willow Springs, Missouri
WWZQ Aberdeen, Mississippi
WAFM Amory, Mississippi
WHKL Crenshaw, Mississippi
WNIX Greenville, Mississippi
WOHT Grenada, Mississippi
WAGR-FM Lexington, Mississippi
WNAU New Albany, Mississippi
WMTI Picayune, Mississippi
WVBG-FM Redwood, Mississippi
WIIN Ridgeland, Mississippi
WAVN Southaven, Mississippi
WGDQ Sumrall, Mississippi
KANA Anaconda, Montana
KKBR Billings, Montana
KOBB-FM Bozeman, Montana
KXTL Butte, Montana
KKGR East Helena, Montana
KIKC Forsyth, Montana
KXGN Glendive, Montana
KLFM Great Falls, Montana
KMTX Helena, Montana
KOFI Kalispell, Montana
KTNY Libby, Montana
KXDR(FM) Pinesdale, Montana
KMXE-FM Red Lodge, Montana
KSEN Shelby, Montana
KWYS West Yellowstone, Montana
KWOL-FM Whitefish, Montana
KVCK Wolf Point, Montana
WZKY Albemarle, North Carolina
WSKY Asheville, North Carolina
WPCM Burlington-Graham, North Carolina
WKQC Charlotte, North Carolina
WCLN Clinton, North Carolina
WERX-FM Columbia, North Carolina
WBLA Elizabethtown, North Carolina
WODR Fair Bluff, North Carolina
WFSC Franklin, North Carolina
WTRG Gaston, North Carolina
WGNC Gastonia, North Carolina
WNCT-FM Greenville, North Carolina
WIZS Henderson, North Carolina
WAIZ Hickory, North Carolina
WCCG Hope Mills, North Carolina
WAAV Leland, North Carolina
WLON Lincolnton, North Carolina
WZAX Nashville, North Carolina
WLWL Rockingham, North Carolina
WSAT Salisbury, North Carolina
WFJA Sanford, North Carolina
WTOE Spruce Pine, North Carolina
KEYA Belcourt, North Dakota
KACL Bismarck, North Dakota
KDVL Devils Lake, North Dakota
KDIX Dickinson, North Dakota
KAUJ Grafton, North Dakota
KEGK Wahpeton, North Dakota
KQWB West Fargo, North Dakota
KCOW Alliance, Nebraska
KCTY Emerson, Nebraska
KGMT Fairbury, Nebraska
KTNC Falls City, Nebraska
KSDZ Gordon, Nebraska
KUVR Holdrege, Nebraska
KKPR-FM Kearney, Nebraska
KLNC Lincoln, Nebraska
KBRL McCook, Nebraska
KOGA Ogallala, Nebraska
KNLV Ord, Nebraska
KSFT-FM South Sioux City, Nebraska
KOAQ Terrytown, Nebraska
KAWL York, Nebraska
WEZS Laconia, New Hampshire
WLTN Littleton, New Hampshire
WQSO Rochester, New Hampshire
WFYX Walpole, New Hampshire
WMID Atlantic City, New Jersey
WIBG-FM Avalon, New Jersey
WBNJ Barnegat, New Jersey
WRNJ Hackettstown, New Jersey
WMTR Morristown, New Jersey
WCTC New Brunswick, New Jersey
WTOC Newton, New Jersey
WTKU-FM Petersburg, New Jersey
WGHT Pompton Lakes, New Jersey
WVLT Vineland, New Jersey
KQEL Alamogordo, New Mexico
KKFG Bloomfield, New Mexico
KCCC Carlsbad, New Mexico
KYVA-FM Church Rock, New Mexico
KRMQ-FM Clovis, New Mexico
KDSK Grants, New Mexico
KVLC Hatch, New Mexico
KEDP Las Vegas, New Mexico
KABG Los Alamos, New Mexico
KLEA-FM Lovington, New Mexico
KRTN-FM Raton, New Mexico
KBCQ Roswell, New Mexico
KCRX Roswell, New Mexico
KBUY Ruidoso, New Mexico
KNYE Pahrump, Nevada
WBAB Babylon, New York
WSEN Baldwinsville, New York
WENI-FM Big Flats, New York
WIYN Deposit, New York
WDOE Dunkirk, New York
WFKL Fairport, New York
WXHC Homer, New York
WHAZ-FM Hoosick Falls, New York
WZCR Hudson, New York
WHVW Hyde Park, New York
WKSN Jamestown, New York
WCKM-FM Lake George, New York
WVOS-FM Liberty, New York
WICY Malone, New York
WCBS-FM New York, New York
WJJL Niagara Falls, New York
WHDL Olean, New York
WZOZ Oneonta, New York
WALK Patchogue, New York
WVTK Port Henry, New York
WTRY-FM Rotterdam, New York
WCDO-FM Sidney, New York
WDLA Walton, New York
WTBQ Warwick, New York
WCIZ-FM Watertown, New York
WLGZ-FM Webster, New York
WJQZ Wellsville, New York
WAKR Akron, Ohio
WRMU-FM Alliance, Ohio
WBCY Archbold, Ohio
WRQN Bowling Green, Ohio
WQCT Bryan, Ohio
WHBC Canton, Ohio
WCHI Chillicothe, Ohio
WZOO-FM Edgewood, Ohio
WZRX-FM Fort Shawnee, Ohio
WLGN Logan, Ohio
WDLW Lorain, Ohio
WMRN Marion, Ohio
WBBG Niles, Ohio
WLKR Norwalk, Ohio
WKSD Paulding, Ohio
WPTW Piqua, Ohio
WSOM Salem, Ohio
WSWR Shelby, Ohio
WDIG Steubenville, Ohio
WKVX Wooster, Ohio
WNIO Youngstown, Ohio
KALV Alva, Oklahoma
KJMZ Cache, Oklahoma
KRVT Claremore, Oklahoma
KKRX Lawton, Oklahoma
KYNZ Lone Grove, Oklahoma
KLOR-FM Ponca City, Oklahoma
KVRO Stillwater, Oklahoma
KSLE Wewoka, Oklahoma
KRAT(FM) Altamont, Oregon
KKBC-FM Baker, Oregon
KXJM Banks, Oregon
KURY Brookings, Oregon
KURY-FM Brookings, Oregon
KRJT Elgin, Oregon
KKNX Eugene, Oregon
KLZS Eugene, Oregon
KCST-FM Florence, Oregon
KLTH Lake Oswego, Oregon
KBZY Salem, Oregon
KSWB Seaside, Oregon
KACI-FM The Dalles, Oregon
WAVL Apollo, Pennsylvania
WNCC Barnesboro, Pennsylvania
WLZS Beaver Springs, Pennsylvania
WALY Bellwood, Pennsylvania
WBWX(AM) Berwick, Pennsylvania
WHLM Bloomsburg, Pennsylvania
WKQL Brookville, Pennsylvania
WCCL Central City, Pennsylvania
WCPA Clearfield, Pennsylvania
WHYP(AM) Corry, Pennsylvania
WOKW Curwensville, Pennsylvania
WKPL Ellwood City, Pennsylvania
WTKT Harrisburg, Pennsylvania
WDAD Indiana, Pennsylvania
WTYM Kittanning, Pennsylvania
WKVA Lewistown, Pennsylvania
WMVL Linesville, Pennsylvania
WBPZ Lock Haven, Pennsylvania
WQZS Meyersdale, Pennsylvania
WBZD-FM Muncy, Pennsylvania
WJST New Castle, Pennsylvania
WYNE North East, Pennsylvania
WKQW Oil City, Pennsylvania
WJAS Pittsburgh, Pennsylvania
WSOX Red Lion, Pennsylvania
WLSW Scottdale, Pennsylvania
WARM Scranton, Pennsylvania
WPHD South Waverly, Pennsylvania
WKBI St. Marys, Pennsylvania
WCDW Susquehanna, Pennsylvania
WTTC Towanda, Pennsylvania
WPKL Uniontown, Pennsylvania
WOWY University Park, Pennsylvania
WRRN Warren, Pennsylvania
WJPA Washington, Pennsylvania
WJPA-FM Washington, Pennsylvania
WBHB-FM Waynesboro, Pennsylvania
WRLC Williamsport, Pennsylvania
WMIA Arecibo, Puerto Rico
WNEL Caguas, Puerto Rico
WTIL Mayaguez, Puerto Rico
WLEO Ponce, Puerto Rico
WIDI Quebradillas, Puerto Rico
WOYE Rio Grande, Puerto Rico
WKVM San Juan, Puerto Rico
WRSS San Sebastian, Puerto Rico
WVIS Vieques, Puerto Rico
WPRV Providence, Rhode Island
WZLA-FM Abbeville, South Carolina
WKSP Aiken, South Carolina
WBSC Bennettsville, South Carolina
WGFG Branchville, South Carolina
WCAM Camden, South Carolina
WPUB-FM Camden, South Carolina
WAHT Clemson, South Carolina
WLFF Georgetown, South Carolina
WPCI Greenville, South Carolina
WKSX-FM Johnston, South Carolina
WKSC Kershaw, South Carolina
WCOO Kiawah Island, South Carolina
WAGL Lancaster, South Carolina
WVCO Loris, South Carolina
WYEZ Murrells Inlet, South Carolina
WKDK Newberry, South Carolina
WXLY North Charleston, South Carolina
WRBK Richburg, South Carolina
WLHH(FM) Ridgeland, South Carolina
WSNW Seneca, South Carolina
WNBK Whitmire, South Carolina
KFMH Belle Fourche, South Dakota
KAWK Custer, South Dakota
KDSJ Deadwood, South Dakota
KUQL Ethan, South Dakota
KXQL Flandreau, South Dakota
KIJV Huron, South Dakota
KBJM Lemmon, South Dakota
KMSD Mibank, South Dakota
KKSD Milbank, South Dakota
KCCR Pierre, South Dakota
KKLS Rapid City, South Dakota
KSQB(AM) Sioux Falls, South Dakota
KVHT Vermillion, South Dakota
WVOL Berry Hill, Tennessee
WBOL Bolivar, Tennessee
WZYX Cowan, Tennessee
WCDZ Dresden, Tennessee
WTRO Dyersburg, Tennessee
WSMG Greeneville, Tennessee
WIRJ Humboldt, Tennessee
WMXX-FM Jackson, Tennessee
WHGG Kingsport, Tennessee
WKOS Kingsport, Tennessee
WKCS Knoxville, Tennessee

WYGO Madisonville, Tennessee
WMSR Manchester, Tennessee
WCMT Martin, Tennessee
WTPR-FM McKinnon, Tennessee
WXMX Millington, Tennessee
WLIK Newport, Tennessee
WOKI Oliver Springs, Tennessee
WTPR Paris, Tennessee
WQKR Portland, Tennessee
WKSR Pulaski, Tennessee
WSDT Soddy-Daisy, Tennessee
WNTT Tazewell, Tennessee
WENK Union City, Tennessee
WQMV Waverly, Tennessee
WWON Waynesboro, Tennessee
KPUR Amarillo, Texas
KBYG Big Spring, Texas
KNEL Brady, Texas
KRVA-FM Campbell, Texas
KCTX Childress, Texas
KEFH Clarendon, Texas
KGAP Clarksville, Texas
KHPT Conroe, Texas
KMXR Corpus Christi, Texas
KIVY Crockett, Texas
KLUV Dallas, Texas
KWMC Del Rio, Texas
KDDD-FM Dumas, Texas
KINL Eagle Pass, Texas
KATX Eastland, Texas
KAMA El Paso, Texas
KOFX El Paso, Texas
KLDE Eldorado, Texas
KGAF Gainesville, Texas
KKDA Grand Prairie, Texas
KCOL-FM Groves, Texas
KONO-FM Helotes, Texas
KTBZ-FM Houston, Texas
KHVL Huntsville, Texas
KRVF Kerens, Texas
KHTC(FM) Lake Jackson, Texas
KITY Llano, Texas
KKCL Lorenzo, Texas
KDAV Lubbock, Texas
KOTY Mason, Texas
KQXX-FM Mission, Texas
KCKM Monahans, Texas
KZRB New Boston, Texas
KEYE-FM Perryton, Texas
KREW Plainview, Texas
KITE Port Lavaca, Texas
KROB Robstown, Texas
KTLU Rusk, Texas
KBPA San Marcos, Texas
KSQX Springtown, Texas
KQXS Stephenville, Texas
KTBB-FM Tyler, Texas
KBGO Waco, Texas
KMQX Weatherford, Texas
KVLL-FM Wells, Texas
KBDX Blanding, Utah
KXBN Cedar City, Utah
KODJ Salt Lake City, Utah
KGNT Smithfield, Utah
KDYL South Salt Lake, Utah
WFOS Chesapeake, Virginia
WDIC-FM Clinchco, Virginia
WKEY Covington, Virginia
WYTT Emporia, Virginia
WGRQ Fairview Beach, Virginia
WZRV Front Royal, Virginia
WZEZ Goochland, Virginia
WHAP Hopewell, Virginia
WSLK Moneta, Virginia
WZFM Narrows, Virginia
WARV-FM Petersburg, Virginia
WBBT-FM Powhatan, Virginia
WRAD Radford, Virginia
WRXL Richmond, Virginia
WXBX Rural Retreat, Virginia
WSVO Staunton, Virginia
WKQY Tazewell, Virginia
WSTA Charlotte Amalie, Virgin Islands
WWOD Hartford, Vermont
WSKI Montpelier, Vermont
WVNR Poultney, Vermont
KEYF-FM Cheney, Washington
KLCK Goldendale, Washington
KBRD Lacey, Washington
KEDO Longview, Washington
KBRC Mount Vernon, Washington
KTRW Opportunity, Washington
KDYM Sunnyside, Washington
KYNR Toppenish, Washington
KCSY Twisp, Washington
KTEL Walla Walla, Washington
WGEZ Beloit, Wisconsin
WISS Berlin, Wisconsin
WWIS Black River Falls, Wisconsin
WOTE Clintonville, Wisconsin
WTTN Columbus, Wisconsin
WRJO Eagle River, Wisconsin
WRKU Forestville, Wisconsin
WDGY Hudson, Wisconsin
WHRY Hurley, Wisconsin
WJBL Ladysmith, Wisconsin
WHIT Madison, Wisconsin
WLTU Manitowoc, Wisconsin
WRJC Mauston, Wisconsin
WCCN Neillsville, Wisconsin
WRCW Nekoosa, Wisconsin
WSFQ Peshtigo, Wisconsin
WPVL-FM Platteville, Wisconsin
WPRE Prairie Du Chien, Wisconsin
WRDB Reedsburg, Wisconsin
WRIG Schofield, Wisconsin
WSBW Sister Bay, Wisconsin
WBOG Tomah, Wisconsin
WJJQ-FM Tomahawk, Wisconsin
WKCH Whitewater, Wisconsin
WVBO Winneconne, Wisconsin
WFGM-FM Barrackville, West Virginia
WUKL Bethlehem, West Virginia
WFGH Fort Gay, West Virginia
WCBC-FM Keyser, West Virginia
WFSP-FM Kingwood, West Virginia
WKAZ-FM Miami, West Virginia
WCLG Morgantown, West Virginia
WDMX Vienna, West Virginia
KBBS Buffalo, Wyoming
KKRR Casper, Wyoming
KMLD Casper, Wyoming
KRRR Cheyenne, Wyoming
KKTY Douglas, Wyoming
KANT Guernsey, Wyoming
KYOY Hillsdale, Wyoming
KMER Kemmerer, Wyoming
KREO Pine Bluffs, Wyoming
KPAD Rawlins, Wyoming
KVOW Riverton, Wyoming
KLMI(FM) Rocky River, Oregon
KQOL Sleepy Hollow, Wyoming
KTHE Thermopolis, Wyoming
KHNA Wamsutter, Wyoming
KKLX Worland, Wyoming
KWOR Worland, Wyoming

Polish

WPNA Oak Park, Illinois
KASM Albany, Minnesota
WRKL New City, New York

Portugese

KIGS Hanford, California
KLBS Los Banos, California
WFHL New Bedford, Massachusetts

Public Affairs

KUCB Unalaska, Alaska
KNAI Phoenix, Arizona
WHDD-FM Sharon, Connecticut
WCSP-FM Washington, District of Columbia
WWNN Pompano Beach, Florida
WKFA St. Catherine, Florida
WKCC Kankakee, Illinois
WVBF Middleborough Center, Massachusetts
WFMR Orleans, Massachusetts
KMSK Austin, Minnesota
KMSU Mankato, Minnesota
KUFL Libby, Montana
KPJH Polson, Montana
WKNS Kinston, North Carolina
WZNB New Bern, North Carolina
KABU Fort Totten, North Dakota
KRAR Espanola, New Mexico
KRRE Las Vegas, New Mexico
KBOM Socorro, New Mexico
WSLG Gouverneur, New York
WXLS Tupper Lake, New York
WGLE Lima, Ohio
WGTE-FM Toledo, Ohio
KZME Brightwood, Oregon
KTCB Tillamook, Oregon
KVRI Blaine, Washington

Reggae

KMSA Grand Junction, Colorado
WQTQ Hartford, Connecticut
WDJA Delray Beach, Florida
KPVS Hilo, Hawaii
KQMQ-FM Honolulu, Hawaii
WGXC Acra, New York
WNYU-FM New York, New York
WVIS Vieques, Puerto Rico
WVJZ Charlotte Amalie, Virgin Islands
WJKC Christiansted, Virgin Islands
WSTX-FM Christiansted, Virgin Islands

Religious

KATB Anchorage, Alaska
KDLG-FM Dillingham, Alaska
KBKO Kodiak, Alaska
KNOM Nome, Alaska
KJNP North Pole, Alaska
KJNP-FM North Pole, Alaska
KRSA Petersburg, Alaska
KUDU Tok, Alaska
WSTF Andalusia, Alabama
WRAB Arab, Alabama
WATV Birmingham, Alabama
WBFR Birmingham, Alabama
WLJR Birmingham, Alabama
WXJC Birmingham, Alabama
WALN Carrollton, Alabama
WYFD Decatur, Alabama
WMBV Dixons Mills, Alabama
WDYF Dothan, Alabama
WGTF Dothan, Alabama
WMOB Mobile, Alabama
WLBF Montgomery, Alabama
WTBJ Oxford, Alabama
WAQG Ozark, Alabama
WJCK Piedmont, Alabama
WAQU Selma, Alabama
WRNF Selma, Alabama
WAKD Sheffield, Alabama
WDLG Thomasville, Alabama
KVMN Cave City, Arkansas
KBDO Des Arc, Arkansas
KVDW England, Arkansas
KARH Forrest City, Arkansas
KAOW Fort Smith, Arkansas
KFSA Fort Smith, Arkansas
KAOG Jonesboro, Arkansas
KUUZ Lake Village, Arkansas
KAAY Little Rock, Arkansas
KCAV Marshall, Arkansas
KWLR Maumelle, Arkansas
KCMH Mountain Home, Arkansas
KSSW Nashville, Arkansas
KANX Sheridan, Arkansas
KMTL Sherwood, Arkansas
KLRC Siloam Springs, Arkansas
KWRB Bisbee, Arizona
KPXQ Glendale, Arizona
KNLB Lake Havasu City, Arizona
KASA Phoenix, Arizona
KFLR-FM Phoenix, Arizona
KPHF Phoenix, Arizona
KRCI Pinetop-Lakeside, Arizona
KNXN Sierra Vista, Arizona
KXXT Tolleson, Arizona
KFLT Tucson, Arizona
KFLT-FM Tucson, Arizona
KWIM Window Rock, Arizona
KYRM Yuma, Arizona
KLFF Arroyo Grande, California
KBRT Avalon, California
KFRB Bakersfield, California
KLHC Bakersfield, California
KWTH Barstow, California
KWTW Bishop, California
KMRO Camarillo, California
KYCJ Camino, California
KHAP Chico, California
KFRJ China Lake, California
KPSH Coachella, California
KFRP Coalinga, California
KFVR Crescent City, California
KSAC-FM Dunnigan, California

RADIO - U.S.

KECR El Cajon, California
KASK Fairfield, California
KYCI Firebaugh, California
KJCU Fort Bragg, California
KJPG Frazier Park, California
KEYQ Fresno, California
KFNO Fresno, California
KGED Fresno, California
KXEX Fresno, California
KXBC Garberville, California
KKMC Gonzales, California
KAXL Greenacres, California
KPJP Greenville, California
KEFR Le Grand, California
KJOP Lemoore, California
KCJH Livingston, California
KLWG Lompoc, California
KLTX Long Beach, California
KHOT Madera, California
KCBC Manteca, California
KADV Modesto, California
KHPY Moreno Valley, California
KHCS Palm Desert, California
KKXX Paradise, California
KPRO Riverside, California
KSGN Riverside, California
KRBP Rock Creek, California
KEBR Rocklin, California
KEAR-FM Sacramento, California
KJAY Sacramento, California
KEZY San Bernardino, California
KWVE-FM San Clemente, California
KSDO San Diego, California
KEAR San Francisco, California
KFAX San Francisco, California
KJDJ San Luis Obispo, California
KPRZ San Marcos-Poway, California
KHFR Santa Maria, California
KGZO Shafter, California
KFRS Soledad, California
KWG Stockton, California
KYCC Stockton, California
KPRA Ukiah, California
KDIA Vallejo, California
KARM Visalia, California
KSMH West Sacramento, California
KJCQ Westwood, California
KLLV Breen, Colorado
KLTT Commerce City, Colorado
KBJD Denver, Colorado
KPOF Denver, Colorado
KCIC Grand Junction, Colorado
KFEL Pueblo, Colorado
KFRY Pueblo, Colorado
KGFT Pueblo, Colorado
KTPL Pueblo, Colorado
KTAD Sterling, Colorado
WADS Ansonia, Connecticut
WFAR Danbury, Connecticut
WJMJ Hartford, Connecticut
WFIF Milford, Connecticut
WCTF Vernon, Connecticut
WXHL-FM Christiana, Delaware
WSWN Belle Glade, Florida
WYFZ Belleview, Florida
WLVJ Boynton Beach, Florida
WRMB Boynton Beach, Florida
WWBC Cocoa, Florida
WHIM(AM) Coral Gables, Florida
WDCF Dade City, Florida
WMFJ Daytona Beach, Florida
WJED Dogwood Lakes Estate, Florida
WKTO Edgewater, Florida
WSEB Englewood, Florida
WMFL Florida City, Florida
WJFP Fort Pierce, Florida
WYFB Gainesville, Florida
WSYR-FM Gifford, Florida
WAPN Holly Hill, Florida
WWWK Islamorada, Florida
WCGL Jacksonville, Florida
WJFR Jacksonville, Florida
WQOP Jacksonville, Florida
WJIR Key West, Florida
WKIZ Key West, Florida
WYBX(FM) Key West, Florida
WKES Lakeland, Florida
WONN Lakeland, Florida
WAPB Madison, Florida
WGSG Mayo, Florida
WCIF Melbourne, Florida
WFRF-FM Monticello, Florida
WJLU New Smyrna Beach, Florida
WRSO(AM) Orlovista, Florida
WJTF Panama City, Florida
WVIJ Port Charlotte, Florida
WFRU Quincy, Florida
WKZM Sarasota, Florida
WKFA St. Catherine, Florida
WUJC St. Marks, Florida
WFTI-FM St. Petersburg, Florida
WTIS Tampa, Florida
WYFE Tarpon Springs, Florida
WPIO Titusville, Florida
WSCF-FM Vero Beach, Florida
WWVO Albany, Georgia
WLTA Alpharetta, Georgia
WFRP Americus, Georgia
WXAG Athens, Georgia
WAEC Atlanta, Georgia
WGUN Atlanta, Georgia
WFAM Augusta, Georgia
WGMI Bremen, Georgia
WCCV Cartersville, Georgia
WRWH Cleveland, Georgia
WFRC Columbus, Georgia
WYFK Columbus, Georgia
WWEV-FM Cumming, Georgia
WDPC Dallas, Georgia
WDCY Douglasville, Georgia
WTJH East Point, Georgia
WMVV Griffin, Georgia
WAKB Hephzibah, Georgia
WGML Hinesville, Georgia
WBML Macon, Georgia
WNEA Newnan, Georgia
WOCE Ringgold, Georgia
WYFS Savannah, Georgia
WHKV Sylvester, Georgia
WRAF Toccoa Falls, Georgia
WGOV Valdosta, Georgia
WASW Waycross, Georgia
WYFA Waynesboro, Georgia
WYFW Winder, Georgia
KTWG Agana, Guam
KSDA-FM Agat, Guam
KCIF Hilo, Hawaii
KHJC Lihue, Hawaii
KFFF-FM Boone, Iowa
KDFR Des Moines, Iowa
KEGR Fort Dodge, Iowa
KCMR Mason City, Iowa
KDCR Sioux Center, Iowa
KNWS Waterloo, Iowa
KNWS-FM Waterloo, Iowa
KGEM Boise, Idaho
KMHR(AM) Boise, Idaho
KBGN Caldwell, Idaho
KBXL Caldwell, Idaho
KZJB Pocatello, Idaho
KYMS Rathdrum, Idaho
KEFX Twin Falls, Idaho
WBJW Albion, Illinois
WXAN Ava, Illinois
WRMS Beardstown, Illinois
WTSG Carlinville, Illinois
WLHW Casey, Illinois
WNTD Chicago, Illinois
WYLL Chicago, Illinois
WDLM East Moline, Illinois
WCBW-FM East St. Louis, Illinois
WRYT Edwardsville, Illinois
WGNN Fisher, Illinois
WJCH Joliet, Illinois
WGSL Loves Park, Illinois
WOTW Monee, Illinois
WAPO Mount Vernon, Illinois
WONC Naperville, Illinois
WWGN Ottawa, Illinois
WCIC Pekin, Illinois
WLWJ Petersburg, Illinois
WSCT Springfield, Illinois
WGNJ St. Joseph, Illinois
WIHM Taylorville, Illinois
WGNR-FM Anderson, Indiana
WGLL Auburn, Indiana
WSPM Cloverdale, Indiana
WFOF Covington, Indiana
WCMR Elkhart, Indiana
WVHI Evansville, Indiana
WBGW Fort Branch, Indiana
WLYV Fort Wayne, Indiana
WHLP Hanna, Indiana
WIWC Kokomo, Indiana
WYTJ Linton, Indiana
WBHW Loogootee, Indiana
WMBL Mitchell, Indiana
WFIA-FM New Albany, Indiana
WSLM Salem, Indiana
WSLM-FM Salem, Indiana
WUBS South Bend, Indiana
WHOJ Terre Haute, Indiana
WKRY Versailles, Indiana
WATI Vincennes, Indiana
WTMK Wanatah, Indiana
WHPL West Lafayette, Indiana
KAXR Arkansas City, Kansas
KBJQ Bronson, Kansas
KHYM Copeland, Kansas
KJIL Copeland, Kansas
KPOR Emporia, Kansas
KVCY Fort Scott, Kansas
KGCR Goodland, Kansas
KBDA Great Bend, Kansas
KPRD Hays, Kansas
KREJ Medicine Lodge, Kansas
KCCV Overland Park, Kansas
KAKA Salina, Kansas
KJTY Topeka, Kansas
KSGL Wichita, Kansas
WYWY Barbourville, Kentucky
WMTA Central City, Kentucky
WKDP Corbin, Kentucky
WCPM Cumberland, Kentucky
WKVO Georgetown, Kentucky
WSGP Glasgow, Kentucky
WJMD Hazard, Kentucky
WKVG Jenkins, Kentucky
WDFB Junction City, Kentucky
WJMM-FM Keene, Kentucky
WYGE London, Kentucky
WMIK-FM Middlesboro, Kentucky
WLCR Mt Washington, Kentucky
WMJR Nicholasville, Kentucky
WPTJ Paris, Kentucky
WJSO Pikeville, Kentucky
WLCK Scottsville, Kentucky
WTHL Somerset, Kentucky
WMTC Vancleve, Kentucky
WMTC-FM Vancleve, Kentucky
WEKC Williamsburg, Kentucky
KAPM Alexandria, Louisiana
KJMJ Alexandria, Louisiana
KAXV Bastrop, Louisiana
WPFC Baton Rouge, Louisiana
WPYR Baton Rouge, Louisiana
KBZE Berwick, Louisiana
KFLO-FM Blanchard, Louisiana
KCKR Church Point, Louisiana
WWRA Clinton, Louisiana
KAJN-FM Crowley, Louisiana
KBAN De Ridder, Louisiana
KVDP Dry Prong, Louisiana
KPAE Erwinville, Louisiana
WCKW Garyville, Louisiana
KKNO Gretna, Louisiana
KAYT Jena, Louisiana
KOJO Lake Charles, Louisiana
KYLC Lake Charles, Louisiana
KAVK Many, Louisiana
KBIO Natchitoches, Louisiana
WLNO New Orleans, Louisiana
WSHO New Orleans, Louisiana
KAPI Ruston, Louisiana
KSJY St. Martinville, Louisiana
WSRO Ashland, Massachusetts
WEZE Boston, Massachusetts
WJWT Gardner, Massachusetts
WVNE Leicester, Massachusetts
WNEB Worcester, Massachusetts
WBMD Baltimore, Maryland
WOLB Baltimore, Maryland
WSRY Elkton, Maryland
WMET Gaithersburg, Maryland
WGTS Takoma Park, Maryland
WWPN Westernport, Maryland
WCRH Williamsport, Maryland
WMDR Augusta, Maine
WHCF Bangor, Maine
WFST Caribou, Maine
WXBP Corinth, Maine
WYFP Harpswell, Maine
WJCX Pittsfield, Maine

WBAE Portland, Maine
WSEW Sanford, Maine
WUFN Albion, Michigan
WAAM Ann Arbor, Michigan
WGCP Cadillac, Michigan
WLJW Cadillac, Michigan
WRQC(FM) East Tawas, Michigan
WLJN Elmwood Township, Michigan
WPHN Gaylord, Michigan
WGDN Gladwin, Michigan
WFUR Grand Rapids, Michigan
WFUR-FM Grand Rapids, Michigan
WDRJ Inkster, Michigan
WJKN Jackson, Michigan
WKPR Kalamazoo, Michigan
WEUL Kingsford, Michigan
WMPC Lapeer, Michigan
WHWL Marquette, Michigan
WNIL Niles, Michigan
KTGG Okemos, Michigan
WMKD Pickford, Michigan
WPCJ Pittsford, Michigan
WNFA Port Huron, Michigan
WNFR Sandusky, Michigan
WTHN Sault Ste. Marie, Michigan
WOFR Schoolcraft, Michigan
WUFL Sterling Heights, Michigan
WHST Tawas City, Michigan
WLJN-FM Traverse City, Michigan
WHWG Trout Lake, Michigan
WGNB Zeeland, Michigan
KJLY Blue Earth, Minnesota
KYCR Golden Valley, Minnesota
WCTS Maplewood, Minnesota
KTIS Minneapolis, Minnesota
KTIS-FM Minneapolis, Minnesota
KBPG Montevideo, Minnesota
KTIG Pequot Lakes, Minnesota
KCFB St. Cloud, Minnesota
KBHZ Willmar, Minnesota
KGNA-FM Arnold, Missouri
KHCR Bismarck, Missouri
KOZO Branson, Missouri
KFUO Clayton, Missouri
KDJR De Soto, Missouri
KJXX Jackson, Missouri
KAUF Kennett, Missouri
KCKV Kirksville, Missouri
KBGM Park Hills, Missouri
KLUH Poplar Bluff, Missouri
KEXS-FM Ravenwood, Missouri
KWFC Springfield, Missouri
KSIV-FM St. Louis, Missouri
KXEN St. Louis, Missouri
KNLN Vienna, Missouri
WJNS-FM Bentonia, Mississippi
WTGY Charleston, Mississippi
WWUN-FM Friar's Point, Mississippi
WBVV Guntown, Mississippi
WAII Hattiesburg, Mississippi
WATP Laurel, Mississippi
WESY Leland, Mississippi
WSJC Magee, Mississippi
WAQL McComb, Mississippi
WASM Natchez, Mississippi
WSEL Pontotoc, Mississippi
WSEL-FM Pontotoc, Mississippi
WATU Port Gibson, Mississippi
WSAO Senatobia, Mississippi
WJZB Starkville, Mississippi
WZKM Waynesboro, Mississippi
KGVW Belgrade, Montana
KBLW Billings, Montana
KEDR(FM) Butte, Montana
KFRD Butte, Montana
KJLF Butte, Montana
KMCJ Colstrip, Montana
KGLE Glendive, Montana
KFRW Great Falls, Montana
KGFC Great Falls, Montana
KXEI Havre, Montana
KVCM Helena, Montana
KLEU Lewistown, Montana
KPLG Plains, Montana
KMBM Polson, Montana
KPGB Pryor, Montana
WCGC Belmont, North Carolina
WCCE Buies Creek, North Carolina
WPTL Canton, North Carolina
WHVN Charlotte, North Carolina
WCLN-FM Clinton, North Carolina
WCKB Dunn, North Carolina
WLOE Eden, North Carolina
WFMO Fairmont, North Carolina
WWOL Forest City, North Carolina
WPFJ Franklin, North Carolina
WNNL Fuquay-Varina, North Carolina
WYCV Granite Falls, North Carolina
WKEW Greensboro, North Carolina
WYFL Henderson, North Carolina
WHPE-FM High Point, North Carolina
WMYN Mayodan, North Carolina
WOTJ Morehead City, North Carolina
WDJS Mount Olive, North Carolina
WAUG New Hope, North Carolina
WGCR Pisgah Forest, North Carolina
WCLY Raleigh, North Carolina
WEED Rocky Mount, North Carolina
WEGG Rose Hill, North Carolina
WYAL Scotland Neck, North Carolina
WVCB Shallotte, North Carolina
WCOK Sparta, North Carolina
WYFQ-FM Wadesboro, North Carolina
WSMY Weldon, North Carolina
WIAM Williamston, North Carolina
WLSG Wilmington, North Carolina
WPOL Winston-Salem, North Carolina
KBFR Bismarck, North Dakota
KHRT Minot, North Dakota
KFNW West Fargo, North Dakota
KPNY Alliance, Nebraska
KJGS Aurora, Nebraska
KNBE Beatrice, Nebraska
KTLX Columbus, Nebraska
KNFA Grand Island, Nebraska
KROA Grand Island, Nebraska
KAYA Hubbard, Nebraska
KNGN McCook, Nebraska
KPNO Norfolk, Nebraska
KJLT-FM North Platte, Nebraska
KOTK Omaha, Nebraska
KGRD Orchard, Nebraska
KCMI Terrytown, Nebraska
WDER Derry, New Hampshire
WVFA Lebanon, New Hampshire
WYGG Asbury Park, New Jersey
WAYV Atlantic City, New Jersey
WTMR Camden, New Jersey
WJPG Cape May Court House, New Jersey
WKVP Cherry Hill, New Jersey
WFME Newark, New Jersey
WXMC Parsippany-Troy Hill, New Jersey
WCHR Trenton, New Jersey
WJPH Woodbine, New Jersey
KYCM Alamogordo, New Mexico
KFLQ Albuquerque, New Mexico
KSVA Albuquerque, New Mexico
KNKT Armijo, New Mexico
KAQF Clovis, New Mexico
KZPI Deming, New Mexico
KRUC Las Cruces, New Mexico
KCKN Roswell, New Mexico
KWFL Roswell, New Mexico
KYCT Ruidoso, New Mexico
KKVV Las Vegas, Nevada
KSOS Las Vegas, Nevada
KXTO Reno, Nevada
WNGN Argyle, New York
WDCX-FM Buffalo, New York
WFBF Buffalo, New York
WLYK Cape Vincent, New York
WCHP Champlain, New York
WJIV Cherry Valley, New York
WYBY Cortland, New York
WSIV E. Syracuse, New York
WLOF Elma, New York
WLNL Horseheads, New York
WFRH Kingston, New York
WYRR Lakewood, New York
WTHE Mineola, New York
WJUX Monticello, New York
WAXQ New York, New York
WWRV New York, New York
WNYK Nyack, New York
WGKV Pulaski, New York
WSFW Seneca Falls, New York
WFRW Webster, New York
WNYV Whitehall, New York
WTOR Youngstown, New York
WJYM Bowling Green, Ohio
WNOC Bowling Green, Ohio
WYFY Cambridge, Ohio
WCVX Cincinnati, Ohio
WCRF-FM Cleveland, Ohio
WHVT Clyde, Ohio
WRFD Columbus-Worthington, Ohio
WCUE Cuyahoga Falls, Ohio
WJJE Delaware, Ohio
WGNZ Fairborn, Ohio
WXMF Marion, Ohio
WFCJ Miamisburg, Ohio
WVML Millersburg, Ohio
WVMS Sandusky, Ohio
WAUI Shelby, Ohio
WOTL Toledo, Ohio
WBBW Youngstown, Ohio
WYTN Youngstown, Ohio
WJIC Zanesville, Ohio
KKWD(FM) Bethany, Colorado
KJHL Boise City, Oklahoma
KNYD Broken Arrow, Oklahoma
KDIM Coweta, Oklahoma
KAYC Durant, Oklahoma
KHEV Fairview, Oklahoma
KSYE Frederick, Oklahoma
KMFS Guthrie, Oklahoma
KALU Langston, Oklahoma
KVRS Lawton, Oklahoma
KMSI Moore, Oklahoma
KLVV Ponca City, Oklahoma
KARG Poteau, Oklahoma
KCFO Tulsa, Oklahoma
KAYM Weatherford, Oklahoma
KGIO Astoria, Oregon
KDJC Baker, Oregon
KJCH Coos Bay, Oregon
KAPK Grants Pass, Oregon
KDOV Medford, Oregon
KYOR Newport, Oregon
KPFR Pine Grove, Oregon
KBVM Portland, Oregon
KAJC Salem, Oregon
KLWJ(AM) Umatilla, Oregon
KGRV Winston, Oregon
WJCS Allentown, Pennsylvania
WUFR Bedford, Pennsylvania
WFKJ Cashtown, Pennsylvania
WPWA Chester, Pennsylvania
WVCH Chester, Pennsylvania
WPGM Danville, Pennsylvania
WISP Doylestown, Pennsylvania
WCOH-FM Du Bois, Pennsylvania
WEFR Erie, Pennsylvania
WHHN Hollidaysburg, Pennsylvania
WPPZ-FM Jenkintown, Pennsylvania
WJSA Jersey Shore, Pennsylvania
WJSA-FM Jersey Shore, Pennsylvania
WJSM-FM Martinsburg, Pennsylvania
WWBJ Martinsburg, Pennsylvania
WRIJ Masontown, Pennsylvania
WVME Meadville, Pennsylvania
WPEL-FM Montrose, Pennsylvania
WRWJ Murrysville, Pennsylvania
WBGM New Berlin, Pennsylvania
WVMN New Castle, Pennsylvania
WPCL Northern Cambria, Pennsylvania
WPHE Phoenixville, Pennsylvania
WLKH Somerset, Pennsylvania
WKDN(FM) State College, Pennsylvania
WRGN Sweet Valley, Pennsylvania
WBMR Telford, Pennsylvania
WLIH Whitneyville, Pennsylvania
WFAB Ceiba, Puerto Rico
WJVP Culebra, Puerto Rico
WCRP Guayama, Puerto Rico
WIVV Island of Vieques, Puerto Rico
WCGB Juana Diaz, Puerto Rico
WRRE Juncos, Puerto Rico
WYEL Mayaguez, Puerto Rico
WPPC Penuelas, Puerto Rico
WBMJ San Juan, Puerto Rico
WKVM San Juan, Puerto Rico
WARV Warwick, Rhode Island
WMIR Atlantic Beach, South Carolina
WVCD Bamberg-Denmark, South Carolina
WAGP Beaufort, South Carolina
WYFV Cayce, South Carolina
WFCH Charleston, South Carolina
WLTQ Charleston, South Carolina
WQXL Columbia, South Carolina
WPDT Coward, South Carolina
WFGN Gaffney, South Carolina
WYFG Gaffney, South Carolina

WLMC Georgetown, South Carolina
WPJF Greenville, South Carolina
WTBI-FM Greenville, South Carolina
WBZF Hartsville, South Carolina
WRIX Homeland Park, South Carolina
WJNI Ladson, South Carolina
WKZK North Augusta, South Carolina
WYFH North Charleston, South Carolina
WKVC North Myrtle Beach, South Carolina
WNMB North Myrtle Beach, South Carolina
WPJK Orangeburg, South Carolina
WCSZ Sans Souci, South Carolina
WFMV South Congaree, South Carolina
WLJI Summerton, South Carolina
WQUL(AM) Woodruff, South Carolina
KKAA Aberdeen, South Dakota
KBRK Brookings, South Dakota
KVCF Freeman, South Dakota
KVFL Pierre, South Dakota
KQFR Rapid City, South Dakota
KQKD Redfield, South Dakota
KNWC Sioux Falls, South Dakota
WBIN Benton, Tennessee
WMBW Chattanooga, Tennessee
WYBK(FM) Chattanooga, Tennessee
WMCH Church Hill, Tennessee
WSGM Coalmont, Tennessee
WWOG Cookeville, Tennessee
WMKW Crossville, Tennessee
WBEJ Elizabethton, Tennessee
WYXE Gallatin, Tennessee
WCLC Jamestown, Tennessee
WCLC-FM Jamestown, Tennessee
WDEB Jamestown, Tennessee
WKXV Knoxville, Tennessee
WMQM Lakeland, Tennessee
WBLC Lenoir City, Tennessee
WAXO Lewisburg, Tennessee
WFLI Lookout Mountain, Tennessee
WYDL Middleton, Tennessee
WFCM-FM Murfreesboro, Tennessee
WENO Nashville, Tennessee
WLAC Nashville, Tennessee
WNQM Nashville, Tennessee
WYFN Nashville, Tennessee
WDNX Olive Hill, Tennessee
WAUV Ripley, Tennessee
WSIB Selmer, Tennessee
WFCM Smyrna, Tennessee
WZYZ Spencer, Tennessee
WYLJ(FM) Tullahoma, Tennessee
WZTH Tusculum, Tennessee
KAQD Abilene, Texas
KDRY Alamo Heights, Texas
KAVW Amarillo, Texas
KJRT Amarillo, Texas
KRGN Amarillo, Texas
KEDR Bay City, Texas
KPDB Big Lake, Texas
KBCX Big Spring, Texas
KMZZ Bishop, Texas
KASV Borger, Texas
KBNR Brownsville, Texas
KBEN Carrizo Springs, Texas
KUZN Centerville, Texas
KAFR Conroe, Texas
KBNJ Corpus Christi, Texas
KCTA Corpus Christi, Texas
KCBI Dallas, Texas
KGGR Dallas, Texas
KDKR Decatur, Texas
KDHN Dimmitt, Texas
KOIR Edinburg, Texas
KVER El Paso, Texas
KVIV El Paso, Texas
KPAS Fabens, Texas
KIJN Farwell, Texas
KIJN-FM Farwell, Texas
KFST Fort Stockton, Texas
KRBL Idalou, Texas
KBJS Jacksonville, Texas
KINE Kingsville, Texas
KHOY Laredo, Texas
KBMD Marble Falls, Texas
KBIB Marion, Texas
KCAS McCook, Texas
KFLB Odessa, Texas
KYFP Palestine, Texas
KAVO Pampa, Texas
KFTG Pasadena, Texas
KPMB Plainview, Texas
KDEI Port Arthur, Texas
KMFM Premont, Texas
KBIC Raymondville, Texas
KRTX Rosenburg-Richmond, Texas
KCRN-FM San Angelo, Texas
KFLB-FM Stanton, Texas
KGLY Tyler, Texas
KVNE Tyler, Texas
KHTA Wake Village, Texas
KANI Wharton, Texas
KPDR Wheeler, Texas
KEZB Beaver, Utah
KEMR Castle Dale, Utah
KEYD Delta, Utah
KRRA Paragonah, Utah
KEYP Price, Utah
KEYR Richfield, Utah
KUFR Salt Lake City, Utah
WLSD Big Stone Gap, Virginia
WAUQ Charles City, Virginia
WJYK Chase City, Virginia
WNLR Churchville, Virginia
WARN Culpeper, Virginia
WOTC Edinburg, Virginia
WKNV Fairlawn, Virginia
WFAX Falls Church, Virginia
WPAK Farmville, Virginia
WYFT Luray, Virginia
WKPA Lynchburg, Virginia
WLVA Lynchburg, Virginia
WRVL Lynchburg, Virginia
WYFI Norfolk, Virginia
WYRM Norfolk, Virginia
WNVA Norton, Virginia
WEQP Pamplin City, Virginia
WGTH-FM Richlands, Virginia
WREJ Richmond, Virginia
WRIS Roanoke, Virginia
WRXT Roanoke, Virginia
WKGM Smithfield, Virginia
WSBV South Boston, Virginia
WXLZ St. Paul, Virginia
WKBA Vinton, Virginia
WYCS Yorktown, Virginia
WGOD-FM Charlotte Amalie, Virgin Islands
WIVH Christiansted, Virgin Islands
WCMD-FM Barre, Vermont
WGLY-FM Bolton, Vermont
WFTF Rutland, Vermont
WTWN Wells River, Vermont
KGNW Burien-Seattle, Washington
KUCC Clarkston, Washington
KSPO Dishman, Washington
KCSH Ellensburg, Washington
KTBI Ephrata, Washington
KARR Kirkland, Washington
KJVH Longview, Washington
KWPZ Lynden, Washington
KOLU Pasco, Washington
KACS Rainier, Washington
KBLE Seattle, Washington
KMBI-FM Spokane, Washington
KAYB Sunnyside, Washington
KSOH Wapato, Washington
KPLW Wenatchee, Washington
KBNO-FM White Salmon, Washington
WDVM Eau Claire, Wisconsin
WVFL Fond Du Lac, Wisconsin
WJTY Lancaster, Wisconsin
WJWD Marshall, Wisconsin
WHJL Merrill, Wisconsin
WMWK Milwaukee, Wisconsin
WVCY-FM Milwaukee, Wisconsin
WMMA Nekoosa, Wisconsin
WVCY Oshkosh, Wisconsin
WRVM Suring, Wisconsin
WVCX Tomah, Wisconsin
WEGZ Washburn, Wisconsin
WJJJ Beckley, West Virginia
WJLS Beckley, West Virginia
WHIS Bluefield, West Virginia
WXAF Charleston, West Virginia
WFSP-FM Kingwood, West Virginia
WOTR(FM) Lost Creek, West Virginia
WELD-FM Moorefield, West Virginia
WRLB Rainelle, West Virginia
WMXE South Charleston, West Virginia
WJYP St. Albans, West Virginia
WBBD Wheeling, West Virginia
KAXG Gillette, Wyoming
KOHR Sheridan, Wyoming
KWCF Sheridan, Wyoming

Rock/AOR

KWHL Anchorage, Alaska
KKED Fairbanks, Alaska
KSUP Juneau, Alaska
WRTT-FM Huntsville, Alabama
KKEG Bentonville, Arkansas
KDJE Jacksonville, Arkansas
KERX Paris, Arkansas
KDKB Mesa, Arizona
KUPD Tempe, Arizona
KBRE Atwater, California
KRRX Burney, California
KFMF Chico, California
KSSI China Lake, California
KCLB-FM Coachella, California
KVHS Concord, California
KRAB Greenacres, California
KURQ Grover Beach, California
KSLG-FM Hydesville, California
KHDR Lenwood, California
KCBS-FM Los Angeles, California
KHWZ Ludlow, California
KAKX Mendocino, California
KJEE Montecito, California
KSFH Mountain View, California
KRQR Orland, California
KROQ-FM Pasadena, California
KQNY Quincy, California
KCAL-FM Redlands, California
KMRQ Riverbank, California
KRXQ Sacramento, California
KZOZ San Luis Obispo, California
KTYD Santa Barbara, California
KRZR Visalia, California
KMKX Willits, California
KBPI Denver, Colorado
KRKV Las Animas, Colorado
WQAQ Hamden, Connecticut
WCCC-FM Hartford, Connecticut
WHCN Hartford, Connecticut
WPLR New Haven, Connecticut
WECS Willimantic, Connecticut
WYYX Bonifay, Florida
WNDN Chiefland, Florida
WJRR Cocoa Beach, Florida
WAAZ-FM Crestview, Florida
WXXJ Jacksonville, Florida
WFEZ(FM) Miami, Florida
WHHZ Newberry, Florida
WHOG-FM Ormond-By-The-Sea, Florida
WTKX-FM Pensacola, Florida
WFKZ Plantation Key, Florida
WGLF Tallahassee, Florida
WQTL Tallahassee, Florida
WWPW(FM) Atlanta, Georgia
WNNX College Park, Georgia
WVRK Columbus, Georgia
WAWH Dublin, Georgia
WBCX Gainesville, Georgia
WRXR-FM Rossville, Georgia
WWRQ-FM Valdosta, Georgia
KQCS Bettendorf, Iowa
KBOB-FM De Witt, Iowa
KRNA Iowa City, Iowa
KAZR Pella, Iowa
KCVI Blackfoot, Idaho
KZDX Burley, Idaho
KZID Culdesac, Idaho
KHTQ Hayden, Idaho
KOZE-FM Lewiston, Idaho
WXRX Belvidere, Illinois
WRXX Centralia, Illinois
WXRT Chicago, Illinois
KPNT Collinsville, Illinois
WKTA Evanston, Illinois
WLSR Galesburg, Illinois
WHPI Glasford, Illinois
WLCA Godfrey, Illinois
WTAO-FM Herrin, Illinois
WCSF Joliet, Illinois
WLTL La Grange, Illinois
WNLF Macomb, Illinois
WLKL Mattoon, Illinois
WDCR Oreana, Illinois
WIXO Peoria, Illinois
WQLZ Taylorville, Illinois
WCVS-FM Virden, Illinois
WDML Woodlawn, Illinois

RADIO - U.S.

WJAA Austin, Indiana
WTFX-FM Clarksville, Indiana
WSFR Corydon, Indiana
WRGF Greenfield, Indiana
WKHY Lafayette, Indiana
WWHI Muncie, Indiana
WXXR(FM) Seelyville, Indiana
WRBR-FM South Bend, Indiana
WISU Terre Haute, Indiana
WBYR Woodburn, Indiana
KACY Arkansas City, Kansas
KQRC-FM Leavenworth, Kansas
KMKF Manhattan, Kansas
KFIX Plainville, Kansas
KDVV Topeka, Kansas
KICT-FM Wichita, Kansas
WCMI-FM Catlettsburg, Kentucky
WGBF-FM Henderson, Kentucky
WKCB-FM Hindman, Kentucky
WIFX-FM Jenkins, Kentucky
WKTG Madisonville, Kentucky
WZZL Reidland, Kentucky
WKCA Salt Lick, Kentucky
WLRS Shepherdsville, Kentucky
KEZP Bunkie, Louisiana
WBMT Boxford, Massachusetts
WKAF Brockton, Massachusetts
WHRB Cambridge, Massachusetts
WIQH Concord, Massachusetts
WLZX Northampton, Massachusetts
WMHC South Hadley, Massachusetts
WWFX Southbridge, Massachusetts
WMVY Tisbury, Massachusetts
WAAF Westborough, Massachusetts
WIYY Baltimore, Maryland
WDLD Halfway, Maryland
WCYY Biddeford, Maine
WTOS-FM Skowhegan, Maine
WCHW-FM Bay City, Michigan
WRIF Detroit, Michigan
WJZJ Glen Arbor, Michigan
WIMK Iron Mountain, Michigan
WKLT Kalkaska, Michigan
WQUS Lapeer, Michigan
WUPK Marquette, Michigan
WKLZ-FM Petoskey, Michigan
WRKR Portage, Michigan
WWBN Tuscola, Michigan
KKLN Atwater, Minnesota
WMIS-FM Blackduck, Minnesota
KUOM Minneapolis, Minnesota
KXXR Minneapolis, Minnesota
KZRV Sartell, Minnesota
KDXL St. Louis Park, Minnesota
KUOM-FM St. Louis Park, Minnesota
KZIO Two Harbors, Minnesota
KSMR Winona, Minnesota
KWXD Asbury, Missouri
KFEB Campbell, Missouri
KBXR Columbia, Missouri
KCMQ Columbia, Missouri
KCOU Columbia, Missouri
KSHE Crestwood, Missouri
KCGQ-FM Gordonville, Missouri
KBBM Jefferson City, Missouri
KRBZ Kansas City, Missouri
KKBL Monett, Missouri
WSMS Artesia, Mississippi
WCPR-FM Wiggins, Mississippi
KRZN Billings, Montana
KDWG Dillon, Montana
KQRK Ronan, Montana
WRCQ Dunn, North Carolina
WTPT Forest City, North Carolina
WXNR Grifton, North Carolina
WXQR-FM Jacksonville, North Carolina
WRFX Kannapolis, North Carolina
WSFL-FM New Bern, North Carolina
KEYA Belcourt, North Dakota
KJKJ Grand Forks, North Dakota
KFNL Kindred, North Dakota
KIBZ Crete, Nebraska
KLPR Kearney, Nebraska
KRNU Lincoln, Nebraska
KOGA-FM Ogallala, Nebraska
KEZO-FM Omaha, Nebraska
KKJK Ravenna, Nebraska
KWSC Wayne, Nebraska
WGIR-FM Manchester, New Hampshire
WPCR-FM Plymouth, New Hampshire
WHEB Portsmouth, New Hampshire
WMGM Atlantic City, New Jersey
WJSV Morristown, New Jersey
WSOU South Orange, New Jersey
WKNJ-FM Union Township, New Jersey
KZRR Albuquerque, New Mexico
KXPZ Las Cruces, New Mexico
KEND Roswell, New Mexico
KOMP Las Vegas, Nevada
KDOT Reno, Nevada
WCDB Albany, New York
WETD Alfred, New York
WZMR Altamont, New York
WGCC-FM Batavia, New York
WHCL-FM Clinton, New York
WQBJ Cobleskill, New York
WKGB-FM Conklin, New York
WKLL Frankfort, New York
WEFX Henderson, New York
WICB Ithaca, New York
WVBR-FM Ithaca, New York
WPDA Jeffersonville, New York
WJJL Niagara Falls, New York
WKRL-FM North Syracuse, New York
WRHO Oneonta, New York
WPOB Plainview, New York
WRUC Schenectady, New York
WHFM Southampton, New York
WOUR Utica, New York
WPNR-FM Utica, New York
WARY Valhalla, New York
WZIP Akron, Ohio
WRMU-FM Alliance, Ohio
WRDL Ashland, Ohio
WBWC Berea, Ohio
WRQK-FM Canton, Ohio
WEBN Cincinnati, Ohio
WENZ Cleveland, Ohio
WTUE Dayton, Ohio
WZRX-FM Fort Shawnee, Ohio
WKET Kettering, Ohio
WCMO Marietta, Ohio
WLFC North Baltimore, Ohio
WUSO Springfield, Ohio
WSTB Streetsboro, Ohio
WIOT Toledo, Ohio
WLHS West Chester, Ohio
KKBS Guymon, Oklahoma
KHIM Mangum, Oklahoma
KATT-FM Oklahoma City, Oklahoma
KMMY Soper, Oklahoma
KMOD-FM Tulsa, Oklahoma
KWDQ Woodward, Oklahoma
KRXF Bend, Oregon
KFLY Corvallis, Oregon
KZZE Eagle Point, Oregon
KROG Grants Pass, Oregon
KUFO-FM Portland, Oregon
WZZO Bethlehem, Pennsylvania
WBUQ Bloomsburg, Pennsylvania
WCAL California, Pennsylvania
WRVV Harrisburg, Pennsylvania
WBSX Hazleton, Pennsylvania
WKVR-FM Huntingdon, Pennsylvania
WVBU-FM Lewisburg, Pennsylvania
WNTE Mansfield, Pennsylvania
WEEO-FM McConnellsburg, Pennsylvania
WTPA Palmyra, Pennsylvania
WMMR Philadelphia, Pennsylvania
WAVT-FM Pottsville, Pennsylvania
WXAC Reading, Pennsylvania
WUSR Scranton, Pennsylvania
WQSU Selinsgrove, Pennsylvania
WZXR South Williamsport, Pennsylvania
WMTT Tioga, Pennsylvania
WWIZ West Middlesex, Pennsylvania
WRKC Wilkes-Barre, Pennsylvania
WQXA-FM York, Pennsylvania
WCAD San Juan, Puerto Rico
WQRI Bristol, Rhode Island
WHJY Providence, Rhode Island
WYBB Folly Beach, South Carolina
WMFX St. Andrews, South Carolina
KVAR Pine Ridge, South Dakota
KDDX Spearfish, South Dakota
WUTK-FM Knoxville, Tennessee
WBUZ La Vergne, Tennessee
KACC Alvin, Texas
KZRK-FM Canyon, Texas
KTUX Carthage, Texas
KLAQ El Paso, Texas
KHFI-FM Georgetown, Texas
KFRQ Harlingen, Texas
KFMX-FM Lubbock, Texas
KKAM Lubbock, Texas
KISS-FM San Antonio, Texas
KNCN Sinton, Texas
KLYD Snyder, Texas
KBAR-FM Victoria, Texas
KBZS Wichita Falls, Texas
KBER Ogden, Utah
WBRW Blacksburg, Virginia
WROX-FM Exmore, Virginia
WFQX Front Royal, Virginia
WZZU Lynchburg, Virginia
WROV-FM Martinsville, Virginia
WNOR Norfolk, Virginia
WRXL Richmond, Virginia
WNRS-FM Sweet Briar, Virginia
WPTE Virginia Beach, Virginia
WEXP Brandon, Vermont
WWLR Lyndonville, Vermont
WNUB-FM Northfield, Vermont
WIZN Vergennes, Vermont
KGRG-FM Auburn, Washington
KISW Seattle, Washington
KATS Yakima, Washington
WAPL Appleton, Wisconsin
WRQT La Crosse, Wisconsin
WMZK Merrill, Wisconsin
WHQG Milwaukee, Wisconsin
WZOR Mishicot, Wisconsin
WSUP Platteville, Wisconsin
WBDL Reedsburg, Wisconsin
WTCX Ripon, Wisconsin
WSHS Sheboygan, Wisconsin
WNLI Sturgeon Bay, Wisconsin
WBCV Wausau, Wisconsin
WAMX Milton, West Virginia
WHBR-FM Parkersburg, West Virginia
WKLC-FM St. Albans, West Virginia
WEGW Wheeling, West Virginia
KIGN Burns, Wyoming
KAZY Cheyenne, Wyoming
KMTN Jackson, Wyoming

Russian

KICY Nome, Alaska
WKTA Evanston, Illinois

Smooth Jazz

WAAX Gadsden, Alabama
KUAP Pine Bluff, Arkansas
KOAS Dolan Springs, Arizona
KJZP Prescott, Arizona
KSSJ(FM) Fair Oaks, California
KJJZ Indio, California
KTWV Los Angeles, California
KIFM San Diego, California
KKXS Shingletown, California
KMYT Temecula, California
WQTQ Hartford, Connecticut
WXJZ Gainesville, Florida
WZJZ Port Charlotte, Florida
WGYL Vero Beach, Florida
WTSM(FM) Woodville, Florida
KKHI Kihei, Hawaii
KQZB Troy, Idaho
WNUA Chicago, Illinois
WARH Granite City, Illinois
WBDC Huntingburg, Indiana
WKYL Lawrenceburg, Kentucky
WJSH Folsom, Louisiana
WEIB Northampton, Massachusetts
WJZQ Cadillac, Michigan
KZWV Eldon, Missouri
WDAF-FM Liberty, Missouri
KQJZ Evergreen, Montana
WCCE Buies Creek, North Carolina
WRMU-FM Alliance, Ohio
KYSJ Coos Bay, Oregon
KZIU-FM Weston, Oregon
WAEB Allentown, Pennsylvania
WFSK-FM Nashville, Tennessee
KERV Kerrville, Texas
KZAL Manson, Washington
WAUN-FM Kewaunee, Wisconsin

Spanish

WWGC Albertville, Alabama
WYAM Hartselle, Alabama

WCRL Oneonta, Alabama
KDXE North Little Rock, Arkansas
KFFK Rogers, Arkansas
KVVA-FM Apache Junction, Arizona
KKMR Arizona City, Arizona
KRMC Douglas, Arizona
KQMR Globe, Arizona
KRIT Parker, Arizona
KNAI Phoenix, Arizona
KOMR Sun City, Arizona
KBFP Bakersfield, California
KPSL-FM Bakersfield, California
KXSB Big Bear Lake, California
KBBF Calistoga, California
KNTO Chowchilla, California
KCVR-FM Columbia, California
KFVR Crescent City, California
KCHJ Delano, California
KLAX-FM East Los Angeles, California
KLMG Esparto, California
KSSD Fallbrook, California
KDAC Fort Bragg, California
KSCA Glendale, California
KSEA Greenfield, California
KHHZ Gridley, California
KMPG Hollister, California
KBHH Kerman, California
KCVR Lodi, California
KIDI-FM Lompoc, California
KSMY Lompoc, California
KBUE Long Beach, California
KQLB Los Banos, California
KHIT-FM Madera, California
KBQF McFarland, California
KLLE North Fork, California
KAAT Oakhurst, California
KATD Pittsburg, California
KLYY Riverside, California
KSOL San Francisco, California
KVVZ San Rafael, California
KVVF Santa Clara, California
KSQL Santa Cruz, California
KTAP Santa Maria, California
KBLA Santa Monica, California
KSES-FM Seaside, California
KMBX Soledad, California
KLOB Thousand Palms, California
KGEN Tulare, California
KUKI Ukiah, California
KSSC Ventura, California
KLLK Willits, California
KMXA Aurora, Colorado
KBJD Denver, Colorado
KRKY-FM Estes Park, Colorado
KNKN(FM) Pueblo, Colorado
KJJD Windsor, Colorado
WLAT New Britain, Connecticut
WJWL Georgetown, Delaware
WTMP-FM Dade City, Florida
WNUE-FM Deltona, Florida
WRLZ Eatonville, Florida
WVOJ Fernandina Beach, Florida
WKIZ Key West, Florida
WQBQ Leesburg, Florida
WUNA Ocoee, Florida
WPSP Royal Palm Beach, Florida
WYUU Safety Harbor, Florida
WIWA St. Cloud, Florida
WGES St. Petersburg, Florida
WWVA-FM Canton, Georgia
WPBS Conyers, Georgia
WPLO Grayson, Georgia
KWSL Sioux City, Iowa
WAIT Crystal Lake, Illinois
WPPN Des Plaines, Illinois
WVIV-FM Highland Park, Illinois
WVIX Lemont, Illinois
WEDJ Danville, Indiana
WSYW Indianapolis, Indiana
KBUZ Topeka, Kansas
KGLA Gretna, Louisiana
WFNO Norco, Louisiana
WMSX Brockton, Massachusetts
WBQH Silver Spring, Maryland
WYGR Wyoming, Michigan
WREY St. Paul, Minnesota
WGSP Charlotte, North Carolina
WTIK Durham, North Carolina
WYMY Goldsboro, North Carolina
WZUP La Grange, North Carolina
WLLN Lillington, North Carolina
WDNJ Hopatcong, New Jersey
WMIZ Vineland, New Jersey
KLMA Hobbs, New Mexico
KGCN Roswell, New Mexico
KSWV Santa Fe, New Mexico
KAVB Hawthorne, Nevada
KRGT Indian Springs, Nevada
KQRT Las Vegas, Nevada
KWID Las Vegas, Nevada
KQLO Sun Valley, Nevada
WBBF Buffalo, New York
WLIM Patchogue, New York
KREU Roland, Oklahoma
KGIO Astoria, Oregon
WHOL Allentown, Pennsylvania
WEST Easton, Pennsylvania
WWNA Aguadilla, Puerto Rico
WNIK-FM Arecibo, Puerto Rico
WBQN Barceloneta-Manati, Puerto Rico
WXRF Guayama, Puerto Rico
WAEL-FM Maricao, Puerto Rico
WIOB Mayaguez, Puerto Rico
WYQE Naguabo, Puerto Rico
WJDZ Pastillo, Puerto Rico
WRIO Ponce, Puerto Rico
WZMT Ponce, Puerto Rico
WKKB Middletown, Rhode Island
WGVL Greenville, South Carolina
WZJY Mount Pleasant, South Carolina
WKMG Newberry, South Carolina
WNFO Sun City-Hilton Head, South Carolina
WBZK York, South Carolina
WKDA Lebanon, Tennessee
KTCY Azle, Texas
KJON Carrollton, Texas
KWOW Clifton, Texas
KGSX Comfort, Texas
KTLZ Cuero, Texas
KLMO-FM Dilley, Texas
KVLY Edinburg, Texas
KOVE-FM Galveston, Texas
KLJA(FM) Georgetown, Texas
KFRO-FM Gilmer, Texas
KBNL Laredo, Texas
KHOY Laredo, Texas
KNEX Laredo, Texas
KYRQ Natalia, Texas
KQLM Odessa, Texas
KFTG Pasadena, Texas
KNVO-FM Port Isabel, Texas
KROB Robstown, Texas
KDAE Sinton, Texas
KAIQ Wolfforth, Texas
KDUT Randolph, Utah
KBJA Sandy, Utah
WVXX Norfolk, Virginia
WKCW Warrenton, Virginia
KMNA Mabton, Washington
KLES Prosser, Washington
KDYM Sunnyside, Washington
KDNA Yakima, Washington
WORT Madison, Wisconsin

Sports

KTZN Anchorage, Alaska
KCBF Fairbanks, Alaska
WBNM Alexander City, Alabama
WAUD Auburn, Alabama
WNSP Bay Minette, Alabama
WJOX-FM Birmingham, Alabama
WSPZ(AM) Birmingham, Alabama
WFMH Cullman, Alabama
WWTM Decatur, Alabama
WZNJ Demopolis, Alabama
WSBM Florence, Alabama
WHEP Foley, Alabama
WTKI Huntsville, Alabama
WUMP Madison, Alabama
WABB Mobile, Alabama
WNTM Mobile, Alabama
WMSP Montgomery, Alabama
WLAY Muscle Shoals, Alabama
WIQR Prattville, Alabama
WELR Roanoke, Alabama
WYTK Rogersville, Alabama
WWIC Scottsboro, Alabama
WBTG Sheffield, Alabama
WBTG-FM Sheffield, Alabama
WFEB Sylacauga, Alabama
WTLS Tallassee, Alabama
WAXU Troy, Alabama
WTBC Tuscaloosa, Alabama
WVNA Tuscumbia, Alabama
WVSA Vernon, Alabama
WKXM Winfield, Alabama
WSLY York, Alabama
KBTA Batesville, Arkansas
KEWI Benton, Arkansas
KREB Bentonville-Bella, Arkansas
KTHS Berryville, Arkansas
KXXA(AM) Conway, Arkansas
KCJF Earle, Arkansas
KELD El Dorado, Arkansas
KOTN Gould, Arkansas
KFFA-FM Helena, Arkansas
KZHS Hot Springs, Arkansas
KAKS Huntsville, Arkansas
KTTG Mena, Arkansas
KVOM Morrilton, Arkansas
KARV Russellville, Arkansas
KUOA Siloam Springs, Arkansas
KHGG Van Buren, Arkansas
KASR Vilonia, Arkansas
KHGG-FM Waldron, Arkansas
KQPN West Memphis, Arkansas
KVNA Flagstaff, Arizona
KGME Phoenix, Arizona
KMVP Phoenix, Arizona
KTAR Phoenix, Arizona
KQNA Prescott Valley, Arizona
KTAN Sierra Vista, Arizona
KDUS Tempe, Arizona
KFFN Tucson, Arizona
KTKT Tucson, Arizona
KATA Arcata, California
KXTK Arroyo Grande, California
KHTY Bakersfield, California
KFPT Clovis, California
KWRM Corona, California
KCBL Fresno, California
KGST Fresno, California
KCKS Hamilton City, California
KOMY La Selva Beach, California
KAVL Lancaster, California
KLAC Los Angeles, California
KSPN Los Angeles, California
KWKW Los Angeles, California
KMFB(FM) Mendocino, California
KESP Modesto, California
KIDD Monterey, California
KLAA Orange, California
KEWE Oroville, California
KPRL Paso Robles, California
KWKU Pomona, California
KVXX Quincy, California
KNRO Redding, California
KWDJ Ridgecrest, California
KHTK Sacramento, California
KLSD San Diego, California
KNBR San Francisco, California
KTRB San Francisco, California
KKJL San Luis Obispo, California
KTCT San Mateo, California
KCNR Shasta, California
KIRN Simi Valley, California
KXPS Thousand Palms, California
KVFG Victorville, California
KEZL(AM) Visalia, California
KCTC West Sacramento, California
KNFO Basalt, Colorado
KSIR Brush, Colorado
KVOR Colorado Springs, Colorado
KRAI Craig, Colorado
KOA Denver, Colorado
KIUP Durango, Colorado
KIIX Fort Collins, Colorado
KTMM Grand Junction, Colorado
KEPN Lakewood, Colorado
KCKK Littleton, Colorado
KKFN Longmont, Colorado
KWUF Pagosa Springs, Colorado
KJMP Pierce, Colorado
KCSJ Pueblo, Colorado
KRGS Rifle, Colorado
KSBV Salida, Colorado
KBCR Steamboat Springs, Colorado
KSPK-FM Walsenburg, Colorado
WINE Brookfield, Connecticut
WPOP Hartford, Connecticut
WTEM Washington, District of Columbia
WDOV Dover, Delaware

WWTX Wilmington, Delaware
WBGF Belle Glade, Florida
WWJB Brooksville, Florida
WKFL Bushnell, Florida
WMEL Cocoa Beach, Florida
WNDB Daytona Beach, Florida
WTJV Deland, Florida
WJSJ Fernandina Beach, Florida
WFLL Fort Lauderdale, Florida
WGGG Gainesville, Florida
WRUF Gainesville, Florida
WNPL Golden Gate, Florida
WNNR Jacksonville, Florida
WJXL Jacksonville Beach, Florida
WKWF Key West, Florida
WHOO Kissimmee, Florida
WBXY La Crosse, Florida
WFFG Marathon, Florida
WLZR(AM) Melbourne, Florida
WQAM Miami, Florida
WNMA Miami Springs, Florida
WTKE-FM Niceville, Florida
WWCN North Fort Myers, Florida
WMOP Ocala, Florida
WYGM Orlando, Florida
WLTG Panama City, Florida
WASJ Panama City Beach, Florida
WHBO Pinellas Park, Florida
WPSL Port St. Lucie, Florida
WMEN Royal Palm Beach, Florida
WSRQ Sarasota, Florida
WSJZ-FM Sebastian, Florida
WHFS(AM) Seffner, Florida
WFOY St. Augustine, Florida
WDAE St. Petersburg, Florida
WSTU Stuart, Florida
WANM Tallahassee, Florida
WNLS Tallahassee, Florida
WJNO West Palm Beach, Florida
WGPC Albany, Georgia
WSRA Albany, Georgia
WRFC Athens, Georgia
WQXI Atlanta, Georgia
WGAC Augusta, Georgia
WFNS Blackshear, Georgia
WMOG Brunswick, Georgia
WSFN Brunswick, Georgia
WBHF Cartersville, Georgia
WYXC Cartersville, Georgia
WRCG Columbus, Georgia
WDMG Douglas, Georgia
WSGC Elberton, Georgia
WGGA Gainesville, Georgia
WHIE Griffin, Georgia
WWWE Hapeville, Georgia
WCEH Hawkinsville, Georgia
WLOP Jesup, Georgia
WLAG La Grange, Georgia
WTRP La Grange, Georgia
WFOM Marietta, Georgia
WMVG Milledgeville, Georgia
WCOH Newnan, Georgia
WCNN North Atlanta, Georgia
WLAQ Rome, Georgia
WJLG Savannah, Georgia
WPTB Statesboro, Georgia
WWNS Statesboro, Georgia
WJAT Swainsboro, Georgia
WJEM Valdosta, Georgia
WVLD Valdosta, Georgia
WVOP Vidalia, Georgia
KHLO Hilo, Hawaii
KPUA Hilo, Hawaii
KKEA Honolulu, Hawaii
KKON Kealakekua, Hawaii
KAOI Kihei, Hawaii
KUPA Pearl City, Hawaii
KMVI Wailuku, Hawaii
KCNZ Cedar Falls, Iowa
KMJM Cedar Rapids, Iowa
WMT Cedar Rapids, Iowa
KBGG Des Moines, Iowa
KWKY Des Moines, Iowa
KXNO Des Moines, Iowa
WDBQ Dubuque, Iowa
KVFD Fort Dodge, Iowa
KQMG Independence, Iowa
KQMG-FM Independence, Iowa
KIFG-FM Iowa Falls, Iowa
KOKX Keokuk, Iowa
KLEM Le Mars, Iowa
KOEL Oelwein, Iowa
KMNS Sioux City, Iowa
KSCJ Sioux City, Iowa
KBFI Bonners Ferry, Idaho
KTIK Nampa, Idaho
KWEI(AM) Payette, Idaho
KWIK Pocatello, Idaho
KRXK Rexburg, Idaho
KSPT Sandpoint, Idaho
WBIG Aurora, Illinois
WBYS Canton, Illinois
WCIL Carbondale, Illinois
WDWS Champaign, Illinois
WCRX Chicago, Illinois
WGN(AM) Chicago, Illinois
WMVP Chicago, Illinois
WSCR Chicago, Illinois
WXLT Christopher, Illinois
WDAN Danville, Illinois
WDZ Decatur, Illinois
WSOY Decatur, Illinois
WXOS East St. Louis, Illinois
WZPN Farmington, Illinois
WGIL Galesburg, Illinois
WGBK Glenview, Illinois
WJPF Herrin, Illinois
WLPO Lasalle, Illinois
WLUV Loves Park, Illinois
WZZT Morrison, Illinois
WVLN Olney, Illinois
WPRS Paris, Illinois
WZOE Princeton, Illinois
WGEM Quincy, Illinois
WKJR Rantoul, Illinois
WTJK South Beloit, Illinois
WHCO Sparta, Illinois
WFMB Springfield, Illinois
WTAX Springfield, Illinois
WSDR Sterling, Illinois
WSPL Streator, Illinois
KFNS Wood River, Illinois
WBIW Bedford, Indiana
WCSI Columbus, Indiana
WKJG Fort Wayne, Indiana
WOWO Fort Wayne, Indiana
WLTH Gary, Indiana
WREB Greencastle, Indiana
WFNI Indianapolis, Indiana
WNDE Indianapolis, Indiana
WXLW Indianapolis, Indiana
WIOU Kokomo, Indiana
WASK Lafayette, Indiana
WYFX Mount Vernon, Indiana
WXFN Muncie, Indiana
WZZB Seymour, Indiana
WSBT South Bend, Indiana
WBOW Terre Haute, Indiana
WAOV Vincennes, Indiana
WRSW Warsaw, Indiana
KKOY Chanute, Kansas
KFH-FM Clearwater, Kansas
KGGF Coffeyville, Kansas
KGNO Dodge City, Kansas
KIUL Garden City, Kansas
KKCI Goodland, Kansas
KVGB Great Bend, Kansas
KFXX-FM Hugoton, Kansas
KWBW Hutchinson, Kansas
KNNS Larned, Kansas
KLWN Lawrence, Kansas
KMAN Manhattan, Kansas
KLKC Parsons, Kansas
KSEK Pittsburg, Kansas
KINA Salina, Kansas
KMAJ Topeka, Kansas
KTOP Topeka, Kansas
WIBW Topeka, Kansas
KFH Wichita, Kansas
KGSO Wichita, Kansas
KKLE Winfield, Kansas
WCBL Benton, Kentucky
WBGN Bowling Green, Kentucky
WXAM Buffalo, Kentucky
WTCO Campbellsville, Kentucky
WNES Central City, Kentucky
WNTC Drakesboro, Kentucky
WIEL Elizabethtown, Kentucky
WCDS Glasgow, Kentucky
WVLK Lexington, Kentucky
WKRD Louisville, Kentucky
WTTL Madisonville, Kentucky
WWXL Manchester, Kentucky
WNBS Murray, Kentucky
WOFC Murray, Kentucky
WVJS Owensboro, Kentucky
WPAD Paducah, Kentucky
WKYH Paintsville, Kentucky
WWKU Plum Springs, Kentucky
WPKY Princeton, Kentucky
WVLK-FM Richmond, Kentucky
KDBS Alexandria, Louisiana
WJBO Baton Rouge, Louisiana
KBZE Berwick, Louisiana
KRRP Coushatta, Louisiana
KNBB Dubach, Louisiana
KRLQ Hodge, Louisiana
KJIN Houma, Louisiana
KFXZ Lafayette, Louisiana
KPEL Lafayette, Louisiana
WWL New Orleans, Louisiana
WWWL New Orleans, Louisiana
WSLA Slidell, Louisiana
KEZM Sulphur, Louisiana
KMBS West Monroe, Louisiana
WARL Attleboro, Massachusetts
WEEI Boston, Massachusetts
WXBR Brockton, Massachusetts
WAMG Dedham, Massachusetts
WEII Dennis, Massachusetts
WSAR Fall River, Massachusetts
WPKZ Fitchburg, Massachusetts
WBOQ Gloucester, Massachusetts
WEEI-FM Lawrence, Massachusetts
WLLH Lowell, Massachusetts
WBSM New Bedford, Massachusetts
WNBH New Bedford, Massachusetts
WESO Southbridge, Massachusetts
WHLL Springfield, Massachusetts
WXTK West Yarmouth, Massachusetts
WORC Worcester, Massachusetts
WVEI Worcester, Massachusetts
WJZ Baltimore, Maryland
WCEM Cambridge, Maryland
WJZ-FM Catonsville, Maryland
WCMD Cumberland, Maryland
WFMD Frederick, Maryland
WQAL(AM) Pikesville, Maryland
WWXT Prince Frederick, Maryland
WICO Salisbury, Maryland
WTGM Salisbury, Maryland
WNST Towson, Maryland
WZON Bangor, Maine
WCME(AM) Brunswick, Maine
WFAU Gardiner, Maine
WIGY Madison, Maine
WTBM Mexico, Maine
WSYY Millinocket, Maine
WOXO-FM Norway, Maine
WRKD Rockland, Maine
WPEI Saco, Maine
WRED Westbrook, Maine
WFYC Alma, Michigan
WTKA Ann Arbor, Michigan
WBRN Big Rapids, Michigan
WBFH Bloomfield Hills, Michigan
WDFN Detroit, Michigan
WXYT-FM Detroit, Michigan
WVFN East Lansing, Michigan
WTRX Flint, Michigan
WGLM Greenville, Michigan
WKMJ-FM Hancock, Michigan
WMPL Hancock, Michigan
WSMB Harbor Beach, Michigan
WCCY Houghton, Michigan
WMIQ Iron Mountain, Michigan
WZAM Ishpeming, Michigan
WIBM Jackson, Michigan
WJNL Kingsley, Michigan
WMBN Petoskey, Michigan
WLUN Pinconning, Michigan
WKNW Sault Sainte Marie, Michigan
WCCW Traverse City, Michigan
KBUN Bemidji, Minnesota
WBJI Blackduck, Minnesota
KLIZ Brainerd, Minnesota
KVBR Brainerd, Minnesota
KDLM Detroit Lakes, Minnesota
KQDS Duluth, Minnesota
WEBC Duluth, Minnesota
KRBT Eveleth, Minnesota
KSUM Fairmont, Minnesota
KDHL Faribault, Minnesota

KDWA Hastings, Minnesota
KDUZ Hutchinson, Minnesota
KYSM Mankato, Minnesota
WCMP-FM Pine City, Minnesota
KOLM Rochester, Minnesota
WBHR Sauk Rapids, Minnesota
KKAQ Thief River Falls, Minnesota
KKDQ Thief River Falls, Minnesota
KXSS Waite Park, Minnesota
KDOM Windom, Minnesota
KDOM-FM Windom, Minnesota
KWNO Winona, Minnesota
KBFL-FM Buffalo, Missouri
KAPE Cape Girardeau, Missouri
KGIR Cape Girardeau, Missouri
KTGR Columbia, Missouri
KYLS Fredericktown, Missouri
KHMO Hannibal, Missouri
KCTE Independence, Missouri
WHB Kansas City, Missouri
KLWT Lebanon, Missouri
KNIM Maryville, Missouri
KXEO Mexico, Missouri
KFMO Park Hills, Missouri
KLID Poplar Bluff, Missouri
KMIS Portageville, Missouri
KTTR Rolla, Missouri
KSMO Salem, Missouri
KGMY Springfield, Missouri
KWTO Springfield, Missouri
KWTO-FM Springfield, Missouri
KFEQ St. Joseph, Missouri
KMOX St. Louis, Missouri
KTRS St. Louis, Missouri
KTUI-FM Sullivan, Missouri
KSAR Thayer, Missouri
KTTN-FM Trenton, Missouri
KFNS-FM Troy, Missouri
KOKO Warrensburg, Missouri
WAMY Amory, Mississippi
WXBD Biloxi, Mississippi
WCJU Columbia, Mississippi
WJWF Columbus, Mississippi
WNMQ Columbus, Mississippi
WFMN Flora, Mississippi
WPBQ Flowood, Mississippi
WMUT Grenada, Mississippi
WFOR Hattiesburg, Mississippi
WDXO Hazlehurst, Mississippi
WJDX Jackson, Mississippi
WSFZ Jackson, Mississippi
WAML Laurel, Mississippi
WXWX Marietta, Mississippi
WAPF McComb, Mississippi
WMOX Meridian, Mississippi
WMLC Monticello, Mississippi
WNAT Natchez, Mississippi
WNAU New Albany, Mississippi
WQMS Quitman, Mississippi
WKOR Starkville, Mississippi
WSSO Starkville, Mississippi
WTUP Tupelo, Mississippi
WQBC Vicksburg, Mississippi
KBLG Billings, Montana
KYSX(FM) Billings, Montana
KMMS Bozeman, Montana
KBOW Butte, Montana
KCAP Helena, Montana
KGEZ Kalispell, Montana
KGRZ Missoula, Montana
KYLT Missoula, Montana
WZKY Albemarle, North Carolina
WISE Asheville, North Carolina
WTKF Atlantic, North Carolina
WYSE Canton, North Carolina
WBCN(AM) Charlotte, North Carolina
WFNZ Charlotte, North Carolina
WWCU Cullowhee, North Carolina
WDNC Durham, North Carolina
WDUR Durham, North Carolina
WGAI Elizabeth City, North Carolina
WGHB Farmville, North Carolina
WFAY Fayetteville, North Carolina
WGNC Gastonia, North Carolina
WMFR High Point, North Carolina
WCMC-FM Holly Springs, North Carolina
WAVQ Jacksonville, North Carolina
WJNC Jacksonville, North Carolina
WLXN Lexington, North Carolina
WLON Lincolnton, North Carolina
WNOS New Bern, North Carolina
WWNB New Bern, North Carolina
WCBT Roanoke Rapids, North Carolina
WRMT Rocky Mount, North Carolina
WCAB Rutherfordton, North Carolina
WFBX Spring Lake, North Carolina
WSIC Statesville, North Carolina
WBLO Thomasville, North Carolina
WMFD Wilmington, North Carolina
WVOT Wilson, North Carolina
KXMR Bismarck, North Dakota
KLXX Bismarck-Mandan, North Dakota
KVOX Fargo, North Dakota
WDAY Fargo, North Dakota
KOVC Valley City, North Dakota
KOZN Bellevue, Nebraska
KICS Hastings, Nebraska
KXPN Kearney, Nebraska
KLMS Lincoln, Nebraska
KSWN McCook, Nebraska
WJAG Norfolk, Nebraska
KOOQ North Platte, Nebraska
KXSP Omaha, Nebraska
WTSV Claremont, New Hampshire
WTSN Dover, New Hampshire
WXEX Exeter, New Hampshire
WTSL Hanover, New Hampshire
WTPL Hillsboro, New Hampshire
WGAM Manchester, New Hampshire
WGIR Manchester, New Hampshire
WGHM Nashua, New Hampshire
WSMN Nashua, New Hampshire
WMYF Portsmouth, New Hampshire
WPKX(AM) Rochester, New Hampshire
WEEY Swanzey, New Hampshire
WNJE Flemington, New Jersey
WSNR Jersey City, New Jersey
WPAT Paterson, New Jersey
KBZU Albuquerque, New Mexico
KDEF Albuquerque, New Mexico
KNML Albuquerque, New Mexico
KCQL Aztec, New Mexico
KNFT Bayard, New Mexico
KCLV Clovis, New Mexico
KENN Farmington, New Mexico
KHOB Hobbs, New Mexico
KYKK Humble City, New Mexico
KPZA-FM Jal, New Mexico
KOBE Las Cruces, New Mexico
KSNM Las Cruces, New Mexico
KRSN Los Alamos, New Mexico
KLEA Lovington, New Mexico
KQTM Rio Rancho, New Mexico
KWES Ruidoso, New Mexico
KRUI Ruidoso Downs, New Mexico
KVSF Santa Fe, New Mexico
KTSN Elko, Nevada
KBAD Las Vegas, Nevada
KENO Las Vegas, Nevada
KLAV Las Vegas, Nevada
KWWN Las Vegas, Nevada
KSHP North Las Vegas, Nevada
KHIT Reno, Nevada
KPLY Reno, Nevada
KBZZ Sparks, Nevada
KUUB Sun Valley, Nevada
WVTL Amsterdam, New York
WYSL Avon, New York
WYOS Binghamton, New York
WPUT Brewster, New York
WBEN Buffalo, New York
WGR Buffalo, New York
WCBA Corning, New York
WELM Elmira, New York
WENE Endicott, New York
WMML Glens Falls, New York
WWSC Glens Falls, New York
WLIR-FM Hampton Bays, New York
WNRS Herkimer, New York
WHCU Ithaca, New York
WJTN Jamestown, New York
WIRD Lake Placid, New York
WIXT Little Falls, New York
WLVL Lockport, New York
WADO New York, New York
WFAN New York, New York
WFUV New York, New York
WTLA North Syracuse, New York
WSLB Ogdensburg, New York
WSGO Oswego, New York
WEAV Plattsburgh, New York
WROC Rochester, New York
WRNY Rome, New York
WGGO Salamanca, New York
WSCP Sandy Creek-Pulaski, New York
WSPQ Springville, New York
WAER Syracuse, New York
WHEN Syracuse, New York
WOFX Troy, New York
WPIE Trumansburg, New York
WIBX Utica, New York
WCJW Warsaw, New York
WNER Watertown, New York
WAKR Akron, Ohio
WARF Akron, Ohio
WFUN Ashtabula, Ohio
WATH Athens, Ohio
WBLL Bellefontaine, Ohio
WQEL Bucyrus, Ohio
WILE Cambridge, Ohio
WCSM-FM Celina, Ohio
WCKY Cincinnati, Ohio
WSAI Cincinnati, Ohio
WKNR Cleveland, Ohio
WTAM Cleveland, Ohio
WBNS Columbus, Ohio
WYTS Columbus, Ohio
WING Dayton, Ohio
WEOL Elyria, Ohio
WFOB Fostoria, Ohio
WMOH Hamilton, Ohio
WJMP Kent, Ohio
WIMA Lima, Ohio
WMOA Marietta, Ohio
WTIG Massillon, Ohio
WJAW-FM McConnelsville, Ohio
WMPO Middleport-Pomeroy, Ohio
WRGM Ontario, Ohio
WKSD Paulding, Ohio
WLEC Sandusky, Ohio
WIZE Springfield, Ohio
WSTV Steubenville, Ohio
WLQR Toledo, Ohio
WBTC Uhrichsville, Ohio
WELW Willoughby, Ohio
WQKT Wooster, Ohio
WKBN Youngstown, Ohio
KADA Ada, Oklahoma
KOKB Blackwell, Oklahoma
KUSH Cushing, Oklahoma
KPNS Duncan, Oklahoma
KADS Elk City, Oklahoma
KFXY Enid, Oklahoma
KXCA Lawton, Oklahoma
KWPN(AM) Moore, Oklahoma
KBIX Muskogee, Oklahoma
KYAL-FM Muskogee, Oklahoma
KREF Norman, Oklahoma
KOKC Oklahoma City, Oklahoma
WKY Oklahoma City, Oklahoma
KOKL Okmulgee, Oklahoma
KOKP Perry, Oklahoma
KOSB Perry, Oklahoma
KYAL Sapulpa, Oklahoma
KSPI Stillwater, Oklahoma
KTLQ Tahlequah, Oklahoma
KAKC Tulsa, Oklahoma
KCFO Tulsa, Oklahoma
KTBZ Tulsa, Oklahoma
KGND Vinita, Oklahoma
KSIW Woodward, Oklahoma
KAST Astoria, Oregon
KBND Bend, Oregon
KICE Bend, Oregon
KLOO Corvallis, Oregon
KUJZ Creswell, Oregon
KSCR Eugene, Oregon
KUIK Hillsboro, Oregon
KFLS Klamath Falls, Oregon
KLAD Klamath Falls, Oregon
KGAL Lebanon, Oregon
KEZX Medford, Oregon
KTIX Pendleton, Oregon
KFXX Portland, Oregon
KXTG Portland, Oregon
KQEN Roseburg, Oregon
KSKR Roseburg, Oregon
KOHI St. Helens, Oregon
KSKR-FM Sutherlin, Oregon
KMBD(AM) Tillamook, Oregon
WSAN Allentown, Pennsylvania
WTKZ Allentown, Pennsylvania
WVAM Altoona, Pennsylvania

WMBA Ambridge, Pennsylvania
WBVP Beaver Falls, Pennsylvania
WBFD Bedford, Pennsylvania
WISR Butler, Pennsylvania
WHYP(AM) Corry, Pennsylvania
WESS East Stroudsburg, Pennsylvania
WEEX Easton, Pennsylvania
WPDC Elizabethtown, Pennsylvania
WFNN Erie, Pennsylvania
WPSE Erie, Pennsylvania
WRIE Erie, Pennsylvania
WFRA Franklin, Pennsylvania
WGET Gettysburg, Pennsylvania
WHGB Harrisburg, Pennsylvania
WTKT Harrisburg, Pennsylvania
WPSN Honesdale, Pennsylvania
WKGE Johnstown, Pennsylvania
WTYM Kittanning, Pennsylvania
WLPA Lancaster, Pennsylvania
WNPV Lansdale, Pennsylvania
WWGE Loretto, Pennsylvania
WGLD Manchester Township, Pennsylvania
WMGW Meadville, Pennsylvania
WJUN Mexico, Pennsylvania
WKST New Castle, Pennsylvania
WIP Philadelphia, Pennsylvania
WPEN Philadelphia, Pennsylvania
WPHB Philipsburg, Pennsylvania
WBGG Pittsburgh, Pennsylvania
WPGB Pittsburgh, Pennsylvania
WYCK Plains, Pennsylvania
WEEU Reading, Pennsylvania
WIOV Reading, Pennsylvania
WEJL Scranton, Pennsylvania
WICK Scranton, Pennsylvania
WKBI St. Marys, Pennsylvania
WQWK(AM) State College, Pennsylvania
WKOK Sunbury, Pennsylvania
WTZN Troy, Pennsylvania
WXVU Villanova, Pennsylvania
WLYC Williamsport, Pennsylvania
WRAK Williamsport, Pennsylvania
WOYK York, Pennsylvania
WGIT Canovanas, Puerto Rico
WALO Humacao, Puerto Rico
WMNT Manati, Puerto Rico
WVOZ San Juan, Puerto Rico
WPRO Providence, Rhode Island
WLKW West Warwick, Rhode Island
WANS Anderson, South Carolina
WROP Belton, South Carolina
WSPO Charleston, South Carolina
WCCP-FM Clemson, South Carolina
WPCC Clinton, South Carolina
WCOS Columbia, South Carolina
WXBT Columbia, South Carolina
WXBT(AM) Columbia, South Carolina
WHSC(AM) Conway, South Carolina
WNKT Eastover, South Carolina
WFIS Fountain Inn, South Carolina
WXJY Georgetown, South Carolina
WFXH(AM) Hilton Head Island, South Carolina
WWFN-FM Lake City, South Carolina
WRHM Lancaster, South Carolina
WRNN Myrtle Beach, South Carolina
WRHI Rock Hill, South Carolina
WOLI Spartanburg, South Carolina
WSPG Spartanburg, South Carolina
WALI Walterboro, South Carolina
KGIM Aberdeen, South Dakota
KBFS Belle Fourche, South Dakota
KDSJ Deadwood, South Dakota
KIJV Huron, South Dakota
KRKI Keystone, South Dakota
KSOO-FM Lennox, South Dakota
KORN Mitchell, South Dakota
KSOO Sioux Falls, South Dakota
KWSN Sioux Falls, South Dakota
KVTK Vermillion, South Dakota
KJJQ Volga, South Dakota
WSAA Benton, Tennessee
WXSM Blountville, Tennessee
WNSR Brentwood, Tennessee
WRKM Carthage, Tennessee
WDEF Chattanooga, Tennessee
WJZM Clarksville, Tennessee
WKFN Clarksville, Tennessee
WMRB Columbia, Tennessee
WCSV Crossville, Tennessee
WEMB Erwin, Tennessee
WCPH Etowah, Tennessee
WEKR Fayetteville, Tennessee
WNML-FM Friendsville, Tennessee
WGFX Gallatin, Tennessee
WWTN Hendersonville, Tennessee
WNRX Jefferson City, Tennessee
WGOC Kingsport, Tennessee
WNML Knoxville, Tennessee
WVLZ Knoxville, Tennessee
WTNQ La Follette, Tennessee
WCOR Lebanon, Tennessee
WLIV Livingston, Tennessee
WMSR Manchester, Tennessee
WKCE Maryville, Tennessee
WHBQ Memphis, Tennessee
WMC Memphis, Tennessee
WREC Memphis, Tennessee
WUMR Memphis, Tennessee
WNFN Millersville, Tennessee
WLIV-FM Monterey, Tennessee
WGNS Murfreesboro, Tennessee
WBFG Parker's Crossroads, Tennessee
WPFT Pigeon Forge, Tennessee
KZQQ Abilene, Texas
KESN Allen, Texas
KACT Andrews, Texas
KVET Austin, Texas
KRUN Ballinger, Texas
KIKR Beaumont, Texas
KGOW Bellaire, Texas
KZRK Canyon, Texas
KGAS Carthage, Texas
KZNE College Station, Texas
KEYS Corpus Christi, Texas
KSIX Corpus Christi, Texas
KZNX Creedmoor, Texas
KRLD-FM Dallas, Texas
KTCK Dallas, Texas
KURV Edinburg, Texas
KULP El Campo, Texas
KHEY El Paso, Texas
KROD El Paso, Texas
KFLC Fort Worth, Texas
KKGM Fort Worth, Texas
WBAP Fort Worth, Texas
KATH Frisco, Texas
KWRD Henderson, Texas
KBME Houston, Texas
KILT Houston, Texas
KTRH Houston, Texas
KHLE Kempner, Texas
KAML Kenedy-Karnes City, Texas
KSET Lumberton, Texas
KMHT Marshall, Texas
KMND Midland, Texas
KOGT Orange, Texas
KNET Palestine, Texas
KLVL Pasadena, Texas
KVOP Plainview, Texas
KBPO Port Neches, Texas
KSOX Raymondville, Texas
KGKL San Angelo, Texas
KKSA San Angelo, Texas
KTKR San Antonio, Texas
KZDC San Antonio, Texas
KTSW San Marcos, Texas
KTDK Sanger, Texas
KJIM Sherman, Texas
KWNX Taylor, Texas
KLTD Temple, Texas
KTEM Temple, Texas
KCMC Texarkana, Texas
KTBB Tyler, Texas
KYZS Tyler, Texas
KRZI Waco, Texas
KMQX Weatherford, Texas
KSL-FM Midvale, Utah
KJQS Murray, Utah
KALL North Salt Lake City, Utah
KLO Ogden, Utah
KOAL Price, Utah
KOVO Provo, Utah
KSVC Richfield, Utah
KFNZ Salt Lake City, Utah
KSL Salt Lake City, Utah
KZNS Salt Lake City, Utah
KHQN Spanish Fork, Utah
KVEL Vernal, Utah
KUNF Washington, Utah
WCBX Bassett, Virginia
WBLT Bedford, Virginia
WKEX Blacksburg, Virginia
WKLV Blackstone, Virginia
WFHG Bristol, Virginia
WINA Charlottesville, Virginia
WKAV Charlottesville, Virginia
WDIC-FM Clinchco, Virginia
WKTR Earlysville, Virginia
WGAT Gate City, Virginia
WMNA-FM Gretna, Virginia
WXTG Hampton, Virginia
WHBG Harrisonburg, Virginia
WREL Lexington, Virginia
WBRG Lynchburg, Virginia
WVGM Lynchburg, Virginia
WJFK-FM Manassas, Virginia
WGH Newport News, Virginia
WTAR Norfolk, Virginia
WRAD Radford, Virginia
WRNL Richmond, Virginia
WXGI Richmond, Virginia
WGMN Roanoke, Virginia
WLOY Rural Retreat, Virginia
WTON Staunton, Virginia
WXTG-FM Virginia Beach, Virginia
WINC Winchester, Virginia
WYVE Wytheville, Virginia
WVWI Charlotte Amalie, Virgin Islands
WSNO Barre, Vermont
WTSA Brattleboro, Vermont
WCAT Burlington, Vermont
WVMT Burlington, Vermont
WFAD Middlebury, Vermont
WRSA St. Albans, Vermont
WDEV-FM Warren, Vermont
WDEV Waterbury, Vermont
KCLK Asotin, Washington
KPUG Bellingham, Washington
KBRO Bremerton, Washington
KELA Centralia-Chehalis, Washington
KXLE Ellensburg, Washington
KULE Ephrata, Washington
KRKO Everett, Washington
KWOK Hoquiam, Washington
KBSN Moses Lake, Washington
KWIQ Moses Lake North, Washington
KIRO Seattle, Washington
KJR Seattle, Washington
KGA Spokane, Washington
KHHO Tacoma, Washington
KIRO-FM Tacoma, Washington
KYNR Toppenish, Washington
KUJ Walla Walla, Washington
KKRT Wenatchee, Washington
WSCO Appleton, Wisconsin
WDUZ-FM Brillion, Wisconsin
WEAQ Chippewa Falls, Wisconsin
WBIZ Eau Claire, Wisconsin
KFIZ Fond Du Lac, Wisconsin
WDUZ Green Bay, Wisconsin
WNFL Green Bay, Wisconsin
WAUK Jackson, Wisconsin
WIZM La Crosse, Wisconsin
WKTY La Crosse, Wisconsin
WTSO Madison, Wisconsin
WMAM Marinette, Wisconsin
WIGM Medford, Wisconsin
WMEQ Menomonie, Wisconsin
WTMJ Milwaukee, Wisconsin
WTLX Monona, Wisconsin
WOSH Oshkosh, Wisconsin
WPVL Platteville, Wisconsin
WEVR River Falls, Wisconsin
WEVR-FM River Falls, Wisconsin
WDTX Rothschild, Wisconsin
WCLB Sheboygan, Wisconsin
WXCX Siren, Wisconsin
WKLJ Sparta, Wisconsin
WOSQ Spencer, Wisconsin
WJJQ Tomahawk, Wisconsin
WJJQ-FM Tomahawk, Wisconsin
WFBZ Trempealeau, Wisconsin
WRRD Waukesha, Wisconsin
WXCO Wausau, Wisconsin
WWNR Beckley, West Virginia
WKEZ Bluefield, West Virginia
WCHS Charleston, West Virginia
WSWW Charleston, West Virginia
WMRE Charlestown, West Virginia
WXKX Clarksburg, West Virginia
WMMN Fairmont, West Virginia
WAMN Green Valley, West Virginia
WMTD-FM Hinton, West Virginia

WRVC Huntington, West Virginia
WEPM Martinsburg, West Virginia
WRNR Martinsburg, West Virginia
WJAW St. Marys, West Virginia
WSLW White Sulphur Spring, West Virginia
KRSV Afton, Wyoming
KBBS Buffalo, Wyoming
KKTL Casper, Wyoming
KVOC Casper, Wyoming
KFBC Cheyenne, Wyoming
KRAE Cheyenne, Wyoming
KODI Cody, Wyoming
KIML Gillette, Wyoming
KHAT Laramie, Wyoming
KOWB Laramie, Wyoming
KYDT Pine Haven, Wyoming

Talk

KBYR Anchorage, Alaska
KENI Anchorage, Alaska
KFQD Anchorage, Alaska
KUDO Anchorage, Alaska
KYUK Bethel, Alaska
KAGV Big Lake, Alaska
KRUP Dillingham, Alaska
KFAR Fairbanks, Alaska
KFBX Fairbanks, Alaska
KUAC Fairbanks, Alaska
KHNS Haines, Alaska
KJNO Juneau, Alaska
KTKN Ketchikan, Alaska
KVOK Kodiak, Alaska
KIAM Nenana, Alaska
KNOM Nome, Alaska
KFSK Petersburg, Alaska
KIFW Sitka, Alaska
KSRM Soldotna, Alaska
KTNA Talkeetna, Alaska
KUDU Tok, Alaska
KVAK Valdez, Alaska
WDNG Anniston, Alabama
WVNN Athens, Alabama
WAPI Birmingham, Alabama
WERC Birmingham, Alabama
WJOX-FM Birmingham, Alabama
WYDE Birmingham, Alabama
WGNQ Bridgeport, Alabama
WRTR Brookwood, Alabama
WACV Coosada, Alabama
WFMH Cullman, Alabama
WXAL Demopolis, Alabama
WWNT Dothan, Alabama
WJLD(AM) Fairfield, Alabama
WHEP Foley, Alabama
WFPA Fort Payne, Alabama
WGEA Geneva, Alabama
WGYV Greenville, Alabama
WGSV Guntersville, Alabama
WBXR Hazel Green, Alabama
WBHP Huntsville, Alabama
WMOB Mobile, Alabama
WNTM Mobile, Alabama
WBAM-FM Montgomery, Alabama
WLWI Montgomery, Alabama
WIJD Prichard, Alabama
WHBB Selma, Alabama
WFEB Sylacauga, Alabama
WTLS Tallassee, Alabama
WVNN-FM Trinity, Alabama
WTBF Troy, Alabama
WTBC Tuscaloosa, Alabama
WUAL-FM Tuscaloosa, Alabama
WVNA Tuscumbia, Alabama
WKXM Winfield, Alabama
KVRC Arkadelphia, Arkansas
KEWI Benton, Arkansas
KREB Bentonville-Bella, Arkansas
KTHS Berryville, Arkansas
KLCN Blytheville, Arkansas
KJMT Calico Rock, Arkansas
KCAB Dardanelle, Arkansas
KCJF Earle, Arkansas
KVDW England, Arkansas
KFAY Farmington, Arkansas
KAYH Fayetteville, Arkansas
KOFC Fayetteville, Arkansas
KBJT Fordyce, Arkansas
KQEW Fordyce, Arkansas
KXJK Forrest City, Arkansas
KFPW Fort Smith, Arkansas
KWHN Fort Smith, Arkansas
KYHN Ft. Smith, Arkansas
KOTN Gould, Arkansas
KURM-FM Gravette, Arkansas
KELD-FM Hampton, Arkansas
KAWW Heber Springs, Arkansas
KXAR Hope, Arkansas
KZHS Hot Springs, Arkansas
KZNG Hot Springs, Arkansas
KBTM Jonesboro, Arkansas
KABZ Little Rock, Arkansas
KARN Little Rock, Arkansas
KLRE-FM Little Rock, Arkansas
KUAR Little Rock, Arkansas
KVMA Magnolia, Arkansas
KTTG Mena, Arkansas
KNBY Newport, Arkansas
KARV-FM Ola, Arkansas
KSMD Pangburn, Arkansas
KFFK Rogers, Arkansas
KARV Russellville, Arkansas
KWCK Searcy, Arkansas
KARN-FM Sheridan, Arkansas
KHGG Van Buren, Arkansas
KHGG-FM Waldron, Arkansas
KWYN Wynne, Arkansas
KZZZ Bullhead City, Arizona
KFNX Cave Creek, Arizona
KVOI Cortaro, Arizona
KAPR Douglas, Arizona
KVNA Flagstaff, Arizona
KPXQ Glendale, Arizona
KTAR-FM Glendale, Arizona
KJAA Globe, Arizona
KDJI Holbrook, Arizona
KAAA Kingman, Arizona
KNTR Lake Havasu City, Arizona
KZXQ Lake of the Woods, Arizona
KFNN Mesa, Arizona
KLPZ Parker, Arizona
KFYI Phoenix, Arizona
KGME Phoenix, Arizona
KKNT Phoenix, Arizona
KMVP Phoenix, Arizona
KPHX Phoenix, Arizona
KZON Phoenix, Arizona
KNKI Pinetop, Arizona
KNAQ Prescott, Arizona
KYCA Prescott, Arizona
KQNA Prescott Valley, Arizona
KVWM Show Low, Arizona
KNXN Sierra Vista, Arizona
KTAN Sierra Vista, Arizona
KGMS Tucson, Arizona
KNST Tucson, Arizona
KUAZ Tucson, Arizona
KUAZ-FM Tucson, Arizona
KAWC Yuma, Arizona
KBLU Yuma, Arizona
KDFC Angwin, California
KIXW Apple Valley, California
KBRT Avalon, California
KAFY Bakersfield, California
KGEO Bakersfield, California
KNZR Bakersfield, California
KSZL Barstow, California
KRXA Carmel Valley, California
KPAY Chico, California
KZFR Chico, California
KHDC Chualar, California
KNWZ Coachella, California
KDVS Davis, California
KRDU Dinuba, California
KGOE Eureka, California
KMUE Eureka, California
KWSW Eureka, California
KWSW(AM) Eureka, California
KJCU Fort Bragg, California
KIRV Fresno, California
KMJ Fresno, California
KMJ-FM Fresno, California
KMUD Garberville, California
KRLA Glendale, California
KKMC Gonzales, California
KNCO Grass Valley, California
KXSR Groveland, California
KCKS Hamilton City, California
KQAB(AM) Lake Isabella, California
KPFZ-FM Lakeport, California
KOSS Lancaster, California
KCAA Loma Linda, California
KSMA Lompoc, California
KABC Los Angeles, California
KFI Los Angeles, California
KPFK Los Angeles, California
KTLK Los Angeles, California
KTNQ Los Angeles, California
KUSC Los Angeles, California
KMYC Marysville, California
KPMO Mendocino, California
KGAM Merced, California
KTIQ Merced, California
KYOS Merced, California
KFIV Modesto, California
KMPH Modesto, California
KIDD Monterey, California
KNRY Monterey Bay, California
KMJC Mount Shasta, California
KVON Napa, California
KTOX Needles, California
KNEW Oakland, California
KNEW(AM) Oakland, California
KWVE(AM) Oildale, California
KLAA Orange, California
KDAR Oxnard, California
KNWQ Palm Springs, California
KPSI Palm Springs, California
KPTR Palm Springs, California
KDOW Palo Alto, California
KKXX Paradise, California
KPRL Paso Robles, California
KZYX Philo, California
KWMR Point Reyes Station, California
KAHZ Pomona, California
KWKU Pomona, California
KVTA Port Hueneme, California
KTIP Porterville, California
KRAC Quincy, California
KSTE Rancho Cordova, California
KQMS Redding, California
KUOR-FM Redlands, California
KFBK Sacramento, California
KION Salinas, California
KTIE San Bernardino, California
KVCR San Bernardino, California
KWVE-FM San Clemente, California
KCBQ San Diego, California
KFMB San Diego, California
KOGO San Diego, California
KPBS-FM San Diego, California
KEST San Francisco, California
KFAX San Francisco, California
KGO San Francisco, California
KNBR San Francisco, California
KSFO San Francisco, California
KJZN San Joaquin, California
KVEC San Luis Obispo, California
KYNS San Luis Obispo, California
KPRZ San Marcos-Poway, California
KCLU Santa Barbara, California
KQSC Santa Barbara, California
KTMS Santa Barbara, California
KZSB Santa Barbara, California
KSCO Santa Cruz, California
KGDP-FM Santa Maria, California
KSMX Santa Maria, California
KUHL Santa Maria, California
KKZZ Santa Paula, California
KSRO Santa Rosa, California
KSMJ Shafter, California
KCNR Shasta, California
KIRN Simi Valley, California
KSVY Sonoma, California
KOWL South Lake Tahoe, California
KWSX Stockton, California
KSUE Susanville, California
KDSC Thousand Oaks, California
KFUT Thousand Palms, California
KXPS Thousand Palms, California
KBDG Turlock, California
KUNX Ventura, California
KVFG Victorville, California
KCEO Vista, California
KFHL Wasco, California
KERN Wasco-Greenacres, California
KZYZ Willits, California
KRCB-FM Windsor, California
KUBA Yuba City, California
KNWH Yucca Valley, California
KNFO Basalt, Colorado
KSIR Brush, Colorado
KSKE Buena Vista, Colorado

KRLN Canon City, Colorado
KRDO Colorado Springs, Colorado
KVOR Colorado Springs, Colorado
KZNT Colorado Springs, Colorado
KVFC Cortez, Colorado
KBJD Denver, Colorado
KCFR-FM Denver, Colorado
KHOW Denver, Colorado
KLZ Denver, Colorado
KNUS Denver, Colorado
KOA Denver, Colorado
KDGO Durango, Colorado
KDEB(AM) Estes Park, Colorado
KFTM Fort Morgan, Colorado
KGLN Glenwood Springs, Colorado
KAFM Grand Junction, Colorado
KEXO Grand Junction, Colorado
KNZZ Grand Junction, Colorado
KFKA Greeley, Colorado
KHNC Johnstown, Colorado
KRKS-FM Lafayette, Colorado
KRCN Longmont, Colorado
KCBR Monument, Colorado
KWUF Pagosa Springs, Colorado
KCSJ Pueblo, Colorado
KGFT Pueblo, Colorado
KRDO-FM Security, Colorado
KKZN Thornton, Colorado
KVLE Vail, Colorado
KCOL Wellington, Colorado
WPRX Bristol, Connecticut
WGCH Greenwich, Connecticut
WGRS Guilford, Connecticut
WQAQ Hamden, Connecticut
WDRC Hartford, Connecticut
WTIC Hartford, Connecticut
WNEZ Manchester, Connecticut
WMMW Meriden, Connecticut
WMRD Middletown, Connecticut
WMNR Monroe, Connecticut
WELI New Haven, Connecticut
WNLK Norwalk, Connecticut
WLIS Old Saybrook, Connecticut
WHDD Sharon, Connecticut
WRXC Shelton, Connecticut
WGSK South Kent, Connecticut
WEDW-FM Stamford, Connecticut
WSTC Stamford, Connecticut
WSNG Torrington, Connecticut
WATR Waterbury, Connecticut
WWCO Waterbury, Connecticut
WCCC West Hartford, Connecticut
WSHU Westport, Connecticut
WKND Windsor, Connecticut
WAMU Washington, District of Columbia
WETA Washington, District of Columbia
WMAL Washington, District of Columbia
WPFW Washington, District of Columbia
WTEM Washington, District of Columbia
WWRC Washington, District of Columbia
WDOV Dover, Delaware
WGMD Rehoboth Beach, Delaware
WDEL Wilmington, Delaware
WILM Wilmington, Delaware
WTMC Wilmington, Delaware
WWTX Wilmington, Delaware
WFLN Arcadia, Florida
WTWB Auburndale, Florida
WTJT Baker, Florida
WJGM(FM) Baldwin, Florida
WSBR Boca Raton, Florida
WWPR Bradenton, Florida
WWJB Brooksville, Florida
WNZF Bunnell, Florida
WKFL Bushnell, Florida
WTAN Clearwater, Florida
WMMV Cocoa, Florida
WWBC Cocoa, Florida
WMEL Cocoa Beach, Florida
WTKS-FM Cocoa Beach, Florida
WJTK Columbia City, Florida
WHIM Coral Gables, Florida
WNDB Daytona Beach, Florida
WTJV Deland, Florida
WYND Deland, Florida
WNWF Destin, Florida
WENG Englewood, Florida
WJNX Fort Pierce, Florida
WFTW Fort Walton Beach, Florida
WDVH Gainesville, Florida
WRUF Gainesville, Florida

WNRP Gulf Breeze, Florida
WXYB Indian Rocks Beach, Florida
WBOB Jacksonville, Florida
WJCT-FM Jacksonville, Florida
WQOP Jacksonville, Florida
WJBW Jupiter, Florida
WYBX(FM) Key West, Florida
WHOO Kissimmee, Florida
WBXY La Crosse, Florida
WWTK Lake Placid, Florida
WLKF Lakeland, Florida
WWAB Lakeland, Florida
WPBR Lantana, Florida
WWBA Largo, Florida
WLBE Leesburg-Eustis, Florida
WFFG Marathon, Florida
WKWM Marathon, Florida
WGUF Marco, Florida
WMMB Melbourne, Florida
WAQI Miami, Florida
WINZ Miami, Florida
WIOD Miami, Florida
WKCP Miami, Florida
WLRN-FM Miami, Florida
WQBA Miami, Florida
WSUA Miami, Florida
WNMA Miami Springs, Florida
WSKY-FM Micanopy, Florida
WFLA-FM Midway, Florida
WEBY Milton, Florida
WEGS Milton, Florida
WPGS Mims, Florida
WNOG Naples, Florida
WSOR Naples, Florida
WPSO New Port Richey, Florida
WTKE-FM Niceville, Florida
WWCN North Fort Myers, Florida
WKAT North Miami, Florida
WMOP Ocala, Florida
WDBO Orlando, Florida
WTLN Orlando, Florida
WELE Ormond Beach, Florida
WFSW Panama City, Florida
WLTG Panama City, Florida
WFLF-FM Parker, Florida
WCOA Pensacola, Florida
WCOA-FM Pensacola, Florida
WAMT Pine Castle Sky Lake, Florida
WFLF Pine Hills, Florida
WINK Pine Island Center, Florida
WTBN Pinellas Park, Florida
WTWD Plant City, Florida
WHSR Pompano Beach, Florida
WPSL Port St. Lucie, Florida
WCCF Punta Gorda, Florida
WZZR Riviera Beach, Florida
WDEO-FM San Carlos Park, Florida
WSDO Sanford, Florida
WLSS Sarasota, Florida
WSRQ Sarasota, Florida
WTMY Sarasota, Florida
WPUL South Daytona, Florida
WTYG Sparr, Florida
WYOO Springfield, Florida
WFOY St. Augustine, Florida
WIWA St. Cloud, Florida
WSTU Stuart, Florida
WFSQ Tallahassee, Florida
WFSU-FM Tallahassee, Florida
WTAL Tallahassee, Florida
WFLA Tampa, Florida
WHNZ Tampa, Florida
WIXC Titusville, Florida
WCZR Vero Beach, Florida
WTTB Vero Beach, Florida
WBZT West Palm Beach, Florida
WJNO West Palm Beach, Florida
WOKB Winter Garden, Florida
WPRD Winter Park, Florida
WZHR Zephyrhills, Florida
WDDQ Adel, Georgia
WALG Albany, Georgia
WLTA Alpharetta, Georgia
WRFC Athens, Georgia
WAOK Atlanta, Georgia
WGKA Atlanta, Georgia
WGST Atlanta, Georgia
WGUN Atlanta, Georgia
WNIV Atlanta, Georgia
WQXI Atlanta, Georgia
WRAS Atlanta, Georgia

WSB Atlanta, Georgia
WGAC Augusta, Georgia
WGIG Brunswick, Georgia
WGRA Cairo, Georgia
WLBB Carrollton, Georgia
WYXC Cartersville, Georgia
WGHC(AM) Clayton, Georgia
WRCG Columbus, Georgia
WJJC Commerce, Georgia
WSRM Coosa, Georgia
WAEF Cordele, Georgia
WBLJ Dalton, Georgia
WSEM Donalsonville, Georgia
WCFO East Point, Georgia
WAEG Evans, Georgia
WDUN Gainesville, Georgia
WGGA Gainesville, Georgia
WDDK Greensboro, Georgia
WHIE Griffin, Georgia
WWWE Hapeville, Georgia
WVCC Hogansville, Georgia
WSIZ-FM Jacksonville, Georgia
WVGA Lakeland, Georgia
WJTP Lithia Springs, Georgia
WIBB Macon, Georgia
WMAC Macon, Georgia
WSBX Ochlocknee, Georgia
WLAQ Rome, Georgia
WRGA Rome, Georgia
WXFO Royston, Georgia
WBMQ Savannah, Georgia
WTKS Savannah, Georgia
WWNS Statesboro, Georgia
WJAT Swainsboro, Georgia
WFSL Thomasville, Georgia
WTIF Tifton, Georgia
WKWN Trenton, Georgia
WZQZ Trion, Georgia
WJEM Valdosta, Georgia
WVLD Valdosta, Georgia
WJSP-FM Warm Springs, Georgia
WWGA(AM) Waycross, Georgia
WPLV West Point, Georgia
WIMO Winder, Georgia
WCGA Woodbine, Georgia
KPRG Agana, Guam
KGUM Hagatna, Guam
KANO Hilo, Hawaii
KHNU Hilo, Hawaii
KPUA Hilo, Hawaii
KGU Honolulu, Hawaii
KHVH Honolulu, Hawaii
KIKI(AM) Honolulu, Hawaii
KKEA Honolulu, Hawaii
KRTR Honolulu, Hawaii
KUMU(AM) Honolulu, Hawaii
KWAI Honolulu, Hawaii
KNUI Kahului, Hawaii
KAOI Kihei, Hawaii
KQNG Lihue, Hawaii
KASI Ames, Iowa
KFFF(AM) Boone, Iowa
KWBG Boone, Iowa
KBUR Burlington, Iowa
KCNZ Cedar Falls, Iowa
KHKE Cedar Falls, Iowa
WMT Cedar Rapids, Iowa
KLNG Council Bluffs, Iowa
KLCD Decorah, Iowa
KWKY Des Moines, Iowa
WHO Des Moines, Iowa
WDBQ Dubuque, Iowa
KGRN Grinnell, Iowa
KQMG Independence, Iowa
KQMG-FM Independence, Iowa
KCJJ Iowa City, Iowa
WSUI Iowa City, Iowa
KOKX Keokuk, Iowa
KFJB Marshalltown, Iowa
KGLO Mason City, Iowa
KRNL-FM Mount Vernon, Iowa
KOEL Oelwein, Iowa
KOJI Okoboji, Iowa
KBIZ Ottumwa, Iowa
KLEE Ottumwa, Iowa
KPVL Postville, Iowa
KIWA Sheldon, Iowa
KMA Shenandoah, Iowa
KSCJ Sioux City, Iowa
KWIT Sioux City, Iowa
KICD Spencer, Iowa

KHOI Story City, Iowa
KNWS Waterloo, Iowa
KXEL Waterloo, Iowa
KBLI Blackfoot, Idaho
KBOI Boise, Idaho
KBSU-FM Boise, Idaho
KBSU-FM Boise, Idaho
KFXD Boise, Idaho
KGEM Boise, Idaho
KSPD Boise, Idaho
KBFI Bonners Ferry, Idaho
KBAR Burley, Idaho
KBSY Burley, Idaho
KBGN Caldwell, Idaho
KBXL Caldwell, Idaho
KBLY Idaho Falls, Idaho
KID Idaho Falls, Idaho
KOZE Lewiston, Idaho
KRFA-FM Moscow, Idaho
KIDO Nampa, Idaho
KTIK Nampa, Idaho
KWEI Notus, Idaho
KEGE Pocatello, Idaho
KISU-FM Pocatello, Idaho
KWIK Pocatello, Idaho
KBYI Rexburg, Idaho
KSPT Sandpoint, Idaho
KWRV Sun Valley, Idaho
KBSW Twin Falls, Idaho
KEZJ Twin Falls, Idaho
KLIX Twin Falls, Idaho
KTRP Weiser, Idaho
WBGZ Alton, Illinois
WCPT-FM Arlington Heights, Illinois
WBIG Aurora, Illinois
WVON Berwyn, Illinois
WTHQ Brookport, Illinois
WBYS Canton, Illinois
WCIL Carbondale, Illinois
WCAZ Carthage, Illinois
WDWS Champaign, Illinois
KSGM Chester, Illinois
WFMT Chicago, Illinois
WGN(AM) Chicago, Illinois
WIND Chicago, Illinois
WLS Chicago, Illinois
WMVP Chicago, Illinois
WRTO Chicago, Illinois
WSSD Chicago, Illinois
WHOW Clinton, Illinois
WYCA Crete, Illinois
WDAN Danville, Illinois
WSOY Decatur, Illinois
WCPY Dekalb, Illinois
WLBK Dekalb, Illinois
WXOS East St. Louis, Illinois
WCRA Effingham, Illinois
WRMN Elgin, Illinois
WFIW Fairfield, Illinois
WZPN Farmington, Illinois
WGNN Fisher, Illinois
WGIL Galesburg, Illinois
WKYX-FM Golconda, Illinois
WJPF Herrin, Illinois
WJIL Jacksonville, Illinois
WLDS Jacksonville, Illinois
WJOL Joliet, Illinois
WKAN Kankakee, Illinois
WKEI Kewanee, Illinois
WLPO Lasalle, Illinois
WSMI Litchfield, Illinois
WGGH Marion, Illinois
WLBH Mattoon, Illinois
WBEQ Morris, Illinois
WCSJ Morris, Illinois
WCSJ-FM Morris, Illinois
WINI Murphysboro, Illinois
WPTH Olney, Illinois
WCMY Ottawa, Illinois
WPRS Paris, Illinois
WCPQ Park Forest, Illinois
WAZU Peoria, Illinois
WMBD Peoria, Illinois
WLWJ Petersburg, Illinois
WPJC Pontiac, Illinois
WZOE Princeton, Illinois
WGEM Quincy, Illinois
WGEM-FM Quincy, Illinois
WTAD Quincy, Illinois
WTRH Ramsey, Illinois
WRHL Rochelle, Illinois
WROK Rockford, Illinois
WAUR Sandwich, Illinois
WPRC Sheffield, Illinois
WHCO Sparta, Illinois
WLUJ Springfield, Illinois
WMAY Springfield, Illinois
WTAX Springfield, Illinois
WGNJ St. Joseph, Illinois
WNIQ Sterling, Illinois
WSDR Sterling, Illinois
WSPL Streator, Illinois
WTIM-FM Taylorville, Illinois
WILL Urbana, Illinois
WGFA Watseka, Illinois
WKRS Waukegan, Illinois
WCPT Willow Springs, Illinois
WGNR Anderson, Indiana
WHBU Anderson, Indiana
WBIW Bedford, Indiana
WGCL Bloomington, Indiana
WHON Centerville, Indiana
WBEW Chesterton, Indiana
WCSI Columbus, Indiana
WCMR Elkhart, Indiana
WTRC Elkhart, Indiana
WVPE Elkhart, Indiana
WGBF Evansville, Indiana
WBOI Fort Wayne, Indiana
WOWO Fort Wayne, Indiana
WFDM-FM Franklin, Indiana
WGVE-FM Gary, Indiana
WLTH Gary, Indiana
WWCA Gary, Indiana
WTRE Greensburg, Indiana
WJOB Hammond, Indiana
WFYI-FM Indianapolis, Indiana
WIBC Indianapolis, Indiana
WNDE Indianapolis, Indiana
WTLC Indianapolis, Indiana
WXLW Indianapolis, Indiana
WXNT Indianapolis, Indiana
WAWK Kendallville, Indiana
WIOU Kokomo, Indiana
WSAL Logansport, Indiana
WLPR-FM Lowell, Indiana
WIMS Michigan City, Indiana
WMRS Monticello, Indiana
WYFX Mount Vernon, Indiana
WFIA-FM New Albany, Indiana
WNDA New Albany, Indiana
WRAY Princeton, Indiana
WETL South Bend, Indiana
WSBT South Bend, Indiana
WHOJ Terre Haute, Indiana
WAOV Vincennes, Indiana
WBAA West Lafayette, Indiana
KFH-FM Clearwater, Kansas
KGGF Coffeyville, Kansas
KGNO Dodge City, Kansas
KBMP Enterprise, Kansas
KCNW Fairway, Kansas
KIUL Garden City, Kansas
KGCR Goodland, Kansas
KLOE Goodland, Kansas
KVGB Great Bend, Kansas
KZAN Hays, Kansas
KZNA Hill City, Kansas
KBUF Holcomb, Kansas
KFXX-FM Hugoton, Kansas
KWBW Hutchinson, Kansas
KARF Independence, Kansas
KJCK Junction City, Kansas
KCVW Kingman, Kansas
KLWN Lawrence, Kansas
KSCB Liberal, Kansas
KMAN Manhattan, Kansas
KNGL McPherson, Kansas
KJRG Newton, Kansas
KCCV-FM Olathe, Kansas
KCCV Overland Park, Kansas
KLKC Parsons, Kansas
KFRM Salina, Kansas
KINA Salina, Kansas
KSAL Salina, Kansas
KYUL Scott City, Kansas
KCVT Silver Lake, Kansas
KMAJ Topeka, Kansas
WIBW Topeka, Kansas
KLEY Wellington, Kansas
KFH Wichita, Kansas
KNSS Wichita, Kansas
KQAM Wichita, Kansas
KSWC Winfield, Kansas
WCBL Benton, Kentucky
WKXO Berea, Kentucky
WKCT Bowling Green, Kentucky
WXAM Buffalo, Kentucky
WSFE Burnside, Kentucky
WNES Central City, Kentucky
WCTT Corbin, Kentucky
WKDP Corbin, Kentucky
WHIR Danville, Kentucky
WHOP Hopkinsville, Kentucky
WVLK Lexington, Kentucky
WFTG London, Kentucky
WFIA Louisville, Kentucky
WFPL Louisville, Kentucky
WGTK Louisville, Kentucky
WHAS Louisville, Kentucky
WKJK Louisville, Kentucky
WUOL-FM Louisville, Kentucky
WTTL Madisonville, Kentucky
WWXL Manchester, Kentucky
WNGO Mayfield, Kentucky
WMST Mt. Sterling, Kentucky
WNBS Murray, Kentucky
WNOP Newport, Kentucky
WKYX Paducah, Kentucky
WKYH Paintsville, Kentucky
WLSI Pikeville, Kentucky
WPRT Prestonsburg, Kentucky
WEKY Richmond, Kentucky
WVLK-FM Richmond, Kentucky
WVKY Shelbyville, Kentucky
WSFC Somerset, Kentucky
WLXO Stamping Ground, Kentucky
KROF Abbeville, Louisiana
KJMJ Alexandria, Louisiana
KSYL Alexandria, Louisiana
WJBO Baton Rouge, Louisiana
WPYR Baton Rouge, Louisiana
WRKF Baton Rouge, Louisiana
KBCL Bossier City, Louisiana
KNBB Dubach, Louisiana
KEUN Eunice, Louisiana
KRLQ Hodge, Louisiana
WWL-FM Kenner, Louisiana
KFXZ Lafayette, Louisiana
KVOL Lafayette, Louisiana
KAOK Lake Charles, Louisiana
KOJO Lake Charles, Louisiana
KMLB Monroe, Louisiana
KBIO Natchitoches, Louisiana
KNOC Natchitoches, Louisiana
WGSO New Orleans, Louisiana
WIST New Orleans, Louisiana
WRNO-FM New Orleans, Louisiana
WVOG New Orleans, Louisiana
WWL New Orleans, Louisiana
KEEL Shreveport, Louisiana
KRMD Shreveport, Louisiana
KNCB Vivian, Louisiana
WPNI Amherst, Massachusetts
WSRO Ashland, Massachusetts
WARL Attleboro, Massachusetts
WNSH Beverly, Massachusetts
WBUR-FM Boston, Massachusetts
WBZ Boston, Massachusetts
WEEI Boston, Massachusetts
WEZE Boston, Massachusetts
WILD Boston, Massachusetts
WRKO Boston, Massachusetts
WTKK Boston, Massachusetts
WXBR Brockton, Massachusetts
WBNW Concord, Massachusetts
WHNP East Longmeadow, Massachusetts
WHTB Fall River, Massachusetts
WSAR Fall River, Massachusetts
WPKZ Fitchburg, Massachusetts
WGAW Gardner, Massachusetts
WAMQ Great Barrington, Massachusetts
WCEC Haverhill, Massachusetts
WEEI-FM Lawrence, Massachusetts
WCAP Lowell, Massachusetts
WMLN-FM Milton, Massachusetts
WNAN Nantucket, Massachusetts
WBSM New Bedford, Massachusetts
WDIS Norfolk, Massachusetts
WPLM Plymouth, Massachusetts
WESO Southbridge, Massachusetts
WHYN Springfield, Massachusetts
WGTX Truro, Massachusetts

RADIO - U.S.

WBUR West Yarmouth, Massachusetts
WXTK West Yarmouth, Massachusetts
WCAI Woods Hole, Massachusetts
WCRN Worcester, Massachusetts
WTAG Worcester, Massachusetts
WCBM Baltimore, Maryland
WEAA Baltimore, Maryland
WJZ Baltimore, Maryland
WYPR Baltimore, Maryland
WCBC Cumberland, Maryland
WKDI Denton, Maryland
WFMD Frederick, Maryland
WYPF Frederick, Maryland
WFRB Frostburg, Maryland
WARK Hagerstown, Maryland
WGMS Hagerstown, Maryland
WHAG Halfway, Maryland
WJSS Havre De Grace, Maryland
WPTX Lexington Park, Maryland
WYPO Ocean City, Maryland
WICO-FM Pocomoke City, Maryland
WICO Salisbury, Maryland
WSCL Salisbury, Maryland
WTHU Thurmont, Maryland
WVQM Augusta, Maine
WZON Bangor, Maine
WBQI Bar Harbor, Maine
WCME(AM) Brunswick, Maine
WVOM Howland, Maine
WBQQ Kennebunk, Maine
WXME Monticello, Maine
WJCX Pittsfield, Maine
WGAN Portland, Maine
WZAN Portland, Maine
WEGP Presque Isle, Maine
WTME Rumford, Maine
WKTQ South Paris, Maine
WBQX Thomaston, Maine
WNZS Veazie, Maine
WRED Westbrook, Maine
WPRR Ada, Michigan
WABJ Adrian, Michigan
WATZ Alpena, Michigan
WUOM Ann Arbor, Michigan
WBCK-FM Battle Creek, Michigan
WMAX Bay City, Michigan
WSJM-FM Benton Harbor, Michigan
WHFB Benton Harbor-St. Jo, Michigan
WAUS Berrien Springs, Michigan
WBRN Big Rapids, Michigan
WODJ Big Rapids, Michigan
WBFH Bloomfield Hills, Michigan
WLJW Cadillac, Michigan
WSGW-FM Carrollton, Michigan
WMKT Charlevoix, Michigan
WDTW Dearborn, Michigan
WDFN Detroit, Michigan
WDTK Detroit, Michigan
WJR Detroit, Michigan
WKAR East Lansing, Michigan
WVFN East Lansing, Michigan
WLJN Elmwood Township, Michigan
WCHT Escanaba, Michigan
WSNL Flint, Michigan
WTRX Flint, Michigan
WWCK Flint, Michigan
WTKG Grand Rapids, Michigan
WVGR Grand Rapids, Michigan
WGLM Greenville, Michigan
WMPL Hancock, Michigan
WHPR-FM Highland Park, Michigan
WHTC Holland, Michigan
WMIQ Iron Mountain, Michigan
WJMS Ironwood, Michigan
WIAN Ishpeming, Michigan
WZAM Ishpeming, Michigan
WKHM Jackson, Michigan
WKMI Kalamazoo, Michigan
WKZO Kalamazoo, Michigan
WJNL Kingsley, Michigan
WILS Lansing, Michigan
WJIM Lansing, Michigan
WKLA Ludington, Michigan
WMTE Manistee, Michigan
WPIQ Manistique, Michigan
WDMJ Marquette, Michigan
WAVC Mio, Michigan
WAZP Munising, Michigan
WKBZ Muskegon, Michigan
WNIL Niles, Michigan
WLUN Pinconning, Michigan
WPHM Port Huron, Michigan
WSGW Saginaw, Michigan
WLBY Saline, Michigan
WMIC Sandusky, Michigan
WKNW Sault Sainte Marie, Michigan
WMMI Shepherd, Michigan
WSJM St. Joseph, Michigan
WIOS Tawas City-East Tawa, Michigan
WICA Traverse City, Michigan
WTCM Traverse City, Michigan
WPON Walled Lake, Michigan
WDEO Ypsilanti, Michigan
WPNW Zeeland, Michigan
KATE Albert Lea, Minnesota
KAUS Austin, Minnesota
WWWI Baxter, Minnesota
KBUN Bemidji, Minnesota
KCRB-FM Bemidji, Minnesota
KKBJ Bemidji, Minnesota
KBPR Brainerd, Minnesota
KLIZ Brainerd, Minnesota
KRWC Buffalo, Minnesota
KSJR-FM Collegeville, Minnesota
KDLM Detroit Lakes, Minnesota
WZFG Dilworth, Minnesota
KDAL Duluth, Minnesota
KDNI Duluth, Minnesota
WEBC Duluth, Minnesota
KBRF Fergus Falls, Minnesota
KCMF Fergus Falls, Minnesota
KKCQ Fosston, Minnesota
KYCR Golden Valley, Minnesota
KDWA Hastings, Minnesota
KLTF Little Falls, Minnesota
KTOE Mankato, Minnesota
KYSM Mankato, Minnesota
KMHL Marshall, Minnesota
KSJN Minneapolis, Minnesota
WCCO Minneapolis, Minnesota
WWTC Minneapolis, Minnesota
KMRS Morris, Minnesota
WNMT Nashwauk, Minnesota
KCHK New Prague, Minnesota
KRLX Northfield, Minnesota
WWWI-FM Pillager, Minnesota
KLOH Pipestone, Minnesota
KKMS Richfield, Minnesota
KROC Rochester, Minnesota
KNSI St. Cloud, Minnesota
WJON St. Cloud, Minnesota
KTNF St. Louis Park, Minnesota
KSTP St. Paul, Minnesota
WIRR Virginia-Hibbing, Minnesota
KWLM Willmar, Minnesota
KDOM Windom, Minnesota
KDOM-FM Windom, Minnesota
KWNO Winona, Minnesota
KRSW Worthington, Minnesota
KWOA Worthington, Minnesota
KNSW Worthington-Marshall, Minnesota
KGNA-FM Arnold, Missouri
KSGF-FM Ash Grove, Missouri
KSWM Aurora, Missouri
KKOZ-FM Ava, Missouri
KBFL-FM Buffalo, Missouri
KZGM Cabool, Missouri
KAPE Cape Girardeau, Missouri
KGIR Cape Girardeau, Missouri
KZIM Cape Girardeau, Missouri
KNLH Cedar Hill, Missouri
KCHR Charleston, Missouri
KRNW Chillicothe, Missouri
KFUO Clayton, Missouri
KCTO Cleveland, Missouri
KFRU Columbia, Missouri
KOPN Columbia, Missouri
KGNN-FM Cuba, Missouri
KREI Farmington, Missouri
KSSZ Fayette, Missouri
KJFF Festus, Missouri
KTBJ Festus, Missouri
KFTK Florissant, Missouri
KHMO Hannibal, Missouri
KMCV High Point, Missouri
KBCV Hollister, Missouri
KCTE Independence, Missouri
KLIK Jefferson City, Missouri
KWOS Jefferson City, Missouri
KZYM Joplin, Missouri
KCMO Kansas City, Missouri
KKFI Kansas City, Missouri
WHB Kansas City, Missouri
KPOW-FM La Monte, Missouri
KBNN Lebanon, Missouri
KLWT Lebanon, Missouri
KCXL Liberty, Missouri
KMAL Malden, Missouri
KWIX Moberly, Missouri
KRMS Osage Beach, Missouri
KFMO Park Hills, Missouri
KCOZ Point Lookout, Missouri
KLID Poplar Bluff, Missouri
KWOC Poplar Bluff, Missouri
KNLP Potosi, Missouri
KAYX Richmond, Missouri
KTTR Rolla, Missouri
KSMO Salem, Missouri
KSIS Sedalia, Missouri
KSIM Sikeston, Missouri
KADI Springfield, Missouri
KSCV Springfield, Missouri
KSGF Springfield, Missouri
KWTO Springfield, Missouri
KWTO-FM Springfield, Missouri
KTTR-FM St. James, Missouri
KFEQ St. Joseph, Missouri
KJSL St. Louis, Missouri
KMOX St. Louis, Missouri
KTRS St. Louis, Missouri
KTUI Sullivan, Missouri
KCRL Sunrise Beach, Missouri
KLPW Union, Missouri
KGNV Washington, Missouri
KWMO Washington, Missouri
KJPW Waynesville, Missouri
KWPM West Plains, Missouri
KUKU Willow Springs, Missouri
WAMY Amory, Mississippi
WTNI Biloxi, Mississippi
WCJU Columbia, Mississippi
WXRZ Corinth, Mississippi
WFMN Flora, Mississippi
WYAB Flora, Mississippi
WDSV Greenville, Mississippi
WMUT Grenada, Mississippi
WHSY Hattiesburg, Mississippi
WURC Holly Springs, Mississippi
WTCD Indianola, Mississippi
WJDX Jackson, Mississippi
WAML Laurel, Mississippi
WMXI Laurel, Mississippi
WJZD-FM Long Beach, Mississippi
WKBB Mantee, Mississippi
WALT Meridian, Mississippi
WMOX Meridian, Mississippi
WRQO Monticello, Mississippi
WBUV Moss Point, Mississippi
WNAT Natchez, Mississippi
WJNT Pearl, Mississippi
WHOC Philadelphia, Mississippi
WWMR Saltillo, Mississippi
WFMM Sumrall, Mississippi
WKMQ Tupelo, Mississippi
WQBC Vicksburg, Mississippi
WTNM Water Valley, Mississippi
KGVW Belgrade, Montana
KBLG Billings, Montana
KBOZ Bozeman, Montana
KMMS Bozeman, Montana
KMPT East Missoula, Montana
KGVA Fort Belknap Agency, Montana
KQDI Great Falls, Montana
KLYQ Hamilton, Montana
KBLL Helena, Montana
KCAP Helena, Montana
KGEZ Kalispell, Montana
KOFI Kalispell, Montana
KBSR Laurel, Montana
KPRK Livingston, Montana
KBGA Missoula, Montana
KGRZ Missoula, Montana
KJJR Whitefish, Montana
WSPC Albemarle, North Carolina
WSKY Asheville, North Carolina
WWNC Asheville, North Carolina
WTKF Atlantic, North Carolina
WCGC Belmont, North Carolina
WFGW Black Mountain, North Carolina
WXIT Blowing Rock, North Carolina
WLTT Bolivia, North Carolina
WSQL Brevard, North Carolina
WZTK Burlington, North Carolina

WCHL Chapel Hill, North Carolina
WBT Charlotte, North Carolina
WFAE Charlotte, North Carolina
WCRU Dallas, North Carolina
WDAV Davidson, North Carolina
WNCU Durham, North Carolina
WRJD Durham, North Carolina
WLOE Eden, North Carolina
WGAI Elizabeth City, North Carolina
WPEK Fairview, North Carolina
WGHB Farmville, North Carolina
WFNC Fayetteville, North Carolina
WIDU Fayetteville, North Carolina
WGBR Goldsboro, North Carolina
WSML Graham, North Carolina
WHNC Henderson, North Carolina
WIZS Henderson, North Carolina
WHKY Hickory, North Carolina
WGOS High Point, North Carolina
WCMC-FM Holly Springs, North Carolina
WAVQ Jacksonville, North Carolina
WJNC Jacksonville, North Carolina
WJRI Lenoir, North Carolina
WLXN Lexington, North Carolina
WYRN Louisburg, North Carolina
WOBX-FM Manteo, North Carolina
WYQS Mars Hill, North Carolina
WMYN Mayodan, North Carolina
WIXE Monroe, North Carolina
WAAE New Bern, North Carolina
WNOS New Bern, North Carolina
WAUG New Hope, North Carolina
WNBU(FM) Oriental, North Carolina
WCBQ Oxford, North Carolina
WPTF Raleigh, North Carolina
WCAB Rutherfordton, North Carolina
WSTP Salisbury, North Carolina
WNCA Siler City, North Carolina
WEEB Southern Pines, North Carolina
WFMI Southern Shores, North Carolina
WBLO Thomasville, North Carolina
WSVM Valdese, North Carolina
WDLX Washington, North Carolina
WTXY Whiteville, North Carolina
WBFJ Winston-Salem, North Carolina
KFYR Bismarck, North Dakota
KLXX Bismarck-Mandan, North Dakota
KFGO Fargo, North Dakota
WDAY Fargo, North Dakota
KNOX Grand Forks, North Dakota
KUND-FM Grand Forks, North Dakota
KNDK Langdon, North Dakota
KQLX Lisbon, North Dakota
KHRT Minot, North Dakota
KEYZ Williston, North Dakota
KCOW Alliance, Nebraska
KWBE Beatrice, Nebraska
KJSK Columbus, Nebraska
KTTT Columbus, Nebraska
KAMI Cozad, Nebraska
KCVN Cozad, Nebraska
KHUB Fremont, Nebraska
KRGI Grand Island, Nebraska
KGFW Kearney, Nebraska
KFOR Lincoln, Nebraska
KLCV Lincoln, Nebraska
KLIN Lincoln, Nebraska
WJAG Norfolk, Nebraska
KODY North Platte, Nebraska
KCRO Omaha, Nebraska
KFAB Omaha, Nebraska
KVNO Omaha, Nebraska
KNEB Scottsbluff, Nebraska
KAWL York, Nebraska
WEVO(FM) Concord, New Hampshire
WKXL Concord, New Hampshire
WDER Derry, New Hampshire
WTSN Dover, New Hampshire
WXEX Exeter, New Hampshire
WEVH Hanover, New Hampshire
WTSL Hanover, New Hampshire
WNNH Henniker, New Hampshire
WTPL Hillsboro, New Hampshire
WEVJ Jackson, New Hampshire
WEVN Keene, New Hampshire
WKBK Keene, New Hampshire
WZBK Keene, New Hampshire
WEMJ Laconia, New Hampshire
WUVR Lebanon, New Hampshire
WGIR Manchester, New Hampshire
WEVS Nashua, New Hampshire
WSMN Nashua, New Hampshire
WNTK-FM New London, New Hampshire
WPKX(AM) Rochester, New Hampshire
WCCM Salem, New Hampshire
WENJ Atlantic City, New Jersey
WNJN-FM Atlantic City, New Jersey
WNJS-FM Berlin, New Jersey
WNJB-FM Bridgeton, New Jersey
WTMR Camden, New Jersey
WNJZ Cape May Court House, New Jersey
WNYM Hackensack, New Jersey
WRNJ Hackettstown, New Jersey
WOBM Lakewood Township, New Jersey
WNJM Manahawkin, New Jersey
WVBV Medford Lakes, New Jersey
WNJY Netcong, New Jersey
WVNJ Oakland, New Jersey
WIBG Ocean City/Somers Po, New Jersey
WVPH Piscataway, New Jersey
WGHT Pompton Lakes, New Jersey
WKMB Stirling, New Jersey
WNJP Sussex, New Jersey
WKXW Trenton, New Jersey
WNJT-FM Trenton, New Jersey
WNJC Vineland, New Jersey
KINN Alamogordo, New Mexico
KABQ Albuquerque, New Mexico
KKIM Albuquerque, New Mexico
KKOB Albuquerque, New Mexico
KUNM Albuquerque, New Mexico
KXKS Albuquerque, New Mexico
KRRT Arroyo Seco, New Mexico
KSVP Artesia, New Mexico
KNFT Bayard, New Mexico
KICA Clovis, New Mexico
KWKA Clovis, New Mexico
KENN Farmington, New Mexico
KNMI Farmington, New Mexico
KTGW Fruitland, New Mexico
KYKK Humble City, New Mexico
KOBE Las Cruces, New Mexico
KSNM Las Cruces, New Mexico
KNMX Las Vegas, New Mexico
KTBL Los Ranchos, New Mexico
KPCV Portales, New Mexico
KSEL Portales, New Mexico
KBIM Roswell, New Mexico
KRUI Ruidoso Downs, New Mexico
KHFM Santa Fe, New Mexico
KKIM-FM Santa Fe, New Mexico
KTRC Santa Fe, New Mexico
KVOT Taos, New Mexico
KNIS Carson City, Nevada
KTSN Elko, Nevada
KELY Ely, Nevada
KDWN Las Vegas, Nevada
KKVV Las Vegas, Nevada
KLAV Las Vegas, Nevada
KMZQ Las Vegas, Nevada
KXNT North Las Vegas, Nevada
KXTE Pahrump, Nevada
KNUU Paradise, Nevada
KJFK Reno, Nevada
KKOH Reno, Nevada
KSVL Smith, Nevada
KBZZ Sparks, Nevada
KQLO Sun Valley, Nevada
KUUB Sun Valley, Nevada
KWNA Winnemucca, Nevada
WAMC-FM Albany, New York
WROW Albany, New York
WVTL Amsterdam, New York
WAUB Auburn, New York
WBTA Batavia, New York
WINR Binghamton, New York
WNBF Binghamton, New York
WXLH Blue Mountain Lake, New York
WXLB Boonville, New York
WBEN Buffalo, New York
WBUF Buffalo, New York
WDCX-FM Buffalo, New York
WNED Buffalo, New York
WNED-FM Buffalo, New York
WWKB Buffalo, New York
WCAN Canajoharie, New York
WCGR Canandaigua, New York
WCKL Catskill, New York
WCHP Champlain, New York
WECK Cheektowaga, New York
WJIV Cherry Valley, New York
WENI Corning, New York
WWLE Cornwall, New York
WFLR Dundee, New York
WDOE Dunkirk, New York
WENY Elmira, New York
WENE Endicott, New York
WEOS Geneva, New York
WGVA Geneva, New York
WWSC Glens Falls, New York
WLEA Hornell, New York
WWLZ Horseheads, New York
WHCU Ithaca, New York
WNYY Ithaca, New York
WJTN Jamestown, New York
WNJA Jamestown, New York
WJFF Jeffersonville, New York
WAMK Kingston, New York
WGHQ Kingston, New York
WLVL Lockport, New York
WOSR Middletown, New York
WABC New York, New York
WFAN New York, New York
WMCA New York, New York
WWRL New York, New York
WXLG North Creek, New York
WSUF Noyack, New York
WQTK Ogdensburg, New York
WOEN Olean, New York
WMCR Oneida, New York
WNYO Oswego, New York
WEBO Owego, New York
WXLU Peru, New York
WCEL Plattsburgh, New York
WEAV Plattsburgh, New York
WTWK Plattsburgh, New York
WAIH Potsdam, New York
WKIP Poughkeepsie, New York
WRHV Poughkeepsie, New York
WGDJ Rensselaer, New York
WFTU Riverhead, New York
WBEE-FM Rochester, New York
WHAM Rochester, New York
WHTK Rochester, New York
WXXI-FM Rochester, New York
WFNP Rosendale, New York
WNBZ Saranac Lake, New York
WSPN Saratoga Springs, New York
WGY Schenectady, New York
WMHT-FM Schenectady, New York
WRLI-FM Southampton, New York
WUSB Stony Brook, New York
WFBL Syracuse, New York
WSYR Syracuse, New York
WANC Ticonderoga, New York
WOFX Troy, New York
WIBX Utica, New York
WUNY Utica, New York
WTBQ Warwick, New York
WATN Watertown, New York
WJNY Watertown, New York
WXZO Willsboro, New York
WARF Akron, Ohio
WHLO Akron, Ohio
WATH Athens, Ohio
WOUB Athens, Ohio
WBLL Bellefontaine, Ohio
WAIS Buchtel, Ohio
WOUC-FM Cambridge, Ohio
WYFY Cambridge, Ohio
WGFT Campbell, Ohio
WILB Canton, Ohio
WBEX Chillicothe, Ohio
WOUH-FM Chillicothe, Ohio
WCVX Cincinnati, Ohio
WGUC Cincinnati, Ohio
WKRC Cincinnati, Ohio
WLW Cincinnati, Ohio
WCPN Cleveland, Ohio
WHK Cleveland, Ohio
WHKW Cleveland, Ohio
WTAM Cleveland, Ohio
WERE Cleveland Heights, Ohio
WTVN Columbus, Ohio
WRFD Columbus-Worthington, Ohio
WWOW Conneaut, Ohio
WOSE Coshocton, Ohio
WDPR Dayton, Ohio
WHIO Dayton, Ohio
WEOL Elyria, Ohio
WFIN Findlay, Ohio
WTKC Findlay, Ohio
WMOH Hamilton, Ohio

WIRO Ironton, Ohio
WOUL-FM Ironton, Ohio
WNIR Kent, Ohio
WFCO Lancaster, Ohio
WLOH Lancaster, Ohio
WIMA Lima, Ohio
WMAN Mansfield, Ohio
WLTP Marietta, Ohio
WMRT Marietta, Ohio
WMRN Marion, Ohio
WMVO Mount Vernon, Ohio
WCLT Newark, Ohio
WMUB Oxford, Ohio
WCCD Parma, Ohio
WEEC Springfield, Ohio
WCWA Toledo, Ohio
WSPD Toledo, Ohio
WBTC Uhrichsville, Ohio
WHKZ Warren, Ohio
WELW Willoughby, Ohio
WASN Youngstown, Ohio
WKBN Youngstown, Ohio
WOUZ-FM Zanesville, Ohio
KWHW Altus, Oklahoma
KWON Bartlesville, Oklahoma
KOKB Blackwell, Oklahoma
KCLI Clinton, Oklahoma
KUSH Cushing, Oklahoma
KPNS Duncan, Oklahoma
KCSC Edmond, Oklahoma
KGWA Enid, Oklahoma
KWXC Grove, Oklahoma
KTJS Hobart, Oklahoma
KOSN Ketchum, Oklahoma
KXCA Lawton, Oklahoma
KBCW-FM McAlester, Oklahoma
KWPN(AM) Moore, Oklahoma
KXMX Muldrow, Oklahoma
KGOU Norman, Oklahoma
KOKC Oklahoma City, Oklahoma
KTLR Oklahoma City, Oklahoma
KTOK Oklahoma City, Oklahoma
KOKL Okmulgee, Oklahoma
KPGM Pawhuska, Oklahoma
KIXR Ponca City, Oklahoma
KRMG-FM Sand Springs, Oklahoma
KSPI Stillwater, Oklahoma
KCFO Tulsa, Oklahoma
KFAQ Tulsa, Oklahoma
KRMG Tulsa, Oklahoma
KSIW Woodward, Oklahoma
KAST Astoria, Oregon
KHSS Athena, Oregon
KBKR Baker, Oregon
KOBK Baker City, Oregon
KBND Bend, Oregon
KBNW Bend, Oregon
KICE Bend, Oregon
KHSN Coos Bay, Oregon
KWRO Coquille, Oregon
KLOO Corvallis, Oregon
KOAC Corvallis, Oregon
KNND Cottage Grove, Oregon
KPPT-FM Depoe Bay, Oregon
KWVR Enterprise, Oregon
KOPB Eugene, Oregon
KPNW Eugene, Oregon
KUGN Eugene, Oregon
KWAX Eugene, Oregon
KZZR Government Camp, Oregon
KAJO Grants Pass, Oregon
KUIK Hillsboro, Oregon
KAGO Klamath Falls, Oregon
KFLS Klamath Falls, Oregon
KLBM La Grande, Oregon
KGAL Lebanon, Oregon
KDOV Medford, Oregon
KMED Medford, Oregon
KBBR North Bend, Oregon
KRBM Pendleton, Oregon
KUMA Pendleton, Oregon
KAPL Phoenix, Oregon
KCMX Phoenix, Oregon
KEX Portland, Oregon
KKPZ Portland, Oregon
KPDQ Portland, Oregon
KPDQ-FM Portland, Oregon
KPOJ Portland, Oregon
KXTG(AM) Portland, Oregon
KDUN Reedsport, Oregon
KQEN Roseburg, Oregon
KOHI St. Helens, Oregon
KFIR Sweet Home, Oregon
KACI The Dalles, Oregon
KMBD(AM) Tillamook, Oregon
KTMK Tillamook, Oregon
KCUP Toledo, Oregon
KPAM Troutdale, Oregon
KLWJ(AM) Umatilla, Oregon
KWLZ-FM West Linn, Oregon
WJCS Allentown, Pennsylvania
WRTA Altoona, Pennsylvania
WMBA Ambridge, Pennsylvania
WILK-FM Avoca, Pennsylvania
WBVP Beaver Falls, Pennsylvania
WBLF Bellefonte, Pennsylvania
WGPA Bethlehem, Pennsylvania
WLFP Braddock, Pennsylvania
WISR Butler, Pennsylvania
WHYL Carlisle, Pennsylvania
WCHA Chambersburg, Pennsylvania
WWCH Clarion, Pennsylvania
WFRM Coudersport, Pennsylvania
WCED Du Bois, Pennsylvania
WRDD Ebensburg, Pennsylvania
WJET Erie, Pennsylvania
WRIE Erie, Pennsylvania
WZSK Everett, Pennsylvania
WSAJ-FM Grove City, Pennsylvania
WHP Harrisburg, Pennsylvania
WITF-FM Harrisburg, Pennsylvania
WAZL Hazleton, Pennsylvania
WHHN Hollidaysburg, Pennsylvania
WRKK Hughesville, Pennsylvania
WLLI(AM) Huntingdon, Pennsylvania
WKFB Jeannette, Pennsylvania
WKGE Johnstown, Pennsylvania
WNTJ Johnstown, Pennsylvania
WFYL King of Prussia, Pennsylvania
WDAC Lancaster, Pennsylvania
WNPV Lansdale, Pennsylvania
WLBR Lebanon, Pennsylvania
WWGE Loretto, Pennsylvania
WJSM-FM Martinsburg, Pennsylvania
WWBJ Martinsburg, Pennsylvania
WEDO McKeesport, Pennsylvania
WMNY McKeesport, Pennsylvania
WMGW Meadville, Pennsylvania
WMLP Milton, Pennsylvania
WFTE Mount Cobb, Pennsylvania
WPLY Mount Pocono, Pennsylvania
WKST New Castle, Pennsylvania
WPHT Philadelphia, Pennsylvania
WURD Philadelphia, Pennsylvania
WWDB Philadelphia, Pennsylvania
WPHB Philipsburg, Pennsylvania
KDKA Pittsburgh, Pennsylvania
WDVE Pittsburgh, Pennsylvania
WPGB Pittsburgh, Pennsylvania
WQED-FM Pittsburgh, Pennsylvania
WWNL Pittsburgh, Pennsylvania
WEMR Pleasant Gap, Pennsylvania
WPAZ Pottstown, Pennsylvania
WECZ Punxsutawney, Pennsylvania
WYBF Radnor Township, Pennsylvania
WEEU Reading, Pennsylvania
WBZU Scranton, Pennsylvania
WPIC Sharon, Pennsylvania
WNTW Somerset, Pennsylvania
WRSC State College, Pennsylvania
WVPO Stroudsburg, Pennsylvania
WKOK Sunbury, Pennsylvania
WTIV Titusville, Pennsylvania
WXVU Villanova, Pennsylvania
WNAE Warren, Pennsylvania
WCHE West Chester, Pennsylvania
WKZN West Hazleton, Pennsylvania
WILK Wilkes-Barre, Pennsylvania
WRAK Williamsport, Pennsylvania
WWPA Williamsport, Pennsylvania
WSBA York, Pennsylvania
WYYC York, Pennsylvania
WCMN Arecibo, Puerto Rico
WBQN Barceloneta-Manati, Puerto Rico
WYAC Cabo Rojo, Puerto Rico
WLEY Cayey, Puerto Rico
WMDD Fajardo, Puerto Rico
WMSW Hatillo, Puerto Rico
WALO Humacao, Puerto Rico
WIVV Island of Vieques, Puerto Rico
WMNT Manati, Puerto Rico
WKJB Mayaguez, Puerto Rico
WPRA Mayaguez, Puerto Rico
WTIL Mayaguez, Puerto Rico
WDEP Ponce, Puerto Rico
WISO Ponce, Puerto Rico
WPAB Ponce, Puerto Rico
WPRP Ponce, Puerto Rico
WUKQ Ponce, Puerto Rico
WAPA San Juan, Puerto Rico
WBMJ San Juan, Puerto Rico
WIPR-FM San Juan, Puerto Rico
WKAQ San Juan, Puerto Rico
WQII San Juan, Puerto Rico
WSKN San Juan, Puerto Rico
WUNO San Juan, Puerto Rico
WRSS San Sebastian, Puerto Rico
WUPR Utuado, Puerto Rico
WXEW Yabucoa, Puerto Rico
WENA Yauco, Puerto Rico
WKFE Yauco, Puerto Rico
WCRI-FM Block Island, Rhode Island
WRNI-FM Narragansett Pier, Rhode Island
WADK Newport, Rhode Island
WHJJ Providence, Rhode Island
WPRO Providence, Rhode Island
WRNI Providence, Rhode Island
WEAN-FM Wakefield-Peacedale, Rhode Island
WBLQ(AM) Westerly, Rhode Island
WNRI Woonsocket, Rhode Island
WAIM Anderson, South Carolina
WZMJ Batesburg, South Carolina
WROP Belton, South Carolina
WSPO Charleston, South Carolina
WBT-FM Chester, South Carolina
WISW Columbia, South Carolina
WXBT(AM) Columbia, South Carolina
WELP Easley, South Carolina
WOLH Florence, South Carolina
WFIS Fountain Inn, South Carolina
WGTN Georgetown, South Carolina
WSCC-FM Goose Creek, South Carolina
WYRD Greenville, South Carolina
WCRS Greenwood, South Carolina
WHGS Hampton, South Carolina
WRIX-FM Honea Path, South Carolina
WRHI Rock Hill, South Carolina
WSNW Seneca, South Carolina
WYRD-FM Simpsonville, South Carolina
WRNN-FM Socastee, South Carolina
WORD Spartanburg, South Carolina
WSPG Spartanburg, South Carolina
WDXY Sumter, South Carolina
KSDN Aberdeen, South Dakota
KBFS Belle Fourche, South Dakota
KIJV Huron, South Dakota
KSOO-FM Lennox, South Dakota
KJAM Madison, South Dakota
KMSD Mibank, South Dakota
KORN Mitchell, South Dakota
KCCR Pierre, South Dakota
KIMM Rapid City, South Dakota
KOTA Rapid City, South Dakota
KTOQ Rapid City, South Dakota
KCSD Sioux Falls, South Dakota
KELO Sioux Falls, South Dakota
KSOO Sioux Falls, South Dakota
KJJQ Volga, South Dakota
KSDR Watertown, South Dakota
WNAX Yankton, South Dakota
WCTA Alamo, Tennessee
WYXI Athens, Tennessee
WSAA Benton, Tennessee
WHCB Bristol, Tennessee
WTBG Brownsville, Tennessee
WGOW Chattanooga, Tennessee
WLMR Chattanooga, Tennessee
WNOO Chattanooga, Tennessee
WMCH Church Hill, Tennessee
WJZM Clarksville, Tennessee
WKFN Clarksville, Tennessee
WBAC Cleveland, Tennessee
WCLE Cleveland, Tennessee
WPWT Colonial Heights, Tennessee
WPTN Cookeville, Tennessee
WZYX Cowan, Tennessee
WAEW Crossville, Tennessee
WMKW Crossville, Tennessee
WTJJ Dyer, Tennessee
WCPH Etowah, Tennessee
WMTY Farragut, Tennessee
WAKM Franklin, Tennessee
WNML-FM Friendsville, Tennessee

WGFX Gallatin, Tennessee
WQZQ Goodlettsville, Tennessee
WCXZ Harrogate, Tennessee
WWTN Hendersonville, Tennessee
WIRJ Humboldt, Tennessee
WNRX Jefferson City, Tennessee
WETS-FM Johnson City, Tennessee
WJCW Johnson City, Tennessee
WETR Knoxville, Tennessee
WITA Knoxville, Tennessee
WKVL Knoxville, Tennessee
WNML Knoxville, Tennessee
WRJZ Knoxville, Tennessee
WCOR Lebanon, Tennessee
WLOD Loudon, Tennessee
WPLN Madison, Tennessee
WRKQ Madisonville, Tennessee
WMSR Manchester, Tennessee
WCMT Martin, Tennessee
WAKI McMinnville, Tennessee
KWAM Memphis, Tennessee
WREC Memphis, Tennessee
WGNS Murfreesboro, Tennessee
WFSK-FM Nashville, Tennessee
WLAC Nashville, Tennessee
WPFT Pigeon Forge, Tennessee
WZNG Shelbyville, Tennessee
WFCM Smyrna, Tennessee
WGOW-FM Soddy-Daisy, Tennessee
WRHA(AM) Spring City, Tennessee
KWKC Abilene, Texas
KZQQ Abilene, Texas
KTEK Alvin, Texas
KIXZ Amarillo, Texas
KXGL Amarillo, Texas
KZIP Amarillo, Texas
KACT Andrews, Texas
KLBJ Austin, Texas
KMFA Austin, Texas
KVET Austin, Texas
KSKY Balch Springs, Texas
KLVI Beaumont, Texas
KTAA Big Sandy, Texas
KBST-FM Big Spring, Texas
KBYG Big Spring, Texas
KWHI Brenham, Texas
KZRK Canyon, Texas
KXYL-FM Coleman, Texas
WTAW College Station, Texas
KTMR Converse, Texas
KCCT Corpus Christi, Texas
KEYS Corpus Christi, Texas
KKTX Corpus Christi, Texas
KAND Corsicana, Texas
KZNX Creedmoor, Texas
KHER Crystal City, Texas
KERA Dallas, Texas
KGGR Dallas, Texas
KLIF Dallas, Texas
KTCK Dallas, Texas
KIXL Del Valle, Texas
KURV Edinburg, Texas
KULP El Campo, Texas
KELP El Paso, Texas
KHRO El Paso, Texas
KQBU El Paso, Texas
KTSM El Paso, Texas
KFCD Farmersville, Texas
KFLC Fort Worth, Texas
KNAF Fredericksburg, Texas
KGAF Gainesville, Texas
KEES Gladewater, Texas
KVCE Highland Park, Texas
KWRD-FM Highland Village, Texas
KCOH Houston, Texas
KILT Houston, Texas
KLAT Houston, Texas
KNTH Houston, Texas
KPRC Houston, Texas
KXYZ Houston, Texas
KMNY Hurst, Texas
KERV Kerrville, Texas
KFRO Longview, Texas
KABA Louise, Texas
KFYO Lubbock, Texas
KJDL Lubbock, Texas
KJTV Lubbock, Texas
KRFE Lubbock, Texas
KAVX Lufkin, Texas
KKHT-FM Lumberton, Texas
KCRS Midland, Texas
KWEL Midland, Texas
KSFA Nacogdoches, Texas
KWBC Navasota, Texas
KNET Palestine, Texas
KIKK Pasadena, Texas
KLVL Pasadena, Texas
KVOP Plainview, Texas
KDEI Port Arthur, Texas
KOLE Port Arthur, Texas
KJCE Rollingwood, Texas
KGKL San Angelo, Texas
KKSA San Angelo, Texas
KCOR San Antonio, Texas
KPAC San Antonio, Texas
KSLR San Antonio, Texas
KTSA San Antonio, Texas
KTSW San Marcos, Texas
KWED Seguin, Texas
KZSP South Padre Island, Texas
KSQX Springtown, Texas
KTEM Temple, Texas
KLUP Terrell Hills, Texas
KKTK Texarkana, Texas
KTFS Texarkana, Texas
KSEV Tomball, Texas
KTBB Tyler, Texas
KTNO University Park, Texas
KBCT Waco, Texas
KWTX Waco, Texas
KKEE Wheelock, Texas
KWFS Wichita Falls, Texas
KSUB Cedar City, Utah
KUSR Logan, Utah
KUSU-FM Logan, Utah
KVNU Logan, Utah
KSL-FM Midvale, Utah
KALL North Salt Lake City, Utah
KLO Ogden, Utah
KOAL Price, Utah
KBYU-FM Provo, Utah
KOVO Provo, Utah
KSVC Richfield, Utah
KCPW-FM Salt Lake City, Utah
KNRS Salt Lake City, Utah
KRCL Salt Lake City, Utah
KSL Salt Lake City, Utah
KZNS Salt Lake City, Utah
KTKK Sandy, Utah
KHQN Spanish Fork, Utah
KCPX Spanish Valley, Utah
KDXU St. George, Utah
KZNU St. George, Utah
KVEL Vernal, Utah
KUNF Washington, Utah
WABN Abingdon, Virginia
WHAN Ashland, Virginia
WBVA Bayside, Virginia
WFNR Blacksburg, Virginia
WKEX Blacksburg, Virginia
WCHV Charlottesville, Virginia
WINA Charlottesville, Virginia
WVAX Charlottesville, Virginia
WMVE Chase City, Virginia
WWVT Christiansburg, Virginia
WMRY Crozet, Virginia
WPIN Dublin, Virginia
WKTR Earlysville, Virginia
WEVA Emporia, Virginia
WFLO Farmville, Virginia
WFFC Ferrum, Virginia
WFVA Fredericksburg, Virginia
WMNA Gretna, Virginia
WKCY Harrisonburg, Virginia
WMRA Harrisonburg, Virginia
WSVA Harrisonburg, Virginia
WCNV Heathsville, Virginia
WMRL Lexington, Virginia
WREL Lexington, Virginia
WBRG Lynchburg, Virginia
WLNI Lynchburg, Virginia
WVGM Lynchburg, Virginia
WKDV Manassas, Virginia
WHEE Martinsville, Virginia
WMVA Martinsville, Virginia
WSVG Mount Jackson, Virginia
WGH Newport News, Virginia
WHRV Norfolk, Virginia
WNIS Norfolk, Virginia
WESR Onley-Onancock, Virginia
WTPS Petersburg, Virginia
WWBU Radford, Virginia
WCVE-FM Richmond, Virginia
WLEE Richmond, Virginia
WRVA Richmond, Virginia
WFIR Roanoke, Virginia
WLOY Rural Retreat, Virginia
WHEO Stuart, Virginia
WRAR Tappahannock, Virginia
WTZE Tazewell, Virginia
WXTG-FM Virginia Beach, Virginia
WKCI Waynesboro, Virginia
WINC Winchester, Virginia
WVGN Charlotte Amalie, Virgin Islands
WVWI Charlotte Amalie, Virgin Islands
WSNO Barre, Vermont
WBTN Bennington, Vermont
WKVT Brattleboro, Vermont
WVMT Burlington, Vermont
WGDR Plainfield, Vermont
WCVR(AM) Randolph, Vermont
WSYB Rutland, Vermont
WRSA St. Albans, Vermont
WDEV-FM Warren, Vermont
KXRO Aberdeen, Washington
KCLK Asotin, Washington
KBAI Bellingham, Washington
KGMI Bellingham, Washington
KPUG Bellingham, Washington
KUGS Bellingham, Washington
KGNW Burien-Seattle, Washington
KELA Centralia-Chehalis, Washington
KOZI Chelan, Washington
KOZI-FM Chelan, Washington
KMAX Colfax, Washington
KKRS Davenport, Washington
KSPO Dishman, Washington
KXLE Ellensburg, Washington
KTBI Ephrata, Washington
KULE Ephrata, Washington
KWOK Hoquiam, Washington
KONA Kennewick-Richland-P, Washington
KLAY Lakewood, Washington
KBSN Moses Lake, Washington
KMWS Mount Vernon, Washington
KSVR Mount Vernon, Washington
KGTK Olympia, Washington
KOMW Omak, Washington
KQWS Omak, Washington
KTRW Opportunity, Washington
KFLD Pasco, Washington
KONP Port Angeles, Washington
KPTZ Port Townsend, Washington
KQQQ Pullman, Washington
KKNW Seattle, Washington
KLFE Seattle, Washington
KNTS Seattle, Washington
KPTK Seattle, Washington
KVI Seattle, Washington
KITZ Silverdale, Washington
KGA Spokane, Washington
KJRB Spokane, Washington
KPTQ Spokane, Washington
KQNT Spokane, Washington
KXLY Spokane, Washington
KIRO-FM Tacoma, Washington
KXOT Tacoma, Washington
KBMS Vancouver, Washington
KGDC Walla Walla, Washington
KUJ Walla Walla, Washington
KWWS Walla Walla, Washington
KPQ Wenatchee, Washington
KIT Yakima, Washington
WHAA Adams, Wisconsin
WXCE Amery, Wisconsin
WLBL Auburndale, Wisconsin
WBEV Beaver Dam, Wisconsin
WDUZ-FM Brillion, Wisconsin
WHSA Brule, Wisconsin
WEAQ Chippewa Falls, Wisconsin
WHAD Delafield, Wisconsin
WDVM Eau Claire, Wisconsin
KFIZ Fond Du Lac, Wisconsin
WHID Green Bay, Wisconsin
WTAQ Green Bay, Wisconsin
WMCS Greenfield, Wisconsin
WHHI Highland, Wisconsin
WKBH Holmen, Wisconsin
WCLO Janesville, Wisconsin
WLIP Kenosha, Wisconsin
WHBY Kimberly, Wisconsin
WHLA La Crosse, Wisconsin
WIZM La Crosse, Wisconsin

WKTY La Crosse, Wisconsin
WLDY Ladysmith, Wisconsin
WHA Madison, Wisconsin
WIBA Madison, Wisconsin
WTDY Madison, Wisconsin
WHWC Menomonie, Wisconsin
WMEQ Menomonie, Wisconsin
WVSS Menomonie, Wisconsin
WJMT Merrill, Wisconsin
WISN Milwaukee, Wisconsin
WTMJ Milwaukee, Wisconsin
WTLX Monona, Wisconsin
WOSH Oshkosh, Wisconsin
WHBM Park Falls, Wisconsin
WPDR Portage, Wisconsin
WRJN Racine, Wisconsin
WJMC Rice Lake, Wisconsin
WRPN Ripon, Wisconsin
WDTX Rothschild, Wisconsin
WHBL Sheboygan, Wisconsin
WCSW Shell Lake, Wisconsin
WHDI Sister Bay, Wisconsin
WXXM Sun Prairie, Wisconsin
KUWS Superior, Wisconsin
WDSM Superior, Wisconsin
WVCX Tomah, Wisconsin
WEGZ Washburn, Wisconsin
WLBL-FM Wausau, Wisconsin
WSAU Wausau, Wisconsin
WXCO Wausau, Wisconsin
WFHR Wisconsin Rapids, Wisconsin
WWNR Beckley, West Virginia
WCST Berkeley Springs, West Virginia
WHIS Bluefield, West Virginia
WBUC Buckhannon, West Virginia
WCHS Charleston, West Virginia
WSWW Charleston, West Virginia
WTCS Fairmont, West Virginia
WVHU Huntington, West Virginia
WFSP Kingwood, West Virginia
WEPM Martinsburg, West Virginia
WRNR Martinsburg, West Virginia
WAJR Morgantown, West Virginia
WVLY Moundsville, West Virginia
WADC Parkersburg, West Virginia
WVNT Parkersburg, West Virginia
WBGS Point Pleasant, West Virginia
WRRL Rainelle, West Virginia
WMOV Ravenswood, West Virginia
WRON Ronceverte, West Virginia
WAJR-FM Salem, West Virginia
WJYP St. Albans, West Virginia
WEIR Weirton, West Virginia
WWVA Wheeling, West Virginia
KUWA Afton, Wyoming
KBBS Buffalo, Wyoming
KTWO Casper, Wyoming
KWYC Cheyenne, Wyoming
KODI Cody, Wyoming
KUYO Evansville, Wyoming
KIML Gillette, Wyoming
KOWB Laramie, Wyoming
KGAB Orchard Valley, Wyoming
KYDT Pine Haven, Wyoming
KPOW Powell, Wyoming
KRKK Rock Springs, Wyoming
KROE Sheridan, Wyoming

Tejano

KAAB Batesville, Arkansas
KSEC Bentonville, Arkansas
KBHC Nashville, Arkansas
KLNZ Glendale, Arizona
KCMT Oro Valley, Arizona
KEVT Sahuarita, Arizona
KXEW South Tucson, Arizona
KCEC-FM Wellton, Arizona
KUKY Wellton, Arizona
KMYX-FM Arvin, California
KWAC Bakersfield, California
KIQQ Barstow, California
KXXZ Barstow, California
KMVE California City, California
KSRT Cloverdale, California
KMQA East Porterville, California
KLBN Fresno, California
KXTS Geyserville, California
KBAA Grass Valley, California
KGEN-FM Hanford, California
KMPG Hollister, California
KESQ Indio, California
KBHH Kerman, California
KEXA King City, California
KSRN Kings Beach, California
KBTW Lenwood, California
KRQK Lompoc, California
KSMY Lompoc, California
KRCX-FM Marysville, California
KIWI McFarland, California
KRAY-FM Salinas, California
KTGE Salinas, California
KLNV San Diego, California
KBUA San Fernando, California
KZSF San Jose, California
KMJV Soledad, California
KXSC(FM) Sunnyvale, California
KFSO-FM Visalia, California
KLOQ-FM Winton, California
KPVW Aspen, Colorado
KFVR-FM Beulah, Colorado
WAFZ-FM Immokalee, Florida
WWRF Lake Worth, Florida
WRUM Orlando, Florida
WAMA Tampa, Florida
WQBN Temple Terrace, Florida
WAUC Wauchula, Florida
WDAL Dalton, Georgia
KPDA-FM Gooding, Idaho
WJZI(AM) Decatur, Indiana
KYQQ Arkansas City, Kansas
KYYS Kansas City, Kansas
WMFN Zeeland, Michigan
WZBO Edenton, North Carolina
WCNC Elizabeth City, North Carolina
WYMY Goldsboro, North Carolina
WWBG Greensboro, North Carolina
WREV Reidsville, North Carolina
KBBX-FM Nebraska City, Nebraska
KRZY Albuquerque, New Mexico
KPZE-FM Carlsbad, New Mexico
KKNS Corrales, New Mexico
KALN Dexter, New Mexico
KJFA Santa Fe, New Mexico
KXMT Taos, New Mexico
KRLV Las Vegas, Nevada
KRRN Moapa Valley, Nevada
KRNV-FM Reno, Nevada
WVKO-FM Johnstown, Ohio
KXTD Wagoner, Oklahoma
KRTA Medford, Oregon
KRDM Redmond, Oregon
KWBY Woodburn, Oregon
WVJP-FM Caguas, Puerto Rico
WGSP-FM Pageland, South Carolina
KOPY-FM Alice, Texas
KBZD Amarillo, Texas
KQQK Beaumont, Texas
KQFX Borger, Texas
KKPS Brownsville, Texas
KTAM Bryan, Texas
KAJP Carrizo Springs, Texas
KBSO Corpus Christi, Texas
KEPS Eagle Pass, Texas
KPSO-FM Falfurrias, Texas
KLNO Fort Worth, Texas
KHMC Goliad, Texas
KQUE Houston, Texas
KLEY-FM Jourdanton, Texas
KJBZ Laredo, Texas
KESS-FM Lewisville, Texas
KBZO Lubbock, Texas
KEJS Lubbock, Texas
KXTQ-FM Lubbock, Texas
KCUL-FM Marshall, Texas
KGBT-FM McAllen, Texas
KBDR Mirando City, Texas
KBED Nederland, Texas
KOKE Pflugerville, Texas
KPIT Pittsburg, Texas
KMIQ Robstown, Texas
KSAB Robstown, Texas
KCLL San Angelo, Texas
KEDA San Antonio, Texas
KROM San Antonio, Texas
KXTN-FM San Antonio, Texas
KESO South Padre Island, Texas
KSTV Stephenville, Texas
KAMZ Tahoka, Texas
KLQB Taylor, Texas
KZMP University Park, Texas
KUVA Uvalde, Texas
KTXZ West Lake Hills, Texas
KXOL Brigham City, Utah
WMYP Frederiksted, Virgin Islands
KZHR Dayton, Washington
KZXR Prosser, Washington
KZML Quincy, Washington
KRCW Royal City, Washington

Triple A

KXLL Juneau, Alaska
KZGL Flagstaff, Arizona
KGHR Tuba City, Arizona
KXCI Tucson, Arizona
KNCA Burney, California
KPYG Cayucos, California
KHUM Cutten, California
KPRI Encinitas, California
KOZT Fort Bragg, California
KRSH Healdsburg, California
KSWD Los Angeles, California
KNSQ Mount Shasta, California
KZAP Paradise, California
KSFN(AM) Piedmont, California
KTKE Truckee, California
KSPN-FM Aspen, Colorado
KZYR Avon, Colorado
KBCO Boulder, Colorado
KSMT Breckenridge, Colorado
KILO Colorado Springs, Colorado
KUTE Ignacio, Colorado
KFMU-FM Oak Creek, Colorado
KPGS Pagosa Springs, Colorado
KSNO-FM Snowmass Village, Colorado
WKZE-FM Salisbury, Connecticut
WOCM Selbyville, Delaware
WZGC Atlanta, Georgia
WAYR-FM Brunswick, Georgia
KLZY Honokaa, Hawaii
KPTL Ankeny, Iowa
KUNI Cedar Falls, Iowa
KICJ(FM) Mitchellville, Iowa
KISU-FM Pocatello, Idaho
KPND Sandpoint, Idaho
WBEL Cairo, Illinois
WBBM Chicago, Illinois
WWHP Farmer City, Illinois
WLCE Petersburg, Illinois
WTTS Bloomington, Indiana
WEEM-FM Pendleton, Indiana
KACY Arkansas City, Kansas
KMUW Wichita, Kansas
WNKU Highland Heights, Kentucky
WUKY Lexington, Kentucky
WKWC Owensboro, Kentucky
WHAY Whitley City, Kentucky
WRNX Amherst, Massachusetts
WXRV Andover, Massachusetts
WBOS Brookline, Massachusetts
WXPL Fitchburg, Massachusetts
WRSI Turners Falls, Massachusetts
WTMD Towson, Maryland
WCLZ North Yarmouth, Maine
WMEA Portland, Maine
WQKL Ann Arbor, Michigan
WLNZ Lansing, Michigan
KUMD-FM Duluth, Minnesota
WTIP Grand Marais, Minnesota
KCMP Northfield, Minnesota
KPRW Perham, Minnesota
KMSE Rochester, Minnesota
KSRQ Thief River Falls, Minnesota
KCLC St. Charles, Missouri
KTBG Warrensburg, Missouri
WUSM-FM Hattiesburg, Mississippi
KMMS-FM Bozeman, Montana
KDTR Florence, Montana
WGWG Boiling Springs, North Carolina
WSGE Dallas, North Carolina
WVOD Manteo, North Carolina
WNCW Spindale, North Carolina
WSIF Wilkesboro, North Carolina
KPPD Devils Lake, North Dakota
KFJM Grand Forks, North Dakota
KPPR Williston, North Dakota
WLKC Campton, New Hampshire
WMWV Conway, New Hampshire
WBJB-FM Lincroft, New Jersey
KUUT Farmington, New Mexico
KTAO Taos, New Mexico
KTHX-FM Dayton, Nevada

WXPK Briarcliff Manor, New York
WGFR Glens Falls, New York
WFUV New York, New York
WSIA Staten Island, New York
WDPS Dayton, Ohio
WYSO Yellow Springs, Ohio
KSMF Ashland, Oregon
KSBA Coos Bay, Oregon
KSKF Klamath Falls, Oregon
KTEE North Bend, Oregon
KINK Portland, Oregon
KLRR Redmond, Oregon
KSYD Reedsport, Oregon
WVMM Grantham, Pennsylvania
WYEP-FM Pittsburgh, Pennsylvania
WDMT Pittston, Pennsylvania
WXLV Schnecksville, Pennsylvania
WFBK Fort Mill, South Carolina
KSQY Deadwood, South Dakota
WSKZ Chattanooga, Tennessee
WDVX Clinton, Tennessee
WRLT Franklin, Tennessee
WFIV-FM Loudon, Tennessee
KEEP Bandera, Texas
KFAN-FM Johnson City, Texas
KRVL Kerrville, Texas
KRTS Marfa, Texas
KNBT New Braunfels, Texas
KSYM-FM San Antonio, Texas
WNRN Charlottesville, Virginia
WCTG Chincoteague, Virginia
WTYD Deltaville, Virginia
WCNR Keswick, Virginia
WVRU-FM Radford, Virginia
WIVI Charlotte Amalie, Virgin Islands
WRSY Marlboro, Vermont
WNCS Montpelier, Vermont
WNUB-FM Northfield, Vermont
WRJT Royalton, Vermont
KOHO-FM Leavenworth, Washington
KMTT Tacoma, Washington
KTRT Winthrop, Washington
WLGE Baileys Harbor, Wisconsin
WYMS Milwaukee, Wisconsin
WMMM-FM Verona, Wisconsin
KBUW Buffalo, Wyoming
KUWC Casper, Wyoming

Urban Contemporary

WJJN Columbia, Alabama
WMGJ Gadsden, Alabama
WHRP Gurley, Alabama
WJUS Marion, Alabama
WBLX-FM Mobile, Alabama
WHWT New Hope, Alabama
WZMG Pepperell, Alabama
WMRK-FM Shorter, Alabama
WZHT Troy, Alabama
WJWZ Wetumpka, Alabama
KAMJ Gosnell, Arkansas
KXHT Marion, Arkansas
KCLT West Helena, Arkansas
KKUU Indio, California
KHHT Los Angeles, California
KDEY(FM) Ontario, California
KDAY Redondo Beach, California
KBMB(FM) Sacramento, California
KDON-FM Salinas, California
KIQI San Francisco, California
KYLD San Francisco, California
KMSA Grand Junction, Colorado
WZMX Hartford, Connecticut
WYBC-FM New Haven, Connecticut
WJBT Callahan, Florida
WMIE-FM Cocoa, Florida
WHNR Cypress Gardens, Florida
WKIQ Eustis, Florida
WRRX Gulf Breeze, Florida
WLLD Lakeland, Florida
WPYO Maitland, Florida
WEDR Miami, Florida
WHBX Tallahassee, Florida
WPRK Winter Park, Florida
WJIZ-FM Albany, Georgia
WVEE Atlanta, Georgia
WSOL-FM Brunswick, Georgia
WWLD Cairo, Georgia
WZBN Camilla, Georgia
WFXE Columbus, Georgia
WQMJ Forsyth, Georgia
WFXM Gordon, Georgia
WHTA Hampton, Georgia
WLZN Macon, Georgia
WPRW-FM Martinez, Georgia
WSTI-FM Quitman, Georgia
WGJK Rome, Georgia
WQBT Savannah, Georgia
WEAS-FM Springfield, Georgia
WBGA St. Simons Island, Georgia
KZGZ Hagatna, Guam
WPCD Champaign, Illinois
WGCI-FM Chicago, Illinois
WIUS Macomb, Illinois
WCZQ Monticello, Illinois
WGZB-FM Lanesville, Indiana
KSDB-FM Manhattan, Kansas
WWTF Georgetown, Kentucky
WBTF Midway, Kentucky
WDXR Paducah, Kentucky
WUBT Russellville, Kentucky
KEDG Alexandria, Louisiana
KMXH Alexandria, Louisiana
KRVV Bastrop, Louisiana
KBCE Boyce, Louisiana
KQLQ Columbia, Louisiana
KBTT Haughton, Louisiana
KJMH Lake Arthur, Louisiana
KZWA Moss Bluff, Louisiana
WQUE-FM New Orleans, Louisiana
KCLF New Roads, Louisiana
KFXZ-FM Opelousas, Louisiana
KMJJ-FM Shreveport, Louisiana
KVMA-FM Shreveport, Louisiana
WERQ-FM Baltimore, Maryland
WXSH Pocomoke City, Maryland
WSBY-FM Salisbury, Maryland
WJLB Detroit, Michigan
WQHH Dewitt, Michigan
WDZZ-FM Flint, Michigan
WVIB Holton, Michigan
WSNX-FM Muskegon, Michigan
WOWE Vassar, Michigan
WPHS Warren, Michigan
KMOJ Minneapolis, Minnesota
WHHL Hazelwood, Missouri
WMBH Joplin, Missouri
KPRS Kansas City, Missouri
WESE Baldwyn, Mississippi
WRBJ-FM Brandon, Mississippi
WAID Clarksdale, Mississippi
WCLD-FM Cleveland, Mississippi
WJXM De Kalb, Mississippi
WJKX Ellisville, Mississippi
WJMG Hattiesburg, Mississippi
WKXI-FM Magee, Mississippi
KJMS Olive Branch, Mississippi
WZLD Petal, Mississippi
WMSU Starkville, Mississippi
WMXU Starkville, Mississippi
WGNG Tchula, Mississippi
WZKS Union, Mississippi
KLSK Great Falls, Montana
WQOK Carrboro, North Carolina
WPEG Concord, North Carolina
WFXC Durham, North Carolina
WRSV Elm City, North Carolina
WCDG(FM) Moyock, North Carolina
WPWZ Pinetops, North Carolina
WMGU Southern Pines, North Carolina
WZFX Whiteville, North Carolina
WMNX Wilmington, North Carolina
KFKX Hastings, Nebraska
WZBZ Pleasantville, New Jersey
WWWS Buffalo, New York
WBLK Depew, New York
WICB Ithaca, New York
WWPR-FM New York, New York
WDKX Rochester, New York
WDPN Alliance, Ohio
WCKX Columbus, Ohio
WRBP Hubbard, Ohio
WCIT(AM) Lima, Ohio
WROU-FM West Carrollton, Ohio
KVSP Anadarko, Oklahoma
KJMM Bixby, Oklahoma
KRMP Oklahoma City, Oklahoma
KJMU Sand Springs, Oklahoma
WAOB-FM Beaver Falls, Pennsylvania
WWLU Lincoln University, Pennsylvania
WRNB Media, Pennsylvania
WUSL Philadelphia, Pennsylvania
WDIN Camuy, Puerto Rico
WJMZ-FM Anderson, South Carolina
WIIZ Blackville, South Carolina
WYNN-FM Florence, South Carolina
WLVH Hardeeville, South Carolina
WXST Hollywood, South Carolina
WCMG Latta, South Carolina
WHXT Orangeburg, South Carolina
WDAI Pawleys Island, South Carolina
WXYY(FM) Port Royal, South Carolina
WZTF Scranton, South Carolina
WWWZ Summerville, South Carolina
WWDM Sumter, South Carolina
WQQK Goodlettsville, Tennessee
WHRK Memphis, Tennessee
WJTT Red Bank, Tennessee
KNDA Alice, Texas
KTCX Beaumont, Texas
KBFB Dallas, Texas
KKDA-FM Dallas, Texas
KBXX Houston, Texas
KMJQ Houston, Texas
KIIZ-FM Killeen, Texas
KPVU Prairie View, Texas
KBBT Schertz, Texas
KBLZ Winona, Texas
KUUU South Jordan, Utah
WUVA Charlottesville, Virginia
WVBE-FM Lynchburg, Virginia
WCDX Mechanicsville, Virginia
WNSB Norfolk, Virginia
WOWI Norfolk, Virginia
WVMA(FM) Norfolk, Virginia
WBTJ Richmond, Virginia
WVBE Roanoke, Virginia
WTOY Salem, Virginia
WWKS Cruz Bay, Virgin Islands
KHHK Yakima, Washington
WJMR-FM Menomonee Falls, Wisconsin
WNOV Milwaukee, Wisconsin

Variety/Diverse

KAUG Anchorage, Alaska
KNBA Anchorage, Alaska
KBRW Barrow, Alaska
KYUK Bethel, Alaska
KCUK Chevak, Alaska
KUAC Fairbanks, Alaska
KZPA Fort Yukon, Alaska
KIYU Galena, Alaska
KIYU-FM Galena, Alaska
KEUL Girdwood, Alaska
KXGA Glennallen, Alaska
KMJG Homer, Alaska
KRNN Juneau, Alaska
KTOO Juneau, Alaska
KALG Kaltag, Alaska
KWJG Kasilof, Alaska
KMXT Kodiak, Alaska
KINU Kotzebue, Alaska
KOTZ Kotzebue, Alaska
KOYU Koyukuk, Alaska
KNOM Nome, Alaska
KCAW Sitka, Alaska
KNSA Unalakleet, Alaska
KCHU Valdez, Alaska
KSTK Wrangell, Alaska
WLJR Birmingham, Alabama
WLJS-FM Jacksonville, Alabama
WHHY-FM Montgomery, Alabama
KVMN Cave City, Arkansas
KHDX Conway, Arkansas
KAVH Eudora, Arkansas
KXUA Fayetteville, Arkansas
KABF Little Rock, Arkansas
KVSA McGehee, Arkansas
KURM Rogers, Arkansas
KXRJ Russellville, Arkansas
KBUX Quartzsite, Arizona
KRMH Red Mesa, Arizona
KRDX Vail, Arizona
KNNB Whiteriver, Arizona
KAHI Auburn, California
KISL Avalon, California
KALX Berkeley, California
KPFA Berkeley, California
KRHV Big Pine, California
KDUP Cedarville, California
KZFR Chico, California
KSPC Claremont, California

KWRM Corona, California
KDVS Davis, California
KECG El Cerrito, California
KMUE Eureka, California
KFCF Fresno, California
KMUD Garberville, California
KTDE Gualala, California
KCRH Hayward, California
KTYM Inglewood, California
KLAI Laytonville, California
KFJC Los Altos, California
KPFK Los Angeles, California
KAKX Mendocino, California
KVMR Nevada City, California
KCSN Northridge, California
KKSM Oceanside, California
KOPA(FM) Pala, California
KZYX Philo, California
KTHM Red Bluff, California
KUCR Riverside, California
KYDS Sacramento, California
KNBX San Ardo, California
KALW San Francisco, California
KPOO San Francisco, California
KMTG San Jose, California
KSJS San Jose, California
KCPR San Luis Obispo, California
KSRH San Rafael, California
KCSB-FM Santa Barbara, California
KFER Santa Cruz, California
KUSP Santa Cruz, California
KZSC Santa Cruz, California
KCSS Turlock, California
KZYZ Willits, California
KGNU-FM Boulder, Colorado
KVCU Boulder, Colorado
KMPB Breckenridge, Colorado
KEPC Colorado Springs, Colorado
KSJD Cortez, Colorado
KZET Cortez, Colorado
KBUT Crested Butte, Colorado
KDUR Durango, Colorado
KRFC Fort Collins, Colorado
KUNC Greeley, Colorado
KWSB-FM Gunnison, Colorado
KZBR La Jara, Colorado
KECC La Junta, Colorado
KRKV Las Animas, Colorado
KRNC Steamboat Springs, Colorado
KOTO Telluride, Colorado
WPKN Bridgeport, Connecticut
WVOF Fairfield, Connecticut
WRTC-FM Hartford, Connecticut
WESU Middletown, Connecticut
WSLX New Canaan, Connecticut
WCNI New London, Connecticut
WBVC Pomfret, Connecticut
WHUS Storrs, Connecticut
WAPJ Torrington, Connecticut
WWEB Wallingford, Connecticut
WWUH West Hartford, Connecticut
WNHU West Haven, Connecticut
WWPT Westport, Connecticut
WVUD Newark, Delaware
WMPH Wilmington, Delaware
WBHQ Beverly Beach, Florida
WBGC Chipley, Florida
WVUM Coral Gables, Florida
WRGP Homestead, Florida
WFCF St. Augustine, Florida
WQBN Temple Terrace, Florida
WREK Atlanta, Georgia
WMLB Avondale Estates, Georgia
WHCJ Savannah, Georgia
WZAT Tybee Island, Georgia
KTUH Honolulu, Hawaii
KURE Ames, Iowa
KROS Clinton, Iowa
WOC Davenport, Iowa
KWLC Decorah, Iowa
KDRB Des Moines, Iowa
KDTH Dubuque, Iowa
KHOE Fairfield, Iowa
KRUI-FM Iowa City, Iowa
KQNU(FM) Onawa, Iowa
KDLS Perry, Iowa
KLCZ Lewiston, Idaho
KBSQ McCall, Idaho
KUOI-FM Moscow, Idaho
WESN Bloomington, Illinois
WJBC Bloomington, Illinois
WDBX Carbondale, Illinois
WEFT Champaign, Illinois
WEIU Charleston, Illinois
WHPK-FM Chicago, Illinois
WIIT Chicago, Illinois
WLUW Chicago, Illinois
WSBC Chicago, Illinois
WZRD Chicago, Illinois
WCFJ Chicago Heights, Illinois
WDGC-FM Downers Grove, Illinois
WEPS Elgin, Illinois
WVKC Galesburg, Illinois
WHPI Glasford, Illinois
WDUK Havana, Illinois
WHSD Hinsdale, Illinois
WLTL La Grange, Illinois
WMXM Lake Forest, Illinois
WAES Lincolnshire, Illinois
WLRA Lockport, Illinois
WHCM Palatine, Illinois
WMTH Park Ridge, Illinois
WSPY-FM Plano, Illinois
WQNA Springfield, Illinois
WILL Urbana, Illinois
WILL-FM Urbana, Illinois
WNTH Winnetka, Illinois
WFWR Attica, Indiana
WFHB Bloomington, Indiana
WPSR Evansville, Indiana
WUEV Evansville, Indiana
WGCS Goshen, Indiana
WTRE Greensburg, Indiana
WJEL Indianapolis, Indiana
WRFT Indianapolis, Indiana
WBRO Marengo, Indiana
WMRS Monticello, Indiana
WBKE-FM North Manchester, Indiana
WECI Richmond, Indiana
WXXR(FM) Seelyville, Indiana
WMHD-FM Terre Haute, Indiana
WVUR-FM Valparaiso, Indiana
WITT Zionsville, Indiana
KVCO Concordia, Kansas
KONQ Dodge City, Kansas
KBTL El Dorado, Kansas
KANZ Garden City, Kansas
KBCU North Newton, Kansas
KTJO-FM Ottawa, Kansas
KKAN Phillipsburg, Kansas
KQMA Phillipsburg, Kansas
WWHR Bowling Green, Kentucky
WKMT Fulton, Kentucky
WCLU Glasgow, Kentucky
WLSK Lebanon, Kentucky
WRFL Lexington, Kentucky
WMKY Morehead, Kentucky
WKMS-FM Murray, Kentucky
WRUS Russellville, Kentucky
WMMT Whitesburg, Kentucky
KLSP Angola, Louisiana
KLSU Baton Rouge, Louisiana
KNWD Natchitoches, Louisiana
KKAY White Castle, Louisiana
WHAB Acton, Massachusetts
WAMH Amherst, Massachusetts
WMUA Amherst, Massachusetts
WERS Boston, Massachusetts
WRBB Boston, Massachusetts
WUMB-FM Boston, Massachusetts
WBIM-FM Bridgewater, Massachusetts
WMBR Cambridge, Massachusetts
WSHL-FM Easton, Massachusetts
WFPB-FM Falmouth, Massachusetts
WHHB Holliston, Massachusetts
WCCH Holyoke, Massachusetts
WUML Lowell, Massachusetts
WWTA Marion, Massachusetts
WMFO Medford, Massachusetts
WMLN-FM Milton, Massachusetts
WNCK Nantucket, Massachusetts
WNEF Newburyport, Massachusetts
WUMD North Dartmouth, Massachusetts
WOZQ Northampton, Massachusetts
WFPB Orleans, Massachusetts
WOCN-FM Orleans, Massachusetts
WBRK Pittsfield, Massachusetts
WMWM Salem, Massachusetts
WSDH Sandwich, Massachusetts
WBSL-FM Sheffield, Massachusetts
WAIC Springfield, Massachusetts
WNEK-FM Springfield, Massachusetts
WSCB Springfield, Massachusetts
WTCC Springfield, Massachusetts
WYAJ Sudbury, Massachusetts
WBRS Waltham, Massachusetts
WORC-FM Webster, Massachusetts
WZLY Wellesley, Massachusetts
WSKB Westfield, Massachusetts
WBPR Worcester, Massachusetts
WCUW Worcester, Massachusetts
WQSR Baltimore, Maryland
WHFC Bel Air, Maryland
WMUC-FM College Park, Maryland
WRNR-FM Grasonville, Maryland
WKHS Worton, Maryland
WERU-FM Blue Hill, Maine
WBOR Brunswick, Maine
WSHD Eastport, Maine
WMPG Gorham, Maine
WUMM Machias, Maine
WSYY-FM Millinocket, Maine
WMEB-FM Orono, Maine
WUPI Presque Isle, Maine
WMHB Waterville, Maine
WVAC-FM Adrian, Michigan
WCBN-FM Ann Arbor, Michigan
WXOU Auburn Hills, Michigan
WMJZ-FM Gaylord, Michigan
WMTU-FM Houghton, Michigan
WION Ionia, Michigan
WIDR Kalamazoo, Michigan
WKDS Kalamazoo, Michigan
WYDM Monroe, Michigan
WBLD Orchard Lake, Michigan
WLSO Sault Ste. Marie, Michigan
WNMC-FM Traverse City, Michigan
KLTA Breckenridge, Minnesota
KDAL Duluth, Minnesota
WELY Ely, Minnesota
KAXE Grand Rapids, Minnesota
KLFD Litchfield, Minnesota
KFAI Minneapolis, Minnesota
KOLV Olivia, Minnesota
WMCN St. Paul, Minnesota
KQAL Winona, Minnesota
KWUR Clayton, Missouri
KXMS Joplin, Missouri
KLUE Poplar Bluff, Missouri
KMNR Rolla, Missouri
KMST Rolla, Missouri
KDHX Saint Louis, Missouri
WMGO Canton, Mississippi
WUSM-FM Hattiesburg, Mississippi
WMPR Jackson, Mississippi
WPRL Lorman, Mississippi
KYPB Big Timber, Montana
KMSM-FM Butte, Montana
KYPC Colstrip, Montana
KINX Fairfield, Montana
KYPR Miles City, Montana
WXDU Durham, North Carolina
WRVS-FM Elizabeth City, North Carolina
WUAW Erwin, North Carolina
WQFS Greensboro, North Carolina
WZMB Greenville, North Carolina
WHKP Hendersonville, North Carolina
WFHE Hickory, North Carolina
WOVV Ocracoke, North Carolina
KDSU Fargo, North Dakota
KABU Fort Totten, North Dakota
KMHA Four Bears, North Dakota
KDCV-FM Blair, Nebraska
KZUM Lincoln, Nebraska
KNCY Nebraska City, Nebraska
WSPS Concord, New Hampshire
WPEA Exeter, New Hampshire
WAJM Atlantic City, New Jersey
WSNJ Bridgeton, New Jersey
WDVR Delaware Township, New Jersey
WFMU East Orange, New Jersey
WGLS-FM Glassboro, New Jersey
WNTI Hackettstown, New Jersey
WRRC Lawrenceville, New Jersey
WMVB Millville, New Jersey
WRSU-FM New Brunswick, New Jersey
WWPH Princeton Junction, New Jersey
WMSC Upper Montclair, New Jersey
KDAZ Albuquerque, New Mexico
KUNM Albuquerque, New Mexico
KRRT Arroyo Seco, New Mexico
KCIE Dulce, New Mexico
KRAR Espanola, New Mexico

KGLP Gallup, New Mexico
KOOT Hurley, New Mexico
KRUX Las Cruces, New Mexico
KRRE Las Vegas, New Mexico
KVSF-FM Pecos, New Mexico
KSIL Rincon, New Mexico
KBOM Socorro, New Mexico
KWPR Lund, Nevada
WCDB Albany, New York
WALF Alfred, New York
WHRW Binghamton, New York
WKRB Brooklyn, New York
WSLU Canton, New York
WHCL-FM Clinton, New York
WSUC-FM Cortland, New York
WXXE Fenner, New York
WCVF-FM Fredonia, New York
WGBB Freeport, New York
WHPC Garden City, New York
WRCU-FM Hamilton, New York
WRHU Hempstead, New York
WSHR Lake Ronkonkoma, New York
WVCR-FM Loudonville, New York
WSLO Malone, New York
WMFU(FM) Mount Hope, New York
WVIP New Rochelle, New York
WVOX New Rochelle, New York
WFUV New York, New York
WKCR-FM New York, New York
WRVO Oswego, New York
WVKR-FM Poughkeepsie, New York
WRUR-FM Rochester, New York
WUMX Rome, New York
WSLL Saranac Lake, New York
WSPQ Springville, New York
WUSB Stony Brook, New York
WKWZ Syosset, New York
WRVD Syracuse, New York
WRPI Troy, New York
WPNR-FM Utica, New York
WRVN Utica, New York
WRVJ Watertown, New York
WSLJ Watertown, New York
WBGU Bowling Green, Ohio
WRUW-FM Cleveland, Ohio
WUDR Dayton, Ohio
WWSU Fairborn, Ohio
WKCO Gambier, Ohio
WFGA Hicksville, Ohio
WMCO New Concord, Ohio
WJCU University Heights, Ohio
WYNS Waynesville, Ohio
WCWS-FM Wooster, Ohio
KDOE Antlers, Oklahoma
KQOB Enid, Oklahoma
KSRG Ashland, Oregon
KWVA Eugene, Oregon
KTEC Klamath Falls, Oregon
KEOL La Grande, Oregon
KLCO Newport, Oregon
KBOO Portland, Oregon
KTCB Tillamook, Oregon
WDIY Allentown, Pennsylvania
WMUH Allentown, Pennsylvania
WLVR-FM Bethlehem, Pennsylvania
WLBS Bristol, Pennsylvania
WDCV-FM Carlisle, Pennsylvania
WMAJ-FM Centre Hall, Pennsylvania
WDNR Chester, Pennsylvania
WESS East Stroudsburg, Pennsylvania
WJRH Easton, Pennsylvania
WRSD Folsom, Pennsylvania
WHHS Havertown, Pennsylvania
WIUP-FM Indiana, Pennsylvania
WKHB Irwin, Pennsylvania
WFNM Lancaster, Pennsylvania
WLCH Lancaster, Pennsylvania
WCNS Latrobe, Pennsylvania
WIXQ Millersville, Pennsylvania
WSFX Nanticoke, Pennsylvania
WPEB Philadelphia, Pennsylvania
WPHE Phoenixville, Pennsylvania
WPTS-FM Pittsburgh, Pennsylvania
WRCT Pittsburgh, Pennsylvania
WYBF Radnor Township, Pennsylvania
WSYC-FM Shippensburg, Pennsylvania
WSRU Slippery Rock, Pennsylvania
WKPS State College, Pennsylvania
WSRN-FM Swarthmore, Pennsylvania
WRDV Warminster, Pennsylvania
WNJR Washington, Pennsylvania
WCUR West Chester, Pennsylvania
WVYC York, Pennsylvania
WOQI Adjuntas, Puerto Rico
WNIK Arecibo, Puerto Rico
WCGB Juana Diaz, Puerto Rico
WJIT Sabana, Puerto Rico
WQBS San Juan, Puerto Rico
WEGA Vega Baja, Puerto Rico
WRIU Kingston, Rhode Island
WJHD Portsmouth, Rhode Island
WELH Providence, Rhode Island
WLTY Cayce, South Carolina
WUSC-FM Columbia, South Carolina
WAVF Hanahan, South Carolina
WLBG Laurens, South Carolina
WLSC Loris, South Carolina
KLND Little Eagle, South Dakota
KVAR Pine Ridge, South Dakota
KCFS Sioux Falls, South Dakota
WQSV Ashland City, Tennessee
WAPX-FM Clarksville, Tennessee
WMTS-FM Murfreesboro, Tennessee
WCFL(FM) Nashville, Tennessee
WUTS Sewanee, Tennessee
WSGI Springfield, Tennessee
KVLF Alpine, Texas
KTXP Bushland, Texas
KNON Dallas, Texas
KGRW Friona, Texas
KWFB Holliday, Texas
KOOP Hornsby, Texas
KPFT Houston, Texas
KTSU Houston, Texas
KRZS Hunt, Texas
KTXT-FM Lubbock, Texas
KLSR-FM Memphis, Texas
KEOM Mesquite, Texas
KZAM Pleasant Valley, Texas
KPVU Prairie View, Texas
KSEY-FM Seymour, Texas
KGWB Snyder, Texas
KSST Sulphur Springs, Texas
KWBU-FM Waco, Texas
KZMU Moab, Utah
KPGR Pleasant Grove, Utah
WUVT-FM Blacksburg, Virginia
WTJU Charlottesville, Virginia
WEHC Emory, Virginia
WMLU Farmville, Virginia
WWHS-FM Hampden-Sydney, Virginia
WHOV Hampton, Virginia
WCLM Highland Springs, Virginia
WCHG Hot Springs, Virginia
WLUR Lexington, Virginia
WWLB Midlothian, Virginia
WVLS Monterey, Virginia
WVST-FM Petersburg, Virginia
WDCE Richmond, Virginia
WWEM Rustburg, Virginia
WCWM Williamsburg, Virginia
WSTA Charlotte Amalie, Virgin Islands
WDHP Frederiksted, Virgin Islands
WRUV Burlington, Vermont
WWPV-FM Colchester, Vermont
WDOT Danville, Vermont
WJSC-FM Johnson, Vermont
WRMC-FM Middlebury, Vermont
WGDR Plainfield, Vermont
WDEV Waterbury, Vermont
WWMP Waterbury, Vermont
KXPA Bellevue, Washington
KCED Centralia, Washington
KCWU Ellensburg, Washington
KSER Everett, Washington
KUBS Newport, Washington
KZUU Pullman, Washington
KSUH Puyallup, Washington
KEXP-FM Seattle, Washington
KWCW Walla Walla, Washington
WBDL Reedsburg, Wisconsin
WXPR Rhinelander, Wisconsin
WRPN-FM Ripon, Wisconsin
WRFW River Falls, Wisconsin
KUWS Superior, Wisconsin
WDRT Viroqua, Wisconsin
WCCX Waukesha, Wisconsin
WVBC Bethany, West Virginia
WVWC Buckhannon, West Virginia
WQWV Fisher, West Virginia
WMUL Huntington, West Virginia
WRSG Middlebourne, West Virginia
WWVU-FM Morgantown, West Virginia
WQAB Philippi, West Virginia
WWYO Pineville, West Virginia
WSHC Shepherdstown, West Virginia
WKWK-FM Wheeling, West Virginia
WVVV Williamstown, West Virginia
KWXR Reliance, Wyoming

Vietnamese

KSJX San Jose, California
KZSJ San Martin, California
KVNR Santa Ana, California
KVVN Santa Clara, California
KYND Cypress, Texas

RADIO - U.S.

Special Radio Programming on Radio Stations in the U.S.

Adult Contemp

KUAC Fairbanks, Alaska
WBHM Birmingham, Alabama
WSGN Gadsden, Alabama
WQPR Muscle Shoals, Alabama
WUAL-FM Tuscaloosa, Alabama
KUAF Fayetteville, Arkansas
KASU Jonesboro, Arkansas
KABF Little Rock, Arkansas
KUAR Little Rock, Arkansas
KCTT-FM Yellville, Arkansas
KVNA Flagstaff, Arizona
KWKM St. Johns, Arizona
KNCA Burney, California
KXLU Los Angeles, California
KSBR Mission Viejo, California
KMPO Modesto, California
KNSQ Mount Shasta, California
KCBX San Luis Obispo, California
KVYN St. Helena, California
KKDV Walnut Creek, California
KRCB-FM Windsor, California
KGNU-FM Boulder, Colorado
KMSA Grand Junction, Colorado
WXCI Danbury, Connecticut
WSHU-FM Fairfield, Connecticut
WGRS Guilford, Connecticut
WMNR Monroe, Connecticut
WYBC-FM New Haven, Connecticut
WQQQ Sharon, Connecticut
WRXC Shelton, Connecticut
WGSK South Kent, Connecticut
WNHU West Haven, Connecticut
WUFT-FM Gainesville, Florida
WOTS Kissimmee, Florida
WKGC Southport, Florida
WFCF St. Augustine, Florida
WVFS Tallahassee, Florida
WUGA Athens, Georgia
WRAS Atlanta, Georgia
WUWG Carrollton, Georgia
KUNI Cedar Falls, Iowa
KCCK-FM Cedar Rapids, Iowa
KNSY(FM) Dubuque, Iowa
KRNI Mason City, Iowa
KICJ(FM) Mitchellville, Iowa
KRNL-FM Mount Vernon, Iowa
KBSU-FM Boise, Idaho
KRFA-FM Moscow, Idaho
KUOI-FM Moscow, Idaho
WSIU Carbondale, Illinois
WEFT Champaign, Illinois
WEIU Charleston, Illinois
WFMT Chicago, Illinois
WNIJ Dekalb, Illinois
WSIE Edwardsville, Illinois
WNUR-FM Evanston, Illinois
WDCB Glen Ellyn, Illinois
WIUM Macomb, Illinois
WGLT Normal, Illinois
WNIU Rockford, Illinois
WFHB Bloomington, Indiana
WVPE Elkhart, Indiana
KANZ Garden City, Kansas
KZNA Hill City, Kansas
KRPS Pittsburg, Kansas
WKUE Elizabethtown, Kentucky
WDCL-FM Somerset, Kentucky
WGBH(FM) Boston, Massachusetts
WAMQ Great Barrington, Massachusetts
WBSL-FM Sheffield, Massachusetts
WMTB-FM Emmitsburg, Maryland
WMHB Waterville, Maine
WBNZ Frankfort, Michigan
WBLU-FM Grand Rapids, Michigan
WLNZ Lansing, Michigan
WNMC-FM Traverse City, Michigan
WBLV Twin Lake, Michigan
WYCE Wyoming, Michigan
KMSK Austin, Minnesota
KBSB Bemidji, Minnesota
WMFG Hibbing, Minnesota
KMSU Mankato, Minnesota
KFAI Minneapolis, Minnesota
KNGA Saint Peter, Minnesota
KVSC St. Cloud, Minnesota
KKFI Kansas City, Missouri
KCOZ Point Lookout, Missouri
KMST Rolla, Missouri
KEMC Billings, Montana
WCQS Asheville, North Carolina
WBUX Buxton, North Carolina
WUNC Chapel Hill, North Carolina
WCKB Dunn, North Carolina
WFQS Franklin, North Carolina
WUND-FM Manteo, North Carolina
WURI Manteo, North Carolina
WNCW Spindale, North Carolina
KCND Bismarck, North Dakota
KDPR Dickinson, North Dakota
KUND-FM Grand Forks, North Dakota
KPRJ Jamestown, North Dakota
KMPR Minot, North Dakota
KPPR Williston, North Dakota
KZUM Lincoln, Nebraska
WEVO Concord, New Hampshire
WEVO(FM) Concord, New Hampshire
WEVH Hanover, New Hampshire
WEVN Keene, New Hampshire
WSNJ Bridgeton, New Jersey
WLFR Pomona, New Jersey
WTSR Trenton, New Jersey
KSJE Farmington, New Mexico
KRWG Las Cruces, New Mexico
KUNR Reno, Nevada
WAMC-FM Albany, New York
WSKG-FM Binghamton, New York
WCAN Canajoharie, New York
WSQE Corning, New York
WSQG-FM Ithaca, New York
WVBR-FM Ithaca, New York
WAMK Kingston, New York
WOSR Middletown, New York
WSUF Noyack, New York
WRHO Oneonta, New York
WSQC-FM Oneonta, New York
WTKV Oswego, New York
WCEL Plattsburgh, New York
WSPN Saratoga Springs, New York
WAER Syracuse, New York
WANC Ticonderoga, New York
WTBQ Warwick, New York
WBGU Bowling Green, Ohio
WGDE Defiance, Ohio
WKSU-FM Kent, Ohio
WGLE Lima, Ohio
WBUK Ottawa, Ohio
WGTE-FM Toledo, Ohio
WKRW Wooster, Ohio
WYSO Yellow Springs, Ohio
WYSU Youngstown, Ohio
KRSC-FM Claremore, Oklahoma
KJKE Newcastle, Oklahoma
KWOX Woodward, Oklahoma
KSMF Ashland, Oregon
KMUN Astoria, Oregon
KSBA Coos Bay, Oregon
KBVR Corvallis, Oregon
KLCC Eugene, Oregon
KSKF Klamath Falls, Oregon
KTEC Klamath Falls, Oregon
KLCO Newport, Oregon
WQLN-FM Erie, Pennsylvania
WZBT Gettysburg, Pennsylvania
WPSX Kane, Pennsylvania
WHYY-FM Philadelphia, Pennsylvania
WXPN Philadelphia, Pennsylvania
WEEU Reading, Pennsylvania
WPSU State College, Pennsylvania
WCRI-FM Block Island, Rhode Island
WJMF Smithfield, Rhode Island
WHHD Clearwater, South Carolina
WPCC Clinton, South Carolina
KAUR Sioux Falls, South Dakota
KCSD Sioux Falls, South Dakota
WTTU Cookeville, Tennessee
KUT Austin, Texas
KAMU-FM College Station, Texas
KEOS College Station, Texas
KTEP El Paso, Texas
KOOP Hornsby, Texas
KNCH(FM) San Angelo, Texas
WNRN Charlottesville, Virginia
WMRY Crozet, Virginia
WMRA Harrisonburg, Virginia
WMRL Lexington, Virginia
WHRV Norfolk, Virginia
WCVE-FM Richmond, Virginia
WVBW Suffolk, Virginia
WNCS Montpelier, Vermont
WRVT Rutland, Vermont
WVPR Windsor, Vermont
KZAZ Bellingham, Washington
KNWR Ellensburg, Washington
KAOS Olympia, Washington
KZUU Pullman, Washington
KFAE-FM Richland, Washington
KAGU Spokane, Washington
KPBX-FM Spokane, Washington
WHSA Brule, Wisconsin
WUEC Eau Claire, Wisconsin
WHWC Menomonie, Wisconsin
WVSS Menomonie, Wisconsin
WHND Sister Bay, Wisconsin
WLBL-FM Wausau, Wisconsin
WHAW Lost Creek, West Virginia
WWVU-FM Morgantown, West Virginia
WWYO Pineville, West Virginia
KUWA Afton, Wyoming
KUWJ Jackson, Wyoming
KUWR Laramie, Wyoming
KUWZ Rock Springs, Wyoming

Agriculture

WKAC Athens, Alabama
WALQ Carrville, Alabama
WZTQ Centre, Alabama
WKUL Cullman, Alabama
WTVY-FM Dothan, Alabama
WNRA Eufaula, Alabama
WKWL Florala, Alabama
WHEP Foley, Alabama
WZOB Fort Payne, Alabama
WWWH Haleyville, Alabama
WERH Hamilton, Alabama
WINL Linden, Alabama
WGMP Montgomery, Alabama
WKEA-FM Scottsboro, Alabama
WHBB Selma, Alabama
WTLS Tallassee, Alabama
WTBF Troy, Alabama
KAAB Batesville, Arkansas
KEWI Benton, Arkansas
KTHS Berryville, Arkansas
KXXA(AM) Conway, Arkansas
KVDW England, Arkansas
KXJK Forrest City, Arkansas
KFIN Jonesboro, Arkansas
KNEA Jonesboro, Arkansas
KVMA Magnolia, Arkansas
KVSA McGehee, Arkansas
KBOA-FM Piggott, Arkansas
KPBQ-FM Pine Bluff, Arkansas
KPOC Pocahontas, Arkansas
KURM Rogers, Arkansas
KARV Russellville, Arkansas
KWCK Searcy, Arkansas
KWAK Stuttgart, Arkansas
KOSE Wilson, Arkansas
KWYN Wynne, Arkansas
KDJI Holbrook, Arizona
KLPZ Parker, Arizona
KVSL Show Low, Arizona
KCFJ Alturas, California
KISV Bakersfield, California
KBHR Big Bear City, California
KJMB-FM Blythe, California
KXO El Centro, California
KRKC King City, California
KUBB Mariposa, California
KYOS Merced, California
KBLF Red Bluff, California
KSTN Stockton, California
KJUG Tulare, California
KWNE Ukiah, California
KUBA Yuba City, California
KGIW Alamosa, Colorado
KRAI Craig, Colorado
KRKY Granby, Colorado
KFKA Greeley, Colorado
KSLV Monte Vista, Colorado
KSTC Sterling, Colorado
KCRT Trinidad, Colorado
KRDZ Wray, Colorado
WGMD Rehoboth Beach, Delaware

WGBG Seaford, Delaware
WBGF Belle Glade, Florida
WLBE Leesburg-Eustis, Florida
WTYS Marianna, Florida
WLVW(FM) Trenton, Florida
WZZS Zolfo Springs, Florida
WAWO Alma, Georgia
WDEC-FM Americus, Georgia
WGAC Augusta, Georgia
WJTH Calhoun, Georgia
WCLA Claxton, Georgia
WDXQ Cochran, Georgia
WRCG Columbus, Georgia
WAEF Cordele, Georgia
WDMG Douglas, Georgia
WHJD Hazlehurst, Georgia
WQCH La Fayette, Georgia
WMCG Milan, Georgia
WHKN Millen, Georgia
WMTM Moultrie, Georgia
WSTI-FM Quitman, Georgia
WJAT Swainsboro, Georgia
WSYL Sylvania, Georgia
WTHO-FM Thomson, Georgia
WTIF Tifton, Georgia
KLGA Algona, Iowa
KJAN Atlantic, Iowa
KWBG Boone, Iowa
KBUR Burlington, Iowa
KCPS Burlington, Iowa
KCNZ Cedar Falls, Iowa
WMT Cedar Rapids, Iowa
KCHE Cherokee, Iowa
KCLN Clinton, Iowa
KCZQ Cresco, Iowa
KDSN Denison, Iowa
WHO Des Moines, Iowa
KDTH Dubuque, Iowa
KDST Dyersville, Iowa
KILR Estherville, Iowa
KIOW Forest City, Iowa
KWMT Fort Dodge, Iowa
KLMJ Hampton, Iowa
KNOD Harlan, Iowa
KHBT Humboldt, Iowa
KKIA Ida Grove, Iowa
KIFG Iowa Falls, Iowa
KOKX Keokuk, Iowa
KLEM Le Mars, Iowa
KMCH Manchester, Iowa
KMAQ Maquoketa, Iowa
KGLO Mason City, Iowa
KCZE New Hampton, Iowa
KCOB Newton, Iowa
KOEL Oelwein, Iowa
KMA Shenandoah, Iowa
KDCR Sioux Center, Iowa
KTFC Sioux City, Iowa
KICD Spencer, Iowa
KKRF Stuart, Iowa
KTLB Twin Lakes, Iowa
KQWC Webster City, Iowa
KMHR(AM) Boise, Idaho
KORT(AM/FM) Grangeville, Idaho
KOZE Lewiston, Idaho
KRLC Lewiston-Clarkston, Idaho
KVSI Montpelier, Idaho
KRPL Moscow, Idaho
KACH Preston, Idaho
KSRA Salmon, Idaho
KLIX Twin Falls, Idaho
KTFI Wendell, Idaho
WQRL Benton, Illinois
WBNQ Bloomington, Illinois
WJBC Bloomington, Illinois
WLMD Bushnell, Illinois
WKRO Cairo, Illinois
WBYS Canton, Illinois
WCIL Carbondale, Illinois
WROY Carmi, Illinois
WDWS Champaign, Illinois
WRJM(AM) Charleston, Illinois
KSGM Chester, Illinois
WDAN Danville, Illinois
WLBK Dekalb, Illinois
WIXN Dixon, Illinois
WDQN Duquoin, Illinois
KUUL East Moline, Illinois
WFIW Fairfield, Illinois
WFIW-FM Fairfield, Illinois
WGIL Galesburg, Illinois
WGEL Greenville, Illinois
WEBQ Harrisburg, Illinois
WDUK Havana, Illinois
WRVY-FM Henry, Illinois
WIJR Highland, Illinois
WJIL Jacksonville, Illinois
WLDS Jacksonville, Illinois
WJBM Jerseyville, Illinois
WJOL Joliet, Illinois
WKAN Kankakee, Illinois
WKEI Kewanee, Illinois
WSMI Litchfield, Illinois
WSMI-FM Litchfield, Illinois
WLUV Loves Park, Illinois
WJEQ Macomb, Illinois
WLRB Macomb, Illinois
WZUS Macon, Illinois
WFXN Moline, Illinois
WRAM Monmouth, Illinois
WCZQ Monticello, Illinois
WCSJ-FM Morris, Illinois
WMIX Mount Vernon, Illinois
WHQQ Neoga, Illinois
WMCI Neoga B, Illinois
WCMY Ottawa, Illinois
WPXN Paxton, Illinois
WMBD Peoria, Illinois
WSPY-FM Plano, Illinois
WZOE Princeton, Illinois
WTAY Robinson, Illinois
WKXQ Rushville, Illinois
WJBD Salem, Illinois
WAUR Sandwich, Illinois
WHCO Sparta, Illinois
WTAX Springfield, Illinois
WSDR Sterling, Illinois
WSQR Sycamore, Illinois
WTIM-FM Taylorville, Illinois
WRAN Tower Hill, Illinois
WILL Urbana, Illinois
WPMB Vandalia, Illinois
WGFA-FM Watseka, Illinois
WRBI Batesville, Indiana
WBIW Bedford, Indiana
WIKY-FM Evansville, Indiana
WILO Frankfort, Indiana
WSHW Frankfort, Indiana
WFLQ French Lick, Indiana
WREB Greencastle, Indiana
WTRE Greensburg, Indiana
WLOI La Porte, Indiana
WASK Lafayette, Indiana
WKOA Lafayette, Indiana
WSAL Logansport, Indiana
WRZR Loogootee, Indiana
WXGO Madison, Indiana
WMYJ Martinsville, Indiana
WEFM Michigan City, Indiana
WRCY Mt. Vernon, Indiana
WLTI(AM) New Castle, Indiana
WMDH-FM New Castle, Indiana
WSEZ Paoli, Indiana
WTCA Plymouth, Indiana
WRIN Rensselaer, Indiana
WKBV Richmond, Indiana
WROI Rochester, Indiana
WIFE-FM Rushville, Indiana
WZZB Seymour, Indiana
WNDI Sullivan, Indiana
WKUZ Wabash, Indiana
WWBL Washington, Indiana
KAIR Atchison, Kansas
KVSV Beloit, Kansas
KSNP Burlington, Kansas
KGNO Dodge City, Kansas
KDNS Downs, Kansas
KIUL Garden City, Kansas
KGCR Goodland, Kansas
KVGB Great Bend, Kansas
KHAZ Hays, Kansas
KNZA Hiawatha, Kansas
KBUF Holcomb, Kansas
KNNS Larned, Kansas
KSCB Liberal, Kansas
KOFO Ottawa, Kansas
KLKC Parsons, Kansas
KKAN Phillipsburg, Kansas
KRSL Russell, Kansas
KSAL Salina, Kansas
KYUL Scott City, Kansas
KMZA Seneca, Kansas
KULY Ulysses, Kansas
KLEY Wellington, Kansas
WANY Albany, Kentucky
WBRT Bardstown, Kentucky
WKDZ Cadiz, Kentucky
WNES Central City, Kentucky
WAIN Columbia, Kentucky
WCPM Cumberland, Kentucky
WHSX Edmonton, Kentucky
WFKN Franklin, Kentucky
WKCM Hawesville, Kentucky
WSON Henderson, Kentucky
WRZI Hodgenville, Kentucky
WFTM Maysville, Kentucky
WMIK Middlesboro, Kentucky
WMST Mt. Sterling, Kentucky
WBKR Owensboro, Kentucky
WVJS Owensboro, Kentucky
WTLO Somerset, Kentucky
WYSB Springfield, Kentucky
WMTC Vancleve, Kentucky
WMTC-FM Vancleve, Kentucky
WLKS West Liberty, Kentucky
WDGL Baton Rouge, Louisiana
KSIG Crowley, Louisiana
WFPR Hammond, Louisiana
WSRY Elkton, Maryland
WICO Salisbury, Maryland
WTTR Westminster, Maryland
WFYC Alma, Michigan
WATZ Alpena, Michigan
WTVB Coldwater, Michigan
WCHT Escanaba, Michigan
WGHN-FM Grand Haven, Michigan
WCSR Hillsdale, Michigan
WKZO Kalamazoo, Michigan
WSGW Saginaw, Michigan
WMIC Sandusky, Michigan
WMLM St. Louis, Michigan
WTCM Traverse City, Michigan
WPNW Zeeland, Michigan
KASM Albany, Minnesota
KATE Albert Lea, Minnesota
KXRA Alexandria, Minnesota
KKCQ-FM Bagley, Minnesota
KBMO Benson, Minnesota
KBEW Blue Earth, Minnesota
KJLY Blue Earth, Minnesota
WGVY Cambridge, Minnesota
KROX Crookston, Minnesota
KDLM Detroit Lakes, Minnesota
KGFK East Grand Forks, Minnesota
KFMC-FM Fairmont, Minnesota
KBRF Fergus Falls, Minnesota
KSNR Fisher, Minnesota
KKCQ Fosston, Minnesota
KDUZ Hutchinson, Minnesota
KKOJ Jackson, Minnesota
KLFD Litchfield, Minnesota
KLTF Little Falls, Minnesota
KEYL Long Prairie, Minnesota
KLQL Luverne, Minnesota
KLQP Madison, Minnesota
KDMA Montevideo, Minnesota
KDIO Ortonville, Minnesota
WCMP Pine City, Minnesota
WQPM Princeton, Minnesota
KROC Rochester, Minnesota
KIKV-FM Sauk Centre, Minnesota
KNSG Springfield, Minnesota
KNSP Staples, Minnesota
KTRF Thief River Falls, Minnesota
KARL Tracy, Minnesota
KWAD Wadena, Minnesota
KDJS Willmar, Minnesota
KWLM Willmar, Minnesota
KAGE Winona, Minnesota
KWOA Worthington, Minnesota
KAAN Bethany, Missouri
KYOO Bolivar, Missouri
KWRT Boonville, Missouri
KMAM Butler, Missouri
KOZX Cabool, Missouri
KRLL California, Missouri
KMRN Cameron, Missouri
KDFN Doniphan, Missouri
KHMO Hannibal, Missouri
KUNQ Houston, Missouri
KWOS Jefferson City, Missouri
KBOA Kennett, Missouri
KIRX Kirksville, Missouri

RADIO - U.S.

KBNN Lebanon, Missouri
KNIM Maryville, Missouri
KMEM-FM Memphis, Missouri
KWWR Mexico, Missouri
KMCR Montgomery City, Missouri
KBTN Neosho, Missouri
KNEM Nevada, Missouri
KBDZ Perryville, Missouri
KSMO Salem, Missouri
KDRO Sedalia, Missouri
KRHW Sikeston, Missouri
KWTO Springfield, Missouri
KFEQ St. Joseph, Missouri
KRWP Stockton, Missouri
KSAR Thayer, Missouri
KTKS Versailles, Missouri
KWRE Warrenton, Missouri
WJNS-FM Bentonia, Mississippi
WLTM Greenville, Mississippi
WROA Gulfport, Mississippi
WTCD Indianola, Mississippi
WJDX Jackson, Mississippi
WMSI-FM Jackson, Mississippi
WIQQ Leland, Mississippi
WRQO Monticello, Mississippi
WWMS Oxford, Mississippi
WHOC Philadelphia, Mississippi
WELO Tupelo, Mississippi
WTYL Tylertown, Mississippi
KFLN Baker, Montana
KBOW Butte, Montana
KXGN Glendive, Montana
KXGF Great Falls, Montana
KOJM Havre, Montana
KPQX Havre, Montana
KXEI Havre, Montana
KXLO Lewistown, Montana
KYUS-FM Miles City, Montana
KATQ Plentywood, Montana
KCGM Scobey, Montana
KSEN Shelby, Montana
KVCK Wolf Point, Montana
KVCK-FM Wolf Point, Montana
WKXR Asheboro, North Carolina
WWNC Asheville, North Carolina
WGAI Elizabeth City, North Carolina
WFMO Fairmont, North Carolina
WQDK Gatesville, North Carolina
WCXL Kill Devil Hills, North Carolina
WKTE King, North Carolina
WHBK Marshall, North Carolina
WPAQ Mount Airy, North Carolina
WWDR Murfreesboro, North Carolina
WCVP Murphy, North Carolina
WPTF Raleigh, North Carolina
WTEL Red Springs, North Carolina
WPTM Roanoke Rapids, North Carolina
WEGG Rose Hill, North Carolina
WRXO Roxboro, North Carolina
WWGP Sanford, North Carolina
WYAL Scotland Neck, North Carolina
WKSK West Jefferson, North Carolina
WENC Whiteville, North Carolina
WTXY Whiteville, North Carolina
KBMR Bismarck, North Dakota
KPOK Bowman, North Dakota
KXPO Grafton, North Dakota
KNDC Hettinger, North Dakota
KSJB Jamestown, North Dakota
KNDK Langdon, North Dakota
KQLX Lisbon, North Dakota
KCJB Minot, North Dakota
KZPR Minot, North Dakota
KUSO Albion, Nebraska
KAAQ Alliance, Nebraska
KCOW Alliance, Nebraska
KWBE Beatrice, Nebraska
KZEN Central City, Nebraska
KCSR Chadron, Nebraska
KQSK Chadron, Nebraska
KKOT Columbus, Nebraska
KTTT Columbus, Nebraska
KGMT Fairbury, Nebraska
KHUB Fremont, Nebraska
KHAS Hastings, Nebraska
KUVR Holdrege, Nebraska
KGFW Kearney, Nebraska
KRVN-FM Lexington, Nebraska
KIOD McCook, Nebraska
KNCY Nebraska City, Nebraska
KNEN Norfolk, Nebraska
KBRX O'Neill, Nebraska
KMCX-FM Ogallala, Nebraska
KOGA Ogallala, Nebraska
KFAB Omaha, Nebraska
KNLV Ord, Nebraska
KNLV-FM Ord, Nebraska
KNEB Scottsbluff, Nebraska
KSID Sidney, Nebraska
KRFS Superior, Nebraska
KTCH Wayne, Nebraska
KTIC-FM West Point, Nebraska
KAWL York, Nebraska
WFAI Salem, New Jersey
KICA Clovis, New Mexico
KOTS Deming, New Mexico
KSEL-FM Portales, New Mexico
KMXQ Socorro, New Mexico
KDSS Ely, Nevada
KWNA Winnemucca, Nevada
WBRV-FM Boonville, New York
WKGB-FM Conklin, New York
WWLE Cornwall, New York
WRWD-FM Highland, New York
WJTN Jamestown, New York
WIXT Little Falls, New York
WLVL Lockport, New York
WLLG Lowville, New York
WICY Malone, New York
WYBG Massena, New York
WEOK Poughkeepsie, New York
WRIV Riverhead, New York
WSPQ Springville, New York
WIBX Utica, New York
WCJW Warsaw, New York
WTNY Watertown, New York
WNCO Ashland, Ohio
WWCD Baltimore, Ohio
WAIS Buchtel, Ohio
WYNT Caledonia, Ohio
WHBC Canton, Ohio
WDOH Delphos, Ohio
WEDI Eaton, Ohio
WFIN Findlay, Ohio
WRAC Georgetown, Ohio
WKTN Kenton, Ohio
WLOH Lancaster, Ohio
WIMA Lima, Ohio
WMOA Marietta, Ohio
WMRN Marion, Ohio
WMPO Middleport-Pomeroy, Ohio
WSEO Nelsonville, Ohio
WHOF North Canton, Ohio
WBUK Ottawa, Ohio
WPTW Piqua, Ohio
WNTO Racine, Ohio
WSOM Salem, Ohio
WEEC Springfield, Ohio
WSPD Toledo, Ohio
WTUZ Uhrichsville, Ohio
WCHO Washington Ct House, Ohio
WBZI Xenia, Ohio
KEYB Altus, Oklahoma
KKBI Broken Bow, Oklahoma
KGWA Enid, Oklahoma
KIHN Hugo, Oklahoma
KMAD Madill, Oklahoma
KYAL-FM Muskogee, Oklahoma
KPNC Ponca City, Oklahoma
KFAQ Tulsa, Oklahoma
KBKR Baker, Oregon
KWVR Enterprise, Oregon
KZZR Government Camp, Oregon
KAGO Klamath Falls, Oregon
KLBM La Grande, Oregon
KSRV Ontario, Oregon
KUMA Pendleton, Oregon
KCKX Stayton, Oregon
KODL The Dalles, Oregon
KLWJ(AM) Umatilla, Oregon
WAEB Allentown, Pennsylvania
WHLM Bloomsburg, Pennsylvania
WFRM Coudersport, Pennsylvania
WDAC Lancaster, Pennsylvania
WWBJ Martinsburg, Pennsylvania
WATS Sayre, Pennsylvania
WMGS Wilkes-Barre, Pennsylvania
WSBA York, Pennsylvania
WSOL San German, Puerto Rico
WVCD Bamberg-Denmark, South Carolina
WJBS Holly Hill, South Carolina
WJAY Mullins, South Carolina
KSDN Aberdeen, South Dakota
KBFS Belle Fourche, South Dakota
KBRK Brookings, South Dakota
KZMX Hot Springs, South Dakota
KJAM Madison, South Dakota
KMSD Mibank, South Dakota
KMIT Mitchell, South Dakota
KORN Mitchell, South Dakota
KOLY Mobridge, South Dakota
KIMM Rapid City, South Dakota
KTOQ Rapid City, South Dakota
KGIM-FM Redfield, South Dakota
KPLO-FM Reliance, South Dakota
KSDR-FM Watertown, South Dakota
KYNT Yankton, South Dakota
WNAX Yankton, South Dakota
WLAR Athens, Tennessee
WHCB Bristol, Tennessee
WMCP Columbia, Tennessee
WEKR Fayetteville, Tennessee
WHIN Gallatin, Tennessee
WMYL Halls Crossroads, Tennessee
WDXI Jackson, Tennessee
WCLC Jamestown, Tennessee
WDEB Jamestown, Tennessee
WJFC Jefferson City, Tennessee
WBUZ La Vergne, Tennessee
WEEN Lafayette, Tennessee
WLIL Lenoir City, Tennessee
WLIV Livingston, Tennessee
WMSR Manchester, Tennessee
WAKI McMinnville, Tennessee
WBMC McMinnville, Tennessee
WREC Memphis, Tennessee
WGNS Murfreesboro, Tennessee
WSM Nashville, Tennessee
WDNX Olive Hill, Tennessee
WRQR(AM) Paris, Tennessee
WUAT Pikeville, Tennessee
WLIJ Shelbyville, Tennessee
WDBL Springfield, Tennessee
WSGI Springfield, Tennessee
WCDT Winchester, Tennessee
KFYN Bonham, Texas
KLXK Breckenridge, Texas
KWHI Brenham, Texas
KMIL Cameron, Texas
KCAR Clarksville, Texas
KSTA Coleman, Texas
KZNE College Station, Texas
KXIT Dalhart, Texas
KDDD-FM Dumas, Texas
KMUL Farwell, Texas
KNAF Fredericksburg, Texas
KGAF Gainesville, Texas
KPIR Granbury, Texas
KGVL Greenville, Texas
KVRP-FM Haskell, Texas
KPAN Hereford, Texas
KWFB Holliday, Texas
KHYI Howe, Texas
KEBE Jacksonville, Texas
KMBL Junction, Texas
KVLG La Grange, Texas
KZZN Littlefield, Texas
KCUL Marshall, Texas
KLRK Mexia, Texas
KSFA Nacogdoches, Texas
KBUS Paris, Texas
KEYE Perryton, Texas
KVOP Plainview, Texas
KITE Port Lavaca, Texas
KGKL San Angelo, Texas
KWED Seguin, Texas
KDAE Sinton, Texas
KSTV Stephenville, Texas
KQQB Stockdale, Texas
KXOX Sweetwater, Texas
KGWU Uvalde, Texas
KBEC Waxahachie, Texas
KWUD Woodville, Texas
KSUB Cedar City, Utah
KYAH Delta, Utah
KVNU Logan, Utah
KMTI Manti, Utah
KOAL Price, Utah
KSVC Richfield, Utah
KVEL Vernal, Utah
WBTX Broadway-Timberville, Virginia
WPAK Farmville, Virginia
WWWJ Galax, Virginia

WXGM Gloucester, Virginia
WMNA Gretna, Virginia
WNRG Grundy, Virginia
WSVA Harrisonburg, Virginia
WHHV Hillsville, Virginia
WKGM Smithfield, Virginia
WSBV South Boston, Virginia
WKDW Staunton, Virginia
WHEO Stuart, Virginia
WKCW Warrenton, Virginia
WKCI Waynesboro, Virginia
WZLF Bellows Falls, Vermont
KOZI Chelan, Washington
KCLX Colfax, Washington
KYSN East Wenatchee, Washington
KTBI Ephrata, Washington
KULE Ephrata, Washington
KONA Kennewick-Richland-P, Washington
KBRC Mount Vernon, Washington
KOMW Omak, Washington
KQQQ Pullman, Washington
KWNC Quincy, Washington
KGA Spokane, Washington
KTEL Walla Walla, Washington
KPQ Wenatchee, Washington
KIT Yakima, Washington
WBEV Beaver Dam, Wisconsin
WXRO Beaver Dam, Wisconsin
WOTE Clintonville, Wisconsin
KFIZ Fond Du Lac, Wisconsin
WTAQ Green Bay, Wisconsin
WAUN-FM Kewaunee, Wisconsin
WKTY La Crosse, Wisconsin
WGLR-FM Lancaster, Wisconsin
WTSO Madison, Wisconsin
WIGM Medford, Wisconsin
WJMT Merrill, Wisconsin
WCCN Neillsville, Wisconsin
WPKR Omro, Wisconsin
WPVL Platteville, Wisconsin
WJUB Plymouth, Wisconsin
WPDR Portage, Wisconsin
WRCO Richland Center, Wisconsin
WRCO-FM Richland Center, Wisconsin
WEVR River Falls, Wisconsin
WRFW River Falls, Wisconsin
WTCH Shawano, Wisconsin
WHBL Sheboygan, Wisconsin
WCSW Shell Lake, Wisconsin
WDOR-FM Sturgeon Bay, Wisconsin
WVRQ Viroqua, Wisconsin
WVRQ-FM Viroqua, Wisconsin
WDUX Waupaca, Wisconsin
WFDL Waupun, Wisconsin
WDEZ Wausau, Wisconsin
WSAU Wausau, Wisconsin
WVMR Frost, West Virginia
WRON-FM Lewisburg, West Virginia
WGGE Parkersburg, West Virginia
WWVA Wheeling, West Virginia
KHAT Laramie, Wyoming
KASL Newcastle, Wyoming
KPOW Powell, Wyoming
KVOW Riverton, Wyoming
KYCN Wheatland, Wyoming

Alternative

KSWH-FM Arkadelphia, Arkansas
KIDE Hoopa, California
WRUF-FM Gainesville, Florida
WXXL Tavares, Florida
KECH-FM Sun Valley, Idaho
WQUB Quincy, Illinois
KBIK Independence, Kansas
KHCA Wamego, Kansas
WIRQ Rochester, New York
WOBN Westerville, Ohio
WFBC-FM Greenville, South Carolina
KWKQ Graham, Texas
KRLF Pullman, Washington
KYVT Yakima, Washington
WSUP Platteville, Wisconsin
KUWS Superior, Wisconsin

Arabic

KLAV Las Vegas, Nevada
WDIY Allentown, Pennsylvania
WMUH Allentown, Pennsylvania
KARI Blaine, Washington

Big Band

KASU Jonesboro, Arkansas
WGRS Guilford, Connecticut
WQUN Hamden, Connecticut
WMNR Monroe, Connecticut
WRXC Shelton, Connecticut
WGSK South Kent, Connecticut
WTAN Clearwater, Florida
KMRY Cedar Rapids, Iowa
WSIU Carbondale, Illinois
WHPO Hoopeston, Illinois
WTAY Robinson, Illinois
WMAY Springfield, Illinois
WXNT Indianapolis, Indiana
KIND Independence, Kansas
KLKC Parsons, Kansas
WESM Princess Anne, Maryland
WHFR Dearborn, Michigan
WBNZ Frankfort, Michigan
WLNZ Lansing, Michigan
WIOS Tawas City-East Tawa, Michigan
KOLV Olivia, Minnesota
KXMS Joplin, Missouri
KPRK Livingston, Montana
WXIT Blowing Rock, North Carolina
WCCE Buies Creek, North Carolina
KUVR Holdrege, Nebraska
WSNJ Bridgeton, New Jersey
WNTI Hackettstown, New Jersey
WDNY-FM Dansville, New York
WDOS Oneonta, New York
WRGR Tupper Lake, New York
WATH Athens, Ohio
WKFI Wilmington, Ohio
WVMM Grantham, Pennsylvania
WNPV Lansdale, Pennsylvania
WLSH Lansford, Pennsylvania
WPHB Philipsburg, Pennsylvania
WJAS Pittsburgh, Pennsylvania
WCRI-FM Block Island, Rhode Island
WHSC Conway, South Carolina
WJMX Florence, South Carolina
KNCT-FM Killeen, Texas
KTBB-FM Tyler, Texas
WVNR Poultney, Vermont
KEYG Grand Coulee, Washington
WVMR Frost, West Virginia
WKLP Keyser, West Virginia

Black

KSUA Fairbanks, Alaska
WNRA Eufaula, Alabama
WGYV Greenville, Alabama
WHMA-FM Hobson City, Alabama
WJAB Huntsville, Alabama
WMGY Montgomery, Alabama
WGOL Russellville, Alabama
WKAX Russellville, Alabama
WHBB Selma, Alabama
KUAF Fayetteville, Arkansas
KFFA Helena, Arkansas
KOSE Wilson, Arkansas
KDVA Buckeye, Arizona
KTKT Tucson, Arizona
KXCI Tucson, Arizona
KHYL Auburn, California
KPFA Berkeley, California
KMUD Garberville, California
KXLU Los Angeles, California
KMPO Modesto, California
KVMR Nevada City, California
KSPB Pebble Beach, California
KZYX Philo, California
KUCR Riverside, California
KYCC Stockton, California
KDIA Vallejo, California
KDYA Vallejo, California
KGNU-FM Boulder, Colorado
KLDC Denver, Colorado
KCSU-FM Fort Collins, Colorado
KMSA Grand Junction, Colorado
WPKN Bridgeport, Connecticut
WFIF Milford, Connecticut
WCNI New London, Connecticut
WVUD Newark, Delaware
WPHK Blountstown, Florida
WVUM Coral Gables, Florida
WRUF Gainesville, Florida
WUFT-FM Gainesville, Florida
WGWD Gretna, Florida
WDSR Lake City, Florida
WLBE Leesburg-Eustis, Florida
WKGC-FM Panama City, Florida
WLTG Panama City, Florida
WPRY Perry, Florida
WKPX Sunrise, Florida
WVFS Tallahassee, Florida
WBVM Tampa, Florida
WDEC-FM Americus, Georgia
WRFC Athens, Georgia
WMOG Brunswick, Georgia
WGRA Cairo, Georgia
WEBS Calhoun, Georgia
WBTR-FM Carrollton, Georgia
WDXQ Cochran, Georgia
WUFF Eastman, Georgia
WYIS McRae, Georgia
WMVG Milledgeville, Georgia
WNEA Newnan, Georgia
WSBX Ochlocknee, Georgia
WTGA Thomaston, Georgia
KLNG Council Bluffs, Iowa
KUOI-FM Moscow, Idaho
WESN Bloomington, Illinois
WEFT Champaign, Illinois
WGN(AM) Chicago, Illinois
WVKC Galesburg, Illinois
WCSF Joliet, Illinois
WMXM Lake Forest, Illinois
WLRA Lockport, Illinois
WFYI-FM Indianapolis, Indiana
WXFN Muncie, Indiana
WWVR West Terre Haute, Indiana
KONQ Dodge City, Kansas
KWBW Hutchinson, Kansas
KSDB-FM Manhattan, Kansas
WWHR Bowling Green, Kentucky
WCPM Cumberland, Kentucky
WNKJ Hopkinsville, Kentucky
WFXY Middlesboro, Kentucky
WEKY Richmond, Kentucky
KLSP Angola, Louisiana
KAJN-FM Crowley, Louisiana
WBSL-FM Sheffield, Massachusetts
WHLL Springfield, Massachusetts
WYAJ Sudbury, Massachusetts
WCHC Worcester, Massachusetts
WKHI Fruitland, Maryland
WUPX Marquette, Michigan
WHLS Port Huron, Michigan
WSJM St. Joseph, Michigan
WNMC-FM Traverse City, Michigan
KFAI Minneapolis, Minnesota
KNOF St. Paul, Minnesota
KMFC Centralia, Missouri
KOPN Columbia, Missouri
KCFV Ferguson, Missouri
KMVC Marshall, Missouri
KLID Poplar Bluff, Missouri
KDRO Sedalia, Missouri
WKCU Corinth, Mississippi
WGRM Greenwood, Mississippi
WNBN Meridian, Mississippi
WRJW Picayune, Mississippi
WJDR Prentiss, Mississippi
WSSO Starkville, Mississippi
WFGW Black Mountain, North Carolina
WRRZ Clinton, North Carolina
WGAI Elizabeth City, North Carolina
WRVS-FM Elizabeth City, North Carolina
WBLA Elizabethtown, North Carolina
WSML Graham, North Carolina
WYRN Louisburg, North Carolina
WHIP Mooresville, North Carolina
WDJS Mount Olive, North Carolina
WNNC Newton, North Carolina
WPJL Raleigh, North Carolina
WRXO Roxboro, North Carolina
KWSC Wayne, Nebraska
WUNH Durham, New Hampshire
WGLS-FM Glassboro, New Jersey
WRRC Lawrenceville, New Jersey
WMSC Upper Montclair, New Jersey
KKIM Albuquerque, New Mexico
WXBA Brentwood, New York
WBNY Buffalo, New York
WSLU Canton, New York
WSIV E. Syracuse, New York
WRCU-FM Hamilton, New York
WHLI Hempstead, New York
WKJY Hempstead, New York

WJJL Niagara Falls, New York
WQKE Plattsburgh, New York
WRNY Rome, New York
WFNP Rosendale, New York
WUSB Stony Brook, New York
WJPZ-FM Syracuse, New York
WOUB Athens, Ohio
WKDC-FM Cedarville, Ohio
WVSG Columbus, Ohio
WWSU Fairborn, Ohio
WDUB Granville, Ohio
WRBP Hubbard, Ohio
WFCJ Miamisburg, Ohio
WNPQ New Philadelphia, Ohio
WCCD Parma, Ohio
WUKV Portsmouth, Ohio
WNTO Racine, Ohio
WEEC Springfield, Ohio
WXUT Toledo, Ohio
KYLV Oklahoma City, Oklahoma
KZBB Poteau, Oklahoma
KKNX Eugene, Oregon
KLCC Eugene, Oregon
KRVM-FM Eugene, Oregon
KWVA Eugene, Oregon
KTEC Klamath Falls, Oregon
KEOL La Grande, Oregon
KSLC McMinnville, Oregon
KLCO Newport, Oregon
KRRC Portland, Oregon
WLVR-FM Bethlehem, Pennsylvania
WFSE Edinboro, Pennsylvania
WKVR-FM Huntingdon, Pennsylvania
WIUP-FM Indiana, Pennsylvania
WFNM Lancaster, Pennsylvania
WNTE Mansfield, Pennsylvania
WARC Meadville, Pennsylvania
WJST New Castle, Pennsylvania
WRCT Pittsburgh, Pennsylvania
WRCT(FM) Pittsburgh, Pennsylvania
WYEP-FM Pittsburgh, Pennsylvania
WVMW-FM Scranton, Pennsylvania
WSYC-FM Shippensburg, Pennsylvania
WXVU Villanova, Pennsylvania
WSBA York, Pennsylvania
WBRU Providence, Rhode Island
WARV Warwick, Rhode Island
WBSC Bennettsville, South Carolina
WCRE Cheraw, South Carolina
WFIS Fountain Inn, South Carolina
WJBS Holly Hill, South Carolina
WRIX Homeland Park, South Carolina
KSDJ Brookings, South Dakota
WYXI Athens, Tennessee
WMBW Chattanooga, Tennessee
WAPX-FM Clarksville, Tennessee
WKBL Covington, Tennessee
WHIN Gallatin, Tennessee
WITA Knoxville, Tennessee
WLIL Lenoir City, Tennessee
WDXL Lexington, Tennessee
WXRQ Mount Pleasant, Tennessee
WGNS Murfreesboro, Tennessee
WLAC Nashville, Tennessee
WUTS Sewanee, Tennessee
WLIJ Shelbyville, Tennessee
KGNZ Abilene, Texas
KAGC Bryan, Texas
KWTS Canyon, Texas
KNES Fairfield, Texas
KOOP Hornsby, Texas
KPFT Houston, Texas
KHVL Huntsville, Texas
KBJS Jacksonville, Texas
KTAI Kingsville, Texas
KVLG La Grange, Texas
KSHN Liberty, Texas
KFRO Longview, Texas
KLVL Pasadena, Texas
KHKZ San Benito, Texas
KOKE-FM Thorndale, Texas
KZMU Moab, Utah
KRCL Salt Lake City, Utah
WKDE-FM Altavista, Virginia
WTJU Charlottesville, Virginia
WKEY Covington, Virginia
WFAX Falls Church, Virginia
WMNA Gretna, Virginia
WVRU-FM Radford, Virginia
WKBA Vinton, Virginia
WKCI Waynesboro, Virginia
KBSG Aberdeen, Washington
KUGS Bellingham, Washington
KZUU Pullman, Washington
KNHC Seattle, Washington
KSFC Spokane, Washington
KUPS Tacoma, Washington
KTCR Yakima, Washington
WMSE Milwaukee, Wisconsin
WVWC Buckhannon, West Virginia
WQAB Philippi, West Virginia
WPHP Wheeling, West Virginia

Blues

KUAC Fairbanks, Alaska
KTNA Talkeetna, Alaska
WVAS Montgomery, Alabama
WQPR Muscle Shoals, Alabama
WVUA-FM Tuscaloosa, Alabama
KFFA Helena, Arkansas
KASU Jonesboro, Arkansas
KERX Paris, Arkansas
KNCA Burney, California
KSPC Claremont, California
KKJZ Long Beach, California
KSBR Mission Viejo, California
KNSQ Mount Shasta, California
KVMR Nevada City, California
KZYX Philo, California
KRXQ Sacramento, California
KXJZ Sacramento, California
KCPR San Luis Obispo, California
KCSM San Mateo, California
KSCU Santa Clara, California
KCLU-FM Thousand Oaks, California
KASF Alamosa, Colorado
KRCC Colorado Springs, Colorado
KDUR Durango, Colorado
KIBT Fountain, Colorado
KWSB-FM Gunnison, Colorado
KWUF-FM Pagosa Springs, Colorado
KVNF Paonia, Colorado
KOTO Telluride, Colorado
WQTQ Hartford, Connecticut
WESU Middletown, Connecticut
WFCS New Britain, Connecticut
WUCF-FM Orlando, Florida
WFCF St. Augustine, Florida
WKPX Sunrise, Florida
WCLK Atlanta, Georgia
WZBN Camilla, Georgia
KUNI Cedar Falls, Iowa
KCCK-FM Cedar Rapids, Iowa
KROS Clinton, Iowa
KNSY(FM) Dubuque, Iowa
KRNI Mason City, Iowa
KICJ(FM) Mitchellville, Iowa
KOJI Okoboji, Iowa
KWIT Sioux City, Iowa
KECH-FM Sun Valley, Idaho
WEFT Champaign, Illinois
WMKB Earlville, Illinois
WIUM Macomb, Illinois
WIUS Macomb, Illinois
WPNA Oak Park, Illinois
WQUB Quincy, Illinois
WNIU Rockford, Illinois
WDML Woodlawn, Illinois
WTTS Bloomington, Indiana
WVPE Elkhart, Indiana
WFYI-FM Indianapolis, Indiana
WCYT Lafayette Township, Indiana
WSND-FM Notre Dame, Indiana
WPUM Rensselaer, Indiana
KANU Lawrence, Kansas
KJHK Lawrence, Kansas
WMKY Morehead, Kentucky
KJMG Bastrop, Louisiana
KGRM Grambling, Louisiana
WGBH(FM) Boston, Massachusetts
WESM Princess Anne, Maryland
WBQI Bar Harbor, Maine
WGTO Cassopolis, Michigan
WHFR Dearborn, Michigan
WDET-FM Detroit, Michigan
WDBM East Lansing, Michigan
WKLT Kalkaska, Michigan
WQUS Lapeer, Michigan
WRKR Portage, Michigan
WPHS Warren, Michigan
WTIP Grand Marais, Minnesota
KOPN Columbia, Missouri
KKFI Kansas City, Missouri
KPOW-FM La Monte, Missouri
KGSP Parkville, Missouri
KBFL Springfield, Missouri
WESE Baldwyn, Mississippi
WROX Clarksdale, Mississippi
WJZD-FM Long Beach, Mississippi
WASU-FM Boone, North Carolina
WNAA Greensboro, North Carolina
WVOD Manteo, North Carolina
WSHA Raleigh, North Carolina
WNCW Spindale, North Carolina
KCND Bismarck, North Dakota
KFJM Grand Forks, North Dakota
KZUM Lincoln, Nebraska
KKCD Omaha, Nebraska
KWSC Wayne, Nebraska
WUNH Durham, New Hampshire
WNEC-FM Henniker, New Hampshire
WKNH Keene, New Hampshire
WPCR-FM Plymouth, New Hampshire
WNTI Hackettstown, New Jersey
WBJB-FM Lincroft, New Jersey
WBFO Buffalo, New York
WICB Ithaca, New York
WVBR-FM Ithaca, New York
WUBJ Jamestown, New York
WZOZ Oneonta, New York
WTKV Oswego, New York
WPDH Poughkeepsie, New York
WSPN Saratoga Springs, New York
WAER Syracuse, New York
WCBE Columbus, Ohio
WUSO Springfield, Ohio
WJUC Swanton, Ohio
WXTS-FM Toledo, Ohio
WXUT Toledo, Ohio
WYSO Yellow Springs, Ohio
KGOU Norman, Oklahoma
KROU Spencer, Oklahoma
KSMF Ashland, Oregon
KSBA Coos Bay, Oregon
KLCC Eugene, Oregon
KMHD Gresham, Oregon
KSKF Klamath Falls, Oregon
KLCO Newport, Oregon
WDCV-FM Carlisle, Pennsylvania
WDNR Chester, Pennsylvania
WPSX Kane, Pennsylvania
WKDU Philadelphia, Pennsylvania
WYEP-FM Pittsburgh, Pennsylvania
WSYC-FM Shippensburg, Pennsylvania
WHYF(AM) Shiremanstown, Pennsylvania
WPSU State College, Pennsylvania
WRDV Warminster, Pennsylvania
WRLC Williamsport, Pennsylvania
WRIU Kingston, Rhode Island
WSSB-FM Orangeburg, South Carolina
KAUR Sioux Falls, South Dakota
WEGR Arlington, Tennessee
WRLT Franklin, Tennessee
WETS-FM Johnson City, Tennessee
KAZI Austin, Texas
KUT Austin, Texas
KLUB Bloomington, Texas
KTRU(FM) Houston, Texas
KXWT Odessa, Texas
KNCH(FM) San Angelo, Texas
KSTX San Antonio, Texas
KSUU Cedar City, Utah
KZMU Moab, Utah
WMRY Crozet, Virginia
WWHS-FM Hampden-Sydney, Virginia
WHOV Hampton, Virginia
WMRA Harrisonburg, Virginia
WCLM Highland Springs, Virginia
WMRL Lexington, Virginia
WCVE-FM Richmond, Virginia
WCWM Williamsburg, Virginia
WRMC-FM Middlebury, Vermont
WIZN Vergennes, Vermont
KMCQ Covington, Washington
KSER Everett, Washington
KKZX Spokane, Washington
KUPS Tacoma, Washington
WBSD Burlington, Wisconsin
WUEC Eau Claire, Wisconsin
WPNE-FM Green Bay, Wisconsin
WMCS Greenfield, Wisconsin
WHND Sister Bay, Wisconsin

WWSP Stevens Point, Wisconsin

Children

KLEF Anchorage, Alaska
KTOO Juneau, Alaska
KRSA Petersburg, Alaska
WMBV Dixons Mills, Alabama
WRWA Dothan, Alabama
WFIX Florence, Alabama
WTSU Montgomery-Troy, Alabama
KFMM Thatcher, Arizona
KYRM Yuma, Arizona
KFRB Bakersfield, California
KZRO Dunsmuir, California
KFNO Fresno, California
KPFK Los Angeles, California
KXLU Los Angeles, California
KWVE-FM San Clemente, California
KFAX San Francisco, California
WIHS Middletown, Connecticut
WJYO Fort Myers, Florida
WJLF Gainesville, Florida
WGNK Pennsuco, Florida
WBVM Tampa, Florida
WTJB Columbus, Georgia
KHMG Barrigada, Guam
KHOE Fairfield, Iowa
KIFG-FM Iowa Falls, Iowa
KTFC Sioux City, Iowa
KTFG Sioux Rapids, Iowa
KCIR Twin Falls, Idaho
WUEV Evansville, Indiana
KJTY Topeka, Kansas
WKHS Worton, Maryland
WHCF Bangor, Maine
WBQX Thomaston, Maine
WDBC Escanaba, Michigan
KJLY Blue Earth, Minnesota
KFSI Rochester, Minnesota
KGNN-FM Cuba, Missouri
KGNV Washington, Missouri
WPAE Centreville, Mississippi
WMBU Forest, Mississippi
KABU Fort Totten, North Dakota
WMVB Millville, New Jersey
KFLQ Albuquerque, New Mexico
KHAC Tse Bonito, New Mexico
WYBG Massena, New York
WRHO Oneonta, New York
WMHR Syracuse, New York
WMHN Webster, New York
WFCJ Miamisburg, Ohio
KIHN Hugo, Oklahoma
KMUN Astoria, Oregon
WFKJ Cashtown, Pennsylvania
WDNR Chester, Pennsylvania
WCOH-FM Du Bois, Pennsylvania
WXPN Philadelphia, Pennsylvania
WCTL Union City, Pennsylvania
WYVL(FM) Youngsville, Pennsylvania
KLND Little Eagle, South Dakota
KPSM Brownwood, Texas
WRR Dallas, Texas
KFST Fort Stockton, Texas
KFST-FM Fort Stockton, Texas
KNLE-FM Round Rock, Texas
KTER Rudolph, Texas
KVNE Tyler, Texas
WTJU Charlottesville, Virginia
WWOD Hartford, Vermont
WCVT Stowe, Vermont
WWMP Waterbury, Vermont
WTWN Wells River, Vermont
KRLF Pullman, Washington
KDNA Yakima, Washington
WGNV Milladore, Wisconsin
WVPG Parkersburg, West Virginia
WQAB Philippi, West Virginia

Chinese

KEST San Francisco, California
KSJX San Jose, California
WJDA Quincy, Massachusetts
WUSB Stony Brook, New York
WJCU University Heights, Ohio
WBZK York, South Carolina
KHCB-FM Houston, Texas
KKER Kerrville, Texas
KHCB League City, Texas
WUVT-FM Blacksburg, Virginia

Christian

KYKD Bethel, Alaska
KNOM Nome, Alaska
WVUA-FM Tuscaloosa, Alabama
KSWH-FM Arkadelphia, Arkansas
KCGS Marshall, Arkansas
KJLH Compton, California
KNCO Grass Valley, California
KFBK-FM Sacramento, California
KFAX San Francisco, California
WEBY Milton, Florida
WMGF Mount Dora, Florida
WZHR Zephyrhills, Florida
WROM Rome, Georgia
KEDB Chariton, Iowa
KGEM Boise, Idaho
KIDO Nampa, Idaho
WDML Woodlawn, Illinois
KBIK Independence, Kansas
WCVK Bowling Green, Kentucky
WHFC Bel Air, Maryland
WYFP Harpswell, Maine
WDBM East Lansing, Michigan
WPHS Warren, Michigan
KGGN Gladstone, Missouri
KWJC Liberty, Missouri
KNEM Nevada, Missouri
KKDY West Plains, Missouri
WQLJ Oxford, Mississippi
WTNM Water Valley, Mississippi
KBZR Billings, Montana
WASU-FM Boone, North Carolina
WLHC Robbins, North Carolina
KTNC Falls City, Nebraska
KKVV Las Vegas, Nevada
WITR Henrietta, New York
WFSO Olivebridge, New York
WRIP Windham, New York
WRDL Ashland, Ohio
WKKI Celina, Ohio
WLFC North Baltimore, Ohio
KKPZ Portland, Oregon
KFIR Sweet Home, Oregon
WCAL California, Pennsylvania
WCOH-FM Du Bois, Pennsylvania
WKVR-FM Huntingdon, Pennsylvania
WCYJ-FM Waynesburg, Pennsylvania
WRLC Williamsport, Pennsylvania
WFIS Fountain Inn, South Carolina
WVCP Gallatin, Tennessee
WNRQ Nashville, Tennessee
KRUN Ballinger, Texas
KHVT Bloomington, Texas
KQTY-FM Borger, Texas
KPSM Brownwood, Texas
KQBZ Brownwood, Texas
KGGR Dallas, Texas
KAVX Lufkin, Texas
KHML Madisonville, Texas
KWMF Pleasanton, Texas
KHKZ San Benito, Texas
KTXZ West Lake Hills, Texas
WVBC Bethany, West Virginia
WELD-FM Moorefield, West Virginia

Classic Rock

KVHS Concord, California
KMMT Mammoth Lakes, California
KVAY Lamar, Colorado
WSGL Naples, Florida
WCSF Joliet, Illinois
WRRG River Grove, Illinois
WBKE-FM North Manchester, Indiana
WECI Richmond, Indiana
KTCC Colby, Kansas
KICT-FM Wichita, Kansas
KHND Harvey, North Dakota
WPSC-FM Wayne, New Jersey
WQKE Plattsburgh, New York
WMAN-FM Fredericktown, Ohio
WFXN-FM Galion, Ohio
WCYJ-FM Waynesburg, Pennsylvania
WDOM Providence, Rhode Island
WVBC Bethany, West Virginia

Classical

KYUK Bethel, Alaska
KCAM Glennallen, Alaska
KRBD Ketchikan, Alaska
KIAM Nenana, Alaska
KNOM Nome, Alaska
KRSA Petersburg, Alaska
KCAW Sitka, Alaska
KSTK Wrangell, Alaska
KESA Eureka Springs, Arkansas
KQSM-FM Fayetteville, Arkansas
KVHS Concord, California
KMMT Mammoth Lakes, California
KSMC Moraga, California
KUCR Riverside, California
KJDX Susanville, California
KCSS Turlock, California
KCIC Grand Junction, Colorado
KSUT Ignacio, Colorado
KVOD Lakewood, Colorado
KVAY Lamar, Colorado
WPKN Bridgeport, Connecticut
WRTC-FM Hartford, Connecticut
WWEB Wallingford, Connecticut
WVUD Newark, Delaware
WIIS Key West, Florida
WKEY-FM Key West, Florida
WSGL Naples, Florida
WUCF-FM Orlando, Florida
WRAS Atlanta, Georgia
WREK Atlanta, Georgia
WMOG Brunswick, Georgia
WNGA Clermont, Georgia
KDFR Des Moines, Iowa
KCMR Mason City, Iowa
KSAS-FM Caldwell, Idaho
KSRA Salmon, Idaho
WESN Bloomington, Illinois
WHPK-FM Chicago, Illinois
WEPS Elgin, Illinois
WVKC Galesburg, Illinois
WDCB Glen Ellyn, Illinois
WJCH Joliet, Illinois
WDSO Chesterton, Indiana
WBKE-FM North Manchester, Indiana
WPUM Rensselaer, Indiana
WECI Richmond, Indiana
WMHD-FM Terre Haute, Indiana
WVUR-FM Valparaiso, Indiana
WVUB Vincennes, Indiana
KTCC Colby, Kansas
KIND Independence, Kansas
KFKF-FM Kansas City, Kansas
WKMS-FM Murray, Kentucky
WYAJ Sudbury, Massachusetts
WMVY Tisbury, Massachusetts
WCHC Worcester, Massachusetts
WKLT Kalkaska, Michigan
WRSR Owosso, Michigan
KNXR Rochester, Minnesota
KQAL Winona, Minnesota
KLJY Clayton, Missouri
KIXQ Joplin, Missouri
KWJC Liberty, Missouri
KMVC Marshall, Missouri
KGNV Washington, Missouri
KMSM-FM Butte, Montana
KNMC Havre, Montana
KALS Kalispell, Montana
WERX-FM Columbia, North Carolina
WFSS Fayetteville, North Carolina
WVOD Manteo, North Carolina
WCVP Murphy, North Carolina
WCPE Raleigh, North Carolina
KHAS Hastings, Nebraska
KLPR Kearney, Nebraska
KCMI Terrytown, Nebraska
WKNH Keene, New Hampshire
WJSE North Cape May, New Jersey
WLFR Pomona, New Jersey
WKNJ-FM Union Township, New Jersey
WPSC-FM Wayne, New Jersey
KUNM Albuquerque, New Mexico
KPCL Farmington, New Mexico
WXLH Blue Mountain Lake, New York
WBFO Buffalo, New York
WHCL-FM Clinton, New York
WRCU-FM Hamilton, New York
WXXY(FM) Houghton, New York
WFSO Olivebridge, New York
WSRK Oneonta, New York
WKWZ Syosset, New York
WPNR-FM Utica, New York
WFRW Webster, New York
WBGU Bowling Green, Ohio

WCUE Cuyahoga Falls, Ohio
WMCO New Concord, Ohio
WUSO Springfield, Ohio
WYTN Youngstown, Ohio
KOSN Ketchum, Oklahoma
KBVR Corvallis, Oregon
KRRC Portland, Oregon
WDIY Allentown, Pennsylvania
WMKX Brookville, Pennsylvania
WSKE Everett, Pennsylvania
WZBT Gettysburg, Pennsylvania
WIUP-FM Indiana, Pennsylvania
WJSA Jersey Shore, Pennsylvania
WJSA-FM Jersey Shore, Pennsylvania
WARC Meadville, Pennsylvania
WJST New Castle, Pennsylvania
WHYY-FM Philadelphia, Pennsylvania
WUSR Scranton, Pennsylvania
WVMW-FM Scranton, Pennsylvania
WQSU Selinsgrove, Pennsylvania
WVYC York, Pennsylvania
WYVL(FM) Youngsville, Pennsylvania
WTPM Aguadilla, Puerto Rico
WMUU-FM Greenville, South Carolina
WHCB Bristol, Tennessee
WOPI Bristol, Tennessee
WVCP Gallatin, Tennessee
WFHU Henderson, Tennessee
WFMQ Lebanon, Tennessee
WDNX Olive Hill, Tennessee
KWTS Canyon, Texas
KNTU McKinney, Texas
KSUU Cedar City, Utah
KPCW Park City, Utah
WVRU-FM Radford, Virginia
WDCE Richmond, Virginia
WIUJ Charlotte Amalie, Virgin Islands
WVPS Burlington, Vermont
WJSC-FM Johnson, Vermont
WWLR Lyndonville, Vermont
WDEV Waterbury, Vermont
KGHP Gig Harbor, Washington
KEYG Grand Coulee, Washington
KMLW Moses Lake, Washington
KAGU Spokane, Washington
WSUP Platteville, Wisconsin
WRJN Racine, Wisconsin
WVBC Bethany, West Virginia
WVTS-FM Dunbar, West Virginia

Comedy

WDJL Huntsville, Alabama
KTCL Wheat Ridge, Colorado
WWHP Farmer City, Illinois
WVSD Itta Bena, Mississippi
WPCR-FM Plymouth, New Hampshire
KFLY Corvallis, Oregon
KJXJ Franklin, Texas

Contemporary Hits/Top 40

WSBB New Smyrna Beach, Florida
WQLF Lena, Illinois
WSGR-FM Port Huron, Michigan
WYGR Wyoming, Michigan
KOLV Olivia, Minnesota
KATQ Plentywood, Montana
WRRV Middletown, New York
WKBO Harrisburg, Pennsylvania
WSBG Stroudsburg, Pennsylvania
WCLM Highland Springs, Virginia

Country

KYUK Bethel, Alaska
KHNS Haines, Alaska
KRBD Ketchikan, Alaska
KSTK Wrangell, Alaska
WQPR Muscle Shoals, Alabama
KRDE Globe, Arizona
KIIM-FM Tucson, Arizona
KPFA Berkeley, California
KSOQ-FM Escondido, California
KFJC Los Altos, California
KVMR Nevada City, California
KCSN Northridge, California
KAZU Pacific Grove, California
KAJX Aspen, Colorado
KOTO Telluride, Colorado
WWEB Wallingford, Connecticut
WAMU Washington, District of Columbia
WWOJ Avon Park, Florida
WTUF Boston, Georgia
WUWG Carrollton, Georgia
WNGA Clermont, Georgia
KSTO Agana, Guam
KIAI Mason City, Iowa
WUIS Springfield, Illinois
WMRS Monticello, Indiana
WPUM Rensselaer, Indiana
WECI Richmond, Indiana
WMHD-FM Terre Haute, Indiana
KFKF-FM Kansas City, Kansas
KANU Lawrence, Kansas
WLVK Fort Knox, Kentucky
WGOH Grayson, Kentucky
WWAG McKee, Kentucky
WMKY Morehead, Kentucky
WKMS-FM Murray, Kentucky
WTKY Tompkinsville, Kentucky
KLSP Angola, Louisiana
WKHS Worton, Maryland
WBPW Presque Isle, Maine
WDBM East Lansing, Michigan
WMUK Kalamazoo, Michigan
WPHS Warren, Michigan
KBEM-FM Minneapolis, Minnesota
WMCN St. Paul, Minnesota
KMST Rolla, Missouri
WKZU Iuka, Mississippi
WSKK Ripley, Mississippi
KXEI Havre, Montana
WASU-FM Boone, North Carolina
WCCE Buies Creek, North Carolina
WZTK Burlington, North Carolina
WUAG Greensboro, North Carolina
WPLW Hillsborough, North Carolina
WMMY Jefferson, North Carolina
WCVP Murphy, North Carolina
WECR Newland, North Carolina
WQDR-FM Raleigh, North Carolina
WLHC Robbins, North Carolina
WEGG Rose Hill, North Carolina
WTQR Winston-Salem, North Carolina
WNEC-FM Henniker, New Hampshire
WDVR Delaware Township, New Jersey
WBJB-FM Lincroft, New Jersey
WBZC Pemberton, New Jersey
KRWG Las Cruces, New Mexico
WBFO Buffalo, New York
WLNL Horseheads, New York
WSQG-FM Ithaca, New York
WUBJ Jamestown, New York
WKCR-FM New York, New York
WGGO Salamanca, New York
WKWZ Syosset, New York
WCNY-FM Syracuse, New York
WUNY Utica, New York
WJNY Watertown, New York
WBGU Bowling Green, Ohio
WVSG Columbus, Ohio
KRSC-FM Claremore, Oklahoma
KRVM-FM Eugene, Oregon
KWVA Eugene, Oregon
KRRC Portland, Oregon
KFIR Sweet Home, Oregon
WWSM Annville-Cleona, Pennsylvania
WFKJ Cashtown, Pennsylvania
WCUC-FM Clarion, Pennsylvania
WSKE Everett, Pennsylvania
WNUZ Mercersburg, Pennsylvania
WRCT Pittsburgh, Pennsylvania
WRCT(FM) Pittsburgh, Pennsylvania
WYEP-FM Pittsburgh, Pennsylvania
WXLV Schnecksville, Pennsylvania
WQSU Selinsgrove, Pennsylvania
WBYO Sellersville, Pennsylvania
WBYX Stroudsburg, Pennsylvania
WRDV Warminster, Pennsylvania
WZZD Warwick, Pennsylvania
WCYJ-FM Waynesburg, Pennsylvania
WCHE West Chester, Pennsylvania
WDOM Providence, Rhode Island
WOPI Bristol, Tennessee
WHRS Cookeville, Tennessee
WEMB Erwin, Tennessee
WVCP Gallatin, Tennessee
WCLC Jamestown, Tennessee
WLAF La Follette, Tennessee
WWLX Lawrenceburg, Tennessee
WEVL Memphis, Tennessee
WUTS Sewanee, Tennessee
WSBI Static, Tennessee
WNTT Tazewell, Tennessee
KQTY-FM Borger, Texas
KETR Commerce, Texas
KSWA Graham, Texas
KSHN Liberty, Texas
KXWT Odessa, Texas
KPCW Park City, Utah
WKDE-FM Altavista, Virginia
WCLM Highland Springs, Virginia
WSIG Mount Jackson, Virginia
WKCW Warrenton, Virginia
WWOD Hartford, Vermont
WJSC-FM Johnson, Vermont
WOJB Reserve, Wisconsin
WVRQ-FM Viroqua, Wisconsin
WHAW Lost Creek, West Virginia

Disco

KSWF Aurora, Missouri

Ethnic

KDLG Dillingham, Alaska
KJHA Houston, Alaska
KJNP North Pole, Alaska
KSAZ Marana, Arizona
KKUP Cupertino, California
KMUD Garberville, California
KMYC Marysville, California
KCSN Northridge, California
KFOG San Francisco, California
KMRB San Gabriel, California
KOBO Yuba City, California
WMRD Middletown, Connecticut
WWPT Westport, Connecticut
WUST Washington, District of Columbia
WKWM Marathon, Florida
WLRN-FM Miami, Florida
WPSO New Port Richey, Florida
KUAI Eleele, Hawaii
KWXX-FM Hilo, Hawaii
KKON Kealakekua, Hawaii
KKUA Wailuku, Hawaii
WCEV Cicero, Illinois
WNKJ Hopkinsville, Kentucky
KEUN Eunice, Louisiana
KEUN-FM Eunice, Louisiana
KVPI Ville Platte, Louisiana
KVPI-FM Ville Platte, Louisiana
WHTB Fall River, Massachusetts
WNBP Newburyport, Massachusetts
WCUW Worcester, Massachusetts
WMPG Gorham, Maine
WCAR Livonia, Michigan
KMSK Austin, Minnesota
KRBT Eveleth, Minnesota
KMSU Mankato, Minnesota
WUMS University, Mississippi
WFMU East Orange, New Jersey
WPRB Princeton, New Jersey
WSOU South Orange, New Jersey
KTAO Taos, New Mexico
KUNR Reno, Nevada
WVOA-FM Mexico, New York
WFUV New York, New York
WMCA New York, New York
WRHV Poughkeepsie, New York
WBEE-FM Rochester, New York
WUSP Utica, New York
WAPS Akron, Ohio
WCPN Cleveland, Ohio
KKRX Lawton, Oklahoma
KBOO Portland, Oregon
WDIY Allentown, Pennsylvania
WMUH Allentown, Pennsylvania
WZUM Carnegie, Pennsylvania
WEDO McKeesport, Pennsylvania
KAGC Bryan, Texas
KGOL Humble, Texas
KTEM Temple, Texas
WWKS Cruz Bay, Virgin Islands
KARI Blaine, Washington
KLFE Seattle, Washington
WGTD Kenosha, Wisconsin
WEKZ Monroe, Wisconsin
WXER Plymouth, Wisconsin
WSHS Sheboygan, Wisconsin

Filipino

KBRW Barrow, Alaska
KECG El Cerrito, California
KMPO Modesto, California

French

KTOO Juneau, Alaska
KSRH San Rafael, California
KVPI-FM Ville Platte, Louisiana
WJIB Cambridge, Massachusetts
WMOU Berlin, New Hampshire
WFEA Manchester, New Hampshire
WCHP Champlain, New York

Gospel

KFAR Fairbanks, Alaska
KSDP Sand Point, Alaska
WSPZ(AM) Birmingham, Alabama
WKNU Brewton, Alabama
WALQ Carrville, Alabama
WTVY-FM Dothan, Alabama
WELB Elba, Alabama
WZOB Fort Payne, Alabama
WJRL-FM Fort Rucker, Alabama
WAOQ Goshen, Alabama
WDJL Huntsville, Alabama
WCKA Jacksonville, Alabama
WIXI Jasper, Alabama
WEBT Langdale, Alabama
WINL Linden, Alabama
WLWI-FM Montgomery, Alabama
WVAS Montgomery, Alabama
WGOL Russellville, Alabama
WFEB Sylacauga, Alabama
WTLS Tallassee, Alabama
WGZZ Waverly, Alabama
KEWI Benton, Arkansas
KMLK El Dorado, Arkansas
KBJT Fordyce, Arkansas
KFFA Helena, Arkansas
KBOK Malvern, Arkansas
KZHE Stamps, Arkansas
KWRF Warren, Arkansas
KCLT West Helena, Arkansas
KDVA Buckeye, Arizona
KXCI Tucson, Arizona
KMVE California City, California
KRML Carmel, California
KJLH Compton, California
KECG El Cerrito, California
KTDE Gualala, California
KSRN Kings Beach, California
KPFK Los Angeles, California
KYOS Merced, California
KAZU Pacific Grove, California
KZYX Philo, California
KEST San Francisco, California
KISQ San Francisco, California
KDIA Vallejo, California
KDYA Vallejo, California
KUBA Yuba City, California
KASF Alamosa, Colorado
KRTZ Cortez, Colorado
KVAY Lamar, Colorado
KSLV Monte Vista, Colorado
KVNF Paonia, Colorado
KGFT Pueblo, Colorado
WQTQ Hartford, Connecticut
WRTC-FM Hartford, Connecticut
WESU Middletown, Connecticut
WYBC-FM New Haven, Connecticut
WCNI New London, Connecticut
WKND Windsor, Connecticut
WHUR-FM Washington, District of Columbia
WAFL Milford, Delaware
WYBT Blountstown, Florida
WWPR Bradenton, Florida
WZEP De Funiak Springs, Florida
WRNE Gulf Breeze, Florida
WWAB Lakeland, Florida
WLBE Leesburg-Eustis, Florida
WQHL Live Oak, Florida
WMAF Madison, Florida
WTYS Marianna, Florida
WLTG Panama City, Florida
WTMY Sarasota, Florida
WANM Tallahassee, Florida
WQLC Watertown, Florida
WFLM White City, Florida
WZZS Zolfo Springs, Florida
WFSH-FM Athens, Georgia
WCLK Atlanta, Georgia
WTUF Boston, Georgia
WJTH Calhoun, Georgia
WZBN Camilla, Georgia
WDXQ Cochran, Georgia
WRDO Fitzgerald, Georgia
WJGA-FM Jackson, Georgia
WNEA Newnan, Georgia
WSBX Ochlocknee, Georgia
WPTB Statesboro, Georgia
WTHO-FM Thomson, Georgia
WGOV Valdosta, Georgia
WVLD Valdosta, Georgia
KSTO Agana, Guam
KROS Clinton, Iowa
KALA Davenport, Iowa
KHOE Fairfield, Iowa
KYTC Northwood, Iowa
KBOE Oskaloosa, Iowa
KIGC Oskaloosa, Iowa
KLEE Ottumwa, Iowa
KTLB Twin Lakes, Iowa
KWIK Pocatello, Idaho
WBGZ Alton, Illinois
WKRO Cairo, Illinois
WSSD Chicago, Illinois
WWHP Farmer City, Illinois
WJRE Galva, Illinois
WDCB Glen Ellyn, Illinois
WHPO Hoopeston, Illinois
WJOL Joliet, Illinois
WMXM Lake Forest, Illinois
WPNA Oak Park, Illinois
WVAZ Oak Park, Illinois
WNTA Rockford, Illinois
WPMB Vandalia, Illinois
WYKT Wilmington, Illinois
WBNL Boonville, Indiana
WIKL(FM) Elwood, Indiana
WFLQ French Lick, Indiana
WKAM Goshen, Indiana
WXLW Indianapolis, Indiana
WYXB Indianapolis, Indiana
WKPW Knightstown, Indiana
WMRS Monticello, Indiana
WRIN Rensselaer, Indiana
WTCJ Tell City, Indiana
WWVR West Terre Haute, Indiana
KDNS Downs, Kansas
KHAZ Hays, Kansas
KINZ Humboldt, Kansas
KWBW Hutchinson, Kansas
KNNS Larned, Kansas
KSDB-FM Manhattan, Kansas
KFNF Oberlin, Kansas
KKAN Phillipsburg, Kansas
KFRM Salina, Kansas
KSKG Salina, Kansas
KMUW Wichita, Kansas
WANY Albany, Kentucky
WLFX Berea, Kentucky
WHVO Hopkinsville, Kentucky
WLBN Lebanon, Kentucky
WFTM Maysville, Kentucky
WWAG McKee, Kentucky
WFXY Middlesboro, Kentucky
WMIK Middlesboro, Kentucky
WTHL Somerset, Kentucky
WTKY Tompkinsville, Kentucky
KRVV Bastrop, Louisiana
WFPR Hammond, Louisiana
KJLO-FM Monroe, Louisiana
WJIB Cambridge, Massachusetts
WAIC Springfield, Massachusetts
WEAA Baltimore, Maryland
WMTB-FM Emmitsburg, Maryland
WKHI Fruitland, Maryland
WAAI Hurlock, Maryland
WESM Princess Anne, Maryland
WGTO Cassopolis, Michigan
WDET-FM Detroit, Michigan
WDZZ-FM Flint, Michigan
WLCM Holt, Michigan
WVHF Kentwood, Michigan
WQUS Lapeer, Michigan
WTLZ Saginaw, Michigan
WMLM St. Louis, Michigan
KDUZ Hutchinson, Minnesota
KLQL Luverne, Minnesota
KYOO Bolivar, Missouri
KBFL-FM Buffalo, Missouri
KRLL California, Missouri
KMFC Centralia, Missouri
KOPN Columbia, Missouri
KUNQ Houston, Missouri
KTTK Lebanon, Missouri
KJAB-FM Mexico, Missouri
KGSP Parkville, Missouri
KMIS Portageville, Missouri
KWND Springfield, Missouri
KTTN-FM Trenton, Missouri
WWZQ Aberdeen, Mississippi
WAMY Amory, Mississippi
WESE Baldwyn, Mississippi
WBKN Brookhaven, Mississippi
WPAE Centreville, Mississippi
WCJU Columbia, Mississippi
WKRA Holly Springs, Mississippi
WKZU Iuka, Mississippi
WNAT Natchez, Mississippi
WNAU New Albany, Mississippi
WWZD-FM New Albany, Mississippi
WOXD Oxford, Mississippi
WSKK Ripley, Mississippi
WKXR Asheboro, North Carolina
WWNC Asheville, North Carolina
WGWG Boiling Springs, North Carolina
WATA Boone, North Carolina
WSQL Brevard, North Carolina
WFXK Bunn, North Carolina
WKYK Burnsville, North Carolina
WQOK Carrboro, North Carolina
WCLN Clinton, North Carolina
WPEG Concord, North Carolina
WCKB Dunn, North Carolina
WFXC Durham, North Carolina
WRVS-FM Elizabeth City, North Carolina
WBLA Elizabethtown, North Carolina
WFSS Fayetteville, North Carolina
WZRU Garysburg, North Carolina
WYCV Granite Falls, North Carolina
WNAA Greensboro, North Carolina
WTZQ Hendersonville, North Carolina
WLNC Laurinburg, North Carolina
WLON Lincolnton, North Carolina
WBRM Marion, North Carolina
WDJS Mount Olive, North Carolina
WIKS New Bern, North Carolina
WECR Newland, North Carolina
WGCR Pisgah Forest, North Carolina
WPJL Raleigh, North Carolina
WEGG Rose Hill, North Carolina
WRXO Roxboro, North Carolina
WNCA Siler City, North Carolina
WEEB Southern Pines, North Carolina
WACB Taylorsville, North Carolina
WKSK West Jefferson, North Carolina
WYNC Yanceyville, North Carolina
KABU Fort Totten, North Dakota
KXPO Grafton, North Dakota
KQLX Lisbon, North Dakota
KTGO Tioga, North Dakota
KINI Crookston, Nebraska
KUVR Holdrege, Nebraska
KRNU Lincoln, Nebraska
KZUM Lincoln, Nebraska
KRFS Superior, Nebraska
WJPG Cape May Court House, New Jersey
WTTH Margate City, New Jersey
WMVB Millville, New Jersey
WTSR Trenton, New Jersey
WMSC Upper Montclair, New Jersey
WJPH Woodbine, New Jersey
KATK Carlsbad, New Mexico
KIOT Los Lunas, New Mexico
KCEP Las Vegas, Nevada
WCDB Albany, New York
WROW Albany, New York
WXLH Blue Mountain Lake, New York
WSLU Canton, New York
WSIV E. Syracuse, New York
WEOS Geneva, New York
WVCR-FM Loudonville, New York
WDKX Rochester, New York
WRUR-FM Rochester, New York
WMYY Schoharie, New York
WAER Syracuse, New York
WHAZ Troy, New York
WRMU-FM Alliance, Ohio
WAIS Buchtel, Ohio

WCVX Cincinnati, Ohio
WEDI Eaton, Ohio
WWSU Fairborn, Ohio
WPOS-FM Holland, Ohio
WXMG London, Ohio
WMPO Middleport-Pomeroy, Ohio
WQIO Mount Vernon, Ohio
WNPQ New Philadelphia, Ohio
WDIG Steubenville, Ohio
WJUC Swanton, Ohio
WERT Van Wert, Ohio
WBZI Xenia, Ohio
KADA Ada, Oklahoma
KYFM Bartlesville, Oklahoma
KKBI Broken Bow, Oklahoma
KDDQ Comanche, Oklahoma
KTNT Eufaula, Oklahoma
KPRV-FM Heavener, Oklahoma
KIHN Hugo, Oklahoma
KFXI Marlow, Oklahoma
KTMC McAlester, Oklahoma
KXMX Muldrow, Oklahoma
KJKE Newcastle, Oklahoma
KRIG-FM Nowata, Oklahoma
KYLV Oklahoma City, Oklahoma
KFAQ Tulsa, Oklahoma
KAJO Grants Pass, Oregon
KGRV Winston, Oregon
KWBY Woodburn, Oregon
WWSM Annville-Cleona, Pennsylvania
WBVP Beaver Falls, Pennsylvania
WCHA Chambersburg, Pennsylvania
WCOH-FM Du Bois, Pennsylvania
WSKE Everett, Pennsylvania
WVMM Grantham, Pennsylvania
WTKT Harrisburg, Pennsylvania
WIUP-FM Indiana, Pennsylvania
WJSA Jersey Shore, Pennsylvania
WJSA-FM Jersey Shore, Pennsylvania
WNUZ Mercersburg, Pennsylvania
WQZS Meyersdale, Pennsylvania
WWBE Mifflinburg, Pennsylvania
WKDU Philadelphia, Pennsylvania
WURD Philadelphia, Pennsylvania
WUSL Philadelphia, Pennsylvania
WPHB Philipsburg, Pennsylvania
WPAM Pottsville, Pennsylvania
WBYO Sellersville, Pennsylvania
WHYF(AM) Shiremanstown, Pennsylvania
WBYX Stroudsburg, Pennsylvania
WZZD Warwick, Pennsylvania
WKZV Washington, Pennsylvania
WRLC Williamsport, Pennsylvania
WRIU Kingston, Rhode Island
WJMF Smithfield, Rhode Island
WZLA-FM Abbeville, South Carolina
WBT-FM Chester, South Carolina
WHSC Conway, South Carolina
WFIS Fountain Inn, South Carolina
WKMG Newberry, South Carolina
KLND Little Eagle, South Dakota
KBHB Sturgis, South Dakota
WATX Algood, Tennessee
WVOL Berry Hill, Tennessee
WFWL Camden, Tennessee
WHUB Cookeville, Tennessee
WZYX Cowan, Tennessee
WSDQ Dunlap, Tennessee
WEMB Erwin, Tennessee
WQQK Goodlettsville, Tennessee
WMYL Halls Crossroads, Tennessee
WTNK Hartsville, Tennessee
WFHU Henderson, Tennessee
WFKX Henderson, Tennessee
WHHM-FM Henderson, Tennessee
WMLR Hohenwald, Tennessee
WDXI Jackson, Tennessee
WLIL Lenoir City, Tennessee
WDXL Lexington, Tennessee
WLIV Livingston, Tennessee
WDIA Memphis, Tennessee
WTRB Ripley, Tennessee
WJLE Smithville, Tennessee
WEPG South Pittsburg, Tennessee
WDBL Springfield, Tennessee
WSGI Springfield, Tennessee
WSBI Static, Tennessee
WNTT Tazewell, Tennessee
KGNZ Abilene, Texas
KIXZ Amarillo, Texas
KAZI Austin, Texas
KQTY-FM Borger, Texas
KNTX Bowie, Texas
KLTR Brenham, Texas
KTAE Cameron, Texas
KCAR Clarksville, Texas
KSTA Coleman, Texas
KEOS College Station, Texas
KCOM Comanche, Texas
KSSM Copperas Cove, Texas
KBHT Crockett, Texas
KDDD-FM Dumas, Texas
KTEP El Paso, Texas
KNES Fairfield, Texas
KSWA Graham, Texas
KHBR Hillsboro, Texas
KHYI Howe, Texas
KOOK Junction, Texas
KRVL Kerrville, Texas
KTAI Kingsville, Texas
KLRK Mexia, Texas
KCKM Monahans, Texas
KJCS Nacogdoches, Texas
KPLT Paris, Texas
KHKZ San Benito, Texas
KXOX Sweetwater, Texas
KTBB Tyler, Texas
KVNE Tyler, Texas
KVWC Vernon, Texas
KALK Winfield, Texas
KWUD Woodville, Texas
KBLQ-FM Logan, Utah
KWCR-FM Ogden, Utah
WKDE Altavista, Virginia
WKDE-FM Altavista, Virginia
WTJU Charlottesville, Virginia
WKEY Covington, Virginia
WPAK Farmville, Virginia
WUKZ(AM) Marion, Virginia
WSIG Mount Jackson, Virginia
WVCV Orange, Virginia
WVST-FM Petersburg, Virginia
WKGM Smithfield, Virginia
WAJL South Boston, Virginia
WXLZ St. Paul, Virginia
WTZE Tazewell, Virginia
WMBG Williamsburg, Virginia
WYVE Wytheville, Virginia
WWOD Hartford, Vermont
WMNV Rupert, Vermont
WTWN Wells River, Vermont
KRKZ Forks, Washington
KNHC Seattle, Washington
KTCR Yakima, Washington
WATK Antigo, Wisconsin
WMCS Greenfield, Wisconsin
WKKV-FM Racine, Wisconsin
WRCO-FM Richland Center, Wisconsin
WRON-FM Lewisburg, West Virginia
WHAW Lost Creek, West Virginia
WELD-FM Moorefield, West Virginia
WVNT Parkersburg, West Virginia
WCWV Summersville, West Virginia
KJUA Cheyenne, Wyoming

Greek

WJOB Hammond, Indiana
WKTX Cortland, Ohio
WCCD Parma, Ohio
WEDO McKeesport, Pennsylvania
WKST New Castle, Pennsylvania
WBZK York, South Carolina
WUVT-FM Blacksburg, Virginia

Italian

WICC Bridgeport, Connecticut
WRYM New Britain, Connecticut
WWUH West Hartford, Connecticut
WDUV New Port Richey, Florida
WRTK Paxton, Illinois
WOSW Fulton, New York
WJTN Jamestown, New York
WRUC Schenectady, New York
WNIO Youngstown, Ohio
WFAX Falls Church, Virginia
WTCS Fairmont, West Virginia
WEIR Weirton, West Virginia

Japanese

KTYM Inglewood, California
KEST San Francisco, California
KCSB-FM Santa Barbara, California
KPUA Hilo, Hawaii
KWVA Eugene, Oregon

Jazz

KBRW Barrow, Alaska
KUAC Fairbanks, Alaska
KIYU Galena, Alaska
KBBI Homer, Alaska
KTOO Juneau, Alaska
KRBD Ketchikan, Alaska
KFSK Petersburg, Alaska
KSTK Wrangell, Alaska
WZEW Fairhope, Alabama
WJRL-FM Fort Rucker, Alabama
WMXB Tuscaloosa, Alabama
KEZA Fayetteville, Arkansas
KXRJ Russellville, Arkansas
KNOT Prescott, Arizona
KXCI Tucson, Arizona
KHSU Arcata, California
KPFA Berkeley, California
KHSR Crescent City, California
KHUM Cutten, California
KMUD Garberville, California
KFGY Healdsburg, California
KFJC Los Altos, California
KPFK Los Angeles, California
KMMT Mammoth Lakes, California
KSMC Moraga, California
KUCR Riverside, California
KZDG(AM) San Francisco, California
KNNN(FM) Shasta Lake City, California
KTHO South Lake Tahoe, California
KCLU-FM Thousand Oaks, California
KCSS Turlock, California
KRCB-FM Windsor, California
KASF Alamosa, Colorado
KGNU-FM Boulder, Colorado
KVCU Boulder, Colorado
KRCC Colorado Springs, Colorado
KDUR Durango, Colorado
KIQX Durango, Colorado
KCSU-FM Fort Collins, Colorado
KMSA Grand Junction, Colorado
KWSB-FM Gunnison, Colorado
KSUT Ignacio, Colorado
KFMU-FM Oak Creek, Colorado
KWUF-FM Pagosa Springs, Colorado
KVNF Paonia, Colorado
KOTO Telluride, Colorado
WPKN Bridgeport, Connecticut
WXCI Danbury, Connecticut
WQTQ Hartford, Connecticut
WZBG Litchfield, Connecticut
WYBC-FM New Haven, Connecticut
WCNI New London, Connecticut
WLIS Old Saybrook, Connecticut
WQQQ Sharon, Connecticut
WNHU West Haven, Connecticut
WECS Willimantic, Connecticut
WKND Windsor, Connecticut
WAMU Washington, District of Columbia
WVUD Newark, Delaware
WGMD Rehoboth Beach, Delaware
WKTO Edgewater, Florida
WJLF Gainesville, Florida
WXCV Homosassa Springs, Florida
WAVV Naples Park, Florida
WSBB New Smyrna Beach, Florida
WMFE-FM Orlando, Florida
WRXB St. Petersburg Beach, Florida
WANM Tallahassee, Florida
WFSU-FM Tallahassee, Florida
WFLM White City, Florida
WPRK Winter Park, Florida
WUGA Athens, Georgia
WREK Atlanta, Georgia
WNGH-FM Chatsworth, Georgia
WMUM-FM Cochran, Georgia
WNGU Dahlonega, Georgia
WPPR Demorest, Georgia
WJWV Fort Gaines, Georgia
WFXM Gordon, Georgia
WGPB Rome, Georgia
WWET Valdosta, Georgia
WJSP-FM Warm Springs, Georgia
WQGA Waycross, Georgia
WXVS Waycross, Georgia

KUAI Eleele, Hawaii
KMXG Clinton, Iowa
KROS Clinton, Iowa
KHOE Fairfield, Iowa
KRNL-FM Mount Vernon, Iowa
KOJI Okoboji, Iowa
KIGC Oskaloosa, Iowa
KSAS-FM Caldwell, Idaho
KBSM McCall, Idaho
KRFA-FM Moscow, Idaho
KUOI-FM Moscow, Idaho
KECH-FM Sun Valley, Idaho
WESN Bloomington, Illinois
WEIU Charleston, Illinois
WFMT Chicago, Illinois
WIIT Chicago, Illinois
WSSD Chicago, Illinois
WEPS Elgin, Illinois
WVKC Galesburg, Illinois
WCSF Joliet, Illinois
WMXM Lake Forest, Illinois
WLRA Lockport, Illinois
WIUM Macomb, Illinois
WIUS Macomb, Illinois
WRRG River Grove, Illinois
WVIK Rock Island, Illinois
WNNS Springfield, Illinois
WGRE Greencastle, Indiana
WNTR Indianapolis, Indiana
WSND-FM Notre Dame, Indiana
WMHD-FM Terre Haute, Indiana
WVUR-FM Valparaiso, Indiana
KNBU Baldwin City, Kansas
KAHS El Dorado, Kansas
KANZ Garden City, Kansas
KZNA Hill City, Kansas
KSDB-FM Manhattan, Kansas
KMUW Wichita, Kansas
KRBB Wichita, Kansas
WKUE Elizabethtown, Kentucky
WMKY Morehead, Kentucky
WDCL-FM Somerset, Kentucky
KLSP Angola, Louisiana
KGRM Grambling, Louisiana
WAMQ Great Barrington, Massachusetts
WHBA Lynn, Massachusetts
WBSL-FM Sheffield, Massachusetts
WYAJ Sudbury, Massachusetts
WMVY Tisbury, Massachusetts
WCHC Worcester, Massachusetts
WLIF Baltimore, Maryland
WHFC Bel Air, Maryland
WARK Hagerstown, Maryland
WBQW Kennebunkport, Maine
WXEX-FM Sanford, Maine
WBQX Thomaston, Maine
WMHB Waterville, Maine
WHFR Dearborn, Michigan
WDET-FM Detroit, Michigan
WKAR-FM East Lansing, Michigan
WVHF Kentwood, Michigan
WUPX Marquette, Michigan
WRKR Portage, Michigan
KFAI Minneapolis, Minnesota
KVSC St. Cloud, Minnesota
KCFV Ferguson, Missouri
KKFI Kansas City, Missouri
KGSP Parkville, Missouri
KMST Rolla, Missouri
KBFL Springfield, Missouri
KSMU Springfield, Missouri
KMOX St. Louis, Missouri
WGNL Greenwood, Mississippi
KMSM-FM Butte, Montana
WSQL Brevard, North Carolina
WFXK Bunn, North Carolina
WXDU Durham, North Carolina
WRVS-FM Elizabeth City, North Carolina
WZRU Garysburg, North Carolina
WKNS Kinston, North Carolina
WIKS New Bern, North Carolina
WTEB New Bern, North Carolina
WNNC Newton, North Carolina
WLHC Robbins, North Carolina
WNCW Spindale, North Carolina
WFDD Winston-Salem, North Carolina
KIOS-FM Omaha, Nebraska
KKCD Omaha, Nebraska
KWSC Wayne, Nebraska
WUNH Durham, New Hampshire
WKNH Keene, New Hampshire
WDER-FM Peterborough, New Hampshire
WPCR-FM Plymouth, New Hampshire
WDVR Delaware Township, New Jersey
WBZC Pemberton, New Jersey
WLFR Pomona, New Jersey
WTSR Trenton, New Jersey
WMSC Upper Montclair, New Jersey
WPSC-FM Wayne, New Jersey
WMCX West Long Branch, New Jersey
KKTC Angel Fire, New Mexico
KSJE Farmington, New Mexico
KGLP Gallup, New Mexico
KTAO Taos, New Mexico
KCEP Las Vegas, Nevada
KNEV Reno, Nevada
WAMC-FM Albany, New York
WCDB Albany, New York
WVIN-FM Bath, New York
WHRW Binghamton, New York
WSKG-FM Binghamton, New York
WXLH Blue Mountain Lake, New York
WBNY Buffalo, New York
WCAN Canajoharie, New York
WSLU Canton, New York
WHCL-FM Clinton, New York
WKGB-FM Conklin, New York
WSQE Corning, New York
WRCU-FM Hamilton, New York
WITR Henrietta, New York
WICB Ithaca, New York
WSQG-FM Ithaca, New York
WAMK Kingston, New York
WOSR Middletown, New York
WRHO Oneonta, New York
WSQC-FM Oneonta, New York
WZOZ Oneonta, New York
WCEL Plattsburgh, New York
WRHV Poughkeepsie, New York
WDKX Rochester, New York
WRUR-FM Rochester, New York
WFNP Rosendale, New York
WMHT-FM Schenectady, New York
WRUC Schenectady, New York
WSFW Seneca Falls, New York
WKWZ Syosset, New York
WCNY-FM Syracuse, New York
WANC Ticonderoga, New York
WPNR-FM Utica, New York
WUNY Utica, New York
WJNY Watertown, New York
WRIP Windham, New York
WRDL Ashland, Ohio
WGBE Bryan, Ohio
WCBE Columbus, Ohio
WGDE Defiance, Ohio
WWSU Fairborn, Ohio
WRBP Hubbard, Ohio
WVKO-FM Johnstown, Ohio
WCIT(AM) Lima, Ohio
WGLE Lima, Ohio
WCLV Lorain, Ohio
WMCO New Concord, Ohio
WLFC North Baltimore, Ohio
WUSO Springfield, Ohio
WGTE-FM Toledo, Ohio
WRVF Toledo, Ohio
WYSO Yellow Springs, Ohio
KRSC-FM Claremore, Oklahoma
KBZQ Lawton, Oklahoma
KCCU Lawton, Oklahoma
KGOU Norman, Oklahoma
KZBB Poteau, Oklahoma
KOAC Corvallis, Oregon
KEOL La Grande, Oregon
KLRR Redmond, Oregon
WLVR-FM Bethlehem, Pennsylvania
WMKX Brookville, Pennsylvania
WDCV-FM Carlisle, Pennsylvania
WDNR Chester, Pennsylvania
WCUC-FM Clarion, Pennsylvania
WESS East Stroudsburg, Pennsylvania
WJRH Easton, Pennsylvania
WMCE Erie, Pennsylvania
WZBT Gettysburg, Pennsylvania
WKVR-FM Huntingdon, Pennsylvania
WPSX Kane, Pennsylvania
WFNM Lancaster, Pennsylvania
WVBU-FM Lewisburg, Pennsylvania
WNTE Mansfield, Pennsylvania
WARC Meadville, Pennsylvania
WIXQ Millersville, Pennsylvania
WVLY-FM Milton, Pennsylvania
WHYY-FM Philadelphia, Pennsylvania
WRCT Pittsburgh, Pennsylvania
WRCT(FM) Pittsburgh, Pennsylvania
WVMW-FM Scranton, Pennsylvania
WSYC-FM Shippensburg, Pennsylvania
WKPS State College, Pennsylvania
WPSU State College, Pennsylvania
WRDV Warminster, Pennsylvania
WPTC Williamsport, Pennsylvania
WVYC York, Pennsylvania
WWNA Aguadilla, Puerto Rico
WUKQ-FM Mayaguez, Puerto Rico
WBRU Providence, Rhode Island
WEGX Dillon, South Carolina
WYNN Florence, South Carolina
WLGI Hemingway, South Carolina
WSSB-FM Orangeburg, South Carolina
WSPA-FM Spartanburg, South Carolina
KSDJ Brookings, South Dakota
KCSD Sioux Falls, South Dakota
WAPX-FM Clarksville, Tennessee
WTTU Cookeville, Tennessee
WFHU Henderson, Tennessee
WEVL Memphis, Tennessee
WMTS-FM Murfreesboro, Tennessee
WUTS Sewanee, Tennessee
KACU Abilene, Texas
KACV-FM Amarillo, Texas
KWTS Canyon, Texas
KEOS College Station, Texas
KNNK Dimmitt, Texas
KODA Houston, Texas
KTRU(FM) Houston, Texas
KFAN-FM Johnson City, Texas
KNCT-FM Killeen, Texas
KMND Midland, Texas
KXWT Odessa, Texas
KQXT-FM San Antonio, Texas
KSTX San Antonio, Texas
KTXK Texarkana, Texas
KWBU-FM Waco, Texas
KBLQ-FM Logan, Utah
KPCW Park City, Utah
WWHS-FM Hampden-Sydney, Virginia
WXJM Harrisonburg, Virginia
WVRU-FM Radford, Virginia
WVCE-FM Richmond, Virginia
WDCE Richmond, Virginia
WCWM Williamsburg, Virginia
WISE-FM Wise, Virginia
WIUJ Charlotte Amalie, Virgin Islands
WIUV Castleton, Vermont
WWLR Lyndonville, Vermont
WEQX Manchester, Vermont
WRMC-FM Middlebury, Vermont
WNCS Montpelier, Vermont
KNWR Ellensburg, Washington
KSER Everett, Washington
KGHP Gig Harbor, Washington
KBRD Lacey, Washington
KWSU Pullman, Washington
KZUU Pullman, Washington
KFAE-FM Richland, Washington
KUOW-FM Seattle, Washington
KAGU Spokane, Washington
KPBX-FM Spokane, Washington
KUPS Tacoma, Washington
WHSA Brule, Wisconsin
WBSD Burlington, Wisconsin
WPNE-FM Green Bay, Wisconsin
WVSS Menomonie, Wisconsin
WMSE Milwaukee, Wisconsin
WSUP Platteville, Wisconsin
WOJB Reserve, Wisconsin
WXPR Rhinelander, Wisconsin
KUWS Superior, Wisconsin
WSUW Whitewater, Wisconsin
WVWC Buckhannon, West Virginia
WQAB Philippi, West Virginia
WPHP Wheeling, West Virginia
KUWA Afton, Wyoming
KUWJ Jackson, Wyoming
KUWR Laramie, Wyoming
KUWZ Rock Springs, Wyoming

Korean

WNKJ Hopkinsville, Kentucky

Light Rock

KTNA Talkeetna, Alaska

Native American

KRUA Anchorage, Alaska
KCAM Glennallen, Alaska
KDLL Kenai, Alaska
KIAM Nenana, Alaska
KABF Little Rock, Arkansas
KNNB Whiteriver, Arizona
KTNN Window Rock, Arizona
KZFR Chico, California
KFCF Fresno, California
KIDE Hoopa, California
KPSI Palm Springs, California
KCSB-FM Santa Barbara, California
KDUR Durango, Colorado
KSUT Ignacio, Colorado
KWIK Pocatello, Idaho
KUEV Evansville, Indiana
WCUP L'Anse, Michigan
WNMC-FM Traverse City, Michigan
KBSB Bemidji, Minnesota
KGVA Fort Belknap Agency, Montana
KEYA Belcourt, North Dakota
KCND Bismarck, North Dakota
KDPR Dickinson, North Dakota
KABU Fort Totten, North Dakota
KMHA Four Bears, North Dakota
KPRJ Jamestown, North Dakota
KMPR Minot, North Dakota
KPPR Williston, North Dakota
KINI Crookston, Nebraska
WNEC-FM Henniker, New Hampshire
KYVA-FM Church Rock, New Mexico
KGLX Gallup, New Mexico
KOAZ Isleta, New Mexico
KTDB Ramah, New Mexico
KXTC Thoreau, New Mexico
KSFR White Rock, New Mexico
WYBG Massena, New York
WNTO Racine, Ohio
KIXR Ponca City, Oklahoma
KIRC Seminole, Oklahoma
KOSU Stillwater, Oklahoma
KWSH Wewoka, Oklahoma
KRVM-FM Eugene, Oregon
KTEC Klamath Falls, Oregon
KOLY Mobridge, South Dakota
KTSD-FM Reliance, South Dakota
KBHB Sturgis, South Dakota
KAOR Vermillion, South Dakota
KUSD Vermillion, South Dakota
KOOP Hornsby, Texas
KZMU Moab, Utah
KRCL Salt Lake City, Utah
WUVT-FM Blacksburg, Virginia
KSER Everett, Washington
KAOS Olympia, Washington
KSFC Spokane, Washington
KYNR Toppenish, Washington
WPNE-FM Green Bay, Wisconsin
WHND Sister Bay, Wisconsin

News

KFBX Fairbanks, Alaska
WOOF-FM Dothan, Alabama
WBPT Homewood, Alabama
WJOU Huntsville, Alabama
WVAS Montgomery, Alabama
WOPP Opp, Alabama
WVNA Tuscumbia, Alabama
KDXE North Little Rock, Arkansas
KBHR Big Bear City, California
KWXY(FM) Cathedral City, California
KHWZ Ludlow, California
KRZA Alamosa, Colorado
KFTM Fort Morgan, Colorado
WOCL Deland, Florida
WOLZ Fort Myers, Florida
WRZN Hernando, Florida
WRGP Homestead, Florida
WCNK Key West, Florida
WONN Lakeland, Florida
WVOI Marco Island, Florida
WOCA Ocala, Florida
WOGK Ocala, Florida
WOKC Okeechobee, Florida
WGHC Clayton, Georgia
WGHC(AM) Clayton, Georgia
WNGA Clermont, Georgia
WWWE Hapeville, Georgia
WLHR-FM Lavonia, Georgia
WALH Mountain City, Georgia
WGMI(FM) Thomasville, Georgia
WOBB Tifton, Georgia
KLGA Algona, Iowa
WOI-FM Ames, Iowa
KIFG-FM Iowa Falls, Iowa
KTFC Sioux City, Iowa
KID Idaho Falls, Idaho
KID-FM Idaho Falls, Idaho
KITT Soda Springs, Idaho
WILY Centralia, Illinois
WPCD Champaign, Illinois
WCGO Evanston, Illinois
WHFH Flossmoor, Illinois
WLTL La Grange, Illinois
WNVR Vernon Hills, Illinois
WBIW Bedford, Indiana
WUZR Bicknell, Indiana
WOCC Corydon, Indiana
WGCS Goshen, Indiana
WORX-FM Madison, Indiana
WSVX Shelbyville, Indiana
WWVR West Terre Haute, Indiana
KCFN Wichita, Kansas
WTUK Harlan, Kentucky
WKMO Lebanon Junction, Kentucky
WFLW Monticello, Kentucky
WCBR Richmond, Kentucky
WODT New Orleans, Louisiana
WOMR Provincetown, Massachusetts
WORC-FM Webster, Massachusetts
WOLB Baltimore, Maryland
WOCQ Berlin, Maryland
WKIK La Plata, Maryland
WSMD-FM Mechanicsville, Maryland
WOLW Cadillac, Michigan
WNWN-FM Coldwater, Michigan
WOMC Detroit, Michigan
WOOD Grand Rapids, Michigan
WOLV Houghton, Michigan
WOCR Olivet, Michigan
WNWN Portage, Michigan
KMAM Butler, Missouri
KMRN Cameron, Missouri
KBNN Lebanon, Missouri
KCXL Liberty, Missouri
KWWR Mexico, Missouri
KSIM Sikeston, Missouri
KRWP Stockton, Missouri
WJNS-FM Bentonia, Mississippi
WQNQ Fletcher, North Carolina
WPLW Hillsborough, North Carolina
WCBQ Oxford, North Carolina
WMPM Smithfield, North Carolina
KHND Harvey, North Dakota
KLIQ Hastings, Nebraska
WSNJ Bridgeton, New Jersey
WOBM Lakewood Township, New Jersey
WJSV Morristown, New Jersey
KCKN Roswell, New Mexico
KDSS Ely, Nevada
WBAZ Bridgehampton, New York
WITC Cazenovia, New York
WKCR-FM New York, New York
WNYC-FM New York, New York
WNYU-FM New York, New York
WJJL Niagara Falls, New York
WOLN Olean, New York
WJZR Rochester, New York
WFNP Rosendale, New York
WOKN Southport, New York
WCII Spencer, New York
WNYR-FM Waterloo, New York
WNYV Whitehall, New York
WONB Ada, Ohio
WRMU-FM Alliance, Ohio
WOMP Bellaire, Ohio
WOHC Chillicothe, Ohio
WONE Dayton, Ohio
WNWV Elyria, Ohio
WRBP Hubbard, Ohio
WCLV Lorain, Ohio
WOBC-FM Oberlin, Ohio
WOBL Oberlin, Ohio
WNXT Portsmouth, Ohio
WNXT-FM Portsmouth, Ohio
KGFY Stillwater, Oklahoma
KSPI Stillwater, Oklahoma
KMHD Gresham, Oregon
KSZN(AM) Gresham, Oregon
KYKN Keizer, Oregon
KBNP Portland, Oregon
WOKW Curwensville, Pennsylvania
WESS East Stroudsburg, Pennsylvania
WOGL Philadelphia, Pennsylvania
WIVV Island of Vieques, Puerto Rico
CFVM-1 Causapscal, Quebec
WLXC Columbia, South Carolina
WOLH Florence, South Carolina
WHYM Lake City, South Carolina
WOLI Spartanburg, South Carolina
WALI Walterboro, South Carolina
WKQK Germantown, Tennessee
WNWS-FM Jackson, Tennessee
WOCV Oneida, Tennessee
WIHG Rockwood, Tennessee
KORA-FM Bryan, Texas
KTAM Bryan, Texas
KCYL Lampasas, Texas
KRFE Lubbock, Texas
WOAI San Antonio, Texas
KSUU Cedar City, Utah
WODI Brookneal, Virginia
WNVZ Norfolk, Virginia
WNVA Norton, Virginia
WNVA-FM Norton, Virginia
WVCV Orange, Virginia
WHEO Stuart, Virginia
WJJR Rutland, Vermont
KASB Bellevue, Washington
KQQQ Pullman, Washington
WOLX-FM Baraboo, Wisconsin
WORQ Green Bay, Wisconsin
WOGO Hallie, Wisconsin
WGLR Lancaster, Wisconsin
WGLR-FM Lancaster, Wisconsin
WNWC-FM Madison, Wisconsin
WORT Madison, Wisconsin
WOMT Manitowoc, Wisconsin
WOKY Milwaukee, Wisconsin
WOBT Rhinelander, Wisconsin
KUWJ Jackson, Wyoming
KMER Kemmerer, Wyoming
KUWR Laramie, Wyoming
KUWZ Rock Springs, Wyoming

News/Talk

WMBV Dixons Mills, Alabama
KIXF Baker, California
KGEO Bakersfield, California
KGBA-FM Holtville, California
KOSS Lancaster, California
KFWB Los Angeles, California
KTOX Needles, California
KVEC San Luis Obispo, California
KGLN Glenwood Springs, Colorado
WILM Wilmington, Delaware
WOTS Kissimmee, Florida
WPBR Lantana, Florida
WWWE Hapeville, Georgia
KFXD Boise, Idaho
WHFH Flossmoor, Illinois
KCFN Wichita, Kansas
WFLW Monticello, Kentucky
KNGT Lake Charles, Louisiana
KKWK Cameron, Missouri
KCMO Kansas City, Missouri
KADI Springfield, Missouri
WQNQ Fletcher, North Carolina
WCBQ Oxford, North Carolina
WMPM Smithfield, North Carolina
WJSV Morristown, New Jersey
WITC Cazenovia, New York
WJJL Niagara Falls, New York
WRMU-FM Alliance, Ohio
WONW Defiance, Ohio
KGWA Enid, Oklahoma
KKBS Guymon, Oklahoma
KBNP Portland, Oregon
KPAM Troutdale, Oregon
WESS East Stroudsburg, Pennsylvania
KBFM Edinburg, Texas
KRFE Lubbock, Texas
KAMX Luling, Texas
WFNR Blacksburg, Virginia
WVBW Suffolk, Virginia
KEDO Longview, Washington

KMER Kemmerer, Wyoming

Oldies

KRSA Petersburg, Alaska
WJRL-FM Fort Rucker, Alabama
WJAB Huntsville, Alabama
KEZA Fayetteville, Arkansas
KSPB Pebble Beach, California
KCWH Weed, California
WQQQ Sharon, Connecticut
WPFW Washington, District of Columbia
WXCV Homosassa Springs, Florida
WMAF Madison, Florida
WGOV Valdosta, Georgia
KMRY Cedar Rapids, Iowa
KCMR Mason City, Iowa
WQUB Quincy, Illinois
WRRG River Grove, Illinois
WKLU Brownsburg, Indiana
WCYT Lafayette Township, Indiana
WXLO Fitchburg, Massachusetts
WEAA Baltimore, Maryland
WKHS Worton, Maryland
WMRX-FM Beaverton, Michigan
WMPX Midland, Michigan
KASM Albany, Minnesota
KXLP Eagle Lake, Minnesota
KNUJ New Ulm, Minnesota
KOLV Olivia, Minnesota
KCHR Charleston, Missouri
KGBX-FM Nixa, Missouri
WVSD Itta Bena, Mississippi
KPRK Livingston, Montana
WLTT Bolivia, North Carolina
WERX-FM Columbia, North Carolina
WZRU Garysburg, North Carolina
WIXE Monroe, North Carolina
KFYR Bismarck, North Dakota
KLIR Columbus, Nebraska
WDVR Delaware Township, New Jersey
KFUN Las Vegas, New Mexico
WVBR-FM Ithaca, New York
WDOS Oneonta, New York
WZOZ Oneonta, New York
WALK-FM Patchogue, New York
WSFW Seneca Falls, New York
WDLA Walton, New York
WRDL Ashland, Ohio
WMBA Ambridge, Pennsylvania
WMKX Brookville, Pennsylvania
WCCS Homer City, Pennsylvania
WLSH Lansford, Pennsylvania
WMNY McKeesport, Pennsylvania
WJAS Pittsburgh, Pennsylvania
WARM Scranton, Pennsylvania
WMGH-FM Tamaqua, Pennsylvania
WYKZ Beaufort, South Carolina
WMXT Pamplico, South Carolina
WSPA-FM Spartanburg, South Carolina
WEGR Arlington, Tennessee
WWLX Lawrenceburg, Tennessee
KULL Abilene, Texas
KFYN Bonham, Texas
KJAS Jasper, Texas
KLSR-FM Memphis, Texas
WEVA Emporia, Virginia
WTSA-FM Brattleboro, Vermont
WIZN Vergennes, Vermont
KITI Chehalis-Centralia, Washington
WECL Elk Mound, Wisconsin
WLKG Lake Geneva, Wisconsin
WFGH Fort Gay, West Virginia

Polish

KCAA Loma Linda, California
WTMY Sarasota, Florida
KZAT-FM Belle Plaine, Iowa
KSKB Brooklyn, Iowa
KMRY Cedar Rapids, Iowa
KDSN Denison, Iowa
KMAQ Maquoketa, Iowa
KLEE Ottumwa, Iowa
WLUV Loves Park, Illinois
WPNA Oak Park, Illinois
WTAY Robinson, Illinois
KRSL Russell, Kansas
WNBH New Bedford, Massachusetts
WHMP Northampton, Massachusetts
WBRK Pittsfield, Massachusetts
WARE Ware, Massachusetts
WIBM Jackson, Michigan
WCUP L'Anse, Michigan
WMTE-FM Manistee, Michigan
WNBY Newberry, Michigan
WUPY Ontonagon, Michigan
WYGR Wyoming, Michigan
KRBT Eveleth, Minnesota
WMFG Hibbing, Minnesota
KDUZ Hutchinson, Minnesota
KLTF Little Falls, Minnesota
WNMT Nashwauk, Minnesota
KWNO Winona, Minnesota
KHND Harvey, North Dakota
KTTT Columbus, Nebraska
WGHT Pompton Lakes, New Jersey
WCVF-FM Fredonia, New York
WKNY Kingston, New York
WXRL Lancaster, New York
WVCR-FM Loudonville, New York
WTLA North Syracuse, New York
WSGO Oswego, New York
WZIP Akron, Ohio
WKTX Cortland, Ohio
WSTV Steubenville, Ohio
WWYC Toledo, Ohio
WELW Willoughby, Ohio
WKBN Youngstown, Ohio
WVAM Altoona, Pennsylvania
WMBA Ambridge, Pennsylvania
WWSM Annville-Cleona, Pennsylvania
WBVP Beaver Falls, Pennsylvania
WGPA Bethlehem, Pennsylvania
WHYL Carlisle, Pennsylvania
WERG Erie, Pennsylvania
WMCE Erie, Pennsylvania
WQFM Forest City, Pennsylvania
WLMI(FM) Kane/Bradford, Pennsylvania
WMNY McKeesport, Pennsylvania
WPHB Philipsburg, Pennsylvania
WYCK Plains, Pennsylvania
WECZ Punxsutawney, Pennsylvania
WHYF(AM) Shiremanstown, Pennsylvania
WCDW Susquehanna, Pennsylvania
WMGH-FM Tamaqua, Pennsylvania
WMBS Uniontown, Pennsylvania
WKZV Washington, Pennsylvania
KYNT Yankton, South Dakota
WMTS-FM Murfreesboro, Tennessee
KWHI Brenham, Texas
KULM-FM Columbus, Texas
KNAF Fredericksburg, Texas
KANI Wharton, Texas
KYKM Yoakum, Texas
WDKM Adams, Wisconsin
WLDY Ladysmith, Wisconsin
WCCN Neillsville, Wisconsin
WVRQ Viroqua, Wisconsin
WSAU Wausau, Wisconsin

Portugese

KSTN-FM Redding, California
WSAR Fall River, Massachusetts
WPHE Phoenixville, Pennsylvania

Public Affairs

KAGV Big Lake, Alaska
KGHR Tuba City, Arizona
KNCA Burney, California
KCRH Hayward, California
KYSR Los Angeles, California
KNSQ Mount Shasta, California
KTYD Santa Barbara, California
KIMN Denver, Colorado
KJJD Windsor, Colorado
WESU Middletown, Connecticut
WILM Wilmington, Delaware
WSTW Wilmington, Delaware
WXTB Clearwater, Florida
WIRA Fort Pierce, Florida
WHKR Rockledge, Florida
WWFR Stuart, Florida
WVOP Vidalia, Georgia
KUUL East Moline, Illinois
WFXN Moline, Illinois
WVAZ Oak Park, Illinois
WSNE-FM Taunton, Massachusetts
WCCY Houghton, Michigan
KQAL Winona, Minnesota
WHHL Hazelwood, Missouri
KCMO Kansas City, Missouri
WWOL Forest City, North Carolina
WKRK Murphy, North Carolina
WHCY Blairstown, New Jersey
WBJB-FM Lincroft, New Jersey
WRPR Mahwah, New Jersey
WTOC Newton, New Jersey
WSOU South Orange, New Jersey
KNCC Elko, Nevada
KSNE-FM Las Vegas, Nevada
KNEV Reno, Nevada
WBSU Brockport, New York
WJYE Buffalo, New York
WNED Buffalo, New York
WAQX-FM Manlius, New York
WDFH Ossining, New York
WUMX Rome, New York
WPPB Southampton, New York
WARY Valhalla, New York
WRQN Bowling Green, Ohio
WKKY Geneva, Ohio
WFCO Lancaster, Ohio
KJSR Tulsa, Oklahoma
KSMF Ashland, Oregon
KSOR Ashland, Oregon
KQAK Bend, Oregon
KSBA Coos Bay, Oregon
KSKF Klamath Falls, Oregon
KLTW-FM Prineville, Oregon
KWPK-FM Sisters, Oregon
KWLZ-FM West Linn, Oregon
WWCH Clarion, Pennsylvania
WSJR Dallas, Pennsylvania
WQLN-FM Erie, Pennsylvania
WIOQ Philadelphia, Pennsylvania
WXTU Philadelphia, Pennsylvania
WSHH Pittsburgh, Pennsylvania
WAGS Bishopville, South Carolina
WKHT Knoxville, Tennessee
KTBZ-FM Houston, Texas
KSWP Lufkin, Texas
KAMX Luling, Texas
KNTU McKinney, Texas
KKYX San Antonio, Texas
KQXT-FM San Antonio, Texas
KVEL Vernal, Utah
WMOO Derby Center, Vermont
WIKE Newport, Vermont
WJJR Rutland, Vermont
KEDO Longview, Washington
WHID Green Bay, Wisconsin
WWSP Stevens Point, Wisconsin

Reggae

WJAB Huntsville, Alabama
KSPC Claremont, California
KSBR Mission Viejo, California
KSPB Pebble Beach, California
KCSB-FM Santa Barbara, California
KSMT Breckenridge, Colorado
KRCC Colorado Springs, Colorado
KWSB-FM Gunnison, Colorado
KTCL Wheat Ridge, Colorado
WXCI Danbury, Connecticut
WIIS Key West, Florida
WFCF St. Augustine, Florida
WANM Tallahassee, Florida
WFLM White City, Florida
WCLK Atlanta, Georgia
WRAS Atlanta, Georgia
KWXX-FM Hilo, Hawaii
WNUR-FM Evanston, Illinois
WSND-FM Notre Dame, Indiana
KJHK Lawrence, Kansas
WLNZ Lansing, Michigan
WVSD Itta Bena, Mississippi
WNAA Greensboro, North Carolina
WVOD Manteo, North Carolina
KKCD Omaha, Nebraska
WBZC Pemberton, New Jersey
WBNY Buffalo, New York
WCVF-FM Fredonia, New York
WEOS Geneva, New York
WITR Henrietta, New York
WICB Ithaca, New York
WPNR-FM Utica, New York
WDUB Granville, Ohio
WVKO-FM Johnstown, Ohio
KEOL La Grande, Oregon
WLVR-FM Bethlehem, Pennsylvania
WJRH Easton, Pennsylvania

WRIU Kingston, Rhode Island
WSSB-FM Orangeburg, South Carolina
KAZI Austin, Texas
KTRU(FM) Houston, Texas
KTSU Houston, Texas
WWHS-FM Hampden-Sydney, Virginia
WHOV Hampton, Virginia
WCWM Williamsburg, Virginia
WIUV Castleton, Vermont
WIZN Vergennes, Vermont
KGHP Gig Harbor, Washington
WBSD Burlington, Wisconsin
WWVU-FM Morgantown, West Virginia

Religious

KHAR Anchorage, Alaska
KYMG Anchorage, Alaska
KBRW Barrow, Alaska
KBKO Kodiak, Alaska
KNOM Nome, Alaska
WKNU Brewton, Alabama
WVPL Dozier, Alabama
WKWL Florala, Alabama
WBFA Fort Mitchell, Alabama
WZOB Fort Payne, Alabama
WRTT-FM Huntsville, Alabama
WLJS-FM Jacksonville, Alabama
WEUP-FM Moulton, Alabama
WGOL Russellville, Alabama
WKEA-FM Scottsboro, Alabama
WTBC Tuscaloosa, Alabama
KMJI Ashdown, Arkansas
KEWI Benton, Arkansas
KLYR Clarksville, Arkansas
KAVV Benson, Arizona
KCUZ Clifton, Arizona
KFYI Phoenix, Arizona
KTKT Tucson, Arizona
KISV Bakersfield, California
KSSB Calipatria, California
KRXA Carmel Valley, California
KCNQ Kernville, California
KLBS Los Banos, California
KDUQ Ludlow, California
KSMC Moraga, California
KAAT Oakhurst, California
KWKU Pomona, California
KVML Sonora, California
KSTN Stockton, California
KSUE Susanville, California
KXPS Thousand Palms, California
KDIA Vallejo, California
KDYA Vallejo, California
KFSO-FM Visalia, California
KUBA Yuba City, California
KSJD Cortez, Colorado
KGLN Glenwood Springs, Colorado
KFKA Greeley, Colorado
KUBC Montrose, Colorado
KCRT Trinidad, Colorado
KSPK-FM Walsenburg, Colorado
KCOL Wellington, Colorado
WECS Willimantic, Connecticut
WILI Willimantic, Connecticut
WJWL Georgetown, Delaware
WYUS Milford, Delaware
WGMD Rehoboth Beach, Delaware
WSTW Wilmington, Delaware
WYBT Blountstown, Florida
WWPR Bradenton, Florida
WLQH Chiefland, Florida
WVUM Coral Gables, Florida
WHNR Cypress Gardens, Florida
WNDB Daytona Beach, Florida
WMGG Egypt Lake, Florida
WENG Englewood, Florida
WIRA Fort Pierce, Florida
WEDM(AM) Fort Walton Beach, Florida
WWRF Lake Worth, Florida
WQHL Live Oak, Florida
WARO Naples, Florida
WPSO New Port Richey, Florida
WHIF Palatka, Florida
WIYD Palatka, Florida
WFLF-FM Parker, Florida
WCOA Pensacola, Florida
WPSL Port St. Lucie, Florida
WSDO Sanford, Florida
WSIR Winter Haven, Florida
WJTH Calhoun, Georgia
WCLA Claxton, Georgia
WBLJ Dalton, Georgia
WDMG Douglas, Georgia
WPLA Dry Branch, Georgia
WAEG Evans, Georgia
WMAC Macon, Georgia
WHKN Millen, Georgia
WNEA Newnan, Georgia
WTHO-FM Thomson, Georgia
WVOP Vidalia, Georgia
KCQQ Davenport, Iowa
KILR Estherville, Iowa
KNOD Harlan, Iowa
KNIA Knoxville, Iowa
KMCH Manchester, Iowa
KFJB Marshalltown, Iowa
KRIB Mason City, Iowa
KYTC Northwood, Iowa
KICD Spencer, Iowa
KTLB Twin Lakes, Iowa
KXEL Waterloo, Iowa
KFXD Boise, Idaho
KVNI Coeur D'Alene, Idaho
KVSI Montpelier, Idaho
KRPL Moscow, Idaho
KIDO Nampa, Idaho
KWIK Pocatello, Idaho
KSPT Sandpoint, Idaho
KTFI Wendell, Idaho
WRMJ Aledo, Illinois
WBGZ Alton, Illinois
WBIG Aurora, Illinois
WDWS Champaign, Illinois
KSGM Chester, Illinois
WIIT Chicago, Illinois
WDKB Dekalb, Illinois
WDQN Duquoin, Illinois
WAIK Galesburg, Illinois
WGIL Galesburg, Illinois
WLSR Galesburg, Illinois
WKYX-FM Golconda, Illinois
WJBM Jerseyville, Illinois
WKEI Kewanee, Illinois
WLBH Mattoon, Illinois
WMOK Metropolis, Illinois
WRAM Monmouth, Illinois
WDQX Morton, Illinois
WINI Murphysboro, Illinois
WLCE Petersburg, Illinois
WKXQ Rushville, Illinois
WJBD Salem, Illinois
WHCO Sparta, Illinois
WTIM-FM Taylorville, Illinois
WRAN Tower Hill, Illinois
WZSR Woodstock, Illinois
WQME Anderson, Indiana
WIFE Connersville, Indiana
WBYT Elkhart, Indiana
WFLQ French Lick, Indiana
WTRE Greensburg, Indiana
WJOB Hammond, Indiana
WXGO Madison, Indiana
WEFM Michigan City, Indiana
WLTI(AM) New Castle, Indiana
WTCA Plymouth, Indiana
WRIN Rensselaer, Indiana
WROI Rochester, Indiana
WZZB Seymour, Indiana
WSBT South Bend, Indiana
WCLS Spencer, Indiana
WCJC Van Buren, Indiana
KABI Abilene, Kansas
KSNP Burlington, Kansas
KVGB Great Bend, Kansas
KFBZ Haysville, Kansas
KHOK Hoisington, Kansas
KNNS Larned, Kansas
KLWN Lawrence, Kansas
KNGL McPherson, Kansas
KLKC Parsons, Kansas
KLEY Wellington, Kansas
WMMG Brandenburg, Kentucky
WFKN Franklin, Kentucky
WHVO Hopkinsville, Kentucky
WRNZ Lancaster, Kentucky
WKYL Lawrenceburg, Kentucky
WFTM Maysville, Kentucky
WFXY Middlesboro, Kentucky
WEKY Richmond, Kentucky
WTLO Somerset, Kentucky
WTKY Tompkinsville, Kentucky
KVVP Leesville, Louisiana
WGAO Franklin, Massachusetts
WBRK Pittsfield, Massachusetts
WHLL Springfield, Massachusetts
WCEM Cambridge, Maryland
WSRY Elkton, Maryland
WMTB-FM Emmitsburg, Maryland
WAYZ Hagerstown, Maryland
WXCY Havre De Grace, Maryland
WHGT Maugansville, Maryland
WVAE Biddeford, Maine
WHOU-FM Houlton, Maine
WATZ Alpena, Michigan
WAUS Berrien Springs, Michigan
WYBR Big Rapids, Michigan
WDBC Escanaba, Michigan
WDZZ-FM Flint, Michigan
WCSR Hillsdale, Michigan
WCCY Houghton, Michigan
WKZO Kalamazoo, Michigan
WFCX Leland, Michigan
WMIM Luna Pier, Michigan
WMTE-FM Manistee, Michigan
WMPX Midland, Michigan
WNIL Niles, Michigan
WUPY Ontonagon, Michigan
WRSR Owosso, Michigan
WJML Petoskey, Michigan
KXRA Alexandria, Minnesota
KXRZ Alexandria, Minnesota
KKCQ-FM Bagley, Minnesota
KDLM Detroit Lakes, Minnesota
KBRF Fergus Falls, Minnesota
KJJK Fergus Falls, Minnesota
WLKX-FM Forest Lake, Minnesota
KKCQ Fosston, Minnesota
WMFG Hibbing, Minnesota
KLFD Litchfield, Minnesota
KLTF Little Falls, Minnesota
KEYL Long Prairie, Minnesota
KQAD Luverne, Minnesota
KMHL Marshall, Minnesota
KYMN Northfield, Minnesota
KDIO Ortonville, Minnesota
KLOH Pipestone, Minnesota
KAGE Winona, Minnesota
KAAN Bethany, Missouri
KCRV Caruthersville, Missouri
KCXL Liberty, Missouri
KMVC Marshall, Missouri
KMEM-FM Memphis, Missouri
KJAB-FM Mexico, Missouri
KMCR Montgomery City, Missouri
KELE-FM Mountain Grove, Missouri
KBDZ Perryville, Missouri
KLID Poplar Bluff, Missouri
KMIS Portageville, Missouri
KDRO Sedalia, Missouri
KWTO Springfield, Missouri
KMOX St. Louis, Missouri
KLPW Union, Missouri
KTKS Versailles, Missouri
KJPW Waynesville, Missouri
WAFM Amory, Mississippi
WAMY Amory, Mississippi
WHJT Clinton, Mississippi
WTCD Indianola, Mississippi
WIQQ Leland, Mississippi
WMOX Meridian, Mississippi
WNBN Meridian, Mississippi
WRQO Monticello, Mississippi
WRJW Picayune, Mississippi
WSKK Ripley, Mississippi
KBOW Butte, Montana
KMSM-FM Butte, Montana
KXTL Butte, Montana
KMSO Missoula, Montana
KATQ Plentywood, Montana
WWNC Asheville, North Carolina
WXIT Blowing Rock, North Carolina
WSQL Brevard, North Carolina
WBAG Burlington-Graham, North Carolina
WRRZ Clinton, North Carolina
WGAI Elizabeth City, North Carolina
WBLA Elizabethtown, North Carolina
WBRM Marion, North Carolina
WHIP Mooresville, North Carolina
WECR Newland, North Carolina
WPTM Roanoke Rapids, North Carolina
WNCA Siler City, North Carolina
WTOE Spruce Pine, North Carolina

WMXF Waynesville, North Carolina
WENC Whiteville, North Carolina
WTXY Whiteville, North Carolina
KEYA Belcourt, North Dakota
KXPO Grafton, North Dakota
KNDK Langdon, North Dakota
KEYZ Williston, North Dakota
KZEN Central City, Nebraska
KJSK Columbus, Nebraska
KINI Crookston, Nebraska
KRVN Lexington, Nebraska
KRFS Superior, Nebraska
WSJO Egg Harbor City, New Jersey
WRDR Freehold Township, New Jersey
WTTH Margate City, New Jersey
WTOC Newton, New Jersey
WGHT Pompton Lakes, New Jersey
WSOU South Orange, New Jersey
WNJC Vineland, New Jersey
KKTC Angel Fire, New Mexico
KARS Belen, New Mexico
KLEA Lovington, New Mexico
KLAV Las Vegas, Nevada
KSNE-FM Las Vegas, Nevada
KNEV Reno, Nevada
WYSL Avon, New York
WBNR Beacon, New York
WHRW Binghamton, New York
WBRV-FM Boonville, New York
WHCL-FM Clinton, New York
WDNY-FM Dansville, New York
WFLR Dundee, New York
WELM Elmira, New York
WGBB Freeport, New York
WMML Glens Falls, New York
WLIE Islip, New York
WKSN Jamestown, New York
WGHQ Kingston, New York
WIXT Little Falls, New York
WLVL Lockport, New York
WLLG Lowville, New York
WOR New York, New York
WGNY Newburgh, New York
WTLA North Syracuse, New York
WDOS Oneonta, New York
WEBO Owego, New York
WQKE Plattsburgh, New York
WEOK Poughkeepsie, New York
WRUR-FM Rochester, New York
WMYY Schoharie, New York
WSPQ Springville, New York
WRGR Tupper Lake, New York
WAJZ Voorheesville, New York
WDPN Alliance, Ohio
WBLL Bellefontaine, Ohio
WMNI Columbus, Ohio
WHIO Dayton, Ohio
WDFM Defiance, Ohio
WZOM Defiance, Ohio
WIRO Ironton, Ohio
WLRX Ironton, Ohio
WVKO-FM Johnstown, Ohio
WCIT(AM) Lima, Ohio
WMOA Marietta, Ohio
WTIG Massillon, Ohio
WMPO Middleport-Pomeroy, Ohio
WMVO Mount Vernon, Ohio
WMCO New Concord, Ohio
WHIZ-FM South Zanesville, Ohio
WCWA Toledo, Ohio
WSPD Toledo, Ohio
WBTC Uhrichsville, Ohio
WTUZ Uhrichsville, Ohio
KWON Bartlesville, Oklahoma
KGYN Guymon, Oklahoma
KICM Healdton, Oklahoma
KTJS Hobart, Oklahoma
KXMX Muldrow, Oklahoma
KJKE Newcastle, Oklahoma
KYLV Oklahoma City, Oklahoma
KZBB Poteau, Oklahoma
KHSS Athena, Oregon
KNND Cottage Grove, Oregon
KAJO Grants Pass, Oregon
KSZN(AM) Gresham, Oregon
KUIK Hillsboro, Oregon
KQIK Lakeview, Oregon
KSLC McMinnville, Oregon
KNPT Newport, Oregon
KACI The Dalles, Oregon
KWBY Woodburn, Oregon
WAEB Allentown, Pennsylvania
WBVP Beaver Falls, Pennsylvania
WHLM Bloomsburg, Pennsylvania
WISR Butler, Pennsylvania
WIOO Carlisle, Pennsylvania
WCCL Central City, Pennsylvania
WCHA Chambersburg, Pennsylvania
WWCH Clarion, Pennsylvania
WFSE Edinboro, Pennsylvania
WVMM Grantham, Pennsylvania
WLLI(AM) Huntingdon, Pennsylvania
WDAD Indiana, Pennsylvania
WTYM Kittanning, Pennsylvania
WNPV Lansdale, Pennsylvania
WCNS Latrobe, Pennsylvania
WWKL Mechanicsburg, Pennsylvania
WJUN Mexico, Pennsylvania
WMSS Middletown, Pennsylvania
WPGR Monroeville, Pennsylvania
WGBN New Kensington, Pennsylvania
WWNW New Wilmington, Pennsylvania
WYCK Plains, Pennsylvania
WHKS Port Allegany, Pennsylvania
WPAZ Pottstown, Pennsylvania
WBZU Scranton, Pennsylvania
WICK Scranton, Pennsylvania
WUSR Scranton, Pennsylvania
WPIC Sharon, Pennsylvania
WSRU Slippery Rock, Pennsylvania
WKBI-FM St. Marys, Pennsylvania
WTRN Tyrone, Pennsylvania
WXVU Villanova, Pennsylvania
WCHE West Chester, Pennsylvania
WKZN West Hazleton, Pennsylvania
WILK Wilkes-Barre, Pennsylvania
WMGS Wilkes-Barre, Pennsylvania
WALO Humacao, Puerto Rico
WEXS Patillas, Puerto Rico
WCRI-FM Block Island, Rhode Island
WJMF Smithfield, Rhode Island
WAGS Bishopville, South Carolina
WQNT Charleston, South Carolina
WHSC Conway, South Carolina
WMUU-FM Greenville, South Carolina
WBHC-FM Hampton, South Carolina
WJDJ Hartsville, South Carolina
WKMG Newberry, South Carolina
WQKI-FM Orangeburg, South Carolina
WSPA-FM Spartanburg, South Carolina
KBFS Belle Fourche, South Dakota
KGIM-FM Redfield, South Dakota
WNAX Yankton, South Dakota
WCTA Alamo, Tennessee
WYXI Athens, Tennessee
WMPS Bartlett, Tennessee
WJZM Clarksville, Tennessee
WYSH Clinton, Tennessee
WKRM Columbia, Tennessee
WZYX Cowan, Tennessee
WAKM Franklin, Tennessee
WMRO Gallatin, Tennessee
WMYL Halls Crossroads, Tennessee
WJFC Jefferson City, Tennessee
WJCW Johnson City, Tennessee
WKTS Kingston, Tennessee
WKGN Knoxville, Tennessee
WLIV Livingston, Tennessee
WREC Memphis, Tennessee
WGNS Murfreesboro, Tennessee
WMGC Murfreesboro, Tennessee
WLIK Newport, Tennessee
WUAT Pikeville, Tennessee
WJTT Red Bank, Tennessee
WLIJ Shelbyville, Tennessee
WZNG Shelbyville, Tennessee
WSMT Sparta, Tennessee
WSGI Springfield, Tennessee
WCDT Winchester, Tennessee
KQIZ-FM Amarillo, Texas
KFYN Bonham, Texas
KWHI Brenham, Texas
KCTX-FM Childress, Texas
KHER Crystal City, Texas
KTDR Del Rio, Texas
KWMC Del Rio, Texas
KTSM El Paso, Texas
KGVL Greenville, Texas
KCLW Hamilton, Texas
KVRP-FM Haskell, Texas
KWFB Holliday, Texas
KTBZ-FM Houston, Texas
KFTX Kingsville, Texas
KVLG La Grange, Texas
KCYL Lampasas, Texas
KSHN Liberty, Texas
KZZN Littlefield, Texas
KCKL Malakoff, Texas
KLSR-FM Memphis, Texas
KBED Nederland, Texas
KNBT New Braunfels, Texas
KEYE Perryton, Texas
KMIQ Robstown, Texas
KDCD San Angelo, Texas
KELI San Angelo, Texas
KQXT-FM San Antonio, Texas
KSTV Stephenville, Texas
KBCY Tye, Texas
KWUD Woodville, Texas
KSUB Cedar City, Utah
KVNU Logan, Utah
KWCR-FM Ogden, Utah
KXRQ Roosevelt, Utah
KHQN Spanish Fork, Utah
KDXU St. George, Utah
KVEL Vernal, Utah
WBNN-FM Dillwyn, Virginia
WFLO Farmville, Virginia
WXGM Gloucester, Virginia
WKCY Harrisonburg, Virginia
WMXH-FM Luray, Virginia
WRAA Luray, Virginia
WZZU Lynchburg, Virginia
WUKZ(AM) Marion, Virginia
WVCV Orange, Virginia
WDCE Richmond, Virginia
WRVA Richmond, Virginia
WYTI Rocky Mount, Virginia
WHEO Stuart, Virginia
WVBW Suffolk, Virginia
WVWI Charlotte Amalie, Virgin Islands
WVVI-FM Christiansted, Virgin Islands
WRMC-FM Middlebury, Vermont
WMNV Rupert, Vermont
KWLE Anacortes, Washington
KGTS College Place, Washington
KYSN East Wenatchee, Washington
KARY-FM Grandview, Washington
KZIZ Pacific, Washington
KRIZ Renton, Washington
KMAS Shelton, Washington
KDNA Yakima, Washington
WATW Ashland, Wisconsin
WRPQ Baraboo, Wisconsin
WCFW Chippewa Falls, Wisconsin
WTTN Columbus, Wisconsin
WJOK Kaukauna, Wisconsin
WAUN-FM Kewaunee, Wisconsin
WJMT Merrill, Wisconsin
WMYX-FM Milwaukee, Wisconsin
WSSP Milwaukee, Wisconsin
WTMJ Milwaukee, Wisconsin
WPFP Park Falls, Wisconsin
WVRQ Viroqua, Wisconsin
WSAU Wausau, Wisconsin
WKEZ Bluefield, West Virginia
WBUC Buckhannon, West Virginia
WVWC Buckhannon, West Virginia
WVMR Frost, West Virginia
WRVC Huntington, West Virginia
WRON-FM Lewisburg, West Virginia
WEPM Martinsburg, West Virginia
WRON Ronceverte, West Virginia
WCWV Summersville, West Virginia
WELC Welch, West Virginia
WZST Westover, West Virginia
KLGT Buffalo, Wyoming
KKTY-FM Glendo, Wyoming
KASL Newcastle, Wyoming

Rock/AOR

KVHS Concord, California
KCPR San Luis Obispo, California
KGRR Epworth, Iowa
WBKE-FM North Manchester, Indiana
WWHR Bowling Green, Kentucky
WQUS Lapeer, Michigan
WTIP Grand Marais, Minnesota
WKNC-FM Raleigh, North Carolina
WLFC North Baltimore, Ohio
WNRN Charlottesville, Virginia
KGRG-FM Auburn, Washington

Russian

KTYM Inglewood, California
KNOF St. Paul, Minnesota
WDCV-FM Carlisle, Pennsylvania
KKNW Seattle, Washington
KLFE Seattle, Washington

Smooth Jazz

WMVB Millville, New Jersey
WVLY-FM Milton, Pennsylvania

Spanish

WTBB Gadsden, Alabama
WTBJ Oxford, Alabama
WRBZ Wetumpka, Alabama
KAAY Little Rock, Arkansas
KABF Little Rock, Arkansas
KXEG Phoenix, Arizona
KINO Winslow, Arizona
KAWC Yuma, Arizona
KKCY Colusa, California
KTHU Corning, California
KCHJ Delano, California
KBIF Fresno, California
KFCF Fresno, California
KKMC Gonzales, California
KXBX Lakeport, California
KEBT Lost Hills, California
KADV Modesto, California
KVON Napa, California
KFPR Redding, California
KPRZ San Marcos-Poway, California
KRZA Alamosa, Colorado
KUVO Denver, Colorado
KLFV Grand Junction, Colorado
KGRE Greeley, Colorado
WFAR Danbury, Connecticut
WYBC New Haven, Connecticut
WHUS Storrs, Connecticut
WDEL Wilmington, Delaware
WJFP Fort Pierce, Florida
WWRF Lake Worth, Florida
WHTY(AM) Riviera Beach, Florida
WTIS Tampa, Florida
WRFG Atlanta, Georgia
WTHV Hahira, Georgia
WGML Hinesville, Georgia
KCHE Cherokee, Iowa
KBGN Caldwell, Idaho
KMHI Mountain Home, Idaho
WPCD Champaign, Illinois
WMBI Chicago, Illinois
WRMN Elgin, Illinois
WWHN Joliet, Illinois
WFEN Rockford, Illinois
WLYV Fort Wayne, Indiana
KVOE Emporia, Kansas
KWKR Leoti, Kansas
KBCU North Newton, Kansas
WFCR Amherst, Massachusetts
WBUR West Yarmouth, Massachusetts
WLEN Adrian, Michigan
WKAR East Lansing, Michigan
WHTC Holland, Michigan
WIBM Jackson, Michigan
WSDS Salem Township, Michigan
WPNW Zeeland, Michigan
KYCR Golden Valley, Minnesota
KYSM-FM Mankato, Minnesota
KCHK New Prague, Minnesota
KRFO Owatonna, Minnesota
KRRW St. James, Minnesota
KSRQ Thief River Falls, Minnesota
KAOL Carrollton, Missouri
KDMO Carthage, Missouri
KCUR-FM Kansas City, Missouri
WMFA Raeford, North Carolina
WSHA Raleigh, North Carolina
KJSK Columbus, Nebraska
KICS Hastings, Nebraska
KJLT North Platte, Nebraska
WFDU Teaneck, New Jersey
KSVA Albuquerque, New Mexico
KCQL Aztec, New Mexico
KLMX Clayton, New Mexico
KVLC Hatch, New Mexico
KFUN Las Vegas, New Mexico
KBUY Ruidoso, New Mexico
KTNM Tucumcari, New Mexico
KKVV Las Vegas, Nevada
KUNV Las Vegas, Nevada
WCVF-FM Fredonia, New York
WLIM Patchogue, New York
WFOB Fostoria, Ohio
WXKR Port Clinton, Ohio
WELW Willoughby, Ohio
KBZQ Lawton, Oklahoma
KTLR Oklahoma City, Oklahoma
KBVR Corvallis, Oregon
KAGI Grants Pass, Oregon
KOHU Hermiston, Oregon
KUIK Hillsboro, Oregon
KAGO Klamath Falls, Oregon
KBVM Portland, Oregon
KKPZ Portland, Oregon
WMCE Erie, Pennsylvania
WKJB Mayaguez, Puerto Rico
WVOZ San Juan, Puerto Rico
KWMG Newberry, South Carolina
WNFO Sun City-Hilton Head, South Carolina
WYPL Memphis, Tennessee
WNQM Nashville, Tennessee
KVLF Alpine, Texas
KVLU Beaumont, Texas
KGSR Cedar Park, Texas
KCTA Corpus Christi, Texas
KEDT-FM Corpus Christi, Texas
KDHN Dimmitt, Texas
KULP El Campo, Texas
KELP El Paso, Texas
KHCB-FM Houston, Texas
KSHU Huntsville, Texas
KKER Kerrville, Texas
KLUX Robstown, Texas
KRRW Rusk, Texas
KEDA San Antonio, Texas
KANI Wharton, Texas
KPDR Wheeler, Texas
WWWJ Galax, Virginia
WHOV Hampton, Virginia
WBTK Richmond, Virginia
KEWU-FM Cheney, Washington
KBSN Moses Lake, Washington
KDNA Yakima, Washington
WMLJ Summersville, West Virginia
KRAE Cheyenne, Wyoming
KUGR Green River, Wyoming

Sports

KRUA Anchorage, Alaska
WMBV Dixons Mills, Alabama
WUMP Madison, Alabama
WMGY Montgomery, Alabama
WZZN Oneonta, Alabama
WZCT Scottsboro, Alabama
KYEL Danville, Arkansas
KFPW Fort Smith, Arkansas
KHOZ Harrison, Arkansas
KBCN-FM Marshall, Arkansas
KWKK Russellville, Arkansas
KDJI Holbrook, Arizona
KAAA Kingman, Arizona
KLVA Maricopa, Arizona
KKNT Phoenix, Arizona
KNOT Prescott, Arizona
KWKM St. Johns, Arizona
KNZR Bakersfield, California
KBHR Big Bear City, California
KIBS Bishop, California
KRKC King City, California
KCAA Loma Linda, California
KLAA Orange, California
KTRB San Francisco, California
KLIV San Jose, California
KKJL San Luis Obispo, California
KVEC San Luis Obispo, California
KSLV-FM Del Norte, Colorado
KIUP Durango, Colorado
KFTM Fort Morgan, Colorado
KPKE Gunnison, Colorado
KUBC Montrose, Colorado
KCOL Wellington, Colorado
WGCH Greenwich, Connecticut
WXDE Lewes, Delaware
WQXM Bartow, Florida
WWBF Bartow, Florida
WSWN Belle Glade, Florida
WVUM Coral Gables, Florida
WJSB Crestview, Florida
WNDB Daytona Beach, Florida
WDSP De Funiak Springs, Florida
WJXL Jacksonville Beach, Florida
WQHL-FM Live Oak, Florida
WEBY Milton, Florida
WFLF Pine Hills, Florida
WTBN Pinellas Park, Florida
WCTH Plantation Key, Florida
WAOC Saint Augustine, Florida
WFNS Blackshear, Georgia
WGMI Bremen, Georgia
WRBN Clayton, Georgia
WFOM Marietta, Georgia
WJAT Swainsboro, Georgia
KCPS Burlington, Iowa
KGGO Des Moines, Iowa
KICB Fort Dodge, Iowa
KLMJ Hampton, Iowa
KOKX-FM Keokuk, Iowa
KRNQ Keokuk, Iowa
KMCH Manchester, Iowa
KFJB Marshalltown, Iowa
KIHK Rock Valley, Iowa
KWDM West Des Moines, Iowa
KID Idaho Falls, Idaho
KID-FM Idaho Falls, Idaho
KTFI Wendell, Idaho
WCDD Canton, Illinois
WGN(AM) Chicago, Illinois
WXEF Effingham, Illinois
WHFH Flossmoor, Illinois
WAIK Galesburg, Illinois
WGIL Galesburg, Illinois
WGBK Glenview, Illinois
WJBM Jerseyville, Illinois
WLTL La Grange, Illinois
WLRA Lockport, Illinois
WFXN Moline, Illinois
WGFA-FM Watseka, Illinois
WETN Wheaton, Illinois
WYKT Wilmington, Illinois
WSCH Aurora, Indiana
WBIW Bedford, Indiana
WUZR Bicknell, Indiana
WGCS Goshen, Indiana
WJOB Hammond, Indiana
WEEM-FM Pendleton, Indiana
WFMG Richmond, Indiana
WAMW-FM Washington, Indiana
KTCC Colby, Kansas
KONQ Dodge City, Kansas
KSEK Pittsburg, Kansas
WTUK Harlan, Kentucky
WKCM Hawesville, Kentucky
WLME Lewisport, Kentucky
WCBR Richmond, Kentucky
WYSB Springfield, Kentucky
KBKK Ball, Louisiana
WDGL Baton Rouge, Louisiana
WTGE Baton Rouge, Louisiana
KMLB Monroe, Louisiana
KSYB Shreveport, Louisiana
WXRB Dudley, Massachusetts
WGFP Webster, Massachusetts
WTAG Worcester, Massachusetts
WNAV Annapolis, Maryland
WXCY Havre De Grace, Maryland
WKIK La Plata, Maryland
WALZ-FM Machias, Maine
WBPW Presque Isle, Maine
WBFH Bloomfield Hills, Michigan
WDMK Detroit, Michigan
WKMI Kalamazoo, Michigan
WZUU Mattawan, Michigan
WRSR Owosso, Michigan
WJML Petoskey, Michigan
KKLN Atwater, Minnesota
WBJI Blackduck, Minnesota
KXDL Browerville, Minnesota
KEYL Long Prairie, Minnesota
KCWJ Blue Springs, Missouri
KDKD-FM Clinton, Missouri
KWWR Mexico, Missouri
KBDZ Perryville, Missouri
KSIM Sikeston, Missouri
KTXR Springfield, Missouri
WMXI Laurel, Mississippi
WZLD Petal, Mississippi
WRJW Picayune, Mississippi
KFLN Baker, Montana
KMON Great Falls, Montana

WATA Boone, North Carolina
WCSL Cherryville, North Carolina
WNCC-FM Franklin, North Carolina
WIZS Henderson, North Carolina
WGOS High Point, North Carolina
WPLW Hillsborough, North Carolina
WELS-FM Kinston, North Carolina
WRNS-FM Kinston, North Carolina
WFLB Laurinburg, North Carolina
WKGX Lenoir, North Carolina
WCBQ Oxford, North Carolina
WQDR-FM Raleigh, North Carolina
WNCA Siler City, North Carolina
WEEB Southern Pines, North Carolina
WRGC Sylva, North Carolina
WTQR Winston-Salem, North Carolina
KLXX Bismarck-Mandan, North Dakota
KDLR Devils Lake, North Dakota
KDIX Dickinson, North Dakota
KCJB Minot, North Dakota
KRRZ Minot, North Dakota
KICS Hastings, Nebraska
KGFW Kearney, Nebraska
KIOD McCook, Nebraska
KNCY Nebraska City, Nebraska
WHTG Eatontown, New Jersey
WJSV Morristown, New Jersey
WCTC New Brunswick, New Jersey
WGHT Pompton Lakes, New Jersey
WKNJ-FM Union Township, New Jersey
WMCX West Long Branch, New Jersey
KICA Clovis, New Mexico
KRSY-FM La Luz, New Mexico
KRSN Los Alamos, New Mexico
KELY Ely, Nevada
KKOH Reno, Nevada
WBTA Batavia, New York
WBAZ Bridgehampton, New York
WBEN Buffalo, New York
WDNY-FM Dansville, New York
WKCR-FM New York, New York
WEBO Owego, New York
WRUC Schenectady, New York
WHEN Syracuse, New York
WFAS White Plains, New York
WZIP Akron, Ohio
WXTQ Athens, Ohio
WCDK Cadiz, Ohio
WBVB Coal Grove, Ohio
WEOL Elyria, Ohio
WFIN Findlay, Ohio
WFCO Lancaster, Ohio
WMOA Marietta, Ohio
WKLM Millersburg, Ohio
WRGM Ontario, Ohio
WBUK Ottawa, Ohio
WPTW Piqua, Ohio
WHIZ-FM South Zanesville, Ohio
WCWA Toledo, Ohio
WFGF Wapakoneta, Ohio
KRVT Claremore, Oklahoma
KEBC Del City, Oklahoma
KOKL Okmulgee, Oklahoma
KGFF Shawnee, Oklahoma
KGFY Stillwater, Oklahoma
KSPI Stillwater, Oklahoma
KGND Vinita, Oklahoma
KITO-FM Vinita, Oklahoma
KPNW Eugene, Oregon
KEX Portland, Oregon
KQEN Roseburg, Oregon
KOHI St. Helens, Oregon
KCKX Stayton, Oregon
WRTA Altoona, Pennsylvania
WBVE Bedford, Pennsylvania
WZWW Bellefonte, Pennsylvania
WFSE Edinboro, Pennsylvania
WCRO Johnstown, Pennsylvania
WFNM Lancaster, Pennsylvania
WNPV Lansdale, Pennsylvania
WBPZ Lock Haven, Pennsylvania
WMSS Middletown, Pennsylvania
WQLV Millersburg, Pennsylvania
WNTP Philadelphia, Pennsylvania
KQV Pittsburgh, Pennsylvania
WDMT Pittston, Pennsylvania
WQSU Selinsgrove, Pennsylvania
WSRU Slippery Rock, Pennsylvania
WMBS Uniontown, Pennsylvania
WWPA Williamsport, Pennsylvania
WMNT Manati, Puerto Rico
WEXS Patillas, Puerto Rico
WLEO Ponce, Puerto Rico
WCVY Coventry, Rhode Island
WDOM Providence, Rhode Island
WVGB Beaufort, South Carolina
WGTR Bucksport, South Carolina
WPCC Clinton, South Carolina
WISW Columbia, South Carolina
WNOW-FM Gaffney, South Carolina
WJKB Moncks Corner, South Carolina
WSNW Seneca, South Carolina
KKSD Milbank, South Dakota
KIMM Rapid City, South Dakota
KSDR-FM Watertown, South Dakota
WNAX Yankton, South Dakota
WHUB Cookeville, Tennessee
WKBQ Covington, Tennessee
WCDZ Dresden, Tennessee
WASL Dyersburg, Tennessee
WTRO Dyersburg, Tennessee
WAKM Franklin, Tennessee
WAEZ Greeneville, Tennessee
WDXI Jackson, Tennessee
WFLI Lookout Mountain, Tennessee
WMSR Manchester, Tennessee
WTNE Trenton, Tennessee
WBOZ Woodbury, Tennessee
KSKY Balch Springs, Texas
KTAM Bryan, Texas
KCAR Clarksville, Texas
KRLD Dallas, Texas
KGAF Gainesville, Texas
KCOH Houston, Texas
KCYL Lampasas, Texas
KSFA Nacogdoches, Texas
KJAK Slaton, Texas
KTBB-FM Tyler, Texas
KVOU-FM Uvalde, Texas
KPGR Pleasant Grove, Utah
WKEX Blacksburg, Virginia
WMNA Gretna, Virginia
WRVL Lynchburg, Virginia
WMEV-FM Marion, Virginia
WYTI Rocky Mount, Virginia
WTON Staunton, Virginia
WTON-FM Staunton, Virginia
WBTN Bennington, Vermont
WVNR Poultney, Vermont
KCED Centralia, Washington
KMNT Chehalis, Washington
KCLX Colfax, Washington
KRKZ Forks, Washington
KONA Kennewick-Richland-P, Washington
KFLD Pasco, Washington
KKNW Seattle, Washington
KXLY Spokane, Washington
KKOV Vancouver, Washington
WBEV Beaver Dam, Wisconsin
WEAQ Chippewa Falls, Wisconsin
WLKG Lake Geneva, Wisconsin
WGLR-FM Lancaster, Wisconsin
WMAM Marinette, Wisconsin
WPVL Platteville, Wisconsin
WRPN-FM Ripon, Wisconsin
WCOW-FM Sparta, Wisconsin
WWSP Stevens Point, Wisconsin
WDUX-FM Waupaca, Wisconsin
WJLS Beckley, West Virginia
WXKX Clarksburg, West Virginia
WTNJ Mount Hope, West Virginia
WGGE Parkersburg, West Virginia
WWYO Pineville, West Virginia
WMOV Ravenswood, West Virginia
KPIN Pinedale, Wyoming

Talk

KFQD Anchorage, Alaska
KTHS-FM Berryville, Arkansas
KVDW England, Arkansas
KBOK Malvern, Arkansas
KXRJ Russellville, Arkansas
KMLE Chandler, Arizona
KCUZ Clifton, Arizona
KFMA Green Valley, Arizona
KFNN Mesa, Arizona
KGME Phoenix, Arizona
KAHI Auburn, California
KJLH Compton, California
KHSR Crescent City, California
KFMI Eureka, California
KFSR Fresno, California
KCRH Hayward, California
KWTM June Lake, California
KXBX Lakeport, California
KIIS-FM Los Angeles, California
KHOT Madera, California
KFIV Modesto, California
KHOP Oakdale, California
KAZU Pacific Grove, California
KXTZ Pismo Beach, California
KTIP Porterville, California
KGGI Riverside, California
KFMB San Diego, California
KIFM San Diego, California
KLCA Tahoe City, California
KKDV Walnut Creek, California
KFTM Fort Morgan, Colorado
KCOL Wellington, Colorado
KRDZ Wray, Colorado
WGCH Greenwich, Connecticut
WJMJ Hartford, Connecticut
WINY Putnam, Connecticut
WEBE Westport, Connecticut
WPFW Washington, District of Columbia
WWPR Bradenton, Florida
WFTW Fort Walton Beach, Florida
WRNE Gulf Breeze, Florida
WHIF Palatka, Florida
WKGC Southport, Florida
WFOY St. Augustine, Florida
WFRC Columbus, Georgia
WJJC Commerce, Georgia
WWWE Hapeville, Georgia
KGUM Hagatna, Guam
KGYM Cedar Rapids, Iowa
KBLY Idaho Falls, Idaho
KIDO Nampa, Idaho
KRVB Nampa, Idaho
WSDZ Belleville, Illinois
WSSD Chicago, Illinois
WEPS Elgin, Illinois
WAIK Galesburg, Illinois
WGBK Glenview, Illinois
WWDV Zion, Illinois
WAMW Washington, Indiana
KHCC-FM Hutchinson, Kansas
KIKS-FM Iola, Kansas
KHCD Salina, Kansas
KCFN Wichita, Kansas
KEYN-FM Wichita, Kansas
WTBK Manchester, Kentucky
WFLW Monticello, Kentucky
WCBR Richmond, Kentucky
WVEZ St. Matthews, Kentucky
WBRP Baker, Louisiana
KPEL-FM Breaux Bridge, Louisiana
KUMX North Fort Polk, Louisiana
WESX Nahant, Massachusetts
WFWM Frostburg, Maryland
WAMS-FM Snow Hill, Maryland
WMDR Augusta, Maine
WTBM Mexico, Maine
WXEX-FM Sanford, Maine
WDZZ-FM Flint, Michigan
WGLI Hancock, Michigan
WNMU-FM Marquette, Michigan
WCSY-FM South Haven, Michigan
WLKX-FM Forest Lake, Minnesota
KFXN Minneapolis, Minnesota
KYMN Northfield, Minnesota
KNXR Rochester, Minnesota
KNSG Springfield, Minnesota
KSWF Aurora, Missouri
KMRN Cameron, Missouri
KFRU Columbia, Missouri
KJXX Jackson, Missouri
KSIM Sikeston, Missouri
WTCD Indianola, Mississippi
WNBN Meridian, Mississippi
WUMS University, Mississippi
KXGN Glendive, Montana
WQNQ Fletcher, North Carolina
WRFX Kannapolis, North Carolina
WMPM Smithfield, North Carolina
WTAB Tabor City, North Carolina
WENC Whiteville, North Carolina
KFJM Grand Forks, North Dakota
KCJB Minot, North Dakota
KHRT Minot, North Dakota
KFOR Lincoln, Nebraska
KAWL York, Nebraska

WMOU Berlin, New Hampshire
WDER-FM Peterborough, New Hampshire
WPNH Plymouth, New Hampshire
WRNJ Hackettstown, New Jersey
WVNJ Oakland, New Jersey
KWKA Clovis, New Mexico
KBCQ Roswell, New Mexico
KMXQ Socorro, New Mexico
KHWK Tonopah, Nevada
WUFO Amherst, New York
WCSS Amsterdam, New York
WSQX-FM Binghamton, New York
WITC Cazenovia, New York
WENT Gloversville, New York
WCKM-FM Lake George, New York
WEOK Poughkeepsie, New York
WJKE(FM) Stillwater, New York
WZIP Akron, Ohio
WPFB Middletown, Ohio
WLRY Rushville, Ohio
WOBN Westerville, Ohio
WCWS-FM Wooster, Ohio
KWOX Woodward, Oklahoma
KHPE Albany, Oregon
KWIP Dallas, Oregon
KYKN Keizer, Oregon
KGAL Lebanon, Oregon
KKPZ Portland, Oregon
KLTW-FM Prineville, Oregon
KOHI St. Helens, Oregon
KFIR Sweet Home, Oregon
KSJK Talent, Oregon
KACI The Dalles, Oregon
WBUQ Bloomsburg, Pennsylvania
WNUZ Mercersburg, Pennsylvania
WBHD Olyphant, Pennsylvania
WPAM Pottsville, Pennsylvania
WPIC Sharon, Pennsylvania
WMBS Uniontown, Pennsylvania
WZAR Ponce, Puerto Rico
WHHD Clearwater, South Carolina
WORG Elloree, South Carolina
WNOW-FM Gaffney, South Carolina
WLMC Georgetown, South Carolina
WRIX-FM Honea Path, South Carolina
KJAM Madison, South Dakota
WPWT Colonial Heights, Tennessee
WZYX Cowan, Tennessee
WRLT Franklin, Tennessee
WQLA La Follette, Tennessee
KIXZ Amarillo, Texas
KMFA Austin, Texas
KAPN Caldwell, Texas
KNES Fairfield, Texas
KTCU-FM Fort Worth, Texas
KMJQ Houston, Texas
KPRC Houston, Texas
KTBZ-FM Houston, Texas
KKBA Kingsville, Texas
KKCL Lorenzo, Texas
KRFE Lubbock, Texas
KSWP Lufkin, Texas
KIKK Pasadena, Texas
KSTX San Antonio, Texas
KBXT Wixon Valley, Texas
KSUB Cedar City, Utah
KLGN Logan, Utah
WFLO Farmville, Virginia
WPCE Portsmouth, Virginia
WRUV Burlington, Vermont
WVPS Burlington, Vermont
WRVT Rutland, Vermont
WVPR Windsor, Vermont
KGMI Bellingham, Washington
KGNW Burien-Seattle, Washington
KELA Centralia-Chehalis, Washington
KPLZ-FM Seattle, Washington
KXLY Spokane, Washington
KVTI Tacoma, Washington
WPFP Park Falls, Wisconsin
WDLS Wisconsin Dells, Wisconsin
WELD-FM Moorefield, West Virginia
WWYO Pineville, West Virginia
KMER Kemmerer, Wyoming
KOVE Lander, Wyoming

Tejano

WCSY-FM South Haven, Michigan
KPAN Hereford, Texas

Triple A

KBBI Homer, Alaska
KOJI Okoboji, Iowa
KWIT Sioux City, Iowa
KMUW Wichita, Kansas
WKMS-FM Murray, Kentucky
WHFC Bel Air, Maryland
WEOS Geneva, New York
WRIP Windham, New York
WEQX Manchester, Vermont

Urban Contemporary

KSWH-FM Arkadelphia, Arkansas
KSPC Claremont, California
KSCU Santa Clara, California
KSMT Breckenridge, Colorado
KCSU-FM Fort Collins, Colorado
WRGP Homestead, Florida
WRSE Elmhurst, Illinois
WVUR-FM Valparaiso, Indiana
WEAA Baltimore, Maryland
WMHB Waterville, Maine
WSGR-FM Port Huron, Michigan
WXDU Durham, North Carolina
WUAG Greensboro, North Carolina
KRNU Lincoln, Nebraska
WBUQ Bloomsburg, Pennsylvania
WCAL California, Pennsylvania
WCUC-FM Clarion, Pennsylvania
WUSR Scranton, Pennsylvania
KCFS Sioux Falls, South Dakota
WTTU Cookeville, Tennessee
KPSM Brownwood, Texas
KGLD Tyler, Texas
WIUV Castleton, Vermont
KGRG-FM Auburn, Washington
KYVT Yakima, Washington
WCCX Waukesha, Wisconsin
WSUW Whitewater, Wisconsin

Variety/Diverse

KRUA Anchorage, Alaska
KSUA Fairbanks, Alaska
WEGL Auburn, Alabama
KNOG Nogales, Arizona
KRLA Glendale, California
KGIL Johannesburg, California
KALW San Francisco, California
KGUM Hagatna, Guam
KIWR Council Bluffs, Iowa
WQNA Springfield, Illinois
KLJY Clayton, Missouri
WNND Pickerington, Ohio
KXTD Wagoner, Oklahoma
KUQL Ethan, South Dakota
KZHN Paris, Texas
KNCN Sinton, Texas

Vietnamese

KSJX San Jose, California
KXMX Muldrow, Oklahoma
KHCB League City, Texas

Canadian Radio Group Ownership

Aboriginal Voices Radio Inc.
PO Box 87,Station E, Toronto ON M6H 4E1
(416) 703-1287; *Fax:*(416) 703-4328
www.aboriginalradio.com
info@aboriginalvoices.com

Acadia Broadcasting Ltd.
Box 2000, Saint John NB E2L 3T4
(506) 648-2100; *Fax:*(506) 632-3407
www.acadiabroadcastinglimited.ca
info@radioabl.ca

Astral Media Inc.
1800 avenue McGill College,Bureau 2700, Montreal PQ H3A 3J6
(514) 939-5000; *Fax:*(514) 939-1515
www.astral.com
Ownership: Abgreen Holdings Ltd., 55.71% vote; 654625 Ontario Inc., 13.63% vote.

Bayshore Broadcasting Corp.
Box 280, Owen Sound ON N4K 5P5
(519) 376-2030; *Fax:*(519) 371-4242
www.bayshorebroadcasting.ca
bayshore@bayshorebroadcasting.ca

Bell Media Inc.
299 Queen Street West, Toronto ON M5V 2Z5
(416) 384-8000
www.bellmedia.ca
bellmediacommunications@bellmedia.ca

Blackburn Group Inc.
140 Fullerton,Suite 1905, London ON N6A 5P2
(519) 679-8680; *Fax:*(519) 679-5321
www.blackburnradio.com

Cogeco Diffusion Inc.
800 rue de la Gauchetiere Ouest,Bureau 1100, Montreal QC H5A 1M1
(514) 787-7799; *Fax:*(514) 787-7979
www.cogecodiffusion.com
Ownership: Cogeco Inc., 100%.

Corus Entertainment Inc.
630 3rd Ave. S.W.,Suite 105, Calgary AB T2P 4L4
(403) 444-4244; *Fax:*(403) 444-4242
www.corusent.com
Ownership: J.R. Shaw controls an aggregate of 80% of the voting rights.

Durham Radio Inc.
1200 Airport Blvd.,Suite 207, Oshawa ON L1J 8P5
(905) 428-9600; *Fax:*(905) 571-1150;

Evanov Communications Inc.
5302 Dundas St. W., Toronto ON M9B 1B2
(416) 213-1035; *Fax:*(416) 233-8617
evanovradiogroup.com

Gestion Appalaches inc.
C.P. 69, Thetford Mines PQ G6G 5S3
(418) 335-7533,; *Fax:*(418) 335-9009,
Ownership: Francois Labbe, 99.9%; Fiducie familiale F. Labbe, .07%; and Annie Labbie, .03%.

Golden West Broadcasting Ltd.
Box 950, Altona MB R0G 0B0
(204) 324-6464; *Fax:*(204) 324-8918
info@cfamradio.com
Ownership: Elmer Hildebrand Ltd., 53.98%; Elmer Hildebrand, 14.91%; and others, 31.11%.

Haliburton Broadcasting Group Inc.
46 Nanton Ave., Toronto ON M4W 2Y9
(416) 925-0488; *Fax:*(416) 925-6256
www.hbgradio.com

Harvard Broadcasting Inc.
Century Plaza,1900 Rose St., Regina SK S4P 0A9
(306) 546-6200; *Fax:*(306) 781-7338
www.harvardbroadcasting.com
Ownership: Harvard Developments Inc., 100%.

Larche Communications Inc.
355 Cranston Crescent, Midland ON L4R 4L3
(705) 720-1991; *Fax:*(705) 526-3060;

Maritime Broadcasting
226 Union St., Saint John NB E2L 1B1
(506) 658-2330; *Fax:*(506) 658-5116
www.mbsradio.com
mailbag@k100.ca

My Broadcasting Corp.
Box 961, Renfrew ON K7V 4H4
(613) 432-6936; *Fax:*(613) 432-1086
www.myfmradio.ca

NewCap Inc.
745 Windmill Rd., Dartmouth NS B3B1C2
(902) 468-7557; *Fax:*(902) 468-7558
www.ncc.ca
Ownership: H.R. Steele, Blavin & Company.

Newfoundland Broadcasting Co.
Box 2020, St. John's NF A1C 5S2
(709) 722-5015; *Fax:*(709) 726-5107
www.ntv.ca
ozfm@ozfm.com,ntv@ntv.com
Ownership: Geoffrey W. Stirling, 89.95%; G. Scott Stirling, 10%; and others, 0.05%.

NL Broadcasting Ltd.
611 Lansdowne St., Kamloops BC V2C 1Y6
(250) 372-2292; *Fax:*(250) 372-2293;

Quinte Broadcasting Ltd.
Box 488, Belleville ON K8N 5B2
(613) 969-5555; *Fax:*(613) 969-8122;

Rawlco Radio Ltd.
715 Saskatchewan Crescent West, Saskatoon SK S7M 5V7
(306) 934-2222; *Fax:*(306) 933-3300
Ownership: Rawlco Inc., 90.1%; and others, 9.9%.

RNC MEDIA Inc.
380 av Murdoch, Rouyn-Noranda PQ J9X 1G5
(819) 762-0741; *Fax:*(819) 762-6331;

RNC Media Saguenay-Lac-Saint-Jean
568 boul. St. Joseph, Roberval QC G8H 2K6
(418) 275-1831; *Fax:*(418) 275-2475
chrlfm.com
malevesque@rncmedia.ca

Rogers Broadcasting Ltd.
One Ted Rogers Way, Toronto ON M4Y 3B7
(416) 935-8200; *Fax:*(416) 935-8288
www.rogersmedia.com
Ownership: Rogers Media Inc., 100%. Note: Rogers Media Inc. is 100% owned by Rogers Communications Inc.

Saskatoon Media Group
366 3rd Ave. South, Saskatoon SK S7K 1M5
(306) 244-1975; *Fax:*(306) 665-8484;

The Jim Pattison Broadcast Group
460 Pemberton Terrace, Kamloops BC V2C 1T5
(250) 372-3322; *Fax:*(250) 374-0445
www.jpbroadcast.com
Ownership: Jim Pattison Group.

Touch Canada Broadcasting (2006) Inc.
5316 Calgary Trail, Edmonton AB T6H 4J8
(780) 466-4930; *Fax:*(780) 469-5335
www.shinefm.com
info@shinefm.com

Vista Broadcast Group Inc.
1940 Third Ave., Prince George BC V2M 1G7
(250) 564-2524; *Fax:*(250) 562-6611
www.vistaradio.ca
Ownership: Jetport Inc., 21.4%; 49 shareholders holding less than 10% each. Note: Group also owns CFFM-FM-2 Quesnel and CIRX-FM-1 Vanderhoof, both BC (both originatingstns).

Radio Stations in Canada

Alberta

Airdrie

CFIT-FM
04-12-2007; 106.1 mhz FM; 60 kw; 40 meters; N51 17 35 W113 59 30
159 B East Lake Blvd., Airdrie, AB Canada
(403) 945-3772, *Fax:* (403) 945-0277
www.therangeonline.ca
contactus@therangeonline.ca
License: Airdrie, AB held by Golden West Broadcasting Ltd *No. News Employees:* 2 *Target Audience:* 25-54.
Bruce Daniels, Operations Dir
Jamie Tiessen, General Manager

Athabasca

CKBA(FM)
08-01-1989; 94.1 mhz FM *Hrs Open:* 24; 9 kw
#1 4902 49 Street, Athabasca, AB T9S 1C2 Canada
(780) 675-5301, *Fax:* (780) 675-4938
www.941theriver.ca
wbetts@newcap.ca
License: Athabasca, AB held by Newcap Inc.
Group Owner: NewCap Inc.; (acq 4-19-2002; grpsl)
Nat'l Reps: Canadian Broadcast Sales *Wire Services:* BN Wire
Population Served: 10,000 *No. News Employees:* 1 *Target Audience:* 25-54.*Adv. Rates:* 33; 26; 26; 20;
Robert Steele, Chairman
Dave Murray, CEO/COO
Robert Steele, President
Dave Schuck, General Manager
Wray Betts, Station Manager
Dave Schuck, General Sales Mgr
Robert Alexander, Programming Director
John Walker, News Director
Abdullah Ismail, Engineering Dir

Blairmore

CJPR-FM
01-01-2004; 94.9 mhz FM; 760 w; N49 38 02 W114 29 30
Box 840, Blairmore, AB T0K 0E0 Canada
(403) 562-2806, *Fax:* (403) 562-8114
www.mountainradiofm.com
bkelly@newcap.ca
License: Blairmore, AB held by Newcap Inc.
Group Owner: NewCap Inc.
Population Served: 2,088 *Arbitron Metro Market:* Blairmore, AB
Format: Country
Barb Kelly, Station Manager
Darryl Ferguson, Programming Director
Randy Spencer, News Director
Linda Huze, Station Manager

Bonnyville

CJEG-FM
05-23-2006; 101.3 mhz FM; 27 kw
Box 8251, Bonnyville, AB T9N 2J5 Canada
(780) 812-3058, *Fax:* (780) 812-3363
www.1013koolfm.com
cjegtraffic@newcap.ca
License: Bonnyville, AB held by NewCap Inc.
Group Owner: NewCap Inc.
Population Served: 6,216 *Arbitron Metro Market:* Bonnyville, AB
Format: Contemporary Hits/Top 40
Lise Lacombe, Station Manager
R.C. Ryder, Programming Director
Robb Hunter, News Director
Raymond Green, Chief Engineer
Cash Kaye, Music Director
Kelli Wispinski, Regional Marketing Executive
Greg Friend, Marketing Consultant
Shannon Vinek, Marketing Consultant

CFNA-FM
01-01-2007; 99.7 mhz FM; 50 kw; N54 10 55 W110 51 59
5316 54th Ave., Suite 102, Bonnyville, AB T9N 2C9 Canada
(780) 573-1745, *Fax:* (780) 573-1746
thegoatrocks.com
License: Bonnyville, AB held by Vista Radio Ltd.
Group Owner: Vista Broadcast Group Inc.; (acq 11-21-2008; C$7.3 million with CKLM-FM Lloydminster)
Population Served: 6,216 *Arbitron Metro Market:* Bonnyville, AB
J. Stewart Dent, General Manager

Brooks

CIXF-FM
10-11-2005; 101.1 mhz FM; 2.2 kw
Unit 8-403 2nd Ave., West Brooks, AB T1R 1S3 Canada
(403) 362-3418, *Fax:* (403) 362-8168
1011thefox@mewcap.ca
License: Brooks, AB held by Newcap Inc.
Group Owner: NewCap Inc.
Population Served: 593,820 *Arbitron Metro Market:* Portland, OR
Format: Adult Contemp
Douglas Kirk, Chairman
Thomas Pippy, CFO
Steve Kassay, Operations Dir
Simon Constam, General Sales Mgr
Cathy Philippo, News Director

CIBQ-FM
02-16-2011; 105.7 mhz FM; 6.6 kw; 45.6 meters
402 2nd Avenue West, Suite 28, Brooks, AB T1R 0S3 Canada
(403) 362-3418
www.q1057.ca
License: Brooks, AB held by New Cap Inc
Group Owner: NewCap, Inc.

John Petrie, Station Manager

Calgary

***CBR**
10-01-1964; 1010 khz AM *Hrs Open:* 20
Mailing Address: CA
Second Address: 1724 Westmount Blvd. N.W., Calgary, AB T2N 3G7
(403) 521-6000, *Fax:* (403) 521-6271
www.cbc.ca
info@cbc.ca
License: Calgary, AB held by CBC.
Format: News, News/Talk, Talk, Variety/Diverse*Hrs. of News Programming:* News progmg 24 hrs wkly
Randy Winczira, Operations Dir
Dan Orchard, General Manager
David Perlich, Programming Director
Michelle Everett, Promotions Manager
Donna McElligott, News Director
Harry Wagter, Marketing Manager
Helen Henderson, ProgrammingDirector

***CBR-FM**
09-29-1975; 102.1 mhz FM; 100 kw; 788 ft
Box 2640, Calgary, AB T2N 3G7 Canada
(403) 521-6000, *Fax:* (403) 521-6271
www.cbc.ca/calgary
info@cbc.ca
License: Calgary, AB held by CBC.
Nat'l Network: CBC Radio Two
Format: Blues
Francois Pageau, General Manager

CFAC
05-01-1922; 960 khz AM *Hrs Open:* 24
CA
(403) 291-0000, *Fax:* (403) 291-4368
www.fan960.com
fan960@rci.rogers.com
License: Calgary, AB held by Rogers Broadcasting Ltd.
Group Owner: Rogers Broadcasting Ltd.; (acq 12-89)
Format: Sports*Special Programming:* Agriculture, rural 10 hrs wkly*Hrs. of News Programming:* news progmg 15 hrs wkly *No. News Employees:* 3 *Target Audience:* 55 plus.
Tony Viner, President
Kevin McKenna, Operations Dir
Jim Dunlop, General Sales Mgr
Kelly Kirch, Programming Director
Paul Williams, Advertising Director
Gary Miles, Executive Vice President

CFFR
01-10-1984; 660 khz AM *Hrs Open:* 24
CA
(403) 291-0000, *Fax:* (403) 291-5342
www.660news.com
tips@660news.com
License: Calgary, AB held by Rogers (Alberta) Ltd.
Group Owner: Rogers Broadcasting Ltd.; (acq 9-10-99; grpsl).
Format: News*Special Programming:* Sports 15 hrs wkly*Hrs. of News Programming:* news progmg 10 hrs wkly *No. News Employees:* 5 *Target Audience:* 25-49.
Kevin McKenna, General Manager
Karen Parsons, Programming Director
Shannon Kotylak, Promotions Manager

***CHFMFM**
08-29-1962; 95.9 mhz FM *Hrs Open:* 24; kw
CA
(403) 291-0000, *Fax:* (403) 291-4368
www.chfm.com
info@chfm.com
License: Calgary, AB held by Rogers Broadcasting Ltd.
Group Owner: Rogers Broadcasting Ltd.
Nat'l Reps: Canadian Broadcast Sales
Format: Adult Contemp *No. News Employees:* 1 *Target Audience:* 35-54; females
Tony Viner, CEO
Tanya Berner, Operations Dir
Kevin McKenna, Station Manager
Vince Cownden, Programming Director
Jennifer Enns, Promotions Manager
David Spence, News Director
Darren Robson, Music Director

CHKF-FM
11-14-1998; 94.7 mhz FM *Hrs Open:* 24; 53 kw
2723-37 Ave. N.E. #109, Calgary, AB T1Y 5R8 Canada
(403) 717-1940, *Fax:* (403) 717-1945
www.fm947.com
general @fm947.com
License: Calgary, Calgary County, AB held by Fairchild Radio (Calgary FM) Ltd.
Population Served: 150,000 *Format:* Ethnic*Hrs. of News Programming:* news progmg 21 hrs wkly *No. News Employees:* 2 *Target Audience:* General.
Christine Leung, General Manager
Perry Chan, Programming Director

CHQR
11-01-1964; 770 khz AM *Hrs Open:* 24
CA
(403) 716-6500, *Fax:* (403) 716-2111
www.qr77.com
john.vos@corusent.com
License: Calgary, AB held by CKIK-FM Ltd.
Group Owner: Corus Entertainment Inc.; (Acq 4-15-70)
Nat'l Reps: Canadian Broadcast Sales; Dora-Clayton
TV Affiliate: CICT-TV affil *Format:* News, News/Talk, Sports, Talk*Hrs. of News Programming:* news progmg 17 hrs wkly *No. News Employees:* 11 *Target Audience:* 35 plus.
Phil Kallsen, Programming Director
Bill Powers, News Director

***CJAQ-FM**
01-26-1993; 96.9 mhz FM *Hrs Open:* 24; kw
CA
(416) 935-8392, *Fax:* (416) 935-8410
www.925jackfm.com
License: Calgary, AB held by Rogers (Toronto) Ltd.
Group Owner: Rogers Broadcasting Ltd.; (acq 9-10-99; grpsl).
Format: Contemporary Hits/Top 40*Hrs. of News Programming:* news progmg 6 hrs wkly *No. News Employees:* 4 *Target Audience:* 25-54.
Gary Miles, CEO
Rael Merson, President
Pat Cardinal, General Manager
Laura Nixon, CFO

***CJAYFM**
06-01-1977; 92.1 mhz FM *Hrs Open:* 24; kw
CA
(403) 240-5800, *Fax:* (403) 242-6956
www.cjay92.com
License: Calgary, AB held by Astral Media Radio G.P.
Group Owner: Astral Media Inc.
Stewart Meyers, General Manager
Sandi Leonard, General Sales Mgr
Bob Harris, Programming Director
Jason Almeida, Promotions Manager
Ken Pasolli, Engineering Dir
Ben Jeffery, Music Director

CJSI-FM
12-01-1997; 88.9 mhz FM; 100 kw; Ant 979 ft; N51 03 54 W114 12 47
4510 Macleod Trail S., Calgary, AB T2G 0A4 Canada
(403) 276-1111, *Fax:* (403) 276-1114
www.cjsi.ca
cameron.harris@shinefm.com
License: Calgary, Canada County, AB held by Touch Canada Broadcasting LP.
Group Owner: Touch Canada Broadcasting (2006) Inc.
Nat'l Reps: Target Broadcast Sales
Format: Christian *Target Audience:* a25-54*Adv. Rates:* 45; 45; 45; 45

Mark Imbach, Operations Dir
Mike Kelly, Programming Director

***CJSWFM**
01-15-1985; 90.9 mhz FM *Hrs Open:* 24; 4 kw
Rm. 312- MacEwan Hall, University Dr. N.W., Calgary, AB Canada
(403) 220-3904, *Fax:* (403) 289-8212
www.cjsw.com
License: Calgary, AB held by The University of Calgary Student Radio Society.
Population Served: 1,000,000*Special Programming:* Fr one hr, Ger 2 hrs, It one, Sp one hr wkly*Hrs. of News Programming:* News progmg 5 hrs wkly *Target Audience:* General; young, trendy & well-heeled
Myke Atkinson, General Manager

CFGQ-FM
04-15-1982; 107.3 mhz FM; 100 kw; Ant 638 ft; N51 03 54 W114 12 47
630 3rd Ave. S.W., Suite 105, Calgary, AB T2P 4L4 Canada
(403) 716-6500, *Fax:* (403) 716-2111
www.q107fm.ca
License: Calgary, AB held by CKIK-FM Ltd.
Group Owner: Corus Entertainment Inc.; (acq 7-6-2000; grpsl).
Population Served: 760,000 *Format:* Classic Rock *Target Audience:* 25-44.
Garry McKenzie, General Manager
Doug Young, General Sales Mgr
Tim Morgan, Programming Director
Natasha Rapchuk, News Director
Wade Wensink, Chief Engineer
Judy Rickleton, Traffic Manager

CKMX
05-18-1922; 1060 khz AM *Hrs Open:* 24
CA
(403) 240-5800, *Fax:* (403) 240-5801
www.classiccountryam1060.com
smeyers@astral.com
License: Calgary, AB held by Astral Media Radio G.P.
Group Owner: Astral Media Inc.; (acq 10-29-2007; grpsl)
Format: Adult Contemp*Special Programming:* Jazz 5 hrs wkly
No. News Employees: 1 *Target Audience:* 45 plus.
Stewart Meyers, General Manager
Sandi Leonard, General Sales Mgr
Ken Rigel, Programming Director
Jason Almeida, Promotions Manager

***CKRYFM**
07-09-1982; 105.1 mhz FM *Hrs Open:* 24; kw
CA
(403) 716-6500, *Fax:* (403) 716-2111
www.country105.com
License: Calgary, Calgary County, AB held by Corus Entertainment Inc.
Group Owner: Corus Entertainment Inc.
Nat'l Reps: Canadian Broadcast Sales
Format: Country*Hrs. of News Programming:* news progmg 7 hrs wkly *No. News Employees:* 6 *Target Audience:* 25-54.
Garry McKenzie, General Manager
Doug Young, General Sales Mgr
Phil Kallsen, Programming Director
Adwoa Yamoah, Promotions Manager

***CBRFFM**
01-01-2002; 103.9 mhz FM; kw*Rebroadcasts:* Rebroadcasts CHFA(AM) Edmonton 100%
Mailing Address: CA
Second Address: 1724 Westmount Blvd. N.W., Calgary, AB T2N 3G7
(866) 306-4636, *Fax:* (780) 468-7849
radio-canada.ca/regions/alberta/index.shtml
License: Calgary, AB held by Canadian Broadcasting Corp.
Nat'l Network: Premiere Chaine
Arbitron Metro Market: Calgary, AB *Format:* French, News, Talk
Francois Pageau, General Manager

CFXL-FM
08-30-2002; 103.1 mhz FM; 100 kw; Ant 482 ft; N51 03 54 W114 12 51
1110 Centre St. N.E., Suite 100, Calgary, AB T2E 2R2 Canada
(403) 271-6366, *Fax:* (403) 278-6772
www.xl103calgary.com
feedback@xl103Calgary.com
License: Calgary, AB held by Newcap Inc.
Group Owner: NewCap Inc.; (acq 4-19-2002; grpsl)
Wire Services: BN Wire
Population Served: 900,000*Hrs. of News Programming:* news progmg 35 hrs wkly *No. News Employees:* 1 *Target Audience:* 35-54.*Adv. Rates:* 114; 131; 114; 35

Vinka Dubroja, General Manager
Steve Ravenhill, General Sales Mgr
Don Stevens, Program Director
Michael Godfrey, Promotions Director
Mike Gratton, Chief Engineer

CIBK-FM
09-06-2002; 98.5 mhz FM; 100 kw
Suite 300, 1110 Cernter St. N., Calgary, AB T2E 2R2 Canada
(403) 240-5800, *Fax:* (403) 240-5801
www.vibe985.com
smeyers@astral.com
License: Calgary, AB held by Astral Media Radio G.P.
Group Owner: Astral Media Inc.; (acq 10-29-2007; grpsl)
Population Served: 1,096,833 *Arbitron Metro Market:* Calgary, AB *Format:* Contemporary Hits/Top 40
Stew Meyers, Operations Dir
Stewart Meyers, General Manager
Sandi Leonard, General Sales Mgr
Chad Martin, Programming Director
Jason Almeida, Promotions Manager
Bill Stovold, Engineering Dir
Sibyl Bigler, PromotionsCoordinator
Angie Beers, Creative Director
Tyler Hall, Music Director / Weekday Afternoon Drive

CBCX-FM
01-01-2003; 89.7 mhz FM; 10 kw
P.O. Box 500 Station A, Toronto, ON M5W 1E6 Canada
(866) 306-4636
www.cbc.ca
License: Calgary, AB held by CBC.
Nat'l Network: Espace Musique
Population Served: 1,096,833 *Arbitron Metro Market:* Calgary, AB *Format:* French
R,mi Racine, Chairman
Hubert T. Lacroix, President & CEO
Don Orchard, General Manager
Henk VanLeeuwen, Programming Director
Maryse Bertrand, Vice-President, Real Estate, Legal Services and Ge
William B. Chambers, Vice-President,Brand, Communications and Corporat
Steven Guiton, Vice-President and Chief Regulatory Officer
Louis Lalande, Executive Vice-President
Suzanne Morris, Vice-President and Chief Financial Officer
Roula Zaarour, Vice-President, People andCulture

CFEX-FM
01-01-2007; 92.9 mhz FM *Hrs Open:* 24; 45 kw
255 17th Ave. S.W., Suite 400, Calgary, AB T2S 2T8 Canada
(403) 670-0210, *Fax:* (403) 212-1399
www.x929.ca
License: Calgary, AB held by Harvard Broadcasting Inc.
Group Owner: Harvard Broadcasting Inc.
Population Served: 1,096,833 *Arbitron Metro Market:* Calgary, AB *Format:* Alternative
Christian Hall, Operations Dir
Cam Cowie, General Manager
Gary Brasil, General Sales Mgr
Christian Hall, Programming Director
Ginette Sowerby, Promotions Manager
James Callsen, News Director
Ginette Ouimet, Marketing Director andAssistant Program Director
Darren Ollinger, Creative Director
Chris McCloy, Production Director
Helene Kolada, Business Manager

CFUL-FM
03-12-2007; 90.3 mhz FM; 100 kw; N51 03 37 W114 10 13
1110 Centre St. N.E., Suite 100, Calgary, AB T2E 2R2 Canada
(403) 271-6366, *Fax:* (403) 278-6772
www.fuelcalgary.com
youshouldplaythis@fuelcalgary.com
License: Calgary, AB held by Newcap Inc.
Group Owner: NewCap Inc.
Population Served: 1,096,833 *Arbitron Metro Market:* Calgary, AB
Murray Brookshaw, Operations Dir
Stephen Peck, General Manager
Michael Godfrey, Promotions Manager

CKCE-FM
03-22-2007; 101.5 mhz FM; 48 kw; N51 03 37 W114 10 13
535 7th Ave. S.W., Calgary, AB T2P 0Y4 Canada
(403) 508-2222, *Fax:* (403) 508-2224
www.calgary1015.com
License: Calgary, AB held by Bell Media Calgary Radio Partnership
Group Owner: Bell Media Inc.; (acq 6-22-2007; grpsl)

James Stuart, General Manager
Gavin Mortimer, General Sales Mgr
Rob Mise, Programming Director
Khazma Tichon, Promotions Manager

CKAV-FM-3
88.1 mhz FM; 33 kw; Ant 1,040 ft; N51 03 54 W114 12 47
PO Box 87, Station E, Toronto, ON M6H 4E1 Canada
(416) 703-1287, *Fax:* (416) 703-4328
aboriginalvoices.com
info@aboriginalvoices.com
License: Calgary, AB held by Aboriginal Voices Radio Inc.
Group Owner: Aboriginal Voices Radio Inc.
Population Served: 2,615,060 *Arbitron Metro Market:* Toronto, ON *Format:* Ethnic
Roy Hennessy, Operations Dir
Patrice Mousseau, Programming Director

CHUP-FM
03-06-2008; 97.7 mhz FM; 100 kw; N51 04 24 W114 15 38
6807 Railway St. S.E., Suite 110, Calgary, AB T2H 2V6 Canada
(403) 385-4000, *Fax:* (403) 385-4001
www.977CalgaryFM.com
win@977CalgaryFM.com
License: Calgary, AB held by Rawlco Radio Ltd.
Group Owner: Rawlco Radio Ltd.
Nat'l Reps: Canadian Broadcast Sales
No. News Employees: 27
Kent Newson, Operations Dir
Rick Burgess, General Sales Mgr
Maranne Vibert, Promotions Manager
Kath Thompson, Assistant Programming Director
Marianne Vibert, Operations Manager
Glen Ruskin, VP, Sales Manager

Camrose

CFCW
11-02-1954; 790 khz AM *Hrs Open:* 24; 50 kw-U, DA-2; N52 57 37 W112 57 33
Mailing Address: 2394 W. Edmonton Mall, 8882 170th St., Edmonton, AB Canada
Second Address: 5708-48 Avenue, Camrose, AB T4V 0K1
(780) 437-4996, *Fax:* (780) 436-9803
www.cfcw.com
License: Camrose, AB held by Newcap Inc.
Group Owner: NewCap Inc.
Nat'l Reps: imsradio
Population Served: 900,000*Special Programming:* Farm 5 hrs wkly*Hrs. of News Programming:* News progmg 11 hrs wkly
Target Audience: 25-54; country music, sports & hockey listeners in Edmonton rgn
Patrick Cardinal, Operations Dir
Randy Lemay, General Manager
Ross Hawse, General Sales Mgr
Jackie Rae-Greening, Programming Director
David Bonneville, Station Accountant

CFCW-FM
10-01-2005; 98.1 mhz FM; 50 kw
5708 48th Ave., Camrose, AB T4V 0K1 Canada
(780) 672-9822, *Fax:* (780) 672-4678
www.981camfm.com
License: Camrose, AB held by Newcap Inc.
Group Owner: NewCap Inc.
Wire Services: BN Wire
Randy Lemay, General Manager
Ron Lehman, General Sales Mgr
John Roberts, Programming Director

Canmore

CHMN-FM
02-01-1998; 106.5 mhz FM; 510 w
749 Railway Ave., Peschl's Corner, Canmore, AB T1W 1P2 Canada
(403) 678-2222, *Fax:* (403) 678-6844
www.mountainfm.ca
License: Canmore, AB held by Rogers Broadcasting Ltd.
Group Owner: Rogers Broadcasting Ltd.
Nat'l Reps: Canadian Broadcast Sales
Format: Adult Contemp
Kevin McKenna, General Manager
Paul Williams, General Sales Mgr
Vince Camden, Programming Director
Jeff Hubbard, Music Director

Cold Lake

CJXK-FM
09-03-2004; 95.3 mhz FM; 100 kw; N54 17 26 W110 28 57

B5412 55th St., Cold Lake, AB T9M 1R5 Canada
(780) 594-2459, *Fax:* (780) 594-3001
www.953krock.com
requests@k-rock953.com
License: Cold Lake, AB held by Newcap Inc.
Group Owner: NewCap Inc.
Population Served: 13,839 *Arbitron Metro Market:* Cold Lake, AB *Format:* Classic Rock
Chad Tabish, General Manager
Carla Beaupre, Station Manager
Jeff Murray, Programming Director
Nola Rudell, Administration/Traffic
Chris Gill, Marketing Consultant
Shannon Vinek, Marketing Consultant
Kelli Wispinski, MarketingConsultant
Greg Friend, Marketing Consultant
Crystal Frey, Marketing Consultant

Drayton Valley

CIBW-FM
01-01-1994; 92.9 mhz FM *Hrs Open:* 24; 7.4 kw
Postal Bag 929, Drayton Valley, AB T7A 1V3 Canada
(780) 542-9290, *Fax:* (780) 542-9319
www.bigwestcountry.ca
bwc929@bigwestcountry.ca
License: Drayton Valley, Brazeau County, AB held by Jim Pattison Broadcast Group Ltd. (the general partner) and Jim Pattison Industries Ltd. (the limited partner) carrying on business as Jim Pattison Broadcast Group L.P.
Group Owner: The Jim Pattison Broadcast Group; (acq 9-7-95).
Nat'l Reps: Canadian Broadcast Sales; Target Broadcast Sales
Wire Services: BN Wire
Population Served: 100,000 *Format:* Country*Hrs. of News Programming:* news progmg 16 hrs wkly *No. News Employees:* 1 *Target Audience:* General.*Adv. Rates:* 32; 29; 29; 20
Paul Mason, General Manager
Bryn James, General Sales Mgr
Trevor Grinde, Programming Director

Drumheller

CKDQ
01-01-1958; 910 khz AM *Hrs Open:* 24
Mailing Address: CA
Second Address: 515 Hwy. 10 E., Drumheller, AB T0J 0Y0
(403) 823-3384, *Fax:* (403) 823-7241
ww.q91country.com
Q91@newcap.ca
License: Drumheller, AB held by Newcap Inc.
Group Owner: NewCap Inc.; (acq 4-19-2002; grpsl)
Nat'l Reps: CBS Radio
Format: Country*Special Programming:* Farm 8 hrs, relg 2 hrs wkly*Hrs. of News Programming:* news progmg 11 hrs wkly *No. News Employees:* 2 *Target Audience:* 25-54.
Rick Walters, General Manager
Linda Scheffelmaier, Station Manager
Al Redel, News Director

Edmonton

CBX
01-01-1948; 740 khz AM *Hrs Open:* 24
Mailing Address: CA
Second Address: Edmonton City Ctr., 10062-102 Ave., Suite 123, Alberta, AB T5J 24G
(780) 468-7500, *Fax:* (780) 468-7419
www.edmonton.cbc.ca
cbx_edmonton@cbc.ca
License: Edmonton, AB held by CBC.
Nat'l Network: CBC Radio One
Format: News, News/Talk, Talk *Target Audience:* 35 plus; college educated
Mike Linden, General Sales Mgr
Judy Piercey, Programming Director

CBX-FM
90.9 mhz FM; 100 kw; Ant 633 ft
Box 555, Edmonton, AB T5J 2P4 Canada
(780) 468-7500, *Fax:* (780) 468-7419
www.edmonton.cdc.ca
License: Edmonton, AB held by CBC
Nat'l Network: CBC Radio Two
Format: News
Mark Sislo, General Manager
Doug MacPherson, Chief Engineer

CFBR-FM
04-25-1951; 100.3 mhz FM; 100 kw; 482 ft
18520 Stony Plain Rd., Suite 100, Edmonton, AB T5S 2E2 Canada
(780) 486-2800, *Fax:* (780) 489-6927
www.thebearrocks.com
info@thebearrocks.com
License: Edmonton, AB held by Astral media Radio G.P.
Group Owner: Astral Media Inc.
Format: Classic Rock
Susan Reade, General Sales Mgr
Ryan Zimmerman, Programming Director
Bob Hunter, Chief Engineer
Park Warden, Music Director

CFRN
01-01-1934; 1260 khz AM
CA
(780) 486-2800, *Fax:* (780) 489-6927
www.cfrn.com
info@cfrn.com
License: Edmonton, AB held by Astral Media Radio G.P.
Group Owner: Astral Media Inc.; (acq 10-29-2007; grpsl)
Format: Sports *Target Audience:* 45 plus.
Stewart Meyers, General Manager
Ryan Zimmerman, Programming Director

CHED
03-03-1954; 630 khz AM
CA
(780) 440-6300, *Fax:* (780) 468-6739
www.630ched.com
info@630ched.com
License: Edmonton, AB held by Corus Premium Television Ltd.
Group Owner: Corus Entertainment Inc.; (acq 7-6-00; grpsl).
Format: Sports, Talk
Doug Rutherford, General Manager
Syd Smith, Programming Director
Tanya Laughren, Promotions Manager
Tom Davies, Chief Engineer

*CHFA
11-20-1949; 680 khz AM *Hrs Open:* 24
Mailing Address: CA
Second Address: 123 Edmonton City Center, Edmonton, AB T5J 2P4
(780) 468-7800, *Fax:* (780) 468-7849
www.radio-canada.ca/alberta
nouvelles.alberta@radio-canada.ca
License: Edmonton, AB held by CBC.
Format: Adult Contemp, News, News/Talk, Talk, Variety/Diverse*Hrs. of News Programming:* news progmg 8 hrs wkly *No. News Employees:* 8 *Target Audience:* 20-60; Fr speaking
Francois Pageau, General Manager
Jack Tyler, Chief Engineer

CHQT
08-19-1965; 880 khz AM
CA
(780) 440-6300, *Fax:* (780) 469-5937
www.inews880.com
news@inews880.com
License: Edmonton, AB held by Corus Radio Co.
Group Owner: Corus Entertainment Inc.
Format: News
Syd Smith, Programming Director
Tanya Laughren, Promotions Manager
Danielle Mattiello, News Director

CIRK-FM
01-01-1949; 97.3 mhz FM; 100 kw
2394 W. Edmonton Mall, 8882 170th St., Edmonton, AB T5T 4M2 Canada
(780) 437-4996, *Fax:* (780) 436-9803
www.k97.fm
License: Edmonton, AB held by NewCap Inc.
Group Owner: NewCap Inc.; (acq 2-17-99; C$10 million)
Nat'l Reps: imsradio
Format: Classic Rock *Target Audience:* 18-54; mobile adults
Patrick Cardinal, Operations Dir
Randy Lemey, General Manager
Kelly Walter, General Sales Mgr
James Gushnowski, Programming Director
Brent Shelton, Promotions Manager
David Bonneville, Station Accountant

CISN-FM
06-05-1982; 103.9 mhz FM; 100 kw; 757 ft
5204 84th St., Edmonton, AB T6E 5N8 Canada
(780) 428-1104, *Fax:* (780) 469-5937
www.cisnfm.com
info@cisnfm.com
License: Edmonton, AB held by Corus Radio Co.
Group Owner: Corus Entertainment Inc.; (acq 7-6-00; grpsl).
Format: Country
Doug Rutherford, General Manager
Devin Gray, General Sales Mgr
Chris Scheetz, Programming Director
Ashtyn Walker, Promotions Manager
Bob Layton, News Director
Tom Davies, Chief Engineer
James Stuart, Programming Director
BryanHall, Sports Commentator
Danielle Mattiello, Traffic Manager

CJCA
05-22-1922; 930 khz AM *Hrs Open:* 24
CA
(780) 466-4930, *Fax:* (780) 469-5335
www.cjca.ca
License: Edmonton, AB held by Touch Canada Broadcasting LP.
Group Owner: Touch Canada Broadcasting (2006) Inc.; (acq 4-12-94)
Format: Christian*Hrs. of News Programming:* News progmg 6 hrs wkly *Target Audience:* 25-54.
Malcolm Hunt, Programming Director
Topher Braithwaite, Promotions Manager
Len Dehek, Disc Jockey
Dean Demitor, Disc Jockey
Johnny Stretch, Disc Jockey

*CJSR-FM
01-01-1984; 88.5 mhz FM *Hrs Open:* 24; 900 w
Room 0-09, Students' Union Bldg., Edmonton, AB T6G 2J7 Canada
(780) 492-2577, *Fax:* (780) 492-3121
www.cjsrfm88.blogspot.com
admin@cjsr.com
License: Edmonton, Canada County, AB held by The First Alberta Campus Radio Association.
Population Served: 1,500,000 *Format:* Alternative*Special Programming:* American Indian 2 hrs, Black 7 hrs, class 2 hrs, f*Hrs. of News Programming:* 8 hrs wkly *No. News Employees:* 1 *Target Audience:* Anyonetired with commercial radio*Adv. Rates:* contact website www.cjsr.com
Heather Hutchinson, Operations Dir
Sarah Edwards, Station Manager
Aaron Levin, Programming Director
Sam Power, News Director

CKER-FM
01-01-1996; 101.7 mhz FM *Hrs Open:* 24; 100 kw
10212 Jasper Ave., Edmonton, AB T5J 5A3 Canada
(780) 424-2222, *Fax:* (780) 401-1600
www.worldfm.ca
feedback@worldfm.ca
License: Edmonton, AB held by Rogers Broadcasting Ltd.
Group Owner: Rogers Broadcasting Ltd.; (acq 11-29-2006; grpsl)
Population Served: 1,000,000 *Format:* Chinese, Ethnic*Special Programming:* It 3 hrs, Sp 8 hrs, Por 2 hrs, Ukrainian 10 hrs, D*Hrs. of News Programming:* news progmg 14 hrs wkly *No. News Employees:* 2 *TargetAudience:* General; ethnic audience (24 languages) & Christian
Stephen Crane, Operations Dir
Tom Bedore, General Manager
Shelley Ruis, General Sales Mgr
Roman Brytan, Programming Director
Susan Reade, Sales Supervisor

CKNG-FM
08-11-1982; 92.5 mhz FM; 100 kw; 900 ft
5204-84 St., Edmonton, AB T6E 5N8 Canada
(780) 469-6992, *Fax:* (780) 469-5937
www.joefm.ca
info@joefm.ca
License: Edmonton, AB held by Corus Premium Television Ltd.
Group Owner: Corus Entertainment Inc.
Format: Contemporary Hits/Top 40
Devin Gray, General Sales Mgr
Greg Johnson, Programming Director
Zac Davis, Promotions Manager

CKRA-FM
11-15-1979; 96.3 mhz FM *Hrs Open:* 24; 100 kw; Ant 757 ft
2394 W. Edmonton Mall, 8882 170th St., Edmonton, AB T5T 4M2 Canada
(780) 437-4996, *Fax:* (780) 435-0844
www.963capitalfm.com
License: Edmonton, AB held by NewCap Inc.
Group Owner: NewCap Inc.
Nat'l Reps: imsradio
Population Served: 800,000 *Format:* Oldies *Target Audience:* 25-54; urban young adults
Patrick Cardinal, Operations Dir
Randy Lemay, General Manager
Kelly Walter, General Sales Mgr
John Roberts, Programming Director

Melanie Harysh, Promotions Manager
David Bonneville, Station Accountant

CKUA
11-21-1927; 580 khz AM *Hrs Open:* 24
CA
(780) 428-7595, *Fax:* (780) 428-7624
www.ckua.com
radio@ckua.com
License: Edmonton, AB held by CKUA Radio Foundation
Format: Variety/Diverse
Tom Cook, General Manager
Don Barnes, General Sales Mgr
Kris Rodts, Engineering Dir
Joe Gurney, Chief Engineer

***CKUA-FM**
06-28-1948; 94.9 mhz FM *Hrs Open:* 24 hrs; 100 kw; 400 ft
10526 Jasper Ave., 4th Fl., Edmonton, AB T5J 1Z7 Canada
(780) 428-7595, *Fax:* (780) 428-7624
www.ckua.com
radio@ckua.com
License: Edmonton, AB held by CKUA Radio Foundation.
Population Served: 3,000,000 *Format:* Jazz, Variety/Diverse*Hrs. of News Programming:* news progmg 6 hrs wkly *No. News Employees:* 4 *Target Audience:* General; Alberta population*Adv. Rates:* 100; 70; 50; 50
Ken Regan, General Manager
Andrea Louie, General Sales Mgr
Brian Dunsmore, Programming Director
Sharon Cross, News Director
Neil Lutes, Chief Engineer
Peter North, Music Director

CJRY-FM
01-01-2004; 105.9 mhz FM; 100 kw; Ant 633 ft
5316 Calgary Tr., Edmonton, AB T6H 4J8 Canada
(780) 466-4930, *Fax:* (780) 469-5335
www.shinefm.com
105.9@shinefm.com?subject=Website_Comments_CJRY
License: Edmonton, AB held by Touch Canada Broadcasting L.P.
Group Owner: Touch Canada Broadcasting (2006) Inc.
Population Served: 817,498 *Arbitron Metro Market:* Edmonton, AB *Format:* Christian
Malcolm Hunt, Programming Director
Johnny Stretch, Disc Jockey
Dean Demitor, Disc Jockey

CHDI-FM
05-09-2005; 102.9 mhz FM *Hrs Open:* 24; 100 kw
5915 Gateway Blvd., Edmonton, AB T6H 2H3 Canada
(780) 423-2005, *Fax:* (780) 437-5129
www.sonic1029.com
al.ford@rci.rogers.com
License: Edmonton, AB held by Rogers Broadcasting Ltd.
Group Owner: Rogers Broadcasting Ltd.; (acq 11-29-2006; grpsl)
Population Served: 817,498 *Arbitron Metro Market:* Edmonton, AB *No. News Employees:* 1
Stephen Crane, Operations Dir
Tom Bedore, General Manager
Shelley Ruis, General Sales Mgr
Al Ford, Programming Director
Brent Shelton, Promotions Manager
Kory Read, News Director

CHBN-FM
02-17-2005; 91.7 mhz FM; 100 kw
10212 Jasper Ave. N.W., Edmonton, AB T5J 5A3 Canada
(780) 424-2222, *Fax:* (780) 401-1600
www.thebounce.ca
License: Edmonton, AB held by Rogers Broadcasting Ltd
Group Owner: Rogers Broadcasting Ltd.
Nat'l Reps: CHUM Radio Sales
Target Audience: 15-39.
James Stuart, General Manager
Giselle Sowa, General Sales Mgr
Dan Tucek, Programming Director
Lamya Asiff, News Director
Trevor Stuart, Chief Engineer

CIUP-FM
12-08-2005; 99.3 mhz FM; 100 kw; 272 meters
5241 Calgary Tr., Suite 700, Centre 104, Edmonton, AB T6H 5G8 Canada
(780) 433-7877, *Fax:* (780) 438-8484
www.magic99.ca
thofer@rawlco.com
License: Edmonton, AB held by Rawlco Radio Ltd.
Group Owner: Rawlco Radio Ltd.
Kurt Leavins, General Manager
Kelly Walter, General Sales Mgr

CKAV-FM-4
01-01-2007; 89.3 mhz FM; 100 kw; N53 30 53 W113 17 07
PO Box 87, Station E, Toronto, ON M6H 4E1 Canada
(416) 703-1287, *Fax:* (416) 703-4328
aboriginalvoices.com
info@aboriginalvoices.com
License: Edmonton, AB held by Aboriginal Voices Radio Inc.
Group Owner: Aboriginal Voices Radio Inc.
Population Served: 2,615,060 *Arbitron Metro Market:* Toronto, ON *Format:* Ethnic
Roy Hennessy, Operations Dir
Patrice Mousseau, Programming Director

CKNO-FM
02-23-2010; 102.3 mhz FM; 51 kw
9894 42 Avenue NW, Suite 102, Edmonton, AB T6E 5V5 Canada
(780) 433-7877
www.1023nowradio.com
License: Edmonton, AB held by Rawlco Radio Ltd
Kurt Leavins, General Manager

CKEA-FM
04-15-2010; 95.7 mhz FM; 47 kw
Centre 104, Suite 700, 5241 Calagry Trail, Edmonton, AB T6H 5G8 Canada
(780) 435-3023
www.lite957.ca
License: Edmonton, AB held by Harvard Broadcasting Inc
Group Owner: Harvard Broadcasting Inc.
Format: Adult Contemp

Edson

CFXE-FM
01-01-2007; 94.3 mhz FM *Hrs Open:* 24; 11 kw; N53 38 47 W116 32 26
Mailing Address: Box 7800, Edson, AB T7E 1V8 Canada
Second Address: 422 50th St., Edson, AB T7E 1T1
(780) 723-4461, *Fax:* (780) 723-3765
www.theeagle.ca
dschuck@fox-radio.ca
License: Edson, AB held by Newcap Inc.
Group Owner: NewCap Inc.
Nat'l Reps: imsradio *Wire Services:* Canadian Press
Population Served: 8,475 *Arbitron Metro Market:* Edson, AB *Format:* Contemporary Hits/Top 40, Adult Contemp*Special Programming:* Farm 2 hrs wkly *No. News Employees:* 3 *Target Audience:* 18-55.
Al Anderson, Operations Dir
Dave Schuck, General Manager
Dave Schuck, General Sales Mgr
Rob Alexander, Programming Director
John Walker, News Director

Falher

***CKRP-FM**
11-02-1996; 95.7 mhz FM; 671 w; N55 44 07 W117 11 34*Rebroadcasts:* Rebroadcasts CITE-FM Montreal 65%
Box 718, Association Canadienne-Francaise de l'Alberta, Falher, AB T0H 1M0 Canada
(780) 837-2346, *Fax:* (780) 837-2092
ckrp_fm@yahoo.ca
License: Falher, AB held by Association canadienne-francaise de l'Alberta-Regionale de Riviere-la-Paix.
Format: Adult Contemp *Target Audience:* Fr population
Julie Cadieux, President

Fort McMurray

CKYX-FM
03-01-1985; 97.9 mhz FM *Hrs Open:* 24; 40 kw
9912 Franklin Ave., Fort McMurray, AB T9H 2K5 Canada
(780) 743-2246, *Fax:* (780) 791-7250
www.rock979.ca
License: Fort McMurray, Canada County, AB held by Rogers Broadcasting Ltd.
Group Owner: Rogers Broadcasting Ltd.; (acq 11-29-2006; grpsl)
Population Served: 60,000 *Format:* Classic Rock*Hrs. of News Programming:* news progmg 5 hrs wkly *No. News Employees:* 3 *Target Audience:* 18-44.*Adv. Rates:* 75; 65; 75; 50
Jim Schneider, General Manager

CJOK-FM
01-01-2003; 93.3 mhz FM *Hrs Open:* 24; 40 kw; N56 41 16 W111 19 55
9912 Franklin Ave., Fort McMurray, AB T9H 2K5 Canada
(780) 743-2246, *Fax:* (780) 791-7250
mymcmurray.com
FortMcMurray@rci.rogers.com
License: Fort McMurray, Canada County, AB held by Rogers Broadcasting Ltd.
Group Owner: Rogers Broadcasting Ltd.; (acq 11-29-2006; grpsl)
Population Served: 64,773 *Arbitron Metro Market:* Fort McMurray, AB *Format:* Country*Hrs. of News Programming:* news progmg 4 hrs wkly *No. News Employees:* 3 *Target Audience:* 25-44.
Jim Schneider, General Manager

CKOS-FM
01-01-2007; 91.1 mhz FM; 35 w; N56 40 11 W111 19 57
P.O. Box 5512, Fort McMurray, AB T9H 3G5 Canada
(780) 791-5911, *Fax:* (780) 743-1526
kaos911.com
info@kaos911.com
License: Fort McMurray, AB held by King's Kids Promotions Outreach Ministries Inc.
Population Served: 64,773 *Arbitron Metro Market:* Fort McMurray, AB *Format:* Christian *Target Audience:* 18-34.
Jill Edwards, Business Manager
Jon Ramer, General Manager
Jonathan Andrews, Music Director
Rick Kirschner, Executive Director
Brittany Pittman, Sales Executive

CFVR-FM
01-01-2008; 103.7 mhz FM; 20 kw; N56 48 29 W111 26 55
9904 Franklin Ave., Fort McMurray, AB T9H 2K5 Canada
(780) 791-0103, *Fax:* (780) 791-1448
www.mix1037fm.com
License: Fort McMurray, AB held by Harvard Broadcasting Inc.
Group Owner: Harvard Broadcasting Inc.
No. News Employees: 3 *Target Audience:* 18-54; women
Jason Huschi, General Manager
Craig Picton, Programming Director

CHFT-FM
06-16-2008; 100.5 mhz FM; 20 kw; N56 44 00 W111 23 04
9904 Franklin Ave., Fort McMurray, AB T9H 2K5 Canada
(780) 791-0810, *Fax:* (780) 791-0811
www.krock.fm
onair@krock.fm
License: Fort McMurray, AB held by Newcap Inc.
Group Owner: NewCap Inc.
Population Served: 64,773 *Arbitron Metro Market:* Fort McMurray, AB *Format:* Classic Rock *No. News Employees:* 1
Ross Jacobs, Sales Manager
James Gushnowski, Music Director
Amanda Purcell, News Director
Brad MacLauchlan, Music Director

Fort Vermilion

CIAM-FM
01-27-2003; 92.7 mhz FM *Hrs Open:* 24; 30 w
Mailing Address: Box 609, 4709 River Road, Fort Vermilion, AB T0H 1N0 Canada
Second Address: 4709 River Rd., Fort Vermilion, AB T0H 1N0
(780)-927-2426, *Fax:* (780) 927-2427
www.ciamradio.com
info@ciamradio.com
License: Fort Vermilion, AB held by Care Radio Broadcasting Association.
Population Served: 727 *Arbitron Metro Market:* Fort Vermilion, AB *Format:* Variety/Diverse
Michael Sandstrom, General Manager
Phil Peters, Programming Director
Kevin Wiebe, News Director

Grand Falls

CBT
07-01-1949; 540 khz AM
CA
(709) 489-2102, *Fax:* (709) 489-1055
www.cbc.ca/nl/
License: Grand Falls, NF held by CBC.
Format: Public Affairs, News
Robert Rabinowitz, CEO
Diane Humber, General Manager
Chris Norman, Station Manager

Grande Prairie

CFGP-FM
06-20-1996; 97.7 mhz FM *Hrs Open:* 24; 70 kw; N55 27 57 W118 45 32
9835 101st Ave., Suite 200, Grande Prairie, AB T8V 5V4 Canada

(780) 539-9700, *Fax:* (780) 532-1600
www.sunfm.com
License: Grande Prairie, AB held by Rogers Broadcasting Ltd.
Group Owner: Rogers Broadcasting Ltd.; (acq 11-29-2006; grpsl)
Format: Contemporary Hits/Top 40*Hrs. of News Programming:* news progmg 4 hrs wkly *No. News Employees:* 4 *Target Audience:* 25-55.
Dave Reid, General Manager
Kevin Becker, Programming Director
Lisa Kirby, Promotions Manager
Daryl Major, News Director
Sam Lowe, Chief Engineer

CJXX-FM
11-01-2000; 93.1 mhz FM *Hrs Open:* 24; 100 kw; N55 03 08 W118 51 59
9817 101st Ave., Suite 202, Grande Prairie, AB T8V 0X6 Canada
(780) 532-0840, *Fax:* (780) 538-1266
www.bigcountryxx.com
info@bigcountryxx.com
License: Grande Prairie, AB held by Jim Pattison Broadcast Group Ltd. (the general partner) and Jim Pattison Industries Ltd. (the limited partner) carrying on business as Jim Pattison Broadcast Group L.P.
Group Owner: The Jim Pattison Broadcast Group; (acq 12-21-2000; grpsl)
Wire Services: BN Wire
Population Served: 55,032 *Arbitron Metro Market:* Grand Prairie, AB *Format:* Country*Hrs. of News Programming:* news progmg 14 hrs wkly *No. News Employees:* 5 *Target Audience:* 25-49; adults who love countrymusic*Adv. Rates:* 93; na; 77; 71
Rick Arnish, President
Ken Norman, General Manager
Anne Graham, General Sales Mgr
Candace Boyne, Promotions Manager
Barbara Shannon, Promotions Director

CFRI-FM
03-30-2007; 104.7 mhz FM; 100 kw
#1 11002 104th Ave., Grande Prairie, AB T8V 7W5 Canada
(780) 357-3733, *Fax:* (780) 830-7815
www.1047freefm.com
gord@1047freefm.com
License: Grande Prairie, Canada County, AB held by Vista Radio Ltd.
Group Owner: Vista Broadcast Group Inc.
Nat'l Reps: Canadian Broadcast Sales
Population Served: 55,032 *Arbitron Metro Market:* Grande Prairie, AB *Format:* Classic Rock *No. News Employees:* 3 *Target Audience:* A 25-54
J.C. Coutts, Operations Dir
Gordon Gauvin, General Manager
Gordon Gauvin, General Sales Mgr
J.C. Coutts, Programming Director
Sara Buchan, News Director
Uncle Scotty, Music Director
Nicole Lester, Retail Sales Supervisor
MartiOltmann, Traffic Manager

CIKT-FM
04-09-2007; 98.9 mhz FM; 100 kw; Ant 842 ft; N55 28 44 W118 45 04
8716 108th St., Suite 104, Grande Prairie, AB T8V 4C7 Canada
(780) 882-6612, *Fax:* (780) 882-6708
www.q99live.com
License: Grande Prairie, AB held by Bear Creek Broadcasting Ltd.
Nat'l Reps: Target Broadcast Sales *Regional Reps:* WTR Media
Population Served: 250,000 *No. News Employees:* 3 *Target Audience:* 35-54.*Adv. Rates:* Available on request
Ken Truhn, President
Ken Truhn, General Manager
Ken Truhn, General Sales Mgr
Paul Ouellette, Programming Director
Cristy Ellen, Promotions Manager
Randy Pike, News Director
Mark Simms, Chief Engineer

CJGY-FM
12-03-2007; 96.3 mhz FM; 70 kw; N55 29 20 W118 44 50
#111, 10530 117 Ave., Grande Prairie, AB T8V 7N7 Canada
(780) 830-7640, *Fax:* (780) 830-7636
www.cjgy.ca
96.3@shinefm.com
License: Grande Prairie, AB held by Grande Prairie Radio Ltd.
No. News Employees: 6
Ed Elias, General Manager
Terry Van Veen, Station Manager
Jane Wheeler, General Sales Mgr
Terry Van Veen, Programming Director
Marco Auriti, Engineering Dir

High Level

CKHL-FM
07-01-1999; 102.1 mhz FM; 8.765 kw
Box 3759, High Level, AB T0H 1Z0 Canada
(780) 926-4530, *Fax:* (780) 926-4564
www.ylcountry.com
sdale@sawridge.com
License: High Level, AB held by 912038 Alberta Ltd.
Population Served: 3,641 *Arbitron Metro Market:* High Level, AB
Format: Country *No. News Employees:* 4
Chris Black, General Manager / Sales Manager
Chris Black, General Manager / Sales Manager
Don Jennings, Programming Director
Karin Koppitz, News Director
Chris Black, General Sales Manager

High Prairie

CKVH-FM
09-12-2011; 93.5 mhz FM; 25 kw
Box 2219, High Prairie, AB T0G 1E0 Canada
(780) 523-5120, *Fax:* (780) 523-3660
www.prairiefm.ca
License: High Prairie, AB held by New Cap Inc
Group Owner: NewCap, Inc.
Format: Contemporary Hits/Top 40, Adult Contemp
Dave Schuck, General Manager

High River

CHRB
12-05-1977; 1140 khz AM *Hrs Open:* 24
CA
(403) 652-2472, *Fax:* (403) 652-7861
www.am1140radio.com
am1140@am1140radio.com
License: High River, AB held by Golden West Broadcasting Ltd.
Group Owner: Golden West Broadcasting Ltd.
Nat'l Reps: Canadian Broadcast Sales
Format: Religious, Country*Special Programming:* Farm 5 hrs hrs wkly*Hrs. of News Programming:* news progmg 10 hrs wkly
No. News Employees: 2 *Target Audience:* General.
Elmer Hildebrand, CEO
Lyndon Friesen, Operations Dir
Keith Leask, Station Manager
Menno Friesen, General Sales Mgr
Don McCracken, News Director
Vern Moores, Chief Engineer

High River-Okotoks

CKUV-FM
01-01-2003; 100.9 mhz FM; 100 kw
2nd Floor, 42 McRae Street, P.O. Box 1889, Okotoks, AB T1S 1B7 Canada
(403) 995-9611, *Fax:* (403) 652-7861
www.theeagle1009.com
pmacdonald@goldenwestradio.com
License: High River-Okotoks, AB held by Golden West Broadcasting Ltd.
Group Owner: Golden West Broadcasting Ltd.
Population Served: 12,920 *Arbitron Metro Market:* High River, AB
Louise Burns, General Sales Mgr
Kristiana Clemmens, Programming Director
Don McCracken, News and Sports Director
Marc Montanchez, Chief Engineer
Juliet Lammers, Promotions Director

CFXO-FM
10-30-2007; 99.7 mhz FM; 18 kw; N50 40 01 W113 58 27
11 5th Ave. S.E., High River, AB T1V 1G2 Canada
(403) 652-2472, *Fax:* (403) 652-7861
sun99radio.com
info@sun99radio.com
License: High River-Okotoks, AB held by Golden West Broadcasting Ltd.
Group Owner: Golden West Broadcasting Ltd.
Population Served: 24,511 *Arbitron Metro Market:* Okotoks, AB
Format: Country
Jeff Young, Station Manager

Hinton

CFXH-FM
07-01-2004; 97.5 mhz FM; 1.2 kw
Newcap Alberta N.W. Division, 2nd Floor, 422-50th Street, Edson, AB T7E 1T1 Canada
(780) 723-4461, *Fax:* (780) 723-3765
www.theeagle.ca
feedback@theeagle.ca
License: Hinton, AB held by Newcap Inc.
Group Owner: NewCap Inc.
Population Served: 9,640 *Arbitron Metro Market:* Hinton, AB
Format: Contemporary Hits/Top 40, Adult Contemp *Target Audience:* 18-54.
Dave Schuck, General Manager
Rob Alexander, Programming Director
John Walker, News Director
Michelle Walsh, Edson and Area Marketing Consultant

Lac La Biche

CFWE-FM
01-01-1990; 89.9 mhz FM *Hrs Open:* 24
13245 146th St., Edmonton, AB T5L 4S8 Canada
(780) 447-2393, *Fax:* (780) 454-2820
www.cfweradio.ca
info@cfweradio.ca
License: Lac La Biche, AB held by Aboriginal Multi-Media Society of Alberta.
Format: Country *Target Audience:* General; Cree, Blackfoot, Stoney, Dene & English language listeners
Bert Crowfoot, CEO
Alan Standerwick, Station Manager

Lacombe

CJUV-FM
06-28-2006; 94.1 mhz FM; 27 kw
4725 49B Ave, Lacombe, AB T4L 1K1 Canada
(403) 786-0194, *Fax:* (403) 786-0199
www.sunny94.com
sonia@laradiogroup.com
License: Lacombe, AB held by L.A. Radio Group Inc.
Population Served: 11,707 *Arbitron Metro Market:* Lacombe, AB
Format: Contemporary Hits/Top 40, Adult Contemp *Target Audience:* 35-54
Troy Stevens, President
Sonia Sawyer, CFO
Darin Clark, Programming Director
Darcy Stingel, Promotions Manager
Kim Kay, News Director
Matt Panelli, Account Manager
Gabi Post, Administrative Assistant

Leduc

CJLD-FM
06-25-2012; 93.1 mhz FM
4111 43a Avenue, Leduc, AB T9E 4S7 Canada
Fax: (780) 986-1244
www.leducfm.com
License: Leduc, AB held by Blackgold Broadcasting Inc
Format: Country
Mark Tamagi, President

Lethbridge

CFRV-FM
01-01-1979; 107.7 mhz FM *Hrs Open:* 24; 100 kw; 600 ft; N49 42 23 W112 43 11
1015 3rd Ave S., Lethbridge, AB T1J 0J3 Canada
(403) 328-1077, *Fax:* (403) 380-1539
www.1077theriver.ca
info@1077theriver.ca
License: Lethbridge, AB held by Rogers Broadcasting Ltd.
Group Owner: Rogers Broadcasting Ltd.
Population Served: 200,000 *Format:* Adult Contemp, Classic Rock*Hrs. of News Programming:* news progmg 2 hrs wkly *No. News Employees:* 1 *Target Audience:* 18-49; males
Terry Voth, General Manager
Robin Haggar, Programming Director
Tanya Wolford, Promotions Manager
Erin Lucas, Music Director

CHLB-FM
01-01-1997; 95.5 mhz FM *Hrs Open:* 24; 100 kw
401 Mayor Magrath Dr. S., Lethbridge, AB T1J 3L8 Canada
(403) 329-0955, *Fax:* (403) 329-0195
www.country95.fm
rbye@country95.fm
License: Lethbridge, AB held by Jim Pattison Broadcast Group Ltd. (the general partner) and Jim Pattison Industries Ltd. (the limited partner) carrying on business as Jim Pattison Broadcast Group L.P.
Group Owner: The Jim Pattison Broadcast Group; (acq 12-21-2000; grpsl)
Format: Country *No. News Employees:* 5 *Target Audience:* 25-54.
Ron Dann, Operations Dir
Terry Regier, General Manager

George Hayes, Programming Director
Larry Gordon, News Director

CJRX-FM
11-03-2000; 106.7 mhz FM; 100 kw; 600 ft.; N49 42 23 W112 43 11
1015 3rd Ave S., Lethbridge, AB T1K 0J3 Canada
(403) 320-1220, *Fax:* (403) 380-1539
www.rock106.ca
info@rock106.ca
License: Lethbridge, AB held by Rogers Broadcasting Ltd.
Group Owner: Rogers Broadcasting Ltd.
Population Served: 83,517 *Arbitron Metro Market:* Lethbridge, AB*Hrs. of News Programming:* news progmg 2 hrs wkly *No. News Employees:* 1 *Target Audience:* 25-44; female
Terry Voth, General Manager

CKVN-FM
04-03-2007; 98.1 mhz FM *Hrs Open:* 24; 20 kw
1277 3rd Ave. S., Lethbridge, AB T1J 0K3 Canada
(403) 327-0981, *Fax:* (403) 328-0095
ckvnradio.com
trowland@goldenwestradio.com
License: Lethbridge, AB held by Golden West Broadcasting Ltd.
Group Owner: Golden West Broadcasting Ltd.; (acq 8-2-2006)
Nat'l Reps: Canadian Broadcast Sales
Population Served: 83,517 *Arbitron Metro Market:* Lethbridge, AB *Format:* Christian*Hrs. of News Programming:* news progmg 6 hrs wkly *No. News Employees:* 2*Adv. Rates:* 33; 27; 33; 23
Deborah Gauger, Operations Dir

CKXU-FM
04-08-2004; 88.3 mhz FM *Hrs Open:* 24; 125 w
SU 164, 4401 University Dr. W., Lethbridge, AB T1K 3M4 Canada
(403) 329-2180, *Fax:* (403) 329-2224
www.ckxu.com
manager@ckxu.com
License: Lethbridge, AB held by CKXU Radio Society.
Population Served: 83,517 *Arbitron Metro Market:* Lethbridge, AB *Format:* Variety/Diverse, French
Aaron Trozzo, Executive Director
Benjamin Maine, Programming Director
Martine M,nard, Music Director
Branden Hamilton, Digital Music Temp
Chris Hibbard, Volunteer Coordinator

CJOC-FM
06-01-2007; 94.1 mhz FM; 100 kw; Ant 433 ft; N49 43 59 W112 57 36
220 Third Ave. S., Suite 400, Lethbridge, AB T1J 0G9 Canada
(403) 388-2910, *Fax:* (866) 841-7971
www.loungeradio.ca
info@loungeradio.ca
License: Lethbridge, AB held by Clear Sky Radio Inc.
Population Served: 83,517 *Arbitron Metro Market:* Lethbridge, AB *Format:* Contemporary Hits/Top 40, Adult Contemp
Paul Larsen, President
Casey Wilson, General Manager

Lloydminster

CKLM-FM
05-18-2001; 106.1 mhz FM *Hrs Open:* 24; 100 kw
Mailing Address: Box 21 Atrium Ctr., 5012 - 49th St, Lloydminster, AB T9V 0K2 Canada
Second Address: 5012 49th St., Lloydminster, AB T9V 0K2
(780) 875-5400, *Fax:* (780) 875-4628
www.borderrock.com
marvin@borderrock.com
License: Lloydminster, AB held by Vista Radio Ltd.
Group Owner: Vista Broadcast Group Inc.; (acq 11-21-2008; C$7.3 million with CFNA-FM Bonnyville)
Population Served: 27,804 *Arbitron Metro Market:* Lloydminster, AB *Format:* Rock/AOR *No. News Employees:* 3 *Target Audience:* 12-54; male*Adv. Rates:* 60; 50; 54; 32
Anita Dent, Operations Dir
Marvin Perry, General Manager/GSM
Doug Zackodnik, General Sales Mgr
JD Anderson, Programming Director
Robin Prebble, News Director
Donnie Atkinson, Account Executive
Aaron Buckingham, AccountExecutive
Chantal Slaney, Account Executive
Vince Angelo, Account Executive
Zelmer, Asst Program Director/Promotions/Drive
Megan Read, Reception/Traffic

CKSA-FM
08-29-2003; 95.9 mhz FM; 100 kw
5026 50th St., Lloydminster, AB T9V 1P3 Canada
(780) 875-3321, *Fax:* (780) 875-4704
www.959lloydfm.com
ctabish@newcap.ca
License: Lloydminster, AB held by NewCap Inc.
Group Owner: NewCap Inc.; (acq 12-22-2004; C$6,246,000 with CILR-FM Lloydminster).
Population Served: 27,804 *Arbitron Metro Market:* Lloydminster, AB *Format:* Country
Chad Tabish, General Manager
Bradley Asselstine, Station Manager
Dean Martin, Creative Director
Heather Klages, Music Director
Rob Anderson, CRM - Senior Marketing Consultant
Susan Hines, Marketing Consultant
Audrey Mushtaler,Marketing Consultant
Erin Stasiuk, Marketing Consultant

Medicine Hat

CFMY-FM
02-01-1999; 96.1 mhz FM; 100 kw
Mailing Address: Division of the Jim Pattison Broadcast Group, Box 1270, Medicine Hat, AB T1A 7H5 Canada
Second Address: Division to the Jim Pattison Broadcast Group, 10 Boundary Rd. S.E., Medicine Hat, AB T0J 2P0
(403) 548-8282, *Fax:* (403) 548-8270
www.my96fm.com
myfm@jpbg.com
License: Medicine Hat, AB held by Jim Pattison Broadcast Group Ltd. (the general partner) and Jim Pattison Industries Ltd. (the limited partner) carrying on business as Jim Pattison Broadcast Group L.P.
Group Owner: The Jim Pattison Broadcast Group; (acq 12-21-2000; grpsl).
Format: Adult Contemp
Rick Arnish, President
Dwaine Dietrich, General Manager
Ed Lundberg, General Sales Mgr
Michael Thibbau, Programming Director
Adrian Bateman, News Director
Carey Downs, Chief Engineer

CKOV-FM
04-01-2003; 93.7 mhz FM *Hrs Open:* 8:30am to 4:30pm; 2.3 kw; N50 02 46 W110 37 11
1201 Kingsway Ave. S.E., Suite 101, Medicine Hat, AB T1A 2Y2 Canada
(403) 529-9599, *Fax:* (403) 529-9282
www.power937.com
rachel@power937.com
License: Medicine Hat, Canada County, AB held by Lighthouse Broadcasting Ltd.
No. News Employees: 6
Pat Lough, President
Rachel Raible, General Manager
John Enns, General Sales Mgr
Darcee Grange, Programming Director

CHAT-FM
01-09-2006; 94.5 mhz FM *Hrs Open:* 24; 100 kw
Mailing Address: Media Centre, 10 Boundary Road, Redcliff, AB T0J 2P0 Canada
Second Address: Division of the Jim Pattison Broadcast Group, 10 Boundary Rd. S.E., Medicine Hat, AB T0J 2P0
(403) 548-8282, *Fax:* (403) 548-8270
www.chat945.com
chat945@jpbg.com
License: Medicine Hat, AB held by Jim Pattison Broadcast Group Ltd. (the general partner) and Jim Pattison Industries Ltd. (the limited partner) carrying on business as Jim Pattison Broadcast Group Ltd.
Group Owner: The Jim Pattison Broadcast Group
Nat'l Reps: Canadian Broadcast Sales
Population Served: 61,000 *Arbitron Metro Market:* Redcliff, AB*TV Affiliate:* CHAT-TV affil *Format:* Country*Hrs. of News Programming:* news progmg 14 hrs wkly *No. News Employees:* 4 *Target Audience:* General.
Rick Arnish, President
Dwaine Dietrich, General Manager

CKMH-FM
02-25-2008; 105.3 mhz FM; 77.9 kw; N50 02 46 W110 37 11
1741 Dunmore Rd. S.E., Suite 206, Medicine Hat, AB T1A 1Z8 Canada
(403) 548-7581
www.rock1053.ca
License: Medicine Hat, AB held by Rogers Broadcasting Ltd.
Group Owner: Rogers Broadcasting Ltd.
Population Served: 61,000 *Arbitron Metro Market:* Medicine Hat, AB *Target Audience:* 25-54.
Tony Marsh, General Manager

CJCY-FM
05-23-2008; 102.1 mhz FM; 100 kw; Ant 686 ft; N50 02 46 W110 37 08
1865 Dunmore Rd. S.E., Suite 104, Medicine Hat, AB T1A 1Z8 Canada
(403) 528-2827, *Fax:* (403) 488-4678
cjcy.loungeradio.ca
info@clearskyradio.com
License: Medicine Hat, AB held by Clear Sky Radio Inc.
Population Served: 61,000 *Arbitron Metro Market:* Medicine Hat, AB *Format:* Contemporary Hits/Top 40, Adult Contemp
Jason Todd, General Sales Mgr
Joe McFarland, News Director

Olds

CKLJ-FM
02-02-2004; 96.5 mhz FM; 35 kw
#6, 4526 49th Ave., Olds, AB T4H 1A4 Canada
(403) 556-2628, *Fax:* (403) 556-2637
cklj@telus.net
License: Olds, AB held by CAB-K Broadcasting Ltd.
Population Served: 8,235 *Arbitron Metro Market:* Olds, AB *Format:* Country
Brian Hepp, General Manager

CKJX-FM
06-02-2008; 104.5 mhz FM; 12 kw; N51 45 30 W114 05 39
4526 49 Ave.#6, Olds, AB T4H 1A4 Canada
(403) 556-2628, *Fax:* (403) 556-2637
www.rock104.ca
bh_cklj@telus.net
License: Olds, AB held by CAB-K Broadcasting Ltd.
Population Served: 8,235 *Arbitron Metro Market:* Olds, AB *Format:* Classic Rock
Brian Hepp, General Manager

Peace River

CKYL
11-01-1954; 610 khz AM; 10 kw-U, DA-2
Bag Service No. 300, Peace River, AB Canada
(780) 624-2535, *Fax:* (780) 624-5424
www.ylcountry.com
License: Peace River, AB held by Peace River Broadcasting Ltd.
Nat'l Reps: Target Broadcast Sales
Terry Babiy, General Manager

CKKX-FM
07-01-1997; 106.1 mhz FM; 990 w
Mailing Address: Bag Service No. 300, Peace River, AB T8S 1T5 Canada
Second Address: 9807 100th Ave, Peace River, AB T8S 1T5
(780) 624-2535, *Fax:* (780) 624-5424
www.kix106.net
reception@ylcountry.com
License: Peace River, AB held by Peace River Broadcasting, LTD.
Terry Babiy, President
Cynthia Babiy, Operations Dir

Red Deer

CIZZ-FM
11-01-1987; 98.9 mhz FM *Hrs Open:* 24; 100 kw; Ant 800 ft
Mailing Address: Box 5339, Red Deer, AB T4N 6W1 Canada
Second Address: 4920 59th St., Red Deer, AB T4N 2N1
(403) 343-1303, *Fax:* (403) 346-1230
www.zedfm.com
zedfm@cnewcap.ca
License: Red Deer, Red Deer County, AB held by Newcap Inc.
Group Owner: NewCap Inc.; (acq 8-10-2005; C$8,392,714 with CKGY-FM Red Deer)
Wire Services: BN Wire
Population Served: 110,000 *Format:* Adult Contemp *No. News Employees:* 6 *Target Audience:* 18-49; male 55%, female 45%
Hilary Montbourquette, General Manager
Al Lucas, General Sales Mgr
Al Tompson, Programming Director
Natasha Eddy, Promotions Manager
Al Redel, News Director

CHUB-FM
01-01-1949; 105.5 mhz FM *Hrs Open:* 24; 100 kw
2840 Bremner Ave., Red Deer, AB T4R 1M9 Canada
(403) 343-7105, *Fax:* (403) 343-2573
www.big105.fm
heydj@big105.fm
License: Red Deer, AB held by Jim Pattison Broadcast Group Ltd. (the general partner) and Jim Pattison Industries Ltd. (the

limited partner) carrying on business as Jim Pattison Broadcast Group L.P.
Group Owner: The Jim Pattison Broadcast Group; (acq 12-21-2000; grpsl).
Nat'l Reps: Target Broadcast Sales *Regional Reps:* WTR Media Sales *Wire Services:* BN Wire
Population Served: 91,877 *Arbitron Metro Market:* Red Deer, AB
Format: Adult Contemp *No. News Employees:* 4 *Target Audience:* Adults 25-49; primary demo-females*Adv. Rates:* 69; 63; 63; 45

Jim Pattison, CEO
Rick Arnish, President
Paul Mason, General Manager
Bryn James, Sales Manager
Jamie Rankin, Programming Director
Tracy Kennedy, Information Director
Jodi Evans, Music Director

CKGY-FM
04-01-2001; 95.5 mhz FM *Hrs Open:* 24; 100 kw; Ant 800 ft.
Mailing Address: Bag 5339, Red Deer, AB T4N 6W1 Canada
Second Address: 4920 59th St., Red Deer, AB T4N 2N1
(403) 343-1170, *Fax:* (403) 346-1230
www.ckgy.com
weekends@kgcountry.ca?subject=General%20Email%20Inquiry
License: Red Deer, Red Deer County, AB held by Newcap Inc.
Group Owner: NewCap Inc.; (acq 8-10-2005; C$8,392,714 with CIZZ-FM Red Deer)
Nat'l Reps: Canadian Broadcast Sales *Wire Services:* BN Wire
Population Served: 91,877 *Arbitron Metro Market:* Red Deer, AB
Format: Country *No. News Employees:* 6 *Target Audience:* 25-54; 50% male, 50% female

Hilary Montbourquette, General Manager
Al Lucas, General Sales Mgr
Abbey White, Programming Director
Natasha Eddy, Promotions Manager
Al Redel, News Director
Sheldon Spackman, Assistant News Director

CFDV-FM
11-08-2004; 106.7 mhz FM; 100 kw
2840 Bremner Ave., Red Deer, AB T4R 1M9 Canada
(403) 343-7105, *Fax:* (403) 343-2573
www.1067thedrive.fm
rock@1067thedrive.fm
License: Red Deer, AB held by Jim Pattison Broadcast Group Ltd. (the general partner) and Jim Pattison Industries Ltd. (the limited partner) carrying on business as Jim Pattison Broadcast Group L.P.
Group Owner: The Jim Pattison Broadcast Group
Nat'l Reps: Target Broadcast Sales *Regional Reps:* WTR Media sales *Wire Services:* BN Wire
Population Served: 90,564 *Arbitron Metro Market:* Red Deer, AB
Format: Classic Rock *Target Audience:* 25-54; adults, primary demo-males

Jim Pattison, CEO
Rick Arnish, President
Tracy Kennedy, Operations Dir
Paul Mason, General Manager
Bryn James, General Sales Mgr
Jim Hall, Programming Director

CKRD-FM
04-04-2011; 90.5 mhz FM; 18.4 kw
27464 Highway 2, Red Deer, AB T4E 1B9 Canada
(403) 356-9052, *Fax:* (403) 356-1745
www.ckrdradio.ca
License: Red Deer, AB held by Touch Canada Broadcasting LP

CKRI-FM
100.7 mhz FM
3617 50th Avenue, Red Deer, AB T4N 3Y5 Canada
(403) 346-8051
www.theriverfm.ca
License: Red Deer, AB held by Harvard Broadcasting Inc
Group Owner: Harvard Broadcasting Inc.

Rocky Mountain House

CHBW-FM
01-01-1997; 94.5 mhz FM; 720 w
4814B 49th St., Rocky Mountain House, AB T4T 1S8 Canada
(403) 844-9450, *Fax:* (403) 844-4770
www.b94.ca
bigshow@telus.net
License: Rocky Mountain House, AB held by Jim Pattison Broadcast Group Ltd. (the general partner) and Jim Pattison Industries Ltd. (the limited partner) carrying on business as Jim Pattison Broadcast Group L.P.
Group Owner: The Jim Pattison Broadcast Group
Population Served: 6,933 *Arbitron Metro Market:* Rocky Mountain House, AB *Format:* Country

Paul Mason, General Manager
Barry Simon, Station Manager

Saint Albert

CFMG-FM
08-29-1994; 104.9 mhz FM *Hrs Open:* 24; 100 kw
18520 Stony Plain Rd., Suite 100, Edmonton, AB T5S 2E2 Canada
(780) 486-2800, *Fax:* (780) 489-6927
www.ezrock1049.com
cfmg@radio.astral.com
License: Saint Albert, Edmonton County, AB held by Astral Media Radio G.P.
Group Owner: Astral Media Inc.; (acq 10-29-2007; grpsl)
Population Served: 870,000 *Format:* Adult Contemp*Hrs. of News Programming:* news progmg 4 hrs wkly *No. News Employees:* 2 *Target Audience:* 25-54; middle to upper income families

Stewart Meyers, Operations Dir
Susan Reade, General Sales Mgr
Rob Vavrek, Programming Director
Karen Paulguaard, Promotions Manager
Bob Hunter, Chief Engineer

Saint Paul

CHSP-FM
97.7 mhz FM; 22 kw; 80.3 meters
4341 50th Avenue, Suite 201, Saint Paul, AB T0A 3A3 Canada
(780) 645-4425, *Fax:* (780) 645-2383
www.977thespur.com
License: Saint Paul, AB held by New Cap Inc
Group Owner: NewCap Inc.

Chad Tabish, General Manager

Siksika

CFXX-FM
01-01-2002; 97.7 mhz FM; 50 w
Box 1490, Siksika, AB T0J 3W0 Canada
(403) 734-5339, *Fax:* (403) 734-5497
siksikamedia@siksikanation.com
License: Siksika, AB held by Siksika Communications Society.

Paul Tallow, General Manager

Slave Lake

CHSL-FM
09-08-2006; 92.7 mhz FM; 5.7 kw; N55 28 18 W114 47 05
Mailing Address: Num 103 229 3rd Ave NW, Slave Lake, AB T0G 2A1 Canada
Second Address: #17 10030 106 Street, Westlock, AB T7P 2K4
(780) 849-2569, *Fax:* (780) 849-4833
www.lakefm.ca
wbetts@newcap.ca
License: Slave Lake, Canada County, AB held by Newcap Inc.
Group Owner: NewCap Inc.
Nat'l Reps: Canadian Broadcast Sales *Wire Services:* BN Wire
Population Served: 10,000 *No. News Employees:* 1

Robert Steele, Chairman
Dave Murray, COO
Robert Steele, President
Dave Schuck, General Manager
Wray Betts, Station Manager
Dave Schuck, General Sales Mgr
Rob Alexander, Programming Director
John Walker, News Director
AbdullahIsmail, Engineering Dir

St. Paul

CHLW
10-01-1974; 1310 khz AM *Hrs Open:* 24
CA
(780) 645-4425, *Fax:* (780) 645-2383
www.1310chlw.com
dwhite@newcap.ca
License: St. Paul, AB held by Newcap Inc.
Group Owner: NewCap Inc.; (acq 4-19-2002; grpsl)
Format: Country*Special Programming:* Farm 5 hrs, relg 5 hrs wkly*Hrs. of News Programming:* news progmg 4 hrs wkly *No. News Employees:* 1 *Target Audience:* 25-54.

Dave Murray, President
Danny White, Station Manager
Jeff Murray, Programming Director

Taber

CJBZ-FM
01-01-2000; 93.3 mhz FM; 50 kw
401 Mayor Magrath Dr., Lethbridge, AB T1J 3L8 Canada
(403) 394-9300, *Fax:* (403) 329-0195
www.b93.fm
info@b93.fm
License: Taber, AB held by Jim Pattison Broadcast Group Ltd. (the general partner) and Jim Pattison Industries Ltd. (the limited partner) carrying on business as Jim Pattison Broadcast Group L.P.
Group Owner: The Jim Pattison Broadcast Group; (acq 12-21-2000; grpsl).
Population Served: 83,517 *Arbitron Metro Market:* Lethbridge, AB *Format:* Contemporary Hits/Top 40, Adult Contemp *No. News Employees:* 4 *Target Audience:* 18-44; adults

Rick Arnish, President
Gary Dorosz, General Manager
Rod Schween, General Sales Mgr
Reid Morgan, Programming Director
Reid Morgan, Promotions Manager
Dori Modney, News Director
Ross Wells, Technical Department

Wainwright

CKKY
02-01-1984; 1080 khz AM *Hrs Open:* 24; 10 kw-D, 9 kw-N
1037 2nd Ave., 2nd fl, Wainwright, AB Canada
(780) 842-4311, *Fax:* (780) 842-4636
ckky@ab.ncc.ca
License: Wainwright, AB held by Newcap Inc.
Group Owner: NewCap Inc.; (acq 5-20-2002; grpsl)
Population Served: 100,000*Special Programming:* Farm 10 hrs wkly*Hrs. of News Programming:* news progmg 14 hrs wkly *No. News Employees:* 2 *Target Audience:* 20-45; agriculture-related working class

Ron Prochner, General Manager

CKWY-FM
01-01-2005; 93.7 mhz FM; 100 kw
1037 2nd Ave., 2nd Fl., Wainright, AB T9W 1K7 Canada
(780) 842-4311, *Fax:* (780) 842-4636
www.waynefm.com
Ctabish@newcap.ca
License: Wainwright, AB held by Newcap Inc.
Group Owner: NewCap Inc.
Population Served: 5,925 *Arbitron Metro Market:* Wainwright, AB
Format: Adult Contemp

Chad Tabish, General Manager
Hugh MacDonald, Station/Sales Manager
Paul O'Neil, Programming Director
Jeff Newland, News Director
Kathy Romanowicz, Administration / Reception / Traffic Coordinator
Anthony Sowan, Music Director
Jeff Murray, Alberta Radio Group - East, Program Director
Erin Stasiuk, Marketing
Brad Asselstine, Marketing
Stephanie Montgomery, Marketing

Westlock

CKWB-FM
09-06-2011; 97.9 mhz FM; 27 kw
10030 106th Street, Westlock, AB T7P 2K4 Canada
(780) 349-4421, *Fax:* (780) 349-6259
www.979therange.ca
License: Westlock, AB held by New Cap Inc
Group Owner: NewCap Inc.

Dave Schuck, General Sales Mgr

Wetaskiwin

CKJR
01-01-1971; 1440 khz AM
CA
(780) 352-0144, *Fax:* (780) 352-5656
www.w1440.com
License: Wetaskiwin, AB held by Newcap Inc.
Group Owner: NewCap Inc.; (acq 4-19-2002; grpsl)
Format: Country*Special Programming:* Greek 2 hrs wkly

Kelly Walter, General Sales Mgr
Larry Donohue, Programming Director

CIHS-FM
12-01-2000; 93.5 mhz FM *Hrs Open:* 24; 5.12 kw; Ant 365 ft
5222 50th Ave., Wetaskiwin, AB T9A 0S8 Canada
(780) 361-0245, *Fax:* (866) 409-2797
www.cihsfm.net
mail@cihsfm.net
License: Wetaskiwin, AB held by 902890 Alberta Ltd.
Target Audience: 0-100.

Dave Dhillon, CEO
Lorelei Dubreuil, Operations Dir
Paula Osha, Station Manager

Whitecourt

CFXW-FM
07-01-2005; 96.7 mhz FM; 9 kw
Mailing Address: Box 2288, Whitecourt, AB T7S 1A1 Canada
Second Address: 5118 50th St., Whitecourt, AB T7S 1A1
(780) 778-5101, *Fax:* (780) 778-5137
www.therig.ca
info@therig.ca
License: Whitecourt, AB held by Newcap Inc.
Group Owner: NewCap Inc.
Population Served: 9,605 *Arbitron Metro Market:* Whitecourt, AB
Format: Classic Rock
Dave Schuck, General Sales Manager
Rob Alexander, Programming Director
John Walker, News Director
Shari Mills, Marketing Consultants, Sales
Magen Steiger, Marketing Consultants, Sales

CIXM-FM
01-01-2006; 105.3 mhz FM; 42.3 kw
Mailing Address: Box 1050, Whitecourt, AB T7S 1N9 Canada
Second Address: 4912A 50th Ave., Whitecourt, AB T7S 1N9
(780) 706-1053, *Fax:* (780) 706-1017
www.xm105.com
info@xm105fm.com

License: Whitecourt, AB held by 1097282 Alberta Ltd.
Nat'l Reps: Target Broadcast Sales
Population Served: 9,605 *Arbitron Metro Market:* Whitecourt, AB
Format: Country
Gene Fabro, President
Ken Singer, Operations Dir
Neil Shewchuk, Station Manager
Neil Shewchuk, General Sales Mgr
Cal Gratton, Programming Director
Nancy Portillo, Promotions Manager
Bayne Opseth, Chief Engineer
Royal Watson,Production Director

British Columbia

Abbotsford

***CFSRFM**
01-01-2001; 92.5 mhz FM; kw
CA
(604) 795-5711, *Fax:* (604) 795-2983
www.starfm.com
starnews@starfm.rogers.com
License: Abbotsford, BC held by Rogers Radio (British Columbia) Ltd.
Group Owner: Rogers Broadcasting Ltd.
Arbitron Metro Market: Chilliwack, BC *Format:* Adult Contemp
Ken Geiger, General Manager
Janis Correia, General Sales Mgr
Murray Olfert, Promotions Manager

CKQC-FM
09-01-2001; 107.1 mhz FM; 215 w
#318-31935 South Fraser Way, Abbotsford, BC V2T 5N7 Canada
(604) 853-4756, *Fax:* (604) 853-1071
www.country1071.com
country.club@country1071.com
License: Abbotsford, BC held by Rogers Radio (British Columbia) Ltd.
Group Owner: Rogers Broadcasting Ltd.
Population Served: 133,497 *Arbitron Metro Market:* Abbotsford, BC *Format:* Country
Ken Geiger, General Manager
Janis Correia, General Sales Mgr
Murray Olfert, Promotions Manager

CIVL-FM
09-01-2007; 88.5 mhz FM *Hrs Open:* 24; 520 watts; 104 meters
33844 King Rd., Abbotsford, BC Canada
(604) 851-6306
www.civl.ca
Bob@civl.ca
License: Abbotsford, BC held by UCFV Campus and Community Radio Society.
Target Audience: 18 plus; campus & community radio
Bob Simpson, Station Manager
Swinder Singh, Programming Director

Big White Ski

***CKIQFM**
05-26-2003; 98.1 mhz FM; kw
Mailing Address: CA
Second Address: 1036 Airport Rd., Iqaluit, NU X0A 0H0
(877)-445-2547, *Fax:* (877) 490-2547
www.ckiq.ca
icefmiqaluit@gmail.com
License: Big White Ski, BC held by Northern Lights Entertainment Inc.
Nat'l Reps: Target Broadcast Sales
Arbitron Metro Market: Iqaluit, NU *Format:* Classic Rock
Terri Chegwyn, General Manager

Boston Bar

CKGO-FM-1
07-04-1980; 106.1 mhz FM; 91 w; -2,871 ft
#520-45715 Hocking Ave., Chilliwack, BC V2P 6Z6 Canada
(604) 795-5711, *Fax:* (604) 702-3212
www.starfm.com
License: Boston Bar, BC held by Rogers Broadcasting Ltd.
Group Owner: Rogers Broadcasting Ltd.; acq 9-10-99; grpsl).
Format: Adult Contemp *No. News Employees:* 3
Ken Geiger, General Manager
Janis Correia, General Sales Mgr
Murray Olfert, Promotions Manager

Burnaby

***CJSF-FM**
02-06-2003; 90.1 mhz FM *Hrs Open:* 7 AM-2AM; 450 w
CJSF Radio, TC 216, Simon Fraser University, Burnaby, BC V5A 1S6 Canada
(604) 291-3727, *Fax:* (604) 291-3695
www.cjsf.ca
cjsfmgr@sfu.ca
License: Burnaby, BC held by Simon Fraser Campus Radio Society.
Population Served: 223,218 *Arbitron Metro Market:* Burnaby, BC
Format: Variety/Diverse*Special Programming:* Persian 2 hrs, Portugese 2 hrs, Sp 4 hrs wkly
Frieda Werden, Operations Dir
Magnus Thyvold, Station Manager
Charlotte Bourne, Programming Director
Ed Blake, Music Director
Sarah Buchanan, Programming Coordinator
Frieda Werden, Public Affairs Coordinator
Bonnie Anderson,Music Coordinator
Dave Swanson, Arts & Entertainment Coordinator
Jordan Mitchell, Production Coordinator

Burns Lake

CFLD
11-01-1965; 760 khz AM
CA
(250) 692-3414, *Fax:* (250) 847-9411
thepeak@bulkley.net
License: Burns Lake, BC held by Vista Radio Ltd.
Group Owner: Vista Broadcast Group Inc.
Format: Adult Contemp
J.C. Brown, General Manager

Campbell River

CIQC-FM
01-01-2008; 99.7 mhz FM; 6 kw; N50 03 15 W125 19 30
470 13th Ave., Campbell River, BC V9W 7J4 Canada
(250) 287-7106, *Fax:* (250) 287-7170
www.997fm.ca
License: Campbell River, BC held by Vista Radio Ltd.
Group Owner: Vista Broadcast Group Inc.
Nat'l Reps: Target Broadcast Sales
Population Served: 31,186 *Arbitron Metro Market:* Campbell River, BC *Format:* Adult Contemp
Raymond Henderson, General Manager

Castlegar

CKQR-FM
01-01-1998; 99.3 mhz FM *Hrs Open:* 24; 333 w; N 49 18 54 W117 37 27
1101 A 4th St., Castlegar, BC V1N 2A8 Canada
(250) 365-7600, *Fax:* (250) 365-8480
www.mountainfm.net
rudy@mountainfm.net
License: Castlegar, BC held by Vista Radio Ltd.
Group Owner: Vista Broadcast Group Inc.
Nat'l Reps: Canadian Broadcast Sales
Format: Classic Rock*Hrs. of News Programming:* news progmg 6 hrs wkly *No. News Employees:* 1 *Target Audience:* 18-49; median target demo
Kevin Einarson, General Manager
TJ Connors, Programming Director
Glen Hicks, News Director

Chase

CFCH-FM
01-10-2005; 103.5 mhz FM *Hrs Open:* 8am - 8pm; 4.7 w
Box 1197, Chase, BC V0E 1M0 Canada
(250) 679-8622, *Fax:* (250) 679-3231
www.cablelan.net/ronfair/CFCH.html
cfchradio@cablelan.net
License: Chase, BC held by Chase and District Community Radio Society
Population Served: 2,409 *Arbitron Metro Market:* Chase, BC
Format: Talk
Ron Fairhurst, General Manager
Susan Parks, Station Manager

Chetwynd

CHET-FM
01-01-1997; 94.5 mhz FM; 25 w
4612 N. Access Rd., Chetwynd, BC V0C 1J0 Canada
(250) 788-9452, *Fax:* (250) 788-9402
www.peacefm.ca
info@peacefm.ca
License: Chetwynd, BC held by Chetwynd Communications Society.
Population Served: 2,635 *Arbitron Metro Market:* Chetwynd, BC
Format: Adult Contemp
Leo Sabulsky, General Manager
Jackie Fowler, Secretary Treasurer
Nancy Atchison, Sales & Promotions
Rhianna Ray, Morning Show Host / Music Director
Adam Perrin, Dawson Creek Representative
Justin Morissette, Swing Announcer /Sports Director
Reinisa MacLeod, Afternoon Host / Volunteer Coordinator

Chilliwack

***CKSRFM**
08-31-2001; 107.5 mhz FM *Hrs Open:* 24; kw
CA
(604) 795-5711, *Fax:* (604) 795-7983
www.starfm.com
starnews@starfm.rogers.com
License: Chilliwack, BC held by Rogers Radio (British Columbia) Ltd.
Group Owner: Rogers Broadcasting Ltd.
Nat'l Reps: Canadian Broadcast Sales
Format: Light Rock*Special Programming:* Farm 2 hrs wkly *No. News Employees:* 3 *Target Audience:* 25-54; general
Ken Geiger, General Manager

CFUN-FM
09-29-1986; 107.5 mhz FM *Hrs Open:* 24; 303 w; N49 06 35 W121 50 52
2440 Ash St., Vancouver, BC V5Z 4J6 Canada
(604) 877-6357, *Fax:* (604) 877-4443
1049greatesthits.com
License: Chilliwack, BC held by Rogers Radio (British Columbia) Ltd.
Group Owner: Rogers Broadcasting Ltd.; (acq 9-10-99; grpsl)
Hrs. of News Programming: News progmg 6 hrs wkly *Target Audience:* 35 plus.
Paul Fisher, Operations Dir
David Larsen, Programming Director

CHWK-FM
02-20-2009; 89.5 mhz FM *Hrs Open:* 6a-6a; 1600 w; Ant 619 ft; N49 06 35 W121 50 52
Box 589 Station Main, Chilliwack, BC V2P 7V5 Canada
(604) 795-2429, *Fax:* (604) 795-9472
www.895thehawk.com
info@895thehawk.com
License: Chilliwack, BC held by Fabmar Communications Ltd.
Nat'l Reps: Target Broadcast Sales *Wire Services:* Canadian Press
Population Served: 77,936 *Arbitron Metro Market:* Chilliwack, BC *Format:* Variety/Diverse*Special Programming:* Chilliwack Bruins Play by Play*Hrs. of News Programming:* 14 *No. News Employees:* 4 *TargetAudience:* 18-54.
Kevin Gemmell, General Manager
Kevin Gemmell, Station Manager and Sales Manager
Glen Slingerland, Program Director and Music Director
Don Lehn, News Director
Marc Fitzgerald, Sports Director
Steve Fanning, PromotionsCoordinator

Matt Wallace, Production Director
Amanda Romaniuk, Creative Director
Shelley Larson, Marketing Representative
Catherine Farrell, Marketing Representative

Cortes Island

CKTZ-FM
12-30-2011; 89.5 mhz FM; 80 watts; 104.3 meters
Box 210, Manson's Landing, BC V0P 1K0 Canada
(250) 935-0200
www.cortesisland.com
cortesradio@gmail.com
License: Cortes Island, BC held by Cortes Community Radio Society

Courtenay

CFCP-FM
01-01-1959; 98.9 mhz FM *Hrs Open:* 24; 2.685 kw
1625-A McPhee Ave., Courtenay, BC V9N 3A6 Canada
(250) 334-2421, *Fax:* (250) 334-1977
www.jetfm.ca
info@jetfm.ca
License: Courtenay, BC held by CFCP Radio Ltd.
Group Owner: Vista Broadcast Group Inc.
Wire Services: BN Wire
Format: Classic Rock*Hrs. of News Programming:* news progmg 16 hrs wkly *No. News Employees:* 4 *Target Audience:* 25-54; women
Raymond Henderson, General Sales Mgr

CKLR-FM
10-01-1998; 97.3 mhz FM *Hrs Open:* 24; 4.7 kw
801B 29th St., Courtenay, BC V9N 7Z5 Canada
(250) 703-2200, *Fax:* (250) 703-9611
www.islandradio.bc.ca
info@973theeagle.com
License: Courtenay, canada County, BC held by Jim Pattison Broadcast Group Ltd. (the general partner) and Jim Pattison Industries Ltd. (the limited partner), carrying on business as Jim Pattison Broadcast Group L.P.
Group Owner: The Jim Pattison Broadcast Group; (acq 6-27-2006; grpsl)
Nat'l Reps: Canadian Broadcast Sales
Population Served: 90,000 *No. News Employees:* 2 *Target Audience:* 25-54; adult*Adv. Rates:* 48; 48; 48; 48
Richard Skinner, Sales Manager
Rob Bye, General Manager
Bob Johnstone, Programming Director
Breana Morgan, Promotions Manager
Bill Nation, News Director
Barry Mandziak, Chief Engineer

Cranbrook

CHBZ-FM
10-01-1995; 104.7 mhz FM *Hrs Open:* 24; 1.26 kw
19 9th Ave. S., Cranbrook, BC V1C 2L Canada
(250) 426-2224, *Fax:* (250) 426-5520
www.b104.ca
info@b104.ca
License: Cranbrook, BC held by Jim Pattison Broadcast Group Ltd. (the general partner) and Jim Pattison Industries Ltd. (the limited partner) carrying on business as Jim Pattison Broadcast Group L.P.
Group Owner: The Jim Pattison Broadcast Group; (acq 2-1-2001; grpsl).
Nat'l Reps: Target Broadcast Sales
Population Served: 65,000 *Format:* Country *No. News Employees:* 3 *Target Audience:* 18-54.
Rick Arnish, President
Rod Schween, General Manager
Dave Walker, General Sales Mgr
Derek Kortschaga, Programming Director
Jeff Johnson, News Director
Dave Walker, Sales Manager

CHDR-FM
01-01-2002; 102.9 mhz FM *Hrs Open:* 24; 1.6 kw
19 9th Ave. S., Cranbrook, BC V1C 2L9 Canada
(250) 426-2224, *Fax:* (250) 426-5520
www.thedrivefm.ca
info@thedrivefm.ca
License: Cranbrook, BC held by Jim Pattison Broadcast Group Ltd. (the general partner) and Jim Pattison Industries Ltd. (the limited partner) carrying on business as Jim Pattison Broadcast Group L.P.
Group Owner: The Jim Pattison Broadcast Group
Nat'l Reps: Target Broadcast Sales
Population Served: 19,364 *Arbitron Metro Market:* Cranbrook, BC *Format:* Rock/AOR *No. News Employees:* 3 *Target Audience:* 25-54.
Rick Arnish, President
Rod Schween, General Manager
Dave Walker, Sales Manager
Derek Kortschaga, Programming Director
Jeff Johnson, News Director
Ross Wells, Chief Engineer

Crawford Bay

*CBTEFM
01-01-1988; 89.9 mhz FM; kw*Rebroadcasts:* Rebroadcasts CBTK-FM Kelowna 100%
CA
(250) 861-3781, *Fax:* (250) 861-6644
www.vancouver.cbc.ca/daybreaksouth
kelowna@cbc.ca
License: Crawford Bay, BC held by Canadian Broadcasting Corp.
Format: News
Charlie Cheffins, Operations Dir

Creston

CFKC
09-21-1968; 1340 khz AM *Hrs Open:* 24
Mailing Address: CA
Second Address: 138-10 Ave. N., Creston, BC V0B 1G0
(250) 368-5510, *Fax:* (250) 368-8471
kbs@radio.astral.com
License: Creston, BC held by Astral Media Radio G.P.
Group Owner: Astral Media Inc.; (acq 10-29-2007; grpsl)
Nat'l Reps: Radio Astral
Format: Adult Contemp
Carissa Donaldson, General Manager
Lea Wilman, Programming Director
David Ford, Engineering Dir

CIDO-FM
97.7 mhz FM; 20 w; Ant 1,092 ft; N49 05 25 W116 22 45
Box 8, Creston, BC V0B 1G0 Canada
(250) 402-6772
www.crestonradio.ca
info@crestonradio.ca
License: Creston, BC held by Creston Community Radio Society.
Population Served: 5,306 *Arbitron Metro Market:* Creston, BC
Format: Variety/Diverse
Bernie LeFrancois, President

Dawson Creek

CJDC
12-15-1947; 890 khz AM *Hrs Open:* 24
CA
(250) 782-3341, *Fax:* (250) 782-3154
cjdccountry.com
License: Dawson Creek, BC held by Astral Media Radio G.P.
Group Owner: Astral Media Inc.; (acq 10-29-2007; grpsl)
Format: Country*Hrs. of News Programming:* 4 hours per week
No. News Employees: 3 *Target Audience:* General.
J. Terrence, Operations Dir
Terry Shepherd, General Manager
Greg Evans, Programming Director
Shaun Briltz, Promotions Manager

CHAD-FM
01-01-2003; 104.1 mhz FM; 50 w*Rebroadcasts:* Rebroadcasts CHET-FM Chetwynd 100%
c/o CHET-FM, Box 214, Chetwynd, BC V0C 1J0 Canada
(250) 788-9452, *Fax:* (250) 788-9402
www.chetchad.com
info@peacefm.ca
License: Dawson Creek, BC held by Chetwynd Communications Society.
Population Served: 11,583 *Arbitron Metro Market:* Dawson Creek, BC *Format:* Adult Contemp, Oldies, Variety/Diverse
Leo Sabulsky, General Manager
Nancy Atchison, Promotions Manager
Mike Sabulsky, Chief Engineer
Jackie Fowler, Secretary Treasurer
Rhianna Ray, Music Director
Justin Morissette, Sports Director
Caghan Perrin, Dawson CreekRepresentative

Duncan

*CJSU-FM
08-01-2000; 89.7 mhz FM *Hrs Open:* 24; kw
CA
(250) 746-0897, *Fax:* (250) 748-1517
www.897sunfm.com
onair@897sunfm.com
License: Duncan, BC held by Vista Radio Ltd.
Group Owner: Vista Broadcast Group Inc.
Nat'l Reps: Target Broadcast Sales; Canadian Broadcast Sales
Arbitron Metro Market: Duncan, BC *Format:* Adult Contemp*Special Programming:* Oldies 8 hrs wkly*Hrs. of News Programming:* news progmg 12 hrs wkly *No. News Employees:* 2 *Target Audience:* 35-54.
Keith James, General Manager
Tracy Hamilton, General Manager and Sales Manager
Jim Jackson, Programming Director
Natasha Riebe, News Director
Andy Beeley, Music Director
Julie Winter, Traffic Manager
Andy Beeley, AssistantProgram Director
Naomi Christie, Production

Egmont

CIEG-FM
07-01-1985; 107.5 mhz FM *Hrs Open:* 24; 50 w; 300 ft*Rebroadcasts:* Rebroadcasts CISQ-FM Squamish 100%
40147 Glenalder Place, Unit 202, Squamish, BC V0N 3G0 Canada
(604) 892-1021, *Fax:* (604) 892-6383
www.mountainfm.com
mountainfm@mountainfm.com
License: Egmont, BC held by Rogers Broadcasting.
Nat'l Reps: Canadian Broadcast Sales
Format: Adult Contemp*Hrs. of News Programming:* news progmg 16 hrs wkly *No. News Employees:* 3 *Target Audience:* 25-44.
Gary Miles, President
Paul Fisher, Operations Dir
Ken Geiger, General Manager
Janis Correia, General Sales Mgr

Fernie

CJDR-FM
08-30-2002; 99.1 mhz FM *Hrs Open:* 24; 470 w*Rebroadcasts:* Rebroadcasts CHOR-FM Cranbrook 66%
19 9th Ave. S., Cranbrook, BC V1C 2L9 Canada
(250) 426-2224, *Fax:* (250) 426-5520
www.thedrivefm.ca
info@thedrivefm.ca
License: Fernie, BC held by Jim Pattison Broadcast Group Ltd. (the general partner) and Jim Pattison Industries Ltd. (the limited partner) carrying on business as Jim Pattison Broadcast Group L.P.
Group Owner: The Jim Pattison Broadcast Group
Nat'l Reps: Target Broadcast Sales
Population Served: 4,217 *Arbitron Metro Market:* Fernie, BC
Format: Rock/AOR *No. News Employees:* 1
Rick Arnish, President
Rod Schween, General Manager
Dave Walker, Sales Manager
Derek Korschaga, Programming Director
Jeff Johnson, News Director
Ross Wells, Chief Engineer

Fort Nelson

CKRX-FM
01-01-1998; 102.3 mhz FM; 1.8 kw
Mailing Address: 5152 Liard St., Fort Nelson, BC V0C 1R0 Canada
Second Address: 5152 Liard St., Fort Nelson, BC V0C 1R0
(250) 774-2525, *Fax:* (250) 774-2577
www.1023thebear.com
kjohnson@astral.com
License: Fort Nelson, BC held by Astral Media Radio G.P.
Group Owner: Astral Media Inc.; (acq 10-29-2007; grpsl)
Format: Contemporary Hits/Top 40
Terry Shepard, General Manager
Kevin Larkin, Programming Director

Fort St. John

CHRX-FM
98.5 mhz FM; 50 kw
10532 Alaska Rd., Fort St. John, BC V1J 1B3 Canada
(250) 785-6634, *Fax:* (250) 785-4544
www.peacesunfm.com
tshepard@astral.com
License: Fort St. John, BC held by Astral Media Radio G.P.
Group Owner: Astral Media Inc.; (acq 10-29-2007; grpsl)
Terry Shepard, Operations Dir
Shaun Briltz, Programming Director

CKFU-FM
09-01-2003; 100.1 mhz FM *Hrs Open:* 24
10423 101st Ave., Fort St. John, BC V1J 2B7 Canada
(250) 787-7100, *Fax:* (250) 263-9749
www.moosefm.ca
reception@moosefm.ca
License: Fort St. John, Canada County, BC held by 663975 B.C. Ltd.
Nat'l Reps: Canadian Broadcast Sales *Wire Services:* BN Wire
Population Served: 30,000*Hrs. of News Programming:* news progmg 5 hours wkly *No. News Employees:* 3 *Target Audience:* 24-45; female
Brad Russell, Programming Director
Adam Reaburn, Promotions Manager

CKNL-FM
01-01-2003; 101.5 mhz FM; 40 kw
10532 Alaska Rd., Fort St. John, BC V1J 1B3 Canada
(250) 785-6634, *Fax:* (250) 785-4544
www.1015thebear.com
peacenews@astral.com
License: Fort St. John, BC held by Astral Media Radio G.P.
Group Owner: Astral Media Inc.; (acq 10-29-2007; grpsl)
Population Served: 18,609 *Arbitron Metro Market:* Fort St. John, BC *Format:* Classic Rock
Angie Cloury, Operations Dir
Terry Shepherd, General Manager
Amy Adkins, Sales Supervisor
Andre da Costa, News Director
Shaun Briltz, Brand Directory
Benji Hajnik, Production
Steve Burden, Production
Dave Lewis, CreativeDirector

Gibsons

***CISCFM**
10-01-1984; 107.5 mhz FM *Hrs Open:* 24; kw*Rebroadcasts:* Rebroadcasts CISQ-FM Squamish
CA
(604) 892-1021, *Fax:* (604) 892-6383
www.mountainfm.com
mountainfm@mountainfm.com
License: Gibsons, BC held by Rogers Broadcasting.
Format: Adult Contemp*Special Programming:* Magazine show 3 hrs wkly*Hrs. of News Programming:* news progmg 16 hrs wkly *No. News Employees:* 3 *Target Audience:* 25-44.
Gary Miles, President
Paul Fisher, Operations Dir
Ken Geiger, General Manager
Janis Correia, Operations Manager

Golden

CKGR-FM
106.3 mhz FM
Box 1403, 825 10th Avenue South, Golden, BC V0A 1H0 Canada
(250) 344-7177, *Fax:* (250) 344-7233
www.golden.myezrock.com
License: Golden, BC held by Astral Media Radio G P
TV Affiliate: 24 Hours
Chris Cameron, Morning Host
Mark Jeffries, Midday Host
Rich Daniels, Afternoon Host

Greenwood

CKGF-FM-2
01-01-2003; 96.7 mhz FM; 40 w horiz; Ant 1,886 ft; N49 05 29 W118 36 36
1101 A 4th St., Castlegar, BC V1N 2A8 Canada
(250) 365-7600, *Fax:* (250) 365-8480
www.mountainfm.net
requests@mountainfm.net
License: Greenwood, BC held by Boundary Broadcasting Ltd.
Population Served: 7,816 *Arbitron Metro Market:* Castlegar, BC *Format:* Classic Rock *Target Audience:* 25-54.
Kevin Einarson, General Manager
Rudy Parachoiak, Programming Director
Heather McGowan, Promotions Manager
Darren McPeake, Senior Program Director
Marcella Chernoff, Senior Account Executive
Dustin Le Page, Account Exective
Christine Smith, Account Executive
Val Maximick, Reception/Traffic
Andrew Baldock, Creative/Production

Invermere

CKIR
12-01-1989; 870 khz AM*Rebroadcasts:* Rebroadcasts CKGR(AM) Golden
CA
(250) 344-7177, *Fax:* (250) 344-7233
www.myezrock.com
ckir@rockies.net
License: Invermere, BC held by Astral Media Radio G.P.
Group Owner: Astral Media Inc.; (acq 10-29-2007; grpsl)
Format: Classic Rock
Ron Langridge, General Manager

Kamloops

***CFFMFM**
08-31-1987; 98.3 mhz FM *Hrs Open:* 24; kw
CA
250-398-6551, *Fax:* (250) 392-4142
www.therushfm.ca
tgard@reachthecariboo.com
License: Kamloops, BC held by Vista Radio Ltd.
Group Owner: Vista Broadcast Group Inc.; (Acq 2006)
Nat'l Reps: Canadian Broadcast Sales
Format: Rock/AOR *No. News Employees:* 2 *Target Audience:* 25-54*Adv. Rates:* 25; 21; 21; 14
Tracey Gard, General Manager

CHNL
05-01-1970; 610 khz AM *Hrs Open:* 24; 25 kw-D, 5 kw-N, DA-N
611 Lansdowne St., Kamloops, BC Canada
(250) 372-2292, *Fax:* (250) 372-2293
www.radionl.com
info@radionl.com
License: Kamloops, BC held by NL Broadcasting Ltd.
Group Owner: NL Broadcasting Ltd.
Regional Network: CRN *Nat'l Reps:* Bell Media Sales *Regional Reps:* Bell Media Sales CHUM Radio Sales *Wire Services:* Canadian Press
Population Served: 160,000*Hrs. of News Programming:* news progmg 15.5 hrs wkly *No. News Employees:* 8 *Target Audience:* 25-54; family oriented, middle-upper class income*Adv. Rates:* 852; 732; 732; 528
Robbie Dunn, General Manager
Jim Reynolds, Operations Dir
Robbie Dunn, General Manager
Gerry Pigeon, General Sales Mgr
Jim Reynolds, Programming Director
Crystal Lilly, Promotions, Events, Web Manager
Jim Harrison, NewsDirector
Dave Coulter, Chief Engineer
Frieda Whitehall, Creative Director
Cheryl Austin, Traffic Manager
Jeff Bolt, Production Manager
Kathy Akins, Controller

CIFM-FM
01-01-1961; 98.3 mhz FM; 4.3 kw
460 Pemberton Terr., Kamloops, BC V2C 1T5 Canada
(250) 372-3322, *Fax:* (250) 374-0445
www.98.3cifm.com
info@98.3cifm.com
License: Kamloops, BC held by Jim Pattison Broadcast Group Ltd. (the general partner) and Jim Pattison Industries Ltd. (the limited partner) carrying on business as Jim Pattison Broadcast Group L.P.
Group Owner: The Jim Pattison Broadcast Group; (acq 1987).
Population Served: 170,000*TV Affiliate:* CFJC-TV affil. *Format:* Rock/AOR*Hrs. of News Programming:* news progmg 9 hrs wkly *No. News Employees:* 6 *Target Audience:* 30-40; baby boomers with disposable income
Rick Arnish, President
Doug Collins, Operations Dir
Bruce Uptigrove, General Sales Mgr
Leo Baggio, Programming Director

CKRV-FM
01-28-1984; 97.5 mhz FM *Hrs Open:* 24; 5 kw
611 Lansdowne St., Kamloops, BC V2C 1Y6 Canada
(250) 372-2197, *Fax:* (250) 372-2293
www.ckrv.com
river@ckrv.com
License: Kamloops, BC held by NL Broadcasting Ltd.
Group Owner: NL Broadcasting Ltd.; (Acq 6-10-93; $925,000.)
Nat'l Reps: CHUM Radio Sales *Regional Reps:* CHUM Radio Sales
Population Served: 80,000 *Format:* Adult Contemp, Contemporary Hits/Top 40*Hrs. of News Programming:* news progmg 5 hrs wkly *No. News Employees:* 1 *Target Audience:* 25-54; professionals, office personnel*Adv. Rates:* 816; 732; 744; 528
Kathy Akins, CFO
Robbie Dunn, President
Jim Reynolds, Operations Dir
Robbie Dunn, General Manager
Peter Angle, General Sales Mgr
Rudy Chase, Programming Director
Crystal Lilly, Promotions Manager
Cheryl Austin, NewsDirector
Dave Coulter, Chief Engineer
Jeff Bolt, Production Director

CKBZ-FM
01-01-2001; 100.1 mhz FM; 3.5 kw
460 Pemberton Terr., Kamloops, BC V2C 1T5 Canada
(250) 372-3322, *Fax:* (250) 374-0445
www.b100.ca
info@b100.ca
License: Kamloops, BC held by Jim Pattison Broadcast Group Ltd. (the general partner) and Jim Pattison Industries Ltd. (the limited partner) carrying on business as Jim Pattison Broadcast Group L.P.
Group Owner: The Jim Pattison Broadcast Group
Population Served: 85,678 *Arbitron Metro Market:* Kamloops, BC*TV Affiliate:* CFJC-TV affil. *Format:* Adult Contemp*Hrs. of News Programming:* news progmg 10 hrs wkly *No. News Employees:* 6 *Target Audience:* 25-44; large, loyal audience with disposable income
Rick Arnish, President
Doug Collins, Operations Dir
Bruce Uptigrove, General Sales Mgr

CFBX-FM
04-02-2001; 92.5 mhz FM; 420 w
900 McGill Rd., House 8, Kamloops, BC V2C 0C8 Canada
(250) 377-3988, *Fax:* (250) 852-6350
www.thex.ca
radio@tru.ca
License: Kamloops, BC held by The Kamloops Campus/Community Radio Society.
Population Served: 85,678 *Arbitron Metro Market:* Kamloops, BC *Format:* Variety/Diverse
Brant Zwicker, Station Manager
Steve Marlow, Programming/Music
Kathy Parkes, Training Coordinator
Julie Niven, Music Librarian

CJKC-FM
01-01-2006; 103.1 mhz FM *Hrs Open:* 24; 5 kw
611 Lansdowne St., Kamloops, BC V2C 1Y6 Canada
(250) 571-1031, *Fax:* (250) 571-5240
www.country103.ca
info@country103.ca
License: Kamloops, BC held by NL Broadcasting Ltd.
Group Owner: NL Broadcasting Ltd.
Nat'l Reps: CHUM Radio Sales *Regional Reps:* CHUM Radio Sales
Population Served: 85,678 *Arbitron Metro Market:* Kamloops, BC *Format:* Country*Hrs. of News Programming:* news progmg 10 hrs wkly *No. News Employees:* 1 *Target Audience:* 25-54.*Adv. Rates:* 756; 672; 672;420
Kathy Akins, CFO
Robbie Dunn, President
Jeff Bolt, Operations Dir
Robbie Dunn, General Manager
Gerry Pigeon, General Sales Mgr
Jim Reynolds, Programming Director
Crystal Lilly, Promotions Manager
Cheryl Austin, NewsDirector
Dave Coulter, Chief Engineer
Frieda Whitehalll, Creative Director
Tim Tyler, Music Director
Howie Reimer, Assistant Program Director

***CHRKFM**
05-27-2008; 97.5 mhz FM; kw
CA
(902) 270-1019, *Fax:* (902) 270-3566
www.giant1019.com
reception@giant1019.com
License: Kamloops, BC held by Newcap Inc.
Group Owner: NewCap Inc.
Arbitron Metro Market: Sydney, NS *Format:* Contemporary Hits/Top 40
Daryl Stevens, Programming Director
Dave Newbury, Sales Manager
Scott Boyd, News Director

Kelowna

***CBTKFM**
11-01-1987; 88.9 mhz FM; kw
CA
(250) 861-3781, *Fax:* (250) 861-6644
www.vancoouver.cbc.ca/daybreaksouth
kelowna@cbc.ca
License: Kelowna, BC held by Canadian Broadcasting Corp.
Nat'l Network: CBC Radio One
Format: News
Charlie Cheffins, Operations Dir

CHSU-FM
09-21-1995; 99.9 mhz FM; 13 kw
435 Bernard Ave., Kelowna, BC V1Y 6N8 Canada
(250) 860-8600, *Fax:* (250) 860-8856
www.thesun.net
info@thesun.net
License: Kelowna, BC held by Astral Media Radio G.P.
Group Owner: Astral Media Inc.
Format: Adult Contemp *No. News Employees:* 3
Don Shafer, General Sales Mgr
Mark Burley, Programming Director
Howard Alexander, News Director
Roy McKenzie, General Sales Manager
Andrew Quinn-Young, Retail Sales Manager

***CILKFM**
06-21-1985; 101.5 mhz FM *Hrs Open:* 24; kw
CA
(250) 860-1010, *Fax:* (250) 860-5754
www.kelowna.myezrock.com
kelownainfo@myezrock.com
License: Kelowna, BC held by Astral Media Radio G.P.
Group Owner: Astral Media Inc.; (acq 10-29-2007; grpsl)
Format: Adult Contemp*Special Programming:* Gospel 3 hrs wkly*Hrs. of News Programming:* news progmg 2 hrs wkly *No. News Employees:* 2 *Target Audience:* 25-54; women
Rick Dyer, General Manager
Dustin Clement, Programming Director

CKFR
11-08-1971; 1150 khz AM
CA
(250) 860-8600, *Fax:* (250) 860-8856
www.am1150.ca
info@am1150.ca
License: Kelowna, BC held by Astral Media Radio G.P.
Group Owner: Astral Media Inc.; (acq 10-29-2007; grpsl)
Format: News, News/Talk, Sports, Talk*Special Programming:* Home improvements 2 hrs, American gold 4 hrs wkly *No. News Employees:* 3 *Target Audience:* 25-54.*Adv. Rates:* 28; 18; 22; 12
Peter Angle, General Sales Mgr
Darren Robertson, Programming Director
Howard Alexander, News Director
Roy McKenzie, General Sales Manager
Andrew Quinn-Young, Retail Sales Manager

CKLZ-FM
01-01-1964; 104.7 mhz FM *Hrs Open:* 24; 3.8 kw; Ant 1,611 ft; N49 46 06 W119 29 59
3805 Lakeshore Rd., Kelowna, BC V1W 3K6 Canada
(250) 763-1047, *Fax:* (250) 762-2141
www.power104.fm
info@power104.fm
License: Kelowna, Central Okanagan County, BC held by Jim Pattison Broadcast Group Ltd. (the general partner) and Jim Pattison Industries Ltd. (the limited partner), carrying on business as Jim Pattison Broadcast Group L.P.
Group Owner: The Jim Pattison Broadcast Group; (acq 6-30-98)
Format: Rock/AOR*Hrs. of News Programming:* news progmg 4 hrs wkly *No. News Employees:* 2 *Target Audience:* 25-49.
Rick Arnish, President
Bruce Davis, General Manager
Don Huculak, General Sales Mgr
Bob Miller, Programming Director
Dan McFarland, Promotions Manager
Jasmin Doobay, News Director
Craig Foster, Chief Engineer

***CHIMFM**
01-01-1996; 104.7 mhz FM; kw
CA
(705) 264-2150
www.chimfm.com
chimfm@vianet.ca
License: Kelowna, BC held by 1158556 Ontario Ltd.
Arbitron Metro Market: Timmins, ON *Format:* Christian
Roger de Brabant, Chairman
Roger deBrabant, General Manager/Founder
Karen Turner, Station Manager
Karen Turner, Sales & Marketing Manager
Angela Sommers, Music Director
Paula Gravel, Weather Announcer, Production
Terry Markovich,Red Deer Manager

CKQQ-FM
08-17-2007; 103.1 mhz FM; 11 kw; N49 46 06 W119 29 59
3805 Lakeshore Rd., Kelowna, BC V1W 3K6 Canada
(250) 762-3331, *Fax:* (250) 762-2141
www.b103.ca
License: Kelowna, BC held by Jim Pattison Broadcast Group Ltd. (the general partner) and Jim Pattison Industries Ltd. (the limited partner), carrying on business as Jim Pattison Broadcast Group L.P.
Group Owner: The Jim Pattison Broadcast Group
Rick Arnish, President
Bruce Davis, General Manager
Don Huculak, General Sales Mgr
Bob Miller, Programming Director
Dan McFarland, Promotions Manager
Jasmin Doobay, News Director
Craig Foster, Chief Engineer

CKKO-FM
01-01-2008; 96.3 mhz FM; 7.1 kw; N49 46 47 W119 30 26
1601 Bertram St., Kelowna, BC V1Y 2G5 Canada
(250) 861-5963
www.k963.fm
License: Kelowna, BC held by New Cap Inc
Dallas Gray, General Manager
Garry Barker, Promotions Manager

CJUI-FM
09-29-2008; 103.9 mhz FM; 5.2 kw; N49 58 00 W119 31 40
1729 Gordon Dr., Kelowna, BC V1Y 3H3 Canada
(250) 980-9009, *Fax:* (250) 980-1038
www.1039thejuice.com
License: Kelowna, BC held by Vista Radio Ltd.
Group Owner: Vista Broadcast Group Inc.
Population Served: 117,312 *Arbitron Metro Market:* Kelowna, BC
Format: Rock/AOR
Ted Farr, General Manager
Charlotte Sault, General Sales Mgr
TJ Connors, Programming Director
Carla Leinemann, Promotions Manager
Fil DeCarvalho, Production Director

Kitimat

CKTK-FM
01-01-2004; 97.7 mhz FM; 170 w
4625 Lazelle Ave., Terrace, BC V8G 1S4 Canada
(250) 635-6316, *Fax:* (250) 638-6320
www.kitimat.myezrock.com
blangston@astral.com
License: Kitimat, BC held by Astral Media Radio G.P.
Group Owner: Astral Media Inc.; (acq 10-29-2007; grpsl)
Population Served: 8,335 *Arbitron Metro Market:* Kitimat, BC
Format: Contemporary Hits/Top 40
Brian Langston, General Manager
John Crawford, News Director
Janine Kraft, Radio Brand Director

Lillooet

CHLS-FM
01-01-2001; 100.5 mhz FM *Hrs Open:* 24; 5 w; lillooet
#415 Main Street, Lillooet, BC V0K 1V0 Canada
(250) 256-2113, *Fax:* (250) 256-2113
www.radiolillooet.ca
station@radiolillooet.ca
License: Lillooet, BC held by Radio Lillooet Society.
Population Served: 2,322 *Arbitron Metro Market:* Lillooet, BC
Format: Variety/Diverse*Special Programming:* First nations 16 hrs wkly*Hrs. of News Programming:* News progmg 5 hrs wkly
Target Audience: All ages;community of Lillooet
Kim North, Operations Dir

MacKenzie

CHMM-FM
10-27-2003; 103.5 mhz FM; 900 w
86 Centennial Ave., Box 547, MacKenzie, BC V0J 2C0 Canada
(250) 997-6277, *Fax:* (250) 997-6222
www.chmm.ca
chmm1035@gmail.com
License: MacKenzie, BC held by MacKenzie and Area Community Radio Society.
Population Served: 4,539 *Arbitron Metro Market:* Mackenzie, BC
Format: Variety/Diverse
J.D. MacKenzie, Station Manager
Bryan Bezo, General Sales Mgr

Merritt

CKMQ-FM
101.1 mhz FM
Box 1630, 201-2196 Quilchena Avenue, Merrit, BC V1K 1B8 Canada
(250) 378-4288, *Fax:* (250) 378-6979
www.q101.ca
info@q101ca
License: Merritt, Thompson-Nicola County, BC held by NL Broadcasting Ltd

Nanaimo

CKWV-FM
01-02-1995; 102.3 mhz FM *Hrs Open:* 24; 1.3 kw; Nanaimo, sc
4550 Wellington Rd., Nanaimo, BC V9T 2H3 Canada
(250) 758-1131, *Fax:* (250) 758-4644
www.1023thewave.com
info@1023thewave.com
License: Nanaimo, BC held by Jim Pattison Broadcast Group Ltd. (the general partner) and Jim Pattison Industries Ltd. (the limited partner), carrying on business as Jim Pattison Broadcast Group L.P.
Group Owner: The Jim Pattison Broadcast Group; (acq 6-27-2006; grpsl)
Nat'l Reps: Canadian Broadcast Sales
Population Served: 125,000 *Format:* Adult Contemp *No. News Employees:* 2 *Target Audience:* 25-54; general*Adv. Rates:* 48; 48; 48; 48
Cathy Johns, Operations Dir
Rob Bye, General Manager
Stu Crouse, General Sales Mgr
Holly Tribble, Promotions Manager
DarylMajor, News Director
Barry Mandziak, Engineering Dir
Barry Mandziak, Chief Engineer
Pam Dogherty, TrafficManager

***CHLY-FM**
09-21-2001; 101.7 mhz FM *Hrs Open:* 24/7/365; 1.3 kw; Ant 312 ft; N49 13 20 W124 00 07
#2-34 Victoria Crescent, Nanaimo, BC V9R 5B8 Canada
(250) 716-3410, *Fax:* (250) 716-1082
www.chly.ca
programdirector@chly.ca
License: Nanaimo, BC held by Radio Malaspina Society.
Population Served: 500,000 *Target Audience:* campus/community
Dylan Perry, Programming Director

CHWF-FM
10-01-2001; 106.9 mhz FM *Hrs Open:* 24 hrs; 1.6 kw; Nanaimo
4550 Wellington Rd., Nanaimo, BC V9T 2H3 Canada
(250) 758-1131, *Fax:* (250) 758-4644
www.1069thewolf.com
info@1069thewolf.com
License: Nanaimo, BC held by Jim Pattison Broadcast Group Ltd. (the general partner) and Jim Pattison Industries Ltd. (the limited partner), carrying on business as Jim Pattison Broadcast Group L.P.
Group Owner: The Jim Pattison Broadcast Group; (acq 6-27-2006; grpsl).
Nat'l Reps: Canadian Broadcast Sales
Population Served: 83,810 *Arbitron Metro Market:* Nanaimo, BC *No. News Employees:* 2 *Target Audience:* 25-54; general*Adv. Rates:* 48; 48; 48; 48
Cathy Johns, Operations Dir
Stu Crouse, General Sales Mgr
Kent Wilson, Programming Director
Katie O'Connor, Promotions Manager
Daryl Major, News Director
Barry Mandziak, Chief Engineer
Pam Dogherty, Traffic Manager
CarlaJohnson, APD/ Director of Listener Engagement
Mike Lang, Music Director
Matt Fogarty, Retail Creative Director
Carolyn Hoare, Account Representative

Nelson

CKKC-FM
01-01-2006; 106.9 mhz FM
1560 Second Ave., Trail, BC V1R 1M4 Canada
(250) 368-5510, *Fax:* (250) 368-8471
www.kbsradio.ca
License: Nelson, BC held by Astral Media Radio G.P.
Group Owner: Astral Media Inc.; (acq 10-29-2007; grpsl)
Nat'l Reps: Radio Astral

Format: Adult Contemp
Nicole Beetstra, General Manager
Lea Wilman, Programming Director
David Ford, Engineering Dir

***CJLY-FM**
01-01-2002; 93.5 mhz FM; 70 w
308a Hall St., Box 767, Nelson, BC V1L 1Y8 Canada
(250) 352-9600, *Fax:* (250) 352-9653
www.kootenaycoopradio.com
km@kootenaycoopradio.com
License: Nelson, BC held by Kootenay Co-operative Radio.
Population Served: 10,203 *Arbitron Metro Market:* Nelson, BC
Format: Variety/Diverse
Bill Metcalfe, Operations Dir
Jay Hannley, Station Manager
Terry Brennan, Operations Manager
Zoe Creighton, Sponsorship Producer

CHNV-FM
04-18-2006; 103.5 mhz FM; 1.1 kw; Ant 1,233 ft
1101 - 4th Street, Castlegar, BC V1N 2A8 Canada
(250) 365-7600, *Fax:* (250) 365-8480
www.mountainfm.net
keinarson@mountainfm.net
License: Nelson, BC held by Vista Radio Ltd.
Group Owner: Vista Broadcast Group Inc.
Population Served: 332 *Arbitron Metro Market:* Crawford Bay, BC *Format:* News *No. News Employees:* 2
Kevin Einarson, General Manager
Darren McPeake, Programming Director
Glenn Hicks, News Director
Marcella Chernoff, Senior Account Executive
Dustin Le Page, Account Exective
Christine Smith, Account Exective
Heather McGowan,Promotion Coordinator

New Denver

CKZX-FM
10-01-1981; 93.5 mhz FM*Rebroadcasts:* Rebroadcasts CKKC(AM) Nelson 100%
1560 2nd Ave., Trail, BC V1R 1M4 Canada
(250) 368-5510, *Fax:* (250) 368-8471
www.kbsradio.ca
License: New Denver, BC held by Astral Media Radio G.P.
Group Owner: Astral Media Inc.; (acq 10-29-2007; grpsl)
Nat'l Reps: Radio Astral
Format: Adult Contemp
Nicole Beetstra, General Manager
Lea Wilman, Programming Director
David Ford, Engineering Dir

New Westminster

CFMIFM
03-22-1970; 101.1 mhz FM; 53 kw; 386.4 meters
700 W. Georgia St., Suite 2000, Vancouver, BC Canada
(604) 331-2808, *Fax:* (604) 331-2727
www.rock101.com
rock101@rock101.com
License: New Westminster, BC held by Corus Premium Television Ltd.
Group Owner: Corus Entertainment Inc.
Target Audience: 25-49.
Linda Pelletier, Station Manager

CKNW
09-01-1944; 980 khz AM *Hrs Open:* 24
CA
(604) 331-2711, *Fax:* (604) 331-2722
www.cknw.com
info@cknw.com
License: New Westminster, BC held by Corus Premium Television Ltd.
Group Owner: Corus Entertainment Inc.; (acq 7-6-2000; grpsl).
Nat'l Reps: Canadian Broadcast Sales
Format: News, News/Talk, Sports, Talk*Hrs. of News Programming:* news progmg 14 hrs wkly *No. News Employees:* 20 *Target Audience:* General.
J.J. Johnson, General Manager
Mike Searson, General Sales Mgr
Chelsea Hobbis, Promotions Manager

One Hundred Mile Hou

CKBX
07-30-1971; 840 khz AM
CA
(250) 395-3848, *Fax:* (250) 395-4147
www.thewolfpack.ca
spence@ckbx.ca
License: One Hundred Mile Hou, BC held by Vista Radio Ltd.
Group Owner: Vista Broadcast Group Inc.; (acq 1981)
Format: Country*Special Programming:* Class one hr wkly
Paul Mann, General Manager
Tracey Gard, Station Manager

Osoyoos

CJOR(AM)
12-01-1966; 1240 khz AM; 1 kw-U, DA-1
203-8309 Main St., Penticton, BC V2A 364 Canada
(250) 492-2800, *Fax:* (250) 493-0370
osoyoo.myezrock.com
License: Osoyoos, BC held by Astral Media Radio G.P.
Group Owner: Astral Media Inc.; (acq 10-29-2007; grpsl)
Nat'l Reps: Canadian Broadcast Sales
Format: Adult Contemp*Special Programming:* Por 3 hrs wkly *No. News Employees:* 1 *Target Audience:* 25-49.
Mike Mlazgar, Operations Dir
Janet Burley, General Manager
Janet Burley, General Sales Mgr
Mark Burley, Programming Director
Karen Davy, Promotions Manager
Jon Ferebee, News Director

Parksville

CIBH-FM
01-01-1999; 88.5 mhz FM *Hrs Open:* 24; 960 w; Parksville, BC
Box 1370, 166 E. Isl Highway, Parksville, BC V9P 2H3 Canada
(250) 248-4211, *Fax:* (250) 248-4210
www.885thebeach.com
info@885thebeach.com
License: Parksville, BC held by Jim Pattison Broadcast Group Ltd. (the general partner) and Jim Pattison Industries Ltd. (the limited partner), carrying on business as Jim Pattison Broadcast Group L.P.
Group Owner: The Jim Pattison Broadcast Group; (acq 6-27-2006; grpsl).
Population Served: 20,479 *Arbitron Metro Market:* Parksville - Qualicum Beach, BC *Format:* Adult Contemp, Oldies *No. News Employees:* 2 *Target Audience:* 25-54; Adults*Adv. Rates:* 24; 24; 24; 24
Cathy Johns, Operations Dir
Rob Bye, General Manager
Rob Bye, General Sales Mgr
Kent Wilson, Programming Director
Felicia Kreutzer, Promotions Manager
Daryl Major, News Director
Barry Mandziak, Chief Engineer
Pam Dogherty,Traffic Manager
Carla Johnson, Creative Director
Cathy Johns, Director of Administration
Stu Crouse, Sales Supervisor
Trish Newton Segal, Account Representative

CHPQ-FM
02-11-2005; 99.9 mhz FM *Hrs Open:* 24; 1.1 kw
Box 1370, Parksville, BC V9P 2H3 Canada
(250) 248-4211, *Fax:* (250) 248-4210
www.thelounge999.com
info@thelounge999.com
License: Parksville, BC held by Jim Pattison Broadcast Group Ltd. (the general partner) and Jim Pattison Industries Ltd. (the limited partner), carrying on business as Jim Pattison Broadcast Group L.P.
Group Owner: The Jim Pattison Broadcast Group; (acq 6-27-2006; grpsl).
Nat'l Reps: Canadian Broadcast Sales
Population Served: 26,501 *Arbitron Metro Market:* Paragould, AR *Format:* Adult Contemp *No. News Employees:* 1 *Target Audience:* 45 plus; adults*Adv. Rates:* 24; 24; 24; 24
Rob Bye, General Manager
Marlow Weldon, News Director
Pam Doherty, Traffic Manager

Pemberton

CISP-FM
10-05-1982; 104.5 mhz FM *Hrs Open:* 24; 400 w; 1,000 ft*Rebroadcasts:* Rebroadcasts CISQ-FM Squamish 100%
Box 1068, Squamish, BC V0N 3G0 Canada
(604) 892-1021, *Fax:* (604) 892-6383
www.mountainfm.com
mountainfm@mountainfm.com
License: Pemberton, BC held by Rogers Broadcasting Ltd.
Group Owner: Rogers Broadcasting Ltd.
Format: Adult Contemp*Hrs. of News Programming:* news progmg 16 hrs wkly *No. News Employees:* 3 *Target Audience:* 25-45.
Gary Miles, President
Paul Fisher, Operations Dir
Ken Geiger, General Manager
Janis Correia, Operations Manager

CFPV-FM
98.9 mhz FM; 420 w
McBride Communications & Media Inc., 10760 Fundy Dr., Pemberton, BC V7E 5K7 Canada
(604) 220-8393, *Fax:* (604) 677-6316
info@cimmfm.com
License: Pemberton, BC held by 0749943 BC Ltd. (Matthew G. McBride).
Population Served: 2,369 *Arbitron Metro Market:* Pemberton, BC
Matthew McBride, President

Pender Harbour

CIPN-FM
10-01-1984; 104.7 mhz FM *Hrs Open:* 24; 750 w; 1,500 ft*Rebroadcasts:* Rebroadcasts CISQ-FM Squamish
Box 1068, Squamish, BC V0N 3G0 Canada
(604) 892-1021, *Fax:* (604) 892-6383
www.mountainfm.com
mountainfm@mountainfm.com
License: Pender Harbour, BC held by Rogers Broadcasting.
Format: Adult Contemp*Hrs. of News Programming:* news progmg 16 hrs wkly *No. News Employees:* 3
Gary Miles, President
Paul Fisher, Operations Dir
Ken Geiger, General Manager
Janis Correia, Operations Manager

Penticton

***CIGVFM**
10-18-1981; 100.7 mhz FM *Hrs Open:* 24; kw
CA
(250) 493-6767, *Fax:* (250) 493-0098
www.giantfm.ca
info@giantfm.ca
License: Penticton, BC held by Great Valleys Radio Ltd.
Nat'l Reps: Target Broadcast Sales *Wire Services:* Broadcast News Ltd.
Format: Adult Contemp, Country*Special Programming:* Class 2 hrs, farm one hr wkly*Hrs. of News Programming:* news progmg 16 hrs wkly *No. News Employees:* 3 *Target Audience:* 18 plus.
James Robinson, CEO
Greg Masson, General Sales Mgr
Troy Scott, Programming Director
Harry Shaw, Chief Engineer

***CJMGFM**
06-01-1965; 97.1 mhz FM; kw
CA
(250) 492-2800, *Fax:* (250) 493-0370
www.sunonline.ca
mburley@astral.com
License: Penticton, BC held by Astral Media Radio G.P.
Group Owner: Astral Media Inc.
Format: Rock/AOR
Janet Burley, General Manager
Karen Davy, Promotions Manager
Jon Ferebee, News Director

CKOR
09-01-1948; 800 khz AM
CA
(250) 492-2800, *Fax:* (250) 493-0370
www.penticton.myezrock.com
License: Penticton, BC held by Astral Media Radio G.P.
Group Owner: Astral Media Inc.; (acq 10-29-2007; grpsl)
Format: Classic Rock
Janet Burley, General Manager
Janet Burley, General Sales Mgr
Karen Davy, Promotions Manager
Jon Ferebee, News Director

Port Alberni

CJAV-FM
09-02-2005; 93.3 mhz FM *Hrs Open:* 24; 6 kw
3296 Third Ave., Port Alberni, BC V9Y 4E1 Canada
(250) 723-2455, *Fax:* (250) 723-0797
www.933thepeak.com
info@933thepeak.com
License: Port Alberni, BC held by Jim Pattison Broadcast Group Ltd. (the general partner) and Jim Pattison Industries Ltd. (the limited partner), carrying on business as Jim Pattison Broadcast Group L.P.
Group Owner: The Jim Pattison Broadcast Group; (acq 6-27-2006; grpsl).

Population Served: 21,376 *Arbitron Metro Market:* Sedalia, MO *Format:* Contemporary Hits/Top 40, Adult Contemp *Target Audience:* 25-54; Adults*Adv. Rates:* 28; 28; 28; 28
Chris Talbot, Operations Dir
Rob Bye, General Manager
Evan Hammond, Programming Director
Pam Doherty, News Director
Cathy Johns, Administration Director

Port Hardy

CFNI
09-01-1979; 1240 khz AM
CA
(250) 949-6500, *Fax:* (250) 949-6580
www.theport.ca
cfniradio@cablerocket.com
License: Port Hardy, BC held by CFCP Radio Ltd.
Group Owner: Vista Broadcast Group Inc.
Format: Adult Contemp *No. News Employees:* 1 *Target Audience:* General.
Paul Mann, CEO

Port Moody

CKPM-FM
98.7 mhz FM
99 Moray Street, Port Moody, BC V3H 3M2 Canada
(604) 917-0188
www.mcmi.ca
info@mcmi.ca
License: Port Moody, Great Vancouver County, BC held by McBride Communications & Media Inc

Powell River

CJMP-FM
01-01-2006; 90.1 mhz FM; 3.6 w
4476 A Marine Ave., Powell River, BC V8A 2K2 Canada
(604) 485-0088, *Fax:* (604) 485-2683
www.cjmp.ca
admin@cjmp.ca
License: Powell River, BC held by Powell River Model Community Project for Persons with Disabilities.
Population Served: 13,165 *Arbitron Metro Market:* Powell River, BC *Format:* Variety/Diverse
Elaine Hill, General Sales Mgr

CFPW-FM
08-27-2008; 95.7 mhz FM; 1.2 kw; N49 41 54 W124 26 05
Suite 101, 7074 Westminster Street, Beach Garden Resort, Powell River, BC V8A 1C5 Canada
(604) 485-4207, *Fax:* (604) 485-4210
www.957sunfm.ca
onair@957sunfm.ca
License: Powell River, BC held by Vista Radio Ltd.
Group Owner: Vista Broadcast Group Inc.
Population Served: 13,165 *Arbitron Metro Market:* Powell River, BC *Format:* Adult Contemp *No. News Employees:* 4
Doug Zackodnik, General Manager
Justin Wilcomes, Programming Director
Jennifer Faerber, News Director
Liz Dick, Account Executive
Jacqueline Leung, Creative Director

Prince George

CBYG-FM
91.5 mhz FM; 100 kw
890 Victoria St., Unit 1, Prince George, BC V2L 5P1 Canada
(250) 562-6701, *Fax:* (250) 562-4777
www.vancouver.cbc.ca/daybreaknorth
daybreaknorth@cbc.ca
License: Prince George, BC held by CBC.
Nat'l Network: CBC Radio One
Format: News
Faydra Aldridge, General Manager

CIRX-FM
10-01-1983; 94.3 mhz FM; 3.5 kw; Ant 1,145 ft
1940 3rd Ave., Prince George, BC V2M 1G7 Canada
(250) 564-2524, *Fax:* (250) 562-6611
www.94xfm.com
info@94xfm.com
License: Prince George, BC held by Vista Radio Ltd.
Group Owner: Vista Broadcast Group Inc.
Target Audience: 18-34.
Gary Russell, General Manager
Sandy Whitwhan, General Sales Mgr
Kev Cotter, Programming Director
Christina Doll, News Director
Chris Terpsma, Chief Engineer

CKKN-FM
03-01-1981; 101.3 mhz FM; 10 kw; Ant 1,000 ft
2nd Fl. 1810 3rd Ave., Prince George, BC V2M 1G4 Canada
(250) 564-8861, *Fax:* (250) 562-8768
www.1013theriver.com
ckpgmail@ckpg.bc.ca
License: Prince George, BC held by Jim Pattison Broadcast Group Ltd. (the general partner) and Jim Pattison Industries Ltd. (the limited partner) carrying on business as Jim Pattison Broadcast Group L.P.
Group Owner: The Jim Pattison Broadcast Group; (acq 12-21-2000; grpsl).
TV Affiliate: CKPG-TV affil. *Format:* Contemporary Hits/Top 40
Rick Arnish, President
Ken Kilcullen, General Manager
Kelli Moorhead, General Sales Mgr
Mike Clotildes, Programming Director
Dave Barry, News Director

***CFUR-FM**
01-01-2002; 88.7 mhz FM; 510 w
University of Northern BC, 3333 University Way, Prince George, BC V2N 4Z9 Canada
(250) 960-7664, *Fax:* (250) 960-5995
www.cfur.ca
fhayes@cfur.ca
License: Prince George, BC held by Education Alternative Radio Society.
Population Served: 71,974 *Arbitron Metro Market:* Prince George, BC *Format:* Variety/Diverse *Target Audience:* Community of Prince George.*Adv. Rates:* 66; 66; 66; 66
Fraser Hayes, Station Manager
Brenden Van Stolk, General Sales Mgr
Joshua Laurin, Programming Director
Glen Yakemchuk, Engineering Dir
Jordan Tucker, Music Director

CKDV-FM
01-01-2003; 99.3 mhz FM *Hrs Open:* 24; 9.3 kw
1810 3rd Ave., 2nd Fl, Prince George, BC V2M 1G4 Canada
(250) 564-8861, *Fax:* (250) 562-8768
www.993thedrive.com
kkilcullen@ckpg.com
License: Prince George, BC held by Jim Pattison Broadcast Group Ltd. (the general partner) and Jim Pattison Industries Ltd. (the limited partner) carrying on business as Jim Pattison Broadcast Group L.P.
Group Owner: The Jim Pattison Broadcast Group
Population Served: 71,974 *Arbitron Metro Market:* Prince George, BC *Format:* Classic Rock
Ken Kilcullen, General Manager
Kelli Moorhead, General Sales Mgr
Ron Polillo, Programming Director
Dave Barry, News Director
Rick Kelly, Music Director

CJCI-FM
08-05-2003; 97.3 mhz FM *Hrs Open:* 24; 12 kw
The Wolf, 1940 3rd Ave., 1940 3rd Ave., Prince George, BC V2M 1G7 Canada
(250) 564-2524, *Fax:* (250) 562-6611
www.97fm.ca
thewolf@97fm.ca
License: Prince George, BC held by Vista Radio Ltd.
Group Owner: Vista Broadcast Group Inc.
Population Served: 71,974 *Arbitron Metro Market:* Prince George, BC *Format:* Country *No. News Employees:* 3 *Target Audience:* 25-54.
Gary Russell, General Manager
Sandy Whitwhan, General Sales Mgr
Bill Fee, News Director
Chris Terpsma, Chief Engineer

CFIS-FM
07-03-2007; 93.1 mhz FM *Hrs Open:* 24; 5 w; N53 54 37 W122 46 34
2880 15th Ave., Prince George, BC V2M 1T1 Canada
(250) 563-2347
www.cfisfm.com
cfisfm@yahoo.ca
License: Prince George, Canada County, BC held by Prince George Community Radio Society.
Population Served: 70,000 *Arbitron Metro Market:* Prince George*Hrs. of News Programming:* 6 hrs wkly *Target Audience:* 55+*Adv. Rates:* $10/30 second ad
Corey Walker, President
Reg Feyer, Operations Dir
Reg Feyer, General Manager
Reg Feyer, Station Manager
Howard Foot, General Sales Mgr
Reg Feyer, Programming Director
Reg Feyer, Promotions Manager

Prince Rupert

***CFPR**
01-01-1936; 860 khz AM *Hrs Open:* 24
CA
(250) 624-2161, *Fax:* (250) 627-8594
www.cbc.ca/daybreaknorth
daybreaknorth@vancouver.cbc.ca
License: Prince Rupert, BC held by CBC.
Nat'l Network: CBC Radio One
Format: News*Special Programming:* Current affrs *Target Audience:* General.
Faydra Aldridge, General Manager

CHTK
01-01-1965; 560 khz AM
CA
(250) 627-8255, *Fax:* (250) 624-3100
www.princerupert.myezrock.com
gsimpson@sri.ca
License: Prince Rupert, BC held by Astral Media Radio G.P.
Group Owner: Astral Media Inc.; (acq 10-29-2007; grpsl)
Format: Contemporary Hits/Top 40
Mike Lunn, General Manager
Janine Kraft, Programming Director

CIAJ-FM
01-01-2000; 100.7 mhz FM; 26.5 w
Box 1, 531 6th Ave. W., Prince Rupert, BC V8J 3P4 Canada

cfirm@citytel.net
License: Prince Rupert, BC held by Aboriginal Christian Voice Network.
Population Served: 12,508 *Arbitron Metro Market:* Prince Rupert, BC *Format:* Christian
Prescott Sandhu, General Manager

CHTK-FM
99.1 mhz FM; 160 watts; 278 meters; 54 17 N55 130 23 W10
4625 Lazelle Avenue, Terrace, BC V8G 1S4 Canada
(250) 635-6316, *Fax:* (250) 638-6320
www.princerupert.myezrock.com
License: Prince Rupert, BC held by Astral Medio Radio G P

Brian Langston, President

Princeton

CIOR(AM)
06-01-1972; 1400 khz AM *Hrs Open:* 6 AM-6 PM; 1 kw-U, DA-1; N49 26 50 W120 30 42
Box 539, 203 8309 Main St., Osoyoos, BC V0H 1V0 Canada
(250) 492-2800, *Fax:* (250) 495-7228
License: Princeton, BC held by Astral Media Radio G.P.
Group Owner: Astral Media Inc.; (acq 10-29-2007; grpsl)
Nat'l Reps: Canadian Broadcast Sales
Population Served: 5,000 *Format:* Adult Contemp
Lee Sterry, General Manager

Quesnel

CKCQ-FM
01-01-2004; 100.3 mhz FM; 1.8 kw
502-410 Kinchant St., Quesnel, BC V2J 7J5 Canada
(250) 992-7046, *Fax:* (250) 992-2354
www.thewolfonline.ca
glong@reachthecariboo.com
License: Quesnel, BC held by Vista Radio Ltd.
Group Owner: Vista Broadcast Group Inc.
Population Served: 10,007 *Arbitron Metro Market:* Quesnel, BC *Format:* Country *No. News Employees:* 4
Tom Tompkins, Operations Dir
Tracey Gard, General Manager
George Henderson, News Director

Revelstoke

CKCR-FM
106.1 mhz FM; 800 watts
Box 1420, 555 Victoria Road, Suite 207, Revelstoke, BC V0E 2SO Canada
(250) 837-2149, *Fax:* (250) 837-5577
www.revelsoke.myezrock.com
License: Revelstoke, BC held by Astral Media Radio G P

Richmond

CHKG-FM
09-06-1997; 96.1 mhz FM *Hrs Open:* 24; 46 kw; N49 21 12 W122 57 18
2090-4151 Hazelbridge Way, Richmond, BC V6X 4J7 Canada
(604) 295-1234, *Fax:* (604) 295-1201
www.fm961.com
general@fm961.com
License: Richmond, BC held by Fairchild Radio (Vancouver FM) Ltd.
Nat'l Reps: Target Broadcast Sales *Regional Reps:* In House
Population Served: 1,300,000 *Format:* Ethnic*Hrs. of News Programming:* news progmg 10 hrs wky *No. News Employees:* 10 *Target Audience:* General.
Thomas Fung, Chairman
Brenda Lo, Operations Dir
Pearl Kwan, General Sales Mgr
Seme Ho, Programming Director
Pearl Kwan, Promotions Manager
Travena Lee, News Director
Alfred Lee, Cantonese Programming
Alan Kwok, OperationsManager
George Lee, Senior Vice President

CISL
05-01-1980; 650 khz AM
CA
(604) 272-6500, *Fax:* (604) 272-0917
www.am650radio.com
rstanton@astral.com
License: Richmond, BC held by Astral Media Radio G.P.
Group Owner: Astral Media Inc.; (acq 10-29-2007; grpsl)
Format: Adult Contemp
Brad Phillips, Operations Dir

Rossland

CHLI-FM
01-01-2009; 101.1 mhz FM; kw
CA
(250) 362-0080
www.rosslandradio.com
radio@rosslandradio.com
License: Rossland, BC held by Rossland Radio Cooperative.
Arbitron Metro Market: Rossland, BC
Yvon Savoes, President
Francois Morache, Operations Dir
George Daviault, General Manager
Mike Mainville, Programming Director
Mark Andre Halle, News Director

Salmo

CFAD-FM
10-11-2008; 91.1 mhz FM; 5 w; N49 11 45 W117 16 51
Box 549, Salmo, BC Canada
(250) 357-2299
www.salmofm.info
info@salmofm.info
License: Salmo, BC held by Salmo FM Radio Society.

Gary Arsenault, General Manager

Salmon Arm

CKXR-FM
06-05-2006; 91.5 mhz FM *Hrs Open:* 24; 400 w
Mailing Address: Box 69, Salmon Arm, BC V1E 4N2 Canada
Second Address: 360 Ross St., Salmon Arm, BC V1E 4N2
(250) 832-2161, *Fax:* (250) 832-2240
www.salmonarm.myezrock.com
License: Salmon Arm, BC held by Astral Media Radio G.P.
Group Owner: Astral Media Inc.; (acq 10-29-2007; grpsl)
Population Served: 17,464 *Arbitron Metro Market:* Salmon Arm, BC *Format:* Adult Contemp *No. News Employees:* 3 *Target Audience:* 25-54.
Ron Langridge, General Manager

Sechelt

CKAY-FM
05-20-2006; 91.7 mhz FM *Hrs Open:* 24; 600 w; Mount Benson-Van. Island
Mailing Address: 1-1877 Field Rd., Sechelt, BC V0N 3A1 Canada
Second Address: 2nd. Floor, 13 Commercial St., Nanaimo, BC
(604) 741-9170, *Fax:* (604) 741-9172
www.ckay.ca
info@ckay.ca
License: Sechelt, Canada County, BC held by Westwave Broadcasting Inc.
Wire Services: BN Wire
Population Served: 4,182 *Arbitron Metro Market:* Gibsons, BC
Format: Contemporary Hits/Top 40, Adult Contemp*Hrs. of News Programming:* news progmg 8 hrs wkly *No. News Employees:* 3
Target Audience: 35 plus;adults
Bob Morris, General Manager and Programming Director
Sean Eckford, News Director
Bob Simpson, Manager, Sales & Marketing
Ed Johnson, Manager, Sales & Marketing
Paul Nattall, VP, Sales & Marketing

Smithers

CFBV
10-25-1963; 870 khz AM
Mailing Address: CA
Second Address: 1139 Queen St., Smithers, BC V0J 2N0
(250) 847-2521, *Fax:* (250) 847-9411
www.thepeak.ca
License: Smithers, BC held by Vista Radio Ltd.
Group Owner: Vista Broadcast Group Inc.
Format: Oldies
Al Collison, General Manager

Squamish

***CISQFM**
11-30-1981; 104.9 mhz FM *Hrs Open:* 24; kw
CA
(604) 892-1021, *Fax:* (604) 892-6383
www.mountainfm.com
mountainfm@mountainfm.com
License: Squamish, BC held by Rogers Broadcasting.
Group Owner: Rogers Broadcasting Ltd.
Nat'l Reps: Canadian Broadcast Sales
Format: Adult Contemp*Special Programming:* Talk 5 hrs wkly*Hrs. of News Programming:* news progmg 5 hrs wkly *No. News Employees:* 3 *Target Audience:* 18-54.
Janis Correia, Operations Dir
Ken Geiger, General Manager

Summerland

CHOR-FM
05-21-2010; 98.5 mhz FM; 20 watts; 348 meters
9901 Main Street, Suite 200, Summerland, BC V0H 1Z0 Canada
(250) 494-0333, *Fax:* (250) 404-0263
www.am1450.ca
License: Summerland, BC held by Astral Media Radio G P
Janet Burley, General Manager

Terrace

CFTK
01-01-1960; 590 khz AM
CA
(250) 635-6316, *Fax:* (250) 638-6320
License: Terrace, BC held by Astral Media Radio G.P.
Group Owner: Astral Media Inc.; (acq 10-29-2007; grpsl)
Format: Adult Contemp
Brian Langston, General Manager

***CJFWFM**
12-01-1983; 103.1 mhz FM; kw
CA
(250) 635-6316, *Fax:* (250) 638-6320
www.cjfw.ca
blangston@astral.com
License: Terrace, BC held by Astral Media Radio G.P.
Group Owner: Astral Media Inc.
TV Affiliate: CFTK-TV affil. *Format:* Country
Brian Langston, General Manager
John Crawford, Programming Director
John Crawford, News Director
Steve Hart, Radio Program Manager

CFNR-FM
01-01-1995; 92.1 mhz FM *Hrs Open:* 24; 43 w
4562 B Queensway Dr., Terrace, BC V8G 3X6 Canada
(250) 638-8137, *Fax:* (250) 638-8027
www.classicrockcfnr.ca
promotions@classicrockcfnr.com
License: Terrace, BC held by Northern Native Broadcasting (Terrace, B.C.).
Population Served: 11,486 *Arbitron Metro Market:* Terrace, BC
Format: Classic Rock*Special Programming:* First nations 9 hrs*Hrs. of News Programming:* News progmg 10 hrs wkly *Target Audience:* General; 35+
Greg Smith, CEO
Barry Wall, General Manager
Craig Ellis, Programming Director
Tara Evans, Promotions Manager
Jillian Milnes, Accounting Manager
Diane Lukasser, Reception
Tania Vance, Assistant Promotions
Brent Halfyard,Creative Director
Denise Halfyard, Website Coordinator

Tofino

CHMZ-FM
01-01-2005; 90.1 mhz FM; 170 w
Box 1092, Tofino, BC V0R 2Z0 Canada
(250) 725-4411, *Fax:* (250) 725-4411
www.chmzfm.com
info@chmzfm.com
License: Tofino, BC held by West Island Radio Enterprises General Partnership.
Population Served: 1,876 *Arbitron Metro Market:* Tofino, BC
Format: Country
Matthew McBride, General Manager

Trail

CJAT-FM
01-01-1996; 95.7 mhz FM; 13.5 kw
1560 2nd Ave., Trail, BC V1R 1M4 Canada
(250) 368-5510, *Fax:* (250) 368-8471
www.kbsradio.ca
License: Trail, BC held by Astral Media Radio G.P.
Group Owner: Astral Media Inc.; (acq 10-29-2007; grpsl)
Nat'l Reps: Radio Astral
Format: Adult Contemp
Nicole Beetstra, General Manager
Lea Wilman, Programming Director
Kirsten Goldstone, Promotions Manager
David Ford, Engineering Dir

Ucluelet

CIMM-FM
09-01-2006; 99.5 mhz FM; 180 w
10760 Fundy Dr., Richmond, BC V7E 5K7 Canada
(250) 725 4411, *Fax:* (604) 677-6316
www.longbeachradio.ca
info@cimmfm.com
License: Ucluelet, BC held by CIMM-FM Radio Ltd.
Population Served: 1,627 *Arbitron Metro Market:* Ucluelet, BC
Format: Variety/Diverse
Matthew McBride, General Manager

Vancouver

***CBU**
01-01-1925; 690 khz AM *Hrs Open:* 24; 50 kw-U, DA-1
Box 4600, 700 Hamilton St., Vancouver, BC Canada
(604) 662-6000, *Fax:* (604) 662-6088
www.cbc.ca/bc
info@cbc.ca/bc
License: Vancouver, BC held by Canadian Broadcasting Corp.
Joan Anderson, General Manager
Joan Athey, Promotions Manager
Brett Ballah, News Director
Dave Newbury, Engineering Dir
Terry Donnelly, News Reporter

CBU-FM
01-01-1947; 105.7 mhz FM *Hrs Open:* 24; 100 kw; 1,823 ft
Box 4600, 700 Hamilton St., Vancouver, BC V6B 4A2 Canada
(604) 662-6000, *Fax:* (604) 662-6088
www..cbc.ca/bc
info@cbc.ca/bc
License: Vancouver, BC held by Canadian Broadcasting Corp

Tod Elvidge, Programming Director

CBUFFM
12-01-1967; 97.7 mhz FM; 50 kw; Ant 1,823 ft
Mailing Address: 700 Hamilton St., Vancouver, BC Canada
Second Address: Box 4600, Vancouver, BC V6B 4A2
(604) 662-6169, *Fax:* (604) 662-6161
www.radio-canada.ca/c-b
License: Vancouver, BC held by CBC.
Nat'l Network: Premiere Chaine
Stephane Boisjoly, General Manager
Mario Deschamps, Programming Director

CFOXFM
10-01-1964; 99.3 mhz FM; 51 kw; 386.4 meters
700 W. Georgia St., Suite 2000, Vancouver, BC Canada
(604) 684-7221, *Fax:* (604) 331-2722
info@cfox.com
License: Vancouver, BC held by Corus Radio Co.
Group Owner: Corus Entertainment Inc.

Bob Mills, Programming Director

***CFROFM**
04-22-1975; 100.5 mhz FM; 5.5 kw; 1,005 ft
110-360 Columbia St., Vancouver, BC Canada
(604) 684-8494
www.coopradio.org
program@coopradio.org
License: Vancouver, BC held by Vancouver Co-Op Radio.
Special Programming: Black 14 hrs, Chinese 2 hrs, Greek one hr, hip hop 17 hrs, jazz 16 hrs, Latin American 7 hrs, Pol 5 hrs wkly *Target Audience:* General; alternative community
Leela Chinniah, Programming Director
Danjel van Tijn, Engineering Dir
Rob Gauvin, Music Director

CFTE
04-20-1922; 1410 khz AM *Hrs Open:* 24; 50 kw-U, DA-2
380 W. 2nd Ave. Suite 300, Vancouver, BC Canada
(604) 871-9000, *Fax:* (604) 871-2901
www.cfun.com
info@cfun.com
License: Vancouver, BC held by Bell Media British Columbia Radio Partnership
Group Owner: Bell Media Inc.
Target Audience: 25-49; upscale, well-educated females
John Hinnen, General Manager

CHMB
12-10-1959; 1320 khz AM *Hrs Open:* 24
CA
(604) 263-1320, *Fax:* (604) 261-0310
www.am1320.com
info@am1320.com
License: Vancouver, BC held by Mainstream Broadcasting Corp.
Nat'l Reps: Canadian Broadcast Sales
Format: Chinese*Special Programming:* American Indian one hr, Japanese 1 hr, Vietnamese*Hrs. of News Programming:* news progmg 30 hrs wkly *No. News Employees:* 8 *Target Audience:* 18-65; multilingual, mainly Chinese
Teresa Wat, CEO
James Ho, President
George Feng, General Sales Mgr
Harry Lee, Programming Director
Trix Chan, News Director
Kay Lai, Sales Manager

CHQMFM
08-10-1960; 103.5 mhz FM *Hrs Open:* 24; 53 kw; Ant 2,026 ft
380 W. 2nd Ave., Suite 300, Vancouver, BC Canada
(604) 871-9000, *Fax:* (604) 871-2901
www.qmfm.com
info@chqm.com
License: Vancouver, BC held by Bell Media British Columbia Radio
Group Owner: Bell Media Inc.; (acq 6-22-2007; grpsl)
Hrs. of News Programming: news progmg 2 hrs wkly *No. News Employees:* 5 *Target Audience:* 25-54.
Neil Gallagher, General Manager
Barry O'Donnell, General Sales Mgr
Clara Carotenuto, Programming Director
Carl LeGrice, Promotions Manager
Dave Youell, Chief Engineer

***CKKSFM**
07-01-1985; 96.9 mhz FM *Hrs Open:* 24; kw*Rebroadcasts:* Rebroadcasts CISQ-FM Squamish
CA
(604) 892-1021, *Fax:* (604) 892-6383
www.mountainfm.com
mountainfm@mountainfm.com
License: Vancouver, BC held by Rogers Broadcasting Ltd.
Group Owner: Rogers Broadcasting Ltd.
Nat'l Reps: Canadian Broadcast Sales
Format: Oldies*Special Programming:* Magazine show 3 hrs wkly*Hrs. of News Programming:* news progmg 16 hrs wkly *No. News Employees:* 3 *Target Audience:* 25-45.
Gary Miles, President
Janis Correia, Operations Dir
Ken Geiger, General Manager
Paul Fisher, General Sales Mgr

***CITRFM**
04-01-1982; 101.9 mhz FM *Hrs Open:* 7:30 AM-4 AM; kw
CA
(604) 822-3017, *Fax:* (604) 822-9364
www.citr.ca
citrmgr@ams.ubc.ca
License: Vancouver, BC held by Student Radio Society of University of British Columbia.
Format: Variety/Diverse*Hrs. of News Programming:* News progmg 5 hrs wkly *Target Audience:* General; campus/community
Brenda Grunau, Station Manager
Robin Alam, Programming Director
Bryce Dunn, Program Coordinator

***CJJRFM**
07-01-1986; 93.7 mhz FM *Hrs Open:* 24; kw
CA
(604) 731-7772, *Fax:* (604) 731-0493
www.jrfm.com
cjjr@jrfm.com
License: Vancouver, BC held by Jim Pattison Broadcast Group Ltd.
Group Owner: The Jim Pattison Broadcast Group
Format: Country *No. News Employees:* 2 *Target Audience:* 25-54.
Bill Jackson, Operations Dir
Gerry Siemens, General Manager
Mark Rogers, General Sales Mgr
Gordon Eno, Programming Director
David Linder, Engineering Dir
Rick Holmes, Creative Director
Mark Patric, Music Director
BrianPritchard, National Sales Manager
Sandra Spence, Office Manager
Tamsin Carling, Promotions Director

CJVB
06-18-1972; 1470 khz AM *Hrs Open:* 24; 50 kw-U, DA-2; N49 11 36 W123 01 17
4151 Hazelbridge Way, Unit 2090 Aberdeen Centre, Richmond, BC Canada
(604) 295-1234, *Fax:* (604) 295-1201
www.am1470.com
general@am1470.com
License: Vancouver, BC held by Fairchild Radio Group Ltd.
Nat'l Reps: Target Broadcast Sales *Regional Reps:* In House
Population Served: 1,300,000*Hrs. of News Programming:* news progmg 23 hrs wkly *No. News Employees:* 10 *Target Audience:* General.
Thomas Fung, Chairman
Brenda Lo, Operations Dir
Pearl Kwan, General Sales Mgr
Alfred Lee, Programming Director
Pearl Kwan, Promotions Manager
Travena Lee, News Director
Seme Ho, AVP International Programming
Alan Kwok,Operations Manager
George Lee, Senior Vice President

CKLG-FM
03-01-1980; 96.9 mhz FM *Hrs Open:* 24; 100 kw; 2,500 ft; N49 21 29 W122 57 09
2440 Ash St., Vancouver, BC V5Z 4J6 Canada
(604) 872-2557, *Fax:* (604) 877-4494
www.jackfm.com
License: Vancouver, BC held by Rogers Broadcasting Ltd.
Group Owner: Rogers Broadcasting Ltd.
Format: Adult Contemp
Barry Taylor, Programming Director
Rick dal Farra, Engineering Dir

CHMJ
06-01-1954; 730 khz AM
CA
(604) 681-7511, *Fax:* (604) 331-2722
www.am730.ca
info@chmj.com
License: Vancouver, BC held by Corus Radio Co.
Group Owner: Corus Entertainment Inc.; (acq 7-6-2000; grpsl).
Format: Talk
J.J. Johnston, General Manager
Shari Wong, General Sales Mgr
Ian Koenigsfest, Programming Director

CKST
01-19-1963; 1040 khz AM *Hrs Open:* 24; 50 kw-U, DA-2
300-380 W. 2nd Ave., Suite 300, Vancouver, BC Canada
(604) 871-9000, *Fax:* (604) 871-2901
www.team1040.ca
info@ckst.com
License: Vancouver, BC held by Bell Media British Columbia Radio Partnership
Group Owner: Bell Media Inc.; acq 6-22-2007;. grpsl)
Nat'l Reps: Canadian Broadcast Sales
Population Served: 2,000,000*Hrs. of News Programming:* news progmg 8 hrs wkly *No. News Employees:* 4 *Target Audience:* 40 plus; intelligent, socially conscious, older demographic
Neil Gallagher, General Manager

CKWX
04-01-1923; 1130 khz AM
CA
(604) 873-2599, *Fax:* (604) 873-0877
www.news1130.com
License: Vancouver, BC held by Rogers Broadcasting Ltd.
Group Owner: Rogers Broadcasting Ltd.; acq 1989).
Nat'l Reps: CBS Radio
Format: News*Hrs. of News Programming:* news progmg 168 hrs wkly *No. News Employees:* 45 *Target Audience:* 35-54; men
Ted Rogers, CEO
Tony Viner, President
Paul Fisher, General Manager
Robert Brimacombe, General Sales Mgr
Jacquie Donaldson, Programming Director
Kattie Bull, Promotions Manager
Rick Dal Farra, Chief Engineer
Gary Miles,Executive Vice President

***CKZZ-FM**
05-01-1991; 95.3 mhz FM; kw
CA
(604) 241-0953, *Fax:* (604) 272-0917
www.virginradio.ca
input@virginradio.ca
License: Vancouver, BC held by Astral Media Radio G.P.
Group Owner: Astral Media Inc.; (acq 10-29-2007; grpsl)
Format: Adult Contemp
Brad Phillips, Operations Dir

CFBT-FM
02-01-2002; 94.5 mhz FM *Hrs Open:* 24; 46 kw
#A301 - 770 Pacific Blvd., Plaza of Nations, Vancouver, BC Canada
(604) 699-2328, *Fax:* (604) 484-4912
www.thebeat.com
info@thebeat.com
License: Vancouver, BC held by Bell Media British Columbia Radio
Group Owner: Bell Media Inc.; (acq 10-12-2007; C$46,006,717)
Hrs. of News Programming: news progmg 2 hrs wkly *No. News Employees:* 1
Jennifer Smith, Operations Dir
Chris Myers, Programming Director

CBUX-FM
09-22-2002; 90.9 mhz FM; 1.28 kw
700 Hamilton St., Vancouver, BC V6B 4A2 Canada
(604) 662-6000, *Fax:* (604) 662-6335
www.radio-canada.ca/c-b
License: Vancouver, BC held by Canadian Broadcasting Corp.
Nat'l Network: Espace Musique

Stephane Boisjoly, General Manager
Mario Deschamps, Programming Director

CKVX
104.9 mhz FM; kw
CA
(306) 463-4411, *Fax:* (306) 882-3037
cjmmnews@goldenwestradio.com
License: Vancouver, BC
Group Owner: Golden West Broadcasting Ltd.
Arbitron Metro Market: Tri-Cities, WA (Richland-Kennewick-Pasco) *Format:* Country
Keith Leask, General Manager

CJRJ
11-01-2006; 1200 khz AM
CA
(604) 299-8863, *Fax:* (604) 299-3088
www.rj1200.com
info@rj1200.com
License: Vancouver, BC held by I.T. Productions Ltd.
Arbitron Metro Market: Albuquerque, NM *Format:* Ethnic
Shushma Datt, CEO
Sudhir Datta, General Manager

CKYE-FM
02-01-2006; 93.1 mhz FM; kw
CA
(604) 598-9311, *Fax:* (604) 599-6063
redfm.ca
info@redfm.ca
License: Vancouver, BC held by South Asian Broadcasting Corp. Inc.
Arbitron Metro Market: Vancouver, BC *Format:* Ethnic
Kulwinder Sanghera, CEO
Bijoy Samuel, General Manager
Harjinder Thind, News Director

CKAV-FM-2
01-01-2007; 106.3 mhz FM; 9 kw; Ant 1,968 ft; N49 21 17 W122 57 25
PO Box 87, Station E, Toronto, ON M6H 4E1 Canada
(416) 703-1287, *Fax:* (416) 703-4328
aboriginalvoices.com
info@aboriginalvoices.com
License: Vancouver, BC held by Aboriginal Voices Radio Inc.
Group Owner: Aboriginal Voices Radio Inc.
Population Served: 2,615,060 *Arbitron Metro Market:* Toronto, ON *Format:* Ethnic
Roy Hennessy, Operations Dir
Patrice Mousseau, Programming Director

CKPK-FM
11-13-2008; 102.7 mhz FM; 2.8 kw; Ant 1,932 ft; N49 21 16 W122 57 30
1401 W. 8th Ave., Suite 300, Vancouver, BC V6H 1C9 Canada
(604) 731-6111, *Fax:* (604) 731-0493
www.thepeak.fm
License: Vancouver, BC held by Jim Pattison Broadcast Group Ltd. (the general partner) and Jim Pattison Industries Ltd. (the limited partner), carrying on business as Jim Pattison Broadcast Group L.P.
Group Owner: The Jim Pattison Broadcast Group
Nat'l Reps: Canadian Broadcast Sales
Target Audience: 25-49; adults
Gerry Siemens, General Manager

CHHR-FM
104.3 mhz FM *Hrs Open:* 24/7; kw
CA
(604) 628-1043, *Fax:* (604) 272-0917
www.shore104.com
rstanton@radio.astral.com?subject=Shore104%20Programming%20Inquiry%2FRandom%20Thoughts
License: Vancouver, Canada County, BC held by Shore Media Group Inc.
Arbitron Metro Market: Vancouver, BC *Format:* Alternative *No. News Employees:* 3 *Target Audience:* 25-54.
Sean Morrison, Chairman
Roy Hennessy, President
Sherri Pierce, General Sales Mgr

CBYKFM
10-09-2012; 84.1 mhz FM; 4.75 kw; 124 meters
218 Victoria Street, Kemloops, BC Canada
(250) 374-6802
www.cbc.ca/kamloops
License: Vancouver, Clark County, BC held by CBC
Nat'l Network: CBC Radio One
Hubert Lacroix, President

Vanderhoof

CIVH
11-01-1973; 1340 khz AM *Hrs Open:* 6-10 AM
CA
(250) 567-4914, *Fax:* (250) 567-4982
thevalleywolf.ca
thewolf@hwy16.com
License: Vanderhoof, BC held by Vista Radio Ltd.
Group Owner: Vista Broadcast Group Inc.
Nat'l Reps: Target Broadcast Sales
Format: Country*Special Programming:* Relg 5 hrs wkly *Target Audience:* General.
Janey VanWinkle, Operations Dir
Gary Russell, General Manager
JC Brown, General Sales Mgr
Jacqui Ryks, Programming Director
Bill Fee, News Director
Karen Fridleifson, Sales

Vernon

CKIZ-FM
11-08-2001; 107.5 mhz FM; 46 kw
3313 32nd Ave., Vernon, BC V1T 2E1 Canada
(250) 545-2141, *Fax:* (250) 545-9008
www.1075kiss.com
kissfm@1075kiss.com
License: Vernon, BC held by Jim Pattison Broadcast Group Ltd. (the general partner) and Jim Pattison Industries Ltd. (the limited partner), carrying on business as Jim Pattison Broadcast Group L.P.
Group Owner: The Jim Pattison Broadcast Group; (acq 10-31-2008; C$4 million)
Nat'l Reps: Canadian Broadcast Sales
Population Served: 38,150 *Arbitron Metro Market:* Vernon, BC *Format:* News
Patrick Nicol, Operations Dir
Gord Wiens, General Sales Mgr
Duane Schindel, Chief Engineer

CICF-FM
01-01-2001; 105.7 mhz FM *Hrs Open:* 8:30 AM-5 PM; 46 kw
2800 31st St., Vernon, BC V1T 5H4 Canada
(250) 545-9222, *Fax:* (250) 542-2083
www.thesunonline.ca
reception@thesunonline.ca
License: Vernon, BC held by Astral Media Radio G.P.
Group Owner: Astral Media Inc.; (acq 10-29-2007; grpsl)
Population Served: 38,150 *Arbitron Metro Market:* Vernon, BC *Format:* Adult Contemp *No. News Employees:* 2
Gord Leighton, General Manager/Sales Manager
Vicki Proulx, Promotions Manager
Larry King, Chief Engineer
Mark Burley, Brand Director
Jeff Winskell, Music Director
Brian Martin, Assistant Brand Manager
Dustin Clement,Production
Mark Baese, Digital Accounts Manager
Tim Weston, Sales

Victoria

***CBCV-FM**
09-28-1998; 90.5 mhz FM; kw
CA
(250) 360-2227, *Fax:* (250) 360-2600
www.vancouver.cbc.ca/ontheisland
victoria@cbc.ca
License: Victoria, BC held by CBC.
Nat'l Network: CBC Radio One
Format: News*Hrs. of News Programming:* news progmg 23 hrs wkly *No. News Employees:* 11
Peter Hutchinson, Station Manager

CFAX
09-04-1959; 1070 khz AM *Hrs Open:* 24
CA
(250) 920-4602, *Fax:* (250) 386-5775
www.cfax1070.com
tspence@cfax1070.com
License: Victoria, BC
Group Owner: Bell Media Inc.; (acq 10-1-2004;. C$7.5 million with co-located FM)
Nat'l Reps: Target Broadcast Sales *Wire Services:* BN Wire
Format: News, News/Talk, Talk*Hrs. of News Programming:* news progmg 21 hrs wkly *No. News Employees:* 7 *Target Audience:* 45 plus; 50% males, 50% females*Adv. Rates:* 169; 106; 115; 53
Terry Spence, General Manager
Kevin Bell, General Sales Mgr
Al Ferraby, Programming Director
Shannon Kowalko, Promotions Manager
Bud Goes, Chief Engineer
Frank Stanford, News Reporter

***CFUVFM**
12-17-1984; 101.9 mhz FM *Hrs Open:* 24; kw
CA
(250) 721-8702
www.cfuv.uvic.ca
cfuvman@uvic.ca
License: Victoria, Canada County, BC held by University of Victoria Student Radio Society.
Format: Variety/Diverse*Special Programming:* It 2 hrs, American Indian one hrs; Fr 2 hrs, Pol o*Hrs. of News Programming:* News progmg 8.5 hrs wkly *Target Audience:* General; people tired of coml radio, on campus & inthe community*Adv. Rates:* 40; 40; 40; 40
Randy Gelling, Station Manager
Jana Grazley, Programming Director
Justin Lanoue, Music Director

CIOC-FM
03-18-1965; 98.5 mhz FM *Hrs Open:* 24; 100 kw; 567 ft
817 Fort St., Victoria, BC V8W 1H6 Canada
(250) 382-0900, *Fax:* (250) 382-4358
www.ocean985.com
License: Victoria, BC held by Rogers Broadcasting Ltd.
Group Owner: Rogers Broadcasting Ltd.
Population Served: 300,000*Hrs. of News Programming:* news progmg 2 hrs wkly *No. News Employees:* 1 *Target Audience:* 35-54; female
Kim Hesketh, Operations Dir
Tony Marsh, General Sales Mgr
Dawn Kaysoe, Programming Director
Dean Fox, Chief Engineer

***CJRQFM**
09-01-1965; 92.1 mhz FM *Hrs Open:* 24; kw
CA
(705) 566-4480, *Fax:* (705) 560-7232
www.q92rocks.com
q92@q92rocks.com
License: Victoria, BC held by Rogers Broadcasting Ltd.
Group Owner: Rogers Broadcasting Ltd.
Hrs. of News Programming: news progmg one hr wkly *No. News Employees:* 5
Terry Callaghan, Programming Director
Kevin Britton, Music Director

CKKQ-FM
12-12-1987; 100.3 mhz FM *Hrs Open:* 24; 100 kw; Ant 1,620 ft; N48 35 41 W123 32 37
2750 Quadra St., Top Fl., Victoria, BC V8T 4E8 Canada
(250) 475-0100, *Fax:* (250) 475-3299
www.theq.fm
thecrew@theQ.fm
License: Victoria, BC held by Jim Pattison Broadcast Group Ltd. (the general partner) and Jim Pattison Industries Ltd. (the limited partner), carrying on business as Jim Pattison Broadcast Group L.P.
Group Owner: The Jim Pattison Broadcast Group; (acq 11-24-2006; C$15.75 million with CJZN-FM Victoria)
Nat'l Reps: Canadian Broadcast Sales
Format: Classic Rock*Hrs. of News Programming:* news progmg 4 hrs wkly *No. News Employees:* 2 *Target Audience:* 25-49.
John Shields, Operations Dir
Dan McAllister, General Manager
Brian Blackburn, General Sales Mgr

CHTT-FM
09-01-2000; 103.1 mhz FM *Hrs Open:* 9 AM-9 PM; 50 w; N48 26 52 W123 19 19
817 Fort St., Victoria, BC V8W 1H6 Canada
(250) 382-0900, *Fax:* (250) 382-4358
www.1031jackfm.ca
don.landels@rci.roger.com
License: Victoria, BC held by Rogers Broadcasting Ltd.
Group Owner: Rogers Broadcasting Ltd.
Nat'l Reps: Canadian Broadcast Sales
Population Served: 200,000 *Format:* Contemporary Hits/Top 40, Adult Contemp*Hrs. of News Programming:* News progmg 5 hrs wkly
Gorde Edlund, General Manager
Tony Marsh, General Sales Mgr

CHBE-FM
08-23-2002; 107.3 mhz FM; 20 kw; N48 25 06 W123 30 35
1420 Broad St., Victoria, BC V8W 2B1 Canada
(250) 382-1073, *Fax:* (250) 386-5775
www.1073kool.fm
koolmornings@1073kool.fm
License: Victoria, Victoria County, BC held by Bell Media British Columbia Radio Partnership
Group Owner: Bell Media Inc.
Population Served: 330,088 *Arbitron Metro Market:* Victoria, BC*Hrs. of News Programming:* News progmg 2 hrs wkly *Target Audience:* 35-49.*Adv. Rates:* 172; 109; 130; 55
Robin Haggar, Programming Director
Murray Langdon, News Director
Carolyn Birch, Promotions / Marketing / Sponsorship Requests
Chris Donnelly, Creative / Production
Carolyn Birch, Contest Questions / Website Maintenance
Kevin Bell,Sales

CJZN-FM
05-01-2000; 91.3 mhz FM; 1.766 kw
Top Floor, 2750 Quadra St., Victoria, BC V8T 4E8 Canada
(250) 475-6611, *Fax:* (250) 475-3299
www.thezone.fm
modernrock@thezone.fm
License: Victoria, BC held by Jim Pattison Broadcast Group Ltd. (the general partner) and Jim Pattison Industries Ltd. (the limited partner), carrying on business as Jim Pattison Broadcast Group L.P.
Group Owner: The Jim Pattison Broadcast Group; (acq 11-24-2006; C$15.75 million with CKKQ-FM Victoria)
Population Served: 80,032 *Arbitron Metro Market:* Victoria, BC *Format:* Rock/AOR *Target Audience:* 25-64.
John Shields, Operations Dir
Dan McAllister, General Manager
Brian Blackburn, General Sales Mgr

CILS-FM
11-07-2007; 107.9 mhz FM; 250 w; N48 25 26 W123 20 10
200-535 Yates St., Victoria, BC V8W 2Z6 Canada

(250) 220-4139, *Fax:* (250) 388-6280
www.cilsfm.ca
radio@francocentre.com
License: Victoria, BC held by Societe radio communautaire Victoria.
Population Served: 80,032 *Arbitron Metro Market:* Victoria, BC
Format: French
Jacques P. Vall,e, President
Jules Desjarlais, Programming Director
Julie Gagnon, Vice President
Fadia Saad, Executive Director
Anne-Marie Breton, Accounting Coordinator
G,rald Montpetit, Brodcasting Chief
William McCarter, ChiefTechnical Officer
Adam Gottlieb, Sales and Promo Counselor

Whistler

***CISWFM**
02-25-1982; 102.1 mhz FM; kw*Rebroadcasts:* Rebroadcasts CISQ-FM Squamish
CA
(604) 892-1021, *Fax:* (604) 892-6383
www.mountainfm.com
mountainfm@mountainfm.com
License: Whistler, BC held by Rogers Broadcasting Ltd.
Group Owner: Rogers Broadcasting Ltd.
Format: Adult Contemp
Gary Miles, President
Paul Fisher, Operations Dir
Ken Geiger, General Manager
Janis Correia, Operations Manager

Williams Lake

CKWL
02-25-1960; 570 khz AM *Hrs Open:* 24
CA
(250) 392-6551, *Fax:* (250) 392-4142
www.thewolfonline.ca
License: Williams Lake, BC held by Vista Radio Ltd.
Group Owner: Vista Broadcast Group Inc.
Nat'l Reps: Canadian Broadcast Sales
Format: Country *No. News Employees:* 1 *Target Audience:* 25-54 plus.*Adv. Rates:* 25; 21; 21; 14
Terry Coles, President
Tom Tomplins, Operations Dir
Tracey Gard, General Manager
Paul Mann, General Sales Mgr

CJLJ-FM
02-11-2012; 100.7 mhz FM; 5 watts; -68.8 meters
2672 Indian Drive, Williams Lake, BC V2G 5K9 Canada
(250) 392-4418, *Fax:* (250) 296-4750
www.williamslakeband.ca
License: Williams Lake, BC held by Sugar Cane Community Diversity Association

Manitoba

Altona

CFAM
03-13-1957; 950 khz AM *Hrs Open:* 24
CA
(204) 324-6464, *Fax:* (204) 324-8918
www.cfamradio.com
cfam@goldenwestradio.com
License: Altona, MB held by Golden West Broadcasting Ltd.
Group Owner: Golden West Broadcasting Ltd.
Nat'l Reps: Canadian Broadcast Sales
Format: Adult Contemp, Agriculture*Special Programming:* Class 15 hrs wkly*Hrs. of News Programming:* news progmg 12 hrs wkly *No. News Employees:* 8 *Target Audience:* General.
Elmer Hildebrand, CEO
Ang Enns, Station Manager

Boissevain

CJRB
01-01-1973; 1220 khz AM *Hrs Open:* 24
CA
(204) 324-6464, *Fax:* (204) 324-8918
License: Boissevain, MB held by Golden West Broadcasting Ltd.
Group Owner: Golden West Broadcasting Ltd.
Wire Services: BN Wire
Format: Agriculture, Religious *No. News Employees:* 1 *Target Audience:* General.
E. Hildebrand, President
Menno Friesen, General Sales Mgr
Al Friesen, Programming Director

Laverne Siemens, Engineering Dir
Lyndon Friesen, Executive Vice President

Brandon

CKLQ
10-01-1977; 880 khz AM *Hrs Open:* 24
CA
(204) 726-8888, *Fax:* (204) 726-1270
www.cklq.com
qcountry@cklq.mb.ca
License: Brandon, MB held by Riding Mountain Broadcasting Ltd.
Nat'l Reps: Target Broadcast Sales
Format: Country*Special Programming:* Farm 18 hrs wkly *No. News Employees:* 7 *Target Audience:* 35 plus.*Adv. Rates:* 63; 50; 50 38
Cam Clark, General Manager
Verna Lenton, General Sales Mgr
Steve Antaya, Programming Director
John Loregio, News Director

CKX-FM
12-16-1963; 96.1 mhz FM; 100 kw; 1,042 ft
2940 Victoria Ave., Brandon, MB R7B 3Y3 Canada
(204) 728-1150, *Fax:* (204) 725-3794
www.kx96online.com
staylor@astral.com
License: Brandon, MB held by Astral Media Radio G.P.
Group Owner: Astral Media Inc.; (acq 10-29-2007; grpsl)
Format: Classic Rock
Janet Trecarten, Operations Dir
Sharon Taylor, General Manager
Darcie Morris, General Sales Mgr
Donna Smith, Promotions Manager
Boyd Kozak, News Director
Angela Greig, Assistant Music Director
Norine Mitchell, Regional SalesManager

CKXA-FM
02-01-2000; 101.1 mhz FM; 100 kw
2940 Victoria Ave., Brandon, MB R7B 3Y3 Canada
(204) 728-1150, *Fax:* (204) 725-3794
www.1011thefarm.com
staylor@astral.com
License: Brandon, MB held by Astral Media Radio G.P.
Group Owner: Astral Media Inc.; (acq 10-29-2007; grpsl)
Population Served: 8,010 *Arbitron Metro Market:* Ruidoso, NM
Format: Country
Sharon Taylor, Operations Dir
Sharon Taylor, General Manager
Darcie Morris, Sales Manager
Tim Black, Programming Director
Donna Smith, Promotions Manager
Boyd Kozak, News Director
Janet Trecarten, Operations Manager
Tim Black,Brand Director
Adam Taylor, Promotions Coordinator
Mike Uhrich, Digital Content Producer
Paul Timm, Digital Accounts Manager
Joanne Barr, Billing

CKLF-FM
06-01-2000; 94.7 mhz FM *Hrs Open:* 24; 100 kw
624 14th St. E., Brandon, MB R7A 7E1 Canada
(204) 726-8888, *Fax:* (204) 726-1270
www.starfmradio.com
Starfm@starfmradio.com
License: Brandon, MB held by Riding Mountain Broadcasting Ltd.
Population Served: 46,061 *Arbitron Metro Market:* Brandon, MB
Format: Adult Contemp *No. News Employees:* 7 *Target Audience:* 25-54; adults*Adv. Rates:* 63; 50; 50; 38
Cam Clark, General Manager
Verna Lenton, General Sales Mgr
Tyler Glen, Programming Director
John LoRegio, News Director
Scott DeMontigny, Rural Sales North
David Simard, Rural Sales South
Jenna MacDonald, Brandon Sales
BrittneeLong, Brandon Sales
Nigel Nolin, Brandon Sales
Trent Bartley, Music Director

CJJJ-FM
05-01-2003; 106.5 mhz FM; 930 w
661 24th St., Brandon, MB R7B 1X8 Canada
(204) 725-4474, *Fax:* (204) 726-7014
www.mediaproacc.ca
sholman@westman.wave.ca
License: Brandon, MB held by Assiniboine Campus-Community Radio Society Inc.
Population Served: 46,061 *Arbitron Metro Market:* Brandon, MB
Format: Variety/Diverse

Jill Ferguson, Station Manager

Cross Lake

CFNC(AM)
01-01-1990; 1490 khz AM; 50 w
Box 129, Cross Lake, MB R0B 0J0 Canada
(204) 676-2331, *Fax:* (204) 676-2911
License: Cross Lake, MB held by Native Communications Inc.
Format: Talk
Dina Monias, President
Joyce Halcrow, General Manager

Dauphin

CKDM
01-06-1951; 730 khz AM *Hrs Open:* 24
CA
(204) 638-3230, *Fax:* (204) 638-8257
www.730ckdm.com
730ckdm@mts.net
License: Dauphin, MB held by Dauphin Broadcasting Co. Ltd.
Format: Country *No. News Employees:* 3
Allan Truman, General Manager
Hector Paulhus, General Sales Mgr

Ebb and Flow

CKEB-FM
10-12-2012; 101.3 mhz FM; 50 watts
520 Arena Road GD, Ebb and Flow, MB R0L 0R0 Canada
(204) 448-2146
www.ebbandflowradio.com
License: Ebb and Flow, MB held by Ebb and Flow Economic Development Corp

Flin Flon

CFAR
11-14-1937; 590 khz AM *Hrs Open:* 24; 10 kw-D, 1 kw-N, DA-2
316 Green St., Flin Flon, MB Canada
(204) 687-3469,(204) 687-8300, *Fax:* (204) 687-6786
www.arcticradio.ca
cfar@arcticradio.ca
License: Flin Flon, MB held by Arctic Radio (1982) Ltd.
Hrs. of News Programming: news progmg 15 hrs wkly *No. News Employees:* 2 *Target Audience:* General.*Adv. Rates:* 60; 55; 60; 48
Tom O'Brien, President
Diane O'Brien, Station Manager
Rob Hart, Programming Director
Joe McCormick, News Director
Danny Porter, Engineering Dir

Marius

CISB-FM
04-23-2011; 106.3 mhz FM
Box 109, Marius, MB R0H 0T0 Canada
(204) 843-2661
www.sandybayradio.com
License: Marius, MB held by Sandy Bay Radio
Sandy Bay, Station Manager

Morden

CKMW
08-01-1980; 1570 khz AM *Hrs Open:* 24
CA
(204) 325-9506, *Fax:* (204) 325-2206
www.ckmwradio.com
country1570@goldenwestradio.com
License: Morden, MB held by Golden West Broadcasting Ltd.
Group Owner: Golden West Broadcasting Ltd.
Nat'l Reps: Canadian Broadcast Sales
Format: Country *No. News Employees:* 2 *Target Audience:* General.
Elmer Hildebrand, CEO
Bill Hildebrand, Station Manager

Portage La Prairie

CFRY
10-18-1956; 920 khz AM
CA
(204) 239-5111, *Fax:* (204) 857-3456
www.cfryradio.ca
wneufeld@goldenwestradio.com
License: Portage La Prairie, MB held by Golden West Broadcasting Ltd.
Group Owner: Golden West Broadcasting Ltd.; (acq 7-26-2000; with co-located FM).

Format: Country*Special Programming:* Farm 4 hrs wkly
Warren Neufeld, Station Manager

Portage la Prairie

CJPG-FM
05-04-2004; 96.5 mhz FM; 24 kw
Mailing Address: 350 River Road, Portage la Prairie, MB R1N 0N6 Canada
Second Address: 350 River Rd., Portage la Prairie, MB R1N 0N6
(204) 239-5111, *Fax:* (204) 857-3456
www.mix965fm.com
rsimpson@goldenwestradio.com
License: Portage la Prairie, MB held by Golden West Broadcasting Ltd.
Group Owner: Golden West Broadcasting Ltd.
Population Served: 12,996 *Arbitron Metro Market:* Portage la Prairie, MB *Format:* Contemporary Hits/Top 40
Warren Neufeld, Station Manager

Pukatawagan

CFPX-FM
09-19-1971; 98.3 mhz FM; 34.8 w
Missinnippi River Native, Communications Inc., Pukatawagan, MB R0B 1G0 Canada
(204) 553-2155, *Fax:* (204) 553-2158
License: Pukatawagan, MB held by Missinnippi River Native Communications Inc.
Format: Country
Rosie Colomb, General Manager

Saint Boniface

CKXL-FM
10-01-1991; 91.1 mhz FM *Hrs Open:* 24; 61 kw
340 Provencher Blvd., Winnipeg, MB R2H 0G7 Canada
(204) 233-4243, *Fax:* (204) 233-3646
www.envol91.mb.ca
info@envol91.mb.ca
License: Saint Boniface, MB held by La Radio Communautaire du Manitoba Inc.
Regional Reps: Target Media; George McKringan
Population Served: 600,000 *Format:* Variety/Diverse*Special Programming:* Folk 2 hrs, jazz 4 hrs, Sp 2 hrs, blues 2 hrs, reg *Target Audience:* 20-50; Francophone*Adv. Rates:* 28; 28; 28; 28
Michel Allard, Operations Dir
Rokhaya Sombounou, General Manager
Rokhaya Soumbounou, General Sales Mgr

Selkirk

CFQXFM
11-09-1981; 104.1 mhz FM *Hrs Open:* 24; 100 kw; 147.5 meters
177 Lombard Ave., 3rd Fl., Winnipeg, MB Canada
(204) 944-1031, *Fax:* (204) 943-7687
www.qx104fm.com
jtrecarten@qx104fm.com
License: Selkirk, MB held by Astral Media Radio G.P.
Group Owner: Astral Media Inc.; (acq 10-29-2007; grpsl)
No. News Employees: 2 *Target Audience:* 25-54.
Sharon Taylor, Operations Dir
Gyl Toshack, General Sales Mgr
Janet Trecarten, Programming Director
Karen Black, Music Director

CICY-FM
01-01-2000; 105.5 mhz FM; kw
CA
(204) 772-8255, *Fax:* (204) 779-5628
www.ncifm.com
info@ncifm.com
License: Selkirk, MB held by Native Communication Inc.
Arbitron Metro Market: Winnipeg, MB *Format:* Variety/Diverse
No. News Employees: 2 *Target Audience:* 25 and up; aboriginal
Dave McLeod, CEO
Rita Ducharme, President

Skownan

CHWN-FM
05-15-2011; 98.7 mhz FM
Box 106, Skownan, MB R0L 1Y0 Canada
(204) 628-3373, *Fax:* (204) 628-3289
skfo.listen2myradio.com
sko987fm@skonanfirstnation.com
License: Skownan, MB held by Skownan Band Development Corp

St Boniface

*CFRMFM
09-01-2002; 101.5 mhz FM *Hrs Open:* 24; kw
CA
(705) 368-1419, *Fax:* (705) 368-1080
www.theislandfm.com
radio@manitoulin.net
License: St Boniface, MB held by Manitoulin Radio Communication Inc.
Arbitron Metro Market: Little Current, ON *Format:* Country *No. News Employees:* 2 *Target Audience:* General; baby boomer
Craig Timmermans, CEO

St. Boniface

*CKSB
05-27-1946; 1050 khz AM *Hrs Open:* 24
CA
(204) 788-3236, *Fax:* (204) 788-3245
www.radiocanada.ca/radio/manitoba
License: St. Boniface, MB held by Societe Radio Canada.
Format: Variety/Diverse *Target Audience:* General.
Robert Rabinovitch, CEO
Rene Fontaine, Programming Director
Huguette Le Gall, Promotions Manager
Marc Babin, News Director
Gilles Frechette, Programming Director

Steinbach

CHSM
03-19-1964; 1250 khz AM *Hrs Open:* 24
CA
(204) 326-3737, *Fax:* (204) 326-2299
www.am1250online.com
License: Steinbach, MB held by Golden West Broadcasting Ltd.
Group Owner: Golden West Broadcasting Ltd.
Nat'l Reps: Canadian Broadcast Sales
Format: Adult Contemp*Hrs. of News Programming:* news progmg 12 hrs wkly *No. News Employees:* 3 *Target Audience:* General.
Elmer Hildebrand, President
Richard Kroeker, General Manager
Al Friesen, Programming Director
Laverne Siemens, Chief Engineer

CILT-FM
09-29-1998; 96.7 mhz FM *Hrs Open:* 24; 50 kw
105-32 Brandt St., Steinbach, MB R5G 2J7 Canada
(204) 346-0000, *Fax:* (204) 326-2299
www.lite967online.com
License: Steinbach, MB held by Golden West Broadcasting Ltd.
Group Owner: Golden West Broadcasting Ltd.
Format: Adult Contemp
Trev Schellenberg, Programming Director

Swan River

CJSB-FM
07-01-2006; 104.5 mhz FM *Hrs Open:* 24; 210 w; N52 06 18 W101 16 10
Box 1268, Swan River, MB R0L 1Z0 Canada
(204) 734-6484, *Fax:* (204) 734-5897
www.cj104radio.ca
onair@cj104radio.com
License: Swan River, Swan Valley County, MB held by Stillwater Broadcasting Ltd.
Nat'l Reps: Target Broadcast Sales *Wire Services:* Canadian Press
Population Served: 390 *Arbitron Metro Market:* Swan River, MB
Format: Contemporary Hits/Top 40*Hrs. of News Programming:* news progmg 20 hrs/week *No. News Employees:* 2
Bill Gade, General Manager

The Pas

CJAR
01-01-1974; 1240 khz AM
CA
(204) 623-5307, *Fax:* (204) 623-5337
www.thepasonline.com
cjar@articradio.ca
License: The Pas, MB held by Arctic Radio Corp. Ltd.
Format: Adult Contemp, Rock/AOR, Country*Special Programming:* Aboriginal 5 hrs wkly
Tom O'Brien, Chairman
Jeremy Wachal, General Manager

Thompson

*CBWK-FM
01-01-1980; 100.9 mhz FM *Hrs Open:* 7 AM-5 PM; 9.4 kw
7 Selkirk Ave., Thompson, MB R8N 0M4 Canada
(204) 677-1680, *Fax:* (204) 677-9517
www.winnipeg.cbc.ca
north@winnwpeg.cbc.ca
License: Thompson, MB held by CBC.
Nat'l Network: CBC Radio One
Population Served: 50,000 *Format:* Talk, Variety/Diverse
Mark Sislo, General Manager
Doug MacPherson, Chief Engineer

CHTM
03-29-1964; 610 khz AM *Hrs Open:* 24; 1 kw-U
103 Cree Road, Thompson, MB Canada
(204) 778-7361, *Fax:* (204) 778-5252
www.thompsononline.ca
chtm@arcticradio.ca
License: Thompson, MB held by Arctic Radio (1982) Ltd.
Population Served: 60,000*Special Programming:* Relg 12 hrs, Cree (American Indian) 10 hrs wkly*Hrs. of News Programming:* news progmg 15 hrs wkly *No. News Employees:* 2 *Target Audience:* General.
Tom O'Brien, President
Sue O'Brien, General Manager
Dave Moore, General Sales Mgr
Tony Taylor, Programming Director
Jaret Schneider, News Director
Danny Parker, Chief Engineer
Don Barkman, Music Director

CINC-FM
01-01-1994; 96.3 mhz FM; 86 w*Rebroadcasts:* rebroadcasts CICY-FM Winnipeg 80%
1507 Inkster Boulevard, Thompson, MB R2X 1R2 Canada
(204) 772-8255, *Fax:* (204) 778-6559
www.ncifm.com
info@ncifm.com
License: Thompson, MB held by Native Communications Inc.
Format: Variety/Diverse
Dave McLeod, CEO
Rosanne Ferguson, Programming Director

Winkler

CJEL-FM
10-04-2000; 93.5 mhz FM *Hrs Open:* 24; 100 kw
Mailing Address: 277 1st, Winkler, MB R6W 4A6 Canada
Second Address: 201-295 Main St., Winkler, MB R6W 4A6
(800) 355-7065, *Fax:* (204) 325-2206
www.eagle935fm.com
bhildebrand@goldenwestradio.com
License: Winkler, MB held by Golden West Broadcasting Ltd.
Group Owner: Golden West Broadcasting Ltd.
Population Served: 10,670 *Arbitron Metro Market:* Winkler, MB
Format: Adult Contemp
Elmer Hildebrand, CEO
Bill Hildebrand, Station Manager

Winnepeg

CHWE-FM
02-27-2011; 106.1 mhz FM; 40 watts
520 Crydon Avenue, Winnpeg, MB R3L 0P1 Canada
(204) 477-1221, *Fax:* (204) 453-8244
www.energy106.ca
License: Winnepeg, MB held by Winnipeg Broadcasting Inc
Format: Contemporary Hits/Top 40
Paul Evenov, Vice President

Winnepeg Beach

CJIE-FM
09-22-2011; 107.5 mhz FM; 1.62 kw
515 Main Street, Gimli, MB R0C 1B1 Canada
(204) 642-4387
www.cj107eradio.com
office@cj107radio.com
License: Winnepeg Beach, MB held by 5777152 Manitoba Ltd
Bill Gade, General Manager

Winnipeg

CBW
09-03-1948; 990 khz AM
CA
(204) 788-3222, *Fax:* (204) 788-3227
www.cbc.ca
License: Winnipeg, MB held by Canadian Broadcasting Corp.
Nat'l Network: CBC Radio One

Format: Variety/Diverse*Special Programming:* Farm 6 hrs, class 8 hrs, C&W one hr wkly
John Bertrand, General Manager

CBW-FM
10-11-1965; 98.3 mhz FM; 354 kw
Box 160, Winnipeg, MB R3C 2H1 Canada
(204) 788-3222, *Fax:* (204) 788-3227
License: Winnipeg, MB held by Canadian Broadcasting Corp
Nat'l Network: CBC Radio Two
TV Affiliate: CBWT(TV) affil
Real Jean, Operations Dir
Marleine Simard, General Manager
Clodine Dorval, News Director

CFWM-FM
06-13-1996; 99.9 mhz FM *Hrs Open:* 24; 100 kw
1445 Pembina Hwy., Winnipeg, MB R3T 5C2 Canada
(204) 477-5120, *Fax:* (204) 453-0815
www.999bobfm.com
info@999bobfm.com
License: Winnipeg, MB held by Bell Media Canada Radio Partnership
Group Owner: Bell Media Inc.; (acq 6-22-2007; grpsl)
Population Served: 672,000*Hrs. of News Programming:* news progmg 5 hrs wkly *No. News Employees:* 1 *Target Audience:* 25-54.
Jim Blundell, General Manager
Chris Brook, Programming Director

CHIQFM
11-01-1963; 94.3 mhz FM; 100 kw; Ant 450 ft; N49 47 58 W97 16 30
1445 Pembina Hwy., Winnipeg, MB Canada
(204) 477-5120, *Fax:* (204) 453-0815
www.curve94.com
info@q94fm.com
License: Winnipeg, MB held by Bell Media Canada Radio Partnership
Group Owner: Bell Media Inc.
Andrew Long, Programming Director

CFRW
11-01-1963; 1290 khz AM; 10 kw-U, DA-2
1445 Pembina Hwy., Winnipeg, MB Canada
(204) 477-5120, *Fax:* (204) 453-0815
License: Winnipeg, MB held by Bell Media Canada Radio Partnership
Group Owner: Bell Media Inc.; (acq 6-22-2007; grpsl)

Jim Blundell, General Manager
Corey Mospanchuk, General Sales Mgr
Ryan Ghidoni, Programming Director

***CITIFM**
01-01-1962; 92.1 mhz FM; kw
CA
(204) 788-3400, *Fax:* (204) 788-3401
www.92citifm.ca
crais@letaawskywinnipegradio.rogers.com
License: Winnipeg, MB held by Rogers Broadcasting Ltd.
Group Owner: Rogers Broadcasting Ltd.; acq 8-20-92).
Format: Classic Rock
Geoff Poulton, General Manager
Gayle Zarbatany, Programming Director
Frank Andrews, Music Director

CJOB
01-01-1946; 680 khz AM *Hrs Open:* 24
CA
(204) 786-2471, *Fax:* (204) 783-4512
www.cjob.com
kwallace@cjob.com
License: Winnipeg, MB held by Corus Premium Television Ltd.
Group Owner: Corus Entertainment Inc.; (acq 7-6-2000; grpsl).
Nat'l Reps: Canadian Broadcast Sales
Format: News, News/Talk, Talk*Hrs. of News Programming:* news progmg 56 hrs wkly *No. News Employees:* 25 *Target Audience:* 25-54.
Garth Buchko, President
Sherrie Johnston, Operations Dir
Steve Dubois, General Sales Mgr
Kevin Wallace, Programming Director
Alexis Teeple, Promotions Manager
Richard Cloutier, News Director
Jack Hoeppner, Chief Engineer
PaulGraham, Music Director
Colin Lougheed, Promotions Director

CJUM-FM
09-04-1998; 101.5 mhz FM *Hrs Open:* 24; 1.2 kw
UMFM, 308 University Center, Winnipeg, MB R3T 2N2 Canada
(204) 474-7027, *Fax:* (204) 269-1299
www.umfm.com
info@umfm.com
License: Winnipeg, MB held by The University of Manitoba Students' Union.
Population Served: 650,000 *Format:* Variety/Diverse*Hrs. of News Programming:* News progmg 12 hrs wkly *Target Audience:* 18-58; all genders, all ages who prefer non-coml music & culture*Adv. Rates:* 18; 18; 18; 18
Jared McKetiak, Station Manager
Michael Elves, Programming Director

***CKISFM**
06-03-1996; 97.5 mhz FM; kw
CA
(416) 935-8392
www.kiss925.com
License: Winnipeg, MB held by Rogers (Alberta) Ltd.
Group Owner: Rogers Broadcasting Ltd.
Format: Classic Rock
Gavin Tucker, Programming Director
Jerry Pendree, Chief Engineer
K. Kirch, Music Director

CKJS
03-25-1975; 810 khz AM; 10 kw-U, DA-1
520 Corydon Ave., Winnipeg, MB Canada
(204) 477-1221, *Fax:* (204) 453-8244
www.ckjs.com
info@ckjs.com
License: Winnipeg, MB held by Newcap Inc.
Group Owner: NewCap Inc.; (acq 4-30-2006; C$2.3 million)
Regional Reps: Direct.
Special Programming: Ger 6 hrs, It 5 hrs, Pol 7 hrs, Sp 3 hrs, Por 8 hr *Target Audience:* General.
Mike Fabian, General Sales Mgr
Gido Gigliotti, Programming Director
Tick Rowson, Promotions Manager

CKMM-FM
02-14-1980; 103.1 mhz FM; 70 kw; Ant 676 ft
177 Lombard Ave., 3rd. Fl., Winnipeg, MB R3B 0W5 Canada
(204) 944-1031, *Fax:* (204) 943-7687
www.hot103live.com
staylor@astral.com
License: Winnipeg, MB held by Astral Media Radio G.P.
Group Owner: Astral Media Inc.; (acq 10-29-2007; grpsl)
Format: Contemporary Hits/Top 40
Sharon Taylor, General Manager
Gyl Toshack, General Sales Mgr
Ace Burpee, Programming Director
Colin Lougheed, Promotions Manager
Chris Love, Music Director

***CKUW-FM**
05-01-1999; 95.9 mhz FM *Hrs Open:* 24; 450 w; N49 52 51 W97 08 56
515 Portage Ave., Rm. 4C M11, Winnipeg, MB R3B 2E9 Canada
(204) 786-9782, *Fax:* (204) 783-7080
www.ckuw.ca
ckuw@uwinnipeg.ca
License: Winnipeg, MB held by The Winnipeg Campus/Community Radio Society.
Population Served: 660,000*Special Programming:* Children 2 hrs, class 4 hrs, folk 2 hrs, jazz 8 hrs*Hrs. of News Programming:* News progmg 5 hrs wkly *Target Audience:* General; Our community*Adv. Rates:* 30; 30;30; 30
Rob Schmidt, Station Manager
Robin Eriksson, Programming Director
Michael Welch, News Director
David Tymoshchuk, Music Director

CHVN-FM
09-14-2000; 95.1 mhz FM *Hrs Open:* 24; 100 kw; N49 46 15 W97 30 35
1-741 St. Mary's Road, Winnipeg, MB R2M 3N5 Canada
(204) 452-9602, *Fax:* (204) 478-6735
www.chvnradio.com
chvn@goldenwestradio.com
License: Winnipeg, MB held by Golden West Broadcasting Ltd.
Group Owner: Golden West Broadcasting Ltd.; (acq 2004)
Nat'l Network: Salem Radio Network
Population Served: 684,100 *Arbitron Metro Market:* Winnipeg, MB *Format:* Christian*Special Programming:* Children one hr, gospel 4 hrs, teens 6 hrs wkly *Target Audience:* 18-49; families*Adv. Rates:* 42; 38; 42;32
Elmer Hildebrand, CEO
Richard Kroeker, General Manager
Trev Schellenbert, Programming Director

CJGV-FM
03-01-2003; 99.1 mhz FM; 63.7 kw; N49 45 20 W97 07 52
99.1 Fresh FM, 1440 Jack Blick Ave. Unit 200, Winnipeg, MB R3G 0L4 Canada
(204) 786-2471, *Fax:* (204) 783-4512
www.991freshfm.com
License: Winnipeg, MB held by Corus Premium Television Ltd.
Group Owner: Corus Entertainment Inc.; (acq 7-6-2007; C$14.5 million with CKBT-FM Kitchener-Waterloo, ON)
Population Served: 684,100 *Arbitron Metro Market:* Winnipeg, MB *Format:* Jazz, Smooth Jazz *No. News Employees:* 1 *Target Audience:* 35-45.
Brian Wortley, Operations Dir
Steve Dubois, Retail Sales Manager
Barry Horne, Programming Director
Jay Thomas, Promotions Manager
Casey Norman, Assistant Program Director
Vanessa Mancini, Promotions Coordinator
Sara Watson,Promotions Coordinator
Lauren Robb, Interactive Content Manager

CFJL-FM
12-07-2002; 100.7 mhz FM *Hrs Open:* 24; 60.9 kw; Ant 578 ft
520 Corydon Ave., Winnipeg, MB Canada
(204) 477-1221
www.thebreezefm.ca
info@hank.fm
License: Winnipeg, MB held by Newcap Inc.
Group Owner: NewCap Inc.; (acq 12-5-2005; C$1,790,000 for stock)
No. News Employees: 1
Randy Skulsky, General Manager
Michelle Pereira, General Sales Mgr
Abbey White, Programming Director
Ami Freeman, Promotions Manager

CFEQ-FM
01-01-2003; 107.1 mhz FM; 100 kw; 223 meters
1-741 St. Mary's Rd., Winnipeg, MB R2M 3N5 Canada
(204) 452-9602, *Fax:* (204) 478-6735
www.ignite107.com
License: Winnipeg, Canada County, MB held by Golden West Broadcasting Ltd.
Group Owner: Golden West Broadcasting Ltd.; (acq 6-27-2008; C$725,000)
Population Served: 750,000
Richard Kroeker, General Manager
Trev Schellenberg, Programming Director

CKY-FM
01-21-2004; 102.3 mhz FM; 70 kw
166 Osborne St., Unit 4, Winnipeg, MB R3L 1Y8 Canada
(204) 788-3400, *Fax:* (204) 788-3401
www.102clearfm.com
crais.letawksy@winnipegradio.rogers.com
License: Winnipeg, MB held by Rogers Broadcasting Ltd.
Group Owner: Rogers Broadcasting Ltd.
Population Served: 663,617 *Arbitron Metro Market:* Winnipeg, MB *Format:* Adult Contemp
Geoff Poulton, Operations Dir
Gayle Zarbatany, Programming Director
Craig Pfeifer, Music Director

CJNU-FM
12-01-2006; 104.7 mhz FM; 40 w
Box 2282, Stn Main, Winnipeg, MB R3C 4A6 Canada
(204) 942-2568
www.cjnu.ca
info@cjnu.ca
License: Winnipeg, MB held by Nostalgia Broadcasting Cooperative.
Population Served: 684,100 *Arbitron Metro Market:* Winnipeg, MB *Format:* Oldies
Bill Stewart, President
Roy Maguire, Chief Engineer

New Brunswick

Balmoral

CIMS-FM
09-14-1994; 103.9 mhz FM; 7.295 kw
1991 Ave. CP2561, des Pionniers, Balmoral, NB E8E 2W7 Canada
(506) 826-1040, *Fax:* (506) 826-2400
www.cimsfm.ca
info@cimsfm.ca
License: Balmoral, NB held by Cooperative Radio Restigouche Ltee.
Format: Variety/Diverse *No. News Employees:* 1
Rico Levesque, President
Annie L. Levesque, General Manager

Christian Labrie, General Sales Mgr
Guy Lavoie, Regional Sales Manager

Bathurst

CKBC-FM
01-22-2004; 104.9 mhz FM *Hrs Open:* 24; 20 kw
640 St. Peter Avenue, Unit 1, Bathurst, NB E2A 2Y7 Canada
(506) 547-1360, *Fax:* (506) 547-1367
www.max1049.ca
maxfm@astral.com
License: Bathurst, NB held by Astral Media Radio Atlantic Inc.
Group Owner: Astral Media Inc.
Nat'l Reps: Canadian Broadcast Sales
Population Served: 12,275 *Arbitron Metro Market:* Bathurst, NB
Format: Adult Contemp*Special Programming:* Fr 9 hrs wkly*Hrs. of News Programming:* news progmg 9 hrs wkly *No. News Employees:* 3 *TargetAudience:* 25-49.*Adv. Rates:* 50; 44; 44; 30
Jacques Parisien, President
Jamie Robichaud, General Manager
Pat Brenan, General Sales Mgr
Jeff Long, Program & Music Supervisor
John LeBlanc, Program & Music Supervisor
John Eddy, Executive Vice President
Glenn States,Advertising Sales
Ken Comeau, Advertising Sales
Caroline Boudreau, Advertising Sales
Kelly Basque, Advertising Sales
Collette Comeau, Specialty Advertising

Blackville

CJFY-FM
01-01-2004; 107.7 mhz FM; 45 w
345 Beaverbrook, Blackville, NB E1V 3L9 Canada
(506) 622-2202, *Fax:* (506) 843-2228
www.liferadio.ca
staff@liferadio.ca
License: Blackville, NB held by Miramichi Fellowship Center Inc.
John Stewart, CEO
Matt Halihan, General Manager
Scott Underhill, Station Manager
Matt Halihan, Programming Director
Scott Underhill, Promotions Manager
Patrick Dunn, News Director

Campbellton

CKNB
01-01-1939; 950 khz AM *Hrs Open:* 24
CA
(506) 753-4415, *Fax:* (506) 789-9505
www.95cknb.ca
cknb@nb.sympatico.ca
License: Campbellton, NB held by Maritime Broadcasting System Ltd.
Group Owner: Maritime Broadcasting
Format: Adult Contemp, Country*Special Programming:* Fr 18 hrs wkly*Hrs. of News Programming:* News progmg 10 hrs wkly *Target Audience:* General.
Merv Russell, President
David Montgomery, General Manager

Caraquet

CJVA
09-15-1977; 810 khz AM *Hrs Open:* 18
CA
(506) 727-4605, *Fax:* (506) 546-6611
www.ckle.fm
superstation@ckle.fm
License: Caraquet, NB held by Radio Acadie Ltd.
Nat'l Reps: Canadian Broadcast Sales
Format: Adult Contemp, Variety/Diverse*Special Programming:* C&W 15 hrs wkly *Target Audience:* 25 plus.
Rufino Landry, President
Armand Roussy, General Manager

Edmundston

***CFAIFM**
01-15-1991; 107.7 mhz FM *Hrs Open:* 24; kw
CA
(506) 737-5060, *Fax:* (506) 737-5084
www.cfai.fm
radio@cfai.fm
License: Edmundston, Madawaska County, NB held by La Cooperative des Montagnes Ltee.
Format: Contemporary Hits/Top 40*Hrs. of News Programming:* News progmg 6 hrs wkly *No. News Employees:* 1 *Target Audience:* 12-50.*Adv. Rates:* 21; 21; 21; 18
Louis G. Plourde, President
Eric Morneault, General Manager
Sheila Desroches, General Sales Mgr

CJEM-FM
07-01-1998; 92.7 mhz FM *Hrs Open:* 24; 40.75 kw; N47 21 47 W68 17 21
64 Rice St., Edmundston, NB E3V 1K2 Canada
(506) 735-3351, *Fax:* (506) 739-5803
www.cjemfm.com
cjem@cjemfm.com
License: Edmundston, Madawaska County, NB held by Radio Edmundston Inc.
Nat'l Reps: Canadian Broadcast Sales
Population Served: 50,000 *Format:* Adult Contemp*Hrs. of News Programming:* news progmg 6 hrs wkly *No. News Employees:* 2 *Target Audience:* 25-54.
Jean Marc Michaud, President
Murillo Soucy, General Manager
Paul Clavette, Programming Director

Fredericton

***CBZ-FM**
01-01-1978; 101.5 mhz FM; 100 kw*Rebroadcasts:* Rebroadcasts CBH-FM Halifax, NS 100%
Mailing Address: Box 2200, Fredericton, NB E3B 5G4 Canada
Second Address: 1160 Regent St., Fredericton, NB E3B 5G4
(506) 451-4000, *Fax:* (506) 451-4170
www.cbc.ca
License: Fredericton, NB held by Canadian Broadcasting Corp.
Nat'l Network: CBC Radio Two
Format: News, News/Talk, Talk
Gary Arsenault, General Manager

CBZF-FM
01-01-2004; 99.5 mhz FM; 3.2 kw
Mailing Address: Box 2200, Fredericton, NB E3B 5G4 Canada
Second Address: 1160 Regent St., Fredericton, NB E3B 5G4
(506) 451-4000, *Fax:* (506) 451-4170
www.cbc.ca
License: Fredericton, NB held by Canadian Broadcasting Corp.
Nat'l Network: CBC Radio One
Format: Variety/Diverse
Faydra Aldridge, General Manager

CHSR-FM
01-24-1961; 97.9 mhz FM *Hrs Open:* 7 AM-3 AM; 250 w; Ant 157 ft
Box 4400, Student Union Bldg., Fredericton, NB E3B 5A3 Canada
(506) 453-4985, *Fax:* (506) 453-4999
www.unb.ca/chsr
chsr@unb.ca
License: Fredericton, York County, NB held by CHSR Broadcasting Inc.
Format: Alternative, Variety/Diverse*Special Programming:* Fr 2 hrs, ethnic 5 hrs, American Indian one hr, cl*Hrs. of News Programming:* News progmg 6 hrs wkly *Target Audience:* General.
Tristis Ward, Station Manager
Linda Pelletier, General Sales Mgr
Mark Kilfoil, Programming Director

CIBX-FM
06-11-1996; 106.9 mhz FM *Hrs Open:* 24; 100 kw
206 Rookwood Ave., Fredericton, NB E3B 2M2 Canada
(506) 455-1069, *Fax:* (506) 452-2345
www.capitalfm.ca
pbrennan@astral.com
License: Fredericton, NB held by Astral Media Radio Atlantic Inc.
Group Owner: Astral Media Inc.; (acq 4-19-2002; grpsl).
Nat'l Reps: Canadian Broadcast Sales
Format: Classic Rock*Hrs. of News Programming:* news progmg 8 hrs wkly *No. News Employees:* 4 *Target Audience:* 25-54.
John Eddy, President
Pat Brennan, General Manager
Ryan Zimmerman, Programming Director

CKHJ(AM)
08-19-1977; 1260 khz AM; 10 kw-U, DA-N
206 Rookwood Ave., Fredericton, NB E3B 2M2 Canada
(506) 451-9111, *Fax:* (506) 452-2345
www.khj.ca
khjnews@astral.com
License: Fredericton, NB held by Astral Media Radio Atlantic Inc.
Group Owner: Astral Media Inc.
Format: Country*Special Programming:* Fr one hr wkly
John Eddy, General Manager
Pat Brennan, General Sales Mgr
Ryan Zimmerman, Programming Director

***CJPN-FM**
08-01-1997; 90.5 mhz FM; 1.56 kw
715 Priestman St., Fredericton, NB E3B 5W7 Canada
(506) 454-2576, *Fax:* (506) 453-3958
www.cjpn.ca
cjpn@nbnet.nb.ca
License: Fredericton, NB held by Radio Fredericton Inc.
Format: Adult Contemp
Pierre Dumas, General Manager

CFXY-FM
07-15-1983; 105.3 mhz FM; 78 kw; 800 ft
206 Rookwood Ave., Fredericton, NB E3B 2M2 Canada
(506) 454-2444, *Fax:* (506) 452-2345
www.foxrocks.ca
khjnews@astral.com
License: Fredericton, NB held by Astral Media Radio Atlantic Inc.
Group Owner: Astral Media Inc.
Format: Country
Pat Brennan, General Manager
Paul Wentzell, General Sales Mgr
Rob Alexander, Programming Director
Jennifer Cox, Promotions Manager
Randy McKeen, News Director

CIXN-FM
04-08-2001; 96.5 mhz FM; 27 w
JoyFM, 1010 Hanwell Rd., Fredericton, NB E3B 6A4 Canada
(506) 443-0991, *Fax:* (506) 443-0991
www.joyfm.ca
welcome@joyfm.ca
License: Fredericton, NB held by The Joy FM Network Inc.
Doug Boyd, General Manager
Doug Boyd, Station Manager
Mike Stackhouse, General Sales Mgr
Nathan Ecker, Programming Director

CFRK-FM
01-01-2005; 92.3 mhz FM; 93 kw
77 Westmoreland St., Suite 400, Fredrickton, NB E3B 6Z3 Canada
(506) 455-0923, *Fax:* (506) 455-3602
www.fredfm.ca
License: Fredericton, NB held by Newcap Inc.
Group Owner: NewCap Inc.
Brad Muir, Operations Dir
Hilary Montbourquette, General Manager

CJRI-FM
05-18-2005; 104.5 mhz FM; 50 w; N45 56 14 W66 39 19
151 Main St., Fredericton, NB E3A 1C6 Canada
(506) 472-0947, *Fax:* (506) 459-8194
www.cjrifm.com
gospel@cjri.fm
License: Fredericton, NB held by Faithway Communications Inc.
Population Served: 34,000 *Arbitron Metro Market:* Fredericton, NB *Format:* Country, Gospel
Ross Ingram, President

CIHI-FM
93.1 mhz FM; 50 kw; 150 meters
77 West Moreland Street, Suite 400, Fredericton, NB E3B 6Z3 Canada
(506) 455-0923, *Fax:* (506) 455-3602
License: Fredericton, NB held by New Cap Inc
Group Owner: NewCap Inc.

Fredericton Centre

CKTP-FM
01-01-2002; 95.7 mhz FM; 50 w
Kchikhusis Commercial Center, 150 Cliffe St., Box R13, Fredericton, NB E3A 0A1 Canada
(506) 474-2795, *Fax:* (506) 206-330
www.cktpradio.com
info@cktpradio.com
License: Fredericton Centre, NB held by Maliseet Nation Radio Inc.
Population Served: 34,000 *Arbitron Metro Market:* Fredericton, NB *Format:* Contemporary Hits/Top 40
Conrad Mead, Station Manager

Grand Falls

CIKX-FM
01-01-2001; 93.5 mhz FM; 5.3 kw
399 Boul. Broadway Blvd, Grand Falls, NB E3Z 2K5 Canada
(506) 473-9393, *Fax:* (506) 473-3893
www.k93.ca
k93@astral.com

License: Grand Falls, NB held by Astral Media Radio Atlantic Inc.
Group Owner: Astral Media Inc.; (acq 2003; grpsl).
Population Served: 5,706 *Arbitron Metro Market:* Grand Falls, NB *Format:* Adult Contemp
Pat Brennan, General Manager
Janice Paradis, Sales Manager
Rick McGuire, Programming Director
Angela Ferguson, News Director
Karen Pare, Advertising Sales Representatives

CKMV-FM
08-01-2000; 95.1 mhz FM *Hrs Open:* 24; 975 w*Rebroadcasts:* Rebroadcasts CJEM-FM Edmundston 100%
174 Church St., Edmundston, NB E3V 1K2 Canada
(506) 735-3351, *Fax:* (506) 739-5803
cjem@nbnet.nb.ca
License: Grand Falls, Victoria County, NB held by Radio Edmundston Inc.
Nat'l Reps: Canadian Broadcast Sales
Target Audience: 25-54.
Murillo Soucy, President
Murillo Soucy, General Manager
Paul Clavette, Programming Director

Inkerman

***CKROFM**
01-01-1988; 97.1 mhz FM; kw
CA
(506) 336-9706, *Fax:* (506) 336-9058
www.ckro.ca
info@ckro.ca
License: Inkerman, NB held by Radio Peninsule Inc.
Format: Adult Contemp *Target Audience:* General.
Rachel Savoie, Operations Dir
Donald Christmas, General Manager
Rejean Hebert, Programming Director
Marilyne McLaughlin, National Sales Manager

Kedgwick

***CFJU-FM**
01-01-1991; 90.1 mhz FM *Hrs Open:* 24; 3 kw; N47 35 05 W67 21 47
C.P. 1043, Kedgwick, NB E8B 1Z9 Canada
(506) 235-9000, *Fax:* (506) 235-9001
www.cfjufm.com
cfjufm@nbnet.nb.ca
License: Kedgwick, NB held by La Radio Communautaire des Hauts-Plateaux Inc.
Population Served: 7,000 *Format:* Variety/Diverse*Special Programming:* Country 12 hrs wkly*Hrs. of News Programming:* News progmg 8 hrs wkly *Target Audience:* 25-55.
M. Victor St- Pierre, President
Lucille Theriault, General Manager

Miramichi

CKMA-FM
93.7 mhz FM; 11 kw; N47 00 37 W65 35 14
300 chemin Beaverbrook, Miramichi, NB E1V 1A1 Canada
(506) 624-9370, *Fax:* (506) 627-4592
www.radiorfa.com/ckma
radio.miracadie@nb.aibn.com
License: Miramichi, NB held by Radio MirAcadie Inc.
Population Served: 18,129 *Arbitron Metro Market:* Miramichi, NB
Format: Variety/Diverse
Rick Arnish, President
Bruce Davis, General Manager
Don Huculak, General Sales Mgr
Bob Miller, Programming Director
Dan McFarland, Promotions Manager
Jasmin Doobay, News Director
Craig Foster, Chief Engineer
Michel Savoie,Director of Operations

Miramichi City

CFAN-FM
01-10-2003; 99.3 mhz FM *Hrs Open:* 24; 17.8 kw
396 Pleasant St., Miramichi City, NB E1V 1X3 Canada
(506) 622-3311, *Fax:* (506) 627-0335
www.993theriver.com
cfan@nb.sympatico.ca
License: Miramichi City, Northumberland County, NB held by Maritime Broadcasting System Ltd.
Group Owner: Maritime Broadcasting
Population Served: 50,000 *Format:* Adult Contemp*Special Programming:* Relg 4 hrs, folk 2 hrs wkly*Hrs. of News Programming:* news progmg 8 hrs wkly *No. News Employees:* 1
Target Audience: General.*Adv.Rates:* 29; 29; 29; 29
Brent Preston, General Manager

Moncton

CBA-FM
03-01-1982; 95.5 mhz FM; 68 kw*Rebroadcasts:* Rebroadcasts CBH-FM Halifax, NS 100%
250 University Ave., Box 950, Moncton, NB E1C 8N8 Canada
(506) 853-6666, *Fax:* (506) 853-6400
www.cbc.ca
infomorning@moncton.cbc.com
License: Moncton, NB held by CBC
Nat'l Network: CBC Radio Two
Format: Talk
Susan Mitton, General Manager

***CBAFFM**
01-01-1982; 98.3 mhz FM; kw
CA
(506) 853-6666, *Fax:* (506) 853-6400
www.cbc.ca/nb
License: Moncton, Westmoreland County, NB held by Radio Canada.
Nat'l Network: Radio Canada
Format: French, News
Susan Mitton, General Manager

***CBAL-FM**
01-01-1983; 98.3 mhz FM; 67.6 kw; Ant 577 ft; N46 08 41 W64 54 14
250 university Ave., Box 950, Moncton, NB E1C 8N8 Canada
(506) 853-6666, *Fax:* (506) 853-6739
www.cbc.radio-canada.ca
License: Moncton, Westmoreland County, NB held by Societe Radio Canada.
Nat'l Network: Espace Musique
Format: Variety/Diverse
Louise Imbeault, General Manager
Claire Hendy, Programming Director

***CFQMFM**
01-01-1976; 103.9 mhz FM; kw
CA
(506) 858-1220, *Fax:* (506) 858-1209
www.radiomoncton.com
magic104@radiomoncton.com,scott.clements@mbsradio.com
License: Moncton, NB held by Maritime Broadcasting System Ltd.
Group Owner: Maritime Broadcasting
Format: Adult Contemp
Scott Clements, General Manager

***CJMOFM**
06-19-1987; 103.1 mhz FM *Hrs Open:* 24; kw
CA
(506) 858-5525, *Fax:* (506) 858-5539
www.c103.com
c103@c103.com
License: Moncton, Canada County, NB held by Newcap Inc.
Group Owner: NewCap Inc.
Nat'l Reps: Canadian Broadcast Sales
Format: Classic Rock*Special Programming:* Jazz 2 hrs wkly*Hrs. of News Programming:* news progmg 5 hrs wkly *No. News Employees:* 4 *Target Audience:* 25-54; adults
Mark Maheu, President
David Murray, Operations Dir
Dan Fagan, General Manager
Nick Addams, Programming Director
Mike Brown, News Director

***CKUM**
01-01-1982; 93.5 mhz FM *Hrs Open:* 24; kw
CA
(506) 858-3750, *Fax:* (506) 858-4524
www.ckum935.com
routierm@umoncton.ca
License: Moncton, NB held by Les Medias Acadiens Universitaires Inc.
Format: Variety/Diverse*Special Programming:* Jazz 4 hrs wkly*Hrs. of News Programming:* News progmg one hr wkly
Target Audience: 15-30.*Adv. Rates:* 14; 13; 14; 11
Brian Gallant, President
Justin Robichaud, Operations Dir
Michele Routier, General Manager
Mylene Dugas, Vice President

CHOY-FM
02-19-2001; 99.9 mhz FM; 9.5 kw
1000 St. George Blvd., Moncton, NB E1E 4M7 Canada
(506) 384-2469, *Fax:* (506) 858-1209
www.radiomoncton.com
magic104@radiomoncton.com,scott.clements@embradio.com
License: Moncton, NB held by CHOY-FM Ltee.
Group Owner: Maritime Broadcasting; (acq 12-19-2005).
Population Served: 138,644 *Arbitron Metro Market:* Moncton, NB
Format: Adult Contemp, Country, French
Scott Clements, General Manager

CJXL-FM
11-01-2000; 96.9 mhz FM *Hrs Open:* 24; 100 kw
27 Arsenault Ct., Moncton Industrial Park, Moncton, NB E1E 4J8 Canada
(506) 858-5525, *Fax:* (506) 858-5539
www.xl96.com
scottyandtony@xl96.com
License: Moncton, NB held by Newcap Inc.
Group Owner: NewCap Inc.
Population Served: 138,644 *Arbitron Metro Market:* Moncton, NB
Format: Country *Target Audience:* 25-54; adults
Mark Maheu, President
Dave Murray, Operations Dir
Dan Fagan, General Manager
Adam McLaren, Programming Director
Sara Goguen, Promotions Manager
Mike Brown, News Director
Cathy Airey, Office Manager
Paul Thomas, PromotionsDepartment
Patricia Crowell, Account Manager
Kenton Dunphy, Account Manager
Greg Wilbur, Account Manager

CKCW-FM
01-01-2001; 94.5 mhz FM; 19 kw
1000 St. George Blvd., Moncton, NB E1E 4M7 Canada
(506) 858-1220, *Fax:* (506) 858-1209
www.radiomoncton.com
magic104@radiomoncton.com,scott.clements@mbsradio.com
License: Moncton, NB held by Maritime Broadcasting System Ltd.
Group Owner: Maritime Broadcasting
Population Served: 138,644 *Arbitron Metro Market:* Moncton, NB
Format: Contemporary Hits/Top 40 *Target Audience:* 18-44; adults
Scott Clements, General Manager

CITA-FM
01-01-2001; 105.1 mhz FM; 880 w
101 Ilsley Ave., Unit 3, Dartmouth, NS B3B 1S8 Canada
(902) 468-8854, *Fax:* (902) 468-8851
www.citafm.com
info@cjlufm.com
License: Moncton, NB held by International Harvesters for Christ Evangelistic Association Inc.
Population Served: 101,343 *Arbitron Metro Market:* Dartmouth, NS *Format:* Christian
Jeff Lutes, President
Jean Brunet, Operations Dir
Rabbi Elmer Grove, Regional Manager

CKOE-FM
11-01-2000; 107.3 mhz FM; 50 w; Ant 82 ft
3030 Mountain Rd., Moncton, NB E1G 2W8 Canada
(506) 384-1009, *Fax:* (506) 383-9699
www.ckoefm.com
info@ckoefm.com
License: Moncton, NB held by Houssen Broadcasting Ltd.
Population Served: 138,074 *Arbitron Metro Market:* Moncton, NB
Format: Christian
James Houssen, General Manager
Jim Houssen, Station Manager
Don Houssen, General Sales Mgr
Steve Raye, News Director
Jason Constantine, Production/Music
Steve Melller, Production/Music
Jimmy D Houssen, WebHead

CKNI-FM
10-11-2005; 91.9 mhz FM; 70 kw
70 Assomption Blvd., Moncton, NB E1C 1A1 Canada
(506) 872-5678
License: Moncton, NB held by Rogers Broadcasting Ltd.
Group Owner: Rogers Broadcasting Ltd.
Population Served: 138,644 *Arbitron Metro Market:* Moncton, NB, Canada *Format:* News, News/Talk, Talk
Rael Merson, President
Jim Hamm, General Manager

CBAM-FM
01-08-2008; 106.1 mhz FM *Hrs Open:* 24; 69.5 kw; N46 08 41 W64 54 11.
Mailing Address: P.O. Box 500, Station A, Toronto, ON M5W 1E6 Canada
Second Address: 250 University Ave., Moncton, NB E1C 8N8
(866) 306-4636, *Fax:* (506) 853-6400
www.cbc.ca
License: Moncton, NB held by CBC.

Nat'l Network: CBC Radio One
Population Served: 138,644 *Arbitron Metro Market:* Moncton, NB
Format: News
R,mi Racine, Chairman
Hubert T. Lacroix, CEO
Jonna Brewer, General Manager
Maryse Bertrand, Vice President/General Counsel
William B. Chambers, Vice-President, Brand, Communications and Corporat
Steven Guiton, Vice-President andChief Regulatory Officer
Louis Lalande, Executive Vice-President

CFBO-FM
01-01-2008; 90.7 mhz FM; 30 kw; N46 11 04 W64 52 52
Cornwall 51, Shediac, NB E4P 8T8 Canada
(506) 532-0080, *Fax:* (506) 532-0120
www.cfbo.ca
cjse@cjse.ca
License: Moncton, NB held by Radio Beausejour Inc.
Population Served: 138,644 *Arbitron Metro Market:* Moncton, NB
Format: Adult Contemp
Serge Parent, General Manager

Sackville

***CHMA-FM**
01-01-1985; 106.9 mhz FM *Hrs Open:* 24; 50 w
62 York Street, Sackville, NB E4L 1B4 Canada
(506) 364-2221
www.mta.ca/chma
chma@mta.ca
License: Sackville, NB held by Attic Broadcasting Ltd.
Population Served: 15,000
Pierre Malloy, Station Manager
Vanessa Blackier, Programming Director

Saint John

CBD-FM
04-01-1981; 91.3 mhz FM; 80 kw
Box 2358, Saint John, NB E2L 3V6 Canada
(506) 632-7744, *Fax:* (506) 632-7761
www.nb.cbc.ca
License: Saint John, Saint John County, NB held by Canadian Broadcasting Corp.
Nat'l Network: CBC Radio One
Format: Talk
Don Orchard, General Manager
Henk VanLeeuwen, Programming Director

CFBC
11-21-1946; 930 khz AM *Hrs Open:* 24
CA
(506) 658-5100, *Fax:* (506) 658-5116
mailbag@k100.ca
License: Saint John, NB held by Maritime Broadcasting System Ltd.
Group Owner: Maritime Broadcasting; (acq 9-29-98; C$2 million with co-located FM).
Format: Oldies
Kelly O'Neill, General Sales Mgr
Donnie Robertson, Programming Director
Brian McLain, News Director

***CHSJ-FM**
01-07-1998; 94.1 mhz FM *Hrs Open:* 24; kw
CA
(506) 633-3323, *Fax:* (506) 644-3485
www.country94.ca
chsj@radioabl.ca
License: Saint John, NB held by Acadia Broadcasting Ltd.
Group Owner: Acadia Broadcasting Ltd.
Nat'l Network: CBS Radio
Format: Country *Target Audience:* 25-54.
Jim MacMullin, General Manager

***CIOK-FM**
08-10-1987; 100.5 mhz FM *Hrs Open:* 24; kw
CA
(506) 658-5100, *Fax:* (506) 658-5116
www.k100.ca
mailbag@k100.ca
License: Saint John, Saint John County, NB held by Maritime Broadcasting System Ltd.
Group Owner: Maritime Broadcasting
Format: Adult Contemp*Special Programming:* Real radio 4 hrs wkly*Hrs. of News Programming:* news progmg 7 hrs wkly *Target Audience:* 25-49; housewives, families, professionals
Scott Clements, Programming Director

***CJYCFM**
03-12-1965; 98.9 mhz FM *Hrs Open:* 24; kw
CA
(506) 658-5100, *Fax:* (506) 658-5116
www.bigjohn.fm
mailbag@989bigjohnfm.com
License: Saint John, NB held by Maritime Broadcasting System Ltd.
Group Owner: Maritime Broadcasting
Format: Classic Rock *Target Audience:* 25-34; young, upwardly, mobile, family oriented
Paul Jensen, Programming Director

CINB-FM
11-16-2000; 96.1 mhz FM; 50 w
NewSong FM, Box 96, Saint John, NB E2L 3X1 Canada
(506) 657-9600, *Fax:* (506) 657-7664
www.newsongfm.com
staff@newsongfm.com
License: Saint John, NB held by New Song Communications Ministries Ltd.
Population Served: 68,000 *Arbitron Metro Market:* Saint John, NB *Format:* Christian
Don Mabee, Station Manager

CHWV-FM
01-01-2001; 97.3 mhz FM *Hrs Open:* 24; 55 kw
Box 2000 58 King St., Saint John, NB E2L 1G4 Canada
(506) 633-3323, *Fax:* (506) 644-3485
www.thewave.ca
mail@thewave.ca
License: Saint John, NB held by Acadia Broadcasting Ltd.
Group Owner: Acadia Broadcasting Ltd.
Population Served: 68,000 *Arbitron Metro Market:* Saint John, NB *Format:* Adult Contemp
Jim MacMullin, Operations Dir

CFMH-FM
01-01-2001; 107.3 mhz FM; 250 w
100 Tucker Park Rd., Thomas J Condon Building RM 235, UNBSJ, Saint John, NB E2L 4L5 Canada
(506) 648-5667, *Fax:* (506) 648-5541
www.localfm.ca
cfmh@unbsj.ca
License: Saint John, NB held by Campus Radio Saint John Inc.
Population Served: 68,000 *Arbitron Metro Market:* Saint John, NB *Format:* Variety/Diverse
June Madeley, Chairman
Brian Cleveland, Station Manager
Jud Crandall, Programming Director
Peter McDonald, Music Director
Stefan Warner, Vice-chair
Anthony Enman, Treasurer
Nick Cameron, Secretary
Darlene Partridge, ExecutiveCommittee Chair, ex-officio
Linda Minor, Programming Committee Representative

CJEF-FM
10-20-2003; 103.5 mhz FM *Hrs Open:* 24; 49.6 w; Ant 200 ft; N45 16 31 W65 04 25
177 King Street East, Saint John, NB E2L 1G9 Canada
(506) 214-7571, *Fax:* (506) 642-7408
www.cjrp.org
OnAir@saintjohnfm.ca
License: Saint John, NB held by TFG Communications Inc.
Population Served: 68,000 *Arbitron Metro Market:* Saint John, NB *Format:* Comedy *Target Audience:* 18-34.*Adv. Rates:* 180; 90; 126; 90
Geoffrey Rivett, CEO
Gary Stackhouse, General Manager
John Kierstead, Sales Manager
Bob Pritchard, Program Director and Owner
John Codner, Program Director and Owner
Graham Brown, News Director
Mark Henwood, Music Director
JudyPritchard, Office Manager
John Codner, Client Relations
Kim Cookson, Sales
John Campbell, Sales
Marc Henwood, Production

CHNI-FM
10-11-2005; 88.9 mhz FM; 79 kw
55 Waterloo St., Saint John, NB E2L 4V9 Canada
(506) 646-5161
License: Saint John, NB held by Rogers Broadcasting Ltd.
Group Owner: Rogers Broadcasting Ltd.
Population Served: 680,004 *Arbitron Metro Market:* Saint John, NB *Format:* News, News/Talk, Talk
Rael Merson, President
Jim Hamm, General Manager

CHQC-FM
01-01-2006; 105.7 mhz FM *Hrs Open:* 24; 1.85 kw
67 Chemin Ragged Point, Saint John, NB E2K 5C3 Canada
(506) 643-6996, *Fax:* (506) 658-3984
chqc.capacadie.com
direction@chqc.ca
License: Saint John, NB held by Cooperative radiophonique - La Brise de la Baie Ltee.
Population Served: 68,000 *Arbitron Metro Market:* Saint John, NB *Format:* Variety/Diverse
Steve Pilotte, President
Nay Saade, General Manager

Saint Stephen

CHTD-FM
05-31-2001; 98.1 mhz FM *Hrs Open:* 24; 40 kw
112 Milltown Blvd., St. Stephen, NB E3L 1G6 Canada
(506) 466-1000, *Fax:* (506) 466-4500
www.thetide.ca
mail@thetide.ca
License: Saint Stephen, NB held by Acadia Broadcasting Ltd.
Group Owner: Acadia Broadcasting Ltd.
Population Served: 61,000 *No. News Employees:* 2 *Target Audience:* 25-54.
Jim MacMullin, General Manager
Dave Boone, Station Manager

Shediac

CJSEFM
07-26-1994; 89.5 mhz FM *Hrs Open:* 24; 20.445 kw; N46 11 04 W64 52 52
96 Rue Providence, Shediac, NB Canada
(506) 532-0080, *Fax:* (506) 532-0120
www.cjse.ca
patricia@cjse.ca
License: Shediac, NB held by Radio Beausejour Inc.

Flavian Babineau, President
Serge Parent, General Manager
Marcel Parker Gallant, Programming Director
Jason Oulette, Promotions Manager

Sussex

CJCW
06-01-1975; 590 khz AM
CA
(506) 432-2529, *Fax:* (506) 433-4900
www.590cjcw.com
cjcw@nbnet.nb.ca
License: Sussex, NB held by Maritime Broadcasting System Ltd.
Group Owner: Maritime Broadcasting
Format: Adult Contemp*Special Programming:* Relg 4 hrs wkly
Target Audience: General.
Robert Pace, CEO
Merv Russell, President
Louis McNamara, General Manager
James Keirstead, News Director

Woodstock

CJCJ-FM
06-01-2001; 104.1 mhz FM; 10 kw
Unit Two, 131 Queen St., Woodstock, NB E7M 2M8 Canada
(506) 325-3030, *Fax:* (506) 325-3031
www.cj104.com
cj104@astral.com
License: Woodstock, Carleton County, NB held by Astral Media Radio Atlantic Inc.
Group Owner: Astral Media Inc.; (acq 4-19-2002; grpsl).
Population Served: 5,254 *Arbitron Metro Market:* Woodstock, NB
Format: Classic Rock
Pat Brennan, General Manager
Bev Whiteway, General Sales Mgr
Rick McGuire, Programming Director
Angela Ferguson, News Director
Mike Robinson, Advertising Representive
Katie Belyea, Advertising Representive
Kelly Simonds,Advertising Representive

Newfoundland

Argentia

CFOZ-FM
01-01-1980; 100.3 mhz FM *Hrs Open:* 24; 5 kw*Rebroadcasts:* Rebroadcasts CHOZ-FM St. John's.
c/o CHOZ-FM, Box 2020, St. John's, NF A1C 5S2 Canada
(709) 726-2922, *Fax:* (709) 726-3300
www.ozfm.com

License: Argentia, Newfoundland County, NL held by Newfoundland Broadcasting Co. Ltd.
Nat'l Reps: Canadian Broadcast Sales
Population Served: 500,000 *Format:* Adult Contemp, Classic Rock, Contemporary Hits/Top 40 *No. News Employees:* 2
Target Audience: 18-49.
Geoff Stirling, Chairman
Scott Stirling, CEO
Doug Neal, General Manager
Lorraine Pope, General Sales Mgr
Jesse Stirling, Promotions Manager
Frank Collins, CFO
Maurice Fitzgerald, Music Director

Baie Verte

CKIM
01-01-1979; 1240 khz AM
CA
(709) 489-2192, *Fax:* (709) 489-8626
www.vocm.com
License: Baie Verte, NF held by NewCap Inc.
Group Owner: NewCap Inc.; (acq 6-00; grpsl).
Format: Country, News, News/Talk, Talk
Dave Hillier, General Manager
Denn Dillion, General Sales Mgr
Richard King, Programming Director
Roger Barnett, News Director
Harold Steele, Chief Engineer

Bonavista Bay

CBGY
08-25-1977; 750 khz AM*Rebroadcasts:* Rebroadcasts CBG(AM) Gander
Mailing Address: CA
Second Address: 98 Sullivan Ave., Gander, NF A1V 1W7
(709) 256-4311, *Fax:* (709) 651-2021
www.cbc.ca/hl/
License: Bonavista Bay, NF held by CBC.
Format: News
Robert Rabinowitz, CEO
Michael Aucoin, Programming Director

CJOZ-FM
01-01-1979; 92.1 mhz FM *Hrs Open:* 24; 50 kw*Rebroadcasts:* Rebroadcasts CHOZ-FM, St John's
c/o CHOZ-FM, 446 Logy Bay Rd., Box 2020, St. John's, NF A1C 5S2 Canada
(709) 726-2922, *Fax:* (709) 726-3300
www.ozfm.com
License: Bonavista Bay, Newfoundland County, NL held by Newfoundland Broadcasting Co.
Group Owner: Newfoundland Broadcasting Co.
Nat'l Reps: Canadian Broadcast Sales
Population Served: 500,000 *Format:* Adult Contemp, Classic Rock, Contemporary Hits/Top 40 *No. News Employees:* 2
Target Audience: 18-49.
Geoff Stirling, Chairman
Scott Stirling, CEO
Doug Neal, General Manager
Lorraine Pope, General Sales Mgr
Jesse Stirling, Promotions Manager
Frank Collins, CFO
Maurice Fitzgerald, Music Director

Burnt Islands

CHBI-FM
01-01-2007; 95.7 mhz FM *Hrs Open:* 9-5 mon - Fri; 50 w; N47 36 18 W58 52 06
Box 101, Burnt Islands, NF A0M 1B0 Canada
(709) 698-3553, *Fax:* (709) 698-3100
www.burntislandsnl.ca
chbi95.7fm@hotmail.com
License: Burnt Islands, Canada County, NL held by Burnt Islands Economic Development Board.
Population Served: 919 *Arbitron Metro Market:* Burnt Islands, NL
Format: Variety/Diverse
Holly Keeping, General Manager

Carbonear

CHVO-FM
01-07-2008; 103.9 mhz FM; 14 kw; N47 43 13 W53 12 50
One CHVO Dr., Carbonear, NF A1Y 1A2 Canada
(709) 596-1560, *Fax:* (709) 596-8626
www.kixxcountry.ca
chavo@vocm.com
License: Carbonear, NL held by Newcap Inc.
Group Owner: NewCap Inc.
Population Served: 4,739 *Arbitron Metro Market:* Carbonear, NL
Format: Country *Target Audience:* 25-54; adults
John Steele, President
John Murphy, General Manager
Aiden Hibbs, Station Manager
Ron Ryan, General Sales Mgr
Mike Campbell, Programming Director
Gerry Phalen, News Director
Harold Steele, Chief Engineer

Churchill Falls

CFLC-FM
01-01-1974; 97.9 mhz FM; 8 w; 50 ft
c/o CFCB(AM), Box 570, Corner Brook, NF A2H 6H5 Canada
(709) 634-3111, *Fax:* (709) 634-4081
www.bigland.fm
info@bigland.fm
License: Churchill Falls, NL held by NewCap Inc.
Group Owner: NewCap Inc.; (acq 4-2-01; grpsl).
Format: Adult Contemp, Country
Michael Murphy, General Manager
Ken Ash, Programming Director

Clarenville

CJKK-FM
01-01-1988; 105.3 mhz FM *Hrs Open:* 24; 2.07 kw
c/o CHOZ-FM, 446 Logy Bay Rd., St. John's, NF A1C 5R6 Canada
(709) 726-2922, *Fax:* (709) 726-3300
www.ozfm.com
License: Clarenville, Newfoundland County, NL held by Newfoundland Broadcasting Co.
Group Owner: Newfoundland Broadcasting Co.
Nat'l Reps: Canadian Broadcast Sales
Population Served: 500,000 *Format:* Adult Contemp, Classic Rock, Contemporary Hits/Top 40 *No. News Employees:* 2
Target Audience: 18-49.
Geoff Stirling, Chairman
Scott Stirling, CEO
Doug Neal, General Manager
Frank Collins, CFO

CKVO
11-15-1974; 710 khz AM*Rebroadcasts:* Rebroadcasts VOCM(AM) St. John's except 9 AM-5 PM (loc progmg)
CA
(709) 726-5590, *Fax:* (709) 726-4633
www.vocm.com
feedback@vocm.com
License: Clarenville, NF held by NewCap Inc.
Group Owner: NewCap Inc.; (acq 6-00; grpsl).
Format: Country
Ken Ash, Operations Dir
John Murphy, General Manager
Dennis Dillon, General Sales Mgr
Paul Raynes, Programming Director
Gerry Phelan, News Director
Harold Steele, Chief Engineer

Corner Brook

***CBY**
04-01-1949; 990 khz AM*Rebroadcasts:* Rebroadcasts CBT(AM) Grand Falls-Windsor
CA
(709) 637-1151, *Fax:* (709) 634-8506
www.cbc.ca/nl/
License: Corner Brook, NF held by CBC.
Nat'l Network: CBC Radio One
Format: News, News/Talk, Talk *Target Audience:* 30 plus; mature
Robert Rabinowitz, CEO
Gordon Lannon, General Manager

CFCB
10-03-1960; 570 khz AM *Hrs Open:* 24
CA
(709) 634-4570, *Fax:* (709) 726-4633
www.vocm.com
License: Corner Brook, NF held by Newcap Inc.
Group Owner: NewCap Inc.; (acq 4-2-01; grpsl).
Nat'l Reps: Canadian Broadcast Sales
Format: Country
Harry Steele, President
J. Steele, Operations Dir
Michael Murphy, General Manager
Darryl Stevens, Operations Manager

CKOZ-FM
01-01-1979; 92.3 mhz FM *Hrs Open:* 24; 50 kw*Rebroadcasts:* Rebroadcasts CHOZ-FM St. John's
c/o CHOZ-FM, 446 Logy Bay Rd., Box 2020, St. John's, NF A1C 5S2 Canada
(709) 726-2922, *Fax:* (709) 726-3300
www.ozfm.com
License: Corner Brook, Newfoundland County, NL held by Newfoundland Broadcasting Co.
Group Owner: Newfoundland Broadcasting Co.
Nat'l Reps: Canadian Broadcast Sales
Population Served: 500,000 *Format:* Adult Contemp, Classic Rock, Contemporary Hits/Top 40 *No. News Employees:* 2
Target Audience: 18-49.
Geoff Stirling, Chairman
Scott Stirling, CEO
Doug Neal, General Manager
Lorraine Pope, General Sales Mgr
Jesse Stirling, Promotions Manager
Frank Collins, CFO
Maurice Fitzgerald, Music Director

CKXX-FM
06-20-1997; 103.9 mhz FM *Hrs Open:* 24; 40 kw
345 O'Connell Dr., P.O. Box 570, Corner Brook, NF A2H6H5 Canada
(709) 634-4570, *Fax:* (709) 634-4081
k-rock1039.com
mastercontrol@k-rock1039.com
License: Corner Brook, NL held by NewCap Inc.
Group Owner: NewCap Inc.; (acq 8-29-90).
Nat'l Reps: Canadian Broadcast Sales
Population Served: 40,000*Special Programming:* Oldies 3 hrs wkly *No. News Employees:* 2 *Target Audience:* 25-54.*Adv. Rates:* 32.4; 32.4; 24.3; 10.8
Daryl Stevens, Operations Dir
Stanley Kruchka, General Manager
Mike Payne, Programming Director

Gander

***CBG**
01-01-1949; 1400 khz AM
Mailing Address: CA
Second Address: 98 Sullivan Ave., Gander, NF A1V 1W7
(709) 256-4311, *Fax:* (709) 651-2021
www.cbc.ca/nl/
gandernews@cbc.ca
License: Gander, NF held by CBC.
Format: Public Affairs, News
Robert Rabinowitz, CEO
Michael Aucion, Programming Director

CKGA
01-01-1969; 650 khz AM
CA
(709) 651-3650, *Fax:* (709) 651-2542
www.vocm.com
License: Gander, NF held by NewCap Inc.
Group Owner: NewCap Inc.; (acq 6-00; grpsl).
Format: Country, News, Talk
Dave Hillier, General Manager
Dennis Dillon, General Sales Mgr
Dean Clarke, Programming Director
Robet Tuck, News Director
Harold Steele, Chief Engineer

CKXD-FM
11-01-2000; 98.7 mhz FM; 6 kw
391 Kenmount Road, P.O. Box 8-590, St. John's, NL A1B 3P5 Canada
(709) 726 - 5590, *Fax:* (709) 726 - 4633
www.vocm.com
vocm.krock.psa@vocm.com
License: Gander, NL held by Newcap Inc.
Group Owner: NewCap Inc.
Population Served: 196,966 *Arbitron Metro Market:* St. John's, NL *Format:* Classic Rock*Special Programming:* Newfoundland & Irish 12 hrs wkly
John Murphy, General Manager
Dennis Dillon, General Sales Mgr
Jay Lawrence, Programming Director
Brian Madore, News Director
Harold Steele, Chief Engineer
Bob Power, CHCM Marystown, News Director, Marystown

Goose Bay

CFLN
08-01-1974; 1230 khz AM
CA

(709) 896-2968, *Fax:* (709) 896-8708
www.vocm.com
License: Goose Bay, NF held by NewCap Inc.
Group Owner: NewCap Inc.; (acq 4-2-01; grpsl).
Format: Adult Contemp
Harry Steele, Chairman
Robert G. Steele, President

CFLN-FM
04-15-2011; 97.9 mhz FM; 1 kw; 25.4 meters
345 O'Connell Drive, Corner Brook, NL A2H 7V3 Canada
(709) 634-6672, *Fax:* (709) 634-4081
www.bigland.fm
License: Goose Bay, NL held by New Cap Inc
Group Owner: NewCap Inc.

Grand Falls

CKCM
10-01-1962; 620 khz AM
Mailing Address: CA
Second Address: 35 A Grenfell Heights, Grand Falls-Windsor, NF A2A 2K2
(709) 489-2192, *Fax:* (709) 489-8626
www.vocm.com
License: Grand Falls, NF held by NewCap Inc.
Group Owner: NewCap Inc.; (acq 6-00; grpsl).
Format: Country
Dave Hillier, General Manager
Dennis Dillon, General Sales Mgr
Richard King, Programming Director
Roger Barnett, News Director
Harold Steele, Chief Engineer

Grand Falls-Windsor

CKXG-FM
01-01-2001; 102.3 mhz FM *Hrs Open:* 24; 17 kw; 96.6 meters
Box 620, Grand Falls-Windsor, NF A2A 2K2 Canada
(709) 489-2192, *Fax:* (709) 489-8626
www.vocm.com
vocm.krock.psa@vocm.com
License: Grand Falls-Windsor, NL held by NewCap Broadcasting Ltd.
Group Owner: NewCap Inc.
Dave Hillier, General Manager
Dennis Dillon, General Sales Mgr
Richard King, Programming Director
Margot pitcher-Hamlyn, News Director
Harold Steele, Chief Engineer

Happy Valley

***CFGB-FM**
02-23-1959; 89.5 mhz FM; 1 kw-w
Box 1029, Stn C, Happy Valley-Goose Bay, NF A0P 1CO Canada
(709) 896-2911, *Fax:* (709) 896-8900
www.cbc.ca/nl/
labmorning@stjohns.cbc.ca
License: Happy Valley, NL held by CBC.
Nat'l Network: CBC Radio One
Format: Public Affairs, News
Diane Humber, General Manager
Cynthia Wall, Programming Director
Conrad Lutes, News Director
Lorne Burry, Engineering Dir

Labrador City

CBDQ-FM
01-01-1997; 96.3 mhz FM; 255 w*Rebroadcasts:* Rebroadcasts CFGB-FM Happy Valley
Box 576, Labrador City, NF A2V 2L3 Canada
(709) 944-3616, *Fax:* (709) 944-5472
www.cbc.ca/nl/
License: Labrador City, NL held by CBC.
Format: Talk
Diane Humber, General Manager

CJRM-FM
09-23-1992; 97.3 mhz FM; 500 w; 1,998 ft; N52 57 01 W66 55 01
C.P. 453, 308 Hudson Dr., Labrador City, NF A2V 2K7 Canada
(709) 944-7600, *Fax:* (709) 944-5125
cjrm@crrstv.net
License: Labrador City, Labrador County, NL held by Radio Communautaire du Labrador Inc.
Population Served: 17,000 *Format:* Variety/Diverse *Target Audience:* General; English & Fr speaking audience in Labrador West

Norman Gillespie, President
linda McLean, Station Manager
Dean Baker, Executive Vice President

Lewisporte

CIFX-FM
01-01-2002; 93.7 mhz FM *Hrs Open:* 24; 50 w; N/A; 37 George Street, Lewisporte, Newfoundland & Labrador,*Rebroadcasts:* N/A
Mailing Address: Box 601, 37 George Street, Lewisporte, NF A0G 3A0 Canada
Second Address: 37 George Street, P.O. Box 601, Lewisporte, NF AOG 3AO
(709) 535-6000, *Fax:* (709) 535-6600
N/A
mixfm@nf.sympatico.ca
License: Lewisporte, N/A County, NL held by Mix FM Inc.
Population Served: 3,312 *Arbitron Metro Market:* Lewisporte, NL *Format:* Talk*Special Programming:* N/A *No. News Employees:* 2 *Target Audience:* 21-52*Adv. Rates:* $8.10
Vicki Fudge, Operations Dir
Koren Hurley, General Sales Mgr
Todd Foss, Programming Director
Angela Brenton, Promotions Manager
Peter Ginn, Engineering Dir
Colleen Harris, Administration/Copy
Terry Spurrell, Software Technician

Marystown

CHCM
01-01-1961; 740 khz AM
CA
(709) 279-2560, *Fax:* (709) 279-3538
www.vocm.com
chem.frontdesk@vocm.com
License: Marystown, NF held by NewCap Inc.
Group Owner: NewCap Inc.; (acq 5-4-00; grpsl).
Format: Country
Russell Murphy, General Manager
Harry Myles, Programming Director
Bob Tower, News Director
Harold Steele, Chief Engineer

CIOZ-FM
01-01-1979; 96.3 mhz FM *Hrs Open:* 24; 25 kw*Rebroadcasts:* Rebroadcasts CHOZ-FM St. John's.
c/o CHOZ-FM, 446 Logy Bay Rd., Box 2020, St. John's, NF A1C 5S2 Canada
(709) 726-2922, *Fax:* (709) 726-3300
www.ozfm.com
License: Marystown, Newfoundland County, NL held by Newfoundland Broadcasting Co.
Group Owner: Newfoundland Broadcasting Co.
Nat'l Reps: Canadian Broadcast Sales
Population Served: 500,000 *Format:* Adult Contemp, Classic Rock, Contemporary Hits/Top 40 *No. News Employees:* 2
Target Audience: 18-49.
Geoff Stirling, Chairman
Scott Stirling, CEO
Doug Neal, General Manager
Lorraine Pope, General Sales Mgr
Jesse Stirling, Promotions Manager
Frank Collins, CFO

Port Au Choix

CFNW
01-01-1960; 790 khz AM *Hrs Open:* 24
CA
(709) 634-4570, *Fax:* (709) 634-4081
License: Port Au Choix, NF held by Newcap Inc.
Group Owner: NewCap Inc.; (acq 4-2-01; grpsl).
Format: Country
Harry Steele, President
Darryl Stevens, Operations Dir
Michael Murphy, General Manager

Rattling Brook

CHOS-FM
01-01-1979; 95.9 mhz FM *Hrs Open:* 24; 50 kw*Rebroadcasts:* Rebroadcasts CHOZ-FM St. John's.
446 Logy Bay Rd., Box 2020, c/o CHOZ-FM, St. John's, NF A1C 5S2 Canada
(709) 726-2922, *Fax:* (709) 726-3300
www.ozfm.com
License: Rattling Brook, Newfoundland County, NL held by Newfoundland Broadcasting Co.
Group Owner: Newfoundland Broadcasting Co.
Nat'l Reps: Canadian Broadcast Sales

Population Served: 500,000 *Format:* Adult Contemp, Classic Rock, Contemporary Hits/Top 40 *No. News Employees:* 2
Target Audience: 18-49.
Geoff Stirling, Chairman
Scott Sterling, CEO
Doug Neal, General Manager
Frank Collins, CFO

Red Rocks

CKSS-FM
01-01-1994; 96.9 mhz FM *Hrs Open:* 24; 520 w*Rebroadcasts:* Rebroadcasts CHOZ-FM St. John's 100%
c/o CHOZ-FM, 466 Logy Bay Rd., Box 2020, St. John's, NF A1C 5S2 Canada
(709) 726-2922, *Fax:* (709) 726-3300
www.ozfm.com
License: Red Rocks, Newfoundland County, NL held by Newfoundland Broadcasting Co.
Group Owner: Newfoundland Broadcasting Co.
Nat'l Reps: Canadian Broadcast Sales
Population Served: 500,000 *Format:* Adult Contemp, Classic Rock, Contemporary Hits/Top 40 *No. News Employees:* 2
Target Audience: 18-49.
Geoff Stirling, Chairman
Scott Stirling, CEO
Doug Neal, General Manager
Lorraine Pope, General Sales Mgr
Jesse Stirling, Promotions Manager
Larry Davis, News Director
Frank Collins, CFO

Saint Andrews

CFCV-FM
01-01-1974; 97.7 mhz FM*Rebroadcasts:* Rebroadcasts CFGN(AM) Port-aux-Basques
Mailing Address: 60 West St., Stephenville, NF A2N 1C6 Canada
Second Address: C/o CFGN(AM), Port-aux-Basques, NF A0M 1C0
(709) 695-2183,(709) 643-2191, *Fax:* (709) 695-9614
www.vocm.com
cfsx@vocm.com
License: Saint Andrews, NL held by NewCap Inc.
Group Owner: NewCap Inc.
Michael Murphy, General Manager
Gerry Murphy, General Sales Mgr
Larry Bennett, Programming Director
Brian O'Keefe, Chief Engineer

Saint John's

***CBN-FM**
07-01-1975; 106.9 mhz FM; 100 kw; 300 ft
Box 12010, Stn A, Saint John's, NF A1B 3T8 Canada
(709) 576-5000, *Fax:* (709) 576-5205
www.cbc.ca/nl
License: Saint John's, NL held by CBC
Nat'l Network: CBC Radio Two
TV Affiliate: *CBNT-TV affil *Format:* News, News/Talk, Talk
Patricia Pleszczynska, Operations Dir
Judith Bleier, Operations Manager

***CHMR-FM**
01-01-1986; 93.5 mhz FM *Hrs Open:* 24; 50 w; -10 ft
Memorial University, MUNSU, South Annex, Rm 2009, Saint John's, NF A1C 5S7 Canada
(709) 737-4777, *Fax:* (709) 737-7688
www.chmr.ca/
chmr@mun.ca
License: Saint John's, NL held by Memorial University of Newfoundland Radio Society Inc.
Population Served: 200,000 *Format:* Alternative, Variety/Diverse*Special Programming:* Fr 2 hrs, jazz 6 hrs, relg 4 hrs, blues 6 hrs, rap*Hrs. of News Programming:* News progmg 7 hrs wkly *Target Audience:* General.
Kathy Rowe, General Manager
Bob Earle, Programming Director
Nancy Earle, Promotions Manager
Ernst Rollmann, Assistant Music Director

CHOZ-FM
06-15-1977; 94.7 mhz FM *Hrs Open:* 24; 100 kw; 821 ft; NN47 31 36 W52 42 50
446 Logy Bay Rd., Box 2050, Saint John's, NF A1C 5R6 Canada
(709) 722-5015, *Fax:* (709) 726-3300
www.ozfm.com
ntvsales@ntv.ca
License: Saint John's, Newfoundland County, NL held by Newfoundland Broadcasting Co. Ltd.
Group Owner: Newfoundland Broadcasting Co.
Nat'l Reps: Canadian Broadcast Sales

Population Served: 500,000*TV Affiliate:* CJON-TV affil. *Format:* Adult Contemp, Classic Rock, Contemporary Hits/Top 40 *No. News Employees:* 2 *Target Audience:* 18-49.
Geoff Stirling, Chairman
Scott Stirling, CEO
Jesse Stirling, Operations Dir
Doug Neal, General Manager
Dave Lawrence, Station Manager
Lorraine Pope, General Sales Mgr
Frank Collins, CFO

CKIX-FM
10-15-1983; 99.1 mhz FM; 100 kw; Ant 930 ft
391 Kenmount Rd., Box 8-590, St. John's, NF A1B 3P5 Canada
(709) 726-5590, *Fax:* (709) 726-4633
www.991hitsfm.com
hitsmail@991hitsfm.com
License: Saint John's, NL held by Newcap Inc.
Group Owner: NewCap Inc.; (acq 1-17-83).
Format: Contemporary Hits/Top 40
John Murphey, General Manager
Randy Snow, Programming Director
Brad Michaels, Music Director

VOCM-FM
09-01-1982; 97.5 mhz FM *Hrs Open:* 24; 100 kw
391 Kenmount Rd., Saint John's, NF A1B 3P5 Canada
(709) 726-5590, *Fax:* (709) 726-4633
www.k-rock975.com
email@krockrocks.com
License: Saint John's, NL
Population Served: 196,966 *Arbitron Metro Market:* St. John's, NL, Canada *Format:* Classic Rock*Hrs. of News Programming:* News progmg 7 hrs wkly *Target Audience:* Adults 25-54.
Ron Ryan, Station Manager

CKSJ-FM
01-01-2004; 101.1 mhz FM; 20 kw
95 Bonaventure Avenue, Suite 201, Saint John's, NF A1B 2X5 Canada
(709) 754-6748, *Fax:* (709) 754-6749
www.coast1011.com
onair@coast1011.com
License: Saint John's, NL held by Coast Broadcasting Ltd.
Population Served: 106,172 *Arbitron Metro Market:* St. John's, NL *Format:* Adult Contemp
Andrew Newman, General Manager

St. John's

***CBN**
04-01-1949; 640 khz AM *Hrs Open:* 19
CA
(709) 576-5000, *Fax:* (709) 576-5205
www.cbc.ca
License: St. John's, NF held by CBC.
Nat'l Network: CBC Radio One
Format: Variety/Diverse*Special Programming:* Fisheries 3 hrs wkly*Hrs. of News Programming:* news progmg 10 hrs wkly *No. News Employees:* 6 *Target Audience:* General.
Larry O'Brien, Operations Dir
Diane Humber, General Manager
Liz Lacey, Programming Director
Lori Wheeler, Promotions Manager

CJYQ
01-01-1951; 930 khz AM
CA
(709) 726-5590, *Fax:* (709) 726-4633
www.thisisnewfoundlandlabrador.ca
info@thisisnewfoundlandlabrador.ca
License: St. John's, NF held by Newcap Inc.
Group Owner: NewCap Inc.
Format: Country
Barb Bell, General Manager

***VOAR**
01-01-1930; 1210 khz AM *Hrs Open:* 24
CA
(709) 745-8627, *Fax:* (709)745-1600
www.voar.org
voar@voar.org
License: St. John's, NF held by Seventh-Day Adventist Church in Newfoundland.
Arbitron Metro Market: St. John's, NL, Canada *Format:* Gospel, Religious*Hrs. of News Programming:* News progmg 12 hrs wkly *Target Audience:* 25-44; individuals interested in family life & traditional values
Gary Hodder, President
Sherry Griffin, Station Manager
Brian Matthews, Chief Engineer
Tina Taylor, Communications Director

VOCM
10-19-1936; 590 khz AM *Hrs Open:* 24
CA
(709) 726-5590, *Fax:* (709) 726-4633
www.vocm.com
feedback@vocm.com
License: St. John's, NF held by NewCap Inc.
Group Owner: NewCap Inc.; (acq 6-00; grpsl).
Nat'l Reps: Canadian Broadcast Sales
Arbitron Metro Market: St. John's, NL, Canada *Format:* Adult Contemp, Country, News, News/Talk, Talk *No. News Employees:* 16 *Target Audience:* 25 plus.
John Steele, President
Ken Ash, Operations Dir
John Murphy, General Manager
Ron Ryan, General Sales Mgr
Paul Magee, Programming Director
Gerry Phelan, News Director
Harold Steele, Engineering Dir
Cathy Ridgely-Ryan, TrafficManager

***VOWR**
06-20-1924; 800 khz AM *Hrs Open:* 24
CA
(709) 579-9233, *Fax:* (709) 579-9232
www.vowr.org
vowr@vowr.org
License: St. John's, NF held by Wesley United Church Radio Board.
Arbitron Metro Market: St. John's, NL, Canada *Format:* Oldies, Variety/Diverse*Special Programming:* Relg 10 hrs, folk 15 hrs wkly *Target Audience:* 40 plus.
Marvin Barnes, Chairman
John Tessier, General Manager

Stephenville

CFSX
11-14-1964; 870 khz AM *Hrs Open:* 24
CA
(709) 643-2191, *Fax:* (709) 643-5025
www.vocm.com
License: Stephenville, NF held by NewCap Inc.
Group Owner: NewCap Inc.; (acq 2001; grpsl).
Format: Country*Special Programming:* Relg one hr wkly *No. News Employees:* 2 *Target Audience:* General.
Harry Steele, Chairman
Robert G. Steele, President
John Murphy, General Manager
Gerry Murphy, Station Manager

CIOS-FM
01-01-1979; 98.5 mhz FM *Hrs Open:* 24; 10 kw*Rebroadcasts:* Rebroadcasts CHOZ-FM St. John's.
c/o CHOZ-FM, 446 Logy Bay Rd., Box 2020, St. John's, NF A1C 5S2 Canada
(709) 726-2922, *Fax:* (709) 726-3300
www.ozfm.com
License: Stephenville, Newfoundland County, NL held by Newfoundland Broadcasting Co.
Group Owner: Newfoundland Broadcasting Co.
Population Served: 500,000 *Format:* Adult Contemp, Classic Rock, Contemporary Hits/Top 40 *No. News Employees:* 2 *Target Audience:* 18-49.
Geoff Stirling, Chairman
Scott Stirling, CEO
Doug Neal, General Manager
Frank Collins, CFO

Northwest Territories

Hay River

CJCD-FM-1
09-15-1986; 100.1 mhz FM; 300 w; 175 ft*Rebroadcasts:* Rebroadcasts CJCD(FM) Yellowknife
Box 218, Yellowknife, NT X1A 2N2 Canada
(867) 920-4636, *Fax:* (867) 920-4033
mix100.ca
info@cjcd.ca
License: Hay River, NT held by CJCD Radio Ltd.
Nat'l Reps: Canadian Broadcast Sales
Format: Adult Contemp *Target Audience:* 25-49.
Eileen Dent, President
Tim Jaworski, General Sales Mgr
Joanne McKenzie, Programming Director
Kirby Marshall, Chief Engineer
Mandy Church, Traffic Manager

CKHR-FM
01-01-1979; 107.3 mhz FM; 32 w; 185 ft
Box 4394, Hay River, NT X0E 1G3 Canada
(867) 874-2547
ckhr@northwestel.nt
License: Hay River, NT held by Hay River Broadcasting Society.
Format: Adult Contemp
Al Erickson, President
Ray Lawson, Station Manager

Inuvik

***CHAK**
11-26-1960; 860 khz AM
CA
(867) 777-7600, *Fax:* (867) 777-7640
www.cbc.ca/north
License: Inuvik, NT held by CBC.
Format: News, News/Talk, Talk*Special Programming:* Inuvialuktun 9 hrs, Gwich'in 9 hrs wkly *Target Audience:* General.
Peter Skinner, General Manager

Iqaluit

CFFB
02-06-1961; 1230 khz AM *Hrs Open:* 24; 1 kw-U, DA-1
Box 490, Iqaluit, NU Canada
(867) 979-6100, *Fax:* (867) 979-6147
cbc.ca/north
nunavut@cbc.ca
License: Iqaluit, NU held by CBC.
Nat'l Network: CBC Radio One
No. News Employees: 9
Patrick Nagle, General Manager
Neville Crabbe, News Director

Tuktoyaktuk

CFCT
01-01-1971; 600 khz AM
CA
(867) 777-7600, *Fax:* (867) 777-7640
License: Tuktoyaktuk, NT held by CBC.
Nat'l Network: CBC Radio One
Format: Variety/Diverse*Special Programming:* Eskimo 5 hrs wkly
Peter Skinner, General Manager

Yellow Knife

***CFYK**
12-13-1958; 1340 khz AM
CA
(867) 920-5400, *Fax:* (867) 920-5410
License: Yellow Knife, NT held by CBC.
Format: News, News/Talk, Talk, Variety/Diverse*Special Programming:* Slavey 8 hrs, Dogrib 4 hrs, Chipewayan 4 hrs wkly *Target Audience:* General.
David McNaughton, Operations Dir
Peter Skinner, General Manager

Yellowknife

CJCD-FM
01-01-1998; 100.1 mhz FM; 400 w; N62 27 00 W114 19 00
Box 218, Yellowknife, NT X1A 2N2 Canada
(867) 920-4636, *Fax:* (867) 920-4033
www.cjcd.ca
info@cjcd.ca
License: Yellowknife, NT held by CJCD Radio Ltd.
Nat'l Reps: Canadian Broadcast Sales
Format: Adult Contemp *Target Audience:* 25-54.
Eileen Dent, President
Joanne McKenzie, Programming Director

CKLB-FM
12-11-1985; 101.9 mhz FM *Hrs Open:* 7 AM-10 PM (M-F); 11 AM-9 PM (S); 130 w; 162 ft*Rebroadcasts:* Rebroadcasts CFWE-FM Lac La Biche, Alberta News
4 Lessard Drive, Box 2193, Yellowknife, NT X1A 2P6 Canada
(867) 873-2977, *Fax:* (867) 920-4205
www.ncsnwt.com
ncs@ncsnwt.com
License: Yellowknife, Canada County, NT held by Native Communications Society of the Western N.W.T.
Population Served: 30,000 *Format:* Country *No. News Employees:* 1*Adv. Rates:* 20; 20; 20; 20
Dane Gibson, Operations Dir
Amos Scott, General Sales Mgr
William Greenland, Programming Director
Andreas Tesfaye, Promotions Manager
Nadira Begg, News Director

Nova Scotia

Amherst

CFTA-FM
07-21-2011; 107.9 mhz FM; 6.5 kw; 123 meters
141 Victoria Street E, Suite S, Amherst, NS B4H 1X9 Canada
(902) 660-1079, *Fax:* (902) 660-1080
www.tantramarfm.ca
ctfa@eastlink.ca
License: Amherst, NS held by Tantramar Community Radio Society

CKDH-FM
07-20-2011; 101.7 mhz FM; 23 kw; 16 meters
Box 670, Amherst, NS B4H 4B8 Canada
(902) 667-3875
www.1017ckdh.com
License: Amherst, NS held by Maritime Broadcasting System
Group Owner: Maritime Broadcasting
Format: Adult Contemp
Ian Hanomansing, News Director

Antigonish

CJFX-FM
01-01-2003; 98.9 mhz FM *Hrs Open:* 24; 75.39 kw
Mailing Address: 85 Kirk St., Box 5800, Antigonish, NS B2G 2R9 Canada
Second Address: 85 Kirk St., Antigonish, NS B2G 2R9
(902) 863-4580, *Fax:* (902) 863-6300
www.989xfm.ca
cjfx@cjfx.ca
License: Antigonish, NS held by Atlantic Broadcasters Ltd.
Nat'l Reps: Canadian Broadcast Sales *Regional Reps:* Canadian Broadcast Sales
Format: Contemporary Hits/Top 40*Hrs. of News Programming:* news progmg 24 hrs wkly *No. News Employees:* 3 *Target Audience:* 18 plus.
Ken Farrell, General Manager
Neil Scribner, General Sales Mgr
Barry Mackinnon, Programming Director
Ken Kingston, News Director

CFXU-FM
01-01-2006; 93.3 mhz FM; 50 w; N45 37 10 W61 59 40
Box 948, St. Francis Xavier University, Antigonish, NS B2G 2W5 Canada
(902) 867-3941
www.radiocfxu.ca
thefox@stfx.ca
License: Antigonish, NS held by Radio CFXU Club.
Population Served: 4,524 *Arbitron Metro Market:* Antigonish, NS
Format: Variety/Diverse
John Sloat, Station Manager
Rose Murphy, Programming Director
John Best, News Director
Cameron Brioux, Music Director
Liam Prost, Program Manager
Brendan Morle, Production Manager

Barrington

CJLS-FM-1
01-01-1982; 96.3 mhz FM; 5.5 kw*Rebroadcasts:* Rebroadcasts CJLS-FM Yarmouth
328 Maint St., Yarmouth, NS B5A 1E4 Canada
(902) 742-7175, *Fax:* (902) 742-3143
www.cjls.com
cjls@cjls.com
License: Barrington, NS held by Radio CJLS Ltd.
Format: Adult Contemp
Ray Zinck, President
Chris Perry, Operations Dir
Dave Hall, General Sales Mgr
Gary Nickerson, News Director
Jim Harris, Engineering Dir

***CJLSFM**
01-01-2003; 96.3 mhz FM *Hrs Open:* 24; kw
CA
(902) 742-7175, *Fax:* (902) 742-3143
www.cjls.com
CJLS@cjls.com
License: Barrington, NS held by Radio CJLS Ltd.
Arbitron Metro Market: Yarmouth, NS *Format:* Adult Contemp
Ray Zinck, General Manager
Dave Hall, General Sales Mgr
Chris Perry, Programming Director
Gary Nickerson, News Director
Jim Harris, Chief Engineer

Sean MacLellan, Sports Director
Carol Sherman, Sales Consultant
Eva Smith, SalesConsultant

Bedford

CHSB-FM
01-01-2007; 99.3 mhz FM; 50 w; N44 44 13 W63 39 13
Box 44073, Bedford, NS B4A 3X5 Canada
(902) 835-5966
www.bedfordbaptist.ca
License: Bedford, NS held by Bedford Baptist Church.
Population Served: 18,274 *Arbitron Metro Market:* Bedford, NS
Format: Religious
Kevin Haggarty, General Manager

Bridgewater

CKBW-FM
02-01-2002; 98.1 mhz FM *Hrs Open:* 24; 32 kw
135 North Street, Suite 200, Bridgewater, NS B4V 2G8 Canada
(902) 543-2401, *Fax:* (902) 543-1208
www.ckbw.ca
hamilton.rick@radioabl.ca
License: Bridgewater, Lunenburg County, NS held by Acadia Broadcasting Ltd.
Group Owner: Acadia Broadcasting Ltd.
Nat'l Reps: Canadian Broadcast Sales *Regional Reps:* Canadian Broadcast Sales
Population Served: 8,241 *Arbitron Metro Market:* Bridgewater, NS *Format:* Adult Contemp*Hrs. of News Programming:* news progmg 11 hrs wkly *No. News Employees:* 15 *Target Audience:* General; rural & small townurban
John Wiles, General Manager
Chris Pearson, General Sales Mgr
Brian Tepper, Promotions Manager
Sheldon MacLeod, News Director
Frank Grayney, Chief Engineer
Pamela Smith, Traffic Manager
Greg Lowe, Advertising
Kerry Oickle,Advertising
Eric Whynot, Advertising
Mel Benoit, Advertising

CJHK-FM
05-15-2010; 100.7 mhz FM; 10 kw
135 North Street, Suite 200, Bridgewater, NS B4V 2V7 Canada
(902) 543-2401, *Fax:* (902) 543-1208
www.hankfm.ca
License: Bridgewater, NS held by Acadia Broadcasting Ltd
Format: Country

Cheticamp

***CKJM-FM**
06-10-1995; 106.1 mhz FM *Hrs Open:* 24; 3 kw; N46 36 55 W61 02 52*Rebroadcasts:* Rebroadcasts CFIM-FM Iles-De-La Madeleine, PQ 5%
Box 699, Les Trois Piqnons, Cheticamp, NS B0E 1H0 Canada
(902) 224-1242, *Fax:* (902) 224-1770
www.ckjm.ca
info@ckjm.ca
License: Cheticamp, Inverness County, NS held by La Cooperative Radio Cheticamp Ltee.
Population Served: 5,000 *Format:* Country*Special Programming:* Gaelic one hr, jazz 3 hrs wkly *Target Audience:* General.*Adv. Rates:* 22; 16; 16; 16
Normand Poirier, President
Angus Lefort, General Manager
Carole Aucoin, General Sales Mgr
Ginette Chiasson, Programming Director

Comeauville

***CIFA-FM**
09-28-1990; 104.1 mhz FM *Hrs Open:* 6am to 10pm; 39.3 w; 475 ft
Box 8, Saulnierville, NS B0W 2Z0 Canada
(902) 769-2432, *Fax:* (902) 769-3101
www.cifa.fm
info@cifafm.ca
License: Comeauville, Digby County, NS held by Association Radio Clare.
Population Served: 60,000 *Format:* News, Variety/Diverse
Target Audience: General.
Albert Geddry, President
Dave LeBlau, General Manager
Paul Lomberd, General Sales Mgr
Emile Blinn, Engineering Dir

Dartmouth

CFDR
12-05-1962; 780 khz AM
CA
(902) 453-4004, *Fax:* (902) 453-3120
www.780kixx.ca
License: Dartmouth, NS held by New Cap Broadcasting Ltd.
Nat'l Reps: Canadian Broadcast Sales
Format: Country
Ted Hyland, General Manager
J. Douglas, Programming Director
Rich Horner, News Director
Steve Lunn, Chief Engineer

***CFRQFM**
11-28-1983; 104.3 mhz FM; kw
CA
(902) 453-4004, *Fax:* (902) 453-3120
www.q104.ca
jcdouglas@newcap.ca
License: Dartmouth, NS held by Newcap Inc.
Group Owner: NewCap Inc.
Format: Classic Rock
Ted Hyland, General Manager
JC Douglas, Programming Director
Rich Horner, News Director
Steve Lunn, Chief Engineer

Digby

CKDY
02-02-1970; 1420 khz AM*Rebroadcasts:* Rebroadcasts CKEN(AM) Kentville and CKAD(AM) Middleton
CA
(902) 678-2111, *Fax:* (902) 678-9894
www.avrnetwork.com
programming@avrnetwork.com
License: Digby, NS held by Maritime Broadcasting System Ltd.
Group Owner: Maritime Broadcasting; (acq 8-79).
Format: Country*Special Programming:* Farm 7 hrs wkly
Mike Mitchell, Operations Dir
Dianne Best, General Manager
Karen Corey, General Sales Mgr
Amanda Misner, Programming Director
Dave Chaulk, News Director
Matthew Povah, Chief Engineer

Eastern Passage

***CFEP-FM**
01-01-2002; 105.9 mhz FM *Hrs Open:* 24; 1.68 kw; 37.6 meters; N44 36 46 W63 29 40
Seaside-FM, Box 196, Eastern Passage, NS B3G 1M5 Canada
(902) 469-9231, *Fax:* (902) 469-1935
www.seasidefm.com
seasidefm@ns.sympatico.ca
License: Eastern Passage, HRM County, NS held by Seaside Broadcasting Organization.
Population Served: 25,000*Hrs. of News Programming:* news progmg 50 hrs wkly *No. News Employees:* 4
Wayne Harrett, Chairman
Wayne Harrett, Operations Dir
Wayne Harrett, General Manager
Wayne Harrett, Station Manager
Jim Coe, General Sales Mgr
Wayne Harrett, Programming Director
George Jordon, News Director
Gordon Hefler,Engineering Dir
George Hefler, Chief Engineer

Eskasoni Indian Reserve

CICU-FM
01-01-1994; 94.1 mhz FM; 1 w
Mailing Address: Box 7100, Eskasoni, NS B1W 1A1 Canada
Second Address: 130 Anslum Rd., Eskasoni Indian Reserve, Eskasoni, NS B1W 1A1
(902) 379-2955, *Fax:* (902) 379-2966
greguj@ns.sympatico.ca
License: Eskasoni Indian Reserve, NS held by Greg Johnson.
Population Served: 3,893 *Arbitron Metro Market:* Eskasoni, NS
Greg Johnson, General Manager
Linda Johnson, Programming Director

Glace Bay

CKOA-FM
12-03-2007; 89.7 mhz FM *Hrs Open:* 24; 6.0 kw; N46 11 59 W59 58 46
106 Reserve St., Glace Bay, NS B1A 4W5 Canada

(902) 849-4301, *Fax:* (902) 849-1272
www.coastalradio.ca
info@coastalradio.ca
License: Glace Bay, Canada County, NS held by Coastal Community Radio Cooperative Ltd.
Nat'l Reps: Target Broadcast Sales
Population Served: 19,076 *Arbitron Metro Market:* Glace Bay, NS *Format:* Country*Hrs. of News Programming:* news progmg 105 hrs wkly *No. News Employees:* 2 *Target Audience:* 40-65; prime demographic
Karen O'Brien, Operations Dir
Bill MacNeil, General Manager
Rose MacNeil, Promotions Manager
Dave Desveaux, News Director
Dennis Chipman, Music Director

Halifax

***CBH-FM**
06-01-1976; 102.7 mhz FM *Hrs Open:* 24; 81 kw; 711 ft
Box 3000, Halifax, NS B3J 3E9 Canada
(902) 420-8311, *Fax:* (902) 420-4429
www.cbc.ca
weekender@halifax.cbc.ca
License: Halifax, NS held by CBC.
Nat'l Network: CBC Radio One
Format: Variety/Diverse *Target Audience:* General.
Susan Mitton, Operations Dir
Nicole Vautour, Programming Director

***CBHAFM**
01-01-1989; 90.5 mhz FM; kw
CA
(902) 420-8311, *Fax:* (902) 420-4357
www.cbc.ca
mainstreet@halifax.cbc.ca
License: Halifax, NS held by CBC.
Nat'l Network: CBC Radio One
Format: Jazz, News, Variety/Diverse
Susan Mitton, Operations Dir
Nicole Vautour, Programming Director

CHFXFM
02-09-1970; 101.9 mhz FM *Hrs Open:* 24; kw
CA
(902) 422-1651, *Fax:* (902) 422-5330
www.fx1019.ca
rpace@mdradio.com
License: Halifax, NS held by Maritime Broadcasting System Ltd.
Group Owner: Maritime Broadcasting; (acq 6-94)
Wire Services: Broadcast News Ltd.
Format: Country*Hrs. of News Programming:* news progmg 6 hrs wkly *No. News Employees:* 5 *Target Audience:* 25-44.
Robert Pace, CEO
Allan Gidyk, Operations Dir
Ian Kent, General Sales Mgr

CKUL-FM
08-01-1990; 96.5 mhz FM *Hrs Open:* 24; 100 kw
3770 Kempt Rd., Suite 200, Halifax, NS B2X 4X8 Canada
(902) 453-4004, *Fax:* (902) 453-3120
www.kool965fm.ca
thyland@newcap.ca
License: Halifax, NS held by Newcap Inc.
Group Owner: NewCap Inc.; (acq 12-17-2001)
Nat'l Reps: Canadian Broadcast Sales
Format: Oldies*Hrs. of News Programming:* news progmg 3 hrs wkly *No. News Employees:* 3 *Target Audience:* 35-54.
Ted Hyland, General Manager
Rob Johnson, Programming Director
Rich Horner, News Director
Steve Lunn, Chief Engineer

CIOOFM
11-01-1977; 100.1 mhz FM *Hrs Open:* 24; 100 kw; 770 ft; N44 39 05 W63 39 51
2900 Agricola St., Halifax, NS Canada
(902) 453-2524, *Fax:* (902) 453-3120
www.c100.net
License: Halifax, Halifax County, NS held by Bell Media Canada Radio Partnership
Group Owner: Bell Media Inc.

Trent McGrath, Promotions Manager
Rob Davidson, News Director

***CKDU-FM**
02-01-1985; 97.5 mhz FM *Hrs Open:* 24; 3.2 kw; Ant 300 ft
Dalhousie SUB, 6136 University Ave., Halifax, NS B3H 4J2 Canada
(902) 494-6479
www.ckdu.ca
info@ckdu.ca
License: Halifax, NS held by CKDU-FM Society Ltd.
Population Served: 250,000 *Format:* Variety/Diverse*Hrs. of News Programming:* news progmg 4 hrs wkly *No. News Employees:* 1 *Target Audience:* General.
Gianna Lauren, Station Manager
Laura Peek, Programming Director

CBAX-FM
09-01-2003; 91.5 mhz FM; 77.5 kw; N44 39 03 W63 39 28
c/o CBAL-FM, 250 University Ave., Moncton, NB E1C 5K3 Canada
(506) 853-6666, *Fax:* (506) 867-8000
www.espace.mu
License: Halifax, NS held by Societe Radio-Canada.
Population Served: 372,858 *Arbitron Metro Market:* Halifax, NS
Format: Classical, Jazz
Benoit Quennecille, General Manager
Andree Girard, Programming Director

CJNI-FM
10-11-2005; 95.7 mhz FM; 65 kw
6080 Young St., Halifax, NS B3K 5L2 Canada
(902) 493-7133
License: Halifax, NS held by Rogers Broadcasting Ltd.
Group Owner: Rogers Broadcasting Ltd.
Population Served: 390,096 *Arbitron Metro Market:* Halifax, NS
Format: News, News/Talk, Talk
Jim Hamm, General Manager

CKHZ-FM
09-01-2006; 103.5 mhz FM *Hrs Open:* 24; 78 kw; N44 38 47 W63 39 40
Evanov Radio Group, 5302 Dundas St. W., Toronto, ON M9B 1B2 Canada
(416) 213-1035, *Fax:* (416) 233-8617
z103halifax.com
info@z103halifax.com
License: Halifax, NS held by HFX Broadcasting Inc.
Group Owner: Evanov Communications Inc.
Population Served: 94,544 *Arbitron Metro Market:* San Angelo, TX *Format:* Contemporary Hits/Top 40*Adv. Rates:* 100; 100; 100; 100
Al Erickson, President
Ray Lawson, Station Manager

CHNS-FM
07-19-2006; 89.9 mhz FM; 100 kw
5121 Sackville St., 3rd Fl., Suite 300, Halifax, NS B3J 1K1 Canada
(902) 422-1651, *Fax:* (902) 422-5330
www.899HALFM.com
rpace@mradio.com
License: Halifax, NS held by Maritime Broadcasting System Ltd.
Group Owner: Maritime Broadcasting
Population Served: 372,858 *Arbitron Metro Market:* Halifax, NS
Format: Classic Rock *Target Audience:* 25-54; adults
Robert Pace, CEO
Allan Gidyk, Operations Dir
Ian Kent, General Sales Mgr

***CKRH-FM**
09-25-2007; 98.5 mhz FM; 2.35 kw; N44 39 03 W63 39 28
5527 Cogswell St., Halifax, NS B3J 1R2 Canada
(902) 490-2574, *Fax:* (902) 429-2574
www.ckrhfm.ca
info@ckrhfm.com
License: Halifax, NS held by Cooperative Radio-Halifax-Metro limitee.
Population Served: 372,858 *Arbitron Metro Market:* Halifax, NS
Format: French *No. News Employees:* 3
Nay Saade, General Manager

CJCH-FM
05-30-2008; 101.3 mhz FM *Hrs Open:* 24; 100 kw; N44 38 47 W63 39 37
2900 Agricola St., Halifax, NS B3K 6B2 Canada
(902) 453-2524, *Fax:* (902) 453-3120,(902) 453-3132
www.1013thebounce.com
License: Halifax, NS held by Bell Media Canada Radio Partnership
Group Owner: Bell Media Inc.

Bob Basile, Programming Director

CKHY-FM
02-26-2012; 105.1 mhz FM; 100 kw; 185.1 meters
5527 Cogswell Street, Halifax, NS B3J 1R2 Canada
(902) 429-1035, *Fax:* (902) 425-8637
www.live105.ca
License: Halifax, NS held by HFX Broadcasting Inc
Format: Rock/AOR

Kentville

CKEN-FM
03-14-1965; 97.7 mhz FM; 18 kw; Ant 680 ft
Mailing Address: 29 Oakdene Ave., Box 310, Kentville, NS B4N 1H5 Canada
Second Address: 29 Oakdene Ave., Kentville, NS B4N 1H5
(902) 678-2111, *Fax:* (902) 678-9894
www.avrnetwork.com
avr@avrnetwork.com
License: Kentville, NS held by Maritime Broadcasting System Ltd.
Group Owner: Maritime Broadcasting; (acq 1998; grpsl).
Nat'l Reps: Canadian Broadcast Sales
Format: Country*Special Programming:* Farm 5 hrs wkly *No. News Employees:* 5 *Target Audience:* 18-49.
Mike Mitchell, Operations Dir
Dianne Best, General Manager
Karen Corey, General Sales Mgr
Amanda Misner, Programming Director
Matthew Povah, Chief Engineer

***CKWMFM**
01-01-2003; 97.7 mhz FM; kw
Mailing Address: CA
Second Address: 29 Oakdene Ave., Kentville, NS B4N 1H5
(902) 678-2111, *Fax:* (902) 678-9894
www.magic949.ca
magic949@magic949.ca
License: Kentville, NS held by Maritime Broadcasting System Ltd.
Group Owner: Maritime Broadcasting
Arbitron Metro Market: Kentville, NS *Format:* Adult Contemp
Mike Mitchell, Operations Dir
Dianne Best, General Manager
Karen Corey, General Sales Mgr
Matthew Povah, Chief Engineer

CIJK-FM
89.3 mhz FM; 9.9 kw; N45 12 12 W64 24 03
8794 Commercial St., Suite 3, New Minas, NS B4N 3C5 Canada
(902) 365-8930, *Fax:* (902) 365-3566
www.k-rock893.com
info@893krock.com
License: Kentville, NS held by Newcap Inc.
Group Owner: NewCap Inc.
Population Served: 5,815 *Arbitron Metro Market:* Kentville, NS
Format: Classic Rock *No. News Employees:* 1 *Target Audience:* 24-54.
Will MacKay, Sales Manager
Curtis Bray, Programming Director
Matt Slaney, Promotions Manager
Dave Chaulk, News Director
Kathryn Fowler, Administrative Assistant
Tony Levy, Creative Copy Director

Micmac

CIPU-FM
10-07-2012; 97.1 mhz FM; 50 watts; 23 meters
522 Church Street, Micmac, NS B0N 1W0 Canada
(902) 236-3636, *Fax:* (902) 758-3637
www.shubiefm.com
shubiefm@gmail.com
License: Micmac, NS held by Shubenacadie Band Council First Nation
Russell Randall Julian, General Manager

Middleton

CKAD
01-01-1962; 1350 khz AM
CA
(902) 678-2111, *Fax:* (902) 678-9894
www.avrnetwork.com
programming@avrnetwork.com
License: Middleton, NS held by Maritime Broadcasting.
Group Owner: Maritime Broadcasting; acq 6-26-79)
Format: Country*Special Programming:* Farm 3 hrs wkly
Mike Mitchell, Operations Dir
Dianne Best, General Manager
Karen Corey, General Sales Mgr
Amanda Misner, Programming Director
Dave Chaulk, News Director
Matthew Povah, Chief Engineer

New Glasgow

CKEC-FM
12-11-2007; 94.1 mhz FM *Hrs Open:* 24; 36.68 kw; N45 32 24 W62 56 44
Mailing Address: Box 519, 84 Provost Street, New Glasgow, NS B2H 5E7 Canada
Second Address: 84 Provost St., New Glasgow, NS B2H 5E7
(902) 752-4200, *Fax:* (902) 755-2468
ckec941.ca
info@ecfm.ca
License: New Glasgow, NS held by Hector Broadcasting Co. Ltd.
Nat'l Network: BN Audio *Nat'l Reps:* Canadian Broadcast Sales
Wire Services: BN Wire
Population Served: 20,876 *Arbitron Metro Market:* New Glasgow, NS *Format:* Adult Contemp*Special Programming:* Scottish*Hrs. of News Programming:* news progmg 15 hrs wkly *No. News Employees:* 3 *Target Audience:* General.
Douglas Freeman, CEO
Michael Freeman, Vice President
Ann MacGregor, Music Director
Lynn MacDonald, Accountant / Office Manager
Tom Buffett, Sales Coordinator
Barbara Weir, Account Executive
Eileen Stinson, Account Executive
Ryan Mader, Creative Director

New Tusket

CJLS-FM-2
01-01-1982; 93.5 mhz FM; 3 kw*Rebroadcasts:* Rebroadcasts CJLS-FM Yarmouth
328 Main St., Suite 201, Yarmouth, NS B5A 1E4 Canada
(902) 742-7175, *Fax:* (902) 742-3143
www.cjls.com
cjls@cjls.com
License: New Tusket, NS held by Radio CJLS Ltd.
Format: Adult Contemp
Ray Zinck, President
Chris Perry, Operations Dir
Dave Hall, General Sales Mgr
Gary Nickerson, News Director
Jim Harris, Engineering Dir

Pictou

CKEZ-FM
97.9 mhz FM
Box 519, New Glasglow, NS B2H 5E7 Canada
(902) 752-4200, *Fax:* (902) 755-2468
License: Pictou, NS held by Hector Broadcasting Co Ltd

Port Hawkesbury

CIGO-FM
01-01-2000; 101.5 mhz FM; 19 kw; N45 39 00 W61 28 00
609 Church St., Ste 201, Port Hawkesbury, NS B9A 2X4 Canada
(902) 625-1220, *Fax:* (902) 625-2664
www.1015thehawk.com
1015thehawk@1015thehawk.com
License: Port Hawkesbury, Inverness County, NS held by MacEachern Broadcasting Ltd.
Wire Services: BN Wire
Population Served: 3,366 *Arbitron Metro Market:* Port Hawkesbury, NS *Format:* Adult Contemp*Special Programming:* East Coast 3 hrs, Scottish 1 hrs, Irish one hr wkl*Hrs. of News Programming:* news progmg 4 hrswkly *No. News Employees:* 2 *Target Audience:* 18-49; blue collar, high school education, married
Bob MacEachern, President
Bob MacEachern, General Manager
Kevin MacEachern, Sales Manager
Kelly MacMillan, Programming Director
Denise Sampson, Promotions Manager
Greg Morrow, News/Sports Director
Scott Oakley, Music Director

Spryfield

CIRP-FM
05-22-2011; 94.7 mhz FM
C/O City Church Halifax, 276 Herring Cove Road, Halifax, NS B3P 1M1 Canada
(902) 479-5433
www.life947.com
License: Spryfield, NS held by City Church Halifax
Format: Christian

Sydney

CBI
11-01-1948; 1140 khz AM
CA
(902) 539-5050, *Fax:* (902) 539-1562
www.cbc.ca/ns
License: Sydney, NS held by CBC.
Nat'l Network: CBC Radio One
Format: Public Affairs, News
Kathy Large, Programming Director

CBI-FM
07-01-1977; 105.1 mhz FM; 20 kw; 400 ft
285 Alexandra St., Sydney, NS B1S 2E8 Canada
(902) 539-5050, *Fax:* (902) 539-1562
www.cbc.ca/ns
License: Sydney, NS held by CBC
Nat'l Network: CBC Radio Two
Format: Adult Contemp, Contemporary Hits/Top 40
Kathy Large, Programming Director

CJCB
02-14-1929; 1270 khz AM *Hrs Open:* 24
CA
(902) 564-5596, *Fax:* (902) 564-1057
www.capebretonradio.com
info@cjcb.com
License: Sydney, NS held by Maritime Broadcasting System Ltd.
Group Owner: Maritime Broadcasting
Format: Country *No. News Employees:* 3 *Target Audience:* General.
Rod Deviller, Operations Dir
Alan Peddle, General Sales Mgr
Phil Thompson, Promotions Manager
Roy MacIntosh, Chief Engineer

CKPE-FM
09-01-1962; 94.9 mhz FM *Hrs Open:* 24; 61 kw; 210 ft
Radio Bldg., 318 Charlotte St., Sydney, NS B1P 1C8 Canada
(902) 564-5596, *Fax:* (902) 564-1873
949thecape.com
info@ckpe.com
License: Sydney, NS held by Maritime Broadcasting System Ltd.
Group Owner: Maritime Broadcasting
Population Served: 109,000 *Format:* Contemporary Hits/Top 40 *No. News Employees:* 3
Joe Purdy, Programming Director
Phil Thompson, Promotions Manager
Roy MacIntosh, Chief Engineer

CJIJ-FM
06-02-2003; 99.9 mhz FM; 50 w; N46 07 01 W60 11 40
Mailing Address: Membertou Radio, 111 Membertou St., Membertou, NS B1S 2M9 Canada
Second Address: 1969 Upper Water St., Suite 1703, Tower II, Purdy's Wharf, Halifax, NS B3J 3R7
(902) 562-0009, *Fax:* (902) 539-6645
c99@membertou.ca
License: Sydney, Cape Breton County, NS held by Membertou Radio Association Inc.
Population Served: 31,597 *Arbitron Metro Market:* Sydney, NS
Format: Classic Rock, Adult Contemp
Jeff Slivocka, CEO
Dawn Wells, General Manager

CHER-FM
01-01-2007; 98.3 mhz FM; 100 kw
318 Charlotte St., Sydney, NS B1P 1C8 Canada
(902) 564-5596, *Fax:* (902) 564-1873
www.capebretonradio.com
info@cherfm.com
License: Sydney, NS held by Maritime Broadcasting System Ltd.
Group Owner: Maritime Broadcasting
Nat'l Reps: Canadian Broadcast Sales
Population Served: 31,597 *Arbitron Metro Market:* Sydney, NS
Format: Contemporary Hits/Top 40, Adult Contemp *No. News Employees:* 3
Fred Denney, Operations Dir
Alan Peddle, General Manager
Phil Thompson, Programming Director
Gary Andrea, News Director
Roy MacIntosh, Chief Engineer

CKCH-FM
06-20-2008; 103.5 mhz FM; 26.5 kw; N46 05 55 W60 18 41
5 Dethridge Dr., Sydney River, NS B1L 1B8 Canada
(902) 563-1035, *Fax:* (902) 270-3566
www.eagle1035.com
reception@eagle1035.com
License: Sydney, NS held by 3221809 Nova Scotia Ltd.
Population Served: 31,597 *Arbitron Metro Market:* Sydney, NS
Format: Country
Dave Newbury, General Manager
Jay Bedford, Programming Director
Jay McNeil, News Director

Truro

*CKTOFM
01-01-1965; 100.9 mhz FM *Hrs Open:* 24; kw
CA
(902) 893-6060, *Fax:* (902) 893-7771
www.bigdog1009.ca
trurecption@astral.com
License: Truro, NS held by Astral Media Radio Atlantic Inc.
Group Owner: Astral Media Inc.; (acq 4-19-2002; grpsl).
Nat'l Reps: Canadian Broadcast Sales
Format: Adult Contemp*Hrs. of News Programming:* news progmg 6 hrs wkly *No. News Employees:* 3 *Target Audience:* 25-49.
John Eddy, President
Mike Worsley, Station Manager
James Cormier, Programming Director
Tim Tucker, News Director
Victor Deveau, Chief Engineer
James Cormier, Music Director

CKTY-FM
01-01-2001; 99.5 mhz FM; 16.75 kw
187 Industrial Ave., Truro, NS B2N 6V3 Canada
(902) 893-6060, *Fax:* (902) 893-7771
www.catcountry995.ca
mworsley@astral.com
License: Truro, NS held by Astral Media Radio Atlantic Inc.
Group Owner: Astral Media Inc.; (acq 4-19-2002; grpsl).
Nat'l Reps: Canadian Broadcast Sales
Population Served: 7,847 *Arbitron Metro Market:* Newcastle, OK
Format: Country
John Eddy, President
Mike Worsley, General Sales Mgr
Chris Van Tassel, Programming Director
Rob De Viller, Music Director
Shaunna Mowatt-Densmore, Advertising Sales Representative
Misti Lamont, Advertising Sales Representative
Alanna Graham, Advertising Sales Representative
Glenn Baker, Advertising Sales Representative
Matthew Mossman, Advertising Sales Representative

CINU-FM
01-01-2004; 98.5 mhz FM; 50 w
Mailing Address: 217 Harmony Ridge Rd, Harmony, NS B6L 3P4 Canada
Second Address: 883 Prince St., Truro, NS B2N 1H2
(902) 843-4673, *Fax:* (902) 662-2879
www.hoperadio.ca
barry@hoperadio.ca
License: Truro, NS held by Hope FM Ministries Ltd.
Population Served: 12,059 *Arbitron Metro Market:* Truro, NS
Format: Christian
Barry Reid, President

Windsor

CFAB
01-01-1945; 1450 khz AM *Hrs Open:* 24
CA
(902) 798-2111, *Fax:* (902) 798-8140
www.avrnetwork.com
avr@avrnetwork.com
License: Windsor, NS held by Maritime Broadcasting System Ltd.
Group Owner: Maritime Broadcasting
Format: Country*Hrs. of News Programming:* news progmg 9 hrs wkly *No. News Employees:* 5 *Target Audience:* 25-54.
Mike Mitchell, Operations Dir
Dianne Best, General Manager
Karen Corey, General Sales Mgr
Amanda Misner, Programming Director
Dave Chaulk, News Director
Matthew Povah, Chief Engineer

Nunavut

Baker Lake

CKQN-FM
01-01-1973; 99.3 mhz FM; 60 w; -50 ft
Box 13, Baker Lake, NU X0C 0A0 Canada
(867) 793-2962, *Fax:* (867-793-2726)
www.tvradioworld.com
License: Baker Lake, NU held by Qamani'tuap Naalautaa Society.
Nat'l Network: CBC Radio One
Format: Ethnic
Eva Elytuk, President

Iqaluit

CFRT-FM
01-01-1994; 107.3 mhz FM; 27 w
C.P. 880, Iqaluit, NU X0A 0H0 Canada
(867) 979-4606, *Fax:* (867) 979-0800
www.franconunavut.ca
cfrt@nunafranc.ca
License: Iqaluit, NU held by Association des francophones de Nunavut.
Population Served: 6,699 *Arbitron Metro Market:* Iqaluit, NU
Format: French
R,jean C"t,, CEO
Daniel Cuerrier, General Manager
Sabrina Bertrand, Programming Director

Rankin Inlet

CBQR-FM
01-01-1988; 105.1 mhz FM *Hrs Open:* 24; 87 w
Box 130, Rankin Inlet, NU X0C 0G0 Canada
(867) 645-2244, *Fax:* (867) 645-2820
www.north.cbc.ca
License: Rankin Inlet, NU held by CBC Radio.
Nat'l Network: CBC Radio One
Format: Adult Contemp, Talk, Variety/Diverse*Special Programming:* Inuktitut 10 hrs wkly
Patrick Nagle, General Sales Mgr
Selma Eccles, Programming Director
Fiona Christensen, News Director

Ontario

Ajax

***CJKX-FM**
01-01-1994; 95.9 mhz FM *Hrs Open:* 24; kw
CA
(905) 571-0949, *Fax:* (905) 571-1150
www.kx96.fm
kx96@kx96.fm
License: Ajax, ON held by Durham Radio Inc.
Group Owner: Durham Radio Inc.
Format: Country*Hrs. of News Programming:* news progmg 1.5 hrs wkly *No. News Employees:* 3 *Target Audience:* 25-54;*Adv. Rates:* 141; 110; 125; 35
Douglas Kirk, President
Steve Kassay, Operations Dir
Steve Macaulay, General Sales Mgr
Steve Kassay, Programming Director
Natalie Fournier, Promotions Manager

Akwesasne

CKON-FM
10-01-1984; 97.3 mhz FM; 150 w; 150 ft
Mailing Address: Box 140, Rooseveltown, NY 13683 Canada
Second Address: Box 1496, Akwesasne, ON K6H 5V5
(613) 575-2100, *Fax:* (613) 575-2566
www.ckonfm.com
ckon@yahoo.com
License: Akwesasne, ON held by Mohawk Nation Council.
Format: Variety/Diverse*Special Programming:* Mohawk *Target Audience:* General.
Larry Edwards, General Manager
Judy Laffin, General Manager

Apsley

CFSH-FM
92.9 mhz FM; 50 w; N44 45 54 W78 05 27
Attn: John Trotter, 299 McFadden Rd., Apsley, ON K0L 1A0 Canada
(705) 656-1510, *Fax:* (705) 656-1510
www.fish929.com
License: Apsley, ON held by Apsley Community Chapel.
Population Served: 324 *Arbitron Metro Market:* Apsley, ON
Format: Christian
Joseph Cormier, President

Aylmer

CHPD-FM
09-01-2003; 105.9 mhz FM *Hrs Open:* 7 AM- 8 AM; 5 PM- 8 PM; 250 w; N42 45 40 W80 56 03
16 Talbot St., Aylmer, ON N5H 1H4 Canada
(519) 773-8555, *Fax:* (519) 773-8606
www.mcson.org
radio@debrigj.org
License: Aylmer, Elgin County, ON held by Mennonite Community Services.
Population Served: 15,000*Hrs. of News Programming:* news progmg one hr wkly *No. News Employees:* 1 *Target Audience:* 5-70; Low German newcomers
Abe Harder, Chairman
Abe Harms, CEO
Abe Harder, Operations Dir
Abe Harms, Station Manager
Jake Wall, Station Manager

Bancroft

CHMS-FM
05-01-2001; 97.7 mhz FM *Hrs Open:* 24; 50 kw
Box 1240, Bancroft, ON K0L 1C0 Canada
(613) 332-1423, *Fax:* (613) 332-0841
www.moosefm.com
moose977@hbgradio.com
License: Bancroft, Hastings County, ON held by The Haliburton Broadcasting Group Inc.
Group Owner: Haliburton Broadcasting Group Inc.
Population Served: 3,880 *Arbitron Metro Market:* Bancroft, ON
Format: Contemporary Hits/Top 40 *Target Audience:* General.
Wendy Gray, Operations Dir
Renzo Rosati, General Manager
Chris Nimigon, National Sales Manager
Steve Scally, News Director
Karen Bonokoski, Operations Support

Barrie

CFJB-FM
10-07-1988; 95.7 mhz FM *Hrs Open:* 24; 41 kw; Ant 500 ft
431 Huronia Rd. Canada
(705) 725-7304, *Fax:* (705) 792-7858
www.rock95.com
dbingley@rock95.com
License: Barrie, ON held by Rock 95 Broadcasting (Barrie-Orillia) Ltd.
Population Served: 280,000 *Format:* Classic Rock*Hrs. of News Programming:* news progmg 4 hrs wkly *No. News Employees:* 3 *Target Audience:* 18-49; broad-based, well-educated, above-average income
Doug Bingley, CEO
Tom Manton, General Sales Mgr
Dave Carr, Programming Director
Todd Palmer, Promotions Manager

***CHAYFM**
05-21-1977; 93.1 mhz FM *Hrs Open:* 24; kw
CA
(705) 737-3511, *Fax:* (705) 737-0603
www.fm93.ca/home/
knoel@corusent.com
License: Barrie, Simcoe County, ON held by Corus Radio Co.
Group Owner: Corus Entertainment Inc.
Format: Adult Contemp*Hrs. of News Programming:* news progmg 13 hrs wkly *No. News Employees:* 3 *Target Audience:* 25-64; general
John Hayes, President
Kim Noel, General Manager
Frank Allinson, General Sales Mgr
Derrick Scott, Programming Director
Dave Pinder, Promotions Manager

CIQB-FM
11-01-1994; 101.1 mhz FM *Hrs Open:* 24; 4.3 kw
Mailing Address: 1125 Bayfield St. N., Box 101, Barrie, ON L4M 4S9 Canada
Second Address: 1125 Bayfield St. N., Barrie, ON L4M 4S9
(705) 726-1011, *Fax:* (705) 726-0022
www.b101fm.com
general@b101fm.com
License: Barrie, ON held by Corus Entertainment, Inc.
Group Owner: Corus Entertainment Inc.; (acq 3-24-2000; grpsl).
Format: Adult Contemp*Hrs. of News Programming:* news progmg 11 hrs wkly *No. News Employees:* 3 *Target Audience:* 25-54; women 35-49 & 25-54 & at work people*Adv. Rates:* 80; 75; 70; 40
John Hayes, President
JJ Johson, General Manager
Mike Patterson, General Sales Mgr
Deb James, Programming Director
Paul Stoutenburg, Promotions Manager
Ian Maclennan, News Director

CJLF-FM
08-15-1999; 100.3 mhz FM; 18.7 kw
115 Bell Farm Rd, Unit 111, Barrie, ON L4M 5G1 Canada
(705) 735-3370, *Fax:* (705) 735-3301
www.lifeonline.fm
License: Barrie, ON held by Trust Communications Ministries.
Scott Jackson, President
Scott Jackson, Station Manager
Cathy Faubert, General Sales Mgr
Steve Jones, Programming Director
Jen Melanson, Promotions Manager
Tim Maaserany, News Director

CKMB
01-01-2006; 107.7 mhz FM *Hrs Open:* 24; kw
CA
(705) 725-7304, *Fax:* (705) 792-7858
www.1075koolfm.com
tmanton@bmts.com
License: Barrie, ON held by Rock 95 Broadcasting (Barrie-Orillia) Ltd.
Arbitron Metro Market: Barrie, ON *Format:* Contemporary Hits/Top 40
Doug Bingley, CEO
Tom Manton, General Sales Mgr
Dave Carr, Programming Director
Helen Mathers, Promotions Manager

Belleville

***CIGLFM**
08-01-1962; 97.1 mhz FM *Hrs Open:* 24; kw
Mailing Address: CA
Second Address: Box 488, Belleville, ON K8N 5B2
(613) 969-5555, *Fax:* (613) 969-8122
www.mix97.com
License: Belleville, ON held by Quinte Broadcasting, LTD
Group Owner: Quinte Broadcasting Ltd.
Format: Adult Contemp
Jody Brooker, General Sales Mgr
Sean Kelly, Programming Director

CJBQ
08-12-1946; 800 khz AM *Hrs Open:* 24
Mailing Address: CA
Second Address: 10 S. Front St., Belleville, ON K8N2Y3
(613) 969-5555, *Fax:* (613) 969-8122
www.cjbq.com
quinte@broadcasting.com
License: Belleville, ON held by Quinte Broadcasting Ltd.
Group Owner: Quinte Broadcasting Ltd.
Format: Country, Talk*Special Programming:* Farm 3 hrs wkly
Bill Morton, General Manager
Jody Brooker, General Sales Mgr
Sean Kelly, Programming Director

CJLX
10-01-1992; 91.3 mhz FM *Hrs Open:* 24; kw
CA
(613) 966-0923, *Fax:* (613) 966-1993
www.91x.fm
contact@91x.fm
License: Belleville, Hastings County, ON held by Loyalist College Radio Inc.
Nat'l Reps: Target Broadcast Sales *Wire Services:* BN Wire
Format: Rock/AOR, Public Affairs*Special Programming:* Folk one hr, jazz 3 hrs, Greek one hr, class 2 hr*Hrs. of News Programming:* news progmg 6 hrs wkly *No. News Employees:* 15 *Target Audience:* 18-34; primary,ages 50 plus secondary*Adv. Rates:* 11; 9; 11; 8
Greg Schatzmann, CEO
Sandi Ramsey, General Sales Mgr
Len Arminio, News Director
Tim Rorabeck, Chief Engineer

CJOJ-FM
12-01-1993; 95.5 mhz FM *Hrs Open:* 24; 42 kw
497 Dundas St. W., Belleville, ON K8P 1B6 Canada
(613) 966-0955, *Fax:* (613) 967-2565
www.classichits955.fm
news@classichits955.fm
License: Belleville, Canada County, ON held by Starboard Communications Ltd.
Nat'l Reps: CHUM Radio Sales
Population Served: 105,000 *Format:* Contemporary Hits/Top 40, Adult Contemp *No. News Employees:* 4 *Target Audience:* 25-54; adults-skewed females 60%, males 40%*Adv. Rates:* 35; 27; 22; 15
John Sherratt, President
Darren Matassa, General Sales Mgr
Paul Ferguson, Programming Director
Cole Nayler, Promotions Manager
Paul Martin, News Director

CHCQ-FM
01-01-2001; 100.1 mhz FM *Hrs Open:* 24; 21 kw
497 Dundas Street West, Belleville, ON K8P 1B6 Canada

(613) 771-0100, *Fax:* (613) 967-2565
www.cool100.fm
darrenm@cool100.ca
License: Belleville, ON held by Starboard Communications Ltd.
Nat'l Reps: CHUM Radio Sales
Population Served: 49,454 *Arbitron Metro Market:* Belleville, ON
Format: Country *No. News Employees:* 4 *Target Audience:* 25-54; adults
John Sherratt, President
Darren Matassa, General Sales Mgr
Mark Philbin, Programming Director
Cole Nayler, Promotions Manager
Tracy Struthers, Senior Account Executive
Sandi Wight, Marketing Specialist

Norah Nelson, MarketingSpecialist
Tracy Patrick, Marketing Specialist
Sharon Fisher, Traffic Manager

CKJJ-FM
10-18-2003; 102.3 mhz FM *Hrs Open:* 24; 45 kw
Mailing Address: Box 23095, Belleville, ON K8P 5J3 Canada
Second Address: 214 Pinnacle St., Belleville, ON K8P 3A6
(613) 966-4822, *Fax:* (613) 966-3211
www.ucbcanada.com
j.hunt@ucbcanada.com
License: Belleville, ON held by United Christian Broadcasters Canada.
Population Served: 49,454 *Arbitron Metro Market:* Belleville, ON
James Hunt, COO
Sean Belfry, Sales Manager
Brad Linnard, Programming Director
James Hunt, Executive Director
Hali Foster, Finance Manager
Anita Geertsma, Traffic Manager
Todd Purvis, Sales Associate
Annette Eastcott, FinanceAssistant
Liz Bozier-Lown, Marketing and Design Coordinator

Bolton

CJFB-FM
03-21-2008; 105.5 mhz FM *Hrs Open:* 24/7; 50 w; N43 52 46 W79 44 18
30 Martha St., Ste. 210, Bolton, ON L7E 5V1 Canada
(905) 951-2899
www.caledonmedia.com
License: Bolton, Canada County, ON held by Rick Sargent.
Population Served: 25,954 *Arbitron Metro Market:* Bolton, ON
Format: Adult Contemp
Rick Sargent, General Manager

Bracebridge

CFBG-FM
05-01-1988; 99.5 mhz FM; 12 kw
Box 960, Haliburton, ON K0M 1S0 Canada
(705) 645-2218, *Fax:* (705) 645-6957
www.hbgradio.com
moose995@hbgradio.com
License: Bracebridge, ON held by The Haliburton Broadcasting Group Inc.
Group Owner: Haliburton Broadcasting Group Inc.; (acq 12-10-97; C$295,000)
Format: Adult Contemp*Special Programming:* Jazz 2 hrs, big band one hr, loc magazine one hr w *Target Audience:* 34-45; older adult contemporary
Christopher Grossman, President
Kimberley Ward, Operations Dir
Sean Connon, General Sales Mgr
Wendy Gray, Operations Manager

Brampton

***CFNYFM**
08-08-1960; 102.1 mhz FM *Hrs Open:* 24; kw
CA
(416) 408-3343, *Fax:* (416) 847-3300
www.edge.ca
License: Brampton, ON held by Corus Radio Co.
Group Owner: Corus Entertainment Inc.; (acq 1995; C$16.75 million)
Nat'l Reps: Canadian Broadcast Sales
Format: Rock/AOR, Alternative*Hrs. of News Programming:* news progmg 3 hrs wkly *No. News Employees:* 2 *Target Audience:* 18-34; self motivated, mus loving, active, young at heart people
Heather Shaw, Chairman
John Cassaday, CEO
Chris Sisam, General Manager
Alan Cross, Programming Director
Tom Peddie, CFO

CIAO
12-23-1953; 790 khz AM *Hrs Open:* 24
CA
(416) 213-1035, *Fax:* (416) 233-8617
www.am530.ca
info@am530.ca
License: Brampton, ON held by CKMW Radio Ltd.
Group Owner: Evanov Communications Inc.; (acq 9-26-83).
Nat'l Reps: Target Broadcast Sales
Format: Ethnic*Adv. Rates:* 100; 100; 100; 100
Bill Evanov, President
Paul Evanov, Executive Vice President

Brantford

CKPC
12-01-1923; 1380 khz AM *Hrs Open:* 24
CA
(519) 759-1000, *Fax:* (519) 753-1470
www.jewel92.com
salesmgr@ckpc.on.ca
License: Brantford, ON held by Telephone City Broadcast Ltd.
Nat'l Reps: Target Broadcast Sales
Format: Contemporary Hits/Top 40, Adult Contemp*Hrs. of News Programming:* news progmg 9 hrs wkly *No. News Employees:* 7 *Target Audience:* 35-64.
Mike Rose, Operations Dir
Randy Reddem, General Sales Mgr
Wendy Rose, Promotions Manager
Warren Beck, News Director

***CKPCFM**
05-01-1949; 92.1 mhz FM *Hrs Open:* 24; kw
CA
(519) 759-1000, *Fax:* (519) 753-1470
www.jewel92.com
salesmgr@ckpc.on.ca
License: Brantford, Brant County, ON held by Telephone City Broadcast Ltd.
Nat'l Reps: Target Broadcast Sales
Format: Adult Contemp*Hrs. of News Programming:* news progmg 7 hrs wkly *No. News Employees:* 7 *Target Audience:* 25-49.
Geoff Stirling, Chairman
Scott Stirling, CEO
Mike Rose, Operations Dir
Doug Neal, General Manager
Randy Reddem, General Sales Mgr
Wendy Rose, Promotions Manager
Warren Beck, News Director
Frank Collins, CFO
MauriceFitzgerald, Music Director

CFWC-FM
01-01-2002; 93.9 mhz FM; 250 w
271 Greenwich St., Brantford, ON N3S 2X9 Canada
(519) 759-2339, *Fax:* (519) 753-1157
www.power93.ca
vicki@power93.ca
License: Brantford, ON held by 1486781 Ontario Ltd.
Format: Christian
Vicki Schleifer, Station Manager
Luke Schleifer, Programming Director

Brockville

CJPT-FM
07-28-1988; 103.7 mhz FM *Hrs Open:* 24; 100 kw; Ant 495 ft; N44 23 58 W75 58 21
601 Stewart Blvd., Brockville, ON K6V 5V9 Canada
(613) 345-1666, *Fax:* (613) 342-2438
www.bob.fm
info@bob.fm
License: Brockville, ON held by Bell Media Ontario Regional Radio
Group Owner: Bell Media Inc.; (acq 6-22-2007; grpsl)
No. News Employees: 3 *Target Audience:* 18-44; male
Paul Ski, President
Greg Hinton, General Manager
Rick Moran, General Sales Mgr
Dan Wylie, Programming Director
Greg Zehr, Promotions Manager

CFJR-FM
01-01-2003; 104.9 mhz FM *Hrs Open:* 24; 5.6 kw
601 Stewart Blvd., Brockville, ON K6V 5V9 Canada
(613) 345-1666, *Fax:* (613) 342-2438
www.hometownradio.ca
comments@hometownradio.ca
License: Brockville, ON held by Bell Media Ontario Regional Radio
Group Owner: CTV Inc.; (acq 6-22-2007; grpsl)
Hrs. of News Programming: news progmg 5 hrs wkly *No. News Employees:* 3 *Target Audience:* 35-54; female slant
Greg Hinton, General Manager
Rick Moran, General Sales Mgr
Dan Wylie, Programming Director
Warren Davies, Chief Engineer

CHXL
06-01-2003; 103.7 mhz FM; kw
CA
(306) 334-3331, *Fax:* (306) 334-2545
info@chxlfm.com
License: Brockville, ON held by O.K. Creek Radio Station Inc.
Arbitron Metro Market: Balcarres, SK *Format:* Variety/Diverse
William Yuzicapi, Station Manager

Burlington

CJXY-FM
09-23-1976; 107.9 mhz FM *Hrs Open:* 24; 26.4 kw; Ant 672 ft; N43 23 12 W79 52 34
875 Main St. West, Hamilton, ON L8S 4R1 Canada
(905) 521-9900, *Fax:* (905) 540-2452
www.y108.ca
jim.mccourtie@corusent.com
License: Burlington, ON held by Corus Radio Co.
Group Owner: Corus Entertainment Inc.
Format: Rock/AOR*Hrs. of News Programming:* news progmg 2 hrs wkly *No. News Employees:* 1 *Target Audience:* 25-39.
Suzanne Carpenter, General Manager
Michael Cassar, General Sales Mgr
Jim McCourtie, Programming Director
Olivia DePetris, Promotions Manager
Jeff Storey, News Director

***CINGFM**
09-14-1964; 107.9 mhz FM *Hrs Open:* 24; kw
Mailing Address: CA
Second Address: 875 Main St. W., Suite 900, Hamilton, ON L8S 4R1
(905) 521-9900, *Fax:* (905) 521-1691
www.vinyl953.com
License: Burlington, ON held by Corus Premium Television Ltd.
Group Owner: Corus Entertainment Inc.
Nat'l Reps: Canadian Broadcast Sales
Format: Country *Target Audience:* 25-54; female
Michael Cassar, General Sales Mgr
Jim McCourtie, Programming Director
Olivia DePetris, Promotions Manager
Ted Townsend, Engineering Dir
Rick Walters, Music Director

Cambridge

CJDV-FM
01-01-1998; 107.5 mhz FM *Hrs Open:* 24; kw
CA
(519) 621-7510, *Fax:* (519) 621-0165
www.davefm.com
lars@davefm.com
License: Cambridge, Waterloo County, ON held by 591989 B.C. Ltd.
Group Owner: Corus Entertainment Inc.; (acq 4-2000; grpsl).
Format: Adult Contemp*Special Programming:* Por 2 hrs wkly *No. News Employees:* 2 *Target Audience:* 18-49.
Lars Wunsche, General Manager
Scott Turner, Programming Director
Patrick Olsen, Promotions Manager
Brian Clemens, Chief Engineer

Cape Croker (Neyaashiinigmiing)

CHFN-FM
01-01-2003; 100.1 mhz FM *Hrs Open:* 24; 72 w
RR 5, Wiarton, ON N0H 2T0 Canada
(519) 534-1003, *Fax:* (519) 534-4916
www.nawash.ca/chfn
chfnradio_station@yahoo.ca
License: Cape Croker (Neyaashiinigmiing), ON held by Jessica Nadjiwon, on behalf of a non-profit corporation to be incorporated.
Population Served: 591 *Arbitron Metro Market:* Neyaashiinigmiing, ON *Format:* Ethnic, News*Hrs. of News Programming:* News progmg 12 hrs wkly *Target Audience:* 18-65; progmg is div
Jake Linklater, President
Peter Akiwenzie, Operations Dir
Jessica Nadjiwon, General Manager
Johnathan Pedoniquotte, Programming Director
Beedahsega Elliott, Promotions Manager

Chatham

CFCO
01-01-1926; 630 khz AM *Hrs Open:* 24
Mailing Address: CA
Second Address: 117 Keil Dr. S., Chatham, ON N7M 5K1
(519) 354-2853, *Fax:* (519) 354-2880
www.630cfco.com
info@630cfco.com
License: Chatham, ON held by Blackburn Groupe, Inc
Group Owner: Blackburn Group Inc.; (acq 3-20-97)
Regional Reps: Rgnl Reps
Format: Country*Special Programming:* Farm 3 hrs, gospel 2 hrs wkly*Hrs. of News Programming:* news progmg 6 hrs wkly *No. News Employees:* 6 *Target Audience:* 35 plus.
Carl Veroba, CEO
Doug Kirk, Operations Dir
Jenna Herdman, Promotions Manager
Walter Ploegman, Operations Manager

CKUE-FM
07-01-1986; 95.1 mhz FM *Hrs Open:* 24; kw
Mailing Address: CA
Second Address: 117 Keil Dr. S., Chatham, ON N7M 5K1
(519) 354-2200, *Fax:* (519) 354-2880
www.canadasrock.ca
info@canadasrock.ca
License: Chatham, Chatham/Kent County, ON held by Blackburn Group, Inc
Group Owner: Blackburn Group Inc.
Format: Rock/AOR *No. News Employees:* 2 *Target Audience:* 18-49.
Carl Veroba, CEO
Doug Kirk, Operations Dir
Walter Ploegman, Programming Director
Jenna Herdman, Promotions Manager
Ron Wilken, Chief Engineer
Justin Oliphant, Promotions Director

*CKSYFM
07-01-1986; 95.1 mhz FM *Hrs Open:* 24; kw
Mailing Address: CA
Second Address: 117 Keil Dr. S., Chatham, ON N7M 5K1
(519) 354-2200, *Fax:* (519) 354-2880
www.943cksy.com
info@cksyfm
License: Chatham, Kent County, ON held by Blackburn Group, Inc.
Group Owner: Blackburn Group Inc.
Format: Adult Contemp*Special Programming:* Gospel 2 hrs wkly*Hrs. of News Programming:* news progmg 5 hrs wkly *No. News Employees:* 5 *Target Audience:* 18-54.
Doug Kirk, Operations Dir
Walter Ploegman, General Manager
Ron Blommers, General Sales Mgr
Jay Poole, Programming Director
Jenna Herdman, Promotions Manager
Bob Becken, News Director
Walter Ploegman, Operations Manager
ShannonSnoes, Promotions Director

CKGW-FM
01-01-2007; 89.3 mhz FM *Hrs Open:* 24; 16.7 kw; Ant 436 ft; N42 26 14 W82 06 23
PO Box 985, Chatham, ON N7M 5L3 Canada
(519) 531-1118, *Fax:* (519) 531-0992
www.ucbchathamkent.com
info@ucbcanada.com
License: Chatham, ON held by United Christian Broadcasters Canada.
Population Served: 44,074 *Arbitron Metro Market:* Chatham, ON *Format:* Christian
James Hunt, COO
Al Baker, Operations Dir
Malcolm Hunt, Station Manager
James Hunt, Executive Director
Matt Reaume, Production Manager/ Web & Social Media Coordinator
Sarah Masters, Administration
Dale Elliott, Sales Executive

Christian Island

CKUN-FM
01-01-2003; 101.3 mhz FM *Hrs Open:* 24; 900 w; Ant 156 ft; N44 49 16 W80 10 24
22 O'Gema Miikean, Christian Island, ON L9M 0A9 Canada
(705) 247-1111, *Fax:* (705) 247-2239
www.chimnissing.ca/xtras/radio.html
2braidz@thunderstar.net
License: Christian Island, Simcoe County, ON held by Chimnissing Communications.
Population Served: 584 *Arbitron Metro Market:* Christian Island, ON *Format:* Variety/Diverse *No. News Employees:* 2
Edna King, General Manager
Richard Sutherland, Announcer/Program Director
Edna King, Manager

Cobourg

CFMXFM
01-01-2008; 103.1 mhz FM *Hrs Open:* 24; kw
Mailing Address: CA
Second Address: Box 1031, One Queen St., Cobourg, ON K9A 1M8
(905) 367-5353, *Fax:* (905) 367-1742
www.classical963fm.com
info@classical963fmx.com
License: Cobourg, Northumberland County, ON held by MZ Media Inc.
Nat'l Reps: imsradio
Format: Classical*Hrs. of News Programming:* news progmg 4 hrs wkly *No. News Employees:* 3 *Target Audience:* 35 plus; well-educated, upscale, owners/managers/professionals
Truus Rosenthal, Operations Dir
John van Driel, General Manager
Al Kingdon, General Sales Mgr
Marissa Colalillo, Promotions Manager
David Franco, News Director
Wassim Saikali, Chief Engineer
Roberta Hunt, Operations Manager
AnnPospischil, Traffic Manager

CKSG-FM
07-18-2002; 93.3 mhz FM *Hrs Open:* 24; kw
Mailing Address: CA
Second Address: 7805 Telephone Rd., Cobourg, ON K9A 4J7
(905) 372-5401, *Fax:* (905) 372-6280
www.star933.com
don.conway@star933.com
License: Cobourg, ON held by Pineridge Broadcasting Inc.
Nat'l Reps: Canadian Broadcast Sales
Arbitron Metro Market: Cobourg, ON *Format:* Adult Contemp*Hrs. of News Programming:* news progmg one hr wkly *No. News Employees:* 3 *Target Audience:* 25-54; predominately female
Don Conway, President
Dave Hughes, General Sales Mgr
Joel Scott, Programming Director
York Bell-Smith, Promotions Manager
Joe Snide, News Director
Tim Hodge, Cruiser Request
Jennifer Daignault, Peterborough Sales Manager

CHUC-FM
08-01-2006; 107.9 mhz FM *Hrs Open:* 24; 6.3 kw
Mailing Address: P.O. Box 520, Cobourg, ON Canada
Second Address: 7805 Telephone Rd., Cobourg, ON K9A 4J7
(905) 372-5401, *Fax:* (905) 372-6280
www.1079thebreeze.com
don.conway@1079thebreeze.com
License: Cobourg, Northumberland County, ON held by Pineridge Broadcasting Inc.
Nat'l Reps: Canadian Broadcast Sales *Wire Services:* Canadian Press
Hrs. of News Programming: news prgmg 3.5 hrs per week *No. News Employees:* 3
Don Conway, President
Joel Scott, Operations Dir
Don Conway, General Manager
Dave Hughes, General Sales Mgr
York Bell Smith, Programming Director
Joe Snider, News Director
Charlie Toner, Engineering Dir

Cochrane

CHPB-FM
01-01-2004; 98.1 mhz FM *Hrs Open:* 24; 50 w
49 Cedar St. South, Timmins, ON P4N 2Q5 Canada
(705) 267-6070, *Fax:* (705) 267-6095
www.moosefm.com
moose981@hbgradio.com
License: Cochrane, ON held by The Haliburton Broadcasting Group Inc.
Group Owner: Haliburton Broadcasting Group Inc.; (acq 11-19-2003; with CFIF-FM Iroquois Falls).
Population Served: 5,340 *Arbitron Metro Market:* Cochrane, ON *Format:* Adult Contemp*Hrs. of News Programming:* news progmg 1.5 hrs wkly *No. News Employees:* 1 *Target Audience:* 18-65.*Adv. Rates:* 22.50;22.50; 22.50; 22.5
Kimberly Ward, Operations Dir
Christopher Grossman, General Manager
Donna Todd, General Sales Mgr
Mike Fry, Programming Director
Wendy Gray, News Director
Kent Matheson, Music Director
Penny Proulx, Traffic Manager
DeborahJacklin-Peters, Accounts Receivable
Chris Nimigon, National Sales Manager

CFDY-FM
01-01-2008; 104.7 mhz FM; 5 w; N49 03 35 W81 01 51
Box 855, Cochrane, ON P0L 1C0 Canada
(705) 272-2774, *Fax:* (705) 272-2783
www.cpbrfm.com
License: Cochrane, ON held by Cochrane Polar Bear Radio Club.
Population Served: 5,487 *Arbitron Metro Market:* Cochrane, ON *Format:* Variety/Diverse*Special Programming:* Fr 5 hrs wkly
Douglas Young, General Manager

Collingwood

CFOS
03-01-1940; 1610 khz AM *Hrs Open:* 24
CA
(519) 376-2030, *Fax:* (519) 371-4242
www.560cfos.ca
bayshore@bayshorebroadcasting.ca
License: Collingwood, ON held by Bayshore Broadcating Corp.
Group Owner: Bayshore Broadcasting Corp.
Nat'l Reps: Target Broadcast Sales *Wire Services:* BN Wire
Format: News, News/Talk, Oldies, Talk*Hrs. of News Programming:* news progmg 12 hrs wkly *No. News Employees:* 7 *Target Audience:* 35 plus.
J.D. Moffat, Operations Dir
Ross Kentner, General Manager
Manny Paiva, News Director

CKCB-FM
03-29-1996; 95.1 mhz FM *Hrs Open:* 24; 350 w
186 Hurontario St., Suite 200, Collingwood, ON L9Y 4T4 Canada
(705) 446-9510, *Fax:* (705) 444-6776
www.thepeakfm.com
jeaton@thepeakfm.com
License: Collingwood, ON held by 591989 B.C. Ltd.
Group Owner: Corus Entertainment Inc.; (acq 3-24-00; grpsl).
Format: Adult Contemp*Hrs. of News Programming:* news progmg 11 hrs wkly *No. News Employees:* 1 *Target Audience:* 25-54.
John Eaton, Operations Dir
JJ Johnston, General Manager
Mike Patterson, General Sales Mgr
Deb James, Programming Director
Matt McLean, Promotions Manager
Ian McLean, News Director

Cornwall

*CFLGFM
01-01-1973; 104.5 mhz FM *Hrs Open:* 24; kw
Mailing Address: CA
Second Address: P.O. 969, Cornwall, ON K6H 5V1
(613) 932-5180, *Fax:* (613) 938-0355
www.variety104.com
scott@seawayvalley.com
License: Cornwall, Stormont County, ON held by Corus Entertainment Inc.
Group Owner: Corus Entertainment Inc.; (acq 11-19-01; grpsl).
Nat'l Reps: Canadian Broadcast Sales
Format: Adult Contemp*Hrs. of News Programming:* news progmg 5 hrs wkly *No. News Employees:* 4 *Target Audience:* 25-54; predominantly female professionals & housewives
Scott Armstrong, General Manager
Angie Baker, General Sales Mgr
Meghan Kyer, Promotions Manager

CHODFM
05-01-1994; 92.1 mhz FM *Hrs Open:* 24; 31.167 kw; 106.7 meters
1111 Montreal Rd., Suite 202, Cornwall, ON Canada
(613) 936-2463, *Fax:* (613) 936-2568
chodfm921@fastmail.fm
License: Cornwall, ON held by Radio Communautaire Cornwall-Alexandria Inc.
Population Served: 45,000*Special Programming:* Class 4 hrs, jazz 4 hrs wkly*Hrs. of News Programming:* news progmg 10 hrs wkly *No. News Employees:* 1 *Target Audience:* 25-54.
Norman Couture, President
Marc Charbonneau, General Manager

CJSS-FM
02-01-2007; 101.9 mhz FM *Hrs Open:* 24; 1.42 kw; N45 03 30 W74 44 45
709 Cotton Mill Street, PO Box 969, Cornwall, ON K6H 5V1 Canada
(613) 932-5180, *Fax:* (613) 938-0355
www.cjssfm.com
License: Cornwall, Stormont County, ON held by Corus Entertainment, Inc.
Group Owner: Corus Entertainment Inc.; (acq 11-19-01; grpsl).
Nat'l Reps: Canadian Broadcast Sales
Special Programming: Relg one hr wkly*Hrs. of News Programming:* news progmg 2 hrs wkly *No. News Employees:* 4
Target Audience: 35 -54; males
JJ Johnston, General Manager
Angie Baker, General Sales Mgr
Darryl Adams, Programming Director
Rob Seguin, Promotions Manager

Dryden

***CJIV-FM**
03-01-2003; 97.3 mhz FM *Hrs Open:* 24; 50 w
Box 112, Dryden, ON P8N 2Y7 Canada
(807) 216-6811, *Fax:* (807) 937-6490
www.cjiv973.net
cjivradio.jacob@gmail.com
License: Dryden, ON held by Way of Life Broadcasting.
Population Served: 7,617 *Arbitron Metro Market:* Dryden, ON
Format: Christian*Hrs. of News Programming:* News progmg 2 hrs wkly *Target Audience:* All ages; interested in Christian radio bcsts
Gordon Robinson, General Manager
Jake Letkeman, Programming Director

CKDR-FM
11-09-2005; 92.7 mhz FM; 36.8 kw
122 King Street, Dryden, ON P8N 1C2 Canada
(807) 223-2355, *Fax:* (807) 223-5090
www.ckdr.net
mail@ckdr.net
License: Dryden, ON held by Northwoods Broadcasting Ltd.
Group Owner: Acadia Broadcasting Ltd.; (acq 5-1-2007; grpsl)
Population Served: 7,617 *Arbitron Metro Market:* Dryden, ON
Format: Adult Contemp *Target Audience:* 25 plus.
Richard McCarthy, Operations Dir
Bruce Walchuk, General Manager
Mike Ebbeling, News Director

Elliot Lake

CKNR-FM
03-03-1997; 94.1 mhz FM; 90 kw
144 Ontario Ave, Elliot Lake, ON P5A-1Y3 Canada
(705) 848-3608, *Fax:* (705) 848-1378
www.moosefm.com
moose941@moosefm.com
License: Elliot Lake, ON held by The Haliburton Broadcasting Group Inc.
Group Owner: Haliburton Broadcasting Group Inc.; (acq 3-12-2004; C$625,000).
Format: Light Rock *No. News Employees:* 1 *Target Audience:* 35-54.
Christopher Grossman, President
Erika MacLellan, Operations Dir
Brian Prokopec, General Manager
Bob Alexander, Programming Director
Kyle Duggan, News Director
Erika MacLellan, Operations Manager
Chris Waschuk, Sales

Englehart

CJBB-FM
01-01-2000; 103.1 mhz FM *Hrs Open:* 24; 1.6 kw
Box 665, 50 Third St., Englehart, ON P0J 1H0 Canada
(705) 544-1121, *Fax:* (705) 544-2286
cjbb@nt.net
License: Englehart, ON held by 1353151 Ontario Inc.
Nat'l Reps: Target Broadcast Sales
Population Served: 1,519 *Arbitron Metro Market:* Englehart, ON
Format: Adult Contemp*Hrs. of News Programming:* news progmg 5 hrs wkly *No. News Employees:* 1 *Target Audience:* 18-54; male & female
Boyd Woods, CEO
Rick Stow, Station Manager
Pat Ferris, News Director

Erin

CHES-FM
01-01-2006; 88.1 mhz FM *Hrs Open:* 24; 250 watts; 63 meters
Mailing Address: Box 881, Erin, ON N0B 1T0 Canada
Second Address: 106 Main St., Erin, ON N0B 1T0
(519) 833-1015
www.erinradio.ca
info@erinradio.ca
License: Erin, ON held by Erin Community Radio.
Population Served: 11,000
Jay Mowat, Chairman

Espanola

CJJM-FM
10-24-2008; 99.3 mhz FM; 794 w; N46 14 16 W81 46 34
90 Gray St., Unit 2, Espanola, ON P2B 3K8 Canada
(705) 869-0578, *Fax:* (705) 869-0578
www.moosefm.com
joco993@yahoo.ca
License: Espanola, ON held by Haliburton Bradcasting Group Inc
Population Served: 5,364 *Arbitron Metro Market:* Espanola, ON
Format: Contemporary Hits/Top 40, Adult Contemp
Joe Cormier, President
Brian Prokopec, General Manager
Chris Nimigon, General Sales Mgr
Kori Rowe, Sales Executive

Fort Erie

CFLZ-FM
05-19-1991; 101.1 mhz FM *Hrs Open:* 24; 19.7 kw; N42 53 52 W78 57 27
4668 St. Clair Ave., Niagara Falls, ON Canada
(905) 356-6710, *Fax:* (905) 356-0696
www.z101.com
robwhite@niagara.com
License: Fort Erie, Niagara County, ON held by Niagara Radio Group Inc.
Population Served: 1,385,000 *Arbitron Metro Market:* Buffalo-Niagara Falls, NY *Target Audience:* 18-44; upper income adults
Robert White, Operations Dir
Elizabeth Lewis, General Manager
John Garey, General Sales Mgr
Dave Universal, Programming Director
Dana Hussman, Promotions Manager
Mike Ridley, Chief Engineer
Andrew Bilous, General Sales Manager

Fort Frances

***CBQTFM**
08-01-1990; 90.5 mhz FM *Hrs Open:* 19; kw
CA
(807) 625-5000, *Fax:* (807) 625-5035
www.cbc.ca
License: Fort Frances, ON held by CBC.
Nat'l Network: CBC Radio One
Format: News*Special Programming:* Canadian Indian one hr wkly *Target Audience:* General; northwestern Ontario residents
Robert Rabinovitch, CEO
Tom Grand, General Manager

CFOB-FM
06-04-2002; 93.1 mhz FM *Hrs Open:* 24; 21 kw
210 Scott Street, Fort Frances, ON P9A 1G7 Canada
(807) 275-5341, *Fax:* (807) 274-2033
www.b93.ca
info@931theborder.ca
License: Fort Frances, ON held by Northwoods Broadcasting Ltd.
Group Owner: Acadia Broadcasting Ltd.; (acq 5-1-2007; grpsl)
Nat'l Reps: TeleRep
Population Served: 7,952 *Arbitron Metro Market:* Fort Frances, ON *Format:* Adult Contemp *No. News Employees:* 2 *Target Audience:* 25-54; International Falls/N. Central MN
Ala Dulas, General Manager

Gananoque

CJGM-FM
10-11-2011; 99.9 mhz FM; 1.49 kw
Box 9, Gananoque, ON K7G 2T6 Canada
(613) 382-6936, *Fax:* (613) 382-8301
www.gananoque.ca
License: Gananoque, ON held by My Broadcasting Corp

Georgina Island

CFGI-FM
01-01-2004; 102.7 mhz FM; 250 w
102.7 Nish Radio, Box N-13, Sutton West, ON L0E 1R0 Canada
(705) 437-3748, *Fax:* (705) 437-3748
nish_cfgi@hotmail.com
License: Georgina Island, ON held by Georgina Island First Nations Communications.
Population Served: 353 *Arbitron Metro Market:* Georgina Island, ON *Format:* Variety/Diverse
Sally Charles, General Manager
Sean Canoe, Programming Director
Morgan Priester, Announcer

Goderich

CHWC-FM
10-15-2007; 104.9 mhz FM *Hrs Open:* 24; 12.55 kw; N43 40 42 W81 42 31
300 Suncoast Dr., Unit E, Goderich, ON N7A 4N7 Canada
(519) 612-1149, *Fax:* (519) 612-1050
www.1049thebeach.ca
thebeach@1049thebeach.ca
License: Goderich, Huron County, ON held by Bayshore Broadcasting Corp.
Group Owner: Bayshore Broadcasting Corp.
Nat'l Reps: Target Broadcast Sales
No. News Employees: 14 *Target Audience:* 18-64
Ross Kentner, President
Ian Solecki, Operations Dir
Kevin Brown, General Sales Mgr
Ally Anderson, Promotions Manager

Guelph

***CFRUFM**
01-28-1980; 93.3 mhz FM *Hrs Open:* 24; kw*Rebroadcasts:* BBC World Service Overnight
CA
(519) 824-4120, *Fax:* (519) 763-9603
www.cfru.ca
info@cfru.ca
License: Guelph, Wellington County, ON held by University of Guelph Radio-Radio Gryphon.
Format: Variety/Diverse*Special Programming:* It one hr, relg one hr, Sp*Hrs. of News Programming:* news progmg 12 hrs wkly *No. News Employees:* 1 *Target Audience:* General.*Adv. Rates:* 21/spot start
Barry Rooke, Operations Dir
Vish Khanna, Programming Director
Peter Bradley, Music Director
Steve Mason, Technical Director

CIMJ-FM
01-01-1969; 106.1 mhz FM *Hrs Open:* 24; 50 kw; 249 ft
75 Speedvale Ave. E., Guelph, ON N1E 6M3 Canada
Fax: (519) 824-7000
www.magic106.com
kevin@magic106.com
License: Guelph, Wellington County, ON held by 591989 B.C., Ltd
Group Owner: Corus Entertainment Inc.
Population Served: 101,000*Hrs. of News Programming:* News progmg 6 hrs wkly *Target Audience:* 25-54.
Chris Sisam, General Manager
Chris Sisam, Station Manager
Ian Clutton, General Sales Mgr
Kevin Kelly, Programming Director
Lisa Richards, Promotions Manager
Neill Clemens, News Director
Rob Brown, Engineering Dir

CJOY
06-14-1948; 1460 khz AM *Hrs Open:* 24
CA
(519) 824-7000, *Fax:* (519) 824-4118
www.cjoy.com
studio@cjoy.com
License: Guelph, ON held by 591989 B.C. Ltd.
Group Owner: Corus Entertainment Inc.; (acq 3-24-00; grpsl).
Format: Oldies*Hrs. of News Programming:* news progmg 8 hrs wkly *No. News Employees:* 4 *Target Audience:* 25-54.
Chris Sisam, General Manager
Ian Clutton, General Sales Mgr
Larry Mellott, Programming Director
Mike Stevens, Engineering Dir

Haldimand County

CKJN-FM
05-15-2006; 92.9 mhz FM; 3.3 kw; Ant 358 ft; N42 56 29 W79 50 45
282 Argyle St. S., Unit 4, Caledonia, ON N3W 1K7 Canada
(289) 284-1070, *Fax:* (289) 284-1072
www.moosefm.com
License: Haldimand County, Haldimand County, ON held by Haliburton Broadcasting Group Inc

Group Owner: Haliburton Broadcasting Group Inc.; (acq 4-18-2007)
Nat'l Reps: imsradio
No. News Employees: 2
Nancy Brown Dacko, President

Haliburton

CKHA-FM
07-01-2003; 100.9 mhz FM; 3.4 kw
Box 1125, Haliburton, ON K0M 1S0 Canada
(705) 457-1009, *Fax:* (705) 457-9522
www.canoefm.com
canoefmadmin@bellnet.ca
License: Haliburton, ON held by Haliburton County Community Radio Association.
Population Served: 17,026 *Arbitron Metro Market:* Haliburton, ON *Format:* Variety/Diverse *Target Audience:* 50 plus.
Paul Cameron, President
Roxanne Casey, Station Manager
Ron Murphy, Chief Engineer
Dave Allen, Sales Representitive
Malcolm MacLean, Vice President
Betty Moffatt, Secretary
Case Bassie, Treasurer/Accounting

CFZN-FM
03-13-2006; 93.5 mhz FM *Hrs Open:* 24 Hours; 6 kw
Mailing Address: Box 960, Haliburton, ON K0M 1S0 Canada
Second Address: 152 Highland St., Upper Level, Haliburton, ON K0M 1S0
(705) 457-3897, *Fax:* (705) 457-3827
www.moosehbgradio.com
moose935@hbgradio.com
License: Haliburton, ON held by The Haliburton Broadcasting Group Inc.
Group Owner: Haliburton Broadcasting Group Inc.
Christopher Grossman, President
Renzo Rosati, General Manager
Renzo Rosati, General Sales Mgr
Dave Newman, Programming Director
Wendy Gray, News Director
Dave Belange, Engineering Dir

Hamilton

*CFMUFM
01-13-1978; 93.3 mhz FM *Hrs Open:* 24; kw
CA
(905) 525-9140, *Fax:* (905) 529-3208
cfmu.mcmaster.ca
cfmumsu@msumcmaster.ca
License: Hamilton, ON held by CFMU Radio Inc.
Format: Variety/Diverse*Special Programming:* Class 5 hrs, Sp one hr, blues 5 hrs, Canadian Indi*Hrs. of News Programming:* News progmg 15 hrs wkly *Target Audience:* General; univ students, people with an adventurousoutlook towards life
Sandeep Bhandari, Operations Dir
James Tennant, Programming Director
Rachel Palmieri, Music Director

CHAM
11-01-1959; 820 khz AM *Hrs Open:* 24
CA
(905) 574-1150, *Fax:* (905) 575-6429
www.820cham.com
info@820cham.com
License: Hamilton, ON held by Astral Media Radio G.P.
Group Owner: Astral Media Inc.; (acq 10-29-2007; grpsl)
Wire Services: BN Wire
Format: Talk*Hrs. of News Programming:* news progmg 26 hrs wkly *No. News Employees:* 4 *Target Audience:* 25-54.*Adv. Rates:* 65; 55; 45; 45
Ian Greenberg, President
Tom Cooke, Operations Dir

CHML
05-27-1927; 900 khz AM *Hrs Open:* 24
CA
(905) 521-9900, *Fax:* (905) 521-2306
www.900chml.com
jstorey@900chml.com
License: Hamilton, ON held by Corus Premium Television Ltd.
Group Owner: Corus Entertainment Inc.; (acq 7-6-2000; grpsl).
Nat'l Reps: Canadian Broadcast Sales
Format: News, News/Talk, Sports, Talk *Target Audience:* 35 plus.
Suzanne Carpenter, General Manager
Greg Hinton, Programming Director
Mike Rose, Music Director

*CIOI-FM
01-01-1998; 101.5 mhz FM *Hrs Open:* 24; 240 w; N43 14 12 W79 53 13
Mohawk College, Ste G108, 135 Fennell Ave. W., Hamilton, ON L8N 3T2 Canada
(905) 575-2175, *Fax:* (905) 575-2385
www.indifm.ca
lespalango@mohawkcollege.ca
License: Hamilton, ON held by The Mohawk College Radio Corp.
Population Served: 400,000 *Format:* Alternative*Hrs. of News Programming:* News progmg 6 hrs wkly *Target Audience:* 17-24; college students & the div communities they represent*Adv. Rates:* 25; 25; 25; 25
Les Palango, Station Manager
Jamie Smith, Programming Director
Jeff Cudahy, Engineering Dir

*CKLHFM
10-07-1986; 102.9 mhz FM; kw
CA
(905) 574-1150, *Fax:* (905) 575-6429
www.k-litefm.com
info@k-litefm.com
License: Hamilton, Wentworth County, ON held by SR L.P.
Group Owner: Astral Media Inc.
Format: Adult Contemp *Target Audience:* 25-54; working women, owners, mgrs, professionals
Tom Cooke, General Manager
Peter Hobbs, General Sales Mgr
Michelle Quinn, Programming Director
Dave DeRocco, Promotions Manager

CKOC
05-20-1922; 1150 khz AM *Hrs Open:* 24
CA
(905) 574-1150, *Fax:* (905) 575-6429
www.oldies1150.com
info@oldies1150.com
License: Hamilton, ON held by Astral Media Radio G.P.
Group Owner: Astral Media Inc.; (acq 10-29-2007; grpsl)
Nat'l Reps: Canadian Broadcast Sales *Wire Services:* Broadcast News Ltd.
Format: Oldies*Hrs. of News Programming:* news progmg 3 hrs wkly *No. News Employees:* 4 *Target Audience:* 25-54.
Paul Fisher, General Manager
Peter Hobbs, General Sales Mgr
Ted Yates, Programming Director
Dave DeRocco, Promotions Manager

CHKX-FM
09-01-2000; 94.7 mhz FM *Hrs Open:* 24; 21.4 kw; Ant 446 ft; N43 12 21 W79 43 50
589 Upper Wellington St., Hamilton, ON L9A 3P8 Canada
(905) 388-8911, *Fax:* (905) 388-7947
www.wave947.fm
smoothjazz@wave947.fm
License: Hamilton, ON held by Durham Radio Inc.
Group Owner: Durham Radio Inc.; (acq 8-31-2007)
Nat'l Reps: Target Broadcast Sales *Wire Services:* Broadcast News Ltd.
Population Served: 3,638,000 *No. News Employees:* 2 *Target Audience:* 35-64.*Adv. Rates:* 100; 80; 60; 40
Douglas Kirk, Chairman
Thomas Pippy, CFO
Steve Kassay, Operations Dir
Simon Constam, General Sales Mgr
Cathy Philippo, News Director

Hanover

CFBW-FM
12-31-2001; 91.3 mhz FM *Hrs Open:* 24; 250 w; Ant 290 ft; N44 08 31 W81 01 47
267 10th St., Hanover, ON N4N 1P1 Canada
(519) 364-0200, *Fax:* (519) 364-5175
www.bluewaterradio.ca
info@blurwaterradio.ca
License: Hanover, Canada County, ON held by Bluewater Community Radio Inc..
Population Served: 150,000*Special Programming:* Scottish Music, Comedy,Gospel,*Hrs. of News Programming:* 2 *No. News Employees:* 3 *Target Audience:* 12-75; Ontario audience rural agricultural/urban*Adv. Rates:* Please Call for details & rate
Gary Smith, Chairman
Andrew McBride, General Manager
Andrew McBride, Station Manager
Carole Plunkett, General Sales Mgr
Andrew McBride, Programming Director
Craig Smith, Chief Engineer

Hawkesbury

CHPR-FM
02-01-1986; 102.1 mhz FM *Hrs Open:* 24; 789 w; 70 ft; N45 35 01 N45 35 01
115 Principale E., Suite 101, Hawkesbury, ON K6A 1A1 Canada
(613) 632-1000, *Fax:* (613) 632-1110
www.radionord.com
infocouleurfmm@radionord.vom
License: Hawkesbury, ON held by RNC MEDIA Inc.
Group Owner: RNC MEDIA Inc.; (acq 8-22-89)
Format: Easy Listening *No. News Employees:* 1 *Target Audience:* 25 plus.
Pierre R. Brosseau, President
M Yves Trottier, Programming Director

CKHK-FM
04-02-2008; 107.7 mhz FM; 875 w; N45 39 24 W74 39 43
1320 Main St. E., Hawkesbury, ON K6A 1C5 Canada
(613) 872-1077, *Fax:* (613) 632-4022
www.jewelradio.com
info@1077thejewel.com
License: Hawkesbury, ON held by Ottawa Media Inc.
Population Served: 10,551 *Arbitron Metro Market:* Hawkesbury, ON *Format:* Easy Listening *No. News Employees:* 1
Aron Goodden, General Sales Mgr
Ted Silver, Administration
Dan Chabot, News Director

Hearst

CHYK-FM-3
01-01-1996; 92.9 mhz FM *Hrs Open:* 24; 140 w*Rebroadcasts:* Rebroadcasts CHYK-FM Timmins
49 Cedar St. S., Timmins, ON P4N 2G5 Canada
(705) 267-6070, *Fax:* (705) 267-6095
www.chycfm.com
chycfm@nbgradio.com
License: Hearst, ON held by LE5 Communications Inc.
Nat'l Reps: Canadian Broadcast Sales
Format: Adult Contemp*Hrs. of News Programming:* news progmg one hrs wkly *No. News Employees:* 1 *Target Audience:* 18-65.*Adv. Rates:* 22.50; 22.50; 22.50; 22.50.
Kimberley Grossman, Operations Dir
Christopher Grossman, General Manager
Sylvie Beaulieu, General Sales Mgr
Sylvain Boucher, Programming Director
Gilles Lafortune, News Director
Penny Proulx, Traffic Manager

*CINN-FM
01-01-1988; 91.1 mhz FM *Hrs Open:* 6 AM-9 PM; kw
CA
(705) 372-1011, *Fax:* (705) 362-7411
www.cinnfm.com
cinnfm@cinnfm.com
License: Hearst, Canada County, ON held by Radio de l'Epinette Noire Inc.
Format: Adult Contemp *No. News Employees:* 2 *Target Audience:* 0-75.
Camire-Lise Laflamme, President
Kathy R. Haberdasher, General Manager

Huntsville

CFBK-FM
09-01-1957; 105.5 mhz FM *Hrs Open:* 24; 5 kw
Unit 2, 15 Main St. E., Huntsville, ON P1H 2C6 Canada
(705) 789-4461, *Fax:* (705) 789-1269
License: Huntsville, Muskoka County, ON held by Muskoka-Parry Sound Broadcasting Ltd.
Group Owner: Haliburton Broadcasting Group Inc.; (acq 11-7-2007)
Nat'l Network: CHUM Radio Network *Wire Services:* BN Wire
Population Served: 30,000 *No. News Employees:* 3 *Target Audience:* 21 plus.
Margaret Byers, Operations Dir

Iroquois Falls

CFIF-FM
12-08-1998; 101.1 mhz FM *Hrs Open:* 24; 50 w
49 Cedar St. S., Timmins, ON P4N 2G5 Canada
(705) 267-6070, *Fax:* (705) 267-6095
www.hbgradio.com
moose1011@hbgradio.com
License: Iroquois Falls, ON held by The Haliburton Broadcasting Group Inc
Group Owner: Haliburton Broadcasting Group Inc.; (acq 11-19-2003; with CHPB-FM Cochrane)

Population Served: 2,500*Hrs. of News Programming:* news progmg 1.5 hrs wkly *No. News Employees:* 1 *Target Audience:* 25-54.*Adv. Rates:* 22.50; 22.50; 22.50; 22.50
Christopher Grossman, President
Shawn McArthur, General Sales Mgr
Mike Fry, Programming Director
Wendy Gray, News Director
Kent Matheson, Music Director
Penny Proulx, Traffic Manager

Kaministiquia

CFQK-FM
01-01-2002; 104.5 mhz FM; 50 w; N48 30 27 W89 27 28
87 Hill St. N., Thunder Bay, ON P7A 5V6 Canada
(807) 346-2600, *Fax:* (807) 345-9923
www.thethunder.ca
thunder@thethunder.ca
License: Kaministiquia, ON held by Northwest Broadcasting Inc.
Nat'l Reps: Target Broadcast Sales
Population Served: 587 *Arbitron Metro Market:* Kaministiquia, ON *Format:* Country
Don Caron, President
Leslie Walker-Larson, National Sales Manager
Bill Malcolm, Programming Director
Cora Cambly, Promotions Manager
Kathy Harris, Director of Local Sales

Kapuskasing

***CKGN-FM**
10-01-1993; 89.7 & 94.7mhz FM *Hrs Open:* 24; 3 000 kw
77 chemin Brunelle Nd., Kapuskasing, ON P5N 2M1 Canada
(705) 335-5915, *Fax:* (705) 335-3508
www.ckgn.ca
ckgnfm@nt.net
License: Kapuskasing, ON held by Radio communautaire KapNord Inc.
Population Served: 20,000 *Format:* Variety/Diverse *No. News Employees:* 1 *Target Audience:* General.
Claude Chabot, General Manager

CKAP-FM
09-01-2001; 100.9 mhz FM; 12 kw
Box 960, Haliburton, ON K0M 1S0 Canada
(705) 335-2379, *Fax:* (705) 337-6391
www.hbgradio.com
License: Kapuskasing, ON held by The Haliburton Broadcasting Group Inc
Group Owner: Haliburton Broadcasting Group Inc.
No. News Employees: 2 *Target Audience:* General.
Christopher Grossman, President
Brent Lecour, Operations Dir

Kemptville

CKKV-FM
11-17-2012; 97.5 mhz FM; kw
CA
(613) 258-1786, *Fax:* (613) 258-1786
www.mystarfin.com
License: Kemptville, ON held by Haliburton Broadcasting Group Inc
Group Owner: Haliburton Broadcasting Group
Format: Adult Contemp

Kenora

CBQXFM
03-28-1978; 98.7 mhz FM; kw*Rebroadcasts:* Rebroadcasts CBW(AM) Winnipeg, Man. & CBQT-FM Thunder Bay
CA
(807) 625-5000, *Fax:* (416) 205-3111
www.nwo.cbc.ca
License: Kenora, ON held by CBC.
Nat'l Network: CBC Radio One
Format: Public Affairs, News
Kelly McInnes, General Manager

CJRL-FM
01-01-2004; 89.5 mhz FM; 40 kw; N49 46 45 W94 27 25
301 1st Ave. S., Kenora, ON P9N 1W2 Canada
(807) 468-3181, *Fax:* (807) 468-4188
www.cjrl.ca
cjrl@cjrl.ca
License: Kenora, ON held by Northwoods Broadcasting Ltd.
Group Owner: Acadia Broadcasting Ltd.; (acq 5-1-2007; grpsl)
Population Served: 15,348 *Arbitron Metro Market:* Kenora, ON *Format:* Adult Contemp *No. News Employees:* 2 *Target Audience:* 25-54.
Jim MacMullin, Operations Dir
Brent Preston, Station Manager

Kettle Point

CKTI-FM
04-26-2004; 107.7 mhz FM *Hrs Open:* 24; 420 w
9111 W. Ipperwash Rd., Unit 6, R.R. 2, Forest, ON N0N 1J0 Canada
(519) 786-3883, *Fax:* (519) 786-2834
www.eaglecountry.ca
info@eaglecountry.ca
License: Kettle Point, ON held by Point Eagle Radio Inc.
Population Served: 936 *Arbitron Metro Market:* Kettle Point, ON *Format:* Classic Rock, Country
Jermey Henry, Operations Dir

Killaloe

CHCR-FM
01-01-1998; 102.9 mhz FM; 33 w
Mailing Address: 14 Lake St. Unit A, PO Box 195, Killaloe, ON K0J 2A0 Canada
Second Address: 14 Lake St., 2nd Fl., Killaloe, ON K0J 2A0
(613) 757-0657, *Fax:* (613) 757-0818
www.chcr.org
stationmanager@chcr.org
License: Killaloe, ON held by Homegrown Community Radio.
Population Served: 2,550 *Arbitron Metro Market:* Killaloe, ON *Format:* Variety/Diverse*Special Programming:* Canadian fiddle 8 hrs, Fr 8 hrs, Pol one hr, trad
Peter Benner, Chairman
Daryl Andermann, General Manager
Peter Benner, Station Manager
Sabrina Radema, Programming Committee
Tim Rivers Garrett, Secretary
Desiree McGlynn, Treasurer
Jude Bivar, Programming Committee
JuneWalterhouse, Station Management Committee
Div Halliday, Station Management Committee

Kincardine

CIYN-FM
03-01-2006; 95.5 mhz FM *Hrs Open:* 24; 5.66 kw
807 Queen St., Kincardine, ON N2Z 2Y2 Canada
(519) 396-7770, *Fax:* (519) 396-7771
www.thecoastfm.ca
info@thecoastfm.ca
License: Kincardine, ON held by Brian Cooper and Daniel McCarthy, on behalf of a corporation to be incorporated.
Format: Adult Contemp *No. News Employees:* 1
Mike Brough, General Manager
Steve Howard, General Sales Mgr
Lynda Cooper, News Director

Kingston

***CBBKFM**
05-21-1979; 92.9 mhz FM *Hrs Open:* 24; kw
CA
(416) 205-3700, *Fax:* (416) 205-6063
www.cbc.ca
info@cbbk.com
License: Kingston, ON held by Canadian Broadcasting Corp.
Nat'l Network: CBC Radio Two
Robert Raeinobitch, CFO

CFLYFM
01-01-1963; 98.3 mhz FM *Hrs Open:* 24; 100 kw; 400 ft
993 Princess St., Suite 10, Kingston, ON Canada
(613) 544-1380, *Fax:* (613) 546-9751
www.flyfmkingston.com
flyfm@flyfmkingston.com
License: Kingston, ON held by Bell Media Ontario Regional Radio Partnership
Group Owner: Bell Media Inc.; (acq 6-22-2007; grpsl)
Hrs. of News Programming: news progmg 5 hrs wkly *No. News Employees:* 2 *Target Audience:* 25-44.
Gary Perrin, General Manager

***CFMKFM**
08-31-1942; 96.3 mhz FM *Hrs Open:* 24; kw
CA
(613) 544-2340, *Fax:* (613) 544-5508
www.fm96.ca
License: Kingston, ON held by 591989 B.C. Ltd.
Group Owner: Corus Entertainment Inc.; (acq 3-24-2000; grpsl)
TV Affiliate: CKWS-TV affil. *Format:* Classic Rock*Hrs. of News Programming:* M-F: 6a, 6:30a, 7a,7:30a, 8a, 8:30a, 12p, 4p, *No. News Employees:* 2 *Target Audience:* 35-64; Male
Mike Ferguson, General Manager
Brad Gibb, Programming Director

***CFRCFM**
10-27-2022; 101.9 mhz FM *Hrs Open:* 24; 3 kw; 295 ft; N44 17 24 W77 25 55
Queens Univ., Lower Carruthers Hall, 62 Fifth Field Company Lane, Kingston, ON Canada
(613) 533-2121, *Fax:* (613) 533-6049
www.cfrc.ca
cfrcops@ams.queensu.ca
License: Kingston, Frontenac County, ON held by Radio Queen's University.
Population Served: 150,000*Hrs. of News Programming:* News progmg 15 hrs wkly *Target Audience:* General.
Kristiana Clemens, Operations Dir
Eric Beers, Station Manager

***CKVI-FM**
01-01-1997; 91.9 mhz FM *Hrs Open:* 8am-6pm; 6.5 w
235 Frontenac St., Kingston, ON K7L 3S7 Canada
(613) 544-7864, *Fax:* (613) 544-8795
www.thecave.ca
ckvi@limestone.on.ca
License: Kingston, Canada County, ON held by KCVI Educational Radio Station Inc.
Format: Variety/Diverse
Fraser Rose, General Manager

CIKR-FM
02-19-2001; 105.7 mhz FM *Hrs Open:* 24; 24 kw
863 Princess St., Suite 301, Kingston, ON K7L 5N4 Canada
(613) 549-1057, *Fax:* (613) 549-5302
www.krock1057.ca
License: Kingston, ON held by Rogers Broadcasting Ltd.
Group Owner: Rogers Broadcasting Ltd.; (acq 5-4-2009; with CKXC-FM Kingston)
Population Served: 123,363 *Arbitron Metro Market:* Kingston, ON*Hrs. of News Programming:* news progmg 2 hrs wkly *No. News Employees:* 2 *Target Audience:* 25-54; adults*Adv. Rates:* 75; 70; 65; 35
Doug Elliot, Operations Dir
John Wright, General Manager
Ross Tirrell, General Sales Mgr
Andrew Revelle, Promotions Manager

CKWS-FM
01-01-2007; 104.3 mhz FM; 4 kw; Ant 813 ft; N44 10 02 W76 25 40
170 Queen St., Kingston, ON K7K 1B2 Canada
(613) 544-2340, *Fax:* (613) 544-5508
www.lite1043.ca
License: Kingston, ON held by 591989 B.C. Ltd.
Group Owner: Corus Entertainment Inc.
TV Affiliate: CKWS-TV affil*Hrs. of News Programming:* Mon-Fri: 6a, 6:30a, 7a, 7:30a, 8a, 8:30a, 12p, 3p, 4p, 5p, 6p; Sat: 8a *No. News Employees:* 2 *Target Audience:* 35-64; female
Mike Ferguson, General Manager
Brad Gibb, Programming Director

CKLC-FM
01-01-2007; 98.9 mhz FM; 8.7 kw; Ant 433 ft; N44 12 36 W76 25 05
993 Princess St., Suite 10, Kingston, ON Canada
(613) 544-1380, *Fax:* (613) 546-9751
www.989.fm
License: Kingston, ON held by Bell Media Ontario Regional Ardio Partnership
Group Owner: Bell Media Inc.
Hrs. of News Programming: news progmg 3 hrs wkly *No. News Employees:* 4
Gary Perrin, General Manager

CKXC-FM
01-01-2007; 93.5 mhz FM; 3.23 kw; Ant 371 ft; N44 17 22 W76 28 50
863 Princess St., Suite 301, Kingston, ON K7L 5N4 Canada
(613) 549-1057, *Fax:* (613) 549-5302
kix935.com
info@1027.com
License: Kingston, Frontenac County, ON held by Rogers Broadcasting Ltd.
Group Owner: Rogers Broadcasting Ltd.; (acq 5-4-2009; with CIKR-FM Kingston)
Population Served: 123,363 *Arbitron Metro Market:* Kingston, ON *Format:* Country *Target Audience:* 35-64.
Doug Elliott, Operations Dir
John Wright, General Manager
Garry McColman, Programming Director
Jacquie Beckett, Music Director

Kirkland Lake

CJKL-FM
01-01-1934; 101.5 mhz FM *Hrs Open:* 24; 23 kw

Box 430, Kirkland Lake, ON P2N 3J4 Canada
(705) 567-3366, *Fax:* (705) 567-6101
www.cjklfm.com
cjkl@cjklfm.com
License: Kirkland Lake, ON held by Connelly Communications Corp.
Nat'l Reps: Canadian Broadcast Sales
Population Served: 8,000 *Arbitron Metro Market:* Kirkland Lake, ON *Format:* Adult Contemp *No. News Employees:* 2*Adv. Rates:* 42; 30; 30; na.
Rob Connelly, President, G.M. & P.D.
Ann Connelly, General Sales Mgr
Elesha Teskey, News Director
Don Elvidge, Engineering Dir
Greg Mackle, News Director
Nathan Evans, Director of Engineering
Corina LaCarte, Sales Manager
PhilHutchinson, Account Executive
Michelle Farstad, Account Executive
Luce Moore, Traffic & Reception

Kitchener

CFCAFM
04-03-1967; 105.3 mhz FM *Hrs Open:* 24; 100 kw; 820 ft; N43 24 15 W80 38 05
255 King St. N., Suite 207, Waterloo, ON Canada

www.koolfm.com
info@koolfm.com
License: Kitchener, Waterloo County, ON held by Bell Media Canada Radio Partnership
Group Owner: Bell Media Inc.
Brant Zwicker, Station Manager
Steve Marlow, Programming Director

CHYM-FM
01-01-1949; 96.7 mhz FM *Hrs Open:* 24; 25 kw; Ant 658 ft
Mailing Address: 305 King St. W., Kitchener, ON N2G 4E4 Canada
Second Address: Box 936, Kitchener, ON N2G 4E4
(519) 743-2611, *Fax:* (519) 743-7510
www.chymfm.com
creative@kitchenerradio.rogers.com
License: Kitchener, ON held by Rogers Broadcasting, Ltd
Group Owner: Rogers Broadcasting Ltd.
Population Served: 500,000 *Target Audience:* A25-54
Mike Collins, General Manager
Mike Collins, General Sales Mgr
Wendy Duff, Programming Director
Christa Hicks, Promotions Manager
Joe Pavia, News Director
Mike McCabe, Engineering Dir
Neil Beaumont, Music Director

CKGL(AM)
01-01-1929; 570 khz AM *Hrs Open:* 24; 10 kw-U, DA-1
305 King St. W., Kitchener, ON N2G 4E4 Canada
(519) 743-2611, *Fax:* (519) 743-7510
www.570news.com
news570@rogers.com
License: Kitchener, ON held by Rogers Broadcasting Ltd.
Group Owner: Rogers Broadcasting Ltd.
Nat'l Network: CBS
Format: News, News/Talk, Sports, Talk *Target Audience:* 35 plus.
Mike Collins, General Manager
Pete Travers, Programming Director

CIKZ-FM
02-06-2004; 99.5 mhz FM; kw
CA
(519) 743-2611, *Fax:* (519) 743-7510
www.kix106online.com
plarche@kicxfm.com
License: Kitchener, ON held by Rogers Broadcasting Ltd.
Group Owner: Rogers Broadcasting Ltd.; (acq 12-24-2007; exchange for CICX-FM Orillia)
Arbitron Metro Market: Kitchener, ON *Format:* Country
Mike Collins, General Manager
Jordan Cooledge, General Sales Mgr
Derm Carnduff, Programming Director
Ron Funnell, General Sales Manager

CKKW-FM
01-01-2009; 99.5 mhz FM; 2.1 kw; Ant 335 ft; N43 24 13 W80 31 54
255 King St. N., Suite 207, Waterloo, ON N2J 4V2 Canada
(519) 884-4470, *Fax:* (519) 884-6482
www.kfun995.com
License: Kitchener, ON
Group Owner: Bell Media Inc.
Population Served: 507,096 *Arbitron Metro Market:* Waterloo, ON *Format:* Oldies
Paul Cugliari, VIce President/General Manager
John Yost, General Sales Mgr
Dave Schneider, Programming Director
Jay Nijhuis, Promotions Manager
Brian Bourke, News Director
Al Douglas, Chief Engineer
Jay Nijhuis, PromotionsManager
Pauline Poole, Account Executive
Jim O'Kane, Account Executive
Tara Parachuk, Advertsing Consultant
Jane Nadeau, Sales Co-Ordinator
Becky Riley, Promotions Assistant

Kitchener-Waterloo

CKBT-FM
01-01-2004; 91.5 mhz FM *Hrs Open:* 24; 3.6 kw
50 Sportsworld Crossing Road, Suite 210, Kitchener, ON N2P OA4 Canada
(519) 772-1212, *Fax:* (519) 772-1213
www.915thebeat.com
david.jutzi@corusent.com
License: Kitchener-Waterloo, ON held by Corus Premium Television Ltd.
Group Owner: Corus Entertainment Inc.; (acq 7-6-2007; C$14.5 million with CJZZ-FM Winnipeg, MB)
Population Served: 204,668 *Arbitron Metro Market:* Kitchener, ON *Format:* Christian *Target Audience:* 18-34.
Lars Wunsche, General Manager
Adelia Dias, General Sales Mgr
Patrick Olsen, Promotions Manager
Tristan Brake, Chief Engineer
Lindsey Martin, Sales
Scott Wilkie, Promotions Coordinator
Vicki Swanton, Interactive AccountManager
Anne Aitken, Interactive Content Coordinator
Danna Ford, Executive Assistant
Kristi McCartney, Receptionist/Administrative Assistant

CJTW-FM
02-01-2004; 94.3 mhz FM *Hrs Open:* 24; 50 w
Mailing Address: Faith FM 94.3, Box 1433, Kitchener, ON N2G 4H6 Canada
Second Address: 659 King St. E., Kitchener, ON N2G 2M4
(519) 575-9090, *Fax:* (519) 575-9119
www.faithfm.org
info@faithfm.org
License: Kitchener-Waterloo, ON held by Sound of Faith Broadcasting.
Special Programming: Religious Spoken Word *Target Audience:* A25-54*Adv. Rates:* 40; 35; 40; 20
Tanya Gafoor, Operations Dir
Dave MacDonald, General Manager
Barbara Dowling, General Sales Mgr
Brad Loveday, Programming Director
Josh Atkinson, Music Director

Leamington

*CHYR-FM
08-23-1993; 96.7 mhz FM *Hrs Open:* 24; kw
CA
(519) 326-6171, *Fax:* (519) 322-1110
www.chyr.com
96.7@chyr.com
License: Leamington, ON held by Blackburn Radio Inc.
Group Owner: Blackburn Group Inc.; (acq 12-19-94; grpsl)
Format: Adult Contemp *Target Audience:* 25-54.
Terry Regier, General Manager
Tim O'Neil, General Sales Mgr
Corey Robertson, Programming Director
Tina Delciancio, Promotions Manager
Kevin Black, News Director
Cathie Morgan, Sales Manager

CJSP
92.7 mhz FM; kw
CA
(519) 944-4400, *Fax:* (519) 322-1110
www.country959.com
96.7@chyr.com
License: Leamington, ON held by Blackburn Radio Inc.
Group Owner: Blackburn Group Inc.
Arbitron Metro Market: Leamington, ON *Format:* Adult Contemp *Target Audience:* 25-64.
Terry Regier, General Manager
Rod Martens, General Sales Mgr

Lindsay (city of Kawartha Lakes)

CKLY-FM
05-16-1998; 91.9 mhz FM *Hrs Open:* 24; 5.27 kw
249 Kent St. W., Lindsay, ON K9V 2Z3 Canada
(705) 324-9103, *Fax:* (705) 324-4149
www.919bobfm.com
y92@y92.net
License: Lindsay (city of Kawartha Lakes), Victoria County, ON held by Bell Media Canada Radio Partnership
Group Owner: Bell Media Inc.; (acq 6-22-2007; grpsl)
Nat'l Reps: Canadian Broadcast Sales
Population Served: 70,000*Hrs. of News Programming:* news progmg 14 hrs wkly *No. News Employees:* 2 *Target Audience:* 30-65.*Adv. Rates:* 45; 35; na; 10
Steve Fawcett, General Manager
Harvey Spry, General Sales Mgr
Dave Illman, Programming Director

London

*CBBLFM
10-01-1978; 100.5 mhz FM *Hrs Open:* 24; kw*Rebroadcasts:* Rebroadcasts CBL-FM Toronto
CA
(416) 205-3700, *Fax:* (416) 205-6063
www.cbc.ca
info@cbbk.com
License: London, ON held by Canadian Broadcasting Corp.
Nat'l Network: CBC Radio Two
Robert Raeinobitch, CFO

*CBCLFM
06-01-1998; 93.5 mhz FM *Hrs Open:* 4 am-6 pm; kw
CA
(519) 667-1990, *Fax:* (519) 667-1557
www.cbc.ca
info@cbbk.com
License: London, ON held by Canadian Broadcasting Corp.
Nat'l Network: CBC Radio One
Special Programming: News 10 hrs wkly
Hubert Lacroix, President

CFPL
09-01-1922; 980 khz AM *Hrs Open:* 24
CA
(519) 931-6000, *Fax:* (519) 438-2415
www.am980.ca
License: London, ON held by Corus Radio Co.
Group Owner: Corus Entertainment Inc.
Format: Adult Contemp, News, News/Talk, Sports, Talk*Hrs. of News Programming:* news progmg 10 hrs wkly *No. News Employees:* 5 *Target Audience:* 35-54.
Dave Farough, General Manager
Rob Chiaramida, General Sales Mgr
Kevin Bernard, Programming Director
Andy Bingle, Engineering Dir
Dave Hopkins, Regional Sales Manager

*CFPLFM
01-01-1948; 95.9 mhz FM *Hrs Open:* 24; kw
CA
(519) 931-6000, *Fax:* (519) 438-2415
www.fm96.com
License: London, Middlesex County, ON held by Corus Radio Co.
Group Owner: Corus Entertainment Inc.
Format: Adult Contemp *Target Audience:* 25-49.
Dave Farough, General Manager
Rob Chiaramida, General Sales Mgr
Kevin Bernard, Programming Director
Andy Bingle, Engineering Dir
Dave Hopkins, Regional Sales Manager

*CHRWFM
09-02-1980; 94.7 mhz FM *Hrs Open:* 24; kw
CA
(519) 661-3601, *Fax:* (519) 661-3372
www.chrwradiio.com
chrwgm@uwo.ca
License: London, London County, ON held by Radio Western Inc.
Format: Alternative, Jazz*Hrs. of News Programming:* news progmg 5 hrs wkly *No. News Employees:* 1*Adv. Rates:* 30; 25; 30; 25
Grant Stein, Station Manager
Michael Brown, Programming Director
Alicks Girowski, Promotions Manager

CIQM-FM
06-01-1986; 97.5 mhz FM *Hrs Open:* 24; 50 kw; 300 ft
743 Wellington Rd. S., London, ON N6C 4R5 Canada

(519) 686-2525, *Fax:* (519) 686-2556
www.975ezrock.com
License: London, ON held by Astral Media Radio G.P.
Group Owner: Astral Media Inc.; (acq 10-29-2007; grpsl)
Wire Services: BN Wire
Format: Adult Contemp *Target Audience:* 25-54; female
Braden Doerr, Operations Dir
Tom Cooke, General Manager
Dan MacGillivray, General Sales Mgr
Ed Wilmott, News Director
Barry Smith, Operations Manager

CIXXFM
10-31-1978; 106.9 mhz FM *Hrs Open:* 24; kw
CA
(519) 453-2810, *Fax:* (519) 452-4153
www.1069thex.com
contact106.9thex@qmail.com
License: London, Middlesex County, ON held by Radio Fanshawe Inc.
Format: Urban Contemporary*Special Programming:* Christian 3 hrs, educ 4 hrs hrs wkly *No. News Employees:* 2 *Target Audience:* 12-34; primarily college, univ., high school
Barry Sutherland, Operations Dir
Steve Andruiak, General Manager
Michael Stoparczyk, Programming Director

CJBC-FM-4
09-03-1978; 99.3 mhz FM; 22.5 kw; 91 ft; N42 57 20 W81 21 20*Rebroadcasts:* Rebroadcasts CJBC(AM) Toronto
Box 500, Stn A, Toronto, ON M5W 1E6 Canada
(416) 205-3311, *Fax:* (416) 205-7795
www.torontocbc.ca
License: London, ON held by Canadian Broadcasting Corp.
Nat'l Network: Premiere Chaine
Format: Variety/Diverse
Claire Margetti, General Manager

CJBK
01-25-1967; 1290 khz AM *Hrs Open:* 24
CA
(519) 686-2525, *Fax:* (519) 686-3658
www.cjbk.com
mailbag@cjbk.com
License: London, ON held by Astral Media Radio G.P.
Group Owner: Astral Media Inc.; (acq 10-29-2007; grpsl)
Format: News, News/Talk, Talk *No. News Employees:* 4 *Target Audience:* 35-54.
Barry Smith, Operations Dir
Tom Cooke, General Manager
Dan MacGillivrey, General Sales Mgr
Ed Wilmott, News Director

CJBXFM
03-03-1980; 92.7 mhz FM *Hrs Open:* 24; kw
CA
(519) 686-2525, *Fax:* (519) 686-3658
www.bx93.com
mailbag@bx93.com
License: London, ON held by Astral Media Radio G.P.
Group Owner: Astral Media Inc.
Format: Country
Barry Smith, Operations Dir
Tom Cooke, General Manager
Dan MacGillivray, General Sales Mgr
Ed Wilmott, News Director

CKSL
06-01-1956; 1410 khz AM *Hrs Open:* 24
CA
(519) 686-2525, *Fax:* (519) 686-2556
www.funny1410.ca
comments@oldies1410.com
License: London, ON held by Astral Media Radio G.P.
Group Owner: Astral Media Inc.; (acq 10-29-2007; grpsl)
Wire Services: BN Wire
Format: Adult Contemp*Hrs. of News Programming:* news progmg one hr wkly *No. News Employees:* 1 *Target Audience:* 35-54; adults
Barry Smith, Operations Dir
Tom Cooke, General Manager
Dan MacGillivray, General Sales Mgr

CHST-FM
09-01-2000; 102.3 mhz FM *Hrs Open:* 24; 20.4 kw
102.3 Bob FM, 1 Communication Rd., London, ON Canada
(519) 690-0102, *Fax:* (519) 686-5942
www.1023bob.com
whatever@1023bob.com
License: London, ON held by Rogers Broadcasting Ltd
Group Owner: Rogers Broadcasting Ltd.; (acq 6-22-2007; grpsl)
Nat'l Network: CHUM Radio Network *Wire Services:* BN Wire
Hrs. of News Programming: weekday mornings *No. News Employees:* 1 *Target Audience:* 25-54; adults
Don Mumford, General Manager
Ann LaRocque, General Sales Mgr
David Jones, Programming Director

CHJX-FM
01-01-2003; 105.9 mhz FM *Hrs Open:* 24; 10 w
100 Fullarton St., London, ON N6A 1K1 Canada
(519) 679-9882, *Fax:* (519) 679-2459
www.gracefm.ca
gracefm_administration@skynet.ca
License: London, ON held by Sound of Faith Broadcasting.
Population Served: 366,151 *Arbitron Metro Market:* London, ON
Format: Christian
Dale Elliott, Station Manager
Carmine Angi, General Sales Mgr

Marathon

***CFNOFM**
07-17-1982; 93.1 mhz FM *Hrs Open:* 24; kw
Mailing Address: CA
Second Address: 93 Evergreen Dr., Marathon, ON P0T 2E0
(807) 229-1010, *Fax:* (807) 229-1686
www.cfno.fm
sales@cfno.fm
License: Marathon, ON held by North Superior Broadcasting Ltd.
Format: Adult Contemp*Special Programming:* C&W 12 hrs wkly
Ian Popple, General Manager
Vince Natomagan, Programming Director

Midland

***CICZ**
09-01-1993; 104.1 mhz FM; kw
CA
(705) 526-2268, *Fax:* (705) 526-3060
www.thedockfm.com
paul.larche@larchecom.com
License: Midland, ON held by Larche Communications Inc.
Group Owner: Larche Communications Inc.
Format: Classic Rock
Marilyn Wideman, CFO
Paul Larche, President
Mora Austin, Operations Dir
Ted Roop, Programming Director
Glen Prinz, Chief Engineer

Mississauga

CJMR
06-17-1974; 1190 khz AM *Hrs Open:* 24
CA
(905) 271-1320, *Fax:* (905) 845-9171
www.cjmr1320.ca
contact@cmjr1320.ca
License: Mississauga, ON held by Trafalgar Broadcasting Ltd.
Nat'l Reps: Target Broadcast Sales
Format: Ethnic*Adv. Rates:* 70 per 30 sec 105 per 60 sec
Michael Caine, President
Harry McDonald, General Manager

CINA
12-22-2008; 1650 khz AM; 5 kw-D, 680 w-N; N43 37 32 W79 37 52
1515 Britannia Rd. E., Suite 315, Mississauga, ON Canada
(416) 777-1650, *Fax:* (905) 795-9030
www.cinaradio.com
cinaradio@gmail.com
License: Mississauga, ON held by Neeti Prakash.
Neeti Ray, President

Moosonee

***CHMO(AM)**
02-29-1976; 1450 khz AM *Hrs Open:* 6 AM-11 PM; 50 w; N51 16 39 W80 38 40
Mailing Address: Box 400, Moosonee, ON P0L 1Y0 Canada
Second Address: 24 First St., Moosonee, ON P0L 1Y0
(705) 336-2466, *Fax:* (705) 336-2186
jbbtcorp@owlink.net
License: Moosonee, ON held by James Bay Broadcasting Corp.
Population Served: 5,000 *Format:* Country, Variety/Diverse*Special Programming:* Cree Indian 5 hrs wkly*Hrs. of News Programming:* news progmg 10 hrs wkly *No. News Employees:* 1 *Target Audience:* General.*Adv. Rates:* 25; 25; 25; 25
John Kirk, President
Ernest Hunter, Station Manager
Jack Williams, Programming Director
George Witham, Chief Engineer

Napanee

CKYM-FM
01-01-2007; 88.7 mhz FM; 5 kw; N44 08 30 W77 04 33
20 Market Sq., Napanee, ON K7R 1J3 Canada
(613) 354-4554, *Fax:* (613) 354-3661
www.myfmradio.ca/887/
napanee@myfmradio.ca
License: Napanee, ON held by My Broadcasting Corp.
Group Owner: My Broadcasting Corp.
Population Served: 15,511 *Arbitron Metro Market:* Greater Napanee, ON *Format:* Adult Contemp
Brad Way, President
Pam Oliver, General Manager
Stafford Murphy, Programming Director
Doug Ritchie, Managing Director

Newmarket

CKDX-FM
09-01-1994; 88.5 mhz FM; 11.3 kw
5312 Dundas St. W., Etobicoke, ON M9B 1B3 Canada
(416) 213-1035, *Fax:* (416) 233-8617
www.jewelradio.com/885
info@885thejewel.com
License: Newmarket, ON held by CKDX Radio Ltd.
Group Owner: Evanov Communications Inc.; (acq 12-21-2000).
Format: Adult Contemp*Adv. Rates:* 100; 100; 100; 100
Bill Evanov, President
Bruce Campbell, General Sales Mgr
Gary Gamble, Programming Director
Grace Pascucci, Promotions Manager

***CHOP-FM**
09-28-2007; 102.7 mhz FM; 5 w; N44 02 49 W79 27 08
Pickering College, 16945 Bayview Ave., Newmarket, ON L3Y 4X2 Canada
(905) 895-1700, *Fax:* (905) 895-9076
www.pickeringcollege.on.ca
info@pickeringcollege.on.ca
License: Newmarket, ON held by Pickering College.
Population Served: 80,400 *Arbitron Metro Market:* Newmarket, ON *Format:* Sports, Talk
Peter Sturrup, General Manager
Kim Bilous, Executive Director of Development

Niagara Falls

CJED-FM
01-01-1996; 105.1 mhz FM *Hrs Open:* 25.?Â ?; 4 kw
Mailing Address: Box 710, Niagara Falls, ON L2E 6X7 Canada
Second Address: 4668 St. Clair Ave., Niagara Falls, ON L2E 3S8
(905) 356-6710, *Fax:* (905) 356-0644
www.river.fm
robwhite@niagara.com
License: Niagara Falls, ON held by Niagara Radio Group Inc.
Nat'l Reps: Target Broadcast Sales
Arbitron Metro Market: Buffalo-Niagara Falls, NY*Hrs. of News Programming:* news progmg 5 hrs wkly *No. News Employees:* 3 *Target Audience:* 25-54.*Adv. Rates:* 45; 42; 40; 42
Robert White, Operations Dir
Elizabeth Lewis, General Manager
Andrew Bilous, General Sales Mgr
Mike Ryan, Programming Director

North Bay

CHUR-FM
01-01-1996; 100.5 mhz FM; 100 kw
743 Main St. E., c/o Rogers Media, North Bay, ON P1B 8K8 Canada
(705) 474-2000, *Fax:* (705) 474-7761
www.ezrocknorthbay.com
andy.wilson@northbayradio.rogers.com
License: North Bay, ON held by Rogers Broadcasting Ltd.
Group Owner: Rogers Broadcasting Ltd.; acq 4-19-2002; grpsl).
Format: Adult Contemp *Target Audience:* 25-54.
Ted Rogers, CEO
Peter Mckeown, General Manager

CKAT(AM)
03-03-1931; 600 khz AM *Hrs Open:* 24; 10 kw-D, 5 kw-N, DA-1
743 Main St. E., North Bay, ON P1B 1C2 Canada
(705) 474-2000, *Fax:* (705) 474-7761
www.600ckat.com
andy.wilson@northbayradio.rogers.com
License: North Bay, ON held by Rogers Broadcasting Ltd.
Group Owner: Rogers Broadcasting Ltd.; acq 4-19-02; grpsl).
Population Served: 56,000 *Format:* Country*Hrs. of News Programming:* news progmg 6 hrs wkly *No. News Employees:* 5 *Target Audience:* 25-54.

RADIO - CANADA

Rick Doughty, Operations Dir
Peter McKeown, General Manager
James Dahlke, General Sales Mgr
Dean Belanger, Programming Director
Peter Tensen, Promotions Manager
Richard Coffin, News Director
Csaba Senyi, Engineering Dir

CKFX-FM
01-19-1967; 101.9 mhz FM *Hrs Open:* 24; 100 kw; Ant 350 ft
Mailing Address: 743 Main St. E., North Bay, ON P1B 1C2 Canada
Second Address: Box 3000, North Bay, ON P1B 8K8
(705) 474-2000, *Fax:* (705) 474-7761
www.foxradio.ca
dean.belanger@northbayradio.rogers.com
License: North Bay, ON held by Rogers Broadcasting Ltd.
Group Owner: Rogers Broadcasting Ltd.

Mike Belanger, Programming Director
Kevin Ochefski, Promotions Manager

CFXN-FM
07-16-2006; 106.3 mhz FM *Hrs Open:* 9am-5pm; 10 kw; N46 18 10 W79 24 39
118 Main St. E., North Bay, ON P1B 1A8 Canada
(705) 475-9991, *Fax:* (705) 475-9058
www.moosefm.com
moose1063@moosefm.com
License: North Bay, ON held by The Haliburton Broadcasting Group Inc.
Group Owner: Haliburton Broadcasting Group Inc.
Population Served: 84,000 *No. News Employees:* 2
Sean Connon, General Sales Mgr
Mike Fry, Programming Director
Amanda Butler, Promotions Manager
Rocco Frangione, News Director
Dave Belanger, Chief Engineer
Toni Ross, Music Director
Mike Monaghan, Programming Director
MikeTrahan, Sales Manager

Oakville

CJYE
11-17-1956; 1250 khz AM *Hrs Open:* 24
CA
(905) 845-2821, *Fax:* (905) 842-1250
www.joy1250.ca
contact@joy1250.ca
License: Oakville, ON held by Trafalgar Broadcasting Ltd.
Nat'l Reps: Western Regional Broadcast Sales
Arbitron Metro Market: Oakville, ON *Format:* Christian
Michael Caine, President
Harry McDonald, General Manager
Michael Caine, Founder

Ohsweken

***CKRZ-FM**
01-01-1991; 100.3 mhz FM *Hrs Open:* 6 AM-11 PM; 250 w
Mailing Address: Box 189, Ohsweken, ON N0A 1M0 Canada
Second Address: 1721 Chiefswood Rd., Oashweken, ON
(519) 445-4140, *Fax:* (519) 445-0177
ckrzinfo@ckrz.com
License: Ohsweken, Haldimond County, ON held by Southern Onkwehon: We Nishinabec Indigenous Communications Society.
Format: Country, Variety/Diverse*Hrs. of News Programming:* news progmg 4.5 hrs wkly *No. News Employees:* 1 *Target Audience:* General.
Loreen Harris, General Sales Mgr
Kathy Montour, Programming Director

Orangeville

***CIDCFM**
05-01-1987; 103.5 mhz FM *Hrs Open:* 24; kw
CA
(416) 213-1035, *Fax:* (416) 233-8617
www.z1035.com
info@z1035.com
License: Orangeville, ON held by Dufferin Communications Inc.
Group Owner: Evanov Communications Inc.; (acq 9-28-94).
Nat'l Reps: Canadian Broadcast Sales
Format: Contemporary Hits/Top 40 *No. News Employees:* 1 *Target Audience:* 18-44.*Adv. Rates:* 180; 180; 180; 180.
Bill Evanov, President
Bruce Campbell, General Manager
Paul Evanov, Programming Director

Orillia

CICX-FM
09-07-1943; 105.9 mhz FM *Hrs Open:* 24; 10.6 kw
7 Progress Dr., Box 550, Orillia, ON L3V 6K2 Canada
(705) 326-3511, *Fax:* (705) 326-1816
www.kicx106.com
mora.austin@larchecom.com
License: Orillia, Simcoe County, ON held by Larche Communications Inc.
Group Owner: Larche Communications Inc.; (acq 1-28-2008; exchange for CIKZ-FM Kitchener-Waterloo)
Format: Country*Hrs. of News Programming:* news progmg 2 hrs wkly *No. News Employees:* 2*Adv. Rates:* 35; 31; 33; 20
Paul Larche, President
Mora Austin, Operations Dir
Linda Young, General Sales Mgr
Jack Latimer, Programming Director
Martin Vanderwoude, News Director

Oshawa

CKDO
01-01-1946; 1580 khz AM *Hrs Open:* 24
CA
(905) 571-0949, *Fax:* (905) 571-1150
www.ckdo.ca
info@ckdo.ca
License: Oshawa, ON held by Durham Radio Inc.
Group Owner: Durham Radio Inc.; (acq 4-23-2003; C$3.9 million with co-located FM).
Format: Contemporary Hits/Top 40, Adult Contemp*Special Programming:* Relg one hr wkly*Hrs. of News Programming:* news progmg 9 hrs wkly *No. News Employees:* 4 *Target Audience:* 45 plus.
Doug Kirk, General Manager
Steve Macaulay, General Sales Mgr
Steve Kassay, Programming Director
Natalie Fournier, Promotions Manager

CKGE-FM
09-12-1957; 94.9 mhz FM *Hrs Open:* 24; 50 kw; 474 ft; N43 57 15 W78 48 24
1200 Airport Blvd., Ste 207, Oshawa, ON L1J 8P5 Canada
(905) 571-0949, *Fax:* (905) 571-1150
www.therock.fm
therock@therock.fm
License: Oshawa, ON held by Durham Radio Inc.
Group Owner: Durham Radio Inc.
Format: Classic Rock*Hrs. of News Programming:* news progmg 5 hrs wkly *No. News Employees:* 4 *Target Audience:* 35-54.
Doug Kirk, General Manager
Doug Elliot, Programming Director

Ottawa

***CBO-FM**
01-07-1991; 91.5 mhz FM; 20 kw
Mailing Address: Box 3220, Station C, Ottawa, ON K1Y 1E4 Canada
Second Address: Ottawa Broadcast Centre, 181 Queen St., Ottawa, ON K1P 1K9
(613) 288-6000, *Fax:* (613) 288-6495
www.ottawa.cbc.ca
License: Ottawa, ON held by CBC.
Nat'l Network: CBC Radio One
Remi Rancine, Chairman
Hubert Lacroix, CEO

***CBOFFM**
09-12-1974; 90.7 mhz FM
Box 3220, Station C, Ottawa, ON Canada
(613) 724-1200,(613) 562-8521, *Fax:* (613) 562-8520
www.cbc.radio-canada.ca/regions/ottawa
License: Ottawa, ON held by Societe Radio-Canada.
Nat'l Network: Radio Canada
Patricia Pleszczynska, Operations Dir
Judith Bleier, Operations Manager

***CBOQ-FM**
02-18-1947; 103.3 mhz FM; 70 kw
Box 3220, Station C, Ottawa, ON K1Y 1E4 Canada
(613) 724-1200,(613) 562-8422, *Fax:* (613) 562-8430,(613) 562-8408
www.ottawa.cbc.ca
License: Ottawa, ON held by CBC.
Nat'l Network: CBC Radio Two
Robert Rabinovitch, CEO
Gilles Tessier, Operations Dir
Miriam Fry, General Manager

***CBOX-FM**
01-01-1990; 102.5 mhz FM; 70 kw; Ant 1,077 ft
Box 3220, Station C, Ottawa, ON K1Y 1E4 Canada
(613) 724-1200,(613) 562-8521, *Fax:* (613) 562-8520
www.radio-canada.ca/regions/ottawa
License: Ottawa, ON held by Societe Radio-Canada.
Nat'l Network: Radio Canada

Robert Rabinovitch, CEO
Gilles Tessier, Operations Dir
Miriam Fry, General Manager

CFGO
06-07-1964; 1200 khz AM *Hrs Open:* 24; 50 kw-U, DA-2
Team 1200, 87 George St., Ottawa, ON Canada
(613) 789-2486, *Fax:* (613) 738-2881
www.team1200.com
License: Ottawa, ON held by Bell Media Ottawa Radio Partnership
Group Owner: Bell Media Inc.; (acq 9-10-99; for 87.5%).
Population Served: 1,000,000 *No. News Employees:* 5 *Target Audience:* 18-34; men
Allan Waters, CEO
Don Holtby, General Sales Mgr
Dave Mitchell, Programming Director
Al Macartney, Promotions Manager
Steve Winogron, News Director
Harrie Jones, Engineering Dir
Jack Derouin, General Sales Manager
Brad Boechler,National Sales Manager
J. R. Ello, Promotions Manager

***CKBYFM**
01-29-1969; 105.3 mhz FM *Hrs Open:* 24; kw
CA
(613) 736-2001, *Fax:* (613) 736-2002
www.y101.fm
License: Ottawa, ON held by Rogers Broadcasting, Ltd.
Group Owner: Rogers Broadcasting Ltd.; (acq 7-2-99; grpsl).
Format: Country*Hrs. of News Programming:* news progmg 6 hrs wkly *No. News Employees:* 2 *Target Audience:* 35-54; female
Scott Parsons, Chairman

CFRA
05-03-1947; 580 khz AM *Hrs Open:* 24; 50 kw-D, 10 kw-N, DA-2
87 George St., Ottawa, ON Canada
(613) 789-2486, *Fax:* (613) 523-6423,(613) 738-5024
www.cfra.com
License: Ottawa, ON held by Bell Media Ottawa Radio Partnership
Group Owner: Bell Media Inc.
Nat'l Network: ABC
Hrs. of News Programming: News progmg 24 hrs wkly *Target Audience:* 35-54.
Jack Derouin, General Sales Mgr
Dave Mitchell, Programming Director
Al Macartney, Promotions Manager
Steve Winogron, News Director
Harrie Jones, Chief Engineer
Daniel Proussalidis, News Reporter
Norman Jack, News Reporter
LindaUlmer, Traffic Manager

***CHEZFM**
03-25-1977; 106.1 mhz FM *Hrs Open:* 24; kw
CA
(613) 736-2001, *Fax:* (613) 736-2002
www.chez106.com
License: Ottawa, ON held by Rogers Broadcasting Ltd.
Group Owner: Rogers Broadcasting Ltd.; (acq 7-2-99; grpsl)
Format: Classic Rock*Hrs. of News Programming:* news progmg 2 hrs wkly *No. News Employees:* 3 *Target Audience:* 25-54; males
Scott Parsons, Chairman

CHRI-FM
03-06-1997; 99.1 mhz FM *Hrs Open:* 24; 25.3 kw; 551 ft; N45 13 01 W75 37 51
1010 Thomas Spratt Pl., Suite 3, Ottawa, ON K1G 5L5 Canada
(613) 247-1440,(613) 247-1886, *Fax:* (613) 247-7128
www.chri.ca
chri@chri.ca
License: Ottawa, Canada County, ON held by Christian Hit Radio Inc.
Population Served: 1,300,000*Special Programming:* Children and Youth Programming*Hrs. of News Programming:* news progmg 2 hrs wkly *No. News Employees:* 1 *Target Audience:* 18-44.*Adv. Rates:* 45; 25; 35; na
Ethel Mahoney, President
Bill Stevens, General Manager
Brock Tozer, Programming Director

***CHUO-FM**
05-31-1991; 89.1 mhz FM *Hrs Open:* 24; 18.2 kw; N45 30 11 W75 51 02
65 University PVT., Suite 0038, Ottawa, ON K1N 9A5 Canada
(613) 562-5965, *Fax:* (613) 562-5969
www.chuo.fm
info@chuo.fm
License: Ottawa, ON held by Radio Ottawa Inc.
Population Served: 900,000 *Format:* French*Special Programming:* Ger 2 hrs, jazz 5 hrs, relg 2 hrs, Sp 3 hrs, Chine *Target Audience:* General.
Marc Gill, General Manager
Emmanuel Sayer, Programming Director

CIWW
06-01-1949; 1310 khz AM *Hrs Open:* 24
CA
(613) 736-2001, *Fax:* (613) 736-2002
1310news.com
tips1310@rogers.com
License: Ottawa, ON held by Rogers Media.
Group Owner: Rogers Broadcasting Ltd.
Format: Oldies
Scott Anderson, General Manager

CJMJ
08-13-1991; 100.3 mhz FM *Hrs Open:* 24; 100 kw
Team 1200, 87 George St., Ottawa, ON Canada
Fax: (613) 750-0100
www.majic100.fm
License: Ottawa, ON held by Bell Media Ottawa Radio Partnership
Group Owner: Bell Media Inc.
Population Served: 1,000,000 *Target Audience:* 25-44; female
Jack Derouin, General Sales Mgr
Kent Newson, Programming Director
Al Macartney, Promotions Manager
Codi Jeffreys, Music Director

CISS-FM
10-29-1969; 105.3 mhz FM; 100 kw; Ant 1,077 ft
2001 Thurston Dr., Ottawa, ON K1G 6C9 Canada
(613) 736-2001, *Fax:* (613) 736-2002
www.1053kissfm.com
License: Ottawa, ON held by Rogers Media
Group Owner: Rogers Broadcasting Ltd.
Format: Adult Contemp, Contemporary Hits/Top 40
Danny Kingsbury, Programming Director

***CKCUFM**
11-15-1975; 93.1 mhz FM *Hrs Open:* 24; kw
CA
(613) 520-2898, *Fax:* (613) 520-4060
www.ckcufm.com
info@ckcufm.com
License: Ottawa, ON held by Radio Carleton Inc.
Format: Variety/Diverse*Special Programming:* Jazz 15 hrs, Black 12 hrs, Fr 2 hrs, Pol one hr, V*Hrs. of News Programming:* news progmg 25 hrs wkly *No. News Employees:* 2 *Target Audience:* General; alternative rock,spoken word, ethnic audience
Matthew Crosier, Station Manager
Dave Sarazin, Programming Director

***CKDJ-FM**
10-03-1994; 107.9 mhz FM; 100 w
1385 Woodroffe Ave., Algonquin College, Ottawa, ON K2G 1V8 Canada
(613) 727-4723, *Fax:* (613) 727-7689
www.ckdj.net
mellond@algonquincollege.com
License: Ottawa, ON held by CKDJ-FM Algonquin Radio.
Population Served: 300,000 *Format:* Alternative *Target Audience:* 17-24; collegel students
Don Crockford, General Manager
Ryan Lindsay, Station Manager

CKKL
01-01-1959; 93.9 mhz FM *Hrs Open:* 24; 95 kw; Ant 1,077 ft
87 George St., Ottawa, ON Canada
Fax: (613) 739-4040
www.939bobfm.com
License: Ottawa, ON held by Bell Media Ottawa Radio Partnership
Group Owner: Bell Media Inc.
Nat'l Network: ABC
Hrs. of News Programming: news progmg one hr wkly *No. News Employees:* 2 *Target Audience:* 18-34.
Steve Gregory, Programming Director
Al Macartney, Promotions Manager
Steve Winogron, News Director

Harrie Jones, Engineering Dir
John Mielke, Disc Jockey
J.R. Rodenburg, Disc Jockey
Sandy Sharkey, Disc Jockey
Louise Seguin,Traffic Manager

***CKQB**
09-01-1994; 106.9 mhz FM *Hrs Open:* 24; kw
CA
(613) 225-1069, *Fax:* (613) 226-3381
www.thebear.fm
License: Ottawa, ON held by Astral Media Radio G.P.
Group Owner: Astral Media Inc.; (acq 10-29-2007; grpsl)
Format: Rock/AOR*Hrs. of News Programming:* news progmg one hr wkly *No. News Employees:* 3 *Target Audience:* 18-49; professionals
Denis Bouchard, Operations Dir
Denis Bouchard, General Manager
Greg Orr, General Sales Mgr
JD Desrosiers, Programming Director
Eric St Louis, Promotions Manager

CIHT-FM
02-01-2003; 89.9 mhz FM; 27 kw
6 Antores Dr., Phase 1, Unit 100, Ottawa, ON K2E 8A9 Canada
(613) 723-8990, *Fax:* (613) 723-7016
www.hot899.com
sbroderick@newcap.ca
License: Ottawa, ON held by NewCap Inc.
Group Owner: NewCap Inc.
Population Served: 812,135 *Arbitron Metro Market:* Ottawa, ON *Format:* Contemporary Hits/Top 40 *Target Audience:* 25-34; females
Scott Broderick, General Manager
Josie Geller, Station Manager

CJLL-FM
01-01-2003; 97.9 mhz FM *Hrs Open:* 24; 6.77 kw
CHIN Radio Ottawa, 30 Murray St., Ottawa, ON K1N 5M4 Canada
(613) 244-0979, *Fax:* (613) 244-3858
www.chinradioottawa.com
chinottawa@chinradio.com
License: Ottawa, ON held by Radio 1540 Ltd.
Population Served: 812,135 *Arbitron Metro Market:* Ottawa, ON *Format:* Ethnic*Hrs. of News Programming:* 12 *No. News Employees:* 2 *Target Audience:* Ethnic 12 plus; mutlicultural*Adv. Rates:* 60; 60; 60; 50
Francesco Di Candia, Operations Dir
Gary Michaels, Programming Director

CILV-FM
12-26-2005; 88.5 mhz FM; 2.3 kw
6 Antares Dr., Phase 1, Unit 100, Ottawa, ON K2E 8A9 Canada
(613) 688-8888, *Fax:* (613) 723-7016
www.livelifelive.fm
sbroderick@newcap.ca
License: Ottawa, ON held by NewCap Inc.
Group Owner: NewCap Inc.
Population Served: 812,135 *Arbitron Metro Market:* Ottawa, ON *Format:* Alternative
Scott Broderick, General Manager
Mark Russett, General Sales Mgr
Dan Youngs, Programming Director
Blair Amyotte, Promotions Manager
Noah Sabourin, Music Director

CJWL-FM
02-01-2006; 98.5 mhz FM; 485 w
127 York St., Ottawa, ON K1N 5T4 Canada
(613) 241-9850, *Fax:* (613) 241-9852
www.985thejewel.com
info@985thejewel.com
License: Ottawa, ON held by Ottawa Media Inc.
Group Owner: Evanov Communications Inc.
Population Served: 812,135 *Arbitron Metro Market:* Ottawa, ON *Format:* Adult Contemp *Target Audience:* 45 plus.
Colin Hunter, Chairman
Bill Evanov, CEO
Doug Large, General Manager
Ted Silver, Programming Director

CKAV-FM-9
01-01-2007; 95.7 mhz FM; 6 kw
PO Box 87, Station E, Toronto, ON M6H 4E1 Canada
(416) 703-1287, *Fax:* (416) 703-4328
aboriginalvoices.com
info@aboriginalvoices.com
License: Ottawa, ON held by Aboriginal Voices Radio Inc.
Group Owner: Aboriginal Voices Radio Inc.
Population Served: 2,615,060 *Arbitron Metro Market:* Toronto, ON *Format:* Ethnic

Roy Hennessy, Operations Dir
Patrice Mousseau, Programming Director

CIDG-FM
06-07-2012; 101.9 mhz FM *Hrs Open:* 24 hours; 1.793 kw; 98 meters
380 Hunt Club Road, Suite 203, Ottawa, ON K1V 1C1 Canada
(613) 730-1019, *Fax:* (613) 7301092
www.dawgfm.com
License: Ottawa, ON held by Todd Bernard Ottawa Inc
Todd Bernard, General Manager
Yves Trottier, Operations Manager
Alyssa Delle Palme, Promotions Manager
J-Man, Music Director

CJFO-FM
11-15-2012; 94.5 mhz FM; 25 kw
245 Avenue McArthur, Ottawa, ON K1L 6P3 Canada
(613) 745-5529, *Fax:* (613) 745-7004
www.cjfofm.com
info@cjfofm.com
License: Ottawa, ON held by La Radio Communautaire Francophone D'Ottawa
Gilles Poulin, CEO
Lucien Bradet, President

CJOT-FM
05-27-2010; 99.7 mhz FM; 100 kw
1504 Merivale Road, Ottawa, ON K2E 6Z5 Canada
(613) 225-1069, *Fax:* (613) 226-3381
www.boom997.com
License: Ottawa, Renfrew County, ON held by Astral Media Radio Inc

Owen Sound

CIXK-FM
01-03-1989; 106.5 mhz FM *Hrs Open:* 24; 100 kw; 555 ft; N44 44 37 W80 54 16
270 9th St. E., Box 280, Owen Sound, ON N4K 5P5 Canada
(519) 376-2030, *Fax:* (519) 371-4242
www.mix106.ca
License: Owen Sound, ON held by Bayshore Broadcasting Corp.
Group Owner: Bayshore Broadcasting Corp.
Nat'l Reps: Target Broadcast Sales *Wire Services:* BN Wire
Format: Adult Contemp *No. News Employees:* 7 *Target Audience:* 18-40.
Ross Kentner, General Manager
J.D. Moffatt, Programming Director
Rob Brignell, Promotions Manager
Manny Paiva, News Director

CKYC-FM
09-04-2001; 93.7 mhz FM *Hrs Open:* 24; 31.6 kw
270 9th St. E., Owen Sound, ON N4K 5P5 Canada
(519) 376-2030, *Fax:* (519) 371-4242
www.radioowensound.com
bayshore@radioowensound.com
License: Owen Sound, ON held by Bayshore Broadcasting Corp.
Group Owner: Bayshore Broadcasting Corp.
Nat'l Reps: Target Broadcast Sales
Population Served: 21,688 *Arbitron Metro Market:* Owen Sound, ON *Format:* Country *Target Audience:* 25-54; adult
Lois Reid, Operations Dir
Ross Kentner, General Manager
Kevin Brown, General Sales Mgr
John Wilson, Promotions Manager
Jim Birchard, News Director
Mariane McLeod, News Director
Peter Jackson, Assistant News Director
MannyPaiva, News Manager
Fred Wallace, Sports Director
Catherine Thompson, News Reporter

CJOS-FM
03-25-2010; 92.3 mhz FM; 9.4 kw; 214 meters
787 9th Avenue East, Owen Sound, ON N4K3E6 Canada
(519) 470-7626, *Fax:* (519) 470-7631
www.923thedock.com
License: Owen Sound, ON held by Larche Communications Inc
Format: Contemporary Hits/Top 40
Paul Larche, President

Paris

CJIQ-FM
01-08-2001; 88.3 mhz FM *Hrs Open:* 24; kw
CA
(519) 748-5220
www.cjiq.fm
mthurnell@conestogac.on.ca

License: Paris, ON held by Conestoga College Communications Corp.
Arbitron Metro Market: Kitchener, ON *Format:* Variety/Diverse
Paul Scott, Operations Dir
Mark Burley, Station Manager
Mike Thurnell, Program Director/CJIQ Coordinator

Parry Sound

CKLPFM
07-01-1986; 103.3 mhz FM *Hrs Open:* 24; 50 kw; 400 ft
60 James St., Suite 301, Parry Sound, ON Canada
(705) 746-2163, *Fax:* (705) 746-4292
www.moosefm.com/cklp
moose1033@hbgradio.com
License: Parry Sound, ON held by The Haliburton Broadcasting Group Inc.
Group Owner: Haliburton Broadcasting Group Inc.; (acq 11-9-01; C$2,025,000).
Nat'l Reps: Target Broadcast
Population Served: 60,000*Special Programming:* Canadian First Nation 1 hr feature*Hrs. of News Programming:* news progmg 12 hrs wkly *No. News Employees:* 2 *Target Audience:* General.
Brian Prokopec, General Manager
Brian Prokopec, General Sales Mgr
Mike Fry, Programming Director
Dave Belanger, Chief Engineer

Pembroke

CHVR-FM
05-06-1996; 96.7 mhz FM; 100 kw
595 Pembroke St. E., Pembroke, ON K8A 3L7 Canada
(613) 735-9670, *Fax:* (613) 735-7748
www.star96.ca
music@star96.ca
License: Pembroke, ON held by Astral Media Radio G.P.
Group Owner: Astral Media Inc.; (acq 10-29-2007; grpsl)
Population Served: 500,000 *Format:* Country *Target Audience:* 25-54.
Al Kennedy, General Manager
Rick Johnston, Programming Director

CIMY-FM
09-01-2005; 104.9 mhz FM; 16.6 kw; 90.5 meters
84 Isabella St., 2nd Fl, Pembroke, ON K8A 5S5 Canada
(613) 735-6936, *Fax:* (613) 732-4054
www.myfmradio.ca/1049/index.htm
info@myfmradio.ca
License: Pembroke, ON held by My Broadcasting Corp.
Group Owner: My Broadcasting Corp.
Andrew Dickson, General Manager
Jon Pole, Programming Director

Penetanguishene

*CFRH-FM
09-24-1999; 88.1 mhz FM *Hrs Open:* 24; 8.6 kw; N44 46 10 W79 59 25
Mailing Address: C.P. 5099, Penetanguishene, ON L9M 2G3 Canada
Second Address: 63 Main, PO box 5099, Penetanguishene, ON L9M 2G3
(705) 549-3116, *Fax:* (705) 549-6463
www.vaguefm.ca
vaguefm@vaguefm.ca
License: Penetanguishene, Simcoe County, ON held by La Cle d'la Baie en Huronie - Association culturel
Regional Reps: Radio Unie Target
Population Served: 50,000 *Target Audience:* Francophone; francophone minority in mid-southern Ontario*Adv. Rates:* 15 per 30 seconds
Pierre Casault, CEO
Michelle Laurin, Operations Dir
Melanie Bouchard, Station Manager
Michel Payment, Host
Marc Lalonde, Host

Perth

CHLK-FM
07-01-2007; 88.1 mhz FM; 2.8 kw; 91.5 meters; N44 54 34 W76 16 51
43 Wilson St. W., Perth, ON Canada
(613) 264-8811, *Fax:* (613) 264-1119
www.lake88.ca
communityradio@perth.igs.net
License: Perth, ON held by Perth FM Radio Inc.
Norm Wright, General Manager

Peterborough

CFFF-FM
01-01-1969; 92.7 mhz FM *Hrs Open:* 24hrs; 700 w
715 George St., N., Peterborough, ON K9H 3T2 Canada
(705) 741-4011
www.trentu.ca/trentradio
info@trentradio.ca
License: Peterborough, Peterborough County, ON held by Trent Radio.
Nat'l Reps: Target Broadcast Sales
Population Served: 120,000 *Target Audience:* General.
John Muir, General Manager
James Kerr, Programming Director

CKQMFM
09-16-1977; 105.1 mhz FM *Hrs Open:* 24; 7.5 kw; Ant 910 ft; N44 17 36 W78 21 20
Box 177, Peterborough, ON Canada
(705) 742-8844, *Fax:* (705) 742-1417
www.country105.fm
country105@chumradio.com
License: Peterborough, Peterborough County, ON held by Bell Media Ontario Regional Radio
Group Owner: Bell Media Inc.; (acq 6-22-2007; grpsl)
Hrs. of News Programming: news progmg 4 hrs wkly *No. News Employees:* 3 *Target Audience:* 25-64.
Ivan Fecan, President
Steve Fawcett, General Manager
Wanda Bergshoeff, General Sales Mgr
Brian Young, Programming Director
Mel Hannah, Promotions Manager
Ed Crompton, Engineering Dir
Ray Hebert, Music Director

CKWF-FM
07-24-1968; 101.5 mhz FM *Hrs Open:* 24; 15.2 kw; Ant 896 ft
159 King St., Peterborough, ON K9J 2R8 Canada
(705) 748-6101, *Fax:* (705) 742-7708
www.thewolf.ca
info@thewolf.com
License: Peterborough, ON held by 591989 B.C. Ltd.
Group Owner: Corus Entertainment Inc.
No. News Employees: 2
Chris Pandof, General Manager
Laurie English, General Sales Mgr
Rob Seguin, Programming Director
Carey Walker, Promotions Manager

CJMB-FM
11-24-2004; 90.5 mhz FM *Hrs Open:* 24; 230 w
993 Talwood Dr., Second Floor, Peterborough, ON K9J 7R8 Canada
(705) 876-0404, *Fax:* (705) 755-0688
www.kaosradio.com
info@kaosradio.com
License: Peterborough, ON held by King's Kids Promotions Outreach Ministries Inc.
Population Served: 112,000 *No. News Employees:* 5 *Target Audience:* 18-40.*Adv. Rates:* 18; 14; 16; 10
Rick Kirschner, General Manager

CKPT-FM
09-10-2007; 99.7 mhz FM *Hrs Open:* 24; 17 kw; Ant 301 ft; N44 17 36 W78 21 20
59 George St. N., Peterborough, ON K9J 6Y8 Canada
(705) 742-8844, *Fax:* (705) 742-1417
www.energy997.ca
energy997@chumradio.com
License: Peterborough, ON held by Bell Media Ontario Regional Radio
Group Owner: Bell Media
Hrs. of News Programming: news progmg 2 hrs wkly *No. News Employees:* 3 *Target Audience:* 18-54; 60% women.
Kevin Crull, President
Steve Fawcett, General Manager
Wanda Bergshoeff, General Sales Mgr
Brian Young, Programming Director
Mel Hannah, Promotions Manager
George Gall, News Director
Ed Crompton, Engineering Dir

Petersborough

CKRU-FM
100.5 mhz FM; 15 kw; 75.3 meters; N44 17 36 W78 21 19
151 King Street, Suite 200, Petersborough, ON K9J 2R8 Canada
(705) 748-6101, *Fax:* (705) 742-7708
www.kruzfm.ca
License: Petersborough, ON held by 591989 B.C. Ltd.
J J Johnston, General Manager

Port Elgin

CFPS-FM
01-01-2005; 97.9 mhz FM *Hrs Open:* 24; 3.8 kw
382 Goderich St., Port Elgin, ON N0H 2C0 Canada
(519) 832-9800, *Fax:* (519) 371-4242
www.98thebeach.ca
License: Port Elgin, ON held by Bayshore Broadcasting Corp.
Group Owner: Bayshore Broadcasting Corp.
Nat'l Reps: Target Broadcast Sales
Population Served: 95,142 *Arbitron Metro Market:* Bryan-College Station, TX *Format:* Adult Contemp *Target Audience:* 18-54.
Ross Kentner, General Manager
Rob Brignell, General Sales Mgr
Don Vail, Programming Director
John Divinski, News Director

Quinte West

CJTN-FM
01-01-2004; 107.1 mhz FM *Hrs Open:* 24; 3.64 kw
31 Quinte St., Quinte West, ON K8V 3S7 Canada
(613) 392-1237, *Fax:* (613) 394-6430
www.rock107.ca
billmorton@mix97.com
License: Quinte West, ON held by Quinte Broadcasting Co. Ltd.
Group Owner: Quinte Broadcasting Ltd.

Bill Morton, CEO/COO
Bill Morton, President
Bob Rowbotham, General Manager
Jody Brooker, General Sales Mgr
Sean Kelley, Programming Director
Lorne Brooker, Promotions Manager
John Spittecs, News Director

Red Lake

CKDR-FM-5
01-01-2008; 97.1 mhz FM; 420 w; N51 01 12 W93 49 51*Rebroadcasts:* Rebroadcasts CKDR-FM Dryden 99%
Mailing Address: 122 King Street, Dryden, ON P8N 1C2 Canada
Second Address: 122 King St., Dryden, ON P8N 2Z3
(807) 223-2355, *Fax:* (807) 223-5090
www.ckdr.net
mail@ckdr.net
License: Red Lake, Sunset County, ON held by Northwoods Broadcasting Ltd.
Group Owner: Acadia Broadcasting Ltd.; (acq 5-1-2007; grpsl)
Population Served: 7,617 *Arbitron Metro Market:* Dryden, ON *Format:* Contemporary Hits/Top 40
Bruce Walchuk, General Manager

Renfrew

CHMY-FM
08-01-2004; 96.1 mhz FM; 7.1 kw; 128.5 meters
Mailing Address: Box 961, Renfrew, ON Canada
Second Address: 321-B Raglan St. S., Renfrew, ON K7V 4H4
(613) 432-6936, *Fax:* (613) 432-1086
www.myfmradio.ca
License: Renfrew, ON held by My Broadcasting Corp.
Group Owner: My Broadcasting Corp.

Andrew Dickson, General Manager

CJHR-FM
12-11-2006; 98.7 mhz FM; kw
CA
(613) 432-9873, *Fax:* (613) 432-9103
www.valleyheritageradio.ca
info@valleyheritageradio.com
License: Renfrew, ON held by Valley Heritage Radio.
Arbitron Metro Market: Renfrew, ON *Format:* Country
Denzil Ferguson, President
Jim Long, Station Manager
Fay Kolpin, Vice President

Richmond Hill

CFMJ
07-01-1957; 640 khz AM *Hrs Open:* 24
CA
(416) 221-6400, *Fax:* (416) 847-3300
www.am640toronto.com
gharris@640toronto.com
License: Richmond Hill, ON held by Corus Premium Television
Group Owner: Corus Entertainment Inc.; (acq 7-6-00; grpsl).
Nat'l Network: Premiere Radio Networks *Nat'l Reps:* Canadian Broadcast Sales *Wire Services:* Broadcast News Ltd.

Format: News, News/Talk, Talk*Special Programming:* NHL hockey*Hrs. of News Programming:* Hourly 24/7 *No. News Employees:* 10 *Target Audience:* 35-64; upscale, mature, male
John Cassaday, CEO
Chris Pandoff, Operations Dir
Chris Sisam, General Manager
Gord Harris, Programming Director
Darren Wasylyk, Promotions Manager
James MacPhee, News Director

Saint Catharines

CFBU-FM
01-01-1997; 103.7 mhz FM *Hrs Open:* 24; 250 w
500 Glenridge Ave., % Brock University, St. Catharines, ON L2S 3A1 Canada
(905) 346-2644
www.cfbu.ca
pd@cfbu.ca
License: Saint Catharines, ON held by Brock University Student Radio.
Population Served: 300,000 *Format:* Variety/Diverse*Special Programming:* American Indian one hr, jazz 4 hrs, Sp 4 hrs, Por*Adv. Rates:* 20; 20; 20; 20.
Deborah Cartmer, Programming Director
Jordy Yack, Music Director

Sarnia

***CBEGFM**
11-27-1977; 90.3 mhz FM; kw*Rebroadcasts:* Rebroadcasts CBE(AM) Windsor
CA
(519) 255-3411, *Fax:* (519) 255-3443
www.windsor.cbc.ca
earlyshift@cbc.ca
License: Sarnia, ON held by CBC.
Nat'l Network: CBC Radio One
Format: Public Affairs, News
Janice Stein, Station Manager

CFGX-FM
09-14-1981; 99.9 mhz FM *Hrs Open:* 24; 27 kw; N42 52 12 W82 23 50
1415 London Rd., Sarnia, ON N7S 1P6 Canada
(519) 542-5500, *Fax:* (519) 542-1520
www.foxfm.com
info@foxfm.com
License: Sarnia, Lambton County, ON held by Blackburn Radio Inc.
Group Owner: Blackburn Group Inc.; (acq 12-19-94; grpsl)
Format: Adult Contemp*Special Programming:* New age 7 hrs wkly *Target Audience:* 25-54; females in the workplace
Ron Dann, Operations Dir
Terry Regier, General Manager
George Hayes, Programming Director
Larry Gordon, News Director

CHOK
07-26-1946; 1070 khz AM *Hrs Open:* 24
CA
(519) 542-5500, *Fax:* (519) 542-1520
www.chok.com
radio@chok.com
License: Sarnia, ON held by Sarnia Broadcasters (1993) Ltd.
Group Owner: Blackburn Group Inc.; (acq 12-18-98; C$902,600)
Nat'l Reps: Canadian Broadcast Sales
Format: Country*Special Programming:* Toronto Blue Jays baseball, Toronto Maple Leaf hoc*Hrs. of News Programming:* news progmg 11 hrs wkly *No. News Employees:* 3 *Target Audience:* 25-54.
Ron Dann, General Manager
Martin Vrolyk, General Sales Mgr
Sue Storr, Programming Director
Jeff Teolis, Promotions Manager
Larry Gordon, News Director

CHKS-FM
01-01-1999; 106.3 mhz FM; kw
CA
(519) 542-5500, *Fax:* (519) 542-1520
www.k106fm.com
rock@k106fm.com
License: Sarnia, ON held by Blackburn Radio Inc.
Group Owner: Blackburn Group Inc.
Arbitron Metro Market: Sarnia, ON *Format:* Rock/AOR
Ron Dann, Operations Dir
Terry Regier, General Manager
George Hayes, Programming Director
Larry Gordon, News Director

Sault Ste Marie

***CHASFM**
05-15-1964; 100.5 mhz FM; kw
CA
(705) 759-9200, *Fax:* (705) 946-3575
www.ezrocksoo.com
License: Sault Ste Marie, ON held by Rogers Broadcasting Ltd.
Group Owner: Rogers Broadcasting Ltd.; acq 4-19-2002; grpsl).
Format: Adult Contemp*Special Programming:* Class 5 hrs, jazz 2 hrs, lt 2 hrs wkly *No. News Employees:* 3 *Target Audience:* 25-54; adults
Scott Sexsmith, General Manager

***CJQMFM**
05-13-1964; 104.3 mhz FM; kw
CA
(705) 759-9200, *Fax:* (705) 946-3575
www.qcountry.ca
License: Sault Ste Marie, ON held by Rogers Broadcasting Ltd.
Group Owner: Rogers Broadcasting Ltd.; acq 4-19-2002; grpsl).
Format: Country*Special Programming:* lt 4 hrs wkly*Hrs. of News Programming:* News progmg 3 hrs wkly *Target Audience:* 25-54; adults
Scott Sexsmith, General Manager

Savant Lake

***CBQLFM**
01-01-1977; 104.9 mhz FM; kw*Rebroadcasts:* Rebroadcasts CBQT-FM Thunder Bay
CA
(807) 625-5000, *Fax:* (807) 625-5035
License: Savant Lake, ON held by CBC.
Nat'l Network: CBC Radio One
Format: Public Affairs, News
Tom Grand, Station Manager

Scarborough

CJVF-FM
02-04-2012; 105.9 mhz FM; 45 watts; 63.4 meters
72-74 Dynamic Drive, Scarborough, ON M1V 4B9 Canada
(416) 299-0118
www.vanakkaradio.com
License: Scarborough, ON held by Subanasiri Vaitilingham
Format: Ethnic
Subanasiri Vaithilingham, General Manager

Simcoe

***CHCD**
01-01-1997; 106.7 mhz FM *Hrs Open:* 24; kw
Mailing Address: CA
Second Address: 55 Park Rd., Simcoe, ON N3Y 4K8
(519) 426-7700, *Fax:* (519) 426-8574
www.cd989.com
webmaster@cd989.com
License: Simcoe, ON held by Radiocorp LTD.
Nat'l Reps: Canadian Broadcast Sales
Format: Adult Contemp *No. News Employees:* 3 *Target Audience:* Women; 25-54*Adv. Rates:* 40; 30; 25; 10
Jim MacLeod, President
Blair Daggett, General Manager
Gerry Hamill, Promotions Manager
Kate Buick, News Director

Sioux Lookout

CKWT-FM
01-01-2007; 89.9 mhz FM; 224 w; N50 05 55 W91 55 08
Mailing Address: Box 1180, Sioux Lookout, ON P8T 1B7 Canada
Second Address: 16 5th Ave., Sioux Lookout, ON P8T 1B7
(807) 737-2951, *Fax:* (807) 737-3224
www.wawataynews.ca
License: Sioux Lookout, ON held by Wawatay Native Communications Society.
Population Served: 5,037 *Arbitron Metro Market:* Sioux Lookout, ON *Format:* Native American
David Neegan, CEO/COO
Adrienne Fox-Keesic, General Manager
Lenny Carpenter, News Director
Tabatha Jourdain, Finance Manager
Evangeline Kanakakeesic, Administration Officer
James Brohm, Sales Administrator

CKDR-FM-2
01-01-2008; 97.1 mhz FM *Hrs Open:* 24; 560 w; N50 06 07 W91 55 17*Rebroadcasts:* Rebroadcasts CKDR-FM Dryden 99%
122 King Street, Dryden, ON P8N 1C2 Canada
(807) 223-2355, *Fax:* (807) 223-5090
www.ckdr.net
mail@ckdr.net
License: Sioux Lookout, ON held by Northwoods Broadcasting Ltd.
Group Owner: Acadia Broadcasting Ltd.; (acq 5-1-2007; grpsl)
Population Served: 7,617 *Arbitron Metro Market:* Dryden, ON *Format:* Oldies *No. News Employees:* 1 *Target Audience:* 25-54.
Richard McCarthy, Operations Dir
Bruce Walchuk, General Manager

Sioux Narrows

***CBQSFM**
05-01-1977; 95.7 mhz FM; kw*Rebroadcasts:* Rebroadcasts CBQT-FM Thunder Bay 100%
CA
(807) 625-5000, *Fax:* (807) 625-5035
www.cbc.ca/ottowa
License: Sioux Narrows, ON held by CBC.
Special Programming: Canadian Indian one hr wkly
Tom Grand, General Manager

Smiths Falls

***CHEQFM**
11-29-1998; 101.1 mhz FM; kw
CA
(418) 387-1013, *Fax:* (418) 387-3757
www.cheqfm.qc.ca
info@cheqfm.qc.ca
License: Smiths Falls, ON held by 9079-3670 Quebec Inc.
Arbitron Metro Market: Sainte-Marie-de-Beauce, PQ *Format:* Adult Contemp
Mario Paquin, CEO
Michel Lambert, President
Mario Paquin, General Manager
Sylvianne Marcoux, Executive Assistant
Marie-Andr,e Poirier, Manager routing business
Side Marco, Copywriter and columnist Arts and Entertainment
LouisLebeau, Animator
Marie-Pier Levesque, Presenter and Journalist
Tommy Fontaine, Producer

CJET-FM
11-01-2000; 92.3 mhz FM; 9.3 kw
Box 430, Smiths Falls, ON K7A 4T4 Canada
(613) 283-4630, *Fax:* (613) 283-7243
www.923jackfm.com
markp.hunter@rci.rogers.com
License: Smiths Falls, ON held by Rogers Broadcasting Ltd., on behalf of CHEZ-FM Inc.
Group Owner: Rogers Broadcasting Ltd.
Population Served: 8,978 *Arbitron Metro Market:* Smiths Falls, ON *Format:* Contemporary Hits/Top 40
Scott Parsons, General Manager
Mark Hunter, General Sales Mgr
Kalum Figura, Retail Sales Manager

St Catharines

***CHREFM**
03-01-1967; 105.7 mhz FM *Hrs Open:* 24; kw
CA
(905) 688-1057, *Fax:* (905) 684-4800
www.1057ezrock.com
info@1057ezrock.com
License: St Catharines, St. Catharines Niagara County, ON held by Astral Media Radio G.P.
Group Owner: Astral Media Inc.; (acq 10-29-2007; grpsl)
Format: Classic Rock *No. News Employees:* 4 *Target Audience:* 25-54.
Rebecca Dunbar, Operations Dir
Madelyn Hamilton, General Manager
Laurie Graham, General Sales Mgr
Sarah Cummings, Programming Director
Michelle Williams, Promotions Manager
Bonnie Heslop, News Director
Joe Gurney, EngineeringDir
Mark Munroe, Music Director

***CHTZFM**
02-01-1949; 97.7 mhz FM; kw
CA
(905) 688-0977, *Fax:* (905) 684-4800
www.htzfm.com
info@htzfm.com
License: St Catharines, ON held by Astral Media Radio G.P.
Group Owner: Astral Media Inc.
Format: Rock/AOR

Bruce Gilbert, Operations Dir
Madelyn Hamilton, General Manager
Laurie Graham, General Sales Mgr
Paul Morris, Programming Director
Michelle Williams, Promotions Manager
Joe Gurney, Engineering Dir
Rebecca Dunbar, BusinessManager

St. Catharines

CKTB
01-01-1930; 610 khz AM
Mailing Address: CA
Second Address: ON
(905) 6840-1174, *Fax:* (905) 684-4800
www.610cktb.com
newsroom@610cktb.com
License: St. Catharines, ON held by Astral Media Radio G.P.
Group Owner: Astral Media Inc.; (acq 10-29-2007; grpsl)
Format: News, News/Talk, Talk *Target Audience:* 35-65.
Rebecca Dunbar, Operations Dir
Bob Harris, General Manager
Laurie Graham, General Sales Mgr
Sarah Cummings, Programming Director
Michelle Williams, Promotions Manager
Tim Parent, News Director
Joe Gurney, Engineering Dir

St. Thomas

CFHK-FM
06-20-1994; 103.1 mhz FM *Hrs Open:* 24; 50 kw; 492 ft; N42 50 57 W81 08 52
380 Wellington St.,Ste. 222, London, ON N6A 5B5 Canada
(519) 931-6000, *Fax:* (519) 679-1967
www.energy103.ca
jeff@energy103.ca
License: St. Thomas, Middlesex County, ON held by Corus Radio Co.
Group Owner: Corus Entertainment Inc.; (acq 8-23-99; grpsl).
Population Served: 600,000 *Format:* Contemporary Hits/Top 40
Target Audience: 18-39.
Dave Farough, General Manager
Bob Fisher, General Sales Mgr
Andy Bingle, Engineering Dir

Stella

CJAI-FM
04-01-2006; 93.7 mhz FM; kw
CA
(613) 384-8282
www.cjai.ca
air@cjai.ca
License: Stella, ON held by Amherst Island Radio Broadcasting Inc.
Arbitron Metro Market: Stella, ON *Format:* Variety/Diverse
Rosemary Richmond, Station Manager

Stratford

CJCS
01-01-1924; 1240 khz AM
CA
(519) 271-2450, *Fax:* (519) 271-3102
www.cjcsradio.com
crae@cjcsradio.com
License: Stratford, ON held by Raedio Inc.
Format: Oldies *Target Audience:* 25-54.
Steve Rae, President
Braden Doerr, General Manager
Eddie Matthews, Programming Director
Kirk Dickson, News Director
Bill Tofflemire, Chief Engineer

CHGK-FM
09-02-2003; 107.7 mhz FM; 2.805 kw
376 Romeo St. S., Stratford, ON N5A 4T9 Canada
(519) 271-2450, *Fax:* (519) 271-3102
www.fm1077stratford.com
news@fm1077stratford.com
License: Stratford, ON held by Raedio Inc.
Population Served: 30,886 *Arbitron Metro Market:* Stratford, ON
Format: Adult Contemp
Steve Rae, President
Braden Doerr, General Manager
Chris Nimigon, National Sales Manager
Eddie Matthews, Programming Director
Kirk Dickson, News Director
Bill Tofflemire, Chief Engineer
Crys Newland, Sales
Dave Elliott,Sales

Ethan Rabidoux, News
Deborah Jacklin, Accounts Receivable
Stewart Cappie, Creative/Producer

Strathroy

CJMI-FM
02-06-2007; 105.7 mhz FM; 1.75 kw
85 Zimmerman St. S., Strathroy, ON N7G 0A3 Canada
(519) 246-6936, *Fax:* (519) 245-6670
www.myfmradio.ca/1057/index.php
License: Strathroy, ON held by My Broadcasting Corp.
Group Owner: My Broadcasting Corp.
Population Served: 20,978 *Arbitron Metro Market:* Strathroy, ON
Format: Adult Contemp
Mike McGuire, Chairman
Denton Hackney, General Manager

Sturgeon Falls

CFSF-FM
04-04-2003; 99.3 mhz FM; 1.35 kw
12006 Hwy. 17, Unit 8, Sturgeon Falls, ON P2B 3K8 Canada
(705) 753-6776, *Fax:* (705) 753-6776
www.moosefm.com
joco@bellnet.ca
License: Sturgeon Falls, ON held by JOCO Communications Inc.
Population Served: 6,672 *Arbitron Metro Market:* Sturgeon Falls, ON *Format:* Adult Contemp, Contemporary Hits/Top 40 *No. News Employees:* 4
Joseph Cormier, President
Mike Trahan, General Manager
Chris Nimigon, National Sales Manager
James Dahlke, Sales Executive
Joanna Landry, Sales Executive
Deborah Jacklin-Peters, Accounts Receivable

Sudbury

***CBCSFM**
06-17-1978; 99.9 mhz FM *Hrs Open:* 24; kw
CA
(705) 688-3200, *Fax:* (705) 688-3220
www.sudbury.cbc.ca
License: Sudbury, ON held by Radio-Canada/CBC.
Nat'l Network: CBC Radio One
Format: News, News/Talk, Talk*Hrs. of News Programming:* news progmg 3 hrs wkly *No. News Employees:* 4 *Target Audience:* 30 plus; College/university educated/professional
Kelly McInnes, Programming Director

CIGM
08-23-1935; 790 khz AM *Hrs Open:* 24
CA
(705) 566-4480, *Fax:* (705) 560-7232
790cigm.com
rick.doughty@sudburyradio.rogers.com
License: Sudbury, ON held by Rogers Broadcasting Ltd.
Group Owner: Rogers Broadcasting Ltd.; (acq 4-19-2002; grpsl).
Format: Country *No. News Employees:* 5 *Target Audience:* Adults 35+.
Nadir Mohamed, President
Rick Doughty, Operations Dir
Gerry Currie, General Sales Mgr
Kevin Britton, Programming Director
Erin McCabe, Promotions Manager
Henri Belanger, Chief Engineer

CJMXFM
01-01-1980; 105.3 mhz FM *Hrs Open:* 24; 100 kw; 285 meters; N46 30 02 W81 01 16
880 Lasalle Blvd., Sudbury, ON Canada
(705) 566-4480, *Fax:* (705) 560-7232
www.ezrocksudbury.com
License: Sudbury, ON held by Rogers Broadcasting Ltd.
Group Owner: Rogers Broadcasting Ltd.; (acq 4-19-2002; grpsl).
Nat'l Reps: Canadian Broadcast Sales
Population Served: 165,000*Hrs. of News Programming:* news progmg 1 hr wkly *No. News Employees:* 6 *Target Audience:* Females 35-44.*Adv. Rates:* 90; 80; 80; 70
Mike Allard, Programming Director

CJTK-FM
01-01-1998; 95.5 mhz FM *Hrs Open:* 24; 1.4 kw
2150 Lasalle Blvd., Sudbury, ON P3A 2A7 Canada
(705) 674-2585, *Fax:* (705) 688-1081
cjtk.com
mail@kfmradio.ca
License: Sudbury, ON held by Eternacom Inc.
Population Served: 240,000 *Format:* Christian, Religious*Hrs. of News Programming:* news progmg 2 hrs wkly *No. News Employees:* 1 *Target Audience:* General.

Curtis Belcher, CEO
Louis Depatie, Operations Dir

***CKLU-FM**
04-30-1997; 96.7 mhz FM *Hrs Open:* 7:30 AM-2:30 AM; 1.3 kw; N46 25 29 W81 00 54
935 Ramsey Lake Rd., Sudbury, ON P3E 2C6 Canada
(705) 673-6538, *Fax:* (705) 675-4878
www.cklu.ca
chef@ckfu.ujyf.ca
License: Sudbury, ON held by Laurentian Student and Community Radio Corp.
Population Served: 150,000 *Format:* Jazz, News, News/Talk, Talk, Variety/Diverse*Special Programming:* It one hr, Pol one hr, Fr 19 hrs, Sp one hr, Ger o*Hrs. of News Programming:* News progmg 3 hrs wkly *TargetAudience:* General.*Adv. Rates:* 26; 26; 26; 26
Dan Welch, President
Lindsey Chrysler, Operations Dir
Carl Jorgensen, Operations Manager

CHNO-FM
02-01-2000; 103.9 mhz FM *Hrs Open:* 24; 11 kw; N46 30 14 W80 58 03
493-B Barrydowne Rd., Sudbury, ON P3A 3T4 Canada
(705) 560-8323, *Fax:* (705) 560-7765
www.rewind1039.ca
news@rewind1039.ca
License: Sudbury, ON held by NewCap Inc.
Group Owner: NewCap Inc.; (acq 11-9-01; C$2,843,000).
Nat'l Reps: CBS Radio
Population Served: 160,274 *Arbitron Metro Market:* Sudbury, ON
Format: Contemporary Hits/Top 40, Adult Contemp*Hrs. of News Programming:* news progmg 4 hrs wkly *No. News Employees:* 25 *Target Audience:* 25-54;middle-income
Rob Steele, CEO
Gerry Currie, General Manager
Rick Tompkins, Programming Director
Suzi Luchi, Promotions Manager
Dave Murray, COO
Karen Bass, Account Manager
Denis Lanteigne, Account Manager
Marcelle Labelle, AccountManager
Kristina Gervais, Account Manager
Michael Neeb, Creative Director

CHYC-FM
01-01-2000; 98.9 mhz FM; 1 kw
336 Pine Street, Suite 301, Sudbury, ON P3C 1X8 Canada
(705) 222-8306, *Fax:* (705) 222-2805
www.leloupfm.com
sboucher@leloupfm.com
License: Sudbury, ON held by LE5 Communications Inc.
Population Served: 160,274 *Arbitron Metro Market:* Sudbury, ON
Format: Adult Contemp, Contemporary Hits/Top 40 *Target Audience:* General.*Adv. Rates:* 18; 15; 12; 9
Christopher Grossman, General Manager
Sylvain Boucher, Engineering Dir
Paul Lefebvre, Owner / Manager
Guy Rouleau, Billing and Routing
Karine Tellier, Sales Representative (Sudbury) - Radio Promotion
Lucie Boudreau, SalesRepresentative
Ron Neault, Sales Representative

CBBX-FM
03-29-2001; 90.9 mhz FM; 50 kw
c/o CBFX-FM, Box 6000, Station centre-ville, Montreal, QC H3C 3A8 Canada
(514) 597-6000
www.cbc.radio-canada.ca
auditoire@radio-canada.ca
License: Sudbury, ON held by Canadian Broadcasting Corp.
Nat'l Network: Espace Musique
Population Served: 160,274 *Arbitron Metro Market:* Greater Sudbury, ON *Format:* Variety/Diverse
R,mi Racine, Chairman
Hubert T. Lacroix, President & CEO
Sylvain LaFrance, Operations Dir
Maryse Bertrand, Vice-President, Real Estate, Legal Services and Ge
William B. Chambers, Vice-President, Brand, Communications and Corporat
Steven Guiton, Vice-President and Chief Regulatory Officer
Louis Lalande, Executive Vice-President French Services
Suzanne Morris, Vice-President and Chief Financial Officer
Roula Zaarour, Vice-President, People and Culture

***CBBSFM**
03-29-2001; 90.1 mhz FM; kw
CA

(866) 306-4636, *Fax:* (705) 688-3220
www.music.cbc.ca/#/radio2
License: Sudbury, ON held by Canadian Broadcasting Corp.
Nat'l Network: CBC Radio Two
Arbitron Metro Market: Greater Sudbury, ON *Format:* Adult Contemp, Triple A
R,mi Racine, Chairman
Hubert T. Lacroix, President & CEO
Kelly McInnes, General Manager
Maryse Bertrand, Vice-President, Real Estate, Legal Services and Ge
William B. Chambers, Vice-President, Brand, Communications and Corporat
Steven Guiton, Vice-President and Chief Regulatory Officer
Louis Lalande, Executive Vice-President French Services
Suzanne Morris, Vice-President and Chief Financial Officer
Roula Zaarour, Vice-President, People and Culture

CKSO-FM
01-01-2002; 101.1 mhz FM *Hrs Open:* 24; 50 w; N46 27 59 W80 58 23
Box 536, Greater Sudbury, ON P0N 1H0 Canada
(866) 799-3072, *Fax:* (705) 235-3921
www.cksofm.netfirms.com
cksofm@vianet.ca
License: Sudbury, ON held by David Jackson, on behalf of a corporation to be incorporated.
Population Served: 160,274 *Arbitron Metro Market:* Greater Sudbury, ON *Format:* Christian
David Jackson, General Manager
Sarah Jackson, Programming Director

CICS-FM
08-18-2008; 91.7 mhz FM; 50 kw; N46 30 14 W80 58 03
60 Elm St., Sudbury, ON P3C 1R8 Canada
(705) 671-7330, *Fax:* (705) 671-7320
www.kicx917.com
License: Sudbury, ON held by Larche Communications Inc.
Group Owner: Larche Communications Inc.
Population Served: 164,000 *Target Audience:* 35-64.
Paul Larche, President
Mick Weaver, General Manager
Mick Weaver, General Sales Mgr
Trinette Atkinson, Programming Director
Shawn McLaren, Promotions Manager
Brian Marth, News Director

Thamesville

CKBK-FM
07-27-2012; 104.3 mhz FM; 45 watts; 25 meters; N42 33 51 W82 52 28
14760 School House Lane, R R 3, Thamesville, ON N0P 2KO Canada
Fax: (519) 692-5522
firstnation.ca/moravian-thames
License: Thamesville, ON held by Delaware Nation Moravian Indian Reserve
Format: Ethnic
Gordon Peters, General Manager

Thunder Bay

***CBQ-FM**
07-05-1984; 101.7 mhz FM *Hrs Open:* 24; 23.5 kw; 900 ft
213 Miles St. E., Thunder Bay, ON P7C 1J5 Canada
(807) 625-5000, *Fax:* (807) 625-5035
www.cbc.ca
License: Thunder Bay, ON held by CBC.
Nat'l Network: CBC Radio One
Format: News, Talk
Robert Rabinovitch, President
Tom Grand, General Manager

***CJSDFM**
10-01-1948; 94.3 mhz FM *Hrs Open:* 24; kw
CA
(807) 346-2600, *Fax:* (807) 345-9923
rock94.com
rock@rock94.com
License: Thunder Bay, ON held by C.J.S.D. Inc.
Nat'l Reps: Target Broadcast Sales
Format: Rock/AOR *Target Audience:* 18-44.
H.F. Dougall, President
K. Harris, General Sales Mgr
Brad Hilgers, Programming Director
Cora Cambly, Promotions Manager
Bryan Wyatt, News Director
D. Caron, Vice President

***CJOA-FM**
12-20-1998; 95.1 mhz FM *Hrs Open:* 24; 50 w
42-63 Carrie Street, Thunder Bay, ON P7A 4J2 Canada
(807) 344-9525, *Fax:* (807) 344-9525
www.cjoa.org
info@cjoa.org
License: Thunder Bay, ON held by Thunder Bay Christian Radio.
Population Served: 108,359 *Arbitron Metro Market:* Thunder Bay, ON *Format:* Christian *Target Audience:* All ages
Ray Gauthier, President
Bonnie Gauthier, General Manager

CJUK-FM
08-01-2001; 99.9 mhz FM; 37 w
180 Park Ave., Suite 200, Thunder Bay, ON P7B6J4 Canada
(807) 344-2000, *Fax:* (807) 345-9939
www.magic999.fm
magicmail@magic999.fm
License: Thunder Bay, ON held by Acadia Broadcasting Inc
Group Owner: NewCap Inc.; (acq 5-10-2005; C$2.3 million).
Dennis Landriault, President

CILU-FM
03-04-2005; 102.7 mhz FM *Hrs Open:* 24; 100 w; N48 25 14 W89 15 37
Mailing Address: 955 Oliver Rd., Thunder Bay, ON P7B 5E1 Canada
Second Address: 707 Oliver Rd., Thunder Bay, ON P7B 2H8
(807) 343-8881
www.luradio.ca
info@luradio.ca
License: Thunder Bay, ON held by LU Campus Radio Inc.
Population Served: 108,359 *Arbitron Metro Market:* Thunder Bay, ON *Format:* Talk
Shawn Hartviksen, Operations Dir
Jason Wellwood, Station Manager
Jenna Piechota, Programming Director
Shawn, Production Manager
Jason, Manager
David Ivany, Music Director

CKPR-FM
06-04-2007; 91.5 mhz FM *Hrs Open:* 24; 100 kw; N48 31 27 W89 06 53
87 N. Hill St., Thunder Bay, ON P7A 5V6 Canada
(888) 218-1428, *Fax:* (807) 345-9923
ckpr.com
License: Thunder Bay, ON held by C.J.S.D. Inc.
Nat'l Reps: Target Broadcast Sales
Population Served: 108,359 *Arbitron Metro Market:* Thunder Bay, ON *Format:* Adult Contemp*Special Programming:* News/talk 10 hrs wkly *Target Audience:* 25-54; families & office workers
H.F. Dougall, President
Cora Cambly, Operations Dir
Kathy Harris, General Sales Mgr
Brad Hilgers, Programming Director
Bryan Wyatt, News Director
D. Caron, Vice President
Leslie Walker-Larson, National Sales Manager
Bill Hogan,Music Director

Tillsonburg

CKOT
04-30-1955; 1200 khz AM *Hrs Open:* Sunrise-sunset
Mailing Address: CA
Second Address: 77 Broadway, Tillsonburg, ON N4G 4H3
(519) 842-4281, *Fax:* (519) 842-4284
www.easy101.com
info@easy101.com
License: Tillsonburg, ON held by Tillsonburg Broadcasting Co. Ltd.
Ross Hawse, General Manager

***CKOTFM**
12-01-1965; 101.3 mhz FM *Hrs Open:* 24; kw
Mailing Address: CA
Second Address: 77 Broadway, Tillsonburg, ON N4G 4H3
(519) 842-4281, *Fax:* (519) 842-4284
www.easy101.com
info@easy101.com
License: Tillsonburg, ON held by Tillsonburg Broadcasting Co. Ltd.
Nat'l Reps: Target Broadcast Sales
Format: Easy Listening*Special Programming:* Gospel one hr wkly *Target Audience:* 30 plus; general
John Lamers, President
Robin Henry, General Sales Mgr

CJDL-FM
08-01-2007; 107.3 mhz FM; 4.5 kw; Ant 538 ft; N43 00 44 W80 50 10
Mailing Address: Box 10, Tillsonburg, ON N4G 4H3 Canada
Second Address: 77 Broadway, Tillsonburg, ON N4G 4H3
(519) 842-4281, *Fax:* (519) 842-4284
www.country1073.ca
info@easy101.com
License: Tillsonburg, ON held by Tillsonburg Broadcasting Co. Ltd.
Nat'l Reps: Target Broadcast Sales
Population Served: 2,000 *Arbitron Metro Market:* Tillsonburg, ON *Format:* Country*Special Programming:* Ger one hr, Hungarian one hr, Belgian one hr, Dutc*Hrs. of News Programming:* news progmg 7 hrs wkly *No. NewsEmployees:* 5 *Target Audience:* 18-50; general
John Lamers, President
Robin Henry, General Sales Mgr

Timmins

***CBON**
06-19-1978; 97.1 mhz FM; kw
CA
(705) 688-3200, *Fax:* (705) 688-3220
www.radio-canada.ca
License: Timmins, ON held by Radio-Canada/CBC.
Nat'l Network: CBC Radio One
Format: French
Gui Babineau, General Manager

CJQQ-FM
09-06-1976; 92.1 mhz FM *Hrs Open:* 24; 40 kw; Ant 400 ft
260 2nd Ave., Timmins, ON P4N 8A4 Canada
(705) 264-2351, *Fax:* (705) 264-2984
www.q92timmis.com
License: Timmins, ON held by Rogers Broadcasting Ltd.
Group Owner: Rogers Broadcasting Ltd.; acq 4-19-02;. grpsl).
Format: Rock/AOR *Target Audience:* 18-44.
Art Pultz, Operations Dir
Angelo Lia, General Sales Mgr

CHYK-FM
01-01-2000; 104.1 mhz FM *Hrs Open:* 24; 3.5 kw
136 Third Avenue, Timmins, ON P4N 1C6 Canada
(705) 269-8307, *Fax:* (705) 269-8305
www.leloupfm.com
plefebvre@leloupfm.com
License: Timmins, ON held by LE5 Communications Inc.
Nat'l Reps: Canadian Broadcast Sales
Population Served: 42,997 *Arbitron Metro Market:* Timmins, ON *Format:* Adult Contemp*Hrs. of News Programming:* news progmg one hr wkly *No. News Employees:* 1 *Target Audience:* 18-65.*Adv. Rates:* 22.50;22.50; 22.50; 22.50
Kimberly Ward, Operations Dir
Christopher Grossman, General Manager
Sylvie Beaulieu, Sales Manager
Sylvain Boucher, Programming Director
Gilles Lafortune, News Director
Jim Whealan, National Sales Manager
Paul Lefebvre, Owner
Penny Proulx, Traffic Manager
Yves Nadeau, Director of Sales
R,jean Tellier, Director General Timmins
Olivier Charbonneau, Animator

CKGB-FM
08-01-2001; 99.3 mhz FM; 40 kw
260 2nd Ave., Timmins, ON P4N 8A4 Canada
(705) 264-2351, *Fax:* (705) 264-2984
www.ezrocktimmins.com
reply@ezrocktimmins.com
License: Timmins, ON held by Rogers Broadcasting Ltd.
Group Owner: Rogers Broadcasting Ltd.; (acq 4-19-2002; grpsl).
Population Served: 42,997 *Arbitron Metro Market:* Timmins, ON *Format:* Classic Rock*Hrs. of News Programming:* news progmg 4 hrs wkly *No. News Employees:* 2 *Target Audience:* 35-55.
Al Campagnola, General Manager
Dave Novak, General Sales Mgr

CHMT-FM
07-12-2001; 93.1 mhz FM *Hrs Open:* 24; 3.6 kw
49 Cedar St. S, Timmins, ON P4N 2G5 Canada
(705) 267-6070, *Fax:* (705) 267-6095
www.hbgradio.com
moose931@hbgradio.com
License: Timmins, ON held by The Haliburton Broadcasting Group Inc.
Group Owner: Haliburton Broadcasting Group Inc.
Nat'l Network: CBS Radio
Hrs. of News Programming: news progmg 1.5 hrs wkly *No. News Employees:* 2 *Target Audience:* 25-54.*Adv. Rates:* 25; 25; 25; 25
Christopher Grossman, President
Kimberly Ward, Operations Dir

Shawn McArthur, General Sales Mgr
Mike Fry, Programming Director
Wendy Gray, News Director
Kent Matheson, Music Director
Penny Proulx, Operations Manager

Toronto

CBL-FM
01-01-1946; 94.1 mhz FM; 55.7 kw; 389 ft
Mailing Address: Box 500, Station A., Toronto, ON M5W 1E6 Canada
Second Address: Box 3220, Station C., Ottawa, ON K1Y 1E4
(416) 205-7400, *Fax:* (416) 205-6336
www.cbc.ca
License: Toronto, ON held by CBC.
Nat'l Network: CBC Radio Two
Robert Rabinovitch, CEO
Tom Grand, General Manager

CBLAFM
04-19-1998; 99.1 mhz FM; 55.1 kw
Box 500, Station A, Toronto, ON Canada
(416) 205-7400, *Fax:* (416) 205-6336
www.cbc.ca
License: Toronto, ON held by CBC.
Nat'l Network: CBC Radio One
Robert Rabinovitch, CEO
Tom Grand, General Manager

CFMZ-FM
01-01-1988; 96.3 mhz FM *Hrs Open:* 24; 24.5 kw; Ant 930 ft; N56 43 38 W55 79 22
550 Queen St. E., Suite 205, Toronto, ON M5A 1V2 Canada
(416) 367-5353, *Fax:* (416) 367-1742
www.classical963fm.com
info@classical1963.com
License: Toronto, York County, ON held by MZ Media Inc.
Nat'l Network: BN Audio *Nat'l Reps:* imsradio *Wire Services:* Standard Broadcast News
Population Served: 4,800,000 *Format:* Classical*Hrs. of News Programming:* news progmg 4 hrs wkly *No. News Employees:* 3 *Target Audience:* 35 plus; well educated, upscale, owners/managers/professionals
George Grant, CEO
John Van Driel, Programming Director

CFRB
02-19-1927; 1010 khz AM *Hrs Open:* 24
CA
(416) 924-5711, *Fax:* (416) 872-8683
www.cfrb.com
comments@cfrb.com
License: Toronto, ON held by Astral Media Radio G.P.
Group Owner: Astral Media Inc.; (acq 10-29-2007; grpsl)
Format: News, News/Talk, Talk*Special Programming:* Class 7 hrs, farm 2 hrs wkly*Hrs. of News Programming:* news progmg 40 hrs wkly *No. News Employees:* 10 *Target Audience:* 25-64; general
Steve Kowch, Operations Dir
Pat Holiday, General Manager
Bill Herz, General Sales Mgr
Nancy Ceneviva, Promotions Manager
Dave Trafford, News Director
Dave Simon, Engineering Dir
G. Johns, Regional Sales Manager

CFTR
08-08-1962; 680 khz AM *Hrs Open:* 24
CA
(416) 935-8468, *Fax:* (416) 935-8480
www.680news.com
680info@680news.com
License: Toronto, ON held by Rogers Broadcasting Ltd.
Group Owner: Rogers Broadcasting Ltd.
Nat'l Network: ABC *Nat'l Reps:* Canadian Broadcast Sales *Wire Services:* BN Wire; Bloomberg News
Format: News*Hrs. of News Programming:* news progmg 168 hrs wkly *No. News Employees:* 50 *Target Audience:* 25-54; owners, managers, professionals
John Hinnen, General Manager

*CHFIFM
02-08-1957; 98.1 mhz FM *Hrs Open:* 24; kw
CA
(416) 935-8298, *Fax:* (416) 935-8480
www.chfi.com
680news@earthci.rodgers.com
License: Toronto, ON held by Rogers Broadcasting Ltd.
Group Owner: Rogers Broadcasting Ltd.
Format: Adult Contemp *Target Audience:* 25-54.
Julie Adam, Operations Dir
Victor Dann, General Sales Mgr
Vicky Belfiore, Promotions Manager
Phyllis Antoniandis, News Director
John Hinnen, Local News Editor
Drew Keith, Music Director
Jim Morris, News Reporter

CHIN
01-01-1966; 1540 khz AM *Hrs Open:* 24
CA
(416) 531-9991, *Fax:* (416) 531-5274
www.chinradio.com
sales@chinradio.com
License: Toronto, ON held by Radio 1540 Ltd.
Format: Ethnic*Hrs. of News Programming:* news progmg 9 hrs wkly *No. News Employees:* 4 *Target Audience:* 30 plus; immigrants in the Toronto census metropolitan area
Johnny Lombardi, CEO
Lenny Lombardi, President
Theresa Lombardi, Operations Dir
Joe Mulvihill, General Manager
Michael Evans, Engineering Dir
Donina Lombardi, Public Affairs Director

CHINFM
01-01-1967; 100.7 mhz FM *Hrs Open:* 24; 8.5 kw; 1,700 ft; N48 38 33 W79 23 15
622 College St., Toronto, ON Canada
(416) 531-9991, *Fax:* (416) 531-5274
License: Toronto, ON held by Radio 1540 Ltd.
Hrs. of News Programming: News progmg 10 hrs wkly *Target Audience:* 30 plus; multi-ethnic, first & second generation immigrants
Roger de Brabant, Chairman
Karen Turner, Station Manager

CHKT(AM)
02-21-1951; 1430 khz AM *Hrs Open:* 24; 50 kw-U, DA-2
135 East Beaver Creek Rd., Units 7 & 8, Richmond Hill, ON L4B 1E2 Canada
(905) 763-3360, *Fax:* (905) 889-9828
www.fairchildradio.com
winniewong@am1430.com
License: Toronto, ON held by Fairchild Radio Group Ltd.
Format: Chinese *Target Audience:* Chinese and other ethnic groups
Cyril Lai, General Manager
Maureen Tang, General Sales Mgr
River Lee, Programming Director
Louisa Lam, News Director
Esther Kwong, Administration
David Choi, Assistant Operations Director

*CHRY-FM
01-01-1987; 105.5 mhz FM *Hrs Open:* 24; 158 w
4700 Keele St., 413 Student Ctr., York University, Toronto, ON M3J 1P3 Canada
(416) 736-5293, *Fax:* (416) 650-8052
www.chry.fm
chryprog@yorku.ca
License: Toronto, ON held by CHRY Community Radio Inc.
Format: Variety/Diverse*Special Programming:* Afghan, African, Caribbean, French, Hebrew, Jazz,*Hrs. of News Programming:* 10 *No. News Employees:* 2 *Target Audience:* General; campus community
Danae Peart, Operations Dir
Matthew Fava, Programming Director

CHUM
10-01-1944; 1050 khz AM; 50 kw-U, DA-2
1331 Yonge St., Toronto, ON Canada
(416) 925-6666, *Fax:* (416) 926-4026
www.tsn.ca/radio
info@1050chum.com
License: Toronto, ON held by Bell Media Toronto Radio Partnership
Group Owner: Bell Media Inc.; (acq 6-22-2007; grpsl)
No. News Employees: 6
Paul Ski, President
Bob McLaughlin, General Manager
Larry Keats, Chief Engineer

CHUMFM
09-15-1963; 104.5 mhz FM; 40 kw; 1,380 ft
1331 Yonge St., Toronto, ON Canada
(416) 925-6666, *Fax:* (416) 926-4026
www.chumfm.com
License: Toronto, ON held by Bell Media Toronto Radio Partnership
Group Owner: Bell Media Inc.
Hrs. of News Programming: News progmg 6 hrs wkly
David Corey, Programming Director
Loretta Tate, Promotions Manager

CFZM(AM)
01-08-2001; 740 khz AM *Hrs Open:* 24; 50 kw-U; N43 34 30 W79 49 02
Mailing Address: Box 740, Station A, Toronto, ON M5W 4K6 Canada
Second Address: Broadcasting Ctr., 284 Church St., Oakville, ON L6J 7N2
(905) 845-2821, *Fax:* (905) 842-1250
www.am740.ca
License: Toronto, ON held by MZ Media Inc.
Population Served: 4,000,000 *Format:* Adult Contemp*Special Programming:* Scottish 2hrs, British 1hr, Irish 1hr*Hrs. of News Programming:* news progmg 9 hrs wkly *Target Audience:* 50 plus.*Adv. Rates:* 120;120; 120; 60
George Grant, CEO
Jacqui Gerrard, Operations Dir
Michael Caine, General Manager

*CILQFM
05-22-1977; 107.1 mhz FM *Hrs Open:* 24; kw
CA
(416) 221-0107, *Fax:* (416) 847-3300
www.q107.com
License: Toronto, ON held by Corus Premium Television Ltd.
Group Owner: Corus Entertainment Inc.; (acq 7-2000; grpsl).
Format: Classic Rock*Hrs. of News Programming:* news progmg 15 hrs wkly *No. News Employees:* 5 *Target Audience:* 18-44.
John Cassaday, CEO
John Hayes, President
Chris Sisam, General Manager
Blair Bartrem, Programming Director

CIRV-FM
01-01-1986; 88.9 mhz FM *Hrs Open:* 24; 1.88 kw
1087 Dundas St. W., Toronto, ON M6J 1W9 Canada
(416) 537-1088, *Fax:* (416) 537-2463
www.cirvfm.com
info@cirvfm.com
License: Toronto, ON held by CIRC Radio Inc.
Format: Ethnic *No. News Employees:* 5
Frank Alvarez, CEO
Alberto Elmir, Operations Dir

*CIUTFM
01-01-1986; 89.5 mhz FM *Hrs Open:* 24; kw
CA
(416) 978-0909, *Fax:* (416) 946-7004
www.ciut.fm
b.burchell@ciut.fm
License: Toronto, ON held by University of Toronto Community Radio Inc.
Wire Services: Canadian Press
Format: Variety/Diverse*Special Programming:* Fr 2 hrs, Sp 4 , Punjabi 5 hrs hrs wkly*Hrs. of News Programming:* News progmg 3 hrs wkly *Target Audience:* General.
Ken Stowar, Station Manager
Ken Stowar, Programming Director

CJBC
01-01-1947; 860 khz AM; 50 kw-U
Box 500, Station A, Toronto, ON Canada
(416) 205-3311, *Fax:* (416) 205-5622
www.cbc.ca
License: Toronto, ON held by CBC.

Alain Dorion, General Manager

CJBCFM
01-01-1993; 90.3 mhz FM; 5.73 kw; 1,414 ft; N43 38 33 W79 23 15
Box 500, Station A, Toronto, ON Canada
(416) 205-2522, *Fax:* (416) 205-7660
License: Toronto, ON held by CBC
Nat'l Network: Radio Canada
Manon Cote, General Manager

CJCL
01-01-1944; 590 khz AM *Hrs Open:* 24; 50 kw-U, DA-1
777 Jarvis St., Toronto, ON Canada
(416) 935-0590, *Fax:* (416) 413-4116
www.sportsnet590.ca
contact@sportsnet590.ca
License: Toronto, ON held by Rogers Broadcasting Ltd.
Group Owner: Rogers Broadcasting Ltd.; acq 4-19-02; grpsl).
Population Served: 4,000,000 *Target Audience:* 25-54; men
Chuck McCoy, General Manager
Don Kollins, Programming Director

CHBM-FM
05-24-1987; 97.3 mhz FM; 28.9 kw; Ant 1,500 ft
2 St. Clair Ave. W., 2nd Fl., Toronto, ON M4V 1L6 Canada
(416) 482-0973, *Fax:* (416) 486-5696
www.ezrock.com
info@ezrock.com
License: Toronto, ON held by Astral Media Radio G.P.
Group Owner: Astral Media Inc.; (acq 10-29-2007; grpsl)
Population Served: 3,000,000 *Target Audience:* 35-54.
Pat Holiday, General Manager

***CJRT**
01-01-1949; 91.1 mhz FM *Hrs Open:* 24; kw
CA
(416) 595-0404, *Fax:* (416) 595-9413
www.jazz.fm
info@jazz.fm
License: Toronto, ON held by CJRT-FM Inc.
Wire Services: Broadcast News Ltd.
Format: Jazz *Target Audience:* 35 plus.
B. Webber, Chairman
Ross Porter, CEO
Brad Barker, Operations Dir
Vince De Lilla, General Sales Mgr
Stacy MacKenzie, News Director
Donnie Tong, Engineering Dir

***CKFMFM**
07-01-1961; 99.9 mhz FM; kw
CA
(416) 922-9999, *Fax:* (416) 872-8683
www.virginradio999.com
info@virginradio999.com
License: Toronto, ON held by Astral Media Radio G.P.
Group Owner: Astral Media Inc.
Format: Adult Contemp *Target Audience:* 25-49.
Pat Holiday, General Manager
Lorie Russell, General Sales Mgr
Martin Tremblay, Programming Director
David Lindores, Promotions Manager
Wayne Webster, Music Director

CFXJ-FM
02-09-2001; 93.5 mhz FM *Hrs Open:* 9 AM-5:30 PM; 1.058 kw; Ant 980 ft
211 Yonge St., Suite 400, Toronto, ON M5B 1M4 Canada
(416) 214-5000, *Fax:* (416) 214-0660
www.flow935.com
info@flow935.com
License: Toronto, ON held by Bell Media Toronto Radio Partnership
Wire Services: BN Wire
No. News Employees: 1 *Target Audience:* 18-35.
Denham Jolly, CEO
Nicole Jolly, Operations Dir
Wayne Williams, Programming Director
Vanessa Santos, Promotions Manager
Scott Palmateer, Chief Engineer

CKAV-FM
12-13-2002; 106.5 mhz FM; 1.1 kw
PO Box 87, Station E, Toronto, ON M6H 4E1 Canada
(416) 703-1287, *Fax:* (416) 703-4328
aboriginalvoices.com
info@aboriginalvoices.com
License: Toronto, ON held by Aboriginal Voices Radio Inc.
Group Owner: Aboriginal Voices Radio Inc.
Population Served: 2,615,060 *Arbitron Metro Market:* Toronto, ON *Format:* Ethnic
Mark MacLeod, Operations Dir
Patrice Mousseau, Programming Director
Roy Hennessy, Operations Manager

CHHA
11-21-2004; 1610 khz AM *Hrs Open:* 30; 6.2 kw-U; N43 42 40 W79 27 11
22 Wenderly Dr., Toronto, ON Canada
(416) 782-2953, ext 225, *Fax:* (416) 782-1219
www.torontohispano.com
sanlorenzo@rogers.com
License: Toronto, ON held by San Lorenzo Latin American Community Centre.
Hrs. of News Programming: News progmg 10 hrs wkly
Herman Astudillo, General Manager

CHOQ-FM
01-01-2005; 105.1 mhz FM *Hrs Open:* 24; 1 kw
425 W. Adelaide St., # 302, Toronto, ON M5V 3C1 Canada
(416) 599-2666, *Fax:* (416) 599-7639
www.choqfm.ca/accueil
info@choqfm.ca
License: Toronto, ON held by La Cooperative radiophonique de Toronto inc.
Population Served: 105,749 *Arbitron Metro Market:* Saint-Denis, RO *Format:* French*Adv. Rates:* 100; 100; 100; 100
Tonia Mori, General Manager

CJSA
01-01-2004; 101.3 mhz FM; kw
CA
(416) 292-4059, *Fax:* (416) 292-4574
www.cmr24.com
info@cmr24.com
License: Toronto, ON held by 3885275 Canada Inc.
Arbitron Metro Market: Tyler-Longview, TX *Format:* Ethnic
Sivakumaran Sivapaphafundaram, General Manager

***CKHC-FM**
01-01-2007; 96.9 mhz FM *Hrs Open:* 24; 60 w; N43 43 43 W79 36 30
Radio Humber 96.9fm, 205 Humber College Blvd., Toronto, ON M5W 5L7 Canada
(416) 675-6622, *Fax:* (416) 675-9730
radio.humber.ca
Dean.Sinclair@Humber.ca
License: Toronto, ON held by Humber Communications Community Corp.
Nat'l Reps: Target Broadcast Sales *Wire Services:* Canadian Press
Population Served: 2,615,060 *Arbitron Metro Market:* Toronto, ON *Format:* French, Country*Special Programming:* All Canadian Music*Hrs. of News Programming:* 9-Sep *Target Audience:* College students*Adv. Rates:* $25/60 $15/30
Jerry Chomyn, Programming Director

CHTO
1690 khz AM
CA
(416) 465-1112, *Fax:* (416) 465-6592
www.am1690.ca
info@am1690.ca
License: Toronto, ON held by Canadian Hellenic Toronto Radio Inc.
Arbitron Metro Market: Toronto, ON *Format:* Ethnic, Greek
Tom O'Brien, President
Sue O'Brien, General Manager
Dave Moore, General Sales Mgr
Tony Taylor, Programming Director
Don Barkman, Music Director

CIRR-FM
04-16-2007; 103.9 mhz FM; kw
CA
(416) 922-1039, *Fax:* (416) 922-3692
www.proudfm.com
info@proudfm.com
License: Toronto, ON held by Rainbow Media Group Inc.
Arbitron Metro Market: Toronto, ON *Format:* Contemporary Hits/Top 40, Talk
Carmela Laurignano, President
Bob Willette, Programming Director
Jaret Sereda, Promotions Manager
Sean Moreman, News Director
Chris Howson, Programming Assistant
Jon Terminesi, Music Director
Sheila Koenig, Creative Director

Vermillion Bay

CKQV-FM
06-01-2004; 103.3 mhz FM; 1.6 kw
Mailing Address: Box 459, Vermillion Bay, ON P0V 2V0 Canada
Second Address: 78 Spruce St., Vermillion Bay, ON P0V 2V0
(807) 227-9988, *Fax:* (807) 227-9985
www.q104fm.ca
info@q104fm.ca
License: Vermillion Bay, ON held by Norwesto Communications Ltd.
Population Served: 1,200 *Arbitron Metro Market:* Vermilion Bay, ON *Format:* Contemporary Hits/Top 40
Rick Doucet, General Manager
Ken O'Neil, Programming Director

Wahta Mohawk Territory near Bala

CFWP-FM
01-01-2003; 98.3 mhz FM *Hrs Open:* 24; 1.06 kw; Ant 96 ft
Canada
(705) 762-1274, *Fax:* (705) 762-2045
www.mohawkradionation.ca
hawk98@mohawknationradio.ca
License: Wahta Mohawk Territory near Bala, ON held by Wahta Communications Society.
Population Served: 716 *Arbitron Metro Market:* Wahta Mohawk Territory, ON *Format:* Variety/Diverse*Adv. Rates:* 5; 5; 5; 5
Cal White, General Manager

Wasaga Beach

CHGB-FM
04-30-2007; 97.7 mhz FM; 200 w
9937 Highway 26, Collingwood, ON L9Z 3Z3 Canada
(705) 422-0970
www.977thebeach.ca
info@977thebeach.ca
License: Wasaga Beach, ON held by Bayshore Broadcasting Corp.
Group Owner: Bayshore Broadcasting Corp.

Rick Ringer, Operations Dir
Ross Kentner, General Manager

Waterloo

***CKMSFM**
10-16-1977; 94.5 mhz FM *Hrs Open:* 6 AM-midnight; kw
CA
(519) 886-2567, *Fax:* (519) 884-3530
www.soundfm.ca
ckmsfm@web.ca
License: Waterloo, ON held by Radio Waterloo Inc.
Format: Variety/Diverse *No. News Employees:* 1 *Target Audience:* General.
Steve Krysak, President
promotion, General Sales Mgr
Mark Green, Programming Director
Carrie Humphries, Promotions Manager

***CKWR**
03-23-1974; 98.5 mhz FM *Hrs Open:* 24; kw
CA
(519) 886-9870, *Fax:* (519) 886-0090
www.ckwr.com
general@ckwr.com
License: Waterloo, Waterloo County, ON held by Wired World Inc.
Nat'l Reps: CHUM Radio Sales *Wire Services:* BN Wire
Format: Adult Contemp*Special Programming:* Romanian 2 hrs, Ger 3 hrs, Greek 2 hrs, Serbian 2*Hrs. of News Programming:* news progmg 8 hrs wkly *No. News Employees:* 2 *Target Audience:* 35-64; mature audience*Adv.Rates:* 46; 40; 42; 24.
Clarence Mascoll, President
Clyde Ross, Station Manager
Marie Hurst, Programming Director

Wawa

CJWA-FM
01-01-1996; 107.1 mhz FM; 210 w
55 Broadway Ave., Wawa, ON P0S 1K0 Canada
(705) 856-4555, *Fax:* (705) 856-1520
License: Wawa, ON held by Labbe Media Incorporated
Nat'l Reps: Canadian Broadcast Sales
Format: Adult Contemp *No. News Employees:* 1 *Target Audience:* 25-54.
Rick Labbe, President
Daniel Walker, News Director
Vern Valois, Chief Engineer

Welland

CIXL-FM
05-20-1999; 91.7 mhz FM *Hrs Open:* 24; 50 kw; N52 42 56 W19 79 16
860 Forks Road West, Welland, ON L3B 5R6 Canada
(905) 732-4433, *Fax:* (905) 732-4780
www.giantfm.com
info@giantfm.com
License: Welland, Niagara County, ON held by R.B. Communications, LTD.
Nat'l Reps: Canadian Broadcast Sales
Population Served: 500,000 *Format:* Classic Rock*Hrs. of News Programming:* news progmg 6 hrs wkly *No. News Employees:* 20 *Target Audience:* 25-54; adults
Pat St. John, President
Peter Morena, Operations Dir
Brian Salmon, Programming Director
Susan Honsberger, News Director

Whitchurch-Stouffville

CIWS-FM
102.7 mhz FM; 50 w
Mailing Address: Box 59, Stouffville, ON L4A 7Z4 Canada
Second Address: 6379 Main St., Stouffville, ON L4A 7Z4

(905) 640-6429
www.whistleradio.com
jim@whistleradio.com
License: Whitchurch-Stouffville, ON held by WhiStle Community Radio.
Population Served: 37,628 *Arbitron Metro Market:* Whitchurch-Stouffville, ON *Format:* Talk
Jim Priebe, CEO

Windsor

***CBE-FM**
10-15-1978; 89.9 mhz FM; 100 kw; 538 ft
825 Riverside Dr. W., Windsor, ON N9A 5K9 Canada
(519) 255-3411, *Fax:* (519) 255-3443
www.cbc.ca
earlyshift@cbc.ca
License: Windsor, ON held by CBC
Nat'l Network: CBC Radio Two
Format: Variety/Diverse
Diane Humber, General Manager

CIDR-FM
01-01-1949; 93.9 mhz FM *Hrs Open:* 24; 100 kw; Ant 700 ft
30100 Telegraph Rd., Suite 460, Bingham Farms, ON 48025 Canada
(313) 961-9811, *Fax:* (313) 961-1603
www.93.9fmradio.com
feedback@93.9fmradio.com
License: Windsor, Essex County, ON held by Bell Media Windsor Radio Partnership
Group Owner: Bell Media Inc.
Nat'l Reps: McGavren Guild
Arbitron Metro Market: Detroit
Murray Brookshaw, Programming Director
Christine Copeland, Promotions Manager

CIMX
07-10-1967; 88.7 mhz FM; 100 kw; 577 ft
1640 Ouellette Ave., Windsor, ON Canada
519-258-888831, *Fax:* 519-258-018231
www.89xradio.com
License: Windsor, ON held by Bell Media Windsor Radio Partnership
Group Owner: Bell Media Inc.
Target Audience: 18-34.
Dave Hunter, Programming Director
Cal Cagno, Promotions Manager

CJAM-FM
11-01-1983; 99.1 mhz FM; kw
CA
(519) 971-3606, *Fax:* (519) 971-3605
www.cjam.ca
news@cjam.ca
License: Windsor, ON held by Student Media, University of Windsor.
Format: Ethnic*Special Programming:* Black 10 hrs, class 4 hrs, folk 4 hrs, jazz 6 hrs, *Target Audience:* General; listeners in Windsor/Detroit area
Josh Kolm, President
Vernon Smith, Station Manager
Sarah Morris, Programming Director

CKLW
06-01-1932; 800 khz AM *Hrs Open:* 24; 50 kw-U, DA-2
1640 Ouellette Ave., Windsor, ON Canada
(519) 258-8888, *Fax:* (519) 258-0182
www.am800cklw.com
info@am800cklw.com
License: Windsor, Essex County, ON held by Bell Media Windsor Radio Partnership
Group Owner: Bell Media Inc.; (acq 6-22-2007; grpsl)
Nat'l Reps: McGavren Guild
Arbitron Metro Market: Detroit *Target Audience:* 25-54.
Eric Proksch, General Manager
Keith Chinnery, Programming Director
Heidi Baiden, Promotions Manager
Jason Moore, News Director
Jim Valvasori, Engineering Dir

CKWW
03-29-1964; 580 khz AM; 500 w-U, DA-1
Mailing Address: 1640 Ouellette Ave., Windsor, ON Canada
Second Address: 30100 Telegraph Rd., Suite 460, Bingham Farms, MI 48025
(519) 258-8888,(313) 961-9811, *Fax:* (519) 258-0182,(313) 961-1603
www.am580radio.com
info@am580radio.com
License: Windsor, ON held by Bell Media Windsor Radio Partnership
Group Owner: Bell Media Inc.; (acq 6-22-2007; grpsl)
Nat'l Reps: McGavren Guild
Arbitron Metro Market: Detroit*Hrs. of News Programming:* News progmg 2 hrs wkly *Target Audience:* 45 plus.
Eric Proksch, General Manager
Charlie O'Brien, Programming Director

CBEW-FM
03-04-2011; 97.5 mhz FM; kw
CA
(519) 225-3411, *Fax:* (519) 255-3443
www.cbc.ca/windsor
License: Windsor, Essex County, ON held by CBC
Nat'l Reps: CBC Radio One

CINA-FM
102.3 mhz FM; 1.9 kw; 55.5 meters
1515 Britannia Road East, Suite 315, Missisauga, ON L4W 4K1 Canada
nettiray@gmail.com
License: Windsor, Essex County, ON held by Neeti P Ray
Neeti P Ray, General Manager

Wingham

CKNX
02-20-1926; 920 khz AM *Hrs Open:* 24
CA
(519) 357-1310, *Fax:* (519) 357-1897
www.1017theone.ca
news@cknxradio.com
License: Wingham, ON held by Blackburn Radio Inc.
Group Owner: Blackburn Group Inc.
Format: Country*Special Programming:* Relg 6 hrs wkly*Hrs. of News Programming:* news progmg 10 hrs wkly *No. News Employees:* 7 *Target Audience:* 35-54.
John Weese, General Manager

CKNXFM
04-17-1977; 101.7 mhz FM *Hrs Open:* 24; kw
CA
(519) 357-1310, *Fax:* (519) 357-1897
www.1017theone.ca
License: Wingham, ON held by Blackburn Radio Inc.
Group Owner: Blackburn Group Inc.
TV Affiliate: CKNX-TV affil. *Format:* Adult Contemp *Target Audience:* 25-49.
Christopher Grossman, President
Kimberly Ward, Operations Dir
John Weese, General Manager
Duana, Duck, General Sales Mgr
Bob Alexander, Promotions Manager
Joe Snider, News Director
Erika MacLellan, Operations Manager
ChrisWaschuk, Sales

CIBU-FM
04-01-2005; 94.5 mhz FM; kw
CA
(519) 357-1310, *Fax:* (519) 357-1897
www.945thebull.ca
License: Wingham, ON held by Blackburn Radio Inc.
Group Owner: Blackburn Group Inc.
Format: Rock/AOR
John Weese, General Manager

Woodstock

***CKDKFM**
07-01-1987; 102.3 mhz FM *Hrs Open:* 24; kw
CA
(519) 539-1040, *Fax:* (519) 679-1967
www.themore1039.ca
dave.farough@corusent.com
License: Woodstock, Oxford County, ON held by Corus Radio
Group Owner: Corus Entertainment Inc.; (acq 1991)
Nat'l Reps: Canadian Broadcast Sales
Format: Classic Rock*Hrs. of News Programming:* news progmg 9 hrs wkly *No. News Employees:* 3 *Target Audience:* 25-54.
John Cassaday, CEO
John Hayes, President
Dave Farough, General Manager
Dennis Tuer, General Sales Mgr
Brad Gibb, Programming Director
Kent Guy, Promotions Manager

CJFH-FM
01-01-2004; 94.3 mhz FM *Hrs Open:* 24; 37 w
Hope FM 94.3, 1038 Parkinson Rd, Woodstock, ON N4S 7W3 Canada
(519) 539-2304, *Fax:* (519) 539-2011
www.hopefm.ca
info@hopefm.ca
License: Woodstock, ON held by Sound of Faith Broadcasting.
Population Served: 37,754 *Arbitron Metro Market:* Woodstock, ON *Format:* Christian*Adv. Rates:* 30, 30, 30, 20
Gary Hill, General Manager
Marci Fess, General Sales Mgr

CIHR-FM
04-10-2006; 104.7 mhz FM *Hrs Open:* 24; 8.95 kw; Woodstock
223 Norwich Ave., Woodstock, ON Canada
(519) 537-8400, *Fax:* (519)537-8600
1047.ca
chris@1047.ca
License: Woodstock, Oxford County, ON held by Byrnes Communications Inc.
Nat'l Reps: Canadian Broadcast Sales
Population Served: 100,000 *No. News Employees:* 4 *Target Audience:* 25-54; adults*Adv. Rates:* 66.50; 50; 61; 44
Chris Byrnes, President
Michael Jones, General Manager
Dan Henry, Programming Director
Adam Nyp, News Director

Prince Edward Island

Charlottetown

***CBCTFM**
01-01-1972; 96.1 mhz FM *Hrs Open:* 24; kw
CA
(902) 629-6400, *Fax:* (902) 629-6518
www.cbc.ca/pei
License: Charlottetown, PE held by CBC.
Nat'l Network: CBC Radio One
Format: Talk*Hrs. of News Programming:* News progmg 11 hrs wkly
Hank van Leeuwen, Operations Dir
Donna Allen, Programming Director
Mitch Cormier, News Director

***CHLQFM**
03-01-1982; 93.1 mhz FM; kw
Mailing Address: CA
Second Address: 5 Prince St., Charlottetown, PE C1A 4P4
(902) 892-1066, *Fax:* (902) 566-1338
www.magic93.fm
requests@magic93.pe.ca
License: Charlottetown, Queens County, PE held by Maritime Broadcasting System Ltd.
Group Owner: Maritime Broadcasting
Format: Adult Contemp
Robert Pace, Chairman
Paul Alan, Operations Dir

CHTN-FM
01-01-2006; 100.3 mhz FM; 33 kw; N46 11 22 W63 09 54
90 University Ave., Suite 320, Atlantic Technology Centre, Charlottetown, PE C1A 4K9 Canada
(902) 569-1003, *Fax:* (902) 569-8693
www.ocean100.com
License: Charlottetown, PE held by Newcap Inc.
Group Owner: NewCap Inc.
Nat'l Reps: Canadian Broadcast Sales
Population Served: 64,487 *Arbitron Metro Market:* Charlottetown, PE *Format:* Contemporary Hits/Top 40, Adult Contemp*Hrs. of News Programming:* news progmg 17 hrs wkly *No. News Employees:* 2 *Target Audience:* 25-54.
Jennifer Evans, General Manager
Corey Tremere, Programming Director
Mandy Dennis, Promotions Manager
Scott Chapman, News Director

CFCY-FM
01-01-2006; 95.1 mhz FM; 100 kw
Mailing Address: 5 Prince Street, Charlottetown, PE C1A 4P4 Canada
Second Address: 5 Prince St., Charlottetown, PE C1A 4P4
(902) 892-1066, *Fax:* (902) 566-1338
cfcy.fm
www.951fmcfcy.com
License: Charlottetown, PE held by Maritime Broadcasting System Ltd.
Group Owner: Maritime Broadcasting
Population Served: 64,487 *Arbitron Metro Market:* Charlottetown, PE *Format:* Country
Robert Pace, Chairman
Paul Alan, Operations Dir

CKQK-FM
07-25-2006; 105.5 mhz FM; 33 kw; N46 12 44 W63 20 32
90 University Ave., Suite 320, Atlantic Technology Centre, Charlottetown, PE C1A 4K9 Canada
(902) 569-1003, *Fax:* (902) 569-8693
www.krock1055.com
License: Charlottetown, PE held by Newcap Inc.
Group Owner: NewCap Inc.
Population Served: 64,487 *Arbitron Metro Market:* Charlottetown, PE *Format:* Classic Rock, Contemporary Hits/Top 40 *Target Audience:* 25-44; male
Jennifer Evans, General Manager
Kate Buick, Programming Director
Whitney Hooper, Promotions Manager
Scott Chapman, News Director

Summerside

CJRW-FM
01-01-2000; 102.1 mhz FM *Hrs Open:* 5:57 AM-12:15 AM; 11 kw
763 Water St. E., Summerside, PE C1N 4J3 Canada
(902) 436-2201, *Fax:* (902) 436-8573
www.spud.fm
spud@mbsradio.com
License: Summerside, PE held by Maritime Broadcasting System Ltd.
Group Owner: Maritime Broadcasting; (acq 8-10-2000; C$650,000 for approximately 92.9% of the common shares).
Population Served: 14,751 *Arbitron Metro Market:* Summerside, PE *Format:* Classical *No. News Employees:* 1 *Target Audience:* General.
Lois Schurman, Chairman
Paul Schurman, President
Brent Schurman, Operations Dir
Don Smith, General Manager
Todd MacEwen, Programming Director
Heather MacCauley, Promotions Manager
Chris Pride, Music Director

Quebec

Acton Vale

CFID-FM
01-01-2004; 103.7 mhz FM *Hrs Open:* 24; kw
CA
(450) 546-1037, *Fax:* (450) 546-7521
www.radio-acton.com
info@radio-acton.com
License: Acton Vale, QC held by Radio-Acton inc.
Arbitron Metro Market: Acton Vale, QC *Format:* Variety/Diverse, French
Gaetan Chevanelle, General Manager
Andr,e-Anne Dubois, General Sales Mgr
Pierre Brousseau, Programming Director
Marie-Pier Roy, Music Manager
Beatrice Trahan, Director General
Jean-Francois Fortier, Sales Representative
MichelMorin, Facilitator and copywriter
Eric Caron, Sales representative, bingo and Webmaster
Carole Chabot, Reception

Alma

CKYK-FM
01-01-1993; 95.7 mhz FM; 100 kw; N48 24 05 W72 05 23
345 Sagueneens Rd., Office 70, Chicoutimi, QC G7H 6K9 Canada
(418) 543-5131, *Fax:* (418) 543-0225
www.kykradiox.com
reception@kykradiox.com
License: Alma, QC held by Groupe Radio Antenne 6 Inc.
Group Owner: RNC Media Saguenay-Lac-Saint-Jean
Format: Oldies, Classic Rock
Marc-Andre Levesque, President

CFGT-FM
03-05-2010; 104.5 mhz FM; 50 kw; 77.6 meters
460 Rue Sacre-Coeur Quest, Suite 200, Alma, QC G8B 1L9 Canada
(418) 662-6888, *Fax:* (418) 662-6070
www.planetradio.ca
License: Alma, QC held by Groupe Radio Antenne 6 Inc

Amos

CHOW-FM
105.3 mhz FM; 5.376 kw; N48 34 25 W78 09 44
43, 1st Ave East, Bureau 100, Amos, QC J9T 1H2 Canada
(819) 732-6991, *Fax:* (819) 732-6988
www.radioboreale.com
infos@radioboreale.com
License: Amos, QC held by Radio Boreale.
Population Served: 12,671 *Arbitron Metro Market:* Amos, QC
Format: Talk
Real Bordeleau, President
Jean Champagne, Vice President
Denis Germain, Administrator
Guylaine Belley, Coordinator

Amqui

CFVM-FM
01-01-2003; 99.9 mhz FM; 23.8 kw
111 rue de l'Hopital, Amqui, QC G5J 2K1 Canada
(418) 629-2025, *Fax:* (418) 629-2599
www.amqui.rougefm.ca
cfvm@globetrotter.net
License: Amqui, QC held by Astral Media Radio inc.
Group Owner: Astral Media Inc.; (acq 5-30-2005; grpsl).
Population Served: 6,322 *Arbitron Metro Market:* Amqui, QC *Format:* Adult Contemp, Classic Rock*Hrs. of News Programming:* news progmg 6 hrs wkly *No. News Employees:* 2 *Target Audience:* 18 plus.
Adalbert Levesque, General Manager
Jean Lemay, Programming Director
Jennifer Gravel, News Director
Jean Fournier, Engineering Dir
Alain Revard, Disc Jockey

Asbestos

CJAN-FM
01-01-2001; 99.3 mhz FM; kw
CA
(819) 879-0993, *Fax:* (819) 879-7922
www.fm993.ca
info@fm993.ca
License: Asbestos, QC held by Radio Plus B.M.D. inc.
Nat'l Reps: Target Broadcast Sales
Arbitron Metro Market: Asbestos, QC *Format:* Adult Contemp *No. News Employees:* 1 *Target Audience:* 35-75; general
Marie-Paule Drouin, President
Marie-Paule G. Drouin, Owner, host
Denis Beaulieu, Aadvertising consultant
Sylvie Pion, Reporter, routing
Lydia Jacques, Moderator, production
Yvon Leblanc, Moderator, production
Jean-MathieuFontaine, Moderator

Baie St Paul

***CIHOFM**
10-10-1986; 96.3 mhz FM *Hrs Open:* 24; kw
CA
(418) 457-3333, *Fax:* (418) 457-3518
www.cihofm.com
ciho@charlevoix.net
License: Baie St Paul, QC held by Radio MF Charlevoix Inc.
Format: Adult Contemp*Special Programming:* Class 2 hrs, jazz 2 hrs wkly
Gervais Desbiens, General Manager
Rene Belanger, General Sales Mgr
Pierre Beauchesne, Programming Director
Dave Kid, News Director

Baie-Comeau

***CBMIFM**
05-28-1974; 93.7 mhz FM; kw*Rebroadcasts:* Rebroadcasts CBVE-FM Quebec 100%
CA
(418) 691-3613, *Fax:* (418) 691-3610
www.cbc.ca/montreal
License: Baie-Comeau, QC held by Canadian Broadcasting Corp.
Nat'l Network: CBC Radio One
Format: Public Affairs
David Kyle, General Manager

***CHLCFM**
01-01-1996; 97.1 mhz FM; kw
CA
(418) 589-3771, *Fax:* (418) 589-9086
www.chlc.com
info@chlc.com
License: Baie-Comeau, QC held by 9022-6242 Quebec Inc.
Format: Adult Contemp *Target Audience:* General.
Yvon Savoes, President
Francois Morache, Operations Dir
George Daviault, General Manager
Mike Mainville, Programming Director
Mark Andre Halle, News Director

Becancour and Nicolet

CKBN
01-01-2008; 90.5 mhz FM; 34 kw; Ant 118 ft; N46 17 04 W72 32 01
10275 Leblanc, Suite 127, Becancour, QC Canada
(819) 294-2526, *Fax:* (819) 294-2527
www.ckbn.ca
License: Becancour and Nicolet, QC held by Cooperative de solidarite radio communautaire Nicolet-Yamaska/Becancour.
Population Served: 25,000
Raymond Noel, President
Raymond Noel, General Manager
Elaine Bolove, Programming Director

Carleton

***CIEUFM**
01-01-1983; 94.9 mhz FM *Hrs Open:* 24; kw
CA
(418) 364-7094, *Fax:* (418) 364-3150
www.cieufm.com
cieufm@cieufm.com
License: Carleton, Bonaventure County, QC held by Diffusion Communautaire Baie des Chaleurs Inc.
Format: Adult Contemp, Contemporary Hits/Top 40*Special Programming:* Blues 5 hrs, class 3 hrs, folk 3 hrs, jazz 3 hrs w*Hrs. of News Programming:* news progmg 7 hrs wkly *No. News Employees:* 2 *Target Audience:* General.
Jacques Veillette, President
Louis St-Laurent, General Manager
Carol Boudreau, Programming Director
Yues Sigouin, News Director
Claude Roy, Local News Editor

Chandler

CFMV-FM
06-08-2005; 96.3 mhz FM; 5.716 kw
Mailing Address: C.P. 99, Chandler, QC G0C 1K0 Canada
Second Address: 141 rue Commerciale Ouest, Chandler, PQ G0C 1K0
(418) 689-4921, *Fax:* (418) 689-3852
www.fm92-1.com
cfmv@fm92-1.com
License: Chandler, QC held by Radio du Golfe inc.
Population Served: 7,703 *Arbitron Metro Market:* Chandler, QC
Format: French
Jacques Vallee, General Manager

Charlesbourg

CIMI-FM
08-10-2001; 103.7 mhz FM; 20 w
4500, Blvd. Henri-Bairassa bur. 103, Charlesbourg, QC G1H 3A5 Canada
(418) 841-4445, *Fax:* (418) 623-2538
www.cimifm.com
License: Charlesbourg, QC
Population Served: 516,622 *Arbitron Metro Market:* Quebec City, QC *Format:* Alternative
Gerald St. Arnaud, President
Francois Beaule, Operations Dir
Eric Veilleux, Programming Director

Chateauguay

CHAI-FM
01-01-1980; 101.9 mhz FM; 100 w
25 boul. St. Francis, Chateauguay, QC J6J 1Y2 Canada
(450) 698-3131, *Fax:* (450) 698-3339
www.101fm.net
chai@videotrom.ca
License: Chateauguay, QC held by Radio Communautaires de Chateauguay Inc.
Population Served: 75,000 *Format:* Adult Contemp*Hrs. of News Programming:* news progmg 4 hrs wkly *No. News Employees:* 2 *Target Audience:* General; all ages
Christian Laberge, President
Sylvain Poirier, Operations Dir

Chibougamau

CKXO-FM
01-01-2007; 93.5 mhz FM; 19.8 kw; N49 56 46 W74 20 57
171-A rue Jean-Proulx, Gatineau, QC J8Z 1W5 Canada
(819) 770-9650
www.chibougamau.planeteradio.ca

License: Chibougamau, QC held by Groupe Radio Antenne 6 Inc.
Group Owner: RNC Media Saguenay-Lac-Saint-Jean
Population Served: 7,541 *Arbitron Metro Market:* Chibougamau, QC *Format:* Adult Contemp
Robert Parent, Operations Dir

Chicoutimi

***CBJX-FM**
09-20-1933; 100.9 mhz FM *Hrs Open:* 24; 98 kw; Ant 294 ft; N48 25 29 W71 06 32*Rebroadcasts:* Rebroadcasts CBF-FM Montreal 95%
500 rue Des Sagueneens, Chicoutimi, QC G7H 6N4 Canada
(418) 696-6600, *Fax:* (418) 696-6689
www.radio-canada.ca/espace_musique/
License: Chicoutimi, QC held by Canadian Broadcasting Corp.
Nat'l Network: Espace Musique
Population Served: 150,000 *Format:* Classical
Patrick Boie, Operations Dir

***CBJEFM**
01-01-1976; 107.9 mhz FM; kw*Rebroadcasts:* Rebroadcasts CBM(AM) Montreal. Weekdays 6 AM-9 AM rebroadcasts CBVE-FM Quebec City
CA
(514) 597-4444, *Fax:* (514) 597-4416
www.cbc.ca/montreal/community
info@cbc.ca/montreal
License: Chicoutimi, QC held by CBC.
Format: Talk
Judith Bleier, Operations Dir
Patricia Pleszczynska, General Manager
Kate Arthur, Promotions Manager
Sally Caudwell, News Director

***CJABFM**
05-25-1979; 94.5 mhz FM *Hrs Open:* 24; kw
CA
(418) 545-9450, *Fax:* (418) 543-7968
www.radioenergie.com
License: Chicoutimi, QC held by Astral Media Radio Inc.
Group Owner: Astral Media Inc.; (acq 8-21-92).
Nat'l Network: Radiomutuel
Format: Contemporary Hits/Top 40
Richard Turcotte, General Manager
Carol Tremblay, General Sales Mgr
Katia Boivin, Programming Director
Jean-Francois Cote, News Director
Stephane Villeneuve, Engineering Dir

***CBJ-FM**
01-01-2001; 93.7 mhz FM *Hrs Open:* 24; kw*Rebroadcasts:* Rebroadcasts CBF-FM Montreal, 70%
CA
(418) 696-6600, *Fax:* (418) 696-6689
www.radio-canada.ca
License: Chicoutimi, QC held by Canadian Broadcasting Corp.
Nat'l Network: Premiere Chaine
Arbitron Metro Market: Chicoutimi, PQ *Format:* Talk *No. News Employees:* 7 *Target Audience:* 35 plus; adlut, news-oriented
Hubert T. Lacroix, President & CEO
Patrick Boie, General Manager
Maryse Bertrand, Vice-President, Real Estate, Legal Services and Ge
William B. Chambers, Vice-President, Brand, Communications and Corporat
Steven Guiton,Vice-President and Chief Regulatory Officer
Louis Lalande, Executive Vice-President, French Services
Kirstine Stewart, Executive Vice-President of CBC's English Services
Roula Zaar, Vice-President, People and Culture

CFIX-FM
07-31-1987; 96.9 mhz FM *Hrs Open:* 24; 43.8 kw
267 est, rue Racine, Chicoutimi, QC G7H 5K3 Canada
(418) 543-9797, *Fax:* (418) 543-7968
www.saguenay.rougefm.ca
cfix@rock-detente.com
License: Chicoutimi, QC held by Astral Media Radio inc.
Group Owner: Astral Media Inc.; (acq 4-19-2002; grpsl).
Population Served: 60,008 *Arbitron Metro Market:* Chicoutimi, PQ *Format:* Adult Contemp
Richard Durcotte, General Manager

Degelis

***CFVD**
01-01-1995; 95.5 mhz FM *Hrs Open:* 24; kw
CA
(418) 853-2370, *Fax:* (418) 853-3321
www.fm95.ca
cfvd@fm95.ca
License: Degelis, QC held by Radio Degelis Inc.
Format: Adult Contemp, Country, Contemporary Hits/Top 40 *No. News Employees:* 10 *Target Audience:* General.*Adv. Rates:* 24; 22; 20; 5
Gilles Caron, President

Dolbeau-Mistassini

CHVD-FM
01-01-2003; 100.3 mhz FM *Hrs Open:* 24; 21.4 kw
1975 Boul Wallberg, Dolbeau, QC G8L 1J5 Canada
(418) 276-3333, *Fax:* (418) 276-6755
www.dolbeau-mistassini.planetradio.ca
License: Dolbeau-Mistassini, QC held by Groupe Radio Antenne 6 Inc.
Group Owner: RNC Media Saguenay-Lac-Saint-Jean; (acq 5-2004)
Format: Adult Contemp
Pierre Broseau, President
Marc Levesque, Operations Dir
Louis Arcand, Programming Director

CKII-FM
01-01-2004; 101.3 mhz FM; 250 w
1709 boul. Wallberg, Dolbeau-Mistassini, QC G8L 1H6 Canada
(418) 239-2544, *Fax:* (418) 239-0842
License: Dolbeau-Mistassini, QC held by L'Alliance Laurentienne des metis et indiens sans statut, Local 30 Mistassini inc.
Population Served: 12,125 *Arbitron Metro Market:* Dolbeau, QC *Format:* French
Michel Bouchard, General Manager

Donnacona

CHXX-FM
01-01-1997; 100.9 mhz FM; 1.585 kw
1134 Grande Allee West, Suite 300, Donnacona, QC G1S 1E5 Canada
(418) 670-1009, *Fax:* (418) 285-5483
www.radiox.com
reception@radiox.com
License: Donnacona, QC held by RNC MEDIA Inc.
Group Owner: RNC MEDIA Inc.; (acq 12-23-2005)
Format: News, News/Talk, Talk
Patrice Denerse, Operations Dir

Drummondville

CHRD-FM
01-01-1997; 105.3 mhz FM *Hrs Open:* 24; 2.9 kw
2070 rue St. Georges, Drummondville, QC J2C 5G6 Canada
(819) 475-1480, *Fax:* (819) 475-5180
www.drummondville.rougefm.ca
chrd@hy.cgocable.ca
License: Drummondville, QC held by Astral Media Radio Inc.
Group Owner: Astral Media Inc.; (acq 8-13-2001).
Format: Adult Contemp, News*Special Programming:* Relg one hr wkly*Hrs. of News Programming:* news progmg 15 hrs wkly *No. News Employees:* 3 *Target Audience:* 18 plus; general
Joel Rioux, President
Martin Tremblay, Programming Director
David Rivet, News Director
Michel Cournoyer, Chief Engineer
Robert Veilleux, Special Events Coordinator

***CJDM-FM**
08-15-1987; 92.1 mhz FM *Hrs Open:* 24; kw
CA
(819) 474-1892, *Fax:* (819) 474-6610
drummondville.radionrj.ca
cjdm@cgocable.ca
License: Drummondville, QC held by Astral Media Radio inc.
Group Owner: Astral Media Inc.; (acq 5-30-2005; grpsl).
Nat'l Reps: Canadian Broadcast Sales
Format: Adult Contemp*Hrs. of News Programming:* news progmg 5 hrs wkly *No. News Employees:* 2 *Target Audience:* 18-44.
Joel Rioux, General Manager
Claude Rene Piette, Programming Director
Martine Pichette, Promotions Manager
Claude Boucher, News Director
Daniel Pelletier, Engineering Dir
Alain Rivard, Music Director

CJRD-FM
12-27-2007; 88.9 mhz FM; 710 w; N45 53 00 W72 29 19
161 rue Marchand, Drummondville, QC J2B 4N3 Canada
(819) 474-2573, *Fax:* (819) 474-0296
www.cjrd.fm
License: Drummondville, QC held by Radio Drummond.
Population Served: 71,852 *Arbitron Metro Market:* Drummondville, QC *Format:* News, Talk
Georges Masse, President
Jean-Pierre Charbonneau, General Manager

Fermont

CBMR-FM
01-01-1982; 105.1 mhz FM; 16 w
1400 Rene Levesque E., c/o CBM(AM) - A 4, Montreal, QC H2L 8M2 Canada
(514) 597-4444, *Fax:* (514) 597-4416
www.cbc.ca
info@cbc.ca/montreal
License: Fermont, QC held by Canadian Broadcasting Corp.
Format: News
Patricia Pleszczynska, Operations Dir
Judith Bleier, Operations Manager

CFMF-FM
01-01-1980; 103.1 mhz FM; 50 w; 100 ft
20 Daviault Place., Box 280, Fermont, QC G0G 1J0 Canada
(418) 287-5147, *Fax:* (418) 287-5776
www.cfmf.ca
cfmf103_1@diffusionfermont.com
License: Fermont, QC held by Radio Communautaire de Fermont Inc.
Format: Contemporary Hits/Top 40, Variety/Diverse*Special Programming:* Jazz one hr, C&W 4 hrs wkly *Target Audience:* 7-55.
Marc Poulin, President
Jocelyn Pelletier, Operations Dir
Nadia Larrivee, General Manager
Karl Gagne-Cote, Programming Director
Carl Champagne, News Director
Genevieve Richard, Music Director

Forestville

CFRP
01-01-1977; 620 khz AM
CA
(418) 589-3771, *Fax:* (418) 589-9086
License: Forestville, QC held by 9022-6242 Quebec Inc.
Format: Adult Contemp
Yvon Savoie, President
George Baviauet, General Manager
Lynn Martin, News Director

Fort-Coulonge

***CHIPFM**
05-02-1981; 101.5 mhz FM *Hrs Open:* 24; kw
Mailing Address: CA
Second Address: 138 Principal St., Fort Coulonge, PQ JOX 1VO
(819) 683-3155, *Fax:* (819) 683-3211
www.chipfm.com
radiopontiac@chipfm.com
License: Fort-Coulonge, QC held by La Radio du Pontiac Inc.
Format: Country*Special Programming:* Oldies, rock, gospel 7 hrs, class 2 hrs wkly*Hrs. of News Programming:* News progmg 5 hrs wkly *Target Audience:* 35 yrs & up; rural people. farming communities, small towns
Chantele Legault, General Manager

Gaspe

***CJRGFM**
12-01-1978; 103.1 mhz FM; kw
CA
(418) 368-3511, *Fax:* (418) 368-1663
www.radiogaspesie.ca
License: Gaspe, QC held by Radio Gaspesie Inc.
Format: Adult Contemp*Special Programming:* Class 2 hrs, jazz 2 hrs wkly
Jacques Chartier, General Manager
Paul Minville, General Sales Mgr
Richard O'Leary, News Director
Yvan DuPuis, Engineering Dir

***CBGA**
01-01-2004; 89.3 mhz FM *Hrs Open:* 5:30 AM-midnight; kw
CA
(514) 597-6000, *Fax:* (418) 562-3555
radio-canada.ca/gaspesie
communications_matane@radiocanada.ca
License: Gaspe, QC held by CBC.
Nat'l Network: Premiere Chaine
Arbitron Metro Market: Matane, QC *Format:* Contemporary Hits/Top 40, Variety/Diverse, News/Talk*Hrs. of News*

Programming: news progmg 3 hrs wkly *No. News Employees:* 5 *Target Audience:* General.
Louis Pelletier, General Manager
Richard Morisset, Programming Director
Johanne LaBrie, Promotions Manager

Gatineau

CHLX-FM
09-23-2002; 97.1 mhz FM; 12.6 kw
125 rue Jean-Proulx, Gatineau, QC J8Z 1T4 Canada
(819) 770-9740, *Fax:* (819) 770-9740
www.gatineau.planeteradio.ca
classique@radionord.com
License: Gatineau, QC held by RNC MEDIA Inc.
Group Owner: RNC MEDIA Inc.; (acq 8-25-2004)
Population Served: 66,246 *Arbitron Metro Market:* Hull, QC
Format: Classical, Jazz
Jean-Pierre Major, General Manager
Diane Pelletier, General Sales Mgr
Yurs Trottier, Programming Director

CJRC-FM
04-16-2007; 104.7 mhz FM; 36 kw; Ant 136 ft; N45 25 09 W75 42 18
150, rue d'Edmonton, Gatineau, QC J8Y 3S6 Canada
(819) 561-8801, *Fax:* (819) 561-9439
www.cjrc1150.com
nouvelles@cjrc1150.com
License: Gatineau, QC held by Cogecodiffusion Aquisitions Inc
Group Owner: Corus Entertainment Inc.
Population Served: 265,349 *Arbitron Metro Market:* Gatineau, QC*Hrs. of News Programming:* news progmg 49 hrs wkly *No. News Employees:* 3 *Target Audience:* 35-64; adult-babyboomers 50% males, 50% females*Adv. Rates:* 90; 75; 90; 50
Sylvie Charette, General Manager
Kathleen Michaud, General Sales Mgr
Louis-Philippe Bruce, News Director

CFTX-FM
01-01-2006; 96.5 mhz FM; kw
CA
(819) 770-9650
www.capitalerock.ca
License: Gatineau, QC held by RNC MEDIA Inc.
Group Owner: RNC MEDIA Inc.
Arbitron Metro Market: Gatineau, QC *Format:* Classic Rock
Robert Parent, Operations Dir
Benoit Vanasse, Programming Director
Eric Brousseau, Promotions Manager

Granby

CFXM
01-01-1997; 104.9 mhz FM; kw
CA
(450) 372-5105, *Fax:* (450) 372-3105
www.m105.ca
License: Granby, QC held by Cooperative de travail de la radio de Granby.
Arbitron Metro Market: Granby, QC *Format:* Adult Contemp
Stephan Roy, General Manager
Luc Normandin, General Sales Mgr
Guy Laporte, Promotions Manager

Harrington Harbour

***CFTH-FM-1**
10-30-1991; 97.7 mhz FM; 180 w; N50 29 36 W59 28 50
Box 88, Harrington Harbour, Duplessis, QC G0G 1N0 Canada
(418) 795-3349, *Fax:* (418) 795-3200
cfth@globetrotter.qc.ca
License: Harrington Harbour, QC held by Radio Communautaire de Harrington Harbour.
Format: Adult Contemp, Country, Oldies *Target Audience:* General; five fishing villages
Kate Nadeau, General Manager
Nancy Bobbitt, Programming Director
Lois Jones, Programming Director
Monica Anderson, Replacement Programming Director

CFTH-FM-2
01-01-1991; 98.5 mhz FM; 70 w
Box 88, Harrington Harbour, QC G0G 1N0 Canada
(418) 795-3349, *Fax:* (418) 795-3200
License: Harrington Harbour, QC held by Radio communautaire de Harrington Harbour.

Kate Nadeau, General Manager
Nancy Bobbitt, Programming Director
Lois Jones, Programming Director

Havre-Saint-Pierre

CILE-FM
01-01-1987; 95.1 mhz FM *Hrs Open:* 24; 1.496 kw; Ant 201 ft
992 Rue du Bouleau, Havre-Saint-Pierre, QC G0G 1P0 Canada
(418) 538-2453, *Fax:* (418) 538-3870
www.cilemf.com
cilemf@globetrotter.net
License: Havre-Saint-Pierre, QC held by Radio & Television Communautaire Havre-St. Pierre.
Format: Adult Contemp
Berchmens Boudreau, General Manager
Catherine Ramoisy, News Director
Gerald Gallant, Engineering Dir

Hull

***CIMFFM**
01-01-1970; 94.9 mhz FM; kw
CA
(819) 770-2463, *Fax:* (819) 770-9338
www.rockdetente.com
cimf@rockdetente
License: Hull, QC held by Astral Media Radio Inc.
Group Owner: Astral Media Inc.; (acq 10-28-2002; grpsl).
Format: Classic Rock*Hrs. of News Programming:* news progmg 3 hrs wkly *No. News Employees:* 2 *Target Audience:* 18-45+
Ian Greenberg, President
Carmen Rodrigue, General Manager
Claude Raymond, General Sales Mgr
Patrice Croteau, Programming Director
Eric St-Louis, Promotions Manager
Mano Aube, News Director
Pierre Sylvestre, Chief Engineer
Jean-Guy Faucher, Music Director

***CKTF**
03-11-1988; 104.1 mhz FM *Hrs Open:* 24; kw
CA
(819) 243-5555, *Fax:* (819) 243-6816
www.radionrj.ca/gatineau
License: Hull, QC held by Astral Media Radio Inc.
Group Owner: Astral Media Inc.
Format: Contemporary Hits/Top 40, Rock/AOR
Carmen Rodrigue, General Manager
Vincent Pons, General Sales Mgr
Astral Musique, Programming Director
Melany Gauvin, Promotions Manager
Pierre Sylvestre, Engineering Dir

Iles-de-la-Madeleine

CFIM-FM
11-15-1981; 92.7 mhz FM *Hrs Open:* 24; 6.3 kw
C.P. 8192, 1172 Chemin Laverniere, Cap-aux-Meules, QC G4T 1R3 Canada
(418) 986-5233, *Fax:* (418) 986-5319
www.cfim.ca
pub@cfim.ca
License: Iles-de-la-Madeleine, QC held by Diffusion Communautaire des Iles Inc.
Format: News, News/Talk, Talk, Variety/Diverse *Target Audience:* General.
Charles Cyr, General Manager
Marjolaine Arseneault, Programming Director
Linda Noel, Promotions Manager
Helen Fauteux, News Director
Paul Turbide, Engineering Dir

Joliette

CJLM-FM
01-01-1996; 103.5 mhz FM *Hrs Open:* 24; 3 kw; N45 59 0 W73 25 52
540 St. Thomas, Joliette, QC J6E 3R4 Canada
(450) 756-1035, *Fax:* (450) 756-8097
www.m1035fm.com
radio@m1035fm.com
License: Joliette, Canada County, QC held by Cooperative de Radiodiffusion MF 103.5 de Lanaudiere.
Format: Adult Contemp*Special Programming:* Oldies 6 hrs wkly *No. News Employees:* 4 *Target Audience:* 25-49.*Adv. Rates:* 42; 42; 40; 39
Normand Masse, General Manager
Benoit Simard, Programming Director
Marie Josee Demera, Promotions Manager
Martin Beaucage, Music Director

Jonquiere

CKAJ-FM
04-11-1977; 92.5 mhz FM *Hrs Open:* 6 AM-midnight; 14.164 kw
Mailing Address: 3877 Harvey Blvd, 2nd Fl., Jonquiere, QC G7X 0A6 Canada
Second Address: Pavillon Manicouagan, 3791, De La Fabrique, Jonquiere, PQ G7X 7W8
(418) 546-2525, *Fax:* (418) 546-2528
www.ckaj.org
ckaj@ckaj.org
License: Jonquiere, QC held by Radio Communautaire du Saguenay Inc.
Format: Country, Variety/Diverse*Hrs. of News Programming:* news progmg 6 hrs wkly *No. News Employees:* 1 *Target Audience:* 25-54.
Johanne Tremblay, President
Pierre Boivin, Programming Director
Henri Girard, Chief Engineer

Kahnawake

***CKRK-FM**
03-30-1981; 103.7 mhz FM *Hrs Open:* 24; kw
CA
(450) 638-1313, *Fax:* (450) 638-4009
www.k103radio.com
info@k103radio.com
License: Kahnawake, QC held by Mohawk Radio Kahnawake Association.
Format: Adult Contemp, Country*Special Programming:* Mohawk 10 wkly*Hrs. of News Programming:* news progmg 3 hrs wkly *No. News Employees:* 2 *Target Audience:* Native community in Kahawake; general audience Montrealregion
Lois Williams, General Sales Mgr
Vince Barrucco, Programming Director
Dino Sisto, News Director
Don Garrett, Disc Jockey
Lance Delisle, Disc Jockey
Thomasina Phillips, News Reporter
Marsha Dailleboust, Traffic Manager

CKKI-FM
06-12-2011; 89.9 mhz FM; kw
CA
(450) 635-2099
www.kkicradio.com
License: Kahnawake, QC held by Brian Moon
Format: Country
Brian Moon, General Manager

Kuujjuaq

CKUJ-FM
01-01-1992; 97.3 mhz FM *Hrs Open:* 10am-12pm; 2-5pm; 394 w
Box 1082, Kuujjuaq, QC J0M 1C0 Canada
(819) 964-2921, *Fax:* (819) 964-2229
License: Kuujjuaq, QC held by Minister Council of Kuujjuaq.
Population Served: 2,375 *Arbitron Metro Market:* Kuujjuaq, PQ
Format: Ethnic
Larry Watt, President
Mary Gordon, Operations Dir

La Baie

CKGS-FM
03-19-2009; 105.7 mhz FM; 2.93 kw; 32.87 meters; N48 21 08 W70 53 56
169 6th St., Saguenay, QC G7B 0A3 Canada
(418) 544-2105
www.ckgsfm.com
info@ckgsfm.com
License: La Baie, QC held by Carl Gilbert.
Carl Gilbert, General Manager

La Malbaie

***CBV-FM-6**
09-20-1979; 99.3 mhz FM *Hrs Open:* 24; 820 w; Ant 108 ft; N47 41 02 W70 08 06*Rebroadcasts:* Rebroadcasts CBV-FM Quebec 100%
888 Saint-Jean St., Quebec, QC G1R 5H6 Canada
(418) 654-1341, *Fax:* (418) 656-8842
www.radio-canada.ca/quebec
License: La Malbaie, QC held by CBC.
Nat'l Network: Premiere Chaine
Format: News
Claude- Saindon, Operations Dir
Susan Campbell, General Manager
Sally Caldwell, News Director
Gaston LeBlanc, Engineering Dir

La Pocatiere

CHOX-FM
04-23-1992; 97.5 mhz FM; 25 kw

601 First St., Suite 50, La Pocatiere, QC G0R1Z0 Canada
(418) 856-1310, *Fax:* (418) 856-3747
www.chox97.com
chox@chox97.com
License: La Pocatiere, QC held by CHOX-FM Inc.
Format: Adult Contemp
Guy Simard, President
Gilles Gosselin, Operations Dir
Diane Bouchard, General Sales Mgr
Renee Giard, Promotions Manager
Jacques Dufour, News Director
Clement Lavoie, Engineering Dir
Maxima Parabas, Music Director
Gabriel Hudon,Promotions Manager
Georgette Charent, Sales VP

La Tuque

CFLM
10-03-1959; 1240 khz AM *Hrs Open:* 24
CA
(819) 523-4575, *Fax:* (819) 676-8000
www.cflm.ca
radio.h-m@sympatico.ca
License: La Tuque, QC held by Radio Haute Mauricie Inc.
Format: Adult Contemp *No. News Employees:* 1 *Target Audience:* General.
Rejean LeClerc, President

Lac Megantic

CJIT-FM
01-01-2002; 106.7 mhz FM *Hrs Open:* 24; 4.25 kw
4766 rue Laval, Lac Megantic, QC G6B 1C7 Canada
(819) 583-0663, *Fax:* (819) 583-0665
www.cjitfm.com
info@cjitfm.com
License: Lac Megantic, QC held by Les Productions du temps perdu inc.
Nat'l Reps: Target Broadcast Sales
Population Served: 5,932 *Arbitron Metro Market:* Lac Megantic, QC *Format:* Adult Contemp, Contemporary Hits/Top 40
Louis Longchamps, Operations Dir
Normand Blondeau, Engineering Dir

Lac-Brome

CIDI-FM
09-20-2007; 99.1 mhz FM; 1.45 kw; Ant 165 ft; N45 11 10 W72 35 20
Box 3611, 305B Knowlton Rd., Knowlton, QC J0E 1V0 Canada
(450) 243-6285, *Fax:* (450) 243-1041
www.sunnymead.org/cidi
deweydurrell@axion.ca
License: Lac-Brome, QC held by Radio Communautaire Missisquoi.
Population Served: 211,000 *Arbitron Metro Market:* Redding, CA
Format: Talk*Hrs. of News Programming:* news progmg 21 hrs wkly *No. News Employees:* 3 *Target Audience:* 18-60.*Adv. Rates:* 160; 160; 160; 160
Lana Littlechief, General Manager

Lac-Etchemin

***CFIN-FM**
03-27-1992; 100.5 mhz FM *Hrs Open:* 24; 6.7 kw; 676 ft; N46 24 41 W70 35 44
201 Claude-Bilodeau St., Lac-Etchemin, QC G0R 1S0 Canada
(418) 625-3737, *Fax:* (418) 625-3730
www.cfinfm.com
cfinfm@sogetel.net
License: Lac-Etchemin, Bellechasse County, QC held by Radio Bellechasse.
Regional Reps: Target.
Population Served: 50,000 *Format:* Adult Contemp, Country*Special Programming:* Class 4 hrs, jazz 6 hrs, relg one hr, country 6 hr*Hrs. of News Programming:* news progmg 30 hrs wkly *No. News Employees:* 2 *TargetAudience:* 35-60.
Marcel Asselin, President
Raymond Boutin, Station Manager
Isabelle Giasson, Programming Director
Norman Poulin, News Director

Lac-Simon (Louvicourt)

CHUT-FM
01-01-2000; 95.3 mhz FM; 97.9 w
1016 rue Wabanonik, Lac-Simon, QC J0Y 3M0 Canada
(819) 736-4501, *Fax:* (819) 736-2333
License: Lac-Simon (Louvicourt), QC held by Radio communautaire MF Lac Simon inc.
Population Served: 984 *Arbitron Metro Market:* Lac-Simon, PQ
Format: Ethnic
Alain Flamand, General Manager

Lachute

***CJLAFM**
12-01-1974; 104.9 mhz FM *Hrs Open:* 24; kw
CA
(450) 562-3733
www.planetlov.ca
fusionfm@citenet.net
License: Lachute, QC held by RNC MEDIA Inc.
Group Owner: RNC MEDIA Inc.; (acq 8-22-89)
Format: Adult Contemp*Hrs. of News Programming:* news progmg 8 hrs wkly *No. News Employees:* 1 *Target Audience:* 25-59.
Pierre Brosseau, President
Marc Dubois, Operations Dir
Jean-Pierre Major, General Manager
Yves Trottier, General Sales Mgr
Olivier Proulx, News Director
Gaston Tousignant, Chief Engineer

Laval

***CFGLFM**
09-01-1968; 105.7 mhz FM *Hrs Open:* 24; kw
CA
(450) 664-1500, *Fax:* (450) 664-4138
www.rythmefm.com
License: Laval, QC held by Cogeco Diffusion inc.
Group Owner: Cogeco Diffusion Inc.
Format: Adult Contemp*Hrs. of News Programming:* news progmg 2 hrs wkly *No. News Employees:* 2 *Target Audience:* 25-54; those preferring soft & easy lstng hits
Sylvain Venne, Operations Dir
Richard LaChance, General Manager
Andre St-Amand, Programming Director
Daniel Brouilette, Promotions Manager
Jean Arcand, Engineering Dir
Lilianne Randall, Music Director

CJLV
01-01-2004; 1570 khz AM; 10 kw-U
Radio Nostalgie, 2040 Autoroute Laval, Laval, QC Canada
(450) 680-1570
www.nostalgie1570.com
avidtoire@nostalgie1570.com
License: Laval, QC held by 759 474 Canada Inc
Colette Chabot, General Manager

Levis

CFEL-FM
01-01-1987; 102.1 mhz FM *Hrs Open:* 24; kw
Mailing Address: CA
Second Address: 5245 Boulevard De La Rive-Sud Levis, Levis, PQ G6V4ZA
(418) 248-1122, *Fax:* (418) 248-1951
www.ckoi.com/quebec
cfel@globetrotter.net
License: Levis, QC held by 5191991 B.C. Ltd.
Group Owner: Corus Entertainment Inc.; (acq 3-24-2000; grpsl).
Format: Adult Contemp *No. News Employees:* 1 *Target Audience:* 25-49.
Michel Montminy, General Manager
Rene Nadeau, Programming Director

CFOM-FM
01-01-1992; 102.9 mhz FM; 16.8 kw
2136.ch.Ste-foy, Quebec, QC G1V 1R8 Canada
(418) 694-1029, *Fax:* (418) 682-8430
www.cfom1029.com
radioflashback@cfom1029.com
License: Levis, QC held by Cogeco Diffusion Aquisitions Inc
Group Owner: Cogeco Diffusion Inc.; (acq 1-21-2005; grpsl).
Target Audience: 25 plus.
Pierre DeMondehare, General Manager
Jean-Paul Lemire, General Sales Mgr
Mario Paquin, Programming Director
Annie Anglehart, Promotions Manager

Listuguj

CFIC-FM
01-01-2000; 105.1 mhz FM; 425 w
Mailing Address: Box 304, 44A Riverside East, Listuguj, QC G0C 2R0 Canada
Second Address: 44A Riverside E., Listuguj, PQ G0C 2R0
(418) 788-5166, *Fax:* (418) 788-3524
www.105hotcountry.com
Gerry@105hotcountry.com
License: Listuguj, QC held by Societe d'Art, de Culture et d'Histoire Micmacs.
Population Served: 399 *Arbitron Metro Market:* Lingwick, QC
Format: Country
Gerald Dedam, President
Jake Dedam, Manager
Linda Gilbert, General Sales Mgr

Longueuil

CHAA-FM
01-01-1987; 103.3 mhz FM *Hrs Open:* 24; kw
CA
(450) 646-6800, *Fax:* (450) 646-7378
www.fm1033.ca
admin@fm1033.ca
License: Longueuil, QC held by Radio Communautaire de la Rive-Sud Inc.
Nat'l Reps: Target Broadcast Sales
Format: Adult Contemp*Special Programming:* Fr 18 hrs, retro oldies 9 hrs, Greek 5 hrs, Vietna*Hrs. of News Programming:* news progmg 5 hrs wkly *No. News Employees:* 2 *Target Audience:* 24-54; general*Adv. Rates:* 34; 30; 34; 30
Eric Tetreault, Chairman
France Dube, Programming Director
Richard Boileau, Promotions Manager

CHMP-FM
04-09-1977; 98.5 mhz FM; 40.8 kw; Ant 623 ft
211 avenue Gordon, Verdun, QC H4G 2R2 Canada
(514) 767-2435, *Fax:* (514) 761-0985
www.fm985.ca
License: Longueuil, QC held by Cogeco Diffusion Aquisition Inc
Group Owner: Cogeco Diffusion Inc.; (acq 2-01-2011; grpsl).
Nat'l Reps: Canadian Broadcast Sales
Hrs. of News Programming: News progmg 5 hrs wkly *Target Audience:* 18-44.*Adv. Rates:* 300; 250; 250; 200
Pierre Beland, President
Pierre Accand, Operations Dir
Jacques Papin, General Manager
David Therrien, General Sales Mgr
Denis Fortin, Programming Director
Pierre Tremblay, Promotions Manager
Real Terrault, Chief Engineer
MichelLacroix, General Sales Manager
Michel Belleau, Music Director
Maurice Tietolman, National Sales Manager

***CIELFM**
12-15-1994; 98.5 mhz FM; kw
CA
(418) 862-8241, *Fax:* (418) 867-4940
www.ciel103.com
clabrie@ciel103.com
License: Longueuil, QC held by Radio CJFP (1986) Ltee.
Format: Adult Contemp
Guy Simard, President
Gilles Lamarre, General Sales Mgr
Daniel St. Pierre, Programming Director
Stephane Gemdrom, News Director
Christian Duchesne, Promotions Director

Louiseville

CHHO-FM
01-22-2007; 103.1 mhz FM; 1.52 kw
50-A de la Fabrique, Louiseville, QC J0K 2W0 Canada
(819) 228-1001, *Fax:* (819) 228-0330
www.ch2ofm.ca
info@ch2ofm.ca
License: Louiseville, QC held by Coop de solidarite radio communautaire de la MRC de Maskinonge.
Population Served: 7,517 *Arbitron Metro Market:* Louiseville, QC
Format: French
Stephane Carbonneau, General Manager

Lourdes-de-Blanc-Sablon

***CFBS-FM**
01-01-1989; 89.9 mhz FM *Hrs Open:* 7 AM-5 PM; 178 w; Blanc Sablon
C.P. 8, 1193 boul. Dr. Camille Marcoux, Lourdes-de-Blanc-Sablon, QC G0G 1W0 Canada
(418) 461-2445, *Fax:* (418) 461-2425
www.cfbsradio.com
cfbs@globetrotter.net
License: Lourdes-de-Blanc-Sablon, QC held by Radio Blanc-Sablon Inc.
Population Served: 5,000 *No. News Employees:* 1

Vicki Driscoll, President
Janice Letemplier, Programming Director
Janice Letemplier, General Director

Magog

***CIMOFM**
01-01-1979; 106.1 mhz FM *Hrs Open:* 6 AM-8 PM; kw
CA
(819) 347-1414, *Fax:* (819) 347-1061
www.radioenergie.com
License: Magog, QC held by Astral Media Radio Inc.
Group Owner: Astral Media Inc.
Format: Contemporary Hits/Top 40 *Target Audience:* 18-34.
Nathalie Johnson, General Manager
Isabelle Gagnon, General Sales Mgr
Anne-Marie Bercier, Promotions Manager
Marc Toussaint, News Director
J.P. Maheu, Chief Engineer

Maliotenam

CKAU-FM
01-01-1993; 104.5 mhz FM; 50 w
C.P. 338, Succ Bureau-chef, Sept-Iles, QC G4R 4K6 Canada
(418) 927-2476, *Fax:* (418) 927-2800
www.ckau.com
info@ckau.com
License: Maliotenam, QC held by Corporation de Radio Kushapetsheken Apetuamiss Uashat.
Population Served: 25,686 *Arbitron Metro Market:* Sept-Iles, PQ
Format: Variety/Diverse
Reginald Steering, CEO
Yves Rock, General Manager
Reginald Thomas, General Sales Mgr
Mathieu McKenzie, Engineering Dir
Guylaine St-Onge, Accounting
Marceline Ambrose, Secretariat
Popoye (George Eugene), Animation andadvertising
Alexander Aster, Animation and journalist

Maniwaki

CBOF-1(AM)
10-22-1973; 990 khz AM; 40 w, DA-1*Rebroadcasts:* Rebroadcasts CBOF-FM Ottawa
Box 3220, Stn C, Ottawa, ON K1Y 1E4 Canada
(613) 288-6000, *Fax:* (613) 288-6560
cbc.ca
License: Maniwaki, QC held by Canadian Broadcasting Corp.
Format: Variety/Diverse
Robert Rabinowitz, CEO
Denis Simard, General Manager

***CHGAFM**
11-01-1980; 97.3 mhz FM *Hrs Open:* 24; kw
CA
(819) 449-3959, *Fax:* (819) 449-7331
www.chga.qc.ca
chga@bellnet.ca
License: Maniwaki, QC held by Radio Communautaire Type B.
Format: Adult Contemp, Variety/Diverse*Special Programming:* Class one hr, jazz 3 hrs, country 8 hrs, folk 5 hr*Hrs. of News Programming:* news progmg 15 hrs wkly *No. News Employees:* 1
Hubert Tremblay, President
Lise Morisette, Operations Dir
Lise Morissette, General Manager
Gaitam Bussiere, General Sales Mgr
Gaetan Bussieres, Programming Director
Georges Vasiloff, Engineering Dir
Kim Lacaille, MusicDirector
Linda Lemieux, Regional Sales Manager

CFOR-FM
08-01-1994; 99.3 mhz FM *Hrs Open:* 24; 2.4 kw
139 South Main, Maniwaki, QC J9E 1Z8 Canada
(819) 441-0993, *Fax:* (819) 441-3488
www.cforfm.com
cfor993@b2b2c.ca
License: Maniwaki, QC held by 9116-1299 Quebec Inc.
Nat'l Reps: Radio Unie Target
Format: Rock/AOR *No. News Employees:* 3 *Target Audience:* 15-45.
Rock Lepine, President
Laure Voilquin, General Sales Mgr

Maniwaki (Kitigan Zibi Anishinabeg

CKWE-FM
01-01-1987; 103.9 mhz FM; 50 w
River Desert Indian Band, Box 309, Maniwaki, QC J9E 3C9 Canada
(819) 449-5170, *Fax:* (819) 449-5673
www.tyendinaga.net
anita.tenasco@kza.qc.ca
License: Maniwaki (Kitigan Zibi Anishinabeg, QC held by Jean-Guy Whiteduck.
Population Served: 3,930 *Arbitron Metro Market:* Maniwaki, PQ
Format: News, Talk
Eleanor Whiteduck, Operations Dir
Anita Penasco, General Manager

Maria (Reserve)

CHRG-FM
01-01-1991; 101.7 mhz FM *Hrs Open:* 24; 10 w
Mailing Address: Box 118, Maria (Reserve), QC G0C 1Y0 Canada
Second Address: 120 School St., Maria (Reserve), PQ G0C 1Y0
(418) 759-8196, *Fax:* (418) 759-8196
www.chrgfm.com
radio@globetrotter.net
License: Maria (Reserve), QC held by Douglas Martin.
Population Served: 1,388 *Arbitron Metro Market:* Maria (Reserve), PQ *Format:* Country, Oldies, Variety/Diverse
Douglas Martin, General Manager
Wes Jones, Programming Director

Mashteuiatsh (Pointe-Bleue)

CHUK-FM
01-01-1996; 107.3 mhz FM *Hrs Open:* 24; 50 w
1491 rue Ouiatchouan, Mashteuiatsh, QC G0W 2H0 Canada
(418) 275-4684, *Fax:* (418) 275-7964
www.chukfm.ca
chuk@chukfm.ca
License: Mashteuiatsh (Pointe-Bleue), QC held by Corporation Mediatique Teuehikan.
Population Served: 2,213 *Arbitron Metro Market:* Mashteuiatsh, PQ *Format:* French
Karl Clary, General Manager
Jean Denis Gill, Programming Director

Matagami

CHEF-FM
01-01-2001; 99.9 mhz FM; 36 w
110 boulevard Matagami, C.P. 39, Matagami, QC J0Y 2A0 Canada
(819) 739-9990, *Fax:* (819) 739-6003
www.chef99.ca
chef99fm@lino.com
License: Matagami, QC held by Radio Matagami.
Population Served: 1,526 *Arbitron Metro Market:* Matagami, PQ
Format: Adult Contemp
Daniel Clich,, Chairman
M. Constantineau, President
Marie-Eve Gallant, General Manager
Daniel Cliche, General Sales Mgr
David Chabot, News Director
Nathalie Poirier, Vice-Chair
Sylvain Cloutier, Secretary-Treasurer
Julie Flag,Director

Matane

CHOE-FM
05-01-1991; 95.3 mhz FM *Hrs Open:* 24; 30 kw
800 Ouest du Phare, Matane, QC G4W 1V7 Canada
(418) 562-8181, *Fax:* (418) 562-0778
www.choefm.com
choe.routage@globetrotter.net
License: Matane, QC held by Les Communications Matane Inc.
Population Served: 20,000 *Format:* Light Rock *Target Audience:* 18-34; young workers
Kenneth Gagne, President
Kenneth Gagne Jr., General Manager
Michel Desrosiers, General Sales Mgr
Carol St-Pierre, News Director
Jacques Tremblay, Chief Engineer

***CHRM-FM**
04-01-2001; 105.3 mhz FM *Hrs Open:* 24; kw
CA
(418) 562-4141, *Fax:* (418) 562-0778
www.chrmfm.com
micheldesrosiers@choefm.com
License: Matane, QC held by Les Communications Matane inc.
Arbitron Metro Market: Matane, PQ *Format:* Adult Contemp
Kenneth Gagne, President
Kenneth Gagne Jr., General Manager
Michel Desrosiers, General Sales Mgr
Carol St-Pierre, News Director
Michel Desrosiers, Commercial director
Carol St-Pierre, Advertising consultant
Romano Quagliano,Advertising consultant
Sylvain Caron, Advertising consultant
Denis L,vesque, Advertising consultant

Mont-Laurier

CFLO-FM
01-01-1995; 104.7 mhz FM; 10.98 kw*Rebroadcasts:* Rebroadcasts CFLO FM-1 L'Annonciation 100%.
332 de la Madone, Mont-Laurier, QC J9L 1R9 Canada
(819) 623-5610, *Fax:* (819) 623-7406
www.cflo.ca
cflofm@cflo.ca
License: Mont-Laurier, QC held by Soneme Inc.
Format: Adult Contemp*Hrs. of News Programming:* News progmg 3 hrs wkly *Target Audience:* 24-54.
Sylvain Lacasse, President
Dominic Bell, Programming Director

Montreal

CBF-FM
01-01-1947; 95.1 mhz FM; 100 kw; 823 ft
Box 6000, Quebec, QC H3C 3A8 Canada
(514) 597-6000
www.cbc.radio-canada.ca
auditore@radio-canada.ca
License: Montreal, QC held by CBC.
TV Affiliate: CBFT(TV) affil. *Format:* Talk
Sylvain LaFrance, Operations Dir
Bertrand Emond, General Manager

CBFX-FM
01-01-1998; 100.7 mhz FM; 100 kw
Box 6000, Montreal, QC H3C 3A8 Canada
(514) 597-6000, *Fax:* (416) 205-3714
www.cbc.radio-canada.ca
License: Montreal, QC held by CBC.
Nat'l Network: Espace Musique
Format: Variety/Diverse
Sylvain LaFrance, Operations Dir
Bertrand Emond, Station Manager
Alain Saulnier, News Director

CBM-FM
01-01-1947; 93.5 mhz FM; 24.6 kw; 823 ft
Box 6000, Montreal, QC H3C 3A8 Canada
(514) 597-6000, *Fax:* (514) 597-4416
www.music.cbc.ca
info@cbc.ca/montreal
License: Montreal, QC held by Canadian Broadcasting Corp.
TV Affiliate: CBMT(TV) affil. *Format:* Talk
Judith Bleier, Operations Dir
Patricia Pleszczynska, Station Manager
Patricia Plesczynska, Programming Director

CBME-FM
01-01-1998; 88.5 mhz FM *Hrs Open:* 24; 16.9 kw
Box 6000, Montreal, QC H3C 3A8 Canada
(514) 597-4444, *Fax:* (514) 597-4142
www.cbc.ca/montreal
License: Montreal, QC held by Canadian Broadcasting Corp.
Nat'l Network: CBC Radio One
Format: News
Judith Bleier, Operations Dir
Patricia Pleszczynska, Station Manager
Sally Caldwell, Programming Director

CFMB
12-21-1962; 1280 khz AM *Hrs Open:* 24
CA
(514) 483-2362, *Fax:* (514) 483-1362
www.cfmb.ca
admin@cfmb.ca
License: Montreal, QC held by CFMB Ltee.
Regional Reps: Direct
Format: Ethnic*Hrs. of News Programming:* news progmg 35 hrs wkly *No. News Employees:* 7*Adv. Rates:* 65; 60; 65; 50
Andrew Mielewczyk, President
Luigi Valente, Station Manager
Ivana Bombardieri, Promotions Manager
Nino Di Stefano, News Director
A.M. St. Germain-Stanczykowski, Executive Vice President
Tony Ferrara, Music Director
Walter Centa,National Sales Manager
Marcello Silveri, Regional Sales Manager

CFQR-FM
11-01-1966; 92.5 mhz FM *Hrs Open:* 24; 41.4 kw; 979 ft

Mailing Address: Box 925, Montreal, QC H4G 3M1 Canada
Second Address: 211 Gordon Ave, Verdum Quebec, PQ H4F-2R2
(514) 767-9250, *Fax:* (514) 787-7979
www.940news.com
info@940news.com
License: Montreal, QC held by Cogeco Diffusion Aquisitions Inc
Group Owner: Corus Entertainment Inc.
Target Audience: 25-54.
Ted Silver, Programming Director
Kathie Murphy, Promotions Manager

***CHOMFM**
07-16-1963; 97.7 mhz FM *Hrs Open:* 24; kw
CA
(514) 989-2523, *Fax:* (514) 989-3868
www.chom.com
infodesk@chom.com
License: Montreal, QC held by Astral Media Radio G.P.
Group Owner: Astral Media Inc.; (acq 10-29-2007; grpsl)
Format: Classic Rock
Bob Harris, Operations Dir
Rob Braide, General Manager
Jacques Bolduc, General Sales Mgr
Ray Scott, Programming Director
Mike Bendixen, News Director
Mark Kavanagh, Engineering Dir

CIBL-FM
04-26-1980; 101.5 mhz FM *Hrs Open:* 24; kw
CA
(514) 526-2581, *Fax:* (514) 526-3583
www.cibl1015.com
administration@cibl1015.com
License: Montreal, QU held by Radio Communautaire Francophone de Montreal Inc.
Format: Talk*Special Programming:* Black 13 hrs, class 4 hrs, jazz 14 hrs, reggae 4 h*Hrs. of News Programming:* news progmg 14 hrs wkly *No. News Employees:* 4 *Target Audience:* General.*Adv. Rates:* 35; 25;35; 20
Genevieve Dore, General Manager
Gilles Labelle, Programming Director
Eric Lefebvre, General Manager

CINQFM
01-27-1975; 102.3 mhz FM *Hrs Open:* 24; 1.29 kw; Ant 180 ft
5212 Boul. St. Laurent, Montreal, QC Canada
(514) 495-2597, *Fax:* (514) 495-2429
www.radiocentreville.com
License: Montreal, QC held by Radio Centre-Ville Saint Louis Inc.
Special Programming: Sp 16, Portugese 13 hrs, Greek 13 hrs, Chinese 5 h *No. News Employees:* 1 *Target Audience:* 25-54; Fr & multilingual
Rene Pluviose, President
Evan Kapetanakis, Station Manager
Daniel Moreau, General Sales Mgr
Miguel Greco (English), Programming Director
Robert Laplante, News Director
Marc Provencher, Chief Engineer
Suzanne Charland (Fr),Programming Director
Ricardo Costa, Programming Director

***CIRA**
05-01-1995; 91.3 mhz FM *Hrs Open:* 24; kw
CA
(514) 382-3913, *Fax:* (514) 858-0965
www.radiovm.com
cira@radiovm.com
License: Montreal, Quebec County, QC held by Radio Ville-Marie.
Nat'l Reps: MPV Radio *Regional Reps:* Gaston Pearson
Format: Religious *No. News Employees:* 15 *Target Audience:* Over 40*Adv. Rates:* 50 to 90 $
Jean-Guy Roy, General Manager
Gaston Pearson, General Sales Mgr
Claudette Lambert, Programming Director
Philippe Vaillancourt, News Director
Joe Pacheco, Engineering Dir
Roger Landry, Chief Engineer

***CISM-FM**
03-01-1991; 89.3 mhz FM; 10 kw
Box 6128, C-1509, Montreal, QC H3C 3J7 Canada
(514) 343-7511, *Fax:* (514) 343-2418
www.cism893.ca
License: Montreal, QC held by Communications du Versant Nord.
Format: Alternative *Target Audience:* 18-24 college students
Jules Hedert, General Manager
Guillaume Vincenot, Programming Director
Patrick Gelinas, Promotions Manager

Catherine Valois, Engineering Dir
Martin Roussy, Music Director

***CITEFM**
05-20-1977; 107.3 mhz FM *Hrs Open:* 24; kw
CA
(514) 845-2483, *Fax:* (514) 288-1073
www.rock-detente.com
cite@rock-detente.com
License: Montreal, QC held by Astral Media Radio Inc.
Group Owner: Astral Media Inc.; (acq 4-19-2002; grpsl).
Format: Adult Contemp *Target Audience:* 25-49.
Jacques Parisien, President
Sylvain Langlois, Operations Dir
Luc Tremblay, General Manager

CJAD
12-08-1945; 800 khz AM *Hrs Open:* 24
CA
(514) 989-2523, *Fax:* (514) 989-3868
www.cjad.com
License: Montreal, QC held by Astral Media Radio G.P.
Group Owner: Astral Media Inc.; (acq 10-29-2007; grpsl)
Format: News, News/Talk, Talk*Hrs. of News Programming:* news progmg 14 hrs wkly *No. News Employees:* 15
Rob Braide, Operations Dir
Jacques Bolduc, General Sales Mgr
Mike Bendixen, Programming Director
Lisa Faoco, Promotions Manager
Derek Conlon, News Director
Mark Kavanagh, Engineering Dir
Bob Harris, Operations Manager

***CJFMFM**
10-01-1962; 95.9 mhz FM; kw
CA
(514) 989-2536, *Fax:* (514) 989-2554
www.montreal.virginradio.ca
License: Montreal, QC held by Astral Media Radio G.P.
Group Owner: Astral Media Inc.
Format: Adult Contemp
Bob Harris, Programming Director
Matthew Wood, Promotions Manager
Mark Kavanagh, Chief Engineer
Ray Scott, Music Director

CJMS
05-01-1999; 1280 khz AM *Hrs Open:* 24
CA
(514) 990-2567, *Fax:* (450) 632-0528
www.cjms10.com
cjms@videotron.ca
License: Montreal, QC held by 3553230 Canada Inc.
Nat'l Network: Radio Unica
Format: Country *No. News Employees:* 2
Dr. David Azoulay, CEO/COO
Alex Azoulay, President

CJPX-FM
06-25-1998; 99.5 mhz FM
124 Chemin du Chenal-Le-Moyne, Iles Notre Dame, Parc Jean-Drapeau, Montreal, QC H3C 1A9 Canada
(514) 871-0995, *Fax:* (514) 871-0990
www.radioclassique.ca
cjpx@radioclassique.ca
License: Montreal, QC held by Radio Classique Montreal Inc.
Format: Classical
Jean-Pierre Coallier, CEO
Pierre Barbeau, Operations Dir
Francois Pare, General Manager
Sebastian Beaulieu, General Sales Mgr

CKAC
09-22-1922; 730 khz AM *Hrs Open:* 24
CA
(514) 845-5151, *Fax:* (514) 845-2229
www.ckac.com
License: Montreal, QC held by 591991 B.C. Ltd.
Group Owner: Cogeco Diffusion Inc.; (acq 1-21-2005; grpsl)
Format: Sports*Hrs. of News Programming:* News progmg 20 hrs wkly *Target Audience:* 35-54.
Julie Gagnon, Operations Dir
Sylvain Chamberland, General Manager

CKGM
12-07-1959; 690 khz AM; 50 kw-U; N45 17 43 W73 43 20
1310 Greene Ave., Montreal, QC Canada
(514) 931-4487, *Fax:* (514) 931-4079
www.tsn.ca/montreal
License: Montreal, QC held by Bell Media Canada Radio Partnership
Group Owner: Bell Media Inc.; (acq 6-22-2007; grpsl)

Lee Hambleton, General Manager
Wayne Bews, General Sales Mgr

***CKMFFM**
05-11-1964; 94.3 mhz FM *Hrs Open:* 24; kw
CA
(514) 529-3229, *Fax:* (514) 529-9308
www.radioenergie.com
Lsabbatini@radio.astral.com
License: Montreal, QC held by Astral Media Radio Inc.
Group Owner: Astral Media Inc.; (acq 1-12-2000; grpsl).
Nat'l Network: Radiomutuel
Format: Contemporary Hits/Top 40*Special Programming:* Disco*Hrs. of News Programming:* News progmg one hr wkly
Target Audience: 18-34.
Jacques Parisien, Chairman
Ian Greenburg, CEO
Charles Benoit, Operations Dir
Luc Tremblay, General Manager
Marie Lefelbvre, General Sales Mgr
Andre Allara, Promotions Manager
Luc Sabbatini, Executive Vice President
MichelTartif, Regional Sales Manager

***CKUT**
11-01-1987; 90.3 mhz FM *Hrs Open:* 24; kw
CA
(514) 448-4041, *Fax:* (514) 398-8261
www.ckut.ca
programming@ckut.ca
License: Montreal, QC held by Radio McGill Inc.
Format: Variety/Diverse*Special Programming:* Black 20 hrs, Fr 9 hrs, Sp 6 hrs, folk 3 hrs, gosp*Hrs. of News Programming:* news progmg 6 hrs wkly *No. News Employees:* 1
Louise Burns, General Sales Mgr
Kristiana Clemmens, Programming Director
Gretchen King, News Director
Marc Montanchez, Chief Engineer
Juliet Lammers, Promotions Director

CJWI
01-01-2002; 1610 khz AM
CA
(514) 287-1288, *Fax:* (514) 287-3299
License: Montreal, QC held by CPAM Radio Union.com inc.
Format: Ethnic
Jean Pierre, General Manager

CKDG-FM
04-18-2004; 105.1 mhz FM *Hrs Open:* 24; 224 w; Ant 722 ft; N45 30 10 W73 35 46
5899 Park Ave., Montreal, QC Canada
(514) 273-2481, *Fax:* (514) 273-3707
www.mikefm.ca
info@mikefm.ca
License: Montreal, Canada County, QC held by CHCR Ltd.
Wire Services: Catholic News Service
Population Served: 1,500,000*Special Programming:* Multicultural*Hrs. of News Programming:* 2 Hours/Day *No. News Employees:* 3 *Target Audience:* 25-54; mostly trilingual
John Daperis, President
Pota Gotsis, Operations Dir
Marie Griffiths, General Manager
Geoffrey Marteng, Station Manager
Mandy Benoualid, Promotions Manager
Tony Choundalas, News Director
Jean Frechette, Engineering Dir
ChrisNucgaud, Music Director
Pota Gotsis, Traffic Manager

CKLX
12-14-2004; 91.9 mhz FM; 1.9 kw; Ant 633 ft; N45 30 12 W73 35 49
200 Avenue Laurier Ouest, Bureau 250, Montreal, QC Canada
(514) 871-0919, *Fax:* (514) 871-8884
www.montrealradiox.com
License: Montreal, QC held by RNC MEDIA Inc.
Group Owner: RNC MEDIA Inc.
Target Audience: 35-64.
Raynald Briere, President
Rene Menard, General Sales Mgr
Annie Belanger, Programming Director
Dominic Plamondon, Programs Director
Marc Giguere, Vice President

CHOU
01-01-2007; 1450 khz AM *Hrs Open:* 24
CA
(514) 790-0002, *Fax:* (514) 745-3475
www.1450am.ca
pdg@1450am.ca

License: Montreal, QC held by 9015-2018 Quebec inc.
Arbitron Metro Market: Montreal, QC *Format:* Arabic, Ethnic
Antoine Karam, General Sales Manager
Zeina Karam, Programming Director

CJLO
01-01-2007; 1690 khz AM
CA
(514) 848-8663, *Fax:* (514) 848-7470
www.cjlo.com
feedback@cjlo.com
License: Montreal, QC held by Concordia Student Broadcasting Corp.
Arbitron Metro Market: Montreal, QC *Format:* Variety/Diverse
Stephanie Saretsky, Station Manager
Amrew Weekes, General Sales Mgr
Brian Joseph, Programming Director
Katie Seline, Promotions Manager
Hannah Besseau, News Director
Omar Husain, Music Director
Kayleigh Jordan-MacGregor,Volunteer Coordinator
Stephanie Doyle, Magazine Editor
Andrew Wieler, RPM Director/Interim Metal Director

CKIN-FM
04-15-2012; 106.3 mhz FM; kw
CA
(514) 273-2481, *Fax:* (514) 273-3707
www.mikefm.ca
License: Montreal, QC held by Canadian Hellenic Cable Radio Inc
Format: Ethnic

Montreal (zone LaSalle)

CKVL-FM
01-08-2008; 100.1 mhz FM *Hrs Open:* 24; 250 w; N45 25 51 W73 35 37
55, ave. Dupras, 3rd Floor, LaSalle, QC H8R 4A8 Canada
(514) 360-2585, *Fax:* (514) 367-4471
www.100-1fm.com
info@radiolasalle.com
License: Montreal (zone LaSalle), QC held by La radio communautaire de LaSalle.
Population Served: 74,276 *Format:* Variety/Diverse
Patrick Coutu, General Manager
Marie-Eve ??Gaudreau, Programming Director
Claudia B,lair, Administrative Assistant

Natashquan

CKNA-FM
01-30-1983; 104.1 mhz FM; 6.56 kw
29 chemin d'en Haut, Natashquan, QC G0G 2E0 Canada
(418) 726-3284, *Fax:* (418) 726-3367
pages.globetrotter.net/ckna/
ckna@globetrotter.net
License: Natashquan, QC held by La Radio Communautaire CKNA Inc.
Population Served: 810 *Arbitron Metro Market:* Natashquan, QC
Format: Adult Contemp
Jean Jaques Landry, General Manager
Renee Lapierre, Promotions Manager

New Carlisle

CHNC-FM
12-23-2008; 107.1 mhz FM *Hrs Open:* 24; 3.9 kw; 200 meters; N48 08 27 W65 14 35*Rebroadcasts:* Carleton, Chandler, PercÃ©, GaspÃ©
Mailing Address: 153 boulevard Gerard-D.-Levesque, New Carlisle, QC G0C 1Z0 Canada
Second Address: 153 boulevard Gerard-D.-Levesque, New Carlisle, PQ G0C 1Z0
(418) 752-2215, *Fax:* (418) 752-6939
www.radiochnc.com
radiochnc@globetrotter.net
License: New Carlisle, QC held by Cooperative des travailleurs CHNC.
Nat'l Reps: MPV Radio *Wire Services:* Canada NewsWire
Population Served: 70,000 *No. News Employees:* 15 *Target Audience:* General; adult
Francis Remillard, General Manager
Michel Morin, News Director

Pikogan

CKAG-FM
01-01-1993; 100.1 mhz FM; 3.738 kw; Ant 126 ft; N48 35 48 W78 07 05
30 rue David Kistabish, Pikogan, QC J9T 3A3 Canada
(819) 727-3237, *Fax:* (819) 727-4432
www.ckagfm.com
ckagfm1001@hotmail.com
License: Pikogan, QC held by Societe de Communication Ikito Pikogan Ltee.
Population Served: 487 *Arbitron Metro Market:* Pikogan, PQ
Format: Variety/Diverse
Brenda Rankin, Operations Dir
Brenda Rankin, General Sales Mgr

Plessisville

***CKYQ**
01-01-1996; 95.7 mhz FM *Hrs Open:* 24; kw
CA
(819) 362-3737, *Fax:* (819) 362-3414
www.kyqfm.com
studi@kyqfm.com
License: Plessisville, QC held by Societe CKYQ Radio Media Enr.
Format: Adult Contemp
Stephane Dion, President
Sebastian Doyon, News Director

Pohenegamook

CFVD-FM-2
09-10-1983; 92.1 mhz FM; 294 w*Rebroadcasts:* Rebroadcasts CFVD-FM Degelis
654 6th St. E., Degelis, QC G5T 1Y1 Canada
(418) 853-3370, *Fax:* (418) 853-3321
www.fm95.ca
cfvd@fm95.ca
License: Pohenegamook, QC held by Radio Degelis Inc.
Format: Variety/Diverse *No. News Employees:* 10 *Target Audience:* General.
Gilles Caron, President

Port-Cartier

CIPC-FM
01-01-1995; 99.1 mhz FM *Hrs Open:* 24; 10kw
Elijah 52-Rochefort, Port-Cartier, QC G5B 1N2 Canada
(418) 766-6868, *Fax:* (418) 766-6870
www.laradioactive.com
info@laradioactive.com
License: Port-Cartier, QC held by Radio Port-Cartier Inc.
Format: Contemporary Hits/Top 40
Yvan Beaulieu, General Manager
Luc Boucher, General Sales Mgr
Matthieu Pineau, Programming Director
Emie jane Dery, News Director
Elizabeth Chevalier, Music Director

Port-Menier

CJBE-FM
01-01-1988; 90.5 mhz FM; 88 w
C.P. 15, Port-Menier (Ile d'Anticosti), QC G0G 2Y0 Canada
(418) 535-0292, *Fax:* (418) 535-0497
www.radiovision.ca/cjbe
info@radio-unie-target.com
License: Port-Menier, QC held by Radio Anticosti Inc.
Population Served: 281 *Arbitron Metro Market:* Anticosti, QC
Format: Public Affairs *No. News Employees:* 1
Francine Ross, Chairman
Francine Ross, President
Julie Lavallee, General Manager
France Dub,, Programming Director
Gervais Desbiens, Vice President
ric Lefebvre, Secretary-Treasurer
Lise Morissette, Administrative Director
Charles Eugene Cyr, Director General
Christian Roy, Member Support
Sylvie Vincent, Accounting Manager

Quebec

***CBV-FM**
01-01-1974; 106.3 mhz FM *Hrs Open:* 24; 100 kw; Ant 541 ft; N46 51 40 W71 04 46
888 Rue Saint-Jean, Quebec, QC GIR 5H6 Canada
(418) 656-8235, *Fax:* (418) 656-8842
www.cbc.ca
License: Quebec, QC held by Societe Radio Canada.
Nat'l Network: Premiere Chaine
Population Served: 500,000*TV Affiliate:* *CBVT-TV affil. *Format:* News, News/Talk, Talk, Variety/Diverse*Hrs. of News Programming:* News progmg 15 hrs wkly *Target Audience:* General.
Robert Rabinovitch, President
Norman LaCombe, News Director
Robert Jacques, Engineering Dir

***CBVEFM**
03-01-1979; 104.7 mhz FM *Hrs Open:* 5:30-8:30 AM; 4-6 PM; kw
CA
(418) 691-3613, *Fax:* (418) 691-3610
www.cbc.ca
quebecam@cbc.ca,breakaway@cbc.ca
License: Quebec, QC held by Canadian Broadcasting Corp.
Nat'l Network: CBC Radio One
Format: News, News/Talk, Talk, Variety/Diverse
Judith Bleier, Operations Dir
Claude Saindon, General Manager
Peter Black, News Director

***CBVX-FM**
01-01-1998; 95.3 mhz FM; 100 kw; 541 ft; N46 51 40 W71 04 46
888 Saint-Jean St., Quebec, QC G1R 5H6 Canada
(418) 654-1341, *Fax:* (418) 656-8212
www.cbc.ca
License: Quebec, QC held by Societe Radio Canada.
Nat'l Network: Radio Canada
Format: Talk*Special Programming:* Jazz 16 hrs, news 7 hrs wkly *Target Audience:* General.
Real Jean, Operations Dir
Marleine Simard, General Manager
Clodine Dorval, News Director

***CHIKFM**
08-01-1982; 98.9 mhz FM; kw
CA
(418) 687-9900, *Fax:* (418) 687-3106
www.radioenergie.com
info@radioenergie.com
License: Quebec, QC held by Astral Media Radio Inc.
Group Owner: Astral Media Inc.
Format: Adult Contemp
Daniel Tremblay, General Manager
Real Marcotte, General Sales Mgr
Jean Alexandre, Programming Director
Julie Durand, Promotions Manager
Rejean Bergeron, News Director
Michel Duval, Engineering Dir

CHRC
04-01-1926; 800 khz AM *Hrs Open:* 24
CA
(418) 688-8080, *Fax:* (418) 670-1234
www.chrc.com
nouvelles@quebec800.com
License: Quebec, QC held by 9183-9084 Quebec Inc.
Format: Sports*Special Programming:* French *Target Audience:* 35 plus.
Elmer Hildebrand, CEO
Lyndon Friesen, Operations Dir
Keith Leask, Station Manager
Menno Friesen, General Sales Mgr
Louis Painchaud, Programming Director
Don McCracken, News Director
Vern Moores, Chief Engineer

***CION**
09-19-1995; 90.9 mhz FM *Hrs Open:* 8 (M-S); 16 (Su); kw
CA
(418) 659-9090, *Fax:* (418) 650-3306
www.radiogalilee.com
cionfm@radiogalilee.qc.ca
License: Quebec, QC held by Radio Galilee.
Format: Adult Contemp, Religious *Target Audience:* General.
Alexandre St. Hilaire, President
Denis Veilleux, General Manager
Berthold Bernier, Programming Director
Jacques Fortin, News Director
Daniel Coulombe, Engineering Dir
Mario Blouin, Music Director

***CITFFM**
07-22-1982; 107.5 mhz FM *Hrs Open:* 24; kw
CA
(418) 527-3232, *Fax:* (418) 687-3106
www.rockdetente.com
info@rockdetente.com
License: Quebec, QC held by Astral Media Radio Inc.
Group Owner: Astral Media Inc.; (acq 4-19-2002; grpsl).
Regional Reps: Radio Plus.
Format: Adult Contemp *No. News Employees:* 2 *Target Audience:* 25-54.
Daniel Tremblay, General Manager
Suzie Baronet, General Sales Mgr
Marc Tanguay, Programming Director

RADIO - CANADA

Julie Durand, Promotions Manager
Michel Duval, Chief Engineer

***CJMFFM**
09-15-1979; 93.3 mhz FM *Hrs Open:* 24; kw
CA
(418) 687-9330, *Fax:* (418) 687-0211
www.le933.com
commentaire@cjmf.com
License: Quebec, QC held by Cogeco Diffusion Inc.
Group Owner: Cogeco Diffusion Inc.; (acq 11-87; $8 million)
Format: Classic Rock, Talk*Hrs. of News Programming:* news progmg 5 hrs wkly *Target Audience:* 25-54; mostly males
Louis Audet, President
Jean-Paul Lemire, General Manager

CKIA-FM
10-31-1984; 88.3 mhz FM *Hrs Open:* 24; 350 w; 700 ft; N46 48 28 W71 12 57
335 St. Joseph St., Suite 200, Quebec, QC G1K 3B4 Canada
(418) 529-9026, *Fax:* (418) 529-4156
www.ckiafm.org
ckiafm@meduse.org
License: Quebec, QC held by Radio Basse-Ville Inc.
Format: Classic Rock, Country, Variety/Diverse*Special Programming:* Class 3 hrs, jazz 4 hrs, Sp 4 hrs, Haitian 2 hrs,*Hrs. of News Programming:* news progmg 2 hrs wkly *No. News Employees:* 1 *Target Audience:* 18-35; general
Bryan St. Louis, President
Ernst Caze, General Manager
Max Raneau, General Sales Mgr
Bryan St. Louis, Programming Director
Denis Roberge, Chief Engineer

***CKRLFM**
02-15-1973; 89.1 mhz FM *Hrs Open:* 24; kw
CA
(418) 640-2575, *Fax:* (418) 640-1588
www.ckrl.qc.ca
ckrl@ckrl.qc.ca
License: Quebec, QC held by CKRL MF 89.1 Inc.
Format: Adult Contemp, Jazz*Special Programming:* Sp 2 hrs, It 2 hrs, Black 6 hrs, Arab 3 hrs wkly *No. News Employees:* 1
Dany Fortin, General Manager
Bastien Gagnon La France, Programming Director
Daniel Deslauriers, Promotions Manager
Daniel Marcoux, Music Director

CJEC-FM
08-01-2003; 91.9 mhz FM; 14.45 kw
815 boulevard, Lebourgneuf, suite 505, Quebec, QC G2J 0C1 Canada
(418) 688-0919, *Fax:* (418) 682-8431
www.wknd.fm
License: Quebec, QC held by Cogeco Diffusion Inc.
Group Owner: Cogeco Diffusion Inc.
Population Served: 516,622 *Arbitron Metro Market:* Quebec City, QC *Format:* Adult Contemp
Louis Audet, President
Jean-Paul Lemire, General Manager
Carole Vezina, General Sales Mgr
Daniel Plante, Promotions Manager
Martin Perkins, Engineering Dir
Lilianne Randall, Music Director

CJSQ-FM
07-25-2007; 92.7 mhz FM; 2.1 kw; N46 49 22 W71 29 41
Radio-Classique Quebec, 2525 BLVD Laurier, Quebec, QC G1V 2L2 Canada
(418) 650-9270, *Fax:* (418) 650-5735
www.radioclassique.ca
cjsq@radioclassique.ca
License: Quebec, QC held by 9147-2605 Quebec inc.
Population Served: 516,622 *Arbitron Metro Market:* Quebec City, QC
Pierre Barbeau, General Manager
Bernard Poitras, General Sales Mgr

***CHOIFM**
11-01-1949; 98.1 mhz FM; kw
CA
(418) 687-9810, *Fax:* (418) 682-8427
www.choiradiox.com
License: Quebec, QC held by RNC MEDIA Inc.
Group Owner: RNC MEDIA Inc.
Arbitron Metro Market: Quebec City, QC *Format:* Talk *Target Audience:* 18-34; young adults
Kenneth Gagne, President
Kenneth Gagne Jr., General Manager
Michel Desrosiers, General Sales Mgr
Carol St-Pierre, News Director
Jacques Tremblay, Chief Engineer

Radisson

CIAU-FM
01-01-1996; 103.1 mhz FM; 17 w
Mailing Address: PO Box 285, 143 rue Joliet, Radisson, QC J0Y 2X0 Canada
Second Address: 143 rue Jolliet, Radisson, PQ J0Y 2X0
(819) 638-7033, *Fax:* (819) 638-1031
www.ciaufm.ca
ciaufm@lino.com
License: Radisson, QC held by Radio communautaire de Radisson
Population Served: 1,303 *Arbitron Metro Market:* Baie-James, QC *Format:* Variety/Diverse*Special Programming:* Fr 8 hrs, Jazz 3 hrs wkly*Hrs. of News Programming:* news progmg 3 hrs wkly *No. News Employees:* 1*Adv. Rates:* 5; 5; 5; 5
Eric Hamel, President
Patrice Maltais, Station Manager

Restigouche

CHRQ-FM
01-01-1991; 106.9 mhz FM; 31 w
Box 180, Restigouche, QC G0C 2R0 Canada
(418) 788-2449, *Fax:* (418) 788-2653
chrq1069@globetrotter.net
License: Restigouche, QC held by Gespegewag Communications Society.
Population Served: 157 *Arbitron Metro Market:* Restigouche, PQ*Hrs. of News Programming:* news progmg one hr wkly *No. News Employees:* 5 *Target Audience:* Community members all ages*Adv. Rates:* 282; 282; 282;282
Sandra Bulmer, Station Manager
Chad Gedeon, General Sales Mgr
Steve Clement, Programming Director
Karen Duguay, Promotions Manager

Rimouski

***CIKIFM**
02-14-1988; 104.5 mhz FM *Hrs Open:* 24; kw
CA
(418) 723-2323, *Fax:* (418) 722-7508
www.ciki.fm
ciki@pqm.net
License: Rimouski, QC held by Astral Media Radio inc.
Group Owner: Astral Media Inc.; (acq 5-30-2005; grpsl).
Format: Rock/AOR
Jean Fournier, Operations Dir
Bertrand Bellavance, General Manager
Ghislain Desgardins, General Sales Mgr
Francois La Fond, Programming Director
Martin Bressard, News Director
Alain Rivard, Music Director

***CBRXFM**
02-28-1959; 101.5 mhz FM; 50 kw; 931 ft
273 rue St-Jean Baptiste Ouest, Rimouski, QC Canada
(418) 723-2217, *Fax:* (418) 723-6126
www.radio-canada.ca/espace_musique/
nouvelles_rimouski@canada.ca
License: Rimouski, QC held by Canadian Broadcasting Corp.
Nat'l Network: Espace Musique
Bernard Labarge, President
Bernard Lebarge, General Manager
Bernard Labarbe, Programming Director

***CKLEFM**
03-29-1990; 96.5 mhz FM *Hrs Open:* 24; kw
CA
(506) 546-4600, *Fax:* (506) 546-6611
www.ckle.fm
superstation@ckle.fm
License: Rimouski, Gloucester County, QC held by Radio De LaBaie Ltd.
Format: Contemporary Hits/Top 40*Special Programming:* Jazz 2 hrs wkly*Adv. Rates:* 26; 23; 18; 14
Armand Roussy, General Manager

CJOI-FM
10-22-2000; 102.9 mhz FM *Hrs Open:* 24; 33.6 kw
287, rue Pierre Saindon, Suite 502, Rimouski, QC G5L9A7 Canada
(418) 723-2323, *Fax:* (418) 722-7508
www.rimouski.rougefm.ca
cjoi@pqm.net
License: Rimouski, QC held by Astral Media Radio inc.
Group Owner: Astral Media Inc.; (acq 5-30-2005; grpsl).
Population Served: 46,860 *Arbitron Metro Market:* Rimouski, PQ
Format: Adult Contemp
Mario Fournier, General Manager/Director of Sales
Francois La Fond, Programming Director
Martin Bressard, News Director
Cathy Pineault, Reception / Administrative Assistant
Guillaume Savard, Promotions and marketing coordinator
Jean Fournier, Technical Director
Bellavance, Webmaster / producer of digital content
Benoit Primeau, Facilitator

***CJBRFM**
01-01-2000; 101.5 mhz FM; kw
CA
(418) 696-6600, *Fax:* (418) 696-6689
www.radio-canada.ca
nouvelles_rimouski@radiocanada.ca
License: Rimouski, QC held by Canadian Broadcasting Corp.
Arbitron Metro Market: Chicoutimi, PQ *Format:* Adult Contemp, News, News/Talk, Talk*Special Programming:* Fr. *Target Audience:* 35 plus; adlut, news-oriented
Hubert T. Lacroix, President & CEO
Bernard Labarge, General Manager
Maryse Bertrand, Vice-President, Real Estate, Legal Services and Ge
William B. Chambers, Vice-President, Brand, Communications and Corporat
Steven Guiton,Vice-President and Chief Regulatory Officer
Louis Lalande, Executive Vice-President, French Services
Kirstine Stewart, Executive Vice-President of CBC's English Services
Roula Zaar, Vice-President, People and Culture

CFYX-FM
10-01-2007; 93.3 mhz FM; 18.197 kw; N48 27 53 W68 12 32
158 Saint-Germain Ouest, Rimouski, QC G5L 4B7 Canada
(418) 722-2848
www.cfyx93.com
direction@cfyx93.com
License: Rimouski, QC held by Radio Rimouski Inc.
Population Served: 6,665 *Arbitron Metro Market:* Mont-Joli, QC
Format: Classic Rock
Pierre-Yves Renaud, General Manager
Rene Girard, General Sales Mgr

Rimouski-Mont Joli

CKMN-FM
06-04-1990; 96.5 mhz FM *Hrs Open:* 24; 6.4 kw; N48 22 32 W68 35 43
323 Montee Industrielle, Rimouski, QC G5M 1A7 Canada
(418) 722-2566, *Fax:* (418) 724-7815
www.ckmn.fm
lemoloche@ckmn.fm
License: Rimouski-Mont Joli, Rimouski County, QC held by La Radio Communautaire du Comte.
Wire Services: CNW Broadcast
Format: Adult Contemp, Country*Special Programming:* Oldies 3 hrs, classical 3 hrs wkly *No. News Employees:* 5 *Target Audience:* 25-55; general*Adv. Rates:* 18; 14; 18; 14
Line Meloche, CEO/COO
Daniel Menard, President
Renie Langlois, Programming Director
Reynald LaPierre, Promotions Manager
Michel Vallee, Chief Engineer
Gabriel Dumont, Executive Vice President

Riviere Au Renar

***CJREFM**
01-01-1979; 97.9 mhz FM *Hrs Open:* 24; kw
CA
(418) 368-3511, *Fax:* (418) 368-1663
License: Riviere Au Renar, QC held by Radio Gaspesie Inc.
Format: Adult Contemp
Jacques Chartier, General Manager
Paul Mainville, General Sales Mgr
Richard O'Leary, News Director
Yvan Dupuis, Engineering Dir

Riviere du Loup

CIBMFM
01-01-1966; 107.1 mhz FM *Hrs Open:* 24; 100 kw; Ant 244 ft
64 Hotel de Ville, Riviere du Loup, QC Canada
(418) 867-1071, *Fax:* (418) 862-7704
www.cibm107.com
License: Riviere du Loup, QC held by CIBM Mont-Bleu.
Nat'l Network: Radiomedia

Guy Simard, General Manager
Renee Giard, General Sales Mgr
Daniel St. Pierre, Programming Director
Daniel St. Pierre, News Director
Clement LaVoie, Engineering Dir

RADIO - CANADA

Roberval

CHRL-FM
03-01-2002; 99.5 mhz FM *Hrs Open:* 24; 16.6 kw; N48 26 25 W72 06 47
568 Blvd. St. Joseph, Roberval, QC G8H 2K6 Canada
(418) 275-1831, *Fax:* (418) 275-2475
www.roberval.planeteradio.ca
chrl@antenne6.com
License: Roberval, QC held by Groupe Radio Antenne 6 inc.
Group Owner: RNC Media Saguenay-Lac-Saint-Jean
Population Served: 10,227 *Arbitron Metro Market:* Roberval, QC *Format:* Variety/Diverse*Hrs. of News Programming:* news progmg 20 hrs wkly *No. News Employees:* 1 *Target Audience:* General; mainly adults
Marc Levesque, General Manager
Lewis Gagnon, General Sales Mgr
Louis Arcand, Programming Director

Rouyn-Noranda

CHOA-FM
09-21-1990; 96.5 mhz FM; 55 kw; 600 ft
380 Ave. Murdoch, Rouyn-Noranda, QC J9X 1G5 Canada
(819) 762-0741, *Fax:* (819) 762-2280
www.abitibi.planetradio.ca
License: Rouyn-Noranda, QC held by RNC MEDIA Inc.
Group Owner: RNC MEDIA Inc.
TV Affiliate: CFEM-TV, CKRN-TV affils. *Format:* Adult Contemp *Target Audience:* 25-54.
Pierre Brosseau, CEO
Raynald Briere, President
Andre Houle, General Manager
Nancy Deschenes, General Sales Mgr
Robert Ashby, Programming Director
Gerald Landry, Chief Engineer

CJMM-FM
06-17-1988; 99.1 mhz FM *Hrs Open:* 24; 3.5 kw; Ant 200 ft
191, avenue Murdoch, Rouyn-Noranda, QC J9X 1E3 Canada
(819) 797-2566, *Fax:* (819) 797-1664
www.radioenergie.com
mtrottier@radioenergie.astral.com
License: Rouyn-Noranda, QC held by Astral Media Radio Inc.
Group Owner: Astral Media Inc.; (acq 1-12-2000; grpsl).
Format: Contemporary Hits/Top 40*Hrs. of News Programming:* news progmg 5 hrs wkly *No. News Employees:* 1 *Target Audience:* 18-44.
Marlene Trottier, General Manager
Chantel Massicotte, General Sales Mgr
Ian Clermont, Promotions Manager
Fanny-Garance Carrier, News Director
Mathieu Barrette, Engineering Dir

CHIC-FM
01-01-2003; 88.7 mhz FM; 300 w
120 rue 9e, Rouyn-Noranda, QC J9X 2B6 Canada
(819) 797-4242, *Fax:* (819) 797-3803
www.chicfm.org
887@chicfm.org
License: Rouyn-Noranda, QC held by Communications CHIC (C.H.I.C.).
Population Served: 41,012 *Arbitron Metro Market:* Rouyn-Noranda, QC *Format:* Christian
Andre Curadeau, General Manager
Vic Cimon, Station Manager
Jocelyn Cote, General Sales Mgr

CHUN-FM
01-01-2005; 98.3 mhz FM; 490 w; N48 18 05 W79 03 08
1016 rue Wabanonic, Lac Simon, QC J0Y 3M0 Canada
(819) 797-5316
www.chunfm.ca
chun98.3@tlb.sympatico.ca
License: Rouyn-Noranda, QC held by Radio communautaire MF Lac Simon Inc.
Population Served: 41,012 *Arbitron Metro Market:* Rouyn-Noranda, QC *Format:* Country
Noe Mitchell, General Manager

Saguenay

CKRS-FM
01-01-2007; 98.3 mhz FM; 51 kw; N48 22 15 W71 10 20
121 rue Racine Est, Chicoutimi, QC G7H 5G4 Canada
(418) 545-2577, *Fax:* (418) 545-9186
www.ckrs.ca
License: Saguenay, QC held by 591991 B.C. Ltd.
Group Owner: Corus Entertainment Inc.
No. News Employees: 6 *Target Audience:* 25-54.
Sylvain Chamberland, President
Sylvain Chamberland, General Manager
Rene Trembley, General Sales Mgr

Saint Augustin

CJAS-FM
01-01-1992; 93.5 mhz FM; 100 w*Rebroadcasts:* Rebroadcasts VOCM(AM) St. John's, NF weekends
Box 100, 558 rue Principal, St. Augustine, QC G0G 2R0 Canada
(418) 947-2239, *Fax:* (418) 947-2664
www.cjasradio.piczo.com
cjasradio@gmail.com
License: Saint Augustin, QC held by La Radio Communautaire de Riviere St-Augustin Inc.
Population Served: 478 *Arbitron Metro Market:* Saint-Augustin, QC *Format:* Adult Contemp
Laurette Gallibois, General Manager
Maria Shattler, Programming Director
Rachel Bilodeau, News Director
Lindsey Durepos, Music Director

Saint Georges-de-Beauce

CKRB-FM
10-01-1953; 103.5 mhz FM *Hrs Open:* 24; 17 kw
Mailing Address: 11760, 3rd Ave., C.P. 100, Saint Georges-de-Beauce, QC G5Y 5C4 Canada
Second Address: 11760 Third Ave., Saint Georges-de-Beauce, PQ G5Y 5C4
(418) 227-0997, *Fax:* (418) 228-0096
www.mix997.com
adminrb@cgocable.ca
License: Saint Georges-de-Beauce, QC held by Radio Beauce Inc.
Format: Adult Contemp*Hrs. of News Programming:* news progmg 11 hrs wkly *No. News Employees:* 2 *Target Audience:* 35 plus.
Guy Simard, President
Maurice Marcotte, General Manager
Claude Girard, General Sales Mgr
Marcel Rancourt, Programming Director
Suzanne Bougie, News Director
Gaston Guay, Chief Engineer
Jacques Goulet, National Sales Manager

Saint Jean-Iberville

CFZZ-FM
01-01-1992; 104.1 mhz FM *Hrs Open:* 24; 1.35 kw
104 rue Richelieu, St. Jean-Sur-Richelieu, QC J3B 6X3 Canada
(450) 346-0104, *Fax:* (450) 348-2274
www.boomfm.com
lstemarie@boomfm.astral.com
License: Saint Jean-Iberville, QC held by Astral Media Radio inc.
Group Owner: Astral Media Inc.; (acq 5-30-2005; grpsl).
Format: Oldies*Adv. Rates:* 65; 65; 65; 65
Leopold Stemarie, General Manager
Ghislaine Plourde, Programming Director
Luc Lalonde, Promotions Manager

Saint Jerome

CIMEFM
03-25-1977; 103.9 mhz FM *Hrs Open:* 24; 39.3 kw
120 Delagare St., Saint Jerome, QC Canada
(450) 431-2463, *Fax:* (450) 565-9755
ventes@cime.fm
License: Saint Jerome, QC held by Cogeco Diffusion Aquisitions Inc
Group Owner: Cogeco Diffusion Inc.; (acq 2-01-2011; grpsl).
No. News Employees: 2 *Target Audience:* 25-54; Adult
John Cassidy, President
Gilbert Cerat, General Manager
Ghislaiu Plourde, Programming Director
Etienne Gregoire, Promotions Manager
Jean Rousseau, News Director

CFND-FM
12-29-2008; 101.9 mhz FM; 49 w; Ant 78 ft; N45 47 04 W73 59 21
Ecole Notre-Dame, 581 rue Ouimet, Saint Jerome, QC J5Z 1R3 Canada
(450) 432-4472, *Fax:* (450) 432-8694
radionotredame@edu.csrdn.qc.ca
License: Saint Jerome, QC held by Amie du Quartier.
Population Served: 68,456 *Arbitron Metro Market:* Saint Jerome, QC *Format:* Talk
Marc Bourcier, General Manager

Saint Pamphile

CJDS-FM
12-07-2001; 94.7 mhz FM; 24 w
109 Route Eagles, Saint Pamphile, QC G0R 3X0 Canada
(418) 356-1303, *Fax:* (418) 356-2586
cjdsradio@globetrotter.net
License: Saint Pamphile, QC held by 3819914 Canada inc.
Population Served: 2,685 *Arbitron Metro Market:* Saint-Pamphile, QC *Format:* Adult Contemp
Jean-Claude Dignard, President
Claire Soulieres, Operations Dir
Ann Dignard, General Sales Mgr
J. Dignard, Public Affairs Director

Saint Remi

***CHOCFM**
01-01-1999; 104.9 mhz FM; 250 w
93 Ruelachapelle Est, Saint Remi, QC Canada
(450) 454-5500, *Fax:* (450) 454-9435
www.chocfm.com
studio@chocfm.com
License: Saint Remi, QC held by Radio Communautaire Intergeneration Jardin du Quebec.
Hrs. of News Programming: news progmg 10 hrs wkly *No. News Employees:* 1
Sylvain Remillard, President
Richard Vegneault, General Manager

Sainte Anne des Monts

CBGN(AM)
01-01-1972; 1340 khz AM; 1 kw-D, 250 w-N
155 St. Sacrament St., Matane, QC G4W 1Y9 Canada
(418) 562-0290, *Fax:* (418) 566-6068
License: Sainte Anne des Monts, QC held by CBC.
Format: News, Talk
Louis Pelletier, General Manager

CJMC-FM
03-01-1996; 100.3 mhz FM *Hrs Open:* 24; 2.51 kw
170 Boul. Ste. Anne, Sainte Anne des Monts, QC G4V 1N1 Canada
(418) 763-5522, *Fax:* (418) 763-7211
cjmc@quebectel.com
License: Sainte Anne des Monts, QC held by Radio du Golfe Inc.
Format: Adult Contemp*Special Programming:* Class 2 hrs, western 2 hrs wkly
Jacques Vallee, President
Stephane Cyr, Programming Director
Olivier Vallee, Promotions Director

Sainte Foy

***CHYZ-FM**
01-29-1997; 94.3 mhz FM *Hrs Open:* 24; 6 kw
Local 0236, Pavillon Pollack, Cite Universitaire, Sainte Foy, QC G1K 7P4 Canada
(418) 656-2131, *Fax:* (418) 656-3660
www.chyz.ca
chyz@public.ulaval.ca
License: Sainte Foy, QC held by Radio Campus Laval.
Population Served: 600,000 *Format:* Variety/Diverse*Special Programming:* Hip-hop/rap 15 hrs wkly*Hrs. of News Programming:* news progmg 10 hrs wkly *No. News Employees:* 4 *Target Audience:* 18-30; univ students
Jean-Philippe Lessard, General Manager
Sebastien Moffet, Programming Director

Senneterre

CIBO-FM
01-01-1982; 100.5 mhz FM *Hrs Open:* 24
C.P. 1150, Senneterre, QC J0Y 2M0 Canada
(819) 737-2222, *Fax:* (819) 737-8599
www.cibofm.com
cibofm@yahoo.ca
License: Senneterre, QC held by Radio communautaire M.F. de Senneterre Inc.
Population Served: 5,600 *Format:* Talk
Guy Bilodeau, President

Sept-Iles

***CBSI-FM**
11-01-1982; 98.1 mhz FM *Hrs Open:* 24; 96.7 kw; 350 ft
350 rue Smith, bur. 30, Sept-Iles, QC G4R 3X2 Canada
(418) 968-0720, *Fax:* (418) 968-9219
www.radio-canada.ca/cote-nord
cbsi@radio-canada.ca
License: Sept-Iles, QC held by CBC.

Population Served: 8,000 *Format:* Talk, Variety/Diverse *Target Audience:* Over 30.
Pierre Lafreniere, Station Manager

CKCN-FM
12-01-1998; 94.1 mhz FM; 4.88 kw
437 Arnaud St., Sept-Iles, QC G4R 3B3 Canada
(418) 962-3838, *Fax:* (418) 968-6662
www.le941.com
le941@le941.com
License: Sept-Iles, QC held by Radio Sept-Iles Inc.
Population Served: 25,686 *Arbitron Metro Market:* Sept-Iles, PQ *Format:* Adult Contemp, News, News/Talk, Talk*Special Programming:* Country 8 hrs wkly*Hrs. of News Programming:* News progmg 16 hrs wkly *TargetAudience:* 25-54.
Pierre Bergeron, President
Dominique Marquis, Station Manager

Shawinigan

CKSM
04-30-1951; 1220 khz AM*Rebroadcasts:* Rebroadcasts CHLN(AM) Trois Rivieres 100%
CA
(819) 378-1023, *Fax:* (819) 378-1360
License: Shawinigan, QC held by Astral Media Radio Inc.
Group Owner: Astral Media Inc.
Format: Adult Contemp, News, News/Talk, Sports, Talk *Target Audience:* 40-55.
Jean Martin, General Manager

CFUT-FM
02-07-2005; 91.1 mhz FM; 5 w
540 Broadway Ave., Shawinigan, QC G9N 1M3 Canada
(819) 537-0911
www.radioshawinigan.com
info@radioshawinigan.com
License: Shawinigan, QC held by La radio campus communautaire francophone de Shawinigan inc.
Population Served: 50,060 *Arbitron Metro Market:* Shawinigan, QC *Format:* French
Pierre-Yves Rousselle, Programming Director

Sherbrooke

CFLXFM
01-01-1984; 95.5 mhz FM *Hrs Open:* 24; kw
CA
(819) 566-2787, *Fax:* (819) 566-7331
www.cflx.qc.ca
commentaire@cflx.qc.ca
License: Sherbrooke, QC held by Radio communautaire de l'Estrie.
Format: News, News/Talk, Talk, Variety/Diverse*Special Programming:* Class 7 hrs, jazz 8 hrs, Sp 3 hrs wkly*Hrs. of News Programming:* news progmg 10 hrs wkly *No. News Employees:* 1 *Target Audience:* 18-35; collegedegree
Jean Comtois, President
Bruno Guillemette, General Manager

CITE-FM-1
09-01-1962; 102.7 mhz FM; 92.8 kw; Ant 1,851 ft
2145 King West, Suite 200, Sherbrooke, QC J1J 2E4 Canada
(819) 566-6655, *Fax:* (819) 566-1011
License: Sherbrooke, QC held by Astral Media Radio Inc.
Group Owner: Astral Media Inc.; (acq 4-19-2002; grpsl).
Natalie Johnson, General Manager

CJMQ-FM
01-01-2004; 88.9 mhz FM *Hrs Open:* 6am-12am; 1.67 kw
184 Queen St., Sherbrooke, QC J1M 1J9 Canada
(819) 822-1838, *Fax:* (819) 822-9682
www.cjmq.fm
cjmqnews@yahoo.ca
License: Sherbrooke, QC held by Radio Bishop's Inc.
Population Served: 170,000 *Format:* Talk*Hrs. of News Programming:* News progmg 5 hrs wkly *Target Audience:* General; campus & community
David Teasdale, Station Manager
Maureen Dillon, Programming Director
Joel Heath, Promotions Manager
David Humble, Engineering Dir
Wayne Stacey, Chief Engineer
Zaheed Bardai, Music Director

CFAK-FM
01-01-2003; 88.3 mhz FM; 490 w
Radio CFAK, 2500 boul. de Universite, Sherbrooke, QC J1K 2R1 Canada
(819) 821-8000, *Fax:* (819) 821-7930
www.cfak.qc.ca
dg.cfak883@usherbrooke.ca
License: Sherbrooke, QC held by Comite de la radio etudiante universitaire de Sherbrooke (CREUS).
Population Served: 154,601 *Arbitron Metro Market:* Sherbrooke, QC *Format:* French
Steve Bazinet, General Manager

CFGE-FM
07-01-2004; 93.7 mhz FM; kw
CA
(819) 822-0937, *Fax:* (819) 562-1666
www.rythmefm.com/estrie
License: Sherbrooke, QC held by Cogeco Diffusion inc.
Group Owner: Cogeco Diffusion Inc.
Arbitron Metro Market: Sherbrooke, QC *Format:* Adult Contemp *No. News Employees:* 1 *Target Audience:* 25-54.
Michel Cloutier, General Manager
Marc Fabi, General Sales Mgr
Jocelyn Proulx, Programming Director
Julie Riendeau, Promotions Manager
Dany Lebeau, Engineering Dir
Lilianne Randall, Music Director
Dave Forest, Producer
NormandGagnon, Production Director
Andr, St-Amand, Vice President of Programming
Jean-Marc Allard, Music Librarian
Denis Desmarchais, Music Librarian

CKOY-FM
01-01-2004; 104.5 mhz FM; 1.3 kw; N45 23 48 W71 49 52
4020 Boul. Portland, Sherbrooke, QC J1L 2V6 Canada
(819) 563-6363, *Fax:* (819) 566-4222
www.fm1077.ca
info@grock.fm
License: Sherbrooke, QC held by Cogeco Diffusion Aquisitions Inc
Group Owner: Cogeco Diffusion Inc.
Population Served: 154,601 *Arbitron Metro Market:* Sherbrooke, QC
Jocelyn Proulx, General Manager

CJRS
01-01-2007; 1510 khz AM
CA
(514) 738-4100
www.radio-shalom.ca
License: Sherbrooke, QC held by Radio Chalom.
Arbitron Metro Market: Montreal, QC *Format:* Ethnic
Robert Levy, President
Greg McLachlan, General Sales Mgr
Jean-No‰l Guenot, Technical Director

Sorel

***CJSO-FM**
09-27-1989; 101.7 mhz FM *Hrs Open:* 24; kw
CA
(450) 743-2772, *Fax:* (450) 743-0293
www.fm1017.ca
cjso@cjso.qc.ca
License: Sorel, QC held by Radio Diffusion Sorel-Tracy Inc.
Format: Classic Rock*Special Programming:* Class 2 hrs wkly*Hrs. of News Programming:* news progmg 5 hrs wkly *No. News Employees:* 2*Adv. Rates:* 30; 30; 30; 30
Jean-Marc Belzile, CEO/COO
Claude St. Germain, General Manager
Jean Lemay, Programming Director
Jean-Marc Lebeau, News Director
Andre Champagne, Disc Jockey
Jocelyne Lambert, Disc Jockey
Valerie Ferland, Music Director
YanickLevesque, Sports Commentator
Marie-Theresee Thibeault, Traffic Manager

St-Gabriel

***CFNJFM**
08-10-1985; 99.1 mhz FM *Hrs Open:* 24; kw
CA
(450) 835-3437, *Fax:* (450) 835-3581
www.cfnj.net
droch@intermonde.net
License: St-Gabriel, QC held by Radio Nord-Joli Inc.
Format: Adult Contemp*Special Programming:* Black one hr, class 2 hrs, C&W 4 hrs, jazz 2 hrs*Hrs. of News Programming:* news progmg 14 hrs wkly *No. News Employees:* 2
Denis Roch, General Manager
Denise LaVoie, General Sales Mgr
Nicolas Bellemare, Promotions Manager

St-George-Beauce

***CHJM-FM**
06-22-1987; 99.7 mhz FM *Hrs Open:* 24; kw
Mailing Address: CA
Second Address: 11760 Third Ave, Saint Georges-de-Beauce, PQ G5Y 5C4
(418) 227-0997, *Fax:* (418) 228-0096
www.mix997.com
adminrb@cgocable.ca
License: St-George-Beauce, QC held by Radio Beauce Inc.
Format: Contemporary Hits/Top 40*Hrs. of News Programming:* news progmg 4 hrs wkly *No. News Employees:* 1 *Target Audience:* 18-44.
Guy Simard, President
Maurice Marcotte, General Manager
Claude Girard, General Sales Mgr
Marcel Rancourt, Programming Director
Gaston Guay, Chief Engineer
Jacques Goulet, National Sales Manager

St-Hyacinthe

***CFEI**
01-01-1988; 106.5 mhz FM *Hrs Open:* 24; kw
CA
(450) 774-6486, *Fax:* (450) 774-7785
www.boomfm.com
jhebert@boomfm.astral.com
License: St-Hyacinthe, QC held by Astral Media Radio Inc.
Group Owner: Astral Media Inc.; (acq 8-13-2001).
Format: News, Oldies
Jacques Parisien, President
Pierre Demondehare, General Manager
Leopold St. Marie, General Sales Mgr
Jean-Francois Hebert, Programming Director
Andre Lalier, Music Director

Tete-a-la-Baleine

CJTB-FM
01-01-2003; 93.1 mhz FM; 49 w; N50 42 12 W59 19 30
C.P. 138, Tete-a-la-Baleine, QC G0G 2W0 Canada
(418) 242-2974
License: Tete-a-la-Baleine, QC held by Radio Communautaire Tete-a-la-Baleine.
Population Served: 129 *Arbitron Metro Market:* T'te-...-la-Baleine, QC *Format:* French
Bertha Monger, President
Mireille Monger, General Manager

Thetford Mines

CFJO-FM
07-15-1989; 97.3 mhz FM *Hrs Open:* 24; 100 kw; Ant 270 ft
Mailing Address: 55 St. Jean Baptiste, Victoriaville, QC G6P 6T3 Canada
Second Address: 327 Rue Labbe, Thetford Mines, PQ G6G 5S3
(418) 338-1009, *Fax:* (418) 338-0386
www.o973.com
License: Thetford Mines, QC held by Reseau des Appalaches (FM) Ltee.
Group Owner: Gestion Appalaches inc.
Nat'l Reps: Target Broadcast Sales
Population Served: 87,913 *Format:* Classic Rock, Rock/AOR *No. News Employees:* 15 *Target Audience:* 18-40.
Annie Labbe, President

CKLD-FM
01-01-1950; 105.5 mhz FM *Hrs Open:* 24; 6 kw
55 Street, St-Jean Baptiste, QC G6G 4E1 Canada
(418) 335-7533, *Fax:* (418) 335-9009
www.passionrock.com
License: Thetford Mines, QC held by Radio Megantic Ltee.
Group Owner: Gestion Appalaches inc.
Nat'l Reps: Target Broadcast Sales
Population Served: 40,384 *Format:* Adult Contemp *No. News Employees:* 5 *Target Audience:* 35-64.
Annie Labbe, General Manager

Toronto

CBF-2
11-28-2011; 98.7 mhz FM; 446 watts; 276.8 meters
34 Kern Road, Toronto, ON Canada
(416) 498-4987
www.g987fm.com
License: Toronto, ON held by Intercity Broadcasting Network Inc
Fitzroy Gordon, President

Trois Rivieres

CBF-FM-1
07-21-1977; 104.3 mhz FM; 100 kw; 1,000 ft; N46 29 27 W72 39 00
Box 6000, Montreal, QC H3C 3A8 Canada
(514) 597-6000, *Fax:* (514) 597-4510
www.cbc.radio-canada.ca
License: Trois Rivieres, QC held by CBC French.
Nat'l Network: Radio Canada
Format: Talk
Sylvain La France, General Manager
Louise Carriere, Programming Director

CHEY-FM
08-22-1990; 94.7 mhz FM; 100 kw
1500 rue Royale, Bur 260, RockDetemte 94.7, Trois Rivieres, QC G9A 6J4 Canada
(819) 376-0947, *Fax:* (819) 373-5555
www.rockdetente.com
License: Trois Rivieres, QC held by Astral Media Radio Inc.
Group Owner: Astral Media Inc.; (acq 4-19-2002; grpsl).
Format: Classic Rock *Target Audience:* 30-40; women
Jean Martin, General Manager
Rene Rivard, General Sales Mgr
Eric Lachapelle, Programming Director
Damien Miville-Deschenes, Promotions Manager

CFOU-FM
09-07-1997; 89.1 mhz FM *Hrs Open:* 24; 3 kw; Trois Rivieres, Quebec, Canada
Universite du Quebec a Trois-Rivieres, 3351, boul. Forges, Pavilion N,r,e-Beauchemin, Trois Rivieres, QC G9A 5H7 Canada
(819) 376-5184, *Fax:* (819) 376-5239
www.cfou.ca
progcfou@uqtr.ca
License: Trois Rivieres, QC held by Radio campus des etudiants de lUniversite du Quebec a Trois-Rivieres.
Nat'l Network: CBC Radio One
Population Served: 131,338 *Arbitron Metro Market:* Trois-RiviŠres, QC *Format:* Variety/Diverse*Hrs. of News Programming:* News progmg one hr wkly *Target Audience:* 18-35.
Fr,d,ric Deru, Chairman
Fran‡ois-Olivier Marchand, CEO
Marc Periard, General Manager
Alain Lefebvre, Programming Director
Francois Marchand, Promotions Manager
Mathieu Plante, Webmaster
Dany Janvier, Producer
Pascal Proulx,Advertising consultant

CJEB-FM
06-08-2004; 100.1 mhz FM; 30.61 kw; Ant 1,177 ft
1350, rue Royale, Suite 1200, Trois Rivieres, QC G9A 4J4 Canada
(819) 691-1001, *Fax:* (819) 691-1002
www.rythmefm.com/mauricie
License: Trois Rivieres, QC held by Cogeco Diffusion Inc.
Group Owner: Cogeco Diffusion Inc.
Population Served: 131,338 *Arbitron Metro Market:* Trois-RiviŠres, QC *Format:* Adult Contemp
Michel Cloutier, General Manager
Pierre Lamontagne, Programming Director
Pierre Lamontagne, Promotions Manager
Gerald Trives, Engineering Dir
Charles Romanos, Programmer/Integrator
Allen ValliŠres, News Media Coordinator
NormandGagnon, Production Director
Jean-Fran‡ois Filion, Producer
Jean-Marc Allard, Music Librarian
Denis Desmarchais, Music Librarian

CKOB-FM
08-20-2007; 106.9 mhz FM; 60 kw; Ant 285 ft; N46 14 21 W72 35 26
1350 rue Royale, Bureau 1200, Trois Rivieres, QC G9A 4J4 Canada
(819) 374-3556, *Fax:* (819) 374-3222
www.1069fm.net
License: Trois Rivieres, QC held by Cogeco Diffusion Aquisitions Inc
Group Owner: Cogeco Diffusion Inc.
Pierre Gaudreau, General Manager
Denis Pratte, Promotions Manager

Trois-Rivieres

*CIGBFM
08-27-1979; 102.3 mhz FM *Hrs Open:* 24; kw
CA
(819) 378-1023, *Fax:* (819) 378-1360
www.radioenergie.com
hmousseau@astral.com
License: Trois-Rivieres, QC held by Astral Media Radio Inc.
Group Owner: Astral Media Inc.; (acq 8-24-90).
Format: Contemporary Hits/Top 40*Hrs. of News Programming:* news progmg 3 hrs wkly *No. News Employees:* 3 *Target Audience:* 18-30.
Jean Martin, General Manager
Mr. Danny Champagne, Programming Director
Mr. Damien Miville-Deschenes, Promotions Manager

Val d'Or

CJMV-FM
06-17-1989; 102.7 mhz FM *Hrs Open:* 24; 96 kw; 156.8 meters
173 Perreault St., Val d'Or, QC J9P 2H3 Canada
(819) 825-2568, *Fax:* (819) 825-2840
www.radioenergie.com
License: Val d'Or, Abitibi-est County, QC held by Astral Media Radio Inc.
Group Owner: Astral Media Inc.; (acq 1-12-2000; grpsl).
Population Served: 50,000 *Target Audience:* 18-49.
Ian Greenberg, President
Marlene Trottier, General Manager

CHGO-FM
01-01-2000; 104.3 mhz FM; 100 kw
380 Avenue Murdoch, Rouyn-Noranda, QC J9X 2G8 Canada
(819) 762-0741, *Fax:* (819) 762-2466
www.abitibi.capitalerock.ca
ndeschenes@rncmedia.ca
License: Val d'Or, QC held by RNC MEDIA Inc.
Group Owner: RNC MEDIA Inc.
Nat'l Network: Radiomedia
Population Served: 41,012 *Arbitron Metro Market:* Rouyn-Noranda, QC *Format:* Classic Rock
Pierre Brosseau, CEO
Ghislain Beaulieu, Operations Dir
Jean-Pierre Major, General Manager
Francis Morin, Programming Director
Nancy Desch^nes, Director and sales
Michelle Desjardins, Representative promotions
Nancy Labont,,Assistant sales and general management
Richard Audet, Advisor advertising
Jean-Paul Proul, Advisor advertising
Marie-Pier Gauthier, Advisor advertising

Valleyfield

CKOD-FM
06-06-1994; 103.1 mhz FM *Hrs Open:* 24; 3 kw; 167 ft; N45 16 08 W74 05 50
249 Victoria St., Suite 103, Valleyfield, QC J6T 1A9 Canada
(450) 373-0103, *Fax:* (450) 854-8103
www.ckod.qc.ca
fm103@ckod.qc.ca
License: Valleyfield, QC held by Radio Express Inc.
Nat'l Reps: Target Broadcast Sales
Format: Adult Contemp*Hrs. of News Programming:* news progmg 7 hrs wkly *No. News Employees:* 1 *Target Audience:* 18-54; general
Robert Brunet, President
Dean Nevins, General Sales Mgr
Martin Leblanc, Programming Director

Vaudreuil-Dorion

CJVD-FM
09-29-2008; 100.1 mhz FM; 550 w; N45 24 55 W74 02 45
2555 rue Dutrisac, Local RC-08 A, Vaudreuil-Dorion, QC J7V 7E6 Canada
(514) 790-1001
cjvd.ca
info@cjvd.ca
License: Vaudreuil-Dorion, QC held by Yves Sauve.
Population Served: 33,305 *Arbitron Metro Market:* Vaudreuil-Dorion, QC *Format:* Oldies, French
Yves Sauve, President

Victoriaville

CFDA-FM
01-01-1999; 101.9 mhz FM *Hrs Open:* 24; 1.35 kw
Mailing Address: Box 490, Victoriaville, QC G6P 6T3 Canada
Second Address: 55 St. Jean Baptiste St., Victoriaville, PQ G6P 6T3
(819) 752-5545, *Fax:* (819) 752-7552
www.passionrock.com
License: Victoriaville, QC held by Radio Victoriaville Ltee.
Group Owner: Gestion Appalaches inc.
Nat'l Reps: Target Broadcast Sales
Population Served: 43,462 *Arbitron Metro Market:* Victoriaville, PQ *Format:* Adult Contemp*Special Programming:* Country 3 hrs, retro/oldies 3 hrs wkly *No. News Employees:* 7 *Target Audience:* 35-65.
Annie Labbe, General Manager

Ville-Marie

CKVM-FM
01-01-2004; 93.1 mhz FM *Hrs Open:* 24; 18.4 kw; N47 19 57 W79 25 38
Mailing Address: 62 Suite Anne, Ville-Marie, QC J9V 2B7 Canada
Second Address: 62 Ste. Anne, Ville-Marie, PQ J9V 2B7
(819) 629-2710, *Fax:* (819) 622-0716
www.ckvm.qc.ca
ckvm@ckvm.qc.ca,dg@ckum.qc.ca
License: Ville-Marie, QC held by Radio Temiscamingue Inc.
Population Served: 2,595 *Arbitron Metro Market:* Ville-Marie, QC *Format:* Adult Contemp*Hrs. of News Programming:* news progmg 11 hrs wkly *No. News Employees:* 1 *Target Audience:* General.
Jacquelin Bastien, President
Patrick Guilbault, Operations Dir
Claude Gagnon, General Manager
Serge Lalonde, Station Manager

Windsor

CIAX-FM
01-01-2000; 98.3 mhz FM; 426 w
49 Sixth Ave., Windsor, QC J1S 1T2 Canada
(819) 845-2692, *Fax:* (819) 845-2692
www.ciaxfm.net
unitewindsor@qc.aira.com
License: Windsor, QC held by La Radio communautaire de Windsor et region inc.
Population Served: 5,239 *Arbitron Metro Market:* Windsor, PQ *Format:* Variety/Diverse
Patrick Levesque, President
Julie Lupien, Programming Director
Marc Savoy, Director of Sales and advertising

Saskatchewan

Blucher

CFAQ-FM
01-01-2006; 100.3 mhz FM; 36 w
2127 St. Andrews Ave., Saskatoon, SK S7M 0M2 Canada
(306) 290-7222
www.saskatoonchristianradio.com
free@radiofree.ca
License: Blucher, SK held by Bertor Communications Ltd.
Population Served: 234,200 *Arbitron Metro Market:* Saskatoon, SK *Format:* Christian
Robert Orr, General Manager

Broadview

CKOO-FM
105.7 mhz FM; 50 watts; 22.7 meters
Box 609, Broadview, SK S0G 0K0 Canada
(306) 696-3291, *Fax:* (306) 696-3201
radio@kahkewistahaw.com
License: Broadview, SK held by Kahkewistahaw Radio Station

Monica Wasacase, General Manager

Cowessess

CIBC-FM
98.1 mhz FM; 49 watts; 25 meters
Box 100, Cowessess, SK S0G 5L0 Canada
(306) 696-2520, *Fax:* (306) 696-3237
carol.lavallee@cowwassessfm.com
License: Cowessess, SK held by Cowassess Community Projects Inc

Cumberland House

CJCF-FM
01-01-1990; 89.9 mhz FM; 30.5 w
Box 100, Cumberland House, SK S0E 0S0 Canada
(306) 888-2176, *Fax:* (306) 888-2103
cjcfradio.com
ken@cjcfradio
License: Cumberland House, SK held by Cumberland House Radio & Television Committee Inc.
Format: Ethnic
Rachel Fiddler, General Manager
Ken Buck, Station Manager

Estevan

CJSL
08-01-1959; 1280 khz AM *Hrs Open:* 24
CA
(306) 634-1280, *Fax:* (306) 634-6364
www.cj1280radio.com
License: Estevan, SK held by Golden West Broadcasting Ltd.
Group Owner: Golden West Broadcasting Ltd.; (acq 3-95)
Nat'l Reps: Canadian Broadcast Sales *Wire Services:* BN Wire
Format: Country*Special Programming:* Farm 4 hrs, relg 10 hrs wkly *Target Audience:* General.
Elmer Hilderbrand, CEO
Laverne Pappel, Station Manager

CHSN-FM
01-01-2001; 102.3 mhz FM; 100 kw
200-1236 Fifth St., Estevan, SK S4A 0Z6 Canada
(306) 634-1280, *Fax:* (306) 634-6364
www.sun102radio.com
License: Estevan, SK held by Golden West Broadcasting Ltd.
Group Owner: Golden West Broadcasting Ltd.
Jim MacMullin, General Manager

CKSE-FM
106.1 mhz FM; 100 kw; 70.85 meters
200-1236 5th Street, Estevan, SK S4A 0Z6 Canada
(306) 634-1280, *Fax:* (306) 634-6364
License: Estevan, SK held by Golden West Broadcasting

Gravelbourg

***CBKF-1(AM)**
01-01-1952; 540 khz AM; 5 kw-U, DA-2
2440 Broad St., Regina, SK S4P 4A1 Canada
(306) 347-9540, *Fax:* (306) 347-9635
www.cbc.ca
License: Gravelbourg, SK held by CBC French.
Format: Variety/Diverse
Robert Rabinowitz, CEO
Rikki Bote, General Manager

CFRG-FM
01-01-2003; 93.1 mhz FM; 48 w
133 5th Avenue East, BP / PO Box 176, Gravelbourg, SK S0H 1X0 Canada
(306) 648-2374, *Fax:* (306) 648-3258
www.cfrg.ca
info@cfrg.ca
License: Gravelbourg, SK held by Association communautaire fransaskoise de Gravelbourg Inc.
Population Served: 1,093 *Arbitron Metro Market:* Gravelbourg, SK *Format:* French
Guylain Bergeron, Director/Station Manager

Humboldt

CHBO-FM
107.5 mhz FM; 59 kw; 164.1 meters
Box 2888, Humboldt, SK S0K 2A0 Canada
(306) 682-2255
www.bolt1075fm.com
License: Humboldt, SK held by Golden West Broadcasting

Island Lake

CIFN-FM
106.5 mhz FM; 33 watts; 15 meters
Box 240, Island Lake, SK S0M 3G0 Canada
(306) 837-2188, *Fax:* (306) 837-2266
License: Island Lake, SK held by Island Lake First Nations Radio Inc

Kindersley

CFYM
07-29-1987; 1210 khz AM*Rebroadcasts:* Rebroadcasts CJYM(AM) Rosetown 95%
CA
(306) 463-4411, *Fax:* (306) 882-3037
www.cjym.com
cjmmnews@goldenwestradio.com
License: Kindersley, SK held by Golden West Broadcasting Ltd.
Group Owner: Golden West Broadcasting Ltd.; (acq 10-21-99).
Nat'l Reps: Target Broadcast Sales
Format: Adult Contemp
Elmer Hildebrand, President

La Ronge

***CBKA-FM**
09-01-1979; 105.9 mhz FM; 80 w
Box 959, La Ronge, SK S0J 1L0 Canada
(306) 347-9540, *Fax:* (306) 425-2270
www.sask.cbc.ca
License: La Ronge, SK held by CBC.
Nat'l Network: CBC Radio One
Format: Public Affairs*Special Programming:* Cree & Dene 20 hrs wkly
David Kyle, General Manager

CJLR-FM
01-01-1990; 89.9 mhz FM *Hrs Open:* 24; 216 w; Ant 151 ft
Box 1529, La Ronge, SK S0J 1L0 Canada
(306) 425-4003, *Fax:* (306) 425-3123
www.mbcradio.com
mbcradio@mbcradio.com
License: La Ronge, SK held by Natotawin Broadcasting Inc.
Population Served: 50,000 *Format:* Country, Ethnic, Variety/Diverse*Special Programming:* Cree & Dene languages
Target Audience: General.
Deborah Charles, CEO
William Dumais, President
Teddy Clark, Operations Dir
Dallas Hicks, Station Manager
Keith Kratchmer, CFO

Marcelin

CICN-FM
01-26-2011; 104.3 mhz FM; 30 watts; 12.1 meters
Box 531, Leask, SK S0J 0M0 Canada
(306) 466-4959, *Fax:* (306) 466-2284
License: Marcelin, SK held by Muskeg Lake Cree Nation Radio Station Corp

Meadow Lake

CJNS
11-01-1977; 1240 khz AM
CA
(306) 236-6494, *Fax:* (306) 236-6141
License: Meadow Lake, SK held by Northwestern Radio Partnership
Group Owner: Rawlco Radio Ltd.; (acq 1-7-2003; grpsl).
Format: Country
David Dekker, General Manager

CFDM-FM
01-01-2001; 105.7 mhz FM; 46.5 w
Box 8168, Flying Dust First Nation, Meadow Lake, SK S9X 1T8 Canada
(306) 236-1445, *Fax:* (306) 236-2861
www.cfdm.sasktelwebhosting.com
cfdmradio@hotmail.com
License: Meadow Lake, SK held by FDB Broadcasting Inc.
Population Served: 4,771 *Arbitron Metro Market:* Meadow Lake, SK *Format:* Contemporary Hits/Top 40, Country
Duwayne Derocher, Station Manager
Josh Derocher, Broadcast Assistant

CJNS-FM
102.3 mhz FM; 45 kw
Box 1460, North Battleford, SK S9A 2Z5 Canada
(306) 236-6494, *Fax:* (306) 236-6141
License: Meadow Lake, SK held by Northwestern Radio Partnership
Group Owner: Rawlco Radio Ltd.
Population Served: 156,929 *Arbitron Metro Market:* Eugene-Springfield, OR
Jim Hamm, General Manager

Melfort

CKJH(AM)
10-08-1966; 750 khz AM *Hrs Open:* 24; 25 kw-U, DA-N; N52 47 57 W104 35 25
Box 750, 611 Main St. N., Melfort, SK S0E 1A0 Canada
(306) 752-2587, *Fax:* (306) 752-5932
www.yourtownnews.ca/news/97
info@cjvr.com
License: Melfort, SK held by Radio CJVR Ltd.
Nat'l Reps: Target Broadcast Sales
Format: Contemporary Hits/Top 40*Special Programming:* Relg 9 hrs wkly*Hrs. of News Programming:* news progmg 15 hrs wkly
No. News Employees: 4 *Target Audience:* General.
Eugene Fabro Sr., Chairman
Eugene Fabro, President
Gary Fitz, Operations Dir
Linda Rheaume, Station Manager
Bill Wood, Programming Director
Lisa Brady, Promotions Manager
Cam Lee, News Director
Bayne Opseth, Chief Engineer
Cal Gratton, Music Director

CJVR-FM
03-01-2002; 105.1 mhz FM; 100 kw
Box 750, 611 Main St., Melfort, SK S0E 1A0 Canada
(306) 752-2587, *Fax:* (306) 752-5932
www.yourtownnews.ca/news/97
info@cjvr.com
License: Melfort, SK held by Radio CJVR Ltd.
Population Served: 5,576 *Arbitron Metro Market:* Melfort, SK
Format: Country
Yves Sauve, President
Linda Rheaume, Station Manager
Dave Marcoux, General Sales Mgr
Bill Wood, Programming Director
Lisa Brady, Promotions Manager
Cam Lee, News Director
Ken Singer, Vice President - Broadcast Operations
CalGratton, Music Director
Branden Crowe, Sports
Alice McFarlane, Agricultural Information Director
Royal Watson, Production Director

Moose Jaw

CHAB
04-22-1922; 800 khz AM *Hrs Open:* 24
CA
(306) 694-0800, *Fax:* (306) 692-8880
www.chabradio.com
greatesthits@goldenwestradio.com
License: Moose Jaw, SK held by Golden West Broadcasting Ltd.
Group Owner: Golden West Broadcasting Ltd.; (acq 8-20-92)
Nat'l Reps: Canadian Broadcast Sales
Format: Contemporary Hits/Top 40 *No. News Employees:* 3
Target Audience: 25-54.
Elmer Hildebrand, CEO
Barry Vice, Station Manager
Abbey White, Promotions Manager
Rob Carnie, News Director

CILG-FM
01-01-2002; 100.7 mhz FM; 100 kw
1704 Main St. N., Moose Jaw, SK S6J 1L4 Canada
(306) 692-1007, *Fax:* (306) 692-8880
www.country100fm.com
jstrom@goldenwestradio.com
License: Moose Jaw, SK held by Golden West Broadcasting Ltd.
Group Owner: Golden West Broadcasting Ltd.
Population Served: 35,629 *Arbitron Metro Market:* Moose Jaw, SK *Format:* Country
Berchmens Boudreau, General Manager
Catherine Ramoisy, News Director
Gerald Gallant, Engineering Dir

CJAW-FM
04-22-2008; 103.9 mhz FM; 100 kw; N50 35 44 W105 04 09
1704 Main St. N., Moose Jaw, SK S6J 1L4 Canada
(306) 694-0800, *Fax:* (306) 692-8880
www.mix1039fm.com
mixmorningshow@goldenwestradio.com
License: Moose Jaw, SK held by Golden West Broadcasting Ltd.
Group Owner: Golden West Broadcasting Ltd.
Population Served: 35,629 *Arbitron Metro Market:* Moose Jaw, SK *Format:* Adult Contemp
Darryl Pisio, Station Manager
Craig Hemingway, Programming Director

Nipawin

CJNE-FM
06-01-2002; 94.7 mhz FM; 14.8 kw
Box 220, Nipawin, SK S0E 1E0 Canada
(306) 862-9478, *Fax:* (306) 862-2334
www.cjnefm.com
pro.cjne@sasktel.net
License: Nipawin, SK held by CJNE FM Radio Inc.
Population Served: 4,061 *Arbitron Metro Market:* Nipawin, SK
Format: Classic Rock, Oldies *No. News Employees:* 1 *Target Audience:* 18-50.
Norm Rudock, General Manager
Treana Rudock, Station Manager
Les Blair, Promotions Manager

CIOT-FM
01-01-2005; 104.1 mhz FM *Hrs Open:* 24; 200 w
Box 1240, Nipawin, SK S0E 1E0 Canada
(306) 862-2468, *Fax:* (306) 862-2660
www.lighthousefm.ca
info@lighthousefm.ca
License: Nipawin, SK held by Wilderness Ministries Inc.

Population Served: 17,000 *No. News Employees:* 1 *Target Audience:* 20-55.*Adv. Rates:* 12; 12; 12; 12
Rod Petersen, Programming Director
Angela Petersen, News Director
Andrew Hildebrandt, Music Director
Andrew Clark, Programming Director

North Battleford

CJHD-FM
01-01-2008; 93.3 mhz FM; 100 kw; N52 48 15 W108 35 18
Box 1460, North Battleford, SK S9A 2Z5 Canada
(306) 445-2477, *Fax:* (306) 445-4599
www.933therock.ca
License: North Battleford, SK held by Northwestern Radio Partnership.
Group Owner: Rawlco Radio Ltd.
David Dekker, General Manager

Pinehouse Lake

CFNK-FM
01-01-1996; 89.9 mhz FM; 7 w
General Delivery, Box 370, Pinehouse Lake, SK S0J 2B0 Canada
(306) 884-2011, *Fax:* (306) 884-2365
www.cfnk.radiok.sympatico.ca
License: Pinehouse Lake, SK held by Pinehouse Communications Society Inc.
Format: Adult Contemp
Peter Smith, General Manager
Vince Natomagan, Programming Director

Prince Albert

CFMM-FM
01-30-1982; 99.1 mhz FM; 100 kw; 606 ft
1316 Central Avenue, Prince Albert, SK S6V 7R4 Canada
(306) 763-7421, *Fax:* (306) 764-1850
www.power99fm.com
power99fm@rawlco.com
License: Prince Albert, SK held by Rawlco Radio Ltd.
Group Owner: Rawlco Radio Ltd.
Format: Classic Rock
Garth Kalin, Operations Dir
Garth Kalin, Programming Director

CKBI
01-01-1934; 900 khz AM
CA
(306) 763-7421, *Fax:* (306) 764-1850
www.900ckbi.com
900ckbi@rawlco.com
License: Prince Albert, SK held by Rawlco Radio Ltd.
Group Owner: Rawlco Radio Ltd.; acq 1946).
Nat'l Reps: Canadian Broadcast Sales
Format: Adult Contemp, Oldies*Special Programming:* Farm 2 hrs wkly *Target Audience:* 34 plus; working women
Jim Scarrow, General Manager
Tyler Kinash, General Sales Mgr
Neil Headrick, Programming Director
Jeff White, News Director
Dale Zimmerman, Engineering Dir

CHQX-FM
06-18-2001; 101.5 mhz FM *Hrs Open:* 24; 100 kw; Ant 606 ft
Box 900, Prince Albert, SK S6V 7R4 Canada
(306) 763-7421, *Fax:* (306) 764-1850
www.mix101fm.com
mix101fm@rawlco.com
License: Prince Albert, SK held by Rawlco Radio Ltd.
Group Owner: Rawlco Radio Ltd.
Population Served: 35,129 *Arbitron Metro Market:* Prince Albert, SK *Format:* Rock/AOR
Jim Scarrow, General Manager
Karl Johnson, General Sales Mgr

Regina

***CBK-FM**
05-01-1977; 96.9 mhz FM; 100 kw; Ant 501 ft
2440 Broad St., Regina, SK S4P 4A1 Canada
(360) 956-7400, *Fax:* (306) 956-7417
www.cbc.ca/sask/
License: Regina, SK held by CBC
Nat'l Network: CBC Radio Two
TV Affiliate: *CBKT(TV) affil *Format:* Classical, Jazz, Variety/Diverse
David Kyle, General Manager

***CBKFFM**
09-01-1973; 97.7 mhz FM *Hrs Open:* 24; kw
Mailing Address: CA
Second Address: 2440 Broad St., Regina, SK S4P-3Z4
(306) 347-9540, *Fax:* (306) 347-9493
www.cbc.ca
License: Regina, SK held by Radio Canada.
Nat'l Network: CBC Radio Two
TV Affiliate: CBKF(TV) affil. *Format:* Variety/Diverse
Rene Fontaine, General Manager
Anne Brochu, News Director
Steve Tomchuk, Engineering Dir

***CFMQFM**
09-15-1994; 92.1 mhz FM *Hrs Open:* 24; kw
CA
(306) 865-3065, *Fax:* (306) 865-2227
cfmq@sasktel.net
License: Regina, SK held by HB Communications Inc.
Format: Country, Variety/Diverse*Hrs. of News Programming:* News progmg one hr wkly *Target Audience:* General.
Mark Brann, President
Dan Brann, General Manager

CFWF-FM
04-15-1982; 104.9 mhz FM; 100 kw; 400 ft
190 Rose St., Regina, SK S4P 0A9 Canada
(306) 546-6200, *Fax:* (306) 781-7338
www.620ckrm.com
info@cwfw.com
License: Regina, SK held by Harvard Broadcasting Inc.
Group Owner: Harvard Broadcasting Inc.; (Acq 8-25-95)
Nat'l Reps: Canadian Broadcast Sales
Format: Classic Rock
Bert Crowfoot, CEO
Alan Standerwick, Station Manager

CHMX-FM
02-04-1966; 92.1 mhz FM *Hrs Open:* 24; 100 kw; 499 ft
1900 Rose St., Regina, SK S4P 0A9 Canada
(306) 546-6200, *Fax:* (306) 781-7338
www.lite92fm.com
jasonh@harvardbroadcasting.com
License: Regina, SK held by Harvard Broadcasting Inc.
Group Owner: Harvard Broadcasting Inc.; (acq 3-1-81)
Format: Adult Contemp
Les Schuster, General Sales Mgr
Greg Morgan, Programming Director

***CIZLFM**
06-01-1982; 98.9 mhz FM; kw
CA
(306) 525-0000, *Fax:* (306) 347-8557
www.z99.com
tmewton@rawlco.com
License: Regina, SK held by Rawlco Radio Ltd.
Group Owner: Rawlco Radio Ltd.; (Acq 4-67).
Format: Adult Contemp, Rock/AOR *Target Audience:* 18-49.
Tom Newton, General Manager
Chris Romanyk, General Sales Mgr
Chris Myers, Programming Director
Amber Morse, Promotions Manager

CKRM(AM)
07-29-1922; 620 khz AM; 10 kw-U, DA-2
1900 Rose St., Regina, SK S4P OA9 Canada
(306) 546-6200, *Fax:* (306) 781-7338
www.620ckrm.com
info@ckrm.com
License: Regina, SK held by Harvard Broadcasting Inc.
Group Owner: Harvard Broadcasting Inc.; (acq 11-30-2001; C$4.2 million with co-located FM)
Format: Country
Mike Olstrom, Station Manager
Karen Broderick, General Sales Mgr
Jason Huschi, Programming Director

CJME
07-27-1926; 760 khz AM *Hrs Open:* 24
CA
(306) 525-0000, *Fax:* (306) 347-8557
www.newstalk980.com
License: Regina, SK held by Rawlco Radio Ltd.
Group Owner: Rawlco Radio Ltd.; acq 11-30-2001).
Format: News, News/Talk, Talk
Tom Newton, General Manager
Russ Bryden, General Sales Mgr
Jay Stone, Programming Director
Marcie Watson, Promotions Manager
Murray Wood, News Director

***CJTR-FM**
11-01-2001; 91.3 mhz FM *Hrs Open:* 24; 480 w; N50 27 18 W104 36 30
Box 334, Station Main, Regina, SK S4P 3A1 Canada
(306) 525-7274, *Fax:* (306) 525-9741
www.cjtr.ca
radius@cjtr.ca
License: Regina, SK held by Radius Communications Inc.
Population Served: 200,000 *Arbitron Metro Market:* Regina, SK *Format:* Variety/Diverse*Special Programming:* American Indian 4 hrs, Black 2 hrs, Chinese one hr*Hrs. of News Programming:* News progmg 10 hrs wkly*Adv.Rates:* 312; 276; 240; 204
Bill Stovin, President
Dave Kuzenko, Operations Dir
Keith Colhoun, General Manager
Norm Sacuta, Vice-President
Joan Beisel, Treasurer
Dave Morgan, Secretary
Brenda Tacik, Past President; co-chair of Fundraising Committee
NadeemNaz, Member at Large
Callan David, Member at Large

CKCK-FM
08-09-2002; 94.5 mhz FM *Hrs Open:* 24; 100 kw
2401 Saskatchewan Dr., Suite 210, Regina, SK S4P 4H8 Canada
(306) 525-0000, *Fax:* (306) 347-8557
www.jackfmregina.com
License: Regina, SK held by Rawlco Radio Ltd.
Group Owner: Rawlco Radio Ltd.
Population Served: 200,000 *Arbitron Metro Market:* Regina, SK
Format: Classic Rock
Gord Rawlinson, President
Tom Newton, General Manager
Ralph Bird, General Sales Mgr
Michael Zaplitny, News Director
Gord Stankey, Engineering Dir
Karen Mains, Traffic Manager

CHBD-FM
02-20-2008; 92.7 mhz FM; 100 kw; N50 28 58 W104 30 20
4303 Albert St., Suite 100 (main floor), Regina, SK S4S 3R6 Canada
(306) 337-2850, *Fax:* (306) 359-0931
www.bigdog927.com
mshannon@bigdog927.com
License: Regina, SK held by Astral Media Radio G.P.
Group Owner: Astral Media Inc.; (acq 9-28-2007; grpsl)
Population Served: 200,000 *Arbitron Metro Market:* Regina, SK
Format: Country *Target Audience:* 25-64.
Michael Olstom, General Manager
Gary Wilson, General Sales Mgr
Heather Prosak, Brand Director
Alison Barton, Brand Director
Dan Jones, Creative Director

Rosetown

CJYM
08-08-1966; 1330 khz AM *Hrs Open:* 24
Mailing Address: CA
Second Address: 208 Hwy.4, Rosetown, SK S0L 2V0
(306) 882-2686, *Fax:* (306) 882-3037
www.cjym.com
cjmmnews@goldenwestradio.com
License: Rosetown, SK held by Dace Broadcasting Corp.
Group Owner: Golden West Broadcasting Ltd.; (acq 10-21-99)
Nat'l Reps: Target Broadcast Sales
Format: Contemporary Hits/Top 40, Adult Contemp *No. News Employees:* 2 *Target Audience:* General.
Barb Bell, General Manager

Saskatoon

CBKF-2(AM)
11-06-1952; 860 khz AM; 10 kw-U, DA-2
144 2nd Ave., Saskatoon, SK S7K 1K5 Canada
(306) 956-7400, *Fax:* (306) 956-7476
www.sask.cbc.ca
License: Saskatoon, SK held by CBC French.
Format: Variety/Diverse *Target Audience:* General.
David Kyle, General Manager
Robert Rabinowitz, Programming Director

***CBKS-FM**
07-01-1978; 105.5 mhz FM *Hrs Open:* 24; 98 kw; Ant 586 ft*Rebroadcasts:* Rebroadcasts CBK-FM Regina
144 2nd Ave. S., Saskatoon, SK S7K 1K5 Canada
(306) 956-7400, *Fax:* (306) 956-7417
www.cbc.ca/sask/
License: Saskatoon, SK held by CBC.
Nat'l Network: CBC Radio Two
Format: Classical, Jazz, Variety/Diverse
David Kyle, Station Manager

RADIO - CANADA

CFCR-FM
01-01-1991; 90.5 mhz FM *Hrs Open:* 6 AM-1 AM; 1.48 kw
103 3rd Ave. N., Box 7544, Saskatoon, SK S7K 4L4 Canada
(306) 664-6678
www.cfcr.ca
cfcr@quadrant.net
License: Saskatoon, SK held by Community Radio Society of Saskatoon Inc.
Population Served: 200,000 *Format:* Variety/Diverse*Special Programming:* Fr one hr, Ger 2 hrs, It one hr, Pol one hr, Sp 2Hrs. *of News Programming:* News progmg one hr wkly *Target Audience:* General.*Adv.Rates:* 20; 20; 20; 15
Dianne Deminchuk, President
Ron Spizziri, General Manager
Bill Jones, General Sales Mgr
Theo Kivol, Programming Director

CFMC-FM
12-12-1965; 95.1 mhz FM; 100 kw; Ant 110 ft
715 Saskatchewan Crescent W., Saskatoon, SK S7M 5V7 Canada
(306) 934-2222, *Fax:* (306) 477-0002
www.c95.com
kwerner@rawlco.com
License: Saskatoon, SK held by Rawlco Radio Ltd.
Group Owner: Rawlco Radio Ltd.

Jamie Wall, General Manager

CKBL-FM
02-06-1995; 92.9 mhz FM; 100 kw
366 3rd Ave. S., Saskatoon, SK S7K 1M5 Canada
(306) 244-1975, *Fax:* (306) 665-7730
www.929thebullrocks.com
cjww.radio@sasktel.com
License: Saskatoon, SK held by 629112 Saskatchewan Ltd.
Group Owner: Saskatoon Media Group
Nat'l Reps: Canadian Broadcast Sales
Format: Country *No. News Employees:* 2 *Target Audience:* General.
Jacques Parisien, President
Jamie Robichaud, General Manager
Pat Brenan, General Sales Mgr
John Eddy, Executive Vice President

CKOM
06-08-1951; 650 khz AM
CA
(306) 934-2222, *Fax:* (306) 477-0002
www.newstalk650.com
License: Saskatoon, SK held by Rawlco Radio Ltd.
Group Owner: Rawlco Radio Ltd.
Format: News, News/Talk, Talk*Hrs. of News Programming:* 10
Kristy Werner, General Manager
Sandee Reed, General Sales Mgr
John Himpe, Programming Director
Vanessa Thomas, Promotions Manager
Angela Hill, News Director

CJWW
01-01-1976; 750 khz AM *Hrs Open:* 24
CA
(306) 938-0600, *Fax:* (306) 665-5501
www.cjwwradio.com
License: Saskatoon, SK held by 629112 Saskatchewan Ltd.
Group Owner: Saskatoon Media Group; (acq 12-21-2000; C$7,450,000)
Nat'l Reps: Canadian Broadcast Sales
Format: Country*Special Programming:* Gospel 3 hrs wkly *No. News Employees:* 7 *Target Audience:* 35-64; central
Elmer Hildebrand, Chairman
Dawn Mann, CFO
Steve Shannon, Operations Dir
V. Dubois, General Manager
Ken McFarlane, General Sales Mgr
Rod Kitter, Programming Director
E. Duchscher, News Director
Kurtis Krwochuk, ChiefEngineer
Jay Richards, Music Director

CJDJ-FM
06-01-1990; 102.1 mhz FM *Hrs Open:* 24; 100 kw
715 Saskatchewan Crescent West, Saskatoon, SK S7M 5V7 Canada
(306) 934-2222, *Fax:* (306) 477-0002
www.rock102rocks.com
License: Saskatoon, SK held by Rawlco Radio Ltd.
Group Owner: Rawlco Radio Ltd.; (acq 12-21-2000; C$870,000 for all the issued and outstanding shares).
Population Served: 200,000*Special Programming:* Relg 6 hrs wkly*Hrs. of News Programming:* news progmg 4 hrs wkly *No. News Employees:* 3 *Target Audience:* 25-49; well educated, well paid professionals
Pam Leyland, President
Kristy Wener, General Manager
Ralph Bird, General Sales Mgr
Chris Myers, Programming Director
Vanessa Thomas, Promotions Manager

CJMK-FM
05-01-2001; 98.3 mhz FM *Hrs Open:* 24; 100 kw
366 3rd Ave. S., Saskatoon, SK S7K 1M5 Canada
(306) 244-1975, *Fax:* (306) 665-5501
www.magic983.fm
magic@magic983.fm
License: Saskatoon, SK held by 629112 Saskatchewan Ltd.
Group Owner: Saskatoon Media Group
Population Served: 234,200 *Arbitron Metro Market:* Saskatoon, SK *Format:* Adult Contemp
Elmer Hildebrand, President
Vic Dubois, General Manager
Ken McFarlane, General Sales Mgr
Steve Chisholm, Programming Director
Eldon Duchscher, News Director
Kurtis Krowchuk, Chief Engineer
Matt Bradley, Music Director

CFWD-FM
01-01-2008; 96.3 mhz FM; 96 kw; N52 10 28 W106 26 04
105 21st St. E., Suite 200, Saskatoon, SK S7K 0B3 Canada
(306) 653-9630
www.wired963.com
info@cfwd.com
License: Saskatoon, SK held by Harvard Broadcasting Inc.
Group Owner: Harvard Broadcasting Inc.
Nat'l Reps: CHUM Radio Sales
Population Served: 234,200 *Arbitron Metro Market:* Saskatoon, SK *Format:* Adult Contemp, Contemporary Hits/Top 40
Carley Caverly, General Sales Manager
Darren Brown, Programming Director
Zoe Vassos, Promotions Manager
Karen Broderick, National Sales Manager
Bonnie Day, Interactive Producer

Shaunavon

CJSN
12-06-1966; 1490 khz AM; 1 kw-U
134 Central Ave North, Shaunavon, SK Canada
(306) 297-2671, *Fax:* (306) 297-3051
www.ckswradio.ca
License: Shaunavon, SK held by Frontier City Broadcasting.
Group Owner: Golden West Broadcasting Ltd.; (acq 1973)
Population Served: 1,200,000
Deborah Gauger, General Manager
Darwin Gooding, Programming Director

Swift Current

CIMG-FM
10-20-1979; 94.1 mhz FM *Hrs Open:* 24; 100 kw; 400 ft
134 Central Ave. N., Swift Current, SK S9H 0L1 Canada
(306) 773-4605, *Fax:* (306) 773-6390
www.eagle94.com
eaglecontrol@goldenwestradio.com
License: Swift Current, SK held by Golden West Broadcasting Ltd.
Group Owner: Golden West Broadcasting Ltd.; (acq 11-8-95; C$97,500).
Nat'l Reps: Canadian Broadcast Sales
Population Served: 48,500 *Format:* Contemporary Hits/Top 40, Adult Contemp*Hrs. of News Programming:* news progmg 4 hrs wkly *No. News Employees:* 3 *Target Audience:* 18-35.
Deborah Gauger, Station Manager
Ryan Switzer, Programming Director

CKSW
06-01-1956; 570 khz AM *Hrs Open:* 24
CA
(306) 773-4605, *Fax:* (306) 773-6390
www.ckswradio.ca
License: Swift Current, SK held by Golden West Broadcasting Ltd.
Group Owner: Golden West Broadcasting Ltd.
Nat'l Reps: Canadian Broadcast Sales
Format: Country*Special Programming:* Farm 5 hrs, Ger one hr wkly*Hrs. of News Programming:* news progmg 9 hrs wkly *No. News Employees:* 5 *Target Audience:* 25-54.
Deborah Granger, General Sales Mgr
Ryan Switzer, Programming Director
Dave Funk, Chief Engineer

CKFI-FM
11-05-2005; 97.1 mhz FM; 100 kw
134 Central Ave. N., Swift Current, SK S9H 0L1 Canada
(306) 773-4605, *Fax:* (306) 773-6390
License: Swift Current, SK held by Golden West Broadcasting Ltd.
Group Owner: Golden West Broadcasting Ltd.
Population Served: 85,118 *Format:* Adult Contemp
Deborah Gauger, General Manager
Ryan Switzer, Programming Director

Watrous

***CBK**
07-29-1939; 540 khz AM *Hrs Open:* 24
CA
(306) 347-9540, *Fax:* (306) 347-9524
www.cbc.ca/sask
kyled@cbc.ca
License: Watrous, SK held by CBC.
Nat'l Network: CBC Radio One
Format: News, Talk, Variety/Diverse*Special Programming:* Farm 5 hrs wkly
Debbie Carpentier, General Manager
David Kyle, Station Manager
Nigel Simms, News Director

Weyburn

CFSL
08-16-1957; 1190 khz AM *Hrs Open:* 24; 10 kw-D, 5 kw-N, DA-N
305 Souris Ave., Weyburn, SK Canada
(306) 848-1190, *Fax:* (306) 842-2720
am1190@coldwestradio.com
License: Weyburn, SK held by Golden West Broadcasting Ltd.
Group Owner: Golden West Broadcasting Ltd.; (acq 2-16-95)
Nat'l Reps: Canadian Broadcast Sales *Wire Services:* BN Wire
Special Programming: Farm 3 hrs, relg 9 hrs wkly *No. News Employees:* 3 *Target Audience:* 25 plus.
Elmer Hildenbrand, CEO
Cameron Birnie, Station Manager

CKRC-FM
103.5 mhz FM; 100 kw
305 Souris Ave., Weyburn, SK S4H 2K2 Canada
(306) 848-1190, *Fax:* (306) 842-2720
License: Weyburn, SK held by Golden West Broadcasting Ltd.
Group Owner: Golden West Broadcasting Ltd.

Guy Simard, President
Maurice Marcotte, General Manager
Claude Girard, General Sales Mgr
Marcel Rancourt, Programming Director
Suzanne Bougie, News Director
Gaston Guay, Chief Engineer
Jacques Goulet, National Sales Manager

CHWY-FM
106.7 mhz FM; 100 kw; 73.7 meters
305 Souris Avenue, Weyburn, SK S4H 0C6 Canada
(306) 848-1190, *Fax:* (306) 842-2720
License: Weyburn, SK held by Golden West Broadcasting Ltd

White Bear Lake Resort

CIDD-FM
01-01-2002; 97.7 mhz FM; 46.5 w
Box 875, Kenosee Lake, SK S0C 2S0 Canada
(306) 577-2450, *Fax:* (306) 577-4313
License: White Bear Lake Resort, SK held by White Bear Children's Charity Inc.
Population Served: 31,612,897 *Arbitron Metro Market:* Carlyle Lake, SK *Format:* Variety/Diverse
Lana Littlechief, General Manager

Yorkton

CJGX
08-19-1927; 940 khz AM
CA
(306) 782-2256, *Fax:* (306) 783-4994
www.gx94radio.com
ykt-reception@harvardbroadcasting.com
License: Yorkton, SK held by Yorkton Broadcasting Ltd. and Walsh Investments Inc., partners of GX Radio, a gen partnership.
Nat'l Reps: CHUM Radio Sales; Target Broadcast Sales
Format: Country
Lyle Walsh, President
Chad Mikals, Operations Dir
Angie Norton, General Manager
Damon Kustra, General Sales Mgr

Brad Bazin, Programming Director
Gina Resler, Promotions Manager
Bryan Mireau, Engineering Dir

CFGW-FM
07-01-2001; 94.1 mhz FM; 100 kw
120 Smith St. E., Yorkton, SK S3N 3V3 Canada
(306) 782-2256, *Fax:* (3006) 783-4994
www.941thefox.com
ykt-reception@harvardbroadcasting.com
License: Yorkton, SK held by Yorkton Broadcasting Ltd.
Population Served: 18,471 *Arbitron Metro Market:* Yorkton, SK
Format: Adult Contemp
Angie Norton, General Manager
Damon Kustra, Sales Manager
Brad Bazin, Programming Director
Gina Resler, Promotions Manager
Natasha Rapchuk, News Director
Wade Wensink, Chief Engineer
Judy Rickleton, Traffic Manager
Mike Wilson,Music Director
Chad Mikals, Production Manager

CJJC-FM
01-02-2006; 98.5 mhz FM; 50 kw; 118 meters
395 Riverview Rd., Yorkton, SK S3N 3V6 Canada
(306) 786-7625, *Fax:* (306) 782-4437
www.1005therock.ca
rocktalk@1005therock.ca
License: Yorkton, SK held by 101056012 Saskatchewan Ltd
No. News Employees: 5
Dennis Dyck, Station Manager
Scott Fitzsimmons, Programming Director

Zenon Park

CKZP-FM
01-01-2002; 102.7 mhz FM; 5.4 w
Box 100, Zenon Park, SK S0E 1W0 Canada
(306) 767-2451, *Fax:* (306) 767-2548
www.thinkfast.ca/tsd/tsdpromo2/zpradio.htm
legeru@tsd53.ca
License: Zenon Park, SK held by Radio Zenon Park Inc.
Population Served: 231 *Arbitron Metro Market:* Zenon Park, SK
Format: French
J. Ulysse Leger, General Manager

Yukon Territory

Dawson City

***CFYT-FM**
10-01-2006; 106.9 mhz FM *Hrs Open:* Fri-Sun, noon to midnight; 5 w; N64 03 27 W139 24 36*Rebroadcasts:* CKRW-FM Whitehorse 86%
Box 689, Dawson City, YT Y0B 1G0 Canada
(867) 993-5152, *Fax:* (867) 993-6834
www.cfyt.ca
cfytradio@gmail.com
License: Dawson City, YT held by Dawson City Community Radio Society.
Population Served: 1,319 *Arbitron Metro Market:* Dawson City, YT *Format:* Alternative
Georgia Hammond, President
John Watt, Vice President
Peter Menzies, Treasurer
Capri Simpson, Secretary
Jen Laliberte, Director
Brendan Reese, Director
Kyle Hammond, Director

Tagish

CFET-FM
06-01-2003; 106.7 mhz FM; 50 w
Mile 234, Tagish, YT Y0B 1T0 Canada
(867) 667-6397, *Fax:* (867) 668-2633
www.tagishtel.ca/radio
cfet@tagishtel.ca
License: Tagish, YT held by Robert G. Hopkins.
Population Served: 206 *Arbitron Metro Market:* Tagish, YT
Format: Classic Rock
Robert Hopkins, General Manager

Whitehorse

***CFWH-FM**
06-01-2012; 94.5 mhz FM *Hrs Open:* 24; 5 kw-U, DA-1
3103 Third Ave., Whitehorse, YT Y1A 1E5 Canada
(867) 668-8400, *Fax:* (867) 668-8408
www.cbc.ca/north
License: Whitehorse, YT held by CBC
Nat'l Network: CBC Radio One
Special Programming: Fr one hr wkly
Frank Fry, Operations Dir

***CHONFM**
02-01-1985; 88.9 mhz FM; kw
CA
(867) 668-6629, *Fax:* (867) 668-6612
www.nnby.net
nnby@nnby.net
License: Whitehorse, Canada County, YT held by Northern Native Broadcasting, YUKON
Format: Classic Rock, Country*Special Programming:* Yukon native language 15 hrs wkly
Shirley Adamason, CEO
Sophie Green, General Manager
Manfred Janssen, General Sales Mgr
Dennis Gerard, Engineering Dir

CKRW-FM
11-17-1969; 96.1 mhz FM
203-4103 4th Ave., Suite 203, Whitehorse, YT Y1A 1H6 Canada
(867) 668-6100, *Fax:* (867) 668-4209
www.ckrw.com
admin@ckrw.com
License: Whitehorse, YT held by Klondike Broadcasting Co. Ltd.
Nat'l Reps: Canadian Broadcast Sales
Rolf Hougen, CEO
Eva Bidrman, General Manager
Keith Ellert, Programming Director

CIAY-FM
01-01-2003; 100.7 mhz FM *Hrs Open:* 24; 50 w
91806 Alaska Hwy., Whitehorse, YT Y1A 5B7 Canada
(867) 393-2429, *Fax:* (867) 393-2439
www.lifewhitehorse.com
info@lifewhitehorse.com
License: Whitehorse, YT held by Bethany Pentecostal Tabernacle.
Population Served: 23,276 *Arbitron Metro Market:* Whitehorse, YT *Format:* Christian
Rod Carby, Station Manager
Theresa Aitcheson, General Sales Mgr
Ian McDonald, Programming Director

Canadian AM Radio Stations by Call Letters

CBG Gander, Newfoundland
CBGN(AM) Sainte Anne des Monts, Quebec
CBGY Bonavista Bay, Newfoundland
CBI Sydney, Nova Scotia
CBK Watrous, Saskatchewan
CBKF-1(AM) Gravelbourg, Saskatchewan
CBKF-2(AM) Saskatoon, Saskatchewan
CBN St. John's, Newfoundland
CBOF-1(AM) Maniwaki, Quebec
CBR Calgary, Alberta
CBT Grand Falls, Alberta
CBU Vancouver, British Columbia
CBW Winnipeg, Manitoba
CBX Edmonton, Alberta
CBY Corner Brook, Newfoundland
CFAB Windsor, Nova Scotia
CFAC Calgary, Alberta
CFAM Altona, Manitoba
CFAR Flin Flon, Manitoba
CFAX Victoria, British Columbia
CFBC Saint John, New Brunswick
CFBV Smithers, British Columbia
CFCB Corner Brook, Newfoundland
CFCO Chatham, Ontario
CFCT Tuktoyaktuk, Northwest Territories
CFCW Camrose, Alberta
CFDR Dartmouth, Nova Scotia
CFFB Iqaluit, Northwest Territories
CFFR Calgary, Alberta
CFGO Ottawa, Ontario
CFKC Creston, British Columbia
CFLD Burns Lake, British Columbia
CFLM La Tuque, Quebec
CFLN Goose Bay, Newfoundland
CFMB Montreal, Quebec
CFMJ Richmond Hill, Ontario
CFNC(AM) Cross Lake, Manitoba
CFNI Port Hardy, British Columbia
CFNW Port Au Choix, Newfoundland
CFOS Collingwood, Ontario
CFPL London, Ontario
CFPR Prince Rupert, British Columbia
CFRA Ottawa, Ontario
CFRB Toronto, Ontario
CFRN Edmonton, Alberta
CFRP Forestville, Quebec
CFRW Winnipeg, Manitoba
CFRY Portage La Prairie, Manitoba
CFSL Weyburn, Saskatchewan
CFSX Stephenville, Newfoundland
CFTE Vancouver, British Columbia
CFTK Terrace, British Columbia
CFTR Toronto, Ontario
CFYK Yellow Knife, Northwest Territories
CFYM Kindersley, Saskatchewan
CFZM(AM) Toronto, Ontario
CHAB Moose Jaw, Saskatchewan
CHAK Inuvik, Northwest Territories
CHAM Hamilton, Ontario
CHCM Marystown, Newfoundland
CHED Edmonton, Alberta
CHFA Edmonton, Alberta
CHHA Toronto, Ontario
CHIN Toronto, Ontario
CHKT(AM) Toronto, Ontario
CHLW St. Paul, Alberta
CHMB Vancouver, British Columbia
CHMJ Vancouver, British Columbia
CHML Hamilton, Ontario
CHMO(AM) Moosonee, Ontario
CHNL Kamloops, British Columbia
CHOK Sarnia, Ontario
CHOU Montreal, Quebec
CHQR Calgary, Alberta
CHQT Edmonton, Alberta
CHRB High River, Alberta
CHRC Quebec, Quebec
CHSM Steinbach, Manitoba
CHTK Prince Rupert, British Columbia
CHTM Thompson, Manitoba
CHTO Toronto, Ontario
CHUM Toronto, Ontario
CIAO Brampton, Ontario
CIGM Sudbury, Ontario
CINA Mississauga, Ontario
CIOR(AM) Princeton, British Columbia
CISL Richmond, British Columbia
CIVH Vanderhoof, British Columbia
CIWW Ottawa, Ontario
CJAD Montreal, Quebec
CJAR The Pas, Manitoba
CJBC Toronto, Ontario
CJBK London, Ontario
CJBQ Belleville, Ontario
CJCA Edmonton, Alberta
CJCB Sydney, Nova Scotia
CJCL Toronto, Ontario
CJCS Stratford, Ontario
CJCW Sussex, New Brunswick
CJDC Dawson Creek, British Columbia
CJGX Yorkton, Saskatchewan
CJLO Montreal, Quebec
CJLV Laval, Quebec
CJME Regina, Saskatchewan
CJMR Mississauga, Ontario
CJMS Montreal, Quebec
CJNS Meadow Lake, Saskatchewan
CJOB Winnipeg, Manitoba
CJOR(AM) Osoyoos, British Columbia
CJOY Guelph, Ontario
CJRB Boissevain, Manitoba
CJRJ Vancouver, British Columbia
CJRS Sherbrooke, Quebec
CJSL Estevan, Saskatchewan
CJSN Shaunavon, Saskatchewan
CJVA Caraquet, New Brunswick
CJVB Vancouver, British Columbia
CJWI Montreal, Quebec
CJWW Saskatoon, Saskatchewan
CJYE Oakville, Ontario
CJYM Rosetown, Saskatchewan
CJYQ St. John's, Newfoundland
CKAC Montreal, Quebec
CKAD Middleton, Nova Scotia
CKAT(AM) North Bay, Ontario
CKBI Prince Albert, Saskatchewan
CKBX One Hundred Mile Hou, British Columbia
CKCM Grand Falls, Newfoundland
CKDM Dauphin, Manitoba
CKDO Oshawa, Ontario
CKDQ Drumheller, Alberta
CKDY Digby, Nova Scotia
CKFR Kelowna, British Columbia
CKGA Gander, Newfoundland
CKGL(AM) Kitchener, Ontario
CKGM Montreal, Quebec
CKHJ(AM) Fredericton, New Brunswick
CKIM Baie Verte, Newfoundland
CKIR Invermere, British Columbia
CKJH(AM) Melfort, Saskatchewan
CKJR Wetaskiwin, Alberta
CKJS Winnipeg, Manitoba
CKKY Wainwright, Alberta
CKLQ Brandon, Manitoba
CKLW Windsor, Ontario
CKMW Morden, Manitoba
CKMX Calgary, Alberta
CKNB Campbellton, New Brunswick
CKNW New Westminster, British Columbia
CKNX Wingham, Ontario
CKOC Hamilton, Ontario
CKOM Saskatoon, Saskatchewan
CKOR Penticton, British Columbia
CKOT Tillsonburg, Ontario
CKPC Brantford, Ontario
CKRM(AM) Regina, Saskatchewan
CKSB St. Boniface, Manitoba
CKSL London, Ontario
CKSM Shawinigan, Quebec
CKST Vancouver, British Columbia
CKSW Swift Current, Saskatchewan
CKTB St. Catharines, Ontario
CKUA Edmonton, Alberta
CKVO Clarenville, Newfoundland
CKWL Williams Lake, British Columbia
CKWW Windsor, Ontario
CKWX Vancouver, British Columbia
CKYL Peace River, Alberta
KCNM Saipan, Guam
V6AH(AM) Pohnpei, 66
V6AI(AM) Yap, 66
V6AK(AM) Truk, 66
VOAR St. John's, Newfoundland
VOCM St. John's, Newfoundland
VOWR St. John's, Newfoundland
WMEJ , Mississippi

Canadian FM Radio Stations by Call Letters

CBA-FM Moncton, New Brunswick
CBAFFM Moncton, New Brunswick
CBAL-FM Moncton, New Brunswick
CBAM-FM Moncton, New Brunswick
CBAX-FM Halifax, Nova Scotia
CBBKFM Kingston, Ontario
CBBLFM London, Ontario
CBBSFM Sudbury, Ontario
CBBX-FM Sudbury, Ontario
CBCLFM London, Ontario
CBCSFM Sudbury, Ontario
CBCTFM Charlottetown, Prince Edward Island
CBCV-FM Victoria, British Columbia
CBCX-FM Calgary, Alberta
CBD-FM Saint John, New Brunswick
CBDQ-FM Labrador City, Newfoundland
CBE-FM Windsor, Ontario
CBEGFM Sarnia, Ontario
CBEW-FM Windsor, Ontario
CBF-2 Toronto, Quebec
CBF-FM Montreal, Quebec
CBF-FM-1 Trois Rivieres, Quebec
CBFX-FM Montreal, Quebec
CBGA Gaspe, Quebec
CBH-FM Halifax, Nova Scotia
CBHAFM Halifax, Nova Scotia
CBI-FM Sydney, Nova Scotia
CBJ-FM Chicoutimi, Quebec
CBJEFM Chicoutimi, Quebec
CBJX-FM Chicoutimi, Quebec
CBK-FM Regina, Saskatchewan
CBKA-FM La Ronge, Saskatchewan
CBKFFM Regina, Saskatchewan
CBKS-FM Saskatoon, Saskatchewan
CBL-FM Toronto, Ontario
CBLAFM Toronto, Ontario
CBM-FM Montreal, Quebec
CBME-FM Montreal, Quebec
CBMIFM Baie-Comeau, Quebec
CBMR-FM Fermont, Quebec
CBN-FM Saint John's, Newfoundland
CBO-FM Ottawa, Ontario
CBOFFM Ottawa, Ontario
CBON Timmins, Ontario
CBOQ-FM Ottawa, Ontario
CBOX-FM Ottawa, Ontario
CBQ-FM Thunder Bay, Ontario
CBQLFM Savant Lake, Ontario
CBQR-FM Rankin Inlet, Nunavut
CBQSFM Sioux Narrows, Ontario
CBQTFM Fort Frances, Ontario
CBQXFM Kenora, Ontario
CBR-FM Calgary, Alberta
CBRFFM Calgary, Alberta
CBRXFM Rimouski, Quebec
CBSI-FM Sept-Iles, Quebec
CBTEFM Crawford Bay, British Columbia
CBTKFM Kelowna, British Columbia
CBU-FM Vancouver, British Columbia
CBUFFM Vancouver, British Columbia
CBUX-FM Vancouver, British Columbia
CBV-FM Quebec, Quebec
CBV-FM-6 La Malbaie, Quebec
CBVEFM Quebec, Quebec
CBVX-FM Quebec, Quebec
CBW-FM Winnipeg, Manitoba
CBWK-FM Thompson, Manitoba
CBX-FM Edmonton, Alberta
CBYG-FM Prince George, British Columbia
CBYKFM Vancouver, British Columbia
CBZ-FM Fredericton, New Brunswick
CBZF-FM Fredericton, New Brunswick
CFAD-FM Salmo, British Columbia
CFAIFM Edmundston, New Brunswick
CFAK-FM Sherbrooke, Quebec
CFAN-FM Miramichi City, New Brunswick
CFAQ-FM Blucher, Saskatchewan
CFBG-FM Bracebridge, Ontario
CFBK-FM Huntsville, Ontario
CFBO-FM Moncton, New Brunswick
CFBR-FM Edmonton, Alberta
CFBS-FM Lourdes-de-Blanc-Sablon, Quebec
CFBT-FM Vancouver, British Columbia
CFBU-FM Saint Catharines, Ontario
CFBW-FM Hanover, Ontario
CFBX-FM Kamloops, British Columbia
CFCAFM Kitchener, Ontario
CFCH-FM Chase, British Columbia
CFCP-FM Courtenay, British Columbia
CFCR-FM Saskatoon, Saskatchewan
CFCV-FM Saint Andrews, Newfoundland
CFCW-FM Camrose, Alberta
CFCY-FM Charlottetown, Prince Edward Island
CFDA-FM Victoriaville, Quebec
CFDM-FM Meadow Lake, Saskatchewan
CFDV-FM Red Deer, Alberta
CFDY-FM Cochrane, Ontario
CFEI St-Hyacinthe, Quebec
CFEL-FM Levis, Quebec
CFEP-FM Eastern Passage, Nova Scotia
CFEQ-FM Winnipeg, Manitoba
CFET-FM Tagish, Yukon Territory
CFEX-FM Calgary, Alberta
CFFF-FM Peterborough, Ontario
CFFMFM Kamloops, British Columbia
CFGB-FM Happy Valley, Newfoundland
CFGE-FM Sherbrooke, Quebec
CFGI-FM Georgina Island, Ontario
CFGLFM Laval, Quebec
CFGP-FM Grande Prairie, Alberta
CFGQ-FM Calgary, Alberta
CFGT-FM Alma, Quebec
CFGW-FM Yorkton, Saskatchewan
CFGX-FM Sarnia, Ontario
CFHK-FM St. Thomas, Ontario
CFIC-FM Listuguj, Quebec
CFID-FM Acton Vale, Quebec
CFIF-FM Iroquois Falls, Ontario
CFIM-FM Iles-de-la-Madeleine, Quebec
CFIN-FM Lac-Etchemin, Quebec
CFIS-FM Prince George, British Columbia
CFIT-FM Airdrie, Alberta
CFIX-FM Chicoutimi, Quebec
CFJB-FM Barrie, Ontario
CFJL-FM Winnipeg, Manitoba
CFJO-FM Thetford Mines, Quebec
CFJR-FM Brockville, Ontario
CFJU-FM Kedgwick, New Brunswick
CFLC-FM Churchill Falls, Newfoundland
CFLGFM Cornwall, Ontario
CFLN-FM Goose Bay, Newfoundland
CFLO-FM Mont-Laurier, Quebec
CFLXFM Sherbrooke, Quebec
CFLYFM Kingston, Ontario
CFLZ-FM Fort Erie, Ontario
CFMC-FM Saskatoon, Saskatchewan
CFMF-FM Fermont, Quebec
CFMG-FM Saint Albert, Alberta
CFMH-FM Saint John, New Brunswick
CFMIFM New Westminster, British Columbia
CFMKFM Kingston, Ontario
CFMM-FM Prince Albert, Saskatchewan
CFMQFM Regina, Saskatchewan
CFMUFM Hamilton, Ontario
CFMV-FM Chandler, Quebec
CFMXFM Cobourg, Ontario
CFMY-FM Medicine Hat, Alberta
CFMZ-FM Toronto, Ontario
CFNA-FM Bonnyville, Alberta
CFND-FM Saint Jerome, Quebec
CFNJFM St-Gabriel, Quebec
CFNK-FM Pinehouse Lake, Saskatchewan
CFNOFM Marathon, Ontario
CFNR-FM Terrace, British Columbia
CFNYFM Brampton, Ontario
CFOB-FM Fort Frances, Ontario
CFOM-FM Levis, Quebec
CFOR-FM Maniwaki, Quebec
CFOU-FM Trois Rivieres, Quebec
CFOXFM Vancouver, British Columbia
CFOZ-FM Argentia, Newfoundland
CFPLFM London, Ontario
CFPS-FM Port Elgin, Ontario
CFPV-FM Pemberton, British Columbia
CFPW-FM Powell River, British Columbia
CFPX-FM Pukatawagan, Manitoba
CFQK-FM Kaministiquia, Ontario
CFQMFM Moncton, New Brunswick
CFQR-FM Montreal, Quebec
CFQXFM Selkirk, Manitoba
CFRCFM Kingston, Ontario
CFRG-FM Gravelbourg, Saskatchewan
CFRH-FM Penetanguishene, Ontario
CFRI-FM Grande Prairie, Alberta
CFRK-FM Fredericton, New Brunswick
CFRMFM St Boniface, Manitoba
CFROFM Vancouver, British Columbia
CFRQFM Dartmouth, Nova Scotia
CFRT-FM Iqaluit, Nunavut
CFRUFM Guelph, Ontario
CFRV-FM Lethbridge, Alberta
CFSF-FM Sturgeon Falls, Ontario
CFSH-FM Apsley, Ontario
CFSRFM Abbotsford, British Columbia
CFTA-FM Amherst, Nova Scotia
CFTH-FM-1 Harrington Harbour, Quebec
CFTH-FM-2 Harrington Harbour, Quebec
CFTX-FM Gatineau, Quebec
CFUL-FM Calgary, Alberta
CFUN-FM Chilliwack, British Columbia
CFUR-FM Prince George, British Columbia
CFUT-FM Shawinigan, Quebec
CFUVFM Victoria, British Columbia
CFVD Degelis, Quebec
CFVD-FM-2 Pohenegamook, Quebec
CFVM-FM Amqui, Quebec
CFVR-FM Fort McMurray, Alberta
CFWC-FM Brantford, Ontario
CFWD-FM Saskatoon, Saskatchewan
CFWE-FM Lac La Biche, Alberta
CFWF-FM Regina, Saskatchewan
CFWH-FM Whitehorse, Yukon Territory
CFWM-FM Winnipeg, Manitoba
CFWP-FM Wahta Mohawk Territory near Bala, Ontario
CFXE-FM Edson, Alberta
CFXH-FM Hinton, Alberta
CFXJ-FM Toronto, Ontario
CFXL-FM Calgary, Alberta
CFXM Granby, Quebec
CFXN-FM North Bay, Ontario
CFXO-FM High River-Okotoks, Alberta
CFXU-FM Antigonish, Nova Scotia
CFXW-FM Whitecourt, Alberta
CFXX-FM Siksika, Alberta
CFXY-FM Fredericton, New Brunswick
CFYT-FM Dawson City, Yukon Territory
CFYX-FM Rimouski, Quebec
CFZN-FM Haliburton, Ontario
CFZZ-FM Saint Jean-Iberville, Quebec
CHAA-FM Longueuil, Quebec
CHAD-FM Dawson Creek, British Columbia
CHAI-FM Chateauguay, Quebec
CHASFM Sault Ste Marie, Ontario
CHAT-FM Medicine Hat, Alberta
CHAYFM Barrie, Ontario
CHBD-FM Regina, Saskatchewan
CHBE-FM Victoria, British Columbia
CHBI-FM Burnt Islands, Newfoundland
CHBM-FM Toronto, Ontario
CHBN-FM Edmonton, Alberta
CHBO-FM Humboldt, Saskatchewan
CHBW-FM Rocky Mountain House, Alberta
CHBZ-FM Cranbrook, British Columbia
CHCD Simcoe, Ontario
CHCQ-FM Belleville, Ontario
CHCR-FM Killaloe, Ontario
CHDI-FM Edmonton, Alberta
CHDR-FM Cranbrook, British Columbia
CHEF-FM Matagami, Quebec
CHEQFM Smiths Falls, Ontario
CHER-FM Sydney, Nova Scotia
CHES-FM Erin, Ontario
CHET-FM Chetwynd, British Columbia
CHEY-FM Trois Rivieres, Quebec
CHEZFM Ottawa, Ontario
CHFIFM Toronto, Ontario
CHFMFM Calgary, Alberta
CHFN-FM Cape Croker (Neyaashiinigmiing), Ontario
CHFT-FM Fort McMurray, Alberta
CHFXFM Halifax, Nova Scotia
CHGAFM Maniwaki, Quebec
CHGB-FM Wasaga Beach, Ontario
CHGK-FM Stratford, Ontario
CHGO-FM Val d'Or, Quebec
CHHO-FM Louiseville, Quebec
CHHR-FM Vancouver, British Columbia
CHIC-FM Rouyn-Noranda, Quebec
CHIKFM Quebec, Quebec
CHIMFM Kelowna, British Columbia
CHINFM Toronto, Ontario
CHIPFM Fort-Coulonge, Quebec
CHIQFM Winnipeg, Manitoba
CHJM-FM St-George-Beauce, Quebec
CHJX-FM London, Ontario
CHKF-FM Calgary, Alberta
CHKG-FM Richmond, British Columbia
CHKS-FM Sarnia, Ontario
CHKX-FM Hamilton, Ontario
CHLB-FM Lethbridge, Alberta
CHLCFM Baie-Comeau, Quebec
CHLI-FM Rossland, British Columbia
CHLK-FM Perth, Ontario
CHLQFM Charlottetown, Prince Edward Island
CHLS-FM Lillooet, British Columbia
CHLX-FM Gatineau, Quebec
CHLY-FM Nanaimo, British Columbia
CHMA-FM Sackville, New Brunswick
CHMM-FM MacKenzie, British Columbia
CHMN-FM Canmore, Alberta
CHMP-FM Longueuil, Quebec
CHMR-FM Saint John's, Newfoundland
CHMS-FM Bancroft, Ontario
CHMT-FM Timmins, Ontario
CHMX-FM Regina, Saskatchewan
CHMY-FM Renfrew, Ontario
CHMZ-FM Tofino, British Columbia
CHNC-FM New Carlisle, Quebec
CHNI-FM Saint John, New Brunswick
CHNO-FM Sudbury, Ontario
CHNS-FM Halifax, Nova Scotia
CHNV-FM Nelson, British Columbia
CHOA-FM Rouyn-Noranda, Quebec
CHOCFM Saint Remi, Quebec
CHODFM Cornwall, Ontario
CHOE-FM Matane, Quebec
CHOIFM Quebec, Quebec
CHOMFM Montreal, Quebec
CHONFM Whitehorse, Yukon Territory
CHOP-FM Newmarket, Ontario
CHOQ-FM Toronto, Ontario
CHOR-FM Summerland, British Columbia
CHOS-FM Rattling Brook, Newfoundland
CHOW-FM Amos, Quebec
CHOX-FM La Pocatiere, Quebec
CHOY-FM Moncton, New Brunswick
CHOZ-FM Saint John's, Newfoundland
CHPB-FM Cochrane, Ontario
CHPD-FM Aylmer, Ontario
CHPQ-FM Parksville, British Columbia
CHPR-FM Hawkesbury, Ontario
CHQC-FM Saint John, New Brunswick
CHQMFM Vancouver, British Columbia
CHQX-FM Prince Albert, Saskatchewan
CHRD-FM Drummondville, Quebec
CHREFM St Catharines, Ontario
CHRG-FM Maria (Reserve), Quebec
CHRI-FM Ottawa, Ontario
CHRKFM Kamloops, British Columbia
CHRL-FM Roberval, Quebec
CHRM-FM Matane, Quebec
CHRQ-FM Restigouche, Quebec
CHRWFM London, Ontario
CHRX-FM Fort St. John, British Columbia
CHRY-FM Toronto, Ontario
CHSB-FM Bedford, Nova Scotia
CHSJ-FM Saint John, New Brunswick
CHSL-FM Slave Lake, Alberta
CHSN-FM Estevan, Saskatchewan
CHSP-FM Saint Paul, Alberta
CHSR-FM Fredericton, New Brunswick
CHST-FM London, Ontario
CHSU-FM Kelowna, British Columbia
CHTD-FM Saint Stephen, New Brunswick
CHTK-FM Prince Rupert, British Columbia
CHTN-FM Charlottetown, Prince Edward Island
CHTT-FM Victoria, British Columbia
CHTZFM St Catharines, Ontario
CHUB-FM Red Deer, Alberta
CHUC-FM Cobourg, Ontario
CHUK-FM Mashteuiatsh (Pointe-Bleue), Quebec
CHUMFM Toronto, Ontario
CHUN-FM Rouyn-Noranda, Quebec
CHUO-FM Ottawa, Ontario
CHUP-FM Calgary, Alberta
CHUR-FM North Bay, Ontario
CHUT-FM Lac-Simon (Louvicourt), Quebec
CHVD-FM Dolbeau-Mistassini, Quebec
CHVN-FM Winnipeg, Manitoba
CHVO-FM Carbonear, Newfoundland
CHVR-FM Pembroke, Ontario
CHWC-FM Goderich, Ontario
CHWE-FM Winnepeg, Manitoba
CHWF-FM Nanaimo, British Columbia

CHWK-FM Chilliwack, British Columbia
CHWN-FM Skownan, Manitoba
CHWV-FM Saint John, New Brunswick
CHWY-FM Weyburn, Saskatchewan
CHXL Brockville, Ontario
CHXX-FM Donnacona, Quebec
CHYC-FM Sudbury, Ontario
CHYK-FM Timmins, Ontario
CHYK-FM-3 Hearst, Ontario
CHYM-FM Kitchener, Ontario
CHYR-FM Leamington, Ontario
CHYZ-FM Sainte Foy, Quebec
CIAJ-FM Prince Rupert, British Columbia
CIAM-FM Fort Vermilion, Alberta
CIAU-FM Radisson, Quebec
CIAX-FM Windsor, Quebec
CIAY-FM Whitehorse, Yukon Territory
CIBC-FM Cowessess, Saskatchewan
CIBH-FM Parksville, British Columbia
CIBK-FM Calgary, Alberta
CIBL-FM Montreal, Quebec
CIBMFM Riviere du Loup, Quebec
CIBO-FM Senneterre, Quebec
CIBQ-FM Brooks, Alberta
CIBU-FM Wingham, Ontario
CIBW-FM Drayton Valley, Alberta
CIBX-FM Fredericton, New Brunswick
CICF-FM Vernon, British Columbia
CICN-FM Marcelin, Saskatchewan
CICS-FM Sudbury, Ontario
CICU-FM Eskasoni Indian Reserve, Nova Scotia
CICX-FM Orillia, Ontario
CICY-FM Selkirk, Manitoba
CICZ Midland, Ontario
CIDCFM Orangeville, Ontario
CIDD-FM White Bear Lake Resort, Saskatchewan
CIDG-FM Ottawa, Ontario
CIDI-FM Lac-Brome, Quebec
CIDO-FM Creston, British Columbia
CIDR-FM Windsor, Ontario
CIEG-FM Egmont, British Columbia
CIELFM Longueuil, Quebec
CIEUFM Carleton, Quebec
CIFA-FM Comeauville, Nova Scotia
CIFM-FM Kamloops, British Columbia
CIFN-FM Island Lake, Saskatchewan
CIFX-FM Lewisporte, Newfoundland
CIGBFM Trois-Rivieres, Quebec
CIGLFM Belleville, Ontario
CIGO-FM Port Hawkesbury, Nova Scotia
CIGVFM Penticton, British Columbia
CIHI-FM Fredericton, New Brunswick
CIHOFM Baie St Paul, Quebec
CIHR-FM Woodstock, Ontario
CIHS-FM Wetaskiwin, Alberta
CIHT-FM Ottawa, Ontario
CIJK-FM Kentville, Nova Scotia
CIKIFM Rimouski, Quebec
CIKR-FM Kingston, Ontario
CIKT-FM Grande Prairie, Alberta
CIKX-FM Grand Falls, New Brunswick
CIKZ-FM Kitchener, Ontario
CILE-FM Havre-Saint-Pierre, Quebec
CILG-FM Moose Jaw, Saskatchewan
CILKFM Kelowna, British Columbia
CILQFM Toronto, Ontario
CILS-FM Victoria, British Columbia
CILT-FM Steinbach, Manitoba
CILU-FM Thunder Bay, Ontario
CILV-FM Ottawa, Ontario
CIMEFM Saint Jerome, Quebec
CIMFFM Hull, Quebec
CIMG-FM Swift Current, Saskatchewan
CIMI-FM Charlesbourg, Quebec
CIMJ-FM Guelph, Ontario
CIMM-FM Ucluelet, British Columbia
CIMOFM Magog, Quebec
CIMS-FM Balmoral, New Brunswick
CIMX Windsor, Ontario
CIMY-FM Pembroke, Ontario
CINA-FM Windsor, Ontario
CINB-FM Saint John, New Brunswick
CINC-FM Thompson, Manitoba
CINGFM Burlington, Ontario
CINN-FM Hearst, Ontario
CINQFM Montreal, Quebec
CINU-FM Truro, Nova Scotia
CIOC-FM Victoria, British Columbia
CIOI-FM Hamilton, Ontario
CIOK-FM Saint John, New Brunswick
CION Quebec, Quebec
CIOOFM Halifax, Nova Scotia
CIOS-FM Stephenville, Newfoundland
CIOT-FM Nipawin, Saskatchewan
CIOZ-FM Marystown, Newfoundland
CIPC-FM Port-Cartier, Quebec
CIPN-FM Pender Harbour, British Columbia
CIPU-FM Micmac, Nova Scotia
CIQB-FM Barrie, Ontario
CIQC-FM Campbell River, British Columbia
CIQM-FM London, Ontario
CIRA Montreal, Quebec
CIRK-FM Edmonton, Alberta
CIRP-FM Spryfield, Nova Scotia
CIRR-FM Toronto, Ontario
CIRV-FM Toronto, Ontario
CIRX-FM Prince George, British Columbia
CISB-FM Marius, Manitoba
CISCFM Gibsons, British Columbia
CISM-FM Montreal, Quebec
CISN-FM Edmonton, Alberta
CISP-FM Pemberton, British Columbia
CISQFM Squamish, British Columbia
CISS-FM Ottawa, Ontario
CISWFM Whistler, British Columbia
CITA-FM Moncton, New Brunswick
CITE-FM-1 Sherbrooke, Quebec
CITEFM Montreal, Quebec
CITFFM Quebec, Quebec
CITIFM Winnipeg, Manitoba
CITRFM Vancouver, British Columbia
CIUP-FM Edmonton, Alberta
CIUTFM Toronto, Ontario
CIVL-FM Abbotsford, British Columbia
CIWS-FM Whitchurch-Stouffville, Ontario
CIXF-FM Brooks, Alberta
CIXK-FM Owen Sound, Ontario
CIXL-FM Welland, Ontario
CIXM-FM Whitecourt, Alberta
CIXN-FM Fredericton, New Brunswick
CIXXFM London, Ontario
CIYN-FM Kincardine, Ontario
CIZLFM Regina, Saskatchewan
CIZZ-FM Red Deer, Alberta
CJABFM Chicoutimi, Quebec
CJAI-FM Stella, Ontario
CJAM-FM Windsor, Ontario
CJAN-FM Asbestos, Quebec
CJAQ-FM Calgary, Alberta
CJAS-FM Saint Augustin, Quebec
CJAT-FM Trail, British Columbia
CJAV-FM Port Alberni, British Columbia
CJAW-FM Moose Jaw, Saskatchewan
CJAYFM Calgary, Alberta
CJBB-FM Englehart, Ontario
CJBC-FM-4 London, Ontario
CJBCFM Toronto, Ontario
CJBE-FM Port-Menier, Quebec
CJBRFM Rimouski, Quebec
CJBXFM London, Ontario
CJBZ-FM Taber, Alberta
CJCD-FM Yellowknife, Northwest Territories
CJCD-FM-1 Hay River, Northwest Territories
CJCF-FM Cumberland House, Saskatchewan
CJCH-FM Halifax, Nova Scotia
CJCI-FM Prince George, British Columbia
CJCJ-FM Woodstock, New Brunswick
CJCY-FM Medicine Hat, Alberta
CJDJ-FM Saskatoon, Saskatchewan
CJDL-FM Tillsonburg, Ontario
CJDM-FM Drummondville, Quebec
CJDR-FM Fernie, British Columbia
CJDS-FM Saint Pamphile, Quebec
CJDV-FM Cambridge, Ontario
CJEB-FM Trois Rivieres, Quebec
CJEC-FM Quebec, Quebec
CJED-FM Niagara Falls, Ontario
CJEF-FM Saint John, New Brunswick
CJEG-FM Bonnyville, Alberta
CJEL-FM Winkler, Manitoba
CJEM-FM Edmundston, New Brunswick
CJET-FM Smiths Falls, Ontario
CJFB-FM Bolton, Ontario
CJFH-FM Woodstock, Ontario
CJFMFM Montreal, Quebec
CJFO-FM Ottawa, Ontario
CJFWFM Terrace, British Columbia
CJFX-FM Antigonish, Nova Scotia
CJFY-FM Blackville, New Brunswick
CJGM-FM Gananoque, Ontario
CJGV-FM Winnipeg, Manitoba
CJGY-FM Grande Prairie, Alberta
CJHD-FM North Battleford, Saskatchewan
CJHK-FM Bridgewater, Nova Scotia
CJHR-FM Renfrew, Ontario
CJIE-FM Winnepeg Beach, Manitoba
CJIJ-FM Sydney, Nova Scotia
CJIQ-FM Paris, Ontario
CJIT-FM Lac Megantic, Quebec
CJIV-FM Dryden, Ontario
CJJC-FM Yorkton, Saskatchewan
CJJJ-FM Brandon, Manitoba
CJJM-FM Espanola, Ontario
CJJRFM Vancouver, British Columbia
CJKC-FM Kamloops, British Columbia
CJKK-FM Clarenville, Newfoundland
CJKL-FM Kirkland Lake, Ontario
CJKX-FM Ajax, Ontario
CJLAFM Lachute, Quebec
CJLD-FM Leduc, Alberta
CJLF-FM Barrie, Ontario
CJLJ-FM Williams Lake, British Columbia
CJLL-FM Ottawa, Ontario
CJLM-FM Joliette, Quebec
CJLR-FM La Ronge, Saskatchewan
CJLS-FM-1 Barrington, Nova Scotia
CJLS-FM-2 New Tusket, Nova Scotia
CJLSFM Barrington, Nova Scotia
CJLX Belleville, Ontario
CJLY-FM Nelson, British Columbia
CJMB-FM Peterborough, Ontario
CJMC-FM Sainte Anne des Monts, Quebec
CJMFFM Quebec, Quebec
CJMGFM Penticton, British Columbia
CJMI-FM Strathroy, Ontario
CJMJ Ottawa, Ontario
CJMK-FM Saskatoon, Saskatchewan
CJMM-FM Rouyn-Noranda, Quebec
CJMOFM Moncton, New Brunswick
CJMP-FM Powell River, British Columbia
CJMQ-FM Sherbrooke, Quebec
CJMV-FM Val d'Or, Quebec
CJMXFM Sudbury, Ontario
CJNE-FM Nipawin, Saskatchewan
CJNI-FM Halifax, Nova Scotia
CJNS-FM Meadow Lake, Saskatchewan
CJNU-FM Winnipeg, Manitoba
CJOA-FM Thunder Bay, Ontario
CJOC-FM Lethbridge, Alberta
CJOI-FM Rimouski, Quebec
CJOJ-FM Belleville, Ontario
CJOK-FM Fort McMurray, Alberta
CJOS-FM Owen Sound, Ontario
CJOT-FM Ottawa, Ontario
CJOZ-FM Bonavista Bay, Newfoundland
CJPG-FM Portage la Prairie, Manitoba
CJPN-FM Fredericton, New Brunswick
CJPR-FM Blairmore, Alberta
CJPT-FM Brockville, Ontario
CJPX-FM Montreal, Quebec
CJQMFM Sault Ste Marie, Ontario
CJQQ-FM Timmins, Ontario
CJRC-FM Gatineau, Quebec
CJRD-FM Drummondville, Quebec
CJREFM Riviere Au Renar, Quebec
CJRGFM Gaspe, Quebec
CJRI-FM Fredericton, New Brunswick
CJRL-FM Kenora, Ontario
CJRM-FM Labrador City, Newfoundland
CJRQFM Victoria, British Columbia
CJRT Toronto, Ontario
CJRW-FM Summerside, Prince Edward Island
CJRX-FM Lethbridge, Alberta
CJRY-FM Edmonton, Alberta
CJSA Toronto, Ontario
CJSB-FM Swan River, Manitoba
CJSDFM Thunder Bay, Ontario
CJSEFM Shediac, New Brunswick
CJSF-FM Burnaby, British Columbia
CJSI-FM Calgary, Alberta
CJSO-FM Sorel, Quebec
CJSP Leamington, Ontario
CJSQ-FM Quebec, Quebec
CJSR-FM Edmonton, Alberta
CJSS-FM Cornwall, Ontario
CJSU-FM Duncan, British Columbia
CJSWFM Calgary, Alberta
CJTB-FM Tete-a-la-Baleine, Quebec
CJTK-FM Sudbury, Ontario
CJTN-FM Quinte West, Ontario
CJTR-FM Regina, Saskatchewan
CJTW-FM Kitchener-Waterloo, Ontario
CJUI-FM Kelowna, British Columbia
CJUK-FM Thunder Bay, Ontario
CJUM-FM Winnipeg, Manitoba
CJUV-FM Lacombe, Alberta
CJVD-FM Vaudreuil-Dorion, Quebec
CJVF-FM Scarborough, Ontario
CJVR-FM Melfort, Saskatchewan
CJWA-FM Wawa, Ontario
CJWL-FM Ottawa, Ontario
CJXK-FM Cold Lake, Alberta
CJXL-FM Moncton, New Brunswick
CJXX-FM Grande Prairie, Alberta
CJXY-FM Burlington, Ontario
CJYCFM Saint John, New Brunswick
CJZN-FM Victoria, British Columbia
CKAG-FM Pikogan, Quebec
CKAJ-FM Jonquiere, Quebec
CKAP-FM Kapuskasing, Ontario
CKAU-FM Maliotenam, Quebec
CKAV-FM Toronto, Ontario
CKAV-FM-2 Vancouver, British Columbia
CKAV-FM-3 Calgary, Alberta
CKAV-FM-4 Edmonton, Alberta
CKAV-FM-9 Ottawa, Ontario
CKAY-FM Sechelt, British Columbia
CKBA(FM) Athabasca, Alberta
CKBC-FM Bathurst, New Brunswick
CKBK-FM Thamesville, Ontario
CKBL-FM Saskatoon, Saskatchewan
CKBN Becancour and Nicolet, Quebec
CKBT-FM Kitchener-Waterloo, Ontario
CKBW-FM Bridgewater, Nova Scotia
CKBYFM Ottawa, Ontario
CKBZ-FM Kamloops, British Columbia
CKCB-FM Collingwood, Ontario
CKCE-FM Calgary, Alberta
CKCH-FM Sydney, Nova Scotia
CKCK-FM Regina, Saskatchewan
CKCN-FM Sept-Iles, Quebec
CKCQ-FM Quesnel, British Columbia
CKCR-FM Revelstoke, British Columbia
CKCUFM Ottawa, Ontario
CKCW-FM Moncton, New Brunswick
CKDG-FM Montreal, Quebec
CKDH-FM Amherst, Nova Scotia
CKDJ-FM Ottawa, Ontario
CKDKFM Woodstock, Ontario
CKDR-FM Dryden, Ontario
CKDR-FM-2 Sioux Lookout, Ontario
CKDR-FM-5 Red Lake, Ontario
CKDU-FM Halifax, Nova Scotia
CKDV-FM Prince George, British Columbia
CKDX-FM Newmarket, Ontario
CKEA-FM Edmonton, Alberta
CKEB-FM Ebb and Flow, Manitoba
CKEC-FM New Glasgow, Nova Scotia
CKEN-FM Kentville, Nova Scotia
CKER-FM Edmonton, Alberta
CKEZ-FM Pictou, Nova Scotia
CKFI-FM Swift Current, Saskatchewan
CKFMFM Toronto, Ontario
CKFU-FM Fort St. John, British Columbia
CKFX-FM North Bay, Ontario
CKGB-FM Timmins, Ontario
CKGE-FM Oshawa, Ontario
CKGF-FM-2 Greenwood, British Columbia
CKGN-FM Kapuskasing, Ontario
CKGO-FM-1 Boston Bar, British Columbia
CKGR-FM Golden, British Columbia
CKGS-FM La Baie, Quebec
CKGW-FM Chatham, Ontario
CKGY-FM Red Deer, Alberta
CKHA-FM Haliburton, Ontario
CKHC-FM Toronto, Ontario
CKHK-FM Hawkesbury, Ontario
CKHL-FM High Level, Alberta
CKHR-FM Hay River, Northwest Territories
CKHY-FM Halifax, Nova Scotia
CKHZ-FM Halifax, Nova Scotia
CKIA-FM Quebec, Quebec
CKII-FM Dolbeau-Mistassini, Quebec
CKIN-FM Montreal, Quebec
CKIQFM Big White Ski, British Columbia
CKISFM Winnipeg, Manitoba
CKIX-FM Saint John's, Newfoundland
CKIZ-FM Vernon, British Columbia
CKJJ-FM Belleville, Ontario
CKJM-FM Cheticamp, Nova Scotia
CKJN-FM Haldimand County, Ontario
CKJX-FM Olds, Alberta

CKKC-FM Nelson, British Columbia
CKKI-FM Kahnawake, Quebec
CKKL Ottawa, Ontario
CKKN-FM Prince George, British Columbia
CKKO-FM Kelowna, British Columbia
CKKQ-FM Victoria, British Columbia
CKKSFM Vancouver, British Columbia
CKKV-FM Kemptville, Ontario
CKKW-FM Kitchener, Ontario
CKKX-FM Peace River, Alberta
CKLB-FM Yellowknife, Northwest Territories
CKLC-FM Kingston, Ontario
CKLD-FM Thetford Mines, Quebec
CKLEFM Rimouski, Quebec
CKLF-FM Brandon, Manitoba
CKLG-FM Vancouver, British Columbia
CKLHFM Hamilton, Ontario
CKLJ-FM Olds, Alberta
CKLM-FM Lloydminster, Alberta
CKLPFM Parry Sound, Ontario
CKLR-FM Courtenay, British Columbia
CKLU-FM Sudbury, Ontario
CKLX Montreal, Quebec
CKLY-FM Lindsay (city of Kawartha Lakes), Ontario
CKLZ-FM Kelowna, British Columbia
CKMA-FM Miramichi, New Brunswick
CKMB Barrie, Ontario
CKMFFM Montreal, Quebec
CKMH-FM Medicine Hat, Alberta
CKMM-FM Winnipeg, Manitoba
CKMN-FM Rimouski-Mont Joli, Quebec
CKMQ-FM Merritt, British Columbia
CKMSFM Waterloo, Ontario
CKMV-FM Grand Falls, New Brunswick
CKNA-FM Natashquan, Quebec
CKNG-FM Edmonton, Alberta
CKNI-FM Moncton, New Brunswick
CKNL-FM Fort St. John, British Columbia
CKNO-FM Edmonton, Alberta
CKNR-FM Elliot Lake, Ontario
CKNXFM Wingham, Ontario
CKOA-FM Glace Bay, Nova Scotia
CKOB-FM Trois Rivieres, Quebec
CKOD-FM Valleyfield, Quebec
CKOE-FM Moncton, New Brunswick
CKON-FM Akwesasne, Ontario
CKOO-FM Broadview, Saskatchewan
CKOS-FM Fort McMurray, Alberta
CKOTFM Tillsonburg, Ontario
CKOV-FM Medicine Hat, Alberta
CKOY-FM Sherbrooke, Quebec
CKOZ-FM Corner Brook, Newfoundland
CKPCFM Brantford, Ontario
CKPE-FM Sydney, Nova Scotia
CKPK-FM Vancouver, British Columbia
CKPM-FM Port Moody, British Columbia
CKPR-FM Thunder Bay, Ontario
CKPT-FM Peterborough, Ontario
CKQB Ottawa, Ontario
CKQC-FM Abbotsford, British Columbia
CKQK-FM Charlottetown, Prince Edward Island
CKQMFM Peterborough, Ontario
CKQN-FM Baker Lake, Nunavut
CKQQ-FM Kelowna, British Columbia
CKQR-FM Castlegar, British Columbia
CKQV-FM Vermillion Bay, Ontario
CKRA-FM Edmonton, Alberta
CKRB-FM Saint Georges-de-Beauce, Quebec
CKRC-FM Weyburn, Saskatchewan
CKRD-FM Red Deer, Alberta
CKRH-FM Halifax, Nova Scotia
CKRI-FM Red Deer, Alberta
CKRK-FM Kahnawake, Quebec
CKRLFM Quebec, Quebec
CKROFM Inkerman, New Brunswick
CKRP-FM Falher, Alberta
CKRS-FM Saguenay, Quebec
CKRU-FM Petersborough, Ontario
CKRV-FM Kamloops, British Columbia
CKRW-FM Whitehorse, Yukon Territory
CKRX-FM Fort Nelson, British Columbia
CKRYFM Calgary, Alberta
CKRZ-FM Ohsweken, Ontario
CKSA-FM Lloydminster, Alberta
CKSE-FM Estevan, Saskatchewan
CKSG-FM Cobourg, Ontario
CKSJ-FM Saint John's, Newfoundland
CKSO-FM Sudbury, Ontario
CKSRFM Chilliwack, British Columbia
CKSS-FM Red Rocks, Newfoundland
CKSYFM Chatham, Ontario
CKTF Hull, Quebec
CKTI-FM Kettle Point, Ontario
CKTK-FM Kitimat, British Columbia
CKTOFM Truro, Nova Scotia
CKTP-FM Fredericton Centre, New Brunswick
CKTY-FM Truro, Nova Scotia
CKTZ-FM Cortes Island, British Columbia
CKUA-FM Edmonton, Alberta
CKUE-FM Chatham, Ontario
CKUJ-FM Kuujjuaq, Quebec
CKUL-FM Halifax, Nova Scotia
CKUM Moncton, New Brunswick
CKUN-FM Christian Island, Ontario
CKUT Montreal, Quebec
CKUV-FM High River-Okotoks, Alberta
CKUW-FM Winnipeg, Manitoba
CKVH-FM High Prairie, Alberta
CKVI-FM Kingston, Ontario
CKVL-FM Montreal (zone LaSalle), Quebec
CKVM-FM Ville-Marie, Quebec
CKVN-FM Lethbridge, Alberta
CKVX Vancouver, British Columbia
CKWB-FM Westlock, Alberta
CKWE-FM Maniwaki (Kitigan Zibi Anishinabeg, Quebec
CKWF-FM Peterborough, Ontario
CKWMFM Kentville, Nova Scotia
CKWR Waterloo, Ontario
CKWS-FM Kingston, Ontario
CKWT-FM Sioux Lookout, Ontario
CKWV-FM Nanaimo, British Columbia
CKWY-FM Wainwright, Alberta
CKX-FM Brandon, Manitoba
CKXA-FM Brandon, Manitoba
CKXC-FM Kingston, Ontario
CKXD-FM Gander, Newfoundland
CKXG-FM Grand Falls-Windsor, Newfoundland
CKXL-FM Saint Boniface, Manitoba
CKXO-FM Chibougamau, Quebec
CKXR-FM Salmon Arm, British Columbia
CKXU-FM Lethbridge, Alberta
CKXX-FM Corner Brook, Newfoundland
CKY-FM Winnipeg, Manitoba
CKYC-FM Owen Sound, Ontario
CKYE-FM Vancouver, British Columbia
CKYK-FM Alma, Quebec
CKYM-FM Napanee, Ontario
CKYQ Plessisville, Quebec
CKYX-FM Fort McMurray, Alberta
CKZP-FM Zenon Park, Saskatchewan
CKZX-FM New Denver, British Columbia
CKZZ-FM Vancouver, British Columbia
KORU Garapan-Saipan, Guam
KPXP Garapan-Saipan, Guam
KRNM Chalan Kanoa-Saipan, Guam
KRSI Garapan-Saipan, Guam
KWAW Garapan-Saipan, Guam
KZMI Garapan-Saipan, Guam
VOCM-FM Saint John's, Newfoundland

Canadian AM Stations by Frequency

1010 khz
CBR Calgary, Alberta
CFRB Toronto, Ontario

1040 khz
CKST Vancouver, British Columbia

1050 khz
CHUM Toronto, Ontario
CKSB St. Boniface, Manitoba

1060 khz
CKMX Calgary, Alberta

1070 khz
CFAX Victoria, British Columbia
CHOK Sarnia, Ontario

1080 khz
CKKY Wainwright, Alberta
KCNM Saipan, Guam

1130 khz
CKWX Vancouver, British Columbia

1140 khz
CBI Sydney, Nova Scotia
CHRB High River, Alberta

1150 khz
CKFR Kelowna, British Columbia
CKOC Hamilton, Ontario

1190 khz
CFSL Weyburn, Saskatchewan
CJMR Mississauga, Ontario
WMEJ , Mississippi

1200 khz
CFGO Ottawa, Ontario
CKOT Tillsonburg, Ontario
CJRJ Vancouver, British Columbia

1210 khz
CFYM Kindersley, Saskatchewan
VOAR St. John's, Newfoundland

1220 khz
CJRB Boissevain, Manitoba
CKSM Shawinigan, Quebec

1230 khz
CFFB Iqaluit, Northwest Territories
CFLN Goose Bay, Newfoundland

1240 khz
CFLM La Tuque, Quebec
CFNI Port Hardy, British Columbia
CJAR The Pas, Manitoba
CJCS Stratford, Ontario
CJNS Meadow Lake, Saskatchewan
CJOR(AM) Osoyoos, British Columbia
CKIM Baie Verte, Newfoundland

1250 khz
CHSM Steinbach, Manitoba
CJYE Oakville, Ontario

1260 khz
CFRN Edmonton, Alberta
CKHJ(AM) Fredericton, New Brunswick

1270 khz
CJCB Sydney, Nova Scotia

1280 khz
CFMB Montreal, Quebec
CJMS Montreal, Quebec
CJSL Estevan, Saskatchewan

1290 khz
CFRW Winnipeg, Manitoba
CJBK London, Ontario

1310 khz
CHLW St. Paul, Alberta
CIWW Ottawa, Ontario

1320 khz
CHMB Vancouver, British Columbia

1330 khz
CJYM Rosetown, Saskatchewan

1340 khz
CBGN(AM) Sainte Anne des Monts, Quebec
CFKC Creston, British Columbia
CFYK Yellow Knife, Northwest Territories
CIVH Vanderhoof, British Columbia

1350 khz
CKAD Middleton, Nova Scotia

1380 khz
CKPC Brantford, Ontario

1400 khz
CBG Gander, Newfoundland
CIOR(AM) Princeton, British Columbia

1410 khz
CFTE Vancouver, British Columbia
CKSL London, Ontario

1420 khz
CKDY Digby, Nova Scotia

1430 khz
CHKT(AM) Toronto, Ontario

1440 khz
CKJR Wetaskiwin, Alberta

1449 khz
V6AH(AM) Pohnpei, 66

1450 khz
CFAB Windsor, Nova Scotia
CHMO(AM) Moosonee, Ontario
CHOU Montreal, Quebec

1460 khz
CJOY Guelph, Ontario

1470 khz
CJVB Vancouver, British Columbia

1490 khz
CFNC(AM) Cross Lake, Manitoba
CJSN Shaunavon, Saskatchewan

1494 khz
V6AI(AM) Yap, 66

1510 khz
CJRS Sherbrooke, Quebec

1540 khz
CHIN Toronto, Ontario

1570 khz
CKMW Morden, Manitoba
CJLV Laval, Quebec

1580 khz
CKDO Oshawa, Ontario

1593 khz
V6AK(AM) Truk, 66

1610 khz
CFOS Collingwood, Ontario
CJWI Montreal, Quebec
CHHA Toronto, Ontario

1650 khz
CINA Mississauga, Ontario

1690 khz
CHTO Toronto, Ontario
CJLO Montreal, Quebec

540 khz
CBK Watrous, Saskatchewan
CBKF-1(AM) Gravelbourg, Saskatchewan
CBT Grand Falls, Alberta

560 khz
CHTK Prince Rupert, British Columbia

570 khz
CFCB Corner Brook, Newfoundland
CKGL(AM) Kitchener, Ontario
CKSW Swift Current, Saskatchewan
CKWL Williams Lake, British Columbia

580 khz
CFRA Ottawa, Ontario
CKUA Edmonton, Alberta
CKWW Windsor, Ontario

590 khz
CFAR Flin Flon, Manitoba
CFTK Terrace, British Columbia
CJCL Toronto, Ontario
CJCW Sussex, New Brunswick
VOCM St. John's, Newfoundland

600 khz
CFCT Tuktoyaktuk, Northwest Territories
CKAT(AM) North Bay, Ontario

610 khz
CHNL Kamloops, British Columbia
CHTM Thompson, Manitoba
CKTB St. Catharines, Ontario
CKYL Peace River, Alberta

620 khz
CFRP Forestville, Quebec
CKRM(AM) Regina, Saskatchewan
CKCM Grand Falls, Newfoundland

630 khz
CFCO Chatham, Ontario
CHED Edmonton, Alberta

640 khz
CBN St. John's, Newfoundland
CFMJ Richmond Hill, Ontario

650 khz
CKOM Saskatoon, Saskatchewan
CISL Richmond, British Columbia
CKGA Gander, Newfoundland

660 khz
CFFR Calgary, Alberta

680 khz
CFTR Toronto, Ontario
CHFA Edmonton, Alberta
CJOB Winnipeg, Manitoba

690 khz
CBU Vancouver, British Columbia
CKGM Montreal, Quebec

710 khz
CKVO Clarenville, Newfoundland

730 khz
CKAC Montreal, Quebec
CKDM Dauphin, Manitoba
CHMJ Vancouver, British Columbia

740 khz
CBX Edmonton, Alberta
CHCM Marystown, Newfoundland
CFZM(AM) Toronto, Ontario

750 khz
CBGY Bonavista Bay, Newfoundland
CKJH(AM) Melfort, Saskatchewan
CJWW Saskatoon, Saskatchewan

760 khz
CFLD Burns Lake, British Columbia
CJME Regina, Saskatchewan

770 khz
CHQR Calgary, Alberta

780 khz
CFDR Dartmouth, Nova Scotia

790 khz
CFCW Camrose, Alberta
CFNW Port Au Choix, Newfoundland
CIAO Brampton, Ontario
CIGM Sudbury, Ontario

800 khz
CHAB Moose Jaw, Saskatchewan
CHRC Quebec, Quebec
CJAD Montreal, Quebec
CJBQ Belleville, Ontario
CKLW Windsor, Ontario
CKOR Penticton, British Columbia
VOWR St. John's, Newfoundland

810 khz
CJVA Caraquet, New Brunswick
CKJS Winnipeg, Manitoba

820 khz
CHAM Hamilton, Ontario

840 khz
CKBX One Hundred Mile Hou, British Columbia

860 khz
CBKF-2(AM) Saskatoon, Saskatchewan
CFPR Prince Rupert, British Columbia
CHAK Inuvik, Northwest Territories
CJBC Toronto, Ontario

870 khz
CFBV Smithers, British Columbia
CFSX Stephenville, Newfoundland
CKIR Invermere, British Columbia

880 khz
CHQT Edmonton, Alberta
CKLQ Brandon, Manitoba

890 khz
CJDC Dawson Creek, British Columbia

900 khz
CHML Hamilton, Ontario
CKBI Prince Albert, Saskatchewan

910 khz
CKDQ Drumheller, Alberta

920 khz
CFRY Portage La Prairie, Manitoba
CKNX Wingham, Ontario

930 khz
CFBC Saint John, New Brunswick
CJCA Edmonton, Alberta
CJYQ St. John's, Newfoundland

940 khz
CJGX Yorkton, Saskatchewan

950 khz
CFAM Altona, Manitoba
CKNB Campbellton, New Brunswick

960 khz
CFAC Calgary, Alberta

980 khz
CFPL London, Ontario
CKNW New Westminster, British Columbia

990 khz
CBOF-1(AM) Maniwaki, Quebec
CBW Winnipeg, Manitoba
CBY Corner Brook, Newfoundland

Canadian FM Stations by Frequency

100.1 mhz

CIOOFM Halifax, Nova Scotia
CJCD-FM Yellowknife, Northwest Territories
CJCD-FM-1 Hay River, Northwest Territories
CKAG-FM Pikogan, Quebec
CHCQ-FM Belleville, Ontario
CKBZ-FM Kamloops, British Columbia
CHFN-FM Cape Croker (Neyaashiinigmiing), Ontario
CKFU-FM Fort St. John, British Columbia
CJEB-FM Trois Rivieres, Quebec
CKVL-FM Montreal (zone LaSalle), Quebec
CJVD-FM Vaudreuil-Dorion, Quebec

100.3 mhz

CFBR-FM Edmonton, Alberta
CFOZ-FM Argentia, Newfoundland
CHVD-FM Dolbeau-Mistassini, Quebec
CJLF-FM Barrie, Ontario
CJMC-FM Sainte Anne des Monts, Quebec
CJMJ Ottawa, Ontario
CKKQ-FM Victoria, British Columbia
CKRZ-FM Ohsweken, Ontario
KWAW Garapan-Saipan, Guam
CKCQ-FM Quesnel, British Columbia
CHTN-FM Charlottetown, Prince Edward Island
CFAQ-FM Blucher, Saskatchewan

100.5 mhz

CBBLFM London, Ontario
CFIN-FM Lac-Etchemin, Quebec
CFROFM Vancouver, British Columbia
CHASFM Sault Ste Marie, Ontario
CHUR-FM North Bay, Ontario
CIBO-FM Senneterre, Quebec
CIOK-FM Saint John, New Brunswick
CHLS-FM Lillooet, British Columbia
CHFT-FM Fort McMurray, Alberta
CKRU-FM Petersborough, Ontario

100.7 mhz

CBFX-FM Montreal, Quebec
CHINFM Toronto, Ontario
CIGVFM Penticton, British Columbia
CIAJ-FM Prince Rupert, British Columbia
CILG-FM Moose Jaw, Saskatchewan
CFJL-FM Winnipeg, Manitoba
CIAY-FM Whitehorse, Yukon Territory
CKRI-FM Red Deer, Alberta
CJHK-FM Bridgewater, Nova Scotia
CJLJ-FM Williams Lake, British Columbia

100.9 mhz

CBJX-FM Chicoutimi, Quebec
CBWK-FM Thompson, Manitoba
CHXX-FM Donnacona, Quebec
CKTOFM Truro, Nova Scotia
CKAP-FM Kapuskasing, Ontario
CKUV-FM High River-Okotoks, Alberta
CKHA-FM Haliburton, Ontario

101.1 mhz

CFMIFM New Westminster, British Columbia
CIQB-FM Barrie, Ontario
CFLZ-FM Fort Erie, Ontario
CKXA-FM Brandon, Manitoba
CHEQFM Smiths Falls, Ontario
CFIF-FM Iroquois Falls, Ontario
CKSJ-FM Saint John's, Newfoundland
CIXF-FM Brooks, Alberta
CKSO-FM Sudbury, Ontario
CHLI-FM Rossland, British Columbia
CKMQ-FM Merritt, British Columbia

101.3 mhz

CKKN-FM Prince George, British Columbia
CKOTFM Tillsonburg, Ontario
CKUN-FM Christian Island, Ontario
CKII-FM Dolbeau-Mistassini, Quebec
CJSA Toronto, Ontario
CJEG-FM Bonnyville, Alberta
CJCH-FM Halifax, Nova Scotia
CKEB-FM Ebb and Flow, Manitoba

101.5 mhz

CBZ-FM Fredericton, New Brunswick
CHIPFM Fort-Coulonge, Quebec
CIBL-FM Montreal, Quebec
CILKFM Kelowna, British Columbia
CIOI-FM Hamilton, Ontario
CBRXFM Rimouski, Quebec
CJUM-FM Winnipeg, Manitoba
CKWF-FM Peterborough, Ontario
CJKL-FM Kirkland Lake, Ontario
CIGO-FM Port Hawkesbury, Nova Scotia
CJBRFM Rimouski, Quebec
CHQX-FM Prince Albert, Saskatchewan
CFRMFM St Boniface, Manitoba
CKNL-FM Fort St. John, British Columbia
CKCE-FM Calgary, Alberta

101.7 mhz

CBQ-FM Thunder Bay, Ontario
CJSO-FM Sorel, Quebec
CKER-FM Edmonton, Alberta
CKNXFM Wingham, Ontario
CHRG-FM Maria (Reserve), Quebec
CHLY-FM Nanaimo, British Columbia
CKDH-FM Amherst, Nova Scotia

101.9 mhz

CFRCFM Kingston, Ontario
CFUVFM Victoria, British Columbia
CHAI-FM Chateauguay, Quebec
CHFXFM Halifax, Nova Scotia
CITRFM Vancouver, British Columbia
CJSS-FM Cornwall, Ontario
CKFX-FM North Bay, Ontario
CKLB-FM Yellowknife, Northwest Territories
CFDA-FM Victoriaville, Quebec
CFND-FM Saint Jerome, Quebec
CIDG-FM Ottawa, Ontario

102.1 mhz

CBR-FM Calgary, Alberta
CFEL-FM Levis, Quebec
CFNYFM Brampton, Ontario
CHPR-FM Hawkesbury, Ontario
CISWFM Whistler, British Columbia
CJDJ-FM Saskatoon, Saskatchewan
CKHL-FM High Level, Alberta
CJRW-FM Summerside, Prince Edward Island
CJCY-FM Medicine Hat, Alberta

102.3 mhz

CIGBFM Trois-Rivieres, Quebec
CINQFM Montreal, Quebec
CKDKFM Woodstock, Ontario
CKRX-FM Fort Nelson, British Columbia
CKWV-FM Nanaimo, British Columbia
CHST-FM London, Ontario
CKXG-FM Grand Falls-Windsor, Newfoundland
CHSN-FM Estevan, Saskatchewan
CKY-FM Winnipeg, Manitoba
CKJJ-FM Belleville, Ontario
CJNS-FM Meadow Lake, Saskatchewan
CKNO-FM Edmonton, Alberta
CINA-FM Windsor, Ontario

102.5 mhz

CBOX-FM Ottawa, Ontario

102.7 mhz

CBH-FM Halifax, Nova Scotia
CITE-FM-1 Sherbrooke, Quebec
CJMV-FM Val d'Or, Quebec
CKZP-FM Zenon Park, Saskatchewan
CFGI-FM Georgina Island, Ontario
CILU-FM Thunder Bay, Ontario
CIWS-FM Whitchurch-Stouffville, Ontario
CHOP-FM Newmarket, Ontario
CKPK-FM Vancouver, British Columbia

102.9 mhz

CFOM-FM Levis, Quebec
CKLHFM Hamilton, Ontario
CJOI-FM Rimouski, Quebec
CHCR-FM Killaloe, Ontario
CHDR-FM Cranbrook, British Columbia
CHDI-FM Edmonton, Alberta

103.1 mhz

CFHK-FM St. Thomas, Ontario
CFMF-FM Fermont, Quebec
CFMXFM Cobourg, Ontario
CJFWFM Terrace, British Columbia
CJMOFM Moncton, New Brunswick
CJRGFM Gaspe, Quebec
CKMM-FM Winnipeg, Manitoba
CHTT-FM Victoria, British Columbia
CKOD-FM Valleyfield, Quebec
CJBB-FM Englehart, Ontario
CIAU-FM Radisson, Quebec
CFXL-FM Calgary, Alberta
CJKC-FM Kamloops, British Columbia
CHHO-FM Louiseville, Quebec
CKQQ-FM Kelowna, British Columbia

103.3 mhz

CBOQ-FM Ottawa, Ontario
CHAA-FM Longueuil, Quebec
CKLPFM Parry Sound, Ontario
CKQV-FM Vermillion Bay, Ontario

103.5 mhz

CHQMFM Vancouver, British Columbia
CIDCFM Orangeville, Ontario
CJLM-FM Joliette, Quebec
CKRB-FM Saint Georges-de-Beauce, Quebec
CJEF-FM Saint John, New Brunswick
CHMM-FM MacKenzie, British Columbia
CKHZ-FM Halifax, Nova Scotia
CHNV-FM Nelson, British Columbia
CKRC-FM Weyburn, Saskatchewan
CFCH-FM Chase, British Columbia
CKCH-FM Sydney, Nova Scotia

103.7 mhz

CFBU-FM Saint Catharines, Ontario
CJPT-FM Brockville, Ontario
CKRK-FM Kahnawake, Quebec
CIMI-FM Charlesbourg, Quebec
CFID-FM Acton Vale, Quebec
CHXL Brockville, Ontario
CFVR-FM Fort McMurray, Alberta

103.9 mhz

CFQMFM Moncton, New Brunswick
CIMEFM Saint Jerome, Quebec
CIMS-FM Balmoral, New Brunswick
CISN-FM Edmonton, Alberta
CKXX-FM Corner Brook, Newfoundland
KZMI Garapan-Saipan, Guam
CKWE-FM Maniwaki (Kitigan Zibi Anishinabeg, Quebec
CHNO-FM Sudbury, Ontario
CBRFFM Calgary, Alberta
CIRR-FM Toronto, Ontario
CJAW-FM Moose Jaw, Saskatchewan
CHVO-FM Carbonear, Newfoundland
CJUI-FM Kelowna, British Columbia

104.1 mhz

CFQXFM Selkirk, Manitoba
CFZZ-FM Saint Jean-Iberville, Quebec
CICZ Midland, Ontario
CIFA-FM Comeauville, Nova Scotia
CKTF Hull, Quebec
CHYK-FM Timmins, Ontario
CKNA-FM Natashquan, Quebec
CJCJ-FM Woodstock, New Brunswick
CHAD-FM Dawson Creek, British Columbia
CIOT-FM Nipawin, Saskatchewan

104.3 mhz

CBF-FM-1 Trois Rivieres, Quebec
CFRQFM Dartmouth, Nova Scotia
CJQMFM Sault Ste Marie, Ontario
CHGO-FM Val d'Or, Quebec
CKWS-FM Kingston, Ontario
CHHR-FM Vancouver, British Columbia
CKBK-FM Thamesville, Ontario
CICN-FM Marcelin, Saskatchewan

104.5 mhz

CFLGFM Cornwall, Ontario
CHUMFM Toronto, Ontario
CIKIFM Rimouski, Quebec
CISP-FM Pemberton, British Columbia
CKAU-FM Maliotenam, Quebec
CFQK-FM Kaministiquia, Ontario
CKOY-FM Sherbrooke, Quebec
CJRI-FM Fredericton, New Brunswick
CJSB-FM Swan River, Manitoba
CKJX-FM Olds, Alberta
CFGT-FM Alma, Quebec

104.7 mhz

CBVEFM Quebec, Quebec
CFLO-FM Mont-Laurier, Quebec
CIPN-FM Pender Harbour, British Columbia
CHBZ-FM Cranbrook, British Columbia
CKLZ-FM Kelowna, British Columbia
CHIMFM Kelowna, British Columbia
CIHR-FM Woodstock, Ontario
CJNU-FM Winnipeg, Manitoba
CJRC-FM Gatineau, Quebec
CFRI-FM Grande Prairie, Alberta
CFDY-FM Cochrane, Ontario

104.9 mhz

CBQLFM Savant Lake, Ontario
CFMG-FM Saint Albert, Alberta
CFWF-FM Regina, Saskatchewan
CISQFM Squamish, British Columbia
CJLAFM Lachute, Quebec
CHOCFM Saint Remi, Quebec
CFJR-FM Brockville, Ontario
CKBC-FM Bathurst, New Brunswick
CKVX Vancouver, British Columbia
CIMY-FM Pembroke, Ontario
CHWC-FM Goderich, Ontario
CFXM Granby, Quebec

105.1 mhz

CBI-FM Sydney, Nova Scotia
CBMR-FM Fermont, Quebec
CBQR-FM Rankin Inlet, Nunavut
CKQMFM Peterborough, Ontario
CKRYFM Calgary, Alberta
CITA-FM Moncton, New Brunswick
CFIC-FM Listuguj, Quebec
CJVR-FM Melfort, Saskatchewan
CJED-FM Niagara Falls, Ontario
CKDG-FM Montreal, Quebec
CHOQ-FM Toronto, Ontario
CKHY-FM Halifax, Nova Scotia

105.3 mhz

CFCAFM Kitchener, Ontario
CKBYFM Ottawa, Ontario
CHRD-FM Drummondville, Quebec
CJKK-FM Clarenville, Newfoundland
CJMXFM Sudbury, Ontario
CISS-FM Ottawa, Ontario
CFXY-FM Fredericton, New Brunswick
CHRM-FM Matane, Quebec
CIXM-FM Whitecourt, Alberta
CKMH-FM Medicine Hat, Alberta
CHOW-FM Amos, Quebec

105.5 mhz

CBKS-FM Saskatoon, Saskatchewan
CFBK-FM Huntsville, Ontario
CHRY-FM Toronto, Ontario
CKLD-FM Thetford Mines, Quebec
CHUB-FM Red Deer, Alberta
CICY-FM Selkirk, Manitoba
CKQK-FM Charlottetown, Prince Edward Island
CJFB-FM Bolton, Ontario

105.7 mhz

CBU-FM Vancouver, British Columbia
CFGLFM Laval, Quebec
CHREFM St Catharines, Ontario
CIKR-FM Kingston, Ontario
CFDM-FM Meadow Lake, Saskatchewan
CICF-FM Vernon, British Columbia
CHQC-FM Saint John, New Brunswick
CJMI-FM Strathroy, Ontario
CKGS-FM La Baie, Quebec
CIBQ-FM Brooks, Alberta
CKOO-FM Broadview, Saskatchewan

105.9 mhz

CBKA-FM La Ronge, Saskatchewan
CICX-FM Orillia, Ontario
CFEP-FM Eastern Passage, Nova Scotia
CHJX-FM London, Ontario
CHPD-FM Aylmer, Ontario
CJRY-FM Edmonton, Alberta
CJVF-FM Scarborough, Ontario

106.1 mhz

CHEZFM Ottawa, Ontario
CIMJ-FM Guelph, Ontario
CIMOFM Magog, Quebec
CKGO-FM-1 Boston Bar, British Columbia
CKJM-FM Cheticamp, Nova Scotia
CKLM-FM Lloydminster, Alberta
CKKX-FM Peace River, Alberta
CFIT-FM Airdrie, Alberta
CBAM-FM Moncton, New Brunswick
CKCR-FM Revelstoke, British Columbia
CHWE-FM Winnipeg, Manitoba
CKSE-FM Estevan, Saskatchewan

106.3 mhz

CBV-FM Quebec, Quebec
CHKS-FM Sarnia, Ontario
CFXN-FM North Bay, Ontario
CKAV-FM-2 Vancouver, British Columbia
CKGR-FM Golden, British Columbia
CISB-FM Marius, Manitoba
CKIN-FM Montreal, Quebec

106.5 mhz

CFEI St-Hyacinthe, Quebec
CIXK-FM Owen Sound, Ontario
CHMN-FM Canmore, Alberta
CKAV-FM Toronto, Ontario
CJJJ-FM Brandon, Manitoba
CIFN-FM Island Lake, Saskatchewan

106.7 mhz

CHCD Simcoe, Ontario
CJRX-FM Lethbridge, Alberta
CJIT-FM Lac Megantic, Quebec
CFET-FM Tagish, Yukon Territory
CFDV-FM Red Deer, Alberta
CHWY-FM Weyburn, Saskatchewan

106.9 mhz

CBN-FM Saint John's, Newfoundland
CHMA-FM Sackville, New Brunswick
CIBX-FM Fredericton, New Brunswick
CIXXFM London, Ontario
CKKC-FM Nelson, British Columbia
CKQB Ottawa, Ontario
CHRQ-FM Restigouche, Quebec
CHWF-FM Nanaimo, British Columbia
CKOB-FM Trois Rivieres, Quebec
CFYT-FM Dawson City, Yukon Territory

107.1 mhz

CIBMFM Riviere du Loup, Quebec
CILQFM Toronto, Ontario
CJWA-FM Wawa, Ontario
CKQC-FM Abbotsford, British Columbia
CFEQ-FM Winnipeg, Manitoba
CJTN-FM Quinte West, Ontario
CHNC-FM New Carlisle, Quebec

107.3 mhz

CITEFM Montreal, Quebec
CKHR-FM Hay River, Northwest Territories
CFGQ-FM Calgary, Alberta
CHBE-FM Victoria, British Columbia
CFMH-FM Saint John, New Brunswick
CHUK-FM Mashteuiatsh (Pointe-Bleue), Quebec
CFRT-FM Iqaluit, Nunavut
CKOE-FM Moncton, New Brunswick
CJDL-FM Tillsonburg, Ontario

107.5 mhz

CKSRFM Chilliwack, British Columbia
CIEG-FM Egmont, British Columbia
CISCFM Gibsons, British Columbia
CITFFM Quebec, Quebec
CJDV-FM Cambridge, Ontario
CFUN-FM Chilliwack, British Columbia
CKIZ-FM Vernon, British Columbia
CJIE-FM Winnepeg Beach, Manitoba
CHBO-FM Humboldt, Saskatchewan

107.7 mhz

CFAIFM Edmundston, New Brunswick
CFRV-FM Lethbridge, Alberta
CKMB Barrie, Ontario
CHGK-FM Stratford, Ontario
CJFY-FM Blackville, New Brunswick
CKTI-FM Kettle Point, Ontario
CKHK-FM Hawkesbury, Ontario

107.9 mhz

CBJEFM Chicoutimi, Quebec
CJXY-FM Burlington, Ontario
CINGFM Burlington, Ontario
CKDJ-FM Ottawa, Ontario
CHUC-FM Cobourg, Ontario
CILS-FM Victoria, British Columbia
CFTA-FM Amherst, Nova Scotia

84.1 mhz

CBYKFM Vancouver, British Columbia

88.1 mhz

CFRH-FM Penetanguishene, Ontario
KRNM Chalan Kanoa-Saipan, Guam
CHES-FM Erin, Ontario
CKAV-FM-3 Calgary, Alberta
CHLK-FM Perth, Ontario

88.3 mhz

CKIA-FM Quebec, Quebec
CJIQ-FM Paris, Ontario
CFAK-FM Sherbrooke, Quebec
CKXU-FM Lethbridge, Alberta

88.5 mhz

CBME-FM Montreal, Quebec
CJSR-FM Edmonton, Alberta
CKDX-FM Newmarket, Ontario
CIBH-FM Parksville, British Columbia
CILV-FM Ottawa, Ontario
CIVL-FM Abbotsford, British Columbia

88.7 mhz

CIMX Windsor, Ontario
CFUR-FM Prince George, British Columbia
CHIC-FM Rouyn-Noranda, Quebec
CKYM-FM Napanee, Ontario

88.9 mhz

CBTKFM Kelowna, British Columbia
CHONFM Whitehorse, Yukon Territory
CIRV-FM Toronto, Ontario
CJMQ-FM Sherbrooke, Quebec
CJSI-FM Calgary, Alberta
CHNI-FM Saint John, New Brunswick
CJRD-FM Drummondville, Quebec

89.1 mhz

CHUO-FM Ottawa, Ontario
CKRLFM Quebec, Quebec
CFOU-FM Trois Rivieres, Quebec

89.3 mhz

CISM-FM Montreal, Quebec
CBGA Gaspe, Quebec
CKGW-FM Chatham, Ontario
CKAV-FM-4 Edmonton, Alberta
CIJK-FM Kentville, Nova Scotia

89.5 mhz

CFGB-FM Happy Valley, Newfoundland
CIUTFM Toronto, Ontario
CJSEFM Shediac, New Brunswick
CJRL-FM Kenora, Ontario
CHWK-FM Chilliwack, British Columbia
CKTZ-FM Cortes Island, British Columbia

89.7 & 94.7mhz

CKGN-FM Kapuskasing, Ontario

89.7 mhz

CJSU-FM Duncan, British Columbia
CBCX-FM Calgary, Alberta
CKOA-FM Glace Bay, Nova Scotia

89.9 mhz

CBE-FM Windsor, Ontario
CBTEFM Crawford Bay, British Columbia
CFNK-FM Pinehouse Lake, Saskatchewan
CFWE-FM Lac La Biche, Alberta
CJCF-FM Cumberland House, Saskatchewan
CJLR-FM La Ronge, Saskatchewan
CFBS-FM Lourdes-de-Blanc-Sablon, Quebec
CIHT-FM Ottawa, Ontario
CHNS-FM Halifax, Nova Scotia
CKWT-FM Sioux Lookout, Ontario
KORU Garapan-Saipan, Guam
CKKI-FM Kahnawake, Quebec

90.1 mhz

CFJU-FM Kedgwick, New Brunswick
CBBSFM Sudbury, Ontario

CJSF-FM Burnaby, British Columbia
CJMP-FM Powell River, British Columbia
CHMZ-FM Tofino, British Columbia

90.3 mhz

CBEGFM Sarnia, Ontario
CJBCFM Toronto, Ontario
CKUT Montreal, Quebec
CFUL-FM Calgary, Alberta

90.5 mhz

CBCV-FM Victoria, British Columbia
CBHAFM Halifax, Nova Scotia
CBQTFM Fort Frances, Ontario
CFCR-FM Saskatoon, Saskatchewan
CJPN-FM Fredericton, New Brunswick
CJBE-FM Port-Menier, Quebec
CJMB-FM Peterborough, Ontario
CKBN Becancour and Nicolet, Quebec
CKRD-FM Red Deer, Alberta

90.7 mhz

CBOFFM Ottawa, Ontario
CFBO-FM Moncton, New Brunswick

90.9 mhz

CBX-FM Edmonton, Alberta
CION Quebec, Quebec
CJSWFM Calgary, Alberta
CBBX-FM Sudbury, Ontario
CBUX-FM Vancouver, British Columbia

91.1 mhz

CINN-FM Hearst, Ontario
CJRT Toronto, Ontario
CKXL-FM Saint Boniface, Manitoba
CFUT-FM Shawinigan, Quebec
CKOS-FM Fort McMurray, Alberta
CFAD-FM Salmo, British Columbia

91.3 mhz

CBD-FM Saint John, New Brunswick
CIRA Montreal, Quebec
CJLX Belleville, Ontario
CJTR-FM Regina, Saskatchewan
CJZN-FM Victoria, British Columbia
CFBW-FM Hanover, Ontario

91.5 mhz

CBO-FM Ottawa, Ontario
CBYG-FM Prince George, British Columbia
CBAX-FM Halifax, Nova Scotia
CKBT-FM Kitchener-Waterloo, Ontario
CKXR-FM Salmon Arm, British Columbia
CKPR-FM Thunder Bay, Ontario

91.7 mhz

CIXL-FM Welland, Ontario
CHBN-FM Edmonton, Alberta
CKAY-FM Sechelt, British Columbia
CICS-FM Sudbury, Ontario

91.9 mhz

CKLY-FM Lindsay (city of Kawartha Lakes), Ontario
CKVI-FM Kingston, Ontario
CJEC-FM Quebec, Quebec
CKLX Montreal, Quebec
CKNI-FM Moncton, New Brunswick

92.1 mhz

CFMQFM Regina, Saskatchewan
CFVD-FM-2 Pohenegamook, Quebec
CHMX-FM Regina, Saskatchewan
CHODFM Cornwall, Ontario
CITIFM Winnipeg, Manitoba
CJAYFM Calgary, Alberta
CJDM-FM Drummondville, Quebec
CJOZ-FM Bonavista Bay, Newfoundland
CJQQ-FM Timmins, Ontario
CJRQFM Victoria, British Columbia
CKPCFM Brantford, Ontario
CFNR-FM Terrace, British Columbia

92.3 mhz

CKOZ-FM Corner Brook, Newfoundland
CJET-FM Smiths Falls, Ontario
CFRK-FM Fredericton, New Brunswick
CJOS-FM Owen Sound, Ontario

92.5 mhz

CFQR-FM Montreal, Quebec
CKAJ-FM Jonquiere, Quebec
CKNG-FM Edmonton, Alberta
CFSRFM Abbotsford, British Columbia
CFBX-FM Kamloops, British Columbia

92.7 mhz

CFFF-FM Peterborough, Ontario
CFIM-FM Iles-de-la-Madeleine, Quebec
CJBXFM London, Ontario
CJEM-FM Edmundston, New Brunswick
CIAM-FM Fort Vermilion, Alberta
CKDR-FM Dryden, Ontario
CHSL-FM Slave Lake, Alberta
CJSQ-FM Quebec, Quebec
CJSP Leamington, Ontario
CHBD-FM Regina, Saskatchewan

92.9 mhz

CBBKFM Kingston, Ontario
CKBL-FM Saskatoon, Saskatchewan
CHYK-FM-3 Hearst, Ontario
CIBW-FM Drayton Valley, Alberta
CKJN-FM Haldimand County, Ontario
CFEX-FM Calgary, Alberta
CFSH-FM Apsley, Ontario

93.1 mhz

CFNOFM Marathon, Ontario
CHAYFM Barrie, Ontario
CHLQFM Charlottetown, Prince Edward Island
CKCUFM Ottawa, Ontario
CJXX-FM Grande Prairie, Alberta
CFOB-FM Fort Frances, Ontario
CHMT-FM Timmins, Ontario
CKVM-FM Ville-Marie, Quebec
CFRG-FM Gravelbourg, Saskatchewan
CKYE-FM Vancouver, British Columbia
CJTB-FM Tete-a-la-Baleine, Quebec
CFIS-FM Prince George, British Columbia
CJLD-FM Leduc, Alberta
CIHI-FM Fredericton, New Brunswick

93.3 mhz

CFMUFM Hamilton, Ontario
CFRUFM Guelph, Ontario
CJMFFM Quebec, Quebec
CJOK-FM Fort McMurray, Alberta
CJBZ-FM Taber, Alberta
CKSG-FM Cobourg, Ontario
CJAV-FM Port Alberni, British Columbia
CFXU-FM Antigonish, Nova Scotia
CFYX-FM Rimouski, Quebec
CJHD-FM North Battleford, Saskatchewan

93.5 mhz

CBCLFM London, Ontario
CBM-FM Montreal, Quebec
CHMR-FM Saint John's, Newfoundland
CJLS-FM-2 New Tusket, Nova Scotia
CKUM Moncton, New Brunswick
CKZX-FM New Denver, British Columbia
CJEL-FM Winkler, Manitoba
CFXJ-FM Toronto, Ontario
CIKX-FM Grand Falls, New Brunswick
CJAS-FM Saint Augustin, Quebec
CJLY-FM Nelson, British Columbia
CIHS-FM Wetaskiwin, Alberta
CKXO-FM Chibougamau, Quebec
CFZN-FM Haliburton, Ontario
CKXC-FM Kingston, Ontario
CKVH-FM High Prairie, Alberta

93.7 mhz

CBMIFM Baie-Comeau, Quebec
CJJRFM Vancouver, British Columbia
CBJ-FM Chicoutimi, Quebec
CKYC-FM Owen Sound, Ontario
CIFX-FM Lewisporte, Newfoundland
CFGE-FM Sherbrooke, Quebec
CKWY-FM Wainwright, Alberta
CKOV-FM Medicine Hat, Alberta
CJAI-FM Stella, Ontario
CKMA-FM Miramichi, New Brunswick

93.9 mhz

CIDR-FM Windsor, Ontario
CKKL Ottawa, Ontario
CFWC-FM Brantford, Ontario

94.1 mhz

CBL-FM Toronto, Ontario
CHSJ-FM Saint John, New Brunswick
CIMG-FM Swift Current, Saskatchewan
CKBA(FM) Athabasca, Alberta
CKNR-FM Elliot Lake, Ontario
CKCN-FM Sept-Iles, Quebec
CICU-FM Eskasoni Indian Reserve, Nova Scotia
CFGW-FM Yorkton, Saskatchewan
CJUV-FM Lacombe, Alberta
CJOC-FM Lethbridge, Alberta
CKEC-FM New Glasgow, Nova Scotia

94.3 mhz

CHIQFM Winnipeg, Manitoba
CHYZ-FM Sainte Foy, Quebec
CIRX-FM Prince George, British Columbia
CJSDFM Thunder Bay, Ontario
CKMFFM Montreal, Quebec
CJTW-FM Kitchener-Waterloo, Ontario
CJFH-FM Woodstock, Ontario
CFXE-FM Edson, Alberta

94.5 mhz

CFWH-FM Whitehorse, Yukon Territory
CJABFM Chicoutimi, Quebec
CKMSFM Waterloo, Ontario
CKCW-FM Moncton, New Brunswick
CHBW-FM Rocky Mountain House, Alberta
CHET-FM Chetwynd, British Columbia
CFBT-FM Vancouver, British Columbia
CKCK-FM Regina, Saskatchewan
CIBU-FM Wingham, Ontario
CHAT-FM Medicine Hat, Alberta
CJFO-FM Ottawa, Ontario

94.7 mhz

CHEY-FM Trois Rivieres, Quebec
CHKF-FM Calgary, Alberta
CHOZ-FM Saint John's, Newfoundland
CHRWFM London, Ontario
CHKX-FM Hamilton, Ontario
CKLF-FM Brandon, Manitoba
CJDS-FM Saint Pamphile, Quebec
CJNE-FM Nipawin, Saskatchewan
CIRP-FM Spryfield, Nova Scotia

94.9 mhz

CIEUFM Carleton, Quebec
CIMFFM Hull, Quebec
CKGE-FM Oshawa, Ontario
CKPE-FM Sydney, Nova Scotia
CKUA-FM Edmonton, Alberta
CJPR-FM Blairmore, Alberta

95.1 mhz

CBF-FM Montreal, Quebec
CFMC-FM Saskatoon, Saskatchewan
CILE-FM Havre-Saint-Pierre, Quebec
CKCB-FM Collingwood, Ontario
CKUE-FM Chatham, Ontario
CKSYFM Chatham, Ontario
CHVN-FM Winnipeg, Manitoba
CJOA-FM Thunder Bay, Ontario
CKMV-FM Grand Falls, New Brunswick
CFCY-FM Charlottetown, Prince Edward Island

95.3 mhz

CBVX-FM Quebec, Quebec
CHOE-FM Matane, Quebec
CKZZ-FM Vancouver, British Columbia
CHUT-FM Lac-Simon (Louvicourt), Quebec
CJXK-FM Cold Lake, Alberta

95.5 mhz

CBA-FM Moncton, New Brunswick
CFLXFM Sherbrooke, Quebec
CFVD Degelis, Quebec
CHLB-FM Lethbridge, Alberta
CJOJ-FM Belleville, Ontario
CJTK-FM Sudbury, Ontario
CKGY-FM Red Deer, Alberta
CIYN-FM Kincardine, Ontario

95.7 mhz

CBQSFM Sioux Narrows, Ontario
CFJB-FM Barrie, Ontario
CJAT-FM Trail, British Columbia
CKRP-FM Falher, Alberta
CKYK-FM Alma, Quebec

CKYQ Plessisville, Quebec
CKTP-FM Fredericton Centre, New Brunswick
CJNI-FM Halifax, Nova Scotia
CKAV-FM-9 Ottawa, Ontario
CHBI-FM Burnt Islands, Newfoundland
CFPW-FM Powell River, British Columbia
CKEA-FM Edmonton, Alberta

95.9 mhz

CFPLFM London, Ontario
CHFMFM Calgary, Alberta
CHOS-FM Rattling Brook, Newfoundland
CJFMFM Montreal, Quebec
CJKX-FM Ajax, Ontario
CKUW-FM Winnipeg, Manitoba
CKSA-FM Lloydminster, Alberta

96.1 mhz

CBCTFM Charlottetown, Prince Edward Island
CFMY-FM Medicine Hat, Alberta
CHKG-FM Richmond, British Columbia
CKRW-FM Whitehorse, Yukon Territory
CKX-FM Brandon, Manitoba
CINB-FM Saint John, New Brunswick
CHMY-FM Renfrew, Ontario

96.3 mhz

CBDQ-FM Labrador City, Newfoundland
CFMKFM Kingston, Ontario
CFMZ-FM Toronto, Ontario
CIHOFM Baie St Paul, Quebec
CINC-FM Thompson, Manitoba
CIOZ-FM Marystown, Newfoundland
CJLS-FM-1 Barrington, Nova Scotia
CKRA-FM Edmonton, Alberta
CJLSFM Barrington, Nova Scotia
CFMV-FM Chandler, Quebec
CFWD-FM Saskatoon, Saskatchewan
CJGY-FM Grande Prairie, Alberta
CKKO-FM Kelowna, British Columbia

96.5 mhz

CHOA-FM Rouyn-Noranda, Quebec
CKUL-FM Halifax, Nova Scotia
CKLEFM Rimouski, Quebec
CKMN-FM Rimouski-Mont Joli, Quebec
CIXN-FM Fredericton, New Brunswick
CKLJ-FM Olds, Alberta
CJPG-FM Portage la Prairie, Manitoba
CFTX-FM Gatineau, Quebec

96.7 mhz

CHVR-FM Pembroke, Ontario
CHYM-FM Kitchener, Ontario
CHYR-FM Leamington, Ontario
CILT-FM Steinbach, Manitoba
CKLU-FM Sudbury, Ontario
CKGF-FM-2 Greenwood, British Columbia
CFXW-FM Whitecourt, Alberta

96.9 mhz

CBK-FM Regina, Saskatchewan
CKKSFM Vancouver, British Columbia
CJAQ-FM Calgary, Alberta
CKLG-FM Vancouver, British Columbia
CKSS-FM Red Rocks, Newfoundland
CJXL-FM Moncton, New Brunswick
CFIX-FM Chicoutimi, Quebec
CKHC-FM Toronto, Ontario

97.1 mhz

CBON Timmins, Ontario
CHLCFM Baie-Comeau, Quebec
CIGLFM Belleville, Ontario
CJMGFM Penticton, British Columbia
CKROFM Inkerman, New Brunswick
CHLX-FM Gatineau, Quebec
CKFI-FM Swift Current, Saskatchewan
CKDR-FM-2 Sioux Lookout, Ontario
CKDR-FM-5 Red Lake, Ontario
CIPU-FM Micmac, Nova Scotia

97.3 mhz

CFJO-FM Thetford Mines, Quebec
CHGAFM Maniwaki, Quebec
CIRK-FM Edmonton, Alberta
CHBM-FM Toronto, Ontario
CJRM-FM Labrador City, Newfoundland
CKLR-FM Courtenay, British Columbia
CKON-FM Akwesasne, Ontario
CHWV-FM Saint John, New Brunswick
CKUJ-FM Kuujjuaq, Quebec
CJCI-FM Prince George, British Columbia
CJIV-FM Dryden, Ontario

97.5 mhz

CHOX-FM La Pocatiere, Quebec
CIQM-FM London, Ontario
CKDU-FM Halifax, Nova Scotia
CKISFM Winnipeg, Manitoba
CKRV-FM Kamloops, British Columbia
VOCM-FM Saint John's, Newfoundland
CFXH-FM Hinton, Alberta
CHRKFM Kamloops, British Columbia
CKKV-FM Kemptville, Ontario
CBEW-FM Windsor, Ontario

97.7 mhz

CBKFFM Regina, Saskatchewan
CBUFFM Vancouver, British Columbia
CFCV-FM Saint Andrews, Newfoundland
CFGP-FM Grande Prairie, Alberta
CFTH-FM-1 Harrington Harbour, Quebec
CHOMFM Montreal, Quebec
CHTZFM St Catharines, Ontario
CKEN-FM Kentville, Nova Scotia
CHMS-FM Bancroft, Ontario
CIDD-FM White Bear Lake Resort, Saskatchewan
CKWMFM Kentville, Nova Scotia
CFXX-FM Siksika, Alberta
CKTK-FM Kitimat, British Columbia
CIDO-FM Creston, British Columbia
CHGB-FM Wasaga Beach, Ontario
CHUP-FM Calgary, Alberta
CHSP-FM Saint Paul, Alberta

97.9 mhz

CFLC-FM Churchill Falls, Newfoundland
CHSR-FM Fredericton, New Brunswick
CJREFM Riviere Au Renar, Quebec
CKYX-FM Fort McMurray, Alberta
KRSI Garapan-Saipan, Guam
CJLL-FM Ottawa, Ontario
CFPS-FM Port Elgin, Ontario
CKWB-FM Westlock, Alberta
CKEZ-FM Pictou, Nova Scotia
CFLN-FM Goose Bay, Newfoundland

98.1 mhz

CBSI-FM Sept-Iles, Quebec
CHFIFM Toronto, Ontario
CKVN-FM Lethbridge, Alberta
CHTD-FM Saint Stephen, New Brunswick
CKBW-FM Bridgewater, Nova Scotia
CHPB-FM Cochrane, Ontario
CKIQFM Big White Ski, British Columbia
CFCW-FM Camrose, Alberta
CHOIFM Quebec, Quebec
CIBC-FM Cowessess, Saskatchewan

98.3 mhz

CBAFFM Moncton, New Brunswick
CBAL-FM Moncton, New Brunswick
CBW-FM Winnipeg, Manitoba
CFFMFM Kamloops, British Columbia
CFLYFM Kingston, Ontario
CIFM-FM Kamloops, British Columbia
CFPX-FM Pukatawagan, Manitoba
CIAX-FM Windsor, Quebec
CJMK-FM Saskatoon, Saskatchewan
CFWP-FM Wahta Mohawk Territory near Bala, Ontario
CHER-FM Sydney, Nova Scotia
CKRS-FM Saguenay, Quebec
CHUN-FM Rouyn-Noranda, Quebec

98.5 mhz

CHRX-FM Fort St. John, British Columbia
CHMP-FM Longueuil, Quebec
CIOC-FM Victoria, British Columbia
CIOS-FM Stephenville, Newfoundland
CIELFM Longueuil, Quebec
CKWR Waterloo, Ontario
CFTH-FM-2 Harrington Harbour, Quebec
CIBK-FM Calgary, Alberta
CINU-FM Truro, Nova Scotia
CJWL-FM Ottawa, Ontario
CJJC-FM Yorkton, Saskatchewan
CKRH-FM Halifax, Nova Scotia
CHOR-FM Summerland, British Columbia

98.7 mhz

CBQXFM Kenora, Ontario
CKXD-FM Gander, Newfoundland
CJHR-FM Renfrew, Ontario
CKPM-FM Port Moody, British Columbia
CBF-2 Toronto, Quebec
CHWN-FM Skownan, Manitoba

98.9 mhz

CFCP-FM Courtenay, British Columbia
CHIKFM Quebec, Quebec
CIZLFM Regina, Saskatchewan
CIZZ-FM Red Deer, Alberta
CJFX-FM Antigonish, Nova Scotia
CJYCFM Saint John, New Brunswick
CHYC-FM Sudbury, Ontario
CFPV-FM Pemberton, British Columbia
CIKT-FM Grande Prairie, Alberta
CKLC-FM Kingston, Ontario

99.1 mhz

CBLAFM Toronto, Ontario
CFMM-FM Prince Albert, Saskatchewan
CFNJFM St-Gabriel, Quebec
CHRI-FM Ottawa, Ontario
CIPC-FM Port-Cartier, Quebec
CJAM-FM Windsor, Ontario
CJMM-FM Rouyn-Noranda, Quebec
CKIX-FM Saint John's, Newfoundland
CJDR-FM Fernie, British Columbia
CJGV-FM Winnipeg, Manitoba
CIDI-FM Lac-Brome, Quebec
CHTK-FM Prince Rupert, British Columbia

99.3 mhz

CBV-FM-6 La Malbaie, Quebec
CFOXFM Vancouver, British Columbia
CJBC-FM-4 London, Ontario
CFOR-FM Maniwaki, Quebec
CKQN-FM Baker Lake, Nunavut
CKQR-FM Castlegar, British Columbia
CJAN-FM Asbestos, Quebec
CKGB-FM Timmins, Ontario
CFAN-FM Miramichi City, New Brunswick
CKDV-FM Prince George, British Columbia
CFSF-FM Sturgeon Falls, Ontario
CIUP-FM Edmonton, Alberta
CHSB-FM Bedford, Nova Scotia
CJJM-FM Espanola, Ontario

99.5 mhz

CBZF-FM Fredericton, New Brunswick
CFBG-FM Bracebridge, Ontario
CJPX-FM Montreal, Quebec
KPXP Garapan-Saipan, Guam
CHRL-FM Roberval, Quebec
CKTY-FM Truro, Nova Scotia
CIKZ-FM Kitchener, Ontario
CIMM-FM Ucluelet, British Columbia
CKKW-FM Kitchener, Ontario

99.7 mhz

CHJM-FM St-George-Beauce, Quebec
CFNA-FM Bonnyville, Alberta
CKPT-FM Peterborough, Ontario
CFXO-FM High River-Okotoks, Alberta
CIQC-FM Campbell River, British Columbia
CJOT-FM Ottawa, Ontario

99.9 mhz

CBCSFM Sudbury, Ontario
CFGX-FM Sarnia, Ontario
CFWM-FM Winnipeg, Manitoba
CHSU-FM Kelowna, British Columbia
CKFMFM Toronto, Ontario
CHOY-FM Moncton, New Brunswick
CHEF-FM Matagami, Quebec
CJUK-FM Thunder Bay, Ontario
CFVM-FM Amqui, Quebec
CJIJ-FM Sydney, Nova Scotia
CHPQ-FM Parksville, British Columbia
CJGM-FM Gananoque, Ontario

Programming on Radio Stations in Canada

Adult Contemp

CIXF-FM Brooks, Alberta
CHFMFM Calgary, Alberta
CKMX Calgary, Alberta
CHMN-FM Canmore, Alberta
CHFA Edmonton, Alberta
CKEA-FM Edmonton, Alberta
CFXE-FM Edson, Alberta
CKRP-FM Falher, Alberta
CKVH-FM High Prairie, Alberta
CFXH-FM Hinton, Alberta
CJUV-FM Lacombe, Alberta
CFRV-FM Lethbridge, Alberta
CJOC-FM Lethbridge, Alberta
CFMY-FM Medicine Hat, Alberta
CJCY-FM Medicine Hat, Alberta
CHUB-FM Red Deer, Alberta
CIZZ-FM Red Deer, Alberta
CFMG-FM Saint Albert, Alberta
CJBZ-FM Taber, Alberta
CKWY-FM Wainwright, Alberta
CFSRFM Abbotsford, British Columbia
CKGO-FM-1 Boston Bar, British Columbia
CFLD Burns Lake, British Columbia
CIQC-FM Campbell River, British Columbia
CHET-FM Chetwynd, British Columbia
CFKC Creston, British Columbia
CHAD-FM Dawson Creek, British Columbia
CJSU-FM Duncan, British Columbia
CIEG-FM Egmont, British Columbia
CISCFM Gibsons, British Columbia
CKBZ-FM Kamloops, British Columbia
CKRV-FM Kamloops, British Columbia
CHSU-FM Kelowna, British Columbia
CILKFM Kelowna, British Columbia
CKWV-FM Nanaimo, British Columbia
CKKC-FM Nelson, British Columbia
CKZX-FM New Denver, British Columbia
CJOR(AM) Osoyoos, British Columbia
CHPQ-FM Parksville, British Columbia
CIBH-FM Parksville, British Columbia
CISP-FM Pemberton, British Columbia
CIPN-FM Pender Harbour, British Columbia
CIGVFM Penticton, British Columbia
CJAV-FM Port Alberni, British Columbia
CFNI Port Hardy, British Columbia
CFPW-FM Powell River, British Columbia
CIOR(AM) Princeton, British Columbia
CISL Richmond, British Columbia
CKXR-FM Salmon Arm, British Columbia
CKAY-FM Sechelt, British Columbia
CISQFM Squamish, British Columbia
CFTK Terrace, British Columbia
CJAT-FM Trail, British Columbia
CKLG-FM Vancouver, British Columbia
CKZZ-FM Vancouver, British Columbia
CICF-FM Vernon, British Columbia
CHTT-FM Victoria, British Columbia
CISWFM Whistler, British Columbia
CFAM Altona, Manitoba
CKLF-FM Brandon, Manitoba
CHSM Steinbach, Manitoba
CILT-FM Steinbach, Manitoba
CJAR The Pas, Manitoba
CJEL-FM Winkler, Manitoba
CKY-FM Winnipeg, Manitoba
KZMI Garapan-Saipan, Guam
CKBC-FM Bathurst, New Brunswick
CKNB Campbellton, New Brunswick
CJVA Caraquet, New Brunswick
CJEM-FM Edmundston, New Brunswick
CJPN-FM Fredericton, New Brunswick
CIKX-FM Grand Falls, New Brunswick
CKROFM Inkerman, New Brunswick
CFAN-FM Miramichi City, New Brunswick
CFBO-FM Moncton, New Brunswick
CFQMFM Moncton, New Brunswick
CHOY-FM Moncton, New Brunswick
CHWV-FM Saint John, New Brunswick
CIOK-FM Saint John, New Brunswick
CJCW Sussex, New Brunswick
CFLN Goose Bay, Newfoundland
VOCM St. John's, Newfoundland
CFOZ-FM Argentia, Newfoundland
CJOZ-FM Bonavista Bay, Newfoundland
CFLC-FM Churchill Falls, Newfoundland
CJKK-FM Clarenville, Newfoundland
CKOZ-FM Corner Brook, Newfoundland
CIOZ-FM Marystown, Newfoundland
CHOS-FM Rattling Brook, Newfoundland
CKSS-FM Red Rocks, Newfoundland
CHOZ-FM Saint John's, Newfoundland
CKSJ-FM Saint John's, Newfoundland
CIOS-FM Stephenville, Newfoundland
CKDH-FM Amherst, Nova Scotia
CJLS-FM-1 Barrington, Nova Scotia
CJLSFM Barrington, Nova Scotia
CKBW-FM Bridgewater, Nova Scotia
CKWMFM Kentville, Nova Scotia
CKEC-FM New Glasgow, Nova Scotia
CJLS-FM-2 New Tusket, Nova Scotia
CIGO-FM Port Hawkesbury, Nova Scotia
CBI-FM Sydney, Nova Scotia
CHER-FM Sydney, Nova Scotia
CJIJ-FM Sydney, Nova Scotia
CKTOFM Truro, Nova Scotia
CJCD-FM-1 Hay River, Northwest Territories
CKHR-FM Hay River, Northwest Territories
CJCD-FM Yellowknife, Northwest Territories
CBQR-FM Rankin Inlet, Nunavut
CHAYFM Barrie, Ontario
CIQB-FM Barrie, Ontario
CIGLFM Belleville, Ontario
CJOJ-FM Belleville, Ontario
CJFB-FM Bolton, Ontario
CFBG-FM Bracebridge, Ontario
CKPC Brantford, Ontario
CKPCFM Brantford, Ontario
CJDV-FM Cambridge, Ontario
CKSYFM Chatham, Ontario
CKSG-FM Cobourg, Ontario
CHPB-FM Cochrane, Ontario
CKCB-FM Collingwood, Ontario
CFLGFM Cornwall, Ontario
CKDR-FM Dryden, Ontario
CJBB-FM Englehart, Ontario
CJJM-FM Espanola, Ontario
CFOB-FM Fort Frances, Ontario
CKLHFM Hamilton, Ontario
CHYK-FM-3 Hearst, Ontario
CINN-FM Hearst, Ontario
CKKV-FM Kemptville, Ontario
CJRL-FM Kenora, Ontario
CIYN-FM Kincardine, Ontario
CJKL-FM Kirkland Lake, Ontario
CHYR-FM Leamington, Ontario
CJSP Leamington, Ontario
CFPL London, Ontario
CFPLFM London, Ontario
CIQM-FM London, Ontario
CKSL London, Ontario
CFNOFM Marathon, Ontario
CKYM-FM Napanee, Ontario
CKDX-FM Newmarket, Ontario
CHUR-FM North Bay, Ontario
CKDO Oshawa, Ontario
CISS-FM Ottawa, Ontario
CJWL-FM Ottawa, Ontario
CIXK-FM Owen Sound, Ontario
CFPS-FM Port Elgin, Ontario
CFGX-FM Sarnia, Ontario
CHASFM Sault Ste Marie, Ontario
CHCD Simcoe, Ontario
CHEQFM Smiths Falls, Ontario
CHGK-FM Stratford, Ontario
CJMI-FM Strathroy, Ontario
CFSF-FM Sturgeon Falls, Ontario
CBBSFM Sudbury, Ontario
CHNO-FM Sudbury, Ontario
CHYC-FM Sudbury, Ontario
CKPR-FM Thunder Bay, Ontario
CHYK-FM Timmins, Ontario
CFZM(AM) Toronto, Ontario
CHFIFM Toronto, Ontario
CKFMFM Toronto, Ontario
CKWR Waterloo, Ontario
CJWA-FM Wawa, Ontario
CKNXFM Wingham, Ontario
CHLQFM Charlottetown, Prince Edward Island
CHTN-FM Charlottetown, Prince Edward Island
CFVM-FM Amqui, Quebec
CJAN-FM Asbestos, Quebec
CIHOFM Baie St Paul, Quebec
CHLCFM Baie-Comeau, Quebec
CIEUFM Carleton, Quebec
CHAI-FM Chateauguay, Quebec
CKXO-FM Chibougamau, Quebec
CFIX-FM Chicoutimi, Quebec
CFVD Degelis, Quebec
CHVD-FM Dolbeau-Mistassini, Quebec
CHRD-FM Drummondville, Quebec
CJDM-FM Drummondville, Quebec
CFRP Forestville, Quebec
CJRGFM Gaspe, Quebec
CFXM Granby, Quebec
CFTH-FM-1 Harrington Harbour, Quebec
CILE-FM Havre-Saint-Pierre, Quebec
CJLM-FM Joliette, Quebec
CKRK-FM Kahnawake, Quebec
CHOX-FM La Pocatiere, Quebec
CFLM La Tuque, Quebec
CJIT-FM Lac Megantic, Quebec
CFIN-FM Lac-Etchemin, Quebec
CJLAFM Lachute, Quebec
CFGLFM Laval, Quebec
CFEL-FM Levis, Quebec
CHAA-FM Longueuil, Quebec
CIELFM Longueuil, Quebec
CHGAFM Maniwaki, Quebec
CHEF-FM Matagami, Quebec
CHRM-FM Matane, Quebec
CFLO-FM Mont-Laurier, Quebec
CITEFM Montreal, Quebec
CJFMFM Montreal, Quebec
CKNA-FM Natashquan, Quebec
CKYQ Plessisville, Quebec
CHIKFM Quebec, Quebec
CION Quebec, Quebec
CITFFM Quebec, Quebec
CJEC-FM Quebec, Quebec
CKRLFM Quebec, Quebec
CJBRFM Rimouski, Quebec
CJOI-FM Rimouski, Quebec
CKMN-FM Rimouski-Mont Joli, Quebec
CJREFM Riviere Au Renar, Quebec
CHOA-FM Rouyn-Noranda, Quebec
CJAS-FM Saint Augustin, Quebec
CKRB-FM Saint Georges-de-Beauce, Quebec
CJDS-FM Saint Pamphile, Quebec
CJMC-FM Sainte Anne des Monts, Quebec
CKCN-FM Sept-Iles, Quebec
CKSM Shawinigan, Quebec
CFGE-FM Sherbrooke, Quebec
CFNJFM St-Gabriel, Quebec
CKLD-FM Thetford Mines, Quebec
CJEB-FM Trois Rivieres, Quebec
CKOD-FM Valleyfield, Quebec
CFDA-FM Victoriaville, Quebec
CKVM-FM Ville-Marie, Quebec
CFYM Kindersley, Saskatchewan
CJAW-FM Moose Jaw, Saskatchewan
CFNK-FM Pinehouse Lake, Saskatchewan
CKBI Prince Albert, Saskatchewan
CHMX-FM Regina, Saskatchewan
CIZLFM Regina, Saskatchewan
CJYM Rosetown, Saskatchewan
CFWD-FM Saskatoon, Saskatchewan
CJMK-FM Saskatoon, Saskatchewan
CIMG-FM Swift Current, Saskatchewan
CKFI-FM Swift Current, Saskatchewan
CFGW-FM Yorkton, Saskatchewan

Agriculture

CFAM Altona, Manitoba
CJRB Boissevain, Manitoba

Alternative

CFEX-FM Calgary, Alberta
CJSR-FM Edmonton, Alberta
CHHR-FM Vancouver, British Columbia
CHSR-FM Fredericton, New Brunswick
CHMR-FM Saint John's, Newfoundland
CFNYFM Brampton, Ontario
CIOI-FM Hamilton, Ontario
CHRWFM London, Ontario
CILV-FM Ottawa, Ontario
CKDJ-FM Ottawa, Ontario
CIMI-FM Charlesbourg, Quebec
CISM-FM Montreal, Quebec
CFYT-FM Dawson City, Yukon Territory

Arabic

CHOU Montreal, Quebec

RADIO - CANADA

Blues

CBR-FM Calgary, Alberta

Chinese

CKER-FM Edmonton, Alberta
CHMB Vancouver, British Columbia
CHKT(AM) Toronto, Ontario

Christian

CJSI-FM Calgary, Alberta
CJCA Edmonton, Alberta
CJRY-FM Edmonton, Alberta
CKOS-FM Fort McMurray, Alberta
CKVN-FM Lethbridge, Alberta
CHIMFM Kelowna, British Columbia
CIAJ-FM Prince Rupert, British Columbia
CHVN-FM Winnipeg, Manitoba
CITA-FM Moncton, New Brunswick
CKOE-FM Moncton, New Brunswick
CINB-FM Saint John, New Brunswick
CIRP-FM Spryfield, Nova Scotia
CINU-FM Truro, Nova Scotia
CFSH-FM Apsley, Ontario
CFWC-FM Brantford, Ontario
CKGW-FM Chatham, Ontario
CJIV-FM Dryden, Ontario
CKBT-FM Kitchener-Waterloo, Ontario
CHJX-FM London, Ontario
CJYE Oakville, Ontario
CJTK-FM Sudbury, Ontario
CKSO-FM Sudbury, Ontario
CJOA-FM Thunder Bay, Ontario
CJFH-FM Woodstock, Ontario
CHIC-FM Rouyn-Noranda, Quebec
CFAQ-FM Blucher, Saskatchewan
CIAY-FM Whitehorse, Yukon Territory

Classic Rock

CFGQ-FM Calgary, Alberta
CJXK-FM Cold Lake, Alberta
CFBR-FM Edmonton, Alberta
CIRK-FM Edmonton, Alberta
CHFT-FM Fort McMurray, Alberta
CKYX-FM Fort McMurray, Alberta
CFRI-FM Grande Prairie, Alberta
CFRV-FM Lethbridge, Alberta
CKJX-FM Olds, Alberta
CFDV-FM Red Deer, Alberta
CFXW-FM Whitecourt, Alberta
CKIQFM Big White Ski, British Columbia
CKQR-FM Castlegar, British Columbia
CFCP-FM Courtenay, British Columbia
CKNL-FM Fort St. John, British Columbia
CKGF-FM-2 Greenwood, British Columbia
CKIR Invermere, British Columbia
CKOR Penticton, British Columbia
CKDV-FM Prince George, British Columbia
CFNR-FM Terrace, British Columbia
CKKQ-FM Victoria, British Columbia
CKX-FM Brandon, Manitoba
CITIFM Winnipeg, Manitoba
CKISFM Winnipeg, Manitoba
KRSI Garapan-Saipan, Guam
CIBX-FM Fredericton, New Brunswick
CJMOFM Moncton, New Brunswick
CJYCFM Saint John, New Brunswick
CJCJ-FM Woodstock, New Brunswick
CFOZ-FM Argentia, Newfoundland
CJOZ-FM Bonavista Bay, Newfoundland
CJKK-FM Clarenville, Newfoundland
CKOZ-FM Corner Brook, Newfoundland
CKXD-FM Gander, Newfoundland
CIOZ-FM Marystown, Newfoundland
CHOS-FM Rattling Brook, Newfoundland
CKSS-FM Red Rocks, Newfoundland
CHOZ-FM Saint John's, Newfoundland
VOCM-FM Saint John's, Newfoundland
CIOS-FM Stephenville, Newfoundland
CFRQFM Dartmouth, Nova Scotia
CHNS-FM Halifax, Nova Scotia
CIJK-FM Kentville, Nova Scotia
CJIJ-FM Sydney, Nova Scotia
CFJB-FM Barrie, Ontario
CKTI-FM Kettle Point, Ontario
CFMKFM Kingston, Ontario
CICZ Midland, Ontario
CKGE-FM Oshawa, Ontario
CHEZFM Ottawa, Ontario
CHREFM St Catharines, Ontario
CKGB-FM Timmins, Ontario
CILQFM Toronto, Ontario
CIXL-FM Welland, Ontario
CKDKFM Woodstock, Ontario
CKQK-FM Charlottetown, Prince Edward Island
CKYK-FM Alma, Quebec
CFVM-FM Amqui, Quebec
CFTX-FM Gatineau, Quebec
CIMFFM Hull, Quebec
CHOMFM Montreal, Quebec
CJMFFM Quebec, Quebec
CKIA-FM Quebec, Quebec
CFYX-FM Rimouski, Quebec
CJSO-FM Sorel, Quebec
CFJO-FM Thetford Mines, Quebec
CHEY-FM Trois Rivieres, Quebec
CHGO-FM Val d'Or, Quebec
CJNE-FM Nipawin, Saskatchewan
CFMM-FM Prince Albert, Saskatchewan
CFWF-FM Regina, Saskatchewan
CKCK-FM Regina, Saskatchewan
CFET-FM Tagish, Yukon Territory
CHONFM Whitehorse, Yukon Territory

Classical

CBAX-FM Halifax, Nova Scotia
CFMXFM Cobourg, Ontario
CFMZ-FM Toronto, Ontario
CJRW-FM Summerside, Prince Edward Island
CBJX-FM Chicoutimi, Quebec
CHLX-FM Gatineau, Quebec
CJPX-FM Montreal, Quebec
CBK-FM Regina, Saskatchewan
CBKS-FM Saskatoon, Saskatchewan

Comedy

CJEF-FM Saint John, New Brunswick

Contemporary Hits/Top 40

CJEG-FM Bonnyville, Alberta
CIBK-FM Calgary, Alberta
CJAQ-FM Calgary, Alberta
CKNG-FM Edmonton, Alberta
CFXE-FM Edson, Alberta
CFGP-FM Grande Prairie, Alberta
CKVH-FM High Prairie, Alberta
CFXH-FM Hinton, Alberta
CJUV-FM Lacombe, Alberta
CJOC-FM Lethbridge, Alberta
CJCY-FM Medicine Hat, Alberta
CJBZ-FM Taber, Alberta
CKRX-FM Fort Nelson, British Columbia
CHRKFM Kamloops, British Columbia
CKRV-FM Kamloops, British Columbia
CKTK-FM Kitimat, British Columbia
CJAV-FM Port Alberni, British Columbia
CKKN-FM Prince George, British Columbia
CHTK Prince Rupert, British Columbia
CKAY-FM Sechelt, British Columbia
CHTT-FM Victoria, British Columbia
V6AH(AM) Pohnpei, 66
V6AI(AM) Yap, 66
CJPG-FM Portage la Prairie, Manitoba
CJSB-FM Swan River, Manitoba
CHWE-FM Winnepeg, Manitoba
CKMM-FM Winnipeg, Manitoba
KPXP Garapan-Saipan, Guam
CFAIFM Edmundston, New Brunswick
CKTP-FM Fredericton Centre, New Brunswick
CKCW-FM Moncton, New Brunswick
CFOZ-FM Argentia, Newfoundland
CJOZ-FM Bonavista Bay, Newfoundland
CJKK-FM Clarenville, Newfoundland
CKOZ-FM Corner Brook, Newfoundland
CIOZ-FM Marystown, Newfoundland
CHOS-FM Rattling Brook, Newfoundland
CKSS-FM Red Rocks, Newfoundland
CHOZ-FM Saint John's, Newfoundland
CKIX-FM Saint John's, Newfoundland
CIOS-FM Stephenville, Newfoundland
CJFX-FM Antigonish, Nova Scotia
CKHZ-FM Halifax, Nova Scotia
CBI-FM Sydney, Nova Scotia
CHER-FM Sydney, Nova Scotia
CKPE-FM Sydney, Nova Scotia
CHMS-FM Bancroft, Ontario
CKMB Barrie, Ontario
CJOJ-FM Belleville, Ontario
CKPC Brantford, Ontario
CJJM-FM Espanola, Ontario
CIDCFM Orangeville, Ontario
CKDO Oshawa, Ontario
CIHT-FM Ottawa, Ontario
CISS-FM Ottawa, Ontario
CJOS-FM Owen Sound, Ontario
CKDR-FM-5 Red Lake, Ontario
CJET-FM Smiths Falls, Ontario
CFHK-FM St. Thomas, Ontario
CFSF-FM Sturgeon Falls, Ontario
CHNO-FM Sudbury, Ontario
CHYC-FM Sudbury, Ontario
CIRR-FM Toronto, Ontario
CKQV-FM Vermillion Bay, Ontario
CHTN-FM Charlottetown, Prince Edward Island
CKQK-FM Charlottetown, Prince Edward Island
CIEUFM Carleton, Quebec
CJABFM Chicoutimi, Quebec
CFVD Degelis, Quebec
CFMF-FM Fermont, Quebec
CBGA Gaspe, Quebec
CKTF Hull, Quebec
CJIT-FM Lac Megantic, Quebec
CIMOFM Magog, Quebec
CKMFFM Montreal, Quebec
CIPC-FM Port-Cartier, Quebec
CKLEFM Rimouski, Quebec
CJMM-FM Rouyn-Noranda, Quebec
CHJM-FM St-George-Beauce, Quebec
CIGBFM Trois-Rivieres, Quebec
CFDM-FM Meadow Lake, Saskatchewan
CKJH(AM) Melfort, Saskatchewan
CHAB Moose Jaw, Saskatchewan
CJYM Rosetown, Saskatchewan
CFWD-FM Saskatoon, Saskatchewan
CIMG-FM Swift Current, Saskatchewan

Country

CJPR-FM Blairmore, Alberta
CKRYFM Calgary, Alberta
CIBW-FM Drayton Valley, Alberta
CKDQ Drumheller, Alberta
CISN-FM Edmonton, Alberta
CJOK-FM Fort McMurray, Alberta
CJXX-FM Grande Prairie, Alberta
CKHL-FM High Level, Alberta
CHRB High River, Alberta
CFXO-FM High River-Okotoks, Alberta
CFWE-FM Lac La Biche, Alberta
CJLD-FM Leduc, Alberta
CHLB-FM Lethbridge, Alberta
CKSA-FM Lloydminster, Alberta
CHAT-FM Medicine Hat, Alberta
CKLJ-FM Olds, Alberta
CKGY-FM Red Deer, Alberta
CHBW-FM Rocky Mountain House, Alberta
CHLW St. Paul, Alberta
CKJR Wetaskiwin, Alberta
CIXM-FM Whitecourt, Alberta
CKQC-FM Abbotsford, British Columbia
CHBZ-FM Cranbrook, British Columbia
CJDC Dawson Creek, British Columbia
CJKC-FM Kamloops, British Columbia
CKBX One Hundred Mile Hou, British Columbia
CIGVFM Penticton, British Columbia
CJCI-FM Prince George, British Columbia
CKCQ-FM Quesnel, British Columbia
CJFWFM Terrace, British Columbia
CHMZ-FM Tofino, British Columbia
CJJRFM Vancouver, British Columbia
CKVX Vancouver, British Columbia
CIVH Vanderhoof, British Columbia
CKWL Williams Lake, British Columbia
V6AI(AM) Yap, 66
CKLQ Brandon, Manitoba
CKXA-FM Brandon, Manitoba
CKDM Dauphin, Manitoba
CKMW Morden, Manitoba
CFRY Portage La Prairie, Manitoba
CFPX-FM Pukatawagan, Manitoba
CFRMFM St Boniface, Manitoba
CJAR The Pas, Manitoba
CKNB Campbellton, New Brunswick
CFXY-FM Fredericton, New Brunswick
CJRI-FM Fredericton, New Brunswick
CKHJ(AM) Fredericton, New Brunswick
CHOY-FM Moncton, New Brunswick
CJXL-FM Moncton, New Brunswick
CHSJ-FM Saint John, New Brunswick
CKIM Baie Verte, Newfoundland

CKVO Clarenville, Newfoundland
CFCB Corner Brook, Newfoundland
CKGA Gander, Newfoundland
CKCM Grand Falls, Newfoundland
CHCM Marystown, Newfoundland
CFNW Port Au Choix, Newfoundland
CJYQ St. John's, Newfoundland
VOCM St. John's, Newfoundland
CFSX Stephenville, Newfoundland
CHVO-FM Carbonear, Newfoundland
CFLC-FM Churchill Falls, Newfoundland
CJHK-FM Bridgewater, Nova Scotia
CKJM-FM Cheticamp, Nova Scotia
CFDR Dartmouth, Nova Scotia
CKDY Digby, Nova Scotia
CKOA-FM Glace Bay, Nova Scotia
CHFXFM Halifax, Nova Scotia
CKEN-FM Kentville, Nova Scotia
CKAD Middleton, Nova Scotia
CJCB Sydney, Nova Scotia
CKCH-FM Sydney, Nova Scotia
CKTY-FM Truro, Nova Scotia
CFAB Windsor, Nova Scotia
CKLB-FM Yellowknife, Northwest Territories
CJKX-FM Ajax, Ontario
CHCQ-FM Belleville, Ontario
CJBQ Belleville, Ontario
CINGFM Burlington, Ontario
CFCO Chatham, Ontario
CFQK-FM Kaministiquia, Ontario
CKTI-FM Kettle Point, Ontario
CKXC-FM Kingston, Ontario
CIKZ-FM Kitchener, Ontario
CJBXFM London, Ontario
CHMO(AM) Moosonee, Ontario
CKAT(AM) North Bay, Ontario
CKRZ-FM Ohsweken, Ontario
CICX-FM Orillia, Ontario
CKBYFM Ottawa, Ontario
CKYC-FM Owen Sound, Ontario
CHVR-FM Pembroke, Ontario
CJHR-FM Renfrew, Ontario
CHOK Sarnia, Ontario
CJQMFM Sault Ste Marie, Ontario
CIGM Sudbury, Ontario
CJDL-FM Tillsonburg, Ontario
CKHC-FM Toronto, Ontario
CKNX Wingham, Ontario
CFCY-FM Charlottetown, Prince Edward Island
CFVD Degelis, Quebec
CHIPFM Fort-Coulonge, Quebec
CFTH-FM-1 Harrington Harbour, Quebec
CKAJ-FM Jonquiere, Quebec
CKKI-FM Kahnawake, Quebec
CKRK-FM Kahnawake, Quebec
CFIN-FM Lac-Etchemin, Quebec
CFIC-FM Listuguj, Quebec
CHRG-FM Maria (Reserve), Quebec
CJMS Montreal, Quebec
CKIA-FM Quebec, Quebec
CKMN-FM Rimouski-Mont Joli, Quebec
CHUN-FM Rouyn-Noranda, Quebec
CJSL Estevan, Saskatchewan
CJLR-FM La Ronge, Saskatchewan
CFDM-FM Meadow Lake, Saskatchewan
CJNS Meadow Lake, Saskatchewan
CJVR-FM Melfort, Saskatchewan
CILG-FM Moose Jaw, Saskatchewan
CFMQFM Regina, Saskatchewan
CHBD-FM Regina, Saskatchewan
CKRM(AM) Regina, Saskatchewan
CJWW Saskatoon, Saskatchewan
CKBL-FM Saskatoon, Saskatchewan
CKSW Swift Current, Saskatchewan
CJGX Yorkton, Saskatchewan
CHONFM Whitehorse, Yukon Territory

Easy Listening

CHPR-FM Hawkesbury, Ontario
CKHK-FM Hawkesbury, Ontario
CKOTFM Tillsonburg, Ontario

Ethnic

CHKF-FM Calgary, Alberta
CKAV-FM-3 Calgary, Alberta
CKAV-FM-4 Edmonton, Alberta
CKER-FM Edmonton, Alberta
CHKG-FM Richmond, British Columbia
CJRJ Vancouver, British Columbia
CKAV-FM-2 Vancouver, British Columbia
CKYE-FM Vancouver, British Columbia
CKQN-FM Baker Lake, Nunavut
CIAO Brampton, Ontario
CHFN-FM Cape Croker (Neyaashiinigmiing), Ontario
CJMR Mississauga, Ontario
CJLL-FM Ottawa, Ontario
CKAV-FM-9 Ottawa, Ontario
CJVF-FM Scarborough, Ontario
CKBK-FM Thamesville, Ontario
CHIN Toronto, Ontario
CHTO Toronto, Ontario
CIRV-FM Toronto, Ontario
CJSA Toronto, Ontario
CKAV-FM Toronto, Ontario
CJAM-FM Windsor, Ontario
CKUJ-FM Kuujjuaq, Quebec
CHUT-FM Lac-Simon (Louvicourt), Quebec
CFMB Montreal, Quebec
CHOU Montreal, Quebec
CJWI Montreal, Quebec
CKIN-FM Montreal, Quebec
CJRS Sherbrooke, Quebec
CJCF-FM Cumberland House, Saskatchewan
CJLR-FM La Ronge, Saskatchewan

French

CBCX-FM Calgary, Alberta
CBRFFM Calgary, Alberta
CKXU-FM Lethbridge, Alberta
CILS-FM Victoria, British Columbia
CBAFFM Moncton, New Brunswick
CHOY-FM Moncton, New Brunswick
CKRH-FM Halifax, Nova Scotia
CFRT-FM Iqaluit, Nunavut
CHUO-FM Ottawa, Ontario
CBON Timmins, Ontario
CHOQ-FM Toronto, Ontario
CKHC-FM Toronto, Ontario
CFID-FM Acton Vale, Quebec
CFMV-FM Chandler, Quebec
CKII-FM Dolbeau-Mistassini, Quebec
CHHO-FM Louiseville, Quebec
CHUK-FM Mashteuiatsh (Pointe-Bleue), Quebec
CFUT-FM Shawinigan, Quebec
CFAK-FM Sherbrooke, Quebec
CJTB-FM Tete-a-la-Baleine, Quebec
CJVD-FM Vaudreuil-Dorion, Quebec
CFRG-FM Gravelbourg, Saskatchewan
CKZP-FM Zenon Park, Saskatchewan

Gospel

CJRI-FM Fredericton, New Brunswick
VOAR St. John's, Newfoundland

Greek

CHTO Toronto, Ontario

Jazz

CKUA-FM Edmonton, Alberta
CJGV-FM Winnipeg, Manitoba
CBAX-FM Halifax, Nova Scotia
CBHAFM Halifax, Nova Scotia
CHRWFM London, Ontario
CKLU-FM Sudbury, Ontario
CJRT Toronto, Ontario
CHLX-FM Gatineau, Quebec
CKRLFM Quebec, Quebec
CBK-FM Regina, Saskatchewan
CBKS-FM Saskatoon, Saskatchewan

Light Rock

CKSRFM Chilliwack, British Columbia
CKNR-FM Elliot Lake, Ontario
CHOE-FM Matane, Quebec

Native American

CKWT-FM Sioux Lookout, Ontario

News

CBR Calgary, Alberta
CBRFFM Calgary, Alberta
CFFR Calgary, Alberta
CHQR Calgary, Alberta
CBX Edmonton, Alberta
CBX-FM Edmonton, Alberta
CHFA Edmonton, Alberta
CHQT Edmonton, Alberta
CBTEFM Crawford Bay, British Columbia
CBTKFM Kelowna, British Columbia
CKFR Kelowna, British Columbia
CHNV-FM Nelson, British Columbia
CKNW New Westminster, British Columbia
CBYG-FM Prince George, British Columbia
CFPR Prince Rupert, British Columbia
CKWX Vancouver, British Columbia
CKIZ-FM Vernon, British Columbia
CBCV-FM Victoria, British Columbia
CFAX Victoria, British Columbia
V6AK(AM) Truk, 66
V6AI(AM) Yap, 66
CJOB Winnipeg, Manitoba
CBZ-FM Fredericton, New Brunswick
CBAFFM Moncton, New Brunswick
CBAM-FM Moncton, New Brunswick
CKNI-FM Moncton, New Brunswick
CHNI-FM Saint John, New Brunswick
CKIM Baie Verte, Newfoundland
CBGY Bonavista Bay, Newfoundland
CBY Corner Brook, Newfoundland
CBG Gander, Newfoundland
CKGA Gander, Newfoundland
CBT Grand Falls, Alberta
VOCM St. John's, Newfoundland
CFGB-FM Happy Valley, Newfoundland
CBN-FM Saint John's, Newfoundland
CIFA-FM Comeauville, Nova Scotia
CBHAFM Halifax, Nova Scotia
CJNI-FM Halifax, Nova Scotia
CBI Sydney, Nova Scotia
CHAK Inuvik, Northwest Territories
CFYK Yellow Knife, Northwest Territories
CHFN-FM Cape Croker (Neyaashiinigmiing), Ontario
CFOS Collingwood, Ontario
CBQTFM Fort Frances, Ontario
CHML Hamilton, Ontario
CBQXFM Kenora, Ontario
CKGL(AM) Kitchener, Ontario
CFPL London, Ontario
CJBK London, Ontario
CFMJ Richmond Hill, Ontario
CBEGFM Sarnia, Ontario
CBQLFM Savant Lake, Ontario
CKTB St. Catharines, Ontario
CBCSFM Sudbury, Ontario
CKLU-FM Sudbury, Ontario
CBQ-FM Thunder Bay, Ontario
CFRB Toronto, Ontario
CFTR Toronto, Ontario
CHXX-FM Donnacona, Quebec
CHRD-FM Drummondville, Quebec
CJRD-FM Drummondville, Quebec
CBMR-FM Fermont, Quebec
CFIM-FM Iles-de-la-Madeleine, Quebec
CBV-FM-6 La Malbaie, Quebec
CKWE-FM Maniwaki (Kitigan Zibi Anishinabeg, Quebec
CBME-FM Montreal, Quebec
CJAD Montreal, Quebec
CBV-FM Quebec, Quebec
CBVEFM Quebec, Quebec
CJBRFM Rimouski, Quebec
CBGN(AM) Sainte Anne des Monts, Quebec
CKCN-FM Sept-Iles, Quebec
CKSM Shawinigan, Quebec
CFLXFM Sherbrooke, Quebec
CFEI St-Hyacinthe, Quebec
CJME Regina, Saskatchewan
CKOM Saskatoon, Saskatchewan
CBK Watrous, Saskatchewan

News/Talk

CBR Calgary, Alberta
CHQR Calgary, Alberta
CBX Edmonton, Alberta
CHFA Edmonton, Alberta
CKFR Kelowna, British Columbia
CKNW New Westminster, British Columbia
CFAX Victoria, British Columbia
CJOB Winnipeg, Manitoba
CBZ-FM Fredericton, New Brunswick
CKNI-FM Moncton, New Brunswick
CHNI-FM Saint John, New Brunswick
CKIM Baie Verte, Newfoundland
CBY Corner Brook, Newfoundland
VOCM St. John's, Newfoundland
CBN-FM Saint John's, Newfoundland
CJNI-FM Halifax, Nova Scotia
CHAK Inuvik, Northwest Territories

RADIO - CANADA

CFYK Yellow Knife, Northwest Territories
CFOS Collingwood, Ontario
CHML Hamilton, Ontario
CKGL(AM) Kitchener, Ontario
CFPL London, Ontario
CJBK London, Ontario
CFMJ Richmond Hill, Ontario
CKTB St. Catharines, Ontario
CBCSFM Sudbury, Ontario
CKLU-FM Sudbury, Ontario
CFRB Toronto, Ontario
CHXX-FM Donnacona, Quebec
CBGA Gaspe, Quebec
CFIM-FM Iles-de-la-Madeleine, Quebec
CJAD Montreal, Quebec
CBV-FM Quebec, Quebec
CBVEFM Quebec, Quebec
CJBRFM Rimouski, Quebec
CKCN-FM Sept-Iles, Quebec
CKSM Shawinigan, Quebec
CFLXFM Sherbrooke, Quebec
CJME Regina, Saskatchewan
CKOM Saskatoon, Saskatchewan

Oldies

CKRA-FM Edmonton, Alberta
CHAD-FM Dawson Creek, British Columbia
CIBH-FM Parksville, British Columbia
CFBV Smithers, British Columbia
CKKSFM Vancouver, British Columbia
CJNU-FM Winnipeg, Manitoba
CFBC Saint John, New Brunswick
VOWR St. John's, Newfoundland
CKUL-FM Halifax, Nova Scotia
CFOS Collingwood, Ontario
CJOY Guelph, Ontario
CKOC Hamilton, Ontario
CKKW-FM Kitchener, Ontario
CIWW Ottawa, Ontario
CKDR-FM-2 Sioux Lookout, Ontario
CJCS Stratford, Ontario
CKYK-FM Alma, Quebec
CFTH-FM-1 Harrington Harbour, Quebec
CHRG-FM Maria (Reserve), Quebec
CFZZ-FM Saint Jean-Iberville, Quebec
CFEI St-Hyacinthe, Quebec
CJVD-FM Vaudreuil-Dorion, Quebec
CJNE-FM Nipawin, Saskatchewan
CKBI Prince Albert, Saskatchewan

Public Affairs

CBG Gander, Newfoundland
CBT Grand Falls, Alberta
CFGB-FM Happy Valley, Newfoundland
CBI Sydney, Nova Scotia
CJLX Belleville, Ontario
CBQXFM Kenora, Ontario
CBEGFM Sarnia, Ontario
CBQLFM Savant Lake, Ontario
CBMIFM Baie-Comeau, Quebec
CJBE-FM Port-Menier, Quebec
CBKA-FM La Ronge, Saskatchewan

Religious

CHRB High River, Alberta
CJRB Boissevain, Manitoba
KCNM Saipan, Guam
VOAR St. John's, Newfoundland
CHSB-FM Bedford, Nova Scotia
CJTK-FM Sudbury, Ontario
CIRA Montreal, Quebec
CION Quebec, Quebec

Rock/AOR

CKLM-FM Lloydminster, Alberta
CHDR-FM Cranbrook, British Columbia
CJDR-FM Fernie, British Columbia
CFFMFM Kamloops, British Columbia
CIFM-FM Kamloops, British Columbia
CJUI-FM Kelowna, British Columbia
CKLZ-FM Kelowna, British Columbia
CJMGFM Penticton, British Columbia
CJZN-FM Victoria, British Columbia
CJAR The Pas, Manitoba
CKHY-FM Halifax, Nova Scotia
CJLX Belleville, Ontario
CFNYFM Brampton, Ontario
CJXY-FM Burlington, Ontario
CKUE-FM Chatham, Ontario
CKQB Ottawa, Ontario
CHKS-FM Sarnia, Ontario
CHTZFM St Catharines, Ontario
CJSDFM Thunder Bay, Ontario
CJQQ-FM Timmins, Ontario
CIBU-FM Wingham, Ontario
CKTF Hull, Quebec
CFOR-FM Maniwaki, Quebec
CIKIFM Rimouski, Quebec
CFJO-FM Thetford Mines, Quebec
CHQX-FM Prince Albert, Saskatchewan
CIZLFM Regina, Saskatchewan

Smooth Jazz

CJGV-FM Winnipeg, Manitoba

Sports

CFAC Calgary, Alberta
CHQR Calgary, Alberta
CFRN Edmonton, Alberta
CHED Edmonton, Alberta
CKFR Kelowna, British Columbia
CKNW New Westminster, British Columbia
CHML Hamilton, Ontario
CKGL(AM) Kitchener, Ontario
CFPL London, Ontario
CHOP-FM Newmarket, Ontario
CKAC Montreal, Quebec
CHRC Quebec, Quebec
CKSM Shawinigan, Quebec

Talk

CBR Calgary, Alberta
CBRFFM Calgary, Alberta
CHQR Calgary, Alberta
CBX Edmonton, Alberta
CHED Edmonton, Alberta
CHFA Edmonton, Alberta
CFCH-FM Chase, British Columbia
CKFR Kelowna, British Columbia
CKNW New Westminster, British Columbia
CHMJ Vancouver, British Columbia
CFAX Victoria, British Columbia
CFNC(AM) Cross Lake, Manitoba
CBWK-FM Thompson, Manitoba
CJOB Winnipeg, Manitoba
CBZ-FM Fredericton, New Brunswick
CBA-FM Moncton, New Brunswick
CKNI-FM Moncton, New Brunswick
CBD-FM Saint John, New Brunswick
CHNI-FM Saint John, New Brunswick
CKIM Baie Verte, Newfoundland
CBY Corner Brook, Newfoundland
CKGA Gander, Newfoundland
VOCM St. John's, Newfoundland
CBDQ-FM Labrador City, Newfoundland
CIFX-FM Lewisporte, Newfoundland
CBN-FM Saint John's, Newfoundland
CJNI-FM Halifax, Nova Scotia
CHAK Inuvik, Northwest Territories
CFYK Yellow Knife, Northwest Territories
CBQR-FM Rankin Inlet, Nunavut
CJBQ Belleville, Ontario
CFOS Collingwood, Ontario
CHAM Hamilton, Ontario
CHML Hamilton, Ontario
CKGL(AM) Kitchener, Ontario
CFPL London, Ontario
CJBK London, Ontario
CHOP-FM Newmarket, Ontario
CFMJ Richmond Hill, Ontario
CKTB St. Catharines, Ontario
CBCSFM Sudbury, Ontario
CKLU-FM Sudbury, Ontario
CBQ-FM Thunder Bay, Ontario
CILU-FM Thunder Bay, Ontario
CFRB Toronto, Ontario
CIRR-FM Toronto, Ontario
CIWS-FM Whitchurch-Stouffville, Ontario
CBCTFM Charlottetown, Prince Edward Island
CHOW-FM Amos, Quebec
CBJ-FM Chicoutimi, Quebec
CBJEFM Chicoutimi, Quebec
CHXX-FM Donnacona, Quebec
CJRD-FM Drummondville, Quebec
CFIM-FM Iles-de-la-Madeleine, Quebec
CIDI-FM Lac-Brome, Quebec
CKWE-FM Maniwaki (Kitigan Zibi Anishinabeg, Quebec
CBF-FM Montreal, Quebec
CBM-FM Montreal, Quebec
CJAD Montreal, Quebec
CBV-FM Quebec, Quebec
CBVEFM Quebec, Quebec
CBVX-FM Quebec, Quebec
CHOIFM Quebec, Quebec
CJMFFM Quebec, Quebec
CJBRFM Rimouski, Quebec
CFND-FM Saint Jerome, Quebec
CBGN(AM) Sainte Anne des Monts, Quebec
CIBO-FM Senneterre, Quebec
CBSI-FM Sept-Iles, Quebec
CKCN-FM Sept-Iles, Quebec
CKSM Shawinigan, Quebec
CFLXFM Sherbrooke, Quebec
CJMQ-FM Sherbrooke, Quebec
CBF-FM-1 Trois Rivieres, Quebec
CIBL-FM Montreal, Quebec
CJME Regina, Saskatchewan
CKOM Saskatoon, Saskatchewan
CBK Watrous, Saskatchewan

Triple A

CBBSFM Sudbury, Ontario

Urban Contemporary

CIXXFM London, Ontario

Variety/Diverse

CBR Calgary, Alberta
CHFA Edmonton, Alberta
CKUA Edmonton, Alberta
CKUA-FM Edmonton, Alberta
CIAM-FM Fort Vermilion, Alberta
CKXU-FM Lethbridge, Alberta
CJSF-FM Burnaby, British Columbia
CHWK-FM Chilliwack, British Columbia
CIDO-FM Creston, British Columbia
CHAD-FM Dawson Creek, British Columbia
CFBX-FM Kamloops, British Columbia
CHLS-FM Lillooet, British Columbia
CHMM-FM MacKenzie, British Columbia
CJLY-FM Nelson, British Columbia
CJMP-FM Powell River, British Columbia
CFUR-FM Prince George, British Columbia
CIMM-FM Ucluelet, British Columbia
CITRFM Vancouver, British Columbia
CFUVFM Victoria, British Columbia
CJJJ-FM Brandon, Manitoba
CKXL-FM Saint Boniface, Manitoba
CICY-FM Selkirk, Manitoba
CKSB St. Boniface, Manitoba
CBWK-FM Thompson, Manitoba
CINC-FM Thompson, Manitoba
CBW Winnipeg, Manitoba
CJUM-FM Winnipeg, Manitoba
KRSI Garapan-Saipan, Guam
CIMS-FM Balmoral, New Brunswick
CJVA Caraquet, New Brunswick
CBZF-FM Fredericton, New Brunswick
CHSR-FM Fredericton, New Brunswick
CFJU-FM Kedgwick, New Brunswick
CKMA-FM Miramichi, New Brunswick
CBAL-FM Moncton, New Brunswick
CKUM Moncton, New Brunswick
CFMH-FM Saint John, New Brunswick
CHQC-FM Saint John, New Brunswick
CBN St. John's, Newfoundland
VOWR St. John's, Newfoundland
CHBI-FM Burnt Islands, Newfoundland
CJRM-FM Labrador City, Newfoundland
CHMR-FM Saint John's, Newfoundland
CFXU-FM Antigonish, Nova Scotia
CIFA-FM Comeauville, Nova Scotia
CBH-FM Halifax, Nova Scotia
CBHAFM Halifax, Nova Scotia
CKDU-FM Halifax, Nova Scotia
CFCT Tuktoyaktuk, Northwest Territories
CFYK Yellow Knife, Northwest Territories
CBQR-FM Rankin Inlet, Nunavut
CKON-FM Akwesasne, Ontario
CHXL Brockville, Ontario
CKUN-FM Christian Island, Ontario
CFDY-FM Cochrane, Ontario
CFGI-FM Georgina Island, Ontario
CFRUFM Guelph, Ontario
CKHA-FM Haliburton, Ontario
CFMUFM Hamilton, Ontario
CKGN-FM Kapuskasing, Ontario

CHCR-FM Killaloe, Ontario
CKVI-FM Kingston, Ontario
CJBC-FM-4 London, Ontario
CHMO(AM) Moosonee, Ontario
CKRZ-FM Ohsweken, Ontario
CKCUFM Ottawa, Ontario
CJIQ-FM Paris, Ontario
CFBU-FM Saint Catharines, Ontario
CJAI-FM Stella, Ontario
CBBX-FM Sudbury, Ontario
CKLU-FM Sudbury, Ontario
CHRY-FM Toronto, Ontario
CIUTFM Toronto, Ontario
CFWP-FM Wahta Mohawk Territory near Bala, Ontario
CKMSFM Waterloo, Ontario
CBE-FM Windsor, Ontario
CFID-FM Acton Vale, Quebec
CFMF-FM Fermont, Quebec
CBGA Gaspe, Quebec
CFIM-FM Iles-de-la-Madeleine, Quebec
CKAJ-FM Jonquiere, Quebec
CKAU-FM Maliotenam, Quebec
CBOF-1(AM) Maniwaki, Quebec
CHGAFM Maniwaki, Quebec
CHRG-FM Maria (Reserve), Quebec
CBFX-FM Montreal, Quebec
CJLO Montreal, Quebec
CKUT Montreal, Quebec
CKVL-FM Montreal (zone LaSalle), Quebec
CKAG-FM Pikogan, Quebec
CFVD-FM-2 Pohenegamook, Quebec
CBV-FM Quebec, Quebec
CBVEFM Quebec, Quebec
CKIA-FM Quebec, Quebec
CIAU-FM Radisson, Quebec
CHRL-FM Roberval, Quebec
CHYZ-FM Sainte Foy, Quebec
CBSI-FM Sept-Iles, Quebec
CFLXFM Sherbrooke, Quebec
CFOU-FM Trois Rivieres, Quebec
CIAX-FM Windsor, Quebec
CBKF-1(AM) Gravelbourg, Saskatchewan
CJLR-FM La Ronge, Saskatchewan
CBK-FM Regina, Saskatchewan
CBKFFM Regina, Saskatchewan
CFMQFM Regina, Saskatchewan
CJTR-FM Regina, Saskatchewan
CBKF-2(AM) Saskatoon, Saskatchewan
CBKS-FM Saskatoon, Saskatchewan
CFCR-FM Saskatoon, Saskatchewan
CBK Watrous, Saskatchewan
CIDD-FM White Bear Lake Resort, Saskatchewan

Special Programming on Radio Stations in Canada

Adult Contemp

CKXL-FM Saint Boniface, Manitoba
CFAN-FM Miramichi City, New Brunswick
VOWR St. John's, Newfoundland
CFGX-FM Sarnia, Ontario
CKUT Montreal, Quebec

Agriculture

CFAC Calgary, Alberta
CFCW Camrose, Alberta
CKDQ Drumheller, Alberta
CFXE-FM Edson, Alberta
CHRB High River, Alberta
CHLW St. Paul, Alberta
CKKY Wainwright, Alberta
CKSRFM Chilliwack, British Columbia
CIGVFM Penticton, British Columbia
V6AH(AM) Pohnpei, 66
CKLQ Brandon, Manitoba
CFRY Portage La Prairie, Manitoba
CBW Winnipeg, Manitoba
CBN St. John's, Newfoundland
CKDY Digby, Nova Scotia
CKEN-FM Kentville, Nova Scotia
CKAD Middleton, Nova Scotia
CJBQ Belleville, Ontario
CFCO Chatham, Ontario
CFRB Toronto, Ontario
CJSL Estevan, Saskatchewan
CKBI Prince Albert, Saskatchewan
CKSW Swift Current, Saskatchewan
CBK Watrous, Saskatchewan
CFSL Weyburn, Saskatchewan

Big Band

CFBG-FM Bracebridge, Ontario

Black

CJSR-FM Edmonton, Alberta
CFROFM Vancouver, British Columbia
CKCUFM Ottawa, Ontario
CJAM-FM Windsor, Ontario
CKUT Montreal, Quebec
CKRLFM Quebec, Quebec
CFNJFM St-Gabriel, Quebec
CIBL-FM Montreal, Quebec
CJTR-FM Regina, Saskatchewan

Blues

CKXL-FM Saint Boniface, Manitoba
KRSI Garapan-Saipan, Guam
CHMR-FM Saint John's, Newfoundland
CFMUFM Hamilton, Ontario
CIEUFM Carleton, Quebec

Children

CHVN-FM Winnipeg, Manitoba
CKUW-FM Winnipeg, Manitoba
CHRI-FM Ottawa, Ontario

Chinese

CFROFM Vancouver, British Columbia
KRNM Chalan Kanoa-Saipan, Guam
CINQFM Montreal, Quebec
CJTR-FM Regina, Saskatchewan

Christian

CIXXFM London, Ontario

Classical

CJSR-FM Edmonton, Alberta
CKBX One Hundred Mile Hou, British Columbia
CIGVFM Penticton, British Columbia
CFAM Altona, Manitoba
CBW Winnipeg, Manitoba
CKUW-FM Winnipeg, Manitoba
CJLX Belleville, Ontario
CHODFM Cornwall, Ontario
CFMUFM Hamilton, Ontario
CHASFM Sault Ste Marie, Ontario
CFRB Toronto, Ontario
CJAM-FM Windsor, Ontario
CIHOFM Baie St Paul, Quebec
CIEUFM Carleton, Quebec
CHIPFM Fort-Coulonge, Quebec
CJRGFM Gaspe, Quebec
CHGAFM Maniwaki, Quebec
CKIA-FM Quebec, Quebec
CKMN-FM Rimouski-Mont Joli, Quebec
CJMC-FM Sainte Anne des Monts, Quebec
CFLXFM Sherbrooke, Quebec
CJSO-FM Sorel, Quebec

Comedy

CFBW-FM Hanover, Ontario

Contemporary Hits/Top 40

CKHC-FM Toronto, Ontario

Country

CBW Winnipeg, Manitoba
CJVA Caraquet, New Brunswick
CFJU-FM Kedgwick, New Brunswick
CFNOFM Marathon, Ontario
CFMF-FM Fermont, Quebec
CFIN-FM Lac-Etchemin, Quebec
CHGAFM Maniwaki, Quebec
CKCN-FM Sept-Iles, Quebec
CFNJFM St-Gabriel, Quebec
CFDA-FM Victoriaville, Quebec

Disco

CKMFFM Montreal, Quebec

Ethnic

V6AI(AM) Yap, 66
CJAR The Pas, Manitoba
CHSR-FM Fredericton, New Brunswick
CKXD-FM Gander, Newfoundland
CKJM-FM Cheticamp, Nova Scotia
CKEC-FM New Glasgow, Nova Scotia
CHAK Inuvik, Northwest Territories
CFCT Tuktoyaktuk, Northwest Territories
CFYK Yellow Knife, Northwest Territories
CBQR-FM Rankin Inlet, Nunavut
CBQTFM Fort Frances, Ontario
CBQSFM Sioux Narrows, Ontario
CJDL-FM Tillsonburg, Ontario
CFZM(AM) Toronto, Ontario
CKWR Waterloo, Ontario
CKDG-FM Montreal, Quebec
CJBRFM Rimouski, Quebec
CBKA-FM La Ronge, Saskatchewan
CJLR-FM La Ronge, Saskatchewan
CHONFM Whitehorse, Yukon Territory

Filipino

V6AI(AM) Yap, 66

French

CJSWFM Calgary, Alberta
CFUVFM Victoria, British Columbia
CKBC-FM Bathurst, New Brunswick
CKNB Campbellton, New Brunswick
CFDY-FM Cochrane, Ontario
CKLU-FM Sudbury, Ontario
CHRY-FM Toronto, Ontario
CIUTFM Toronto, Ontario
CHRC Quebec, Quebec
CFCR-FM Saskatoon, Saskatchewan
CFWH-FM Whitehorse, Yukon Territory

Gospel

CILKFM Kelowna, British Columbia
V6AH(AM) Pohnpei, 66
CHVN-FM Winnipeg, Manitoba
CFCO Chatham, Ontario
CKSYFM Chatham, Ontario
CFBW-FM Hanover, Ontario
CKOTFM Tillsonburg, Ontario
CHIPFM Fort-Coulonge, Quebec
CJWW Saskatoon, Saskatchewan

Greek

CKJR Wetaskiwin, Alberta
CFROFM Vancouver, British Columbia
CJLX Belleville, Ontario
CKWR Waterloo, Ontario
CHAA-FM Longueuil, Quebec
CINQFM Montreal, Quebec

Italian

CJSWFM Calgary, Alberta
CKER-FM Edmonton, Alberta
CFUVFM Victoria, British Columbia
CKJS Winnipeg, Manitoba
CFRUFM Guelph, Ontario
CJQMFM Sault Ste Marie, Ontario
CKLU-FM Sudbury, Ontario
CKRLFM Quebec, Quebec
CFCR-FM Saskatoon, Saskatchewan

Japanese

CHMB Vancouver, British Columbia
V6AI(AM) Yap, 66

Jazz

CKMX Calgary, Alberta
CKXL-FM Saint Boniface, Manitoba
CKUW-FM Winnipeg, Manitoba
KRSI Garapan-Saipan, Guam
CJMOFM Moncton, New Brunswick
CKUM Moncton, New Brunswick
CHMR-FM Saint John's, Newfoundland
CKJM-FM Cheticamp, Nova Scotia
CJLX Belleville, Ontario
CFBG-FM Bracebridge, Ontario
CHODFM Cornwall, Ontario
CHUO-FM Ottawa, Ontario
CKCUFM Ottawa, Ontario
CFBU-FM Saint Catharines, Ontario
CHASFM Sault Ste Marie, Ontario
CHRY-FM Toronto, Ontario
CJAM-FM Windsor, Ontario
CIHOFM Baie St Paul, Quebec
CIEUFM Carleton, Quebec
CFMF-FM Fermont, Quebec
CJRGFM Gaspe, Quebec
CFIN-FM Lac-Etchemin, Quebec
CHGAFM Maniwaki, Quebec
CBVX-FM Quebec, Quebec
CKIA-FM Quebec, Quebec
CIAU-FM Radisson, Quebec
CKLEFM Rimouski, Quebec
CFLXFM Sherbrooke, Quebec
CFNJFM St-Gabriel, Quebec
CIBL-FM Montreal, Quebec

Korean

KRNM Chalan Kanoa-Saipan, Guam

Native American

CJSR-FM Edmonton, Alberta
CHMB Vancouver, British Columbia
CFUVFM Victoria, British Columbia
CHTM Thompson, Manitoba
CHSR-FM Fredericton, New Brunswick
CKON-FM Akwesasne, Ontario
CFBU-FM Saint Catharines, Ontario
CKRK-FM Kahnawake, Quebec
CJTR-FM Regina, Saskatchewan

News

CBCLFM London, Ontario
CKPR-FM Thunder Bay, Ontario
CBVX-FM Quebec, Quebec

News/Talk

CISCFM Gibsons, British Columbia
CFPR Prince Rupert, British Columbia
CKKSFM Vancouver, British Columbia
CIOK-FM Saint John, New Brunswick
CFBG-FM Bracebridge, Ontario
CKPR-FM Thunder Bay, Ontario

Oldies

CJSU-FM Duncan, British Columbia
CKXX-FM Corner Brook, Newfoundland
CHIPFM Fort-Coulonge, Quebec
CJLM-FM Joliette, Quebec
CHAA-FM Longueuil, Quebec
CKMN-FM Rimouski-Mont Joli, Quebec
CFDA-FM Victoriaville, Quebec

Polish

CKJS Winnipeg, Manitoba
CKLU-FM Sudbury, Ontario
CFCR-FM Saskatoon, Saskatchewan

Portugese

CJSF-FM Burnaby, British Columbia
CJOR(AM) Osoyoos, British Columbia
CJDV-FM Cambridge, Ontario
CINQFM Montreal, Quebec

Reggae

KRSI Garapan-Saipan, Guam
CIBL-FM Montreal, Quebec

Religious

CKDQ Drumheller, Alberta
CHLW St. Paul, Alberta
CIVH Vanderhoof, British Columbia
V6AH(AM) Pohnpei, 66
CHTM Thompson, Manitoba
CFAN-FM Miramichi City, New Brunswick
CJCW Sussex, New Brunswick
VOWR St. John's, Newfoundland
CFSX Stephenville, Newfoundland
CHMR-FM Saint John's, Newfoundland
CJSS-FM Cornwall, Ontario
CFRUFM Guelph, Ontario
CJTW-FM Kitchener-Waterloo, Ontario
CKDO Oshawa, Ontario
CHUO-FM Ottawa, Ontario
CKNX Wingham, Ontario
CHRD-FM Drummondville, Quebec
CFIN-FM Lac-Etchemin, Quebec
CJSL Estevan, Saskatchewan
CKJH(AM) Melfort, Saskatchewan
CJDJ-FM Saskatoon, Saskatchewan
CFSL Weyburn, Saskatchewan

Spanish

CJSWFM Calgary, Alberta
CKER-FM Edmonton, Alberta
CKJS Winnipeg, Manitoba
CFRUFM Guelph, Ontario
CFMUFM Hamilton, Ontario
CHUO-FM Ottawa, Ontario
CIUTFM Toronto, Ontario
CKRLFM Quebec, Quebec
CFLXFM Sherbrooke, Quebec

Sports

CFFR Calgary, Alberta
CHWK-FM Chilliwack, British Columbia
CFMJ Richmond Hill, Ontario
CHOK Sarnia, Ontario

Talk

CKFR Kelowna, British Columbia
CHLS-FM Lillooet, British Columbia
CISQFM Squamish, British Columbia
CFNR-FM Terrace, British Columbia
CIXXFM London, Ontario
CKLPFM Parry Sound, Ontario
CKPR-FM Thunder Bay, Ontario

Urban Contemporary

CHYZ-FM Sainte Foy, Quebec

Vietnamese

CHMB Vancouver, British Columbia
CHAA-FM Longueuil, Quebec

Rank	Company	Subs
1	Comcast Corporation	22,118,000
2	DIRECTV (U.S. Only)	19,981,000
3	DISH Network Corporation	14,061,000
4	Time Warner Cable Inc.	12,484,000
5	Cox Communications, Inc.	4,660,675
6	Verizon Communications Inc.	4,473,000
7	Charter Communications, Inc.	4,269,000
8	AT&T Inc.	4,146,000
9	Cablevision Systems Corporation	3,257,000
10	Bright House Networks, LLC	2,058,667
11	Cequel Communications, LLC d/b/a Suddenlink Communications	1,230,100
12	Mediacom Communications Corporation	1,037,000
13	Cable One, Inc.	612,729
14	WideOpenWest Networks, LLC d/b/a WOW!	455,881
15	RCN Corporation	331,661
16	Knology, Inc.	254,856
17	Atlantic Broadband Group, LLC	251,718
18	Armstrong Utilities, Inc. d/b/a Armstrong Cable Services	237,349
19	Midcontinent Communications	229,359
20	Service Electric Cable TV Incorporated	215,679
21	MetroCast Cablevision	177,806
22	Blue Ridge Cable Technologies, Inc. d/b/a Blue Ridge Communications	166,824
23	WaveDivision Holdings, LLC	158,820
24	General Communication, Inc.	143,700
25	Buckeye CableSystem	132,565

Top 25 Cable Networks by Estimated Year End 2011 Subscribers

Rank	Network	Subs (mil.)
1	CNN	101.0
2	The Weather Channel	100.6
3	Discovery Channel	100.4
4	Nickelodeon/Nick At Nite/NickMom	100.2
5	Food Network	100.1
6	USA	100.0
7	TNT	99.9
8	A&E	99.7
9	ESPN	99.7
10	ESPN2	99.5
11	Lifetime Television	99.5
12	HGTV	99.4
13	Spike TV	99.4
14	Disney Channel	99.4
15	Cartoon Network	99.3
16	TLC	99.3
17	C-SPAN	99.3
18	MTV	99.2
19	Comedy Central	98.9
20	HLN	98.9
21	History	98.8
22	FOX News	98.7
23	Syfy	98.7
24	VH1	98.7
25	FX Network	98.4

Top 25 Cable Companies by Basic Video Penetration of Homes Passed as of Q2 2012

Rank	Network	Basic Vid./HP
1	Adams CATV, Inc.	73.1%
2	Blue Ridge Cable Technologies, Inc. d/b/a Blue Ridge Communications*	69.1%
3	Massillon Cable TV, Inc.	66.4%
4	TV Service Incorporated*	64.3%
5	Armstrong Utilities, Inc. d/b/a Armstrong Cable Services	59.9%
6	Arvig Communication Systems	59.8%
7	General Communication, Inc. (GNCMA)	59.3%
8	Rainbow Communications	59.2%
9	Cablevision Systems Corporation (CVC)	58.0%
10	BendCable Communications, LLC d/b/a BendBroadband	53.6%
11	Mid-Hudson Cablevision Inc.	52.4%
12	Cass Cable TV, Inc.	50.6%
13	Hector Communications Corporation*	49.1%
14	Schurz Communications, Inc.*	49.0%
15	Atlantic Broadband Group, LLC	48.8%
16	Bright House Networks, LLC*	48.2%
17	Allen's TV Cable Service Inc.*	47.0%
18	Cox Communications, Inc.*	45.6%
19	Buckeye CableSystem*	45.4%
20	Sweetwater Cable Television	45.2%
21	Comporium Communications	44.1%
22	MetroCast Cablevision	43.2%
23	Tele-Media Corporation of Delaware	43.1%
24	Midcontinent Communications	42.9%
25	Cable One, Inc.	42.7%

Top 10 Cable Programs

RANK	PROGRAM	NETWORK	US AA % LIVE + SD
20	BCS CHAMPIONSHIP L	ESPN	14.0
37	ROSE BOWL L	ESPN	10.2
59	NFL REGULAR SEASON L	ESPN	8.4
59	FIESTA BOWL L	ESPN	8.4
128	SUGAR BOWL L	ESPN	6.2
245	ORANGE BOWL L	ESPN	4.5
259	REPUBLICAN PRES DEBATE(S)-12/15/2011	FOXNC	4.4
306	REPUBLICAN PRES DEBATE(S)-09/22/2011	FOXNC	4.0
317	REPUBLICAN PRES DEBATE(S)-09/22/2011	FOXNC	3.9
362	NBA ALLSTAR SAT NIGHT(S)-02/25/2012	TNT	3.6

Source: Television Bureau of Advertising, based on data from Nielsen Galaxy Lightning. Ranked by average audience percentage of the total number of homes in the U.S. with TV sets. Full Season: 9/19/11-5/23/12. Reprinted with permission.

National Cable Networks

A&E Network
on 10,000 Cable Systems
235 E. 45th St., New York, NY 10017
(212) 210-1400, *Fax:* (212) 210-9755
www.aetv.com
Satellite: Galaxy V*Transponder:* 23
Mel Berning, President
David Zagin, Operations Dir
A&E Network offers discerning viewers a unique blend of original progmg featuring its signature series BIOGRAPHY, original movies, dramas, series & documentaries.

ABC Family Channel
500 S. Buena Vista St., Burbank, CA 91521
(818) 560-1000, *Fax:* (818) 560-1930
www.abcfamily.com
Satellite: Galaxy V*Transponder:* 11
Anne Sweeney, Chairman
Basic cable network available in over 87 million homes nationwide 24 hours; delivers a dynamic mix of quality entertainment with original series & movies, classics from Disney.
1422 W. Main St, Suite 201, Lewisville, TX 75067-3388
(972) 436-2217; *Fax:* (972) 436-0209
Mark Solow, Dir Southwest Rgn
660 Newport Center Dr, Suite 770, Newport Beach, CA 92660-6401
(714) 759-7685; *Fax:* (714) 759-9491
Janice Slipp, Dir Western Rgn
5445 DCT Pkwy, Suite 525, Englewood, CO
(303) 220-8901; *Fax:* (303) 220-9102
Tracy Jenkins, J.D., Dir Rocky Mountain Rgn
1301 W. 22nd St, Suite 902, Oakbrook, IL 60523-2006
(630) 990-0437; *Fax:* (630) 990-0463
Ralph Trentadue, Natl Dir Lcl Adv Sls
Shirley Hill, Vp Western Division
Box 2050, 2877 Guardian Ln, Virginia Beach, VA
(757) 459-6281; *Fax:* (757) 459-6429
Craig Sherwood, Sr Vp/Mgng Dir
Box 492347, Atlanta, GA 30349-9338
(770) 461-4929; *Fax:* (770) 461-8678
Russell A. Breault, Vp Eastern Division
1133 Ave. of the Americas, 36th Fl, New York, NY 10036-6710
(212) 782-1860; *Fax:* (212) 782-1865
Steve Israelsky, Vp Northeast Rgn

ABS-CBN (The Fiilipino Channel)
859 Cowan Rd., Burlingame, CA 94010
(650) 697-3700, *Fax:* (650) 697-3500
www.abs-bn.com
Augusto Almeda-Lopez, Chairman
A 24-hour all Filipino premium svc ch delivered via satellite from the Philippines. Serving 35,000 subs on 11 systems. Satellite: Galaxy 11, transponder 24.

ABS-CBN International
100,000 Subscribers served on 144 Cable Systems
Div/DBA: (formerly 14BS-CBN International)
150 Shoreline Dr., Redwood City, CA 94065-1400
(650) 508-6000, *Fax:* (650) 551-1062
www.abs-cbni.com
tfc@abs-cbni.com
Rafael Lopez, President
Jun del Rosario, Operations Dir
A 24-hour svc for Filipinos worldwide. Progmg originates at ABS-CBN, the Philippines top-rated net. Time-shifted for North America.
Satellite: Galaxy 11, PAS-2 for Pacific delivery, Telstar 5 (ku) transponder 22 for North America.

Access Television Network Inc.
40 million Subscribers served on 650 Cable Systems
2600 Michelson Dr., Suite 1650, Irvine, CA 92612
(949) 263-9900, *Fax:* (949) 622-6295
www.accesstv.com
info@accesstv.com
Transponder: 9
Robert T. Tyler, CFO
Mark R. Russo, President
Organized natl marketplace for paid progmg on loc cable systems. Galaxy 11.
1020 15th St., Unit 30, Denver, CO 80202-2300

African Independent Television (AIT)
One AIT Rd., PMB 1309, Apapa, Alagbado-Lagos, Nigeria
(212) 213-2070
www.aittv.com
Satellite: Telstar 5*Transponder:* 5
Ladi Lawal, COO
AIT is a Pan-African gen entertainment ch offering news, talk show, soap opera, sports, Afician culture & music 24 hours a day. Areas: United States & Afica.

AMC
85 million Subscribers served
Div/DBA: (Rainbow Programming Service Holdings Inc.)
200 Jericho Quadrangle, Jericho, NY 11753
(516) 803-2300
www.amctv.com
Satellite: Satcom C-4*Transponder:* 1
Charlie Collier, President
David Sehring, Operations Dir
AMC is a 24 hour, movie-based mix or original series, documentaries & specials.

America's Collectibles Network (ACNTV)
10001 Kingston Park, Suite 57, Knoxville, TN 37922
(865) 693-8471, *Fax:* (865) 560-3298
www.acntv.com
F. Robert Hall, President
Harris Bagley, Operations Dir
ACNT offers a wide var of jewelry & gemstones at reduced prices, 24 hours a day home shopping, in the United States & Canada. Serving more than 63 million subs. Satellite: Telstar7, Transponder 21, Galaxy 11, Transponder 19.

AmericanLife TV Network
Div/DBA: (formerly GoodLife TV Network)
650 Massachusetts Ave. N.W., Suite 202, Washington, DC 20001
(202) 289-6633, *Fax:* (202) 289-6632
www.americanlifetv.com
Mark Ringwald, Programming Director
Shera Higgs Thompson, Promotions Manager
Speaks to the interests & values of the unstopable Baby Boomer delivering enteraining classic programs & awarding-winning originals.

Animal Planet
One Discovery Pl., Silver Spring, MD 20910
(240) 662-2000, *Fax:* (240) 662-1854
www.animalplanet.com
first_last@discovery.com
Marjorie Kaplan, President
Available in more than 94 million homes in the U.S., online assets, the ultimate online destination for all things animal, 24/7 broadband ch, Animal Planet Beyond, Petfinder.com, pet adoption, PetsIncredible, a major producer & distributorof pet-training videos & web svc & other media platforms, a robust VOD svc, mobile content & merchandising extensions.

Anime Network
10114 West Sam Houston Pkwy. S., Suite 200, Houston, TX 77099
(713) 341-7200, *Fax:* (713) 341-7199
www.theanimenetwork.com
John Ledford, Chairman
Anime is an exploration of Western pop culture. Anime reaches males 18-35 demographic with four different genres, including martial arts, comedy, science fiction & drama 24 hours a day, basic ad-supported. Serving more than 84 million subs.

ART (Arab Radio & Television)
315 Arden Ave., Suite 26, Glendale, CA 91203
(818) 243-0278, *Fax:* (818) 243-9278
www.art.tv.net
Michael Scott, Operations Dir
ART's foundation is based on the largest gen entertainment library in the Middle East. Available 24 hours a day in North America, has progmg targeted to second generation Arab Americans. Satellite: Galaxy 11, transponder 24.

Automotive Networks Corp.
Div/DBA: WheelsTV
289 Great Rd., Acton, MA 01720
(978) 264-4333, *Fax:* (978) 264-9547
www.wheelstv.net
jimbar@wheelstv.net
Automotive entertainment & info via video on demand, worldwide web & dir mktg.
Serving 9.1 million subs.

AYM Sports
Avenida Chapultepac 405, Colonia Juarez, Delegacion Cuauhtemoc, Mexico, 06600

www.aymsports.tv
Benjamin Hinojosa, President
Carlos Carrillo, Programming Director
Available 24 hours a day, 100% Mexican network consisting of soccer, basketball, rodeo charreadas, horse racing, boxing, kick boxing, jujitsu, karate, tae kwon do, swimming, driving, truck series, rallies and much more. Satellite: Telestar7, transponder 12.

BabyFirstTV
Box 25639, Los Angeles, CA 90025
(888) 251-2229
www.babyfirsttv.com
Guy Oranim, CEO
Sharon Rechter, President
Arik Kerman, Operations Dir

Bandamax
5999 Center Dr., Los Angeles, CA 90045
(301) 348-3371
www.tutv.tv
Carlos Madrazo, CFO
Chris Fager, President
Ariela Nerobay, General Sales Mgr
Bandamax features a 24-hour a day country music video, including best artists in Tex-Mex, Norteno, Banda & Manachi genres. De Pelicula Sp-language films, De Pelicula Clasico films of Mexico's golden era.

BBC America
37 million Subscribers served
747 3rd Ave., Fl. 6, New York, NY 10017-2871
(301) 347-2222, (212) 705-9387
www.bbcamerica.com
Satellite: Galaxy VII*Transponder:* 22
Bill Hilary, President
Kathryn Mitchell, General Manager
BBC America is a 24 hour award-winning TV featuring razor-sharp comedies, provocative dramas & life changing makeovers. Digital, Analog & DBS. Satellite: Satcom C3.

BET (Black Entertainment Television)
78 million Subscribers served
1235 W St. N.E., Washington, DC 20018
(202) 608-2000, *Fax:* (202) 608-2631
www.bet.com
bet-tv_bizdev@bet.com
Satellite: Galaxy V*Transponder:* 20
Scott Mills, COO
BET is the nation's leading TV network providing 24 hour for African-American audience in the United States, Canada & the Caribbean. BET Digital Networks-BET jazz, BET Gospel & BET Hip-Hop.
BET/Los Angeles - Production
2801 W. Olive Ave, Burbank, CA 91505-4578
(818) 566-9940; *Fax:* (818) 566-1655
BET Film Production Facility
2000 West Pl. N.E., Washington, DC 20018-1226
(202) 608-2800; *Fax:* (202) 608-2629
BET/New York
380 Madison Ave, 20th Fl, New York, NY 10017-2513
(212) 716-5600; *Fax:* (212) 697-2050
Network Operations
1899 Ninth St. N.E., Washington, DC 20018-1001
(202) 608-2800;
BET/Chicago
180 N. Stetson Ct, Suite 4350, Chicago, IL 60601-6710
(312) 819-8600;

BET Jazz: The Jazz Channel
9 million Subscribers served
1235 W St. N. E., Washington, DC 20018
(202) 608-2000, *Fax:* (202) 608-2631
www.bet.com
Satellite: Galaxy VII*Transponder:* 21
Robert L. Johnson, Chairman
The Jazz Channel is a 24-hour TV progmg svc dedicated exclusively to jazz through in-studio performances, documentaries,concert coverage & celebrity interviews.

BLACK BELT TV/The Martial Arts Network
880 Calle Primavera, San Dimas, CA 91773
(909) 971-9300, *Fax:* (909) 854-9329
www.blackbelttv.com
info@blackbelttv.com
Erik D. Jones, President
A 24/7 cable TV net that targets demographics highly desired by advertisers. Our appeal focuses on all income level individuals & families. Provides progmg for advertisers seeking to attract martial arts practitioners/enthusiasts,health/fitness-minded individuals, as well as sports enthusiasts, suppliers of exercise equipment, & other companies & product manufacturers that can directly reach their target audience. Our progmg includes martial arts movies, martial artstraining/self-defense, self-improvement programs, sports, women, & children-oriented programs, martial arts news, & much more.

Bloomberg Television
499 Park Ave., New York, NY 10022
(212) 893-3331, *Fax:* (202) 522-2400
www.bloomberg.com/media/tv
Kenneth Kohn, Operations Dir
Betsy Alekman, Promotions Manager
A sophisticated 24-hour business & financial news ch. Serving over 200 million subs worldwide, United States, Canada, Central & South America, Europe,& Asia/Pacific. Satellite: Galaxy 11, HITS, C3.

BlueHighways TV
111 Shivel Dr., Hendersonville, TN 37075
(615) 264-3292, *Fax:* (615) 264-3308
www.bluehighwaystv.com
feedback@bluehighwaystv.com
Stan Hitchcock, Chairman
BlueHighways TV is a multi-platform progmg svc featuring roots music, American culture & back roads exploration. Satelite: AMC-10. Transponder 15.

The Boating Channel (TBC)
Box 1148, Sag Harbor, NY 11963
(631) 725-4440, *Fax:* (631) 725-0748
www.boatingchannel.com
service@baotingchannel.com
Daniel E. London, COO
Barbara London, President
Gregory Hahn, Programming Director
Marine news & weather, entertainment, info & educ for the recreational, professional boater & cruise vacationer.

Boston Kids & Family TV
43 Hawkins St., Suite 1B, Boston, MA 02114
(617) 635-3112, *Fax:* (617) 635-4475
www.cityofboston.gov/cable
cable@ci.boston.ma.us
Michael Lynch, General Manager
David Burt, Station Manager
A partnership between the City of Boston & WGBH. Available 24 hour a day , edu TV progmg. PBS Kids from WGBH in Boston.

Bravo
Div/DBA: NBCUniversal
30 Rockefeller Plaza, 14th Fl. E., New York, NY 10112
(212) 664-4444
www.bravotv.com

Buzztime Entertainment, Inc.
5966 La Place Ct., Suite 100, Carlsbad, CA 92008
(760) 476-1976, *Fax:* (760) 438-3505
www.buzztime.com
Stanley Kinsey, Chairman
Buzztime is the only 24-hour interactive entertainment bcst created exclusively for TV audiences. Featuring play-along trivia games for players of all interests & ability levels.

C-SPAN (Cable Satellite Public Affairs Network)
87 million Subscribers served
400 N. Capitol St. N.W., Suite 650, Washington, DC 20001
(202) 737-3220, *Fax:* (202) 737-3323
www.c-span.org
Satellite: Satcom C-3 *Transponder:* 7
Brian P. Lamb, Chairman
C-SPAN progmg includes live coverage of the House of Representatives, National Pres Club speeches & congressional hearings. C-SPAN 2 live coverage of the U.S. Senate & C-SPAN 3 pub affrs TV.

c/net: the computer network
235 Second St., San Francisco, CA 94105
(415) 344-2000
www.cnet.com
Shelby Bonnie, CEO
CNET news.com, airs weekly on CNBC & CNET tv.com airs on syndication.

The California Channel
5.8 million Subscribers served on 114 Cable Systems
1121 L St., Suite 110, Sacramento, CA 95814
(916) 444-9792, *Fax:* (916) 444-9812
www.calchannel.com
contactus@calchannel.com
Transponder: 3 C
John Hancock, President
Televised coverage of California state legislature & govt agency proceedings. M-F, 9 AM-3:30 PM. Satellite: Galaxy 15.

Canal 24 Horas
1100 Ponce de Leon Blvd., Coral Gables, FL 33134
(305) 444-4402, *Fax:* (305) 444-6301
www.rtve.es
aragon@tveamerica.com
Mariano Aragon, General Manager
A 24 hour news network from TVE which offers a Headline News fromat with 30 minute blocks. The network also produces 17 different 30 minutes daily & wkly news magazines. Areas: United States, Mexico, Caribbean,

Cartoon Network
1050 Techwood Dr. N.W., Altanta, GA 30318
(404) 827-4700, (404) 827-1700
www.cartoonnetwork.com
Satellite: Galaxy IR *Transponder:* 8 (East)
Gary Albright, Operations Dir
Bob Higgins, Programming Director
Dennis Adamovich, Promotions Manager
A Turner Broadcasting System. Inc.'s 24-hour Cartoon Network offers the best in animated entertainment. Drawing from the world's largest cartoon library, also showcases unique original ventures such as Johnny Bravo, Cow and Chicken, Dexter'sLaboratory, Ed, Edd n Eddy, and Cartoon Cartoon. Serving 86 million subs around the world. Satellite: Galaxy 1, transponder 15 (West).

Cartoon Network Latin America
1050 Techwood Dr., N.W., Atlanta, GA 30318
(404) 885-4398, (404) 827-1700, *Fax:* (404) 885-2157
www.cartoonnetworkla.com
larissa.pissarra@turner.com
The first global 24-hour cable ch programmed entirely with cartoons. Available in Sp, Portuguese or English.
Serving more than 10.9 million subs. Satellite: PanAmSat 3R.

CBS College Sports Network
15 million Subscribers served
85 10th Ave., 3rd Fl., New York, NY 10011
(212) 342-8700, *Fax:* (212) 342-8899
www.cstv.com
Satellite: Galaxy IR *Transponder:* 22
The network televises regular season & championship events coverage from every major collegiate athletic conference & televises nine NCAA Championships available 24-hour, ad-supported..

CCTV 4
11 Fuxing Rd., Beijing, 100859 China
(310) 414-2110, 011-86-10-6-850-6517, *Fax:* (310) 141-2101, 011-86-10-6-851-4993
www.cctv-4.com
Michael Scott, Operations Dir
China Central TV (CCTV) China's only national bcstg network. Provide Info about China's politics, economy, society, culture, science, edu & history, also Chinese viewers, living outside of China, 24 hours a day. Serving more than 100 millionsubs. Satellite: Galaxy 11, transponder 24.

Channel One Russia Worldwide Network
20 Frunzenskaya Daberezhmaya, Suite D, Moscow, 119146
(310) 414-2110, *Fax:* (310) 414-2101
www.firstchannel.tv
David Quinn, General Manager
A 24-hour Russian language ch for Russian communities throughout the United States. The ch consists of dramas, movies, news, children progmg, sports, talk show and more. Satellite: Galaxy 11, transponder 24.

Chronicle DTV
one million Subscribers served
53 W. 36th St., Suite 203, New York, NY 10018
(212) 337-9700 ext.105, *Fax:* (212) 352-1190
www.chronicledtv.com
Satellite: Telstar 5 *Transponder:* 22
David Peipers, Chairman
A 24-hour digital TV progmg network offering diverse selection of feature length non-fiction & documentary programs. Chronicle is seen in 35 cities in the United States, Los Angeles, Miami, West Palm Beach & Orlando.

Cinemax
Div/DBA: (Home Box Office)
1100 Ave. of the Americas, New York, NY 10036
(212) 512-1000, *Fax:* (212) 512-5637
www.cinemax.com
Cinemax is a 24-hour digital pay-TV svc designed to provide viewers with the most movies & fewest repeats. Multiplex chs: Cinemax, MoreMAX, ActionMAX, ThrillerMAX, WMAX, @MAX, 5StarMAX, OuterMAX. Cinemax is seen in the U.S. & Puerto Rico.

Classic Arts Showcase
Box 828, Burbank, CA 91503
(323) 878-0283, *Fax:* (323) 878-0329
www.classicartsshowcase.org
casmail@sbcglobal.net
James Rigler, President
Charlie Mount, General Manager
CAS is a non-profit arts progmg svc that include 16 art disciplines. The svc also features classic video from independent producers with the right to show clips. We require copies from masters on BetaCam-SP Tap. Available 24 hour.
Serving60 million subs. Satellite: Galaxy 1R, transponder 5.

CMT: Country Music Television
330 Commerce St., Nashville, TN 37201
(615) 335-8400, *Fax:* (615) 335-8615
www.cmt.com
CMT, America's # one country music network, 24 hours a day. CMT, owned & operated by MTV networks. Serving 80 million subs. Satellite: Satcom C-4, transponder 24, Satcom C3, transponder 18 west coast.

CNBC
900 Sylvan Ave., Englewood Cliffs, NJ 07632
(201) 735-2622
www.cnbc.com
Mark Hoffman, President
CNBC set the standard for up-to-the-minute business news & incisive analysis of global financial markets. During primetime, the network presents broad-base news, talk, interview & entertainment progmg.
Serving 86 million subs. Satellite:Galaxy 5, transponder 13.

CNN en Espanol
One CNN Ctr., Atlanta, GA 30303
(404) 878-1555, *Fax:* (404) 878-0050
espanol.mesa@turner.com
Christopher Crommett, Operations Dir
A 24-hour Sp-language news network in the United States & Latin America. The network keeps its loyal viewers connected with the events, issues trends that matter most to them & their families.
Serving more than 24 million subs.

CNN Headline News
One CNN Ctr., Atlanta, GA 30348-5366
(404) 827-1500, *Fax:* (404) 827-1995
www.cnn.com/hln
Roland Santo, President
Provides viewers with a 30-minute news, 24-hours. Each half-hour covers major news stories as well as business, sports, medicine, entertainment, weather & human interest topics. Areas: United States, Canada, Mexico & Caribbean.

CNN-Cable News Network
1 CNN Ctr., Atlanta, GA 30303
(404) 827-2300
www.cnn.com
Mich Gelman, President
David Payne, General Manager
Susan Grant, News Director
CNN provides coverage of major breaking stories, business, weather, sports & special reports, worldwide audience, 24 hours.

CNNI (CNN International)
One CNN Ctr., 3rd Flr., Atlanta, GA 30348
(404) 827-1500, *Fax:* (404) 827-1995
www.cnn.com/cnni
Debra Kocker, Operations Dir
Chris Cramer, General Manager
A 24-hour global news & info, with live, breaking world news, sports, features & weather. Serving 170 million worldwide.

College Entertainment Network
10 million Subscribers served
6255 Sunset Blvd., Suite 611, Hollywood, CA 90028
(323) 465-9880, *Fax:* (323) 465-9881
www.collegeentertainment.com
Robert Artura, President
Georgina Montalvan, Promotions Manager
College Entertainment Network is a world of college TV stn on one network, it features block of programs, from extreme sports to entertainment.

Comedy Central
345 Hudson St, New York, NY 10014
(212) 767-8600, *Fax:* (212) 767-8592
www.comedycentral.com
Michele Ganeless, President
A 24-hour all comedy TV network that covers stand-up, sketch comedy, movies, talk shows, sitcoms, specials & classics TV shows. Serving 84.8 million subs. Satellites: Satcom C-3, transponder 21 (east), Galaxy 1R, transponder 1 (west).
2049 Century Park E, Suite 4250, Los Angeles, CA 90067-3101

(310) 201-9500; *Fax:* (310) 201-9488

The Crime Channel
78206 Varner Rd., Suite D131, Palm Desert, CA 92211
(760) 360-6151, *Fax:* (760) 360-3258
crimechannel@dcrr.com
Arnie Frank, President
The Crime Channel offers series, movies, documentaries, original productions, on the spot crime news & foreign programs. Satellite: Satcom C-1, transponder 11.

CTI Zhong Tian Channel
1255 Corporate Center Dr., Suite 212, Monterey Park, CA 91754
(323) 415-0068
Andy Chung, General Manager
A 24-hour Mandarin-Chinese ch, consists of progmg derived from Chinese TV Int'l reputable Zhong Tian news. Satelite: Galaxy 11, transponder 24.

Daystar Television Network
4201 Pool Rd., Colleyville, TX 76034
(817) 571-1229, *Fax:* (817) 571-7458
www.daystar.com
comments@daystar.com
David Troxel, Operations Dir
Janice Smith, Programming Director
Our progmg is multi-ch & interdenominational. Christian TV net, is available from DirectTV, Dish Network 24-hours a day.

De Pelicula
750,000 Subscribers served
5999 Center Dr., Los Angeles, CA 90045
(301) 348-3371
www.tutv.tv
Carlos Madrazo, CFO
Mark Feldman, President
A 24-hour contemporary & classic movie ch featuring the best Sp language films.
Multiplex ch: De Pelicula Clasico is a 24-hour movie ch featuring the best films of Mexico's golden era.
TeleHit is a young, hip & cutting-edge, trendsetting lite-style & music ch.

Deep Dish TV
339 Lafayette St., New York, NY 10012
(212) 473-8933, *Fax:* (212) 420-8223
www.deepdishtv.org
deepdish@igc.org
Satellite: Galaxy IR*Transponder:* 15
Ron Davis, Chairman
Educational progmg (one hour a wk) distributed to PBS & pub access chs.

Discovery Channel
74.9 million Subscribers served
One Discovery Pl., Silver Springs, MD 20910
(240) 662-2000, *Fax:* (240) 662-1854
www.discovery.com
first_last@discovery.com
Satellite: Satcom C-4*Transponder:* 13
John Ford, President
Joe Abruzzese, General Sales Mgr
Billy Goodwyn, Promotions Manager
The United States largest cable TV net, the nation's premier provider of real-world entertainment, offering a signature mix of compelling, high-end production values & vivid cinematography that consistently represents qulity for viewers.Primetime progmg features science & technology, exploration, adventure, history and in-depth, behind-the scenes glimpses at the people, places, organizations that shape, share our world & is dedicated to creating the highest quality TV & media toinspire audiences by delivering knowledge about the world in an energizing way; evolving a timeless brand for a changing world.

Discovery en Espanol
One Discovery Place, Silver Spring, MD 20910
(240) 662-2000, *Fax:* (240) 662-1854
www.discovery.com
first_last@discovery.com
Luis Silberwasser, President
Bill Goodwyn, General Sales Mgr
Provider of high quality nonfiction entertainment for Sp-speaking audiences in the United States. Offering original progmg, some of the best Discovery content from around the world, the portfolio includes Discovery en Espanol & DiscoveryFamilia.

Discovery HD Theater
One Discovery Pl., Silver Spring, MD 20910
(240) 662-2000, *Fax:* (240) 662-1854
www.dhd.discovery.com
first_last@discovery.com
Patrick Younge, President
Bill Goodwyn, General Sales Mgr
Provide viewers with the hightest-quality TV experience available with spectacular images, dynamic sound & compelling stories from across the globe. A broad array of rich, original HD content across several progmg categories such as worldcultures, wildlife, high-end auto & adventure.

Discovery Kids Channel
Div/DBA: (Discovery Communications)
One Discovery Pl., Silver Spring, MD 20910
(240) 662-2000, *Fax:* (240) 662-1854
www.discoverykids.com
first_last@discovery.com
Marjorie Kaplan, President
Bill Goodwyn, General Sales Mgr
Provides entertaining, engaging & high-quality real-world progmg that kids enjoy & parent trust. Kids can learn about science, adventure, exploration & natural history through documentaries, reality shows, scripted dramas & animated stories.

Discovery Kids en Espanol
One Discovery Pl., Silver Spring, MD 20910
(240) 662-2000, *Fax:* (240) 662-1854
www.discovery.com
first_last@discovery.com
Luis Silberwasser, President
Bill Goodwyn, General Sales Mgr
Offering original progmg develop for Sp-speaking audiences, in addition to some of the best Discovery content from around the world, the portfolio includes Discovery en Espanol & Discovery Familia.

Disney Channel
3800 W. Alameda Ave., Burbank, CA 91505
(818) 569-7500, *Fax:* (818) 566-1358
www.disneychannel.com
Rich Ross, President
A 24-hour gen entertainment network for kids & families through original series, movies & contempary acquired progmg. Serving over 87 million subs. Satellite: Galaxy 5, transponder 1 east, Galaxy 1-R, transponder 7 west.

The Dream Network
9300 Georgia Ave., Suite 206, Silver Springs, MD 20910
(301) 587-0000, *Fax:* (301) 587-7464
www.thedreamnetwork.com
Alvin Augustus Jones, President
The Dream Network is the urban family choice for news, talk, sports & gospel music. Seen in the United States, Canada, Caribbean, Europe, Africa & Asia. Serving 25 million subs on 10 million cable systems. Satellite: DirecTV.

Ecology Communications
10 million Subscribers served
9171 Victoria Dr., Ellicott City, MD 21042
(410) 465-0480, *Fax:* (410) 461-5152
www.ecology.com
Shelley Duvall, Chairman
Ecology Communications focuse on ecology & enviroment in a var of entertainment-driven formats wkly.

eSignal
3955 Point Eden Way, Hayward, CA 94545
(510) 266-6000, *Fax:* (510) 266-6100
www.esignal.com
Chuck Thompson, President
Grant Mader, Operations Dir
Real-time stock, option, commodity quotation service & sports service delivered via cable TV, FM frequency & bcst VBI to end user PC.
Serving more than 20,000 subs on more than 850 systems. Satellites: Satcom F3, transponder 11; Galaxy 3,transponder 24.

ESPN
88 million Subscribers served
ESPN Plaza, Bristol, CT 06010-9454
(860) 766-2000, *Fax:* (860) 766-2400
www.espn.com
Satellite: Galaxy V*Transponder:* 9
Chris Driessen, CFO
Edward Erhardt, President
Ed Durso, Operations Dir
Lee Ann Daly, Promotions Manager
A 24-hour svc covering sports events, news, info, & lifestyle progmg.
ESPN CLASSIC is a 24-hour, all sports network devoted to telecasting the greatest games, stories, heroes & memories in the history of sports. ESPN DEPORTE offers a widevar of domestic & intl sports progmg 24-hours. ESPN HD offers a 24-hours high definition TV svc from ESPN, features high profile telecast. ESPNEWS, the nation's only 24-hours TV sports news svc, provides an expanded window for news & highlights,aswell as live coverage of beaking news.
605 3rd Ave, New York, NY 10158-0180
(212) 916-9200;

ESPN2
86 million Subscribers served
ESPN Plaza, Bristol, CT 06010-9454
(860) 766-2000, *Fax:* (860) 766-2400
www.espn.com
Satellite: Galaxy V*Transponder:* 14
George Bodenheimer, President
Sean Bratches, General Sales Mgr
A 24-hour sports net features a progmg line-up on par with ESPN.

ESPNU
c/o ESPN Regional Television, 11001 Rushmore Dr., Charlotte, NC 28277
(704) 973-5000, *Fax:* (704) 973-5090
www.espn.com
Rosalyn Durant, General Manager
ESPNU is a TV ch that specializes in college sports & is produced by affil with & owned by parent Network ESPN.

EUROCINEMA
Div/DBA: European Movies on TV
387 Park Ave., 3rd Fl., New York, NY 10016
(212) 763-5533
robert.richer@snet.net
Robert E. Richer, President
Broker specializing in the sale of overseas media properties.

EWTN
53 million Subscribers served
Div/DBA: The Global Catholic Network
5817 Old Leeds Rd., Irondale, AL 35210
(205) 271-2900, *Fax:* (205) 271-2925
www.ewtn.com
Satellite: Galaxy IR*Transponder:* 11
R. William Steltemeier, Chairman
America's largest relg cable network offers coml-free family-oriented progmg in English & Sp. EWTN features documentaries, music, drama, live talk shows, animated children shows & special church events from around the world.

FamilyNet Television & Radio
6350 West Fwy., Fort Worth, TX 76116
(800) 832-6638, (817) 570-1423, *Fax:* (817) 737-7853
www.familynet.com
info@familynet.com
Martin Coleman, COO
Randy Singer, President
R. Chip Turner, Promotions Manager
Ray Raley, Engineering Dir
FamilyNet TV is a full-time cable network, including original values-based programs & operates Christian talk ch 161 on sirius statellite radio. Reliable, safe TV for today's family.

FitTV
One Discovery Pl., Silver Spring, MD 20910
(240) 662-2000, *Fax:* (240) 662-1854
www.fittv.com
first_last@discovery.com
Eileen O'Neill, President
Bill Goodwyn, General Sales Mgr
FitTV is the premier, interactive fitness brand that inspires consumers to improve their fitness & well-being-on their terms. FitTV features approachable experts & entertaining shows that help real people learn how to incorporate fitness into their busy lives.

Food Network
82 million Subscribers served
1180 6th Ave., 12th Fl., New York, NY 10036
(212) 398-8836, *Fax:* (212) 736-7716
www.foodnetwork.com
Satellite: Galaxy IR*Transponder:* 4
Brooke Johnson, President
Adam Rockmore, Promotions Manager
A 24-hour net committed to exploring new, different & interesting ways to approach food.

Fox Business Network
1211 Avenue of the Americas, New York, NY 10036
(888) 369-4762, (212) 601-7000, *Fax:* (212) 601-7990
www.foxbusiness.com
Roger Ailes, Chairman

Fox Movie Channel
Div/DBA: (FX Networks Inc.)
10201 W. Pico Blvd., Bldg. 103, 4th Fl., Los Angeles, CA 90035

(310) 369-0586, *Fax:* (310) 969-4687
www.foxmoviechannel.com
Chuck Saftler, General Manager
The network is dedicated to preserving Hollywood history through original series & specials.

Fox Net
10201 W. Pico Blvd., Bldg. 100, Los Angeles, CA 90064
(310) 369-1000
www.fox.com
Steve Nazar, Operations Dir
Keith Goldberg, General Manager
Julie Allen, General Sales Mgr
Dwayne Bright, Programming Director
Betty Wang, Promotions Manager
A 24-hours basic cable affil to Fox Broadcasting Co.
FOX Broadcasting Co
10201 W. Pico Blvd., Los Angeles, CA 90064-2606
(310) 369-5153; *Fax:* (310) 969-0316
Susan Kiel, Vp, Network Distribution & Cable Operations

Fox News Channel: See listing in Major National TV News Organizations, this section.

Free Speech TV
Box 44099, Denver, CO 80201
(303) 442-8445, *Fax:* (303) 442-6472
www.freespeech.org
jon@freespeech.org
Jon Stout, General Manager
FSTV airs primarily social, political, cultural & environmental documentaries & news programs, 24-hours a day. Serving 30 million subs, on 180 cable systems & DISH Network.

Fuel
1440 S. Sepulveda Blvd., Suite 1900, Los Angeles, CA 90025
Fax: (310) 444-8559
www.fuel.tv
hookup@fuel.tv
Kelsey Martinez, General Manager
Cj Olivares, Programming Director
A 24-hour sports network featuring snowboarding, wakeboarding, surfing, BMX, motorcross & skateboading. Serving 5 million subs. Satellite: Galaxy II, transponder 5.

Fuse
11 Penn Plaza, 15th Fl., New York, NY 10001
(212) 324-8500, *Fax:* (212) 324-3445
www.fuse.tv
Kim Martin, President
Theano Apostolou, Operations Dir
Norman Schoenfeld, Programming Director
Fuse is the only all-music, viewer-influenced TV network, featuring music videos, exclusive artist interviews, live concerts & specials. Serving 35 million subs. Satellite; Loral Skynet Telstar 7, transponder 14.
Chicago Office
205 N. Michigan, Suite 803A, Chicago, IL 60601-5927
(312) 938-4222;
Joseph Glennon, Sr. Vp
The Water Garden
2425 W. Olympic Blvd., Suite 5050, Santa Monica, CA 90404-4030
(310) 998-9300;
John Pezzini, Vp

FX Networks Inc.
Div/DBA: (A subsidiary of Fox, Inc.)
1440 S. Sepulveda Blvd., Los Angeles, CA 90025
(310) 444-8777, *Fax:* (310) 444-8266
www.fxnetworks.com
Lindsay Gardner, President
Eric Shiu, Operations Dir
Steve LeBlang, General Sales Mgr
Chuck Saftler, Programming Director
An entertainment basic cable net from Fox Television involving hit series, daily films, original programs & sports.
Serving more than 53 million subs on 3,293 cable systems.
Satellite: Hughes Communications Galaxy 7, transponder 4 & 5.

Galavision
37 million Subscribers served
605 3rd Ave., 12th Fl., New York, NY 10158
(212) 455-5200, *Fax:* (212) 867-6710
www.univision.com
Satellite: Satcom C-4 *Transponder:* 4
Tim Krass, President
Timothy Spillane, Operations Dir
A 24-hr Sp language cable network for United States Hispanics in distribution & viewership.
2323 Bryan St., Suite 1900, Dallas, TX 75201-2603
(214) 758-2300;
6701 Center Dr. W, Suite 650, Los Angeles, CA 90045-1535
(310) 348-3600;
541 N. Fairbanks Ct, Suite 1240, Chicago, IL 60611-3319
(312) 494-5101;

Game Show Network
2150 Colorado Ave., Santa Monica, CA 90404
(310) 255-6800, *Fax:* (310) 255-6810
www.gsn.com
distribution@gsn.com
Game Show Network (GSN) is the only U.S. television network dedicated to game progmg and interactive game playing, featuring over 65 hours per week of original progmg & enhanced classics.
Reaching 50 million subs.
The Republic Center, 325 N. St. Paul St. Suite 1500, Dallas, TX 75201-3891
(214) 965-8500; *Fax:* (214) 965-8576
680 Fifth Ave. 11th Fl., New York, NY 10019-5429
(212) 333-2510; *Fax:* (646) 557-2996
515 N. State St. Suite 2120, Chicago, IL 60654-4864
(312) 261-4500; *Fax:* (312) 261-4521

The Golf Channel
7580 Commerce Center Dr., Orlando, FL 32819
(407) 355-4653, *Fax:* (407) 363-7976
www.thegolfchannel.com
Page H. Thompson, President
A 24-hour ch offering a blend of tournament coverage from the PGA, LPGA, Sr Tour, Nike, EPGA Tours, as well as instruction, interactive talk, news, profiles, classics, travel & more.
Serving 30 million subs on 2,200 cable systems.Satellite: Galaxy VI, Transponder 7.

Great American Country
24 million Subscribers served
49 Music Sq. W., Suite 301, Nashville, TN 37203
(615) 327-7525, *Fax:* (615) 329-8770
www.gactv.com
Satellite: Satcom C-3 *Transponder:* 20
Ed Hardy, President
GAC is a country music video net, features natl & loc adv, also featuring a broad var of videos programs.

Guthy-Renker Television
41-550 Eclectic St., Suite 200, Palm Desert, CA 92260
(760) 773-9022, *Fax:* (760) 773-9016
www.guthy-renker.com
Direct-response TV.

Hallmark Channel
56 million Subscribers served
12700 Ventura Blvd., Suite 200, Studio City, CA 91604-2463
(818) 755-2400, *Fax:* (818) 755-2564
www.hallmarkchannel.com
Satellite: Satcom C-3 *Transponder:* 5
David Kenin, Programming Director
A 24-hour basic cable ch that provides high quality entertainment progmg to a national audience.

HBO (Home Box Office)
1100 Ave. of the Americas, New York, NY 10036
(212) 512-1000
www.hbo.com
info@hob.com
Bill Nelson, Chairman
Features 24-hour var progmg including theatrical films, original movies, specials, documentaries, sports, & series. Multiplex chs. HBO, HBO 2, HBO Latino, HBO Signature, HBO Family, HBO Comedy, HBO Zone - known collectively as HBO The Works.MoreMAX.

HDNET
2400 N. Ulster St., Denver, CO 80238
(303) 388-8500, *Fax:* (303) 388-9600
www.hd.net
info@hd.net
Mark Cuban, Chairman
HDNET, the leader in high-indefinition bcstg, produces & televises 24-hour a day. Satellite: Galaxy 9, transponder 19C. HDNET Movies is a 24-hour coml-free schedule of full-length feature films. Satellite: Galaxy 9, transponder 19C.

Home & Garden Television Network (HGTV)
9721 Sherrill Blvd., Knoxville, TN 37932
(865) 694-2700, *Fax:* (865) 531-1588
www.hgtv.com
Satellite: Galaxy IR *Transponder:* 4
Jim Samples, President
Mike Boyd, Promotions Manager
HGTV is a 24-hour network that provides practical info & creative ideas to help the viewers to make the most of their lives at home & is designed to appeal to all ages & lifestyles.

HSN, The Home Shopping Network
81 million Subscribers served
One HSN Dr., St. Petersburg, FL 33729
(727) 872-1000, *Fax:* (727) 872-7356
www.hsn.com
Satellite: Satcom C-4 *Transponder:* 10
Tom McInerney, CEO
Peter Ruben, President
HSN offers live, 24-hour video retailing.

I.M.A.G.E. LLC
Div/DBA: (Interactive Meet and Greet Entertainment)
Box 702, 67 River St., Hudson, MA 01749-0702
(508) 788-5474
www.allcollectors.com
wexrex@aol.com
Gary Sohmers, Chairman
Basic svc, 24-hour progmg targeted to collectors of various merchandise & memorabilia, educ & entertaining progmg with a shopping element, with patent pending interactive applications.

IFC
11 Penn Plaza, New York, NY 10001
(917) 542-6320, *Fax:* (917) 542-6395
www.ifc.com
help@ifcentetainment.com
Satellite: Galaxy VII
Jonathan Sehring, President

iN DEAMAND
Div/DBA: (formerly Viewers Choice)
345 Hudson St., 17tt Fl., New York, NY 10014
(646) 638-8200
www.indemand.com
Rob Jacobson, President
Pay-Per-View (PPV), Video-On-Demand (VOD) & high-definition (HD) progmg 24-hrs. National Cable Program Services.
Programming genres: gen entertainment.
1888 Century Park E, Los Angeles, CA 90067-1702
(310) 785-9094, (310) 785-9194; *Fax:* (310) 785-9195, (310) 785-9769
1117 Perimeter Ctr. W, Suite 500 E, Atlanta, GA 30338-5451
(404) 399-3119; *Fax:* (404) 399-3014
26677 W. Twelve Mile Rd, Southfield, MI
(810) 354-3375; *Fax:* (810) 358-9693

The Independent Film Channel (IFC)
Div/DBA: (A division of Rainbow Media Programming Holdings)
11 Penn Plaza, 18th Fl., New York, NY 10001
(917) 542-6200, *Fax:* (917) 542-6395
www.ifc.com
webmaster@ifctv.com
A 24-hour uncut coml-free ch, capturing the true spirit of ind film, original series, live events & enchanced new media progmg.

The Inspiration Network INSP
21 million Subscribers served
Box 7750, Charlotte, NC 28241
(803) 578-1000
www.insp.com
Satellite: Galaxy IR *Transponder:* 17
David Cerullo, CEO
Rod Tapp, President
Tom Hohman, Operations Dir
Larry Simms, General Sales Mgr
Ron Shuping, Programming Director
INSP blends ministry programs with family-oriented movies, dramas, music & children's programs along with concerts & specials.

Inspirational Life Television
6 million Subscribers served
Div/DBA: (I-Lifetv)
7910 Crescent Executive Dr., 5th Fl., Charlotte, NC 28217
(704) 525-9800, *Fax:* (704) 525-9899
Satellite: Galaxy IR *Transponder:* 7
David Cerullo, President
Tom Hohman, Operations Dir
Larry Sims, General Sales Mgr
TV net which distributes life-enriching, edu entertainment progmg & digital, 24-hours.

International Networks
14 Million Subscribers served
4100 E. Dry Creek Rd., Centennial, CO 80122
(303) 712-5400, *Fax:* (303) 712-5401
internationalnetworks.com
Transponder: 24

Scott Wheeler, President
Victor Perez, Operations Dir
Rod Shanks, General Manager
Offer in-language progmg from a var of international sources: Arabic Radio & Television, ATV (Cantonese), China Central Television-4 (Mandarin), Channel One Russia, CTI-Zhong Tian Channel (Mandarin), Deutsche Welle (German), MYX (AsianAmerican), Phoenix North America Chinese Channel (Mandarin), Phoenix InfoNews (Mandarin), ProSiebenSat.1 Welt (German), RAITALIA (Italian), Russian Television Network (Russian), Saigon Broadcasting Television Network (Vietnamese), STAR India GOLD,STAR India NEWS, STAR India ONE & STAR India PLUS (all Hindi), The Filipino Channel, TV Asia (South Asian), TV JAPAN, tvK (Korean), TV5MONDE (French), TV Polonia (Polish) & VIJAY (Tamil).
12100 W. Olympic Blvd., Suite 200, Los Angeles, CA 90064-1048
(310) 979-2246;
1114 Ave. of the Americas, 22nd Fl., New York, NY 10036-7703
(917) 934-1558;

Investigation Discovery
One Discovery Pl., Silver Spring, MD 20910
(240) 662-2000, *Fax:* (240) 662-1854
www.investigationdiscovery.com
first_last@discovery.com
Vivian Schiller, President
Bill Goodwyn, General Sales Mgr
Provides the highest quality investigative progmg focused on dynamic stories of human nature from the past to the present.

The Irish Channel (CelticVision)
179 Amory St., Brookline, MA 02445
(617) 731-8566
eric@hilding.com
Eric Hilding, President
FM ch studies, complex FM substitution proposals, site locations, 301 applications engrg, gen bcst consulting.

Jewelry Television By ACN
10001 Kingston Pike, Knoxville, TN 37922
(865) 692-6000, *Fax:* (865) 692-6050
www.jtv.com
Harry Bagley, Operations Dir
Jewerly TV the only network that focuses exclusively on the sls of fine jewelry & gemstones, 24-hours a day. Satellite: Telstar 5. Serving 32 milion subs, on 11 million cable systems, transponder 19.

Jewish Television Network
13743 Ventura Blvd., Suite 200, Sherman Oaks, CA 91423
(818) 789-5891
www.arcta.org
info@arcta.org
Directors: Mike Wilson, Dennis Yocum, Garry Bowman, Harold Kimmel, Rick Smith, Harvey Oxner, Jay Butler, Doug Martin.

The Jones Companies
9697 E. Mineral Ave., Centennial, CO 80112
(303) 792-3111, *Fax:* (303) 784-8454
www.jones.com
publicrelations@jones.com
Glenn R. Jones, President
Timothy J. Burke, Operations Dir
A 24-hour revenue providing svc that features full-length product demonstrations & introduction of new products in a hands-on demonstration format.

KTLA
1 million Subscribers served on 220 Cable Systems
Div/DBA: United Video (a company of the United Video Satell
5800 Sunset Blvd., Los Angeles, CA 90028
(323) 460-5500, *Fax:* (323) 460-5333
www.ktla.com
ktla-am-news@tribune.com
Transponder: 15
John Reardon, General Manager
Los Angeles CW stn offers movies, news, specials & live sporting events, featuring the Los Angeles Clippers basketball. Services offered: Ind satellite carrier serving CATV, SMATV & MMDS distributing WGN, WPIX, KTLA & WFMT (FM) Networksvcs. Satellite: Spacenet 6E.

The Learning Channel (TLC)
Div/DBA: (Discovery Communications)
One Discovery Pl., Silver Spring, MD 20910
(240) 662-2000, *Fax:* (240) 662-1854
www.tlc.com
first_last@discovery.com
David Abraham, President
Bill Goodwyn, General Sales Mgr
TLC's themed nights that focus on real families , relationship, careers & entertaining consist of perennial fashion favorite, makeover sensation, humorous & fun workplace competion. Real-life progmg portrays relatable people with compellingstories in the blockbuster hits Jon & Kate Plus 8, Little People, Big World & LA Ink.

Lifetime
86 million Subscribers served
Div/DBA: (A&E Television Networks)
309 West 49th St., 17th Fl., New York, NY 10019
(212) 424-7000, *Fax:* (212) 957-4264
www.mylifetime.com
morgenstein@lifetimetv.com
Satellite: Satcom C-3*Transponder:* 12
Nickolas Davatzes, President
Charles Maday, Operations Dir
Dan Davids, General Manager
Offering the highest quality entertainment, info progmg & advocating a wide range of issues affecting women & their families.

Lifetime Movie Network
309 W. 49th St., New York, NY 10019
(212) 424-7000, *Fax:* (212) 957-4264
www.lifetimetv.com
James Wesley, CFO
Andrea Wong, President
Rick Haskins, General Manager
Offering the highest quality entertainment & info progmg 24-hours.

LIFETIME Television
309 W. 49th St., New York, NY 10019
(212) 424-7000, *Fax:* (212) 957-4264
www.lifetimetv.com
Satellite: Galaxy V*Transponder:* 21
James Wesley, CFO
Richard Basso, President
Gwynne McConkey, Operations Dir
Tim Brooks, General Sales Mgr
Offering the highest quality entertainment, info progmg & advocating a wide range of issues affecting women & their families, 24 hours nationwide .

The Locomotion Channel
420 Lincoln Rd., Suite 235, Miami Beach, FL 33139
(786) 276-1140, *Fax:* (786) 276-1141
Rodrigo Piza, General Manager
The Locomotion features the best intl productions created specifically for viewers ages 18-35, combining electronic music & digital culture 24-hrs a day.

Military Channel
One Discovery Pl., Silver Spring, MD 20910
(240) 662-2000, *Fax:* (240) 662-1854
www.military.discovery.com
first_last@discovery.com
Deborah Adler Myers, President
Bill Goodwyn, General Sales Mgr
Real-world stories of heroism, military strategy, technological breakthroughs & turning points in history. Takes viewers 'behind the lines' to hear the personal stories of servicemen & women & offers in-depth explorations of militarytechnology, battlefield strategy, aviation & history. It also provides unique access to this world, allowing viewers to experience & understand a world full of human drama, courage, innovation & long-held military traditions.

MLB Network
40 Hartz Way, Suite 10, Secaucus, NJ 07094
(201) 520-6400
mlb.mlb.com/network/
Bill Morningstar, President

The Movie Channel (TMC)
Div/DBA: (Showtime Networks Inc.)
1633 Broadway, New York, NY 10019
(212) 708-1600, *Fax:* (212) 708-1212
www.sho.com
TMC features daily movie marathons, overnight & double vision weekends & Movie Channel Xtra, offers more of viewers favorite movies, 24-hours a day. Serving 34.8 million subs. Satellites: Satcom C-3, transponder 19 east; Satcom G-9,transponder 5 west.

MSNBC
82 million Subscribers served
One MSNBC Plaza, Secaucus, NJ 07094
(201) 583-5000, *Fax:* (201) 583-5179
www.msnbc.com
Satellite: Galaxy IR*Transponder:* 10
Dan Abrams, General Manager
Val Nicholas, Promotions Manager
MSNBC is an all news net 24-hours.

MTV Networks
1515 Broadway, New York, NY 10036
(212) 258-8000, *Fax:* (212) 258-8100
www.mtvn.com
MTV2 is the premier destination to find the hottest mix of music videos, long form music programs, exclusive access to their favorite bands, and ground-breaking music before it hits mainstream.

MTV Networks Latin America
Div/DBA: (formerly MTV Latino)
1111 Lincoln Rd., 6th Fl., Miami Beach, FL 33139
(305) 535-3700, *Fax:* (305) 535-8388
www.mtvla.com
MTV's sixth global network, 24-hour progmg, advertiser supported & available in Latin America & the United States. Serving over 8.5 million subs. Satellite: Satcom C3, transponder 19 (USA); PanAm Sat 3, transponder 5C & 6C (Latin America).

MTV: Music Television
Div/DBA: MTV Networks Inc.
1515 Broadway, New York, NY 10036
(212) 258-8000, *Fax:* (212) 258-8100
www.mtv.com
Judy McGrath, Chairman
A 24-hrs music video ch in stereo, with 22 worldwide music on the web, original, innovative online music & entertainment progmg to each net. Also includes 14 international destinations throughout Europe, Asia, & Latin America.

National Geographic Channel
47 million Subscribers served
1145 17th St. N.W., Washington, DC 20036-4688
(202) 912-6500, *Fax:* (202) 912-6603
www.natgeotv.com
comments@natgeochannel.com
Satellite: Satcom C-3*Transponder:* one
David Haslingden, CEO
Kiera Hynninen, President
John Ford, Programming Director
NGC provides the spectacular imagery that the National Geographic is know for in stunning high-dedinition.

National Jewish Television Network
Box 480, Wilton, CT 06897
(203) 834-3799
www.kedaradio.com
kedakid@aol.com
Comprises three stns in Texas, three affiliates. Represented by Caballero Spanish Media.

Nationality Broadcasting Network
Div/DBA: (Radio-WKTX 830 AM/NBN TV)
11906 Madison Ave., Lakewood, OH 44107
(216) 221-0330, *Fax:* (216) 221-3638
Jim Georgiades, Operations Dir
Provides internationally & locally-produced nationality TV & radio progmg, special programs & comls; also full-svc production house. Serving one cable system. On SCOLA TV network.

Newsworld International
Div/DBA: (North American Television Inc.)
1230 Ave. of the America, New York, NY 10020
(212) 413-5000
www.nwitv.com
nwifeedback@indtvholdings.com
John Bernbach, Chairman
Intl progmg covering top stories from around the world plus current affrs, documentaries, the latest business, financial & sports news, 24-hours.

NFL Network
10950 Washington Blvd., Culver City, CA 90232
(310) 840-4635, *Fax:* (310) 280-1132
www.nfl.com/nflnetwork/home
krista.ostensen@la.nfl.net
Steve Bornstein, President
Adam Shaw, Operations Dir
A national cable & satellite ch telecasting NFL content 24 hrs a day. Satellites: Galaxy 11, Transponder 9. Serving 30 million subs. On more than 60 cable systems.

NICK at NITE: See Nickelodeon.

Nickelodeon
Div/DBA: (MTV Networks Inc.)
1515 Broadway, New York, NY 10036

CABLE - U.S.

(212) 258-8000, *Fax:* (212) 258-6284
www.nickelodeon.com
Tom Freston, Chairman
Nickelodeon cable net targets kids. NICK at NITE provides entertainment svc for the TV generation. NICKTOONS is the 24-hours digital destination for the next generation of animation. NICK2 gives viewers the convenience of watching theirfavorite Nickelodeon & NICK at NITE shows at different times of the day.

Noah's World International
11448 Kanapali Ln., Boynton Beach, FL 33437
(561) 732-2108, *Fax:* (516) 732-5108
www.noahsworldtv.com
Ilan Klein, President
Noah's World Internation profiles & present enlightened countries around the globe, 24-hours a day.

Noggin/The N
1633 Broadway, 7th Fl., New York, NY 10019
(212) 654-7707, *Fax:* (212) 654-4867
www.noggin.com
Satellite: Satcom C-3*Transponder:* 15
Tom Ascheim, General Manager
Kenny Miller, Programming Director
The N, the nighttime net for teens, 24-hours.

OASIS TV
1.8 million Subscribers served on 16 Cable Systems
1875 Century Park E., Suite 600, Los Angeles, CA 90067-2507
(310) 553-4300, *Fax:* (310) 553-4300
www.oasistv.com
service@oasistv.com
Azim Khamisa, Chairman
Independent content provider of branded Body-Mind-Spirit video progmg. Range of topics: Health, Healing, Metaphysics, Spirituality, Earth, Environment, World Peace, Visionary Arts & Personal Growth.

Open TV
350 5th Ave., Fl. 59, New York, NY 10118-5999
(212) 601-2719
David Reese, President
Individualized TV progmg for educ & entertainment.
3040 Rte 22 W., Suite 210, Branchburg, NJ
(908) 252-3800;
David Reese, Chairman

The Outdoor Channel
43445 Business Park Dr., Suite 103, Temecula, CA 92590
(800) 770-5750
www.outdoorchannel.com
Roger Werner, President
Outdoor Channel offers progmg such as fishing, hunting, hiking, competitive shooting & motor sports, 24-hours.

OVATION-The Arts Network
6.6 million Subscribers served
5801 Duke St., Suite D-112, Alexandria, VA 22304
(703) 813-6310, *Fax:* (703) 813-6336
www.ovationtv.com
info@ovationtv.com
Satellite: Galaxy VII*Transponder:* 13
Edward J. Mathias, Chairman
The net covers arts news from around the world & children's arts programs, 20 hours a day.

OWN: The Oprah Winfrey Network
9150 Wilshire Blvd., Suite 240, Beverly Hills, CA 90212
(424) 204-1800
Christina Norman, CEO
Robin Schwartz, President

Oxygen Media Inc.
75 9th Ave., 7th Fl., New York, NY 10011
(212) 651-2070, *Fax:* (212) 651-2099
www.oxygen.com
feedback@oxygen.com
Mary G. Murano, President
Oxygen Media is a 24-hour cable network for women.

Pennsylvania Cable Network (PCN)
401 Fallowfield Rd, Camp Hill, PA 17011
(717) 730-6000, *Fax:* (717) 730-6005, (717) 441-4540
www.pcntv.com
pcntv@pcntv.com
Brian Lockman, President
Michelle Harter, Operations Dir
William J. Bova, Programming Director
Rick Cochran, Promotions Manager
The nation's preeminent state pub affrs net, with live & same-day coverage of the Pennsylvania General Assembly. PCN also covers significant state events, such as high school sports finals.

Serving 3.3 million subs on 150 cable systems,transponder 13C.
Satellite: AMC-6.
400 N. Broad St., Philadelphia, PA 19130-4015
(215) 854-4455;
Corey Clarke, Bureau Chief
Pittsburgh Post Gazette Bldg, 34 Blvd., Pittsburgh, PA
(412) 263-1300;
Doug Sicchitano, Bureau Chief

Pentagon Channel
5.3 million Subscribers served
601 North Fairfax St., Alexandria, VA 22314
(703) 428-0265, *Fax:* (703) 428-0466
pentagonchannel@hq.afis.osd.mil
Gene Brink, General Manager
Pentagon Channel is a gov owned TV of the Department of Defense, providing internal communications to svc members, families, the National Guard, the Reserve & military retirees, available 24-hours.

Planet Green
Div/DBA: (formerly Discovery Home Channel)
One Discovery Pl., Silver Spring, MD 20910
(240) 662-2000, *Fax:* (240) 662-1854
www.planetgreen.com
first_last@discovery.com
Laura Michalchyshyn, President
Planet Green will provide entertaining, authentic & quality info for such categories as eco-design, organic food & green architecture, progmg for a green lifestyle.

Plato Learning Inc.
10801 Nesbitt Ave. S., Bloomington, MN 55437
(800) 447-5286
www.plato.com
info@plato.com
Terri Reden, Promotions Manager
Interactive TV progmg for children.

Playboy TV
Div/DBA: (Playboy Entertainment Group)
2706 Media Center Dr., Los Angeles, CA 90065
(323) 276-4000, *Fax:* (323) 276-4500
www.playboytv.com
Jeff Jenest, President
Craig Simon, Operations Dir
Entertainment targeted to adults. Schedule consists of nearly 100% original Playboy programs with the balance comprised of acquired programs & feature films. Serving 4.5 under PPV svc. Satellite: Galaxy 5, transponder 2.
Hot Zone is a24-hour Pay-Per-View ch for adults. Satellite: Telstar 7, transponder 5.
Hot Networks is a 24-hour Pay-Per-View ch for adults. Satellite: Telstar 7, transponder 5.

Praise Television
28059 US Hwy. 19 N., Suite 300, Clearwater, FL 33761
(800) 921-9692, *Fax:* (727) 530-0671
Satellite: GE-1*Transponder:* 7
Dustin Rubeck, President
A 24-hours, Christian music for family entertainment.

Product Information Network (PIN)
35 million Subscribers served
9697 East Mineral Ave., Englewood, CO 80155-3309
(303) 784-8321, *Fax:* (303) 784-8549
Satellite: Satcom C-3*Transponder:* 20
Jon Shaver, COO
Richard Steele, General Sales Mgr
Tom Cahill, Promotions Manager
A 24-hours info net, ad-supported.

Puma TV
2.7 million Subscribers served
2029 S.W. 105th Ct., Miami, FL 33165-7937
(305) 554-1876, *Fax:* (305) 554-6776
Satellite: Telstar 5
Jose Luis Rodriguez, President
Osvaldo Rodriguez, Operations Dir
Puma TV offers a wide var of info programs on fashion, modeling & entertainment, music ch by Hispanic for Hispanic, 24-hours.

QVC
85.4 million Subscribers served
Studio Park, West Chester, PA 19380
(484) 701-1000
www.qvc.com
webmaster@qvc.com
Satellite: Satcom C-4*Transponder:* 9
Douglas S. Briggs, President
Tim Megaw, Operations Dir

Preeminent electronic retailer mktg a wide var of brand name products, categories as home furnishings, licensed products, fashions, beauty, electronics & fine jewelry.

The Real Estate Network-TREN
325 Sharon Park Dr., Suite 512, Menlo Park, CA 94025
(650) 361-1000, *Fax:* (650) 332-1605
kevintren@yahoo.com
Ronald D. Keithley, COO
Niche advertiser-supported entertainment progmg & interactive svc focusing on mdse real estate listings & related products & svcs throughout America.

Recovery Network
1411 5th St., Suite 250, Santa Monica, CA 90401
(310) 393-3979
www.sbca.com
info@sbca.org

Sci-Fi Channel
Div/DBA: (USA Networks)
30 Rockefeller Plaza, New York, NY 10112
(212) 644-4444, *Fax:* (212) 703-8533
www.scifi.com
David Howe, General Manager
Dedicated to a broad range of science fiction & fact, fantasy, & horror programs, 24-hours.

The Science Channel
One Discovery Pl., Silver Spring, MD 20910
(240) 662-2000, *Fax:* (240) 662-1854
www.sciencechannel.com
first_last@discovery.com
Deborah Adler Myers, President
Bill Goodwyn, General Sales Mgr
Scientific topics ranging form string theory & futuristic cities to accidental discoveries & outrageous inventions. Reaching more than 50 million homes nationwide.

SCOLA
21557 270th St., McClelland, IA 51548-0619
(712) 566-2202, *Fax:* (712) 566-2502
www.scola.org
scola@scola.org
Satellite: Telstar 5
Francis Lajba, President
John Millar, Operations Dir
Foreign language news & educ progmg, 24-hours a day.

Scripps Networks
25 million Subscribers served
9721 Sherrill Blvd., Knoxville, TN 37932
(865) 694-2700, *Fax:* (865) 690-9281
www.scrippsnetworks.com
Satellite: Galaxy IR*Transponder:* 4
Bob Baskerville, President
Jeff Sears, Operations Dir
Robyn Ulrich, Promotions Manager
DIY cable TV net operated by Scripps Networks, providing in depth demonstrations & tips for categories such as home improvement, home bldg, tools, products, gardening, landscaping, automotive, boating, decorating, design, arts, crafts,cooking, hobby & recreations, 24-hours.

ShopNBC
on 1900 Cable Systems
ValueVision Media Inc., 6740 Shady Oak Rd., Eden Prairie, MN 55344
(952) 943-6000, *Fax:* (952) 943-6011
www.shopnbc.com
Frank Elsenbast, CFO
ValueVision Media (Nasdaq: VVTV) operates in the rapidly growing converged world of TV, the Internet & e-commerce. The company flagship media property, ShopNBC, the nation's fastest growing shoppng network, is bcst into 70 million homes 24hrs a day. GE Equity & NBC own approximately 27% of ValueVision Media. Satellite used and transponder: Galaxy 15, transponder 12.

Short TV
2.5 million Subscribers served
580 Broadway, Suite 1104, New York, NY 10012
(212) 226-6258, *Fax:* (212) 925-5802
www.shorttv.com
info@shorttv.com
Roland Dib, President
Short films, available 24-hours, ad-supported.

Showtime Networks Inc.
34.8 million Subscribers served
1633 Broadway, New York, NY 10019

(212) 708-1600, *Fax:* (212) 708-1212
www.sho.com
Satellite: Satcom C-3*Transponder:* 19 (east)
Matthew C. Blank, Chairman
THE MOVIE CHANNEL & FLIX. SNI also operates & manages the premium TV net SUNDANCE CHANNEL, SHOWTIME on Espanol, a separate audio feed of SHOWTIME, available for the Sp-speaking audience. SNI also markets & distributes sports &entertainment events for exhibition to Subscribers on a pay-per-view basis. Multiplex chs: SHOWTIME BEYOND, SHOWTIME PAY-PER-VIEW. SHOWTIME EXTREME, SHOWTIME FAMILY ZONE, SHOWTIME NEXT, targeting gen young adults 18-24, SHOWTIME SHOWCASE, SHOWTIMETOO, SHOWTIME WOMEN.

Si TV
3030 Andrita St., Bldg. A, Los Angeles, CA 90065
(323) 256-8900, *Fax:* (323) 256-9888
www.sitv.com
Jeff Valdez, Chairman
SiTV is a Latino-themed network in English that features original progmg, comedy, drama, var shows, talk-format strips, music & style shows, available 24-hours.

The Ski Channel
NSS Data: TV-CATV only
881 Alma Real Dr., Terrace 8, Pacific Palisades, CA 90272
(310) 230-2050
dcski.com
connielawn@aol.com
Covers major natl, international & specialty stories for radio & TV stns in the U.S. & around the world. Also do live talk-back features. Serves radio, TV & write ski reports.

Skyview World Media
100,000 Subscribers served
Two Executive Dr., Suite 6000, Fort Lee, NJ 07024
(201) 242-3000, *Fax:* (201) 944-5961
www.skyviewmedia.com
info@kskyviewmedia.com
John Lunsford, President
James Helfott, Operations Dir
Skyview World Media is North America's leading provider of foreign ethnic progmg.

Sleuth
NBC Universal Cable, 900 Sylvan Ave., 1 CNBC Plaza, Englewood Cliffs, NJ 07632
(201) 735-3604
www.sleuthchannel.com

Soapnet
3800 West Alameda Ave., Burbank, CA 91505
(818) 569-7500, *Fax:* (818) 566-1358
www.soapnet.com
Deborah Blackwell, Operations Dir
Mary Ellen DiPrisco, Programming Director
Sherri York, Promotions Manager
Soapnet features today's soaps tonight, classic soaps, news & info from the world of soaps, 24-hours. Serving 35.7 million subs. Satellite: Galaxy 10 R.

Sorpresa
6125 Airport Fwy., Suite 200, Fort Worth, TX 76117
(817) 222-1234, *Fax:* (817) 222-9809
www.sorpresatv.net
Satellite: Telstar 5*Transponder:* 24
Leonard Firestone, Chairman
The nation's first network dedicated to America's Hispanic children, available 24-hours, ad-supported, Digital Premium.

SourceSuite, LLC
400,000 Subscribers served
5601 MacArthur Blvd., Suite 201, Irving, TX 75038
(469) 524-0116, *Fax:* (469) 417-0314
www.intchan.com
Charlie Barnes, General Manager
SourceSuite is a leading provider of interactive TV products, available 24-hours.

SPEED
57.1 million Subscribers served
9711 Southern Pines Blvd., Charlotte, NC 28273
(704) 731-2222, (704) 731-2285, *Fax:* (704) 731-2197
www.speedtv.com
Satellite: Satcom C-4*Transponder:* 11
Hunter Nickell, President
Francois McGillicuddy, Operations Dir
Bob Ecker, Programming Director
Providing insight & action, number one authority for anything motorsports.

Spice 1
11,000 Subscribers served
2706 Media Center Dr., Los Angeles, CA 90065
(323) 276-4000, *Fax:* (323) 276-4500
www.spicetv.com
Satellite: Telstar 5
James English, President
An erotic adult-theme movie net, Premium, Pay-Per-View, available 24-hours. Multiplex ch: Spice 2.

Spike TV
87.2 million Subscribers served
Div/DBA: (division of MTV Networks)
1775 Broadway, 37th Fl., New York, NY 10019
(212) 846-8705, (212) 767-4275
www.spiketv.com
Satellite: Satcom C-3*Transponder:* 18
Kevin Kay, President
Network for men.
2806 Opryland Dr., Nashville, TN 37214-1209
(615) 457-7230;

The Sportsman Channel
10.7 million Subscribers served
2855 S. James Dr., Suite 101, New Berlin, WI 53151
(262) 432-9100, *Fax:* (262) 432-9101
www.thesportsmanchannel.com
Satellite: Telstar 5*Transponder:* 1
C. Michael Cooley, President
Todd D. Hansen, Operations Dir
Darrell Lake, General Sales Mgr
Jim Seley, Programming Director
The Sportsman Channel provides continuous hunting & fishing progmg 24-hours a day.

STARNET
1332 Enterprise Dr., Suite 200, West Chester, PA 19380
(610) 427-4163
Joy Tartar, CFO
Jerry Lenfest, President
Automatic cross-ch tune-in promotion svc for basic, PPV delivered via satellite. Nu-Star - automatic cross ch tune-in promotion svc for basic PPV delivered via satellite. The Promoter-individualized tune-in promotion for PPV delivered viasatellite.

Starz Entertainment LLC
Div/DBA: (formerly Encore Media Corp.)
8900 Liberty Cir., Englewood, CO 80112
(720) 852-7700, *Fax:* (720) 852-7710
www.starz.com
Robert B. Clasen, CEO
Bill Myers, President
Jerry Maglio, Promotions Manager
Offers 16 movie channels including the flagship Starz & Encore brands with approximately 16.8 million & 31.4 million subs. Advanced svcs including Starz HD, Encore HD, Starz On Demand, Encore On Demand, MoviePlex On Demand, Starz HD OnDemand, Encore On HD Demand, MoviePlex HD On Demand, Starz Play & Vongo.
southeast region
5775 Peachtree Dunwoody Rd, Suite D-620, Atlanta, GA 30342-1556
(404) 531-7060; *Fax:* (404) 531-7075
Cindy Feinberg, Rgnl Vp
Founders
5445 DTC Pkwy, Suite 600, Englewood, CO 80111-3045
(303) 771-7700; *Fax:* (303) 267-4001
Robin Feller, Rgnl Vp
eastern region
70 Hudson St, Hoboken, NJ 07030-5630
(201) 239-9020; *Fax:* (201) 239-2290
Shanita Evans, Rgnl Vp
central region
111 E. Wacker Dr., Suite 1300, Chicago, IL 60601-3713
(312) 938-8900; *Fax:* (312) 938-8902
Susan LeVarsky, Rgnl Vp
International Channel
11766 Wilshire Blvd, Suite 710, Los Angeles, CA 90025-6538
(310) 477-9922; *Fax:* (310) 477-4544
Victoria Kent, Rgnl Vp
New Media
5445 DTC Pkwy, Suite 600, Englewood, CO 80111-3045
(303) 771-7700; *Fax:* (303) 267-4098
Leslie Nittler, Vp Sls & Mktg
Time Warner & Central region office
2340 E. Trinity Mills Rd, Suite 300, Carrollton, TX 75006-1942
(972) 417-2866; *Fax:* (972) 417-2806
Paige Holmes, Chairman

Starz!
Div/DBA: See Encore Media Corp

The Style Network
34 million Subscribers served
5750 Wilshire Blvd., Los Angeles, CA 90036-3709
(323) 954-2400, *Fax:* (323) 954-2500
www.eonline.com
Style Network covers the gamut of the lifestyle genre.

Sun TV
2245 Godby Rd., Atlanta, GA 30349
(404) 766-9197, *Fax:* (404) 767-5264
David C. Simon, President
Virgil Scott, Operations Dir
Sun TV network features news, sports, entertainment, sitcoms, soaps, talk shows from 6:30 AM-midnight Saturday-Sunday (EST). Original progmg from the Caribbean, Central & South America. Serving 700,000 subs. Satellite: Galaxy 4-13.

Sundance Channel
17 million Subscribers served
1633 Broadway, 8th Fl., New York, NY 10019
(212) 654-1500, (212) 708-8025
www.sundancechannel.com
Satellite: Satcom C-4*Transponder:* 20
Larry Aidem, President
Kim Gabelmann, Operations Dir
Sundance Channel is a 24-hours a day ch, featuring uncut coml-free programs, providing TV viewers daring & engaging feature films, short, documentaries, world cinema & animation.

Talk Internetwork, Inc.
9662 E. Volture Dr., Scottsdale, AZ 85260
(480) 551-9774
www.tribuneradio.com
bpabst@tribune.com
Kurt Vanderan, Operations Dir
Network comprised of: Chicago Cubs Network (50 stns), National Farm Report (260 stns), Farming America (200 stns), Agri-Voice Network (95 stns), Samuelson's Soapbox (150 stns). Represented by Eastman.

Talkline Communications Television Network
Box 20108, Park West Stn., New York, NY 10025-1510
(212) 769-1925, *Fax:* (212) 799-4195
www.talklinecommunications.com
info@talklinecommunications.com
Zev Brenner, President
Nationally acclaimed Jewish TV programs carried on NBC digital and cable systems in New York as well as nationwide and online.

TBN-Trinity Broadcasting Network
49 million Subscribers served on 43.4 million Cable Systems
Div/DBA: (TBN Cable Network)
2823 W. Irving Blvd., Irving, TX 75061
(972) 313-9500, (800) 735-5542, *Fax:* (972) 313-1010
www.tbn.org
comments@tbn.org
Satellite: Galaxy V*Transponder:* 3
Paul Crouch, President
Robert Higley, Promotions Manager
TBN is America's most watched relg network, offering 24-hours of coml-free inspiritional original programs, that appeal to viewers in many denominations. Progmg includes Nashville gospel concerts, health & fitness, talk shows & svcs fromAmerica's largest Churches. Multiplex ch: TBN Enlace USA is a 24-hour multi-faith Hispanic ch from Trinity Broadcasting Network. The Church Channel is a new digital network from TBN features church svc program from Protestant, Catholic & Jewish faithgroups, 24-hours.

TBS
90.9 million Subscribers served
1050 Techwood Dr. N.W., Atlanta, GA 30318
(404) 885-4339, *Fax:* (404) 885-4319
tbs.com
Satellite: Galaxy V*Transponder:* 6
Steve Koonin, President
Ken Schwab, Programming Director
TBS is TV top-rated comedy network. It serves as home to such original comedy series (just name a few) as MY Boys, The Bill Engvall Show, Tyler Perry's House of Payne, Tyler Perry's Meet The Browns & George Lopez's Lopez Tonight, blockbustermovies; & hosted movie showcases.

TechTV
43 milion Subscribers served
650 Townsend St., 3rd Fl., San Francisco, CA 94103
(415) 355-4000, *Fax:* (415) 355-4670
techtvinfo@techtv.com
Satellite: Satcom C-4*Transponder:* 12

Joseph Gillespie, President
Greg Brannan, Operations Dir
Peter Gochis, General Sales Mgr
TechTV intrigues viewers with everything from help & info to cutting-edge factual progmg to outrageous late-night fun.

Telemundo
2290 W. 8th Ave., Hialeah, HI 10019
(305) 889-7200, *Fax:* (305) 889-7205
Don Brown, CFO
Ramon Escobar, President
Telemundo, a United States Sp-language TV network, available 24-hours. Multiplex ch: Telemundo Internacional. Serving 32 million subs. Satellite: Satcom, transponder 20 east, AMC-4, transponder 8 west.

TEN-The Erotic Network
7007 Winchester Cir., Suite 200, Boulder, CO 80301
(303) 786-8700, *Fax:* (303) 938-8388
www.noof.com
Michael Weiner, CEO
Ken Boenish, President
William Mossa, Promotions Manager
TEN is a network that uses the 'un-inhibited' editing standard, 24-hours a day. Multiplex chs: TEN On Demand, TENBlox, TENBlue, TENClips & TENXtsy, PLEASURE. Serving 13.7 million subs. Satellite: Telstar 7-24, TUN, G10R-7.

The Tennis Channel
3 million Subscribers served
2850 Ocean Park Blvd., Santa Monica, CA 90405
(310) 314-9400, *Fax:* (310) 314-9433
www.thetennischannel.com
Satellite: Telstar 5*Transponder:* 15
Ken Solomon, Chairman
The Tennis Channel is the 24-hour cable TV network devoted to tennis & other racquet sports, ad-supported.

The Theatre Channel
NSS Data: Radio Only
Box 2676, Venice, CA 90294
(310) 823-6508
www.dcski.com
connielawn@aol.com
Connie Lawn, President
Covers major natl, international & ski stories for radio & TV stns in the United States & around the world. Also live 'inserts' into radio & TV shows.

Time Warner Cable
One Time Warner Ctr., New York, NY 10019
(212) 598-7200
www.timewarner.com
Jeffrey L. Bewkes, President
Cable svc. Serving over 1.3 million subs.
41-61 Kissena Blvd, Flushing, NY 11355-3181

TNT (Turner Network Television)
90.3 million Subscribers served
1050 Techwood Dr. N.W., Atlanta, GA 30318
(404) 885-4339, *Fax:* (404) 885-4319
www.tnt.tv
Satellite: Galaxy V*Transponder:* 17
Steve Koonin, President
Top-rated networks, offers original series, also home to powerful one-hr dramas, bcst premiere movies, compelling prime-time specials & championship sports coverage. Available in high definition.

TNT Latin America
1050 Techwood Dr. N.W., Atlanta, GA 30318
(404) 827-1700, *Fax:* (404) 575-5341
www.tntla.com
patricia.brito@turner.com
Rick Perez, General Manager
Cable network bcst in Sp, Portuguese, English featuring contemp, original movies, NBA coverage & exclusive premieres, 24-hours a day. Serving more than 8.5 million subs in 39 countries in the rgn. Satellite: PanAmSat 1, transponder 3.

Toon Disney
3800 W. Alameda Ave., Burbank, CA 91505
(818) 569-7500, *Fax:* (818) 566-1358
www.toondisney.com
Ann Sweeney, President
Toon Disney is a var of acquired animated programs, 24-hours a day. Serving more than 43 million subs. Satellite: Galaxy 10R.

TR!O
1230 Ave. of the Americas, New York, NY 10020
(212) 413-5000, *Fax:* (212) 413-6552
www.triotv.com
Lauren Zalaznick, President
TR!O is an entertainment cable TV ch reflecting pop culture, 24-hours a day. Serving 20 million subs. Satellite: Galaxy 1R, transponder 24, Satcom C3, transponder 8.

Travel Channel
5425 Wisconsin Ave., Suite 500, Chevy Chase, MD 20815
(301) 244-7500, *Fax:* (301) 244-7507
www.travelchannel.com
Patrick Younge, President
Bill Goodwyn, General Sales Mgr
Bringing knowledge, insight & info to a community of people who want to experience their world & satisfy their curiosity.

truTV
600 3rd Ave., 2nd Fl., New York, NY 10016
(212) 973-2800, *Fax:* (212) 973-3210
www.courttv.com
Ira Fields, CFO
Art Bell, President
Marc Juris, General Manager
Court TV telecast trails day by day & high profile original programs 24-hours. Serving 80 million subs.

Turner Classic Movies (TCM)
63.9 million Subscribers served
1050 Techwood Dr. N.W., Atlanta, GA 30318
(404) 885-5535
www.turnerclassicmovies.com
Mark Lazarus, President
Tom Karsch, General Manager
Features Hollywood's greatest movies of all time, presented 24-hours, coml-free.

TV Asia
Div/DBA: (Asian Star Broadcasting Network Inc.)
76 National Rd., Edison, NJ 08817
(732) 650-1100, *Fax:* (732) 650-1112
www.tvasiausa.com
info@tvasiausa.com
TV Asia provides a wide range of prgmg produced for South Asian Americans, 24-hrs.

TV Games (TVG) Network
12 million Subscribers served
6701 Center Dr. W., Los Angeles, CA 90045
(310) 242-9500
www.tvgnetwork.com
Satellite: GE-1*Transponder:* 23
Ryan O'Hara, COO

TV Guide Channel
70 million Subscribers served
6922 Hollywood Blvd., Los Angeles, CA 90028
(323) 817-4600, *Fax:* (323) 762-8815
www.tvguide.com
Satellite: Satcom C-4
Ray Hopkins, President
The network combines original etertaining long-form progmg with comprehensive listing info 24-hours a day.
708 Third Ave., 21st Fl., New York, NY 10017-4201
(212) 370-1799; *Fax:* (212) 370-7575
Chris Manning, Eastern Sls Mgr

TV Japan
Div/DBA: (Japan Network Group Inc.)
100 Broadway, 15th Fl., New York, NY 10005
(212) 262-3377, *Fax:* (212) 262-5577
www.tvjapan.net
takeuchi@tvjapan.net
Koki Matsumoto, President
TV Japan is a Japanese language ch, available 24-hours a day. Satellite: Galaxy II, transponder 24.

TV Land
82.1 million Subscribers served
1515 Broadway, New York, NY 10036
(212) 258-8000, *Fax:* (212) 846-1775
Satellite: Satcom C-3*Transponder:* 18
Larry W. Jones, General Manager
TV Land is the only network dedicated to the best of everything TV from the past 50 years, available 24-hours.

Univision Television Group
605 3rd Ave., 12th Fl., New York, NY 10158
(212) 455-5200, *Fax:* (212) 867-6710
www.univision.com
Satellite: Galaxy IR
Univision Network, the most-watched Spanish-language broadcast television network in the U.S. reaching 97% of U.S. Hispanic households.
Serving 34.5 million subs. Satellite: Galaxy 1R.
TeleFutura Network, a general-interestSpanish-language broadcast television network, which was launched in 2002 and now reaches 85% of U.S. Hispanic households. Serves 7.2 million subs. Satellite: Galaxy 1.
Central
2323 Bryan St., Suite 1900, Dallas, TX 75201-2603
(214) 758-2405; *Fax:* (214) 758-2395
Deanna Andaverde, Vp Affl Rel
East
605 Third Ave, 26 Fl., New York, NY 10158-0180
(212) 455-5342; *Fax:* (212) 986-4731
John Heffron, Vp Affl Rels

Urban Television Network Corp.
300 Radio Shack Cir., Suite T3-381, Fort Worth, TX 76102
(817) 415-4816
www.ddgtv.com
contacts@ddgtv.com
Dan Devlin, CEO
News sets, softset, virtual set environments, promotions, newsrooms, facility planning, lighting direction, consultation, Videssence Integration & softset (Virtual Reality Sets).

USA Network
30 Rockefeller Plaza, c/o NBC, New York, NY 10112
(212) 664-4444, *Fax:* (212) 413-6509
www.wnbc.com
Jeff Wachtel, President
Nework featuring movies, original series, sports specials, teen & children's progmg, 24-hours.

Versus
on 4,893 Cable Systems
One Comcast Ctr., 27th Fl., Philadelphia, PA 19103
(215) 665-1700
www.versus.com
Offers collegiate sports featuring nationally-ranked teams from top conference, features the best field sports progmg on TV & is a destination for sports fans, athletes & sportsmen to find exclusive, competitive events that audiences can'tfind elsewhere.
90 Park Ave., 2nd Fl., New York, NY 10016-1301
(212) 883-4000; *Fax:* (212) 687-1819
11835 W. Olympic Blvd., Suite 980, Los Angeles, CA 90064-5001
(310) 473-5404; *Fax:* (310) 473-6525

VH1 (Music First)
86.3 million Subscribers served
Div/DBA: (MTV Networks Inc.)
1515 Broadway, New York, NY 10036
(212) 846-7840
www.vh1.com
Satellite: Satcom C-4*Transponder:* 23
VH1 is a 24-hours ch that features new, current & classic music video, for viewers ages 18-49 who grew up with music videos. Multiplex chs: VH1 Classic, VH1 Country, VH1 Megahits, VH1 Soul & VH Uno.

WE-Women's Entertainment
11 Penn Plaza, 19th Fl., New York, NY 10001
(516) 803-4400
www.wetv.com
Kim Martin, General Manager
A 24-hours cable net featuring classic movies & TV progmg devoted entirely to romance.

The Weather Channel
300 Interstate North Pkwy., Atlanta, GA 30339
(770) 226-0000, *Fax:* (770) 226-2950
www.weather.com
Terry Connelly, President
All-weather progmg 24-hours a day; natl, international, rgnl & loc weather forecasts & features. Multiplex ch: WeatherScan. Serving 87.5 million subs. Satellite: GE Satcom C-3, transponder 13.
845 Third Ave., 11th Floor, New York, NY 10022-6601
(212) 893-2245;
Lyn Andrews, Pres. Twc Media Solutions

WGN America
2501 W. Bradley Pl., Chicago, IL 60618-4718
(773) 528-2311, (773) 883-3241, (212) 210-5900, *Fax:* (773) 883-6299
WGNAmerica.com
Sean Compton, President
Chris Manning, General Sales Mgr
Broad scope entertainment network offering blockbuster movies & series, including MLB baseball & NBA basketball in HD. Total Subscribers: 72 million. Satellite used and transponder: Galaxy 14. transponder 13C.

CABLE - U.S.

Worship Network
66 million Subscribers served
Box 428, Safe Harbor, FL 34695-0365
(727) 536-0036
www.worship.net
Transponder: 7
Bruce Kobish, President
Worship Network features, scenery from around the world with words of wisdom from scriptures & inspirational music. Available 24 hours a day.

WSBK-TV
Div/DBA: (Boscom)
1170 Soldiers Field Rd., Boston, MA 02134
(617) 787-7000, *Fax:* (617) 254-6383
www.boston.cbs.com
Satellite: GE-3*Transponder:* 3
Ed Piette, President
WSBK-TV is a 24-hours ind ch from Boston featuring sports, movies, news & specials.

Regional Cable News Networks

Allbritton Communications
1000 Wilson Blvd., Suite 2700, Arlington, VA 22209
(703) 647-8745, *Fax:* (703) 647-8746
www.newschannel8.net
jkillen@allbrittontv.com
James Killen, General Sales Mgr
There are 8 stns: WJLA. Newschannel 8. WHTM, WSET, WCIU, WBMA, KATV, KTUL.

The Arizona News Channel
5555 N 7th Ave., Phoenix, AZ 85013
(602) 207-3762, *Fax:* (602) 379-2459
www.azfamily.com
advertising@azfamily.com
Arizona's first & only 24-hour loc news svc built on a unique partnership; live loc breaking coverage gives viewers the latest news from around the Valley; NewsChannel 3's 'Good Morning Arizona,' 'Good Day Arizona,' 'Good Evening Arizona' &'The News Show' replay throughout the day on the AZ News Channel, Cox Cable Channel 14; progmg also includes loc productions exclusive to cable, such as 'Project Parenting.'

Bay News 9
700 Carillon Pkwy., Ste. 9, St. Petersburg, FL 33716
(727) 329-2300, *Fax:* (727) 329-2434
www.baynews9.com
viewer@baynews9.com
Elliott Wiser, General Manager
Mike Gautreau, News Director
Bay News 9 is a 24-hour ch owned & operated by Bright House Network. The ch serves over 1 million cable customers in Tampa Bay. Also programs a 24-hour Sp & sports ch.

Bay TV
Div/DBA: (KRON 4)
1001 Van Ness Ave., San Francisco, CA 94109
(415) 441-4444
gerald.rourke@comast.net

CablePulse (CP 24)
299 Queen St. W., Toronto, ON M5V 2Z5 Canada
(416) 591-5757, *Fax:* (416) 593-6397
www.pulse24.com
info@cp24.com
David Kirkwood, Operations Dir
Stephen Hurlbut, General Manager
Allan Schwebel, General Sales Mgr
Karen Reid, News Director
Rgnl 24-hour a day English language news & information channel.

The California Channel
1121 L St, Suite 110, Sacramento, CA 95814
(916) 444-9792, *Fax:* (916) 444-9812
www.calchannel.com
John Hancock, President
The California Channel is an independent, nonprofit, public affairs cable television network. Programming includes coverage of California Assembly and Senate floor sessions and committee meetings, capitol press conferences, and proceedingsof regulatory boards and state commissions. 33.5 hours/week, serving 5,800,000 subs.

CBS News 4
8900 N.W. 18th Terr., Doral, FL 33172
(305) 591-4444
www.cbs4news.com

Central Florida News 13
20 N. Orange Ave., Suite 13, Orlando, FL 32801
(407) 513-1300, *Fax:* (407) 513-1310
www.cfnews13.com
newsdesk@cfnews13.com
Robin A. Smythe, General Manager
Central Florida News 13 is Orlando & the Central Florida Region's only 24-hour loc cable news ch seen only on Bright House Networks.

CLTV News (ChicagoLand Television News)
2000 York Rd., Suite 114, Oak Brook, IL 60523
(630) 368-4000, *Fax:* (630) 571-0489
www.cltv.com
Steve Farber, General Manager
Covers Chicago loc & rgnl news, sports, news, weather & traf info, serving 1.9 million subs.

CN8 - The Comcast Network
1500 Market St., 28th Fl., W. Tower, Philadelphia, PA 19102
(215) 981-7750, *Fax:* (215) 981-8420
www.cn8.com
Michael A. Doyle, President
Melissa Kennedy, Promotions Manager
CN8, The Comcast Network, is an award-winning, 24-hours news, talk, sports & entertainment cable net created by Comcast Cable Communications, that has steadily won viewers, awards & accolades since its inception in 1996. CN8 provides qualitylocally-produced progmg in four main areas-live, interactive television; rgnl news; entertainment; coverage of high school, college & professional sports. CN8 continues to expand its compelling mix of news, talk, sports & entertainment progmgthrough the eastern seaboard, from Washington DC, to the new England area, broadcasting to 6.2 million viewers everyday.

Country Television Network San Diego
1600 Pacific Hwy., Rm. 208, San Diego, CA 92101-2422
(619) 595-4600, *Fax:* (619)557-4027
www.ctn.org
ctn@sdcountry.ca.gov
Janice McGee, President
Michael Workman, General Manager
Country Television Network San Diego makes country govt more accessible & understandable to the citizens of San Diego County through informational progmg focusing on the svcs, programs & current issues of county gov, 24 hr a day, serving708,700 subs.

Las Vegas One
3228 Channel 8 Dr., Las Vegas, NV 89109
(702) 792-8888, *Fax:* (702) 792-2977
www.klas-tv.com
Emily Neilson, President
Robert Stoldal, Operations Dir
Las Vegas One is a 24-hours loc news ch serving the Las Vegas area.

Michigan Government Television
111 S. Capitol Ave., 4th Fl., Romney Bldg., Lansing, MI 48909
(517) 373-4250, *Fax:* (517) 335-7342
www.mgtv.org
mgtv@mgtv.org
Bill Trevarthen, General Manager
Cable network covering all branches of Michigan's state government.

Neighborhood News 12
111 New South Rd., Hicksville, NY 11801
(516) 393-3378
www.news12.com
Barry J. Romanski, General Manager
Neighborhood News 12 is a 24-hrs news ch for individual communities.

New England Cable News
160 Wells Ave., Newton, MA 02459
(617) 630-5000, *Fax:* (617) 630-5057, (617) 630-5055
www.necn.com
Charles J. Kravetz, President
Tom Melville, News Director
A 24-hour rgnl news net.

New York 1 News
75 9th Ave., 6th Fl., New York, NY 10011
(212) 691-6397, *Fax:* (212) 563-7154
www.ny1.com
ny/news@ny1.com
Steve Paulus, Operations Dir
Brad Shapiro, General Manager
Kevin Dugan, Programming Director
Bernie Han, News Director
A 24-hour, all-news cable ch devoted primarily to coverage of New York City & its neighborhoods.

News 10 Now
815 Erie Blvd. E., Syracuse, NY 13210
(315) 234-1000, *Fax:* (315) 234-0635
www.news10now.com
info@news10now.com
Ron Lombard, General Manager
A 24-hour loc/rgnl news ch serving 560,000 Time Warner cable Subscribers throughout central/upstate New York.

News 12 Bronx
930 Soundview Ave., Bronx, NY 10473
(718) 861-6800
rattiganjack@aol.com
Jack M. Rattigan CRMC, CEO
Specializes in 'mktg to the 50+ demographic' (baby boomers & beyond). Customized sls training & seminars for stns programmed to the mature & wealthiest audience.

News 12 Connecticut
28 Cross St., Norwalk, CT 06851
(203) 849-1321, *Fax:* (203) 849-1327
www.news12.com
news12.ct@news12.com
Carmela Williams, News Director
24 hour, 7 day week reg news ch featuring hyper-loc news coverage including sports & weather.

News 12 Long Island
One Media Crossways, Woodbury, NY 11797
(516) 393-1200, *Fax:* (516) 393-1456
www.news12.com
new12li@news12.com
Patrick Dolan, News Director
A 24-hours rgnl news svc.

News 12 New Jersey
450 Raritan Ctr. Pkwy., Edison, NJ 08837-3994
(732) 346-3200, *Fax:* (732) 417-5155
www.news12.com
news12nj@news12.com
Larry Meyrowitz, Operations Dir
Randal W. Stanley, General Manager
Laura Johnson, General Sales Mgr
Patrick O. Young, Promotions Manager
Provides 24-hour coverage of breaking news & events throughout New Jersey, in addition to pub affrs, info & lifestyle progmg of loc interest. Serving 1.8 million households in 14 northern & central counties in New Jersey .

News 12 Westchester
6 Executive Plaza, Yonkers, NY 10701
(914) 378-8916, *Fax:* (914) 378-8938
www.news12.com
news12wc@news12.com
Marguerite Tolliver, General Manager
24-hour news organization covering Westchester County.

News 14 Carolina
316 East Morehead St., Suite 100, Charlotte, NC 28202
(704) 973-5800, *Fax:* (704) 731-2760
www.news14.com
feedback@news14.com
New 14 Carolina offers 24-hours loc news & weather every ten minutes on the Ones.

News Channel 8
1100 Wilson Blvd., 6th Fl., Arlington, VA 22209
(703) 236-9555, *Fax:* (703) 236-2331
www.news8.net
A 24-hour news svc offered in the Washington, DC metropolitan area over all cable svcs. It is available to cable subs in Alexandria, Arlington County, Fairfax City, Fairfax County & Loudoun County in Virginia, Montgomery & Prince George'sCounties in Maryland & Washington, DC.

News Now 53
777 Northwest Grand Blvd., Suite 600, Oklahoma City, OK 73118
(405) 600-6600, *Fax:* (405) 600-0670
www.kotv.com

News On One
3501 Farnam, Omaha, NE 68131
(402) 346-6666, *Fax:* (402) 233-7888
www.wowt.com
sixonlin@wowt.com
Dir of prom & production & tech opns.

NewsChannel 5+
474 James Robertson Pkwy., Nashville, TN 37219
(615) 248-5371, *Fax:* (615) 248-5394
www.newschannel5.com
mbonnett@newschannel5.com
Michelle Bonnett, General Manager
NewsChannel 5+ is a loc news & info stn, serving 550,000 homes in Middle Tennessee & Southern Kentucky.

Ohio News Network
770 Twin Rivers Dr., Columbus, OH 43215
(614) 280-3700, *Fax:* (614) 280-6305
www.ohionewsnow.com
Vince Jones, Operations Dir
Tom Griesdorn, General Manager
Chuck DeVendra, General Sales Mgr
Jason Pheister, Programming Director
Frank Willson, Promotions Manager
Greg Fisher, News Director
A 24-hour cable news ch featuring loc news, weather & sports for the people of Ohio. Currently seen in over 1.5 million homes.

Orange County Newschannel
625 North Grand Avenue, Santa Ana, CA 92701
(714) 565-3850
www.rtnda.org
Mike Sweeney, General Manager
Mya Bulwa, Programming Director
Susanne Lysak, News Director
Don Engelhardt, Chief Engineer
Orange County Newschannel features exclusive coverage of loc news, sports, weather & traf in southern California's Orange County, 24 hours serving over 575,000 subs.

Pennsylvania Cable Network (PCN)
401 Fallowfield Rd., Camp Hill, PA 17011
(717) 730-6000, *Fax:* (717) 730-6005
www.pcntv.com
pcntv@pcntv.com
Brian Lockman, President
Michelle Harter, Operations Dir
William Bova, Programming Director
Richard Cochran, Promotions Manager
PCN is the nation's pre-eminent state pub affrs network, with live & same day coverage of the Pennsylvania Senate/House & other govt activities. PCN televises significant state events (such as high school sports championships), toursmuseums & mfg facilities in the state & distributes educ progmg.

Pittsburgh Cable News Channel (PCNC)
4145 Evergreen Rd., Pittsburgh, PA 15214
(412) 237-1190, *Fax:* (412) 237-1286
www.wpxi.com
mbarash@wpxi.com
Brian Abzanka, Operations Dir
Mark W. Barash, Station Manager
Paul Curran, General Sales Mgr
Loc & rgnl news, talk & info.

R News/Time Warner Communications
71 Mt. Hope Ave., Rochester, NY 14620
(585) 756-2424, *Fax:* (585) 756-1673
www.rnews.com
assignment@rnews.com
Ed Buttaccio, News Director
Loc news 24-hours 7 days per week. Interactive daily call-in show. Nightly loc Sp newscast.

Regional News Network (RNN)
721 Broadway, Kingston, NY 12401
(914) 417-2700
Richard French, General Manager
RNN is a 24 hour provider of news & pub info targeted to suburban New York, Connecticut & and New Jersey serving over 250,000 subs.

Rhode Island News Channel
10 Orms St., Providence, RI 02904
(401) 453-8000, *Fax:* (401) 331-4431
www.abc6.com
radeszkoza@abc6.com
Ronald Adeszko, General Manager
Rhode Island News Channel is a simulcast & rebroadcast of WLNE newscasts for Rhode Island.

San Diego's Newschannel 15
Box 85347, San Diego, CA 92186
(619) 237-1010, *Fax:* (619) 527-0369
www.10news.com
San Diego's Newchannel 15 provides original newscasts, repeats of KGTV-10 newscasts & live break-ins 24 hours.

SNN News 6
1741 Main St., Sarasota, FL 34236
(941) 361-4600, *Fax:* (941) 361-4699
www.snn6.com
Linda DesMarais, General Manager
A 24-hour cable news ch with focus on loc news & info. The Sarasota Herald -Tribune newspaper owned by the New York Times Co.

Texas Cable News
570 Young St., Dallas, TX 75202
(214) 977-4500
www.txcn.com
James T. Aitken, General Manager
News ch covering the state of Texas, 24-hours loc & rgnl.

Tri-State Media News (TSM news)
2215 DuPont Pkwy., New Castle, DE 19770
(877) TSM-NEWS
www.tsmnews.com
Stanley H. Green, President

WJLA-TV/Newschannel 8
1100 Wilson Blvd., 6th Fl., Arlington, VA 22209
(703) 647-8745, *Fax:* (703) 647-8746
www.newschannel8.net
jkillen@allbrittontv.com
James Killen, General Sales Mgr
A 24-hours rgnl news svc for Washington, DC, suburban Maryland & northern Virginia. On 15 cable systems serving 1,125,000 subs.

Regional Cable Sports Networks

Big Ten Network
444 N. Michigan Ave., Suite 1200, Chicago, IL 60611
(312) 665-0700, *Fax:* (312) 665-0740
www.bigten.org
Mark Silverman, President

CBS College Sports Network
Chelsea Piers, Pier 62, Suite 316, New York, NY 10011
(212) 342-8700, *Fax:* (212) 342-8899
www.cstv.com
customerservice@website.cstv.com
Eric Krasnoo, Operations Dir

Channel 4 San Diego
350 10th Ave., Suite 500, San Diego, CA 92101
(619) 683-1900, *Fax:* (619) 876-4993
4sd.com
Craig Nichols, General Manager
San Diego Padres baseball, etc.

Comcast SportsNet
3601 South Broad St., Philadelphia, PA 19148
(215) 336-3500, *Fax:* (215) 952-5996
www.comcastsportsnet.com
askcsn@comcastsportsnetwork.com
Jack Williams, President
Rgnl TV progmg svcs includes live coverage of Philadelphia Flyers ice hockey, Philadelphia '76ers basketball, Philadelphia Phillies baseball, pro boxing, college basketball, football, indoor lacross, ABL, loc sports news & sports talkprograms.
Serving 3 million subs on MSOS(16).

Comcast SportsNet Mid-Atlantic
7700 Wisconsin Ave., Suite 200, Bethesda, MD 20814
(301) 718-3200, *Fax:* (301) 718-3300
midatlantic.comcastsportsnet.com
viewmail@comcastsportsnet.com
Rgnl sports net serving mid-Atlantic. Progmg includes Orioles baseball, Capitals, hockey, Wizards, basketball, ACC & CAA.
Serving 4.4 million subs on over 200 cable systems.
Satellite: Spacenet III, transponder 12-H, ch 23 (scrambled).

Connecticut Sports Network
1049 Asylum Ave., Hartford, CT 06105
(860) 278-5310
Anthony Meliso, General Manager

Cox Sports AZ
20401 N. 29th Ave., Phoenix, AZ 85027
(623) 322-8001, *Fax:* (623) 322-7424
phoenix.cox.net
Phoenix Suns basketball, sports specials, high school sports & high school championships, etc. Phoenix metropolitan area serving over 500,000 subs. Loc microwave/fiber distributed regionally to additional operators.

Cox Sports Television
2121 Airline Dr., Metairie, LA 70001
504-304-2740, *Fax:* 504-304-2243
www.coxsportstv.com
coxsportstv@cox.com
Rod Mickler, Operations Dir
Cox Sports TV is an innovated, 24 hours net providing compelling & rgnl sports progmg. Satellite: Galaxy 23. Serving 1.3 million sub, on 79 cable systems, transponder one.

CSS - Comcast/Charter Sports Southeast
2995 Courtyards Dr., Norcross, GA 30071
(770) 559-7800, (770) 559-2742 (Jeff Miller), *Fax:* (770) 559-2329
www.csssports.com
css@csssports.com

ESPN Classic
ESPN Plaza, 545 Middle St., Bristol, CT 06010
(860) 766-2000, *Fax:* (860) 766-2400
www.espn.com
Classic sporting events, sports series, documentaries & movies; home shopping for sports merchandise & interactive sports games.
Serving 20 million subs on 400 plus cable systems.
Satellite: Galaxy 7, transponder 13 (compressed).

ESPN Inc.
ESPN Plaza, 545 Middle St., Bristol, CT 06010
(860) 766-2000, *Fax:* (860) 766-2400
www.espn.com
ESPN offers a var of professional & amateur sports, including NFL, college basketball, NHL major league baseball, the woman's NCAA tournament.
On 28,000 affiliating cable systems serving over 77 million subs.

ESPNews
ESPN Plaza, 545 Middle St., Bristol, CT 06010-9454
(860) 585-2000, *Fax:* (860) 766-2400
www.espn.com

Fox Soccer Channel
over 30 million Subscribers served on 550+ Cable Systems
1440 S. Sepulveda Blvd., 2nd Fl., Los Angeles, CA 90025
(310) 444-8642, *Fax:* (310) 444-8445
www.foxsoccer.com
ben.alkaly@fox.com
David Sternberg, President
Fausto Ceballos, Operations Dir
David Stenberg, General Manager
Mike Petruzzi, General Sales Mgr
Frank Uddo, Programming Director
Veronica Alvarez, Promotions Manager
Fox Soccer Channel is the nation's leading TV destination for young, passionate & affluent soccer fans. The best in exclusive coverage of professional, college & youth soccer. Satellite: Galaxy 11, transponder 8.

Fox Sports en Espanol
1440 S. Sepulveda Blvd., Los Angeles, CA 90025
(310) 444-8658, *Fax:* (310) 444-8445
www.fse.tv, patrick.ilabaca@fox.com
Live, exclusive coverage in Sp of the Copa Toyota Libertadores & Major League Baseball's All-Star game & World Series postseason, boxing & nightly sports news. Serving 7.9 million subs on 1,321 cable systems. Satellite: Satcom C1,Transponder 1, ch 8 (SA Power VU IRD D9225).
1211 Ave. of the Americas, New York, NY 10036-8701
(212) 822-7000;
Tom Maney, Vp Adv Sls

Fox Sports Net
10201 W. Pico Blvd., FNC/Bldg. 101, 5th Fl., Los Angeles, CA 90035
(310) 369-6000, *Fax:* (310) 969-6700
www.foxsports.com
Jeff Shell, CFO
Randy Freer, President
Arthur Smith, Programming Director
A natl, rgnl & loc supplier of sports progmg.
Serves 68 million subs through 22 rgnl sports nets.

Fox Sports Net Bay Area
77 Geary St., 5th Fl., San Francisco, CA 94108
(415) 296-8900, *Fax:* (415) 296-9198
www.fsnbayarea.com, fsnbayinfo@fsnbayarea.com
Jeff Krolik, General Manager
Michael McCright, General Sales Mgr
Ted Griggs, Programming Director
Programing: San Francisco Giants, Oakland Athletics, Golden State Warriors, San Jose Sharks, San Jose Saber Cats & San Jose Stealth.

Serving more than 4 million households in Northern California & Northern Nevada.
Satellite:Compressed, AMC 1, T 18 Channel 110.

Fox Sports Net Detroit
26555 Evergreen Rd., Suite 90, Southfield, MI 480276
(248) 226-9700, *Fax:* (248) 226-9725
www.foxsports.com/detroit, detroit@foxsports.net
Greg Hammaren, General Manager
John Tuohey, Programming Director
Cable sports net featuring Detroit Pistons, Red Wings, Tigers, Fury, Shock, CCHA hockey & Michigan High School Association championship contests.
Serving 3.2 million subs on more than 70 cable systems.

Fox Sports Net Midwest
700 St. Louis Union Station, Suite 300, St. Louis, MO
(314) 206-7020, *Fax:* (314) 206-7070
www.foxsports.com, midwest@foxsports.net
Jack Donovan, General Manager
Fox Sports Net Midwest reaches more than 5.4 million cable & satellite TV homes in six Midwest states. It telecasts more that 2,000 hours of loc progmg each year, including coverage of St. Louis Cardinals baseball, St. Louis Blues hockey,Indiana Pacers basketball, Indiana Fever basketball, Kansas City Royals baseball, Cincinnati Reds baseball, Big 12: football, women's basketball & showcase, Univ. of Missouri athletics, Kansas State Univ. athletics, Univ. of Nebraska Basketball,Missouri Valley Conference basketball, championship events, Gateway Conference football, & loc high school sports programs, collegiate coaches shows.
FSN Indiana
135 N. Pennsylvania St., Suite 720, Indianapolis, IN 46204-2400

Fox Sports Net New England
42 3rd Ave., Burlington, MA 01803-4414
(781) 270-7200
www.foxsportsnewengland.com
Boston Celtics basketball, New York Mets (Connecticut only), college basketball, golf, football, hockey, professional tennis, soccer & auto racing.
On 215 cable systems serving 2.9 million subs.
Satellite: GE1, transponder 14.

Fox Sports Net New York
Two Penn Plaza, 4th Fl., New York, NY 10001
(212) 465-6000, *Fax:* (212) 465-6024
msn.foxsports.com
A two-ch rgnl sports network that delivers approximately 300 live games of the New York Islanders, Mets, New Jersey Nets & Devils, in addition to horse racing, college football, basketball & variety of sports specials.
On 128 affil cablesystems serving more than 2.7 million subs.
Satellite: GE SpaceNet 2, transponders 1.

Fox Sports Net North
1 Main St. S.E., #600, Minneapolis, MN 55414-1036
(612) 330-2468, (612) 486-9500
www.foxcable.com
Rgnl Sports Network: Minnesota, Iowa, Wisconsin, South Dakota & North Dakota. MLB & Brewers, NBA Timberwolves & Bucks, University of Minnesota hockey, & women's athletics, University of Wisconsin men's & women's athletics, MarquetteUniversity athletics.
Serving 3 million subs.
Satellite: GE 3, transponder 6.

Fox Sports Net Northwest
3626 156th Ave. S.E., Bellevue, WA 98006
(425) 641-0104, *Fax:* (425) 641-9811
www.foxsports.com/northwest
Mike Smith, CFO
Liz Serrette, Operations Dir
Julie McCormack, General Manager
Brett Bibby, General Sales Mgr
Amy Affeld, Programming Director
Coverage of PAC-10, Big Sky, other collegiate conference athletic events; Mariners, SuperSonics & other professional & high school events in the Pacific Northwest rgn.
Serving 2.4 million subs on 100 cable systems.
Satellite: G7,transponder 4.

Fox Sports Net Ohio
9200 S. Hills Blvd., Suite 200, Broadview Heights, OH 44147
(440) 746-8000, *Fax:* (440) 746-9480
www.foxsports.com
Steve Pawlowski, Promotions Manager
Live sports progmg: Cleveland Indians, Cleveland Cavaliers, Cincinnati Reds, Columbus Blue Jackets, college football, basketball & sports news.
Serving 4.5 million subs on 206 cable systems.
Satellite: Satcom GE1, transponder T4.Alternate: GE1 T17.
11311 Cornell Park Dr., Suite 406, Cincinnati, OH 45242-1889
(513) 469-2006; *Fax:* (513) 469-2007
www.foxsports.net

Fox Sports Net Rocky Mountain
2300 15th St., Suite 300, Denver, CO 80202
(720) 898-2700, *Fax:* (720) 898-2735
www.foxsports.com
Amy Turner, General Manager
Rgnl sports net serving 8 states. Progmg includes Denver Nuggets, Utah Jazz, Colorado Avalanche, Colorado Rockies, Univ of Denver & Big 12 conference. Serving 2.2 million subs on 300 cable systems.
Satellites: G7.

Fox Sports Net Southwest
100 E. Royal Ln., Suite 200, Irving, TX 75039
(972) 868-1800, *Fax:* (972) 868-1678
www.foxsports.com
Jon Heidtke, General Manager
Mike Ibanez, General Sales Mgr
Mike Anastassiou, Programming Director
Rgnl sports net serving Texas, Oklahoma, Arkansas, Louisiana & parts of New Mexico. Serving 9 million subs on 1,300 cable and satellite systems. Satellite: Galaxy 11, transponder 4 (digitally compressed).

FSN Arizona
2 North Central Ave., Suite 1700, One Renaissance Sq., Phoenix, AZ 85004
(602) 257-9500, *Fax:* (602) 257-0848
www.foxsports.com/arizona
Mike Connelly, General Manager
Jen Baker, General Sales Mgr
Michael Bardess, Programming Director
Brett Hansen, Promotions Manager
Provides rgnl coverage of loc interest sports progmg. Serving 2.3 million subs in Arizona & Mexico. Satellite: C-1/16.

FSN Florida
1550 Sawgrass Corporate Pkwy., Suite 350, Sunrise, FL 33323
(954) 845-9994
www.fsnflorida.com
Jeff Genthner, General Manager
FSN Florida progmg includes Major League Baseball's Marlins, Tampa Bay Devil Rays & National Hockey League's Florida Panthers.

FSN Pittsburgh
2.3 million Subscribers served on 60 Cable Systems
323 North Shore Dr., Suite 200, Pittsburgh, PA 15212
(412) 316-3800, *Fax:* (412) 316-3892
www.fsninsider.com
Ted Black, General Manager
FSN Pittsburgh telecasts more than 2,000 hours loc progmg each year including the Pittsburgh Pirates, Penguins & Steelers. Also carries athletic contsts & progmg from the University of Pittsburgh, West Virginia & the WPIAL, among others.Satellite: Galaxy 17.

FSN South
1175 Peachtree St. N.E., Bldg. 100, Suite 200, Atlanta, GA 30361
(404) 230-7300, *Fax:* (404) 230-7399
www.foxsports.com
Cheryl Raiford, CFO
Jeff Genthner, Operations Dir
Jamie Kimbrough, General Manager
Brian Hogan, General Sales Mgr
Bill Irish, Programming Director
NCAA sports, Atlanta Hawks, Memphis Grizzlies basketball, Atlanta Braves, Baltimore Orioles, Cincinnati Reds, St. Louis Cardinals baseball, Carolina Hurricanes, Nashville Predators hockey, NASCAR, golf, tennis & much more.
Serving 11.3million subs on more than 1,100 cable systems.
Satellite: Galaxy 11, transponder 4, ch 2.

FSN West
1100 S. Flower St. #2200, Los Angeles, CA 90015
(213) 743-7800, *Fax:* (213) 743-7841
msn.foxsports.com/regional/west
Steve Simpson, General Manager
Los Angeles Lakers basketball, Kings hockey, Lazers indoor soccer, Strings tennis, San Diego Soccers soccer & collegiate sports, etc.

FSN West 2
4,800,000 Subscribers served
1100 S. Flower St., #2200, Los Angeles, CA 90015
(213) 743-7800, *Fax:* (213) 743-7841
msn.foxsports.com/regional/west
Steve Simpson, General Manager
Lisa Laky, General Sales Mgr
Alex Tevllin, Programming Director
Amy Wilson, Promotions Manager
Greg Dowling, News Director
Rgnl sports net featuring the Los Angeles Dodgers, Los Angeles Clippers, Los Angeles Galaxy, Mighty Ducks of Anaheim, USC & UCLA athletic events & other sports.
Serving 3 million subs.
Satellite: G1, transponder 21.

Madison Square Garden Network
Two Penn Plaza, 4th Fl., New York, NY 10001
(212) 465-6000, *Fax:* (212) 465-6024
www.msgnetwork.com, mscnetpr@msgnetwork.com
New York Knicks, Rangers & Yankees; college football & basketball games; boxing. Exclusive Garden events as well as original series progmg.
Serving more than 6.1 million subs on more than 250 cable systems.
Satellite: Satcom 4,transponder 6.

Mid-Atlantic Sports Network
333 W. Camden St., Baltimore, MD 21201
(410) 625-7100
www.masnsports.com

New England Sports Network (NESN)
480 Arsenal St. #1, Watertown, MA 02472-2805
(617) 536-9233, *Fax:* (617) 536-7814
www.boston.com/sports.nesn
NESN is a cable sports svc that delivers Boston Bruins, Red Sox, New England college sports as well as boxing, tennis, fishing, bowling & wrestling.
Serving 3.5 million subs on 28 cable systems.
Satellites: Satcom F-4, transponder 13;GE C-3, transponder 14.

The Sports Network
2200 Byberry Rd., Hatboro, PA 19040
(215) 441-8444, *Fax:* (215) 441-5767
www.sportsnetwork.com
kzajac@sportsnetwork.com
International real-time sports wire svc providing content, branded web pages, satellite and/or computer feeds directly to broadcasters (radio & TV), print, Internet sites, wireless with state of the art technology.

SportsNet New York
75 Rockefeller Plaza, 29th Fl., New York, NY 10019
(212) 485-4800, *Fax:* (212) 485-4802
www.sny.tv
Jon Litner, President

Sun Sports
1000 Legion Place, Suite1600, Orlando, FL 32801-1060
(407) 648-1150, *Fax:* (407) 245-2571
www.sunsportstv.com, askus@foxsports.net
Cathy Weeden, General Manager
Rgnl sports cable net. Progmg includes Orlando Magic & Miami Heat NBA basketball, Tampa Bay Lightning NHL hockey, Florida State, Univ. of Florida, SEC, & FHSAA, athletics, as well as a wide var of loc & rgnl sports events plus Chevy TailgateSaturday, In My Own Words, Chevy FL Fishing Report. Serving 6.3 million subs.
Satellites: Galaxy II, transponder 4.
1550 Sawgrass Corp. Pkwy., Suite 350, Sunrise, FL 33323-2818

Victory Sports One
60 S. 6th St., Suite 3700, Minneapolis, MN 55403
(612) 661-3778
www.news12.com, customerservice@news12.com
News 12 Bronx is a 24-hours rgnl news progmg svc (a News 12 Regional Network).

VideoSeat Pay-Per-View
Div/DBA: (A division of Host Communications Inc.)
546 E. Main St., Lexington, KY 40508
(859) 226-4678, *Fax:* (859) 226-4391
www.hostcommunications.com, dossd@hcionline.com
Lawthon Logan, General Sales Mgr
VideoSeat handles turnkey pay-per-view syndication of several top schools in college football, including: Kentucky, Mississippi State, South Carolina, & Tennessee. Systems in Kentucky, Georgia, Mississippi, South Carolina & Tennessee.

Yankees Entertainment and Sports Network LLC
The Chrysler Bldg., 405 Lexington Ave., 36th Fl., New York, NY 10174-3699
(646) 487-3600, *Fax:* (646) 487-3612
www.yesnetwork.com, info@yesnetwork.com
Michael Wach, President

VCR,DVD,CABLE,SATELLITE
PENETRATION TRENDS
Source:BBM Canada Fall Surveys

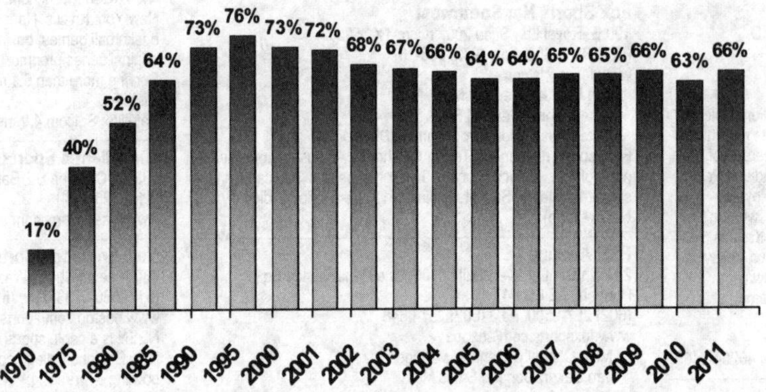

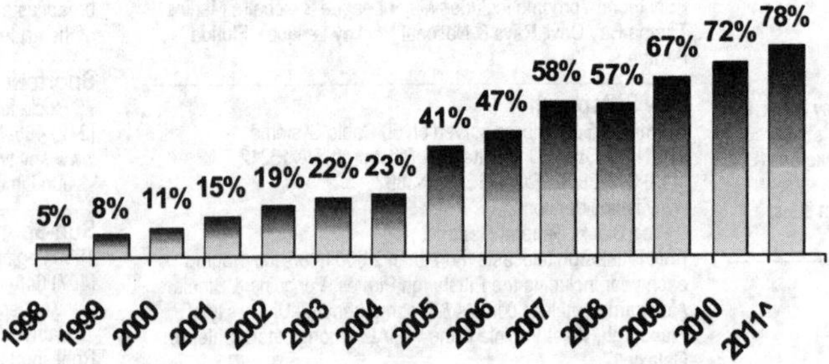

^Media Stats

"TV Basics, 2012-2013," *Television Bureau of Canada*, accessed November 9, 2012, http://www.tvb.ca/page_files/pdf/InfoCentre/TVBasics.pdf.

BBM Extended Market Area - All Persons 2+ (Mo-Su 6a-2a, Fall 2011)

Markets	2+ Pop (000)	2+ Total Wkly Hrs (000)	Cable (%)	Satellite (%)	PVR (%)	Wkly 2+ Hrs/Cap
St John's-Corner Brook	449	9,894	68	31	18	22.0
Charlottetown	139	2,689	50	42	21	19.3
Sydney-Glace Bay	135	3,146	58	38	14	23.3
Halifax	666	13,678	71	24	26	20.5
Saint John-Moncton	608	13,025	54	41	23	21.4
Carleton	141	3,570	47	49	7	25.3
Rim-Mat-Sept Iles	214	5,854	71	28	19	27.3
Rivière du Loup	130	3,695	54	42	13	28.4
Saguenay	262	7,361	69	30	28	28.1
Québec	1,054	24,990	75	21	22	23.7
Sherbrooke	560	13,997	65	29	17	25.0
Montréal Anglo	976	18,225	61	31	21	18.7
Trois Rivières	298	8,181	66	29	19	27.5
Rouyn-Noranda	140	3,675	60	38	14	26.3
French Canada	6,951	158,278	71	24	19	
Ottawa-Gatineau	1,442	26,829	62	33	28	18.6
Ottawa-Gatineau Anglo	1,009	17,947	59	36	31	17.8
Ottawa-Gatineau Franco	433	8,881	67	27	22	20.5
Pembroke (CM)	100	2,056	13	78	16	20.6
Kingston	265	5,586	42	49	22	21.1
East Central Ont.	726	15,997	35	59	20	22.0
Peterborough	301	6,520	32	62	20	21.7
Barrie	482	10,179	48	47	24	21.1
Kitchener-London	1,968	38,839	55	38	22	19.7
Kitchener	1,025	19,573	58	35	22	19.1
London	835	16,732	55	40	22	20.0
Windsor	402	8,546	53	28	15	21.3
Sudbury-Timmins-North Bay/S.S. Marie	513	11,844	49	47	18	23.1
Thunder Bay	146	3,256	56	42	23	22.3
Kenora	58	1,133	46	46	23	19.5
Winnipeg	961	18,277	69	25	37	19.0
Yorkton	78	1,778	25	70	14	22.8
Regina-Moose Jaw	306	6,226	67	30	38	20.3
Saskatoon	330	5,965	63	30	26	18.1
Prince Albert	105	2,118	35	57	15	20.2
Medicine Hat	83	1,557	58	36	43	18.8
Lloydminster	91	1,717	24	70	26	18.9
Edmonton	1,674	32,877	59	35	48	19.6
Dawson Creek	63	987	25	59	30	15.6
Kelowna	349	7,359	74	22	41	21.1
P. George-Kamloops	355	7,626	48	46	34	21.5
Terrace Kitimat	69	1,384	43	44	18	20.1
Total Canada	**33,593**	**678,062**	**66**	**28**	**29**	**20.2**

Source: BBM TV Diary EM Statistics, Fall 2011

Meter Markets						
Toronto-Hamilton	7,337	137,458	73	21	26	18.7
Montreal	4,642	95,100	75	19	33	20.5
Vancouver-Victoria	3,506	67,459	84	10	49	19.2
Calgary	1,672	28,014	72	22	49	17.2

Source: BBM Fall 2011

"TV Basics, 2012-2013," *Television Bureau of Canada*, accessed November 9, 2012, http://www.tvb.ca/page_files/pdf/InfoCentre/TVBasics.pdf.

CABLE - CANADA

Canadian Cable Networks

Aboriginal Peoples Television Network
339 Portage Ave., Winnipeg, MB R3B 2C3 Canada
(204) 947-9331, *Fax:* (204) 947-9307
www.aptn.ca
info@aptn.ca
Jean LaRose, CEO

Alliance Broadcasting
Div/DBA: (dba Showcase TV & History TV)
121 Bloor St. E., Toronto, ON M4W 3M5 Canada
(416) 967-1174, *Fax:* (416) 960-0971
www.allianceatlantis.com
Phyllis Yaffe, President
Best of Canadian & international TV series & movies. Serving 5 million subs on 100 cable systems. Satellite: ANIK-E2.

ARTV
1400 boul. Rene-Levesque Est, Bureau A-53-1, Montreal, QC H2L 2M2 Canada
(514) 597-3636, *Fax:* (514) 597-3633
www.artv.ca
Catherine Dupont, Operations Dir
Marie Cote, General Manager
Marc Pichette, Promotions Manager
ARTV is a French-language channel dedicated entirely to arts and culture. Twenty-four hours a day of great performances, films, documentaries, dramas & design. The pleasure of capturing the art and culture of Quebec, Canada & the whole world.

Atlantic Satellite Network (ASN)
2885 Robie St., Halifax, NS B3K 5Z4 Canada
(902) 453-4000, *Fax:* (902) 454-3302
www.ctv.ca
bt@ctv.ca
L. Wartman, Operations Dir
Rich Marchand, General Sales Mgr
Movies & news, educ programs weekend mornings.
Serves 51 cable systems. Satellite: Anik C-1.

BookTelevision: The Channel
299 Queen St. W., Toronto, ON M5V 2Z5 Canada
(416) 591-5757
slatterb@natchez.net
Talent coaching.

Bravo!
299 Queen St. W., Toronto, ON M5V 2Z5 Canada
(416) 591-5757, *Fax:* (416) 591-8497
www.bravo.ca
bravomail@bravo.ca
Bravo! NewStyle Arts Channel is dedicated to entertaining, stimulating & enlightening veiwers who have a taste for more complex TV. Bravo! delivers a wide array of fine arts progmg, balancing longer-form structured shows & shorter piecesthat appear in a more random way as 'flow' to create a fluid mix of distinctive music, dance, opera, drama, literature, cinema, visual art, the art of TV & the art of talk. Serving 5.8 million subs on 700 cable systems.

Canadian Satellite Communications Inc. (CANCOM)
2055 Flavelle Blvd., Mississauga, ON L5K 1Z8 Canada
(905) 403-2020, *Fax:* (905) 403-2022
www.cancom.ca
Don Fletcher, Operations Dir
Expert in evaluating, selecting, integrating & implementing satellite-based solutions for business. Cancom operates in four main lines of business: broadcast solutions, tracking solutions, learning solutions & data solutions.

CBC Newsworld
Box 500, Station A, Toronto, ON M5W 1E6 Canada
(416) 205-2409, *Fax:* (416) 205-8684
www.newsworld.com
maria_mirowicz@cbc.ca
Maria Mirowicz, Programming Director
Live 24-hours news & info net on basic cable, satellite & wireless in Canada.
On 1500 cable systems serving 8 million subs. Satellite: Anik E2 (Ku-band).

The Comedy Network
Box 1000, Station O, Toronto, ON M4A 2W3 Canada
(416) 332-5300, *Fax:* (416) 332-5283
Rick Brace, President
Brent Haynes, Programming Director
A 24-hour service featuring Canadian & international programs devoted exclusively to comedy sketches, standup comedy, & ongoing comedy series. Coverage area: national.

Country Music Television (Canada)
64 Jefferson Ave, Unit 18, Toronto, ON M6K 3H4 Canada
(416) 534-1191, *Fax:* (416) 530-2215
www.cmtcanada.ca
info@cmt.ca
Michael Harris, CEO
A 24-hour mus & entertainment net that combines mus videos with programs and features that focus on the artists and their mus.
Serving 7 million subs on 1,487 cable systems in Canada.
Satellite: Anik E2 (Ku-Band), transponder T4.

Court TV Canada
10212 Jasper Ave., Edmonton, AB T5J 5A3 Canada
(780) 440-7777, *Fax:* (780) 440-8899
www.courttvcanada.ca
info@courttvcanada.ca
Jill Bonenfant, Programming Director
Court TV Canada, in partnership with the U.S. based Court TV, combines Court TV's compelling daytime live trial coverage, legal analysis from inside U.S. courts with legal & police dramas, movies, documentaries & series from Canada & abroad.

CPAC-Cable Public Affairs Channel
Div/DBA: (A subsidiary of Consortium of Canadian Cable Comp
1750-45 O'Connor St., Ottawa, ON K1P 1A4 Canada
(613) 567-2722, *Fax:* (613) 567-2741
www.cpac.ca
comments@cpac.ca
Uncut, unfiltered coverage of Canadian pub affrs issues including LIVE bcsts of the House of Commons & its Standing Committees. Serving 7.2 million subs.

CTV News Channel
Box 9, Station O, Toronto, ON M4A 2M9 Canada
(416) 332-5000, *Fax:* (416) 291-5337
www.ctv.ca
news@ctv.ca
Jana Juginovic, Programming Director
Continually updated headline news, business, sports, weather & entertainment, every 15 minutes.

Discovery Channel
#9 Channel 9 Ct., Toronto, ON M1S 4B5 Canada
(416) 332-5000
www.ctv.ca
Ivan Fecan, President
Corrie Coe, Programming Director
Non-fiction documentary TV progmg focusing on the themes of nature, science & technology, adventure.
On 385 cable systems serving 5.6 million subs.
Satellite: Anik E2, Channel 210.

DMX Music-Canada
7260 12th St. S.E., Suite 120, Calgary, AB T2H 2S5 Canada
(403) 640-8527, *Fax:* (403) 253-2788
www.dmx.ca
brad.trumble@dmxmusic.com
Brad Trumble, Operations Dir
Formerly a residential svc, now a coml svc exculsively.
Considering a return to the Canadian market. DMX commercial audio svc; 102 formats digital audio.
Serving 8000 subs. Satellites: C3 Bank, TBA (Ku-band) delivered by satellite ant.

Drive-In Classics
299 Queen St. W., Toronto, ON M5V 2Z5 Canada
(416) 591-5757
nj@jewishmail.com
Joel A. Levitch, President
NJT offers documentaries, children's programs, news magazines, Info, cultural & relg progmg for the Jewish community, presented 3-hours every Sunday.

Fairchild Television Ltd.
#3300-415, Hazelbridge Way, Aberdeen Centre, Richmond, BC V6X 4J7 Canada
(604) 295-1313, *Fax:* (604) 295-1300
www.fairchildtv.com
info@fairchildtv.com
Joseph Chan, President
The only Chinese language specialty TV across Canada. Serving 360,000 subs on 8 cable systems & DTH.

The Family Channel Inc.
Box 787, BCE Place, 181 Bay St., Suite 100, Toronto, ON M5J 2T3 Canada
(416) 956-2030, *Fax:* (416) 956-2035
www.family.ca
info@family.ca
Barbara Bailie, General Manager
Kevin Wright, Programming Director
Premium TV net offering family entertainment based on 60% from the Disney Channel, 25% Canadian & 15% international progmg.
Serving 5.4 million subs, on 300 cable systems, transponder T20.

FashionTelevisionChannel
299 Queen St. W., Toronto, ON M5V 2Z5 Canada
(416) 591-5757
www.dougholland.com
dougholland@att.net
Doug Holland, President
Turnkey opns, allocation studies, due diligence, transmitter installations, upgrades & coverage maps

Food Network Canada
121 Bloor St. E., Toronto, ON M4W 3M5 Canada
(416) 967-1174
tvisk@yahoo.com
Promotional concepts, scripts & publications for the bcstg & entertainment industries.

HGTV Canada
121 Bloor St. E., Suite 200, Toronto, ON M4W 3M5 Canada
(866) 967-4488, (416) 967-0022, *Fax:* (416) 960-0971
www.hgtv.ca
feedback@hgtv.ca
Norm Bolen, President
A 24-hour Canadian home & garden progmg resource.
Serving 5.2 million subs.
Satellite: F1, transponder T19.

History Television
121 Bloor St. E., Suite B1, Toronto, ON M4W 3M5 Canada
(416) 967-1174, *Fax:* (416) 960-0971
www.allianceatlantis.com
Marc Etkind, Programming Director
A 24-hour program svc featuring current & world history told in documentaries, mini-series & feature films.
Satellite: Launching September 1997. On 350 cable systems serving 4 million subs.
Satellite: Anik e-2, transponder 19.

La Magnetotheque
1055 Rene Levesque E., Suite 501, Montreal, QC H2L 4S5 Canada
(514) 282-1999, *Fax:* (514) 282-1676
www.lamagnetotheque.qc.ca
info@lamagnetotheque.qc.ca
Majorie Theodore, General Manager
French-language reading svc for persons who are blind, visually impaired, or print-handicapped.

Le Canal Nouvelles
1600 boul. de Maisonneuve est, Montreal, QC H2L 4P2 Canada
(514) 598-2869, *Fax:* (514) 598-6037
www.tva.canoe.ca
Martin Cloutier, General Manager

Le Reseau des sports (RDS)
1755 Blvd. Rene-Levesque Est, Suite 300, Montreal, QC H2K 4P6 Canada
(514) 599-2244, *Fax:* (514) 599-2299
www.rds.ca
webmaster@rds.ca
Jerry Frappier, General Manager
Provides 24-hour sports TV in Fr.
Satellite: ANIK E-2, transponder T-18.

Les Chaines Tele Astral
Les Chaines Tele Astral, Une division d'Astra Media, 2100, Ste-Catherine St. W., Rm. 700, Montreal, QC H3H 2T3 Canada
(514) 939-3150, *Fax:* (514) 939-3151
www.astral.com
Pierre Roy, President
Johanne Saint-Laurent, Operations Dir
Progmg includes Super Écran, the Fr pay-TV stn; Canal Famille, children's progmg stn devoted to children from ages 3 to 14; Canal D, a specialty ch featuring mainly documentaries.
Serving 245,000 subs (Super Ecran); 2,110,000 subs(Canal Famille), &1,705,000 subs (Canal D).
Serving 370 cable systems.
Satellite: Anik E-2, transponder 11-A.

Life Network
121 Bloor St. E., Suite 200, Toronto, ON M4W 3M5 Canada
(416) 967-0022, *Fax:* (416) 960-0971
www.lifenetwork.ca
info@lifenetwork.ca
Kirstine Layfield, General Manager
Offers lifestyle entertainment progmg about the people, places & experiences that make the journey of life worthwhile &

interesting.
Serving 26 million English & Fr subs on 100 cable systems.
Satellite: Anik E2 (Ku-band), transponderT19 (horizontal).

Movie Central
5324 Calgary Tr., Suite 200, Edmonton, AB T6H 4J8 Canada
(780) 430-2800, *Fax:* (780) 437-3188
www.moviecentral.com
Andrew Eddy, General Manager
Sandy Perkins, Programming Director
Coml-free premium pay TV svc including movies, mus & comedy specials, major sports events & boxing (Superchannel, Movie Max!, Viewers Choice, Pay-Per-View).
Serving 300,000 subs on 170 cable systems.
Satellite: Anik E2.

MuchLOUD
299 Queen St. W., Toronto, ON M5V 2Z5 Canada
(416) 591-5757
www.jewishtvnetwork.com
jewishtv@earthlink.net
Jay Sanderson, CEO
Production & cablecasting of net quality Jewish progmg in news, pub affrs, educ, arts, PBS & entertainment.

MuchMoreMusic
299 Queen St. W., Toronto, ON M5V 2Z5 Canada
(416) 591-5757, *Fax:* (416) 926-4026
www.muchmoremusic.com
muchmoremail@muchmoremusic.com
David Kines, General Manager
Brings music fans Hot AC MusicVideo, top international specials, documentaries, movies and a growing roster of exclusive, original programming they can't find anywhere else.

MuchMoreRetro
299 Queen St. W., Toronto, ON M5V 2Z5 Canada
(416) 591-5757, *Fax:* (416) 926-4026
www.muchmoreretro.com
request@muchmoreretro.com
David Kines, General Manager
Source for 24/7 classic videoflow from artists including The Police, Madonna, Bon Jovi, Corey Hart, Prince, Aerosmith, Duran Duran, Janet Jackson, Rush, Nirvana and Alanis Morissette and more.

MuchMusic
299 Queen St. W., Toronto, ON M5V 2Z5 Canada
(416) 591-5757
www.jnproductions.bc.ca
jnproductions@telus.net
Jakob Nortman, President
For all your voice-over needs, including narration, corporate videos, on-hold telephone messages & announcements for GPS systems. Radio production facilities available.

MuchVibe
299 Queen St. W., Toronto, ON M5V 2Z5 Canada
(416) 591-5757
www.vradio.com
joel@virtualradio.com
Joel Easton, General Manager
Virtual Radio is the oldest music website providing a new radio format, content & internet expertise to bcstrs world wide.

MusiMax & MusiquePlus
355 rue Ste- Catherine O., Montreal, QC H3B 1A5 Canada
(514) 284-7587, *Fax:* (514) 284-1889
www.musiqueplus.com
Pierre Marchand, General Manager
Musimax is a French-language speciality svc owned equally by Astral Media Inc. of Montreal and CHUM Ltd. of Toronto. MusiquePlus is MuchMusic's French-language counterpart in Quebec. Serving 2.078 million subs on approximately 120 cablesystems . Satellite: Anik F1, transponder 9B.

OLN
Div/DBA: Outdoor Life Network
9 Channel Nine Crt., Scarborough, ON M1S 4B5 Canada
(416) 332-5000, *Fax:* (416) 332-5861
www.tsn.ca/oln
Anna Stamboic, General Manager
Canada's destination for adventurous entertainment. Going beyond the comforts of home, OLN's progmg reveals the onsatible human drive for adventure.

Prime TV
5 million Subscribers served
2100 One Lombard Pl., Winnipeg, MB R3B-OX3 Canada
(204) 926-4800
www.globaltv.com
Tim Schellenberg, General Manager
The best of TV. Classy & classic entertainment & informational progmg for those moving on from youth-skewed traditional TV fare.

RDI-Le Reseau de l'information
9.2 million Subscribers served
Div/DBA: (Formerly RDI-Le Reseau de l'information de Radio 1400 Blvd. Rene-Levesque E., Montreal, QC H2L 2M2 Canada
(514) 597-7224, *Fax:* (514) 597-5226
www.radio-canada.ca/rdi
gilles.desjardins@radio-canada.ca
RDI-Le Reseau de l'information is Canada's French-language news network. RDI provide live of coverage major events, newscasts every 15 minutes, sports, financial news, as well as info programs on a wide range of topics.

Report on Business Television
720 King St. W., 10th Fl., Toronto, ON M5V 2T3 Canada
(416) 957-8100, *Fax:* (416) 957-8180
www.robtv.com
Jack Fleischmann, General Manager

The Score Television Network
370 King St. W., Suite 304, Toronto, ON M5V 1J9 Canada
(416) 977-6787, *Fax:* (416) 977-0238
www.thescore.ca
info@thescore.ca
John Levy, CEO
David Errington, General Manager
Delivers the most comprehensive svc of professional & amateur sports news & info from Canada & around the world & is in every major Canadian cable market. Available in more than 5 million cable homes.
Serving 5.4 million subs on 370 cablesystems.
Satellite: Anik F1, transponder 19.

Sex TV: The Channel
299 Queen St. W., Toronto, ON M5V 2Z5 Canada
(416) 591-5757
www.tankersleyproductions.com
randy@tankersleyproductions.com
Randy Tankersley, President
Full-bcst svcs. ENG/EFP Beta SP crews with/without producers, avid nonlinear editing.

The Shopping Channel
59 Ambassador Dr., Mississauga, ON L5T 2P9 Canada
(905) 565-3500, (905) 565-2600 (voicemail), *Fax:* (905) 565-2641
www.theshoppingchannel.ca
Ted Starkman, General Manager
Live, shop-at-home televised retail svc, offering a var of consumer products.
Serving 5.7 million subs across Canada via cable & satellite.
Satellite: Anik E2, transponder 5.

SPACE: The Imagination Station
299 Queen St. W., Toronto, ON M5V 2Z5 Canada
(416) 591-5757
www.dickburden.com
rwburden@pacbell.net
Richard W. Burden, Engineering Dir
Bcst tech svcs, facilities design, Traveller's Information Service (TIS) & Educational FM (EDFM) FCC applications, Part 15 AM & FM bcst systems engrg.

Star! The Entertainment Information Station
299 Queen St. W., Toronto, ON M5V 2Z5 Canada
(416) 591-7400
www.cameraplanet.com
archive@cameraplanet.com
Steve Rosenbaum, President

Talk TV
Box 9, Station O, Toronto, ON M4A 2M9 Canada
(416) 332-5030, *Fax:* (416) 332-5283
www.talktv.ca
Ed Robinson, General Manager
Patrick Patterson, General Sales Mgr

TELETOON
6 Million Subscribers served on 1000 Cable Systems
Box 787, 181 Bay St., Toronto, ON M5J 2T3 Canada
(416) 956-2060, *Fax:* (416) 956-2070
www.teletoon.com
info@teletoon.com
Darrell Atherley, General Sales Mgr
Leslie Kruger, Promotions Manager
This specialty net shows the best in animation from Canada & around the planet.
Serving 6 million subs on 1,000 cable systems.
Satellite: Anik E2, transponder 20.

TMN—The Movie Network/MOVIEPIX
Box 787, BCE Place, 181 Bay St., Suite 100, Toronto, ON M5J 2T3 Canada
(416) 956-2010, *Fax:* (416) 956-2018
www.movienetwork.ca
kwright@tv.astral.com
Kevin Wright, Programming Director
Two English-language, gen interest, pay TV nets featuring recent movie titles on the multi-channeled TMN, & new classics on MOVIEPIX.
Serving 350,000 subs on 200 cable systems.
Satellite: Anik E1 (Ku-band), transponder T31 (TMN); AnikE2 (Ku-band), transponder T27 (MOVIEPIX).

Treehouse TV
64 Jefferson Ave., Unit 18, Toronto, ON M6K-3H4 Canada
(416) 534-1191
www.treehousetv.ca
Susan Ross, General Manager
Phil Piazza, Programming Director
Treehouse TV is a specialty net dedicated to providing a variety of imaginative, stimulating and coml-free progmg for preschoolers from morning until bedtime.
Serving 4 million subs on 180 cable systems.
Satellite: Anik E-2,transponder 5.

TSN—The Sports Network
9 Channel Nine Crt., Toronto, ON M1S 4B5 Canada
(416) 332-5000, *Fax:* (416) 332-7656
www.tsn.ca
Phil King, President
Rick Chisholm, Operations Dir
Nikki Moffat, General Manager
Adam Ashton, Promotions Manager
TSN's flagship news program, SportsCentre, NHL & first three rounds of the Stanley Cups Playoffs, Toronto Maple Leafs hockey, International Hockey including the IIHF World Junior Championship, the Olympic Games through 2012. CFL, NFL, PGATour & all four golf Majors, Season of Champions Curling, NASCAR. A 24-hour sports ch distributed on cable in Canada. Covers all major professional & amateur sports.
Serving 8.8 million subs on more than 2,000 cable systems.
Satellite: Anik E1,transponder 18 KU-H.

TVOntario
2180 Yonge St., Toronto, ON M4T 2T1 Canada
(416) 484-2600, *Fax:* (416) 484-6285
www.tvontario.org
jjavet@tvontario.org
Ray Newell, Operations Dir
Lee Robock, General Manager
Provides educ progmg in English & Fr off air & via cable systems throughout Ontario.
TVO network (English) serves 98% of Ontario households. (Fr) serves 75% of Ontario households & 300,000 households in Quebec. Together the nets are on327 cable systems.
Satellites: Anik F1, transponder 21.

Viewer's Choice Canada
Box 787, BCE Place, 181 Bay St., Suite 100, Toronto, ON M5J 2T3 Canada
(416) 956-2010, *Fax:* (416) 956-2055
www.viewerschoice.com
John Riley, President
Eastern Canada's pay-per-view network.
On 50 cable systems serving 600,000 addressable subs.
Satellites: Anik E1; Anik E2.

Vision TV: (Canada's Multi Faith Network)
80 Bond St., Toronto, ON M5B 1X2 Canada
(416) 368-3194, *Fax:* (416) 368-9774
www.visiontv.ca
estella@visiontv.ca
Mark Prasuhn, COO
Bill Roberts, President
Programs presented by 30 plus faith groups, British comedies, movies dramas, documentaries, pub affrs, music & performance.
Serving 7.8 million subs on 12 cable systems. Satellite: Anik F1, transponder 5.

VIVA
Corus Specialty Television, 64 Jefferson Ave., Unit 18, Toronto, ON M6K 3H4 Canada
(416) 534-1191, *Fax:* (416) 588-9341
www.myviva.ca

VoicePrint(TM)
Div/DBA: (A division of The National Broadcast Reading Serv
1090 Don Mills Rd., Suite 303, Toronto, ON M3C 3R6 Canada
(416) 422-4222, *Fax:* (416) 422-1633
www.voiceprintcanada.com
nbrs@nbrscanada.com

Robert S. Trimbee, President
Mike Hanson, General Manager
Read published news in audio format for blind, vision-restricted & sr Canadians.

W Network
64 Jefferson Ave., Unit 18, Toronto, ON M6K 3H4 Canada
(416) 534-1191
www.wnetwork.com

The Weather Network/MeteoMedia Inc.
Div/DBA: (A division of Pelmorex Communications Inc.)
1755 Rene-Levesque Blvd. E., Suite 251, Montreal, QC H2K 4P6 Canada
(514) 597-1700, *Fax:* (514) 597-2981
www.theweathernetwork.com
Pierre L. Morrissette, President
Luc Perreault, Operations Dir
Natl satellite-to-cable TV network bcstg in Fr (MétéoMédia) & English (The Weather Network) offering weather & environmental info 24-hours a day, 7 days a week.
Serving 8.2 million subs on 752 head ends.
Satellite: Anik E2, transponder 1A.

YTV Canada Inc.
64 Jefferson Ave., Unit 18, Toronto, ON M6K 3H4 Canada
(416) 534-1191, *Fax:* (416) 533-0346
www.ytv.ca
info@ytv.ca
Phil Piazza, Programming Director
Susan Schaefer, Promotions Manager
English language basic cable specialty svc dedicated to children, teens & their families.
On approximately 1,200 cable systems serving an estimated 8.1 million subs.
Satellite: ANIK E1 East/West-DVC, transponder 7 (nationwide), 111degrees (Ku-band), vert polarization, 11900 MHZ.

Major TV Program Syndicators / Distributors

CBS Television Distribution
2401 Colorado Avenue, Suite 110, Santa Monica, CA 90404
(310) 264-3300, *Fax:* (310) 264-3301
Armando Nunez, CBS Global, President
Scott Koondel, Distribution President
Aaron Meyers, President, Programming/Development
Steven LoCascio, EVP/CFO
Joseph DiSalvo, President, Sales
New York Office
1700 Broadway, New York, NY 10019; Tel: 212-315-4000; Fax: 212-582-9255.
Major First-Run Programming
Judge Judy, Dr. Phil, Wheel of Fortune, Jeopardy!, Inside Edition, Judge Joe Brown, The Jeff Probst Show, Rachael Ray, Entertainment Tonight.
Major Off-Net Programming
Everybody Loves Raymond, CSI, Frazier, Criminal Minds, NCIS, NCIS: Los Angeles, The Good Wife, Blue Bloods, Hawaii Five-O, Hot in Cleveland.

Disney-ABC Domestic Television
500 South Buena Vista Street, Burbank, CA 91521
(818) 560-9300
Janice Marinelli, President
Tom Malanga, SVP/Finance
Howard Levy, EVP, New York Office
Irv Schulman, SVP, New York Office
Sal Sardo, EVP/Marketing
New York Office
Advertising/Media Sales: 1133 Avenue of the Americas, 33rd floor, New York, NY 10036; Tel: 212-625-5100; Fax: 212-625-5140.
Major First Run Programming
Who Wants to be a Millionaire, Live! with Kelly and Michael, Katie.
Major Off-Net Comedies
According to Jim, Scrubs, Tyler Perry's Meet the Browns.

MGM Domestic Television
245 North Beverly Drive, Beverly Hills, CA 90210
(310) 449-3000
John Bryan, President
Vicky Gregorian, vice President
New York Office
655 Third Avenue, 27th floor, New York, NY 10017; Tel: (646) 744-3782.
Off-Network Syndication
Cash Cab, Jeremiah, Dead Man's Gun.

NBC Universal Domestic Television Distribution
30 Rockefeller Plaza, 11th Floor West, New York, NY 10112
(212) 664-4444
Barry Wallach, President
Domestic Syndication Programming
Access Hollywood, Access Hollywood Live, The Jerry Springer Show, Maury, The Steve Wilkos Show.
First-Run Syndicated Programming
The Chris Matthews Show, The Wall Street Journal Report with Maria Bartiromo.
Off-Network Distribution
30 Rock, Friday Night Lights, House, Law and Order, Monk, The Office, The Real Housewives franchise.

Sony Pictures Television
Mailing Address: 9336 Washington Blvd, Culver City, CA 90232
Second Address: Sony Pictures Entertainment, 10202 West Washington Blvd, Culver City, CA 90232
(310) 244-4000
Steve Mosko, President
Chris Elwell, EVP, US Distribution
Jeffrey Reyna, SVP, Business Affairs
New York Office
550 Madison Avenue, New York, NY 10022; Tel: (212) 833-8500.
Daytime Dramas
The Young and the Restless, Days of Our Lives.
First-Run Syndication
The Dr. Oz Show, The Queen Latifah Show.
Off-Network Syndication
Rules of Engagement, Community, Seinfeld, The King of Queens.

Twentieth Television
2121 Avenue of the Stars, 21st Floor, Los Angeles, CA 90067
(310) 369-1000, *Fax:* (310) 369-3899
www.20thtv.com
Greg Meidel, President
First-Run Programming
The Ricki Lake Show, Dish Nation, The Wendy Williams Show, Family Feud, The Jeremy Kyle Show, Divorce Court, Judge Alex.
Major Off-Network Programming
Glee, Modern Family, Burn Notice, Family Guy, 24, Cops, The Simpsons, My Name is Earl, The Unit, How I met Your Mother, American Dad, The Cleveland Show.

Warner Brothers Domestic Television Distribution
4000 Warner Blvd, Burbank, CA 91522
(818) 954-6000, *Fax:* (212) 636-5300
Kenneth Werner, President
Andy Lewis, EVP/General Manager
Micheal Teicher, EVP, Media Sales
Roseann Cacciola, SVP, General Asales Manager
New York Office
1325 Avenue of the Americas, 31st floor, New York, NY 10019; Tel: (212) 636-5300.
Syndicated Shows
The Ellen DeGeneres Show, Extra.
Syndicated Off-Net Programming
The Big bang Theory, Two and a Half Men, Friends, The New Adventures of Old Christine, George Lopez, Without a Trace, The Closer, Cold Case.

Major National TV News Organizations

ABC News
77 West 66th Street, New York, NY 10023
(212) 456-2777, *Fax:* (212) 456-2795
abcnews.go.com
customerservice@abcnews.go.com
Anne Marie Sweeney, President-Disney ABC
Ben Sherwood, President ABC
Barbara Fedida, VP/Talent
Joe Ruffalo, VP/News Digital
Susan Mercandetti, VP/Business Development
Andrew Kubitz, VP/Programming
Kevin Brockman, VP/GlobalCommunications
Ownership: Walt Disney Company
7 West 66th Street, New York, NY 10023; Tel: (212) 456-2777; Fax: (212) 456-2796; Executives: David Weston, President; Dave Davis, EVP; Paul Mason, SVP/Politics; Phyliis McGrady, vP/Creative Development.
Domestic Bureau: (Atlanta)
25810 Cumberland Parkway, SE, Suite 160, Atlanta, GA; Tel: (770) 431-2380.
Domestic Bureau: (Chicago)
190 North Sate Street, Chicago, IL 60601; Tel: (312) 899-4015; Suzanne Caraher, Assignment Editor.
Domestic Bureau: (Los Angeles)
4151 Prospect Ave., Los Angeles, CA 90027; Tel: (323) 671-5210; David Hernson, Bureau Chief; Mark Lima, Deputy Bureau Chief; Michael Ray Gammon, Assignment Editor; Roger Scott, Correspondent.
Domestic Bureau: (New York)
47 West 66th Street, 3rd Floor, New York, NY 10023; Tel: (212) 456-2700; Wendy Fisher, Director/Domestic News; John Berman, Correspondent.
Domestic Bureau: (Washington)
1717 DeSales Street, Washington, DC 20036; Tel: (202) 222-7777; Robin Sproul, VP/Bureau Chief; Jane Aylor, Director/Bureau Operations; David Chalian, Director/Political Unit.
Domestic Bureau: (Dallas)
606 Young Street, Dallat, TX 75202; Tel: (214) 749-7013.
Domestic Bureau: (Denver)
123 East Speer Blvd., Denver, CO 80203; Tel: (303) 832-7777.
Domestic Bureau: (Miami)
1320 South Dixie Highway, Coral Gables, FL 33146; Tel: (305) 662-2116.
Primetime Shows Exec. Producers:
20/20: David Sloan; Good Morning America: Tom Cibrowski; Nightline: Jeanmarie Condon; Primetime: Eric Strauss; World News Tonight with Diane Sawyer: Michael Corn.
Affiliate News Service:
ABSAT, 47 West 66th Street, 3rd Floor, Room 303, New York, NY 10023; Tel: (212) 456-1700; Mike Huitt, Director; Nac@abc.com

CBS News
555 West 57th Street, New York, NY 10019
(212) 975-4114
www.cbs.com
Jeff Fager, Chairman
David Rhodes, President
John Frazee, SVP/News Services
Sonya McNair, SVP/Communications
Anthony Mason, Sr Business Correspondent
Domestic Bureau: (Atlanta)
260 14th Street NE, Atlanta, Ga 30309; Tel: (404) 685-2400.
Domestic Bureau: (Dallas)
10111 North Central Expressway, Dallas, TX 75231; Tel: (817) 451-1111.
Domestic Bureau: (Los Angeles)
7800 Beverly Blvd., Los Angeles, CA, 90036; Tel: (323) 575-2345.
Domestic Bureau: (Miami)
4700 Biscane Blvd., Suite 1170, Miami, FL 33101; Tel: (305) 571-4400.
Domestic Bureau: (San Francisco)
825 Battery Street, San Francisco, CA 94111; Tel: (415) 362-8177.
Domestic Bureau: (Washington)
2020 M Street NW, Washington, DC 20036; Tel: (202) 457-4444.
CBS News Programming:
The Early Show, Evening News, Up tot he Minute, Morning News, 60 Minutes, 48 Hours Mystery, Sunday Morning, The Saturday Early Show, Face the Nation.

CNBC Inc
900 Sylvan Avenue, Englewood Cliffs, NJ 07632
(201) 735-2622, *Fax:* (2012) 735-3200
www.cnbc.com
Patricia Fill-Kruschel, Chairman
Mark Hoffman, CEO
Satpal Brainch, President
Tom O'Brien, Chief Revenue Officer
Thomas Clendenin, SVP/Marketing
Nikhil Deogun, SVP/Editor-in-Chief
David Fabor, Anchor/Reporter
Melissa Francis,Anchor/Reporter
Maria Bartiromo, Anchor/Reporter
Bertha Coombs, Anchor/Reporter
Domestic Bureau: (Washington)
1025 Connecticut Avenue NW, Suite 800, Washington, DC 20036; Tel: (202) 467-5400; Alan Murray, Bureau Chief/Anchor.
Domestic Bureau: (Los Angeles)
3000 West Almeda Avenue, Burbank, CA 91523; Tel: (818) 840-3214; Lacy O'Toole, Bureau Chief.
Programming:
Worldwide Exchange, Squawk Box, Squawk on the Street, Power Lunch, Street Signs, Closing Bell, Fast Money, The Kudlow Report.
Weekend Programming:
The Suze Orman Show, The Wall Street Journel Report.

CNN
One CNN Center, Atlanta, GA 30303
(404) 827-1700
www.cnn.com
Greg Dalba, President
Jonathan Davies, EVP/CNN International
Richard Davis, EVP/News Standards
Susan Grant, EVP/News Services
Katherine Green, EVP/Managing Editor
Janet Rolle, EVP/Chief Marketing Officer
Domestic Bureau: (New York)
One Time Warner Center, New York, NY 10019; Tel: (212) 275-7800; Darius Walker, Bureau Chief.
Domestic Bureau: (Boston)
637 Washington Stree, Suite 200, Brookline, MA 02446; Tel: (617) 264-9905.
Domestic Bureau: (Chicago)
435 North Michigan Avenue, Chicago, IL 60611; Tel: (312) 645-8555.
Domestic Bureau: (Los Angeles)
6430 West Sunset Blvd., Los Angeles, CA 90028; Tel: (323) 993-5000.
Domestic Bureau: (Miami)
12000 Biscayne Blvd., Miami, FL 33181; Tel: (305) 892-5100; John Zarella, Bureau Chief.
Domestic Bureau: (Washington)
820 First Street NE, Washington, DC 20022; Tel: (202) 898-7900; Sam Feist, Bureau Chief.
Morning Programming:
Starting Point, Anderson Cooper 360, Early Start, CNN Newsroom, The Situation Room.
Evening Programming:
The Situation Room, Lou Dobbs, CNN Election Center, Piers Morgan, Anderson Cooper 360.
Overnight Programming:
Piers Morgan Tonight, Anderson Cooper 360.

Fox News Channel
1211 Avenue of the Americas, New York, NY 10036
(212) 301-3000
www.foxnews.com
Robert Murdoch, Chairman
Chase Casey, Deputy Chairman/President
James Murdoch, Deputy COO/CEO
David Devoe, SVP/CFO

Gerson Zweifach, SVP/General Counsel
John Nallen, Deputy CFO
Ownership: News Corp.
Domestic Bureau: (Atlanta)
260 14th Street, Atlanta, GA 30318; Tel: (404) 685-2280; John Boswell, Bureau Chief.
Domestic Bureau: (Denver)
999 18th Street, Suite 1665, Denver, CO 80202; Tel: (303) 383-1170; Dennis King, Bureau Chief.
Domestic Bureau: (Dallas)
301 North Market Street, Suite 450, Dallas, TX 75202; Tel: (214) 742-5005; Russell Cosby, Bureau Chief.
Domestic Bureau: (Los Angeles)
2044 Armocast Avenue, Los Angeles, CA 90025; Tel: (310) 571-2000; Nancy Harmeyer, Bureau Chief.
Domestic Bureau: (Miami)
1440 79th St. Causeway, Suite 208, North Bay Village, FL 33141; Tel: (305) 866-8007.
Domestic Bureau: (Washington)
2201 C Street NW, Washington, DC 20520; Tel: (202) 496-0109.
Primetime Shows:
Fox and Friends, Special Report with Bret Baier, The O'Reilly Factor, Hannity; On Record with Greta Van Susteren, Your World with Cavuto.

MSNBC
1 MSNBC Plaza, Seacaucus, NJ 07094
(201) 583-5000, *Fax:* (201) 583-5453
www.msnbc.com
Phil Griffin, President
Shannon High-Bassilik, Managing Editor/VP
Jeffrey Zucker, CEO/NBC
Steve Capus, President/NBC
Val Nochols, VP/Business Development
Programming:
Today Show, Nightly News, Dateline, Meet the Press, MSNBC TV.

NBC News
30 Rockefeller Plaza, New York, NY 10112
(212) 664-4444, *Fax:* (212) 664-4085
www.nbc.com
Patricia Fill-Krushel, Chairman
Steve Capus, President
Marianne Gambelli, President/Net Advertising
Vivian Schiller, SVP/Chief Digital Officer
Chris Penna, Executive Editor
Executive Producer, Promotions Manager
Ownership: NBC Universal
Domestic Bureau: (Midwest)
454 North Columbus Drive, 1st Floor, Chicago, IL 60611.
Programming:
Nightly News, TODAY, Dateline NBC, Meet the Press, Weekend Today, Weekend Nightly News, NBC Sports.

TV News Services

AccuWeather Inc.
NSS Data: TV-CATV only
385 Science Park Rd., State College, PA 16803
(814) 235-8600, (800) 566-6606, *Fax:* (814) 235-8609
www.accuweather.com
sales@accuweather.com
Evan Myers, President
TV, radio, weather progmg & systems, plus turnkey solutions to take your loc news to the mobile web.

Agence France-Presse
1500 K St. N.W., Suite 600, Washington, DC 20005
(202) 289-0700, *Fax:* (202) 414-0632
www.afp.com
afp-usa@afp.com
Philipe Raater, Operations Dir
Produces a variety of international news svcs for radio & TV, including text wires in six languages, photo wires, graphics & financial wires plus video svcs.

All Africa Global Media
920 M Street S.E., Washington, DC 20003
(202) 546-0777, *Fax:* (202) 546-0676
www.allafrica.com
newsdesk@allafrica.com
Reed Kramer, CEO
Amadou Mahtar Ba, President
A news & info svc on African affrs for TV, radio & print news svcs.

American Academy of Dermatology
NSS Data: Radio Only
Div/DBA: Communications Dept., American Academy of Dermatol
Box 4014, Schaumburg, IL 60168-4014
(847) 330-0230, *Fax:* (847) 330-8907
www.aad.org
mediarelations@aad.org
Expert physicians available for TV & radio interviews, audio & video tapes on skin cancer pevention & detection, as well as info on skin, hair & nail conditions.

American Heart Association National Center
7272 Greenville Ave., Dallas, TX 75231
(214) 706-1330, (800) 242-8721 (aha-usa1), *Fax:* (214) 706-5243
www.americanheart.org
Julie Del Barto, Programming Director
Periodic satellite news feeds of medical rsch stories.

APTN Productions
The Interchange, Oval Rd., Camden Lock, London, NW1 7DZ United Kingdom
(0) 20 7482 7400, *Fax:* (0) 20 7413 8312
www.aptn.com
Nigel Baker, General Manager
International TV svcs company, daily satellite news feeds to bcstrs worldwide, tech facilities, camera crew hire worldwide.
Serves TV.
1995 Broadway, New York, NY 10023-5882
(212) 362-4440;

The Associated Press
NSS Data: TV-CATV only
AP Broadcast News Center, 1100 13th St., Suite 700, Washington, DC 20005
(202) 736-1100, (800) 821-4747, *Fax:* (202) 736-1124
www.apbroadcast.com
James R. Williams III, Operations Dir
AP Services for TV: Video: APTN Video News. Wires: APTV Wire, AP News Tickers, AP NewsPower, AP Data Stream. AP Alert Graphics: AP GraphicsBank. Software: AP NewsCenter; AP NewsDesk; AP NewsDesk (LAN), ENPS, SNAPfeed Satellite Delivery: APExpress. Elections: ENPS Stats, AP Politics, AP Election Wire. Online content: CustomNews, AP Online, Online Video Network, AP Spanish Online. Photos: Photo Archive, Photo Stream.

Audio-Video News
3622 Stanford Cir., Falls Church, VA 22041
(703) 354-6795
fboylebrkr@aol.com
Frank Boyle, President
Radio & TV media brokerage, mergers & acquisitions/appraisals.

Bloomberg Financial L.P.
Div/DBA: (formerly Bloomberg L.P.
731 Lexington Ave., New York, NY 10022
(212) 318-2200, EXT. 2201, *Fax:* (917) 369-5000
www.bloomberg.com
John Meehan, Programming Director
Offers business & news reports for radio & TV stns. 24-hours a day. Full news svc.

British Information Services
845 3rd Ave., New York, NY 10022
(212) 745-0277, *Fax:* (212) 745-0359
www.britianusa.com
Mark Hopkinson, Operations Dir
Sarah Kendall, Promotions Manager
Assists radio & TV crews visiting the United Kingdom.
Serves radio & TV.

Broadcast Interview Source
2233 Wisconsin Ave. N.W., Washington, DC 20007
(202) 333-5000, *Fax:* (202) 342-5411
www.expertclick.com
expertclick@gmail.com
Mitchell P. Davis, Operations Dir
Free source of interview contacts

Camera Planet
253 Fifth Ave., New York, NY 10016
(212) 779-0500
Jeffberke@yahoo.com

Canada NewsWire Ltd.
NSS Data: TV-CATV only
1500, 20 Bay St., WaterPark Pl., Toronto, ON M5J 2N8 Canada
(416) 863-9350, (866) 805-9530, *Fax:* (416) 863-9429
www.newswire.ca
cnwtor@newswire.ca
Sylvia Kavanagh, General Manager
Tim Griffin, Programming Director
Carolyn McGill, Promotions Manager
Offers a range of industry leading communication products & svcs for companies looking to maximize the strength of their news. Whether you are an investor rel off, or a specialist in PR, CNW offers the right tools for your communications.

The Canadian Press
36 King St. E., Toronto, ON M5C 2L9 Canada
(416) 364-3172, *Fax:* (416) 364-1325
www.thecanadianpress.com
broadcast@thecanadianpress.com
David Ross, CFO
Wayne Waldroff, General Manager
Terry Scott, News Director
Full wire & audio svcs (news agency), satellite delivery for radio program syndicators.
Serves radio & TV.

Capital Television News Service (CTNS)
NSS Data: TV-CATV only
1629 S. St., Sacramento, CA 95811
(916) 446-7890, *Fax:* (916) 446-7893
www.pacsat.com
pacsat@pacsat.com
Video wire svc providing daily news coverage, via satellite, of California's capitol for subscribing TV stns throughout the state.

CBS News: See CBS listing in Major National TV News Organizations, this section.

CNN and CNN Headline News: See listing in Major National TV News Organizations, this section.

Compu-Weather Inc.
NSS Data: TV-CATV only
2566 Rt. 52, Hopewell Junction, NY 12533
(800) 284-7246, *Fax:* (845) 226-1918
www.compuweather.com
sales@compuweather.com
Jeff Wimmer, President
TV & radio svc providing weather forecasts, features, info & actualities.

Congressional Quarterly Inc.
1255 22nd St. NW, Washington, DC 20037
(202) 419-8500, (800) 432-2250, *Fax:* (202) 419-8760
www.cq.com
marketing@cq.com
David Rapp, Operations Dir
Congressional Quarterly Weekly Report & News Service, editorial rsch reports, newsletters, seminars, rsch, reference volumes, paperbacks; daily & wkly congressional info publications.

Connecticut Weather Center Inc.
NSS Data: Radio Only
18 Woodside Ave., Danbury, CT 06810-7123
(203) 730-2899, *Fax:* (203) 730-2839
www.ctweather.com
weatherlab@ctweather.com
William Jacquemin, President
Weather forecasts for all media. Custom intros/outros/lives. Accurate forecasts. Barter or cash arrangement available.

CW11.com WPIX-TV New York
220 E. 42nd St., 10th Fl., New York, NY 10017
(212) 949-1100, *Fax:* (212) 210-2591
www.cw11.com
jziegler@tribune.com
Betty Ellen Berlamino, General Manager
John Ziegler, Promotions Manager

Feature Story News
NSS Data: Radio Only
1730 Rhode Island Ave. N.W., Suite 405, Washington, DC 20036
(202) 296-9012, *Fax:* (202) 296-9205
www.featurestorynews.com
markss@featurestory.com
Simon Marks, President
Ind supplier of radio & TV news to English-language bcstrs worldwide. Bureaus in Washington, Moscow, London, New York, Orlando & San Francisco.

Fox News Channel: See listing in Major National TV News Organizations, this section.

Golden Lamb Productions
NSS Data: TV-CATV only
Box 47, Schoolhouse Rd., Nassau, NY 12123
(866) 457-2739
www.glpvideoproduction.com
Dow Haynor, President

ENG, EFP crews, HD & SD, SNG available. Serves the Northeast, 24-hour call, packages, live remotes, camera crane news & sports.

Hollywood News Service
13636 Ventura Blvd., Suite 303, Sherman Oaks, CA 91423
(818) 986-8168, (818) 990-5945, *Fax:* (818) 789-8047
www.newscalendar.com
editor@newscalender.com
A wire svc to the entertainment media. Publisher of Hollywood News Calendar in Los Angeles; Entertainment News Calendar in New York.

Independent Television News of London Ltd.
400 N. Capital St., Suite 850, Washington, DC 20001
(202) 429-9080, *Fax:* (202) 429-8948
www.itn.co.uk
michael.herrod@itn.co.uk
Other branches: South Africa, Moscow, London. Hong Kong. British TV news, Washington bureau.
ITN House, 200 Grays Inn Rd, London,
011-441-637-2424, 2017-833-3000;
Stewart Purvis, Editor

Israel Broadcasting Service
800 2nd Ave., New York, NY 10017
(212) 499-5402, *Fax:* (212) 499-5425
www.israel.org
yonih@newyork.mfa,gov.il
Yoni Heilman, Operations Dir
Free radio & TV programs & footage about Israel.

Kyodo News New York Bureau
747 Third Ave., Suite 1801, New York, NY 10017
(212) 508-5460, *Fax:* (212) 508-5461
www.kyodo.co.jp
Japan's leading newsgathering organization serving virtually all media in all parts of the world. The combined circulation of nwspr Subscribers is about 50 million.

Medialink
708 Third Ave., New York, NY 10017
(212) 682-8300, (800) 843-0677, *Fax:* (212) 682-5260
www.medialink.com
info@medialink.com
Larry Thomas, COO
Michele Wallace, Operations Dir
International video & audio PR, satellite feed & news advisory service. Accessible by computer/newswire in U.S. & European newsrooms.
Serves radio & TV.
6430 Sunset Blvd, Suite 1100, Los Angeles, CA 90028-7901
(323) 465-0111; *Fax:* (323) 465-9230
One Maritime Plaza, Suite 1670, San Francisco, CA
(415) 296-8877; *Fax:* (415) 296-9929
The Time & Life Bldg, 541 N. Fairbanks Ct, Suite 1910, Chicago, IL 60611-3706
(312) 222-9850; *Fax:* (312) 222-9810
Natl. Press Bldg., 529 14th St. N.W., Suite 1230-A, Washington, DC 20045-2520
(202) 628-3800; *Fax:* (202) 628-2377
5000 Quorum, Suite 450, Dallas, TX 75254-7063
(972) 774-0200; *Fax:* (972) 774-0222
7 Fitzroy Sq., London,
44-207 554 2700; *Fax:* 44-207 554 2710

MediaOne Services
NSS Data: TV-CATV only
901 Battery Street, Suite 220, San Francisco, CA 94111
(415) 262-4222, *Fax:* (415) 693-5005
www.mediaoneservices.com
info@mediaoneservices.com
Benjamin Schick, CEO
Danny Skarka, Operations Director
Nelson Ferreira, Briadcast Director
Full HD Studio and Remote Production for Broadcast and Web, Branded Spots, Conferences, Theatercasts. Two insert studios for news channel live shots. Media Training, Fiber transmission, and Satellite downlink.

Metro Weather Service Inc.
NSS Data: TV-CATV only
132 Franklin Place, Suite 385, Woodmere, NY 11598
(800) 488-7866, *Fax:* (516) 568-8853
www.metrowx.com
metrowx@aol.com
Pat Pagano, President
Tailored weather forecasts for TV & briefings to weathercasters. Serves radio & TV.

Miami News Net
NSS Data: TV-CATV only
2641 S.W. 27th St., Miami, FL 33133
(305) 285-0044, *Fax:* (305) 285-0074
www.miaminewsnet.com
mnn@bellsouth.net
Catherine A. Scull, President
A 24-hour TV news, sports & entertainment svc that provides crews, video archive, avid, beta edit & feed facilities. Live talkback studio facilities, dual path digital KU uplink trunk.

Mountain News Corporation
50 Vashell Way, Suite 400, Orinda, CA 94563
(925) 254-4456, *Fax:* (925) 254-7923
www.mountainnews.com
info@mountainnews.com
Rob Brown, Programming Director
Mountain News Corporation, formally AMI News, is the largest & oldest producer of winter & summer progmg for media. We deliver the most accurate & timely news & info covering mountain activities.

The Nasdaq Stock Market
1 Liberty Plaza, New York, NY 10006
(212) 858-5211, (212) 401-8700, *Fax:* (646) 625-6548
www.nasdaq.com
petersos@nasdaq.com
Robert Greifeld, President
Customized loc data for the stock market.
Serves radio & TV.

NBC News: See NBC listing in Major National TV News Organizations, this section.

Nielsen Entertainment News Wire
NSS Data: TV-CATV only
101 Federal St., Suite 600, Boston, MA 02110
(617) 478-5500, *Fax:* (617) 478-5501
www.nielsenenw.com
donald.gallagher@nielsen.com
Donald Gallagher, Operations Dir
Advance news from Nielsen-owned publications serving radio, TV, nwsprs & online.

Nippon TV Network Corp.
645 5th Ave., Suite 303, New York, NY 10022
(212) 660-6900, *Fax:* (212) 660-6998, (212) 265-8495
www.ntv.co.jp
motoko@ntvic.com
Jusaburo Hayashi, President
Motoko Hasegawa, Operations Dir
International media svcs.

NOAA/National Weather Service Headquarters
1325 East-West Hwy., Silver Spring, MD 20910
(301) 713-0700, *Fax:* (301) 713-1598
www.nws.noaa.gov
Weather & flood warnings, forecasts & related info for the media & gen public.
7220 N.W. 101 Terr., Kansas City, MO 64153-2371
(816) 891-8914;
Sandy Boyse, Dir Central Rgn
630 Johnson Ave., Bohemia, NY 11716-2618
(516) 244-0101;
Dean Gulezian, Dir Eastern Rgn
Grosvenor Ctr. Mauka Tower, 737 Bishop St., Suite 2200, Honolulu, HI 96813-3212
(808) 532-6416; *Fax:* (808) 532-5569
James Weyman, Dir Pacific Rgn
819 Taylor St., Rm. 10A06, Fort Worth, TX 76102-6124
(817) 978-1000;
Erma Nations, Dir Southern Rgn
Federal Bldg., 125 S. State St., Rm. 1311, Salt Lake City, UT
(801) 524-5122;
Vickie L. Nadolski, Dir Western Rgn
222 W. Seventh Ave, 23, Rm. 517, Anchorage, AK 99513-7500
(907) 271-5136;

NorthStar Studios Inc.
NSS Data: TV-CATV only
3201 Dickerson Pike, Nashville, TN 37207
(615) 650-6000, *Fax:* (615) 650-6300
www.northstarstudios.tv
grant.barbre@northstarstudios.tv
Grant Barbre, President
Complete TV production svcs: 7 stages, mobile production/uplink trucks, network origination, transmissions, digital archiving, Avid/DS, linear editing, graphics/animations & ENG crews.

Potomac Television - News & Video Service
1510 H. St. N.W., Suite 202B, Washington, DC 20005
(202) 783-6464, *Fax:* (202) 783-1132
www.ptpngroup.com
jnorins@potomactv.com
Jamie Norins, News Director
Washington, DC, news coverage, studios, editing facilities, live shots, crews, satellite capability & duplications.

Presson Perspectives
600 Druid Rd. E., Clearwater, FL 33756
(800) 249-4521, *Fax:* (727) 443-1984
gpresson@tampabayrr.com
Gina Presson, President
Specializing in TV news & documentary production & electronic publishing. Svcs include rsch, field production, videography, postproduction, & satellite feeds for radio & TV.
Serves radio & TV.

Reuters America
3 Times Sq., New York, NY 10036
(646) 223-4000
www.reuters.com
boblagrassa@reuters.com
Bob Lagrassa, Operations Dir
Worldwide TV news production & transmission svcs for loc TV stns/producers. Camera crews, production facilities, news bureaus, satellite svcs, video/slide archives.

The Seattle Video Bureau
Box 99218, Seattle, WA 98199
(206) 448-2500, *Fax:* (206) 378-1700
www.seattlevideo.com
dave@seattlevideo.com
David Oglevie, President
ENG/EFP crews with BETACAM SP kits. Net experienced.

Skywatch Weather Center
NSS Data: TV-CATV only
347 Prestley Rd., Bridgeville, PA 15017
(412) 221-6000, (800) 759-9282, *Fax:* (412) 221-3160
www.skywatchweather.com
airsci@skywatchweather.com
Dr.Stanley J. Penkala, President
Harry Green, Operations Dir
Weather forecasts targeted to the viewing area, & comprehensive briefings for on-air talent. Serves radio & TV.

Skyways Communications, L.L.C.
89 Access Rd., Suite 20, Norwood, MA 02062
(781) 551-9960, *Fax:* (781) 551-5956
www.skyways.net
scott@skyways.net
LuAnn Reeb, President
Kate Kenney, Programming Director
Custom TV news gathering, producing & mobile satellite uplinking svcs. Provides bcst-experienced crews, producers, reporters & technicians for breaking news, live-event coverage & webcasting.

The Sports Network
2200 Byberry Rd., Suite 200, Hatboro, PA 19040
(215) 441-8444, *Fax:* (215) 441-5767
www.sportsnetwork.com
kzajac@sportsnetwork.com
Mickey Charles, President
Ken Zajac, General Sales Mgr
International real-time sports wire svc providing content, branded web pages, satellite and/or computer feeds directly to broadcasters (radio & TV), print, Internet sites, wireless with state of the art technology.

U.S. Conference of Catholic Bishops
NSS Data: TV-CATV only
Div/DBA: Department of Communication, Film/TV Review Svcs. Office for Film & Broadcasting, 1011 First Ave., New York, NY 10022
(212) 644-1880, *Fax:* (212) 644-1886
www.usccb.org
ofb@msn.com
Harry Forbes, General Manager
Publishes wkly reviews of movies, TV with artistic & moral observations.

The Washington Bureau
NSS Data: TV-CATV only
400 N. Capitol St. N.W., Suite 775, Washington, DC 20001
(202) 347-6396, *Fax:* (202) 628-6295
www.twbnews.com
rtillery@twbnews.com
Julia Rockler, CEO
Custom TV news coverage: ENG crews, producers & talent. Prod svcs: editing, studio, remote & satellite capabilities. Two live studios. Teleconference capability. Fiber Optic connectivity with Capital, White House & other locations.

WeatherData Inc.
245 N. Waco St., Suite 310, Wichita, KS 67202
(316) 265-9127, *Fax:* (316) 265-1949
www.weatherdata.com
ceo@weatherdata.com
Mike Smith, CEO
Forecasts for radio & TV, meteorology training, slides & videotape of weather & related phenomena. Nexrad radar interpretation seminar; distributor of Nexrad weather display systems. Meteorologist 24/7, storm monitoring & customer svc.

WSI (Weather Services International)
400 Minuteman Rd., Andover, MA 01810
(978) 983-6300, *Fax:* (978) 983-6400
www.wsi.com
Mark Gildersleeve, President
Linda Maynard, Promotions Manager
WSI is the leading source of professional on-air weather systems, solutions & forecasting svc for TV, including TrueView, the most innovative weather storytelling tool available.

Radio News Services

ABC News Radio
NSS Data: TV-CATV only
125 West End Ave., New York, NY 10023
(212) 456-5100, *Fax:* (212) 456-5150
www.abcradionetworks.com
customerservice@abc.com
Steve Jones, Operations Dir
Robert Garcia, General Manager
Serves 2,500 affiliates & 92.5 million wkly listeners nationwide, with bcst facilities in New York City & Washington, DC.

AccuWeather Inc.
NSS Data: Radio Only
385 Science Park Rd., State College, PA 16803
(814) 235-8600, *Fax:* (814) 235-8609
www.accuweather.com
info@accuweather.com
Dr. Joel N. Myers, President
Gary Kemp, General Sales Mgr
World's most accurate svc provides products & svcs for TV, radio, internet, mobile web & all new media platforms.

Agence France-Presse
1500 K St. N.W., Suite 600, Washington, DC 20005
(202) 289-0700, *Fax:* (202) 414-0632
www.afp.com
afp-usa@afp.com
Pierre Louette, CEO
Jean-Pierre Vignolle, General Manager
Produces a var of international news svcs, including text wires in six languages, photo wires, graphics & financial wires.

Alaska Public Radio Network
3877 University Dr., Anchorage, AK 99508
(907) 550-8400, *Fax:* (907) 550-8401
www.aprn.org
aprn@alaska.net
Bede Trantina, Station Manager
Duncan Moon, News Director
Satellite-delivered news/info programs to 26 member stn across Alaska from state-of-the-art studios, hqtr in Anchorage.

American Academy of Dermatology
NSS Data: Radio Only
Div/DBA: Communications Dept., American Academy of Dermatol
Box 4014, Schaumburg, IL 60168-4014
(847) 330-0230, *Fax:* (847) 330-8907
www.aad.org
mediarelations@aad.org
Expert physicians available for TV & radio interviews, audio & video tapes on skin cancer pevention & detection, as well as info on skin, hair & nail conditions.
1350 I Street NW, Suite 870, Washington, DC 20005-3305
(202) 842-3555; *Fax:* (202) 842-4355
1350 I Street NW, Suite 870, Washington, DC 20005-3305
(202) 842-3555; *Fax:* (202) 842-4355

American Heart Association
7272 Greenville Ave., Dallas, TX 75231-4596
(214) 706-1330, (800) 242-8721 (aha-usa1), *Fax:* (214) 706-5243
www.americanheart.org
M. Cass Wheeler, CEO
Rsch & lifestyle reports, distributed via podcast.

American Urban Radio Networks
960 Penn Ave., Suite 200, Pittsburgh, PA 15222
(412) 456-4000, *Fax:* (412) 456-4040
www.aurn.com
jlopes@aurn.com
Ronald Davenport, Chairman
Jerry Lopes, President Program Operations
Howard Eisen2, President Sales
Ty Miller, Manager News/Sports
Baob Sharkey, Engineering Dir
Info, news, sports & entertainment of special interest to Blacks & other minorities.
432 Park Ave. S., 14th Fl., New York, NY 10016-8013
(212) 883-2100; *Fax:* (212) 297-2571
jay@aurn.com
E.J. ""Jay"" Williams, Pres

AMI News
50 Vashell Way, Suite 200, Orinda, CA 94563
(925) 254-4456
www.theamigroup.com
Chad Dyer, Operations Dir
MP3 Wave phone- & tape-supplied features focusing on skiing, fishing, camping, travel & beach conditions with related news & information. Offered seasonally. Available on the Internet.
Eastern Bureau,
(800) 736-0370;

Associated Press Broadcast Services
NSS Data: TV-CATV only
1825 K St. N.W., Suite 800, Washington, DC 20006-1202
(202) 641-9281
www.apbroadcast.com
Audio: PrimeCuts, Sound Bank. On Air: Radio News. On Line: News Tickers, Online Video Network; Custom News, Sp Online. Prep: Power Prep. Software: News Desk, APENPS. Sound Desk, News Center. Text Headlines, Sp, Sports Power, News Power,Images & Multimedia: asap, all AP.

Associated Press Network News: See Associated Press listing in Major National Radio Networks, this section.

Audio-Video News
3622 Stanford Cir., Falls Church, VA 22041
(703) 354-6795
fboylebrkr@aol.com
Frank Boyle, President
Radio & TV media brokerage, mergers & acquisitions/appraisals.

The Berns Bureau
Box 2939, Washington, DC 20013-2939
(202) 314-5165
Matt Kaye
Complete localized coverage of Washington, DC. Satellite ISDN & telephone transmission. Audio news releases. Govt, politics, farm, relg & other progmg for radio. Audio svc for TV.

Black Radio Network Inc. (BRN)
166 Madison Ave., New York, NY 10016
(212) 686-6850, *Fax:* (212) 686-7308
news@blackradionetwork.com
Roy Thompson, Operations Dir
Provides a daily actuality news service emphasizing minority-oriented items.

British Information Services
845 Third Ave., New York, NY 10022
(212) 745-0395, *Fax:* (212) 745-0463
www.britainusa.com
Provides daily audio news feed svc filed by digital line from London at no cost to stns. Assists radio & TV crews visiting the United Kingdom.

Canada NewsWire Ltd.
NSS Data: TV-CATV only
1500, 20 Bay St., WaterPark Pl., Toronto, ON M5J 2N8 Canada
(416) 863-9350, (866) 805-9530, *Fax:* (416) 863-9429
www.newswire.ca
cnwtor@newswire.ca
Sylvia Kavanagh, General Manager
Tim Griffin, Programming Director
Carolyn McGill, Promotions Manager
Offers a range of industry leading communication products & svcs for companies looking to maximize the strength of their news. Whether you are an investor rel off, or a specialist in PR, CNW offers the right tools for your communications.
Gulf Canada Sq, 401 Ninth Ave. S.W., Suite 835, Calgary, AB Canada
(403) 269-7605; *Fax:* (403) 263-7888, TWX: 03-824872
Michle.dauphine@newswire.ca
Krista Wightman, Mgr
Gulf Canada Sq, 401 Ninth Ave. S.W., Suite 835, Calgary, AB Canada
(403) 269-7605; *Fax:* (403) 263-7888, TWX: 03-824872
Michle.dauphine@newswire.ca
Krista Wightman, Mgr
Sun Tower, 1550 Bedford Hwy., Suite 410, Halifax, NS Canada
(902) 422-1411; *Fax:* (902) 422-3507, TWX: 019-21534
jgallant@newswire.ca
Robert Moffatt, Mgr Atlantic Canada
Sun Tower, 1550 Bedford Hwy., Suite 410, Halifax, NS Canada
(902) 422-1411; *Fax:* (902) 422-3507, TWX: 019-21534
jgallant@newswire.ca
Robert Moffatt, Mgr Atlantic Canada
255 Albert St., Suite 460, Ottawa, ON Canada
(613) 563-4465; *Fax:* (613) 563-0548, TWX: 053-3292
Hugh Johnson, Vp Natl Capital Rgn
255 Albert St., Suite 460, Ottawa, ON Canada
(613) 563-4465; *Fax:* (613) 563-0548, TWX: 053-3292
Hugh Johnson, Vp Natl Capital Rgn
1155 Rene Levesque Blvd. W, Suite 3310, Montreal, PQ Canada
(514) 878-2520; *Fax:* (514) 878-4451, TWX: 055-60936
scmtl@newswire.ca
Elaire Carr, Vp Quebec
1155 Rene Levesque Blvd. W, Suite 3310, Montreal, PQ Canada
(514) 878-2520; *Fax:* (514) 878-4451, TWX: 055-60936
scmtl@newswire.ca
Elaire Carr, Vp Quebec
650 West Georgia St., Suite 1103, Vancouver, BC Canada
(604) 669-7764; *Fax:* (604) 669-4356, TWX: 04-508529
Larry Cardy, Vp Western Canada
650 West Georgia St., Suite 1103, Vancouver, BC Canada
(604) 669-7764; *Fax:* (604) 669-4356, TWX: 04-508529
Larry Cardy, Vp Western Canada

The Canadian Press
NSS Data: Radio Only
36 King St. E., Toronto, ON M5C 2L9 Canada
(416) 364-3172, *Fax:* (416) 364-8896
www.thecanadianpress.com
broadcast@thecanadianpress.com
Full wire & audio svcs (news agency), satellite delivery for radio program syndicators.

CBS News: See CBS listing in National Radio Programming Services, this section.

The Church of Jesus Christ of Latter-day Saints (Mormons)
50 East North Temple, Salt Lake City, UT 84150
(801) 240-1000
corberlaw@aol.com

CNN Radio News
One CNN Ctr., 4 S.W., Atlanta, GA 30303
(404) 827-2751, *Fax:* (404) 827-5363
www.westwoodone.com
Fred Bennett, Operations Dir
Top- & bottom-of-the-hour radio newscasts 24-hours a day plus business, sports & lifestyle updates.

Compu-Weather Inc.
NSS Data: Radio Only
2566 Rt. 52, Hopewell Junction, NY 12533
(800) 284-7246, *Fax:* (845) 226-1918
www.compuweather.com
sales@compuweather.com
Jeff Wimmer, President
Weather forecasts, features, info & actualities for TV & radio.

Congressional Quarterly Inc.
1255 22nd St. N.W., Washington, DC 20037
(202) 419-8500, *Fax:* (202) 419-8760
www.cq.com
customerservice@cq.com
David Rapp, Operations Dir
Keith A. White, General Manager
Print & Web-based info products & svcs on govt, politics & current interest topics. Daily & wkly publications, reference books & newsletters.

Connecticut Weather Center Inc.
NSS Data: Radio Only
18 Woodside Ave., Danbury, CT 06810-7123
(203) 730-2899, *Fax:* (203) 730-2839
www.ctweather.com
weatherlab@ctweather.com
William Jacquemin, President
Weather forecasts for all media. Custom intros/outros/lives. Accurate forecasts. Barter or cash arrangement available.

Corus Radio Network
700 W. Georgia St., Suite 2000, Vancouver, BC V7Y 1K9
Canada
(604) 331-2830, *Fax:* (604) 331-2722
www.corusent.com
akrueger@cknw.com
John P. Hayes, President
Allan Krueger, Operations Dir
Live & pre-recorded info & entertainment program production & satellite delivery to rgnl & natl Canadian radio stns.

Dairyline Radio
1843 Front St., Suite A, Lynden, WA 98264
(360) 354-5596, EXT. 101, *Fax:* (360) 354-7517
www.dairyline.com
bbaker@dairyline.com
Lee Mielke, President
Bill Baker, Promotions Manager
Five minute & 9 1/2 minute Dairy Report- weekdays. Daily updates of news affecting the dairy industry.
DairyBusiness Communications
7225 Wrightsville Ave, 204, Wilmington, NC 28403-7224
Lynden, WA

Entertainment News Calendar
NSS Data: Radio Only
13636 Ventura, Suite 303, Sherman Oaks, CA 91423
(212) 421-1370, (818) 990-5945, *Fax:* (818) 789-8047, (212) 563-3488
www.newscalendar.com
editor@newscalendar.com
Evelyn Heyward, Operations Dir
Daily entertainment news svc.
Hollywood News Calender
15030 Ventura Blvd., Ste 742, Sherman Oaks, CA 91403-5470
(818) 990-5945;
Carolyn Fox, Publisher

Evan Weiner Productions
NSS Data: TV-CATV only
Box 1656, Mount Vernon, NY 10552
(914) 667-9070, (203) 288-2597 (producer)
www.bickley.com/evan_weiner.html
evan4256@aol.com
Evan Weiner, Programming Director
Sports commentaries & reporting. Current program: The Business of Sports, commentaries on Metro Source.

Fairchild Broadcast News
NSS Data: TV-CATV only
Box 535, Hewlett, NY 11557
(212) 686-6850, *Fax:* (212) 686-7308
www.fairchildgroup.com/news
Gathers & disseminates news around the world.

Feature Story News
NSS Data: Radio Only
1730 Rhode Island Ave. N.W., Suite 405, Washington, DC 20036
(202) 296-9012, *Fax:* (202) 296-9205
www.featurestorynews.com
markss@featurestory.com
Simon Marks, President
Ind supplier of radio & TV news to English-language bcstrs worldwide. Bureaus in Washington, Moscow, London, New York, Orlando & San Francisco.
1133 Broadway, Suite 1420, New York, NY 10010-7903
(917) 330-3806;
Nathan King, Correspondent
1133 Broadway, Suite 1420, New York, NY 10010-7903
(917) 330-3806;
Nathan King, Correspondent
1103 Palmer St., Orlando, FL 32801-4048
(407) 898-1929;
Steve Mort, Correspondent
1103 Palmer St., Orlando, FL 32801-4048
(407) 898-1929;
Steve Mort, Correspondent

Hollywood News Calendar
NSS Data: Radio Only
13636 Ventura Blvd., #303, Sherman Oaks, CA 91423
(818) 990-5945, (818) 986-8186, *Fax:* (818) 789-8047
www.newscalendar.com
editor@newscalendar.com
Carolyn Fox, Publisher
Daily entertainment news svc. Publisher of Hollywood News Calendar in Los Angeles & Entertainment News Calendar in New York.
Entertainment News Calender
250 W. 57th St, #1431, New York, NY 10107-0001
(212) 421-1370; *Fax:* (212) 563-3488
Carolyn Fox, Publisher

Israel Broadcasting Service
800 Second Ave., New York, NY 10017
(212) 499-5402
Free radio & TV programs, features from & about Israel.

Medialink
708 3rd Ave., 9th Fl., New York, NY 10017-5345
(212) 682-8300, *Fax:* (212) 682-5260
www.medialink.com
Larry Thomas, COO
Laurence Moskowitz, President
Mary C. Buhhay, Operations Dir
International video & audio PR, satellite feed & news advisory svc. Advisories accessible by computer/newswire in United States & Europe.
37/38 Golden Sq., London,
44-71-240-3923;
Jim Gold, Chairman
One Maritime Plaza, San Francisco, CA
(415) 296-8877; *Fax:* (415) 296-9929
1401 New York Ave. N.W., Suite 520, Washington, DC 20005-2102
(202) 628-3800;
6430 Sunset Blvd., Suite 1100, Los Angeles, CA 90028-7901
(323) 465-0111;
The Time & Life Bldg., 541 N. Fairbanks Ct., Suite 1910, Chicago, IL 60611-3706
(312) 222-9850;
3340 Peachtree Rd. N.E., Suite 1520, Atlanta, GA 30326-1000
(404) 848-7500;
4851 LBJ Fwy., Suite 605, Dallas, TX 75244-6004
(972) 774-0200;

Metro Networks/Shadow Broadcast Services, a Westwood One Co.
2800 Post Oak, Suite 4000, Houston, TX 77056
(713) 407-6000, (713) 407-6911, *Fax:* (713) 407-6849
www.westwoodone.com
Peter Kosann, President
Provider of traf reporting svcs & leading supplier of loc news, sports, weather & video news svcs to the TV & radio bcst industries.

Metro Weather Service Inc.
NSS Data: TV-CATV only
788 Franklin Ave., Valley Stream, NY 11580
(516) 568-8844, *Fax:* (516) 568-8853
www.metroweather.com
metrowx@aol.com
Pat Pagano, President
Brettt Zueiback, General Manager
Tailored weather forecasts for radio & TV. Feature reports farming, marine, ski, long-range forecasts via phone, computer, fax, ISDN, MP3 & Skype.

News Broadcast Network
75 Broad St., 15th Fl., New York, NY 10004
(212) 684-8910, (800) 920-6397, *Fax:* (212) 684-9650
www.newsbroadcastnetwork.com
info@newbroadcastnetwork.com
Michael J. Hill, President
Robert Hill, Programming Director
Production & distribution of electronic news releases, actualities & pub affrs programs distributed by satellite, telephone & tape.
Seattle, WA
(206) 624-7505; *Fax:* (206) 624-7556
Milwaukee, WI
(414) 321-6210; *Fax:* (414) 321-3608
Chicago, IL
(603) 963-4455; *Fax:* (603) 963-4487
Los Angeles, CA
(909) 621-6903; *Fax:* (909) 621-9492
Washington,
(703) 893-4577, (202) 638-1603; *Fax:* (703) 893-6967, (202) 638-1607

Nielsen Entertainment News Wire
Div/DBA: (formerly VNU Entertainment News Wire)
101 Federal St., Suite 600, Boston, MA 02110
(617) 478-5500, *Fax:* (617) 478-5501
www.vnuenw.com
Advance news from Nielsen owned publications.

NOAA/National Weather Service
1325 East-West Hwy., Silver Spring, MD 20910
(301) 713-0622, *Fax:* (301) 713-1292
www.nws.noaa.gov
George Hernandez, Operations Dir
Jack F. Kelly, General Manager
Weather & flood warnings, forecasts & related info for the media & general pub.

North American Network
5335 Wisconsin Ave. N.W., Washington, DC 20015
(301) 654-9810, *Fax:* (301) 654-9828
www.radiospace.com
Tom Sweeney, President
Audio news releases & talk show interviews. On-site coverage for corps, govt agencies & assns.

PA-SportsTicker
NSS Data: Radio Only
989 6th Ave., 2nd Fl., New York, NY 10018
(212) 738-5611, *Fax:* (212) 695-8560
www.pa-sportsticker.com
newsroom@sportsticker.com
Jim Morganthaler, General Manager
Jay Imus, General Sales Mgr
Provides 24-hr sports news, info, instant scores & complete sports news coverage on all professional & major college events.
19 E 34th St., New York, NY 10016-4304
(212) 515-1000; *Fax:* (212) 515-1211
Boston Fish Pier, West Bldg. #1, Suite 302, Boston, MA
(617) 951-0070; *Fax:* (617) 737-9960

Radio America
NSS Data: TV-CATV only
1100 N. Glebe Rd., Suite 900, Arlington, VA 22201
(703) 302-1000, (800) 807-4703, *Fax:* (571) 480-4140
www.radioamerica.org
radio@radioamerica.org
Michael Paradiso, COO
Rich McFadden, News Director
Short & long-form programs, special series, documentaries, daily one hr news show & conservative talk radio.

Radio Press News Services
8633 Arbor Dr., El Cerrito, CA 94530-2728
(510) 524-9559
www.driveinclassics.ca
driveinclassics@driveinclassics.ca
Drive-In classics is a movie ch that celebrates the funny, entertaining & sometimes thought-provoking drive-in movies of the 50s, 60s & 70s.

Radio Pulsebeat News
NSS Data: TV-CATV only
Box 418, Hewlett, NY 11557
(212) 686-6850, *Fax:* (212) 686-7308
Jay R. Levy, President
Gen actuality news svc.

RadioTour.com
NSS Data: TV-CATV only
2233 Wisconsin Ave. N.W., Washington, DC 20007
(202) 333-4904, *Fax:* (202) 342-5411
www.expertclick.com
expertclick@gmail.com
Publisher of free Yearbook of Experts, Authorities & Spokespersons.

Reuters America Inc.
1333 H St. N.W., #500, Washington, DC 20005
(202) 898-8300, *Fax:* (202) 898-8383
www.reuters.com
Mitch Koppelman, Operations Dir
The Reuter Broadcast Report & Reuter Broadcast PLUS, features natl & international news, sports, business news, entertainment & weather.

Skywatch Weather Center
NSS Data: Radio Only
347 Prestley Rd., Bridgeville, PA 15017
(800) SKY-WATCH, *Fax:* (412) 221-3160
www.skywatchweather.com
airsci@skywatchweather.com
Dr.Stanley Penkala, President
Taped, live & MP3 weathercasts targeted to the listening area, in stn-specified formats. Featuring accuracy, clarity & mature voices.

The Sports Network
NSS Data: Radio Only
2200 Byberry Rd., Hatboro, PA 19040
(215) 441-8444, *Fax:* (215) 441-5767
www.sportsnetwork.com
kzajac@sportshetwork.com
Mickey Charles, CEO
Ken Zajac, General Sales Mgr

International real-time sports wire svc providing content, branded web pages, XML feeds directly to bcstrs (radio & TV), print, Internet sites, wireless with state of the art technology.

Studio M Productions
4032 Wilshire Blvd., Ste 403, Los Angeles, CA 90010
(213) 389-7372
www.cocabletv.com
pboyle@rbwpolicy.com

Texas State Networks
NSS Data: TV-CATV only
4131 N. Central Expwy., Suite 500, Dallas, TX 75204-2175
(214) 525-7400, *Fax:* (214) 525-7372
www.tsnradio.com
tsnnews@cbs.com
Brian Purdy, General Manager
Dan Bell, General Sales Mgr
News svc of the Texas State Networks. Provides Texas news, sports, agriculture, business & weather, Texas Rangers Radio Network & special features & long form programs.
Austin News Bureau
502 E. 11th, Suite 320, Austin, TX 78701-2650
(512) 474-5264 (NEWS), (512) 474-5275 (SALES);
Robert Wood, Dir

Trans World Communications Inc.
NSS Data: TV-CATV only
Box 418, Hewlett, NY 11557
(212) 686-6850, *Fax:* (212) 686-7308
Jay Levy, Operations Dir
Produces audio news svcs for radio & TV bcstg.

United Press International Inc.
1510 H St. N.W., Washington, DC 20005
(202) 898-8000, *Fax:* (202) 898-8048
www.upi.com
editorforms@upi.com
Nicholas Chiaia, COO
Christopher Ching, Operations Dir
Full global text, audio, photo news , info svcs, morning drive progmg, world, natl news, sports, weather, features & financial reports 24 hours.

The Wall Street Journal Radio Network
1155 Avenue of Americas, 8th Fl., New York, NY 10017
(800) 828-6397, (212) 659-1208, *Fax:* (212) 659-1908
www.wsjradio.com
wsjradio@dowjones.com
Nancy Abramson, General Manager
Hourly business & financial news reports transmitted live via satellite 18 times daily from the Journal's New York newsroom. Dow Jones Money Report also transmitted 18 times daily.

The Weather Center
Div/DBA: (a broadcast service of Aviation Weather Inc.)
701 Gervais St., Suite 224, Columbia, SC 29201
(803) 422-4823
thomashendrickson@yahoo.com
Liam Ferguson, President

Weather-One
Div/DBA: (A wholly-owned division of Liberty Hill Broadcast
5829 West Maple Rd., Suite 115, West Bloomfield, MI 48322
(248) 737-3000, *Fax:* (248) 737-3555
bzate@imageteleproducts.com
Barry Zate, Operations Dir
Provides weather forecasting svcs, advanced storm warnings, agricultural & ski info to radio stns.

WeatherData Inc.
245 N. Waco, Suite 310, Wichita, KS 67202
(316) 265-9127, *Fax:* (316) 265-1949
www.weatherdata.com
ceo@weatherdata.com
Mike Smith, CEO
Weather radar, graphic & info display systems, training, on air forecast & storm warning svcs. Select Warn, Storm Hawk, 24/7 storm monitoring, & customer svc. Complete system integration & training.

Westwood One
Div/DBA: Radio New Services
40 W. 57th St., 5th Fl., New York, NY 10019
(212) 641-2000, *Fax:* (212) 641-2185
www.westwoodone.com
Steven Kalin, COO
Gary Schonfeld, President
Producer & distributor of radio progmg including CNN, NBC, Mutual, CNBC Business Radio, 24-hours music formats, long-short-form talk, music & news programs.

WINGS: Women's International News Gathering Service
Box 95090, Vancouver, BC BC V5T 4T8 Canada
(604) 876-6994
www.wings.org
wings@wings.org
Frieda Werden, Programming Director
Syndicate audio news & current affrs program, both produced in-house & acquired, focus on women & hard news. Distribution CD, satellite, & FTP.
Box 33220, Austin, TX 78764-0220
Stacy Pettigrew, Bureau Mgr

World Radio Network
Box 1212, London, SW8 2ZF United Kingdom
44-20-7896-9000, *Fax:* 44-20-7896- 9007
www.wrn.org
contactus@wrn.org
Karl Miosga, Chairman
Jeff Cohen, General Sales Mgr
Tim Ashburner, Engineering Dir
World Radio Network (via Galaxy 25) news & features ch, comprising live progmg segments in English & languages from more than 20 international bcstrs. WRN can also supply many customized progmg feeds to radio stns as well as progmgdistribution, satellite uplink & internet streaming.

Radio Format Providers

ABC Radio Networks
13725 Montfort Dr., Dallas, TX 75240
(972) 991-9200, *Fax:* (972) 448-3378
www.abcradionetwork.com
James Robinson, President
Julie Atherton, Promotions Manager
Bcsts five full-service line nets, Paul Harvey News & Comment, ESPN Radio, long-form progmg, 24-hour formats, ABC News, ABC Sports, & d/wkly features.

American Comedy Network & Onion Radio News
91 River St., Milford, CT 06460
(203) 877-8210, *Fax:* (203) 877-8242
www.americancomedynetwork.com
acn@americancomedynetwork.com
Kurt Luchs, General Manager
Adrienne Munos, General Sales Mgr
Ben Churchill, Programming Director
Comedy svc providing daily topical audio sound bites, song parodies, fake comls. Comedy CD, e-mail prep & gold library. Onion Radio News 10 features every week via web and more.

Beethoven Satellite Network
Div/DBA: (BSN Around the Clock)
5400 N. St. Louis Ave., Chicago, IL 60625
(773) 279-2112, *Fax:* (773) 279-2199
www.wfmt.com
cmartinez@wfmt.com
David Schmidt, President
Steve Robinson, General Manager
Carol Martinez, Station Relations Manager
Tony Macaluso, Director/Network/Marketing
Satellite-delivered classical music format svc 12-hours overnight serving over 300 outlets nationwide. Produced by WFMT-FM Chicago. Since 1986.
Satellite: Galaxy 6, Digital frequency B72.4.

CBS Radio Networks
524 West 57th St., New York, NY 10019
(212) 975-2044, *Fax:* (212) 974-0615
www.westwoodone.com
barobinson@cbs.com
Andrew Zaref, CFO
Peter Kosann, President
Beth Robinson, Programming Director
This division currently offers NFL Football, NCAA Basketball & College Football. Also syndicates David Letterman's Top Ten List.

Creative Radio Network
Box 7749, Thousand Oaks, CA 91359
(818) 991-3892, *Fax:* (818) 991-3894
Darwin Lamm, President
Radio music program for A/C—country & modern. Elvis international forum magazine.

CRN International Inc.
One Circular Ave., Hamden, CT 06514
(203) 288-2002, *Fax:* (203) 281-3291
www.crnradio.com
info@crnradio.com
S. Richard Kalt, President
Patrick Kane, Operations Dir
Doug Harris, General Manager
Features include Ski Watch, a 60-second, daily ski conditions update. Summer-oriented progmg includes Beach Watch & Summer Watch. Small business programs include the Small Business Report & Small Business Profile. All programsavailable on a barter basis.

Dialogue
One Woodrow Wilson Plaza, 1300 Pennsylvania Ave., N.W., Washington, DC 20004-3027
(202) 691-4146, *Fax:* (202) 691-4141
www.wilsoncenter.org/dialogue
dialogue@wwic.si.edu
George Liston Seay, Programming Director
Wkly half-hour program of conversations on natl, internatl affrs, history & culture. Available to pub & coml stns free of charge on CD. Progmg produced by the Woodrow Wilson International Center for Scholars.

Eagle Media Productions Ltd.
Box 580, Northford, CT 06472
(203) 294-1190, *Fax:* (203) 294-9512
www.louadler.com
lou.adler@sbcglobal.net
Louis Adler, President
Thalia Adler, Operations Dir
Offers Medical Journal, 90-second feature-barter; CD delivery.

Excelsior Radio Networks
220 W. 42nd St., New York, NY 10036-7202
(212) 419-2929, *Fax:* (212) 681-1952
www.exradio.com
robscolaro@aol.com
Jonathan Goldman, President
Sports talk 24-hours a day. Sports analysis & commentary on AOL & the internet.
1445 E. Tropicana Ave., Las Vegas, NV
Phil Hall, Gen Mgr

Executive Broadcast Services
30 Mobray Ct., Colorado Springs, CO 80906
(719) 579-6676, *Fax:* (719) 579-6664
skip@executivebroadcast.com
Skip Joeckel, President
Markets & sells a select line of programs, products & svcs to U.S. radio stns.

Hispanic Communications Network
1126 16th St., N.W., Suite 350, Washington, DC 20036
(202) 637-8800, *Fax:* (202) 637-8801
www.hcnmedia.org
info@hcnmedia.com
Jeff Kline, Chairman
Produces six daily Spanish radio programs & distributes them to Hispanic Radio net affiliates.

J J McKay Productions Inc.
800 Pennsylvania St., Suite 305, Denver, CO 80203
(303) 880-6926
www.jjmckay.com
J.J. McKay, President
Maximum-impact production & versatile voice-over talent. All formats. Choose the voice for today AND tomorrow! Delivered via analog tape, DAT, ISDN/Zephyr, MP3, DCI.

Jameson Broadcast Inc.
1644 Hawthorne St., Sarasota, FL 34239
(941) 906-8800
www.eurocinema.com
eurocinema@envrocinema.com
Sebastiaen Perioche, Chairman
Non-Hollywood movies service for Broadband & Digital TV

Miller Broadcast Management
616 W. Fulton St., Suite 516, Chicago, IL 60661
(312) 454-1111, *Fax:* (312) 454-0044
info@millerbroadcast.com
Lisa Miller, President
Matt Miller, Operations Dir

MRN Radio (Motor Racing Network)
555 MRN Dr., Concord, NC 28027
(704) 262-6700, *Fax:* (704) 262-6811
www.mrnradio.com
David Hyatt, President
Cheryl Knight, General Manager
Live bcsts of NASCAR stock car racing & related programs via satellite.

Musical Starstreams
Box 12685, LaJolla, CA 92039-2685
(619) 276-8989
www.baytv.com
4listens@kron4.com
A 24-hour loc news, sports & info cable ch.

Orange Productions
523 Righters Ferry Rd., 1st Fl., Bala Cynwyd, PA 19004
(610) 667-8620, *Fax:* (610) 667-8939
www.soundsofsinatra.com
orange@snip.net
Sid Mark, President
Jon Harmelin, General Manager
Production & distribution of a wkly two-hour program Sounds of Sinatra.

Premiere Radio Networks Inc.
15260 Ventura Blvd., 4th Fl., Sherman Oaks, CA 91403-5339
(818) 377-5300, *Fax:* (818) 377-5333
www.premrad.com
webmaster@premradio.com
Kraig T. Kitchin, President
Premiere Radio features the following personalities: Rush Limbaugh, Delilah Ryan Seacrest, Steve Harvey, Jim Rome, Glenn Beck, Ty Pennington, Blair Garner, Whoopi Goldberg, Dr. Laura Schlessinger, Maria Bartiromo, George Noory, Casey Kasem,Ben & Brian, Bill Handel, Bob (Kevoian) & Tom (Griswold), Jeff Foxworthy, Jay Leno, Hohn Boy & Billy, T.D. Jakes, Matt Drudge, Big Tigger, Art Bell, Big D & Bubba, & Dr. Dean Edell.
1270 Ave. of the Americas, New York, NY 10020-1700
(212) 445-3900;
Catherine Mongarella, Sr Vp/Eastern Sls
15260 Ventura Blvd., 5th Fl., Sherman Oaks, CA 91403-5307
(818) 377-5300;
Theresa Gage, Sr Vp/Western Sls
875 N. Michigan Ave., Suite 1450, Chicago, IL 60611-1803
(312) 266-3870;
Susan McDonald, Vp/Chicago Rgnl Sls Mgr
3405 Piedmont Rd., Suite 500, Atlanta, GA 30305-1745
(404) 870-5070;
Alexandra Fenech, Vp/Southern Sls
14001 N. Dallas Pkwy., Suite 500, Dallas, TX 75240-4346
(972) 239-6220;
Jeff Steele., Sr Vp/Natl Music Syndication
306 S. Washington Ave., Suite 214, Royal Oak, MI 48067-3845

Radio Center for People with Disabilities (RCPD)
230 E. Ohio St., Suite 101, Chicago, IL 60611
(312) 640-5000, *Fax:* (312) 640-5010
www.rcpd.org
rc4pd@aol.com
Brad Saul, CEO
PCPD is a non-profit agency founded to recruit, train & place people with disabilities in paying, off-air jobs in the radio business.

Radio Express Inc.
1415 W. Magnolia Blvd., Suite 201, Burbank, CA 91506
(818) 295-5800, *Fax:* (818) 295-5801
www.radioexpress.com
radioinfo@radioexpress.com
Tom Rounds, CEO
John Fleck, President
Distributors outside the United States: The World Chart Show, Rick Dees Weekly Top 40, Country Countdown, Hot Mix, Hitdisc, Golddisc, Supercharger Production tool kit & Production libraries by firstcom music. Programs available by cash orbarter, libraries & products cash only.

Radio Spirits
Box 3107, Wallingford, CT 06492
(203) 265-8044
www.radiospirits.com
Hakan Lindskog, President
Radio producers of the nationally-syndicated old time radio program When Radio Was. Complete digital recording studio features Sonic Solutions Digital Work Station with No-Noise.

RPM Radio Programming and Management Inc.
1133 West Long Lake Rd., Bloomfield Hills, MI 48302
(800) 521-2537, (248) 647-1068, *Fax:* (248) 647-3936, (888) 776-0006
www.tophitsusa.com
info@tophitsusa.com
Thomas M. Krikorian, President
Top Hits USA wkly CD svc & CD libraries including Solid Gold, Spectrum A/C & Country One. Classic rock, CD Christmas library.

Salem Music Network Inc.
Div/DBA: (A division of Salem Music Networks/Salem Radio Ne
402 BNA Dr., Suite 400, Nashville, TN 37217
(615) 367-2210, *Fax:* (615) 367-0758
www.salemmusicnetwork.com
info@salemmusicnetwork.com
Michael S. Miller, General Manager
Provider of three different 24-hour Christian music formats via digital satellite to 230 plus radio stns throughout the US, Canada & operator of two greater Nashville (TN) radio stns.

SFX Radio Network
Clear Channel Entertainment, 220 W. 42nd St., New York, NY 10036
(917) 421-4000
www.sfxnet.com
Offers both wkly & mthy shows featuring classic rock, country, urban contemp & live concerts in addition to stn prep svcs.

Sheridan Broadcasting Corp.
960 Penn Ave., Suite 200, Pittsburgh, PA 15222
(412) 456-4008, (800) 456-4211, *Fax:* (412) 456-4040 (progmg), (412) 457-4077 (admin)
Ronald Davenport, Chairman
Provides hourly news & sports, longform talk & mus progmg as well as USA Music Magazine. Other alternative progmg includes Coming Soon movie review, Straight Up with Bev Smith & White House Report with White House correspondent April Ryan.

Sirius Satellite Radio
1221 Ave. of the Americas, 36th Fl., New York, NY 10020
(212) 584-5100, *Fax:* (212) 584-5200
www.sirius.com
rshnall@siriusradio.com
Rebecca Schnall, Operations Dir

Southcott Productions
Box 33185, Granada Hills, CA 91394
(818) 368-4938, *Fax:* (818) 368-4938
www.chucksouthcott.com
chucksongs@aol.com
Chuck Southcott, President
Adult pop standards format; 'This is Music' fully hosted adult atandards program available through ftp or on CD for use from one hour per week to up to three hours daily, Monday through Friday.
4605 Lankershim Blvd., Suite 702, North Hollywood, CA 91602-1818
(818) 755-9952;
Chuck Southcott, Program Dir

Talkline Communications Network
Box 20108, Park West Station, New York, NY 10025-1510
(212) 769-1925, *Fax:* (212) 799-4195
www.talkline communication.com
tcntalk@aol.com
Zev J. Brenner, President
National Jewish radio net featuring news, interviews with newsmaker guests & celebrities; live call-in format; live segments from Israel; satellite delivered. Available on barter.

TM Century Inc.
2002 Academy, Dallas, TX 75234
(972) 406-6800, *Fax:* (972) 406-6890
www.tmcentury.com
tmci@tmcentury.com
David Graupner, President
Erik Hastings, Programming Director
Eve Mayer Orsburn, Promotions Manager
GoldDisc music libraries, HitDisc wkly mus svc, music on hard drive, jingles, mus libraries production, special programs, CD-ROM.

Toby Arnold & Associates
3234 Commander Dr., Carrollton, TX 75006
(972) 661-8201, (800) 527-5335, *Fax:* (972) 250-6014
www.taamusic.com
toby@taamusic.com
Toby Arnold, President
Lawrence Mangiameli, Operations Dir
Audio Production libraries for radio. Station Imaging, Morning show promo sweeper, stager packages for all formats. Cash or Barter.

United Press International
1510 H St. N.W., Washington, DC 20005
(202) 898-8111, (202) 898-8100, *Fax:* (202) 898-8057
www.upi.com
editorforms@upi.com
Michael Marshall, Operations Dir
Tobin C. Beck, News Director

Full-svc company offers a number of short-form info features to its affil radio stns.

Virtual Radio
4521 Campus Dr., Suite 579, Irvine, CA 92612
(800) 601-6923
www.mbaa.org
info@mbaa.org

The Weather Center
Div/DBA: (a broadcast service of Aviation Weather Inc.)
701 Gervais St., Suite 224, Columbia, SC 29201
(803) 422-4823
thomashendrickson@yahoo.com
Liam Ferguson, President

WFMT Fine Arts Radio
5400 N. St. Louis Ave., Chicago, IL 60625
(773) 279-2000, *Fax:* (773) 279-2199
www.wfmt.com
guide@networkchicago.com
Daniel Schmidt, President
Peter Whorf, Programming Director
Classical, opera & folk mus, news & fine art progmg 24-hours per day through United Video Inc. Serving 200 cable systems in 30 states with 850,000 subs.

Cable Audio Services

The Classical Station, WCPE
Box 897, Wake Forest, NC 27588
(919) 556-5178, *Fax:* (919) 556-9273
theclassicalstation.org
wcpe@wcpe.org
Deborah S. Proctor, General Manager
Free 24-hour classical music progmg with live announcers for radio, cable, other distributors. Weekly request programs, opera and features. Satellite: AMC 1, Transponder 12 k, Vert, 1,1942 MHz.

CRN Digital Talk Radio
10487 Sunland Blvd., Sunland, CA 91040
(818) 352-7152, *Fax:* (818) 352-3229
www.crntalk.com
info@crni.net
Michael Horn, CEO
Jennifer Horn, General Sales Mgr
Premier provider for radio syndication. CRN develops the hottest new, unique talk talent & distributes it worldwide via cable TV audio, radio, satellite audio & the internet. ON 125 cable systems nationwide serving 26 million subs.Satellite: IA 13, transponder 15, virtual ch 521-526. CRN 1-8 with 8 talk networks, featuring Sp & world talk radio.

DMX, Inc.
600 Congress Ave., Fl. 14, Austin, TX 78701
(512) 380-8500, *Fax:* (512) 380-8501
www.dmx.com
Steve Hicks, Chairman
Offers uninterrupted premium digital audio music progmg via satellite & cable to residential & coml subs.

Moody Radio
Div/DBA: (Formerly Moody Broadcasting Network)
820 N. LaSalle Blvd., Chicago, IL 60610
(800) 621-7031, (312) 329-4433, *Fax:* (312) 329-4339
www.whereyouturn.org
moodyradio@moody.edu
Scott Krus, President
Wayne Pederson, Operations Dir
Provides 24-hours format of relg & educ progmg; music, drama, talk, news & pub affrs.
On 461 radio stns nationwide.
Satellites: AMC-3, transponder 17H (DVB-stereo digital) on AMC-8 (SCPC, digital stereo).

Music Choice
110 Gibraltar Rd., Suite 200, Horsham, PA 19044
(215) 784-5840, *Fax:* (215) 784-5869
www.musicchoice.com
David J. Del Beccaro, President
Damon Williams, Operations Dir
Music Choice is the premier music television network, reaching U.S .households through digital cable and satellite television. Music Choice programs interruption-free music for homes and businesses and distributes televised concerts andmusic shows. The Music Choice music channels reach 33 million households and the Music Choice Concert Series airs in 44 million homes nationally. Music Choice is a partnership among subsidiaries of Microsoft Corporation, Motorola, Inc., SonyCorporation of America, Warner Music Group, Inc., EMI Music and several

PROGRAMMING & PRODUCTION SERVICES

leading U.S. cable providers: Adelphia Cable Communications, Comcast Cable Communications, Cox Communications, and Time Warner Cable.

The Weather Center
Div/DBA: (a broadcast service of Aviation Weather Inc.)
701 Gervais St., Suite 224, Columbia, SC 29201
(803) 422-4823
thomashendrickson@yahoo.com
Liam Ferguson, President

WFMT Radio Network
5400 N. St. Louis Ave., Chicago, IL 60625
(773) 279-2112, (773) 279-2114, *Fax:* (773) 279-2199
www.wfmt.com
cmartinez@wfmt.com
Daniel Schmidt, President
Steve Robinson, Genral Manager/VP
Carol Martinez, Station Relations Manager
Tony Macaluso, Director/Syndication/Marketing
Classical music, spoken arts & fine arts program series & specials. Satellite- & tape-delivered. Major symphony orchestras, opera, jazz, exclusive BBC & Radio Deutsche Welle progmg, WFMT-produced archival & spoken-word progmg, live studioperformances, folk music. Since 1976.
Serving more than 900 radio outlets worldwide.
Satellite: Galaxy 4, digital frequeney B72.0.

Yesterday U.S.A.
2001 Plymouth Rock, Richardson, TX 75081
(972) 889-8255, *Fax:* (972) 889-4415
www.yesterdayusa.com
yesterdayusa@mail.com
William J. Bragg, Chairman
A 24-hour natl radio voice of the National Museum of Communication of Irving, TX. Presenting public domain old-time radio shows & vintage music free of charge & without comls.
Satellites: Galaxy 11, transponder 18, Ku verticel, frequency12060, audio PID 1620 left ch.

PROGRAMMING & PRODUCTION SERVICES

Producers, Distributors and Production Services Subject Index

PROGRAMMING & PRODUCTION SERVICES

PROGRAMMING & PRODUCTION SERVICES

PROGRAMMING & PRODUCTION SERVICES

Distribution, Music

Distribution, Radio & TV Programming

Distribution, Radio Programming

Distribution, TV Programming

Dubbing Services

Duplication Services

Editing Services

Educational Programming, Radio

Educational Programming, Radio & TV

Educational Programming, TV

Entertainment Programming, Radio

Juravic Entertainment
Lakeside TV Co.
Limelight Communications Inc.
MacNeil/Lehrer Productions
Marty Stouffer Productions Ltd.
Montgomery Community Television Inc.
Soldiers Radio & Television, U.S. Army Public Affairs
Southern STAR
Tapestry International, Ltd.
The Worship Network
Thomas Horton Associates Inc.
Tomwil Inc.
Wide Eye Productions, Inc.

News Programming, Radio

C N R Radio
Call For Action Inc.
Canadian Broadcasting Corp.
Chinamerica Hit Radio
Clear Channel Broadcasting Inc.
Eagle Media Productions Ltd.
Ecumedia News Service
FamilyNet Radio
Hometown Illinois Radio Network
KCSN 88.5 FM
Launch Radio Networks
Maryknoll Productions
MediaTracks Inc.
Moody Radio
National Council of Churches Communications Unit
National Public Radio
North American Network, Inc.
North Shore Productions
RPM Media Enterprises-The Relic Rack Review
Radio America
Ray Sports Network
Talk America Radio Networks
The Image Generators
Traffic Scan Network, Inc
United Stations Radio Network
WCTD AM 1620
Washington Korean Broadcasting Co.

News Programming, Radio & TV

Accuracy in Media Inc.
American Farm Bureau Inc.
CompuWeather Inc.
GlobeCast
Gordon Productions
John Driscoll/VoiceOver America
Medialink
News Broadcast Network
Presson Perspectives
SCOLA
Soldiers Radio & Television, U.S. Army Public Affairs
Traffic Scan Network, Inc
Ukrainian Melody Hour
University of Kentucky Public Relations & Radio-TV News Bureau
Warren Only Media Group

News Programming, TV

Asia Pacific Productions USA, Ltd.
Bell Foto Art Productions
Call For Action Inc.
CelebrityFootage
Daley Video
Devillier Donegan Enterprises L.P.
E! Entertainment Television
Evergreen Entertainment Group
Hamilton Productions Inc.
Health Net Productions & Pet Talk
Ivanhoe Broadcast News Inc.
J. Arnold Productions
KCRA-TV
Litton Entertainment
Midwest Video Communications Inc.
Mobile Video Services Ltd.
P. Allen Smith Gardens
PACSAT
PBS Video
Parrot Communications International Inc.
Planet Pictures Ltd.
Potomac TV/Communications
Prime Cut Productions Inc.
Primo Newservice Inc.
Reuters Media
Seven Network Australia Inc.
Sullivan Video Services Inc.
Telepros
The Television Syndication Company, Inc.

U.S. Plan B Inc.
Video Techniques Inc.
Wide Eye Productions, Inc.
Yorkshire Television

Original Music Scoring

Carriage House Studios
Continental Recordings Inc.
Groove Addicts
JAM Creative Productions Inc.
Metro Music Productions Inc.
Shelly Palmer Productions
Smith/Lee Productions, Inc.
SoperSound Music Library
Studio Center Total Production
TS James & Associates

Performing Arts Programming, Radio

KCSN 88.5 FM
National Public Radio
RPM Media Enterprises-The Relic Rack Review
WFMT Radio Network
WQXR

Performing Arts Programming, Radio & TV

Arthur Henley Productions
The Classical Station, WCPE
WQED Multimedia

Performing Arts Programming, TV

Arkadia Entertainment Corp.
CABLEready Corp.
CABLEready Corp.
Crystal Pictures Inc.
E! Entertainment Television
Free Speech TV (FSTV)
Global Entertainment Media
Kultur International Films
M C Stuart & Associates Pty Ltd.
MacNeil/Lehrer Productions
Myriad Pictures
Reid/Land Productions Inc.
Tapestry International, Ltd.
VIEW Video Inc.
Video-Cinema Films Inc.
WTOB—Community/Government Access TV
Yorkshire Television

Photographic Services

CompuWeather Inc.
Maslow Media Group Inc.
RAD Marketing & Cabletowns
Sandy Zimmerman Productions
Videosmith Inc.
White Rabbit Productions

Postproduction Facilities

Agora TV
Anderson Productions Ltd. (APL)
Ascent Media Network
CFP Video Productions
CN8, The Comcast Network
Catholic Communications Corp.
Center City Film & Video
Cinecraft Productions Inc.
Cinema Concepts Animation Studio
Crawford Communications
Daley Video
ESPI Video
Eagle Eye Film Company
GVI
Highland Laboratories
Horizons Television Inc.
MPL Media
MVI Post
Matchframe Video
NRS Group PTY Ltd.
North by Northwest Productions
Northwest Imaging & FX
Palace Producers
Point 360
Power Play Music Video L.L.C.
Rampion Visual Productions L.L.C.
Seraphim Communications Inc.
Studio Babelsberg GmbH
TYG Media
Tankersley Productions, Inc., St. Louis
Telenium Studios
The Audio Department Inc.
The Saturday Evening Post Television Department
The Transfer Zone
Thomas Horton Associates Inc.

University of Colorado Television
Video I-D Teleproductions Inc.
Video Techniques Inc.
Videographic West
Vyvx
WKMG Productions
Work Edit

Postproduction Services

Advanced Digital Services, Inc.
Agora TV
Alan Weiss Productions
CFP Video Productions
CN8, The Comcast Network
Carleton Productions International Inc.
CineGroupe Corporation
Cinema Concepts Animation Studio
Cookie Jar Group
Cornell University Video Production Group
Darino Films/Library of Special Effects
DeLuxe Laboratories
Eagle Eye Film Company
GTN
Getty Images
Gordon Productions
HAVE Inc.
Henninger Media Services, Inc.
KJD Teleproductions
Limelight Communications Inc.
MPL Media
MVI Post
Magno Sound & Video
Manhattan Transfer Miami
Masai Films Inc.
Maysles Films, Inc.
Media Access Group at WGBH
Montgomery Community Television Inc.
NTV International Corp.
NYSE Amex
National Collegiate Athletic Association (NCAA)
Northwest Imaging & FX
Oppix Productions Inc
PACSAT
PostWorks, New York
Quality Film & Video
RAD Marketing & Cabletowns
Rex Post
Rockwell Audio Media
Seraphim Communications Inc.
Soundtrack
Studio Center Total Production
TR Productions
TRI-COMM Productions
The Transcription Company
The WPA Film Library
VA-Tech Video/Broadcast Services
VTTV Videothek Electronic TV-Production GmbH + Co Kopier KG
WKMG Productions
White Rabbit Productions
William Mauldin Productions Inc.
ZBS Foundation

Processing Labs

DeLuxe Laboratories

Producers, Documentaries

American Farm Bureau Inc.
Bell Foto Art Productions
Brillig Productions Inc.
Broadview Media
Charlie Spencer Productions
Daniel Wilson Productions Inc.
David Finch Distribution Ltd.
Ecumedia News Service
Evangelical Lutheran Church in America
FTC/Orlando
FamilyNet
Free Speech TV (FSTV)
GRB Entertainment
GVI
Great North Productions
Horizons Television Inc.
International Television Corp.
Janson Media
Jordan Klein Film & Video
MRC Films
MacNeil/Lehrer Productions
Make It Happen Productions Inc.
Maryknoll Productions
Maryland Public Television

Producers, Film

Producers, Multimedia

Producers, Radio Programming

Producers, TV Programming

Producers, Video

Production Music Libraries

Production Services

Promotion Design

Teleconferences

Traffic Reporting

Training Film Productions

Training Films

Travel Programming, TV

Travelogues

Video Conferences

Videotape Editing

Voice-Overs

Weather Programming

Weather Programming, Radio

Producers, Distributors & Production Services

A-1 Entertainment
611 Cedar Lane, Teaneck, NJ 7666 USA
(201) 394-1849, *Fax:* (201) 357-8482
www.a-one-entertainment.com
mlrfilms@aol.com,alanmacademy@aol.com
Al Leifer, President
Alan Miller, President
Distribution of film, TV & video progmg worldwide.

ABC Family
3800 W. Alameda Ave., Burbank, CA 91521 USA
(818) 560-1000, *Fax:* (818) 840-1922
www.abcfamily.com
ABC Family features quality, contemporary entertainment for all members of the family including original series, movies & specials. Available in over 97 million homes via basic cable.

ACC Entertainment
Bavariafilmplatz 7, 82031 Greenwald, Munich,
49-89 64981-332,49-89 64981-232
accficm@acc.com
Film & TV producers, distributors.

Accuracy in Media Inc.
4455 Connecticut Ave. N.W., Suite 330, Washington, DC 20008 USA
(202) 364-4401, *Fax:* (202) 364-4098
www.aim.org
info@aim.org
Don Irvine, Chairman
Cliff Kincaid, Programming Director
Roger Aronoff, Media Analyst
Nationwide media monitoring organization produces documentary TV films, radio and podcast commentaries, bi-monthly printed publications, daily website updates, and programs that critique media coverage.

Acme
9976 W. Wanda Dr., Beverly Hills, CA 90210 USA
(310) 276-5509, *Fax:* (310) 276-1183
acmetoys@yahoo.com
Fred Wietzchz, CEO
Bradley Friedman, President
David Temianka, General Manager
Feature film & TV production, music videos, childrens progmg, commercials, robotics, scripting, tin toy props, rock music stock footage, space stock footage.

ACTV Inc.
233 Park Ave., 10th Floor, New York, NY 10020 USA
(212) 497-7000, *Fax:* (212) 459-9548
info@actv.com
David Reese, Chairman
Christopher Cline, CFO
Interactive TV progmg for educ & entertainment.

ADM—International Film & TV Distribution
Drienerwolde House, Drienerwoldeweg, Hengelo, IL 7552 PC NLD
31 74 250 6843, *Fax:* 31 74 250 1874
Herman Melzer, Chairman
Carole Hodson, General Manager
Sarah Mydlak, Promotions Manager
International distributor of film & TV programs including features, classics, documentaries, children's, plus much more.

Advanced Digital Services, Inc.
948 N. Cahuenga Blvd., Hollywood, CA 90038 USA
(323) 468-2200, *Fax:* (323) 468-2211
www.adshollywood.com
Andrew McIntyre, Chairman
Kevin Yates, COO
Jack Fleming, President
Video duplication, standard conversion, digital post-production.

Adventist Media Center
101 W. Cochran, Simi Valley, CA 93065 USA
(805) 955-7777, *Fax:* (805) 522-1082
info@faithfortoday.tv
Marshall Chase, General Manager
TV program production & distribution.

African Family Film Foundation
Box 630, Santa Cruz, CA 95061-0630 USA
(831) 426-3133
www.africanfamily.org
taale@africanfamily.org
Taale Rosellini, General Manager
Production & distribution of films & videotapes promoting African family life & culture.

Agency for Instructional Technology (AIT)
Box A, Bloomington, IN 47402-0120 USA
(800) 457-4509,(812) 339-2203, *Fax:* (812) 333-4218
www.ait.net
info@ait.net
Chuck Wilson, General Manager
Produces, acquires & distributes technology-based learning resources including video, videodisc, software & printfor all K-12 curricular areas, vocational educ/tech prep, early childhood, & professional dev.
1800 N. Stonelake Dr, Bloomington, IN 47404 United States

Agora TV
195 Hicks Dr. S.E., Marietta, GA 30060 USA
(404) 226-4503, *Fax:* (678) 581-3750
www.agoratv.tv
joe@agoratv.tv
Joseph Gora, President
TV production & equipment rental; Fly packages.

Agrinet Farm Radio Network
176 Radio Rd., Powell's Point, NC 27966 USA
(252) 491-2414, *Fax:* (252) 491-2959
www.agrinetradio.com
Gary Gross, Operations Dir
Bill Ray, General Manager
Lisa Ray, General Sales Mgr
State, rgnl & natl agricultural news, mkts & weather.

Airwaves Audio Inc.
150 Mutual St., Toronto, ON M5B 2M1 CAN
(416) 977-1098, *Fax:* (416) 997-5701
Audiovisual & industrial postproduction. Audio recording & mixing for radio & TV.

Alan Weiss Productions
355 W. 52nd St., 3rd Fl., New York, NY 10019 USA
(212) 974-0606, *Fax:* (212) 974-0976
www.awptv.com
myacoub@awptv.com
Alan Weiss, President
Tania Wilk, Operations Dir
Fourteen Emmys for video production. We handle any broadcast, PR or corporate from concept to distribution.

Alden Films
Box 449, Clarksburg, NJ 8510 USA
(732) 462-3522, *Fax:* (732) 294-0330
www.aldenfilms.com
info@aldenfilms.com
Paul Weinberg, President
Fran Fried, Operations Dir
Distributes nearly 200 DVD's & CD's on Israel & Judaica. Official distributor for state of Israel.

Alfred Haber Distribution Inc.
111 Grand Ave., Suite 203, Palisades Park, NJ 7650 USA
(201) 224-8000, *Fax:* (201) 947-4500
www.alfredhaber.com
info@haberinc.com
George Scanlon, COO
Alfred Haber, President
TV program distribution.

ALIN TV
149 Madison Ave., Suite 602, New York, NY 10016 USA
(212) 889-1327, *Fax:* (212) 213-6968
www.alintv.com
Alan Cohen, President
Unwired TV natl network, syndication, digital media sls & mktg.

All Media Productions Inc.
12261 Cleveland Ave. Ste F, Nunica, MI 49448-9309 USA
(616) 837-0899, *Fax:* (616) 837-0897
www.allmediaproductions.com
linda@allmediaproductions.com
Linda Langs, President
Web dev, internet mktg & film distribution.

All My Features Inc.
9190 Clearstream Terr., Mechanicsville, VA 23111 USA
(804) 730-1534, *Fax:* (804) 559-4809
Provides daily entertainment news, entertainment-related features via audio & computer feeds.

All Productions
7025 Regner Rd., Suite 5, San Diego, CA 92119 USA
(619) 284-2566, *Fax:* (619) 460-6160
www.allproductions.com
mikeall@eudoramail.com
Michael All, CEO
Jean All, President
George Kay, Programming Director
Stephen All, CFO
Tony Stevens, Producer Director
TV & radio program production, distribution; cable-ready TV progmg; promotion film production, production svcs; TV, radio spots & coml announcers.
7025 Regner Rd, San Diego, CA 92119-1941 United States
(619) 460-4837 (619) 286-7733; *Fax:* (619) 460-6160

Allegro Productions Inc.
1000 Clint Moore Rd., Suite 108, Boca Raton, FL 33487 USA
(800) 275-4636, *Fax:* (888) 329-3737; (561) 241-0707
www.ssrvideo.com
allegro@ssrvideo.com
Scott Forman, President
Educational & corporate progmg, including documentary/bcst. From concept to completion, offering full service video post production, CD-ROM/DVD authoring, multi-format duplication, 3D animation & effects.

Alliance for Christian Media / Day1
644 W. Peachtree St., Suite 300, Atlanta, GA 30309-1925 USA
(404) 815-9110, *Fax:* (404) 815-0495
http://day1.org
info@day1.org
Louis Schueddig, President
Peter Wallace, Operations Dir
Radio program production & distribution; relg ecumenical media.

Allumination FilmWorks, LLC
21250 Califa St., Suite 102, Woodland Hills, CA 91367 USA
(818) 712-9000, *Fax:* (818) 712-9074
www.alluminationfilmworks.com
info@alluminationfilmworks.com
Cheryl Freeman, CEO
Distribution, dev, production documentaries, TV series, kids, specials.

Aloha Productions
Box 33648, San Diego, CA 92163 USA
(619) 275-7357,(800) 223-2564, *Fax:* (619) 296-5909
jhal@alohajingles.com
Hal Hodgson, Programming Director
Original coml music production, scoring, jingles, long-form; movie & TV scores.

Alternative Programming
4215 Brendenwood Rd., Rockford, IL 61107
(815) 229-3995, *Fax:* (815) 229-5043
www.alternative-programming.com
altprog@sbcglobal.net
Gary Knoll, President
Complete music formats for radio - current music for various formats - custom CD svc.

Altman Productions
3401 Macomb St. N.W., Washington, DC 20016 USA
(202) 362-3088
itsacademicquiz@aol.com
Susan Altman, Programming Director
Susan Lechner, Editor
TV & radio program production. Producers of It's Academic, the high school quiz program, longest running TV quiz program in the world.

Altruist Media
2601A Wilson Blvd., Arlington, VA 22201 USA
(703) 812-8813, *Fax:* (703) 812-9710
www.altruistmedia.com
info@altruistmedia.com
Jan Dearth, President
A full-svc visual communications firm. Staff producers, writers & dirs provide full creative direction & project mgmt from concept dev, treatment, scripting & graphics design to production & delivery. Offers videotape, live eventproduction, consulting svcs for organizational communications. Provides comprehensive production svcs for videotape, special event & live business TV-video conference progmg. Also offers media training, VNR production, video press tours, consultingfor private networks, new media svcs including distributed multimedia, WWW design & CD-ROM dev.

Americ Disc
2525 Canadien, Drummondville, QC J2C 7W2 Canada

(819) 474-2655; (800) 263-0419, *Fax:* (819) 478-4575
www.americdisc.com
info@americdisc.com
CD & DVD replication and fulfillment.

America On The Road Inc.
1767 Lakewood Ranch Blvd., #183, Bradenton, FL 34211 USA
(941) 750-6590, *Fax:* (941) 708-6523
www.americaontheroad.com
info@americaontheroad.com
Al Herskovitz, Operations Dir
Jack Nerad, Programming Director
Mike Anson, Co-Host
One hour wkly, 2.5-minute daily automotive consumer show.

America One Television Network
6125 Airport Freeway, Suite 100, Ft. Worth, TX 76117 USA
(817) 546-1400, *Fax:* (682) 647-0756
www.americaone.com
Matt Reiff, President
Preston Bornman, Operations Dir
24 hour gen entertainment bcst network.

America's Most Wanted
2 Bethesda Metro Center, Suite 800, Bethesda, MD 20814 USA
(240) 482-1100, *Fax:* (240) 482-1181
www.amw.com
feedback@amw.com
Marc Kaplan, President
Wkly reality-based program for Fox TV.

American Blues Network
Box 6216, Gulfport, MS 39506
(800) 896-5307, *Fax:* (228) 896-5703
www.americianbluesnetwork.com
info@americianbluesnetwork.com
Stan Daniels, CEO
The only 24-hour blues syndication.

American Chiropractic Association Inc.
1701 Clarendon Blvd., Arlington, VA 22209 USA
(703) 276-8800, *Fax:* (703) 243-2593
www.acatoday.org
memberinfo@acatoday.org
Professional membership organization.

American Farm Bureau Inc.
600 Maryland Ave., SW, Suite 1000W, Washington, DC 20024 USA
(202) 406-3600, *Fax:* (202) 406-3602
www.fb.org
Don Lipton, General Manager
AGFeed, mthy video feed of news stories about food & agriculture, Newsline radio svc, Focus on Agriculture commentary, stock footage.

American Foundation for the Blind
11 Penn Plaza, Suite 300, New York, NY 10001 USA
(212) 502-7600,(800) 232-5463, *Fax:* (212) 502-7777
www.afb.org
afbinfo@afb.net
Carl Augusto, President
Liz Greco-Rocks, General Manager
Provides consultation & referrals, social & technological rsch, publications, info svcs, public educ, govt rel & talking books.

American Heart Association
7272 Greenville Ave., Dallas, TX 75231-4596 USA
(214) 706-1330, *Fax:* (214) 706-5243
americanheart.org
Julie Del Barto, Promotions Manager
Video news releases, podcasts, stock footage, limited animation related to heart & disease for news programs.

American Public Television
55 Summer St., Boston, MA 2110 USA
(617) 338-4455, *Fax:* (617) 338-5369
www.aptonline.org
info@aptonline.org
Cynthia Fenneman, CEO
Major distributor of high quality TV programs to all U.S. public TV stns. Also distributor of programs to international media.

American TelNet
855 SW 78th Ave., Plantation, FL 33324 USA
(954) 453-7000, *Fax:* (954) 453-7809
success@americantelnet.com
An 800/900 Interactive svc bureau offering a wide var of turnkey pay-per-call entertainment & business programs.

AmericaNurse TV Productions
Box 7717, Romeoville, IL 60446 USA
(815) 773-4497
www.americantvproductions.com; www.americanurse.com
asktvnurse@yahoo.com
Karon Gibson, Programming Director
Consumer educ shows on health, safety & other self-help titles. Entertaining introduction to optional alternative & mainstream medicine & Rx. Travel, entertainment, legal, and reality tv. Also, internet programming on ustream.tv,'Outspoken' with Karon.

ANA Television Network
1510 H St. N.W., Suite 400, Washington, DC 20005
(202) 898-8222
Satellite: Galaxy V*Transponder:* 11
Angelyn Adams, CFO
Arabic-language TV net bcstg to the Arab-American community 24 hours via cable, wireless cable. Satellite: DIRECTV Plus.

Anderson Productions Ltd. (APL)
55 W. 39th St., Suite 800, New York, NY 10018 USA
(212) 414-9220, *Fax:* (212) 206-0279
www.apltv.com
steveanderson@apltv.com
Steven Anderson, Programming Director
TV program production for bcst, cable TV & nonprofit orgs..

Angel Films Co.
967 Hwy. 40, New Franklin, MO 65274-9778 USA
(573) 698-3900, *Fax:* (573) 698-3900
phoeenix@phoeenix.org
William Hoehne, Chairman
Joyce Chow, CEO
Arlene Hulse, President
Leana Le Gee, General Sales Mgr
Matthew Eastman, Programming Director
Production, distribution, syndication of progmg for adults & children.

Animated Production Services
321 W. 44th St., New York, NY 10036 USA
(212) 265-2942, *Fax:* (212) 265-2944
www.digitaltofilm.com
info@digitaltofilm.com
TV program, coml, promotional film production, distribution & production svcs, digital film.

Antenne 2 - French TV 2
1290 Ave. of the Americas, Suite 3410, New York, NY 10104 USA
(212) 581-1771, *Fax:* (212) 541-4309
www.france2.fr
TV program production.

APA International Film Distributors Inc.
7152 SW 47th St., Miami, FL 33155 USA
(305) 666-0020, *Fax:* (305) 666-1725
apafilm@bellsouth.net
Rafael Fusaro, President
TV program production & distribution.

APM/Associated Production Music LLC
6255 Sunset Blvd., Suite 820, Hollywood, CA 90028 USA
(323) 461-3211,(800) 543-4276, *Fax:* (323) 461-9102
www.apmmusic.com
sales@apmmusic.com
Sixteen Libraries: KPM, Bruton, Sonoton, Carlin, Castle, NFL. Over 5,000 CDs, Personalized Packages, Music Search, 15-20 New CD releases mthy.
342 Madison Ave., Suite 1200, New York, NY 10173
(800) 276-6874;
Craig Giummarra, Sls Mgr

The Arabic Channel
366 86 St., 1st Fl., Brooklyn, NY 11209-5002 USA
(718) 238-2450, *Fax:* (718) 238-2465
gmt@ethnicnet.com
Gamil M. Tawfik, CEO
Marguerite Moore, Operations Dir
Arabic language progmg bcst Time Warner Cable.

Archive Films/Archive Photos
75 Varick St., 5th Floor, New York, NY 10013 USA
(646) 613-4000,(800) 462-4379, *Fax:* (646) 613-4140
www.gettyimages.com
sales@gettyimages.com
Stock footage/photo library providing all types of historical footage & photos for use in products for TV/CATV.
Archive Films/Archive Photos
17 Conway St, London W1P 6EE,
44 171 312 0300; *Fax:* 44 171 391 9123
Chris Blakeston, Contact
Archive Films GMBH
Bremstrasse 12, Cologne 50969,
49 221 936 4080; *Fax:* 49 221 360 4112
Craig Burns, Contact
Archive Films/Archive Photos
Italy Via Terraggio 17, Milan 20123,
39 2 874 693; *Fax:* 39 2 805 7739
Guido Rossi, Contact
Archive Films/Archive Photos
Scandinavia Birger Jarlsgatan 55, 111 45 Stockholm,
46 8 20 89 20; *Fax:* 46 8 20 89 33
Lennert Karlsson, Contact
Archive Films/Archive Photos
4 Boulevard Poissonniere, Paris Ducaud, 75009 France
33 1 55 77 00 00; *Fax:* 33 1 55 77 00 66
Sylvie Ducaud, Contact

Arkadia Entertainment Corp.
34 E. 23rd St., 3rd Fl., New York, 10010
(212) 533-0007, *Fax:* (212) 979-0266
www.arkadiarecords.com
arkadian@aol.com
Bob Karcy, CEO
CD, DVD, video production & distribution worldwide. A broad range of exclusive progmg.

Armedia Communications
307-3219 Yonge St., Toronto, ON M4N 2L3 CAN
(905) 889-0076, *Fax:* (905) 889-0078
http://david-mazmanian.vpweb.com
armedia@msn.com
David Mazmanian, President
Audio, video, music production & bcst svcs.

Arthur Henley Productions
101 W. 23rd St., #2462, New York, NY 10011 USA
(718) 263-0136
ah55@webtv.net
Arthur Henley, President
TV & radio program production; radio program distribution.

Artisan PictureWorks Ltd.
800 Forrest St. N.W., Atlanta, GA 30318 USA
(404) 355-3398, *Fax:* (404) 350-0302
www.artisanpictureworks.com
info@artisanpicture.com
Bryan Gartman, President
Ben Smart, Station Manager
Amy Thompson, Programming Director
Studio facilities feature Ultimatte, fiber optics to satellite uplink. Live multicam specialists. Remote & in-house production facilities.

Artist View Entertainment Inc.
4425 Irvine Ave., Studio City, CA 91502-1919 USA
(818) 752-2480, *Fax:* (818) 752-9339
www.artistviewent.com
info@artistviewent.com
Scott Jones, President
Jay Joyce, Operations Dir
Worldwide distribution in all media specializing in feature films.

Ascent Media Group
520 Broadway, 5th Fl., Santa Monica, CA 91401 USA
(310) 434-7000
www.ascentmedia.com
Network services, syndication, advertising solutions, satellite bcst distribution, & net construction & maintenance.

Ascent Media Management East
235 Pegasus Ave., Northvale, NJ 7647 USA
(201) 767-3800, *Fax:* (201) 784-2769
www.apvi.com
agavin@apvi.com,tgreff@apvi.com
Don Buck, President
Tony Beswick, Operations Dir
Al Gavin, General Sales Mgr
Standards & aspect ratio conversion, international duplication, PAL/NTSC editing, film-to-tape transfers, 16 X 9 audio layback, restoration & satellite svcs, dud authoring, compression, streaming.
Audio Plus Video West
200 S. Flower St, Burbank, CA 91502 United States
(818) 841-7100;
Larry Kingen, Vp/Gen Mgr

Ascent Media Network
250 Harbor Dr., Stamford, CT 6902 USA
(203) 965-6000, *Fax:* (203) 965-6405
www.ascentmedia.com
Peter Brickman, General Manager
Video transmission, origination; tech consulting, new media products; private networks, post production, studio, graphics; bcst event svcs & satellite svcs.

PROGRAMMING & PRODUCTION SERVICES

GWNS Minneapolis
6845 20th Ave., Minneapolis, MN 55038
(612) 330-2639;
Joel Helseth, Sls & Mktg
Asia Bcst Centre
Singapore,
(612) 330-2639
vhendra@abc.gwns.com
Vincent Helseth, Chairman

Ascent Media Network Services
2901 W. Alameda Ave., Burbank, CA 91505 USA
(818) 840-7174, *Fax:* (818) 567-1131
www.ascentmedia.com
Sharon Pyne, Operations Dir
Jodynne Wood, General Sales Mgr
Lennis Schwartz, VP Operations
AM NS powers the bcst-cable nets around the world. We distribute progmg content over our integrated fiber & satellite net.
48 Charlotte St., London, WIT 2NS United Kingdom

Asia Pacific Productions USA, Ltd.
19698 S.E. Cottonwood St., Portland, OR 97267 USA
(503) 723-6456
approd.com
info@approd.com
Thomas Hopkins, President
Miyuki Shigeji, Operations Dir
Provides news, documentary & program production; coml production; business/promotional film & video production; production svcs for TV/CATV.
Asia-Pacific Productions
Japan - 3-17 Higashi Maruyama Cho, Kobe 653-086 Japan -, 81 78 691 2450;

Associated Press Television News
The Interchange, Oval Road, Camden Lock, London, DC NW17DZ United Kingdom
+44(0)20 7482 7400, *Fax:* +44(0)20 7413 8302
www.ap.org,www.aptn.com
aptninfo@ap.org
TV news production, news library, video editing & ENG production.

Associated Television International
4401 Wilshire Blvd., Los Angeles, CA 90010 USA
(323) 556-5600, *Fax:* (323)
556-5610,www.associatedtelevision.com
atiwest@aol.com
David McKenzie, President
Justin Pierce, Operations Dir
Jim Romanovich, President/World Media
Full-svc production, distribution & syndication company in business for over 20 years.

Association of Islamic Charitable Projects
4431 Walnut St., Philadelphia, PA 19104 USA
(215) 387-8888
www.aicp.org
Islamic services providing Education with a Full Time Elementary school for metro Philadelphia.

At a Glance
6350 W. Freeway, Fort Worth, TX 76116 USA
(817) 570-1400,(800) 266-1837,(800) 433-5757, *Fax:* (817) 737-9436
www.familynetradio.com
info@familynet.com,lbratton@familynetradio.com,dsenn@familynetradio.com,cries@familynetradio.com
Chuck Ries, Programming Director
Donna Senn, Promotions Manager
Lisa Bratton, Radio Marketing & Dist.
Variety of topics: health, fitness, character, parenting, etc. 60 second spots, 10 per month, on CD.

ATA Trading Corp.
Box 307, Massapequa Park, NY 11762 USA
(516) 541-5336, *Fax:* (516) 541-5336
atat@verizon.net
Harold Lewis, President
Susan Lewis, Operations Dir
Worldwide distributors for ind producers in all areas of feature films, made-for-TV productions, series, documentaries & children's programs.

Atlantic Video Inc.
650 Massachusetts Ave. N.W., Washington, DC 20001 USA
(202) 408-0900, *Fax:* (202) 408-8496
www.atlanticvideo.com
questions@atlanticvideo.com
Edward Milligan, President
John Sommers, Operations Dir
Amy Schwab, Promotions Manager
Soundstages, postproduction, graphics, duplication, remote, satellite uplink, videoconferencing, film-to-tape, D-2, digital 110 pathways & audio sweetening.
150 S. Gordon St, Alexandria, VA 22304 United States
(703) 823-2800;

Auburn Television Satellite Uplink
Auburn University, Admin.Bldg, Auburn, AL 36849-5423 USA
(334) 844-5707, *Fax:* (334) 844-5708
www.auburn.edu
taylody@auburn.edu
Deborah Howard, Operations Dir
Bliss Bailey, Station Manager
John Gober, Chief Engineer
Tape/CD/DVD Duplication, satellite uplink/downlink facilities, & CATV. Affiliate Studio production facilities (Broadview Media) are available in Montgomery Alabama via microwave link to the uplink.

The Audio Department Inc.
119 W. 57th St., 4th Fl., New York, NY 10019 USA
(212) 586-3503, *Fax:* (212) 245-1675
www.theaudiodepartment.com
Aimee Mitchaud, General Manager
Lola Norarevian, Manager
Audio & audio for video, adv & media promotion.

Audio Production Services, University of Colorado
Campus Box 379, 312 Stadium Bldg., Boulder, CO 80309 USA
(303) 492-2675, *Fax:* (303) 492-7017
Radio program production.

Auritt Communications Group
555 8th Ave., Suite 709, New York, NY 10018 USA
(212) 302-6230, *Fax:* (212) 302-2969
www.auritt.com
info@auritt.com
Joan Auritt, President
Satellite media tours, event coverage, video news releases, B-roll packages, radio tours, audio news releases, sls/corporate videos, web casting & print tours.

Avid
One Park West, Tewksbury, MA 1876 USA
(800) 949-2843,(978) 640-6789, *Fax:* (978) 640-3366
www.avid.com
ugdiva@avid.com
Avid is a leading supplier of newsroom computer, editing, playback & effects systems. Implemented as stand-alone or networked systems, Avid solutions provide speed, creativity & operating efficiencies throughout the newsroom.

Axcess Broadcast Services Inc.
4801 Spring Valley, Suite 105-B, Dallas, TX 75244 USA
(972) 386-6847, *Fax:* (972) 386-5207
Sls consulting for new businesses in the top 100 markets. CD production library, radio, TV promotions & IDs.

Bardel Entertainment Inc.
548 Beatty St., Vancouver, BC V6B 2L3 CAN
(604) 669-5589, *Fax:* (604) 669-9079
www.bardelentertainment.com
info@bardel.ca
Delna Bhesania, CEO
Barry Ward, President
Michael Remedios, Co-CEO
High quality 3D, Maya, Flash, Harmony & hybrids of digital & traditional animation for feature film, television, interactive media, internet & commercials. Interactive and New Media services, specializing in virtual worlds and online casualgames.

Bavaria Film GmbH
Bavariafilmplatz 7, D-82031Geiselgasteig/Munich, GU Germany
49 89 6499 0, *Fax:* 49 89 6492 507
www.bavaria-film.de
presse@bavaria-film.de
Dieter Frank, President
Peter Kussius, General Sales Mgr
Thilo Kleine, President
Dubbing, film laboratories, film & tape transfers, film & TV production, production svcs, multimedia svcs.

Bayliss
208 Good Hill Rd., Weston, CT 06883-2326 USA
(203) 227-7521, *Fax:* (203) 454-1032
www.genebayliss.com
Gene Bayliss, Consultant
Produces, directs video conferences, videotapes for corporations & industries, meetings & special events.

BBC Worldwide Americas Inc.
747 3rd Ave., 7th Fl., New York, NY 10017-2803 USA
(212) 705-9300, *Fax:* (212) 888-0576
www.bbcamerica.com
help@ecnext.com
Radio & TV broadcaster, TV program production & distribution, home video, library sls, licensing.

BBC Worldwide Television Ltd.
Woodlands, 80 Wood Lane, London, AL W12 0TT
Fax: (181) 749-0538,(181) 576-2000
www.bbc.co.uk
www.bbc.co.uk/feedback/
Program licensing to international bcstrs & generation of co-production business. Dev of BBC branded satellite & cable channels worldwide.

Beckmann International
Meadow Ct., West St., Ramsey, Isle of Man, AL IM8 1AE
4 401 624 816 585, *Fax:* 4 401 624 816 777
www.beckmanngroup.co.uk
sales@beckmanngroup.co.uk
International sls distributor specializing in non-fiction progmg.

Beethoven Satellite Network
c/o WFMT Fine Arts Radio, 5400 N. St. Louis Ave., Chicago, IL 60625 USA
(773) 279-2000,(800) USA-WFMT, *Fax:* (773) 279-2199
www.wfmt.com
Steve Robinson, Operations Dir
Carol Martinez, Programming Director
Terry Medina, Promotions Manager
Peter Vandegraaff, Programming Director
Program production & distribution; 84 hour-a-week classical music format with program hosts in one-hour modules, loc sound included.

Bell Foto Art Productions
2577 S. Pennsylvania St., Denver, CO 80210-5722 USA
(303) 377-4606, *Fax:* (303) 322-2443
www.bellfoto.tv
bellfoto@att.net
Chris Bell, President
Award winning High Definition video production: VNR, corporate, news, sports, medical, training & legal. Story tellers with AJ-HDX 900, HVX-200, Sony Z1-U, Sony EX-3 and now the Sony XD-HD. The future of HD production in the real world! Allowed and operated with the additional toys and hugely experienced crew. We want to work for you.

Bellon Entertainment Inc.
14 Vandervенter Ave, Suite L3A, Port Washington, NY 11050 USA
(516) 883 - 1810
www.bellonentertainment.com
webmail@bellonentertainment.com
Gregory Bellon, President
Represent and develop TV formats for worldwide distribution.

Ben Cromer Communications
Box 526, Round Hill, VA 20142 USA
(540) 678-5539
info@bencromer.com
Ben Cromer, President
Feature writing & script preparation for print & bcst media; specializing in the music & entertainment industry; telecommunications; business/economics & travel/history.

Ben Manilla Productions
3361 20th St., San Francisco, CA 94110-2627 USA
(415) 970-8020, *Fax:* (415) 970-8024
www.bmpaudio.com
info@bmpaudio.com,benm@bmpaudio.com,info@bmpaudio.com
J. Ben Manilla, President
Devon Strolovitch, Programming Director
Erik Beith, Producer
Audio production & progmg for a var of formats.

Best Film & Video Corp.
108 New South Road, Hicksville, NY 11801 USA
(516) 931-6969, (800) 526-2189, *Fax:* (516) 931-5959
Roy Winnick, President
Jeff Miller, General Sales Mgr
Dana Miller, Promotions Manager
TV program production & distribution of home video.
242 N. Canon Dr, Beverly Hills, CA 90210 United States
(310) 274-9944; *Fax:* (310) 274-9960

Bill Melendez Productions Inc.
13400 Riverside Dr., Suite 201, Sherman Oaks, CA 91423 USA

PROGRAMMING & PRODUCTION SERVICES

(818) 382-7382, *Fax:* (818) 382-7377
www.billmelendez.tv
generalinquiries@billmelendez.tv
Steven C. Melendez, President
TV program, coml animation production.

Billy Graham Evangelistic Association
Radio Department, Box 1270, Charlotte, NC 28201 USA
(704) 401-2432, (877) 247-2426, *Fax:* (704) 401-3028
www.billygraham.org
had@bgea.org
Franklin Graham, President
Roger Flessing, General Manager

Black Audio Devices
Box 106, Ventura, CA 93002-0106 USA
(805) 653-5557, *Fax:* (805) 653-5557
www.blackaudio.com

Blackbird Productions
6 Molasses Row, Plantation Wharf - Battersea, London, AL SWI1 3UX GBR
+44(0)20 7924 6440, *Fax:* +44(0)20 7924 4778
www.blackbirdproductions.co.uk
enquiries@blackbirdproductions.co.uk
Program production & distribution.

Blackstone Stock Footage
509 Upsall Drive, Antioch, TN 37013 USA
(615) 731-5310, *Fax:* (615) 731-5232
www.blackstonestockfootage.com
g.clifford@worldnet.att.net
Glenda Clifford, President
We offer: Archival newsreel footage, medical, extreme sports, landmarks from around the world, food, people, animals, underwater, timelapse cities & nature.

Blanc Communications Corp.
171 Pier Ave., Suite 517, Santa Monica, CA 90405 USA
(310) 278-2600, *Fax:* (310) 396-8434
TV program production; TV & radio coml production & distribution.

Blue Canyon Productions
Box 6622, Santa Fe, NM 87502 USA
(505) 989-9298
www.bluecanyonproductions.com
Jim Terr, President
Award-winning, nationally-bcst jingle, PSA & radio spot production, voice-overs, video production, as well as music production, scoring & scripting.

Blue Heaven Productions
11 Glenwood Rd., Toms River, NJ 08753-4117 USA
(732) 349-8569
raynorman3@juno.com
Ray Norman, President
Nostalgia music production library, CD masters made

Blue Sky Studios
One American Lane, Greenwich, CT 6831 USA
(203) 992-6000, *Fax:* (203) 992-6001
www.blueskystudios.com
info@blueskystudios.com
Brian Keane, General Manager
Dev & production of CG animated films.

Blue Star Media
Dallas Cowboys Football Club, One Cowboys Pkwy., Irving, TX 75063 USA
(972) 556-9345, *Fax:* (972) 556-9339
dallascowboys.com
Scott Purcel, General Manager
Radio play by play, wkly sports TV for NFL Dallas Cowboys & show for Dallas Cowboys.

Bonneville Communications
5 Triad Ctr., Suite 700, Salt Lake City, UT 84180-1121 USA
(801) 237-2600, *Fax:* (801) 237-2614
www.bonneville.com
bonneville@bonneville.com
Gregg Garber, General Manager
Paul Yates, Controller
Marc Lee, Director
A values-driven adv agency engaged in communications for quality life.

Boston Symphony Orchestra
Symphony Hall, 301 Massachusetts Ave., Boston, MA 2115 USA
(617) 266-1492, *Fax:* (617) 638-9367
www.bso.org
Mark Volpe, Station Manager
Evening at Pops TV series & other special TV productions.
Originates regular radio bcst of BSO concerts.

Brillig Productions Inc.
770 Amalfi Dr., Pacific Palisades, CA 90272 USA
(310) 459-4450, *Fax:* (310) 459-4456
brilligprod@cooliwk.net
Barry Brown, President
Joy Brown, Operations Dir
Feature films, TV features, TV comls, documentaries.

British Broadcasting Corp.
c/o WFMT Radio Network, 5400 N. St. Louis Ave., Chicago, IL 60625 USA
(773) 279-2112,(773) 279-2114, *Fax:* (773) 279-2199
www.wfmt.com
finearts@wfmt.com
Steve Robinson, Operations Dir
Carol Martinez, Station Manager
Terry Medina, Promotions Manager
Distribute wkly series My Music, & My Word for coml & public stns in the United States by WFMT Fine Arts Network.

Broadcast News Service
Box 919, Norwood, MA 02062-0919 USA
(781) 344-6988, *Fax:* (781 344-8928
P. Romano, General Manager
Radio, TV features & productions, audio news & features.

Broadview Media
4455 W. 77th St., Minneapolis, MN 55435 USA
(952) 835-4455, *Fax:* (952) 835-0971
redw@broadviewmedia.com
Red White, President
Full-svc production.

Bruder Releasing Inc. (BRI)
2020 Broadway, Santa Monica, CA 90404 USA
(310) 829-2222, *Fax:* (310) 829-0202
www.4bri.net and www.4ced.com
bruder@brivideo.com
Marc Bruder, President
Celena Perkins, Operations Dir
Alex Hill, General Manager
Studio, producer representative for worldwide broadcast distribution to IPTV platforms, pay-per-view channels, satellite netwroks, cable operators, lodging systems, internet streaming venues and mobile-cellular and hand-held-devicetransmission venues. CED is the leading broadcast program supplier of adult content worldwide. BRI is a major supplier of independent movies, specials, events and shows of all catagories.
BRI & CED headquarters
2020 Broadway-Santa Monica, CA 90404

Bulbeck & Mas SL
Quinones, 2, 28015 Madrid,
34 91 594 2709, *Fax:* 34 91 445 7212
bymfilms@bulbeckymas.com
Specialists in libraries of Spanish features.

Burrud Productions Inc.
468 N. Camden Dr., 2nd Flr, Beverly Hills, CA 90210 USA
(310) 860-5158, *Fax:* (562) 595-5986
www.burrud.com
info@burrud.com
Shannon Mead, CEO
John Burrund, President
Drew Horton, Operations Dir
Linda Karabin, Vice President
Valerie Chow, Vice President
Feature film & TV production of reality, wildlife, oceanic, human adventure, documentary & world exploration progmg.

Buzzco Associates Inc.
33 Bleecker St., Suite 5A, New York, NY 10012 USA
(212) 473-8800, *Fax:* (212) 473-8891
www.buzzzco.com
info@buzzzco.com
Candy Kugel, General Manager
Vincent Cafarelli, Director
A full range of animation from traditional to innovative computer 2-D.

C 2 Productions Inc.
15430 Catalpa Cove Ln., Fort Myers, FL 33908 USA
(239) 437-4222, *Fax:* (239) 437-2042
chriscorley.com
chris@chriscorley.com
Chris Corley, President
Voice-overs delivered digitally or in person.

C N R Radio
Box 27532, Minneapolis, MN 55427-0532 USA
(763) 537-5868
www.cnradio.notlong.com
CNRadio@comcast.net
George Carden, President
News interviews, soundbites & features with newsmakers for primarily Christian radio stns & nets.

CA Media Development
1144 Hooper Ave., Suite 208, Toms River, NJ 8753 USA
(732) 797-1965, *Fax:* (732) 797-1260
ca.media@comcast.net
Gregory Koziar, President
Full svc adv agency, as well as coml production, for radio & cable TV.

Cable Films & Video
Box 7171, Country Club Station, Kansas City, MO 64113 USA
(913) 362-2804,(800) 514-2804, *Fax:* (913) 362-2804
www.onlineworld.com/movies
cablesfilms@kc.rr.com
Herbert Miller, CEO
Classic films, all formats: one inch BETA SP, CD-ROM, U-Matic, PAL, NTSC, SECAM, DVD. Over 300 motion pictures & classic cartoons, clips available.

CABLEready Corp.
98 East Ave., Norwalk, CT 06851-5029 USA
(203) 855-7979, *Fax:* (203) 855-8370
www.cableready.net
info@cableready.net
Gary Lico, President
Lou Occhicone, Operations Dir
Liz Levenson, General Manager
Sabrina Toledo, General Sales Mgr
Dev & sls of programs to U.S. cable TV networks & systems & all international telecasters.

Call For Action Inc.
5272 River Rd., Suite 300, Bethesda, MD 20816 USA
(301) 657-8260, *Fax:* (301) 657-2914
www.callforaction.org
Shirley Rooker, President
International hotline svc, affiliated with the bcst media, that provides info, assistance to individuals & small businesses with consumer problems.

Camera Group International
3920 N. 29th Ave., Hollywood, FL 33020 USA
(954) 925 - 3776, *Fax:* (954) 925 - 3760
www.cameragroupinternational.com
garcia2020@aol.com
Eileen Garcia, President
Rental, sls, svc & maintenance of motion picture, TV & video production equipment (16mm, 35mm & digital matte cameras).

CamMate Systems
425 E. Comstock, Chandler, AZ 85225 USA
(480) 813-9463, *Fax:* (480) 813-9292
www.cammate.com
Linda Mitchell, CEO
James Mitchell, Promotions Manager
Camera cranes, telescopic cranes & mini cranes.

Campbell-Ewald Advertising
30400 Van Dyke Ave., Warren, MI 48093 USA
(586) 574-3400, *Fax:* (586) 558-5891
www.campbell-ewald.com
lturk@campbell-ewald.com
Anthony Hopp, Chairman
Anthony Hopp, CEO
S.H. Gilbert, President
D.A. Karnowsky, Operations Dir
J.T. Seregny, Vice President
L.M. Schultz, Vice President
W.J. Ludwig, Vice President
TV programs, TV radio coml, promotion film production.
One Dag Hammarskjold Plaza, New York, NY 10017 United States
(212) 605-8000;
11100 Santa Monica Blvd, 6th Fl, Los Angeles, CA 90025 United States
(213) 914-2200;
11444 W. Olympic Blvd, 11th Flr, Los Angeles, CA 90064-1549 United States
(310) 231 - 2900;
One Magnificent Mile, 930 N. Michigan Ave, Suite 1060, Chicago, IL 60611 United States
(312) 587-2650;

PROGRAMMING & PRODUCTION SERVICES

Canadian Broadcasting Corp.
Box 6000, Montreal, QC H3C 3A8 CAN
(514) 597-7656, *Fax:* (514) 597-6607
www.rcinet.ca
rci@montreal.src.ca
Jean Larin, Station Manager
Daily shortwave & internet, seven languages, 24-hour eutelsat F6 Europe, intelsat 707 Africa, asiasat 2. Recorded & live program placement on foreign stns.

Canamedia Inc.
381 Richmond St. E., Suite 200, Toronto, ON M5A 1P6 CAN
(416) 483-7446, *Fax:* (416) 483-7529
www.canamedia.com
canamed@canamedia.com
Les Harris, President
Andrea Stokes, General Sales Mgr
Canamedia offers production & international distribution svcs. It also exclusively represents in Canada the ITN source Archive & Natural History New Zealand Archives as well as the PUMP audio music archive.

CanLib Inc.
4819 Galendo St., Woodland Hills, CA 91364-4326 USA
(818) 888-6005, *Fax:* (818) 888-2505
canlibinc@adelphia.net
Carol Stevens, President
Gene Accas, President
Bcstg & media consulting: rsch for producers, distributors, advertisers, agencies & law firms (legal expert witness).

Cannell Studios
7083 Hollywood Blvd., Suite 600, Hollywood, CA 90028 USA
(323) 465-5800, *Fax:* (323) 856-7390
www.cannell.com
questions@cannell.com
Stephen Cannell, Chairman

Capital Communications
2357-3 South Tamiami Trl., Venice, FL 34293 USA
(941) 492-4688, *Fax:* (941) 492-4923
www.isp.com
cap5678@isp.com
James Springer, CEO
International distributor of pre-packaged TV programs.

Carden & Cherry Syndication Inc.
1220 McGavock St., Nashville, TN 37203 USA
(615) 255-6694, *Fax:* (615) 255-8345
TV & radio coml production & distribution; production svcs.

Careco Television Productions
5717 N.W. Pkwy., Suite 104, San Antonio, TX 78249 USA
(800) 668-8081, *Fax:* (210) 697-0150
www.outdooraction.com
Charles Goodloe, President
Lavonne Kacalek, Operations Dir
Producer of American Outdoors & Fishing Texas, weekly half hour series.

Caridi Entertainment
250 W. 57th St., Suite 1326, New York, NY 10107 USA
(212) 581-2277, *Fax:* (212) 581-2278
c.caridi@att.net
Full-svc international distributor & production company.

Carleton Productions International Inc.
1500 Merivale Rd., 5th Fl., Nepean, ON K2E 6Z5 CAN
(613) 224-9666, *Fax:* (613) 224-9074
www.carletonproductions.com
cpi@magi.com
Mark Ross, President
TV & radio programs, coml production & distribution & production svcs.

Carlton International Media Inc.
11145 N.W. 1st Pl., Coral Springs, FL 33071 USA
(954) 345-1620, *Fax:* (954) 345-1490
www.carltonint.co.uk
clarea@msn.com
Rupert Dillnot-Cooper, CEO
Claire Alter, Operations Dir
Louise Pedersen, General Manager
British TV distributor, licenses a wide range of programs worldwide.
Studio City, CA 91604 United States
(818) 753-6363;
Jeri Sacks, Vp/Us Sls

Carpel Video Inc.
429 E. Patrick St., Frederick, MD 21701 USA
(800) 238-4300,(301) 694-3500, *Fax:* (301) 694-9510
www.carpelvideo.com
Andy Carpel, President
Videotape recyclers; production svcs, video tape to DVD duplication.

Carriage House Studios
119 Westhill Rd., Stamford, CT 6902 USA
(203) 358-0065, *Fax:* (203) 964-4988
chstudios@optonline.net
John Montagnese, President
Recording studio.

Carsey-Werner Distribution
16027 Ventura Blvd. 6th Flr, Encino, CA 91436 USA
(818) 464 - 9600, *Fax:* (818) 464 - 9654
www.carseywerner.com
Herbert Lazarus, President
TV program distribution.

Castle Hill Productions Inc.
36 W. 25th St., 2nd Fl., New York, NY 10010 USA
(212) 242-1500, *Fax:* (212) 414-5737
www.castlehillproductions.com
mm@castlehillproductions.com
Julian Schlossberg, President
Movie distribution for theater, TV, cable, and video.
2385 Executive Center Dr., Suite 100, Boca Raton, FL 33431

Catholic Communications Corp.
65 Elliot St., Springfield, MA 1105 USA
(413) 732-3175, (800) 854-0003
www.diospringfield.org
m.dupont@diospringfield.org
Mark E. Dupont, CEO
TV & radio production svcs.

Catholic Television Network
Box 430, 9531 Akron-Canfield Rd., Canfield, OH 44406-0430 USA
(330) 533-2243, *Fax:* (330) 533-1907
www.doy.org
judyctny@aol.com
Bob Gavalier, General Manager
24-hour ecumenical TV ch.

CBC International Sales
Audience Relations, CBC, Box 500, Stn. A, Toronto, ON M5W 1E6 CAN
(416) 205-3500, (866) 306-4636, *Fax:* (416) 205-3482
www.cbc.ca/toronto
cbcis@toronto.cbc.ca
Susan Hewitt, Head of International Sales
CBC is Canada's natl bcstr. Produces & distributes TV progmg in both English & French.
1950 Sawtelle Blvd, Suite 333, Los Angeles, CA 90025 United States
43/51 Great Titchfield St, London W1P 8DD,

CBS Studios International
7800 Beverly Blvd., Los Angeles, CA 90036 USA
(323) 575-5460, *Fax:* (323) 575-5469
www.cbscorporation.com
firstname.lastname@cbs.com
Armando Nunez, President
Barry Chamberlain, General Sales Mgr
Joe Lucas, Promotions Manager
International television distribution, co-production, local production formats, channel management.

CBS Television Distribution
2401 Colorado Ave., Suite 110, Santa Monica, CA 90404 USA
(310) 264-3300, *Fax:* (310) 264-3301
www.cbstvd.com
John Nogawski, President
Terry Wood, Promotions Manager
Robert Madden, Senior Executive VP
TV program production, distribution, mktg to domestic syndication & other TV venues.

CCI Entertainment Ltd.
18 Dupont St., Toronto, ON MSR 1V2 CAN
(416) 964-8750, *Fax:* (416) 964-1980
www.ccientertainment.com
info@ccientertainment.com
Charles Falzon, Chairman
Arnie Zipursky, CEO
Annette Frymer, President
Distributor & co-producer, producer

CDC United Network Brussels
127, rue Marconi, 1190 Brussels, AL Belguim
32 2 502 66 40, *Fax:* 32 2 502 66 56
www.cdcun.com/en/home
alexandre@cdc.skynet.beMOBILE:3275713057
Alexandre Lippens, CEO
Maximillian Weiner, President
TV distribution & merchandising in Latin America.

CDR Communications Inc.
9310-B Old Keene Mill Rd., Burke, VA 22015 USA
(703) 569-3400, *Fax:* (703) 569-3448
www.cdrcommunications.com
chris@cdrcommunications.com
Christopher Rogers, President
Nancy Rogers, Operations Dir
Film, TV, video & radio production: teleconferences, documentaries, adv campaigns, PSAs; graphics, animation, syndication, promotion, publishing, distribution, postproduction & mktg.
9302 C Old Keene Mill Rd., Burke, VA 22015

Celebrities Productions
230 S. Bemiston Ave., Suite 1400, St. Louis, MO 63105 USA
(314) 862-7800, *Fax:* (314) 721-5171
I.J. Davis, President
David Dovich, Operations Dir
Walt Williams, Vice President
Creation, production of radio, TV spots, programs, audio visuals; arrangement for celebrity talent, music, syndication & video conference production.

CelebrityFootage
320 South Almont Dr., Beverly Hills, CA 90211 USA
(310) 360-9600, *Fax:* (310) 360-9696
www.celebrityfootage.com
michael@celebrityfootage.com
Michael Goldberg, President
Provides media outlets with celebrity entertainment news from the Los Angeles area, including movie premieres, award shows & charity benefits.

Celluloid Dreams
2 Rue Turgot, 75009 Paris, AL France
(33) 1 49 70 03 70, *Fax:* (33) 1 49 70 03 71
www.celluloid-dreams.com
info@celluloid-dreams.com
International distribution of ind features, documentaries & animation films.

Center City Film & Video
1503-05 Walnut St., Philadelphia, PA 19102 USA
(215) 568-4134, *Fax:* (215) 568-6011
www.ccfv.com
centercity@ccfv.com
Jordan Schwartz, Chairman
Brian Isely, Operations Dir
John Gillespie, Programming Director
Award winning production staff, video; film production, studio; remote camera packages including ultimatte, digital audio suite, flint, complete post production.

Central City Productions, Inc.
212 East Ohio St. #3, Chicago, IL 60611 USA
(312) 654-1100, *Fax:* (312) 654-0368
www.ccptv.com
Don Jackson, Chairman
Don Jackson, CEO
Erma Gray Davis, President
Rosemary Jackson, Operations Dir
Jennifer Jackson, General Manager
Heather Davis, General Sales Mgr
Production & mktg of bcst & cable TV progmg targeted towards minority viewers.

Central Park Media Corp.
331 W. 57th St., Suite 554, New York, NY 10019 USA
(646) 957-8301 (X-8303), *Fax:* (646) 957-8316
www.centralparkmedia.com
jod@teamcpm.com
John O'Donnell, General Manager
Over 200 Japanese Anime titles available for TV & cable.

Century III at Universal Studios Florida
2000 Universal Studios Plaza, Orlando, FL 32819-7606 USA
(407) 354-1000, *Fax:* (407) 352-8662
www.century3.com
rcibella@century3.com
Full-svc production & postproduction facility, audio department, custom graphics, digital editing capabilities, film transfers, interactive department, satellite uplink svcs.

CFP Video Productions
Box 86, Caldwell, NJ 07006-0086 USA

(973) 226-2481, *Fax:* (973) 226-2480
cfpvideo.com
don.spitzmiller@verizon.net
Donald Spitzmiller, President
Full video, audio svcs for TV & industrial productions. Avid edit svc/post production.

Channel Four Television
124 Horseferry Rd., London, AL SW1P 2TX
44 (0)845 076 0191
www.channel4.com
righttoreply@channel.4.com
Andy Duncan, CEO
UK bcstr.

Charles H Stern Agency Inc.
1999 Ave. of the Stars, Suite 1400, Los Angeles, CA 90267 USA
(310) 788-4570
Radio coml production & distribution. Represents a variety of TV & radio personalities.

The Charles Morrow Associates Company LLC
307 7th Ave., Suite 1402, New York, NY 10001 USA
(212) 989-2400, *Fax:* (212) 989-2697
www.cmorrow.com
cmorrow@cmorrow.com
Charlie Morrow, President
Sound design, audio production, music production, audio/visual service, music composition, multimedia producers, surround sound studio, public service announcements.

Charlie Spencer Productions
107 Jensen Cir., West Springfield, MA 01089-4451 USA
(413) 737-7600, *Fax:* (413) 737-7600 (Voice First)
cspencer@mail.map.com
Charlie Spencer, General Manager
Specializes in nature & environmental progmg, as well as outdoor recreation & nature travel. Svcs include consulting, producing, directing, rsch, writing & narration. Progms include Gardening with Wildflowers, The Urban Canoeist & AmericanWaste.

Chicago Radio Syndicate Inc.
15003 Lemay St., Van Nuys, CA 91405 USA
(800) 621-6949, *Fax:* (818) 376-8529
www.sandyorkin-crs.com
sandyo@earthlink.net
Sandy Orkin, President
Syndication of Dick Orkin comedy featuresChickenman, Tooth Fairy & Mini-People & commercial camgaigns.

Children's Media Productions
Box 40400, Pasadena, CA 91114-7400 USA
(626) 797-5462
www.childrensmedia.com
childrensmedia@yahoo.com
C. Carlson, President
Joy Carlson, Promotions Manager
Producer & distributor of children's progmg, dvds & feature films, worldwide.

Chinamerica Hit Radio
Box 683, Times Square Station, New York, NY 10108 United States
(800) 827-1722, *Fax:* (212) 868-5663
www.chinamericahitradio.com
programming@chinamericahitradio.com
Steve Warren, Programming Director
24 Hour Pop-Contemporary Chinese hit music. Hosted in English

24-20 Jackson Ave., Suite 209, Long Island City, NY 11101

Christian Children's Associates Inc.
Box 446, Toms River, NJ 8754 USA
(732) 240-3003, *Fax:* (732) 286-4244
www.adventurepals.com
adventurepals@juno.com
Jean Donaldson, President
Frank Troilo, Operations Dir
William Cook, General Manager
Production, distribution of radio & TV progmg for children.

Christian Media Network
Box 448, Jacksonville, OR 97530 USA
(541) 899-8888
www.christianmedianetwork.com

Christian Science Sentinel - Radio Edition
210 Massachusetts Ave., Boston, MA 02115-3122 USA
(617) 450-2000, *Fax:* (617) 450-2893
www.sentinelradio.com
sentinelradio@csps.com
Susan Kerr, Programming Director
Religious radio programs.

Christian TV Services of Ellicottville Inc.
P. O. Box 209, Ellicottville, NY 14731-0209 USA
(716) 699-2549
www.christiantvservices.com
geothayer@yahoo.com
Rev. George Thayer, CEO
Christian media consultants Ministering to ministries around the world; locally linked area worship places, internet listing places; svcs inc. since 1974.

The Christophers Inc.
12 E. 48th St., New York, NY 10017 USA
(212) 759-4050, *Fax:* (212) 838-5073
www.christophers.org
mail@christophers.org
Tony Rossi, Programming Director
We produce and distribute only our own media (radio, print)

Chrysalis Distribution
13 Bramley Rd., London, WI0 6SP
(44) 207 4674, *Fax:* (44) 207 221 6286
distribution@chrysalis.co.uk
Christina Willoughby, General Manager
International sale of TV programs to all media worldwide.

The Chuck Blore Co.
17428 Tarzana St., Encino, CA 91316 USA
(818) 784-5104, *Fax:* (818) 986-1196
www.chuckblore.com
bloregroup@aol.com
Chuck Blore, CEO
TV programs & coml production svcs. Radio coml production svcs. TV programs consultation.

Chuck Fries Productions Inc.
9903 Santa Monica Blvd., Ste 870, Beverly Hills, CA 90212 USA
(310) 203-9520, *Fax:* (310) 203-9519
chuckfries@aol.com
Domestic & international TV, home video, & feature film production & distribution.

CIFEX International Inc.
One Peconic Hills Ct., Southampton, NY 11968-1618 USA
(631) 283-9454, *Fax:* (631) 283-4210
cifex@prodigy.net
Gerald Rappoport, President
Beulah Rappoport, Operations Dir
Shirley Clarke, Promotions Manager
Distributor of foreign-language feature films, animated & live-action short films & documentaries.

Cimarron Group
6855 Santa Monica Blvd., Hollywood, CA 90038 USA
(323) 337-0300, *Fax:* (323) 337-0333
www.cimarrongroup.com
Bob Farina, President
TV promotions, spec shoots, graphics, sls presentations, trade & consumer print design, title treatment & image campaigns.

Cinecraft Productions Inc.
2515 Franklin Blvd., Cleveland, OH 44113 USA
(216) 781-2300, *Fax:* (216) 781-1067
www.cinecraft.com
info@cinecraft.com
Neil McCormick, Chairman
Maria Keckan, President
Neil MCCormick, General Manager
Betacam field production; 60' x 70' sound stage with hard cyc; AVID MC1000NT; Animation with Soft Image; interactive DVD & CD-R dev.

CineFilm
2156 Faulkner Rd. N.E., Atlanta, GA 30324 USA
(404) 633-1448,(800) 633-1448, *Fax:* (404) 633-3867
www.cinefilmlab.com
csr@cinefilmlab.com
William Thorton, President
Jim Ogburn, General Manager
16mm, super 16mm, 35mm color negative processing & printing. Dailies thru release prints. State-of-the-art video dailies & scene-to-scene transfers. Spirit Data Cini, all HD Formats

CineGroupe Corporation
1151 Alexandre-DeSeve St., Montreal, QC H2L 2T7 CAN
(514) 524-7567, *Fax:* (514) 849-5001
www.cinegroupe.com
distribution@cinegroupe.ca
Jacques Pettigrew, CEO
Linda Caron, President
Elaine Bigras, General Sales Mgr
Michel Lemire, Executive Vice President
Animation, TV production, postproduction, paint & trace studio, distribution of animation TV series for children.

Cinema Concepts Animation Studio
2030 Powers Ferry Rd., #214, Atlanta, GA 30339 USA
(770) 956-7460, *Fax:* (770) 956-8358
www.cinemaconcepts.com
info@cinemaconcepts.com
Stewart Harnell, CEO
Sharron Harnell, Operations Dir
Theresa Dickey, General Manager
John Price, Station Manager
Animated corporate IDs, presentation/policy trailers for TV, cable & motion picture theatres, theatrical trailer fulfillment.

The Cinema Guild Inc.
130 Madison Ave., 2nd Fl., New York, NY 10016-7038 USA
(212) 685-6242, *Fax:* (212) 685-4717
www.cinemaguild.com
info@cinemaguild.com
Mary Hobel, Chairman
Philip Hobel, CEO
Gary Crowdus, General Manager
Film & video distribution to theatrical, non-theatrical, TV & home video mkts, worldwide.

Circle Oak Productions Inc.
33 N. Birch Hill Rd., Patterson, NY 12563 USA
(845) 878-9017, *Fax:* (845) 878-9018
Educ film production.

Citadel Media
261 Madison Ave., 3rd Fl., New York, NY 10016 USA
(212) 735-1700, *Fax:* (212) 735-1799
www.citadelmedianetworks.com
Dan Formento, Operations Dir
Tom Powell, Vice President
Producers of natl & international radio features, such as Flashback, Flashback Pop Quiz & Rock Slides.

Citadel Media
13725 Montfort Dr., Dallas, TX 75240 USA
(972) 991-9200, *Fax:* (972) 991-9890
www.citadelmedianetworks.com
Jim Robinson, President
Michael Knize, General Sales Mgr
Carl Anderson, Programming Director
Omar Thompson, Promotions Manager
Live 24-hour-a-day premium progmg available featuring 9 radio formats. Other media svcs. include advanced digital media platforms with online interactive advertising, streaming audio & podcasts, syndicated music and talk programs includingFlashback, format-specific e-PREP, production libraries.

Classic Media
860 Broadway, 6th Fl., New York, NY 10003 USA
(212) 659-3011, *Fax:* (212) 659-1958
Bob Higgins, Promotions Manager
Douglas Schwalbe, Head of International Sales
Classic Media is a New York-based entertainment company that manages some of the most recognizable family oriented properties across all media including feature film, television, home video & consumer products.
8640 Wilshire Blvd., Beverly Hills, CA 90211
(310) 659-6004; *Fax:* (310) 659-4599
Leslie Levine, Dorothy Schecter

The Classical Station, WCPE
Box 897, Wake Forest, NC 27588
(919) 556-5178, *Fax:* (919) 556-9273
theclassicalstation.org
wcpe@wcpe.org
Curtis Brothers, Operations Dir
Deborah Proctor, General Manager
Peter Blume, General Sales Mgr
Dick Storck, Programming Director
Rae Weaver, Development Director
Free 24-hour classical music progmg with live announcers for radio, cable, other distributors. Wkly request programs, opera & features.

Clayton-Davis & Associates Inc.
230 S. Bemiston Ave., Suite 1400, St. Louis, MO 63105 USA
(314) 862-7800, *Fax:* (314) 721-5171
www.claytondavis.com
Jennifer Jermak, President
Steve Pezold, Operations Dir
Program production, syndication & barter.

Clear Channel Broadcasting Inc.
55 Music Sq. West, Nashville, TN 37203 USA
(615) 664-2400, *Fax:* (615) 664-2457
www.clearchannel.com
webmaster@clearchannel.com
Randall Mays, CFO
State radio networking, collegiate radio & TV networking.

Clear Channel Entertainment Television
220 W. 42nd St., 9th Fl., New York, NY 10036 USA
(917) 421-5206, *Fax:* (917) 421-5239
www.clearchannelentertainment.com
Joe Townley, President
Dawn Olejar, Operations Dir
Marc Forest, Programming Director
Steve Stern, Executive Producer
Produces TV programs & promotion films, documentary film production, sports event TV production.

Clever Cleaver Productions
4718 N. Placita Ventana Del Rio, Tucson, AZ 85750 USA
(520) 615-1582, *Fax:* (520) 615-1586
www.clevercleaver.com
clevercook@comcast.net
Lee Gerovitz, President
Steve Cassarino, Operations Dir
Offers 260 3-minute entertaining cooking vignettes; 27 30-minute entertaining cooking shows, 90-second high-definition cooking vignettes (cash or barter) & 2-minute tailgate cooking vignettes (free licensing fee).

CMT
330 Commerce St., Nashville, TN 37201 USA
(615) 335-8400, *Fax:* (615) 335-8615
www.cmt.com
Brian Philips, President
Jay Frank, Operations Dir
Bob Kusbit, General Sales Mgr
Mary Beth Cunin, Programming Director
Neil Holt, SVP/Ad Sales
John Hamlin, SVP/Production
Suzanne Norman, SVP/Strategy
Martin Clayton, VP DigitalMedia
America's #1 country music net, provides original progmg, live concerts, events, music videos by established & cutting edge artists, news & info.

CN8, The Comcast Network
Penns Landing Studio, 1351 S. Columbus Blvd., Philadelphia, PA 19147 USA
(215) 468-2222, *Fax:* (215) 468-3812
www.cn8.tv
Stephanie Millagranna, COO
Buck Dopp, Operations Dir
Brian McLendon, General Manager
Mark Dudzinski, Station Manager
Denise Pettyford, General Sales Mgr
Alex Soumbenioits, Promotions Manager
Rich Frantz, Engineering Dir
ScottClark, Chief Engineer
Larry Watzman, Creative Services Director
Jon Gurevitch, VP Sports
CN8, The Comcast Network, is a rgnl cable net offering news, sports, & entertainment progmg to 3.9 million cable homes.
New Castle Studio
2215 N. Dupont Hwy., New Castle, DE 19720
(302) 661-4202; *Fax:* (302) 661-4201

CNBC Syndication
900 Sylvan Ave., Englewood Cliffs, NJ 7632 USA
(201) 735-2622, *Fax:* (201) 585-3365
www.cnbc.com
Pamela Thomas Graham, CEO
Syndicated TV program, Wall Street Journal Report, business events.

CNN Newsource Sales Inc.
One CNN Center, 12 North, Atlanta, GA 30303 USA
(404) 827-5475, *Fax:* (404) 827-4466
http://newsource.cnn.com
cnn.newsource@turner.com
Ed Stephen, President
Taylor Fuller, Operations Dir
Provider of news & info content to the loc bcst news industry.

Coe Film Associates Inc.
70 E. 96th St., New York, NY 10128 USA
(212) 831-5355, *Fax:* (212) 996-6728
cfainc@juno.com
TV program distribution.

Colon & Associates Inc.
7100 Blvd. East, Guttenberg, NJ 7093 USA
(201) 869-4615, *Fax:* (201) 869-6217
www.saptv.com
rei616@aol.com,saptv@saptv.com
Reinaldo Colon, CEO
Program distribution, production, Sp language dubbing.

ComBridges
70 Irwin St., San Rafael, CA 94901 USA
(415) 454-5505, *Fax:* 888-530-5505
www.combridges.com
info@combridges.com
Shelah Norman, General Manager
Jon Leland, Programming Director
Source of videos, seminars & interactive media. Producer, websites.

Combs Music
636 W 4th Street, Winston-Salem, NC 27101 USA
(800) 932-6627, *Fax:* (336) 723-1611
www.combsmusic.com
dave@combsmusic.com
Composes, produces, publishes & distributes easy lstng instrumental music, e.g., Rachel's Song.

Comcast Media Center
4100 E. Dry Creek Rd., Littleton, CO 80122 USA
(303) 486-3800, *Fax:* (303) 486-3891
www.comcast.com
Network origination, production, postproduction, uplinking, compression, remote production, audio production.

Command Productions
Box 3000, Sausalito, CA 94966-3000 USA
(415) 332-3161, *Fax:* (415) 332-1901
www.commandproductions.com
audio@commandproductions.com
Warren Weagant, President
Kitt Weagant, Operations Dir
Radio-TV, CATV audio voice identification and promotion production.
480 Gate Five Rd., Suite 107, Sausalito, CA 94965

Communications III Inc.
921 Eastwind Dr., Suite 104, Westerville, OH 43081 USA
(614) 901-7720, *Fax:* (614) 901-7721
www.comIII.com
shalliday@comiii.com
Scott Halliday, President
Central Ohio C-band satellite & Teleport svc, with access to studio, edit suites, at Ohio State University & various downtown locations.

CompuWeather Inc.
2566 Rt. 52, Hopewell Junction, NY 12533 USA
(800) 825-4445, *Fax:* (800) 825-4441
www.compuweather.com
forecasts@compuweather.com
Jeff Wimmer, General Manager
Todd Gross, Principal
Weather, environmental features, actualities, forecasts, info, worldwide weather consulting svc, forecast, outcodes, studies, advice, site specific, 24/7 & 31 years experience.

Concept Videos
5371 Punta Alta, Apt.1E, Laguna Hills, CA 92653 USA
(800) 333-8252, *Fax:* (877) 523-5592
www.preschoolpower.com
wjconnell@preschoolpower.com
William Connell, President
Gold medal winning children's series, Pre-School Power, (13 x 30) recently telecast on 190 public TV stns.

Consolidated Film Industries (CFI)
959 N. Seward St., Hollywood, CA 90038 USA
(323) 960-7444, *Fax:* (323) 960-7573
www.technicolor.com
Film processing; titles & opticals; videotape transfers; office rentals.

Continental Recordings Inc.
23 Mirimichi Street, Plainville, MA 02762-1710 USA
(508) 699- 0003, *Fax:* (617) 699-0005
danf31@earthlink.net
L. Daniel Flynn, President
Coml jingles, stn IDs, original music creation & production, cassette duplication & bcstg adv consultation, CD & DVD duplicator.

CONUS Archive
3415 University Ave., St. Paul, MN 55114 USA
(651) 642-4576, *Fax:* (651) 642-4669
www.conus.com
Jim Richter, Operations Dir
Chris Bridson, General Sales Mgr
Video archive svcs to natl & international program producers.

Cookie Jar Group
266 King St. West, 2nd Floor, Toronto, ON M5V 1H8 CAN
(416) 977-3238, *Fax:* (416) 977-4526
www.cookiejarentertainment.com
Katarina Dietrich, CEO
Kirk Bloomgarden, President
Michael Hirsh, CEO
Scott McCaw, CFO
Tom Mazza, EVP, Head of Worldwide Sales
Toper Taylor, President/COO
International dev, production, postproduction & distributer of live action, animated and educational programming. Worldwide consumer products and licensing division including ownership of CPLG.
Cookie Jar Entertainment
4100 W Alameda Ave, Burbank, CA 91505
818-955-5454;
Cookie Jar Entertainment
11 Rue Torricelli - 75017 Paris, France
011 331 45 74 30 50;
CPLG
3 Shortlands - London W6 8PP UK - 44 20 8563 6400,

Coote Communications
568 Carver Hill, Milton, ON LQT 5K5 CAN
(905) 203-0065
amcoote@hotmail.com
Morgan Coote, President
Donald Coote, Operations Dir
Complete film & videotape production from script to screen.

Cornell University Video Production Group
312 College Avenue, Ithaca, NY 14853-6601 USA
(607) 255-8162, *Fax:* (607) 255-1563
www.DLS.cornell.edu
grp2@cornell.edu
Glen Palmer, General Manager
Satellite uplinks, Betacam DvcPro video production & postproduction, audio production

Country Crossroads
6350 W. Freeway, Fort Worth, TX 76116 USA
(817) 570-1491,(800) 292-2287, *Fax:* (817) 737-9436
www.countrycrossroadsradio.com
cries@familynetradio.com,kteegarden@familynetradio.com
Chuck Ries, Programming Director
Kirk Teegarden, Producer
Country music with interviews. Program hosted by Brother Jon Rivers, 30 minute wkly on CD or download.

Cramer
425 University Ave., Norwood, MA 2062 USA
(781) 278-2300, *Fax:* (781) 255-0721
www.crameronline.com
info@crameronline.com
Tom Martin, CEO
Rich Sturchio, President
T.J. Martin, Executive Vice President
Film & video production svcs from design to presentation; staging svcs; video duplications. Web-casting, interactive media.

Crawford Communications
3845 Pleasantdale Rd., Atlanta, GA 30340 USA
(404) 876-7149, *Fax:* (678) 421-6717
www.crawford.com
Jesse Crawford, President
Bill Thompson, General Sales Mgr
Jessica Moore, Promotions Manager
Paul Hansel, President
Computer graphics, animation, production & postproduction svcs domestic & international teleport.

Creative International Activities Ltd.
372 Central Park W., New York, NY 10025 USA
(212) 663-8944, *Fax:* (212) 865-8486
ciaklaus@aol.com
Klaud Lehmann, President
International TV program syndication & consultation.

Creative Marketing & Communications Corp.
7633 Athenia Dr., Cincinnati, OH 45244 USA
(513) 624-8301,(800) 845-8477, *Fax:* (513) 624-8302
www.cmcideas.com
Terry Dean, President
Susan Dean, Operations Dir
Syndicated 30-60-second coml wraparounds.

Creative Radio Network
Box 7749, Thousand Oaks, CA 91359 USA
(818) 991-3892, *Fax:* (818) 991-3894
Darwin Lamm, President
Radio program production & syndicationall formats; holiday & artist specials.

Crest National Digital Media Complex
1000 N. Highland Ave., Hollywood, CA 90038 USA
(323) 466-0624, *Fax:* (323) 461-8901
www.crestnational.com
info@crestnational.com
Ron Stein, President
John Walker, General Sales Mgr
Full videotape postproduction including film transfer, processing, sweetening & duplication.

The Crime Channel
78206 Varner Rd. (D131), Palm Desert, CA 92211 USA
(760) 360-6151, Ext. 3, *Fax:* (760) 360-3258
crimechannel.com
crimechannel@dc.rr.com
Arnie Frank, President
TV program distribution & bcstg.

Critical Mass Releasing Inc.
77 Mowat Ave., Suite 110, Toronto, ON M6K 3E3 CAN
(416) 538-2535, *Fax:* (416) 538-3367
cmass@netcom.ca
William Alexander, President
Lisa-Marie Doorey, Director, International Sales
International TV & domestic distribution, TV & film, film & series production, theatrical & video releasing.

CRM Learning
2215 Faraday Ave., Suite 110, Carlsbad, CA 22182 USA
(800) 421-0833, *Fax:* (760) 931-5792
www.crmlearning.com
Peter Jordan, CEO
Production & distribution of business training films.

CRN International
One Circular Ave., Hamden, CT 6514 USA
(203) 288-2002, *Fax:* (203) 281-3291
www.crnradio.com
Barry Berman, President
S. Kalt, Executive Vice President
Short-form customized radio progms & promotions; SkiWatch BeachWatch & small business reports.

Crossroads Christian Communications Inc.
Box 5100, Burlington, ON L7R 4M2 CAN
(905) 335-7100
www.crossroads.ca
Doug McKenzie, CEO
Ron Mainse, President
Produces 100 Huntley Street program.

Crown International Pictures Inc.
8701 Wilshire Blvd., Beverly Hills, CA 90211 USA
(310) 657-6700, *Fax:* (310) 657-4489
www.crownintlpictures.com
crown@crownintlpictures.com
Mark Tenser, CEO
Scott Schwimer, Operations Dir
Lisa Agay, General Manager
Film production & distribution.

Crystal Pictures Inc.
200 Riverside Dr., Bldg. 22 1st Fl., Asheville, NC 28804 USA
(828) 285-9995, *Fax:* (828) 285-9997
cryspic@aol.com
Joshua Tager, President
Jane Rolston, General Sales Mgr
Distribution of feature film & svcs to all TV outlets in United States & abroad.

CS Associates
200 Dexter Ave, Watertown, MA 02472-4236 USA
(617) 923-0077, *Fax:* (617) 923-0025
programs@csassociates.com
Charles Schuerhoff, President
Lisa Carey, Operations Dir
Brian Gilbert, General Sales Mgr
Jason Redmond, Manager, Acquisitions
Program distribution, specializing in documentaries, foreign & domestic TV & cable; broker co-productions.

CTV Television Inc.
Box 9, Stn. O, Toronto, ON M4A 2M9 CAN
(416) 332-5000, *Fax:* (416) 332-5065
www.ctv.ca
Susanne Boyce, Programming Director
TV bcstg, program production & distribution.

CTVC Hillside Studios
Merry Hill Rd., Bushey, Watford, Herts, WD23 1DR
2 089 504 426, *Fax:* 2 089 501 437
www.ctvc.co.uk
barrie.allcott@ctvc.co.uk
Barrie Allcott, General Manager
Ray Bruce, Programming Director
Producers of programs with humanitarian values, especially relg. Also full bcst facilities available for hire.

Cube International
Box 307, Lehi, UT 84043-0307 USA
(801) 722-1000, *Fax:* (801) 722-1000
www.cubeinternational.com
phillcatheral@earthlink.net
Olivier de Courson, General Manager
Phillip Catherall, Managing Director
Film & TV distribution to all worldwide markets & media.

Curb Entertainment International Corp.
3907 W. Alameda Ave., Burbank, CA 91505 USA
(818) 843-8580, *Fax:* (818) 566-1719
www.curbentertainment.com
info@curbentertainment.com
Mike Curb, Chairman
Eddie Francis, COO
Carole Curb, President
Mona Kirton, General Manager
Conor Barrett, Promotions Manager
International sales company.

Custom Productions Inc.
1334 3rd St. Promenade, Suite 300, Santa Monica, CA 90401 USA
(310) 393-4144, *Fax:* (310) 393-1143
www.customproductions.TV
Steve Stockman, President
Creation & production of custom TV campaigns for radio stns and TV news stns in the top 25 markets.

D'Ocon Films Productions
C/Calaf.3 Bajos, Barcelona, 8021 ESP
34-93-240-41-22, *Fax:* 34-93-240-41-24
docon@docon.es
Principally an animation company offering full range of pre-production, production & postproduction svcs either developing our own concepts or co-producing.

D-Squared Media
210 E. 38th St., Suite 5H, New York, NY 10016 USA
(212) 254-3489, *Fax:* (212) 254-3489
www.dsquaredmedia.com
solutions@dsquaredmedia.com
Adriana Davis, Programming Director
Film, video, & radio production svcs from script to screen.

D-V-X International
1038 Bay Ridge Ave., Brooklyn, NY 11219 USA
(718) 680-7234, *Fax:* (718) 680-7234
Video recording, creative production & postproduction svcs.

The D.L. Dykes Jr. Foundation
111 E. Capitol St., Jackson, MS 39201 USA
(601) 354-0767
David Dyker, CEO
Joe Todaro, Programming Director

Daley Video
4095 Hitchcock Rd., Concord, CA 94518 USA
(925) 676-7260, *Fax:* (413) 541-8354
gadaley@aol.com
Greg Daley, CEO
Betacam SP, D1 digital betacom editing & 3/4-inch postproduction; TV production.

Daniel Wilson Productions Inc.
300 W. 55th St. Ste 8V, New York, NY 10019 USA
(212) 765-7148, *Fax:* (212) 765-7916
wilprod@verizon.net
Daniel Wilson, President
TV & theatrical film production & distribution.

Danny Thomas Productions
10100 Santa Monica Blvd., Suite 950, Los Angeles, CA 90067 USA
(310) 277-4866, *Fax:* (310) 286-1963
anita@dethomasbobo.com
Anita De Thomas, President
TV programs, features, coml production.

Dargaud-Marina
15-27 rue Moussorgski, Paris, 75018 FRA
331-5326-3100, *Fax:* 331-5326-3113
sales@dargaudmarina.fr
Claude De Saint Vincent, President
Patrick Desiev, Operations Dir
Gaspard De Chavagnac, General Manager
G. Guillot, General Sales Mgr
Distribution & production company specialized in children's progmg, mainly animation.

Darino Films/Library of Special Effects
222 Park Ave. S., New York, NY 10003 USA
(212) 228-4024
edarino@hotmail.com
Ed Darino, President
Distributors of TV programs, video, CD, animation, educationals, effects libraries, stock footage libraries, production CD & DVD.

Daro Film Distribution
Le Victoria, 13 Blvd. Princess Charlotte, MC, 98000
(377) 979-1600, *Fax:* (377) 979-1590
daro@meditnet.com
International distribution, co-production, co-financing of TV programs & films.

Dave Bell Associates Inc.
3211 Cahuenga Blvd. W., Hollywood, CA 90068 USA
(323) 851-7801, *Fax:* (323) 851-9349
dbmovies@aol.com
Dave Bell, President
Fred Putman, Operations Dir
Kitty Stallings, General Manager
Ted Weiant, Vice President
Dev & production of TV movies, reality series, feature films, documentaries & game shows.

David Finch Distribution Ltd.
Box 264, Walton-on-Thames, KT12 3YR GBR
44-1932-882733, *Fax:* 44-1932-882108
sales@david-finch.com
David Finch, CEO
Supply of programs for home video & TV worldwide. Acquisition for United Kingdom home video.

David Kaye Productions Inc.
1361 Paseo Redondo Ave., Burbank, CA 91501 USA
(800) 843-3933,(310) 403-1714, *Fax:* (604) 921-1926
www.davidkaye.com
info@davidkaye.com
David Kaye, President
Stephan Sisk, Operations Dir
Full svc voice-over production company, providing radio & TV imaging & branding around the world.

DaviSound
Box 521, 1504 Sunset, Newberry, SC 29108 USA
(803) 276-0639
www.davisound.com
davisound@hotmail.com
Annette Davis, Operations Dir
Coml & promotional writing & producing for radio, jingles & program production & distribution. Also provides DaviSound Tool Boxes, custom fabricated pro audio equipment.

DC Audio
1783 Lanier Pl. N.W., Suite B, Washington, DC 20009 USA
(202) 667-1234, *Fax:* (202) 667-5578
www.dailyfeed.com
dfeed@dailyfeed.com
John Dryden, President
Produces The Daily Feed, a 90-second political, social satire radio commentary. Markets cash and bartered radio inventory to 18 + demos.

De Wolfe Music Library Inc.
25 W. 45th St., New York, NY 10036 USA
(212) 382-0220, *Fax:* (212) 382-0278
www.dewolfemusic.com
info@dewolfmusic.com
Andrew Jacobs, President
Jamie Gillespie, General Sales Mgr
The largest independant production music library in the world!

DeLuxe Laboratories
1377 N. Serrano Ave., Hollywood, CA 90027 USA
(323) 462-6171, *Fax:* (323) 461-0608
www.bydeluxe.com
Cyril Drabinsky, President
Steve Van Anda, General Sales Mgr
Full svc motion picture processing lab with labs in Toronto, London, Rome.

Design Partners Inc.
2919 W. Burbank Blvd., Suite B, Burbank, CA 91505 USA
(818) 845-9191, *Fax:* (818) 845-9258
www.dpi-ld.com
designpartners@dpi-ld.com
Greg Brunton, President
TV, lighting design, industrial production & TV production & tech supervision svcs.

Devillier Donegan Enterprises L.P.
4401 Connecticut Ave. N.W., 6th Floor, Washington, DC 20008 USA
(202) 686-3980, *Fax:* (202) 686-3999
www.ddegroup.com
Ronald Devillier, CEO
Brian Donegan, President
Joan Lanigan, Operations Dir
Gregory Diefenbach, General Sales Mgr
Linda Ekizian, Promotions Manager
Worldwide distribution of progmg: international & ind documentaries, Hollywood profiles, science series, drama, natural history progmg & the performing arts.

Devlin Design Group Inc.
12526 High Bluff, # 300, San Diego, CA 92130 USA
(760) 634-6515, *Fax:* (760) 634-6929
www.ddgtv.com
creative@ddgtv.com
Designs, builds & installs news sets & newsrooms. Facility planning, broadcast consulting, tech & lighting direction. Virtual Reality Rsch & Dev Ctr. Virtual sets, soft sets.

DG Systems
750 W. John Carpenter Fwy., Irving, TX 75039 USA
(972) 581-2000, *Fax:* (972) 581-2001
www.dgsystems.com
Marty Melody, General Sales Mgr
Duplication & distribution of corporate training & educ, TV & radio programs. Distribution of syndicated TV programs via satellite & videotape.

Dial Global
Candler Tower, 220 W. 42nd Street, New York, NY 10036 USA
(212) 967-2888
www.dial-global.com
Independent, full-service radio network, offering formats, prep, programming, jingles & imaging as well as national advertising sales representation.

DIC Entertainment
4100 W. Alameda Ave., Burbank, CA 91505 USA
(818) 955-5400, *Fax:* (818) 955-5696
www.dicentertainment.com
Andy Heyward, Chairman
Andy Heyward, CEO
Brad Brooks, President
Jedd Gold, Promotions Manager
DIC Entertainment, a leading children's entertainment company, is a full-service studio dedicated to creating, developing, producing, distributing, mktg & mdsg children's & family-based intellectual properties.

Dick Brescia Associates
164 Garfield St., Haworth, NJ 7641 USA
(201) 385-6566, *Fax:* (201) 385-6449
www.ictx.com/dba
dbasyndicators@prodigy.net
Radio shows: When Radio Was, Stan Freberg Here. Radio movie classics, radio super heroes.

The Dick Clark Productions
9200 W Sunset Blvd., Loa Angeles, CA 90069-3502 USA
(818) 841-3003, *Fax:* (818) 954-8609
www.dickclarkproductions.com
Dick Clark, Chairman
Bill Simon, CFO
Francis C. La Maina, President
TV production for networks, cable & syndication. Produces series, specials & movies for TV.

Dick Orkin's Amazing Radio
15003 Lemay St., Van Nuys, CA 91405 USA
(800) 621-6949, *Fax:* (818) 376-8529
www.sandyorkin-crs.com
sandyo@earthlink.net
Sandy Orkin, President
Syndicated packages of Dick Orkin comls customized for loc advertisers. Available in six categories.

Digital Brewery L.L.C.
3820 Packard, Suite 150, Ann Arbor, MI 48108 USA
(800) 572-0098,(734) 975-8880, *Fax:* (734) 975-8915
www.digitalbrewery.com
Sal Calabrese, Co-President
Terry Dollhoff, Co-President
Packaged animations include backgrounds, holidays, corporate, adv & globes, maps & flags.

Digital Force
149 Madison Ave., 12th Fl., New York, NY 10016 USA
(212) 252-9300, *Fax:* (212) 252-7377
www.digitalforce.com
info@digitalforce.com
Jerome Bunke, President
Arthur Crumlish, Operations Dir
Vanessa Towle-Mullin, Programming Director
Compact disc, CD-ROM & DVDproduction service to meet the needs of bcstrs, cable networks, & small labels/ind artists. Clients include the National Football League (NFL) & National Hockey League (NHL) on Fox TV as well as PSAs & promotionaldiscs from bcstrs nationwide, ABC-TV & NBC, Westwood One & CBS.

Dimension 3 Corp
5240 Medina Rd., Woodland Hills, CA 91364-1913 USA
(818) 592-0999, *Fax:* (818) 592-0987
www.d3.com
info@d3.com
Daniel Symmes, President
Supplies 3-D bcst TV process & 3-D film; equipment, consultation & 3-D glasses.

Disney Channel
3800 W. Alameda Ave., Burbank, CA 91505 USA
(818) 569-7700, *Fax:* (818) 845-8249
www.disneychannel.com
Anne Sweeney, President
Original TV program production & distribution.

Diversified Communications Inc.
2000 M St. N.W., Suite 340, Washington, DC 20036 USA
(202) 775-4300, *Fax:* (202) 775-4363
www.dciteleport.com
Al Levin, President
Nelson Crumling, Operations Dir
Complete mobile facilities, Ku-band uplink trucks, extensive loc & global connectivity; internationally compliant, fully redundant Ku-band air transportable uplink.

DLT Entertainment Ltd.
124 E. 55th St., New York, NY 10022-4501 USA
(212) 245-4680, *Fax:* (212) 315-1132
www.dltentertainment.com
John Fitzgerald, CEO
Donald Taffner, President
Donald Taffner Jr., Operations Dir
Jeff Cotugno, Vice President
TV program production & distribution.

DMX Music
900 E. Pine St., Seattle, WA 98122 USA
(800) 831-8001, *Fax:* (206) 329-9952
www.dmxmusic.com
Liberty Media, President
Programmer & supplier of satellite-delivered music svcs for business & cable TV. Available satellite direct or through FM subcarrier.

The Dolmatch Group Ltd.
Box 3298, 19697 Glen Brae Dr., Saratoga, CA 95070 USA
(408) 741-8620, *Fax:* (408) 741-8620
tdgdolmatch@yahoo.com
Murray Dolmatch, President
Sandra Dolmatch, Operations Dir
Represents producers in the United States, United Kingdom, Germany, France & Italy; distributes feature films, documentaries & animation; active in co-production & co-financing.

Domain Communications L.L.C.
289 S. Main Pl., Carol Stream, IL 60188-2425 USA
(630) 668-5300, *Fax:* (630) 668-0158
www.domaincommunications.com
dmorris@domaincommuications.com
David Morris, President
Jim Draper, General Sales Mgr
Recording audio studios, production, CD replication, high-speed cassette duplicating, fulfillment.

Dome Productions
1 Blue Jays Way, Suite #3400, Toronto, ON M5V1J3 CAN
(416) 341-2001,(514) 731-3663, *Fax:* (416) 341-2020,(514) 731-4646
www.domeproductions.com
mcarlyle@domeprod.com
Mary Carlyle, Operations Dir
Mobile production trucks/airpacks (High Definition, Digital, Analog), telecommunications (Fibre/Satellite transmission, satellite media tours, playouts), Host bcst (Design, production, engrg, opons).
5647 Ferrier, Mont-Royal, PQ Canada

Donnelly & Associates
7507 Sunset Blvd., Suite 205, Los Angeles, CA 90046 USA
(323) 850-5861, *Fax:* (323) 850-5866
wpdonnelly@earthlink.net
W.P. Donnelly, President
Mktg & licensing films to pay-TV, network & syndication packages.

Dorling Kindersley Vision
80 Strand, London, WC2R 0RL
442 070 103 000, *Fax:* 442 070 106 636
www.dk-uk.com
dkvision@dk-uk.com
Produces programs for the international TV & video markets, incorporating visual design with universally appealing subjects.

Duke International
Box 46, Douglas, Isle of Man, IM99 1DD
(+44) 1624 640020, *Fax:* (+44) 1624 640001
www.dukesales.com
info@dukesales.com
Jon Quayle, General Sales Mgr
A wide range of powersport progmg, documentaries, clips; also production & editing facilities.

DWJ Television
One Robinson Ln., Ridgewood, NJ 7450 USA
(201) 445-1711, *Fax:* (201) 445-8352
www.dwjtv.com
dwjinfo@dwjtv.com
Daniel Johnson, President
Cynthia Boseski, Operations Dir
Michael Friedman, Executive Vice President
Provides TV, radio progmg, production; promotional video production & production svcs.

E! Entertainment Television
; 84 million SUbscribers served
5750 Wilshire Blvd., Los Angeles, CA 90036-3709
(323) 954-2400, *Fax:* (323) 954-2500
www.eonline.com
Satellite: Satcom C-3*Transponder:* 23
Ken Bettsteller, CEO
Ted Harbert, President
Neil Baker, General Sales Mgr
A 24-hours progmg net covering celebrities, entertainment news, gossip & pop-culture, feature behind the scenes with today's biggest stars.
11 W. 42nd St, New York, NY 10036-8002
(212) 852-5100, (212) 852-5151;
Dave Cassaro, Exec Vp
11 W. 42nd St, New York, NY 10036
(212) 852-5100 (212) 852-5151;
Dave Cassaro, Exec Vp

Eagle Eye Film Company
824 N. Victory Blvd., Burbank, CA 91502 USA
(818) 506-6100, *Fax:* (818) 506-4313
www.eagleyepost.com
Chuck Spatariu, President
Joel Minnich, Operations Dir
Editing facility, editing rentals & RAID storage solutions.

Eagle Media Productions Ltd.
Box 580, Northford, CT 6472 USA
(203) 294-1190, *Fax:* (203) 294-9512
louadler@sbcglobal.net
Louis Adler, President
Thalia Adler, Operations Dir
Radio program syndication, program & news consultant. Producers of Medical Journal.

Eaton Films Ltd.
10 Holbein Mews, London, SW1W 8NN
(44) 207-823-6173, *Fax:* (44) 207-823-6017
eaton.films@talk21.com
Judith Bland, General Manager
Liz Cook, General Sales Mgr
TV & video distribution.

Echo Radio Productions Inc.
44895 Hwy. 82, Aspen, CO 81611 USA
(800) 385-4612,(970) 925-2640, *Fax:* (970) 925-9369
www.echoradio.com
kayla@echoradio.com

Rodney Jacobs, CEO
Kayla Hoffman-Cook, Operations Dir
Syndicator & producer of radio vignette progmg.

Ecumedia News Service
Box 358, Ridgefield, CT 6877 USA
(203) 431-6092, *Fax:* (212) 870-2030
roy.lloyd@ecunet.org
Roy Lloyd, General Manager
News stories, features & actualities about ethics & relg produced for radio.

Ecumenical Communications
48 Eastview Rd., Terryville, CT 6786 USA
(860) 585-5090
www.ecucomm.ro
info@ecucomm.ro
Robert Geckler, President
Radio, podcast program production, distribution; production, restoration svcs, internet, website & podcast svcs.

Eddie Kessler Productions Publications & Promotions
Box 6243, Martinsburg, WV 25402 USA
(302) 399-8690
Eddie Kessler, CEO
Extensive film library, props and photo library.

Educational Technologies Network (ETN)
9300 Imperial Hwy., Rm. 126, Los Angeles County Office of Education, Downey, CA 90242-2890 USA
(562) 922-6641, *Fax:* (562) 922-8841
www.lacoe.edu
ENT_Productions@lacoe.edu
Rodney Conner, COO
Richard Quinones, Station Manager
ETN provides multimeda production svcs to LACOE division & school districts throughout Los Angeles county. Include: studio & remote video production, distance learning & vitual meetings, video streaming, videoconferencing, interactive CD-ROM& DVD authoring & live event video coverage,

Edward Sarson Productions
30 Duke St., Suite 511, Kitchener, ON N2H 3W5 CAN
(519) 576-1824, *Fax:* (519) 740-6766
George Sarson, President
Producers for the Toad Patrol TV series.

Ellis Entertainment
1300 Yonge St., Suite 300, Toronto, ON M4T 1X3 CAN
(416) 924-2186, *Fax:* (416) 924-6115
www.ellisent.com
sales@ellisent.com
Stephen Ellis, President
Grace Lo, Operations Dir
Producers and distributors of 1000+ hrs of non-fiction and family entertainment for TV and video for four decades.

Empire Burbank Studio
1845 Empire Ave., Burbank, CA 91504 USA
(818) 840-1400, *Fax:* (818) 567-1062
Sound stage studio rental, audience rated TV studios, full-svc production facilities & equipment, ultimate stage.

Encore Video Productions Inc.
811 Main St., Myrtle Beach, SC 29577 USA
(843) 448-9900, *Fax:* (843) 448-9235
www.encorevideo.biz
frank@encorevideo.biz
Rik Dickinson, President
Frank Payne, Operations Dir
Location & studio production, specializing in EFP/ENG 1-Camera productions, full script to screen svc, VNR, EPK satellite media tours, teleconferences, & magazine TV production. Betagami SP, non-linear editing.

Enoki Films U.S.A. Inc.
16430 Ventura Blvd., Suite 308, Encino, CA 91436 USA
(818) 907-6503, *Fax:* (818) 907-6506
www.enokifilmsusa.com
info@enokifilmsusa.com
Madoka Koike, COO
Yoshi Enoki, President
Ricki Ames, Operations Dir
Producer & distributor of children's animation for TV & video.

Envoy Productions
660 Mason Ridge Ctr. Dr., St. Louis, MO 63141-8557 USA
(314) 317-4216, *Fax:* (314) 317-4299
www.envoyproductions.com
sandi.clement@lhm.org
Kurt Klaus, President
Sandi Clement, General Manager
TV, radio production, distribution (English & Sp). Syndicates 30-minute wkly radio shows, The Lutheran Hour & TV holiday specials.

Episcopal Church Center
815 2nd Ave., New York, NY 10017 USA
(212) 716-6102, *Fax:* (212) 949-8059
www.episcopalchurch.org
Spokespersons for church & society issues.

ESPI Video
4801 Spring Valley Rd., Suite 116, Dallas, TX 75244 USA
(214) 522-6699, *Fax:* (214) 522-7699
www.espivideo.com
gsleeper@espivideo.com
Gary Sleeper, President
Full-svc production company specializing in corporate video production. Postproduction facilities & on-location svcs also available.

ESPN Radio Network
ESPN Plaza, Bristol, CT 6010 USA
(860) 766-2661, *Fax:* (860) 860-5523
www.espnradio.com
John Martin, Programming Director
John Walsh, Exec Editor
Len Weiner, Programming Director
NBA On ESPN Radio; College Game Day (Sat); ESPN Radio weekends; Brent Musburger afternoon drive sportscasts; AM & PM drive commentaries; NFL Gameday (Sun)

ESPN Regional Television
11001 Rushmore Dr., Charlotte, NC 28277 USA
(704) 973-5000, *Fax:* (704) 973-5090
www.espn.com
Chuck Gerber, President
Producer & distributor of TV sports events including college & professional basketball, boxing & auto racing for over-the-air & cable.

Essence Television Productions Inc.
135 W. 50th St., Frnt 4, New York, NY 10020-1201 USA
(212) 642-0600, *Fax:* (212) 921-5173
www.essence.com
Edward Lewis, Chairman
Edward Lewis, CEO
TV program production.

Ethnic-American Broadcasting Co.
Two Executive Drive, Fort Lee, NJ 7024 USA
(201) 242-3000, *Fax:* (201) 944-5961
info@skyview
Provides ethnic radio & TV language svcs via DBS & through cable systems throughout North America.
2 Executive Dr, Suite 600, Fort Lee, NJ 07024 United States
(201) 242-3000;

EUE Screen Gems Studios
222 E. 44th St., New York, NY 10017 USA
(212) 450-1600, *Fax:* (212) 450-1610
Mitchell Brill, President
Ed Brancaccio, Chief Engineer
TV program, coml production & distribution.
1223 N. 23rd St., Wilmington, NC 28405
(910) 343-3500;

Eurocine
33 Ave. Des Champs Elysees, Paris, 75008 FRA
33.1.42.25.6492, *Fax:* 33.1.42.25.7338
www.eurocine.net
eurocine@club-internet.fr
Production & distribution in all media.

Europe Images International
1 Rond-Point Victor Hugo, F-92130, Issy-Les-Moulineaux, FRA
(33) 1 55 95 58 00, *Fax:* (33) 1 55 95 58 10
www.europeimages.com
Europe-Images@europeimages.com
John Rouilly, CEO
Acquires, distributes & invests in international TV progmg. Catalog close to 5 hours broken into three categories, drama, children's documentaries.

Evangelical Lutheran Church in America
8765 W. Higgins Rd., Chicago, IL 60631 USA
(773) 380-2941, *Fax:* (773) 380-2406
www.elca.org
ava.martin@elca.org
Ava Martin, General Manager
TV & radio progmg, promotional film production, distribution, production svcs & news.

Evergreen Entertainment Group
1825 Ponce De Leon Blvd., Suite 450, Coral Gables, FL 33134-3626 USA
(305) 460-4448
evergreenenter@juno.com
Migdalia Inocencio, President
Worldwide programs distribution; international co-production liaison; mktg & progmg cable/satellite.

Expand Images
7 Rue Taylor, Paris, 75010
(33) 0148-0305-44, *Fax:* (33) 0148-0345-04
www.expand.fr
communication@expand.fr
Production & distribution company.

Eye in the Woods
Box 89, Brewton, AL 36427 USA
(251) 809-1909, *Fax:* (251) 809-0729
www.sportsmanshowcase.com,www.eyeinthewoods.com
Dale Faust, Programming Director
Produce a weekly show viewed on The Outdoor Channel.

Eyewitness Kids News, LLC
182 Sound Beach Ave., Old Greenwich, CT 06870-0116 USA
(203) 637-0044, *Fax:* (203) 698-0812
www.educationtelevisionfund.org
primonews@aol.com
Albert T. Primo, President
Coaching of TV news, program talent, strategic planning & production svcs.
355 W 52nd St, 3rd FL, New York, NY 10019

Faith for Today
101 W. Cochran St., Simi Valley, CA 93065 USA
(805) 955-7606, *Fax:* (805) 522-1082
www.faithfortoday.tv,www.theevidence.org
info@faithfortoday.tv
Michael Tucker, Chief Engineer
Producer & distributor of Lifestyle Magazine, McDougall M.D. & The Evidence.

Family Stations Inc.
290 Hegenberger Rd., Oakland, CA 94621 USA
(510) 568-6200,(800) 543-1495, *Fax:* (510) 633-7983
www.familyradio.com
famradio@familyradio.com
William Thornton, Operations Dir
Harold Camping, General Manager
W. Craig Hulsebos, Programming Director
Rick Prime, Engineering Dir
Radio program production & distribution.

FamilyNet
6350 W. Freeway, Fort Worth, TX 76116 USA
(817) 737-4011, *Fax:* (817) 377-4372
www.familynet.com
ddavis@familynet.com
David Clark, President
Glenn McEowen, Operations Dir
Darin Davis, General Sales Mgr
Martin Coleman, Programming Director
Chip Turner, Promotions Manager
FamilyNet is a 24/7 cable net. In addition, FamilyNet produces 5 syndicated radio progms. Values based, family oriented progmg.

FamilyNet Radio
6350 W. Freeway, Fort Worth, TX 76116-4511 USA
(817) 570-1416,(800) 266-1837, *Fax:* (817) 735-1790
www.familynetradio.com
smiller@familynet.com
Dale Weller, COO
Scott Miller, General Manager
FamilyNet Radio is SIRIUS 161, Christian talk. We produce Mornings which airs only on SIRIUS .

Faraone Communications Inc.
75 West End Ave., R-9A, New York, NY 10023 USA
(212) 489-1313, *Fax:* (212) 489-8978
www.worldwidepublicrelations.com
ted.faraone@verizon.net
Ted Faraone, President
Randolph Nader, Operations Dir
Media rel svcs to producers, distributors of radio, TV programs, talent & home video.
Valley Village
4804 Laurel Canyon Blvd., Ste 516, Valley Village, CA 91607

Federal Citizen Information Center
1800 F St. N.W., Rm. G-142, Washington, DC 20405 USA

(202) 501-1794, *Fax:* (202) 501-4281
www.pueblo.gsa.gov, www.usa.gov
nancy.tyler@gsa.gov
Nancy Tyler, Promotions Manager
Teresa Nasif, Chief Engineer
TV & radio PSAs promoting USA.gov, the official web portal of the federal government.

Festival de Television de Monte-Carlo
4, Boulevard du Jardin Exotique, Monte Carlo, 98000
377 93 10 40 60, *Fax:* 377 93 50 70 14
www.tvfestival.com
info@tvfestival.com
Competition of TV films & miniseries; news programs; producers. Conferences, panels & other market-related activities.

Film House Inc.
810 Dominican Dr., Nashville, TN 37228 USA
(615) 255-4000, *Fax:* (615) 255-4111
results@filmhouse.com
Andy Cohen, CFO
Ron Routson, President
Wayne Campbell, Operations Dir
Curt Hahn, CEO
Creates & produces TV mktg campaigns for radio & TV stns worldwide.

Film Roman Inc.
12020 Chandler Blvd., Suite 200, North Hollywood, CA 91607 USA
(818) 761-2544, *Fax:* (818) 985-2973
www.filmroman.com
John Hyde, CEO
Animation production studio.

Filmoption International Inc.
3401 St. Antoine St., Westmount, QC H3Z 1X1 CAN
(416) 598-1557, *Fax:* (416) 593-0013
www.filmoption.com
mrosilo@filmoption.com
Maryse Rouillard, President
Lizanne Rouillard, Operations Dir
Evangelia Ozek, General Sales Mgr
Muriel Rosilio, Senior Executive Sales
International distribution of TV programs.
3401 St-Antoine, Westmount, PQ H3Z 1X1 Canada
(215) 931-6180; *Fax:* (514) 939-2034
mrouilla@filmoption.com
Maryse Rouillard, Pres
144 Front St. West, Suite 760, Toronto, ON M5J 2L7 Canada
(416) 598-1557; *Fax:* (416) 593-0013
mrosilio@filmoption.com
Muriel rosilio, Sr Exec Sls Co-Productions

Films Media Group
Box 2053, Princeton, NJ 08543-2053 USA
(609) 671-0266,(800) 257-5126, *Fax:* (609) 671-5772
www.films.com
custserv@films.com
Amy Bevilacqua, President
Diane Bilello, General Sales Mgr
Distributes programs for bcst & cable industries to non-theatrical, educ, institutional, home video & business markets.

Films of the Nations
Box 449, Clarksburg, NJ 8510 USA
(732) 462-3522, *Fax:* (732) 294-0330
www.aldenfilms.com
aldfilms@bellatlantic.net
Paul Weinberg, President
TV program, promotion & educ film distribution.

Financial Media Services, Inc.
Box 870928, Stone Mountain, GA 30087 USA
(770) 413-2258, *Fax:* (770) 465-0180
charles@charlesross.com
Produces & syndicates nationally syndicated radio show Your Personal Finance.

Finger Lakes Productions International
119 S. Cayuga St., Ithaca, NY 14850 USA
(607) 275-9400, *Fax:* (607) 277-0961
www.flpradio.com
info@flpradio.com
Paul Bartishevich, CEO
Full-service radio mktg, production & syndication of short-form radio features. International mktg, sls & consulting.

First Marketing
3300 Gateway Dr., Pompano Beach, FL 33069 USA
(954) 979-0700,(800) 641-9251, *Fax:* (954) 971-4707
www.first-marketing.com
Ronald Drenning, President
Neil Rosenblum, Operations Dir
First Marketing offers 30 yrs of experience partnering with marketing professionals to dev custom communications programs designed to enhance custom relationships & profitability.

First Run/Icarus Films
32 Court St., 21st Fl., Brooklyn, NY 10201 USA
(718) 488-8900, *Fax:* (718) 488-8642
www.frif.com
info@frif.com
Jonathan Miller, President
International TV program distribution: documentaries, current affrs, music, arts, cultural programs.

FirstCom Music
1325 Capital Pkwy., Suite 109, Carrollton, TX 75006 USA
(800) 858-8880, *Fax:* (972) 242-6526
www.firstcom.com
info@firstcom.com
Carol Riffert, Operations Dir
Ken Nelson, Programming Director
FirstCom's 18 spectacular libraries deliver the combined power of 186,000 compositions & growing by 6,000 new tracks a year. Delivery options include DVD, CD, Hard-drive & online. Guaranteed to add creativity to your production!
8750 Wilshire Blvd., 2nd Fl., Beverly Hills, CA 90211

Fischer Broadcast Services
10841 Bittersweet Lane, Fishers, IN 46038-2203
(317) 514-5757, *Fax:* (317) 578-3884
www.superfisch.com
superfisch@midspring.com
Scott Fischer, President
SUPERFISCH—VOICE IMAGING & BRANDING. Scott Fischer voice artist for radio & TV loc, cable, Netw. Promax & Emmy award voice. A versitile-VO-value! Yes you CAN afford me-can you afford not to check me out?

Forde Motion Picture Labs
1001 Lenora St., Seattle, WA 98121-2706 USA
(206) 682-2510,(800) 682-2510, *Fax:* (206) 682-2560
www.fordelabs.com
Richard Vedvick, President
Overnight processing of 35mm/16mm Eastman color negative dailies; release printing.

Fox 17 Studio Productions
631 Mainstream Dr., Nashville, TN 37228 USA
(615) 244-1717, *Fax:* (615) 259-3962
www.wztv.com,www.fox17.com,www.citysepach.com
production@fox17.com
Bill Zuckerman, Promotions Manager
Full range video & film production facility; 25 x 40 studio & 60 x 60 studio soundstage; betacams & a var of tape formats for TV/CATV.

Fox 29 WUTV Sinclair
951 Whitehaven Rd., Grand Island, NY 14072 USA
(716) 773-7531, *Fax:* (716) 773-5753
www.wutv.com
Jon May, COO
Don Moran, General Manager
TV coml production; U.S. rep, Katz; Canadian rep, Airtime.

Fox Digital
Fox Network Ctr., 10201 W. Pico Blvd., Los Angeles, CA 90035 USA
(310) 369-6622, *Fax:* (310) 969-6125
www.fox.com
Videotape production facilities, stages & equipment.

Fox Sports West
1100 S. Flower St., Los Angeles, CA 90015 USA
(213) 743-7800, *Fax:* (213) 743-7835
www.foxsports.com
Dennis Johnson, Operations Dir
Steve Simpson, General Manager
TV program production & distribution.

Fred Wolf Films
4222 W. Burbank Blvd., Burbank, CA 91505 USA
(818) 846-0611, *Fax:* (818) 846-0979
www.fredwolffilms.com
administration@fredwolffilms.com
Fred Wolf, President
TV program production & distribution.

Free Speech TV (FSTV)
Box 44099, Denver, CO 80201 USA
(303) 442-8445, *Fax:* (303) 442-6472
www.freespeech.org
ops@freespeech.org,viewercomments@fstv.org
John Schwartz, President
Nathaniel Reeder, Operations Dir
Jason McKain, General Manager
Eric Galatas, Programming Director
Jon Stout, General Manager
Acquires works from activists, independent film/video artists & community based media; providing exposure to progressive ideas.

Freewheelin' Films Ltd.
44895 Hwy. 82, Aspen, CO 81611 USA
(970) 925-2640, *Fax:* (970) 925-9369
www.fwf.com
kalyla@fwf.com
Rodney Jacobs, CEO
Kayla Hoffman-Cook, Operations Dir
25-yr old production company specializing in entertainment, sports & lifestyle specials.

The Fremantle Corp.
25 Lesmill Road, #5, Toronto, ON M3B 2T3 Canada
416-443-9204, *Fax:* 416-443-8685
www.fremantlecorp.com
Marshall Kesten, CEO
Randy Zalken, President
Diane Tripp, General Sales Mgr
Irv Holender, Principal
Lisa Dunn, VP Sales
International TV program distribution & co-production.
New York Office
(212) 840-6269 LA Office: (310) 445-0700;

Fremantle Media Ltd.
1 Stephen St., London, W1T 1AL GBR
44 (0)20 7691-6000, *Fax:* 44 (0)20 7691-6100
www.pearsontv.com
feedback@freemantlemedia.com
Greg Dyke, CEO
Tony Cohen, General Manager
James Bennet, CEO
TV production & distribution.

FremantleMedia North America Inc.
2700 Colorado Ave., Suite 450, Santa Monica, CA 90404 USA
(310) 255-4700, *Fax:* (310) 255-4800
www.fremantlemedia.com
Cecile Coutaz, COO
David Lyle, President
TV production.
1540 Broadway, New York, NY 10036 United States
Catherine V MacKay, Deputy Ceo

FTC/Orlando
324 DeSota Cir., Orlando, FL 32804 USA
(407) 422-8246, *Fax:* (407) 843-0738
www.ftcorlando.com
ftcorlando@aol.com
A.J. Foresta, President
Full-svc film & TV production company, specializing in coml & feature production. Area specialty: steadicam.

Galavision
605 Third Ave., 12th Fl., New York, NY 10158-0180 USA
(212) 455-5300, *Fax:* (212) 953-0198
www.univision.com
Ray Rodriguez, COO
Cesar Conde, Operations Dir
Joanne Lynch, General Manager
Spanish TV program distribution, cable.
541 N. Fairbanks Ct., 12th Fl., Suite 1240, Chicago, IL 60611
(312) 494-5100; *Fax:* (312) 494-5115
2323 Bryan St, Suite 1900, Dallas, TX 75201 United States
(214) 758-2420; *Fax:* (214) 758-2430
9405 N.W. 41st St., Miami, FL 33178
(305) 471-4022; *Fax:* (305) 471-3977
5999 Center Dr., Los Angeles, CA 90045 United States
(310) 348-3621; *Fax:* (310) 348-3619

Gedeon Programmes
44-50 av du Capitaine Glarner, Saint-Quen, 93585
33 01 49 48 65 00, *Fax:* 33 01 49 48 65 03
www.gedeonprogrammes.com
Films, TV movies, TV series, interactive fiction.

General Broadcasting Co. Inc.
8 N. Bothwell St., Suite 103, Palatine, IL 60067 USA
(847) 202-8804, *Fax:* (847) 202-8834
Robert Potter, President
Charles Maples, Operations Dir

Eric Edgerton, General Manager
Dean Mulchaey, Programming Director
Background music, environmental music progmg.

George Carlson & Associates
323 First Ave. W., Seattle, WA 98119 USA
(206) 213-0562, *Fax:* (206) 213-0562
George Carlson, Programming Director
Producers/distributors of 1/2-hour color, true life, travel adventure series to all parts of the world called The Traveler & Northwest Traveler.

Georgia Film, Video & Music Office
Georgia Department of Economic Dev, 75 Fifth St. N.W., Atlanta, GA 30308
(404) 962-4052, *Fax:* (404) 962-4053
www.georgia.org
film@georgia.org
Bill Thompson, General Manager
Location scouting & preproduction svcs provided to feature film, TV movie, coml & multimedia production companies.

Getty Images
601 N. 34th St., Seattle, WA 98103 USA
(206) 925-5000, *Fax:* (206) 925-5001
www.gettyimages.com
sales@gettyimages.com
Getty Images is an imagery company creating and providing still and moving images to communications professionals around the globe.

Ghostwriters/Radio Mall
2412 Unity Ave. N., Dept BCY, Minneapolis, MN 55422-3450
(800) 759-4561, *Fax:* (763) 522-6256
www.radiomall.com
info@radio-mall.com
David Dworkin, President
Over 23 years experience with products sold to more than 7,300 radio stns worldwide as well as TV stns, audio-video producers & cable operators. If you have a product that you'd like to mkt to radio or TV stns, contact us.

Gladney Communications Ltd.
101 Reni Rd., Manhasset, NY 11030 USA
(516) 627-3016, *Fax:* (516) 767-1957
Marion Gladney, President
Norman Gladney, President
TV & radio production & distribution.

Glenray Productions Inc.
Box 40400, Pasadena, CA 91114-7400 USA
(626) 797-5462
www.childrensmedia.com
2glenray@sbcglobal.net
C. Ray Carlson, President
Films, TV series, DVD distribution & production, primarily for family & children.

GLL TV Enterprises Inc.
8009 Via Fiore, Sarasota, FL 34238 USA
(941) 925-4339, *Fax:* (941) 925-3976
glltv@pobox.com
Gunther Less, President
Ellen Less, Operations Dir
TV program, coml, promotional film production & distribution. Journey to Adventure, the longest-running syndicated travel show on TV.

Global Entertainment Media
1200 N.W. 78th Ave., Suite 104, Miami, FL 33126 USA
(786) 206-4873, *Fax:* (786) 206-4889
www.gem-media.com
sales@gem-media.com
Alexander A. Fiore, CEO
Mercedes M. Fiore, President
Production & distribution company.

Global Telemedia Inc.
1698 Post Rd. E., Suite 1B, Westport, CT 6880 USA
(203) 259-9985, *Fax:* (203) 259-9986
www.globaltelemedia.com
anne@globaltelemedia.com
Greg Kimmelman, President
Anne Corsak, Operations Dir
Production & distribution of broadcast TV & DVD programming worldwide.

GlobeCast
1270 Avenue of the Americas, Ste 2800, New York, NY 10020 USA
(212) 373-5140, *Fax:* (212) 399-1949
www.globecast.com
info@globecastna.com
David Sprechman, CEO
Jonathan Feldman, Operations Dir
Mary Frost, General Sales Mgr
Keven Cahoon, Promotions Manager
GlobeCast Audio division supports a comprehensive package of audio transmission svcs:ABC/Keystone Ventures provides Satcom C5 DATS/SEDAT distribution svcs to 7,000 radio stns.3D2, a high-quality digital net designed to svc the entertainmentindustry, connections post-production facilities, recording studios & voice-over talent worldwide.A/FX Network utilizing Telos Zephyr code located at venues for sports backhauls & special events.Hybrid bridging svcs to simplify a digital world fullof different flavored audio codecs.Remote Production Packages for single or multi-stn remote bcsts.
GlobeCast Washington/DC
1120 G Street, NW - 2nd Floor, Washington, DC 20005 United States
1-202-383-2745; *Fax:* 1-202-393-4914
GlobeCast Miami Headquarters America/Florida
7291 NW 74th St., Miami, FL 33166 United States
1-310-687-1600; *Fax:* 1-305-341-4424
GlobeCast Los Angeles/California
10525 W. Washington Blvd., Culver City, CA 90232 United States
1-310-845-3900; *Fax:* 1-310-845-3904
GlobeCast Salt Lake City/Utah
1193 West 2400 South, Suite A, Salt Lake City, UT 84119 United States
1-801-908-1100; *Fax:* 1-801-954-0991

GlobeCast North America
10525 W. Washington Blvd., Culver City, CA 90230 USA
(310) 845-3900, *Fax:* (310) 845-3904
www.globecast.com,www.globecast.net
Ken Drake, Operations Dir
In the center of Hollywood, GlobeCast North America's Sunset facility provides studio production second audio progmg (SAP), & related client facility svcs on an as-scheduled or contractual basis. GlobeCast's studio is completely integratedw/GlobeCast's network of global, end-to-end connectivity via satellite, fiber optics & microwave.GlobeCast North America, provides the bcstg industry with a unique combination of both recognized expertise & extensive inter-continental svcs. ThroughGlobeCast's vast global infrastructure of over 100 transponders, 30 teleports & interconnect facilities, the company provides instant access to the world's major media markets. GlobeCast North America is part of France Telecom, one of the worldslargest telecommunications companies.

GMI Media L.L.C.
325 Washington Ave S, #399, Kent, WA 98032 USA
(206) 374-8889, *Fax:* NA
www.gmimedia.com
http://www.gmimedia.com/contact.htm
Ron Erak, President
Richard Germaine, Operations Dir
Custom ID jingle packages for all radio & TV formats as well as commercial jingles for local adsales. CD production libraries. Voice overs & production for promotions & spots.

Golden Gate Studios
400 Tamal Plaza, Suite 428, Corte Madera, CA 94925 USA
(415) 945-7500, *Fax:* (415) 924-0264
www.goldengatestudios.com
2 Studios, Green Screen Options, Full Production Packages

Good Life Associates
Box 82808, Lincoln, NE 68501-2808 USA
(402) 464-6440, *Fax:* (402) 464-6880
www.goodlifeassociates.org
martinj@backtothebible.org
Thomas Schindler, President
Martin Jones, General Manager
Radio program, coml production & distribution svcs.

Good News Broadcasting Association Inc.
6400 Cornhusker Hwy., Lincoln, NE 68501 USA
(402) 464-7200, *Fax:* (402) 464-7474
www.backtothebible.org
info@backtothebible/backtothebible.com
Woodrow Kroll, President
Radio & TV program production & distribution.

Gordon Productions
1557 Pine St., San Francisco, CA 94109 USA
(415) 776-7484, *Fax:* (415) 776-7822
www.gpvideo.com
john@gpvideo.com
Jerry Gordon, CEO
John Gordon, President
Les Lieurance, Operations Dir
Broadcast pub rels svcs include: B-roll & VNR production & distribution, TV, radio PSA's & audio news releases. Corporate video production include: trade shows, patient educ, training & employee presentations.

GPN Inc & Destination Education Inc.
Box 6124, Lincoln, NE 68506 USA
(402) 435-0110, *Fax:* (402) 435-0119
www.shopdei.com
serevice@shopdei.com
Stephen Lenzen, President
Acquires, produces, promotes & distributes videotaped instructional videos for bcst, cablecast & audiovisual use.

Granada America
15303 Ventura Blvd., Suite C-800, Sherman Oaks, CA 91403 USA
(818) 455-4600, *Fax:* (818) 455-4700
www.granadaamerica.com
Emily Brecher, CFO
Sam Zoda, President
Paul Buccieri, CEO
Worldwide distribution, production of TV series & made-for-TV movies.
609 Greenwich St., 9th Fl., Granada, NY 10014

GRB Entertainment
13400 Riverside Dr., 3rd Fl., Studio City, CA 91423 USA
(818) 728-7697, *Fax:* (818) 728-7601
www.grbtv.com
gbenz@grbtv.com
Gary Benz, CEO
Production & distribution (TV).

Great Chefs Television/Publishing
747 Magazine St., New Orleans, LA 70156 USA
(504) 581-5000, *Fax:* (504) 581-1188
www.greatchefs.com
info@greatchefs.com
John Shoup, CEO
Production, distribution of cooking, jazz TV programs, videos, CDs, CD-ROMs & books.

Great North Productions
3720-76 Ave., Edmonton, AB T6B 2N9 CAN
(780) 440-2022, *Fax:* (403) 440-3400
www.greatnorth.ab.ca
Penny Ritco, Operations Dir
A full-svc international production & distribution company, providing worldwide distribution for bcst home video, non-theatrical markets & co-production opportunities.

The Griffin Group
130 S. El Camino Dr., Beverly Hills, CA 90212 USA
(310) 385-2700, *Fax:* (310) 358-2701
www.merv.com
Larry Cohen, CEO
Full-svc dev & production company; slate includes series, specials & films. Also real estate & hotel ownership.

Grinberg Film Libraries Inc.
21011 Itasca St., Unit D, Chatworth, CA 91311 USA
(818) 709-2450, *Fax:* (818) 709-8540
www.grinberg.com
W. 'Bill' Brewington, CEO
Stock footage & news library.

Groove Addicts
12211 West Washington Blvd., Los Angeles, CA 90066 USA
(310) 572-4646, *Fax:* (310) 572-4647
www.grooveaddicts.com
info@grooveaddicts.com
Dain Blair, CEO
Bill Stolier, Operations Dir
Adward winning custom scoring & syndicated branding & ID packages for bcsts & entertainment projects worldwide.
Groove Addicts Chicago
108 W. Hubbard St., Chicago, IL 60610 United States
(312) 467-7047; *Fax:* (312) 467-7049

Groove Addicts Production Music Catalog
12211 West Washington Blvd., Los Angeles, CA 90066 USA
(310) 572-4644, *Fax:* (310) 572-4647
www.grooveaddicts.com
info@groveaddicts.com
Bill Stolier, Operations Dir
Continuously updated, sound design & SFX. Annual blanket license & custom music packages. 17 library collection with over 750 releases.

Grove Television Enterprises Inc.
46216 Dry Creek Dr., Badger, CA 93603 USA
(559) 337-2595, *Fax:* (559) 337-1334
Brett Coker, CEO
TV production & distribution international & domestic.

GTN
13320 Northend Ave., Oak Park, MI 48237 USA
(248) 548-2500, *Fax:* (248) 548-1916
www.gtninc.com
Doug Cheek, President
Studios, remote equipment, multi-format editing, film transfer, audio & duplication svcs, on-site satellite svcs & graphics.

GVI
1775 K St. N.W., Suite 220, Washington, DC 20006 USA
(202) 293-4488, *Fax:* (202) 293-3293
www.g-v-i.com
Andy Hemmindinger, President
Bob Burnett, Operations Dir
Full creative script-to-screen production, camera crews, Avid editing, DVD authoring & equipment rental.

Halland Broadcast Services
2412 Unity Ave. N. Dept BCY, Minneapolis, MN 55422 USA
(763) 522-6256, *Fax:* (763) 522-6256
www.h-b-s.com
info@radio-mall.com
Dave Dworkin, General Manager
Rock 'n' Roll Graffiti oldies library on compact disc, The Eighties Plus AC/CHR library on compact disc & The Seventies AC/CHR gold library on compact disc. Country music libraries on compact disc. Also available on hard drive.

Hamilton Productions Inc.
7732 Georgetown Pike, McLean, VA 22102 USA
(703) 734-5444, *Fax:* (703) 734-5449
jah@dgsys.net
John Hamilton, President
Anne Deger, Operations Dir
Jay Hamilton, Vice President
Ind TV production firm.

Hanna-Barbera Productions Inc.
15303 Ventura Blvd., Suite 1400, Sherman Oaks, CA 91403 USA
(818) 977-7500, *Fax:* (818) 977-7510
www.hanna-barbera.com
William Hanna, Chairman
William Hanna, Co-Chairman
TV program production.

Happi Associates
Box 110892, Nashville, TN 37222 USA
(615) 220-6050,(615) 604-1981
doddrace@aol.com
Skeeter Dodd, General Manager
Radio program & mgmt; country formats; motivational speaking, jingles ID & coml, production music, features, customized productions.

Harmony Gold U.S.A. Inc.
7655 Sunset Blvd., Los Angeles, CA 90046 USA
(323) 851-4900, *Fax:* (323) 851-5599
www.harmonygold.com
sales@harmonygold.com
Frank Agrama, Chairman
Frank Agrama, CEO
Melissa Wohl, General Sales Mgr
TV production, international TV distribution.

Harpo Productions
110 N. Carpenter St., Chicago, IL 60607 USA
(312) 633-1000
www.oprah.com
Produces The Oprah Winfrey Show.

Harvey Sheldon Productions
7855 E. Horizon View Dr., Anaheim Hills, CA 92808 USA
(714) 281-5929, *Fax:* (714) 281-5929
Harvey Sheldon, President
Daily or wkly classic rock/swing video format for TV & cable stns. On Century Cable available for syndication serving 150,000 TV/cable households in Los Angeles/Orange county.

HAVE Inc.
350 Power Ave., Hudson, NY 12534-2448 USA
(518) 828-2000,(800) 999-4283, *Fax:* (518) 828-2008
www.haveinc.com
have@haveinc.com
Nancy Gordon, President
Paul Swedenburg, Operations Dir
Distribution of cable connected products, equipment, accessories & supplies, featuring BELDEN, CANARE, MOGAMI & GEPCO cable. Duplication, video/audio postproduction svcs & CD-Audio & CD-ROM, DVD & Blu-ray replication & duplication, DVD &Blu-ray authoring. Digital Archiving & file delivery & order fulfillment svcs.
HAVE, Inc.
Lancaster, CA 93536
phone 661-722-2957
email dherrera@haveinc.com

HEA Productions
313 Gahbauer Rd., Hudson, NY 12534 USA
(518) 822-1717, *Fax:* (518) 822-1042
susan@susanhamilton.com
Susan Hamilton, President
Radio & TV music production.

Health Net Productions & Pet Talk
185 N. New Ballas Rd., St. Louis, MO 63141 USA
(314) 997-5422, *Fax:* (314) 997-5422
judyleven@aol.com
Judy Leventhal, President
Chuck LeRoi, Operations Dir
Distributes 90-second pharmacy vignettes, 45 to 60-second pet care vignettes & 90-second sports medicine vignettes.

Hearst Entertainment, Inc.
300 W. 57th St., 15th Fl., New York, NY 10019 USA
(212) 969-7553, *Fax:* (646) 280-1553
www.hearstent.com
Bruce Paisner, President
Stacey Valenza, General Sales Mgr
Leading producer & distributor of made-for-television movies, first-run entertainment, animated series, reality & documentary progmg for the global marketplace.

Hearts of Space Inc.
454 Las Gallinas #333, San Rafael, CA 94903 USA
(415) 499-9901, *Fax:* (415) 499-9903
www.hos.com
help@hos.com
Stephen Hill, President
Leyla Hill, Operations Dir
Slow Music for Fast Times. Syndicated one-hour progmg of ambient, electronic, multi-cultural & contemplative spacemusic via NPR satellite transmission & by direct subscription online at www.hos.com.

Heil Enterprises
Box 1372, Lancaster, PA 17608-1372 USA
(717) 898-9100, *Fax:* (717) 898-6600
www.thegospelgreats.com
radio@thegospelgreats.com
Paul Heil, President
Shelia Heil, General Manager
Radio program (The Gospel Greats)

Henninger Media Services, Inc.
2601-A Wilson Blvd., Arlington, VA 22201 USA
(703) 243-3444,(888) 243-3444, *Fax:* (703) 243-5697,(703) 243-4023
www.henninger.com
Rob Henninger, CEO
TV postproduction, film & video, film processing, 2-D & 3-D graphics, TV progmg dev, distribution; multi-media & DVDs.
Henninger Media Services
1150 17th St, Suite 401, Washington, DC 20036 United States
(202) 833-3444; *Fax:* (202) 833-3995
Robert Anderson, Facility Mgr
Henninger Capitol
2121 Wisconsin Ave. N.W., Washington, DC 20007 United States
(202) 965-7800; *Fax:* (202) 965-7815
Bobby Wright, Gen Mgr
Commonwealth Film Labs
1500 Brook Rd, Richmond, VA 23220 United States
(804) 649-8611; *Fax:* (804) 648-7715
Roger Robison, Gen Mgr
Henninger Elite
Metro Center 50 Vantage Way, Suite 100, Nashville, TN 37228 United States
(615) 256-7678; *Fax:* (615) 255-7212
Roy Giorgio, Gen Mgr
Henninger Richmond
1901 E. Franklin St, Suite 103, Richmond, VA 23223 United States
(804) 644-5006; *Fax:* (804) 783-0820
Scott Witthaus, Gen Mgr

Heritage/Baruch Television Distribution
1025 Connecticut Ave. N.W., Suite 1012, Washington, DC 20036-5417 USA
(202) 833-1777, *Fax:* (202) 496-0162
Ed Baruch, President
Steve Smallwood, Operations Dir
Valerie Cooley-Elliott, Promotions Manager
Mktg, syndication & production/distribution of progmg to network syndication international.

Highland Laboratories
Administration Bldg., Pier 96, San Francisco, CA 94124 USA
(415) 981-5010, *Fax:* (415) 981-5019
www.highlandlab.com
B.J. Brose, President
Video, audio, film duplication, film transfers: D-2, Betacam, 2 inches, 1 inch, 3/4 inch, 1/2 inch.

The History Makers
1900 S. Michigan Ave., Chicago, IL 60616 USA
(312) 674-1900, *Fax:* (312) 674-1915
www.thehistorymakers.com
Video production.

HIT Entertainment P.L.C.
Maple House, 149-150 Tottenham Ct. Rd., 5th Fl., London, W1T 7NF GBR
20-7554-2500, *Fax:* 20-7388-9321
www.hitentertainment.com
contactus@hitentertainment.com
Peter Orton, Chairman
Rob Lawes, CEO
Charles Caminada, General Sales Mgr
Steve Ruffini, CFO
Distributor, co-producer & financier of quality animiation, children's & natural history progmg.
9300 Wilshire Blvd., 2nd Fl., Beverly Hills, CA 90212 United States
(301) 724-8979;
830 Greenville Ave., Allen, TX 7500-3320 United States
(972) 390-6000;

Holigan Investment Group Ltd.
15950 N. Dallas Pkwy., Suite 750, Dallas, TX 75248 USA
(972) 387-7999, *Fax:* (972) 387-1685
www.michael.holigan.com
Michael Holigan, Programming Director
Tim Dickey, Executive Producer
Production & syndication of YOUR NEW HOUSE and THE REALITY OF SPEED; 30 minute TV programs.
6029 Beltline, Suite 110, Dallas, TX 75240 United States

Home Improvement Television Network
3441 Baker St., San Diego, CA 92117
(858) 273-0572, *Fax:* (858) 273-8410
www.hometvnet.com
homefix@hometvnet.com
Bruce Lamb, President
Providers of home improvement progmg & 90-second video vignettes.

Hometown Illinois Radio Network
Box 169, 918 E. Park, Taylorville, IL 62568-0169 USA
(217) 824-3395, *Fax:* (217) 824-3301
www.hometownillinoisradio.com
Randal Miller, President
Wired network providing loc reports & podcasts from Illinois State Fair, Illinois Farm Bureau Convention, Commodity Classic & Farm Progress Show.

Hope Channel
12561 Old Columbia Pike, Silver Spring, MD 20914 USA
(301) 680-6689, *Fax:* (301) 680-6312
www.hopetv.org
info@hopetv.org
Gary Gibbs, Operations Dir
Brad Thorp, General Manager
Family friendly TV progmg, 24/7.

Horizon Audio Creations
Box 486, Hudson Heights, QC J0P 1J0 CAN
(928) 684-1113, *Fax:* (928) 684-1113
reachcraigcutler@mac.com
Craig Cutler, President
Mary-Lou Dodd, Operations Dir
Marguerite Blais, Programming Director
Radio program, coml production; production svcs; inflight audio progmg & adv, feature film & short subject provisioning.

Horizons Television Inc.
9305 Monalaine Ct., Great Falls, VA 22066 USA

(703) 759-7500, *Fax:* (703) 759-1620
www.horizonstv.com
admin@horizonstv.com
Leesa Kelly, President
Timothy Donner, Station Manager
Creative dev & full-svc production of reality-based TV programs & commissioned videos for diverse major & community-based organizations & assns. Avid media composer.

Host Communications Inc.
546 E. Main St., Lexington, KY 40508-2300 USA
(859) 226-4678, *Fax:* (859) 226-4419
www.hostcommunications.com
James Host, CEO
Gordon Whitner, President
TV & radio production & syndication.

Hot Box Digital
367 N. Hwy. 101, Solana Beach, CA 92075 USA
(858) 292-8520, *Fax:* (858) 292-8520
Cam MacMillan, Programming Director
Design & production of bcst 3-D computer graphics. Logo animation, stn packages. All tape formats supported. Productions of Subito Studio Video Graphics Volumes.

Huntridge Video Productions Inc.
Box 3813, Greenville, SC 29608-3813 USA
(864) 271-3348, *Fax:* (864) 232-4462
www.huntridge.com
mat@huntridge.com
TV production & postproduction.

The Idea Channel
2002 Filmore Ave., Suite 1, Erie, PA 16506 USA
(814) 464-9068, *Fax:* (814) 464-9069
www.ideachannel.com
info@ideachannel.com
Bob Chitester, CEO
Rick Platt, Operations Dir
Discussions 20-40 minutes in length, featuring two or three leading scholars on a wide variety of subjects. Internet offerings also.

The Image Generators
18156 Darnell Dr., Olney, MD 20832 USA
(301) 924-5700, *Fax:* (301) 570-8916
www.imagegenerators.com
mweiner@imagegenerators.com
Michael J. Weiner, CEO
Voice-overs, radio spot & program production; media training, progmg concept to completion; ISDN-equipped (TELOS).

Imagers Inc.
1575 Northside Dr., Suite 490, Atlanta, GA 30318 USA
(404) 351-5800, *Fax:* (404) 351-9020
www.imagers.com
TV coml production & distribution; production svcs.

In-Motion Pictures
5 Percy St., London, AL W1T 1DG GBR
(207) 467-6880, *Fax:* (207) 467-6890
www.jment.com
Sales@jment.com
Dr. Hilmar Siebert, Chairman
Julian Freeston, CFO
Film & TV production & distribution.
412 S. Beverly Dr., 5th Fl., Beverly Hills, CA 90212 United States
(301) 789-4500;

Independent Edge Films
719 52nd St. N., St. Petersburg, FL 33710 USA
(727) 321-2898
www.indi-edge.com
michaelfox@indi-edge.com
Michael Fox, General Manager
Ind motion picture/TV/web production & distribution.

Integrity Media
401 E. Corpoorate Dr., #222, Lewisville, TX 75057 USA
(214) 222-7878, *Fax:* (214) 222-7838
schalupka@integritymedia.net
Douglas Neece, President
Sandy Chalupka, Operations Dir
TV & radio program distribution, time buying & media planning.

International Broadcasting Network
Box 691111, 5206 FM 1960 W., Suite 105, Houston, TX 77269 USA
(281) 587-8900, *Fax:* (281) 774-9923
ibn@ev1.net
Paul Broyles, President
Network of ten low power stns; including loc produced progmg.

International Program Consultants Inc.
52 E. End Ave., New York, NY 10028 USA
(212) 734-9096, *Fax:* (212) 734-6495
Russell Kagan, General Manager
International TV distribution, TV progmg & home video acquisition consultation, co-production consultation.

International Tele-Film
41 Horner Ave., Unit #3, Toronto, ON M8Z 4X4 CAN
(416) 252-1173, *Fax:* (416) 252-1676
www.itf.ca
info@itf.ca
Distributor for documentaries, features, series & specials, in Canada & worldwide.

International Television Corp.
4380 N.W. 128th St., Miami, FL 33054 USA
(305) 688-7475, *Fax:* (305) 685-5697
www.coralintl.com
Guadalupe D'Agostino, Operations Dir
Jose Escalante, General Manager
TV progmg distribution & production. Worldwide distribution, co-productions.

International Television Broadcasting Inc.
36-01 36th Ave., 2nd Fl., Long Island City, NY 11106 USA
(718) 784-8555, *Fax:* (718) 784-8901
www.itvgold.com
info@itvgold.com
Dr. Sathya Viswanath, President
Full time Indian TV program for cable & bcst TV.

Ion Weather Network
13 B East Main St., Denville, NJ 7834 USA
(973) 983-8222, *Fax:* (973) 983-1390
www.ionweather.com
steve@ionweather.com
Stephen Pellettiere Sr., President
Stephen Pellettiere Jr., Consultant
Gen weather forecasts, science info.

Irving Productions Inc.
3202 E. 21st, Tulsa, OK 74114 USA
(918) 744-1221, *Fax:* (918) 744-1223
www.irvingproductions.com
irving@irvingproductions.com
Dick Schmitz, President
Audio recording & production svcs for all media.

ISL Television Ltd.
Seymour News House, Seymour News, London, W1H 9PE
(44) 171 616 11 11, *Fax:* (44) 171 616-1110
www.islworld.com
TV program sls & distribution, bcst sponsorship, events & TV program production & TV consultancy.

It Is Written Television
Box O, Thousand Oaks, CA 91360 USA
(805) 955-7733, *Fax:* (805) 955-7734
www.iiw.org
iiw@iiw.org
Mark Finley, General Manager
Shawn Boonstra, Associate Speaker
TV & radio program production & distribution; internet.

Italtoons Corp.
32 W. 40th St., New York, NY 10018 USA
(212) 730-0280, *Fax:* (212) 730-0313
www.italtoons.com
salesinfo@italtoons.com
Giuliana Nicodemi, President
Ken Priester, General Manager
Luisa Rivosecchi, General Sales Mgr
TV program production & distribution. Children's animation.

Ivanhoe Broadcast News Inc.
2745 W. Fairbanks Ave., Winter Park, FL 32789 USA
(407) 740-0789, *Fax:* (407) 740-5320
www.ivanhoe.com
jcherry@ivanhoe.com
Majorie BeKaert Thomas, President
John Cherry, General Sales Mgr
Marsha Hitchcock, News Director
Producer & syndicator of targeted new series. Medical breakthroughs, Inside Science, Prescription Health & Smart Woman.

J&H Music Programming
5814 Fleming Terrace Rd., Greensboro, NC 27410 USA
(336) 218-8052, *Fax:* (336) 218-8052
Joseph Gelo, President
Helen Gelo, Operations Dir
Radio program distribution.

J. Arnold Productions
363 Massachusetts Ave., Lexington, MA 2420 USA
(781) 674-2277, *Fax:* (781) 674-0272
jarpro@aol.com
James Arnold, President
Eric Fisher, Programming Director
Lori Arnold, Production Manager
Full-svc on location video production. ENG-EFP crews & Betacam equipment packages.
147 Cove Creek Rd., Charlotte, NC 28117
(704) 663-4444; *Fax:* (704) 663-6696
James Arnold, Pres

J.N. Productions
902-1790 Bayshore Dr., Vancouver, BC V6G 3G5 Canada
604-331-0690
www.fmaynard.com
info@fmaynard.com
Jakob Nortman, President
Radio & TV engrg svcs & applications.

Jack Hilton Inc.
230 Park Ave., Suite 1530, New York, NY 10169 USA
(212) 687-2002, *Fax:* (212) 697-9008
TV & video productions.

Jack Rourke Productions
Box 1705, Burbank, CA 91507 USA
(818) 843-4839
TV & radio program production.

JAM Creative Productions Inc.
5454 Parkdale Dr., Dallas, TX 75227 USA
(214) 388-5454, *Fax:* (214) 381-4647
www.jingles.com
sales@jingles.com
Jonathan Wolfert, President
Mary Lyn Wolfert, Operations Dir
Cary Bass, General Sales Mgr
Randy Bell, Sales
Tom Parma, Sales
ID jingle & coml production for radio & TV, custom music & production svcs.

Jameson Broadcast Inc.
1644 Hawthorne St., Sarasota, FL 34239 USA
(941) 906-8800, *Fax:* (941) 906-8801
www.jamesonbroadcast.com
radio@jamesonbcast.com
Jamie Jameson, President
Trulee Jameson, Operations Dir
Radio program production, syndication & special projects.

Janson Media
88 Semmens Rd., Harrington Park, NJ 7640 USA
(201) 784-8488, *Fax:* (201) 784-3993
www.janson.com
info@janson.com
Stephen Janson, President
Zara Janson, Operations Dir
Betsy Van Ost, General Manager
Lynne Warshavsky, Director
International TV & video/ DVD program distribution & production; video/DVD publishing.

JC Productions Inc.
1851 Murray Hill Station, New York, NY 10016 USA
(212) 213-0455, *Fax:* (212) 532-2820
www.jc-productions.com
jcpro@bellatlantic.net
Joe Conforti, General Manager
Live action coml production; CD-ROM multimedia production; 3D animation & graphic design.

Jeff Davis Productions Inc.
6166 Mulholland Hwy., Los Angeles, CA 90068 USA
(323) 464-3500, *Fax:* (323) 464-1414
www.jeffdavis.com
jeffdavies@jeffdavies.com
Jeff Davies, CEO
Voiceover, production, TV & radio.

Jeff Gold Productions Inc.
13900 Panay Way, Marina del Rey, CA 90292 USA
(310) 827-9165
Jeff Gold, General Manager

JGT Media Productions
12408 86th Pl., N.E., Kirkland, WA 98034-2601 USA
(425) 820-4523, *Fax:* (425) 820-4523

PROGRAMMING & PRODUCTION SERVICES

TV program, promotion film production & distribution; production svcs; rgnl award program, ARBY Awards; film & video production.

Jim Owens Entertainment
624 Grassmere Park, Suite 16, Nashville, TN 37211 USA
(615) 256-7700, *Fax:* (615) 242-9735
www.crookandchase.com
Jim Owens, President
Jennifer Anderson, Programming Director
Radio program production company for syndication. TV production for cable & home video.

Joe Jones Productions
10556 Arnwood Rd., Lake View Terrace, CA 91342 USA
(818) 899-4457, *Fax:* (818) 899-4457
jojones@jojonesnetcom.com
Marion Jones, Operations Dir
Joe Jones, Programming Director
TV, radio coml & program production; jingle production & production svcs.

John Driscoll/VoiceOver America
PO box 1996, Studio City, CA 91614 USA
(888) 766-2049,(818-373-9849)
www.johndriscoll.com
johndriscoll@voiceoveramerica.com
John Moore, CEO
Voice Over America, as heard on TNT,VH-1,NBC-TV,FOX-TV ,Spike TV,NBA,NFL,MLB and NHL affiliates. Comcast ,HBO/Cinemax, Global,Corus,Rogers,RTE, CBC, CTV. Direct TV.
Represented by AT&A
(818) 760-6688;

John Lemmon Films
1325 Rock Point Rd., Charlotte, NC 28270 USA
(704) 532-1944, *Fax:* (704) 566-1984
www.jlf.com
jlemmon@jlf.com
John Lemmon, President
Mike Rosinski, Head Animator
Clay, cel & stop-motion animation for TV specials, comls, program openings & on-air IDs.

The Johnson Group
6800 Fleetwood Rd, Suite 100, McLean, VA 22101 USA
(703) 356-4004, *Fax:* (703) 356-6969
www.thejgroup.com
rmjcameron@aol.com
Robert Johnson, President
Joe Fab, Operations Dir
Video, film, multimedia & radio creative svcs & production.

Jordan Klein Film & Video
10197 S.E. 144th Pl., Summerfield, FL 34491 USA
(352) 288-3999, *Fax:* (352) 288-5538
www.jordy.com
jkfv01@gate.net,jordy@jordy.com
Jordan Klein, President
Underwater, on-the-water production; rental film, video housing & crews; Bahamas specialist.

Juravic Entertainment
620 Glenridge Dr., Glenview, IL 60025 USA
(847) 998-5998, *Fax:* (847) 998-6013
dljuravic@aol.com
TV program syndication.

The Kay Arnold Group
34 Kramer Dr., Paramus, NJ 7652 USA
(201) 652-6037, *Fax:* (201) 612-8578
Kay Arnold, President
Production & distribution of film & tape programs for TV, satellite, cable, home video & non-theatrical.

Kazmark Entertainment Group
14320 Ventura Blvd., Suite 601, Sherman Oaks, CA 91423 USA
(818) 981-4410, *Fax:* (818) 501-2211
jkazmark@earthlink.net
Jeffrey Kazmark, President
Progmg distribution.

KCRA-TV
3 Television Cir., Sacramento, CA 95814-0794 USA
(916) 446-3333, *Fax:* (916) 325-3731
www.thekcrachannel.com
Elliott Troshinsky, General Manager
TV program & coml production; production svcs.

KCSN 88.5 FM
California State University, Northridge, 18111 Nordhoff St., Northridge, CA 91330-8312 USA
(818) 677-3090
www.kcsn.org
frederick.d.johnson@csun.edu
Fred Johnson, General Manager
Laura Kelly, General Sales Mgr
Martin Perlich, Programming Director
Keith Goldstein, News Director
Michael Worrall, Chief Engineer
Public radio serving parts of Los Angeles, CAclassical weekdays, eclectic weeknights & weekends. PRI, AP affil. The best of public radio.

The Kenwood Group
75 Varney Pl., San Francisco, CA 94107-1922 USA
(415) 957-5333, *Fax:* (415) 957-5311
www.kenwoodgroup.com
Christina Crowley, President
Creative svcs & production of comls & corporate communications, film, video, multimedia, meetings & events.

Killer Tracks
8750 Wilshire Blvd., FL 2, Beverly Hills, CA 90211-2715 USA
(323) 957-4455, *Fax:* (323) 957-4470
www.killertracks.com
sales@killertracks.com
Provides production music library & sound effects.

Kipany Productions Ltd.
32 E. 39th St., New York, NY 10016 USA
(212) 883-8300, *Fax:* (212) 883-0409
share82308@aol.com
K. Colligan, CEO
T. Hendry, President
Video production, bcst progmg, mktg, sls & communications experts/web designers specializing in Telcom, event mgmt.

KJD Teleproductions
30 Whyte Dr., Voorhees, NJ 8043 USA
(856) 751-3500, *Fax:* (856) 751-7729
www.kjdteleproductions.com
mactoday@earthlink.net
Larry Scott, CEO
TV, radio program, coml, promotion film production & distribution; production svcs; TV processing lab.

Klein &
20530 Pacific Coast Hwy., Malibu, CA 90265 USA
(310) 317-9599, *Fax:* (310) 456-7701
www.kleinand.com
imagedoctor@kleinand.com
Bob Klein, President
Mktg consulting, creative svcs for bcst, cable & Internet companies.

Knowledge In A Nutshell Inc.
1420 Centre Ave., Suite 2213, Pittsburgh, PA 15219 USA
(800) 688-7435,(412) 765-2020, *Fax:* (412) 765-3672
www.knowledgeinanutshell.com
audrey@knowledgeinanutshell.com
Charles Reichblum, President
Syndicates radio/TV program, Knowledge in a Nutshell & Knowledge minute.

KPTS-TV
320 West 21st St. N., Wichita, KS 67203-2499 USA
(316) 838-3090, *Fax:* (316) 838-8586
www.kpts.org
dchecots@kpts.org
Dave McClintock, Operations Dir
Don Checots, General Manager
Industrial video production for corporate training & mktg communications.

KTOO-TV & Radio Station
360 Egan Dr., Juneau, AK 99801 USA
(907) 586-1670, *Fax:* (907) 586-3612
www.ktoo.org
info@ktoo.org
Jeff Brown, General Manager
A radio program highlighting diversified music & stories for children.

Kultur International Films
195 Hwy. 36, West Long Branch, NJ 7764 USA
(732) 229-2343, *Fax:* (732) 229-0066
www.kultur.com
info@kultur.com
Dennis Hedlund, Chairman
Pearl Lee, Operations Dir
Ronald Davis, General Manager
Suppliers of programs on DVD in North America. Selection includes documentaries, opera, ballet, classical music, profiles, theater, comedy, fitness, country music, rock & roll.

KUSA Television
500 Speer Blvd., Denver, CO 80203 USA
(303) 871-9999, *Fax:* (303) 698-4700
www.9news.com
kusa@9news.com
Asa Darrow, Programming Director
News production only.

Lakeside TV Co.
300 Highpoint Dr., Suite 712, Hartsdale, NY 10530 USA
(914) 946-7806, *Fax:* (914) 946-7806 (fax/phone)
bernshu@msn.com
Bernard Schulman, President
Diane Ross, Operations Dir
TV program distribution, production & syndication.

Lambert Television
100 N. Crescent Dr., 2nd Flr., Beverly Hills, CA 90210 USA
(310) 385-4288, *Fax:* (310) 385-4004
www.lamberttv.com
jones@lamberttv.com
Michael Jones, President
Sam Englebardt, Operations Dir
Lambert Television owns and operates a television station group.

Lapco Communications
437 E. Beil Ave., Nazareth, PA 18064 USA
(610) 759-9444, *Fax:* (610) 759-8589
www.lapcocom.com,www.visualpizzazz.com
sales@lapcocom.com
P. Pagilaro, President
L. Van Winkle, Operations Dir
TV progmg & production, computer graphics, producers of original progmg, TV comls, TV promotion production, production mgmt, computer stock background library.

Larry Harmon Pictures Corp.
7080 Hollywood Blvd., Suite 202, Hollywood, CA 90028 USA
(323) 463-2331, *Fax:* (323) 463-7219
www.bozo.com
tellbozo@aol.com
Larry Harmon, President
Marci Breth, Operations Dir
Susan Harmon, Executive Vice President
Owner & distributor of Bozo cartoons & live show franchise, & Laurel & Hardy cartoons.

Larry John Wright Inc.
1045 E. University Dr., Suite 1, Mesa, AZ 85203 USA
(480) 833-8111, *Fax:* (480) 969-2895
www.larryjohnwright.com
jessica@LarryJohnWright.com
Larry F. John, CEO
John N. Wright, President
Own & operate production studios; produce film & video comls, radio comls & jingles, TV shows & industrial videos.

Launch Radio Networks
Div/DBA: (a division of United Stations Radio Network)
1065 Ave. of the Americas, 3rd Fl., New York, NY 10018
(212) 536-3600, *Fax:* (212) 536-3601
www.launchradionetworks.com
ccolombo@launchradionetworks.com
Dave Ankers, Operations Dir
Charlie Colombo, General Manager
Launch Radio Networks produces, distributes music, entertainment news & svcs for radio stns as well as other media worldwide.

Leadem to Water Production Inc.
Box 279, Oregon City, OR 97045 USA
(503) 631-7661, *Fax:* (503) 631-7672
www.horsemansworld.com
info@horsemansworld.com
Produces syndicated radio show Horseman's World, coml video narrations, produces World bcst for A.Q.H.A. on 250 + stn, cable TV houses northwest & cowboy cooking.

Leo Productions
1 Rond Point Victor Hugo, 92130-Issy-Les-Moulineaux, FRA
(331) 55 95 57 00, *Fax:* (331) 55 95 57 01
www.leoproductions.com
leo@leoproductions.com
Jean-Louis Brugat, General Manager
TV production, progmg consultants, live bcsts.

Leukemia & Lymphoma Society
1311 Mamaroneck Ave., White Plains, NY 10605 USA

PROGRAMMING & PRODUCTION SERVICES

(914) 949-5213, *Fax:* (914) 949-6691
www.leukemia-lymphoma.org
lanereg@lls.org
Geralyn Laneve, Operations Dir
Nancy Klein, Promotions Manager
Produces & distributes educational ideas to inform & educate viewers about leukemia & related diseases & available treatment.

Liberty Studios Inc.
238 E. 26th St., New York, NY 10010 USA
(212) 532-1865, *Fax:* (212) 779-2207
email@libertystudios.us
Anthony Lover, President
John Sawyer, Operations Dir
TV program, coml, film & video production.

Lifestyle Magazine/The Evidence
101 W. Cochran St., Simi Valley, CA 93065 USA
(805) 955-7606, *Fax:* (805) 522-1082
www.faithfortoday.tv,www.theevidence.tv,www.lifestyle.org
info@faithfortoday.tv
Michael Tucker, Chief Engineer
TV program production & distribution.

Lightbridge Production & Distribution
1051 Broadway, Sonoma, CA 95476 USA
(707) 939-4920, *Fax:* (707) 939-4919
Roy Walkenhorst, CEO
Judy Brooks, President
TV & video progmg.

Lighthouse Productions
118 S. Main St., Goshen, AL 46526
(574) 533-1400, *Fax:* (661) 760-8775
www.audicolabels.com
audicolabels@audicolabels.com
Bill Landow, President
Audio, video full production svc, documentaries, training, audio & video recording svcs.

Lightyear Entertainment L.P.
434 Ave of the Americas, 6th flr., New York, NY 10111 USA
(212) 353-5084, *Fax:* (212) 353-5083
www.lightyear.com
mail@lightyear.com
Arnold Holland, CEO
TV program production & distribution. Audio & video distribution.

Limelight Communications Inc.
2812 Roesh Way, Vienna, VA 22181 USA
(703) 242-4596, *Fax:* (703) 991-0616
www.limelightdc.com
moreinfo@limelightdc.com
Kenneth Reff, President
Writing, producing & editing svcs for bcst & industrial clients. Available as sub-contractors for specific svcs, or to fully produce complete shows.

Lindberg Productions Inc.
24 Mulford Ave., East Hampton, NY 11937 USA
(212) 599-1239,(917) 696-1826
ctimany@aol.com
Larry Lindberg, President
Erika Shapeero, Programming Director
Video production for business & industry.

Lion and Fox Recording Studios
9517 Baltimore Ave., College Park, MD 20740-1321 USA
(301) 982-4431
www.lionfox.com
mail@lionfox.com
James Fox, President
Digital audio production for TV & radio; music & EFX libraries; CD and CD-ROM & cassette duplication; location audio.

Lions Gate Entertainment
2700 Colorado Ave., Suite 200, Santa Monica, CA 90404 USA
(310) 449-9200, *Fax:* (310) 392-0252
www.lionsgatefilms.com
Don Feltheimer, CEO
Domestic & international TV, film, video distribution & adv sls firm. Builds, manages, invests in domestic & foreign bcst networks.

Litton Entertainment
884 Allbritton Blvd., Suite 200, Mount Pleasant, SC 29464 USA
(843) 883-5060, *Fax:* (843) 883-9957
www.litton.tv
sara@litton.tv
David Morgan, CEO
TV distribution (TV program sls & mktg).

Lon Gibby Productions, Inc./ Gibby Media Group
1213 S Pines Rd., Ste C, Spokane Valley, WA 99206-5485 USA
(509) 467-1113,(800) 200-1113, *Fax:* (509) 467-4763
www.longibby.com
lon@longibby.com
Lon Gibby, CEO
Multimedia productions, video, CD-Rom, CD-I, producers of bcst TV programs, comls, infomercials, corporate videos & webcasting

London Weekend Television International
South Bank TV Ctr., Upper ground, London, SE1 9LT GBR
(020) 7620-1620
www.lwt.co.uk
images@lwt.co.uk
Steve Morrison, Operations Dir
Charles Allen, General Manager
TV program production & distribution.
500 Fifth Ave, Suite 1710, New York, NY 10110 United States
(212) 682-3055; *Fax:* (212) 869-3693
Ellis Bell, Cpa

Longhorn Radio Network
1 University Station, (A0704) University of Texas, Austin, TX 78712-1090 USA
(512) 471-1631, *Fax:* (512) 471-3700
www.kut.org
J. Stewart Vanderwilt, General Manager
Hawk Mendenhall, Programming Director

Loral Skynet
2440 Research Blvd. #200, Rockville, MD 20850 USA
(301) 258-8101, *Fax:* (301) 258-8119
www.loralskynet.com
Terry Hart, CEO
Gayle Armstrong, Operations Dir
International satellite communications company that leases capacity for video transmissions for TV & other program distributors. Also provides Internet access & private net svcs directly to Internet Service Providers & multinationalbusinesses worldwide. Svcs include data networking, voice, video, teleconferencing & news distribution to multiple points worldwide.
Loral Cyberstar-Europe
Inc. 131-151 Great Titchfield St, London W1P 8AE,
+44 171 892 3700;

M C Stuart & Associates Pty Ltd.
2/34 Power St., Balwyn Victoria, AL 3103 AUS
61 3 9888 5830,61 409 885 831 (mobile), *Fax:* 61 3 9888 5831
maxstuart@ecomtel.com.au
Max Stuart, General Manager
Worldwide TV & feature film distributors.

MacNeil/Lehrer Productions
2700 S. Quincy St., Suite 250, Arlington, VA 22206 USA
(703) 998-2170, *Fax:* (703) 998-5707
www.pbs.org/newshour
pbs@newshour.org
Dan Werner, President
David Sit, Operations Dir
Pam Wyatt, General Manager
Susan Mills, Programming Director
Harold Crawford, Controller
Produces news & info programs for public TV & other coml & cable networks. Production of The News Hour with Jim Lehrer.

Madison Square Garden Network
4 Penn Plaza, 4th Floor, New York, NY 10001 USA
(212) 465-5926, *Fax:* (212) 465-6024
www.msgnetwork.com
msgnetpr@thegarden.com
Mike McCarthy, President
Neil Davis, General Sales Mgr
Leon Schwier, Programming Director
NY Knicks, NY Rangers & NY Mets, NY MetroStars, NY Power, NY Islanders & NY Liberty; boxing, college football & basketball; exclusive Garden events; original series.

Magno Sound & Video
729 7th Ave., New York, NY 10019 USA
(212) 302-2505, *Fax:* (212) 819-1282
www.magnosound.com
david@magnosound.com
Robert Friedman, President
David Friedman, Operations Dir
Complete film, TV & radio production & postproduction svcs for agency, feature, network, corporate & industrial clients.

Make It Happen Productions Inc.
5925 Troost Ave., No. Hollywood, CA 91601 USA
(323) 851-6444, *Fax:* (323) 851-6465
bfrank@mihpitv
Billy Frank, President
Ind & co-productions, dev of projects, package projects, production svcs, post production.

Makedwde Publishing
10556 Arnwood Rd., Lake View Terrace, CA 91342 USA
(818) 899-4457, *Fax:* (818) 890-4050
mjones@verizon.com
Music publishing.

Man From Mars Productions
159 Orange St., Manchester, NH 03104-4217 USA
(603) 668-0652, *Fax:* (603) 666-4878
www.manfrommars.com
brouder@juno.com
Ed Brouder, President
Aircheck sls for radio collectors; coml production.

MAN QC Creations
123 E. Dania Beach Blvd., Dania, FL 33004 USA
(954) 921-1111

Manhattan Production Music
355 W. 52nd St., 6th Fl., New York, NY 10019 USA
(212) 333-5766,(800) 227-1954, *Fax:* (212) 262-0814
www.mpmmusic.com
info@mpmmusic.com
Norman Chesky, President
Five music libraries Apple Trax, Live Trax, MPM, AMM, BRg containing over 450 CDs, including the Audiophile Sound effects series & the Chesky Classical Library.

Manhattan Transfer Miami
2850 Tiger Tail, Coconut Grove, FL 33133 USA
(800) 826-8864,(305) 857-0350, *Fax:* (305) 857-0175
www.bvinet.com
George O'Neil, Operations Dir
Full-svc video post-production including film transfer, on-line, off-line editing, audio, graphics, progmg, voice dubbing translation, sound stage & new media dev.
2028 N.E. 15th Ct., Miami, FL 33179 United States
(305) 652-5762;

Mar Vista Entertainment
12519 Venice Blvd., Los Angeles, CA 90066 USA
(310) 737-0950, *Fax:* (310) 737-9115
www.marvista.com
info@marvista.net
Ferdando Szew, COO
George Port, President
Joseph Szew, CEO
Michael Jacobs, President
Domestic & international distribution of children's animation & live action features & series, films & documentaries.
310 Grant Street, Suite 711, Pittsburgh, PA 15219

Marathon International
74 rue Bonaparte, 75006 Paris,
331-53-1091-00, *Fax:* 331-43-2504-66
www.marathon.fr
marathon@marathon.fr
Distributor of TV programs worldwide; series, documentaries, animation, wildlife, TV movies.

Marie Hoy Film & TV
18 Bruton Pl. Berkeley Sq., Mayfair, London, W1X 7AA
020-7851-6666, *Fax:* 017-1493-3997
mariehoy@cocoon.co.uk
Co-production Funding & Financial Packaging.

Mark Druck Productions Inc.
300 E. 40th St., New York, NY 10016 USA
(212) 682-5980, *Fax:* (212) 682-5981
markdruck@aol.com
Mark Druck, President
Lisa Dodenhoff, Programming Director
TV & video tape industrial progmg, prom film production & distribution.

Marty Stouffer Productions Ltd.
44190 Hwy. 82 E., Aspen, CO 81611 USA
(970) 925-5536, *Fax:* (970) 920-3820
mary@stoufferoffice.com
TV program production.

Maryknoll Productions
75 Ryder Rd., Maryknoll, NY 10545-0308 USA
Fax: (914) 762-6567
www.maryknollmall.org
nkeel@maryknoll.com

PROGRAMMING & PRODUCTION SERVICES

Lawrence M. Rich, Programming Director
Offers a library of video & film productions featuring Third World countries; radio & TV programs also available.

Maryland Public Television
11767 Owings Mills Blvd., Owings Mills, MD 21117 USA
(410) 356-5600, *Fax:* (410) 581-4338
www.mpt.org
Robert Shuman, CEO
Larry Unger, President
Eric Eggleton, Operations Dir
TV program production & distribution.

Masai Films Inc.
6922 Hollywood Blvd., Suite 401, Hollywood, CA 90028 USA
(323) 466-5451, *Fax:* (323) 466-2440
TV & radio program & coml producers; production svcs.

Maslow Media Group Inc.
2233 Wisconsin Ave. N.W., Suite 400, Washington, DC 20007-4104 USA
(202) 965-1100, *Fax:* (202) 965-6171
www.maslowmedia.com
cneubecker@lmaslowmedia.com
Linda Maslow, CEO
Video production, production support svcs, staffing (freelance & fulltime), factors, creative & tech people, camera crews anywhere in the world, cable, film, multimedia, animators, payroll & paymaster svcs nationwide for bcst studio, field &new media.

Mason Video
9632 N. 34th St., Omaha, NE 68112 USA
(402) 455-9422, *Fax:* (402) 455-0707
www.masonvideo.com
melemason@aol.com
Mele Mason, President
Offers bcst video productions. Equipment includes Ikigami HLV55 Betacam, DVcam & HDV.

MasterControl FamilyNet Radio
6350 W. Freeway, Fort Worth, TX 76116 USA
(817) 570-1400, *Fax:* (817) 737-9436
www.familynetradio.com
lbratton@familynet.com,lbratton@familynet.com,dsenn@familynetradio.com
Chuck Ries, Programming Director
Donna Senn, Promotions Manager
Lisa Young, Radio Marketing & Dist.
Total health program featuring interviews with experts on physical, mental, financial, and spiritual health, hosts Ralph Baker & Terri Barrett.

Matchframe Video
610 N. Hollywood Way, Suite 101, Burbank, CA 91505 USA
(818) 840-6800, *Fax:* (818) 840-2726
George Francisco, CEO
Pam Hollander, President
Michael Levy, Operations Dir
Rand Gladden, President
In-house editing suites; audio sweetening; portable on-line/off-line (AVID/HD and SD) editing systems; graphics; telecine; tape to tape color connection.

Maximum Marketing Services Inc.
833 W. Jackson, Ste 300, Chicago, IL 60607 USA
(312) 226-4111, *Fax:* (312) 226-5765
www.maxmarketing.com
John McGowan, President
TV & radio program, production & distribution; public relation services.

Maysles Films, Inc.
250 W. 54th St., New York, NY 10019 USA
(212) 582-6050, *Fax:* (212) 586-2057
www.mayslesfilms.com
info@mayslesfilms.com
Albert Maysles, President
Full production svcs for theatrical & TV non-fiction films; adv comls; industrial films, including pre- & postproduction.

McClain Enterprises Inc.
4405-B Belmont Park Terrace, Nashville, TN 37215-3609 USA
(615) 269-6517, *Fax:* (615) 269-6648
www.mcclaintv.com
carolyn@mcclaintv.com
Carolyn McClain, President
Custom & syndicated TV mktg for radio, sls consulting, sls & promotional projects for radio & TV stns.

Media Access Group at WGBH
One Guest St., Boston, MA 2135 USA
(617) 300-3600, *Fax:* (617) 300-1020
access.wgbh.org
access@wgbh.org
Larry Goldberg, General Manager
Provides real-time & off-line captioning, subtitling, descriptive narration & consulting.
Media Access Group West
300 E. Magnolia Blvd., 2nd Fl., Burbank, CA 91502 United States
(818) 562-3344;

The Media Group of Connecticut Inc.
17 Maple St., Weston, CT 06883-1026 USA
(203) 544-0018
mediagr@aol.com
Harvey Bellin, President
TV, video production, writing, directing & editing; digital animation; dramatization & documentary; TV, corporate & govt svcs offered.

Media Planning Group (MPG)
195 Broadway, 12th Fl., New York, NY 10007 USA
(646) 587-5000, *Fax:* (646) 587-5005
www.mpgsite.com
Bob Riordan, General Manager
Producers, distributors & TV program packagers; videocassette producer/distributor. Full svc media buying & planning company.

Media Visions
8430 Terminal Rd., Newington, VA 22079 USA
(703) 550-1500,(800) 628-3556, *Fax:* (703) 550-9711
www.mediavisions.net
mrock@mediavisions.net
Provides full-svc video duplication, packaging, warehousing & complete order fulfillment. CD, DVD.

Medialink
708 3rd Ave., 8th Fl., New York, NY 10017 USA
(212) 682-8300, *Fax:* (212) 682-2370
www.medialink.com
mwallace@medialink.com
Mary Buhay, Operations Dir
Monica Jennings, Senior VP
Video & audio news release distributor & producer to TV & radio stns throughout the United States & Europe.

MediaTracks Inc.
2250 E. Devon Ave., Suite 150, Des Plaines, IL 60018-4507 USA
(847) 299-9500, *Fax:* (847) 299-9501
www.mediatracks.com
slustig@mediatracks.com
Shel Lustig, President
Reed Pence, Operations Dir
Produce, syndicate & distribute radio progmg, news, comls & PSAs. Specialists in health & medicine, news & pub affrs.

Megatrax Production Music Inc.
7629 Fulton Ave., North Hollywood, CA 91605 USA
(818) 255-7100,(888) 634-2555, *Fax:* (818) 255-7199
www.megatrax.com
megatrax@megatrax.com
John Dwyer, President
Ron Mendelsohn, Owner
Production music for bcst promotion & adv. Custom scoring & news music packages available.

Message on Hold
Box 747, Hendersonville, NC 28793-0747 USA
(828) 692-7200,(800) 223-1930, *Fax:* (828) 692-9147
molton.ad@bellsouth.net
J. Ellis Molton, President
Randy Molton, Operations Dir
Producers of high-quality comls for telephone hold lines. Specializing in automotive, financial, medical & pharmacies.

Metro Music Productions Inc.
37 W. 20th St., Suite 906, New York, NY 10011 USA
(212) 229-1700,(800) 697-7392, *Fax:* (212) 229-9063
www.metromusicinc.com
info@metromusicinc.com
Mitch Coodley, President
Katrina Haskell, General Manager
Original music scoring for TV progmg, prom, news, sports, comls. Production music library geared toward bcst.

Metro Networks
300 Bridge St., New Cumberland, PA 17070 USA
(717) 774-8150, *Fax:* (717) 774-8160
www.metronetworks.com
elaine.konkle@metronetworks.com
Elaine Konkle, General Manager
TV & radio net; radio production/distribution.

Metro Weather Service Inc.
132 Franklin Place, Suite 385, Woodmere, NY 11598 USA
(516) 568-8844,(800) 488-7866, *Fax:* (516) 568-8853
www.metrowx.com
metrowx@aol.com
Pat Pagano, President
Provides accurate & understandable weather forecasts. Serves any part of the nation; live consultations.

MG/Perin Inc.
110 Green St. Suite 304, New York, NY 10012 USA
(212) 941-9750, *Fax:* (212) 941-9122
mgperin@aol.com
Richard Perin, President
TV program production & distribution.

MGC The Multimedia Group of Canada
415-A Mount Pleasant, Montreal Westmount, QC H3Y 3G9 CAN
(514) 844-3636, *Fax:* (514) 844-4990
www.the-mgc.com
mgc@the-mgc.com
Jacques Bouchard, CEO
David Seeler, General Sales Mgr
Roselyne Brovillet, Sales
Participates in the dev & distribution of progmg in the intl mkt.

MGM Inc.
2500 Broadway, Santa Monica, CA 90404 USA
(310) 449-3000, *Fax:* (310) 264-1244
www.mgm.com
TV program distribution.

MGM TV Canada
20 Queen St. West #3500, Toronto, ON H5H 3R3 CAN
(416) 260-9680, *Fax:* (416) 260-9993
www.mgm.com
Film distribution for all UA, Polygram & Orion film library (features, series & animated).

Midwest Video Communications Inc.
Box 11627, Omaha, NE 68111 USA
(402) 991-2981, *Fax:* (402) 933-8990
midwestvideo@msn.com
John S. Turner, President
Artes Johnson, General Manager
John Lott, Programming Director
TV program & distribution; coml production, satellite teleconference productions; business & promotion film productions; production svcs, TV news features production.

Miller Broadcast Management
616 W. Fulton St., Suite 516, Chicago, IL 60661 USA
(312) 454-1111, *Fax:* (312) 454-0044
www.millerbroadcast.com
info@millerbroadcast.com
Lisa Miller, President
Matt Miller, Operations Dir
Produces & syndicates natl progmg including KidsRadio.

Miss Universe, L.P.
4111 W. Alameda, Suite 605, Burbank, CA 91505 USA
(818) 972-9202, *Fax:* (818) 972-9001
www.missuniverse.com
Paula M. Shugart, President
Tony Santomauro, Operations Dir
TV program production.

Mobile Video Services Ltd.
1620 I St. N.W., Washington, DC 20006 USA
(202) 331-8882, *Fax:* (202) 331-9064
www.mobilevideo.net
bookfeed@mobilevideo.net
Lawrence VanderVeen, President
Christine Baber, Operations Dir
Bcst production svcs, best Official Washington, live shot, remote crews, studio svcs, editing, graphics suites, satellite & fiber transmission svcs.

Modern Entertainment
Box 8075, Van Nuys, CA 91409-8075 USA
(818) 386-0444, *Fax:* (818) 728-3677
Michael Weiser, CEO
Allyson Hall, Operations Dir
Ken Du Bow, General Sales Mgr
Distribution of movies world wide, CD, DVD.

Modern Sound Pictures Inc.
1402 Howard St., Omaha, NE 68102 USA
(402) 341-8476, *Fax:* (402) 341-8487
www.modernsoundpictures.com
mspi1@att.net
Sandra L. Smith, President

Non-theatrical 16mm film, video rental library & retail audiovisual equipment for rental & sls.

Molton Advertising Inc.
Box 747, Hendersonville, NC 28793-0747 USA
(828) 692-7200,(800) 223-1930, *Fax:* (828) 692-9147
www.moltonad.com
molton@bellsouth.net
Ellis Molton, President
Randy Molton, Operations Dir
Syndicated radio & nwspr series for loc use.

Mondo TV
Via G. Gatti 8/A, 00162 Rome, ITA
39-6-86320364,39-06-86323293, *Fax:* 39-06-86209836
mondotv@mondotv.it
Orlando Corradi, CEO
Gian Claudio Galatoli, General Manager
Roberto Farina, Head of International Sales
Animated TV series.

Montgomery Community Television Inc.
7548 Standish Pl., Rockville, MD 20855 USA
(301) 424-1730, *Fax:* (301) 294-7476
www.montgomerycommunitytv.com
Don Katzen, Promotions Manager
Full-svc video production & postproduction, 2,400 sq ft. studio including complete control room, GVG200 switcher, DVE, on- & off-line editing. Also, opn of two cable chs reaching 220,000 subs.

Moody Radio
820 N. LaSalle Blvd., Chicago, IL 60610-3284 USA
(312) 329-4433,(800) 621-7031, *Fax:* (312) 329-4339
www.moodyradio.org
moodyradio@moody.com
Scott Krus, General Manager
Denny Nugent, Programming Director
Radio program production, full-svc relg digital stereo audio progmg via, satellite internet file download & syndicated tape distribution & ACCUWatch radio transmitter monitoring.

Moonstone Entertainment
Box 7400, Studio City, CA 91614-7400 USA
(818) 985-3003, *Fax:* (818) 985-3009
www.moonstonefilms.com
Ernst 'Etchie' Stroh, CEO
Luz Moretti, President
Michael Grant, Station Manager
Shahar Stroh, Chief Engineer
Yael Stroh, President
Greg Majerus, Vice President
International distribution and production.

MotorNet
Box 69, Farmingdale, NJ 07727-0069 USA
(732) 751-1020, *Fax:* (732) 751-1038
www.motorsportsreport.com
motornet@iop.com
Charlie Roberts, President
Ken Stout, Programming Director
Jack Schultz, Promotions Manager
Radio program production & distribution.

Mountain News Corporation
50 Vashell Way, Suite 200, Orinda, CA 94563-3020 USA
(925) 254-4456, *Fax:* (925) 254-7923
www.theamigroup.com
admin@aminews.com
Rob Brown, President
Chad Dyen, Operations Dir
Produce & package outdoor recreation reports of 30, 60 & 90-seconds in length. Also deliver ski reports via phone, computer, facsimilie for on-air, phone lines & web sites.
Eastern Bureau
(800) 736-0370;

MPL Media
621 Mainstream Dr., Ste 260, Nashville, TN 37228 USA
(615) 256-1675, *Fax:* (615) 256-0757
www.mplmedia.com
daviddeeb@mplmedia.com
Peggy Shedlock, Operations Dir
David Deeb, Promotions Manager
16/35 color negative processing, rank cintel & ursagold transfer, video edit, graphics, DVD authoring & fulfillment, HD video editing.

MRC Films
Box 697, Plainview, NY 11803 USA
(516) 796-7568
jlmollot3@verizon.net
Larry Mollot, Programming Director
Producers of original progmg for bcst, cablecast, TV comls & PSAs.

MRN Radio
1801 International Speedway Blvd., Daytona Beach, FL 32114 USA
(386) 947-6400, *Fax:* (386) 947-6716
www.mrnradio.com
David Hyatt, General Manager
Steve Harrison, General Sales Mgr
Cheryl Knight, Director Affiliates
Live coverage of NASCAR stock car racing plus NASCAR LIVE wkly telephone talk, NASCAR Today daily news program, via satellite.

MSE
540 Toby Hill Rd., Westbrook, CT 6498 USA
(860) 399-0191, *Fax:* (860) 399-0196
www.mseusa.com
marcia@mseusa.com
Marcia Simon, President
Short form programs: Health/Medical, Green/Eco-Friendly, podcast production

MTI The Image Group
885 2nd Ave., Level C, New York, NY 10017 USA
(212) 548-7700, *Fax:* (212) 759-7465
www.image-group.com
jromano@image-group.com
Nine studios, 25 Digital online suites, 10 Avids, four infernos, 63 D platforms, NIT/MAC platforms, URSA Diamond/c-Reality, Digital Sound mixing Duplication.
727 11th Ave, New York, NY 10019 United States
(212) 649-6333;
Jerry Romano, Dir Business Dev
401 Fifth Ave., New York, NY 10016 United States
(212) 592-0600;

MTM Entertainment Inc.
12700 Ventura Blvd., Studio City, CA 91604 USA
(818) 755-2400
TV program production & distribution.

Munhwa Broadcasting Corp. (MBC)
National Press Bldg., Suite 1131, Washington, DC 20045 USA
(202) 347-0078, *Fax:* (202) 347-0079
www.imbc.com
mgchoi@imbc.com
Chang-Young Choi, Station Manager
Korean natl TV net news.

Munz
2470 W. 8th Ave., Hialeah, FL 33010 USA
(305) 884-8200, *Fax:* (305) 889-7212
www.mun2television.com
Don Browne, COO
Maria Acosta, Operations Dir
Joe Bernard, General Sales Mgr
Yolanda Foster, Programming Director
Laura Dergal, Promotions Manager
Tracy McDonough, Director, Business Operations
Alvaro Krupkin, Director, CreativeServices
English language cable network targeting young U.S. Hispanics.

Musical Starstreams
Box 12685, La Jolla, CA 92039-2685 USA
(619) 276-8989
www.starstreams.com
forest@starstreams.com
Two-hour wkly or nightly syndicated exotic electronica music progmg also available as a full-time format; radio adv production.

Musivision Inc.
185 E. 85th St., New York, NY 10028 USA
(212) 860-4420

Muzak
3318 Lakemont Blvd., Fort Mill, SC 29708 USA
(803) 396-3000,(800) 331-3340, *Fax:* (803) 396-3136
www.muzak.com
feedback@muzak.com
Bill Boyd, CEO
Bcsts 60 chs of business mus, adv parting audio messages, ZNET data bcstg & video via direct bcst satellite.

MVI Post
6320 Castle Pl., Falls Church, VA 22044 USA
(703) 536-7678, *Fax:* (703) 536-9490
www.mvipost.com
m.kohn@mvipost.com
Frank Maniglia, President
Craig Maniglia, Operations Dir
Full-svc video, audio & graphics postproduction; features screensound digital audio system 601 component digital video suite, high definition digital postproduction facility.

Myriad Pictures
3015 Main St., Suite 400, Santa Monica, CA 90405 USA
(310) 279-4000, *Fax:* (310) 279-4001
www.myriadpictures.com
info@myriadpictures.com
An ind TV co-production & distribution company specializing in music series, features, documentaries & drama for the international market.

N W Media
106 SE 11th Avenue, Portland, OR 97214 USA
(503) 223-5010, *Fax:* (503) 223-4737
www.nwmedia.com
info@nwmedia.com
Jeanne Alldredge, President
Mitchell Harris, General Sales Mgr
Audio/videotape duplication; CD/DVD Duplication, multimedia authoring, graphic design, mastering svcs & messaging.

NAHB Production Group
1201 15th St. N.W., 5th Fl., Washington, DC 20005 USA
(202) 822-0200 ext 8543, *Fax:* (202) 266-8054
cgoldweber@nahb.org
Cary Goldweber, Programming Director
Complete video production/editing facility with large stock library. Productions include Scripps/DIY series, webisodes, political spots, PSA, & instructional/marketing programs.

NASA Broadcast & Imaging Branch
NASA Headquarters (PMD), 300 E. St. S.W., Rm. CL78, Washington, DC 20546 USA
(202) 358-0000, *Fax:* (202) 358-4333
Mike Crnkovic, Chief Printing & Des
Aeronautics & Space Report, an hour magazine quarterly (Betacam SP) to media & producers only.

National Church Broadcasting
Box 8263, Haledon, NJ 7508 USA
(973) 956-2900, *Fax:* (973) 956-0600
Samuel Cummings, President
June Young, Operations Dir
Distributor of church & children's religious progmg to radio stns.

National Collegiate Athletic Association (NCAA)
P.O. Box 6222, Indianapolis, IN 46206-6222 USA
(317) 917-6222, *Fax:* (317) 917-6807
www.NCAA.com
Dr. Myles Brand, President
Greg Weitekamp, Programming Director
Chris Fitzpatrick, Chief Engineer
Televise and produce selected NCAA championships. Manage TV programming and production, including broadcast rights, for all 88 NCAA championships.

National Council of Churches Communications Unit
475 Riverside Dr., Rm. 850, New York, NY 10115 USA
(212) 870-2227, *Fax:* (212) 870-2030
www.ncccusa.org
news@ncccusa.org
Carol Fouke, General Manager
Shirley Struchen, Programming Director
Wesley Pettillo, Promotions Manager
Bcst production, distribution & assistance to reporters, networks, stns; prepared radio reports & actualities without charge from bcst news professionals.

National Film Board of Canada
350 Fifth Ave., Suite 4820, New York, NY 10118 USA
(212) 629-8890, *Fax:* (212) 629-8502
www.nfb.ca
newyork@nfb.ca
Christina Rogers, Promotions Manager
TV program distribution.

National Mobile Television
2740 California St., Torrance, CA 90503 USA
(310) 782-9945,(800) 242-0642, *Fax:* (310) 782-9949
www.nmtv.com
Stephanie Hampton, Operations Dir
Kevin Sublette, General Manager
Mobile TV facilities for remote production of multi-camera events.
12698 Gateway Dr., Seattle, WA 98168 United States
(206)-242-0642;

National Public Radio
635 Massachusetts Ave. N.W., Washington, DC 20001-3753 USA

PROGRAMMING & PRODUCTION SERVICES

(513) 414-2000, *Fax:* (513) 414-3329
www.npr.org
Jim Elder, CFO
Ken Stern, President
Kathleen Jackson, Operations Dir
Barbara Hall, General Sales Mgr
Jay Kernis, Programming Director
Mike Starling, Chief Engineer
Jeffrey Dvorkin, Omsbudman
Maria Thomas, VP Online
Radio program production & distribution.

NBD Television Ltd.
2, Royalty Studios, 105 Lancaster Rd., London, W11 1QF GBR
44 (0) 20 7243 3646, *Fax:* 44 (0) 7243 3656
www.nbdtv.com
distribution@nbdtv.com
Nicky Williams, CEO
Andrew Winter, General Sales Mgr
International TV progmg sls distribution.

NCAA
Box 6222, Indianapolis, IN 46206-6222 USA
(317) 917-6222, *Fax:* (317) 917-6807,(317) 917-6856
www.ncaasports.com,www.ncaa.org
jrinebold@ncaa.org
Chris Farrow, General Manager
Ron Schwartz, Director
Frank Rhodes, Manager
Greg Weitekamp, Manager
Jeramy Michiaels, Manager
NCAA championship progmg, distribution & footage requests.
19 West 57th St, New York, NY 10019 United States
(212) 541-8840; *Fax:* (212) 262-4647
Ron Schwartz, Dir Ncaa Tv New Svcs

NDR Media
Rothenbaumchaussee 159+161, Hamburg, 20149 DEU
(040) 44 1920
www.ndrtv.de
info@ndrtv.de
Horst Bennit, General Manager
Ulla Lamas-Torres, General Sales Mgr
Hans-Stefan Heyne, Head International A
Distribution of TV plays, dramas, wildlife, educ, children's & documentary programs.

NEP Studios
1 Dag Hammarskjold Plaza, Concourse Level, New York, NY 10017-2201 USA
(212) 548-7700, *Fax:* (212) 355-0523
www.nepinc.com
wsheehy@nepstudios.com
William Sheehy, Operations Dir
Shooting stage, Filmor tape, duplication all standards editing & DVD-R duplication.

Network Music
8750 Wilshire Blvd., Beverly Hills, CA 90211 USA
(800) 854-2075, *Fax:* (310) 358-4311
www.networkmusic.com
sales@networkmusic.com
Gary Gross, President
Chuck Ansel, Operations Dir
Carl Peel, General Manager
Dennis Dunn, General Sales Mgr
Todd Kern, Promotions Manager
Produces music, sound effects & production elements libraries.

New City Releasing Inc.
5959 Topanga Canyon Blvd, Suite 255, Woodland Hills, CA 91367 USA
(818) 348-2500, *Fax:* (818) 348-3022
www.newcityreleasing.com
Alan Burnsteen, President
Cathy Goodman-Robbins, Operations Dir
Producer & distributor of motion pictures to cable TV.

New Dimensions Radio
Box 569, Ukiah, CA 95482 USA
(800) 935-8273,(707) 468-5215
www.newdimensions.org
info@newdimensions.org
Justine Toms, President
Michael Toms, Co-President
Radio program production & distribution.

New Films International
8484 Wilshire Blvd., Suite 510, Beverly Hills, CA 90211 USA
(323) 655-1050, *Fax:* (323) 655-1070
www.newfilmsint.com
newfilms@newfilmsint.com,sezin@newfilmsint.com
Nesin Hason, President
Sezin Sonar, Operations Dir
U.S.-based distribution company specialized in Romania, Bulgaria, & Turkey.

New Line Television
888 Seventh Ave., 20th Fl., New York, NY 10106 USA
(212) 649-4900, *Fax:* (212) 956-1936
www.newline.com
David Spiegelman, President
Robin Seidner, Operations Dir
Jim Rosenthal, President
TV program production & distribution.
116 N. Robetson, Los Angeles, CA 90048 United States

New Visions Syndication Inc.
44895 Hwy. 82, Aspen, CO 81611 USA
(970) 925-2640, *Fax:* (970) 925-9369
www.newvisionssyndication.com
kayla@nvs.com
Kayla Hoffman-Cook, Operations Dir
International & domestic syndicator of specials & series; sports, lifestyle & entertainment.

New Zoo Revue
6399 Wilshire Blvd., Suite 816, Los Angeles, CA 90048 USA
(323) 782-3525, *Fax:* (323) 782-3530
www.newzoorevue.com
newzoo@aol.com
Barbara Atlas, President
TV program production & distribution.

News Broadcast Network
451 Park Ave. S., 7th Fl., New York, NY 10016 USA
(212) 684-8910, *Fax:* (212) 684-9650
www.newsbroadcastnetwork.com
Jill Hill, Chairman
Mike Hill, President
Produce & distribute news & feature material to TV & radio stns.

NFL Films
1 NFL Plaza, Mt. Laurel, NJ 8054 USA
(856) 222-3500, *Fax:* (856) 722-6779
www.nflfilms.com
Barry Wolper, COO
Steve Sabol, President
Jeff Howard, Operations Dir
Rick Angeli, General Manager
William Driber, Programming Director
Phil Tuckett, VP Entertainment
Teleproduction facility: digital editing suites, 16mm & 35mm film processing, film-to-tape transfer, studio & remote production, sound studios, animation & flame.

NHK Japan Broadcasting Corp.
2030 M St. N.W., Suite 706, Washington, DC 20036 USA
(202) 828-5180, *Fax:* (202) 828-4571
www.nhk.or.jp/englishtop/
Ryuichi Teshima, Station Manager
TV & radio program distribution.

Nicole Jouve
54 Avenue du Roule, Neuilly Sur Seine, 92200 FRA
33 1 47 22 43 27, *Fax:* 33 1 47 22 43 27
interamany@aol.com
Nicole Jouve, President
Distribution of French films (non-theatrical, TV & video), documentaries (Jean Rouch) childrens programs.

Nightingale-Conant Corp.
6245 W. Howard St., Niles, IL 60714 USA
(847) 647-0300, *Fax:* (847) 647-7145
www.nightingale.com
Vic Conant, President
Radio program production & distribution.

Nine Network Australia
6255 Sunset Blvd., Suite 1500, Los Angeles, CA 90028 USA
(323) 461-3853, *Fax:* (323) 462-4849
Studio production facility, standard conversion & all format tape facilities.

No Soap Productions
936 Broadway, 4th Fl., New York, NY 10010 USA
(212) 581-5572, *Fax:* (212) 586-0045
www.nosoap.net
dan@nosoap.net
Dan Aron, President
Radio comls, sound design for radio & TV, voicecasting, production studio-digital.

North American Network, Inc.
5335 Wisconsin Ave., Suite 305, Washington, DC 20015 USA
(301) 654-9810, *Fax:* (301) 654-9828
www.radiospace.com,www.radioespacio.net
info@nanradio.com
Thomas Sweeney, President
Tammy Lemley, Operations Dir
Full-svc radio P.R. providing progmg, news PSAs, promotional campaigns & sls opportunities to stns nationwide in English & Spanish.

North by Northwest Productions
903 W. Broadway, Spokane, WA 99201 USA
(509) 324-2949, *Fax:* (509) 324-2959
www.nxnw.net
marcdahlstrom@nxnw.net
Marc Dahlstrom, President
High end video & film production; D1/D2 postproduction; Paint/3D animation; sound design/production; HD ediiting.
601 W. Broad St, Boise, ID 83702 United States
(208) 345-7870;
Shane Jibben, Opns Mgr

North Shore Productions
Box 1308, Detroit Lakes, MN 56502 USA
(218) 846-1936, *Fax:* (218) 846-1936
www.agriculture.com/sfradio,www.thecareerclinic.com
nspsfrm@tekstar.com,info@thecareerclinic.com
Produces & distributes The Career Clinic & the Successful Farming Radio Magazine, two-minute features with affil sharing natl revenues.

North Star Music
338 Compass Cir., Unit A1, North Kingstown, RI 2852 USA
(401) 886-8888, *Fax:* (401) 886-8886
www.northstarmusic.com
info@northstarmusic.com
Richard Waterman, President
Production, distribution, mktg & promotion of recorded music.

Northwest Imaging & FX
2339 Columbia St., Suite 100, Vancouver, BC V5Y 3Y3 CAN
(604) 873-9330, *Fax:* (604) 873-9339
nwfx@nwfx.com
Alex Tkach, Operations Dir
Shooting, visual effects, animation, digital editing suites, audio sweetening, Digital Betacam Sp. D-1, 1 inch, duplication Cintel Diamond Film transfer.

NRS Group PTY Ltd.
9-13 Lawry Pl., Macquarie, Canberra, Act 2614 AUS
(61) 2-6251-6333, *Fax:* 61 2-6251-6240
grahampatrick@nrsgroup.com.au,admin@nrsgroup.com.au
Graham Patrick, General Manager
Produces range of quality TV series & documentaries, full TV & audio production facility with qualified personnel, international program distributor.

NTN Communications Inc.
5966 La Place Ct., Suite 100, Carlsbad, CA 92008-8830 USA
(888) PLAYNTN, *Fax:* (760) 438-3505
www.ntn.com
Stanley Kinsey, Chairman
James Frakes, CFO
Mark deGorter, President
Tyrone Lam, President, Buzztime Entertainment
NTN Communications, Inc., a leading producer & distributor of live interactive TV entertainment, bcsts exciting multi-player games to hospitality venues.

NTV International Corp.
645 Fifth Ave., Suite 303, New York, NY 10020 USA
(212) 660-6900, *Fax:* (212) 660-6998
www.ntvic.com
Jusaburo Hayashi, President
Complete video production & postproduction facility; satellite transmission capabilities worldwide; ENG package international TV coord, program sls & acquisitions.

NVC Arts
The Forum, 74-80 Camden St., London, NW1 0EG GBR
44 (0) 7388 3833, *Fax:* 44 (0)20 7388 7174
www.nvcarts-tv.com
mia_fjox-non@nvcarts.com
John Kelleher, General Manager
Elfyn Morris, Station Manager
Producers & distributors of opera, ballet & performing arts programs for world TV.

NYSE Amex
11 Wall St., New York, NY 10005 USA

(212) 656-3000
www.nyx.com
TV studio location on a trading floor, teleprompters, access to industry analysts, production and postproduction svcs.

O'Grady & Associates
8431 Sabal Palm Ct., Vero Beach, FL 32963-4296 USA
(772) 234-4177, *Fax:* (772) 231-9819
jfogjr@juno.com
James O'Grady Jr., President
Brokerage/consulting.

O. Atlas Enterprises Inc.
327 North Palm Dr., Beverly Hills, CA 90210 USA
(323) 782-3525, *Fax:* (323) 782-3530
www.newzoorevue.com
newzoo@aol.com
International licensing, distribution of progmg for TV, all media.

Oasis International
6 Pardee Ave., Suite 103, Toronto, ON M6K 3H5 CAN
(416) 588-6821, *Fax:* (416) 588-7276
www.oasisinternational.com
info@oasisinternational.com
Peter Emerson, President
Prentiss Holman, General Manager
Ben Bishop, General Sales Mgr
Valerie Cabrera, Executive Vice President
Worldwide TV & format distribution.

Oasis TV Inc.
9887 Santa Monica Blvd., Suite 200, Beverly Hills, CA 90212 USA
(310) 553-4300, *Fax:* (310) 553-1159
www.oasistv.com
24-hours cable/satellite net providing a broad, well-branded var of new age/human potential progmg.

OGM Production Music
6464 Sunset Blvd., Suite 790, Hollywood, CA 90028 USA
(323) 461-2701,(800) 421-4163 (Sales), *Fax:* (323) 461-1543
www.ogmmusic.com
ogmmusic@ogmmusic.com
Ole Georg, President
Video, cable, films, CD-ROM, bcst, multimedia, infomercials, satellite program, interactive TV, electronic publishing, theatrical features.

Omnimusic
52 Main St., Port Washington, NY 11050 USA
(800) 828-6664,(516) 883-0121, *Fax:* (516) 883-0271
www.omnimusic.com
bring@omnimusic.com
Doug Wood, President
Patti Wood, Operations Dir
Barbara Ring, Promotions Manager
Dynamic production music with four great libraries that deliver the sounds you need for maximum impact. Easy search and download on the web 24/7. We are always just a phone call or email away, ready to help you with your music needs.

On Track
6350 W. Freeway, Fort Worth, TX 76116 USA
(817) 570-1400,(800) 266-1837, *Fax:* (817) 737-9436
www.familynetradio.com
info@familynet.com,lbratton@familynetradio.com,dsenn@familynetradio.com,cries@familynetradio.com
Chuck Ries, Programming Director
Donna Senn, Promotions Manager
Lisa Bratton, Radio Marketing & Dist.
Contemporary Christian music with artist interviews, 30 minutes wkly, on CD.

One Hundred Biblemen & Women of the U.S.A.
Box 8263, Haledon, NJ 7508 USA
(973) 956-2900, *Fax:* (973) 956-0600
Sam Cummings, President
Low-cost bcstg & buying net for churches.

1st Miracle Productions
3439 W. Cahuenga Blvd., Hollywood, CA 90068 USA
(323) 874-6000, *Fax:* (323) 874-4252
www.1stmiracleproductions.com
sales@1stmiracleproductions.com
Moshe Bibiyan, CEO
Simon Bibiyan, President
International distribution, co-production, postproduction finance.

Oppix Productions Inc
3531 Laurel Leaf Ln, Fairfax, VA 22031-3212 USA
(703)280-8200, *Fax:* (703) 280-9292
www.oppix.com
info@oppix.com
James Oppenheimer, President
Full-svc video internet, DVD production & post, serving bcst, corporate assns, nonprofit & gov. All formats.

Orange Productions Inc.
523 Righters Ferry Rd., 1st floor, Bala Cynwyd, PA 19004 USA
(610) 667-8620, *Fax:* (610) 667-8939
www.soundsofsinatra.com
orange@snip.net
Sid Mark, President
Brian Mark, Operations Dir
Production & distribution of a wkly two-hour program Sounds of Sinatra.

Outdoor Media Group
Box 2151, Lake Oswego, OR 97035 USA
(503) 675-7345, *Fax:* (503) 675-7820
www.aojtv.com
omg@aojtv.com
Russell Cameron, President
TV program, coml production & distribution; production svcs.

P. Allen Smith Gardens
Box 7347, Little Rock, AR 72217 USA
(501) 376-1894, *Fax:* (501) 376-1896
www.pallensmith.com
P. Allen Smith, President
Nationally syndicated gardening & lifestyle news inserts reported by professional garden designer Allen Smith.

PACSAT
1629 S St., Sacramento, CA 95811 USA
(916) 446-7890, *Fax:* (916) 446-7893
www.pacsat.com
pacsat@pacsat.com
Steve Mallory, President
Marcia Calvin, Operations Dir
Video, audio & satellite professionals. Ku-HD satellite trucks. ENG crews. Fly pack with CCU'S. Post production & graphics.

Palace Producers
29 N. Main St., South Norwalk, CT 6854 USA
(203) 853-1740, *Fax:* (203) 855-9608
www.palaceproductions.tv
wendy@palacedigital.com
Wendy Lambert, President
Soundstage w/Cyc; HD Production Services;HD Editorial;Broadcast Design & Animation;Audio Record & Mixing;DVD Authoring & Duplication

Pan American Video
3144 Broadway, Suite 4, Eureka, CA 95501 USA
(707) 822-3800, *Fax:* (707) 822-0800
www.panamvideo.com
panam@panamvideo.com
Teri Lane, President
Sheila McQuillen, Operations Dir
Public domain movies & TV shows, bcst quality & stock footage.

Pantomime Pictures Inc.
12144 Riverside Dr., North Hollywood, CA 91607 USA
(818) 980-5555, *Fax:* (818) 984-3470
Fred Crippen, General Manager
Matt Crippen, Programming Director
Animation production & design for TV comls, educ & industrial use. Animation camera for 35 mm & 16 mm.

Parrot Communications International Inc.
2917 N. Ontario St., Burbank, CA 91504 USA
(818) 567-4700, *Fax:* (818) 567-4600
www.parrotmedia.com
info@parrotmedia.com
Rae Mertz, President
Blanca Pineda-Villanueva, Operations Dir
Karol L. Wagner Loy, Promotions Manager
Database mgmt, direct mail svcs, promotional fulfillment, warehousing, contest fulfillment, bcst faxing, high speed duplication & videotape duplication.

Pathe International
21 rue Francois 1 er, 75008 Paris, FRA
Fax: 33-1-40-76-9169,33-1-40-76-9194
www.pathe.fr
christine.hayet@pathe.com
Eduardo Malone, Chairman
Michel Crepon, COO
Emma Rami, Operations Dir
Production & distribution of TV films & documentaries. Production of multimedia programs.

PAULAR Entertainment L.L.C.
13700 Marina Pointe Dr., Suite 901, Marina del Rey, CA 90292 USA
(310) 821-0430, *Fax:* (310) 821-3793
thirdwayv@aol.com
Larry Friedricks, President
Paula Fierman, Partner
World-wide distribution of feature films, video & TV including movies, series & mini-series.

Paulist Media Works
3055 4th St. N.E., Washington, DC 20017 USA
(202) 269-6064, *Fax:* (202) 269-4304
www.paulist.org/pmw
info@paulist.org
Sue Donovan, President
Support for non-profit organization in internet svcs/website/web design distribution of relg radio programs, video/documentary production

Paulist Productions
Box 1057, Pacific Palisades, CA 90272 USA
(310) 454-0688, *Fax:* (310) 459-6549
www.paulistproductions.org
paulistmail@paulistproductions.org
Enid Sevilla, CFO
Frank Desiderio, President
Joseph Kim, Operations Dir
Barbara Gangi, Programming Director
TV program production.

PBS Video
2100 Crystal Dr., Arlington, VA 22202 USA
(703) 739-5000, *Fax:* (703) 739-8487
www.pbs.org
Barbara Landes, CFO
Paula Kerger, President
John Boland, Programming Director
John McCoskey, Chief Engineer
Wayne Godwin, COO
Katherine Lauderdale, General Counsel
A trusted provider of classroom resources for more that 25 years, PBS Video extends the reach of public TV by distributing meda throughout the United States & Canada, making valuable resources available to educators, librarians & trainersthrough Shop PBS for Teacher.

Peckham Productions
50 S. Buckhout Street, Irvington, NY 10533 USA
(914) 591-4140, *Fax:* (914) 591-4149
www.peckhampix.com
info@peckhampix.com
Peter Peckham, President
Russell Peckham, General Manager
Waldine Peckham, Production Manager
Full-svc film & video producer of TV comls, TV programs & TV net promos.

Perception Media Group
1848 Clay St., Roanoke, VA 24013 USA
(540) 563-5225, *Fax:* (540) 563-0117
Ben Peyton, President
TV & radio coml program production, distribution & jingles. Religious programs & distribution.

PETER RODGERS ORGANIZATION
6513 Hollywood Blvd., #201, Hollywood, CA 90028 USA
(323) 962-1778, *Fax:* (323) 962-7174
www.profilms.com
info@profilms.com
Stephen Rodgers, CEO
Pavel Miller, Operations Dir
Ron Adler, Chief Engineer
Consultants, Distributors, Reps. Celebrating over 35 years representing productions, companies & independent producers with over 2,000 hours of progmg .

Peters Communications
1555 Berenda Pl., El Cajon, CA 92020
(619) 444-6984, *Fax:* (619) 440-1481
edpeters@cox.net
Edward J. Peters, President
Media mktg consultants, providing rsch, concept, mktg plan, music, graphics & animation.

Philadelphia Flyers Hockey Club
3601 S. Broad St., Philadelphia, PA 19148 USA
(215) 465-4500, *Fax:* (215) 952-4103
www.philadelphiaflyers.com
rryan@comcast-spectacor.com
Ed Snider, Chairman
Bob Clarke, President
Shawn Tilger, Operations Dir
TV & radio program production.

Phoebus Communications Inc.
10905 Ft. Washington Rd., Suite 300, Fort Washington, MD 20744 USA
(301) 292-9800, *Fax:* (301) 292-0829
www.phoebusinc.net
phoebuscom@aol.com
Gail Arnall, Ph.D., President
Full scale distance learning net mgmt.

Phoenix Communications Group
3 Empire Blvd., South Hackensack, NJ 7606 USA
(201) 807-0888, *Fax:* (201) 807-0272
www.phoenixcomm.com
Joe Podesta, Chairman
Jim Holland, President
Trish Ferreri, General Manager
Geoff Belinfante, Programming Director
Rich Domich, Promotions Manager
Major League Sports Newsatellite; TV & video production & distribution; stock footage licensing.

Pied Piper Films Ltd.
825941 Mel-Nott TL, R. R. 2, Shelburne, ON L0N 1S6 CAN
(519) 925-6558, *Fax:* (519) 925-9015
thefallsfarm@yahoo.ca
Allan Wargon, Programming Director
Motion picture production.

Pike Productions Inc.
Box 300, 11 Clarke St., Newport, RI 2840 USA
(401) 846-8890, *Fax:* (401) 847-0070
info@pikefilmtrailers.com
James Pike, President
Cornelia Pike, General Sales Mgr
Custom ads & special announcement trailers produced & distributed in all formats35mm, 185x1, Scope, stereo, 70mm stereo.

Planet Pictures Ltd.
4222 Kingfisher Rd., Suite 208, Calabasas, CA 91302 USA
(818) 344-4493, *Fax:* (818) 344-4493
www.planetpictures.com
info@planetpictures.com
Jim Hayden, President
Peter Torvik, Operations Dir
Jennifer Hayden, General Manager
Production & distribution for documentary, informational, reality-based TV programs.

Playboy Entertainment Group Inc.
2706 Media Center Dr., Los Angeles, CA 90065 USA
(323) 276-4000, *Fax:* (323) 276-4500
Jim English, President
James Griffith, Operations Dir
TV program production, distribution & video.
Andrita Studios
3030 Andrita St., Los Angeles, CA 90065
Sol Weisel, Vp Production

Playhouse Pictures
Box 2089, Los Angeles, CA 90078-2089 USA
(323) 851-2112, *Fax:* (323) 851-2117
playpix@aol.com
Gerry Woolery, General Manager
Ted Woolery, Programming Director
Todd Shalter, Director
Animated TV coml production & short films.

Point 360
1133 North Hollywood Way, Burbank, CA 91505 USA
(818) 556-5700, *Fax:* (818) 556-5753
www.point360.com
Dennis Imbler, General Manager
Paul Ponzio, General Sales Mgr
Postproduction & duplication, film-to-tape transfers, audio svcs. Digital editing, distribution & syndication.
1220 N. Highland Ave, Hollywood, CA 90038 United States
(323) 957-5500;
Rich Appel, Gen Mgr
VP business dev, President
12421 W. Olympic Blvd, Los Angeles, CA 90064 United States
(310) 207-7079;
Carl Segal, Gen Mgr
Brian Grant, Vp Business Dev
1025 N. McCadden Pl, Hollywood, CA 90038 United States
(323) 461-8383;
Fabian Sanchez, Gen Mgr
Brian Grant, Vp Business Dev
712 N. Seward St, Hollywood, CA 90038 United States
(323) 462-5330;
Yvonne Parker, Gen Mgr
Brian Grant, Vp Business Dev

PorchLight Entertainment Inc.
11777 Mississippi Ave., Los Angeles, CA 90025 USA
(310) 477-8400, *Fax:* (310) 477-5555
www.porchlight.com
William Baumann, CFO
Bruce Johnson, President
Produces & distributes family entertainment progmg including animation, TV movies & interactive multimedia progmg, licensing & merchandising.

Ports of Paradise
Box 33648, San Diego, CA 92163 USA
(619) 275-7357,(800) 223-2564, *Fax:* (619) 296-5909
www.portparadise.com
aloharn@portparadise.com
J. Hal Hodgson, Programming Director
Hour-long radio program with Hawaiian music & info. Available on a barter basis.

PostWorks, New York
100 Ave. of the Americas, New York, NY 10013 USA
(212) 557-4949, *Fax:* (212) 983-4083
www.pwny.com
Film-to-tape or data in standard or Hi-Definition; editing: digital, Hi-Definition, non-linear; duplication, conversion, satellite & fibre transmissions.

Potomac TV/Communications
15110 H St. N.W., Suite 202, Washington, DC 20005 USA
(202) 783-8000, *Fax:* (202) 783-1132
www.potomactv.com
www.sgreenaway@potomactv.com
Nick Chiaia, President
New content & video svcs production facility. C- & Ku-band satellite transmitters/receive svcs.

Power Play Music Video L.L.C.
223-225 Washington St., Newark, NJ 7102 USA
(973) 642-5132, *Fax:* (973) 642-5747
www.powerplay-mvtv.com
powerplaytv@cs.com
Greg Ferguson, President
TV & radio program; coml production & distribution; production svcs.

Powerline
6350 W. Fwy., Fort Worth, TX 76116 USA
(817) 570-1491,(800) 292-2287, *Fax:* (817) 737-9436
www. powerlineradio.com
cries@familynetradio.com,kteegarden@familynetradio.com
Chuck Ries, Programming Director
Kirk Teegarden, Producer
Adult contemp music blended with brief commentaries about life by host Brother Jon Rivers, 30 min wkly on CD or download.

Powersports/Millenium International
14242 Ventura Blvd., Ste 300, Sherman Oaks, CA 91423-2757 USA
(818) 708-9995, *Fax:* (818) 708-0598
www.ps-mill.com
intl@ps-mill.com
Tal McAbian, President
William McAbian, President
Production & distribution of special interest & documentaries for TV, cable & home video.

PPM Multimedia
Brezo 4 - URB Los Robles, Torrelodones, Madrid, 28250 ESP
(34) 91 859 1913, *Fax:* (34) 91 859 0932
www.ppmm.es
multimedia@ppmm.es
Paco Rodriguez, General Manager
Distribution of animation, feature films, documentaries, co-production setting.

Prairie Dog Entertainment
12827 Corte Dorotea, Poway, CA 92064 USA
(800) 448-7664
www.buckhowdy.com
Steve Vaus, Programming Director
Exclusively offering Buck Howdy's Cow Pie Radio, the fastest growing wkly kids radio program.

Praxis Media Inc.
9 Twilight Pl., South Norwalk, CT 6854 USA
(203) 866-6666, *Fax:* (203) 853-8299
praxiscc@aol.com
Christopher Campbell, General Manager
Deborah Weingrad, Director
TV program, coml, promotional film production; production svcs.

Premiere Radio Networks Inc.
15260 Ventura Blvd., 5th Fl., Sherman Oaks, CA 91403-5339 USA
(818) 377-5300, *Fax:* (818) 377-5333
www.premrad.com
webmaster@premrad.com
Kraig Kitchin, President
Dan Yukelson, Operations Dir
Rich Meyer, President
Eileen Thorgusen, Vice President
Nancy Deitemeyer, VP Operations
Line-up includes Bcst Results Group (BRG) features, Olympia, Premiere Comedy Networks Formats, Long-form features, Mediabase rsch formats, music svcs, online, plain-wrap formats, prep & short-form. All features & svcs offered on a barterbasis are available via satellite, disc, tape, script or phone, depending on the program.

Presbyterian Church (U.S.A.)
100 Witherspoon St., Louisville, KY 40202-1396 USA
(502) 569-5211,(502) 569-5493, *Fax:* (502) 569-8845
Jerry Marter, News Director
Radio & TV production, video, audio production, distribution, mktg & Internet svcs.

Presson Perspectives
600 Druid Rd. E., Clearwater, FL 33756 USA
(727) 461-1885, *Fax:* (727) 443-1984
www.medforum.com
gpresson@tampabay.rr.com
Gina Presson, Programming Director
News, documentary & internet production ranging from turnkey pieces to any segment.

Prime Cut Productions Inc.
11909 E. Trail, San Fernando, CA 91342 USA
(818) 897-7321, *Fax:* (818) 834-9889
www.primecutproductions.com
janicekaplan@primecutproductions.com,edwardflaherty@yahoo.com(France)
Jan Kaplan, President
Edward Flaherty, Operations Dir
NTSC Betacam European producers for American TV; bilingual location professionals; distribution, co-production, stock footage, TV script consultant/writer & editing.

Primedia Workplace Learning
4101 International Pkwy., Carrollton, TX 75007 USA
(800) 848-1717, *Fax:* (972) 309-5666
www.pwpl.com
Josh Karin, CEO
Gina Valencia, Promotions Manager
Video-based, interactive tech training programs for industry, utilities, govt relating to maintenance, opns & safety.

Primo Newservice Inc.
Box 116, 182 Sound Beach Ave., Old Greenwich, CT 06870-0116 USA
(203) 637-0044, *Fax:* (203) 698-0812
www.teenkidsnews.com
primonews@aol.com
Albert Primo, CEO
TV news consulting, strategic news positioning talent & mgmt, coaching. Cable news training; Internet broadband svc.
355 W 52nd St. 3rd FL, New York, NY 10019

Pro Video
2904-A Colorado Ave., Santa Monica, CA 90404 USA
(310) 828-2292
provideo1@earthlink.net
Joel Webb, President
Commercials mastered to DVD & 3/4 inches.

Producers Group, Ltd.
713 S. Pacific Coast Hwy., Suite B, Redondo Beach, CA 90277-4233 USA
(310) 316-0481, *Fax:* (310) 316-1482
lee.gluckman@producers-group.tv
Lee Gluckman Jr., President
Dev & production of theatrical, TV films & series.

Production Garden Music Libraries
510 E. Ramsey Rd., Suite 4, San Antonio, TX 78216 USA
(800) 247-5317, *Fax:* (210) 530-5230
www.productiongarden.com
sales@productiongarden.com
Mel Taylor, President
Ten distinct music libraries featuring production music, including production elements, sound effects; both lease & buy-out options available.

Productions La Fete
387 St. Paul W., Montreal, QC H2Y 2A7 CAN
(514) 848-0417, *Fax:* (514) 848-0064
info@lafete.com
Rock Demers, President
Daniel Proulx, Operations Dir
Xiao Zhou, VP Distribution
Production of children/family feature films, drama series, documentaries, multimedia, etc.

The Program Exchange
375 Hudson St., New York, NY 10014 USA
(212) 463-3500, *Fax:* (212) 463-2662
www.programexchange.com
info@programexchange.com
Allen Banks, President
Chris Hallowell, Operations Dir
TV program distribution.

Promark Television
323 S. Doheny Dr., Suite 308, Los Angeles, CA 90048 USA
(310) 276-3020, *Fax:* (310) 276-3208
www.promarktv.com
hdlevine@promarktv.com
David Levine, CEO
TV program production & distribution.

Promusic
941-A Clint Moore Rd., Boca Raton, FL 33487 USA
(561) 995-0331,(800) 322-7879, *Fax:* (561) 995-8434
www.promusiclibrary.com
mail@promusiclibrary.com
Alain Leroux, President
Mike Spitz, General Sales Mgr
Production music for film, TV & more. Vast CD catalog to choose from with extensive classical & opera.

PSSI Global Services-Strategic Television
15315 Magnolia Blvd., Suite 423, Sherman Oaks, CA 91403 USA
(310) 575-4400, *Fax:* (310) 575-4451
www.pssiglobal.com
pssi@pssiglobal.com
Robert Lamb, President
Brian Nelles, Operations Dir
Clayton Packard, Promotions Manager
Matt Bridges, Pres-Strategic Television
Full service production & satellite transmission company with 25 fully redundant C- & Ku-band satellite trucks located nationwide. Available for news, sports, corporate, entertainment events, media tours, video conferencing, webcasting &downlinks. Additional svcs include Standard, High Definition digital transmission, encryption, multiple camera productions, event coordination & a C/Ku Flyaway system for international & domestic transmission. skIP Broadband also available forinternet, voice connectivity, & webcasting via satellite, ideal in remote areas with little or no connectivity.

Public Media Incorporated
1560 Sherman Ave. Ste 440, Evanston, IL 60201-4803 USA
(773) 878-2600, *Fax:* (773) 878-8406
www.homevision.net
webmasters@homevision.com
Adrianne Furniss, CEO
Carole Little, Operations Dir
Sls to all TV outlets in North America, foreign & classic cinema distribution.

Quality Film & Video
232 Cockeysville Rd., Hunt Valley, MD 21030 USA
(410) 785-1920
www.qualityfilmvideo.com
qfv@qualityfilmvideo.com
Peter Garey, President
Guy Garey, Operations Dir
Video production, postproduction svcs, videotape, CD-ROM & DVD duplication.

Questar
680 N. Lake Shore Dr., Suite 900, Chicago, IL 60611 USA
(312) 266-9400, *Fax:* (312) 266-9523
www.questar1.com
Jason Nader, President
Producer, distributor of travel documentaries, children's cultural historical & natural history.

RAD Marketing & Cabletowns
167 Crary-on-the-Park, Mount Vernon, NY 10550 USA
(914) 668-3563, *Fax:* (914) 668-4247
cabletown@verizon.net
Bob Dadarria, President
Adele Dadarria, General Sales Mgr
Consumer list, individuals & household lifestyles. Svcs include: cable TV subs with addressable box direct TV buyers with Tel # scrubbed mailing lists, rgnl area mkts, natl area mkts, sweepstakes entrants list, children lists, donors,travel.

Radio & TV Roundup Productions
653 Sunhaven Dr., Clayton, NJ 08312-1955 USA
(856) 881-2570, *Fax:* (856) 307-9506
www.nanes.com
delfon@att.net
Bill Bertenshaw, CEO
B.C. Slachofsky, General Manager
Bobbi Cherrelle, Programming Director
Richard Nanes, Director
Production, placement of TV & radio progmg including comls & PSAs. Distribute free classical CDs & TV progmg.
Box 108, Cape May, NJ 08204-0108
Bobbi Cherrelle, Exec Producer

The Radio Almanac
107 Jensen Cir., West Springfield, MA 01089-4451 USA
(413) 737-7600, *Fax:* (413) 737-7600
cspencer@mail.map.com
Charles Spencer, Operations Dir
Lifestyle info; special rsch; writing, voice & production projects. Monthly filler material publication, featuring events, sports, biographical sketches & other info.

Radio America
1030 15th St. N.W., Suite 1040, Washington, DC 20005 USA
(202) 408-0944, *Fax:* (202) 408-1087
www.radioamerica.org
radioa@radioamerica.org
Mike Paradiso, COO
James Roberts, President
Greg Corombos, Programming Director
Rich McFadden, Producer
News & feature svc providing daily, wkly & special programs (90 seconds to one hr) & multi-part documentaries.

Radio City Entertainmement
2 Penn Plaza, New York, NY 10021 USA
(212) 465-6000,(212) 485-7000
www.thegarden.com,www.radiocity.com
Katie Schroeder, General Manager
TV program producers; production svcs.
2049 Century Park E, Suite 1200, Los Angeles, CA 90067 United States
(310) 551-2721;

Radio Express Inc.
1415 W. Magnolia Blvd., Burbank, CA 91506 USA
(818) 295-5800, *Fax:* (818) 295-5801
www.radioexpress.com
radioinfo@radioexpress.com
Tom Rounds, CEO
Christian Jones, Operations Dir
Anita Antonio, General Manager
Jessica D'Agostin, General Sales Mgr
Christopher DiMatteo, Promotions Manager
Radio Express exports Radioplay, the best music svc for radio, production music & progmg to enhance any music format, worldwide.

Radio Production Services Inc.
201 Lena Dr., Easley, SC 29640-9647 USA
(864) 855-7191, *Fax:* (864) 855-7191, EXT 2
kenroy2@aol.com
W.L. Ames, CFO
R. Kenneth Rogers, President
E.C. Rogers, Operations Dir
Nan Cohen, General Manager
Jason Gold, General Sales Mgr
Ron Rackley, Chief Engineer
Radio program production specializing in early rhythm and blues & oldies formats. Radio, TV coml production & distribution. Stn ID packages, jingles, consultation svcs in sls & progmg.
Radio Production Services Inc.
Box 26, Cold Spring Harbor, NY 11724 United States
(516) 246-9182;
Alex Silvers, A&R Dir
Radio Production Services Inc.
206 Union St, Nashville, TN 37201 United States
(615) 227-1947;
Fred James, Vp
Radio Production Services Inc.
27 Congress Street, Salem, MA 01970 United States
(978)-740-0990; *Fax:* (978)-740-0660

Radio Sound Network
605 S. Front St., Columbus, OH 43215
(614) 460-3850, *Fax:* (614) 621-5620
www.radiohio.com
steve.clawson@radiohio.com
Tony Miller, General Manager
Steve Clawson, Chief Engineer
Full-svc digital satellite audio & data distribution, including affil rel & net bldg. for new & existing sports, news/talk, music & specialty networks.

Radio Spirits
2 Ridgedale Ave., Cedar Knolls, NJ 7927 USA
(800) 359-0570, ext.236,(973) 539-7557, *Fax:* (973) 539-1273
www.radiospirits.com
wholesale@radiospirits.com
Hakan Lindskog, President
David Carroll, General Sales Mgr
Syndicated radio production specializing in Golden Age of Radio. Production of When Radio Was with Stan Freberg, bartered to 300 affls.

Radio Television Espanola (RTVE)
Edificio Prado Del Rey/ Desp. 3/023, Prado Del Rey, Madrid, 28223
(34 91) 581-54 91, *Fax:* (34 91) 581-77 41
www.rtve.es
contratos_canales_inter.ep@rtve.es
Production & distribution of its own productions as well as some 250 feature films in co-production with independent Sp & Latin American film producers.

Radioguide People Inc.
Box 880, Novi, MI 48376 USA
(248) 926-1234
www.vuolovideo.com
artvuolo@aol.com
Arthur Vuolo Jr., President
Publishers of radio stn guides for the gen public, co-sponsored by loc stns & natl advertisers. Produces videos of radio stns, radio events for educational & entertainment purposes.

RAI Corp.
32 Avenue of the Americas Bldg 1, New York, NY 10013-2473 USA
(212) 468-2500, *Fax:* (212) 765-1956
www.raicorp.net
Mario Bona, CEO
Guido Corso, President
Italian natl radio & TV.

Rampion Visual Productions L.L.C.
125 Walnut St., Watertown, MA 2472 USA
(617) 972-1777, *Fax:* (617) 972-9157
www.rampion.com
info@rampion.com
Michael Garneau, President
Steven Tringali, General Manager
Full Digital Component Editing (BetaSP & DigiBeta), Computer Graphics (2D & 3D), Green Screen Studio, Digital Compositing & DVD creation.

Ray Sports Network
176 Radio Rd., Powell's Point, NC 27966 USA
(252) 491-2414, *Fax:* (252) 491-2959
Bill Ray, President
TV & radio program & coml production, distribution. Sports syndication.

Raycom Sports
1900 W. Morehead St., Charlotte, NC 28208 USA
704 378-4400, *Fax:* (704) 374-3859
www.raycomsports.com
Ken Haines, President
Colin Smith, Operations Dir
Jim Ford, General Sales Mgr
Charles Moye, Engineering Dir
Laura Hager, Controller
Jimmy Rayburn, VP, Production
George Johnson, VP, Programing
Wyatt Hicks, VP, Sponsorship
TV, marketing, sports production & syndication.

Raycom Sports
1900 West Morehead Street, Charlotte, NC 28208 USA
(704) 378-4400, *Fax:* (704) 373-3324
www.raycomsports.com
khaines@raycomsports.com
Ken Haines, CEO
Colin Smith, Operations Dir
Jim Ford, General Sales Mgr
Peter Rolfe, Programming Director
Wyatt Hick, Promotions Manager

Laura Hager, Controller
Jimmy Rayburn, VP Production
Production trucks and HD uplink, sls distribution, produce, market, distribute sports, entertainment progmg nationally & internationally.

RBC Ministries
Box 2222, Grand Rapids, MI 49501-2222 USA
(616) 942-6770, *Fax:* (616) 957-5741
www.rbc.net
rbc@rbc.org
Martin De Haan II, President
TV & radio production & distribution. Programs: TV Day of Discovery, Radio-Discover the Word, Words To Live By, Our Daily Bread, Sports Spectrum, My Utmost for His Highest & Walk In The Wood.

RBC Ministries/Midwest Media Managers
Box 2606, Grand Rapids, MI 49501-2606 USA
(877) 245-0550,(616) 942-6360, *Fax:* (616) 957-5741
www.rbc.net/mmm
mmm@rbc.net
Martin De Haan, President
John Nasby, General Manager
Rod McNany, Director
In-house agency for RBC Ministries; providing TV/Radio placement & promotional support of RBC resources including the devotional, Our Daily Bread.

RDF Media
Kensington Village, Avonmore Road, London, AL W14 8TS GBR
44 (0)20 7 013 4000
www.rdfmedia.com
sales@rdfmedia.com
David Frank, CEO
Joely Fether, Programming Director
Production & distribution of TV & radio programs.

Reel Media International Inc.
7000 Independence Parkway, Suite 160-7, Plano, TX 75025 USA
(214) 521-3301, *Fax:* (214) 522-3448
www.reelmediaintl.com
reelmedia@aol.com
Tom T. Moore, President
Worldwide distributor of motion pictures, copyrighted documentaries, Public Domain Library of 2,000 movies, series & documentaries. Servicing all rights.

Reid/Land Productions Inc.
425 E. 58th St., Suite 46H, New York, NY 10022 USA
(212) 754-3348, *Fax:* (212) 754-7034
reidland@rcn.com
Allen Reid, President
Mady Land, Executive Vice President
Packaging, creation & production of TV programs: variety, entertainment, music, games, sports how-to & cooking.

Reizner & Reizner Film & Video
7179 Via Maria, San Jose, CA 95139 USA
(408) 226-6339, *Fax:* (408) 226-6403
dick@reizner.com
Dick Reizner, President
Bcst & industrial production in all formats. Certified Legal Video Specialist. Gyrozoom rental.

Reliance Audio Visual Corp.
575 Lexington Ave., New York, NY 10022 USA
(212) 586-5000, *Fax:* (914) 237-1004
rav@aol.com
Gil Meyer, President
Norma Matthews, Executive Vice President
Audio & video permanent installations, design, video & teleconferencing, consultation, rentals, staging multimedia, video projection, dealerships, leasing & display design.

Response Reward Systems L.C.
1850 Bay Rd., 2-C, Vero Beach, FL 32963 USA
(772) 234-5449, *Fax:* (772) 234-5949
marcyuk@mpinet.net
Henry Von Kohorn, MBA, Ph.D., CEO
Patented technology enablling TV viewers in the United States to legally bet, cost-free and risk-free, on the outcome of sports events, from their homes via the Internet.

Reuters Media
3 Times Sq., 18th Fl., New York, NY 10036 USA
(646) 223-4300, *Fax:* (646) 223-4390,(646) 223-4370
www.reuters.com
Richard Sabreen, President
International news for interactive multimedia news archive for CD-ROM & on-demand applications. Stock photos & film footage.

Reuters Television
1333 H St. N.W., Washington, DC 20005 USA
(202) 898-0056, *Fax:* (202) 898-1236
www.reuters.com
John Clarke, Programming Director
Reuters news & sports svcs include 128 Reuters bureaus, camera crews & a comprehensive satellite network. It serves more than 200 bctrs & their affils in 84 countries. Satellite & news production svcs feature satellite delivery networks.International bcst centers in Moscow, Washington, DC & London. Offers live positions, studio facilities & direct access to the satellite network. Library & program packages cover major news & sporting events.

Rex Post
610 S.W. 17th Ave., Portland, OR 97205 USA
(503) 238-4525, *Fax:* (503) 236-8347
www.rexpost.com
info@rexpost.com
Tara Krick, Operations Dir
Russell Gorsline, General Manager
Lee Rooklin, General Sales Mgr
TV & radio production, audio recording, video production, CD-ROM & DVD, website. Audio/video production & post, ISDN digital patch, DVD authoring & web design.

Richter Productions Inc.
330 W. 42nd St., Suite 2410, New York, NY 10036 USA
(212) 947-1395, *Fax:* (212) 643-1208
www.richtervideos.com
richter330@aol.com
Robert Richter, President
Amy Kessler, Programming Director
TV program, promo film production, distribution, film & video.

Riden International Inc.
6024 Paseo Palmilla, Goleta, CA 93117 USA
(805) 964-7041, *Fax:* (805) 964-1338
www.rideninc.com
rideninc@aol.com
Richard Dennison, President
Motion Picture , TV program production & distribution.

Rigel Entertainment
4201 Wilshire Blvd., Suite 555, Los Angeles, CA 90010 USA
(323) 954-8555, *Fax:* (323) 954-8592
www.rigel.tv
info@rigel.tv
John Laing, CEO
Kristie Smith, Operations Dir
Bryan Hambleton, General Sales Mgr
Laura Hoffman, Sales
Offers international TV, video rights to TV series, MOWs, specials & feature films.

River City Video Productions
Box 310601, New Braunfels, TX 78131-0601 USA
(830) 625-3474, *Fax:* (830) 625-3710
www.fishingandoutdoor.com
Deborah Dougherty, President
Mktg, instructional & promotional videos & TV commercials.

RMD & Assoc. Inc.
534 Rosemary Cir., Media, PA 19063 USA
(610) 566-3799, *Fax:* (610) 566-3799
rmdassociates@yahoo.com
Celeste Walsh, Programming Director
Hank Shaw, Engineering Dir
Dick D'Anjolell, Executive Producer
Program creative svcs, production & distribution, specializing in promotion & business info.

Robert L. Bocchino
264 Montgomery Ave., Haverford, PA 19041-1531 USA
(610) 649-0993, *Fax:* (610) 649-0895
Robert Bocchino, President
Voice over artist, coml spokesperson.

Robert Michelson Inc.
508 3rd Ave., San Francisco, CA 94118 USA
(415) 386-6862, *Fax:* (415) 386-2714
www.rmitv.com
rm@rmitv.com
Robert Michelson, President
David Alexander, General Manager
TV coml production; custom & syndicated TV spots for radio stns. Leading producer of TV spots for rock radio.

Robert Wold Co.
88 Three Vines Ct., Ladera Ranch, CA 92694 USA
(949) 363-0993
robertnwold@cox.net
Robert Wold, President
Special-interest & entertainment progmg for bcst & cable TV. Production, mktg & distribution of syndicated programs.

Roberts Communications Network Inc.
4175 Cameron St., Suite B-10, Las Vegas, NV 89103 USA
(702) 227-7500, *Fax:* (702) 227-7501
Tommy Roberts, Chairman
Todd Roberts, CEO
C-Bond satellite transponder capacity, uplinking, encoding & decoding. 50 Ch Direct To Home Platform

Robin Miller, Filmaker Inc.
606 W. Broad St., Bethlehem, PA 18018 USA
(610) 691-0900, *Fax:* (610) 691-0952
www.filmaker.com
mail@filmaker.com
TV program, promotion film production; production svcs.

Rockey Hill and Knowlton
221 Yale Ave. N., Ste 530, Seattle, WA 98109-5490 USA
(206) 728-1100, *Fax:* (206) 728-1106
www.rockey-seattle.com
Corporate & financial film production. Public relations.

Rockwell Audio Media
56 W. 45th St., Suite 1503, New York, NY 10036 USA
(212)840-9200, *Fax:* (212)840-9203
www.rockwellaudiomedia.com
john@rockwellaudiomedia.com
John Rockwell, President
Audio editing & production-spoken word & educational.

Romano & Associates Inc.
5094 Dorsey Hall Dr., Suite 104, Ellicott City, MD 21042 USA
(410) 730-4133, *Fax:* (410) 730-2219
www.racommunications.com
Jim Carroll, Operations Dir
Neil Romano, General Manager
Full-svc production company specializing in issue-oriented short-feature films & documentaries, PSAs; professional of children's educ videos & comls.

Rose Entertainment
5529 McLennan Ave., Encino, CA 91436 USA
(818) 817-7554, *Fax:* (818) 817-7585
rosenter@pacbell.net
Rosamaria Gonzalez, President
Flory Quiroa, Operations Dir
TV progmg distribution company for Latin America.

Rosler Creative
88 Howard St., #2307, San Francisco, CA 94105 USA
(415) 896-1414, *Fax:* (415) 896-1616
www.roslercreative.com
Peter@RoslerCreative.com
Peter Rosler, President
TV comls, creative dev & production.TV-CATV only.

Rosnay International
6 Rue Robert Estienne, Paris, 75008 FRA
01.42.89.18.54, *Fax:* 01.42.25.34.39
fronet3038@aol.com
Distribution & production company.

ROZON
2101 Blvd St. Laurent, Montreal, H2X 2T5
(514) 845-3155, *Fax:* (514) 845-4140
www.hahaha.com
Bruce Hills, COO
Gilbert Rozon, President
Christos Sourligas, General Sales Mgr
Producer/distributor of comedy programs, standup comedy & nonverbal light entertainment.

RPM Media Enterprises-The Relic Rack Review
108 Holmes Oval, New Providence, NJ 07974-1425 USA
(908) 464-2222
www.relic-rack.com
richardjlorenzo@relicrack.com
Margaret Lorenzo, CFO
Richard Lorenzo, President
Jack Kratoville, Operations Dir
Four-hour wkly rock & roll oldies syndicated entertainment program called the Relic Rack Review, that includes music, news & nostalgia entertainment. Prep svcs including Relic Rack Fast Facts. Multi format radio program consulting svcs.

RPM-Radio Programming & Management Inc.
1133 W. Long Lake Rd., Ste 200, Bloomfield Hills, MI 48302 USA
(248) 647-1068,(800) 521-2537, *Fax:* (888) 776-0006
www.tophitsusa.com
rpmorlk@aol.com
Thomas Kirkorian, President
Wkly CD svc top hits U.S. & CD music libraries. Full CD format svcs & progmg consultation.

Russ Reid Company
2 N. Lake Ave., Suite 600, Pasadena, CA 91101 USA
(626) 449-6100, *Fax:* (626) 463-0028
www.russreid.com
Gene Gee, Operations Dir
David Stuart, General Sales Mgr
David DeBetta, Programming Director
Mark McIntyre, SVP/Government Relations
Kevin White, VP Media
Full service agency specializing in fund-raising, govt rels, adv & PR for nonprofit organizations via mutiple chs, including: TV, radio, interactive/online, direct mail, nwspr, magazines, out-of-home & other media. Partners with loc & natlclients to help them thrive, supporting theirs efforts to change the world.
Government Relations
2000 L St. N.W., Suiter 350, Washington, DC 20036
(202) 912-8600;
Radio Division
25195 S.W. Parkway Ave., Suite 200, Wilsonville, OR 97070
(503) 682-7227;

S. Banks Group Inc.
174 Johnston Ave., Toronto, ON M2N 1H3 CAN
(416) 224-0296, *Fax:* (416) 224-8542
Sydney Banks, President
Feature film and TV program production.

Sak Entertainment
398 W. Amelia St., Orlando, FL 32801 USA
(407) 648-0001, *Fax:* (407) 648-1333
www.sak.com
info@sak.com
David Russell, Programming Director
Professional comedy actors, dirs, producers & writers. Entertainment consultants for WDW, Universal Studio, Harrahs Corp. & Busch Gardens.

Salem Publishing
750 Old Hickory Blvd Ste 150-1, Brentwood, TN 37027 USA
(615) 312-4244, *Fax:* (615) 312-4266
www.salempublishing.com
jcharles@salempublishing.com
Publisher of Homecoming, Preaching, YouthWorker Journal, Singing News & Townhall magazines
Salem Communications
Santa Rosa Blvd, Camarillo, CA 93012

Sam Shad Productions
Box 10853, Reno, NV 89510 USA
(775) 857-2244, *Fax:* (775) 857-2272
www.bestofreno.tv
sam@shad.reno.nv.us
Sam Shad, President
Bonnie McCorkle, Programming Director
Radio progmg & coml production, TV progmg & coml production, TV & radio progmg concepts dev from start to finish, internet design & adv, public relations.

The Samuel Goldwyn Films
9570 W. Pico Blvd., Suite 400, Los Angeles, CA 90035-6405 USA
(310) 860-3100, *Fax:* (310) 860-3195
Samuel Goldwyn Jr., Chairman
Samuel Goldwyn Jr., CEO
Meyer Gottlieb, President
Movie acquisition & distribution.

Sanctuary Records Group Ltd.
Sanctuary House, 45-53 Sinclair Rd., London, W14 0NS GBR
44-020-7602-6351, *Fax:* 44-020-7603-5941
www.sanctuarygroup.com
info@sanctuarygroup.com
Program production & sls.

Sandra Carter Global, Inc.
230 W. 79th St., Suite 102, New York, NY 10024 USA
(212) 875-1811, *Fax:* (212) 875-0088
www.sandra-carter.com
sales@sandra-carter.com
Sandra Carter, President
Ettore Botta, General Sales Mgr
Distribution to all media, co-production deals, production, principle product in factual series.

Sandy Frank Entertainment Inc.
954 Lexington Ave., Suite 255, New York, NY 10021 USA
(212) 772-1889, *Fax:* (212) 772-2297
www.sandyfrankent.com
filmsfe@aol.com
Sandy Frank, Chairman
Sandy Frank, CEO
Maury Shields, Operations Dir
Barbara Kalicinska, General Sales Mgr
Rosalie Perrone, Controller
Sophia Evans, Sales
Susan Piscitello, Sales
Nora Maria Diaz, Sales Director
Sandi Spidell,VP Operations
TV production & syndication.

Sandy Zimmerman Productions
4800 Black Bear Rd., Suite 204, Las Vegas, NV 89149 USA
(702) 731-6491
sandyzimm@go.com
Sandy Zimmerman, President
Robert Gonzales, Programming Director
Develops, produces & distributes TV programs, documentaries, infomercials, travel specials, TV comls, & industrial & corporate videos. Syndicates one- to five-minute program fillers.

The Saturday Evening Post Television Department
1100 Waterway Blvd., Indianapolis, IN 46202 USA
(317) 634-1100, *Fax:* (317) 637-0126
www.satevepost.org
q.lee@satevepost.com,satevepst@aol.com
Quinton Lee, General Manager
Producers & distributors of health shows for radio & TV; coml production.

SB Management
890 Monterey, Box 12837, San Luis Obispo, CA 93406 USA
(805) 543-9214, *Fax:* (805) 543-9243
www.mikehesser.com
michael@mikehesser.com
Mike Hesser, President
Consulting & coaching for sls & mgmt.

SCOLA
21557 270th St, McClelland, IA 51548 USA
(712) 566-2202, *Fax:* (712) 566-2502
www.scola.org
scola@scola.org
Francis Lajba, President
John Millar, Operations Dir
SCOLA progmg from more than 100 countries in more than 90 languages. These programs are available via internet, satellite, cable to learners of languages study, ethnic communities & anyone seeking a global perspective. Mission is to helpthe people of the world learn about one another.

Seattle Video Crew
Box 99218, Seattle, WA 98199 USA
(206) 448-2500, *Fax:* (206) 378-1700
www.seattlevideo.com
crew@seattlevideo.com
David Oglevie, President
Location video production for bcst news, corporate & industrial, mktg, & medical. BETACAM SP, & DVCAM, NTSC or PAL formats.

Semaphore Entertainment Group
32 E. 57th St., New York, NY 10022 USA
(212) 371-8650, *Fax:* (212) 888-8650
www.seg.com
TV program production, radio program production & distribution.

SeniorVision Productions Inc.
418 North Central St., East Bridgewater, MA 2333 USA
(508) 350-9700
Noah Brookoff, President
Steve Brown, Co-Owner

Seraphim Communications Inc.
1568 Eustis St., St. Paul, MN 55108 USA
(651) 645-9173, *Fax:* (651) 645-3515
www.seracomm.com
info@seracomm.com
Hal Dragseth, President
Kristin Wiersma, Operations Dir
Full-svc video & AV capabilities. Emphasis on video production from concept through final product. In-house grahics, interactive Web, CD-ROM/DVD.

SESAC Inc.
55 Music Sq E, Nashville, TN 37203 USA
(615) 320-0055, *Fax:* (615) 329-9627
www.sesac.com
Pat Collins, COO
SESAC is a service organization created to assist both the creators & users of music through royalty collection & efficient music licensing.
152 W 57th St, 57th Fl, New York, NY 10019
(212) 484-0600; *Fax:* (212) 489-5699
Stephen Swid, Chairman
Freddie Gershon, CEO/COO
Ira Smith, Co-Chmn
67 Upper Berkeley St, London W1H 3FF,
020 7616 9284; *Fax:* 020 7563 7029
Dr. Wayne Bickerton, Chairman
420 Lincoln Rd, Ste 502, Miami, FL 33139
(305) 534-7500; *Fax:* (305) 534-7578
501 Santa Monica Blvd, Ste 450, Santa Monica, CA 90401
(310) 393-9671; *Fax:* (310) 393-6497
981 Joseph E Lowery Blvd NW, Ste 111, Atlanta, GA 30318
(404) 897-1330; *Fax:* (404) 897-1306

Sesame Workshop
One Lincoln Plaza, New York, NY 10023 USA
(212) 595-3456, *Fax:* (212) 875-6111
www.sesameworkshop.org
Gary Knell, President
TV program production.

Seven Network Australia Inc.
10100 Santa Monica Blvd., Suite 1750, Los Angeles, CA 90067 USA
(310)-553-3345, *Fax:* (310) 553-4812
www.seven.com.au
Zane Bair, General Manager
Mike Amor, Station Manager
U.S. office & news bureau of ch 7, Australiaa major coml TV network of Australia. Producing news. Purchasing TV programming.

Seville Pictures
150 Eglington Ave. E., Suite 804, Toronto, ON M4P 1E8 CAN
(416) 480-0453, *Fax:* (416) 480-0501
www.seville.com
1ufor@seville.com
David Reckziegel, President
Andrew Austin, Operations Dir
Pierre Brousseau, President
Seville pictures is involved in production and distribution of multimedia content for film, TV, video & on-line communication marketplace.

SFP Productions
2 Ave. de L' Europe, 94360 Bry-Sur-Marne Cedex, FRA
33 169 833 602, *Fax:* 331 149 833 604
www.sfp.fr
distribution@sfr.fr
Roland Fiszel, CEO
Sophie Vtueite, General Sales Mgr
Distribution worldwide rights (TV movies, series, mini-series documentaries).

Shelly Palmer Productions
P. O. Box 1877, New York, NY 10156-1877 USA
(212) 532-3880
www.shellypalmer.com
info@shellypalmer.com
Shelly Palmer, President
Music, video, TV, film production & creative svcs. Adv & mktg. Music libraries, sound design, sls videos & post-production.

Shield Productions Inc.
11964 N Lake Dr., Boynton Beach, FL 33436 USA
(561) 734-5599, *Fax:* (561) 734-8176
James Dolan, President
Creation & production of radio & TV comls.

Shukovsky English Entertainment
4605 Lankershim Blvd., Suite 510, North Hollywood, CA 91602 USA
(818) 763-9191, *Fax:* (818) 763-9878
Joel Shukovsky, President
Diane English, Programming Director
Producer & distributor of TV progmg, especially half-hour comedy.

Sidewater Enterprises Inc.
2647 Laurel Pass, Los Angeles, CA 90046 USA
(310) 358-4960, *Fax:* (323) 656-7853
fredericsid@aol.com

PROGRAMMING & PRODUCTION SERVICES

Frederic Sidewater, President
Rosalyn Sidewater, Executive Vice President
Consulting regarding financing & distribution for independent productions.

Silverline Pictures
22837 Ventura Blvd., Ste. 205, Woodland Hills, CA 91364 USA
(818) 225-9032, *Fax:* (818) 225-9053
www.silverlinepictures.com
silverline@earthlink.net
Leman Cetiner, CEO
Axel Munch, President
Full-svc production & distribution company producing theatrical, TV & kids series.

Silverman Stock Footage Inc.
210 Douglass St., Suite 1-D, Brooklyn, NY 11217 USA
(917) 470-9104, *Fax:* (718) 764-4411
www.silvermanstockfootage.com
donald@silvermstockfootage.com
Donald Silverman, President
Stock footage.

Sing For Joy
St. Olaf College, 1520 St. Olaf Avenue, Northfield, MN 55057 USA
(507) 786-8596, *Fax:* (507) 786-3033
www.singforjoy.org
singforjoy@stolaf.edu
Miriam Mueller, COO
Jeffrey O'Donnell, Programming Director
Joshua Wyatt, Associate Producer
John Ferguson, Music Advisor
Pastor Bruce Benson, Program Host
Sacred choral works with host commentary relating the music to the scriptural lessons during each week of the church year.

Skywatch Weather Center
347 Prestley Rd., Bridgeville, PA 15017 USA
(412) 221-6000,(800)-SKYWATCH, *Fax:* (412) 221-3160
www.skywatchweather.com
airsci@skywatchweather.com
Stanley Penkala, President
Daniel Krzywiecki, Operations Dir
Specially formatted weathercasts produced in the Skywatch Weather Center.

Smith/Lee Productions, Inc.
7420 Manchester Rd., St. Louis, MO 63143 USA
(314) 647-3900, *Fax:* (314) 647-3959
www.smithlee.com
global@smithlee.com
David Smith, President
Barry Lee, Operations Dir
TV & radio coml promotional film production; production svcs; studio specializing in Audio Post; music production, voice recording & multimedia.

Soldiers Radio & Television, U.S. Army Public Affairs
Box 31, 2511 Jefferson Davis Hwy., Arlington, VA 22202 USA
(703) 602-4675, *Fax:* (703) 602-5220
www.army.mil/srtv,www.soldiersradio.com
armynewswatch@smc.army.mil
Jim Ryan, Operations Dir
George McNamara, General Manager
Melody Day, Promotions Manager
Gene Gunderson, Chief Engineer
Paul Schultz, Operations Manager
Radio, TV news bureau, soldiers radio network & Army Newswatch a biweekly TV newscast.

Solid Gospel Network (Reach Satellite Network, Inc.)
402 BNA Drive, Suite 400, Nashville, TN 37217 USA
(615) 367-2210
www.solidgospel.com
info@SalemMusicNetwork.com
Wade Schoenemann, Operations Dir
Jim Black, General Manager
Don Burns, Programming Director
Michael Miller, General Manager
Ed Evensen, Local Traffic Manager
Rick Shelton, Manager
24-hour, satellite delivered, Christian country & southern gospel network, featuring artists like Bill Gaither, The Isaacs, Gold City, Jeff & Sheri Easter & The Martins, live from Nashville, the Christian music capital of the world.

Sony Pictures
10202 West Washington Blvd., Culver City, CA 90232 USA
(310) 244-4000, *Fax:* (310) 244-2626
www.spe.sony.com
Michael Lynton, CEO
550 Madison Ave., New York, NY 10022 United States
(212) 883-8500;
3500 Maple Ave., Suite 205, Dallas, TX 75219 United States
(214) 520-7070;
455 N. Cityfront Plaza Dr., Suite 2520, Chicago, IL 60611 United States
(312) 644-0770;
2859 Paces Ferry Rd., Suite 1130, Atlanta, GA 30339 United States
(770) 434-5400;

SoperSound Music Library
Box 869, Ashland, OR 97520 USA
(800) 227-9980, *Fax:* (541) 552-0832
www.sopersound.com
info@sopersound.com
Dennis Reed, President
Contemp music library for all production needs. Available on CDs & direct digital down load online.

Sound Idea Productions
417 Nursery St., Nevada City, CA 95959 USA
(510) 832-5178, *Fax:* (510) 832-4829
soundidea@oro.net
Glenn Davidson, President
Archival Service. Radio production & syndication.
405 14th St, Suite 612, Oakland, CA 94612 United States
(530) 478-9770;

Sound Ideas
105 W. Beaver Creek Rd., Suite 4, Richmond Hill, ON L4B 1C6 CAN
(905) 886-5000,(800) 387-3030, *Fax:* (905) 886-6800
www.sound-ideas.com
info@sound-ideas.com
Brian Nimens, CEO
Royalty free sound effects, imaging elements, music for the professional audio industry; including bcst, cable, film, multimedia & internet applications.

Sound of Birmingham Productions
3625 5th Ave. S., Birmingham, AL 35222 USA
(205) 595-8497
soundofbirmingham.com
don@soundofbirmingham.com
Don Mosley, President
Betty Mosley, Operations Dir
Radio & TV voice-overs, jingles, video sweetening, custom music, recording studios, full-svc studios, ISDN.

Sound Source Networks
2 St. Clair Ave. W., Suite 1101, Toronto, ON M4V 1L6 CAN
(416) 922-1290, *Fax:* (416) 323-6819
www.soundsource.ca
info@soundsource.ca
Lesley Soldat, Operations Dir
Jean Marie Heimrath, General Manager
Radio net that produces, markets & distributes radio programs nationally.

Sound*Bytes
1425 Hopkins St. N.W., Suite 401, Washington, DC 20036 USA
(202) 296-2022
www.soundbytesradio.com
press@soundbytesradio.com
Jan Ziff, President
Computer audio show production & syndication.

Soundshop Recording Studio LLC
1307 Division St., Nashville, TN 37203 USA
(615) 244-4149, *Fax:* (615) 242-8759
soundshopstudio@aol.com
Don Cook, President
Mike Bradley, Owner
Music production, recording studios, 2-48 track digital or 24 track analog studios.

Soundtrack
162 Columbus Ave., Boston, MA 02116-5222 USA
(617) 303-7500, *Fax:* (617) 303-7555
www.soundtrackboston.com
Jeanne Priest, General Manager
Production, postproduction & custom music of all kinds; specializing in sound designs.
936 Broadway, New York, NY 10010
(212) 420-6010;
Chris Rich, Opns Mgr

Southcott Productions
Box 33185, Granada Hills, CA 91394 USA
(818) 368-4938, *Fax:* (818) 368-4938
chucksongs@aol.com
Chuck Southscott, President
Radio program, coml production & distribution.

Southern STAR
61 295 192 677, *Fax:* 61 295 172 530
www.southern-star.com.au
info@duplitek.com.au
Robyn Watts, General Sales Mgr
Errol Sullivan, Programming Director
Southern Star is an integrated film & TV production distribution & manufacturing group. Southern Star is a public listed company.

Spanish Broadcasting System
26 W. 56th St., New York, NY 10019 USA
(212) 541-9200, *Fax:* (212) 541-6904
www.lamusica.com
Joseph Garcia, CFO
Carey Davis, Operations Dir
Raul Alarcon, CEO
Spanish progmg syndication.

Spelling Television Inc.
5700 Wilshire Blvd., Suite 575, Los Angeles, CA 90036 USA
(323) 965-5700, *Fax:* (323) 965-5895
E. Vincent, Chairman
Jonathan Levin, President
E. Vincent, Vice Chairman
TV program production.

SPI International
55 White St., Suite 1A, New York, NY 10013 USA
(212) 673-5103, *Fax:* (212) 673-5183
www.spiintl.com
Loni Farhi, President
Stacey Sobel, Operations Dir
For over nineteen years SPI International, Inc. has been a leading supplier of theatrical films and a wide variety of television programming to the international market. To further exploit its vast library SPI established its own cablestations on pay and basic cable level in Poland , Czech Republic ,Slovakia and Hungary. SPI will open additional channels throughout Eastern Europe during 2009.

Sport International Inc.
Villa del Mar East, 14 J Ave. Isla Verde, Carolina, PR 979 USA
(787) 268-8751, *Fax:* (787) 726-7683
www.hjfsport.com
hector@hjfsport.com
Juliet Giamartino, Chairman
Jennifer Marin, Operations Dir
Juliet Giamartino, Co-Chairman
Global mktg, distribution, bcstg, sports events, Pay-Per-View & special entertainment progmg. Current properties include: This Day in Sports, Wide World of Bloopers, live buying & buying documentaries.

Sports Byline U.S.A.
300 Broadway, Suite 8, San Francisco, CA 94133 USA
(415) 434-8300, *Fax:* (415) 391-2569
www.sportsbyline.com
webmaster@sportsbyline.com
Ron Barr, Chairman
Darren Peck, President
Satellite-delivered nationwide radio sports talk net, listener 800 number, 7days (West Coast), barter.

StarDate/Universo Productions
2609 University Ave., # 3.118, Austin, TX 78712 USA
(512) 471-5285, *Fax:* (512) 471-5060
www.stardate.org
perez@stardate.org
Damond Benningfield, Programming Director
Sandra Preston, Executive Producer
Syndicated two-minute radio programs on stars & planets visible in the night sky. Each program is date-specific. English/Spanish.

Steve Rotfeld Productions Inc.
610 Old Lancaster Rd., Suite 210, Bryn Mawr, PA 19010 USA
(610) 520-0671, *Fax:* (610) 520-0681
www.rotfeldproductions.com
Steve Rotfeld, Programming Director
A TV production company that produces & syndicates TV shows.

Steven B. Stevens
7400 Sweetwater Branch, West Chester, OH 45069 USA
(513) 755-7300, *Fax:* (513) 755-7507
sbstevens@aol.com
Steven Stevens, President
Accomplished narrator/voice talent with deep warm authoratative voice.

Strand Media Group Inc.
12240 Venice Blvd., Suite 23, Los Angeles, CA 90066 USA
(310) 390-2248, *Fax:* (310) 390-2857
www.somethingyoushouldknow.net
strandmg@aol.com
Mike Carruthers, President
Radio programs, coml production & distribution; media buying agent.

Strength for Living
6350 W. Freeway, Fort Worth, TX 76116 USA
(817) 570-1400,(800) 266-1837, *Fax:* (817) 737-9436
www.familynetradio.com
info@familynet.org,lbratton@familynetradioccom,dseen@familynetradio.com,drkaren@familynetradio.com
Chuck Ries, Programming Director
Donna Senn, Promotions Manager
Lisa Bratton, Radio Marketing & Dist.
Offers audiences relevant messages of hope & spiritual encouragement in their search to find strength for living. Host Bob Reccord.

Studio Babelsberg GmbH
August-Bebel-St. 26-53, 14482 Potsdam, DEU
49 (0) 331-72 -13151, *Fax:* 49 (0) 331-72-12525
www.studiobabelsberg.de
info@studiobabelsberg.com
Gerhard Bergfried, CEO
Studio area, studio technology, set design & construction, film laboratory, postproduction, dubbing theatres for films, TV & video.

Studio Center Total Production
161 Business Park Drive, Virginia Beach, VA 23462 USA
(866) 515-2111, *Fax:* (757) 623-5512
www.studiocenter.com
info@studiocenter.com
William Prettyman, CEO
Radio & TV commmercials, station promotions, voice-over services, original music, copywriting, on hold & website audio.
3875 S. Jones Blvd., Las Vegas, CA 89103
(702) 248-2777; *Fax:* (702) 248-5400
2693 Union Ave. Ext., Memphis, TN 38112
(901)323-7060; *Fax:* (901) 320-0003
5245 Cleveland St., Ste. 204, Virginia Beach, VA 23462
(757)622-2111;
315 Madison Ave., 11th Floor, New York, NY 10017
(212)986-1929;
7033 W. Sunset Blvd., Suite 318, Los Angeles, CA 90028
(323)466-9673;

Studio M Productions Unlimited
4032 Wilshire Blvd., Suite 403, Los Angeles, CA 90010 USA
(213) 389-7372, *Fax:* (213) 389-3299
www.mandy.com/stu001.html
mixer@sound4film-tv.com
Mike Michaels, President
Robert Dickerson, Chief Engineer
TV & radio program production, tape, film & live production svcs. Live remotes for TV, radio, news & sports. (888) 389-7372.
Jim Walters Co
4224 Waialae #201, Honolulu, HI 96816-5330
808-373-2701;

STV Central Ltd.
Pacific Quay, Glasgow, G51 1PQ
1 413 003 704
Bcstr & production company.

Suite Audio
21 Stone Wall Ln., Clinton, CT 6413 USA
(860) 664-9499
www.suiteaudio.com
info@suiteaudio.com
Bob Nary, President
Facility: ProTools HDII/TDM, Waves restoration & Platinum, Sonic Solutions. Commercial - Program - surround production. CD mastering - authoring - duplication. Cassette duplication.
Clinton
CT 21 Stonewall Ln, Clinton, CT 06413 United States
Bob Nary, Owner

Sullivan Entertainment Inc./Sullivan Entertainment International
110 Davenport Rd., Toronto, ON M5R 3R3 CAN
(416) 921-7177, *Fax:* (416) 921-7538
www.sullivan-ent.com
Production, distribution, home video, dev series & feature film.
Sullivan Entertainment Europe Ltd
Savant House, 63-65 Camden High St., London United Kingdom,
(207) 383-5192;
Muriel Thomas, Sr Vp Intl Sls

Sullivan Video Services Inc.
7 Pickman Dr., Bedford, MA 1730 USA
(781) 271-1720, *Fax:* (781) 271-1740
www.sullivanvideo.com
johnsul@sull
John Sullivan, President
Full-svc video production company. Provides ENG/EFP news crews & Ku-band satellite svcs, Fiber Optic Studio Tape feeding capabilities.

The Summit Media Group Inc. (Sub 4 Kids Entertainment)
1414 Ave. of the Americas, New York, NY 10019 USA
(212) 754-4900, *Fax:* (212) 754-5480
shirsch@4kidsent.com
Alfred Kahn, Chairman
Sheldon Hirsch, CEO
Distribution of programs in the United States with emphasis on programs for children.

Sunbow Entertainment
100 5th Ave., Fl. 3, New York, NY 10011 USA
(212) 893-1600, *Fax:* (212) 893-1630
www.tvloonland.com
Rebecca Gallivan, Operations Dir
Suzanne Berman, General Manager
Developers, producers & distributors of quality children's & family programs, licensors & merchandise.

Sundial Productions
275 Huyler St., S. Hackensack, NJ 7606 USA
(201) 525-0100, *Fax:* (201) 525-5111
David Lapidus, President
Jack Kreismer, Principal
Voice production company; radio & telephone feature production.

SunGard Output Solutions
350 Automation Way, Irondale, AL 35210 USA
(205) 307-6713, *Fax:* (205) 307-6813
www.sungard.com
jamey.vella@sungard.com
Joseph Harper, President
Jamey Vella, General Sales Mgr
SunGard's document distribution output channels include: paper, electronic (ebill/email), optical and/ or magnetic media.

Swell Pictures Inc.
455 N. City Front Plaza, 18th Fl., Chicago, IL 60611 USA
(312) 464-8000, *Fax:* (312) 464-8020
www.swellinc.com
Brian Clark, President
Dave Mueller, Operations Dir
Joe Flores, Chief Engineer
Radi Akel, Operations Manager
Michael Topel, President
Film-to-tape transfer, videotape editing, digital sound editing & original music. Avid, 3-D graphics & compositing, audio & new media.

System TV
45/47 rue Paul Bert, 92100 Boulogne, Paris, FRA
(33)-1-55-38-2020, *Fax:* (33)-1-55-38-20-30
www.systemtv.fr
daniel@systemtv.fr
Daniel Renoug, President
TV program production, press agency, produce weather & info svcs.

Talco Productions
279 E. 44th St., New York, NY 10017 USA
(212) 697-4015, *Fax:* (212) 697-4827
alaw1@mindspring.com
Alan Lawrence, President
Marty Holberton, Operations Dir
TV, radio progmg, documentaries, ind, educ production, PR consultation & production.

Talk America Radio Networks
520 Broad St., Newark, NJ 7102 USA
(973) 438-3026, *Fax:* (973) 438-1637
www.talkamerica.com
Trang Nguyen, COO
Maurice Bortz, Operations Dir
24-hour talk seven days a week offering live call-in programs. All programs barter & every minute is covered.

Talk Radio Network
Box 3755, Central Point, OR 97502 USA
(541) 664-8827, *Fax:* (541) 664-6250
www.talkradionetwork.com
Mark Masters, President
Full-svc live talk radio format 24 hours daily. Serving more than 400 affils nationwide.

Talkline Communications Radio Network
Box 20108, Park West Station, New York, NY 10025-1510 USA
(212) 769-1925, *Fax:* (212) 799-4195
www.talklinecommunications.com
tcntalk@aol.com
Zev J. Brenner, Programming Director
Natl Jewish radio net. Carried in over 2,500 markets. Contemp Jewish progmg; interview & call-in format with newsmaker guests from politics, entertainment & Israel. Live segments from Israel. Available on barter. Satellite delivered.

Tamouz Media
37 W. 20th, Suite 1007, New York, NY 10011 USA
(212) 463-7437, *Fax:* (212) 463-7409
www.tamouz.com
tamouzmedia@aol.com
Ilan Ziv, Programming Director
TV program & documentary production.

Tankersley Productions, Inc., St. Louis
858 Hanley Industrial Ct., St. Louis, MO 63144
(314) 725-0116
www.tlgdc.com
mail@tlgdc.com
Randy Tankersley, President

Tapestry International, Ltd.
11 Hanover Sq., 14th Fl., New York, NY 10005 USA
(212) 505-2288, *Fax:* (212) 505-5059
tunein@tapestry.tv
Nancy L. Walzog, President
Karen Carlson, General Manager
Laura Ibanez, General Sales Mgr
Production & distribution company working in the international TV marketplace.

Technisonic Studios
500 S. Ewing Ave., Suite G, St. Louis, MO 63103 USA
(314) 533-1777, *Fax:* (314) 533-6527
www.technisonic.com
mstroot@technisonic.com
16 & 35 mm film production, full-sound studios, video production, film & video editing.

Tel-A-Cast Productions
1016 Everee Inn Rd., Griffin, GA 30224 USA
(770) 233-4200, *Fax:* (770) 233-4247
mrenew@osmose.com
Michael Renew, Programming Director
From concept to execution, produces TV & radio comls, training videos, mktg videos & other projects quickly & efficiently.

Tel-Air Interests Inc.
2040 Sherman St., Hollywood, FL 33020 USA
(954) 924-4949, *Fax:* (954) 924-4980
www.telairint.com
telair@aol.com
Grant Gravitt, President
M. Gravitt, Operations Dir
Syndicated TV specials (sports & music), contract production, theatrical short subjects & documentary TV & films, infomercials. Digital recording studio, digital & linear editing.

TeleCom Productions Inc.
5875 Peachtree Industrial Blvd., Suite 150, Norcross, GA 30092 USA
(770) 455-3569, *Fax:* (770) 455-3938
www.tcpatlanta.com
Roger Clark, Chairman
Budd O. Libby, President
Roger Clark, Co-Chairman
Production & syndicator of Let's Go to the Races, Free Cash Lotto, Daily Race Game & Post Time retail prize promotions; random animated digital drawing systems (RADDS).

Telegenic Programs Inc.
161 Forest Hill Rd., Toronto, ON M5P 2N3 CAN
(416) 484-8000, *Fax:* (416) 484-8001
telegenic@aol.com
H. Fein, Chairman
H. Fein, CEO
Ronda Taylor, Operations Dir
One of Canada's leading TV distribution companies now in its 30th successful year.

Telenium Studios
525 Mildred Ave., Primos, PA 19018 USA
(610) 626-6500, *Fax:* (610) 626-2638
www.telenium.com

Todd Strine, CEO
Peter Hayes, General Manager
Cathie Hunt, General Sales Mgr
Studio & location production & postproduction for networks, syndication & cable. Full facilities, production mgmt & creative svcs.
Telenium Post
520 N. Columbus Blvd., Suite 204, Philadelphia, PA 19123
United States
(215) 629-2000; *Fax:* (219) 625-8353
Mark Reidenaver, Dir of Post Prod

Telepros
Box 1116, Belmont, CA 94002 USA
(650) 345-0505
telepros@comcast.net
Niels Melo, President
Producers of live entertainment, sports, news, performing arts, corporate videos and webcasts.

Televents Ltd.
2450 Virginia Ave. N.W., Washington, DC 20037 USA
(202) 296-0541, *Fax:* (202) 296-0541
James Avis, General Manager
TV program production & distribution.

Television & Radio Features Inc.
Box 237, Lincolnshire, IL 60069-0327 USA
(847) 541-7600, *Fax:* (847) 541-2600
Morton A. Small, President
Promotions, prize svcs; mktg.

Television Representatives Inc.
9720 Wilshire Blvd., Suite 202, Beverly Hills, CA 90212-2006 USA
(310) 278-4050, *Fax:* (310) 278-3350
heyalans@aol.com
Alan Silverbach, President
TV program distribution, United States & international.

The Television Syndication Company, Inc.
520 Sabal Lake Dr., Suite 108, Longwood, FL 32779 USA
(407) 788-6407, *Fax:* (407) 788-4397
www.tvsco.com
cassie@tvsco.com
Cassie Yde, President
A full-svc TV syndication & distribution organization offering TV progmg to bcstrs worldwide.

Televix Entertainment Inc.
449 S. Beverly Dr., 3rd Fl., Suite 300, Beverly Hills, CA 90212 USA
(310) 788-5500, *Fax:* (310) 286-0207
www.televix.com
postmaster@televix.com
Hugo Rose, CEO
Pamela Popp, Operations Dir
Distribution of TV programs in the Latin American & Spanish U.S. markets.

Telfax Inc.
3305 Pleasant Valley Ln., Arlington, TX 76015 USA
(817) 468-0070, *Fax:* (817) 468-0111
ts4telfax@aol.com
Tony Symanovich, President
Remote TV production svcs.

Tepuy
2745 Ponce de Leon Blvd., Coral Gables, FL 33134 USA
(305) 774-0033, *Fax:* (305) 774-7372
www.tepuy.com
Marcos Santana, Chairman
Marcos Santana, CEO
Igancio Barrera, President
Esperanza Garay, Operations Dir
Fernando Espejo, General Manager
Program distribution.
Via Dos Castillas
9C-P2, 2B, Pozuelo de Alarcon, 28224 Spain
(3491) 351-7107;
Fernando Espeto, Chairman
Ave. Libertador Torre E, EXA PH-1, Caracas, 1060 Venezuela
(58212) 953-3363;

Thomas Craven Film Corp.
5 W. 19th St., New York, NY 10011-4216 USA
(212) 463-7190, *Fax:* (212) 627-4761
www.cravenfilms.com
michael@cravenfilms.com
Michael Craven, President
Ernest Barbieri, Operations Dir
Complete film & video production svcs from scripting through shooting & editing to distribution.

Thomas Horton Associates Inc.
408 Bryant Cir., Suite K, Ojai, CA 93023 USA
(805) 646-7866, *Fax:* (805) 646-3600
www.sharktv.com
tha@sharktv.com
Thomas Horton, President
Jean Garner, Operations Dir
Garry R. Garner, Promotions Manager
TV program full-svc production, postproduction, international & domestic distribution, specializing in award-winning documentaries.

Thompson Creative
4141 Office Parkway, Dallas, TX 75204 USA
(214) 559-4000, *Fax:* (214) 521-8578
www.thompsoncreative.com
info@thompsoncreative.com
J. Larry Thompson, CEO
Susan Price Thompson, President
Contemp radio ID jingles for all formats.

Tim Cissell Music
1120 Grassmere Dr., Richardson, TX 75080-2909 USA
(972) 680-0817, *Fax:* (972) 680-0866
www.web.wt.net/~tcissell
tcissell@wt.net
Tim Cissell, President
Offers music composition & production for all media (TV/CATV & radio)jingles, IDs, film & video.

Time Capsule, Inc.
124 Cottonwood Lane, Centerville, MA 02632-1911 USA
(800) 822-7785, *Fax:* (508) 637-3333
www.tcapsule.com/radio
tc@tcapsule.com
Richard Teimer, President
Bill Stephens, Operations Dir
Nancy Q. Proctor, VP/Affiliates Relations
System to bring 1,000 more cash ads per year; daily quizzes fit all formats.

TM Studios
2002 Academy Ln., Suite 110, Dallas, TX 75234 USA
(972) 406-6800, *Fax:* (972) 406-6890
www.tmstudios.com
info@tmstudios.com
Chris Long, Operations Dir
TMC creates, produces & distributes music-based products for bcst, including compilation libraries, production music, I.D. packages & coml jingles.

Toby Arnold and Associates Inc.
3234 Commander Dr., Carrollton, TX 75006 USA
(800) 527-5335,(972) 661-8200, *Fax:* (972) 250-6014
www.taamusic.com
toby@taamusic.com
Dolly Arnold, COO
Toby Arnold, President
Lawrence Mangiameli, Promotions Manager
Audio production libraries for TV & radio. Station Imaging, Morning show promo sweeper, stager packages for all formats.

Today Video
475 10th Ave. 10th Fl., New York, NY 11024 USA
(212) 239-3999, *Fax:* (212) 239-2999
David Seeger, CEO
Production svcs.

Toes Production Inc.
22 Hickory Dr., Maplewood, NJ 7040 USA
(973) 793-5440, *Fax:* (973) 363-7798
phonepatch@aol.com
Brad Abelle, President
Brad is a radio talk show host and voice artist.

Tom Jones Recording Studios
1620 Greenview Dr. S.W., Rochester, MN 55902-1034 USA
(507) 288-7711, *Fax:* (507) 288-4531
Thomas Jones, President
Aaron Manthei, Chief Engineer
Recording studio, compact disc duplication recording svcs. Radio program & coml production.

Tomwil Inc.
4905 Gentry Ave., Valley Village, CA 91607 USA
(818) 769-0883, *Fax:* (818) 769-0887
tomwil@earthlink.net
James Rokos, President
Wilda Rokos, Operations Dir
Distributors of features, light entertainment, sports, series & documentaries to all media in the world market.

Toucan Productions
60 Fiddlers Elbow Rd., Margaretville, NY 12455 USA
(212) 580-4882,(845) 586-1746, *Fax:* (845) 586-4623

Tourism Australia
6100 Center Drive, Ste 1150, Los Angeles, CA 90045 USA
(310) 695-3200, *Fax:* (310) 695-3201
www.tourism.australia.com
Various Marketing divisions.

TR Productions
209 W. Central St., Suite 108, Natick, MA 1760 USA
(508) 650-3400, *Fax:* (508) 650-3455
www.trprod.com
Cary Benjamin, President
Production svcs.

Traffic Pulse Networks (A Unit of Mobility Technologies)
Moblity Technology - Traffic Pluse Network, 851 Duportail Rd., Wayne, PA 19087 USA
(610) 725-9700, *Fax:* (610) 725-0530
www.mobilitytechnologies.com
info@mobilitytechnologies.com
Doug Alexander, CEO
Al McGowan, Operations Dir
Robert Pollan, COO/CFO
Jim Brown, Vice President
Traffic Pulse Networks provides digital & traditional traffic data to radio, TV & CATV. It also provides an inventory rep service.

Traffic Scan Network, Inc
7707 Waco Ave., Baton Rouge, LA 70806-1440 USA
(225) 926-7152, *Fax:* (225) 923-0704
www.trafficscannetwork.com
johnny@trafficscannetwork.com
Johnny Ahysian, President
Traf, news, sports, weather reports for radio, TV & cable systems.

The Transcription Company
4100 W. Burbank Blvd., 3rd Flr., Burbank, CA 91505 USA
(818) 848-6500, *Fax:* (818) 556-4150
www.transcripts.net,www.transcripts.tv,www.captioningcompany.com,www.rapidtext.com
customerservice@transcripts.net
Michele Bartmon, General Manager
Samantha Somers, Manager, Entertainment
Transcribe all media: TV shows, films, news, sports, documentaries, meetings interviews. Provide closed captioning. Provide translations. Sell ABC News transcripts.
Rapidtext Inc.
1801 Dove St., Suite 101, Newport Beach, CA 92660
(949) 399-9200;
Glory Johnson, Coo & Vp

The Transfer Zone
13251 Northend, Oak Park, MI 48237-3261 USA
(248) 548-7580, *Fax:* (248) 548-0924
thetransferzone.com
transferzone@juno.com
Roxane B. Newhouse, Promotions Manager
International video standard conversions, duplication, film/slide transfers: A-B roll editing, video slide/film. Video to CD & DVD & duplication.

TRF Production Music Libraries
One International Blvd., Suite 212, Mahwah, NJ 7495 USA
(800) 899-MUSIC, *Fax:* (201) 335-0004
www.trfmusic.com
info@trfmusic.com
Michael Nurko, CEO
Largest collection of contemporary, retro and traditional production music. Every category available including all types of ethnic and specialty music.

TRI-COMM Productions
11 Palmetto Pkwy., Suite 201, Hilton Head Island, SC 29926-3703 USA
(843) 681-5000, *Fax:* (843) 681-2945
www.tri-comm.tv
William J. Robinson, CEO
A full-svc production company specializing in film HD & digital betacam production, sound design, graphics/animation. Also offers sugar sand beaches & the best golf courses around.

Triage Entertainment Inc.
6701 Center Dr. W., Suite 1111, Los Angeles, CA 90045-1552 USA

(818) 386-6800, *Fax:* (818) 386-9889
www.triageinc.com
Stu Schreiberg, President
John Bravakis, Operations Dir
Chris Greenleaf, General Sales Mgr
Steve Kroonpnick, Executive Director
Independent, full-svc production company with extensive experience in the production of TV & film; post-production facilities & motion control/graphics department.

Tribune Entertainment Co.
5800 Sunset Blvd., Los Angeles, CA 90028 USA
(323) 460-5800, *Fax:* (323) 460-3858
www.tribtv.com
David Berson, Operations Dir
George NeJame, General Manager
Jon Krobot, General Sales Mgr
Karen Corbin, Programming Director
Natalie Sackin, Promotions Manager
Gina Brittle-Mackey, Director
Seth Howard, Director
Taylor Fuller,Director
Larry Hutchings, Vice President
Richard Inouye, Vice President
Acquires, develops, produces & distributes progmg for TV including Gene Roddenberry's Andromeda, Gene Roddenberry's Earth: Final Conflict, BeastMaster, Malibu, CA, Soul Train, U.S. Farm Report, Soul Train Music Awards, Soul Train Lady ofSoul Awards, Soul Train Christmas Starfest, & Live from the Academy Awards.
435 N. Michigan Ave., Suite 1800, Chicago, IL 60611 United States
(312) 222-4000; *Fax:* (312) 222-3815
Michael Adinamis, Vp Bcst Opns
Dick Bailey, Dir Midwest Adviser Sls
Jennifer Dreyer, Acc Exec Midwest Rgnl Sls
Jeff McElheney, Acc Exec Midwest Rgnl Sls
1580 Warsaw Rd., Suite 210, Roswell, GA 30076 United States
(770) 643-4504; *Fax:* (770) 643-2549
Samuel K. Fuller, Dir
SE rgnl sls, CEO/COO
220 E. 42nd St., Suite 400, New York, NY 10017 United States
(212) 210-1000; *Fax:* (212) 210-1056
Liz Koman, Sr Vp Adv Sls
Steve Mulderrig, Sr Vp/Gen Sls Mgr

Tribune Radio Networks
435 N. Michigan Ave., Chicago, IL 60611 USA
(312) 222-3342, *Fax:* (312) 222-4876
www.tribuneradio.com
Barbara Pabst, Operations Dir
Tom Langmyer, General Manager
Wendi Power, Manager
Tape & internet digital delivered farm, sports & specialty programs including: Chicago Cubs Network, Agri-Voice, National Farm Report, Farming America, Samuelson's Sez.

Trident Releasing
8401 Melrose Pl., 2nd Fl., Los Angeles, CA 90069 USA
(323) 655-8818, *Fax:* (323) 655-0515
tridents@aol.com
Jean Ovrum, Chairman
Victoria Plummer, President
Kristi Mailing, General Sales Mgr
Acquire feature films in the postproduction & completed stages.

Troma Entertainment, Inc.
733 Ninth Ave., New York, NY 10019 USA
(212) 757-4555, *Fax:* (212) 399-9885
www.troma.com
Troma is one of the oldest ind film companies in the world. We produce & distribute films & offer stock footage.

TS James & Associates
83 Christopher St., New York, NY 10014-4246 USA
(212) 331-0186, *Fax:* (212) 505-0959
tom@jandasound.com
Thomas James, President
Original scoring for film & TV.

Turner Entertainment Co.
1888 Century Park E., 10th Fl., Los Angeles, CA 90067 USA
(310) 788-6801, *Fax:* (310) 788-6810
roger.mayer@turner.com
Robert Mayer, COO
Sls, licensing & servicing of major film & TV library.

TVOntario
Box 200, Stn Q, Toronto, ON M4T 2T1 CAN
(416) 484-2600, *Fax:* (416) 484-2662
www.tvo.org
Lee Robock, COO
Yuonne Carey-Le, General Manager
Educ production, educ bcst international program sls, coproduction.

Twentieth Century Fox Television Distribution
Box 900, Beverly Hills, CA 90213-0900 USA
(310) 369-1000, *Fax:* (310) 369-8892
www.foxnow.com
Marion Edwards, President
Mark Kaner, President
Peter Levinshon, President
Production & distribution.
Fox Film Do Brasil Ltda.
Rua Dr. EDuardo De Souza Arrrrranha, 387-3o Andar, Sao Paulo, 04543-121 Brazil
5511-3365-5205; *Fax:* (5511) 3365-5177
Twentieth Century Fox France, Inc.
TV Division 21 bis rue Lord Byron, Paris, 75008 France
33-1-5393-9398; *Fax:* 33-1-5393-9397
Fox/Incendo
101 Bloor Street West, Suite #400, Toronto, ON M5S 2Z7 Canada
416-643-3897; *Fax:* 416-643-3907
Twentieth Century Fox Television Distribution
31-32 Soho Square..., London WID 3AP,
44-20-7437-7766; *Fax:* 44-20-7439-1806
Fox Studios Austrailia
Driver Avenue, Moore Park, 1363 Australia
61-8353-2200; *Fax:* 61-2-835-2205
Twentieth Century Fox Television Distribution
2000 N.W. 150th Avenue, Suite 1110, Pembroke Pines, FL 33028-2867 United States
954-322-5000; *Fax:* 954-322-5275

Twentieth Television
2121 Ave. of the Stars, Suite 2100, Los Angeles, CA 90067 USA
(310) 369-3924, *Fax:* (310) 369-1506
www.fox.com
Bob Cook, COO
Bob Cesa, President
David Shall, Executive Vice President
Mark Kaner, President
Robb Dalton, President
Produces, distributes progmg for net TV, domestic & international TV markets.
Twentieth Television
1211 Avenue of the Americas, 16th Fl., New York, NY 10036 United States
Bob Cesa, Exec Vp Adv Sls & Cable Progmg Sls

Two Oceans Entertainment Group
2017 Lemoyne St., Suite 800, Los Angeles, CA 90026 USA
(818) 501-6550, *Fax:* (818) 501-6558
twoceans@aol.com
Meryl Marshall, President
Susan Whittaker, General Sales Mgr
Domestic & international TV production. Most recentWhen Danger Follows You Home, Baby Monitor, Sound of Fear, Happily Ever After, Fairy Tales For Every Child.

20th Century Fox/Incendo Television Distribution Ltd.
2 Bloor St. W., Suite 1700, Toronto, ON M4W 3E2 CAN
(416) 643-3897, *Fax:* (416) 643-3898
www.foxincendo.com
Michael Murphy, Operations Dir
David Heath, General Sales Mgr
Kimberley Ball, Promotions Manager
TV program distribution.

TYG Media
6525 Babcock St., SE, Malabar, FL 32950-5002 USA
(321) 725-0014, *Fax:* 3(21) 725-0098
www.musicofyourlife.com
info@musicofyourlife.com
Kerry Fink, CEO
Full Service Production Facility 30 ft Green Screen 3 High Def Cameras HD Edit Suite

U.S. Air Force Recruiting Service
Randolph AFB, 550 D Street W., Universal City, TX 78150-5421 USA
(210) 652-3937, *Fax:* (210) 652-4892
www.airforce.com
rspsa@rs.af.mil
Ted Northrup, General Manager
Gary Quesenberry, Broadcasting
Custom production of radio & TV PSAs for Air Force recruiting for local communities.

U.S. Conference of Catholic Bishops
3211 4th St. N.E., Washington, DC 20017 USA
(202) 541-3204, *Fax:* (202) 541-3129
www.usccb.org/ccc
pgarcia@usccb.org
Pat Garcia, General Manager
TV & radio pub svc programs.

U.S. Plan B Inc.
466 Orange St., Suite 280, Redlands, CA 92374 USA
(818) 998-8833,(888) 877-5262, *Fax:* (702) 926-2532
www.usplanb.com
office@usplanb.com
Marc Curtis, Programming Director
TV news gathering & production crews, stock footage, rsch.

UBC Radio
230 Ohio St., Suite 101, Chicago, IL 60611 USA
(312) 640-5000,(312) 751-0135, *Fax:* (312) 640-5010
Bradley Saul, CEO
Ron Gleason, President
Talk radio long form progmg plus short form features.

Ukrainian Melody Hour
Box 2257, Washington, DC 20013 USA
(202) 529-7606,(202) 269-1824, *Fax:* (202) 638-5995
Odile Marynowych, Operations Dir
Roman Marynowych, General Manager
Ukrainian radio, TV & cable program productions.

United Learning Co.
1560 Sherman Ave., Suite 100, Evanston, IL 60201 USA
(800) 323-9084, *Fax:* (847) 328-6706
www.unitedlearning.com
joel.altschul@unitedlearning.com
Joel Altschul, Chairman
Educ programs, series & documentaries, videos & curriculums, streaming.

United Methodist Communications
810 - 12th Ave. S., Nashville, TN 37203 USA
(615) 742-5400, *Fax:* (615) 742-5125
www.umcom.org
lalexander@umcom.org,jjones@umcom.umc.org
Larry Hollon, Operations Dir
Jeneane Jones, General Manager
TV & radio production & distribution.

United Sound Systems Inc.
15849 Wyoming St., Detroit, MI 42838 USA
(313) 340-4200, *Fax:* (313) 832-5666
Audio & duplicating recording, postproduction audio facilities & svcs, & music production.

United Stations Radio Network
25 W. 45 St., New York, NY 10036 USA
(212) 869-1111, *Fax:* (212) 869-1115
www.unitedstations.com
info@unitedstations.com
Nick Verbitsky, CEO
Entertainment & comedy. Progmg for radio stns, news, business & weather features.
11400 W. Olympic Blvd., # 200, Los Angeles, CA 90064 United States
(310) 914-0188;
Anne Martinez, Mgr
Dallas, TX United States
(972) 506-8776;
Rob Ellis, Mgr
333 W. Weeker Dr., # 700, Chicago, IL 60606 United States
(312) 444-2034;
Rich Baum, Vp Midwest

University of Colorado Television
Campus Box 379, Boulder, CO 80309 USA
(303) 492-1857, *Fax:* (303) 492-7017
kathleen.albers@colorado.edu
Kate Albers, General Manager
TV & radio program production & distribution; production svcs.

University of Detroit Mercy
4001 W. McNichols, Communication Studies Dept., Detroit, MI 48221-3038 USA
(313) 578-0311,(313) 993-2005, *Fax:* (313) 993-1166
www.udmercy.edu
Michael Jayson, Chief Engineer
Radio program syndication.

University of Kentucky Public Relations & Radio-TV News Bureau
Mathews Bldg., Rm. 4, Lexington, KY 40506 USA

(859) 257-1754, *Fax:* (859) 257-4017
www.uky.edu
cnath1@email.uky.edu
Carl Nathe, General Manager
TV & radio program & coml, promotional film production & distribution.

Univision Communications Inc.
5999 Center Drive, Los Angeles, CA 90045 USA
(310) 556-7676, *Fax:* (310) 556-7615
www.univision.net
A. Perenchio, Chairman
A. Perenchio, CEO
Ray Rodriguez, President
Sp language bcst & cable TV net radio stns, music record labels & an internet destination.

VA-Tech Video/Broadcast Services
285 Whittemore Hall, Blacksburg, VA 24061 USA
(540) 231-5930, *Fax:* (540) 231-4622
www.vbs.vt.edu
Mark Harden, General Manager
Complete video & audio production & postproduction svcs. Uplink, downlink & CATV opn. Telephone & data communication.

Valentino Music & Sound Effect Libraries
500 Executive Blvd., Elmsford, NY 10523 USA
(914) 347-7878,(800) 223-6278, *Fax:* (914) 347-4764
www.tvmusic.com
tvmusic@ibm.net
Thomas Valention, President
Francis Valentino, Operations Dir
Compact disc music & sound effects libraries.

Van Vliet Media
420 E. 55th St., Suite 6L, New York, NY 10022 USA
(212) 486-6577, *Fax:* (212) 980-9826
vanvlietmedia.com
vanvlietmedia@att.net
Rochelle Bebell, President
Harlan DeBell, Operations Dir
Digital transfers, dup cardiac angiography.

Venevision International
121 Alhambra Plaza, Suite 1400, Coral Gables, FL 33134 USA
(305) 442-3411, *Fax:* (305) 448-4762
www.venevisionintl.com
info@venevisionintl.com
Manuel Perez, CFO
Luis Villanueva, President
Jose Antonio Espinal, Operations Dir
Cesar Diaz, General Sales Mgr
Cristobal Ponte, Sales Director
Daniel Rodriguez, Sales Director
Miguel Somoza, Sales Director
Distribution of progmg.

Venice Media Services
299 W. Houston, 10th Fl., New York, NY 10014-3620 USA
(212) 859-5100, *Fax:* (212) 727-9495
Peggy Green, President
TV program distribution.

Viacom Inc.
1515 Broadway, New York, NY 10036 USA
(212) 258-6000, *Fax:* (212) 258-6465
www.viacom.com
Sherry Lansing, Chairman
Matthew Blank, CEO
Al Weber, President
Carl Folta, Operations Dir
Sherry Lansing, Chairman
Michael Fricklas, Executive Vice President
Herb Scannell, President
Jack Ramanos, President
Carol Melton,Senior VP
Martin Shea, Senior VP
TV program production & distribution, motion pictures production & distribution, book publishing, video production & distribution, theme parks.
Showtime Networks Inc.
1633 Broadway, New York, NY 10019 United States
Simon & Schuster
1230 Ave. of the Americas, New York, NY 10020 United States
MTV Networks
1515 Broadway, New York, NY 10036 United States
Paramount Parks
8720 Red Oak Blvd., Suite 375, Charlotte, NC 28217 United States
Blockbuster Entertainment
1201 Elm St., Dallas, TX 75270 United States
Paramount Pictures
5555 Melrose Ave., Hollywood, CA 90038 United States

Viacom Video Services
524 W. 57th St., New York, NY 10019-2924 USA
(212) 975-8139, *Fax:* (212) 975-7272
www.viacom.com
mjeffers@cbs.com
Mark Jeffers, General Manager
Duplicate & distribute syndicated TV progmg via tape & satellite, coml integration, international standards conversion, uplink/downlink, tape duplication, space segment; high definition.
10877 Wilshire Blvd, Los Angeles, CA 90024 United States
(310) 446-6051; *Fax:* (310) 446-6066
Lee Salas, Vp & Natl Sls Mgr

Video Enterprises Inc.
575 29th St., Manhattan Beach, CA 90266-3430 USA
(310) 796-5555, *Fax:* (310) 546-2921
hambrose@earthlink.net
Heidi Lane-Ambrose, President
Renska Somers, General Manager
Natl placement of ten-second promotional spots on game shows, talk, var & sports programs.

Video I-D Teleproductions Inc.
105 Muller Rd., Washington, IL 61571 USA
(800) 333-9123, *Fax:* (309) 444-4333
www.videoid.com
videoid@videoid.com
Sam Wagner, President
Larry Strantz, General Sales Mgr
Gwen Howarter, Promotions Manager
Full Teleproduction Svcs, Location Production, HD Editing, 3D graphics, Custom DVD Authoring, Branding Pkgs - Documentary, Corporate Image, Sales, Marketing, Safety, Training - Police Training - Turnkey Kiosks - Internet Streaming - Webbased instruction - Medical In Service Training

Video One Inc.
4952 Nagle Ave., Sherman Oaks, CA 91423 USA
(818) 781-9824, *Fax:* (818) 753-4704
Robert Kaufmann, President
Kevin Hamburger, Operations Dir
Remote TV production facilities.

Video Services
1033 Elm Hill Pike, Nashville, TN 37210 USA
(615) 248-1010, *Fax:* (615) 244-5712
www.siffordvideoservices.com
info@siffordvideoservices.com
Joel Covington, President
CD, DVD, videotape duplication, standard conversions.

Video Techniques Inc.
Box 9649, Bradenton, FL 34206-9649 USA
(941) 758-3077, *Fax:* (941) 758-4896
www.videotechniques.com
vti@videotechniques.com
Bob Lorentzen, President
Beta SP & MII field & postproduction facilities. CD, DVD authoring & duplication, VHS duplication, streaming video hosting.

Video-Cinema Films Inc.
510 E. 86th St., New York, NY 10028 USA
(212) 734-1632, *Fax:* (212) 734-1632
Larry Stern, President
Distribution/licensor of motion pictures & excerpts for all forms of TV & allied media in US and worldwide.

Video/Media Distribution Inc.
1050 N. State St., Chicago, IL 60610 USA
(312) 944-4700, *Fax:* (312) 944-1582
shelvm@aol.com
Shel Beugen, President
Program sls & syndication svcs to bcst, cable stns & networks.

VideoActive Productions (VAP)
1560 Broadway, Suite 610, New York, NY 10036 USA
(212) 541-6592
www.videoactiveprod.com
Steven Garrin, President
Digital video, audio production & post production.

Videographic West
Box 1093, 30 Benchmark Rd., Avon, CO 81620 USA
(970) 949-5593, *Fax:* (970) 949-6331
www.skitv.com,www.videographicwest.com
video@colorado.net
Michael Billingsley, President
Stephanie Billingsley, Principal
Specializing in cable sports progmg & distribution, extensive stock footage of action sports, mountain lifestyle, sking, golf, family & travel. Full-svc production house, field crews, two SD/component pinnacle Liquid uncompressed NLEworkstations, complete multimedia suite with DVD authoring/encoding, 2D animation suite with talented artists.

Videomedia
C/Jose Isbert, 2, Ciudad de la Imagen, Madrid, 28223 ESP
34-91-512.8000, *Fax:* 34-91-518.8017
www.videomedia.es
videomedia@videomedia.es
Jorge Arque, CEO
Daniel Acuna, Programming Director
Mireia Acosta, Fiction manager
Fernanda Montoro, International Division
Independent production company. Entertainment formats & programs, documentaries, fiction.

Videosmith Inc.
100 Spring Garden St., Philadelphia, PA 19123 USA
(215) 238-5070, *Fax:* (215) 238-5075
www.videosmith.com
info@videosmith.com
Steven Smith, President
TV progmg, equipment rentals & production mgmt.

VIEW Video Inc.
34 E. 23rd St., New York, NY 10010 USA
(212) 674-5550, *Fax:* (212) 979-0266
www.view.com
viewvid@aol.com
Bob Karcy, President
Stephen Kates, Promotions Manager
International home video production & distribution of special interest progms in the areas of art, jazz, pop music, opera, dance, children's interactive sports & modern lifestyle progms.

Virginia Tech, CNS (Communications Network Services)
1770 Forecast Dr., Blacksburg, VA 24061-0506 USA
(540) 231-6460, *Fax:* (540) 231-8418
www.cns.vt.edu
Judy Lilly, General Manager
Video & Audio Service to campus - faculty staff & students.

Vision Broadcasting - KVBA TV 19
1017 New York Ave., Alamogordo, NM 88310-6921 USA
(505) 437-1919
kvba@kvbatv.com
William Oechsner Jr., General Manager
Bcst of Christian, loc TV, sports & public interest TV.

Vision Maker Media
1800 North 33rd Street, Lincoln, NE 68503-1409 USA
(402) 472-3522, *Fax:* (402) 472-8675
www.visionmakermedia.org
visionmaker@uni.edu
Mary Koehler, Operations Dir
Shirley Sneve, Station Manager
Georgiana Lee, Chief Engineer
Native stories for public broadcasting. Also, your premier source for quality Native American educational and home videos.

VRI (Video Rentals Inc.)
100 Stonehurst Ct., Northvale, NJ 7647 USA
(800) 255-2874,(201) 750-3200, *Fax:* (201) 784-2795
www.rentvri.com
info@rentvri.com
Tom Canavan, Operations Dir
Full-svc rental facility with a complete inventory of bcst & industrial video equipment.

VTTV Videothek Electronic TV-Production GmbH + Co Kopier KG
Havelchaussee 161, Berlin, 14055 DEU
(030) 300 95-3, *Fax:* (030) 300 95-500
www.vttv.de
info@vttv.de
Paul Bielicki, President
Friedel Lux, General Sales Mgr
Herbert Bauermeister, Promotions Manager
Complete production service: studios (600/225 m2), professional equipment for production & postproduction, high definition production units. Commercials, documentaries, features, pop promos, TV.

Vuolo Video Air-Chex
Box 880, Novi, MI 48376 USA
(248) 926-1234
www.vuolovideo.com
artvuolo@aol.com

Arthur Vuolo Jr., Programming Director
Video air checks of American radio stns & An Inside Look.

Vyvx
One Technology Center, Tulsa, OK 74103 USA
(800) 364-0807, *Fax:* (918) 547-2989
www.vyvx.com
Derek Smith, Operations Dir
Distributor of TV comls/traf via satellite by remote VTR control to 600 stns; radio coml distribution; production, postproduction. Multi-format duplication.

Wade Productions Inc.
493 High Cliffe Lane, Tarrytown, NY 10591 USA
(212) 286-9111
wade@1cj@aol.com
Carolyn Wade, President
Meetings, video, entertainment, staging & teleconferencing for corporations & assns.

Walt Disney Company
500 S. Buena Vista St., Burbank, CA 91521-0990 USA
(818) 560-1000, *Fax:* (818) 560-1930
Zenia Mucha, Promotions Manager
The Walt Disney Company subsidiary; devs & syndicates first-run adult & children's progmg, off-net progmg & feature film packages.

The Walt Disney Company
500 S. Buena Vista St., Burbank, CA 91521 USA
(818) 560-1000, *Fax:* (818) 560-1930
www.disney.com
Michael Eisner, Chairman
Michael Eisner, CEO

Warner Bros.
Bldg. 140, 300 Television Plaza, Burbank, CA 91505 USA
(818) 954-7500, *Fax:* (818) 954-7322
Peter Ross, President
TV program production & distribution.

Warner Bros. Animation
15301 Ventura Blvd., Suite 115301, Unit E, Sherman Oaks, CA 91403 USA
(818) 977-8700, *Fax:* (818) 382-6056
www.warnerbros.com
Sander Schwartz, President
Andy Lewis, Operations Dir
Dev & produces animated progmg for TV, video & other media.

Warner Bros. Domestic Television Distribution
4000 Warner Blvd., Burbank, CA 91522 USA
(818) 954-5877, *Fax:* (818) 954-5820
www.warnerbros.com
Dick Robertson, President
Jacqueline Hartley, Operations Dir
Jim Paratore, Executive Vice President
Mark O'Brien, Senior VP
Jeff Hufford, Vice President
Print DepartmentBurbank: Bud Rowe, foreign TV print administrator. (818) 954-3731.TV program syndication.

Warner Bros. International Distribution Inc. (Canada)
5000 Yonge St., Suite 1503, Toronto, ON M2N 6P1 CAN
(416) 250-8384, *Fax:* (416) 250-8598
www.wbitv.com
Leslie Hibbins, Operations Dir
Mickie Steinmann, General Manager
TV progm distribution & promotions for Canada.

Warner Bros. International Television
4000 Warner Blvd., Burbank, CA 91522 USA
(818) 954-6000, *Fax:* (818) 954-4040
Jeffrey Schlesinger, President
Catherine Malatesta, Operations Dir
James Marrinan, Senior VP
Malcolm Dudley-Smith, Senior VP
Susan Kroll, Senior VP
Josh Berger, Vice President
Marsha Armstrong, Vice President
Matthew Robinson,Vice President
TV program production & distribution.
Warner Bros. PTY. Ltd.
8-20 Napier St, North Sydney, NSW 2060
011-61-2-9957-3899; *Fax:* 011-61-2-9956-7788
Wayne Broun, Vp Mgng Dir Australia, Asia Pacific
Greg Robertson, Vp Asia
Time Warner Entertainment Japan
1-2-4 Hamamatsu-cho, Minato-ku, Tokyo, 105 Japan
011-81-3-5472-8341; *Fax:* 011-81-3-5472-6343
Teruji Mochimaru, Mgng Dir Japan
Warner Bros. International TV
Artuto Soria, 336 1, Madrid 28033,
011-34-1-384-06-40; *Fax:* 011-34-1-384-06-41
Jose Abad, Sls Exec Sp Territories
Warner Bros. International TV
67 Avenue Dewagram, Paris, 75017 France
011-33-1-5537-5933; *Fax:* 011-33-1-5537-4968
Michel Lecourt, Vp Fr Territories
Warner Bros. (Mexico) S.A.
Colonea Codesa, Acapulco 37 06140,
011-525-211-3353-211-0293 211-0298-211-0466; *Fax:* 011-525-553-2822-553-2002
Jorge Sanchez, Vp Latin America
Warner Bros. International TV
135 Wardour St, London W1V 4AP,
011-44-171-494-3710; *Fax:* 011-44-171-287-9086
Richard Milnes, Vp Uk Territories, Turkey, Israel

Warner Bros. Television Production
4000 Warner Blvd., Burbank, CA 91522 USA
(818) 954-6000, *Fax:* (818) 954-7048
www.warnerbros.com
Robert Rosenbaum, Programming Director
Julie Waxman, Senior VP Business Affairs
David Sacks, Senior VP Current Programming
Steve Pearlman, Senior VP Current Programming
Greg Maday, SVP Movies
Paul Stager, SVE Studio Gen Counsel
Mary Buck, SVP Talent & Casting
TV program production.

Warren Miller Entertainment
2540 Frontier Ave., Suite 104, Boulder, CO 80301 USA
(303) 442-3430, *Fax:* (303) 442-3402
www.warrenmiller.com
Tim Malone, General Manager
Josh Haskins, Programming Director
Second unit feature, coml, TV program, promotion; film production & distribution specializing in snow & outdoor adventure sports.

Warren Only Media Group
Box 2372, Times Square Station, New York, NY 10036 USA
(856) 507-9368, *Fax:* (856) 507-9368
www.warrenonly.com
warrenonly@90.com
Satellite program distribution, syndication, playout, back hauling, film & video production.

Washington Korean Broadcasting Co.
7004 - K Little River Tpke., Annandale, VA 22003 USA
(703) 354-4900, *Fax:* (703) 658-1500
wkbcwashington@yahoo.com
Yong Chan Pak, President
All ethnic radio progmg offered in Korean language featuring news, music, drama & talk show.

Wawatay Native Communication Society
Box 1180, 16 Fifth Ave., Sioux Lookout, ON P8T 1B7 CAN
(807) 737-2951, *Fax:* (807) 737-3224
www.wawataynews.ca
Mike Metatawabin, President
Christine Chisel, Station Manager
Radio & TV (Cree, Ojibway & English) net, bilingual nwspr, aboriginal language translations, multi-track audio recording.

Wax Music, Sound Design & Mix
18 W. 21st St., 10th Fl., New York, NY 10010-6903 USA
(212) 989-9292, *Fax:* (212) 989-5195
www.waxnyc.com
chris@waxnyc.com
James Wolcott, Programming Director
Chris Arbisi, Chief Engineer
Original music, sound design & mixing for all media. Three digital studios.

WCTD AM 1620
244 Post Rd., Westerly, RI 2891 USA
(401) 322-1743,(401) 322-9091, *Fax:* (401) 322-1645
www.wblq.org/htm.wctd
Chris DiPaola, President
J.J. MacDade Nunez, General Manager
Traveler information.

We the People to BNK Kids
41 Madison Ave., New York, NY 10010 USA
(212) 213-2700, *Fax:* (212) 685-8332
www.amazin.com
Entertainment & media company specializing in the youth market. Hqtrs in New York & offices in Chicago, Los Angeles & Paris, France.

The Weather Center
Div/DBA: (a broadcast service of Aviation Weather Inc.)
701 Gervais St., Suite 224, Columbia, SC 29201
(803) 422-4823
thomashendrickson@yahoo.com
Liam Ferguson, President

WeatherVision Inc.
NSS Data: TV-CATV only
916 Foley St., Jackson, MS 39202-3406
(601) 948-7018, (800) 353-9177, *Fax:* (601) 948-6052
www.weathervision.com
edward@weathervision.com
Edward Saint-Pe', President
Jason McCleave, Operations Dir
Customized, localized TV weathercasts with or without meteorologists. Barter/cash via Ku-band satellite. Complete studio teleport for use by news media on site. Avid editing available on site. Serves radio, TV & 3-D branding animation svcs.

Wellspring
419 Park Ave. S., 20th Fl., New York, NY 10016 USA
(212) 686-6777, *Fax:* (212) 685-2625
www.wellspring.com
Sheri Levine, Operations Dir
Marie Guirgis, General Manager
Worldwide distributors of film & video properties for home video, standard & non-standard TV.

Welwood International Film Production
160 Washington S.E., Suite 138, Albuquerque, NM 87108-2731 USA
(505) 265-1899
welwoodint@aol.com
Barbara Ferrel, CEO
Bill Swortwood, President
Works with consultants, rsch companies & client stns to create effective TV campaigns since 1986.

Westar Music
105 West Beaver Creek Rd. Suite 5, Richmond Hill, ON L4B 1C6 CAN
(905) 886-3100, *Fax:* (905) 886-6800
www.westarmusic.com
info@westarmusic.com
Brian Nimens, CEO
High caliber production music in a wide var of categories for bcst, cable, film, corporate video & multimedia applications.

Western International Syndication
12100 Wilshire Blvd., Suite 150, Los Angeles, CA 90025 USA
(310) 820-8485, *Fax:* (310) 820-8376
www.wistelevision.com
info@wistelevision.com
Chris Lancey, CEO
Danielle Valdivia, General Sales Mgr
Distributes wkly & special progmg nationwide as well as internationally.

Westwood One
Div/DBA: Radio New Services
40 W. 57th St., 5th Fl., New York, NY 10019
(212) 641-2000, *Fax:* (212) 641-2185
www.westwoodone.com
Steven Kalin, COO
Gary Schonfeld, President
Producer & distributor of radio progmg including CNN, NBC, Mutual, CNBC Business Radio, 24-hours music formats, long-short-form talk, music & news programs.

WFMT Radio Network
5400 N. St. Louis Ave., Chicago, IL 60625 USA
(773) 279-2112,(773) 279-2114, *Fax:* (773) 279-2119
www.wfmt.com
Steve Robinson, Operations Dir
Produces wkly series including Chicago Symphony Orchestra & the New York Philharmonic This Week for coml & pub stns. Broad range of symphonic, opera & class music documentary progmg, jazz & folk music, including exclusive features from BBC &Radio Deutsche Welle, Germany.

White Rabbit Productions
1587 S. Main St., Salt Lake City, UT 84115 USA
(800) 549-3115,(801) 463-9292, *Fax:* (801) 463-7226
www.whiterabbitproductions.com
info@whiterabbitproductions.com
Sam Prigg, President
Complete film & video production svcs; two Ikegami HL-V55 Beta Sp camera packages, digital video point-of-view cam, non-linear editing.

Wide Eye Productions, Inc.
686 N. 9th, Boise, ID 83702 USA
(208) 336-0391, *Fax:* (208) 336-6644
www.wideeye.tv
info@wideeye.tv
Tom Hadzor, General Manager
Jennifer Isenhart, Programming Director
Full-service bcst & industrial video production. ENG/EFP. High definition & Sony B-600.

William F. Cooke Television Programs
307-23 Lesmill Rd, Toronto, ON M3B 3P6 CAN
(416) 967-6141, *Fax:* (416) 967-5133
info@cooketv.com
William F. Cooke, CEO
Alex McWilliams, Promotions Manager
TV program production & distribution.

William Mauldin Productions Inc.
1010 Canonero Dr., Greensboro, NC 27410-3804 USA
(336) 632-9801, *Fax:* (540) 301-0399
www.mauldin.net
productions@mauldin.net,bill@mauldin.tv
William Mauldin, CEO
Major market talent for narrations & voice overs, documentaries, stn IDs, program intros, comls for any media market. Let us provide the voice & production for your projects. We can offer finished products via CD, MP3, or via the web. Checkour website for samples of our work!

Witt/Thomas Productions
11901 Santa Monica Blvd., Suite 596, W. Los Angeles, CA 90025 USA
(310) 472-6004, *Fax:* (310) 476-5015
Susan Harris, President
Tony Thomas, Partner
TV & film production company.

WKMG Productions
4466 N. John Young Pkwy., Orlando, FL 32804 USA
(407) 291-6000, *Fax:* (407) 521-1204
www.local6.com
Laura Genette, Operations Dir
Skip Valet, General Manager
TV program, coml, promotional film production; production svcs, post production & field production. WKMG production resources primarily dedicated to stn use.

WMAQ-TV
NBC Tower, 454 N. Columbus Dr., Chicago, IL 60611-5555 USA
(312) 836-5555, *Fax:* (312) 527-4290
www.nbc5.com
Larry Wert, President
Patricia Golden, General Sales Mgr
TV program production; production svcs.

WNN Health and Wealth Motivation
6699 N. Federal Hwy., Boca Raton, FL 33487 USA
(561) 997-0074, *Fax:* (561) 997-0476
www.wnnhealthtalkradio.com
Robert Morency, Operations Dir
Worldwide 24-hour format of motivational speakers & self-help info.

Work Edit
270 W. 39th St., 11th Floor, New York, NY 10018 USA
(212) 719-4577, *Fax:* (212) 719-4380
www.workedit.com
Dalton Helms, President
Ken Sackheim, Owner
Post production svcs, DVD authoring.

World Events Productions Ltd.
One Memorial Dr., St. Louis, MO 63102 USA
(314) 345-1000, *Fax:* (314) 345-1091
www.wep.com
wep@wep.com
Edward Koplar, President
Tiffany Ilardi, General Manager
TV program production & distribution.

World Radio Network
Box 1212, London, SW8 2ZF United Kingdom
44-20-7896-9000, *Fax:* 44-20-7896- 9007
www.wrn.org
contactus@wrn.org
Karl Miosga, Chairman
Jeff Cohen, General Sales Mgr
Tim Ashburner, Engineering Dir
World Radio Network (via Galaxy 25) news & features ch, comprising live progmg segments in English & languages from more than 20 international bcstrs. WRN can also supply many customized progmg feeds to radio stns as well as progmgdistribution, satellite uplink & internet streaming.

Worldview Entertainment Inc.
145 W. 55th St., Suite 7-D, New York, NY 10019 USA
(212) 582-6997, *Fax:* (212) 925-2314
birnhardt@aol.com
Sandra Birnhak, CEO
Glenn Shealey, President
Archival stock footage library, distribution to international bcstrs.

Worldvision NY
143 W. 29th St., New York, NY 10001 USA
(212) 736-2997, *Fax:* (212) 736-9755
www.worldvision.org
John Claus, Station Manager
TV program distribution for ind productions.

Worldvision Enterprises U.K. Ltd
54 Pont St, London SW1X OAE,
011-441-71-584-5357; *Fax:* 011-441-71-581-3483
Bill Peck, Chairman
Janice Wilson, CEO/COO
Zsuzsanna Jung, Operations Dir

Worldvision Enterprises S.A.R.L.
28, Rue Bayard, Paris, 75008 France
011-33-1-4723-3995; *Fax:* 011-33-1-4070-9269
Mary Jane Fourniel, Chairman
Catherine Molinier, CEO/COO
John Hernan, President

Worldvision Enterprises of Australia PTY Ltd.
5-13 Northcliff St, Sydney, Milsons Point, 02061
011-61-2-9922-4722; *Fax:* 011-61-2-9955-8207 TWX: (790) 70474
Brian Rhys-Jones, Chairman
Paul Stuart, CEO/COO
Karen Zylstra, President
22270 Rua Voluntarios Da Patria N, Gr.604, Rio de Janeiro, CEP 22270 Brazil
011-55-21-539-2992; *Fax:* 011-55-21-266-4737
Raymundo Rodriguez, Chairman
Maria Alice Freire, CEO/COO
Tsukiji Hamarikyu Bldg, 7th Fl, 5-3-3 Tsukiji, Chou-ku, Tokyo, 104 Japan
011-81-3-3545-3978; *Fax:* 011-81-3-5550-8316
Mie Horasawa, Chairman
Yukie Kumagai, CEO/COO

Adalia Anstalt
Via del Corso, 22/Int 10, 00186 Rome
011-39-6-322-5190; *Fax:* 011-39-6-322-6450
Michael Kiwe, Dorothy Shaw

The Worship Network
28059 U.S. Hwy. 19 N., Suite 300, Clearwater, FL 33761 USA
(727) 536-0036, *Fax:* (727) 530-0671
www.worship.net
ken@worship.net
Bruce Koblish, CEO
Tim Brown, Operations Dir
Inspirational music set to nature scenes, overlaid with scripture 24 hours a day. Progmg is interspersed with short devotional teachings.

The WPA Film Library
16101 S. 108th Ave., Orland Park, IL 60467 USA
(708) 460-0555, *Fax:* (708) 460-0187
www.wpafilmlibrary.com
sales@wpafilmlibrary.com
Diane Paradiso, General Sales Mgr
One of the largest stock footage libraries in the U.S. WPA offers holdings in newsreels, music, pop culture & stock shots.

WQED Multimedia
4802 5th Ave., Pittsburgh, PA 15213 USA
(412) 622-1300, *Fax:* (412) 622-6413
www.wqed.org, info@wqed.org
Patricia Walker, CFO
Deborah Acklin, General Manager
Rosemary Martinelli, Station Manager
Lilli Mosco, General Sales Mgr
Steven Reubi, Controller
Susan Johnson Radlo, Executive Director
TV & radio program/production, distribution; production svcs & web, publishing.

WQXR
122 5th Ave., 3rd Fl., New York, NY 10011 USA
(212) 633-7600, *Fax:* (212) 633-7666
www.wqxr.com, listener.mail@wqxr.com
Thomas Bartunek, General Manager
Penny Gaffney, General Sales Mgr
Radio program production. The classical Radio Station of the New York Times.

WRS/Channel One
1000 Napor Blvd., Pittsburgh, PA 15205 USA
(412) 937-7700, *Fax:* (412) 922-1020
www.wrslabs.com
jackn@wrslabs.com
F. Napor, President
Complete syndication & distribution svcs via satellite & tape. Integration, AMOL encoding, duplication, uplink/downlink fulfillment, audio, film-to-tape transfer; replication of CD/DVD.

WSI Corp.
400 Minuteman Rd., Andover, MA 1810 USA
(978) 983-6300, *Fax:* (978) 983-6400
www.wsi.com
World leader in providing real-time weather data, imagery, forecasting & weather progmg for bcst stns, cable operators & cable nets.

WTOB—Community/Government Access TV
300 S. Main St., Blacksburg, VA 24062 USA
(540) 961-1199, *Fax:* (540) 961-1875
www.blacksburg.gov
wtob@blacksburg.gov
Carlton Herman, Station Manager
Public interest video, live Town Council & Planning Commission meeting, live & archived streaming video.

WWE Entertainment Inc.
Titan Tower, 1241 E. Main St., Stamford, CT 6902 USA
(203) 352-8600, *Fax:* (203) 352-8699
www.wwe.com
Vincent McMahon, Chairman
Linda McMahon, CEO
Donna Goldsmith, Operations Dir
Phil Livingston, CFO
James Rothschild, Senior VP
Exclusive worldwide distributor of WWF events, TV programs (bcst network/syndication, PPV & basic cable) & other sports/entertainment properties.

The Wyland Group
101 W. Cochran St., Simi Valley, CA 93065 USA
(805) 955-7680, *Fax:* (805) 522-1082
www.lifestyle.org
Linda Walter, General Manager
Chauncey Smith, General Sales Mgr
Production of health related, family values progmg.

XL Media Solutions
110 N. Ditmar St., Oceanside, CA 92054 USA
(760) 722-8284, *Fax:* (888) 722-8234
www.exxelaudio.com
staff@exxelaudio.com
William Kottcamp, General Manager
Radio program, coml production & distribution.

Yada/Levine Video Productions
1253 Vine St., Suite 21A, Los Angeles, CA 90038 USA
(323) 461-1616, *Fax:* (323) 461-2288
www.yadalevine.com
video@yadalevine.com
Michael Yada, President
Full-service video productions. Crews & equipment including HD, DV & Betacam SP.

Yale Video Inc.
2441 W. La Palma Ave., Suite 530, Anaheim, CA 92801 USA
(714) 693-5300, *Fax:* (714) 693-5395
www.webcastingtv.com
burty@webcastingtv.com
Burton Yale, CEO
Offers the latest in editing technology; from D-2 to Hi8.

Yorkshire Television
Television Centre, 104 Kirkstall Rd., Leeds, LS3 IJS GBR
0113-243-8283, *Fax:* 0113-244-5107
www.granada.co.uk,www.yorkshiretv.co.uk
communications@granadamedia.com
Charles Allen CBE, Chairman
Independent TV program maker & bcstr.

Zachry Associates
500 Chestnut, Suite 2000, Abilene, TX 79602 USA
(325) 677-1342, *Fax:* (325) 672-2001
H.C. Zachry, President
Produces & distributes TV & radio programs & comls as well as promotional films & production svcs.

ZBS Foundation
174 N. River Rd., Fort Edward, NY 12828 USA
(518) 695-6406, *Fax:* (518) 695-4041
www.zbs.org, info@zbs.org
Thomas Lopez, President
Producer of audio drama.

Equipment Manufacturers and Distributors Subject Index

EQUIPMENT MANUFACTURERS

Audio Compressors
Alesis
Circuit Research Labs Inc. (CRL Systems, Inc.)
Furman
Sascom Marketing Group
Sescom Inc.
TC Electronic

Audio Consoles
Arrakis Systems Inc.
Autogram Corp.
Euphonix Inc.
Harris Corp., Broadcast Communications, HQ
Henry Engineering
Logitek Electronic Systems Inc
Ward-Beck Systems Ltd.
Wheatstone Corp.

Audio Equipment
Audio Implements/GKC
Audio Precision Inc.
BBE Sound Inc.
Bexel
Bogen Communications Inc.
Broadcast Store Inc.
Burlington A/V Recording Media Inc.
Comprehensive Video Group
Comrex Corp.
Countryman Associates Inc.
DBX Professional Products
Film/Video Equipment Service Co. Inc.
FitzCo. Inc.
Full Compass Systems Ltd.
Galaxy Audio Inc.
Geneva Aviation Inc.
Group One Ltd.
Industrial Equipment Representatives (IER)
Jensen Transformers Inc.
Lectrosonics Inc.
Memorex Products Inc.
Nady Systems Inc.
National Video Services Inc.
Opamp Labs Inc.
Peavey Electronics
Photomart Cine-Video Inc.
ProAudio.com/Crouse-Kimzey Company
Professional Sound Corp.
Protech Audio Corp.
QSC Audio Products Inc.
Samson Technologies Corp.
Sanyo Fisher Co.
Sascom Marketing Group
Sennheiser Electronic Corp.
Servoreeler Systems
Systems Wireless Ltd.
TAI Audio
TC Group Americas Inc.
TEAC America Inc.
Thomson, Inc, (RCA/GE)
Visual Sound Inc.
Whirlwind

Audio Jackfields, Pre-Wired
Audio Accessories Inc.
Farrtronics Ltd.
Furman
Glentronix
Milestek Corp.
Penny & Giles Inc.
Seger Electronics
Switchcraft Inc.

Audio Limiters
Amek U.S.A.
Circuit Research Labs Inc. (CRL Systems, Inc.)
Harman International Industries Inc.
Symetrix Inc.

Audio Mixers and Recorders
ATI-Audio Technologies Inc.
Alesis
Amek U.S.A.
Audio-Technica U.S., Inc.
Location Sound Corp.
Martinsound Inc.
Micro Technology Unlimited
Nady Systems Inc.
Otari USA Sales Inc.
Penny & Giles Inc.
Professional Sound Corp.
Professional Sound Services Inc.
Protech Audio Corp.
Radio Design Labs. (RDL)
Shure Inc.
Superscope Technologies Professionals
The Image Group Post, LLC.
United States Broadcast
Yamaha Corp. of America

Audio Monitoring Systems
AKG Acoustics, U.S.
B&B Systems
Dorrough Electronics
Fostex USA
Furman
IRIS Technologies Inc.
Martinsound Inc.
McCurdy Radio Ltd.
Renkus-Heinz Inc.
Westlake Audio

Audio Noise Reduction Systems
Allen Avionics, Inc.
Digidesign
Dolby Laboratories Inc.
Image Video
Noise Control Corp.
Symetrix Inc.

Audio Processors
Audioarts Engineering
BBE Sound Inc.
Inovonics Inc.
Linear Acoustic Inc.
Modulation Sciences Inc.
Nady Systems Inc.
Peavey Electronics
Protech Audio Corp.
Samson Technologies Corp.
Sascom Marketing Group
Symetrix Inc.

Audio Replacement Heads
International Electro-Magnetics (IEM)
Sprague Magnetics Inc.

Audio Routing Switches
Burst Electronics Inc.
Logitek Electronic Systems Inc
NTV International Corporation
NVISION Products
Omicron Video
Radio Design Labs. (RDL)
Richmond Sound Design Ltd.
Sierra Automated Systems & Engineering Corp.
Sigma Electronics Inc.
The ISIS Group
Utah Scientific Inc.

Audio Signal Processing Systems
Alesis
Aphex Systems Ltd.
BBE Sound Inc.
Broadcasters General Store Inc.
Circuit Research Labs Inc. (CRL Systems, Inc.)
Communications Specialties Inc.
Dolby Laboratories Inc.
G Prime Ltd.
Group One Ltd.
International Datacasting Corp.
Lectrosonics Inc.
Pixel Instruments Corp.
Sabine Inc.
Shure Inc.
Symetrix Inc.
TC Electronic

Audio Systems and Components
Audio Implements/GKC
Gefen Inc.
Parsons Audio
Protech Audio Corp.
VidCAD Documentation Programs (VDP Inc.)
Visual Sound Inc.

Audio Test Tapes, Gauges & Equipment
Audio Precision Inc.
Leader Instruments Corp.
Tentel

Audio Transmission Equipment
Artel Video Systems
Audio Processing Technology Ltd./APT
Fiber Options
Intelligent Media Technology
International Datacasting Corp.
MUSICAM U.S.A.
Neutrik U.S.A. Inc.
TFT Inc.

Audio/Video Cartridges
CoarcVideo
Memorex Products Inc.

Audiotape
Burlington A/V Recording Media Inc.
CoarcVideo
Maxell Corp. of America
Memorex Products Inc.
Moviola
National Video Services Inc.
Sony BMG Music Entertainment

Audiotape Cartridge Machines
A.C.C. Electronix, Inc.

Audiotape Duplicating Equipment
National Audio Co. Inc.

Automated Newsroom Systems
Avid Broadcast
CEA-Computer Engineering Associates
Comprompter Inc.
Computer Concepts Corp.
Dalet Digital Media Systems
Harris Automation Solutions
Thomson Reuters
WireReady NSI

Automated Radio
Dalet Digital Media Systems
ENCO Systems Inc.
Encoda Systems Inc.
Marketron Broadcast Solutions
Marketron International
Radio Computing Services (RCS)
Register Communications
Spotcat Software
WireReady NSI

Automated Tape Winders
Otari USA Sales Inc.

Automated Telephone & Voice Mail
Aspect Software
Microlog Corp.
TALX Corp.

Automatic Cassette Loaders
Otari USA Sales Inc.

Automatic Transmission Systems
Encoda Systems Inc.
Harris Automation Solutions

Automation Systems
ADTEC Inc.
Arrakis Systems Inc.
Broadcast Electronics Inc.
CEA-Computer Engineering Associates
Computer Concepts Corp.
ENCO Systems Inc.
Encoda Systems Inc.
Harris Automation Solutions
Harris Corp., Broadcast Communications, HQ
Leightronix Inc.
Marketron International
Media Computing Inc.
Mediastar-SG
Orban
Radio Computing Services (RCS)
Register Communications
Spotcat Software
Sundance Digital Inc.
Technicolor SA
Time Logic Inc.
WireReady NSI

Automation, Switching and Control
ADTEC Inc.
FloriCal Systems Inc.
Harris Automation Solutions
Leightronix Inc.
MATCO Inc.
Register Communications
Richmond Sound Design Ltd.
Sierra Automated Systems & Engineering Corp.

Wescam Inc.

Broadcast Video Products
360 Systems
ADC
Abekas, Incorporated
Alpine Optics Inc.
Analog Digital International Inc.
Battery Pros Inc.
Belden
Bitcentral Inc.
Broadcast Electronic Services
Canon U.S.A. Inc.
Fast Forward Video
Glentronix
Hitachi Kokusai Electric America, Ltd.
Hotronic Inc.
LINK Electronics Inc.
MATCO Inc.
Matrox Video Products Grp
Maxell Corp. of America
Roscor Corp.
Sencore Inc.
Snell & Wilcox Inc.
Telemetrics Inc.
The Tiffen Company
Videomagnetics Inc.
WEGENER
Wiltronix Inc.
teletech.ca

Bulktape DeGausser
Audiolab Electronics Inc.
Data Security Inc.
Garner Products
Glentronix
Paulmar Industries Inc.
Sprague Magnetics Inc.

Bulktape, Audio Cassette
CoarcVideo
National Audio Co. Inc.

CATV Equipment and Supplies
ADSCO Line Products Inc.
AVCOM of Virginia Inc.
Advanced Media Technologies, Inc.
Alpha Technologies Inc.
Andrew Corp.
Arista Information Systems
Benner-Nawman Inc.
Blonder Tongue Laboratories Inc.
C I S Inc.
C-COR/ Arris
CADCO Systems Inc.
CATV Services Inc.
Cable Prep
Cable Services Company Inc.
Cable Technologies International
Channell Commercial Corp.
Charles Industries Ltd.
Comtech Antenna Systems Inc.
Condux International
Convergys Inc.
DST Innovis
Ditch Witch
Eagle Comtronics Inc.
Electroline Equipment Inc.
Emerson Network Power-Viewsonics
FM SYSTEMS Inc.
Gefen Inc.
General Atomics
Harmonic Inc.
Hogg & Davis Inc.
ICM Corporation
JDS Uniphase Corp.
Kalun Communications Inc.
Kathrein Inc., Scala Division
Keywest Technology
Lemco Tool Corp.
Lindsay Broadband Inc.
Mega Hertz
Motorola Broadband Communications Sector
Ortel
Qintar Technologies Inc.
R.L. Drake Holdings LLC
Ripley Company
Scientific Atlanta
Sencore Inc.
Telecrafter Products
Texscan MSI
Thomas & Betts
Thomas & Betts Corp.
Times Fiber Communications Inc.
Toner Cable Equipment Inc.
Transtector Systems Inc.
Trilogy Communications Inc.
Vermeer Manufacturing Co.
WEGENER
Zenith Electronics Corp.

CATV Hybrid Modules
Narragansett Imaging

CATV Power Supplies
Alpha Technologies Inc.
Electroline Equipment Inc.
Lindsay Broadband Inc.

CD Players
Sanyo Fisher Co.
Stanton Group
Superscope Technologies Professionals

Cabinets, Racks, Panels
ADTEC Inc.
APW Mayville/Stantron
Allied Electronics Inc.
Atlas Sound
Benner-Nawman Inc.
Bud Industries Inc.
CMP Enclosures Inc.
Calzone Case Co.
Emcor Enclosures
Emerson Network Power
Fusion Consoles
Gepco International Inc.
Hardigg Cases
High Tech Industries
IMS/AMCO Engineering Products
Mega Hertz
Murphy Studio Furniture
National Video Services Inc.
Neumade Products Corp.
Newark Electronics
Parsons Manufacturing Corp.
Penn Elcom Inc.
Seger Electronics
Seton Identification Products
Stahl, A Scott & Fetzer Co.
Star Case Manufacturing Co. Inc.
Storeel Corp.
Thermodyne International LTd
Ultimate Precision/GKM
Winsted Corp.
Zack Electronics Inc.

Cable Security Systems
Electroline Equipment Inc.
Emerson Network Power-Viewsonics

Cable Termination Equipment, A/V
Clark Wire & Cable Co. Inc.
Vecima Networks Inc.
Videotron Ltee
Zack Electronics Inc.

Cable and Accessories
Allied Electronics Inc.
Belden
CCI Systems Inc.
Canare Corp.
Channel Master
Clark Wire & Cable Co. Inc.
Communications Specialties Inc.
Comprehensive Video Group
Corning Cable Systems
Cortland Cable Co. Inc.
Emcor Enclosures
Gefen Inc.
General Cable
Gepco International Inc.
HAVE Inc.
Insulated Wire Inc. Microwave Products Division
James Thomas Engineering Inc.
LEMO USA Inc.
M/A-COM
Marshall Electronics
Milestek Corp.
Mohawk
Nemal Electronics International Inc.
Newark Electronics
Phillystran Inc.
Prysmian Communications Cables and Systems USA, LLC
Radio Frequency Systems
Servoreeler Systems
Stage Equipment & Lighting Inc.
Stanley Supply & Services
Times Fiber Communications Inc.
Trilogy Communications Inc.
Trompeter Semflex
WIREMAX Ltd.
Whirlwind
Wireworks Corporation
Zack Electronics Inc.

Calibrators, TV Cameras/Monitors
Commercial Radio Monitoring Co.
Dage-MTI Inc.

Camera Mounts
Alan Gordon Enterprises Inc.
Alpha Video & Electronics (AVEC)
CamMate Studios/Systems
Interlogix
Matthews Studio Equipment Inc. (MSE)
Sachtler Corp. of America
Wescam Inc.

Camera Pan/Tilt Heads
ARRI Inc.
Alan Gordon Enterprises Inc.
Allen Osborne Associates Inc.
Arri Canada Ltd.
Bogen Imaging Inc.
Broadcast Sports Technologies
Camera Dynamics
Canon U.S.A. Inc.
Hitachi Kokusai Electric America, Ltd.
Innovision Optics Inc.
Isaia & Co.
Miller Camera Support, LLC USA
O'Connor Professional Camera Support Systems
Quick-Set International Inc.
Telemetrics Inc.
Vinten Inc.

Camera Tubes
Aydin Displays Inc.
Daily Electronics Corp.
Narragansett Imaging

Cameras, Projectors & Accessories
Alan Gordon Enterprises Inc.
Arri Canada Ltd.
Band Pro Film & Digital Inc.
Broadcast Store Inc.
Camera Service Center
Camplex Corporation
Eastman Kodak Co.
General Electrodynamics Corp.
Ikegami Electronics (U.S.A.) Inc.
Innovision Optics Inc.
International Cinema Equipment
JVC Professional Products Company
Northrup Grumman
Schneider Optics Inc.
Tamron U.S.A. Inc.
Television Engineering Corp.
The J-Lab Co.
Toshiba America Consumer Products
Vicon Industries Inc.

Capacitors
Allied Electronics Inc.
Chicago Condenser Corp.
Jennings Technology Co.
Motor Capacitors Inc.
NWL Capacitors
Peter W. Dahl Co. Inc.
Skytec, Inc.

Captioning Equipment
Broadcast Video Systems Corp.
Cheetah International
Image Logic Corp.

Cartridge Automatic Tape
National Video Tape Co. Inc.

Cartridge Storage Racks
Murphy Studio Furniture
Russ Bassett Corporation

Cases
Alpack Associates, Inc.

EQUIPMENT MANUFACTURERS

EQUIPMENT MANUFACTURERS

Milestone Technologies Inc.
Mohawk
O'Connor Professional Camera Support Systems
Panasonic Broadcast & Television Systems Co.
Professional Communications Systems
Sarnoff Corp.
Sencore Inc.
Sharp Electronics Corp., CCD Products Div.
SyntheSys Research Inc.
TANDBERG Television Inc.
Teleplex Inc.
Thomson Broadcast & Media Solutions
Toshiba America Consumer Products
Utah Scientific Inc.
WEGENER
Ward-Beck Systems Ltd.
Winsted Corp.

Headend Systems
ADC
Alpha Technologies Inc.
Beyond Broadband Technology LLC
Blonder Tongue Laboratories Inc.
C-COR/ Arris
CCI Systems Inc.
ComSonics Inc.
D.H. Satellite
General Atomics
Kalun Communications Inc.
Mega Hertz
Norsat International Inc.
North American Cable Equipment Inc.
Ortel
Scientific Atlanta
Sitco Antenna Company/Simplicity Tool Corp
Standard Communications Corp.
TANDBERG Television Inc.
Toner Cable Equipment Inc.

Heads, Magnetic Film & Tape, Disk
AheadTek
International Electro-Magnetics (IEM)
Polyline
Sprague Magnetics Inc.

Heads, Refurbishing
International Electro-Magnetics (IEM)
Sprague Magnetics Inc.
Videomagnetics Inc.

Headsets, Headphones
AKG Acoustics, U.S.
ATI-Audio Technologies Inc.
Anchor Audio Inc.
Audio-Technica U.S., Inc.
COMTEK Inc.
Clear-Com Communication Systems
Fostex USA
Henry Engineering
Production Intercom Inc./Technical Projects
RAM SYSTEMS, LLC
RTS Systems Telex Communications Inc
Sacramento Theatrical Lighting (STL)
Sennheiser Electronic Corp.
Stanton Group
Telex Communications Inc.

Helicopters
American Eurocopter Corp.
Geneva Aviation Inc.
Gyrocam Systems
Wescam Inc.

High Definition Television (HDTV)
Beyond Broadband Technology LLC
Cintel Inc.
Hitachi Kokusai Electric America, Ltd.
LARCAN USA Inc
Leitch Inc.
Miranda Technologies Inc.
Moseley Associates Inc.
Sarnoff Corp.
Sencore Inc.
Telecast Fiber Systems Inc.
Toshiba America Consumer Products

ISO Couplers (AM & FM)
Phasetek Inc.

Image Enhancers, TV
Colorado Video Inc.
Xintekvideo Inc.

Infrared Transmission Systems
Sennheiser Electronic Corp.
Sound Associates

Installation Services
180 Connect
American Antenna Inc.
B&B Systems
Broadcast Store Inc.
CBT Systems
Professional Communications Systems
Quality Tower Erectors Inc.
Superior Tower Services Inc.
Teletech Inc.
VidCAD Documentation Programs (VDP Inc.)

Instruments Cases
A & S Case Co. Inc.
Atlas Case Corp.
Calzone Case Co.
Hardigg Cases
Penn Elcom Inc.
Stanley Supply & Services
Star Case Manufacturing Co. Inc.
Thermodyne International LTd

Interactive Television
Avid Broadcast
BIAP Inc.
TANDBERG Television Inc.
Tribune Media Services
Vidiom Systems Inc.

Intercom Systems
Anchor Audio Inc.
Bogen Communications Inc.
Clear-Com Communication Systems
Farrtronics Ltd.
Fuller Manufacturing
HME
ITI Electronics Inc.
Olesen
Production Intercom Inc./Technical Projects
RTS Systems Telex Communications Inc
Sacramento Theatrical Lighting (STL)
Setcom Corporation
Sierra Automated Systems & Engineering Corp.
Stage Equipment & Lighting Inc.
Studio Technologies Inc.
Swintek Enterprises Inc.
Systems Wireless Ltd.
Talk-A-Phone Co.
Telex Communications Inc.
Wiltronix Inc.

Jack Panels and Accessories
ADC
Audio Accessories Inc.
Auernheimer Labs Corp.
Clark Wire & Cable Co. Inc.
Gepco International Inc.
ITI Electronics Inc.
Kings-Winchester Electronics Corp.
NVISION Products
Penn Elcom Inc.
Penny & Giles Inc.
Trimm Inc.

Jibs
Matthews Studio Equipment Inc. (MSE)

Klystron Amplifiers/Lead Oxide Vidicon
Penta Laboratories
e2v Inc.

Klystrons
Communication & Power Industries
Daily Electronics Corp.
LARCAN USA Inc
MRPP Inc.
Penta Laboratories
e2v Inc.

LED, VU and S Panel Meters
Dorrough Electronics
Logitek Electronic Systems Inc
Sescom Inc.
Weschler Instruments

Labels
Audico Labels
Memorex Products Inc.
National Audio Co. Inc.
Seton Identification Products
Techni-Tool Inc.
U.S. Tape & Label Corp.
Veriad

Lenses, Optical and Camera
Alpine Optics Inc.
Band Pro Film & Digital Inc.
Canon U.S.A. Inc.
Dimension 3
Film/Video Equipment Service Co. Inc.
Fujinon Inc.
Homalite
Innovision Optics Inc.
Marshall Electronics
Navitar Inc.
Pentax Imaging Co.
Schneider Optics
Schneider Optics Inc.
Tamron U.S.A. Inc.

Library Storage Systems
Hollywood Vaults Inc.
Imagine Products Inc.
Neumade Products Corp.
Paulmar Industries Inc.

Lighting Design
DeSisti Lighting/Desmar Corp
Devlin Design Group Inc.
L.E. Nelson Sales Corp.
New York City Lites
Packaged Lighting Systems Inc.
Sachtler Corp. of America
The Express Group
Videssence L.L.C.

Lighting Equipment
ARRI Inc.
AVAB America Inc.
Allen Osborne Associates Inc.
Anton/Bauer Inc.
Arri Canada Ltd.
Atlantic Sound Systems
Automatic Devices Company
Band Pro Film & Digital Inc.
Bend-A-Lite Flexible Neon
CECO International Corp.
Camera Service Center
Channel One Lighting Systems Inc.
Comprehensive Video Group
DEDOTEC USA Inc.
DeSisti Lighting/Desmar Corp
Dove Systems
Electronic Theatre Controls Inc.
Emerson Network Power
Film/Video Equipment Service Co. Inc.
Flash Technology Corporation of America
Frezzolini Electronics Inc.
Full Compass Systems Ltd.
GAMPRODUCTS Inc.
Group One Ltd.
Honeywell Lighting & Electronics
Illumination Dynamics Inc.
James Thomas Engineering Inc.
L.E. Nelson Sales Corp.
LTM Corp. of America
Leviton NSI Colortran
Lowel-Light Manufacturing Inc.
Matthews Studio Equipment Inc. (MSE)
Mole-Richardson Co.
Musco Mobile Lighting Ltd.
Neutrik U.S.A. Inc.
New York City Lites
Olesen
PC & E
Packaged Lighting Systems Inc.
Panavision New York
Photomart Cine-Video Inc.
Pro Video & Film Equipment Co. Inc.
Rosco Laboratories Inc.
Sachtler Corp. of America
ScreenLight & Grip
Sinar Bron Inc.
Skytec, Inc.
Stage Equipment & Lighting Inc.
Strand Lighting Inc.
Strong International
Teatronics/Entertainment Lighting Control
Theatre Service & Supply Corp.

EQUIPMENT MANUFACTURERS

Equipment Manufacturers & Distributors

A & S Case Co. Inc.
5260 Vineland Ave., N. Hollywood, CA 91601 USA
(818) 509-5920, *Fax:* (818) 509-1397
www.ascase.com
billw@ascase.com
Bill Waskey, Operations Dir
Denise Berry, General Manager
Elden Boice, Purchasing
Since 1976, A&S Case Company, Inc. has been the leader in the design & manufacture of ATA Spec 300 Category one compliant reusable shipping & carrying cases. Our ability to innovate has put us at the cutting edge of the industry, allowing usto provide custom solutions for customers in a wide var of fields with spefific needs.

A R T Applied Research and Technology
215 Tremont St., Rochester, NY 14608 USA
(585) 436-2720, *Fax:* (585) 436-3942
www.artproaudio.com
sales@artproaudio.com
Philip Betette, President
Digital audio signal processors & enhancement devices.

A.C.C. Electronix, Inc.
420 Wylie Drive, Normal, IL 61761-4315 USA
(309) 888-9990, *Fax:* (309) 452-0893
www.accelectronix.com
acc@accelectronix.com
Andy Rector, Owner
John Franklin, Finance Executive
Repair cartridge tape recorders & reproducers.

Abekas, Incorporated
1090 O'Brien Drive, Menlo Park, CA 94025 USA
(650) 470-0900, *Fax:* (650) 470-0913
www.abekas.com
info@abekas.com
Junaid Sheikh, CEO
Douglas Johnson, Operations Dir
Phil Bennett, Chief Engineer
Abekas, Incorporated (www.abekas.com) is a privately-held company headquartered in Menlo Park, California. Abekas designs, manufactures, sells, and supports a complete line of digital video/audio delay devices, disk recorders, digitalspecial effects and editing tools for use in the worldwide professional television marketplace â€" encompassing the production, post production, broadcasting and computer video markets.

Abroyd Communications Ltd.
3-360 Montrose St.North, Cambridge, ON N3H 2H8 CAN
(519) 650-5093, (888) 658-5100, *Fax:* (519) 650-9546
www.abroyd.com
info@abroyd.com
Ryan Schindler, President
Paul Firminger, Sales/Marketing
Designers, manufacturers & installers of communication towers; manufacturer for Lightning Dissipation Arrays Chem-Rod from LEC.

Access Intelligence LLC
4 Choke Cherry Rd., 2nd Fl., Rockville, MD 20850 USA
(301) 354-2000, *Fax:* (301) 309-3847
www.accessintel.com
info@accessintel.com
Michael E W Jackson, Chairman
Donald Pazour, CEO
Ed Pinedo, CFO
Macy Fecto, Executive Vice President
Magazines, trade shows, seminars & cable publication.

AccuWeather Inc.
385 Science Park Rd., State College, PA 16803-2215 USA
(814) 235-8500, (814) 235-8770, *Fax:* (814) 235-8639
www.accuweather.com
sales@accuweather.com
Barry Myers, CEO/COO
Dr. Joel Myers, President
Dr. Joe Sobel, Senior VP/Director Forensics
Michael R. Smith, CEO/Weather Data Services
Elliot Abrams, SVP/Chief Meteorologist
Justin Robert, Communications Manager
Dr. R. Lee Rainy,VP of Marketing
AccuWeather, Inc. offers a broad new menu of powerful integrated, muturally supporting weather content & weather brand-building solutions.

Acme Electric Corp., Aerospace Division
528 W. 21st St., Suite 6, Tempe, AZ 85282 USA
(480) 894-6864, *Fax:* (480) 921-0470
www.acme-electric.com/aerospace
John Gleason, General Manager
Gary Lesser, General Sales Mgr
Sealed fiber nickel-cadmium batteries, battery chargers, battery control units, & AC/DC & DC/OC converters.

Acoustic Systems/ETS-Lindgren HQ
1301 Arrow Point Dr., Cedar Park, TX 78613 USA
(512) 531-6400, (512) 531-6498, *Fax:* (512) 531-6500
www.acousticsystems.com
sales@ets-lingren.com
Bruce Butler, CEO/COO
Glen Watkins, General Manager
Mark Mawdsley, General Sales Mgr

Acoustical Solutions Inc.
2420 Grenoble Rd., Richmond, VA 23294 USA
(800) 782-5742, *Fax:* (804) 346-8808
www.acousticalsolutions.com
info@accousticalsolutions.com
Michael Binns, President
David Ingersoll, General Sales Mgr
Sound & noise control materials including products for the bcst/recording industry, telecommunications industry, architectural acoustics & industrial noise control.

Acrodyne Industries Inc. (Ai)
200 Schell Ln., Phoenixville, PA 19460 USA
(610) 917-1300, *Fax:* (610) 917-8148
www.acrodyne.com
ellen.rainey@acrodyne.com
Nat Ostroff, Chairman
Richard Murray, CEO
Dan Traynor, General Sales Mgr
Ellen Rainey, Marketing Executive
AiR series of ATSC UHF on-channel repeaters that provide the ideal solution for broadcasters to fill in areas of their Authorized Digital Service area that are not sufficiently covered by their main transmitter; Mobile360 system thatprovides all components or equipment necessary, both at studio and transmitter, to integrate ATSC Mobile DTV transmission into any DTV broadcast facility; Universal XD Exciter/Driver system for analog to digital conversions; Quantum standard IOT andmaximum efficiency depressed collector technology; complete line of liquid and air-cooled Solid-State transmitters.

ADC
Box 1101, Minneapolis, MN 55440-1101 USA
(952) 938-8080,(800) 366-3889, *Fax:* (952) 917-1717
www.adc.com
Will Cadogan, Chairman
Robert Switz, CEO/COO
Jo Anne Anderson, President
Lois Martin, Operations Dir
Charles Oswald, Director
ADC provides the connections for wireline, wireless, cable, bcst & enterprise nets around the world. ADC's equipment & svcs enable high-speed Internet, data, video & voice svcs.

Adcom, LLC
8541 E Anderson Drive, Scottsdale, AZ 83225 USA
(480) 607-2277, *Fax:* (480) 348-9876
www.adcom.com
service@adcom.com
Night Suite DI, non-linear editing systems, bcst control systems, video conferencing. Room control systems 1 room.

ADCOUR, Inc.
623 Main St., Woburn, MA 1801 USA
(781) 937-0011, *Fax:* (781) 937-3499
adcourrj@aol.com
Richard Jacobs, President
Batteries, chargers, power supplies & power conditioning.

Adrienne Electronics Corp.
7225 Bermuda Rd., Unit G, Las Vegas, NV 89119 USA
(702) 896-1858, *Fax:* (702) 896-3034
www.adrielec.com
info@adrielec.com
Tracey Ruesch, President
Time code reader/generator products with PCI, PCI Express, USB and serial interfaces

ADSCO Line Products Inc.
3500 Washington Ave., Houston, TX 77007 USA
(713) 880-2424,(800) 247-6484, *Fax:* (713) 880-2456
www.adscoline.com
ajackd@dscoline.com
Linda Schmuck, President
Nancy Wallace, Marketing Manager
Outside plant line hardware for CATV: guy strand, messengers, lashing wire/rods, formed grips/dead-ends & related line hardware. Stainless steel poleline hardware.

ADTEC Inc.
408 Russell St., Nashville, TN 37206 USA
(615) 256-6619 ext. 113, *Fax:* (615) 256-6593
www.adtecinc.com
sales@adtecinc.com
Ron Johnson, Operations Dir
Kevin Ancelin, General Sales Mgr
Products offered: Loc origination controllers & systems, coml insertion controllers & systems, network delay recording.
2231 Corporate Square Blvd., Jacksonville, FL 32216 United States
(904) 720-2003;
Kevin Ancelin, Pres

Advanced Designs Corp.
1169 W. 2nd St., Bloomington, IN 47403 USA
(812) 333-1922, *Fax:* (812) 333-2030
www.doprad.com
adc@doprad.com
Matt McGrath, President
Martin Riess, Owner
DOPRAD™ 32 doppler radar system, weather data display system, storm path analyzer, street-level maps, lightning, low-cost remoting & composite live doppler.

Advanced Media Inc.
Box 599, 80 Orville Drive, Bohemia, NY 11716-0599 USA
(631) 244-1616, *Fax:* (631) 244-1415
www.advancemedia.com
team@advancedmedia.com
Haas Kaemmlein, President/CEO
Alan Schoenbart, VP/CFO
Kiosk-interactive technology.

Advanced Media Technologies, Inc.
720 S. Powerline Rd., Suite G, Deerfield Beach, FL 33442-8156 USA
(888) 293-5856, *Fax:* (954) 427-9688
www.amt.com
sales@amt.com
Ken Mosca, President
AMT offers a complete line of broadband products from the world's most recognized manufacturers. Products include CATV QAM IP set-tops, digital, analog & IP headend electronics, Digcipher receivers, off-air 8-vsb receivers, RF & fibertransport, digital encoders, ad insertion, line gear, modems & much more.

Advent Communications Ltd.
Nashleigh Hill, Chesham, Buckinghamshire, HP5 3HE GBR
44 1494 774400, *Fax:* 44 1494 791127
www.adventcomms.com
sales@adventcomms.com
Stephen Rudd, General Manager
George Koumblis, General Sales Mgr
Provides satellite communication solutions for bcst, telecommunications, military & coml applications-design, manufacture & integrating a complete range of digital SNG flyaway & vehicle mounted terminals, a complete range of subsystemsupconverters, downconverters, DVB modulators, MPEG II Video Exciters, equalizers & remote control systems.

Aeroflex
35 South Service Rd., P.O. Box 6022, Plainview, NY 11803 USA
(516) 694-6700, (800) 843-1553, *Fax:* (516) 694-2562
www.aeroflex.com
info-test@aeroflex.com
Leonard Borow, CEO
Test & measurement instrumentation.
49 Trophy Club Rd., Trophy Club, TX 76262 United States
(817) 430-5842;
Carlos Blanco, Sls Mgr - South America

AheadTek
6410 Via Del Oro, San Jose, CA 95119 USA
(408) 226-9800 (408) 226-9991 (800) 971-9191, *Fax:* (408) 226-9195
www.aheadtek.com
patj@aheadtek.com
Tim Higgins, President
Patrick Johnston, General Sales Mgr
Cost effective solutions for your specialty magnetic head applications.

AKG Acoustics, U.S.
8500 Balboa Blvd., Northridge, CA 91329 USA
(818) 920-3212, *Fax:* (818) 920-3208
www.akg.com
akgusamarketing@harman.com
Kim Temple Holmes, President
Doug Mac Callum, Operations Dir
Brendan Stead, Vice President
Microphones, headphones, wireless microphones, in-ear monitoring systems, wireless loudspeakers, conferencing products.

Alan Gordon Enterprises Inc.
5625 Melrose Ave., Hollywood, CA 90038 USA
(323) 466-3561, *Fax:* (323) 871-2193
www.alangordon.com
info@alangordon.com
Don Sahlein, President
Wayne Loucks, General Manager
Tom Austin, Finance Director
Rental, Sale, Equipment Training and Repair Services for professional motion picture HD, film and video equipment.

Alesis
200 Scenic View Dr., Suite 201, Cumberland, RI 2864 USA
(401) 658-5760
www.alesis.com
marketing@alesis.com
Digital tape recording system, mixing consoles, digital & analogue signal processing, amplification, drum machines, keyboards.

Alexander Technologies
1511 South Garfield Pl., Mason City, IA 50401 USA
641) 423-8955, *Fax:* (641) 423-1644
www.alexandertechnologies.com
cservice@alexenergy.com
John Casey, CEO
Jay Miller, SVP
Rechargeable nicad in-board, on-board & battery belts; nicad battery chargers & analyzer/conditioners; portable radio & pager batteries.

All Mobile Video Inc.
221 W. 26th St., New York, NY 10001 USA
(212) 727-1234, *Fax:* (212) 255-6644
www.allmobilevideo.com
Anton Duke, CEO
Eric Duke, President
Bcst video equipment rental including truck remotes & total carry-in packages, complete studio facilities.
10490 Gandy Blvd., Saint Petersburg, FL 33742 United States
(813) 579-8902;
Bary Spencer, Dir Teleport Opns
9670 Aero Dr, San Diego, CA 92123 United States
(619) 569-8451;
N. Tabkum, Dir West Coast Opns

Allen Avionics, Inc.
255 E. Second St., Mineola, NY 11501 USA
(516) 248-8080, *Fax:* (516) 747-6724
www.allenavionics.com
jim@allenavionics.com
Jim Lyons, Operations Dir
A broad line of standard Passive Electronic Components that include Precision LC Filters of all types from 20 Hz to 5GHz, Microwave filters, Coaxial adapters and wave guide components to 40GHz, general purpose analog and digitalelectromagnetic delay lines, filters for NTSC and pal, Video Delay lines and Attenuators, Amplitude Phase Equalizers, audio and video, isolation transformers for NTSC, SDI, and HD-SDI, Hum eliminators, diplaxers, networks, and electronic timingproducts up to to 2 minutes.

Allen Osborne Associates Inc.
756 Lakefield Rd., Westlake Village, CA 91361 USA
(805) 495-8420, *Fax:* (805) 373-6067
www.aoa-gps.com
j_osborne@aoa-gps.com
Jim Osborne, Operations Dir
Pneumatic masts systems for remote E.N.G., fixed or mobile radio communications, etc.

Allied Electronics Inc.
7151 Jack Newell Blvd. S., Fort Worth, TX 76118 USA
(817) 595-3500, (866) 433-5722, *Fax:* (817) 595-8530
www.alliedelec.com
Lee Davidson, President
Broad line distributor of electronic components.

Allied Tower Co. Inc.
4646 Mandale, Alvin, TX 77511 USA
(281) 331-9627, *Fax:* (281) 331-9822
www.alliedtower.com
Max Bowen, CEO
Jeff Bowen, President
Doug Moore, Operations Dir
Jerry Moore, General Manager
Design, fabrication & erection of FM, AM, TV & communication towers.

Allison Payments Systems L.L.C.
2200 Production Dr., Indianapolis, IN 462414912 USA
(317) 808-2400,(800) 755-2440, *Fax:* (317) 808-2477
www.apsllc.com
sales@apsllc.com
Coupon payment billing systems.

Allsop Inc.
4201 Meridian Street, Bellingham, WA 98226-5512 USA
(360) 734-9090, *Fax:* (360) 733-4302
www.allsop.com
info@allsop.com
Jim Allsop, President
Brett Allsop President, President
Ryan Allsop, Vice President
Linda Pilon, HR Executive
Cleaning accessories for audio & video, record care products & compact discs, computer accessories.

Allstate Tower Company Inc.
Div/DBA: (formerly Nationwide Tower Company Inc.)
232 Heilman Drive, Henderson, KY 42420
(270) 830-8512, *Fax:* (270) 830-8475
www.allstatetower.com
sales@allstatetower.com
William Johnston, CEO
Sam Dorris, Operations Dir
Andy Denton, CFO
Kevin Roth, General Sales Mgr
Tower Manufacturing Co. including: Tower inspections, painting, repair re-guy, lighting, antennas, feedlines, analysis, erect, dismantle, line sweeping, site monitoring, & tower tracker svcs.

Alpack Associates, Inc.
6 High Point Dr., Wayne, NJ 7470 USA
(973) 694-5510, *Fax:* (973) 694-7080
www.alpack-pic.com
info@alpack-pic.com
Les Weinstock, President
Dante Cuoco, Manager
Standard & custom carrying & shipping cases for all bcst equipment. Both hard & soft case styles.

Alpha Technologies Inc.
3767 Alpha Way, Bellingham, WA 98226 USA
(360) 647-2360, *Fax:* (360) 392-2144
www.alpha.com
alpha@alpha.com
Fred Kaiser, Chairman
Drew Zogby, President
Jeff Lechtanski, Chief Marketing Officer
Develops power conversion, protection and standby products for telecommunications and broadband cable industries, including custom, application-specific power solutions.

Alpha Video & Electronics (AVEC)
200 Mingo Church Rd., Finleyville, PA 15332 USA
(724) 348-8280, *Fax:* (724) 348-8600
www.aveceng.com
henry@aveceng.com
Henry Lassige, Sr., President
O.B. vans, eng vans, DSNG vans, ENG mast safety device, turnkey systems, camera transporter.

Alpine Optics Inc.
9913 N.W. 20th St., Pompano Beach, FL 33071 USA
(954) 344-9871, *Fax:* (954) 344-3665
www.alpine-optics.com
toalpine_optics@bellsouth.net
Horst Stahl, President
Gabrielle Jung, Director
Repair, maintenance of all Canon, Fujinon, Nikon, Schneider & JVC lenses.

Altronic Research Inc.
621 Highway 202 West, Yellville, AR 72687 USA
(800) 482-5623,(870) 449-4093, *Fax:* (870) 449-6000
www.altronic.com
info@altronic.com
John Dyess, President
Gary James, Engineering
Jim Keyes, Engineering
Billie Heenan, Finance
Omegaline RF coaxial load resistors (dummy loads).

Aluma Tower Company Inc.
Box 2806, 1639 Old Dixie Hwy., Vero Beach, FL 32961-2806 USA
(772) 567-3423, *Fax:* (772) 567-3432
www.alumatower.com
atc@alumatower.com
Robert Main, President
Theodore Gottry, Vice President
Aluminum telescoping towers combined with trailers & optional shelters provides mobile units. Vehicle mounted towers for installation on customer's vehicle.

Amdocs
1390 Timberlake Manor Pkwy., Chesterfield, MO 63017
(314) 212-7000
www.amdocs.com
info@amdocs.com
Eli Gelman, CEO
Guy Dubois, President
Amdocs is the market leader in customer experience systems innovation, enabling world-leading svc providers & integrated, innovative & intentional customer experience at every point of svc.

Amek U.S.A.
1449 Donelson Pike, Nashville, TN 37217 USA
(615) 360-0488, *Fax:* (615) 360-0273
amekusa@harman.com
Allan Nichols, Contact
Josh Thomas, Contact
Amek, TAC (Total Audio Concepts) & Langley audio consoles for production, postproduction, audio recording, sound reinforcement & Medici signal processing equipment.

American Antenna Inc.
4707 Roosevelt St., Glen Park, IN 46408 USA
(219) 985-4000, *Fax:* (219) 985-4001
www.americanantenna.com
sales@americanantenna.com
Nick Michels, President
Rick Gard, Operations Dir
Chuck Forsyth, General Sales Mgr
Manufactuer, Distributor & installer of Earth Station Antennas up to 6.1m. Motorized, actuators, receivers, controllers, feeds, multi-beam feed system, LNB's & accessories.

American Eurocopter Corp.
2701 North Forum Drive, Grand Prairie, TX 75052-7099 USA
(972) 522-4780, *Fax:* (972) 641-3419
www.eurocopterusa.com
Marc Paganini, President/CEO
Brenda Revland, Promotions Manager
Servicing North American market; manufactures & sells complete line of single- & twin-engine turbine helicopters.

American Tower Corp.
116 Huntington Avenue, Boston, MA 02116 USA
(781) 926-4772, *Fax:* (781) 926-4755
www.americantower.com
lisa.poston@americantower.com
James Taillett Sr, President/Chairman
Tom Barlett, Chief Financial Officer
Owners & operators of TV, FM & other bcst towers & specialty structures.

Ampex Data Systems -America
500 Broadway, Redwood City, CA 94063-3199 USA
(650) 367-3365, *Fax:* (650) 367-4669
www.ampexdata.com
info@ampexdata.com
Larry Chiarelli, CEO/President
Donald Downing, Business Dev Manager
John Hardy, Business Dev Manager
Data recorders, data systems, mass data storage, instrumentation recorder products; 19 mm scanning recorders, library systems (DST & DIS products), related tape, after-market parts & video recorder support.

Amplivox Portable Sound Systems
3995 Commercial Ave., Northbrook, IL 60062 USA
(847) 498-9000, (800) 267-5486, *Fax:* (800) 267-5489
www.ampli.com
droth@ampli.com
Don Roth, CEO
Ron Stelzer, Financial Executive
Portable sound systems/lecterns/wireless/indoor-outdoor, made in USA, UL, CSA, CE, 6 years warranty.

Amtel Network
431 Myrtle St., Suite 6, Glendale, CA 91203 USA

EQUIPMENT MANUFACTURERS

(818) 842-8088, (800) 893-4509, *Fax:* (818) 551-4999
www.amtelsystems.com
amtel@amtel.com,support@amtel.com
Mike Takamatsu, President
Text-visual intercom system.

Analog Digital International Inc.
20 E. 49th St., 2nd Fl., New York, NY 10017-1023 USA
(212) 688-5110, *Fax:* (212) 688-5405
www.analogdigitalinc.com
info@analogdigitalinc.com
Ayres D'Cunha, President
Sls & rentals of professional /bcst-NTSC/PAL equipment. Post production svcs. DVD authoring replication. AVID/FCP editing.

Anchor Audio Inc.
2565 W. 237th St., Torrance, CA 90505 USA
(310) 784-2300,(800) 262-4671, *Fax:* (310) 784-0066
www.anchoraudio.com
sales@anchoraudio.com
Janet Jacobs, COO
David Jacobs, President
Alicia Gariby, Manufacturing Director
Portable public address sound systems and wired and wireless intercom equipment.

Andrew Corp.
10500 W 153rd Street, Orlando, IL 60462 USA
(779) 435-6500,(800) 255-1479, *Fax:* (779) 435-8579, (800) 349-5444
www.andrew.com
Jonas Aleska, Manager
Nancy Lawrence, Manager
VHF & UHF-TV transmitting, microwave & ESA's; coaxial cable; waveguides; towers; equipment shelters; instal svcs, combiners & pressurization equipment.
10500 W. 153rd St., Orland Park, IL 60462 United States
(708) 349-3300;
Paul Cox, Group Pres
sls, President
George Tong, Govt Antennas & Esas

Antenna Concepts Inc.
6626 Merchandise Way, Diamond Springs, CA 95619 USA
(530) 621-2015, *Fax:* (530) 622-3274
www.antennaconcepts.com
sales@antennaconcepts.com
Mark Cunningham, CEO
Dave Bolls, Principal
Custom & standard low-, medium- and high-power omni or directional digital & analog UHF, VHF, FM, & MMDS bcst antennas. Full power Broadcast antennas. TV: UHF/VHF analog/digital antennas including full-UHF band CP panel. Fm: Ultra Trackersingle-lobe.

Anton/Bauer Inc.
14 Progress Drive, Shelton, CT 6484 USA
(203) 929-1100, *Fax:* (203) 929-9935
www.antonbauer.com
Michael Accardi, President
Pat Loch, Chief Administrative Officer
Shin Minowa, Chief Marketing Officer
NiCad, NIMH & Li-ion cameras batteries, chargers, lighting & diagnostic accessories for the professional video industry.

Anvil Cases
15730 Salt Lake Ave., City of Industry, CA 91745 USA
(626) 968-4100, *Fax:* (626) 968-1703
www.anvilcase.com
web.sales@anvilcase.com
Joseph Calzone, President
Vince Calzone, Vice President
Deb Visckay, General Manager
Heavy-duty reuseable, custom, standard shipping cases & containers for all bcst equipment.

APC by Schneider Electric
132 Fairgrounds Rd, West Kingston, RI 2892 USA
(877) 272-2722, *Fax:* (401) 789-3710
www.apc.com
info@mgeups.com
Laurent Vernerey, CEO
Manufacturers of uninterruptible power systems (UPS) power conditioners & inverters that protect equipment from power related problems.
520 8th Ave., 21st Fl., New York, NY 10018 United States
(212) 594-9333; *Fax:* (212) 594-3691
2895 Greenspoint Pkwy. #350, Hoffman Estates, IL 60195 United States
(847) 585-1113; *Fax:* (847) 585 1125

Aphex Systems Ltd.
11068 Randall St., Sun Valley, CA 91352 USA
(818) 767-2929, *Fax:* (818) 767-2641
www.aphex.com
sales@aphex.com
Marvin Caesar, President
Rick McClenden, General Manager
Wayne La Farr, Programming Director
Model 2020 MKIII, Compellor-intelligent AGC, Dominator II precision multi-band peak limiter, Aural Exciter, Expressor, remote controlled mic preams, TVGS MIC/instrument, preamplifiers, analog to digital converters.

APM Music
6255 Sunset Blvd., Suite 820, Los Angeles, CA 90028 USA
(323) 461-3211,(212) 856-9800, *Fax:* (323) 461-9102
www.apmmusic.com
accountservices@apmmusic.com
Adam Taylor, President
George Macias, Sales Executive
Craig Giummarra, General Sales Mgr
Sharon Jennings, Promotions Manager
George Macias, EVP Sales
George Maloian, Key Account Director
Giselle Vasconez, Key Account Director
Matthew Gutknecht, Key Account Director
Over 300,000 tracks, 30 production music libraries, over 4,000 CDs, personalized packages, music search svcs, 20-25 new CD releases mthy & fantastic music dir who can assist in searches for all productions.
381 Park Ave. S., Suite 1101, New York, NY 10016 United States

APW Mayville/Stantron
403 Degner Ave., Mayville, WI 53050-1513 USA
(800) 558-7297,(920) 387-3000, *Fax:* (920) 387-7196
www.apwmayville.com
customerservice@mayvilleproducts.com
Daniel Eder, President
Rich Runnels, General Sales Mgr
Stantron racks, cabinets, enclosures, & related accessories for bcst integrators & professional audio video installations.

Argo Systems
2964 Peachtree Rd., Suite 400, Atlanta, GA 30305
(404) 869-4575, *Fax:* (404) 844-9009
www.argosys.com
info@argosys.com
Doug Callahan, President
Catherine Dunn, Operations Dir
An integrated affil mgmt software solution providing functionality, data mgmt, reporting & SOX compliance across a network's Affiliate Finance, Sales Operations, IT & Engineering departments.

Argraph Corp.
111 Asia Place, Carlstadt, NJ 7072 USA
(201) 939-7722, *Fax:* (201) 939-7782
www.argraph.com
info@argraph.com
Irvine Roth, CEO
Mark Roth, President
Martin Lipton, General Sales Mgr
Anti-stat cleaning cloths, samigron video tripods.

Argraph West
2710 McCone, Hayward, CA 94545 United States
(510) 298-0575;

Aries Industries Inc.
Corporate Office, 550 Elizabeth St., Waukesha, WI 53186 USA
(262) 896-7205,(800) 234-7205, *Fax:* (262) 246-7099
www.ariesind.com
sales@ariesind.com
James Lenahan, CEO
Lisa Meissner, Chief Marketing Officer
Claire Schaefier, Chief Technical Officer
Manufacture pipeline inspection televising test & seal equipment.
5748 E. Shields, Fresno, CA 93727 United States
(800) 671-0383; *Fax:* (559) 291-0463
J. Lenahan, Ceo

Arista Information Systems
2220 Morth Mart Parkway, Suite 100, Duluth, GA 30096 USA
(678) 473-1885, *Fax:* (678) 473-1051
www.aristainfo.com
bgreer@aristainfo.com
Bob Greer, CEO
Tom Baglive, Manufacturing Executive
Cable TV subscriber & statement printing.

Arrakis Systems Inc.
6604 Powell St., Loveland, CO 80538-8714 USA
(970) 461-0730, *Fax:* (970) 663-1010
www.arrakis-systems.com
sales@arrakis-systems.com
Michael Palmer, President
Roderic Graham, Operations Dir
Jon Young, General Sales Mgr
Audio consoles, digital audio, satellite, live-assist, hard drive automation & production systems, studio furniture.

Arri Canada Ltd.
415 Horner Ave., Unit 11, Etobicoke, ON M8W 4W3 CAN
(416) 255-3335, *Fax:* (416) 255-3399
www.arri.com
Sebastien Laffoux, Programming Director
Hinwai Sheffield, Finance Manager
ARRI camera, lightning equipment & all professional accessories, sales & service.

ARRI Inc.
600 North Victory Blvd, Burbank, CA 91502 USA
(818) 841-7070, *Fax:* (818) 848-4028
www.arri.com
info@arri.com
Charles Davidson, COO
Volker Bahnemann, President
Bill Russell, Operations Dir
Juergen Schwinzer, VP, Camera Division
Glenn Kennel, VP, CTO
John Gresch, VP, Lighting Division
Ted Kampel, VP, Finance
Manufacturer of professional motion picture film cameras & accessories, lighting equipment & post-production tools.

ARRI Inc.
2385 Stirling Road Ft. Lauderdale, FL 33312
(954) 322-4545; *Fax:* (818) 954-4188

ARRI Inc.
617 Route 303, Blauvelt, CA 10913
(845) 353-1400; *Fax:* (845) 425-1250

Arris
Corporate Headquarters, 3871 Lakefield Dr., Suwanee, GA 30024 USA
(866) 362-7747 (in US),(678) 473-5656, *Fax:* (678) 473-8470
www.arris.com
Andrew T. Heler, Director
CMTS, cable modems, telephony voice ports & modems, oss/provisioning systems, HFC infrastructure products.

Artel Video Systems
237 Cedar Hill Street, Marlborough, MA 01752 USA
(508) 303-8200, *Fax:* (508) 303-8197
www.artel.com
info@artel.com
Richard Dellacanonica, CEO
Since 1981 Artel Video Systems has been an industry leading developer of carrier class, bcst quality video over fiber-optic transport hardware. Our products deliver video, audio & data in real time with reliability meeting the most demandingrequirements for 24/7/365 opn in harsh environments.

Ascent Media Creative Services Inc.
6344 Fountain Ave., Hollywood, CA 90028 USA
(323) 466-7663, *Fax:* (323) 466-5539
www.encorehollywood.com
info@encorehollywood.com
Steven Fuset, Creative Director
Bill Royeo, SVP
Josh Ouber, SVP/Technical

Asia Broadcast Centre
(65) 548-0388;
Jim Crowe, Mgng Dir

Ascent Media Management Services
2901 W. Alameda Ave., Burbank, CA 91505 USA
(818) 840-7000, *Fax:* (818) 840-7129
www.ascentmedia.com
William Humphrey, President
Andre Macaluso, Operations Dir
Chris Van Duyn, Director
Beth Simon, General Sales Mgr
Postproduction video & film svcs: editing, telecine, sound, duplication, satellite svcs, film lab, standard conversion tape to film transfers & digital asset mgmt.
235 Pegasus Ave., Northvale, NJ 07647
(201) 767-3800; *Fax:* (201) 767-4568
Beth Simon, Sr Vp Sls/Mktg

Ascent Media Services
520 Broadway, 5th Fl., Santa Monica, CA 90401-2420 USA

(310) 434-7000, *Fax:* (310) 434-7111
www.ascentmedia.com
William Fitzgerald, CEO
William Niles, EVP/General Counsel
John Orr, SVP
A transmission company specializing in video switching, quality control, last mile connections, remote transmissions, production & audiovisual svcs to the bcst, cable & corporate TV industries.

Aspect Software
300 Apollo Dr., Chelmsford, MA 1824 USA
(978) 250-7900,(888) 412-7728, *Fax:* (978) 244-7420
www.aspect.com
info@aspect.com
Mohammed Ali, President
Automated telephone call processing products for inbound & outbound call centers.
3778 Realty Rd, Dallas, TX 75238 United States
(609) 235-1771;
Randy Pugh, Natl Acct Exec
1010 Northern Blvd., Suite 208, Great Neck, NY 11021 United States
(516) 829-0390;
Rich Bogner, Sls Rep
1300 Bristol St. N., Suite 100, Newport Beach, CA 92660 United States
(714) 261-9330;
Roy Rich, Sls Rep
5001 LBJ Fwy., Suite 727, Dallas, TX 75244 United States
(214) 387-5210;
Nick Pollard, Western Rgnl Sls Mgr

Aspera Inc.
5900 Hollis St. - Suite E, Emeryville, AL 94608
(510) 849-2386, *Fax:* (510) 868-8392
www.asperasoft.com
info@asperasoft.com
Michelle Munson, President
Cary Capece, Operations Dir
Chris Markle, Engineering Dir
Serban Simu, VP Engineering/Co-Founder
Software developer of high speed file transfer technology, fasp.

Associated Press Broadcast Services
1100 13th St., Suite 700, Washington, DC 20005 USA
(800) 342-5127
www.apbroadcast.com
Jon Petrovich, Operations Dir
Lee Perryman, General Manager
Andy Wormser, Technical Operations
Greg Groce, Director/Business Operations
AP NewsDesk: Newsroom computer software program for mgng TV, radio news & info resources.

ATCI/Antenna Technology Communications Inc.
450 N. McKemy Ave., Chandler, AZ 85226 USA
(480) 844-8501, (480) 308-4599, *Fax:* (480) 898-7667
www.atci.com
Gary Hatch, CEO
Ron Kahle, COO/CFO
Simulsat multibeam earth stns; parabolic antennas from 1.8 m to 32 m. Headend electronics, design & maintenance, used/refurbished equipment.

ATI-Audio Technologies Inc.
223 Peppermill Road, West Berlin, NJ 8091 USA
(856) 626-3480, *Fax:* (856) 504-0220
www.atiaudio.com
sales@atiaudio.com
Contact Officer, Promotions Manager
Bcst audio, products: Mic, Line & Distribution Amps, AD/DA & Sample Rate Converters, AES Clock Generator, Portable Field Mixers & Audio Test Equipment.

Atlantic Inc.
10018 Santa Fe Springs Rd., P.O. Box 2399, Sante Fe Springs, CA 90670-2922 USA
(562) 903-9550, *Fax:* (562) 903-9053
www.atlantic-inc.com, www.theatlanticstore.com
customer_relations@atlantic-inc.com
Leo Dardashti, President
Don Dolliver, General Sales Mgr
Mary Jo Schrader, Sales Executive
Brian Hilby, Purchasing Executive
Manufacturer of metal storage systems for DVDs, CDs, & VHS.

Atlantic Sound Systems
R.R. 2 Station Main, New Glasgow, Pictou County, NS B2H 5C5 CAN
(902) 752-8527
plann@wisic.com
Peter W Lann, President
Professional bcstg, sound & lighting equipment. Rental & PA Installations.

Atlantic Video Inc.
650 Massachusetts Ave. N.W., Washington, DC 20001 USA
(202) 408-0900, (877) 777-1118, *Fax:* (202) 408-8496
www.atlanticvideo.com
questions@atlanticvideo.com
Ed Milligan, President
Gary Purviance, General Manager
Werner Seubert, Chief Financial Officer
Atlantic video is a full svc bcst production svc facility, from studio, remote, post & transmission.

Atlas Case Corp.
1380 S. Cherokee St., Denver, CO 80223 USA
(888) 325-2199, (303) 778-7058, *Fax:* (877) 525-2339, (303) 778-7102
www.atlascases.com
sales@atlascases.com
Randy Sabey, President
Airline-approved shipping & carrying cases. Local transport cases, custom or from stock.

Atlas Sound
4545 E. Baseline Rd., Phoenix, AZ 85042 USA
(800) 876-3332,(602) 438-4545, *Fax:* (800) 765-3435
www.atlassound.com
atlascustser@atlassound.com
Lloyd Ivey, CEO
Ken Peck, General Sales Mgr
Steve Young, Promotions Manager
Manny Kitagawa, General Sales Manager
Atlas Sound brand microphone & equipment stands, accessories; equipment consoles, racks & cabinets; loudspeaker systems; a/v monitoring devices.
Atlas Sound Manufacturing
1601 Jack McKay, Ennis, TX 75119 United States

Audico Labels
118 South Main St., Goshen, IN 46526 USA
(800) 252-5667, (574) 533-6688, *Fax:* (661) 760-8775
www.audicolabels.com
audicolabels@audicolabels.com
Bill Landow, President
Claudia Landow, Owner/President
Media pressure sensitive labels.

Audio Accessories Inc.
25 Mill St., P.O. Box 360, Marlow, NH 3456 USA
(603) 446-3335, *Fax:* (603) 446-7543
www.patchbays.com
audioacc@patchbays.com
M.B. Hall, President
T.J. Symonds, Operations Dir
Michael Hart, Operations Executive
Jack panels, (audio & video patchbays) patch cords, telephone jacks & plugs, pre-wired jack panels (miniature & full-size) & video panels.

Audio Implements/GKC
1703 Pearl St., Waukesha, WI 53186-5626 USA
(262) 524-2424, *Fax:* (262) 524-7898
www.audioimplements.com
info@audioimplements.com
Walter Kolb, President
Anita Kolb, Operations Dir
Acoustic coiled earpiece, receivers & cords, microphone line & monitor amplifiers, used in conjunction with IFB system.

Audio Precision Inc.
5750 S.W. Arctic Dr., Beaverton, OR 97005 USA
(503) 627-0832, (800) 231-7350, *Fax:* (503) 641-8906
www.audioprecision.com
sales@ap.com
David Schmoldt, President
John Scoles, General Sales Mgr
Tom Williams, Promotions Manager
2700 Series, Portable One & ATS-1, ATS-2 audio test sets for bcst & satellite use.

Audio Processing Technology Ltd./APT
Whitehouse Business Park, 729 Springfield Rd., Belfast, AL BT12 7FP IRL
44 0 28 9067 7200, *Fax:* 44 0 28 9067 7201
www.aptx.com
sales@aptodecs.com
Digital (apt-X) audio compression system for professional applications such as storage & transmission of audio over low capacity digital circuits such as ISDN.
6255 Sunset Blvd., Suite 1025, Los Angeles, CA 90028 United States
(323) 463-2963; *Fax:* (323) 463-8878
Simav Factor, Chairman

Audio-Technica U.S., Inc.
1221 Commerce Dr., Stow, OH 44224 USA
(330) 686-2600, *Fax:* (330) 686-0719
www.audio-technica.com
pro@atus.com
Tamara Hoffman, Chief Financial Officer
Greg Pinto, VP Marketing
Microphones, wireless microphones, headphones, automatic microphone mixers, phono cartridges, turntables, audio & video accessories.

Audio-Video Engineering Co.
One Pineapple Ln., Stuart, FL 34996 USA
(772) 219-3623, *Fax:* (772) 219-3624
Olga Drucker, President/Chairman
Rolf Dracker, Director
Video hum stop coil (hum bucker).

Audioarts Engineering
600 Industrial Dr., New Bern, NC 28562 USA
(252) 638-7000, *Fax:* (252) 635-4857
www.audioartsengineering.com,www.wheatstone.com
sales@wheatstone.com
Gary Snow, President
Andrew Calvanese, Operations Dir
Jay Tyler, General Sales Mgr
Manufacturer of digital & analog broadcast audio mixing consoles & processing equipment.

Audiolab Electronics Inc.
620 Commerce Street, Suite100, Roseville, CA 95678 USA
(916) 784-0200, (800) 624-1903, *Fax:* (916) 784-1425
www.audiolabelectronics.com
info@audiolabelectronics.com
Ronald Stofan, CEO
Professional line of bulk tape degaussers for all formats of tape including: Beta SP, DAT 2 reels up to 16 diameters, hard drives, DLT media & degaussing svc.

Auernheimer Labs Corp.
4561 E. Florence Ave., Fresno, CA 93725 USA
(559) 442-1048
Clarence Auernheimer, President
Warren Auernheimer, Operations Dir
Dwayne Auernheimer, Sec/Treasurer
Manufactures household audio & video equipment; wholesales chemicals & allied products.

Austin Insulators Inc.
7510 Airport Rd., Mississauga, ON L4T 2H5 CAN
(905) 405-1144, *Fax:* (905) 405-1150
www.austin-insulators.com
sales@austin-insulators.com
Beverly O'Brien, President
Patrick Warr, President
Base/guyline insulators, static drain devices, tower lighting transformers, replacements for obsolete insulators & LED lighting for AM(MW), LW antennas .

Autodesk
10 Duke St., Montreal, QC H3C 2L7 CAN
(514) 393-1616, *Fax:* (514) 393-0110
www.autodesk.com
med-ent@autodesk.com
Marc Petit, Operations Dir
Stig Gruman, VP, Digital Entertainment
Autodesk solutions for creating, mgng & distributing digital content, so artists can create once & use anywhere.

Autodesk
11 Mc Innis Parkway, San Rafael, CA 94903
(415) 507-5000, *Fax:* (415) 507-5100
www.autodesk.ca
Carl Boss, CEO
Andrew Anagnost, SVP
Ken Bado, General Sales Mgr
2D & 3D computer graphic imaging & animation software for professionals in entertainment & industrial markets.

Autogram Corp.
Box 456, 1500 Capital Ave., Plano, TX 75074-8113 USA
(972) 424-8585,(800) 327-6901, *Fax:* (972) 423-6334
www.autogramcorp.com
info@autogramcorp.com
Ernest Ankele, CEO
Delores Ankele, Operations Dir
John Stanley Jr., Promotions Manager
Pacemaker IIk audio consoles, Pacemaker 6, 8, 10 Slide Pot, Mini-Mix 8 & Mini-Mix 12 Economy Consoles.Solution 20 audio

systems, CYA-4 emergency switchers. Autoclock clock/timer/thermometer.

Automatic Devices Company
2121 S. 12th St., Allentown, PA 18103 USA
(610) 797-6000, (800) 360-2321, *Fax:* (610) 797-4088
www.automaticdevices.com
info@automaticdevices.com
Dennis Lopez, COO
John Samuels, President
Elwood Hausman, Purchasing Executive
Cyclorama tracks, lighting tracks, lift & draw machines, electronic limit switches.

Autoscript
16 Progress Drive, Shelton, CT 6484 USA
(203) 926-2900, *Fax:* (203) 338-8359
www.autoscript.tv
support@autoscript.tv
Brian Larter, President
Joanne Pizzaferro, General Manager
Greg Prentiss, Sales Director
George Andros, Consultant
Design & manufacture of digital teleprompting systems, maintain a high level of new product dev.

Autoscript (UK)
Unit 2, Heathlands Close., Twickenham, TW1 4BP United Kingdom
44 0 208 891 8900; *Fax:* 44 0 208 891 8901
b.larter@autoscript.tv
Brian Larter, Mgng Dir

AVAB America Inc.
434 Payran Street, Petaluma, CA 94952 USA
(707)778-8990
www.avab.com
sales@avab.com
Frantz Lau, CEO/COO
Hans Lain, General Manager
Joe Dupre, Design Engineer, Tech Manager
Manufacturer of studio & theatrical lighting equipment; lighting controllers, dimmers, fixtures.

AVCOM of Virginia Inc.
7730 Whitepine Rd., Richmond, VA 23237 USA
(804) 794-2500, *Fax:* (804) 794-8284
www.avcomofva.com
Jay Evans, President
Manufactures high quality low cost spectrum analyzers.

AVerMedia Technologies Inc.
423 Dixon Landing Rd., Milpitas, CA 95035 USA
(800) 863-2332,(408) 263-3828, *Fax:* (408) 263-8132
www.aver.com, www.avermedia.com
Sinar Pait, CEO
Arthur Pait, President
Julie Lange, Finance Executive
John Hall, Sales Executive
Ted Pepping, Executive Officer
Aside from TV Turner/Desktop TV Personal Video Recorder products, AVerMeida also provides digital camera picture TV display devices, Document Camera & PC-to-TV Converters.

AVI Systems
7270 Trade St., Suite 102, San Diego, CA 92121 USA
(858) 695-7888, *Fax:* (858) 695-7844
www.avisystems.com
brad.sousa@avisystems.com
Joseph Stoebner, Chairman
Jeffrey Stoebner, President
Bradley Sousa, Operations Dir
Randi Borth, Treasurer
Dealer & systems Integrator for video, audio, presentation distance learning & video conferencing, svc.

Avid Broadcast
1 Park West, Tewksbury, MA 1876 USA
(978) 640-6789, (800) 949-2843, *Fax:* (978) 640-1366, (978) 640-3366
www.avid.com
Gary Greenfield, CEO
Beth Martinko, Operations Dir
Tex Schenkkan, General Manager
Automated bcst newsroom systems. Non-linear video editing systems, media storage & networking systems, video server, content mgmt systems & asset mgmt systems.
6400 Enterprise Ln., Suite 200, Madison, WI 53719
(608) 274-8686; *Fax:* (608) 273-5876
Robert Long, Cto
115 N. First St., Burbank, CA 91502
(818) 557-2520; *Fax:* (818) 557-2558
John Steinhauer, Dir Bcst Group Sls
575 Lexington Ave., 14th Fl., New York, NY 10022
(212) 983-2424; *Fax:* (212) 983-8718
Michael Wright, Dir Sls

Avid Technology Inc.
65 Newton Drive, Burlington, MA 1876 USA
(800) 949-AVID,(978) 640-6789, *Fax:* (978) 640-3366
www.avid.com
info@avid.com
Gary Greenfield, President/CEO
Ken Sexton, EVP/CFO
Glover Lawrence, VP/Corporate Development
W Sean Ford, VP/Marketing
Ken Sexton, CFO
Avid's networked bcst news productions are designed to facilitate the process of digital news gathering (DNG).
317 Madison Ave., Suite 521, 5th Fl, New York, NY 10017 United States
(212) 983-2424;
Michael Wright, Dir Strategic Sls
115 N. 1st St., Suite 100, Burbank, CA 91502 United States
(818) 557-2520;
John Steinhauer, Dir Strategic Sls America

AVS Graphics & Media Inc.
963 Autumn Ave, Salt Lake City, UT 84116-2243 USA
(801) 975-9799, *Fax:* (801) 975-0970
www.avsgmedia.com
sales@avsgmedia.com
Gavin Hunter, CEO
Bcst & production character generators & Still stores.

Avtech Systems Inc.
141 Ayers Ct., Suite 1B, Teaneck, NJ 7666 USA
(201) 833-8777, *Fax:* (201) 833-4995
www.avtechsystems.com
sales@avtechsystems.com
Fred Samuel, President
David Samuel, General Sales Mgr
Closed circuit video equipment, components & accessories security video systems.

AVX Corp.
One Avx Blvd, Fountain Inn, SC 29644-9039 USA
864-967-2150
www.avxcorp.com, www.avx.com
gib@avxcorp.com,
John Gilbertson, CEO/COO
Kurt Cummings, VP/CFO/Secretary
Jimmy White, General Sales Mgr
Craig Hunter, Promotions Manager
Electronic component.

Axcera
103 Freedom Drive, PO Box 525, Lawrence, PA 15055 USA
1-800-215-2614, *Fax:* (724) 873-8105
www.axcera.com
info@axcera.com
Dave Neff, President
Richard Schwartz, Operations Dir
Mike Rosso, General Sales Mgr
Low Medium & High Power Solid State TV Transmitters, High Power Transmitters, Liquid-Cooled Solid State Transmitters, Mobile Multimedia Base Stations, MMDS/BRS/MDS & WCS Transmitters, DOCSIS(r) Based Broadband Wireless Access, Analog &Digital, UHF, VHF, L-Band & S-Band.

Aydin Displays Inc.
One Riga Lane, Birdsboro, PA 19508 USA
(610) 404-7400,(866) 367-2934, *Fax:* (610) 582-0851
www.teltrontech.com
sales1@aydindisplays.com
Ronald Ordway, CEO
Arthur Mengel, President
Clyde Mock, General Sales Mgr
Camera tubes for monochrome, color, special purpose applications & view finder CRTs.

AZCAR U.S.A. Inc.
121 Hillpointe Dr., Suite 700, Canonsburg, PA 15317 USA
(724) 873-0800, (888) 873-0800, *Fax:* (724) 873-4770
www.azcar.com
info@azcar.com
Stephen Pumple, CEO
Gavin Schutz, President
Tom Deyo, Operations Dir
Karl Paulsen, Chief Engineer
Bcst engrg, systems integration.
3235 14th Ave., Markham, ON L3R 0H3 Canada
(905) 470-2545; *Fax:* (905)470-2556
S. Pumple, Pres/Ceo

#1 College Business Park, Coldhams Lane, Cambridge, CB1 3HD United Kingdom
44 1223 414101; *Fax:* 44 123 414102
F. Jarvis, Dir

B&B Systems
9420 Lurine Ave., Unit C, Chatsworth, CA 91311 USA
(818) 998-9500, *Fax:* (818) 998-9106
www.bandbsystems.com
lou@broadcaststore.com
Design & instal of production & postproduction systems, vans & mobile units, manufacturer of audio monitoring products.

Bald Mountain Laboratory
222 Bellevue Rd., Troy, NY 12180 USA
(518) 279-9753
hambob@highstream.net
Robert Henry, President
Frequency readings.

Baldor Linear
25026 Anza Dr., Santa Clarita, CA 91355-3413 USA
(661) 257-0216, *Fax:* (661) 257-2037
www.baldor.com
John McFarland, Chairman
John McFarland, CEO
Ronald Tucker, President
Randall Breaux, Operations Dir

Band Pro Film & Digital Inc.
3403 W. Pacific Ave., Burbank, CA 91505 USA
(818) 841-9655, *Fax:* (818) 841-7649
www.bandpro.com
sales@bandpro.com
Amnon Band, CEO
Renee Contreras, President
Band Pro Film and Digital, Home of HD, offers cinemtographers the highest level of expertise & finest equipment available.

Band Pro Munich GmbH
Karl-Hammerschmidt Str. 38, Dornach, 85909 Germany
49 89-945 48 490;
Gerhard Baieir, Mgmg Dir

Band Pro Israel
Hasolelim 3, Tel Aviv 67897 Israel,
(972) 3-562-1631; *Fax:* (972) 3-562-1632
Ofer Menashe, Mgng Dir

Barco Inc.
3059 Premiere Pkwy., Suite 100, Duluth, GA 30097 USA
(678) 475-8000, *Fax:* (678) 475-8100
www.barco.com
bpsmarketing@barco.com
Eric Van Zele, CEO
Dave Scott, General Manager
Carl Peeters, Chief Financial Officer
Jacqu Bertrand, Chief Marketing Officer
Offers complete monitoring solutions for control rooms in telecom traf, surveillance, pub utilities, process control & financing.

Baron Telecom
2355 Industrial Park Blvd., Cumming, GA 30041 USA
(678) 847-5015
www.barantelecom.com
Ran Bukshpan, CEO
Ross Kruchten, President
Ron Raviv, CFO
Project mgmt & turn-key construction of communications towers, including erection, maintenance & inspection of tall towers.
10430 Rogers Rd., Houston, TX 77070 United States
(713) 973-6904; *Fax:* (713) 973-0205
Ross Kruchten, Chairman
11112 117th Pl. N.E., Kirkland, WA 98033 United States
(425) 739-9342; *Fax:* (425) 739-9314
Russ Stromberg, Chairman
4640 Wedgewood Blvd., Frederick, MD 21703 United States
(301) 663-9300; *Fax:* (301) 663-9584
Tom Cureton, Chairman

Battery Pros Inc.
PO Box 54, 161 First Street, Horseshoe Beach, FL 32648-0054 USA
(352) 498-2477,(800) 451-7171, *Fax:* (770) 498-2482
www.batteryprosinc.com
sales@batteryprosinc.com
Patti Novak, President
Maria Arce, Operations Dir
Battery recelling/rebuilding for Bricks & Belts, primary & secondary batteries, custom battery pack design & manufacture.

Bauer Transmitters
1644 Lamaland Drive, El Paso, TX 79935 USA

EQUIPMENT MANUFACTURERS

(915) 595-1048, *Fax:* (915) 595-1840
www.bauertx.com
paul@bauertx.com
Paul Gregg, President
Remanufactured Bauer-Sparta & Elcom Bauer AM/FM transmitters, AM combining & antenna coupling equipment.

BBE Sound Inc.
5381 Production Dr., Huntington Beach, CA 92649 USA
(714) 897-6766, (800) 233-8346, *Fax:* (714) 895-6728
www.bbesound.com
info@bbesound.com
John McLaren, Chairman
John McLaren, CEO
David McLaren, President
Paul Gagon, Operations Dir
Steve Hase, VP Licensing
Audio/video signal processors to eliminate phase & amplitude distortion.

BEI Duncan Electronics
170 Technology Dr., Irvine, CA 92618-2401 USA
(949) 341-9500, *Fax:* (949) 453-2700
www.beiduncan.com
sales@beiducan.com
Philippe Roux, General Manager
Manufacturer of motion & position sensors

Belar Electronics Laboratory Inc.
Box 76, 119 Lancaster Ave., Devon, PA 19333 USA
(610) 687-5550, *Fax:* (610) 687-2686
www.belar.com
sales@belar.com
Arno Meyer, President
AM, FM, FM stereo, SCA, RDS/RBDS, shortwave, TV, TV stereo modulation & frequency monitors.

Belden
2200 U.S. Hwy. 27 S., Richmond, IN 47374 USA
(765) 983-5200, *Fax:* (765) 983-5294
www.belden.com
info@belden.com
Precision video coaxial, triaxial cables, professional music cables, ENG cables, audio snakes, RGB cables & 50 ohm transmission cables.

Bencher Inc.
241 E. Depot St., Antioch, IL 60002 USA
(847) 838-3195, *Fax:* (847) 838-3479
www.bencher.com
bencher@bencher.com
Tere Benedict, President
Photographic & video vertical camera copystands & accessories, including Motion Picture Maker movable copy stage.

Benchmark Media Systems Inc.
203 East Hampton Pl., Suite 2, Syracuse, NY 13206-1707 USA
(315) 437-6300,(800) 262-4675, *Fax:* (315) 437-8119
www.benchmarkmedia.com
sales@benchmarkmedia.com
Allen Burdick, President
Ruth Burdick, President
R. Rall, Sales Manager
Richard Kalinowski, Purchasing Manager
Audio processing & distribution systems, VU/PPM meters, interface/headphone amplifiers, microphone pre-amplifiers; digital to analog & analog to digital converters.

Bend-A-Lite Flexible Neon
905 G St., Hampton, VA 23661 USA
(757) 245-7675,(800) 236-3254, *Fax:* (757) 244-4819,(877) 445-7298
www.bendalite.com
cs@bendalite.com
Hugh Jones, President
Ron Koppel, Promotions Manager
Flexible neon that can be cut with scissors, cut section can be re-electrified. 110v, 12v, 220v, 24v, indoor/outdoor. Lengths up to 300 ft., brilliant neon colors.

Benner-Nawman Inc.
3450 Sabin Brown Rd., Wickenburg, AZ 85390 USA
(800) 992-3833,(928) 684-2813, *Fax:* (928) 684-7041
www.bnproducts.com
mail@bnproducts.com
Edward Kientz, President/CEO
Angel Bourne, Controller
Lon Brown, General Manager
Mel Kientz, Chief Marketing Officer
Daniel Sibiga, Business Development
Specialty tools for CATV, cable termination & distribution boxes (cabinets).

Bexel
2701 N. Ontario St., Burbank, CA 91504 USA
(818) 841-5051 (818) 847-8670, *Fax:* (818) 841-1572
www.bexel.com
rentals@bexel.com
Andy Crist, CEO
Greg Bragg, General Manager
Joyce Bente, General Sales Mgr
Scott Nardelli, Bexel1bfs/Broadcast
Craig Schiller, Worldwide Live Event
Bexel has delivered the finest customer svc & best audio/video production equipment rentals for over 30 years & remains the world leader. Real 24/7/365 emergency svc/tech natl offices/experts in solutions/custom engrg, systems design &application/sound tech advice, also used equipment sls.

Bexel Seattle Office
3314 Fourth Ave. South, Seattle, WA 98134 United States
(206) 628-7000;
Chris Hunter, Account Executive

Bexel Miami Office.
20239 N.E. 15th Ct., Miami, FL 33179 United States
(305) 653-5051; *Fax:* (305) 655-6209
Andrea Rosenkrans, Accountant Exec

Bexel Atlanta Office
5555 Oak Brook Pkwy., Suite 160, Norcross, GA 30093 United States
(770) 448-3000; *Fax:* (770) 449-5747
Frank Zamor, Rental Mgr

Bexel Dallas Office
1001 N. Union Bower, Suite 130, Irving, TX 75061 United States
(214) 946-5051; *Fax:* (972) 831-9860
Jim Barrett, Rental Mgr

Bexel New York Office
625 W. 55th St., New York, NY 10019 United States
(212) 246-5051; *Fax:* (212) 246-6373
Mke King, Rental Mgr

Bexel DC Office
555 Herndon Pkwy., Suite 135, Herndon, VA 20170
(703) 437-5559; *Fax:* (703) 437-6931

Bexel Corporation
5555 Oak Brook Pkwy., Suite 160, Norcross, GA 30093 USA
(770) 448-3000, (800) 225-6185
www.bexel.com
Julia Rodgers, Manager
John McCorell, Manager

BEXT Inc.
1045 10th Ave., San Diego, CA 92101 USA
(619) 239-8462, (888) 239-8462, *Fax:* (619) 239-8474
www.bext.com
bext@bext.com
Claudio Tilesi, CFO
Dennis Pieri, CEO
Radio & Digital TV Transmitters, Antennas, Amplifiers, Receivers, Boosters, STLs, RF Combiners, RF Filters, Stereo Generators, FmExtra Digital Radio Encoders & Receivers.

Beyerdynamic
56 Central Ave., Farmingdale, NY 11735 USA
(631) 293-3200,(800) 293-4463, *Fax:* (631) 293-3288
www.northamericanbeyerdynamic.com
info@beyerdynamic.com
Nel Keinz, General Manager
Alan Feckanin, General Sales Mgr
Bob Lowig, Sales
Microphones, headsets, monitor headphones, studio & on-location UHF & VHF wireless systems.

Beyond Broadband Technology LLC
6125 Paluxy Dr., Tyler, TX 75703-5976 USA
(903) 561-4411, *Fax:* (903) 561-4031
www.bbtsolution.com
info@bbtsolution.com
Bennett Hooks, President
William Bauer, Partner/CEO
Tony Swain, Partner/COO
DCAS-open standard downloadable conditional access & MPEG 4 Transport.
8477 Trail Lake Dr., Powell, OH 43065 United States
1140 10th St., Gering, NE 69341

BGW Systems, Amplifier Technologies, Inc.
1749 Chapin Rd., Montebello, CA 90640 USA
(323) 278-0001, *Fax:* (310) 323-0083
www.bgw.com
info@bgw.com
Morris Kessler, President
Angie Scott, Operations Dir
Professional, bcst, coml audio power amplifiers & self-powered subwoofer systems.

BHP Inc.
4700 Chase Ave., Lincolnwood, IL 60712-1689 USA
(847) 677-3000, (800) 323-7520, *Fax:* (847) 677-1311, (800) 784-6733
www.bhpinc.com
sales@rtico.com
Ray Short, CEO
Jonathan Banks, President
Tom Boyle, SVP/Sales
Bill Wolouka, VP/Sales
Motion picture laboratory equipment, film printers & accessories.

BIAP Inc.
5800 Granite Pkwy., Suite 480, Plano, TX 75024 USA
(972) 464-5880, *Fax:* (972) 464-5881
www.biap.com
mpruneau@biap.com
Timothy Peters, CEO
John Gregoire, President

Bird Electronic Corp.
30303 Aurora Rd., Solon, OH 44139-2794 USA
(866) 695-4569, *Fax:* (866) 546-4306
www.bird-technologies.com
sales@bird-technologies.com
David Hessler, Chairman
Bird Technologies Group is a global, innovative supplier of RF products, systems, svcs & educ solutions.

Birns and Sawyer Inc.
5273 Craner Avenue, North Hollywood, CA 90028 USA
(323) 466-8211, *Fax:* (323) 466-1868
www.birnsandsawyer.com
info@birnsandsawyer.com
William Meurer, President
Jason Stuckey, General Manager
Kathie Dugan, Business Acct Manager
Camera and support, lighting, grip rental and sales

Bitcentral Inc.
18872 Bardeen Ave., Irvine, CA 92612 USA
(949) 253-9003, *Fax:* (949) 253-9027
www.bitcentral.com
sales@bitcentral.com
Fred Fourcher, CEO/Owner
Bicentral is in the business of providing innovative solutions that transform the mgmt, production & distribution of the news.

Blimpy Floating Signs/Bend-A-Lite
905 G St., Hampton, VA 23661 USA
(757) 245-7675,(800) 448-2014, *Fax:* (757) 244-4819
www.blimpy.com
cs@blimpy.com
Hugh Jones, President
Ron Koppel, Promotions Manager
Giant blimps, hot air balloons & rooftop balloons. Complete custom department for any shape or size, flexible neon in seven brilliant colors.

Blonder Tongue Laboratories Inc.
Box 1000, One Jake Brown Rd., Old Bridge, NJ 08857-1000 USA
(732) 679-4000,(800) 523-6049, *Fax:* (732) 679-4353
www.blondertongue.com
information@blondertongue.com
James Lukson, CEO/COO
John Lynon, Information Technology
Norman Westcott, General Sales Mgr
Manufacturer of private cable equipment, including satellite receivers, modulators, processors, amplifiers, combiners & passives.

Bogen Communications Inc.
50 Spring Street, Suite 1, Ramsey, NJ 7446 USA
(201) 934-8500,(800) 999-2809, *Fax:* (201) 934-9832
www.bogen.com
info@bogen.com
Jonathan Guss, CEO
Michael Fleischer, President
David Chambers, General Sales Mgr
Audio amplifiers, mixer-preamplifiers, power amplifiers; FM/AM tuners & receivers; intercom systems; pub address & sound reinforcement systems; digital repeater products & speakers.

Bogen Imaging Inc.
565 E. Crescent Ave., Ramsey, NJ 7446 USA
(201) 818-9500, *Fax:* (201) 818-9177
www.bogenimaging.us
info@bogenimaging.com

Stev Romanick, CEO/COO
Paul Wild, President
Kriss Brumgardener, General Manager
Mark Bender, General Sales Mgr
Paul Wagner, Sales Director
Professional video products including tripods, fluid heads, dollies, stands & accessories. Grip equipment & lighting filters.

Boonton Electronics Corp.
25 Eastmans Rd., Parsippany, NJ 07054-3702 USA
(973) 386-9696, *Fax:* (973) 386-9191
www.boonton.com
boonton@boonton.com
Edward Garcia, CEO
John Kenneally, General Sales Mgr
Wolfgang Damm, Programming Director
Brent Hessen-Schmidt, Promotions Manager
Richard Blackwell, Chief Engineer
Monty Johnson, CEO
Marc Wolfsohn, CFO
Larry Henderson, CMO
Electronic test & measuring equipment: microwave/RF power, RF voltmeters, capacitance/inductance & modulation meters.

Bradley Broadcast and Pro Audio
7309-D Grove Rd., PO Box 756, Frederick, MD 21704 USA
(800) 732-7665,(301) 682-8700, *Fax:* (301) 682-8377
www.bradleybroadcast.com
info@bradleybroadcast.com
David Matthews, President
Art Reed, General Manager
Your source for all major brands of radio & professional audio equipment. The friendly personal svc of a family-owned company, the tech experience of many years in the business & very compteitive pricing too.

Broadcast Data Consultants
3980 E. State Rd. 64, Bradenton, FL 34208 USA
(800) 275-6204, *Fax:* (941) 749-5566
www.broadcastdata.com
bdc@broadcastdata.com
Scott Wachtler, President
Neil Edwards, Operations Dir
The Traffic C.O.P. for windows traffic billing progm. Free CD Rom demo available.

Broadcast Electronic Services
4825 Trawler Ct., Jacksonville, FL 32225 USA
(904) 646-1630, *Fax:* (904) 641-1443
Tim Derstine, President
Betabox/GPI net 410, video-editing interface products for E.N.G. & postproduction; T.B.C. remote devices.

Broadcast Electronics Inc.
4100 N. 24th St., Quincy, IL 62305 USA
(217) 224-9600, *Fax:* (217) 224-9607
www.bdcast.com
bdcast@bdcast.com
Joseph Roam, CEO
Debra Huttenburg, Operations Dir
Brenne Ormone, Chief Marketing Officer
Kevin Maider, General Sales Mgr
Ray Miklius, Vice President
Tim Bealor, Vice President
Radio bcst equipment including digital studio systems, AM, FM transmitters, RPUs & STLs.

Broadcast Engineering
9800 Metcalf Ave., Overland Park, KS 66212 USA
(913) 967-1737, *Fax:* (913) 967-1905
www.broadcastengineering.com
brad.dick@penton.com
Jon Chalon, Operations Dir
Brad Dick, Programming Director
Broadcast Engineering: Published for mgmt & engrg personnel working in bcst, production, postproduction, cable facilities in North America.
335 Court St., 9, Brooklyn, NY 11231 United States
(718) 802-0488; *Fax:* (718) 522-4751
Josh Gordon, Chairman
Orient Echo Inc.
1101 Grand Maison, Shimomiyabi-cho 2-18, Shinjuku-ku, Tokyo, 162-0822
(03) 3235-5961; *Fax:* (03) 3235-5852
Mashy Yoshikawa, Chairman
Box 250, Banbury, Oxon, OX16 8YJ
+44-129-527-8407; *Fax:* +44-129-527-8408
Richard Woolley, Chairman

Broadcast Equipment Sales and Engineering
119 South Oak Street, Raymond, MS 39154 USA
(601) 857-8573, *Fax:* (601) 857-2346
corkren@netdoor.com
Jeffrey Corkren, Operations Dir
Represents bcst equipment manufacturers; sls, svc, instal, turnkey designs, engrg; new & used equipment.

Broadcast International Group
10458 N.W. 31st Terr., Doral, FL 33172 USA
(305) 599-2112, *Fax:* (305) 599-1133
www.bigmiami.com
sales@bigmiami.com
Ana Maria Sagastegui, President
Bcst TV equipment.

Broadcast Microwave Services Inc.
12367 Crosthwaite Circle, Dock 10, Poway, CA 92064 USA
(858) 391-3050,(800) 669-9667, *Fax:* (858) 391-3049
www.bms-inc.com
sales@bms-inc.com
Graham Bunney, President
Tim Macy, Contractor
COFDM wireless microwave, transmitters, receivers & antenna systems for ENG vehicles, helicopters, autotrackers, central receive sites.
293 Sycamore Grove, Los Angeles, CA 93065 United States
(805) 581-4566; *Fax:* (805) 527-8263
Jim Kubit, Sls Engr
105A Lew Dewitt Blvd., #278, Waynesboro, VA 22980 United States
(540) 932-3660; *Fax:* (858) 391-3049
Russell Murphy, Sls Engr

Broadcast Sports Technologies
1360 Blair Dr., Suite A, Odenton, MD 21113-1343 USA
(410) 672-3900, *Fax:* (410) 672-3906
www.wescam.com
Peter Larsson, General Manager
Supply microwave, camera & cable equipment for large sporting events. Supply remote control cameras & communication systems.

Broadcast Store Inc.
9420 Lurline Ave., Unit C, Chatsworth, CA 91311 USA
(818) 998-9100, *Fax:* (818) 998-9106
www.broadcaststore.com
sales@broadcaststore.com
Lou Claude, President
Buy, sell, consign new & preowned Audio/Video bcst equiptment for production & post-production needs.
500 W. 37th St., New York, NY 10018
(212) 268-8800; *Fax:* (212) 268-1858
1031 Ives Dairy Rd., Miami, FL 33179
305-266-2112; *Fax:* 305-266-2113

Broadcast Supply Worldwide
2237 S. 19th St., Tacoma, WA 98405 USA
(800) 426-8434, *Fax:* (800) 231-7055
www.bswusa.com
sales@bswusa.com
Irv Law, Chairman
Tim Schwieger, President
Audio bcst equipment distributor. Representing over 200 manufacturers worldwide.

Broadcast Video Systems Corp.
25 Forest Ridge Rd., Richmond Hill, ON L4E 3L8 CAN
(905) 305-0565, *Fax:* (416) 946-1964
www.bvs.ca
bvs@bvs.ca
Bert Verwey, President
SDI, analog video keyers, chroma keyers, closed captioning, encoders/decoders, positioner, bridge, V-chip, data transmission, encoders & transcoders.

Broadcasters General Store Inc.
2480 S.E. 52nd St., Ocala, FL 34480 USA
(352) 622-7700, *Fax:* (352) 629-7000
www.bgs.cc
info@bgs.cc
David Kerstin, President
Lee Freshwater, Sales Executive
Professional audio, video & RF equipment, Telco interfaces, digital codecs, 400+ vendor line card. Axia Opx
BGS IN Office
765-935-6707;
Gary Tibbot, Chairman
BGS NC Office
828-698-2893;
Cindy Edwards, Chairman
BGS KY Office
Cecile Gibson - 270-928-1151,

Bryston Ltd.
Box 2170, 677 Neal Dr., Peterborough, ON K9J 6X7 CAN
(705) 742-5325, *Fax:* (705) 742-0882
www.bryston.ca
contact@bryston.ca
Micah Sheveloff, General Manager
Audio amplifiers, pre-amplifiers, crossovers, & microphone pre-amps.

Bud Industries Inc.
4605 E. 355 St., Willoughby, OH 44094 USA
(440) 946-3200, *Fax:* (440) 951-4015
www.budind.com
saleseast@budind.com
Blair Haas, President
Josian Haas, General Sales Mgr
Open & welded racks; cabinets & accessories.
Box 41190, Phoenix, AZ 85080 United States
(623) 516-9494;

Burk Technology
7 Beaver Brook Rd., Littleton, MA 1460 USA
(978) 486-0086, *Fax:* (978) 486-0081
www.burk.com
sales@burk.com
Peter Burk, President
Nathan Burk, Marketing Executive
Bill Irvine, Engineering Dir
Bcst transmitter remote control & monitoring.

Burle Industries Inc.
1000 New Holland Ave., Lancaster, PA 17601-5688 USA
(717) 295-6888, (800) 366-2875, *Fax:* (717) 295-6096
www.burle.com
burlesls@burle.com
E. Burlefinger, CEO
Carl Rintz, President
Kirk Jenne, General Counsel
VHF/FM power tubes, photomultipliers & imaging devices.

Burlington A/V Recording Media Inc.
106 Mott St., Oceanside, NY 11572-5823 USA
(516) 678-4414,(800) 331-3191, *Fax:* (516) 678-8959
www.burlington-av.com
sales@burlington-av.com
Jan Alan, President
Ruth Schwartz, Operations Dir
Wholesale distributor for all formats of recording media, blank audio/video tape, CD-R, DVD-RR, diskettes, data media, A/V recording equipment.

Burst Electronics Inc.
Box 65947, Albuquerque, NM 87193 USA
(505) 898-1455, *Fax:* (505) 898-0159
www.burstelectronics.com
sales@burstelectronics.com
Brad Hamlin, President
CG, DA's, HD/analog video switchers, video mixers, decoders, logo generator, video generators, TBC & GPI converters.

C I S Inc.
3360 Martin Farm Rd., Suwanee, GA 30024 USA
(678) 482-2000, *Fax:* (678) 482-2007
www.cisfocus.com
sales@cisfocus.com
Jeffery Eichler, President
Lynn Hamlin, General Sales Mgr
Integrated broadband & fiber design software products. Software solutions for network mapping, planning, design, & management of the outside plant.

C-COR/ Arris
60 Decibel Rd., State College, PA 16801 USA
(814) 238-2461, *Fax:* (814) 238-4065
www.arrisi.com
David Woodle, Chairman
David Woodle, CEO
Globally-tailored fiber optic, RF & digital video transport telecommunications products, OSS mgmt solutions & high-end tech field svcs for broadband networks.
Broadband Management Soultions Software Divison He
5673 Gibraltar Dr., Suite 100, Pleasanton, CA 94588 United States
(925) 251-3000; *Fax:* (925) 467-0600
Douglas W. Engerman, Chairman
Broadband Communication Products Product Division
999 Research Pkwy, Meriden, CT 06450 United States
(203) 630-5700; *Fax:* (203) 630-5701
John O. Caezza, Chairman
Broadband Network Services Services Division
300 Union Blvd., Suite 515, Lakewood, CO 80228 United States

(303) 980-8058;
Paul E. Janson, Chairman

Cable Leakage Technologies
940 Hensley Ln., Wylie, TX 75098 USA
(972) 907-8100,(800) 783-8878, *Fax:* (972) 907-2950
www.wavetracker.com
support@wavetracker.com
Perry Havens, President
Digital RF tracking/mapping system used in CLI monitoring.

Cable Prep
Box 373, 207 Middlesex Ave, Chester, CT 06412-0373 USA
(860) 526-4337, *Fax:* (860) 526-2291
www.cableprep.com
toolmaker@cableprep.com
Deborah Morrow, President
David Morrow, Operations Dir
Cable Prep TerminX, hex crimp, coring & stripping, drop wire stripping, jacket strippers, messenger removal & tools.

Cable Serv Inc.
4560 Eastgate Pkwy., Mississauga, ON L4W 3W6 CAN
(905) 629-1111, (800) 668-2033, *Fax:* (905) 629-1115
www.cableserv.com
inquiries@cableserv.com
Audley Alexander, President
TV Exciters, 5-10-20 watt LPTV trans & transmitters, TV modulators, demodulators, processors, & satellite receivers.

Cable Services Company Inc.
2113 Marydale Ave., Williamsport, PA 17701 USA
(570) 323-8518,(800) 326-9444, *Fax:* (570) 322-5373
www.cable-services.com
Ken R. Michaels, CEO
John M. Roskowski, President
Eugene S. Welliver, Operations Dir
Harland W. Bergstrom, General Manager
Neal W. Kimberling, Vice President
Turnkey fiber-optic & coaxial construction; distributor of CATV products.

Cable Technologies International
460 Oakdale Ave., Hatboro, PA 19040 USA
(215) 672-5400, *Fax:* (215) 672-0440
www.cabletechnologies.com
sales@cabletechnologies.com
Paul Morse, President
Your #1 Co. for buying/selling/repairing/new/used/surplus-digital products-DCT's/parts/cables/universal remotes, advanced analog converters, headend/distribution equipment, test equipment including signal level meters, character generators,cables, HDTV/cables/modems/audio components/home theater/coax, remotes & batteries.
75 S. Central Ave., Mechanicville, NY 12118

Cable Yellow Pages
20917 Higgins Ct., Torrance, CA 90501 USA
(800) 777-4320, *Fax:* (310) 212-5392
www.cableyellowpages.com
Neal Schnog, President
Glenn Schrader, Manager
Wade Pierce, VP/Associate Publisher
Phone directory for cable TV systems.

CableReady Inc.
6260 Downing St., Denver, CO 80216 USA
(303) 288-8107,(800) 222-2142, *Fax:* (303) 288-4769
www.icmcorp.net
sales@icmcorp.net
Randy Holliday, President
Gary Williams, General Sales Mgr
Painted galvolume molding with custom fittings backed by a 15-year warranty, U.L. listed and Class A fire rated.

CableTek Wiring Products Inc.
1150 Taylor St., Elyria, OH 44035 USA
(440) 365-3889,(800) 562-9378, *Fax:* (440) 322-0321
www.cable-tek.com
treilly@apk.net
Tim Reilly, General Manager
Interior & exterior surface wiring products; terminal enclosures, residential enclosures, security products.

Cablynx, Inc.
28 Tower Office Park, Woburn, MA 01801-6552 USA
(781) 933-2000, (877) 222-5969, *Fax:* (781) 933-4641
sales@nova-sys.com
Shintaro Asano, President
Routing switchers, distribution amplifiers, time code, component video, PC accessories, compugraphics to video, frame synchronizer.

CADCO Systems Inc.
3401 Wynwood Dr., Plano, TX 75074 USA
(972) 271-3651,(800) 877-2288, *Fax:* (972) 271-3654
www.cadcosystems.com
carmen@cadcosystems.com
Steven Johnson, Chairman
Steven Johnson, CEO
Carmen Howard, Station Manager
Manufacturer of CATV & broadband communication products such as modulators, demodulators, signal processors, ch converters, translators & special application headend equipment, fixed-channel & frequency agile.

Calculated Industries Inc.
4840 Hytech Dr., Carson City, NV 89706 USA
(775) 885-4900,(800) 854-8075, *Fax:* (775) 885-4949
www.calculated.com
info@calculated.com
Steve Kennedy, President
Time code calculators work in & convert between all time formats; drop/non-drop, multiple EPS rates for all SMPTE/PAL equations.

California Amplifier
1401 N. Rice Ave., Oxnard, CA 93030 USA
(805) 987-9000, *Fax:* (805) 987-8359
www.calamp.com
sales@calcamp.som
Michael Burdick, President
Rick Vitalle, Chief Financial Officer
Manufacturer of mesh & offset satellite antennas ranging in size from 18 to 16'.

Calumet Photographic
1111 N. Cherry Ave., Chicago, IL 60642 USA
(312) 440-4920, *Fax:* (800) 577-3686
www.calumetphoto.com
custserv@calumetphoto.com
Peter Biasotti, President
Don Ernest, Vice President

Calzone Case Co.
225 Black Rock Ave., Bridgeport, CT 6605 USA
(800) 243-5152, *Fax:* (203) 336-4406
www.calzonecase.com
vin.calzone@calzonecase.com
Joseph Calzone, President
Vincent Calzone, General Sales Mgr
Manufacturers of custom & standard shipping cases for all industries featuring Escort, LD-ATA, Military, X series, Titan
75006 Luna Rd., Suite 126, Carrollton, TX 75007 United States
(972) 241-3900; *Fax:* (972) 241-3998
Tom Mackno, Vp
15730 Salt Lake Ave., City of Industry, CA 91745 United States
(626) 968-4100; *Fax:* (626) 968-1703
Mike Herman, Vp Admin/Sls

Camera Dynamics
709 Executive Blvd., Ste. A, Valley Cottage, NY 10989-2024 USA
(845) 268-2113 (888) 284-6836, *Fax:* (845) 268-9324
www.vinten.com
info-cd-usa@vitecgroup.com
Bob Carr, President
Best quality studio camera robotics, Parliamentary camera robotics & virtual sets.

Camera Service Center
25 Enterprise Ave. N., Secaucus, NJ 7094 USA
(212) 757-0906, *Fax:* (212) 713-0075
www.arricsc.com
Simon Broad, President
David Lamadrio, CFO
James Alexander, Operations Manager
The largest full-svc film equipment rental company, carrying a complete line of camera & lighting products.
2385 Stirling Rd., Fort Lauderdale, FL 33312
(954) 322-4545; *Fax:* (954) 322-4188
Ed Stamm, Chairman

CamMate Studios/Systems
425 E. Comstock, Chandler, AZ 85225 USA
(480) 813-9500, *Fax:* (480) 813-9292
www.cammate.com
cammate@cammate.com
Linda Mitchell, CEO
Exclusive sls & rental of the CamMate, a single operator remote camera crane in various configurations for video & film. Now offering Telescoping Jips.

Camplex Corporation
3302 W. 6th Ave., Suite C, Emporia, KS 66801 USA
(620) 342-7743, *Fax:* (620) 342-7405
www.camplex.com,www.pro-x1.com
jtwebb@camplex.com
J. Webb, CEO
C. Woodmas, President
CAMPLEX is a universally adaptable video/audio signals multiplexing system for ENG/EFP/SNG Prosamer cameras, camcorders used in remote applications.

Canare Corp.
45 Commerce Way, Unit C, Totowa, NJ 7512 USA
973-837-0070, *Fax:* 973-837-0080
www.canare.com
sales@canare.com
Kazuo Urata, CEO
Larry Cano, General Sales Mgr
Professional Audio & Video Cable, 75 ohm connectors, patchbays, snake systems, assemblies, strip & crimp tools, SMPTE 311 Hybrid and Single Mode fiber optical products.

Canon U.S.A. Inc.
65 Challenger Rd., Ridgefield Park, NJ 7660 USA
(800) 321-4388, *Fax:* (201) 807-3333
www.canonbroadcast.com
bctv@cusa.canon.com
John Rose, General Sales Mgr
Patrick Breheny, Sales
Rich Eiles, Sales
The Canon Broadcast & Communications (BCTV) division a part of the larger Canon U.S.A. Inc. The BCTV lens products is squarely based on the highly advanced optical, mechanical & digital technologies for which Canon became legendary. Studio,field & ENG lenses & svc, (HDTV/SDTV) video, audio, data optical beam transmission, remote control P/T/Z camera system.
15955 Alton Pkwy., Irvine, CA 92618 United States
(949) 753-4330; *Fax:* (949) 753-4337
Tom Bender, Sls
Joe Patton, Sls
Stephanie Franz, Sls
100 Park Blvd., Itasca, IL 60143 United States
(630) 250-6236; *Fax:* (630) 250-0399
Dave Pavlik, Sls
5625 Oakbrook Pkwy., Norcross, GA 30093 United States
(770) 849-7890; *Fax:* (770) 849-7888
Jim Dobbins, Sls
3200 Regent Blvd., Irvine, TX 75063 United States
(972) 409-8871; *Fax:* (972) 409-8869
Mark Parks, Sls

Capstone Communications Inc.
15 Wilson St., Markham, ON L3P 1M9 USA
(905) 472-2330
www.capstonecomm.com
Brokerage, rsch consultation & bcst equipment brokerge.

Carpel Video Inc.
429 E. Patrick St., Frederick, MD 21701 USA
(800) 238-4300,(301) 694-3500, *Fax:* (301) 694-9510
www.carpelvideo.com
Andy Carpel, President
Videotape wholesalers. Mail order post production in MD; store: DVD production and duplication. Lowest prices on 6 blank video tapes. 800-238-4300.

CATV Services Inc.
12099 N.W. 98th Ave., Hialeah Gardens, FL 33018-2927 USA
(305) 512-5601,(800) 227-1200, *Fax:* (305) 512-5606
www.catvservices.com
info@catvservices.com
Richard Richmond, President
Excess inventory professionals, buy & sell.

CBT Systems
10115 Carroll Canyon Rd., San Diego, CA 92131 USA
(858) 536-2927, *Fax:* (858) 536-2354
www.cbt.net
Darrell Wendhardt, President
Rachel Barnes, CFO
TV bcst studio systems & mobile unit design, engrg & integration.

CCI Systems Inc.
105 Kent Street, Iron Mountain, MI 49801 USA
800-338-9299, *Fax:* (906) 774-6117
www.ccisystems.com
John Jamar, President
CCI Systems designs, builds and integrates communication networks. With over 50 years of experience engineering, constructing, and integrating complex networks, CCI Systems has the unique expertise required to deliver carrier-class turnkeysolutions for all network platforms.

CEA-Computer Engineering Associates
7526 Connelley Dr., Suite H, Hanover, MD 21076 USA
(410) 787-9250,(800) 888-3922, *Fax:* (410) 787-9254
www.ceanews.com
sales@ceanews.com
Paul Keys, President
CEA newsroom system—complete automation systems for radio & TV newsrooms.
5465 Rt. 8, Gibsonia, PA 15044 United States
(412) 443-2600;
Bill Interthal, Mgr
600 Heron Dr, Bridgeport, NJ 08014 United States
(800) 888-3922;
Steve McKemy, Vp

CECO International Corp.
440 W. 15th St., New York, NY 10011 USA
(212) 206-8280, *Fax:* (212) 727-2144
www.cecostudios.com
info@ceostudios.com
Remey Burke, CEO
Donald Kline, President
Motion picture & TV equipment; sound stages; location trucks with generators.

Celco
8660 Red Oak Ave., Rancho Cucamonga, CA 91730 USA
(909) 481-4648, *Fax:* (909) 481-6899
www.celco.com
info@celco.com
Michael Constantine, Financial Executive
Design & manufacture of motion picture film recorders.

Center City Film & Video
1501-1503 Walnut St., Philadelphia, PA 19102 USA
(215) 568-4134, *Fax:* (215) 568-6011
www.ccfv.com
info@ccfv.com
Jordan Schwartz, Chairman
Brian Tsely, Operations Dir
Studio/remote/postproduction D-2, D-3, 1 - Beta - 3/4 - ADO - Paint Box/Abekas 62/GV300 with E-Mem; film/tape DaVinci color correction, ADO repositioning & interactive motion control; D-s, D-3; AVID, Digital Betacam.

Channel Master
1331 Industrial Park Dr., Smithfield, NC 27577 USA
(919) 934-7078, *Fax:* (919) 934-2809
www.channelmaster.com
Coty Youtsey, President
Joe Bingochea, Programming Director
Manufacturer of TV Antennas and Accessories, Cable, Connectors and Amplifiers

Channel One Lighting Systems Inc.
1522 E. 6th St., Tulsa, OK 74120-4026 USA
(800) 651-8869, *Fax:* (623) 934-5160
W. Blair Powell, President
Complete line of lighting equipment for TV, theatre & industrial applications; specializes in the design & manufacture of electrical distribution, grid & cyclorama systems, curtain & track & manufactures radio & TV communications equipment.

Channell Commercial Corp.
Box 9022, 26040 Ynez Rd., Temecula, CA 92589-9022 USA
(951) 719-2600, *Fax:* (951) 296-2322
www.channellcomm.com
uscustsrv@channellcorp.com
William Channell, CEO
Gary Marge, President
John Kaiser, General Sales Mgr
Andrew Zogby, Chief Marketing Officer
Global designer & manufacturer of equipment, offers a complete line of enclosures for CATV & telecommunication

Charles Industries Ltd.
5600 Apollo Dr., Rolling Meadows, IL 60008 USA
(847) 806-6300, *Fax:* (847) 806-6231
www.charlesindustries.com
Joseph Charles, President
Pedestals, custom security boxes, amplifier & TAP brackets-hardware, splicing vaults, taps, splitters & couplers.

Cheetah International
847 Sherman Street, Suite 1, Denver, CO 80203 USA
(720) 536-3618, (800) 869-6986, *Fax:* (720) 293-0017
www.cheetahinternational.com
sales@cheetahinternational.com
Donald Miller, President
Closed captioning software on-line & postproduction & related hardware.

Chicago Condenser Corp.
6455 N. Avondale Ave., Chicago, IL 60631 USA
(773) 774-6666, *Fax:* (773) 774-6690
www.capacitorindustries.com
info@capacitorindustries.com
Terry Noone, President
High Voltage Filter Capacitors for radio & TV bcst transmission.

Chrono-Log Corp.
2 W. Park Rd., Havertown, PA 19083 USA
(610) 853-1130, (800) 247-6665, *Fax:* (610) 853-3972
www.chronolog.com
chronlog@chronolog.com
Paula Freilich, President
GPS Receiver (time only), WWV synchronizer, digital clocks & time display systems, time code generators.

Chyron Corp.
5 Hub Dr., Melville, NY 11747 USA
(631) 845-2000, *Fax:* (631) 845-3895
www.chyron.com
Kevin Prince, COO
Michael Wellesley-Wesley, President
Mark Bachmore, Kathleen Pauger
SVP/Sales, Programming Director
A leading provider of broadcast hardware, software & services spanning television & the Internet. Provides a broad range of leading edge hardware & software products, including paint & animation systems, character generators, master controlswitches, & bcst, automation & media mgmt packages.
One CNN Ctr., South Towers, Suite 558, Atlanta, GA 30303 United States
(404) 880-9004; *Fax:* (404) 880-9104
Ryad Kahale, Chyron Rgnl Sls

Chryon Corp. West
10121 Miller Ave., Suite 201, Cupertino, CA 95014 United States
(408) 873-3800; *Fax:* (408) 986-0452
Denise Gallant, Product Mgr

Cine 60 Inc.
P.O. Box 770631, Woodside, NY 11377 USA
(917) 239-8119
www.cine60newyork.com
info@cine60newyork.com
Paul Wildum, President
Richard Ortiz, General Manager
Vidal Ortiz, Station Manager
Nickel-Cadmium battery belts, battery packs, chargers, sun-guns, kits, dir chair, dir viewfinders, slates, cables & snaplocks.

Cintel Inc.
28910 Ave. Penn, Suite 202, Valencia, CA 91355 USA
(661) 294-2310, *Fax:* (661) 294-1019
www.cintel.co.uk
sales@cintel.co.uk
Curtis Christianson, Operations Dir
Adam Welsh, General Manager
David Saville, General Sales Mgr
Flying spot telecines, DVE system, keycode system, high-resolution scanner, color correctors.
80 Red Schoolhouse Rd., Suite 103, Chestnut Ridge, NY 10977 United States
(914) 371-7220; *Fax:* (914) 371-6896
David Saville, Sls Dir

Circuit Research Labs Inc. (CRL Systems, Inc.)
8350 E. Evans Rd., Suite C-4, Scottsdale, AZ 85260 USA
(480) 403-8300, *Fax:* (480) 403-8302
www.crlsystems.com,www.orban.com
sales@orban.com
Robert McMartin, CEO
Charles Jayson Brentlinger, President
Bob Orban, Operations Dir
Multiband audio AGCs, compressors & limiters for AM/FM; MTS processors, stereo generators, shortwave, AES/EBU digital audio tester.

Clark Wire & Cable Co. Inc.
1355 Armour Blvd., Mundelein, IL 60060-4401 USA
(847) 949-9944, *Fax:* (847) 949-9595
www.clarkwire.com
sales@clarkwire.com
Shane Collins, President
Patti Stickler, Operations Dir
Javier Juarez, General Manager
Dan Collins, Promotions Manager
Audio, video, camera & speciality cable products for bcst industry, available in bulk or assembled harnesses, connectors, panels, reels, & boxes.

Clear-Com Communication Systems
850 Marina Village Pkwy, Alameda, CA 94501 USA
(510) 337-6600, *Fax:* (510) 337-6699
www.clearcom.com
CustomerServicesUS@vitecgroup.com
Jake Dodson, Operations Dir
Matt Danilowicz, General Manager
Michael Shreve, Programming Director
Jiou-Pahn Lee, Chief Engineer
Single & multi-ch hardwire intercom systems for use in teleproduction. Wired & wireless partyline & digital matrix intercom systems.
Box 302, Walnut Creek, CA 94596 United States
(925) 932-8134;
Peter Giddings, Asia/Pacific Dir of Sls

Eastleigh
England Eastleigh, England,
44-23-8090-7000;
Patrick Woolcocks, Emea Direct Sales

Clearone Communications Corp.
5225 Wiley Post Way, Suite 500, Salt Lake City, UT 841196 USA
(801) 975-7200,(800) 945-7730, *Fax:* (801) 977-0087
www.clearone.com
sales@clearone.com
Zee Hakimoglu, CEO
Joe Sorrentino, Operations Dir
Tracy Bathurst, Chief Engineer
Professional audio & teleconferencing.

CMP Enclosures Inc.
3901 Grove Ave., Gurnee, IL 60031 USA
(847) 244-3230, *Fax:* (847) 244-3257
www.enclosures.com
cmpencl@aol.com
Mike Gober, President
Wendi Lee, Operations Dir
Manufacturers of electronic enclosures for rack mounting equipment.

CoarcVideo
Box 2, Rt. 217, Mellenville, NY 12544 USA
(800) 888-4451,(518) 672-4451, *Fax:* (518) 672-4048
coarc@aol.com
Alva Stalker, Programming Director
Bob Spiewak, Promotions Manager
Used by bcstrs, cable systems, duplicating houses, production companies for environmentally-designed videotape reloaded products & standard video tape products; provides Umatic & Betacam VHS tape, program fulfillment svcs. CoarcVideo is partof the Coarc organization, which trains employees & provides various programs for the disabled.

COASTCOM
1141 Harbor Bay Pkwy., Alameda, CA 94502 USA
(510) 523-6000 (510) 521-2708, *Fax:* (510) 523-6150
www.coastcom.com
info@coastcom.com
Tracy Sutherland, President
Manufacturer of T1 voice data network systems specializing in T3 cross connecting, T1 multiplexing & digital program channels for audio bcstg.
1151 Harbor Bay Pkwy., Alameda, CA 94502 United States
(510) 523-6000;
Mark Packwood, Rgnl Sls Mgr
5000 Sharonwoods Ln., Charlotte, NC 28210 United States
(704) 643-7221;
Duane Hardie, Rgnl Sls Mgr
562 Continental Dr., Lewisville, TX 75067 United States
(972) 316-3611;
Mike Walsh, Rgnl Sls Mgr
19 Harding St., Pearl River, WY 10965 United States
(914) 980-3703;
Tom McCafferty, Rgnl Sls Mgr

Coaxial Dynamics
6800 Lake Abram Dr., Middleburg Hts., OH 44130 USA
(440) 243-1100, *Fax:* (440) 243-1101
www.coaxial.com
coaxial@apk.net
Joe Kluha, General Manager
RF wattmeters, terminations, RF load resistors, RF couplers & accessories.

Cohu Inc.
12367 Crossthwaite Circle, Poway, CA 92064 USA
(858) 277-6700, *Fax:* (858) 277-0221
www.cohu.com/cctv
info@cohu.com

Joe Olmstead, General Sales Mgr
Jeff Tyler, Promotions Manager
CCTV cameras & camera control systems, color, CCD, B/W.

Colorado Video Inc.
Box 928, Boulder, CO 80306 USA
(303) 530-9580, *Fax:* (303) 530-9569
www.colorado-video.com
sales@colorado-video.com
Kirk Fowler, President
Image transmission for UBI system; time-division video multiplexing/demultiplexing system.

Comex Worldwide Corp.
Box 8, Aldie, VA 20105-0008 USA
(703) 327-1520, *Fax:* (703) 327-1540
www.comexworldwide.com
cwcmmds@hotmail.com
Jack Rickel, CEO
Susan Rose, General Manager
CWC develops bcst & pay TV systems, VHF/UHF bcsts, satellite communications, MMDS & cable systems & turnkey communication systems.

Commercial Electronics Ltd.
1335 Burrard St., Vancouver, BC V6Z 1Z7 CAN
(604) 669-5525, *Fax:* (604) 669-6347
www.commercialelectronics.ca
pro@cemail.ca
H.H. von Tiesenhausen, President
Audio video equipment, systems designs.

Commercial Radio Monitoring Co.
103 S.W. Market St., Lee's Summit, MO 64063 USA
(816) 524-3777, *Fax:* (816) 524-3777
www.commercialradio.us
W. R. Thorsen, President
Ronald Thorsen, Operations Dir
Frequency measurements & equipment calibration.

CommScope Inc.
1100 CommScope Pl. S.E., Hickory, NC 28603 USA
(800) 982-1708,(828) 324-2200, *Fax:* (828) 328-3400
www.commscope.com
communications@commscope.com
Frank Drendel, CEO
Coaxial & fiber-optic cables including CRD & NEC approved drop cables, QR, P3 & CableGuard.

Communication & Power Industries
607 Hansen Way, Palo Alto, CA 94304 USA
(650) 846-2900, *Fax:* (650) 846-3276
www.cpii.com
Joel A. Littman, CFO
Robert Fikett, President
Andrew E. Tafler, Operations Dir
John R. Beighley, General Sales Mgr
Manufactures a complete line of power grid tubes, klystrons & klystrode IOTs, traveling wave tubes, satellite communication transmitters, microwave components.
811 Hansen Way, Palo Alto, CA 94304 United States
(415) 846-2800 (415) 846-3700;
Armand Staprans, Pres Microwave Products
Jim Commendatore, Pres Satcom

Beverly Microwave Division
150 Sohier Rd, Beverly, MA 01915 United States
(978) 922-6000;
Dennis Gleason, Division Pres
45 River Dr, Georgetown, ON L7G-2J4 Canada
(905) 877-0161;
Joseph Caldarelli, Pres Communications & Medical Products
301 Industrial Way, San Carlos, CA 94070 United States
(415) 592-1221;
H. Frederick Koehler, Pres Eimac Div
607 Hansen Way, Palo Alto, CA 94304 United States
(415) 846-2900;
Al Ferriera, Pres Traveling Wave Tube Products

Communication Graphics, Inc.
1765 N. Juniper, Greenway Business Park, Broken Arrow, OK 74012 USA
(800) 331-4438,(918) 258-6502, *Fax:* (918) 251-8223
www.cgilink.com
info@cgilink.com
Dave Cleveland, President
Choose the company MORE radio stations have selected for printing decals, event stickers, statics, concert patches, magnets, media kits and more!

Communications General Corp.
2685 Alta Vista Dr., Fallbrook, CA 92028-9739 USA
(760) 723-2700
r.gonsett@ieee.org
Robert Gonsett, President
Monthly AM, FM & TV frequency measurements in the Southern California area & spectral measurements.

Communications Specialties Inc.
55 Cabot Ct., Hauppauge, NY 11788 USA
(631) 273-0404, *Fax:* (631) 273-1638
www.commspecial.com
info@commspecial.com
John Lopinto, CEO
Paul Seiden, General Sales Mgr
Manufacturer of fiber-optic transmission sytems, including the Pure Digital Fiberlink line for professional quality video, audio and data.
100 Bencoolen Rd., # 22-09, Shaw Tower, 189702 Singapore
(+665) 656 391-8790; *Fax:* (+656) 656 396-0138
Jeohan Tohkingkeo, Rgnl Mgr Asia Pacific

Comprehensive Video Group
55 Ruta Ct., South Hackensack, NJ 7606 USA
(800) 526-0242, *Fax:* (201) 814-0510
www.comprehensiveinc.com
sales@comprehensiveinc.com
Scott Schaefer, Operations Dir
Digital HDTV UpConverter, High Resolution bulk cable, Video/Audio Multi media & Data Cable assemblies (lifetime warranty), connectors, adaptors, wallplates, distribution amps, switches, convertors, etc.

Comprompter Inc.
1601 Caledonia St., Suite E, La Crosse, WI 54603-3606 USA
(800) 785-7766, *Fax:* (608) 784-5013
www.enrnews.com
enrnews@enrnews.com
Ralph King, President
Offers PC-compatible prompting & networked computerized newsroom & newsroom automation systems for radio, TV, corporate & industrial use.

Computer Concepts Corp.
13375 Stemmons Fwy., Suite 400, Dallas, TX 75234 USA
(800) 255-6350,(913) 541-0900, *Fax:* (913) 541-0169
www.ccc-dcs.com
Greg Dean, Chairman
Total digital integration improves sound, progmg production & scheduling. Business software includes traf & billing for radio.

Computer Resolutions
35 Benham Ave., Suite 1, Bridgeport, CT 6605 USA
(203) 384-0742, *Fax:* (203) 384-0473
Carl Palmieri, CEO
PC- & mainframe-based traf systems; both offer multistation capability.

Comrex Corp.
19 Pine Rd., Devens, MA 1434 USA
(978) 784-1776, *Fax:* (978) 784-1717
www.comrex.com
info@comrex.com
Kris Bobo, General Manager
Chris Crump, General Sales Mgr

Comsearch
19700 Janelia Farm Blvd., Ashburn, VA 20147 USA
(703) 726-5500; (800) 318-1234, *Fax:* (703) 726-5595
www.comsearch.com
customersupport@comsearch.com
Chris Hardy, Vice President
Janeka Carlisle, Chief Marketing Officer
Melissa Wagner, Human Resources Director
Communication engrg svcs for mobile, microwave & satellite systems, including frequency, propagation & integrations svcs.

ComSonics Inc.
1350 Port Republic Rd., Box 1106, Harrisonburg, VA 22801 USA
(540) 434-5965,(800) 336-9681, *Fax:* (540) 432-9794
www.comsonics.com
info@comsonics.com
Dale Lann, CFO
Dennis A. Zimmerman, President
Donald J. Sommerville, General Sales Mgr
Donn E. Meyerhoeffer, COO
Manufacture RF signal level meter & RF leakage detector, CATV repair facility.

Comtech Antenna Systems Inc.
3100 Communications Rd., St. Cloud, FL 34769 USA
(407) 892-6111, *Fax:* (407) 892-0994
www.comtechantenna.com
info@comtechantenna.com
Thomas Christy, President
Ronnie Hamilton, General Sales Mgr
Satellite antenna systems, sizes 1.8-7.3 meters; Offsat(tm), 2 degree spacing antenna; 3.8, 5.0m & Offsat(tm) transportables.

Comtech EF Data
2114 West 7th Street, Tempe, AZ 85281 USA
480-333-2200, *Fax:* (602) 437-4811
www.comtechefdata.com
sales@comtechefdata.com
Brenda Wyatt, General Manager
Comtech EF Data Corp. manufactures a broad spectrum of satellite communications products, including Satellite Modems, Bandwidth & Capacity Management, TCP/IP Performance Enhancement Proxies, Encapsulators, Receivers, Converters, Amplifiers,Transceivers and Terminals.

COMTEK Inc.
357 West 2700 South, Salt Lake City, UT 84115 USA
(801) 466-3463,(800) 496-3463, *Fax:* (801) 484-6906
www.comtek.com
service@comtek.com
Laurel Robertson, General Sales Mgr
Jon Belgique, Promotions Manager
Ralph Belgique, Chief Engineer
COMTEK manufactures synthesized & fixed frequency wireless communication equipment & accessories, including cuing systems (IFB) & wireless microphones.

Condor D C Power Supplies Inc.
6050 King Ddr., Bldg. A, Ventura, CA 93033 USA
(800) 235-5929, *Fax:* (858) 712-2040
www.slpower.com
info@slpower.com
Jim Taylor, President
Mike Shaw, Promotions Manager
Multiple outlet strips, surge & noise suppressors, & uninterruptible power supplies.

Condux International
Box 247, 145 Kingswood Rd., Mankato, MN 56002 USA
(800) 533-2077,(507) 387-6576, *Fax:* (507) 387-1442
www.condux.com
cndxinfo@condux.com
Eric Cope, CEO
Tom Ortolano, Global Sales Manager
Tony Stockman, International Sales Manager
Underground & aerial construction tools & equipment for coaxial cable, telephone & fiber.

Connectronics Corp.
Box 3355, 2745 Avondale Ave., Toledo, OH 43607 USA
(419) 537-0020,(800) 965-0020, *Fax:* (419) 537-0007
www.connectronicscorp.com
info@connectronicscorp.com
Tom Ricketts, President
Al Mocek, Operations Dir
Audio wire & cable, special wire & cable assys. Interconnect products for audio, video, data & telephone.
California Box 2047, Morgan Hill, CA 95037
(408) 779-8888; *Fax:* (408) 778-0722

Conrac Systems Inc.
5124 Commerce Dr., Baldwin Park, CA 91706 USA
(626) 480-0095, *Fax:* (626) 480-0077
www.conrac.com
monitors@conrac.com
Bill Moeller, President
Manufacturer of a var of color & monochrome video monitors for bcst & computer graphic display.

Continental Electronics Corporation
4212 S. Buckner Blvd., Dallas, TX 75227 USA
(214) 381-7161, *Fax:* (214) 381-3250
www.contelec.com
sales@contelec.com
Adil Mina, Operations Dir
Michael Troje, General Sales Mgr
Continental is the premier manufacturer of radio frequency (RF) bcst transmission equipment. We specialize in the design, dev & manufacture of leading-edge digital & analog transmitter systems for the global market. We offer a full range ofproducts for high-power FM, HF, VHF, UHF, LF & VLP application including particle accelerators & fusion rsch, defense communications, radar & industrial heating.
2280 Rockcreek Tr., Birmingham, AL 35226 United States
(205) 822-1078;
Dave Hultsman, Regional Sales Manager
1230 Rugged Oaks Rd., Glen Rose, TX 76043 United States

(254) 898-9200;
Steve Schott, Rgnl Sls Mgr

Convergent Media Systems Corp.
190 Bluegrass Valley Pkwy., 190 Bluegrass Valley Pkwy., Alpharetta, GA 30005 USA
(770) 369-9000, *Fax:* (770) 369-9100
www.convergent.com
convergent@convergent.com
Murray Holland, CEO
Bryan Allen, President
Transportable satellite uplinking & downlinking svcs. Includes facilities & transponder time for Ku- & C-band applications.

Convergys Inc.
201 E. 4th St., Cincinnati, OH 45202 USA
(513) 723-7000,(888) 284-9900, *Fax:* (513) 241-1543
www.convergys.com
Dave Daugherty, President/CEO
Erik Schumann, General Sales Mgr
Cablemaster/Icoms customer mgmt & billing system running on IBM as/400 platform; solution for the convergent cable TV/Telephone industry.
4170 Ashford Dunwoody Rd, Suite 525, Atlanta, GA 30319 United States
(404) 845-4400;

Cooper Sound Systems Inc.
1241 Knollwood Dr., PMB 106, Cambria, CA 93428 USA
(805) 772-1007, *Fax:* (805) 456-1631
www.coopersound.com
coopersoundsystems@att.net
Andrew Cooper, President
Janet Cooper, Operations Dir
Spare parts & tech asst.

Copperweld Fayetteville Division
254 Cotton Mill Rd., Fayetteville, TN 37334-7249 USA
(931) 433-7177, *Fax:* (931) 433-0419
www.fushicopperweld.com
fayetteville@copperweld.com
Li Fu, Chairman
Li Fu, CEO
Wenbing Christopher Wang, President
Copper-clad aluminium wire, copper-clad steel wire, & aluminum-clad steel wire.

Coptervision
7625 Hayvenhurst Ave., #36, Van Nuys, CA 91406 USA
(818) 782-6673, *Fax:* (818) 782-6636
www.coptervision.com
info@coptervision.com
Sarita Spiwak, CEO

Corning Cable Systems
800 17th St. N.W., P.O. Box 489, Hickory, NC 28603 USA
(828) 901-5000; (800) 743-2671, *Fax:* (828) 325-5060
www.corning.com/cablesystems
Clark Kendall, President
Mike Genovese, Operations Dir
Manufacturer of optical fiber cables & accessories for video, data, voice communications applications.

Corning Gilbert Inc.
5310 W. Camelback Rd., Glendale, AZ 85301 USA
623) 245-1050, *Fax:* (623) 931-0684,(800) 334-6358
www.corning.com
info-gilbert@corning.com
Kathy Murphy, CEO
Barbara Metcalf, Vice President
Trunk, distribution & F connectors for CATV.

Corning Incorporated
One Riverfront Plaza, Corning, NY 14831 USA
(607) 248-2000
www.corning.com/opticalfiber
cofic@corning.com
Martin J. Curran, President
Single-mode & multimode optical fibers including: ClearCurve single-mode and multimode fibers, InfiniCor laser-optimized multimode fibers, SMF-28e fibers, LEAF fiber, & Vascade submarine fibers.

CORPLEX Inc.
915 Sherwood Dr., Lake Bluff, IL 60044 USA
(847) 582-8800,(888) 673-5400, *Fax:* (847) 582-8730
www.corplex.tv
carter@corplex.tv
Carter Ruehrdaz, CEO
Scott West, President
Video production equipment, postproduction equipment, rental & mobile TV.

Cortana Corp.
Box 2548, 1170 Valentine Road, Farmington, NM 87499-2548 USA
(888) 325-5336, *Fax:* (505) 326-2337
cortana@cyberport.com
Evelyn Nott, President
Henry Bond, Operations Dir
Stati-Cat Lightning Prevention System.

Cortland Cable Co. Inc.
Box 330, 44 River St., Cortland, NY 13045-0330 USA
(607) 753-8276, *Fax:* (607) 753-3183
www.cortlandcable.com
cortlandcable@cortlandcable.com
John Stidd, President
Rick Nye, Operations Dir
Kevlar fiber antenna guys & ropes, including eye splice end terminations-potted sockets.

Costume Armour Inc./Christo Vac
2 Mill St., Bldg 1 - Suite 101, Cornwall, NY 12518 USA
(845) 534-9120, *Fax:* (845) 534-8602
www.costumearmour.com
info@costumearmour.com
Nino Novellino, President
Period armor & weapons, vacuum-formed background panels, custom made props & sculpture.

Countryman Associates Inc.
195 Constitution Dr., Menlo Park, CA 94025 USA
(800) 669-1422,(650) 364-9988, *Fax:* (650) 364-2794
www.countryman.com
sales@countryman.com
Carl Countryman, Chief Engineer
Very small precision electret condenser microphones for wide applications & the Type-85 Direct Box.

CPC-Computer Prompting & Captioning Co.
1010 Rockville Pike, Suite 306, Rockville, MD 20852 USA
(301) 738-8487,(800) 977-6678, *Fax:* (301) 738-8488
www.cpcweb.com
Dilip Som, President
Sidney Hoffman, Operations Dir
Closed captioning & subtitling systems & svc for HD, DVD, NLE, webcasts & ipod. Plus teleprompting systems.

Crossed Field Antennas Inc.
48 Mountain Rd., Farmington, CT 60322 USA
(860) 676-0051, *Fax:* (860) 677-9639
cfaricher@snet.net
Robert Richer, President
Alec Thomas, Engineering Dir
Maurice Hately, Chief Engineer
Company mkts medium wave & long wave antennas.
97 Foxwood Close, Hansworth, Middlesex, NO TW13 7 United Kingdom
(1) 44 0797 085;
Alex Thomas, Head Engrg

Crown Broadcast IREC
Box 2000, 25166 Leer Dr., Elkhart, IN 46515-2000 USA
(574) 262-8900, (877) 262-8900, *Fax:* (574) 262-5399
www.crownbroadcast.com
kkoselke@irecl.com
Clyde Moore, CEO/President
Kent Kaselle, General Sales Mgr
Alvaro Matina, Engineering Dir
Bcst RF equipment, FM radio transmitters. Supplier to the Natl weather svc for emergency weather radio transmitters.

CS Communications Inc.
9825 Bridleridge Ct., Vienna, VA 22181 USA
(703) 938-5365, *Fax:* (703) 938-5823
chazsamp@aol.com
Charles Sampson, President
Engrg & consulting svcs for wireless and satellite systems. System design, feasibility & economic analysis.

CSG Systems
9555 Maroon Cir., Englewood, CO 80112 USA
(303) 796-2850,(800) 366-2744, *Fax:* (303) 804-4088
www.csgsystems.com
sales@csgsystems.com
Randy Wiese, CFO
Peter Kalan, President
Robert Scott, Operations Dir
Complete sub info mgmt & data processing systems for the cable TV & telephone industries.
6303 Blue Lagoon Dr., Miami, FL 33126 United States
(305) 421-8900 (305) 421-8934;
1-11 John Adams St., London WC2N6HT United Kingdom,
44 20 7004 1840 44 20 7004 1841;
6 Temasek Blvd., 038986 Singapore
65 6883 1900 65 6883 1990;

Cygnal Technologies
120 East Beaver Creek Rd., Richmond Hill, ON L4B 4V1 CAN
(905) 944-6500, (866) 429-4625, *Fax:* (905) 944-6520
www.connexservice.ca
central@connexservice.ca
Jos Wintermans, Chairman
Brian Pedlar, CFO
John Challinor, Promotions Manager
Mgmt, instal & maintenance svcs for studios, radio-TV transmitters, satellite systems & CATV.

D.H. Satellite
Box 239, 600 N. Marquette Rd., Prairie du Chien, WI 53821 USA
(608) 326-8406, *Fax:* (608) 326-4233
www.dhsatellite.com
mdoll@mhtc.net
Mike Doll, Operations Dir
Manufacturer of solid spun aluminum antennas & mounts. Antennas range from .6m (24) to 5m (16') with various mounting options. Delivery & instal is available from DH for all of our antenna equipment.

Da-Lite Screen Company, Inc.
3100 N. Detroit St., P.O. Box 137, Warsaw, IN 46581-0137 USA
(574) 267-8101, (800) 622-3737, *Fax:* (574) 267-7804, (877) 325-4832
www.da-lite.com
info@da-lite.com
Blake Brubaker, VP Sales
Collin Boggs, Sales Manager
Mobile projector, TV & video, tables & cabinets, wall & ceiling mount brackets.

Dage-MTI Inc.
701 N. Roeske Ave., Michigan City, IN 46360 USA
(219) 872-5514, *Fax:* (219) 872-5559
www.dagemti.com
sales@dagemti.com
Arthur Sterling, President
Peggy Moore, Promotions Manager
Closed circuit TV cameras & accessories.

Daily Electronics Corp.
Box 822437, 19311 NE 91st Street, Vancouver, WA 98682-0053 USA
(360) 896-8856,(800) 346-6667, *Fax:* (360) 896-5476
www.dailyelectronics.net
daily@worldaccessnet.com
Jim Grimes, President
Produces vacuum tubes—transmitting, camera, industrial & receiving. Tube rebuilding.

Dalet Digital Media Systems
110 Wall St., 2nd Fl., New York, NY 10005 USA
(212) 269-6700, *Fax:* (212) 269-6709
www.dalet.com
sales@dalet.com
Stephane Guez, COO
Fred Roux, Operations Dir
Benjamin Desbois, General Manager
Luc Comeau, General Sales Mgr
Software for radio & TV. Newsroom computer systems, acquisition, cataloging, producing, sharing, archiving, distribution of video & audio assets.

Data Security Inc.
729 Q St., Lincoln, NE 68508 USA
(800) 225-7554,(402) 434-5959, (877) 326-6630, *Fax:* (402) 434-3291
www.datasecurityinc.com
rschafer@telesis-inc.com
Brian Boles, CEO
Eric Schafer, Operations Dir
Tape Enhancement Series features bulk tape deguassers & videotape cleaner/evaluators.

DBX Professional Products
8760 S. Sandy Pkwy., Sandy, UT 84070 USA
(801) 568-7660, *Fax:* (801) 568-7662
www.dbxpro.com
support@dbxpro.com
Robert Benson, General Sales Mgr
Audio signal processing devices: compressor/limiters, De-essers, equalizers, gates & noise reduction.

DEDOTEC USA Inc.
48 Sheffield Business Park, Ashley Falls, MA 1222 USA

(413) 229-2550, *Fax:* (413) 229-2556
www.dedolight.com
info@dedeolight.com
Paul Tepper, President
Dedolight precision lighting instruments for film, TV, ENG/EFP, still photo & architectural applications. Portable location lighting kits & studio equipment. Special effects attachments & accessories.

Delta Electronics Inc.
Box 11268, 5730 General Washington Dr., Alexandria, VA 22312 USA
(703) 354-3350, *Fax:* (703) 354-0216
www.deltaelectronics.com
sales@deltaelectronics.com
William Fox, President
Joseph Novak, Operations Dir
RF instrumentation including Single & Dual Scale RF Ammeters, Operating Impedance Bridges, Common Point Bridges, Receiver/Generators, AM Stereo Exciters & Monitors, High Power Coaxial Transfer Switches, Toroidal Current Transformers, DigitalRF Ammeters, Splatter Monitor, Stero Noise Generator & Meter Panels.

DeSisti Lighting/Desmar Corp
1101 US Highway 22, Suite 3, Mountainside, NJ 07092 USA
(908) 317-0020, *Fax:* (201) 319-1104
Mario Desigto, Chairman
Frank Kosuda, General Manager
Complete professional lighting equipment & svcs. Quartz fresnels, softlights & cyc lights; HMI fresnels, softlights & sunguns; motorized studio lighting.
World Headquarters (Desisti Lighting, Spa)
Via Cancelliera 10/A, 00040 Cecchina, Albano Laziale, Rome, Italy
01139-06934991; *Fax:* 01139-069343489
Fabio Desisti, Gen Mgr

Devlin Design Group Inc.
625 Broadway, Ste. 1101, Box 5208, Frisco, CO 80443-5208 USA
(970) 688-2772, *Fax:* (970) 688-2772
www.ddgtv.com
ddgemail@ddgtv.com
Dan Devlin, CEO
Kristina Jones, Programming Director
Judy Parker, Promotions Manager
Specializes in bcst news productions. News sets, newsrooms, turnkey & design only. Set design, virtual sets, hard set construction, consultation.

Dialogic Communications Corp.
730 Cool Springs Blvd., Suite 300, Franklin, TN 37067 USA
(615) 790-2882,(800) 723-3207, *Fax:* (615) 790-1329
www.dccusa.com
marketing@dccusa.com
Gene Kirby, President
Charles Smith, Operations Dir
Interactive audio response voice processing equipment & software for pay-per-view, appointment confirmation, outage reporting, etc.

Dictaphone Corp.
3191 Broadbridge Ave., Stratford, CT 6614 USA
(203) 381-7000, *Fax:* (203) 386-8597
www.dictaphone.com
Rob Schwager, Chairman
Multi-ch voice communications tape recorders (loggers).

Dielectric Communications
Box 949, 22 Tower Rd., Raymond, ME 4071 USA
(207) 655-8100, *Fax:* (207) 655-8177
www.dielectric.com
dcsales@spx.com
Garrett VanAtta, President
Anna Morton, Operations Dir
Roger Cote, General Sales Mgr
Cory Edwards, Sales
Matt Leland, Sales
Antennas, inside equipment, waveguide, transmission line, switches, loads, filters, combiners, pressurization, lighting for TV, Radio, mobile media, mobile broadcasting.

DiGi Co. Ltd.
Box 2260, Keller, TN 76244 USA
(877) 292-1623
www.digiconsoles.com
David Webster, Operations Dir
Taidus Vallandi, General Sales Mgr
Digital audio mixing consoles

Digidesign
2001 Junipero Serra Blvd., Daly City, CA 94014-3886 USA
(650) 731-6300, *Fax:* (650) 731-6399
www.digidesign.com
prodinfo@digidesign.com
David Lebolt, General Manager
Christopher Bock, General Sales Mgr
France Office
44 Ave. Georges Pompidou, 92300 Levallois-Perret France,
33 1 41 49 40 10; *Fax:* 33 1 47 49 40 10
UK Office West Complex Pinewood Studios
Pinewood Rd., Iver Heath, Bucks, SLO ONH United Kingdom
44 1753 653322; *Fax:* 44 1753 658501
Japan Office
4F ATT Bldg., 2-11-7 Akasaka, Minato-ku, Tokyo, 107-0052 Japan
81-3-3505-7963; *Fax:* 81-3-3505-3417
New York Office
1650 Broadway, Suite 1113, New York, NY 10019 United States
(212)664-7627;
France Office
44 Ave. Georges Pompidou, 92300 Levallois-Perret France,

Dimension 3
5240 Medina Rd., Woodland Hills, CA 91364 USA
(818) 592-0999
www.d3.com
info@d3.com
Daniel Symmes, CEO
Provides 3-D bcst TV processes. Supplies equipment, consultation & 3-D glasses.

Direct Broadcast Services Inc.
3 Rose Ave., Chestnut Ridge, NY 10977 USA
(845) 267-2800, *Fax:* (845) 267-2123
www.directbroadcast.com
dbs@directbroadcast.com
Leo Rosenberg, President
Transmission svcs & rentals: Ku-band uplinking/downlinking, portable microwave, newsvan opns.

DISH Network Corp.
9601 S. Meridian Blvd., Englewood, CO 80211 USA
(303) 723-1000, *Fax:* (303) 723-1046
www.dishnetwork.com
Charlie Ergen, Chairman
Joseph Clayton, CFO
Mark Jackson, Operations Dir
Jim Defranco, EVP
Satellite TV reception systems.
5701 S. Santa Fe Rd, Littleton, CO 80120 United States
(303) 723-1000; *Fax:* (303) 723-1099
Charles Ergen, Ceo/Chman of Bd
Brent Gale, Dir Bcst Engrg

The Display & Exhibit Source
4715 McEwen St., Dallas, TX 75244 USA
(972) 239-0061, *Fax:* (972) 239-0089
www.displaysource.com
sales@displaysource.com
Dan South, General Sales Mgr
Designs, manufacturer modular, portable backdrops, displays, signal & graphic systems.

Display Devices Inc.
5880 N. Sheridan Blvd., Arvada, CO 80003 USA
(303) 412-0399, *Fax:* (303) 412-9346
www.displaydevices.com
Merv Perkins, President
Ruth Perkins, Operations Dir
Eric Perkins, General Manager
Rich Nichols, Marketing Executive
CRT, LCD, slide projector motorized lifts & stationary mounts. Custom applications.

Display Systems International Inc.
2214 Hanselman Ave., Saskatoon, SK S7L 6A4 CAN
(306) 934-6884, *Fax:* (306) 934-6447
www.displaysystemsintl.com
sales@displaysystemsintl.com
Dale Lemke, President
Electronic progmg guide to display on-screen scrolling TV listing. Also info display software & systems for bulletin boards & adv.

Ditch Witch
Box 66, 1959 W. Fir Ave., Perry, OK 73077 USA
(800) 654-6481, *Fax:* (580) 572-3523
www.ditchwitch.com
info@ditchwitch.com
Manufacturer of trenching, vibratory plow, trenchless technology equipment, electronic locating & tracking equipment, mini-skid steers, excavators tool-carriers & the Zahn family of power utility equipment..

DMT USA, Inc.
109 Gibraltar Rd., Horsham, PA 19044 USA
(267) 961-USA1, *Fax:* (267) 961-1020
www.dmtonline.us
sales@dmtonline.us
Alberto Giorgini, CEO
Stephen Blasetti, Enrinco Marantonio
SVP, Operations Dir
DMT USA specializes in digital television transmitters & Mobile TV. We manufacture UHF & VHF DTV transmitters, antennas & custom RF systems. All models are solid state & environmentally safe. Look to DMT USA for cutting edge technology &true customer service. We are your clear choice for turnkey DTV transmission equipment.

Dolby Laboratories Inc.
100 Potrero Ave., San Francisco, CA 94103 USA
(415) 558-0200, *Fax:* (415) 642-4000
www.dolby.com
Ray Dolby, Chairman
Bill Jasper, CEO
Michael Rockwell, Information Technology
Audio noise reduction & signal processing equipment; digital audio coding for ISDN, cable, satellite & other applications; dolby surround equipment.
Wootton Bassett, Wiltshire, SN4 8QJ
1793 842 100;
Tony Spath, Bcst Projects Mgr

Dorrough Electronics
5221 Collier Pl., Woodland Hills, CA 91364 USA
(818) 998-2824, *Fax:* (818) 998-1507
www.dorrough.com
dorroughel@aol.com
Mike Dorrough, President
Dorrough Electronics manufactures Audio Loudness Meters featuring Peak & Average signals ballistically set for a highly accurate reading.
20434 Corisco St, Chatsworth, CA 91311 United States
(818) 998-4886;

Doty-Moore Tower Services
1570 W. Beltline Rd., Cedar Hill, TX 75104 USA
(972) 293-1200, *Fax:* (972) 293-1255
www.stainlessllc.com
services@stainlessllc.com
Don Doty, President
Jon Marcusse, General Sales Mgr
Thomas Hoenninger, Chief Engineer
Full spectrum of tower maintenance, costruction & inspections. RF svcs include RF mapping of tower & facilities. 24 hr emergency svcs.
Corp. Office
1140 Welsh Road, #250, North Wales, PA 19454

Dove Systems
3563 Sueldo St., Suite E, San Luis Obispo, CA 93401-7590 USA
(805) 541-8292, *Fax:* (805) 541-8293
www.dovesystems.com
dove@dovesystems.com
Gary Dove, President
Denise Calder, Purchasing Executive
Brandon Dove, Sales Executive
Studio & stage lighting control equipment.

Dow-Key Microwave Corp.
4822 McGrath, Ventura, CA 93003 USA
(805) 650-0260, *Fax:* (805) 650-1734
www.dowkey.com
askdk@dowkey.com
Mark Mandrell, President
Dow-Key is specialized in a broad range of RF coaxial relays operating from DC to 40 GHZ, waveguide switches (operating up 70 GHz), electromechanical & solid state switch matrices, Fiber

EQUIPMENT MANUFACTURERS

optics switching network, PXI moduless & CustomSolutions. Both 75 ohm & 50 ohm styles are available.

DPA Microphones, Inc.
1500 Kansas Avenue, Suite 3A, Longmont, CO 80501 USA
(303) 485-1025, *Fax:* (303) 485-6470
www.dpamicrophones.com
info-usa@dpamicrophones.com
Bruce Myers, President
Martin Stove, Director/Business Development
Paul Koza, Sales/Marketing Director
DPA Microphones features a complete line of cardioid & omnidirectional microphones & accessories for all applictions.

DSC Laboratories
3565 Nashua Dr., Mississauga, ON L4V 1R1 CAN
(905) 673-3211, *Fax:* (905) 673-0929
www.dsclabs.com
dsc@dsclabs.com
D. Corley, President
S. Corley, Promotions Manager
Combi Optical Signal Generators (OSGs) & CamAlign chip charts for camera alignment & matching-deal for studio, shop & stadium.

DST Innovis
1104 Investment Blvd., Eldorado Hills, CA 95762
(800) 835-8389, *Fax:* (916) 934-7054
www.dstinnovis.com
Michael McGrail, President
Anthony Piniella, General Manager
Customer mgmt & billing solutions for communications & utilities industries. Clients include providers of CATV, telephony, DBS, wireless, electricity, water, gas, waste mgmt, utility & multi-svcs in over 20 countries.
CableData (Latin America)
Andar, Suite 81, Ave. Eng Luis Carlos Berrini, 1297, Sao Paulo, +55 11.5505.6799; *Fax:* +55 11.5505.8691
CableData (Asia Pacific)
Level 4, 44 Miller St, Suite 404, North Sydney, +61 29.460.2250; *Fax:* +61 29.460.2238
CableData (Latin America) Andar
Suite 81, Ave. Eng Luis Carlos Berrini, Sao Paulo, 1297, 04571-010 Brazil
+55 11.5505.6799; *Fax:* +55 11.5505.8691
CableData (Asia Pacific) Level 4
44 Miller St, Suite 404, North Sydney, NSW 2061
+61 29.460.2250; *Fax:* +61 29.460.2238

Dubner International Inc.
13 Westervelt Pl., Westwood, NJ 7675 USA
(201) 664-6434, *Fax:* (201) 358-9377
www.dubner.com
rdubner@compuserve.com
Robert Dubner, President
Frank Brescher, Vice President

Dynamic Solutions 2000
50 Conyngham St., Ashley, PA 18706 USA
(717) 825-0306, *Fax:* (570) 824-0556
www.ds2000.net
jpgibbons@prodigy.net
John Gibbons, President
Convergent billing solutions for the communications & utility industries.

E-N-G Mobile Systems Inc.
2245 Via De Mercados, Concord, CA 94520 USA
(925) 798-4060, *Fax:* (925) 798-0152
www.e-n-g.com
info@e-n-g.com
Dick Glass, President
Rex Reed, General Manager
Bob Capps, Information Technology
Custom-designed ENG & DSNG vehicles, rack-ready & turnkey systems. Other mobile electronic systems & ENG system components.
119 Lloyd Rd., West Grove, PA 19390 United States
(610) 659-2640;
John Watkins, Opns Mgr

E-Z Trench Manufacturing Co. Inc.
2315 S. Hwy. 701, Loris, SC 29569 USA
(843) 756-6444, *Fax:* (843) 756-6442
www.eztrench.com
Gail Porter, President
Lightweight trenchers—digs trench, lays cables & covers all in one pass.

E.F. Johnson Co.
229 Johnson Avenue, Waseca, MN 56093 USA
(507) 835-6367, *Fax:* (507) 835-6283
www.efjohnson.com
Michael Jalbert, CEO
Andrew Adams, President
A leading provider of two way radios and communications systems.

e2v Inc.
Suite 450, 520 White Plains Road, Tarrytown, NY 10591 USA
(914) 592-6050, *Fax:* (914) 592-5148
www.e2v.com
enquiries@e2v.com
Vijay Patel, Operations Dir
Keith Atwood, Chief Financial Officer
Mark Strohecker, General Sales Mgr
Manufacturer of Digital & Analog IOTs, ESCiors, Klystrons for UHF TV transmitters, Stellar range of satellite uplink amplifiers.
Box 29667, Mississauga, ON L5A 4H2 Canada
(905) 848-6430; *Fax:* (905) 848-9343
Ann Au-Yong, Chairman

Eagle Comtronics Inc.
7665 Henry Clay Blvd., Liverpool, NY 13008 USA
(315) 622-3402,(800) 448-7474, *Fax:* (315) 622-3800
www.eaglecomtronics.com
sales@eaglecomtronics.com
Timothy Devendorf, President
CATV manufacturer & designer of security traps, decoders, & tier traps. Custom OEM filter designs.

Eastman Kodak Co.
343 State St., Rochester, NY 14650 USA
(800) 698-3324, *Fax:* (585) 724-0663
www.kodak.com
Antonio Perez, Chairman
Antonio Perez, CEO
Cameras, projectors, graphic & entertainment imaging products.

EDCOR Electronics Corp.
7130 National Parks Hwy., Carlsbad, NM 88220 USA
(800) 854-0259, *Fax:* (575) 887-6880
www.edcorusa.com
sales@edcorusa.com
Brian Weston, President
Phyllis Weston, Finance Executive
Audio mic/line, audio transformers, custom transformers & power transformers.

Eddie Egan & Associates
6138 West Washington Blvd, Culver City, CA 90232 USA
(310) 278-0370, *Fax:* (310) 559-4348
eddieegan@bcglobal.net
Daniel Egan, President
Armand Egan, Operations Dir
Floor coverings for video stages including wood, vinyl & carpeting.

EDX Wireless
101 East Broadway, MS 305, Eugene, OR 97401 USA
(541) 345-0019, *Fax:* (541) 345-8145
www.edx.com
info@edx.com
RF Planning software for FM, TV & DTV.

EEG Enterprises Inc.
586 Main St., Farmingdale, NY 11735 USA
(516) 293-7472, *Fax:* (516) 293-7417
www.eegent.com
sales@eegent.com,sales@eeg.tv
Philip McLaughlin, CEO
Eric McErlain, General Sales Mgr
TV closed captioning technology; HDTV & SDTV, closes caption encoders, decoders; V-chip encoders, decoders & systems; affil communications.
EEG Enterprises
20 Jay Street, Suite 736, Brooklyn, NY 11201

EFI Electronics Corp.
1751 S. 4800 W., Salt Lake City, UT 84104 USA
(800) 877-1174, *Fax:* (801) 977-0200
www.efielectronics.com
Terry O'Neal, President
Levi Below, Operations Dir
Craig Pluemer, General Sales Mgr
Aaron Davis, Promotions Manager
Manufacturer of industrial & coml Surge Protective Devices for all electrical distribution systems & configurations, both externally & internally mounted.

Eigen
13366 Grass Valley Ave., Grass Valley, CA 95945 USA
(530) 274-1240,(888) 924-2020, *Fax:* (530) 265-2792
www.eigen.com
sales@eigen.com
David Franco, CFO
Michael Castorino, President
Digital image processors with storage & High-resolution video disc recorders.

Elan Enterprises Ltd.
506 E. St. Charles Rd., Carol Stream, IL 60188 USA
(800) 331-8382, *Fax:* (630) 690-6618
www.generator-inverter.com
eeljim8720@aol.com
Jim Johnsen, President
Joe Johnsen, Operations Dir
Redi-line electric generators. Tripp Lite inverters & sure power isolators.

Elcom Systems Inc.
20423 State Rd. 7, Boca Raton, FL 33498-6797 USA
(561) 883-1945, *Fax:* (561) 883-1945
www.elcomsystems.com
sales@elcomsystems.com
Leonard Pollachek, President
RF coaxial attenuators, terminations, couplers, double balanced mixers, detectors, DC-4.2 Ghz, impedance transformers.

Electro Impulse Laboratory Inc.
Box 278, 1805 Rt. 33, Neptune, NJ 07754-0278 USA
(732) 776-5800, *Fax:* (732) 776-6793
www.electroimpulse.com
sales@electroimpulse.com
Mark Rubin, President
Peter Ferraro, Engineering
Manufacturer of dry, forced, air-cooled FM dummy loads & RF calorimeters.

Electro Rent Corp.
6060 Sepulveda Blvd., Van Nuys, CA 91411 USA
(818) 787-2100, *Fax:* (818) 787-4354
www.electrorent.com
Daniel Greenberg, President
Craig Birgi, General Sales Mgr
Test rental equipment including CATV sweep analyzers, signal level meters, video generators/monitors & cable fault locators, data equipment-desktops & laptops to rent, lease or purchase.
3500 Corporate Way, Duluth, GA 30096 United States
(770) 813-7000 (800) 688-1111;
Rich Curry, Eastern Rgnl Sls Mgr

Electroline Equipment Inc.
11035 Louis H. Lafontaine, Anjou, QC H1J 3AE CAN
(514) 374 6335, *Fax:* (514) 374-2257
www.electroline.com
info@electroline.com
John Vincent, CEO
Alain Servant, Operations Dir
Jay Staiger, Promotions Manager
Cable TV equipment, off-premises addressable systems, passive devices, filters, amplifiers, headend RF signal mgnt equipment, transponders, optical nodes & FTTH.

Electronic Script Prompting
6129 Western Ave., Willowbrook, IL 60527 USA
(630) 887-0346, *Fax:* (630) 887-0389
www.prompting.com
Frank Warner, CEO
Teleprompting rental & sale.

Electronic Theatre Controls Inc.
3031 Pleasant View Rd., Middleton, WI 53562 USA
(608) 831-4116, *Fax:* (608) 836-1736
www.etcconnect.com
Fred Foster, CEO
Entertainment & Architectural lighting systems, including control consoles, dimming equipment, interface products & elipsoidals.
Film Center Bldg.
630 Ninth Ave., Suite 1001, New York, NY 10036 United States
(212) 397-8080;
Joe DiNardo, Northeast Rgnl Mgr
4201 Vineland Rd., Suite I-1, Orlando, FL 32811 United States
(407) 843-7770;
Rob Raff, Southeast Rgnl Mgr

Electronology, Inc.
508 Lakeland Blvd., Mattoon, IL 61938 USA
(800) 278-2050 (217) 235-2035, *Fax:* (217) 258-5558
www.einc.com
info@einc.com
Jay Martin, General Manager
Jim Remkel, Consultant
John Sullivan, President

Emcor Enclosures
1600 4th Ave. N.W., Rochester, MN 55901 USA
(507) 287-3535, *Fax:* (507) 287-3405
www.emcorenclosures.com
emcor@emcorenclosures.com
Lance Fleming, President
Ed Doran, Vice President
Conventional & Flat Panel Display Consoles, modification/custom capabilities, EMI/RFI shielded & Seismic qualified enclosures, a full range of component accessories.

Emerson Network Power
Box 1380, 328 Water St., Binghamton, NY 13902-1380 USA
(607) 731-8865,(800) 288-6169, *Fax:* (607) 722-8713
www.control-concepts.com
info@control-concepts.com
Bill Fierle, President
Sarah Beadle, Promotions Manager
Power protection products for transmitters, studios, CATVs from transients & lightning induced voltages.

Emerson Network Power
Box 610, 23123 E. Mission Ave., Liberty Lake, WA 99019 USA
(509) 927-0401, *Fax:* (509) 927-0435
www.emersonnetworkpower.com
webmaster@northern-tech.com
David N. Farr, President
Craig W. Ashmore, Operations Dir
Scott Barbour EVP, Station Manager
Ed Feeney, Executive Vice President
Full line of transient control systems for AC, dataline & telephone, including UPS systems & regulators.

Emerson Network Power
4350 Weaver Pkwy., Warrenville, IL 60555 USA
(630) 579-5000, *Fax:* (630) 579-5050
www.marconi.com
Dusty Becker, Operations Dir
34 Grosvenor, London WIK2HD United Kingdom,
44 (0) 20 7493 8484; *Fax:* 44 (0) 20 7493 1974

Emerson Network Power-Viewsonics
3103 N. Andrews Ave. Ext, Pompano Beach, FL 33064-2118 USA
(954) 971-3439, *Fax:* (954) 971-4422
www.emersonnetworkpower.com/connectivity
David N. Farr, CEO
Edward K. Feeney, President
Jay Goldmacher, EVP
Jerry Patton, General Sales Mgr
One GHz amplifiers, security systems, apartment boxes, combiners, LAN, CATV, one GHz splitters, taps, custom design systems & products, head end signal coupler/splitter system.

ENCO Systems Inc.
29444 Northwestern Hwy., Southfield, MI 48034 USA
(248) 827-4440, *Fax:* (248) 827-4441
www.enco.com
sales@enco.com
Neil Price, COO
Eugene Novacek, President
Don Backus, Operations Dir
DAD and Presenter digital audio delivery systems, custom software engineering for the broadcast industry.

Encoda Systems Inc.
1999 Broadway, Suite 4000, Denver, CO 80202-3050 USA
(303) 237-4000, *Fax:* (303) 237-0085
www.encodasystems.com
info@encodasystems.com
Wiliam Cox, CEO
Eileen Hardin, Director, Professional Services
Rob McConnell, COO
Encoda is the authority in seamless automation for the business of media. Encoda is the only company offering end-to-end technological solutions to buyers & sellers of adv time within the electronic media marketplace (bcst, cable, wireless,& DBS).

Energy-Onix Broadcast Equipment Co. Inc.
Box 801, 1306 River St., Valatie, NY 12184 USA
(518) 758-1690, *Fax:* (518) 758-1476
www.energy-onix.com
energy-onix@energy-onix.com
Bernard Wise, President
Transmitters:AM solid state to 10 kw, ,grounded grid triode to 50 kw & AM & SW to 100 kw. STL, Translator & remote pick up. FM, Shortwave,

Enghouse Systems Limited
80 Tiverton Ct., Suite 800, Markham, ON L3R 0G4 CAN
(905) 946-3200, *Fax:* (905) 946-3201
www.enghouse.com
info@enghouse.com
Stephen Sadler, CEO
Anthony Pearlman, President
Sunil Diaz, General Sales Mgr
Networks™—automated mapping/facilities mgmt software with integrated design capabilities for fiber, copper & coax solutions.

Engineered Electric Company
141 North Ave., Bridgeport, CT 6606 USA
(203) 366-5211, *Fax:* (203) 367-3642
www.drspowersolutions.com
John Uvodich, Operations Dir
Tactical Quiet Generators Sets for military applications.

Ensemble Designs
Box 993, Grass Valley, CA 95945 USA
(530) 478-1830, *Fax:* (530) 478-1832
www.ensembledesigns.com
info@ensembledesigns.com
David Wood, President
Mondae Hott, General Sales Mgr
Cindy Zuelsdorf, Promotions Manager
Video, audio conversion distribution, HD/down conversion, fiber satellite & desktop video applications.

Enterprise Electronics Corp.
128 S. Industrial Blvd., Enterprise, AL 36330 USA
(334) 347-3478, *Fax:* (334) 393-4556
www.eecradar.com
sales@eecradar.com
William Collins, CEO
Larry Sabourin, President
Tim Thompson, Director
Chris Goode, Chief Marketing Officer
Gary Bruce, General Sales Mgr
Frank Sloan, Promotions Manager
Doppler weather radar systems (rain & wind measurements) with PC-based graphics display & control.

Entertainment Communications Network (ECN)
4370 Tujunga Ave., Studio City, CA 91604 USA
(818) 752-1400, *Fax:* (818) 752-1443
www.ecnmedia.com
csd@ecnmedia.com
Angela Tietze, President
Deb Washington, Client Services Manager
Dianne Charves, Media Services Manager
Tom Skoblicki, Sales Director
Bcst faxing to entertainment data bases, online resources, E-mail networks, digital graphics-delivery.
1628 Dubac Rd., Wall, NJ 07719 United States
(732) 280-7107;

EON Corporation
360 Herndon Pkwy., Herndon, VA 20170 USA
(703) 467-0230, *Fax:* (703) 467-0232
Ted Tarr, Operations Dir
Tom Macleod, General Sales Mgr
Dev & mfg of wireless two-way interactive technology for consumers & businesses which operate via radio frequency.

Equipment Technology LLC.
341 NW 122nd Street, Oklahoma City, OK 73114 USA
(405) 748-3841, *Fax:* (405) 755-6829
www.eti1.com
sales@eti1.com
Chris Neuberger, President
Aerial buckets: articulating & telescoping; truck & van mounted; working height ranges 33 to 43 ft.
341 N.W. 122, Oklahoma City, OK 73114 United States
Glenn Smith, Vp Mktg/Sls

ERI - Electronics Research, Inc.
7777 Gardner Rd., Chandler, IN 47610 USA
(812) 925-6000, *Fax:* (812) 925-4030
www.eriinc.com
sales@eriinc.com
Jim Meleski, COO
Thomas Silliman, President
Todd Forbes, CFO
RF and structural engineering, field, and installation services

ESE
142 Sierra St., El Segundo, CA 90245 USA
(310) 322-2136, *Fax:* (310) 322-8127
www.ese-web.com
ese@ese-web.com
William Kaiser, President
Brian Way, Operations Dir
Fernando Vallin, International Sales
Master clocks, digital clocks, programmable timers, time code generators & readers, distribution amplifiers, programmable clocks.

ETS-Lindgren
1301 Arrow Point Dr., Cedar Park, TX 78613 USA
(512) 531-6400, *Fax:* (512) 531-6500
www.ets-lindgren.com
info@ets-lindgren.com
Bruce Butler, CEO
Dave Baron, General Sales Mgr
Glenn Warren, Chief Marketing Officer
Mark Mawdsley, VP Sales
Non-ionizing radiation test equipment; low frequency survey meters; RF/microwave broadband field strength meters; calibration svcs, software & training.

Euphonix Inc.
220 Portage Ave., Palo Alto, CA 94306 USA
(650) 855-0400, *Fax:* (650) 855-0410
www.euphonix.com
mailman@euphonix.com
Martin Kloiber, CEO
Manufactures the Euphonix CSII digitally-controlled analog audio mixing system.
Euphonix Sales & Marketing
11112 Ventura Blvd., #301, Studio City, CA 91604 United States
(818) 766-1666; *Fax:* (818) 766-3401
Euphonix NYC
424 West 33rd St., # 560, New York, NY 10001

Even Technologies Inc.
601 West Cordova St., #490, Vancouver, BC V6B 1G1 CAN
(604) 689-1858, *Fax:* (604) 689-1758
www.eventechnologies.com
info@eventechnologies.com
Nick Ringma, CEO
Glen Simpson, CFO
Peter Koat, Chief Technical Officer
Video compression technology, sofware & hardware for streaming media & real time delivery of IPTV & pre-corded video.

Eventide Inc.
One Alsan Way, Little Ferry, NJ 7643 USA
(201) 641-1200, *Fax:* (201) 641-1640
www.eventide.com
audio@eventide.com
Richard Factor, Chairman
Jason Beck, President
Ray Maxwell, Chief Marketin Officer
Gordon Moore, General Manager
Tony Agnello, Chief Engineer
Audio delay lines, time compression/expansion, pitch change effects, digital reverb, effects processor & digital audio logger.

Evertz Microsystems Ltd.
5288 John Lucas Dr., Burlington, ON L7L 5Z9 CAN
(905) 335-3700, *Fax:* (905) 335-3573
www.evertz.com
sales@evertz.com
Joe Cirincione, General Manager
Orest Holyk, General Sales Mgr
Evertz provides the most comprehensive line of Fiber Optic Transport equipment, the most advanced line of Multi-Image Display, Monitoring Systems, SDTV & HDTV conversion, synchronization products for use in satellite, cable & bcstapplications.
9250 Mosby St., Suite 201, Manassas, VA 20110 United States
212 N. Evergreen St., Burbank, CA 91505 United States
59 Suttons Business Park, Reading, RG6 1AZ United Kingdom

The Express Group
3360 Thorn St., San Diego, CA 92104 USA
(619) 280-9061, *Fax:* (619) 280-9030
www.theexpressgroup.com
egmail@theexpressgroup.com
Byron Andrus, President
Robin Andrus, General Manager
George Andrus, Consultant
Design, fabrication, lighting of custom news sets, newsrooms, interview sets; custom & modular radio cabinetry.

F&F Productions, L.L.C.
14333 Myerlake Cir., Clearwater, FL 33760 USA
(727) 535-6776, *Fax:* (727) 577-5011
www.fandfhd.tv
George Orgera, CEO
Ryan Hatch, Operations Dir
Bill McKechney, Chief Engineer
Remote production svcs & TV mobile units.

F-Conn Industries
6260 Downing St., Denver, CO 80216 USA
(303) 288-8107, *Fax:* (303) 288-4769
www.icmcorp.net
sales@icmcorp.net
Randy Holliday, President
Susan Stockstill, General Sales Mgr

Faroudja Laboratories
180 Baytech Dr., Ste.110, San Jose, CA 95134 USA
(408) 635-4200, *Fax:* (408) 957-0364
www.faroudja.com
Eric Erdman, President
NTSC Encoder; NTSC & PAL/NTSC Decoder (RGB or D1 output); Bidirectional Transcoder; NTSC & PAL/NTSC Line Doublers & Line Quadruplers.

Farrtronics Ltd.
39 Kent Ave., Kitchener, ON N2G 3R2 CAN
(519) 741-1010, *Fax:* (519) 578-2044
Audio & video patchfields; intercom systems, IFB systems, audio distribution amplifiers, beltpack party line systems, monitor packages.

Fast Forward Video
1151 Duryea Avenue, Irvine, CA 92614 USA
(949) 852-8404, *Fax:* (949) 852-1226
www.ffv.com
sales@ffv.com
Dennis Mallon, COO
Hal Reisiger, CEO
Kevin McNally, Sales Executive
Paul Dekeyser, Chief Engineer
Fast Forward Video is committed to providing cutting edge DVR technology in both award-winning finished goods & board-levl products along with engrg supports to a variety of industries including bcstg, sports, military, film production,surveillance & many more.

Feldmar Watch and Clock Center
9000 W. Pico Blvd., Los Angeles, CA 90035 USA
(310) 274-8016, *Fax:* (310) 274-2081
www.feldmarwatch.com
sales@feldmarwatch.com
Sol Meller, President
Stopwatches, clocks, watches, timers, sls & repairs.

Ferno-Washington Inc.
70 Weil Way, Wilmington, OH 45177-9371 USA
(937) 382-1451, *Fax:* (937) 382-1191
www.ferno.com
Joe Bourgraf, CEO
Tim Schroeder, Promotions Manager
Tim Wells, Chief Marketing Officer
Paul Rankin, Chief Financial Officer
Carts designed to aid in the movement of heavy & bulky equipment.

Fiber Options
4575 Research Way, Suite 250, Corvallis, OR 97333 USA
(800) 469-1676,(541) 754-9134, *Fax:* (541) 752-9097
cvovideosales@ge.com
John Collins, President
Vic Milani, Operations Dir
Fred Scott, General Sales Mgr
Manufactures fiber-optic video, data, and audio transmission systems for security, bcst, educ, teleconferencing, ITS, and industrial markets.

Fiber Options Europe Ltd.
Unit 7, Cliff Pk, Morley, Leeds, West Yorkshire, L527 OLQ
44-1132-3816668; *Fax:* 44-1132-2588121
Steve Clarke, Mgng Dir

Film/Video Equipment Service Co. Inc.
800 S. Jason St., Denver, CO 80223 USA
(303) 778-8616, *Fax:* (303) 778-8657
www.fvesco.com
dschnieder@fvesco.com
Dean D. Schneider, President
Film & video equipment rentals-cameras, lenses, lighting, grip, pro audio, camera support & specialty gear for quality production.

FitzCo. Inc.
Box 710, 4300 W. Wall, Bldg. B, Midland, TX 79702 USA
(432) 684-0861, *Fax:* (432) 682-9978
www.fitzcosound.com
fitzcosound@mac.com
Milt Hathaway, President
Speakers, recorders, amplifiers, mixers, tapes, microphones, & headphones; sound reinforcement & bcst equipment.

Flash Technology Corporation of America
332 Nichol Mill Ln., Franklin, TN 37067 USA
(615) 261-2000, *Fax:* (615) 261-2600
www.flashtechnology.com
info@flashtechnology.biz
Mark Joss, Operations Dir
Aviation high-intensity obstruction lights for tall structures & medium intensity for structures up to 500 ft.
55 Lake St, Nashua, NH 03060 United States
(603) 883-6500;

FloriCal Systems Inc.
1500 NW 27th Avenue, Gainesville, FL 32609 USA
(352) 372-8326, *Fax:* (352) 375-0859
www.florical.com
sales@florical.com
Shawn Maynard, Operations Dir
Jim Berry, General Sales Mgr
Kim McKnight, Promotions Manager
TV Automation, complete on-air management and presentation systems include; asset mgmt, material acquisition, variable multi ch control systems, BXF traffic interface, e-mail reports, AssetDispatcher (HD central ingest tool) optional accessthrough web svcs. Dynamic, highly configurable, scalable & reliable.

Fluke Corp.
Box 9090, Everett, WA 98206-9090 USA
(800) 443-5853, *Fax:* (206) 446-5116
www.fluke.com
fluke-info@fluke.com
H. Lawrence Culp, CEO
Barbara Hulit, President
Electronic test, measurement & control instrumentation.

FM Atlas—Publishing and Electronics
Box 336, Esko, MN 55733-0336 USA
(218) 879-7676, *Fax:* (218) 879-8333
www.user.aol.com/fmatlas
fmatlas@aol.com
Bruce Elving, President
Tunable FM/SCS & SAP-modified TV audio radios, adaptor kits with LED display. Brailled radios for the blind.

FM SYSTEMS Inc.
3877 South Main Street, Santa Ana, CA 92707 USA
(714) 979-3355,(800) 235-6960, *Fax:* (714) 979-0913
www.fmsystems-inc.com
fmsystemsinc@sbcglobal.net
Don McClatchie, COO
Frank McClatchie, CEO
Digital test & measurement equipment & digital audio gain control for AES, HD & SD TV singles. Stereo performance meter, audio level masters, digital video volt meters, video & audio modulation meters, multichannel subcarriers & video gaincontrols (VM771).

Focus Enhancements
931 Benecia Avenue, Sunnydale, CA 94085 USA
(650) 230-2400, *Fax:* (408) 739-1706
www.focusinfo.com
info@focusinfo.com
Peter Mor, SVP
Michael Conway, Chief Technical Officer
Tam Chiang, VP Marketing

FOR- A Corp. of America
11125 Knott Ave., Suite A, Cypress, CA 90630 USA
(714) 894-3311, *Fax:* (714) 894-5399
www.for-a.com
Chuck Bocan, General Sales Mgr
Video & audio bcst & postproduction equipment; TBCs, color correctors, production switchers, de/encoders, complete video editing systems, virtual studio & multiviewers.

Fostex USA
9 Mars Ct., Boonton, NJ 7005 USA
(973) 394-0015, *Fax:* (973) 394-0800
www.fostexusa.com
ed@fostexusa.com
Steven Savvides, President
Ed Alstrom, General Sales Mgr
Manufacturer & marketer of innovative digital recorders, field recorders, headphones & monitoring solutions for bcst environments, musicians, producers, personal & professional studios.

Four Seasons Solar Products Corp.
5005 Veterans Memorial Hwy., Holbrook, NY 11741 USA
(631) 563-4000, *Fax:* (631) 563-4010
www. oikos.com
Patrick Marron, CEO
David Ewing, President
Peter Allen, Chief Marketing Officer

Fred A. Nudd Corp.
Box 577, 1743, Rt. 104, Ontario, NY 14519 USA
(315) 524-2531, *Fax:* (315) 524-4249
www.nuddtowers.com
Tom Nudd, President/Owner
Tim Wilson, Sales Executive
Design, manufacture, instal, maintenance & analysis of communication towers.

Frequency Measuring Service Inc.
Box 353, Commerce City, CO 80037 USA
(303) 288-1482, *Fax:* (303) 289-8006
Howard Eldridge, President
Frequency measurements, modulation calibration, field intensity measurements, spectrum analysis.

Frezzolini Electronics Inc.
5-7 Valley St., Hawthorne, NJ 07506 USA
(973) 427-1160, *Fax:* (973) 427-0934
www.frezzi.com
info@frezzi.com
James Crawford, President
High-capacity NIMH, Lithium Ion & Nickel Zinc rechargeable batteries for professional cameras & camcorders; advanced charger & power supplies, location lighting with Frezzi Mini & Micro-fill tungsten quartz & Micro-Sun-Guns, LED MR-19replacement lamps for Mini & Micro fill lighting.

Frontline Communications
12770 44th St. N., Clearwater, FL 33762 USA
(727) 361-9392, *Fax:* (727) 571-3295
www.frontlinecomm.com
dmckay@frontlinecomm.com
John Sherk, SVP
Andy Callaway, General Manager
Steve Williamson, General Sales Mgr

FUJIFILM Recording Media U.S.A. Inc.
200 Summit Lake Dr., Valhalla, NY 10595-1356 USA
(914) 789-8100, *Fax:* (914) 789-8530
www.fujifilmusa.com
Peter Faulhaber, Operations Dir
Gene Kern, General Manager
Professional recording media & data media for bcst, production, cinematography & industrial applications.
1100 King George Post Rd., Edison, NJ 08837 United States
(732) 857-3000;
45 Crosby Drive, Bedford, MA 01730 United States
(781) 271-4400;

Fujinon Inc.
10 High Point Dr., Wayne, NJ 7470 USA
(973) 633-5600, *Fax:* (973) 633-5216
www.fujinon.com
lens.sales@fujinon.com
H. Hayashi, President
John Newton, Operations Dir
Tom Calabro, General Sales Mgr
HDTV, CTV, ENG, EFP lenses, optical systems, accessories.
4951 Airport Pkwy, Suite 802A, Addison, TX 75001 United States
(972) 385-8902;
David Waddell, Mktg Mgr
4101 N. 48th Terr, Hollywood, FL 33021 United States
(954) 966-0484;
Kelly Nelson, Southeast Rgnl Sls Mgr
West Bay Business Park, 2621A Manhattan Beach Blvd, Redondo, CA 90278 United States
(310) 536-0800;
Miles Shozuya, West Coast Sls Mgr
Chuck Lee, Mktg Mgr

Full Compass Systems Ltd.
9770 Silicon Prarie Parkway, Madison, WI 53593-3194 USA
(800) 356-5844,(608) 831-7330, *Fax:* (608) 831-6330
www.fullcompass.com
customerservice@fullcompass.com
Jonathan Lipp, CEO
Over 300 product lines for bcst recording, entertainment, video & sound reinforcement industries.

Fuller Manufacturing
695 S. Glenwood Pl., Burbank, CA 91506 USA
(818) 500-0116, *Fax:* (818) 238-9959
Ron Fuller, Chief Engineer
IFB for news & satellite trunks.

Furman
1690 Corporate Cir., Petaluma, CA 94954 USA
(707) 763-1010, *Fax:* (707) 763-1310
www.furmansound.com
info@furmansound.com

John Humphrey, CFO
Dave Keller, General Sales Mgr
Analog, digital, video monitor systems, power conditioning/distribution, mixers, equalizers, compressors, crossovers, patch bays, voltage regulators, headphone amplifiers & distribution systems.

Fusion Consoles
107 West Valencia Avenue, Burbank, CA 91504 USA
(818) 847-0200, *Fax:* (888) 262-1726
www.marketec.com
info@marketec.com
Penny Russell, President
Technical Furniture & Accessories including ready-to-assemble NLE console desks, racks & full custom tech furniture fabrication complete with CAD drawing for the bcst & cable, post production, audio & multimedia applications.

Future Productions Inc.
100 Industrial Ave., Little Ferry, NJ 07643-1913 USA
(201) 727-0903, *Fax:* (201) 727-0908
members.aol.com/futureprd/video.html
Manufactures & svcs audio/video distribution amplifiers, video duplication control systems, bcst camera control systems, computer graphic systems; & video duplication svc.

FWT Inc.
Box 8597, 5750 E. I-20, Fort Worth, TX 76124 USA
(817) 255-3060, *Fax:* (817) 255-2957
www.fwtinc.com
info@fwtinc.com
Fred Moore, CEO
David Savage, Chief Financial Officer
Bill Sales, General Sales Mgr
Monopoles, self supporting towers, guyed towers, communications bldgs, standby power systems, mobile communications bldgs, COWS, fiber optics, & splicing trailers.

G Prime Ltd.
Radio City Sn., Box 1525, New York, NY 10101 USA
(212) 765-3415, *Fax:* (212) 581-8938
www.gprime.com
info@gprime.com
Russ Hamm, President
Phil Kapp, General Sales Mgr
Importer & distributor of European professional audio equipment for the bcst & recording industries.

Gala
3185 First Street, St. Hubert, QC J3Y 8Y6 CAN
(450) 678-7226, *Fax:* (450) 678-4060
www.galasystems.com
info@pacocorp.com
Philippe Laforest, President
Philippe Desmarais, General Sales Mgr
Theatrical rigging, revolving stages & orchestra lifts.
655 Calle Ladra, Es Condido, CA 92025 United States
(760) 738-5555;
Richard R. Haller, Chairman

Galaxy Audio Inc.
601 East Pawnee Sreet, Wichita, KS 67216-0285 USA
(316) 263-2852, *Fax:* (316) 263-0642
www.galaxyaudio.com
sales@galaxyaudio.com
Brock Jabara, President/CEO
Yule Jabara, General Sales Mgr
Wireless speakers & microphones, headset mics, personal monitors power & unpowered, combiners, splitters SPL meters & audio test equipment.

GAMPRODUCTS Inc.
4975 W. Pico Blvd., Los Angeles, CA 90019 USA
(323) 935-4975, *Fax:* (323) 935-2002
www.gamonline.com
Joseph Tawil, President
Heidi Vessels, Operations Dir
Jeff Davis, General Sales Mgr
Lighting equipment, portable, studio special effects, projections, control console, dimming, color, correction, diffusion filters & patterns (gobos).

Garner Products
10620 Industrial Avenue, Suite 100, Roseville, CA 95678
(916) 784-0200 (800) 624-1903, *Fax:* (916) 784-1425
www.garner-products.com
info@garner-products.com
Ronald Stofan, President
Professional line of bulk tape degaussers for all formats of tape including: Beta SP, DAT 2 reels up to 16 diameters, hard drives, DLT media & degaussing svc.

Geac Libra
1193 West 2400 South, Suite C, Salt Lake City, UT 84119 USA
(800) 453-3827, *Fax:* (801) 974-1900
www.gcs.geac.com
info@geac.com
Eric Schlor, General Sales Mgr
Accounting software for radio, including billing affidavits & sls analysis.

Gefen Inc.
20600 Nordhoff Street, Chatsworth, CA 91311 USA
(800) 545-6900,(818) 772-9100, *Fax:* (818) 772-9120
www.gefen.com
gsinfo@gefen.com
Hagai Gefen, CEO
Robert Lemer, General Sales Mgr
Gefen supplies a wide selection of signal switchers,splitters, extenders, scalers, converters, and accessories that enable audio/video and computer systems to be easily integrated, extended, distributed, and optimized to maximizeperformance. The GefenPRO line suppies 24/7 technical support and valuable features for demanding broadcast industries.

General Atomics
4949 Greencraig Ln., San Diego, CA 92123 USA
(858) 522-8300, *Fax:* (858) 522-8301
www.ga-esi.com
Phil Arneson, President
Carol Ann Mantz, Sales/Marketing Director
Terminal automation products, radiation, monitoring system, triqq and manufacturer of Maxwell high voltage capactiors & power supplies.

General Cable
4 Tesseneer Dr., Highland Heights, KY 41076 USA
(859) 572-8000, *Fax:* (859) 572-8458
www.generalcable.com
info@generalcable.com
Greg Lampert, President/CEO
Copper, aluminum and fiberoptic wire, cable products for communications, energy & electrical markets.

General Electric Co.
3135 Easton Tpke., Fairfield, CT 6431 USA
(800) 626-2004,(203)373-2039, *Fax:* (203) 373-3198
www.ge.com
geinfo@www.ge.com
NBC bcstg; CNBC & MSNBC; lighting products; Americom satellite; electrical distribution & control; intercast; MSNBC desktop video.

CNBC & MSNBC
2200 Fletcher Ave, Fort Lee, NJ 07024 United States
Bill Bolste, Pres

NBC
30 Rockefeller Plaza, New York, NY 10020 United States
(212) 664-4444;
Robert C. Wright, Pres
4338 Nela Park, Cleveland, OH 44112 United States
(216) 362-5600; *Fax:* (216) 266-2310
Keith T.S. Ward, Quartz-Stage Studio Production Mgr

General Electrodynamics Corp.
8000 Calendar Rd., Arlington, TX 76001 USA
(817) 572-0366, *Fax:* (817) 572-0373
www.gecscales.com
Dick Davis, President
George Lindlonger, General Manager
Tubes, TV cameras, electronics, aircraft weighing equipment, contract weighing svcs, truck scales, load scales.

Geneva Aviation Inc.
19717 Grand Avenue, Suite E101, Kent, WA 98032 USA
(253) 395-9105, *Fax:* (253) 395-9150
www.genevaaviation.com
info@genevaaviation.com
Jeff Shapiro, President
Steve Cudnosskey, Chief Engineer
Design, manufacture & instal of E.N.G. & microwave equipment for news helicopters.

Gennum Corp.
4281 Harvester Rd., Burlington, ON L7L 5M4 CAN
(905) 632-2996, *Fax:* (905) 632-2055
www.gennum.com
Franz fINK, CEO
High performance integrated circuits, including switches & processing functions, for analog & digital video applications.

Gepco International Inc.
1770 Birchwood Ave., Des Plaines, IL 60018 USA
(847) 795-9555, *Fax:* (847) 795-8770
www.gepco.com
gepco@gepco.com
David Mecklenburger, CFO
Gary Geppert, President
Jay Lahman, General Manager
Ken Bernd, General Sales Mgr
Audio cable & video cable in bulk or cut to length. Assemblies, boxes, connectors, patchbays. ADC, Kings Neutrik & switchcraft
1000 N. Lake St, Burbank, CA 91502 United States
(818) 569-5222; *Fax:* (818) 569-5226

Glentronix
90 Nolan Ct., Unit 7, Markham, ON L3R 4L9 CAN
(905) 475-8494, *Fax:* (905) 475-0955
www.glentronix.com
Studio video equipment, audio jackfield & test equipment.

Global Microwave Systems Inc.
1916 Palomar Oaks Way, Suite 100, Carlsbad, CA 92008 USA
(760) 496-0055, *Fax:* (760) 496-0057
www.gmsinc.com
gms@gmsinc.com
Sam Nasiri, President
Ursula Meinhard, Operations Dir
Wayne Rogers, General Sales Mgr
James Henderson, Sales Executive
The latest in microwave communications equipment.

Globecomm Systems Inc.
45 Oser Ave., Hauppauge, NY 11788-3816 USA
(631) 231-9800, *Fax:* (631) 231-1557
www.globecommsystems.com
David Hershberg, CEO/Chairman
Keith Hall, President/COO
Matthew Byron, SVP
Tom Coyne, SVP/General Manager
Earth stn ground segements. Video Broadcasting Service & Content Delivery Service.

Gorman-Redlich Manufacturing Co.
257 W. Union St., Athens, OH 45701 USA
(740) 593-3150, *Fax:* (740) 592-3898
www.gorman-redlich.com
jimg@gorman-redlich.com
James Gorman, President
EAS encoders & decoders, EAS with built-in character generator for TV; digital antennas monitors; NOAA weather radios with SAME decoding.

Grant Tower, Inc.
13064 Wisner Ave., Grant, MI 49327 USA
(231) 834-5665, *Fax:* (231) 834-7870
www.granttower.com
Terry Sharp, President
Walter Knoch, General Manager
Bcst tower erection & maintenance svc.

Gray Engineering Laboratories Inc.
2118 W. Collins Ave., Orange, CA 92867 USA
(714) 997-4151, *Fax:* (714) 997-1939
www.grayengineeringlabs.com
Scott Gray, President
SMPTE time-code generators & readers, safe area generators, video-assisted film editing components.

Great Lakes Data Systems, Inc.
5954 Priestly Dr., Carlsbad, CA 92008 USA
(760) 753-1024, *Fax:* (760) 753-2538
www.cablebilling.com,www.glds.com
sales@cablebilling.com
J. Alonzo Rosado, President
Garrick Russell, Vice President
Laura Rosado, General Sales Mgr
Affordable PC/Network billing & subscriber mgmt systems. Addressable interface, PPV, ARU, ANI, Hotel PPV. Training, data conversion & toll-free support.
Box 295, Beaver Dam, WI 53916 United States
(920) 887-7651; *Fax:* (920) 887-7653

Greenberg Teleprompting
115 S. Olive St., Orange, CA 92866 USA
(818) 838-4437, *Fax:* (818) 838-0447
www.greenprompt.com
info@greenprompt.com
Jim Estochin, President
Camera mounted teleprompting, speech prompting, nationwide clients.

Group One Ltd.
70 Sea Ln., Farmingdale, NY 11735 USA

EQUIPMENT MANUFACTURERS

(561)249-1399, *Fax:* (516-) 249-8870
www.g1limited.com
sales@g1limited.com
Jack Kelly, President
Chris Fichera, General Sales Mgr
Exclusive distributor for a number of prominent audio & lighting products including : BlueSky, Digico, Junger, MC, RTW, VanDamme, Elektalite, and Pulsar.

Gyrocam Systems
7345 16th Street East, Suite 101, Sarasota, FL 34243 USA
(941) 355-3206, *Fax:* (941) 355-3417
www.gyrocamsystems.com
info@gyrocamsystems.com
Ken Sanborn, President/CEO/Founder
Stefanie Kowitt, Station Manager
Joe Stark, General Sales Mgr
Manufacturer of the Gyrocam-gyrostablized camera systems for aircraft, boats or vehicles. High Definition Cameras & V700 watt searchlight also available.

Hardigg Cases
Box 201, 147 N. Main St., South Deerfield, MA 01373-0201 USA
(800) 542-7344, *Fax:* (413) 665-8330
www.hardigg.com,www.stormcase.com
cases@hardigg.com
James Hardigg, President
Alice Hardigg, Vice President
With our rugged, dependable shipping cases, we have a video bcst solution for you. Design to protect everything form consumer-grade cameras & lenses to LCD panels & professional studio units, our video bcst cases ensure that all yoursensitive, delicate & valuable gear arrives at its destination intact & ready to go.

Harman International Industries Inc.
8500 Balboa Blvd., Northridge, CA 91329 USA
(818) 893-8411, *Fax:* (818) 892-9590
www.harman.com
Dinesh Paliwal, Chairman
Herbert K. Parker, CFO
Susan Bercovivi, General Manager
Manufacturer of audio signal processing equipment designed for sound reinforcement, recording & bcstg.

Harmonic Inc.
549 Baltic Way, Sunnyvale, CA 94089 USA
(408) 542-2500, *Fax:* (408) 542-2511
www.harmonicinc.com
Patrick Harshman, President
Fiber-optic & digital transmission systems for cable TV, including transmitters, receivers, return path equipment & net mgmt hardware & software.

Harris Automation Solutions
1025 West Nasa Blvd, Melbourne, FL 32919 USA
(408) 990-8200, *Fax:* (408) 990-8250
www.harris.com
sales@harris.com
Howard Lance, General Manager
Louth is a supplier of media mgmt, automation system: for bcst & cable TV.
700 NW Gilman Blvd, 133-227, Issaquah, WA 98027 United States
(425) 837-3799;
Brian Lay, Dir Sls, Western & Central Rgn
Bos 3200, Wantagh, NY 11793 United States
(516) 783-6022;
Martin Frange, Dir Sls

Harris Broadcast Communications
4393 Digital Way, Mason, OH 45040 USA
(800) 231-9673, *Fax:* (513) 701-5301
www.broadcast.harris.com
Harris Morris, President
Richard Scott, Operations Dir
Bruce Allan, General Manager
Bob Jennett, VP Operations
Manufacturer of test/measurement equipment, video demodulators, routing switchers, color correctors/processors, related equipment for professional video/TV bcst markets.

Harris Corp., Broadcast Communications, HQ
1025 West Nasa Blvd, Melbourne, FL 32919 USA
1(800)231-9673, *Fax:* (321)727-9100
www.broadcast.harris.com
Harris Morris, President
Harris Broadcast Communications offers products, systems and services that provide interoperable workflow solutions for broadcast, cable, satellite and out-of-home networks. The Harris ONEâ„¢ solution brings together highly integrated andcost-effective products that enable advanced media workflows for emerging content delivery business models.

Harris Corp., Broadcast Division
Box 4290, 3200 Wismann Ln., Quincy, IL 62305-4290 USA
(217) 222-8200, *Fax:* (217) 221-7085
www.harris.com
Phil Timmons, COO
Bob Weirather, Operations Dir
Jack O'Dear, General Sales Mgr
Gaylen Evans, Dir N.American Field
Jeri Hilgert, Purchasing Executive
Digital radio & TV transmission equipment, svc, tower studies, training, turnkey RF systems.
Box 1179, 10373 Saratoga Rd., South Glens Falls, NY 12803 United States
(518) 793-2181; *Fax:* (518) 793-7423
Rich Redmond, Sls Mgr
33430 13th Pl. S., Suite 205A, Federal Way, WA 98003 United States
(206) 874-7444; *Fax:* (206) 874-8866
Cal Vandegrift, Sls Rep

Harris Corporation
1025 W. NASA Blvd., Melbourne, FL 32919-0001 USA
(321) 727-9100
Gary L. McArthur, CFO
Howard L. Lance, Chairman
R. Kent Buchanan, Chief Engineer
Robert K. Henry, EVP/COO
Provides a wide range of products & svcs for coml & govt communications markets such as wireless, bcst, & govt.
Box 867717, Plano, TX 75023 United States
(214) 612-2053 (800) 729-0494; *Fax:* (214) 612-2145
Doc Masoomian, Chairman

Harris-Farinon
350 Twin Dolphin Dr., Redwood Shores, CA 94065 USA
(650) 594-3000, *Fax:* (650) 594-3110
www.harris.com
Microwave for intercity relay & STLs.

Harrison Consoles
1024 Firestone Pkwy., LaVergne, TN 37086 USA
(615) 641-7200, *Fax:* (615) 641-7224
www.harrisonconsoles.com
info@harrisonconsoles.com
Gary Thielman, Station Manager
Charley White, General Sales Mgr
Ben Loftis, Promotions Manager
David Ives, Contact
Analog & digital audio mixing consoles for on-air bcst, production, video, film sound postproduction, live sound & music recording.

HAVE Inc.
350 Power Ave., Hudson, NY 12534-2448 USA
(518) 828-2000,(800) 999-4283, *Fax:* (518) 828-2008
www.haveinc.com
have@haveinc.com
Nancy Gordon, President
Paul Swedenburg, Operations Dir
Canare, Belden, Gepco, Flexygy, Mogami Cable; Network connectors & adaptors. Professional blank media, equipment & accessories. DVD, CD duplication & postproduction svcs.
HAVE, Inc.
West Coast Office - 661-722-2957,

Henry Engineering
503 Key Vista Dr., Sierra Madre, CA 91024 USA
(626) 355-3656, *Fax:* (626) 355-0077
www.henryeng.com
info@henryeng.com
Hank Landsberg, President
The Matchbox, and other digital and analog interface, distribution, mixing, control, and power conditioning products.

Hessler Enterprises Inc.
106 Susan Dr., #1, Elkins Park, PA 19027 USA
(215) 379-2300, *Fax:* (215) 663-8839
www.hessler.com
Ed Hessler, President
Brian Hessler, Operations Dir
Produces bcstg forms including script sets, contracts, program logs, invoices, labels, A/R statements & computer stock paper.

Hewlett Packard Co.
3000 Hanover St., Palo Alto, CA 94304 USA
(650) 857-1501, *Fax:* (650) 857-5518
www.hewlettpackard.com

High Tech Industries
27636 Ynez Rd., L7-209, Temecula, CA 92591 USA
(888) 747-9817, *Fax:* (951) 279-5773
www.customstudio.com
Douglas Kanczuzewski, General Manager
Bcst TV & radio equipment consoles, rack, cabinetry both standard & custom for edit suites, control rooms & machine rooms.

Highway Information Systems, Inc.
4021 Stirrup Creek Dr., Suite 100, Durham, NC 27703 USA
(919) 361-2479,(800) 849-4447, *Fax:* (800) 849-2947
www.highwayinfo.com,www.qttinc.com
sales@highwayinfo.com
Mike Corbett, Operations Dir
Bruce Reimer, General Manager
Mark Holland, General Sales Mgr
Manufacturer of travelers info stns & hwy advisory bcst systems on low-power AM radio for motorists.

Hignite Tower Service
9945 Arkansas St., Bellflower, CA 90706 USA
(562) 925-1951, *Fax:* (562) 925-6171
jhighnite@ca.rr.com
John Hignite, President
Jackie Hignite, General Manager
Tower erection, maintenance & painting.

Hipotronics Inc.
Box 414, 1650 Rt. 22, Brewster, NY 10509 USA
(845) 279-8091, *Fax:* (845) 279-2467
www.hipotronics.com
sales@hipotronics.com
Richard Davies, Principal
Christopher Faust, Sales Executive
Michelle Gulkins, HR Executive
High-voltage DC power supplies & industrial grade voltage regulators for medium-to-high-power applications.

Hitachi Kokusai Electric America, Ltd.
150 Crossway Park Dr., Woodbury, NY 11797 USA
(516) 921-7200, *Fax:* (516) 496-3718
www.hitachikokusai.us
info@hitachikokusai.us
Masahiko Momose, President
Bob Johnston, Operations Dir
Sean Moran, General Sales Mgr
Bcst, professional & industrial TV cameras, MPEG Codecs, microware links & RF telecommunication equipment.
371 Van Ness Way, Torrance, CA 90501 United States
(310) 328-6116;
David Morris, Rgnl Sls Mgr

HME
Pro Audio Division, 14110 Stowe Dr., Poway, CA 92064-7147 USA
(858) 535-6060, *Fax:* (858) 391-2814
www.hme.com
jkowalski@hme.com
John Kowalski, General Sales Mgr
Wireless Intercoms

Hoagland Instrument, Inc.
120 Eastern Ave., Chelsea, MA 2150 USA
(617) 887-9492, *Fax:* (617) 887-9493
www.hoagland-instrument.com
Jacob Burke, President
Thermal & electronic time delay relays.

Hogg & Davis Inc.
Box 405, 3800 Eagle Loop, Odell, OR 97044 USA
(541) 354-1001, *Fax:* (541) 354-1080
www.hoggdavis.com
info@hoggdavis.com
F. Hogg, President
Cable reels, cable reel trailers, pole tongs, cable sheaves, break-away reels, 36 & 52 tensioners underground puller, 4 drum puller.

Hollywood Rentals Production Services
22800 Foothill Road, Sylmar, CA 91342 USA
(818) 407-7800, *Fax:* (818) 407-7875
www.hollywoodrentals.com
Kelly Koskella, President
Production equipment & vehicles for film & video (rental); sale of new equipment & expendable items.
9100-C Perimeter Woods Dr, Charlotte, NC 28216 United States
(740) 597-1308;
Jeff Pentek, Chairman

Hollywood Vaults Inc.
742 North Seward Street, Hollywood, CA 90038 USA

EQUIPMENT MANUFACTURERS

(323) 461-6464, (800) 569-5336, *Fax:* (323) 461-6479
www.hollywoodvaults.com
vault@hollywoodvaults.com
David Wexler, President
Julianna Wexler, Operations Dir
State-of-the-art film & tape storage vault. Secure, climate-controlled, 24-hours self svc access.

Corporate office of Hollywood Vaults Inc.
1780 Prospect Ave., Santa Barbara, CA 93103 United States
(800) 569-5336;

Homalite
11 Brookside Dr., Wilmington, DE 19804 USA
(302) 652-3686, *Fax:* (302) 652-4578
www.homalite.com
Robert Cahill, President
Manufactures low-reflectance, contrast enhancement filters for use on CRTs, LEDs & other forms of info display.

Honeywell Lighting & Electronics
550 State Rte. 55, Urbana, OH 43078 USA
(877) 285-4466,(937) 484-2056, *Fax:* (602) 822-8015
www.oblighting.com
oblighting@honeywell.com
Steve Sortillion, Site Leader
Tower, obstruction lighting & controls.

Hoodman Corp.
20445 Gramercy Pl., Suite 201, Torrance, CA 90501 USA
(310) 222-8608,(800) 818-3946 (US), *Fax:* (310) 222-8623
www.hoodmanusa.com
lou@hoodmanusa.com
Mike Schmidt, President
Louis Schmidt, Operations Dir
Bob Schmidt, General Sales Mgr
WristShot camcorder support systems, moniter hoods, RAW CF & SD memory cards.

Horita
Box 3993, Mission Viejo, CA 92690 USA
(949) 489-0240, *Fax:* (949) 489-0242
www.horita.com
horita@horita.com
Gerald Hester, President
Christopher Lovallo, General Sales Mgr
SMPTE time code readers, generators, inserters, PC tape logging software; color bar, black, sync generators; titler, distribution amplifiers, audio meter & matte generator.

Hotbox Digital
367 N. Hwy. 101, Solana Beach, CA 92075 USA
(858) 292-8520, *Fax:* (858) 292-1812
Cam MacMillan, President
Design & production of bcst 3-D computer graphics. Logo animation, stn packages. All tape formats supported. Producers of Subito Studio Video Graphic Library.

Hotronic Inc.
1875 S. Winchester Blvd., Campbell, CA 95008 USA
(408) 378-3883, *Fax:* (408) 378-3888
www.hotronics.com
sales@hotronics.com
Andy Ho, President
Linda Chang, General Sales Mgr
HD/SD/Analog Audio/Video delay from 1 video frame to 5 hrs. Test Signal Generator. HD/SD 8x2 or 4X1 Asynchronized Router with live quad, A/V Multiplexer/Demultiplexer, audio or video converter, Uncompressed digital video recorder/player/TBC/Frame Synchronizer etc.

ICM (International Crystal Mfg.Co.)
10 N. Lee Ave., Box 1768, Oklahoma City, OK 73101 USA
(405) 236-3741, *Fax:* (405) 235-1904
www.icmfg.com
info@icmfg.com
Royden Freeland, CEO
Precision electronic crystals, crystal filters, clock oscillators, TCXO's, VCXO's.

ICM Corporation
6260 Downing St., Denver, CO 80216 USA
(303) 288-8107, (800) 222-2142, *Fax:* (303) 288-4769
www.icmcorp.net
sales@icmcorp.net
Ramon Dempers, President/CEO
Doug Burgess, Co-Founder/CFO
Doug Marcotte, EVP/Sales/Marketing
CablePro's attention to design, material & workmanship produces the highest quality for instal tools.

ICX Global
8206 E. Park Meadows Dr., Lone Tree, CO 80134 USA
(720) 873-8400 (800) 777-2259
www.icxglobal.com
Matt Morgan, Operations Dir
Johhny Iverson, General Manager
Jerry Greenwald, Chief Engineer
ICX Global designs, manufactures & markets a wide range of remote control products for bcst, satellite, cable, & consumer electronics devices.
3960 Harlem Rd., Amherst, NY 14226 United States
(716) 839-3803;

Identix
5600 Rowland Road, Minnetonka, MN 55343 USA
(952) 932-0888, *Fax:* (952) 932-7181
www.identix.com
Bob MacCashin, CEO
Robert Brigum, Principal
Identix is a leading biometrics solutions provider with proven & cost-effective verification security for applications including banking, healthcare, government, & access control.

Ikegami Electronics (U.S.A.) Inc.
37 Brook Ave., Maywood, NJ 7607 USA
(201) 368-9171, *Fax:* (201) 569-1626
www.ikegami.com
sales@ikegami.com
Alan Keil, Chief Engineer
Bcst/professional video cameras, monitors, microwave equipment.
2631 Manhattan Beach Blvd., Manhattan Beach, CA 90273 United States
(310) 297-1900; *Fax:* (310) 536-9550
747 Church Rd., Unit C1, Elmhurst, IL 60126 United States
773 Bearden, Waxahachie, TX 75167 United States
5200 N.W. 33rd Ave., Suite 111, Ft. Lauderdale, FL 33309

Illumination Dynamics Inc.
13571 Vaughn Street, Building D, San Fernando, CA 91340 USA
818-686-6400, *Fax:* 818-686-6776
www.illuminationdynamics.com
Jeff Pentek, COO
Carly Barber, President
Craig Chiapuzio, Operations Dir
Maria Carpenter, Chief Marketing Officer
Complete line of lighting, grip, generators & power distribution for Feature Film, Television, Commercials, Broadcast & Special Events.
3823 Barringer Drive - Charlotte, NC 28217
704-679-9400;

The Image Group Post, LLC.
885 2nd Ave., New York, NY 10017 USA
(212) 592-0600, *Fax:* (212) 355-0523
www.image-group.com
Charles Pontillo, Chairman
Willie Sheehy, President
Production & postproduction svcs, including remotes, computer animation, scenic svcs, satellite transmissions & networking.
305 E. 46th St., New York, NY 10017 United States
(212) 548-4400;

Image Logic Corp.
6807 Brennon Ln., Chevy Chase, MD 20815 USA
(301) 907-8891, *Fax:* (301) 652-6584
www.imagelogic.com
info@imagelogic.com
Woodrow Landay, President/CEO
AutoCaption desktop closed captioning & subtitling system for analog, DTV, HDTV, DVD & Web applications. Also Log Producer for video logging.

Image Video
1620 Midland Ave., Toronto, ON M1P 3C2 CAN
(416) 750-8872, *Fax:* (416) 750-8015
www.imagevideo.com
sales@imagevideo.com
Andy Vanags, President
Dave Russell, Operations Dir
Under monitor tally display systems, tally mappers, multi-video display systems & alarm systems..

Imagine Products Inc.
1052 Summit Dr., Carmel, IN 46032 USA
(317) 843-0706, *Fax:* (317) 843-0807
www.imagineproducts.com
sales@imagineproducts.com
Dan Montgomery, CEO
M. Jane Montgomery, Operations Dir
Mac and Win software/hardware for logging and video libraries and web sharing. Offloading and proxy creation software.

IMS (Interactive Market Systems Inc.)
770 Broadway, 15th Fl., New York, NY 10003 USA
(646) 654-5900, *Fax:* (646) 654-5901
www.imsms.com
sales@imsusa.com
George Wishart, CEO
James O Hara, Chief Financial Officer
Barbara Kardas, VP/National Sales
IMS is the leading international provider of info systems & solutions for the media industry. IMS systems & software form an integral part of media & mktg decisions around the world. Media professionals trust IMS for innovative technologies,an unparalled global perspective & valuable insights.

IMS/AMCO Engineering Products
1 Innovation Dr., Des Plaines, IL 60016 USA
(847) 391-8100, *Fax:* (847) 391-8354
www.amcoengineering.com
sales@imsmfg.com
Thomas Anderson, CEO/COO
Thomas Anderson, President
Dave Presi, Chief Techinical Officer
Angela Oliver, Director Of Human Resources
Data/Communications, monitoring & EMI cabinets, single or multiple bay. Inline or curved configurations, standard or custom.

Industrial Acoustics Co., Inc.
1160 Commerce Ave., Bronx, NY 10462 USA
(718) 931-8000, *Fax:* (718) 863-1138
www.industrialacoustics.com
info@industrialacoustics.com
Kenneth DeLasho, President
Complete accu-tone II acoustical environments for bcst industry plus noise-lock sound control doors, windows, walls & silencers.
Walton House, Central Trading Estate, Staines, Middlesex, TW18 4XB
Simon White, Dir Mktg

Hopewell Centre
183 Queen's Rd. E, Rm. 2501, 25/F, Wanchai,
557-8633;
Alvin Leung Jr, Chairman

Industrial Equipment Representatives (IER)
1685 Precision Park Ln., Suite E, San Diego, CA 92173 USA
(619) 428-2261, *Fax:* (619) 428-3483
www.ier-broadcast.com
ierbroadcast@sbcglobal.net
Juan Biosca, General Manager
Alex Rodriguez, General Sales Mgr
Bcst, TV & recording studios equipment & supplies.

Innovision Optics Inc.
1719 21st Street, Santa Monica, CA 90404 USA
(310) 453-4866, *Fax:* (310) 453-4677
www.innovisionoptics.com
innovision@innovision-optics.com
Mark Centkowski, President
Remote-controlled Camera Tracking Systems, Specialized HD Lens, HD Cine SpeedCam. Remote controlled camera systems

Inovonics Inc.
1305 Fair Ave., Santa Cruz, CA 95060-5372 USA
(831) 458-0552, *Fax:* (831) 458-0554
www.inovon.com
info@inovon.com
Ben Barber, Operations Dir
Manufacturers of bcst audio signal processing, encoding/decoding, sound recording & instrumentation equipment.

Inscriber Technology Corporation
26 Peppler St., Waterloo, ON N2J 3C4 CAN
(519) 570-9111, *Fax:* (519) 570-9140
www.inscriber.com
info@inscriber.com
Randy Fowlie, COO
Dan Mance, President
Mike Bernhardt, General Sales Mgr
Software for desktop & bcst video markets, including Character generators, digital stores & Video Server/Sequencers

Inscriber Technology-European Rep Office
Zijdsraat 72, 1431 EE Aalsmeer,
+31-297-362030; *Fax:* +31-297-380939
David Hughes, Dir European Oper

Inscriber Technology-Asian Rep Office
Level 9, AIG Bldg, 1-1-3 Marunouchi, Chiyoda-ky, Tokyo, 100-0005 Japan
81-3-5288-5237; *Fax:* 81-3-5288-5111
Doug Strable, Dir Oper - Asia Pacific

EQUIPMENT MANUFACTURERS

EQUIPMENT MANUFACTURERS

Insulated Wire Inc. Microwave Products Division
20 E. Franklin St., Danbury, CT 6810 USA
(203) 791-1999, *Fax:* (203) 748-5217
John Moredli, President
Ed Lagato, Sales Manager
High-frequency, low-loss microwave cable & cable assemblies featuring IW's Tuf-Flex Series to 60 GHz.

Integrys Holdings L.L.C.
770 Pelham Rd., Suite 220, Greenville, SC 29615 USA
(864) 297-9290, *Fax:* (864) 297-9213
www.integrysllc.com
William Cox, CEO
Subscriber mgmt & billing system.

Intelligent Media Technology
4407 Vineland Rd., Suite D-18, Orlando, FL 32811 USA
(407) 428-1071, *Fax:* (407) 428-1075
www.intelligentmedia.us
salesl@intelligentmedia.us
Bob Proctor, Chief Engineer
Digital audio snakes, A/D conversion & transmission, D/A conversion receiver/repeaters, multimedia fiber optic transmission systems (audio/video/voice/data).

Intelliprompt
9037 Lucerne Avenue, Culver City, CA 90232 USA
(310) 837-0389, *Fax:* (310) 837-0806
www.intelliprompla.com
tony@intellipromptla.com
Tony Finetti, Owner
Computerized teleprompting svcs.
630 9th Ave., Suite. 907 (corner of 44th & 45th), New York, NY 10036
(212) 765-0555; *Fax:* (888) 504-5047
prompt@intelliprompt.com
Trish Devine, Chairman
44 Tecumseth St., Toronto, ON M5V 2R8 Canada
(888) 504-9535; *Fax:* (888) 504-5047
prompt@intelliprompt.com
Trish Devine, Chairman

Interface Media Group
1233 20th St. N.W., Washington, DC 20036 USA
(202) 861-0500, *Fax:* (202) 296-4492
www.interfacevideo.com
info@interfacevideo.com
Jeff Weingarten, President
Adam Hurst, EVP
Steve Yerman, Director, Client Services
FACILITY: film transfer/location/studio/motion control, Avid/interformat digital edit, audio, graphics, dubs, Vyvx/3D2/DGS/satellite, standards conversion.

Interlogix
280 Huyler St., South Hackensack, NJ 7606 USA
(201) 489-9595, *Fax:* (201) 489-0111
Closed circuit TV cameras, monitors & accessories, specializing in covert surveillance cameras.

International Cinema Equipment
1998 N.E. 150th St., North Miami, FL 33181 USA
(305) 573-7339, *Fax:* (305) 573-8101
www.iceco.com
iceco@aol.com
Steve Krams, President
Dara Reusch, Operations Dir
Julio Urbay, VP/International Sales
Offered 16mm, 35mm, 70mm film projection equipment, film-to-tape transfer equipment, sound systems & editing equipment.

International Datacasting Corp.
50 Frank Nighbor Pl., Kanata, ON K2V 1B9 CAN
(613) 596-4120, *Fax:* (613) 596-4863,(613) 596-9208
www.datacast.com
corporate@datacast.com
Denzil Doyle, Chairman
Ron Clifton, CEO
Barry Grout, General Sales Mgr
Gary Carter, Chief Engineer
Rsch, dev, manufacture & mktg of value added high speed digital data transmission net & svcs.

International Electro-Magnetics (IEM)
350 N. Eric Drive, Unit B, Palatine, IL 60067 USA
(847) 358-4622, *Fax:* (847) 358-4623
www.iemmag.com
mail@iemmag.com
Anthony Pretto, President
Standard replacement & custom recording heads for audio, video & film.

Intersil Corp.
1001 Murphy Ranch Rd., Milpitas, CA 95035 USA
(408) 432-8888, *Fax:* (408) 432-0640
www.intersil.com
Dave Zinsner, CFO
Dave Bell, President
David Loftos, Chief Marketing Officer
ICs for wireless networking, high performance analog-flat panel displays, optical storage (CD,DVD recordaable) & power mgmt.
2401 Palm Bay Rd., Palm Bay, FL 32905 United States
(321) 724-7000 (888) 486-3774
www.intersil.com
investor@intersil.com
Queen Tower A, 12F 2-3-1, Minato-Mirai, Nishi-ku, Yokohama, 220-5820 Japan
+81 45 682 5820; *Fax:* +81 45 682 5821
The Gateway, 9 Canton Rd., Suite 1506, 15F Tower 6, Tsimshatsui, Kowlon, Hong Kong
+852 2709 7600;

IPITEK
2330 Faraday Ave., Carlsbad, CA 92008 USA
(760) 438-1010, *Fax:* (760) 438-2462
www.ipitek.com
sales@ipetk.com
Michael Salour, Chairman
Michael Salour, CEO
Horace Tsiang, General Sales Mgr
Ralph Weeks, Tech Support

IRIS Technologies Inc.
104 Industrial Park Rd., Greensburg, PA 15601 USA
(724) 832-9855 (412) 867-1017, *Fax:* (724) 832-8999
www.iristech.com
sales@iristech.com
Jerry Salandro, CEO
Video Commander icon based routing, iNED & SmartPort product lines which allow complete headend control from anywhere in the world.
563 W 500 South, Bountiful, VT 84010 United States
(801) 296-8250; *Fax:* (801) 296-8248

Isaia & Co.
PO Box 668, Hermosa Beach, CA 90254 USA
(310) 466-9858, *Fax:* (310) 798-2146
www.isaia.com
matt@isaia.com
Matt Isaia, President
Angenieux Film & Digital Lenses, Runford Baker tripods & heads, Badger camera support, Tango & blue mod accessories.

The ISIS Group
119 E. McKnight Way, Unit A, Grass Valley, CA 95949-9503 USA
(888) 622-4747,(530) 477-2984, *Fax:* (530) 477-2986
www.gpsys.com
info@isis-group.com
Bob Stillwaugh, President
Manufacturer of routing switchers and signal processing equipment.

ITI Electronics Inc.
32 Stonewall Dr., Livingston, NJ 07039-1822 USA
(973) 890-7888, *Fax:* (973) 992-0459
itielect@aol.com
Robert Stein, President/Owner
Connectorized & Prewired jackfields; patch panels; telephone line amplifiers; other series 400 & 10 line cards.

ITT Cannon Electric
666 East Dyer Road, Santa Ana, CA 92705 USA
(714) 628-8722, *Fax:* (714) 628-2249
www.ittcannon.com
William Taylor, President
Keith Teichmann, General Sales Mgr
Electronic connectors & interconnect systems & info card technology suppliers to a var of industries, including bcst & data communications companies.

J and R Moviola Inc.
1135 N. Mansfield Ave., Los Angeles, CA 90038 USA
(323) 467-3107, *Fax:* (213) 466-2201
www.movieola.com
Joe Paskal, CEO
Chief Technical Officer, General Sales Mgr
Randy Paskal, Executive Vice President
Film editing equipment, film & video shipping & storage, film-to-video transfer machine.
8000 E. 40th Ave., Denver, CO 80238 United States
(303) 321-1099;
Randy Urlik, Exec VP
636 11th Ave., New York, NY 10036 United States
(212) 247-0972;
Bob Herman, VP
416 W. Ontario, Chicago, IL 60610 United States
(312) 787-0622;
Jeff McNeir, VP

The J-Lab Co.
Box 6530, Malibu, CA 90264 USA
(310) 457-4090, *Fax:* (310) 457-4494
www.j-lab.com
sales@j-lab.com
Jerry LaBarbera, President
Component accessories, battery-operated video, audio DAs, LCD monitors & portable switchers.

J.A. Taylor & Associates
Box 331, Boyertown, PA 19512-0331
(610) 754-6800, *Fax:* (610) 754-9766
www.broadcastassociates.com
jataylor@broadcastassociates.com
John Taylor, President
Appraisers & brokers of TV production equipment. Serves video production companies, TV stns & financial institutions.

James Thomas Engineering Inc.
10240 Caneel Dr., Knoxville, TN 37931 USA
(865) 692-3060, *Fax:* (865) 692-9020
www.jthomaseng.com
salesus@jthomaseng.com
Mike Garl, President
Manufacturer of structural aluminum truss, towers & ground supported roof systems. Truss range includes: superlite, supertruss, gen purpose truss, ground support towers, speaker support towers, truss circles & custom fabricated structures.Also manufactures spun aluminum PAR fixtures, pre-wired lighting bars, spot baks & accessories. Distributor of CEEP Multipin connectors, Multicable, Kee Safety pipe fittings, CM Chain Hoists & rigging accessories.

Jampro Antennas Inc.
6340 Sky Creek Dr., Sacramento, CA 95828 USA
(916) 383-1177, *Fax:* (916) 383-1182
www.jampro.com
jampro@jampro.com
Doug McCabe, COO
Alex Perchevitch, President
Cyndi Sanderson, Operations Dir
Manufacturers of TV & FM bcst antennas, combiners, filters & a complete line of rigid coaxial transmission line.

JBL Professional
Box 2200, 8500 Balboa Blvd., Northridge, CA 91329 USA
(818) 894-8850, *Fax:* (818) 830-1220
www.jblpro.com
info@jblpro.com
Mark Terry, CEO
John Carpanini, President
Chief Marketing Officer, Operations Dir
John Sager, Operations
Ed Kamp, Director
Manufacturers of loudspeaker systems for bcstg, recording studios, theaters, concerts, stadiums & other applications.

JC Sound Stages
6670 Lexington Ave., Hollywood, CA 90038 USA
(323) 467-7870, *Fax:* (323) 467-7832
www.jcband.com/jcsoundstages.html
J.C. Belanger, President
Cable-controlled camera booms equipped for film or video, rehearsal pre-production recording all in classiest vibe avail anywhere.

JDS Uniphase Corp.
430 N. McCarthy Blvd., Milpitas, CA 95035 USA
(408) 546-5000, *Fax:* (408) 546-4300
www.jdsu.com
Martin Kaplan, Chairman
Thomas Waechter, CEO
Test equipment for video nets, including broadband RF & fiber optics. (SLMs, system analyzers, leakage, sweeps & OTDRs) software.

Jennings Technology Co.
970 McLaughlin Ave., San Jose, CA 95122 USA
(408) 282-0363, *Fax:* (408) 286-1789
www.jenningstech.com
sales@jenningstech.com
Steve Randazzo, President
High-voltage vacuum & gas capacitors; relays, switches, single- & three-phase contactors & instruments.

Jensen Transformers Inc.
9304 Deering Ave., Chatsworth, CA 91311-5857 USA
(818) 374-5857, *Fax:* (818) 374-5856
www.jensen-transformers.com
sales@jensen-transformers.com
Bill Whitlock, President
Audio transformers, ISO-MAX audio & video ground isolation boxes

Jewell Instruments LLC
850 Perimeter Rd., Manchester, NH 3103 USA
(800) 638-3771, *Fax:* (603) 669-5962
www.triplett.com
wjh@triplett.com
Carlo Carluccio, President/CEO
Tim Cetto, General Manager
Panel instruments & test equipment. Electrical, electronic, telecommunication & railroad testers.

JNJ Industries Inc.
290 Beaver Street, Suite 303, Franklin, MA 02038 USA
(508) 553-0529, *Fax:* (508) 553-9973
www.jnj-industries.com
sales@jnj-industries.com
Jack Volpe, President
Gail Howe, Operations Dir
Bob Enterkin, Promotions Manager
CFC & HCFC free solvents, presaturated cloth wipes, spray bottles, dry cloth wipes, lens wipes; aqueous chemistries ; industrial & precision cleaning products.

JOA Cartridge Service
448 E. Hancock St., Lansdale, PA 19446 USA
(215) 362-8796, *Fax:* (215) 368-2336
www.joaonline.com
mark@joaonline..com
Mark Molyneaux, President
Bcst audiotape cartridges, audio, videotape, cassettes, tape accessories, DAT tape, cassettes, data storage diskettes, cassettes, optical disks, recordable CDs & reloading svc.

JSB Service Co.
204 S. Bayard Ave., Waynesboro, VA 22980 USA
(540) 949-5899, *Fax:* (540) 949-5863
www.jsbservice.com
Joseph Brumbelow, CEO
Paul Bosak, Operations Manager
Repair, resale of microwave communication devices, receivers, transmitters, solid state sources, amplifiers.

JVC Professional Products Company
1700 Valley Road, Wayne, NJ 07470 USA
(973) 317-5000, *Fax:* (973) 317-5030
www.jvc.com/pro
proinfo@jvc.com
Bob Mueller, CEO
Kirk Hirota, President
Plasmas; full line of professional video equipment including digital VTRs cameras, monitors & projectors.
705 Enterprise St., Aurora, IL 60504-8149 United States
(630) 851-7809;
Chris Dalaly, Branch Mgr
1700 Valley Rd., Wayne, NJ 07470 United States
(973) 317-5000;
Paul Kasparian, Branch Mgr
5665 Corporate Ave., Cypress, CA 90630 United States
(714) 229-8024;
Eric Rosenberg, Rgnl Sls Mgr

Kahn Communications Inc.
338 Westbury Ave., Suite 2, Carle Place, NY 11514 USA
(516) 222-2221, *Fax:* (516) 338-1942
www.wrathofkahn.org
radio221@aol.com
Leonard Kahn, President
To build bcstg & communications equipment.
767 3rd Ave., New York, NY 10017 United States
(212) 983-6765;
Leonard R. Kahn, Pres

Kalun Communications Inc.
44 Larkfield Dr., Toronto, ON M3B 2H1 CAN
(416) 410-4138, *Fax:* (416) 410-4138
www.kalun.4t.com
postmaster@kalun.4t.com
Paul Wong, Chief Engineer
RF test equipment including wideband sweep generators, sweep comparator, switched attenautor, return loss bridge, detector & headend equipment for ATSC

Kangaroo Products Inc.
10845 Wheatlands Ave., Suite C, Santee, CA 92071-2856 USA
(619) 562-9696, *Fax:* (619) 449-7244
www.kangarooproducts.com
sales@kangarooproducts.com
Steve Leiserson, President
Nancy Byrd, VP, Human Resources
Custom contract carrying cases.

Kathrein Inc., Scala Division
555 Airport Rd., Medford, OR 97504 USA
(541) 779-6500, *Fax:* (541) 779-3991
www.kathrein-scala.com
broadcast@kathrein.com
Manfred Muenzel, President
Judy Young, General Sales Mgr
Michael Bach, Sales Engineer
Antennas & filters, low to full power, includes STL/TSL, LPTV, CATV, RPU, translator & FM/TV monitoring. Custom patterns our specialty.

Kay Industries Inc.
7834 Queen Road, Plymouth, IN 46617 USA
(574) 936-9374, *Fax:* (574) 289-5932
www.kayind.com
phasemaster@kayind.com
John Colage, Managing Executive
Rotary phase converters for single phase to three phase power.

Keywest Technology
14563 W. 96th Terr., Lenexa, KS 66215 USA
(800) 331-2019,(913) 492-4666, *Fax:* (913) 322-1864
www.keywesttechnology.com
info@keywesttechnology.com
Wes Dixon, General Sales Mgr
Markus Lubick, Contact
Manufacturer of automated media servers, loc origination ch, LO ch, media player, CATV character generators, logo & ID inserters.

Kidde-Fenwal Inc.
400 Main St., Ashland, MA 01721 USA
(508) 881-5102, *Fax:* (508) 881-7619
www.kidde-fenwal.com
John Sullivan, President
Kevin Barron, Operations Dir
Kate Houghton, Chief Marketing Officer
Jim Livingstone, Chief Technical Officer
High-speed fire protection systems.

Kings-Winchester Electronics Corp.
1685 Overview Drive 2, Suite B, Rock Hill, SC 29730 USA
(803) 909-5000,(203) 741-5400, *Fax:* (803) 909-5092
www.kingselectronics.com,www.winchesterelectronics.com
Robert Dock, President
Allen Trustman, Operations Dir
Holli Mills, Chief Marketing Officer
Virginia King, General Sales Mgr
Video patch panels, patch cords, coaxial connectors, triaxial connectors & twinaxial connectors.
62 Barnes Industrial Rd. N., Wallingford, CT 06492
(203) 741-5400 (203) 741-5500;

Kintronic Labs Inc.
Box 845, Bristol, TN 37621-0845 USA
(423) 878-3141, *Fax:* (423) 878-4224
www.kintronic.com
ktl@kintronic.com
Louis King, CEO
Tom King, President, General Manager
Gwen King, Operations Dir
AM matching & directional antenna phasing systems, AM multiplexers, transmitter combiners, AM dummy loads, isocouplers, passive RF components & transmission lines.

Knox Video
8547 Grovemont Cir., Gaithersburg, MD 20877 USA
(301) 840-5805, *Fax:* (301) 840-2946
www.knoxvideo.com
Ted Neiman, President
Ken Nottingham, Promotions Manager
Electronic bulletin bd for video messages. VCR control units. Full matrix routing switches.

Konica Minolta Corp. USA Inc
100 Williams Drive, Ramsey, NJ 07446 USA
(201) 825-4000, *Fax:* (201) 529-6070
www.minoltausa.com
isddisplay@minolta.com
Masatoshi Matsuzaki, President/CEO
CRT & LCD color analyzing instrumentation.

Kuhnel Co. Inc.
155 Harmony Rd., Mickleton, NJ 8056 USA
(856) 423-4277, *Fax:* (856) 423-5105
Mary Kuhnel, President
Jennifer Elentrio, Business Development
Installation & maintenance of antennas & towers.

L-3 Communications Telemetry East
1515 Grundy Lane, Bristol, PA 19007-0729 USA
(267) 545-7000, *Fax:* (267) 545-0100
www.l-3com.com
Frank Lanza, CEO
Marc Lienard, President
Doug Crawford, Business Development
Todd Warton, Business Development
Robert Holland, Engineering/Technical
Manufacturer of satellite receiving systems, antennas, telemetry receiving systems, ancillary equipment, communications for aerospace & defense.

L.E. Nelson Sales Corp.
4800 W. University Ave., Las Vegas, NV 89103 USA
(702) 367-3656, *Fax:* (702) 367-7058
Heidi Nelson, President
D.R. Imfeld, Operations Dir
H.F. Nelson, VP Western Region
Studio lamps, quartz (tungsten-halogen) from 25 w to 10 kw & projection lamps. Exculsive importer of Thorn Lamps.
18-02 River Rd., Fair Lawn, NJ 07410 United States
(201) 794-6700;
Dan Imfeld, Vp Eastern Rgn

LARCAN
228 Ambassador Dr., Mississauga, ON L5T 2J2 CAN
(905) 564-9222, *Fax:* (905) 564-9244
www.larcan.com
sales@larcan.com
Jim Adamson, General Sales Mgr
LARCAN is a full service Broadcast Solutions company. LARCAN innovates, designs, and manufactures superior Analog and Digital television transmitters for wireless and broadcast markets worldwide. We specialize in Custom Network Planning andRF Synergies for Broadcast and Mobile Video / DVB-H technologies. LARCAN offers 'End to End' engineering solutions in Solid State VHF, UHF, High Power IOT transmitters, as well as Low Power transmitters / translators and FM Solutions. We offer thebest in broadcast innovations and transmitters from 1W to 100kW strong, and provide a wealth of broadcast solutions and services designed with the right fit for you. Look to LARCAN for Truly Made to Measure Solutions.
LARCAN USA
1360 Overlook Dr., #2, Lafayette, CO 80026

LARCAN USA Inc
1390 Overlook Dr., Lafayette, CO 80026 USA
(303) 665-8000, *Fax:* (303) 673-9900
www.larcan.com
David Hale, Chairman
Jim Adamson, President
Repair & sls of high power UHF TV transmitters, low power TV transmitters & translators, FM transmitters & translators & AC line surge protectors.

Laser Diode Inc.
4 Olsen Avenue, Edison, NJ 8820 USA
(732) 549-9001, *Fax:* (732) 906-1559
www.laserdiode.com
laserdiodes.sales@macomtechcom
Steve Lerner, Operations Dir
Rollin Ball, General Manager/Director
Peggy Scarillo, General Sales Mgr
George Minakas, Programming Director
Manufacture FP, high power pulsed & CW lasers along with high sensitivity detectors, FDDI/SONET modules for short/long haul transmission, test DWDM, military & coml fiber optic systems. Also offer Hi-Reliability custom packaging svcs.

LBA Technology Inc.
Box 8026, 3400 Tupper Drive, Greenville, NC 27835-8026 USA
(800) 522-4464,(252) 757-0279, *Fax:* (252) 752-9155
www.lbagroup.com
lbatech@lbagroup.com
Lawrence Behr, CEO
Jerry Brown, President
Javier Castillo, Operations Dir
Design & manufacture medium wave antenna systems marketed worldwide, including folded unipole antennas, tuning units, transmitter combiners, diplexers, triplexers, RF components & collocation equiptment.

LEA International
4726 Eisenhower Blvd, Tampa, FL 33634 USA
(813) 621-1324, *Fax:* (813) 621-8980
www.leaintl.com

Shawn Thompson, President
Travis Coffey, General Manager
Dave Stimmel, Chief Financial Officer
Manufacturers of transient voltage surge suppression & power conditioning equipment.
10701 Airport Dr., Hayden Lake, ID 83835
(800) 881-8506; *Fax:* (208) 762-6099

Leader Instruments Corp.
6484 Commerce Dr., Cypress, CA 90630 USA
(714) 527-9300, *Fax:* (714) 527-7490
www.leaderusa.com
lopez@leaderusa.com
Hiro Sawa, President
Maria Magbanua, Chief Administrative Officer
Electronic test equipment for video, audio, RF, microwave, oscilloscopes & gen use.
6484 Commerce Dr, Cypress, CA 90630 United States
(714) 527-9300;

Lectrosonics Inc.
581 Laser Rd. NE, Rio Rancho, NM 87124 USA
(505) 892-4501, *Fax:* (505) 892-6243
www.lectrosonics.com
sales@lectrosonics.com
Larry Fisher, President
Wes Herron, Station Manager
Gordon Moore, General Sales Mgr
Bruce Jones, Promotions Manager
Bob Cunnings, Chief Engineer
Wireless microphone & IFB systems for bcst, motion picture & tele-product applications. Automatic sound mixers & audio signal processing equipment.

Leightronix Inc.
2330 Jarco Dr., Holt, MI 48842 USA
(800) 243-5589, *Fax:* (517) 694-1600
www.leightronix.com
sales@leightronix.com
David Leighton, President
Video Servers & TV Automation.

Leitch Inc.
920 Corporate Lane, Burbank, CA 91505 USA
(757) 548-2300,(800) 231-9673, *Fax:* (757) 548-2300
www.leitch.com
leitch@leitch.com
Paula Moore, General Manager
Tom Jordan, General Sales Mgr
Don Thompson, Promotions Manager
Audio & video distribution amplifiers, sync generators, clock systems & timers, synchronizers, test equipment, still storage, scramblers & descramblers. Audio, video, digital & data routing switchers, terminations, serial digital products.

Leitch Technology Corp.
150 Ferrand Dr., Suite 700, Toronto, ON M3C 3E5 Canada
(416) 445-9640 (800) 387-0233;
John Nielson, South Central Rgnl Sls Mgr

Lemco Tool Corp.
1850 Metzger Ave., Cogan Station, PA 17728 USA
(570) 494-0620, *Fax:* (570) 494-0860
www.lemco-tool.com
toolinfo@lemco-tool.com
Mike Miller, President
Designers & manufacturers of mechanical tools, for the construction & maintenance of CATV systems. Also coaxial cables and cell tower networks.

LEMO USA Inc.
635 Park Court, Rohnert Park, CA 94927-2408 USA
(707) 578-8811, *Fax:* (707) 578-0869
www.lemo.com
info@lemousa.com
Julie Carson, General Manager
Michael Greico, General Sales Mgr
Julie Carlson, Promotions Manager
LEMO designs & manufactures precision custom connection solutions. LEMO developed the 3K.93C series connector which is now the SMPTE standard for natl & international bcst companies.

Leviton NSI Colortran
20497 S.W. Teton, Tualatin, OR 97062 USA
(503) 404-5500,(800) 576-6060, *Fax:* (503) 404-5600
pauls@leviton.com
Harold Leviton, President
Paul Sherbo, General Sales Mgr
Lighting fixtures & control devices for theater, TV & architectural applications.

Lightning Eliminators & Consultants Inc.
6687 Arapahoe Rd., Boulder, CO 80303 USA
(303) 447-2828,(800) 521-6101, *Fax:* (303) 447-8122
www.lecglobal.com
info@lecglobal.com
Avram Saunders, CEO
Peter Carpenter, President
Joanna Silberman, Marketing
Designers & manufacturers of lightning strike prevention, grounding & power conditioning systems.

Lightning Master Corp.
1351 N. Arcturas Ave., Clearwater, FL 33765 USA
(727) 447-6800, *Fax:* (727) 499-0138
www.lightningmaster.com
RBEATIE@lightningmaster.com
Bruce A. Kaiser, Owner
Tom Lewellyn, Sales Executive
Richard Beatie, Chief Engineer
Structural lightning protection equipment, dissipator technology, transient voltage surge suppression, bonding & grounding products, consulting svcs; site survey, analysis & training.

Lightning Prevention Systems
154 Cooper Rd., Suite 1201, West Berlin, NJ 08091-9116 USA
(856) 767-7806,(888) 667-8745, *Fax:* (856) 767-7547
www.lpsnet.com
info@lpsnet.com
Pat McLaughlin, CEO
Ian E. Fawthrop, President
Manufactures equipment utilizing point discharge technology to remove the lightning attractive static charge on towers or structures that they're on, preventing lightning strikes.

Lindsay Broadband Inc.
2035 Fisher Dr., R.R. #5, Peterborough, ON K9J 6X6 CAN
(705) 742-1350, *Fax:* (705) 742-7669
www.lindsaybroadbandinc.com
sales@lindsaybroadbandinc.com
Linda Curtin, CFO
David Atman, President
David Hayford, Operations Dir
Jonathan Haight, General Sales Mgr
Laurie Matthews, Customer Support
A diverse range of last mile communication products, including Wi-Fi & mesh wireless systems, hard line passives, trunk, distribution amplifiers, free space optic systems, headend & subscriber passives, a range of MDU amplifers with UPSoptions, mini optical nodes, WDM fiber optic equipment & NRBS/MEF compliant media converters. Markets & sell to the worldwide telecommunications market.

Linear Acoustic Inc.
108 Foxshire Drive, Suite 110, Lancaster, PA 17603 USA
(717) 735-3611, *Fax:* (717) 735-3612
www.linearacoustic.com
sales@linearacoustic.com
Tim Carroll, President
Christina Carroll, General Sales Mgr
Guy Huffard, Marketing Director

LINK Electronics Inc.
2137 Rust Ave., Cape Girardeau, MO 63703 USA
(573) 334-4433, *Fax:* (573) 334-9255
www.linkelectronics.com
sales@linkelectronics.com
Bob Henson, President/CEO
Dave Aufdenberg, Operations Dir
Ellen Henson, Executive Vice President
James Timberlake, VP Operations
Manufacturer of Sync Generators, system timing, audio & video DAs, power amps, encoders, decoders, video processing, test equipment & video presence detectors, closed caption encoders, decoders, video switchers, routers for analog, SDI HD,digital distribution & conversion. Closed caption encoders for analog SD HD SDI, Up/Down/Cross Conversion, frame syncs.

LINK Electronics Inc.-Northeast & Southeast Rgnl S
2 W. Laurelwood Dr., Lawrenceville, NJ 08648 United States
(573) 257-9473
raybouchard@aol.com
Ray Bouchard, Rgnl Mgr-N.E. & S.W. Rgns

Lipsner Smith Co.
4700 Chase Ave., Lincolnwood, IL 60712 USA
(847) 677-3000,(800) 323-7520, *Fax:* (847) 677-1311,(800) 784-6733
www.lipsner.com
sales@lipsner.com
Ray Short, Owner
Jonathan Banks, Sales Executive
Motion Picture Film Laboratory Equipment.

Listec Corp.
2001 Palm Beach Lakes Blvd., Suite 502-I, West Palm Beach, FL 33409 USA
(561) 683-3002, *Fax:* (561) 683-7336
www.listec.com
sales@listec.com
Joanne Camarda, President
Raymond Blumenthal, Operations Dir
Fully professional range of flat-panel, prompters for studio, field & conferencing applications complemented by Windows prompting software. PRO-Motion light & medium duty tripods. Brick House Video compact production switcher. USRepresentatives for IPV.
40-3 Oser Ave., Hauppauge, NY 11788 United States
(631) 273-3029; *Fax:* (631) 435-4544
Lisa Grunert, Sls & Product Support

Location Sound Corp.
10639 Riverside Dr., North Hollywood, CA 91602 USA
(818) 980-9891, *Fax:* (818) 980-9911
www.locationsound.com
information@locationsound.com
Robert Noone, General Manager
Steve Joachim, General Sales Mgr
Angelica Dewlow, Marketing Director
Dealer of professional audio & communications solutions for film, video, broadcast, business, institutional & recording applications. Over 30 years experience.

Logica Inc.
655 3rd Ave., Suite 2900, New York, NY 10017 USA
(212) 682-7411, *Fax:* (212) 682-0715
Consulting.

Logitek Electronic Systems Inc
5622 Edgemoor Dr., Houston, TX 77081 USA
(713) 664-4470,(800) 231-5870, *Fax:* (713) 664-4479
www.logitekaudio.com
inorthamericansales@logitekaudio.com
Tag Borland, President
Frank Grundstein, General Sales Mgr
Digital audio consoles, digital audio routers & audio level indicators (meters).

Lowel-Light Manufacturing Inc.
140 58th St., Brooklyn, NY 11220 USA
(718) 921-0600, *Fax:* (718) 921-0303
www.lowel.com
info@lowel.com
Dale Marks, General Sales Mgr
Toni Pearl, Dealer Liaison
Eric Drucker, Eastern Sales Executive
Don Youngberg, Midwest Sales
Lights, controls, mounts & kits for imaging professionals, innovatively designed & built for rugged dependable use, ease of operation and portability.

LTM Corp. of America
7755 Haskell Ave., Van Nuys, CA 91406-1906 USA
(818) 780-9828, *Fax:* (818) 780-9848
www.ltmlighting.com
info@ltmlighting.com
Richard Espinosa, President
HMI & quartz lighting fixtures for film & video production; fresnels, open face, fiber optic, soft lights & fluorescents from 18w to 18,000 w. Also complete line of microphone poles, windscreens & muffs.

Luxor
2245 Delany Rd., Waukegan, IL 60087 USA
(847) 244-1800,(800) 323-4656, *Fax:* (800) 327-1698,(847) 244-1818
www.luxorfurn.com
sales@luxorfurn.com
Robert Raw, General Manager
Bill Gamber, General Sales Mgr
Randy Douglas, Director
Computer stands, A/V equipment stands, conference room furniture, TV stands, library, office furniture, ceiling, wall universal & projector mounts.

M. Ducommun Co.
58 Main St., Warwick, NY 10990 USA
(845) 986-5757, *Fax:* (845) 986-7720
M. Ducommun, President
M. Ducommon, Jr.
Stopwatches for radio, TV, sls, svc & repair.

M/A-COM
100 Chelmsford Street, Lowell, MA 01851 USA
(978) 442-5000,(800) 366-2266, *Fax:* (978) 442-5350
www.macom.com

Rick P. Hess, CEO
Tim Emery, General Manager
RF microwave & mm wave components & subsystems.

M2 America
470 Riverside St., Portland, ME 4103 USA
(508) 485-4880, *Fax:* (207) 797-2604
www.m2america.com
info@m2america.com
CD, CD-R, DVD-R & optical disk duplicators.

Macrovision Corp.
2830 De La Cruz Blvd., Santa Clara, CA 95050-8594 USA
(408) 562-8400, *Fax:* (408) 567-1800
www.macrovision.com
info@macrovision.com
John Ryan, Chairman
Bill Krepick, CEO
Copy protection & rights mgmt for videocassettes, pay-per-view cable, satellite TV, & video conferencing.

Macrovision UK Ltd.
14-18 Bell St., Maiden Head, Beeshire, SL 61 BR United Kingdom
(44) 870 871 1111;
Martin Brooker, Chairman

Macrovision Japan
K.K. Takaba Bldg. 2F, 6-18-5, Jingumae, Shibuya-Ku, Tokyo, 150-0001 Japan
81-35-774-6253;
Masao Kumei, Chairman

Magna-Tech Electronic Co. Inc.
1998 N.E. 150th St., North Miami, FL 331481 USA
(305) 573-7339, *Fax:* (305) 573-8101
www.magna-tech.com
magnatech@iceco.com
Allen Lasky, CEO
Steven Krams, President
Barnet Kaufman, Operations Dir
Manufactures professional motion picture sound recording, reproducing & projection equipment, film recorders & reproducers; 16 & 35mm recorders, telecine followers, counters, pre amps, dubbers & looping systems.readers.

Magni Systems Inc.
22965 N.W. Evergreen Pkwy., Hillsboro, OR 97124 USA
(503) 615-1900, *Fax:* (503) 615-1999
www.magnisystems.com
sales@magnisystems.com
Victor Kong, CEO
Chuck Barrows, General Sales Mgr
Video Test Equipment and Scan Converters. Automated video test & monitoring equipment, waveform monitors, vectorscopes, test signal generators, VIT inserter, PC graphics to video encoders & video overlay scan converters.

Magnum Towers Inc.
9370 Elder Creek Rd., Sacramento, CA 95829 USA
(916) 381-5053, *Fax:* (916) 381-2144
magnumtowers.com
office@magnumtowers.com
Ron Craig Kardokus, President
Jeff Styler, Operations Dir
Lori Morris, General Manager
Radio, TV & microwave towers.

Marathon Norco Aerospace, Inc.
8301 Imperial Drive, Waco, TX 76712 USA
(254) 776-0650, *Fax:* (254) 776-6558
www.mnaerospace.com
marathon@mptc.com
Jack Stiffer, President
Clay Collins, General Manager
Deanne Hollenback, General Sales Mgr
CASP universal battery support systems & AC/DC power supplies.

Marietta Design Group
82 Plantation Point, Suite 200, Fairhope, AL 36532 USA
(251) 990-3558, *Fax:* (360) 838-9046
www.mariettadesign.com
support@mariettadesign.com
AccuPrompt— & QuickPrompt— teleprompting software for MacIntosh.
QuickPrompt 1.7.2—for professional video prompting.

Maritz Inc.
1355 North Highway Dr., Fenton, MO 63099 USA
(877) 462-7489,(636) 827-4000, *Fax:* (636) 827-8605
www.maritz.com
Christine Duffy, CEO
Scott Wingenbach, Vice President
Steve Bowen, Operations Dir
Communications, film/video training, business meetings & mktg.

Marketron Broadcast Solutions
101 Empty Saddle Trail, Hailey, ID 83333 USA
(208) 788-6800, *Fax:* (208) 788-5786
www.marketron.com
Gary Coats, COO
Tony Gaughan, Chief Technical Officer
Jerome Hollus, Sales/Marketing
Pete D'Acosta, CEO
Marketron is the media industry's leading provider of business software solutions and services. Marketron develops and supports advanced software systems for radio operations, traffic, billing, and reporting functions.
Toronto, ON Canada
Opelika, AL
San Francisco, CA
Denver, CO

Marketron Broadcast Solutions
Box 3078, 508 S. 7th St., Opelika, AL 36803 USA
(888) 239-8878, *Fax:* (334) 749-5666
www.marketron.com
sales@datacount.com
Pete D'Acosta, CEO
Bill Price, General Manager

Marketron International
700 Airport Blvd., Suite 130, Burlingame, CA 94010-2001 USA
(800) 788-9245, *Fax:* (650) 548-2295
www.marketron.com
lcarpenter@marketron.com
Mike Jackson, CEO
Keith Winter, President
Don Hansen, VP Finance
Software applications for radio, TV, networks, syndicators, traf, accounting, mgmt, demand pricing, inventory control, rsch & proposals.
101 Empty Saddle Trail, Hailey, ID 83333 United States
(208) 788-6272;
Gary Coats, Gen Mgr
5075 Yonge St., Suite 404, Toronto, ON M2N 6C6 Canada
(416) 221-9944;
Les Bridgen, Gen Mgr
3000 Riverchase Galleria, 8th Fl., Birmingham, AL 35244 United States
(205) 987-7456; *Fax:* (205) 733-4535
tvsales@marketron.com
Michael Hunter, Gen Mgr

Marshall Electronics
1910 E. Maple Ave., El Segundo, CA 90245 USA
(310) 333-0606,(800) 800-6608, *Fax:* (310) 333-0688
www.marshall-usa.com
sales@lcdracks.com
Leonard Marshall, CEO
Nathan Mordukhay, President
Rob Foster, Sales Director
Provides the hightest quality products to the bcst, video & music recording markets. Products include cable, connectors, Mogami superflex wire, cable, Tajimi connectors & LCD bcst monitors. Marshall also specializes in mfg optics microphones& multimedai devices.

Marti Electronics
4100 N. 24th St., Quincy, IL 62305 USA
(217) 224-9600, *Fax:* (217) 224-9607
www.martielectronics.com
sales@martielectronics.com
Tim Bealor, Operations Dir
George Marti, General Manager
Composite, dual mono & digital STL systems, remote pickup systems, telemetry links, studio to transmitter links, FM exciters, transmitters & pots remote pickup systems.

Martinsound Inc.
1151 W. Valley Blvd., Alhambra, CA 91803-2440 USA
(626) 281-3555, *Fax:* (626) 284-3092
www.martinsound.com,(800) 582-3555
info@martinsound.com
Joe Martinson, President
Sharon Michael, Operations Dir
Doug Osborne, General Manager
Complete line of audio control consoles for music recording, bcst, & video postproduction applications. MultiMax surround monitor control system, flying faders console automation, Martech MSS-10 precision microphone preamplifier.

Masterclock, Inc.
2484 W. Clay St., St. Charles, MO 63301 USA
(800) 940-2248, *Fax:* (636) 724-3776
www.masterclock.com
sales@masterclock.com
William Clark, President
Masterclock systems! Accurate gps time! Network time, Power Over Ethernet & Time Code. Industrial grade generators, pci cards, analog & digital clocks. Extensive experience in the bcst industry. Designed & products in the U.S.A.

MATCO Inc.
15000 Stetson Rd., Los Gatos, CA 95033-9770 USA
(408) 353-2670,(800) 348-1843, *Fax:* (408) 353-8781
www.matco-video.com
sales@matco-video.com
David Harbert, President
Rita Harbert, General Manager
Playback automation, coml insertion, & machine control systems for bcst, cable & coml, industrial & medical. MPEG 2 video servers with automation software options.

Matrox Video Products Grp
1055 St. Regis Blvd., Dorval, QC H9P 2T4 CAN
(514) 822-6364, *Fax:* (514) 685-2853
www.matrox.com/video
video.info@matrox.com
Amantha Citia, Sales Director
Emmy award-winning technology & mktg leader in the field of digital video hardware for accelerated H.264 encoding, realtime editing, DVD/Blu-ray authoring & web streaming.

Matthews Studio Equipment Inc. (MSE)
4250 West Valerio Street, Burbank, CA 91505 USA
(818) 843-6715, *Fax:* (323) 843-7419
www.msegrip.com
info@msegrip.com
Ed Phillips, President
Robert Kulesh, General Sales Mgr
TV camera support dollies, land tripods, studio pedestals, pan/tilt heads, cases.

MAVRIC Media Inc.
117 Church St., Roseville, CA 95678
(800) 804-7756, *Fax:* (888) 453-8870
www.mavricmedia.com
dana@mavricmedia.com
Don Smith, President
Garland Bell, VP/COO
Gene Marcucci, CFO
Hosted, web-based asset mgmt & content delivery tools.

Maxell Corp. of America
3 Garrett Mountain Plaza, 3rd Floor, Suite 300, Woodland Park, NJ 07424 USA
(201) 794-5900, *Fax:* (201) 796-8790
www.maxellpromedia.com
Masaru Kanemoto, President
Blank audio & video recording tape for professional bcstrs & duplicators.

Maze Corporation
3867 Rock Ridge Rd., Irondale, AL 35210-3797 USA
(205) 706-2080, *Fax:* (205) 956-6328
www.mazecorp.com
mazecorp@charger.net
Vira Maze, President
Tamara Syinn, Secretary
Remarketers of TV & video equipment.

McCurdy Radio Ltd.
30 Kelfield Street, Unit 6, Toronto, ON M9W 5T4 CAN
(416) 248-6155, *Fax:* (416) 248-6755
www.mcradio.com
sales8800@mcradio.com
Paul Hudson, President
Bob Hudson, General Manager
Audio monitors & meters.
1051 Clinton St., Buffalo, NY 14206 United States

MCG Surge Protection
12 Burt Dr., Deer Park, NY 11729 USA
(631) 586-5125, *Fax:* (631) 586-5120
www.mcgsurge.com
info1@mcgsurge.com
Christine Jelley, CEO
Sue Baron, General Sales Mgr
Diane Lanciotti, CFO
Surge protectors for AC power lines, telephone/signal & data lines. Protecting industry since 1967.

MCL Inc.
501 S. Woodcreek Dr., Bolingbrook, IL 60440-4999 USA
(630) 759-9500, *Fax:* (630) 759-5018
www.mcl.com
sales@mcl.com
David Krautheimer, President
John Harrington, Vice President
Satellite communication fixed & mobile High Power Amplifiers in C-band, X-Band, Ku-band, DBS, V-Band, Ka-Band & Multi-Band.

Media Computing Inc.
Box 4169, Cave Creek, AZ 85327-4169 USA
(480) 575-7281
www.mediacomputing.com
info@mediacomputing.com
Michael Rich, CEO
Kathryn Hulka, Operations Dir
ANGIS-PC-based software automatically updates displays on characters generators & web pages with real-time data like elections, news tickers, closing.

Media Concepts Inc.
200 Spring Garden, Unit B, Philadelphia, PA 19123 USA
(215) 928-1820, *Fax:* (215) 928-0750
mediacon@libertynet.org
Bob Weissman, President
Video duplication, international video standards conversion, CD-Rom duplication, DVD duplication authoring. Macrovision copy-protection.

Mediasoft Inc.
7301 N. Broadway Ext., Suite 120, Oklahoma City, OK 73116 USA
(405) 607-2000, *Fax:* (405) 607-2071
www.mediasoftusa.com
info@mediaofusa.com
Bob Alfson, CEO
Dave Easley, General Sales Mgr
Microcomputer products & svcs.

Mediastar-SG
702 Mangrove Ave., #221, Chico, CA 95926 USA
(530) 826-3342, *Fax:* (530) 898-9588
www.mediastar-sg.com
corporate@mediastar-sg.com
Ken Danner, Promotions Manager
Multimedia production systems for cable TV, bcst, PEG & corporate TV. Pre & post-launch consulting, training & sls seminars. Repair & support svcs for all competitors' products. Data recovery svcs.

Mega Hertz
4100 International Plaza, Suite 150, Fort Worth, TX 76109 USA
(800) 883-8839, *Fax:* (817) 529-0745
www.go2mhz.com
sales@go2mhz.com
Doug Sherar, Promotions Manager
Mega Hertz is a Value-Added-Reseller of Unique Multi-Vendor System Solutions that support the deployment of advanced technologies in hybrid Fiber/Coax Braodband Networks. MHz â€œEngineering & Integration Groupâ€ provides pre-saleEngineering, Design, Project Management, Installation, Activation & Training, as well, as Level 1 product support for MHz advanced video, voice and data end2end solutions.

Megastar Inc.
4709 Compass Bow Ln., Las Vegas, NV 89130 USA
(702) 386-2844, *Fax:* (702) 388-1250
www.1megastar.com
Jim Foy, CEO
Nigel Macrae, President
Reseller, earth stations & all support equipment, c band transceivers.

MEGGER
2621 Van Buren Ave., Norristown, PA 19403 USA
(610) 676-8500, *Fax:* (610) 676-8610
www.megger.com
sales@megger.com
Keiser Carvel, CEO/COO
Mark Snopek, President
Greame Thomson, Vice President
Cable fault-locating equipment & other electrical testing instruments.

Memorex Products Inc.
17777 Center Court Dr., Suite 800, Cerritos, CA 90703 USA
(562) 653-2800, *Fax:* (562) 653-2900
www.memorex.com
generaling@memorex.com
Michael Golacingki, CEO
Brad Yeager, Director, Product Marketing
Scott Stroup, Operations Dir
Memorex is a manufacturer, marketer of consumer media & computer products.

Meridian Design Associates, Architects
1140 Broadway, New York, NY 10001 USA
(212) 431-8643, *Fax:* (212) 431-8775
www.meridiandesign.com
info@meridiandesign.com
Antonio Argibay, Founder
Bice C Wilson, Founder
Luis Rogers, Principal
Robert Milkie, Principal
Architectural firm specializing in the design of bcst & media facilities.
907 S.W. 79th Ave., Miami, FL 33144 United States
(305) 262-7663; *Fax:* (305) 262-7675
Antonio Argibay, Chairman

Merlin Engineering Works Inc.
1888 Embarcadero Rd., Palo Alto, CA 94303 USA
(650) 856-0900,(800) 227-1980, *Fax:* (650) 858-2302
www.merlineng.com
sales@merlineng.com
Debbie Dirickson, General Manager
Bcst VTRs, custom VTRs & accessories, VTR automation systems, stereo audio encoders, standards converters.

Metz Engineering
15684 Old Mormon Bridge Rd., Crescent, IA 51526-4138 USA
(712) 545-3222, *Fax:* (712) 545-9111
Joanne M. Metz, President
John P. Metz III, General Manager
Machine & welding shop plus construction.

Michael Stevens & Partners Ltd.
Invicta Works, Elliott Rd., Bromley, Kent, BR2 9NT GBR
44 0 020 8460 7299, *Fax:* 44 0 020 8460 0499
www.michael-stevens.com
simon@michael-stevens.com
Simon Adamson, Engineering Dir
Bcst equipment, audio mktg, processing & monitoring video production.
149 Dillard Ct., Suite E, Kingston Springs, TN 37082
(615) 952-2345; *Fax:* (615) 952-2342
Megan McCullough, Sls Office Mgr

Micro Rymsa Communications Inc.
Box 4365, 438 Kelley Ave., Grenier Field, Manchester, NH 03108-4365 USA
(603) 624-4351,(800) 545-0608, *Fax:* (603) 624-4822
www.mcibroadcast.com
frank.malanga@mcibroadcast.com
Paul Smith, CEO
Al Kula, General Sales Mgr
Sam Matthews, Promotions Manager
Kim Blackford, Branch Manager
Waveguide & coaxial transmission line; complete RF system packages for UHF, VHF, FM & LPTV panel antennas; antennas for UHF, VHF & FM.

Micro Technology Unlimited
9390 Six Forks Rd., Suite 101, Raleigh, NC 27615 USA
(919) 870-0344, *Fax:* (919) 870-7163
www.mtu.com
info@mtu.com
David B. Cox, President
Lynn Cox, Marketing
Karaoke software products & pro workstations.

Microlog Corp.
20270 Goldenrod Ln., Germantown, MD 20876 USA
(301) 540-5500, *Fax:* (301) 540-5557
www.mlog.com
sales@mlog.com
Richard Meccarielli, CEO
Janet Turner, SVP Sales/Marketing
Call and contact Center Solutions, Speech Recognition, IVR, Outbound Marketing Solutions and custom application development.

Micron Audio Products Ltd.
216 Little Falls Rd., Cedar Grove, NJ 7009 USA
(973) 857-8150, *Fax:* (973) 857-3756
micronaudio@cs.com
Paul Tepper, President
TRAM lavalier microphones, sls & svc.

Microspace Communications Corp.
3100 Highwoods Blvd., Suite 120, Raleigh, NC 27604 USA
(919) 850-4500, *Fax:* (919) 850-4518
www.microspace.com
uplink@microspace.com
Joseph Amor, Operations Dir
Greg Hurt, General Sales Mgr
Ron Burns, Chief Engineer
Providing video, data & audio transmission svcs designed for antennas as small as 30 inches. Operates on domestic satellites for coverage of North America. Also providing fixed C- & Ku-band uplink svcs for video transmissions supportingapplications such as news, sports, program origination (live or taped); & business TV. Remote & studio production available. Turnaround svc to & from domestic & international satellites.

Microwave Filter Co. Inc.
6743 Kinne St., East Syracuse, NY 13057 USA
(315) 438-4700,(800) 448-1666, *Fax:* (315) 463-1467
www.microwavefilter.com
mfcsales@microwavefilter.com
Carl Fahrenkrug, President
Scott Parsell, General Sales Mgr
Richard Jones, Chief Financial Officer
Filters, traps, combiners & custom networks for TV, radio, CATV, wireless cable, LAN & mobile radio.

Milestek Corp.
1506 I-35W, Denton, TX 76207-2402 USA
(940) 484-9400,(800) 524-7444, *Fax:* (940) 484-9402
www.milestek.com
salesinfo@milestek.com
David McCarthy, President
Mike Guidry, General Manager
Leticia Hill, Finance
Lisa Daniels, Sales
Connectors including both 50 ohm & 75 ohm BNCs, cabling, patching & tools for coaxial cable.

Milestone Technologies Inc.
3101 Skyway Court, Fremont, CA 94539 USA
(510) 651-2454
www.milestonetechnologies.com
info@milestonetechnologies.com
Prem Chand, President/CEO
Tony Silveria, EVP
Jim Schultz, Chief Financial Officer
Data bcstg file transfer software (SATX). Bcst binary files over one-way data nets (DBS, VSAT, TV, FM, VBI, RDS, MPEG2, etc.). Consulting & system integration svcs.

Miller Camera Support, LLC USA
218 Little Falls Rd., Cedar Grove, NJ 7009 USA
(973) 857-8300, *Fax:* (973) 857-8188
www.millertripods.com
info@millertripods.us
Gus Harilaou, General Sales Mgr
Pan & tilt fluid heads, tripods & camera support systems & accessories for DV, ENG & EFP (OB).

Miranda Technologies Inc.
3499 Douglas B. Floreani, Montreal, QC H4S 2C6 CAN
(514) 333-1772,(800) 224-7882, *Fax:* (514) 333-9828
www.miranda.com
ussales@miranda.com
Strath Goodship, CEO
Spiro Plagakis, General Sales Mgr
Digital video interface products for bcstg & postproduction: serializers, digital-to-analog converters, NTSC encoders, computer video interfaces.

Miranda Asia
Unit 1706, Tai Tung Bldg., 8 Fleming Rd., Wanchai, Hong Kong
+852-2539-6987; *Fax:* +852-2539-0804
asiasales@miranda.com

Miranda China
Rm. 2402, Sichuan Bldg., E. Tower, 1 Fuchengmenwai St., Xicheng District, Beijing, 100037 China
+86 10-68364818; *Fax:* +81 10-68364817
chinasales@miranda.com

Miranda Europe
Hithercroft Rd., Wallingford, Oxfordshire, OX10 9DG United Kingdom
+44 (0) 1491 820 000; *Fax:* +44 (0) 1491 820 001
europesales@miranda.com

Miranda France
216 rue de Rosny, 931000 Montreuil, Montreuil, 93100 France
+33 (0) 1 55 86 87 88; *Fax:* +33 (0) 1 55 86 00 29
francesales@miranda.com

Miranda USA
195 Mountain Ave., Springfield, NJ 07081 United States
(973) 379-0089; *Fax:* (973) 379-1953
usssales@miranda.com

EQUIPMENT MANUFACTURERS

Miranda Japan
3-1-17 Nihombashi Ningyacho, Ishii Bldg. 2F, Cjuo-ku, Tokyo, 103-0013 Japan
+81 (0) 3-5644-7533; *Fax:* +81 (0) 3-3662-7555

Mitsubishi Digital Electronics America Inc.
9351 Jeronimo Rd., Irvine, CA 92618 USA
(949) 465-6000, *Fax:* (949) 465-6046
www.mitsubishi-tv.com
Frank De Martin, Operations Dir
David Noranjo, General Sales Mgr
Shoichi Suwa, SVP/General Manager
Portable videotape recorder systems, consumer VCR's & audio visual big screen TV's.

Mobile Video Services Ltd.
1620 Eye St. N.W., Washington, DC 20006 USA
(202) 331-8882, *Fax:* (202) 331-9064
www.mobilevideo.net
Bookfeed@mobilevideo.net
Lawrence VanderVeen, President
Christine Baber, Operations Dir
Complete EFP & ENG svcs, multi-camera remote packages, editing teleco & satellite transmission svcs available. CBS & CNN news feeds available.

MODCOMP Inc.
1500 S. Powerline Rd., Suite A, Deerfield Beach, FL 33442 USA
(954) 571-4600, *Fax:* (954) 571-4700
www.modcomp.com
info@modcomp.com
John P Clary, CEO
Victor Dellovo, President
Ron Cook, Operations Dir
Christina Luis, Promotions Manager
Minicomputer systems, hardware & software for ground stn monitoring & control. SCADA applications & website enabling software.

Modulation Sciences Inc.
12A World's Fair Dr., Somerset, NJ 8873 USA
(732) 320-3090, *Fax:* (732) 302-0206
www.modsci.com
sales@modsci.com
Eric Small, CEO
Judy Mueller, President
With 20+ years experience in the bcst industry, we manufacture full line of FM & TV equipment including: composite clipper, STL's distribution amplifiers, SteroMaxx—Spatial image englarger, modulation monitors, SCA & Data SCA equipment, TVstereo reference decoder, SAP & PRO generators, PRO ch receivers, SAP receivers, NTSC precision video demodulators.

Mohawk
324 Clark Street, Leominster, MA 1453 USA
(978) 537-9961, *Fax:* (978) 537-4358
www.mohawk-cable.com
info@mohawk-cable.com
Jenna Desimone, General Sales Mgr
Joe Barry, Engineering Dir
Leslie Hicks, National Broadcast Sales
Mohawk offers an end to end solution for your HDTV cabling needs. We use LEMO stainless connectors & have many varieties of SMPTE cable. Mohawk is the OEM for fiber & copper camera cable assemblies for all of the major camera manufacturers.

Mole-Richardson Co.
937 N. Sycamore Ave., Hollywood, CA 90038-2384 USA
(323) 851-0111, *Fax:* (323) 851-5593
www.mole.com
info@mole.com
Larry Parker, President
Don Phillips, General Sales Mgr
Michael Parker, President/CEO
Lighting equipment for the motion picture, TV, video & still photographic industries.

Moseley Associates Inc.
82 Coromar Dr., Santa Barbara, CA 93117-3024 USA
(805) 968-9621, *Fax:* (805) 685-9638
www.moseleysb.com
info@moseleysb.com
Bruce Tarr, CFO
Jamal Hamdani, President
Larry Sollecito, General Manager
AM & FM stereo STLs, TV Digital STLs, data transmission systems & telecommunications, digital transmission systems.

Motion Picture Enterprises Inc.
Box 276, Tarrytown, NY 10591-0276 USA
(212) 245-0969, *Fax:* (212) 245-0974
www.mpe.net
mpeny@aol.com
Neal Pilzer, President
Shipping cases, cabinets & cans for film & tape; custom made fibre cases, film & video equipment, supplies, sls, rental & repairs.

Motor Capacitors Inc.
6455 Avondale Ave., Chicago, IL 60631 USA
(773) 774-6666, *Fax:* (773) 774-6690
www.capacitorindustries.com
info@capacitorindustries.com
Terence Noone, President
Liam D, General Manager
Motor-run, motor-start, metalized, oil-filtered, high voltage, film, electrolytic & power capacitors, & R.C. networks.

Motorola Broadband Communications Sector
101 Tournament Dr., Horsham, PA 19044 USA
(215) 674-4800, *Fax:* (215) 323-0242
www.motorola.com/broadband
broadband@motorola.com
Daniel M. Moloney, President
CATV headend & distribution equipment; sub terminals, addressable systems & interactive products.
1330 Capital Pkwy., Lewisville, TX 75057 United States
(972) 323-4100;
Tim Roberti, Rgnl Mgr
6400 S. Fiddler-Green Cir., Englewood, CO 80111 United States
(303) 740-6118;
Pete Wornski, Vp

Motorola Digital Media Systems
1303 E. Algonquin Rd., Schaumburg, 60196
(847) 576-5000
www.motorola.com
Greg Brown, CEO
Patricia B Morrison, President
Karen P. Tandy, Operations Dir
Eduardo Courado, SVP/ Chief Marketing Officer
Gene Delaney, EVP
Mark Moon, EVP

Moviola
Mailing Address: 545 W. 45th St., New York, NY 10036 USA
Second Address: Mavikola Los Angeles, 1135 N Mansfield Ave, Hollywood, CA 90038
(212) 581-7111,(800) 327-3724, *Fax:* (212) 581-7977
Joe Pascal, CEO
Robert Schoenberg, Operations Dir
Michael Blorn Blakstad, Communications Director
Full-svc supplier of videotape, accessories & digital data storage products.

MRPP Inc.
201 W. Chatham St., Suite 202, Cary, NC 27511 USA
(919) 468-1000, *Fax:* (919) 468-1956
www.mrppinc.com
Sheila Ogle, CEO
Sue Toth, President
Procuring, servicing, instal, & sale of bcstg & satellite equipment. Leasing plans available.

Murphy Studio Furniture
4153 N. Bonita St., Spring Valley, CA 91977 USA
(619) 698-4658, *Fax:* (619) 698-1268
www.murphystudiofurniture.com
dennismurphy@cox.net
Dennis Murphy, President/Owner
Design/construction of studio furniture for radio, TV & production facilities. Five modular lines. Custom designs.

Murray Company
1807 Park 270 Dr., Suite 460, St. Louis, MO 63146 USA
(314) 576-2818, *Fax:* (314) 434-5780
www.murray-company.com
Dick Arnold, Founder
John O'Hara, President
Gen construction, design, program mgmt, space planning, project budgeting & consolidation planning.
7300 College, Suite 210, Kansas City, KS 66210
(913) 451 1884; *Fax:* (913) 451-3761

Murry Rosenblum Sound Assoc., Inc.
21-36 33rd Rd., Long Island City, NY 11106 USA
(718) 728-2654, *Fax:* (718) 728-2654
murryrosenblum2@nyc.rr.com
Murry Rosenblum, President
Audio limited wireless microphones—two switchable frequencies—small UHF standard or diversity receiver—pocket transmitter or handhold transmitter.

Musco Mobile Lighting Ltd.
Box 808, 100 First Ave. W., Oskaloosa, IA 52577 USA
(641) 673-0411, *Fax:* (641) 672-1996
www.musco.com
Joe Crookham, President
Jeff McNulty, Operations Dir
Jerome Fynaardt, General Sales Mgr
Leo Kirk, Manager
Jeff Rogers, Sales Executive
Mobile location lighting utilizing 6K HMIs; remote control of pan, tilt & focus.

MUSICAM U.S.A.
Bldg. 4, 670 N. Beers St., Holmdel, NJ 7733 USA
(732) 739-5600, *Fax:* (732) 739-1818
www.musicamusa.com
sales@musicamusa.com
Cindy DeVito, Promotions Manager
Digital Audio codecs for remote bcstg with Bandwidth up to 20 khz for ISDN, POTS or IP.

MYAT Inc.
360 Franklin Tpke., Mahwah, NJ 7430 USA
(201) 684-0100, *Fax:* (201) 684-0104
www.myat.com
sales@myat.com
Philip Cindrich, President
Derek Small, General Manager
Dennis Heymans, General Sales Mgr
Transmision line systems, filters, combiners, UHF & L-band antenna.

Nady Systems Inc.
6701 Shellmound St., Emeryville, CA 94608 USA
(510) 652-2411, *Fax:* (510) 652-5075
www.nady.com
ussales@nady.com
John Nady, CEO
Scott Wunschel, General Sales Mgr
Wireless VMP & AMF products for bcst, film, video, stage, fixed instals. Consumer audio & communication equipment.

Nalpak
1267 Vernon Way, El Cajon, CA 92020-1838 USA
(619) 258-1200, *Fax:* (619) 258-0925
www.nalpakcom.com,www.cases4less.com
nalpaak@nalpak.com
Robert Kaplan, President
Debra Kaplan, Operations Dir
Packaging & Material Handling Products; teffpak,Torm, Magliner, Leatherman, Gerber, Buck, Surefire, Steamlight.

Narda - An L-3 Communications Co.
435 Moreland Rd., Hauppauge, NY 11788 USA
(631) 231-1700, *Fax:* (631) 231-1711
nardamicrowave.com
nardaeast@l-3com.com
Jihn Mega, President
Michael Sanator, Executive Vice President
Portable RF/microwave test instruments, power density meters, coaxial power monitors & meters.

Narda Satellite Networks
435 Moreland Road, Hauppauge, NY 11788 USA
(631) 231-1700, *Fax:* (631) 272-5500
www.nardiamicroware.com
sn.mktg@l-3com.com
John Mega, CEO
Ken Leighton, Operations Dir
Margaret Pawetto, Administration
Turnkey satellite earth stns & networks, SNG & Fly Away electronics, ground communications equipment & M&C systems. Manufactures & implements a full line of earth stn network monitors & control systems.

Narragansett Imaging
51 Industrial Dr., North Smithfield, RI 2896 USA
(401) 762-3800, *Fax:* (401) 767-4407
www.nimaging.com
Bill Ulmschneider, President
Keith Cowling, General Manager
Camera tubes, CCD camera modules.

National Audio Co. Inc.
Box 7100, 309 Water Street, Springfield, MO 65801 USA
(417) 863-1925, *Fax:* (417) 863-7825
www.nationalaudiocompany.com
nac@nactape.com
Steve Stepp, President
Audio Pro-blank audio cassettes, Audio cassette custom duplication, printing & packaging, CDR & DVD blank media,

CDR/DVD custom duplication, printing & packaging, CDR/DVD duplicating & printing equipment, CDR/DVD packing.

National Mobile Television
2740 California St., Torrance, CA 90503 USA
(800) 242-0642,(206) 782-9945, *Fax:* (206) 782-9949
www.nmtv.com
Mark Howorth, Chairman
Mark Howorth, CEO
Frank Coll, VP Operations
Equipment includes: 40' & 34' trailers. Philips LDK-26 cameras with 44X lenses, Ikegami HL-79EAL cameras, Grass Valley switchers, Sony BVH-2000 & BVH-3100 1 VTR's, Chyron 4100 EXB with CCM, Abekas A-53D, Yamaha audio mixers, RTS intercom &IFB, Sony BVE-900 edit on bd.

National Mobile TV - Houston
10 Greenway Plaza, Houston, TX 77046 USA
(713) 627-9270, *Fax:* (713) 871-9617
Tim Jopplin, Operations Dir
Bob Robinson, General Manager
Multi-camera location production company with 4-48' & 1-36' location production trucks. Eng Package & full-service offices in Houston & Dallas. Additional permanent facilities at the Summit in Houston.
6 Communications Complex, 6221 N. O'Connor, Suite 117, Irving, TX 75039 United States
(972) 556-1816; *Fax:* (972) 556-2543

National Steel Erectors Corp.
Box 709, 3315 South Cherokee, Muskogee, OK 74402 USA
(918) 683-6511, *Fax:* (918) 683-0888
www.nsec.com
B.R. Bayless, President
Neal Bayless, Executive Vice President
Bob Scroggins, Contact
Erection of radio, TV & microwave towers, including turnkey construction, from design to completion.

National Video Services Inc.
18 Commerce Rd., Newtown, CT 6470 USA
(203) 270-0677, *Fax:* (203) 270-9619
www.intermedvideo.com
sales@intermedvideo.com
Harry Davies, President
Terry Cavalier, Purchasing Executive
Distribution of video equipment for corporate & industrial use; design & install of TV studios; mfg of video equipment; rsch & engrg.

National Video Tape Co. Inc.
845 N. Church Ct., Elmhurst, IL 60126 USA
(925) 803-1440,(630) 834-3113, *Fax:* (630) 758-0930
nationalvideotape.com
jlittlefield@nationalvideotape.com
Mike Cullen, President
Custom length VHS cassettes; Sony, Fuji, Maxell Panasonic video & data media products. CD/DVD printing & duplication.
1471 Elliott Ave. W., Seattle, WA 98199 United States
(206) 284-3340;
Mari Scimeca, Chairman

Nautel Ltd.
10089 Peggy's Cove Rd., Hackett's Cove, NS B3Z 3J4 CAN
(902) 823-2900, *Fax:* (902) 823-3183
http://www.nautel.com
info@nautel.com
Peter Conlon, President
Time Hardy, Head of Development
Edward Lannotti, General Manager
John Whyte, Promotions Manager
Kevin Rodgers, Customer Service
Solid state AM/FM bcst transmitters.

Nautel Maine Inc.
201 Target Industrial Cir., Bangor, ME 04401 United States

Navitar Inc.
200 Commerce Dr., Rochester, NY 14623 USA
(585) 359-4000, *Fax:* (585) 359-4999
www.navitar.com
info@navitar.com
Julian Goldtein, CEO
Thomas McCune, COO
Jeremy Goldstein, President
Mark Smith, Chief Financial Officer
Projection lenses, LCD, slide & overhead projectors.

NEC America Inc.
6555 N. State Hwy. 161, Irving, TX 75039 USA
(214) 262-2000,(214) 262-6299, *Fax:* (214) 262-2586
www.nec.com
Bruce Blain, General Sales Mgr

VUES on-line digital editing system (video).

Nemal Electronics International Inc.
12240 N.E. 14th Ave., North Miami, FL 33161 USA
(305) 899-0900, *Fax:* (305) 895-8178
www.nemal.com
info@nemal.com
Benjamin Nemser, President
Manufacturer of electronic cable, connectors, assemblies, & interconnect products for use in bcst applications.
Av. Morumbi 7948, Sao Paulo, Brazil
011-5535-2368;
Carlos Heckmann Jr., Gen Mgr

Neumade Products Corp.
30 Pecks Lane 40, Newtown, CT 6470 USA
(203) 270-1100, *Fax:* (203) 270-7778
www.neumade.com
neumadels@aol.com
R.N. Jones, CEO
Gregory Jones, Operations Dir
Film handling & editing equipment; storage facilities for film, slides, videotape, overhead & opaque projectors, motion picture projection systems.

Neutrik U.S.A. Inc.
195 Lehigh Ave., Suite 1, Lakewood, NJ 8701 USA
(732) 901-9488, *Fax:* (732) 901-9608
www.neutrikusa.com
info@neutrikusa.com
James Cowan, President
Julie Applegate, Station Manager
Audio connectors, plugs & jacks, patch panels, patch cord assemblies, circular, industrial connectors & accessories, knobs, BNC jacks & plugs, RJ45, 3-5 mm plugs.

New York City Lites
122 W. 27th St., 12th Floor, New York, NY 10001 USA
(212) 366-9800, *Fax:* (212) 366-5040
www.newyorkcitylites.tv
nycl@nycl.tv
Deke Hazirjian, President/CEo
Lighting design for video & TV.

Newark Electronics
4801 N. Ravenswood Ave., Chicago, IL 60640 USA
(773) 784-5100, *Fax:* (888) 551-4801
www.newark.com
Peter Costello, Chairman
Mike Ruprich, CEO
Paul Buckley, Operations Dir
Barry Litwin, Promotions Manager
Distributor of bcst cable, assemblies, connectors voice/data networking & electronic component parts. Branches throughout the U.S., Canada, U.K. & Germany.

Newdoll Enterprises
3515- B Edison Way, Menlo Park, CA 94025 USA
(650) 365-2843, *Fax:* (650) 365-3057
www.newdollenterprises.com
ron@newdollenterprises.com
Ronald Newdoll, President
High-speed tape duplicating & recording equipment, digital audio logging recorders, audio & videotape conditioners, audio recorders. CD-R recorders for audio & ROM.

Noise Control Corp.
2160 Mars Court, Bakersfield, CA 93308 USA
(800) 606-6473
www.noisecontrol.com
ncc@noisecontrol.com
Steve Anderson, President
Acoustical noise control products.

Norlight Telecommunications Inc.
13935 Bishops Dr., Brookfield, WI 53005 USA
(262) 792-9700, *Fax:* (262) 792-7276
www.norlight.com
Al Cinelli, Chairman
John Cinelli, CEO
John Iber, VP Operations
Robert Rogers SVP, Station Manager
Fiber-optic & microwave transmission of bcst level video.
3617 Oakton St., Skokie, IL 60076 United States
(847) 674-7476;
Dave Pritchard, Dir

Norpak Corporation
10 Hearst Way, Kanata, ON K2L 2P4 CAN
(613) 592-4164, *Fax:* (613) 592-6560
www.norpak.ca
sales@nordak.ca,info@norpak.ca
James Carruthers, President
Michael Dobson, Operations Dir
TV Data Broadcast; Interactive TV; Financial, News, Weather Radar Information Broadcast; HDTV Data Encoding; Closed Captioning; V-Chip; NABTS

Norsat International Inc.
110-4020 Viking Way, Richmond, BC V6V 2L4 CAN
(604) 821-2800,(800) 644-4562, *Fax:* (604) 821-2801
www.norsat.com
Aimee Chan, CEO
Randy Witten, General Sales Mgr
High speed, reliable data transmission products & networks, microware products & worldwide installations of opns STDs, DVB & SAT networks.
The Old School, South Carlton, Lincoln, LN1 2RL
(011) 44 1522 730 800; *Fax:* 011- 44 1522 730 927
smullery@noisat.com
Stan Mullery, Chairman

Beijing Broadcasting Institute
1704-A Union Plaza, 20 Chao Wai Plaza, Beijing, 100029 China
(011) 86 10 65871281; *Fax:* (011) 86 10 65871081

North American Cable Equipment Inc.
1085 Andrew Dr., Suite A, West Chester, PA 19380 USA
(800) 688-9282, *Fax:* (800) 230-1793
www.northamericancable.com
sales@northamericancable.com
Aaron Starr, President
Kirk Davies, General Sales Mgr
Manufacturer of CATV, RF modulators, demodulators & processors.

North Dakota Television L.L.C.
200 N. Fourth St., Bismarck, ND 58501 USA
(701) 255-5757, *Fax:* (701) 255-8220
www.kfyrtv.com
Jim Sande, Programming Director

North Hills Signal Processing
6851 Jericho Tpke., Suite 170, Syosset, NY 11791 USA
(516) 682-7700, *Fax:* (516) 682-7704
www.northhills-sp.com
info@northills-sp.com
Richard Schwarz, General Manager
Manufactures of MIL-STDT553 data bus products & wideband/video transformer. Our standard & custom product, offer unmatched performance & reliability for a wide range of applications in the military, aerospace & industrial OEM markets.

Northeast Towers Inc.
199 Brickyard Rd., Farmington, CT 6032 USA
(860) 677-1999, *Fax:* (860) 677-1300
netowers@ctl.nai.net
Stephen Savino Jr, President
HDTV, TV, Cellular, PCS, AM, FM, CATV & microwave towers; ground systems; maintenance, materials, turnkey instals, specialty coatings, & strobes.

Northeastern Communications Concepts Inc.
40 Benford Dr., Princeton Junction, NJ 8550 USA
(609) 936-0006
www.nccnewyork.com
webmaster@nccnewyork.com
Alfred D'Alessio, President
Bcst design svcs, studio furniture, custom audio equipment, custom data systems/components, cabinets, racks, panels, recording studios construction & prefab.

Northern Power Systems
182 Mad River Park, Waitsfield, VT 5673 USA
(802) 496-2955, *Fax:* (802) 496-2953
www.nothernpower.com
info@northernpower.com
Clint Coleman, President
Remote power systems based on renewable energy inputs (wind/solar); hybrid power systems.

Northrup Grumman
1840 Century Park E., Los Angeles, CA 90067 USA
(310) 553-6262, *Fax:* (310) 553-2076
Ronald Sugar, President
Darryl Fraser, Operations Dir
Film & video cameras for military; video-to-film recorders; optics & optical systems.

Northwest Monitoring Service
Box 70144, Eugene, OR 97401 USA
(541) 345-2236
James Bradley, President
Mthy frequency measurements for AM-FM-TV. Mobile svc includes California, Oregon, Washington, Idaho & Nevada.

NSI
9050 Red Branch Rd., Columbia, MD 21045 USA
(410) 964-8400, *Fax:* (410) 964-9661
www.nsystems.com
sales@nsystem.com
Stephen Neuberth, President
Robert Boshka, Operations Dir
Microwave antennas & remote controls for ENG applications.

NTV International Corporation
645 5th Ave., Suite 303, New York, NY 10022 USA
(212) 660-6900, *Fax:* (212) 660-6998
www.ntvic.com
Jusaburo Hayahii, President
Leo Lahm, Engineering Dir
Yorihosha Kono, VP/Finance

NUCOMM Inc.
101 Bilby Rd., Hackettstown, NJ 7840 USA
(908) 852-3700, *Fax:* (908) 813-0399
www.nucomm.com
Dr. John Payne, CEO
Alan Conen, Sales Engineering Manager
Microwave transmitters, receivers including digital video microwave systems & accessories for both portable & fixed line of sight applications. Modulators/demodulators & color bar generators.

NVISION Products
125 Crown Point Ct., Grass Valley, CA 95945 USA
(530) 265-1000, *Fax:* (530) 265-1021
www.nvision.tv
nvsales@nvision1.com
Charles Meyer, President
Jay Kuca, General Manager
Doug Buterbaugh, General Sales Mgr
Birney Dayton, Chief Engineer
Digital audio & data distribution, conversion, routing & transmission equipment for production/postproduction applications for bcstg industry.

NWL Capacitors
Box 10416, 8550 Monterey Drive, Riviera Beach, FL 33419-0416 USA
(561) 848-9009, *Fax:* (561) 848-9011
www.nwl.com
David Seitz, Owner
Robert Seitz, President
Manufacturers.

O'Connor Professional Camera Support Systems
100 Kalmus Dr., Costa Mesa, CA 92626 USA
(714) 979-3993, *Fax:* (714) 957-8138
www.ocon.com
sales@ocon.com
Joel Johnson, Operations Dir
Robert Low, General Sales Mgr
Jeannine McQuilliam, Chief Engineer
Manufacturer of camera support equipment including fluid heads, tripods & accessories.

Olesen
12800 Foothill Blvd, Sylmar, CA 91342 USA
(818) 407-7800, *Fax:* (818) 407-7868
www.hollywoodrentals.com
info@hollywoodrentals.com
Kelly Koskella, President
Joe Dougherty, Operations Dir
Victor Duran, Chief Engineer
Steve Antman, Chief Marketing Executive
All production supplies, equipment for TV, theater, both live & taped.

Omicron Video
22251 Roscoe Blvd., West Hills, CA 91304 USA
(818) 704-0704, *Fax:* (818) 704-0475
www.omicronvideo.com
sales@omicronvideo.com
Kimiharu Akiyama, Owner
Video/audio distribution equipment. Computer graphics/HDTV distribution equipment.

Omnimount Systems
8201 S. 48th St., Phoenix, AZ 85044 USA
(480) 829-8000, *Fax:* (480) 756-9000
www.omnimount.com
info@omnimount.com
Garrett Weyand, Chairman
Raymond Nakano, CEO
Geoff Miller, President
Mitch Jones, Chief Technical Officer
Loudspeaker mounts-omnidirectional adjustability supporting ounces to hundreds of pounds. Also, flexible, refined mounting systems for TV's/computer monitors & peripherals.

180 Connect
6365 N.W. 6th Way, Suite 200, Ft. Lauderdale, FL 33309 USA
(800) 683-0253, *Fax:* (954) 671-8619
Dalia Rodborne, General Manager
Have been providing Turkey residential/commercial inside premise wiring & outside plant construction svcs for 20 yrs.

Opamp Labs Inc.
1033 N. Sycamore Ave., Los Angeles, CA 90038-2398 USA
(323) 934-3566, *Fax:* (323) 462-6490
www.opamplabs.com
opamplabs@gmail.com
B. Losmandy, President
Amplifiers: audio, video, microphone, line & power. Audio oscillators & transformers. Power supplies, network audio/video feed boxes, audio/video routing switches.

Open Text Digital Media Group
700 King Farm Blvd, One Irvington Circle, Suite 600, Rockville, MD 20850 USA
(519) 888-7111, (800) 499-6544 (in N. America), *Fax:* (519) 888-0677
www.opentext.com
digtalmedia.opentext.com
D Scott Bowen, President/COO
John Schlipp, Vice President

Optical Disc Corp.
10415 Shusher Drive, Sante Fe Springs, CA 90670 USA
(562) 946-3050, *Fax:* (562) 946-6030
www.optical-disc.com
James Wu, President
John Brown, Operations Dir
Ken Shrimplin, Senior VP
Recordable laser video discs, videodisc recording systems & other auxiliary equipment. Compact disc & videodisc mastering systems.

Orban
1525 Alvarado St., San Leandro, CA 94577 USA
(510) 351-3500, *Fax:* (510) 351-0500
www.orban.com
info@orban.com
Charles Jayson Brentlinger, CEO
Bob Orban, Operations Dir
Orban manufacturers bcst audio equipment for radio & TV including processors for TV, FM, AM & HF & the Audicy digital audio workstation, & the Airtime digital audio delivery system.

Ortel
2015 W. Chestnut St., Alhambra, CA 91803 USA
(626) 293-3400, *Fax:* (626) 293-3428
www.emcore.com
docmaster@agere.com
Reuben F. Richards, Chairman
Hong Q. Hou, CEO
Gyo Shinozaki, Promotions Manager
John Ianelli, Chief Engineer
Steven Rizzone, Contact
Signal transmission products, specializing in opto electronics & RF electronics technologies.

Otari USA Sales Inc.
21110 Nordhoff St., Suite G/H, Chatsworth, CA 91311 USA
(818) 734-1785, *Fax:* (818) 734-1786
www.otari.com
sales@otario.com
Nick Higashino, President
Tim Murray, General Sales Mgr
Manufacturer of audio & video cassette loaders & duplicators. Manufacturer of audio mixing consoles, hard disk audio recorders, tape recorders, DAT recorders, minidisc recorders & players, CD changers, digital audio format converters.

Pace Micro Technology P.L.C.
3701 FAU Blvd., Suite 200, Boca Raton, FL 33431 USA
(561) 995-6000, *Fax:* (561) 995-6001
www.pace.com
info@pace.com
Mike McTighe, Chairman
David McKinney, COO
Michael Pulley, President
Tim O'Loughlin, Chief Marketing Officer
Chief Financial Officer, General Sales Mgr
Neil Gaydon, CEO
First DVB MPEG-2 set-top boxes, the first to integrate DOCSIS into a digital cable set-top box & launching the first ever H.264 DVB-S2 high definition set-top box.

Packaged Lighting Systems Inc.
Box 285, 29 Grant St., Walden, NY 12586 USA
(845) 778-3515,(800) 836-1024 (orders), *Fax:* (845) 778-1286
www.packagedlighting.com
info@packagedlighting.com
Hy Hilzen, President
Factory prewired, self-contained TV studio systems complete with lighting/dimming/grid/power distribution.

Panasonic Broadcast & Television Systems Co.
One Panasonic Way, Panazip 2E-7, Secaucus, NJ 7094 USA
(201) 348-5300, *Fax:* (201) 348-5318
www.panasonic.com/broadcast
Don Iwatani, Chairman
Don Iwatani, CEO
John Baisley, President
Robert Harris, Operations Dir
Steve Beck, Principal
MII VCR, D3 ½ digital VCRs, digital processed cameras, Carts (MARC) analog & digital, tapes, DVC pro, D5, Post Box, RAMJA products, monitors, projectors.
One Panasonic Way, 4E-7, Secaucus, NJ 07094 United States
(201) 348-7621;
3330 Cahuenga Blvd. W., Los Angeles, CA 90068 United States
(323) 436-3500;

Panavision New York
540 W. 36th St., New York, NY 10018 USA
(212) 606-0700, *Fax:* (212) 244-4457
www.panavisionnewyork.com
Peter Schnitzler, President
Ira Goodman, Operations Dir
16mm & 35mm motion picture & video equipment, lighting & grip equipment, generators, trucks, dollies & cranes.

Panel Authority Inc.
411 New Ave., Lockport, IL 60441 USA
(815) 838-0488, *Fax:* (815) 838-7852
www.panelauthority.com
preston@panelauthority.com
Preston Wakeland, President
Custom made engraved aluminum connector panels & enclosures.

Paragon Towers Inc.
Box 270655, 3820 North 8th Street, Oklahoma City, OK 73137 USA
(405) 948-3335, *Fax:* (405) 948-3358
www.paragontowersinc.com
charlene@paragontowersinc.com
Melvyn Lieberman, Chairman
Joe James, President
Competitively priced tower mfg, complete line of broadcasting, communications, cellular, microwave, turn-key, bundle package design, full range of tower accessories, guarantee of company's products.
3820 N.W. 8th St., Oklahoma City, OK 73107 United States

Parsons Audio
192 Worcester St., Wellesley, MA 02481 USA
(781) 431-8708, *Fax:* (781) 431-8783
www.paudio.com
sales@paudio.com
Mark Parsons, CEO
Christopher Stabach, General Sales Mgr
Les Arnold, Sales
Rick Scott, Sales
Lenore Fauliso, Sales Support
Equipment & courses for audio recording, production, broadcast, performance, etc. 200+ product lines: Yamaha, Dolby, Digidesign, Tascam, etc. Also, training courses for professionals, taught by masters.

Parsons Manufacturing Corp.
1055 O'Brien Dr., Menlo Park, CA 94025 USA
(650) 324-4726, *Fax:* (650) 324-3051
www.pmccases.com
pmccase@aol.com
Alan Parsons, CEO
Alan Hall, Operations Dir
Instrument carrying cases, shipping cases molded plastic, retracting wheels & recessed hardware.

Paulmar Industries Inc.
39804 North Stonebridge Court, Antioch, IL 60002 USA
(847) 395-2080, *Fax:* (847) 589-2070
www.paulmar.com
sales@paulmar.com
Robert Menary, President
Automatic film, video inspection machines, film & video supplies, DVD repair & rejuvenation equipment.

PC & E
2235 Defoor Hills Rd., Atlanta, GA 30318 USA
(404) 609-9001, *Fax:* (404) 609-9926
www.pce-atlanta.com
Doug Smith, President
Randy Nappier, Operations Dir
Mark Wofford, Promotions Manager
Lighting, grip, camera, stage & generator rental. Full svc sls department with expendables.

Peavey Electronics
5022 Hartley Peavey Dr., Meridian, MS 39305 USA
(601) 483-5365, *Fax:* (601) 486-1278
www.peavey.com
marketing@peavey.com
Hartley Peavey, CEO
Recording & audio products, SMPTE/MIDI synchronization signal processing, reference monitors, microphones & production mixing consoles.

Peerless Industries Inc.
3215 W. North Ave., Melrose Park, IL 60160 USA
(708) 865-8870, *Fax:* (708) 865-0760
www.peerlessindustries.com
info@peerlessindustries.com
Mike Campagna, President
John Potts, Vice President
Joe Mitchell, General Manager
Larry Zabinski, Finacial Executive
Adrian Czornik, Engineering Dir
Video Mounting hardware including stands, carts & brackets for floor, furniture, wall & ceiling applications.

Penn Elcom Inc.
12691 Monarch St., Garden Grove, CA 92841 USA
(714) 230-6200, *Fax:* (714) 230-6222
www.penn-elcom.com
california@penn-elcom.com
Roger Williams, Chairman
Frank McCourt, President
Phil Stratford, General Manager
Zon Mendoza, HR Executive
Hardware & accessories for flightcases, racks, speaker cabinets, stagelights & trussing.

Penny & Giles Inc.
665 Baldwin Park Blvd, City of Industry, CA 91746 USA
(562) 531- 6500, *Fax:* (562) 531-4020
www.pgcontrols.com
u.s.sales@pennyandgiles.com
Chris Thomson, Operations Dir
Neil Parker, Principal
Studio faders; joystick controllers; T-Bar controllers for video effects generators; MIDI mgr & D.A.W. interface.
Cwmfelinfach, Gwent, NP1 7HZ
(44) 1495-202024;

Penta Laboratories
9740 Cozycroft Ave., Chatsworth, CA 91311 USA
(818) 882-3872,(800) 421-4219, *Fax:* (818) 882-3968
www.pentalabs.com
Veronica Calderon, CFO
Steve Sanett, President
Marianne Griego, General Sales Mgr
Electron tubes distribution & mfg.
PENTA LABS OF BRASIL-NOVO ENDEREÇO
Av. Vicente Rao, 1636 -Jd Petrópolis - São Paulo - CEP 04636-001,
Tel.: 55 11 5181-5555;

Pentax Imaging Co.
663 17th Street, Suite 2600, Denver, CO 80202 USA
(303) 799-8000, *Fax:* (303) 728-0226
www.pentaxusa.com
Ned Bunnel, President
Bill Zani, General Sales Mgr
Manufacture camera lens.

Performance Power Technologies
Box 947, Roswell, GA 30077 USA
(770) 475-3192
www.performance-power.com
poweringcatv@yahoo.com
Jud Williams, President
Standby power supplies, AC power supplies & battery testers.

PerkinElmer
35 Congress St., Salem, MA 1970 USA
(978) 745-3200, *Fax:* (978) 745-0894
www.perkinelmer.com
opto@perkinelmer.com
John Pautler, Operations Dir

High-medium-intensity aviation obstruction lighting & beacons. FAA-approved; StrobeGuard & FlashGuard.

Pesa Headquarters
103 Quality Cir., Suite 210, Huntsville, AL 35806 USA
(256) 726-9200, *Fax:* (256) 726-9271
www.pesa.com
sales@qustream.com
Howard Sutton, Chairman
Chuck Tillett, President
Ricky Ng, Chief Financial Officer
Manufacturer of HD/SD video/audio Routing switchers, signal processing & distribution.
Atlanta Branch
3305 Breckinridge Blvd., Suite 118, Duluth, GA 30096 United States
(770) 806-0234;

Peter Albrecht Company Inc.
6250 Industrial Ct., Greendale, WI 53129-2432 USA
(414) 421-6630, *Fax:* (414) 421-9091
www.peteralbrecht.com
sales@peteralbrecht.com
T.C. Ziolkowski, President/Owner
Don Lemoine, Engineering Tech
Motorized studio battens, plaks & other rigging systems. Tension Grids, Chandelier Hoist, Banner Hoists designed & installed.

Peter W. Dahl Co. Inc.
5869 Waycross, El Paso, TX 79924 USA
(915) 751-2300, *Fax:* (915) 751-0768
www.pwdahl.com
pwdco@pwdahl.com
Peter Dahl, President
Gary Komassa, Operations Dir
Heavy duty plate, power, filament, modulation transformers & reactor; single- & three-phase rectifiers, vacuum & oil filled capacitors.

Phasetek Inc.
550 California Road, Unit 11, Quakertown, PA 18951 USA
(215) 536-6648, *Fax:* (215) 536-7180
www.phasetekinc.com
sales@phasetekinc
David Gorman, President
Robin Nelson, Operations Dir
Matthew Nelson, Purchasing Executive
Kurt Gorman, President
Manufactures AM/MW antenna, phasing equipment, antenna tuning units, diplexers, dummy loads, RF inducters & components.

Philip-Cooke Co.
132 N. 11th St., Allentown, PA 18102 USA
(800) 887-0950,(610) 437-2251, *Fax:* (610) 437-1610
www.philipcooke.com
kentk@philipcooke.com
Kent Kjellgren, President
Distribute video cassette duplications equipment & CDs.

Phillystran Inc.
151 Commerce Dr., Montgomeryville, PA 18936 USA
(215) 368-6611, *Fax:* (215) 362-7956
www.phillystran.com
info@phillystran.com
Wynne Wister III, President
Kenneth Knight, General Sales Mgr
Robert Lombardo, Managing Director
Phillystran HPTG; electrically transparent, maintenance free tower guy system; specially designed systems for high-power applications.

Phoenix E N G, Inc.
6832 Foxhill Ln., Cincinnati, OH 45236 USA
(513) 891-1444, *Fax:* (513) 891-3453
engphoenix@aol.com
Kevin Jordan, President
Bob Braun, Operations Dir
One man band live trucks, vans, 4-wheel-drive. On-location radio vehicles & production trucks.

Photo Research
9731 Topanga Canyon Pl., Chatsworth, CA 91311 USA
(818) 341-5151, *Fax:* (818) 341-7070
www.photoresearch.com
Francis Dominic, President/CEO
Mike Klein, Chief Marketing Officer
George Ward, Engineering Tech
Brightness photometers, footcandle meters, telephotometers, spectroradiometers, spectral & spatial scanners.

Photomart Cine-Video Inc.
6327 S. Orange Ave., Orlando, FL 32809 USA
(407) 851-2780,(800) 443-2901, *Fax:* (407) 851-2553
www.photomartusa.com
info@photomartusa.com
Jeffrey Bova, President
Sls, svc, of professional support equipment, supplies for video, film & still photography.

Pinnacle Systems Inc.
385 Rovendale Drive, Mountain View, CA 94043 USA
(650) 526-1600, *Fax:* (650) 526-1601
www.pinnaclesys.com
sales@pinnaclesys.com
Sharad Rastogi, General Manager
Tanguy Leborgne, Promotions Manager
Manufacturer of a complete set of home video editing & PCTV viewing tools for the consumer market.

Pinta Acoustic Inc.
2601 49th Ave. N., Suite 400, Minneapolis, MN 55430 USA
(612) 520-3620,(800) 662-0032, *Fax:* (612) 521-5639
www.pinta-acoustic.com
sales@pinta-acoustic.com
Mark Frederick, CFO
Sonex accoustical products including wall panels & ceiling tiles.

Pinzone Engineering Group Inc.
10142 Fairmount Rd., Newbury, OH 44065 USA
(304) 368-7950, *Fax:* (440) 729-5591
www.pinzone.com
systemsengineering@pinzone.com
Basil Pinzone, President
Bernadette Pinzone, Vice President
Satellite Uplinks Systems, Turnkey, Site Engineering, AM Broadcast Antenna- Anti-Skywave Antenna.

Pirod Inc.
1200 N Oak Drive, Plymouth, IN 46563 USA
(574) 936-4221, *Fax:* (574) 936-6796
www.pirod.com
pirod@pirod.com
Myron Noble, CEO
Hillary Asher, General Sales Mgr
Frank Epps, Engineering Dir
Solid-rod towers, monopoles & tower accessories for cellular, PCs, bdcst, microwave & two-way communication.

Pixel Instruments Corp.
20526 Prospect Road, Saratoga, CA 95032 USA
(408) 871-1975, *Fax:* (408) 871-1976
www.pixelinstruments.tv
info@pixelinstruments.tv
Mirko Vojnovic, President
Designs & manufactures innovative audio & video signals processing products with an emphasis on the measurement & correction of lips sync errors. These products are used in a wide range of bcst, cable TV, video production & relatedapplications. Current products include the LipTracker Lip Sync Analyer, Audio Delay Synchronizers for automatic lip sync correction & Tally/GPI Interfaces.

Plastic Reel Corp. of America
40 Triangle Blvd., Carlstadt, NJ 7072 USA
(201) 933-5100, *Fax:* (201) 933-9468
info@prcofamerica.com
Benjamin Zuk, President
Pat Baccarella, Executive Vice President
Carole Pinker, President
Videotape, audiotape reels, boxes, video cassette mailing, storage boxes, video supplies, recording media, video & audio.
5410 W. Roosevelt Rd., Chicago, IL 60644 United States
(800) 929-0356;
Edwin Santani, Office Mgr
8140 Webb Ave., North Hollywood, CA 91605 United States
(818) 504-0400;
Carole Pinker, Vp

PMTV Producers Management Television
681 Moore Rd., Suite 100, King of Prussia, PA 19406
(610) 768-1770, *Fax:* (610) 768-1773
www.pmtv.com
mailto.pmtv@pmtv.com
Brian Powers, President
Danna Doo, Operations Dir
Rob Schmoll, SVP
Full-svc mobile TV production company, providing mobile units, crews, satellite svcs, lighting, staging, etc. for sports, entertainment & teleconferences worldwide.

Polyline
845 N Church Ct., Elmhurst, IL 60126 USA

(800) 701-7689, *Fax:* (800) 816-3330
www.polylinecorp.com
sales@polylinecorp.com
Edwin Kaiser, President
Ray Kaiser, Marketing Executive
Michael Sandborn, Manager
Stock media packaging for DVD, CD, VHS & audio plus bulk CD-R, DVD-R, Blu-ray media. Disc publishing equipment & supplies are also available.

Polyline West Coast Distribution Ctr.
4408 W. Vanowen St., Burbank, CA 91505 United States

PortaBrace
940 Water Street, North Bennington, VT 5257 USA
(802) 442-8171, *Fax:* (802) 442-9118
www.portabrace.com
info@portabrace.com
Gregg Haythorn, President
Mike D'Angelo, Station Manager
Soft carrying cases for professional portable video/audio equipment.

Potomac Instruments, Inc.
932 Philadelphia Avenue, Silver Springs, MD 21704-7258 USA
(301) 696-5550, *Fax:* (301) 696-5553
www.pi-usa.com
sales@pi-usa.com
David Harry, COO
Euy Berry, Manager, Special Projects
Antenna monitors, field strength meters, repairs and calibration.

Power & Telephone Supply Co.
2673 Yale Ave., Memphis, TN 38112 USA
(901) 324-6116, *Fax:* (901) 320-3082
www.ptsupply.com
Jim Pentecost, President
Laburn Dye, Operations Dir
Larry Smith, Vice President
Full-line supplier of communication products, including telecom, data & cable TV.
16666 S.W. 72nd, Bldg. 12, Tigard, OR 97224 United States
(503) 620-4909; *Fax:* (503) 620-9074
Andy Baker, Chairman
Box 244, Rt. 272, Reamstown, PA 17567 United States
(215) 267-4991; *Fax:* (215) 267-4367
Don Skinner, Chairman
Box 1856, 2950 Greensboro St., Lexington, NC 27292 United States
(704) 249-0256; *Fax:* (704) 249-7475
Don Skinner, Chairman
3107 S.W. 61st St., Bldg. D, Des Moines, IA 50321 United States
(515) 244-4375; *Fax:* (515) 244-4757
Doug McPhee, Chairman
12314 Bell Ranch Rd., Los Angeles, CA 90670 United States
(310) 903-1701; *Fax:* (310) 903-1705
Sonny Dickinson, Chairman
7535 N.W. 52nd St., Miami, FL 33166 United States
(305) 597-0091; 597-0262;
Tommy Browder, Chairman

Powr-Ups Corp.
One Roned Rd., Brookhaven Red Plaza, Shirley, NY 11967 USA
(631) 345-5700, *Fax:* (631) 345-0060
Steven Summer, President
DC-motor controls.

Precision Microproducts of America
#1 Comac Loop, Unit 13, Ronkonkoma, NY 11779 USA
(631) 580-3456, *Fax:* (631) 580-3003
www.p-m-a.com
sales@p-m-a.com
Carlos Fernades, President
Photographic processing machines & accessories.

Prime Image, Inc.
662 Giguere Ct., Suite C, San Jose, CA 95133-1742 USA
(408) 867-6519, *Fax:* (408) 926-7294
www.primeimageinc.com
ssales@primeimageinc.com,adrienne@primeimageinc.com
Walter Lornak Jr, CEO
Rodney Hampton, Operations Dir
Richard Detore, Chief Financial Officer
Bob Waligunda, Promotions Manager
Provides digital progmg time reduction/editingequipment; audio & video delays; transcoding time base correctors; synchronizers; digital standards converters; computer video products.

Prisma Packaging
2302 West Claibourn Street, Milwaukee, WI 53188 USA
(414) 342-6464, *Fax:* (414) 342-0932
www.prismapkg.com
info@prismapkg.com
Richard Schmaelzle, President
Printer manufacturer specializing in presentation folders, media kits, sls kits & videocassette packaging.

Pro Video & Film Equipment Co. Inc.
11425 Mathis Ave., Studio 40, Dallas, TX 75234 USA
(972) 869-9990,(888) 869-9998, *Fax:* (972) 869-0145
www.provideofilm.com,www.provideofilm.com
providfilm@aol.com
Bill Reiter, President
Stephanie Fox, Promotions Manager
Used equipment dealer specializing in video, bcst, film, lighting, audio. Consignment, sales, leasing & appraisal svcs available. Service & repairs.

ProAudio.com/Crouse-Kimzey Company
1320 Post & Paddock Rd, Ste 200, Grand Prairie, TX 75050 USA
(800) 433-2105, *Fax:* (972) 623-2800
www.proaudio.com
sales@proaudio.com
John Paul Kimzey, President
Mark Bradford, Operations Dir
Broadcast & Pro Audio Equipment Sales

Crouse Kimzey/Mid-America
9170 South U.S. Hwy. 27, Lynn, IN 47355 United States
(877) 223-2221; *Fax:* (765) 874-2540
Barry Pike, Acct Mgr

Crouse-Kimzey of Missouri
381 Molly Ln., Rockaway Beach, MO 65740
(417) 561-1050 (800) 955-6800; *Fax:* (417) 561-1052
Bill Wallace, Acct Mgr

Crouse-Kimzey of Colorado
4125 Novia Dr., Colorado Springs, CO 80911 United States
(800) 257-6233; *Fax:* (719) 392-8876
Lee Edwards, Acct Mgr

Production Intercom Inc./Technical Projects
Box 3247, Barrington, IL 60011-3247 USA
(800) 562-5872, *Fax:* (847) 381-4360
www.beltpack.com
info@beltpack.com
Glenn mullis, President
Sibbelina Mullis, Operations Dir
Unique talent receiver (IFB), small to large intercom systems, headsets for cameras & new half-duplex wireless system.

Products International Inc.
9030 Junction Circle, Annapolis Junction, MD 20723 USA
(800) 638-2020, *Fax:* (240) 568-3948,(800) 545-0058
info@prodintl.com
William Siegel, President
Equipment, instruments, tools, supplies for electronic production, maintenance & svc.

Professional Communications Systems
5426 Beaumont Center Blvd., Suite 350, Tampa, FL 33634 USA
(800) 447-4714, *Fax:* (813) 886-9477
www.pcomsys.com
info@pcomsys.com
Tony Stephens, President
William Blush, VP Sales
Consulting, design, procurement, systems integration, training & support.
8930 State Road 84, #315, Davie, FL 33324 United States
(954) 472-9400; *Fax:* (954) 424-6065
Charles Ross, Chairman
340 Summer Cover Circle, St. Augustine, FL 32086 United States
(904) 797-7133; *Fax:* (904) 797-7135
Ed Kothera, Chairman
2001 Augusta Ave., Pensacola, FL 32507
(850) 455-9800;
Hardy Morris, Chairman
2800 Old Dawson Road, Suite 2, PMB 206, Albany, GA 31707 United States
(229) 439-4954; *Fax:* (229) 434-0719
Karl Laster, Chairman
11921 S.W. 144th St., Miami, FL 33186 United States
(305) 253-4900; *Fax:* (305) 253-2551
Lloyd Hicks, Chairman
7051 University Blvd., Suite 310, Winter Park, FL 32792 United States
(407) 657-6421; *Fax:* (407) 657-6475

Professional Sound Corp.
28085 Smyth Dr., Valencia, CA 91355 USA
(661) 295-9395, *Fax:* (661) 295-8398
www.professionalsound.com
sales@professionalsound.com
Ron Meyer, President
Debby Meyer, Promotions Manager
Design, manufacture of portable sound recording products for film & video industries

Professional Sound Services Inc.
311 W. 43rd St., Suite 1100, New York, NY 10036 USA
(212) 586-1033, *Fax:* (212) 586-0970
www.pro-sound.com
Rich Topham, President
Wireless microphones, wireless, wired intercoms, IFB, telephone interfaces, analog, digital recorders, mixers, lavaliers, boompoles.Sls, rentals & svc.

Prophet Systems Innovations
214 Spruce Street, Ogallala, NE 69153 USA
(877) 774-1010, *Fax:* (308) 284-4181
www.prophetsys.com
prophetsales@prophetsys.com
Kevin Lockhart, President
Tim Gieschen, President/Operations
Tanya Gieschen, Director/Information Services

Protech Audio Corp.
1158 Cedar River Road, Indian Lake, NY 12842 USA
(518) 648-6410, *Fax:* (518) 648-6395
sales@protechaudio.com
Bill Murphy, President
Dugan Automatic Mixing Controllers, Audio Distribution Amplifiers, Dugan Automatic Mixers

Prysmian Communications Cables and Systems USA, LLC
700 Industrial Dr., Lexington, SC 29072-3755 USA
(803) 951-4800, *Fax:* (803) 951-4898
www.prysmianusa.com
Martin Hanchard, CEO
Brian DiLascia, Operations Dir
ISO 9001-registered manufacturer of fiber-optic cables & Fiber to the Home (FTTH) solutions.

QEI Corporation
Box 805, One Airport Drive, Williamstown, NJ 8094 USA
(856) 728-2020, *Fax:* (856) 629-1751
www.qei-broadcast.com
qeisales@qei-broadcast.com
Bruce Sadzean, President
Rick Harvey, Vice President
John Turzanski, Purchasing Executive

Qintar Technologies Inc.
827 Pleasant Dale Place, Westlake Village, CA 91362 USA
(818) 991-7300, *Fax:* (818) 889-7400
www.qintar.com
sales@qintar.com
Randall Tishkoff, President
Active & passive devices for CATV, amplifiers, filters, connectors, wall plates & wiring products. We also make OEM and custom products.

QSC Audio Products Inc.
1675 MacArthur Blvd., Costa Mesa, CA 92626-1440 USA
(714) 754-6175, *Fax:* (714) 754-6174
www.qscaudio.com
Pat Quilter, Chairman
Barry Andrews, CEO
Gregg McLogan, General Sales Mgr
John Andrews, COO
Professional power amplifiers, dual monaural power amplifiers, plug-in accessory products, integrated amplifiers, music & paging system.

QTV
306 Fifth Ave., 3rd Fl., New York, NY 10001 USA
(212) 929-7755, *Fax:* (212) 929-2105
www.qtv.com
sales@qtv.com
Aaron Brady, General Sales Mgr
Steven Carofone, Manager
Computer prompter software. 9, 12 & 15 on-camera prompters. Lightweight flat panel prompters.
19 W. 21st St., New York, NY 10010
(212) 929-7755; *Fax:* (212) 929-2105
Steve Carofalo, Gen Mgr
5919 W. 3rd St., Los Angeles, CA 90036 United States
(213) 936-6195;
Steve Hulkower, Gen Mgr

Quality Tower Erectors Inc.
2280 10th St. S.E., Largo, FL 33771 USA

EQUIPMENT MANUFACTURERS

(727) 585-6176, *Fax:* (727) 581-3277
Robert Diamond, President/Owner
QTE offers a full line of tower services in addition to our other offerings. Now more than ever, QTE is the complete soloution for your communication site & asset needs. Turn Key civil services, erection, antenna systems, microwave,cellular, painting, turnkey service & tower site rental services included.

Quantel Inc.
1950 Old Gallows Rd., Suite 101, Vienna, VA 22182 USA
(703) 448-3199, *Fax:* (703) 448-3189
www.quantel.com
Tom McGowan, CEO
Steve Owen, Promotions Manager
Quantel is the world's leading designer & manufacturer of digital image processing & manipulation products for video, film & print.
5 Concourse Pkwy., Suite 330, Atlanta, GA 30338 United States
(770) 804-5470; *Fax:* (770) 804-5479
Dan Wingard, Chairman
111 W. 57th St., 10th Fl., New York, NY 10019 United States
(212) 977-4877; *Fax:* (212) 977-6539
Dave Saadatmandi, Chairman
8501 Wilshire Blvd., Suite 340, Los Angeles, CA 90212 United States
(310) 652-9227; *Fax:* (310) 657-8869
Mark Grasso, Chairman
1Yonge St., Suite 1100, Toronto, ON M5E 1E5 Canada
(416) 362-9522;
Mark Northeast, Chairman
100 Bush St., Suite 1910, San Francisco, CA 94104 United States
(650) 225-9036 (415) 263-1300; *Fax:* (650) 225-9091
Tom McGowan, Chairman
541 N. Fairbanks, Suite 1225, Chicago, IL 60611 United States
(312) 755-1766; *Fax:* (312) 755-1767

Quick-Set International Inc.
3650 Woodhead Dr., Northbrook, IL 60062-1895 USA
(847) 498-0700, *Fax:* (847) 498-1258
www.quickset.com
Andy Lareau, President
Jim Fenning, General Sales Mgr
Dan Clove, Sales
Don Zeilenga, Finance Executive
Instrument positioning equipment. Tripods, pan & tilts.

R.L. Drake Holdings LLC
9900 Springboro Avenue, Miamisburg, OH 45342 USA
(937) 746-4556, *Fax:* (937) 806-1510
www.rldrake.com
bcyearbook@rldrake.com
Ron Wysong, CEO
Andy Ruffin, General Sales Mgr
Philip Hawkins, Sales
Analog, digital cable headend equipment including receivers, modulators, processors, accessories for reception & distribution of progmg.
655 The Queensway, Peterborough, ON K9J 7M1 Canada
(705) 742-3122;
Steve Roe, Sls Mgr

Radian Communication Services Inc
461 Cornwall Rd., Box 880, Oakville, ON L6J 5C5 CAN
(905) 844-1242, *Fax:* (905) 844-8837
www.radiancorp.com
info@radiancorp.com
H Douglas Tipple, President/CEO
David Hahn, Vice President
Design, supply, instal of bcst transmitters, antennas & towers.

Radio Aids Inc.
313 Kintzele Rd., Michigan City, IN 46350 USA
(219) 879-2215, *Fax:* (219) 874-8239
John Carpenter, President
Measurement of occupied bandwidth, TV aural & visual, radio carriers, subcarriers, pilots, STL/TSL links.

Radio Computing Services (RCS)
445 Hamilton Ave., White Plains, NY 10601 USA
(914) 428-4600, *Fax:* (914) 428-5922
www.rcsworks.com
info@rcsworks.com
Philippe Generali, President
Mike Powell, Operations Dir
Digital studio automation & digital audio ripping/analysis, music scheduling, traf, sls, newsroom & talk show software/hardware, internet/streaming tools.
10 Anson Rd, 10-10 International Plaza, Singapore, 079903 Sin
+65 6324 6658; *Fax:* 65-6324-6659
cfawell@attglobel.net
Colin Fawell, Gen Mgr
Borsigallee 37, Frankfurt, 60388
49-610-973-4450; *Fax:* 49-610-973-4499
info@rcseurope.de
Karl Kessler, Gen Mgr
262 Hart Niwas, 30th Rd., Bandra Mumboi (West), 400050 India
+91 22 697 1600; *Fax:* +91 22 695 5760
Elliot Stechman, Chairman
83 Ave. Philippe Auguste, Paris, 75011 France
33-1-53-27-36-36; *Fax:* 33- 1-53- 27- 36-60
Eric Vanryckeghem, Chairman

RCS (NZ) Ltd.
33 Sir William Pickering Dr., Christchurch, 8005 New Zealand
+64.3.358.4333; *Fax:* +64.3.358.4330
info@rcs.co.nz www.rsc.co.nz
Ian Campbell, Chairman
Box 32060, 410 #5 Rd., Richmond, BC V6X 3R9 Canada
(604) 986-4468; *Fax:* (604) 986-4469
Ross Langbell, Chairman

Radio Design Labs. (RDL)
659 N. 6th St., Prescott, AZ 86301 USA
(805) 684-5415, *Fax:* (805) 684-9316
www.rdlnet.com
sales@rdlnet.com
Joel Bump, President
Daniel Bump, General Sales Mgr
Full line of microphone & line level amplifiers, mixers, DAs & processors.

Radio Engineering Industries Inc.
6534 L St., Omaha, NE 68117 USA
(402) 339-2200, *Fax:* (402) 339-1704
www.radioeng.com
sales@radioeng.com
Terry Jukes, CEO
Dave Ruback, President
Gunnar Guenette, Promotions Manager
Sls, svc of bcst equipment, amplifiers, paging systems, SCA & coml sound equipment.

Radio Frequency Systems
200 Pondview Dr., Meriden, CT 06450-7195 USA
(203) 630-3311, *Fax:* (203) 634-2272
www.rfsworld.com
sales.americas@rfsworld.com
Bill Bayne, President
Bob Braun, Operations Dir
Rick Kluesner, Controller
John Gu, Chief Technical Officer
Rigid coaxial line (7/8 to 9 3/16), FM antennas, FM, VHF/UHF IFTS, MMDS, TV antennas, dehydrators, instal accesories, RF, microwave antenna subsystems, instal & field svc.

Radio Research Instrument Co. Inc.
584 N. Main St., Waterbury, CT 6704 USA
(203) 753-5840, *Fax:* (203) 754-2567
www.radioresearch.thomasregister.com
radiores@prodigy.net
E. Doyle, President
Sy Chaimovich, Chief Engineer
P. Plishner, President
Provides radar systems, threat emitters & spare parts; complete maintenance facility for repair.

Radio Systems Inc.
601 Heron Dr., Logan Township, NJ 08085-1741 USA
(856) 467-8000, *Fax:* (856) 467-3044
www.radiosystems.com
sales@radiosystems.com
Daniel Braverman, President
Gerrett Conover, Operations Dir
Analog, digital & Live-wire-compatible audio consoles, distribution amplifiers, low-power TIS/HAR AM transmitters, clock & timer systems, telephone hybrids, the StudioHub+wiring system & IP-Connect, a licensed 18 GHz digitalstudio-to-transmitter link.

Radiodetection/Riser Bond
154 Portland Rd., Bridgton, ME 4009 USA
(207) 647-9495, *Fax:* (207) 647-9496
www.dielectrictechnologies.com
bridgton@radiodetection.spx.com
Zenya Brackett, Operations Dir
Paul Sherman, General Sales Mgr
Electronic test equipment; cable fault locators; time domain reflectometer.

RAM SYSTEMS, LLC
Box 278, Wauconda, IL 60084-0277 USA
(800) 779-7575,(847) 487-0910, *Fax:* (847) 487-2440
WWW.RAMSYSTEMSONLINE.COM
SALES@RAMSYSTEMSONLINE.COM
Ron Mitchell, President
Switchers (audio & video) mixers, intercom systems, audio/video DAs, systems engrg & custom cabinetry.

Raven Screen Corp.
112 Spring St., Monroe, NY 10950 USA
(212) 534-8408,(845) 782-1844, *Fax:* (845) 782-1840
www.ravenscreen.com
info@ravenscreen.com
Martin Soss, President
Manual, motorized & custom projection screens & materials.

Record/Play Tek Inc.
Box 790, 112 E. Vistula St., Bristol, IN 46507-0790 USA
(574) 848-5233, *Fax:* (574) 848-5333
www.recordplaytek.com
stoll@recordplaytek.com
Michael Stoll, CEO
Voice logging recorders 911, cassette, reel-to-reel, VHS, computer CDR & DVD+ R.

Recortec Inc.
1650 Berryessa Rd., San Jose, CA 95133-1026 USA
(408) 928-1480, *Fax:* (408) 729-3661
www.recortec.com
info@recortec.com
George Walls, COO
Lester Lee, President
Manufacturer of coml disc players & LCD players.

Reel-O-Matic Inc.
6408 S. Eastern Ave., Oklahoma City, OK 73149 USA
(405) 672-0000,(888) 873-4000, *Fax:* (405) 672-7200
www.reel-o-matic.com
Terry Simmons, President
Mark Zercher, Operations Dir
Russell Maddox, Engineering Tech
Equipment to re-spool, coil, measure & distribute cable.

Rees Associates Inc.
9211 Lake Hefner Pkwy., Suite 300, Oklahoma City, OK 73120 USA
(405) 942-7337, *Fax:* (405) 948-1261
www.rees-associates.com
C. Leroy James, COO
Frank Rees, President
Ralph S. Blackman, Operations Dir
William Yost, Vice President
Steven Lawson, Vice President
Bcst & production facility design; architectural svcs; studio design; equipment planning; facility business plans; interior design & consulting.
1801 N. Lamar St., Suite 600, Dallas, TX 75202 United States
(214) 522-7337;
951 Peachtree St. N.E., Atlanta, GA 30309
(404) 351-6869;
7810 N. Forker Rd., Spokane, WA 99217
(509) 921-1057;

Register Communications
1691 Forsyth St., Macon, GA 31201 USA
(478) 745-5500, *Fax:* (478) 745-0500
www.registerdata.com
sales@registerdata.com
Lowell Register, President
Ricky Lockerman, General Sales Mgr
Digital audio automation systems for live assist, satellite, traf & billing software packages for radio & TV.

Renkus-Heinz Inc.
4700 West Chase Avenue, Foothill Ranch, CA 92610-3510 USA
(949) 588-9997, *Fax:* (949) 588-9514
www.renkus-heinz.com
sales@renkus-heinz.com
Harro Heinz, President
Carl Dorwaldt, Promotions Manager
Reference point arrays, powered network loudspeakers, R-control remote supervision network. Reference point arrays, powered network loudspeakers.

Research Technology International Inc.
4700 Chase Ave., Lincolnwood, IL 60712-1689 USA
(847) 677-3000,(800) 323-7520, *Fax:* (847) 677-1311
www.rtico.com
sales@rtico.com
Ray Short, President
Thomas Boyle, Operations Dir
Bill Wolavka, General Sales Mgr
Videotape evaluator/cleaners; degaussers; storage & care, supplies, film cleaners. CD/DVD cleaners-restorers inspectors.

RF Specialties Group
22406 N.E. 159th St., Kearney, MO 64060 USA

(800) 467-7373, *Fax:* (816) 628-4508
www.rfspec.com
rfmo@uniteone.net
Patricia Kreger, Chairman
Chris Kreger, Operations Dir
John Sims, General Sales Mgr
Full-line radio bcst equipment suppliers. AM & FM transmitters, towers, lines, antenna systems, studios, microwave & digital systems.

RF Specialties of Missouri, Inc.
22406 N.E. 159th St., Kearney, MO 64060 United States
(800) 467-7373 (816) 628-5959; *Fax:* (816) 628-4508
rfmo@uniteone.net
Chris Kreger, Chairman
John Sims, CEO/COO

RF Specialties of Asia Corporation
4958 Guerrero St., Poblacion, Makati City, Metro Manila, 15239 Philippines
+63-2-412-4327; *Fax:* +63-2-895-6509
eedmiston@rfsasia.com
Ed Edmiston, Chairman

RF Specialties of Missouri, Inc.
1651 Capri Lane, Richmond, IN 47374-1501 United States
888-966-1990; *Fax:* 800-859-5481
rf@insightbb.com
Rick Funk, Chairman

RF Specialties of Pennsylvania, Inc.
40 Settlement Hill, New Ipswich, NH 03071 United States
(603) 878-0618 (800) 485-8684; *Fax:* (603) 878-1527
sam_on_the_hill@Monad.net
S.A. Matthews, Chairman

RF Specialties of California
3463 State St., Suite 229, Santa Barbara, CA 93105 United States
(805) 682-9429 (800) 346-6434; *Fax:* (805) 682-5170
rfsca@aol.com
Sam Lane, Chairman

RF Specialties of Florida
4706 Young Rd., Crestview, FL 32539 United States
(850) 423-7335 (800) 476-8943; *Fax:* (850) 423-7331
rfoffl@aol.com
William Hoisington, Chairman

RF Technologies Corp.
1 Gendron Dr., Lewiston, ME 4240 USA
(207) 777-7778, *Fax:* (207) 777-7784
www.rftechnologies.net
George Harris, President
Peter Robicheau, Operations Dir
Bill Ammons, General Sales Mgr
Designs & manufactures high-power bcst RF nets, components for FM & TV bcstrs. Products include antennas, diplexers, combiners, filters, switches, coax, waveguides & coaxal.

Richardson Electronics
PO Box 393, 40W267 Keslinger Rd., LaFox, IL 60147 USA
(630) 208-2200, *Fax:* (630) 208-2662
broadcast.rell.com
broadcast@rell.com
Edward Richardson, CEO
Robert Prince, Operations Dir
Global provider of power tubes, TV, radio transmitters, IP, digital satellite systems, NLE video systems & studio pakages.
Box 393, 40W267 Keslinger Rd., LaFox, IL 60147-0393 United States
(630) 208-2200 (800) 882-3872; *Fax:* (630) 208-2550
broadcast@rell.com broadcast.rell.com

Richmond Sound Design Ltd.
5264 Rose St., Vancouver, BC V5W EK7 CAN
(604) 715-9441, *Fax:* (604) 628-3391
www.richmondsounddesign.com
sales@richmondsounddesign.com
C.B. Richmond, President
M. Williams, General Manager
Virtual Sound System & show control software.

RIO Steel & Tower, LTD
12017 Mitchell Drive, Alvarado, TX 76009 USA
817-225-0890, *Fax:* 817-225-0895
www.riosteel.com
info@riosteel.com
Keith Cendrick, President
Vance Happerman, General Sales Mgr
Tower mf, Erection, maintenance, true turn-key installation, foundations, emergency svcs, antenna & transmission line replacement, site acquistion.

Ripley Company
46 Nooks Hill Rd., Cromwell, CT 6416 USA
(860) 635-2200,(800) 528-8665, *Fax:* (860) 635-3631
www.ripley-tools.com
info@ripley-tools.com
Kenneth McCormath, President
Tom Lindenmuth, General Manager
Keith D'Amato, General Sales Mgr
Ripley's Cablematic, Miller & Utility tool lines offer manufacturers cable preparation tools for CATV telecomm data & electric utiliy.

Rodelco Electronics Corp.
111 Haynes Ct., Ronkonkoma, NY 11779 USA
(631) 981-0900, *Fax:* (631) 981-1792
rodelco@erols.com
Joseph Rodgers, President
John Mellon, Engineering Dir
Peter Nister, Chief Engineer
TV translators, VHF & UHF.

Rohn Industries Inc.
6718 W. Plank Rd., Peoria, IL 61604 USA
(309) 697-4400, *Fax:* (309) 697-5612
www.rohnnet.com
mail@rohnnet.com
Horace Ward, CEO
Dave Ramsey, General Sales Mgr
Towers (up to 2,000 feet) monopoles, antenna mounts for communication industry. Turnkey construction & installation avaible worldwide.

Roland Corp. U.S.
Box 910921, 5100 S. Eastern Ave., Los Angeles, CA 90091-0921 USA
(323) 890-3700, *Fax:* (323) 890-3701
www.rolandus.com
Dennis Houlihan, CEO
Vince Landuca, Chief Marketing Executive
Mark Malbon, Executive Vice President
Electronic musical instruments, signal processors, sound reinforcement, hard disk editors, noise eliminators, bcst production equipment & post production equipment.

Rosco Laboratories Inc.
52 Harbor View Ave., Stamford, CT 6902 USA
(203) 708-8900, *Fax:* (203) 708-8919
www.rosco.com
info@rosco.com
Stan Miller, President
Ed Donahue, General Sales Mgr
Stan Schwartz, Executive Vice President
Lighting filters & diffusers, studio floor covering, connectors & digital (or rental & custom) backdrops.
1120 N. Citrus Ave, Hollywood, CA 90038 United States
(323) 462-2233; *Fax:* (323) 462-3338
Jim Meyer, Mgr

Roscor Corp.
1061 Feehanville Dr., Mount Prospect, IL 60056 USA
(847) 299-8080, *Fax:* (847) 299-4206,(847) 803-8089
www.roscor.com
sales@roscor.com
Mitch Roston, Vice President
Edward Jones, Operations Dir
Tom Voigts, General Sales Mgr
Paul Roston, President
Professional audio/video/RF/presentation equipment. Turnkey engrg & instal svcs.
27280 Haggerty Rd., Suite C2, Farmington Hills, MI 48331 United States
(248) 489-0090;
Paul Niehaus, Branch Mgr
600 W. Virginia St., Milwaukee, WI 53204 United States
(414) 223-2600;
Steve Olson, Branch Mgr
2868 E. Kemper Rd., Cincinnati, OH 45241
(513) 772-3393;
Tim Navaro, Branch Mgr

Ross Video Ltd.
Box 220, 8 John St., Iroquois, ON K0E 1K0 CAN
(613) 652-4886, *Fax:* (613) 652-4425
www.rossvideo.com
solutions@rossvideo.com
David Ross, CEO
Jeff Poapst, Operations Dir
Jeff Moore, General Sales Mgr
Joe Lalonde, CFO
Ross Video's product line includes Vision & Synergy Multi-Definition Video production switchers, openGear, RossGear & GearLite Terminal Equipment, SoftMetal Video Servers & the OverDrive Production Control System.

Royal Consumer Information Products
379 Campus Dr., Somerset, NJ 8875 USA
(732) 627-9977, *Fax:* (800) 232-4769
www.olivettiofficeusa.com
Salomon Suwalsky, President
Todd Althoff, Operations Dir

RTS Systems Telex Communications Inc
2550 N. Hollywood Way, Suite 207, Burbank, CA 91505-1055 USA
(818) 566-6700, *Fax:* (818) 843-7953
www.telex.com
Ralph Strader, Operations Dir
Britt Bowers, General Sales Mgr
Murray Porteous, National Sales Manager
Ken Smalley, Regional Sales Manager New York
Michael Brown, Regional Sales Manager NE
Rick Fisher, Regional Sales ManagerSouth
Dave Richardson, Regional Sales Manager West
Intercommunication systems, IFB systems, pro-audio amplifiers, microphones & phono preamplifiers.
10927 FM 1565, Terrell, TX 75160 United States
(972) 524-6047;
Britt Bowers, Rgnl Sls
Box 866, 10 Park Pl. Bldg. 1, Butler, NJ 07405 United States
(973) 283-6200;
Ken Smalley, Rgnl Sls
311 Stillwater Cove, Destin, FL 32541 United States
(850) 654-4058;
Rick Fisher, Sls Regl Mgr
15463 Waters Creek, Centerville, VA 20120 United States
(703) 867-8333;
Michael Brown, Sls Regnl
3807 Sunrise Lakes, Milford, PA 18337 United States
(570) 686-5444;
Chuck Roberts, Tech Support/Engrg

Russ Bassett Corporation
8189 Byron Rd., Whittier, CA 90606 USA
(562) 945-2445, *Fax:* (562) 698-8972
www.russbassett.com
info@russbassett.com
Ed Bassett, Owner
High density storage solutions for all media type.

S W R Inc.
619 Industrial Park Rd., Ebensburg, PA 15931 USA
(814) 472-5436, *Fax:* (814) 472-5552
www.swr-rf.com
davide@swr-rf.com
Edward Edmiston, President
David Edmiston, General Sales Mgr
Manufacturers of TV & FM transmit antennas, rigid coax, waveguide & associated accessories.
31-E Scout Bayoran, Timog, Quezon City, 011-632-411-0068;
Edward J. Edmiston, Pres

S&L Plastics Inc.
2860 Bath Pike, Nazareth, PA 18064 USA
(610) 759-0280, *Fax:* (610) 759-0650
www.slpinc.cc
John Bungert, President
Thermo plastic products.

Sabine Inc.
13301 Hwy. 441, Alachua, FL 32615 USA
(386) 418-2000, *Fax:* (386) 418-2001
www.sabine.com
sabine@sabine.com
Doran Oster, CEO
Kim Kelley, Finance Director
Manufacturers of digital signal processing equipment for sound systems. Makers of the patented FBX Feedback Exterminator & True MobilityTM wireless microphones.

Sachtler Corp. of America
709 Executive Blvd., Valley Cottage, NY 10989 USA
(845) 268-2113, *Fax:* (845) 268-9324
www.sachtler.com
sales@sachtler.com
Bob Carr, President
Ali Ahmadi, Promotions Manager
Complete line of camera support equipment for ENG, EFP, O.B. & the new generation of studio cameras. Lighting for news, production & studio open-face technology & fresnel.
3316 W. Victory Blvd., Burbank, CA 91505 United States
(818) 854-4446;

Sacramento Theatrical Lighting (STL)
950 Richards Blvd., Sacramento, CA 95814 USA

(800) 283-2785, *Fax:* (916) 447-5012
saclight@aol.com
Steve Odehnal, General Manager
Specialists in studio & location lighting, grip equipment, draperies, rigging & grid work. Consultation & production svcs. Sls, rentals & svcs.

Sadelco Inc.
75 W. Forest Ave., Englewood, NJ 7631 USA
(201) 569-3323, *Fax:* (201) 569-6285
www.sadelco.com
sadelco@aol.com
Les Kaplan, President
Robert Bradin, General Manager
Signal level meters, calibrators & leakage detectors.

SAIC (Science Applications International Corp.)
1710 Saic Dr., Suite B, Mclean, VA 22102
(703) 821-4300
Kenneth C. Dahlberg, Chairman & CEO
Natl security, energy, environment, critical infrastructure, health , rsch & dev.

SAIC Inc.
10260 Campus Point Dr., San Diego, CA 92121 United States
(858) 826-6000 (800) 430-7629; *Fax:* (858) 826-6800

Samson Technologies Corp.
45 Gilpin Ave., Hauppauge, NY 11788 USA
(516) 364-2244, *Fax:* (516) 364-3888
www.samsontech.com
sales@samsontech.com
Scott Goodman, CEO
Douglas Bryant, Operations Dir
Mark Wilder, Promotions Manager
Jack Knight, VP Operations
Manufacturer of wireless microphones, mixing consoles, power amplifiers & audio products. Behringer audio processing, Hartke speakers & Zoom effects processors.

Sanyo Fisher Co.
21605 Plummer St., Chatsworth, CA 91311 USA
(818) 998-7322, *Fax:* (818) 998-3533
www.sanyo.com
Paul D'Arcy, President
David Berkus, Operations Dir
Audio amplifiers & receivers, CD players, audiotape recorders, turntables, dictation machines, cordless telephones, TVs, VTRs & LCD projectors.

Sarnoff Corp.
201 Washington Rd., Princeton, NJ 08543-5300 USA
(609) 734-2553, *Fax:* (609) 734-2221
www.sarnoff.com
Dr. John Newsome, CEO
John P. Riganati, Operations Dir
video, Promotions Manager
Peter J. Burt, Vision Technologies
Contract rsch & dev facility for electronic, biomedical, & info technologies, specializing in digital video.

Sascom Marketing Group
34 Nelson St., Oakville, ON L6L 3H6 CAN
(905) 469-8080, *Fax:* (905) 469-8081
www.sascom.com
c.smith@sascom.com
Curt Smith, President
Sascom Represents: Cube-Tec Plugins for Pro Tools, Nuendo and Sequoia, and Doremi Labs digital video products

Satellite Systems Corp.
101 Malibu Dr., Virginia Beach, VA 23452 USA
(757) 463-3553, *Fax:* (757) 463-3891
www.satsyscorp.com
Bob Kite, President
SCPC & video subcarrier satellite systems for radio, SNG & data bcst networks.

Schafer International
220 Surrey Dr., Bonita, CA 91902 USA
(619) 267-9000, *Fax:* (619) 267-9003
www.schaferinternational.com
schaferpc@gmail.com
Paul Schafer, President
Equipment & parts, for radio & TV stns, primarily in Mexico.

Schafer World Communications Corp.
Box 1047, Marion, VA 24354-1047 USA
(276) 783-2000, *Fax:* (276) 783-2064
Bob Dix, President
Ann Dix, Operations Dir
Kevin Soos, Promotions Manager
Schafer offers two levels of sophistication in hard disk audio systems, GENESIS Digital Studio: touch screen & remote control interface; excellent live assist & full automation capability (complete music scheduling software included);cut-to-cut mixing on hard disk including editing; simultaneous record/playback from hard disk; can connect to external machines & CD multi-players.

Schneider Optics
7701 Haskell Ave., Van Nuys, CA 91406 USA
(818) 766-3715, *Fax:* (818) 505-9865
www. schneideroptics.com
info@schneideroptics.com
Bill Turner, Operations Dir
Wide angle & telephoto lens for video & motion picture cameras; lens accessories; lens service; schneider filters.

Schneider Optics Inc.
285 Oser Ave., Hauppauge, NY 11788 USA
(631) 761-5000, *Fax:* (631) 761-5090
www.schneideroptics.com
info@schneideroptics.com
Dwight Lindsay, CEO
Dawn Tenny, Manager
Manufacturer/distributor of high quality optical filters for video, still photography & motion picture. Product line also includes a wide range of lenses for CCTV, large format photography, darkroom enlarging, slide & film projection.
7701 Haskell Ave., Van Nuys, CA 91506
(818) 766-3715;

Scientific Atlanta
5030 Sugarloaf Pkwy., Lawrenceville, GA 30044 USA
(770) 236-5000, *Fax:* (770) 902-2591
www.sciatl.com
gregg.echols@sciatl.com
James McDonald, Chairman & CEO
Dwight Duke, President
Michael Harney, President
Patrick Tylka, President
A complete line of cable TV & broadband communications systems, products. and professional services.

Scientific Atlanta Canada Inc. Nexus Division
Satellite TV Networks, 100 Middlefield Rd. Unit 1, Scarborough, ON M1S 4M6 CAN
(416) 299-6888, *Fax:* (416) 299-7145
www.scientificatlanta.com
Evan Sloves, President
Dwight Duke, Operations Dir
Dean Rockwell, General Manager
Patrick Tylka, Senior VP
Michael Harney, SVP, Sub Net
TV RF signal processing equipment, transmission products & cable TV amplifiers.

Scott Studios Corporation
701 Canyon Drive, Suite 120, Dallas, TX 75234 USA
(972) 620-2211
David Blythe, President
Business svcs, computer integrated systems & design.

Scotts Valley Group Inc
540 Hauer Apple Way, Aptos, CA 95003-9315 USA
(831) 768-8668, *Fax:* (831) 768-7810
www.mar-com.com
marty@mar-com.com
Martin Jackson, President
FM, AM, TV & microwave transmitting equipment; sls engrg, instal & maintenance.

ScreenLight & Grip
502 Sprague St., Dedham, MA 2026 USA
(781) 326-5088, *Fax:* (781) 326-4751
www.screenlightandgrip.com
lightsne@aol.com
Guy Holt, President
Location lighting & production svcs, equipment rental, trucks, vans, etc.

Seger Electronics
97 Libbey Pkwy, Weymouth, MA 2189 USA
(781) 682-4844
www.seger.com
Ray Norton, CEO
Frank Flynn, President
Largest inventory of electromechanical components. No mimimums. Liberal sampling. 24-hours order check. Custom assembly, engraving & printing.

Selco Products Co.
605 S. East Street, Anaheim, CA 92805 USA
(714) 717-1333,(800) 527-3526, *Fax:* (714) 917-1355
www.selcoproducts.com
sales@selcoproducts.com
Tim Wilkinson, President
Michelle Blakeslee, Promotions Manager
A full range of product lines are offered by selco including thermal products, control knobs, electronic controls & digital panel meters.

Sencore Inc.
3200 W Sencore Dr., Sioux Falls, SD 57107 USA
(605) 339-0100, *Fax:* (605) 339-0317
www..sencore.com
sales@sencore.com
John Suranyi, CEO
Chuck Robertson, Operations Dir
Ken Christensen, Promotions Manager
Tom Stingley, EVP, Marketing & Sales
Dana Nachreiner, VP Operations
Electronic test equipment for servicing & performance testing of consumer electronics & CATV/MATV equipment.

Senior Aerospace
790 Greenfield Dr., El Cajon, CA 92021 USA
(619) 442-3451, *Fax:* (619) 440-1456
Ron Case, General Manager
Design build-to-print aerospace products, cryogenic lines, valves, burst discs, electric motors, actuators.

Sennheiser Electronic Corp.
One Enterprise Dr., Old Lyme, CT 6371 USA
(860) 434-9190, *Fax:* (860) 434-1759
www.sennheiserusa.com
info@sennheiserusa.com
John Falcone, CEO
Jeff Alexander, General Sales Mgr
Lachlan Brennan, Manager
Microphones, headphones, boomsets, wireless microphones & infrared products as well as Neumann mucrophone, Klein+Hummel loudspeakers & HHB recorders.
Av. Xola No. 613 PH6, Col. Del Valle, 3100 D.F. Mexico
(525) 639-0956; *Fax:* (525) 639-9482

Servoreeler Systems
218-31 97th Ave., Queens Village, NY 11429 USA
(718) 464-9400, *Fax:* (718) 464-9435
www.servoreelers.com
srsystems@servoreelers.com
Claude Karczmer, President
Eileen Karczmer, General Sales Mgr
SUSPENDED MICROPHONE SERVOREELERS - deploy, retract & position suspended microphones by remote pushbutton or computer control. They are used for Teleconferencing, Corporate board rooms, Houses of Worship, Concert halls, Sports arenas &Universities.

SES Americom Inc.
4 Research Way, Princeton, NJ 8540 USA
(609) 987-4000, *Fax:* (609) 987-4517
www.ses-americom.com
Robert Bednarek, CEO
Bryan mcGurik, President
Satellite distribution svcs for coml bcst & cable TV; prog syndicators, SNG & bcst radio distribution svcs.

Sescom Inc.
608 Main St., wellsville, KS 66092 USA
(785) 883-3009, *Fax:* (785) 883-4422
www.sescom.com
sescom@sescom.com
Bryan McGuirk, President
Jodi Morelli, Promotions Manager
Audio interfacing equipment, audio transformers & modules.

Setcom Corporation
3019 Alvin Devane Blvd., Suite 560, Austin, TX 78741 USA
(888) 673-8266, *Fax:* (650) 965-1193
www.setcomcorp.com
sales@setcomcorp.com
James Roberts, President
Police motorcycle communication equipment.

Seton Identification Products
20 Thompson Road, Branford, CT 6405 USA
(203) 488-8059, *Fax:* (203) 488-7259
www.seton.com
comments@seton.com
Richard Fisk, President
Tracy Carpenter, Manager
Signs, tags, labels, pipe markers, valve tags, & nameplates to meet OSHA/ANSI specifications.

Shallco Inc.
Box 1089, 308 Components Dr., Smithfield, NC 27577 USA
(800) 876-3135 (USA only),(919) 934-3298 (outside, *Fax:* (919) 934-3135 (outside USA only)
www.shallco.com
sales@shallco.com
John Shallcross, President
Jason Shallcross, President
Mark Francis, Manager
Variable & fixed audio attenuators.

Sharp Electronics Corp., CCD Products Div.
Sharp Plaza, Mail Stop One, Mahwah, NJ 07430-2135 USA
(201) 529-8200,(866) 4-VISUAL, *Fax:* (201) 529-9636
www.SharpLCD.com,www.sharp-usa.com
ProLCD@SharpSEC.com
Doug Koshima, Chairmsn & CEO
Ron Colgan, Operations Dir
Fred Krazeisze, General Manager
Bob Soucy, General Sales Mgr
Bruce Pollack, Promotions Manager
Judah Zeilger, Associate VP, Marketing
Data/video projection systems for portable and permanent installation applications; LCD video monitors, TVs, VCRs, TV/VCRs and Viewcam Camcorders.

Shively Labs
Box 389, 188 Harrison Rd., Bridgton, ME 4009 USA
(207) 647-3327, *Fax:* (207) 647-8273
www.shively.com
sales@shively.com
Paul Wescott, President
David Allen, Operations Dir
Angela Gillespie, General Sales Mgr
Joe Rohrer, Regional Sales Manager
FM antennas, FM translators, branched & balanced combiners, coax, patch panels, filters, compressor dehydrators, & related RF equipment, pattern work & field svcs.

Shook Mobile Technology, LP
7451 FM 3009, Schertz, TX 78154 USA
(210) 651-5700, *Fax:* (210) 651-5220
www.shook-usa.com
shook@shook-usa.com
John Heaney, CEO
Ronald Crockett, Promotions Manager
Mobile TV production, ENG, SNV vehicles. Rack ready or turnkey delivery. HD/SD Systems integration.

Shure Inc.
5800 W. Touhy Ave., Niles, IL 60714 USA
(847) 600-2000, *Fax:* (847) 600-1212
www.shure.com
info@shur.com
R.L. Shure, Chairman
S. LaMantia, President
World-standard microphones, wireless audio systems, phonograph cartridges, mixers, digital signal processors, & personal monitors.

Siemens Dematic Limited
167 Hunt St., Ajax, ON L1S 1P6 CAN
(905) 683-8200, *Fax:* (905) 683-0186
www.siemens.ca
Solid state FM transmitters to 5 kw, automatic coaxial changeover units, shortwave transmitters.

Sierra Automated Systems & Engineering Corp.
2821 Burton Ave., Burbank, CA 91504 USA
(818) 840-6749, *Fax:* (818) 840-6751
www.sasaudio.com
Edward Fritz, President
Al Salci, Operations Dir
Giovanni Morales, General Manager
Cam Eicher, General Sales Mgr
Mike Hagans, Engineering Dir
Audio switching & mixing systems maunufacturer.
Mix-Minus/IFB, satellite distribution/switching, automated switching & distribution, studio intercom, on-air routing, teleconferencing.

Sigma Electronics Inc.
1027 Commercial Ave., Box 448, East Petersburg, PA 17520-0448 USA
(717) 569-2681, *Fax:* (717) 569-4056
www.sigmaelectronics.com
sales@sigmaelectronics.com
Billy Swilley, CEO
Routing switchers for audio & video; distribution amplifiers; sync & test signal generators; encoders, decoders, transcoders, converters.

Western rgnl office
Santa Rosa, CA United States
(707)539-5314;
Randy Smith, Western Rgnl Sls Mgr

Signal Monitoring Service
773 Upper Fredricktown Rd., Mt. Vernon, OH 43050 USA
(888) 449-5643, *Fax:* (740) 397-2769
Robert (Bob) Bowman, President
AM/FM/TV frequency & modulation documentation - NRSC proof for AM.

Sinar Bron Inc.
17 Progress St., Edison, NJ 8820 USA
(908) 754-5800, *Fax:* (908) 754-5807
www.sinarbron.com
Michael Hejtmanek, President
Pro-Cyc prefabricated coves for infiniti walls in video & photo studios; & studio lighting/HMI.

Sitco Antenna Company/Simplicity Tool Corp
Box 20456, 10330 N.E. Marx St., Portland, OR 97220-1139 USA
(503) 253-2000, *Fax:* (503) 253-2009
www.simplicitytool.com
sitco@simplicitytool.com
Markus Burcker, President
CATV, MATV antennas.

SiteSafe Inc.
200 N. Glebe Rd., Suite 1000, Arlington, VA 22203-3728 USA
(703) 276-1100, *Fax:* (703) 276-1169
www.sitesafe.com
info@sitesafe.com
Wesley McGee, President
Elizabeth Nash, Operations Dir
Ed Katz, Chief Financial Officer
Winston Smith, Information Technology
Engrg software & wireless telecom engrg consulting svcs.

Skotel Corp.
92094 CSP Portobello, Brossard, QC J4W 3K8 CAN
(514) 806-2340
stephenscott@videotron.ca
Stephen Scott, President
Switching Equipment: Distribution switchers, Video equipment: Time code generators & time code readers.

Skytec, Inc.
23 Inland Farm Rd., Windham, ME 4062 USA
(207) 893-1700, *Fax:* (207) 893-1717
www.skytecinc.com
skytecinc@aol.com
Rick Sullivan, President
Manufacturer of skystrobe obstruction lighting systems - ETL certified, FAA approved. Parts, sls, svc & training seminars for obstruction lighting.

Snell & Wilcox Inc.
3519 Pacific Ave., Burbank, CA 91505 USA
(818) 556-2616, *Fax:* (818) 556-2626
www.snellwilcox.com
americas@snellwilcox.com
John Poulter, Chairman
Simon Derry, CEO
Jonathan Goldstein, President
Roderick Snell, General Sales Mgr
Snell & Wilcox is one of the world's largest manufacturers of bcst electronics. The complete product family includes a full range of video & audio processing equipment consisting of Decoding, Encoding, High Definition Format Conversion, MPEGCompression & Pre-processing, Display, Noise Reduction, Post Production Switchers (both SDTV & HDTV), Standards Conversion, Synchronization, Test & Measurement & IQ Modular products.

Snell & Wilcox Ltd.
Durford Mill, Petersfield, Hampshire, GU33 5AZ
44-0-730-821-188 44-0-730-821-199;
David Youlton, Chmn

Smith & Wilcox Ltd.
Southleigh Park House, Eastleigh Rd., Havant, Harts, P09 2PE

Solid State Logic Inc.
320 W. 46th St., New York, NY 10036 USA
(212) 315-1111, *Fax:* (212) 315-0251
www.solid-state-logic.com
nysales@solidstatelogic.com
Steve Zaretsky, President
Don Wershba, SVP
Bryon Engke, CFO
SSL is a leading manufacturer of digital audio broadcast consoles for on-air and live-to-tape production. New for 2009, the C10 brings a new level of price/performance to digital audio broadcast consoles
5757 Wilshire Blvd., Los Angeles, CA 90036 United States
(323) 549-9090;
Phil Wagner, Pres

Solutec Ltd. (HA)
4360 D'Iberville, Montreal, QC H2H 2L8 CAN
(514) 522-8960, *Fax:* (450) 437-8572
gilles.fortin@sympatico.ca
Gilles Fortin, President
Closed caption encoders (analog & SDI) & software, wireless communications.

Sony BMG Music Entertainment
550 Madison Ave., New York, NY 10022 USA
(212) 833-8000
www.bmg.com
Rolf Schmidt Hotz, Chairman
Hartwig Mason, CEO
Lauren Hubert, President/Creative Marketing
Produce, market & distribute recorded musics.

Sound Associates
424 W. 45th St., New York, NY 10036-3565 USA
(212) 757-5679, *Fax:* (212) 265-1250
T. Richard Fitzgerald, President
Domonic Sack, Operations Dir
Electronic equipment racking systems, console automation systems & digital recording facilities.

SOUND ASSOCIATES INC.
979 Saw Mill River Road, Yonkers, NY 10710
914-963-3452;

Soundcraft U.S.A.
8500 Balboa Blvd., Northridge, CA 91329 USA
(818) 920-3212, *Fax:* (818) 920-3208
www.soundcraft.com
soundcraft-usa@harman.com
Tom Der, General Sales Mgr
Dave Neal, Promotions Manager
Kathy Templeman Holmes, US Sales/Marketing
Audio mixing consoles for recording, theater, concert sound reinforcement & bcstg.

Southern Broadcast Services
80 Commerce Dr., Suite B, Pelham, AL 35124 USA
(800) 256-9235, *Fax:* (205) 663-7108
www.southernbroadcastservices.com
Jim Coleman, President
Tower erection, antenna instal, maintenance svcs.

Spacenet Services Inc.
1750 Old Meadow Rd., McLean, VA 22102 USA
(703) 848-1000, *Fax:* (703) 848-1010
www.spacenet.com
Glenn Katy, President
David Shiff, Operations Dir
Robert Turner, Business Development
Satellite-based interactive data, bcst data & bcst video for coml companies worldwide.

Specialized Communications Corp.
20940 Twin Springs Dr., Smithsburg, MD 21783-1510 USA
(800) 359-1858, *Fax:* (301) 790-0173
www.spec-comm.com
service@spec-comm.com
David Linetsky, President
Andrew Hoffman, Operations Dir
Judy Hoffman, Promotions Manager
Emily Hoffman, Service Coordinator
Factory Authorized Service Center providing repair & maintenance of bcst video equipment. Factory Integrator & Dealer for distinctive industry brands, such as Panasonic, Sony, JVS, Cannon. Also manufacturer of Digital Signage systems &provider of digital signage installation, integraton, content creation & content management.

Spotcat Software
1734 Green Valley Rd., Havertown, PA 19083 USA
(610) 446-1515
support@spotcat.com

Sprague Magnetics Inc.
12806 Bradley Ave., Sylmar, CA 91342 USA
(818) 364-1800,(800) 553-8712, *Fax:* (818) 364-1810
www.spraguemagnetics.com
smiav@spraguemagnetics.com
Dorothy Sprague, President/Finance Executive
Gary Moore, General Manager
Long-wearing cart, film, reel-to-reel tape heads, refurbishment svcs, replacement parts, alignment tapes, accessories.

Stage Equipment & Lighting Inc.
12250 N.E. 13th Ct., North Miami, FL 33161 USA
(305) 891-2010, *Fax:* (305) 893-2828,(800) 597-2010
www.seal-fla.com
mail@seal-fla.com
Rick Rudolph, President
Michael Grosz, Operations Dir
Stephen Grieco, Engineering Dir
Vivian Gill, President
Film, video & theatrical lighting & grip, & related support equipment.
9207 Palm River Rd., Suite 108, Tampa, FL 33619 United States
(813) 626-8500; *Fax:* (813) 620-1404
Adam Vidaurri, Manager
4600 S.W. 36th St., Orlando, FL 32811 United States
(407) 425-2010; *Fax:* (407) 648-2604
Curt Contrata, Manager

Stahl, A Scott & Fetzer Co.
3201 Old Lincoln Way, Wooster, OH 44691 USA
(330) 264-7441, *Fax:* (330) 264-3319
www.stahl.cc
info@stahl.cc
Jim Kraschinsky, President
Brad Yocheim, General Sales Mgr
Cardington, OH 43315 United States
(419) 864-6871;
Eric McNaly, Plant Mgr
Durant, OK 74701 United States
(405) 924-5575;
Steve Shepard, Plant Mgr
Merced, CA 95340 United States
(209) 383-4336;

Stainless LLC
1140 Welsh Rd., Suite 250, North Wales, PA 19454 USA
(215) 631-1400, (800) 486-3333, *Fax:* (215) 631-1425
www.stainlessllc.com
sales@stainlessllc.com
Donald T. Doty, CEO
Duane MacEntee, President/COO
Patrick Moore, SVP Technical Services
Jon Marcusse, General Sales Mgr
Tom Hoenninger, Chief Engineer
Ed Deetscreek, Sales Engineer
Design, engrg, fabrication of communications & bcst towers. Existing tower engrg studies & analysis. Full spectrum of tower maintenance, construction & inspections. RF services include RF mapping of tower & facilities. 24-HR EMERGENCYSERVICES.
Stainless Doty Moore
213 E. Louisiana St., Ste. 250, McKinney, TX 75069
(214) 585-0117
Doty Moore Stainless
1570 W. Beltline Rd., Cedar Hill, TX 75104
(972) 637-5000

Stancil Corp.
2644 S. Croddy Way, Santa Ana, CA 92704 USA
(714) 546-2002 ext. 4316,(800) 782-6245, *Fax:* (714) 546-2092
www.stancilcorp.com
guy.churchouse@stancilcorp.com
Michael Custer, CEO
Sharon Stancil, President
Simon Farrow, Engineering Tech
Voice logging recorders, multichannel, 4-144 channels, 24-hour recording time; digital format, instant recall recorders, windows 2000 voiceXP.

Standard Communications Corp.
6260 Sequence Dr., San Diego, CA 92121 USA
(858) 546-5300, *Fax:* (858) 546-5301
www.standardcom.com
SatcommSales@stdcom.com
Ron Blanchard, CEO
Broadband TV receivers & cable headend products for broadcast and CATV.

Stanley Supply & Services
7815 S. 46th St., Phoenix, AZ 85044 USA
(602) 453-3169,(800) 366-9662, *Fax:* (877) 372-5108
www.stanleysupplyservices.com
sales@stanleyworks.com
Holly Tsourides, President
Electronic tool kits & cases, tools, test equipment.

Stanton Group
3000 S.W. 42nd St., Ft. Lauderdale, FL 33312 USA
(954) 316-1500, *Fax:* (954) 316-1590
www.stantonmagnetics.com
info@stantonmagnetics.com
Timothy Dorwart, CEO
Mike Quandt, President
Jim Moore, Principal
Turntables, professional cartridges, CD players, final scratch, monitors, speakers.

KRK
5242 Business Dr., Huntington, CA 92649 United States
(714) 373-4600 (714) 373-0421;

Kerwin Vega
555 Fast Easy Street, Simi Valley, CA 93065 United States

Star Case Manufacturing Co. Inc.
648 Superior Ave., Munster, IN 46321 USA
(219) 922-4440,(800) 822-STAR, *Fax:* (219) 922-4442
www.starcase.com
star@starcase.com
Dennis Toma, President
Ralph Hoopes, Operations Dir
Flight cases (protective casement)—Carry Star, ATA Star, Super Star, Ultra Star, Star Light.

StarGuide Digital Networks Inc.
750 W. John Carpenter Fwy., Suite 700, Irving, TX 75039 USA
(972) 581-2000, *Fax:* (972) 581-2001
www.starguidedigital.com
hq@starguidedigital.com
High speed internet networking of digital audio, video & web. Software, satellite, terrestrial & DSL systems.

Storeel Corp.
Box 80523, Atlanta, GA 30366 USA
(770) 458-3280, *Fax:* (770) 457-5585
reely@mindspring.com
Carolyn Galvin, President
Elizabeth Galvin, General Sales Mgr
Michael Valerio, General Sales Manager
Steven Albright, Marketing Consultant
Space-efficient storage for all formats of tape & film; double-drive systems for longer lengths; set-up trucks; CD storage.

StorerTV Inc.
1361 W. Towne Square Rd., Mequon, WI 53092 USA
(262) 241-9005, *Fax:* (262) 241-9036
www.storertv.com
storer@storertv.com
Peter Storer, President
Doug Knight, Operations Dir
SIMS-Multi-Station/Network program rights, scheduling & finance system. Manages non-linear rights and scheduling as well.

Strand Lighting Inc.
6603 Darin Way, Cypress, CA 90630 USA
(714) 230-8200, *Fax:* (714) 899-0042
www.strandlight.com
sales@strandlight.com
Peter Rogers, Sales Executive
Studio & remote lighting, & control equipment.
928 Broadway, New York, NY 10010-6008
(212) 242-1042;

Strong International
c/o Ballantyne of Omaha Inc., 4350 McKinley St., Omaha, NE 68112 USA
(402) 453-4444, *Fax:* (402) 453-7238
www.ballantyne-omaha.com
John Wilmers, President
Ray Boegner, Operations Dir
35/70mm projection equipment, Xenon lamphouse systems, platters, Xenon bulbs, follow spotlights.

Structural System Technology Inc.
6867 Elm Street, Suite 200, McLean, VA 22101 USA
(703) 356-9765, *Fax:* (703) 448-0979
www.sst-towers.com
contact@sst-towers.com
Fred Purdy, CEO
Kaveh Mehrnama, President
Bryan Burton, Operations Dir
Monty Beck, Vice President
Mary Acker, Finance Executive
Structural engrg studies, analysis, design, modifications, inspections, fabrication, erection of towers & antenna.

Studio Technologies Inc.
5520 W. Touhy Ave., Suite 1, Skokie, IL 60077 USA
(847) 676-9177, *Fax:* (847) 982-0747
www.studio-tech.com
stisales@studio-tech.com,cgage@studio-tech.com
Gordon Kapes, President
Carrie Gage, Promotions Manager
Joe Urbanczyk, Sales Executive
Microphone pre-amplifiers, stereo simulators & recognition units, telephone & hard-wired IFB communications systems on-air announcer's consoles. Accessories for digital audio workstations.

Studio Technology
529 Rosedale Road, Suite 103, Kenneth Square, PA 19348 USA
(610) 925-2785, *Fax:* (610) 925-2787
www.studiotechnology.com
sales@studiotechnology.com
Vince Fiola, CEO
Bcst furniture, design & instal svcs.

Summit Software Systems Inc.
777 Main Ave., 217, Durango, CO 81301 USA
(800) 771-1824
www.summitsoftware.com
sales@summitsoft
Paul Adams, President
PC-based traf, sls, billing, accounts receivable, accounts payable, payroll & gen ledger for single or multi-stns & single or multi-users.

Sundance Digital Inc.
545 E. John Carpenter Fwy., Suite 200, Irving, TX 75062 USA
(972) 444-8442, *Fax:* (972) 444-8450
www.sundancedigital.com
sales@sundig.com
Jacque Durocher, General Manager
Rick Stora, Promotions Manager
Eric Harrington, Engineering Dir
Sundance Digital a part of Avid is an award-winning leader in TV automation solutions for individual & multistation bcstrs.

Superior Satellite Engineers Inc.
1743 Middle Rd., Columbia Falls, MT 59912 USA
(406) 257-9590, *Fax:* (406) 257-9599
www.superiorsatelliteusa.com
superior@superiorsatelliteusa.com
Doyle Catlett, President
Steve Catlett, Operations Dir
Navigator steerable & fixed antenna systems; multiple satellite feed systems & LNBs for cable bcst IPTV.

Superior Tower Services Inc.
5757 FM 1696, Iola, TX 77861 USA
(936) 394-9925 (800) 306-4504, *Fax:* (936) 394-4020
Edward Carter, President/Owner
For all your tower & antenna needs: antenna, transmission line analysis, emergency repairs, two way, microwave, cellular, AM/FM, installations, tower erections, inspections, & maintenance.

Superscope Technologies Professionals
2640 White Oaks Circle, Suite A, Aurora, IL 60504 USA
(630) 820-4800, *Fax:* (630) 820-8103
www.superscopetechnologies.com
Fred Hackendahl, President
Products include portable cassette recorders, single & dual cassette recorders, CD players, multi-track recorders, compact recorders, portable, & rackmount.

Swager Communications Inc.
Box 656, Fremont, IN 46737 USA
(260) 495-2515, *Fax:* (260) 495-4205
www.swager.com
tim@swager.com
Dan Swager, President
Lee Swager, Operations Dir
Tim Swager, Sec/Treasurer
Designs, fabricates, installs & maintains AM/FM, TV/CATV & microwave communication towers.

Swintek Enterprises Inc.
965 Shulman Ave., Santa Clara, CA 95050 USA
(408) 727-4889,(408) 727-7544, *Fax:* (408) 727-3025
www.swintek.com
ssales@swintek.com
William Swintek, President
18 ch wireless intercom, 1 w IFB with wireless EAR piece receiver, complete linear headsets.

Switchcraft Inc.
5555 N. Elston Ave., Chicago, IL 60630 USA
(773) 792-2700, *Fax:* (773) 792-2129
www.switchcraft.com
David K. Dunmead, President
Keith Bandolik, President
Jim Hoffman, Chief Marketing Executive
Judy Pulliam, Sales
Offers a variety of products including audio patchbays, connectors, adapters, jacks & plugs, and video patchbays.

Symetrix Inc.
6408 216th St. S.W., Suite A, Mountlake Terrace, WA 98043 USA
(425) 778-7728, *Fax:* (425) 778-7727
www.symetrixaudio.com
symetrix@symetrixaudio.com
Dane Butcher, President/CEo
Jennifer Anderson, Financial Executive
Paul Roberts, General Sales Mgr
John Harris, Engineering Dir
Digital & analog audio signal processing.

Symmetricom
2300 Orchard Pkwy., San Jose, CA 95131 USA
(949) 598-7500, *Fax:* (949) 598-7524
Erik Van derKay, President
Bob Krist, Operations Dir
Time code generators, readers, displays, encoders, search systems, distribution amplifiers, transmitters & receivers; design & manufacture of precision frequency products & timing instruments.

Datum-Irvine
3 Parker, Irvine, CA 92718 United States
(714) 770-5000;
Heinz Badura, Pres

Datum-Austin
Box 14766, Austin, TX 78761 United States
(512) 251-2341;
Jack Rice, Pres

Symmetricom
Mailing Address: 3750 Westwind Blvd, Santa Rosa, CA 95403 USA
Second Address: 2300 Orchard Parkway, San Jose, CA 95131
(707) 528-1230, *Fax:* (707) 527-6640
www.symmetricom.com
Thomas Steipp, CEO
Gurdip Jande, Operations Dir
Paul Chermak, General Sales Mgr
Doug Arnold, Chief Engineer
Time & frequency receivers traceable to NIST & USNO. Complete line of time code instrumentation.

Syntellect Inc.
2095 W Pinnacle Peak Road, Suite 110, Phoenix, AZ 85053 USA
(800) 788-9733,(800) 347-9907, *Fax:* (770) 587-0589
www.syntellect.com
Steve Dodenhoff, President
J.R. Sloan, Chief Marketing Officer
ARUs for automated customer svc, ANI svcs for PPV order processing, predictive dialing systems for telemarketing & collections.
20401 N. 29th Ave, Phoenix, AZ 85027 United States
(602) 789-2800;
Scott Coleman, Pres

SyntheSys Research Inc.
3475-D Edison Way, Menlo Park, CA 94025 USA
(650) 364-1853, *Fax:* (650) 364-5716
www.synthesysresearch.com
info@synthesysresearch.com
Dr Lute Henckels, CEO
Jim Waschura, President
Bob Hayes, Founder
John Ryan, General Sales Mgr
Charlie Schaffer, VP Marketing
SyntheSys is a leading manufacturer of test & measurement specializing in serial digital video analyzers for SDI & high definition.

System Associates
4848 W Seldon Lane, Glendale, AZ 85312 USA
(866) 937-0209, *Fax:* (866) 435-0160
www.systemsassociates.tv
video@systemsassociates.com
Mike Ferguson, President
Used bcst TV equipment, to buy and sell, appraisals, auctions

Systems Wireless Ltd.
555 Herndon Pkwy., Ste. 135, Herndon, VA 20170 USA
(703) 471-7887, *Fax:* (703) 437-1107
www.swl.com
Bill Sien, General Sales Mgr
Ron Gallihugh, Finance
Sls, service & rental of wireless microphones, wireless intercom, wireless listening devices, wireless video & Clear Com cabled intercom systems.

T-C Specialties Co.
Box 192, Coudersport, PA 16915 USA
(814) 274-8060,(800) 458-6074, *Fax:* (814) 274-0690
www.tcspecialties.com
tcsmail@adelphia.net
Daniel Major, President
Bill Crown, Operations Dir
Judi Tucker, Secretary
Mike Harris, VP Operations
Coupon billing systems & related forms; large volume dir mail inkjetting, presort/barcoding mailing

T.T. Technologies Inc.
2020 E. New York St., Aurora, IL 60502 USA
(800) 533-2078,(630) 851-8200, *Fax:* (630) 851-8299
www.tttechnologies.com
info@tttechnologies.com
Chris Brahler, President/CEO
Dave Holcomb, Operations Dir
Grundomat Pneumatic piercing tools, Grundoram pipe ramming system, Grundocrack Preumatic pipe bursting systems & Grundoburst Static Pipe Bursting.
3701 N.E. 36th Ave., Suite C, Ocala, FL 34479 United States
(352) 622-2077;
Tom Garner, Gen Mgr

TAI Audio
5828 Old Winter Garden Rd., Orlando, FL 32835 USA
(407) 296-9959,(800) 486-6444, *Fax:* (407) 648-1352
www.taiaudio.com
sales@taiaudio.com
Joseph Guzzi, President
Rental, sls & svc of professional audio for film, video, TV & postproduction. Specializes in wireless communication equipment.

Talk-A-Phone Co.
7530 N. Natchez Ave., Niles, IL 60714 USA
(773) 539-1100, *Fax:* (773) 539-1241
www.talkaphone.com
info@talkaphone.com
S. Shanes, Chairman
Robert Shanes, Operations Dir
Intercommunication systems, ADA compliant emergency phones, ADA areas of rescue, apartment access systems.

TALX Corp.
1850 Borman Ct., St. Louis, MO 63146 USA
(314) 214-7000, *Fax:* (314) 214-7588
www.talx.com
Michael Smith, Operations Dir
William Canfield, General Manager
Interactive communications; more specific svc; Interactive voice response, Interactive web, employment verification (work # for everyone) & Outsource svc.

Tamron U.S.A. Inc.
10 Austin Blvd., Commack, NY 11725 USA
(631) 858-8400, *Fax:* (631) 543-5666
www.tamron.com
feedback@tamron.com
Tak Inoue, President
Bert Krank, Operations Dir
Keiki Warashina, General Manager
John VanSteenberg, Station Manager
Gregg Maniaci, General Sales Mgr
Stacie Errera, Promotions Manager
Lenses for 35mm SLR digital & film cameras, & CCTV lenses.

TANDBERG Television Inc.
4500 River Green Pkwy., Duluth, GA 30096 USA
(678) 812-6300, *Fax:* (678) 812-6400
www.tandbergtv.com
Eric Cooney, CEO
Staffan Pehrson, President
Video compression, content distribution, video on-demand solutions, content management systems, advanced advertising

Tapeswitch Corp.
100 Schmitt Blvd., Farmingdale, NY 11735 USA
(631) 630-0442, *Fax:* (631) 630-0454
www.tapeswitch.com
sales@tapes.com
Michael Steele, President
Patrick Falbo, Operations Dir
April Sabbatini, Promotions Manager
Safety light curtains, sensing mats, edges, ribbon switches, electronic zone controllers, sensing bumpers, safety & protection equipment.
Mission, CA 92692 United States
(949) 588-9387;
Jeff Johnson, Rgnl Sls Mgr
Franklin, TN 37064 United States
(615) 591 7399;
Tim DePeri, Rgnl Sls Mgr
Fishers, IN 46038 United States
(317) 570-6178;
Tom Bertellotti, Rgnl Sls Mgr
New Bern, NC 28562 United States
(252) 637-7728;
Vinnie Colucci, Rgnl Sls Mgr

TC Electronic
5706 Corsa Ave., Suite 107, Westlake Village, CA 91362 USA
(818) 665-4900, *Fax:* (818) 665-4901
www.tcbroadcast.com
info@tcus.com
Ed Simeone, Chairman
John Maier, CEO
Digital compressor/limiter expander, digital signal processors, DTV audio processors & high-resolution digital delays.

TC Group Americas Inc.
335 Gage Ave., Suite 1, Kitchener, ON N2M 5E1 CAN
(519) 745-1158, *Fax:* (519) 745-2364
http://www.tcgroup-americas.com/
inquiries@tcg-americas.com
Marc Bertrand, CEO
Brands offered: Tannoy, Lab.gruppen, tc electronic, TC Helicon, dynaudio acoustics, Linn

TC Group Americas

TDK Electronics Corp.
3190 E. Miraloma Ave., Anaheim, CA 92806 USA
(714) 238-7900, *Fax:* (714) 632-1868
www.tdk.com
Hajime Sawabe, Chairman & CEO
Takehiro Kamigama, President

TEAC America Inc.
7733 Telegraph Rd., Montebello, CA 90640 USA
(323) 726-0303, *Fax:* (323) 727-7656
www.teac.com
Koichiro Nakamura, President
Jim Savage, CFO
Les Luzar, General Sales Mgr
Hitomi Down, Controller
Consumer audio/video & professional recording equipment, airborne video recorder, instrumentation data recorders, computer peripherals/floppy disks, tape backup & industrial optical disk recorders & playback.

Teatronics/Entertainment Lighting Control
P.O. Box 508, Santa Mangarita, CA 93453 USA
(805) 438-4000, *Fax:* (805) 438-5400
www.teatronics.com
sales@teatronics.com
Gary Beckerman, President
Lighting control & power distribution systems for stage, studio & remote applications.

Tech Laboratories Inc.
955 Belmont Ave., North Haledon, NJ 7508 USA
(973) 427-5333, *Fax:* (973) 427-5455
www.techlabsinc.com
corporate@techlabs.com
Bernard Ciongoli, President
Earl Bjorndal, Operations Dir
Rotary switches; electrical/electronic subcontract, attenuators, transformers, pcb assembly & infrared security systems.

TECH-SA-PORT
Box 5372, 120 S. Whitfield St., Pittsburgh, PA 15206-0372 USA
(412) 661-1620,(800) 543-2233
www.tech-sa-port.com
tech-sa-port@juno.com
Lewis Scheinman, President
Computer & electronic equipment cleaning supplies, including lint-free wipers, contamination-free chemicals, & spray dusters. All types of wiping materials.

EQUIPMENT MANUFACTURERS

Technet Systems Group
20 Chester Turnpike, Auburn, NH 3032 USA
(603) 483-5365, *Fax:* (603) 483-0512
www.technetsystems.com
svanni@technetsystems.com
Steve Vanni, President
Bcst equipment supplier & distributor for radio & TV, specializing in complete turnkey packages including planning, design, equipment, instal, towers & FCC licensing.

Techni-Tool Inc.
1547 N. Trooper Rd., PO Box 1117, Worcester, PA 19490-1117 USA
(800) 832-4866,(610) 825-4990, *Fax:* (610) 828-5623,(800) 854-8665
www.techni-tool.com/comm
sales@techni-tool.com
Paul Weiss, President
Michael Ryan, General Sales Mgr
David Weitner, Promotions Manager
Steven Weiss, Executive Vice President
Master distributor of hand tools, kits & cases, test equipment, supplies & safety products for the Communications Field Techician working with fiber optic, coaxial & twisted pair cabling. As well as for the bench tech working on electronicsproduction/repair & cable assemby.

Technicolor SA
2300 S. Decker Lake Blvd., Salt Lake City, UT 84119 USA
(801) 972-8000, *Fax:* (801) 972-6304
www.thomsonmultimedia.com
Frederic Rose, CEO
13 Kevin Ct, Wyomissing, PA 19610 United States
(215) 678-8711; *Fax:* (215) 678-8784
Jeff Rosica, Sls Mgr

Technologies for Worship
3891 Holburn Rd., Queensville, ON L0G 1R0 CAN
(905) 473-9822, *Fax:* (905) 473-9928
www.tfwm.com
bc@tfwm.com
Shelagh Rogers, President
Barry Cobus, Operations Dir
Kevin Rogers-Cobus, Programming Director
Trade magazine & tech directory for houses of worship involved in audio, AV, bcst, computers, film, video & music. Owner of Inspiration Conferences & Expositions.

Tekskil Industries Inc.
#102-998 Harbourside Dr., North Vancouver, BC V7P 3T2 CAN
(604) 985-2250, *Fax:* (604) 985-2248
www.tekskil.com
tekskilprompters2008@tekskil.com
John Veenstra, President
Manufacturer of video, speech & computer prompting equipment.

Tektronix Inc.
13975 SW Karl Braun Dr., Beaverton, OR 97077 USA
(800) 835-9433,(503) 627-7111, *Fax:* (503) 627-6108
www.tektronix.com
Jim Lico, President
Arif Kareem, Operations Dir
Larry Brown, Information Tech
Jane Elliot, Information Tech
Tim Anderson, Information Tech

Telcom Research
3375 N. Service Rd., A7, Burlington, ON L7N 3G2 CAN
(905) 336-2450, *Fax:* (905) 336-1487
www.timecode.com
dougl@tecomresearch.com
Douglas Finch, President
Brian Weppler, Operations Dir
SMPTE/EBU time code generators, readers; character inserters, LTC-VITC & VITC-LTC trans. Logging/offline/EDL software.

Tele-Measurements Inc.
145 Main Ave., Clifton, NJ 07014-1078 USA
(973) 473-8822,(800) 223-0052, *Fax:* (973) 473-0521
www.tele-measurements.com
tmcorp@aol.com
William Endres, President
W. Chris Endres, General Manager
Bcst video equipment, tapes TV systems, teleconferencing, maintenance support, CCTV & rentals, distance learning.

Telecast Fiber Systems Inc.
102 Grove St., Worcester, MA 1605 USA
(508) 754-4858, *Fax:* (508) 752-1520
www.telecast-fiber.com
sales@telecast-fiber.com
Richard Cerny, President
Eugene Baker, Operations Dir
Joseph Commare, Promotions Manager
Mark Borezo, Financial Executive
Fiber-optic video & audio systems for TV bcst production.
3009 Bentwillow Dr., Fuquay-Varina, NC 27526
(919) 557-6059; *Fax:* (919) 557-5206
Bryan Keen, Southeast Sls
16 Rock River Ct., Naperville, IL 75231
(630) 717-9384; *Fax:* (630) 717-1844
Bill Hollis, Midwest Sls
280 Ferry Rd., Saco, ME 04072
(207) 282-9772; *Fax:* (207) 282-8666
Steve Nelson, Northeast & Gvt Sls
835 Autumn Ln., Mill Valley, CA 94941
(415) 383-5388; *Fax:* (650) 745-3711
James Hurwitz, Western U.S/Sls & Camera Systems

Telecrafter Products
12687 W. Cedar Dr., Suite 100, Lakewood, CO 80228-2031 USA
(303) 986-0086, *Fax:* (303) 986-1042
www.telecrafter.com
mail@telecrafter.com
Drop installation products for broadband telecommunications delivery svc, including cable clips, cablemakers, cable guard, house boxes, fitting savers, & more.

Telemetrics Inc.
6 Leighton Pl., Mahwah, NJ 7430 USA
(201) 848-9818, *Fax:* (201) 848-9819
www.telemetricsinc.com
Anthony Cuomo, President
Camera pan, tilt systems & triax camera control systems.

Teleplex Inc.
4801 Industrial Pkwy., Suite A, Indianapolis, IN 46226 USA
(317) 895-8800, *Fax:* (317) 895-2900
www.teleplexcorp.com
Tom Fitch, CEO
Lois Clark, Operations Dir
Stephen Yelton, SVP
Produces precision electronics, components, FM stn combiners, custom FM radio antenna arrays, TV antenna systems, & HDTV monitor antennas. Supports all Alford products & antenna products.

Telescript Inc.
445 Livingston St., Norwood, NJ 7648 USA
(201) 767-6733, *Fax:* (201) 784-0323
www.telescript.com
info@telescript.com
John McGrath, Station Manager
Andrew Wischmeyer, General Sales Mgr
IBM & compatibles prompting programs & equipment. Lightweight, high-resolution 12 & 17 monitor prompters. Flat panel prompters, window based prompting software for bcst & video productions applications, comprehensive line of LCD prompters.

Telescript West
7801 N. Lamar Blvd., Austin, TX 78752 United States
(512) 302-0766;
Jim Stringer, Mgr

Teletech Inc.
38235 Executive Drive, Westland, MI 48185 USA
(734) 641-2300, *Fax:* (734) 641-2323
www.teletech-inc.com
Keith Johnson, Operations Dir
Todd Osment, General Manager
Kevin Beltramo, Engineering Dir
Richard Humphrey, Chief Engineer
Facility construction, antenna instal for AM, FM, TV, LPTV & microwave; antenna site mgmt; FCC applicacations; EME studies; Aeronautical studies.

teletech.ca
3-211 Telson Rd, Markham, ON L3R 1E7 CAN
(905) 475-5646, *Fax:* (905) 475-5684
www.teletech.ca
admin@teletech.ca
Jack Kirkpatrick, President
Total bcst, postproduction, audio & video sls, service, & rentals of equipment & supplies.

Television Engineering Corp.
2647 Rock Hill Industrial Ct., Saint Louis, MO 63144 USA
(314) 961-2800, *Fax:* (314) 961-2808
www.tvengineering.com
Jack Vines Jr., General Sales Mgr
Jack Vines Sr., Chief Engineer
Manufacturer of news vans, satellite vehicles, Eagle Eye camera, IFB controller & turnkey systems.

Television Equipment Assoc. Inc./Matthey
Box 404, Brewster, NY 10509-0404 USA
(845) 278-0960, *Fax:* (845) 278-0964
Bill Pegler, President
Joseph Tocidlowski, General Manager
Serial digital interface products, NTSC/PAL Decoders, analog & digital DAs, video & pulse delays, video filters, A/D & D/A converters, headsets, serial digital/Fiberoptic links, Routing switches for digital video and radio.

Telex Communications Inc.
12000 Portland Ave. S., Burnsville, MN 55337 USA
(952) 884-4051, *Fax:* (952) 884-0043
www.telex.com
prosound@telex.com
Ned Jackson, CEO
Wired & wireless microphones; headphones/headsets; wired & wireless intercoms; audio duplicators/copiers.
2550 Hollywood Way, Suite 207, Burbank, CA 91505 United States
(818) 566-6700;

TELLABS
1415 W. Diehl Rd., Naperville, IL 60563 USA
(630) 798-8800, *Fax:* (630) 798-2000
www.tellabs.com
Teleconferencing systems, digital echo cancellers, data over voice multiplexers, signaling systems, video conferencing, audio systems.
60 Commerce Dr., Hauppauge, NY 11788 United States
(516) 231-1550;
29 The Quandrant, Abingdon, Oxfordshire 0X14 3Y3, 011-44-235-524-400;

Telos Systems
1241 Superior Ave., Cleveland, OH 44114 USA
(216) 241-7225, *Fax:* (216) 241-4103
www.telos-systems.com
Frank Foti, President
Denny Sanders, Chief Engineer
Michael Dosch, President/Axia Audio
Steve Church, President/CEO/Founder
Telos Systems, is the leading global manufacturer of coded audio, ISDN, telephone interface and networked audio products for talk-shows, teleconferencing, audio production, remote broadcasts, and intercom applications. Omnia Audio, a Teloscompany, is world-renowned for its digital audio signal processing expertise. Omnia audio processors for FM, AM, TV, HD Radio & DAB, Internet, and audio production are setting new standards for professional audio quality. Axia Audio, a Telos company,builds Ethernet-based professional IP-Audio products for broadcast, production, sound-reinforcement and commercial audio applications. Products include digital audio routers, on-air control surfaces, DSP mixers and processors, audio logging devices,and software for configuring, managing, and interfacing networked audio systems.

Tenco Tower Co.
9647 Folsom Blvd., Sacramento, CA 95827-1326 USA
(916) 638-8833, *Fax:* (916) 366-7383
donald.tenn@towerguys.com,donald@towerman.net
Donald Tenn, CEO
Instal, maintenance, sls of towers, antennas, hardware for the bcst, cable & communications industry.

Tentel
333 Industrial Drive, Suite 4, Placerville, CA 95667 USA
(530) 344-0183, *Fax:* (530) 344-0186
www.tentel.com
info@tentel.com
John Chavers, General Manager

Texas Electronics Inc.
Box 7225, Dallas, TX 75209 USA
(214) 631-2490, *Fax:* (214) 631-4218
www.texaselectronics.com
info@texaselectronics.com
Carol Westlund, President
Jane Hansen, Operations Dir
Jason Burson, General Sales Mgr
Manufacturer of meteorological instruments & controls.

Texscan MSI
2210 W. Alexander Street, Suite A, Salt Lake City, UT 84119 USA
(801) 956-0000, *Fax:* (801) 956-0750
www.texscan.com
Leonard Fabiano, President

Character generators, digital, analog commercial insertion systems, audio/video playback systems, weather data svc, multimedia graphics production systems & VCR controllers.

TFT Inc.
1953 Concourse Dr., San Jose, CA 95131-1708 USA
(408) 943-9323, *Fax:* (408) 432-9218
www.tftinc.com
info@tftinc.com
Darryl Parker, Operations Dir
Digital, analog STLs, Reciters, synchronous boosters, modulation monitors & emergency alert systems(EAS).

Thales Broadcast & Multimedia S.A.
1 rue de l'Hautil, Z.A. les Bountries, Conflans Sainte Honorine Cedex, 78702 FRA
1 34 90 31 00, *Fax:* 1 34 90 30 00
www.thomsongrassvalley.con
Bill Patrizio, President
Jeff Rosica, Operations Dir
Handling everything from video, audio to data signals & control systems.

Theatre Service & Supply Corp.
1792 Union Ave., Baltimore, MD 21211 USA
(410) 467-1225, *Fax:* (410) 467-1289
www.stage-n-studio.com
sales@stage-n-studio.com
Richard Antisdel, President
Jacauelin Keleman, General Sales Mgr
Manufacturer of studio, theatrical curtains, track systems, distributor of lighting & theatrical hardware.

Theatrical Services Inc.
128 S. Washington Street, Wichita, KS 67202 USA
(316) 263-4415, *Fax:* (316) 263-9927
www.theatricalservices.com
tsi@theatricalservices.com
Stephen Wolf, President
Manufacturers & distributors of studio lighting & control equipment, studio cycloramas, curtains & track.

Thermodyne International LTd
1841 Business Pkwy., Ontario, CA 91761 USA
(909) 923-9945, *Fax:* (909) 923-7505
www.thermodyne-online.com
Gary Ackerman, President
Josh Ackerman, Chief Marketing Officer
Reusable shipping cases; rack-mounted operating cases. Provides protection for all electronic equipment during transit.

Thomas & Betts
700 Thomas Ave., Saint-Jean-sur Richelieu, QC J2X 2M9 CAN
(450) 347-5318, *Fax:* (450) 347-1976
www.tnb.com
Dominic Pileggi, Chairman & CEO
Michael Kenney, President
Manufacturer of quality products for aerial construction & subscriber instal hardware for the Cable TV & telephone industry.

Thomas & Betts Corp.
8155 T&B Blvd., Memphis, TN 38125 USA
(800) 816-7809,(901) 252-8000, *Fax:* (800) 816-7810,(901) 252-1354
www.tnb.com
elec_custserv@tnb.com
Manufacturer of Poleline hardware aerial & drop systems, fiber-optic hand holes, MMDS antenna mounting hardware.

Thomson
104 Feeding Hills Rd., Southwick, MA 1077 USA
(413) 998-1100, *Fax:* (413) 569-0679
www.thomson.net
joseph.turbolski@thomson.net
Joseph Turbolski, Operations Dir
Richard Fiore, Programming Director
Thomson manufuctures, markets equipment sytems & solutions in the fields of terrestrial transmission, digital videl processing & multimedia distribution.

Thomson Broadcast & Media Solutions
Box 599000, 400 Providence Mine Road, Nevada City, CA 95959-5900 USA
(800) 824-5127, *Fax:* (530) 478-3166
www.thomsongrassvalley.com
Tim Thorsteinson, CEO
Russ Johnson, General Sales Mgr
Stephen Wong, Pacific Region sales
Video servers/disk recorders, media platforms, video production centers (switchers), signal mgmt systems (routers, modular), DVEs & HDTV equipment.

Thomson Reuters
3 Times Square, New York, NY 10036 USA
(646) 223-4000
www.thomsonreuters.com
Chris Ahearn, President
Supplier of natl, world, business news, info to media & professionals.
165 Sparks St., Booth Bldg., Ottawa, ON K1P 5P8 Canada
(613) 235-6745;
Antony Parry, Financial Correspondent
John Rogers, Gen News
1333 H St. N.W., Suite 410, Washington, DC 20005 United States
(202) 898-8300;
Bruce Russell, Chief
311 S. Wacker Dr., Suite 1100, Chicago, IL 60606 United States
(312) 922-6038;
Geoffrey Atkins, Chief
445 S. Figueroa, Suite 2100, Los Angeles, CA 90071 United States
(213) 380-2014;
Ronald Clarke, Chief
Standard Life Centre
121 King St. W., 20th Fl, Toronto, ON M5H 3T9 Canada
(416) 869-3600;
Peter Thomas, Mgr Canada
2020 Rue Universite, Suite 1020, Montreal, PQ H3A 2A5 Canada
(514) 282-0705;
William Miller, Chairman

Thomson, Inc, (RCA/GE)
10330 N. Meridian St., Indianapolis, IN 46290 USA
(317) 587-3000, *Fax:* (317) 587-6708
www.rca.com
dave.arland@thomson.net
Richard Huser, President
Manufactures mkt audio, video communications & accessories products.
Thomson S.A. (parent co.)
46 Quai Alphonse Le Gallo, Boulogne, Cedex, 92045
3301-418650;

360 Systems
31355 Agoura Road, Westlake Village, CA 91361-4610 USA
(818) 991-0360, *Fax:* (818) 991-1360
www.360systems.com
info@360systems.com
Phil Cox, President
Robert Easton, President
Image Server Maxx Video & Graphics servers in standard and High Defintion, Time Delay servers, DigiCart/E, Instant Replay2 and Short/Cut audio editors and players.

3M
3M Product Information Center, St. Paul, MN 55144-1000 USA
(651) 737-6501,(888) 3m-helps, *Fax:* (800) 713-6329,(651) 737-7117
www.3m.com
innovation@mmm.com
George Buckley, President
Robert MacDonald, Promotions Manager
Fault locators; cable & cabling equipment & supplies; Post-it notes & flags; Telephony: copper & fiber optic networks; Vikuiti display enhancement films; splicing kts; volition fiber optics; electrical tubing, tapes, terminations &connectors.

The Tiffen Company
90 Oser Ave., Hauppauge, NY 11788 USA
(631) 273-2500,(800) 645-2522, *Fax:* (631) 273-2557
www.tiffen.com
Michael Cannatta, COO
Steve Tiffen, President
Jeff Cohen, Operations Dir
Hilary Araujo, Promotions Manager
Photographic filters, lens accessories for motion picture, still photography, digital video, Davis & Sanford tripods, Domke Bags, support systems; steadicam camera stabilizing systems..

Time Logic Inc.
1914 Palomar Oaks Way, Suite 150, Carlsbad, CA 92008 USA
(760) 517-0445, *Fax:* (760) 431-1351
www.timelogic.com
jiml@timelogic.com
Rick MacDonald, CEO
Automation systems for TV bcstrs & radio stns. Custom software dev for Tektronix Profile disks, HDTV time delay systems, using disk or tape.

Time Manufacturing Co.
1200 Texes Central Parkway, Waco, TX 76702-0368 USA
(254) 399-2100, *Fax:* (254) 399-2651
www.timemfg.com
Charles Wiley, President
Amber Pierce, Promotions Manager
Truck mounted aerial lifts ranging from 29' to 210' in height.

Times Fiber Communications Inc.
358 Hall Ave., Wallingford, CT 6492 USA
(203) 265-8500, *Fax:* (203) 265-8422
www.timesfiber.com
Timothy Cohane, COO
Stan VonFeldt, General Sales Mgr
Chris Huffman, Promotions Manager
Diana Reardon, Chief Financial Officer
Coaxial, twisted pair composite cables for broadband, cellular/PCS applications, semiflex, svc entry, drop cables & connectors.
Box 14975, Phoenix, AZ 85063 United States
(602) 278-5576;
Les Judd, Chairman
Box 430, Renfrew, ON Canada
(613) 432-8557;
Box 119A, Rt. 2, Chatham, VA 24531 United States
(804) 432-1800;

Tinsley Laboratory Inc.
4040 Lakeside Dr., Richmond, CA 94806 USA
(510) 222-8110, *Fax:* (510) 223-4534
Dan Desmond, President
John Kincaid, General Manager
Gyrozoom image stabilizing lens, GX3 integrated CCD camera/stabilizing system.

TOA Electronics Inc.
601 Gateway Blvd., Suite 300, South San Francisco, CA 94080 USA
(650) 588-2538, *Fax:* (650) 588-3349
info@toaelectronics.com
Hisayuki Okvoka, CEO
Allan Lamberti, General Sales Mgr
Sound, communication equipment for coml sound & audio/video industries. Manufacturer, distributor of high quality, reliable audio & security products.

Toner Cable Equipment Inc.
969 Horsham Rd., Horsham, PA 19044 USA
(215) 675-2053,(800) 523-5947, *Fax:* (215) 675-7543
www.tonercable.com
info@tonercable.com
Robert Toner, President/CEO
B.J. Toner, Operations Dir
Steve Beasley, General Sales Mgr
International distributor & manufacturer of a complete line of cable TV & wireless cable equipment.
UK Ltd.
Unit 9 Berinsfield Business Park, Tower Industrial Estate, Fane Dr., Berinsfield, Oxfordshire, OX10 7LN United Kingdom
0186 534 1222;

Torpey Time
580 Danforth Road, Toronto, ON M1v 1E1 CAN
(416) 298-7788,(800) 387-6141, *Fax:* (416) 298-7789
www.torpeytime.com
torpey@attglobal.net
Bob Torpey, President
Master clock systems, digital & analog slave clocks, timers, video time & temperature equipment.

Toshiba America Consumer Products
1420 Toshiba Dr., Lebanon, TN 37087 USA
(615) 444-8501, *Fax:* (615) 443-3810
www.toshiba.com
Yoshirio Matsumoto, President
Jodi Sally, Operations Dir
Marcia Repole, VP/Communications
HDTV products: HD-VCR (Analog-UniHi), HD monitor (projection & CRT), NTSC to HDTV upconverter, HD-CCD color camera, HD horizon system.
82 Totowa Rd., Wayne, NJ 07470 United States
(973) 628-8000; *Fax:* (973) 628-1875

Tower Innovations
2855 Hwy. 261, Newburgh, IN 47630 USA
(812) 853-0595,(800) 664-8222, *Fax:* (812) 853-6652
www.towerinnovations.net
towers@towerinnovations.net
David Nicholson, COO
Josh Bridgeman, General Manager
Melissa Nicholson, Promotions Manager
Manufacture towers for broadcast (up to 2000'), cellular & PCS Communications Innovative engrg solutions, fabrication, construction planning, tower erection & turnkey systems.

2855 Hwy 261, Newburgh, IN 47630

Tower Inspection Inc.
3317 S Cherokee Drive, Muskogee, OK 74402-0709 USA
(918) 683-8915, *Fax:* (918) 683-0888
www.towerinspection.com
sales@towerinspection.com
Gary Lehman, President
Inspection svcs during construction; maintenance inspection, painting, repairs of radio, microwave & TV towers.

Tower Network Services
900 RR 6205, Suite C206, Austin, TX 78734 USA
(512) 266-6200, *Fax:* (512) 266-6210
www.towernetwork.com
Svc tower, antenna. RF testing & tower structural analysis. Tower elevator repair and upgrading.

Towers-R-Us
Box 1255, 3304 Wadley Road, Waycross, GA 31502 USA
(912) 283-6317, *Fax:* (912) 283-6318
towersrus2008@yahoo.com
Velvet Beard, CEO
Grant Balwanz, President
Design, engineer, fabricate, erect, maintain, and paint high radio towers

Transcom Corp.
2655 Philmont Avenue, Suite 1500, Huntington Valley, PA 19027 USA
(215) 938-7304, *Fax:* (215) 938-7361
www.fmamtv.com
transcom@fmamtv.com
Martin Cooper, President
New digital (8VSB/DVB-T/H), angle TV transmitters, microwave links, antenna, cable & select used TV, AM, FM transmitters.
2655 Philmont Ave., Suite 200, Huntington Valley, PA 19006 United States
(215) 938-7304 (800) 441-8454; *Fax:* (215) 938-7361
Martin Cooper, Pres

Transcrypt International
3900 N.W. 12th St., Suite 200, Lincoln, NE 68521 USA
(800) 228-0226
www.ecjohnstontechnologies.com
Massoud Safavi, COO
Technological assst for installation, application in all types & brands of land mobile radios. Transcrypt ensures you the best value in the industry

Transit and Rail Design Inc.
Valley Forge Corporate Center, 1010 Adams Ave., Audubon, PA 19403-2402 USA
(610) 650-7730, *Fax:* (610) 650-8190
www.rsdconsulting.com
Bob Dietz, CEO
Walter Clarke, President
Esther McGinnis, Operations Dir
Consulting engrs, tower engrg, design & construction mgmt.

Transtector Systems Inc.
10701 Airport Drive, Hayden, ID 83835 USA
(800) 882-9110,(208) 772-8515, *Fax:* (208) 762-6133
www.transtector.com
sales@transtector.com
David Stimmel, CFO
Shawn Thompson, President/Director
James E. Harless, Operations Dir
Linda Johnson, Promotions Manager
Steve Pare, CFO
Transient overvoltage protective devices, power quality consulting svcs; college-accredited, power-quality assurance education courses.

Transvision/Vision Accomplished Inc.
550 Maulhardt Ave., Oxnard, CA 93030 USA
(805) 981-8740, *Fax:* (805) 981-8738
www.txvision.com
info@txvision.com
Transportable, flyaway satellite transmission; mobile/TVROs; studio/remote production & transmission mgmt.

Tribune Media Services
40 Media Drive, Queensbury, NY 12801 USA
(800) 833-9581 (518) 792-9914, *Fax:* (518) 761-7118
www.tvdata.com
tvdata@tvdata.com
Lanna Langlois, CFO
James McCormick, Operations Dir
John Kelleher, General Manager
Ken Carter, Station Manager
Kathleen Tolstrup, General Sales Mgr
International source for TV info. Clients include interactive on-screen & on-line guides, nwsprs, print publications, cable companies, telephone companies, rsch organizations, producers, syndicators of TV programs & advertisers.

Trident Media Group/ Spector Entertainment Group Inc.
2441 Impala Dr., Carlsbad, CA 92008 USA
(760) 438-9080, *Fax:* (760) 438-0968
Eric Spector, President
Evan Spector, President
International audio, video, data & telephone communications svcs between United States/Canada & Mexico/Latin America; private TV networks; 12 C-band uplinks; teleports; satellite space segment; encryption; organization svcs; closed circuitTV & security systems.

Trilogy Communications Inc.
2910 Highway 80 East, Pearl, MS 39208 USA
(601) 932-4461,(800) 874-5649, *Fax:* (601) 939-6637
www.trilogycoax.com
info@trilogycoax.com
John Kaye, Chairman
Sidney Shinn Lee, President
Bill Lee, Operations Dir
Jim Oldham, General Sales Mgr
Fei Wei, Promotions Manager
World leading manufacturer of advanced technology coaxial cables for wireless networks for cellular, paging, PCS, SMR and in- building networking applications application, ISO-9001 certified.

Trimm Inc.
407 Railroad St., Butner, NC 27509 USA
(800) 298-7466, *Fax:* 919) 575-6200
www.trimminc.com
trimminc@frontiernet.net
Will Newton, President
Ricky Brummet, General Sales Mgr
Manufacturer of fuse panel s& terminal blocks.

Trompeter Semflex
55550 E. McDowell Rd., Mesa, AZ 85215 USA
(480) 985-9000, *Fax:* (480) 985-0334
www.trompeter.com
sales@trompeter.com
Joe Norwood, President
Dale Reed, Vice President
DS3 interconnection & DSX products for central office.

TTE Inc.
11652 W. Olympic Blvd., Los Angeles, CA 90064 USA
(310) 478-8224, *Fax:* (800) 473-2791
www.tte.com
sls@tte.com
Stephen Sodaro, General Sales Mgr
Dave Zavac, Manager
LC filters to 18 GHz, balun, matching transformers, combiners, active filters to 1 MHz. RF, microwave filters DC-18ghz & video splitters.

Tulsat/An Addvantage Technologies Co.
1221 E. Houston St., Broken Arrow, OK 74012 USA
(800) 331-5997, *Fax:* (918) 251-1138
www.tulsat.com
tulsat@tulsat.com
David Chymiak, Chairman
Ken Chymiak, President
Mark Schumacher, General Sales Mgr

Turner Studios Field Operations
1065 Williams Street NW, Atlanta, GA 30318 USA
(404) 885-4746, *Fax:* (404) 885-2175
charli.whitfield@turner.com
Charli Whitfield, Operations Dir
Bob McGee, Director, Technical Operations
Scott Marks, Vice President
Steve Wench, Operations Executive
Glen Bohete, Manager
Ken Brady, Chief Technical Officer
Two 53 ft expandable mobile units with or without crews; 12 cams, 9 VTRs, EVS, DVEous, Infinit & Deko; FFV Omega DDRs.

TWR Lighting Inc.
4300 Windfern, Suite 100, Houston, TX 77041-0943 USA
(713) 973-6905, *Fax:* (713) 973-9352
www.twrlighting.com
info@twrlightinc.com
Edwin Wahler Jr, Chairman
Ken Meador, CEO
Jeff Huchlefeld, Operations Dir
Raymond Kraemer, General Sales Mgr
Aviation obstruction lighting manufacturer, sls & svc of low, medium, LED products & High Intensity systems.

Tyco Electronics
300 Constitution Dr., Menlo Park, CA 94025 USA
(650) 361-3333,(717) 564-0100, *Fax:* (650) 361-2288
www.tycoelectronics.com
Thomas Lynch, CEO
Dennis Conway, General Sales Mgr
Coaxial connectors, environmental sealing products & antenna de-icers.

U.S. Tape & Label Corp.
2092 Westport Ctr. Dr., St. Louis, MO 63146 USA
(314) 824-4444, *Fax:* (314) 824-4400
www.ustl.com
Jim Eiseman, President/Owner
Debbie Reed, Engineering
Bob Rubin, Finance
Custom printed bumper strips & window labels for the bcst industry. Industrial labels, direct mail printing & label-aire equipment.

U.S. Traffic & Display Solutions
9603 John St., Santa Fe Springs, CA 90670 USA
(562) 923-9600, *Fax:* (562) 923-7555
www.displaysolutionsinc.com
dsi@dsiusa.com
Glen Hirami, President
Changeable outdoor electronic adv displays.

Ultimate Precision/GKM
200 Finn Ct., Farmingdale, NY 11735 USA
(631) 249-7816, *Fax:* (631) 777-1828
www.gkmbroadcastracks.com
kmerrigan@afcosystems.com
Michael Mallia, CEO
Gerard Becker, President
GKM is the source for Bcst Racks & Communication Products featuring a comprehensive line of bcst racks, frames & enclosure solutions for the bcst industry. A division of Ultimate Precision Metal Products, Inc.-part of the AFCO Systems Group.Ultimate has been a recognized leader precision sheet metal mfg for over 30 years

Ultimate Support Systems Inc.
5836 Wright Dr., Loveland, CO 80538 USA
(800) 525-5628, *Fax:* (970) 776-1941
www.ultimatesupport.com
custserv@ultimatesupport.com
Mike Belitz, CEO/President
Doug Towne, Manager
Jeff Moore, President
Strong, lightweight speaker & lighting tripods. Microphone stands for nearly any application.

Ultimatte Corp.
20945 Plummer St., Chatsworth, CA 91311 USA
(818) 993-8007, *Fax:* (818) 993-3762
www.ultimatte.com
Lynne Sauve, President
Reid Baker, General Sales Mgr
Alan Dadourian, Chief Engineer
Max Portillo, Engineering
Video compositing devices for coms, live bcst, production, postproduction & computerized tripod head.

Uni-Set Corp.
449 Ave. A, Rochester, NY 14621-4501 USA
(585) 544-3820, *Fax:* (585) 544-1110
www.unisetcorp.com
info@unisetcorp.com
Ronald Kniffin, President
Modular studio staging systems for studio settings; news setting; 7 top talent tables, & UNI-CYC anywhere cyclorama.

Union Connector Co.
40 Dale St., West Babylon, NY 11704-1104 USA
(631) 753-9550, *Fax:* (631) 753-9560
www.unionconnector.com
Richard Wolpert, President
Alan Wolpert, Operations Dir
Electrical connectors, power distribution systems, portable power cabinets, custom switchgear, cases, carts & grip equipment.

Unique Business Systems
2901 Ocean Park Drive, Santa Monica, CA 90401 USA
(310) 396-3929, *Fax:* (310) 396-6114
www.unibiz.com
pbatra@unibiz.com

Pradeep Batra, President/Co-Founder
Stan Sugimoto, Co-Founder
Asset management software to track equipment sales and rentals, service and repair, and labor planning. Single system from quote to invoice. Two products: 'R2' software for Entertainment Rental companies and 'CR2' software for ConstructionEquipment Dealers.

Unisys Corp.
801 Lakeview Drive, Suite 100, Blue Bell, PA 19424 USA
(215) 986-4011
www.unisys.com
Joseph W. McGrath, CEO
Kevin Kern, Operations Dir
Barbara Harris, Programmer
Adam Brodman, Member
Nancy S. Sundheim, Senior VP & Gen Counsel
Cable info business systems. Unisys hardware: A1, A4, A6, A10, A12, A17 & IBM PC compatibles.

United Media Inc.
4771 E. Hunter, Anaheim, CA 92807 USA
(714) 227-7183, *Fax:* (714) 777-2434
www.unitedmediainc.com
umi@unitedmediainc.com
United Media Inc is a developer & manufacturer which recognizes the ongoing need for high quality, affordable professional video equipment, developer of the On-Line Express non-linear editing system for Windows NT and multicom. The On-LineExpress offers uncompromised digital editing, compositing, digital audio editing, titling, 2D & 3D realtime effects & sophisticated media mgmt.

United States Broadcast
1371 Production Dr., Burlington, KY 41005 USA
(859) 282-1802, *Fax:* (859) 282-1804
www.usbroadcast.com
info@usbroadcast.com
Pete Beckett, President
New, used TV, audio equipment, bcst batteries & chargers.

UniVision Inc.
2801 S. Russell, Missoula, MT 59801 USA
(406) 721-8876, *Fax:* (406) 721-0810
www.univision-computers.com
sales@univision-computers.com
Jim Green, President
Sell & repair computers. Program software, fiberoptics & wiring.

Utah Scientific Inc.
4750 Wiley Post Way, Suite 150, Salt Lake City, UT 84116 USA
(800) 453-8782, *Fax:* (801) 537-3099
www.utahscientific.com
info@utahscientific..com
David Burland, COO
Tom Harmon, CEO
Routing, master control switchers & control systems. Industry's best warranty-10 years!

Utility Tower Company
Box 12369, 3200 N.W. 38th, Oklahoma City, OK 73157 USA
(405) 946-5551, *Fax:* (405) 947-8466
utctower@aol.com,utctower@utilitytower.com
Gloria Nelson, President
Joe James, Operations Dir
Ron Nelson Jr., Vice President
Tower structures, accessories for bcstg & wireless applications; tower design, engrg analysis, turnkey instals; modifications, maintenance & inspections.

V-Soft Communications
401 Main Street, Suite 213, Cedar Falls, IA 50613 USA
(319) 266-8402, *Fax:* (319) 266-9212
www.v-soft.com
info@v-soft.com
Doug Vernier, President
John Gray, Operations Dir
Kate Michler, Engineering Dir
Best engineering software for AM, FM, TV & general communications. Signal propagation, allocation work, path profiles, custom mapping & more.

Valmont Specialty Structures
3575 25th St. S.E., Salem, OR 97302-1190 USA
(503) 363-9267,(800) 547-2151, *Fax:* (503) 363-4613
www.valmont.com
custoinfo@microflect.com
Bret Davis, Station Manager
Towers, microwave passive repeaters, waveguide support systems & tech svcs.

Van Nostrand Radio Engineering Service
256 Strickland Pasture Rd., Jackson, GA 30233-4019 USA
(770) 775-7575
vnres@bellsouth.com
Samuel Boor, Co-Owner
Frequency measurements up to 26 GHz.
Box 510458, Melbourne Beach, FL 32951-0458 United States
(321) 723-1250;
Samuel B. Boor, Co-Owner

Vantage Lighting Inc.
175 Paul Dr., Suite E, San Rafael, CA 94903 USA
(800) 445-2677 (415) 507-0402, *Fax:* (415) 507-0502
www.vanltg.com
eight@vanltg.com
Arlene Allsman, President
Peter Allsman, General Manager
Replacement lamps including stage, studio, projection audiovisual, HMI, Xenon, 3D video & laser system. Electronic ballasts for HID lighting.

Vecima Networks Inc.
150 Cardinal Place, Victoria, BC V87 6N6 CAN
Fax: (250) 881-1982,(250) 881-1974
wwwvecima.com
invest@vecima.com
Dr Surinder Kumar, Chairman
Dr Hugh Wood, COO
Sumit Kumar, President
Dr. Surinder Kumar, CEO
Mr. Mike Barry, CFO
Designer, manufacturer & seller of products that enable broadband access to cable, wireless & telephony networks.
150 Cardinal Pl., Saskatoon, SK 57L 6H7 Canada
(306) 955-7075;
Dr. Hugh Wood, COO

Veetronix Inc.
Box 480, 1311 W. Pacific, Lexington, NE 68850 USA
(308) 324-6661, *Fax:* (308) 324-4985
www.veetronix.com
sales@veetronix.com
James Longley, President
Roger Teeters, General Sales Mgr
Ladonna Kwiatkowski, Purchasing Executive
Keyboard & panel reed switches & keycaps with in-house tooling.

Vega
8601 Cornhusker E. Hwy., Lincoln, NE 68505-5321 USA
(402) 467-5324, *Fax:* (402) 467-3279
www.vega-signaling.com
vega@telex.com
Don Poysa, General Sales Mgr
Dispatch control consoles, amplifiers & monitoring products.

Veriad
650 Columbia St., Brea, CA 92821 USA
(800) 423-4643 (714) 990-2700, *Fax:* (800) 962-0658
info@veriad.com
Videotape & audiotape format labels, CD & DVD labels tape mgmt labels, labeling software, packaging products & production supplies.

Vermeer Manufacturing Co.
1210 Vermeer Rd. E., Pella, IA 50219 USA
(515) 628-3141,(888) 837-6337, *Fax:* (515) 621-7734
www.vermeer.com
salesinfo@vermeermfg.com
Robert Vermeer, Chairman
Mary Andringa, CEO
Steve Heap, Sr Director/International Sales
Cable plows, trenchers, backhoes, stump cutters & hyraulic boring equipment.

Vertex Communications Corp.
1104 Energy Dr., Kilgore, TX 75662-5536 USA
(903) 984-7811, *Fax:* (903) 984-1826
www.tripointglobal.com
vertexrsi@gdsatcom.com
Chris Marzizzi, President
Gary Kanipe, Operations Dir
Jeff Porter, General Manager
John Sciberras, Promotions Manager
Antennas, control systems, passive microwave devices, field svcs, satcom net equipment, custom engrg solutions, SSPAs, LNAs, RF components/subsystems.

Vertex Beijing Office
COFCO Plaza, Suite 411, Tower B, N. 8 Jian Guo Men Nei Ave, Be, 100005
(+86-10) 6528-7258; *Fax:* (+86-10) 6528-7261
info@vertex.com.cn

Vertex Antennentechnik GmbH
Baumstr. 50, Duisburg, D-47198
49-2066-20960; *Fax:* 49-2066-209611
info@vertexant.com

Vertex International Ltd.
37 Kinghorn Rd., Burntisland, Fife, KY3 9EA
44-1592-873-956
vertes@mbox3.singnet.com.sg

Vertex Asia (Singapore Representative Office)
21-03 Suntec Tower One, 7 Temasek Blvd., 038987 Singapore
65-430-9524; *Fax:* 65-430-9516
vertex@pacific.net.sg

Vertex Antenna Systems LLC
2211 Lawson Ln., Santa Clara, CA 95054 United States
(408) 654-5600; *Fax:* (408) 654-5613/5614
bernard@tiw.com

Vertex Microwave Products Inc.
3111 Fujita St., Torrance, CA 90505 United States
(310) 539-6704; *Fax:* (310) 539-7463
info@vertexmpi.com

Vicon Industries Inc.
89 Arkay Dr., Hauppauge, NY 11788 USA
(631) 952-2288, *Fax:* (631) 951-9288
www.vicon-cctv.com
John Badke, CFO
Larry Greenwald, President
Peter Horn, Operations Dir
Yacov Pshtissky, General Sales Mgr
Bret McGowan, Promotions Manager
Guy Arazi, Engineering Dir
Closed circuit TV equipment, systems for the security & surveillance industry.

VidCAD Documentation Programs (VDP Inc.)
2010 E. Lohman Ave., Suite 2Suite D9, Las Cruces, NM 88001 USA
(505) 522-0003, *Fax:* (505) 522-0009
www.vidcad.com
sales@vidcad.com
Walter Black, CEO
John Weadock, Training Manager
VidCAD software connects your idea from diagram design & rack planning to installation, maintenance & rebuilds-on time & on budget.

Video Accessory Corp.
1243 Salerman Drive, Suite 8, Longmount, CO 80301 USA
(800) 821-0426, *Fax:* (303) 440-8878
www.vac-brick.com
vac@vac-brick.com
Frank S. Barnes, President
Amy Barnes Frey, CEO
Bruce Wallingford, Promotions Manager
Richard Frey, Chief Engineer
Black Burst generators, video & audio distribution amplifiers, video line isolators, video & audio switches.

Video International Development Corp.
Box 349, 21 Winans Place, Locust Valley, NY 11560 USA
(516) 671-6765, *Fax:* (516) 671-6771
www.videointernational.com
info@videointernational.com
Bernd Bressel, President/Broadcast Media Executive
HD & SD Digital TV standards converters with motion compensated interpolation for bcst & industrial use as well as audio/video processors for production & post-production.

X-Form Systems-Spechtweg 1
Braunschweig, 38108 Germany
(0531) 30292890;

Videomagnetics Inc.
3970 Clearview Frontage Rd., Colorado Springs, CO 80911 USA
(719) 390-1313, *Fax:* (719) 390-1316
www.videomagnetics.com
vmi@csprings.com
Tony Korte, President/CEO
Jane Pennie, General Sales Mgr
Full service specialists in betacam camera & recorders. Refurbished video heads & scanners.

Videotron Ltee
300 Viger Avenue East, Montreal, QC H28 3W4 CAN
(514) 281-1711, *Fax:* (514) 985-8652
Robert Depatie, CEO
Manon Brouillette, Operations Dir
Saro Saroyan, General Manager
Bernard Bricallt, Vice President
Cable TV, digital TV, interactive TV and telecommunications.

LeGroupe Videotron Ltee.
300 ave Viger est, Montreal, PQ H2X 3W4 Canada

EQUIPMENT MANUFACTURERS

Videssence L.L.C.
10768 Lower Azusa Rd., El Monte, CA 91731 USA
(626) 579-0943, *Fax:* (626) 579-6803
www.videssence.tv
contact@videssence.tv
Toni Swarens, President
Lauri Maines, Operations Dir
Energy-efficient fluorescent and LED, studio lighting products for TV, film, stage, commercial broadcasting and communications applications.

Vidiom Systems Inc.
10901 W. 120th Ave., Suite 230, Broomfield, CO 80021 USA
(303) 604-0800, *Fax:* (303) 604-0080
www.vidiom.com
mmalcy@vidiom.com
Timothy Wahlers, CEO
David Housman, Operations Dir
Michael Malcy, Promotions Manager
Travis Paranto, Finance Director
Software engrg & design, software testing, application development, technical writing, training for OCAP, ETV, headends.

Viking Cases
10480 Oak St. N.E., St. Petersburg, FL 33716 USA
(800) 237-8560, *Fax:* (727) 577-2082
www.vikingcases.com
sales@vikingcases.com
Arthur Stemler, CEO
Bruce Stemler, President
Reese Autry, Operations Dir
Heavy-duty reusable shipping cases, lightweight carrying cases & EIA rack cases.

Vinten Inc.
709 Executive Blvd., Suite B, Valley Cottage, NY 10989 USA
(845) 268-0100, *Fax:* (845) 268-0113
www.vinten.com
mike.denicola@vinten.com
Bob Carr, President
Ali Ahmadi, Promotions Manager
Joan Frison, Financial Executive
Remote control camera systems. Pneumatic studio pedestals, pan & tilt heads, lightweight tripods & heads.
50 Moberly Ave., Toronto, ON M4CC 2B1 Canada
(416) 693-8578; *Fax:* (416) 693-9489
Sam Duncan, Canadian Rgnl Sls Mgr
4 Birch Ct., Shamong, NJ 08088 United States
(609) 268-2405; *Fax:* 609-268-3204
Len Donovan, Northeast Rgnl Sls Mgr
10208 N.W. 47th St., Sunrise, FL 33351 United States
(945) 572-4344; *Fax:* (945) 572-4565
Joseph Lantowski, Southern Rgnl Sls Mgr
G 95 S. Glenwood, Suite B, Burbank, CA 91506 United States
(818) 843-5244; *Fax:* (818) 843-5176
Mark Playdon, West Rgn Sls Mgr

Vision Database Systems
1095 Jupiter Park Dr., Suite 3, Jupiter, FL 33458 USA
(561) 748-0711, *Fax:* (561) 748-0712
www.visiondatabase.com
Emil Bonaduce, President
Photo image software.

Visual Sound Inc.
485 Park Way, Broomall, PA 19008 USA
(610) 544-8700,(800) 523-7525, *Fax:* (610) 544-3385
www.visualsound.com
info@visualsound.com
Karen Bogosian, President
John Greene, General Sales Mgr
Audio-video sls, svcs, installation, maintainance of teleconferencing rooms, interactive white boards, training rooms; ENG, production vans, studios, events production & rentals.
490 S. St. John's Church Rd., Camp Hill, PA 17011 United States
(717) 730-6651 (800) 382-1301; *Fax:* (717) 761-0874
Beltsville
3919 Vero Rd. # J, Halethorpe, MD 21227 United States
(410) 242-4216;

Vortek
7200 Rawson Road, Victor, NY 14564 USA
(585) 924-5000, *Fax:* (585) 924-0545
www.vortekrigging.com
Scott Seeman, President
David Ross, Operations Dir
Robin Allen, Purchasing Executive
Engineer manufacture rigging systems, motorized hoists & controls.

VSG Inc.
1033 Elm Hill Pike, Nashville, TN 37210 USA
(615) 248-1010, *Fax:* (615) 244-5712
www.vsginc.com
Chris Ramsey, President
Greg Shriner, General Sales Mgr
CD & DVD replication, CD DVD duplication, packaging & fulfillment.

VTECH Communications
9590 S.W. Gemini Drive, Suite 120, Beaverton, OR 97008-7109 USA
(503) 596-1200, *Fax:* (503) 644-9887
www.vtechphones.com
Bruce Garfield, CEO
Doug Vernier, President
Matt Ramage, Operations Dir
Tom Bacon, Marketing VP
Kate Michler, Engineering Dir
900 mhz cordless analog digital telephones.

Ward-Beck Systems Ltd.
Unit 10, 455 Milner Ave., Toronto, ON M1B 2K4 CAN
(416) 335-5999, *Fax:* (416) 335-5202
ward-beck.com
request@ward-beck.com
Eugene Johnson, General Manager
Michael Jordan, General Sales Mgr
Gerald Bell, Manager
Doug Bascombe, Chief Engineer
Distribution metering, monitoring, conversion of AES & analog audio, video & serial digital bcstg signals. Radio consoles.

Wearguard
141 Longwater Dr., Norwell, MA 2061 USA
(781) 871-4100, *Fax:* (800) 867-7160
www.wearguard.com
George McNaughton, President
Offers a comprehensive line of work clothing & identity apparel serving the cable industry.

WeatherBank Inc.
1015 Waterwood Pkwy., Suite J, Edmond, OK 73034 USA
(405) 359-0773,(800) 687-3562, *Fax:* (405) 341-0115
www.weatherbank.com
sroot@weatherbank.com
Steven Root, CEO
Michael R. Root, Operations Dir
Satellite-delivered weather info, audio forecasting svcs & consulting to all industries.

WEGENER
11350 Technology Cir., Johns Creek, GA 30097 USA
(770) 814-4000, *Fax:* (770) 623-0698
www.wegener.com
globalsales@wegener.com
Robert Placek, CEO/Chairman
Ned L. Mountain, President
Elias J. Livaditis, Chief Engineer
Troy Woodbury, CEO
Jim Traicoff, CFO
WEGENER is an international provider of digital video and audio solutions for broadcast television, radio, telco, private and cable networks. With over 30 years experience in optimizing point-to-multipoint multimedia distribution oversatellite, fiber, and IP networks, WEGENER offers a comprehensive product line that handles the scheduling, management and delivery of media rich content to multiple devices, including video screens, computers and audio devices. WEGENER focuses onlong- and short-term strategies for bandwidth savings, dynamic advertising, live events and affiliate management.

Wescam Inc.
649 N. Service Rd. W., Burlington, ON L7P 5B9 CAN
(905) 633-4000, *Fax:* (905) 633-4100
www.wescam.com
Mark Chamberlain, CEO
John Dehne, President
Larry Spanier, Vice President
Featuring Wescam Helicopter film, video, HD system, new & ultimately stable XR for all group applications.
7150 Hayvenhurst Ave., Van Nuys, CA 91406-3823 United States
(818) 785-9282; *Fax:* (818) 785-9787
Chris White, Chairman

Weschler Instruments
16900 Foltz Parkway, Cleveland, OH 44149 USA
(440) 238-2550, *Fax:* (440) 238-0660
www.weschler.com
sales@weschler.com
David Hughes, President
Gary Lanham, Operations Dir
Michael Dorman, Executive Vice President
Mark Norquest, Manager
Digital & analog panel meters, RF ammeters, process indicators, digital multimeters, circuit tracers, power analyzers & test equipment.

Westcott
1447 Summit Street North, Toledo, OH 43603 USA
(419) 243-7311, *Fax:* (419) 243-8401
www.fjwestcott.com
info@fjwestcott.com
Thomas Waltz, President
Robin Wilson, Manager
Kelly Mendora, Marketing Executive
Lightweight, portable & collapsible light control equipment: silks & solids, scrims, Illuminator™ reflectors, umbrellas, light modifiers, & Scrim Jim modular light panels.

Westlake Audio
2696 Lavery Ct., Unit 18, Newbury Park, CA 91320 USA
(805) 499-3686, *Fax:* (805) 498-2571
www.westakeaudio.com
barbarab@westlakeaudio.com
Glenn Phoenix, President
Barbara Born, Sales Manager/Marketing
Ken Centrofante, Promotions Manager
Sherwood Davies, Finance
Audio monitors & accessories.

Westlake Audio, Professional Sales Group
7265 Santa Monica Blvd., Los Angeles, CA 90046 USA
(323) 851-9800, *Fax:* (323) 851-0182
www.westlakeaudio.com
Steve Burdick, Operations Dir
Deborah Rally, General Manager
David Logan, General Sales Mgr
Professional audio equipment repairs, professional recording equipment sales, rentals, studio design. Westlake can provide all your Pro Audio needs, from Pro Audio equipment sls to full tracking & mixing.
2696 Lavery Ct., Unit 18, Newbury Park, CA 91320 United States
(805) 499-3686; *Fax:* (805) 498-2571
Glenn Phoenix, Pres
8447 Beverly Blvd., Los Angeles, CA 90048 United States
(323) 654-2155; *Fax:* (323) 655-0478

Wheatstone Corp.
600 Industrial Dr., New Bern, NC 28562 USA
(252) 638-7000, *Fax:* (252) 635-4857
www.wheatstone.com
sales@wheatstone.com
Gary Snow, President
Andrew Calvanese, Operations Dir
Jay Tyler, General Sales Mgr
Dan Murdoch, Chief Technical Officer
Manufacturer of analog & digital bcst audio mixing consoles, processing equipment, radio & TV products since 1976.

Whirlwind
99 Ling Rd., Greece, NY 14612 USA
(585) 663-8820, *Fax:* (585) 865-8930,(888) 733-4396
www.whirlwindusa.com
sales@whirlwindusa.com
Michael Laiacona, President
Al Keltz, General Manager
Mix-6 audio mixers, presspower 2 active pressbox, active splitters; P-12 & power amplifiers, MD-1 MIC/line driver.

Wil-Can Electronics Ltd.
8560 Torbram Rd., Unit #35, Brampton, ON L6T 5C9 CAN
(905) 790-2711, *Fax:* (905) 790-8861
www.powersurges.com
wilcan@lightningtvss.com
William Black, President
Gregory Black, VP/General Manager
Designers, manufacturers & consultants. Lightning & high energy transient control including protection for telephone, signal & data lines.
2316 Delaware Ave., Suite 285, Buffalo, NY 14216 United States
(888) 596-2020; *Fax:* (888) 866-7775
Gregory J. Black, Gen Mgr/Sec Treas

WILL-BURT Co.
401 Collins Blvd, Orrville, OH 44667 USA
(330) 682-7015, *Fax:* (330) 684-1190
www.willburt.com
contact_us@willburt.com
Jeff Evans, CEO
Steven Pinkley, General Sales Mgr
John Mayles, Programming Director

Telescoping mast used to position antennas, lights & cameras to heights of 20 to 134 ft.

Wiltronix Inc.
Box 364, 16850 Oakmont Ave., Washington Grove, MD 20880 USA
(301) 258-7676, *Fax:* (301) 963-8624
www.wiltronix.com
equipsales@wiltronix.com
Dwight Wilcox, President
Ellen Packard, Operations Dir
Manufacturers rep for digital HD, SD, video, audio, signal processing, transmission for bcst production & govt video facilities.
6927R Mink Hollow Rd., Highland, MD 20777

Winsted Corp.
10901 Hampshire Ave. S., Minneapolis, MN 55438 USA
(952) 944-9050 (800) 447-2257, *Fax:* (952) 944-1546
www.winsted.com
info@winsted.com
G.R. Hoska, Chairman
Stephen Hoska, CEO
Randy Smith, President
Editing, Production & Post production consoles, space saving tape & data storage systems. Multimedia & Lan/Wan server workstations. Console installations.

Winsted Technical Interiors
1750 Breckinridge Pwky., Suite 100, Duluth, GA 30096
Phone # 800-237-5606 or 770-840-0880;

Wireless Accessories Group
1840 County Line Rd., Suite 301, Huntingdon Valley, PA 19006 USA
(888) 233-0202,(215) 322-4600, *Fax:* (215) 322-4606
www.wirexgroupl.com,www.wirexgroup.com
Two-way radio equipment.

WIREMAX Ltd.
Box 3336, 705 Wamba Ave., Toledo, OH 43607
(800) 843-9479, *Fax:* (419) 531-9503
Al Mocek, President
Tom Ricketts, Operations Dir
Mark Robinson, General Manager
Manufacturer of high temp, wire, cable, high voltage wire & cable.

WireReady NSI
56 Hudson St., Northboro, MA 1532 USA
(800) 833-4459 (508) 393-0200, *Fax:* (508) 393-0255
www.wireready.com
sales@wireready.com
David Gerstmann, President/CEO
NewsReady 32, CartReady, ControlReady, NewsReady, StormReady & SalesReady software. Cart replacement, satellite, music on HD, newsrooms & sls automation. All windows/pc.

Wireworks Corporation
380 Hillside Avenue, Hillside, NJ 7205 USA
(908) 686-7400 (800) 642-9473, *Fax:* (908) 686-0483
www.wireworks.com
sales@wireworks.com
Gerald Krulewicz, President
Larry Williams, Operations Dir
Susan Cochrane, Business Development
Audio, video, & audio/video combination cabling assemblies for bcst market; cable testers, transformer isolated mic splitters; multi-pin connectors & perfect custom panels.

Wohler Technologies Inc.
31055 Huntwood Ave., Hayward, CA 94544 USA
(510) 870-0810, *Fax:* (510) 870-0811
www.wohler.com
Carl Dempsey, CEO
Dave Johnson, COO
Kim Templeman-Holmes, General Sales Mgr
Tom Belford, Director, Marketing

WOIO & WUAB TV
1717 E. 12th St., Cleveland, OH 44114 USA
(216) 771-1943, *Fax:* (216) 515-7152
www.hometeam19.com,www.hometeam43.com
Sharon Ohlson, COO
Paul McTear, President
Wayne Daugherty, EVP
Jim Stunek, General Manager
Full studio facilities; GVG 300 switcher, CMX 3100B edit, 1-inch, 3/4-inch, Beta formats; Abekas digital F/X; Artstar graphics; remote packages.

Wolf Coach Inc.
7 B St., Auburn Industrial Park, Auburn, MA 1501 USA
(508) 363-3489, *Fax:* (508) 799-2384
www.wolfcoach.com
sales@wolfcoach.com
Richard Wolf, Operations Dir
Emeric Feldmar, General Manager
Mark A. Leonard, General Sales Mgr
Thomas Jennings, National Sales Rep
News vans, satellite vehicles, production trailers, vehicle based microwave, satellite uplink, digital SNG, audio/video systems & turnkey systems.
2451 South 600 W., 200, Salt Lake City, UT 84115 United States
(801) 977-9533;
Rex A. Reed, Systems Mgr/Engr
chief engr, President

World Tower Co. Inc.
Box 508, 1213 Compressor Dr., Mayfield, KY 42066 USA
(270) 247-3642, *Fax:* (270) 247-0909
www.worldtower.com
worldtow@ldd.net
Doug Walker, President/Owner
Brent Walker, Vice President
Keith Scoggins, Operations Executive
Keith Scoggins, Senior Operations Director
Manufactures & erects bcst & CATV towers, microwave & cellular.

World Video Sales Co.
625 Hoffmansville Road, Unit 3, Bechtelville, PA 19512 USA
(610) 754-6800, *Fax:* (610) 754-9766
sales@mivs.com
John Taylor, President/Owner
Manufacturers of: video timers/titlers, screen splitters, pattern generators, routing systems, distribution amplifiers & other special purpose video equipments.

Xintekvideo Inc.
56 W. Broad St., Stamford, CT 6902 USA
(203) 348-9229, *Fax:* (203) 348-9266
www.xintekvideo.com
jrossi@xintekvideo.com
John Rossi, President
Video processing equipment, including transcoders, color correctors, image enhancers, noise reducers, co-channel filters, ghost removers & impulse noise eliminators.

Yamaha Corp. of America
6600 Orangethorpe Ave., Buena Park, CA 90620 USA
(714) 522-9011
www.yamaha.com
Richard Hinsz, Chief Operating Officer
Hogen Osawa, President
Tom Sumner, Operations Dir
Paul Calvin, Chief Marketing Officer
Vomal Thomas, Chief Technical Officer
Portable keyboards, synthesizers & drums. Manufactures a complete line of professional audio products targeted to the project studio, coml studio, postproduction, bcst & sound reinforcement markets.

Yanchar Design & Consulting Group
26741 Portola Pkwy., Suite 1E, Foothill Ranch, CA 92610-1713 USA
(949) 770-6601, *Fax:* (949) 770-6575
www.yanchardesign.com
info@yanchardesign.com
Carl Yanchar, President
Acoustical design, facility design, consultation, systems design, studio construction & instal.

Zack Electronics Inc.
1070 Hamilton Rd., Duarte, CA 91010 USA
(626) 303-0655,(800) 466-0449, *Fax:* (626) 303-8694
www.zackelectronics.com
jlomas@zackelectronics.com
Dennis Awad, President
Judi Lomas, General Manager
Darren Godoy, Economic Manager
Cable, connectors, & comprehensive core products for the bcst industry, custom audio/video/data cable assemblies. Featuring: Belden, Neutrik, Switchcraft, Pomona & avbcable.com.

Zenith Electronics Corp.
2000 Millbrook Dr., Lincolnshire, IL 60069 USA
(847) 941-8000, *Fax:* (847) 941-9200
www.zenith.com
David Penski, CEO
T J Lee, President
Hyon Ick Jo, VP/Chief Financial Officer
Kathryn Wolfe, President/Sales
Michael Thomas, SVP
Full line of CATV converters; MMDS systems; cable & pay TV systems for PAL & SECAM international markets; PC-based system controllers; accessories.

Ziehl Electronic Service
8611 Dale Rd., Gasport, NY 14067 USA
(716) 772-7800, *Fax:* (716) 772-7985
Richard Ziehl, President
Frequency measurement svc.

Zomax Inc.
7001 Discovery Blvd., Dublin, OH 43017 USA
(888) 638-2832,(614) 761-2000, *Fax:* (614) 766-3176
www.zomax.com
Ellis Kern, Chairman
Arun Kurana, CEO/COO
Melodie Gee, COO
Vice President, General Manager
CD manufacturer specializing in printing fulfillment svcs, & custom work in CD entertainment & CD-ROM.

Satellite & Transmission Services

ABC Family Worldwide
Div/DBA: (a subsidiary of International Family Entertainmen
500 S. Buena Vista, Burbank, CA 91521-0001
(818) 560-1000
www.abcfamily.com
Haim Saban, Chairman
Basic cable net available in over 76 million homes nationwide; delivers a dynamic mix of quality entertainment with original movies, specials & series in prime time & a fun-filled daytime lineup of newly produced & classic series for kids.
12700 Ventura Blvd, Studio City, CA 91604-2469
(818) 755-2400;
Tony Thomopoulos, Ceo Mtm Entertainment
1133 Ave. of the Americas, 37th Fl., New York, NY 10036-6710
(212) 782-0600;
Rick Sirvaitis, Pres Adv Sls
Barbara Bekkedahl, Exec Vp/ Adv Sls

Agri Net Ray Communications Inc.
104 Radio Rd., Powells Point, NC 27966-9601
(252) 491-2414, *Fax:* (252) 491-2939
www.agrinetradio.com
info@agrinetradio.com
William S. Ray, President
Bob Yanacek, Operations Dir
Lisa Ray, General Sales Mgr
Turnkey satellite transmission service for radio news, sports, syndicated program distribution, audio conferencing; transportable bcst studio/uplinks for remote bcsts & domestic back hauling; network coord svcs & space segment bookingsavailable.

American Microwave & Communications
Div/DBA: (A division of Western Tele-Communications)
4616 N. Grand River Ave., Suite D, Lansing, MI 48906-2576
(517) 327-3000, (517) 331-3719, *Fax:* (517) 327-4706
albronson@sbcglobal.net
Microwave delivery of distant signals to cable systems; net TV & radio service to bcst stns; networking among TV stations.

AMV Gateway Teleport
Div/DBA: Williams Communications Group
27 Randolph St., Carteret, NJ 07008
(732) 969-3191, *Fax:* (732) 541-2007
www.allmobilevideo.com
info@amvchelsea.com
Michael Carberry, General Manager
Operates teleport facilities serving New York City. Videotape svcs; satellite transmission for the bcst, CATV & videoconferencing industries. International wideband voice, data & videoconferencing svcs overseas.

Arqiva Inc.
Div/DBA: (formerly BT North America, Broadcast Services)
2025 M St. N.W., Suite 450, Washington, DC 20036
(202) 721-8886, *Fax:* (202) 721-8595
www.arqiva.com
karen.foster@arqiva.com
Simon Thrush, Operations Dir
Operates international bcst center; 24-hour satellite rooftop teleport, digital compression & encryption svcs.
12950 Culver Blvd., Los Angeles, CA 90066-6781
(310) 577-6643;

Arqiva Limited
Crawley Ct., Winchester, Hampshire, S021 2QA United Kingdom

01962 823434, *Fax:* 01962 822378
www.kingstoninmedia.com
inmedia@kcom.com
Peter Douglas, Chairman
Satellite svcs company providing data bcst, business TV, international VSAT nets & uplink facilities.

Ascent Media
Div/DBA: (formerly Ascent Media Network Services)
250 Harbor Dr., Stamford, CT 06902
(203) 965-6000
www.ascentmedia.com
Peter Brickman, General Manager
C- & Ku-band domestic & international transmission service; fiber-optic connectivity to metropolitan New York. Cable origination, bcst, business TV, transponder availability, studio & postproduction.

Teleport Minnesota
90 S. 11th St, Minneapolis, MN 55403-2414
(612) 330-2645; *Fax:* (612) 330-2603
Kelly Gordon, Mgr

AT&T Alascom
505 E. Bluff Dr., Anchorage, AK 99501-1100
(907) 264-7274, (907) 223-7184, *Fax:* (907) 274-5029
www.attalascom.com
Mike Felix, President
Kay Witt, Operations Dir
Telecommunications, long-distance telephone carrier for the state of Alaska offering bcst, voice, data, WATS, Alaskanet & dedicated private line long-distance svcs.

BAF Satellite & Technology Corp.
200 S.harbor City Blvd., Suite 201, Melbourne, FL 32901
(800) 966-3822, (800) 223-1860 (24 hr), *Fax:* (800) 486-5983, (800) 223-1866 (24 hr)
www.bafsat.com
info@bafsat.com
Jim Vautrot, President
Long-term, short-term & occasional analog & digital KU & C band satellite space, full or partial transponder or transponders for domestic or international video, voice or data transmissions.

CATV Services Inc.
Div/DBA: (Penn Service Microwave Co. Inc.)
115 Mill St., Danville, PA 17821
(570) 275-1431, (570) 275-8410, *Fax:* (570) 275-3888
www.catvservice.com
Video distribution of TV signals to various CATV companies in Pennsylvania.

Communications III
921 Eastwind Dr., Suite 104, Westerville, OH 43081
(614) 901-4420, *Fax:* (614) 901-7721
www.comiii.com
shalliday@comiii.com
Scott Halliday, President
Common carrier/C-band uplink svcs. ISDN, IP, & satellite videoconferencing, Polycom & First Virtual.

Crawford Communications
Div/DBA: (formerly Crawford Satellite Services)
3845 Pleasantdale Rd., Atlanta, GA 30340
(404) 876-7149, *Fax:* (678) 421-6717
www.crawford.com
info@crawford.com
Greg West, CFO
Jesse Crawford, President
Domestic/international satellite trasmission, net origination/playback, satellite uplink trucks, IP-media, fiber ooptics, studio & remote video production, HD/SD post production, DVD.

DCT Transmission L.L.C.
10040 E. Happy Valley Rd., Unit 454, Scottsdale, AR 85255
(480) 515-0913, *Fax:* (480) 515-4632
wiesenberg@spacedata.net
Jim Wiesenberg, General Manager
Broadband microwave provider.

Detroit Public Television
7441 Second Ave., Detroit, MI 48202
(313) 874-1801, (313) 873-7200
www.detroitpublictv.org
email@dptv.org
Daniel Alpert, General Manager
Detroit Public Television (WTVS-Analog 56 & Digital 43) offers Ku-band uplinking to any satellite; uplink, fiberlink, downlink, production, postproduction & teleconference svcs available.

DIRECTV Latin America
1211 Ave. of the Americas, 6th Fl., New York, NY 10036
(212) 462-5000, *Fax:* (212) 462-5081
www.directvla.com
webmaster@directvla.com
Bruce Churchill, President
Provides direct TV for Latin America.

GlobeCast America
10525 Washington Blvd., Culver City, CA 90232
(310) 845-3900, *Fax:* (310) 845-3904
www.globecastamerica.com
Paul Rush, Operations Dir
GlobeCast America provides the bcstg industry with a unique combination of both recognized expertise & extensive inter-continental svcs. Through GlobeCast's vast global infrastructure of over 100 transponders, 30 teleports & interconnectfacilities, the company provides instant access to the world's major media markets. GlobeCast America is part of France Telecom, one of the world's largest telecommunications companies.

GlobeCast Hero Productions
7291 N.W. 74 St., Miami, FL 33166-2407
(305) 887-1600; *Fax:* (305) 391-4424

Home Shopping Network
1 HSN Dr., St. Petersburg, FL 33729
(727) 872-1000, *Fax:* (727) 872-6615
www.hsn.com
grossmanm@hsn.met
Mindy Grossman, CEO
Rob Solomon, Engineering Dir
Svcs include C- & Ku-band transmissions from Tampa, FL, C-band transmissions from New York, NY, & Los Angeles, CA, & postproduction.

International Telecommunications Satellite Organization (INTELSAT)
3400 International Dr. N.W., Washington, DC 20008-3098
(202) 944-6800, *Fax:* (202) 944-8125
www.intelsat.com
John Romm, President
Intelsat supplies video, data & voice connectivity in approximately 200 countries & territories for over 1,800 customers worldwide. Intelsat provides svcs on a global fleet of 53 satellites & 7 owned teleports & terrestrial facilities.

Kaufman Broadcast Services
3655 Olive St., St. Louis, MO 63108
(314) 533-6633, *Fax:* (314) 533-1113
www.kaufmanbroadcast.com
info@kaufmanbroadcast.com
Bill Kaufman, President
Transmission svcs via satellite or fiber optics, production & editing facilities.

MCI
500 Clinton Center Dr., Clinton, MS 39056
(601) 460-5600, (800) 644-news
www.mci.com
Tammy McLean, Promotions Manager
Data, internet, international long distance & telecom svcs throughout the United States.

MCI Tampa
3608 Queen Palm Dr., Tampa, FL 33619-1311
(813) 829-0011
www.mci.com
Michael Capellas, President
Serves Pennsylvania Public Television Network, Pennsylvania, Ohio, New Jersey, Vermont, New Hampshire, New York & Massachusetts. CATV systems with a variety of svcs.

Megastar Inc.
4709 Compass Bow Ln., Las Vegas, NV 89130
(702) 386-2844, *Fax:* (702) 388-1250
www.1megastar.com
Nigel Macrae, President
Houston, TX Teleport svcs, C-band & Ku-band, fiber-optic & microwave interconnect. 11M Intelsat antenna, PanAmSat, etc. Other svcs available.

Microwave Networks Inc.
4000 Greenbriar St. #100A, Stafford, TX 77477
(281) 263-6500, (888) 225-6429, *Fax:* (281) 263-6400
www.microwavenetworks.com
Jim Gordon, General Manager

Microwave Service Co.
1359 Rd. 681, Saltillo, MS 38866
(662) 842-7620, *Fax:* (662) 844-7061
lharris@wtba.com
Jane Spain, CEO
Larry Harris, General Sales Mgr
Point-to-point transmission of video by microwave.

Multicomm Sciences International Inc. (MSI)
266 W. Main St., Denville, NJ 07834
(973) 627-7400, *Fax:* (973) 215-2168
www.multicommsciences.com
Victor J. Nexon Jr., President
Serves satellite, microwave, lightwave, radio & cable industries. Market info, field surveys, system design, feasibility studies, frequency coordination & project mgmt.

Norlight Telecommunications
13935 Bishops Drive, Brookfield, WI 53005
(888) 210-3100, *Fax:* (812) 759-1465
www.norlight.com
mjt@norlight.com
James Ditter, President
Michael J. Turnbull, General Manager
Design, installation & maintenance of custom network solutions, including HDTV transport, on-site data center - secure co-location svc, off-site video file servers & managed router svc.

Novanet Communications Ltd.
725 Westney Rd. S., Suite 4, Ajax, ON L1J 7J7 Canada
(905) 686-6666, *Fax:* (905) 619-1053
www.novanetcomm.com
getinfo@novanetcomm.com
Joseph Uyede, President
Stewart Sheriff, Operations Dir
Debbie MacLeod, General Sales Mgr
Provides info distribution svcs; audio svcs from 3.5 khz to 20 khz in analog or digital formats, also a line of data bcst offerings ranging in speed from 75 baud to T-1; & 'Satpac,' a packet-switched data net using receiver technology.

NPR Satellite Services
635 Massachusetts Ave. N.W., Washington, DC 20001
(202) 513-2626, *Fax:* (202) 513-3035
www.nprss.org
linkup@npr.org
George Gimourginas, General Manager
Comprehensive satellite solutions for audio & video distribution: space segment, equipment, systems design, engrg support 24-hrs customer svc.

PanAmSat
20 Westport Rd., Suite 270, Wilton, CT 06897
(203) 210-8000, *Fax:* (203) 210-8001
www.panamsat.com
Joseph R. Wright, Jr., CEO
Owns & operates private global network of communications satellites providing bcst, business communications, telephony & data svcs to customers worldwide.

Potomac Television-News & Video Services
529 14th St. N.W., Suite 480, Washington, DC 20045
(202) 783-6464, *Fax:* (202) 783-1132
www.potomac.com
jnorins@potomactv.com
Jamie Norins, News Director
TV production facilities include studios, on-line & non-linear editing & transmission facilities to Ku-band & C-band satellites. Interconnect to major news-gathering points in Washington, DC, at the National Press Bldg.

Production & Satellite Services Inc. (PSSI)
11860 Mississippi Ave., Los Angeles, CA 90025
(310) 575-4400, *Fax:* (310) 575-4451
www.pssi-global.com
Robert Lamb, President
Joseph A. Kittrell, General Sales Mgr
Full service production & satellite transmission company specializing in coordination, production & transmission of international live-event progmg. Own & operate 12 fully redundant transportable upling/production trucks which are maintainedin Los Angeles, San Francisco, Seattle, Las Vegas, Denver, Phoenix & Chicago. Entire Western region of the United States is covered including Albuquerque, Salt Lake City & Portland. Also subcontract with vendors throughout U.S. to provide uplink,downlink & production svcs and production svcs for teleconferences & other events.

Reuters Television Internationale
3 Times Sq., 4th Fl., New York, NY 10036
(646) 223-6600, *Fax:* (646) 223-6615
www.reuters.com
Bob LaGrasso, General Sales Mgr
Satellite svcs for news departments. Satellite production & communication departments handle satellite feed requirements from anywhere in the world. Satellite coordinates, video crews & major studios on six continents. Standards conversion.

SES Americom
4 Research Way, Princeton, NJ 08540
(609) 987-4000, *Fax:* (609) 987-4517
www.ses-americom.com
Bryan A. McGuirk, President
Operates GE-1-3, SATCOM, GSTAR & SPACENET domestic satellites (C-band & six Ku-band). The fleet svcs the cable TV, bcst, radio & educ market & govt businesses. Supports net of earth stns, central terminal offices & TT&C facilities.

SpaceCom Systems
Div/DBA: A TV Guide Company
1950 E. 71st St., Tulsa, OK 74136
(800) 950-6690, *Fax:* (918) 477-6861
www.spacecom.com
David Pollack, President
Ruth Ann Odom, Promotions Manager
Satellite transmission svcs, equipment & space segment on C- & Ku-Band for point-to-multipoint applications. Also two-way high-speed Satellite Broadband for remote locations, quick connects, disaster recovery, Internet.

Spacenet Inc.
Div/DBA: (formerly Spacenet Services Inc.)
1750 Old Meadow Rd., McLean, VA 22102
(703) 848-1000, *Fax:* (703) 245-5426
www.spacenet.com
Glenn Katz, COO
Jim Norton, Operations Dir
Comprehensive range of satellite-based communication svcs for video & data; digital video networks for business applications.

Teleglobe
1555 Rue Carrie-Derick, Montreal, QC H3C 6W2 Canada
(514) 868-7272, *Fax:* (514) 868-7234
www.teleglobe.com
jean-louis-houde@vsnlinternational.com
Vinod Kumar, President
Jean-Louis Houde, Operations Dir
International satellite transmission svcs from Lawrentides/Lake Cowichan earth stns in Canada. Signatory on Intelsat, Immarsat. Full range of svcs to world satellite systems.
Two Pacifco Place, 88 Queensway, Hong Kong,
852-2530-8500; *Fax:* 852-2-537-7417
Andrew Kwok, Dir

Telemundo Network
2470 W. 8th Ave, Hialeah, FL 33010
(305) 884-8200, *Fax:* (305) 882-8765
www.telemundo.com
James McNammara, President
Production capabilities & svcs. Uplink & video transmission. C- & Ku-band uplink & downlink. Fiber & microwave also available.

Telenor Satellite Services
1101 Wooton Pkwy, Rockville, MD 20852
(301) 838-7800, *Fax:* (301) 838-7801
www.telenor.com/satellite
customer.care@telenor.com
Bob Baker, President
Dave Farmer, Promotions Manager
Telenor is a global provider of satellite svcs, inmarsat, intelsat, new skies, satmex, digital networking svcs & technology.

Teleport Chicago
3617 Oakton St., Rear, Skokie, IL 60076
(847) 674-7476, (888) 255-8755, *Fax:* (847) 674-1991
www.norlight.com
sales@norlight.com
Dave Pritchard, General Manager
A full-svc teleport serving the upper Midwest via the Norlight Telecommunications microwave & fiber-optic transmission system.

Telesat
Div/DBA: (formerly Loral Skynet Inc.)
500 Hills Dr., Bedminster, NJ 07921
(908) 719-0094
www.telesat.ca
Daniel S. Goldberg, President

Telesat Canada
1601 Telesat Ct., Gloucester, ON K1B 5P4 Canada
(613) 748-0123, *Fax:* (613) 748-8712
www.telesat.ca
info@telesat.ca
Communications via satellite, consulting, & satellite earth stn nets.
1780 Centre Ave. N.E., Calgary, AB Canada
(403) 235-5751; *Fax:* (403) 273-3337
1200 Papineau Ave., Suite 140, Montreal, PQ Canada
(514) 521-7862; *Fax:* (514) 527-6429

Time Warner Cable
290 Harbor Dr., Stamford, CT 06902
(800) 479-0624
www.timewarnercable.com
Landel C. Hobbs, COO
Robert Marcus, President
Time Warner Cable is committed to in-home entertainment, communications, info, customer care & quality products that create the best possible customer experience.
75 Rockerfeller Plaza, New York, NY 10019-6908
(212) 484-8000;

Transvision Inc.
550 Maulhardt Ave., Oxnard, CA 93030
(805) 981-8740, *Fax:* (805) 981-8738
www.txvision.com
info@txvision.com
Kimithy Vaughan, General Sales Mgr
Vince Waterson, Engineering Dir
Twelve transportable & satellite transmission facilities (video, audio, voice, data); flypack production & SNG svcs; digital compression; domestic & international. Facilities in Brazil, Australia, Phillipines & Western Europe.

TV Guide Inc.
7140 S. Lewis Ave., Tulsa, OK 74136
(918) 488-4000, *Fax:* (918) 488-4979
www.tvguide.com
Mike Burks, Operations Dir
Josh Axelrod, Programming Director
Diversified communications company serving cable, home satellite TV, radio/data networks, private businesses; operating companies: UVTV, Prevue Networks, Superstar Satellite Entertainment, SpaceCom Systems.

Verestar Inc.
3040 Williams Dr., Suite 600, Fairfax, VA 22031
(703) 206-9000, *Fax:* (703) 573-3522
www.verestar.com
info@verestar.com
Raymond J. O'Brien, President
Satellite svcs for bcstrs & communication net.

Videocom Media Services, LLC
Box 212, Boston, MA 02137
(781) 329-4080, *Fax:* (781) 329-8534
www.videocom.com
Ownership: Private.
Daniel V. Swartz, General Manager
Steerable C- & Ku-band antennas interconnected via private microwave & telco loops co-located with single- & multiple-camera program origination facility. Receives & transmits all formats of videotape; transportable uplinks; bcst newsdistribution; link with Canadian satellites. Digital video transmission & net mgmt svcs.

Warren Only Media Group
19 West Almond St., Vineland, NJ 08360
(856) 507-9368, *Fax:* (856) 507-9368
www.warrenonly.com
Warren Only, President
Program playout, turnarounds, uplink services.
Box 2372, New York, NY
(917) 339-0036;

WGVU-TV
301 W. Fulton, Grand Rapids, MI 49504-6492
(616) 331-6666, *Fax:* (616) 331-6625
www.wgvu.org
wgvu@gvsu.edu
Michael Walenta, General Manager
Ken Kolbe, Station Manager
Bob Lumbert, Engineering Dir
Provides multiple studio post production, teleconferencing & satellite uplink svcs.

WHYY Inc.
Independence Mall W., 150 N. 6th St., Philadelphia, PA 19106
(215) 351-1200, *Fax:* (215) 351-0398
www.whyy.org
pgluck@whyy.org
Paul Gluck, Operations Dir
Occasional video, encryption svcs, transponder time available. Interconnect with Telco, on-site production facilities, & teleconferencing for up to 1,000 people. Transportable Ku-band earth stn; C- or Ku-band uplinking.

Williams Communications
111 E. 1st St., Vyvx Services, Tulsa, OK 74103
(918) 547-5760, *Fax:* (918) 547-5760
Jeff Storey, CEO
Provider of integrated fiber-optic, satellite, teleport multimedia, data gathering, mgmt & transmission svcs.
1802 Briarcliff Rd., Atlanta, GA 30329-4008
(800) 648-3333;
One Maynard Dr., Park Ridge, NJ
(800) 746-3019;
200 Oceangate, Suite 570, Long Beach, CA 90802-4302
(800) 747-7074;

Teleports

Ascent Media
250 Harbor Dr., Stamford, CT 06902
(203) 965-6000
www.ascentmedia.com
Ownership: Stamford
Peter Brickman, General Manager
C- & Ku-band domestic & international transmission service; connectivity to metro New York via proprietary fiber origination, bcst, business TV, transponder availability; studio & postproduction svcs.

Atlanta International Teleport
3530 Bomar Rd., Douglasville, GA 30135
(770) 949-6600, *Fax:* (770) 942-6653
www.atlantateleport.com
sales@atlantateleport.com
Adam Grow, III, Chief Engineer
Internet, private business networks, VSAT Hub, C/Ku Up/down, audio, video, data, telephony, TDMA, SCPC, VCII+, fiber, standards conversion, Intelsat-B Station.

Crawford Communications Inc.
3845 Pleasantdale Rd., Atlanta, GA 30340
(404) 876-7149, (800) 831-8027, *Fax:* 678) 421-6717
www.crawford.com
info@crawford.com
Jesse Crawford, Chairman
Network origination & playback, domestic/international satellite transmissions, streaming media/webcasting, online svcs, fiber optics, satellite uplink trucks, studios, post production & DVD.

Echostar
6723 W. Steger Rd., Monee, IL 60449
(708) 534-2400, *Fax:* (708) 534-0060
www.echostar.com
lawrence.baer@echostar.com
Ownership: Chicago, IL.
Larry Baer, General Manager
C- & Ku-band satellite transmission svcs. Audio, video, data, uplink/downlink communication.

Edmonton Teleport. Telesat Canada
5311 Allard Way, Edmonton, AB T6H 5B8 Canada
(780) 437-6167, *Fax:* (780) 436-5667
www.telesat.ca
Major bcst teleport offering full North American arc at C-band, & Anik E1 & E2 at Ku-band for occasional use needs.

GlobeCast North America
10525 W. Washington Blvd., Culver City, CA 90232
(310) 845-3900 (sales), (310) 845-3939, *Fax:* (310) 845-3903
www.globecast.com
america.booking@globecast.com
Mary Frost, CEO
GlobeCast Hero Productions
7291 N.W. 74 St., Miami, FL 33166-2407
(305) 887-1600; *Fax:* (305) 887-7076
110 E. 42nd St., 11th Fl., New York, NY 10017-5611
(212) 885-8700; *Fax:* (212) 885-8701
400 North Capitol St. N.W, Suite 880, Washington, DC 20001-1511
(202) 737-4440; *Fax:* (202) 737-1476
1825 K St. N.W., 9th Fl., Washington, DC 20006-1202
(202) 861-0894; *Fax:* (202) 861-3107

GlobeCast North America
5 Teleport Dr., Staten Island, NY 10311
(718) 983-2600, *Fax:* (718) 983-2615
www.globecast.com
robert.marking@globecastna.com
Mary Frost, CEO
Offers a transmission network of leased domestic & international satellite transponders providing radio & TV origination svcs for more than 1,000 U.S. & international clients every year, including news, sports, program distribution &business TV clientele.

ICG Telecom Group
161 Inverness Dr., West Englewood, CO 80112

Alternative Access Carrier. Bay Area Teleport provides communications svcs at DS0, T1 or T3 levels for primary or alternative access applications. Bay Area Teleport's system connects 12 counties in northern California. Includes a fiber-opticnetwork in San Francisco, CA & across to Oakland, CA, as well as access to satellite svcs through its earth stn complex in Niles Canyon.

Jackson Teleport Inc.
916 Foley St., Jackson, MS 39202
(800) 353-9177, (601) 352-6673, *Fax:* (601) 948-6052
www.weathervision.com
edward@weathervision.com
Edward Saint Pe, President
Jason McCleave, Operations Dir
Fixed 7-meter earth stn on site. Video satellite transmission & reception. Videoconferencing, business TV, news, sports & weathercast feed, origination, program distribution & syndication svcs.

Megastar Inc.
4709 Compass Bow Ln., Las Vegas, NV 89130
(702) 386-2844, *Fax:* (702) 388-1250
www.1megastar.com
Nigel Macrae, President

Network Teleports Inc.
3200 Chartres St., New Orleans, LA 70117
(504) 942-9200, *Fax:* (504) 942-9204
www.networkteleports.com
uplink@networkteleports.com
Ownership: New Orleans.
C.E. Feltner, Chairman
C-band voice/video & data, Ku-band data/voice, B-MAC encryption, newsfeeds, production, fiber-optic links, audio-subcarrier & C- & Ku-band 5CPC, satellite telephones, IP multicasting, webcasting.

Norlight Teleport Chicago
3617 Oakton St., Skokie, IL 60076
(847) 674-7476, *Fax:* (847) 674-1991
www.norlight.com
drp@norlight.com
Dave Pritchard, General Manager
Full-svc teleport, domestic & international, satellite uplink, downlink, turnaround, encryption, rgn access on Norlight Telecommunications Interstate Network, VYVX ant AT&T fiber access.
275 N. Corporate, Brookfield, WI 53045-5825

Pittsburgh International Telecommunications
Box 14070, Pittsburgh, PA 15239
(724) 337-1888, *Fax:* (724) 337-1754
www.pitcomm.com
info@pitcomm.com
Al Stem, President
Bill Sciolla, General Manager

Potomac Television-News & Video Services
529 14th St. N.W., Suite 480, Washington, DC 20045
(202) 783-6464, *Fax:* (202) 783-1132
www.potomac.com
jnorins@potomactv.com
Jamie Norins, News Director
TV production facilities include studios, on-line & non-linear editing & transmission facilities to Ku-band & C-band satellites. Interconnect to major news-gathering points in Washington, DC, at the National Press Bldg.

Rainbow Network Communications
620 Hicksville Rd., Bethpage, NY 11714
(516) 803-0355, (516) 803-0300, *Fax:* (516) 918-6940
www.rncnetwork.com
togreco@rainbow-media.com
Steve Pontillo, President
Thomas A. Greco, Operations Dir
Multiple 11-meter & 9-meter uplinking antennas, multiple downlinking ants, both servicing the entire satellite arc. Connectivity in & out of New York & metropolitan area, Ku-band transportable, origination/editing svcs, & full, longterm &occasional transponder leasing. Compression svcs.

Telesat
1601 Telesat Ct., Gloucester, ON K1B 5P4 Canada
(613) 748-0123, *Fax:* (613) 748-8712
www.telesat.ca
info@telesat.ca
Ownership: Montreal.
Daniel Goldberg, President/CEO
Pat Enright, VP Network Operations
Paul Bush, VP Business Development
Access to all Telesat Anik and Nimiq satellites & most U.S. domestic satellites.

Toronto Teleport. Telesat Canada
1601 Telesat Ct., Gloucester, ON K1B 5P4 Canada
(613) 748-0123, *Fax:* (613) 748-8712
www.telesat.ca
info@telesat.ca
Ownership: Toronto.
Access to all Telesat Anik & Nimiq satellites & most united states domestic satellites.

Turner Teleport Inc.
Box 105366, One CNN Ctr., Atlanta, GA 30348-5366
(404) 827-1500
Satellite uplink & downlink svcs for Turner Broadcasting Services.

Vancouver Teleport. Telesat Canada
1601 Telesat Ct., Gloucester, ON K1B 5P4 Canada
(613) 748-0123, *Fax:* (613) 748-8712
www.telesat.ca
info@telesat.ca
Ownership: Vancouver.
Access to all Telesat Anik & Nimiq satellites & most North American satellites.

Verestar Inc.
3040 Williams Dr., Suite 600, Fairfax, VA 22031
(703) 206-9000, *Fax:* (703) 573-3522
www.verestar.com
info@verestar.com
Raymond J. O'Brien, President
Satellite svcs for bcstrs & communication net.

Videocom Media Services, LLC
Box 212, Boston, MA 02137
(781) 329-4080, *Fax:* (781) 329-8534
www.videocom.com
Ownership: Private.
Daniel V. Swartz, General Manager
Steerable C- & Ku-band antennas interconnected via private microwave & telco loops co-located with single- & multiple-camera program origination facility. Receives & transmits all formats of videotape; transportable uplinks; bcst newsdistribution; link with Canadian satellites. Digital video transmission & net mgmt svcs.

VYVX Level 3 Teleport Denver
9174 S. Jamaica St., Englewood, CO 80112
(303) 397-4100, *Fax:* (303) 799-8325
Ownership: Denver.
Theran Davis, Operations Dir
Domestic & international uplink, downlink & transponder service for video & date communications. Regional Fiber & microwave interconnectivity to broadcast affiliates, PoPs & sports venues

VYVX Teleport Atlanta
1802 Briarcliff Rd., Atlanta, GA 30329
(404) 325-0818
www.oabok.org
harrison@oabok.org
Vance Harrison, pres.

Willliams Services/VYVX Steele Valley Teleports
20021 Santa Rosa Mine Rd., Perris, CA 92570
(909) 943-5399, *Fax:* (909) 943-3459
gene.brookhart@wcg.com
Gene Brookhart, General Manager
Offers domestic U.S. & international uplink, downlink & transponder svc for video (analog or compressed), image, data & voice telecommunication. Fiber-optic & microwave links to points of presence for major bcst & telco locations in the LosAngeles metropolitan area. Direct access to all C- & Ku-band satellites in domestic U.S. arc & POR; include program origination; tape playback, recording & editing; standards conversion; encryption; & turnarounds.
58 Inverness Dr. E., Englewood, CO 80112-5104
(303) 397-4100, (800) 424-9757 (full-time svcs);

WLWT-TV
1700 Young St., Cincinnati, OH 45202
(513) 412-5000, *Fax:* (513) 412-6100
www.wlwt.com
rdyer@hearst.com
Richard Dyer, General Manager
Mark Diangelo, General Sales Mgr
On-line. Provides occasional C-band uplinking svcs.

Employment & Executive Search Services

Barry Skidelsky, Esq.
655 Madison Ave., Fl. 19, New York, NY 10065
(212) 832-4800
dganske@charter.net
Dale A. Ganske, President
Complete radio/TV brokering, consulting, FCC rules & regulations.

Bishop Partners
708 Third Ave., Suite 2200, New York, NY 10017
(212) 986-3419, *Fax:* (212) 986-3350
www.bishop partners.com
info@bishoppartners.com
Susan K. Bishop, President
A retained exec search firm specializing in cable, bcst, telecommunications, wireless, entertainment, publishing & multimedia.

Brad Marks International
15233 Ventura Blvd., PH 16, Sherman Oaks, CA 91403
(818) 382-6300, *Fax:* (818) 386-0050
www.bradmarks.com
bodysnatcher@bradmarks.com
Brad Marks, Chairman
Exec search at sr mgmt levels for communications, bcst, cable & multimedia companies. Areas include TV & film production, progmg, sls, mktg, news, gen mgmt, financial svcs, postproduction & adv/promotion.

California Broadcasters Association
915 L St., Sacramento, CA 95814
(916) 444-2237, *Fax:* (916) 444-2043
www.cabroadcasters.org
cbaberry@aol.com
Stan Statham, President
Lobbyist for coml radio & TV for the state of California & other legal issues.

Eatman Media Services Inc.
5901 N. Cicero Ave., Suite 307, Chicago, IL 60646
(773) 777-5463, *Fax:* (773) 777-7106
emstalent@aol.com
Representation of TV newspersons, TV personalities, & radio talent in job placement & contract negotiation.
Box 102, Bedford, NY 10506-0102
(914) 234-4748;
Ross Eatman, Esq
Box 102, Bedford, NY 10506-0102
(914) 234-4748;
Ross Eatman, Esq
Box 853, Pacific Palisades, CA 90272-0853
(310) 459-3728;
Robert Eatman, Pres
Box 853, Pacific Palisades, CA 90272-0853
(310) 459-3728;
Robert Eatman, Pres

Entertainment Employment Journal (T.M.)
5632 Van Nuys Blvd., Suite 320, Van Nuys, CA 91401
(800) 335-4335, (818) 776-2800
www.eej.com
sales@eej.com
Bimonthly magazine providing career information & job listings with major & independent motion picture, TV & cable companies.

Filcro Media Staffing
521 Fifth Ave., Suite 1801, New York, NY 10175
(212) 599-0909, *Fax:* (212) 599-1023
www.ExecutiveSearch.tv
tony@filcro.com
Tony Filson, CEO/COO
Retained Global Media & broadcasting executive search

The Howard-Sloan-Koller Group
300 E. 42nd St., New York, NY 10017
(212) 661-5250, *Fax:* (212) 490-5322
www.hsksearch.com
ekoller@hsksearch.com
Edward R. Koller Jr., President
Exec search & consulting in the cable, digital, entertainment & publishing industries.
9701 Wilshire Blvd., Beverly Hills, CA 90212-2020
(310) 601-7114; *Fax:* (310) 601-7110
Edward R. Koller Jr., President

JOBPHONE
Box 5048, Newport Beach, CA 92662
(949) 721-9280, *Fax:* (949) 721-8478
www.infoguru.com
jobphone@aol.com
Keith Mueller, President
Natl TV/radio employment hotline.To hear job openings nationwide: (900) 726-5627-JOBS.

Keystone America
38 Thomas St., Exeter Plaza, Exeter, PA 18643
(570) 655-7143, *Fax:* (570) 654-5765
keystoneamerica.com
usmail@keystoneamerica.com
Alan Kornish, Operations Dir
Ntl Employment svc for bcst employers & candidates, placement of engrs & technicians. Serving all USA states. See our website: keystoneamerica.com.

Korn/Ferry International
1900 Avenue of the Stars, Suite 2600, Los Angeles, CA 90067
(310) 552-1834
www.kornferry.com
Gregg Kvochak, CFO
William D. Simon, General Manager
Worldwide sr level mgmt exec search firm servicing all sectors of the entertainment industry.

Lipson & Co.
1900 Ave. of the Stars, Suite 2810, Los Angeles, CA 90067
(310) 277-4646, *Fax:* (310) 277-8585
www.lipsonco.com
inquiries@lipsonco.com
Howard R. Lipson, President
Harriet Lipson, Operations Dir
Specialists in international & domestic bcstg (TV & radio), cable & entertainment, & related financial, professional audio/video & electronic recruiting. Svcs also for TV & film production, merchandising, licensing, & computers.

Maslow Media Group Inc.
2134 Wisconsin Ave. N.W., Washington, DC 20007
(202) 965-1100, *Fax:* (202) 965-6171
www.maslowmedia.com
lmaslow@maslowmedia.com
Linda Maslow, CEO
Carl Neubecker, Operations Dir
Freelance & fulltime staffing, crewing & payroll svcs for bcst, corporate, & federal govt. Find a job @ www.tvgigsonline.com

Media Management Resources Inc.
6890 S. Tuscon Way, Englewood, CO 80112
(303) 290-9800, *Fax:* (303) 290-9596
bwein@mediamanagement.com
Michael S. Wein, President
David Reiber, General Manager
Full-svc consulting practice providing business support & technology svcs to select media & technology companies.

Media Staffing Network
6518 East Shooting Star Way, Scottsdale, AZ 85266
(312) 944-9194, *Fax:* (312) 944-9195
www.mediastaffingnetwork.com
laurie@mediastaffingnetwork.com
Laurie Kahn, President
Media Staffing Network the only full-service staffing company that specializes in media adv sls & associated departments, offering both temporary & full-time positions nationwide. Clients include radio & TV stns, rep firms, Internet, cablesystems, networks, syndication, magazines & adv agencies. Openings range from entry-level support to sr mgmt positions in sls, prom, buying, planning, traf, continuity, customer svc & rsch.

MediaLine
Box 51909, Pacific Grove, CA 93950
(800) 237-8073, *Fax:* (831) 648-5204
www.medialine.com
medialine@medialine.com
Mark Shilstone, CEO
Adrienne Laurent, President
Job listings for TV news, production & promotions; streaming video of resume tapes on the Internet; daily eletronic newsletter.

Miller Broadcast Management Inc.
616 W. Fulton St., Suite 516, Chicago, IL 60661
(312) 454-1111, *Fax:* (312) 454-0044
www.millerbroadcasts.com
info@millerbroadcast.com
Lisa Miller, President
Matt Miller, Operations Dir
Representing radio personalities.

R.A. Stone & Associates
5495 Belt Line Rd., Suite 103, Dallas, TX 75254-7671
(972) 233-0483, *Fax:* (972) 991-4995
stonesearch@aol.com
Robert Stone, President
Retainer based exec search svcs for the domestic & international TV, radio, cable, multimedia, production & related communications/entertainment industries.

Ron Sunshine Associates
2404 Clear Field Dr., Plano, TX 75025
(972) 618-3670, (214) 509-3778, *Fax:* (972) 599-9583
www.ronsunshineassociates.com
Ron@Ronsunshineassociates.com
Ron Sunshine, President
Barbara Blake, Operations Dir
Radio, TV & cable middle & upper mgmt.

RTNDA's Career Services
Div/DBA: (formerly RTNDA Job Services)
1025 F St, Suite 700, Washington, DC 20004
(800) 80-RTNDA, *Fax:* (202) 223-4007
www.rtnda.org
rtnda@rtnda.org
Barbara Cochran, President
Sarah Stump, Operations Dir
We offer current career opportuunties in electronic journalism, as well as a wealth of resources for job seekers. We also have the most accurate & current industry rsch on salaries, newsroom staffing, newsroom profitability & woman/minorityrepresentation in the newsroom.

Search Source Inc.
Box 1161, Granite City, IL 62040-1161
(618) 931-6060, *Fax:* (618) 876-6071
search@norcom2000.com
James R. McKechan, President
Search & recruitment of bcst professionals.

Warren & Morris Ltd.
463 15th St., Del Mar, CA 92014
(858) 481-3388, *Fax:* (858) 481-6221
www.warrenmorrisltd.com
swarren@warrenmorrismltd.com
Scott Warren, Operations Dir
Natl & international exec/mgmt-level recruitment svcs in the cable TV, wireless communications & digital media industries.
132 Chapel St, Portsmouth, NH 03801-3848
(603) 431-7929; *Fax:* (603) 431-3460
Scott Warren., Sr Ptn
Arron Chaffee, Ptn

Youngs, Walker & Co.
1605 Colonial Pkwy., Inverness, IL 60067
(847) 991-6900, *Fax:* (847) 934-6607
www.youngswalker.com
info@youngswalker.com
Carl Youngs, President
Exec recruitment on a retained basis for TV & radio stn mgmt levels & corporate positions.

Engineering & Technical Consultants

Advanced Technology Systems Corp.
4000 Legato Road, Suite 600, Fairfax, VA 22033
(703) 891-8200, *Fax:* (703) 891-8201
www.salientfed.com
inquiries@salientfed.com
Bill Parker, COO
Brad Antile, President
Tricia Long, Promotions Manager
Software & systems dev, lifecycle mgmt, systems integration, testing IT, infrastructure outsourcing mgmt, business process improvement, info sharing, consulting, wireless svcs & specialized functional expertise.

AF Associated Inc./Ascent Media
235 Pegasus Ave., Northvale, NJ 07647
(201) 767-3800, *Fax:* (201) 784-8637
www.afassoc.com
consulting@ascentmedia.com
Tom Canavan, President
Chris Summey, Operations Dir
Andre Macaluso Sr., General Manager
Mgmt & distribution of content to major motion picture studios, ind producers, bcst networks, cable channels, adv agencies & other companies that produce, own/or distribute entertainment, adv, news, sports, corporate, educ & industrialcontent.

AZCAR U.S.A. Inc.
121 Hillpointe Dr., Suite 700, Canonsburg, PA 15317

(724) 873-0800, *Fax:* (724) 873-4770
www.azcar.com
info@azcar.com
Stephen Pumple, President
Bcst, video & audio system consultation, design, instal & training; serving cable systems, corporate & teleproduction facilities.

Bernard Associates
143 Palmers Hill Rd., Stamford, CT 06902-2111
(203) 348-0804, *Fax:* (203) 921-1016
Bernard Eishwald, P.E

Broadcast Engineering & Equipment Maintenance Co.
Div/DBA: (BEEM Co.)
2322 S. 2nd Ave., Arcadia, CA 91006
(626) 446-3468, *Fax:* (626) 445-8028
www.beemco.com
joel@beemco.com
Joel T. Saxberg, President
Site studies, applications, AM directional arrays, allocation studies, field work, mobile signal analysis, bcst consulting & radiofrequency electromagnetic field measurements.

Broadcast Services Inc.
Box 6418, Brattleboro, VT 05302-6418
(802) 258-3000, (802) 258-4500 Svc, *Fax:* (802) 258-2500
www.markhutchins.com
mh@markhutchins.com
Mark F. Hutchins, President
Field studies: Spectrum analysis, NRSC/RFR compliance. Propagation analysis, coverage maps, path profiles & shadowing studies.

Broadcast Signal Lab, LLP
64 Richdale Ave., Cambridge, MA 02140-2629
(617) 864-4298, *Fax:* (617) 661-1345
www.broadcastsignallab.com
information@broadcastsignallab.com
David P. Maxson, Operations Dir
RF safety evaluation, expert testimony, coverage analysis, license engrg & applications, interference & spectrum analysis, frequency monitoring, tech due diligence.

Bromo Communications Inc.
Box 191747, Atlanta, GA 31119-1747
(404) 636-2257, *Fax:* (404) 636-2256
www.bromocom.com
bill@bromocom.com
Gil Moor, Engineering Dir
Consulting engrg for bcst stns. AM/FM & TV allocations, including field instals.
Washington, DC
(202) 429-0600;

C.P. Crossno & Associates
Div/DBA: Consulting Engineers
Box 180312, Dallas, TX 75218
(214) 031-9140, *Fax:* (214) 321-9146
c.crossno@ieee.org
Charles Paul Crossno, President
Aeronautical issues; antenna design.

Carl E. Smith Consulting Engineers
Box 807, 2324 N. Cleveland-Massilon Rd., Bath, OH 44210-0807
(330) 659-4440, *Fax:* (330) 659-9234
Al Warmus, President
Roy Stype III, Operations Dir
AM, FM, TV & LPTV engrg, FCC applications, ant systems adjustments. Sls: towers, ants, transmission line, phasing equipment. Turnkey instal.

Carl T. Jones Corp.
7901 Yarnwood Ct., Springfield, VA 22153
(703) 569-7704, *Fax:* (703) 569-6417
www.ctjc.com
hhurst@ctjc.com
*C. Thomas Jones Jr., President
*Herman E. Hurst, General Manager
Carl Gluck, Engineering Dir
Consulting engrs specializing in AM, FM & TV tech design & regulatory filings.

Cavell, Mertz & Associates, Inc.
7839 Ashton Ave., Manassas, VA 20109
(703) 392-9090, *Fax:* (703) 392-9559
www.cavellmertz.com
office@cavellmertz.com
Gary Cavell, President
Richard H. Mertz, Operations Dir
Broadcast & Communications Consulting Engineers located in suburban Washington, DC. Experts in radio/TV ch searches, upgrades, transmission, coverage studies, interference evaluation, RF safety, strategic planning, both bcst (AM/FM radio,TV, digital TV, microwave/satellite) & industrial.

Cecil Lynch Consulting Engineers
2460 Illinois Ave., Modesto, CA 95358
(209) 523-3955, *Fax:* (209) 522-5287
Cecil Lynch, CEO
Bcst engrg, stn appraisals, customized computer progmg svc, GPS surveying & RFR measurements.

Charles A. Hecht & Associates Inc.
16 Doe Run, Pittstown, NJ 08867
(908) 730-7959
Charles A. Hecht, President
Charles J. Hecht, Engineering Dir
Bcst engrg svcs including FCC studies & applications, directional antenna design, fieldwork, tech litigation; specialists in AM studies for telecommunications companies.

Charles S. Fitch, P.E.
45 Sarah Dr., Avon, CT 06001
(860) 673-7260, *Fax:* (860) 675-7269
fitchpe@comcast.net
*Charles S. Fitch, P.E., President
FCC allocations & applications, facility design, system design, construction supervision, field surveys, facility appraisals & inspections, computer progmg.

Chenevert Architects LLC
6767 Perkins Rd., Suite 100, Baton Rouge, LA 70808
(225) 757-0955, *Fax:* (225) 757-0765
www.chenevertarchitects.com
chenevert@architects.com
Norman J. Chenevert, President
Architects, planners, & technical designers, specializing in new & renovated bcst/cable production facilities.

Chevalier Aviation Associates, LLC
928 Via Panorama, Palos Verdes, CA 90274
(310) 375-2979, *Fax:* (310) 791-7181
jack.chevalier@verizon.net
Jack Chevalier, President
L. Gene Garrett, General Manager
Part 77 studies, FCC registrations, EMI analysis, legal assistance & representation before FAA, state & loc aeronautical & zoning agencies.

Clear Channel Communications
1834 Lisenby Ave., Panama City, FL 32405
(850) 769-1408, *Fax:* (850) 769-0659
www.clearchannel.com
contactus@clearchannel.com
Turnkey installations (AM, FM studios & transmitters), tech appraisals, emergency repairs, upgrades. International startups & upgrades.

Cohen, Dippell and Everist, P.C.
1300 L St. N.W., Suite 1100, Washington, DC 20005
(202) 898-0111, *Fax:* (202) 898-0895
http://www.broadcast-consulting-engineers.com
cde@attgobal.net
*Donald G. Everist, P.E., President
*Ross Heide, P.E., Engineering Dir
Professional engrg svcs to the bcstg industry, United States & worldwide.

Commercial Radio Co.
One Duttonsville School Dr., Cavendish, VT 05142
(802) 226-7582, *Fax:* (802) 226-7738
commercialradiocompany.us
Daniel W. Churchill, PE, President
Centura L. Churchill, Operations Dir
Andre S. LaPlante, General Sales Mgr
William E. Ford, Engineering Dir
Custom bcst engrg; AM, FM & shortwave bcst equipment sls & svce, specializing in transmitting components.

Communications Design Associates Inc.
437 Turnpike St., Canton, MA 02021-2702
(339) 502-6551, *Fax:* (781) 502-6569
www.cdaconsultants.com
information@cdaconsultants.com
Greg Vincent, Operations Dir
Ind consultants to radio, TV, corporate & govt clients. Designers of studios, production, presentation & multimedia facilities.

Communications General Corp.
2685 Alta Vista Dr., Fallbrook, CA 92028-9739
(760) 723-2700
www.rockabillyhall.com/joeleonard.html
lin45@ntin.net
Joe M. Leonard Jr., President
Brokerage of radio & TV.

Communications Technologies Inc.
Box 1130, 65 Country Club Ln., Marlton, NJ 08053
(856) 985-0077, *Fax:* (856) 985-8124
www.commtechrf.com
info@commtechrf.com
Clarence M. Beverage, President
Laura M. Mizrahi, Operations Dir
James W. Pollock, P.E., Engineering Dir
Bcst engrg consulting svcs with emphasis on AM, FM & TV RF systems design & FCC application preparation consistent with FCC rules & policies.

Comsearch
19700 Janellia Farm Blvd., Ashburn, VA 20147
(703) 726-5500, *Fax:* (703) 726-5600
www.comsearch.com
Doug Hall, President
A complete communications engrg svc organization, specializing in frequency mgmt & propagation engrg.

ComSonics Inc.
Box 1106, 1350 Port Republic Rd., Harrisonburg, VA 22801
(540) 434-5965, *Fax:* (540) 432-9794
www.comsonics.com
info@comsonics.com
Dennis A. Zimmerman, President
Donn E. Meyerhoeffer, Operations Dir
Don J. Sommerville, Promotions Manager
Microprocessor controlled signal level meters, RF leakage detection & CATV repair facility.

Contemporary Communications
9408 Grand Gate St., Las Vegas, NV 89143
(702) 898-4669, *Fax:* (208) 567-6865
www.radioguys.net
larryfuss@cox.net
Larry G. Fuss, President
FM, TV, STL & RPU applications; FM upgrades; computerized frequency searches; site selection assistance.

Crown Castle
2000 Corporate Dr., Cannonsburg, PA 15317
(724) 416-2000, *Fax:* (724) 416-2200
www.crowncastle.com
Communications engrg consultants & site/tower mgrs.

CSI Telecommunications Inc.
750 Battery St., Suite 350, San Francisco, CA 94111-1555
(415) 751-8845, *Fax:* (415) 292-9981
www.csitele.com
info@csitele.com
Michael S. Newman, CEO
Philip M. Kane, P.E., Esq, Operations Dir
D. Doon, P.E., Engineering Dir
Telecommunications, radio & microwave engrg, feasibility studies, FCC applications, systems engrg; equipment specifications, project mgmt & lab measurements.

D.L. Markley & Associates Inc.
2104 W. Moss Ave., Peoria, IL 61604
(309) 673-7511, *Fax:* (309) 673-8128
www.dlmarkley.com
dlm@dlmarkley.com
*Donald L. Markley, President
Keith A. Turcot, Engineering Dir
AM/FM, TV, microwave applications, construction & measurements. Allocation studies, non-ionizing radiation measurements.

D.W. Sargent Broadcast Inc.
804 Richard Rd., Cherry Hill, NJ 08034
(856) 667-8573, *Fax:* (856) 667-1409
Dean W. Sargent, President
Ant system design & measurements for FM & TV. FM & TV master ant system design.

Dettra Communications Inc.
7906 Fox Hound Rd., McLean, VA 22102
(703) 790-1427, *Fax:* (703) 790-0497
John E. Dettra Jr., President
Exhibits for bcst, mobile telephone, cellular, microwave & private radio svcs, FCC rsch & consulting.

Devlin Design Group Inc.
Box 5208, Frisco, CO 80443
(970) 453-9360
nkeng@insightbb.com
Frank Hertel, President

RF & frequency measurements for AM-FM-TV coml users via air or on location. Audio/video svc & instals.

Diversified Systems
Div/DBA: (formerly Diversified Systems Inc.)
363 Market St., Kenilworth, NJ 07033
(908) 245-4833, *Fax:* (908) 245-0011
www.divsysinc.com
info@divsysinc.com
Alfred D'Alessandro, President
Full-svc engrg, specializing in video & RF systems.

Doug Holland Inc.
1871 Sweet Briar Ln., Birmingham, AL 35235-3357
(205) 229-5628
jwishnow@yahoo.com
Jerrold D. Wishnow, President
Position bcst clients as community service leaders.

Doug Vernier Telecom Consultants
401 Main St., Suite 213, Cedar Falls, IA 50613
(319) 266-8402, *Fax:* (319) 266-9212
www.v-soft.com
consulting@v-soft.com
Doug Vernier, President
Kate Michler, Engineering Dir
Tech consulting for AM, FM, & TV. Coverage mapping, frequency searches, applications, site evaluations, stn watches, stn audits & more.

The Downtown Group
236 W. 27th St., New York, NY 10001
(212) 675-9506, *Fax:* (212) 675-3276
www.downtowngroup.com
info@downtowngroup.com
Mark Winkleman, Operations Dir
Design of tech facilities: architecture, acoustics, engrg, testing. Typical projects include edit rooms, stages, recording studios & support facilities.

DSI RF Systems Inc.
26H World's Fair Dr., Somerset, NJ 08873
(732) 563-1144, *Fax:* (732) 563-1818
www.dsirf.com
jmueller@dsirf.com
Tim Carroll, President
Herb Squire, Engineering Dir
Joseph Giardina, Chief Engineer
Radio & TV system design, transmitter & studio instal, microwave & satellite engrg & instal, remote control camera systems.

du Treil, Lundin & Rackley Inc.
201 Fletcher Ave., Sarasota, FL 34237-6019
(941) 329-6000, *Fax:* (941) 329-6030
www.dlr.com
bobjr@dlr.com
Tech consulting for the communications industry.

ERI - Electronics Research Inc.
7777 Gardner Rd., Chandler, IN 47610
(812) 925-6000, *Fax:* (812) 925-4030
www.eriinc.com
sales@eriinc.com
*Thomas B. Sillman, President
David White, Engineering Dir
Antennas, transmission line, filters-combiners & towers for FM, AM TV BR'S-EBS, mobile media bcstrs, also related engng, field & installations svcs.

Evans Associates Consulting
216 Green Bay Rd., Suite 205, Thiensville, WI 53092
(262) 242-6000, *Fax:* (262) 242-6045
www.evansassoc.com
info@evansassoc.com
*B. Benjamin Evans, P.E., Operations Dir
Telecommunications consulting engrs, net design, FCC applications, digital bcstg strategic planning, fieldwork for AM, FM, TV, CATV, ITFS, microwave relay facilities & fiber, wireless, & PCS networks.

Federal Engineering Inc.
Redwood Plaza II, 10600 Arrowhead Dr., Fairfax, VA 22030
(703) 359-8200, *Fax:* (703) 359-8204
www.fedeng.com
info@fedeng.com
Ronald F. Bosco, President
John E. Murray, Operations Dir
Strategic planning, coverage analysis, new product definition, market rsch, competitive analysis, rates & tariffs, bcst stn design, mergers & acquisitions, expert testimony, regulatory support.

Frank J. Maynard
44683 Mansfield Dr., Novi, MI 48375
(248) 344-2965
www.cdc.net/~bba
bba@cdc.net
Alfred C. Dick, Broker
Media broker & consultant for radio, TV & cable systems.

Frederick A. Smith Engineers
1123 Old River Rd., Elloree, SC 29047
(803) 897-2815, *Fax:* (803) 897-2816
Frederick A. Smith, P.E., President
Cameron E. Smith, Operations Dir
Communications systems design, microwave path surveys, ant impedance measurements. United States & foreign.

Freedman, Mel
2612 Portsmouth Ln., Modesto, CA 95355
(209) 522-1180, *Fax:* (209) 522-1750
melengr@sbcglobal.net
Mel Freeman, Engineering Dir

GeoMart
516 Villanova Ct., Fort Collins, CO 80525
(970) 416-8340, *Fax:* (970) 416-8345
www.geomart.com
sales@geomart.com
Chuck Cotherman, President
All USGS & DMA digital & paper maps. All NOS/NOAA charts, international topographic series, aerial photography, raised relief maps, digital products, business & mktg maps, travel maps, globes, etc.

George Jacobs & Associates Inc.
3210 N. Leisure World Blvd., Suite 1001, Silver Spring, MD 20906-7605
(301) 598-1282, *Fax:* (301) 598-7788
www.gjainc.com
broadcaster@gjainc.com
*George Jacobs, P.E., President
Specialists in conceptional design, application filing & frequency mgmt for FCC-licensed International Broadcast Stations (shortwave). Consultative liaison with foreign bcst stns & organizations.

George M. Frese, P.E.
1011 Denis Ct., East Wenatchee, WA 98802
(509) 884-4558, *Fax:* (509) 884-9170
frese@genext.net
*George M. Frese, President
AM Antenna design. Short, DA & Multiplexing.

Graphic Enterprises Inc.
3874 Highland Park N.W., North Canton, OH 44720
(800) 842-8448, *Fax:* (800) 358-7767
www.geiwideformat.com
sales@geiwideformat.com
Large-format digital printing systems.

Hammett & Edison Inc.
Box 280068, San Francisco, CA 94128-0068
(707) 996-5200, (202) 396-5200 (DC), *Fax:* (707) 996-5280
www.h-e.com
engr@h-e.com
William F. Hammett, P.E., President
Rajat Mathur, P.E., Engineering Dir
Design & FCC filings: AM, FM, TV, STL, wireless cable. Specialties: computerized coverage studies, AM directionals / diplexers, RF radiation predictions / measurements / mitigations, field strength measurements, due diligence technicalsurveys, FAA EMI analysis.

Hatfield & Dawson, Consulting Engineers L.L.C.
9500 Greenwood Ave. N., Seattle, WA 98103
(206) 783-9151, *Fax:* (206) 789-9834
www.hatdaw.com
hatdaw@hatdaw.com
Benjamin F. Dawson, President
Telecommunications, radio physics engrg, including bcst, electromagnetic compatibility, NIER measurement/analysis, antenna/propagation analysis & design.

Hilding Communications
Box 1700, Morgan Hill, CA 95038-2222
(408) 842-2222
mkrafcisin@hotmail.com
Michael H. Krafcisin, President
Mgmt, progmg, production, scriptwriting, talent, voice-over svcs, opns & engrg consultation

HN Telecom Inc.
1160 Douglas Rd., ., Burnaby, BC V5C 4Z6 Canada
(604) 294-3401, *Fax:* (604) 299-6712
www.hntelecom.com
contact@hntelecom.com
Bruce W. Grantholm, President
P. Hostinsky, Operations Dir
Telecommunications tech consulting svcs for AM, FM, TV bcst & CATV systems, studio-to-transmitter links & studio systems.

Independent Broadcast Consultants Inc.
110 County Rd. 146, Trumansburg, NY 14886
(607) 273-2970, *Fax:* (607) 273-5125
www.trumansburgchamber.com
ibcengineering@juno.com
William J. Sitzman, President
M.F. Sitzman, Operations Dir
R.A. Lynch, Engineering Dir
AM, FM & SW applications, specializing in AM allocation studies & broadband AM directional antenna design & AM diplexer design.

J. Boyd Ingram & Associates
Box 1528, Batesville, MS 38606
(662) 563-4007
www.radiobroker.com
garland@radiobroker.com
David Garland, President
Broker of radio stn properties in Texas & surrounding states.

J.M. Stitt & Associates Inc.
621 E. Mehring Way, Suite 1907, Cincinnati, OH 45202
(513) 621-9292, *Fax:* (513) 651-9622
www.jmstittassociates.com
towerjimsk@gmail.com
James Stitt, President
Engrg consultants, facility design & instal, contract engrg svcs, acoustical consultants, tower site mgmt.

Jenel Systems and Design Inc./Smalling Systems
6700 Spokane, Plano, TX 75023
(972) 491-1442, *Fax:* (972) 491-1442
smalling@smallingsystems.com
Elmer Smalling III, President
Howard Halcomb III, General Sales Mgr
Erin Day Loyd III, Promotions Manager
Digital bcstg solutions; studio, post, acoustic & earth stn, design; trucks; TV system design from planning to turnkey construction.

John F.X. Browne & Associates P.C.
38710 Woodward Ave., Suite 220, Bloomfield Hills, MI 48304
(248) 642-6226, *Fax:* (248) 642-6027
www.jfxb.com
consultants@jfxb.com
*John F.X. Browne, P.E., President
Leonard W. Eden, Engineering Dir
Bcst consulting AM/FM/TV/DTV, MMDS/ITFS, PCS & satellite systems. FCC/FAA applications, filings & studies. Field measurement vehicle AM/FM/TV/DTV.

John H. Battison, P.E. & Associates
Div/DBA: Consulting Radio Engineers
2684 State Rt. 60, Loudonville, OH 44842
(419) 994-3849, *Fax:* (419) 994-5419
batcom@bright.net
John H. Battison, Engineering Dir
All FCC svcs: AM, FM, TV, LPTV, applications, licensing, DA-proofs, ITFS & MMDS expert witness svcs.

John J. Davis & Associates
Box 128, Sierra Madre, CA 91025-0128
(626) 355-6909, *Fax:* (626) 355-4890
www.socaltowers.com
johnjdavis@roadrunner.com
*John J. Davis, President
Primary focus on FM & TV ch allocation studies & applications; facility upgrades, FM & TV translator applications, tower site mgmt.

KCI Technologies Inc.
4601 Six Forks Rd., Landmark Center II, Suite 220, Raleigh, NC 27609
(919) 783-9214, *Fax:* (919) 783-9266
www.kci.com
corpcom@kci.com
Tom Donohue, P.E., Operations Dir
James Blake, Engineering Dir
Full engrg svcs to the communications industry, including tower analysis & remediation, design of standard & non-standard sites, 'stealth' engrg, photo realistic renderings & turnkey construction.

Kessler & Gehman Associates Inc.
507 N.W. 60th St., Suite C, Gainesville, FL 32607

(352) 332-3157, *Fax:* (352) 332-6392
www.kga.bz
rwilhour@bellsouth.net
*Robert Gehman, P.E. Jr., President
William Kessler, P.E. Jr., Operations Dir
William T. Godfrey, P.E. Jr., Engineering Dir
Studies, system design, FCC applications, bidding documents & contract monitoring for bcst, ITFS, wireless cable, microwave & mobile communications systems & digital TV.

Lawrence Behr Associates Inc.
Box 8026, Greenville, NC 27835-8026
(252) 757-0279, *Fax:* (252) 752-9155
www.lbagroup.com
lbagrp@lbagroup.com
Lawrence Behr, CEO
*Jerry E. Brown, Operations Dir
Provides wireless svcs: site acquisition, construction mgmt, AM detuning, AM tower colocation, RF hazard mgmt, RF shielding, due diligence, facility mgmt, dev, maintenance, support svcs.

Lawrence L. Morton Associates
3234 Greenwich Drive, Shasta Lake, CA 96019
(503) 275-4020
larry@radiotv.biz
*Lawrence L. Morton, P.E., President
Telecommunications engrg consulting svcs for AM, FM, TV & LPTV. Computerized engrg svcs, field svcs, FCC applications.

Lightning Eliminators & Consultants Inc.
6687 Arapahoe Rd., Boulder, CO 80303
(303) 447-2828 ext 107, *Fax:* (303) 447-8122
www.lightningprotection.com
info@lecglobal.com
Avram Saunders, President
Peter Carpenter, General Manager
JoOnna Silberman, Promotions Manager
JoOnna Silberman, News Director
Darwin Sletten, Engineering Dir
Kirk Chynoweth, Chief Engineer
Lightning protection, grounding solutions. protection consulting, design and installation, engineering and design.

Lohnes and Culver
8309 Cherry Ln., Laurel, MD 20707-4830
(301) 776-4488, *Fax:* (301) 776-4499
locul@locul.com
*Robert D. Culver, Operations Dir
Communication consulting engrg svc for bcst & related fields. Design, application, optimization, system evaluation & expert representation svcs.

Mahlum Architects
71 Columbia, Suite 400, Seattle, WA 98104
(206) 441-4151, *Fax:* (206) 441-0478
www.mahlum.com
info@mahlum.com
John Mahlum, President
Architect interiors & planning.

Marsand Inc.
Box 485, 6100 IH 35W, Alvarado, TX 76009
(817) 783-5566, *Fax:* (817) 783-5577
www.marsand.com
tvcowboy@marsand.com
*Matthew A. Sanderford, Jr., P.E., President
David Sanderford, Operations Dir
Turnkey installation, CAD-VIDCAD wiring documentation, Digital FM & TV proof-of-performance, FCC consulting & applications, RF troubleshooting, installations & conversions, RF site safety.

McClanathan & Associates Inc.
Box 939, Portland, OR 97207
(503) 246-8080, *Fax:* (503) 246-6304
*Robert A. McClanathan, P.E., President
Professional electrical engrs for radio & TV FCC applications, computer svcs, field engrg & construction svcs.

Meintel, Sgrignoli, & Wallace
1282 Smallwood Dr., Suite 372, Waldorf, MD 20603
(202) 251-7589, *Fax:* (301) 645-1426
www.mswdtv.com
wallacedtv@aol.com
Gary Sgrignoli, Operations Dir
Specializing in digital & analog TV & Radio technical software, consumer electronics.

MidAmerica Electronics Service Inc.
410 Mt. Tabor Rd., New Albany, IN 47150
(812) 945-1209, *Fax:* (812) 945-1859
peterclb@aol.com
AM & FM field engrg svcs, antenna measurements, AM stereo instal & proof of performance, AM & FM spectrum analysis, NRSC compliance measurement, new construction & rebuilding.

Morgan, Angel & Associates LLC
1601 Connecticut Ave. N.W., Suite 601, Washington, DC 20009
(202) 265-1833, *Fax:* (202) 265-8022
www.morganangel.com
luis@morganangel.com
Luis A. Blandon Jr., Promotions Manager
Consulting research firm specializing in Section 106 showings and environmental assessments for proposed towers and project sites.
3605 Nelson St., Wheat Ridge, CO 80033-5565
(303) 425-9170;
Dr. Edward Angel, Principal Owner

Mueller Broadcast Design
613 S. La Grange Rd., La Grange, IL 60525
(708) 352-2166, *Fax:* (708) 352-2170
www.muellerbroadcastdesign.com
mark@muellerbroadcastdesign.com
Mark A. Mueller, President
Karen S. Mueller, General Manager
AM/FM tech consultant, AM directional systems.

Mullaney Engineering Inc.
9049 Shady Grove Court, Gaithersburg, MD 20877
(301) 921-0115, *Fax:* (301) 590-9757
www.mullengr.com
mullaney@mullengr.com
John J. Mullaney, President
Timothy Z. Sawyer, Engineering Dir
Alan E Gearing, Chief Engineer
Mullaney Engineering, Inc., and its predecessor firms have been providing consulting engineering services to the radio and television industry since 1948. In the early 1970's, the firm pioneered the computer aided design and optimization ofAM directional arrays which minimizes construction costs through the elimination of unnecessary towers. The firm was also one of the first to provide a computer analysis of the allocation conditions for FM, TV, and MDS facilities. With theestablishment of its in-house computer facilities in 1974, the firm prides itself on remaining on the leading edge of technology. Mullaney Engineering, Inc., currently provides services in: AM, FM, TV, DTV, MDS/ITFS, LPTV, Cellular, and environmentalradiation analysis.

Multicomm Sciences International Inc.
266 W. Main St., Denville, NJ 07834
(973) 627-7400, *Fax:* (973) 215-2168
www.multicommsciences.com
victor@multicommsciences.com
Victor J. Nexon Jr., President
Frequency coord, site surveys, earth stn interference studies, FCC license, radiation hazard testing.

Munn-Reese Inc.
Box 220, 385 Airport Dr., Coldwater, MI 49036-0220
(517) 278-7339, *Fax:* (517) 278-6973
www.munn-reese.com
wayne@munn-reese.com
Wayne S. Reese, President
Christine Reese, Operations Dir
Rick Grizebik, Engineering Dir
AM, FM, TV, low power TV & engrg consulting service, including applications, field tuning & problem solving.

Newman-Kees Frequency Measurements, Engineering, & Installations
8611 Slate Rd., Evansville, IN 47720
(812) 963-3294
www.kepffbarr.com
kempffcc@aol.com
Ron Kempff, President
Aurelia Serna, Operations Dir
Broker & consultant also offering financial & mgmt svcs, court ordered sale of stns.

Owl Engineering & EMC Test Labs, Inc.
5844 Avenue N., Shoreview, MN 55126
(651) 784-7445, *Fax:* (651) 784-7541
www.owleng.com
info@owleng.com
*Garrett G. Lysiak, P.E., President
Diane Stewart Lysiak, Operations Dir
Telecommunications consulting engrg svcs, applications, facilities specifications svcs, field engrg svcs, maintenance & FCC compliance svcs, EMC testing.

Pacific Radio Electronics
969 N. La Brea, Los Angeles, CA 90038
(323) 969-2035, (800) 634-9476, *Fax:* (323) 969-2053
www.pacrad.com
info@pacrad.com
Joseph Phillips, President
Distributor of racks, patch bays, cable, adaptors, connectors, handtools, outlet strips & many other products for the bcst industry.

Paul Dean Ford
3881 West Dugger Avenue, West Terre Haute, IN 47885
(812) 535-3828
www.worldpower.us/
wpfr@joink.com
Paul Dean Ford, P.E., President
Engineering consultant.

R.L. Hoover Consulting Telecommunications
Div/DBA: Consulting Telecommunications Engineer
11704 Seven Locks Rd., Potomac, MD 20854
(301) 983-0054
*Robert Lloyd Hoover, P.E., President
Professional engrg consulting for AM, FM & TV applications & testimony. Radiation hazard analyses & testimony. Ex-owner AM & FM stns. Patent agent.

Radio/TV Engineering Co.
1416 Hollister Ln., Los Osos, CA 93402
(805) 528-1996, *Fax:* (805) 528-1982
Norwood J. Patterson, President
G. Dawn Patterson, Engineering Dir
AM, FM, FCC applications, directional ant design. Serving bcstrs for over 35 years.

Radiotechniques Engineering, LLC
Box 367, 402 10th Ave., Haddon Heights, NJ 08035-0367
(856) 546-8008, *Fax:* (856) 546-1841
www.radiotechniques.com
ted@radiotechniques.com
*Edward A. Schober, P.E., Operations Dir
AM, FM, TV, digital bcst, boosters, FCC, equipment, field, & systems engrg. RF, financial, opns, & acoustical design.

RF Technologies Corp.
1 Gendron Dr., Lewiston, ME 04240
(207) 777-7778, *Fax:* (207) 777-7784
www.rftechnologies.net
info@rftechnologies.net
Designs & manufactures high-power bcst RF networks & components for FM & TV bcstrs. Products include ants, diplexers, combiners, filters, switches, coaxial & waveguides.

Richard L. Vega Group Inc.
1245 W. Fairbanks Ave., #380, Winter Park, FL 32789
(407) 539-6540
Richard L. Vega Jr., Chairman
Engrg svcs & business consulting svcs.

Richard S. Becker & Associates, Chartered
7128 Fair Fax Rd., Bethesda, MD 20814
(301) 986-9005, *Fax:* (301) 986-8496
beckereng@aol.com
Richard Becker, Operations Dir
Siamak Harandi, Engineering Dir
Legal & engrg svc for bcstg, cable TV, cellular, paging, microwave & private radio.

Richard W. Burden Associates
20944 Sherman Way, Suite 213, Canoga Park, CA 91303
(818) 340-4590
www.fcc.gov
mwilhelm@fcc.gov

Rimma Posin
3712 Carmel Ave., Irvine, CA 92606
(949) 857-9639, *Fax:* (949) 857-9639
Rimma Posin, President

Consulting for cable; FCC applications.

RKF Engineering, LLC
1229 19th St., N.W., Washington, DC 20036
(202) 463-1565, *Fax:* (202) 463-0344
www.rkfengineering
prubin@satpar.com
Jeffrey Freedman, CFO
*Philip A. Rubin, P.E., President
Alex Latker, General Manager
William Meeker, Engineering Dir
MSS, FSS & BSS satellite experts, TV & radio cellular & other new media technologies. Experts in FCC rules & regulations. International experience, experts in ITU regulation. Software developers, simulation & modeling. In business over 20years.

Rogers Cable Systems
35-73 Wolfdale, Mississauga, ON L5C 3T6 Canada
(905) 273-8000, *Fax:* (905) 273-9661
www.rogers.com
Consulting engrg svcs with emphasis on design, instal & testing of CATV systems, fiber-optic nets.

Sellmeyer Engineering
Box 356, McKinney, TX 75070
(972) 542-2056, *Fax:* (214) 636-5940
www.sellmeyer.com
*J.S. Sellmeyer, P.E., President
AM, FM, TV applications, hearing support, directional ant design & adjustment; facilities planning & specialized equipment design.

Serge Bergen, P.E.
7503 Amkin Ct., Clifton, VA 22024
(703) 250-2691
www.aviationweatherinc.com
wxcenter@aviationweatherinc.com
Liam Richard Ferguson, President
Regional Radio Broadcast/Weathercast Network across the Carolinas & Georgia in over 20 bcst markets. Weather forecasting, site-specific bcst svc for stns all across America. 100% barter.

SiteSafe Inc.
200 N. Glebe Rd., Suite 1000, Arlington, VA 22203-3728
(703) 276-1100, *Fax:* (703) 276-1169
www.sitesafe.com
info@sitesafe.com
Wesley McGee, President
Bill Zlotnick, Operations Dir
Bcst & land mobile & wireless engrg consulting svcs.

Smith and Fisher, LLC
2237 Tackett's Mill Dr., Suite A, Woodbridge, VA 22192
(703) 494-2101, *Fax:* (703) 494-2132
www.smithandfisher.com
kevin@smithandfisher.com
Kevin Fisher, President
Kyle Fisher, Engineering Dir
Engrg consultants to FM, TV, & LPTV stns, FCC applications, allocation studies, RFR measurements, coverage/ interference mapping & field studies.

Southern Broadcast Services
80 Commerce Dr., Suite B, Pelham, AL 35124
(205) 663-3709, (800) 256-9235, *Fax:* (205) 663-7108
www.southernbroadcastservices.com
jwcoleman@southernbroadcastservices.com
Jim Coleman, President
Tower erection, ant & line instal additional , cellular & maintenance svcs.

Steve Vanni Associates Inc.
Box 422, Auburn, NH 03032
(603) 483-5365, *Fax:* (603) 483-0512
svanni@techsystems.com
Steve Vanni, President
Tech consulting, systems design, project mgmt; complete turnkey svcs including equipment & towers through Technet Systems Group.

T.Z. Sawyer Technical Consultants LLC
9049 Shady Grove Ct., Gaithersburg, MD 20877
(301) 921-0115, *Fax:* (301) 590-9757
www.tzsawyer.com
info@tzsawyer.com
Timothy Z. Sawyer, President
FCC applications for AM, FM, TV, LPTV & aux svcs; AM directional ant design; AM, FM, & TV ant measurements; allocation studies; site surveys & inspections.

Technet Systems Group
Div/DBA: (A division of Steve Vanni Associates Inc)
Box 422, Auburn, NH 03032
(603) 483-5365, (800) 329-4767, *Fax:* (603) 483-0512
www.technetsystems.com
sales@technetsystems.com
Steve Vanni, President
Bcst equipment supplier/distributor for radio & TV, specializing in complete 'turnkeyed' packages including planning, design, equipment, instal, towers & FCC licensing.

Teletech Inc.
38235 N. Executive Dr., Westland, MI 48185
(734) 641-2300
www.teletech-inc.com
Susan Dobronski, President
Keith Johnson, Operations Dir
Engrg consultants: AM, FM, TV, LPTV; FCC applications/filings; FAA filings, aeronautical studies; tower erection, maintenance & inspections; antenna site dev & mgmt; directorial antenna design & proof of performance; contract engrg svcs.
Box 4221, Scottsdale, AZ 85261-4221
(480) 367-1500;

TransVision
550 Maulhardt Ave., Oxnard, CA 93030
(805) 981-8740, *Fax:* (805) 981-8738
www.txvision.com
info@txvision.com
Kimithy Vaughn, General Sales Mgr
Twelve transportable & satellite transmission facilities (video, audio, voice, data). Flypack production & SNG svcs. Facilities in Brazil, Australia, Phillipines & Western Europe.

Vir James, P.C.
965 S. Irving St., Denver, CO 80219
(303) 937-1900, *Fax:* (303) 937-1902
*Timothy C. Cutforth, P.E., President
AM/FM/TV allocation studies & applications, AM directional ant design & tune-up, conductivity measurements.

W.L. Pritchard & Co. L.C.
4405 E.W. Hwy., Suite 501, Bethesda, MD 20814
(301) 654-1144, *Fax:* (301) 654-1814
www.wlpco.com
wlpritchard-co@verizon.net
Ellen Hoff, President
Paul Schrantz, Engineering Dir
Professional engrg, business problem solving in telecommunications, competitor analysis, satellite communications, earth stns, & launch vehicles.

William Culpepper & Associates Inc.
900 Jefferson Dr., Charlotte, NC 28270
(704) 365-9995, *Fax:* (704) 364-4823
*William A. Culpepper, President
AM & FM applications & feasibility studies, specializing in applications for AM power increases & transmitter relocation.

William F. Pohts Telecommunications
225 Denfield Dr., Alexandria, VA 22309
(703) 360-7193, *Fax:* (703) 360-0309
bill@pohts.com
*William F. Pohts, P.E., Engineering Dir
Consulting engr specializing in the emerging technologies in telecommunications & electronic systems.

Willoughby & Voss, LLC
Box 701190, San Antonio, TX 78270-1190
(210) 490-2778, (210) 525-1111, *Fax:* (210) 490-2779
willvoss@satx.rr.com
Lyndon H. Willoughby, President
AM, FM, TV, STL, trans applications, directional ant design, field svcs, allocations, site studies, system planning, frequency searches, facility inspection & non-ionized radiation studies.

Wireless Systems Engineering Inc./MLJ
Div/DBA: (formerly JMS/MLJ Worldwide Inc.)
15713 Crabbs Branch Way, Suite 140, Rockville, MD 20855
(301) 840-2030, *Fax:* (301) 840-2031
info@wse-mlj.com
IT & software engrg, wireless engrg & internet svcs needs.

Legal Services

A. Chavis Vanias, Attorney at Law
P.O. Box 9612, Columbia, SC 29209
(803) 256-1244, *Fax:* (803) 753-0007
acvanias@scbar.org

Abacus Communications Company
1801 Columbus Rd. N.W., Suite 101, Washington, DC 20009-2031
(202) 462-3680, *Fax:* (202) 462-3781
abacuscommco@covad.net

Akerman & Senterfitt
Citrus Center, 255 South Orange Ave., 17th Fl., Orlando, FL 32801
(407) 843-7860, *Fax:* (407) 843-6610

Akin Gump Strauss Hauer & Feld LLP
Robert S. Strauss Bldg., 1333 New Hampshire Ave. N.W., Washington, DC 20036
(202) 887-4000, *Fax:* (202) 887-4288
akingump.com
sturner@akinggump.com

Anderson, Kill & Olick L.L.P.
2100 M St. N.W., Suite 650, Washington, DC 20037
(202) 416-6500, *Fax:* (202) 416-6555
www.andersonkill.com

Arent & Fox, PLLC
1050 Connecticut Ave. N.W., Washington, DC 20036-5339
(202) 857-6000, *Fax:* (202) 857-6395
www.arentfox.com
delorey.denise@arentfox.com

Arnold & Porter LLP
555 12th St. N.W., Washington, DC 20004-1206
(202) 942-5000, *Fax:* (202) 942-5999
www.arnoldporter.com
norman.sinel@aporter.com

Asbury, Philip S.
309 S. Broad St., Philadelphia, PA 19107-5813
(215) 985-0911, *Fax:* (215) 985-1195
pasburypir@ol.com

Attorney At Law
2154 Wisconsin Ave., N.W., Suite 250, Washington, DC 20007-2280
(202) 223-3772, *Fax:* (202) 315-3587
kenhardman@att.net

Ausley & McMullen
Box 391, 227 S. Calhoun St., Tallahassee, FL 32302
(850) 224-9115, *Fax:* (850) 222-7560

Baker & Hostetler LLP
1050 Connecticut Ave. N.W., Suite 1100, Washington, DC 20036
(202) 861-1500, *Fax:* (202) 861-1783
www.bakerlaw.com
khoward@bakerlaw.com

Baker Botts L.L.P.
1299 Pennsylvania Ave. N.W., Washington, DC 20004
(202) 639-7700, *Fax:* (202) 639-7890
laurie.spielman@bakerbotts.com

Baker, Ravenel & Bender
Box 8057, 1730 Main St., Columbia, SC 20292
(803) 799-9091, *Fax:* (803) 779-3423

Barron & Newburger, P.C.
1212 Guadalupe St., Suite 104, Austin, TX 78701
(512) 476-9103, *Fax:* (512) 476-9253
bbarron@bnpdaw.com

Barry Skidelsky, Esq.
18 E. 41st St., New York, NY 10017
(212) 832-4800
bskidelsky@mindspring.com
Barry Skidelsky, Consultant
Consults lenders, investors, owners & mgmt on M&A, strategy & opns, FCC ownership, bankruptcy, trustee, arbitrator & expert witness.

Bass, Berry & Sims
315 Deaderick St., South Center Suite 2700, Nashville, TN 37238-0002
(615) 742-6200, *Fax:* (615) 742-6293

Beitchman & Hudson
215 14th St. N.W., Atlanta, GA 30318
(404) 897-5252, *Fax:* (404) 874-4270
leebeebee@aol.com

Bell, Boyd & Lloyd
1615 L St. N.W., Suite 1200, Washington, DC 20036
(202) 466-6300, *Fax:* (202) 463-0678

Berkowitz, Trager & Trager, P.C.
8 Wright St., Westport, CT 06880
(203) 226-1001, *Fax:* (203) 226-3801

Bingham McCuthen, LLP
2020 K St. N.W., Washington, DC 20006
(202) 373-6033, *Fax:* (202) 373-6001
www.bingham.com
andrew.lipman@bingham.com

Birch, Horton, Bittner & Cherot
1155 Connecticut Ave. N.W., Suite 1200, Washington, DC 20036
(202) 659-5800, *Fax:* (202) 659-1027
www.birchhorton.com

Bishop, Payne, Harvard & Kaitcer, L.L.P.
500 W. Seventh St., Suite 1800, Fort Worth, TX 76102-4782
(817) 335-4911, *Fax:* (817) 870-2631

Blank, Rome, LLP
405 Lexington Ave., 23rd Floor, New York, NY 10174
(212) 885-5000, *Fax:* (212) 885-5001
www.blankrome.com

Bleiweiss, Irene
U.S. FCC, Audio Services Division, 445 12th St. S.W., Rm. 2B450, Washington, DC 20554
(202) 418-2700, *Fax:* (202) 418-1411
www.fcc.gov/mb/audio
irene.bleiweiss@fcc.gov

Blooston, Mordkofsky, Dickens, Duffy & Prendergast, LLP
2120 L St. N.W., Suite 300, Washington, DC 20037
(202) 659-0830, *Fax:* (202) 828-5568
www.bloostonlaw.com
halmor@bloostonlaw.com

Blumberg, Grace Ganz
UCLA School of Law, 405 Hilgard Ave., Los Angeles, CA 90095
(310) 825-1334, *Fax:* (310) 206-6489
www.law-ucla.edu
blumberg@law-ucla.edu

Blume & Associates LLC
10 Ellsworth Rd., Suite 209, West Hartford, CT 06107
(860) 231-8777, *Fax:* (860) 231-8763
www.blumelegal.net
db@blumelegal.net

Boelter & Perry
330 Washington Blvd., Suite 310, Marina Del Rey, CA 90292
(310) 882-5037, *Fax:* (310) 823-4325
boltperr@comcast.net

Boies, Schiller & Flexner, LLP
100 S.E. 2nd St., Suite 2800, Miami, FL 33131
(305) 539-8400, *Fax:* (305) 539-1307
www.bsfllp.com

Bone McAllester Norton PLLC
511 Union St., Suite 1600, Nashville, TN 37219
(615) 238-6330, *Fax:* (615) 238-6301
www.bonelaw.com
mnorton@bonelaw.com

Boose, Casey, Ciklin, Lubitz, Martens, McBane & O'Connell
Northbridge Tower, 515 N. Flagler Dr., Suite 1900, West Palm Beach, FL 33401
(561) 832-5900, *Fax:* (561) 833-4209
rcrump@boosecasey.com

Booth, Freret, Imlay & Tepper P.C.
14356 Cape May Rd., Silver Spring, MD 20904-6011
(301) 384-5525, *Fax:* (301) 384-6384
bfitpc@aol.com

Bordelon, Hamlin & Theriot
701 S. Peters St., Suite 100, New Orleans, LA 70130-1661
(504) 524-5328, *Fax:* (504) 523-1071

Borsari & Paxson
4000 Albemarle St. N.W., Suite 100, Washington, DC 20016
(202) 296-4800, *Fax:* (202) 296-4460
www.baplaw.com
bap@baplaw.com

Borsari and Assoc., P.L.C.
Box 100009, Arlington, VA 22210
(703) 524-5800, *Fax:* (703) 524-4329
www.borsari.com
John@borsari.com

Boult, Cummings, Conners & Berry, PLC
1600 Division St., Suite 700, Nashville, TN 37219
(615) 244-2582, *Fax:* (615) 252-6380
www.boultcummings.com

Bramson, Plutzik, Mahler, Birkhaeuser, LLP
2125 Oak Grove Rd., Suite 120, Walnut Creek, CA 94598
(925) 945-0200, *Fax:* (925) 945-8792
rbramson@bramsonplutzik.com

Brann & Isaacson
Box 3070, 184 Main St., Lewiston, ME 04243
(207) 786-3566, *Fax:* (207) 783-9325
www.brannlaw.com
gisaacson@brannlaw.com

Brenner, Daniel L.
National Cable Telecommunications Association, 25 Massachusetts Ave. N.W., Washington, DC 20001
(202) 775-3664, (202) 775-2300, *Fax:* (202) 775-3603
www.ncta.com
dbrenner@ncta.com

Brickfield, Burchette, Ritts & Stone
1025 Thomas Jefferson St. N.W., Suite 800 West Tower, 8th Fl., Washington, DC 20007
(202) 342-0800, *Fax:* (202) 342-0807
www.bbrslaw.com

Brighton , Runyon & Callahan
45 Main St., Suite 22, Peterborough, NH 03458-0674
(603) 924-7276, *Fax:* (603) 924-9764

Brooks, Pierce, McLendon, Humphrey & Leonard
150 Fayetteville St., Suite 1600, Raleigh, NC 27602
(919) 839-0300, *Fax:* (919) 839-0304
www.brookspierce.com
whargrove@brookspierce.com

Brown, Dean, Wiseman, Lisert, Proctor & Hart, L.L.P.
306 W. 7th St., Suite 200, Fort Worth, TX 76102
(817) 332-1391, *Fax:* (817) 870-2427
www.browndean.com

Brown, Nietert, & Kaufman, Chartered
1301 Connecticut Ave., Suite 450, Washington, DC 20036
(202) 887-0600, *Fax:* (202) 223-8685
david@bnkcomlaw.com

Brown, Steven Ames
69 Grand View Ave., San Francisco, CA 94114-2741
(415) 647-7700, *Fax:* (415) 285-3048
sabrown@entertainmentlaw.com

Bryan Cave L.L.P.
700 13th St. N.W., Suite 700, Washington, DC 20005
(202) 508-6000, *Fax:* (202) 508-6200
jwilner@bryancave.com
1290 Ave. of the Americas, New York, NY 10104-0101
(212) 541-2000; *Fax:* (212) 541-4630
www.bryancave.com
Jerome S. Boros, Renee E. Frost
Andrew Irving, Alan Pearce
Michael Rosen, President
3500 One Kansas City Pl., Kansas City, MO 64105-2158
(816) 474-7400; *Fax:* (816) 374-3300
www.bryancave.com
John R. Wilner, Chairman

Bubar, James S., Attorney at Law
1776 K St. N.W., Suite 800, Washington, DC 20006
(202) 223-2060, *Fax:* (202) 223-2061
www.lawyers.com/jamesbubar/
jbubar@aol.com

Bullivant, Houser, & Bailey
300 Pioneer Tower, 888 S.W. 5th Ave., Suite 300, Portland, OR 97204
(503) 228-6351, *Fax:* (503) 295-0915
www.bullivant.com

Byelas & Neigher
1804 Post Rd. E., Westport, CT 06880
(203) 259-0599, *Fax:* (203) 255-2570

Cades Schutte
1000 Bishop St., Honolulu, HI 96813
(808) 521-9221, *Fax:* (808) 540-5040
jportnoy@cades.com

Cahill, Gordon & Reindel LLP
1990 K St. N.W., Suite 950, Washington, DC 20006
(202) 862-8900, *Fax:* (202) 862-8958
mulvid@cgrdc.com
80 Pine St, New York, NY 10005-1702
(212) 701-3000;
Floyd Abrams, Chairman

Calfee, Halter & Griswold
800 Superior Ave., Suite 1400 MacDonald Investment Ctr., Cleveland, OH 44114
(216) 622-8200, *Fax:* (216) 241-0816
www.calfee.com
cbowers@calfee.com

Callister, Nebeker & McCullough
Gateway Tower E., Suite 900, Salt Lake City, UT 84133
(801) 530-7300, *Fax:* (801) 364-9127
www.cnmlaw.com

Cameron & Mittleman LLP
56 Exchange Terr., Providence, RI 02903-1766
(401) 331-5700, *Fax:* (401) 331-5787
www.cm-law.com

Caridi, Carmella, Esq.
Caridi Video Inc., 250 W. 57th, New York, NY 10107-1722
(212) 581-2277, *Fax:* (212) 581-2278

Carr, Morris & Graeff
1120 G St. N.W., Suite 930, Washington, DC 20005
(202) 789-1000, *Fax:* (202) 628-3834

Carter Ledyard & Milburn LLP
1401 Eye St. N.W., Suite 300, Washington, DC 20005
(202) 898-1515, *Fax:* (202) 898-1521
www.clm.com
info@clm.com

Cavallo, Robert M.
400 Park Ave., 21st Fl., New York, NY 10022-4406
(212) 753-2224, *Fax:* (212) 753-7113
rcavallo@jtjsys.com

Chadbourne & Parke
1200 New Hampshire Ave. N.W., Suite 300, Washington, DC 20036
(202) 974-5600, *Fax:* (202) 974-5602
www.chadbourne.com
info@chadbourne.com
30 Rockefeller Plaza, New York, NY 10112-0015
(212) 408-5100;
601 S. Figueroa St, Los Angeles, CA 90017-5704
(213) 892-1000;

Chetkof, Gary H.
Box 367, 293 Tinker St., Woodstock, NY 12498
(845) 679-7600, *Fax:* (845) 679-5395
www.wdst.com

Clark Hill P.L.C.
500 Woodward Ave., Suite 3500, Detroit, MI 48226-3435
(313) 965-8300, *Fax:* (313) 962-4348, (313) 965-8252
www.clarkhill.com
dlee@clarkhill.com

Clifford, Chance, LLP
31 West 52 St., New York, NY 10019-6131
(212) 878-8000, *Fax:* (212) 878-8375
www.cliffordchance.com

Cohn and Marks LLP
1920 N St. N.W., Suite 300, Washington, DC 20036-1622
(202) 293-3860, *Fax:* (202) 293-4827
www.cohnmarks.com
richard.helmick@cohnmarks.com

Colby, Lauren A.
Box 113, 10 E. Fourth St., Frederick, MD 21705-0113
(301) 663-1086, *Fax:* (301) 695-8734
www.lcolby.com
lac@lcolby.com

Cole, Raywid & Braverman, L.L.P.
1919 Pennsylvania Ave. N.W., Suite 200, Washington, DC 20006
(202) 659-9750, *Fax:* (202) 452-0067
www.crblaw.com
info@crblaw.com

Cooke, James R.
2821 Beachwood Cir., Arlington, VA 22207
(703) 841-1001, *Fax:* (703) 841-1004
jrcde@comcast.net
130 E. Main St., Rochester, NY 14604-1610
(716) 232-4440; *Fax:* (716) 232-1925

Gunther Buerman, Mgng Ptnr
One Grimsby Dr., Hamburg, NY
(716) 646-5050; *Fax:* (716) 648-8204
Raymond Stapell, Mgng Ptnr
119 E. Seneca St., Ithaca, NY 14850-4359
(607) 273-6444; *Fax:* (607) 273-6802
Mark Wheeler, Chairman
20 Corporate Woods Blvd., Albany, NY 12211-2396
(518) 427-9706; *Fax:* (518) 427-0235
Terence Burke, Chairman
300 S. State St., 4th Fl., Syracuse, NY 13202-2024
(315) 423-7100; *Fax:* (315) 426-9331
Thomas E. Taylor, Chairman
2 University Plaza, 2nd Fl., Hackensack, NJ 07601-6202
(201) 488-2200; *Fax:* (201) 342-6677
Vincenzo Taparo, Chairman
530 Fifth Ave., New York, NY 10036-5101
(212) 687-0100; *Fax:* (212) 997-7868
William O'Connor, Chairman

Cooper, White & Cooper, L.L.P.
201 California St., 17th Fl., San Francisco, CA 94111
(415) 433-1900, *Fax:* (415) 433-5530
www.cwclaw.com
whansell@cwclaw.com

Cooter, Mangold, Tompert & Wayson
5301 Wisconsin Ave N.W., Suite 500, Washington, DC 20015
(202) 537-0700, *Fax:* (202) 364-3664
mterry@cootermangold.com

Corberlaw
Box 4656, Panorama City, CA 91412-0212
(818) 786-7133
jboyd@panola.com
J. Boyd Ingram, A.E., President
Tech consultation, facility construction & repair.

Corn-Revere, Robert
Davis Wright Tremaine LLP, 1919 Pennsylvania Ave. N.W., Washington, DC 20006
(202) 973-4225, (202) 973-4200, *Fax:* (202) 973-4499
www.dwt.com
bobcornrevere@dwt.com

Couzens, Michael
Box 3642, Oakland, CA 94609
(510) 658-7654, *Fax:* (510) 654-6741
www.lptv.tv

Covington & Burling
1201 Pennsylvania Ave. N.W., Washington, DC 20004
(202) 662-6000, *Fax:* (202) 662-6291
www.cov.com
mrosentein@cov.com

Craven Law Office
1005 N. 7th St., Springfield, IL 62702
(217) 544-1777, *Fax:* (217) 544-0713
www.cravenlawoffice.com
presslaw@aol.com

Creative Industry Law Group
Div/DBA: (Formerly Hasse / Molesky P.C.)
155 Sansome St., Suite 500, San Francisco, CA 94104
(415) 433-4380, *Fax:* (415) 433-6580
www.creativelawgroup.com
lhasse@creativelawgroup.com

Crowell & Moring
1001 Pennsylvania Ave. N.W., Washington, DC 20004-2595
(202) 624-2500, *Fax:* (202) 628-5116
www.crowell.com
sthomas@crowell.com

Cuni, Ferguson, Levay & Bergmann
10655 Springfield Pike, Cincinnati, OH 45215
(513) 771-6768, *Fax:* (513) 771-6781
pmusgrove@cfl-law.com

David L. Maddox & Associates, P.C.
1207 17 Ave. S., Suite 300, Nashville, TN 37212
(615) 329-0086, *Fax:* (615) 320-7150
david@dmaddox.com

Davis Wright Tremaine LLP
(206) 622-3150, *Fax:* (206) 628-7699
www.dwt.com
seattle@dwt.com
999 Main St, Suite 911, Boise, ID 83702-9000
(208) 338-8200; *Fax:* (208) 338-8299
Deborah Kristensen, Chairman
2300 First Interstate Tower, 1300 S.W. 5th Ave, Portland, OR 97201-5630
(503) 241-2300; *Fax:* (503) 778-5299
Duane A. Bosworth, Chairman
1000 Wilshire Blvd, Suite 600, Los Angeles, CA 90017-2457
(213) 633-6800; *Fax:* (213) 633-6899
Kelli L. Sager, Chairman
1155 Connecticut Ave. N.W., Washington, DC 20036-4306
(202) 508-6600; *Fax:* (202) 508-6699

Davis Wright Tremaine LLP
1919 Pennsylvania Ave. N.W., Suite 200, Washington, DC 20006
(202) 973-4200, *Fax:* (202) 973-4499
www.dwt.com

Day & Associates
1812 Waterfront Plaza, 325 W. Main, Louisville, KY 40202-4251
(502) 585-4131, *Fax:* (502) 581-1210
dayandassociates@bellsouth.net

Day, Berry & Howard L.L.P.
CityPlace I, Hartford, CT 06103-3499
(860) 275-0122, *Fax:* (860) 275-0343
www.dbh.com
mwelsass@dbh.com

Debevoise & Plimpton LLP
919 3rd Ave., New York, NY 10022
(212) 909-6000, *Fax:* (212) 909-6836
www.debevoise.com
rdbohm@debevoise.com
21 Ave. George V, Paris,
33-1-40-73-12-12;
James A. Kiernan III, Chairman
Antoine F. Kirry, CEO/COO
Bolshoi Palashevsky Per 13/2, Moscow,
7503-956-3858;
Dmitri V. Nikiforov, Chairman
555 13th St. N.W., Suite 1100-E, Washington, DC 20004-1109
(202) 383-8000;
Jeffrey P. Cunard, Chairman
13/F Entertainment Bldg, 30 Queen's Rd. Central, Hong Kong,
852-2810-7918;
Jeffrey S. Wood, Chairman
The International Financial Centre, 25 Old Broad St, London,
44-171-786-9000;
Robert R. Bruce, Chairman

Decker, Jones, McMackin, McClane, Hall & Bates
801 Cherry St., Suite 2000, Unit 46, Fort Worth, TX 76102
(817) 336-2400, *Fax:* (817) 332-3043
www.deckerjones.com

Del, Shaw, Moonves, Tanaka, Finkelstein & Lezcano
2120 Colorado Ave., Suite 200, Santa Monica, CA 90404
(310) 979-7900, *Fax:* (310) 979-7999

Denechaud & Denechaud
1010 Common St., Suite 3010 & 1207, New Orleans, LA 70112-2483
(504) 522-4756, *Fax:* (504) 568-0783
cidlaw@bellsouth.net

Dennis Ardi Attorney at Law Professional Corporation
Div/DBA: (formerly Ardi Dennis)
340 N. Camden Dr., Third Fl., Beverly Hills, CA 90210
(310) 271-6900, *Fax:* (310) 271-6963

Devine & Millimet
Box 719, 111 Amherst St., Manchester, NH 03101
(603) 669-1000, *Fax:* (603) 669-8547
www.devinemillimet.com
kmcginley@dm.com

Dewey & LeBoeuf LLP
Div/DBA: (formerly LeBoeuf, Lamb, Greene & MacRae)
1101 New York Ave., Suite 1100, Washington, DC 20005
(202) 346-8000, *Fax:* (202) 986-8102
www.deweyleboeuf.com
One Embarcadero Ctr., Suite 400, San Francisco, CA
(415) 951-1100; *Fax:* (415) 951-1180
99 Washington Ave., Albany, NY 12210-2822
(518) 626-9000; *Fax:* (518) 626-9010
260 Franklin St., Boston, MA 02110-3112
(617) 748-6800; *Fax:* (617) 439-0341
125 W. 55th St., New York, NY 10019-5369
(212) 424-8000; *Fax:* (212) 424-8500

DeWitt, Ross & Stevens
2 E. Mifflin St., Suite 600, Madison, WI 53703
(608) 255-8891, *Fax:* (608) 252-9243
www.dewittross.com
info@dewuttriss.com

Dickstein Shapiro LLP
Div/DBA: (Formerly Dickstein Shapiro Morin and Oshinsky LLP
1825 Eye St., N.W., Washington, DC 20006-5403
(202) 420-2200, *Fax:* (202) 420-2201
www.dicksteinshapiro.com
info@dicksteinshapiro.com
1177 Ave. of the Americas, 41st Fl, New York, NY 10036-2714

Dieguez, Richard P.
192 Garden St., Suite 2, Roslyn Heights, NY 11577-1012
(516) 621-6424, *Fax:* (516) 621-6508
www.rpdieguez.com
rpdieguez@rpdieguez.com

DLA Piper Rudnick Gray Cary US LLP
1200 19th St. N.W., Suite 700, Washington, DC 20036
(202) 861-3913, *Fax:* (202) 689-7626
www.dlapiper.com
1251 Ave. of the Americas, New York, NY 10020-1104
(212) 835-6000; *Fax:* (212) 835-6001
mmccabe@piperrudnick.com
Monica McCabe, Chairman

Don Buchwald & Associates
10 E. 44 St., 7th Fl., New York, NY 10017-3606
(212) 867-1200, *Fax:* (212) 972-3209
www.buchwald.com
richard@buchwald.com

Donald E. Martin, P.C.
Box 8433, Falls Church, VA 22041
(703) 642-2344, *Fax:* (703) 642-2357
dempc@prodigy.net

Dorsey & Whitney, L L P
50 S. 6th St., Suite 1500, Minneapolis, MN 55402-1498
(612) 340-2873, *Fax:* (612) 340-2868
www.dorsey.com
cattanach.robert@dorsey.com
666 Burrard St., Suite 1300, Park Pl., Vancouver, BC Canada
(604) 687-5151; *Fax:* (604) 687-8504
1031 West 4th Ave., Suite 600, Anchorage, AK 99501-5900
(907) 276-4557; *Fax:* (907) 276-4152
Republic Plaza Bldg., Suite 4400, 370 Seventeenth St., Denver, CO 80202-5608
(303) 629-3400; *Fax:* (303) 629-3450
50 S. 6th St., Minneapolis, MN 55402-1540
(612) 340-2600; *Fax:* (612) 340-2868
Dakota Ctr., 51 N. Broadway, Suite 402, Fargo, ND
(701) 235-6000; *Fax:* (701) 235-9969
Veritas House, 125 Finsbury Pavement, London,
011-44-171-588-0800; *Fax:* 011-44-171-588-0555
38 Technology Dr, Irvine, CA 92618-5310
(714) 424-5555; *Fax:* (714) 424-5554
1001 Pennsylvania Ave. N.W., Suite 200 South, Washington, DC 20004-2505
(202) 824-8800; *Fax:* (202) 824-8990
US Bank Building Ctr., 1420 5th Ave., Suite 400, Seattle, WA 98101-2613
(206) 654-5400; *Fax:* (206) 654-5500
250 Park Ave, New York, NY 10177-0001
(212) 415-9200; *Fax:* (212) 953-7201
125 Bank St., Suite 600, Missoula, MO
(406) 721-6025; *Fax:* (406) 543-0863
507 Davidson Bldg., 8 Third St., Great Falls, MO
(406) 727-3632; *Fax:* (406) 727-3638
Wells Fargo Plaza, 170 S. Main St., Suite 925, Salt Lake City, UT 84101-1666
(801) 350-3581; *Fax:* (801) 350-3585

Dow Lohnes PLLC
1200 New Hampshire Ave. N.W., Suite 800, Washington, DC 20036
(202) 776-2000, *Fax:* (202) 776-2222
www.dowlohnes.com
info@dowlohnes.com
One Ravinia Dr., Suite 1600, Atlanta, GA
(770) 901-8800;

Downs, Bertis E.
170 College Ave., Athens, GA 30601
(706) 353-6689, *Fax:* (706) 546-6069

Drinker Biddle & Reath L.L.P.
1500 K St. N.W., Suite 1100, Washington, DC 20005-1209
(202) 842-8800, *Fax:* (202) 842-8465
www.dbr.com
joe.edge@dbr.com

Duane Morris LLP
30 S. 17th St., Philadelphia, PA 19103
(215) 979-1000, *Fax:* (215) 979-1020
www.duanemorris.com

Eaton, Peabody
Box 1210, 80 Excahange St., Bangor, ME 04402-1210
(207) 947-0111, *Fax:* (207) 942-3040
www.eatonpeabody.com
eaton@eatonpeabody.com

Eckert, Seamans, Cherin & Mellott
1515 Market St. 9th Fl., Philadelphia, PA 19102
(215) 851-8400, *Fax:* (215) 851-8383
www.escm.com

Edelstein, Laird & Sobel, L.L.P.
9255 Sunset Blvd., Suite 800, Los Angeles, CA 90069
(310) 274-6184, *Fax:* (310) 274-6185
elsentlaw.com
laird@elsentlaw.com

Edmund W. Turnley III
30 Music Square W., Suite 302, Nashville, TN 37203
(615) 321-8600, *Fax:* (615) 321-8602

Edward de R. Cayia, P.A.
432 N.E. 3rd Ave., Fort Lauderdale, FL 33301
(954) 765-1400, *Fax:* (954) 765-1421

Edwards Angell Palmer & Dodge L.L.P.
111 Huntington Ave., Boston, MA 02199
(617) 951-2233, *Fax:* (888) 325-9120
www.eapdlaw.com
smeredith@eapdlaw.com

Elam & Burke, P.A.
251 E. Front St., Suite 300, Boise, ID 83702-7311
(208) 343-5454, *Fax:* (208) 384-5844
mag@elamburke.com

Epstein, Levinsohn, Bodine, Hurwitz & Weinstein, P.C.
1790 Broadway, 10th Fl., New York, NY 10019
(212) 262-1000, *Fax:* (212) 262-5022
entlawfirm.com

Ezor, A. Edward
201 S. Lake Ave., Suite 505, Pasadena, CA 91101
(626) 568-8098, *Fax:* (626) 568-8475

Faegre & Benson, L.L.P.
801 Grand , Suite 3100, Des Moines, IA 50309-8002
(515) 248-9000, *Fax:* (515) 248-9010
www.faegre.com
mgiudicessi@faegre.com

Farmer, Shirley Stewart
One Lincoln Plaza, Suite 19S, New York, NY 10023-7149
(212) 787-6566, *Fax:* (212) 787-6567
www.shirleystewartfarmeronline.com
stewfar@rcn.com

Farrand, Cooper P.C.
235 Montgomery St., Suite 905, San Francisco, CA 94104
(415) 399-0600, *Fax:* (415) 677-2950
www.fcblaw.com

Federal Communications Comission Public Safety & Homeland Security Bureau
Public Safety & Homeland Security Bureau, 445 12th St., S.W., Washington, DC 20554
(202) 418-0680
www.kba.org
kba@kba.org
Gary White, pres; Patti L. Pollen, exec asst.

Ferris & Britton
401 West A St., Suite 1600, San Diego, CA 92101
(619) 233-3131, *Fax:* (619) 232-9316
www.ferrisbritton.com
aferris@ferrisbritton.com

Fine & Associates, P.L.C.
335-337 Decatur St., Vieux Carre, New Orleans, LA 70130-1023
(504) 581-5152, *Fax:* (504) 581-5152, EXT. 124
dnfinelaw@aol.com

Fine & Block
2060 Mt. Paran Rd. N.W., Suite 106, Atlanta, GA 30327
(404) 261-6800, *Fax:* (404) 261-6960
www.fineandblock.com

Finkelstein, Thompson & Loughran
1050 30th St. N.W., Washington, DC 20007
(202) 337-8000, (866) 592-1960, *Fax:* (202) 337-8090
www.ftllaw.com
lks@stllaw.com

Fleischman & Walsh, L.L.P.
1919 Pennsylvania Ave. N.W., 6th Fl., Washington, DC 20006
(202) 939-7900, *Fax:* (202) 745-0916
www.fw-law.com
fw@fw-law.com

Fletcher, Heald & Hildreth, P.L.C.
1300 N. 17th St., 11th Fl., Arlington, VA 22209
(703) 812-0400, *Fax:* (703) 812-0486
www.fhhlaw.com
office@fhhlaw.com

Foley & Lardner
150 E. Gilman St., Madison, WI 53703
(608) 257-5035, *Fax:* (608) 258-4258
dwalsh@foleylaw.com

Forrest, Herbert E.
Federal Programs Br., U.S. Dept. of Justice, 20 Massachusetts Ave. N.W., Civil Division, Rm. 7112, Washington, DC 20530
(202) 514-2809, *Fax:* (202) 616-8470
herbert:forrest@usdoj.gov

Fowler, Measle & Bell
300 W. Vine St., Suite 600, Lexington, KY 40507-1660
(859) 252-6700, *Fax:* (859) 255-3735
www.fmblaw.com
fmb@fmb.com

Fox & Film Entertainment
10201 W. Pico Blvd., Los Angeles, CA 90035
(310) 369-1000, *Fax:* (310) 369-3333
www.fox.com

Frederic E. Brown, Attorney at Law
Box 71718, Fairbanks, AK 99707
(907) 452-3452, *Fax:* (907) 452-3733
fbrown@mosquitonet.com

Frost, Mark E.
Box 153, Glens Falls, NY 12801-0153
(518) 792-1126, *Fax:* (518) 793-1587
mfrost@loneoak.com

Gammon & Grange, P.C.
8280 Greensboro Dr., 7th Fl., McLean, VA 22102-3807
(703) 761-5000, *Fax:* (703) 761-5023
www.gg-law.com
awf@gg-law.com

Ganz & Hollinger
1394 3rd Ave., New York, NY 10021
(212) 517-5500, *Fax:* (212) 772-2720
www.ganzhollinger.com

Gardere Wynne Sewell LLP
1601 Elm St., Thanksgiving Tower, Suite 3000, Dallas, TX 75201-4761
(214) 999-3000, *Fax:* (214) 999-4667
www.gardere.com
mwebb@gardere.com

Gardner, Carton & Douglas
1301 K St. N.W., Suite 900 E. Tower, Washington, DC 20005
(202) 230-5000, *Fax:* (202) 230-5300
www.gcd.com

Garvey, Schubert & Barer
100 Wall St., 20th Fl., New York, NY 10005-3708
(212) 431-8700, *Fax:* (206) 464-0125
www.gsblaw.com
kdavis@gsblaw.com
1000 Potomac St. N.W., 5th Fl., Washington, DC
(202) 965-7880; *Fax:* (202) 965-1729
www.gsblaw
jking@gsblaw.com
Matthew R. Schneider, D.C. Mgng Dir
John Wells King, Counsel
599 Broadway, 10th Fl., New York, NY
(212) 431-8700; *Fax:* (212) 334-1278
www.gsblaw.com
Matthew R. Schneider, Ny Mgng Dir
121 S. W. Morrison St., Portland, OR 97204-3117
(503) 228-3939; *Fax:* (503) 226-0259
www.gsblaw.com
Larry Brant, Steve Connolly
Bob Weaver, Portland Mgmt Comm

Gary P. Schonman
445 12th St. S.W., Rm. 3A660, Federal Communications Commision, Washington, DC 20554
(202) 418-1795, *Fax:* (202) 418-2080
www.fcc.gov

Gibbs & Associates, P.C.
146 Central Park W., Suite 19E, New York, NY 10023
(212) 787-2828, *Fax:* (212) 787-2886
bhg1cg2@aol.com

Gibson, Dunn & Crutcher
333 S. Grand Ave., Suite 4600, Los Angeles, CA 90071-3197
(213) 229-7000, *Fax:* (213) 229-7520
www.gdclaw.com
agravit@gibsondunn.com
1050 Connecticut Ave. N.W., Suite 900, Washington, DC 20036-5320
(202) 955-8500;
Jill Sterner, Chairman

Glenn A. Goldstein, Attorney at Law
1650 Market St., Suite 4900, Philadelphia, PA 19103
(215) 981-5922, *Fax:* (215) 981-5959
glenn802@aol.com

Gold & Pyle
526 Superior Ave. E., 1140 Leader Bldg., Cleveland, OH 44114
(216) 696-6122, *Fax:* (216) 696-3214

Goldberg, Godles, Wiener & Wright
1229 19th St. N.W., Washington, DC 20036
(202) 429-4900, *Fax:* (202) 429-4912
g2w2.com
general@g2w2.com

Golden & Golden, P.C.
10627 Jones St., Suite 101B, Fairfax, VA 22030
(703) 691-0117, *Fax:* (703) 691-1367
www.gglawva.com
k8los@aol.com

Golob, Bragin & Sassoe
1990 S. Bundy Dr., Suite 540, Los Angeles, CA 90025-5245
(310) 979-0321, *Fax:* (310) 979-0366

Goodkind, Labaton, Rudoff & Sucharow, L.L.P.
100 Park Ave., New York, NY 10017
(212) 907-0700, *Fax:* (212) 818-0477
www.glrs.com
rrosenblum@labton.com

Gray & Robinson
301 E. Pine St., Suite 1400, Orlando, FL 32802
(407) 843-8880, *Fax:* (407) 244-5690
www.gray-robinson.com
llee@gray-robinson.com

Greensfelder, Hemker & Gale, P.C.
10 S. Broadway, Suite 2000, St. Louis, MO 63102-1774
(314) 516-2662, *Fax:* (314) 345-5499
www.greensfelder.com
mlw@greensfelder.com

Greiter, Pegger, Kofler & Partner
Maria Theresien-Strasse 24, A-6020, Innsbruck,
43 512-57-1811, *Fax:* 43 512-5849-25, 43 512-5711-52

Groveman, Amy S.
Cablevision Systems Corp., 111 Stewart Ave., Bethpage, NY 11714
(516) 803-2300, *Fax:* (516) 803-2575
www.cablevision.com
agrovema@cablevision.com

Grubb, Jay G.
12 Forrest Edge Dr., Titusville, NJ 08560
(410) 329-2108, *Fax:* (410) 329-2109

Grubman, Indursky & Shire, P.C.
152 W. 57th St., 31st Fl., New York, NY 10019
(212) 554-0400, *Fax:* (212) 554-0444

Gullett, Sanford, Robinson & Martin
315 Deadrick St., Suite 1100, Nashville, TN 37238
(615) 244-4994, *Fax:* (615) 256-6339

Gust Rosenfeld P.L.C.
201 E. Washington, Suite 800, Phoenix, AZ 85004-2327
(602) 257-7422, *Fax:* (602) 254-4878
www.gustlaw.com
chauncey@gustlaw.com

Hall, Dickler, Kent, Goldstein & Wood
909 3rd Ave., 27th Fl., New York, NY 10022
(212) 339-5409
www.halldickler.com

Handman, Stanley H.
10160 Cielo Dr., Beverly Hills, CA 90210-2037
(310) 276-7503, *Fax:* (310) 276-1559
www.fleischerstudios.com
stanhandman@yahoo.com

Hansen, Jacobson, Teller, Hoberman, Newman, Warren & Sloan, L.L.P.
450 N. Roxbury Dr., 8th Fl., Beverly Hills, CA 90210-4222
(310) 248-3105/248-3101, *Fax:* (310) 275-2329/550-5209
sdecker@hjth.com

Harris, Wiltshire & Grannis, L.L.P.
1200 Eighteenth St. N.W., Washington, DC 20036
(202) 730-1300, *Fax:* (202) 730-1301
www.harriswiltshire.com
sharris@harris

Head, Johnson & Kachigian
228 W. 17th Pl., Tulsa, OK 74119
(918) 587-2000, *Fax:* (918) 584-1718
www.hjklaw.com
hjk@law.com

Hearn, Edward R. A Professional Law Corporation
Div/DBA: (formerly Hearn, Edward R)
84 W. Santa Clara St., Suite 660, San Jose, CA 95113
(408) 998-3400, *Fax:* (408) 297-1104
www.internetmedialaw.com
nedhearnml@aol.com

Hebert, Spencer, Cusimano & Fry, LLP
701 Laurel St., Baton Rouge, LA 70802
(225) 344-2601, *Fax:* (225) 387-1714
clsatty@aol.com

Heller Ehrman LLP
275 Middlefield Rd., Menlo Park, CA 94025
(650) 324-7000, *Fax:* (650) 324-0638
www.hellerehrman.com

Hendrickson, Thomas
203 Alderwood Dr., N. Potomac, MD 20878
(301) 519-0085
www.spacecast.com
space@spacecast.com
Cable-delivered, national, 24 hour, English-language Science Fiction, Science Fact, Speculation and Fantasy channel. The program mix includes memorable sci-fi classics and current popular series, plus feature films, documentaries, specialsand daily original productions with a tilt to information and new age speculation.

Hewitt Katz Stepp and Wright Attorney at Law
945 E. Paces Ferry Rd., Resurgens Plaza Ste. 2610, Atlanta, GA 30326
(404) 240-0400, *Fax:* (404) 240-0401
www.robertnkatz.com
khewitt@atllawofc.com

Hill & Welch
1330 New Hampshire Ave. N.W., Suite 113, Washington, DC 20036
(202) 775-0070, *Fax:* (202) 775-9026
welchlaw@earthlink.net

Hinshaw & Culbertson
333 S. 7th St., Suite 2000, Minneapolis, MN 55402
(612) 333-3434, *Fax:* (612) 334-8888
www.hinshawculbertson.com

Hogan & Hartson
Columbia Sq., 555 13th St. N.W., Washington, DC 20004
(202) 637-5600, *Fax:* (202) 637-5910
www.hhlaw.com
1040 Brussels,

Holland & Knight LLC
131 S. Dearborn St., 30 Fl., Chicago, IL 60603
(312) 263-3600, *Fax:* (312) 578-6666
www.hklaw.com

Holland & Knight LLP
2099 Pennsylvania Ave. N.W., Suite 100, Washington, DC 20006
(202) 955-3000, *Fax:* (202) 955-5564
www.hklaw.com

Horgan, Michael Owen
407 E. Robert Toomb Ave., Washington, GA 30673
(706) 678-1987, *Fax:* (706) 678-1999
mhorgan@nu-z.net

Ice Miller LLP
One American Sq., Suite 2900, Indianapolis, IN 46282-0002
(317) 236-2100, *Fax:* (317) 236-2219
www.icemiller.com
info@icemiller.com

Inghram & Inghram
529 Hampshire St., Suite 409, Bank of America Bldg., Quincy, IL 62301
(217) 222-7420, *Fax:* (217) 222-1653
inghram@inghramlaw.com

Irwin, Campbell & Tannenwald, P.C.
1730 Rhode Island Ave. N.W. #200, Washington, DC 20036-3120
(202) 728-0400, *Fax:* (202) 728-0354
www.ictpc.com

Isaacman, Kaufman & Painter
8484 Wilshire Blvd., Suite 850, Beverly Hills, CA 90211
(323) 782-7700, *Fax:* (323) 782-7744
www.ikplaw.com
zucker@ikplaw.com

Jackson & Campbell, P.C.
1120 20th St. N.W., Suite 300-S, Washington, DC 20036
(202) 457-1600, *Fax:* (202) 457-1678
www.jacksoncampbell.com
jmatteo@jackscamp.com

Jacobs & Associates
11 North Washington St., Suite 640, Rockville, MD 20850
(301) 251-5470, *Fax:* (301) 251-5481
jacobs@internet-law-firm.com

James A. Hatcher
Cox Communications Inc., 1400 Lake Hearn Dr. N.E., Atlanta, GA 30319
(404) 843-5000, *Fax:* (404) 843-5845

Jeffer, Mangels, Butler & Marmaro LLP
1900 Ave. of the Stars, 7th Fl., Los Angeles, CA 90067-5010
(310) 203-8080, *Fax:* (310) 203-0567
www.jmbm.com

Jenner & Block
601 13th St. N.W., 12th Fl., Washington, DC 20005
(202) 639-6000, *Fax:* (202) 639-6066
www.jenner.com
mstull@jenner.com

John D. Pellegrin P.C.
10515 Dominion Valley Dr., Fairfax Station, VA 22039
(703) 250-1595, *Fax:* (703) 250-1597
www.pellegrin-law.com
jd@lawpell.com

John Hearne
715 Broadway, Suite 320, Santa Monica, CA 90401
(310) 451-4430, *Fax:* (310) 451-1423

Johnson, Andrea L.
225 Cedar St., California Western School of Law, San Diego, CA 92101
(800) 255-4252, EXT. 1474, *Fax:* (619) 696-9999
www.cwsl.edu
ajohnson@cwsl.edu

Johnston & Buchan LLP
275 Slater St., Suite 1700, Ottawa, ON K1P 5H9 Canada
(613) 236-3882, *Fax:* (613) 230-6423/230-6762, (613) 230-6762
www.johnstonbuchan.com

Jon M. Waxman Associates
302 W. 12th St., New York, NY 10014
(212) 929-2562, *Fax:* (212) 229-1625
jon@jonwaxman.com

Jones, Day
51 Louisiana Ave. N. W., Washington, DC 20001
(202) 879-3939, *Fax:* (202) 626-1700
www.jonesday.com

Joseph E. Dunne III, Attorney at Law
P.O. Box 9203, Durango, CO 81302-9203
(970) 385-7312, *Fax:* (970) 385-7343
lawman@animas.net

Kass, Mitek & Kass
1050 17th St. N.W., Suite 1100, Washington, DC 20036
(202) 659-6500, *Fax:* (202) 293-2608
www.kmklawyers.com

Katten Muchin Rosenman LLP
1025 Thomas Jefferson St. NW, 700 East Lobby, Washington, DC 20007
(202) 625-3500, *Fax:* (202) 298-7570
www.kattenlaw.com
howard.braun@kattenlaw.com

Kay, Sheldon L.
30445 Northwestern Hwy., Suite 320, Farmington Hills, MI 48334
(248) 539-1111, *Fax:* (248) 539-1114
www.myspace.com/mrlawyershow
sllaw@hotmail.com

Kaye, Scholer, L.L.P.
901 15th St. N.W., Washington, DC 20005
(202) 682-3500, *Fax:* (202) 682-3580
kayescholer.com
jshrinsky@kayescholer.com

Keller & Heckman
1001 G St. N.W., Suite 500 W, Washington, DC 20001
(202) 434-4100, *Fax:* (202) 434-4646
www.khlaw.com

Kelley, Drye Collier Shannon
3050 K St. N.W., Washington, DC 20007
(202) 342-8400, *Fax:* (202) 342-8451
www.colliershannon.com

Kenkel & Associates
9908 Sorrel Ave., Potomac, MD 20854
(301) 299-6260, *Fax:* (301) 299-0720
jngkenkel@aol.com

Kilpatrick & Stockton L.L.P.
1100 Peach Tree St., Suite 2800, Atlanta, GA 30309
(404) 815-6500, (404) 745-2492, *Fax:* (404) 815-6555
www.kilpatrickstockton.com
rbuttram@kilpatrickstockton.com

King & Ballow
1100 Union St. Plaza, 315 Union St., Nashville, TN 37201
(615) 259-3456, *Fax:* (615) 254-7907
www.kingballow.com
lawfirm@kingballow.com

Kirkpatrick & Lockhart L.L.P.
75 State St., Boston, MA 02109
(617) 261-3100, (617) 951-9230, *Fax:* (617) 261-3175
www.klng.com
bmorrissey@klng.com

Kleinberg, Lopez, Lange, Cuddy, Edel & Klein L.L.P.
2049 Century Park E., Suite 3180, Los Angeles, CA 90067-3205
(310) 286-9696, *Fax:* (310) 277-7145, (310) 286-6445
www.kllcek.com
lawyers@kllcek.com

Kletter, Matthew L.
183 Madison Ave., Penthouse, New York, NY 10016
(212) 726-0090

Klitzman, Stephen
Div/DBA: Office of Legislative & Inter-Govt Affairs
U.S. Federal Communications Commission, 445 12th St., SW, Office of General Counsel, Washington, DC 20554
(202) 418-1763, *Fax:* (202) 418-7540
steve.klitzma@fcc.gov

Koerner & Olender, P.C.
11913 Grey Hollow Ct., North Bethesda, MD 20852
(301) 468-3336, *Fax:* (301) 468-3343
bkofcclaw@erols.com

Kraditor & Haber, P.C.
1212 Ave. of the Americas 3rd Fl., New York, NY 10036
(212) 768-2100, *Fax:* (212) 768-2450
www.fcc.gov

Lang, Richert & Patch
5200 N. Palm Ave., Suite 401, Fresno, CA 93704-2225
(559) 228-6700, *Fax:* (559) 228-6727
www.www.lrplaw.net

Larry D. Perry, Attorney at Law
11464 Saga Ln., Suite 110, Knoxville, TN 37931-2819
(865) 927-8474, *Fax:* (865) 927-4912
larryperry@att.net

Latham & Watkins
555 11th St. N.W., Suite 1000, Washington, DC 20004
(202) 637-2200, *Fax:* (202) 637-2201
www.lw.com
eric.bernthal@lw.com

Law Offices of Martin J. Barab & Associates
3rd Fl., 9606 Santa Monica Blvd., Beverly Hills, CA 90210-4427
(310) 859-6644, *Fax:* (310) 859-6650

Law Firm of Rosalind Lichter
Tribeca Film Ctr., 375 Greenwich St., New York, NY 10013
(212) 941-4075, *Fax:* (212) 941-4076

Law Office of Dan J. Alpert
2120 N. 21st Rd., Arlington, VA 22201
(703) 243-8690, *Fax:* (703) 243-8692
www.commlaw.tv
dja@commlaw.tv

Law Office of David Honig
3636 16th St. N.W., Suite B-366, Washington, DC 20010
(202) 332-7005, *Fax:* (202) 332-7511
dhonig@crosslink.net

Law Office of Dennis J. Kelly
Box 41177, Washington, DC 20018
(202) 293-2300, 888-FCC-LAW-1, *Fax:* (410) 626-1794
dkellyfcclaw1@comcast.net

Law Office of Edward M. Kelman
100 Park Ave., 20th Fl., New York, NY 10017
(212) 371-9490, *Fax:* (212) 750-1356
emknyc@aol.com

Law Office of George Edward Regis
121 W. 27th St., Suite 1001, New York, NY 10001-6207
(212) 645-8800
info@theskichannel.com
Steve Bellamy, Chairman

Law Offices of Bernard R. Corbett
6312 Barrister Pl., Alexandria, VA 22307-1214
(703) 686-1880

Law Offices of Douglas W. Harold Jr.
109 Southdown Cir., Stephens City, VA 22655
(540) 869-0040, *Fax:* (540) 869-0041
douglasharoldjr@yahoo.com

Law Offices of Edward L. Weidenfeld
888 17th St. N.W., Suite 900, Washington, DC 20006
(202) 785-2143, *Fax:* (202) 452-8938
julie@weidenfeldlaw.com

Law Offices of George E. Darby
Box 893010, Mililani, HI 96789-3010
(808) 626-1300, *Fax:* (808) 626-1350
www.teleport-asia.com
darbylaw@teleport-asia.com

Law Offices of Henry W. Root, P.C.
1541 Ocean Ave., Suite 200, Santa Monica, CA 90401-2104
(310) 395-6800, *Fax:* (310) 393-7777
henry@grrlaw.com

Law Offices of James L. Oyster
108 Oyster Ln., Castleton, VA 22716
(540) 937-4800, *Fax:* (540) 937-2148
joyster@crosslink.net

Law Offices of Jeff Berke
12400 Wilshire Blvd., Suite 400, Los Angeles, CA 90025-6538
(310) 312-9221
www.foodtv.ca
info@alliancealantis.com
Bill Kossman, Programming Director

Law Offices of Jeffrey L. Graubart
350 W. Colorado Blvd., Suite 200, Pasadena, CA 91105
(626) 304-2800
wtranavitch@cox.net
William V. Tranavitch Jr., Operations Dir
Engrg svcs: AM, FM, TV, translators, LPTV.

Law Offices of Joel Weisman, P.C.
1901 Raymond Dr., Suite 6, Northbrook, IL 60062
(847) 400-5900, *Fax:* (847) 400-5534
www.weismanmedialaw.com

Law Offices of Lawrence Bernstein
3510 Springland Ln., N.W., Washington, DC 20008
(202) 296-1800, *Fax:* (202) 296-1800
lawberns@verizon.net

Law Offices of Lee Sacks
23852 Pacific Coast Hwy., Suite 157, Malibu, CA 90265-4879
(310) 451-3113, *Fax:* (310) 451-0089

Law Offices of Michael R. Gardner, P.C.
1150 Connecticut Ave. N.W., Suite 710, Washington, DC 20036
(202) 785-2828, *Fax:* (202) 785-1504
mrgpc@aol.com

Law Offices of Patrice Lyons, Chartered
910 17th St. N.W., Suite 800, Washington, DC 20006
(202) 293-5990, *Fax:* (202) 293-5121
palyons@bellatlantic.net

Law Offices of Philip L. Schwartz PA
2000 Glades Rd., Suite 208, Boca Raton, FL 33431
(954) 760-7770, *Fax:* (954) 524-4169
phil@philipschwartz.com

Law Offices of Richard J. Hayes
Box 200, Lincolnville, ME 04849
(207) 336-3333, *Fax:* (202) 478-0048
www.rjhayes.com
fcclaw@rjhayes.com

Law Offices of Robert J. Buenzle
11710 Plaza America Dr., Suite 2000, Reston, VA 20190
(703) 430-6751, *Fax:* (703) 430-4994
buenzle@buenzlelaw.com

Law Offices of Ruth S. Baker-Battist
5600 Wisconsin Ave., Chevy Chase, MD 20815
(301) 718-0955, *Fax:* (301) 718-8867
rbattist@aol.com

Law Offices of Thomas G. Shack Jr.
1150 Connecticut Ave. N.W., Suite 900, Washington, DC 20036
(202) 293-5900, *Fax:* (202) 659-3493

Law Offices of Timothy K. Brady
Box 930, Johnson City, TN 30605-0930
(423) 477-7619
kaij.us
studio@kaij.us
George McClintock, General Manager
John McClintock, Programming Director
Ted Randall, Promotions Manager
KAIJ Dallas, TX.

Law Offices of William D. Silva
5335 Wisconsin Ave. N.W., Suite 400, Washington, DC 20015-2003
(202) 362-1711, *Fax:* (202) 686-8282
wmsilvalaw.com
bill@luselaw.com

Lawrence & Eason
14000 Quail Spgs Pkwy, Suite 200, Oklahoma City, OK 73134-2638
(405) 841-6000, *Fax:* (405) 841-6006

Leibowitz & Associates, P.A.
One S.E. 3rd Ave., Suite 1450, Miami, FL 33131-1715
(305) 530-1322, *Fax:* (305) 530-9417
mleibowitz@broadlaw.com

Leopold, Petrich & Smith
2049 Century Park E., Suite 3110, Los Angeles, CA 90067-3274
(310) 277-3333, *Fax:* (310) 277-7444
www.lpsla.com
dmayeda@lpsla.com

Lerman Senter PLLC
Div/DBA: (Formerly Leventhal Senter & Lerman PLLC)
2000 K St. N.W., Suite 600, Washington, DC 20006-1809
(202) 429-8970, *Fax:* (202) 293-7783
www.lermansenter.com
slerman@lermansenter.com

Lewis, Lewis & Ferraro
28 N. Main St., West Hartford, CT 06107-1928
(860) 521-1500, *Fax:* (860) 521-4500
attorney@lewislewisferraro.com

Lindsey S. Feldman, Attorney at Law
4551 Glencoe Ave., Suite 300, Marina del Rey, CA 90292
(310) 823-1600, *Fax:* (310) 775-8775
lfeldman@bergerkahn.com

Loeb & Loeb L.L.P.
345 Park Ave., New York, NY 10154
(212) 407-4000, (212) 407-4987, *Fax:* (212) 407-4990
www.loeb.com
jmanton@loeb.com
10100 Santa Monica Blvd, Los Angeles, CA 90067-4003
(310) 282-2475; *Fax:* (310) 282-2192
Mickey Mayerson, Chairman
1000 Wilshire Blvd, Los Angeles, CA 90017-2457
(213) 688-3400; *Fax:* (213) 688-3460

Loftus & Borgstrom
One Court St., Suite 320, Lebanon, NH 03766
(603) 448-6420, *Fax:* (603) 448-6147
wrlpc@valley.net

Lommen Abdo, Cole, King & Stageberg, P. A.
2000 IDS Ctr., 80 S. 8th St., Minneapolis, MN 55402
(612) 339-8131, *Fax:* (612) 339-8064
www.Lommen.com

London, Michael B.
10452 Oletha Ln., Los Angeles, CA 90077-2420
(310) 474-0577, *Fax:* (310) 474-5413

Lowndes, Drosdick, Doster, Kantor & Reed, P.A.
Box 2809, 215 N. Eola Dr., Orlando, FL 32801
(407) 843-4600, *Fax:* (407) 843-4444
karen.plunkett@lowndes-law.com

Lukas, Nace, Gutierrez & Sachs Chartered
1650 Tysons Blvd., Suite 1500, McLean, VA 22102
(703) 584-8678, *Fax:* (703) 584-8696
www.fcclaw.com
rlucas@fcclaw.com

Madigan & Getzendanner
30 N. LaSalle St., Suite 3906, Chicago, IL 60602
(312) 346-4321, *Fax:* (312) 346-5619

Magee Law Firm, PLLC
6845 Elm St., Suite 205, McLean, VA 22101
(703) 356-7500, *Fax:* (703) 356-6863
jmagee@mageelawfirm.com

Margolin Law Firm
5502 High Dr., Mission Hills, KS 66208-1121
(816) 753-3838

The Marshall Firm
271 Madison Ave., 20th Fl., New York, NY 10016
(212) 382-2044, *Fax:* (212) 382-3610
tmf@marshallfirm.com

Mary A. McReynolds, P.C.
1050 Connecticut Ave. N.W., Suite 1000, Washington, DC 20036
(202) 429-1770, *Fax:* (202) 772-3101

McDonald, Hopkins, L.P.A.
2100 Bank One Ctr., 600 Superior Ave. E., Cleveland, OH 44114-2653
(216) 348-5400, *Fax:* (216) 348-5474
www.mhbh.com
attorneys@mhbh.com

Mensch, Linda Susan
200 S. Michigan Ave., Suite 1240, Chicago, IL 60604
(312) 922-2910, *Fax:* (312) 922-1865
menschlaw@yahoo.com

Messerli & Kramer
150 S. 5th St., Suite 1800, Minneapolis, MN 55402-4246
(612) 672-3600, *Fax:* (612) 672-3777
www.messerlikramer.com
djohnson@mandklaw.com

Meyers & Meyers
360 E. Randolph St., Suite 3104, Chicago, IL 60601
(312) 616-1500, *Fax:* (312) 616-1737
www.petermeyers.net
peterarbme@aol.com

Midlen Law Center
7618 Lynn Dr., Chevy Chase, MD 20815-6043
(301) 656-3000, *Fax:* (301) 656-8262
www.midlen.com
john@midlen.com

Miller & Van Eaton, P.L.L.C.
1155 Connecticut Ave. N.W., Suite 1000, Washington, DC 20036

(202) 785-0600, *Fax:* (202) 785-1234
www.millervaneaton.com
info2@millervaneaton.com

Miller and Neely, P.C.
Div/DBA: (Miller & Neely, P.C.)
6900 Wisconsin Ave., Suite 704, Bethesda, MD 20815
(301) 986-4160, *Fax:* (301) 986-4162
mandnlaw@gmail.com

Miller, Balis and O'Neil
1140 19th St. N.W., Suite 700, Washington, DC 20006
(202) 296-2960, *Fax:* (202) 296-0166
mgrossman@mbolaw.com

Miller, Canfield, Paddock & Stone, P.L.C.
150 W Jefferson Ave., Suite 2500, Detroit, MI 48226
(313) 963-6420, *Fax:* (313) 496-7500
www.millercanfield.com
houser@millercanfield.com

Mintz, Levin, Cohn, Ferris, Glovsky & Popeo, P.C.
701 Pennsylvania Ave. N.W., Suite 900, Washington, DC 20004
(202) 434-7300, *Fax:* (202) 434-7400
www.mintzlevin.com
One Financial Center, Boston, MA
(617) 542-6000; *Fax:* (617) 542-2241
Irwin Heller, Chairman

Mirowski & Associates
757 W. Ivy St., San Diego, CA 92101
(619) 702-5300, *Fax:* (619) 702-4666
www.mirlaw.com
pmirowski@mirlaw.com

Mitchell Silberberg & Knupp
11377 W. Olympic Blvd., Los Angeles, CA 90064
(310) 312-2000, *Fax:* (310) 312-3100
www.msk.com
info@msk.com

Mitchell, Charles D.
1601 N. Frontage Rd., Suite F, Vicksburg, MS 39180
(601) 636-4545, EXT. 123, *Fax:* (601) 634-0897
www.vicksburgpost.com
fysadm@vicksburgpost.com

Mizrack & Gantt
Suite 850, 555 11th St. N.W., Washington, DC 20004-1304
(202) 628-1717, *Fax:* (202) 628-1919
jbgantt@att.global.net

Morris, Rathnau & De La Rosa
39 La Salle St., Fl 500, Chicago, IL 60603
(312) 606-0876, *Fax:* (312) 606-0879
mdlrlawchicago@aol.com

Morrison & Foerster L.L.P.
2000 Pennsylvania Ave. N.W., Suite 5500, Washington, DC 20006
(202) 887-1500, *Fax:* (202) 887-0763
www.mofo.com

Moss & Barnett, A Professional Assn
4800 Wells Fargo Ctr., 90 S. 7th St., Minneapolis, MN 55402-4129
(612) 877-5000, *Fax:* (612) 877-5999
www.moss-barnett.com
weinstockd@moss-barnett.com

Myman, Abell, Fineman, Greenspan & Light
11601 Wilshire Blvd., Suite 2200, Los Angeles, CA 90025
(310) 820-7717, *Fax:* (310) 207-2680

Nadel, Mark S.
U.S. Federal Communications Commission, 445 12th St. S.W., Rm. 5B 551, Washington, DC 20554
(202) 418-7385, *Fax:* (202) 418-7361
www.fcc.gov
mnadel@fcc.gov

Naphtali, Ashirah S.
130-33 217 St., Suite B, Laurelton, NY 11413-1230
(718) 481-7236, *Fax:* (718) 481-7236
anaphml@aol.com

Nathan M. Nickolaus
320 E. McCarthy St., Jefferson City, MO 65101-3115
(573) 634-6313, *Fax:* (573) 634-6504
nnickolaus@jeffcity.mo.org
Nathan M. Nickolaus, Consultant

National Exchange Carrier Association, N.E.C.A.
80 S. Jefferson Rd., Whippany, NJ 07981-1009
(973) 884-8000, (800) 228-8597, *Fax:* (973) 884-8469
www.neca.org

NBC Universal Television Group
100 Universal City Plaza, Bldg #1320, Suite 3E, Universal City, CA 91608
(818) 777-6968, *Fax:* (818) 866-7597
tracy.rich@nbcuni.com

Nemeth, Valerie A., Attorney at Law
191 Calle Magadalena, Suite 270, Encinitas, CA 92024-3750
(760) 944-4130, (310) 471-7648 (L.A.), *Fax:* (760) 944-3325
www.entlawyer.com
vanemeth@entlawyer.com

Neuland, Nordberg, Andrews & Whitney
22502 Avenida Empresa, Rancho Santa Margarita, CA 92688
(949) 766-4700, *Fax:* (949) 766-4712
www.nnalaw.com
dottieneuland@nnawlaw.com

Nilsson, Kent R.
U.S. Federal Communications Commission, 445 12th St. S.W., Washington, DC 20554
(202) 418-2478, *Fax:* (202) 418-2345
www.fcc.gov

Nixon Peabody L.L.P.
401 9th St. NW, Suite 900, Washington, DC 20004
(202) 585-8000, *Fax:* (202) 585-8080
www.nixonpeabody.com
aprilsteffan@nixonpeabody.com
Box 1051, Clinton Sq, Rochester, NY
(716) 263-1000;
Richard D. Rochford Jr, Chairman

Nixon, Wilbert E. Jr.
Div/DBA: Wireless Telecommunications Bureau, Police & Rules Federal Communications Commission, 445 12th St. S.W. Rm. 4-A207, Washington, DC 20554
(202) 418-7240, *Fax:* (202) 418-7447
www.fcc.gov
wnixon@fcc.gov

Nossaman, L.L.P.
50 California St., 34th Fl., San Francisco, CA 94111
(415) 398-3600, *Fax:* (415) 398-2438
www.nossaman.com
mmattes@nossaman.com

O'Connell & Aronowitz PC
54 State St., Albany, NY 12207
(518) 462-5601, *Fax:* (518) 462-2670
www.oalaw.com
o'connell@albany.net

O'Connell, Susan Lee
U.S. Federal Communications Commission, 445 12th St. S.W., Rm. 6A847, Washington, DC 20554
(202) 418-1484, *Fax:* (202) 418-2824
soconnell@fcc.gov

O'Connor & Hannan
1666 K St. N.W., Suite 500, Washington, DC 20006
(202) 887-1400, *Fax:* (202) 466-2198
gadler@oconnorhannan.com

O'Melveny & Myers
1625 Eye St. N.W., Washington, DC 20006
(202) 383-5300, *Fax:* (202) 383-5414
www.omm.com
jbeisner@omm.com

O'Neil, Cannon, Hollman, DeJong S.C.
Chase Tower, 111 E. Wisconsin Ave., Suite 1400, Milwaukee, WI 53202-4803
(414) 276-5000, *Fax:* (414) 276-6581
www.wilaw.com

O'Neill, Athy & Casey
1310 19th St. N.W., Washington, DC 20036
(202) 466-6555, *Fax:* (202) 466-6596
oacpc.com
aathy@oacpc.com

O'Reilly, Rancilio, Nitz, Andrews, Turnbull, & Scott P.C.
12900 Hall Rd., Suite 350, Sterling Heights, MI 48313-1151
(586) 726-1000, *Fax:* (586) 726-1560
www.orlaw.com

Ogden Murphy Wallace, P.L.L.C.
1601 5th Ave., Suite 2100, Westlake Ctr. Tower, Seattle, WA 98101-1686
(206) 447-7000, *Fax:* (206) 447-0215
www.omwlaw.com
nparks@omwlaw.com

OPASTCO
21 Dupont Cir. N.W., Suite 700, Washington, DC 20036
(202) 659-5990, *Fax:* (202) 659-4619
www.opastco.org
vlf@opastco.org

Orr & Reno
Box 3550, One Eagle Sq., Concord, NH 03302-3550
(603) 224-2381, *Fax:* (603) 224-2318
www.orr-reno.com
mmclean@orr-reno.com

Overton, John B.
14 Manzanita Pl., Mill Valley, CA 94941
(415) 331-2889, *Fax:* (415) 331-5837
overton@plownet.com

Pankopf, Arthur
7819 Hampden Ln., Bethesda, MD 20814-1108
(301) 657-8790, *Fax:* (301) 657-3296
apankopf@worldnet.att.net

Pardo & Pardo P.A.
Box 398646, Miami Beach, FL 33239
(305) 673-1515, *Fax:* (305) 673-9359

Patton Boggs L.L.P.
2550 M St. N.W., Suite 900, Washington, DC 20037
(202) 457-6000, *Fax:* (202) 457-6315
www.pattonboggs.com

Paul T. Julian Esq.
Div/DBA: (formerly Julian & Associates)
1038 N. LaSalle Dr., Chicago, IL 60610
(312) 266-1500, *Fax:* (312) 337-1972
pjulian302@aol.com

Paul, Hastings, Janofsky & Walker LLP
1299 Pennsylvania Ave. N.W., 10th Fl., Washington, DC 20004-2400
(202) 508-9500
www.paulhastings.com

Paul, Weiss, Rifkind, Wharton & Garrison, L.L.P.
1615 L St. N.W., Suite 1300, Washington, DC 20036
(202) 223-7300, *Fax:* (202) 223-7427
www.paulweiss.com

Pearce & Durick
Box 400, 314 E. Thayer Ave., Bismarck, ND 58502-0400
(701) 223-2890, *Fax:* (701) 223-7865
www.pearce-durick.com
law.office@pearce-durick.com

Pepper Hamilton LLP
3000 Two Logan Sq., Eighteenth & Arch St., Philadelphia, PA 19103-2799
(215) 981-4000, *Fax:* (215) 981-4750
www.pepperlaw.com
phinfo@pepperlaw.com
600 14th St. N.W., Washington, DC 20005-2008
(202) 220-1200; *Fax:* (202) 220-1665
David A. Wormser, Chairman

Perkins, Jr., Roy F.
1724 Whitewood Ln., Herndon, VA 20170
(703) 435-9700, *Fax:* (703) 435-9701

Peter A. Casciato P.C.
335 Bryant St., Suite 410, San Francisco, CA 94107
(415) 291-8661, *Fax:* (415) 291-8165
www.petercasciato.com
pacasciato@gmail.com

Peterson Law Firm
2033 Walnut St., Philadelphia, PA 19103
(215) 557-9001

Phillips Nizer LLP
666 5th Ave., 28th Fl., New York, NY 10103-0084
(212) 977-9700, *Fax:* (212) 262-5152
www.phillipsnizer.com
marketing@phillipsnizer.com

PROFESSIONAL SERVICES

Pierce & Robinson P A
Div/DBA: (Formerly Pierce, Robinson & Greene P A)
600 W. 4th St., North Little Rock, AR 72114-5360
(501) 372-3131, *Fax:* (501) 372-3825
www.prg-law.com

Pillsbury Winthrop Shaw Pittman LLP
2300 N St. N.W., Washington, DC 20037
(202) 663-8000, *Fax:* (202) 663-8007

Pillsbury, Winthrop Shaw Pittman LLP
1540 Broadway, New York, NY 10036-4039
(877) 323-4171, *Fax:* (415) 983-1200
www.pillsburylaw.com

Powell, Goldstein, Frazer & Murphy
1201 W. Peachtree St. N.W., Fl. 14, Atlanta, GA 30309
(404) 572-6600, *Fax:* (404) 572-6999
www.pgfm.com
wmoeling@pgfm.com
1001 Pennsylvania Ave. N.W., 6th Fl, Washington, DC 20004-2505
(202) 347-0066; *Fax:* (202) 624-7222
Jerome S. Breed, Chairman

Pratcher & Associates P.C.
1133 Kensington Ave., Buffalo, NY 14215-1611
(716) 838-4612, *Fax:* (716) 838-4828
frpratcher@pratcher.com
Town Gardens Plaza, 447 Williams St, Suite H, Buffalo, NY 14204-1896
(716) 847-0145;

Preston, Gates, Ellis & Rouvelas Meeds L.L.P.
1735 New York Ave. N.W., Suite 500, Washington, DC 20006
(202) 628-1700, *Fax:* (202) 331-1024
www.prestongates.com
robert@prestongates.com

Proskauer Rose L.L.P.
1585 Broadway, New York, NY 10036
(212) 969-3000, *Fax:* (212) 969-2900
www.proskauer.com
lbudish@proskauer.com

Provosty, Sadler Delaunay, Fiorenza & Sobel
Box 1791, Hibernia National Bank, 8th Fl., Alexandria, LA 71309-1791
(318) 445-3631, *Fax:* (318) 445-9377

Pulis, Gregory M.
Div/DBA: (Creative Artists Agency)
2000 Avenue of the Stars, Los Angeles, CA 90067
(424) 288-4545, (424) 288-2000, *Fax:* (424) 288-4800, (424) 288-2900
gpulis@caa.com

Putbrese, Hunsaker & Trent, P.C.
200 S. Church St., Woodstock, VA 22664
(540) 459-7646, *Fax:* (540) 459-7656
phtlaw@mindspring.com

Reddy, Begley & McCormick, L.L.P.
1156 15th St. N.W., Suite 610, Washington, DC 20005-1770
(202) 659-5700, *Fax:* (202) 659-5711
www.rbmfcclaw.com
rbm@rbmfcclaw.com

Reed Smith LLP
3110 Fairview Park Dr., Suite 1400, Falls Church, VA 22042-4503
(703) 641-4200, *Fax:* (703) 641-4340
www.reedsmith.com
reedsmith@reedsmith.com

Rees, Broome & Diaz
8133 Leesburg Pike, 9th Fl., Vienna, VA 22182
(703) 790-1911, *Fax:* (703) 848-2530
www.rbdlaw.com
info@rbdlaw.com

Renouf & Polivy
1532 16th St. N.W., Washington, DC 20036
(202) 265-1807, *Fax:* (202) 265-1810
thamber@aol.com

Resnick, Bernard Max, Esq, P.C.
Two Bala Plaza, Suite 300, Bala Cynwyd, PA 19004-1501
(610) 660-7774, *Fax:* (610) 668-0574
www.bernardresnick.com
bmresnick@aol.com

Reynolds & Manning, P.A.
Box 2809, Prince Frederick, MD 20678
(410) 535-9220, *Fax:* (410) 535-9171
www.lawyers.com/reynoldsandmanning
calvertlawyer@comcast.net

Richard N. Clarvit, P.A.
1313 N.E. 125th St., Suite 200, North Miami, FL 33161
(305) 893-4135, *Fax:* (305) 893-4173
richsongs@aol.com

Richard S. Becker & Associates
7128 Fairfax Rd., Bethesda, MD 20814
(301) 986-9005, *Fax:* (301) 986-8456
Beckereng@aol.com

Richards, Mary Beth
U.S. Federal Communications Commission, 445 12th St. S.W., Rm. 8-C750, Washington, DC 20554
(202) 418-1000, *Fax:* (202) 418-2801
www.fcc.gov
marybeth.richards@fcc.gov

Riezman & Berger
7700 Bonhomme Ave., 7th Fl., St. Louis, MO 63105
(314) 727-0101, *Fax:* (314) 727-6458
www.riezmanberger.com
jacobs@riezmamberger.com

Riker Danzig Scherer Hyland & Perretti LLP
One Speedwell Ave., Headquarters Plaza, Morristown, NJ 07962-1981
(973) 538-0800, *Fax:* (973) 538-1984
www.riker.com
info@riker.com
50 W. State St, Suite 1010, Trenton, NJ 08608-1220

Robert A. DePont, Attorney at Law
140 South St., Annapolis, MD 21401
(410) 263-0632, *Fax:* (410) 280-8624
www.robertdeport.com
robertade@msn.com

Robins, Kaplan, Miller & Ciresi
2800 LaSalle Plaza, 800 LaSalle Ave., Minneapolis, MN 55402-2015
(612) 349-8500, *Fax:* (612) 339-4181
www.rkmc.com
kamarron@rkmc.com

Rosenfeld, Meyer & Susman L.L.P.
9601 Wilshire Blvd., Suite 710, Beverly Hills, CA 90210-5225
(310) 858-7700, *Fax:* (310) 860-2430
www.rmslaw.com

Ross Eatman
Box 102, Bedford, NY 10506-0102
(914) 234-4748, *Fax:* (914) 234-4750
emstalent@aol.com

Rourke, Gerald S.
76 Northwood Rd., Madison, CT 06443
(203) 421-3424
wstacey@stacey.ca
Wayne A. Stacey, President
Govt rels, CRTC/IC applications, bcst rsch, bcst consulting, engrg svcs, demographic studies.

Rubin, Winston, Diercks, Harris & Cooke, L.L.P.
1155 Connecticut Ave. N.W., 6th Fl., Washington, DC 20036
(202) 861-0870, *Fax:* (202) 429-0657
www.rwdhc.com
jwinston@rwdhc.com

Ryan, Swanson & Cleveland P.L.L.C.
1201 3rd Ave., Suite 3400, Seattle, WA 98101-3034
(206) 464-4224, (800) 458-5973, *Fax:* (206) 583-0359
www.ryanlaw.com
collette@ryanlaw.com

Sahl, Jack
School of Law, University of Akron, Akron, OH 44325-2901
(330) 972-6753, *Fax:* (330) 258-2343
www.uakron.edu/law
jps@uakron.edu

Sanchez Law Firm
2300 M. St., N.W., Suite 800, Washington, DC 20037
(202) 237-2814, *Fax:* (202) 237-5614
esanchez@bellatlantic.net

Sapronov & Associates, P. C.
3 Ravinia Dr., Suite 1455, Atlanta, GA 30346
(770) 399-9100, *Fax:* (770) 395-0505
www.wstelecomlaw.com
info@wstelecomlaw.com

Schuman, Felts, Chartered
4804 Moorland Ln., Bethesda, MD 20814
(301) 986-0200, *Fax:* (301) 986-7960

Schuster & Associates
3594 Armourdale Ave., Long Beach, CA 90808
(562) 596-5900, *Fax:* (562) 431-4540
www.flightlaw.com
attorney@flightlaw.com

Schwaninger & Associates, P.C.
Schwaninger and Associates Inc, 6715 Little River Tnpk, Suite 204, Annandale, VA 220033
(703) 256-0637, *Fax:* (703) 256-3578
www.sa-lawyers.net
rschwaninger@sa-lawyers.net

Schwartz, Woods & Miller
1233 20th St., N.W., Suite 610, Washington, DC 20036
(202) 833-1700, *Fax:* (202) 833-2351
www.swmlaw.com
[last name]@swmlaw.com

The Seale Law Firm
Bryton Tower, 1271 Poplar Ave., Memphis, TN 38104
(901) 521-9958

Sell & Melton
Box 229, 577 Mulberry St., Suite 1400, Macon, GA 31202-0229
(478) 746-8521, *Fax:* (478) 745-6426
www.sell-melton.com
eds@sell-melton.com

Severaid, Ronald H.
1805 Tribute Rd., Suite J, Sacramento, CA 95815
(916) 929-8383, *Fax:* (916) 925-4763
rhseveraid@earthlink.net

Seyfarth Shaw
2029 Century Park E., 33rd Fl., Los Angeles, CA 90067-3063
(310) 277-7200, *Fax:* (310) 201-5219
www.seyfarth.com

Seyfarth Shaw LLP
55 E. Monroe St., Chicago, IL 60603
(312) 781-8655, *Fax:* (312) 269-8869
www.seyfarth.com
aunikel@seyfarth.com

Shapiro, Burton J.
2147 N. Beachwood Dr., Los Angeles, CA 90068-3462
(323) 469-9452, *Fax:* (603) 710-8109
www.burtshapiro.com
burtjay@mail.com

Shine and Hardin L.L.P.
2810 Beaver Ave., Fort Wayne, IN 46807
(260) 745-1970, *Fax:* (260) 744-5411
www.shineandhardin.com
sshine@shineandhardin.com

Shukat, Arrow, Hafer & Weber, L.L.P.
111 W. 57th St., Suite 1120, New York, NY 10019-2211
(212) 245-4580, *Fax:* (212) 956-6471
Peter@musiclaw.com

Shulman, Rogers, Gandal, Pordy & Ecker, P.A.
11921 Rockville Pike, 3rd Fl., Rockville, MD 20852
(301) 230-5200, *Fax:* (301) 230-2891
www.shulmanrogers.com
atilles@srgpe.com

Siegal, Joel H.
703 Market St., San Francisco, CA 94103
(415) 777-5547

Siegel, Kelleher & Kahn
426 Franklin St., Buffalo, NY 14202
(716) 881-5800, *Fax:* (716) 885-3369
www.skklaw.com
info@skklaw.com

Silver, Garvett & Henkel P.A.
18001 Old Cutler Rd., Suite 600, Miami, FL 33157
(305) 377-8802, *Fax:* (305) 377-8804

Skadden, Arps, Slate, Meagher & Flom L.L.P.
1440 New York Ave. N.W., Washington, DC 20005

(202) 371-7000, *Fax:* (202) 393-5760
www.skadden.com

Smith & Metalitz LLP
1747 Pennsylvania Ave. N.W., Suite 825, Washington, DC 20006
(202) 833-4198
www.lds.org
russelldg@chq.byu.edu
Gordon Hinckley, President
Donald G. Russell, Operations Dir
Offers free pub affrs, news & feature progmg for TV & radio; also guests for talk shows. Pub affrs progmg is not church-oriented.

Smith, Dianne
Div/DBA: (formerly Pauker, Molly)
Fox Television Stations Inc., 5151 Wisconsin Ave., N.W., Washington, DC 20016-4124
(202) 895-3088, *Fax:* (202) 895-3222
dianne.smith@foxtv.com

Smithwick & Belendiuk, P.C.
Suite 301, 5028 Wisconsin Ave. N.W., Washington, DC 20016
(202) 363-4050, *Fax:* (202) 363-4266
fccworld.com
gsmithwick@fccworld.com

Sodos & Kafkas
16985 Bluemount Rd., Suite 202, Brookfield, WI 53005
(262) 785-5500, *Fax:* (262) 785-1100
office@sodos.com

Sommers, Schwartz, Silver & Schwartz, P.C.
2000 Town Ctr., Suite 900, Southfield, MI 48075
(248) 355-0300, *Fax:* (248) 746-4001
www.sommerspc.com

Sonneman & Sonneman, P.A.
111 Riverfront, Suite 202, Winona, MN 55987
(507) 454-8885, *Fax:* (507) 454-8887
sonneman@luminet.net

Sonnenschein, Nath & Rosenthal LLP
8000 Sears Tower, 233 S. Wacker Dr., Chicago, IL 60606
(312) 876-3114, *Fax:* (312) 876-7934
www.sonnenschein.com
sfifer@sonnenschein.com

Southmayd & Miller
1220 19th St. N.W., Suite 400, Washington, DC 20036
(202) 331-4100
www.lawyers.com
graubart@gte.net

Spawn, Coy U.
1815 Bering Dr., Houston, TX 77057-3109
(713) 782-2977, *Fax:* (713) 782-2977

Spiegel & McDiarmid, LLP
1333 New Hampshire Ave. N.W., Washington, DC 20036
(202) 879-4000, *Fax:* (202) 393-2866
www.spiegelmcd.com
jim.horwood@spiegelmcd.com

Springman, Braden, Wilson & Pontius, P.C.
1022 Bannock St., Denver, CO 80204
(303) 685-4897/685-4633, *Fax:* (303) 685-4627
sbwp@indra.com

Squire, Sanders & Dempsey
Box 407, 1201 Pennsylvania Ave. N.W., Washington, DC 20044-0407
(202) 626-6600, *Fax:* (202) 626-6780
www.ssd.com
jnadler@ssd.com
4900 Key Tower, 127 Public Sq, Cleveland, OH 44114-1217
(216) 479-8500; *Fax:* (216) 479-8780
Terrence J. Clark, Ptnr

Stennett, Wilkinson & Peden
401 Legacy Park, Ridgeland, MS 39157
(601) 206-1816, *Fax:* (601) 206-9132
www.swplaw.com
swplaw@attorney.net

Stephens Media LLC
P.O. Box 70, Las Vegas, NV 89125
(702) 477-3830, *Fax:* (702) 383-0230
www.stephensmedia.com

Steptoe & Johnson
1330 Connecticut Ave. N.W., Washington, DC 20036
(202) 429-3000, *Fax:* (202) 429-3902
www.steptoe.com
amamlet@steptoe.com

Stevens, Sally L.
Box 41, Lumberville, PA 18933
(215) 297-8245, *Fax:* (215) 297-5106

Stewart & Irwin P.C.
251 E. Ohio St., Suite 1100, Indianapolis, IN 46204
(317) 639-5454, *Fax:* (317) 632-1319
www.stewart-irwin.com
raikman@silegal.com

Stewart, Estes & Donnell PLC
424 Church St., Fifth Third Ctr., Suite 1401, Nashville, TN 37219
(615) 244-6538, *Fax:* (615) 256-8386
www.sedlaw.com

Strichartz, James L.
200 W. Mercer St., Suite 511, Seattle, WA 98119
(206) 282-8020
www.booktelevision.com
info@booktelevision.com
BookTelevision: The Channel spotlights all the writing that informs & entertains us in our daily lives.

Stroock, Stroock & Lavin
180 Maiden Lane, New York, NY 10038-4982
(212) 806-5400, *Fax:* (212) 806-6006
www.stroock.com
speters@stroock.com

Stryker, Tams & Dill LLP
2 Penn Plaza E., Newark, NJ 07105-2293
(973) 491-9500, *Fax:* (973) 491-9692
www.strykertams.com
dlinken@strykertams.com

Taylor, Jack
1289 Lincoln Rd., Yuba City, CA 95991
(530) 671-6800, *Fax:* (530) 671-6447

Taylor, Ray L.
11608 Chayote St., Los Angeles, CA 90049
(310) 476-6493, *Fax:* (310) 471-2763

Technology Law Group L.L.C.
5335 Wisconsin Ave. N.W., Suite 440, Washington, DC 20015
(202) 895-1707
www.victorysports.com
info@victorysports.com

Teitelbaum, Israel
11301 Amherst Ave., Suite 202, Silver Spring, MD 20902
(301) 933-3373, *Fax:* (301) 933-3651

Thelen Reid & Priest LLP
Div/DBA: Washington, D.C.
701 Pennsylvania Ave. N.W., Suite 800, Washington, DC 20004
(202) 508-4000, *Fax:* (202) 508-4321
www.thelenreid.com
101 2nd St., Suite 1800, San Francisco, CA 94105-3672
(415) 371-1200; *Fax:* (415) 371-1211

Thiemann, Aitken & Vohra
908 King St., Suite 300, Alexandria, VA 22314
(703) 836-9400, *Fax:* (703) 836-9410
ajthiemann@ttalaw.com

Thomas, Ballenger, Vogelman & Turner
124 S. Royal St., Alexandria, VA 22314
(703) 836-3400, *Fax:* (703) 836-3549

Thompson Hine LLP
1920 N St. N.W., Suite 800, Washington, DC 20036
(202) 331-8800, *Fax:* (202) 331-8330
www.thompsonhine.com
barry.friedman@thompsonhine.com
10 W. Broad St., Suite 700, Columbus, OH 43215-3418
(614) 469-3200; *Fax:* (614) 469-3361
www.thompsonhine.com
tom.lodge@thompsonhine.com
Thomas E. Lodge, Chairman

Thrasher, Dinsmore & Dolan
100 7th Ave., Suite 150, Chardon, OH 44024-1079
(440) 285-2242, *Fax:* (440) 285-9423
dmoore@dolan.law.pro

Todd W. Musburger, Ltd.
142 E. Ontario St., Suite 500, Chicago, IL 60611
(312) 664-2600, *Fax:* (312) 664-4137
todd@musburger.com

Troutman Sanders L.L.P.
600 Peachtree St., Suite 5200, Atlanta, GA 30308
(404) 885-3000, *Fax:* (404) 885-3900
www.troutmansanders.com

Troy & Gould, PC
1801 Century Park E., 16th Fl., Los Angeles, CA 90067
(310) 553-4441, *Fax:* (310) 201-4746
www.troygould.com

Trugman, Richard S.
9200 Sunset Blvd., Suite 206, Los Angeles, CA 90069
(310) 273-8834, *Fax:* (310) 273-8345
trulaw@sbcglobal.net

Turtle, Joel S.
55 Santa Clara Ave., Suite 120, Oakland, CA 94610
(510) 763-7600, *Fax:* (510) 763-7894
www.riotmedia.com
joelturtle@yahoo.com

Umansky, Barry D.
Irwin, Campbell & Tannerwald, 1730 Rhode Island Ave. N.W., Suite 200, Washington, DC 20036-3101
(202) 728-0400
www.ictpc.com

Van Cott, Bagley, Cornwall & McCarthy
36 S. State St., Suite 1900, Salt Lake City, UT 84111-1478
(801) 532-3333, *Fax:* (801) 534-0058
www.vancott.com
info@vancott.com

Varnum LLP
Div/DBA: (Formerly Varnum, Riddering, Schmidt & Howlett LL
Box 352, Bridgewater Pl., Grand Rapids, MI 49501-0352
(616) 336-6000, *Fax:* (616) 336-7000
www.varnumlaw.com
generalinfo@varnumlaw.com

Venable LLP
1800 Mercantile Bank Bldg., 2 Hopkins Plaza, Baltimore, MD 21201
(410) 244-7400, *Fax:* (410) 244-7742
mscott@venable.com
1201 New York Ave. N.W, Suite 1000, Washington, DC 20005-3917
(202) 962-4800, (202) 962-8300;

Veryl Miles/Professor at Law School
Cardinal Stn., Columbus School of Law, /Catholic Univ. America, Washington, DC 20064
(202) 319-5140, *Fax:* (202) 319-4459
www.law.edu

Vorys, Sater, Seymour and Pease LLP
Box 1008, 52 E. Gay St., Columbus, OH 43216-1008
(614) 464-6400, *Fax:* (614) 464-6350
www.vorys.com
bcschmidt@vorys.com
1828 L St. N.W, Suite 1111, Washington, DC 20036-5104
(202) 467-8800; *Fax:* (202) 467-8900
Mark J. Palchick, Robert E. Levine

Wagner, Michael Francis
Mass Media Bureau, 445 12th St. S.W., Rm. 2-A523, Washington, DC 20554
(202) 418-2700, *Fax:* (202) 418-1410
www.fcc.gov/mb/audio

Waller Lansden Dortch & Davis, PLLC
511 Union St., Suite 2700, Nashville, TN 37219
(615) 244-6380, *Fax:* (615) 244-6804
www.wallerlaw.com

Weil, Gotshal & Manges, L.L.P.
1300 I St. N.W., Suite 900, Washington, DC 20005
(202) 682-7000, *Fax:* (202) 857-0940
www.weil.com
bruce.turnbull@weil.com

Weissmann, Wolff, Bergman, Coleman, Grodin & Evall
9665 Wilshire Blvd., 9th Fl., Beverly Hills, CA 90212-2345
(310) 858-7888, *Fax:* (310) 550-7191
www.weissmannwolff.com
seisner@wwllp.com

Westervelt, Johnson, Nicholl & Keller, LLC
Associated Bank Bldg., 411 Hamilton Blvd., 14th Fl., Peoria, IL 61602
(309) 671-3550, *Fax:* (309) 671-3588
westervelt@westerveltlaw.com

WGBH Educational Foundation
125 Western Ave., Boston, MA 02134-1098
(617) 300-2000, *Fax:* (617) 300-1014
www.wgbh.org

Wheeler Wolf Law Firm
Box 2056, 220 N. 4th. St., Bismarck, ND 58502-2056
(701) 223-5300, *Fax:* (701) 223-5366
jackmcdonald@wheelerwolf.com

Wildman, Harrold, Allen & Dixon
225 W. Wacker Dr., Suite 3000, Chicago, IL 60606
(312) 201-2000, *Fax:* (312) 201-2555
www.wildmanharrold.com

Wiley Rein LLP
1776 K St. N.W., Washington, DC 20006
(202) 719-7000, *Fax:* (202) 719-7049
www.wileyrein.com
dcorini@wileyrein.com

Wilkinson Barker Knauer, L.L.P.
2300 N St. N.W., Suite 700, Washington, DC 20037
(202) 783-4141, *Fax:* (202) 783-5851
www.wbklaw.com

Willcox & Savage, P.C.
One Commercial Pl., Suite 1800, Norfolk, VA 23510
(757) 628-5500, *Fax:* (757) 628-5566
www.willcoxsavage.com
mshearon@wilsav.com
Box 61888, One Columbus Ctr, Suite 1010, Virginia Beach, VA 23466-1888
Fax: (757) 628-5659
Jeffrey H. Gray, Chairman

William Morris Agency
151 El Camino Dr., Beverly Hills, CA 90212-2704
(310) 859-4000, *Fax:* (310) 859-4462

Willkie Farr & Gallagher LLP
1875 K St. N.W., Washington, DC 20006
(202) 303-1000, *Fax:* (202) 303-2000
www.willkie.com

Wilmer Cutler Pickering Hale and Dorr LLP
1875 Pennsylvania Ave., N.W., Washington, DC 20006-3642
(202) 663-6000, *Fax:* (202) 663-6363
william.richardson@wilmerhale.com

Winkler, Bevacqua & Simmons, P.C.
60 Park Pl., 19th Fl., Newark, NJ 07102
(973) 676-1200, *Fax:* (973) 624-5980

Winston & Strawn
35 W. Wacker Dr., Chicago, IL 60601-9703
(312) 558-5600, *Fax:* (312) 558-5700
www.winston.com
jneis@winston.com
1400 L St. N.W., 8th Fl, Washington, DC
(202) 371-5700; *Fax:* (202) 371-5950
Deborah C. Costlow, Chairman

Wolf, Block, Schorr, & Solis-Cohen
250 Park Ave., New York, NY 10177-0030
(212) 986-1116, *Fax:* (212) 986-0604
www.wolfblock.com

Womble, Carlyle, Sandridge & Rice, PLLC
1401 I St. N.W., 7th Fl., Washington, DC 20005
(202) 467-6900, *Fax:* (202) 467-6910
www.wcsr.com

Wood, Maines & Nolan, Chartered
4121 Wilson Blvd., Suite 101, Arlingtron, VA 22203
(703) 465-2361, *Fax:* (703) 465-2365
legalcompass.com
wmb@legalcompass.com

Wright & Talisman, P.C.
1200 G St. N.W., Suite 600, Washington, DC 20005
(202) 393-1200, *Fax:* (202) 393-1240
www.wright.com
statman@wrightlaw.com

WTTW Channel 11/Chicago
5400 N. St. Louis Ave., Chicago, IL 60625
(773) 583-5000, *Fax:* (773) 583-3046
www.wttw.com

Young, Clement & Rivers L.L.P.
25 Callahan Street, Suite 400, Charleston, SC 29401
(843) 577-4000, (803) 254-2238, *Fax:* (843) 724-6600
www.ycrlaw.com
email@ycrlaw.com

Young, Williams, Kirk & Stone PC
First Tennessee Plaza, Suite 2021, Box 550, Knoxville, TN 37901-0550
(865) 637-1440, *Fax:* (865) 546-9808
www.tn-attorneys.com
bob@tn-attorneys.com

Management & Marketing Consultants

A.G. Visk
2973 Evans Oaks Ct., Atlanta, GA 30340
(770) 939-5657
www.news-directions.com
tony@news-direction.com
Tony Windsor, President
Professional dev & career mktg for TV news reporters, anchors & producers.

Abt Associates Inc.
55 Wheeler St., Cambridge, MA 02138
(617) 492-7100, *Fax:* (617) 492-5219
www.abtassoc.com
webmaster@abtassociated.com
John Shane, Chairman
Mktg rsch, strategic planning, mgmt consulting, audience rsch & segmentation; customer satisfaction programs, quality of svc programs, social science survey rsch, publ policy rsch, economical rsch.
4800 Montgomery Ln., Suite 600, Bethesda, MD 20814-3429
(301) 913-0500; *Fax:* (301) 652-3618
640 N. LaSalle, Chicago, IL 60654-3781
(312) 867-4000; *Fax:* (312) 867-4200
1110 Vermont Ave. N.W., Washington, DC 20005-3544
(202) 263-1800, (202) 263-1801;

Alan Burns & Associates
27250 Perdido Beach Blvd, Suite G, Gulf Shores, AL 32507-7866
(251) 980-7070, *Fax:* (251) 980-7090
www.burnsradio.com
alan@burnsradio.com
Donna Burns, COO
Alan Burns, President/CEO
Jeff Johnson, SVP
Mollie Allen, Assistant
Progmg & mktg consultants.

Anderson Productions Ltd.
55 W. 39th St., Suite 800, New York, NY 10018
(212) 414-9220, *Fax:* (212) 206-0279
www.apltv.com
steveanderson@apltv.com
Steven C.F. Anderson, President
TV documentary, pub affrs production & short films for non-profits.

The Aspen Institute Communications & Society Program
1 Dupont Cir. N.W., Suite 700, Washington, DC 20036
(202) 736-5818, *Fax:* (202) 467-0790
www.aspeninstitute.org/c&s
firestone@aspeninstitute.org
Charles M. Firestone, General Manager
Pub policy seminars & reports.

Associated Broadcasters, Inc.
Box 42566, Cincinnati, OH 45242 45242
(513) 791-5982, *Fax:* (513) 891-5727
irvschwartz@aol.com
Irv Schwartz, President
Legal & filing svcs in turnkey packages; consulting & appraisal svcs available.

Audience Research & Development (AR&D)
2440 Lofton Terr., Fort Worth, TX 76109
(817) 924-6922, *Fax:* (817) 924-7539
www.ar-d.com
jgumbert@ar-d.com
Jerry Gumbert, President
Rsch-based, full-svc, new media consulting firm serving TV stns, cable systems, internet companies, nwsprs & program syndicators.

The Austin Company
6095 Parkland Blvd., Cleveland, OH 44124
(440) 544-2600, *Fax:* (440) 544-2690
www.theaustin.com
Austin.info@theaustin.com
Patrick Flanagan, President
Michael G. Pierce, General Sales Mgr
Consulting, architectural design, engrg & construction svcs for TV, cable & radio bcstg facilities.
6410 Oak Canyon, #150, Irvine, CA 92618-5213
(949) 451-9000;
Ken Stone, Chairman
3500 Piedmont N.E., #725, Atlanta, GA 30305-1507
(404) 564-3950;
Matt Eddleman, Chairman

AVI Communications Inc.
517 Huffines Blvd., Lewisville, TX 75056
(214) 637-5464, (800) 221-2842, *Fax:* (214) 637-6285
www.avi-communications.com
info@avi-communications.com
Patrick Shaughnessy, President
Matthew Price, Operations Dir
TV sls training, new business dev svcs & Butch Harmon golf tips for TV & radio.

AZCAR
121 Hillpointe Dr., Suite 700, Canonsburg, PA 15317
(724) 873-0800, *Fax:* (724) 873-4770
www.azcar.com
info@azcar.com
Richard Bisignano, President
Mary Nahra, Operations Dir
Video & audio system consultation, systems integration, design, instal & training; serving cable systems, cable mfg, corporate, bcst & teleproduction facilities & engng.

Barry Skidelsky, Esq.
18 E. 41st St., New York, NY 10017
(212) 832-4800
bskidelsky@mindspring.com
Barry Skidelsky, Atty/Consultant
Employment contact; EEO compliance, training, audits, litigation & arbitration.

Bayliss Broadcast Foundation
Box 51126, Pacific Grove, CA 93950
(831) 655-5229, *Fax:* (831) 655-5228
www.baylissfoundation.org
khfranke@baylissfoundation.org
Carl Butrum, President
Kit Hunter Franke, General Manager
Bayliss Radio Intern program & scholarships for college students studying for a career in radio are primary focus of Foundation.

The Benchmark Co.
907 S. Congress, Suite 207, Austin, TX 78704-1700
(512) 707-7500, *Fax:* (512) 707-7757
www.thebenchmarkcompany.net
thebenc@earthlink.net
Rob Balon, President
Full-svc bcst consulting & rsch company featuring benchmark perceptual phone surveys & the Focus 100 system, which replaces focus groups.

The Benton Group
Box 5076, Vancouver, WA 98668
(360) 574-7369, *Fax:* (360) 576-6866
www.donbenton.com
Donald Benton, President
Yellow-page & nwspr experts, specialized sls training programs & seminars.

Beveridge Institute of Sales & Sales Management
113 North Grant St., Barrington, IL 60010
(847) 381-7797, (800) 227-4332, *Fax:* (847) 381-7301
www.beveridgeinc.com
info@beveridgeinc.com
Dick Beveridge, President
Sls & sls mgmt performance & productivity improvement programs; training workshops.

BIA Financial Network
15120 Enterprise Ct., Suite 100, Chantilly, VA 20151
(703) 818-2425, *Fax:* (703) 803-3299
www.bia.com
info@bia.com
Thomas J. Buono, Chairman
Financial & strategic consultants to communications industries offering fair market valuations, expert tax appraisals, due diligence, acquisition consulting, business plans, internal

operational audits, litigation support, investmentbanking, venture funding, capital, industry rsch & analysis publications & software.

Big Blue Dot
124 Watertown St., Suite F, Watertown, MA 02472
(617) 600-1100, *Fax:* (617) 923-0002
www.bigblue.com
bigbluedot@bigblue.com
Jan Craige Singer, President
Trend tracking resources for the kids' market, consulting, & newsletter via e-mail; creative svcs.

Bill Hennes & Associates
5009 Crosswinds Dr., Wilmington, NC 28409
(910) 264-6006, *Fax:* (910) 313-0228
www.allaboutcountry.com
bhennes105@aol.com
Bill Hennes, President
Progmg & mgmt consulting.

Bill Slatter & Associates
423 Main St., Natchez, MS 39120
(601) 442-1828
www.commnow.com
research@commnow.com
Robert Daigle, Promotions Manager
Telecommunications, high-technology, mktg rsch.

Blackburn & Co. Inc.
201 N. Union St., Suite 340, Alexandria, VA 22314
(703) 519-3703, *Fax:* (703) 519-9756
rblack4@aol.com
James W. Blackburn Jr., Chairman
Acquisition svcs of all kinds including appraisals, brokerage & financing for radio & TV stations and communications towers.

Blair Productions
4801 Connecticut Ave. N.W., Washington, DC 20008
(202) 364-1019
Full-svc mgmt & financial counseling to the bcst industry with emphasis on radio turnarounds, problems & start-ups; investment banking svc.

Block Communications Group Inc.
2910 Neilson Way, Suite 503, Santa Monica, CA 90405-5368
(310) 452-3355, *Fax:* (310) 452-4077
www.blockcommunicationsgroup.com
dblock@earthlink.net
Richard C. Block, President
Consultants specializing in new cable svcs, bcstg stns, syndicated progmg, distribution & mktg serving U.S. & international clients since 1974.

Bond & Pecaro Inc.
1920 N St. N.W., Suite 350, Washington, DC 20036
(202) 775-8870, *Fax:* (202) 775-0175
www.bondpecaro.com
bp@bondpecaro.com
Timothy Pecaro, Operations Dir
Economic & financial consulting, valuation studies, asset allocations, appraisals, feasibility studies, fairness opinions, Internet valuations & expert testimony.

Bortz Media & Sports Group
4582 S. Ulster St., Ste 1340, Denver, CO 80237
(303) 893-9902, *Fax:* (303) 893-9913
www.bortz.com
info@bortz.com
James M. Trautman, General Manager
TV stn mgmt consulting, cable financial & market analysis; corporate strategic planning.

Bowman Valuation Services
706 Duke St., Alexandria, VA 22314
(703) 549-5681, *Fax:* (703) 549-5682
www.bowmanvaluation.com
bowman@bowmanvaluation.com
Chip Snyder, Operations Dir
Appraisals, asset allocations, specialized studies.

Broadcast Media Associates
Box 1233, Santa Maria, CA 93456
(805) 937-1553, *Fax:* (805) 937-7212
broadcastmediabroker.com
cliffhunter@cliffhunter.com
Clifford M. Hunter, President
Mgmt consulting, mktg studies & bcst investment analysis.

Broadcast Services Inc.
Box 6418, Brattleboro, VT 05302-6418
(802) 258-3000, (802) 258-4500 svc, *Fax:* (802) 258-2500
www.markhutchins.com
mh@markhutchins.com
Mark F. Hutchins, President
Predicted-coverage mapping, signal-improvement studies, interference mitigation, satellite & microwave facilities inter-connection, RF radiation safety/compliance.

Broadcasting Asset Management Corp.
1323 Forest Glen Dr. N., Winnetka, IL 60093
(847) 446-8882, *Fax:* (847) 446-4855
jmink@ix.netcom.com
Jack Minkow, General Manager
Merger & feasibility studies; acquisition analyses; capital structuring, brokerage, mgmt procurement & consulting; sr, subordinated & equity placement.

Broadcasting Unlimited Inc.
35 Main St., Wayland, MA 01778
(508) 653-7200
www.recoverynetwork.org
info@recoverynetwork.com
Progmg addresses behavioral & alternative health care issues & treatments for eating disorders, addictions, depression, sexual addictions, substance abuse, etc.
Serving 5 million subs on 36 systems. Satellite: Galaxy 7. Launched Spring1996.

Broward Alliance
110 E. Broward Blvd., #1990, Fort Lauderdale, FL 33301-2248
(954) 524-3113 ext 220, (800) 741-1420, *Fax:* (954) 524-3167
www.browardalliance.org/film
info@browardalliance.org
Resource for film, TV & print industry production and business relocation.

BTMI (Broadcast Trustee Management Inc.)
1090 Vermont Ave. N.W., Suite 800, Washington, DC 20005
(202) 408-7036, *Fax:* (202) 408-1590
www.btmi.com
Probinson@aol.cin
Financial-asset mgmt, valuation, mktg, restructuring & recovery consultation svcs.

Cable Audit Associates Inc.
5340 So. Quebec St., Suite 100, Greenwood Village, CO 80111
(303) 694-0444, *Fax:* (303) 694-2559
www.cableaudit.com
blazarus@cableaudit.com
Bruce N. Lazarus, CEO
Mitch Walker, Operations Dir
Progmg license fee audits of cable operators, MMDS, SMATVs & TVRO middlemen.

Cameo Wind Creative Management
225 W. 34th St., Suite 1100, New York, NY 10122
(212) 947-1998, *Fax:* (212) 221-7386
jijulien@aol.com

Carolina Media Professionals Inc.
Box 3325, Spartanburg, SC 29304
(864) 597-1301, *Fax:* (864) 596-7539
www.carolinamedia.com
rachel@upstate.net
Rachel Greene, President
Specializes in the placement of natl adv through radio, TV for products, svs and programs. Print: natl adv. Production: audio & video.

The Center for Sales Strategy, Inc.
610 W. DeLeon St., Tampa, FL 33606-2720
(813) 254-2222, *Fax:* (813) 254-9222
www.csscenter.com
Jim Hopes, CEO
Comprehensive consulting & training svcs for radio & TV, cable, and nwspr, in sls, mktg & mgmt, exclusively on a long-term, multi-year basis.

Chenevert Songy Rodi Soderberg
Div/DBA: (An Engrg/Architectural Corp.)
6767 Perkins Rd., Suite 200, Baton Rouge, LA 70808
(225) 769-0546, *Fax:* (225) 767-0060
www.csrsonline.com
csrs@csrsonline.com
Architects, planners & tech designers specializing in new & renovated bcst/cable production facilities.

Christian Television Services
9775 S.W. 87th Ave., Miami Beach, FL 33141
(305) 592-7642, *Fax:* (305) 596-4564
www.citv.com
webmaster@citv.com
Russell Thorne, CEO
Relg media buying.

Christian TV Services
18 Elizabeth St., P.O. Box 209, Ellicottville, NY 14731-0209
(716) 699-2549, *Fax:* (716) 699-2590
www.christiantvservices.com
george@christianservices.com
George A. Thayer, President
Joyce E. Thayer, Operations Dir
Russell A. Thayer, General Manager
Roger A. Thayer, Programming Director
Randall A. Thayer, Promotions Manager
TVRO consultant for Christian media started: 1974; affil: TBN/TCT/CTS Ministering to Ministries, listing media organizations & Internet places of worship. (800) 982-8823.

Chubb Group of Insurance Companies
15 Mountain View Rd., Warren, NJ 07059
(908) 903-2000, *Fax:* (908) 903-2027
www.chubb.com
info@chubb.com
Endorsed multi-natl property/casualty carrier by the Bcst Financial Mgrs Assns.
Branches in more than 115 offices in 30 countries.

Claritas Inc.
1525 Wilson Blvd., Suite 1000, Arlington, VA 22209
(703) 812-2700, *Fax:* (703) 812-2701
www.claritas.com
info@claritas.com
Mktg data, software & consulting designed for cable, TV, radio & other new media companies.
332 S. Michigan Ave, Suite 200, Chicago, IL 60604-4434
(312) 986-2650;
Margie Lymperis, Vp Electronic Media

Clark-Mann & Associates Inc.
1714 Stockton St., Suite 300, San Francisco, CA 94133
(415) 421-0220, *Fax:* (415) 421-0417
wclarkmann2@msn.com
William D. Clark, CEO
Ken Erickson, Operations Dir
Helen Butler, General Sales Mgr
Full-svc adv agency & PR firm with background in bcst & print.

Clear Channel Satellite
76 Inverness Dr. E., Suite B, Englewood, CO 80112
(303) 925-1708, *Fax:* (303) 925-1714
www.clearchannelsatellite.com
sales@clearchannelsatellite.com
Don Harms, President
Monty Dent, General Sales Mgr
Satellite space-time; audio distribution via satellite; WAN protection svcs; DSNG svcs; satellite equipment sls; Satellite installation svcs.

Clifton Gardiner & Company, L.L.C.
2437 S. Chase Ln., Denver, CO 80227
(303) 758-6900, *Fax:* (303) 757-5005
www.cliftongardiner.com
cliff@cliftongardiner.com
Clifton H. Gardiner, President
Brokerage, consulting, financial svcs for the bcst & cable TV industries.

Colorado Springs Film Commission
515 S. Cascade Ave., Colorado Springs, CO 80903
(719) 635-7506 x127, *Fax:* (719) 635-4968
www.filmcoloradosprings.com
kgriffis@experiencecoloradosprings.com
Free location svcs, Production Resource Guide, location guide available for the Colorado Springs, CO area; help with crews, hotels & permits.

Coltrin & Associates Inc.
1212 Ave. of the Americas, 10th Fl., New York, NY 10036
(212) 221-1616, *Fax:* (212) 221-7718
www.coltrin.com
steve_coltrin@coltrin.com
Consultant svcs to bcst mgmt, mktg sls, promotional rsch; New York, NY, & Washington, DC representation in corporate, govt & PR.
801 Floral Vale Blvd., Yardley, PA 19067-5513
(215) 497-3188;
Gwen Coltrin, Coo
433 Airport Blvd, Suite 414, Burlingame, CA 94010-2017
(650) 373-2005;
Benoit Rungeard, Dir
50 Raffles Pl., 37th Fl., Singapore, Indonesia
+65 6829 7149;
Chan Chee Pong, Vp

215 Celebration Pl., Suite 500, Celebration, FL 34747-5400
(321) 559-1112;
215 S. State St, Suite 675, Salt Lake City, UT 84111-2319
(801) 350-9412;
35 Picadilly, 3rd Fl., London, United Kingdom
+44 20 7494 4748;

Columbia Management Advisors
One S. Wacker Dr., Chicago, IL 60606
Fax: (312) 855-2552
William Rarkin, President
Investment counsel & mutual fund mgmt. Offices in Chicago, IL; Cleveland, OH; New York, NY; San Francisco, CA; & Puerto Rico.

ComBridges
70 Irwin, San Rafael, CA 94901
(415) 454-5505, *Fax:* (888) 530-5505
www.combridges.com
info@combridges.com
Jon Leland, President
Complete creative & production svcs including: animation, special effects, video production, video streaming, web site design, & computer-based production system design. Experience with creative svc departments & corporate communications.

CommNOW
15 Random Farm Rd., Chappaqua, NY 10514
(914) 944-0216
www.muchloud.com
muchloud@muchmusic.com
For fans of hard music everywhere - MuchLOUD delivers. Alternative, metal and punk music videos, featured alongside exclusive artist interviews, specials, classic archival material and up-to-the-minute concert info.

Communication Trends Inc.
6120 Powers Ferry Rd. N.W., Suite 140, Atlanta, GA 30339
(404) 843-8717, *Fax:* (404) 843-6869
Mktg & adv for cable, direct bcst, bcst communications industries & related technologies.

Communications Design Associates Inc.
437 Turnpike St., Canton, MA 02021-2702
(339) 502-6551, *Fax:* (339) 502-6595
www.cdaconsultants.com
srandall@cdaconsultants.com
Stewart R. Randall
Ind consultants to radio, TV, corp & govt clients. Designers of studios, production, presentation & multi-media facilities.

Communications Equity Associates
101 E. Kennedy Blvd., Suite 3300, Tampa, FL 33602
(813) 226-8844, *Fax:* (813) 225-1513
www.ceaworldwide.com
spark@ceaworldwide.com
J. Patrick Michaels Jr., CEO
Provides investment banking, brokerage, regulatory affrs & mgmt svcs for bcst, CATV & related communications industries.
54 Thompson St., 4th Fl., New York, NY 10012-4308
(212) 218-5085;

Comsearch
19700 Janelia Farm Blvd., Ashburn, VA 20147
(703) 726-5500, *Fax:* (703) 726-5600
www.comsearch.com
info@comsearch.com
Douglass R. Hall, President
Provides frequency coord, site selection, RFI measurements, path surveys, protection for satellite earth stn dishes & terrestrial microwave facilities & wireless engrg svcs & data.

Conley & Associates, LLC
1459 Interstate Loop, Bismarck, ND 58503-5560
(701) 222-3902, *Fax:* (701) 222-4815
www.conleyassociates.net
info@conleyassociates.net
Candace Christianson, Operations Dir
Consultants in the areas of strategic planning, appraisals, finance, opns, engrg, mktg, human resources & pub/govt rel.

Connecticut Film Video & Media Office
One Constitution Plaza, 2nd Fl., Hartford, CT 06103
(800) 392-2122, (860) 256-2800, *Fax:* (860) 256-2811
www.CTfilm.com
info@ctfilm.com
Karen Senich, General Manager
A film commission eager to respond to any situation or need.

Connelly Co. Inc.
17909 Holly Brook Dr., Tampa, FL 33647-2245
(813) 991-9494, *Fax:* (813) 991-9494
connellyradiotv@verizon.net
Robert J. Connelly, President
Brokers, consultants & recovery units to assist banks & financial institutions.

Connelly Co. Inc. (Summer only)
Bailey Rd, South Effingham, NH
(603) 522-6462; *Fax:* (603) 522-6348
R.J. Connelly, Pres
198 S. Main St, New Market, NH
(603) 659-3648; *Fax:* (603) 659-3681
Rob Connelly, Chairman

Consolidated Communications Consultants
1837 S.E. Harold St., Portland, OR 97202-4932
(503) 232-9787, (800) 929-5119, *Fax:* (503) 232-9787, (800) 929-5119
www.acmusicresearch.com
acmrl@myexcel.com
Eric Norberg, General Manager
Provide progmg, sls & mktg assistance for radio stns (AM mass-appeal, A/C stns a specialty).

Contemporary Communications
9408 Grand Gate St., Las Vegas, NV 89143
(702) 898-4669, *Fax:* (208) 567-6865
www.radioguys.net
larryfuss@cox.net
Larry G. Fuss, President
Progmg, opns & mgmt consulting for small- & medium-market radio stns; tech svcs; FCC compliance; computer software svcs.

Convergent Media Systems
190 Bluegrass Valley Pky., Suite 800, Alpharetta, GA 30305
(770) 369-9000, *Fax:* (770) 369-9100
www.convergent.com
convergent@convergent.com
William Wheless Jr., CFO
Bryan Allen, President
Provider of video & data technologies to support the communication & training needs of companies. Svcs include consultation, design, instal, net & systems mgmt; systems integration in the following areas: special event TV, business TV,desktop video, video production, videoconferencing, & interactive multimedia.

Cox & Cox, LLC
2454 Shiva Ct., St. Louis, MO 63011 63011
(636) 458-4780, *Fax:* (636) 273-1312
www.coxandcoxllc.com
bc@coxandcoxllc.com
Robert Cox, President
Linda Cox, Operations Dir
Media mergers & acquisitions, appraisals, consulting, expert testimony, receivership & workout.

Cross-Country Communications Inc.
Box 535, Suffern, NY 10901
(917) 652-3850, *Fax:* (208) 692-2181
www.cross-country.com
cccomm@aol.com
Joe Capobianco, President
Strategic planning, business dev, new product launches in media/entertainment & production for Radio-TV-Web.

Dave Gifford International
1142 Tano Del Este, Santa Fe, NM 87506
(505) 989-7007, *Fax:* (505) 988-1991
giff@talkgiff.com
Sls & sls management training, sls turnarounds & troubleshooting. Sls, mgmt & adv seminars. New account sls & client dev., creator of graduate school of sls.

David Tait Appraisal
1848 Laurel Canyon Rd, Los Angeles, CA 90046-2029
(323) 654-8420, *Fax:* (323) 656-1854
dta87@earthlink.net
David M. Tait, BCBA, President
Fair market value appraisals of radio/TV/CATV for purchase allocation, finance, estate planning, ESOPs, bankruptcy.

DDS Sales Training
6904 W. Sagamore Cir., Sioux Falls, SD 57106
(605) 361-9923, *Fax:* (605) 361-1828
ddssales@sio.mideo.net
Darrell Solberg, President
Billy Solberg, Operations Dir
Radio sls training /consulting, mgmt training/consulting & mktg/adv seminars for businesses.

Direct Mail Express Inc.
2441 Bellevue Ave., Daytona Beach, FL 32114
(386) 257-2500, *Fax:* (386) 271-3001
www.dmenet.com
tpanaggio@dmenet.com
Mike Panaggio, CEO
Mike Waither, President
High-impact, direct-mail campaigns, data base mgmt, audience rsch via cluster-targeted mktg, market exclusive.

DIS Consulting Corp.
10 Waterside Plaza, #33D, New York, NY 10010-2608
(212) 213-6872, *Fax:* (212) 213-6876
www.disconsultingcorporation.com
dougsheer@aol.com
Douglas I. Sheer, CEO
Regina C. Sheer, General Manager
Mktg consultants to 1,000 equipment manufacturers since 1982. Mktg consultation, business plan writing, financial & market rsch, mktg & distribution plans.

Donald A Perry & Associates Inc.
Box 1275, Newport News, VA 23601
(757) 877-4367, *Fax:* (757) 693-2885
dperry@cablefirst.net
Donald A. Perry, President
Mgmt, brokerage & appraisal svcs to the cable TV industry.

E. Alvin Davis & Associates Inc.
35 Hampton Ln., Cincinnati, OH 45208
(513) 325-5600, (513) 321-9661, *Fax:* (513) 272-2303
www.ealvin.com
ealvin@ealvin.com
E. Alvin Davis, President
Ted McAllister, Operations Dir
Provides expert counsel to oldies stns.

Edwin Tornberg & Co. Inc.
8917 Cherbourg Dr., Potomac, MD 20854
(301) 983-8700, *Fax:* (301) 299-2297
Edwin Tornberg, President
Negotiators for purchase & sale of radio, TV stns & CATV systems; appraisers & financial advisers; mgmt consultants.

Electronicast Corp.
9959 Old Orchard Ln., Upper Lake, CA 95485
(707) 275-9397, *Fax:* (707) 257-9502
www.electronicast.com
massaf@electronicast.com
Market forecast consulting concern for the fiber-optic, optoelectronic, telecommunication & CATV industries. Multi-client & custom reports available.

Enterprise Appraisal Co.
489 Devon Park Dr., Suite 320, Wayne, PA 19087
(610) 687-5855, *Fax:* (610) 971-0760
www.enterpriseappraisal.com
Evaluates communications-oriented assets, such as equipment & real estate, for TV, CATV, radio, cellular systems, & satellites.
Washington, DC
(202) 887-0948;
New York, NY
(212) 517-8037;

EnVest Media, LLC
6802 Patterson Ave., Richmond, VA 23226 23226
(804) 282-5561, *Fax:* (804) 282-5703
www.envestmedia.com
mitt@envestmedia.com
Mitt Younts, General Manager
Nationwide radio, TV acquisition, valuation, financing & consulting firm. The company provides brokerage svcs to stn transaction, appraisal svcs to stn owners & financial institutions. The group secures debt & equity acquisition financing,offers consulting & asset mgmt svcs, acting as court appointed receivers or trustees for bcst stns.

Equidata
724 Thimble Shoals Blvd., Newport News, VA 23606
(757) 873-3395, (757) 873-0519, *Fax:* (800) 873-9752, (757) 873-1224
www.equidata.net
Mary Emmett, President
Nationwide collection agency/credit reporting agency.

Evalueserve, Inc.
Box 2037, Saratoga, CA 95070-0037
(408) 872-1078, *Fax:* (720) 294-0943
evalueserve.com
alok.aggarwal@evalueserve.com
Alok Aggarwal, Chairman
Telecommunications, high-technology, businessrsch, data anaylsis.

Executive Broadcast Services
30 MoBray Ct., Colorado Springs, CO 80906
(719) 579-6676, *Fax:* (719) 579-6664
www.executivebroadcast.com
skip@executivebroadcast.com
Skip Joeckel, President
Offers talk progmg & sports guides.

Executive Decision Systems Inc.
6421 W. Weaver Dr., Littleton, CO 80123-3815
(303) 795-9090, *Fax:* (303) 795-1970
www.retailinsights.com
dlenoble@comcast.net
Provide sls & mgmt training, focusing on generating long-term, loc direct revenues. Provides academic approach to media mktg to stns around the United States & abroad. System 21 is guaranteed to return 12 times the revenues within 150 daysor your money is refunded.

Executive Media Services
138 E. Waterford Dr., Seneca, SC 299672
(864) 985-1133, *Fax:* (864) 985-1137
www.executivecomm.com
excomm@bellsouth.net
Loc sls consulting for TV & radio stns, cable TV systems. Provides source for sls strategy & sls support, sls seminars; start-up & turnaround specialists. New revenue dev & sls, training, using the internet, the home of one-on-one sls &training.

The Exline Company
388 Lowell Avenue, Mill Valley, CA 94941
(415) 381-5473, *Fax:* (415) 381-5473
www.exlinecompany.com
exline@pacbell.net
Andrew P. McClure, President
Mgmt, financial rsch, appraisal, receiverships & bankruptcies. Station brokerage.

The Express Group
3175 Dwight St., San Diego, CA 92104
(619) 280-9061, *Fax:* (619) 280-9030
www.theexpressgroup.com
egmail@theexpressgroup.com
Byron Andrus, President
Roberta Andrus, Operations Dir
Design, fabrication, instal & lighting of news environments, newsrooms, interview & talkshow sets.

Eyewitness Newservice Inc.
Box 116, 182 Sound Beach Ave., Old Greenwich, CT 06870-0116
(203) 637-0044, *Fax:* (203) 698-0812
www.teenkidsnews.tv
primonews@aol.com
Albert Primo, President
TV news strategic planning, focus group rsch talent & mgmt, coaching. Cable news training; Internet Broadband Svc; TV production.
355 W. 52nd St., New York, NY 10019-6239
(212) 974-0606;
Al Primo, Exec Producer

Faraone Communications Inc./dba Worldwide Public Relations
75 West End Ave., Suite R-9A, New York, NY 10023
(212) 489-1313, *Fax:* (212) 489-8978
www.worldwidepublicrelations.com
ted.faraone@verizon.net
Ted Faraone, Chairman
PR svc to bcst, cable, radio, TV & other entertainment properties & media companies.

Faries & Associates
67 Central Ave., Los Gatos, CA 95030
(408) 354-7308, *Fax:* (408) 395-6670
www.fariesinc.com
David A. Faries, Operations Dir
Business forcasting & analysis.

Federal Engineering Inc.
Redwood Plaza II, 10600 Arrowhead Dr., Fairfax, VA 22030
(703) 359-8200, *Fax:* (703) 359-8204
www.fedeng.com
info@fedeng.com
Ronald F. Bosco, President
John E. Murray, Operations Dir
Strategic planning, coverage analysis, new product definition, market rsch, competitive analysis, rates & tariffs, bcst stn design, mergers & acquisitions, expert testimony, regulatory support.

Ferraro Communications Inc.
39 Byron Rd., Weston, MA 02493
(781) 235-5556, *Fax:* (781) 235-5558
Tom Ferraro, President
Concept, script & production/direction for coml, radio, film & videotape productions.

Florical Systems
4581 N. W. 6th St., Gainesville, FL 32609
(352) 372-8326, *Fax:* (352) 375-0859
www.florical.com
sales@florical.com
Jim Berry, General Sales Mgr
Manufacturer of TV automations, controls & effects.

FM Atlas - Publishing and Electronics
Box 336, Esko, MN 55733-0336
(218) 879-7676, *Fax:* (218) 879-7676
users.aol.com/fmatlas
fmatlas@aol.com
Bruce F. Elving, President
FM radio directory, rsch on FM-SCS & FM trans, FM-SCS receivers & newsletter.

Focal Press
30 Corporate Dr., Suite 400, Burlington, MA 01803
(781) 212-2212, *Fax:* (781) 313-4880
www.focalpress.com
j.tracy@elsevier.com
Joanne Tracy, General Manager
Chris Mebegon, Promotions Manager
Publishes professional tech books in bcstg, film, video, multimedia, theatre & photography.
Linacre House, Jordan Hill, Oxford,
011-44-1-865-310366;
Jennifer Welham, Chairman

Ford Foundation
Media, Arts, & Culture, 320 E. 43rd St., New York, NY 10017
(212) 573-5000, *Fax:* (212) 351-3649
www.fordfound.org

Franey, Muha & Alliant Inc.
9901 Business Pkwy., Suite B, Lanham, MD 20706
(301) 459-0055
www.franeymuhaalliant.com
Bill Franey, CEO
Insurance, bonding & benefits admin.
13921 Park Central Rd, Suite160, Herndon, VA
(703) 397-0977; *Fax:* (703) 397-0995
John Muha, Chairman

Frank Boyle & Co., L.L.C.
2001 W. Main St., Suite 280, Stamford, CT 06902 6902
(203) 969-2020
fboylebrkr@aol.com
Robert E. Richer, CEO
Frank Boyle, President
Radio & TV media brokerage, mergers & acquisitions/appraisals.

Frank N. Magid Associates Inc.
One Research Ctr., Marion, IA 52302
(319) 377-7345, *Fax:* (319) 377-5861
www.magid.com
mailia@magid.com
Brent Magid, CEO
Steve Ridge, President
Specialists in rsch-driven consultation to traditional & new media firms; svcs include strategic planning, web site evaluation & dev, program evaluation, talent search, coaching, TMI, & the Magid Network.
15260 Ventura Blvd, Suite 2130, Sherman Oaks, CA 91403-5307
(818) 263-3300; *Fax:* (818) 263-3311
Jack MacKenzie, Exec Vp
1775 Broadway, Suite 1401, New York, NY 10019-1903
(212) 974-2310; *Fax:* (212) 515-4540
Vicki Cohen, Exec Vp

Gary Stevens & Co.
Box 4880, Stamford, CT 06907-0880
(203) 966-6465, *Fax:* (203) 966-6522
deelmakur@aol.com
Gary Stevens, General Manager
Bcst mergers, acquistions & investment banking svcs.

George Moore & Associates Inc.
6918 Wildglen Dr., Suite 100 W, Dallas, TX 75230
(214) 369-5665, (800) 220-3287, *Fax:* (214) 369-5667
W. James Moore, President
Brokerage of radio, TV & CATV properties; asset & market appraisals; introduction to institutional financing sources.

George Rodman Associates
100 Christwood Blvd., Apt. 119, Covington, LA 70433-4601
(831) 626-1630, *Fax:* (831) 626-8662
grodman@viaworldwide.com
George T. Rodman, President
Sally M. Rodman, Operations Dir
Provides stns, networks, groups & program suppliers with mktg counseling & promotional materials, including adv campaigns, logos, on-air design, TV spots & animation.

Getty Images
601 N. 34th St., Seattle, WA 98103
(206) 925-5000, *Fax:* (206) 925-5001
www.gettyimages.com
feedback@gettyimages.com
Jonathan Klein, CEO
Business & mgmt consulting, training, long-term strategic planning, organizations analysis, mktg positioning; seminars on goal setting, leadership, mgmt skills, sls training. Retail training.

Gilbert Communications
4101 Legends Way, Maryville, TN 37801
(865) 982-2889, *Fax:* (865) 977-6633
rwgilbert@charter.com
Robert W. Gilbert, President
Full-svc radio/TV news consulting, writing seminars, staff motivation, news policy formulation, profit center strategy & Broadcast News Handbook.

Greenwood Performance Systems LLC
907 S. Detroit, Suite 720, Tulsa, OK 74120
(800) 331-9115, (918) 665-7252, *Fax:* (918) 665-7233, (800) 378-2544
www.greenwoodperformance.com
info@greenwoodperformance.com
Jena Rhea, President
Bcst-specific sls & mgmt training, seminars & courses including sls mgmt consultation, strategic planning, compensation, selection & evaluation.

Guidestar Corp.
10600 Arrowhead Dr., Fairfax, VA 22030
(703) 352-5700, *Fax:* (703) 359-8204
www.fedeng.com
info@fedeng.com
Ronald F. Bosco, General Manager
Mktg communications & PR specifically tailored to serve the telecommunications & info processing marketplaces.

Halper & Associates
550 Adams St. #365, Quincy, MA 02169
(617) 786-0666, *Fax:* (617) 786-1809
www.donnahalper.com
dlh@donnahalper.com
Donna L. Halper, President
Radio progmg & mgmt consulting, market studies, format changes, music library software. Staff training, motivation. Specialize in small & medium markets, new owners, turnarounds. Also bcst historian.

Hoffman Schutz Media Capital Inc.
2044 West California St., San Diego, CA 92110
(619) 291-7070
www.hs-media.com
Anthony M. Hoffman, President
David E. Schutz, Operations Dir
Strategic planning for lender & investor appraisals & litigation support.

Host Communications Inc.
546 E. Main St., Lexington, KY 40508
(859) 226-4678, *Fax:* (859) 226-4391
www.hostcommunications.com
College sports bcstg & TV syndications; publishing & sports mktg.

Howard Burkat Communications
16 Drake Rd., Scarsdale, NY 10583
(914) 723-9043, (914) 723-1581, *Fax:* (914) 472-6225
www.burkat.com
hburkat@burkat.com
Sls, mktg & mgmt consulting for TV, cable, radio, domestic & international. Planning analysis, rsch & recruiting.

The Howard-Sloan-Koller Group
300 E. 42nd St., New York, NY 10016
(212) 661-5250, *Fax:* (212) 557-9178
www.hsksearch.com
hsk@hsksearch.com
Edward R. Koller Jr., President
Exec search & consulting in the cable, infotechnology, entertainment, new media & publishing industries.

The Image Generators
Div/DBA: (A division of Voicelines Inc.)
18156 Darnell Dr., Olney, MD 20832
(301) 924-5700, *Fax:* (301) 570-8916
www.imagegenerators.com
mweiner@imagegenerators.com
Michael J. Weiner, CEO
Mktg & mgmt issues; talent training workshops & coaching.

Inergize Digital Media
1600 Utica Ave. S., Suite 400, Minneapolis, MN 55416
(952) 417-3294, *Fax:* (952) 417-3407
www.ingerizedigitalmedia.com
Jason Gould, General Manager
Website hosting & dev, platforms, multimedia.

International Media Consulting, Inc.
48 Mountain Rd., Farmington, CT 06032-2341
(860) 677-9688
www.muchvibe.ca
muchvibe@muchmusic.com
The source for top music videos, interviews, concert specials, concert listings and classic clips from the CHUM music video archive. Hip Hop, Rap, R&B, Old School, Reggae and more.

IPI Report
Div/DBA: The International Journalism Magazine
320 Lee Hills Hall, Columbia, MO 65211
(573) 884-7542, *Fax:* (573) 884-1870
ipi-report@missouri.edu
Shawn Donnelly, Operations Dir
IPI Report defends, celebrates, relects & explores the international media & freedom of expression.
132A Neff Annex, Columbia, MO
(573) 884-7542;
Stuart H. Loory, Editor

J.M. Miller
Box 190, Ashburn, VA 20146
703-729-7745, *Fax:* 703-729-7745
broadcastappraisal@yahoo.com
Jan M. Miller, President
Bcst TV, DTV, AM, FM, production, satellite, microwave facility & equipment inspection, asset appraisal reports, engrg evaluation overviews & consulting svcs. For valuation, acquisition, finance, purchase price allocation, ad valorem tax,insurance, leasing, liquidation & litigation.

Jay Mitchell Associates Inc.
4 Ventana, Aliso Viejo, CA 92656
(949) 533-4912, *Fax:* (949) 666-5045
www.jaymitchell.com
mitchell @jaymitchell.com
Jay Mitchell, President
Mgmt, mktg, progmg, promotions consulting; market analysis, web site design & consulting.

John P. Allen Airspace Consultants Inc.
290 Marsh Lakes Dr., Fernandina Beach, FL 32034
(904) 261-6523, *Fax:* (904) 277-3651
johnpallenairspace.com
maryjpa@bellsouth.net
Mary C. Lowe, President
Conducts FAA aeronautical evaluations as specified in Subpart C of Part 77 of the Federal Aviation Regulations.

Jon Ulmer & Associates
2176 Highpoint Rd., Snellville, GA 30078
(770) 979-3031, *Fax:* (770) 979-3789
julmercpa@comcast.net
John R. Ulmer, President
Accounting, computer & financial mgmt consulting.

Jones TM, Inc.
2002 Academy, Dallas, TX 75234
(972) 406-6800, *Fax:* (972) 406-6890
www.jonestm.com
jtm@jonestm.com
David Graupner, CEO
Jay Noble, General Sales Mgr
The world's leading supplier of jingles, production & imaging libraries, wkly music svc & music libraries on hard drive.

Kagan Media Appraisals, a division of Media Central/Primedia
One Lower Ragsdale Dr., Building One, Suite 130, Monterey, CA 93940
(831) 624-1536, *Fax:* (831) 625-3225
www.Kagan.com
info@kagan.com
Robin Flynn, Programming Director
Specializes in the valuation & appraisal of media & communications properties. As part of the Media Central Group of Companies, we maintain the industry's most comprehensive data base of stn values, so we know what yesterday's stns sold for,what buyers are paying today & what they are likely to pay tomorrow. Svcs include: Fair market valuations, expert witness testimony, asset appraisals, ESOP valuations, fairness opinions, minority interest valuations, financial feasibility studies,strategic planning, custom rsch & reports & consulting.

Kagan World Media/Primedia, Inc.
One Lower Ragsdale Dr., Building One, Suite 130, Monterey, CA 93940
(831) 624-1536, *Fax:* (831) 625-3225
www.kagan.com
Larry Gerbrandt, COO
Sandie Borthwick, Operations Dir
Strategic conferences on media & communications topics, including interactive, multimedia, telecommunications, entertainment deals & financing.

Kalba International Inc.
116 McKinley Ave., New Haven, CT 06515
(203) 397-2199, *Fax:* (781) 240-2657
www.kalbainternational.com
kalba@comcast.net
Kas Kalba, President
F. Roberts, Operations Dir
Consulting & advisory svcs on telecommunications, bcstg & cable TV, including international ventures, due diligence, litigation support.

Kane Reece Associates Inc.
822 South Ave. W., Westfield, NJ 07090-1460
(908) 317-5757, *Fax:* (908) 317-4434
www.kanereece.com
info@kanereece.com
Norval D. Reece, Operations Dir
Asset appraisals, business valuations, due diligence, expert testimony, property tax compliance & control, system mgmt & mgmt/engrg consulting.

Kempff Communications Co.
3301 Bayshore Blvd., Suite 1407, Tampa, FL 33629 33629
(813) 258-3433
www.kepffbarr.com
kempffcc@aol.com
Cheryl Beach, CEO
Ron Kempff, President
Aurelia Serna, VP
Pat McMahon, Programming Director
Broker & consultant also offering financial & mgmt svcs, court ordered sale of stns.

Kent Burkhart's Office Inc.
133 East End Dr., Key Biscayne, FL 33149
(305) 439-8871, *Fax:* (305) 361-0650
radiokent@aol.com
Kent Burkhart, President
Media consultant to radio stns, networks, the Internet, cable TV, audio & product mktg. LMA liaisons & negotiators.

The Kompas Group
Box 250813, Milwaukee, WI 53225-6513
(262) 781-0188, *Fax:* (262) 781-5313
www.yourlptvsource.com
kompasgroup@toast.net
John Kompas, President
Jackie Kompas, Operations Dir
Financial & mktg svcs for LPTV, audience demographic reports, stn coverage maps, financial & strategic planning.

Kovsky & Miller Research
37 Sawmill River Rd., Hawthorne, NY 10532
(914) 347-3606, *Fax:* (914) 347-3976
kovskymiller.com
hkkmrresearch@aol.com
Harry Kovsky, President
Specialists in content & format analysis of loc & network TV news & entertainment programs, promotional analysis, ratings analysis, audience promotional rsch & audience survey rsch.

Kozacko Media Services
Box 948, Elmira, NY 14902
(607) 733-7138, *Fax:* (607) 733-1212
www.kozackomediaservices.com
rkozacko@stny.rr.com
Richard L. Kozacko, President
Appraisals, current market evaluations of radio/TV stns & bcst acquisition planning.
6890 E. Sunrise Dr., Box 120-40, Tucson, AZ 85732-2040
(520) 299-4869; *Fax:* (520) 844-8559
George W. Kimble, Assoc
1071 Club Dr., Keswick, VA 22947-2613
(434) 244-2653; *Fax:* (434) 244-2666
W. Donald Roberts Jr., Assoc

KSL 5 Television
55 N. 300 W., Salt Lake City, UT 84180
(801) 575-5555, *Fax:* (801) 575-5830
www.ksl.com
Bruce Christensen, President
Greg James, Operations Dir
An advertiser-supported NABTS news & info svc available through TV decoders or personal computers equipped with modems. Modem number is (801) 575-5911.

Lawson & Associates Architects
7939 Norfolk Ave., Suite 200, Bethesda, MD 20814
(301) 654-1600, *Fax:* (301) 654-1601
www.lawsonarch.com
blawson@lawsonarch.com
Bruce Lawson, Operations Dir
Consulting architectural design & construction mgmt svcs for the TV & cable industry; facility planning, design & coordination of construction svcs.

Liberty Hill Corp.
Box 253003, West Bloomfield, MI 48325
(248) 737-3000, *Fax:* (248) 737-3555
barryzate@aol.com
Ronald Zate, President
Barry Zate, Operations Dir
Consulting for radio progmg, talent & admin svcs; on-site seminars, problem targeting & complete strategic planning for the communications industry.

Lipson & Co.
1900 Ave. of the Stars, Suite 2810, Los Angeles, CA 90067
(310) 277-4646, *Fax:* (310) 277-8585
www.lipsonco.com
inquries@lipsonco.com
Howard R. Lipson, President
Executive recruiting for international & domestic bcstg, cable, entertainment, adv, mktg, finance, mdse, licensing & digital medai.

Locations Tasmania Pty. Ltd.
Box 537, Sandy Bay, Tasmania, 07005
61-362-243578, *Fax:* 61-362-24248211
wildangels@bigpond.com
Coordination svcs for international film & TV production. Second unit svcs stock footage library.

Loral Skynet
2400 Research Blvd., Suite 200, Rockville, MD 20850
(301) 258-8101, *Fax:* (301) 258-3222
www.loralskynet.com
info@loralskynet.com
Terry Hart, President
International telecommunication svcs in Asia Pacific rgn, specializing in private networks via satellite.

Lund Consultants to Broadcast Management Inc.
840 Hinckley Rd., Suite 123, Burlingame, CA 94010-1505
(650) 692-7777, *Fax:* (650) 692-7799
www.lundradio.com
lundradio@aol.com
John C. Lund, President
Dan R. Spice, Operations Dir
Experts in progmg consulting; multiopoly strategy. Adult contemp, country, top 40, rock, classic rock, oldies, news-talk, music, formatics, proms, talent dev & perceptual rsch.

Mahlum Architects
71 Columbia, Suite 400, Seattle, WA 98104
(206) 441-4151, *Fax:* (206) 441-0478
www.mahlum.com
info@mahlum.com
Design; tech consulting; feasibility & facilities studies; cost analysis & construction admin for TV/radio stns, production & equipment storage facilities, & film studios.

Margret Haney Media Brokerage & Consultants
2995 Woodside Rd., Bldg. 400, Woodside, CA 94062-2446
(408) 557-8887, *Fax:* (408) 557-0808
www.margarethaney.com
hhmargret@yahoo.com
Margret Haney, CEO
Media brokerage/consulting, adv, media buyers.

Mark Blinoff Inc.
1837 S.E. Harold St., Portland, OR 97202-4932

(503) 232-9787, (800) 929-5119, *Fax:* (503) 232-9787
acmrl@myexcel.com
Eric Norberg, General Manager
Consulting firm for radio bcstrs, including sls dev, mgmt training & progmg.

Marketing & Creative Services
Div/DBA: (Division of Frank N. Magid Associates Inc.)
One Research Ctr., Marion, IA 52302
(319) 377-7345, *Fax:* (319) 377-5861
www.magid.com
mailia@magid.com
Brent Magid, CEO
Steve Ridge, President
Bill Hague, Operations Dir
Rsch & consultation.
15260 Ventura Blvd., Suite 2130, Sherman Oaks, CA 91403-5307
(818) 263-3300; *Fax:* (818) 263-3311
Jack MacKenzie, Exec Vp
1775 Broadway, Suite 1401, New York, NY 10019-1903
(201) 974-2310; *Fax:* (212) 515-4540
Vicki Cohen, Exec Vp

Marshall & Stevens Inc.
355 S. Grand Ave, Ste 1759, ste. 1750, Los Angeles, CA 90017
(213) 612-8000, *Fax:* (213) 612-8010
www.marshall-stevens.com
info@marshall-stevens.com
Fred Thomas, Operations Dir
Natl appraisal firm with extensive bcstg client base. Value real estate, equipment, intangible assets & overall business valuations. Assist in financing sls, purchase price allocation, & cast segregation.
701 Market Street, # 370, St. Louis, MO 63101-1830
(800) 325-7337, (800)-325-7337;
Raymond Essma, Vp Central Div
1156 Ave. of the Americas, #703, New York, NY 10036-2702
(212) 425-4300;
Wiley Scott, Vp Sls

Maxagrid
3939 Belt Line Rd., Suite 250, Addison, TX 75001
(972) 241-2110, *Fax:* (972) 241-2174
www.maxagrid.com
maxagrid@maxagrid.com
Jim Tiller, President
Karen Brian, General Manager
Yield mgmt systems for bcst in USA, Australia, & Canada. Systems & strategies that help mgrs improve yields on adv revenues.

Maxwell Media Group
6053 Bunker Hill, Pittsburgh, PA 15206
(412) 441-2020, *Fax:* (412) 661-9377
Bill Maxwell, President
Consultant.

Mayo Communications Inc.
Box 82784, Tampa, FL 33682
(813) 264-5050, *Fax:* (813) 264-5353
Lincoln A. Mayo, President
Media brokerage, appraisals for bcst & print. Consulting, concerning media sls & acquisitions.

Mazer & Associates
3452 Grayton Rd., Detroit, MI 48224
(313) 885-5686
John Mazer, J.D. Jr., President
Radio & TV progmg svcs, market rsch, format design, talent evaluation, license renewal preparation, labor rel, mgmt & admin consulting.

McVay Media
2001 Crocker Rd., Suite 260, Cleveland, OH 44145
(440) 892-1910
www.jamesonbroadcast.com/radio
jamie@jamesonbcast.com
Specializes in short-form entertainment, info programs & promotions.

Media & Marketing
4245 Sarah St., Burbank, CA 91505
(818) 753-9510, (818) 558-3924
www.mediaandmarketing.com
mel.lambert@mediaandmarketing.com
Mel Lambert, General Sales Mgr
Consulting svc for the audio & multimedia industries.

Media Communications Group Inc.
Box 335, 11 Spiral Dr., Suite 3, Florence, KY 41042
(859) 647-0055, *Fax:* (859) 647-2611
www.paragoncomm.com
jpierce@paragoncomm.com
John L. Pierce, President
Rebecca Neal, Operations Dir
Representing, consulting & mgmt svcs to radio stns nationwide.

Media Economics
69 N. Sheridan Ave., Bethpage, NY 11714
(516) 931-0248
jdsouthmayd@msn.com

Media Perspectives
127 Greensward Ln., Cherry Hill, NJ 08002
(856) 482-7979, *Fax:* (856) 482-0957
Steven G. Apel, President
Progmg & mktg counseling through applied audience & advertiser rsch.

Media Sales Management
Potsdamer Strasse 31, Berlin, 10783
49-30-215-30300, *Fax:* 49-30-215-1182
Offers a complete package of bcst svcs, finance, acquisition, progmg sls mgmt, rsch & valuations. German & European specialists.
Sthamerstrasse 58, Hamburg,
49-40-605-2114; *Fax:* 49-40-605-1762
Norbert Schmidt, Pres

The Mediacenter
1500 Harbor Blvd., Weehawken, NJ 07086
(866) 412-0866, *Fax:* (201) 348-1761
www.mediacenteronline.com
info@mediacenteronline.com
Barbara Zeiger, President
Russell Sands, General Manager
Promote increased mktg professionalism among TV execs & mgrs; provide sls support tools that identify & dev new adv budgets.

Mercer Capital Management Inc.
5860 Ridgeway Center Pkwy., 4th Fl., Memphis, TN 38120
(901) 685-2120, *Fax:* (901) 685-2199
www.mercercapital.com
mcm@mercercapital.com
Lisa Doble, Operations Dir
Mercer Capital provides high-quality independent business appraisals & other financial advisory svcs for all types of media including radio.
206 Kentuckey Towers, Louisville, KY
(502) 585-6340;
James E. Graves, Vp

Metro Orlando Film & Television Commission
301 E. Pine St., Suite 900, Orlando, FL 32801
(407) 422-7159, *Fax:* (407) 841-9069
www.filmorlando.com
suzy@filmorlando.com
Suzy Allen, Operations Dir
One stop permitting, locations library, location scouting, community familiarization tours, Filmbook with complete listings of crews, technicians & production support vendors.

Multimedia Research Group Inc. (MRG, Inc.)
1754 Technology Dr., Suite 132, San Jose, CA 95110
(408) 453-5553, *Fax:* (408) 453-5559
www.mrgco.com
info@mrgco.com
Gary Schultz, President
Provides strategic consulting & published market intelligence on content dev, content distribution, channels & networks.

Nashville Mayor's Office of Film
222 2nd Ave., Suite 418, Nashville, TN 37201
(615) 880-1827, *Fax:* (615) 862-6025
www.filmnashville.com
andyvr@nashville.org
Tessa Atkins, General Manager
Location scouting, permits, produce annual production directory, assist with all logistics of TV/film/video projects, liaison to media & govt.

Nathan M. Nickolaus
320 E. McCarthy St., Jefferson City, MO 65101-3115
(573) 634-6313, *Fax:* (573) 634-6504
nnickolaus@jeffcity.mo.org
Nathan M. Nickolaus, Consultant

National Strategies Inc.
1100 H St. N.W., Suite 1200, Washington, DC 20005
(202) 349-7001, *Fax:* (202) 783-1041
www.nationalstrategiesinc.com
daylward@natstrat.com
Al Gordon, CFO
Pub policy strategies & implementation, business & investment dev.
Via San Senatore 10, Milan, Italy
+39 02 720 94266; *Fax:* +39 02 720 94759
14 E. 60th St., Suite 1002, New York, NY 10022-1006
(212) 758-0690, (212) 750-6518;

Navigant International
945 Hornet Dr., Suite 101, Hazelwood, MO 63042
(314) 592-3800, *Fax:* (314) 592-3900
Mike Million, Operations Dir
Corporate & leisure travel, specializes in promotional packages & incentive programs.

New England Media L.L.C.
Box 594, Willimantic, CT 06226
(860) 456-7400, *Fax:* (860) 456-5688
mcrice@prodigy.net
Michael Rice, Operations Dir
Media brokers, consultants & appraisers specializing in radio in the Northeast.
50 Kaya Lane, Mansfield Center, CT 06250-1332
(860) 455-1414;
Michael Rice, Mgng Ptnr

Newbrough Associates Inc.
Box 1822, Des Moines, IA 50305-1822
(515) 244-8909, *Fax:* (515) 244-8909
wbn@att.net
Bill Newbrough, President
Provides alternative advisory consultaions worldwide, focusing on communications. Forty years of mass media & mgmt experiences. WISDOM+RESEARCH=SUCCESS.

NEWSDirections
1521 Rocky Knoll Ln., Dacula, GA 30019-6754
(770) 569- 2277
www.bravotv.com
support@bravotv.com
Lauren Zalaznick, President
Bravo offers innovative arts & entertainment progmg with a unique point of view featuring original series, theater, dance, music & documentaries 24 hours.

Nick Anthony & Associates Inc.
1795 W. Market St., Akron, OH 44313
(330) 864-2268, *Fax:* (330) 864-2261
www.nickanthony.com
nick@nickanthony.com
Nick Anthony, President
Mktg, progmg & motivational consultant.

Noll & Associates
20 Sunnyside Avenue, Suite I, Mill Valley, CA 94941
(415) 888-8460, *Fax:* (415) 888-8462
www.nollmedia.com
kennen@nollmedia.com
Kennen Williams, President
Bcst mktg/sls training, new business dev & organizational dev.

Norman Fischer & Associates Inc.
Box 5308, Austin, TX 78763
(512) 476-9457, *Fax:* (512) 476-0540
www.nfainc.com
terrill@nfainc.com
Terrill Fischer, President
Brokerage in radio, TV & cable, consultation in mgmt & opns, appraisals, feasibility studies, expert testimony, financial planning & assistance.

Northwest Broadcasting Co.
Box 332, Dallastown, PA 17313-0332
(815 308-7613
www.level3.com
jeff.huffman@level3.com
Jeff Huffman, General Manager
VYVX's UpSouth Teleport offers domestic U.S. & international uplink, downlink & transponder service for video (analog or compressed), data, & voice telecommunication. Fiber-optic & microwave links to points of presence for major bcst & telcolocations in the Atlanta, GA, metropolitan area. Direct access to all C- & Ku-band satellites in domestic U.S. arc & AOR. Svcs include program origination; tape playback, recording & editing; standards conversion; encryption; & turnarounds.

The Omnia Group
601 South Blvd., Tampa, FL 33606

PROFESSIONAL SERVICES

(800) 525-7117, *Fax:* (813) 254-8558
www.omniagroup.com
mcleveland@omniagroup.com
Same-day response on best industry-validated selection tools that help hire the right person the first time.

Ott & Associates
9225 Chatham Grove Ln., Suite D, Richmond, VA 23236
(804) 276-7202, *Fax:* (804) 745-7778
www.rickott.com
rick@rickott.com
Rick Ott, President
Problem solving, consultation in complete confidentiality. Mgmt consulting.

Palazzo Intercreative
308 Occidental Ave. South, Suite 200, Seattle, WA 98104
(206) 328-5555, *Fax:* (206) 324-4348
www.palazzo.com
palazzo@palazzo.com
Richard Roberts, President
Stn identity design & consultation svcs, including on-air, print, outdoor, graphics, syndicated animation packages, movie & news opns, & radio spots.

Paragon Media Strategies
12345 W. Alameda Pkwy., Suite 325, Denver, CO 80228
(303) 922-5600, *Fax:* (303) 922-1589
www.paragonmediastrategies.com
info@paragonmediastrategies.com
Mike Henry, CEO
Media rsch & consulting.

Patrick Communications L.L.C.
6805 Douglas Legum Dr., Suite 100, Elkridge, MD 21075 21075
(410) 799-1740, *Fax:* (410) 799-1705
www.patcomm.com
larry@patcomm.com
Larry Patrick, Managing Partner
Susan Patrick, Managing Partner
Grey Guy, Managing Partner
Jason James, Vice President
David Benton, Analyst
Stn brokerage, investment banking, mgmt consulting svcs, appraisals & opns consulting.

PMA Marketing Inc.
4359 S. Howell, Suite 106, Milwaukee, WI 53207
(414) 482-2638, *Fax:* (414) 483-1980
www.amfmtv.com
patrick@amfmtv.com
Patrick Martin, President
Buy & sell new & used bcst equipment, radio stn start-ups & turnarounds, problem solving for difficult bcst situations.

Point Broadcasting Company
Div/DBA: Point 3G
715 Broadway, Suite 320, Santa Monica, CA 90401
(310) 451-4430, *Fax:* (310) 451-1423
John Hearne, General Manager
Operating, technical & financial mgmt.

Pollack Media Group Inc.
860 Via De La Paz, Suite D2, Pacific Palisades, CA 90272
(310) 459-8556, *Fax:* (310) 454-5046
www.pollackmedia.com
hq@pollackmedia.com
Jeff Pollack, Chairman
Worldwide bcst progmg advisory firm, all facets of progmg, positioning, mktg, adv, rsch, music. All formats.

Poorman & Group
143-147 E. Main St., Suite 2C, Lock Haven, PA 17745
(570) 748-7000, *Fax:* (570) 748-7700
www.lockhaven.com
Stephen P. Poorman, President
Pennsylvania & Texas-based mgmt consulting firm offers 'no-charge' interviews to radio & TV stns relating to business & real estate issues. Specializes in organizing & mgng financially distressed businesses.

PR/PR
775 S. Kirkman Rd., Suite 104, Orlando, FL 32811
(407) 299-6128, *Fax:* (407) 299-2166
www.prpr.net
pam@prpr.net
Pam Lontos, President
Rick Dudnick, Operations Dir
Publicity in Radio, TV, print for speakers & authors.

Price Waterhouse Coopers
1 North Wacker Drive, Chicago, IL 60606
(312) 298-2000, *Fax:* (312) 298-2001
www.pwc.com
Provides valuation consulting svcs for acquisitions, swaps, estate planning & litigation.

The R Corp.
2477 Stickney Point Rd., Suite 201 B, Sarasota, FL 34231
(941) 924-2400, *Fax:* (941) 924-1650
rcorp@comcast.net
Consulting to electronic media, cable, wireless, & bcstg.

R. Miller Hicks & Co.
1011 W. 11th St., Austin, TX 78703
(512) 477-7000, *Fax:* (512) 477-9697
www.rmhicks.com
millerhicks@rmhicks.com
R. Miller Hicks, President
Brokerage, financing, mgmt consulting.

R.F. Technologies Corp.
12 Foss Rd., Lewiston, ME 04240
(207) 777-7778, *Fax:* (207) 777-7784
www.rftechnologies.net
info@rftechnologies.net
George M. Harris, President
Provides file engrg & svc for TV & FM antennas, transmission lines, diplexers & combiners.

Rattigan Resources
3409 Wilshire Rd., Portsmouth, VA 23703
(757) 484-3017
www.mcvaymedia.com
mcvaymedia@aol.com
Doris McVay, General Manager
Consultant radio stns in progmg various formats.
Atlanta
628 Braidwood Dr., Atlanta, GA
Fax: (770) 795-1022

Ray H. Rosenblum Sales & Management Consultant
Box 38296, Pittsburgh, PA 15238
(412) 362-6311, *Fax:* (412) 362-6317
rayhrosenblum@hotmail.com
Ray H. Rosenblum, Consultant
Consultant & appraiser for radio & TV stns & political candidates, with focus on mgmt, sls, proms, news & PR.

RBC Daniels L.P.
3200 Cherry Creek S. Dr., Suite 500, Denver, CO 80209
(303) 778-5555, *Fax:* (303) 778-5599
www.rbcdaniels.com
info@rbcdaniels.com
Brian Deevy, Chairman
Provides both mergers & acquisitions, corporate financial svcs to the cable telecommunications, media & technology industries.
711 5th Ave, Suite 405, New York, NY 10022-3111
(212) 935-5900; *Fax:* (212) 863-4859
Greg Ainsworth, Sr Mgng Dir
David Tolliver, Mgng Dir, Media Bcst Group

Rees Associates Inc.
Rees Plaza at East Wharf, 9211 Lake Hefner Pkwy, Suite 300, Oklahoma City, OK 73120
(405) 942-7337, (888) 942-7337, *Fax:* (405) 948-1261
www.rees.com
rees@rees.com
Leroy James Jr., President
Kristina Dover Jr., Promotions Manager
Bcst & production facility design; architectural svcs; facility business plans; interior design; studio design; equipment planning, consulting.
1801 N. Lamar St., Suite 600, Dallas, TX 75202-1712
(214) 522-7337; *Fax:* (214) 522-0444
Frank Rees Jr., Pres
The Metropolis Bldg.
951 Peachtree St. N.E., Atlanta, GA 30309-3918 United Kingdom
(404) 351-6869; *Fax:* (404) 351-8343

Restivo Communications/Starstruck Entertainment Company
73 Widdicombe Hill Blvd., Suite 1515, Toronto, ON M9R 4B3 Canada
(416) 242-7009
www.prmediaconnection.com
Peter J. Restivo, President
Bcst & media consultants; media training, MOW development.

Richard A. Foreman Associates Inc.
330 Emery Dr. E., Stamford, CT 06902-2210
(203) 327-2800, *Fax:* (203) 967-9393
www.rafamedia.com
raf@rafamedia.com
Richard A. Foreman, President
Fair market evaluations & asset appraisals, media brokerage, stn financing, & mgmt/production consultation.

Roehling Broadcast Services Ltd.
7340 Oak Knoll Dr., Indianapolis, IN 46217 46217
(317) 887-1945, *Fax:* (317) 887-1947
roehlingbroadcast.com
edradiobr@aol.com
Edward W. Roehling, President
Sandra Roehling, Operations Dir
Bcst appraisers, brokers, consultants, also financing, sls, mgmt consultation.

RPM Radio Programming & Management
1133 W. Longlake Rd., Suite 200, Bloomfield Hills, MI 48302
(888) 776-0006, *Fax:* (248) 647-2663
www.tophitsusa.com
info@tophitsusa.com
Thomas M. Krikorian, President
Top Hits U.S. wkly CD svc & CD libraries including Solid Gold, Spectrum A/C & Country One; CD Christmas library.

Rumbaut & Co.
555 N.E. 34th St., Suite 2701, Miami, FL 33137-4060
(305) 868-0000, *Fax:* (305) 571-0433
www.rumbaut.com
julio@rumbaut.com
Julio Rumbaut, President
Media brokers & consultants in all facets of the TV & radio industries.

S C Research International Inc.
1317 Third Ave., Suite 100, New York, NY 10021
(212) 867-6060, *Fax:* (212) 867-6579
www.scri.com
info@scri.com
Desmond C. Chaskelson, General Manager
Syndicated reports & custom rsch for manufacturers & investors in bcstg, professional video & audio; publishers of Broadcast Equipment Marketplace (BEM), Professional Video Marketplace (PFM), Professional Multi-Media Marketplace (PMM),European Telemedia Marketplace (ETM), Asian Telemedia Marketplace (ATM).

San Antonio Film Commission
203 S. St. Mary's St., 2nd Fl., San Antonio, TX 78298
(210) 207-6730, *Fax:* (210) 207-6843
www.filmsanantonio.com
filmsa@filmsanantonio.com
Drew Mayer-Oakes, General Manager
City film commission. Photo Library. Liaison with all city offices. Filming permits. Parking assistance.

SATMAGAZINE.COM
800 Siesta Way, Sonoma, CA 95476
(707) 939-9306, *Fax:* (707) 939-9235
www.satnews.com
design@satnews.com
Publishers of the mthy Satmagazine online magazine on coml satellite systems. Also available on a CD-ROM & through the web at http://www.satnews.com.

Satterfield & Perry Inc.
7211 Fourth Ave. S., St. Petersburg, FL 33707
(727) 345-7338, *Fax:* (727) 345-3809
www.satterfieldandperry.com
eraust@prodigy.net
Robert Austin, President
John Willis, Operations Dir
Radio, TV, broker, mgmt & sls consultant, FDIC-approved appraiser & expert witness.
2020 S. Monroe St., Suite 302, Denver, CO 80210-3700
Al Perry, Pres Emeritus
Joe Benkert, Vp
Jim Birschbach, Vp
Box 362, Coos Bay, OR 97420-0041
(541) 751-0043, (541) 256-5553;
Dick McMahon, Vp
4918 W. 101st Terr., Overland Park, KS 66207-3431
(913) 649-5103; *Fax:* (913) 649-5103
Doug Stephens, Vp
131 Inwood Dr., Suite 302, Aiken, SC 29803-5613
(803) 649-0031, (803) 649-7786;
John Willis, Vp
169 Mountain Meadows Ln., Wetumpa, AL 36093-3855
(334) 514-2241, (334) 514-2291;
Ken Hawkins, Vp

SB Management
PO Box 12837, San Luis Obispo, CA 93401
(805) 543-9214
www.mikehesser.com
Michael@mikehesser.com
Michael Murray, CEO
Todd Marcelle, COO
Norm Bogan, VP Global Research
Dan Mahoney, Advisor
Assist in finding, evaluating, financing & structuring acquisitions. Also, consult mgmt & sls.

Seabrook Travel Consultants
4225 Sawgrass Dr., Summerville, SC 29420
(843) 552-0702, *Fax:* (843) 552-3717
larry@thekirbycompanies.com
Larry Kirby, CEO
Bcst incentive trips worldwide; all major sporting events; owned & operated by bcstrs.

Shane Media Services
2500 Tanglewilde, Suite 106, Houston, TX 77063
(713) 952-9221, *Fax:* (713) 952-1207
www.shanemedia.com
smsofc@shanemedia.com
Ed Shane, CEO
Renee Revett, Programming Director
Radio progmg and mgmt consultation, custom designed perceptual and qualitative rsch for electronic media outlets.

Shotmakers, Inc.
One Horizon Rd., Fort Lee, NJ 07024
(201) 886-0287, *Fax:* (201) 886-0287
www.shotmakers.org
info@shotmakers.org
Dan Robinson, President
Media consultant, original film & TV productions; novelist. Represent historic photos & film of New York City & Atlanta.

Skywatch Weather Center
347 Prestley Rd., Bridgeville, PA 15017
(412) 221-6000, (800) SKY-WATCH, *Fax:* (412) 221-3160
www.skywatchweather.com
airsci@skywatchweather.com
Dr.Stanley J. Penkala, President
Daniel Krywiecki, Operations Dir
Specially formatted weathercasts from the Skywatch Weather Center.

Smart Target Marketing
6800 Southwest 40th St., #304, Miami, FL 33155
(305) 667-6665, *Fax:* (305) 667-3508
www.smarttarget.com
contact@smarttarget.com
Custom strategic direct-mktg programs; complete promotional & adv svcs including direct mail/targeted mailing lists, telemarketing, data base, custom publishing, sls training, & interactive phone/prom, smart targets & prizm targeting svcs.

Soundtrack
162 Columbus Ave., Boston, MA 02116-5222
(617) 303-7500, *Fax:* (617) 303-7555
www.soundtrackgroup.com
Amy Blankenship, Operations Dir
Production, postproduction & custom music of all kinds; specializing in sound designs.
936 Broadway, New York, NY 10010-6013
(212) 420-6010;
Chris Rich, Opns Mgr

Southern Surveys
1551 Olde Mill Pl., Marietta, GA 30066
(678) 467-8650, *Fax:* (770) 924-3584
www.streetlevelviews.com
rick@streetlevelviews.com
Rick Phillips, President
Natl qualitative moderator for one-on-one rsch. Nationwide recruiting for auditorium music tests since 1986. Video market rsch.

SRCS/Markits
17 Royal Rd., Bangor, ME 04401
(207) 942-5548, *Fax:* (207) 942-9164
www.markits99.com
Steve Robbins, President
Client-directed mktg program for coml bcst properties (radio & TV).

Stonick Recruitment Inc.
1230 Lake Deeson Pointe, Lakeland, FL 33805
(863) 680-1379, *Fax:* (863) 680-1397
www.stonickrecruitment.com
stonick@gate.net
Chris Stonick, President
A natl radio sls consulting firm bringing 'recruitment adv' to radio (strictly new business dev).

StorerTV Inc.
Div/DBA: (formerly Peter Storer & Associates Inc.)
1361 W. Towne Sq. Rd., Mequon, WI 53092
(262) 241-9005, *Fax:* (262) 241-9036
www.storertv.com
doug@storertv.com
Peter Storer Jr., President
Doug Knight, General Sales Mgr
Storer Info System (SIMS): Multi-ch, multi-user, PC based TV program schedule, amortization & liability system, for linear & non-linear scheduling.

Structural System Technology Inc.
6867 Elm St., McLean, VA 22101
(703) 356-9765, *Fax:* (703) 448-0979
www.sst-towers.com
fred.purdy@sst-towers.com
Fred Purdy, P.E., President
Kaveh Mehrnama, P.E., Operations Dir
Structural engrg studies, analysis, design, modifications, inspections, fabrication & erection of towers & antenna structures.

Synovate
8600 N.W. 17th St., Suite 100, Miami, FL 33126
(305) 716-6800, *Fax:* (305) 716-6756
www.synovate.com
Richard Tobin, President
Full-svc mktg rsch company, specializing in the Hispanic market; focus group testing, awareness usage tracking studies, media ratings.
23151 Alde Dr, Suite C4, Laguna Hills, CA
(714) 598-9055;
Dave Thomas, VP/Gen Mgr

Szabo Associates Inc., Media Collection Professionals
3355 Lenox Rd. NE, 9th Fl., Atlanta, GA 30326
(404) 266-2464, *Fax:* (404) 266-2165
www.szabo.com
info@szabo.com
C. Robin Szabo, President
Experts in creditor & debtor rights; consulting media properties in the accounts receivable process; domestic & international collections.

TalentTrainers
10807 Waring Pl., Charlotte, NC 28277
(704) 541-0892, *Fax:* 1-800-787-4284
www.talenttrainers.com
brice@talenttrainers.com
Shirley Brice, President
Talent coaching for TV stns & newspapers. Media trainer for corporate executives. One-on-one sessions, small workshops & individual critiques. Weekly 'live' coaching chat on www.talent trainers.com.

The Ted Hepburn Co.
325 Garden Rd., Palm Beach, FL 33480 33480
(561) 863-8995, *Fax:* (561) 863-8997
tedhep2@mac.com
Ted Hepburn, President
Radio, TV & cable brokerage; appraisals.

Tele-Measurements Inc.
145 Main Ave., Clifton, NJ 07014-1078
(973) 473-8822, *Fax:* (973) 473-0521
www.tele-measurements.com
contact@telemeasurements.com
William E. Endres, President
Douglas W. Cook, General Sales Mgr
Bcst, professional video equipment, videotape, TV systems, teleconferencing, ongoing maintenance support, CCTV, equipment rentals.

Teletech Inc.
Box 85567, Westland, MI 48185
(734) 641-2300, *Fax:* (734) 641-2323
www.teletech-inc.com
Keith Johnson, Operations Dir
Antenna site mgmt; tower, studio & antenna construction & maintenance; frequency searches; FCC application preparation; EMI, radiation & microwave studies.

Television by Design Inc.
3277 Roswell Rd., Suite 714, Atlanta, GA 30305
(404) 873-3277, *Fax:* (404) 873-7900
www.tvbd.com
jay@tvbd.com
Jay Antzakas, President
Creators of electronic graphic design; consultants on visual design, equipment & opns for TV stns.

Tenner & Associates Inc.
121 Quail Run Rd., Henderson, NV 89014
(702) 792-9430, *Fax:* (702) 792-5748
www.tennerandassoc.com
Lisa Tenner, President
Event & conference producers for the entertainment industry.

3-H Cable Communications Consultants
502 E. Main St., Auburn, WA 98002-5502
(253) 833-8380, *Fax:* (253) 833-8430
Cable franchise admin, negotiation, renewal, tech evaluation, community needs assessment & franchise fee audits.

Tony Lease Incentive Tours
500 S. Palm Canyon Dr., Suite 215, Palm Springs, CA 92264-7454
(760) 325-9799, *Fax:* (760) 325-9755
www.tonylease.com
info@tonylease
Five star sls incentive tours for media. Also has Media Sports Tours for Superbowl, Final Four OLympic packages. Forty years experience; world wide contacts.

Laguna Niguel
Box 7531, Laguna Niguel, CA 92607-7531
(949) 249-6867;
Becky Cerato, Exec Asst Mgr

Transcomm Inc.
Box 2845, Fairfax, VA 22031
(703) 323-5150, *Fax:* (703) 426-4527
www.transcommusa.com
transcommusa@msn.com
Dr. Norman C. Lerner, Engineering Dir
Financial/economic analysis, market rsch, pricing studies & regulatory economics.

Vanguard Media Corp.
310 N. Westlake Blvd., Suite 230, Westlake Village, CA 91362
(805) 446-4100, *Fax:* (805) 446-4111
www.vanmedia.com
info@vanmedia.com
Rick Newberger, President
Advisory firm to media companies, specializing in planning, & dev of new progmg svcs (e.g., The Golf Channel) & distribution systems (e.g., DBS).

Veronis, Suhler
350 Park Ave., New York, NY 10022
(212) 935-4990, *Fax:* (212) 381-8168
www.veronissuhler.com
John J. Veronis, Chairman
Merchant bankers to media, communications & info industries, with focus on mergers & acquisitions, valuations, joint ventures & private equity.

VIP Research Inc.
5700 Broadmoor St., Suite 200, Mission, KS 66202
(888) 384-9494, *Fax:* (913) 677-2727
www.vipresearch.net
clark@vipresearch.net
Clark Roberts, CFO
Mike Heydman, General Sales Mgr
Provides hook-tape production, listener screening, fielding & tabulation for all music testing, perceptual studies, focus groups & promotional telemarketing.

W.L. Pritchard & Co. L.C.
4405 E.W. Hwy., Suite 501, Bethesda, MD 20814
(301) 654-1144, *Fax:* (301) 654-1814
www.wlpco.com
wlpritchard-co@verizon.net
Ellen Hoff, President
Paul Schrantz, Engineering Dir
Professional engrg, business problem solving in telecommunications, competitor analysis, satellite communications, earth stns, & launch vehicles.

Walter Wulff & Associates
Div/DBA: FAA Consultants
Box 914, Point Clear, AL 36564
(251) 990-2502, *Fax:* (334) 990-2503
wulff@zebra.net
Walter H. Wulff, CEO

Conducts FAA tower studies & EMI evaluations.

Warren Only Media Group
19 W. Almond St., Vineland, NJ 08360
(856) 507-9368, *Fax:* (856) 507-9368
www.warrenonly.com
sales@warrenonly.com
Warren Only, Consultant
Bcstg radio & TV consultants, telecommunications, FCC applications.

Washington Information Group Ltd.
1655 N. Ft. Meyer Dr., Suite 800, Arlington, VA 22209
(202) 463-7334, *Fax:* (703 527-4586
www.winfogroup.com
Douglas House, President
Customized business rsch. Competitive intelligence, pub & private company rsch, industry & market studies. Strictly confidential; free consultation.

Wayne A. Stacey & Assoc. Ltd.
2145 Hubbard Cr., Ottawa, ON K1J 6L3 Canada
(613) 745-9151
www.aviationweatherinc.com
wxcenter@aviationweatherinc.com
Rgnl Radio Bcst/Weathercast Network across the Carolinas & Georgia in over 20 bcst markets. Weather forecasting, site-specific bcst svcs for stns all across America.

The Weather Center
NSS Data: TV-CATV only
Div/DBA: (A bcst svc of Aviation Weather Inc.)
701 Gervais St., Suite 224, Columbia, SC 29201
(803) 422-4823
www.aviationweatherinc.com
wxcenter@aviationweatherinc.com
Liam Richard Ferguson, President
Regional Radio Broadcast/Weathercast Network across the Carolinas & Georgia in over 20 bcst markets. Weather forecasting, site-specific bcst svc for stns all across America. 100% barter.

The Wexler Group
1317 F St. N.W., Suite 600, Washington, DC 20004
(202) 638-2121, *Fax:* (202) 638-7045
www.wexlergroup.com
Anne Wexler, Chairman
Consulting firm, specializing in govt rel & pub affrs with strong emphasis on mass media, telecommunications, copyright, trade.

William Russell & Associates Inc.
305 W. Masonic View Ave., Alexandria, VA 22301
(703) 739-6277, *Fax:* (703) 797-7584
www.wmrussellassociates.com
russell@williamrussellassociates.com
William A. Russell Jr., President
Govt rel & pub rel consultants specializing in telecommunications & international trade issues.

Wind River Broadcast Center
117 E. 11th St., Loveland, CO 80537
(800) 669-3993, (970) 669-3442, *Fax:* (970) 663-6081
www.windriverbroadcast.com
jim@windriverbroadcast.com
Jim McDonald, CEO
TV/FM/AM tech & regulatory consulting; publishers of The Bigbook Project, a radio/TV stn tech & regulatory workbook system. FCC applications, engrg.

Wishnow Group Inc.
82 Bubier Rd., Marblehead, MA 01945-3640
(781) 631-2444
www.smimetlaw.com
info@smimetlaw.com

Wolfe Media
10755-F Scripps Poway Pkwy., #612, San Diego, CA 92131
(858) 530-8787, (888) 965-3226, *Fax:* (858) 530-9974
www.wolfemedia.com
dw@wolfemedia.com
David Wolfe, President
Media consultants.

WW Associates
10040 East Happy Valley Rd. unit 454, Scottsdale, AZ 85255
(480) 515-0913, *Fax:* (480) 515-4632
jwiesenberg@mba1977.hbs.edu
International new media dev, strategic planning & acquisition assistance, cable & wireless MMDS expertise, PPV event & movie studio liaison.

Music Licensing

American Society of Composers, Authors & Publishers (ASCAP)
One Lincoln Plaza, New York, NY 10023
(212) 621-6000, *Fax:* (212) 724-9064
www.ascap.com
info@ascap.com
Marilyn Bergman, Chairman
A membership assn of more than 275,000 composers, lyricists, & music publishers, ASCAP licenses the pub performances of its members' works. ASCAP has reciprocal agreements with foreign societies representing virtually every country that haslaws protecting copyright.
ASCAP - Atlanta
PMB 400, 541 Tenth St. N.W., Atlanta, GA 30318-5713
(404) 351-1224; *Fax:* (404) 351-1252
ASCAP - Los Angeles
7920 W. Sunset Blvd., 3rd Fl., Los Angeles, CA 90046-3300
(323) 883-1000; *Fax:* (323) 883-1049
Todd Brobeck, Sr Vp
ASCAP - Miami
420 Lincoln Rd., Suite 385, Miami Beach, FL 33139-3019
(305) 673-3446; *Fax:* (305) 673-2446
ASCAP - Midwest
1608 N. Milwaukee Ave., Suite 1007, Chicago, IL 60647-5456
(773) 394-4286; *Fax:* (773) 394-5639
ASCAP - Nashville
2 Music Sq. W., Nashville, TN 37203-3204
(615) 742-5000; *Fax:* (615) 742-5020
ASCAP - London
8 Cork St., London,
01-44-207-439-0909; *Fax:* 001-44-207-434-0073

APM Music
6255 Sunset Blvd., Suite 820, Hollywood, CA 90028
(323) 461-3211, *Fax:* (323) 461-9102
www.apmmusic.com
accountservices@apmmusic.com
Adam Taylor, President
George Mecias, General Sales Mgr
Sharon Jennings, Promotions Manager
Sixteen libraries: KPM, Bruton, Sonoton, Carlin, Castle, NFL. Over 3,000 CDs, personalized packages, music search, 15-20 new CD releases mthy.
381 Park Ave. S., Suite 1101, New York, NY 10016-8806
(212) 856-9800; *Fax:* (212) 856-9807
George Macisa, Natl Sls Mgr

BMI-Broadcast Music Inc.
320 W. 57th St., New York, NY 10019
(212) 586-2000, *Fax:* (212) 582-5972
www.bmi.com
John E. Cody, COO
Del Bryant, President
Licenses the pub performance rights of musical compositions for more than 300,000 songwriters, composers & music publishers; maintains reciprocal arrangements with more than 40 licensing organizations worldwide.
1691 Michigan Ave., Suite 350, Miami, FL
(305) 266-3636;
Tower Pl. 100, 3340 Peachtree Rd. N.E., Suite 570, Atlanta, GA 30326-1059
(404) 261-5151;
Bank Trust Plaza, 255 Ponce de leon Ave, East Wing, Suite A-262, Hato Rey, PR
(787) 754-6490;
84 Harley House, Marlebone Rd., London, NO United Kingdom
0114420 7486 2036;
8730 Sunset Blvd., Los Angeles, CA 90069-2210
(310) 659-9109;
10 Music Sq. E., Nashville, TN 37203-4321
(615) 401-2000;

European American Music Distributors L.L.C.
254 W. 31st St., 15th Fl., New York, NY 10000
(212) 461-6940, *Fax:* (212) 810-4565
www.eamdllc.com
info@eamdllc.com
Jim Kendrick, President
Music publisher & distributor.

The Harry Fox Agency Inc.
40 Wall Street, 6th Floor, New York, NY 10001
(212) 922-3297, (212) 834-0100, *Fax:* (646) 487-6711
www.harryfox.com
press@harryfox.com
Mechanical licensing, mechanical royalty collection and distribution, rights management solutions.

SESAC Inc.
55 Music Sq. E., Nashville, TN 37203
(615) 320-0055, *Fax:* (615) 329-9627
www.sesac.com
dhoughton@sesac.com
Performing rights organization representing a diversity of copyrighted music.
420 Lincoln Rd., Suite 502, Miami, FL
(305) 534-7500; *Fax:* (305) 534-7578
501 Santa Monica Blvd., Suite 450, Santa Monica, CA 90401-2431
(310) 393-9671; *Fax:* (310) 393-6497
981 Joseph E. Lowery Blvd. N.W., Suite 11, Atlanta, GA 30318-5286
(404) 897-1330; *Fax:* (404) 897-1306
152 W. 57th St., 57th Fl., New York, NY 10019-3386
(212) 586-3450; *Fax:* (212) 489-5699
67 Upper Berkeley St., London, United Kingdom

Society of Composers, Authors & Music Publishers of Canada (SOCAN)
Div/DBA: Societe Canadienne des auteurs, compositeurs et ed
41 Valleybrook Dr., Toronto, ON M3B 2S6 Canada
(416) 445-8700, (866) 307-6226, *Fax:* (416) 445-7108
www.socan.ca
socan@socan.ca
SOCAN licenses the public performance of music in Canada & distributes performance royalties to copyright holders worldwide.
600, boul. de Maisonneuve Ouest, Bureau 500, Montreal, (514) 844-8377; *Fax:* (514) 849-8446
1201 W. Pender St., Suite 400, Vancouver,
(604) 669-5569; *Fax:* (604) 688-1142
1145 Weber Centre, 5555 Calgary Tr., Edmonton,
(780) 439-9049; *Fax:* (780) 432-1555
Queen Sq., 45 Alderney Dr., Suite 802, Dartmouth,
(902) 464-7000; *Fax:* (902) 464-9696

Warner Bros. Publications
15800 N.W. 48th Ave., Miami, FL 33014
(305) 620-1500
www.warnerbros.com
Full-line music publishers of popular, standard & educ music as well as instructional videos from influential musicians. International market.

Research Services

American Media Services L.L.C.
Box 20696, Charleston, SC 29413 29413
(843) 972-2200, *Fax:* (843) 881-4436
www.americanmediaservices.com
ams@ams.fm
Ed Seeger, Chairman
Frank McCoy, President
Developers & brokers of radio properties. Also appraisals, search svcs (buyer's agent), upgrade studies.
Chicago office
24180 N. Forest Dr., Forest Lake, IL 60047-8825
(847) 540-5410;
Frank McCoy, Exec Vp/Engrg
Dallas office
9208 Timbercreek Dr., Bonham, TX 75418-5134
(903) 640-5857; *Fax:* (903) 640-5859
David Reeder, Rgnl Broker
Austin office
303 Avenue Q, Marble Falls, TX 78654-5426
(877) 267-2636;
Patrick McNamara, Rgnl Broker

Associated Broadcasters, Inc.
Box 42566, Cincinnati, OH 45242 45242
(513) 791-5982, *Fax:* (513) 891-5727
irvschwartz@aol.com
Irv Schwartz, President
Legal & filing svcs in turnkey packages; consulting & appraisal svcs available.

Barger Broadcast Brokerage, Ltd.
8023 Vantage Dr., Suite 840, San Antonio, TX 78230 78230
(210) 340-7080, *Fax:* (210) 341-1777
jwbarger@sbcglobal.net
John W. Barger, President
Media brokerage, loc mktg agreements, financial placements, appraisals & mgmt/financial consulting.

Barry Skidelsky, Esq.
185 E. 85th St., 23D, New York, NY 10028 10028
(212) 832-4800
Barry Skidelsky, President

Acquisitions, divestitures, mergers, time brokerage, financing.

Blackburn & Co. Inc.
201 N. Union St., Suite 340, Alexandria, VA 22314 22314
(703) 519-3703, *Fax:* (703) 519-9756
rblack4@aol.com
James Blackburn, Chairman
Richard F. Blackburn, President
Tony Rizzo, Broker
Radio, TV stns , communications tower brokerage, financing & appraisals.

Broadcast Media Associates
Box 1233, Santa Maria, CA 93456 93456
(805) 937-1553, *Fax:* (805) 937 7212
broadcastmediabroker.com
cliffhunter@cliffhunter.com
Clifford M. Hunter, President
Radio/TV/cable brokerage in the western states. Confidential mktg for radio, TV & LPTV properties; valuation packages & financial analysis; consultants to sellers & buyers.

Broadcasting Asset Management Corp.
1323 Forest Glen, Winnetka, IL 60093 60093
(847) 446-8882, *Fax:* (847) 446-4855
Jack Minkow, President
Radio stn & group stn brokerage, mergers, acquisition analysis, appraisals, feasibility studies; subdebt & equity placement.

BroadcastStations4Sale.com
512 Jones St., Graham, NC 27253 27253
(336) 570-9133, *Fax:* (336) 570-3464
www.broadcaststations4sale.com
tedjgray@netzero.net
Ted J. Gray, President & Broker
Buy or sell radio stns or TV stns. List to sell yourself or let BroadcastStations4Sale.com sell it for you.

Bruce Houston Associates, Inc.
2251 Hunter Mill Rd., Vienna, VA 22181 22181
(703) 938-1016, *Fax:* (703) 938-6078
bruceahouston@aol.com
Bruce Houston, President
Joan Houston, Operations Dir
Media brokers for radio & TV.

Bulkley Capital, L.P.
5949 Sherry Ln., #1370, Dallas, TX 75225 75225
(214) 692-5476, *Fax:* (214) 692-9309
www.bulkleycapital.com
info@bulkleycapital.com
Bradford Bulkey, President
Oliver Cone, Operations Dir
Lisa Bulkley, VP
Investment banking: mergers, acquisitions, private placements of debt & equity capital.

Burt Sherwood & Associates Inc.
6415 Midnight Pass Rd., Suite 206, Sarasota, FL 34242 34242
(941) 349-2165, *Fax:* (941) 312-0974
bohica1@comcast.net
Burt Sherwood, President
Brokerage radio, TV & LPTV; appraisals.

Business Broker Associates
Box 4757, Chattanooga, TN 37405-0757 37405-0757
(423) 756-7635
www.cdc.net/~bba
bba@cdc.net
Alfred C Dick, Broker
Media broker & consultant for radio, TV & cable systems.
500 E. 77th St, Suite 1909, New York, NY 10162-0025
(212) 288-0737;
Hugh Ben LaRue, Pres
Joy Thomas, Vp

Chaisson & Company Inc.
154 Indian Waters Dr., New Canaan, CT 06840 6840
(203) 966-6333, *Fax:* (203) 966-1298
rchaisco@aol.com
Robert A. Chaisson, President
Brokerage of radio/TV sls & acquisitions.

Chapin Enterprises
1248 O St., Suite 751, Lincoln, NE 68508 68508
(402) 475-5285, *Fax:* (402) 475-5293
dchapin@inetnebr.com
R.W. Chapin, President
Stn sls, consulting, financial counseling, per location & receiver. Media broker, consulting.

Clifton Gardiner & Company, L.L.C.
2437 S. Chase Ln., Lakewood, CO 80227 80227
(303) 758-6900, *Fax:* (303) 757-5005
www.cliftongardner.com
cliff@cliftongardiner.com
Clifton H. Gardiner, President
Brokerage & financial svcs for the bcst & cable industries.

CobbCorp, LLC
7400 Tamiami Trail North, Suite 102, Naples, FL 34108-2855 34108-2855
(212) 960-8468, *Fax:* (239) 596-0660
www.cobbcorp.com
briancobb@cobbcorp.com
Brian E. Cobb, President
Dennis LeClair, Vice President
Mergers, acquisitions, investment & merchant banking.

Communication Resources Media Brokers
5343 E. 22nd St., Tulsa, OK 74114 74114
(918) 743-8300, *Fax:* (918) 749-3348
tbelc@cox.net
Tom Belcher, President
Brokerage svc to radio & TV stns, cable TV companies, & individual telephone companies.

Communications Equity Associates
101 E. Kennedy Blvd., Suite 3300, Tampa, FL 33602 33602
(813) 226-8844, *Fax:* (813) 225-1513
www.ceaworldwide.com
J. Patrick Michaels Jr., Chairman
Ming Jung Sr., CFO-CEA
Robert Berger, General Manager
Carsten Philipson, Managing Director
Ken Jones, Sr. VP & General Counsel
Donald Russell, Managing Director
Investment & merchant banking, corporate finance & private equity firm specializing in the cable, bcstg, telecommunications, media, & entertainment industries.
1270 Avenue of the Americias, Suite 1818, New York, NY 10020-1700
(212) 218-5085; *Fax:* (212) 218-5099
Alexander Rossi, Mgng Director
Bob Ennis, Mgng Director
Waldo Glasman, Mgng Director
Paul Miller, Mgng Director
Evan Blum, Dir
Jason Donnell, Dir
191 Post Rd. W., Westport, CT 06880-4625
(203) 221-2662; *Fax:* (203) 221-2663
Dave Moyer, Pres

The Connelly Co.
17909 Holly Brook Dr., Tampa, FL 33647-2245 33647-2245
(813) 907-0017, *Fax:* (813) 991-9444
connellyradiotv@verizon.net
Robert J. Connelly, President
Brokers, consultants & recovery unit to assist banks & financial institutions.
Effingham (Summer only)
Bailey Rd., South Effingham, NH
(603) 522-6462; *Fax:* (603) 522-6348
198 S. Main St., New Market, NH
(603) 659-3648;

Cox & Cox, LLC
2454 Shiva Ct., St. Louis, MO 63011 63011
(636) 458-4780, *Fax:* (636) 273-1312
www.coxandcoxllc.com
bc@coxandcoxllc.com
Robert Cox, President
Linda Cox, Operations Dir
Media mergers & acquisitions, appraisals, consulting, expert testimony, receivership & workout.

Dave Garland Media Brokerage
NSS Data: Radio Only
1007 Shadow Cir., League City, TX 77573 77573
(713) 882-2402
www.radiobroker.com
garland@radiobroker.com
David Garland, President
Robert Miles Master, Operations Dir
Broker of radio stn properties in Texas & surrounding states.

Diversified Investment Services, Inc.
17146 S.E. 23rd Dr., Suite 58, Vancouver, WA 98683 98683
(503) 221-1122, (800) 635-1772, *Fax:* (360) 882-4760
a.stilli@yahoo.com
Armand J. Santilli, President
Media brokers/finders, real estate investment bankers & brokers.

Earl Reilly Enterprises
550 Aloha St., Suite 404, Seattle, WA 98019 98019
(206) 282-6914
www.tvspotnet.com
earlcant@comcast.net
Earl F. Reilly, President
Bcst rep, representing U.S. TV stns in Canada. Also licensed bcst stn brokers.
Box 1000, Freeland, WA
(206) 331-7223; *Fax:* (206) 331-7223

Ed Walters & Associates
1170 Clearwater Ct., Palatine, IL 60067 60067
(847) 359-6117, *Fax:* (847) 359-6167
www.edwaltersandassoc.com
radiobroker@msn.com
Ed Walters, President
Michael Walters, Operations Dir
Karrol Walters, Secretary
Nationwide brokers, specializing in radio, TV & cable systems, acquisition searches with confidentiality ensured.

Edwin Tornberg & Co. Inc.
8917 Cherbourg Dr., Potomac, MD 20854 20854
(301) 983-8700, *Fax:* (301) 299-2297
Edwin Tornberg, President
Appraisals, brokerage, financial & mgmt consulting for radio, TV & cable.

EnVest Media, LLC
6802 Patterson Ave., Richmond, VA 23226 23226
(804) 282-5561, *Fax:* (804) 282-5703
www.envestmedia.com
mitt@envestmedia.com
Mitt Younts, General Manager
Nationwide radio, TV acquisition, valuation, financing & consulting firm. The company provides brokerage svcs to stn transaction, appraisal svcs to stn owners & financial institutions. The group secures debt & equity acquisition financing,offers consulting & asset mgmt svcs, acting as court appointed receivers or trustees for bcst stns.

The Exline Company
4340 Redwood Hwy., Suite F-230, San Rafael, CA 94903 94903
(415) 479-3484, *Fax:* (415) 479-1574
www.exline.com
exline@pacbell.net
Andrew P. McClure, President
Complete brokerage, consulting & appraisal svcs for radio & TV properties.

Explorer Communications Inc.
3615 W. Treyburn Path, Lecanto, FL 34461 34461
(352) 746-0505, *Fax:* (352) 746-4255
jfhoff@tampabay.rr.com
Jim Hoffman, President
Bcst media brokerage svcs. Specialists in medium & small market entrepreneurial transactions.

Frank Boyle & Co., L.L.C.
2001 W. Main St., Suite 280, Stamford, CT 06902 6902
(203) 969-2020
fboylebrkr@aol.com
Robert E. Richer, CEO
Frank Boyle, President
Radio & TV media brokerage, mergers & acquisitions/appraisals.

Fugatt Media Services
9214 Butternut Dr., Crystal Lake, IL 60014 60014
(815) 546-1470, (815) 788-7481
fugattmediaservices@comcast.net
Michael L. Fugatt, President
Media brokerage firm specialing in radio & cable svcs including appraisals.

Gammon Miller L.L.C.
Div/DBA: (Formerly Gammon Media Brokers L.L.C.)
4806 Vue Du Lac Pl., Suite B, Manhattan, KS 66503-8688 66503-8688
(785) 539-1700, *Fax:* (785) 565-0437
www.gammonmiller.com
cmiller@gammonmiller.com
Christopher D. Miller, President/CEO
Brokerage & strategy advice to sellers, buyers of radio stns, TV stns, nwspr & cable TV systems. Gammon Miller Revenue Travel as a division Gammon Miller LLC, is a media based incentive travel provider for radio hstns, TV stns, nwspr andcable TV systems.

Gary Stevens & Co.
Box 4880, Stamford, CT 06907-0880 06907-0880

PROFESSIONAL SERVICES

(203) 966-6465, *Fax:* (203) 966-6522
deelmakur@aol.com
Gary Stevens, President
Bcst mergers, acquisitions & investment banking svcs.

George Moore & Associates Inc.
6918 Wildglen Dr., Suite 100 W, Dallas, TX 75230 75230
(214) 369-5665, *Fax:* (214) 369-5667
jimmoore@texan.net
W. James Moore, President
Brokerage of radio, TV, asset & market appraisals prepared for owners, buyers & lenders.

Gordon P. Moul & Associates Inc.
Box 42, York Haven, PA 17370 17370
(717) 266-4212, *Fax:* (717) 266-0780
gpmassociatesinc@netscape.com
Gordon P. Moul, President
Bcst broker & consultant. Specializing in East Coast AM-FM & TV.

Gordon Rice Associates
Box 20398, Charleston, SC 29413 29413
(843) 884-3590, *Fax:* (843) 881-0358
gordon@gordonriceassociates.com
Gordon Rice, Broker
Brokerage svcs, appraisals & investment analysis for radio & TV.

H.B. LaRue, Media Brokers
9454 Wilshire Blvd., Suite 628, Beverly Hills, CA 90212 90212
(310) 275-9266
hblarue@sbcglobal.net
Media brokerage; TV, radio & CATV. Appraisals & feasibility studies.
500 E. 77th Street, New York, NY
(212) 288-0737;
Hugh Ben LaRue, President
Joy Thomas, VP

Hadden & Associates
Div/DBA: Media Brokers - Orlando
147 Eastpark Dr., Celebration, FL 34447 34447
(321) 939-3141, *Fax:* (321) 939-3142
www.haddenonline.com
haddenws@aol.com
Doyle Hadden, President
Ryan P. Hadden, Operations Dir
Communications broker, acquisitions, divestitures; financial assistance and appraisal to the broadcasting industry.

Hawkeye Radio Properties Inc.
3325 Conservancy Ln., Middleton, WI 53562 53562
(608) 831-8708
dganske@charter.net
Jay Williams, CEO
Dale A Ganske, President
Complete radio/TV brokering, consulting, FCC rules & regulations.

Henson Media Inc.
455 S. Fourth Ave., Suite 494, Louisville, KY 40202-2508 40202-2508
(502) 589-0060, *Fax:* (502) 589-0058
www.hensonmedia.com
edhenson1@bellsouth.net
Edward Henson, President
Radio & TV brokers. Radio stations owned and operated.
7811 Saloma Rd., Campbellsville, KY 42718-8008
(270) 789-9513;
Bryan McForland, Chairman

Holt Media Group
2178 Industrial Dr., Suite 914, Bethlehem, PA 18017 18017
(610) 814-2821, *Fax:* (610) 814-2826
www.holtmedia.com
artholt@holtmedia.com
Christine E. Borger, Executive VP
Brokerage, consulting, appraisals.

Howard E. Stark
575 Madison Ave., 10th Fl., New York, NY 10022 10022
(212) 355-0405
Howard E. Stark, President
Media broker; mergers & acquisitions in the communications field.

HPC Puckett & Co.
Box 9063, Rancho Santa Fe, CA 92067 92067
(858) 756-4915, *Fax:* (858) 756-4534
www.hpcpuckett.com
Thomas F. Puckett, CEO
Hunter T. Puckett, Operations Dir
Jason A. Meyer, General Manager
Communications brokerage & investment banking.

International Media Consulting
48 Mountain Rd., Farmington, CT 06032-2341 06032-2341
(860) 677-9688
robert.richer@snet.net
Robert E. Richer, President
Broker specializing in the sale of overseas media properties.

Jack Maloney Inc.
28 Shore Dr., Huntington, NY 11743 11743
(631) 549-2656, *Fax:* (631) 549-2656
JFMINC@AOL.COM
Jack Maloney, President
Provides confidential svcs to buyers, sellers in the radio & TV business.

Joe M. Leonard Jr. & Associates Inc.
Box 222, Gainesville, TX 76241 76241
(940) 665-4076
www.rockabillyhall.com/joeleonard.html
lin45@ntin.net
Jacob R. Miles III, CEO
Joe M. Leonard Jr., President
Brokerage of radio & TV.

John Pierce & Company L.L.C.
11 Spiral Dr., Suite 3, Florence, KY 41042 41042
(859) 647-0101, *Fax:* (859) 647-2616
www.johnpierceco.com
jpierce@johnpierceco.com
Rebecca Grizovic, Finance Director
Radio, TV, & cable sls & appraisals.

John W. Saunders, Media Broker
1207 Woodhollow Dr., Suite 3101, Houston, TX 77057 77057
(713) 789-4222, *Fax:* (713) 789-4322
www.theradiobroker.com
theradiobroker@aol.com
John W. Saunders, President
Nationwide radio brokerage & appraisals. Buyers or sellers represented on a confidential, professional & personal basis. Top 10 to small markets.

Johnson Communication Properties Inc.
375 Waycliffe Dr. S., Wayzata, MN 55391 55391
(952) 404-1104, *Fax:* (952) 404-1102
johncomm88@aol.com
Jerry Johnson, President
Christina Bowers, Operations Dir
Radio & TV broker for 25 years.

Jorgenson Broadcast Brokerage Inc.
426 S. River Rd., Tryon, NC 28782-7879 28782-7879
(828) 859-6982, *Fax:* (828) 859-6831
www.radiotvbrokerage.com
goradiotv@aol.com
Mark W. Jorgenson, President
Confidential, nationwide brokerage of bcst properties.

Kalil & Co. Inc.
6363 N. Swan Rd., Suite 200, Tucson, AZ 85718 85718
(520) 795-1050, *Fax:* (520) 322-0584
www.kalilco.com
kalil@kalilco.com
Frank Kalil, President
Steve Backerman, COO
Fred Kalil, VP
Max Drachman, VP
Frank Higney, VP
Todd Hartman, VP
Louis McDermott, VP
Tom Ziaket, VP
Media brokerage firm dealing in radio, TV & cable. Handles exclusive listings & confidential searches.

Kempff Communications Co.
3301 Bayshore Blvd., Suite 1407, Tampa, FL 33629 33629
(813) 258-3433
www.kepffbarr.com
kempffcc@aol.com
Cheryl Beach, CEO
Ron Kempff, President
Aurelia Serna, VP
Pat McMahon, Programming Director
Broker & consultant also offering financial & mgmt svcs, court ordered sale of stns.

Kepper, Tupper & Company
112 High Ridge Ave., Ridgefield, CT 06877 6877
(203) 431-3366, *Fax:* (203) 431-3864
www.kepper-tupper.com
jtupper@kepper-tupper.com
John B. Tupper, President
Brokerage & investment banking svcs for the cable & bcst TV industries. Please visit our website kepper-tupper.com.

Knowles Media Brokerage Services
Box 9698, Bakersfield, CA 93389 93389
(661) 833-3834, *Fax:* (661) 833-3845
www.media-broker.com
gregg.knowles@netzero.com
Gregg K. Knowles, Broker
Daily & wkly nwsprs, print publications/sls, consultation. Sls, mergers, acquistions, appraisals.

Kozacko Media Services
Box 948, Elmira, NY 14902 14902
(607) 733-7138, *Fax:* (607) 733-1212
www.kozackomediaservices.com
dick@kozacko.com
Richard L. Kozacko, President
Appraisals & current market evaluations of radio & TV stns; bcst stn acquisition brokers.
6890 E. Sunrise Dr., Box 120-40, Tucson, AZ 85732-2040
(520) 299-4869; *Fax:* (520) 844-8559
George W. Kimble, Assoc
1071 Club Dr., Keswick, VA 22947-2613
(434) 244-2653; *Fax:* (434) 244-2666
W. Donald Roberts Jr., Assoc

Lattice Communications, L.L.C.
441 Vine St., Suite 3900, Cincinnati, OH 45202 45202
(513) 381-7775, *Fax:* (513) 381-8808
www.latticecommunications.com
R. Dean Meiszer, President
Acquisition, merger, appraisal & financial svcs to radio, TV, nwspr, cable & other media-related industries.

Lazard L.L.C.
30 Rockefeller Plaza, New York, NY 10020 10020
(212) 632-6000
www.lazard.com
Bruce Wasserstein, CEO
Robert Hougie, General Manager
Michael Castellano, CFO
Lazard's broad range of svcs includes: gen financial advice; domestic, cross-border mergers & acquisitions; divestitures; privatizations; special committee assignments; takeover defenses; corporate restructurings; strategicpartnerships/joint ventures; & debt/equity underwriting.

Legacy Securities Corp.
4060 Peachtree Rd., N.E., Atlanta, GA 30019 30019
(404) 965-2420
www.legacysecurities.com
Michael D. Easterly, Chairman
Chris Battel, President

Mayo Communications Inc.
Box 82784, Tampa, FL 33682 33682
(813) 264-5050, *Fax:* (813) 264-5353
Lincoln A. Mayo, President
Media brokerage, & appraisals for bcst & print. Consulting concerning media sls & acquisitions.

Media Services Group Inc.
3948 S. Third St. #191, Jacksonville Beach, FL 32250 32250
(904) 285-3239, *Fax:* (904) 285-5618
www.mediaservicesgroup.com
reedmsconsulting@cs.com
George R. Reed, General Manager
One of the nation's leading full svc media brokerage, valuation & consulting firms with in-depth industry knowledge & market expertise.

Providence, RI
170 Westminster St., Suite 701, Providence, RI 02903-2101
(401) 454-3130; *Fax:* (401) 454-3131
rmaccini@ cox.net; scs@scsloan.com
Robert J. Maccini, Dir
Stephan Sloan, Assoc
Ted Clark, Analyst

Kansas City, KS
5225 W. 122nd Street, Overland Park, KS 66209-3547
(913) 498-0040; *Fax:* (913) 498-0041
75767.3151@compuserve.com
Bill Lytle, Dir
Mike Lytle, Assoc

Dallas, TX

1131 Rockingham Dr., Suite 209, Richardson, TX 75080-4354
(972) 231-4500; *Fax:* (972) 231-4509
whitelytx@cs.com
Bill Whitley, Dir

St. Simons Island, GA
205 Marina Dr., St. Simons Island, GA 31522-2243
(912) 634-6575; *Fax:* (912) 634-5770
edwesser@adlphia.net
Eddie Esserman, Dir

Salt Lake City
1289 North 1500 E., Logan, UT 84341-2848
(435) 753-8090; *Fax:* (435) 753-2980
ggm@cache.net
Greg Merrill, Dir

Colorado Springs, CO
2910 Electra Drive, Colorado Springs, CO 80906-1073
(719) 630-3111; *Fax:* (719) 630-1871
jbmccoy@adelphia.net
Jody McCoy, Dir

New York Metro
45 Park Pl. S. #146, Morristown, NJ 07960-3924
(973) 631-6612; *Fax:* (973) 631-6613
rtmck2515@aol.com
Tom McKinley, Dir
147 Oak Knoll Terr., Highland Park, IL 60035-5320
(847) 266-9822; *Fax:* (847) 266-9826
Robet L. Heymann, Dir

Media Venture Partners
244 Jackson St., 4th Fl., San Francisco, CA 94111 94111
(415) 391-4877, *Fax:* (415) 391-4912
www.mediaventurepartners.com
pcanberryharris@mediaventurepartners.com
Brian Pryor, General Manager
Elliot Evers, Managing Director
Greg Widroe, Managing Director
Radio & TV brokerage svcs; mergers & acquisitions; telecom; investment banking.
75 State St., Suite 2500, Boston, MA 02109-1827
(617) 345-7316; *Fax:* (617) 507-5667
Jason Hill, Mgng Dir
6314 Brookside Plaza, Suite 203, Kansas City, MO 64113-1765
(816) 523-8566; *Fax:* (816) 817-0570
R. Clayton Funk, Mgng Dir

Michael Fox International, Inc.
Div/DBA: (A division of Goldnustry)
11425 Cronhill Dr., Owings Mills, MD 21117 21117
(410) 654-7500, *Fax:* (410) 654-5876
www.michaelfox.com
info@michaelfox.com
William Z. Fox, Chairman
David S. Fox, CEO
Auction sls of bcst properties.

Montcalm
Box 4608, Rolling Bay, WA 98061-0608 98061-0608
(206) 780-1700, *Fax:* (206) 842-7151
jerden@aol.com
Gerald B. Dennon, President
Radio & TV brokerage svcs, mergers, acquisitions & investment banking.

MyMediaBroker.com
407 Broadmoor Acres, Portales, NM 88130 88130
(575) 356-2000, *Fax:* (575) 356-2003
www.mymediabroker.com
sandibergman@mymediabroker.com
Sandi Bergman, President
Full svc media brokerage firm.

Norman Fischer & Associates Inc.
Box 5308, Austin, TX 78763-5308 78763-5308
(512) 476-9457, *Fax:* (512) 476-0540
www.nfainc.com
terrill@nfainc.com
Terrill Fischer, President
Brokerage in radio, TV & cable. Consultation in mgmt & opns, appraisals, feasibility studies, expert testimony, financial planning & assistance.

Nutmeg Broadcasting
Div/DBA: (formerly New England Media L.L.C.)
720 Main St., Willimantic, CT 06226 6226
(860) 456-1111, *Fax:* (860) 456-9501
www.wili.com
Radio stn.

Patrick Communications L.L.C.
6805 Douglas Legum Dr., Suite 100, Elkridge, MD 21075 21075
(410) 799-1740, *Fax:* (410) 799-1705
www.patcomm.com
larry@patcomm.com
Larry Patrick, Managing Partner
Susan Patrick, Managing Partner
Grey Guy, Managing Partner
Jason James, Vice President
David Benton, Analyst
Stn brokerage, investment banking, mgmt consulting svcs, appraisals & opns consulting.

Questcom Media Services Inc.
10130 Mallard Creek Rd., Suite 300, Charlotte, NC 28262-6001 28262-6001
(704) 948-9800, *Fax:* (704) 948-9888
drbussell@aol.com
Donald R. Bussell, President
Radio & TV stn brokerage specialists concentrating in top 150 markets; offering asst with mergers & consolidations.

R. Miller Hicks & Co.
1011 W. 11th St., Austin, TX 78703 78703
(512) 477-7000, *Fax:* (512) 477-9697
millerhicks@rmhicks.com
R. Miller Hicks, President
Business dev & consulting svcs since 1957.

R.E. Meador & Associates, Inc.
Box 36, Lexington, MO 64067 64067
(660) 259-2544, *Fax:* (660) 259-6424
Remeador1@embarqmail.com
Ralph E. Meador, President
Acquisitions, sls, mktg studies & appraisal svcs in central & midwestern states.
69 Ussery Dr., Lexington, MO 64067-1530
(660) 259-2544;

RadioStationsForSale.net
Div/DBA: (formerly SalesGroup)
41 Herbert Rd., Braintree, MA 02184 2184
(781) 848-4201, *Fax:* (781) 848-4715
www.radiostationsforsale.net
radio@beld.net
Harold Bausemer, President
Stn brokers, USA.

Ray H. Rosenblum, Media Broker / Appraiser / Consultant
Box 38296, Pittsburgh, PA 15238 15238
(412) 362-6311
Ray H. Rosenblum, Broker
Media brokering, appraising, financing & consulting for radio & TV stns in 50 states plus territories.

RBC Daniels
Div/DBA: (Formerly RBC Daniels, L.P.)
3200 Cherry Creek Dr. S., Suite 500, Denver, CO 80209 80209
(303) 778-5555, *Fax:* (303) 778-5599
www.rbcdaniels.com
info@rbcdaniels.com
Provides mergers, acquisitions, corporate finance & financial advisory svcs to the cable, telecommunications media & technology industries.

3 World Financial Center
200 Vesey St., 9th Fl., New York, NY 10285-0002
(212) 935-5900; *Fax:* (212) 863-4859
David Tolliver, Mgng Dir
11150 Santa Monica Blvd., Suite 1230, Los Angeles, CA 90025-3380
(310) 473-2300; *Fax:* (310) 943-2052

Richard A. Foreman Associates, Inc.
330 Emery Dr. E., Stamford, CT 06902-2210 06902-2210
(203) 327-2800, *Fax:* (203) 967-9393
www.rafamedia.com
raf@rafamedia.com
Richard A. Foreman, President
Specializing in cash-positive radio & TV stns in major growth mkts.

Riley Representatives
14330 Midway Rd., Dallas, TX 75244 75244
(972) 788-1630
Jack Riley, President

Roehling Broadcast Services Ltd.
7340 Oak Knoll Dr., Indianapolis, IN 46217 46217
(317) 887-1945, *Fax:* (317) 887-1947
roehlingbroadcast.com
edradiobr@aol.com
Edward W. Roehling, President
Sandra Roehling, Operations Dir

Bcst appraisers, brokers, consultants, also financing, sls, mgmt consultation.

Rumbaut & Company
555 N.E. 34th St., Suite 2701, Miami Beach, FL 33137-4060 33137-4060
(305) 868-0000, *Fax:* (305) 571-0433
www.rumbaut.com
julio@rumbaut.com
Julio Rumbaut, President
Media brokers, advisors, and consultants in all sectors of the media industry including television, radio, and the new media.

S.R. Chanen & Co. Inc.
Div/DBA: (Media Technology Capital Corp.)
3300 N. 3rd Ave., Phoenix, AZ 85013 85013
(602) 266-2160
Steven R. Chanen, Chairman
Investment banking, brokerage & financial advisory svcs for the communications & entertainment industries.

Satterfield & Perry Inc.
7211 Fourth Ave. S., St. Petersburg, FL 33707 33707
(727) 345-7338, *Fax:* (727) 345-3809
www.satterfieldandperry.com
eraust@prodigy.net
Robert Austin, President
John Willis, Operations Dir
Radio & TV broker, mgmt & sls consultant, FDIC-approved appraiser & expert witness.
2020 S. Monroe St. #302, Denver, CO 80210-3767
(303) 758-1876; *Fax:* (303) 756-1865
Al Perry, Chmn Emeritus
4918 W. 101st Terr., Overland Park, KS 66207-3431
(913) 649-5103; *Fax:* (913) 649-5103
Douglas Stephens, Sr Vp
PO Box 362, Coos Bay, OR 97420-0041
(541) 751-0043; *Fax:* (541) 751-0043
Dick McMahon, Vp
20456 E. Orchard Pl., Centennial, CO 80016-3891
(303) 400-5150; *Fax:* (303) 400-5063
Jim Birschbach, Vp
Box 620308-B, Littleton, CO
(303) 948-2200; *Fax:* (303) 948-3468
Joe Benkert, Vp
131 Inwood Dr., Aiken, SC 29803-5613
(803) 270-5613; *Fax:* (803) 649-7786
John Willis, Vp
169 Moumtain Meadows La., Wetumpka, AL
(334) 514-2241; *Fax:* (334) 514-2291
Ken Hawkins, Vp

Serafin Bros. Inc.
Box 262888, Tampa, FL 33685 33685
(813) 885-6060, *Fax:* (813) 885-6857
gserafin@tampabay.rr.com
Glenn M. Serafin, Director
Bcst brokerage, finance & valuation svcs.
4212 Deepwater Ln., Tampa, FL 33615-5618

Snowden Associates
Box 1966, One Commerce Sq., Suite 200, Washington, NC 27889 27889
(252) 940-1680, *Fax:* (252) 940-1682
zophsnowden@embarqmail.com
C. Zoph Potts, Chairman
Brokers, consultants & appraisers to the bcst industry in the Southeast.

Stan Raymond & Associates Inc.
Box 8231, Longboat Key, FL 34228 34228
(941) 383-9404, *Fax:* (941) 383-9132
stanraymond.com
stnray@aol.com
Stan Raymond, President
Financial svcs, media brokers, appraisers & consultants specializing in the Southeast.

The Ted Hepburn Co.
325 Garden Rd., Palm Beach, FL 33480 33480
(561) 863-8995, *Fax:* (561) 863-8997
tedhep2@mac.com
Ted Hepburn, President
Radio, TV & cable brokerage; appraisals.

The Thorburn Company
6625 Hwy. 53 E., Suite 410-72, Dawsonville, GA 30534 30534
(678) 513-1363, *Fax:* (678) 513-1615
www.thorburncompany.com
thorburnco@aol.com
Robert M. Thorburn, President

Appraisals, brokerage, financial, mgmt consulting for radio, TV & cable.

Van Huss Media Services Inc.
4239 Heyward Pl., Indianapolis, IN 46250 46250
(317) 813-0106, *Fax:* (317) 813-0107
vanhussmediaservices@aol.com
William Van Huss, President
Brokerage, financial consulting & appraisals for radio, TV & cable.

The Whittle Agency
12716 Lindley Dr., Raleigh, NC 27614 27614
(919) 848-3596, *Fax:* (919) 848-0519
thewhittleagency@nc.rr.com
Gary L. Whittle, President
Total media brokerage svcs, including sls/appraisals of radio stns in the Carolinas, Virginia & Southeast.

Willis Broadcasting
645 Church St., Suite 400, Norfolk, VA 23510 23510
(757) 624-6500, *Fax:* (757) 624-6515
www.wpce1400.com
willisbroadcasting@yahoo.com
L. E. Willis Sr., President

Wood & Co. Inc.
431 Ohio Pike, Suite 200, Cincinnati, OH 45255 45255
(513) 528-7373, *Fax:* (513) 528-7374
Larry C. Wood, President
Nationwide brokerage service to buyers & sellers of TV & radio properties.

Station & Cable System Brokers

American Media Services L.L.C.
Box 20696, Charleston, SC 29413 29413
(843) 972-2200, *Fax:* (843) 881-4436
www.americanmediaservices.com
ams@ams.fm
Ed Seeger, Chairman
Frank McCoy, President
Developers & brokers of radio properties. Also appraisals, search svcs (buyer's agent), upgrade studies.

Associated Broadcasters, Inc.
Box 42566, Cincinnati, OH 45242 45242
(513) 791-5982, *Fax:* (513) 891-5727
irvschwartz@aol.com
Irv Schwartz, President
Legal & filing svcs in turnkey packages; consulting & appraisal svcs available.

Barger Broadcast Brokerage, Ltd.
8023 Vantage Dr., Suite 840, San Antonio, TX 78230 78230
(210) 340-7080, *Fax:* (210) 341-1777
jwbarger@sbcglobal.net
John W. Barger, President
Media brokerage, loc mktg agreements, financial placements, appraisals & mgmt/financial consulting.

Barry Skidelsky, Esq.
185 E. 85th St., 23D, New York, NY 10028 10028
(212) 832-4800
Barry Skidelsky, President
Acquisitions, divestitures, mergers, time brokerage, financing.

Blackburn & Co. Inc.
201 N. Union St., Suite 340, Alexandria, VA 22314 22314
(703) 519-3703, *Fax:* (703) 519-9756
rblack4@aol.com
James Blackburn, Chairman
Richard F. Blackburn, President
Tony Rizzo, Broker
Radio, TV stns , communications tower brokerage, financing & appraisals.

Broadcast Media Associates
Box 1233, Santa Maria, CA 93456 93456
(805) 937-1553, *Fax:* (805) 937 7212
broadcastmediabroker.com
cliffhunter@cliffhunter.com
Clifford M. Hunter, President
Radio/TV/cable brokerage in the western states. Confidential mktg for radio, TV & LPTV properties; valuation packages & financial analysis; consultants to sellers & buyers.

Broadcasting Asset Management Corp.
1323 Forest Glen, Winnetka, IL 60093 60093
(847) 446-8882, *Fax:* (847) 446-4855
Jack Minkow, President
Radio stn & group stn brokerage, mergers, acquisition analysis, appraisals, feasibility studies; subdebt & equity placement.

BroadcastStations4Sale.com
512 Jones St., Graham, NC 27253 27253
(336) 570-9133, *Fax:* (336) 570-3464
www.broadcaststations4sale.com
tedjgray@netzero.net
Ted J. Gray, President & Broker
Buy or sell radio stns or TV stns. List to sell yourself or let BroadcastStations4Sale.com sell it for you.

Bruce Houston Associates, Inc.
2251 Hunter Mill Rd., Vienna, VA 22181 22181
(703) 938-1016, *Fax:* (703) 938-6078
bruceahouston@aol.com
Bruce Houston, President
Joan Houston, Operations Dir
Media brokers for radio & TV.

Bulkley Capital, L.P.
5949 Sherry Ln., #1370, Dallas, TX 75225 75225
(214) 692-5476, *Fax:* (214) 692-9309
www.bulkleycapital.com
info@bulkleycapital.com
Bradford Bulkey, President
Oliver Cone, Operations Dir
Lisa Bulkley, VP
Investment banking: mergers, acquisitions, private placements of debt & equity capital.

Burt Sherwood & Associates Inc.
6415 Midnight Pass Rd., Suite 206, Sarasota, FL 34242 34242
(941) 349-2165, *Fax:* (941) 312-0974
bohica1@comcast.net
Burt Sherwood, President
Brokerage radio, TV & LPTV; appraisals.

Business Broker Associates
Box 4757, Chattanooga, TN 37405-0757 37405-0757
(423) 756-7635
www.cdc.net/~bba
bba@cdc.net
Alfred C Dick, Broker
Media broker & consultant for radio, TV & cable systems.

Chaisson & Company Inc.
154 Indian Waters Dr., New Canaan, CT 06840 6840
(203) 966-6333, *Fax:* (203) 966-1298
rchaisco@aol.com
Robert A. Chaisson, President
Brokerage of radio/TV sls & acquisitions.

Chapin Enterprises
1248 O St., Suite 751, Lincoln, NE 68508 68508
(402) 475-5285, *Fax:* (402) 475-5293
dchapin@inetnebr.com
R.W. Chapin, President
Stn sls, consulting, financial counseling, per location & receiver. Media broker, consulting.

Clifton Gardiner & Company, L.L.C.
2437 S. Chase Ln., Lakewood, CO 80227 80227
(303) 758-6900, *Fax:* (303) 757-5005
www.cliftongardner.com
cliff@cliftongardiner.com
Clifton H. Gardiner, President
Brokerage & financial svcs for the bcst & cable industries.

CobbCorp, LLC
7400 Tamiami Trail North, Suite 102, Naples, FL 34108-2855 34108-2855
(212) 960-8468, *Fax:* (239) 596-0660
www.cobbcorp.com
briancobb@cobbcorp.com
Brian E. Cobb, President
Dennis LeClair, Vice President
Mergers, acquisitions, investment & merchant banking.

Communication Resources Media Brokers
5343 E. 22nd St., Tulsa, OK 74114 74114
(918) 743-8300, *Fax:* (918) 749-3348
tbelc@cox.net
Tom Belcher, President
Brokerage svc to radio & TV stns, cable TV companies, & individual telephone companies.

Communications Equity Associates
101 E. Kennedy Blvd., Suite 3300, Tampa, FL 33602 33602
(813) 226-8844, *Fax:* (813) 225-1513
www.ceaworldwide.com
J. Patrick Michaels Jr., Chairman
Ming Jung Sr., CFO-CEA
Robert Berger, General Manager
Carsten Philipson, Managing Director
Ken Jones, Sr. VP & General Counsel
Donald Russell, Managing Director
Investment & merchant banking, corporate finance & private equity firm specializing in the cable, bcstg, telecommunications, media, & entertainment industries.

The Connelly Co.
17909 Holly Brook Dr., Tampa, FL 33647-2245 33647-2245
(813) 907-0017, *Fax:* (813) 991-9444
connellyradiotv@verizon.net
Robert J. Connelly, President
Brokers, consultants & recovery unit to assist banks & financial institutions.

Cox & Cox, LLC
2454 Shiva Ct., St. Louis, MO 63011 63011
(636) 458-4780, *Fax:* (636) 273-1312
www.coxandcoxllc.com
bc@coxandcoxllc.com
Robert Cox, President
Linda Cox, Operations Dir
Media mergers & acquisitions, appraisals, consulting, expert testimony, receivership & workout.

Dave Garland Media Brokerage
NSS Data: Radio Only
1007 Shadow Cir., League City, TX 77573 77573
(713) 882-2402
www.radiobroker.com
garland@radiobroker.com
David Garland, President
Robert Miles Master, Operations Dir
Broker of radio stn properties in Texas & surrounding states.

Diversified Investment Services, Inc.
17146 S.E. 23rd Dr., Suite 58, Vancouver, WA 98683 98683
(503) 221-1122, (800) 635-1772, *Fax:* (360) 882-4760
a.stilli@yahoo.com
Armand J. Santilli, President
Media brokers/finders, real estate investment bankers & brokers.

Earl Reilly Enterprises
550 Aloha St., Suite 404, Seattle, WA 98019 98019
(206) 282-6914
www.tvspotnet.com
earlcant@comcast.net
Earl F. Reilly, President
Bcst rep, representing U.S. TV stns in Canada. Also licensed bcst stn brokers.

Ed Walters & Associates
1170 Clearwater Ct., Palatine, IL 60067 60067
(847) 359-6117, *Fax:* (847) 359-6167
www.edwaltersandassoc.com
radiobroker@msn.com
Ed Walters, President
Michael Walters, Operations Dir
Karrol Walters, Secretary
Nationwide brokers, specializing in radio, TV & cable systems, acquisition searches with confidentiality ensured.

Edwin Tornberg & Co. Inc.
8917 Cherbourg Dr., Potomac, MD 20854 20854
(301) 983-8700, *Fax:* (301) 299-2297
Edwin Tornberg, President
Appraisals, brokerage, financial & mgmt consulting for radio, TV & cable.

EnVest Media, LLC
6802 Patterson Ave., Richmond, VA 23226 23226
(804) 282-5561, *Fax:* (804) 282-5703
www.envestmedia.com
mitt@envestmedia.com
Mitt Younts, General Manager
Nationwide radio, TV acquisition, valuation, financing & consulting firm. The company provides brokerage svcs to stn transaction, appraisal svcs to stn owners & financial institutions. The group secures debt & equity acquisition financing,offers consulting & asset mgmt svcs, acting as court appointed receivers or trustees for bcst stns.

The Exline Company
4340 Redwood Hwy., Suite F-230, San Rafael, CA 94903 94903
(415) 479-3484, *Fax:* (415) 479-1574
www.exline.com
exline@pacbell.net
Andrew P. McClure, President

Complete brokerage, consulting & appraisal svcs for radio & TV properties.

Explorer Communications Inc.
3615 W. Treyburn Path, Lecanto, FL 34461 34461
(352) 746-0505, *Fax:* (352) 746-4255
jfhoff@tampabay.rr.com
Jim Hoffman, President
Bcst media brokerage svcs. Specialists in medium & small market entrepreneurial transactions.

Frank Boyle & Co., L.L.C.
2001 W. Main St., Suite 280, Stamford, CT 06902 6902
(203) 969-2020
fboylebrkr@aol.com
Robert E. Richer, CEO
Frank Boyle, President
Radio & TV media brokerage, mergers & acquisitions/appraisals.

Fugatt Media Services
9214 Butternut Dr., Crystal Lake, IL 60014 60014
(815) 546-1470, (815) 788-7481
fugattmediaservices@comcast.net
Michael L. Fugatt, President
Media brokerage firm specialing in radio & cable svcs including appraisals.

Gammon Miller L.L.C.
Div/DBA: (Formerly Gammon Media Brokers L.L.C.)
4806 Vue Du Lac Pl., Suite B, Manhattan, KS 66503-8688 66503-8688
(785) 539-1700, *Fax:* (785) 565-0437
www.gammonmiller.com
cmiller@gammonmiller.com
Christopher D. Miller, President/CEO
Brokerage & strategy advice to sellers, buyers of radio stns, TV stns, nwspr & cable TV systems. Gammon Miller Revenue Travel as a division Gammon Miller LLC, is a media based incentive travel provider for radio hstns, TV stns, nwspr andcable TV systems.

Gary Stevens & Co.
Box 4880, Stamford, CT 06907-0880 06907-0880
(203) 966-6465, *Fax:* (203) 966-6522
deelmakur@aol.com
Gary Stevens, President
Bcst mergers, acquisitions & investment banking svcs.

George Moore & Associates Inc.
6918 Wildglen Dr., Suite 100 W, Dallas, TX 75230 75230
(214) 369-5665, *Fax:* (214) 369-5667
jimmoore@texan.net
W. James Moore, President
Brokerage of radio, TV, asset & market appraisals prepared for owners, buyers & lenders.

Gordon P. Moul & Associates Inc.
Box 42, York Haven, PA 17370 17370
(717) 266-4212, *Fax:* (717) 266-0780
gpmassociatesinc@netscape.com
Gordon P. Moul, President
Bcst broker & consultant. Specializing in East Coast AM-FM & TV.

Gordon Rice Associates
Box 20398, Charleston, SC 29413 29413
(843) 884-3590, *Fax:* (843) 881-0358
gordon@gordonriceassociates.com
Gordon Rice, Broker
Brokerage svcs, appraisals & investment analysis for radio & TV.

H.B. LaRue, Media Brokers
9454 Wilshire Blvd., Suite 628, Beverly Hills, CA 90212 90212
(310) 275-9266
hblarue@sbcglobal.net
Media brokerage; TV, radio & CATV. Appraisals & feasibility studies.

Hadden & Associates
Div/DBA: Media Brokers - Orlando
147 Eastpark Dr., Celebration, FL 34447 34447
(321) 939-3141, *Fax:* (321) 939-3142
www.haddenonline.com
haddenws@aol.com
Doyle Hadden, President
Ryan P. Hadden, Operations Dir
Communications broker, acquisitions, divestitures; financial assistance and appraisal to the broadcasting industry.

Hawkeye Radio Properties Inc.
3325 Conservancy Ln., Middleton, WI 53562 53562
(608) 831-8708
dganske@charter.net
Jay Williams, CEO
Dale A Ganske, President
Complete radio/TV brokering, consulting, FCC rules & regulations.

Henson Media Inc.
455 S. Fourth Ave., Suite 494, Louisville, KY 40202-2508 40202-2508
(502) 589-0060, *Fax:* (502) 589-0058
www.hensonmedia.com
edhenson1@bellsouth.net
Edward Henson, President
Radio & TV brokers. Radio stations owned and operated.

Holt Media Group
2178 Industrial Dr., Suite 914, Bethlehem, PA 18017 18017
(610) 814-2821, *Fax:* (610) 814-2826
www.holtmedia.com
artholt@holtmedia.com
Christine E. Borger, Executive VP
Brokerage, consulting, appraisals.

Howard E. Stark
575 Madison Ave., 10th Fl., New York, NY 10022 10022
(212) 355-0405
Howard E. Stark, President
Media broker; mergers & acquisitions in the communications field.

HPC Puckett & Co.
Box 9063, Rancho Santa Fe, CA 92067 92067
(858) 756-4915, *Fax:* (858) 756-4534
www.hpcpuckett.com
Thomas F. Puckett, CEO
Hunter T. Puckett, Operations Dir
Jason A. Meyer, General Manager
Communications brokerage & investment banking.

International Media Consulting
48 Mountain Rd., Farmington, CT 06032-2341 06032-2341
(860) 677-9688
robert.richer@snet.net
Robert E. Richer, President
Broker specializing in the sale of overseas media properties.

Jack Maloney Inc.
28 Shore Dr., Huntington, NY 11743 11743
(631) 549-2656, *Fax:* (631) 549-2656
JFMINC@AOL.COM
Jack Maloney, President
Provides confidential svcs to buyers, sellers in the radio & TV business.

Joe M. Leonard Jr. & Associates Inc.
Box 222, Gainesville, TX 76241 76241
(940) 665-4076
www.rockabillyhall.com/joeleonard.html
lin45@ntin.net
Jacob R. Miles III, CEO
Joe M. Leonard Jr., President
Brokerage of radio & TV.

John Pierce & Company L.L.C.
11 Spiral Dr., Suite 3, Florence, KY 41042 41042
(859) 647-0101, *Fax:* (859) 647-2616
www.johnpierceco.com
jpierce@johnpierceco.com
Rebecca Grizovic, Finance Director
Radio, TV, & cable sls & appraisals.

John W. Saunders, Media Broker
1207 Woodhollow Dr., Suite 3101, Houston, TX 77057 77057
(713) 789-4222, *Fax:* (713) 789-4322
www.theradiobroker.com
theradiobroker@aol.com
John W. Saunders, President
Nationwide radio brokerage & appraisals. Buyers or sellers represented on a confidential, professional & personal basis. Top 10 to small markets.

Johnson Communication Properties Inc.
375 Waycliffe Dr. S., Wayzata, MN 55391 55391
(952) 404-1104, *Fax:* (952) 404-1102
johncomm88@aol.com
Jerry Johnson, President
Christina Bowers, Operations Dir
Radio & TV broker for 25 years.

Jorgenson Broadcast Brokerage Inc.
426 S. River Rd., Tryon, NC 28782-7879 28782-7879
(828) 859-6982, *Fax:* (828) 859-6831
www.radiotvbrokerage.com
goradiotv@aol.com
Mark W. Jorgenson, President
Confidential, nationwide brokerage of bcst properties.

Kalil & Co. Inc.
6363 N. Swan Rd., Suite 200, Tucson, AZ 85718 85718
(520) 795-1050, *Fax:* (520) 322-0584
www.kalilco.com
kalil@kalilco.com
Frank Kalil, President
Steve Backerman, COO
Fred Kalil, VP
Max Drachman, VP
Frank Higney, VP
Todd Hartman, VP
Louis McDermott, VP
Tom Ziaket, VP
Media brokerage firm dealing in radio, TV & cable. Handles exclusive listings & confidential searches.

Kempff Communications Co.
3301 Bayshore Blvd., Suite 1407, Tampa, FL 33629 33629
(813) 258-3433
www.kepffbarr.com
kempffcc@aol.com
Cheryl Beach, CEO
Ron Kempff, President
Aurelia Sema, VP
Pat McMahon, Programming Director
Broker & consultant also offering financial & mgmt svcs, court ordered sale of stns.

Kepper, Tupper & Company
112 High Ridge Ave., Ridgefield, CT 06877 6877
(203) 431-3366, *Fax:* (203) 431-3864
www.kepper-tupper.com
jtupper@kepper-tupper.com
John B. Tupper, President
Brokerage & investment banking svcs for the cable & bcst TV industries. Please visit our website kepper-tupper.com.

Knowles Media Brokerage Services
Box 9698, Bakersfield, CA 93389 93389
(661) 833-3834, *Fax:* (661) 833-3845
www.media-broker.com
gregg.knowles@netzero.com
Gregg K. Knowles, Broker
Daily & wkly nwsprs, print publications/sls, consultation. Sls, mergers, acquistions, appraisals.

Kozacko Media Services
Box 948, Elmira, NY 14902 14902
(607) 733-7138, *Fax:* (607) 733-1212
www.kozackomediaservices.com
dick@kozacko.com
Richard L. Kozacko, President
Appraisals & current market evaluations of radio & TV stns; bcst stn acquisition brokers.

Lattice Communications, L.L.C.
441 Vine St., Suite 3900, Cincinnati, OH 45202 45202
(513) 381-7775, *Fax:* (513) 381-8808
www.latticecommunications.com
R. Dean Meiszer, President
Acquisition, merger, appraisal & financial svcs to radio, TV, nwspr, cable & other media-related industries.

Lazard L.L.C.
30 Rockefeller Plaza, New York, NY 10020 10020
(212) 632-6000
www.lazard.com
Bruce Wasserstein, CEO
Robert Hougie, General Manager
Michael Castellano, CFO
Lazard's broad range of svcs includes: gen financial advice; domestic, cross-border mergers & acquisitions; divestitures; privatizations; special committee assignments; takeover defenses; corporate restructurings; strategicpartnerships/joint ventures; & debt/equity underwriting.

Legacy Securities Corp.
4060 Peachtree Rd., N.E., Atlanta, GA 30019 30019
(404) 965-2420
www.legacysecurities.com
Michael D. Easterly, Chairman
Chris Battel, President

Mayo Communications Inc.
Box 82784, Tampa, FL 33682 33682
(813) 264-5050, *Fax:* (813) 264-5353

PROFESSIONAL SERVICES

Lincoln A. Mayo, President
Media brokerage, & appraisals for bcst & print. Consulting concerning media sls & acquisitions.

Media Services Group Inc.
3948 S. Third St. #191, Jacksonville Beach, FL 32250 32250
(904) 285-3239, *Fax:* (904) 285-5618
www.mediaservicesgroup.com
reedmsconsulting@cs.com
George R. Reed, General Manager
One of the nation's leading full svc media brokerage, valuation & consulting firms with in-depth industry knowledge & market expertise.

Media Venture Partners
244 Jackson St., 4th Fl., San Francisco, CA 94111 94111
(415) 391-4877, *Fax:* (415) 391-4912
www.mediaventurepartners.com
pcanberryharris@mediaventurepartners.com
Brian Pryor, General Manager
Elliot Evers, Managing Director
Greg Widroe, Managing Director
Radio & TV brokerage svcs; mergers & acquisitions; telecom; investment banking.

Michael Fox International, Inc.
Div/DBA: (A division of GoIndustry)
11425 Cronhill Dr., Owings Mills, MD 21117 21117
(410) 654-7500, *Fax:* (410) 654-5876
www.michaelfox.com
info@michaelfox.com
William Z. Fox, Chairman
David S. Fox, CEO
Auction sls of bcst properties.

Montcalm
Box 4608, Rolling Bay, WA 98061-0608 98061-0608
(206) 780-1700, *Fax:* (206) 842-7151
jerden@aol.com
Gerald B. Dennon, President
Radio & TV brokerage svcs, mergers, acquisitions & investment banking.

MyMediaBroker.com
407 Broadmoor Acres, Portales, NM 88130 88130
(575) 356-2000, *Fax:* (575) 356-2003
www.mymediabroker.com
sandibergman@mymediabroker.com
Sandi Bergman, President
Full svc media brokerage firm.

Norman Fischer & Associates Inc.
Box 5308, Austin, TX 78763-5308 78763-5308
(512) 476-9457, *Fax:* (512) 476-0540
www.nfainc.com
terrill@nfainc.com
Terrill Fischer, President
Brokerage in radio, TV & cable. Consultation in mgmt & opns, appraisals, feasibility studies, expert testimony, financial planning & assistance.

Nutmeg Broadcasting
Div/DBA: (formerly New England Media L.L.C.)
720 Main St., Willimantic, CT 06226 6226
(860) 456-1111, *Fax:* (860) 456-9501
www.wili.com
Radio stn.

Patrick Communications L.L.C.
6805 Douglas Legum Dr., Suite 100, Elkridge, MD 21075 21075
(410) 799-1740, *Fax:* (410) 799-1705
www.patcomm.com
larry@patcomm.com
Larry Patrick, Managing Partner
Susan Patrick, Managing Partner
Grey Guy, Managing Partner
Jason James, Vice President
David Benton, Analyst
Stn brokerage, investment banking, mgmt consulting svcs, appraisals & opns consulting.

Questcom Media Services Inc.
10130 Mallard Creek Rd., Suite 300, Charlotte, NC 28262-6001 28262-6001
(704) 948-9800, *Fax:* (704) 948-9888
drbussell@aol.om
Donald R. Bussell, President
Radio & TV stn brokerage specialists concentrating in top 150 markets; offering asst with mergers & consolidations.

R. Miller Hicks & Co.
1011 W. 11th St., Austin, TX 78703 78703
(512) 477-7000, *Fax:* (512) 477-9697
millerhicks@rmhicks.com
R. Miller Hicks, President
Business dev & consulting svcs since 1957.

R.E. Meador & Associates, Inc.
Box 36, Lexington, MO 64067 64067
(660) 259-2544, *Fax:* (660) 259-6424
Remeador1@embarqmail.com
Ralph E. Meador, President
Acquisitions, sls, mktg studies & appraisal svcs in central & midwestern states.

RadioStationsForSale.net
Div/DBA: (formerly SalesGroup)
41 Herbert Rd., Braintree, MA 02184 2184
(781) 848-4201, *Fax:* (781) 848-4715
www.radiostationsforsale.net
radio@beld.net
Harold Bausemer, President
Stn brokers, USA.

Ray H. Rosenblum, Media Broker / Appraiser / Consultant
Box 38296, Pittsburgh, PA 15238 15238
(412) 362-6311
Ray H. Rosenblum, Broker
Media brokering, appraising, financing & consulting for radio & TV stns in 50 states plus territories.

RBC Daniels
Div/DBA: (Formerly RBC Daniels, L.P.)
3200 Cherry Creek Dr. S., Suite 500, Denver, CO 80209 80209
(303) 778-5555, *Fax:* (303) 778-5599
www.rbcdaniels.com
info@rbcdaniels.com
Provides mergers, acquisitions, corporate finance & financial advisory svcs to the cable, telecommunications media & technology industries.

Richard A. Foreman Associates, Inc.
330 Emery Dr. E., Stamford, CT 06902-2210 06902-2210
(203) 327-2800, *Fax:* (203) 967-9393
www.rafamedia.com
raf@rafamedia.com
Richard A. Foreman, President
Specializing in cash-positive radio & TV stns in major growth mkts.

Riley Representatives
14330 Midway Rd., Dallas, TX 75244 75244
(972) 788-1630
Jack Riley, President

Roehling Broadcast Services Ltd.
7340 Oak Knoll Dr., Indianapolis, IN 46217 46217
(317) 887-1945, *Fax:* (317) 887-1947
roehlingbroadcast.com
edradiobr@aol.com
Edward W. Roehling, President
Sandra Roehling, Operations Dir
Bcst appraisers, brokers, consultants, also financing, sls, mgmt consultation.

Rumbaut & Company
555 N.E. 34th St., Suite 2701, Miami Beach, FL 33137-4060 33137-4060
(305) 868-0000, *Fax:* (305) 571-0433
www.rumbaut.com
julio@rumbaut.com
Julio Rumbaut, President
Media brokers, advisors, and consultants in all sectors of the media industry including television, radio, and the new media.

S.R. Chanen & Co. Inc.
Div/DBA: (Media Technology Capital Corp.)
3300 N. 3rd Ave., Phoenix, AZ 85013 85013
(602) 266-2160
Steven R. Chanen, Chairman
Investment banking, brokerage & financial advisory svcs for the communications & entertainment industries.

Satterfield & Perry Inc.
7211 Fourth Ave. S., St. Petersburg, FL 33707 33707
(727) 345-7338, *Fax:* (727) 345-3809
www.satterfieldandperry.com
eraust@prodigy.net
Robert Austin, President
John Willis, Operations Dir
Radio & TV broker, mgmt & sls consultant, FDIC-approved appraiser & expert witness.

Serafin Bros. Inc.
Box 262888, Tampa, FL 33685 33685
(813) 885-6060, *Fax:* (813) 885-6857
gserafin@tampabay.rr.com
Glenn M. Serafin, Director
Bcst brokerage, finance & valuation svcs.

Snowden Associates
Box 1966, One Commerce Sq., Suite 200, Washington, NC 27889 27889
(252) 940-1680, *Fax:* (252) 940-1682
zophsnowden@embarqmail.com
C. Zoph Potts, Chairman
Brokers, consultants & appraisers to the bcst industry in the Southeast.

Stan Raymond & Associates Inc.
Box 8231, Longboat Key, FL 34228 34228
(941) 383-9404, *Fax:* (941) 383-9132
stanraymond.com
stnray@aol.com
Stan Raymond, President
Financial svcs, media brokers, appraisers & consultants specializing in the Southeast.

The Ted Hepburn Co.
325 Garden Rd., Palm Beach, FL 33480 33480
(561) 863-8995, *Fax:* (561) 863-8997
tedhep2@mac.com
Ted Hepburn, President
Radio, TV & cable brokerage; appraisals.

The Thorburn Company
6625 Hwy. 53 E., Suite 410-72, Dawsonville, GA 30534 30534
(678) 513-1363, *Fax:* (678) 513-1615
www.thorburncompany.com
thorburnco@aol.com
Robert M. Thorburn, President
Appraisals, brokerage, financial, mgmt consulting for radio, TV & cable.

Van Huss Media Services Inc.
4239 Heyward Pl., Indianapolis, IN 46250 46250
(317) 813-0106, *Fax:* (317) 813-0107
vanhussmediaservices@aol.com
William Van Huss, President
Brokerage, financial consulting & appraisals for radio, TV & cable.

The Whittle Agency
12716 Lindley Dr., Raleigh, NC 27614 27614
(919) 848-3596, *Fax:* (919) 848-0519
thewhittleagency@nc.rr.com
Gary L. Whittle, President
Total media brokerage svcs, including sls/appraisals of radio stns in the Carolinas, Virginia & Southeast.

Willis Broadcasting
645 Church St., Suite 400, Norfolk, VA 23510 23510
(757) 624-6500, *Fax:* (757) 624-6515
www.wpce1400.com
willisbroadcasting@yahoo.com
L. E. Willis Sr., President

Wood & Co. Inc.
431 Ohio Pike, Suite 200, Cincinnati, OH 45255 45255
(513) 528-7373, *Fax:* (513) 528-7374
Larry C. Wood, President
Nationwide brokerage service to buyers & sellers of TV & radio properties.

Station Financing Services

ABN AMRO
Park Ave. Plaza 55 E. 52nd St., New York, NY 10055
(212) 409-1000, (212) 251-3524, *Fax:* (212) 409-7291
www.abnamro.com
Joost Kuiper, Chairman

Allied Capital Corp.
1919 Pennsylvania Ave. N.W., 3rd Fl., Washington, DC 20006
(202) 331-1112, *Fax:* (202) 659-2053
www.alliedcapital.com
wrichardson@alliedcaptial.com
William Walton, Chairman
Subordinated debt, deal size $3 million to $8 million, natl & international.

Alta Communications
200 Clarendon St., 51st Fl., Boston, MA 02116

(617) 262-7770, *Fax:* (617) 262-9779
www.altacomm.com
clarason@altacomm.com
Brian McNeill, CEO
Provide equity & subordinated debt for acquisitions, buyouts, recapitalizations, etc. for companies in radio, TV, cable TV & related industries.

Bank of America Illinois
231 S. LaSalle St., Chicago, IL 60697
(312) 828-2345, *Fax:* (312) 828-7397
www.bankofamerica.com
pat.mendrik@bankofamerica.com
John Brennan, President

The Barclays Group
200 Park Ave., New York, NY 10166
(212) 412-4000, *Fax:* (212) 412-7300
www.barcap.com
Bob Diamond, President

Barry Skidelsky, Esq.
185 E. 85th St., 23 D, New York, NY 10028
(212) 832-4800
Barry Skidelsky, President
Full svc assistance to investors, owners, mgmt, aquisition, divestiture, start-up, improvement, trustee (bankruptcy & FCC ownership), expert witness & arbitrator.

Berkery, Noyes & Co.
1 Liberty Plaza, 13th Fl., New York, NY 10006
(212) 668-3022, *Fax:* (212) 747-9092
www.berkerynoyes.com
cathy@berkerynoyes.com
Joseph Berkery, CEO
Mai-Anh Tran, Operations Dir
Assists with mergers, acquisitions, divestitures; financial analysis & counsel; debt or equity financing through private or pub chs, including LBOs, ESOPs & valuations.
40 Kirkstall Rd., Newton, MA 02460-2218
(617) 969-7935;
Marlowe G. Teig, Mgng Dir
580 California St., 5th Fl., San Francisco, CA 94104-1000
(415) 440-5001;

BIA Capital Strategies LLC
15120 Enterprise Ct., Suite 100, Chantilly, VA 20151
(703) 818-8115, *Fax:* (703) 803-3299
www.bia.com
info@bia.com
Mark Giannini, COO
Investment banking svc, including placement of debt & equity, advice in capital structure & merger, & acquisition issues.

BIA Digital Partners, L.P.
15120 Enterprise Ct., Suite 100, Chantilly, VA 20151
(703) 227-9600, *Fax:* (703) 803-3299
www.biadigitalpartners.com
gjohnson@bia.com
Lloyd R. Sams, Operations Dir
Provides subordinated debt & preferred equity for communications companies in amounts from 4-25 million.

BIA Financial Network
15120 Enterprise Ct., Suite 100, Chantilly, VA 20151-1102
(703) 818-2425, *Fax:* (703) 803-3299
www.bia.com
info@bia.com
Mark Giannini, COO
Financial consultants to the communications industry; fair market valuations, tax appraisals, acquisition consulting, business plans, internal operational audits, litigation support, investment, publications, & database software, venturefunding, capital.

Blackburn & Co. Capital Markets Group
201 N. Union St., Suite 340, Alexandria, VA 22314
(703) 519-3703, *Fax:* (703) 519-9756
rblack4@aol.com
James W. Blackburn Jr., Chairman
Brokerage of radio & TV stns.

BMO Nesbitt Burns (Bank of Montreal)
3 Times Sq., New York, NY 10036
(212) 605-1424, *Fax:* (212) 605-1648
www.bmo.com
yvonne.bos@bmo.com
Provides lending & other capital raising svcs, derivatives, & cash mgmt to the bcst & cable industries.

BNP Paribas
9787 Seventh Ave., New York, NY 10019
(212) 841-2000, *Fax:* (212) 841-3251
Leading underwriting & syndicating time-sensitive, non-investment grade debt financing; often requiring complex & creative capital structures; also financing & equity co-investments.
Branch offices located in Los Angeles, London, New York,& Paris.

Bulkley Capital L.P.
5949 Sherry Ln., Suite 1370, Dallas, TX 75225
(214) 692-5476, *Fax:* (214) 692-9309
www.bulkleycapital.com
info@bulkleycapital.com
Oliver Cone, Operations Dir
Investment banking; mergers, acquisitions, private placements of debt & equity capital.

Chaisson & Company Inc.
154 Indian Waters Dr., New Canaan, CT 06840 6840
(203) 966-6333, *Fax:* (203) 966-1298
rchaisco@aol.com
Robert A. Chaisson, President
Brokerage of radio/TV sls & acquisitions.

CIBC World Markets
300 Madison Ave., New York, NY 10017
(212) 856-4000, *Fax:* (212) 856-3996
www.cibcwm.com
Gary W. Brown, President
Investment banking & asset mgmt.

Clifton Gardiner & Company L.L.C.
2437 S. Chase Ln., Denver, CO 80227
(303) 758-6900, *Fax:* (303) 757-5005
www.cliftongardiner.com
cliff@cliftongardiner.com
Clifton H. Gardiner, President
Consulting svcs on debt & equity placements.

Communicaions Equity Associate
Div/DBA: (Formerly CEA Inc.)
54 Thompson St., 4th Fl., New York, NY 10012
(212) 218-5085, *Fax:* (212) 334-3063
www.ceaworldwide.com
J. Patrick Michael Jr., CEO
Investment banking, brokerage & private equity.
101 Kennedy Blvd., #3300, Tampa, FL 33602-5151
(813) 226-8844;

Communications Equity Associates
101 E. Kennedy Blvd., Suite 3300, Tampa, FL 33602
(813) 226-8844, *Fax:* (813) 225-1513
www.ceaworldwide.com
rmichaels@ccceaworldwide.com
J. Patrick Michaels Jr., Chairman
Investment banking, corporate finance & private equity, firm specializing in cable, bcstg, new media & entertainment industries.
Prinzregentenstrasse 56, Muenchen,
49-(0)89 290 7250; *Fax:* 49 (0)89 290 725 200
Dr. Stephan Goetz, Stefan Sanktjohanser
mgng ptnrs, Dr. Gemot Wunderle
mgng dir, President
1270 Avenue of the Americas, Suite 1818, New York, NY 10020-1700
(212) 218-5085; *Fax:* (212) 218-5099
Alexander Rossi, Mgng Director
Bob Ennis, Mgng Director
Waldo Glasman, Mgng Director
Paul Miller, Mgng Director
Evan Blum, Dir
Jason Donnell, Dir
191 Post Rd. W., Westport, CT 06880-4625
(203) 221-2662; *Fax:* (203) 221-2663
David Moyer, Mktg Dir

Cox & Cox, LLC
2454 Shiva Ct., St. Louis, MO 63011 63011
(636) 458-4780, *Fax:* (636) 273-1312
www.coxandcoxllc.com
bc@coxandcoxllc.com
Robert Cox, President
Linda Cox, Operations Dir
Media mergers & acquisitions, appraisals, consulting, expert testimony, receivership & workout.

The Deer River Group
888 16th St., N.W., Suite 400, Washington, DC 20006
(202) 939-9090, *Fax:* (202) 939-9091
robin.martin@earthlink.net
Robin B. Martin, President
Assist bcst execs in acquiring stns, securing financing; financial consultant to single stns & group owners; investment banking svcs.

Dresdner Kleinwort
1301 Ave. of the Americas, New York, NY 10019
(212) 969-2700
www.dresdnerkleinwort.com
Integrated investment bank offering premier mergers & acquisitions advising as well as private equity investment & placement, structuring, underwriting & advisory for global debt & equity.

Edwin Tornberg & Co. Inc.
8917 Cherbourg Dr., Potomac, MD 20854
(301) 299-6661, *Fax:* (301) 299-2297
Edwin Tornberg, President

EnVest Media, LLC
6802 Patterson Ave., Richmond, VA 23226 23226
(804) 282-5561, *Fax:* (804) 282-5703
www.envestmedia.com
mitt@envestmedia.com
Mitt Younts, General Manager
Nationwide radio, TV acquisition, valuation, financing & consulting firm. The company provides brokerage svcs to stn transaction, appraisal svcs to stn owners & financial institutions. The group secures debt & equity acquisition financing,offers consulting & asset mgmt svcs, acting as court appointed receivers or trustees for bcst stns.

GE Capital Inc.
500 W. Monroe St., Chicago, IL 60661
(312) 463-2300, *Fax:* (312) 441-6728
www.gecapital.com
Kim Gutierrez, Promotions Manager
Coml financial svcs.

GE Commercial Finance Global Media and Communications
201 Main Ave., 4th Fl., Norwalk, CT 06851
(203) 956-4000, *Fax:* (203) 956-4528
www.geglobalmediacomm.com
Michael E. Chen, President
Leading provider of capital to the bcstg, cable, entertainment, movie theater, outdoor adv, publishing, technology, towers, wireless & wireline industries. Locations in Atlanta, Chicago, Delhi, London, New York, Norwalk, & San Francisco.

Gleacher Partners
660 Madison Ave., New York, NY 10021
(212) 418-4200, *Fax:* (212) 752-2711
www.gleacher.com
William Payne, Chairman
Provide advice & capital to companies in the media & telecommunications industries.

Great Hill Partners
One Liberty Sq., Boston, MA 02109
(617) 790-9400, *Fax:* (617) 790-9401
www.greathillpartners.com
sgormley@greathillpartners.com
Laurie Gerber, CEO
Private equity for media & communications companies.

Hoffman Schutz Media Capital Inc.
2044 W. California St., San Diego, CA 92110
(619) 291-7070
1needham@ribroadcasters.com
Directors:
Lori Neeham, exec dir

HSBC
One HSBC Ctr., Buffalo, NY 14203
(716) 841-7212, *Fax:* (716) 854-2751
www.us.hsbc.com
Postproduction & radio/TV equipment financing.

Hungerford, Aldrin, Nichols & Carter, CPAs
2910 Lucerne Dr. S.E., Grand Rapids, MI 49546
(616) 949-3200, *Fax:* (616) 949-7720
www.hanc.com
charper@hanc.com
Jerry Nichols, Shareholder
Confidential radio & TV market revenue share reports for the bcst industry.

J P Morgan and Co. Inc.
60 Wall St., New York, NY 10260
(212) 483-2323
www.jpmorgan.com
Jamie Dimon, CEO

Mergers & acquisitions; debt & equity capital raising; swaps & derivatives; credit arrangement & loan syndication; securities sls & trading; asset mgmt.
333 S. Hope St, 35th Fl, Los Angeles, CA 90071-1406
(213) 437-9300;
227 W. Monroe St, Suite 2800m, Chicago, IL 60606-5055
(312) 541-3300;
101 California St, 38th Fl, San Francisco, CA 94111-5802
(415) 954-3200;

KeyBanc Capital Markets
127 Public Sq., 6th Fl., Cleveland, OH 44114-1306
(216) 689-3000, *Fax:* (216) 689-4666
www.key.com/media
kmayher@keybanccm.com
Kathleen Mayher, President
Financing for media—TV, radio, cable, nwsprs, bcstg & telecommunications.

The Kompas Group
Box 250813, Milwaukee, WI 53225-6513
(262) 781-0188, *Fax:* (262) 781-5313
www.yourlptvsource.com
kompasgroup@toast.net
John Kompas, President
Jackie Kompas, Operations Dir
Financial & mktg svcs for LPTV, audience demographic reports, stn coverage maps, financial & strategic planning.

M/C Venture Partners
75 State St., Suite 2500, Boston, MA 02109
(617) 345-7200, *Fax:* (617) 345-7201
www.mcventurepartners.com
jwade@mcventurepartners.com
David Croll, Operations Dir
Provides equity financing & strategic guidance to entrepreneurial ventures in the media & telecommunications industries.

The MFR Group
Box 1184, Rancho Mirage, CA 92270
(760) 324-1516, *Fax:* (760) 324-8255
www.mfrgroup.net
bfenmore@mfrgroup.net
Bart Fenmore, President
Accounts receivable funding for radio/TV stns.

Multimedia Broadcast Investment Corp.
3101 South St. N.W., Washington, DC 20007
(202) 293-1166, *Fax:* (202) 293-1181
wthreadgill@comcast.net
Walter Threadgill, President
Provides sr, subordinated debt, equity for telecommunications & bcst ventures.

National Broadcast Finance Corp.
Box 3167, 27 Harrison St., New Haven, CT 06515-0267
(203) 389-6000, *Fax:* (203) 389-6020
cherhoniak@sbcglobal.net
David C. Cherhoniak, President
Specialized investment banking & financial consulting, including raising debt & equity for bcst acquisitions & refinancings; also brokerage for acquisitions & divestitures.

Nautic Partners
50 Kennedy Plaza, Providence, RI 02903
(401) 278-6770, *Fax:* (401) 278-6387
www.nauticpartners.com
bwheeler@nautic.com
Habib Gorgi, Operations Dir
Source of equity capital to well-managed, positive cash flowing companies.

Norman Fischer & Associates Inc.
Box 5308, Austin, TX 78763
(512) 476-9457, *Fax:* (512) 476-0540
www.nfainc.com
terrill@nfainc.com
Terrill Fischer, President
Brokerage in radio, TV & cable; consultation in mgmt & opns; appraisals; feasibility studies; expert testimony; financial planning & assistance.
1330 Biafore Ave, Bethlehem, PA 18017-1006
(610) 317-2424;
Bernhard Fuhrmann, East Coast/Atlantic Assoc

Patrick Communications L.L.C.
6805 Douglas Legum Dr., Suite 100, Elkridge, MD 21075 21075
(410) 799-1740, *Fax:* (410) 799-1705
www.patcomm.com
larry@patcomm.com
Larry Patrick, Managing Partner
Susan Patrick, Managing Partner
Grey Guy, Managing Partner
Jason James, Vice President
David Benton, Analyst
Stn brokerage, investment banking, mgmt consulting svcs, appraisals & opns consulting.

Phoenix Cable Inc.
17 S. Franklin Tpke., Ramsey, NJ 07446
(201) 825-9090, *Fax:* (201) 825-8794
James Feeney, General Manager
Cable TV systems ownership, system mgmt svcs, lease & debt financing svcs.
2401 Kerner Blvd, San Rafael, CA 94901-5569
(415) 485-4500;
Gus Constantin, Pres

PK World Media
126 Clock Tower Pl., Carmel, CA 93923-8734
(831) 624-5100, *Fax:* (831) 625-3225
www.pkworldmedia.com
info@pkworldmedia.com
Paul Kagan, CEO
Specializing in financial & investment rsch. Media financial newsletters & database reports. Strategic consulting, seminars & conferences.

Premier Capital Group
670 106 St., Suite 200, Urbandale, IA 50322
(515) 698-9600, *Fax:* (515) 698-9699
Equipment financing for business owners or financing of customers of a broker or distributor.

R. Miller Hicks & Co.
1011 W. 11th St., Austin, TX 78703
(512) 477-7000, *Fax:* (512) 477-9697
millerhicks@rmhicks.com
Business consultant & dev firm.

RBC Daniels L.P.
Div/DBA: (formerly Daniels & Associates)
3200 Cherry Creek S. Dr., Suite 500, Denver, CO 80209
(303) 778-5555, *Fax:* (303) 778-5599
www.danielsonline.com
info@rbcdaniels.com
Brian Deevy, Chairman
Provides mergers, acquisitions, corporate finance & financial advisory svcs to the tcable, telecom, media & internet industries.
711 5th Ave., Suite 405, New York, NY 10022-3111
(212) 935-5900; *Fax:* (212) 8634859
David Tolliver, Vp

Richard A. Foreman Associates Inc.
330 Emery Dr. E., Stamford, CT 06902-2210
(203) 327-2800, *Fax:* (203) 967-9393
www.rafamedia.com
raf@rafamedia.com
Richard A. Foreman, President
Debt & equity placement for radio & TV stn acquisitions in major growth markets.

Rodgers Broadcasting
2301 W. Main St., Richmond, IN 47375
(765) 962-6533, *Fax:* (765) 966-1499
David A. Rodgers, President
Financing particulary for small operators.

SB Management
Div/DBA: (formerly Media Capital Inc.)
890 Monterey St., Suite G, San Luis Obispo, CA 93401
(805) 543-9214, *Fax:* (805) 543-9243
michael@mikehesser.com
Michael B. Hesser, President
Assist in finding, evaluating, financing & structuring acquisitions. Also, consult mgmt & sls.

Schroder Investment Management North America Inc.
Div/DBA: (formerly Schroder Investment Management)
875 Third Ave., 22nd Fl., New York, NY 10022
(212) 641-3800, (212) 641-3830, *Fax:* (212) 641-3985
www.schroders.com/us
Jamie Dorrien-Smith, CEO

Silicon Valley Bank
185 Berry St., Lobby 1, Suite 3000, San Francisco, CA 94107
(415) 512-4227, (415) 512-4200, *Fax:* (415) 348-0258, (415) 856-0810
www.svb.com
moleary@svbank.com
Ken Wilcox, President
Meghan O'Leary, Operations Dir
Comprehensive finance svcs for middle market bcst & cable operators.

Syndicated Communications Inc. (SYNCOM)
8401 Colesville Rd., Suite 300, Silver Spring, MD 20910
(301) 608-3203, *Fax:* (301) 608-3307
www.syncomfunds.com
Terry L. Jones, General Manager

Veronis Suhler Stevenson
350 Park Ave, New York, NY 10022
(212) 935-4990, *Fax:* (212) 381-8168
www.veronissuhler.com
stevenson@veronissuhler.com
James P. Rutherfurd, President
Jeffrey T. Stevenson, Operations Dir
Private equity/media buyout affil of Veronis, Suhler, established in 1987 & investing in companies across the spectrum of communications industry segments.
London
St. James Square, Buchanan House, 8th Fl, London, United Kingdom
44-207-484-1440; *Fax:* 44-207-484-1415
Nigel Stapleton, Chmn Veloms Schler International

Wachovia Securities
Wachovia Securities, 301 S. College St., Charlotte, NC 28288
(704) 348-9500, *Fax:* (704) 715-1997
www.wachovia.com
info@wachovia.com
Ben Jenkins, President
Secured financing for acquisition &/or recapitalization of bcst properties.

Waller Capital Corp.
30 Rockefeller Plaza, Suite 4350, New York, NY 10112
(212) 632-3600, *Fax:* (212) 632-3607
www.wallercc.com
info@wallercc.com
John Waller, III, Chairman
Financing & investment svcs to cable TV industry, specializing in cable TV mergers & acquisitions, buyout financing, raising debt & equity.

Wells Fargo Equipment Finance Inc.
530 Fifth Ave., 15th Fl., New York, NY 10036
(212) 805-1000, *Fax:* (212) 805-1050
www.wellsfargo.com
wfefi@wellsfargo.com
John Crum, President
Leading provider of equipment leasing & financing, intermediate term lending & specialty finance products to the bcst industry.
100 Mill Plain Rd., 3rd Fl., Danbury, CT 06811-5178
(203) 791-3944;
Brian Rodden, Vp
14081 Yorba St., Suite 205, Tustin, CA 92780-2010
(714) 544-4190;
Deborah Anderson, Vp

Wood & Co. Inc.
431 Ohio Pike, Suite 200, Cincinnati, OH 45255
(513) 528-7373, *Fax:* (513) 528-7374
Larry C. Wood, President

Talent Agents & Managers

Abrams Artists Agency
9200 Sunset Blvd., 11th Fl., Los Angeles, CA 90069
(310) 859-0625, *Fax:* (310) 276-6193
www.abramsart.com
harry.abrams@abramsart.com
Harry Abrams, President
Robert Attermann, Operations Dir
Performing artists rep talent agency.
Abrams Artists Agency
275 7th Ave, 26th Fl., New York, NY 10001-6708
(646) 486-4600; *Fax:* (646) 486-0100
Neal Altman, Sr Vp
Robert Attermann, Vp

Barry Skidelsky, Esq.
185 East 85th St., 23D, New York, NY 10028
(212) 832-4800
Barry Skidelsky, Esq., President
Personal mgmt & representation. Contract negotiations, counsel, etc.

Burt Shapiro Management
2147 N. Beachwood Dr., Los Angeles, CA 90068

(323) 469-9452, *Fax:* (801) 653-6571
www.burtshapiro.com
burtjay@mail.com
Burt Shapiro, President
Represents on-air talent including anchors, reporters, hosts, & sports anchor/reporters, as well as producers & news directors.

Eatman Media Services Inc.
5901 N. Cicero Ave., Suite 307, Chicago, IL 60646
(773) 777-5463, *Fax:* (773) 777-7106
emstalent@aol.com
Representation of TV newspersons, TV personalities, & radio talent in job placement & contract negotiation.

Ephraim & Associates, P.C.
108 W. Grand Ave., Chicago, IL 60654-4206
(312) 321-9700, *Fax:* (312) 321-3655
www.ephraim.com
eliot@ephraim.com
Donald M. Ephraim, President
David M. Ephraim, Operations Dir
Talent representation, including contract negotiation, legal & career consulation, tax, estate & pension planning. Elliot Ephraim, atty/agent.

Goldstein Management Group, Inc.
1601 N. Sepulveda Blvd., Suite 357, Manhattan Beach, CA 90266
(310) 545-8530, *Fax:* (310) 943-1569
glenn802@aol.com
Glenn A. Goldstein, President
Full-svc representation of bcst talent & bcst journalists.

The Image Generators
18156 Darnell Dr., Olney, MD 20832
(301) 924-5700, *Fax:* (301) 570-8916
www.imagegenerators.com
Michael J. Weiner, President
Valle Bonhag, General Manager
Voiceover talent, audition svc, online demos of pro voices.

International Creative Management Inc.
825 Eighth Ave., New York, NY 10019
(212) 556-5600, *Fax:* (212) 556-5665
www.ICMtalent.com
Jeff Berg, Chairman
10250 Constellation Blvd., Los Angeles, CA 90067-6200
(310) 550-4000;
61 Frith Street, London,
+44 207 851 4853;

Ken Fishkin & Associates
50 Milk St., 20th Fl., Boston, MA 02109-5002
(617) 423-5800, *Fax:* (617) 426-2674
cindy@kfishkin.com
Kenneth R. Fishkin, President
Contract negotiation & job placement, TV & radio.

Miller Broadcast Management Inc.
616 W. Fulton St., Suite 516, Chicago, IL 60661
(312) 454-1111, *Fax:* (312) 454-0044
www.millerbroadcast.com
info@millerbroadcast.com
Lisa Miller, President
Representing radio & TV personalities.

N S Bienstock Inc.
250 W. 57th St., Suite 333, New York, NY 10107
(212) 765-3040, *Fax:* (212) 757-6411
www.nsbtalent.com
nsb@nsbtalent.com
News & syndication talent specialists—loc & net—on & off camera. Packager of talk & reality progmg—MOWs.

Paradigm
360 N. Crescent Dr., N. Bldg., Beverly Hills, CA 90210-6818
(310) 288-8000, *Fax:* (310) 288-2000
www.paradigmagency.com
info@paradigm-agency.com
Sam Gores, President
124 12th Ave. S., Suite 410, Nashville, TN 37203-3146
(831) 375-4889; *Fax:* (831) 375-2623
509 Hartnell St., Monterey, CA 93940-2825
(615) 251-4400; *Fax:* (615) 251-44001

Rebel Entertainment
5700 Wilshire Blvd., Ste 456, Los Angeles, CA 90038
(323) 935-1700, *Fax:* (323) 932-9901
www.arltalent.com
rlawre8075@aol.com
Richard Lawrence, President
Debra Goldfarb, Operations Dir
Talent placement & TV show packaging.

Reece Halsey Agency
8733 Sunset Blvd., Suite 101, West Hollywood, CA 90069
(415) 789-9191, *Fax:* (415) 789-9177
Reece Halsey Agency
Box 704, 98 Main St, Tiburon, CA 94920-0704
(415) 789-9191;
Kimberly Cameron, Chairman

Screen Children's Casting
4000 Riverside Dr., Suite A, Burbank, CA 91505
(818) 846-4300, *Fax:* (818) 846-3745
Irene B. Gallagher, President
Full-svc children's casting representing babies (especially twins), children & teenagers up to age 18, extra work.

Shirley Hamilton Inc.
333 E. Ontario, Chicago, IL 60611
(312) 787-4700, *Fax:* (312) 787-8456
www.shirleyhamilton.com
shamilton@att.net
Shirley Hamilton, President
Lynne Hamilton, General Manager
Representing talent for TV, PRINT, RADIO, ON CAMERA, FILM, LIVE, THEATRICAL, VOICEOVER, INDUSTRIALS. Audition facilities for OnCamera, Digital voiceover, Print.

The Voicecaster
1832 W. Burbank Blvd., Burbank, CA 91506
(818) 841-5300, *Fax:* (818) 841-2085
www.voicecaster.com
casting@voicecaster.com
Huck Liggett, President
Voice casting for comls, films, animation, theme parks, audiovisual projects, etc.

Weisman, P.C., Law Offices of Joel
1901 Raymond Dr., Northbrook, IL 60062
(847) 400-5900, *Fax:* (847) 400-5534
www.weismanmedialaw.com
joel@weismanmedialaw.com
Joel Weisman, President
Bcst contract drafting & negotiation, career & performance counseling, for anchors, reporters & producers.

William Morris Agency Inc.
1325 Ave. of the Americas, New York, NY 10019
(212) 586-5100, *Fax:* (212) 246-3583
www.wma.com
Cara Stein, COO
Jim Griffin, Operations Dir

National Associations

Academy of Canadian Cinema & Television
49 Ontario Street, Suite 501, Toronto, ON M5A 2V1
416-366-2227, *Fax:* 416-366-8454
www.academy.ca
info@academy.ca
Helga Stevenson, Chief Executive Officer
Suzan Ayscough, Director, Communications
Andrea McGrath, Coordinator, Communications
Jennifer Stewart, Director, Marketing
Ellen Benjamin, Director, Finance
Mission: A national non-profit, professional association dedicated to the promotion, recognition, and celebration of exceptional achievements in Candian film, television, and digital media.

Academy of Television Arts and Science
5200 Lankershim Blvd, North Hollywood, CA 91601-3155
818-754-2800, *Fax:* 818-761-2827
www.emmys.com
John Shaffner, Chairman
Todd Leavitt, President
Founded: 1957 *Number of Members:* 12000 *Mission:* Nonprofit corporation devoted to the advancement of telecommunications arts and sciences and to fostering creative leadership in the telecommunications industry. In additionto recognizing outstanding programming and individual achivements for Primetime and Los Angeles area programming, ATAS sponsors meetings, conferences and activities for collaboration on a variety of topics involving traditional broadcast interests,new media and emerging digital technology.

Accrediting Council on Education in Journalism and Mass Communications
1435 Jayhawk Blvd, Lawrence, KS 66045-7594
785-864-3973, *Fax:* 785-864-5225
www.ukans.edu
Susanne Shaw, Executive Director
Jan Dates, VP
Founded: 1945 *Number of Members:* 113 *Mission:* ACEJMC members are journalism and media departments, education associations and professional organizations.

Accuracy in Media
4455 Connecticut Ave NW, Suite 330, Washington, DC 20008-2372
202-364-4401, *Fax:* 202-364-4098
www.aim.org
info@aim.org
Don Irvine, Chairman
Deborah Lambert, Director of Special Projects
Roger Aronoff, Executive Secretary
Founded: 1969 *Number of Members:* 3500 *Mission:* Accuracy in Media is a non-profit, grassroots citizens watchdog of the news media that critiques botched and bungled news stories and sets the record straight on importantissues that have received slanted coverage.

Acoustical Society of America
2 Huntington Quadrayle, Suite 1N01, Melville, NY 11747-4502
(516) 576-2360, *Fax:* (516) 576-2377
asa.aip.org
asa@aip.org

Ad Council
815 2nd Ave, 9th Floor, New York, NY 10017-4503
212-922-1500, *Fax:* 212-962-1676
www.adcouncil.org
info@adcouncil.org
Peggy Conlon, President/CEO
Jon Fish, CFO
Founded: 1942 *Number of Members:* 100 *Mission:* Our mission is to identify a select number of significant public issues and stimulate action on those issues through communications programs that make a measurable difference inour society.

Advanced Television Systems Committee
1776 K Street, 8th Floor, Washington, DC 20006-2304
202-872-9160, *Fax:* 202-872-9161
www.atsc.org
atsc@atsc.org
Mark Richer, President
Jerry Whitaker, Vice President
Lindsay Shelton Gross, Director, Communications
Daro Bruno, Office Manager
Mission: ATSC is an international, non-profit organzation developing voluntary standards for digital television.

Advertising Council Inc
1707 L Street NW, Suite 600, Washington, DC 20036
202-331-9153, *Fax:* 202-331-9186
www.adcouncil.org
info@adcouncil.org
Peggy Conlon, President, CEO
John Fish, EVP, Chief Financial Officer
Barbara Leshinsky, EVP, Development
Priscilla Natkins, Director, Client Services
Paula Veale, Corporate Communications
Mission: The Ad Council marshals volunteer talent from the advertising and communications industries, the facilities of the media, and the resources of the business and non-profit communities to create awareness, foster understandingand motivate action.

Advertising Educational Foundation
220 E 42nd St, Suite 3300, New York, NY 10017-5813
212-986-8060, *Fax:* 212-986-8061
www.aef.com
pa@aef.com
Paula Alex, CEO
John Follis, President
Founded: 1983 *Number of Members:* 48 *Mission:* The advertising industry's provider and distributor of educational content to enrich the understanding of advertising and its role in culture, society and the economy.

Advertising Photographers of America
PO Box 725146, Atlanta, GA 31139
800-272-6264, *Fax:* 888-889-7190
www.apanational.com
ceo@apanational.com
Theresa Raffetto, President
Stephen Best, National CEO
Founded: 1981 *Mission:* Our goal is to establish, endorse and promote professional practices, standards and ethics in the photographic and advertising community.

Advertising Research Foundation
432 Park Ave S, 6th Floor, New York, NY 10016-8013
212-751-5656, *Fax:* 212-319-5265
www.thearf.org
info@thearf.org
Robert Barocci, President/CEO
Leslie Hutchings, Marketing Director
Rachael Feigenbaum, Program Director
Founded: 1936 *Mission:* An open forum where the best and the brightest from every avenue of advertising can gather to exchange ideas and research strategies

Advertising Specialty Institute
4800 Street Rd, Langhorne, PA 19053-6698
215-953-4000, *Fax:* 215-953-3045
www.asicentral.com
info@asicentral.com
Timothy M Andrews, CEO
Susanne Curry, SVP Marketing
Founded: 1950 *Number of Members:* 26000 *Mission:* Advertising Specialty Institute provides distributors, suppliers and decorators in the advertising specialty industry with catalogs, information directories, newsletters,magazines, web sites and databases, and offers interactive e-commerce, marketing and selling tools.

Agricultural Communications in Education
Mowry Road, Building 16, Gainesville, FL 32611
352-392-9588, *Fax:* 352-392-8583
www.aceweb.org
ace@ifas.ufl.edu
Kristina Boone, President
Steve Dodrill, VP
Hugh Maynard, Associate Director
Founded: 1970 *Number of Members:* 700+ *Mission:* Members are writers, editors, broadcasters and communicators who are involved in the dissemination of agricultural, food sciences and natural resource information in land-grantcolleges, federal and state agencies, international agencies and other private communications work.

The Alliance for Community Media
1760 Old Meadow Road, Suite 500, McLean, VA 22102
703-506-2889, *Fax:* 703-506-3266
www.allcommunitymedia.org
info@allcommunitymedia.org
Sylvia Strobel, Executive Director
Gregory Morrison, Manager, Membership
Founded: 1976 *Number of Members:* 1000 *Mission:* Promotes civic engagement through community medias.

Alliance for Telecommunication Industry
1200 G St NW, Suite 500, Washington, DC 20005-6706
202-628-2070, *Fax:* 202-393-5453
www.atis.org
atispr@artis.org
Susan Miller, President/CEO
Kelly Weiss, Director Information Services
Bill Klein, VP Finance/Operations
Founded: 1983 *Number of Members:* 1400 *Mission:* Membership organization that provides the tools necessary for the industry to identify standards, guidelines and operating procedures that make the inoperability of existingand emerging telecommunications products and services possible.

Alliance for Women in Media
1760 Old Meadow Rd, Suite 500, Mc Lean, VA 22102-4306
703-506-3290, *Fax:* 703-506-3266
www.allwomeninmedia.org
info@allwomeninmedia.org
Erin Fuller, President
Amy Lotz, EVP
Founded: 1951 *Mission:* Leverages the promise, passion, and power of women in all forms if media. One of the longest established professional association dedicated to advancing women in the media and entertainment. Still strongafter 60 years, carrying forth with its mission by educating, advocating, and acting as a resource to its members and the industry at large via inspired thought leadership that illuminates areas od social need.

Alliance of Motion Picture and Television Producers
15503 Ventura Boulevard, Encino, CA 91436
818-995-3600, *Fax:* 818-382-1793
www.amptp.org
Nick Counter, President
Founded: 1982 *Number of Members:* 350 *Mission:* Trade association with respect to labor issues in the motion picture and television industry. We negotiate 80 industry wide collective bargaining agreements that cover actors,craftspersons, directors, musicians, technicians and writers — virtually all of the people who work on theatrical motion pictures and television programs. In these negotiations, the AMPTP represents over 350 production companies and studios.

American Advertising Federation
1101 Vermont Ave NW, Suite 500, Washington, DC 20005-6306
202-898-0089, *Fax:* 202-898-0159
www.aaf.org
aaf@aaf.org
James Edmund Datri, President & CEO
Steve Pacheco, Chairman
John Osborn, Vice Chairman
Andy Narrai, Treasurer
Greg D'Alba, Secretary
Founded: 1967 *Number of Members:* 40000 *Mission:* The AAF is the oldest national advertising trade association, and protects and promotes the well-being of advertising. The AAF accomplishes this through a unique, nationallycoordinated grassroots network of advertisers, agencies, media companies, local advertising clubs and college chapters.

American Agricultural Editors' Association
120 Main Street W, PO Box 156, New Prague, MN 56071
952-758-6502, *Fax:* 952-758-5813
www.ageditors.com
aaea@gardnerandgardnercommunications.com
Den Gardner, Executive Director
Karen Simon, President
Kenna Rathai, Associate Executive Director
Mission: National professional development member association for agricultural communicators.

American Association of Advertising Agencies (AAAA)
405 Lexington Ave., 18th Fl., New York, NY 10174-1801
(212) 682-2500, *Fax:* (212) 682-8391
www.aaaa.org

American Association of Sunday & Feature Editors
1921 Gallows Road, Suite 600, Vienna, VA 22182-3900
703-902-1639, *Fax:* 703-620-4557
www.aasfe.org
nahan@naa.org
Chris Beringer, President
Gina Seay, VP
Denise Joyce, VP
Kim Marcum, Secretary-Treasurer
Mission: An organization of editors from the United States and Canada dedicated to the quality of features in newspapers and the craft of feature writing.

American Auto Racing Writers and Broadcasters
922 N Pass Ave, Burbank, CA 91505-2703
818-842-7005, *Fax:* 818-842-7020
www.aarwba.org
dusty.brandel@gmail.com
Dusty Brandel, President/Executive Director
Kathy Seymour, National VP

Dr. George Peters, Secretary/Treasurer
Ron Lemasters, Sr., Midwest VP
Joe Jennings, Southern VP
Founded: 1955 *Number of Members:* 400 *Mission:* Members are professional journalists who regularly cover auto racing and related sports events.

American Center for Children and Media
5400 North St Louis Avenue, Chicago, IL 60623
703-509-5510, *Fax:* 773-509-5303
www.centerforhildrenandmedia.org
info@centerforchildrenandmedia.org
James Fellows, Founder
David Kleeman, President
Mission: Mission is to support a vibrant children's media industry by convening key constituencies to develop, implement and promote policies and practices that respect young people's well being, and are sustainable.

American Cinema Editors Inc.
100 Universal City Plaza, Bldg. 2282, Rm. 234, Universal City, CA 91608
(818) 777-2900, *Fax:* (818) 733-5023
www.ace-filmeditors.org

American Composers Alliance (ACA)
648 Broadway, Rm. 803, New York, NY 10012-2301
(212) 362-8900, (212) 925-0458, *Fax:* (212) 925-6798
www.composers.com
info@composers.com

American Copy Editors Society (ACES)
7 Avenida Vista Grande, Suite B7 #467, Santa Fe, NM 87508

www.copydesk.org
info@copydesk.org
Teresa Schmedding, President
Lisa McLendon, Vice President Conferences
Sara Hendricks, Vice President Membership
Rudy Bahr, Executive Director
Gerri Berendzen, Content Editor
Founded: 1997 *Mission:* ACES is a professional organization working toward the advancement of editors. Their aim is to provide opportunities through training, discussion and advocacy that promote the editing profession.

American Disc Jockey Association
20118 N 67th Avenue, Suite 300-605, Glendale, CA 85308

www.adja.org
office@adja.org
Rob Snyder, Director
Mission: An association of professional mobile entertainers. Encourages success for its members through continuous education, camaraderie, and networking. The primary goal is to educate Disc Jockeys so that each member acts ethicallyand responsibly.

American Electronics Association
5201 Great America Pkwy., Suite 520, Santa Clara, CA 95054
(408) 987-4200, *Fax:* (408) 987-4298
www.aeanet.org
601 Pennsylvania Ave, Washington, DC
(202) 682-9110; *Fax:* (202) 682-9111
William Archey, Pres

American Federation of Television and Radio Artists
260 Madison Ave, Suite 7, New York, NY 10016-2401
212-532-7633, *Fax:* 212-532-2242
www.aftra.com
info@aftra.com
Steven Burrow, Executive Director
Bob Edwards, First VP
Roberta Reardon, Second VP
Founded: 1952 *Number of Members:* 80000 *Mission:* Represents its members in four major areas: news and broadcasting; entertainment programing; the recording business; and commercials and non-broadcast, industrial, educationalmedia.

American Marketing Association
311 S. Wacker Dr., Suite 5800, Chicago, IL 60606
(312) 542-9000, (800) 262-1150, *Fax:* (312) 542-9001
www.marketingpower.com
info@ama.org

American Medical Writers' Association
40 W Gude Dr, Suite 525, Rockville, MD 20850-1152
301-294-5303, *Fax:* 301-294-9006
www.amwa.org
ronnie@amwa.org
Donna Munari, Executive Director
Founded: 1940 *Number of Members:* 3.4M *Mission:* Concerned with the advancement and improvement of medical communications.

American Meteorological Society
45 Beacon St., Boston, MA 02108-3693
(617) 227-2425, *Fax:* (617) 742-8718
www.ametsoc.org/ams
amsinfo@ametsoc.org

American Newspaper Representatives
2075 W Big Beaver Rd, Suite 310, Troy, MI 48084-3439
248-643-9910, *Fax:* 248-643-9914
www.anrinc.net
Hilary Howe, President
Robert Sontag, Executive VP/COO
John Jepsen, Controller
Melanie Cox, Regional Sales Manager
Mission: Supports those newspaper representatives and distributors in the United States. Hosts annual trade show.

American Press Institute (API)
11690 Sunrise Valley Drive, Reston, VA 20191-1498
703-620-3611, *Fax:* 703-620-5814
www.americanpressinstitute.org
info@americanpressinstitute.org
Thomas A. Silvestri, Chairman
Peter Bhatia, Editor
James Moroney, III, Publisher and CEO
Katharine Weymouth, Chief Executive Officer
Founded: 1946 *Mission:* API is the trusted source for career leadership development for the newsmedia industry in North America and around the world. They help companies innovate and leaders realize their full potential.

American Private Radio Association (APRA)
PO Box 4221, Scottsdale, AZ 85261-4221
480-661-5000
Mission: Association members are from private radio stations.

American Radio Relay League
225 Main St., Newington, CT 06111
(860) 594-0200, *Fax:* (860) 594-0259
www.arrl.org
hg@arrl.org
Directors:
Joel Harrison, 1st VP

American Society of Business Publication
214 North Hale Street, Wheaton, IL 60187
630-510-4588, *Fax:* 630-510-4501
www.asbpe.org
info@asbpe.org
Amy Florence Fischbach, President
Erin Erickson, Vice President
Tina Grady Barbaccia, Secretary/Treasurer
Janet Svazas, Executive Director
Robin Sherman, Associate Dir. & Newsletter Editor
Founded: 1964 *Mission:* ASBPE is the professional association for full-time and freelance editors and writers employed in the business, trade, and specialty press. It is widely known for its annual Awards of Excellencecompetition, which recognizes the best editorial, design, and online achievement.

American Society of Composers, Authors & Publishers (ASCAP)
One Lincoln Plaza, New York, NY 10023
(212) 621-6000, *Fax:* (212) 724-9064
www.ascap.com
info@ascap.com
(See listing under Music Licensing, Section G.)
ASCAP - Nashville
Two Music Square W., Nashville, TN
(615) 742-5000; *Fax:* (615) 742-5020
ASCAP - Miami
420 Lincoln Rd., Suite 385, Miami Beach, FL 33139-3036
(305) 673-3446; *Fax:* (305) 673-2446
ASAP - Los Angeles
7920 W. Sunset Blvd., 3rd Fl., Los Angeles, CA 90046-3300
(323) 883-1000; *Fax:* (323) 883-1049
ASCAP - Atlanta
541 Tenth St. N.W., PMB400, Atlanta, GA 30318-5713
(404) 351-1224; *Fax:* (404) 351-1252
ASCAP - Chicago
1608 N. Milwaukee, Suite 1007, Chicago, IL 60647-5456
(773) 394-4286; *Fax:* (773) 394-5639
ASCAP - Puerto Rico
654 Ave. Munoz Rivera, IBM Plaza Suite 1101 B, Hato Rey, PR
(787) 281-0782; *Fax:* (787) 767-2805
ASCAP - London
8 Cork St., London, United Kingdom
011 44-207-439-0909; *Fax:* 011 44-207-434-0073

American Society of Journalists and Authors
1501 Broadway, Suite 302, New York, NY 10036-5505
212-997-0947, *Fax:* 212-937-2315
www.asja.org
webeditor@asja.org
Alexandra Owens, Executive Director
Lisa Collier Cool, President
Barbara DeMarco Barrett, Newsletter Editor
Founded: 1948 *Number of Members:* 1000+ *Mission:* For freelance nonfiction writers whose bylines appear in periodicals and in books.

American Society of Magazine Editors
810 Seventh Avenue, 24th Floor, New York, NY 10019
212-872-3700, *Fax:* 212-906-0128
www.magazine.org
asme@magazine.org
Sid Holt, Chief Executive
Nina Fortuna, Program Coordinator
Larry Hackett, President
Peggy Northrop, Vice President
Lucy Danziger, Secretary
Founded: 1963 *Number of Members:* 700 *Mission:* ASME is the principal organization for magazine journalists in the United States. ASME works to defend the First Amendment, protect editorial independence and support thedevelopment of journalism.

American Society of Media Photographers
150 North 2nd Street, Philadelphia, PA 19108
215-451-2767
www.asmp.org
info@asmp.org
Jim Cavanaugh, President
Gail Mooney, First Vice President
Eugene Mopsik, Executive Director
Elena Goertz, General Manager
Khaisha Allford, Member Services Coordinator
Founded: 1944 *Mission:* ASMP is the premier trade association for the world's most respectd photograhers. ASMP is the leader in promoting photographers' rights, providing education in better business practices, producing businesspublications for photographers, and helping to connect purchasers with professional photographers.

American Society of News Editors (ASNE)
11690B Sunrise Valley Drive, Reston, VA 20191
703-453-1122
www.asne.org
asne@asne.org
Cristal Williams Chancellor, Director of Public Relations
Richard Karpel, Executive Director
Diana Mitsu Klos, Senior Project Director
Connie Southard, Project Coordinator
Founded: 1922 *Mission:* ASNE is a membership organization for editors, producers or directors in charge of journalistic organizations or departments, deans or faculty at university journalism schools, and leaders and faculty ofmedia-related foundations and training organizations.

American Society of TV Cameramen Inc.
Div/DBA: (U.S. affll of International Society of Videograph
2520 Lotus Hill Dr., Las Vegas, NV 89134-7855
(702) 228-6704, *Fax:* (702) 228-6714
ruzwe7@aol.com
Directors:
Tom Jocelyn, Peter Basil, Gino Guarna & Sol Bress
Box 296, Sparkill, NY 10976-0296
Nicole Zweck-Spanos, Production Planning

American Sportscasters Association
225 Broadway, Suite 2030, New York, NY 10007
(212) 227-8080, *Fax:* (212) 571-0556
americansportscastersonline.com
lschwa8918@aol.com
Directors:
Lou Schwartz, Jon Miller, Jim Nantz, Dick Enberg & Bill Walton

American Sportscasters Association
225 Broadway, Suite 2030, New York, NY 10007-3742
212-227-8080, *Fax:* 212-571-0556
www.americansportscastersonline.com
lschwa8918@aol.com
Louis O Schwartz, President/Founder
Dick Enberg, Chairman
Founded: 1980 *Number of Members:* 500 *Mission:* National Association of Sportscasters, radio, television and cable covering the US, Puerto Rico and Canada. Very active web site. Offers

seminars, compiles statistics andoperates a placement service, maintains a Hall of Fame and biographical archives and library.

American Sportscasters Hall of Fame Trust
225 Broadway, Suite 2030, New York, NY 10007
(212) 227-8080, *Fax:* (212) 571-0556
www.americansportscastersonline.com
lschwa8918@aol.com

American Women in Radio and Television Inc.
8405 Greenboro Dr., Suite 800, McLean, VA 22102
(703) 506-3290, *Fax:* (703) 506-3266
www.awrt.org
info@awrt.org

Armed Forces Communications and Electronics Association
4400 Fair Lakes Ct., Fairfax, VA 22033-3899
(703) 631-6100, (800) 336-4583, *Fax:* (703) 631-6130
www.afcea.org
promo@afcea.org
Al Grasso, Chairman
Kent Schneider, President/CEO
Becky Nolan, Executive Vice President
Pat Miorin, EVP/Chief Financial Officer
AFCEA International, established in 1946, is a non-profit organization serving its members by providing a forum for the ethical exchange of information, and dedicated to increasing knowledge through the exploration of issues relevant to itsmembers in information technology, communications and electronics for the defense, homeland security and intelligence communities.

Asian American Journalists Association
5 Third Street, Suite 1108, San Francisco, CA 94103
415-346-2051, *Fax:* 415-346-6343
www.aaja.org
national@aaja.org
Kathy Chow, Executive Director
Antonia M. Salas, MDIV, MA, Membership & Chapter Dev. Manager
Nao Vang, Student Programs Coordinator
Marcia K. Santillan, Professional Programs Coordinator
Doris Truong, National President
Founded: 1981 *Number of Members:* 1400 *Mission:* AAJA provides support among Asian American and Pacific Islander journalists. It provides encouragement, information, advice and scholarship assistance to Asian American andPacific Islander students who aspire to professional journalism careers.

Associated Press Broadcasters
1825 K Street NW, Suite 800, Washington, DC 20006-1202
202-968-8150, *Fax:* 202-736-1107
www.apbroadcast.com
James R Williams III, VP Broadcast Services
Greg Groce, Director Business Operations
Brad Kalbfeld, Deputy Director\Managing Editor
Roger Lockhart, Director Marketing/Communications
George Galt, Director Business Affairs
Founded: 1941 *Number of Members:* 5.9m *Mission:* Seeks to advance journalism through radio and television, and cooperates with the AP to promote accurate and impartial news.

Associated Press Managing Editors
450 W 33rd St, New York, NY 10001-2647
212-621-1849, *Fax:* 212-833-7574
www.apme.com
apme@ap.org
Collins Munro, Manager
Deanna Sands, VP
Bill Felber, Treasurer
Mark Mittelstadt, Executive Director
Founded: 1933 *Mission:* Members are managing editors or executives of Associated Press News Executives.

Associated Press Media Editors (APME)
450 West 33rd Street, New York, NY 10001
212-621-7007
www.apme.com
sjacobsen@ap.org
Bob Heisse, President
Brad Dennison, Vice President
Alan D. Miller, Journalism Studies Chair
Founded: 1933 *Mission:* APME is an association of U.S. and Canadian editors, broadcasters and educators whose entitites are members of The Associated Press.

Association for Education in Journalism & Mass Communication (AEJMC)
234 Outlet Point Blvd., Suite A, Columbia, SC 29210
(803) 798-0271, *Fax:* (803) 772-3509
www.aejmc.org
aejmc@aejmc.org

Association for Educational Communication
1800 N Stonelake Drive, Suite 2, Bloomington, IN 47404
812-335-7675, *Fax:* 812-335-7678
www.aect.org
Mary Herring, President
Mary Beth Jordan, Secretary/Treasurer
Founded: 1923 *Number of Members:* 2200 *Mission:* For audiovisual and instructional materials specialists, educational technologists, audiovisual and television production personnel, school media specialists.

Association for Education in Journalism
234 Outlet Pointe Boulevard, Columbia, SC 29210-5667
803-798-0271, *Fax:* 803-798-3509
www.aejmc.org/
aejmchq@aol.com
Jennifer McGill, Executive Director
Felicia Greenlee Brown, Production Manager
Richard Burke, Business Manager
Mission: AEJMC promotes the highest possible standards for education in journalism and mass communication, encouraging the widest possible range of communication research and the implementation of a multi-cultural society in theclassroom and curriculum, defending and maintaining the freedom of expression in day-to-day living.

The Association for International Broadcasting
Box 141, Cranbrook, TN17 9AJ United Kingdom
+44 (0) 20 7993 2557, *Fax:* +44 (0) 20 7993 8043
Directors: Tom Walters, mktg; Tim Keeler, pub affrs.

Association for Interactive Marketing
1430 Broadway Avenue, 8th Floor, New York, NY 10018
Fax: 212-391-9233
www.interactivehq.org
info@interactivehq.org
Kevin Noonan, Executive Director
Mission: AIM is a non-profit trade association for interactive marketers and service providers.

The Association for Maximum Service Television
4100 Wisconsin Avenue NW, PO Box 9897, Washington, DC 20016
202-966-1956, *Fax:* 202-966-9617
www.mstv.org
lmillory@mstv.org
Craig Dubow, CEO
Mission: Formed in 1956, MSTV has endeavored to insure that American public receive the highest quality, interference free, over-the-air local television signals. Recognized as the industry leader in broadcasting technology andspectrum policy issues.

Association for Service Managers
11031 Via Frontera, Suite A, San Diego, CA 92127
239-275-7887, *Fax:* 239-275-0794
www.afsmi.org
info@afsmi.org
John Schoenewald, Executive Director
Jb Wood, President/Ceo
Founded: 1975 *Number of Members:* 3000+ *Mission:* A global organization dedicated to furthering the knowledge, understanding, and career development of executives, managers and professionals in the high technology serviceindustry.

Association for Women in Communications
3337 Duke Street, Alexandria, VA 22314
703-370-7436, *Fax:* 703-370-7437
www.womcom.org
info@womcom.org
Pamela Valenzuela, National Administrator
Founded: 1909 *Number of Members:* 3500 *Mission:* Supports all those professional women in the fields of journalism online media, public relations, advertising, marketing, educational communications, graphic and web design,photography and film. Hosts bi-annual conference.

Association of American Railroads
American Railroads Bldg., 50 F St. N.W., Washington, DC 20001
(202) 639-2100, *Fax:* (202) 639-2558
www.aar.org
twhite@www.aar.org

Association of Cable Communicators
25 Massachusetts Ave NW, Suite 100, Washington, DC 20013-5007
202-222-2370, *Fax:* 202-222-2371
www.cablecommunicators.org
services@cablecommunicators.org
Steven R Jones, Executive Director
Michelle L Butler, Associate Executive Director
Mission: ACC is the only national, professional organization specifically addressing the issues, needs and interests of the cable industry's communications and public affairs professionals.

Association of Canadian Advertisers
99 St Clair Avenue West, Suite 1103, Toronto, ON M4V 1N6
416-964-3805, *Fax:* 416-964-0771
www.acaweb.ca
rlund@acaweb.ca
Ron Lund, President, CEO
Susan Charles, Vice President, Member Services
Paul Hetu, Vice President, Montreal
Bob Reaume, Vice President, Policy and Research
Randy Scotland, Vice President, Communications
Mission: Industry organization exclusively dedicated to client-marketers, helping them maximize the full value of their investments in all forms of marketing communications.

Association of Federal Communications Consulting Engineers (AFCCE)
PO Box 19333, 20th Street Station, Washington, DC 20036-0333
941-329-6000, *Fax:* 703-591-0115
www.afcce.org
Thomas Silliman, President
Alan R Rosner, VP
Founded: 1948 *Number of Members:* 250 *Mission:* An organization of professional engineering consultants serving the telecommunications industry.

Association of Independent Commercial Producers
3 W 18th St, New York, NY 10011
212-929-3000, *Fax:* 212-929-3359
www.aicp.com
info@aicp.com
Matt Miller, President & CEO
Renee Paley, VP Communications
Founded: 1972 *Number of Members:* 500 *Mission:* The national trade association of television commercial producers who account for in excess of 80% of the commercial production done in the United States annually.

Association of Local Television Stations
1320 19th Street NW, Washington, DC 20036
202-887-1970
www.altv.com

Association of National Advertisers Inc. (ANA)
708 3rd Ave., New York, NY 10017
(212) 697-5950, *Fax:* (212) 661-8057
www.ana.net
bduggan@ana.net
Directors:
Donald F. Calhoun, Jocelyn Carter-Miller, J. Andrea Alstrup, Catherine D. Constable, Christopher Fraleigh, James J. Garrity, David B. Green, John D. Hayes, Stephen C. Jones, Dawn Hudson, David N. Iauco, Abby F. Kohnstamm, Ann Lewnes, Eric W.Leininger, Robert D. Liodice, Paula S. Sneed, Gary E. McCullough, James R. Stengel, James D. Speros, Allan H. Stefl, Stephen G. Sullivan, Joseph V. Tripodi, Rebecca Saeger, James L. McDowell, Nancy J. Wiese, Robert J. Gamgort & Robert C Lachky
Washington,

Association of Public Television Stations
2100 Crystal Drive, Suite 700, Arlington, VA 22202
202-654-4200, *Fax:* 202-654-4236
www.apts.org
Mark Erstling, Acting President/CEO
Lonna Thompson, Senior VP/General Counsel
Debra Tica Sanchez, VP, Government Relations
Jeffrey Davis, VP, Communications
Founded: 1980 *Number of Members:* 153 *Mission:* Nonprofit membership organization that supports the continued growth and development of a strong and financially sound noncommercial television service for the American public.Provides advocacy for public television interests at the national level, as well as consistent leadership and information in marshaling grassroots and congressional support for its members: the nation's public television stations.

Audio Engineering Society
60 E 42nd St, Room 2520, New York, NY 10165
212-661-8528, *Fax:* 212-682-0477
www.aes.org
HQ@aes.org
Roger Furness, Executive Director
Jim Anderson, President
Robert E Lee, Jr, Secretary
Louis Fielder, Treasurer

Mission: Professional society devoted to audio technology. Membership includes leading engineers, scientists and other authorities in the field. Serves its members, the industry and the public by stimulating and facilitating advancesin the constantly changing field of audio.

Baptist Communicators Association
PO Box 270187, Nashville, TN 37227
615-329-7543
baptistcommunicators.org
bca.office@comcast.net
Jan Kelley, President
Teresa Dickens, Communications VP
Ele Clay, Missions VP
Jerilynn Armstrong, Treasurer
Founded: 1953 *Number of Members:* 300 *Mission:* PR and journalism profesionals.

BMI Broadcast Music Inc.
320 W. 57th St., New York, NY 10019-3790
(212) 586-2000, *Fax:* (212) 246-2163
www.bmi.com
abooth@bmi.com
Directors:
Philip A. Jones, Frances W. Preston, James G. Babb, Harold C. Crump, N. John Douglas, Frank E. Melton, George V. Willoughby, K. James Yager, G. Neil Smith, David Sherman, Donald A. Thurston, Cecil L. Walker, Catherine L. Hughes, Craig A.Dubow, Amador Bustos & John L. Sander
8730 Sunset Blvd, 3rd Fl. W., West Hollywood, CA 90069-2210
(310) 659-9109;
10 Music Sq. E, Nashville, TN 37203-4321
(615) 401-2000;

Broadcast Cable Credit Association Inc. (BCCA)
550 W. Frontage Rd., Suite 3600, Northfield, IL 60093
(847) 881-8757, *Fax:* (847) 784-8059
www.bccacredit.com
info@bccacredit.com

Broadcast Designers' Association
145 W 45th Street, Room 1100, New York, NY 10036-4008
212-376-6222, *Fax:* 212-376-6202
Mission: Association for manufacturers or suppliers of broadcast design equipment, supplies and services.

Broadcast Education Association
1771 N St. N.W., Washington, DC 20036-2891
(202) 429-3935, *Fax:* (202) 775-2981
www.beaweb.org
beainfo@beaweb.org
Directors:
Mary Alice Molgard, Thomas R. Berg, Rustin Greene, Joe Misiewicz, David Byland, Robert K. Avery, Gary Martin, Greg Luft, D'Artagnan Bebel, Stephen J. Cohen, Larry Patrick, Alan R. Albarran, Gary Corbitt, Steven Anderson, Norman Pattiz &Jannette L. Dates

Broadcast Education Association
1771 N St NW, Washington, DC 20036-2800
202-429-5355, *Fax:* 202-429-4199
www.beaweb.org
beamemberservices@nab.org
Heather Birks, Executive Director
Staven D. Anderson, VP Academic Relations
Gary Corbitt, VP Professional Relations
Founded: 1955 *Number of Members:* 1400 *Mission:* Serves as a higher education association of professors and industry professionals who teach college students worldwide and prepares them to go into the broadcasting and relatedemerging technologies professions upon graduation from college.

Broadcast Pioneers
320 W 57th St, Suite 3, New York, NY 10019-3705
212-586-2000, *Fax:* 212-246-2163
www.bmi.com
Del Bryant, President & CEO
Founded: 1942 *Number of Members:* 1.4M *Mission:* Honors radio or television stations for excellence in art and community service. Maintains library documents on television broadcasting history.

Broadcasters Foundation of America
125 West 55th Street, 21st Floor, New York, NY 10019
212-373-8250, *Fax:* 212-373-8254
www.broadcastersfoundation.org
info@thebfoa.org
Jim Thompson, President
Carl Butrum, Vice President
Mission: Provides financial assistance to radio and television broadcasters who are in financial need.

The Broadcasters Hall of Fame
1240 Ashford Lane, 1A, PO Box 8247, Akron, OH 44320
330-867-3779, *Fax:* 330-867-4907
www.broadcastershalloffame.com
info@briadcastershalloffame.com
C S (Doc) Williams, Founder, CEO
Henry Dunn, Chairman
Mission: A wealth of memorabilia from the early days of broadcasting, clippings from newspapers and magazines, taped recorded portions of early radio shows and other gems of broadcasting history.

Cable & Telecommunications Association
201 N Union Street, Suite 440, Alexandria, VA 22314-2642
703-549-4200, *Fax:* 703-684-1167
www.ctam.com
info@ctam.com
Char Beales, President/CEO
Daniel Cassidy, SVP/Finance/Administration
Founded: 1976 *Number of Members:* 5500 *Mission:* Dedicated to the discipline and development of consumer marketing excellence in cable television, new media and telecommunications services. As a member, you have the advantageof progressive research, insightful publications and forward thinking conferences all designed to help you and your company gain a competitive edge.

Cable & Television Association for Marketing
Div/DBA: Cable & Telecommunications Association
201 N. Union St., Suite 440, Alexandria, VA 22314
(703) 549-4200, *Fax:* (703) 684-1167
www.ctam.com
info@ctam.com

The Cable Center
2000 Buchtel Blvd., Denver, CO 80210
(303) 871-4885, *Fax:* (303) 871-4514
www.cablecenter.org
info@cablecenter.org

Cable in the Classroom
25 Massachussetts Ave NW, Suite 100, Washington, DC
202-222-2335, *Fax:* 202-222-2336
www.ciconline.org
help@ciconline.org
Frank Gallagher, Executive Director
Helen Dimsdale, Deputy Executive Director
Kat Stewart, Director, Strategic Initiatives
Beverly Hicks, Assistant Director
Mission: Promotes the visionary, sensible, responsible and effective use of cable's broaband technology, services, and content in teaching and learning. CIC also advocates digtial citizenship and supports the complimentary provision,by cable industry companies, of broadband and multichannel video services and educational content to the nation's schools.

Cable Television Laboratories Inc.
858 Coal Creek Cir., Louisville, CO 80027-9750
(303) 661-9100, *Fax:* (303) 661-9199
www.cablelabs.com
m.schwartz@cablelabs.com
Broadband dev for cable system operators.
Directors:
Brian L. Roberts, chmn

Cabletelevision Advertising Bureau Inc. (CAB)
830 3rd Avenue, 2nd Floor, New York, NY 10022 USA
(212) 508-1200, *Fax:* (212) 832-3268
www.thecab.tv
Bill Abbott, President/CEO
CAB's member organizations include virtually all of the national and regional ad-supported cable networks; system operators and interconnects representing more than 90 percent of all U.S. cable subscribers; and suppliers to the cableadvertising business. All of these organizations actively work together through CAB to further increase awareness of the power of cable as an advertising medium; and to make cable an increasingly effective marketing environment for advertisersthroughout the U.S.-nationally, regionally and locally.

Canadian Association of Broadcast Consultants
130 Cree Crescent, Winnepeg, MB R3J 3W1
204-889-9202, *Fax:* 204-831-6650
www.cabc-accr.ca
jsadoun@yrh.com
Joseph Sadoun, Ing P Eng, President
Kerry Pelser, Secretary/Treasurer
Mission: Prepares technical briefs, coverage studies and frequencies.

Canadian Association of Broadcasters
700-45 O'Connor Street, PO Box 627, Station B, Ottawa, ON K1P 1A4
613-233-4035, *Fax:* 613-233-6961
www.cab-acr.ca
sbissonette@cab-acr.ca
Paul Ski, Chief Executive Officer
Rick Arnish, President
Charles Benoit, EVP
Sylvie Bissonette, Vice President
Mission: Serves as the eyes and ears of the private broadcasting community to advocate and lobby on its behalf and to act as a cebtral point on matters of joint interest.

Canadian Association of Ethnic Broadcaster
622 College Street, Toronto, ON M6G 1B6
416-531-9991, *Fax:* 416-531-5274
www.chinradio.com
info@chinradio.com
Johnny Lombardi, Founder, President
Mission: Pioneer in multicultural radio broadcasting and has lead the way for similar briadcast operations to be established.

Canadian Film and Television Production Association (CFTPA)
160 John St., Toronto, ON M5C 2E5 Canada
(416) 304-0280, *Fax:* (416) 304-0499
www.cftpa.ca
toronto@cftpa.ca
Directors:
Cara Martin
151 Slater St., Suite 605, Ottawa, ON
(613)-233-1444; *Fax:* (613)-233-0073

CanWest Media Sales
121 Bloor Street East, Suite 1500, Toronto, ON M4W 3M5
416-967-1174, *Fax:* 416-967-1285
www.shawmedia.ca
info@shawmedia.ca
Chris McDowell, Director, Publicity
Grace Park, Publicity Manager
Nick Porter, Publicist
Mission: Televison and newspaper advertising, marketing, and sales company.

Caribbean Broadcasting Union
Suite 1B, Building 6A, Harbor Industrial Estate, St Michael, BB 11145
246-430-1006, *Fax:* 242-228-9524
www.caribunion.com
patrick.cozier@caribsurf.com
Patrick Cozier, President
Mission: Stimulates the flow of broadcast material among the radio and television systems in the Caribbean region.

Catholic Academy for Communication Arts Professionals
1645 Brook Lynn Dr., Suite 2, Dayton, OH 45432-1944
(937) 458-0265, *Fax:* (937) 458-0263
www.catholicacademy.org
admin@catholicacademy.org
Directors:
Jeanean Merkel, 1st VP; Vicki Bedard, 2nd VP

Center for Communication Inc.
561 Broadway, Suite 12 B, New York, NY 10012
(212) 686-5005, *Fax:* (212) 504-2632
www.cencom.org
info@cencom.org
Directors:
Edward Bleier, chmn; Frank Stanton, dir emeritus. Timothy Barry, William F. Baker, Robert M. Batscha, Patricia T. Carbine, Antoinette Cook Bush, John A. Dimling, David R. Drobis, Michael Eigner, Peter R. Ezersky, Charles B. Fruit, RalphGuild, Andrew Heyward, Peter Jennings, Gerald M. Levin, Kate McEnroe, Martin Nisenholtz, Herbert Scannell, Alan Siegel, Alfred C. Sikes, Kenneth Stoddard, Howard Stringer, Alberto Vitale, Stephen A. Weiswasser, David Westin, Bob Wright, Lois Wyse,Mortimer B. Zuckerman, Simon Michael Bessie, Louis D. Boccardi, David W. Burke, Henry A. Grunwald, Irwin Segelstein, Burton B. Staniar & Loet A. Velmans

Coalition Opposing Signal Theft
1724 Massachusetts Avenue NW, Washington, DC 20001
202-222-2300
www.ncta.com
webmaster@ncta.com
Nilda Cid Gumbs, Director
Mission: Acts as a clearinghouse of information regarding cable signal theft.

Collegiate Press Association
330 21st Avenue S, Minneapolis, MN 55455-0480
612-625-3500, *Fax:* 612-626-0720
Tom Rolnicki, Manager
Mission: Supports all those involved in the development and betterment of collegiate press. Hosts annual trade show.

Commonwealth Broadcasting Assn
CBA Secretariat, 17 Fleet St., London, EC4Y 1AA United Kingdom
011-44-171-5835550, *Fax:* 011-44-171-5835549
www.cba.org.uk
cba@cba.org.uk
Directors:
George Valarino, Ronald Abraham, Roger Grant, Robert O'Rielly, Tombong Saidy, Sharon Crosbie & Cecilia Khuzwayo

Community Antenna Television Association
PO Box 1005, Fairfax, VA 22030-1005
202-775-3550
Number of Members: 3M *Mission:* An association of over 3,000 cable television systems serving over 30 million subscribers.

Cooperative Communicators Association
174 Crestview Dr, Bellefonte, PA 16823-8516
806-795-2783, *Fax:* 806-795-5289
www.communicators.coop
CCA@communicators.coop
Susie Bullock, Executive Director
Greg Brooks, Director Media/Public Relations
Chuck Lay, Board Member
Leta Mach, Board Member
Sheryl Meshke, Board Member
Founded: 1953 *Number of Members:* 350 *Mission:* A teaching and news tool for the Cooperative Communicators Association, CCA consists of 310 communicators, editors, photographers, graphics, designers, public relationsspecialists who work for cooperatives in 35 states, Canada and Poland.

Corporation for Public Broadcasting
401 9th St NW, Washington, DC 20004
202-879-9600, *Fax:* 202-879-9700
www.cpb.org
oigemail@cpb.org
Patricia de Stacy Harrison, President & CEO
Vincent Curren, EVP & COO
Michael Levy, EVP, Corporate & Public Affairs
William P. Tayman Jr., CFO & Treasurer
Ernest J. Wilson III, Chairman
Founded: 1967 *Mission:* A private, nonprofit corporation created by Congress in 1967. Its mission is to facilitate the development of, and ensure universal access to, non-commercial high-quality programming and telecommunicationsservices. It does this in conjunction with non-commercial educational telecommunications licensees across the country.

Council of Better Business Bureaus Inc.
4200 Wilson Blvd., 8th Fl., Arlington, VA 22203-1838
(703) 276-0100, *Fax:* (703) 525-8277
www.bbb.org
bbb@bbb.org
44 Byward Market Sq., Suite 220, Ottawa, ON Canada

Country Music Association Inc.
One Music Cir. S., Nashville, TN 37203
(615) 244-2840, *Fax:* (615) 726-0314
www.cmaworld.com

Country Radio Broadcasters
819 18th Ave S, Nashville, TN 37203-3218
615-327-4487, *Fax:* 615-329-4492
www.crb.org
info@crb.org
Ed Salamon, Executive Director
Chasity Crouch, Business Manager
Bill Mayne, VP
Gary Krantz, Secretary
Jeff Walker, Treasurer
Mission: Broadcasting forum.

Education Writers Association
2122 P St NW, Suite 201, Washington, DC 20037-1037
202-452-9830, *Fax:* 202-452-9837
www.ewa.org
ewa@ewa.org
Lisa Walker, Executive Director
Lori Crouch, Assistant Director
Lesley Dahlkemper, VP
Linda Lenz, Secretary
Founded: 1947 *Number of Members:* 800 *Mission:* The Education Writers Association is the national professional organization of education reporters and intent of improving education reporting to the public.

Educational Broadcasting Association
450 W 33rd St, New York, NY 10001-2605
212-560-3063, *Fax:* 212-560-3199
www.thirteen.org
programming@thirteen.org
William F. Bakerns, President & CEO
Stella Giammasi, VP Communication
Daisy Pommer, Manager
Number of Members: 500 *Mission:* Association members are producers and directors of public educational programming, channel 13, PBS.

Electro Federation Canada
5800 Explorer Dr., Suite 200, Mississauga, ON L4W 5K9 Canada
(866) 602-8877, *Fax:* (905) 602-5686
www.electrofed.com
info@electrofed.com

Electronic Industries Alliance (EIA)
2500 Wilson Blvd., Arlington, VA 22201
(703) 907-7500, *Fax:* (703) 907-7501
www.eia.org
dmccurdy@eia.org

Electronic Retailing Association (ERA)
200 N. 14th St., Suite 300, Arlington, VA 22201
(703) 841-1751, (800) 987-6462, *Fax:* (703) 841-1751
www.retailing.org
contact@retailing.org
Directors:
Stephen F. Breimer, Esq.; Jeffrey Knowles, Esq.. Linda Goldstein, Mike Ackerman, Rick Cesari, Dan Danielson, Denise Dubarry Hay, Rollie Froehlig, Larry Jellen, Jack Kirby, Mark Lavin, Shigeru Ohashi, Rick Petry, Steve Pittenridgh, RichardProchnow, Randy Ronning, Robert Rosenblatt, Bret Saxton, Mark Thornton & Reiner Weihofen

Electronic Service Dealers Association
4927 W. Irving Park Rd., Chicago, IL 60641
(773) 282-9400

Electronics Representatives Association
300 W. Adams St., Suite 617, Chicago, IL 60606
(312) 527-3050, *Fax:* (312) 527-3783
www.era.org
info@era.org
Directors:
Tom Shanahan

FCBA (Federal Communications Bar Association)
1020 19th St. N.W., Suite 325, Washington, DC 20036-6101
(202) 293-4000, *Fax:* (202) 293-4317
www.fcba.org
fcba@fcba.org

Forest Industries Telecommunications
1565 Oak St, Eugene, OR 97401-4008
541-485-8441, *Fax:* 541-485-7556
www.landmobile.com
license@landmobile.com
Kevin Mc Carthy, President
Founded: 1947 *Number of Members:* 600 *Mission:* Organized to assist the forest industry in radio matters before the FCC.

Forestry Conservation Commuications
Po Box 3217, Gettysburg, PA 17325
717-338-1505, *Fax:* 717-334-5656
www.fcca-usa.org
nfc@fcca-usa.org
Ralph Haller, Executive Director
Paul Leary, President
Founded: 1944 *Number of Members:* 200 *Mission:* Certified by the FCC as the radio frequency coordinator for the Forestry Conservation Radio Service.

Foundation for American Communications
44 Avenue Road South, Suite 1200, Arlington, VA 22203
703-276-0100, *Fax:* 703-525-8277
www.facsnet.org
info@facsnet.org
John E Cox, CEO, President
Peter C McCarthy, Senior VP, COO
Paul Davis, Senior VP, Programs
Randy Reddick, Director
Christina Gardner, VP, Operations
Mission: A national non-profit educational organization with the mission of improving the quality of information reaching the public through the news.

Free TV Australia Ltd.
Div/DBA: (formerly Commercial Television Australia CTVA)
44 Avenue Rd., Mosman, N.S.W., 02088 Australia
61 2 8968 7100, *Fax:* 61 2 9969 3520
www.freevaust.com.au
contact@freetv.com.au
Provides a forum for discussion of industry matters by its members & is the pub voice of the industry on a wide range of issues & has represented the coml free-to-air TV industry for over 40 years.

Gay and Lesbian Press Association
PO Box 8185, Universal City, CA 91618-8185
Fax: 818-902-9576
Mission: Supports those gay and lesbian professionals in the field of journalism. Publishes quarterly newsletter.

Geospatial Information and Technology
14456 E Evans Ave, Aurora, CO 80014-1409
303-337-0513, *Fax:* 303-337-1001
www.gita.org
bsamborski@gita.org
Bob Samborski, Executive Director
Lisa Connor, Membership Services Manager
Wilma Kumar-Rubock, Secretary
Susan Ancel, Treasurer
Founded: 1960 *Number of Members:* 2200 *Mission:* Provides unbiased educational programs, forums and publications for professionals involved with geospatial information and technology.

Hollywood Foreign Press Association
646 N Robertson Blvd, West Hollywood, CA 90069-5022
310-657-1731, *Fax:* 310-939-9034
www.hfpa.org
info@hfpa.org
Phillip Berk, President
Mike Goodridge, VP
Lawrie Masterson, VP
Chantal Dinnage, Managing Director
Mission: Foreign correspondents covering Hollywood and the entertainment industry.

Hollywood Radio and Television Society
13701 Riverside Dr, Suite 205, Sherman Oaks, CA 91423
818-789-1182, *Fax:* 818-789-1210
www.hrts.org
info@hrts.org
Dave Ferrara, Executive Director
Jennie Nevin, Director of Operations
Ruzzo Martinelli, Events
Meshak Vallesillas, Marketing & Communications
Elvia Gonzalez, Member Services
Founded: 1947 *Number of Members:* 100 *Mission:* Sponsors monthly luncheons featuring top industry and government speakers and seminars about broadcasting, maintains film and audio library.

Independent Film & Television Alliance (IFTA)
10850 Wilshire Blvd., 9th Fl., Los Angeles, CA 90024-4321
(310) 446-1000, *Fax:* (310) 446-1600
www.ifta-online.org
info@ifta-online.org
Directors:
Glen Basner, Steve Bickel, Alison Thompson, Nicolas Chartier, Roger Corman, Pierre David, Peter Elson, Kimberly Ferguson, Antony Ginnane, Peter Graham, Robert Hayward, Avi Lerner, Mark Lindsay, Nicole Mackey, Nicholas Meyer, Bobby Meyers,Michael Weiser, Kevin Williams & Andrew Stevens

Institute of Electrical and Electronics Engineers
445 Hoes Ln., Piscataway, NJ 08854-1331
(732) 981-0060, *Fax:* (732) 981-1721
www.ieee.org
3 Park Ave. 17th Fl., New York, NY 10016-5902
(212) 419-7900; *Fax:* (212) 752-4929

Interactive & Newsmedia Financial
14237 Bookcliff Ct, Purcellville, VA 20132-1771
703-421-4060, *Fax:* 703-421-4068
www.infe.org
Jeff Hood, President
Founded: 1947 *Number of Members:* 1000 *Mission:* Focuses on newspaper financial management, with members representing most North American newpaper companies, as well as many offshore. INFE's activities include publishing,conferences, workshops, industry surveys and studies, and offers members networking opportunities.

Intercollegiate Broadcasting Systems
367 Windsor Highway, New Windsor, NY 12553-7900

845-565-0003, *Fax:* 845-565-7446
www.ibsradio.org
ibs@ibsradio.org
Norman Prusslin, President
Fritz Kass, Chief Operating Officer
Founded: 1940 *Number of Members:* 800 *Mission:* Nonprofit association of student staffed radio stations based at schools and colleges across the country. Some 800 member stations operate all sizes and types of facilitiesincluding Internet-Webcasting, closed circuit, AM carrier-current, cable radio and FCC-licensed FM and AM stations.

International Academy of Television Arts and Sciences
25 West 52nd Street, New York, NY 10019
212-489-6969, *Fax:* 212-489-1946
www.iemmys.tv
iemmys@iemmys.tv
Camille Bidermann-Roizen, Executive Director
Gerry Brahney, Advertising Director
Nathaniel Brendel, Judging Director
Eva Obadia, Communications Director
Tracy Oliver, General Manager
Mission: Member based organization comprised of leading media and entertainment figures from over 50 countries and 500 companies from all sectors of television including internet, mobile and technology.

International Advertising Association
Div/DBA: (The global partnership of advertisers, agencies &
521 Fifth Ave., Suite 1807, New York, NY 10175
(212) 557-1133, *Fax:* (212) 983-0455
www.iaaglobal.org
iaa@iaaglobal.org
Directors:
Wendy Burrell, mgng dir. Richard Corner

International American Press Association
1801 Sw 3rd Ave, Miami, FL 33129-1487
305-634-2465, *Fax:* 305-635-2272
www.sipiapa.org
info@sipiapa.org
Julio Nunoz, Executive Director
Alejo Miro Cisneros, First VP
Diana Daniels, Second VP
Earl Maucker, Treasurer
Mission: Supports all those involved in the media and journalism industry. Hosts annual trade show.

International Animated Film Society
ASIFA-Hollywood, 2114 Burbank Blvd., Burbank, CA 91506
(818) 842-8330, *Fax:* (818) 842-5645
www.asifa-hollywood.org
asifaalert-subscribe@yahoogroups.com
Directors:
Jerry Beck, Stephen Worth, Bob Miller, Tom Knott, Frank Gladstone, David Derks, Margaret Kerry-Wilcox, Larry Loc & Will Ryan

International Association of Audio Information Services
c/o NBRS, 1090 Don Mills Rd., Suite 303, Toronto, ON M3C 3R6 Canada
(416) 422-4222, ext 224, *Fax:* (416) 422-1633
www.iaais.org
hlusignan@nbrscanada.com

International Association of Broadcast Monitors
PO Box 986, Irmo, SC 29063
803-749-9833, *Fax:* 888-732-9004
www.iabm.com
iabm@iabm.com
Lisa Smith, Executive Director
Kevin Repka, President
Ron Coucil, VP International
John Croll, Secretary
Holly Wine, Treasurer
Founded: 1981 *Mission:* Worldwide trade association made up of news retrieval services which monitor television, radio, internet and print news mediums. It acts as a clearinghouse or forum for discussion on topics of collectiveconcerns and acts as a united voice for the news monitoring industry.

International Association of Audio Information
1090 Don Mills Road, Suite 303, Toronto, ON M3C 3R6
416-422-4222, *Fax:* 416-422-1622
www.iaais.org
info@iaais.org
Kim Walsh, President
Lori Kessinger, Chairperson
Stuart Holland, 1st Vice President
Mission: Encourages and supports the establishment and maintenance of audio information services that provide access to printed information for individuals who cannot read conventional print because of blindness or any other visual,physical, or learning disability.

International Association of Audio Visual
57 West Palo Verde Avenue, PO Box 250, Ocotillo, CA 92259-0250
760-358-7000, *Fax:* 760-358-7569
www.cindys.com
sheemonw@cindys.com
Sheemon Wolfe, Contact
Founded: 1957 *Number of Members:* 5200 *Mission:* Members are audio-visual professionals using the media of film, video, slides, filmstrips, multi-image and interactive media to communicate information

International Communication Agency Network (ICOM)
1649 Lump Gulch Rd., Rollinsville, CO 80474
(303) 258-9511, *Fax:* (303) 484-4087
www.icomagencies.com
info@icomagencies.com
Directors:
Frank G. Weyforth

International Communications Industry
11242 Waples Mill Road, Suite 200, Fairfax, VA 22030
703-273-7200, *Fax:* 703-278-8082
www.infocomm.org
customerservice@infocomm.org
Randy Pagnan, Chairman
Jay Armand, President
Randy Lemke, Executive Director
Mission: Centers on the technologies, products and systems for visual display, audio reproduction, video and audio production, interfacing and signal distribution, lighting, control systems, interactive display and audio presentationsystems, remote video and web conferencing.

International Communications Association
1500 21st St Nw, Washington, DC 20036-1000
202-955-1444, *Fax:* 202-530-9851
www.icahdq.org
icahdq@icahdq.org
M Haley, Executive Director
Founded: 1950 *Number of Members:* 3400 *Mission:* Supports all students and professionals in the international communications industry. Publishes bi-monthly newsletter.

International Council-National Academy
142 West 57th Street, New York, NY 10019-3300
212-489-6969, *Fax:* 212-489-6557
www.iemmys.tv
gl@iemmys.tv
Georges Leclere, Executive Director
Camille Bidermann-Roizen, General Manager
Kim Czaplinski, Accounting/Membership
MJ Sorenson, Director Marketing
Founded: 1969 *Number of Members:* 250+ *Mission:* Furthers the arts and sciences by bestowing International Emmy Awards, George Movshon Fellowship and the Joan Wilson memorial scholarship.

International Institute of Communications
35 Porland Pl., 3rd. Fl., Westcott, London, WIB IAE United Kingdom
(44) 207- 323-9622, *Fax:* (44) 207- 323- 9623
www.iicom.org
enquiries@iicom.org

International Newspaper Marketing
10300 North Central Expressway, Suite 467, Dallas, TX 75231
214-373-9111, *Fax:* 214-373-9112
www.inma.org
inma@inma.org
Eivind Thomsen, President
Ross McPherson, VP
Scott C Schurz, Treasurer
Earl Wilkinson, Executive Director
Founded: 1930 *Number of Members:* 1100 *Mission:* Individuals in marketing, circulation, research and public relations of newspapers.

International Radio and Television Society Foundation Inc.
420 Lexington Ave, Suite 1601, New York, NY 10170
212-867-6650, *Fax:* 212-867-6653
www.irts.org
jim.cronin@irts.org
Joyce M. Tudrynff, President
Jim Cronin, Dir, Member Prgms & Development
Marilyn L. Ellis, Director, Program Administration
Lauren Kruk-Winokur, Dir, Academic Prgms & Communication
Tom Kane, Chairman
Founded: 1939 *Number of Members:* 750 *Mission:* The lines between broadcast televison and radio, cable, telephony and the computer industry may be blurring, but one thing remains clear, we all have an affinity for a businessthat entertains, informs, educates and serves the American public in a meaningful way. The foundation provides a unique common forum for all segments of the communication industry. Members can enjoy sharing insight and ideas with colleagues duringthe season's numerous events.

International Recording Media Association
182 Nassau Street, Suite 204, Princeton, NJ 08542
609-279-1700, *Fax:* 609-279-1999
info@recordingmedia.org
www.recordingmedia.org
Charles Van Horn, President
Thomas Van Sickle, Director
Mission: International trade association dealing with every facet of recording, media and related industries. Membership includes raw material providers, manufacturers, replicators, duplicators, packagers, and copyright holders.

International Television Academy
888 Seventh Avenue, 5th Floor, New York, NY 10019
212-489-6969, *Fax:* 212-489-6557
www.iemmys.tv
zoe.dyck@iemmys.tv
Bruce Paisner, President
Fred Cohen, Chairman
Founded: 1969 *Mission:* Organization of global broadcasters, with representatives from over 50 countries based outside of the US, and represents the world's largest production, distribution and broadcast companies.

Investigative Reporters and Editors
138 Neff Annex, Missouri School of Journalism, Columbia, MO 65211
573-882-2042, *Fax:* 573-882-5431
www.ire.org
info@ire.org
Brant Houston, Executive Director
Len Bruzzese, Deputy Director
John Green, Membership Coordinator
Evelyn Ruch-Graham, Conference Coordinator
Heather Feldman, Financial Officer
Founded: 1975 *Number of Members:* 3300 *Mission:* For individuals involved in investigative journalism.

Jones/NCTI-National Cable Television
Po Box 3309, Englewood, CO 80155
303-792-3111, *Fax:* 303-797-0829
www.jones.com
info@ncti.com
Glenn R Jones, CEO
Michael Guilfoyle, Director Market Strategy
Jerry Neese, Director Sales
Ken Ziel, VP/CFO
Mark Johnson, VP Business Development
Founded: 1968 *Number of Members:* 30 *Mission:* Workforce performance products, services and education.

Land Mobile Communications Council
8484 Westpark Drive, Suite 630, McLean, VA 22102-5117
703-528-5115, *Fax:* 703-524-1074
www.lmcc.org
donald.vasek@enterprisewireless.org
Alfred Ittner, President
Ralph Haller, VP
Donald Vasek, Secretary/Treasurer
Founded: 1967 *Mission:* A nonprofit association of organizations representing land mobile radio carriers and manufacturers equipment; LMCC membership represents diverse telecommunications sectors such as public safety,industrial/land transportation, private radio, specialized mobile radion and critical infrastructure.

League of Advertising Agencies
915 Clifton Avenue, Clifton, NJ 07013
973-473-6643, *Fax:* 973-473-0685
www.weinrichadv.com
info@weinrichadv.com
Andy Weinrich, Executive Vice President
Robert Weinrich, Marketing Director
Mission: Provides marketing solutions that maximize success.

Library of American Broadcasting Foundation Inc.
Box 2749, Alexandria, VA 22301

(703) 548-6090, *Fax:* (703) 549-4349
www.labfoundation.org
westsqn@aol.com
Directors:
Donald H. Kirkley, Jr.. James L. Greenwald, Vincent Curtis, Arthur W. Carlson, Erwin Krasnow, Jerry Lee, Larry Taishoff, Jim Morley, Susan Ness, Don West, Richard Buckley, Perre Bouvard, Russ Withers, Carl Brazell, Michael Carter, TimCookerly, Sam Donaldson, James E. Duffy, Erica Farber, Skip Finley, Gary Fries, Marc Guild, Dr. Judy Kuriansky, David Kennedy, Dawson B. Nail, Allen Shaw, Ramsey Woodworth & Millard Younts
University of Maryland, College Park, Maryland, NO
(301) 405-9160; *Fax:* (301) 314-2634
www.lib.umd.edu/umcp/lab

Library of American Broadcasting
University of Maryland, College Park, MD 20742-7011
301-405-9160, *Fax:* 301-314-2634
www.lib.umd.edu
bp50@umail.umed.edu
Founded: 1972 *Mission:* Holds a wide ranging collection of audio and video recordings, books, pamphlets, periodicals, personal collections, oral histories, photographs, scripts and vertical files devoted exclusively to the historyof broadcasting.

MAGNET: Marketing & Advertising Global
1017 Perry Hwy, Suite 5, Pittsburgh, PA 15237-2173
412-366-6850, *Fax:* 412-366-6840
www.magnetglobal.org
cheri@magnetglobal.org
Jim Nash, President
Cheri Gmiter, Executive Director
Founded: 1999 *Number of Members:* 40 *Mission:* A group of non-competing, independently owned advertising agenices in major markets throughout the world. Provides a way for member agencies to share their experience, knowledgeand ideas with other agencies in other parts of the world.

Manufacturers Radio Frequency Advisory
899-A Harrison St SE, Leesburg, VA 20175
703-669-0320
www.mrfac.com
jpakla@mrfac.com
Mary McKinley, President
Stan Jenkins, First VP
Clark Hart, Second VP
Dan Fiest, Secretary
Jim Pakla, Manager
Number of Members: 14000 *Mission:* Representing the voice of the manufacturing industry and private land mobile radio users before the Federal Communications Commision, the responsible federal regulatory agency for the nation'sindustrial communications. The leaders of the manufacturing industry, individually and collectively, have an obligation to influence the policies, plans, and procedures which govern the growth, structure and use of our national radio spectrum andtelecommunications systems.

Media Access Group at WGBH
One Quest St., Boston, MA 02135
(617) 300-2000, *Fax:* (617) 300-1020
access.wgbh.org
access@wgbh.org

Media Alliance
1904 Franklin St, Suite 500, Oakland, CA 94612-2926
510-832-9000, *Fax:* 510-238-8557
www.media-alliance.org
Tracy Rosenberg, Executive Director
Eloise Rose Lee, Program Director
Mission: A nonprofit training and resource center for media workers, community organizations and political activists.

Media Communications Association
PO Box 5135, Madison, WI 53705-0135
608-836-0722, *Fax:* 888-899-6224
www.mca-i.org
loiswei@aol.com
Gary Shifflet, President
Lois Weiland, Executive Director
Mike Brown, Treasurer
Jim Powell, Secretary
John Coleman, Board Member
Founded: 1968 *Mission:* Global community that provides its members opportunities for networking, learning and career advancement. Members work in video, film, collaborative communication, distance learning, web design andcreation, and all forms of interactive visual communication, along with associated crafts; serving businesses, nonprofit organizations, the government, educational institutions, the medical field, and electronic media. Chapters are throughout the US,with affiliates in Asia and Europe. It also provides professional development seminars and events, opportunities for networking, members-only benefits, forums for education and information resources for media communications professionals.

Media Financial Management Association (MFM)
550 W Frontage Road, Suite 3600, Northfield, IL 60093-1243
847-716-7000, *Fax:* 847-716-7004
www.mediafinance.org
info@mediafinance.org
Mary M Collins, President/CEO
Jamie Smith, Director of Operations
Founded: 1961 *Number of Members:* 1300 *Mission:* Professional society of more than 1,300 media's top financial, MIS Credit and HR executives, plus associates in auditing, data processing, software development, law, tax andcredit and collections

The Media Institute
2300 Clarendon Blvd, Suite 602, Arlington, VA 22201
703-243-5700, *Fax:* 703-243-8808
www.mediainstitute.org
info@mediainstitute.org
Patrick Maines, President
Richard Kaplar, Vice President
Susanna Coto, Director, Public Events
Mission: Non-profit research foundation specializing in communications policy isssues.

Minority Media and Telecommunications Council
3636 16th Street NW, Suite B 366, Washington, DC 20010
202-332-0500, *Fax:* 202-332-0503
www.mmtconline.org
info@mmtconline.org
Hon Julia L Johnson, Chairperson
Hon Deborah Taylor Tate, Vice Chair
Erwin Krasnow, Vice Chair
Ari Fitzgerald, Secretary
Ronald Johnson, Treasurer
Mission: national non-profit organization dedicated to promoting and oreserving equal opportunity and civil rights in the mass media, telecommunications and broadband industries, and closing the digital divide.

Motion Picture Association of America
15503 Ventura Blvd., Encino, CA 91436
(818) 995-6600, *Fax:* (818) 382-1795
www.mpaa.org
15503 Ventura Blvd, Encino, CA 91436-3114
(818) 995-6600; *Fax:* (818) 382-1778

The Museum of Broadcast Communications
360 North State Street, Chicago, IL 60654-5411
312-245-8200, *Fax:* 312-245-8207
www.museum.tv
info@museum.tv
Bruce DuMont, President, CEO
Marc Glick, Executive Producer
Wally Podrazik, Consulting Curator
Adam Yenkin, Archives Clerk
Bert Gall, Project Manager
Mission: Collects, preserves, and presents historic and contemporary radio and television content as well as educate, inform , and entertain the public through its archives, public programs, screenings, exhibits, publications, andonline access to its resources.

MZTV Museum of Television
550 Queen St. E., Toronto, ON M5A 1V2 Canada
(416) 599-7339, *Fax:* (416) 599-3572
www.mztv.com
mztv@MZTV.com

The National Academy of Television Arts & Sciences
111 W. 57th St., Suite 600, New York, NY 10019
(212) 586-8424, *Fax:* (212) 246-8129
www.emmyonline.org

The National Academy of Television Journalists Inc.
Box 289, Salisbury, MD 21803-0289
(410) 251-2511, *Fax:* (410) 543-0658
www.goldenviddyawards.com
infi@goldenviddyawards.com
Directors:
Dr.Catherine North & Dr.Cathy Roche

National Academy of Television Arts and
111 W 57th St, Suite 600, New York, NY 10019-2271
212-586-8424, *Fax:* 212-246-8129
www.emmyonline.tv
Herb Granath, Chairperson
Darryl Cohen, 1st Vice Chair
Malachy Wienges, 2nd Vice Chair
Carolyn Grippi, COO/CFO
Paul Pillitteri, CAO
Founded: 1957 *Number of Members:* 12M *Mission:* Dedicated to the advancement of the arts and sciences of television and the promotion of creative leadership for artistic, educational and technical achievements within thetelevision industry. It recognizes excellence in television with the coveted Emmy Award.

National Association of Accredited Preventive Entities
C/CastellÃ³, 59 bis, Madrid, 28001 Spain
91 575 53 81, *Fax:* 91 435 66 53
www.anepa.net
anepa@anepa.net
Dancausa Juan Roa, President/CEO
The National Association of Accredited Preventive Entities (ANEPA), founded in 1998, is a nonprofit organization that brings together major preventive accredited institutions of our country. It is a full member of the CEOE, being therepresentative of the business sector in the prevention of occupational hazards.occupational hazards .

National Association of Black Owned Broadcasters Inc. (NABOB)
1201 Connecticut Avenue NW, Suite 200, Washington, DC 20036
202-463-8970, *Fax:* 202-429-0657
www.nabob.org
nabobinfo@nabob.org
Pierre Sutton, Chairman
Bennie Turner, President
Michael Carter, Vice President
James Winston, Executive Director
Mission: Largest trade organization representing the interests of African-American owners of radio and television stations across the country.

National Association of Broadcasters
1771 N St Nw, Washington, DC 20036-2800
202-429-5300, *Fax:* 202-429-4199
www.nab.org
nab@nab.org
David K Rehr, CEO
Philip J Lombardo, Chairman
Dean Goodman, COO
Ann Young-Orr, Executive Director
Michelle Duke, Development Director
Founded: 1923 *Number of Members:* 7000 *Mission:* Full service trade association that represents the interests of free, over-the-air radio and television broadcasters. Offers seminars and workshops to members and holds localmeetings that offer support on legal and industry issues. Sponsors the National Association of Broadcasters Educational Foundation, dedicated to serving the public interest via education and training programs, strategies to increase diverseinitiatives, community support and philanthropy.

National Association of Black Journalists
8701-A Adelphi Rd, Adelphi, MD 20783-1716
301-445-7100, *Fax:* 301-445-7101
www.nabj.org
nabj@nabj.org
Karen Wynnfreeman, Executive Director
Ernie Suggs, Director
Stephanie Jones, Director
Elliott Lewis, Director
Marsha J. Eaglin, Director
Victor W. Vaughan, Director
Founded: 1975 *Number of Members:* 3300 *Mission:* An organization of journalists, students and media-related professionals that provides quality programs and services and advocates on behalf of black journalists worldwide.

National Association of College Radio/TV
71 George Street, Providence, RI 02912-1824
401-863-2225, *Fax:* 401-863-2221
nacb@aol.com
Founded: 1988 *Number of Members:* 1600 *Mission:* Members are student radio/TV stations and interested individuals. Has an annual budget of approximately $300,000.

National Association of Farm Broadcasters
PO Box 500, Platte City, MO 64079-2294
816-431-4032, *Fax:* 816-431-4087
www.nafb.com
info@nafb.com
Bill Oneill, Executive Director
Jeremy Povenmire, Member Service Manager
Rose Marie Lawrence, Secretary
Gene Millard, Director Marketing & Promotion

Founded: 1944 *Number of Members:* 600 *Mission:* Works to improve quantity and quality of farm programming and serves as a clearinghouse for new ideas in farm broadcasting.

National Association of Hispanic
1050 Connecticut Avenue NW, Washington, DC 20036
202-662-7145, *Fax:* 202-662-7144
www.nahj.org
nahj@nahj.org
Anna M. Lopez Buck, Interim Executive Director
Kevin Olivas, Recruitment and Guidance Manager
Founded: 1984 *Number of Members:* 2300 *Mission:* NAHJ is dedicated to the recognition and professional advancement of Hispanics in the news industry. NAHJ created a national voice and unified vision for all Hispanicjournalists.

National Association of Television Program Executives International
See listing under Major National Associations, this section.

National Association of Telecommunications Officers and Advisors
1800 Diagonal Rd., Suite 495, Alexandria, VA 22314
(703) 519-8035, *Fax:* (703) 519-8036
www.natoa.org
info@natoa.org

National Association of Television
5757 Wilshire Blvd, Penthouse 10, Los Angeles, CA 90036-5810
323-937-4465, *Fax:* 310-453-5258
www.natpe.org
info@natpe.org
Rick Feldman, President/CEO
Wayneston Harbeson, Operations Manager
Jon Dobkin, CFO
Founded: 1963 *Number of Members:* 2800 *Mission:* A global, non-profit organization dedicated to the creation, development and distribution of televised programming in all forms across all mature and emerging media platforms.

National Black Media Coalition
145 Alderson Ave., Billings, MT 59101
(406) 248-4450, *Fax:* (301) 593-3604
www.nbmc.org
webmaster@nbm.org

National Cable and Telecommunications Association(NCTA)
25 Massachusetts Ave Nw, Suite 100, Washington, DC 20001-1434
202-222-2300, *Fax:* 202-775-3604
www.ncta.com
webmaster@ncta.com
Michael Powell, President And CEO
James Assey, Executive VP
Founded: 1952 *Number of Members:* 3189 *Mission:* Members are cable TV systems; associate members are manufacturers, distributors, suppliers of hardware, programmers and other services Association forthose interested in programs about cable television.

National Captioning Institute
3725 Concorde Parkway, Suite 100, Chantilly, VA 20151
703-917-7600, *Fax:* 703-917-9853
www.ncicap.org
tcalkins@ncicap.org
Gene Chao, CEO, President
Drake Smith, Chief Technology Officer
Marc Okrand, Director, Administration
Tony Calkins, Director, National Sales
Jay Feinberg, Director, Marketing
Mission: Non-profit organization whose primary purposes are to deliver effective captioning services and encourage, develop and fund the continuing development of captioning, subtitling, and other media access services for the benefitof peopl who require additional access to the auditory and visual information.

National Council for Families & TV
3801 Barham Boulevard, Los Angeles, CA 90068-1000
323-953-7300, *Fax:* 310-208-5984
www.salonprofessionals.org
Mission: Advances and promotes television awareness for family television shows.

National Education Association
1201 16th St. N.W., Washington, DC 20036-3290
(202) 833-4000, *Fax:* (202) 822-7974
www.nea.org
editorial@list.nea.org

National Federation of Community Broadcasters (NFCB)
1970 Broadway, Suite 1000, Oakland, CA 94612
510-451-8200, *Fax:* 510-451-8208
www.nfcb.org
comments@nfcb.org
Maxie C Jackson III, President/CEO
Brian Terhorst, Board Chair
Kim Bosler, Secretary
Peggy Berryhill, Treasurer
Mission: A national alliance of stations, producers, and others committed to community radio. NFCB advocates for national public policy, funding, recognition, and resources on behalf of its membership while providing services toempower and strengthen community broadcasters through the core values of localism, diversity, and public service.

National Federation of Press Women Inc.-NFPW
Mailing Address: PO Box 34798, Alexandria, VA 22334-0798
Second Address: PO Box 5556, Arlington, VA 22205
800-780-2715, *Fax:* 703-237-9808
www.nfpw.org
presswomen@aol.com
Ella Robinson, President
June Mathews, VP
Founded: 1937 *Number of Members:* 2000 *Mission:* Members are writers, editors and other communication professionals for newspapers, magazines, wire services, agencies and freelance.

National League of Cities
1301 Pennsylvania Ave. N.W., Suite 550, Washington, DC 20004
(202) 626-3000, *Fax:* (202) 626-3043
info@nlc.org
Directors:
James C. Hunt, pres; Bart Peterson, VP; Cynthia McCollum, 2nd VP. R. Michael Amyx, Tommy Baker & Vickie Barnett

National Lesbian and Gay Journalists
2120 L Street NW, Suite 850, Washington, DC 20037
202-588-9888
www.nlgja.org
info@nlgja.org
Bach Polakowski, National Office Administrator
Matthew Rose, Membership Coordinator
Michael Tune, Executive Director
David Steinberg, President
Jen Christensen, Vice President/Broadcast
Founded: 1990 *Number of Members:* 220 *Mission:* NLGJA is an organization of journalists, media professionals, educators and students working within the news industry to foster fair and accurate coverage of LGBT issues. NLGJAopposes all forms of workplace bias and provides professional development to its members.

National Museum of Communications Inc.
2001 Plymouth Rock Dr., Richardson, TX 75081
(972) 889-9872, *Fax:* (972) 889-2329
www.yesterdayusa.com
bill46@yesterdayusa.com
Directors:
William J. Bragg, Betty Lewis & Kim Bragg

National Newspaper Association
Mailing Address: PO Box 7540, Columbia, MO 65205-7540
Second Address: PO Box 5737, Arlington, VA 22205
800-829-4ANNA, 573-77-4890, 703-237-9802, *Fax:* 573-777-4985, 703-237-9808
www.nnaweb.org
lynn@nna.org
Lynn Edinger, Associate Director
Founded: 1885 *Number of Members:* 2000 *Mission:* To protect, promote and enhance America's community newspapers.

National Press Club
529 14th St NW, 13th Floor, Washington, DC 20045-2393
202-662-7500, *Fax:* 202-662-7512
www.npcpress.org
contact through website
William Mc Carren, Manager
Donna Leinwand, Vice President
Maureen Groppe, Secretary
Alan Bjerga, Treasurer
Mark Hamrick, Membership Secretary
Number of Members: 4.6M *Mission:* A private organization composed of professional journalists who are directly related to the media. Persons must qualify to be admitted.

National Press Foundation
1211 Connecticut Ave NW, Suite 310, Washington, DC 20036-2709
202-530-5355, *Fax:* 202-662-1232
www.nationalpress.org
maha@nationalpress.org
Bob Meyers, President
Gerald Seib, Vice Chairman
Founded: 1976 *Mission:* Supports all those involved with national press and the media. Publishes bi-weekly newsletter.

National Public Radio Association
635 Massachusetts Ave Nw, Suite 1, Washington, DC 20001-3753
202-686-0516, *Fax:* 202-513-3329
www.npr.org
Gary E Knell, President/CEO
Joyce MacDonald, Chief of Staff/Vice President
Jeff Perkins, Chief People Officer
Robert Kempf, General Manager
Deborah Cowan, VP/Chief Financial Officer
Founded: 1970 *Number of Members:* 750 *Mission:* Works in partnership with member stations to create a more informed public, one challenged and invigorated by a deeper understanding and appreciation of events, ideas, andcultures.

National Religious Broadcasters
9510 Technology Dr, Manassas, VA 20110-4149
703-330-7000, *Fax:* 703-330-7100
www.nrb.org
info@nrb.org
Frank Wright, President
Linda Smith, President Assistant
David Keith, VP Operations
Number of Members: 1700 *Mission:* Represents more than 1500 evangelical Christian radio and television stations, program producers, multimedia developers and related organizations around the world. Members are responsible for muchof the world's Christian radio and television.

National Retail Federation
325 7th St. N.W., Suite 1100, Washington, DC 20004
(202) 783-7971, (800) nrf-how2, *Fax:* (202) 737-2849
www.nrf.com

National Scholastic Press Association
2221 University Ave SE, Suite 121, Minneapolis, MN 55414-3074
612-625-8335, *Fax:* 612-626-0720
www.studentpress.org
Logan Aimone, Executive Director
Ann Akers, Associate Director
Jesse Rinkenberger, Business Manager
Mission: Supports all those involved in yearbook printing and photographic services, college journalism departments and video yearbook production services. Hosts annual trade show.

National Sportscasters and Sportswriters
PO Box 1545, Salisbury, NC 28145-1545
704-633-4275, *Fax:* 704-633-2027
www.nssahalloffame.com
nssahalloffame@aol.com
Bob Setzer, President
Dennis White, Vice President
Founded: 1959 *Number of Members:* 1000 *Mission:* Meet annually.

National Telemedia Council
1922 University Avenue, Madison, WI 53726
608-218-1182, *Fax:* 608-218-1183
www.nationaltelemediacouncil.org
ntelemedia@aol.com
Marieli Rowe, Editor of the Journal of Media Literacy
Karen Ambrosh, President
Mission: Promotes media literacy through workshops and telemediun.

National Translator Association
5611 Kendall Court, Suite 2, Arvada, CO 80002
303-378-8209, *Fax:* 303-940-8442
www.tvfmtranslators.com
stcl@comcast.net
Byron St. Clair, President
Arnold Cruze, VP
Paul Burkholder, Secretary/Treasurer
Arnold Cruze, Director
Dave Sunderman, Director
Founded: 1967 *Mission:* Dedicated to the preservation of free over-the-air TV in all geographical areas. It works to improve the technology of rebroadcast translators and regulatory climate which governs them. It continouslypromotes the concept of universal free over-the-air TV and reprsents the ineterests of translator operators before the FCC and other government agencies such as the Forest Service and the Bureau of Land Management. Membership is open to allindividuals and organizations that are interested.

Native American Journalists Association
University of Oaklahoma, Gaylor College, 395 W Lindsey Street, Norman, OK 73019-4201
405-325-9008, *Fax:* 405-325-6945
www.naja.com
Jeff Harjo, Executive Director
Heather Dutcher, Marketing Director
Rhonda LeValdo, President
Jolene Schonchin, Secretary
Founded: 1983 *Mission:* NAJA serves and empowers Native journalists through programs and actions designed to enrich journalism and promote Native cultures. NAJA educates and unifies its membership through journalism programs thatpromote diversity and defends challenges to free press.

New England Cable & Telecommunications
10 Forbes Road, Suite 440W, Braintree, MA 02184-2648
781-843-3418, *Fax:* 781-849-6267
www.necta.info
info@necta.info
Mission: NECTA is a six state regional trade association representing sbtstantially all private cable telecommunications companies in Connecticut, Maine, Massachusetts, New Hampshire, Rhode Island and Vermont.

New England Press Association
360 Huntington Avenue 428CP, Boston, MA 02115
617-254-4880, *Fax:* 617-373-5615
www.nepa.org
info@nepa.org
Brenda Reedtani, Executive Director
Lynn Delaney, Second VP
Marlene Switzer, Secretary
Founded: 1950 *Number of Members:* 460 *Mission:* This organization offers a publication about the newspaper industry specifically focusing on New England newspapers and the issues that affect them, which goes to everynewspaper in New England.

New Jersey Collegiate Press Association
840 Bear Tavern Rd, Suite 305, Ewing, NJ 08628-1019
609-406-0600, *Fax:* 609-406-0300
www.njpa.org
foundation@njpa.org
John O'Brien, Executive Director
Founded: 1952 *Number of Members:* 49 *Mission:* Supports all those involved in the development and betterment of collegiate press. Hosts annual trade show.

Newseum
1101 Wilson Blvd., Arlington, VA 22209
(703) 284-3544, (888) new-seum
www.newseum.org
newseum@freedomforum.org

Newspaper Association Managers
70 Washington Street, Salem, MA 01970-3518
978-744-8940, *Fax:* 978-744-0333
Bob New, Owner
Morley Piper, Executive Director
Founded: 1923 *Number of Members:* 65 *Mission:* Executives of state, regional, national and international newspaper associations.

Newspaper Association of America
4401 Wilson Blvd, Suite 900, Arlington, VA 22203-4195
571-366-1000, *Fax:* 571-366-1195
www.naa.org
joan.mills@naa.org
Reggie Hall, Senior VP
Rebecca Albers, VP
Paula Hummel, Director
Joan Mills, Marketing Manager
Charles Pittman, Director
Donna Barrett, Director
Susan Clark-Johnson, Director
Paul Boyle, Director
Su Lin Nichols, Director
Randy Bennett, Director
Founded: 1992 *Number of Members:* 2000 *Mission:* Newspaper Association of America maintains close, cooperative relations with other newspaper and journalism organizations.

Newspaper Guild: CWA
501 3rd St Nw, 6th Floor, Washington, DC 20001-2760
202-434-1254, *Fax:* 202-434-1426
www.nabetcwa.org
guild@cwa-union.org
John Clark, President
Carol D Rothman, Secretary/Treasurer
Andy Zipser, Guild Reporter
Founded: 1937 *Mission:* Organization covering the newspaper industry, its employment practices, press freedom and labor movement.

North American Broadcasters Association (NABA)
Box 500, Stn A, Rm. 6C 300, Toronto, ON M5W 1E6 Canada
(416) 598-9877, *Fax:* (416) 598-9774
www.nabanet.com
info@nabanet.com
Directors:
Joseph Flaherty, Felix Arauji Ramirez, Ignacio Suarez, Andy Setos & Peter Smith

North American Broadcasters Association (NABA)
205 Wellington Street West, Suite 6C300, Toronto, ON M5V 3G7
416-598-9877, *Fax:* 416-598-9774
www.nabanet.com
contact@nabanet.com
Michael McEwan, Director General
Anh Ngo, Director, Administration
Jason Paris, Senior Coordinator
Mission: A non-profit association of broadcasting organizations in the United States, Mexico, and Canada committed to advancing the interests of broadcasters at home and internationally.

North American Network
3700 Crestwood Pkwy NW, Suite 350, Duluth, GA 30096-7154
770-279-4560, *Fax:* 770-279-4566
www.pkfnan.org
rbeilfuss@pkfnan.org
Terry Snyder, President
Mission: Radio broadcasting agency that provides news and programming services to radio stations and organizations. Programming is sponsored by the corporations, government angencies, associations and nonprofit organizations who areindentified in the program notes and scripts.

North American Retail Dealers Association
10 E. 22nd St., Suite 310, Lombard, IL 60148-6191
(630) 953-8950, (800) 621-0298, *Fax:* (630) 953-8957
www.kwmu.com
nardahdq@narda.com

Overseas Press Club of America
40 W 45th St, New York, NY 10036
212-626-9220, *Fax:* 212-626-9210
www.opcofamerica.org
sonya@opcofamerica.org
Sonya Fry, Executive Director
David Andelman, President
Jacqueline Albert-Simon, Treasurer
Founded: 1939 *Number of Members:* 600 *Mission:* OPC is a private non-profit membership organization of journalists engaged in international news.

Pacific Pioneer Broadcasters
Box 4866, Valley Village, CA 91617-4866
(323) 461-2121, *Fax:* (818) 768-8251
www.ppbwebsite.org

The Paley Center for Media
Mailing Address: 25 West 52nd Street, New York, NY 10019
Second Address: 465 N. Beverly Dr., Beverly Hills, CA 90210
212-621-6800, 212-621-6600; 310-786-1000
www.paleycenter.org
coman@paleycenter.org
Pat Mitchell, President, CEO
John Wolters, Vice President, CFO
Jennifer Juzaitis, Vice President, Development
Diane Lewis, Vice President, Public Affairs
Mission: Leads the discussion about the cultural, creative, and social significance of television, radio, and emerging platforms for the professional community and media-interested public.

PCIA- The Wireless Industry Association
6355 Walker Ln, Suite 700, Alexandria, VA 22310-3247
703-971-7100, *Fax:* 703-922-5518
www.pcia.com
andrewd@pcia.com
Andrea Burns, Director Gov't Relations
Connie Durcksak, Sr Director Industry Relations
Rick Harris, Sr Director Press/Public Relations
Founded: 1949 *Number of Members:* 3000 *Mission:* Represents companies that develop, own, manage and operate towers, commercial rooftops and other facilities for the provision of all types of wireless, broadcasting andtelecommunications services.

PROMAX&BDA
9000 W. Sunset Blvd., Suite 900, Los Angeles, CA 90069
(310) 788-7600, (800) 977-6629, *Fax:* (310) 788-7616
www.promax.tv
jim@promax.tv
Directors:
David Snapp, George Pierson, Lisa Fengler, Leslie Celia, Jeannine Chanin, Tony Cleave, Ann Epstein-Cohen, Steve Delaney, Miguel Muelle, Karen Olcott, Jan Phillips, Abel Sanchez, Robin Skirboll, Anne White, Mark Stroman, Glynn Brailsford,Brian Blum, Judy Braune, Alan Cohen, Scott Danielson, C.J. Fredricksen, Lee Hunt, Kay Hutchison, Tony Lakin, Vince Manze, Brigitte McCray, Rob Middleton, Nick Miller, Michael Mischler, David Muscari, Billy Pittard, Sal Sardo, George Schweitzer,Curtis Symonds & Donna Weston

Synapse Pacific LTD
49 Hollywood Rd., 19th Fl., Hong Kong, China

Promax & BDA Europe
61 Webber St., London, NO United Kingdom

Promotion Marketing Association Inc.
257 Park Ave. S., Suite 1102, New York, NY 10010
(212) 420-1100, *Fax:* (212) 533-7622
www.pmalink.org
pma@pmalink.org

Public Radio in Mid-America (PRIMA)
3651 Olive Street, St Louis, MO 63108
314-516-5968, *Fax:* 314-516-6397
www.kmwu.org
info@kmwu.org
Tim Eby, General Manager
Terrence Dupuis, Chief Engineer
Shelley Kerley, Director, Development
Mission: Trusted source of information and entertainment that opens minds and mourishes the spirit

Public Radio News Directors Incorporated
821 University Ave., Madison, NY 53706
(608) 265-3378, *Fax:* (608) 263-5838
walker@wpr.org
Directors:
Dave Piznanelli, Martha Foley, Jonathan Ahl & Christine Paige-Diers

Public Relations Society of America
33 Maiden Ln., 11th Fl., New York, NY 10038
(212) 460-1400, *Fax:* (212) 995-0757
www.prsa.org
hq@prsa.org

Pulic Radio News Directors Incorporated
PO Box 838, Sturgis, SD 57785
605-490-3033, *Fax:* 605-490-3085
www.prndi.org
info@prndi.org
George Bodarky, President
Bob Beck, Treasurer
Naomi Starobin, Large Station Rep
Matt Schaffer, Medium Station Rep
Aaron Selbig, Small Station Rep
Mission: A non-profit professional association that exists to improve local news and information programming by serving public radio journalists.

Radio & Television News Directors Foundation
1600 K St. NW, Suite 700, Washington, DC 20006
(202) 659-6510, *Fax:* (202) 223-4007
www.rtndf.org
rtndf@rtndf.org

Radio & Television Research Council
c/o MSA, Attn: R. Sharpe, 152 Madison Ave., Suite 801, New York, NY 10016
(212) 481-3038, *Fax:* (212) 481-3071
rtrcny@aol.com

Radio Advertising Bureau
1320 Greenway Dr, Suite 500, Irving, TX 75038-2547
972-753-6700, *Fax:* 972-753-6727
www.rab.com
jhaley@rab.com
Mike Mahone, VP
Leah Koman, SVP Marketing
Number of Members: 7000 *Mission:* Our mission is to lead industry initiatives and provide organizational, educational, research and advocacy programs and services that benefit the RAB membership and the Radio industry as a whole.

Radio and Television Museum
2608 Mitchellville Rd., Bowie, MD 20716
(301) 390-1020, *Fax:* (301)947-3338
www.radiohistory.org
radiobelanger@comcast.net
Directors:
Brian Belanger, exec dir. Kenneth Mellgren, Ed Walker, Peter Eldridge, William McMahon, William Goodwin, Tony Young, Rob

Huddleston, Chris Sterling, Don Ross, Gerald Schneider, Paul Courson, Charles Grant & Michael Rubin

Radio and Television Research Council
245 5th Avenue, New York, NY 10016-8728
212-028-8933, *Fax:* 212-481-3071
Robert M Purcell, Executive Director
Founded: 1941 *Number of Members:* 200 *Mission:* Members are professionals actively engaged in radio/television research.

Radio Information Service
600 Forbes Ave, Suite 140, Pittsburgh, PA 15219-3016
412-488-3944, *Fax:* 412-488-3953
www.readingservice.org
info@readingservice.org
Andy Ai, President
Erica Hacker, Vice President
Number of Members: 10000 *Mission:* Membership is offered to radio reading and information services for the blind or print handicapped.

Radio Marketing Bureau
175 Bloor St. E., Suite 316 North Tower, Toronto, ON M4W 3R8
Canada
(416) 922-5757, (800) 667-2346, *Fax:* (416) 922-6542
www.rmb.ca
info@rmb.ca

Radio Television Digital News Association
529 14th Street NW, Suite 425, Washington, DC 20045
Fax: 202-223-4007
www.rtdna.org
mikec@rtdna.org
Mike Cavender, Executive Director
Ryan Murphy, Communications
Katie Switchenko, Programs
Mission: An association dedicated to setting new standards for newsgathering and reporting.

Radio Television News Directors
1025 Thomas Jefferson St, 7th Floor, Washington, DC 20007-5214
202-625-3500, *Fax:* 202-223-4007
www.rtnda.org
barbarac@rtnda.org
Barbara Cochran, President
Founded: 1946 *Number of Members:* 3000+ *Mission:* Largest professional organization exclusively serving the electronic news profession. Dedicated to setting standards for newsgathering and reporting. Represents electronicjournalists in radion, television and all digital media, as well as journalism educators and students.

Radio Television News Directors Association(Canada)
2175 Shepherd Avenue E, Suite 310, Toronto, ON M2J 1W8
Canada
416-756-2126, *Fax:* 416-364-8896
www.rtndacanada.com
info@rtndacanada.com
Ian Koenigsfest, President
Mission: Progressive organization offering a forum for open discussion and action in the broadcast news industry. Speaks for the leaders of Canada's radio and television news operations on the issues that impact the newsroom.

Radio-Television Correspondents' Association
S-325, U.S. Capitol, Washington, DC 20510
(202) 224-6421, *Fax:* (202) 224-4882
www.senate.gov/galleries.radiotv.com
Directors:
Jerry Bodlander, Bob Fuss, Edward O'Keefe, Dave McConnell, Richard Tillery & David Welna

Recording Industry Association of America Inc. (RIAA)
1330 Connecticut Ave. N.W., Suite 300, Washington, DC 20036
(202) 775-0101, *Fax:* (202) 775-7253
www.riaa.com

Royal Television Society, North America Inc.
Box 870501, Arizona State University, Tempe, AZ 85287-0501
(480) 965-7661, *Fax:* (480) 965-1371
royaltv@asu.edu

Satellite Broadcasting & Communications Association
1100 17th St NW, Suite 1150, Washington, DC 20036
202-349-3620, *Fax:* 202-349-3621
www.sbca.com
info@sbca.org
Joseph Widoff, Executive Director
Benjamin Rowan, Education Manager
Joy O'Brien, Director Government Affairs
Pat Andrews, Senior VP
Brian Lynch, Director Program Development
Founded: 1986 *Number of Members:* 1000 *Mission:* National trade organization representing all segments of the satellite consumer services industry. The association is committed to expanding the utilization of satellitetechnology for the delivery of video, data, voice, interactive and broadband services.

Society for News Design
1130 Ten Rod Rd, Suite D-202, North Kingstown, RI 02852-4168
401-294-5233, *Fax:* 401-294-5238
www.snd.org
snd@snd.org
Scott Goldman, President
Gayle Grin, Vice President
Matt Mansfield, Secretary/Treasurer
Elise Burroughs, Executive Director
Founded: 1979 *Number of Members:* 2600 *Mission:* An international professional organization that encourage high standards of journalism through design. An international forum and resource for all those interested in newsdesign, SND works to recognize excellence and strengthen visual journalism as a profession.

Society of American Business Editors and Writers
ASU, Walter Cronkite School of Journalism, 555 North Central Ave, Suite 416, Phoenix, AZ 85004-1248
602-496-7862
www.sabew.org
sabew@sabew.org
Carrie Paden, Executive Director
Rex Seline, VP
Jon Lansner, Secretary/Treasurer
Brant Houston, Executive Director
Founded: 1964 *Number of Members:* 3200 *Mission:* Members are financial and economic news writers and editors for print and broadcast outlets.

Society of Broadcast Engineers
9102 N Meridian St, Suite 150, Indianapolis, IN 46260-1896
317-846-9000, *Fax:* 317-846-9120
www.sbe.org
mclappe@sbe.org
John Poray, Executive Director
Vincent A Lopez, VP
Founded: 1964 *Number of Members:* 5500 *Mission:* SBE provides members with the opportunity to network and share ideas and information in keeping current with the ongoing changes within the industry. Members can attend annualconferences and expositions, have access to educational opportunities and obtain professional certification.

Society of Cable Telecommunications Engineers Inc.
140 Philips Rd., Exton, PA 19341-1318
(610) 363-6888, *Fax:* (610) 363-5898
www.scte.org
scte@scte.org
Professional membership assn offering information, professional dev resources, standards to cable telecommunications engineers & other professional.
Directors:
Joel E. Welch, Thomas Russell & Joan Hagelin

The Society of Environmental Journalists
PO Box 2492, Jenkintown, PA 19046
215-884-8174, *Fax:* 215-884-8175
www.sej.org
sej@sej.org
Beth Parke, Executive Director
Linda Knouse, Records Manager
Jeanne Scanlon, Assistant
Mission: Mission is to strengthen the quality. reach and viability of journalism across all media to advance public understanding of environmental issues.

Society of Environmental Journalists(SEJ)
PO Box 2492, Jenkintown, PA 19046
215-884-8174, *Fax:* 215-884-8175
www.sej.org
bparke@sej.org
Beth Parke, Executive Director
Tim Wheeler, President
Linda Knouse, Records Manager
Jeanne Scanlon, Assistant
Founded: 1990 *Mission:* To advance public understanding of environmental issues by improving the quality, accuracy, and visibility of environmental reporting. To strengthenthe quality, reach and viability of journalism across allmedia to advance public understanding of environmental issues.

Society of Motion Picture & Television Engineers(SMPTE)
3 Barker Ave, 5th Floor, White Plains, NY 10601-1509
914-761-1100, *Fax:* 914-761-3115
www.smpte.org
contact through website
Barbara Lange, Executive Director
June M. Sobrito, Executive Assistant
Peter Symes, Engineering Director
Founded: 1916 *Number of Members:* 6000 *Mission:* More than 10,000 members are spread throughout 85 countries. Also, over 250 corporate members belong to SMPTE, allowing networking and contacts to occur on a larger scale.Touching on every discipline, our members include engineers, technical directors, cameramen, editors, technicians, manufacturers educators, and consultants.

Society of Professional Journalists
3909 N Meridian Street, Indianapolis, IN 46208
317-927-8000, *Fax:* 317-920-4789
www.spj.org
webmaster@spj.org
Gordon McKerral, President
David E Carlson, Secretary/Treasurer
James Highland, VP
Founded: 1909 *Number of Members:* 9000 *Mission:* Broad-based journalism organization, dedicated to encouraging the free practice of journalism and stimulating high standards of ethical behavior.12 regional directors, national officials elected annually, two students reps, two directors at-large and two campus advisors at-large

Society of Satellite Professionals International
New York Information Technology Center, 250 Parke Ave, 7th Floor, New York, NY 10004-2501
212-809-5199, *Fax:* 212-825-0075
www.sspi.org
Robert Bell, Executive Director
Louis Zacharilla, Director Development
Founded: 1983 *Number of Members:* 1700 *Mission:* Members are individuals in the fields of businesss, education, entertainment, media, science and industry who share common interests in satellite technology.

Society of Telecommunications Consultants
13275 State Highway 89, PO Box 70, Old Station, CA 96071
530-335-7313, *Fax:* 530-335-7360
www.stcconsultants.org
Cathy Cimaglia, Administrative Manager
Founded: 1976 *Number of Members:* 180 *Mission:* The STC is an international organization of independent telecommunications and information technology consultants who serve clients in business and government

The Songwriters Guild of America
1560 Broadway, Suite 408, New York, NY 10036
(212) 768-7902, *Fax:* (212) 768-7902
www.songwritersguild.org
ny@songwritersguild.com
6430 Sunset Blvd, Hollywood, CA 90028-7901
(213) 462-1108;
Aaron Meza, Rgnl Dir
1222 16th Ave. St, Suite 25, Nashville, TN
(615) 329-1782;
Rondi Regan, Rgnl Dir
6430 Sunset Blvd., Los Angeles, CA 90028-7901

Special Industrial Radio Service
8484 Westpark Drive, # 630, Mc Lean, VA 22102-3590
703-528-5115
www.ita-relay.com
Mark Crosby, President/CEO
Founded: 1953 *Number of Members:* 15 *Mission:* Provides a license renewal reminder service. Maintains liaison with major radio manufacturers and mediates problems between licensees.

Statenets National Association of State Radio Networks Inc.
17911 Harwood Avenue, Homewood, IL 60430
708-799-6676, *Fax:* 708-799-6698
www.statenets.com
tdobrez@statenets.com
Tom Dobrez, Executive Director
Sharon Kitchell, Deputy Director
Mission: Works with hundreds of regional and national marketers and political campaigns solve marketing challenges.

Syndicated Network Television Association
One Penn Plaza, Suite 5310, New York, NY 10119

212-259-3740, *Fax:* 212-259-3770
www.snta.com
mburg@snta.com
Mitch Burg, President
Jordan Harris, Director, Marketing
Hadassa Gerber, Director. Research
Mission: Communicates to advertisers, their agencies and media planners and buyers the benefits of syndication, from the wide range of programming choices to their high ratings and national reach, and the reliability and costeffectiveness of advertising in syndicated programming.

Telecommunications Industry Association
2500 Wilson Blvd., Arlington, VA 22201
(703) 907-7700, *Fax:* (703) 907-7727
www.tiaonline.org
tia@tiaonline.org
Directors:
Grant Seiffert, Bill Belt, John Derr, Derek Khlopin, Jason Leuck, Anna Amselle, Henry Wieland, Maryann Lesso, David Smith, Dan Bart & Henry Cuschieri

USITO
Rm. 332, 3/f Lido Office Tower, Lido Place, Jichang Rd., Jiang Tai Rd., Beijing 100004, China
(8610) 6430-1368/69/70/71/72; *Fax:* (8610) 6430-1367
www.usito.org
usito@usito.org
Anne Stevenson-Yang, Mgng Dir

Telecommunications Research and Action Center (TRAC)
Box 27279, Washington, DC 20005
(202) 263-2950, *Fax:* (202) 263-2960
www.trac.org
trac@trac.org

Television Bureau of Advertising
3 E 54th St, Suite 1000, New York, NY 10022-3139
212-486-1111, *Fax:* 212-935-5631
www.tvb.org
info@tvb.org
Steve Lanzano, President
Abby Auerbach, Executive VP/CMO
Scott Roskowski, SVP/Business Development
Stacey Lynn Schulman, SVP/Research
Founded: 1954 *Number of Members:* 600 *Mission:* Not-for-profit trade association of America's broadcast television industry. TVB provides a diverse variety of tools and resources to support its members and to help advertisersmake the best use of local television.

Television Bureau of Canada
160 Bloor St. E, Suite 1005, Toronto, ON M4W 1B9 Canada
(416) 923-8813, *Fax:* (416) 413-3879
www.tvb.ca
tvb@tvb.ca

Television Bureau of Canada
160 Bloor Street East, Suite 1005, Toronto, ON M4W 1B9
416-923-8813, *Fax:* 416-413-3879
www.tvb.ca
tvb@tvb.ca
Theresa Treutler, President, CEO
Duncan Robertson, Director, Media Insights
Rhonda Lynn Bagnall, Director, Telecaster Services
Mission: TVB markets the benefits and effectiveness of the TV medium in all its forms to advertisers and agencies. TVB collects, interprets, develops, identifies, and communicates information and data to be used.

Television Critics Association
825 East Douglas Avenue, Witchita, KS 67202
316-268-6394, *Fax:* 316-288-6627
www.tvcritics.org
info@tvcritics.org
Candy Havens, President
Scott Pierce, Vice President
Amber Dowling, Secretary
Brian Gianelli, Treasurer
Mission: Represents more than 220 journalists writing about television for print and online outlets.

Television Operators Caucus
1176 K Street NW, 9th Floor, Washington, DC 20006
202-719-7090, *Fax:* 202-719-7548
Margita White, President
Mission: Non-profit group of memebers that support television issues and its impacts on the world today.

Trade Promotion Management Association
51 Cragwood Road, Suite 200, South Plainfield, NJ 07080
646-442-3703, *Fax:* 908-755-7451
www.tpmaww.com
bhouk@tpmaww.com
Bob Houk, Executive Director
Susan Haupt, Operations Director
Founded: 1989 *Number of Members:* 90 *Mission:* Dedicated specifically to the practice of trade promotion marketing in all its forms. Serve as a resource for information and education on trade promotion programs as well asprovides strategies for developing, implementing and evaluating such programs.

Traffic Audit Bureau for Media Measurement
271 Madison Ave, Suite 1504, New York, NY 10016-1012
212-972-8075, *Fax:* 212-972-8928
www.tabonline.com
inquiry@tabonline.com
Joseph Philport, President
Sean McCarthy, VP Information Technology
Founded: 1933 *Number of Members:* 450 *Mission:* Acts as an independent third party provider of standardized and valid circulation measures for out of home media.

U.S. Conference of Catholic Bishops, Dept. of Communications
3211 4th St. N.E., Washington, DC 20017-1194
(202) 541-3000, *Fax:* (202) 541-3173
www.usccb.org

United Telecom Council
1901 Pennsylvania Ave Nw, 5th Floor, Washington, DC 20006-3406
202-872-0030, *Fax:* 202-872-1331
www.utc.org
bill.moroney@utc.org
William R Moroney, President/CEO
Jill Lyon, VP and General Counsel
Founded: 1948 *Number of Members:* 1500 *Mission:* Represents organizations using telecommunications in their operations before various federal and state legislative and regulatory agencies, particularly the FCC

Veteran Wireless Operators Association Inc.
Box 1003, Peck Slip, New York, NY 10272-1003

www.vwoa.org
vwoa@interactive.net
Directors:
Richard T. Kenney & D. I. Temple

Veterans Bedside Network
Div/DBA: (The Veterans Hospital Radio & TV Guild.)
10 Fiske Pl., Rm. 301, Mount Vernon, NY 10550
(914) 699-6069, *Fax:* (914) 667-0405

WGBH Educational Foundation
One Guest Street, Boston, MA 2135
617-300-5400
www.wgbh.org
Jonathan Abbott, President/CEO
Benjamin Godley, Executive Vice President and Chief
David Bernstein, VP/Gneral Manager
Melinda Braithwate, VP for Human Resources
Margaret Drain, VP for National Programming
Founded: 1836 *Mission:* Make knowledge and the creative life of the arts, sciences, and humanities available to the widest possible public

Wireless Communications Association International, Inc.
1333 H St. N.W., Suite 700, Washington, DC 20005-4754
(202) 452-7823, *Fax:* (202) 452-0041
www.wcai.com
sonu@wcai.com
Directors:
John T. von Harz III, William Andrie Jr., T. Lauriston Hardin III, Chris Farnworth & Patrick J. Gossman III

Women in Cable & Telecommunications
14555 Avion Pkwy., Suite 250, Chantilly, VA 20151
(703) 234-9810, *Fax:* (703) 817-1595
www.wict.org
info@wict.org
Directors:
Mary Busby, Robin Burke Zahory, Lisa McBee & Lisa Vega

Women In Film
8857 W. Olympic Blvd., Suite 201, Beverly Hills, CA 90211
(310) 657-5144, *Fax:* (310) 657-5154
www.wif.org
info@wif.org

World Broadcasting Unions (WBU)
Box 500, Stn. A, Rm. 6C 300, Toronto, ON M5W 1E6 Canada
(416) 598-9877, *Fax:* (416) 598-9774
www.nabanet.com/wbu
info@nabanet.org

World Teleport Association
55 Broad St., 14th Fl., New York, NY 10004
(212) 825-0218, *Fax:* (212) 825-0075
www.worldteleport.org
wta@worldteleport.org
Directors:
Chris Russell, David Sprechman, Gary Hatch, Oliver Badard, Nick Thompson, Yoshihiro Yohoyama & tohm Tahahasin

State & Regional Broadcast Associations

Advertising Women of New York
25 W 45th St, Suite 1001, New York, NY 10036-4910
212-221-7969, *Fax:* 212-221-8296
www.awny.org
awny@awny.org
Liz Schroeder, Executive Director
Mary Morgan, President
Founded: 1912 *Number of Members:* 1300 *Mission:* AWNY is a professional organization comrising over 1,300 women and men in the advertising/communications industry. Its man focus is to provide a forum foe personal andfrofessional grouth; to serve as an catalyst for the advancement of women in the communications field; and to promote and support philanthropic endeavors through th AWNY foundation.

Alabama Broadcasters Association
2180 Pkwy. Lake Dr., Hoover, AL 35244
(205) 982-5001, *Fax:* (205) 982-0015
www.al-ba.com

Alaska Broadcasters Association
700 W 41st Street, Suite 102, Anchorage, AK 99503
907-258-2424, *Fax:* 907-258-2414
www.alaskabroadcaster.org
akba@gci.net
Laurie Prax, President
Founded: 1964 *Mission:* To provide assistance, which enables members to serve their communities of license through education, representation and advocacy.

Arizona Broadcasters Association
426 N. 44th St., Suite 310, Phoenix, AZ 85008
(602) 252-4833, *Fax:* (602) 252-5265
www.azbroadcasters.org
aba3@mindspring.com

Arkansas Broadcasters Association
2024 Arkansas Valley Dr., Suite 403, Little Rock, AR 72212
(501) 227-7564, *Fax:* (501) 223-9798
www.arkbroadcasters.org
mail@arkbroadcasters.org

California Broadcasters Association
915 L St., Suite 1150, Sacramento, CA 95814
(916) 444-2237, *Fax:* (916) 444-2043
www.cabroadcasters.org
jberry@yourcba.com
Directors:
Kathy Baker, chmn

Colorado Broadcasters Association
Box 2369, Breckenridge, CO 80424
(970) 547-1388, *Fax:* (970) 547-1384
www.coloradobroadcasters.org
cobroadcasters@earthlink.net
Directors:
Wick Rowland, sec/treas

Connecticut Broadcasters Association
90 South Park St., Willimantic, CT 06226
(860) 633-5031, *Fax:* (860) 456-5688
www.ctba.org
mcrice@prodigy.net

Festival of Nouveau Cinema Montreal
3805 Blvd. Saint-Lavrent, Montreal, QC H2W 7X9 Canada
(514) 282-0004, *Fax:* (514) 282-6664
www.nouveaucinema.ca
ngirard@nouveaucinema.ca

Florida Association of Broadcasters
201 S. Monroe St., #201, Tallahassee, FL 32301

(850) 681-6444, *Fax:* (850) 222-3957
www.fab.org

Georgia Association of Broadcasters Inc.
8010 Roswell Rd., Suite 150, Atlanta, GA 30350
(770) 395-7200, *Fax:* (770) 395-7235
www.gab.org
piguej@gab.org

Idaho State Broadcasters Association
270 N. 27th St., Suite B, Boise, ID 83702-3167
(208) 345-3072, *Fax:* (208) 343-8046
www.idahobroadcasters.org
isba@qwestoffice.net

Illinois Broadcasters Association
200 Missouri Ave., Carterville, IL 62918
(618) 985-5555, *Fax:* (618) 985-6070
www.ilba.org
ilbrdcst@neondsl.com

Indiana Broadcasters Association Inc.
3003 E. 98th St., Suite 161, Indianapolis, IN 46280
(317) 573-0119, *Fax:* (317) 573-0895
www.indianabroadcasters.org
indba@aol.com
Directors: Sally Brown, Arthur Angotti III, Roger Diehm, Tasha Mann, Lundy, Phil Hoover, Leigh Ellis, James Conner, Earl Metzger, Chuck Williams, Paulette Lees. Directors at Large: Marty Pieratt, Steve Lindell, Jeff Smulyan, Dr. JoeMisiewicz, Matt Jaquint, William Van Huss, Ron Miller, Scott Uecker, Brett Beshore.

Iowa Broadcasters Association
Box 71186, Des Moines, IA 50325
(515) 224-7237, *Fax:* (515) 224-6560
www.iowabroadcasters.com
iowaiba@dwx.com

Kansas Assn of Broadcasters
2709 S.W. 29th St., Topeka, KS 66614
(785) 235-1307, *Fax:* (785) 233-3052
www.kab.net
kent@kab.net

Kentucky Broadcasters Association
101 Enterprise Dr., Frankfort, KY 40601
(502) 848-0426
www.starstreams.com
info@starstreams.com
Musical Starstreams is a wkly two-hour program of "exotic electronica" targeted to adults age 25-54.

Louisiana Association of Broadcasters
660 Florida St., Baton Rouge, LA 70801
(225) 267-4522, *Fax:* (225) 267-4329
www.broadcasters.org
lab@broadcasters.org
Directors: George Sirven; Charles Spencer, legal counsel; Mike Barras; Tom Gay, treas; Bob Holladay; Irene Robinson; Irene Robin, vice chmn-radio; Larry Delia, vice chmn-TV. Louise Munson, pres/CEO.

Maine Assn of Broadcasters
69 Sewall St., Augusta, ME 04330
(207) 623-3870, (800) 664-6221, *Fax:* (207) 621-0585 (call first)
www.mab.org

Maryland-District of Columbia-Delaware Broadcasters Association
106 Old Court Rd., Suite 300, Baltimore, MD 21208-4038
(410) 653-4122, *Fax:* (410) 486-7354
www.mdcdd.com
info@mdcd.com

Massachusetts Broadcasters Association Inc.
PMB 401, 43 Riverside Ave., Medford, MA 02155
(800) 471-1875, *Fax:* (800) 471-1876
www.massbroadcasters.org
info@massbroadcasters.org

Michigan Association of Broadcasters
819 N. Washington Ave., Lansing, MI 48906
(517) 484-7444, *Fax:* (517) 484-5810
www.michmab.com
mab@michmab.com
Directors: Duane Alverson, Don Backus, Al Blinke, James Lutton, Bob Sliva, Paul Grzebik, Michael J. King, Ken Radant, Trey Fabacher, Gayle Olson, Bob Peters, W. Palmer Pyle, Jeffrey J. Scarpelli, Robert Stricer Diane Kniowski, MarioIacbelli, Bart Brandmiller, Tom Mogush. Honorary Board Members: Ed Christian, Alan Frank, Bruce Goldsen. Legal/Legislative Counsel: Rob Elhenicky, John J. Ronayne III.

Minnesota Broadcasters Association
3033 Excelsior Blvd., Suite 440, Minneapolis, MN 55416
(612) 926-8123, *Fax:* (612) 926-9761
www.minnesotabroadcasters.com
jdubois@minnesotabroadcasters.com
Directors: Mike Neudecker, chmn; Rosanne Rybak; Steve Woodbury; Brett Paradis; John J. Sowada; Mike Iazzo; Dennis Wahlstrom; Ed Smith. Legal Counsels: Terry Moore; Gregg Skall.

Mississippi Association of Broadcasters
855 S. Pear Orchard Rd., Suite 403, Ridgeland, MS 39157
(601) 957-9121, *Fax:* (601) 957-9175
www.msbroadcasters.org
jlett2@earthlink.net

Missouri Broadcasters Association
1025 Northeast Dr., Jefferson City, MO 65109
(573) 636-6692, *Fax:* (573) 634-8258
www.mbaweb.org
dhicks@mbaweb.org
Directors: Rick McCoy, Dave Alpert, Gary Exline, Mike Smythe, Dennis Lamme, Craig Allison, Mike Mera, Mike Harbit, Richard Womack, Mark Gordon, Don Hicks, Mark Sableman, Spencer Koch, John Caran, Danny Thomas.

Montana Broadcasters Association
1914 Rainbow Bend Dr., Bonner, MT 59823
(406) 244-4622, *Fax:* (406) 244-5518
www.mtbroadcasters.org
mba@mtbroadcasters.org

Nebraska Broadcasters Association
11414 West Center Road, Suite 324, Omaha, NE 68154
(402) 933-5995, *Fax:* (402) 933-0059
www.ne-ba.org
marty@ne-ba.org
Directors:
Marty Riemenschneider, pres; Marty Riemenschneider, exec dir

Nevada Broadcasters Association
1050 E. Flamingo Rd., Suite S-102, Las Vegas, NV 89119
(702) 794-4994, *Fax:* (702) 794-4997
www.nevadabroadcasters.org
rdfnba@aol.com
Directors:
Mary Ozer, chmn; Tony Bonnici, chmn elect

New Hampshire Association of Broadcasters
707 Chestnut St., Manchester, NH 03104
(603) 627-9600, *Fax:* (603) 627-9603
www.nhab.org
asprague@bggadvertising.com

New Jersey Broadcasters Association
348 Applegarth Rd., Monroe Twp., NJ 08831
(609) 860-0111, *Fax:* (609) 860-0110
www.njba.com
njba@njba.com
Directors:
Arthur Camiolo, Josh Gertzog, Charles McCreery, Joseph M. Bilotta, Dan Spears, Richard Swetits, John F. Garziglia & Thomas R. Ray

New Mexico Broadcasters Association
2333 Wisconsin N.E., Albuquerque, NM 87110
(505) 881-4444, *Fax:* (505) 881-5353
www.nmba.org
info@nmba.org
Directors:
Matt Martinez, Gene Dow & Milt McConnell

New York Market Radio Broadcasters Association (NYMRAD)
261 Madison Ave., 23rd Fl., New York, NY 10016
(646) 254-4493, *Fax:* (646) 254-4498
www.nymrad.org
db@nymrad.org

New York State Broadcasters Association Inc.
1805 Western Ave., Albany, NY 12203
(518) 456-8888, *Fax:* (518) 456-8943
www.nysbroadcasters.org
info@nysbroadcasters.org

North Carolina Assoc of Broadcasters
Box 627, Raleigh, NC 27602
(919) 821-7300, *Fax:* (919) 839-0304
www.ncbroadcast.com
Directors: Don

North Dakota Broadcasters Association
Box 3178, Bismarck, ND 58502-3178
(701) 258-1332, *Fax:* (701) 250-6372
www.ndba.org
bethh@ndba.org
Directors: Syd Stewart, Barry Schumaier, Larry Timpe, Tim Ost, Carol Anhorn, Darren Lenertz, George Smith.

Northern California Broadcasters Association
50 Francisco St., Suite 450, San Francisco, CA 94133
(415) 292-5700, *Fax:* (415) 292-5790
www.ncbaradio.com
tdevoto@ncradio.com

Ohio Association of Broadcasters
88 E. Broad St., Suite 1180, Columbus, OH 43215-3525
(614) 228-4052, *Fax:* (614) 228-8133
www.oab.org
oab@oab.org

Oklahoma Association of Broadcasters
6520 N. Western, Suite 104, Oklahoma City, OK 73116
(405) 848-0771
james@plancktech.com
KIMF Pinon, NM Broadcasts on 5.835 mhz and 11.885 mhz with two 50 kw transmitters.

Oregon Assn of Broadcasters
9020 SW Washington Square Road, Suite 140, Portland, OR 97223-8366
(503) 443-2299, *Fax:* (503) 443-2488
www.theoab.org
theoab@theoab.org
Bill Johnstone, President

Pennsylvania Association of Broadcasters
8501 Paxton St., Hummelstown, PA 17036
(717) 482-4820, *Fax:* (717) 482-1111
www.pab.org
rwyckoff@pab.org

Rhode Island Broadcasters Association
11 S. Angell St., Providence, RI 02920
(401) 255-8200
georgeregis@yahoo.com

South Carolina Broadcasters Association
One Harbison Way, Suite 112, Columbia, SC 29212
(803) 732-1186, *Fax:* (803) 732-4085
www.scba.net
scba@scba.net

South Dakota Broadcasters Association
Box 1037, 106 W. Capital Ave., Pierre, SD 57501
(605) 224-1034, *Fax:* (605) 224-7426
www.sdba.org
info@sdba.org

Tennessee Association of Broadcasters
Two International Plaza Dr., Suite 507, Nashville, TN 37217
(615) 945-4061, *Fax:* (615) 824-0054
www.tabtn.org
tabtn@bellsouth.net
Directors: Bryan Kell, Scott Walker, Ed Brantley, Chuck Wilkins, Sheri Sawyer, Paul Tinkle, Mason Hunter, assoc. Director at Large: Lee Meredith, TV; Dan Phillippi, TV; Doug Combs, Radio; Lacy Ennis, Radio. Debbie Turner, chmn; Whit Adamson,pres; Tom English, chmn elect; Larry Wood, past chmn; Mike Costa, vice-chmn TV; Jeff Shaw, vice-chmn Radio; George DeVault, sec/treas; Jack Mayer, Emeritus; Doug Pierce, legal counsel.

Think LA
Div/DBA: (formerly Los Angeles Advertising Agencies Associa
4223 Glencoe Ave., Suite C-100, Marina del Rey, CA 90292
(310) 823-7320, *Fax:* (310) 823-7325
www.thinkla.org
info@thinkla.org

Utah Broadcasters Association
1600 S. Main St., Salt Lake City, UT 84115
(801) 486-9521
www.utahbroadcasters.com

Vermont Association of Broadcasters
Box 4489, Burlington, VT 05406
(802) 655-5768
www.vab.org
Directors:
Jim Condon, exec dir

Virginia Association of Broadcasters
600 Peter Jefferson Pkwy., Suite 300, Charlottesville, VA 22911

(434) 977-3716, *Fax:* (434) 979-2439
www.vabonline.com
doug.easter@easterassociates.com
Directors: Nick Nicholson; Harrison Pittman; Larry Saunders; Randy Smith; Jack Dempsey; Tex Meyer; Robert Scutari; Doris Newcomb; Bob Peterson; Linda Forem; Bob Willloughby; Francis Wood; John Schick; Kenneth Hill; Warren Fihr.
Directors:
Michael Guild

Washington State Association of Broadcasters
724 Columbia St., Suite 310, Olympia, WA 98501-1249
(360) 705-0774, *Fax:* (360) 705-0873
www.wsab.org
wa-broadcasters@earthlink.net

West Virginia Broadcasters Association
140 7th Ave., South Charleston, WV 25303-1452
(304) 744-2143, *Fax:* (304) 744-1764
www.wvba.com
wvba@wvba.com
Mike Buxser, pres; Michele Crist, exec dir; Jay Phillipone, treas; Tim D'Fazio, past pres.

Wisconsin Broadcasters Association
44 E. Mifflin St., Suite 900, Madison, WI 53703
(608) 255-2600, (800) 236-1922, *Fax:* (608) 256-3986
www.wi-broadcasters.org
mvetterkind@wi-broadcasters.org
Directors: Gregg Albert, Edward Allen III, Scott Chorski, Kira Lafond, Dean Maytag, Malcolm Brett, Kelly Radandt, Jeff Robinson, Jill Sommers, Cuyanne Taylor, Jeff Tyler. Michelle Vetterkind, pres; Linda Baun, VP/admin. Officers: Doug Kiel(immediate past chair), Wendy Oberc (chair of bd), Al Lancaster (vice chair-TV), Tom Koser (vice chair), Juli Buehler (treas), Bill Hurwitz (sec).
Box 2048, Wausau, WI 54402-2048
Bob Jung, Midwest Communications
1908 Grand Ave., Wausau, WI 54403-6870
Laurin Jorstad, Waow-Tv
Box 933, West Bend, WI 53095-0933
Jim Hodges, Wbkv/Wbwi

Wyoming Association of Broadcasters
7217 Hawthorne Dr., Cheyenne, WY 82009
(307) 632-7622, *Fax:* (307) 638-3469
www.wyomingbroadcasting.org
grottski@aol.com
Directors: Larry Cross, chmn; Roger Gelder, vice chmn; Steve Core, vice chmn.

State & Regional Cable Associations

Alabama Cable Telecommunications Association
Box 230666, Montgomery, AL 36123-0666
(334) 271-2281, *Fax:* (334) 271-2260
www.alcta.com
alacable@aol.com

Arizona-New Mexico Cable Telecommunications Association
3875 N. 44th St., Suite 300, Phoenix, AZ 85018
(602) 955-4122, *Fax:* (602) 955-4505
www.azcable.org
info@azcable.org
Directors: Susan Bitter Smith, exec dir; Chris Dunkeson, pres

Arkansas Cable Telecommunications Association
411 South Victory, Suite 201A, Little Rock, AR 72201
(501) 907-6440
celtictv@aol.com
Serving 140,000 subs on 2 cable systems.

Broadband Cable Association of Pennsylvania
127 State St., Harrisburg, PA 17101
(717) 214-2000, *Fax:* (717) 214-2020
www.pcta.com

Broadband Communications Association of Washington
216 First Ave. S., Suite 260, Seattle, WA 98104
(206) 652-9303, *Fax:* (206) 652-8297
www.broadbandwashington.org
rmain@broadbandwashington.org
Directors: Janet Turpen, Steve Kipp, Steve Holmes, Bob Rubery, Jim Penney, Carlos Gutierrez, Bruce Gladner.
Directors:
Janet Turpen, Steve Kipp, Jerry Rotondo, Bob Lam, Matt Zavala, Bruce Gladner & Carlos Gutirrez

Cable Telecommunications Assn. of Maryland, Delaware & District of Col.
2530 Riva Rd., #316, Annapolis, MD 21401
(410) 266-9111, *Fax:* (410) 266-6133
ctaofmd-de-dc@msn.com

Cable Telecommunications Association of New York Inc.
54 State St., Suite 800, Albany, NY 12207
(518) 463-6676, *Fax:* (518) 463-0574
www.cabletvny.com
clany@cabletv.com
Directors: Mary Cotter, chmn.

Cable Television & Communications Association of Illinois
2400 E. Devon Ave., Suite 317, Des Plaines, IL 60018
(847) 297-4520, *Fax:* (847) 297-3865
ctc2400@aol.com

Cable Television Association of Georgia
9 Dunwoody Park, Suite 121, Atlanta, GA 30338
(404) 252-4371, *Fax:* (404) 252-0215
www.gacable.com
info@gacable.com
Directors: Kim Gage, chmn; Michael Clemons.

California Cable & Telecommunications Assn.
1001 K St., 2nd Fl., Sacramento, CA 95814
(916) 446-7732, *Fax:* (916) 446-1605
www.calcable.org
mel@cable.org
Director: Bernie Orozco, govt affairss; Jerry Yanowitz, VP, fedeal affairs, Lesla Lehtonen, VP legal & regulatory affairs; Jerome Candelaria, VP & counsel, regulatory affairs. Carolyn McIntyre, pres.
1121 L St., Suite 400, Sacramento, CA 95814-3926
(916) 446-7732; *Fax:* (916) 446-1605

Colorado Cable TV Association
1410 Grant St., Suite A-101, Denver, CO 80203
(720) 379-3623
www.kepffbarr.com
kempffcc@aol.com
Ron Kempff, President
Aurelia Serna, Operations Dir
Broker & consultant also offering financial & mgmt svcs, court ordered sale of stns.

Hawaii Cable Television Association
200 Akamainui St., Mililani, HI 96789
(808) 625-8359, *Fax:* (808) 625-5888
kbeuret@oceanic.com

Idaho Cable Telecommunications Association
1015 W. Hays Street, Boise, ID 83702
(208) 344-6633, *Fax:* (208) 344-0077
www.idahocable.com
Directors: Michelle Cameron, pres, Russ Young, past pres.

Indiana Cable Telecommunications Association Inc.
201 N. Illinois St., Suite 1560, Indianapolis, IN 46204
(317) 237-2288, *Fax:* (317) 237-2290
www.incable.org
toakes@incable.org
Directors:
Rachel McKay & Nicole Roenl

Iowa Cable & Telecommunications Association
Box 3627, Des Moines, IA 50322
(515) 276-0006, *Fax:* (515) 309-3779
www.iowacable.org
tomgraves@mchsi.com
Paul Johnson, pres; Steve Purcell, VP; Thomas P. Graves, exec VP.

Kansas Cable Telecommunications Association
815 S.W. Topeka Blvd., 2nd Floor, Topeka, KS 66612
(785) 290-0018, *Fax:* (785) 232-1703
www.cableinkansas.org
johnfed@cox.net
Directors: Jay Allbaugh Cox Communications; Kevin Collins Time Warner Cable; Mike Flood Cable ONE; Scott Schneider Cox Communications; Tom Krewson Comcast; Clarence Matlock Cable ONE; Joe Michael Cox Communications. Association Officer:Roger Ponder (chair) Gary Shorman (immediate past chair); Patrick Knorr (vice-chair); Coleen Jennison (sec/treas); John Federico, pres; Dan Murray, Legislative dir.

Kentucky Cable Telecommunications Association
Box 415, Burkesville, KY 42717
(270) 864-5352, *Fax:* (270) 864-3110
www.kycable.com
randawright@mchsi.com
Directors:
Jim Finch, assoc dir; Jim Hays III, assoc dir; Robert Thacker III, assoc dir

Louisiana Cable & Telecommunications Association
763 North St., Baton Rouge, LA 70802
(225) 387-5960, *Fax:* (225) 383-6705
www.lacable.com
lcta@lacable.com
Cheryl P. McCormick, CEO

Michigan Cable Telecommunications Association
412 W. Ionia St., Lansing, MI 48933
(517) 482-2622, *Fax:* (517) 482-1819
www.michcable.org
Directors: Colleen M. McNamara, exec dir; Bob McCann, sec; Rick Clark, treas; Tim Ransberger, pres, Ron Orlando, VP.

Mid-America Cable Telecommunications Association
Box 2138, Jefferson City, MO 65102-2138
(573) 635-5588, *Fax:* (573) 635-5510
www.midamericacable.tv
info@midamericacable.tv
Directors: Tony Bolton; Mary Marshall Burr; Eric Claytor; Kevin Colins; Bill Copeland; Art Cunningham; Vic Davis; Mike Drahota; Debby Exon; Bridget Farley; John Federico; Scott Grim; Lori Hansen; Greg Harrison; Gail Hastings; Christina Hill;Oscar Ordaz; Amie Hinderlifter; DeMaris Johnson; Denise Lewis; Dale Laine; Deirdre LaVerdiere; Tyler Leach; Charlotte McClure; Dan Mulvenon; Oscar Ordaz; Len Pitock; Mark Ronek; Joe Scott; Mike Slyman; Larry Stiffelman; Brian Thompson; Jim Walker;George Wilburn.

Minnesota Cable Communications Association
1885 University Ave., Suite 320, St. Paul, MN 55104
(651) 641-0268, *Fax:* (651) 641-0319
www.mncca.com
mmartin@mncca.com

Mississippi Cable Telecommunications Association
1501 Lakeland Dr., Suite 301, Jackson, MS 39216
(601) 981-3646, *Fax:* (601) 981-5547
www.mctaweb.com
mcta@bellsouth.net
Directors:
Lee Ann Hayes, exec dir

Missouri Cable Telecommunications Association
223 E. Capitol Ave., Box 1895, Jefferson City, MO 65102-1895
(573) 635-1915, *Fax:* (573) 635-1778
www.missouricabletv.com
info@missouricable.tv
Directors:
Roger Ponder, chmn; Greg Harrison, pres

Nebraska Cable Communications Association
1233 Lincoln Mall, Suite 203, Lincoln, NE 68508
(402) 474-3242
www.ftchannel.com
infoft@ftchannel.com
Bev Nenson, Operations Dir
Marcia Martin, General Manager
Allan Schwebel, General Sales Mgr
Ellen Baine, Programming Director
Scott Greig, Promotions Manager
Canada's first & only 24-hour English language fashion channel dedicated to the world of art, architecture, photgraphy & designb with a celebration of style. Designer TV 24-hours a day.

Nevada State Cable Telecommunications Association
2210 Sugar Bowl Ct., Reno, NV 89511-9175
(775) 852-2253, *Fax:* (775) 852-2403
nscta@aol.com
Steve Schorr; Leon Brennan, VP; Scott Dockery, sec/treas; Marsha Berkbigler.

New England Cable Telecommunications Association Inc. (NECTA)
10 Forbes Rd., Suite 440W, Braintree, MA 02184
(781) 843-3418, *Fax:* (781) 849-6267
info@necta.info
Directors:
Paul R. Cianelli, pres

New Jersey Cable Telecommunications Association
124 W. State St., Trenton, NJ 08608
(609) 392-3223, *Fax:* (609) 394-0074
www.cablenj.org

Elizabeth Murray, chmn; Dante Di Pirro, sr VP.

North Carolina Cable Telecommunications Association
Box 1347, Raleigh, NC 27602
(919) 834-7113, *Fax:* (919) 839-0304
www.nccta.com
lreynolds@nccta.com
Joanne Higgins, dir communications.

North Central Cable Television Association
1885 University Ave., Suite 320, St. Paul, MN 55104
(651) 641-0268, *Fax:* (651) 641-0319
www.mncca.com
mncableassc@comcast.net
Bill Wright, pres; John Growley, VP.

Ohio Cable Telecommunications Association
50 W. Broad St., Suite 1118, Columbus, OH 43215
(614) 461-4014, *Fax:* (614) 461-9326
www.octa.org
octa@octa.org
Ed Kozelek, pres; Kevin Flanigan, VP; Pat Eltzroth, treas; Ann Doris, sec.

Oklahoma Cable and Telecommunications Association
301 N.W. 63rd, Suite 400, Oklahoma City, OK 73116
(405) 843-8855, *Fax:* (405) 843-8934
www.okcta.org
octa@coxatwork.com
Directors:
Dave Bialis, chmn; Andy Dearth, vice chmn; George Wilburn, sec/treas. Bill Drewry, Nicole Evans, Johnny Bowen, David Wall, Leon Pfeifer, Danny Thompson, Ed Perry, Holly Henderson & Tim Easley

Oregon Cable Telecommunications Association
1249 Commercial St. S.E., Salem, OR 97302
(503) 362-8838, *Fax:* (503) 399-1029
www.oregoncable.com
mdewey@oregoncable.com

Tennessee Cable Telecommunications Association
611 Commerce St., Suite 2706, Nashville, TN 37203
(615) 256-7037, *Fax:* (615) 254-9710
www.tcta.net
info@tcta.net
Stacey B. Briggs, pres, exec dir; Curtis Person III, chmn.

Texas Cable Association
Div/DBA: (Formerly Texas Cable & Telecommunications Associa
919 Congress Ave., Suite 1350, Austin, TX 78701
(512) 474-2082, *Fax:* (512) 474-0966
www.txcable.com
txcable@txcable.com

Virginia Cable Telecommunications Association
1001 E. Broad St., Suite 210, Richmond, VA 23219
(804) 780-1776, *Fax:* (804) 225-8036
www.vcta.com
rlamura@vcta.com
Ray Lamura, pres; Barbara Davis, VP pub affrs; Kirby Brooks, chmn; Danita Bowman, dir govt rels.

West Virginia Cable Telecommunications Association
117 Summers St., Charleston, WV 25301
(304) 345-2917, *Fax:* (304) 342-1285
www.wvcta.com
mpolen@arnoldagency.com
Michael Kelemen, pres; Peter Brown, treas (Suddenlink Communications); Gordon Waters, VP (Armstrong Cable Services).

Wisconsin Cable Communications Association
22 East Mifflin Street, Suite 1010, Madison, WI 53703
(608) 256-1683, *Fax:* (608) 256-6222
www.wicable.com
wcca@charterinternet.com
Directors: Mike Fox; Robert Ryan; Bev Greenberg; Emmett Coleman; Lisa Washa. Director at large: Doug Nix; Dave Seyora. Associate Directors: Kenneth Mullane; Kate Schroeder; Jeff Fischer. Advisory Committee: Christy Benson; Randy Bunnell;Wendy Gross; Charlie Mullen; Randy Scott; JackHerbert, pres, Tim Vowell, VP; Bob Steichen, past pres; Thomas E. Moore, exec dir; Adam M. Raschka, dir regulatory/external affrs; Nancy Magestro, office admin, Bev Kautzky, accounting mgr.

Wyoming Cable Telecommunications Association-WCTA
Div/DBA: (formerly Wyoming CATV Association)
1113 Lucky Ct., Cheyenne, WY 82001
(307) 637-3933, (307) 733-3081, *Fax:* (307) 637-5399
wyocable.org
Executive Director: H.L. Jensen. Board Members: Dan Higgins, Darlene Raymond, Wes Frost, Shawn Beqaj, Sara Viard-assoc bd member, Elizabeth Davis-assoc bd member. Clint Rodeman, pres; Marty Carollo, VP; Mary Johnson, sec/treas.

Major Broadcasting & Cable Awards

AAAS Science Journalism Awards
1200 New York Ave. N.W., Washington, DC 20005
(202) 326-6440, (202) 326-6421, *Fax:* (202) 789-0455
www.aaas.org/aboutaaas/awards/sja/index.shtml
media@aaas.org
Award Description:
Awards of distinction for professional journalists in the science writing field.

Academy of Television Arts and Sciences Emmy Awards
Academy of Television Arts & Sciences, 5220 Lankershim Blvd., North Hollywood, CA 91601
(818) 754-2800, (818) 754-2874, *Fax:* (818) 754-2836
www.emmys.org
shore@emmys.org
Award Description:
Award for excellence in TV progmg.

Alfred I. duPont-Columbia University Awards
Div/DBA: duPont Center for Broadcast Journalism
Columbia Univ Graduate School of Journalism, 2950 Broadway, Rm. 709B, New York, NY 10027
(212) 854-5047, *Fax:* (212) 854-3148
www.dupont.org
dupontawards@jrn.columbia.edu
Award Description:
These awards are now regarded as the most prestigious prizes in TV & radio news, the bcst equivalent of the Pulitzer Prizes.

Alliance for Community Media Hometown Video Festival Awards
666 11th St. N.W., Suite 740, Washington, DC 20001-4542
(202) 393-2650, *Fax:* (202) 393-2653
www.alliancecm.org
dvinsel@tctv.net
Award Description:
Award for excellence & innovation among original public access TV.

The American Legion Fourth Estate Award
Attn: Public Relations, The American Legion National Hqtrs., 700 N Pennsylvania St., Indianapolis, IN 46204
(317) 630-1253, *Fax:* (317) 630-1368
www.legion.org
pr@legion.org
The Fourth Estate Award is presented annually by The American Legion National Public Relations Commission to an individual, publication or bcst organization for outstanding achievement in the field of journalism. A 2,000 dollar stipendaccompanies the award to defray expenses of recipent accepting award in August.
Award Description:
The Fourth Estate Award is presented annually to an individual, publication or bcst organization for outstanding achievement in the field of journalism. A 2,000 dollar stipend accompanies the award to defray expenses of recipent acceptingaward.

American Women in Radio and Television Inc. Awards
8405 Greensboro Dr., Suite 800, McLean, VA 22102
(703) 506-3290, *Fax:* (703) 506-3266
www.awrt.org
info@awrt.org
Award Description:
Honors progmg & individuals of the highest caliber in all facets of radio, TV, cable & web-based media.

Armstrong Awards
Armstrong Foundation, Columbia Univ., 500 W. 120th St., Rm. 1312 S.W. Mudd Bldg., New York, NY 10027
(212) 854-3121, *Fax:* (212) 854-7837
www.armstrongfoundation.org
kkg1@columbia.edu

Association of Cable Communicators
Beacon Awards, 25 Massachusetts Ave. N.W., Suite 100, Washington, DC 20001
(202) 222-2370, *Fax:* (202) 222-2371
www.cablecommunicators.org
services@cablecommunicators.org
Award Description:
Recognize individuals who have made outstanding contributions to cable communcations & pub affrs.

Bart Richards Award for Media Criticism
302 James Bldg., Pennsylvania State Univ., University Park, PA 16801-3867
(814) 865-8801, *Fax:* (814) 863-6134
www.comm.psu.edu/bart
sws102@psu.edu
Award Description:
Recognnizes distinguished contributions to the improvement of print & bcst journalism through responsible journalism.

Batten Fellows Program
Box 6550, The Darden School, University of Virginia, Charlottesville, VA 22906
(434) 924-7739, *Fax:* (434) 243-8708
www.darden.virginia.edu
ahs4c@virginia.edu
Award Description:
Awarded to pursuants in areas of enterpreneurship & corporate innovation.

BDA International Design Award
9000 W. Sunset Blvd., Suite 900, Los Angeles, CA 90069
(310) 788-7600, *Fax:* (310) 788-7616
www.bda.tv
adrienne@promax.tv
Award Description:
Presented for outstanding achievement in electronic & bcst media.

Christopher Video Contest for College Students
The Christophers, 5 Hanover Sq., New York, NY 10005
(212) 759-4050, *Fax:* (212) 838-5073
www.christophers.org/contests.html
youth@christophers.org
Award Description:
Awarded to 10 college students upon presentation of a short video depicting ways 'One Can Make a Difference'.

The CLIO Awards Ltd.
770 Broadway, 6th Fl., New York, NY 10001
(212) 683-4300, *Fax:* (212) 683-4796
www.clioawards.com
Award Description:
Excellence awards for Advertising, Design & Interactive Media.

Corporation for Public Broadcasting
401 9th St. N.W., Washington, DC 20004
(202) 879-9600, *Fax:* (202) 879-9700
www.cpb.org
press@cpb.org
Award Description:
Various grants throughout the year.

DGA Awards
Directors Guild of America Inc., 7920 Sunset Blvd., Los Angeles, CA 90046
(310) 289-5333, *Fax:* (310) 289-5384
www.dga.org
laraine@dga.org
Award Description:
Adward for outstanding directorial achievement.

EDGE Awards - Entertainment Industries Council Inc.
1760 Reston Pkwy., Suite 415, Reston, VA 20190-3303
(703) 481-1414, *Fax:* (703) 481-1418m (818) 333-5005 (West Coast)
www.prismawards.com
eiceast@eiconline.org
Award Description:
Recognizes feature films, TV movies, reality programs that effectively promote firearm safety & discourage gun violence.

Freedoms Foundation National Awards
Freedoms Foundation at Valley Forge, 1601 Valley Forge Rd., Valley Forge, PA 19482-0706
(610) 933-8825, *Fax:* (610) 935-0522
www.ffvf.org
csantangelo@ffvf.org
Award Description:
Awarded to individuals or organizations which have made an impact on a loc, rgnl or natl level to teach, foster the principles & olbigations of freedom.

Gabriel Awards
Catholic Academy for Communications Arts Professionals, 1645 Brook Lynn Dr., Suite 2, Dayton, OH 45432-1944
(937) 458-0265, *Fax:* (937) 458-0263
www.catholicacademy.org
admin@catholicacademy.org
Award Description:
Honoring execellence in film, network & cable TV programs that uplift & enrich the human spirit.

George Foster Peabody Award
H.W. Grady College of Journalism, University of Georgia, Athens, GA 30602-3018
(706) 542-3787, *Fax:* (706) 542-9273
www.peabody.uga.edu
peabody@uga.edu
Award Description:
Annual international awards for distinction & achievement within the fields of bcst journalism documentary film making & educ progmg .

George Polk Awards
Long Island Univ.,The English Dept, University Plaza, Brooklyn, NY 11201
(718) 488-1115, *Fax:* (718) 243-0766, (718) 246-6302
www.liu.edu/cwis/bklyn/polk/polk.html
A plaque.
Award Description:
A plaque.

Global Media Awards
Div/DBA: (For Excellence in Population Reporting)
The Population Institute, 107 2nd St. N.E., Washington, DC 20002
(202) 544-3300, *Fax:* (202) 544-0068
www.populationinstitute.org
web@populationinstitute.org
Award Description:
Honors those who have contributed to creating awareness of population programs through their outstanding journalistic endeavors. Presented in developing countries.

Golden Mike Award
Broadcasters Foundation of America, 7 Lincoln Ave., Greenwich, CT 06830
(203) 862-8577, *Fax:* (203) 629-5739
www.broadcastersfoundation.org
ghastings@broadcastersfoundation.org
Award Description:
Broadcast industry excellent svc.

Golden Viddy Award
Box 289, National Academy of TV Journalists Inc., Salisbury, MD 21803
(410) 548-5343, *Fax:* (410) 543-0658
goldenviddyawards.com
nbayne@shore.intercom.net
Award Description:
Honors members of the working media especially those making contributions to their communities.

Heywood Broun Award
The Newspaper Guild-CWA, 501 Third St. N.W., 6th Fl., Washington, DC 20001
(202) 434-7177, *Fax:* (202) 434-1472
www.newsguild.org
guild@cwa-union.org
Award Description:
Recognizes individual journalistic achievement by members of the working media in the advancement of social issues.

Hugo Awards
Chicago International TV Competition, 77 E. Randolph St., 2nd Fl., Chicago, IL 60601
(312) 683-0121, *Fax:* (312) 683-0122
www.chicagofilmfestival.com
info@chicagofilmfestival.com
Award Description:
Gold HUGO to best overall production. Silver HUGO, Gold Plaque, Silver Plaque, certificate of Merit to best production with a specific category.

Ida B. Wells Award
Northwestern Univ., Medill School of Journalism, 1845 Sheridan Rd., Evanston, IL 60208
(847) 467-2579, *Fax:* (847) 491-2370
m-awards@northwestern.edu
Award Description:
Presented annually to a media exec or mgr who has provided leadership in increasing access & opportunities to people of color in journalism. Sponsored jointly by the (NABJ) National Association of Black Journalists & the (NCEW) NationalConference of Editorial Writers.
Sam Adams (Curator)
Ida B.Wells Award, 1552 Alvamar Dr., Lawrence, KS 66047-1606

International Broadcasting Awards
Hollywood Radio & TV Society, 13701 Riverside Dr., Suite 205, Sherman Oaks, CA 91423
(818) 789-1182, *Fax:* (818) 789-1210
www.hrts.org
info@hrts.org
Award Description:
Recognition for best radio & TV comls.

International Emmy Awards
The International Academy of Television Arts & Sciences, 888 7th Ave., Suite 506, New York, NY 10019
(212) 489-6969, *Fax:* (212) 489-6557
www.iemmys.tv
info@iemmys.tv
Award Description:
Awarded for excellence in TV programs produced & intially aired outside of the U.S.

International Radio & Television Society Foundation Gold Medal
420 Lexington Ave., Suite 1601, New York, NY 10170
(212) 867-6650 ext. 301, *Fax:* (212) 867-6653
www.irts.org
Award Description:
Presented annually for significant career long contributions to the integrity, health & success of the electronic media industry.

IRE Annual Awards for Investigative Reporting
138 Neff Annex, Missouri School of Journalism, Columbia, MO 65211
(573) 882-6668, *Fax:* (573) 884-8151
www.ire.org/contest
beth@ire.org
Award Description:
The annual IRE Awards recognize outstanding investigative work across all media.

IRE Tom Renner Award for Crime Reporting
138 Neff Annex, UMC-Journalism, Columbia, MO 65211
(573) 882-2042, *Fax:* (573) 882-5431
www.ire.org
info@ire.org
Award Description:
For outstanding crime reporting.

The John Bayliss Broadcast Foundation Internships, Scholarships Programs
Box 51126, Pacific Grove, CA 93950
(831) 655-5229, *Fax:* (831) 655-5228
www.baylissfoundation.org
khfranke@baylissfoundation.org
Award Description:
Scholarships & internship opportunities for college students preparing for a career in radio bcstg.

John Chancellor Award
Columbia Univ Graduate School of Journalism, 2950 Broadway, MC 3805, New York, NY 10027
(212) 854-5047, *Fax:* (212) 854-3148
www.jrn.colummbia.edu
chancelloraward@jrn..columbia.edu
Award Description:
The $25,000 annual prize honors the legacy of John Chancellor. This award is intended to honor the sustained achievement of a single journalist, who may not be well-known nationally, but whose cumulative accomplishments are exemplary

Knight-Wallace Journalism Fellows
Wallace House, 620 Oxford Rd., Ann Arbor, MI 48104
(734) 998-7666, *Fax:* (734) 998-7979
www.kwfellows.org
wpalms@umich.edu
Award Description:
Awarded to full-time journalists with a minimum of 5 years professional experience, $70,000.

The Livingston Awards for Young Journalists
Wallace House, 620 Oxford Rd., Ann Arbor, MI 48104
(734) 998-7575, *Fax:* (734) 998-7979
www.livawards.org
LivingstonAwards@umich.edu
Award Description:
For the best examples of print, online or bcst journalism, three $10,000 awards.

Mark of Excellence
3909 N. Meridian St., Society of Professional Journalists, Indianapolis, IN 46208-4011
(317) 927-8000, *Fax:* (317) 920-4789
www.spj.org
awards@spj.org
Award Description:
Awards honors the best in student journalism. Print, radio, TV & online collegiate journalism.

Missouri Honor Medal
Missouri School of Journalism, 120 Neff Hall, Columbia, MO 65211
(573) 882-1908, *Fax:* (573) 884-5400
journalism.missouri.edu
dukesb@missouri.edu
Award Description:
Awarded for distinguished svc in Journalism.

The Mobius Advertising Awards
713 S. Pacific Coast Hwy., Suite A, Redondo Beach, CA 90277-4233
(310) 540-0959, *Fax:* (310) 316-8905
www.mobiusawards.com
mobiusinfo@mobiusawards.com
Award Description:
Honoring creative excellence in mixed media.

NAB Crystal Radio Awards
NAB Radio, 1771 N St. N.W., Washington, DC 20036-2891
(202) 775-3511, *Fax:* (202) 775-3523
www.nab.org
csuever@nab.org
Award Description:
Recognizes radio stns for outstanding year-round commitment to community svc.

NAB Marconi Radio Awards
NAB Radio, 1771 N St. N.W., Washington, DC 20036
(202) 775-3511, *Fax:* (202) 775-3523
www.nab.org
csuever@nab.org
Award Description:
Recognizes overall excellence in radio.

NAB National Radio Award
1771 N St. N.W., Washington, DC 20036-2891
(202) 775-3511, *Fax:* (202) 775-3523
www.nab.org
csuever@nab.org
Award Description:
Presented annually to an individual who is an outstanding leader in the radio industry.

National Academy of Television Arts and Sciences ""Emmy"" Awards
111 W. 57th St., Suite 600, New York, NY 10019
(212) 586-8424, *Fax:* (212) 246-8129
www.emmyonline.org
Recognizes outstanding achievements in all phases of TV, including progmg, directing, writing, performing, etc. The National Academy of TV Arts & Sciences also presents the Sports Emmy , The Technology, Engineering, New & Documentary, DayEntertainment, Humanitarian & Public Service Awards.
Award Description:
Recognizes outstanding achievements in all phases of TV, including progmg, directing, writing, performing, etc. The National Academy of TV Arts & Sciences also presents the Sports Emmy, The Technology, Engineering, New & Documentary, DayEntertainment, Humanitarian & Public Service Awards.

National Association of Broadcasters (NAB)
International Bcstg Excellence Award, 1771 N St., N.W., Washington, DC 20036-2891
(202) 429-5360, *Fax:* (202) 429-5461
www.nab.org/lag/international/award.asp
edorey@nab.org
Award Description:
Recognized international bcst organizations that have demonstrated exceptional leadership in advancing the bcst industry & svcs.

National Association of Broadcasters (NAB) Engineering Achievement Awards
1771 N St. N.W., Washington, DC 20036-2891
(202) 429-5300, *Fax:* (202) 429-5461
www.nab.org
nab@nab.org
Award Description:
Awarded for individual outstanding achievement in significant contributions in advancement of the State of the Art of Broadcast Engineering.

National Awards for Education Reporting
Education Writers Association, 2122 P St. N. W. # 201, Washington, DC 20037
(202) 452-9830, *Fax:* (202) 452-9837
www.ewa.org
ewa@ewa.org
Award Description:
This prestigious contest awards prizes in 18 different categories & is the only independently judged educ writing competition of its kind in the United States.

National Headliner Awards
Box 239, 226 Mt. Vernon Ave., Northfield, NJ 08225
(609) 646-8896, *Fax:* (609) 646-8826
www.nationalheadlinerawards.com
infoheadliners@aol.com
Award Description:
Recognizes excellence in journalism.

The New York Festivals Advertising Awards
260 W. 39th St., 10 th Fl., New York, NY 10018
(212) 643-4800, *Fax:* (212) 643-0170
www.newyorkfestivals.com
info@newyorkfestivals.com
The New York Festivals Advertising Awards celebrates the best & most creative adv in the world.
Award Description:
The New York Festivals Advertising Awards celebrates the best & most creative adv in the world.

The New York Festivals Radio Broadcasting Awards
260 W. 39th St., 10 th Fl., New York, NY 10018
(212) 643-4800, *Fax:* (212) 643-0170
www.newyorkfestivals.com
info@newyorkfestivals.com
Recognizes 'The World's Best Work' (TM) in radio bcstg. Entries are judged by a panel of radio experts from stns & companies throughtout the world.
Award Description:
Recognizes 'The World's Best Work' (TM) in radio bcstg. Entries are judged by a panel of radio experts from stns & companies throughtout the world.

NPPA Annual TV News Photography & Editing Competition
3200 Croasdaile Dr., Durham, NC 27705
(919) 383-7246, *Fax:* (919) 383-7261
www.nppa.org
info@nppa.org
Award Description:
Contest showcases the best news photography, editing in print, TV & on the website.

The Ollie Awards
American Center for Children and Media, 5400 N. Saint Louis Ave., Chicago, IL 60625
(773) 509-5510, *Fax:* (773) 509-5303
www.centerforchildrenandmedia.org
dkleeman@atgonline.org
Award Description:
Award for excellence in children's TV

Overseas Press Club of America Awards
40 W. 45th St., New York, NY 10036
(212) 626-9220, *Fax:* (212) 626-9210
www.opcofamerica.org
sonya@opcofamerica.org
Overseas Press Club of Americia has 21 awards for nwsprs, magazines, photography, cartoons, radio, TV, human rights & environment.
Award Description:
Overseas Press Club of Americia has 20 awards for nwsprs, magazines, photography, cartoons, radio, TV, human rights & environment.

Paul Miller Washington Reporting Fellowships
National Press Foundation, 1211 Connecticut Ave. N.W., Suite 310, Washington, DC 20036
(202) 663-7280, *Fax:* (202) 530-2855
www.nationalpress.org
nolan@nationalpress.org
Award Description:
Fellowship dedicated to itensive study sessions on subjects such as the Federal Budget, other Federal & Congressional matters.

PRISM Awards, Entertainment Industries Council Inc.
PRISM Awards, Entertainment Industries Council Inc., 1760 Reston Pkwy., Suite 415, Reston, VA 20190-3303
(703) 481-1414, *Fax:* (703) 481-1418m (818) 333-5005 (West Coast)
www.prismawards.com
eiceast@eiconline.org
Award Description:
Recognize actors for outstanding performances in portrayal of substance abuse, addiction & mental illness onscreen, in TV & feature films.

PROMAX & BDA Awards
9000 W. Sunset Blvd., Los Angeles, CA 90069-2906
(310) 788-7600, *Fax:* (310) 788-7616
www.promax.tv
awards@promax.tv
Award Description:
Recognizes the best in promotion & mktg.

Radio-Mercury Awards
22 Cortland St., 17th Fl., New York, NY 10001
(212) 681-7208, *Fax:* (212) 681-7223
www.radiomercuryaward.com
mercury@rab.com
Award Description:
Honors individuals, their employers who create, produce memorable, successful radio comls & pub svc announcements.

Robert F. Kennedy Journalism Awards
1367 Connecticut Ave. N.W., Suite 200, Washington, DC 20036
(202) 463-7575, *Fax:* (202) 463-6606
www.rfkmemorial.org
info@rfkmemorial.org
Award Description:
Awarded for outstanding coverage of Social Justice issues.

RTNDA Edward R. Murrow Awards
1600 K St., Suite 700, Washington, DC 20006-2838
(202) 659-6510, 800-80-RTNDA, *Fax:* (202) 223-4007
www.rtnda.org
rtnda@rtndf.org
Award Description:
Awarded for outstanding achievement in electronic journalism.

Scripps Howard Foundation - National Journalism Awards
Scripps Howard Foundation, 312 Walnut St., Cincinnati, OH 45202-4067
(513) 977-3030, *Fax:* (513) 977-3800
www.scripps.com/foundation
sue.porter@scripps.com
Award Description:
Since 1953 the Scripps Howard Foundation has recognized the best work in journalism through the National Journalism Awards. Cash prizes totaling $195,000 will be awarded in 19 categories for work January through December 2009. Most categoriesare open to staff and freelance journalists at radio, television and cable outlets. Online work also eligible. Entry deadline January 30; winners announced March 12; awards dinner April 23 in Tampa, FL. Review last year's winning entries and obtainofficial rules and entry form online after October 15: www.scripps.com/foundation

Sigma Delta Chi Distinguished Service Awards Society of Professional Journalists
3909 N. Meridian St., Indianapolis, IN 46208
(317) 927-8000, *Fax:* (317) 920-4789
www.spj.org
awards@spj.org
Award Description:
Recognizes the best in professional journalism covering prints, radio, TV newsletters, photography online & rsch.

Silver Anvil Awards
Public Relations Society of America Inc., 33 Maiden Ln., 11th Fl., New York, NY 10003-5150
(212) 460-1456, *Fax:* (212) 995-0757
www.prsa.org
awards@prsa.org
Award Description:
Recognizes excellence in PR, annually awarded to organization which have successfully addressed a contemporary issue.

Silver Gavel Awards
American Bar Association, Div for Pub Education, 541 N. Fairbanks Ct., Chicago, IL 60611
(312) 988-5738, *Fax:* (312) 988-5494
www.abanet.org /publiced/gavel
howardkaplan@staff.abanet.org
Award Description:
Recognizes outstanding contributions to the pub info & understanding the roles of law & courts in our society.

Society of Motion Picture & Television Engineers Awards
3 Barker Ave., 5th Fl., White Plains, NY 10601
(914) 761-1100, *Fax:* (914) 761-3115
www.smpte.org
Award Description:
Citation for Outstanding Svc to the Society recognizes individuals for dedicated svc to the society. The Presidential Proclamation recognizes individuals of established & outstanding status & reputation in the motion picture & TV industriesworldwide. Eastman Kodak Medal Award recognizes outstanding contributions that lead to new or unique educ programs using motion pictures, TV, high-speed & instrumental photography or other photographic sciences. The award recognizes dev in equipment,systems or instructional applications that advance the educ process at any or all levels. The John Grierson International Gold Medal Award recognizes significant tech achievements related to the production of documentary motion picture films.
Additional Awards
The Journal Award recognizes the outstanding paper originally published in the Journal of the Society during the previous calendar year. The Technicolor/Herbert T. Kalmus Gold medal Award recognizes outstanding contributions in the dev ofcolor films, processing, techniques or equipment useful in making color motion pictures for theater or TV use. The Fuji Gold Medal Award recognizes outstanding engrg achievements in the design & dev of new or enhanced techniques &/or equipment thathave contributed significantly to the advancement of photographic or electronic image origination.

Sunscan Award, Entertainment Industries Council Inc.
1760 Reston Pkwy, Suite 415, Reston, VA 20190-3303
(703) 481-1414, *Fax:* (703) 481-1418m (818) 333-5005 (West Coast)
www.eiconline.org
eiceast@eiconline.org
Award Description:
Recognition for entertainment production that address sun safety.

Voice of Democracy Scholarship Program
VFW National Hqtrs., 406 W. 34th St., Kansas City, MO 64111
(816) 968-1117, *Fax:* (816) 968-1149
www.vfw.org
kharmer@vfw.org
Award Description:
Awarded to winner of audio essay competition based on their opinion of Civic Responsiblity, $30,000 scholarship. Open to high school students, ages 15-18.

Western Heritage Awards-The Wrangler
National Cowboy & Western Heritage Museum, 1700 N.E. 63rd St., Oklahoma City, OK 73111
(405) 478-2250, *Fax:* (405) 478-4714
www.nationalcowboymuseum.org
lyndahaller@nationalcowboymuseum.org
Award Description:
Honors works in Literature, Music Film & TV reflecting significant stories of the American West.

Trade Shows

AAF National Conference
1101 Vermont Avenue NW, Suite 500, Washington, DC 20005
202-898-0089, *Fax:* 202-898-0159
www.aaf.org
conference@aaf.org
James Edmund Datri, President & CEO
Number of Attendees: 807 *Description:* Provides a forum for all issues that concern constituents of the advertising industry. Share ideas and strategies for surviving and thriving, learn new strategies, network with clients,creatives, executives and students.

ADMERICA!
1101 Vermont Ave NW, Suite 500, Washington, DC 20005-6306
202-898-0089, *Fax:* 202-898-0159
www.aaf.org
aaf@aaf.org
Wally Snyder, President
Joanne Schecter, Executive Director
Description: Connects all aspects of the advertising industry. Influential agencies, clients, media companies, suppliers, and colleges from across the country will address how to thrive in a recovering economy and how the changingculture of business and consumers is impacting our industry.

Advertising Law & Public Policy Conference
708 Third Avenue, 33 Floor, New York, NY 10017
212-697-5950, *Fax:* 212-661-8057
www.ana.net
info@ana.net

Bob Liodice, President & CEO
William Zengel, EVP, Member Relations
Duke Fanelli, SVP, Marketing & Communications
Description: Discuss new policy initiatives and how they will transform advertising; recent court decisions, regulatory changes reshaping the legal environment for advertising. Hear from FCC, FTC, and FDA experts and representatives.Registration begins at $795.

Advertising Media Credit Executives
PO Box 433, Louisville, KY 40201
502-582-4327, *Fax:* 502-582-4330
www.amcea.org
amcea@amcea.org
Cheryl E Szluzer, President
Sheila Wroten, Vice President
Number of Attendees: 400 *Description:* Media credit managers, editors, business mangers and other professionals gather for exhibits of advertising media such as newspapers, magazines, radio and television.

AES Convention
60 E 42nd Street, Room 2520, New York, NY 10165-2520
212-661-8528, *Fax:* 212-682-0477
www.aes.org
HQ@aes.org
Bob Moses, Executive Director
Roger Furness, Deputy Director
Jan Pederson, President
Frank Wells, President-Elect
Robert Breen, Vice President
Description: An international organization that unites audio engineers, creative artists, scientists and students worldwide by promoting advances in audio and disseminating new knowledge and research.

Alaska Broadcasters Association Conference
700 W 41st Street, Suite 102, Anchorage, AK 99503
907-258-2424, *Fax:* 907-258-2414
www.alaskabroadcaster.org
akba@gci.net
Gary Donovan, President
Matt Wilson, Vice President
Charlie Ellis, Secretary/Treasurer
Chris Fry, Director
Number of Attendees: 225 *Description:* Provides assistance which enables members to serve their communities of license through educations, representation and advocacy.

American Public Communications Council
625 Slaters Lane, Suite 104, Alexandria, VA 22314
703-739-1322, *Fax:* 703-739-1324
www.apcc.net
Willard Nichols, President
Description: Conference, luncheon and 100 exhibits of public communications equipment and information including, pay phones, internet, atm, multimedia and more. Discussions include lobbying, the political climate, legal regulatory andlegislative updates.

American Society of Journalists and Authors
1501 Broadway, Suite 302, New York, NY 10036-5501
212-997-0947, *Fax:* 212-937-2315
www.asja.org
director@ajsa.org
Alexandra Owens, Executive Director
Salley Shannon, President
Barbara DeMarco- Barrett, Newsletter Editor
Stephen Morril, Web Editor
Bruce Miler, Web Master
Number of Attendees: 700 *Description:* A forum for the exchange of ideas between journalists.

American Society of News Editors (ASNE)
Washington Marriott Wardman Park, 2660 Woodley Road, NW, Washington, DC 20008
703-453-1122
www.asne12.org
registrar@naa.org
Cristal Williams Chancellor, Director of Public Relations
Richard Karpel, Executive Director
Diana Mitsu Klos, Senior Project Director
Connie Southard, Project Coordinator
Description: ASNE's annual convention is the largest annual gathering of newsroom leaders from daily newspapers and other news organizations. Editors and leaders in the field of journalism education will gather to refresh their spiritsand create a roadmap to transform their newsrooms and shape the future of professional journalism.

ANA Annual Conference - The Masters of Marketing
708 Third Avenue, 33 Floor, New York, NY 10017
212-697-5950, *Fax:* 212-661-8057
www.ana.net
info@ana.net
Bob Liodice, President & CEO
William Zengel, EVP, Member Relations
Duke Fanelli, SVP, Marketing & Communications
Description: The conference offers an opportunity to learn from and engage with the leaders of the industry as they build brands, leverage the expanding array of media, make marketing more accountable and improve the quality of theirmarketing organizations.

ANA Digital & Social Media Conference
708 Third Avenue, 33 Floor, New York, NY 10017
212-697-5950, *Fax:* 212-661-8057
www.ana.net
info@ana.net
Robert Liodice, President & CEO
William Zengel, EVP, Member Relations
Duke Fanelli, SVP, Marketing & Communications
Description: Discussing how to use social media to impact the consumer decision journey and how to effectively partner with other companies to maximize social media reach and more.

ANA TV & Everything Video Forum
708 Third Avenue, 33 Floor, New York, NY 10017
212-697-5950, *Fax:* 212-661-8057
www.ana.net
info@ana.net
Bob Liodice, President & CEO
William Zingel, EVP, Member Relations
Duke Fanelli, SVP, Marketing & Communications
Description: The forum recognizes that the role of television in the media mix is being redefined and broadened. In addition to traditional television, the TV & Everything Video Forum will explore the use of video on any type of screenor device: the computer, Internet, mobile, point-of-purchase, gaming, and more. Registration starts at $595.

ANA/WFA Global Marketing Conference
708 Third Avenue, 33 Floor, New York, NY 10017
212-697-5950, *Fax:* 212-661-8057
www.ana.net
info@ana.net
Robert Liodice, President & CEO
William Zengell, EVP, Member Relations
Duke Fanelli, SVP, Marketing & Communications
Description: Offers tips on marketing on a worldwide scale.

Annual Community Radio Conference
1970 Broadway, Suite 1000, Oakland, CA 94612
510-451-8200, *Fax:* 510-451-8208
www.nfcb.org
comments@nfcb.org
Carol Pierson, President/CEO
Virginia Z Berson, VP Federation Services
Number of Attendees: 300 *Description:* National conference for public community radio stations offering opportunities for staff development, skill building, networking, affinity group, inspiration, new ideas, discussion andexchanges; exhibit area; programming awards. Business meetings for National Federation of Community Broadcasters.

Annual Conference for Catalog & Multichannel Merchants
1120 Avenue of Americas, New York, NY 10036
212-768-7277, *Fax:* 212-768-4547
www.the-dma.org
Julie Hogan, SVP Conference & Events
Number of Attendees: 10M *Description:* Adding all the best of digital and direct marketing, this even will provide a robust marketing tool box for attendees looking for innovative content that maximizes customer experience andROI.

Annual IBS Broadcasting & Webcasting
367 Windsor Highway, New Windsor, NY 12553-7900
845-565-0003, *Fax:* 845-565-7446
www.ibsradio.org
ibshq@aol.com
Norman Prusslin, President
Fritz Kass, Chief Operating Officer
Number of Attendees: 1.2M *Description:* Over 110 seminars, live music, over 250 top broadcasting professionals, and 1,200 student radio & webcasters from around the world. Live webstream during conference.

Annual Multimedia Convention & Career Expo
Disney's Coronado Spings Resort, 1000 W Buena Vista Drive, Lake Buena Vista, FL 32830

www.nahjconvention.org
Michele Salcedo, President
Manuel De La Rosa, Vice President/Broadcast
Russell Contreras, VP Print/Financial Officer
Description: NAHJ is dedicated to the recognition and professional advancement of Hispanics in the news industry. NAHJ created a national voice and unified vision for all Hispanic journalists.

Associated Press Media Editors (APME)
The John Seigenthaler Center, Vanderbilt Univ., 1207 18th Avenue S., Nashville, TN 37212
615-727-1600
www.apme.com
sjacobsen@ap.org
Bob Heisse, President
Brad Dennison, Vice President
Alan D. Miller, Journalism Studies Chair
Description: APME is an association of U.S. and Canadian editors, broadcasters and educators whose entitites are members of The Associated Press.

Association for Education in Journalism
234 Outlet Pointe Boulevard, Suite A, Columbia, SC 29210-5667
803-798-0271, *Fax:* 803-772-3509
www.aejmc.org/
aejmchq@ad.com
Fred Williams, Communications & Convention Manager
Richard Burke, Business Manager/Convention Manager
Jennifer McGill, Executive Director
Number of Attendees: 2000 *Description:* Annual show of publishers and educational groups. Exhibits include publications, information retrieval services and special programs.

Audio Engineering Society Meeting
60 E 42nd Street, Room 2520, New York, NY 10165-2520
212-661-8528, *Fax:* 212-682-0477
www.aes.org
Roger K Furness, Executive Director
Number of Attendees: 5M *Description:* 250 booths, held in the fall and spring of each year.

AWC National Conference
3337 Duke Street, Alexandria, VA 22314
703-370-7436, *Fax:* 703-370-7437
www.womcom.org
info@womcom.org
Patricia Valenzuela, National Administrator
Description: Annual conference and exhibits of journalism, public relations, advertising, marketing, educational communications and film.

Broadcast Designers' Association
145 W 45th Street, Room 1100, New York, NY 10036-4008
212-376-6222, *Fax:* 212-376-6202
Description: Annual show and exhibits of broadcast design equipment, supplies and services.

Broadcast Engineering Conference (BEC)
9102 N Meridian Street, Suite 150, Indianapolis, IN 46260
317-846-9000, *Fax:* 317-846-9120
www.sbe.org
mclappe@sbe.org
John Poray, Executive Director
Vincent A Lopez, President
Number of Attendees: 500 *Description:* Offers broadcast engineers the opportunity to attend educational sessions, see the latest equipment and supplies, and meet with peers.

Cable Advertising Conference
830 3rd Avenue, 2nd Floor, New York, NY 10022
212-508-1200, *Fax:* 212-832-3268
www.thecab.tv
Sean Cunningham, President
Number of Attendees: 2000 *Description:* Annual conference and exhibits of advertising-supported cable television networks and services to support local advertising sales.

Cable and Satellite: European
255 Washington Street, Newton, MA 02458-1637
617-584-4900, *Fax:* 617-630-2222
Elizabeth Hitchcock, International Sales
Number of Attendees: 7.9M *Description:* Communications forum for professionals in the broadcasting industry.

Cable Television Trade Show and Convention: East
6175 Barfield Road NE, Suite 220, Atlanta, GA 30328-4327
404-252-2454, *Fax:* 404-252-0215
Nancy Horne, Show Manager
Number of Attendees: 6M *Description:* NCTA also hosts the industry's annual trade show, which serves as a national showcase for the cable industry's innovative services, including quality television programming, interactivetelevision services,

ASSOCIATIONS, EVENTS, EDUCATION & AWARDS

high-speed Internet access, and competitive local telephone service.

Co-Creation and the Future of Agencies
1065 Avenue of the Americas, 16th Floor, New York, NY 10018
212-682-2500, *Fax:* 212-682-8391
www.aaaa.org
kipp@aaaa.org
Nancy Hill, President
Michel D. Donahue, Executive Vice President
Laura J. Bartlett, CFO & COO
Michele Adams, Board Secretary
Description: Your Agency's New Role as Curator, Not Just Creator. As part of the trend toward the disintermediation of agents, marketers are increasing going around agencies to work directly with the media, production companies, andeven directly to creative talent via crowdsourcing.

Collegiate Press Association Trade Show
330 21st Avenue S, Minneapolis, MN 55455-0480
612-625-3500, *Fax:* 612-626-0720
Tom Rolnicki, Show Manager
Number of Attendees: 1.2M *Description:* 20 booths including learning sessions and press conferences.

Comprehensive CRM & Database Marketing
1120 Avenue of the Americas, New York, NY 10036-6700
212-768-7277, *Fax:* 212-302-6714
www.the-dma.org
customerservice@the-dma.org
Lawrence M Kimmel, CEO
Description: In an increasingly digital marketing landscape, metrics and ROI are being scrutinized and recalibrated like never before. Whether interested in classic database statistics or emerging trends in web analytics, the insightsgained in our classes will add up to success.

CRS - Country Radio Show
819 18th Avenue South, Nashville, TN 37203
615-327-4487, *Fax:* 615-329-4492
www.crb.org
info@crb.org
Ed Salamon, Executive Director
Chasity Crouch, Business Manager
Number of Attendees: 2,000 *Description:* Jams, discussions, introduction of new comers, Hall of Fame presentations.

DMA Annual Conference & Exhibition
1120 Avenue of Americas, New York, NY 10036-6700
212-768-7277, *Fax:* 212-302-6714
www.the-dma.org
dmaconferences@the-dma.org
Lawrence M Kimmel, CEO
Julie A Hogan, SVP Conferences/Education Services
Number of Attendees: 12000 *Description:* Offers a progressive marketers to help better engage customers and improve bottom line results in all channels, including social, search, monile, video and more.

IAB Annual Leadership Meeting
116 E 27th Street, 7th Floor, New York, NY 10016
212-380-4700
www.iab.net
Randall Rothenberg, President/CEO
Description: IAB Annual Leadership Meeting-three days of intense networking among the most influential brand marketers, agency executives, and publishers, paired with powerful debate and discussion. Focused on the theme 'Beyond Timeand Space,' the speakers and audience, together, tackled the most pressing challenges facing the advertising industry and addressed breaking down the complexity of the evolving marketplace in order to continue share shift.

INFE's Annual Conference
14237 Bookcliff Court, Suite 200, Purcellville, VA 20132
703-421-4060, *Fax:* 703-421-4068
www.infe.org
Jeff Hood, President
Description: Offers attendees unparalleled opportunities to plug into their industry and profession. Exhibitors, networking sessions, and CPE classes.

Integrated Marketing Members Only
99 Bedford Street, Floor 5, Boston, MA 02111
617-457-3938
www.ana.net
ksweet@pohlyco.com
Kristina Sweet, Assoc Publisher, Dir Sales & Mktg
Description: The development of new communications and the evolution of traditional communications have shifted power from the marketer to the consumer, which created enormous opportunities, providing marketers with the ability tobetter target their customers. Discover how top marketers develop, execute, and evaluate their overall marketing communications strategy based on consumer insight.

International American Press Association
2911 NW 39th Street, Miami, FL 33142-5148
305-634-2465
Julio Munoz, Executive Director
Number of Attendees: 500 *Description:* 12 booths.

International Newspaper Marketing
World-Herald Square, Omaha, NE 68102
402-734-7632, *Fax:* 402-444-1370
Terry Ausenbaugh, Chairman
Number of Attendees: 100 *Description:* 20 booths.

Magazine Media Factbook
810 Seventh Avenue, 24th Floor, New York, NY 10019
212-872-3700, *Fax:* 212-906-0128
www.magazine.org
info@magazine.org
Sid Holt, Chief Executive
Nina Fortuna, Program Coordinator
Larry Hackett, President
Peggy Northrop, Vice President
Lucy Danziger, Secretary
Description: A comprehensive guide of magazine media facts for advertisers, advertising agencies, media planners and consumer magazine marketers.

MFMA/BCCA Annual Conference
550 W Frontage Road, Suite 3600, Northfield, IL 60093
847-716-7000, *Fax:* 847-716-7004
www.bcfm.com
info@mediafinance.org
Mary Collins, President/CEO
Jamie Smith, Director of Operations
Number of Attendees: 800 *Description:* Offers professional education targeting media financial and business executives; CPE opportunities; exhibitors; roundtables; and networking opportunities.

MIP-TV: International Television
255 Washington Street, Newton, MA 02458-1637
617-584-4900, *Fax:* 617-630-2222
Elizabeth Hitchcock, International Sales
Number of Attendees: 9M *Description:* Spring market for the television industry to buy, sell and distribute television programming.

MIXX Conference & Expo
116 E 27th Street, 7th Floor, New York, NY 10016
212-380-4700
www.iab.net
lisa@iab.net
Lisa Milgram, Events Director
Margaret Southwell, Events Coordinator
Description: The preeminet event for marketing and agency professionals-and the publishers and technology firms who help drive their efforts. Brings together the industry's most prominent and influential figures to share insights onthe most pressing topics in advertising.

NAB Radio Show
1771 N Street NW, Washington, DC 20036
202-429-5300, *Fax:* 202-429-4199
www.nabshow.com
NABSHOW@expressreg.net
David Wharton, EVP Media Relations
Jennifer Landry-Jackson, Exhibit Sales
Kelly Bryant, Event Operations
Description: A unique networking opportunity for station professionals representing all format and market sizes, with exhibits showcasing technologies, tools and solutions for the industry.

NAB Show
1771 N Street NW, Washington, DC 20036
202-429-5300, *Fax:* 202-429-4199
www.nabshow.com
NABSHOW@expressreg.net
David Wharton, EVP Media Relations
Jennifer Landry-Jackson, Exhibit Sales
Kelly Bryant, Event Operations
Number of Attendees: 85M *Description:* A global event for boradcasting news, legislation, networking, education and technology. Over 150 countries represented by 85,000+ attendees and exhibitors; conferences, and trainingsessions, and over 1,500 exhibitors.

NAMIC Conference
320 West 37th Street, 8th Floor, New York, NY 10018
212-594-5985, *Fax:* 212-594-8391
www.namic.com
info@namic.com
Kathy A Johnson, President
James Jones, VP Programs
Number of Attendees: 700 *Description:* Educational forum focused on leadership development, corporate diversity and inclusion, digital media and multi-ethnic content and programming. Content emphasizes diversity as a strategicbusiness imperative

National Cable Television Association
25 Massachusetts Avenue NW, Suite 100, Washington, DC 20001
202-222-2300
www.ncta.com
webmaster@ncta.com
Robert Sachs, CEO
Number of Attendees: 14M *Description:* Convention newsletter and programs concerning cable television. 2,000 booths.

National Conference of the American Copy
Sheraton New Orleans Hotel, 500 Canal Street, Nw Orleans, LA 70130
504-525-2500, *Fax:* 504-595-5552
www.sheratonneworleans.com
Teresa Schmedding, President
Lisa McLendon, Vice President Conferences
Sara Hendricks, Vice President Membership
Rudy Bahr, Executive Director
Gerri Berendzen, Content Editor
Description: ACES is a professional organization working toward the advancement of editors. Their aim is to provide opportunities through training, discussion and advocacy that promote the editing profession.

National Convention & Annual LGBT Media
2120 L Street NW, Suite 850, Washington, DC 20037
202-588-9888
www.nlgja.org
info@nlgja.org
Bach Polakowski, National Office Administrator
Matthew Rose, Membership Coordinator
Michael Tune, Executive Director
David Steinberg, President
Jen Christensen, Vice President/Broadcast
Description: NLGJA is an organization of journalists, media professionals, educators and students working within the news industry to foster fair and accurate coverage of LGBT issues. NLGJA opposes all forms of workplace bias andprovides professional development to its members.

National Editorial Conference
The Gleacher Center, 450 N. Cityfront Plaza Drive, Chicago, IL 60611
312-464-8787, *Fax:* 312-464-8683
www.gleachercenter.com
info@asbpe.org
Amy Florence Fischbach, President
Erin Erickson, Vice President
Tina Grady Barbaccia, Secretary/Treasurer
Janet Svazas, Executive Director
Robin Sherman, Associate Dir. & Newsletter Editor
Description: The National Editorial Conference focuses on the skills and ideas you need to weather the down economy and thrive in the new B2B publishing landscape.

National Magazine Awards
810 Seventh Avenue, 24th Floor, New York, NY 10019
212-872-3700, *Fax:* 212-906-0128
www.magazine.org
info@magazine.org
Sid Holt, Chief Executive
Nina Fortuna, Program Coordinator
Larry Hackett, President
Peggy Northrop, Vice President
Lucy Danziger, Secretary
Description: The National Magazine Awards honor magazines, published in print and on digital platforms, that consistently demonstrate superior execution of editirial objectives, innovative techniques, noteworthy journalistic enterpriseand imaginative art direction.

National Public Radio Association
635 Massachusetts Avenue NW, Washington, DC 20001-3753
202-513-2000, *Fax:* 202-513-3329
www.npr.org
Vivian Schiller, President & CEO
Howard Stevenson, Chair of the Board of Directors
Mitch Praver, COO

Number of Attendees: 1.2M *Description:* Seventy five booths for public radio professionals and providers of resource materials for public radio.

National Religious Broadcasters Annual
9510 Technology Drive, Manassas, VA 20110
703-330-7000, *Fax:* 703-330-7100
www.nrb.org
info@nrb.org
Dr Frank Wright, President/CEO
Linda Smith, President Assistant
David Keith, VP Operations
Number of Attendees: 5,700 *Description:* Containing 280 exhibits. Broadcast and communications emphasis.

National Scholastic Press Association
330 21st Avenue S, Suite 620, Minneapolis, MN 55455-0479
612-625-8335, *Fax:* 612-626-0720
Tom Rolnicki, Executive Director
Number of Attendees: 1800 *Description:* Annual conference and exhibits of information on yearbook printing and photographic services, college journalism departments and video yearbook production services.

NATPE Market & Conference
5757 Wilshire Boulevard, Penthouse 10, Los Angeles, CA 90036-3681
310-453-4440, *Fax:* 310-453-5258
www.natpe.org
info@natpe.org
Nick Orfanopoulos, Senior VP Exhibitions
Beth Braen, Senior VP Marketing
Number of Attendees: 8000 *Description:* The National Association of Television Program Executives (NATPE) is a global alliance of business professionals engaged in the creation, development and distribution of content as well asadvertising and financial activities. NATPE is the world's largest non-profit association dedicated to facilitating the continued growth and convergence of all content across all distribution platforms.

NATPE: The Alliance of Media Content
6868 Wilshire Boulevard, Penthouse 10, Los Angeles, CA 90036-3681
310-453-4440, *Fax:* 310-453-5258
www.natpe.org
info@natpe.org
Pam Silverman, Exhibition & Advertising
Linda Nichols, Exhibitor Services
Eric Low, Registration & Membership
Number of Attendees: 1000 *Description:* The National Association of Television Program Executives (NATPE) is a global alliance of business professionals engaged in the creation, development and distribution of content as well asadvertising and financial activities. NATPE is the world's largest non-profit association dedicated to facilitating the continued growth and convergence of all content across all distribution platforms.

NECTA Convention & Exhibition
10 Forbes Road, Suite 440W, Braintree, MA 02184-2648
781-843-3418, *Fax:* 781-849-6267
www.necta.info
info@necta.info
Paul Cianelli, President
William Durand, Executive Vice President
Donna Nolan, Office Manager
Number of Attendees: 1.1M *Description:* A six state regional trade association representing substantially all private cable telecommunications companies in Connecticut, Maine, Massachusetts, New Hampshire, Rhode Island, andVermont.

Newspaper Association of America
1921 Gallows Road, Suite 600, Vienna, VA 22182-3995
703-902-1600, *Fax:* 703-902-1600
James Abbott, VP
Number of Attendees: 1M *Description:* NAA mediaXchange, the largest annual gathering of newspaper media industry executives in North America, offers unprecedented networking opportunities that combine an exchange of informationand ideas with programming designed to generate results. The conference is designed to provide valuable ideas and insights to help newspaper professionals grow audience and revenue for their print and digital products. Sessions highlight leading-edgethinking about media strategies, successes in product and revenue development, new ideas and innovation inside and outside the industry, and tactics and techniques to employ in print and digital.

NRF Annual Convention & EXPO
325 7th Street NW, Suite 1100, Washington, DC 20004
202-661-3052, *Fax:* 202-737-2849
www.rama-nrf.org
Mike Gatti, Executive Director
Megan Zatko, Marketing Manager
Number of Attendees: 400 *Description:* RAMA is undertaking in important transformation to become an organization that's representative of the changes that are affecting the retail marketing community with a strategic view thatincludes the integration of mobile, digital and traditional media.

OAB Broadcast Engineering Conference
9102 N Meridian Street, Suite 150, Indianapolis, IN 46260
317-846-9000, *Fax:* 317-846-9120
www.sbe.org
mclappe@sbe.org
Vincent A Lopez, President
John Poray, Executive Director
Description: Offers broadcast engineers the opportunity to attend educational sessions, see the latest equipment and supplies, and meet with peers.

RAB2009 Conference
1320 Greenway Drive, Suite 500, Irving, TX 75038
972-536-6700, *Fax:* 972-753-6727
www.rab.com
jhaley@rab.com
Jeff Haley, President
Leah Kamon, SVP Marketing
Number of Attendees: 1600 *Description:* Learn about new media opportunities from new digital platforms and monetizing streams to HD strategies that will empower you to compete at a new level and be an innovator at your station.

RAC: The Show
325 7th Street NW, Suite 1100, Washington, DC 20004
202-661-3052, *Fax:* 202-737-2849
www.rama-nrf.org
Mike Gatti, Executive Director
Megan Zatko, Marketing Manager
Number of Attendees: 700 *Description:* Event for advertising agencies, media partners, consultants and retailers seeking fresh ideas and lasting solutions to their marketing and advertising challenges.

Recruiting Conference and Expo
1 Phoenix Mill Lane, Floor 3, Peterborough, NH 03458
603-924-1006
www.recruiting2006.com
conferences@kennedyinfo.com
Matt Lyons, Director, Recruiting Group
Description: Learn about the winning strategies, best practices, and tools ou will need to succeed in a challenging talent market.

Reinventing Account Management
1065 Avenue of the Americas, 16th Floor, New York, NY 10018
212-682-2500, *Fax:* 212-682-8391
www.aaaa.org
kipp@aaaa.org
Nancy Hill, President
Michael D. Donahue, Executive Vice President
Laura J. Bartlett, CFO & COO
Michele Adams, Board Secretary
Description: Next Practices for Senior Agency Professionals. The traditional account management function at advertising agencies and other marketing communications firms is changing dramatically to meet the needs of a 24/7 digitallyconnected multichannel marketplace.

Response Expo
201 Sandpointe Ave, Suite 500, Santa Ana, CA 92707-8700
714-338-6700, *Fax:* 714-513-8482
www.responsemagazine.com
thaire@questex.com
Thomas Haire, Editor
Don Rosenberg, VP
Kristina Kronenberg, Marketing Director
Description: Focuses on the evolution of consumers from passive watchers to active and empowered brand evangelists. Technology and social media have enabled and encouraged consumers to engage and interact with content. Learn how totake DR marketing from traditional campaign management to the future of customer engagement.

SABEW Annual Conference
ASU, Walter Cronkite School of Journalism, 555 North Central Ave, Suite 416, Phoenix, AZ 85004-1248
602-496-7862
www.sabew.org
sabew@sabew.org
Warren Watson, Executive Director
Lacey Clements, Marketing Director
Mark Scarp, Membership Director
Brant Houston, Executive Director
Description: Defines and inspires excellence in business journalism.

Satellite Broadcasting and Communication
900 Jorie Boulevard, Suite 200, Oak Brook, IL 60523-3835
Fax: 630-990-2077
Diana Bubalo, Show Manager
Number of Attendees: 2.5M *Description:* Join thousands of communications professionals in the satellite community to explore next generation products and technology on the Exhibit Floor and discuss tomorrow's solutions for today'schallenges with experts, thought leaders and veterans from the field. Our mission is to keep you up-to-date on recent developments and challenges in the satellite community. The SATELLITE Conference and Exhibition is led by professionals in thecommunity who have their finger on the pulse of satellite-enabled communications to ensure you experience the most relevant topics and receive actionable solutions.

SCTE Cable-Tec EXPO
140 Philips Road, Exton, PA 19341-1318
610-363-6888, *Fax:* 610-363-5898
www.scte.org
scte@scte.org
Lori Bower, Director
John Clark, CEO
Number of Attendees: 12M *Description:* Five hundred booths and, exhibits featuring telecommunications and programming equipment; dozens of workshops, with new technologies showcased.

SMPTE Annual Tech Conference & EXPO
3 Barker Avenue, 5th Floor, White Plains, NY 10601
914-761-1100, *Fax:* 914-761-3115
www.smpte.org
smpte@smpte.org
Sally-Ann D'Amato, Director of Operations
Peter Symes, Director of Engineering & Standards
Joel Welch, Director, Professional Development
Description: SMPTE annual Technical Conference & Exhibition-THE premier annual event for motion imaging and media technology, production and operations. Join us and network with world-renowned technology thought-leaders in the motionpicture studios, broadcast and distribution networks, production and post-production community, software companies, systems integrators, manufacturers, display technologies and distribution providers. As an accredited industry standards-setting body,SMPTE is also the industry's leading nonprofit association providing technology education and information to the motion imaging industry. We're all about creation, management, distribution and display of the moving image. We offer three days ofhighly technical sessions, a high-tech exhibition hall and unparalleled networking opportunities.

Television Bureau of Advertising Annual
3 E 54th Street, New York, NY 10022
212-486-1111, *Fax:* 212-935-5631
www.tvb.org
info@tvb.org
Chris Rohrs, President
Abby Auerbach, EVP
Gary Bellis, VP/Communications
Description: Annual show of 20-25 exhibitors of services for television stations, including research, sales and management training programs, incentives, collection agencies, advertiser contests and computer software.

West Coast Practicum
550m Ritchie Highway #271, Severna Park, MD 21146
888-664-0428, *Fax:* 410-544-4640
www,aipparl.org
aip@aipparl.org
Mary Remson, CP-T, President
Alison Wallis, Vice President
Sadie Boles, Treasurer
Jim Jones, CPP-T, Accrediting Director
Jeanette Williams, CP-T, Education Director
Description: Topics being covered are convention committees, boards and problems related to boards, reference committees and the parliamentarian's role in consulting with boards.

Western Cable Television Conference and
11820 Parklawn Drive, Suite 250, Rockville, MD 20852-2505
301-519-1610
Susan Rosenstock, Expo Director
Number of Attendees: 10M *Description:* One thousand three hundred booths featuring exhibits of programming, mobile aerial devices, video equipment and products and services for the communications and related industry fields.

Western Show
11820 Parklawn Drive, Suite 250, Rockville, MD 20852-2505

301-519-1610, *Fax:* 301-468-3662
Susan Rosenstock, Director
Number of Attendees: 10M *Description:* One thousand booths featuring exhibits from cable operators and suppliers to the cable industry. The California Cable Television Association and the Arizona Cable Television Associationsponsor this annual event.

Union/Labor Groups

Actors' Equity Association (AEA)
Div/DBA: (AFL-CIO)
165 W. 46th St., New York, NY 10036
(212) 869-8530, *Fax:* (212) 719-9815
www.actorsequity.org
Mark Zimmerman, President
John Connolly, General Manager
Labor Union for Theatrical Actors & Stage mgrs.
10319 Orangewood Blvd, Orlando, FL 32821-8239
(407) 345-8600; *Fax:* (407) 345-1522
Brian Spitler, Business Rep
350 Sansome St., Ste 900, San Francisco, CA 94104-1316
(415) 391-3838; *Fax:* (415) 391-0102
Joel Reamer, Business Rep
125 S. Clark St., Chicago, IL 60603-5200
(312) 641-0393; *Fax:* (312) 641-6365
Kathryn Lamkey, Central Rgnl Dir
5757 Wilshire Blvd, Suite 1, Los Angeles, CA 90036-5810
(323) 634-1750; *Fax:* (323) 634-1777

Affiliated Property Craftsperson (IATSE Local 44)
Div/DBA: (IATSE, AFL-CIO)
12021 Riverside Dr., North Hollywood, CA 91607
(818) 769-2500, *Fax:* (818) 769-3111
www.local44.org
ejennings@local144.org
Elliott Jennings, Operations Dir

American Federation of Labor-Congress of Industrial Organizations (AFL-CIO)
815 16th St. N.W., Washington, DC 20006
(202) 637-5000, *Fax:* (202) 637-5058
www.aflcio.org
bholton@afleio.org
Linda Chavez-Thompson, President

American Federation of Musicians, United States & Canada
1501 Broadway, Suite 600, New York, NY 10036
(212) 869-1330, *Fax:* (212) 764-6134
www.afm.org
Thomas F. Lee, President
Sam Folio, Operations Dir
Representing 110,000 professional musicians throughout the United States & Canada.
75 The Donway W, Suite 1010, Don Mills, ON Canada
(416) 391-5161; *Fax:* (416) 391-5165
Bobby Herriot, Chairman
1717 K St. NW, Suite 500, Washington, DC 20036-5342
(202) 463-0772; *Fax:* (202) 466-9009
Hal Ponder, Chairman
Los Angeles
3550 Wilshire Blvd., Suite 1900, Los Angeles, CA 90010-2401
(213) 251-4510; *Fax:* (213) 251-4520

American Federation of Television & Radio Artists (AFTRA)
Div/DBA: (AFL-CIO)
260 Madison Ave., New York, NY 10016
(212) 532-0800, *Fax:* (212) 532-2242
www.aftra.com
Roberta Reardon, President
AFTRA represents 77,000 professional actors, singers, dancers, announcers, newspersons, sportscasters & disc jockeys throughout the country who work in TV, radio, comls, industrial & educ videos, interactive media & the recording industry.
5757 Wilshire Blvd., 9th Fl., Los Angeles, CA 90036-5810
(323) 634-8100; *Fax:* (323) 634-8194
John Russum, Chairman

American Guild of Musical Artists
1430 Broadway, 14th Fl, New York, NY 10018-3308
(212) 265-3687, *Fax:* (212) 262-9088
www.musicalartists.org
agma@musicalartists.org
James Odom, President

American Guild of Variety Artists
Div/DBA: (AFL-CIO)
363 7th Ave 17th Fl., New York, NY 10001
(212) 675-1003, *Fax:* (212) 633-0097
www.agva.com
agva@aol.com
Rod McKuen, President
David Cullum, Operations Dir
Labor Union for performers in live venues.
4741 Laurel Canyon Blvd, Los Angeles, CA
(818) 508-9984; *Fax:* (818) 508-3029

The Animation Guild (IATSE Local 839)
4729 Lankershim Blvd., North Hollywood, CA 91602
(818) 766-7151, *Fax:* (818) 506-4805
www.animationguild.org
info@animationguild.org
The labor union for animation & CG artists & technicians in southern CA.

Art Directors Guild & Scenic Title and Graphic Artists (IATSE Local 800)
11969 Ventura Blvd., Suite 200, Studio City, CA 91604
(818) 762-9995, *Fax:* (818) 762-9997
www.artdirectors.org
lydia@artdirectors.org
Tom Walsh, President
Scott Roth, General Manager

Broadcast-Television Recording Engineers (IBEW Local 45)
6255 Sunset Blvd., Suite 721, Hollywood, CA 90028
(323) 851-5515, *Fax:* (323) 466-1793
www.ibew45.org
feedback@ibew45.org
Represents radio, TV, cable engirs, federal, county, city electronic tech.

Communications Workers of America (CWA)
Div/DBA: (AFL-CIO)
501 3rd St. N.W., Washington, DC 20001-2797
(202) 434-1100, *Fax:* (202) 434-1279
www.cwa-union.org
jmiller@cwa-union.org
Larry Cohen, President
Jeff Miller, Promotions Manager

Directors Guild of America Inc. (DGA)
7920 Sunset Blvd., Los Angeles, CA 90046
(310) 289-2000, *Fax:* (310) 289-2029
www.dga.org
Michael Apted, President
Jay Roth, General Manager
110 W. 57th St, New York, NY 10019-3319
(212) 581-0370; *Fax:* (212) 581-1441
Chris Lomdino, Eastern Exec Dir
400 N. Michigan Ave, Suite 307, Chicago, IL 60611-4130
(312) 644-5050; *Fax:* (312) 644-5775

Illustrators & Matte Artists (IATSE Local 790)
13245 Riverside Dr., Suite 300-A, Sherman Oaks, CA 91423
(818) 784-6555, *Fax:* (818) 784-2004
local790@earthlink.net
Joseph Musso, President
Marjo Bernay, Operations Dir

International Alliance of Theatrical Stage Employees, Moving Picture (IATSE)
1430 Broadway, 20th Fl, New York, NY 10018
(212) 730-1770, *Fax:* (212) 730-7809
www.iatse-intl.org
Thomas Short, President
10045 Riverside Dr., Toluca Lake, CA 91602-2543
(818) 980-3499; *Fax:* (818) 980-3496
Joseph Aredas, Chairman
258 Adelaide St E, Suite 403, Toronto, ON Canada
(416) 362-3569; *Fax:* (416) 362-3483

International Association of Machinists and Aerospace Workers (IAM)
9000 Machinists Pl, Upper Marlboro, MD 20772-2687
(301) 967-4500
www.iamaw.org
websteward@goiam.org
R. Thomas Buffenbarger, President
Warren Mart, Operations Dir

International Brotherhood of Electrical Workers (IBEW)
Div/DBA: (AFL-CIO)
900 7th St. N.W., Washington, DC 20001
(202) 728-6026, *Fax:* (202) 728-6295
www.ibew.org
broadcasting@ibew.org
Edwin D. Hill, President
Peter Homes, General Manager
Represent worker in all areas of bcstg & cable.

International Cinematographers Guild
7715 Sunset Blvd., Suite 300, Los Angeles, CA 90046
(323) 876-0160, *Fax:* (323) 876-6383
www.cameraguild.com
Gary Dunham, President
Bruce C. Doering, General Manager
Represents our members' contracts & activities.
80 Either Ave, 14th Fl, New York, NY
(212) 647-7300; *Fax:* (212) 647-7317
1411 Peterson Ave, Suite 102, Park Ridge, IL 60068-5000
(847) 692-9900; *Fax:* (847-692-5607
7463 Conroy-Windermere Rd, Suite A, Orlando, FL 32835-2761
(407) 295-5577; *Fax:* (407) 295-5335

International Sound Technicians (IATSE Local 695)
Div/DBA: (IATSE, MPMO)
5439 Cahuenga Blvd., North Hollywood, CA 91601
(818) 985-9204, (323) 877-1052, *Fax:* (818) 760-4681
www.695.com
local695@695.com
Mark Ulano, President
James Osburn, Operations Dir

International Union of Electronic & Communications Workers of America
501 3rd St. N.W., Washington, DC 20001
(202) 434-1100
iue-cwa.org
James Clark, President
Bill Gray, Operations Dir

Laboratory Film/Video Technicians & Cinetechnicians (IATSE Local 683)
Box 7429, Burbank, CA 91510-7429
(818) 252-5628, *Fax:* (818) 252-4962
scottgeorge@mindsprings.com
Bill Milano, President
Scott George, Operations Dir
Serves the Labor Union.
IATSE
1515 Broadway, Suite 601, New York, NY 10036-8901

Make-Up Artist & Hairstylists Guild (IATSE Local 706)
828 N. Hollywood Way, Burbank, CA 91505
(818) 295-3933, *Fax:* (818) 295-3930
www.local706.org
info@ialocal706.org
Susan Cabral-Ebert, President
Tommy Cole, Operations Dir
Union for make-up artists, hair stylist's in motion picture industry.

Motion Picture Costumers (IATSE Local 705)
4731 Laurel Canyon Blvd., Suite 201, Valley Village, CA 91607
(818) 487-5655, *Fax:* (818) 487-5663
www.motionpicturecostumers.org
mpc705@aol.com
Sandra Berke Jordan, President
Buffy Snyder, Operations Dir
The gathering (by rental or puchase) of costumes for film & TV. The construction of new costumes (wardrobe). The fitting & handling of costumes (wardrobe) during filming.

Motion Picture Editors Guild (IATSE Local 700)
7715 W. Sunset Blvd., Suite 200, Hollywood, CA 90046
(323) 876-4770, *Fax:* (323) 876-0861
www.editorsguild.com
mail@editorsguild.com
Labor union representin post-production employees.
New York
145 Hudson St., Suite 201, New York, NY 10013-2103
(212) 302-0700; *Fax:* (212) 302-1091
Paul Moore, Asst Exec Dir
Chicago
6317 N. Northwest Hwy, Chicago, IL 60631-1669
(773) 594-6598; *Fax:* (773) 594-6599

Motion Picture Set Painters & Sign Writers (IATSE Local 729)
1811 W. Burbank Blvd., Burbank, CA 91506-1314
(818) 842-7729, *Fax:* (818) 846-3729
www.ialocal729.com
Kirk Hansen, President
George Palazzo, Operations Dir

National Association of Broadcast Employees & Technicians
Div/DBA: (Communications Workers of America, AFL-CIO)
501 3rd St. N.W., 5th Fl., Washington, DC 20001
(202) 434-1254, *Fax:* (202) 434-1426
www.nabetcwa.org
nabet@cwa-union.org
John Clark, President
Representing employees in the bcstg, cable TV & related industries.
Local 11, 888 7th Ave., Suite 4511, New York, NY 10106-0001
(212) 757-3065;
John S. Clark, Pres Nabet-Cwa

The Newspaper Guild
Div/DBA: (CWA)
501 3rd St. N.W., Washington, DC 20001
(202) 434-7177, *Fax:* (202) 434-1472
www.newsguild.org
guild@cwa-union.org
Linda K. Foley, President
Bernie Lunzer, Operations Dir
Represents newsroom & other media workers in U.S., Canada & Puerto Rico.
Baxter Centre, 1050 Baxter Rd, Unit 7B, Ottawa, ON Canada
(613) 820-9777;
Arnold Amber, Canadian Dir

Office & Professional Employees International Union
265 W 14th St, 6th Fl, New York, NY 10011
(212) 675-3210
Michael Goodwin, President

Professional Musicians, Local 47, AFM
817 N. Vine St., Hollywood, CA 90038-3779
(323) 462-2161, *Fax:* (323) 461-5260
www.promusic47.com
Hal Espinosa, President
Serena Kay Williams, Operations Dir
Musicians, vocalists, orchestrators, copyists, composers, conductors, contractors & librarians, referral service & recording studio.

Screen Actors Guild
5757 Wilshire Blvd., Los Angeles, CA 90036
(323) 954-1600, *Fax:* (323) 549-6656
www.sag.org
Alan Rosenberg, President
Contract administration, negotiation & enforcement, residual payment processing, regulation franchising of talent agents, membership, record-keeping & communication.

Script Supervisors/Continuity & Allied Prodution Specialists Guild Local 871, IATSE
Div/DBA: (IATSE)
11519 Chandler Blvd., North Hollywood, CA 91601
(818) 509-7871, *Fax:* (818) 506-1555
www.ialocal871.org
ialocal871@aol.com
We think for a living. Script Supervisors/Continuity. Teleprompter Operators, Production Office Coordinator, Art Department Coordinator, Production Accountants & Assistants.

Service Employees International Union (SEIU)
1313 L St NW, Washington, DC 20005
(202) 898-3200, *Fax:* (202) 350-6614
www.seiu.org
burgera@seiu.org
Andrew Stern, President
Anna Burger, Operations Dir

Set Designers & Model Makers (IATSE Local 847)
13245 Riverside Dr., Ste 300-A, Sherman Oaks, CA 91423
(818) 784-6555, *Fax:* (818) 784-2004
Local847@earthlink.net
Jim Wallace, President
Marjo Bernay, Operations Dir

Studio Electrical Lighting Technicians (IATSE Local 728)
14629 Nordhoff St., Panorama City, CA 91402
Fax: (818) 891-5288
www.iatse728.org
loc728@iatse728.org
Patric J. Abaravich, President

United Electrical, Radio & Machine Workers of America (UE)
One Gateway Ctr., Suite 1400, Pittsburgh, PA 15222-1416
(412) 471-8919, *Fax:* (412) 471-8999
www.ranknfile-ue.org
ue@ranknfile-ue.org
John H. Hovis, President
Bruce Klipple, Operations Dir

United Scenic Artists (IATSE Local USA 829)
29 W. 38th St. 15th Fl., New York, NY 10018
(212) 581-0300, *Fax:* (212) 977-2011
www.usa829.org
administrator@usa829.org
Michael McBride, Operations Dir
Representing designers of set, costume, lighting, sound, scenic artists, computer arts and art dept coordinators in the entertainment industry.
5225 Wilshire Blvd, Suite 506, Los Angeles, CA 90036-4301
(323) 965-0957; *Fax:* (323) 965-0958
Charles Berliner, Rgnl Business Rep
203 N. Wabash, Suite 1210, Chicago, IL 60601-2406
(312) 857-0829; *Fax:* (312) 857-0819
Chris Phillips, Rgnl Business Rep
10459 SW 78th St, Miami, FL 33173-2908
(305) 596-4772; *Fax:* (305) 596-6095
David Goodman, Rgnl Business Rep

Writers Guild of America, East Inc. (WGAE)
555 W. 57th St., Suite 1230, New York, NY 10019
(212) 767-7800, *Fax:* (212) 582-1909
www.wgaeast.org
info@wgaeast.org
Warren Leight, President

Writers Guild of America, West Inc. (WGAW)
7000 W. Third St., Los Angeles, CA 90048-4329
(323) 951-4000, *Fax:* (323) 782-4800
www.wga.org
gscott@wga.org
Patrick Verrone, President
Gabriel Scott, Operations Dir
WGAW represents writers primarily for the purpose of collective bargaining in the motion picture, bcst, cable & new technologies industries.

Vocational & Career Development Schools

The Art Institute of Pittsburgh
420 Blvd. of the Allies, Pittsburgh, PA 15219
(412) 263-6600, *Fax:* (412) 263-3715
www.aip.aii.edu
admissions-aip@aii.edu
Hans Westman, Promotions Manager
Courses offered include audio recording & production, engrg, EFP video production, bcst media, feature writing, scriptwriting, legal issues, non-linear editing, image manipulation, filmmaking & multicamera field production.

Broadcast Center
2360 Hampton Ave., St. Louis, MO 63139
(314) 647-8181, *Fax:* (314) 647-1575
www.broadcastcenterinfo.com
jberry@yourcba.com
Douglas H. Huber, President
Linda Hoy, Operations Dir
Training in mktg & time sls, coml & program production, bcst journalism & bcst performance. Training includes voice training & dev for bcstg; announcing training including news, comls, DJ & sportscasting; news & coml copywriting.

Broadcasting Institute of Maryland
7200 Harford Rd., Baltimore, MD 21234
(410) 254-2770, (800) 942-9246, *Fax:* (410) 254-5357
www.bim.org
info@bim.org
John C. Jeppi Sr., President
John I. Perry Sr., Operations Dir
Lois Carringan Sr., General Manager
Courses offered include comprehensive course in radio & TV bcstg; majors available in radio, TV production, news & sports.

Brown College
1440 Northland Dr., Mendota Heights, MN 55120
(651) 905-3400, *Fax:* (651) 905-3550
www.browncollege.edu
lwright@browncollege.edu
Lisa Wright, Dept Chair School Of
The Associate of Applied Science degree in Radio Broadcasting is designed to help develop an on-air presence as well as the technical-hands on, and writing skills needed for positions in this growing industry. The Associate of AppliedScience degree in Television Production is designed to prepare students for an entry level position in a number of areas including: broadcast TV stations, industrial video firms, cable companies and satellite operations.

Carolina School of Broadcasting
3435 Performance Rd., Charlotte, NC 28214
(704) 395-9272, *Fax:* (704) 395-9698
www.csbradiotv.com
csbnc@bellsouth.net
Courses offered include a non-tech bcstg group session & an in-stn training lab course; announcing, production, copywriting, news, digital coml production, sls & administration. Day & night sessions. In-stn training, full- or part-time asdetermined by stn & student. TV facilities & stereo control room; resident training in studio & stn opns at coml radio & TV stns worldwide. Digital audio & non-linear editing for TV.

Cleveland Institute of Electronics
1776 E. 17th St., Cleveland, OH 44114
(216) 781-9400, (800) 243-6446, *Fax:* (216) 781-0331
www.cie-wc.edu
instruct@cie-wc.edu
Paul Valvoda, CFO
John R. Drinko, President
Scott D. Katzenmeyer, Operations Dir
Offers associate in applied science degree in electronics engrg technology, bsct engrg. FCC license preparation & cable technician training.

World College
5193 Shore Dr., Suite 105, Virginia Beach, VA 23455-2500
(757) 464-4600, (800) 696-7532; *Fax:* (757) 464-3687
www.worldcollege.edu
instruct@cie-wc.edu
John R. Drinko, Pres

Clover Park Technical College
4500 Steilacoom Blvd. S.W., Lakewood, WA 98499-4098
(253) 589-5800, *Fax:* (253) 589-5797
www.cptc.edu
Bcst training since 1954. Comprehensive Associate degree program in all aspects of radio stn opn prepares students for entry-level employment. Course includes staff experience at 51-kw *KVTI(FM). A two-year state college. Assoc of AppliedTechnology degree programs.

Columbia College Hollywood
18618 Oxnard St., Tarzana, CA 91356-1411
(818) 345-8414, *Fax:* (818) 345-9053
www.columbiacollege.edu
info@columbiacollege.edu
Jan Stanley Mason, President
Mark J. Stratton, Operations Dir
Courses offered in TV/video production & cinema; degree program includes classes in directing, studio lighting, camera opns, videotape editing, scriptwriting, film editing, sound mixing, asst camera & script supervision. A.A. degree inTV/video production; B.A. degree in TV/video, cinema, and cinema/TV combination.

Columbia School of Broadcasting
Metro Washington DC Communications Ctr., 3947 Univ. Dr. 2nd Fl, Fairfax, VA 22030-2506
(800) 362-0660, *Fax:* (703) 591-6147
www.csbamerica.com
bill@csbamerica.com
William Butler, President
Courses offered include radio, TV announcing, radio, TV sls, internet bcstg, digital journalism & production.

Columbia School of Broadcasting
Div/DBA: (Washington, DC Metro Area)
3947 University Dr., 2nd Fl., Fairfax, VA 22030-2506
(703) 591-6000, *Fax:* (703) 591-6147
www.columbiaschoolbroadcas.com
djtrain@columbiaschoolbroadcas.com
William Butler, President
Courses offered include English & Sp radio announcing (voice-over, newscaster, DJ, sportscaster, traffic/weather reporter & interviews/talk show host), TV announcing, radio play-by-play sportscasting & basic radio production. Distance educ &resident courses offer comprehensive training for entry-level bcstg positions. Founded in 1964.

Connecticut School of Broadcasting, Inc.
63 Bay State Rd., Boston, MA 02215
(617) 267-2006, *Fax:* (617) 267-2004
www.800tvradio.com
btilden@gocsb.com
David Banner, COO
Scott Knight, President

Jason Muth, Operations Dir
Katie MacKay, Promotions Manager
Courses (day & evening): On-air performance: Radio, TV, Internet bcst. Production courses: Digital audio & video, linear & non-linear avid editing. Other communications courses: Sports, voice-overs, sls, proms, mktg, wireless & multi-mediatechnology.

GCP Pawcatuck LLC
185 S. Broad St., 3rd Fl. #303, Pawcatuck, CT
(860) 599-1108; *Fax:* (860) 599-5915
Mwlanie Mariano, Campus Coord

GCP Davie LLC
3538 S. University Dr., University Park Plaza, Davie, FL 33328-2003
(954) 474-3700; *Fax:* (954) 474-7404
Angie Lopez, Dir

GCP Hasbrouck Heights
377 Rt. 17 S., #140, Hasbrouck Heights, NJ
(201) 288-5800; *Fax:* (201) 288-7966
Janet Hutsebaut, Dir
Kevin Foley, Career Svcs, (Nyc Area)

GCP Cherry Hill LLC
One Cherry Hill, #201, Cherry Hill, NJ
(856) 755-1200; *Fax:* (856) 755-0865
Tom DeFranco, Dir
Nicole McClintock, Campus Coord, (Philadelphia Area)

GCP Atlanta LLC
1117 Perimeter Ctr W., Suite N-301, Atlanta, GA 30338-5451
(770) 522-8803; *Fax:* (770) 522-9876
Aarib Elya, Dir
Peter Bernier, Campus Coord

GCP Stratford LLC
80 Ferry Blvd., Stratford, CT 06615-6079
(203) 378-5155; *Fax:* (203) 378-4330
Joe LaChance, Dir

GCP Tampa LLC
3901 Coconut Palm Dr., Sabal Business Center II, Suite 105, Tampa, FL 33619-8362
(813) 740-0990; *Fax:* (813) 663-0085
Kelly Crain, Dir

GCP Westbury LLC
1400 Old Country Rd., Suite 211, Westbury, LI, NY
(516) 338-1000; *Fax:* (516) 338-1170
Marty Herstein, Dir

GCP Arlington
2170 Crystal Plaza Arcade, #38, Arlington, VA 22202-4601
(703) 415-7600; *Fax:* (703) 415-0238
R.J. Narsavage, Dir
Marcella Jones, Campus Coord

GCP CSB Austin LLC
9600 Great Hills Tr., Suite 200-E, Austin, TX 78759-6387
(512) 340-1420; *Fax:* (512) 340-1430
Randy Ahrens, Dir
Jason Seale, Campus Coord

GCP CSB Dallas LLC
5605 N. MacArthur Blvd., Suite 220, Irving, TX 75038-2617
(214) 441-9941; *Fax:* (214) 441-9942
Scott Powell, Dir
Kristin Tran, Campus Coord

GCP Farmington
Media Park, 130 Birdseye Rd., Farmington, CT
(860) 677-7577; *Fax:* (860) 677-1141
Stacey Buba, Dir

GCP Needham LLC
73 TV Pl., Needham, MA 02494-2302
(781) 235-2050; *Fax:* (781) 444-0406
Steve Williams, Dir
Matt Sawyer, Office Mgr

GCP Palm Beach Gardens LLC
3450 Northlake Blvd., Suite 110, FL
(561) 842-2000; *Fax:* (561) 775-8390
Dave Duran, Rgnl Dir
Skip Kelly, Campus Coord

Dunwoody College of Technology
818 Dunwoody Blvd., Minneapolis, MN 55403
(612) 374-5800, *Fax:* (612) 374-4128
www.dunwoody.edu
info@dunwoody.edu
C. Ben Wright, President
Brian Seviola, Promotions Manager
Courses offered include assoc in electronics tech degree, computer technician, radio-TV, industrial electronics technician, digital electronics specialists, electronics technician, TV specialists, certificate programs, aviation electronics,& info mgmt systems.

Education Direct
925 Oak St., Scranton, PA 18515
(570) 342-7701, *Fax:* (570) 961-4888
www.educationdirect.com
info@educationdirect.com
Dan Conrad, General Manager
Diploma courses include basic electronics, electronics technology, basic computer progmg, TV/VCR repair or personal computer repair, Java progmg, internet web page design, electricians, telecommunications technician. Center for DegreeStudies: specialized assoc degree in electronics technology & electrical, mechanical, civil & industrial engrg technology; specialized assoc degree in business mgmt, mktg, finance, accounting or applied computer science; Internet technology in webprogmg, Internet technology multimedia, Internet technology in e-commerce administration, graphic design, DC maintenance technology.

Grantham University
2101 Wilson Blvd, Suite 110, Arlington, VA 22201
Fax: (703) 465-1273
www.grantham.edu
info@grantham.edu
Roy Winter, President
Joanna Boldt, General Manager
Courses offered include computer science, electronics engrg tech & computer engrg tech by correspondence, leading to A.S. & B.S. degrees.

The Illinois Center for Broadcasting
55 West 22nd St., Suite 240, Lombard, IL 60148
(630) 916-1700, *Fax:* (630) 916-1764
www.beonair.com
director.chicago@beonair.com
Patrick Johnson, School Dir
10-month, hands-on course in radio & TV bcstg procedures & techniques.

International College of Broadcasting
6 South Smithville Road, Dayton, OH 45431
(937) 258-8251, *Fax:* (937) 258-8714
www.icb.edu
admissions@icb.edu
J Michael LeMaster, CEO/COO
J Michael LeMaster, President
Courses offered include radio, TV, cameraman, CATV, disc jockey, news, sports & audio/recording engrg. Assoc degree in communication arts available in radio/TV & video production/recording audio engrg. Diploma programs offered inaudio/recording engrg & bcstg.

Madison Media Institute-College of Media Arts
2702 Agriculture Dr., Madison, WI 53718
(608) 663-2000, *Fax:* (608) 442-0141
www.madisonmedia.edu
swh@madisonmedia.com
Chris Hutchings, President
Steve Hutchings, Operations Dir
Courses offered include digital media design, production, video, motion graphics, recording & music technology. Accredited by Accrediting Commission of Career Schools & Colleges of Technology.

The New England Institute of Art
10 Brookline Pl. W., Boston, MA 02445
(617) 739-1700, *Fax:* (617) 582-4500
www.artinstitutes.edu/boston
neiaadm@aii.edu
Fran Berger, Operations Dir
Debra Leahy, General Manager
Programs offered: Bachelor's Degree in Graphic Design, Photography, Digital Film & Video Production, Interactive Media Design, Media Arts & Animation, Interior Design, Audio & Media Technology. Associate's Degrees in Audio Production,Broadcasting,

New England School of Communications
One College Cir., Bangor, ME 04401
(207) 941-7176, *Fax:* (207) 947-3987
www.nescom.edu
info@nescom.edu
Courses offered include announcing, bcst sls, writing for bcst, TV production, sound recording, voice/diction, news/sports reporting, adv & PR, pub speaking, video graphics, desktop publishing, print journalism & web design.

New School University
2 W. 13th St., New York, NY 10011
(212) 229-8903, *Fax:* (212) 229-5357
www.newschool.edu
baronej@newschool.edu
Dawnja Burris, Chairman
Courses offered include TV writing workshop; writing for TV, films & radio; TV production workshop; voice & speech for theater & TV; seminars on TV comls; writing TV comls. Offers certificate in film/TV studies, B.A., B.A./M.A., M.A. inmedia studies.

Northland Community & Technical College (KSRQ-FM)
1101 Hwy. 1 E., Thief River Falls, MN 56701
(218) 681-0701, (800) 959-6282, *Fax:* (218) 681-0774
www.northlandcollege.edu
Julie Olson, Operations Dir
Courses offered include a diploma-earning program in radio bcstg working on a 24,000 kw educ FM stn.

The Ohio Center for Broadcasting-Cleveland
9000 Sweet Valley Drive, Valley View, OH 44125
(216) 447-9117, *Fax:* (216) 642-9232
www.beonair.com
ocb@beonair.com
Robert Mills, President
10-month, hands-on course on radio & TV bcstg & techniques. Fully accredited by ACCSCT. Graduates earn 36 quarter credit hrs with diploma. Instructors are professional bcstrs. Nationally accredited by ACCSCT. Full time placement assistance.
1310 Wadsworth Blvd., Denver, CO
(303) 937-7070;

The Ohio Center for Broadcasting-Cincinnati
6703 Madison Rd., Cincinnati, OH 45227
(513) 271-6060, *Fax:* (513) 271-6135
www.beonair.com
Eric Armstrong, Operations Dir
10-month, hands-on course in Radio & TV procedures & techniques.

The Poynter Institute for Media Studies
801 3rd St. S., St. Petersburg, FL 33701
(727) 821-9494, *Fax:* (727) 821-0583
www.poynter.org
oseifert@poynter.org
Karen Brown Dunlap, President
Seminars & conferences for print & bcst & online journalists. Courses for TV/radio include stn leadership, new leaders in the newsroom, newsroom mgmt, ethical decision-making, anchors as newsroom leaders investigative reporting, powerreporting, computer-assisted journalism, visual storytelling & ethics, & producing newscasts.

Specs Howard School of Media Arts Inc.
19900 W. Nine Mile Rd., Southfield, MI 48075-3953
(248) 358-9000, *Fax:* (248) 746-9772
www.specshoward.edu
info@specshoward.edu
Lisa Zahodne, COO
Dick Kernen, Operations Dir
Courses offered include Radio-TV-Film & video production graphic design. Accredited by ACCSCT.

Technical Career Institutes
320 W. 31st St., New York, NY 10001
(212) 594-4000, *Fax:* (212) 629-3937
www.tcicollege.net
admissions@tcicollege.edu
James Melville, President
Bonnie Price, Operations Dir
Tech courses offered include electronics engrg, EETT & IETC office technology, computerized accounting, bldg maintenance, air conditioning, heating & refrigeration technology. Assoc degree available.

Western Technical College
304 6th St. N., La Crosse, WI 54601
(608) 785-9200, *Fax:* (608) 785-9407
www.westerntc.edu
westpfahlr@westertc.edu
Lee Rasch, President
Joan Pierce, Promotions Manager
Courses in the Visual Communications associates's degree include design fundamentals, audio production, media technologies, digital photography, Adobe Photoshop & illustrator, video production & web design.

Federal Communication Commission Executives & Staff

Federal Communications Commission (FCC)
445 12th Street SW, Washington, DC 20554
(888) 225-5322
www.fcc.gov
Julius Genachowski, Chairman
Maria Gaglio, Confidential Assistant
Zachary Katz, Chief of Staff
Sherrese Smith, Sr Legal Advisor
Renee Wetzel, Legal Advisor
Charles Matias, Special Counsel
Michael Steffen, Legal Advisor
Commissioner: Robert McDowell
Tel: (202) 418-2200; Angela Giancarlo, Chief of Staff; Christine Kurth, Policy Director; Erin McGGrath, Legal Advisor/Media; Brigid Calamis, Deputy Chief of Staff; Tasha Kinney, Staff Assistant.
Commissioner: Mignon Clyburn
Tel: (202) 418-2000; Dave Grimaldi, Chief of Staff; Drema Johnson, Deputy Chief of Staff; Rick Chessan, Legal Advisor; Angela Kronenberg, Legal Advisor; Louis Peraertz, Legal Advisor; DeeAnn Smith, Staff Assistant.
Commissioner: Jessica Rosenworcel
Tel: (202) 418-2300; Valarie Galasso, Confidential Assistant; David Goldman, Senior Legal Advisor; Priscilla Delgado, Legal Advisor; Alex Hoehn-Saric, Policy Director; Tajuana Dill, Staff Assistant.
Commissioner: Ajit Pai
Tel: (202) 418-2500; Lori Alexiou, Confidential Assistant; Matthew Berry, Legal Advisor; Nicholas Degani, Legal Advisor; Courtney Reinhard, Legal Advisor.
Office of Administrative Law Judges
Richard Sippel, Chief Administrative Law Judge; Mary Gosse, Administrative law Judge.
Office of the Secretary
Marlene Dortch, Secretary; William Caton, Deputy Secretary.
Office of Communications Business
Thomas Reed, Director.
Office of Engineering Technology
Julius Knapp, Director; Ira Keltz, Deputy Chief; Jennifer Manner, Deputy Chief; Ron Repasi, Deputy Chief; Bruce Romano, Associate Chief (Legal).
Office of General Counsel
Matthew Berry, General Counsel; Paula Michelle Ellison, Deputy General Counsel; Ajit Pai, Deputy General Counsel; Jacob Lewis, Associate General Counsel.
Office of the Inpsector General
David Hunt, Inspector General.
Office of Legislative Affairs
Greg Guice, Director; Chris Lewis, Deputy Director; David Toomey, Deputy Director; Lori Holy Maarbjerg, Advisor.
Office of Managing Director
Anthony Dale, Managing Director; Mindy Ginsburg, Deputy Managing Director; Joseph Hall, Deputy Managing Director; Mark Stone, Deputy Managing Director.
Office of Media Relations
Tammy Sun, Director; Vacant, Deputy Director; Maribeth McCarrick, Associate Director; Neil Grace, Press Secretary.
Enforcement Bureau
Kris Monteith, Bureau Chief; Michael Carowitz, Chief of Staff; Ellen Conners, Senior Deputy Bureau Chief; Robert Ratcliffe, Deputy Bureau Chief; Susan McNeil, Deputy Bureau Chief; Gene Fullano, Deputy Bureau Chief; George Dillon, AssociateBureau Chief; William Davenport, Assistant Bureau Chief.
International Bureau
Mindel De La Torre, Bureau Chief; Roderick Porter, Deputy Bureau Chief; Troy Tanner, Deputy Bureau Chief; Tom Sullivan, Chief of Staff; Gardner Foster, Assistant Bureau Chief; Robert Somers, Outreach Coordinator.
Media Bureau
William Lake, Bureau Chief; Robert Ratcliffe, Sr Deputy Bureau Chief; Kris Monteith, Deputy Bureau Chief; Michelle Carey, Deputy Bureau Chief; Thomas Horan, Chief of Staff; Nancy Murphy, Associate Bureau Chief.
Wireline Competition Bureau
Julie Veach, Bureau Chief; Carol Mattey, Deputy Bureau Director; Kirk Burgee, Chief of Staff; Lisa Gelb, Deputy Bureau Chief; Deena Shelter, Associate Bureau Chief; Eric Ralph, Chief Economist.
Wireless Telecommunications Bureau
Ruth Milkman, Bureau Chief; James Schlichting, Sr Deputy Bureau Chief; Jane Jackson, Associate Bureau Chief; Jessica Almond, Chief of Staff; Tom Peters, Chief Engineer.

US Government Agencies

Department of Agriculture
1400 Independence Ave. S.W., Washington, DC 20250
(202) 720-4623, *Fax:* (202) 720-5043
www.usda.gov
larry.quinn@usda.gov
Ed Lloyd, President
Terri Teuber, Promotions Manager
Wkly TV satellite newsfeed. Daily radio newsline. Wkly radio features on CD.

Department of Commerce
1401 Constitution Ave. N.W., Suite 5040, Washington, DC 20230
(202) 482-2000, *Fax:* (202) 482-2639
www.doc.gov/opa
Ranjit DeSilva, Operations Dir

Department of Defense
1400 Defense, Pentagon, Washington, DC 203011400
(703) 545-6700, *Fax:* (703) 695-4299
www.defense.gov

Department of Energy
1000 Independence Ave. S.W., Washington, DC 20585
(800) dial-DOE, *Fax:* (202) 586-4403
www.energy.gov
Craig Stevens, President
Five business lines encompass everything that DOE does: energy, resouces, natl security, environmental quality, science & technology, & economic productivity.

Department of Health and Human Services
200 Independence Ave. S.W., Washington, DC 20201
(202) 619-0257, (287) 696-6775
www.hhs.gov
Ellen Field, Operations Dir

Department of Justice, Office of Public Aff.
950 Pennsylvania Ave. N.W., Washington, DC 20530
(202) 514-2007, (202) 514-2000
www.justice.gov
AskDOJ@usdoj.gov
Tasia Scolinos, General Manager

Department of Labor
200 Constitution Ave. N.W., Frances Perkins Bldg., Washington, DC 20210
(202) 693-5000, (202) 693-4676
www.dol.gov
Elaine L. Chao, Operations Dir
Fosters, promotes, & develops the welfare of working people.

Department of State
2201 C St. N.W., Washington, DC 20520
(202) 647-4000
www.state.gov

Department of the Treasury
1500 Pennsylvania Ave. N.W., Washington, DC 20220
(202) 622-2000, (202) 622-2960 (press off.), *Fax:* (202) 622-6415
www.treasury.gov
Christopher Smith, Chairman

Department of Transportation
1200 New Jersey St. S.E., Washington, DC 20590
(202) 366-4000
www.dot.gov
Robert Johnson, Operations Dir
Mission: To serve the United States by ensuring a fast, safe, efficient, accessible and convenient transportation system that meets our vital natl interests and enhances the quality of life of the American people, today & into the future.

Executive Office of the President
The White House, 1600 Pennsylvania Ave. N.W., Washington, DC 20500
(202) 456-1414, *Fax:* (202) 456-2461
www.whitehouse.gov
comments@whitehouse.gov
Tony Snow, President

Federal Communications Commission
445 12th St. S.W., Washington, DC 20554
(888) 225-5322, *Fax:* (866) 418-0232
www.fcc.gov
david.fiske@fcc.gov
Kevin J. Martin, Chairman
(For full listing of commissioners & staff, see FCC Executives & Staff.)

Federal Emergency Management Agency
Office of Policy & Regional Operations, 500 C St. S.W., Washington, DC 20472
(800) 621-FEMA(3362), *Fax:* (800) 827-8112
www.fema.gov
FEMAOPA@dhs.gov
R. David Paulison, Operations Dir
Comprehensive info source on emergency preparedness, federal disaster response & recovery.

Federal Trade Commission
600 Pennsylvania Ave. N.W., Washington, DC 20580
(877) 382-4357
www.ftc.gov
webmaster@ftc.gov
Deborah Platt Majoras, Chairman

House Appropriations Committee
Rm. H218, Capitol Bldg, Washington, DC 20515
(202) 225-2771
http://appropriations.house.gov/
Dave Obey, Chairman
Funds government agencies.

House Committee on Energy and Commerce
2125 Rayburn House Office Bldg., Washington, DC 20515-6115
(202) 225-2927
energycommerce.house.gov
Joe Barton, Chairman
Laws to improve the quality of the air we breathe, to clean up toxic waste sites, to provide health care to senior citizens & children, to protect the safety of our food & drugs, to promote a vibrant telecommunications industry, to preventfraud in our financial markets & much mor

House Committee on the Judiciary
2138 Rayburn House Office Bldg., Washington, DC 20515-6216
(202) 225-3951
www.house.gov/judiciary
judiciary@mail.house.gov
F. James Sensenbrenner, Jr., Chairman
Matters relating to the administration of justice in Federal courts, administrative bodies & law enforcement agencies. Its infrequent but important role in impeachment proceedings has also brought it much attention.

National Aeronautics & Space Administration (NASA)
300 E St. S.W., Washington, DC 20546
(202) 358-0001, *Fax:* (202) 358-3469
www.nasa.gov
public-inquiries@hq.nasa.gov
Michael Griffin, Operations Dir

National Labor Relations Board
1099 14th St. N.W., Washington, DC 20570-0001
(202) 273-1991, *Fax:* (202) 273-1789
www.nlrb.gov
dparker@nlrb.gov
The NLRB adjudicates unfair labor practice charges & conducts union representation elections under the Natl Labor Rel Act.

National Science Foundation
4201 Wilson Blvd., Arlington, VA 22230
(703) 292-5111, (800) 877-8339, *Fax:* (703) 292-9087
www.nsf.gov
info@nsf.gov
Dr. Arden L. Bement, Jr., General Manager

National Telecommunications and Information Administration
14th & Constitution N.W., Washington, DC 20230
(202) 482-7002, *Fax:* (202) 219-2077
www.ntia.doc.gov
Sara Morris, Operations Dir
James Wasllewski, General Manager
Eric T. Werner, General Sales Mgr
William Cooperman, Programming Director
NTIA serves as the principal advisor to the exec branch on domestic & international communication & info issues.

Securities and Exchange Commission
100 F St. N.E., Washington, DC 20549
(202) 942-8088, (202) 551-5400 (sec), *Fax:* (202) 942-9628
www.sec.gov
Christopher Cox, Chairman
Administers federal securities laws that protect investors. These laws ensure that securities markets are fair & provide sanctions for enforcement.

Senate Appropriations Committee
The Capitol S-131, Washington, DC 20510

(202) 224-7363
http://appropriations.senate.gov/

Senate Committee on Commerce, Science, and Transportation
Dirksen Senate Office Bldg., Suite 508, Washington, DC 20510-6125
(202) 224-0411, *Fax:* (202) 224-1259 (majority)
http://commerce.senate.gov/
Ted Stevens, Chairman
Jurisdiction includes communications, aviation, consumer affairs, foreign commerce & tourism, oceans & fisheries, science, technolgy & space, surface transportion & merchant marine, manufactruring & competiveness.

Senate Judiciary Committee
224 Dirksen Senate Office Bldg, Washington, DC 20510
(202) 224-5225 (R), (202) 224-7703 (D), *Fax:* (202) 224-9102
http://judiciary.senate.gov/
Arlen Specter, Chairman

U.S. Advisory Commission on Public Diplomacy
301 4th St. S.W., Washington, DC 20547
(202) 203-7880, *Fax:* (202) 203-7886
http://www.state.gov/r/adcompd/
Jamice Clayton, Operations Dir
Athena Katsoulos, General Manager
A bipartisan presidentially appointed panel created by Congress to oversee U.S. government activities intended to understand, inform & influence foreign publics.

U.S. Court of Appeals for the District of Columbia Circuit
333 Constitution Ave. N.W., Washington, DC 20001
(202) 216-7000, *Fax:* (202) 216-7200
www.cadc.uscourts.gov
Appeals from District Court cases. Appeals from federal agency decisions.

U.S. Department of Education
400 Maryland Ave. S.W., Washington, DC 20202
(202) 401-2000, (800) 872-5327
www.ed.gov
Provides daily audio svc for radio news; arranges bcst interviews with sr department officials.

U.S. District Court for the District of Columbia
333 Constitution Ave. N.W., Rm. 4826, Washington, DC 20001
(202) 354-3000
www.dcd.uscourts.gov
Sheldon Snook, Operations Dir
Hears civil & criminal cases that arise under federal law, cases involving the U.S. Constitution, disputes between two states, or cases in which the United States is a party.

U.S. Supreme Court
One First St. N.E, Washington, DC 20543
(202) 479-3211, (202) 479-3030 (visitor info)
www.supremecourtus.gov/
pio@sc-us.gov
John G. Roberts, Jr., Chief Justice

US State Cable Regulatory Agencies

Connecticut Department of Public Utility Control
10 Franklin Sq., New Britain, CT 06051
(860) 827-1553, *Fax:* (860) 827-2613
www.state.ct.us/dpuc
dpuc.information@po.state.ct.us

Delaware Public Service Commission
861 Silver Lake Blvd. Cannon Bldg., Suite 100, Dover, DE 19904
(302) 736-7500, *Fax:* (302) 739-4849
www.state.de.us/delpsc
ronnette.brown@state.de.us
Bruce Burcat, General Manager

Hawaii Cable Television Division
Box 541, Dept. of Commerce & Consumer Affairs, Honolulu, HI 96809
(808) 586-2620, *Fax:* (808) 586-2625
www.hawii.gov/dcca/catv
cabletv@dcca.hawaii.gov
Clyde S. Sonobe, Operations Dir
Mark Recktenwald, General Manager

Massachusetts Department of Telecommunications & Energy
Div/DBA: (Cable Television Division)
Two South Station, 4th Fl., Boston, MA 02110
(617) 305-3580, *Fax:* (617) 478-2591
www.state.ma.us/dpu/catv
Alicia C. Matthews, Programming Director

New Jersey Office of Cable Television
2 Gateway Center, Newark, NJ 07102
(973) 648-2670, *Fax:* (973) 648-3135
www.nj.gov/bpu/divisions/cable/
Charles A. Russell, President
Celeste Fasone, General Manager

New York State Department of Public Service
3 Empire State Plaza, Albany, NY 12223-1350
(518) 474-7080
www.dps.state.ny.us
Robert Mayer, General Manager

Regulatory Commission of Alaska
701 W. 8th Ave., Suite 300, Anchorage, AK 99501-3469
(907) 276-6222, (800) 390-2782, *Fax:* (907) 276-0160
www.state.ak.us/rca
G. Nanette Thompson, Chairman

Rhode Island Division of Public Utilities and Carriers
89 Jefferson Blvd., Warwick, RI 02888
(401) 780-2130, *Fax:* (401) 941-9248
http://www.ripuc.org/
eric.palazzo@ripuc.org
Eric A. Palazao, Operations Dir

Vermont Public Service Board
Chittenden Bank Bldg., 4th Fl., 112 State St., Drawer 20, Montpelier, VT 05620-2701
(802) 828-2358, *Fax:* (802) 828-3351
www.state.vt.us/psb
clerk@psb.state.vt.us
James Volz, Chairman

Canadian Regulatory Agencies

Canadian Radio Television and Telecommunications Commission
Central Building One, Promenade du Portage, Les Terrasses de la Chaudiere, Gatineau, QC J8X 4B1 Canada
(819) 997-0313, *Fax:* (819) 994-0218
www.crtc.gc.ca
Konrad W von Finckenstein, Chairman
Leonard Katz, Vice-Chair/Communications
Namir Anani, Executive Director/Policy Development
Scott Hutton, Executive Director/Broadcasting
John Traversy, Executive Director/Telecommunications
The CRTC is vested with the authority to regulate and supervise all aspects of the Canadian broadcasting system, as well as to providers that fall under federal jursidiction. Reports to parliament through the Minister of Canadian Heritage.

Industry Canada/Industrie Canada
C D Howe Building, 235 Queen Street, Ottawa, ON K1A 0H5 Canada
(800) 328-6189, *Fax:* (613) 954-2340
www.ic.gc.ca
info@ic.gc.ca
Hon Christian Paradis, Miniser/Industry/State
John Knubley, Deputy Minister
The mission of Industry Canada is to help make Candians more productive and competitive in a global knowledge based economy. The departments policies, programs, and services assist in the creation of an economy that provides more and betterpaying jobs for Canadians; supports stronger buisness growth through sustained improvements in productivity and gives consumers, businesses, and investors confidence that the marketplace is fair, efficient, and competitive. To reach its clients,Industry Canada collaborates extensively with partners at all levels of government and private sector.